1‑

6/14

12/13

WEBSTER'S
NEW
EXPLORER
DESK
ENCYCLOPEDIA

WEBSTER'S NEW EXPLORER DESK ENCYCLOPEDIA

Created in Cooperation with the Editors of
MERRIAM-WEBSTER

FEDERAL
STREET
PRESS

A Division of Merriam-Webster, Incorporated
Springfield, Massachusetts

Copyright © 2003 by Merriam-Webster, Incorporated

Federal Street Press and New Explorer are trademarks of
Federal Street Press, a division of Merriam-Webster, Incorporated.

All rights reserved. No part of this book covered by the copyrights hereon
may be reproduced or copied in any form or by any means—graphic,
electronic, or mechanical, including photocopying, taping, or
information storage and retrieval systems—without
written permission of the publisher.

This edition published by
Federal Street Press
A Division of Merriam-Webster, Incorporated
P.O. Box 281
Springfield, MA 01102

Federal Street Press books are available for bulk purchase for sales promotion
and premium use.
For details write the manager of special sales,
Federal Street Press, P.O. Box 281, Springfield, MA 01102

ISBN 10 1-59695-015-3

ISBN 13 978-1-59695-015-3

Printed in the United States of America

06 07 08 09 5 4 3 2 1

Preface

WEBSTER'S NEW EXPLORER DESK ENCYCLOPEDIA is a new reference work created especially for Federal Street Press. With over 17,000 brief articles ranging in length from about 40 to over 500 words, and a total of about 1.5 million words of text, it endeavors to cover every area of human knowledge.

This new encyclopedia is intended as a convenient reference source not only for students—from middle school through college—but also for the general adult public. The user who needs a detailed map of *Ireland* or *Iran*, a diagram of an *ice hockey* rink or the human *circulation* system, or a table listing every *pope* or *chemical element* will find it here. So will the reader seeking a brief account of the history of *Harvard University*, the development of the *swastika,* or the life of *Mohandas Gandhi.* The student confused about the difference between a *jackal* and a *hyena,* the *Baltic States* and the *Balkan Peninsula,* an *electrode* and a *diode, Édouard Manet* and *Claude Monet,* a *concerto* and a *sonata, Slovakia* and *Slovenia,* or even a *fruit* and a *vegetable* will quickly find his or her question answered. Unlike most encyclopedias, this volume provides pronunciations for such often-mispronounced words and names as *prion, Tanzania,* and *Marcel Proust.* And, of course, it is packed with small, surprising facts: how the *ladybug* got its name, why *Macy & Co.* has a red star as a symbol, what feats *Charles Blondin* accomplished on his tightrope above Niagara Falls, and how the "couple" in *Grant Wood*'s famous painting *American Gothic* are actually related. These and hundreds of thousands of other facts are waiting to be discovered by the curious reader—and discovered much faster than it would take to boot up a computer. We hope this volume—with its comprehensive coverage, authoritative accuracy, and unmatched convenience of use—will continue to serve its users as a valuable reference tool for many years to come.

A number of editors took part in creating this volume. First and foremost, Jocelyn White Franklin and C. Roger Davis had principal responsibility for such tasks as creating the entry list, editing existing articles, writing new ones, fact-checking, and proofreading. Four freelance editors contributed to the project: Orin K. Hargraves, Elizabeth Stevens, Amy Fass, and especially Helen Downs Haller. The major task of keyboarding the extensive text alterations was undertaken by Florence A. Fowler and Joan Matteson. The whole text was given a late-stage reading by Diane Caswell Christian, Christopher Chapin Connor, Allison S. Crawford, Ilya A. Davidovich, Kathleen M. Doherty, Daniel J. Hopkins, Benjamin T. Korzec, Joan I. Narmontas, Michael D. Roundy, Maria Sansalone, Adrienne M. Scholz, and Judy Yeh, several of whom contributed useful critiques of individual articles. And finally, Robert D. Copeland's electronic expertise repeatedly proved invaluable throughout the course of the project.

Mark A. Stevens
Editor

Explanatory Notes

Alphabetization This encyclopedia's articles are alphabetized letter-by-letter, with any spaces between words being ignored. Entries with a comma indicating an inversion of the headword (as in *Vienna, University of*) precede entries in which the same initial word or combination of words is followed by another word without an intervening comma (e.g., *Vienna Circle*). The following ordering illustrates the letter-by-letter principle:

> bird
> Bird, Larry
> bird-of-paradise
> bird of prey
> Birdseye, Clarence
> birdsong
> bird-watching

Further alphabetization rules include the following: (1) Diacritics, apostrophes, hyphens, dashes, periods, and ampersands are ignored in alphabetization. (2) Names of monarchs and popes that are identical except for the Roman numeral following the name are ordered numerically. (3) Names beginning with *Mac-* and *Mc-* are ordered literally, all names beginning with *Mac-* preceding (by a number of pages) all names beginning with *Mc-*.

Entry headword style Variant spellings or versions of the encyclopedia's entry headwords are printed in boldface type when they are in common use; more obscure variants are printed in ordinary roman type and are not provided with pronunciations. No effort has been made to be exhaustive in listing variants, and rare variants have been ignored.

Several italicized terms are used to discriminate among the variants. The label *or* simply indicates a common alternative name or spelling. The label *orig.* precedes the birth name of a person who is entered under a name that was adopted or acquired subsequently. The label *known as* precedes a common way of referring to a person that may never have had formal status. The label *later*

generally precedes a title bestowed on a person in the course of his or her lifetime. The label *formerly* indicates an older and generally discarded name for an entity, usually a geographical locale. The label *officially* indicates a formal or legal version of a name. The label *in full* precedes a fully spelled-out version of a name that is usually encountered in its shorter form. A label consisting of a language name precedes a native version or spelling of a name or term.

Biographical entry headwords in particular may employ parentheses in several ways. Parentheses may enclose portions of a person's name that are rarely used, a person's original given name or names, or translations of titles or epithets. When a person's original surname is different from the name in the principal headword, the entire birth name is given, not enclosed in parentheses.

petroleum *or* **crude oil**
Mao Zedong *or* **Mao Tse-tung**
Le Corbusier *orig.* Charles-Édouard Jeanneret
Medici, Lorenzo de' *known as* **Lorenzo the Magnificent**
Drake, Francis (*later* **Sir Francis**)
Ankara *formerly* **Angora**
Libya *officially* **Socialist People's Libyan Arab Jamahiriya**
CD-ROM *in full* compact disc read-only memory
Moluccas *Indonesian* **Maluku**
Eliot, T(homas) S(tearns)
Hoffa, Jimmy (*orig.* James Riddle)
Jackson, Stonewall (*orig.* Thomas Jonathan)
Radetsky, Joseph, Graf (Count)
Stowe, Harriet Beecher *orig.* Harriet Elizabeth Beecher

Pronunciations Entries for terms and names whose pronunciation the encyclopedia's likely users might hesitate over are supplied with pronunciations. Foreign names or terms that are pronounced in a markedly different way by native speakers and English-speakers are frequently provided with two pronunciations, one of them preceded by a language label (*Engl, Fr, Span,* etc.). Thus, for the name of the French actress Sarah Bernhardt we provide the pronunciations "\ber–'när, *Engl* 'bərn-ˌhärt\." The symbols employed and the sounds they represent are listed on page x.

Romanization of foreign languages Words from languages that do not use the Western (Roman) alphabet generally reflect the spellings most commonly seen in English-language contexts.

Chinese names are almost always transcribed according to the pinyin system. Where a Chinese name or term appears as a headword, the older Wade-Giles spelling is given as an *or* variant. Taiwanese place-names and biographical names, however, are generally listed in their Wade-Giles spelling, with the pinyin spelling as a variant. A few Chinese words widely used in English (e.g., *Taoism*) retain their traditional English spelling.

Japanese names and terms are generally transcribed according to the Hepburn system but without macrons to indicate vowel length.

Russian names and terms generally observe traditional Western spellings and follow the diacriticless system employed by the U.S. Board on Geographic Names.

Arabic names and terms generally follow the best-established Western usage. 'Ayns (') and hamzas (') have generally been omitted. Except in a few cases, the *l* in the article *al-* or *el-* ("the") is not assimilated to a following consonant (thus, we employ the spelling *Harun al-Rashid*, not *Harun ar-Rashid*), even though such assimilation reflects Arabic pronunciation.

Cross-references Cross-references to other articles are indicated by having the alphabetized element of the name or term (and everything that follows it) set in small capitals. Thus, "John VON NEUMANN" sends the reader to the V's, "J. W. von GOETHE" to the G's; "CAPE BRETON ISLAND" sends the reader to the C's, "Cape of GOOD HOPE" to the G's; and so on.

A term is generally set in small capitals only when it is likely that the reader of the article within which the cross-reference appears might want to be notified about the additional article. Hence many terms for which there are corresponding entries are not bulleted. (As a special case, the names of countries, U.S. states, and Canadian provinces are never set as cross-references, since most readers will correctly assume that the encyclopedia contains articles on them.) The reader should not assume that a noun lacks its own entry simply because it does not appear in small capitals within a given article.

Over 2,000 cross-references are provided at their own alphabetical place (for example, "**ADD** See ATTENTION DEFICIT DISORDER"), to direct the reader who has looked up an alternative version of the name or has expected an entry to be alphabetized according to an element other than the one actually used.

Abbreviations

A.D.	anno Domini	Ga.	Georgia	N.J.	New Jersey
Adm.	Admiral	Gen.	General	N.M.	New Mexico
Ala.	Alabama	Ger	German	Nov.	November
Apr.	April	Gov.	Governor	NW	northwestern
Ariz.	Arizona	i.e.	id est (that is)	N.W.	Northwest
Ark.	Arkansas	Ill.	Illinois	N.Y.	New York
Assn.	Association	in.	inch(es)	Oct.	October
Aug.	August	Ind.	Indiana	Okla.	Oklahoma
b.	born	Jan.	January	Ore.	Oregon
B.C.	before Christ	Jap	Japanese	orig.	originally
C	Celsius	Jr.	Junior	O.S.	Old Style
c.	circa	K	Kelvin	oz	ounce(s)
Cal.	California	Kan.	Kansas	Pa.	Pennsylvania
Capt.	Captain	kg	kilogram(s)	PhD	Doctor of
cc	cubic	km	kilometer(s)		Philosophy
	centimeter(s)	kph	kilometers per	pop.	population
cent.	century,		hour	Pres.	President
	centuries	Ky.	Kentucky	r.	reigned, ruled
cm	centimeter(s)	La.	Louisiana	Rev.	Reverend
Co.	Company,	lb, lbs	pound, pounds	R.I.	Rhode Island
	County	m	meter(s)	S	southern
Col.	Colorado,	MA	Master of Arts	S.	South
	Colonel	Maj.	Major	S.C.	South Carolina
Conn.	Connecticut	Mar.	March	S.D.	South Dakota
Corp.	Corporation	Mass.	Massachusetts	SE	southeastern
cu	cubic	Md.	Maryland	S.E.	Southeast
d.	died	Me.	Maine	Sen.	Senator
D.C.	District of	mi	mile(s)	Sept.	September
	Columbia	Mich.	Michigan	Span	Spanish
Dec.	December	Minn.	Minnesota	sq	square
Del.	Delaware	Miss.	Mississippi	St.	Saint
Dr.	Doctor	ml	milliliter(s)	SW	southwestern
E	eastern	mm	millimeter(s)	S.W.	Southwest
E.	East	Mo.	Missouri	Tenn.	Tennessee
ed.	edition	Mont.	Montana	U.N.	United Nations
e.g.	exempli gratia	mph	miles per hour	Univ.	University
	(for example)	Mt.	Mount	U.S.	United States
Engl	English	Mtn.,	Mountain,	Va.	Virginia
est.	estimate,	Mtns.	Mountains	vols.	volumes
	estimated	N	northern	vs.	versus
F	Fahrenheit	N.	North	Vt.	Vermont
Feb.	February	N.C.	North Carolina	W	western
fl.	flourished	N.D.	North Dakota	W.	West
Fla.	Florida	NE	northeastern	W.V.	West Virginia
Fr	French	N.E.	Northeast	Wash.	Washington
ft	foot, feet	Neb.	Nebraska	Wisc.	Wisconsin
Ft.	Fort	Nev.	Nevada	Wy.	Wyoming
g	gram(s)	N.H.	New Hampshire		

Pronunciation Symbols

ə	banana, collide, abut, humdrum
˙ə	preceding \l\, \n\, \m\, \ŋ\, as in battle, mitten, eaten, lock and key \-ᵊŋ-\; following \l\, \m\, \r\, as in French table, prisme, titre
ər	further, merger, bird
a	mat, gag
ā	day, fade, aorta
ä	bother, cot, father, cart
ȧ	father as pronounced by speakers who do not rhyme it with *bother*; French patte
au̇	now, loud, out
b	baby, rib
ch	chin, nature \ˈnā-chər\
d	did, adder
e	bet, bed, peck
ē	beat, easy
f	fifty, cuff
g	go, big
h	hat, ahead
i	tip, banish
ī	site, buy
j	gem, judge
k	kin, cook, ache
k̲	German ich, Buch
l	lily, pool
m	murmur, dim
n	no, own
ⁿ	indicates that a preceding vowel or diphthong is pronounced with the nasal passages open, as in French un bon vin blanc \œⁿ-bōⁿ-vaⁿ-bläⁿ\
ŋ	sing \ˈsiŋ\, singer \ˈsiŋ-ər\, finger \ˈfiŋ-gər\, ink\ˈiŋk\

ō	bone, know, beau
ȯ	saw, all, caught
œ	French boeuf, German Hölle
œ̄	French feu, German Höhle
ȯi	coin, destroy
p	pepper, lip
r	red, car, rarity
s	source, less
sh	shy, mission, machine, special
t	tie, attack, late, latter
th	thin, ether
th̲	then, either, this
ü	rule, youth, union \ˈyün-yən\, few \ˈfyü\
u̇	pull, wood, book
ue	German füllen, hübsch
ūe	French rue, German fühlen
v	vivid, give
w	we, away
y	yard, cue \ˈkyü\, union \ˈyün-yən\
ʸ	indicates that during the articulation of the sound represented by the preceding character the front of the tongue has substantially the position it has when pronouncing *y*, as in French digne \dēnʸ\
z	zone, raise
zh	vision, azure \ˈa-zhər\
ˈ	precedes a syllable with primary (strongest) stress: \ˈpen-mən-ˌship\
ˌ	precedes a syllable with secondary (medium) stress: \ˈpen-mən-ˌship\
-	marks syllable division

A

Aachen \\'ä-ḵən\\ *French* **Aix-la-Chapelle** \\ˌeks-lȧ-shȧ-'pel\\ City (pop., 2001: 241,000), W Germany, southwest of Cologne. It was inhabited by Romans in the 1st cent. A.D. The second city of CHARLEMAGNE's empire, it was the site of his great palace. The cathedral built by Charlemagne about 800 saw the coronation of most German kings of the 10th–16th cent. Aachen was part of France 1801–15. It is famous for its many spas.

Aaiun, El See EL AAIUN

Aalto \\'äl-tȯ\\, **(Hugo) Alvar (Henrik)** (1898–1976) Finnish architect and designer. His distinctive style blends classic modernism and informal regional character, often employing indigenous materials (especially timber). It was perhaps best expressed in his civic center at Säynätsalo (1950–52), with its simple forms in red brick, wood, and copper. He remains one of the Modern movement's most popular architects; reproductions of his bent laminated wood furniture appear in households worldwide. His wife Aino Marsio (d.1949) long served as his collaborator.

aardvark *or* **African ant bear** Heavily built mammal (*Orycteropus afer*) of sub-Saharan forests and plains. Its stout, piglike body ("aardvark" is Afrikaans for "earth pig") may be as long as 6 ft (1.8 m), including a 2-ft (60-cm) tail. It has a long snout, rabbitlike ears, short legs, and long toes with large, flattened claws. It feeds at night by ripping open ant and termite nests and lapping up the insects with a long (1-ft, or 30-cm), sticky tongue.

Aare River \\'är-ə\\ *or* **Aar River** River, central and N Switzerland. The longest river entirely within Switzerland, it flows northwest from the BERNESE ALPS and passes by the city of BERN before entering the RHINE at Koblenz, after 183 mi (294 km).

Aarhus See ARHUS

Aaron (fl.c.13th cent. B.C.) Brother of MOSES and first high priest of ancient Israel. Acting as a spokesman for Moses, he played a central role in forcing the pharaoh to allow the Israelites to leave Egypt. God charged Aaron and Moses with commemorating the event at Passover. Later, he is mentioned as the one responsible for the Israelites' idolatrous worship of the golden calf while Moses was on Mt. Sinai. His death at 123 is noted in Numbers.

Aaron, Hank (*orig.* Henry Louis) (b.1934) U.S. baseball player, one of the greatest hitters of all time. Born in Mobile, Ala., he played briefly in the Negro and minor leagues before joining the Milwaukee (later Atlanta) Braves in 1954. He would play outfield most of his career. In 1974 he hit his 715th home run, breaking Babe RUTH's record. His records for career home runs (755), extra-base hits (1,477), and runs batted in (2,297) remain unbroken, and only Ty COBB and Pete ROSE exceeded him in career hits (3,771).

abacus Calculating instrument that uses beads that slide along a series of wires or rods set in a frame to represent the decimal places. Probably of Babylonian origin, it was used by merchants in the Middle Ages throughout Europe and the Arabic world. It was gradually replaced by arithmetic based on HINDU-ARABIC NUMERALS.

Abakanowicz \\ˌä-bä-'kän-ō-ˌwits\\, **Magdalena** (b.1930) Polish sculptor. A descendant of nobility, she became the pioneer of sculpture made of woven fabrics, calling her three-dimensional weavings "Abakans" (from her surname). She produced series of fabric forms called *Heads* (1975), *Backs* (1976–80), *Embryology* (1980), and *Catharsis* (1986). She has exhibited paintings, drawings, and sculptures internationally, and has been widely imitated in Europe and the U.S.

abalone \\ˌa-bə-'lō-nē\\ Any of several marine SNAIL species (genus *Haliotis,* family Haliotidae), found in warm seas worldwide. The outer surface of the single shell has a row of small holes, most of which fill in as the animal grows. Abalones generally range from 4 to 10 in. (10–25 cm) across and up to 3 in. (8 cm) deep. The largest (*H. rufescens*) is 12 in. (30 cm) across . The shell's lustrous, iridescent interior is used in ornaments, and the large muscular foot is eaten as a delicacy.

Abbado \\ä-'bä-dō\\, **Claudio** (b.1933) Italian conductor. Born in Milan, he studied piano before beginning to conduct in Vienna. He was long associated with the La Scala opera house (1968–86), ultimately as artistic director, as well as with the Vienna Philharmonic. In 1989 he succeeded Herbert von KARAJAN as head of the Berlin Philharmonic, a post he held until 2002. He is known for his commitment to adventurous programming, including much modern music.

Abbas, Ferhat (1899–1985) Algerian political leader, first president of the provisional government of the Algerian Republic (1958). Disillusioned with France, during World War II he issued a demand for a constitution that would grant equality to all Algerians. He joined the National Liberation Front (FLN), which helped achieve independence from France 1958–62. He was elected president of the Algerian Constituent Assembly in 1962, but resigned in 1963.

Abbas I *known as* **Abbas the Great** (1571–1629) Shah of Persia 1587–1629. Succeeding his father, Sultan Muhammad Shah, he strengthened the SAFAVID DYNASTY by expelling Ottoman and Uzbek troops and creating a standing army. Under Abbas ESFAHAN became Persia's capital and one of the world's most beautiful cities. Persian artistic achievement and international trade reached a high point during his reign. Although tolerant in public life (he granted privileges to Christian groups) and concerned for his people's welfare, his fear for his personal

Abbas I Painting, Mughal school of Jahangir, c.1620

security and ruthlessness led him to blind or execute many of his immediate family.

Abbasid dynasty \\ə-'ba-səd\\ (750–1258) Second dynasty of the Muslim Empire of the Caliphate, succeeding the UMAYYAD DYNASTY. It was named after al-Abbas (566–c.633), uncle of MUHAMMAD, from whom all its CALIPHS were descended. The Abbasids refocused their attention to the east of Arabia, moving the capital city to BAGHDAD. Under their rule, Arab culture and empire reached new heights and Islam gained non-Arab converts. The greatest Muslim contributions to science and philosophy were made during this "golden age." The Abbasids' hold on power began to weaken when invaders from the east demanded civil autonomy. Gradually the caliphate's power became largely spiritual. The dynasty fell to the MONGOLS after a siege of Baghdad.

Abbate \äb-'bä-tā\, **Niccolo dell'** (1509/12–1571) Italian painter. He developed his mature style under the influence of CORREGGIO and PARMIGIANINO in Bologna (1544–52). There he painted portraits and decorated palaces with frescoes of landscapes and Mannerist figure compositions. In 1552 he was invited by Henry II of France to work under Francesco PRIMATICCIO at the palace of FONTAINEBLEAU, where he executed immense murals (most now lost). His mythological landscapes were a principal source of the French classical landscape tradition.

abbey Complex of buildings housing a MONASTERY or convent directed by an abbot or abbess. The first abbey was MONTE CASSINO in Italy, founded in 529. The CLOISTER linked the abbey together. The dormitory was often built over the dining hall on the E side of the cloister and joined to the central church. The W side of the cloister provided for public dealings; the gatehouse controlled the only opening to the outer, public courtyard. On the S side were a central kitchen, brewery, and workshops. The novitiate and infirmary were housed in a building with its own chapel, bathhouse, dining hall, kitchen, and garden. In the 12th–13th cent., many abbeys were built throughout Europe.

Abbey Theatre Dublin theater. It developed from the Irish Literary Theatre, founded in 1899 by W. B. YEATS and Lady Augusta GREGORY to foster Irish drama. After moving the troupe to a renovated theater on Abbey Street in 1904, they codirected its productions with J. M. SYNGE, staged their own plays, and commissioned works by Sean O'CASEY and others. Important premieres included Synge's *The Playboy of the Western World* (1907) and O'Casey's *The Plough and the Stars* (1926). A fire destroyed the original playhouse in 1951, and a new theater was built in 1966.

Abbott, Berenice (1898–1991) U.S. photographer. Born in Springfield, Ohio, she left in 1918 to study in New York, Paris, and Berlin. In Paris she became an assistant to Man RAY and Eugène ATGET. In 1925 she set up her own studio and made portraits of artists and writers. In the 1930s, she photographed New York's architecture for the WPA FEDERAL ART PROJECT; many of the photographs were published in *Changing New York* (1939).

Abbott, George (Francis) (1887–1995) U.S. theater director and playwright. Born in Forestville, N.Y., he began in 1913 as an actor in Broadway plays. As a writer and director, he achieved the first of many hits with *The Fall Guy* (1925). He also wrote, directed, or produced the popular musicals *The Boys from Syracuse* (1938), *Pal Joey* (1940), *Wonderful Town* (1953), and *Damn Yankees* (1955). He directed a revival of *On Your Toes* at age 95, and lived to be 107.

Abbott, Lyman (1835–1922) U.S. minister. Born in Roxbury, Mass., he became editor of H. W. BEECHER's weekly *Christian Union* (later *Outlook*) in 1881. In 1888 he succeeded to Beecher's pulpit in Brooklyn. A leading exponent of the Social Gospel reform movement, he worked to apply Christianity to social and industrial problems and sought to interpret rather than condemn the effect of the theory of evolution on religion, in such books as *Christianity and Social Problems* (1897).

Abbott and Costello U.S. comedy team. Bud (born William Alexander) Abbott (1895–1974) was born in Asbury Park, N.J.; Lou (born Louis Francis) Costello (1906–1959) in Paterson, N. J. Initially stars of vaudeville and radio, their first successful film, *Buck Privates* (1941), was followed by over 30 other SLAPSTICK comedies, with tall, thin Abbott playing straight man to short, plump Costello, the buffoon. Their famous routine "Who's on First?" was first performed in the film *The Naughty Nineties* (1945).

ABC *in full* **American Broadcasting Co.** Major U.S. broadcasting network. It began when the expanding radio company NBC was forced to sell one of its two networks in 1941. Its buyer was Edward J. Noble, maker of Life Savers candies. ABC expanded into the emerging television industry and soon became one of the three top networks. It specialized in sports broadcasting and developed the instant replay in 1961. It was bought by the Walt Disney Co. in 1995.

Abd al-Krim \ˌab-dəl-'krēm\, *in full* Muhammad ibn Abd al-Karim al Khattabi (1882–1963) BERBER resistance leader against Spanish and French rule in N Morocco. While a judge, he became disillusioned with Spanish policies and

eventually led a resistance movement. He set up the Republic of the Rif in 1921. In 1926 France and Spain amassed 250,000 men to force his surrender. Exiled to Réunion, in 1947 he received permission to live in France, but went to Egypt instead. When Morocco became independent (1956), he was invited to return, but refused because of the continued presence of French troops in N. Africa.

Abd al-Malik ibn Marwan \ˌab-dəl-'mal-ik-ˌib-ən-mär-'wan\ (646/67–705) Fifth caliph (685–705) of the UMAYYAD DYNASTY. Raised in Medina, he was forced out with his father in 683 by rebels. Two years later he succeeded to the caliphate and began a seven-year campaign to defeat all rebellions against the Umayyads and reunify the Muslim world. He resumed the conquest of N. Africa, winning the Berbers to his side and capturing Carthage (697). He made Arabic the language of government throughout his domains, struck new, Islamic gold coins to replace Byzantine ones, and built the DOME OF THE ROCK in Jerusalem.

Abd al-Mumin ibn Ali \ˌab-dəl-'mù-min-ˌib-ən-à-'lē\ (d.1163) BERBER caliph (1130–63) of the ALMOHAD DYNASTY. Around 1117 he fell under the sway of Ibn Tumart, founder of the Almohad religious movement, and joined him to oppose the ruling ALMORAVID DYNASTY. He succeeded Ibn Tumart on the latter's death in 1130 and carried on the struggle against the Almoravids. After defeating them at Marrakech in 1147, he massacred the city's inhabitants, then made Marrakech his home base and conquered all of N. Africa west of Egypt.

Abd al-Rahman III \ˌab-dəl-räk̲-'män\ (891–961) First CALIPH and greatest ruler of the Spanish Umayyad dynasty. He succeeded his grandfather Abdullah as emir of CÓRDOBA in 912. He set out immediately to subdue Muslim rebels, which became an annual task until the fall of Toledo in 933. He led the campaigns of Muez (920) and Navarre (924) against Christians in the north. In 928 he declared himself caliph. During his rule, Córdoba was exemplary for its social, political, and cultural development; Christian and Jewish communities flourished, and the city's fame rivaled that of Constantinople.

Abdelqadir al-Jazairi \ˌab-dəl-'käd-ər-al-jaz-'a-i-rē\ (1808–1883) Founder of Algeria and leader of its struggle against the French, who invaded Algeria in 1830. Abdelqadir succeeded his father, Mahieddin, as emir in 1832; by 1837 he had established his rule over most of Algeria's interior, leaving the French in control of some port cities. He imposed equal taxes, suppressed the privileges of the warlike tribes, fortified the interior towns, opened arsenals and workshops, and expanded education. The French overpowered him by 1846. Revered for his exemplary life and ideals, he died respected by both French and Algerians, and he remains the Algerian national hero.

Abdera \ab-'dir-ə\ City of ancient THRACE on the Aegean Sea. First settled in the 7th cent. B.C., it was colonized again around 540 B.C. A prosperous member of the DELIAN LEAGUE, it was the home of DEMOCRITUS and PROTAGORAS.

abdominal cavity Largest hollow space of the body, between the DIAPHRAGM and the top of the pelvic cavity and surrounded by the spine and the abdominal muscles and others. It contains most of the ALIMENTARY CANAL, the LIVER, PANCREAS, SPLEEN, KIDNEYS, and ADRENAL GLANDS. The membrane lining it is the peritoneum.

Abdulhamid II \ˌab-dəl-ha-'mēd\ (1842–1918) Ottoman sultan (1876–1909) under whose rule the TANZIMAT reform movement reached its climax. After initially promoting the first Ottoman constitution, he suspended it 14 months later and ruled as a despot. He used Pan-Islamism to rally Muslim opinion outside his empire. Discontent with his absolutist rule and resentment over European intervention in the Balkans resulted in his overthrow by the YOUNG TURKS in 1908. See also M. K. ATATURK, ENVER PASA.

Abdul-Jabbar \ˌab-dəl-jə-'bär\, **Kareem** *orig.* **(Ferdinand) Lew(is) Alcindor** (b.1947) U.S. basketball player. Born in New York City, he reached a height of 7 ft 1³/₈ in. (2 m 17 cm). He led UCLA to three national championships (1966–68), then joined the Milwaukee Bucks; in 1975 he was traded to the Los Angeles Lakers. The dominant center of his time, in 1984 he surpassed Wilt CHAMBERLAIN's career scoring total of 31,419 points, and by the time he retired in

1989 he had scored 38,387 points. He also holds the record for most field goals (15,837) and ranks second for most blocked shots (3,189) and games played (1,560). He was voted Most Valuable Player a record six times.

Abel See CAIN AND ABEL

Abelard, Peter (1079–1142) French theologian and philosopher. The son of a knight, he abandoned his inheritance to study philosophy. Sometime around 1114, he became private tutor to Héloïse, niece of a canon in Paris; they fell in love and married secretly. Her wrathful uncle had Abelard castrated, after which he became a monk and Héloïse became a nun. Abelard's *Theologia* was condemned as heretical in 1121. From around 1135 Abelard taught and wrote at Mont-Sainte-Geneviève, where he wrote *Ethica,* in which he analyzed the notion of sin. In 1140 he was again condemned for heresy, and he withdrew to the monastery at CLUNY. His other works include *Sic et non,* a collection of contradictory writings by church fathers.

Aberdeen City (pop., 2000 est.: 211,000) and commercial port on the North Sea, E Scotland. Situated at the mouths of the Dee and Don rivers, it is the chief port of N Scotland. It was a royal burgh from the 12th cent. and a Scottish royal residence in the 12th–14th cent. It supported ROBERT I the Bruce in wars for Scottish independence, and for a time was the headquarters of EDWARD I. From the 1970s Aberdeen developed rapidly as the principal British center of the North Sea oil industry.

Aberhart \'ā-bər-ˌhärt\, **William** (1878–1943) Canadian politician. Born in Kippen, Ontario, he was a high-school principal in Calgary (1915–35) and a lay preacher. In 1932 he used his evangelical rhetoric to promote monetary-reform theories to solve Alberta's Depression-era problems, proposing to issue dividends (social credit) to each person, based on the real wealth of the province. When his Social Credit party won a majority in 1935, he became Alberta's premier, but his social-credit proposals were disallowed by the federal government.

Abernathy \'ab-ər-ˌnath-ē\, **Ralph David** (1926–1990) U.S. pastor and civil rights leader. Born in Linden, Ala., he was ordained a Baptist minister and led a church in Montgomery, Ala., where he met M. L. KING. In 1955–56 the two men organized a nonviolent boycott of the city bus system, which marked the beginning of the CIVIL RIGHTS MOVEMENT. In 1957 they founded the SOUTHERN CHRISTIAN LEADERSHIP CONFERENCE; Abernathy served as its president 1968–77.

abhijna \ə-'bij-nə\ In Buddhist philosophy, the miraculous powers obtained through meditation and wisdom. They include the ability to travel any distance or take any form at will, to see and hear everything, to read minds, and to recall former existences. The powers are signs of spiritual progress, but their indulgence is a distraction from the path toward Enlightenment.

Abidjan \ˌä-bē-'jän\ Largest city (pop., 2001 est.: 2,900,000) and chief port of Ivory Coast. Abidjan was a rail terminus from 1904; after its lagoon was opened to the sea to create a port (1950), the city became the financial center of FRENCH W. AFRICA. Though it was once the country's capital and remains its seat of government, the official capital was moved to YAMOUSSOUKRO in 1983.

Abilene Town (pop., 1998 est.: 6,000), Kansas. It lies on the Smoky Hill River east of Salina. Settled in 1858, it became the railway terminus for Texas cattle drives and acquired a reputation for lawlessness; Wild Bill HICKOK was its marshal in 1871. Pres. Dwight EISENHOWER grew up there and is buried at the Eisenhower Center.

ABM See ANTIBALLISTIC MISSILE

abnormal psychology *or* **psychopathology** Psychology of mental and emotional disorders (e.g., NEUROSIS, PSYCHOSIS, mental deficiency) and certain incompletely understood normal phenomena (such as DREAMS and HYPNOSIS). The chief tool used in classifying psychological disorders is the American Psychiatric Assn.'s *Diagnostic and Statistical Manual of Mental Disorders,* 4th ed. *(DSM–IV).*

ABO blood-group system Classification of human BLOOD according to whether red blood cells (ERYTHROCYTES) have or lack the inherited ANTIGENS called A (including A1 and A2) and B on their surface. Blood can be type O (lacking both), type A (having only A), type B (having only B), or type AB (having both). The ABO antigens make certain blood types incompatible for BLOOD TRANSFUSION. The frequencies of blood groups vary among racial groups and geographic areas. Certain diseases are rarer in persons with particular blood groups.

abolitionism (c.1783–1888) Movement to end the SLAVE TRADE and emancipate slaves in W Europe and the Americas. Antislavery sentiment gradually gained support in England in the 18th cent., but initially had little impact on the centers of slavery—the W. Indies, S. America, and the S U.S. In 1807 British and U.S. abolitionists successfully banned the importation of African slaves, and turned their attention to winning the emancipation of slaves already in captivity. The 11 Southern states of the U.S., however, clung to slavery as a social and economic institution. The AMERICAN ANTI-SLAVERY SOCIETY fueled the abolitionist movement in the North; leaders included W. L. GARRISON, Frederick DOUGLASS, and H. B. STOWE. The election of Abraham LINCOLN, who opposed the spread of slavery into the West, marked the issue's turning point; the AMERICAN CIVIL WAR led to the EMANCIPATION PROCLAMATION (1863) and the 13th Amendment to the U.S. Constitution (1865), freeing all slaves in the nation. Slavery was finally abolished in Latin America by 1888.

Abominable Snowman *Tibetan* **Yeti** Mythical monster believed to inhabit the HIMALAYAS near the snow line. The Yeti is thought to resemble an oversized man covered with shaggy fur. Reported sightings are rare; evidence of its existence consists largely of unusual footprints left in the snow, probably the overlapping footprints of bears.

Aborigine See AUSTRALIAN ABORIGINE

abortion Expulsion of a FETUS from the UTERUS before it can survive on its own. Induced abortions today are performed to preserve the mother's life or health, to prevent the completion of a pregnancy resulting from rape or incest, to prevent the birth of a child with serious medical problems, or because the mother does not believe she is in a position to rear a child properly. During the first 12 weeks of pregnancy, abortions are performed by sucking or scraping out the contents of the uterus. The drug RU 486, if taken within a few weeks of conception, will trigger a MISCARRIAGE. Up to about 19 weeks of pregnancy, injections of saline solutions or hormones may be used. Surgical removal of the contents of the uterus may be used in the second trimester or later. The social acceptability of abortion as a means of population control has varied from time to time and place to place throughout history. It was apparently a common method of family limitation in the Greco-Roman world, but Christian theologians early and vehemently condemned it. It became widely accepted in Europe in the Middle Ages. Severe criminal sanctions to deter abortion became common in the 19th cent., but in the 20th cent. those sanctions were gradually modified in many countries. See also *Roe vs. Wade.*

Abraham (fl. early 2nd millennium B.C.) First of the Hebrew PATRIARCHS, revered in JUDAISM, CHRISTIANITY, and ISLAM. GENESIS tells how Abraham, at 75, left UR with his barren wife Sarai (later SARAH) and others to found a new nation in CANAAN. There God made a COVENANT with him, promising that his descendants would inherit the land and become a great nation. Abraham fathered Ishmael by Sarah's maidservant Hagar; Sarah herself bore ISAAC, who inherited the covenant. Abraham's faith was tested when God ordered him to sacrifice Isaac; he was prepared to obey but God relented. In Judaism he is a model of virtue, in Christianity he is the father of all believers, and in Islam he is an ancestor of MUHAMMAD.

Abraham, Plains of Plateau located southwest of the old walled city of QUEBEC, Canada. On Sept. 13, 1759, it was the scene of the decisive battle of the FRENCH AND INDIAN WAR, in which the British under James WOLFE defeated the French under the Marquis de MONTCALM. U.S. forces held the plateau (1775–76) in their siege of Quebec during the AMERICAN REVOLUTION.

abrasives Sharp, hard materials used to wear away the surface of softer, less resistant materials. Abrasives are indispensable to the manufacture of the highly precise compo-

nents and ultrasmooth surfaces required in automobiles, airplanes and space vehicles, electrical appliances, and machine tools. Abrasives may be natural (e.g., DIAMOND, CORUNDUM, emery) or synthetic (e.g., silicon CARBIDE or Carborundum, synthetic diamond). They range from the relatively soft particles used in household cleansers and jeweler's polish to diamonds.

Abruzzi \ä-'brüt-sē\ Autonomous region (pop., 2001: 1,294,000), central Italy. Its capital is L'AQUILA. It includes the APENNINES. The ancient Italic tribes of the region long resisted conquest by the Romans. The Normans established themselves in the 12th cent., and the region later sided with the HOHENSTAUFENS against the papacy. The area became part of the Kingdom of Italy in 1861.

Absalom (fl.c.1020 B.C.) In ancient Israel, the third and most beloved son of DAVID. His story is told in II Samuel 13–19. He killed his half-brother Amnon as revenge for the latter's rape of Tamar, Absalom's sister, and was banished for a time. He later raised a rebellion against his father but met defeat in the forest of Ephraim, where he was killed by his cousin Joab, who found him caught by the hair in an oak tree. Despite Absalom's treachery, David greatly lamented his death.

abscess \'ab-ˌses\ Localized collection of pus in a cavity on the skin or within the body, formed in response to INFLAMMATION caused by bacteria. A wall develops, separating the thick yellowish pus (formed from broken-down tissues, dead bacteria, and LEUKOCYTES) from the extracellular fluid of nearby healthy tissues. Rupture of the abscess allows the pus to escape and relieves swelling and pain. Treatment consists of cutting to drain the pus and giving antibiotics. If infective contents enter the bloodstream, they may seed new abscesses. See also BOIL.

absolute value Measure of the magnitude of a REAL NUMBER, COMPLEX NUMBER, or VECTOR. Geometrically, the absolute value of any real number is its distance from zero. Thus if the number a is positive or zero, its absolute value is itself; if a is negative, its absolute value is $-a$. The absolute value of the complex number $a + bi$ is the real number $\sqrt{a^2 + b^2}$. The absolute value of a vector is its length. In all three cases, absolute value is symbolized by vertical bars, as in $|x|$, $|z|$, or $|v|$. Such expressions are always nonnegative and obey the properties $|a \cdot b| = |a| \cdot |b|$ and $|a + b| \leq |a| + |b|$.

absolute zero Temperature at which a thermodynamic system (see THERMODYNAMICS) has the lowest ENERGY, 0 kelvin (0 K), corresponding to $-459.67°F$ ($-273.15°C$). A gas at constant pressure contracts as the temperature is decreased. An IDEAL GAS would reach zero volume at absolute zero. However, a real gas condenses to a liquid or a solid at a temperature higher than absolute zero. At absolute zero, the system's molecular energy is minimal and none is available for transfer to other systems.

absolution In Christianity, a pronouncement of forgiveness of SINS made to a person who has repented. This rite is based on the forgiveness that JESUS extended to sinners during his ministry. In ROMAN CATHOLICISM penance is a SACRAMENT, and the priest has the power to absolve a contrite sinner who promises to make satisfaction to God during CONFESSION. In Protestant churches, the confession of sin is usually made in a formal prayer by the whole congregation, after which the minister announces their absolution.

absolutism Political doctrine of centralized authority and absolute sovereignty, especially as vested in a monarch. The ruling power is not subject to regular challenge or check by any judicial, legislative, religious, or electoral agency. Though it has been used throughout history, the form that developed in Europe in the 16th–18th cent. became the prototype, exemplified by LOUIS XIV. The monarch became the head of the church as well as the state, on the basis that the right to rule came from God. See also AUTHORITARIANISM, DICTATORSHIP.

absorption Transfer of ENERGY from a wave to the medium through which it passes. (In general, a wave's energy can be reflected, transmitted, or absorbed.) If the medium absorbs only a fraction of the energy, it is said to be transparent to that energy. When all energy is absorbed, the medium is opaque. All substances absorb energy to some extent, and absorb specific types of RADIATION completely. Rubber is transparent to INFRARED RADIATION and X RAYS, but opaque to visible LIGHT. Green glass is transparent to green light but absorbs red and blue light. Absorption of SOUND is fundamental to ACOUSTICS.

abstract art Art, including painting, sculpture, and graphic art, that does not represent recognizable objects. In the late 19th cent., the traditional European conception of art as the imitation of nature was abandoned in favor of the imagination and the unconscious. Abstraction developed in the early 20th cent. with such movements as FAUVISM, EXPRESSIONISM, CUBISM, and FUTURISM. Vasily KANDINSKY is credited as the first modern artist to paint purely abstract pictures (c.1910). The DADA group in Zurich and Piet MONDRIAN and the De STIJL group widened the spectrum (c.1915–20). After the 1930s abstraction was the most characteristic feature of 20th-cent. art. After World War II, ABSTRACT EXPRESSIONISM had a great influence on European and American painting and sculpture.

Abstract Expressionism Movement in U.S. painting that began in the late 1940s. It had two notable forerunners, Arshile GORKY and Hans HOFMANN, and the arrival of many European avant-garde artists greatly influenced the New York painters, most prominent among them Jackson POLLOCK, Willem DE KOONING, Franz KLINE, and Mark ROTHKO. The movement comprised many styles but shared several characteristics. The works were usually abstract (see ABSTRACT ART); they emphasized freedom of emotional expression and execution; they displayed a single unified field or image in unstructured space; and the canvases were large, projecting monumentality and power. The movement had a great impact on U.S. and European art in the 1950s; it marked the shift of the creative center of modern painting from Paris to New York.

absurd, theater of the Body of dramatic works of the 1950s and '60s that expressed the existentialist philosophy of the absurdity of life. Such playwrights as Edward ALBEE, Samuel BECKETT, Jean GENET, Eugène IONESCO, and Harold PINTER created absurdist plays without traditional plots and with characters who engaged in circular, purposeless conversations. Beckett's *Waiting for Godot* (1953) is a classic of the genre.

Abu Bakr \ə-ˌbü-'bä-kər\ (573?–634) MUHAMMAD's father-in-law, adviser, and close companion. He became the first CALIPH after Muhammad's death in 632, and during his two-year reign he consolidated central Arabia under Muslim control, ending the resistance to Muslim hegemony. He also realized the urgency of rapidly expanding the regions under Muslim control if peace was to be maintained among Arab tribes.

Abu Dhabi Largest emirate (pop., 1999 est.: 1,127,000) of the United Arab Emirates. Its rich oil fields make it, after DUBAYY, the federation's most prosperous emirate. It fronts the PERSIAN GULF and borders Qatar, Saudi Arabia, and Oman. Since the 18th cent. the Al bu Falah clan has held power. In 1761 they found potable water at the site of ABU DHABI city, and they made their headquarters there from 1795. Territorial conflicts with MASQAT and Oman and the ancestors of Saudi Arabia's rulers led to border disputes, most still unsettled. An agreement with Britain in 1892 placed foreign affairs under British control. When Britain withdrew from the Persian Gulf in 1968, Abu Dhabi and the other Trucial States formed the United Arab Emirates.

Abu Dhabi City (pop., 1995: 398,000), capital of ABU DHABI emirate and national capital of the United Arab Emirates. It occupies a small island. Settled in 1761, it was of little importance until the discovery of the emirate's rich oil fields in 1958. Oil royalties revolutionized its political and economic position, and it has ambitiously modernized.

Abuja \ä-'bü-jä\ City (pop., 1995 est.: 423,000), federal capital of Nigeria. Construction of the city, about 300 mi (480 km) northwest of LAGOS, began in 1976 under the architect Kenzo TANGE. It officially replaced Lagos as capital in 1991.

Abu Muslim \ə-ˌbü-'mu̇s-lim\ (d.755) Leader of a revolutionary movement that brought down the UMAYYAD DYNASTY. Born a Muslim of humble origins, he met an Abbasid agent while in prison (741). After his arranged release he was sent

to Khorasan, Persia (745–46), to instigate a revolt. He succeeded in overthrowing the last Umayyad caliph, Marwan II, and was rewarded with the governorship of Khorasan. His popularity led the second Abbasid caliph, Abu al-Mansur, to view him as a threat and have him put to death. See also ABBASID DYNASTY.

Abu Simbel Site of two temples built by RAMSES II in the 13th cent. B.C. The area, anciently at the S frontier of pharaonic Egypt, lies near the modern Sudanese frontier. The temples were discovered in 1813. The larger temple displays four 67-ft (20-m) seated figures of Ramses; the smaller was dedicated to Queen Nefertari. When the ASWAN HIGH DAM project threatened to submerge the site in the early 1960s, an international team disassembled and reconstructed both temples 200 ft (60 m) above the riverbed.

Abu Simbel Sandstone figures of Ramses II

Abydos Ancient Anatolian town northeast of modern Canakkale, Turkey, on the E side of the DARDANELLES. It was colonized about 670 B.C. by the Milesians (see MILETUS). Abydos is celebrated for its resistance to PHILIP V of Macedon in 200 B.C. and for the legend of HERO AND LEANDER.

Abydos \ə-'bī-dəs\ Sacred city, one of the most important archaeological sites of ancient Egypt. It was a royal necropolis of the first two dynasties, and later a pilgrimage center for the worship of OSIRIS. The pharaohs, embellished the temple to Osiris, and some pharaohs had CENOTAPHS at Abydos. The temple of Seti I, one of the most beautiful, helped decode Egyptian history through a long relief, the so-called Abydos list of kings.

abyssal plain \ə-'bis-əl\ Flat seafloor area at a depth of 10,000–20,000 ft (3,000–6,000 m), generally adjacent to a continent. The larger plains, hundreds of miles wide and thousands of miles long, are most common in the Atlantic Ocean; in the Pacific Ocean, plains occur mainly as small, flat floors of marginal seas or as long, narrow bottoms of trenches. They are thought to be the upper surfaces of land-derived sediment that accumulates in abyssal depressions.

Abyssinia See ETHIOPIA

AC See ALTERNATING CURRENT

acacia \ə-'kā-shə\ Any of the approximately 800 species of trees and shrubs that make up the genus *Acacia,* of the MIMOSA family, native to tropical and subtropical regions of the world, particularly Australia and Africa. Acacias have distinctive, finely divided leaflets, and their leafstalks may bear thorns or sharp spines. Their small, often fragrant, yellow or white flowers have many stamens apiece, giving each a fuzzy appearance. Several species are important economically, yielding substances such as gum arabic and tannin, as well as valuable timber.

academic degree See academic DEGREE

Académie Française \à-kà-dā-'mē-frä^n-'sez\ French literary academy founded by Cardinal de RICHELIEU in 1634 to maintain standards of literary taste and to set the literary language. In modern times it has tried to purify French of foreign words. It is limited to 40 members. Many of France's great writers, including Jean RACINE, VOLTAIRE, and Victor HUGO, have been members.

academy Learned society organized to advance some cultural or intellectual area of endeavor. The word comes from the name of an olive grove outside ancient Athens, the site of PLATO's famous school of philosophy in the 4th cent. B.C. Academies appeared in Italy in the 15th cent. and reached their greatest influence in the 17th–18th cent. Most European countries now have at least one academy sponsored by or otherwise connected with the state. See also ACADÉMIE FRANÇAISE.

Academy Awards Annual awards of merit presented by the Academy of Motion Picture Arts and Sciences. Formed in 1927 by L. B. MAYER and others to raise the standards of film production, it presented its first awards in 1929. The awards (nicknamed Oscars when an Academy librarian joked that the gold-plated statuette looked like her Uncle Oscar) recognize excellence in acting, directing, screenwriting, and other activities related to film production.

Acadia N. American possession of France in the 17th–18th cent., centered in what is now NOVA SCOTIA. The first European settlement was made by the French colonizer Sieur de Monts in 1604. The area was contested often in the 18th-cent. colonial wars; in 1713 Nova Scotia came under British rule. In 1755 many French-speaking Acadians were deported by the British because of imminent war with France; several thousand settled in French-ruled Louisiana, where their descendants were known as CAJUNS. The event was the theme for H. W. LONGFELLOW's *Evangeline.*

acanthus \ə-'kan-thəs\ Any of the plants that make up the family Acanthaceae. Most are herbaceous forest plants or shrubs; some are climbers (vines) or trees. Most grow in damp tropical forests. Acanthus have simple leaves arranged in opposite pairs on the twigs, and bilaterally symmetrical, bisexual flowers usually crowded together in clusters and individually enclosed by leaflike bracts, often colored and large. They are mainly of horticultural interest and include some ornamentals. The acanthus leaf was a prominent motif in classical art and architecture.

Acapulco (de Juárez) Seaport (pop., 2001: 640,000), SW Mexico. Situated on a deep semicircular bay, it has the best harbor on Mexico's Pacific coast. It was discovered by Hernán CORTÉS in 1531, and a settlement was founded in 1550. Until 1815 it was a main depot for Spanish colonial fleets going to E. Asia. It has become a major international resort.

acceleration Rate of change of VELOCITY. Acceleration, like velocity, is a VECTOR quantity: it has both magnitude and direction. The velocity of an object moving on a straight path can change in magnitude only, so its acceleration is the rate of change of its speed. On a curved path, the velocity may or may not change in magnitude, but it will always change in direction. If velocity is stated in meters per second (m/s) and the time interval in seconds (s), then the units of acceleration are meters per second per second (m/s/s, or m/s^2). See also CENTRIPETAL ACCELERATION.

accelerator, particle See PARTICLE ACCELERATOR

accelerometer \ik-,se-lə-'rä-mə-tər\ Instrument that measures ACCELERATION. Because it is difficult to measure acceleration directly, the device measures the FORCE exerted by restraints placed on a reference mass to hold its position fixed in an accelerating body. Accelerometers are used in varied applications: control of industrial vibration test equipment, detection of earthquakes (seismographs), and input to navigational and inertial guidance systems.

acclimatization Any gradual, long-term response of an individual organism to changes in its environment. The responses are more or less habitual and reversible. These criteria differentiate acclimatization from HOMEOSTASIS; from growth and development (which cannot be reversed); and from evolutionary adaptation (which occurs in a population over generations). Examples include adaptations to seasonal changes and adjustments to changes in altitude.

accordion Portable musical instrument that uses a hand-pumped bellows and two keyboards to sound free reeds, small metal tongues that vibrate when air flows past them. The right-hand keyboard plays the treble line or lines. Most of the keys on the left-hand (bass) keyboard sound three-note chords; "free-bass" accordions permit the playing of single-note lines. A prototype accordion was patented in 1822 by Friedrich Buschmann, inventor of the HARMONICA. The instrument gained wide popularity in dance bands and as a folk instrument.

accounting Systematic development and analysis of information about the economic affairs of an organization. The actual recording and summarizing of financial transactions is known as BOOKKEEPING. Abstracting such data into reports for outside use is called financial accounting. Three reports are typically generated in financial accounting: the BALANCE SHEET, which summarizes the firm's assets and liabilities; the income statement, which reports the firm's gross proceeds, expenses, and profit or loss; and the statement of cash flow, which analyzes the flow of cash into and out of the firm. The creation of reports (usually monthly) for internal managerial use is called managerial accounting; its aim is to provide managers with reliable cost information to assist in budgeting.

Accra \'ä-krə, ə-'krä\ Capital and largest city (pop., 1995 est.: 1,000,000) of Ghana, on the Gulf of GUINEA. The Portuguese first settled on the coast in 1482. In 1650–80 the English, the Danes, and the Dutch built fortified trading posts. The Danes and Dutch left the region in 1850 and 1872, respectively, and in 1877 Accra became the capital of the British GOLD COAST colony. Today it is Ghana's administrative, economic, and educational center.

acetaminophen \ə-ˌsē-tə-'min-ə-fən\ Organic compound, an ANALGESIC drug. Unlike ASPIRIN, it has no anti-inflammatory effect. It is also less likely to irritate the stomach, is not linked with REYE'S SYNDROME, and can be taken by persons using ANTICOAGULANTS or allergic to aspirin. Overdoses can cause fatal liver damage. The most familiar brand name in the U.S. is Tylenol. See also IBUPROFEN.

acetic acid \ə-'sē-tik\ Most important CARBOXYLIC ACID. Pure ("glacial") acetic acid is a clear, syrupy, corrosive liquid that mixes readily with water. VINEGAR is its dilute solution, from FERMENTATION and oxidation (see OXIDATION-REDUCTION) of natural products. Its SALTS and ESTERS are acetates. It occurs naturally in body fluids and plant juices. Industrial production is either synthetic, from ACETYLENE, or biological, from ETHANOL. Plastics, photographic films, textiles, and solvents are made from it.

acetone \'a-sə-ˌtōn\ *or* **dimethyl ketone** \dī-'me-thəl-'kē-ˌtōn\ Simplest and most important KETONE. It is a colorless, flammable liquid. Many materials dissolve easily in it, so it is used to make artificial fibers, explosives, resins, paints, inks, cosmetics (including nail-polish remover), coatings, and adhesives. Acetone is an important industrial raw material.

acetylene \ə-'se-tᵊl-ən\ *or* **ethyne** \'e-ˌthīn\ Simplest alkyne, C_2H_2. A colorless, flammable, explosive gas, it is used as a fuel in welding and cutting metals and as a raw material for many organic compounds and plastics. Decomposing it liberates heat. An acetylene torch reaches about 6,000°F (3,300°C), hotter than combustion of any other known gas mixture. See also HYDROCARBON.

Achaean League \ə-'kē-ən\ 3rd-cent.-B.C. confederation of towns of Achaea, an area in the N Peloponnese of ancient Greece. Twelve cities had joined together by the 4th cent. B.C. to combat piracy, but they disbanded after the death of ALEXANDER THE GREAT. Ten cities renewed the league in 280 B.C., later admitting non-Achaean cities to defend themselves against Macedonia, then Sparta, and finally Rome. Rome dissolved the league after defeating it in 146 B.C. A later league existed into the Roman imperial age.

Achaemenian dynasty \ˌa-kə-'mē-nē-ən\ (7th cent. B.C.–330 B.C.) Persian dynasty. Achaemenes, its founder, is thought to have lived in the early 7th cent. B.C. From his son Teispes were descended two lines of kings. The older line included Cyrus I, Cambyses I, CYRUS II (the Great), and Cambyses II; the junior line began with DARIUS I and ended with the death of Darius III after his defeat by ALEXANDER THE GREAT (330 B.C.). Its other great ruler was XERXES I, who completed many of Darius's public works. At its

height, the Achaemenian empire reached from Macedonia to N India and from the Caucasus Mtns. to the Persian Gulf. The ruins of PERSEPOLIS survive from its golden age.

Achebe \ä-'chā-bā\, **(Albert) Chinua(iumogu)** (b.1930) Nigerian Igbo novelist. He is acclaimed for showing the disorienting effects of imposing Western customs and values on traditional African society. *Things Fall Apart* (1958) and *Arrow of God* (1964) portray traditional Igbo life as it clashes with colonialism. *No Longer at Ease* (1960), *A Man of the People* (1966), and *Anthills of the Savannah* (1988) deal with corruption and other aspects of postcolonial African life.

Acheson \'a-chə-sən\, **Dean (Gooderham)** (1893–1971) U.S. secretary of state (1949–53). Born in Middletown, Conn., he practiced law in Washington, D.C., before joining the State Department (1941). In 1947 he helped design the TRUMAN DOCTRINE and the MARSHALL PLAN. As secretary of state under Harry TRUMAN, he promoted the formation of NATO and was a principal creator of U.S. foreign policy in the Cold War. He established the policies of nonrecognition of Red China and aid to the regime of CHIANG KAI-SHEK in Taiwan, and he supported U.S. aid to the French colonial regime in Indochina. After leaving office, he continued to advise successive presidents. His memoir *Present at the Creation* (1969) won a Pulitzer Prize.

Acheson, Edward Goodrich (1856–1931) U.S. inventor. Born in Washington, Pa., he helped develop the INCANDESCENT LAMP, and in 1881 installed the first electric lights for Thomas EDISON in Italy, Belgium, and France. Attempting to produce artificial diamonds, he created instead the highly effective ABRASIVE material Carborundum. This discovery led to his patenting a GRAPHITE-making process in 1896.

Achilles \ə-'ki-lēz\ In GREEK MYTHOLOGY, the bravest and strongest of the Greek warriors in the TROJAN WAR. Because his mother dipped him into the River STYX, he was invulnerable except at the heel by which she held him. During the war against Troy Achilles took 12 nearby cities, but after a quarrel with AGAMEMNON he refused further service. The death of Achilles' beloved cousin Patroclus at the hands of HECTOR prompted Achilles to return to battle, kill Hector, and drag his body around the walls of Troy. According to one poet, PARIS killed Achilles with an arrow guided by APOLLO.

Achilles Painter (fl.5th cent. B.C.) Greek vase painter, named for an amphora decorated with a painting of Achilles and Briseis attributed to him. He was active in Athens in the time of PERICLES, and was a contemporary of PHIDIAS. His Achilles vase (c.450 B.C.) is among the finest surviving examples of RED-FIGURE POTTERY. His *lekythoi* (funerary vases with colored figures on a white background) are regarded as the most reliable documentation of monumental Greek paintings.

Achinese \ˌa-chə-'nēz\ One of the main ethnic groups on the island of Sumatra, Indonesia. In the 13th cent. they became the first people in the archipelago to adopt Islam. After expelling the Portuguese in the 17th cent., the sultanate of Acheh was dominant in N Sumatra until conquered by the Dutch in 1904. Now part of the Indonesian republic, they are restive and are administered within a special district. They number about 2.1 million.

acid Any substance that in water solution tastes sour, changes the color of acid-base indicators (e.g., LITMUS), reacts with some METALS (e.g., iron) to yield HYDROGEN gas, reacts with BASES to form SALTS, and promotes certain CHEMICAL REACTIONS. Acids contain one or more hydrogen atoms that, in solution, dissociate as positively charged hydrogen IONS. Inorganic acids include SULFURIC ACID, NITRIC ACID, and HYDROCHLORIC ACID. Organic acids include CARBOXYLIC ACIDS and PHENOLS. Broader definitions of acids cover situations in which water is not present (see ACID-BASE THEORY).

acid and basic rocks Division of IGNEOUS ROCKS on the basis of their SILICATE MINERAL content. Rocks are described as acid, intermediate, basic, and ultrabasic, in order of decreasing silica content, because it was earlier thought that silica is present in rock MAGMAS in the form of silicic acid. Today the terms do not refer to acidity in the chemical sense. In general, the gradation from acid to basic corresponds to an increase in color (light to dark).

acid-base theory Any of several theories that give rise to alternative definitions of ACIDS and BASES. The original theory, based on Svante ARRHENIUS's electrolytic theory of solutions, involved the dissociation of water into hydrogen and hydroxide IONS. To explain certain chemicals' behavior, other theories were developed. One is the Brønsted-Lowry definition (1923): An acid is a chemical that tends to lose a PROTON (H⁺), and a base is a chemical that tends to gain a proton. Another is the Lewis definition (also 1923): An acid (see ELECTROPHILE) is a chemical that can accept an ELECTRON pair from a base (see NUCLEOPHILE), which they share to form a COVALENT BOND. The three theories have superficial similarities but subtle and important differences for certain applications.

acid rain Any precipitation, including snow, that contains a heavy concentration of SULFURIC and NITRIC ACIDS. Automobiles, factories, and power plants that burn FOSSIL FUELS emit sulfur dioxide and nitrogen oxides into the atmosphere, where they combine with water vapor to form acids. The resultant highly acidic precipitation may contaminate lakes and streams, harming fish and other aquatic species; damage vegetation, including agricultural crops and trees; and corrode the outsides of buildings. Most severe around large urban and industrial areas, it can also occur at great distances from the source of the pollutants.

ACLU See AMERICAN CIVIL LIBERTIES UNION

acne \'ak-nē\ Any of some 50 inflammatory diseases of the oil glands of the SKIN. Acne vulgaris, probably the most frequent chronic skin disorder, results from an interplay of hereditary factors, hormones, and bacteria, beginning in the teen years when overactive SEBACEOUS GLANDS are stimulated by high levels of ANDROGENS. The primary lesion (blackhead) consists of a plug of skin oil (sebum), cell debris, and microorganisms in a hair follicle. Acne has four grades of severity, with increasing degrees of spread, inflammation, pustule formation, and scarring. Lower grades generally respond to treatment (skin medication, sunlight, antibiotics, and hormones); many cases eventually resolve spontaneously.

Acoma \'ä-kō-mə\ Indian pueblo, W central New Mexico. Located west of ALBUQUERQUE, the "Sky City," with its terraced dwellings made of stone and adobe, lies atop a sandstone butte 357 ft (109 m) high. Settled in the 10th cent., it is believed to be the oldest continuously inhabited place in the U.S. In 1540 Spanish explorer Francisco CORONADO described it as the strongest defensive position in the world.

Aconcagua \ˌä-kōn-'kä-gwä\, **Mt.** Mountain, W Argentina, on the Chilean border. At 22,834 ft (6,960 m) high, it is the highest peak of the ANDES and of the Western Hemisphere. The summit was first reached in 1897.

acoustics \ə-'kü-stiks\ Science of production, control, transmission, reception, and effects of SOUND. Its principal branches are architectural, environmental, musical, and engineering acoustics, and ULTRASONICS. Environmental acoustics focuses on controlling noise produced by aircraft engines, factories, construction machinery, and general traffic. Musical acoustics deals with the design and use of musical instruments and how musical sounds affect listeners. Engineering acoustics concerns sound recording and reproduction systems.

acquired immunodeficiency syndrome See AIDS

Acre \'ä-krə, 'ä-kər\ *or* **Akko** \'ä-kō\ Seaport city (pop., 1994 est.: 45,000), NW Israel on the Mediterranean coast. First mentioned in the 19th cent. B.C., it was ruled by Egyptians, Romans, Persians, and Arabs. The crusaders captured it from the SELJUQ Turks in 1104 and made it their capital as St. Jean d'Acre (see CRUSADES). It was chiefly ruled by Ottoman Turks from 1516 until British forces took it in 1918. It was part of Palestine under the British mandate and became part of Israel in 1948. Notable structures include the Great Mosque and the Crypt of St. John.

acropolis (Greek: "city at the top") Central, defensively oriented district in ancient Greek cities, located on the highest ground and containing the chief municipal and religious buildings. The renowned Athens Acropolis (5th cent. B.C.) is home to four main marble edifices—the Propylaea, PARTHENON, Erechtheum (Ionic temple noted for its CARYATID porch), and Temple of Athena Nike.

Acropolis, Athens

acrylic compound Any of a class of synthetic plastics, resins, and oils used to manufacture many products. With different starting reagents (such as acrylic acid or acrylonitrile) and processes, a material may be produced that is hard and transparent, soft and resilient, or a thick liquid. Acrylic compounds are used to make molded structural and optical parts, jewelry, adhesives, coating compounds, and textile fibers. Lucite and Plexiglas are familiar trademarks.

acting Art of representing a character on a stage or before a camera. Acting in the Western tradition originated in Greece in the 6th cent. B.C.; THESPIS is traditionally regarded as the first actor. ARISTOTLE defined acting as "the right management of the voice to express various emotions" and declared it a natural gift that he doubted could be taught. Acting declined as an art in the Middle Ages, then emerged in the 16th cent. with Italy's COMMEDIA DELL'ARTE troupes. It flourished during the era of William SHAKESPEARE. Not until the 18th cent., however, was acting considered a serious profession, through the efforts in England of the actor-manager David GARRICK and the talents of such actors as Sarah SIDDONS and Edmund KEAN. Modern acting styles have been influenced by K. STANISLAVSKY's emphasis on the actor's identification with his role and by Bertolt BRECHT's insistence on the objectivity and discipline of the actor. The STANISLAVSKY METHOD was adapted in the U.S. by Lee STRASBERG and Stella Adler (1901–1992) and is the basis of most contemporary training.

actinide \'ak-tə-ˌnīd\ Any of 15 consecutive chemical ELEMENTS in the PERIODIC TABLE from actinium to lawrencium (ATOMIC NUMBERS 89–103). All are radioactive heavy METALS; and only the first four occur in nature in appreciable quantities. The other 11 (the transuranium elements) are unstable and are produced only artificially. Actinides are TRANSITION ELEMENTS; the most usual VALENCES are 3 and 4.

actinomycete \ˌak-ti-nō-'mī-sēt\ Any of a group of gram-positive (see GRAM STAIN) BACTERIA identified by a growth pattern that results in large threadlike structures. The filaments may break into fragments. Some actinomycetes can form spores. Many species occur harmlessly in soil; others are important disease-causing agents. Many ANTIBIOTICS (e.g., TETRACYCLINE, streptomycin) come from actinomycetes, especially STREPTOMYCES.

action painting Dynamic style of painting that involves the spontaneous application of vigorous, sweeping brush strokes and the chance effects of dripping and spilling paint onto the canvas. A major force in ABSTRACT EXPRESSIONISM in the 1950s, it characterizes the work of Jackson POLLOCK, Willem DE KOONING, and Franz KLINE. The "automatic" techniques developed earlier in Europe by the Surrealists influenced U.S. artists, who regarded a picture not merely as a finished product but as a record of the process of its creation.

action potential Brief (about one-thousandth of a second) reversal of electric polarization of the membrane of a nerve or muscle cell. Stimulation of the cell by certain chemicals or by sensory receptor cells causes depolarization of the membrane, permitting an impulse to move along the nerve fiber (in nerve cells) or causing the cell to contract (in muscle cells).

Actium \'ak-shē-əm\, **Battle of** (31 B.C.) Naval battle off Acarnania, W Greece, between Octavian (later AUGUSTUS) and Mark ANTONY. Deserted by allies, lacking supplies, and outmaneuvered on land, Antony attacked Octavian at sea from his camp at Actium. Antony's larger fleet included his own and CLEOPATRA's ships. In the heat of battle Cleopatra fled with her galleys, and Antony followed with a few ships. His fleet surrendered immediately, his army a week later. Octavian's victory left him undisputed ruler of the Roman world.

activation energy Minimum amount of ENERGY (HEAT, ELECTROMAGNETIC RADIATION, or electrical energy) required to activate ATOMS or MOLECULES to a condition in which it is equally likely that they will undergo chemical reaction or transport as it is that they will return to their original state. Supposing there is a transition state between the initial conditions and the product conditions, the activation energy is the amount of energy required to boost the initial materials "uphill" to the transition state; the reaction then proceeds "downhill" to form the products. CATALYSTS (including ENZYMES) lower the activation energy by altering the transition state. Activation energies are measured in experiments that study the dependence of REACTION RATE on temperature, proposed by Svante ARRHENIUS. See also ENTROPY.

active galactic nucleus Small region at the center of a GALAXY that emits a prodigious amount of energy as radio, optical, X-ray, or gamma radiation or high-speed particle jets. Many classes of "active galaxies" have been identified; they have many similarities to QUASARS. The observed energy may be generated as matter accretes onto a BLACK HOLE millions or billions of times as massive as the sun. This matter can outshine the rest of the galaxy as it is heated in very high-speed collisions outside the EVENT HORIZON. Many galaxies may harbor central black holes and might once have been quasars but now appear to be dormant unless orbiting matter is accreting onto the black hole.

Act of Union See Act of UNION

actor-manager system Method of theatrical production prevalent in 19th-cent. England and the U.S. An actor formed a theater company, chose the plays, played the leading roles, and managed the company's business arrangements. In the 18th cent. actor-managers such as Colley CIBBER and David GARRICK gained prominence. The system produced high performance standards, typified by such 19th-cent. figures as William MACREADY. It waned as actor-managers were replaced first by stage managers and later by directors.

Actors Studio Professional actors' workshop based in New York. Founded in 1947 by the directors Cheryl Crawford, Elia KAZAN, and Robert Lewis as a leading center of the STANISLAVSKY METHOD, it was directed by Lee STRASBERG from 1948 to 1982. Actors work together without the pressures of commercial production. Six or seven new members are chosen yearly from 1,000 auditions. Members have included Marlon BRANDO, Marilyn MONROE, Paul NEWMAN, and Robert DE NIRO.

actuary One who calculates insurance risks and premiums. Actuaries compute the probability of the occurrence of such events as birth, marriage, illness, accidents, and death. They also evaluate the hazards of property damage or loss and the legal liability for the safety and well-being of others. Usually employed by insurance companies, actuaries set premium rates based on statistical studies, establish underwriting procedures, and determine the amounts of money required to assure the payment of benefits.

Acuff \'ā-kəf\, **Roy (Claxton)** (1903–1992) U.S. singer, songwriter, and fiddler. Born in Maynardsville, Tenn., he turned to music after an aborted baseball career and gained immediate popularity with "The Great Speckled Bird" and "The Wabash Cannonball." He became a national radio star on the GRAND OLE OPRY, and in 1942 he and Fred Rose (1897–1954) founded the first publishing house exclusively for country music. In 1962 Acuff was elected the first living member of the Country Music Hall of Fame.

acupressure *or* **shiatsu** \shē-'ät-sü\ ALTERNATIVE-MEDICINE practice, developed in ancient China, in which pressure is applied to points on the body aligned along 12 main meridians (pathways), usually for a short time, to improve the flow of vital force (QI). A single point may be pressed to relieve a specific symptom or condition, or a series of points can be worked on to promote overall well-being. Some studies suggest that acupressure can be effective for certain health problems, including nausea, pain, and stroke-related weakness. See also ACUPUNCTURE.

acupuncture ALTERNATIVE MEDICINE technique, developed in ancient China, in which needles are inserted into the skin and underlying tissues at precise points along 12 meridians (pathways) in the body, through which the vital life force (QI) is believed to flow, in order to restore YIN–YANG balance and treat disease. Acupuncture appears to relieve pain and is used as an ANESTHETIC for surgery. Theories to explain its effects include stimulation of release of natural opiates, blockage of pain-signal transmission, and a placebo effect. See also ACUPRESSURE.

Ada \'ā-də\ High-level computer PROGRAMMING LANGUAGE whose development was initiated in 1975 by the U.S. Dept. of Defense and standardized in 1983. Ada was intended to be a common language for use on computers produced by many different manufacturers. It is similar to PASCAL but contains additional features convenient for the development of large-scale, multiplatform programs. The 1995 revision, Ada 95, supports object-oriented design methodology (see OBJECT-ORIENTED PROGRAMMING).

Adalbert \'ad-əl-ˌbərt\, **St.** *orig.* Vojtech (956–997) Czech prelate. Descended from the princes of Bohemia, he was trained in theology at Magdeburg (Germany). Elected the first native bishop of Prague in 982, he promoted the political aims of the Bohemian prince by extending the influence of the church beyond the Czech kingdom. Failing to convert his people, he left Bohemia in 994 to become a missionary along the Baltic coast, where he was martyred in 997. An account of his life was written by his friend and disciple St. BRUNO OF QUERFURT.

Adam, Robert (1728–1792) Scottish architect and designer. He traveled in Europe 1754–58, studying architectural theory and Roman ruins. With his brother James (1730–1794), he developed a decorative style that synthesized elements from various sources and employed classical forms with a new lightness and freedom. Their style is noted for its contrasting room shapes and delicate classical ornaments. Adam's work focused on the remodeling of houses, including Osterley Park (1761–80) in Middlesex and Kedleston Hall (c.1765–70) in Derbyshire. Other works included the Adelphi development in London (1768–72) and the Univ. of Edinburgh (1789). Adam was also a leading furniture designer; his style was popularized by George HEPPLEWHITE.

Adam and Eve In Jewish, Christian, and Islamic traditions, the parents of the human race. GENESIS contains the tale of their creation in the Garden of Eden and their subsequent banishment after disobeying God by eating the fruit of the forbidden tree of knowledge of good and evil. CAIN AND ABEL were their children. Christian theologians developed the doctrine of ORIGINAL SIN based on the story of their transgression; in contrast, the QURAN teaches that Adam's sin was his alone and did not make all people sinners.

Adamawa \ˌä-dä-'mä-wä\ Traditional emirate centered in what is now Adamawa state, E Nigeria. It was founded by Modibbo Adama in the early 19th cent. The colonialist British established trading posts and in 1901 captured Yola, the capital. Adamawa was partitioned in 1901 between British Northern Nigeria and German Kamerun (Cameroon); in 1919 the latter was divided between the French and the British. The emirate's territories eventually came to form almost all of N Cameroon and part of E Nigeria.

Adamawa-Ubangi languages \ˌad-ə-'mä-wə-ü-'baŋ-gē\ Branch of the NIGER-CONGO superfamily of languages, with two divisions, Adamawa in the west and Ubangi in the east. Adamawa may comprise more than 70 languages, most of them poorly known and with fewer than 100,000 speakers, in E Nigeria, N Cameroon, SW Chad, and W Central African Republic. Ubangi includes about the same number of languages as Adamawa and extends across a much broader region, from N Cameroon to S Sudan and N Congo. Ubangi languages with over half a million speakers include

Banda, Gbaya, Ngbaka, and Zande. Sango, based on the Ngbandi group of Ubangi, has become a lingua franca.

Adams, Abigail *orig.* Abigail Smith (1744–1818) U.S. first lady. Born in Weymouth, Mass., she married John ADAMS in 1764 and raised four children, including J. Q. ADAMS, in Quincy, Mass. In 1774 she began a prolific correspondence with her husband when he was at the Continental Congress in Philadelphia, describing daily life and discussing public affairs during the American Revolution with wit and political acuity. She continued her letters to family and friends while in Europe (1784–88) and Washington, D.C. (1789–1801), during her husband's diplomatic and presidential careers.

Adams, Ansel (1902–1984) U.S. photographer. Born in San Francisco, in 1927 he published *Parmelian Prints of the High Sierras*, photographs that imitated Impressionist painting with soft, misty effects achieved in the darkroom. Known for his dramatic images of mountain landscapes, he also was an outstanding technician; *Making a Photograph* (1935) was the first of his many books on photographic technique. He worked consistently to foster public awareness of photography as a fine art; in 1940 he helped organize the first public collection of photographs, at the Museum of Modern Art, and in 1946 he established, at the Calif. School of Fine Arts, the first academic photography department.

Adams, Gerry (*orig.* Gerard) (b.1948) Irish nationalist and leader of SINN FÉIN. Allegedly commander of the IRISH REPUBLICAN ARMY (IRA) in Belfast, he was interned as a suspected terrorist in 1972 and 1973–77. He became vice president of Sinn Féin in 1978 and persuaded the group to enter candidates in the 1981 elections. Elected to Parliament in 1983, he refused to take the oath of allegiance and never took his seat. As Sinn Féin president (from 1983), in 1991 he began to shift its strategy toward negotiation; his efforts led to a 1993 agreement by the British and Irish prime ministers to consider Northern Ireland's future. He continues to lead Sinn Féin in talks to establish a power-sharing executive under the terms of the 1998 peace agreement.

Adams, Henry (Brooks) (1838–1918) U.S. historian and man of letters. A descendant of two presidents, he was disgusted by American politics of his own time. As a young newspaperman, he called for social and political reforms but later lost faith with a world he considered devoid of principle. This was reflected in his novel *Democracy* (1880). His concern culminated in the nine-volume *History of the United States of America* (1889–91), which gained instant acclaim. In *Mont-Saint-Michel and Chartres* (1913) he described the medieval worldview as reflected in its architecture. *The Education of Henry Adams* (1918) is his best-known work and one of the outstanding autobiographies of Western literature.

Adams, John (Coolidge) (b.1947) U.S. composer. He has worked as a professional clarinetist, taught at the San Francisco Conservatory, and conducted widely. His style, strongly influenced by minimalism, has become richer with time. His *Nixon in China* (1987) and *The Death of Klinghoffer* (1991) are two of the best-known operas of recent decades. Other celebrated works include *Harmonium* (1980) and *Harmonielehre* (1985).

Adams, John (1735–1826) First vice president (1789–97) and second president (1797–1801) of the U.S. Born in Braintree, Mass., he practiced law in Boston. In 1764 he married Abigail Smith (Abigail ADAMS). Active in the American independence movement, he served as a delegate to the CONTINENTAL CONGRESS (1774–78), where he was appointed to many committees, including one with Thomas JEFFERSON and others to draft the DECLARATION OF INDEPENDENCE. He served as a diplomat in France, the Netherlands, and England (1778–88). In the first U.S. presidential election, he received the second-

John Adams

largest number of votes and became vice president under George WASHINGTON. Adams's term as president was marked by controversy over his signing the ALIEN AND SEDITION ACTS in 1798 and by his alliance with the conservative FEDERALIST PARTY. In 1800 he was defeated for reelection by Jefferson and retired to live a secluded life in Massachusetts. In 1812 he was reconciled with Jefferson, with whom he began an illuminating correspondence. Both men died on July 4, 1826, the Declaration's 50th anniversary. J. Q. ADAMS was his son.

Adams, John Quincy (1767–1848) Sixth president of the U.S. (1825–29). Born in Braintree, Mass., he was the eldest son of John ADAMS and Abigail ADAMS. He served as U.S. minister to the Netherlands (1794), Prussia (1797), Russia (1809–11), and Britain (1815–17), and served in the U.S. Senate (1803–8). As secretary of state (1817–24), he was instrumental in acquiring Florida from Spain and in drafting the MONROE DOCTRINE. In the 1824 presidential election, he was one of three candidates; none received a majority of the electoral votes, though Andrew JACKSON received a plurality. The decision went to the House of Representatives, where

John Quincy Adams

Adams received crucial support from Henry CLAY and the electoral votes necessary to elect him president. He appointed Clay secretary of state, which further angered Jackson. Adams's presidency was unsuccessful; when he ran for reelection, Jackson defeated him. In 1830 he was elected to the U.S. House, where he served until his death. Outspoken in his opposition to slavery, he led the effort to repeal gag rules passed by Southern congressmen to prevent discussion of antislavery petitions. In 1841 he successfully defended the slaves in the AMISTAD MUTINY case.

Adams, Samuel (1722–1803) American Revolutionary leader. Born in Boston, a cousin of John ADAMS, he became a strong opponent of British taxation measures and organized resistance to the STAMP ACT. In 1772 he helped found the COMMITTEES OF CORRESPONDENCE. In reaction to the TEA ACT of 1773, he organized the BOSTON TEA PARTY, and he led opposition to the INTOLERABLE ACTS. A delegate to the CONTINENTAL CONGRESS (1774–81), he continued to call for separation from Britain and signed the DECLARATION OF INDEPENDENCE. He served as governor of Massachusetts 1794–97.

Adamson, Joy *orig.* Joy-Friederike Victoria Gessner (1910–1980) Czech-British naturalist. Educated in Vienna, she moved to Kenya in 1939. She became known worldwide for books describing how she and her husband raised a lion cub, Elsa, and returned it to its natural habitat: *Born Free* (1960), *Living Free* (1961), and *Forever Free* (1962). She repeated her success with cheetah and leopard cubs. She founded the Elsa Wild Animal Appeal conservation fund (1961).

Adam's Peak Mountain, S central Sri Lanka. Standing 7,360 ft (2,243 m) high, it is sacred and a place of pilgrimage to Buddhists, Muslims, and Hindus. On its summit is a large hollow, 5 ft (1.5 m) long, that is venerated as the footprint of BUDDHA, ADAM, and SHIVA, respectively.

Adana \ˌä-dä-ˈnä\ City (pop., 1996: 1,099,000), S central Turkey, on the Seyhan River. An agricultural and industrial center, it probably overlies a HITTITE settlement of around 1400 B.C. Conquered by ALEXANDER THE GREAT in 335–334 B.C., it later fell to the Romans, then the ABBASID Arabs and others until the establishment of the TURKMEN dynasty in 1378. Adana's prosperity has long derived from the fertile valleys behind it and its position as a bridgehead on the Anatolian–Arabian trade routes.

Adanson \ˈa-dän-ˌsōⁿ\, **Michel** (1727–1806) French botanist. He returned from several years in Senegal with a large col-

lection of plant specimens, now in the National Museum of Natural History. His classification system of plants was opposed by Carolus LINNAEUS, whose system eventually prevailed. He was the first to classify mollusks. He also studied electricity in torpedo fish and the effects of electrical current on regenerating frog legs and heads. He is now known mainly for introducing the use of statistical methods in botanical studies.

adaptation In biology, the process by which an organism becomes fitted to its environment. It is the result of NATURAL SELECTION acting on inherited VARIATION. Even simple organisms must be adapted in many ways, including structure, physiology, and genetics; movement or dispersal; means of defense and attack; and reproduction and development.

ADD See ATTENTION DEFICIT DISORDER

Addams, Charles (Samuel) (1912–1988) U.S. cartoonist. Born in Westfield, N.J., he sold his first cartoon to *The New Yorker* in 1933. He became famous for cartoons depicting morbid behavior by sinister-looking characters, especially a family of ghouls whose activities travestied those of a conventional family. These evolved into *The Addams Family*, a 1960s television series that generated two Hollywood films.

Addams, Jane (1860–1935) U.S. social reformer. Born in Cedarville, Ill., she became interested in social reform and in 1889 cofounded Hull House in Chicago, one of the first SETTLEMENT HOUSES in N. America. She championed such social reforms as juvenile-court law, justice for immigrants and blacks, workers' rights and compensation, and the women's suffrage movement. In 1910 she became the first female president of the National Conference of Social Work. An ardent pacifist, she served in 1915 as chair of the International Congress of Women and helped form the Women's International League for Peace and Freedom. In 1931 she shared the Nobel Peace Prize with N. M. BUTLER.

Adda River \'äd-dä\ River, LOMBARDY region, Italy. It flows southward 194 mi (313 km) through Lake COMO and across the Lombardy Plain before joining the PO RIVER above Cremona. It provides hydroelectric power and irrigation. It has served as a strategic defense line in wars dating back to the Roman period.

adder Any of several venomous snakes of the VIPER family (Viperidae) and the viperlike death adder. Common adders, puff adders, and night adders occur in Europe, Asia, Africa, and Australia. They range in length from 18 in. to 5 ft (45 cm–1.5 m). A bite from the puff adder of Africa or the death adder of Australia is often lethal. The name is also used for the HOGNOSE SNAKE and others.

Addis Ababa \'äd-dis-'ä-bä-,bä, 'a-dəs-'a-bə-bə\ Capital and largest city (pop., 1994: 2,113,000), Ethiopia. It lies on a central plateau at an altitude of about 8,000 ft (2,450 m). It has become the national center for higher education, banking and insurance, and trade. Several international organizations have their headquarters there, including the ORGANIZATION OF AFRICAN UNITY. In recent decades it has suffered extensive damage as a result of political instability.

Addison, Joseph (1672–1719) English essayist, poet, and dramatist. His poem on the Battle of Blenheim, *The Campaign* (1705), gained the attention of the Whigs and led to important government posts (including secretary of state) and literary fame. With Richard STEELE, he was a leading contributor to the periodicals *The Tatler* (1709–11) and *The Spectator* (1711–12, 1714). A master of English prose, he brought to perfection the periodical essay. His play *Cato* (1713) is one of the important tragedies of the 18th cent.

Addison's disease Disease in which gradual shrinking of the cortex of the ADRENAL GLANDS causes them to produce insufficient quantities of the STEROID hydrocortisone while causing the PITUITARY GLAND to produce excess quantities of pituitary hormones. Most of the cortex tissue is destroyed by the time symptoms appear. Hydrocortisone replacement therapy is often successful. Many cases are believed to be due to an AUTOIMMUNE DISEASE; the remainder are caused by destruction of the adrenal gland by granuloma (e.g., TUBERCULOSIS).

Adelaide City (pop., 1998: 1,088,000) and capital, S. Australia state. The city lies at the base of the Mt. Lofty Ranges on the Torrens River. Founded in 1837, it was incorporated in 1840 as Australia's first municipal government. It grew from an agricultural market with nearby mineral deposits to an industrial center with petroleum refineries and connections to natural-gas fields. Landmarks include the Univ. of Adelaide, parliament houses, and two cathedrals.

Aden \'ä-dən, 'ā-dən\ Seaport city (pop., 1994: 398,000), S Yemen, on the Gulf of ADEN. It was a terminus of the spice road of W Arabia for about 1,000 years before the 3rd cent. A.D. It then became a trading center under Yemeni, Ethiopian, and Arab control. The Turks captured the city in 1538, and the British governed it as part of India 1839–1937. Its importance grew after the opening of the SUEZ CANAL. Made a crown colony in 1937, it was part of the Federation of South Arabia (1963–67), and later the capital of S. Yemen (1967–90) and Yemen (from 1990).

Aden, Gulf of Arm of the Indian Ocean between the ARABIAN PENINSULA and Somalia. To the west, it connects with the Red Sea; its E limit is the tip of Somalia. It is about 550 mi (885 km) long. It was controlled by the British after their occupation of Aden (1839) and SOCOTRA (1876). Its coastline supports many fishing towns and the major ports ADEN and DJIBOUTI.

Adenauer \'a-d°n-aủr\, **Konrad** (1876–1967) German statesman, first chancellor of the Federal Republic of Germany (W. Germany). Lord mayor of Cologne 1917–33, he was elected to the Prussian Staatsrat (state council) in 1920 and served as its speaker 1928–33. He lost his posts when the Nazis came to power, and in 1944 he was sent to a concentration camp. A founder and chairman of the CHRISTIAN DEMOCRATIC UNION, he became chancellor in 1949. He stressed individualism under the rule of law, was a strong supporter of NATO, and worked hard to reconcile Germany with its former enemies, especially France and Russia. He retired in 1963.

adenine \'a-d°n-,ēn\ Organic compound of the PURINE family, consisting of two rings, each containing both nitrogen and carbon atoms, and an amino group. It occurs free in tea and in combined form in NUCLEIC ACIDS, ATP, vitamin B_{12}, and several coenzymes. In DNA its complementary base is THYMINE. It or its corresponding NUCLEOSIDE or NUCLEOTIDE is made from nucleic acids by HYDROLYSIS.

adenoids \'a-d°n-,ȯidz\ *or* **pharyngeal tonsils** \,far-ən-'jē-əl, fə-'rin-jē-əl\ Mass of LYMPHOID TISSUE, similar to the TONSILS, on the back of the PHARYNX. Infected, inflamed adenoids can obstruct breathing and SINUS drainage (promoting SINUSITIS) and block the eustachian tubes that connect to the middle ear (promoting OTITIS); their surgical removal is frequently recommended.

adenosine triphosphate See ATP

adenovirus \,a-d°n-ō-'vī-rəs\ Any of a group of spheroidal VIRUSES, made up of DNA wrapped in a protein coat, that cause sore throat and fever in humans and several diseases in other mammals and birds. An adenovirus develops within the nucleus of an infected cell. Like cold viruses, adenoviruses are often found in inactive infections in clinically healthy persons.

ADHD See ATTENTION DEFICIT DISORDER

Adige River \'ä-dē-jä\ River, 255 mi (410 km) long, the longest in Italy after the PO. It rises below the Resia Pass and flows southeast through the Venosta Valley. After receiving the Isarco River at Bolzano, it turns south across the Po lowlands to enter the ADRIATIC SEA south of Chioggia. It supplies hydroelectric power and irrigation; its floods do great damage. The Adige has been the scene of many battles, notably in the Austrian–Italian campaign of 1916.

Adi Granth \,ä-dē-'grănth\ (Punjabi: "First Book") Sacred scripture of SIKHISM. Composed of nearly 6,000 hymns of the Sikh GURUS and Hindu and Islamic saints, it is the central object of worship in all GURDWARAS (temples). First compiled in 1604 by ARJAN, it included hymns and the devotional songs of saints. In 1704 the last Guru, GOBIND SINGH, added more hymns and decreed that after his death the Granth would take the place of the Guru. Written mostly in Punjabi or Hindi, it contains the *Mul Mantra* (basic prayer), *Japji* (the most important scripture, written by NANAK), and hymns arranged by their RAGAS.

adipose tissue *or* **fatty tissue** CONNECTIVE TISSUE consisting mainly of FAT cells, specialized to synthesize and contain large globules of fat with a structural network of fibers. It is found mainly under the skin but also in deposits between the muscles, among the intestines and in their membrane folds, around the heart, and elsewhere. The stored fat acts as a fuel reserve, helps conserve body heat, and forms pads between organs.

Adirondack Mountains \ˌa-də-ˈrän-ˌdak\ Mountains in NE New York state. They extend south from the ST. LAWRENCE RIVER valley and Lake CHAMPLAIN to the MOHAWK RIVER valley. They include more than 40 summits higher than 4,000 ft (1,219 m); the tallest, Mt. Marcy (5,344 ft, or 629 m), is the state's highest. Samuel de CHAMPLAIN was the first European to sight the Adirondacks (1609). In 1892 the state created Adirondack Park; it has become the largest U.S. state or national park outside of Alaska, with over 5 million acres (2 million hectares).

Adler, Alfred (1870–1937) Austrian psychiatrist. A student and associate of Sigmund FREUD (1902–11), he eventually broke with Freud over the importance of early-childhood sexual conflicts in the development of psychopathology. He developed the school of individual psychology, the humanistic study of drives, feelings, emotions, and memory in the context of the individual's overall life plan. Advancing the theory of the INFERIORITY COMPLEX, he sought to direct patients emotionally disabled by inferiority feelings toward maturity, common sense, and social usefulness. He established the first child-guidance clinic in 1921 in Vienna. He taught in the U.S. from 1927 until his death. His works include *Understanding Human Nature* (1927) and *What Life Should Mean to You* (1931).

Adler, Mortimer J(erome) (1902–2001) U.S. philosopher, educator, and editor. Born in New York City, he taught philosophy of law at the Univ. of Chicago from 1930, where he joined Robert M. HUTCHINS to promote the idea of liberal education based on great books. Together they edited the 54-volume *Great Books of the Western World* (1952). In 1969 he became director of planning for ENCYCLOPAEDIA BRITANNICA, and he served as chairman of its board of editors 1974–95. His works include *How to Read a Book* (1940).

administrative law Law regulating the powers, procedures, and acts of public administration. It applies to all public officials and public agencies. As distinguished from legislative and judicial authority, administrative authority entails the power to issue rules and regulations based on statutes, grant licenses and permits to facilitate the conduct of government business, initiate investigations and provide remedies for complaints or problems, and issue orders directing parties to conform to governing statutes or rules.

Admiralty Islands Extension of the BISMARCK ARCHIPELAGO. The group lies about 190 mi (300 km) north of Papua New Guinea in the SW Pacific Ocean and comprises about 40 islands (pop., 1995: 35,000). Manus Island contains most of its land area. First sighted by the Dutch explorer Willem Schouten in 1616, it was named by the British captain Philip Carteret in 1767. Subsequently ruled by the Germans, Australians, and Japanese, the islands became part of the U.N. Trust Territory of New Guinea in 1946, and of Papua New Guinea in 1975.

adobe \ə-ˈdō-bē\ Handmade sun-dried bricks made of heavy clay and straw. Adobe dates back thousands of years; molds for shaping the bricks were brought to the New World by the Spanish. Excellent insulating properties make adobe an ideal material for both dwellings and ovens. The adobe buildings at Taos, N.M., are typical of Native American PUEBLO dwellings.

adolescence Period of life from PUBERTY to ADULTHOOD (roughly ages 12–20) characterized by marked physiological changes, development of sexual feelings, efforts toward the construction of identity, and a progression from concrete to abstract thought. In adolescence youths begin to separate themselves from their parents but still lack a clearly defined role in society. It is generally regarded as an emotionally intense and often stressful period.

Adonis \ə-ˈdä-nəs\ In GREEK MYTHOLOGY, a youth of remarkable beauty, the favorite of APHRODITE. He was put in the care of PERSEPHONE, who refused to allow him to return from the underworld. ZEUS ruled that he should spend a third of the year with Persephone, a third with Aphrodite, and a third on his own. After he was killed by a boar, Zeus allowed him to spend half the year with Aphrodite and half in the underworld. He is identified with the Babylonian god TAMMUZ and represents the seasonal cycle of death and resurrection.

adoption Act of transferring parental rights and duties to someone other than a minor's biological parents. The practice is ancient and occurs in all cultures. Traditionally, its goal was to continue the male line for the purposes of inheritance and succession; most adoptees were male (and sometimes adult). Contemporary laws and practices aim to promote child welfare and the development of families. Traditional restrictions, such as those on level of income and placement across religious and ethnic lines, have loosened over time. Single-parent adoptions and adoptions by same-sex couples have also become more acceptable.

Adorno \ä-ˈdȯr-nō\, **Theodor (Wiesengrund)** (1903–1969) German philosopher. He taught briefly at the Univ. of Frankfurt before emigrating to England in 1934 to escape Nazism. He lived 10 years in the U.S. (1938–48) before returning to head the Frankfurt Institute for Social Research (see FRANKFURT SCHOOL). His brilliant but demanding works on philosophy, literature, psychology, sociology, and music have become highly influential since his death. For Adorno, the great task of music, literature, and art was to keep alive social alternatives to capitalism, which philosophy and political theory could no longer imagine. His works include *Dialectic of Enlightenment* (1947; with Max Horkheimer), *Minima Moralia* (1951), and *Notes to Literature* (4 vols., 1958–74).

adrenal gland \ə-ˈdrē-nᵊl\ *or* **suprarenal gland** \ˌsü-prə-ˈrē-nᵊl\ Either of two small, triangular endocrine GLANDS over the kidneys. In humans, each gland weighs about 0.15 oz (4.5 g) and consists of an inner medulla, which produces the HORMONES EPINEPHRINE and NOREPINEPHRINE, and an outer cortex (about 90% of the gland), which secretes the STEROID hormones aldosterone, cortisol, and ANDROGENS (the last two in response to ACTH from the PITUITARY GLAND). See also ADDISON'S DISEASE, CUSHING'S SYNDROME.

adrenaline See EPINEPHRINE

Adrian, Edgar Douglas, *later* Baron Adrian of Cambridge (1889–1977) British electrophysiologist. He amplified electrical potential variations in nerve impulses from sense organs, eventually recording impulses from single sensory endings and motor NEURONS. His work clarified the physical basis of sensation and the mechanism of muscular control. Adrian later studied epilepsy and the location of cerebral lesions. He shared a 1932 Nobel Prize with Charles SHERRINGTON.

Adrian IV \ˈā-drē-ən\ *orig.* Nicholas Breakspear (1100?–1159) Pope (1154–59), the only Englishman ever to hold the office. He served in France and Italy before a successful mission to Scandinavia led to his election as pope. Adrian crowned FREDERICK I Barbarossa emperor in 1155, but his policy toward the Normans of S Italy soon aroused the emperor's anger. His controversial bull *Laudabiliter* supposedly gave Ireland to HENRY II of England, a claim that was later refuted.

Adrianople, Battle of *or* **Battle of Hadrianopolis** (A.D. 378) Battle fought in present-day Edirne, Turkey, that marked the beginning of serious Germanic incursions into Roman territory. It pitted the Roman army under the emperor Valens (A.D. 328–378) against the horsemen of the VISIGOTHS, OSTROGOTHS, and other Germanic tribes. The Roman army was annihilated and Valens died on the battlefield. His successor, THEODOSIUS I, and the GOTHS agreed in 382 that the Goths would help with imperial defenses in exchange for food subsidies. The treaty set the pattern for later barbarian intrusions.

Adriatic Sea Arm of the MEDITERRANEAN SEA, lying between Italy and the Balkan Peninsula. It is about 500 mi (800 km) long, with an average width of 110 mi (175 km), and a maximum depth of 4,035 ft (1,324 m). The Italian coast is relatively straight and continuous, but the Balkan coast is full of islands. The Strait of Otranto at its southeasterly limit links it with the Ionian Sea.

adsorption Capability of a SOLID substance to attract to its surface MOLECULES of a GAS or SOLUTION with which it is in contact. Physical adsorption depends on VAN DER WAALS FORCES of attraction between molecules. In chemical adsorption (chemisorption; see CATALYSIS), the gas is held to the surface by chemical forces specific to the chemicals involved, and formation of the bond may require an ACTIVATION ENERGY.

adult education See CONTINUING EDUCATION

adultery Sexual relations between a married person and someone other than the spouse. Prohibitions against adultery are found in virtually every society; Jewish, Islamic, and Christian traditions all condemn it. Attitudes toward adultery in different cultures have varied widely. In ancient Rome, for example, an offending female could be killed, but men were not severely punished. In Western Europe and N. America, adultery by either spouse is a ground for divorce. The spread of Western ideas of equality in marriage has resulted in pressure for equal marital rights for women in traditional African and S.E. Asian societies.

adulthood Period in the human life span in which full physical and intellectual maturity have been attained. Adulthood is thought of as beginning at age 20 or 21. It includes middle age (from around age 40) and old age (from about 60). Physically, it is characterized by the peaking (around age 30) and gradual decline of bodily functioning; the post-peak phase includes diminished acuity of the senses, reduction in muscular and skeletal mass, weakening of the heart muscle, and diminished production of hormones. Some slowing of central-nervous-system processing begins with middle age, but is generally compensated for by an increased capacity to retain practical information and apply cultural knowledge. Old age usually brings a significant decline in physical capacity, and often impaired mental function.

Advent In the Christian calendar, the first season of the church year, a period of preparation for the birth of JESUS. Advent begins on the Sunday nearest to November 30 and continues until CHRISTMAS. Viewed as a penitential season, it is also considered a time of preparation for the Second Coming of Christ. Advent was observed as early as the 6th cent.

Adventist Member of any of a group of Protestant churches that arose in the U.S. in the 19th cent. and assert that the Second Coming of Christ is close at hand. Adventism was founded by William Miller (1782–1849) during a period marked by MILLENNIALISM. Miller asserted that Christ would return to separate saints from sinners and inaugurate his 1,000-year kingdom on earth sometime in the year before March 21, 1844. The "Great Disappointment" after that date passed was followed by an Adventist conference in 1845. Those who persisted concluded that Miller had misinterpreted the signs and that, though Christ had begun the "cleansing of the heavenly sanctuary," he would not appear until its completion. These Millerites founded the Seventh-Day Adventists in 1863; other Adventist groups include the Evangelical Adventists and the Advent Christian Church. Seventh-Day Adventists observe Saturday as the SABBATH and avoid eating meat and using narcotics and other stimulants.

adversary procedure In Anglo-American law, the principal method of offering evidence in court. It requires the opposing sides to present pertinent information and to introduce and cross-examine witnesses before a jury and/or a judge. In criminal proceedings, the prosecution represents the government and has at its disposal the police department with its investigators and laboratories; the defense must arrange and pay for its own investigation. (Legal aid is available for the poor.) In civil (noncriminal) proceedings, both sides engage private attorneys. Skillful questioning often produces testimony that can be interpreted in various ways; in cross-examination, lawyers seek to alter the jury's initial perception of the testimony.

advertising Techniques and practices used to bring products, services, opinions, or causes to public notice to evoke a desired response. London newspapers first carried advertisements in the 17th cent. The first advertising agencies were established in the 19th cent. to broker for space in newspapers, and by the early 20th cent. agencies were producing the advertising message itself. Most advertising promotes goods for sale, but similar methods are used to promote causes, charities, or political candidates. Advertising is normally the most important source of income for the media through which it is conducted. In addition to newspapers, magazines, and broadcast media, advertising media include direct mail, billboards and posters, transit advertising, and promotional items such as matchbooks or calendars. Advertisers attempt to choose media that are favored by the advertisers' target audience.

adze *or* **adz** Hand tool for shaping wood. A handheld stone chipped to form a blade, it is one of the earliest tools, and was used widely in the PALEOLITHIC and NEOLITHIC periods. By Egyptian times, it had acquired a wooden haft (handle) with a copper or BRONZE blade set flat at the top of the haft to form a T. In this form but with a steel blade, it continued to be the prime hand tool for shaping and trimming wood; the carpenter stands on or astride a log or other piece of timber, swinging the adze like a pick, down and between the legs.

Aegean civilizations \i-'jē-ən\ BRONZE AGE civilizations around 3000–1000 B.C. in the area of the Aegean Sea. They included CRETE, the CYCLADES, the Greek mainland south from Thessaly, including the Peloponnese, and MACEDONIA, THRACE, and W Anatolia. The most significant were the MINOAN and MYCENAEAN civilizations. The term also sometimes refers to NEOLITHIC PERIOD civilizations in the same region around 7000–3000 B.C.

Aegean Islands Greek islands, AEGEAN SEA, particularly the CYCLADES, Sporades, and Dodecanese groups. The Cyclades consist of about 220 islands. The Dodecanese, or Southern Sporades, include 12 main islands, among them Patmos and RHODES; some geographers also include SAMOS, CHIOS, and LESBOS. The Sporades, or Northern Sporades, include Skyros, Skopelos, and Skiathos.

Aegean Sea Arm of the MEDITERRANEAN SEA, lying between Greece and Turkey. About 380 mi (610 km) long and 190 mi (300 km) wide, it has a total area of some 83,000 sq mi (214,000 sq km) and a maximum depth of 11,627 ft (3,543 m). The straits of the DARDANELLES, the Sea of MARMARA, and the BOSPORUS connect it with the BLACK SEA. The Aegean was the cradle of the great early civilizations of Crete and Greece.

Aegina \ē-'jī-nə\ Island in the Saronic group of Greece. Located 16 mi (26 km) southwest of Piraeus, it has an area of 32 sq mi (83 sq km). Inhabited since about 3000 B.C., it gradually became a maritime power; its period of glory, reflected in PINDAR's poetry, was in the 5th cent. B.C. Its economic rivalry with Athens led to frequent warfare, and in 431 B.C. the Athenians deported all its population. It came under Roman rule in 133 B.C. It was briefly the capital of Greece (1826–28).

Aegospotami \ˌē-gə-'spä-tə-ˌmī\, **Battle of** (405 B.C.) Naval victory of Sparta over Athens in the final battle of the PELOPONNESIAN WAR. The Spartans under LYSANDER surprised the Athenians at anchor off Aegospotami, in Thrace, and defeated them decisively. The Spartans put almost 4,000 captured Athenians to death. The victory led to the Spartan march on Athens and the Athenian surrender in 404.

Aeneas \i-'nē-əs\ Mythical hero of Troy and Rome. He was the son of APHRODITE and Anchises, a member of Trojan royal family. According to HOMER, he was second only to his cousin HECTOR in defending Troy during the TROJAN WAR. VIRGIL's *Aeneid* tells of Aeneas's escape after Troy's fall, carrying his elderly father on his back, and of his journey to Italy, where his descendants became the rulers of Rome. See also DIDO.

Aeolus \'ē-ə-ləs\ Greek god of the winds. In the *Odyssey*, Aeolus is the mortal ruler of the floating island of Aeolia. He gave ODYSSEUS a favorable wind for his voyage and also a bag containing the unfavorable winds. Odysseus' greedy companions opened the bag, releasing the winds and driving their ship back to shore. Later writers depicted Aeolus as a minor god rather than a human being.

aerial See ANTENNA

aerobics System of physical conditioning for increasing the efficiency of the body's intake of OXYGEN. Aerobic exercises (e.g., running, jogging, swimming, dancing) stimulate heart and lung activity. To produce a benefit, aerobic training must raise the heart rate (PULSE) to the exerciser's training level for at least 20 minutes and include at least three sessions a week.

aerodynamics Branch of physics concerned with the forces acting on bodies passing through air and other gaseous FLUIDS. It explains the principles of flight of aircraft, rockets, and missiles. It is also involved in the design of automobiles, trains, and ships, and even stationary structures such as bridges and tall buildings, which must withstand high winds. See also TURBULENCE.

aerosol System of tiny liquid or solid particles evenly distributed in a finely divided state through a gas, usually air. Aerosol particles participate in chemical processes and influence the electrical properties of the atmosphere. Though true aerosol particles range in diameter only up to about 1 micrometer, the term is commonly used to refer to fog droplets and dust particles, which can have diameters of more than 100 micrometers. See also COLLOID, EMULSION.

aerospace medicine Branch of medicine dealing with atmospheric flight (aviation medicine) and space flight (space medicine). Intensive preflight simulator training and attention to design of equipment and spacecraft promote the safety and effectiveness of humans exposed to the stresses of flight. The world's first unit for space research was established in the U.S. in 1948.

Aeschines \ˈes-kə-ˌnēz\ (390–314? B.C.) Athenian orator and advocate of PHILIP II of Macedonia's expansion into Greece. He and DEMOSTHENES, who later became his bitter opponent, participated in 346 B.C. in forging a peace between Athens and Macedonia. Demosthenes later accused Aeschines of treason because he had promoted the Macedonian cause during the negotiations, but Aeschines was acquitted in 343. In 339 he helped incite the war that led to Macedonian control of central Greece. In 336 he opposed as illegal a motion to honor Demosthenes, but he suffered an overwhelming defeat.

Aeschylus \ˈes-kə-ˌləs\ (525–456 B.C.) Greek tragic dramatist. He won the first of several major dramatic competitions in Athens in 484 B.C. He wrote over 80 plays, but only seven survive; the earliest of these, the *Persians,* was performed in 472 B.C. Others are the *Oresteia* trilogy (*Agamemnon, The Libation Bearers,* and *The Eumenides), Seven Against Thebes, The Suppliants,* and *Prometheus Bound.* Considered the father of Greek tragic drama, he added a second actor to the performance, which enabled the later development of dialogue. He was the first of the three great Greek tragedians, preceding SOPHOCLES and EURIPIDES.

Aesculapius See ASCLEPIUS

Aesir \ˈā-zir\ In GERMANIC RELIGION, one of the two main groups of deities, the other being the VANIR. ODIN, FRIGG, Tyr (the god of war), and THOR were the four Aesir common to the Germanic nations. BALDER and LOKI were considered Aesir by other peoples. The Aesir were a warlike race and were originally dominant over the Vanir, but after numerous defeats in battle they granted the Vanir equal status.

Aesop \ˈē-ˌsäp\ Supposed author of a collection of Greek FABLES, almost certainly a legendary figure. Though HERODOTUS said he was a real person, "Aesop" was probably no more than a name invented to provide an author for fables about beasts. The 200 or so Aesopian fables treat human social interactions, and their morals offer advice on how to deal with the competitive realities of life. The Western fable tradition effectively begins with these tales.

Aestheticism \es-ˈthet-ə-ˌsiz-əm\ Late-19th-cent. European arts movement based on the belief that art exists for the sake of its beauty alone. It began in reaction to prevailing utilitarian social thought and to the perceived ugliness of the industrial age. Its philosophical foundations were laid by Immanuel KANT, who proposed that aesthetic standards could be separated from morality, utility, or pleasure. J. M. WHISTLER, Oscar WILDE, and Stéphane MALLARMÉ were principal figures. Aestheticism had affinities with French SYMBOLISM and was a precursor of ART NOUVEAU.

aesthetics \es-ˈthet-iks\ Philosophical study of the nature and evaluation of art, also concerned with beauty and taste.

Though aesthetics is broader than the philosophy of art, art is often taken as the prime example of its nature. G. W. F. HEGEL considered the study of the various forms of art and the spiritual content of each to be the main task of aesthetics. Seminal works include Edmund BURKE's *On the Sublime and Beautiful* (1757), Immanuel KANT's *Critique of Judgment* (1790), and Ludwig WITTGENSTEIN's *Philosophical Investigations* (1953).

Aethelberht I See ETHELBERT I

Aethelred Unraed See ETHELRED II

Aetolia \ē-ˈtō-lē-ə\ District north of the Gulf of Corinth, ancient Greece. Aetolia figures prominently in early legend. By 367 B.C. it had joined the AETOLIAN LEAGUE. Coming under Roman rule, it was incorporated into the province of Achaea (see ACHAEAN LEAGUE) in 27 B.C. by Caesar AUGUSTUS. Governed later by Albania and Venice, it came under Turkish rule in A.D. 1450. It was the scene of fierce fighting in the War of GREEK INDEPENDENCE (1821–29).

Aetolian League \ē-ˈtō-lē-ən\ Federal state of AETOLIA in central ancient Greece. A leading power by around 340 B.C., it resisted invasions by Macedonia (322 and 314–311) and the Gauls (279). The league's power in central Greece was confirmed with the defeat of the Boeotians (245). From the late 3rd cent. Aetolia began to lose power and territory to Macedonia, culminating in the sacking of the league's federal capital, Thermum (220). The league then allied with Rome against Macedonia; Rome later forced it into a permanent alliance (189) that cost it territory, power, and independence.

Afars and Issas, French Territory of the See DJIBOUTI

affective disorder Mental disorder presenting dramatic changes of mood, often including manic or depressive episodes less severe than those of BIPOLAR DISORDER. Symptoms include elevated, expansive, or irritable mood, with hyperactivity, pressured speech, and inflated self-esteem; and/or dejected mood, with sleep disturbances, agitation, and feelings of worthlessness or guilt.

affirmative action In the U.S., an active effort to improve employment or educational opportunities for women and minority groups. It was undertaken at the federal level following passage of the landmark CIVIL RIGHTS ACT OF 1964. Designed to counteract the effects of past discrimination, it consists of policies and programs that give preferences to minorities and women especially in job hiring, college admissions, and government contract awards. The main criteria are race, sex, ethnic origin, religion, disability, and age. The most important challenge to the program came in the U.S. Supreme Court's 1978 ruling in *Regents of the Univ. of California vs. Bakke.* Several recent decisions placed further restrictions on these programs, as in *Adarand Constructors vs. Pena* (1995) and *Texas vs. Hopwood* (1996).

afforestation See DEFORESTATION

Afghan hound Breed of dog developed as a hunter in the hill country of Afghanistan. It was brought to Europe in the late 19th cent. by British soldiers returning from the Indian–Afghan border wars. It has been used to pursue leopard and gazelle. It stands 24–28 in. (61–71 cm) high and weighs 50–60 lbs (23–27 kg). It has floppy ears, a long topknot, and a long silky coat of various colors.

Afghanistan Nation (Islamic state), S central Asia. Area: 251,825 sq mi (652,225 sq km). Population (2000 est.): 25,889,000. Capital: KABUL. About half the people are PASHTUNS; other ethnic groups include Tajiks, Uzbeks, and Hazaras. Languages: Pashto, Dari (a form of Persian) (official). Religion: Islam (official). Currency: Afghani. Afghanistan has three distinctive regions: the N plains are the major agricultural area; the SW plateau consists primarily of desert and semiarid landscape; the central highlands, including the HINDU KUSH, separates these regions. Afghanistan has a developing economy based largely on agriculture; its significant mineral resources remain largely untapped because of the AFGHAN WARS of the 1980s and subsequent extended fighting. Traditional handicrafts remain important; woolen carpets are a major export. The area was part of the Persian empire in the 6th cent. B.C. and was conquered by ALEXANDER THE GREAT in the 4th cent. B.C. Hindu influence entered with the Hephthalites and SASANIANS; Islam became entrenched during the rule of the Saffarids, about A.D. 870.

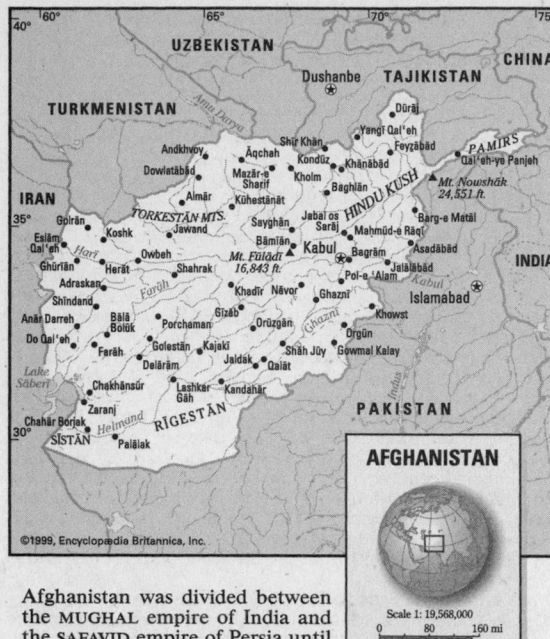

60° 65° 70° 75°

40°

UZBEKISTAN CHINA

Dushanbe TAJIKISTAN

TURKMENISTAN

Amu Darya Dūrāj

Shīr Khān Yangī Qal'eh PAMIRS
Andkhvoy Āqchah Konduz Khānābād Feyzābād Qal'eh-ye Panjeh
Dowlatābād Mazār-e Kholm Baghlān Mt. Nowshāk
Sharīf 24,551 ft.
IRAN Almār Kūhestānāt *HINDU KUSH*
35° *TORKESTĀN MTS.* Jabal os Barg-e Matāl
Gowr̄ Koshk Jawand Sarāj Mahmūd-e Rāqī
Eslām Bāmiān Kabul Bagrām INDIA
Qal'eh Owbeh Shahrak Mt. Fūlādī Jalālābād
Ghūrīān Herāt 16,843 ft. Asadābād
Adraskan *Harī* Khadir Nāvor Pol-e 'Ālam Islamabad
Anār Darreh Bālā Porchaman Gīzāb Orūzgān Khowst
Do Qal'eh Farāh Golestān Kajakī Jaldak Qalāt PAKISTAN
Delārām Lashkar Shāh Jūy Gowmal Kalay
30° Chakhānsūr Gāh Kandahār Orgūn
Zaranj *RĪGESTĀN*
Chahār Borjak *Helmand* SĪSTĀN Pālālak

Lake
Sāberī

©1999, Encyclopædia Britannica, Inc.

AFGHANISTAN

Scale 1: 19,568,000
0   80   160 mi
0 120   240 km

Afghanistan was divided between the MUGHAL empire of India and the SAFAVID empire of Persia until the 18th cent., when other Persians under Nadir Shah took control. Britain and Russia fought several wars in the area in the 19th cent. From the 1930s the country had a stable monarchy; it was overthrown in the 1970s. The rebels' intention was to institute Marxist reforms, but the reforms sparked rebellion and Soviet troops invaded to establish order. Afghan guerrillas prevailed, and the Soviets withdrew in 1988. In 1992 rebel factions overthrew the government and established an Islamic republic, but fighting among factions continued. In 1996 the government was taken over by the TALIBAN army. The Taliban's religious extremism led to its welcoming the fugitive Osama BIN LADEN, who set up terrorist training camps. The terrorist attacks on the U.S. in 2001 were followed by a two-month war and the replacement of the Taliban by a broad-based government.

Afghan Wars Wars in Afghanistan from the 19th to the 21st cent. In the 19th cent. Britain and Russia twice competed indecisively for influence in central Asia by fighting there (1838–42, 1878–81). In the 20th cent., the Third Afghan War resulted in the country's full independence (Treaty of Rawalpindi, 1919). From 1978 Afghanistan engaged in a civil war that provoked a military intervention by the former Soviet Union. After the Soviet withdrawal, the various rebel groups (see MUJAHIDIN) began competing with one another again for power. In 1994 the TALIBAN displaced them, capturing Kabul in 1996. They were in turn displaced in 2001 by a U.S.-led military coalition pursuing Osama BIN LADEN and his AL-QAEDA terrorist network, and a coalition government was installed.

AFL-CIO *in full* **American Federation of Labor–Congress of Industrial Organizations** U.S. federation of labor unions formed by the merger of the AFL and the CIO. The AFL was founded in 1886 as a loose federation of craft unions under Samuel GOMPERS. Member unions retained autonomy and received protection of their workers and jurisdiction over a certain industrial territory. The CIO was founded in 1935 as the Committee for Industrial Organization by AFL leaders who believed in organizing skilled and unskilled workers across entire industries. In 1938 it elected John L. LEWIS president. At first bitter rivals, the two groups formed an alliance in the conservative, antilabor postwar era, and in 1955 they merged under George MEANY. Membership reached 17 million in the late 1970s but declined in the 1980s and '90s as the U.S. manufacturing sector shrank. AFL-CIO activities include recruiting members, conducting educational campaigns, and supporting political candidates and legislation deemed beneficial to labor.

Afonso I *known as* **Afonso the Conqueror** (c.1110–1185) First king of Portugal (1139–85). He defeated his mother to take the throne (1128), ruling first as a vassal of his cousin Alfonso VII of León but later securing Portuguese independence and gaining the title of king (1139). He took Lisbon (1147) from the Moors and eventually extended Portugal beyond the TAGUS RIVER. He left his son SANCHO I a stable, independent monarchy.

Afonso the Great See Afonso de ALBUQUERQUE

Africa Second-largest continent on earth. It is bounded by the Mediterranean Sea, the Atlantic Ocean, the Red Sea, and the Indian Ocean; it is divided almost equally by the equator. Area: 11,724,300 sq mi (30,365,700 sq km). Population (2001 est.): 818,000,000. Elevations range from 19,340 ft (5,895 m) at Mt. KILIMANJARO to 515 ft (157 m) below sea level at Lake Assal. The SAHARA, the world's largest contiguous desert, occupies more than one-fourth of the total land area. The continent's hydrology is dominated by the NILE RIVER in the north and the CONGO in central Africa. Only about 6% of the continent is arable, while nearly one-fourth is forested or wooded. The peoples of Africa probably speak more languages than those of any other continent. Arabic is predominant from Egypt to Mauritania and in the Sudan. In sub-Saharan Africa, the BANTU and KHOISAN LANGUAGES are particularly important. Peoples of European descent are found in the south; Dutch (Boer) migrations began in the 17th cent., and the English first settled in what is now Zambia and Zimbabwe in the 19th cent. Agriculture is the most important sector of the economy in most countries. Diamond and gold mining are important in the south; other areas produce petroleum and natural gas. Most African governments are controlled by a single clique. African leaders have sought to develop pan-African cooperation through the ORGANIZATION OF AFRICAN UNITY. Human beings are widely thought to have originated in Africa. The oldest known hominids, members of the genus *AUSTRALOPITHECUS*, date from about 8 million years ago. *HOMO HABILIS* and *HOMO ERECTUS* inhabited Africa before and during the Pleistocene epoch (1.6 million–10,000 years ago), and forms of *HOMO SAPIENS* began appearing 500,000–300,000 years ago. Africa's first great historical kingdom, Egypt, arose along the Nile about 3000 B.C. and flourished for nearly 3,000 years. The PHOENICIANS established a colony at CARTHAGE and controlled the W Mediterranean for nearly 600 years. While N Africa was dominated by the Romans for several centuries, the first known empire in W Africa was GHANA (5th–11th cent. A.D.). Muslim empires included those of MALI (c.1250–1400) and the SONGHAI of Gao (c.1400–1591). In E and central Africa the emphasis was on trade with Arabia, and several powerful city-states, including MOGADISHU and MOMBASA, were established. The Portuguese explored the coast in the 15th cent. Before the late 19th cent., Europe showed little interest in colonizing Africa, but by 1884 European countries had begun a scramble to partition the continent, and by 1920 much of it was under colonial rule. Anticolonial sentiment developed gradually, becoming widespread after 1950, and one by one the colonies became independent.

Africa, Roman Proconsular Roman province. It was founded after the Roman defeat of CARTHAGE in 146 B.C. It expanded to include NUMIDIA and the N part of modern Libya, and between 30 B.C. and A.D. 180 other parts of N Africa became part of the Roman empire. The region was taken by the VANDALS in the 5th cent. and by the Muslims in 641.

African architecture Building styles of Africa. Most of Africa's 5,000 peoples build in grasses, wood, and clay. A prevalent form in S and W. Africa is the cylindrical house with conical thatched roof. A common method of construction uses a ring of posts with mud infill (see POLE CONSTRUCTION). Where wood is less available, houses may be constructed of mud in a coil pottery technique. In some areas the KRAAL serves a defensive function. The characteristic settlement form in W. Africa is the walled compound, including dwellings, granaries, and pens for animals. Rec-

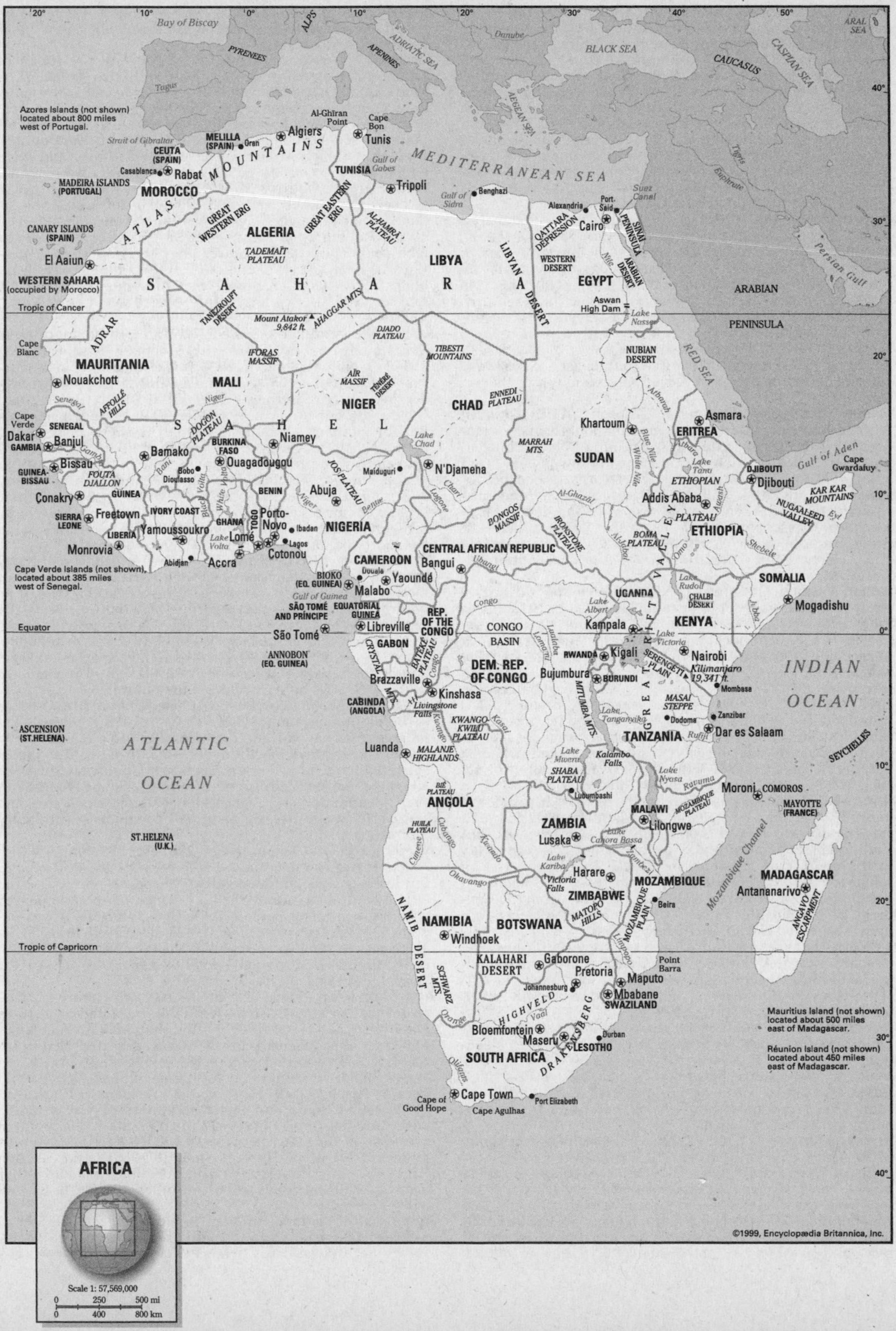

tangular houses with pitched roofs covered with thatch (or corrugated iron) are used by many rain-forest peoples. Many pastoral nomads build tent structures. The MASAI construct rectangular huts using stick frames plastered with cattle dung. Earlier urban civilizations were often influenced by Arab and N. African traditions, erecting rectilinear, flat-roofed buildings of mud and stone. The great palace of Benin City, Nigeria, was as large as a European town, with galleried buildings, shingled roofs, and high towers sporting bronze birds. Yoruba towns maintain the traditional *afin* (palace) at the center, from which broad roads radiate. Prominent in many W. African towns are the mosques, bristling with wood reinforcement.

African languages Languages indigenous to sub-Saharan Africa that belong to the NIGER-CONGO, NILO-SAHARAN, KHOISAN, and AFROASIATIC LANGUAGE phyla. Africa is thought to have 1,000 to 1,200 languages, more than any other continent. Distinctions in TONE play a significant role in nearly all sub-Saharan languages. Contact between people with different languages has necessitated the development of LINGUA FRANCAS such as SWAHILI in E. Africa, Lingala in the Congo River basin (see BANTU LANGUAGES), Sango in the Central African Republic (see ADAMAWA-UBANGI LANGUAGES), and ARABIC across much of the SAHEL.

African Methodist Episcopal Church (AME Church) African-American Methodist denomination, formally organized in 1816. It originated with a group of black Philadelphians who, led by Richard ALLEN, withdrew in 1787 from a local Methodist church (see METHODISM) because of racial discrimination and built Bethel African Methodist Church. In 1816 Allen became bishop of the new African Methodist Episcopal Church. From the Northern states, it spread rapidly in the South after the Civil War, founding many colleges and seminaries. Today it has 3,600 churches worldwide.

African National Congress (ANC) S. African political party and black nationalist organization. Founded in 1912, it was long dedicated to the elimination of APARTHEID. In response to government massacres of demonstrators at Sharpeville (1960) and Soweto (1976), it promoted guerrilla warfare, but with little effect, owing to stringent S. African internal-security measures, including an official ban on the ANC 1960–90. In 1991 Nelson MANDELA became ANC president. In 1994 the party swept the country's first all-race elections; the ANC led a coalition government including its longtime rival the NATIONAL PARTY, and Mandela became S. Africa's president. In 1999 Thabo MBEKI succeeded him as president of the ANC and of S. Africa.

African religions Indigenous religions of the African continent. The introduced religions of Islam (in N Africa) and Christianity are now the continent's major religions, but traditional religions still play an important role, especially in the interior of sub-Saharan Africa. Traditional African religions share the notion of a creator god, who made the world and then withdrew, remaining remote from the concerns of human life. Prayers and sacrificial offerings are usually directed toward secondary divinities, who are intermediaries between the human and sacred realms. Ancestors also serve as intermediaries. Rituals are aimed at maintaining a harmonious relationship with cosmic powers. ANIMISM is a common feature, and misfortune is often attributed to WITCHCRAFT AND SORCERY.

African violet Any plant of the genus *Saintpaulia,* of the gesneriad family, especially *S. ionantha.* Native to high elevations in tropical E Africa, they are small, hairy, usually stemless herbaceous plants with crowded, long-stalked leaves. The violet, white, or pink flowers bloom most of the year. They are popular houseplants, and hundreds of varieties have been developed.

Afrikaans language \ˌaf-ri-'känz\ Language of the Republic of S. Africa developed from 17th-cent. Dutch by descendants of European settlers, indigenous KHOISAN-speaking peoples, and African and Asian slaves of the Dutch. It differs from Dutch in its sound system, and in grammar and vocabulary. Afrikaans is the first language of close to 6 million S. Africans, both AFRIKANERS and people of mixed race, and a second or third language of several million

more, some in Namibia. Standard Afrikaans was made an official language in S. Africa in 1925; today it is one of 11 official S. African languages.

Afrikaner \ˌaf-ri-'kän-ər\ *formerly* **Boer** Any S. African of Dutch or Huguenot descent whose native language is AFRIKAANS. Originally called Boers ("farmers"), since many early Dutch and Huguenot settlers became frontier farmers in the TRANSVAAL and the ORANGE FREE STATE, they established self-sufficient, patriarchal Calvinist communities, developed their own language and subculture, and were committed to APARTHEID. They fought a bitter war with the British (the S. AFRICAN WAR, 1899–1902) over the right to govern the frontier territories. Though defeated, they retained their language and culture and eventually attained political domination throughout S. Africa for most of the 20th cent. They yielded power after the first all-race elections in 1994. Much of the country's economic wealth remains in Afrikaner hands. Today they number about 6.4 million. See also GREAT TREK, NATIONAL PARTY OF S. AFRICA.

Afroasiatic languages *formerly* **Hamito-Semitic languages** Superfamily of about 250 languages spoken by an estimated 250–300 million people in N. Africa and parts of sub-Saharan African and in SW Asia. The major branches of Afroasiatic are SEMITIC, Berber, EGYPTIAN, Cushitic, Omotic, and Chadic. Berber is a group of closely related languages spoken by perhaps 15 million people in enclaves scattered across N. Africa. Cushitic is a family of about 30 languages spoken by more than 30 million people in countries of NE Africa. Omotic is a cluster of some 30 languages spoken by 2–3 million people near the Omo River in SW Ethiopia. Chadic comprises about 140 languages spoken in N Nigeria, S Niger, S Chad, and N Cameroon; except for HAUSA, none has more than half a million speakers.

Afrocentrism Ideology that promotes the study of history from an African standpoint, viewing Africans as shapers of history and not merely subjects of investigation. One of its controversial tenets is that ancient Greek culture, especially philosophy, derives from Egypt, an idea promoted by Martin Bernal's *Black Athena* (1989). Extremist pronouncements in the debate on Afrocentrism have sparked charges and countercharges of racism. A number of urban schools in the U.S. offer an Afrocentric curriculum.

afterburner Second combustion chamber in a TURBOJET or turbofan engine, immediately in front of the engine's exhaust nozzle. The injection and combustion of extra fuel in this chamber provide additional thrust for takeoff or supersonic flight; the afterburner may nearly double the thrust of a turbojet engine. Because the afterburner sharply increases fuel consumption and is generally less effective at subsonic speeds, its use is usually restricted to supersonic military aircraft.

Agadir \ˌä-gä-'dir\ Seaport (pop., 2001 est.: 599,000), SW Morocco. It was occupied in the 16th cent. by the Portuguese, but later became an independent Moroccan port. After the 1911 MOROCCAN CRISIS when a German gunboat appeared offshore to protect perceived German interests, it was occupied by French troops in 1913. Destroyed in 1960 by earthquakes, tidal wave, and fire, the port was rebuilt south of its original location and serves as a marketplace for the surrounding agricultural area.

Aga Khan \ˌä-gə-'kän\ Title of the IMAMS of the Nizari ISMAILI sect of SHIITE Islam. It was first granted in 1818 to Hasan Ali Shah (1800–1881) by the shah of Iran. Aga Khan I later revolted against Iran (1838) and, defeated, fled to India. His eldest son, Ali Shah (d.1885), was briefly Aga Khan II; Ali Shah's son Sultan Sir Mohammed Shah (1877–1957) became Aga Khan III. He served as president of the All-India Muslim League, and played an important part in Indian constitutional reform (1930–32); in 1937 he was appointed president of the LEAGUE OF NATIONS. His successor was his grandson Karim al-Hussain Shah (b.1936), who, as Aga Khan IV, founded the Aga Khan Foundation and other agencies offering educational and other services in S. Asia and E. Africa.

Agamemnon \ˌa-gə-'mem-ˌnän\ In Greek legend, the son of ATREUS, king of MYCENAE and commander of the Greek forces that attacked Troy. When PARIS carried off Menelaus's wife, HELEN, Agamemnon called for a war of revenge against the Trojans. When ARTEMIS prevented the Greek fleet from sailing, Agamemnon sacrificed his daughter IPHIGENEIA to appease the goddess. After the TROJAN WAR he returned home, where he was killed by his wife, Clytemnestra, and her lover, Aegisthus. His murder was avenged by his son ORESTES. These events formed the basis of AESCHYLUS' great *Oresteia.*

agaric \'a-gər-ik\ Any FUNGUS of the family Agaricaceae, including the familiar commercially grown MUSHROOM. Agarics have SPORE-bearing cells (basidia) located on thin sheets called gills. The best-known genus is *Agaricus (Psalliota),* which includes the edible meadow or field mushroom, *A. campestris,* and the common cultivated mushroom, *A. bisporus.*

Agassi \'a-gə-sē\, **Andre (Kirk)** (b.1970) U.S. tennis player. Born in Las Vegas, he won the Wimbledon men's singles in 1992, the U.S. Open in 1994, and the Australian Open in 1995. By 1997 he had dropped to 122 in the international rankings, but he recovered to win the U.S. Open (1999), the French Open (1999), and the Australian Open three times (2000, 2001, 2003).

Agassiz \'a-gə-sē\, **Alexander (Emmanuel Rodolphe)** (1835–1910) Swiss-U.S. marine zoologist, oceanographer, and mining engineer. The son of Louis AGASSIZ, he emigrated in 1849 to the U.S., where he conducted significant systematic zoology work on ECHINODERMS (e.g., STARFISH) and later challenged Charles DARWIN's theory of CORAL-REEF formation. He developed and supervised what became the world's foremost copper mine (Calumet, Mich.).

Agassiz, Elizabeth Cabot *orig.* Elizabeth Cabot Cary (1822–1907) U.S. naturalist and educator. Born in Boston, in 1850 she married Louis AGASSIZ. She helped manage his field trips, and together they founded a marine laboratory. After his death she pursued her idea of a college for women to be taught by the HARVARD UNIV. faculty. She cofounded (1882) and headed the Society for the Collegiate Instruction of Women; in 1894 it was renamed Radcliffe College, and she continued as president until 1899.

Agassiz \'a-gə-sē\, **(Jean) Louis (Rodolphe)** (1807–1873) Swiss-U.S. naturalist. After teaching in Switzerland (1832–46), where he did landmark work on glaciers and extinct fishes, he moved to the U.S. He became famous for his innovative teaching methods, which encouraged learning through direct observation of nature, and his teaching at Harvard Univ. revolutionized the study of natural history in the U.S. He was also an outstanding science administrator, promoter, and fund-raiser. He was a lifelong opponent of Charles DARWIN's theory of evolution. His second wife, E. C. AGASSIZ, and his son, Alexander AGASSIZ, were also noted naturalists.

agate \'a-gət\ Common semiprecious silica mineral, a variety of CHALCEDONY that occurs in bands of varying color and transparency. Varieties (see ONYX) are characterized by peculiarities in the shape and color of the bands. Agate is essentially QUARTZ and is found throughout the world, commonly in cavities in eruptive rocks and in GEODES. Brazil and Uruguay are major producers of agates;

Banded agate

they are also found in W U.S. states. Much commercial agate is artificially dyed to make the naturally dull-gray stones more colorful.

Agathocles \ə-'ga-thə-klēz\ (361–289 B.C.) Tyrant of SYRACUSE (317–304?) and self-styled king of Sicily (304?–289). He served in the Syracusan army and, after two failed attempts, overthrew the Syracusan oligarchy (317). He waged wars with other Sicilian Greek cities (316–313?) and with Carthage (311), effectively curtailing Carthaginian expansion in Sicily. He restored Syracusan liberty in his will, but his death was followed by a renewal of Carthaginian power in Sicily.

agave family \ə-'gä-vē\ Family Agavaceae of the order Liliales, composed of short-stemmed, often woody plants found in tropical, subtropical, and temperate areas. They have narrow, lance-shaped, sometimes fleshy or toothed leaves clustered at the base of the plant. Most species have large flower clusters. Plants of the genus *Agave* are important primarily for their leaf fibers, especially the valuable sisal HEMP, from *A. sisalana.* Some species contain a sap that is fermented to produce the intoxicating drinks pulque and mescal. Many species of YUCCA are popular as ornamentals.

Agee \'ā-jē\, **James** (1909–1955) U.S. writer. Born in Knoxville, Tenn., he attended Harvard Univ. In the 1930s and '40s, his film reviews in *Time* and the *Nation* made him a pioneer in serious film criticism. His lyrical *Let Us Now Praise Famous Men* (1941) documents the daily lives of poor sharecroppers. His screenplays include *The African Queen* (1951) and *The Night of the Hunter* (1955). He is best known for his autobiographical novel *A Death in the Family* (1957, Pulitzer Prize).

agency In law, a relationship in which one party (the agent) acts on behalf of and under the control of another (the principal) in dealing with third parties. Agency becomes a legal issue when the agent injures or wrongs a third party. In Anglo-American law, principals are bound by and liable for the acts of such agents as stockbrokers, contractors, real-estate agents, and lawyers. See also REGULATORY AGENCY.

Agent Orange Mixture of HERBICIDES. It contains approximately equal amounts of ESTERS of 2,4-D (2,4-dichlorophenoxyacetic acid) and 2,4,5-T (2,4,5-trichlorophenoxyacetic acid) with traces of DIOXIN. About 13 million gallons were sprayed by U.S. military forces onto Vietnam's forests and crops during the Vietnam War, with the dual purpose of destroying cover for enemy movements and destroying food sources. Exposure to Agent Orange has been blamed for abnormal numbers of miscarriages, skin diseases, cancers, birth defects, and malformations among Vietnamese and of cancers and other disorders in U.S. servicemen and their families.

Agesilaus II \ə-,je-sə-'lā-əs\ (444?–360 B.C.) King of SPARTA (399–360) and commander of its army during most of the era of Spartan supremacy (404–371). He took the throne with LYSANDER's help while Sparta was fighting Persia and defeated the allied Thebes, Athens, Argos, and Corinth in the Corinthian War (395–387). He dissolved the Boeotian League, but battles against the Boeotian Confederacy (371) and Thebes (370, 361) ended Sparta's ascendancy. He died returning from a mercenary engagement in Egypt.

agglomerate \ə-'glä-mə-rət\ Large, coarse, angular rock fragments that are ejected during explosive volcanic eruptions. Although they resemble sedimentary CONGLOMERATES, agglomerates are IGNEOUS ROCKS that consist of angular or rounded lava fragments. Some geologists sort agglomerates into bombs, blocks, and BRECCIA. Bombs are ejected in a molten state, becoming rounded upon solidification, and blocks are erupted as solid fragments.

Agincourt \'a-jin-kōrt\, **Battle of** (Oct. 25, 1415) Battle resulting in the decisive victory of the English over the French in the HUNDRED YEARS' WAR. In pursuit of his claim to the French throne, HENRY V invaded Normandy with an army of 11,000 men in August 1415. The English took Harfleur in September, but with their forces cut in half by battle and disease, they resolved to return to England. At Agincourt they were cornered by a French army of 20,000–30,000 men, including many mounted knights in heavy armor. On the cramped battlefield, Henry made skillful use of his lightly equipped, mobile archers. The French lost over 6,000 men, while the English lost fewer than 450.

aging Gradual change in an organism that leads to increased risk of weakness, disease, and death. It takes place in a cell, an organ, or the total organism over the entire adult life span. There is a decline in biological functions and in ability to adapt to metabolic stress. Overall effects of aging include reduced immunity, loss of muscle strength, decline in memory and other aspects of cognition, and loss of color in the hair and elasticity in the skin. In women, the process accelerates after MENOPAUSE. See also GERONTOLOGY AND GERIATRICS.

Agnes, St. (fl. early 4th cent.) Legendary Christian martyr, the patron saint of girls. According to tradition, she was a

beautiful virgin in Rome who turned away all suitors, declaring that she could have no spouse but Jesus. The rejected suitors informed Roman officials that she was a Christian, and she was punished by being exposed in a brothel. The only man who attempted to violate her there was struck blind, and she healed him with prayer. She was murdered during DIOCLETIAN's persecutions.

Agnew, Spiro T(heodore) (1918–1996) U.S. vice president (1969–73), the only one forced to resign. Born in Baltimore, he served as county executive (1962–67) and governor of Maryland (1967–69). In 1968 and 1972 he was elected vice president on the Republican ticket headed by Richard NIXON. His speeches denouncing Vietnam War protesters and television news coverage brought him much attention. Investigated for extortion, bribery, and income-tax violations during his governorship, he resigned in 1973 and was fined $10,000 and sentenced to three years of unsupervised probation. Disbarred in 1974, he became a consultant to foreign businesses.

Agni Hindu god of fire, second only to INDRA in Vedic mythology. He is the fire of the sun, of lightning, and of the hearth of worship, and he personifies the fire of sacrifice. Agni is described as ruddy-hued and with two faces, one beneficent and one malignant. In the RIG VEDA he is sometimes identified with Rudra, the forerunner of SHIVA.

Agnon \äg-ˈnōn\, **S. Y.** *orig.* Shmuel Yosef Halevi Czaczkes (1888–1970) Ukrainian-Israeli writer. Born into a Polish Galician family, he moved to Palestine in 1907 and chose to write in Hebrew. His novel *The Day Before Yesterday* (1945) examines the problem facing the westernized Jew who emigrates to Israel. Other novels include *The Bridal Canopy* (1919) and *A Guest for the Night* (1938). He is regarded as one of the greatest modern Hebrew writers. In 1966 he and Nelly SACHS shared the Nobel Prize.

agnosticism \ag-ˈnäs-tə-ˌsiz-əm\ Doctrine that one cannot know the existence of anything beyond what one can experience. It is popularly equated with religious skepticism, and especially with the rejection of traditional Christian beliefs under the impact of modern scientific thought. T. H. HUXLEY coined the term agnostic (as opposed to gnostic) in 1869, to designate one who rejected traditional Judeo-Christian THEISM but was not an atheist (see ATHEISM). Agnosticism may mean no more than a suspension of judgment, or it may constitute a rejection of traditional Christian tenets.

agora \ˈa-gə-rə\ In ancient Greek cities, an open space serving as an assembly area and backdrop for commercial, civic, social, and religious activities. Use of the agora varied in different periods. Located in the middle of the city or near the harbor, it was often enclosed by public buildings, COLONNADES containing shops, and stoas for protection from sun and bad weather.

Agora Model of the Agora, Athens, as it might have appeared in the 2nd cent. A.D.

agouti \ə-ˈgü-tē\ Any of about half a dozen species of rabbit-sized rodents (genus *Dasyprocta*) that occur in the American tropics (S Mexico to N S. America). Agoutis are 16–24 in. (40–60 cm) long and have a long body, small ears, vestigial tail or none at all, and slender feet with long, hooflike claws. Their wiry fur has individual hairs banded in what is called the agouti pattern. Agoutis eat roots, leaves, and fruit.

Agra \ˈä-grə\ City (pop., 2001: 1,082,000), W central Uttar Pradesh, India. Founded in the early 18th cent. on the Yumana River southeast of New Delhi, it was intermittently the MUGHAL capital. The city fell to the British in 1803. It is the site of the TAJ MAHAL and the imperial palace of AKBAR.

Agricola \ə-ˈgri-kə-lə\, **Georgius** *orig.* Georg Bauer (1494–1555) German scientist, the father of MINERALOGY. A physician in Saxony (1527–33), he was among the first to found a natural science upon observation as opposed to speculation. His *De natura fossilium* (1546), considered the first mineralogy textbook, presented the first scientific classification of minerals (based on their physical properties). His *De re metallica* (1556) dealt chiefly with mining and smelting.

Agricola \ə-ˈgrik-ə-lə\, **Gnaeus Julius** (A.D. 40–93) Roman general. After serving as TRIBUNE and QUAESTOR in Britain and Asia, and as governor of Britain (77/78–84), he conquered parts of Wales and N England, then advanced into Scotland. In 83 he defeated the Caledonians at Mons Graupius; he then occupied Scotland to the fringe of the highlands. Recalled to Rome, Agricola was offered the proconsulship of Asia, but chose retirement. His life is known through the writings of his son-in-law TACITUS.

Agricultural Revolution Gradual transformation of the traditional agricultural system that began in Britain in the 18th cent. Not completed until the 19th cent., it included the reallocation of land ownership to make farms more compact and an increased investment in technical improvements, such as new machinery, better drainage, scientific methods of breeding, and experimentation with new crops and systems of crop rotation. It was an essential prelude to the INDUSTRIAL REVOLUTION.

agriculture Science or art of cultivating the SOIL, growing and harvesting crops, and raising livestock. Agriculture probably first developed in SW Asia and Egypt, then spread to Europe, Africa, the rest of Asia, the islands of the central and S. Pacific, and finally to N. and S. America. Agriculture in the Middle East is believed to date from 9000–7000 B.C. Early cultivated crops include wild barley (Middle East), domesticated beans and water chestnuts (Thailand), and pumpkins (the Americas). Domestication of animals occurred during roughly the same period. Steady improvements in tools and methods over the centuries increased agricultural output, as did mechanization, selective breeding and hybridization, and, in the 20th cent., the use of HERBICIDES and INSECTICIDES. More of the world's aggregate manpower is devoted to agriculture than to all other occupations combined.

Agriculture, U.S. Department of (USDA) Federal executive division in charge of programs and policies relating to the farming industry and the use of NATIONAL FORESTS and grasslands. Formed in 1862, the USDA works to stabilize or improve domestic farm income, develop foreign markets, protect soil and water resources, make credit available for rural development, and ensure the quality of food supplies.

Agrippa \ə-ˈgrip-ə\, **Marcus Vipsanius** (63?–12 B.C.) Powerful deputy of AUGUSTUS. He helped Octavian (later Augustus) take power after Julius CAESAR's murder (44), defeating Sextus Pompeius (c. 67–35 B.C.) in 36 and Mark ANTONY at the Battle of ACTIUM in 31. He went on to quell rebellions, found colonies, administer parts of the empire, and give funds for public works and buildings to Rome. In 23 Augustus seemed to make him heir, and Agrippa married Augustus' daughter JULIA, but he died during the emperor's lifetime. Agrippa's writings (now lost) influenced STRABO and PLINY THE ELDER. His daughter Agrippina the Elder (14? B.C.–A.D. 33) was the wife of GERMANICUS CAESAR, mother of CALIGULA and AGRIPPINA THE YOUNGER, and grandmother of NERO.

Marcus Vipsanius Agrippa Marble bust, early 1st cent. B.C.

Agrippina the Younger \ˌag-ri-ˈpī-nə\ (A.D. 15–59) Mother of NERO and a major influence in the early years of his reign. She was exiled (A.D. 39–41) for conspiring against her brother CALIGULA. Accused of poisoning her second husband (49), she married CLAUDIUS, her uncle, and had him adopt Nero as his heir instead of his own son. She poisoned her son's rivals, and when Claudius died in 54 she was suspected of having poisoned him. She became regent when Nero took the throne at 16, but gradually lost power; he finally had her put to death at her country house.

agrochemical Any chemical used in AGRICULTURE, including chemical FERTILIZERS, HERBICIDES, and INSECTICIDES. Together with other technological advances, including tractors, mechanical harvesters, and irrigation pumps, agrochemicals have increased the per-acre productivity of regions such as the Great Plains by 200–300% since the 1930s. Their long-term effects on the environment and the stability of agricultural systems that use them are hotly debated.

agronomy Branch of AGRICULTURE that deals with field crop production and soil management. Agronomists generally work with major cereal crops that require relatively little management. Agronomic experiments focus on a variety of factors relating to crop plants, including yield, diseases, cultivation, climate, and soil.

Aguascalientes City (pop., 1995: 537,000), capital of AGUASCALIENTES state, Mexico. Founded as a mining settlement in 1575, it became the state capital in the 1850s. Sometimes called "The Perforated City," it contains an underground pre-Columbian labyrinth of tunnels. It is an agricultural center, with growing industries. Several churches exhibit outstanding examples of colonial religious art.

Aguascalientes \ˌä-gwäs-käl-ˈyen-tās\ State (pop., 2000: 943,000), central Mexico. A small state (2,112 sq mi, or 5,471 sq km), it occupies part of the central plateau. Explored by Spaniards in the 16th cent., it became a coal-mining center. During the revolution of 1919–20 it was the scene of bitter fighting. It is a fertile agricultural area, and is noted for its mineral production. Its capital is AGUASCALIENTES.

Aguinaldo \ˌä-gē-ˈnäl-dō\, **Emilio** (1869–1964) Philippine independence leader. He became a leader of the Katipunan, a revolutionary society that fought the Spanish for Philippine independence (see PHILIPPINE REVOLUTION). After Spain signed a treaty ceding the islands to the U.S. (1898), Aguinaldo fought U.S. forces until he was captured in 1901. After taking an oath of allegiance to the U.S., he retired from public life. For collaborating with the Japanese during World War II, he was briefly imprisoned; released by presidential amnesty, he was appointed to the Council of State in 1950. In his later years he promoted nationalism, democracy, and improvement of relations between the U.S. and the Philippines.

Agulhas \ə-ˈgəl-əs\, **Cape** Southernmost point of the African continent. Its name, Portuguese for "needles," refers to the rocks and reefs that have wrecked many ships. The cape's meridian of 20°E is the official boundary between the Indian and Atlantic oceans.

Ahab \ˈā-ˌhab\ (fl.9th cent. B.C.) Seventh king of the N kingdom of ISRAEL (r.c.874–853 B.C.). His marriage to JEZEBEL revived an alliance with the PHOENICIANS, but her efforts to establish BAAL worship provoked bitter opposition from ELIJAH. Ahab's reign was dominated by a fierce border war with Syria; he died in an attempt to recover Ramoth-Gilead from the Syrians.

ahimsa \ə-ˈhim-sä\ (Sanskrit: "noninjury") Fundamental ethical virtue of JAINISM, also respected in BUDDHISM and HINDUISM. In Jainism ahimsa is the standard by which all actions are judged. Those observing the small vows (anuvrata) must refrain from killing any animal life. Ascetics observing the great vows (mahavrata) must take the greatest care not to injure any living substance, even unknowingly. In the 20th cent. Mohandas GANDHI extended ahimsa into the political sphere as SATYAGRAHA.

Ahmadabad \ˈä-mə-də-ˌbäd\ City (metro. area pop., 2001: 4,519,000), Gujarat state, W central India, 290 mi (467 km) north of Bombay. Founded in 1411 by Sultan Ahmad Shah, it flourished as a capital, declined 1512–72, revived under MUGHAL rule in the 17th cent., and fell to the British in 1818. With the opening of cotton mills in 1859, it became India's largest inland industrial center. Mohandas GANDHI's nationalist political agitation began there in 1930.

Ahmadiya \ˌäh-mə-ˈdē-ə\ Modern Islamic sect, founded in India in 1889 by Mirza Ghulam Ahmad (1839–1908). It holds that JESUS feigned death and resurrection and escaped to India, and that JIHAD is a peaceful battle against nonbelievers. After 1914, the Ahmadiya split. The Qadianis, based in Rabwah, Pakistan, recognize Ghulam Ahmad as a prophet; they zealously preach Ahmadi beliefs as the one true ISLAM. A Lahore-based sect regards Ghulam Ahmad merely as a reformer of Islam. The term Ahmadiya is also used to describe various Sufi orders (see SUFISM), particularly that founded by Ahmad al-Badawi (d.1276).

Ahmad Shah Durrani \ˈäk-məd-ˈshä-dùr-ˈä-nē\ (1722?–1772) Founder of Afghanistan. The son of an Afghan chief, he became shah in 1747. He proceeded to invade India repeatedly in an attempt to control the trade routes to central and W Asia, and became ruler of an empire that extended from the AMU DARYA to the Indian Ocean and from Khorasan to present-day N India. His hold on the Punjab was weakened by his distractions in the west, and he ultimately lost control of it to the Sikhs. Much of his empire disintegrated after his death.

Ahura Mazda \ˈä-hùr-ə-ˈmäz-də\ Supreme god of ancient Iranian religion, especially ZOROASTRIANISM. ZOROASTER taught that Ahura Mazda created the universe and maintains the cosmic order, and that the history of the world consists of the battle between two spirits he created—the beneficent Spenta Mainyu and the destructive Angra Mainyu. The AVESTA identifies Ahura Mazda himself with the beneficent spirit and represents him as bountiful, all-knowing, and the creator of everything good. In late sources, Zurvan ("Time") is the father of the twins Ormazd (Ahura Mazda) and Ahriman (Angra Mainyu), who reign alternately over the world until Ormazd's ultimate victory.

AI See ARTIFICIAL INTELLIGENCE

AIDS in full **acquired immunodeficiency syndrome** Fatal transmissible disorder caused by HIV. AIDS, the last stage of HIV infection, is defined by the appearance of potentially lethal opportunistic infections. The first AIDS cases were identified in 1981, HIV was isolated in 1983, and blood tests were developed by 1985. In 2000, more than 35 million people worldwide were living with HIV, and over 15 million had died of AIDS. In the U.S., some 2 million people had been infected with HIV, 800,000 had been diagnosed with AIDS, and 450,000 had died. Sub-Saharan Africa remains the focus of infection, but the number of cases in S. and S.E. Asia and elsewhere continues to mount at an alarming rate as well. An initial acute illness usually resolves within weeks. Infected persons then generally have few or no symptoms for about 10 years. As the IMMUNE SYSTEM deteriorates, they develop diseases such as *Pneumocystis carinii* PNEUMONIA, CYTOMEGALOVIRUS, LYMPHOMA, or KAPOSI'S SARCOMA.

Aiken \ˈā-kən\, **Conrad (Potter)** (1889–1973) U.S. writer. Born in Savannah, Ga., he was traumatized as a child when his father killed his mother and then himself. Educated at Harvard Univ., he wrote most of his psychoanalysis-influenced fiction in the 1920s and '30s, most notably such short stories as "Strange Moonlight" from *Bring! Bring!* (1925) and "Silent Snow, Secret Snow" from *Among the Lost People* (1934). His poems include "Preludes to Definition."

aikido \ˌī-ki-ˈdō, ī-ˈkē-dō\ Japanese art of self-defense utilizing the principle of nonresistance to cause an opponent's own momentum to work against him. Aikido was developed to subdue rather than (as in JUJITSU and KARATE) to maim or kill. It especially emphasizes the importance of achieving complete mental calm and control of one's own body. There are no offensive moves. It originated in Japan, probably in the 14th cent.; its modern form was developed by Ueshiba Morihei.

Ailey \ˈā-lē\, **Alvin, Jr.** (1931–1989) U.S. dancer and choreographer. Born in Rogers, Texas, he moved to Los Angeles in 1942, where he studied dance and choreography. After moving to New York, in 1958 he founded the Alvin Ailey American Dance Theater, composed primarily of blacks. The numerous works he choreographed for the company included its signature *Revelations* (1960), set to black spirituals. The company toured worldwide, making Ailey one of the best-known U.S. choreographers. After his death from AIDS, Judith JAMISON became artistic director.

Alvin Ailey, 1960

Ainu \ˈī-nü\ People of Japan, originally residing throughout its four major islands. The few remaining pure Ainu today live principally in N Hokkaido, Sakhalin, and the Kuril Islands. Originally physically and culturally distinct from the Japanese, their language and origins have been the subject of scholarly debate. The Ainu were traditionally hunters, fishermen, and trappers; their religion centered on spirits believed to be present in animals and the natural world.

air Mixture of gases constituting the earth's atmosphere. Gases that occur in steady concentrations include molecular nitrogen, 78% by volume, and molecular oxygen, 21%. Small amounts of argon, neon, helium, methane, krypton, hydrogen, nitrous oxide, and xenon are also present in almost constant proportions. Other gases occur in variable concentrations: water vapor, ozone, carbon dioxide, sulfur dioxide, and nitrogen dioxide. Air also contains trace amounts of ammonia and hydrogen sulfide. The variable constituents are important for maintaining life. Water vapor is the source for all forms of precipitation and is an important absorber and emitter of infrared radiation, as is carbon dioxide, which is also necessary for photosynthesis. Ozone (see OZONE LAYER) is an effective absorber of ultraviolet radiation from the sun, but at ground-level is a major constituent of smog.

air brake Either of two kinds of braking systems. The first, used by trains, trucks, and buses, operates by a piston driven by compressed air from reservoirs connected to BRAKE cylinders. When air pressure in the brake pipe is reduced, air is automatically admitted into the brake cylinder. The first practical air brake for railroads was invented in the 1860s by George WESTINGHOUSE. The second type, used by aircraft and race cars, consists of a flap or surface that can be mechanically projected into the airstream.

airbrush Pneumatic device for developing a fine, small-diameter spray of paint, protective coating, or liquid color (see AEROSOL). The airbrush can be a pencil-shaped atomizer used for various highly detailed activities such as shading drawings and retouching photographs; in contrast, a spray gun is usually used for covering large surfaces with paint.

air-conditioning Control of temperature, humidity, purity, and motion of air in an enclosed space. In a self-contained air-conditioning unit, air is cooled by being blown across a refrigerant-filled coil and then distributed to a controlled indoor environment. Central air-conditioning in a large building generally consists of a main plant located on the roof or mechanical floor and intermittently spaced fans that deliver air through ducts to zones within the building. The air then returns to the central machinery through spaces called plenums to be recooled (or reheated) and recirculated. Alternative systems of cooling use chilled water propelled by pumps to units with fans that circulate air locally.

aircraft carrier Naval vessel equipped with a platform that allows airplanes to take off and land. Takeoffs are facilitated by using catapults. For landing, retractable hooks on the aircraft engage transverse wires on the deck to achieve a quick stop. The British navy developed the first true aircraft carrier near the end of World War I, and carriers first saw combat in World War II. The Japanese attack on Pearl Harbor was conducted by carrier-based planes, and the carrier played leading roles in the Battles of MIDWAY and the Coral Sea.

air-cushion vehicle *or* **hovercraft** Vehicle supported above the surface of land or water by an air cushion, produced by downwardly directed fans, enclosed within a flexible skirt beneath the hull. Though first proposed in the 1870s, a working model was not produced until 1955, when Christopher Cockerell solved the problem of keeping the air cushion from escaping from under the vehicle, and formed Hovercraft Ltd. Today hovercraft are used mainly as ferries.

Airedale terrier Dog breed, the largest of the TERRIERS. It stands about 23 in. (58 cm) high, weighs 40–50 lbs (18–23 kg), and has a boxy appearance, with a long, squared muzzle. Its coat is dense and wiry, with a black saddle and tan legs, muzzle, and underparts. Intelligent and courageous, powerful and affectionate, the Airedale has been used as a wartime dispatch carrier, police dog, guard, and big-game hunter.

air force Military organization with responsibility for AIR WARFARE. The air force must gain control of the air, support ground forces, and accomplish strategic-bombing objectives. Its basic weapons are FIGHTER AIRCRAFT, BOMBERS, attack aircraft (which operate at lower altitudes than bombers), and reconnaissance craft. The air forces of some of the world's major powers are responsible for land-based ICBMS and nuclear-armed long-range bombers. The army and naval branches may also operate aircraft.

air mass Large body of air having nearly uniform conditions of temperature and humidity at any given altitude. It may extend hundreds or thousands of miles horizontally and sometimes as high as the top of the TROPOSPHERE. An air mass forms whenever the atmosphere remains in contact with a large, relatively uniform land or sea surface long enough to acquire its temperature and moisture properties. The earth's major air masses originate in polar or subtropical latitudes; the middle latitudes constitute a zone of modification and mixing.

airplane Fixed-wing aircraft that is heavier than air, driven by a propeller or a high-velocity JET ENGINE and supported by the dynamic reaction of the air against its wings. An airplane's essential components are the body or fuselage, a flight-sustaining wing system, stabilizing tail surfaces, altitude-control devices such as rudders, a thrust-providing power source, and a landing support system. Beginning in the 1840s, several British and French inventors produced designs for engine-powered aircraft, but the first powered, sustained, and controlled flight was only achieved by Wilbur and Orville WRIGHT in 1903. Most airplanes today have a long nose section, swept-back wings with jet engines placed behind the plane's midsection, and a tail stabilizing section. SEAPLANES are adapted to touch down on water, and carrier-based planes are modified for high-speed short takeoff and landing. See also AVIATION. See diagram on next page.

air pollution Release into the atmosphere of gases, finely divided solids, or finely dispersed liquid aerosols at rates that exceed the capacity of the atmosphere to dissipate them or to dispose of them through incorporation into the BIOSPHERE. Dust storms in desert areas and smoke from forest and grass fires contribute to particulate and chemical air pollution. Volcanic activity is the major natural source of air pollution, pouring huge amounts of ash and toxic fumes into the atmosphere. Air pollution may affect humans directly as SMOG, or indirectly as ACID RAIN. Still less direct are possible effects on global climates (see GLOBAL WARMING).

airship *or* **dirigible** Lighter-than-air aircraft with steering and propulsion systems. Airships could be nonrigid (blimps), semirigid, or rigid. They all included a large cigar-shaped bag or balloon filled with a gas such as HYDROGEN or HELIUM, a car or gondola suspended below the balloon that held the crew and passengers, engines to drive the propellers, and rudders for steering. The first propeller-driven airship flew in 1852 in France; design improvements led to construction of the rigid ZEPPELIN (1900). The nonrigid helium-filled blimp was principally developed by Alberto Santos-Dumont (1873–1932). In 1928 Germany began regular transatlantic airship passenger service. Several explosions, particularly the 1937 *HINDENBURG* DISASTER, and AIRPLANE developments made the airship commercially obsolete.

air warfare Military operations conducted by airplanes, helicopters, or other aircraft. Hot-air balloons were used in the 19th cent. to observe enemy troop movements. By World War I, the British, French, German, Russian, and Italian

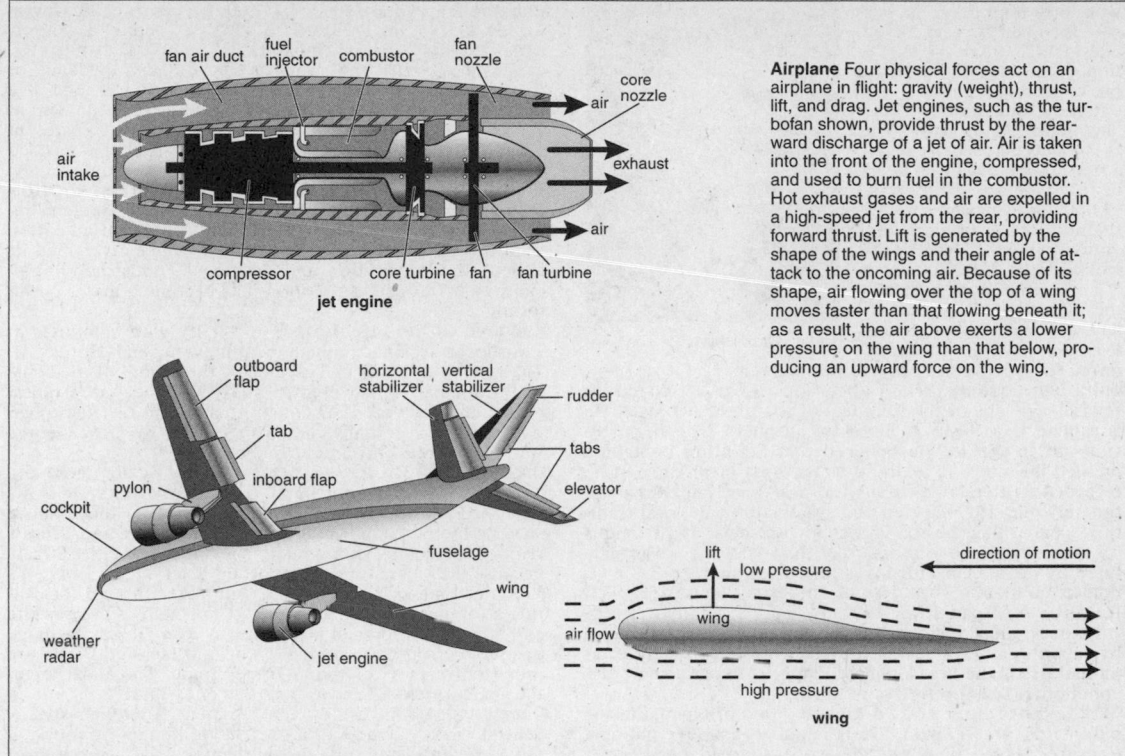

Airplane Four physical forces act on an airplane in flight: gravity (weight), thrust, lift, and drag. Jet engines, such as the turbofan shown, provide thrust by the rearward discharge of a jet of air. Air is taken into the front of the engine, compressed, and used to burn fuel in the combustor. Hot exhaust gases and air are expelled in a high-speed jet from the rear, providing forward thrust. Lift is generated by the shape of the wings and their angle of attack to the oncoming air. Because of its shape, air flowing over the top of a wing moves faster than that flowing beneath it; as a result, the air above exerts a lower pressure on the wing than that below, producing an upward force on the wing.

jet engine

wing

armed forces had flying units, including biplanes made of wood and fabric and armed with machine guns for "dogfights" with enemy FIGHTER AIRCRAFT. Zeppelins and Allied airplanes also carried out bombing raids. The 1920s and '30s saw development of the monoplane, the all-metal fuselage, and the AIRCRAFT CARRIER. The scale of air warfare in World War II remains unparalleled. The Battle of BRITAIN (1940) was the first fought exclusively in the air, and the Battle of the Coral Sea (1942) was the first between aircraft carriers. The Hiroshima and Nagasaki bombings (1945) ended the war.

Aitken, William Maxwell See Baron BEAVERBROOK

Aix-en-Provence \ˌeks-äⁿ-prō-ˈväⁿs\ City (pop., 1999: 137,000), SE France. Founded as a military colony by the Romans about 123 B.C., it was the scene of the defeat of the Teutons by MARIUS in 102 B.C. It was plundered successively by Visigoths, Franks, Lombards, and Spanish Muslims. As the capital of PROVENCE, it was a center of culture during the Middle Ages; it became part of France in 1486. A cosmopolitan university town that has inspired many artists, it is known for its fountains.

Aix-la-Chapelle See AACHEN

Ajax Greek hero of the TROJAN WAR. HOMER describes him as of great stature and second only to ACHILLES as a warrior. He fought HECTOR and rescued Achilles' body from the Trojans. When Achilles' armor was awarded to ODYSSEUS, he was so enraged that he went mad. According to several poets, Ajax slaughtered a flock of sheep he mistook for his enemies, then returned to his senses and killed himself out of shame.

Ajodhya \ə-ˈjōd-yə\ *or* **Ayodhya** \ə-ˈyōd-yə\ Former city, N India. Now part of Faizabad, Ajodhya in ancient times was one of India's greatest cities, and it is one of the seven holy cities of HINDUISM. It became a Buddhist center in the 6th–4th cent. B.C.; the BUDDHA is said to have lived there. The founder of JAINISM was born there as well. In the 16th cent. the Muslim emperor BABUR built a mosque on a site associated with an ancient Hindu temple marking the birthplace of the god RAMA. The mosque was stormed by Hindus in

1990; riots followed, and the ensuing crisis brought down the government. In 1992 the mosque was demolished by Hindu fundamentalists; more than 1,000 people may have died in related rioting.

Akbar *in full* Abu-ul-Fath Jalal-ud-Din Muhammad Akbar (1542–1605) Greatest of the Mughal emperors (see MUGHAL DYNASTY) of India (r.1556–1605). Initially his rule extended only over the Punjab and the area around Delhi. The RAJPUTS acknowledged his overlordship from 1562. Akbar included Rajput princes and other Hindus in the highest ranks of his government and reduced discrimination against non-Muslims. He continued his conquests, taking Gujarat (1573), Bengal (annexed in 1576), and Kashmir (1586), and moved south into the Deccan. Administratively, he strengthened central power, establishing that all military officers and civil administrators were to be appointed by the emperor. He encouraged scholars, poets, painters, and musicians, making his court a center of culture. His reign was often portrayed as a model by later governments—strong, benevolent, tolerant, and enlightened.

Akhenaton *or* **Akhnaton** \äk-ˈnä-tᵊn\ *orig.* **Amenhotep IV** \ˈä-mən-ˈhō-ˌtep\ (r.1353–36 B.C.) Egyptian pharaoh of the 18th dynasty (1539–1292 B.C.). He came to power when Egypt controlled Palestine, Phoenicia, and Nubia. He encouraged the exclusive worship of the little-known sun deity ATON. Assuming the name Akhenaton ("One Useful to Aton"), he moved his capital from Thebes to present-day Tell el-Amarna to escape established religious powers and make a fresh start. In government, Akhenaton tried to recapture the old authority of the ruler from bureaucrats and officials, but his focus on his new religion and neglect of affairs of state resulted in the disintegration of Egypt's Asian empire. He was succeeded by two of his sons-in-law, Smenkhkare and TUTANKHAMEN, and the old religion was soon restored.

Akhmatova \ək-ˈmä-tə-və\, **Anna** *orig.* Anna Andreyevna Gorenko (1889–1966) Russian poet. She won fame with her first poetry collections (1912, 1914). Soon after the Revolution of 1917, Soviet authorities condemned her work for what they considered its narrow focus on love and God, and in 1923, after the execution of her former husband on conspiracy charges, she entered a long period of literary silence. After World War II she was again denounced. After Joseph STALIN's death in 1953, she was slowly rehabilitated and became the influential center of a circle of younger poets. Her longest work, *Poem Without a Hero,* is one of the great poems of the 20th cent. Regarded today as one of the greatest Russian poets, she is also admired for her translations and her memoirs.

Anna Akhmatova

Akiba ben Joseph \à-'kē-vä-ben-'jō-zəf\ (c.A.D. 40–c.135) Jewish sage, one of the founders of RABBINIC JUDAISM. He is said to have been an illiterate shepherd who began to study after age 40. He believed that Scripture contained implied meanings in addition to its overt meaning, and he regarded written law (Torah) and oral law (Halakah) as ultimately one. He collected and systematized the oral traditions concerning the conduct of Jewish social and religious life, thus laying the foundation of the MISHNA. He was martyred by the Romans for his public teaching.

Akihito \à-'kē-hē-,tō\ *or* **Heisei emperor** \'hā-'sā\ (b.1933) Emperor of Japan from 1989. Because his father, HIROHITO, renounced the quasi-divine status previously enjoyed by Japan's emperors, Akihito's role has been largely ceremonial. He is the first Japanese emperor to have married a commoner. See also HEISEI PERIOD.

Akita \ə-'kē-tə\ Breed of working dog that originated in the mountains of N Japan. Designated a Japanese national treasure, it is a powerful dog with a broad head, erect pointed ears, and a large curved tail carried over the back or curled against the flank. All but the white akitas have a dark area around the muzzle. They stand 24–28 in. (60–71 cm) high.

Akkad \'a-kad\ Ancient region, central Iraq. The N division of ancient BABYLONIA (SUMER was the S division), its name was taken from the city of Agade, founded by the conqueror SARGON around 2300 B.C. Sargon and Naram-Sin extended the empire to much of MESOPOTAMIA. The empire waned in the 22nd cent. B.C. Under the kings of Akkad, their Semitic language, AKKADIAN, became a literary language, and great art was fostered.

Akkadian language \ə-'kā-dē-ən\ *or* **Assyro-Babylonian language** SEMITIC LANGUAGE spoken in Mesopotamia in the 3rd–1st millennium B.C. and known from many inscriptions, seals, and clay tablets in CUNEIFORM WRITING. It replaced Sumerian as the major spoken language of S Mesopotamia by 2000 B.C. and then split into an Assyrian dialect in the northeast and a Babylonian dialect in the south. In the first half of the 1st millennium B.C., Akkadian gave way to ARAMAIC in Mesopotamia.

Akko See ACRE

Akmola See ASTANA

Akron City (pop., 2000: 217,000), NE Ohio, on the CUYAHOGA RIVER. Akron was named for its "high place" (Greek: *acros*) on the watershed between the MISSISSIPPI RIVER and the GREAT LAKES. Laid out in 1825, the town was assured substantial growth by the completion of two canals (1827, 1840). B. F. Goodrich (1841–1888) moved a rubber factory here in 1871. With the increasing demand for automobile tires, Akron became known as "rubber capital of the world."

Aksum *or* **Axum** \'äk-,süm\ Ancient kingdom, N Ethiopia. At its peak (3rd–6th cent. A.D.), Aksum merchants traded as far as ALEXANDRIA and beyond the NILE RIVER. The modern town of Aksum (pop. 2001: 33,000), once the kingdom's capital, is a religious and tourist center best known for its antiquities. According to tradition, King Menilek I, son of SOLOMON and the Queen of SHEBA, brought the ARK OF THE COVENANT there from Jerusalem.

Alabama State (pop., 2000: 4,447,000), S central U.S. Covering 51,705 sq mi (133,916 sq km), its capital is MONTGOMERY. Its original inhabitants included CHEROKEE, CHICKASAW, CHOCTAW, and CREEK Indians; evidence of their activity can be found near Tuscaloosa. Hernando DE SOTO traveled here, and the French founded a settlement at Ft. Louis in 1702. The Alabama Territory was created in 1817, and statehood was granted in 1819. Alabama seceded from the Union in 1861, becoming part of the Confederacy; it was readmitted in 1868. Efforts during RECONSTRUCTION to include blacks in government failed, and Alabama remained segregationist until the 1960s. Dependent on cotton until the early 20th cent., the state has since diversified its agricultural production and developed industrially, especially at BIRMINGHAM; MOBILE has become a major ocean terminal.

Alabama, University of State university with campuses at Tuscaloosa (main campus), Birmingham, and Huntsville. The school of law is in Tuscaloosa, the school of medicine in Birmingham. Chartered in 1831, it is the state's oldest public university. A 1963 court order to end racial segregation there was initially met with protest by Gov. George WALLACE. Total enrollment is about 38,000.

Alabama River River, S Alabama. Formed by the Coosa and TALLAPOOSA rivers northeast of MONTGOMERY, it flows westward and south for 318 mi (512 km). It is joined above MOBILE by the TOMBIGBEE to form the Mobile and Tensaw rivers. Mobile and Montgomery became major cities largely because they were on this important artery.

alabaster Fine-grained GYPSUM that has been used for centuries for statuary and carvings. It normally is snow-white and translucent but can be artificially dyed; it may be made opaque by heat treatment. Florence, Milan, and Berlin are important centers of the alabaster trade. The alabaster of the ancients was a brown or yellow onyx marble.

Alacahoyuk \,ä-lä-'jä-hō̄e-,yūēk\ Ancient Anatolian site, N central Turkey. Traces of a HITTITE building were found in the early 20th cent., and below them a royal necropolis of tombs dating from about 2500 B.C. Copper Age jewelry, bowls, and jugs have been found. The inhabitants probably belonged to the non-Indo-European population that preceded the Hittites.

Aladdin Hero of a well-known story in *The THOUSAND AND ONE NIGHTS.* The son of a poor widow, he is a lazy, careless boy who meets a magician claiming to be his uncle. The magician sends him into a cave to find a magic lamp and shuts him in when he refuses to turn over the lamp while still in the cave. The trapped Aladdin discovers that he can summon powerful genies (jinn) by rubbing the lamp. The genies grant his every wish, and he becomes rich, marries the sultan's daughter, and reigns for many years.

Alamein, Battles of El See Battles of EL ALAMEIN

Alamo (Spanish: "cottonwood") 18th-cent. mission in San Antonio, Texas, site of a historic resistance in 1836 by a small group of Texans besieged by a Mexican army. At the start of the Texas war for independence in Dec. 1835, volunteers occupied the Alamo, an abandoned mission, and vowed to fight to the death any attempt to recapture it. In Feb. 1836 a

Alamo

Mexican army of several thousand began a siege that lasted 13 days. The Texas force of about 180, led by Jim BOWIE and including Davy CROCKETT as well as women and Mexicans, was overrun; all were killed. "Remember the Alamo!" became a rallying cry in Texas's fight for independence.

Alanbrooke, Viscount See A. F. BROOKE

Åland Islands \'ō-,län\ Archipelago, SW Finland. It consists of about 35 inhabited islands (pop., 1998 est.: 25,000) and over 6,000 uninhabited ones, with a total land area of 590 sq mi (1,527 sq km). The islands were Christianized by 12th-cent. Swedish missionaries. When Finland declared its independence in 1917, the Ålanders sought to become part of Sweden. The islands remain with Finland but have been given unique autonomy.

alanine \\'a-lə-nēn\ Either of two organic compounds. Alpha-alanine is a nonessential AMINO ACID, found in most PROTEINS, particularly the protein in SILK. It is used in research and as a dietary supplement. Beta-alanine is a naturally occurring amino acid not found in proteins. It is an important constituent of the vitamin pantothenic acid and is used in research, electroplating, and organic synthesis.

Alaric I \\'a-lə-rik\ (c.370–410) Chief of the VISIGOTHS (395–410). After commanding Gothic troops in the Roman army, he led his tribe into Greece, sacking cities until placated by the Eastern Roman emperor (397). He twice led invasions of Italy, the second time extorting a large payment from the Roman Senate. Alaric's forces grew after the Romans massacred the wives and children of Visigoths serving in the Roman army. He besieged Rome (408, 409), then in 410 occupied and plundered it, the first time the city had been captured by a foreign enemy in 800 years.

Alaska State (pop., 2000: 627,000) of the U.S., lying at the extreme northwest of N. America. It is the largest in area of the U.S. states and covers 591,004 sq mi (1,530,700 sq km), most of it in land. Facing SIBERIA across the Bering Strait and Sea to the west, it has the highest point on the continent, Mt. MCKINLEY. Its capital is JUNEAU. The original inhabitants, Indians and Eskimos, are thought to have migrated over the Bering Land Bridge as well as from the Arctic. The first European settlement was established in the late 18th cent. by Russian fur traders on KODIAK ISLAND. HUDSON'S BAY CO. traders were also interested in the same area, and Russian–Canadian trade rivalry lasted well into the 19th cent. In 1867 William SEWARD negotiated Alaska's sale from the Russians to the U.S., and the subsequent discovery of gold stimulated American settlement. Alaska was a U.S. Territory from 1912 until it was admitted as the 49th state in 1959. Its economy has become increasingly centered on oil and natural gas: since the opening of the TRANS-ALASKA PIPELINE in 1977, Alaska has become second only to Texas in the U.S. production of crude oil.

Alaska, Gulf of Gulf, S Alaska. Situated between the Alaska Peninsula and the ALEXANDER ARCHIPELAGO, it receives the Susitna and Copper rivers. Capt. James COOK, its European discoverer, first entered the gulf in 1778. Its ports include ANCHORAGE, Seward, and Valdez, the terminus of the TRANS-ALASKA PIPELINE.

Alaskan malamute Sled dog developed by the Malemiut Eskimos. It is a strongly built dog with a broad head, erect ears, and a plumelike tail carried over its back. Its thick coat is usually gray and white or black and white. It stands 23–25 in. (58–64 cm) high and weighs 75–85 lbs (34–39 kg). It is characteristically loyal and friendly.

Alaska Pipeline See TRANS-ALASKA PIPELINE

Alaska Purchase Acquisition in 1867 by the U.S. from Russia of 586,412 sq mi (1.5 million sq km) at the NW tip of N. America, comprising the current state of Alaska. Pres. Andrew JOHNSON's secretary of state, William SEWARD, negotiated its purchase for $7.2 million, or about two cents an acre. Critics labeled the purchase "Seward's Folly." Congressional opposition delayed the appropriation until 1868, when extensive lobbying and bribes by the Russians secured the required votes.

Alaska Range Mountain range, S Alaska. An extension of the Coast Mtns., it extends in a semicircle from the Alaska Peninsula to the YUKON TERRITORY. Mt. MCKINLEY, in DENALI NATIONAL PARK, is the highest point in N. America. Many nearby peaks exceed 13,000 ft (3,960 m), including Mts. Silverthrone, Hunter, Hayes, and Foraker.

Alaungpaya dynasty \ä-ˌlä-ùṇ-ˈpī-ə\ or **Konbaung dynasty** \ˌkȯn-bȧ-ˈùṇ\ (1752–1885) Last ruling dynasty of Myanmar (Burma). As the TOUNGOO DYNASTY ended, Alaungpaya (1714–1760), headman in a village near Mandalay, raised an army and subdued the separatist MON people in S Myanmar and then conquered the NE Shan states. He attacked the Siamese capital of Ayutthaya (now in Thailand), but was mortally wounded. Hsinbyushin, the third king of the dynasty (r.1763–76), sent armies into neighboring kingdoms and successfully rebuffed four retaliatory Chinese invasions. The sixth king, Bodawpaya (r.1782–1819), mounted unsuccessful campaigns against the Siamese but conquered the kingdom of Arakan. His incursions in Assam aroused the ire of the British, and under Bagyidaw (r.1819–37) Myanmar was defeated in the first ANGLO–BURMESE WAR. From then on the dynasty's hold gradually declined, ending in total annexation by the British in 1885.

al-Azhar University See al-AZHAR UNIV.

Alba, Fernando Álvarez de Toledo (y Pimentel), duque (Duke) de (1507–1582) Spanish soldier. He commanded CHARLES V's imperial armies to defeat the Protestant Schmalkaldic League in 1547. As a chief minister to Philip II, Alba became notorious for his tyranny as governor-general of the Netherlands (1567–73); he instituted the Council of Troubles, a court that condemned some 12,000 people for rebellion. Recalled to Spain in 1573, he later conducted a brilliant campaign against Portugal (1580) but never regained Philip's favor.

albacore Large oceanic TUNA (*Thunnus alalunga*) noted for its fine flesh. The streamlined bodies of these voracious predators are adapted to fast and continuous swimming. They occur in both the Atlantic and Pacific oceans and migrate long distances.

Albania officially **Republic of Albania** Nation, W Adriatic coast of the BALKAN PENINSULA. Area: 11,000 sq mi (28,700 sq km). Population (2000): 3,490,000. Capital: TIRANE. Ethnic Albanians are the Ghegs and the Tosks. Language: Albanian (official). Religions: Islam; minority, Christianity

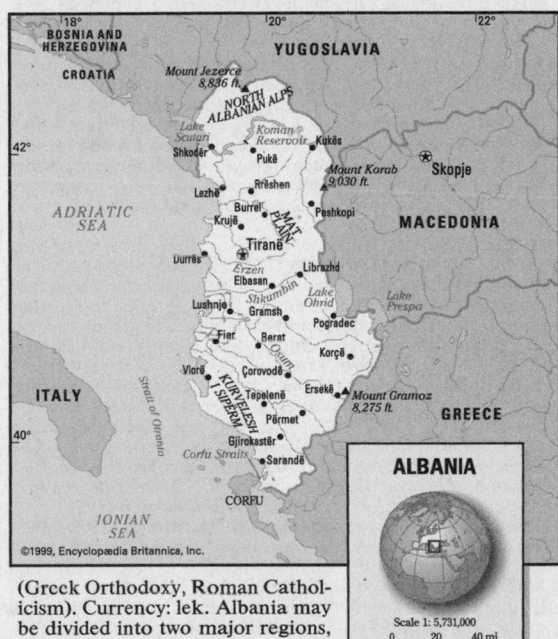

(Greek Orthodoxy, Roman Catholicism). Currency: lek. Albania may be divided into two major regions, a mountainous highland region and a W coastal lowland region that contains the country's agricultural lands and most of its population. It has a developing economy that until 1991 was shaped by a socialist system of state ownership. In 1992 the government introduced economic reforms encouraging a free-market economy. The Albanians are descended from the Illyrians, an ancient Indo-European people who lived in central Europe and migrated south by the beginning of the Iron Age (see ILLYRIA). Of the two major Illyrian migrating groups, the Ghegs settled in the north and the Tosks in the south, along with Greek colonizers. The area was under Roman rule by the 1st cent. B.C.; after A.D. 395 it was connected administratively to Constantinople. Turkish invasion began in the 14th cent. and continued into the 15th cent.; though the national hero, SKANDERBEG, was able to resist them for a time, after his death (1468) the Turks consolidated their rule. The country achieved independence in 1912 and was admitted into the League of Nations in 1920. It was briefly a republic (1925–28), then became a monarchy under ZOG I, whose initial alliance with Benito MUSSOLINI led to Italy's invasion of Albania in 1939. After the war a so-cialist government under Enver HOXHA was installed, and gradually Albania cut itself off from the nonsocialist inter-national community, and eventually from all nations, in-cluding China, its last political ally. By 1990 economic hard-ship had produced antigovernment demonstrations, and in 1992 a non-Communist government was elected and Alba-nia's international isolation ended. In 1997 it plunged into chaos with the collapse of pyramid investment schemes. In 1999 it was overwhelmed by ethnic Albanians seeking refuge from Yugoslavia.

Albany \'ȯl-bə-nē\ City (pop., 2000: 96,000), capital of New York state. It lies along the HUDSON RIVER 145 mi (230 km) north of New York City. Settled by the Dutch (1624), it was renamed by the British (1664) to honor the Duke of York and Albany. In 1754 the ALBANY CONGRESS adopted Ben-jamin FRANKLIN's "Plan of Union." In the 19th cent. Al-bany became a major transportation center. Its focal point today is the Empire State Plaza complex.

Albany Congress Conference in 1754 at Albany, N.Y., that advocated a union of the British colonies in N. America. It was convened by the British colonial government in part to secure a defensive union against the French before the out-break of the FRENCH AND INDIAN WAR. Colonial delegates such as Benjamin FRANKLIN supported a plan to unify the seven colonies, but it was never adopted. The plan became a model for later proposals made during the AMERICAN REVOLUTION.

albatross Any of more than a dozen species of large seabirds (family Diomedeidae). Albatrosses are spectacular gliders; in windy weather they can stay aloft for hours without flap-ping their wings. They drink seawater and usually eat squid. Albatrosses come ashore only to breed, in colonies typically established on remote oceanic islands. Adults attain wing-spans of 7–11 ft (200–350 cm). Long-lived birds, they were once held in awe by seamen, who held that killing one would bring bad luck.

albedo \al-'bē-dō\ Fraction of light reflected by a PLANET, natural SATELLITE, or ASTEROID. "Normal" albedo (the rel-ative brightness of a surface when illuminated and observed from directly above) is often used to determine the surface compositions of satellites and asteroids. The albedo, diame-ter, and distance of such objects determine their brightness.

Albee \'ȯl-bē\, **Edward (Franklin)** (b.1928) U.S. playwright. Born in Virginia, he was the adopted grandson and name-sake of a well-known vaudeville theater manager. His first one-act play, *The Zoo Story* (1959), and other early plays were characteristic of the theater of the ABSURD. His *Who's Afraid of Virginia Woolf* (1962; film, 1966) was widely ac-claimed. He won Pulitzer Prizes for *A Delicate Balance* (1966), *Seascape* (1975), and *Three Tall Women* (1991).

Albéniz \äl-'bā-nēs\, **Isaac (Manuel Francisco)** (1860–1909) Spanish composer. A piano prodigy by age 4, he later stud-ied in Leipzig and Brussels, taught in Barcelona and Madrid, then moved to France in 1893. His fame rests on his piano pieces, which draw on the style of Spanish folk music. *Iberia* (1905–9) is a set of 12 virtuoso piano pieces; other piano works include the *Suite española* and five sonatas. He also wrote several operas.

Albers, Josef (1888–1976) German-U.S. painter and theoreti-cian. He studied and taught at the BAUHAUS, and in 1933 emigrated to the U.S., where he taught at Black Mtn. Col-lege and later at Yale. He developed a painting style characterized by abstract rec-tilinear patterns and primary colors as well as black and white. He is known for his se-ries of paintings titled *Hom-age to the Square*, begun in 1950. His research into color theory was published in the influential *Interaction of Col-or* (1963).

Joseph Albers Photo by Arnold Newman, 1948

Albert *orig.* Franz Albrecht August Karl Emanuel, Prinz (Prince) von Sachsen-Coburg-Gotha *known as* **Prince Al-**bert (1819–1861) Prince consort of Queen VICTORIA of Britain and father of EDWARD VII. Albert married Victoria, his first cousin, in 1840 and became in effect her private secretary and chief confidential adviser. Their domestic happiness helped assure the continuation of the monarchy, which had been somewhat uncertain. Though the German-born Albert was undeservedly unpopular, the British public belatedly recognized his worth after his death at 42 from ty-phoid fever.

Albert, Lake Lake, E central Africa. Lying at an altitude of 2,021 ft (616 m), it is 100 mi (160 km) long and has an aver-age width of about 20 mi (32 km). In the southwest, the Semliki River brings into the lake the waters of Lake ED-WARD; at its NE corner, it receives the Victoria Nile from Lake VICTORIA. In 1864 its first European visitor, Samuel Baker (1821–1893), named it after Queen Victoria's con-sort. It now forms part of the Uganda–Congo border.

Albert I (1875–1934) King of the Belgians (1909–34). He suc-ceeded his uncle, King LEOPOLD II, in 1909. He reaffirmed Belgian neutrality in 1914, rejecting WILLIAM II's demand (Aug. 2, 1914) for free passage of German troops across Bel-gium. Following the German invasion on August 5, Albert assumed leadership of the Belgian army and remained with his troops throughout World War I. He later guided the country's postwar rebuilding effort.

Alberta Province (pop., 2001: 2,962,000), Canada, western-most of three Prairie Provinces. Alberta is bounded by Saskatchewan, British Columbia, the Northwest Territories, and the U.S. Its capital is EDMONTON. Long inhabited by various Indian peoples, the area was explored by Europeans in the 1750s. It eventually came under the rule of the HUD-SON'S BAY CO., which transferred it to the Dominion of Canada in 1870. It was made part of the Northwest Territo-ries in 1882 and named for a daughter of Queen Victoria. Its population grew with the coming of the railroads, and the expansion of wheat farming. Alberta was made a province in 1905. Once dependent on agriculture, it underwent eco-nomic growth with the discovery of oil in 1947, and the en-suing discovery of other major oil and gas deposits.

Alberta, University of Public university in Edmonton, Al-berta. Opened in 1908, it is one of Canada's five largest re-search universities. It offers programs in liberal arts, agri-culture and forestry, science and engineering, business, law, education, the health professions, and native studies. Total enrollment is about 30,000.

Alberti, Leon Battista (1404–1472) Italian architect, art the-orist, and humanist. His Palazzo Rucellai (c.1445–51) and facade of Santa Maria Novella (1456–70), both in Florence, are noted for their harmonic proportions. His central-plan church of Sant'Andrea, Mantua (begun 1472), with its tri-umphal-arch motif, is an early Renaissance masterpiece. Al-berti was one of the foremost theorists on Renaissance ar-chitecture and art, known for codifying the principles of linear perspective (in *On Painting,* 1436). A prototype of the Renaissance man, he also made contributions to moral phi-losophy, cartography, and cryptography.

Albert the Great, St. See ALBERTUS MAGNUS

Albertus Magnus, St. (c.1200–1280) German cleric and philosopher. Son of a wealthy German lord, he joined the Dominican order in Padua (1223). At the Univ. of Paris he was introduced to the works of ARISTOTLE and to AVERR-OËS' commentaries. For 20 years he worked on his *Physica,* which encompassed natural science, logic, rheto-ric, mathematics, astronomy, ethics, economics, politics, and metaphysics. In 1248 he organized a seminary at Co-logne, where THOMAS AQUI-NAS was his chief disciple. His works represented the entire body of European knowledge of his time, and he contributed greatly to the development of natural sci-ence.

Albertus Magnus Fresco by Tommaso da Modena, c.1352

Albigensian Crusade \ˌal-bə-ˈjen-shən\ (1209–29) Crusade called by Pope INNOCENT III against the heretical CATHARI of S France. The war pitted the nobility of N France against that of S France; it virtually destroyed the Albigensian heresy (named for the town of Albi) but at the price of much devastation and injustice, which Innocent came to regret. The Treaty of Paris (1229) took away the independence of the S princes and largely destroyed the culture of PROVENCE. The heresy lingered on into the 13th–14th cent. and became the object of the INQUISITION.

Albigensians See CATHARI

albinism \ˈal-bə-ˌni-zəm, al-ˈbī-ˌni-zəm\ Absence of the pigment MELANIN in the eyes, skin, hair, scales, or feathers. It arises from a genetic defect and occurs in humans and other vertebrates. Because they lack the pigments that provide protective coloration and screen against the sun's ultraviolet rays, albino animals rarely survive in the wild. Humans have long intentionally bred certain albino animals (e.g., rabbits) for their appearance. In humans with generalized, or total, albinism, the affected person has milk-white skin and hair; the iris of the eye appears pink, the pupil red. Generalized albinism occurs in all races in about one in 20,000 persons.

Albinoni \ˌal-bə-ˈnō-nē\, **Tomaso (Giovanni)** (1671–1751) Italian composer. Born to a wealthy Venetian family, he was not obliged to work for a living, and he became a highly prolific composer. He had more than 50 operas successfully produced between 1694 and 1741, though few survive. His 60 concertos became popular; he also wrote more than 80 sonatas for various instruments and over 40 solo cantatas.

Albright, Ivan (Le Lorraine) (1897–1983) U.S. painter. Born in North Harvey, Ill., he studied at various institutions, developing a meticulously detailed style and often spending several years of painstaking work on a single painting. With hallucinatory hyperclarity, he repeatedly depicted decay, corruption, and the wreckage of age, often with great emotional intensity. His important works include *That Which I Should Have Done I Did Not Do* (1931–41) and *The Picture of Dorian Gray* (1943), painted for a film of Oscar WILDE's story, which brought him fame.

albumin \al-ˈbyü-mən\ Any of a diverse class of PROTEINS. They are readily coagulated by heating. Examples include serum albumin, a major component of PLASMA; α-lactalbumin, found in milk; and ovalbumin, the predominant protein of egg white. Ovalbumin is used in the food, wine, adhesives, paper coatings, pharmaceutical, and other industries.

Albuquerque \ˌäl-bü-ˈkər-kə\, **Afonso de** or **Afonso the Great** (1453–1515) Portuguese soldier. He gained early military experience in N. Africa, but his reputation came from his service in S. and S.E. Asia, where he conquered Goa (1510) and Melaka (1511). His efforts to gain control of all the main maritime trade routes of the East and to build permanent fortresses with settled populations paved the way for Portuguese domination in S.E. Asia.

Albuquerque \ˈal-bə-ˌkər-kē\ City (pop., 2000: 448,000), New Mexico. The state's largest city, it lies on the RIO GRANDE southwest of Santa Fe. Founded in 1706, it was named for the viceroy of NEW SPAIN. After 1800 the SANTA FE TRAIL brought an influx of settlers; an army post was established; and with the coming of the railroad in 1880, the population expanded. The Spanish "old town" and mission church have survived. Since the 1930s Albuquerque has welcomed many defense-related federal agencies and technology research facilities.

Alcatraz Island Rocky island in SAN FRANCISCO BAY, California. It has an area of 22 acres (9 hectares) and is located 1.5 mi (2 km) offshore. It was the site of the California's first lighthouse (1854), an army garrison (1859) and a military prison (1868). From 1934 to 1963 it served as a federal prison for dangerous civilian prisoners. Its famous inmates included Al CAPONE, George "Machine Gun" Kelly, and Robert Stroud, the "Birdman of Alcatraz."

alcázar \al-ˈkä-zər\ Form of military architecture of medieval Spain, generally rectangular with defensible walls and massive corner towers. Inside was an open space surrounded by chapels, salons, hospitals, and gardens. The finest surviving example is Seville's Alcázar Palace; begun

in 1181 under the ALMOHADS and continued by the Christians, it exhibits both Moorish and Gothic features.

Alcestis \al-ˈses-təs\ In Greek legend, the beautiful daughter of Pelias, king of Ioclos. Admetus, son of the king of Pherae, sought her hand, which he won with the aid of APOLLO. When Apollo learned that Admetus had not long to live, he persuaded the FATES to prolong his life, on condition someone else die in his stead. As a loyal wife Alcestis consented to do so, but was rescued by HERACLES, who wrestled with Death at her grave.

alchemy Pseudoscience focused on the attempt to change base metals into gold. Ancient alchemists believed that, under the correct astrological conditions, lead could be "perfected" into gold. They tried to hasten this transformation by heating and refining the metal in a variety of mostly secret chemical processes. Alchemy was practiced from China and India to Greece and Egypt. It was revived in 12th-cent. Europe through translations of Arabic texts. Medieval European alchemists made some useful discoveries, including mineral acids and alcohol. The revival led to the development of PHARMACOLOGY and the rise of modern CHEMISTRY. Not until the 19th cent. were alchemy's gold-making processes discredited.

Alcibiades \ˌal-sə-ˈbī-ə-ˌdēz\ (c.450–404 B.C.) Brilliant but unscrupulous Athenian politician and commander. PERICLES was his guardian, and he became associated with SOCRATES, with whom he served in the PELOPONNESIAN WAR. By 420 he was a general. Recalled from a Sicilian expedition in 415 on charges of sacrilege for mutilating statues of Hermes, he fled to Sparta. Though he aided the Spartan cause against Athens, he was eventually rejected and sought haven with the Persian king. The Athenian fleet recalled him, and he directed Athenian victories 411–408. Though he achieved hero status, his enemies again forced him to leave, and he was eventually murdered by the Spartans. His political agitation was a decisive factor in Athens's defeat in the Peloponnesian War. His notorious behavior helped strengthen the charges brought against Socrates in 399.

Alcindor, Lew See Kareem ABDUL-JABBAR

Alcmaeon or **Alcmeon** \alk-ˈmē-ən\ In GREEK MYTHOLOGY, the son of the seer Amphiaraus. The seer had been persuaded by his wife to join the expedition of the Seven Against THEBES. On realizing that he would die, he charged Alcmaeon and his other sons to avenge him. Alcmaeon led the sons of the seven in the destruction of Thebes and then obeyed his father's injunction to kill his mother, for which the FURIES drove him mad. He was purified by King Phegeus of Psophis, whose daughter he married but subsequently killed. He fled, but was found and killed by Phegeus and his sons.

Alcoa U.S. company, the world's largest producer of aluminum. Established in Pittsburgh in 1888, it adopted the name Aluminum Co. of America in 1907. Alcoa introduced aluminum foil in 1910 and found uses for aluminum in the emerging aviation and automobile industries. In 1913 it established the town of Alcoa in E Tennessee as a planned industrial community. In 1998 Alcoa acquired Alumax Inc.; the combined companies have 140,000 employees and an annual output of nearly 4 million tons of aluminum.

alcohol Any of a class of common organic compounds that contain one or more hydroxyl groups (–OH) attached to one or more of the carbon atoms in a HYDROCARBON chain. Depending on the number of other substituent groups on that carbon atom, the alcohol can be primary, secondary, or tertiary. Many alcohols occur naturally and are valuable intermediates because of the characteristic CHEMICAL REACTIONS of the hydroxyl group. Oxidation (see OXIDATION-REDUCTION) of primary alcohols yields ALDEHYDES and (if taken further) CARBOXYLIC ACIDS; oxidation of secondary alcohols, KETONES. Tertiary alcohols break down on oxidation. Alcohols generally react with carboxylic acids to produce ESTERS. They may also be converted to ETHERS and olefins. Products of these numerous reactions include fats and waxes, detergents, plasticizers, emulsifiers, lubricants, emollients, and foaming agents. ETHANOL and METHANOL (wood alcohol) contain one hydroxyl group. GLYCOLS (e.g., ethylene glycol, or antifreeze)

contain two hydroxyl groups, GLYCEROL three, and polyols three or more. See also ALCOHOLIC BEVERAGE, ALCOHOLISM.

alcoholic beverage Any fermented liquor, such as WINE, BEER, or DISTILLED LIQUOR, that contains ETHANOL as an intoxicating agent. When an alcoholic beverage is drunk, the alcohol is rapidly absorbed (rather than digested) in the stomach and intestines and then distributed to the rest of the body through the blood. Under the influence of alcohol, the drinker is less alert, less able to discern objects in the environment, slower in reacting to stimuli, and generally prone to sleep.

Alcoholics Anonymous (AA) Voluntary fellowship of people suffering from ALCOHOLISM who seek to become and stay sober through mutual self-help by meeting in local, independent groups to share their common experience. Anonymity, confidentiality, and understanding of alcoholism as a disease free members to speak frankly. Many consider AA to be the most successful method of coping with alcoholism. Its 12 steps to recovery include acknowledgment of the problem, faith in a "higher power" as understood by each individual, self-examination, and a desire to change for the better and to help others recover. Begun in 1935 by two alcoholics, AA has grown to some 2 million members worldwide.

alcoholism Excessive habitual consumption of alcoholic beverages despite physical, mental, social, or economic harm. It is usually considered an addiction and a disease. The causes are unclear, but there may be a genetic predisposition. Alcoholism occurs in about 4.2% of adults in the U.S. It is more common in men, but women are more likely to hide it. Treatment may be physiological (with drugs that cause vomiting and a feeling of panic when alcohol is consumed), psychological (with therapy and rehabilitation), and/or social (with group therapies). Suddenly stopping heavy drinking can lead to withdrawal symptoms, including DELIRIUM TREMENS. See also CIRRHOSIS, ALCOHOLICS ANONYMOUS.

Alcott, (Amos) Bronson (1799–1888) U.S. teacher and philosopher. Born in Wolcott, Conn., he worked as a peddler before founding a series of innovative but unsuccessful schools for children. He went to Britain with money borrowed from R. W. EMERSON and returned with the mystic Charles Lane, with whom he founded the short-lived utopian community Fruitlands outside Boston. As superintendent of schools in Concord, Mass., he set up the first parent-teacher association. A prominent member of the Transcendentalists, he wrote a number of books, but did not become financially secure until his daughter L. M. ALCOTT achieved success.

Alcott, Louisa May (1832–1888) U.S. author. Born in Germantown, Pa., the daughter of Bronson ALCOTT, she grew up in Transcendentalist circles in Boston and Concord, Mass. An ardent abolitionist, she began writing to help support her family. Typhoid, contracted while volunteer nursing during the American Civil War, permanently damaged her health, but her book *Hospital Sketches* (1863) brought her fame. The autobiographical *Little Women* (1868–69) enjoyed huge success; it was followed by *An Old-Fashioned Girl* (1870), *Little Men* (1871), and *Jo's Boys* (1886).

Louisa May Alcott Portrait by George Healy

Alcuin \ˈal-ˌkwēn\ (732?–804) Anglo-Latin poet, educator, and cleric. As head of the Palatine school established by CHARLEMAGNE at AACHEN, he introduced the traditions of Anglo-Saxon humanism into W Europe and spearheaded the revival of learning known as the Carolingian Renaissance. He also made important reforms in the Roman Catholic liturgy and left over 300 Latin letters, a valuable historical source.

aldehyde Any of a class of organic compounds that contain a carbonyl group (–C=O; see FUNCTIONAL GROUP) in which the carbon atom is bonded to at least one hydrogen atom. Oxidation (see OXIDATION-REDUCTION) of aldehydes yields ACIDS; reduction produces ALCOHOLS. They participate in many CHEMICAL REACTIONS and readily undergo POLYMERIZATION into very long chains. The combination of aldehydes (e.g., FORMALDEHYDE) with other molecules results in several familiar PLASTICS. Many aldehydes are large-scale industrial materials, useful as solvents, monomers, perfume ingredients, and intermediates. Many SUGARS and several natural and synthetic HORMONES and other important biochemical compounds are aldehydes.

Alden, John (1599?–1687) American (British-born) colonist. He was hired as a cooper for the *Mayflower's* expedition to the New World in 1620. Alden signed the MAYFLOWER COMPACT and served as assistant to the governor 1623–41 and 1650–86. He was mythologized in H. W. LONGFELLOW's poem as the stand-in for Myles STANDISH in his suit for Priscilla Mullins's hand in marriage. Alden in fact married Mullins in 1623.

alder Any of about 30 species of ornamental shrubs and trees in the genus *Alnus*, of the BIRCH family, found throughout the Northern Hemisphere and W S. America on cool, wet sites. Unlike birches, alders have CONES that remain on the branches after the winged nutlets are released, scaly bark, and oval leaves that fall without changing color. Alder wood is fine-textured and durable, even under water; it is useful for furniture, cabinetry, lathe work, and in charcoal manufacture. Alders' spreading root systems and tolerance of moist soils make them useful on stream banks for flood and erosion control.

Aldrich \ˈȯl-drich\, **Robert** (1918–1983) U.S. film director and producer. Born in Cranston, R.I., he held various jobs at RKO from 1941. After directing his first feature film, *The Big Leaguer* (1953), he formed his own production company and earned a reputation for tough, often violent films, including *Apache* (1954), *The Big Knife* (1955), *Hush . . . Hush, Sweet Charlotte* (1964), and *The Dirty Dozen* (1967).

Aldrin \ˈȯl-drən\, **Edwin Eugene, Jr.** *known as* **Buzz Aldrin** (b.1930) U.S. astronaut. Born in Montclair, N.J., he flew 66 combat missions in the Korean War and was chosen as an astronaut in 1963. In 1966 he joined James A. Lovell, Jr. (b.1928) on the four-day Gemini 12 flight. Aldrin's 5 1/2-hour walk in space proved that humans can function in space. In July 1969, on the APOLLO 11 mission, he became the second human on the moon.

ale Fermented beverage made from malted grain, with a strong flavor of HOPS. Until the 17th cent. it was made only with YEAST, water, and malt, BEER being the same brew with hops added. Modern ale is largely synonymous with beer but processed at higher temperatures than lager beer. Pale ale has up to 5% alcohol content; the darker strong ale contains up to 6.5%.

aleatory music \ˈā-lē-ə-ˌtōr-ē\ (from Latin, *alea:* "dice game") Any music whose composition or performance incorporates elements of chance. Such aspects as the ordering of a piece's sections, its rhythms, and even its pitches are decided at the moment of performance. When not purely improvising, players follow lists of arbitrary rules or "graphic" notation that merely suggest the sounds. Charles IVES and Henry COWELL had used such techniques, but John CAGE became the principal figure in aleatory.

Aleichem, Sholem See SHOLEM ALEICHEM

Aleixandre \ˌä-lā-ˈsän-drä\, **Vicente** (1898–1984) Spanish poet. A member of the group of Spanish writers called the Generation of 1927, he was strongly influenced by Surrealism. *Destruction or Love* (1935) was his first major book. Other works include *Historia del corazón* (1954; "History of the Heart") and *En un vasto dominio* (1962; "In a Vast Domain"). He received the Nobel Prize in 1977.

Aleksandrovsk See ZAPORIZHZHYA

Alembert \ä-län-ˈber\, **Jean Le Rond d'** (1717–1783) French mathematician, scientist, philosopher, and writer. In 1743 he published a treatise on DYNAMICS containing "d'Alembert's principle," relating to Isaac NEWTON's laws of motion. He developed partial differential equations and published findings of his research on INTEGRAL CALCULUS. He was associated with the *ENCYCLOPÉDIE* of Denis DIDEROT from about 1746 as editor of its mathematical and scientific articles. He was elected to the French Academy in 1754.

Aleppo \ə-'le-pō\ *Arabic* **Halab** \'hȧ-lȧb\ City (pop., 1994 est.: 1,591,000), NW Syria. It lies about 30 mi (48 km) from the Turkish border. Situated at the crossroads of great commercial routes, it has come under the control of many kingdoms. First mentioned at the end of the 3rd millennium B.C. it fell to the HITTITES (17th–14th cent. B.C.), the Persians (6th–4th cent. B.C.), the SELEUCID DYNASTY, the Romans (1st cent. B.C.), and the Arabs (A.D. 637). The city successfully defended itself from the Crusaders (1124), fell to the MONGOLS (1260), and finally was incorporated into the OTTOMAN EMPIRE (1516). Modern Aleppo is an industrial and intellectual center rivaling DAMASCUS.

Aleut \ˌa-lē-'üt\ Native of the Aleutian Islands and W portion of the Alaska Peninsula. Aleuts are physically and culturally closely related to the ESKIMO. Traditional Aleut villages were located on the seashore near fresh water, where the people hunted marine mammals, fish, birds, caribou, and bear. Aleut women wove fine grass basketry; stone, bone, and ivory were also worked. After the arrival of the Russians in the 18th cent., their population declined, and today the Aleut number only about 3,500.

Aleutian Islands \ə-'lü-shən\ Chain of 200 small islands (pop., 1990: 12,000), Alaska. They form a border of the BERING SEA, extending in an arc about 1,100 mi (1,800 km) west from the tip of the Alaska Peninsula to Attu Island. The main settlements are on Unalaska and Adak. Originally inhabited by ALEUTS, the islands were explored by Russia in 1741. As Siberian fur hunters moved eastward through the islands, the Russians gained a foothold in N. America but nearly caused the extinction of the Aleuts. Russia sold the islands, with the rest of Alaska, to the U.S. in 1867. The islands, which endure frequent earthquakes and volcanic eruptions, are now the site of research stations and military bases.

alewife Important N. American food fish (*Pomolobus*, or *Alosa, pseudoharengus*) of the HERRING family. The alewife grows to about 1 ft (30 cm). Most populations spend several years along the Atlantic coast before ascending freshwater streams to spawn each spring.

Alexander, Harold (Rupert Leofric George) *later* **Earl Alexander (of Tunis)** (1891–1969) British field marshal in World War II. In 1940 he helped direct the DUNKIRK EVACUATION and was the last man to leave the beaches. Appointed British commander in chief in the Mediterranean theater in 1942, he helped lead the N. AFRICA CAMPAIGNS against the Germans, and directed the invasions of Sicily and Italy. He later served as governor-general of Canada (1946–52) and as Britain's minister of defense (1952–54).

Alexander, Severus See SEVERUS ALEXANDER

Alexander, William *later* **Earl of Stirling, Viscount of Canada** (1576?–1640) Scottish poet and colonizer of Canada. He was a member of the court of JAMES I, where he wrote his sonnet sequence *Aurora* (1604). In 1621 he obtained a grant for territory in N. America that he named New Scotland (Nova Scotia), despite French claims to part of the land, but the region was not colonized until 1629. Alexander was compelled to surrender the territory under a 1629 treaty that ended an Anglo-French conflict. Scottish settlers were ordered to withdraw by 1631.

Alexander I *Russian* Aleksandr Pavlovich (1777–1825) Czar of Russia (1801–25). He became czar in 1801 after the assassination of his father, PAUL I. He and his advisers corrected many of the injustices of the preceding reign, but retained serfdom. During the NAPOLEONIC WARS he alternately fought and befriended Napoleon and helped form the coalition that finally defeated him, participating in the Congress of VIENNA (1814–15). After his sudden death, a legend sprang up that he had simply "departed" to a Siberian retreat.

Alexander II *Russian* Aleksandr Nikolayevich (1818–1881) Czar of Russia (1855–81). Succeeding to the throne at the height of the CRIMEAN WAR, which was demonstrating Russia's backwardness, he responded to a general desire for drastic change with such reforms as the emancipation of the serfs (1861). He also improved communications and administrative institutions. His reforms fostered humanitarian progress and economic development, but he remained a firm upholder of autocratic principles. An assassination attempt in 1866 led to a period of repression and a reaction in the form of revolutionary terrorism, and in 1881 he was killed in a plot sponsored by the terrorist organization People's Will.

Alexander III See ALEXANDER THE GREAT

Alexander III *orig.* Rolando Bandinelli (c.1105–1181) Pope (1159–81). A member of the group of cardinals who feared the growing strength of the HOLY ROMAN EMPIRE, he angered FREDERICK I Barbarossa by referring to the Empire as a "benefice," implying that it was a gift of the pope. On Alexander's election as pope in 1159, a minority of cardinals supported by Frederick elected the first ANTIPOPE, and imperial opposition obliged Alexander to flee to France (1162). He returned to Rome in 1165 but was exiled again the following year. He supported the LOMBARD LEAGUE, which defeated Frederick at Legnano in 1176; Alexander was then acknowledged as the true pope. A reformer, he presided at the third LATERAN COUNCIL (1179).

Alexander III *Russian* Aleksandr Aleksandrovich (1845–1894) Czar of Russia (1881–94). Succeeding his father, ALEXANDER II, he instituted internal reforms to correct what he saw as the too-liberal tendencies of his father's reign. He ardently supported Russian nationalism; his political ideal was a nation containing a single nationality, language, religion, and form of administration. Accordingly he instituted programs such as the Russification of national minorities in the Russian empire and the persecution of non-Orthodox religious groups.

Alexander VI *orig.* Rodrigo de Borja y Doms (1431–1503) Pope (1492–1503). Born into the Spanish branch of the Borgia family, he lived scandalously, fathering four illegitimate children prior to his election as pope, which resulted chiefly from Spanish influence. He warred against the Ottoman Turks and forced the French to abandon their effort to seize Naples. The murder of his son Juan (1497) prompted Alexander's short-lived attempt to restrain the corruption of the papal court. He concluded an alliance with Spain and negotiated the Treaty of TORDESILLAS (1494). A patron of the arts, he embellished the Vatican palaces.

Alexander Archipelago Group of about 1,100 islands (pop., 1991 est.: 39,000), SE Alaska, extending southward from GLACIER BAY. The chief towns are Sitka (on Baranof) and Ketchikan (on Revillagigedo). The islands are separated from the mainland by the deep, narrow channels of the INSIDE PASSAGE. The archipelago's name, given in 1867, honors Czar ALEXANDER II.

Alexander Island Island in Bellingshausen Sea, separated from the Antarctica mainland by George VI Sound. An extremely rugged region with peaks as high as 9,800 ft (3,000 m), it is 270 mi (435 km) long and up to 125 mi (200 km) wide, with an area of 16,700 sq mi (43,250 sq km). The Russian F. G. von Bellingshausen (1778–1852) discovered the land in 1821 and named it after Czar ALEXANDER. It is connected to the continent by a huge floating ice shelf. It has been claimed by Britain (since 1908), Chile (1940), and Argentina (1942).

Alexander Nevsky \'nev-skē\, **St.** (c.1220–1263) Prince of Novgorod (1236–52) and Kiev (1246–52) and grand prince of Vladimir (1252–63). He fought off invading Swedes in 1240 at the Neva River (resulting in the epithet Nevsky), defeated the TEUTONIC ORDER on the ice of Lake Peipus in 1242, and also won victories over the Lithuanians and Finns. He collaborated with the GOLDEN HORDE in imposing Mongol rule on Russia, and the Great Khan made him grand prince of Vladimir. He helped the Mongols impose taxes, interceding with the Khan to prevent reprisals when rebellions broke out. A national hero, he was canonized by the Russian Orthodox Church.

Alexander the Great *or* **Alexander III** (356–323 B.C.) Greatest military leader of antiquity. The son of PHILIP II of Macedonia, he was taught by ARISTOTLE. He succeeded his assassinated father in 336 and promptly conquered Thessaly and Thrace; he brutally razed Thebes. Such destruction was to be his standard method, and other Greek states submit-

ted meekly. In 334 he defeated a Persian army at the Granicus River. He is said to have cut the Gordian knot in Phrygia (333), by which act, according to legend, he was destined to rule all Asia. In 333, he defeated the army of the Persian king Darius III (r.336–330 B.C.), then took Syria and Phoenicia. In 332 he completed a seven-month siege of Tyre, considered his greatest military achievement, and reached and took Egypt. There he founded AL-EXANDRIA and visited the oracle of the god AMON, the basis of his claim to divinity. In control of the E Mediterranean coast, in 331 he defeated Darius in a decisive battle at Gaugamela. He next took the province of Babylon. In Persia he burned XERXES' palace at PERSEPOLIS in 330, and he envisioned an empire ruled jointly by Macedonians and Persians. He continued eastward, taking control to the Oxus and Jaxartes rivers and founding cities (most named Alexandria) to hold the territory. Taking present-day Tajikistan, he married the princess Roxana and embraced Persian absolutism, adopting Persian dress and enforcing Persian court customs. By 326 he reached the Hyphasis in India, where his weary men mutinied; he turned back, marching and pillaging down the Indus, and reached Susa with much loss of life. He continued to promote his unpopular policy of racial fusion, a seeming attempt to form a Persian-Macedonian master race. He fell ill at Babylon after long feasting and drinking and died at 33. His empire, the greatest that had existed to that time, extended from Thrace to Egypt and from Greece to the Indus Valley.

Alexander the Great

Alexandra *Russian* Aleksandra Fyodorovna *orig.* Alix, Prinzessin (Princess) von Hesse-Darmstadt (1872–1918) Consort of Russia's Czar NICHOLAS II. A granddaughter of Queen VICTORIA, she married Nicholas in 1894. Desperate for help for her hemophiliac son, Alexis, she turned to the hypnotic powers of Grigory RASPUTIN. In 1915 Nicholas left Moscow to command Russian forces in World War I, and Alexandra dismissed capable ministers and replaced them with nonentities favored by Rasputin. Her misrule contributed to the collapse of the imperial government. After the RUSSIAN REVOLUTION OF 1917, the royal family was imprisoned and later executed.

Alexandria City (metro. area pop., 1996 est.: 3,700,000) and chief seaport, N Egypt. The ancient island of Pharos, whose lighthouse was one of the SEVEN WONDERS OF THE WORLD, is now a peninsula just east of Alexandria's modern harbor. The city was founded in 332 B.C. by ALEXANDER THE GREAT and was noted as a center of Hellenistic culture; its library was the greatest in ancient times. The city was captured by the Arabs in A.D. 640 and by the Turks in 1517. After a long decline, Alexandria was revived commercially when joined by a canal to the Nile in the early 19th cent. Today cotton is its chief export and important oil fields lie nearby. See also MUSEUM OF ALEXANDRIA.

Alexandria, Library of Most famous library of classical antiquity. Part of the Alexandrian Museum, a research institute at Alexandria, Egypt, founded and maintained by a succession of Ptolemies from the early 3rd cent. B.C., the library aspired to incorporate all Greek literature and also translations into Greek, but it is uncertain how close to this ideal it came. A catalog compiled by CALLIMACHUS was a standard reference until lost in the Byzantine period. The museum and library were destroyed in the late 3rd cent. A.D.; a subsidiary library was destroyed in A.D. 391.

alexandrine \\al-ek-'zan-drən\ Most popular measure in French poetry. It consists of a line of 12 syllables with a pause after the sixth syllable, major stresses on the sixth and the last syllables, and one secondary accent in each half line. A flexible form, adaptable to a wide range of subjects, it became the preeminent French verse form in the 17th cent. with the tragedies of Pierre CORNEILLE and Jean RACINE.

Alexeyev \ə-lyi-'ksyä-yif\, **Vasily** (b.1942) Soviet weightlifter. A superheavyweight, he broke 80 world records between 1970 and 1977 and won Olympic gold medals in 1972 and 1976. He was the first man ever to lift more than 500 lbs (227 kg) in the clean and jerk.

Alexis *Russian* Aleksey Mikhaylovich (1629–1676) Czar of Russia (1645–76). Son of MICHAEL, the first ROMANOV monarch of Russia, Alexis acceded to the throne at 16. During his reign the peasants were enserfed, the land assemblies fell into gradual disuse, the bureaucracy and army grew in importance, and NIKON's reforms of the Russian Orthodox church were adopted. Though popular, Alexis was a weak ruler who entrusted matters of state to sometimes incompetent favorites.

Alexius I Comnenus \käm-'nē-nəs\ (1048–1118) Byzantine emperor (1081–1118). An experienced military leader, he seized the Byzantine throne in 1081, driving back the invading NORMANS and Turks and founding the Comnenian dynasty. Alexius increased Byzantine strength in the E Mediterranean but failed to curb the power of the landed magnates. He protected the Eastern Orthodox church but seized its assets when in financial need. His appeal for Western support in 1095 led to Pope URBAN II's call for the First CRUSADE. Alexius's relations with the crusaders were difficult and, from 1097 onward, the Crusades frustrated his foreign policy.

alfalfa Perennial, CLOVER-like LEGUME (*Medicago sativa*), widely grown primarily for HAY, pasturage, and silage. It is known for its tolerance of drought, heat, and cold, and for its value in soil improvement. The plant, which grows 1–3 ft (30–90 cm) tall, develops numerous stems at soil level, each bearing many three-leaved leaflets. Its long primary root accounts for its unusual ability to tolerate drought. It can yield as many as 13 crops of hay in one growing season. Alfalfa hay is very nutritious and palatable, high in protein, minerals, and vitamins.

Alfasi \äl-'fä-sē\, **Isaac ben Jacob** (1013–1103) Moroccan Jewish scholar. He spent most of his life in Fez, but in 1088 he was denounced to the government and was obliged to flee to Spain. There he established a noted Talmudic academy, provoking a rebirth of Talmudic study in Spain. His codification of the Talmud, *Sefer ha-Halakhot* ("Book of Laws"), was crucial in establishing the primacy of the Babylonian Talmud over the Palestinian Talmud.

Alfonso I (Portugal) See AFONSO I

Alfonso V *known as* **Alfonso the Magnanimous** (1396–1458) King of ARAGON (1416–58) and of NAPLES (as Alfonso I, 1442–58). He followed a policy of Mediterranean expansion, pacifying Sardinia and Sicily and attacking Corsica (1420). Taken prisoner by the Genoese (1435) while preparing to attack Naples, he persuaded his captors into an alliance and conquered Naples (1442), to which he transferred his court. He engaged in much diplomatic and military activity in order to protect his commerce with the East and defend Christendom against the Turks.

Alfonso VI *known as* **Alfonso the Brave** (1040–1109) King of LEÓN (1065–70) and of CASTILLA Y LEÓN (1072–1109). He inherited León from his father, Ferdinand I, and Castile from his brother Sancho. He also occupied Galicia and imprisoned his brother García, its rightful ruler. In 1077 Alfonso proclaimed himself emperor of all Spain. He took Toledo from the Muslims, but his demands for tribute led to invasion by the ALMORAVIDS, and he was defeated at Zallaqah (1086). El CID became an ally and defended E Spain, but Alfonso continued to lose ground against the Berber armies.

Alfonso X *known as* **Alfonso the Wise** (1221–1284) King of Castilla y León (1252–84). He crushed revolts by Muslims (1252) and nobles (1254), and he annexed Murcia after repelling an invasion by Morocco, Granada, and Murcia (1264). He claimed the title of Holy Roman Emperor, but Pope Gregory X persuaded him to renounce the claim (1275). Alfonso's court was a center of culture, producing an influential law code, the *Siete partidas,* and establishing the form of modern Castilian Spanish.

Alfonso XIII (1886–1941) Spanish king (1886–1931). The posthumous son of Alfonso XII, he was immediately proclaimed king under his mother's regency and assumed full authority at 16. After World War I he moved toward a system of more autocratic rule. He associated himself with the dictatorship of Miguel PRIMO DE RIVERA (1923–30), but after the latter's fall, he was forced to leave Spain. His grandson became JUAN CARLOS I.

Alfred *known as* **Alfred the Great** (849–899) King of WESSEX (871–99). He joined his brother Ethelred I in confronting a Danish army in Mercia (868). Succeeding his brother as king, Alfred fought the Danes in Wessex (871) and defeated them at the Battle of Edington (878); he saved Kent from another Danish invasion in 885. The next year he took the offensive and captured London, a success that brought all the English not under Danish rule to accept him as king. Alfred drew up an important code of laws and promoted literacy and learning, personally translating Latin books into Anglo-Saxon. The compilation of the Anglo-Saxon Chronicle was begun under his reign.

algae \'al-jē\ Any of a group of mostly aquatic, photosynthetic organisms (see PHOTOSYNTHESIS) that defy precise definition. They range in size from the microscopic flagellate *Micromonas* to giant KELP that reach 200 ft (60 m) in length. Algae provide much of the earth's oxygen, serve as the food base for almost all aquatic life, and provide foods and industrial products. Their cells have features not found among plants and animals. The classification of algae is changing rapidly as new taxonomical information is discovered. Algae are classified based on the type of pigment molecules in their CHLOROPLASTS. Algae are not closely related to each other in an evolutionary sense. Specific groups can be distinguished from PROTOZOANS and fungi (see FUNGUS) only by the presence of chloroplasts and their ability to carry out photosynthesis. Use of algae is perhaps as old as mankind; seaweeds are eaten by coastal societies, and algae are served in many restaurants. They are common on "slimy" rocks in streams (see DIATOMS) and as green sheens on pools and ponds.

algebra, linear See LINEAR ALGEBRA

algebra and algebraic structures Generalized version of arithmetic that uses VARIABLES to stand for unspecified numbers. Its purpose is to solve ALGEBRAIC EQUATIONS or SYSTEMS OF EQUATIONS. An example of such solutions is the quadratic formula (for solving a QUADRATIC EQUATION). In higher mathematics, an "algebra" is a structure consisting of a class of objects and a set of rules (analogous to addition and multiplication) for combining them. Basic and higher algebraic structures share two essential characteristics: (1) calculations involve a finite number of steps and (2) calculations involve abstract symbols (usually letters) representing more general objects (usually numbers).

algebraic equation Mathematical statement of equality between algebraic expressions. An expression is algebraic if it involves a finite combination of numbers and VARIABLES and algebraic operations (addition, subtraction, multiplication, division, raising to a power, and extracting a root). Two important types of such equations are linear equations, in the form $y = ax + b$, and QUADRATIC EQUATIONS, in the form $y = ax^2 + bx + c$. A solution is a numerical value that makes the equation a true statement when substituted for a variable. Algebraic equations are particularly useful for modeling real-life phenomena.

Alger \'al-jər\, **Horatio** (1832–1899) U.S. writer. Born in Chelsea, Mass., he graduated from Harvard with honors, then earned a degree from its divinity school. Forced to leave his pulpit after allegations of improper activities with youths, he took up writing. Beginning with *Ragged Dick* (1868), he wrote over 100 books preaching that through honesty, cheerful perseverance, and hard work, a poor but virtuous lad would have his just reward (though good luck almost always played a part). Despite his books' weak plots and dialogue, Alger was one of the century's most popular and socially influential writers.

Algeria *officially* **Democratic and Popular Republic of Algeria** Nation, N Africa. Area: 918,497 sq mi (2,378,907 sq km). Population (2000): 30,554,000. Capital: ALGIERS. Most of the population is Arabic; Berbers are the main minority group. Languages: Arabic (official), French, Berber. Religion: Islam (official). Currency: Algerian dinar. Algeria has the second-largest land area (after Sudan) on the continent.

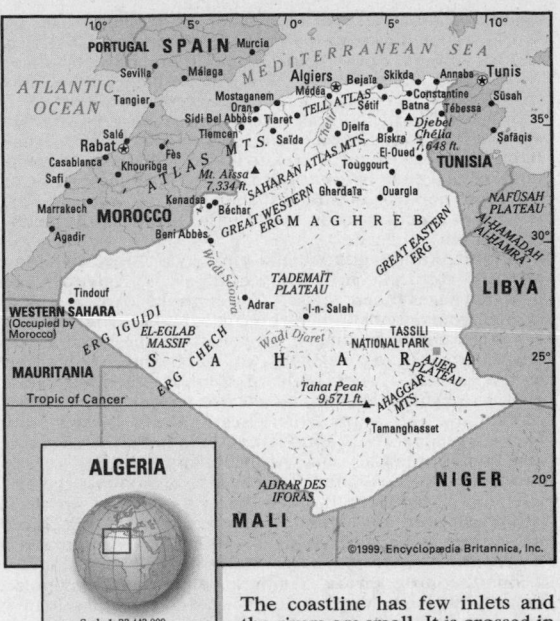

The coastline has few inlets and the rivers are small. It is crossed in the north by the Saharan Atlas and ATLAS MTNS.; its highest peak is Djebel Chélia, at 7,648 ft (2,331 m). Central and S Algeria occupy much of the N SAHARA Desert. Phoenician traders settled the Algeria region early in the 1st millennium B.C.; several centuries later the Romans invaded, and by A.D. 40 they had control of the Mediterranean coast. The fall of Rome in the 5th cent. led to invasion by the VANDALS, and later by Byzantium. The Islamic invasion began in the 7th cent; by 711 all of N Africa was under the control of the UMAYYAD caliphate. Several Islamic Berber empires followed, most prominently the ALMORAVID (c.1054–1130), which extended its domain to Spain, and the ALMOHAD (c.1130–1269). The BARBARY COAST pirates, operating in the area, had menaced Mediterranean trade for centuries, and France seized this pretext to enter Algeria in 1830. By 1847 France had established control in the region, and by the late 19th cent. had instituted civil rule. Popular movements resulted in the bloody ALGERIAN WAR (1954–61); independence was achieved following a referendum in 1962. Algeria has a centrally planned developing economy based primarily on the production and export of oil and natural gas. Since achieving independence, the country has nationalized much of its economy. It is a republic with two legislative bodies; its chief of state is the president, and its head of government is the prime minister. In the 1990s Islamic fundamentalists opposing the military brought Algeria to a state of virtual civil war.

Algerian War (1954–1962) War for Algerian independence from France. The movement for independence gained momentum after promises of greater self-rule went unfulfilled after World War II. In 1954 the National Liberation Front (FLN) began a guerrilla war against France. In 1959 Charles DE GAULLE declared that the Algerians had the right to determine their own future. Despite terrorist acts by European Algerians opposed to independence, a truce was signed in 1962 and Algeria became independent.

Algiers *French* **Alger** \al-'zhā\ City (pop., 1998: 1,519,000), chief seaport, and capital of Algeria. First settled by Phoenicians, it was later ruled by the Romans. It was destroyed by the VANDALS (5th cent. A.D.) but revived under the Berbers (10th cent.). When the Spanish threatened it in the early 16th cent., the emir appealed to BARBAROSSA, who expelled the Spanish and placed Algiers under the OTTOMAN sultanate. For 300 years Algiers was home to the BARBARY COAST pirates; their activities were finally curtailed in 1818 by Stephen DECATUR. The French took the city in 1830 and made it headquarters for their African colonial empire. In World War II, it became the Allied headquarters in N Africa and for a time the provisional capital of France. After Algeria achieved independence (1962), Algiers grew as the country's political, economic, and cultural center.

ALGOL \'al-ˌgȯl\ High-level algebraic computer PROGRAMMING LANGUAGE developed in the late 1950s as an international language for the expression of ALGORITHMS between humans as well as between humans and machines. ALGOL was more popular in Europe than in the U.S., but it was an important precursor of PASCAL and it influenced the development of C language.

Algonquian languages \al-ˈgän-kwē-ən\ *or* **Algonkian languages** \al-ˈgäŋ-kē-ən\ Family of 25–30 N. American Indian languages found across E and central N. America, and divided conventionally into three geographic groups. Eastern Algonquian languages, spoken from the Gulf of St. Lawrence south to coastal N. Carolina, include Micmac, E. and W. Abenaki, and Delaware. Central Algonquian languages include Shawnee, Sauk, Kickapoo, Potawatomi, Menominee (all around the Great Lakes), Ojibwa, and Cree-Montagnais-Naskapi. Plains Algonquian includes the languages of the Cheyenne, Arapaho, and Blackfeet.

algorithm \'al-gə-ˌri-thəm\ Procedure that produces the answer to a question or the solution to a problem. An algorithm that produces a yes or no answer is called a decision procedure; one that leads to a solution is a computation procedure. A mathematical formula and the instructions in a computer program are examples of algorithms. Manipulation of lists (searching for, inserting, and removing items) can be done efficiently by using algorithms.

Algren \'ȯl-grən\, **Nelson** *orig.* Nelson Ahlgren Abraham (1909–1981) U.S. writer. Born in Detroit, the son of a machinist, he grew up in Chicago and worked his way through college during the Depression. His novels about the city's underside are lifted from routine naturalism by his vision of his characters' pride, humor, and unquenchable yearnings. Among his popular successes were *The Man with the Golden Arm* (1949; film, 1956) and *A Walk on the Wild Side* (1956; film, 1962).

Alhambra \äl-ˈäm-brə\ Palace of the Moorish monarchs of Granada, Spain, built 1238–1358 on a plateau above the city. Its name (Arabic: "the red") may refer to the color of the bricks in its outer walls. Its intact portions consist of rooms and gardens clustered around courts with fountains and water basins. Its surfaces are astoundingly ornate and varied, with outstanding examples of stalactite work.

Ali (ibn Abi Talib) (c.600–661) Son-in-law of the prophet MUHAMMAD and fourth CALIPH. Ali had been a ward of Muhammad, just as Muhammad had been a ward of Ali's father. An early convert to Islam, he helped Muhammad foil an assassination plot and fought beside him. The controversy over Ali's claim to the caliphate resulted in the first FITNAH (656–61). His brief reign as caliph (656–61) was spent fighting corruption and rebellions. See also HUSAYN IBN ALI, Battle of KARBALA, al-MUAWIYAH I.

Ali, Muhammad *orig.* **Cassius (Marcellus) Clay** (b.1942) U.S. boxer. Born in Louisville, Ky., he won the Olympic light heavyweight crown in 1960. His first professional heavyweight title win was against Sonny Liston in 1964. After defending the title nine times (1965–67), he was stripped of it for refusing induction into the armed forces following his conversion to Islam. He regained it in 1974 after defeating Joe Frazier and the then-current champion George FOREMAN. In 1978 he lost and regained the title a third time, becoming the first heavyweight ever to do so. He retired in 1979, having lost only three of 59 fights. Ali was known for his aggressive charm, invincible

Muhammad Ali (right) fighting Ernie Terrell, 1967

attitude, and colorful boasts, often expressed in doggerel verse. He was diagnosed in 1984 with Parkinson's disease.

Alice Springs Town (pop., 1991: 26,000), Northern Territory, Australia. It lies between DARWIN and ADELAIDE, virtually in the center of the continent. It originated in the 1870s as a telegraph station. Because of its location, it has become a major shipping point for cattle and minerals and a popular winter tourist destination.

alien In law, one who resides in a country without becoming naturalized, retaining instead the citizenship of another country. Under U.S. law, all aliens have had to register since 1940. Registration cards ("green cards") entitle them to obtain employment. Like citizens, aliens are protected by the U.S. Constitution, including the Bill of Rights and the due-process clause of the 14th Amendment. They remain subject to limitations under local laws.

Alien and Sedition Acts Four laws passed by the U.S. Congress in 1798, in anticipation of war with France after the XYZ AFFAIR, which restricted aliens and curtailed press criticism of the government. The laws, aimed at French and Irish immigrants (who were mostly pro-France), increased the waiting period for naturalization and authorized expulsion of aliens considered dangerous. Opposition to the laws helped propel Thomas JEFFERSON to the presidency. They were repealed or had expired by 1802.

alimentary canal *or* **digestive tract** Pathway along which food travels when it is eaten and from which solid wastes are expelled. It includes the MOUTH, PHARYNX, ESOPHAGUS, STOMACH, SMALL and LARGE INTESTINES, and anal canal. See also DIGESTION.

alimony See MARRIAGE LAW

Alkalai \ˌal-kə-ˈlī\, **Judah ben Solomon Hai** (1798–1878) Bosnian-born Sephardic rabbi. Raised in Jerusalem, he became rabbi at Semlin, Croatia. He argued that a physical return to Israel, rather than a symbolic return through repentance and practice, was necessary for the salvation of the Jewish people, a view that put him at odds with Jewish orthodoxy. Unsuccessful in gaining support for emigration, he himself settled in Palestine in 1871. His writings helped pave the way for ZIONISM.

alkali \'al-kə-ˌlī\ Inorganic compound, any soluble HYDROXIDE (–OH) of the ALKALI METALS, the ALKALINE EARTH METALS, or AMMONIA. Strong BASES that turn LITMUS paper blue, they react with ACIDS to yield SALTS, are caustic, and in concentrated form corrode tissues. Sodium hydroxide (CAUSTIC SODA) and potassium hydroxide (caustic potash) are very important industrial chemicals, used in the manufacture of soaps, glass, and many other products.

alkali metal Any of the six chemical ELEMENTS in the leftmost group of the PERIODIC TABLE (LITHIUM, SODIUM, POTASSIUM, rubidium, CESIUM, and francium). They form ALKALIES when they combine with other elements. Because their ATOMS have only one ELECTRON in the outermost shell, they react rapidly, even violently, with water, form numerous compounds, and are never found free in nature.

alkaline earth metal Any of the six chemical ELEMENTS in the second leftmost group of the PERIODIC TABLE (BERYLLIUM, MAGNESIUM, CALCIUM, STRONTIUM, BARIUM, and RADIUM). Their ATOMS have two ELECTRONS in the outermost shell, so they react readily, form numerous compounds, and are never found free in nature.

alkaloid Basic (see BASE) organic compounds of plant origin. Alkaloids are AMINES, so their names usually end in "ine" (e.g., CAFFEINE, NICOTINE, MORPHINE, QUININE). Most have complex chemical structures of multiple ring systems. They have diverse, important physiological effects on humans and other animals, but their functions in the plants that produce them are poorly understood. Some plants (e.g., OPIUM POPPY, ERGOT fungus) produce many different alkaloids, but most produce only one or a few. Alkaloids are extracted from plants by dilute ACID.

alkane *or* **paraffin** Any of a class of HYDROCARBONS whose MOLECULES consist only of carbon and hydrogen atoms joined by single COVALENT BONDS. The simplest is METHANE (CH_4). Alkanes with more than three carbon atoms may have straight and branched ISOMERS. Cycloalkanes have ring structures (but are not AROMATIC COMPOUNDS); many have more than one ring. Commercial sources include PETROLEUM and NATURAL GAS. Uses, often as mixtures, include as fuels, SOLVENTS, and raw materials.

al-Khwarizmi \al-'kwär-iz-mē\ *Arabic* Muhammad Ibn Musa al-Khwarizmi (c.780–c.850) Muslim mathematician and astronomer. He lived in Baghdad during the first golden age of Islamic science and wrote books that collected the discoveries of earlier mathematicians. His *Kitab al-jabr wa al-muqabalah* ("The Book of Integration and Equation") compiled rules for solving linear and QUADRATIC EQUATIONS, as well as problems of geometry and PROPORTION. Its translation into Latin in the 12th cent. provided the link between the great Hindu and Arab mathematicians and European scholars. The word *algebra* derives from the book's title; the term *algorithm* derives from the author's name.

Allah Standard Arabic word for God, used by Arab Christians as well as by Muslims. According to the QURAN, Allah is the creator and judge of mankind, omnipotent, compassionate, and merciful. The Muslim profession of faith affirms that there is no god but Allah and emphasizes that "nothing is like unto him." Everything that happens occurs by his commandment; submission to God is the basis of ISLAM.

Allahabad \'ä-lä-hä-ˌbäd\ City (metro. area pop., 2001: 1,049,000), N India, on the YAMUNA and GANGES RIVERS. An ancient holy city sacred to Hindu pilgrims, it was under Muslim rule 1194–1801, then ceded to the British. It was the scene of a serious outbreak in the 1857 INDIAN MUTINY. As the home of the NEHRU family, it was later a center of the Indian independence movement. It is the site of the Pillar of Asoka (erected 240 B.C.), the Jama Masjid (Great Mosque), and the Univ. of Allahabad.

Allegheny Mountains \ˌal-ə-'gā-nē\ Part of the APPALACHIAN MTNS. in Pennsylvania, Maryland, Virginia, and W. Virginia, west of the BLUE RIDGE MTNS. They extend some 500 mi (800 km) south-southwestward, reaching heights of over 4,800 ft (1,450 m). The Allegheny Plateau spans the entire upland area from the CUMBERLAND PLATEAU to the Mohawk Valley in New York.

Allegheny River River in Pennsylvania and New York. It rises in Potter Co., Pa., loops northwest into New York, turns back into Pennsylvania, and unites with the MONONGAHELA to form the OHIO RIVER at Pittsburgh. It is 325 mi (523 km) long. Several dams make the river navigable from Pittsburgh to E. Brady.

allegory Written, oral, or visual work using symbolic figures, objects, and actions to convey generalizations about human conduct. It encompasses such forms as the FABLE and parable. Characters represent abstract concepts or types, and the narrative action stands for something not explicitly stated. Symbolic allegories, where characters have an identity apart from the message they convey, have often been used to represent historical situations and are popular as vehicles for SATIRE. Edmund SPENSER's long poem *The Faerie Queen* is a famous example.

allele \ə-'lēl\ Any one of two or more alternative forms of a GENE that may occur alternatively at a given site on a CHROMOSOME. Alleles may occur in pairs, or there may be multiple alleles affecting the expression of a particular trait. If paired alleles are the same, the organism is said to be homozygous for that trait; if they are different, the organism is heterozygous. A dominant allele will override the traits of a recessive allele in a heterozygous pairing (see DOMINANCE, RECESSIVENESS). An individual cannot possess more than two alleles for a given trait.

Allen, Ethan (1738–1789) American soldier and frontiersman. Born in Litchfield, Conn., he fought in the FRENCH AND INDIAN WAR, then settled in what is now Vermont. In 1770 he organized a force he called the Green Mountain Boys, which in the AMERICAN REVOLUTION helped win the Battle of Ticonderoga, N.Y. (1775). Later that year he was captured by the British and held prisoner until 1778. He returned to Vermont, where he worked for statehood.

Allen, Fred *orig.* John Florence Sullivan (1894–1956) U.S. comedian. Born in Cambridge, Mass., he appeared in comedy revues in the 1920s. He entered radio in 1932 and created the popular *Fred Allen Show* (1939–49). He and his wife, Portland Hoffa (1906–1990), played the principal roles in "Allen's Alley." He wrote nearly all the 273 episodes,

which displayed his laconic style, dry wit, and flawless timing.

Allen, Richard (1760–1831) U.S. religious leader. He was born to slave parents in Philadelphia. A Methodist convert, he was licensed to preach at 22. By 1786 he had purchased his freedom, and he joined St. George's Methodist Episcopal Church. Racial discrimination prompted him to withdraw in 1787, and he turned an old blacksmith shop into the first black church in the U.S. With his followers he built the Bethel African Methodist Church. In 1816 he convened black leaders to form the AFRICAN METHODIST EPISCOPAL CHURCH.

Allen, Steve (*orig.* Stephen Valentine Patrick William) (1921–2000) U.S. entertainer. Born in New York City, he appeared as a comedian on radio before moving to late-night television, where he created and hosted *The Tonight Show* (1953–57) and *The Steve Allen Show* (1957–60). He hosted several other shows, including *Meeting of Minds* (1977–81). He composed over 3,000 songs, including "This Could Be the Start of Something Big," and "Impossible," and appeared in several films.

Allen, Woody *orig.* Allen Stewart Konigsberg (b.1935) U.S. film director, screenwriter, and actor. His Jewish family in Brooklyn and his chronic neuroticism became the source of much of his comic material. After writing routines for comedians, he wrote the Broadway play *Don't Drink the Water* (1966). His first film, *What's New, Pussycat?* (1965), was followed by *Take the Money and Run* (1969), *Bananas* (1971), and *Sleeper* (1973), combining highbrow comedy and slapstick. Later romantic comedies such as *Annie Hall* (1977), which won him three Academy Awards, and *Manhattan* (1979) offered a bittersweet view of New York life. His other films include *Zelig* (1983), *Hannah and Her Sisters* (1986, Academy Award), *Crimes and Misdemeanors* (1989), and *Bullets over Broadway* (1994).

Allenby, Edmund (Henry Hynman) *later* **Viscount Allenby (of Megiddo and of Felixstowe)** (1861–1936) British field marshal. In World War I, he commanded with distinction in the Middle East. His victory over the Turks at Gaza (1917) led to the capture of Jerusalem, and his victory at Megiddo, along with his capture of Damascus and Aleppo, ended Ottoman power in Syria. He is remembered as the last great British leader of mounted cavalry. As high commissioner for Egypt (1919–25), he steered that country to recognition as a sovereign state (1922).

Allende (Gossens) \ä-'yen-dä\, **Salvador** (1908–1973) Socialist president of Chile (1970–73). A physician, Allende helped found Chile's Socialist Party in 1933. He ran for president three times before winning narrowly in 1970. He attempted to restructure Chilean society along socialist lines while retaining democracy, civil liberties, and due process of law, but his efforts to redistribute wealth resulted in stagnant production, food shortages, inflation, and widespread strikes. His policies dried up foreign credit and led to a covert campaign by the U.S. CENTRAL INTELLIGENCE AGENCY to destabilize the government. He was overthrown and died in a violent military coup and was replaced by Gen. Augusto PINOCHET.

allergy Hypersensitive reaction by the body to foreign substances (allergens or ANTIGENS), such as pollens, drugs, dusts, and foods, that are harmless to most people. Immediate allergic reactions result from genetic predisposition or previous sensitization; blood vessels dilate and bronchial air passages constrict. Delayed allergic responses (e.g., contact DERMATITIS) appear 12 hours or more after exposure. When avoidance is not feasible and ANTIHISTAMINES do not relieve symptoms, desensitization can be attempted. See also ANAPHYLAXIS, HIVES.

alliance In international politics, a union for joint action of various powers or states. Many alliances rest on the principle of collective security, through which an attack on one member is considered an attack on all members. Major 20th–cent. alliances have included the ANZUS PACT, ARAB LEAGUE, ASSN. OF S.E. ASIAN NATIONS, NATO, ORGANIZATION OF AMERICAN STATES, and WARSAW PACT.

Alliance for Progress International development program initiated by the U.S. and joined by 22 Latin American countries in 1961 to strengthen democratic government and pro-

mote social and economic reforms in Latin America. The program of loans and aid built some schools and hospitals but was widely viewed as a failure. Significant LAND REFORM was not achieved, population growth outstripped gains in health and welfare, and the U.S. willingness to support military dictators who opposed communism sowed distrust and undermined the intended reforms.

Allied Powers *or* **Allies** Nations allied in opposition to the CENTRAL POWERS in WORLD WAR I or to the AXIS POWERS in WORLD WAR II. The original Allies in World War I—the British empire, France, and the Russian empire—were later joined by such countries as Portugal, Japan, and Italy. (The U.S. entered the war in 1917 as one of the Associated Powers.) In World War II, the major Allied Powers were Britain, France, the Soviet Union, the U.S., and China. More generally, the Allies included all the wartime members of the UNITED NATIONS, the 1942 signatories to the Declaration of the U.N.

alligator Either of two species of long-snouted reptiles constituting the genus *Alligator* (family Alligatoridae, order Crocodilia). Alligators differ from CROCODILES in snout shape and tooth placement. Living in lakes, swamps, and rivers, these lizardlike carnivores use their powerful tail for defense and swimming. The eyes, ears, and nostrils project above the water's surface. Alligators dig burrows in which they shelter from danger and hibernate in cold weather. The once-endangered American alligator of the SE U.S. usually ranges from 6 to 12 ft (2–3.5 m long). The smaller Chinese alligator is considered endangered or extinct.

allosaurus \ˌal-ə-ˈsȯr-əs\ Large carnivorous dinosaur (genus *Allosaurus*) found in fossils in Late Jurassic to Early Cretaceous rocks of N. America, Africa, and Australia. It weighed 2 tons (1,800 kg) and grew to 34 ft (10.4 m) long. Its tail was half of its total body length. Allosaurs walked on their two hind limbs and probably used their much smaller forelimbs for grasping. Equipped with powerful, flexible jaws, they likely preyed on dead or dying dinosaurs.

allosteric control \ˌa-lō-ˈster-ik\ Inhibition or activation of an ENZYME by a small regulatory molecule that interacts with the enzyme at a site other than the active site (at which catalytic activity occurs). The interaction changes the shape of the enzyme, affecting the active site. As a result, the enzyme's ability to catalyze a reaction (see CATALYSIS) is either inhibited or enhanced. Feedback inhibition occurs if the regulatory molecule inhibits an enzyme in the pathway of its own synthesis. Allosteric control enables the cell to regulate needed substances rapidly.

alloy Metallic substance composed of two or more elements, as either a mixture, compound, or solid solution. The components of alloys are ordinarily themselves METALS, though CARBON is an essential nonmetal component of STEEL. Alloys are usually produced by melting the mixture of ingredients. The value of alloys was discovered in very ancient times; BRASS (copper and zinc) and BRONZE (copper and tin) were especially important. Today the most important are the alloy steels, which have a wide range of special properties, including hardness, corrosion resistance, and workability.

All Saints' Day In Christianity, a day commemorating all the saints of the church, known and unknown. It is celebrated on November 1 in the Western churches and on the first Sunday after PENTECOST in the Eastern churches. The first general observance was in 837. In medieval England it was called All Hallows, and the preceding day ("eve") is still known as HALLOWEEN.

All Souls' Day In the Roman Catholic church, a day commemorating all the Christians believed to be in PURGATORY. Celebrated on November 2, it was first established by Odilo (d.1048), abbot of Cluny, and it was widely celebrated by the 13th cent. The date follows ALL SAINTS' DAY. Roman Catholic doctrine holds that the prayers of the faithful will help cleanse these souls in order to prepare them for heaven.

allspice Tropical EVERGREEN tree (*Pimenta dioica*) of the MYRTLE family, native to the W. Indies and Central America and valued for its berries, the source of a highly aromatic spice. The flavor of the dried berry resembles a combination of cloves, cinnamon, and nutmeg. It is widely used in baking. The name is applied to such other aromatic shrubs as Carolina allspice (*Calycanthus floridus*) and wild allspice, or spicebush.

alluvial deposit Material deposited by rivers. It consists of SILT, SAND, CLAY, and GRAVEL, as well as much organic matter. Alluvial deposits usually form floodplains and DELTAS at the mouths of rivers, but they may form at any point where the river overflows its banks or slows down. They yield very fertile soils, such as those of the deltas of the Mississippi, Nile, and Huang (Yellow) rivers. They contain most of the world's tin ore.

Almagro \äl-ˈmä-grō\, **Diego de** (1475–1538) Spanish soldier who played a leading role in the Spanish conquest of what is now Peru. He arrived in S. America in 1524 and, with Francisco PIZARRO, led the expedition that conquered the INCA empire. Enmity arose between the two men, and Almagro imprisoned Pizarro's two brothers for insubordination. Pizarro then defeated Almagro's army and had his former friend killed.

almanac Book or table containing a calendar of a given year, with a record of various astronomical phenomena, often with weather predictions, seasonal tips for farmers, and other information. The first printed almanac appeared in the mid-15th cent. Benjamin FRANKLIN began his famous *Poor Richard's* series in 1732. A form of folk literature, 18th-cent. almanacs furnished useful and entertaining reading matter where it was scarce; a surviving example is the *Old Farmer's Almanac.*

Al-Manamah See MANAMA

Alma-Tadema \ˈal-mə-ˈta-də-mə\, **Lawrence** (*later* **Sir Lawrence**) (1836–1912) Dutch-British painter. After studies at the Antwerp Academy, he visited Italy (1863) and became enamored of Greco-Roman antiquity and Egyptian archaeology; the ancient world was to provide his primary themes. He settled in London in 1870. He excelled at the accurate re-creation of ancient scenes, exotic costumes, and the sensuous depiction of beautiful women. He enjoyed immense popularity and flaunted a sumptuous personal style. He was elected to the Royal Academy in 1879 and knighted in 1899. His work went out of favor after his death, only to be revived in the late 20th cent.

Almaty \əl-ˈmä-tē\ *or* **Alma-Ata** \əl-ˈmä-ə-ˈtä\ City (pop., 1997 est.: 1,064,000), SE Kazakstan. The modern city was founded in 1854 when the Russians established a fortification on the site of the ancient city of Almaty, destroyed by the MONGOLS in the 13th cent. With the coming of the railroad in 1930, its population grew rapidly. In World War II, heavy industry expanded widely as factories were evacuated to there from Russian Europe. The city remains a major industrial center.

Almendros \äl-ˈmen-drōs\, **Nestor** (1930–1992) Spanish cinematographer. In 1948 he emigrated from Spain to Cuba, where he worked with documentary filmmakers. After moving to France in 1961, he collaborated with Eric Rohmer on *My Night at Maud's* (1969) and with François TRUFFAUT on *The Wild Child* (1970). His many films in the U.S. include *Days of Heaven* (1978, Academy Award), *Sophie's Choice* (1982), and *Billy Bathgate* (1991).

Almohad dynasty \ˈal-mō-ˌhad\ (1130–1269) Dynasty created by a BERBER confederation that opposed the ALMORAVIDS. The Almohad leader, Ibn Tumart, began his rebellion in the 1120s. Marrakech was captured in 1147 under the leadership of his successor ABD AL-MUMIN. By the 1170s all of the MAGHREB was under unified control for the only time in its history, along with Muslim Spain. Almohad rule was marked by the cultivation of science and philosophy and efforts at compelling Jews and Christians to convert or leave. They lost control of Spain to the Christians in 1212, and their N. African provinces to the Hafsid dynasty in Tunis (1236) and the Marinids in Marrakech (1269).

almond Tree (*Prunus dulcis*) in the ROSE family, native to SW Asia; also its edible seed, or NUT. The tree, which resembles the PEACH, is strikingly beautiful when in flower. The nuts are either sweet or bitter. Sweet almonds are consumed as nuts and used in baking and cooking. The extracted oil of bitter almonds is used to make flavoring extracts.

Almoravid dynasty \ˌal-mə-ˈrä-vəd\ (1056–1147) BERBER dynasty that succeeded the FATIMID DYNASTY in the MAGHREB.

Its founder, Abdallah ibn Yasin, was a religious scholar and reformer who gained followers in the mid-11th cent. As the Fatimids lost political control in the aftermath of the Arab invasion, the Almoravids took over Morocco, the rest of the Maghreb, and eventually Muslim Spain. Christians there began to win back territory in 1118. In the 1120s the ALMOHADS began their rebellion, eventually displacing the Almoravids.

aloe Any SUCCULENT plant of the genus *Aloe* in the LILY FAMILY, containing about 200 species native to Africa. Most aloes have a rosette of leaves at the base but no stem. Several species are cultivated as ornamentals. The juice of some species, especially the true aloe *(Aloe vera)*, is used in cosmetics and as a treatment for burns.

Alonso, Alicia *orig.* Alicia Martínez Hoyo (b.1921) Cuban ballerina and choreographer. She studied in Havana and New York, where she danced with the Ballet (later AMERICAN BALLET) THEATRE in the 1940s and '50s. In 1948 she formed her own company, Ballet Alicia Alonso (renamed Ballet Nacional de Cuba in 1959), with which she performed frequently on tour in Latin America. Despite failing eyesight, she long continued to dance as a guest artist with leading companies.

alpaca \al-'pa-kə\ S. American species *(Lama pacos)* in the CAMEL family (Camelidae). It is one of the lamoids, which include the closely related guanaco, LLAMA, and VICUÑA. The alpaca has a slender body, long neck and legs, small head, short tail, and large, pointed ears. Alpacas stand about 35 in. (90 cm) at the shoulder and weigh 120–145 lbs (54–65 kg). Found in the Andes Mtns. of Peru and Bolivia, they are the most important of the lamoids for wool production.

Alpaca *(Lama pacos)*

Alp-Arslan \'älp-är-'slän\ (c.1030–1072/73) Second sultan of the SELJUQ DYNASTY, who added Georgia, Armenia, and much of Asia Minor to his domains of Khorasan and W Iran. He preferred conquest to governing, and left the administration of his empire to his viziers. In 1071 his victory over the Byzantines resulted for the first time in a Byzantine emperor being held captive by the Muslims. Alp-Arslan's Byzantine expeditions paved the way for the Turkish conquest of Asia Minor.

alphabet Set of symbols or characters that represent language's sounds in WRITING. Each character usually represents a VOWEL, a diphthong (two vowels), or one or two CONSONANTS. The first alphabet is believed to have been the N. Semitic, which originated in the E Mediterranean between 1700 and 1500 B.C. Alphabets that arose in the next 500 years included the Canaanite and Aramaic, from which the modern Hebrew and Arabic alphabets descended, and the Greek (ancestor of the LATIN ALPHABET), the first alphabet to include both CONSONANTS and VOWELS. Scholars have developed new alphabets such as the INTERNATIONAL PHONETIC ALPHABET to represent the sounds in all languages.

Alpha Centauri Triple star in the constellation Centaurus, whose faintest component, Proxima Centauri, is currently the closest star to the sun (about 4.3 light-years away). The other two stars are about 0.1 light-year farther; the three cannot be distinguished as separate stars by the unaided eye. As seen from earth, the system is the third-brightest star (after SIRIUS and Canopus) and is visible only from south of about 40° N latitude.

alpha decay Type of radioactive disintegration (see RADIOACTIVITY) by which some unstable atomic nuclei dissipate excess energy. An alpha particle, with two positive charges and a MASS of four atomic mass units (identical to a helium nucleus), is spontaneously ejected. Though emitted at speeds about one-tenth that of light, alpha particles are not very penetrating and have ranges in air of about 1–4 in. (2.5–10 cm). Alpha decay commonly occurs in elements with ATOMIC NUMBERS greater than 83 (bismuth).

Alpha decay half-lives range from about a microsecond (10^{-6} second) to billions of years (10^{17} seconds).

Alpheus River \al-'fē-əs\ River, S Greece. About 75 mi (120 km) long, it is the longest river in the PELOPONNESE, flowing from Arcadia into the Ionian Sea. OLYMPIA is on its N bank. It shares its name with the ancient river god, and it figures in Greek legend, including Hercules' cleaning of the Augean stables.

Alps Mountain system, S central Europe. The Alps extend in a crescent about 750 mi (1,200 km) from the Mediterranean coast between France and Italy to Vienna, and cover more than 80,000 sq mi (200,000 sq km). Several peaks rise above 10,000 ft (3,000 m); the highest is Mont BLANC. The Alps form a divide between the Atlantic, the Mediterranean, and the Black Sea, and give rise to several major European rivers, including the RHÔNE, DANUBE, and PO. Glaciers cover about 1,500 sq mi (4,000 sq km). The ST. GOTTHARD PASS is one of the Alps' notable tunnels. GRENOBLE, INNSBRUCK, and Bolzano are major alpine cities.

Al-Qaeda \ˌäl-'kī-də\ (Arabic: "the Base") Terrorist network organized by Osama BIN LADEN. Formed in the early 1990s, it initially consisted largely of militant Muslims who bin Laden had met in Afghanistan. The network funded and organized several terrorist attacks, including detonating truck bombs against American targets in Saudi Arabia (1996), killing tourists in Egypt (1997), and simultaneously bombing the U.S. embassies in Kenya and Tanzania (1998), killing almost 300. From its base in Afghanistan, Al-Qaeda trained and equipped terrorists while directing thousands of members in such countries as Saudi Arabia, Yemen, Libya, Bosnia, Russia, and the Philippines. After the SEPTEMBER 11 ATTACKS against the U.S., Al-Qaeda became the main target of a worldwide campaign against terrorism.

Alsace-Lorraine \al-'sas-lò-'rän\ Area, E France. It includes the present-day French departments of Haut-Rhin, Bas-Rhin, and Moselle. The area was ceded by France to Germany in 1871 after the FRANCO–PRUSSIAN WAR. It was returned to France after World War I, occupied by the Germans in World War II, then again restored to France. Both French and German are taught in the schools; the German dialect known as Alsatian remains the mutually understood tongue.

Alsatian See GERMAN SHEPHERD

Altaic languages \al-'tā-ik\ Group of about 40 languages, comprising the TURKIC, MONGOLIAN, and Manchu-Tungus families, spoken across Eurasia by more than 140 million people (most of whom speak Turkic languages). Some scholars consider Altaic itself to be a superfamily. A remote relationship with KOREAN and JAPANESE is regarded by some as probable but not proven.

Altamira \ˌal-tə-'mir-ə\ Cave near SANTANDER, N Spain, famous for its magnificent prehistoric paintings and engravings dating to 14,000–12,000 B.C., first described in 1880. The cave is 890 ft (270 m) long. The roof of the main chamber is covered with paintings, chiefly of bison, in vivid red, black, and violet. There are also wild boars, horses, eight engraved anthropomorphic figures, and various handprints and hand outlines. The site may have been a center for seasonal gatherings. See also MAGDALENIAN CULTURE, ROCK ART.

altar Raised structure or place used for sacrifice, worship, or prayer. Altars probably originated with the belief that objects or places (e.g., a tree or spring) were inhabited by spirits or deities worthy of prayers or gifts. Blood SACRIFICE to deities required a structure on which the animal or person could be killed and blood channeled off or flesh burned. In ancient Israel, the altar was a rectangular stone with a hollowed-out basin on top. The ancient Greeks placed altars in homes, marketplaces, public buildings, and sacred groves. Roman altars were similarly ubiquitous. Christians at first did not use altars, but by the 3rd cent. the table on which the EUCHARIST was celebrated was regarded as an altar.

altarpiece Painting, sculpture, screen, or decorated wall standing on or behind an altar in a Christian church. The images depict holy personages, saints, and biblical subjects. The reredos type rises from the floor behind the altar; the retable type stands on the altar itself or on a pedestal behind it. A diptych is an altarpiece consisting of two panels; a trip-

tych, three panels; and a polyptych, four or more panels. Altarpieces vary greatly in size, and some have movable wings that can be opened and closed. Sculptural altarpieces date from the 11th cent.; altar paintings became common in the 14th cent.

Altay Shan \al-ˈtī-ˈshän\ *or* **Altay Mountains** Mountain system, central Asia. The mountains extend about 1,200 mi (2,000 km) southeast-northwest from the GOBI DESERT to the W Siberian plain, through Chinese, Mongolian, Russian, and Kazak territory. The highest point is the Russian peak Belukha, at approx. 15,000 ft (4,600 m). The mountains are the source of the Irtysh and OB rivers.

Altdorfer \ˈält-ˌdȯr-fər\, **Albrecht** (c.1480–1538) German painter and printmaker, the leading artist of the Danube School. Most of his works depict religious subjects, but he was one of the first artists to develop landscape painting as an independent genre, specializing in sunset lighting and ruins in twilight. The influence of Albrecht DÜRER is evident in his miniature engravings and woodcuts. From 1526 he was town architect of Regensburg.

alternating current (AC) Flow of ELECTRIC CHARGE that reverses periodically. It starts from zero, grows to a maximum, decreases to zero, reverses, reaches a maximum in the opposite direction, returns to zero, and repeats the cycle indefinitely. The time to complete one cycle is called the period and the number of cycles per second is the FREQUENCY; the maximum value in either direction is the current's amplitude. Low frequencies (50–60 cycles per second) are used for domestic and commercial power, but frequencies of around 100 million cycles per second (100 megahertz) are used in television, and of several thousand megahertz in RADAR and MICROWAVE communication. A major advantage of alternating current is its efficient transmission over long distances. See also DIRECT CURRENT, ELECTRIC CURRENT.

alternation of generations In biology, alternation of a sexual phase (GAMETOPHYTE) and a nonsexual phase (SPOROPHYTE) in the life cycle of an organism. The two phases are often distinct in structure. Alternation of generations is common in ALGAE, fungi (see FUNGUS), MOSSES, FERNS, and SEED PLANTS. The character and extent of the two phases vary greatly. In higher (VASCULAR) plants, the sporophyte is the dominant phase; in more primitive plants, the gametophyte is dominant. Many invertebrates (e.g., PROTOZOANS, jellyfish, flatworms) also have an alternation of sexual and asexual generations.

alternative education Education that diverges in some way from that offered by conventional schools. The focus may be on alternative structures (e.g., open classrooms), alternative subject matter (e.g., religious instruction), or alternative relationships (e.g., more informal relations between students and teachers or between students of different ages). Alternative education, including homeschooling, may supply desired moral or ethical principles or recognition of children's individual learning styles and innate creativity.

alternative energy Any of various renewable POWER sources to use in place of FOSSIL FUELS and URANIUM. Fusion devices (see NUCLEAR FUSION) are believed by some to be the best long-term option, because their primary energy source would be DEUTERIUM, abundant in ordinary water. Other technologies include solar energy, WIND POWER, tidal power, wave power, HYDROELECTRIC POWER, and GEOTHERMAL ENERGY. The amount of energy in such renewable and virtually pollution-free sources is large in relation to world energy needs, yet at present only a small portion of it can be converted to electric power at reasonable cost.

alternative medicine *or* **complementary medicine** Any of a broad range of healing approaches not used in conventional Western MEDICINE, including HOLISTIC MEDICINE, ACUPUNCTURE, AROMATHERAPY, Ayurveda medicine, CHINESE MEDICINE, CHIROPRACTIC, HOMEOPATHY, MASSAGE, MEDITATION, and YOGA. Though considered alternative in the West, such medicine is the main source of health care for up to 80% of people in less-developed countries. Some alternative-medicine practices are useless or harmful; others are effective and may help where conventional approaches have not succeeded (e.g., chronic disorders).

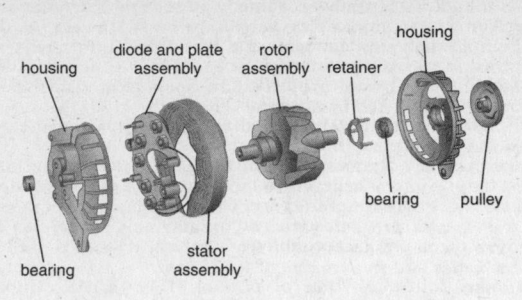

Alternator Exploded view of an automotive alternator. The engine's turning crankshaft, connected to the alternator's pulley by a belt, turns the magnetic rotor inside the stationary stator assembly, generating an alternating current. The diode assembly rectifies the alternating current, producing direct current, which is used to meet the demands of the vehicle's electrical system, incl. recharging the battery.

alternator Source of direct ELECTRIC CURRENT in modern vehicles for ignition, lights, fans, and other uses. The electric power is generated by an alternator mechanically coupled to the engine, with a rotor field coil supplied with current through slip rings, and a stator with a three-phase winding. A rectifier converts the power from alternating to direct form. A regulator ensures that the output voltage is properly matched to the battery voltage as engine speed varies.

Altgeld, John Peter (1847–1902) U.S. (German-born) governor of Illinois (1893–97). In the 1870s he moved to Chicago, where he became active in Democratic Party politics, winning the governorship as a reformist candidate. In 1893, at the insistence of Clarence DARROW and labor leaders, he pardoned participants in the HAYMARKET RIOT, which provoked an outcry from conservatives and contributed to his defeat for reelection in 1896. Altgeld's decision later gained wide approval in judicial circles.

altimeter \al-ˈtim-ət-ər\ Instrument that measures the altitude of the land surface or of any object, such as an airplane. The mechanical pressure altimeter measures atmospheric pressure relative to sea level through a series of bellows, gears, and springs, which move pointers on a dial. Radio altimeters measure the distance of an aircraft above the ground by indicating the time a pulse of RADIO energy takes to travel from the aircraft to the ground and back.

Altiplano \ˌal-ti-ˈplä-nō\ Region, SE Peru and W Bolivia. Comprising a series of high plains, it originates northwest of Lake TITICACA in S Peru and extends southeast to SW Bolivia. The region's wildlife originally included the alpaca and the llama, both now bred for wool. The city of LA PAZ (Bolivia) lies along the lake's shores. The area has been populated since ancient times.

altitude and azimuth \ˈaz-məth\ Coordinates of the position of an object above earth in the altazimuth, or horizon, system. In this COORDINATE SYSTEM, used in astronomy, gunnery, navigation, surveying, and other fields, altitude is expressed as angle of elevation (up to 90°) above the horizon and azimuth, in astronomical measurement, as the number of degrees clockwise from due north to the point on the horizon most directly below the object.

altitude sickness *or* **mountain sickness** Acute reaction to a change from low altitudes to altitudes above 8,000 ft (2,400 m). Most people gradually adapt, but some have a severe reaction that can be fatal unless they return to low altitude. Symptoms include breathlessness, racing heartbeat, headache, gastrointestinal upsets, and weakness. Pulmonary EDEMA is quickly reversed with oxygen and evacuation to a lower area.

Altman \ˈȯlt-mən\, **Robert (B.)** (b.1925) U.S. film director. Born in Kansas City, Mo., he directed several television series before making his first feature film, *Countdown* (1967).

The successful antiwar comedy *M*A*S*H* (1970) established his reputation as an independent director whose work emphasizes character and atmosphere over plot. His other films include *Brewster McCloud* (1970), *McCabe and Mrs. Miller* (1971), *Nashville* (1976), *Popeye* (1980), *The Player* (1992), and *Gosford Park* (2001).

Altman, Sidney (b.1939) Canadian-U.S. molecular biologist. Born in Montreal, he has taught at Yale Univ. since 1971. Altman and Thomas CECH independently discovered that RNA, previously believed to be a passive carrier of genetic codes between different parts of the living cell, could also initiate and carry out some reactions, opening up new fields of research and biotechnology. The two shared a 1989 Nobel Prize.

alto *or* **contralto** Voice or register that extends approximately from the F below middle C to the second D above. The second-highest part in four-part music, it is normally sung by women. The name derives from *contratenor altus*, the part above the tenor part. It is used for some instruments that play principally in the alto range (alto saxophone, alto flute, etc.).

altruism Ethical theory that regards the good of others as the end of moral action. The term was coined by Auguste COMTE and adopted generally as a convenient antithesis to EGOISM. Most altruists have held that each person has an obligation to further the pleasures or happiness, and alleviate the pains, of other people.

alum \ˈa-ləm\ Inorganic compound, usually consisting of ALUMINUM sulfate, water of hydration (essential to the CRYSTAL makeup), and the SULFATE of another element. The most important alums are potassium alum (potash alum, $K_2SO_4 \cdot Al_2(SO_4)_3 \cdot 24H_2O$) and those of ammonium sulfate and sodium sulfate. Alums occur naturally in various minerals; most are white crystals with an astringent, acid taste. They are used in paper sizing, water treatment, and dyeing, and in pickles, baking powder, fire extinguishers, and medicines.

aluminum Chemical ELEMENT, chemical symbol Al, atomic number 13. A lightweight, silvery-white METAL, it is so reactive chemically that it always occurs in compounds. It is the most abundant metallic element in the earth's crust, chiefly in BAUXITE (its principal ORE), FELDSPARS, MICAS, CLAY MINERALS, and laterite. It also occurs in gemstones, such as TOPAZ and GARNET; emery, CORUNDUM, RUBY, and SAPPHIRE are crystalline aluminum OXIDE. Aluminum was first isolated in 1825, became commercially available in the late 19th cent., and is now the most widely used metal after IRON. Uses include building and construction, corrosion-resistant chemical equipment, auto parts, power transmission lines, photoengraving plates, magnets, and tubes for ointments and pastes. Important compounds include ALUMS; alumina (aluminum oxide), aluminum chloride, and aluminum hydroxide.

Alvarez \ˈal-və-ˌrez\, **Luis W(alter)** (1911–1988) U.S. experimental physicist. Born in San Francisco, he taught at UC–Berkeley 1936–78. In 1938 he discovered a form of BETA DECAY. In 1939 he and Felix Bloch (1905–1983) made the first measurement of the magnetic moment of the NEUTRON. During World War II he developed a radar guidance system for landing aircraft and participated in the MANHATTAN PROJECT. He later helped construct the first proton linear accelerator and constructed the liquid hydrogen bubble chamber. With his son, the geologist Walter Alvarez (b.1940), he helped develop the theory that links the dinosaurs' extinction with a giant asteroid or comet impact. For work that included the discovery of many subatomic particles, he received a Nobel Prize in 1968.

alveolus See PULMONARY ALVEOLUS

Alzheimer's disease \ˈälts-ˌhī-mərz\ Degenerative brain disorder of middle to late adult life that destroys neurons and connections in the CEREBRAL CORTEX, resulting in significant loss of brain mass. The most common form of DEMENTIA, Alzheimer's disease progresses from short-term memory impairment to further memory loss; deterioration of language, perceptual, and motor skills; mood instability; and, in advanced stages, unresponsiveness, with loss of mobility and control of body functions; death typically ensues in 5–10 years. Alzheimer's disease is now recognized as ac-

counting for much of the SENILE DEMENTIA once thought normal with aging. The 10% of cases that begin before age 60 result from an inherited mutation. No cure has been found. Most treatment targets the depression, behavioral problems, and sleeplessness that often accompany the disease. Ibuprofen, folic acid, antioxidants, exercise, and mental exercise may all help prevent Alzheimer's.

AM *in full* amplitude modulation. Variation of the amplitude of a radio wave in correspondence to fluctuations in the audio or video signal being transmitted. AM is the oldest method of broadcasting radio programs. Commercial AM stations operate in the frequency range of 535–1705 kilohertz (kHz). Radio waves of these frequencies can be detected by receivers hundreds of miles away. In addition to commercial radio broadcasting, AM is also employed in transmitting the video portion of television programs. See also FM.

Amadeus VI \ˌam-ə-ˈdā-əs\ *known as* **Amadeus the Green Count** (1334–1383) Count of SAVOY (1343–83). Ruler of Savoy from age 9, he significantly extended his kingdom's territory and power. In the 1350s he held nearly the entire W Alps, and added lands on the Italian side. He joined a crusade against the Turks (1366) and restored JOHN V PALAEOLOGUS to the Byzantine throne. A mediator of quarrels among Italian powers, he set out to rescue Queen JOAN I of Naples from her enemies (1382) but died of plague during the expedition.

Amado \ä-ˈmä-dü\, **Jorge** (1912–2001) Brazilian novelist. Born and reared on a cacao plantation, he published his first novel at 20. His early works, including *The Violent Land* (1942), show the exploitation of plantation workers. Imprisoned and exiled for leftist activities, he kept writing, though his books were banned in Brazil and Portugal. Works such as *Gabriela, Clove and Cinnamon* (1958), *Dona Flor and Her Two Husbands* (1966), and *The War of the Saints* (1993) express his politics in more subtle satire.

Amalfi \ä-ˈmäl-fē\ Town (pop., 1993 est.: 6000), S Italy, on the Gulf of Salerno. It grew into one of the first Italian maritime republics in the 9th cent., becoming a rival of VENICE and GENOA. Annexed by ROGER II of Sicily in 1131, it was sacked by PISA in 1135 and 1137 and rapidly declined in importance, though its maritime code, the Tavola Amalfitano, was recognized in the Mediterranean until 1570. Amalfi is now a notable tourist resort.

amalgam \ə-ˈmal-gəm\ ALLOY of MERCURY and one or more other METALS. Those of silver, gold, and palladium occur naturally. Those with a very high mercury content are liquid. Amalgams of silver and tin, with minor amounts of copper and zinc, are used to fill decayed teeth. Amalgams are used to recover silver and gold from their ores: The ore is shaken with mercury, and the amalgam is separated and heated until the mercury distills off (see DISTILLATION), leaving the precious metal behind. Amalgams are also used to silver mirrors and apply other metal coatings.

amanita \ˌam-ə-ˈnē-tə\ Any MUSHROOM of the genus *Amanita,* containing about 100 species, some of which are poisonous to humans. Among the deadliest of all mushrooms are the large white destroying angels (*A. bispongera, A. ocreata, A. verna,* and *A. virosa*), which are found in forests during wet periods in summer and autumn. The green or brown death cap (*A. phalloides*) and the fly agaric (*A. muscaria*) are also poisonous. Common edible species include *A. caesarea, A. rubescens,* and *A. vaginata.*

amaranth family \ˈa-mə-ˌranth\ Family Amaranthaceae, of more than 800 species of plants native to tropical America and Africa. Globe amaranth (*Gomphrena*) and cockscomb (*Celosia*) are cultivated as ornamentals. The

Amanita muscaria, or fly agaric

large genus *Amaranthus* contains the ornamentals love-lies-bleeding (*A. caudatus*) and Joseph's-coat (*A. tricolor*), as well as many weedy plants known as pigweed. Some *Amaranthus* species are TUMBLEWEEDS, and some are potential grain crops.

Amar Das \'əm-är-'däs\ (1479–1574) Third Sikh GURU. Much revered for his wisdom and piety, he became Guru at age 73. He was noted for his missionary efforts to spread SIKHISM and for the division of the PUNJAB into 22 dioceses. He required that anyone wanting to see him must first eat at the casteless *langar* ("community kitchen"). Advocating a middle way between the extremes of asceticism and sensuous pleasure, he purified Sikhism of Hindu practices, encouraged intercaste marriages, allowed widows to remarry, and prohibited suttee.

Amarillo City (pop., 2000: 173,000), N Texas. The chief city of the Texas Panhandle, it originated in 1887 with the coming of the railroad. It grew after 1900 with the agriculture industry, then, from the 1920s, petroleum and natural gas.

Amarna, Tell el- See TELL EL-AMARNA

amaryllis family \ˌam-ə-'ril-əs\ Family Amaryllidaceae of the order Liliales, containing about 65 genera and at least 835 species of perennial herbaceous plants, found mostly in tropical and subtropical regions and prized for their showy flowers, which are borne on smooth, hollow stalks with few or no leaves. Many species are cultivated as garden ornamentals and houseplants.

Amaterasu (Omikami) \ˌam-ə-'ter-ə-sü\ In SHINTO, the sun goddess from whom the Japanese royal family traditionally claimed descent. She ruled over heaven while her brother, the storm god Susanoo, ruled over the sea. When Susanoo began to behave rudely and destructively, Amaterasu withdrew in protest into a cave, plunging the world into darkness. After she was lured out, a rope was placed over its entrance to prevent her return. Her chief place of worship is the Grand Shrine of Ise, Shinto's most important shrine.

Amazon In GREEK MYTHOLOGY, a member of a race of women warriors. One of the labors of HERACLES was to obtain the girdle of the Amazon queen Hippolyte. In another tale, THESEUS attacked the Amazons, and they responded by invading Attica, where they were defeated; Theseus married the Amazon Antiope.

Amazonia National Park Park, N central Brazil, between MANAUS and BELÉM, along the TAPAJÓS RIVER. Established in 1974, it now covers 2.5 million acres (1 million hectares) and contains an immense diversity of flora and fauna.

Amazon River *Portuguese* **Rio Amazonas** River, N S. America. It is the largest river in the world in volume and area of drainage basin, and second only to the NILE in length. It originates within 100 mi (160 km) of the Pacific Ocean in the Peruvian ANDES and flows almost 4,000 mi (6,400 km) across N Brazil into the Atlantic Ocean. Its more than 1,000 known tributaries rise in the Guiana Highlands, the Brazilian Highlands, and (principally) the Andes; seven are longer than 1,000 mi (1,600 km), and the MADEIRA RIVER is longer than 2,000 mi (3,200 km). The Amazon can accommodate large freighters as far as MANAUS, 1,000 mi (1,600 km) upriver. The first European descent was made by Francisco de Orellana (c.1490–c.1546) in 1541; he is said to have given the river its name after reporting battles with tribes of women, whom he likened to the AMAZONS. Pedro Teixeira (c.1575–1640) achieved the first ascent in 1637–39. The river was opened to world shipping in the 1860s; traffic increased exponentially with the rubber trade, which reached its height around 1910. It is the site of the world's greatest rain forest and hosts an extraordinary variety of birds and wildlife. Since the 1960s, the ecological effects of economic exploitation, including the clearing of some 5 million acres per year, have generated worldwide concern.

ambassador Highest-ranking diplomatic representative of one government to another or to an international organization. As defined at the Congress of VIENNA (1815), ambassadors were representatives of their country's chief executive rather than of the whole country, and their rank entitled them to meet personally with the head of state of the host country. Originally, only the principal monarchies exchanged ambassadors; the U.S. did not appoint ambassadors until 1893. Since 1945 all nations have sent ambassadors or their equivalents to all countries with which diplomatic relations are maintained, though they are no longer entrusted with extensive powers.

amber Fossil tree resin that occurs as irregular nodules, rods, or droplike shapes in all shades of yellow with nuances of orange, brown, and, rarely, red. Hundreds of species of insects and plants are found as fossils in amber. Deeply colored translucent amber is prized as gem material, and numerous ornamental carved objects and beads are made from amber. It is found throughout the world; the largest deposits occur around the Baltic Sea.

ambergris \'am-bər-ˌgris, 'am-bər-ˌgrē\ Waxy substance (about 80% CHOLESTEROL) formed in the intestine of SPERM WHALES, used chiefly as a spice in the East and for fixing the scent of fine PERFUMES in the West. Fresh ambergris is soft, black, and smelly; exposed to sun, air, and seawater, it hardens, fades, and develops a pleasant scent. It may wash ashore or be found floating or in the bodies of slaughtered whales.

Ambon \äm-'bòn\ Island of the MOLUCCAS, Indonesia. Located in the MALAY ARCHIPELAGO, it is 31 mi (50 km) long and 10 mi (16 km) wide. Its chief port is also called Ambon (pop., 1995 est.: 249,000). The island is subject to volcanic activity; Mt. Salhatu (3,405 ft, or 1,038 m) is its highest point. The clove trade first attracted the Portuguese, who founded a settlement in 1521. The Dutch ousted the Portuguese in 1605, and in 1623 killed English settlers in the Amboina Massacre. An independence movement in 1950 was suppressed. The late 1990s were marked by ethnic conflicts.

Ambrose, St. (339?–397) Bishop of Milan. Born in Gaul, he was raised in Rome and became a Roman provincial governor. He was unexpectedly elevated from unbaptized layman to bishop of Milan in 374. He established the medieval concept of the Christian emperor as subject to episcopal advice and censure, and he opposed tolerance for ARIANISM. His treatises included *On the Holy Spirit* and *On the Duties of Ministers*. His sermons converted St. AUGUSTINE.

AMC See AMERICAN MOTORS CORP.

AME Church See AFRICAN METHODIST EPISCOPAL CHURCH

Amen See AMON

amen Expression of agreement or confirmation used in worship by Jews, Christians, and Muslims. The Greek Old Testament usually translates it as "so be it"; in the English Bible it is often translated as "verily" or "truly." By the 4th cent. B.C., it was a common prayer response in the Jewish temple liturgy. By the 2nd cent. A.D., Christians had adopted it in the liturgy of the Eucharist, and a final amen now often concludes Christian prayers or HYMNS.

Amenemhet I \'ä-mə-nəm-'het\ Egyptian pharaoh (r.1938–1908 B.C.) who founded the 12th dynasty and, with provincial governors, restored unity to Egypt after a civil war. He moved the capital from Thebes to near modern-day al-Lisht, south of Memphis. He extended Egyptian control up the Nile and fortified the delta, while also enlarging the Temple of AMON at Thebes. In 1918 B.C. he made his son, Sesostris I, his coruler. He was assassinated 10 years later.

Amenhotep II \'ä-mən-'hō-ˌtep\ Egyptian pharaoh (r.1514–1493 B.C.), son and successor of Ahmose I. He extended Egyptian rule southward to the Third Cataract of the Nile while also maintaining rule in the northeast. He pioneered the transition away from pyramidal tombs to rock-cut tombs in the Valley of the Kings in W Thebes, though the location of his own tomb is unknown.

Amenhotep III Egyptian pharaoh (r.1390–1353 B.C.) during a time of prosperity and peace. His reign is noted for the expansion of diplomacy with Syria, Cyprus, Babylon, and Assyria, and the construction of public buildings in Memphis, Thebes, and Nubia, including portions of the temples at Luxor and Karnak. He broke with tradition by marrying Tiy, a commoner, with whom he shared his rule. He was succeeded by his son AKHENATON.

Amenhotep IV See AKHENATON

America See CENTRAL AMERICA, NORTH AMERICA, SOUTH AMERICA

American Airlines Major U.S. airline. American was created through a merger of several smaller U.S. airlines and incorporated in 1934. It continued to buy the routes of other airlines, becoming an international carrier in the 1970s and eventually uniting some 85 companies; its routes today include S. America, the Caribbean, Europe, and the W Pacific. In 2001 it acquired TRANS WORLD AIRLINES.

American Anti-Slavery Society Activist arm of the U.S. abolition movement. Cofounded in 1833 by W. L. GARRISON, it promoted the formation of state and local auxiliaries to agitate for abolition. Despite violent opposition, by 1840 the group had 2,000 auxiliaries and over 150,000 members, including Theodore WELD and Arthur TAPPAN. Its most effective public meetings featured testimony of former slaves, including Frederick DOUGLASS and W. W. BROWN. In 1839 it split into two factions: a radical group led by Garrison and a moderate faction led by Tappan.

American Ballet Theatre Ballet company based in New York. It was founded in 1939 as the Ballet Theatre (the name was changed in 1958) by Lucia Chase and Richard Pleasant to promote works "American in character." Mikhail BARYSHNIKOV served as artistic director (1980–89) after dancing with the company. New ballets were created for the company by Agnes DE MILLE, Jerome ROBBINS, and Twyla THARP; Michel FOKINE revived many of his earlier works for them as well. Principal dancers have included Alicia ALONSO, Anton DOLIN, and Natalia MAKAROVA.

American Bar Association (ABA) Voluntary association (founded 1878) of U.S. lawyers, judges, and other legal professionals. It seeks to improve the legal profession, ensure the availability of legal services to all citizens, and improve the administration of justice. It conducts educational and research projects, sponsors professional meetings, and publishes a monthly journal. Currently it has about 375,000 members.

American Broadcasting Co. See ABC

American Civil Liberties Union (ACLU) Organization founded by Roger BALDWIN and others in 1920 to champion constitutional liberties in the U.S. It works for three basic concepts: freedom of expression, conscience, and association; DUE PROCESS of law; and EQUAL PROTECTION under the law. From its founding it has initiated test cases and intervened in cases already in the courts. The SCOPES TRIAL was one of its test cases; it provided counsel for the SACCO-VANZETTI CASE. In the 1950s and '60s it opposed the blacklisting of supposed left-wing subversives and worked to guarantee freedom of worship and the rights of the accused. See also CIVIL LIBERTY.

American Civil War *or* **Civil War** *or* **War Between the States** (1861–65) Conflict between the U.S. federal government and 11 Southern states that fought to secede from the Union. It arose out of disputes over the issues of slavery, trade and tariffs, and the doctrine of states' rights. In the 1840s and '50s, Northern opposition to slavery in the W territories caused the Southern states to fear a threat to their slaveholdings, the economic base of their large cotton plantations. By the 1850s ABOLITIONISM was growing in the North, and when the antislavery Abraham LINCOLN was elected president in 1860, the Southern states seceded and organized as the CONFEDERATE STATES OF AMERICA under Jefferson DAVIS. The war began when Confederate artillery fired on FORT SUMTER on April 12, 1861. In July 1861, 30,000 Union troops marched toward the Confederate capital at Richmond, Va., but were stopped by Confederate forces at BULL RUN and forced to retreat to Washington, D.C. The defeat shocked the Union, which called for 500,000 more recruits. The war's first major campaign began in February 1862, when Union troops under U. S. GRANT captured Confederate forts in W Tennessee. Union victories at the Battles of SHILOH and New Orleans followed. Gen. R. E. LEE won several Confederate victories in the SEVEN DAYS' BATTLES and, after defeat at ANTIETAM, in the Battle of FREDERICKSBURG (Dec. 1862). After the Confederate victory at CHANCELLORSVILLE, Lee invaded the North and engaged Union forces at the momentous Battle of GETTYSBURG. In July 1863 Grant's success in the VICKSBURG CAMPAIGN brought the entire Mississippi River under Union control. After the Union defeat at CHICKAMAUGA, Lincoln gave Grant supreme command of the Union armies. He began a strategy of attrition and, despite heavy Union casualties at the Battles of the Wilderness and Spotsylvania, began to surround Lee's troops in Petersburg, Va.

(see PETERSBURG CAMPAIGN). Meanwhile Gen. W. T. SHERMAN captured Atlanta in September (see ATLANTA CAMPAIGN), set out on a destructive march through Georgia, and soon captured Savannah. Grant captured Richmond on April 3, 1865, and accepted Lee's surrender on April 9 at APPOMATTOX COURT HOUSE. On April 26 Sherman received the surrender of Joseph Johnston, thereby ending the war. The mortality numbers were staggering—about 620,000 deaths out of a total of 2.4 million soldiers. The South was devastated. But the Union was preserved, and slavery was abolished.

American Express Co. U.S. financial-services company. Founded in 1850 as an express-transportation company, American Express originally provided rapid transport of goods across New York and the Midwest. It introduced traveler's checks in 1891 and opened its first European office in Paris in 1895. Today it offers credit cards, provides services for travelers, and owns banking and investment-services firms.

American Federation of Labor-Congress of Industrial Organizations See AFL-CIO

American Federation of Teachers (AFT) Trade union for classroom teachers in the U.S., formed in 1916. Through COLLECTIVE BARGAINING and strikes, it has obtained better wages, pensions, sick leaves, academic freedom, and other benefits. Under Albert Shanker (1928–97; pres. 1974–97), it instituted national certification tests. Membership is about 940,000. See also NATIONAL EDUCATION ASSN.

American Indian *or* **Native American** *or* **Amerindian** Member of any of the aboriginal peoples of the Western Hemisphere, with the exception of the ESKIMOS and ALEUTS. The ancestors of the American Indians were nomadic hunters of NE Asia who migrated over the Bering Strait land bridge into N. America probably during the last glacial period (20,000–30,000 years ago). By around 10,000 B.C. they had occupied much of N., Middle, and S. America. See also ANASAZI CULTURE, CLOVIS COMPLEX, EASTERN WOODLANDS INDIANS, FOLSOM COMPLEX, HOHOKAM CULTURE, HOPEWELL CULTURE, MESOAMERICAN CIVILIZATION, MISSISSIPPIAN CULTURE, MOGOLLON CULTURE, NORTHWEST COAST INDIANS, PLAINS INDIANS, PUEBLO INDIANS, WOODLAND CULTURES.

American Indian languages Languages spoken by the original inhabitants of the Americas and the W. Indies and by their modern descendants. They display a wide structural range, and no attempt to unite them into a small number of families has succeeded. Before Columbus, more than 300 distinct languages were spoken in N. America north of Mexico by about 2–7 million people. Today there are fewer than 170 languages, mostly spoken fluently only by older adults. A few widespread language families (ALGONQUIAN, Iroquoian, SIOUAN, Muskogean, ATHABASKAN, UTO-AZTECAN, Salishan) account for many of the languages of E and interior N. America, though the far west was an area of extreme diversity (see HOKAN). In Mexico and N Central America, an estimated 15–20 million people spoke more than 300 languages before Columbus. The MAYAN and other families and a single language, NAHUATL, dominated this area. More than 10 of these languages still have over 100,000 speakers. S. America and the W. Indies had an estimated pre-Columbian population of 10–20 million, speaking more than 500 languages. Important language families include QUECHUAN and Aymaran in the Andean region, and ARAWAKAN in N and central lowland S. America. Most remaining S. American Indian languages have very few speakers, and some face extinction before linguists can document them.

American League With the NATIONAL LEAGUE, one of two associations in the U.S. and Canada of professional, major-league BASEBALL teams. The league was founded in 1900. There are now three divisions: Eastern (comprising the Baltimore Orioles, Boston Red Sox, New York Yankees, Tampa Bay Devil Rays, and Toronto Blue Jays), Central (Chicago White Sox, Cleveland Indians, Detroit Tigers, Kansas City Royals, and Minnesota Twins), and Western (Anaheim Angels, Oakland Athletics, Seattle Mariners, and Texas Rangers).

American Legion Organization of U.S. war veterans. Founded in 1919, it focuses on the care of disabled and sick

veterans; its membership requirement is honorable service and an honorable discharge. Instrumental in establishing veteran hospitals, it sponsored the creation of the U.S. Veterans Administration (see U.S. Department of VETERANS AFFAIRS). It played an important role in the passage of the GI BILL. The Legion has about 3 million members in 15,000 local posts, or groups.

American Motors Corp. (AMC) U.S. automobile manufacturer. AMC was formed in 1954 from Nash-Kelvinator Corp. (successor to Nash Motor Co., founded 1916) and Hudson Motor Car Co. (founded 1909). AMC produced compact cars, trucks and buses, and, until 1968, Kelvinator appliances. AMC purchased the Kaiser-Jeep Corp. (dating to 1903) in 1970. In 1987 AMC became a subsidiary of CHRYSLER CORP., which merged with DAIMLER-BENZ in 1998.

American Museum of Natural History Major center of research and education in the natural sciences, established in New York City in 1869. It pioneered in staging field expeditions and in creating dioramas and other lifelike exhibits. Its research collections, including its huge fossil and insect collections, contain tens of millions of specimens. It conducts research in such fields as anthropology, astronomy, ichthyology, invertebrate biology, and vertebrate paleontology, and maintains permanent research stations in the Bahamas, New York, Florida, and Arizona. It also contains one of the world's largest planetariums.

American Party See KNOW-NOTHING PARTY

American Renaissance *or* **New England Renaissance** Period from the 1830s through the American Civil War, in which U.S. literature came of age. The literary scene was led by New Englanders, notably H. W. LONGFELLOW, O. W. HOLMES, and J. R. LOWELL. Also influential were the Transcendentalists (see TRANSCENDENTALISM), including R. W. EMERSON and H. D. THOREAU, as well as the great imaginative writers Nathaniel HAWTHORNE, Herman MELVILLE, Walt WHITMAN, and E. A. POE.

American Revolution *or* **United States War of Independence** (1775–83) War that won political independence for 13 of Britain's N. American colonies, forming the United States of America. After the end of the costly FRENCH AND INDIAN WAR (1763), Britain imposed new taxes on the colonies (see STAMP ACT, SUGAR ACT) and trade restrictions, which fueled growing resentment and added to the colonists' objection to their lack of representation in the British Parliament. Determined to achieve independence, the colonies formed the Continental Army, composed chiefly of MINUTEMEN, to challenge Britain's large, organized militia. The war began when Britain sent a force to destroy rebel military stores at Concord, Mass. After fighting broke out on April 19, 1775 (see Battles of LEXINGTON AND CONCORD), rebel forces began a siege of Boston (see Battle of BUNKER HILL) that ended when American forces forced out the British troops on March 17, 1776. Britain's offer of pardon in exchange for surrender was refused by the Americans, who declared themselves independent on July 4, 1776. British forces retaliated by driving the army of George WASHINGTON from New York to New Jersey. On Christmas night, Washington crossed the Delaware River to win the Battles of TRENTON AND PRINCETON. The British army split to cover more territory, a fatal error; in engaging the Americans in Pennsylvania, notably in the Battle of the BRANDYWINE, they left the troops in the north vulnerable (see Battle of SARATOGA; Oct. 17, 1777). Washington quartered his 11,000 troops through a bleak winter at VALLEY FORGE, where they received training from Frederick STEUBEN that gave them victory in Monmouth, N.J., on June 28, 1778. France, which had been secretly furnishing aid to the Americans since 1776, finally declared war on Britain in June 1778. French troops assisted American troops in the south, culminating in the successful Siege of YORKTOWN, where Charles CORNWALLIS's forces surrendered on October 19, 1781, bringing an end to the war on land. War continued at sea, fought chiefly between Britain and the U.S.'s European allies; Spain and the Netherlands contained most of Britain's navy near Europe. The last battle of the war was won by the American navy under John BARRY in March 1783 in the Straits of Florida. With the Treaty of Paris (Sept. 3, 1783), Britain recognized the independence of the U.S. east of the Mississippi River and ceded Florida to Spain.

American saddlebred *or* **American saddle horse** Breed of light HORSE that originated in the U.S., formed by crossing THOROUGHBREDS, Morgans, and STANDARDBREDS on native mares having an easy gait. It stands 15–16 hands (5–5.3 ft, or 1.5–1.6 m) high. There are two distinct types, three-gaited and five-gaited. The three natural gaits are walk, trot, and canter; the five-gaited horse also has two trained gaits, the rack and the slow gait, or running walk. The American saddlebred is used as a fine harness horse mainly for show.

American Samoa *officially* **Territory of American Samoa** Unincorporated U.S. territory (pop., 2000: 57,000), SW central Pacific Ocean, including the islands of Tutuila (with over two-thirds of the territory's land area and 95% of the population), Aunuu, Rose, Swains, and the Manua group. Area: 77 sq mi (199 sq km). Capital: PAGO PAGO (on Tutuila). Languages: Samoan, English (both official). Currency: U.S. dollar. Most of the islands are rocky, were formed from extinct volcanoes, and are surrounded by coral reefs. Fishing and tourism are major industries. Most of the population is of Samoan ancestry. The islands were probably inhabited by Polynesians 2,500 years ago. Dutch explorers became the first Europeans to visit the islands in 1722. A haven for runaway sailors and escaped convicts, the islands were ruled by native chiefs until about 1860. The U.S., Britain, and Germany administered a tripartite protectorate in 1889–99. The high chiefs ceded the E islands to the U.S. in 1904 (Britain ceded Swains in 1925). Its first constitution was approved in 1960, and in 1978 its first elected governor took office.

American Stock Exchange (AMEX) Second-largest stock exchange in the U.S. Originally known as "the Curb," it began as an outdoor marketplace in New York City about 1850. Once a market for SECURITIES not reputable enough for the NEW YORK STOCK EXCHANGE, it eventually became equally respectable. In 1999 it merged with NASDAQ to form the Nasdaq-Amex Market Group.

American System of manufacture Production of many identical parts and their assembly into finished products. Though Eli WHITNEY has been credited with this development, the ideas had appeared earlier in Europe and were part of U.S. armory practice. Marc BRUNEL, while working for the British Admiralty (1802–8), devised a process for producing wooden pulley blocks by sequential machine operations, whereby 10 men (rather than 110) could make 160,000 pulley blocks per year. Not until London's CRYSTAL PALACE exhibition (1851) did British engineers, viewing exhibits of machines used in the U.S. to produce interchangeable parts, begin to apply the system. Within 25 years, the American System was being widely used in making a host of industrial products. See also ASSEMBLY LINE.

American Telephone and Telegraph Co. See AT&T

American University Private university in Washington, D.C. It was incorporated by act of Congress in 1891 as a graduate school and research center, but courses did not begin until 1914. An undergraduate division was founded in 1925. It includes schools of law, business, international service, and public affairs. Total enrollment is about 11,000.

America Online (AOL) Company that provides online services and Internet access. Founded in 1985 by Steve CASE as Quantum Computer Services, it offered e-mail, electronic bulletin boards, and news and information services. Adopting its new name in 1991, it became the world's largest online service, with over 25 million members by 2000. It acquired such other companies as CompuServe (1997), Netscape (1998), and Digital Marketing Services (1999). In 2001 AOL merged with Time Warner Inc. to create AOL Time Warner, with combined revenues of over $300 billion. A steep decline in the online service's revenues led to a sharp drop in the company's valuation by 2003.

America's Cup Most prestigious trophy in international yachting competition. First offered in Britain in 1851, the cup was won easily by the *America* from New York and became known as the America's Cup. The 22.6-mi (36.4-km) America's Cup race, held about every four years, is between one defending vessel and one challenging vessel, each designed and built in the country it represents. The U.S. completely dominated the competition until it was defeated by Australia (1983) and later New Zealand (1995). From 1936 until 1983 the race was held off Newport, R.I.; the more recent U.S. site has been San Diego.

americium \\,am-ə-'ri-shē-əm\\ Synthetic radioactive chemical ELEMENT, chemical symbol Am, atomic number 95. The fourth transuranium element discovered, it was first produced in 1944 in a nuclear reactor. The ISOTOPE americium-241 has been prepared in kilogram quantities and is used in measuring applications that utilize its gamma radiation, such as in household smoke detectors.

Amerindian See AMERICAN INDIAN

Ames, Fisher (1758–1808) U.S. politician. Born in Dedham, Mass., he initially worked as a teacher and lawyer. Supporting a strong central government and arguing for property rights and protection of commercial interests, he was elected to the U.S. House of Representatives (1789–97), where he was active as a Federalist. His eloquent support of the treaty negotiated by John JAY to preserve peace with England (1794) convinced the House to pass an enabling appropriation.

amethyst Transparent, coarse-grained variety of QUARTZ, valued as a semiprecious gem for its violet color. Its color probably arises from its iron content; heating removes the color or changes it to the yellow of CITRINE. Notable deposits are found in Brazil, Uruguay, Ontario, and N. Carolina. The birthstone for February, amethyst has been used since ancient times for carved intaglios.

AMEX See AMERICAN STOCK EXCHANGE

Amhara \\am-'hä-rə\\ Agricultural people of the Ethiopian central highlands numbering about 17 million. Their language is AMHARIC, their religion Ethiopian Orthodox. The Amhara, who have dominated the history of their country, descend from ancient Semitic conquerors who mingled with indigenous Cushitic peoples.

Amharic language \\am-'hä-rik\\ SEMITIC LANGUAGE of Ethiopia, spoken by over 17 million people as a first language, and used as a LINGUA FRANCA in central Ethiopia. It became a national language because of the long line of AMHARA sovereigns. Amharic is written in a modified form of a partly syllabic, partly alphabetic script. Though manuscripts in Amharic are known from the 14th cent., the language has only recently been used as a general medium for literature, journalism, and education.

Amherst, Jeffery later **Baron Amherst** (1717–1797) British army commander. In the FRENCH AND INDIAN WAR, he took the French fort at Louisbourg, Cape Breton Island, in 1758, and was promoted to chief of command in America. He directed the campaign that captured Quebec and Montreal (1760); having secured Canada for Britain, he remained there as governor-general until 1763. Returning to England, he served as commander in chief of the British army (1772–95), but his tenure was marred by failure in the war with the American colonies. Several U.S. towns and AMHERST COLLEGE are named for him.

Amherst College \\'am-ərst\\ Private liberal-arts college in Amherst, Mass., chartered in 1825. Noah WEBSTER was one of its founders. Originally a men's college, it became coeducational in 1975. It is consistently ranked as one of the finest colleges in the U.S. It shares resources with nearby Hampshire, MOUNT HOLYOKE, and SMITH colleges and the Univ. of Massachusetts. Enrollment is about 1,600.

amicus curiae \\ə-'mē-kəs-'kyúr-ē-ī, ə-'mī-kəs-'kyúr-ē-ē\\ (Latin: "friend of the court") One who assists a court by furnishing information or advice regarding questions of law or fact. A person (or other entity, such as a state government) who is not a party to a particular lawsuit but nevertheless has a strong interest in it may be allowed to file an amicus curiae brief, a statement of particular views on the subject matter of the lawsuit. Such briefs are often filed in cases involving public-interest matters (e.g., consumer protection, civil rights).

amide \\'a-,mīd\\ Any member of either of two classes of NITROGEN-containing organic compounds related to AMMONIA and AMINES and also containing a carbonyl group ($-C=O$; see FUNCTIONAL GROUP). In the first class, covalent amides, the hydroxyl group (–OH) of an ACID is replaced by

an amino group ($-NR_2$, in which R may represent a HYDROGEN atom or an organic combining group. If formed from CARBOXYLIC ACIDS, they are called carboxamides. They do not conduct electricity, have high boiling points, and (when liquid) are good SOLVENTS. There are no practical natural sources of simple covalent amides, but PEPTIDES and PROTEINS are long chains (POLYMERS) with amide linkages. UREA is an amide with two amino groups. Commercially important covalent amides include several used as solvents; others are the SULFA DRUGS and NYLON. The second class, ionic amides (see IONIC BOND), are made by treating a covalent amide, an amine, or ammonia with a reactive metal (e.g., sodium) and are strongly alkaline.

Amiens \\äm-'yeⁿ\\ ancient Samarobriva later Ambianum. City (pop., 1999: 136,000), N France. Located on the SOMME RIVER, it became a Roman stronghold, passed to BURGUNDY in 1435, and was captured by the Spanish in 1597. Recovered by HENRY IV, it served as the capital of PICARDY until 1790. It has been a major center of the French textile industry since the 16th cent. and is the site of the Gothic cathedral of Notre Dame, the largest church in France.

Amin (Dada Oumee) \\ä-'mēn\\, **Idi** (b.1924/25) Military officer and president (1971–79) of Uganda. In 1971 he staged a coup against Milton OBOTE, Uganda's first prime minister and president. He expelled all Asians from Uganda in 1972 and reversed Uganda's amicable relations with Israel. He was involved in the 1976 ENTEBBE INCIDENT. He ordered the torture and murder of 100,000–300,000 Ugandans. When nationalist and Tanzanian troops invaded in 1979, Amin fled to Libya and eventually settled in Saudi Arabia.

amine \\ə-'mēn\\ Any of a class of NITROGEN-containing organic compounds derived from AMMONIA (NH_3). Almost all their chemical names end in "ine." Replacement of one, two, or all three of the HYDROGEN atoms in ammonia with organic groups yields primary, secondary, or tertiary amines, respectively. Naturally occurring amines include ALKALOIDS, present in certain plants; some NEUROTRANSMITTERS, including DOPAMINE and EPINEPHRINE; and HISTAMINE. Industrially important amines include ANILINE, ethanolamine, and others, used in making rubber, dyes, pharmaceuticals, synthetic resins and fibers, and many other products. A nitrogen atom with one or two hydrogens is often referred to as an amino group.

amino acid \\ə-'mē-nō\\ Any of a class of organic compounds in which a CARBON atom has bonds to an amino group ($-NH_2$), a carboxyl group (–COOH), a hydrogen atom (–H), and an organic side group (called –R). They are therefore both CARBOXYLIC ACIDS and AMINES. The properties unique to each result from the properties of the R group. Amino acids joined linearly by peptide bonds in a particular order make up PEPTIDES and PROTEINS. Of over 100 natural amino acids, each with a different R group, only 20 make up the proteins of all living organisms. Humans can synthesize 10 of them, but the other 10 (essential amino acids: arginine, histidine, isoleucine, leucine, LYSINE, methionine, phenylalanine, threonine, TRYPTOPHAN, and valine) must be consumed in the diet.

Amis, Kingsley (William) (later **Sir Kingsley**) (1922–1995) British novelist and poet. His first novel, the comic masterpiece Lucky Jim (1954; film, 1957), was a huge success. Often called an ANGRY YOUNG MAN, he wrote more than 40 books, notably the mordantly humorous That Uncertain Feeling (1955; film, Only Two Can Play, 1962), The Green Man (1959; film, 1957), Jake's Thing (1978), and The Old Devils (1986, Booker Prize). He was the father of Martin AMIS.

Amis \\'ā-mis\\, **Martin** (b.1949) British writer and critic. The son of Kingsley AMIS, he worked as a journalist and critic before becoming a full-time author. His works—including the novels Money (1984), London Fields (1989), Time's Arrow (1991), The Information (1995), and Night Train (1998)— satirize the horrors of city life and feature inventive word play and harsh black humor.

Amish \\'ä-mish\\ Member of a conservative Christian group in N. America known as the Old Order Amish Mennonite Church. The Amish originated in 1693–97 as followers of the MENNONITE elder Jakob Ammann (1644?–c.1730) in Switzerland, Alsace, and Germany. He taught that lying was

grounds for excommunication (which meant being shunned by all other Mennonites), that clothing should be uniform and beards untrimmed, and that the state church should be avoided. Immigrants to N. America settled in Pennsylvania in the 18th cent. After 1850 they split into "Old Order" (traditional) and "New Order" (now the Mennonite churches). Old Order Amish now live in Pennsylvania, Ohio, Indiana, Iowa, Illinois, and Kansas. Adults are baptized and admitted to formal church membership at age 17 to 20. Amish wear modest, old-fashioned clothing and reject modern technology, including automobiles and telephones.

Amistad Mutiny Revolt by 53 African slaves aboard the schooner *Amistad* near Cuba in 1839. The slaves, abducted from Africa, seized control of the ship, killed the captain, and ordered the navigator to sail for Africa. He secretly sailed northward instead, and the ship was intercepted off New York. Despite attempts by Pres. Martin VAN BUREN to send the Africans to Cuba, abolitionists demanded a trial, contending the men were free under international law. A federal judge agreed, and the government appealed to the U.S. Supreme Court, where in 1841 J. Q. ADAMS successfully argued that the men should be freed.

Amman \ä-'man\ Largest city (pop., 1994: 969,000) and capital of Jordan. It lies 25 mi (40 km) northeast of the DEAD SEA. Its earliest settlements date from the Chalcolithic period (c.4000–3000 B.C.). As Rabbah, it became the capital of the Ammonites. It was conquered by Egypt's PTOLEMY II PHILADELPHUS, who renamed it Philadelphia. Taken by the Arabs in A.D. 635, it declined and subsequently disappeared. In 1878 the Ottoman Turks resettled it. When the British set up Transjordan in 1921, Amman became its capital. Its modern development was furthered by Jordanian independence in 1946. Amman has since often had to deal with refugee problems exacerbated by the continuing unrest between Israelis and Palestinians.

ammonia \ə-'mō-nyə\ Colorless, pungent gas composed of NITROGEN and HYDROGEN, chemical formula NH_3. Easily liquefied by compression or cooling for use in refrigerating and air-conditioning equipment, it is manufactured in huge quantities. Ammonia is made by the HABER-BOSCH PROCESS. Its major use is as a FERTILIZER. SALTS of ammonia, including ammonium phosphate and ammonium nitrate (a high explosive), are used as fertilizers too. Ammonia has many industrial uses as a raw material, CATALYST, and ALKALI. It dissolves readily in water to form ammonium hydroxide, familiar as a household cleaner.

ammonia-soda process See SOLVAY PROCESS

ammonoid \'am-ə-,nȯid\ *or* **ammonite** Any of a group of extinct shelled CEPHALOPODS. Related to the modern pearly NAUTILUS, they are commonly found as FOSSILS in marine rocks of the DEVONIAN to the CRETACEOUS PERIODS (410–65 million years ago). The shells, either straight or (more often) coiled, enabled the animals to compensate for varying water depths. Ammonoids are important index fossils for dating because of their wide geographic distribution in shallow marine waters and the rapid evolution of individual species.

Ammonoid Polished cross section

amnesia \am-'nē-zhə\ Loss of MEMORY as a result of brain injury or deterioration, shock, fatigue, senility, drug use, alcoholism, anesthesia, illness, or neurotic reaction. Amnesia may be anterograde (in which events following the onset are forgotten) or retrograde (events preceding the onset are forgotten). It can often be traced to a severe emotional shock, in which case personal memories (e.g., identity) rather than less-personal material (e.g., language skills) are affected. Such amnesia offers an escape from disturbing memories, and is thus an example of REPRESSION; these memories can often be recovered through PSYCHOTHERAPY or HYPNOSIS.

Amnesty International (AI) International HUMAN-RIGHTS organization. Founded in 1961 by Peter Benenson (b.1921),

a London lawyer who organized a letter-writing campaign calling for amnesty for "prisoners of conscience," AI seeks to inform the public about violations of human rights, especially abridgments of freedom of speech and religion and the imprisonment and torture of political dissidents. Its members and supporters are said to number 1 million in 162 countries. Its first director, Sean MACBRIDE, won the 1974 Nobel Peace Prize; AI itself won the award in 1977.

amniocentesis \,am-nē-ō-sen-'tē-səs\ Surgical insertion of a hollow needle through the abdominal wall into the UTERUS of a pregnant female to extract fluid for analysis of fluid and fetal cells. This can reveal the fetus's sex (important when sex-linked genetic disease is possible), chromosomal disorders, and other problems. It is generally done under local anesthesia in the 15th–17th week of gestation.

amoeba \ə-'mē-bə\ One-celled PROTOZOAN that can form temporary extensions of CYTOPLASM (pseudopodia) in order to move about. Some are found in streams and ponds. Others live in the digestive system; one type causes amebic DYSENTERY in humans. Each amoeba contains a small mass of cytoplasm with VACUOLES and a NUCLEUS. Food is taken in and material is excreted at any point on the cell surface.

Amon \'ä-,män\ *or* **Amen** Egyptian deity revered as king of the gods. Amon may have originated as a local deity at Khmun in Middle Egypt. He became patron of the pharaohs by Mentuhotep I's reign (2008–1957 B.C.) and was identified with the sun god RE but represented as a human or ram. AKHENATON directed his reforms against the cult of Amon, but with little success. In the New Kingdom, Amon came to be seen as one of a triad with PTAH and Re, and in the 11th–10th cent. B.C. as a universal god who intervened in affairs of state by speaking through oracles.

amortization \,am-ər-ti-'zā-shən\ In finance, the systematic repayment of a debt; in accounting, the systematic writing off of some account over a period of years. An example of the first meaning is a home mortgage, which may be repaid in monthly installments that include interest and a gradual reduction of the principal. In the second sense, a firm may gradually reduce the balance-sheet valuation of a depreciable asset such as a building, machine, or mine. The U.S. government has sometimes permitted accelerated amortization of assets, which encourages industrial development by decreasing a company's tax burden in the years immediately after a purchase.

Amos (fl.8th cent. B.C.) Earliest Hebrew PROPHET (one of the 12 Minor Prophets) to have a biblical book named for him. A shepherd, he traveled from Judah to Israel to preach his visions of divine destruction and the message that God's absolute sovereignty required justice for rich and poor alike and that God's chosen people were not exempt from the moral order. He foretold the destruction of the N kingdom of Israel and anticipated the predictions of doom by later prophets.

Amos 'n' Andy See Freeman GOSDEN AND CHARLES CORRELL

Ampère \äⁿ-'per\, **André Marie** (1775–1836) French physicist, founder of the science of ELECTROMAGNETISM. A prodigy who mastered the entire known field of mathematics by age 12, he became a professor of physics, chemistry, and mathematics. He formulated a law of electromagnetism, called Ampère's law, that describes the magnetic force between two electric currents. An instrument he devised to measure the flow of electricity was later refined as the GALVANOMETER. The ampere (A) unit of electric current was named for him.

amphetamine \am-'fe-tə-,mēn\ Organic compound, typical of a class of drugs (e.g., Benzedrine, Dexedrine, methamphetamine) that stimulate the central NERVOUS SYSTEM. Amphetamines cause wakefulness, euphoria, decreased fatigue, and increased ability to concentrate. Since they dull the appetite, they have been used for weight reduction. Often called "speed," they are used (often illicitly) to stay awake. In hyperactive children, they have a calming effect, helping them concentrate. Undesirable effects include overstimulation, with restlessness, insomnia, tremor, and irritability, and a deep DEPRESSION when the drug wears off. This, along with rapid development of tolerance requiring increased doses, can lead to DRUG ADDICTION. Large doses can bring on a psychosis.

amphibian Any member of a class (Amphibia) of cold-blooded VERTEBRATE animals that includes more than 4,400 species in three groups: FROGS and TOADS (order Anura), SALAMANDERS (order Caudata), and CAECILIANS (order Apoda). Probably evolved from fishes of the Early DEVONIAN PERIOD (410–391 million years ago), amphibians were the first vertebrates to move from water to land. Most species have an aquatic larval, or tadpole, stage that meta-morphoses into a terrestrial adult, but a few species spend their entire life in water.

amphibious warfare Military operations directed against hostile shores and characterized by attacks launched from the sea by naval and landing forces. The Greeks attacking Troy (1200 B.C.) had to make a shore landing, as did the Persian invaders of Greece prior to the Battle of MARA-THON (490 B.C.). The British-led landings at GALLIPOLI (1915) were the main amphibious assault in World War I. The Allies of World War II used amphibious tactics in the Pacific campaign against numerous Japanese-held islands. The NORMANDY CAMPAIGN (1944) ranks as the greatest am-phibious assault in history. Amphibious warfare's greatest advantages are mobility and flexibility; its greatest limita-tion is the need to start from nothing to build up strength ashore.

Amphion and Zethus \\'am-fē-ən...'zē-thəs\\ In GREEK MY-THOLOGY, twin sons of ZEUS by the mortal Antiope. Left to die on Mt. Cithaeron, the infants were found and raised by a shepherd. Amphion grew up to become a great musician and singer, while Zethus became a hunter and herdsman. They built the city of THEBES after the stone blocks ar-ranged themselves into walls at the sound of Amphion's lyre. Amphion became king of Thebes, but committed sui-cide when his children were killed by the gods as punish-ment for the thoughtless boast of his wife, NIOBE.

amphitheater Freestanding, open-air round or oval struc-ture with a central arena and tiers of concentric seats. The amphitheater originated in ancient Italy (Etruria and Cam-pania) and reflects the entertainment forms popular there, including gladiatorial games and contests of animals. The earliest extant amphitheater is one built at POMPEII (c.80 B.C.). The most famous surviving example is Rome's COLOSSEUM.

amplifier Device that responds to a small input signal (volt-age, current, or power) and delivers a larger output signal with the same waveform features. Amplifiers are used in ra-dio and television receivers, audio equipment, and comput-ers. Amplification can be provided by electromechanical devices (e.g., TRANSFORMERS and GENERATORS) and VAC-UUM TUBES, but most electronic systems now employ solid-state microcircuits. One amplifier is usually insufficient, so the output is fed into successive amplifiers until its level is satisfactory.

amplitude modulation See AM

amputation Removal of any part of the body, usually surgi-cal removal of part or all of a limb. Surgical amputation may be a lifesaving measure to prevent excessive blood loss from injury or to check the spread of infection, gangrene, or malignant soft-tissue or bone tumors. Reconstructive surgery and rehabilitation have made amputation rarer than in the past. Prostheses reduce handicaps for amputees, whose surgery may have been designed with the PROSTHE-SIS in mind.

Amr ibn al-As \\'äm-ər-,ib-ən-əl-'äs\\ (d.663) Arab conqueror of Egypt. After accepting Islam his first mission was in Oman, where he converted its rulers. He also gained SW Palestine in the 630s before setting out to conquer Egypt, succeeding (642) after a two-year campaign. Late in his ca-reer he aided the governor of Syria, al-MUAWIYAH I, against ALI, Islam's fourth caliph. He was the governor of Egypt at the beginning of the UMAYYAD DYNASTY (661).

Amritsar \\,əm-'rit-sər\\, **Massacre of** (1919) Incident in which British troops fired on a crowd of Indian protesters. In 1919 the British government of India enacted the Rowlatt Acts, extending its World War I emergency powers to combat subversive activities. On April 13th a large crowd gathered to protest the measures and troops opened fire,

killing about 380 and wounding about 1,200. The massacre was the prelude to Mohandas GANDHI's noncooperation movement of 1920–22.

Amsterdam City (pop., 1999 est.: 727,000), W Netherlands. It lies at the head of the IJSSELMEER. It is the nominal cap-ital of the Netherlands, whose seat of government is at The HAGUE. Originally a fishing village, it received its charter as a town in 1300. It joined the HANSEATIC LEAGUE in 1369 and grew steadily in the 14th–15th cent. The center for the Dutch E. INDIA and W. India companies, it became the lead-ing trade metropolis of Europe. It became part of the King-dom of Holland, which entered the Kingdom of the Nether-lands in 1815. Its prosperity increased when it was connected by canal to the North Sea in 1875. The city is now a major European port and the main wholesale and in-dustrial center of the Netherlands.

Amtrak *formally* **National Railroad Passenger Corp.** Feder-ally supported corporation that operates nearly all intercity passenger trains in the U.S. It was established by Congress in 1970 in the face of private railroads' heavy financial losses. Routes were cut back severely, and service is now maintained only in highly populated areas and between the largest cities. Amtrak pays the railroads to run passenger trains and compensates them for the use of tracks and ter-minals, while bearing all administrative costs and managing scheduling, route planning, and ticket sales. Amtrak still re-quires large federal subsidies to cover its operating losses. See also CONRAIL.

Amu Darya \\'ä-mü-'där-yə\\ *ancient* **Oxus** River, central Asia. It is one of the longest rivers in central Asia, at 1,578 mi (2,540 km). From the Pamirs plateau it flows west-north-west to its mouth on the ARAL SEA. It forms part of Afghan-istan's border with Tajikistan, Uzbekistan, and Turkmeni-stan, and of Uzbekistan's border with Turkmenistan.

Amundsen \\'ä-mun-sən\\, **Roald (Engelbregt Gravning)** (1872–1928?) Norwegian explorer, leader of the first group to reach the South Pole. In 1903–5 he was the first to navi-gate the Northwest Passage. He planned an expedition to the North Pole, but after learning that Robert PEARY had reached that goal, he sailed for the South Pole in 1910. He prepared his trip carefully and in October 1911 set out with four men, 52 dogs, and four sledges. He reached the South Pole in December 1911, one month before R. F. SCOTT's ill-fated attempt. In 1926 he and Umberto Nobile (1885–1978) passed over the North Pole in a dirigible. Amundsen disap-peared in 1928 while flying to rescue Nobile from a dirigi-ble crash.

Amur River \\ä-'mür\\ *Chinese* **Heilong** or **Hei-lung** \\'hä-'lung\\ River, NE Asia. The Amur begins at the confluence of the Shilka and Argun rivers and is 1,755 mi (2,824 km) long. It flows east-southeast along the Russian–Chinese border to Khabarovsk, Siberia, then northeast across Rus-sian territory to empty into the Tatar Strait. From the 18th cent., Russians have settled to the north of the river and Chinese to the south, at times provoking border clashes.

amyotrophic lateral sclerosis (ALS) \\,ā-,mī-ə-'trō-fik...sklə-'rō-səs\\ *or* **Lou Gehrig's disease** Degenerative NERVOUS-SYSTEM disorder causing muscle wasting and paralysis. The disease usually occurs after age 40, more often in men. Most victims die within two to five years from respiratory muscle atrophy. ALS affects motor NEURONS; the muscles they control become weak and atrophied, usually beginning in the hands and creeping slowly up to the shoulders. The lower limbs become weak and spastic. In 1993 the defective gene that accounts for 5–10% of cases was discovered.

Anabaena \\,an-ə-'bē-nə\\ Genus of blue-green algae (CYANO-BACTERIA) that are capable of NITROGEN FIXATION. Found as PLANKTON in shallow water and on moist soil, they occur in both solitary and colonial forms. In N latitudes in sum-mer, extensive growth of *Anabaena* may form water blooms that remain suspended instead of forming a surface scum.

Anabaptist Member of a radical movement of the 16th-cent. Protestant REFORMATION characterized by adult BAPTISM. Following Huldrych ZWINGLI, Anabaptists held that infants were not punishable for SIN since they had no awareness of good and evil. The first adult baptisms took place outside Zurich in early 1525. Confident of living at the end of time, most Anabaptists were pacifists and refused to swear civil

oaths. They were expelled from one city after another, and many were martyred. Many settled in Moravia, where they modeled their communitarian life on the primitive church at Jerusalem. This branch continues as the HUTTERITE movement. Increasingly persecuted throughout Europe, Anabaptists in the Netherlands and N Germany rallied under the leadership of MENNO SIMONSZ. and survive as the MENNONITES.

anabolic steroids \ˌa-nə-ˈbä-lik\ STEROID HORMONES that increase tissue growth. They are given to elderly or postoperative patients to promote muscle growth and tissue regeneration. Use by athletes to build muscle and improve strength can have harmful effects, including heart disease, sexual and reproductive disorders, immunodeficiencies, liver damage, stunted growth, aggressive behavior, susceptibility to injury, and (in girls) irreversible masculinization.

anaconda Either of two S. American snake species in the genus *Eunectes* (family Boidae) that constrict their prey. The heavily built giant anaconda, or great water boa, can be longer than 24 ft (7.5 m), rivaling the largest PYTHONS in length. The yellow anaconda is much smaller. The giant anaconda lives along tropical rivers east of the Andes and in Trinidad. It kills at night; it constricts prey as large as young pigs and occasionally forages in trees for birds. It may bear 75 live young at a time.

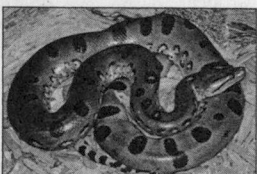

Giant anaconda (*Eunectes murinus*)

Anacreon *or* **Anakreon** \ə-ˈnak-rē-ən\ (582?–485? B.C.) Last great lyric poet of Asian Greece. Only fragments of his poetry have survived—quoted by later writers—and they are chiefly in praise of love and wine. His style was widely imitated, and anacreontic poetic meter was named for him.

Anaheim City (pop., 2000: 328,000), SW California. Lying 25 mi (40 km) southeast of Los Angeles, it was founded by German immigrants in 1857 as a cooperative agricultural community. By 1950 its citrus groves and vineyards had been displaced by urban-industrial expansion. Walt DISNEY's first amusement park, Disneyland, opened there in 1955. Today Anaheim is a prominent convention site.

Analects See LUNYU

analgesic \ˌan-əl-ˈjē-zik\ Drug that relieves pain. Two classes are defined by the type of pain-relieving action. Opioids (opiates and synthetic narcotics; see OPIUM) may be used for short- or long-term pain relief, usually by prescription, but carry a risk of DRUG ADDICTION. Nonopioids, used mostly for short-term relief, are available without prescription. They include NSAIDs (including ASPIRIN and IBUPROFEN), ACETAMINOPHEN, and phenacetin.

analog computer COMPUTER in which variable physical quantities such as fluid pressure or mechanical motion are represented by quantities that correspond to them in the problem to be solved. The analog system is set up according to initial conditions and then allowed to change freely. Analog computers are especially well suited to working with problems in DYNAMICS. They have been widely used in simulating the operation of aircraft, nuclear power plants, and industrial chemical processes. See also DIGITAL COMPUTER.

analysis In chemistry, the determination of the properties and composition of samples of materials. Qualitative analysis establishes what is there, and quantitative analysis measures how much. Systematic procedures have evolved in close association with other branches of the physical sciences. A sample of a single COMPOUND may be analyzed to establish its elemental composition (see ELEMENT, MOLECULAR WEIGHT) or molecular structure; many measurements use SPECTROSCOPY and SPECTROPHOTOMETRY. A mixed sample is usually analyzed by separating, detecting, and identifying its components by methods that depend on differences in their properties. The many types of CHROMATOGRAPHY are increasingly useful, particularly with biological and biochemical samples.

analytic geometry *or* **Cartesian geometry** Investigation of geometric objects using COORDINATE SYSTEMS. It springs from the idea that any point in two-dimensional space can be represented by two numbers and any point in three-dimensional space by three. Because objects like lines, circles, ellipses, and spheres can be thought of as collections of points in space that satisfy certain equations, they can be explored via equations and formulas rather than graphs. Most of analytic geometry deals with the CONIC SECTIONS.

analytic philosophy Tradition that defines the primary goal of philosophy as analysis of concepts and language. Predominantly Anglo-American, it is commonly, if dubiously, opposed to. CONTINENTAL PHILOSOPHY. Analytic philosophers primarily pursue issues in logic, language, EPISTEMOLOGY, and the philosophy of mind. The tradition, rooted in British EMPIRICISM, began in the early 20th cent., with work by G. E. MOORE, Alfred North WHITEHEAD, and Bertrand RUSSELL. It has strong connections to the VIENNA CIRCLE, LOGICAL POSITIVISM, Gottlob FREGE, and the early work of Ludwig WITTGENSTEIN. Later contributions include those of A. J. Ayer, Gilbert RYLE, and W. V. O. QUINE.

analytic psychology Psychoanalytic method of C. G. JUNG as distinguished from that of Sigmund FREUD. Jung attached less importance than did Freud to the role of childhood sexual conflicts in NEUROSIS. He defined the UNCONSCIOUS to include both the individual's own unconscious and that inherited from ancestors (the "collective unconscious"). He classified people into INTROVERT AND EXTROVERT types, and further according to which of four primary functions of the mind—thinking, feeling, sensation, and intuition—predominated in any given person.

Ananda \ˈä-nən-də\ (fl.6th cent. B.C.) First cousin and disciple of the BUDDHA. A monk who served as the Buddha's personal attendant, he became known as the "beloved disciple." It was Ananda who persuaded the Buddha to allow women to become nuns. By tradition, he was the only intimate disciple of the Buddha who had not attained enlightenment before his master's death; he attained that state just before the first Buddhist Council (c.544 or 480 B.C.).

anaphylaxis \ˌan-ə-fī-ˈlak-sis\ Severe, immediate, often fatal bodily reaction to contact with a substance (ANTIGEN) to which the individual has become sensitized. It is often triggered by antiserum, antibiotics, and insect stings; symptoms include skin flushing, bronchial swelling (with difficulty breathing), and loss of consciousness. SHOCK may follow. Milder cases may involve HIVES and severe headache. Treatment, consisting of injection of EPINEPHRINE, followed by ANTIHISTAMINES, CORTISONE, or similar drugs, must begin within minutes.

anarchism \ˈan-ər-ˌkiz-əm\ Political theory holding all forms of government authority to be unnecessary and undesirable and advocating a society based on voluntary cooperation of individuals and groups. The word was used only pejoratively until Pierre-Joseph PROUDHON, now regarded as the founder of anarchism, adopted it in *What Is Property?* (1840). The anarchist Mikhail BAKUNIN clashed with Karl MARX at the FIRST INTERNATIONAL; when it was dissolved in 1872, Bakunin's followers retained control of workers' organizations in Spain and Italy. Even anarchists who believed that the transition to a government-free society required violent revolution disagreed on the nature of the transition (see SYNDICALISM). In the 19th and 20th cent., anarchism also inspired experimental communities, including New Lanark in Britain and BROOK FARM in the U.S. Anarchism lost ground after World War II to a host of libertarian and communitarian variations.

Anasazi culture \ˌä-nə-ˈsä-zē\ N. American civilization that developed from around A.D. 100 to historic times, centering on the area where the boundaries of Arizona, New Mexico, Colorado, and Utah now intersect. *Anasazi* (Navajo for "Ancient Ones") is used to refer to the ancestors of contemporary PUEBLO INDIAN peoples. As among present-day Pueblo peoples, religion was highly developed and centered on rites partly conducted in underground KIVAS. The best-known Anasazi ruins are the great cliff dwellings at MESA VERDE (Col.) and Chaco Canyon (N.M.).

Anastasia *Russian* Anastasiya Nikolayevna (1901–1918) Youngest daughter of Czar NICHOLAS II. She was executed at age 17 with her family by the Bolsheviks in the RUSSIAN REVOLUTION OF 1917. Several women outside Russia later claimed her identity, making her the subject of periodic popular conjecture and publicity. The most famous was Anna Anderson (d.1984), a Pole married to a U.S. history professor; her claim was rejected in 1970, and later genetic tests proved there was no connection between Anderson and the Romanovs.

Anastasius I \,an-ə-'stā-zhəs\ (430?–518) Byzantine emperor (491–518). Succeeding Zeno as emperor, he reformed the monetary and taxation systems and expelled rebel tribes from Constantinople, building a wall to protect the capital against raiders. He recognized THEODORIC's rule in Italy (497) but later sent a fleet to ravage the Italian coast. War with Persia (502–5) ended when he agreed to pay tribute to the Persian king. Anastasius accepted the MONOPHYSITE doctrine, which caused unrest in Byzantium but fostered peace with Egypt and Syria.

Anath \'an-ath\ Chief W. Semitic goddess of love and war, sister and helpmate to the BAAL, whom she retrieved from the land of the dead. Famous for her youthful vigor and ferocity in battle, in Egypt she was depicted nude holding flowers and standing on a lion. During the Hellenistic Age, Anath and ASTARTE were merged into the deity Atargatis.

Anatolia See ASIA MINOR

anatomy Biological field that deals with body structures as revealed by dissection. HEROPHILUS first described gross anatomy, the study of structures large enough to see without a microscope. GALEN's ideas, dominated anatomy in Europe until Andreas VESALIUS' methods placed it on a firm foundation of observed fact. Tiny structures (e.g., capillaries and cells) are the subject of microscopic anatomy. Advances in this area led to the new fields of CYTOLOGY and HISTOLOGY. ELECTRON MICROSCOPY opened up the study of subcellular structures, and X-RAY DIFFRACTION gave rise to molecular anatomy. Comparative anatomy compares similar structures in different animals to see how they have changed with EVOLUTION.

Anaxagoras \,an-ak-'sag-ə-rəs\ (c.500–428? B.C.) Greek philosopher, remembered for his cosmology and for his discovery of the true cause of eclipses. His cosmology grew out of the efforts of earlier PRE-SOCRATICS. According to his doctrine of *nous* ("mind"), the growth of living things depends on the power of *nous* that enables them to extract nourishment from surrounding substances.

Anaximander \ə-'nak-sə-,man-dər\ (610–546/545 B.C.) Greek philosopher, first thinker to develop a COSMOLOGY, often called the founder of astronomy. He apparently wrote treatises on geography, astronomy, and cosmology that survived for several centuries and made a map of the known world. His use of geometry and mathematical proportions to help map the heavens departed from earlier, more mystical conceptions and foreshadowed the achievements of later astronomers. Anaximander asserted that the earth remained unsupported at the center of the universe because it had no reason to move in any direction, rather than being suspended or supported from elsewhere in the heavens.

Anaximenes \,an-ak-'sim-ə-,nēz\ (fl.c.545 B.C.) Greek philosopher of nature. With THALES and Anaximander, he is one of three Milesian thinkers (see MILETUS) traditionally considered the first Western philosophers. He defined the essence of matter as *aer* ("air") and explained the densities of various types of matter in terms of varying degrees of condensation of moisture.

ANC See AFRICAN NATIONAL CONGRESS

ancestor worship Religious beliefs or practices that involve addressing prayers or offerings to the spirits of dead relatives. It existed among the ancient Greeks and the ancient Europeans; it also plays a major role in traditional AFRICAN RELIGIONS. The dead, including mythical ancestors, are related to the family, clan, tribe, or village. They may be friendly, or they may be displeased and require propitiation. Worship of individual ancestors may be combined with communal forms of worship, as in the case of the Roman emperor cult. An ancestor whose deeds are heroic may attain the status of a god. In E. Asia, ancestor worship (or reverence) has declined with the decline in the size and importance of kinship groups.

Anchorage Seaport, largest city (pop., 2000: 260,000), and chief commercial center of Alaska. It lies at the head of Cook Inlet. It was founded in 1914 to support construction of a railroad to FAIRBANKS. It became a key aviation and defense center in World War II and is now a regular stop on air routes from the U.S. to E. Asia. Anchorage grew rapidly in the late 20th cent. In 1964 a severe earthquake caused extensive damage.

anchovy Any of more than 100 species of schooling saltwater fishes (family Engraulidae) related to the HERRING. Anchovies are distinguished by a large mouth, almost always extending behind the eye, and by a pointed snout. Adults are 4–10 in. (10–25 cm) long. Temperate-water species such as the northern and European anchovies are important food fishes; tropical species such as the tropical anchovy, or anchoveta, are important bait fishes.

ancien régime \äⁿs-yaⁿ-rā-'zhēm\ (French: "old order") Political and social system of France before the FRENCH REVOLUTION. Under the regime, everyone was a subject of the king of France as well as a member of an estate and province. All rights and status flowed from the social institutions, divided into three orders (estates): clergy, nobility, and others (the THIRD ESTATE). France was not truly a unit of government until after 1789.

Andalusia \,an-də-lü-'sē-ə\ Autonomous community (pop., 1996 est.: 7,235,000) and historic region, S Spain. It occupies an area of 33,694 sq mi (87,267 sq km); the capital is SEVILLE. It is crossed by the Sierra Morena and Sierra Nevada mountains and the GUADALQUIVIR RIVER. It was home to the Phoenicians (at what is now Cádiz, c.1100 B.C.), the Carthaginians (480 B.C.), and the Romans. When the UMAYYAD DYNASTY established its court at CÓRDOBA, this area became an intellectual and political center. It returned to Spanish rule in 1492. In 1833 it was divided into eight provinces. A mining and agricultural region, its beaches along the Costa del Sol attract a growing tourist trade.

Andaman and Nicobar Islands \'an-də-mən...'nik-ō-,bär\ Union territory (pop., 1994 est.: 322,000), India. It consists of two groups of islands in the Bay of BENGAL about 400 mi (650 km) west of Myanmar. Most of the population lives in the Andaman group. The first European settlement was at Port Blair, S. Andaman, now the union territory capital. In the Nicobar group there are remnants of inhabitation dating to A.D. 1050.

Andean civilization Complex of aboriginal cultures that evolved in the Andean region (see ANDES) of W S. America before the arrival of the Spanish CONQUISTADORES in the 16th cent. None of the aboriginal Andean peoples developed a system of writing, though the INCAS devised a sophisticated system of recording numbers. In its overall cultural development, however, this civilization constitutes a New World counterpart to those of ancient Egypt, China, and Mesopotamia. See also TIAHUANACO.

Andersen, Hans Christian (1805–1875) Danish writer of FAIRY TALES. Though born poor, he attended a university. In his many collections of tales (1835–72) he broke with literary tradition and used the idioms of speech. His stories, including such favorites as "The Ugly Duckling" and "The Emperor's New Clothes," combine elements from folk legend. Some reveal a belief in the ultimate triumph of good ("The Snow Queen"), but others are deeply pessimistic; they often identify with the unfortunate and outcast. He also wrote plays, novels, poems, travel books, and several autobiographies.

Anderson, Marian (1897–1993) U.S. singer. Born in Philadelphia, she was immediately recognized for the beauty of her voice and her artistry at her New York debut in 1924, but the fact that she was black made a concert or opera career in the U.S. impossible. She worked ex-

Marian Anderson

clusively in Europe until 1935, when she was convinced to return to her native land. When she was denied use of Constitution Hall in Washington, D.C., by the Daughters of the American Revolution in 1939, Eleanor ROOSEVELT arranged for her to sing at the Lincoln Memorial, and the concert was broadcast to great acclaim. Her 1955 debut at the Metropolitan Opera was the first performance there by a black singer.

Anderson, (James) Maxwell (1888–1959) U.S. playwright. Born in Atlantic, Pa., he worked as a journalist before cowriting his first successful play, *What Price Glory?* (1924). His verse dramas *Elizabeth the Queen* (1930) and *Mary of Scotland* (1933) were later adapted for film. He returned to prose for *Both Your Houses* (1933, Pulitzer Prize) and *Winterset* (1935). He collaborated with Kurt WEILL on the musicals *Knickerbocker Holiday* (1938) and *Lost in the Stars* (1949). *Key Largo* (1939), *Anne of the Thousand Days* (1948), and *The Bad Seed* (1954) became successful films.

Anderson, Sherwood (1876–1941) U.S. author. Born in Camden, Ohio, he started a family but abruptly left them to become a writer in Chicago. His first mature book, *Winesburg, Ohio* (1919), a collection of interrelated tales about the obscure lives of small-town citizens made his reputation. His prose style, based on everyday speech and influenced by the experimental writing of Gertrude STEIN, in turn influenced such writers as Ernest HEMINGWAY and William FAULKNER.

Andersonville Village, SW central Georgia. It was the site of a Confederate military prison in 1864–65 during the AMERICAN CIVIL WAR, notorious for its dreadful conditions. The Andersonville National Cemetery, which includes the prison site, contains the graves of 12,912 Union prisoners who perished there. In 1865 Capt. Henry Wirz, commander of the prison, was tried by a military commission and hanged.

Andes Mountain system, W S. America. One of the great natural features of the globe, the Andes extend north-south about 5,500 mi (8,850 km). They run parallel to the Caribbean coast in Venezuela before turning southwest and entering Colombia. In Ecuador they form two parallel cordilleras, one facing the Pacific and the other descending toward the Amazon basin. These ranges continue southward into Peru; the highest Peruvian peak is Mt. Huascarán, at 22,205 ft (6,768 m), in the Cordillera Blanca. In Bolivia, the Andes again form two distinct regions; between them lies the ALTIPLANO. Along the Chile–Argentina border, they form a complex chain that includes their highest peak, Mt. ACONCAGUA. The Andes are studded with numerous volcanoes that form part of the RING OF FIRE. They also are the source of many rivers, including the ORINOCO, AMAZON, and PILCOMAYO.

andesite \'an-də-ˌzīt\ Any member of a large family of rocks that occur in most of the world's volcanic areas, mainly as surface deposits. The Andes, where the name was first applied, and most of the cordillera (parallel mountain chains) of Central and N. America consist largely of andesites. They also occur in abundance in volcanoes around the Pacific basin. Andesites are most often porphyritic (having distinct crystals in a fine-grained base) rocks.

Andorra *officially* **Principality of Andorra** Independent coprincipality, SE Europe. Lying on the S slopes of the PYRENEES, it consists of a cluster of mountain valleys bounded by Spain and France. Area: 180 sq mi (480 sq km). Population (2000): 67,000. Capital: ANDORRA LA VELLA. Much of the population is Spanish; a minority is Andorran. Language: Catalan (official). Religion: Roman Catholicism. Currency: euro. Andorra's independence is traditionally ascribed to CHARLEMAGNE, who recovered the region from the Muslims in 803. It was placed under the joint suzerainty of the French counts of Foix and the Spanish bishops of the See of Urgell in 1278, and it was subsequently governed jointly by the Spanish bishop of Urgell and the French head of state. This feudal system of government, the last in Europe, lasted until 1993, when a constitution was adopted that transferred most of the coprinces' powers to the Andorran General Council, a council elected by universal suffrage. Andorra has long had a strong affinity with CATALONIA; its institutions are based in Catalonian law and it is part of the diocese of the See of Urgell (Spain). The tradi-

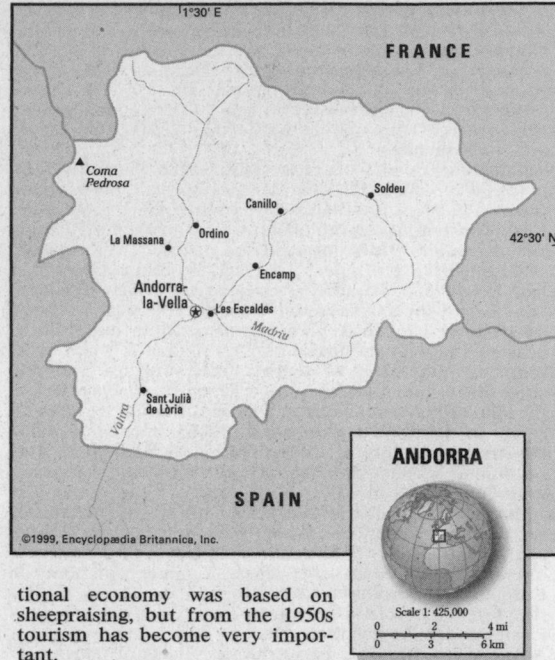

©1999, Encyclopædia Britannica, Inc.

ANDORRA
Scale 1: 425,000
0   2   4 mi
0   3   6 km

tional economy was based on sheepraising, but from the 1950s tourism has become very important.

Andorra la Vella \an-ˈdȯr-ə-lä-ˈvel-yä\ Town (pop., 1995: 22,000), capital of Andorra. It lies near the confluence of the Valira and Valira del Norte rivers. Long isolated, the town grew after World War II as tourists began arriving at the nearby sports areas. Because of its country's duty-free status, the town has become a retail shopping center for other Europeans.

Andrada e Silva \aⁿ-ˈdrä-thȧ-ē-ˈsil-vä\, **José Bonifácio de** *known as* **José Bonifácio** \zhü-ˈze-ˌbō-ni-ˈfä-sē-ō\ (1763?–1838) Chief architect of Brazil's independence from Portugal. Born in Brazil and educated in Portugal, in 1819 he became chief minister of the Portuguese prince regent (later the emperor PEDRO I) and the leading intellectual advocate of independence. After Pedro I declared Brazil independent in 1822, Andrada served as prime minister and as tutor to PEDRO II, who became an effective and enlightened monarch.

Andrassy \ˈän-ˌdrä-sē\, **Gyula, Grof (Count)** (1823–1890) Hungarian politician. He helped lead the unsuccessful revolt of 1848–49, then fled into exile until 1857. He supported the creation of an Austro-Hungarian dual monarchy and played a major role in negotiating the COMPROMISE OF 1867. As Hungary's first prime minister (1867–71), and later as foreign minister (1871–79), he helped strengthen Austria-Hungary's international position. Just before resigning, he signed the fateful Austro-German alliance that linked those two powers until 1918.

Andre, Carl (b.1935) U.S. sculptor. He grew up in Quincy, Mass., and moved to New York in 1957. He soon was producing large-scale horizontal configurations out of steel plates, slabs of granite, styrofoam planks, bricks, and cement blocks, using a grid system based on simple mathematical principles. In the late 1960s he was among the pioneers of MINIMALISM. In 1988 he was tried for murder after his wife, the sculptor Ana Mendiata, fell to her death from their apartment window, but was acquitted.

André \ˈan-drē\, **John** (1750–1780) British army officer and spy. As chief intelligence officer to the British commander at New York, André corresponded with Gen. Benedict ARNOLD, who had become disillusioned with the American cause and in 1780 agreed to surrender the West Point fort. André was captured and incriminating papers were found in his boot; he was found guilty of espionage and hanged.

Andrea del Sarto \än-ˈdrā-ə-del-ˈsär-tō\ *orig.* Andrea d'Agnolo (1486–1530) Italian painter active in Florence. His name derives from his father's profession (*del sarto,* "of the tailor"). After an apprenticeship with PIERO DI COSIMO, he became one of the outstanding painters of the city, most notably as a fresco decorator and painter of altarpieces. His feeling for color and atmosphere was unrivaled among Florentine painters. His most striking achievements include the frescoes on the life of St. John the Baptist (1511–26) in the Chiostro dello Scalzo.

Andreanof Islands \ˌan-drē-ˈa-nȯf\ Group of the ALEUTIAN ISLANDS, SW Alaska. Lying between the Pacific Ocean and the BERING SEA, the islands extend east to west about 270 mi (430 km). They were strategically important in World War II. Islands in the group include Adak, Atka, Tanaga, and Kanaga.

Andreini family \ˌän-drä-ˈē-nē\ Italian actors. After their marriage, Francesco Andreini (1548–1624) and Isabella Canali Andreini (1562–1604) founded the Compagnia dei Gelosi, one of the earliest and most famous of the COMMEDIA DELL'ARTE troupes. Their son Giovambattista Andreini (1579?–1654) formed his own troupe, the Compagnia dei Fedeli, around 1601. The troupe was invited to the French court in Paris, where Andreini wrote the play *Adamo* (1613), supposedly the inspiration for John MILTON's *Paradise Lost.*

Andreotti, Giulio (b.1919) Italian politician who was several times prime minister during 1972–92. Elected to the national assembly in 1947, he served in cabinet posts from 1954. A leader of the Christian Democratic Party, he cofounded its newspaper *Il Populo.* As prime minister, he formed seven coalition governments and became one of Italy's most powerful politicians. After his party lost in 1992, he resigned but was investigated for various charges of corruption. In 2002 he was convicted for complicity in the 1979 murder of a journalist.

Andretti, Mario (Gabriel) (b.1940) Italian-U.S. automobile racing driver. He moved to the U.S. in 1955. His notable wins include the USAC championship-car race (1965–66, 1969), the Daytona Beach stock-car race (1967), the Sebring Grand Prix sports-car race (1967, 1970), the INDIANAPOLIS 500 race (1969), and the Formula I world driving championship (1978). He retired in 1994.

Andrew, St. (d.A.D. 60/70) One of the 12 APOSTLES, brother of St. PETER, and patron saint of Scotland and Russia. According to the Gospels, he was a fisherman and a disciple of JOHN THE BAPTIST. He and Peter were called from their fishing by JESUS, who promised to make them fishers of men. Early church legends tell of Andrew's missionary work around the Black Sea. A 4th-cent. tradition says he was crucified; 13th-cent. tradition states that the cross was X-shaped.

Andrews, Julie (*later* **Dame Julie**) *orig.* Julia Elizabeth Wells (b.1935) British-U.S. actress and singer. She made her New York stage debut in *The Boy Friend* (1954). A major star of the Broadway musical, she originated the roles of Eliza Doolittle in *My Fair Lady* (1956) and Guinevere in *Camelot* (1960). She also starred in such films as *Mary Poppins* (1964, Academy Award), *The Sound of Music* (1965), and *Victor/Victoria* (1982).

Andrews, Roy Chapman (1884–1960) U.S. naturalist, explorer, and author. Born in Beloit, Wis., in 1906 he joined the staff of the American Museum of Natural History, where he would eventually become director (1935–42). He led expeditions to Tibet, SW China, and Burma (1916–17); N China and Outer Mongolia (1919); and central Asia. Important discoveries included the first known dinosaur eggs, skeleton parts of *Baluchitherium* (the largest known land mammal), and evidence of prehistoric human life. His many books include *Across Mongolian Plains* (1921) and *This Amazing Planet* (1940).

androgen \ˈan-drə-jən\ Any of a group of HORMONES that mainly influence the development of the male REPRODUCTIVE SYSTEM. The main and most active androgen is TESTOSTERONE, produced in the TESTES. Other androgens are produced in smaller quantities, mainly by the ADRENAL GLAND but also by the testes. Androgens cause the normal changes of PUBERTY in boys' bodies and then influence sperm-cell formation, sexual interest and behavior, and male pattern baldness. Females produce trace quantities.

Andromeda \an-ˈdrä-mə-də\ In GREEK MYTHOLOGY, the wife of PERSEUS. Her mother boasted that Andromeda was more beautiful than the NEREIDS, and POSEIDON punished her by sending a sea monster to devastate her father's kingdom. To appease the gods, Andromeda was chained to a rock and left to be devoured. Perseus flew by on PEGASUS, fell in love with Andromeda, and slew the monster. She married him and bore him six sons and a daughter. After her death she became a constellation.

Andromeda galaxy \an-ˈdrȯ-mə-də\ *or* **M31** Great spiral galaxy in the constellation Andromeda, nearest spiral galaxy outside the MILKY WAY, and one of the few visible to the unaided eye, appearing as a milky blur. About 2 million light-years from earth, it has a diameter of about 200,000 light-years, making it the largest galaxy in the Local Group. Until Edwin HUBBLE determined in the 1920s that it was a separate galaxy, it was considered part of the Milky Way.

Andronicus I Comnenus \ˌan-drə-ˈnī-kəs...käm-ˈnē-nəs\ (1118–1185) Byzantine emperor (1183–85), the last of the Comnenus dynasty. He raised an army and seized power in 1182, causing a massacre of Westerners in Constantinople. Crowned co-emperor with Alexius II in 1183, he had Alexius strangled and married his 13-year-old widow. Andronicus asserted the independence of the Eastern Church, provoking a Sicilian Norman invasion. News of the Normans' approach led to a revolt, in which Andronicus was killed by a mob.

Andronicus II Palaeologus \ˌpā-lē-ˈäl-ə-gəs\ (1260–1332) Byzantine emperor (1282–1328). The son of MICHAEL VIII PALAEOLOGUS, he was an intellectual and theologian rather than a soldier and statesman, and during his reign the BYZANTINE EMPIRE declined to the status of a minor state. Ottoman Turks controlled Anatolia by 1300, and Serbs dominated the Balkans. By siding with Genoa in its war with Venice, he provoked an attack by the Venetian navy. Despite the rising political disorder, he promoted Byzantine art and the independence of the Eastern Orthodox Church. Deposed by his grandson, he entered a monastery.

anemia Condition in which ERYTHROCYTES (red blood cells) are reduced in number or volume or are deficient in HEMOGLOBIN. The patient is usually noticeably pale. Close to 100 varieties exist (including PERNICIOUS ANEMIA and SICKLE-CELL ANEMIA), distinguished by cause; erythrocyte size, shape, and hemoglobin content; and symptoms. Anemia may result from blood loss; increased destruction, reduced production, or inhibited formation of red cells; or hormone deficiency. Treatment may involve nutrition, toxin removal, drugs, surgery, or transfusion.

anemometer \ˌan-ə-ˈmä-mə-tər\ Instrument for measuring the speed of airflow. The most familiar instruments for measuring wind speeds are the revolving cups that drive an electric generator. For very low airspeeds, a unit in which revolving vanes operate a counter is used. For strong, steady wind speeds (in wind tunnels and aboard aircraft in flight), a PITOT-TUBE anemometer is often used; the pressure difference between the interior of the tube and the surrounding air can be measured and converted to airspeed.

anemone \ə-ˈne-mə-nē\ Any of about 120 species of perennial plants that make up the genus *Anemone,* in the BUTTERCUP family, many of which are cultivated for their colorful flowers. Anemones occur most commonly in woodlands and meadows of the N temperate zone. Many varieties of *A. coronaria* are grown for the garden and florist trade. Other species, such as the Japanese anemone (*A. hupehensis),* are favorite border plants for autumn flowering. The European wood anemone, *A. nemorosa,* causes blistering of the skin and was once used in medicines. Anemones are also known colloquially as pasqueflowers or windflowers.

anesthesiology \ˌa-nəs-ˌthē-zē-ˈäl-ə-jē\ Medical specialty dealing with anesthesia and related matters. Originally concerned only with general anesthesia, anesthesiology now includes epidural anesthesia (injection of local ANESTHETICS into the spinal fluid, cutting off feeling below the point of injection); artificial respiratory support during operations requiring paralyzing drugs that render patients unable to breathe; clinical management of all unconscious patients; management of pain relief, and cardiac and respiratory resuscitation problems; respiratory therapy; and treatment of

various metabolic disturbances. Progress in anesthesiology has made possible more complex operations.

anesthetic \,an-es-'thet-ik\ Agent that produces a local or general loss of sensation, including pain, and therefore is useful in SURGERY and DENTISTRY. General anesthesia induces loss of consciousness; familiar general anesthetics include cyclopropane, ethylene, CHLOROFORM, ethyl chloride, trichloroethylene, ETHERS, tribromoethanol, NITROUS OXIDE, and BARBITURATES. Local anesthesia induces loss of sensation in one area of the body by blocking nerve conduction (see NERVOUS SYSTEM, NEURON), usually with ALKALOIDS such as COCAINE or synthetic substitutes. See also ANESTHESIOLOGY.

aneurysm \'an-yə-,riz-əm\ Blood-filled protrusion in the wall of a blood vessel (usually an ARTERY, and particularly the AORTA). Disease or injury weakens the wall so that normal BLOOD PRESSURE makes it balloon out. Symptoms vary with size and location. Aneurysms tend to enlarge over time, and blood-vessel walls weaken with age. Many aneurysms eventually burst, causing serious internal bleeding; aortic aneurysm rupture causes severe pain and immediate collapse. Rupture of an aneurysm in the brain is a major cause of STROKES. Treatment can consist of simply tying off a small vessel; more serious aneurysms require surgery to replace the diseased section of artery with a plastic graft.

angel Primarily in Western religions, any of numerous benevolent spiritual beings who mediate between heaven and earth. They often serve as messengers or servants of God or as guardians of an individual or nation. JUDAISM and CHRISTIANITY base their notion of angels on Old Testament references to divine servants and to the heavenly hosts. ISLAM's hierarchy of angels descends from the four throne bearers of Allah to the cherubim, archangels, and lesser angels such as the *hafazeh* (guardian angels). See also CHERUB, SERAPH.

Angel Falls Waterfall, SE Venezuela. It lies on the Churún River, southeast of Ciudad Bolívar. The highest waterfall in the world, it drops 3,212 ft (979 m) and is 500 ft (150 m) wide at its base. It was named for James Angel (1899?–1956), an American who crash-landed his plane nearby in 1937.

Angel Falls

angelfish Any of various unrelated fishes of the order Perciformes. The best-known are freshwater CICHLIDS popular in home aquariums (genus *Pterophyllum*): thin and deep-bodied fishes that are usually silver with vertical dark markings but may be solid or partially black. These species may grow to 6 in. (15 cm) long. Brightly colored marine angelfishes (family Pomacanthidae) are found among tropical reefs in the Atlantic and the Indo-Pacific.

Angelico \an-'jel-i-kō\, **Fra** *orig.* Guido di Piero (c.1395–1455) Italian painter active in Florence. He entered the convent of San Domenico at Fiesole sometime between 1417 and 1425 and began his artistic career by painting illuminated manuscripts and altarpieces. Among his earliest masterpieces is a large triptych, the Linaiuoli Altarpiece (1433–36). His most notable works are frescoes at the convent of San Marco, Florence (c.1440–45), and in the chapel of Pope Nicholas V in the Vatican (c.1448–49). One of the outstanding fresco painters of the 15th cent., he influenced such masters as Fra Filippo LIPPI; Benozzo GOZZOLI was among his students.

Angelou \'an-jə-,lō\, **Maya** *orig.* Marguerite Johnson (b.1928) U.S. poet. Born in St. Louis, she was raped at age 8 and was mute for a time. Before becoming a writer she was a waitress, prostitute, cook, dancer, and actress. Her autobiographical works, which explore economic, racial, and sexual oppression, include *I Know Why the Caged Bird Sings* (1970), *The Heart of a Woman* (1981), and *All God's Children*

Need Traveling Shoes (1986). Her poetry collections include *And Still I Rise* (1978) and *I Shall Not Be Moved* (1990). Her recitation at William CLINTON's first inauguration (1993) brought her widespread fame.

Angevin dynasty \'an-jə-vən\ Descendants of a 10th-cent. count of ANJOU (the source of the adjective Angevin). It overlaps with the House of PLANTAGENET, but is usually said to consist of only the English kings HENRY II, RICHARD I, and JOHN. When Henry took control of Normandy, Anjou, Maine, and Aquitaine, he extended the Angevin empire from Scotland to the Pyrenees. English claims to French territory led to the HUNDRED YEARS' WAR; by 1558 the English had lost all their former French lands.

angina pectoris \an-'jī-nə-'pek-tə-rəs\ Spasm of chest pain, caused when the heart's oxygen demand temporarily outpaces its blood supply, usually because of CORONARY HEART DISEASE. A deep, viselike pain in the heart and stomach area commonly spreads to the left arm. Exertion or stress can bring on angina, obliging the victim to rest until the pain subsides. Drugs (e.g., NITROGLYCERIN) can dilate the blood vessels. As heart disease worsens, angina recurs with less exertion.

angiography \,an-jē-'äg-rə-fē\ *or* **arteriography** \är-,tir-ē-'äg-rə-fē\ X-RAY examination of ARTERIES and VEINS with a CONTRAST MEDIUM to differentiate them from surrounding organs. Angiography of diseased leg, brain, or heart arteries is necessary before corrective surgery.

Angiolini \,an-jə-'lē-nē\ **Gasparo** *or* **Angelo Gasparini** (1731–1803) Italian choreographer, among the first to integrate dance, music, and plot in dramatic ballets. In 1757 he became ballet master of the Vienna court opera house; in 1761 he collaborated with Christoph Willibald GLUCK to produce *Don Juan*, and he later choreographed other ballets to Gluck's music. In 1765 he became ballet master of the Imperial Theatre in St. Petersburg. He maintained a rivalry with Jean-Georges NOVERRE and disagreed with his interpretation of the innovative *ballet d'action*.

angioplasty \'an-jē-ə-,plas-tē\ Opening of a blocked blood vessel, often by flattening plaques (see ARTERIOSCLEROSIS) against an artery's wall by inflation of a balloon near the end of a catheter (see CATHETERIZATION). Angioplasty is a less invasive alternative to CORONARY BYPASS surgery in the treatment of CORONARY HEART DISEASE. Results are generally excellent, but plaques tend to recur. Angioplasty is also used to expand a severely obstructed heart valve.

angiosperm See FLOWERING PLANT

Angkor Archaeological site, NW Cambodia. Located 4 mi (6 km) north of the modern town of Siem Reap, it was the capital of the KHMER (Cambodian) empire in the 9th–15th cent. Its most imposing monuments are ANGKOR WAT, a temple complex built in the 12th cent. by King SURYAVARMAN II, and Angkor Thom, a temple complex built about 1200 by King JAYAVARMAN VII. Construction continued over 300 years. After the Siamese conquest of the Khmers in the 15th cent., the ruined city and its temples were buried in the jungle. When the French colonial regime was established in 1863, the entire site became the focus of scholarly interest. Cambodia's political upheavals of the late 20th cent. resulted in some war damage and serious neglect.

Angkor Wat \'aŋ-kòr-'wät\ Temple complex in Angkor (now in NW Cambodia), the crowning work of Khmer architecture. About 1,700 yards (1,550 m) long by 1,500 yards (1,400 m) wide, it is the world's largest religious structure. It was built in the 12th cent. by SURYAVARMAN II. The Wat, an artificial mountain, rises in three enclosures toward a flat summit. The five remaining towers (shrines) at the summit are composed of the repetitive diminishing tiers typical of Asian architecture.

angle In geometry, a pair of rays (see LINE) sharing a common endpoint (the vertex). An angle may be thought of as the rotation of a single ray from an initial to a terminal position, and may be measured in degrees (one full rotation = 360°) or radians (one full rotation = 2π rad). A 90° angle is called a right angle. Any angle less than 90° is an acute angle; any angle between 90° and 180° is an obtuse angle.

anglerfish Any of about 210 species of marine fishes (order Lophiiformes) named for their method of "angling" for prey. The foremost spine of the dorsal fin is located on the head and is modified into a "fishing rod" tipped with a fleshy "bait." Prey fishes attracted come close enough for the anglerfish to swallow them. Often bizarre in form, most species inhabit the sea bottom. In some species the small male bites into the larger female's body, his mouth fuses with the skin, and the bloodstreams of the two become permanently connected.

Angles Germanic people who, with the Jutes and SAXONS, invaded England in the 5th cent. A.D. According to BEDE, their homeland was Angulus, traditionally identified as the Angeln district in Schleswig. They abandoned this area when they invaded Britain. Their language is known as Englisc, and they gave their name to England.

Anglesey \'aŋ-gəl-sē\ *ancient* Mona. Island (pop., 1995 est.: 67,000), Wales. The largest island in England or Wales, at 276 sq mi (715 sq km). By 100 B.C. the Celts had colonized the island, which became a famous DRUID center and later a stronghold of resistance to the Romans. It finally fell to Suetonius Paulinus in A.D. 78. It was ruled by the princes of Wales in the 9th–13th cent., when it was taken by EDWARD I. Tourism is now an important part of the economy.

Anglia See ENGLAND

Anglican Communion See Church of ENGLAND

Anglo–Afghan Wars See AFGHAN WARS

Anglo–Burmese Wars (1824–26, 1852, 1885) Conflicts between the British and the Burmese in present-day Myanmar. The Burmese king Bodawpaya's conquest of the kingdom of Arakan, which bordered on British-controlled territory in India, led to border conflicts. When the Burmese crossed into Bengal, the British responded in force, taking Rangoon. The resulting two-year conflict ended with a treaty that gave Britain Arakan and Assam and required the Burmese to pay an indemnity. Another war erupted 25 years later when a British naval officer seized a ship of the Burmese king; this war resulted in the British occupation of Lower Burma. The third war was sparked by threats to the British teak monopolies and Burmese overtures to the French; it resulted in the British annexation of Upper Burma, ending Burmese independence.

Anglo–Dutch Wars *or* **Dutch Wars** Four naval conflicts between England and the Dutch Republic. The First (1652–54), Second (1665–67), and Third (1672–74) Anglo–Dutch Wars all arose from commercial rivalry between the two nations, and victories by England established its naval might. The Fourth (1780–84) broke out over Dutch interference in the AMERICAN REVOLUTION. By 1784 the Dutch Republic had declined dramatically in power and prestige.

Anglo–French Entente See ENTENTE CORDIALE

Anglo–French War See OPIUM WARS

Anglo-Saxon See OLD ENGLISH

Anglo-Saxon literature Literature written in OLD ENGLISH from around 650 to around 1100. Anglo-Saxon poetry survives largely in four manuscripts. *Beowulf* is the longest of the poems; other great works include *The Wanderer, The Seafarer,* and *The Battle of Maldon.* The stressed words in each line tend to start with the same sound; another feature is the use of poetic formulas (kennings) for common nouns (e.g., "swan road" for "sea"). Notable prose includes the *Anglo-Saxon Chronicle,* a historical record of more than three centuries, begun about the time of King ALFRED's reign (871–99). See also CAEDMON, CYNEWULF.

Angola *officially* **Republic of Angola** *formerly* **Portuguese West Africa** Nation, SW Africa. Area: 481,351 sq mi (1,246,700 sq km). Population (2000): 10,145,000. Capital: LUANDA. The population is made up of mostly BANTU PEOPLES; the main ethnic groups are the Ovimbundu and the Mbundu, while the Khoisan-speaking SAN (Bushmen) inhabit SE Angola. Languages: Portuguese (official), indigenous languages. Religions: Christianity (Roman Catholicism, Protestantism), traditional beliefs. Currency: kwanza. Angola's northernmost section of coastland, the Cabinda exclave, is separated from Angola proper by a narrow corridor of Congo territory. The country contains several plateau regions, which separate it into three distinct drainage systems. One in the northeast drains into the CONGO RIVER basin; another in the SE sector drains into the ZAMBEZI system; the remaining drainage, westward into the At-

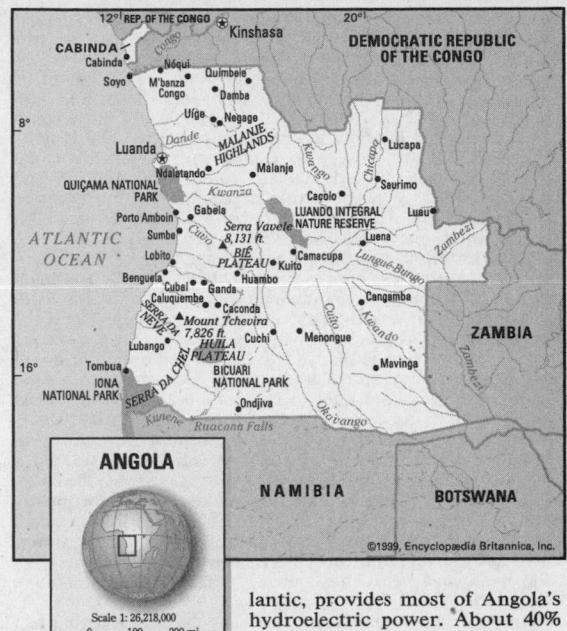

ANGOLA

Scale 1: 26,218,000

0   100   200 mi
0   120   240 km

©1989, Encyclopædia Britannica, Inc.

lantic, provides most of Angola's hydroelectric power. About 40% of the land area is forest; less than 10% is arable. Despite substantial petroleum reserves, Angola's economy has been unable to take advantage of its resources because of the devastation caused by its protracted civil war. It is nominally a republic with one legislative house; its head of state and government is the president assisted by the prime minister. An influx of Bantu-speaking peoples in the 1st millennium A.D. led to their dominance in the area by about 1500. The most important Bantu kingdom was the KONGO; south of the Kongo was the Ndongo kingdom of the Mbundu people. Portuguese explorers arrived in 1483 and over time gradually extended their rule. Angola's frontiers were largely determined with other European nations in the 19th cent., not without severe resistance by the indigenous peoples. Its status as a Portuguese colony was changed to that of an overseas province in 1951. Resistance to colonial rule led to the outbreak of fighting in 1961, which led ultimately to independence in 1975. Rival factions continued fighting after independence; though a peace accord was reached in 1994, forces led by Jonas SAVIMBI continued to resist government control.

Angora See ANKARA

Angoulême \äⁿ-gü-ˈläm\ City (pop., 1990: 46,000), SW France. CLOVIS I captured the town from the VISIGOTHS in 507, and from the 9th cent. it was the center of a countship. Fought over by the French and English in the HUNDRED YEARS' WAR, it passed to the house of Orleans in 1394. The city is noted for papermaking and is the site of the 12th-cent. cathedral of St. Pierre.

angry young men Description of mid-20th-cent. young British writers whose works express lower-class bitterness toward the establishment and its mediocrity and hypocrisy. The label was a press agent's term for John OSBORNE, whose play *Look Back in Anger* (1956) is the most representative work. The group was said to include John Wain (1925–1994), Kingsley AMIS, and Alan Sillitoe (b.1928). A dominant literary force in the 1950s, its influence faded in the early 1960s.

Ångström \ˈäŋ-strœm\, **Anders Jonas** (1814–1874) Swedish physicist. He devised a method of measuring thermal conductivity, showing it to be proportional to electrical conductivity. A founder of SPECTROSCOPY, he discovered that hydrogen is present in the sun's atmosphere, published a map of the normal solar spectrum, and was the first to examine the spectrum of the aurora borealis. The angstrom (10^{-10} m), a unit of length, was named in his honor.

Anguilla \aŋ-ˈgwi-lə\ Island (pop., 1995 est.: 7,000), LEE-WARD ISLANDS, W. Indies. A dependent territory of the United Kingdom, it is the most northerly of the Leeward Islands, and covers about 35 sq mi (90 sq km). Most of its people are descendants of African slaves. The official language is English, and most of the population is Protestant. First colonized in 1650, it was administered by the British. From 1825 it was closely associated with St. Kitts, a situation Anguilla protested. It was united with St. Kitts and Nevis in 1882. When a nation consisting of all three was formed in 1967, Anguilla proclaimed its independence. The British intervened, and Anguilla was separated in 1980.

angular momentum VECTOR property that describes the rotary INERTIA of a system in motion about an axis. The magnitude of the angular momentum of an object is the product of its linear MOMENTUM (mass m × velocity v) and the perpendicular distance r from the center of rotation, or mvr. The direction is that of the axis of rotation. The angular momentum of an isolated system is constant, so a rigid spinning object continues to spin at a constant rate unless acted upon by an external TORQUE. See also GYROSCOPE.

anhinga *or* **snakebird** Any fish-eating bird of the family Anhingidae (order Pelecaniformes), sometimes considered a single species *(Anhinga anhinga)*. Anhingas are about 35 in. (90 cm) long, slender, and long-necked. They are mostly black, with silvery wing markings. Anhingas live in small colonies along lakes and rivers in tropical to warm temperate regions except in Europe. They swim nearly submerged; the head and neck show above water, darting snakelike from side to side.

anhydride \ˌan-ˈhī-ˌdrīd\ Any chemical COMPOUND obtained by eliminating WATER (H_2O) from another compound. Examples of inorganic anhydrides are sulfur trioxide, SO_3, which is derived from sulfuric acid, H_2SO_4; and calcium oxide, CaO, which is derived from calcium hydroxide, $Ca(OH)_2$. The most important organic anhydride is acetic anhydride, $(CH_3CO)_2O$, ACETIC ACID minus water, an important raw material for cellulose acetate (the base of magnetic tapes), textile fibers, and ASPIRIN. Organic anhydrides are important starting materials for organic synthesis, as they can give rise to CARBOXYLIC ACIDS, ESTERS, or AMIDES.

anhydrite Rock-forming mineral, anhydrous calcium sulfate, which differs chemically from GYPSUM (to which it changes in humid conditions) by having no water of crystallization. Anhydrite occurs most often with salt deposits in association with gypsum, as in the Texas-Louisiana salt domes. It is used in plasters and cement as a drying agent.

aniline \ˈa-nə-ˌlīn\ One of the most important organic BASES. Pure aniline is a highly poisonous, oily, colorless liquid with a distinctive odor. First obtained (1826) from indigo, it is now made synthetically. It is used to make chemicals used in producing rubber, dyes and intermediates, photographic chemicals, urethane foams, pharmaceuticals, explosives, herbicides, and fungicides.

animal Any member of the kingdom Animalia (see TAXONOMY), a group of many-celled organisms that differ from members of the two other many-celled kingdoms, the PLANTS and the fungi (see FUNGUS), in several ways. Animals have developed muscles, making them capable of spontaneous movement (see LOCOMOTION), more elaborate sensory and nervous systems, and greater levels of general complexity. Unlike plants, animals cannot manufacture their own food, and thus are adapted for securing and digesting food. In animals, the cell wall is either absent or composed of material different from that of the plant cell wall. Animals account for about three-quarters of all living species. Some one-celled organisms display both plant and animal characteristics. See also ALGAE, ARTHROPOD, BACTERIA, CHORDATE, INVERTEBRATE, PROTIST, PROTOZOAN, VERTEBRATE.

animal communication Transmission of information from one animal to another. Most animal communication uses sound (e.g., birds calling, crickets chirping). Visual communication usually indicates an animal's identity (species, sex, age, etc.) or other information through specific characteristics (e.g., horns, patches of color) or behavior (e.g., the bee's "dance" describing a source of food). Chemical communication involves pheromones (chemical signals) produced by the animal's endocrine system. EELS and some other fishes use electrical impulses to communicate.

animal-rights movement Organized social effort promoting the humane treatment of animals (see cruelty to ANIMALS). The movement is rooted in the teachings of PYTHAGORAS. What may have been the world's first anticruelty law was part of the legal code of the Massachusetts Bay Colony (1641). Animal advocacy groups beginning in the late 20th cent. have sought to protect ENDANGERED SPECIES, ban painful or brutal methods of trapping and killing animals, and reduce the use of animals in medical and scientific research and in product testing (e.g., of cosmetics).

animals, cruelty to Willful or wanton infliction of pain, suffering, or death upon an animal or the intentional or malicious neglect of an animal. The world's first animal welfare society, the Society for the Protection of Animals, was established in England in 1824; the American Society for the Prevention of Cruelty to Animals was chartered in 1866. In varying degrees, cruelty to animals is illegal in most countries, and interest in ENDANGERED SPECIES gave further impetus to the anticruelty movement in the late 20th cent. Acts of cruelty throughout time have ranged from the mistreatment of domesticated animals to BULLFIGHTING and VIVISECTION. Factory farming, which involves various evidently cruel practices, has remained largely exempt from legal scrutiny. See also ANIMAL-RIGHTS MOVEMENT.

animation Process of giving the illusion of movement to drawings or inanimate objects. From the mid-1850s, such optical devices as the zoetrope produced the illusion of animation. Stop-action photography enabled the production of cartoon films. The innovative design and assembly techniques of Walt DISNEY soon moved him to the forefront of the animation industry, with such classic animated films as *Snow White and the Seven Dwarfs* (1937). In reaction against the naturalistic style of Disney's cartoons, a group of artists formed United Productions of America (UPA) and created such characters as Mr. Magoo and Howdy Doody. The first fully computer-generated animated feature, *Toy Story* (1995), moved the art to a new level.

animism Belief in the existence of spirits separable from bodies. Such beliefs are traditionally identified with small-scale ("primitive") societies, though they also occur in major world religions. As surveyed by E. B. TYLOR in *Primitive Culture* (1871), classic animism consists of attributing conscious life to natural objects or phenomena, a practice that eventually gave rise to the notion of a SOUL. See also SHAMAN.

anion \ˈa-ˌnī-ən\ Atom or group of atoms carrying a negative ELECTRIC CHARGE, indicated by a superscript minus sign after the chemical symbol. Anions in a liquid subjected to an electric field migrate toward the positive electrode (ANODE). Examples include hydroxyl ($-OH^-$; see HYDROXIDE), CARBONATE ($-CO_3{}^{2-}$), and PHOSPHATE ($-PO_4{}^{3-}$). See also ION.

anise Annual herb *(Pimpinella anisum)* of the PARSLEY family, cultivated chiefly for its fruit, called aniseed, which tastes like LICORICE. Native to the E Mediterranean, anise is cultivated throughout the world. Aniseed is used as a flavoring and as a soothing herbal tea. Star anise is the dried fruit of the EVERGREEN tree *Illicium verum* (MAGNOLIA family), native to SE China and Vietnam. Its flavor and uses are similar to those of anise.

Anjou \ˈan-jü\ Historical region, lower Loire valley, NW France. Organized in the Gallo-Roman period as the Civitas Andegavensis, it later became the countship, and from 1360 the duchy, of Anjou. Under the CAROLINGIAN DYNASTY, it was administered by a count representing the French king. The area came under the English king HENRY II when he married ELEANOR OF AQUITAINE in 1152, thus founding the Anglo-Angevin empire of the PLANTAGENET dynasty. The French recovered Anjou in 1259, and it was united with France in 1487.

Anjou, House of See House of PLANTAGENET

Ankara \ˈäŋ-kə-rə\ *formerly* **Angora** City (pop., 1996: 2,890,000), capital of Turkey. Located about 220 mi (355 km) southeast of ISTANBUL, Ankara has been inhabited since the Stone Age. Conquered by ALEXANDER THE GREAT in 334 B.C., it was incorporated into the Roman empire by AUGUSTUS. It was a city of the Byzantine empire until it came under Ottoman rule in 1403. After World War I, M. K.

ATATURK made Ankara the center of resistance to both the Ottomans and the invading Greeks, and it became the capital of Turkey in 1923. The city today is Turkey's chief industrial center after Istanbul. Its history is displayed in Roman, Byzantine, and Ottoman architecture and ruins and in important museums.

ankh \\'äŋk\\ Ancient Egyptian HIEROGLYPH signifying life, consisting of a cross surmounted by a loop. In tomb inscriptions, gods and pharaohs are often pictured holding the ankh, which forms part of the hieroglyph for concepts such as health and happiness. It is used as a cross in the COPTIC ORTHODOX CHURCH.

Anna *in full* Anna Ivanovna (1693–1740) Empress of Russia (1730–40). After the death of Peter II, the Supreme Privy Council offered Anna the throne (as the daughter of Ivan V) if she agreed to place the real power in the council's hands. She initially agreed but later abolished the council and reestablished the autocracy, countenancing a severely repressive regime. She occupied herself primarily with extravagant amusements and relied on her lover, Ernst Johann Biron (1690–1772), and a group of German advisers to manage the state.

Annaba \\à-'nä-bə\\ *formerly* **Bône** \\'bōn\\ Seaport (pop., 1998: 348,000), NE Algeria. Identified with the port of ancient Hippo (or Hippo Regius) to the south, it was a rich city of Roman Africa until about A.D. 300. It was home to St. AUGUSTINE 396–430. Severely damaged by the VANDALS in 431, it was rebuilt by the Arabs in the 7th cent. and named Bona. It was occupied by the French in 1832. Modern Annaba is Algeria's chief exporter of minerals.

Annales school \\ä-'näl\\ Influential school of history led by Lucien Febvre (1878–1956) and Fernand BRAUDEL, and rooted in the journal *Annales*, Febvre's new version of his earlier journal formed with Marc Bloch (1886–1944). Under Braudel the Annales school promoted a form of history that replaced the study of leaders with the lives of ordinary people and emphasized climate, agriculture, commerce, technology, and social groups and their beliefs instead of politics, diplomacy, and wars. While aiming at a "total history," it also yielded dazzling studies of villages and regions. Its international influence has been enormous.

Annam \\a-'nam\\ Historic kingdom, E Vietnam. The area was conquered around 200 B.C. by the Chinese. It became independent in the 15th cent. A.D., opening the way for steady Vietnamese movement toward the MEKONG RIVER delta. When Vietnam was united in 1802, HUE became the capital, and the area was ruled by the emperor of Annam. Central Vietnam gradually came under French control; it became a protectorate in 1883–85, leaving the court at Hue with only nominal power. The area was partitioned between N. and S. Vietnam in 1954, and Annam's last emperor was deposed in 1955.

Annan \\'a-,nan\\, **Kofi (Atta)** (b.1938) Seventh secretary-general of the UNITED NATIONS (from 1997). Born in Ghana, the son of a provincial governor and hereditary paramount chief of the Fanti people, he did graduate work at Geneva's Institute for Advanced International Studies and at MIT. His career with the U.N. began at the WORLD HEALTH ORGANIZATION (1962). As undersecretary-general for peacekeeping (from 1993), he transferred peacekeeping operations in Bosnia from the U.N. to NATO. In 1996 he became the first U.N. secretary-general from sub-Saharan Africa. His priorities have included a comprehensive program of reform, efforts to restore public confidence in the organization, and work to strengthen the U.N.'s activities for peace and development.

Annapolis Convention Meeting in Annapolis, Md., in 1786 that led to the convening of the CONSTITUTIONAL CONVENTION. Delegates from five states gathered to discuss problems in maritime commerce but found they could not solve them without changes in the ARTICLES OF CONFEDERATION. They issued a call to all states to meet in Philadelphia in 1787 to resolve the difficulties.

Annapurna Mountain range, Nepal. It forms a ridge 30 mi (48 km) long and contains four main summits. Annapurna I (26,545 ft, or 8,091 m) was first scaled in 1950 by a French expedition. In 1970 an all-woman Japanese team climbed Annapurna III (24,786 ft, or 7,555 m).

Ann Arbor City (pop., 2000: 114,000), SE Michigan. Founded in 1824, it became an agricultural center with the coming of the railroad in 1839. Since 1837 the Univ. of MICHIGAN has played a major role in Ann Arbor's growth. Private industrial research and the university's institutes of science and technology make the city a major Midwest center for space and nuclear research.

Anne (1665–1714) Queen of Great Britain (1702–14) and the last STUART monarch. Second daughter of JAMES II, who was overthrown by WILLIAM III in 1688, Anne became queen on William's death (1702). Her intellectual limitations and poor health led her to rely on advisers, including the duke of MARLBOROUGH. Her reign was marked by the Act of UNION with Scotland (1707) and by bitter rivalries between Whigs and Tories.

annealing Treatment of a METAL, ALLOY, or other material by heating to a predetermined temperature, holding for a certain time, and then cooling to room temperature, done to improve DUCTILITY and reduce brittleness. Process annealing is carried out intermittently during the working of a piece of metal if several cold-forming operations are required but the metal is so hardened after the first operation that further cold working would cause cracking (see HARDENING). Full annealing is done to give workability to such parts as forged blanks. Annealing is also done for relief of internal stresses in metal and glass. Annealing temperatures and times differ for different materials and with properties desired; steel is usually held for several hours at about 1,260°F (680°C). See also HEAT TREATING.

annelid \\'a-nə-,lid\\ Any member of a phylum (Annelida) of INVERTEBRATES with a body cavity (coelom), movable bristles (setae), and a body divided into segments by crosswise rings. Known as segmented WORMS, annelids include ma-

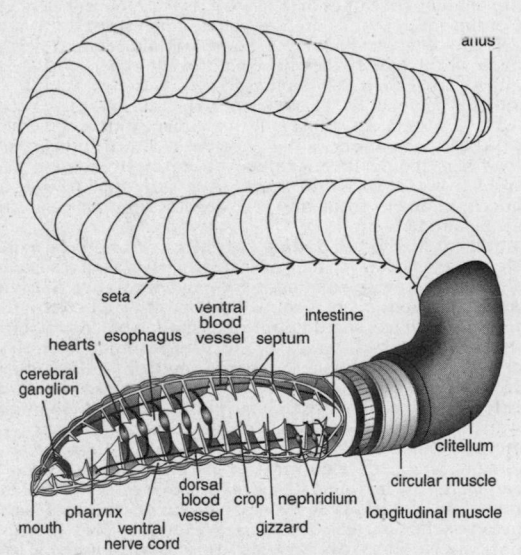

Annelid Body plan of an earthworm. Partitions (septa) divide the body cavity (coelom) into more than 100 segments. The circular and longitudinal muscles work with the setae to move the worm forward. Soil is pulled into the mouth by the sucking action of the pharynx; the crop releases food slowly into the gizzard, where the soil is ground to release and break up any organic matter. The cerebral ganglion or brain controls all body functions and movement via a ventral nerve cord. Contraction of the hearts (aortic arches) and ventral blood vessel forces blood through the body, which returns via the dorsal blood vessel. Nitrogenous waste is eliminated through the tubules of the nephridia. The clitellum secretes mucus for mating and a cocoon in which eggs are deposited.

rine worms (Polychaeta), EARTHWORMS (Oligochaeta), and LEECHES (Hirudinea).

Anne of Austria (1601–1666) Queen consort (1615–43) of LOUIS XIII of France and regent (1643–51) for her son LOUIS XIV. Daughter of Philip III of Spain and Margaret of Austria, Anne married the 14-year-old Louis XIII in 1615. He treated her coolly, and the powerful Cardinal de RICHELIEU attempted to limit her influence. As regent after Louis's death, she strove to ensure that her son would succeed to the absolute power Richelieu had won for Louis XIII. Together with her first minister, Cardinal MAZARIN, she faced the series of revolts known as the FRONDE.

Anne of Cleves (1515–1557) Fourth wife of HENRY VIII of England. In January 1540 Henry married Anne to form an alliance with her brother William, duke of Cleves, a leader of the Protestants of W Germany. The alliance, arranged by Thomas CROMWELL, seemed necessary because it appeared that the major Roman Catholic powers, France and the Holy Roman Empire, intended to attack Protestant England. When that threat dissipated, the marriage of six months was annulled.

Anne's War, Queen See QUEEN ANNE'S WAR

annual Any plant that completes its life cycle in a single growing season. The dormant SEED is the only part of an annual that survives from one growing season to the next. Annuals include many WEEDS, WILDFLOWERS, garden flowers, and VEGETABLES. See also BIENNIAL, PERENNIAL.

annuity Payment made at a fixed interval. A common example is the payment received by retirees from their PENSION plan. There are two main classes of annuities: annuities certain and contingent annuities. Under an annuity certain, a specified number of payments are made, after which the annuity stops. With a contingent annuity, each payment depends on the continuance of a given status; for example, a life annuity continues only as long as the recipient survives. Contingent annuities such as pension plans or LIFE INSURANCE depend on shared risk. Some will die before receiving back all the money they have paid, while others will live to collect more than they have paid.

anode Terminal or ELECTRODE from which ELECTRONS leave a system. In a BATTERY or other source of DIRECT CURRENT, the anode is the negative terminal. In a passive load it is the positive terminal. In an electron tube, electrons from the CATHODE travel across the tube toward the anode; in an electroplating cell, negative ions are deposited at the anode.

anodizing Method of coating metal for corrosion resistance, electrical insulation, thermal control, abrasion resistance, sealing, improving paint adhesion, and decorative finishing. Anodizing consists of electrically depositing an OXIDE film from an aqueous solution onto the surface of a metal, often ALUMINUM, which serves as the ANODE in an electrolytic cell. In the most common type of anodizing, which uses a 15% sulfuric-acid bath, dyes can be introduced to achieve a colored surface. Colored aluminum is used widely in giftware, home appliances, and architectural decoration.

anorexia nervosa \ˌa-nə-ˈrek-sē-ə-nər-ˈvō-sə\ Extreme emaciation caused by emotional or psychological aversion to eating, mostly in young women who believe that they are fat and must lose weight. They do not feel hungry. Extreme cases involve schizophrenic delusions. Weight may drop to half of normal. No causative organic defects are known. Usual symptoms are digestive disturbances, with spontaneous vomiting and ceasing of menstruation. Treatment requires cooperation among patient, physician, and psychiatrist. See also BULIMIA.

anorthosite Type of IGNEOUS ROCK composed predominantly of calcium-rich FELDSPAR. It is less abundant than either basalt or granite, but the complexes in which it occurs are often immense. All anorthosites found on the earth consist of coarse crystals, but some from the moon are finely crystalline.

Anouilh \ä-ˈnüy\, **Jean (-Marie-Lucien-Pierre)** (1910–1987) French playwright. His first play, *The Ermine* (1932), was followed by the successful *Traveler Without Luggage* (1937). He is best remembered for *Antigone* (1944), *The Lark* (1953), and *Becket* (1959), in which he used such techniques as the play within the play, flashbacks and flash-forwards,

and the exchange of roles. A skillful exponent of the WELL-MADE PLAY, he rejected naturalism and realism.

Anschluss \ˈän-ˌshlús\ (German: "union") Political union of Austria with Germany. In March 1938 the Austrian chancellor Kurt von SCHUSCHNIGG was bullied into canceling a plebiscite on union with Germany, which he expected Austrians to oppose. He resigned and ordered the Austrian army not to resist the Germans. The Germans invaded on March 12, and the enthusiasm shown by Austrians persuaded Adolf HITLER to annex Austria the next day. Though France and Britain protested, they accepted the fait accompli.

Anselm of Canterbury, St. (1033–1109) Founder of SCHOLASTICISM. Born in Lombardy, Anselm became abbot of the Benedictine monastery at Bec (in Normandy) in 1078. In 1077 he wrote the *Monologium* to demonstrate God's existence and attributes by reason alone. In his *Proslogium*, he presented his "ontological argument" for the existence of God, which claimed that the human ability to imagine God proved his existence. In 1093, Anselm became archbishop of Canterbury. In the INVESTITURE CONTROVERSY, he asserted that only an ecclesiastical authority—not a secular one—could invest him with the symbols of office. Anselm was declared a Doctor of the Church in 1720.

Ansgar \ˈans-ˌgär\, **St.** (801?–865) Missionary and patron saint of Scandinavia. Sent by LOUIS I the Pious to help Christianize Denmark and Sweden, he initiated a mission to all Scandinavians and Slavs and was appointed first archbishop of Hamburg (832). But Sweden and Denmark returned to paganism by 845 and Ansgar had to repeat all his work. He thwarted another pagan rebellion and was canonized soon after his death.

Anshan *or* **An-shan** \ˈän-ˈshän\ City (pop., 1999 est.: 1,285,000), Liaoning province, NE China. Established as a post station in 1387, it was fortified in 1587 by the MING DYNASTY against the MANCHUS. It was destroyed by fire during the BOXER REBELLION and badly damaged during the RUSSO–JAPANESE WAR (1904–5). The city was bombed by U.S. aircraft in 1944 and looted by the Soviets following World War II. The Chinese later redeveloped it into an industrial center.

ant Any member of approximately 8,000 species of the social insect family Formicidae. Ants range from 0.1 to 1 in. (2–25 mm) long and are usually yellow, brown, red, or black. They eat both plant and animal substances; some even "farm" fungi for food or "milk" APHIDS. Ant colonies consist of three castes (queens, males, and workers) interacting in a highly complex society paralleling that of HONEYBEES. Well-known species are the carpenter ants of N. America, the voracious army ants of tropical America, and the stinging FIRE ANT.

Antakya See ANTIOCH

Antananarivo \ˌän-tä-ˌnä-nä-ˈrē-vō\ *formerly* **Tananarive** \tä-ˌnä-nä-ˈrēv\ City (pop., 1993: 1,103,000), capital of Madagascar. Located in central Madagascar Island, at an elevation of 4,100 ft (1,250 m), the city was founded in the 17th cent. and was the capital of the Hova chiefs. The Imerina kings captured it in 1794 and ruled until the end of the 19th cent.

Antarctica Fifth-largest continent on earth. Antarctica lies concentrically about the SOUTH POLE, its landmass almost wholly covered by a vast ice sheet averaging 6,500 ft (2,000 m) thick. Its land area is about 5.5 million sq mi (14.2 million sq km). The S portions of the Atlantic, Pacific, and Indian oceans form the surrounding Antarctic Ocean (see ANTARCTIC REGIONS). Antarctica would be circular except for the outflaring Antarctic Peninsula and two principal bays, the Ross Sea and the Weddell Sea. E. and W. Antarctica are defined by the long chain (1,900 mi, or 3,000 km) of the Transantarctic Mtns. The ice sheet overlaying the continent represents about 90% of the world's glacial ice. By far the coldest continent, it has the world's lowest recorded temperature, –128.6°F (–89.2°C), measured in 1983. The climate supports scant vegetation, but the rich offshore food supply promotes immense seabird rookeries. The Russian F. G. von Bellingshausen (1778–1852), the Englishman Edward Bransfield (1795?–1852), and the American Nathaniel Palmer (1799–1877) all claimed first sightings of the conti-

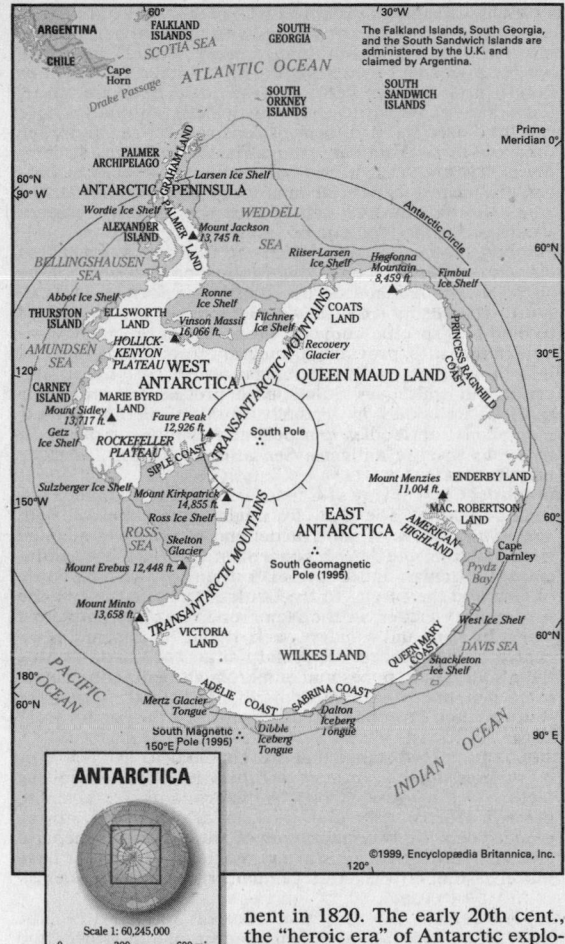

ARGENTINA
FALKLAND ISLANDS
SOUTH GEORGIA
CHILE
Cape Horn
SCOTIA SEA
ATLANTIC OCEAN
Drake Passage
SOUTH ORKNEY ISLANDS
SOUTH SANDWICH ISLANDS

The Falkland Islands, South Georgia, and the South Sandwich Islands are administered by the U.K. and claimed by Argentina.

Prime Meridian 0°

PALMER ARCHIPELAGO
Larsen Ice Shelf
60°N 90°W
ANTARCTIC PENINSULA
WEDDELL
Wordie Ice Shelf
ALEXANDER ISLAND
Mount Jackson 13,745 ft.
SEA
60°N
BELLINGSHAUSEN SEA
Ritser-Larsen Ice Shelf
Hognonna Mountain 8,459 ft.
Fimbul Ice Shelf
Abbot Ice Shelf
Ronne Ice Shelf
THURSTON ISLAND
ELLSWORTH LAND
Filchner Ice Shelf
COATS LAND
Vinson Massif 16,066 ft.
Recovery Glacier
AMUNDSEN SEA
HOLLICK-KENYON PLATEAU
WEST ANTARCTICA
30°E
120°
CARNEY ISLAND
MARIE BYRD LAND
QUEEN MAUD LAND
Mount Sidley 13,717 ft.
Faure Peak 12,926 ft.
South Pole
Getz Ice Shelf
ROCKEFELLER PLATEAU
SIPLE COAST
TRANSANTARCTIC MOUNTAINS
Sulzberger Ice Shelf
Mount Kirkpatrick 14,855 ft.
Mount Menzies 11,004 ft.
ENDERBY LAND
150°W
EAST ANTARCTICA
MAC. ROBERTSON LAND
ROSS SEA
Skelton Glacier
AMERICAN HIGHLAND
60°
Cape Darnley
Mount Erebus 12,448 ft.
South Geomagnetic Pole (1995)
Prydz Bay
Mount Minto 13,658 ft.
West Ice Shelf
VICTORIA LAND
60°N
180°
PACIFIC OCEAN
60°N
WILKES LAND
QUEEN MARY COAST
DAVIS SEA
Shackleton Ice Shelf
Mertz Glacier Tongue
ADÉLIE COAST
SABRINA COAST
Dalton Iceberg Tongue
INDIAN OCEAN
South Magnetic Pole (1995)
150°E
Dibble Iceberg Tongue
90°E

©1999, Encyclopædia Britannica, Inc.
120°

ANTARCTICA

Scale 1: 60,245,000
0 300 600 mi
0 400 800 km

nent in 1820. The early 20th cent., the "heroic era" of Antarctic exploration, produced expeditions deep into the interior by R. F. SCOTT and later Ernest SHACKLETON. The South Pole was reached by Roald AMUNDSEN in Dec. 1911, and by Scott in Jan. 1912. Seven nations claimed sectors of the continent, while many other nations carried out explorations. In the International Geophysical Year of 1957–58, 12 nations established over 50 stations on the continent for cooperative study. In 1961 the Antarctic Treaty, reserving Antarctica for free and nonpolitical scientific study, entered into full force. A 1991 agreement imposed a ban on mineral exploitation for 50 years.

Antarctic Circle Parallel of latitude approximately 66.5° south of the equator. It marks the N limit of the area within which, for one day or more each year, the sun does not set or rise. The length of continuous day or night increases southward from the Antarctic Circle, mounting to six months at the SOUTH POLE.

Antarctic Regions ANTARCTICA and the S waters of the Pacific, Atlantic, and Indian oceans (the term *Antarctic Ocean* is sometimes used, inappropriately). Ice shelves and sea ice extend well beyond the borders of the continent. The greatest recorded depth is 21,043 ft (6,414 m). Water cooled by the coastal ice masses sinks and flows northward along the ocean bottom and is replaced at the surface by warmer water flowing south from the Indian, Pacific, and Atlantic oceans. The meeting point of these currents is the Antarctic Convergence, an area rich in phytoplankton and krill, which are important to various species of fish and seabirds.

anteater Any of four species of toothless, insect-eating placental mammals. Found from Mexico to N Argentina and

Uruguay, anteaters have a long tail, dense fur, a long skull, and a tubular muzzle. They feed mainly on ants and termites, obtained by inserting their sticky wormlike tongue into a nest torn open by the long, sharp, curved claws of their forefeet. The species range in length from 15 in. (37 cm) to 6 ft (1.8 m). Anteaters are no longer grouped with the ECHIDNAS and PANGOLINS.

Lesser anteater (*Tamandua tetradactyla*)

antelope Any of numerous species of grazing or browsing BOVIDS that typically are swift, slender, and graceful plains dwellers. Most are African; the others are Eurasian, except for the N. American PRONGHORN, also sometimes called an antelope. The male, and sometimes the female, bears distinctive, backwardly curved horns. See also BONGO, DIK-DIK, DUIKER, ELAND, GAZELLE, GNU, HARTEBEEST, IMPALA, KUDU, ORYX, SPRINGBOK.

antenna *or* **aerial** Component of RADIO, TELEVISION, and RADAR systems that directs incoming and outgoing radio waves. Usually of metal, antennas range in shape and size from the mastlike devices used for radio and television broadcasting to the large parabolic reflectors used to focus satellite signals and the radio waves generated by distant astronomical objects and reflect them toward the centrally located receiver.

antenna In zoology, one of a pair of slender, segmented sensory organs on the head of INSECTS, myriapods (e.g, CENTIPEDES, MILLIPEDES), and CRUSTACEANS. Antennae of insects are believed to serve as both tactile and smell receptors; in some species, they may also serve for hearing. Evidence supports this idea only for the MOSQUITO, whose antennae are attached to structures stimulated by vibrations of the antennal shaft. In social insects (e.g., ANTS), antennae movements may serve as communication.

Anthony, Susan B(rownell) (1820–1906) U.S. pioneer in the WOMEN'S SUFFRAGE MOVEMENT. Born in Adams, Mass., she taught at a female academy in upstate New York (1846–49). Discouraged by the limited public role for women, from 1852 she joined E. C. STANTON and Amelia BLOOMER in campaigning for women's rights, helping found the Woman's New York State Temperance Society. In 1872, demanding equal voting rights, she twice led a group of women to the polls, and was arrested and fined for violating voting laws. A founder (1869) and president (1892–1900) of the National American Woman Suffrage Assn., she lectured throughout the country for a federal women's-suffrage amendment.

Anthony of Egypt, St. (A.D. 251?–356) Egyptian hermit, considered the founder of organized Christian MONASTICISM. He began his practice of asceticism at age 20 and lived in solitude on Mt. Pispir from 286 to 305. He emerged from his retreat to organize the monastic life of the hermits who had settled nearby. He later moved to the desert between the Nile and the Red Sea. His monastic rule was still observed in the 20th cent. by Coptic and Armenian monks. The hellish temptations he endured as a hermit became a popular subject for artists.

Anthony of Padua, St. (1195–1231) Franciscan friar, Doctor of the Church, and patron saint of Portugal. Born in Lisbon, he joined the Augustinian order in 1210. He joined the Franciscans in 1220, hoping for martyrdom among the Saracens, but instead became a teacher of theology at Bologna and in S France. The most beloved of the followers of St. FRANCIS, he was known as a great preacher and miracle worker. He was buried in Padua, Italy.

anthracite *or* **hard coal** COAL containing more fixed carbon than any other form of coal and the lowest amount of volatile (quickly evaporating) material, giving it the greatest heat value. The most valuable of the coals, it is also the least

A

plentiful, making up less than 2% of U.S. coal reserves; most of them in the East. Anthracites are black, with a brilliant luster; they can be polished and used for decorative purposes. They are difficult to ignite but burn with a pale-blue flame and require little attention to sustain combustion. They are sometimes mixed with BITUMINOUS COAL to heat commercial buildings.

anthracnose \an-'thrak-ˌnōs\ Plant disease of warm humid areas, caused by a FUNGUS (usually *Colletotrichum* or *Gloeosporium*), that infects various plants from trees to grasses. Symptoms include sunken spots of various colors in leaves, stems, fruits, or flowers, often leading to wilting and dying. Dogwood anthracnose, which thrives in cool climates, has caused severe losses to natural stands of DOGWOODS. It is controlled by destroying diseased tree tissue, applying FUNGICIDES, and controlling insects and mites that spread anthracnose fungi from plant to plant.

anthrax \'an-ˌthraks\ Infectious disease of warm-blooded animals, caused by *Bacillus anthracis*, a bacterium that, in spore form, can retain its virulence in contaminated soil or other material for many years. A disease chiefly of herbivores, the infection may be acquired by the products of affected animals. In humans, anthrax occurs as a cutaneous, pulmonary, or intestinal infection. Skin infection may lead to fatal septicemia (blood poisoning). Pulmonary infection is usually fatal. In recent decades, various countries have attempted to develop anthrax as a weapon of BIOLOGICAL WARFARE; many factors, including its extreme potency (vastly greater than any chemical-warfare agent), make it the preferred biological-warfare agent. Concerns about anthrax mounted in 2001 after it was found in letters mailed to members of the U.S. government and news agencies.

anthropology Study of human beings, particularly their evolutionary history, biological variation, social relationships, and cultural history. Established as an academic discipline in the early 20th cent., anthropology as practiced in the U.S. consists of four major disciplines: PHYSICAL ANTHROPOLOGY, ARCHAEOLOGY, CULTURAL ANTHROPOLOGY, and anthropological LINGUISTICS. Some specialists use the term ethnology to refer to comparative and historical anthropology.

anthroposophy \ˌan-thrə-'pä-sə-fə\ Philosophy based on the view that the human intellect has the ability to contact spiritual worlds. It was formulated in the early 20th cent. by Rudolf STEINER and was influenced by THEOSOPHY. Steiner wanted to develop a faculty for spiritual perception independent of the senses, which he believed was latent in all people. His Anthroposophical Society, founded in 1912, has branches and schools worldwide.

antiaircraft gun ARTILLERY piece fired from the ground or shipboard in defense against aerial attack. In World War I, field artillery was converted to antiaircraft use by mountings that enabled nearly vertical firing. RANGE FINDERS and searchlights, developed in the 1920s and '30s, enhanced results. World War II saw rapid-firing and automatic weapons, RADAR for target tracking, and radio-operated fuses. Heavy GUNS, up to 120 mm, were used against high-flying bombers. The most effective was the German 88-mm *Fliegerabwehrkanone*; its abbreviated name, flak, became a universal term for antiaircraft fire. In the 1950s and '60s, heavy guns gave way to guided missiles, though lighter radar-guided automatic guns remained effective against low-flying aircraft and helicopters.

antiballistic missile (ABM) Weapon designed to intercept and destroy ballistic MISSILES. In the late 1960s both the U.S. and the Soviet Union developed two-part, nuclear-armed ABM systems that combined a high-altitude interceptor missile with a terminal-phase interceptor. Such systems were limited by the 1972 ABM Treaty, under which each side was allowed one ABM location with 100 interceptor missiles. See also STRATEGIC DEFENSE INITIATIVE.

Antibes \äⁿ-'tēb\ *ancient* Antipolis. Seaport (pop., 1990: 71,000), SE France. Located on the Mediterranean coast southwest of NICE, it was established by Phocaean traders about 340 B.C. It became a Roman town and eventually a fief of the Grimaldi family (see MONACO) from 1384 to 1608. It is a noted winter resort.

antibiotic Chemical substance that can inhibit the growth of microorganisms or destroy them with minimal harm to the infected host. Early antibiotics were natural microbial products (made by ACTINOMYCETES, other bacteria, or fungi); now semisynthetic and synthetic ones are made. Since the discovery of PENICILLIN (1928), antibiotics have revolutionized the treatment of bacterial, fungal, and some other diseases. Familiar ones include penicillin, streptomycin, TETRACYCLINE, and bacitracin. Drawbacks include activity against beneficial microorganisms, often causing DIARRHEA; ALLERGIES; and development of drug-resistant strains of the targeted microorganisms.

antibody Protective molecule in the IMMUNE SYSTEM that circulates in BLOOD and LYMPH in response to invasion by an ANTIGEN. Antibodies are GLOBULINS formed in LYMPHOID TISSUES by B CELLS, whose receptors are specialized to bind to a specific antigen. Antibodies have widely varying binding sites, providing protection from a wide range of infectious agents and toxic substances. In 1975 César MILSTEIN and colleagues developed a process for producing specific antibodies in virtually limitless amounts; these monoclonal antibodies can deliver radiation or drugs directly to specific antigens. See also ANTITOXIN, RETICULOENDOTHELIAL SYSTEM.

Antichrist Chief enemy of Christ, first mentioned in the epistles of St. JOHN. The idea of a mighty ruler who will fight against the forces of good at the end of time was adapted from Judaism; the Jewish concept in turn had been influenced by Iranian and Babylonian myths of the final battle of God and the DEVIL. In the Book of DANIEL the evil one is a military leader; in the New Testament, the Antichrist works by signs and wonders, seeks divine honors, and is accepted by Jews because they did not accept Christ. During the Middle Ages, popes and emperors struggling for power often denounced each other as the Antichrist; during the Reformation, Protestant leaders identified the papacy itself as the Antichrist.

anticoagulant Substance that prevents BLOOD from clotting by suppressing the synthesis or function of various clotting factors (see COAGULATION). Anticoagulants are given to prevent THROMBOSIS and used in drawing and storing blood. There are two main types of anticoagulants: heparin and VITAMIN K antagonists (e.g., warfarin); the latter have longer-lasting effects. Anticoagulant therapy carries a risk of HEMORRHAGE.

antidepressant Any drug used to treat DEPRESSION. The three main types inhibit the metabolism of SEROTONIN and NOREPINEPHRINE in the brain. The aim is to keep these NEUROTRANSMITTERS from dropping to levels associated with depression. The drugs may take a few weeks to show any effect. The first type, tricyclic antidepressants, help more than 70% of patients. The second type, monoamine oxidase (MAO) inhibitors, have unpredictable side effects and are usually given only when tricyclic drugs do not help. The third type, selective serotonin reuptake inhibitors (SSRIs), includes the best-known and most widely used antidepressant, fluoxetine (trade name Prozac): it often helps with depression unrelieved by tricyclics or MAO inhibitors and has milder side effects.

antidote Remedy to counteract the effects of a POISON or TOXIN. Administered by mouth, intravenously, or sometimes on the skin, it may work by directly neutralizing the poison; causing an opposite effect in the body; binding to the poison; or binding to a receptor to prevent the poison's binding there. Some poisons are not active until converted to a different form in the body; their antidotes interrupt that conversion.

Antietam \an-'tē-təm\, **Battle of** (Sept. 17, 1862) Decisive and bloody battle of the AMERICAN CIVIL WAR that halted the Confederate advance. Following victory at the Second Battle of BULL RUN, Gen. R. E. LEE moved his troops into Maryland with an eye to capturing Washington, D.C. They were stopped by Union troops under George MCCLELLAN at Antietam Creek, Md. Over 13,000 Confederate troops died. The victory encouraged Pres. Abraham LINCOLN to issue a preliminary EMANCIPATION PROCLAMATION.

Anti-Federalists U.S. leaders who opposed the strong central government envisioned in the U.S. CONSTITUTION of

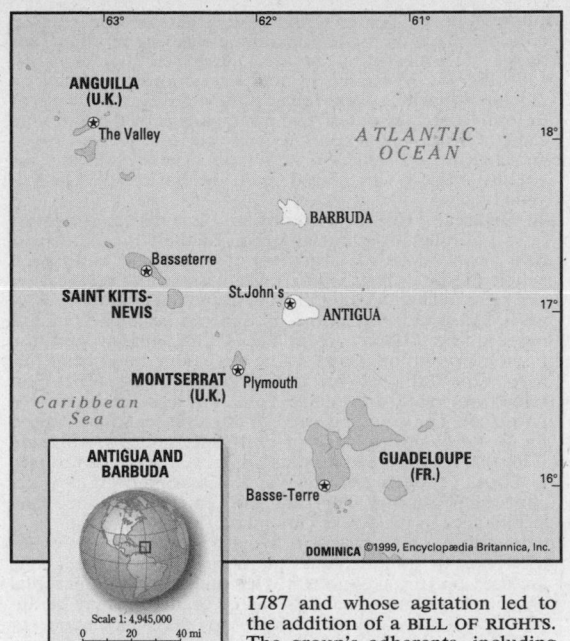

Map showing ANGUILLA (U.K.), The Valley, ATLANTIC OCEAN, BARBUDA, Basseterre, SAINT KITTS-NEVIS, St.John's, ANTIGUA, MONTSERRAT (U.K.), Plymouth, Caribbean Sea, ANTIGUA AND BARBUDA, GUADELOUPE (FR.), Basse-Terre, DOMINICA ©1999, Encyclopædia Britannica, Inc. Scale 1: 4,945,000

1787 and whose agitation led to the addition of a BILL OF RIGHTS. The group's adherents, including George MASON, Patrick HENRY, Thomas PAINE, and Samuel ADAMS, were as numerous as the FEDERALISTS, but their influence was weak in urban areas, and only Rhode Island and N. Carolina voted against ratification. Powerful during Thomas JEFFERSON's presidency, they formed the nucleus of what later became the DEMOCRATIC PARTY.

antifreeze Any substance that lowers the FREEZING POINT of WATER, protecting a system from the ill effects of freezing. In automobile cooling systems, mixing water with ETHYLENE GLYCOL or propylene glycol works down to 0°F (−17.8°C) and does not damage radiators. Creatures protect themselves with GLYCEROL or dimethyl sulfoxide (insects), glycerol or trehalose (other invertebrates), and PROTEINS (antarctic fishes).

antigen \'an-ti-jən\ Foreign substance in the body that induces an immune response by stimulating LYMPHOCYTES to produce ANTIBODIES or to attack the antigen directly (see IMMUNITY). Virtually any large foreign molecule can act as an antigen, including those of bacteria, viruses, parasites, foods, venoms, blood components, and cells and tissues of various species, including humans. Sites on the antigens' surface fit and bind to receptor molecules on the lymphocytes' surface.

Antigone \an-'ti-gə-nē\ In Greek legend, the daughter born of the incestuous relationship between OEDIPUS and his mother. After Oedipus had blinded himself in self-punishment, Antigone and her sister served as his guides, following him into exile. When he died, Antigone returned to THEBES, where her brothers Eteocles and Polyneices were at war. Both were killed, and Creon, the new king, declared that because Polyneices was a traitor, his corpse should remain unburied. Antigone defied the decree and buried him; when Creon condemned her to death, she hanged herself.

Antigonus I Monophthalmus ("One-Eyed") \an-'tig-ə-nəs...-ˌmän-əf-'thal-məs\ *or* **Antigonus I Cyclops** (382–301 B.C.) Founder of the Macedonian dynasty of the Antigonids. He served as a general under ALEXANDER THE GREAT. From the plots, alliances, and wars among Alexander's successors, he emerged in control of Asia Minor and Syria, though he soon relinquished the lands east of the Euphrates to SELEUCUS I NICATOR. With the help of his son, Demetrius I, he gained control of the E Mediterranean, the Aegean, and Asia Minor. In 306 he was proclaimed king of the empire by the assembled army. His dreams of taking Macedonia itself and Alexander's entire former empire died with him at the Battle of Ipsus (301), the only battle he ever lost.

Antigua and Barbuda \an-'tə-gə...bär-'byü-də\ Island nation, Lesser ANTILLES. It consists of three islands, Antigua, Barbuda, and Redonda. Area: 171 sq mi (443 sq km). Population (2000): 71,000. Capital: ST. JOHN's (on Antigua). The majority of the population are descendants of African slaves brought in during colonial times. Language: English (official). Religion: Christianity. Currency: Eastern Caribbean dollar. The largest of the islands is Antigua (108 sq mi, or 280 sq km). It lacks forests, mountains, and rivers, and is subject to droughts. The main anchorage is the deepwater harbor of St. John's. Barbuda, 25 mi (40 km) north of Antigua, is a 62-sq-mi (161-sq-km) game reserve inhabited by a variety of wildlife, including wild deer; its only settlement is Codrington, on its W coast. Redonda, an uninhabited rock (0.5 sq mi, or 1.3 sq km), lies southwest of Antigua. Tourism is the mainstay of the country's economy; offshore banking is growing. Christopher COLUMBUS visited Antigua in 1493 and named it after a church in SEVILLE, Spain. It was colonized by English settlers in 1632, who imported African slaves to grow tobacco and sugarcane. Barbuda was colonized by the English in 1678. In 1834 its slaves were emancipated. Antigua (with Barbuda) was part of the British colony of the Leeward Islands from 1871 until that colony was defederated in 1956. The islands achieved independence in 1981. See map in left column.

antihistamine \ˌan-ti-'his-tə-ˌmēn, ˌan-ti-'his-tə-mən\ Synthetic drug that counteracts the effects of released HISTAMINE in the body, preventing allergic attacks (see ALLERGY) or INFLAMMATION. Some antihistamines also prevent MOTION SICKNESS and VERTIGO. Drowsiness is a frequent side effect. H_2 antihistamines, which bind to a different receptor type, are used to control gastric-acid secretion (see STOMACH) and treat PEPTIC ULCERS.

Antilles \an-'til-ēz\, **Greater and Lesser** Two groups of islands in the W. INDIES, bounding the Caribbean Sea on the north and east, respectively. The Greater Antilles include the largest islands (Cuba, Jamaica, Hispaniola, and Puerto Rico), the Lesser Antilles all being much smaller.

Anti-Masonic Movement Popular movement in the U.S. opposed to FREEMASONRY. The disappearance and presumed murder, in New York in 1826, of a former Mason who had supposedly revealed the order's secrets ignited reaction against the secret society in the NE U.S. In 1831 the Anti-Masonic Party became the first U.S. third party and the first party to hold a national convention. Its candidate won Vermont in the 1832 election. By the late 1830s it had been absorbed into the WHIG PARTY.

antimatter Substance composed of elementary particles having the MASS and ELECTRIC CHARGE of ordinary matter (such as ELECTRONS and PROTONS), but for which the charge and related magnetic properties are opposite in sign. The existence of antimatter was a consequence of the electron theory of Paul DIRAC. In 1932 the POSITRON (antielectron) was detected in COSMIC RAYS, followed by the antiproton and the antineutron using PARTICLE ACCELERATORS. When matter and antimatter are in close proximity, annihilation occurs within a fraction of a second, releasing large amounts of ENERGY.

antimony \'an-tə-ˌmō-nē\ Semimetallic to metallic chemical ELEMENT (see METAL), chemical symbol Sb, atomic number 51. Its most common form is a lustrous, bluish, brittle, flaky solid. In nature antimony occurs chiefly as the mineral stibnite. Pure antimony has no important uses, but its ALLOYS and COMPOUNDS are extremely useful. Some antimony alloys expand on solidifying; these are used for castings and for type metal. Alloys with lead are used in car BATTERIES, bullets, and cable sheaths; alloys with tin and lead are used in machine bearings. Antimony compounds are widely used as flame retardants or as paint pigments.

antinovel Type of avant-garde novel that departs from tradition by ignoring such elements as plot, dialogue, and human interest. Seeking to overcome readers' habits and challenge their expectations, antinovelists avoid revealing their own personality and values. Though the term was coined by J.-P. SARTRE in 1948, the approach goes at least as far back as the 18th-cent. writer Laurence STERNE. Antinovelists include Nathalie SARRAUTE, Claude SIMON and Alain ROBBE-GRILLET.

Antioch \\'an-tē-ˌäk\ *Turkish* **Antakya** \ˌän-tä-'kyä\ City (pop., 1994 est.: 137,000), S Turkey. Founded in 300 B.C. by Greeks, Antioch was the center of the SELEUCID kingdom until 64 B.C., when the Romans made it the capital of Syria. An early center of Christianity, the city was the headquarters of St. PAUL about A.D. 47–55. It fell to the Persians in the 6th cent., the Arabs in the 7th cent., and the Crusaders in 1098; Ottoman Turks held it from 1517 until World War I.

Antioch University Private university founded in 1852 as Antioch College in Yellow Springs, Ohio. Horace MANN was its first president (1853–59). From its founding it was coeducational, nonsectarian, and open to black students. It is noted for its experimental curricula. Students alternate between academic work and full-time jobs. In 1978 Antioch consolidated its programs and far-flung campuses and adopted the name Antioch Univ. Total enrollment is about 3,200.

Antiochus I Soter \an-'tī-ə-kəs...'sō-ter\ (324–262/261 B.C.) King of SELEUCID Syria in the east (292?–281 B.C.) and later overall (281–261). Son of SELEUCUS I, he consolidated the Seleucid kingdom, founded numerous cities, and expanded its trade routes. In 281 he contended with revolts in Syria and N Anatolia and fought a war with Antigonus II Gonatas. He defeated the Gauls in Greece (279) and Asia Minor (275), after which he was hailed as Soter ("Savior") by appreciative Ionians. He settled Greeks in Asia Minor and Persia to counter invasions, and worked to revive Babylonian culture. Though he won Phoenicia and the coast of Asia Minor from Egypt, he soon lost them, and in 261 he lost much of N Asia Minor to Pergamum.

Antiochus III *known as* **Antiochus the Great** (242–187 B.C.) SELEUCID king of the Syrian empire (223–187 B.C.). After quelling a rebellion in Asia Minor (213), he marched east to India (212–205). He forged alliances with Armenia, Parthia, and Bactria, stilling resistance to his campaign. Following Ptolemy IV's death, he and PHILIP V of Macedonia divided most of Ptolemy's empire. He then marched against Egypt, concluding a peace in 195, through which he acquired S Syria and Ptolemy's territories in Asia Minor. Rome eventually defeated him at Magnesia (189). He gave up lands in Europe and W Asia Minor but kept Syria, Mesopotamia, and W Iran. He was murdered while exacting much-needed tribute near Susa.

Antiochus IV Epiphanes \i-'pif-ə-ˌnēz\ ("God Manifest") (c.215–164 B.C.) SELEUCID king of the Hellenistic Syrian kingdom (175–164 B.C.). Son of ANTIOCHUS III, he was taken hostage in Rome (189–175). On his release, he ousted a usurper to take over Syria. He conquered Egypt except Alexandria (169) and ruled Egypt as regent for his nephew Ptolemy VI. The Roman defeat of his Macedonian allies forced him to leave Cyprus and Egypt. He took Jerusalem (167) and enforced its Hellenization; Jewish rites were forbidden on pain of death. In 164 JUDAS MACCABAEUS and the anti-Greek Jews conquered Judaea except for the Acra in Jerusalem. Antiochus then turned to defending his empire against the Parthians in the east, regained Armenia, and went on to the Arabian coast before dying in Persis.

antioxidant Any of various COMPOUNDS added to products to retard combination with OXYGEN and resultant ill effects. AROMATIC COMPOUNDS such as aromatic AMINES, PHENOLS, and aminophenols delay loss of elasticity in rubber and gummy deposits in gasoline. Preservatives such as tocopherol (VITAMIN E), propyl gallate, butylated hydroxytoluene (BHT), and butylated hydroxyanisole (BHA) prevent rancidity in FATS, OILS, and fatty foods. In the body, antioxidants such as VITAMINS C and E and SELENIUM may reduce oxidation caused by FREE RADICALS.

Antiphon \\'an-ti-ˌfän\ (c.480–411 B.C.) Orator and statesman. The first Athenian known to practice rhetoric professionally, he wrote speeches for others to give in court. He may have instigated the revolution of the oligarchic Council of the Four Hundred, an attempt to seize the Athenian government in the midst of war. When the oligarchy fell, he defended himself in a speech called by THUCYDIDES the greatest defense ever made, but he was nonetheless executed.

antipope In ROMAN CATHOLICISM, a person who tries to take the place of the legitimately elected pope. Some antipopes were elected by factions in doctrinal disagreements, and others were chosen in double elections arbitrated by secular authorities or picked as third candidates in an effort to resolve such disputes. The principal age of the antipope came after the papal court was moved from Rome to Avignon in the 14th cent. (see AVIGNON PAPACY). During this era, the antipopes are considered to be those elected in Avignon.

anti-Semitism Hostility toward or discrimination against Jews as a religious or racial group. By the 4th cent., Christians saw Jews as the crucifiers of Christ and as an alien people (despite Christ's own Jewishness) whose repudiation of Christ had condemned them to perpetual migration. Jews were denied citizenship and its rights in large parts of Europe in the Middle Ages. The Enlightenment and the French Revolution brought a new religious freedom to Europe in the 18th cent., but in the 19th cent. race rather than religion became a primary basis for anti-Semitism (see POGROM). The economic and political dislocations caused by World War I intensified anti-Semitism. An estimated 5,700,000 Jews were exterminated in Nazi death camps (see HOLOCAUST) during World War II. Anti-Semitism later declined in Western Europe and the U.S., but it gained new significance in the Soviet Union and the Middle East.

antiseptic Agents applied to living tissue to destroy or inhibit growth of infectious microorganisms. Disinfectants are used on surfaces; ANTIBIOTICS and other antimicrobial agents are usually given in shots or orally but may be applied locally. An antiseptic's efficiency depends on concentration, time, and temperature. Many antiseptics destroy specific types or forms of microorganisms (e.g., BACTERIA but not SPORES). Major types include ALCOHOLS, PHENOLS, CHLORINE and IODINE compounds, MERCURY-based tinctures, certain DYES, and some ESSENTIAL OILS.

Anti-Slavery Society, American See AMERICAN ANTI-SLAVERY SOCIETY

antitoxin ANTIBODY formed in reaction to a bacterial TOXIN, which it can neutralize. People who have recovered from bacterial diseases often develop specific antitoxins that give them IMMUNITY. Injecting an animal (usually a horse) with increasing doses of toxin produces a high concentration of antitoxin in the blood: the resulting preparation is called an antiserum. The first antitoxin developed (1890) was specific to DIPHTHERIA; today, antitoxins are also used to treat BOTULISM, DYSENTERY, gas GANGRENE, and TETANUS.

antitrust law Any law restricting business practices considered unfair or monopolistic. Among U.S. laws, the best known is the SHERMAN ANTITRUST ACT of 1890, which declared illegal "every contract, combination . . . or conspiracy in restraint of trade or commerce." The Clayton Antitrust Act of 1914, as amended in 1936 by the Robinson-Patman Act, prohibits discrimination among customers through prices or other means; it also prohibits mergers or acquisitions whenever the effect may be "to substantially lessen competition." Labor unions are also subject to antitrust laws.

antlion Insect (family Myrmeleontidae) known in its larval stage for its aggressive capture of prey. The antlion LARVA digs a funnel-shaped sandy pit, then waits within. Any small insect slipping into the pit is seized by the antlion, which sucks the contents of its victim and throws out the empty skin. The best known of the 65 described species, *Myrmeleon formicarius*, occurs in N. America and Europe.

Antonello da Messina \ˌan-tō-'nel-ō-dä-mā-'sē-nə\ (c.1430–1479) Italian painter. Born in Messina, Sicily, and trained in Naples, then a cosmopolitan art center, he studied the Flemish artists, notably Jan van EYCK. He introduced oil painting into Venetian art. His major works were altarpieces and portraits. His portrait busts in three-quarter view combine Flemish detail with Italian grandeur.

Antonine Wall Roman frontier barrier in Britain. It ran 37 mi (59 km) across Scotland between the Clyde River and the Firth of Forth. Ordered by ANTONINUS PIUS and built in A.D. 142, it was about 15 ft (5 m) wide and 10 ft (3 m) high; a ditch 40 ft (12 m) wide and 12 ft (4 m) deep ran in front of it and a road behind. It was controlled by 19 forts. Its construction moved the N boundary of Roman Britain into Scotland, providing defense against the N tribes beyond HADRIAN'S WALL. The wall was abandoned by 196, but traces remain.

Antoninus Pius \ˌan-tə-ˈnī-nəs-ˈpī-əs\ *in full* Caesar Titus Aelius Hadrianus Antoninus Augustus Pius (A.D. 86–161) Roman emperor (A.D. 138–61). Of Gallic origins, he served as consul (120) and later governed the province of Asia (c.134). An adviser to HADRIAN, he was made his heir in 138. On accession, he had the deceased emperor declared a god; for such dutiful acts he was named Pius ("pious"). He quelled rebellions in Britain and in other provinces and built the ANTONINE WALL.

Antonioni \ˌan-ˌtō-nē-ˈō-nē\, **Michelangelo** (b.1912) Italian film director and producer. His first major film, *The Girl Friends* (1955), was followed by the international successes *L'avventura* (1960), *Eclipse* (1962), and *Blow-up* (1966). His other films include *The Red Desert* (1964), *Zabriskie Point* (1970), and *The Passenger* (1974). In Antonioni's films, plot and dialogue are subordinated to the visual image, which becomes a metaphor of human existence rather than a record of it.

Antony, Mark *Latin* Marcus Antonius (82/81–30 B.C.) Roman general. He helped Julius CAESAR drive POMPEY from Italy in 49, and in 44 was made co-consul. After Caesar's assassination, Octavian (later AUGUSTUS) initially opposed Antony, but later formed the Second TRIUMVIRATE with Antony and Lepidus. Antony helped defeat republican forces at PHILIPPI. On a mission to Egypt to question CLEOPATRA about her loyalty, he became her lover (41–40). He returned to Italy in 40 to settle differences with Octavian, whereupon he received command of the E provinces. To

Mark Antony

strengthen his position, he agreed to marry Octavian's sister Octavia. When relations with Octavian again collapsed, he headed for Syria and sent for Cleopatra for aid. Octavian sent Octavia to him, and when Antony ordered her back to Rome a fatal breach opened. The triumvirate ended in 32, leaving Antony little support in Rome. He divorced Octavia, and Octavian declared war on Cleopatra. Antony lost the Battle of ACTIUM, and he and Cleopatra fled to Egypt pursued by Octavian. When resistance became futile, they committed suicide.

Antwerp *French* **Anvers** \äⁿ-ˈver\ *Flemish* **Antwerpen** \ˈänt-ˌver-pən\ City (pop., 1998: 450,000), capital of Antwerp province, Belgium. Lying in the Flemish-speaking region, it is also the unofficial capital of FLANDERS. Situated on the Schelde River, it is one of the world's major seaports. It received municipal rights in 1291 and was a member of the HANSEATIC LEAGUE by 1315. It became the commercial and financial capital of Europe in the 16th cent. Following destructive invasions it went into decline, but began to revive after NAPOLEON's improvement of the harbor about 1803. Its current economic life centers around shipping, port-related activities, and major manufacturing.

antyesti \ant-ˈyes-tē\ Hindu funeral rites. They generally involve cremation followed by disposal of the ashes in a sacred river. As soon as possible after death, the body is removed to the cremation grounds, usually on the riverbank. For 10 days, the mourners perform rites intended to provide the soul of the deceased with a new spiritual body for the next life. At a prescribed date, the remains are buried or immersed in a river.

Anu \ˈä-ˌnü\ Mesopotamian sky god. He belonged to a triad that included Bel and EA. Though he was the highest god, his role in mythology, hymns, and cult was small. The father of all gods, evil spirits, and demons, and the god of kings and the calendar, he was depicted with headdress and horns signifying strength.

Anubis \ə-ˈnü-bəs\ Ancient Egyptian god of the dead, represented as a jackal or as a man with the head of a jackal. He was originally preeminent as lord of the dead, but he was later overshadowed by OSIRIS. Associated with the care of the dead, he was credited with the invention of embalming, an art he first practiced on the corpse of Osiris. Later he was assigned the role of conducting souls into the underworld.

Anuradhapura \ə-ˈnur-ə-də-ˌpur-ə\ Sinhalese kingdom in Sri Lanka (3rd cent. B.C.–A.D. 10th cent.). Though plagued by invasions from S India (which took actual control of the kingdom several times) and internal strife among warring clans, the kingdom developed a high degree of culture. Its complex irrigation system is often considered its major achievement. The city of Anuradhapura contains vast Buddhist ruins.

Anvers See ANTWERP

anxiety In psychology, a feeling of dread, fear, or apprehension, often with no clear justification. It is marked by physiological signs such as sweating, tension, and increased pulse, by doubt concerning the reality and nature of the perceived threat, and by self-doubt about one's capacity to cope with it. Some anxiety inevitably arises in the course of daily life and is normal; but persistent, intense, chronic, or recurring anxiety not justified by real-life stresses is usually regarded as a sign of an emotional disorder. See also STRESS.

Anzio \ˈänt-sē-ˌō\ Seaport and resort town (pop., 1991: 32,000) southeast of Rome, Italy. Conquered by Rome in 338 B.C., it became a resort for wealthy Romans. NERO and CALIGULA were born there. Destroyed by the SARACENS in the 9th–10th cent., it remained virtually deserted until 1698, when Pope Innocent XII built a port nearby. In 1944 it was the scene of a bloody but successful amphibious landing by Allied forces.

ANZUS Pact *officially* **Pacific Security Treaty** Security pact for the S. Pacific, signed in 1951 by Australia, New Zealand, and the U.S. (hence its acronym). The signatories agreed to maintain a consultative relationship for their collective security. In the 1980s New Zealand refused to let ships carrying nuclear weapons dock at its ports; the U.S., refusing to identify its nuclear-armed ships, suspended its treaty obligations to New Zealand in 1986, and the treaty has since been nonoperative with reference to New Zealand.

AOL See AMERICA ONLINE

aorta ARTERY that carries blood leaving the heart. Where the left ventricle opens into the aorta, a valve prevents backflow of blood. The aorta ascends from the heart, arches over it to the left, then descends into the trunk. Arteries branch off along its length until it divides at hip level into arteries that go to the legs.

AP See ASSOCIATED PRESS

A&P See GREAT ATLANTIC & PACIFIC TEA CO.

Apache American Indians of the SW U.S. Culturally, they are divided into Eastern Apaches, which were predominantly HUNTING AND GATHERING SOCIETIES, and Western Apaches, which relied more on farming. The Apache attempted to be friends of the Spanish, the Mexicans, and later the Americans. In 1861, however, there began a quarter-century confrontation between U.S. military forces and the Apache and NAVAJO. The Apache wars were among the fiercest fought on the frontier. The last ended in 1886 with the surrender of GERONIMO. The Apache today total about 11,000 and live largely on or near reservations in Arizona and New Mexico. See also COCHISE.

apartheid \ə-ˈpär-ˌtāt\ (Afrikaans: "apartness" or "separateness") Policy of segregation and political and economic discrimination against non-European groups in S. Africa. The term was first used for the official policy of the NATIONAL PARTY in 1948. The Group Areas Act of 1950 established residential and business sections in urban areas for each race and strengthened the existing "pass" laws requiring nonwhites to carry identification papers. Other laws forbade most social contacts between the races, authorized segregated public facilities, restricted each race to certain types of jobs, curtailed nonwhite labor unions, and established various black African "homelands," partly self-governing units dependent on S. Africa. Apartheid led to many

violent protests, strikes, acts of sabotage, and international censure. In 1990–91 most apartheid legislation was repealed, though segregation remains deeply entrenched in S. African society.

apatite Member of the PHOSPHATE group of minerals, the world's major source of phosphorus, found as variously colored, glassy crystals, masses, or nodules. If not for its softness, apatite would be a popular gemstone; some of the material found is clear, but it is fragile and difficult to cut and polish.

apatosaurus See BRONTOSAURUS

ape Any of the tailless, anthropoid PRIMATES of two families: Hylobatidae (the lesser apes: GIBBONS and siamangs) and Pongidae (the great apes: CHIMPANZEES, BONOBOS, ORANGUTANS, and GORILLAS). Apes are found in the tropical forests of W and central Africa and SE Asia. They are distinguished from monkeys by having no tail, having an appendix, and having a more complex brain. Apes typically move about by swinging, and they tend to stand erect. Highly intelligent animals, apes are more closely related to humans than are any other living primates. All apes are now regarded as endangered.

APEC *in full* **Asia-Pacific Economic Cooperation** Trade group established in 1989 to promote the economic development of its members. The original members were Australia, Brunei, Canada, China, Indonesia, Japan, Malaysia, New Zealand, the Philippines, Singapore, S. Korea, Thailand, and the U.S., as well as Taiwan and Hong Kong. Mexico, Chile, and Papua New Guinea joined APEC in 1994. The APEC group now represents about 40% of the world's population, 40% of global trade, and 50% of the world's gross national product.

Apennines \'a-pə-ˌnīnz\ Mountain range, central Italy. It stretches some 840 mi (1,350 km) from near Savona in the northwest to REGGIO DI CALABRIA in the south. Monte Corno is its highest peak, at 9,560 ft (2,915 m). The range is the source of most of Italy's rivers. It is famous for its hill towns, including FLORENCE, Arezzo, L'AQUILA, and Benevento.

Apgar Score System Rating procedure to identify newborns needing life-sustaining medical assistance. It was developed in 1952 by Virginia Apgar (1909–1974). Five signs, keyed to her name—Appearance (color), Pulse, Grimace (reflex irritability), Activity (muscle tone), and Respiration—are measured. The maximum score is 10. If the score at one and five minutes after birth is less than 7, the infant is reevaluated every five minutes for 20 minutes or until two consecutive scores of 7 or more are obtained.

aphasia \ə-'fā-zhə\ *or* **dysphasia** \dis-'fā-zhə\ Brain-generated defect in saying words, unrelated to physical ability to produce sounds. Symptoms vary with the brain area involved: the ability to say words in a specific category or to put words in a meaningful order may be lost. The term also covers related disturbances, including inability to write and inability to recognize what is perceived through one of the senses, such as DYSLEXIA.

aphid \'ā-fəd', a-fəd\ Any of several species of sapsucking, soft-bodied INSECTS (order Homoptera) that are about the size of a pinhead. Serious plant pests, they stunt plant growth, produce plant GALLS, transmit plant viral diseases, and deform leaves, buds, and flowers. ANTS may protect aphids from enemies and transfer them from wilted to healthy plants. The ants in turn obtain honeydew, a sweet product excreted by aphids, by "milking" them (stroking their abdomens).

aphorism Generally accepted truth or sentiment expressed in a short, memorable way. The term was first used in the *Aphorisms* of HIPPOCRATES, a series of statements about disease and the art of healing, and aphorisms were originally used to deal with such subjects as art, agriculture, medicine, jurisprudence, and politics. In the modern era they have usually been vehicles of wit and pithy wisdom. Celebrated modern aphorists include Friedrich NIETZSCHE and Oscar WILDE.

aphrodisiac \ˌa-frə-'dē-zē-ˌak\ Any of various forms of stimulation thought to arouse sexual excitement. They may be psychophysiological (arousing the senses) or internal (e.g., foods, alcoholic drinks, drugs, love potions, medicinal prep-

arations). Most foods traditionally believed to be aphrodisiacs have no chemical components that would have such an effect. The reputation of some may be based on a supposed resemblance to genitalia. Drugs such as alcohol or marijuana may lead to sexual excitation by lessening the user's inhibitions. The only substances medically recognized as aphrodisiacs are extremely hazardous.

Aphrodite \ˌa-frə-'dī-tē\ Greek goddess of sexual love and beauty. She is also associated with the sea and, according to legend, was born of sea foam arising from the genitals of URANUS. Sparta, Thebes, and Cyprus honored her as a goddess of war. Her cult was probably Semitic rather than Greek in origin. According to Homer, she was the daughter of ZEUS and his consort Dione, and she married HEPHAESTUS, but betrayed him with ARES. VENUS is her Roman counterpart.

Apia \ä-'pē-ä\ Seaport town (pop., 1999: 38,000) and capital, Samoa. It lies on the N coast of Upolu Island. Its economy centers on the export of goods to AMERICAN SAMOA. R. L. STEVENSON is buried nearby; his former home is now the residence of the head of state.

apiculture See BEEKEEPING

Apis \'ā-pəs\ In ancient Egypt, a sacred bull deity worshiped at Memphis from at least the 1st dynasty (c.2925–c.2775 B.C.). Originally a fertility god, Apis became associated with gods of the dead. When an Apis bull died, it was buried with great pomp, and the calf that was to be its successor was installed. Apis's priests drew omens from its behavior, and his ORACLE had a wide reputation. The worship of Serapis (a combination of OSIRIS and Apis) probably arose in the 3rd cent. B.C. and became one of the most widespread oriental cults in the Roman empire.

apocalypse \ə-'pä-kə-ˌlips\ In many Western religious traditions, the period of catastrophic upheaval expected to occur just before the end of the world. The belief that the world will come to a violent and cataclysmic end exists in Judaism and Christianity. Several prophetic works of the Old Testament, notably the Book of DANIEL, include visions of the apocalypse. The Book of REVELATION gives a dark and dramatic picture of the end of time. The approach of the Last Days is expected to be marked by famines, wars, earthquakes, and plagues, along with signs in the heavens. Today apocalyptic themes are emphasized by fundamentalist Christians. See also ESCHATOLOGY, MILLENNIALISM.

Apocrypha \ə-'pä-krə-fə\ In biblical literature, works outside an accepted canon of SCRIPTURE. In modern usage the Apocrypha refers to ancient Jewish books that are not part of the Hebrew BIBLE but are considered canonical in ROMAN CATHOLICISM and EASTERN ORTHODOXY, including Tobit, Judith, Baruch, Maccabees, Ecclesiasticus, and Wisdom of Solomon. Protestant churches follow Jewish tradition in judging these works apocryphal or noncanonical.

Apollinaire \ˌa-pò-lē-'ner\, **Guillaume** *orig.* Guillelmus (*or* Wilhelm) Apollinaris de Kostrowitzky (1880–1918) Italian?-French poet. He arrived in Paris at 20, but kept his early life obscure. He took part in all the avant-garde movements that flourished at the beginning of the 20th cent. His poetry featured daring technical experiments, and because it creates surprise through unusual verbal associations and word patterns, he is often considered the herald of SURREALISM. His poetic masterpiece was *Alcools* (1913). He died of a head wound in World War I.

Apollo Most widely revered of the Greek gods. He communicated the will of his father ZEUS, made humans aware of their guilt and purified them of it, presided over religious and civil law, and foretold the future. As a patron of the arts, he was often associated with the MUSES.

Apollo Statue, "Apollo Belvedere," from a Greek original, 4th cent. B.C.

He became associated with the sun, and was even identified with HELIOS, the sun god. Also associated with healing, he was the father of ASCLEPIUS. ARTEMIS was his twin sister. Apollo's oracle was established at DELPHI; the PYTHIAN GAMES commemorated his killing (while still an infant) of the serpent Python to take the shrine. His many lovers fared poorly: the fleeing DAPHNE became a laurel tree; the unfaithful Coronis was shot by Artemis, and CASSANDRA, who rejected him, was doomed to utter true prophecies no one would believe.

Apollo NASA moon-landing project of the 1960s and '70s. The Apollo spacecraft, supplied with their own low-powered rockets, could brake to orbit the MOON and release a lunar module, with its own rocket power, to land ASTRONAUTS on the moon and bring them back to the lunar orbiter. In July 1969 Apollo 11 made the first lunar landing (see Edwin ALDRIN, Neil ARMSTRONG). In 1970 Apollo 13 was damaged by an explosion but returned safely. Later missions explored the lunar surface extensively, collecting samples and installing instruments for research. Apollo 17, the program's final flight, took place in 1972.

Apollo asteroid See EARTH-CROSSING ASTEROID

Apollonius Dyscolos \ˌap-ə-ˈlō-nē-əs-ˈdis-kə-ləs\ (fl.2nd cent. A.D.) Greek grammarian considered the founder of the systematic study of GRAMMAR. PRISCIAN based his work on the writings of Apollonius. Four of Apollonius' works survive: *On Syntax, On Pronouns, On Conjunctions,* and *On Adverbs.*

Apollonius of Perga (262?-c.190 B.C.) Anatolian mathematician known as "The Great Geometer." His *Conics,* one of the greatest scientific treatises of the ancient world, built on the work of EUCLID. In it he introduced the terms parabola, ellipse, and hyperbola; he also improved on ARCHIMEDES' approximation of π (see PI).

Apollonius of Rhodes (b.c.295 B.C.) Greek poet and grammarian. He served as librarian of the famous Library of ALEXANDRIA. His romantic epic about the ARGONAUTS, *Argonautica,* is derived from HOMER but noted for its fresh handling of the old stories, original similes, and vivid descriptions of nature.

apoptosis \ˌa-pəp-ˈtō-səs\ *or* **programmed cell death** Mechanism that allows CELLS to self-destruct when stimulated by the appropriate trigger. It may be initiated when a cell is no longer needed, when a cell becomes a threat to the organism's health, or for other reasons. The aberrant inhibition or initiation of apoptosis contributes to many disease processes, including CANCER. Apoptosis is distinguished from necrosis, a form of cell death that results from injury.

a posteriori See A PRIORI

Apostle Any of the 12 disciples chosen by JESUS. They were PETER, JAMES and JOHN (sons of Zebedee), ANDREW, Philip, BARTHOLOMEW, MATTHEW, THOMAS, James (son of Alphaeus), Thaddaeus or Judas (son of James), Simon the Cananaean or Zealot, and JUDAS ISCARIOT. The 12 were privileged to attend Jesus continually and receive his teaching. After the defection and death of Judas Iscariot, Matthias was elected an Apostle. PAUL also claimed the title on the ground that he had seen the Lord and been commissioned by him.

Apostolic succession \ˌa-pə-ˈstä-lik\ In Christianity, the doctrine that BISHOPS represent an uninterrupted line of descent from the APOSTLES of JESUS. This succession gives bishops the right to confirm church members, ordain priests, consecrate other bishops, and rule over the clergy and church members of a diocese. Clement, bishop of Rome, stated the doctrine as early as A.D. 95, and it is accepted by Roman Catholic, Eastern Orthodox, Old Catholic, and several other churches.

apotheosis \ə-ˌpä-thē-ˈō-səs\ Elevation to the status of a god. The term recognizes that some individuals cross the dividing line between human and divine. In ancient GREEK RELIGION, historical figures were sometimes worshiped as gods. Until the end of the republic the Romans accepted only one apotheosis, identifying the god QUIRINUS with ROMULUS. When AUGUSTUS ordered Julius CAESAR recognized as a god, he began a tradition of deifying emperors.

Appalachian Mountains Mountain system, E N. America. Among the oldest mountains on earth, the Appalachians extend almost 2,000 mi (3,200 km) from Newfoundland, Quebec, and New Brunswick southwest to Alabama, and include the WHITE MTNS. in New Hampshire, the GREEN MTNS. in Vermont, the CATSKILL MTNS. in New York, the ALLEGHENY MTNS. in Pennsylvania, the BLUE RIDGE MTNS. in Virginia and N. Carolina, the GREAT SMOKY MTNS. in N. Carolina and Tennessee, and the CUMBERLAND PLATEAU in Tennessee. Their highest peak is Mt. MITCHELL. See also APPALACHIAN NATIONAL SCENIC TRAIL.

Appalachian National Scenic Trail Footpath, APPALACHIAN MTNS. Extending over 2,000 mi (3,200 km) along the crest of the mountains from Maine to Georgia, the trail passes through 14 states, eight national forests, and two national parks. Volunteers maintain the shelters and campsites. Originally established by hikers in the 1930s, it became part of the National Trail System established in 1968.

appeal Resort to a higher court to review the decision of a lower court, or to any court to review the order of an administrative agency. In the U.S., the higher court will review only matters in the record of the original trial; no new evidence can be presented. The U.S. Supreme Court hears some important appellate cases, but appeal usually stops with the U.S. COURTS OF APPEALS.

appeasement Foreign policy of pacifying an aggrieved nation through negotiation in order to prevent war. In the prime example, Britain's Neville CHAMBERLAIN sought to accommodate Fascist Italy's invasion of Ethiopia in 1935 and took no action when Nazi Germany absorbed Austria in 1938. When Adolf HITLER prepared to annex ethnically German portions of Czechoslovakia, Chamberlain negotiated the notorious MUNICH AGREEMENT.

Appel \ˈä-pel\, **Karel** (b.1921) Dutch painter and sculptor. A cofounder of the Cobra group of N European Expressionists, in 1950 he moved to Paris and by the 1960s he had settled in New York. He developed a painting style of expressive abstraction characterized by thick layering of pigment, violent color and brushwork, and crude figures. His figurative sculptures are executed in metal and wood. He painted portraits of jazz musicians and a number of public works, including a mural in the Paris UNESCO building.

appendix *in full* **vermiform appendix** Vestigial hollow tube attached to the LARGE INTESTINE. The human appendix, usually 3-4 in. (8-10 cm) long and less than 0.5 in. (1.3 cm) wide, has no digestive function. Its muscular walls expel their own mucous secretions or any intestinal contents that enter it. Blockage of the opening may cause appendicitis: fluids collect, bacteria propagate, and the appendix becomes distended and inflamed; tissue in the appendix begins to die, and it may burst, causing PERITONITIS. Symptoms may begin with moderate pain in the upper abdomen, about the navel, or all over the abdomen, followed by FEVER, nausea, and vomiting. The LEUKOCYTE count is high (12,000-20,000). Differentiating acute appendicitis from other causes of abdominal pain requires careful examination. Treatment is removal of the appendix (appendectomy).

Appian Way \ˈa-pē-ən\ *Latin* Via Appia. First and most famous of the ancient Roman roads, running from Rome to Campania and S Italy. Begun in 312 B.C. by Appius Claudius Caecus, the road originally ran 132 mi (212 km) to ancient Capua; by 244 B.C. it extended 230 mi (370 km) to the port of Brundisium (Brindisi). Built of smoothly fitted blocks of lava on a heavy stone foundation, the road provided a long-lasting surface for transporting merchandise to these seaports. Remains can be seen today outside Rome.

apple Widely cultivated tree and fruit of the genus *Malus,* in the ROSE family, the most widely cultivated tree fruit. *Malus* species are native to the temperate zones of both hemispheres. Since apples do not breed true, cultivated apples are always grafted. They require well-drained soil, careful pruning, and a rigorous pest-management program for mature trees. Most apples are roundish and some shade of red or yellow. The thousands of varieties fall into three broad classes: cider, cooking, and dessert. Varieties that ripen in late autumn may be stored for as long as a year. The largest producers of apples are the U.S., China, France, Italy, and Turkey. Apples provide vitamins A and C, carbohydrates, and fiber.

Apple Computer, Inc. Microcomputer design and manufacturing company, the first successful PERSONAL-COMPUTER company. It was founded in 1976 by Steven JOBS and Stephen WOZNIAK. The Apple II (1977), with its plastic case and color graphics, earned Apple over $100 million by 1980, the year the company first offered stock to the public. The 1981 introduction of IBM's PC marked the beginning of long-term competition for Apple in the personal-computer market. The Macintosh, introduced in 1984, was the first personal computer to use a GRAPHICAL USER INTERFACE and a MOUSE. The "Mac" initially sold poorly, but eventually it found its niche in the desktop publishing market. Stiff competition from Microsoft's Windows hurt Apple's market share. In 1997 Jobs formed an alliance with Microsoft, and in 1998 he helped introduce the iMac, which quickly became the best-selling of all the Macs.

Appleseed, Johnny *orig.* John Chapman (1774–1845) U.S. pioneer and folk hero. Born in Leominster, Mass., he was trained as a nurseryman and began (c.1800) collecting apple seeds from cider presses in Pennsylvania, then traveled west to the Ohio River valley, planting apple seeds along the way. He tended 1,200 acres of his own orchards and sold or gave away thousands of apple seedlings to pioneers. His kind and generous nature, devout spirituality, affinity for the Indians, and eccentric appearance (including bare feet, a coffee-sack garment and a mush pan for a hat) helped make him a legendary hero.

applied psychology Branch of psychology concerned with solving practical problems of human behavior. Intelligence testing, legal problems, industrial efficiency, motivation, and delinquency were among the first areas of application in the early 20th cent. World Wars I and II fostered work on vocational testing, teaching methods, evaluation of attitudes and morale, performance under stress, propaganda and psychological warfare, and rehabilitation. Other areas include engineering psychology (the study of human–machine relationships), consumer psychology, school psychology, and community psychology.

appliqué See QUILTING

Appomattox Court House \ˌa-pə-ˈma-təks\ Former town, S central Virginia, site of the surrender of Robert E. LEE to Ulysses S. GRANT on April 9, 1865, effectively ending the AMERICAN CIVIL WAR. It became a national historical monument in 1940 and a national historical park in 1954.

apprenticeship Training in an art, trade, or craft under a legal agreement defining the relationship between master and learner and the duration and conditions of their relationship. Known from antiquity, apprenticeship became prominent in medieval Europe with the emergence of the craft GUILDS. The standard apprenticeship lasted seven years. During the Industrial Revolution, in a new kind of apprenticeship, the employer was the factory owner, and the apprentice trained to become a factory worker. The increasing need for semiskilled workers led to the development of vocational and technical schools, especially after World War II. Today in the U.S. some industries, such as the building industry, continue to employ apprenticeship schemes, the trainee advancing by passing exams.

apricot Fruit of the tree *Prunus armeniaca,* in the ROSE family, cultivated generally throughout the temperate regions of the world and used fresh, cooked in pastries, or preserved by canning or drying. Apricot trees have heart-shaped, dark green leaves and white flowers. The fruit is generally similar to the PEACH in shape, but smaller and with little to no ripeness when ripe. Apricots are a good source of vitamin A; dried apricots are an excellent source of iron.

a priori \ˌä-prē-ˈōr-ē, ˌä-prī-ˈōr-ī\ In EPISTEMOLOGY, knowledge that is independent of all particular experiences, as opposed to a posteriori (or empirical) knowledge, which derives from experience. The terms have their origins in the medieval Scholastic debate over Aristotelian concepts (see SCHOLASTICISM). Immanuel KANT initiated their current usage.

apse Semicircular or polygonal termination to the choir, chancel (see CATHEDRAL), or aisle of a public building, first used in pre-Christian Roman architecture. Originally a large niche to hold the statue of a deity in a temple, the apse also appeared in ancient baths and BASILICAS.

Apuleius \ˌa-pə-ˈlā-əs\, **Lucius** (A.D. 124?–after 170?) Roman Platonic philosopher, rhetorician, and author. *The Golden Ass*, a novel of the ribald adventures of a young man changed into an ass, describes ancient manners and is especially valuable for its revelations about ancient religious mysteries. Apuleius' philosophical treatises included three books on PLATO, two of which survive.

Apulia See PUGLIA

Aqaba \ˈä-kə-bə\, **Gulf of** NE arm of the RED SEA penetrating between Saudi Arabia and the SINAI Peninsula. It is 100 mi (160 km) long and 12–17 mi (19–27 km) wide. Its head touches Egypt, Israel, Jordan, and Saudi Arabia. Jordan and Israel created the ports of Aqaba and Elat, respectively, as outlets to the Red Sea and the INDIAN OCEAN.

Aqmola See ASTANA

aquamarine Pale greenish blue or bluish green variety of BERYL, valued as a gemstone. The most common variety of gem beryl, it occurs in PEGMATITES and forms larger and clearer crystals than EMERALD, the dark green variety of beryl. Aquamarine occurs in Brazil, the chief source, and in such other sites as the Ural Mtns., Madagascar, Sri Lanka, India, and Maine, New Hampshire, Connecticut, N. Carolina, and Colorado.

aquarium Receptacle for maintaining aquatic organisms, either freshwater or marine, or a facility in which a collection of aquatic organisms is displayed or studied. The first display aquarium opened in Regent's Park, England, in 1853. Many principal cities now have public aquariums; other aquarium facilities serve as research institutions. Regardless of size—whether a one-gallon jar or a million-gallon tank—aquariums must be constructed with care; many substances nontoxic to humans are toxic to water-breathing animals. The primary requirement for maintaining aquatic organisms is water quality.

aquatint Method of ETCHING that produces finely granulated tonal areas rather than lines, so that finished prints often resemble WATERCOLORS. A copper plate is exposed to acid through a layer of granulated resin or sugar, which yields a finely speckled gray tone when the plate is inked and printed. The tone is controlled by the strength of the acid baths and the exposure time. Aquatint became the most popular method of producing toned prints in the late 18th cent.; its most notable practitioner was Francisco de GOYA. In the 20th cent. the sugar aquatint was employed by Pablo PICASSO, Georges ROUAULT, and André MASSON.

aqueduct Conduit built to carry water from its source to a main distribution point. Ancient Rome's extraordinary aqueduct system brought water to the city from as far as 57 mi (92 km) away. Though a portion utilized the familiar stone arch, most Roman aqueducts were underground conduits of stone or terra-cotta pipe. Modern aqueduct systems employ cast iron or steel. See also WATER-SUPPLY SYSTEM.

aquifer \ˈä-kwə-fər\ Rock layer or sequence that contains water and releases it in appreciable amounts. The rocks contain water-filled pores that, when connected, allow water to flow through their matrix. A confined aquifer is overlain by a rock layer that is mainly impermeable; there probably are few truly confined aquifers. In an unconfined aquifer the upper surface (WATER TABLE) is open to the atmosphere through permeable overlying material.

Aquino \ə-ˈkē-nō\, **(Maria) Corazon** *orig.* Maria Corazon Cojuangco (b.1933) President of the Philippines (1986–92). Born into a politically prominent family, she married Benigno S. Aquino, Jr. (1932–1983), who became the most prominent opponent of Pres. Ferdinand MARCOS. Benigno was assassinated in 1983 on his return from exile, and Corazon ran for president in 1986. Though Marcos was officially reported the winner, he fled following widespread allegations of voting fraud and military support for Aquino. As president, Aquino oversaw a popular new constitution. Over time her popularity declined amid charges of corruption and economic injustice.

Aquinus, St. Thomas See St. THOMAS AQUINAS

Aquitaine Historical region, SW France. It was roughly equivalent to Aquitania, the Roman division of SW Gaul, the area between the PYRENEES and the GARONNE RIVER. Conquered by CLOVIS I in A.D. 507, it was later made a subkingdom by CHARLEMAGNE in the 8th cent., then became a

feudal duchy, which by the 10th cent. controlled much of France south of the LOIRE RIVER. It passed to the Capetian line when ELEANOR OF AQUITAINE married Louis VII (1137); on her second marriage, to HENRY II of England (1152), it passed to the English Plantagenets. Its later history is merged with that of GASCONY and Guienne.

AR-15 See M16 RIFLE

Arab Any member of the ARABIC-speaking peoples of the Middle East and N. Africa. Before the spread of Islam in the 630s, the term referred to the largely nomadic Semitic peoples of the ARABIAN PENINSULA; it came to apply to other peoples of N Africa and W Asia after their acceptance and promotion of Islam. Traditionally, some Arabs are desert nomads (see BEDOUIN), whereas others live by oases and in small, isolated farming villages. While most Arabs are Muslims, some are Christian. The term may also be used in an ethnic or sociolinguistic sense.

Arabian Desert Desert region, ARABIAN PENINSULA. It covers about 900,000 sq mi (2,330,000 sq km), occupying nearly the entire peninsula. It lies largely within Saudi Arabia but extends into Jordan, Iraq, Kuwait, Qatar, the United Arab Emirates, Oman, and Yemen. While sand covers at least one-third of the desert, two water systems, the TIGRIS and EUPHRATES RIVERS in the northeast and the Wadi Hajr in Yemen, flow continually.

Arabian Desert Rub al-Khali sand desert

Arabian horse Earliest improved breed of HORSE, valued for its speed, stamina, beauty, intelligence, and gentleness. Its long history has been obscured by legend, but it was developed in Arabia by the 7th cent. A.D. It is compact and relatively small, with a small head, protruding eyes, wide nostrils, marked withers, and a short back. Its average height is about 15 hands (60 in., or 152 cm), its average weight 800–1,000 lbs (360–450 kg). Gray is its usual color.

Arabian Nights' Entertainment See The THOUSAND AND ONE NIGHTS

Arabian Peninsula or **Arabia** Peninsular region, SW Asia. With its offshore islands, it covers about 1 million sq mi (2.6 million sq km). It is divided among Bahrain, Kuwait, Oman, Qatar, United Arab Emirates, Yemen, and principally Saudi Arabia. Its population (1998) is about 44,000,000. The modern economy is dominated by oil production. Its political consolidation was begun by MUHAMMAD and extended after his death. It was the center of the orthodox caliphate until 661, when the UMAYYAD caliphate, ruling from DAMASCUS, took over. After 1517 much of the region was dominated by the Ottoman Turks, though revolts occurred repeatedly into the 20th cent. See also ARABIAN DESERT.

Arabian Sea NW part of the Indian Ocean, lying between India and the Arabian Peninsula. It has an area of about 1,491,000 sq mi (3,862,000 sq km) and an average depth of 8,970 ft (2,734 m). The Gulf of OMAN connects it with the PERSIAN GULF via the Strait of HORMUZ, while the Gulf of ADEN connects it with the RED SEA via the Strait of Bab el-Mandeb. Chief ports are BOMBAY, KARACHI, and ADEN. The sea was part of the principal trade route between Europe and India for centuries.

Arabic alphabet Script used to write ARABIC and a number of other languages whose speakers are Muslims. The 28-character Arabic alphabet developed from a script used to write ARAMAIC. Because Arabic had more consonants, and diacritical dots were used to distinguish some letters, and these remain a feature of the script. Arabic is written from right to left. The letters denote only consonants, though the sym-

bols for some letters do double duty as vowel letters. Other marks, representing short vowels and double consonants, are normally employed only for the text of the QURAN. Most letters have slightly different forms depending on whether they occur in the beginning, middle, or end of a word. Non-Semitic languages that use the Arabic alphabet include PERSIAN, Pashto, URDU, MALAY, SWAHILI, and HAUSA.

Arabic language SEMITIC LANGUAGE spoken across a broad region of SW Asia and in N. Africa from Egypt and the Sudan west to Morocco and Mauritania. Though Arabic words and proper names are found in ancient Middle Eastern inscriptions, abundant documentation of the language only begins with the rise of ISLAM. Grammarians from the 8th cent. on codified it into the form known as Classical Arabic. In the 19th–20th cent., Classical Arabic was modified to create Modern Standard Arabic, which serves as a LINGUA FRANCA in the Arab world. Spoken Arabic has long diverged from the classical language, and the more than 200 million speakers of today use many dialects, which at their furthest extremes are mutually unintelligible. See also ARABIC ALPHABET.

Arabic literary renaissance 19th-cent. movement to develop a modern Arabic literature, inspired by contacts with the West and a renewed interest in classical Arabic literature. It began in Egypt with Syrian and Lebanese writers who sought the freer environment there. It spread to other Arab countries with the dismemberment of the OTTOMAN EMPIRE after World War I and the coming of independence after World War II. Its success is related to the spread and modernization of education and the emergence of an Arabic press.

Arab–Israeli Wars Wars fought between various Arab countries and Israel between 1948 and 1982. The first war (1948–49) began when Israel declared its independence following the U.N. partition of PALESTINE. Protesting this move, Egypt, Iraq, Jordan, Lebanon, and Syria attacked Israel. The conflict ended with Israel gaining much territory. The 1956 Sinai campaign began after Egypt nationalized the SUEZ CANAL. The 1967 engagement was known as the SIX-DAY WAR. An undeclared war of attrition was fought along the Suez Canal (1969–70) and was ended with the help of U.S. diplomacy. Egypt and Syria made a surprise attack in 1973 (the Yom Kippur War), which resulted in an indecisive exchange of border territories. In 1979 Egypt made peace with Israel. In 1982 Israel invaded Lebanon with the aim of expelling the PALESTINE LIBERATION ORGANIZATION, with which it began peace talks in 1993. See also Yasir ARAFAT, Hafiz al-ASSAD, Menachem BEGIN, David BEN-GURION, CAMP DAVID ACCORDS, Moshe DAYAN, HIZBULLAH, G. A. NASSER, Yitzhak RABIN, Anwar al-SADAT.

Arab League or **League of Arab States** Regional organization formed in 1945 and based in Cairo. It initially included Egypt, Syria, Lebanon, Iraq, Transjordan (now Jordan), Saudi Arabia, and Yemen; today Libya, Sudan, Tunisia, Morocco, Kuwait, Algeria, Bahrain, Oman, Qatar, the United Arab Emirates, Mauritania, Somalia, the PALESTINE LIBERATION ORGANIZATION, and Djibouti are also members. The league's original aims were to coordinate political, cultural, economic, and social programs and to mediate disputes, to which it later added military defense coordination. Members have often split on political issues. See also PAN-ARABISM.

Arachne \ə-ˈrak-nē\ In GREEK MYTHOLOGY, a weaver who challenged ATHENA to a contest. Athena wove a tapestry showing the gods in majesty, while Arachne depicted them in their amorous adventures. Enraged at the perfection of her rival's work, Athena tore it to shreds, whereupon Arachne hanged herself. Out of pity Athena loosened the rope, which became a cobweb, and Arachne became a spider.

arachnid \ə-ˈrak-nid\ Any member of the class Arachnida, primarily carnivorous ARTHROPODS having a well-developed head, hard external skeleton, and four pairs of walking legs. Most species have a segmented body (but see DADDY LONGLEGS); they range in size from the MITE (0.003 in., or 0.08 mm, long) to the 8-in. (21-cm) black SCORPION of Africa. As arachnids grow, they molt several times. Most inject their prey with digestive fluids, then suck the liquefied remains. Arachnids are found worldwide. Some mites and TICKS are parasitic; these can carry serious animal and human diseases. Venomous SPIDERS and scorpions also may pose a danger to humans, but most arachnids are harmless and prey on insect PESTS.

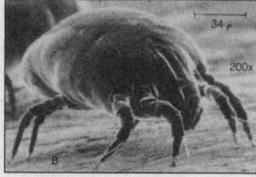

Arachnid Protonymph of the N. American house-dust mite, magnified over 100x

Arafat \ˌar-ə-ˈfat\, **Yasir** orig. Muhammad Abd al-Rauf al-Qudwah al-Husayni (b.1929) Palestinian leader. Born in Jerusalem, he studied engineering at the Univ. of Cairo and served in the Egyptian army during the 1956 war with Israel. That year he cofounded the guerrilla organization FATAH, which became the leading military component of the PALESTINE LIBERATION ORGANIZATION (PLO), which he led from 1969. In 1988 he acknowledged Israel's right to exist, and in 1993 he formally recognized Israel during direct talks regarding land controlled by Israel since the SIX-DAY WAR. In 1994 he shared the Nobel Peace Prize with Yitzhak RABIN and Shimon PERES. In 1996 he became president of the new Palestinian Authority. He was fiercely condemned for his failure to control the wave of Palestinian suicide bombings that began in 2000.

Aragon \ˈar-ə-ˌgän\ Autonomous community (pop., 1996 est.: 1,188,000), NE Spain. It occupies an area of 18,398 sq mi (47,651 sq km); its capital is SARAGOSSA. Mountains, including the PYRENEES, dominate the relief north and south of the EBRO RIVER, which bisects Aragon. Established in 1035 by Ramiro I, the historical kingdom of Aragon grew as land was retaken from the Moors: Saragossa, the capital of the ALMORAVID kingdom, fell to Alfonso I of Aragon in 1118, and the reconquest of present-day Aragon was completed by the late 12th cent. In the 13th–14th cent., it came to rule Sicily, Sardinia, Naples, and Navarre. In the 15th cent. FERDINAND married ISABELLA of Castile, uniting the kingdoms of Aragon and Castile and forming the nucleus of modern Spain.

Aragon \à-rà-ˈgōⁿ\, **Louis** orig. Louis Andrieux (1897–1982) French poet and novelist. He and André BRETON cofounded the Surrealist review *Littérature* in 1919. From 1927 Aragon was increasingly a communist activist and spokesman, which resulted in a break with the Surrealists. His novel *Le monde réel* (4 vols., 1933–44) describes the class struggle of the proletariat. Other works include the huge novel *Les communistes* (6 vols., 1949–51), several novels of veiled autobiography, and poetry expressing patriotism and love for his wife. He was editor of the communist arts weekly *Les lettres françaises* 1953–72.

aragonite \ə-ˈrag-ə-ˌnīt\ A CARBONATE MINERAL, the stable form of calcium carbonate at high pressures. Aragonite is found in recent deposits formed at low temperatures near the surface of the earth, as in caves as stalactites, with ore minerals, in serpentine and other basic rocks, and in sediments. Aragonite is the mineral normally found in pearls, and it occurs in some animal shells. It is polymorphous (same chemical formula but different crystal structure) with CALCITE and vaterite, and, with geologic time, changes to calcite.

Araguaia River \ˌar-ə-ˈgwī-ə\ River, central Brazil. Rising in the Brazilian highlands, it flows north some 1,600 mi (2,620 km) to join the TOCANTINS RIVER at São João do Araguaia. It divides into two channels at Bananal Island, which is about 200 mi (320 km) long and the site of the National Park of Araguaia. The river drains a vast area of interior Brazil.

arahant See ARHAT

Araks River \ä-ˈräks\ or **Aras River** \ä-ˈräs\ River in Turkey, Armenia, and Azerbaijan. It rises in the mountains of Turkish Armenia south of Erzurum and flows east to join the Kura River near its mouth. Since a flood in 1897, a separate distributary of the Araks has also emptied into the Caspian Sea. About 570 mi (915 km) long, it forms the boundary between Armenia and Azerbaijan (north) and Turkey and Iran (south).

Aral Sea Large saltwater lake between KAZAKSTAN and UZBEKISTAN. It once covered 25,659 sq mi (66,457 sq km) and was the fourth-largest inland body of water in the world, but diversion of incoming waters for irrigation has shrunk its surface area by half since 1960, and its volume by 75%. It has a salinity of 10.7%.

Aram \ˈar-əm\ Ancient country, SW Asia. It extended from the Lebanon Mtns. to beyond the EUPHRATES RIVER. It was named after the ARAMAEANS, who invaded Syria and Upper MESOPOTAMIA (c.14th cent. B.C.) and built DAMASCUS. It lends its name to the ARAMAIC LANGUAGE.

Aramaeans \ˌar-ə-ˈmē-ən\ Tribal people that migrated from the Arabian Peninsula to the FERTILE CRESCENT around 1500–1200 B.C. Among them were the biblical matriarchs Leah and Rachel, wives of Jacob. The ARAMAIC LANGUAGE and culture spread through international trade. By 500 B.C., Aramaic had become the universal language of commerce, culture, and government throughout the Fertile Crescent and remained so through the time of JESUS and into the 7th cent. in some areas.

Aramaic language \ˌar-ə-ˈmā-ik\ SEMITIC LANGUAGE, originally spoken by the ancient ARAMAEANS. The earliest Aramaic texts are inscriptions in a Phoenician alphabet found in the N Levant dating from c.850–600 B.C. The period 600–200 B.C. saw a dramatic expansion of Aramaic, leading to the development of a standard form known as Imperial Aramaic. Late (or Classical) Aramaic (c.A.D. 200–1200) has an abundant literature. With the rise of Islam, Arabic rapidly replaced Aramaic as a vernacular in SW Asia. Modern Aramaic (Neo-Aramaic) comprises two main dialects spoken by several hundred thousand people in scattered areas of the Middle East and elsewhere.

Aran Islands \ˈar-ân\ Islands (pop., 1991: 600), Galway Bay, W Ireland. They total about 18 sq mi (47 sq km) in area. Their main town is Kilronan on Inishmore. The islands contain impressive prehistoric and early Christian forts. Liam O'FLAHERTY was born on Inishmore.

Arany \ȯr-ˈȯnⁱ\, **Janos** (1817–1882) Hungarian poet. Considered Hungary's greatest epic poet, his main work is the *Toldi* trilogy (1847–79). Telling the adventures of a 14th-cent. youth of great physical strength, it was embraced by a public craving an accessible national literature. Other works include an epic fragment, *Bolond Istok* (1850; "Stephen the Fool"), and *The Death of King Buda* (1864), the first part of a projected Hun trilogy. The *Oszikek*, written just before he died, poignantly reflects a sense of failure and isolation.

Arapaho \ə-ˈra-pə-ˌhō\ PLAINS INDIAN people who lived along the Platte and Arkansas rivers in the 19th cent. Like other Plains groups, the Arapaho were nomadic, living in TEPEES and depending on the buffalo for subsistence. They were highly religious and practiced the SUN DANCE. Long allied with the CHEYENNE, they fought with them against Col. G. A. CUSTER at LITTLE BIGHORN in 1876. Today about 2,000 Arapaho live in Wyoming and another 3,000 Arapaho-Cheyenne in Oklahoma.

arap Moi, Daniel See Daniel arap MOI

Ararat \ˈar-ə-ˌrat\, **Mt.** Mountain, E Turkey. It has two peaks, Great Ararat, at almost 17,000 ft (5,300 m) the highest in Turkey, and Little Ararat, almost 13,000 ft (4,000 m). Ararat is traditionally cited as the mountain where Noah's ark came to rest at the end of the biblical flood. Until 1840 a village existed on its slopes where Noah is said to have built an altar.

Aras River See ARAKS RIVER

Araucanians \ə-ˌraȯ-ˈkä-nē-ənz\ S. American Indians now living near the Bío Bío River in S central Chile. When the Spanish CONQUISTADORES arrived in Chile, they encountered three Araucanian populations: the Picunche, the Huilliche, and the Mapuche. The first two were soon assimilated, but the Mapuche resisted Spanish and Chilean control for 350 years. Finally subdued in the late 19th cent., they were settled on reservations, but now live independently.

Arawak \ˈar-ə-ˌwäk\ American Indians of the Greater Antilles and S. America, including the TAINO. The Arawak were apparently the people who Christopher COLUMBUS first encountered in 1492. The S. American Arawak inhab-

ited N and W areas of the Amazon basin, where they farmed, hunted, and fished. The Campa Arawak lived in the foothills of the Andes.

Arawakan languages \ˌar-ə-ˈwä-kən\ *or* **Maipuran languages** \mī-ˈpü-rən\ Largest family of American Indian languages, comprising an estimated 65 known languages, of which at least 30 are now extinct. They occur all over the N half of S. America. Taino, a now extinct Arawakan language of the Antilles, was the first American Indian language encountered by Europeans. Arawakan languages spoken today include Guajiro in Colombia and Venezuela; Amuesha and the Campa languages in Peru; and Terena in Brazil.

Arbenz (Guzmán) \ˈär-bāns\, **Jacobo** (1913–1971) Soldier and president of Guatemala (1951–54). Arbenz joined the leftist army officers who overthrew the dictator Jorge Ubico (1878–1946) in 1944. Elected president in 1951, he focused on LAND REFORM. His efforts to expropriate UNITED FRUIT CO. land and his alleged Communist links led to an invasion sponsored by the U.S. CENTRAL INTELLIGENCE AGENCY. When the army refused to defend Arbenz, he went into exile, and the CIA installed Col. Carlos Castillo Armas (1914–1957) as president.

Arber, Werner (b.1929) Swiss microbiologist. He shared a 1978 Nobel Prize with Daniel Nathans (1928-1997) and Hamilton O. SMITH for the discovery and use of restriction enzymes that break the giant molecules of DNA into pieces small enough to be separated for individual study but large enough to retain meaningful amounts of genetic information. He also observed that BACTERIOPHAGES cause mutation in their bacterial hosts and undergo hereditary mutations themselves.

arbitrage \ˈär-bə-ˌträzh\ Business operation involving the purchase of foreign CURRENCY, gold, financial SECURITIES, or commodities in one market and their almost simultaneous sale in another market, in order to profit from price differentials. In so-called risk arbitrage, one seeks to buy STOCK in companies targeted for takeover and sell it at a profit when the takeover is announced and the company's stock rises in value.

arbitration Process of resolving a dispute or a grievance outside the court system by presenting it to an impartial third party or panel for a decision. Both sides usually must agree in advance as to the choice of arbitrator and must certify that they will abide by the arbitrator's decision. It is commonly used in commercial, labor-management, and international disputes. The procedures differ from those used in the courts, especially regarding burden of proof and presentation of evidence. Arbitration avoids costly litigation and offers a relatively speedy resolution as well as privacy for the disputants, but setting guidelines is difficult. See also MEDIATION.

arboretum \ˌär-bə-ˈrē-təm\ Place where trees, shrubs, and sometimes herbaceous plants are cultivated for scientific and educational purposes. An arboretum may be a collection in its own right or a part of a botanical garden. The U.S. National Arboretum is in Washington, D.C.

arbovirus \ˌär-bə-ˈvī-rəs\ Any of a large group of viruses that develop in arthropods (chiefly mosquitoes and ticks), in which they cause no apparent harm. Arboviruses are transmitted by bites to vertebrate hosts, in which they establish infections and complete their growth cycle; they include the agents responsible for YELLOW FEVER and equine ENCEPHALITIS.

Arbus, Diane *orig.* Diane Nemerov (1923–1971) U.S. photographer. Born in New York City, the sister of Howard NEMEROV, she worked with her husband, Allan Arbus, as a fashion photographer in the 1950s, and published her first photo essay, for *Esquire*, in 1960. She is best known for her striking photographs of the unusual and the extraordinary, including nudists, sideshow freaks, inmates of mental hospitals, and transvestites. Her suicide followed years of increasing depression.

Arbuthnot \är-ˈbəth-nət\, **John** (1667–1735) Scottish mathematician, physician, and satirist. Among his satires was a political allegory, *The History of John Bull* (1712), that established John Bull as a personification of England. A founding member of the famous Scriblerus Club, which aimed to ridicule bad literature and false learning, he was also chief contributor to the *Memoirs of Martinus Scriblerus* (1713–14), a mocking exposure of pedantry.

arbutus \är-ˈbyü-təs\ Any of about 14 species (genus *Arbutus*) of broad-leaved EVERGREEN shrubs or trees, in the HEATH FAMILY. Native to S Europe and W N. America, they are characterized by loosely clustered white or pink flowers and red or orange berries. Some are cultivated as ornamentals. The trailing arbutus belongs to the genus *Epigaea*.

Arcadia Ancient country, central PELOPONNESE, Greece. Mountainous and landlocked, its isolation and its pastoral character partly explain why it was represented as a paradise in Greek and Roman bucolic poetry. It was the scene of conflict during the War of GREEK INDEPENDENCE (1821–29). The modern Greek department of Arkadhía is nearly coextensive with the ancient country.

Arcadian League Confederation of ancient Greek city-states of Arcadia. Arcadian towns had been forced to ally with SPARTA by 550 B.C., and most remained faithful to Sparta during the PELOPONNESIAN WAR (431–404 B.C.). In an effort to contain Sparta, EPAMINONDAS of Thebes founded MEGALOPOLIS in 371–368 B.C. as the seat of the Arcadian League. The League united the Arcadians for a few decades until internal discord crippled their confederation.

Arcaro, Eddie (*orig.* George Edward) (1916–1997) U.S. jockey. Born in Cincinnati, he became the first jockey to ride five KENTUCKY DERBY winners (1938, 1941, 1945, 1948, 1952) and the first to ride two TRIPLE CROWN champions. In 31 years of riding Thoroughbreds (1931–61), he won 549 stakes events and 4,779 races.

Arc de Triomphe \ˈärk-də-trī-ˈōⁿf\ Largest TRIUMPHAL ARCH in the world. A masterpiece of Romantic classicism, it stands at the W terminus of the CHAMPS-ÉLYSÉES. Initiated by NAPOLEON, designed by J. F. T. CHALGRIN, and constructed 1806–36, this monument to Napoleon's military victories is 164 ft (50 m) high and 148 ft (45 m) wide. Decorative relief sculptures cover its surfaces.

arc furnace Type of electric furnace in which heat is generated by an arc between carbon ELECTRODES above the surface of the material being heated. William SIEMENS first demonstrated the arc furnace in 1879 at the Paris Exposition by melting iron in crucibles; horizontally placed carbon electrodes produced an electric arc above the container of metal. Modern furnaces range in heat size from a few tons up to 400 tons (360 metric tons), and the arcs strike directly into the metal bath from vertically positioned, graphite electrodes to remelt scrap steel or refine briquettes of direct-reduced iron ore.

arch Curved structure that spans the opening between two piers or columns and supports loads from above. The masonry arch provides the stepping stone from the POST-AND-BEAM SYSTEM to the evolution of the VAULT, and was first widely used by the Romans. Its construction depends on a series of wedge-shaped blocks (voussoirs) set side by side in a semicircular curve or along two intersecting arcs (as in a pointed arch). The central voussoir is called the keystone, and the two points where the arch rests on its supports are known as the spring points. An arch can carry a much greater load than a horizontal beam of the same size and material, because downward pressure forces the voussoirs together instead of apart. The resulting outward thrust must be resisted by the arch's supports.

archaebacteria \ˌär-kē-ˌbak-ˈtir-ē-ə\ Group of BACTERIA whose members differ from the EUBACTERIA in certain physical, physiological, and genetic features (e.g., cell-wall components). Archaebacteria may be aquatic or terrestrial, and exhibit a diversity of shapes; they survive in various extreme environments, including very hot or salty ones. Some require oxygen; some do not. Some produce methane; others depend on sulfur for their metabolism.

archaeology Scientific study of material remains (including fossil relics, artifacts, and monuments) of past human life and activities. Archaeological investigations are a principal source of our knowledge of prehistoric, ancient, and extinct cultures. The field emerged as an academic discipline in the late 19th cent. Among the archaeologist's principal activities are the locating, surveying, and mapping of sites and

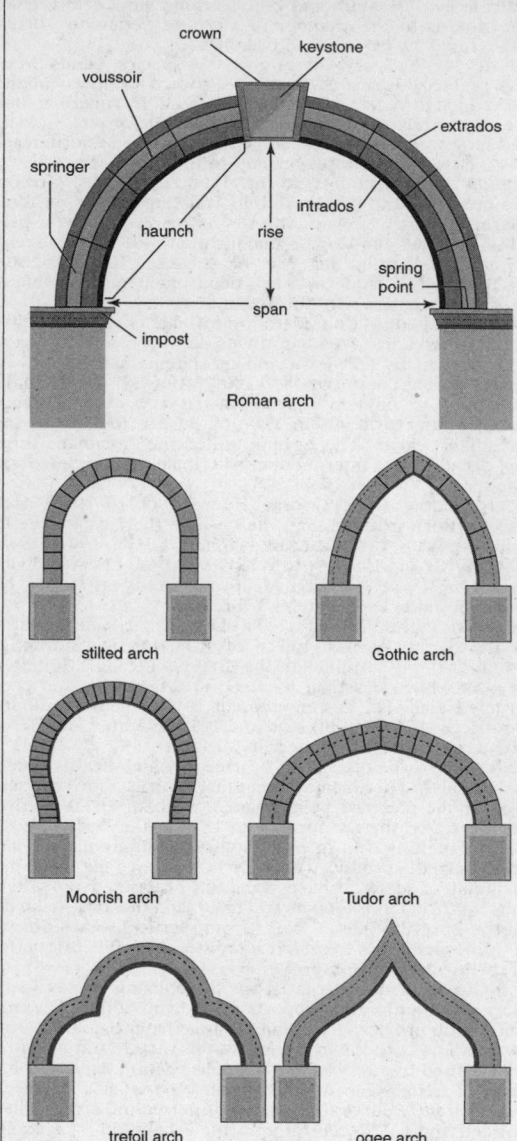

Roman arch

stilted arch Gothic arch

Moorish arch Tudor arch

trefoil arch ogee arch

Arch The arch supports a vertical load primarily by axial compression of its wedge-shaped voussoirs. As shown on the Roman arch, the first voussoir, or springer, rests on the impost, at the top of the abutment or pier. The haunch, rising from the impost to the crown (highest point), is defined by the inner curve, or intrados, and outer curve, or extrados. The Roman arch, with its semicircular intrados, has a rise exactly half the width of the span. Below it are shown examples of the curved arch (left) and the pointed arch (right). The stilted arch has vertical sides. A Moorish arch widens above the spring points. The trefoil arch's intrados has three indentations, or foils. A Gothic arch is a pointed arch usually having two haunches of equal radii of curvature. A Tudor arch has greater curvature near the springers than near the point. Each haunch of the ogee arch consists of a double curve.

the EXCAVATION, classification, DATING, and interpretation of materials to place them in historical context. See also AN-THROPOLOGY, STONE-TOOL INDUSTRY.

archaeopteryx \ar-kē-'äp-tə-riks\ Oldest known fossil animal that is generally accepted as a bird. It flourished during the Late JURASSIC PERIOD (163–144 million years ago). It ranged in size from as small as a blue jay to as large as a chicken. It had well-developed wings, a birdlike skull, and, like THEROPOD dinosaurs, well-developed teeth and a long tail.

Archangel See ARKHANGELSK

archbishop In Christianity, a BISHOP who has jurisdiction, but not superiority, over the other bishops in a province. Introduced as an honorary title in the Eastern churches in the 4th cent., the office did not become common in Western churches until the 9th cent. It is now most widely used in the Roman Catholic and Eastern Orthodox churches. The Church of England has archbishops of Canterbury and York.

Archean eon or **Archaean eon** \är-'kē-ən\ Earliest eon of geologic history. The Archean begins with the formation of the earth's CRUST about 3.8 billion years ago and extends to about 2.5 billion years ago, or the start of the PROTEROZOIC EON. The earliest and most primitive forms of life (BACTERIA and CYANOBACTERIA) originated in the middle of the Archean (its alternative name, Archeozoic, means "ancient life"). See table at GEOLOGIC TIME.

archer fish Any of five species (family Toxotidae) of Indo-Pacific fishes noted for their ability to knock their insect prey off overhanging vegetation by shooting it with drops of water expelled from their mouth. Archer fishes have deep, flat bodies. The head is pointed, and the mouth is large. Different species are spotted or vertically banded with black. They live in both fresh and salt water, usually near the surface. One well-known species *(Toxotes jaculator,* or *jaculatrix)* grows to about 7 in. (18 cm) long.

archery Sport of shooting with BOW AND ARROW. As the bow began to be replaced by the gun as the principal weapon of warfare and the hunt in the 16th cent., it increasingly became a sporting device. Competitions including target-shooting were held at the Olympic Games in the early 20th cent., but were then suspended until 1972. Other varieties of archery include field archery (a simulation of hunting) and flight shooting (a distance event).

Arches National Park Preserve, E Utah. Located on the COLORADO RIVER north of Moab, it was established as a national park in 1971. Its area is 115 sq mi (298 sq km). Its red limestone has been eroded into unusual shapes, including Devils Garden, site of Landscape Arch, at 291 ft (89 m) the longest natural rock bridge in the world.

archetype \'är-ki-ˌtīp\ Image, character, or pattern of events that recurs in literature and thought consistently enough to be considered universal. Literary critics adopted the term from Carl JUNG's theory of the collective UNCONSCIOUS. Originating in pre-logical thought, archetypes are held to evoke startlingly similar feelings in everyone. Archetypal symbols include the snake, whale, eagle, and vulture. An archetypal theme is the passage from innocence to experience; archetypal characters include the blood brother, rebel, and wise grandparent.

Archimedean screw \ˌär-kə-'mēd-ē-ən\ Machine for raising water, said to have been invented by ARCHIMEDES for removing water from the hold of a large ship. One form consists of a circular pipe enclosing a helix and inclined at an angle of about 45°, with its lower end dipped in the water; rotation of the device lifts the water in the pipe.

Archimedes \ˌär-kə-'mē-ˌdēz\ (c.290–212 B.C.) Legendary Greek inventor and mathematician. His principal discoveries were the Archimedes screw (an ingenious device for raising water) and ARCHIMEDES' PRINCIPLE. His mathematical proofs show boldly original thought and impeccable rigor. His approximation of π (see PI) was not improved on until after the Middle Ages, and translations of his works were important influences on 9th-cent. Arab and 16th- and 17th-cent. European mathematicians. In his native city, Syracuse, he was known as a genius at devising siege and countersiege weapons. He was killed by a Roman soldier during the storming of the city.

Archimedes' principle Law of buoyancy, discovered by ARCHIMEDES, which states that any object submerged in a fluid at rest is acted on by an upward, or buoyant, FORCE. The magnitude of this force is equal to the WEIGHT of the fluid displaced by the object. The volume of fluid displaced is equal to the volume of the portion of the object submerged.

Archipenko \ˌär-kə-ˈpeŋ-kō\, **Alexander** (1887–1964) Ukrainian-U.S. sculptor and painter. In 1908 he moved to Paris and soon became active in the Cubist movement. His abstract sculptures reduced the human figure to geometrical forms with holes and concavities, producing contrasting solids and voids, which revolutionized modern sculpture. From 1923 he worked and taught in New York City.

archives Repository for an organized body of records produced or received by an institution in the course of its affairs and preserved by it or its successors. The modern type of archives dates from the late 18th cent., when national and departmental archives were established in France. In the U.S. the National Archives was established in 1934 to house retired federal records; the Federal Records Act of 1950 set up regional repositories. Each state also has an archival agency. Archivists in the 20th cent. increasingly handled computer-kept records and those of nongovernment institutions and individuals.

Archon \ˈär-ˌkän\ In GNOSTICISM, any of various world-governing powers created by the DEMIURGE. Because the Gnostics regarded the material world as evil, Archons were considered forces of evil who had imprisoned the divine spark of human souls in material creation. Seven or 12 in number, they were identified with the seven planets of antiquity or the 12 signs of the ZODIAC. The knowledge sent from the realms of divine light through Jesus enabled Gnostic initiates to transcend the spheres of the Archons.

archon In ancient Greece, the chief magistrate or magistrates in a city-state, from the Archaic period onward. In ATHENS, archons headed the BOULE and ECCLESIA, commanded troops, presided over legal cases involving foreigners, headed state religion, and handled various judicial matters. At first only elected aristocrats could serve, and their term was for life; later, terms were limited to a year. Archons were chosen by a combination of election and lot. In the 5th cent. B.C., the archons' authority declined as elected generals took most of their powers.

archosaur \ˈär-kə-ˌsȯr\ Any of the various advanced REPTILES in the subclass Archosauria ("ruling reptiles"), including all thecodonts, PTEROSAURS, DINOSAURS, bird ancestors, and crocodilians, the only living order. Early archosaurs appeared just before the TRIASSIC PERIOD (248–208 million years ago). All early archosaurs possessed an ankle specialization that aided in upright posture. The teeth of archosaurs were (and are) set not in a groove, but in sockets.

Archytas \är-ˈkī-təs\ (c.430–350 B.C.) Greek scientist, philosopher, and Pythagorean mathematician, sometimes called the founder of mathematical mechanics. PLATO, a close friend, made use of his work in mathematics, and EUCLID probably borrowed from him for the eighth book of his *Elements*. He served seven years as commander in chief of his city, Tarentum.

Arcimboldo \ˌär-chēm-ˈbōl-dō\, **Giuseppe** (1527?–1593) Italian painter. He began his career as a painter and designer of stained-glass windows for Milan Cathedral. In 1562 he moved to Prague and became court painter to the emperors Ferdinand I and Rudolf II, also painting scenery for the court theater. He is known for his eccentric and grotesque symbolical compositions of fruits, vegetables, animals, landscapes, and implements arranged into human forms. The style was regarded as being in poor taste until the Surrealists revived the art of visual punning in the 1920s.

Arctic Archipelago Group of Canadian islands, Arctic Ocean. They lie north of the Canadian mainland and have an area of about 550,000 sq mi (1,424,500 sq km). The archipelago includes Prince of Wales, Devon, BAFFIN, ELLESMERE, VICTORIA, and BANKS ISLANDS.

Arctic Circle Parallel of latitude approximately 66.5° north of the equator. It marks the S limit of the area within which, for one day or more each year, the sun does not set or rise. The length of continuous day or night increases northward from the Arctic Circle, mounting to six months at the NORTH POLE.

Arctic fox Northern FOX (*Alopex lagopus*) found throughout the Arctic. Its short, rounded ears and short muzzle reduce its exposure to cold, and it has fur-covered soles. It is 20–24 in. (50–60 cm) long (excluding the 12-in, or 30-cm, tail) and weighs 7–17 lbs (3–8 kg). An individual fox may change color from grayish brown to white to gray-blue. It dwells in burrows and feeds on any available animal or vegetable material.

Arctic National Park, Gates of the See GATES OF THE ARCTIC NATIONAL PARK

Arctic Ocean Ocean centering approximately on the NORTH POLE. Smallest of the world's oceans, it is surrounded by the landmasses of Eurasia and N. America, and is distinguished

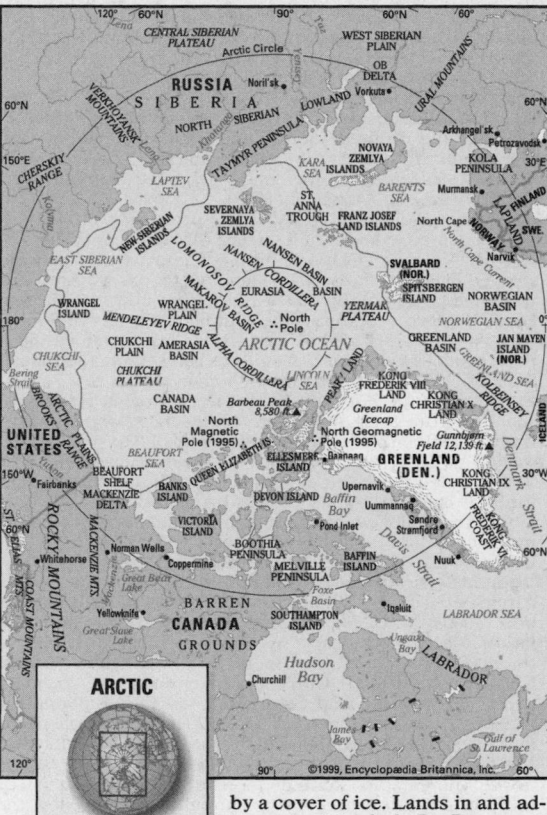

by a cover of ice. Lands in and adjacent to it include Pt. Barrow in Alaska, the ARCTIC ARCHIPELAGO, two-thirds of GREENLAND, SVALBARD, FRANZ JOSEF LAND, and N SIBERIA. The ocean covers about 5,427,000 sq mi (14,056,000 sq km) and reaches a maximum depth of about 18,000 ft (5,500 m). Various sections are known by specific names, including the Chukchi, Greenland, Kara, BARENTS, and BEAUFORT SEAS. Areas within the ARCTIC CIRCLE were first explored in the 9th–12th cent. by the Norse. Martin FROBISHER discovered the S part of BAFFIN ISLAND (1576–78), and Henry HUDSON navigated the E coast of HUDSON BAY (1610–11). Later explorers included Roald AMUNDSEN, Fridtjof NANSEN, Robert PEARY, and Richard BYRD.

Arctic tern TERN species (*Sterna paradisaea*) that makes the longest annual migration of any bird. It breeds in the southerly reaches of the Arctic and winters in the Antarctic, making its migration a round-trip of nearly 22,000 mi (over 35,000 km). It is white with a black cap and grayish wings.

Ardennes \är-'den\ *or* **Forest of Ardennes** Wooded plateau region, NW Europe. It covers over 3,860 sq mi (10,000 sq km) and includes parts of Belgium, Luxembourg, and the MEUSE RIVER valley of France; its average height is about 1,600 ft (488 m). Half of it is covered with forests. It lies within the populous PARIS–BRUSSELS–COLOGNE triangle. The area was the scene of severe fighting in 1914, 1918, and 1944 (see Battle of the BULGE).

Arecibo Observatory \,ar-ə-'sē-bō\ Astronomical OBSERVATORY near Arecibo, Puerto Rico, site of the world's largest single-unit RADIO TELESCOPE (as opposed to multiple telescope arrays such as the VERY LARGE ARRAY). The telescope dish, 1,000 ft (300 m) across, is built into a valley; celestial sources are tracked by moving secondary structures about 500 ft (150 m) above it. The observatory has produced detailed radar maps of Venus and near-earth asteroids, made detailed studies of the ionosphere, and contributed to studies of PULSARS and hydrogen gas in galaxies.

Arendt \ə-'rent, 'ä-rənt\, **Hannah** (1906–1975) German-U.S. political theorist. She obtained her doctorate from the Univ. of Heidelberg. Forced to flee the Nazis in 1933, she settled in Paris, then fled again, to New York, in 1941. In her major work, *Origins of Totalitarianism* (1951), she related totalitarianism to 19th-cent. anti-Semitism, imperialism, and the disintegration of the traditional nation-state. She taught at the Univ. of Chicago and the New School for Social Research. Her other books included the controversial *Eichmann in Jerusalem* (1963).

Arequipa \,ä-rā-'kē-pä\ City (pop., 1998 est.: 710,000), S Peru. Located at an altitude of 7,557 ft (2,303 m) at the foot of Misti Volcano (19,031 ft, or 5,801 m), it was largely destroyed by an earthquake in 1868. For the INCAS, Arequipa was an important point on the route from CUZCO to the seacoast. Modern Arequipa is the commercial center of S Peru.

Ares \'ar-ēz\ Greek god of war. Unlike his Roman counterpart, MARS, his worship was not extensive. From the time of HOMER, he was one of the Olympian deities, the son of ZEUS and HERA, but disliked by the other gods. He was associated from early times with APHRODITE, who was portrayed as either his legitimate wife or his lover.

Aretino \,ä-rā-'tē-nō\, **Pietro** (1492–1556) Italian poet, prose writer, and dramatist. Celebrated throughout Europe in his time for insolent literary attacks on the powerful, his bold letters and dialogues are of great historical interest. His dramas include five comedies and a tragedy, *Orazia* (1546), perhaps the best 16th-cent. Italian tragedy.

Argentina *officially* **Argentine Republic** Federal republic, S. America. Area: 1,072,156 sq mi (2,776,884 sq km). Population (2000): 37,032,000. Capital: BUENOS AIRES. The population is largely ethnically Spanish, with other European influences. Language: Spanish (official). Religion: Roman Catholicism (official). Currency: Argentine peso. Argentina can be divided into four general regions: the NE plains, the PAMPAS, PATAGONIA, and the ANDES. The NE plains in the northeast are divided by the PARANÁ RIVER into Mesopotamia to the east and GRAN CHACO to the west and north. The Pampas, south and west of the Paraná, is one of the world's most productive agricultural areas and the country's most populous region. Patagonia lies south of the Colorado River. The Argentine Andes include the continent's highest peak, Mt. ACONCAGUA. Argentina's hydrology is dominated by the Paraná, URUGUAY, and PILCOMAYO RIVERS that drain into the Río de la PLATA. Argentina has a developing economy based largely on manufacturing and agriculture; it is Latin America's largest exporter of beef and beef products. It is a republic with two legislative houses; its head of state and government is the president. Little is known of the indigenous population before the Europeans' arrival. The area was explored for Spain by Sebastian Cabot 1526–30; by 1580, ASUNCIÓN, Santa Fe, and Buenos Aires had been settled. At first attached to the viceroyalty of PERU (1620), it was later included with regions of modern Uruguay, Paraguay, and Bolivia in the viceroyalty of La Plata, or Buenos Aires (1776). With the establishment of the United Provinces of the Plate River in 1816, Argentina achieved its independence from Spain, but its boundaries were not set until the early 20th cent. In 1943 the government was overthrown by the military; Col. Juan

©1999, Encyclopædia Britannica, Inc.

ARGENTINA

Scale 1: 40,101,000

0   200   400 mi
0   300   600 km

PERÓN took control in 1946. He in turn was overthrown in 1955. He returned in 1973 after two decades of turmoil. His second wife, Isabel, became president on his death in 1974, but lost power after a military coup in 1976. The military government tried to take the FALKLAND ISLANDS in 1982 but was defeated by the British, with the result that the government returned to civilian rule in 1983. The government of Raúl Alfonsín (b.1926/27) worked to end the human-rights abuses that characterized the former regimes. Hyperinflation led to public riots. His Peronist successor, Carlos MENEM (1989–99) was linked to an arms scandal. Argentina continued to struggle with recession and debt surpassing half its annual economic output.

Argerich \'är-ger-ich\, **Martha** (b.1941) Argentine pianist. A prodigy, she began concertizing before she was 10. She won the Busoni and Geneva competitions at 16, and the Chopin competition in 1965. The exceptionally brilliant technique, emotional depth, and élan displayed in the Romantic works in which she specializes have won her perhaps the most enthusiastic international following of any pianist in the world.

argon Chemical ELEMENT, chemical symbol Ar, atomic number 18, the most abundant NOBLE GAS on earth and the one most used in industry. It constitutes about 1% of air and is obtained by DISTILLATION of liquid air. Argon provides an inert gas shield in welding, in special bulbs and lasers, in Geiger counters, and in the production of certain metals. Because it is formed by decay of naturally occurring radioactive POTASSIUM, it can be used to date samples over 100,000 years old.

argon-argon dating See POTASSIUM-ARGON DATING

Argonauts In Greek legend, a band of 50 heroes who went with JASON in the ship *Argo* to retrieve the Golden Fleece from the grove of ARES at Colchis. They included such figures as HERACLES, ORPHEUS, and THESEUS. They had many adventures before arriving at Colchis, from which they were eventually forced to flee, pursued by MEDEA's father, Aeëtes.

Árgos Ancient city-state, NE PELOPONNESE, Greece. Under the Argive king Pheidon, it was the dominant city-state in the PELOPONNESE in the 7th cent. B.C. until the rise of SPARTA. Árgos joined the ACHAEAN LEAGUE in 229 B.C., later came under Roman rule, flourished in Byzantine times, and in the 16th cent. fell to the OTTOMAN EMPIRE. During the War of GREEK INDEPENDENCE (1821–29), the first free Greek Parliament was convened at Árgos. The modern town (pop., 1991 est.: 22,000) is an agricultural center.

arhat \'är-hət\ *or* **arahant** \'a-rə-hant\ In BUDDHISM, one who has gained insight into the true nature of existence, has achieved NIRVANA, and will not be reborn again. THERAVADA Buddhism regards becoming an arhat as the goal of spiritual progress. MAHAYANA Buddhism criticizes the goal of becoming an arhat and considers becoming a BODHISATTVA to be a higher goal, one of the fundamental differences between Theravada and Mahayana Buddhism.

Århus *or* **Aarhus** \'òr-ˌhüs\ Seaport (pop., 1999 est.: 283,000), E Jutland, Denmark. It became a bishopric in A.D. 948 and, with its many religious institutions, prospered during the Middle Ages. In modern times, industrialization and harbor expansion have made it Denmark's second-largest city.

aria Solo song with instrumental accompaniment in OPERA, CANTATA, or ORATORIO. The strophic or stanzaic aria, in which each new stanza might represent a melodic variation on the first, appeared in opera in Claudio MONTEVERDI's *Orfeo* (1607) and was widely used for decades. The standard early aria form (c.1650–1775) was the da capo aria, in which the opening melody and text are repeated after an intervening section (often in a different key, tempo, and meter); the return of the first section was often virtuosically embellished by the singer. Comic operas never limited themselves to da capo form. Even in serious opera, from around 1750 a variety of forms were used; Gioacchino ROSSINI and others often expanded the aria into a complete musical scene in which two or more conflicting emotions were expressed. Richard WAGNER's operas largely abandoned the aria in favor of a continuous musical texture, but arias have never ceased to be written.

Ariadne \ˌar-ē-'ad-nē\ In GREEK MYTHOLOGY, the daughter of King MINOS of Crete. She fell in love with THESEUS, who had promised to slay the MINOTAUR confined in Minos's Labyrinth. She gave Theseus a ball of thread or glittering jewels that enabled him to mark his path and thus emerge after killing the monster. Endings to the legend vary. In one, Theseus abandons Ariadne and she hangs herself; in others, he carries her to Naxos, where she either dies or marries the god DIONYSUS.

Arianism Christian HERESY that declared JESUS to be not truly divine but a created being. According to the Alexandrian presbyter ARIUS (4th cent.), God alone is immutable and self-existent, and the Son is not God, but a creature with a beginning. The Council of Nicaea (A.D. 325) condemned Arius and declared the Son to be "of one substance with the father." The Council of CONSTANTINOPLE (381) approved the NICENE CREED and proscribed Arianism. Similar beliefs are held today by the JEHOVAH'S WITNESSES and some adherents of UNITARIANISM.

Arias Sánchez \ˈär-ē-əs-ˈsán-chəs\, **Oscar** (b.1941) President of Costa Rica (1986–90). Arias worked for the moderate socialist National Liberation Party from the 1960s. He became president at a time when Central America was torn by civil war. His 1987 Central American peace plan, signed by the leaders of El Salvador, Guatemala, Honduras, and Nicaragua, provided for cease-fires, free elections, and amnesty. He was awarded the 1987 Nobel Peace Prize.

Arion \ə-ˈrī-ən\ Semilegendary Greek poet and musician. A native of LESBOS, he is identified as the inventor of the DITHYRAMB. He was sailing homeward after a performing tour when the sailors decided to kill him and steal his wealth. After singing a dirge for himself, he jumped overboard, but a dolphin charmed by his music carried him to shore. Arion's lyre and the dolphin were placed in the heavens as the constellations Lyra and Delphinus.

Ariosto \ˌär-ē-ˈò-stō\, **Ludovico** (1474–1533) Italian poet. His highly influential epic poem *Orlando Furioso* (1516) is regarded as the finest literary expression of the Italian Renaissance. His five comic plays based on Latin classics but inspired by contemporary life were among the first of a type that would long characterize European comedy. He also wrote seven satires modeled on HORACE.

Aristide \ˌar-i-ˈstēd\, **Jean-Bertrand** (b.1953) First president of Haiti (1991, 1994–96, 2001–) elected in free democratic elections. A priest, he aligned himself with the poor and courageously opposed the harsh regime of Jean-Claude Duvalier, son of François DUVALIER. In 1990 progressive-center forces united behind Aristide and swept him into power. He initiated dramatic reforms but was soon ousted in a military coup. Though restored to office in 1994 with the help of U.S. occupying troops, he received little aid to solve his country's ills. Constitutionally prohibited from a consecutive second term, he stepped down in 1996 but has remained Haiti's most potent political figure. In 2000 he was reelected president amid charges of electoral fraud.

Aristides the Just (5th cent. B.C.) Athenian statesman and general. He helped defeat the Persians at the battles of SALAMIS (480) and PLATAEA (479). In 478 he helped Sparta's E allies form the DELIAN LEAGUE; based on Athenian naval power and the trust Aristides inspired, the league effectively became the Athenian empire.

aristocracy \ˌar-ə-ˈstä-krə-sē\ Originally, leadership by a small privileged class or a minority thought to be best qualified to lead. PLATO and ARISTOTLE considered aristocrats to be those who were morally and intellectually superior, and therefore fit to govern in the interests of the people. The term has come to mean the upper layer of a stratified group. Many European societies stratified their aristocratic classes by formally titling their members, thereby making the term roughly synonymous with nobility.

Aristophanes \ˌar-ə-ˈstä-fə-ˌnēz\ (c.450–388? B.C.) Greek playwright. An Athenian, he began his career as a comic dramatist in 427 B.C. He wrote about 40 plays, of which 11 survive, including *The Clouds* (423 B.C.), *The Wasps* (422), *The Birds* (414), *Lysistrata* (411), and *The Frogs* (405). Most of the plays typify the Old Comedy, in which mime, chorus, and burlesque were important features. His satire, wit, and merciless topical commentary made him the greatest comic dramatist of ancient Greece.

Aristotle (384–322 B.C.) Greek philosopher and scientist. Son of the court physician to ALEXANDER THE GREAT's grandfather, he became a student of PLATO in Athens and taught at Plato's Academy for 20 years. He went back to Macedonia about 342 to tutor the young Alexander, then returned to Athens in 335 to found his own school, the Lyceum. Aristotle distinguished his philosophy from Plato's by declaring that the assumption of the existence of a separate realm of transcendent Ideas (see FORM) is unnecessary and that the world of perceived things is the real world. His major surviving works include the *Organon*, *De Anima, Physics, Metaphysics, Nicomachean Ethics, Eudemian Ethics, Magna Moralia, Politics, Rhetoric*, and *Poetics*. Aristotle divides philosophical topics into

Aristotle Marble bust, from a Greek original, late 4th cent. B.C.

ETHICS, PHYSICS, and LOGIC. To him, logic was required for the study of every other topic. He postulated an unmoved mover (God) as a necessary element of physics. In ethics, he argued that "good" lies in fulfilling one's purpose or function, a view that came to be known as TELEOLOGY. With Plato, Aristotle is considered a founder of Western philosophy, and his scientific works exerted a vast influence on later Western science.

arithmetic Branch of mathematics that deals with the properties of NUMBERS and ways of combining them through addition, subtraction, multiplication, and division. Initially, it dealt only with the counting numbers, but its definition has broadened to include not only RATIONAL NUMBERS but also IRRATIONAL and COMPLEX NUMBERS. Of primary importance in arithmetic is the establishment of the order of operations—multiplication and division before addition and subtraction—and the properties of the operations. In multiplication and addition, for example, order does not matter (the COMMUTATIVE LAW), and grouping is arbitrary (the ASSOCIATIVE LAW). Subtraction and division do not share these properties.

Arius \'ar-ē-əs\ (c.250–336) Christian priest and heretic, whose teachings gave rise to the doctrine of ARIANISM. As leader of a Christian community near Alexandria, he preached doctrines that combined NEOPLATONISM with a literal, rationalist interpretation of biblical texts. By asserting the absolute oneness and immutability of God, he called into question the divinity of Christ. His views were publicized through his major work, *Thalia* (c.323). In 325 the Council of Nicaea declared him a heretic. The Arian heresy posed a threat to Christian orthodoxy for several centuries.

Arizona State (pop., 2000: 5,130,000), SW U.S. It covers 114,000 sq mi (295,260 sq km); its capital is PHOENIX. Its highest point is Humphrey's Peak, at 12,633 ft (3,850 m). Site of the GRAND CANYON and PETRIFIED FOREST NATIONAL PARK, Arizona also has almost 40% of U.S. Indian tribal lands. Humans settled the area more than 25,000 years ago. Nomadic APACHE and NAVAJO Indians arrived after the collapse of the ANASAZI and HOHOKAM CULTURES. They were followed in the 16th cent. by Spanish treasure seekers from Mexico, including Francisco de CORONADO, establishing Mexico's claim to the area. In 1776 the Mexican army built the first presidio at TUCSON. After the MEXICAN WAR, Arizona was ceded to the U.S. as part of New Mexico in 1848; the GADSDEN PURCHASE was added in 1853. Organized as a territory in 1863, Arizona became the 48th state in 1912. Though still lightly populated, it has grown rapidly in recent decades, largely because of its attractive climate. About one-sixth of the population is Spanish-speaking; another 5% is Indian, including Navajo, HOPI, Apache, Papago, and Pima. Its diverse economy includes agriculture, mining, aerospace, electronics, and tourism.

Arjan \'ər-jən\ (1563–1606) Fifth GURU of the Sikhs (1581–1606) and SIKHISM's first martyr. He compiled the volume of Sikh scripture on which the ADI GRANTH is based, and he completed the GOLDEN TEMPLE at Amritsar. The first Guru to serve as both temporal and spiritual head of Sikhism, he built up Amritsar as a commercial center. He prospered under the tolerant Mughal emperor AKBAR, but was tortured to death by Akbar's successor for not removing from the Adi Granth passages that gave offense to Hinduism or Islam.

Arjuna \'ər-jü-na\ One of the five brothers who are the heroes of the *MAHABHARATA*. His reluctance to go into battle prompts KRISHNA, manifested as his friend and charioteer, to deliver the discourse on duty that constitutes the BHAGAVADGITA. An exemplar of skill, duty, and compassion, Arjuna is a central figure in Hindu myth and theology.

Arkansas State (pop., 2000: 2,673,000), S central U.S. It covers 53,187 sq mi (137,754 sq km). Its capital is LITTLE ROCK, while its highest point is Magazine Mtn., at 2,753 ft (839 m). The earliest inhabitants were Indian bluff dwellers along the Mississippi River around A.D. 500. Mound-building cultures later left burial mounds along the river. Spanish and French explorers traversed the region in the 16th–17th cent.; the first permanent European settlement was founded at Arkansas Post in 1686. Acquired by the U.S. as part of the LOUISIANA PURCHASE, Arkansas Territory was formed in 1819; the state's current boundaries were fixed in 1828. Arkansas became the 25th state in 1836. It seceded in 1861 to join the Confederacy in the AMERICAN CIVIL WAR; it was readmitted to the Union in 1868. Following RECONSTRUCTION, a rigid policy of segregation lasted until 1957, when court-ordered desegregation of the schools was imple-

mented. Once dominated by agriculture, the state's economy now also includes mining and manufacturing. Tourism is promoted especially by the mineral springs at HOT SPRINGS NATIONAL PARK and resorts in the OZARK MTNS.

Arkansas River River, rising in central Colorado. At 1,450 mi (2,333 km) long, it flows east through S Kansas and southeast across NE Oklahoma and bisects Arkansas, where it empties into the MISSISSIPPI RIVER. Its largest tributaries are the Cimarron and the CANADIAN RIVER. It is believed to have been crossed by Francisco de CORONADO in 1541.

Arkhangelsk \,ər-'kän-gilsk\ *English* **Archangel** City (pop, 1994 est.: 374,000), NW Russia. It has a large harbor kept open in winter by icebreakers. The area was settled by Norsemen in the 10th cent. A.D. In 1553 it was visited by the English who were looking for the NORTHEAST PASSAGE. Founded in 1584 as a monastery of MICHAEL the archangel, the city was opened to European trade by Boris GODUNOV, and flourished as the sole Russian seaport until ST. PETERSBURG was built in 1703. It was the scene of British, French, and U.S. support of the N Russian government against the BOLSHEVIKS, 1918–19. Now Russia's major timber exporting port, it also has extensive shipbuilding facilities.

Ark of the Covenant In Judaism and Christianity, the ornate, gold-plated wooden chest that in biblical times housed the two tablets of the Law given to MOSES by God. Following the conquest of CANAAN, it was kept at Shiloh, but was sometimes carried into battle. DAVID took it to Jerusalem, and SOLOMON placed it in the Temple of JERUSALEM, where it rested in the Holy of Holies and was seen only by the high priest on YOM KIPPUR.

Arkwright, Richard (*later* **Sir Richard**) (1732–1792) British textile industrialist and inventor. His first spinning machine was patented in 1769. His water frame (operated by waterpower) produced a cotton YARN suitable for warp, stronger than thread made on the SPINNING JENNY, which proved suitable only for weft. He introduced all-cotton calico in 1773. He opened several factories equipped to carry out the phases of textile manufacturing from CARDING through spinning.

Arlen, Harold *orig.* Hyman Arluck (1905–1986) U.S. songwriter. Born in Buffalo, N.Y., Arlen left school to form a band. In 1929 he began a successful collaboration with lyricist Ted Koehler (1894–1973) with "Get Happy"; their later songs were featured in shows at Harlem's Cotton Club. Arlen's Broadway musicals included *Bloomer Girl* (1944); *St. Louis Woman* (1946), with Johnny MERCER; and *House of Flowers* (1954), with Truman CAPOTE. For Hollywood, Arlen wrote "It's Only a Paper Moon" and "That Old Black Magic." His most famous song is perhaps "Over the Rainbow" from *The Wizard of Oz* (1939).

Arles \'ärl, 'ärlz\ City (pop, 2001: 51,000), SE France. Occupied by the Romans in the 1st cent. B.C., Arles became, through commerce, a leading city of the ROMAN EMPIRE. In the 10th cent. A.D. it became the capital of BURGUNDY, known also as the Kingdom of Arles. Portions of the Roman wall around the old town remain, along with a Roman arena. The city was home to Vincent VAN GOGH during one of his most productive periods. Arles is still a river port, but its economy is based largely on tourism and agriculture.

Arlington Unincorporated settlement (pop., 2000: 189,000), N Virginia. The city was once part of Washington, D.C. (1789–1846), which lies across the POTOMAC RIVER. It is the site of Arlington National Cemetery (on the former estate of Robert E. LEE), Ronald Reagan National Airport, and the PENTAGON.

Armada, Spanish Great fleet of about 130 ships sent by PHILIP II of Spain in 1588 to invade England in conjunction with a Spanish army from Flanders. Philip was motivated by a desire to restore Roman Catholicism in England and by English piracies against Spanish trade and possessions. In the weeklong battle, the Spanish suffered defeat after the English launched fire ships into the Spanish fleet, breaking its formation and making it susceptible to the English ships' heavy guns. Many Spanish ships were also lost during the long voyage home. The defeat of the Armada, in which Francis DRAKE played a principal role, saved England and the Netherlands from possible absorption into the Spanish empire.

armadillo Any of 20 species of armored mammals (family Dasypodidae) related to SLOTHS and ANTEATERS. Armadillos are stout and short-legged, with strong, curved claws and a protective covering of armor composed of solid plates separated by movable bands. They occur in tropical and subtropical regions, primarily in S. America. The species range in size from about 6 in. (16 cm) to 5 ft (1.5 m) long. They feed on termites or other insects, vegetation, small animals, and carrion.

Armageddon \ˌär-mə-'ged-ən\ In the NEW TESTAMENT, the place where the kings of the earth under demonic leadership will wage war on the forces of God at the end of history. Armageddon is mentioned only in the Book of REVELATION. The name may mean "Mountain of Megiddo," a reference to the strategic city of Megiddo.

Armagnac \ˌär-mȧ-'nyȧk\ Small territory in historical GASCONY, SW France. A portion was part of the Roman province of Aquitania (see AQUITAINE). From about 960 it was the separate countship of Armagnac, and grew to occupy a buffer zone between French and English lands. It led the resistance to the English king HENRY V's invasion of France, but lost at the Battle of AGINCOURT. First annexed to France in 1497, it returned finally by descent through the Navarre family in 1607. It was again a countship 1645–1789. It produces the famous Armagnac brandy.

Armenia *officially* **Republic of Armenia** Nation, SW Asia. Area: 11,500 sq mi (29,800 sq km). Population (2000): 3,810,000 (de jure); about 3,000,000 (de facto). Capital: YEREVAN. Armenians constitute nine-tenths of its population; there are also small numbers of Azerbaijanis, Kurds,

Russians, and Ukrainians. Languages: Armenian (official), Russian. Religion: Christianity (Armenian Apostolic, Armenian Catholic). Currency: dram. Armenia is a mountainous country with an average elevation of 5,900 ft (1,800 m). The Lesser CAUCASUS MOUNTAINS lie across its N portion, and Lake Sevan lies in the E central part. Armenia has a dry and continental climate that changes dramatically with elevation. Though it has become highly industrialized (as a result of the development of hydroelectric power during Soviet rule) and increasingly urbanized, agriculture is still important. Armenia is a successor state to a historical region in SW Asia. Historical Armenia's boundaries have varied considerably, but old Armenia extended over what is now NE Turkey and the Republic of Armenia. The area was equivalent to the ancient kingdom of URARTU, which ruled around 1270–850 B.C. It was later conquered by the Medes (see MEDIA) and MACE-

DONIA, and still later allied with the Roman empire. Armenia adopted Christianity as its national religion in A.D. 301. For centuries the scene of strife among Arabs, Seljuqs, Byzantines, and Mongols, it came under the rule of the Ottoman Turks in 1514. Over the next centuries, as parts were ceded to other rulers, nationalism arose among the scattered Armenians; by the late 19th cent. it was causing widespread disruption. Fighting between Turks and Russians escalated when part of Armenia was ceded to Russia in 1878, and it continued trough World War I, leading to Armenian deaths on a genocidal scale (see ARMENIAN MASSACRES). With the Turkish defeat, the Russian part was set up as a Soviet republic in 1921. Armenia became a constituent republic of the U.S.S.R. in 1936. With the latter's dissolution in the late 1980s, Armenia declared its independence in 1990. In the years that followed, it fought Azerbaijan for control over NAGORNO-KARABAKH until a cease-fire in 1994. About one-fifth of the population has left the country since 1993 because of an energy crisis. Political tension escalated, and in 1999 the prime minister and some legislators were killed in a terrorist attack on the legislature.

Armenian massacres GENOCIDE of Turkish Armenians by the Ottomans under ABDULHAMID II in 1894–96 and by the YOUNG TURKS in 1915–16. In 1894, when the Armenians began resisting Turkish authority, Turkish troops and Kurdish tribesmen killed thousands. In 1896, hoping to call attention to their plight, Armenian revolutionaries seized the Ottoman Bank in Istanbul. Mobs of Muslim Turks and government agents killed more than 50,000 Armenians in response. Sporadic killings occurred over the next two decades. In 1915, in response to the formation of anti-Turkish Armenian battalions, the Turkish government deported 1.75 million Armenians south to Syria and Mesopotamia, in the course of which 600,000 Armenians were killed or died of starvation.

Armenians Indo-European people first recognized in the early 7th cent. B.C. when they moved into an area conquered by BABYLONIA and MEDIA. Armenian culture reached a high point in the 14th cent., producing highly regarded sculpture, architecture, and fine art. Armenians have always struggled for independence from foreign domination, first by the BYZANTINE EMPIRE, then by the SELJUQ DYNASTY, the OTTOMAN EMPIRE, Persia, and Russia. The most recent period of foreign domination (1922–90) ended with the collapse of the Soviet Union. Until the 20th cent., Armenians were primarily agricultural; now they are highly urbanized. Traditionally they are Christians; Armenia was considered the first Christian state. Over 3.5 million live in Armenia, and there is a large population in the West. See also ARMENIAN MASSACRES.

Armistice (1918) Agreement between Germany and the Allies ending WORLD WAR I. Allied representatives met with a German delegation in a railway carriage at Rethondes, France, to sign an agreement on November 11, and the war ended at 11 a.m. that day ("the 11th hour of the 11th day of the 11th month"). The principal term was that Germany would evacuate Belgium, France, and Alsace-Lorraine. Negotiations formalizing the armistice were conducted at the PARIS PEACE CONFERENCE. Later, a "stab in the back" legend developed in Germany asserting that the German military situation had not been hopeless and that traitorous politicians had signed the Armistice.

armor *or* **body armor** Protective clothing that can shield a wearer from weapons and projectiles. Prehistoric war-

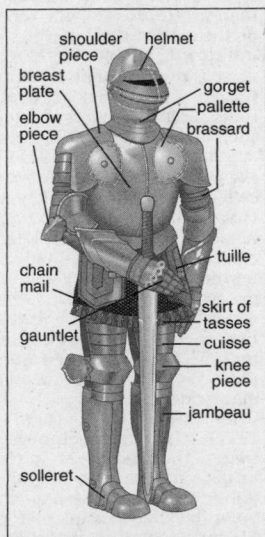

Armor Suit of 15th-cent. European plate armor.

Map labels:

REPUBLIC OF GEORGIA

DZHAVAKHET RANGE

LESSER CAUCASUS RANGE

Alaverdi
Stepanavan
Debed
Gyumri
Spitak
Vanadzor
Artik
Dilijan
Sevan
Hrazdan
SHAKHDAG RANGE
Aragats 13,418 ft.
Charentsavan
Abovyan
Kamo
Ejmiadzin
Hrazdan
GEGHAMA RANGE
Lake Sevan
ARMENIAN HIGHLAND
Hoktemberyan
Yerevan
VARDENIS RANGE
Artashat
Ararat
Arpa
KARABAKH UPLAND
Goris
ZANGEZUR RANGE
Kapan

AZERBAIJAN
Ijevan
Lake Mingächevir
Kuru
SHIRAK STEPPE
ARMENIA
MTS.
AZERBAIJAN
AZERBAIJAN
TURKEY
IRAN
44°
46°
40° N

ARMENIA

©1999, Encyclopædia Britannica, Inc.

Scale 1: 4,429,000
0   20   40 mi
0   30   60 km

Armor labels: shoulder piece, helmet, breast plate, gorget, pallette, brassard, elbow piece, tuille, chain mail, skirt of tasses, gauntlet, cuisse, knee piece, jambeau, solleret

riors used leather hides and helmets. Chinese warriors used rhinoceros skin in the 11th cent. B.C.; Greek infantry wore multilayered metal-and-linen cuirasses in the 5th cent. B.C. CHAIN MAIL was worn throughout the Roman Empire and in Western Europe until the 14th cent. Ancient Greeks and Romans used armor made of rigid metal plates, which reappeared in Europe from the 13th cent. until the 17th cent., when firearms began to make it obsolete. The helmet reappeared in World War I. Today's bulletproof vest, now often made of KEVLAR, covers the chest and sometimes the groin.

Armory Show *formally* International Exhibition of Modern Art. Exhibition of painting and sculpture held in 1913 at the 69th Regiment Armory in New York City. Conceived as a selection of works exclusively by U.S. artists, it evolved into a comprehensive look at current European art movements. Of the 1,300 works assembled, one-third were European, with works representative of IMPRESSIONISM, SYMBOLISM, POSTIMPRESSIONISM, FAUVISM, and CUBISM. The U.S. works featured the younger, more radical artists of the ASH CAN SCHOOL and The EIGHT. The show traveled to Chicago and Boston, introducing the public to advanced European art and establishing itself as a decisive event in the development of U.S. art and art collecting.

arms, coat of Heraldic device dating to the 12th cent. in Europe. It was originally a cloth tunic worn over or in place of armor to establish identity in battle. Consisting of a shield, or escutcheon, and surface, or field, it is divided into nine parts, or points. It is ornamented with a crest, motto, crown, wreath, or symbols in bold colors. Shields of arms were used to record personal or family history, property ownership, or profession, and were later adopted as emblems for schools, churches, guilds, and corporations to reflect their mottoes or histories. See also HERALDRY.

arms control Concept of limiting the development, production, or use of weapons through international agreements. Arms control did not arise in international diplomacy until the first HAGUE CONVENTION (1899). The Washington Conference (1921–22) to limit the naval arms race was broken without much fear of sanction. U.S.–Soviet treaties to control nuclear weapons were taken more seriously. See also NUCLEAR TEST-BAN TREATY, SALT, START.

Armstrong, Edwin H(oward) (1890–1954) U.S. inventor. Born in New York City, he studied at Columbia Univ., where he devised a feedback circuit that greatly amplified radio signals (1912). At its highest amplification, the circuit shifted from being a receiver to being a generator of radio waves, and as such it is at the heart of all radio and television broadcasting. It earned him the Franklin Medal, the highest U.S. scientific honor. His 1933 invention of circuits that produced FM carrier waves made possible the first high-fidelity broadcasting.

Armstrong, Gillian (b.1950) Australian film director. She received international acclaim as the director of *My Brilliant Career* (1979). Her subsequent works include Australian films such as *Oscar and Lucinda* (1997) as well as U.S. films such as *Mrs. Soffel* (1984) and *Little Women* (1994).

Armstrong, Lance (b.1971) U.S. cyclist and four-time winner of the TOUR DE FRANCE. Born in Plano, Texas, he excelled in swimming and cycling from his youth. He won the U.S. amateur cycling championship in 1990 and began professional road racing in 1992. In 1996 he was diagnosed with testicular cancer that had spread to his lungs and brain. After months of surgery and chemotherapy, he resumed training, winning a race in 1998. Originally a specialist in one-day races, he changed his training to win the 22-day Tour de France in 1999, and went on to win it the next three years, in 2002 finishing seven minutes ahead of the second-place rider.

Armstrong, Louis (1901–1971) U.S. trumpeter and singer, the first great soloist in jazz and its most popular public figure. Armstrong was born in New Orleans, where he participated in marching, riverboat, and cabaret bands. In 1922 he moved to Chicago

Louis Armstrong

to join King OLIVER's Creole Jazz Band; he made his first records the following year. In 1924 he joined the Fletcher HENDERSON Orchestra in New York and recorded with Bessie SMITH and Ma RAINEY. In 1925 he began recording under his own name with his Hot Five and Hot Seven ensembles. In these recordings the prevailing emphasis on collective improvisation gives way to his developing strength as soloist and vocalist. By the time of his 1928 "West End Blues," Armstrong had established the preeminence of the virtuoso soloist in jazz. His vibrant melodic phrasing, inventive harmonic improvisation, and swinging rhythmic conception established the vernacular of jazz music. His powerful tone, great range, and dazzling velocity set a new technical standard. As solo attraction, bandleader, film actor, and musical ambassador to the world, he achieved fame and eminence unmatched by any other jazz musician.

Armstrong, Neil (Alden) (b.1930) U.S. astronaut. Born in Wapakoneta, Ohio, he became a pilot at 16, studied aeronautical engineering, and won three Air Medals in the Korean War. He joined the space program in 1962 with the second group of astronauts. In 1966, in Gemini 8, he and David Scott completed the first manual space docking, with an unmanned Agena rocket. On July 20, 1969, as part of the APOLLO 11 mission, he became the first person to step onto the moon, announcing "That's one small step for a man, one giant leap for mankind."

army Large, organized force armed and trained for war, especially on land. Armies have variously been built around infantry soldiers or mounted warriors (e.g., CAVALRY) or men in machines, professionals or amateurs, MERCENARIES fighting for pay or for plunder, or patriots fighting for a cause. See also AIR FORCE, CONSCRIPTION, GUERRILLA, MILITARY UNIT, MILITIA, UNITED STATES ARMY.

Arne, Thomas Augustine (1710–1778) British composer. Son of a London upholsterer, he secretly taught himself instrumental skills and composition. He had an early success with his first opera, *Rosamond* (1733), and thereafter concentrated almost exclusively on the theater. As composer to Drury Lane Theatre and London's great pleasure gardens, he became Britain's leading theatrical composer. Of some 90 theatrical works, the best known are *Comus* (1738), *The Judgment of Paris* (1740), and *Artaxerxes* (1762). His song "Rule, Britannia" became an unofficial national anthem.

Arnhem Land \'är-nəm\ Region, NE NORTHERN TERRITORY, Australia. It extends south from Van Diemen Gulf to the Gulf of CARPENTARIA and Groote Eylandt. Its 37,000 sq mi (96,000 sq km) area contains important bauxite and uranium deposits. Named for the ship of its Dutch discoverer, Arnhem Land is now known for its large reserves of AUSTRALIAN ABORIGINES.

Arnold, Benedict (1741–1801) U.S. army officer and traitor. Born in Norwich, Conn., he joined the American Revolutionary army in 1775. He led the victories at Ft. Stanwix, N.Y., and at the Battle of SARATOGA, where he was seriously wounded. He was placed in command of Philadelphia, where he lived extravagantly and socialized with wealthy Loyalist sympathizers, marrying one in 1779. After receiving command of the fort at West Point, N.Y. (1780), he offered to surrender it to the British for £20,000. The plot was uncovered after his British contact, John ANDRÉ, was captured. Arnold escaped to England, where he died penniless.

Arnold, Hap (*orig.* Henry Harley) (1886–1950) U.S. air force officer. Born in Gladwyne, Pa., he attended West Point, then volunteered as a flyer and received instruction from Orville WRIGHT. After World War I, he became an eloquent advocate of an expanded air force, and rose through the ranks of the U.S. Army Air Corps to become its chief in 1938. He commanded the Army Air Forces worldwide during World War II, greatly influencing air bombardment strategy. He was named general of the army in 1944 and later general of the newly independent U.S. Air Force.

Arnold, Matthew (1822–1888) English poet and literary and social critic. Son of Thomas ARNOLD, after attending Oxford he worked as an inspector of schools. His best-known poem is "Dover Beach"; others include "Sohrab and Rustum," "The Scholar Gipsy," and "Thyrsis." *Culture and Anarchy* (1869), his main critical work, is a searching analysis of Victorian society. He thought the critic's role was to promote high culture as an antidote to the crass materialism ("philistinism") of industrial society.

Arnold, Thomas known as **Dr. Arnold** (1795–1842) British educator. A classical scholar, he became headmaster in 1828 of Rugby School, which was in a state of decline. He revived Rugby by reforming its curriculum, athletics program, and social structure, becoming in the process the preeminent figure in British education. In 1841 he was named Regius Professor of Modern History at Oxford. His works include a three-volume *History of Rome* (1838–43). He was the father of Matthew ARNOLD.

Arnolfo di Cambio (c.1245–1302?) Italian sculptor and architect active in Florence. He studied under Nicola PISANO. In 1277 he went to Rome, where he worked for Charles of Anjou. His portrait statue of Charles is one of the earliest since ancient times. A document from 1300 praises Arnolfo as designer of Florence's Duomo (1296) and sculptor of the statues for its facade. Other buildings in Florence attributed to him include the Palazzo Vecchio and the church of Santa Croce.

Arno River River, central Italy. It is 150 mi (240 km) long, flowing west from the APENNINES through FLORENCE and into the Ligurian Sea below PISA. Near Arezzo it is connected with the TIBER RIVER. Prone to disastrous floods, in 1966 it inundated Florence and caused extensive damage.

aromatherapy Therapy using ESSENTIAL OILS and water-based COLLOIDS extracted from plant materials to promote physical, emotional, and spiritual health and balance. Extracts may be diffused into inhaled air, used in massage oil, or added to bathwater. The inhaled molecules stimulate the olfactory nerve, sending messages to the brain's limbic system (the seat of memory, learning, and emotion) that are said to trigger physiological responses (e.g., eucalyptus relieves congestion, lavender promotes relaxation). Mainstream medical practitioners question the claim of independent physiological effects; they consider many of the benefits more likely due to conditioned responses. The few risks involved include allergic reactions.

aromatic compound Any of a large class of ORGANIC COMPOUNDS whose molecular structure includes one or more planar rings of atoms, usually but not always six CARBON atoms. The rings' carbon-carbon bonds (see BONDING) are neither single nor double but a type characteristic of these compounds. The term was first applied around 1860 to a class of HYDROCARBONS having unusually strong odors. In modern chemistry, aromaticity denotes the chemical behavior, especially low reactivity, of this class of molecules related to their bonding. The parent aromatic compound is BENZENE. See also HYDROGENATION.

Aron \är-'ōⁿ\, **Raymond (-Claude-Ferdinand)** (1905–1983) French sociologist and historian. After receiving his doctorate, he taught at the Univ. of Toulouse until 1939. During World War II he joined the FREE FRENCH and edited their newspaper. He later taught at the Sorbonne and the Collège de France. As a columnist for *Le Figaro* (1947–77), his opposition to Marxism put him at odds with France's left-wing intellectuals. His books often discuss violence and war from a rationalist humanist point of view.

Arp, Jean known as **Hans Arp** (1886–1966) French painter and sculptor. After studying in Germany and Paris, he became involved in the most important movements of early 20th-cent. art, including DADA, SURREALISM, and Abstraction-Creation. He produced polychrome relief carvings in wood, cut-paper compositions, and, in the 1930s, his most distinctive works in sculpture: abstract forms that suggest animals and plants.

arrest Restraint and seizure of a person by someone (e.g., a police officer) acting under legal authority. An officer may arrest a person who is committing or attempting to commit a crime in the officer's presence. Arrest is also permitted if the officer reasonably believes that a crime has been committed and that the person arrested is the guilty party. A court or judicial officer may issue an arrest warrant on a showing of probable cause. Most states restrict or prohibit arrest in civil (noncriminal) cases. In the U.S., suspects must be warned of their rights when arrested (see *MIRANDA VS. ARIZONA*). See also GRAND JURY, INDICTMENT.

Arrhenius \är-'ā-nē-əs\, **Svante (August)** (1859–1927) Swedish chemist, one of the founders of physical chemistry. His theories on dissociation of substances in solution into ELECTROLYTES or IONS (1884) were initially met with skepticism. He also did important work on REACTION RATES; the equation describing the dependence of reaction rates on temperature is often called the Arrhenius law, and he was the first to recognize the GREENHOUSE EFFECT. He received the third Nobel Prize for Chemistry (1903).

arrhythmia See CARDIAC ARRHYTHMIA

arrow See BOW AND ARROW

arrowroot Any of several plant species of the genus *Maranta* (family Marantaceae), whose RHIZOMES yield an edible starch. Chief among these is the herbaceous perennial *M. arundinacea*. The powder obtained from the harvested roots is used in cookery as a thickener. Arrowroot is easily digested and is used in diets requiring bland, low-salt, and low-protein foods. Its name is sometimes applied to plant starches used as substitutes for true arrowroot. Brazilian arrowroot, from the CASSAVA plant, is the source of tapioca.

Arrow War See OPIUM WARS

Ars Antiqua \'ärs-an-'tē-kwə\ (Latin: "the Old Art") Musical style of the 13th cent., as distinguished from that of the 14th cent. (ARS NOVA), beginning with the NOTRE-DAME SCHOOL. It employs the six rhythmic modes, each being a rhythmic pattern that would recur throughout a piece, such as long–short (first mode) or short–long (second). Akin to the "feet" of poetry (see PROSODY), the relative lengths of long and short depended on the mode. The system broke down as composers began to use subdivisions of the short note. The musical genres of the Ars Antiqua included ORGANUM and the early MOTET.

arsenic Nonmetallic to semimetallic chemical ELEMENT, chemical symbol As, atomic number 33. It exists uncombined in two stable forms, one gray and one yellow, but is more usually found in nature as the sulfide or OXIDE. Elemental arsenic is used to form ALLOYS of METALS (especially lead), and SEMICONDUCTORS are made from crystals of gallium arsenide. Arsenious oxide (arsenic trioxide), is used in pesticides, as a pigment, and as a preservative of hides and wood; this is the poisonous "arsenic" in detective stories. Arsenic pentoxide is also used in insecticides, herbicides, metal adhesives, and pigments.

Arsinoe II \är-'sin-ō-ē\ (316?–270 B.C.) Daughter of PTOLEMY I SOTER and queen of THRACE (300–281) and of Egypt (277–270). She married the king of Thrace (300) and tried to have her son made heir instead of Agathocles, the king's son by an earlier marriage. Agathocles sought help from the SELEUCIDS, causing a war in which Arsinoe's husband was killed in battle. Her half brother, who took power in Thrace and Macedonia, married her and then promptly killed her two younger sons. She fled to Alexandria, ousted the wife of her brother PTOLEMY II, and married him (c.277). She wielded great power and shared many honors with Ptolemy, including deification while alive.

Ars Nova \'ärs-'nō-və\ (Latin: "the New Art") Musical style of the 14th cent. As composers began to use ever shorter notes in their music, the old system of rhythmic modes (see ARS ANTIQUA) ceased to be adequate to describe it. In 1323, in his treatise *Ars nova*, Philippe de Vitry (1291–1361) proposed a way of relating longer and shorter notes by a metrical scheme, the ancestor of time signatures, whereby each note value could be subdivided into either two or three of the next-shorter note. This innovation enabled composers to better control the relative motion of several voices. Guillaume de MACHAUT and Francesco Landini (c. 1325–1397) are the principal composers of the Ars Nova. See also FORMES FIXES.

arson Crime of willfully, wrongfully, and unjustifiably setting property on fire, often for the purpose of committing fraud (e.g., on an insurance company). In nearly all countries, the arsonist may be charged with murder if arson causes death. A fire caused by accident or ordinary carelessness is not arson, but people who act in reckless disregard of the consequences of their actions may be guilty of arson.

art Combination of skill and imagination in the creation of objects, environments, or experiences. The term also designates modes of expression such as PAINTING, drawing,

SCULPTURE, filmmaking, MUSIC, DANCE, POETRY, THE-ATER, ARCHITECTURE, CERAMICS, and decorative arts, collectively known as the arts.

Artaud \är-ˈtō\, **Antonin** (1896–1948) French poet, actor, and drama theorist. He wrote surrealist poetry from 1925 and made his acting debut in surrealist productions in Paris. He described his theory of drama in the *Manifesto of the Theatre of Cruelty* (1932) (see theater of CRUELTY) and *The Theatre and Its Double* (1938), which influenced playwrights of the theater of the ABSURD. Lifelong mental illness confined him periodically to asylums from 1936.

Art Deco \ˌärt-ˈde-kō, ˌär-dā-ˈkō\ Movement in design, interior decoration, and architecture in the 1920s and '30s in Europe and the U.S. The name derives from the Exposition Internationale des Arts Décoratifs et Industriels Modernes in Paris in 1925. It was initially a luxury style featuring sleek, streamlined geometric shapes and expensive materials that expressed wealth and sophistication. During the Great Depression, emphasis was also given to materials that could be economically mass-produced, such as Bakelite. Typical motifs included stylized animals, foliage, nude female figures, and sun rays.

Artemis \ˈär-tə-məs\ In GREEK RELIGION, the goddess of wild animals, the hunt, vegetation, chastity, and childbirth. Daughter of ZEUS and LETO and twin sister of APOLLO, she both killed game and, as Mistress of the Animals, protected it. Stories of her NYMPHS' love affairs may originally have been told of herself, but poets after Homer stressed her chastity. Artemis may have developed out of ISHTAR in the East. Her Roman counterpart was DIANA.

Artemisia II (d.c.350 B.C.) Sister and wife of King Mausolus (r.377?–353? B.C.) of Caria, SW Anatolia, and sole ruler for about three years after his death. She built his tomb, the Mausoleum, considered one of the SEVEN WONDERS OF THE WORLD. She was also known as a botanist and medical researcher; the plant genus *Artemisia* is named for her.

arteriography See ANGIOGRAPHY

arteriosclerosis \är-ˌtir-ē-ō-sklə-ˈrō-səs\ *or* **hardening of the arteries** Chronic disease characterized by abnormal thickening of the walls of the ARTERIES. In atherosclerosis, its major form, fatty deposits of CHOLESTEROL form on arterial inner walls. These thicken, forming plaques that narrow the vessel channel and impede blood flow. Scarring and calcification make the walls less elastic, raising blood pressure. Eventually, plaques may completely block a vessel, or a blood clot (thrombus) may obstruct a narrowed channel. Atherosclerosis of coronary arteries is called CORONARY HEART DISEASE In the brain, arteriosclerosis may result in STROKE. In leg arteries, it may cause intermittent lameness, pain, and ulceration, with increased risk of infection.

artery Vessel that carries blood from the heart to other parts of the body (see CARDIOVASCULAR SYSTEM). Arterial blood carries oxygen and nourishment to tissues; the one exception is the pulmonary artery (see PULMONARY CIRCULATION). Arteries are muscular, elastic tubes that transport blood under the pressure of the heart's pumping action, which can be felt as the PULSE. Large arteries branch off from the AORTA and give rise to smaller arteries, down to the threadlike arterioles, which branch into CAPILLARIES. See also ARTERIOSCLEROSIS, VEIN.

arthritis \är-ˈthrī-təs\ INFLAMMATION of the JOINTS and its effects. Acute arthritis is marked by pain, redness, and swelling. The principal forms are OSTEOARTHRITIS, RHEUMATOID ARTHRITIS, and septic arthritis (caused by bacterial, viral, or fungal infection). Several forms of arthritis are part of the symptom complexes of AUTOIMMUNE DISEASES.

arthropod Any member of the largest phylum (Arthropoda) in the ANIMAL kingdom, consisting of more than a million known INVERTEBRATE species in four subphyla: Uniramia (five classes, including INSECTS), Chelicerata (three classes, including ARACHNIDS and HORSESHOE CRABS), Crustacea (CRUSTACEANS), and Trilobita (TRILOBITES). All arthropods are bilaterally symmetrical and possess a segmented body covered by an exoskeleton; each body segment may bear a pair of jointed appendages. The phylum includes CARNIVORES, HERBIVORES, OMNIVORES, detritus feeders, filter feeders, and parasites (see PARASITISM) in nearly all environments. See diagram on following page.

Arthur, Chester A(lan) (1829–1886) 21st president of the U.S. (1881–85). Born in N. Fairfield, Vt., he practiced law in New York City. A close associate of Roscoe CONKLING, he was appointed customs collector for the port of New York (1871–78), an office long known for its use of the SPOILS SYSTEM. Though not personally corrupt, he continued to pad the payroll with Conkling loyalists. Arthur was the compromise choice for vice president on the Republican ticket with James GARFIELD in 1880, and became president on Garfield's assassination. As president, Arthur displayed unexpected inde-

Chester A. Arthur Photo by C. M. Bell, 1882

pendence by vetoing measures that rewarded political patronage; he also signed the reform PENDLETON CIVIL SERVICE ACT. He and his navy secretary recommended the appropriations that initiated the rebuilding of the U.S. Navy. He failed to win his party's nomination for a second term.

Arthurian legend Body of medieval stories centering on the legendary English king Arthur. It chronicles the adventures of his knights, including the adulterous love between Sir LANCELOT and Arthur's queen, Guinevere. Popular in Wales before A.D. 1100, it was brought into literature by GEOFFREY OF MONMOUTH and adapted by other medieval writers, including Thomas MALORY, becoming entwined with legends of the GRAIL. The revived legend has figured in major works by Alfred TENNYSON and T. H. WHITE. It is uncertain whether there was a real Arthur. Medieval sources say he was a 6th-cent. warrior and champion of Christianity, who united the British tribes against Saxon invaders, died in battle at Camlann around 539, and was buried at Glastonbury. See also GALAHAD, MERLIN, TRISTAN AND ISOLDE.

artichoke Large thistlelike perennial plant (*Cynara scolymus*) of the COMPOSITE FAMILY. The thick edible scales and bottom part (heart) of the immature flower heads are a culinary delicacy. Native to the Mediterranean, it is cultivated extensively in other regions with rich soil and a mild, humid climate. The JERUSALEM ARTICHOKE is unrelated.

Articles of Confederation Early U.S. constitution (1781–89) that bridged the initial government by the CONTINENTAL CONGRESS and the federal government provided under the U.S. CONSTITUTION of 1787. It provided for a confederation of sovereign states and gave the Congress power to regulate foreign affairs, war, and the postal service, to control Indian affairs, and to borrow money; it also enabled the Congress to enact the NORTHWEST ORDINANCES. But the Congress had no power to enforce its requests to the states for money or troops, and governmental effectiveness broke down by late 1786. Delegates to the ANNAPOLIS CONVENTION called a meeting to amend the Articles.

artificial heart Machine or mechanical pump that maintains BLOOD CIRCULATION in the body. The heart-lung machine, a mechanical pump, can maintain circulation while the heart is stopped for surgery. It shunts blood away from the heart, oxygenates it, and returns it to the body. No device has yet been developed for total, long-term replacement of the heart; existing ones reduce the heart's workload and are suitable only as temporary replacements in patients awaiting transplant. See also PACEMAKER.

artificial insemination Introduction of SEMEN into a female's vagina or cervix by means other than SEXUAL INTERCOURSE. First developed for animal breeding, it is now also used to induce pregnancy in women whose partners cannot impregnate them. The partner's (or other donor's) semen is inserted with a syringe. In livestock, deep-frozen semen can be stored for long periods without losing its fertility, thus allowing a single bull to sire as many as 10,000 calves a year.

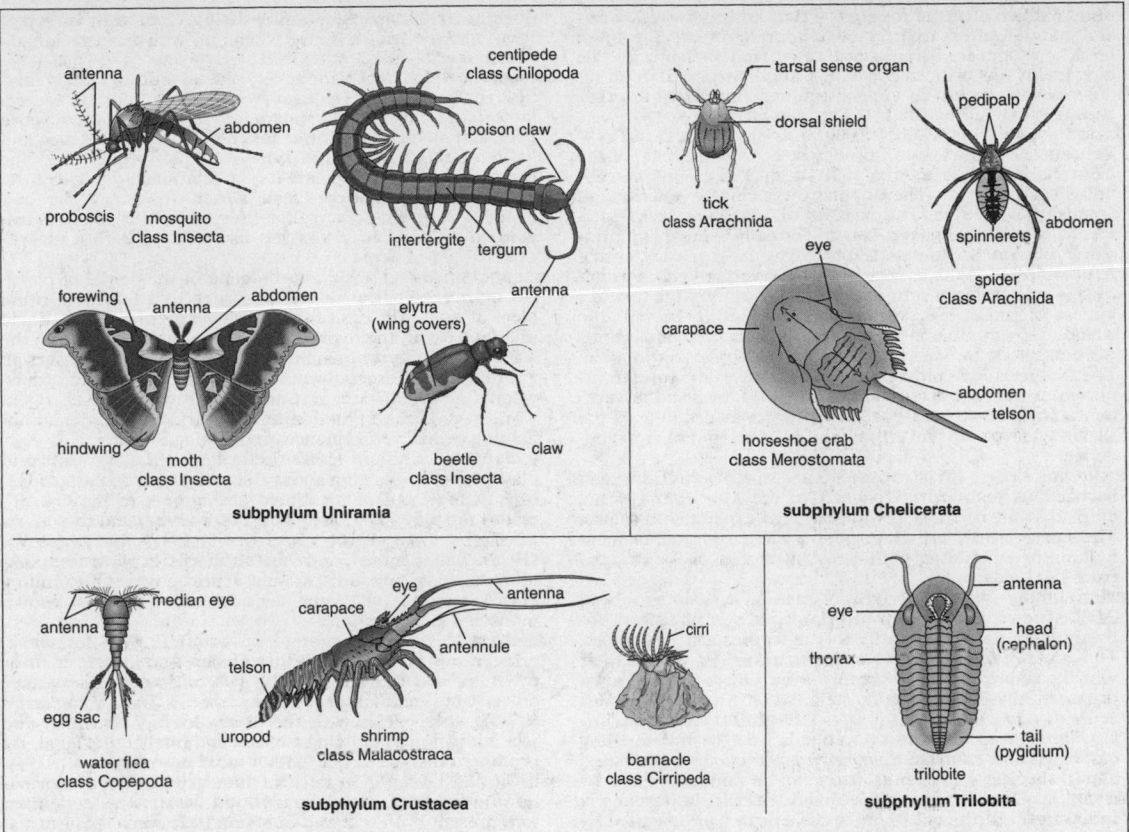

Arthropod Representative arthropods. Uniramia, the largest of the arthropod subphyla, contains mostly terrestrial insects and myriapods (incl. centipedes and millipedes). The insects, the largest arthropod class, differ from other arthropods in that they are usually winged and have only three pairs of legs. Members of the Crustacea subphylum are mostly marine-dwelling and include the shrimp, lobsters, crabs, and barnacles. The microscopic water fleas are chiefly found in freshwater, and along with other minute members of this subphylum are part of the zooplankton. Most members of the Chelicerata subphylum are arachnids (class Arachnida), incl. the spiders, scorpions, ticks, and mites. The trilobites are extinct marine arthropods that flourished during the Cambrian period. Fossilized remains show a body having three longitudinal lobes divided into three regions consisting of a head, thorax, and tail region.

artificial intelligence (AI) Ability of a machine to perform tasks thought to require human intelligence. Typical applications include game playing, language translation by computers, and ROBOTICS. AI research began in the 1940s. It has grown and developed at about the same rate as computer speed and sophistication, which are its main limiting factors. Computer memories containing circuits as numerous as the connections in the human brain have brought about the most striking advances in the field. AI research today aims to understand how computer capabilities must be organized in order to reproduce humanlike thinking, such as visual PATTERN RECOGNITION, complex decision making, and the use of natural language. See also TURING TEST.

Artigas \är-'tē-gàs\, **José Gervasio** (1764–1850) Soldier and revolutionary leader regarded as the father of Uruguayan independence. A GAUCHO, he allied himself with the Buenos Aires junta, fought for independence from Spain, and won a brilliant victory at Las Piedras. His subsequent insistence on federalism against the domination of Buenos Aires led to civil war. He ruled over a portion of what is now Uruguay and central Argentina until a Portuguese invasion forced him into exile in 1820. Uruguay achieved independence in 1828.

artillery Big GUNS, howitzers, or MORTARS of a caliber greater than 15 mm. The earliest artillery, introduced in the 14th cent., were CANNON and mortars of bronze, brass, or iron mounted on two-wheeled carriages. Advances in the later 19th cent. included steel gun barrels, more powerful gunpowders, and piston mountings to limit recoil. Encasing powder and projectile in a SHELL allowed faster loading. Since World War II, artillery has been ranked as light (up to 105 mm, for support of ground troops), medium (106–155 mm, for bombardment), and heavy (over 155 mm, for attacking rear installations). See also ANTIAIRCRAFT GUN.

Art Nouveau \ˌärt-nü-'vō, ˌär-nü-'vō\ ("New Art") Decorative style that flourished in Western Europe and the U.S. about 1890–1910. The term was derived in 1895 from a gallery in Paris called L'Art Nouveau. Characterized by sinuous, asymmetrical lines based on plant forms, the style was used in architecture, interior design, graphic art and design, jewelry, and glass. It was international in scope, with celebrated exponents in England (Aubrey BEARDSLEY), Paris (Alphonse MUCHA), the U.S. (L. C. TIFFANY), Scotland (C. R. MACKINTOSH), Spain (Antoni GAUDÍ), and Belgium (Victor HORTA). See also ARTS AND CRAFTS MOVEMENT, JUGENDSTIL.

Arts and Crafts Movement English social and aesthetic movement of the late 19th cent., dedicated to reestablishing the importance of craftsmanship in an era of mechanization and mass production. The name derives from the Arts and Crafts Exhibition Society (1888). Inspired by John RUSKIN and other writers who deplored the effects of industrialization, William MORRIS founded a firm of interior designers and manufacturers to produce handcrafted textiles, printed books, wallpaper, furniture, jewelry, and metalwork. The movement was criticized as elitist and impractical in an industrial society, but its appeal widened and spread to other countries, including the U.S. See also ART NOUVEAU.

Aruba Island (pop., 2000: 96,000), Lesser ANTILLES, off NW Venezuela. Aruba is an internally self-governing part of the Netherlands. It has an area of 70 sq mi (180 sq km). Its capital is ORANJESTAD. The population is chiefly Amerindian, Spanish, and Dutch. Dutch is its official language; Papiamento, a creole language, is used for daily affairs. The principal religion is Roman Catholicism. Its currency is the Aruban florin. Aruba's lack of water severely limits agriculture. Its petroleum-refining complex, among the world's largest, closed in 1985. Since then, tourism has become the island's economic mainstay. Aruba's earliest inhabitants were ARAWAK Indians; the Dutch took possession in 1636. The Netherlands controls Aruba's defense and foreign affairs, but internal affairs are handled by an island government. In 1986 Aruba seceded from the Federation of NETHERLANDS ANTILLES, an initial step toward independence.

arugula \ə-'rü-gə-lə\ *or* **rocket** Yellowish-flowered European herbaceous plant *(Eruca sativa)* of the MUSTARD FAMILY cultivated for its foliage, which is used especially in salads. The leaves taste sharp and peppery when young and succulent but become bitter with age. A medicinal oil is extracted from the seeds.

arum family \'ar-əm\ Family Araceae, containing about 2,000 species, that is rich in popular ornamentals and foliage plants native primarily to the tropics and subtropics. The genera *Philodendron* and *Monstera* are grown for their vinelike habit and large green leaves. Other arums grown ornamentally include the florist's CALLA lily and the water arum *(Calla palustris)*. JACK-IN-THE-PULPIT *(Arisaema triphyllum)* is well known in woodlands, and the foul-smelling eastern skunk cabbage *(Symplocarpus foetidus)* in marshes. Sap in species of the genus *Arum* can be poisonous.

Aryan \'ar-ē-ən\ Prehistoric people that settled in Iran and N India. In the 19th cent. there arose a notion, propagated by the comte de Gobineau (1816–1882) and Houston Stewart Chamberlain (1855–1927), of an "Aryan race": people who spoke INDO-EUROPEAN, especially GERMANIC, languages, lived in N Europe, and were superior to all other races. Though repudiated by scholars, including Franz BOAS, the notion was seized on by Adolf HITLER and made the basis of the Nazi policy of exterminating Jews, Gypsies, Slavs, and other "non-Aryans."

Asad, Hafiz al- See Hafiz al-ASSAD

Asam \'äz-äm\, **Cosmas Damian and Egid Quirin** (1686–1739, 1692–1750) Bavarian architects, decorators, and brothers. Cosmas Damian became a prolific fresco painter and Egid Quirin a sculptor and stuccoist. Working as a team, they produced magnificent illusionistic decoration, combining dramatic lighting and color, in ecclesiastical buildings. Their most notable collaboration, the church of St. John Nepomuk in Munich (1729–46)—known as the Asamkirche, as it was owned by them and attached to Egid Quirin's house—is a masterpiece of Bavarian Rococo style.

asbestos Any of several minerals that separate readily into long, flexible fibers. Chrysotile, the fibrous form of SERPENTINE, accounts for about 95% of all asbestos still in commercial use. Asbestos fiber was used in brake linings, insulation, roofing shingles, floor and ceiling tiles, cement pipes, and other building materials. Asbestos fabrics were used for safety apparel and theater curtains. In the 1970s, it was found that prolonged inhalation of the tiny asbestos fibers causes ASBESTOSIS and lung cancer. In 1989 the U.S. government instituted a gradual ban on the manufacture, use, and export of most products made with asbestos.

asbestosis \,as-bes-'tō-səs\ Lung disease caused by long-term inhalation of ASBESTOS fibers, found primarily in asbestos workers. Asbestosis is also seen in people living near asbestos industries. Fibers remain in the lungs, and symptoms such as shortness of breath emerge many years later; advanced cases include a dry cough. There is no effective treatment. The associated increased cardiac effort may in-

duce heart disease. Smoking greatly exacerbates its symptoms. LUNG CANCER is more common with asbestos inhalation and asbestosis.

Ascension In Christian belief, the ascent of JESUS into heaven 40 days after the Resurrection. The Book of Acts relates that, after several appearances to the APOSTLES over a period of 40 days, Jesus was taken up in their presence and hidden behind a cloud, a symbol of God's presence. The event is thought to indicate a new relationship between Jesus and God and between Jesus and his followers. The feast of the Ascension, universally observed by Christians, is celebrated 40 days after EASTER and 10 days before PENTECOST.

asceticism \ə-'set-ə-,siz-əm\ Practice of the denial of physical or psychological desires in order to attain a spiritual ideal or goal. The desire for ritual purity in order to come in contact with the divine, the need for atonement, and the wish to earn merit or gain access to supernatural powers all are reasons for ascetic practice. Christian monastic orders, wandering Hindu ascetics, and Buddhist monks all reject worldly goods and practice various forms of self-denial, including celibacy, abstinence, and fasting.

Asch \'äsh\, **Sholem** (1880–1957) Polish-U.S. novelist and playwright. His writing about the village life of Eastern European Jews and of his fellow immigrants to the U.S. includes the play *The God of Vengeance* (1907) and the novels *Mottke the Thief* (1916), *Uncle Moses* (1918), and *Judge Not* (1926). Later, more controversial works explore the common heritage of Judaism and Christianity. Outstanding both for output and impact, he is one of the best-known modern Yiddish writers.

Ascham \'as-kəm\, **Roger** (1515–1568) English humanist, scholar, and writer. The future Queen ELIZABETH I's tutor in Greek and Latin (1548–50), he continued to serve her during her reign. His best-known book is *The Scholemaster* (1570), which deals with the psychology of learning, and sees education as molding a moral and intellectual ideal. He promoted the vernacular with a lucid prose style.

ASCII \'as-kē\ *in full* American Standard Code for Information Interchange. Standard DATA-TRANSMISSION code used to represent both text and commands. It converts information into standardized digital formats that allow computers to communicate with each other and to process and store data efficiently. Standard ASCII uses seven-digit bytes (see BIT), and can represent 128 characters. Extended ASCII, which uses an eight-bit encoding system, can represent 256 characters, including many useful characters such as letters with accents.

Asclepius \as-'klē-pē-əs\ *Latin* **Aesculapius** \,es-kyə-'lā-pē-əs\ Greco-Roman god of medicine. Son of APOLLO and the nymph Coronis, he learned the art of healing from the centaur CHIRON. Fearful that Asclepius would make humans immortal, ZEUS slew him with a thunderbolt. Because Asclepius was said to cure the sick in dreams, sleeping in his temples became common. He was often represented holding a staff with a serpent coiled around it.

ascorbic acid See VITAMIN C

ASEAN See ASSOCIATION OF S.E. ASIAN NATIONS

Asgard \'as-,gärd\ In Norse mythology, the dwelling place of the gods. It consisted of 12 or more realms, including VALHALLA, home of ODIN, and Thrudheim, home of THOR. Each Norse god had his own palace in Asgard. It could only be reached from earth via the rainbow bridge called Bifrost.

ash Any tree of the genus *Fraxinus,* in the OLIVE family. The genus includes about 70 species of trees and shrubs found mostly in the Northern Hemisphere. The U.S. boasts 18 species of ash, five of which furnish most of the ash cut as lumber. White ash *(F. americana)* and green ash *(F. pennsylvanica),* yield wood that is stiff, strong, and resilient, yet lightweight. They are used for baseball bats, hockey sticks, paddles and oars, tennis and other racket frames, and the handles of agricultural tools. Black ash *(F. nigra),* blue ash *(F. quadrangulata),* and Oregon ash *(F. latifolia)* are used for furniture, interior paneling, and barrels.

Ashanti People of S Ghana and adjacent areas of Togo and the Ivory Coast. A section of the Akan peoples, they number about 5 million. Though some Ashanti now live and work in urban centers, they remain primarily an agricultural people. The Ashanti supplied slaves to British and Dutch traders in exchange for firearms, which they used to build a large empire in the 18th–19th cent. They fought several wars against the British (1824, 1863, 1869, 1874), finally losing their capital, KUMASI, in 1896. Thereafter Ashanti influence declined. Ashanti goldwork and kente cloth remain desired items of trade.

Ashbery, John (Lawrence) (b.1927) U.S. poet. Born in Rochester, N.Y., he initially became well known as an art critic. His elegant, original, and obscure poems are characterized by arresting images, exquisite rhythms, intricate form, and sudden shifts in tone and subject. His collections include *Some Trees* (1956), *Rivers and Mountains* (1966), *Self-Portrait in a Convex Mirror* (1975, Pulitzer Prize), *Houseboat Days* (1977), *A Wave* (1984), *Flow Chart* (1991), and *Wakefulness* (1998).

Ash Can school Group of U.S. realist painters active in New York City about 1908–18, who specialized in scenes of everyday urban life. Inspired by Robert HENRI, the core group included William GLACKENS, George Luks (1867–1933), Everett Shinn (1876–1953), and John SLOAN. As artist-reporters on the *Philadelphia Press* before moving to New York, they had developed a quick eye and a memory for detail. They often depicted slums and outcasts of the city, hence the group's name. George BELLOWS and Edward HOPPER were also associated with the group. See also The EIGHT.

ash cone See CINDER CONE

Ashcroft, Peggy (*orig.* Edith Margaret Emily) (*later* **Dame Peggy**) (1907–1991) British actress. She appeared from 1932 with the OLD VIC company, winning acclaim in *Romeo and Juliet* (1935). She starred in more than 100 stage productions, playing comedy and tragedy with equal success. One of the great actresses of the British stage, she was a founding member of the ROYAL SHAKESPEARE CO. (1961). She acted in such films as *The Thirty-nine Steps* (1935) and *A Passage to India* (1984, Academy Award) and in the television series *The Jewel in the Crown* (1984).

Ashe, Arthur (Robert), Jr. (1943–1993) U.S. tennis player. Born in Richmond, Va., he was recognized early as a tennis prodigy. After a stellar career at UCLA and victory at the U.S. Open (1968), he turned professional. The first black member of the U.S. DAVIS CUP team, he helped win five championships (1963, 1968, 1969, 1970, 1978). In 1975 he received top world ranking. He retired in 1980 and became captain of the U.S. Davis Cup team (to 1985). In 1985 he became the first black male inducted into the International Tennis Hall of Fame. Off the court he was a critic of racial injustice. In 1992 he revealed that he had been infected with the AIDS virus by a transfusion, and he thereafter worked to increase awareness of the disease. The U.S. Open is now played at Arthur Ashe Stadium in Flushing, N.Y.

Ashford, Evelyn (b.1957) U.S. sprinter. Born in Shreveport, La., she attended UCLA, where she won four national collegiate championships and competed in the 1976 Olympics. She won world championship matches (100- and 200-m sprints) in 1979 and 1981, and was named Woman Athlete of the Year both years. She won two gold medals in the 1984 Olympics (100-m dash, 4 × 100-m relay), and a silver and a gold in the 1988 Olympics. At her fifth Olympics (1992), she became the oldest woman (at 35) to win a gold medal in track and field (4 × 100-m relay).

Ashgabat \ˈäsh-gä-ˌbät\ *or* **Ashkhabad** \ˈash-kə-ˌbad\ City (pop., 1999 est.: 525,000), capital of Turkmenistan. Founded in 1881 as a Russian military fort, it was the capital of Turkmenistan S.S.R. 1924–90. A violent earthquake destroyed the city in 1948; it was rebuilt on the same plan. It is now an industrial, transportation, and cultural center.

Ashikaga family \ˌä-shē-ˈkä-gä\ Japanese warrior family that established the ASHIKAGA SHOGUNATE in 1338. The founder, Ashikaga Takauji (1305–1358), turned on the emperor GO-DAIGO and set up an emperor from another branch of the imperial family, who granted Takauji the title of SHOGUN. Takauji's grandson Yoshimitsu (1358–1408), the third Ashikaga shogun, ended the dual imperial courts that had resulted from his grandfather's actions, reorganized civil government, reopened formal trade with China, and commissioned the famous Golden Pavilion (Kinkaku-

ji) in Kyoto. Ashikaga Yoshimasa (1436–1490), the eighth Ashikaga shogun, was also a great patron of the arts and a devotee of the TEA CEREMONY; he commissioned the Silver Pavilion (Ginkaku-ji), whose understated elegance contrasts with the opulence of the Golden Pavilion. Yoshimasa's tenure as shogun coincided with an increasing loss of control over the countryside as Japan headed toward a century of civil war.

Ashikaga shogunate Military government of Japan established in 1338 by the warrior Ashikaga Takauji. It lasted in name until 1573, when the last of the Ashikaga SHOGUNS was deposed, but in fact lost control of Japan during the ONIN WAR (1467–77). Also known as the Muromachi period, it was a time of great cultural growth; it saw the flourishing of ZEN Buddhism, NO DRAMA, and Chinese-style ink painting. See also ASHIKAGA FAMILY, DAIMYO, SAMURAI.

Ashkenazi \ˌäsh-kə-ˈnä-zē\ Any of the historically Yiddish-speaking European Jews who settled in central and N Europe, or their descendants. They lived originally in the Rhineland valley, and their name is derived from the Hebrew word *Ashkenaz* ("Germany"). After the start of the CRUSADES, many migrated east to Poland, Lithuania, and Russia to escape persecution. In later centuries Jews who adopted the German-rite synagogue ritual were called Ashkenazim to differentiate them from the Sephardic, or Spanish-rite, Jews (see SEPHARDI). Today they constitute more than 80% of the world's Jews.

Ashley, William Henry (1778?–1838) U.S. fur trader. Born in Powhatan, Va., he arrived in Missouri about 1802. With Andrew Henry (1771–1833), he organized the Rocky Mountain Fur Co. in 1822 and established a trading post at the junction of the Missouri and Yellowstone rivers. Forced to abandon the post by Indians, in 1825 he instituted the annual rendezvous, where trappers would trade their furs to him for supplies for the next year. By 1827 he had made a fortune and retired. Elected to the U.S. House of Representatives (1831–37), he championed Western interests.

Ashoka \ə-ˈshō-kə\ *or* **Asoka** \ə-ˈsō-kə\ (d.238? B.C.) Last major emperor (c.265–238 B.C.) of the MAURYAN EMPIRE in India and a patron of BUDDHISM. After his bloody conquest of Kalinga in the eighth year of his reign, Ashoka renounced military aggression and resolved to live according to the DHARMA. He spoke of Buddhism only to fellow Buddhists and adopted a policy of toleration for other religions. He enjoined officials to be aware of the needs of common people and to dispense justice impartially; he also erected stupas and monasteries, developed a course of study for adherents, and sent missionaries to Ceylon. He is remembered as the ideal Buddhist ruler.

Ashqelon \ˈash-kə-ˌlän\ *formerly* Ascalon. Archaeological site, Israel. The historic coastal city-state of Ascalon was traditionally the key to the conquest of SW PALESTINE. Its name appears in Egyptian texts around 1800 B.C. It was conquered by ALEXANDER THE GREAT in 332 B.C. and the Arabs in A.D. 636. It was taken by Crusaders in 1153 and became one of their principal ports. It was retaken by SALADIN in 1187 and destroyed by BAYBARS I in 1270. Modern Ashqelon (pop., 1990 est.: 57,000) is now a resort and industrial center.

Ashtart See ASTARTE

Ashton, Frederick (William Mallandaine) (*later* **Sir Frederick**) (1904–1988) Principal choreographer and director of England's ROYAL BALLET. He joined the Vic-Wells (later Royal) Ballet in 1933, becoming principal choreographer, assistant director (1953–63), and director (1963–70). At least 30 of his works remain in its repertoire, including *Façade* (1931), *Symphonic Variations* (1946), and *Birthday Offering* (1956).

Ashur Archaeological site and ancient religious capital of ASSYRIA, on the TIGRIS RIVER, 60 mi (97 km) south of Mosul, N Iraq. The name Ashur was applied to the city, to Assyria itself, and to Assyria's principal god. The area was originally occupied around 2500 B.C., and later became part of AKKAD. By the late 12th cent. B.C. it was under Assyrian control. In 614 B.C. it was destroyed by BABYLONIA.

Ashurbanipal \ˌä-sər-ˈbä-ni-ˌpäl\ (r.668–627 B.C.) Last great Assyrian king. He was appointed crown prince of Assyria in 672 B.C. On his father's death, Ashurbanipal assumed full

power. He quelled a rebellion in Egypt and successfully besieged Tyre. His half-brother, who ruled Babylonia, joined a coalition of peoples from outlying areas of the Assyrian empire and plotted rebellion, but Ashurbanipal discovered the plots and later took Babylon. By 639 B.C. he had the whole known world under his control. A religious zealot, he rebuilt or adorned most of the major shrines of Assyria and Babylonia. In Nineveh he created the first systematically organized library in the Middle East; the clay tablets collected there preserved omens, epics, prayers, scientific and lexicographical texts, and folktales.

Ashurbanipal Stone bas-relief, 650 B.C.

Ash Wednesday See LENT

Asia Largest continent on earth. It is bounded by the Arctic Ocean, the Pacific Ocean, and the Indian Ocean; the W boundary, with Europe, runs roughly north-south along the E Ural Mtns.; the Caspian, Black, Aegean, and Mediterranean seas; the Suez Canal; and the Red Sea. The islands of Sri Lanka and Taiwan and the archipelagoes of Indonesia, the Philippines, and Japan also form part of Asia. Area: 17,139,445 sq mi (44,391,162 sq km). Population, excluding Asian Russia and the countries of former Soviet Central Asia (1996 est.): 3,499,626,000. Asia's elevations include the earth's highest (Mt. EVEREST) and the lowest (the DEAD SEA). The largest of its many desert regions are the Thar and the GOBI DESERT. Its hydrology is dominated by some of the longest rivers in the world, including the EUPHRATES, TIGRIS, INDUS, GANGES, CHANG (Yangtze), HUANG (Yellow), OB, YENISEY, and LENA RIVERS. The CASPIAN, ARAL, and Dead seas are major saltwater lakes. Asia's principal language groups include SINO-TIBETAN, INDO-ARYAN, JAPANESE, AUSTRONESIAN, AUSTROASIATIC, SEMITIC, and KOREAN. E. Asia contains three main ethnic groups: Chinese, Japanese, and Korean. The Indian subcontinent contains a vast diversity of people. Because of the influence of China and the former Soviet Union, Mandarin and Russian are widespread. Asia is the birthplace of all the world's major religions and hundreds of minor ones. HINDUISM is the oldest; JAINISM and BUDDHISM emerged in the 6th and 5th cent. B.C., respectively. SW Asia was the cradle of JUDAISM and its offshoots, CHRISTIANITY and ISLAM. TAOISM and CONFUCIANISM originated in the 6th or 5th cent. B.C. Asia is marked by great disparities in wealth, both between and within its countries. Asia's culture is the result of the interaction of five main influences: Chinese, Indian, Islamic, European (including Russia), and Central Asian. China has had great influence in E. Asia as the source of Confucianism, a style of art, and the Chinese script. Indian influence has been expressed through Hinduism and Buddhism, affecting Tibet, Indonesia, Cambodia, and Central Asia. Islam spread from its original Arabian home to SW Asia and elsewhere, along with the Arabic alphabet. Writing developed in the Tigris and Euphrates river valleys about 3500–3000 B.C. (see MESOPOTAMIA). Civilization in the Indus valley and in N Syria followed around 2500 B.C. Chinese urban civilization began with the SHANG DYNASTY (traditionally, 1766–1122 B.C.) and continued under the ZHOU DYNASTY (1122–221 B.C.). Indo-European-speaking peoples (ARYANS) began to invade India from the west about 1700 B.C. and developed the VEDIC RELIGION. A succession of empires and charismatic rulers, including ALEXANDER THE GREAT, followed. In the 13th cent. A.D., GENGIS KHAN and his MONGOL successors united much of Asia under their rule. In the 14th cent. TIMUR conquered much of Central Asia. Muslim Turks destroyed the remnants of the Byzantine empire in the 15th cent. In the 19th cent., European imperial-

ism began to replace Asian imperialism. Czarist Russia pushed to the Pacific Ocean, the British gained control of India, the French moved into Indochina, the Dutch occupied the E. Indies, and the Spanish and later the U.S. ruled the Philippines. After World War II, European imperialism largely vanished as former colonies gained independence.

Asia Minor *or* **Anatolia** *Turkish* **Anadolu** \ˌä-nä-ˈdō-lü\ The part of Turkey in Asia. The peninsula forms the W extremity of Asia, between the Black Sea and the Mediterranean Sea; it also borders on the Aegean Sea. It was the original location of the Kingdom of HITTITES (c.1950–1200 B.C.). Later, Indo-European races, possibly Greeks, established the kingdom of PHRYGIA. In the 6th cent. B.C., CYRUS THE GREAT ruled the area; it was invaded by ALEXANDER THE GREAT in 334 B.C. In the 1st cent. B.C., the Romans won control; in A.D. 395 the area fell to the Byzantine empire. It endured invasions by Arabs, Turks, Mongols, and the Turkic army of TIMUR before Ottoman power was established in the 15th cent.; its later history to 1920 is that of the OTTOMAN EMPIRE.

Asimov \ˈa-zi-ˌmóf\, **Isaac** (1920–1992) U.S. (Russian-born) author and biochemist. He arrived in the U.S. at age 3, earned a doctorate from Columbia Univ., then taught for many years at Boston Univ. He began publishing his stories while in college. "Nightfall" (1941) is often called the finest science-fiction short story ever written. His *I, Robot* (1950) greatly influenced writing about intelligent machines, and the *Foundation* trilogy (1951–53) is a classic. Asimov's nonfiction is popular for its clarity and humor. Immensely prolific, he published over 300 books.

Asmara \ˈäs-mȧ-rä\ City (pop., 1995 est.: 431,000), capital of Eritrea. It lies on the Red Sea at the N tip of the Ethiopian Plateau at an elevation of 7,765 ft (2,367 m). Asmara became the capital of the Italian colony of Eritrea in 1900. It was under British control from 1941 until Eritrea's federation with Ethiopia in 1952. It became the capital of independent Eritrea in 1993. It is an agricultural marketplace.

Asoka See ASHOKA

asp Venomous snake, originally probably the Egyptian COBRA (*Naja haje*). The asp was the symbol of royalty in Egypt, and its bite was used to execute criminals in Greco-Roman times. CLEOPATRA is said to have killed herself with an asp.

asparagus Any plant of the genus *Asparagus* (LILY FAMILY), which contains about 300 species native from Siberia to S Africa. The best-known is the economically important garden asparagus, *A. officinalis*, whose stalks are harvested as a green VEGETABLE. Several African species are grown as ornamental plants. The poisonous species prized for their delicate and graceful foliage are *A. plumosus* (called asparagus fern, or florists' fern), *A. sprengeri*, and *A. asparagoides*.

aspartame \ˈas-pər-ˌtām\ Synthetic organic compound of phenylalanine and aspartic acid. It is 150–200 times as sweet as cane SUGAR and is used as a nonnutritive tabletop sweetener and in low-calorie prepared foods (brand names NutraSweet, Equal) but is not suitable for baking. Because it contains phenylalanine, persons with PHENYLKETONURIA must avoid it. See also SACCHARIN.

Aspen City (pop., 2000: 6,000), W central Colorado. It is located on the Roaring Fork River at the edge of the White River National Forest, at an altitude of 7,907 ft (2,410 m). Founded about 1878, it was a booming silver-mining town by 1887 but declined when silver prices collapsed in the early 1890s. It has become a popular tourist town and ski resort, also known for its cultural festivals, notably the Aspen Music Festival.

aspen Any of three trees of the genus *Populus*, of the WILLOW family: *P. tremula* (European aspen), *P. tremuloides* (quaking aspen), and *P. grandidentata* (big-tooth aspen). Native to the Northern Hemisphere, aspens are known for the fluttering of their leaves in the slightest breeze. Aspens grow farther north and higher up the mountains than other *Populus* species. All aspens have a smooth, whitish bark, random branching, and rich green leaves that turn brilliant yellow in fall.

aspergillus \ˌas-pər-ˈjil-əs\ Any FUNGUS of the genus *Aspergillus* of the Fungi Imperfecti. *A. niger* causes black mold of foodstuffs; *A. niger, A. flavus,* and *A. fumigatus* cause as-

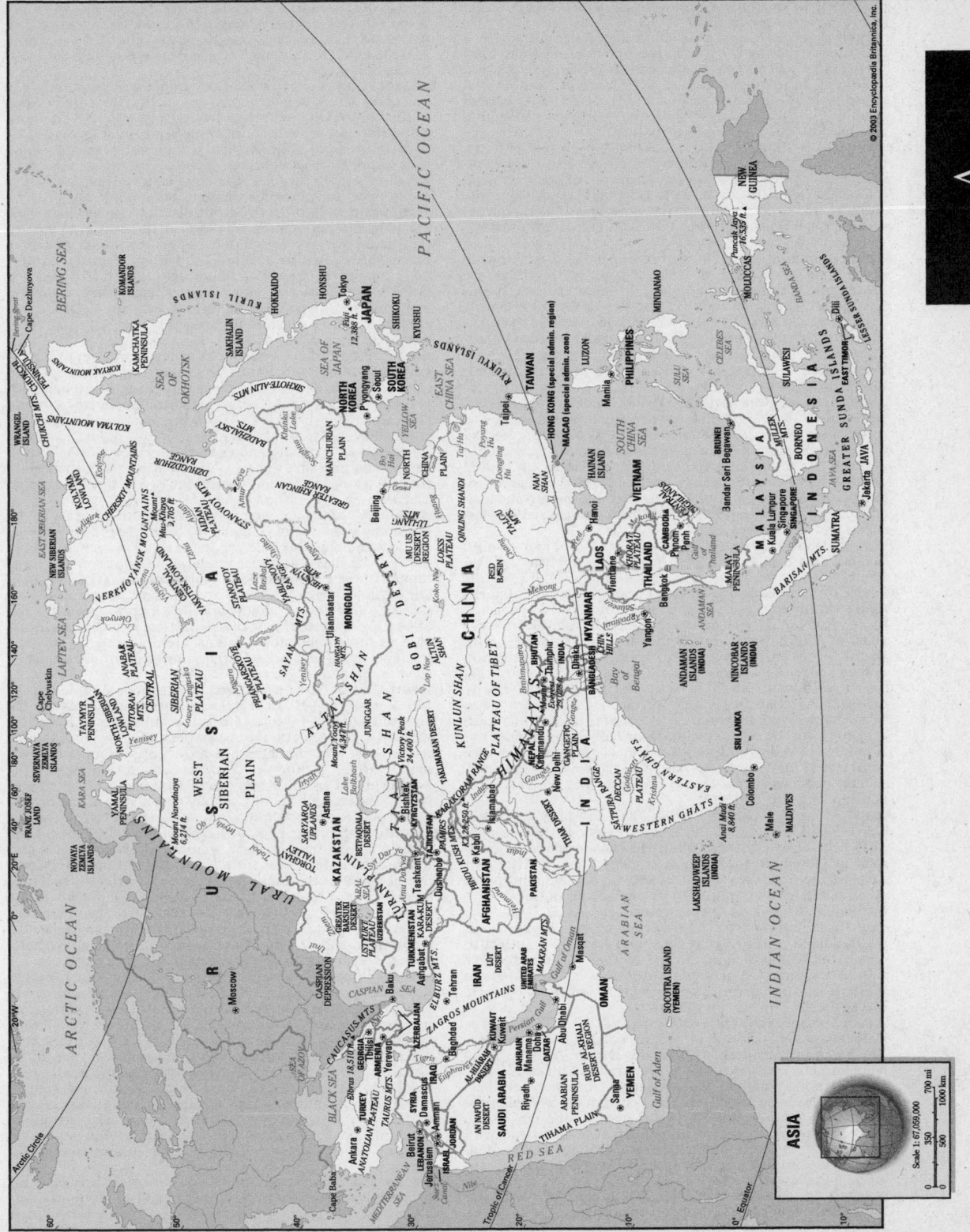

PACIFIC OCEAN

ARCTIC OCEAN

INDIAN OCEAN

RUSSIA

CHINA

INDIA

MONGOLIA

KAZAKSTAN

SIBERIA

WEST SIBERIAN PLAIN

CENTRAL SIBERIAN PLATEAU

GOBI DESERT

PLATEAU OF TIBET

HIMALAYAS

SAUDI ARABIA

IRAN

JAPAN

NORTH KOREA

SOUTH KOREA

TAIWAN

VIETNAM

LAOS

THAILAND

CAMBODIA

MYANMAR

BANGLADESH

NEPAL

BHUTAN

PAKISTAN

AFGHANISTAN

TURKMENISTAN

UZBEKISTAN

TAJIKISTAN

KYRGYZSTAN

MALAYSIA

INDONESIA

PHILIPPINES

BRUNEI

SINGAPORE

SRI LANKA

OMAN

YEMEN

UNITED ARAB EMIRATES

QATAR

BAHRAIN

KUWAIT

IRAQ

SYRIA

TURKEY

GEORGIA

ARMENIA

AZERBAIJAN

LEBANON

ISRAEL

JORDAN

ASIA

Scale 1: 67,059,000

0 350 700 mi
0 500 1000 km

© 2003 Encyclopædia Britannica, Inc.

A

pergillosis in humans. *A. oryzae* is used to ferment SAKE, and *A. wentii* to process SOYBEANS.

asphalt Black or brown petroleum-like material that has a consistency varying from viscous liquid to glassy solid. Consisting chiefly of HYDROCARBONS, it is obtained either as a residue from the distillation of petroleum or from natural deposits. It softens when heated and is elastic under certain conditions. Used principally in road surfacing, asphalt is also used for roofs and waterproofing.

asphyxia \as-'fik-sē-ə\ Lack of exchange of oxygen and carbon dioxide due to respiratory failure or disturbance, resulting in insufficient brain oxygen, which leads to unconsciousness or death. Causes include strangulation, drowning, choking, and CARBON MONOXIDE poisoning. Emergency resuscitation usually includes CARDIOPULMONARY RESUSCITATION.

aspirin Common name of acetylsalicylic acid, an organic compound introduced in 1899. Its primary effects are ANALGESIC, fever-reducing, and anti-inflammatory. It also has ANTICOAGULANT activity, and low doses are taken by CORONARY HEART DISEASE patients to prevent MYOCARDIAL INFARCTION. Prolonged use may cause stomach bleeding and PEPTIC ULCER, and its use in children with fever has been linked to REYE'S SYNDROME. See also ACETAMINOPHEN, IBUPROFEN, NSAIDS.

Asplund, (Erik) Gunnar (1885–1940) Swedish architect. His work shows the transition from neoclassical architecture to modernism. By 1928, influenced by LE CORBUSIER, he had turned from a reminiscent style to the new architecture. He planned the Stockholm Exposition of 1930, an influential collection of futuristic, glassy pavilions. His Woodland Crematorium, Stockholm (1935–40), with its spare Neoclassical colonnade surrounded by meadows, is admired by classicists and modernists alike.

Asquith, H(erbert) H(enry) *later* Earl of Oxford and Asquith (1852–1928) British politician and prime minister (1908–16). Elected to the House of Commons in 1886, he became leader of the Liberal Party and prime minister in 1908. His plan to limit the powers of the House of Lords was enacted by the Parliament Act of 1911. He led Britain in the early years of World War I, but domestic crises combined with British losses in the war led to widespread dissatisfaction and he resigned in 1916.

ass *or* **wild ass** Either of two species of small, sturdy EQUINES. Asses are 3–5 ft (90–150 cm) high at the shoulder. The African wild ass, or true ass (*Equus asinus*), is bluish gray to fawn; the Asiatic wild ass, or half-ass (*E. hemionus*), is reddish to yellow-gray, with extremely long, slender legs, shorter ears, and larger hooves. The true ass has the alternating "hee-haw" bray. Desert dwellers, they are very swift runners. See also DONKEY.

Assad \'ä-säd\, **Hafiz al-** (1930–2000) President of SYRIA (1971–2000). He joined the BAATH PARTY in 1946 and in 1955 became an air-force pilot. He became air-force commander (1963) after the Baathists gained power. After participating in a military coup in 1966, he became minister of defense. He led a coup in 1970 to replace his political mentor, Salah al-Jadid, as Syria's leader. He joined Egypt in a surprise attack on Israel (1973), but nearly 20 years later (1991) joined peace negotiations with Israel in an effort to regain the Golan Heights, taken by Israel in the SIX-DAY WAR. A longtime foe of Saddam HUSSEIN, he supported the Western Alliance against Iraq in the PERSIAN GULF WAR. He was succeeded by his son Bashar.

Assam \a-'sam\ State (pop., 1994 est.: 24,200,000), NE India. With an area of 30,318 sq mi (78,524 sq km), Assam borders Bhutan and Bangladesh; its capital is Dispur. A strong independent kingdom was founded there in the 13th cent. by invaders from Myanmar (Burma) and China; it reached its zenith in the early 18th cent. The British took control in the early 19th cent. Beginning in the 1960s, four new states were created from land within Assam. The BRAHMAPUTRA RIVER valley is its dominant physical feature. The population is Indo-Iranian and Asian; the most widely spoken language is Assamese.

Assassin Islamic sect of the 11th–13th cent. that regarded killing its enemies as a religious duty. The sect's leader, Hasan-e Sabbah (d.1124), commanded a network of strong-

holds from Alamut, Iran, and a corps of terrorists who murdered generals and statesmen of the ABBASID DYNASTY. The MONGOLS finally ended Assassin power when they captured Alamut in 1256. Present-day ISMAILIS are descended from the Assassins.

assassin bug Any of about 4,000 insect species (family Reduviidae) with a thin structure connecting the narrow head to the body. Ranging in size from 0.5 to 1 in. (13–25 mm), assassin bugs use their short, three-segmented beak to suck body fluids from their victims, usually other insects; some suck blood from vertebrates, including humans, and transmit diseases. One species, the large assassin bug, can accurately "spit" saliva toxic enough to blind a human.

assault and battery Related but distinct crimes. Battery is the unlawful application of physical force to another; assault is an attempt to commit battery or an act that may reasonably cause fear of imminent battery. Battery requires no minimum degree of force, nor does it need to be applied directly; administering poison and transmitting a disease may both be battery. Accidents and ordinary NEGLIGENCE are not, nor is reasonable force used in the performance of duty (e.g., by a police officer). See also RAPE.

assault rifle Military firearm chambered for ammunition of reduced size or propellant charge that can switch between semiautomatic and fully automatic fire. Light and portable, yet able to deliver accurate high-volume fire at combat ranges of 1,000–1,600 ft (300–500 m), assault rifles have become the standard infantry weapon of modern armies. Their ease of handling makes them ideal for mobile assault troops and guerrilla fighters. Widely used assault rifles are the U.S. M16, the Soviet Kalashnikov (AK-47), the Belgian FAL and FNC, and the German G3.

assaying \'a-sā-iŋ\ In chemical ANALYSIS, the process of determining proportions of metal, particularly precious metal, in ORES and metallurgical products. Precious metals tend to occur as scattered particles randomly distributed, so a large sample of ore is required. Such large samples (typically containing gold, silver, and lead) are still most economically assayed by this ancient method, which involves several steps of heating and cooling. More sophisticated recent methods, such as spectrochemical analysis, are not suited to assaying precious metal ores because the samples of ore that must be used are too large.

Assemblies of God Largest Pentecostal denomination in the U.S. Formed in 1914 in Hot Springs, Ark., it emphasizes the centrality of the Bible in Christian faith and worship. Instead of SACRAMENTS, the Assemblies have two ordinances, BAPTISM by total immersion and the Lord's Supper. Millennial doctrines dealing with Christ's Second Coming and the establishment of the Kingdom of God are of great importance. The Assemblies of God have been very active in mission work. See also MILLENNIALISM, PENTECOSTALISM.

assembly language Type of low-level PROGRAMMING LANGUAGE consisting mostly of symbolic equivalents of a particular computer's MACHINE LANGUAGE. Computers produced by different manufacturers have different machine languages and require different assembly languages. Some assembly languages convert the code that programmers write (source code) into machine language (readable by the computer), and also facilitate programming (e.g., by combining a sequence of several instructions into one).

assembly line Industrial arrangement of machines, equipment, and workers for continuous flow of workpieces in MASS-PRODUCTION operations. It is designed by determining the sequences of operations for manufacture of each component as well as the final product. Each movement of material is made as simple and short as possible, with no cross flow or backtracking. Work assignments, numbers of machines, and production rates are programmed so that all operations performed along the line are compatible. Automated assembly lines (see AUTOMATION) consist entirely of machines run by other machines and are used in petroleum refining, chemical manufacture, and automobile-engine plants.

assessment Process of setting a value on real or personal property, usually for the purpose of taxation. Property may be assessed on the basis of its annual rental value, as in Britain, or its capital value, as in the U.S. Methods used to determine capital value include analysis of market data to estimate the property's current market price, estimation of the cost of reproducing the property minus accrued DE-PRECIATION, and capitalization of the property's earnings.

Assiniboin \ə-ˌsin-ə-ˈbȯi-ən\ PLAINS INDIAN people who inhabited an area between the upper Missouri and middle Saskatchewan rivers. Generally friendly with whites, they moved their camps frequently in pursuit of migrating buffalo. Prowess in war consisted of taking scalps and horses and of touching the enemy ("counting coups") during battle. Their numbers were severely reduced by smallpox in the 1820s and '30s, after which most were placed on reservations. Today they number about 1,000 in Canada and about 4,000 in the U.S.

Assiniboine River \ə-ˈsin-ə-ˌbȯin\ River, S Canada. Rising in Saskatchewan, it flows into the RED RIVER OF THE NORTH at WINNIPEG. It is about 590 mi (950 km) long. Explored by Pierre de LA VÉRENDRYE in 1736, it later served as a route to the plains by colonists from Red River Settlement.

Assis, Joaquim Maria Machado de See J. M. MACHADO DE ASSIS

Assistance, Writs of General search warrants used in the American colonies by the British. The warrants authorized customhouse officers, with the assistance of a sheriff, to search any house or ship indiscriminately for smuggled goods. Their legality was challenged by such colonists as James OTIS in the 1760s, and the writs became a major grievance in the years leading up to the AMERICAN REVOLUTION.

Associated Press (AP) Cooperative NEWS AGENCY, the oldest in the U.S. and the largest in the world. It began in 1848, when six New York newspapers financed a telegraphic pool of foreign news brought by ships to Boston. In 1892 the modern AP was set up. Its restrictive controls on new memberships were ended with federal antitrust prosecution in the 1940s, and it now serves more than 15,000 news outlets worldwide.

association In psychology, the process of forming mental connections between sensations, ideas, or memories. The "association of ideas" was first proposed by John LOCKE and later examined by David HUME, Herbert SPENCER, and William JAMES. Ivan PAVLOV's study of association resulted in his identification of the conditioned reflex (see CONDITIONING). Within PSYCHOANALYSIS, the therapist encourages "free association" to help identify latent conflicts. Practitioners of GESTALT PSYCHOLOGY have criticized associationist theory as too all-embracing, while some theorists of COGNITIVE PSYCHOLOGY have made it central to their theory of MEMORY.

association football See SOCCER

Association of Caribbean States (ACS) Trading bloc composed of 25 nations of the Caribbean basin. Responding to a 1994 proposal for a hemisphere-wide Free Trade Area of the Americas (FTAA), existing Caribbean-area trading blocs joined forces in 1995 to strengthen their economic position and ease future integration into the FTAA. Prominent in the ACS are the Caricom nations (13 English-speaking countries and Suriname), which have been struggling toward a single market and economy along the lines of the European Union.

Association of Southeast Asian Nations (ASEAN) International organization established by Indonesia, Malaysia, the Philippines, Singapore, and Thailand in 1967 to accelerate economic growth, social progress, and cultural development and to promote peace and security in the region. Brunei became a member in 1984, Vietnam in 1995, Laos and Myanmar in 1997, and Cambodia in 1999. In 1992 member nations created the ASEAN Free Trade Area.

associative law Two closely related laws of number operations. In symbols, they are stated: $a + (b + c) = (a + b) + c$, and $a(bc) = (ab)c$. Stated in words: The terms or factors may be associated in any way desired and the result will be the same. This holds for the numbers generally encountered: positive and negative, integral and fractional, RATIONAL and IRRATIONAL, and REAL and IMAGINARY NUMBERS. See also COMMUTATIVE LAW, DISTRIBUTIVE LAW.

Assyria Ancient empire, W Asia. It grew from a small region around ASHUR (N Iraq) to extend from Palestine to Turkey.

Its greatest period began in the 9th cent. B.C., when its conquests reached the Mediterranean under Ashurnasipal II, and around 745–626 B.C., when it conquered Israel, Damascus, Babylon, and Samaria. Its greatest rulers during the latter period were TIGLATH-PILESER III, SARGON II, SENNACHERIB, and ASHURBANIPAL. Famous for their cruelty and fighting prowess, the Assyrians were also monumental builders, as shown by archaeological finds at NINEVEH, ASHUR, and Calah, noted for their stone bas-reliefs. The opulence of Ashurbanipal's court at Nineveh became legendary. Assyria fell to the kings of MEDIA and BABYLONIA (Chaldea) 626–612 B.C.

Assyro-Babylonian language See AKKADIAN LANGUAGE

Astaire, Fred orig. Frederick Austerlitz (1899–1987) U.S. dancer and singer of stage and movies. Born in Omaha, at age 7 he and his sister Adele began their popular vaudeville dance act, making their Broadway debut in 1917; they continued dancing in stage hits until Adele retired in 1932. Astaire's legendary film appearances with Ginger Rogers (1911–1995) began with *Flying Down to Rio* (1933) and continued until 1939. In the 1940s and '50s he danced on-screen with such stars as Judy GARLAND. His singing, though untrained, was widely admired. His sophisticated, effortless grace and technical virtuosity revolutionized popular-dance performance.

Astana formerly (1992–99) **Aqmola** or **Akmola** \ȧk-ˈmō-lə\, (1961–92) **Tselinograd** \ˈtsi-nə-ˌgrät\ City (pop., 1997 est.: 270,000) and capital of Kazakstan. Founded in 1824 as a Russian military outpost, it gained importance as the junction site of the Trans-Kazakstan and S. Siberian railways and center of a mineral-rich steppe region. In 1994 the Kazakh government began to transfer the national capital from ALMATY to Astana, changing the city's name in 1999.

Astarte \a-ˈstär-tē\ or **Ashtart** \ˈash-ˌtärt\ Goddess of the ancient Near East. Astarte shared many qualities, and perhaps a common origin, with her sister ANATH. The goddess of love and war, she was worshiped in Egypt and among the Hittites as well as in Canaan. Her Akkadian counterpart was ISHTAR. She is often mentioned in the Bible as Ashtaroth, and JOSIAH destroyed the shrines dedicated to her.

aster Any of various chiefly fall-blooming, leafy-stemmed herbaceous plants (*Aster* and closely related genera) in the COMPOSITE FAMILY, often with showy flowers. Included among the asters are many perennial WILDFLOWERS and hundreds of garden varieties.

asteroid or **minor planet** Any of the many small rocky astronomical objects found mainly in a "belt" between the orbits of Mars and Jupiter. They are thought to have been kept from aggregating into a single planet while the SOLAR SYSTEM was forming by the gravitational influence of what became Jupiter. Only about 30 are more than 125 mi (200 km) across. Ceres is the largest known asteroid. Millions of boulder-sized asteroids are thought to exist in the solar system. A few strike the earth, plunging through the atmosphere as METEORS. Asteroids appear to be composed of carbonaceous, stony, and metallic (mainly iron) materials. See also EARTH-CROSSING ASTEROID.

asthenosphere \as-ˈthe-nə-ˌsfir\ Zone of the earth's MANTLE lying beneath the LITHOSPHERE. Believed to be much hotter and more fluid than the lithosphere, the asthenosphere is thought to extend from about 60 mi (100 km) to about 450 mi (700 km) below the earth's surface.

asthma \ˈaz-mə\ Chronic disease with attacks of shortness of breath, wheezing, and coughing from constriction and mucous-membrane swelling in the air passageways in the lungs. It is caused primarily by ALLERGY respiratory infection, diesel fumes, or secondhand smoke. Asthma is common, runs in families, and affects all races; predisposition may be hereditary. Exercise, stress, and sudden changes in temperature or humidity can bring on attacks, lasting from a half hour to several hours; severe attacks can be fatal. Corticosteroids can control asthma; injections of EPINEPHRINE can relieve acute attacks.

astigmatism \ə-ˈstig-mə-ˌti-zəm\ Lack of symmetry in the curvature of the cornea or, rarely, the lens of the EYE. The unequal curvatures prevent light rays from being sharply focused at a point on the RETINA, causing blurring of part

of the image. Astigmatic vision is corrected by eyeglasses or CONTACT LENSES.

Astor, John Jacob (*orig.* Johann Jakob) (1763–1848) German-U.S. fur magnate and financier. After emigrating from Germany at 17, he opened a fur-goods shop in New York about 1786. He established the American Fur Co. (1808) and controlled the fur trade with China and in the Mississippi and Missouri valleys before selling his interests in 1834. He invested lucratively in New York real estate. At his death Astor was the wealthiest person in the U.S.; he willed $400,000 to found what became the NEW YORK PUBLIC LIBRARY. His son, William B. Astor (1792–1875), greatly expanded the family real-estate holdings, building over 700 stores and dwellings in the city.

Astrakhan \'as-trə-ˌkan\ City (pop., 1997 est.: 490,000), SW Russia. It is situated on several islands in the delta of the VOLGA RIVER. It was a trading center and the capital of a TATAR khanate independent of the GOLDEN HORDE in the 13th cent. IVAN IV the Terrible conquered Astrakhan in 1556, giving Russia control of the Volga. The Turks burned the city in 1569. It served as the base for PETER I the Great's campaign against Persia and was given special trade privileges by CATHERINE II.

astrolabe Type of early scientific instrument used for reckoning time and for observational purposes. Invented in the 6th cent. A.D., it came into wide use in Europe and the Islamic world, and was adopted by mariners by the mid-15th cent. The planespheric astrolabe, a kind of basic analog computer, let astronomers calculate the positions of the sun and major nearby stars with respect to both the horizon and the meridian.

astrology DIVINATION that consists of interpreting the influence of stars and planets on earthly affairs and human destinies. In ancient times it was inseparable from ASTRONOMY. It originated in Mesopotamia (c.3rd millennium B.C.) and spread to India, but it developed its Western form in Greek civilization during the Hellenistic period. According to the Greek tradition, the heavens are divided according to the 12 constellations of the ZODIAC, and the bright stars that rise at intervals cast a spiritual influence over human affairs. Astrology was also important in ancient China, where a HOROSCOPE was cast for each newborn child and at all decisive junctures of life. Interest in astrology has continued into modern times, and astrological signs are still widely believed to influence personality.

astronaut Person trained to pilot a SPACECRAFT, operate any of its systems, or conduct research aboard it during spaceflights, usually to participate in U.S. space missions (cosmonaut is the Russian equivalent). Training includes study of technical subjects; practice in simulators and full-sized mock-ups of spacecraft to experience FREE FALL; and learning to use the control, communication, and life-support systems of spacecraft and to conduct difficult flight operations. See also Edwin ALDRIN, Neil ARMSTRONG, Yury GAGARIN, John GLENN, Sally RIDE, Alan B. SHEPARD.

astronomical unit (AU) Unit of distance equal to the average distance of the earth from the sun: 92,955,808 mi (149,597,870 km). It cannot be measured directly through the PARALLAX method, because the sun overwhelms the light of the background stars necessary to make the measurement. The most precise values have been obtained since 1958 by timing radar reflections from Venus. This indirect method is based on Kepler's law relating the relative size of the planets' orbits; thus, if the distance to one planet can be determined, then the distance to the sun can be calculated.

astronomy Science dealing with the origin, evolution, composition, distance, and motion of all matter in the UNIVERSE. The most ancient of the sciences, it has existed since the dawn of recorded civilization. Much of the earliest knowledge of celestial bodies is often credited to the Babylonians. The ancient Greeks' cosmological ideas included theories about the earth in relation to the rest of the universe. PTOLEMY's model of an earth-centered universe (2nd cent. A.D.) influenced astronomical thought for over 1,300 years. In the 16th cent., Nicolaus COPERNICUS assigned the central position to the sun (see COPERNICAN SYSTEM), ushering in modern astronomy. The 17th cent. saw Johannes KEPLER's discovery of the principles of planetary motion,

GALILEO's use of the TELESCOPE for astronomical observation, and the formulation of Isaac NEWTON's laws of motion and gravitation. ASTROPHYSICS was developed in the 19th cent. In 1927 Edwin HUBBLE proved the concept of the EXPANDING UNIVERSE. In 1937 the first RADIO TELESCOPE was built. The first man-made satellite, SPUTNIK, was launched in 1957, and the first deep-space probes (see PIONEER) were launched in the 1960s. See also BIG BANG, GAMMA-RAY ASTRONOMY, INFRARED ASTRONOMY, RADIO AND RADAR ASTRONOMY, ULTRAVIOLET ASTRONOMY, X-RAY ASTRONOMY.

astrophysics Branch of ASTRONOMY concerned with the properties and structures of cosmic objects, including the universe as a whole. Once SPECTROSCOPY and photography were used to study the brightness, temperature, and chemistry of cosmic objects in the 19th cent., it was clear that their properties must be understood in terms of the physics of their atmospheres and interiors. X-RAY ASTRONOMY, GAMMA-RAY ASTRONOMY, INFRARED ASTRONOMY, ULTRAVIOLET ASTRONOMY, and RADIO AND RADAR ASTRONOMY have extended the portion of the electromagnetic spectrum emitted by astronomical objects that can be measured.

Asturias \äs-'tûr-ē-əs\, **Miguel Ángel** (1899–1974) Guatemalan poet, novelist, and diplomat. He moved to Paris in 1923 and became a Surrealist under the influence of André BRETON. He began his diplomatic career in 1946. His writings combine a Mayan mysticism and a magic-realist style with an epic impulse toward social protest, especially against U.S. and oligarchic power. In his masterpiece, *Men of Maize* (1949), he depicts the seemingly irreversible wretchedness of the Indian peasant. Other major novels are *El Señor Presidente* (1946), a fictional denunciation of Guatemala's dictator; *The Cyclone* (1950); *The Green Pope* (1954); and *The Eyes of the Interred* (1960). He won the Nobel Prize in 1967.

Miguel Ángel Asturias

Asunción \ä-ˌsün-'syōn\ *in full* Nuestra Señora de la Asunción. Capital city (pop., 1992: 502,000) of Paraguay. It lies on the PARAGUAY RIVER. Founded in 1537 by Spanish conquistadores, it replaced BUENOS AIRES as the headquarters of Spanish colonial activities in E S. America 1541–80. In 1731 Asunción was the site of one of the first major rebellions against Spanish rule. The city declared independence from both Spain and Argentina in 1811. Today it is the social, cultural, and economic center of Paraguay.

Aswan High Dam Dam across the NILE RIVER, north of Aswan, Egypt. Built 4 mi (6 km) upstream from the earlier Aswan Dam (1902), it is 364 ft (111 m) high and 12,562 ft (3,830 m) long. Differences with Gamal Abdel NASSER led the U.S. and Britain to withdraw support of the project in 1956, whereupon Nasser turned to the Soviet Union. The dam, completed in 1970, impounds the reservoir Lake NASSER and controls the annual Nile flood, releasing floodwaters when needed for irrigation; it also produces great amounts of electric power.

asylum Protection from arrest and extradition given to political refugees by a nation or by an embassy that has diplomatic immunity. Its traditional use has been to protect those accused of such political offenses as TREASON, desertion, SEDITION, and ESPIONAGE. It may now also be granted to those who can demonstrate a reasonable fear of politically motivated persecution in their home country.

asymptote \'a-səm-ˌtōt\ In mathematics, a line or curve that acts as the LIMIT of another line or curve. For example, a descending CURVE that approaches but does not reach the horizontal axis is said to be asymptotic to that axis, which is the asymptote of the curve.

Atahuallpa \ä-tä-'wäl-pä\ (1502?–1533) Last free-reigning emperor of the INCAS. Having defeated his half brother in what may have been the greatest military engagement in Inca history, he was met by the CONQUISTADOR Francisco

PIZARRO just before his triumphal entry into Cuzco and invited to a feast. When he and his retainers arrived, Pizarro ambushed them on horseback with cannons and guns and slaughtered thousands. Pizarro accepted Atahuallpa's ransom offer of a roomful of gold, then, having received 24 tons of gold and silver, ordered him burned at the stake. The sentence was changed to death by garrote when Atahuallpa agreed to convert to Christianity.

Atalanta \ˌa-tᵊl-ˈan-tə\ In GREEK MYTHOLOGY, a swift-footed huntress. She was left to die at birth but was suckled by a bear. She took part in the famous Calydonian boar hunt and drew first blood. She offered to marry any man who could outrun her, but the losers paid with their lives. One contestant, Hippomenes, obtained three golden apples from APHRODITE to carry in the race. As he dropped them, Atalanta stooped to pick them up, and thus lost the race. The two were later turned into lions after they desecrated a shrine.

Ataturk \ˈat-ə-ˌtərk\, **Mustafa Kemal** *orig.* Mustafa Kemal (1881–1938) Founder of modern Turkey. Born in Ottoman-controlled Greece, he graduated near the top of his class in military school. As a young officer, he criticized the government and became involved with Turkish nationalists. He nevertheless fought for the government during World War I, defeating the Allies at GALLIPOLI. The eventual Allied victory brought British, French, and Italian troops to Anatolia; appointed to restore order there, he used the opportunity to incite the people against the Allied invaders. He overcame foreign opposition to Turkish nationalism, and the Turkish republic was established in 1932. He was given the name Ataturk ("father of the Turks") in 1934. He pursued a policy of Westernization, deemphasizing religion, emancipating women, overhauling the legal system, and replacing the Arabic alphabet with the Roman. See also ENVER PASA, YOUNG TURKS.

Atchison, Topeka and Santa Fe Railroad Co. Former railway. Chartered in Kansas in 1860 by Cyrus K. Holliday, the founder of Topeka, as the Atchison and Topeka Railroad Co., it was built along the SANTA FE TRAIL and became known as the Santa Fe Railway. Its main line, completed in 1872, extended to the Colorado state border. With further expansion west, by 1941 it owned 13,000 mi (21,000 km) of track. In 1971 its famously luxurious passenger service was sold to AMTRAK. In the 1990s it merged with Burlington Northern to become Burlington Northern Santa Fe Railway.

Aten See ATON

Atget \àt-ˈzhe\, **(Jean-) Eugène (-Auguste)** (1857–1927) French photographer. After working as an itinerant actor, he settled in Paris and became a photographer. With an eye for strange images, he recorded shop fronts, trees, monuments, and poor tradespeople. After World War I he received a commission to document the brothels of Paris. Man RAY published four of Atget's photographs in *La révolution surréaliste* (1926), the only recognition he received in his lifetime. After his death, Berenice ABBOTT helped buy his remaining collection, which is now in the Museum of Modern Art.

Athabasca, Lake Lake, W central Canada. It extends 208 mi (335 km), crossing the Alberta–Saskatchewan boundary. It receives the ATHABASCA RIVER and discharges into the Slave River. It is important for commercial fishing.

Athabasca River River, W central Canada. A tributary of the MACKENZIE RIVER in Alberta, it rises in the Rocky Mtns. in JASPER NATIONAL PARK, and flows northeast and north 765 mi (1,231 km) into Lake ATHABASCA. Extensive petroleum deposits lie in oil-impregnated sands along a 70-mi (113-km) stretch of the river.

Athabaskan languages *or* **Athapaskan languages** Family of N. American Indian languages, with perhaps 200,000 speakers today. Northern Athabaskan includes more than 20 languages scattered across Alaska and W and central Canada. Pacific Coast Athabaskan consisted of four to eight nearly extinct languages. Apachean consists of eight closely related languages spoken in the SW U.S. and N Mexico, including Navajo. Navajo now has close to 150,000 speakers, far more than any other indigenous language of the U.S. or Canada. The Athabaskan family may be related to Tlingit

and Haida (languages of Alaska and British Columbia, respectively).

Athanasius \ˌa-thə-ˈnā-zhəs\, **St.** (293?–373) Early defender of Christian orthodoxy against ARIANISM. He studied philosophy and theology at Alexandria, Egypt, and in 325 he attended the Council of Nicaea, which condemned the Arian heresy. In 328 he was appointed patriarch of Alexandria, but theological disputes led to the first of several banishments in 336. After being banished by Constantius II in 356, he lived in a remote desert in Upper Egypt and wrote theological treatises, including his *Four Orations Against the Arians*. A controversy with JULIAN's heathen subjects forced him to flee into the Theban desert. At the time of his death he again possessed the see at Alexandria.

atheism \ˈā-thē-ˌiz-əm\ Critique and denial of metaphysical beliefs in God or divine beings. Unlike AGNOSTICISM, atheism is a positive denial of God's existence. Ancient Greek philosophers such as DEMOCRITUS and EPICURUS argued for it in the context of MATERIALISM. Atheists such as Ludwig Feuerbach (1804–1872) held that God was a projection of human ideals and that recognizing this fiction made self-realization possible. MARXISM exemplified modern materialism. Beginning with Friedrich NIETZSCHE, existentialist atheism proclaimed the death of God and the human freedom to determine value and meaning.

Athena \ə-ˈthē-nə\ *or* **Athene** \ə-ˈthē-nē\ In ancient GREEK RELIGION, the goddess of war, handicraft, and wisdom, and patroness of Athens. Her Roman counterpart was MINERVA. HESIOD told how Athena sprang in full armor from ZEUS's forehead. In the *Iliad*, she fought alongside the Greek heroes, and she represented the virtues of justice and skill in warfare as opposed to the blood-lust of ARES. She was associated with birds, especially the owl and the snake, and she was usually represented as a virgin goddess.

Athena Roman marble copy of Phidias' gold-and-ivory statue (438 B.C.)

Athens *Greek* **Athínai** \ä-ˈthē-ne\ City (pop., 1991: 772,000), capital of Greece. The source of many of the West's intellectual and artistic conceptions, including that of democracy, Athens is generally considered the birthplace of Western civilization. An influential city-state by the 6th cent. B.C. it was destroyed by XERXES I in 480 B.C., but by 450 B.C., led by PERICLES, it was at its height, and over the following 40 years many major building projects, including the ACROPOLIS and PARTHENON, were completed. Athens' "Golden Age" saw the works of the philosophers SOCRATES, PLATO, and ARISTOTLE; the dramatists SOPHOCLES, ARISTOPHANES, and EURIPIDES; the historians HERODOTUS, THUCYDIDES, and XENOPHON; and the sculptors PRAXITELES and PHIDIAS. The PELOPONNESIAN WAR with SPARTA ended in Athens' defeat in 404, but it quickly recovered its independence and prosperity. After 338 B.C. Athens came under MACEDONIA's hegemony, which was lifted with the aid of Rome in 197 B.C. It became subject to Rome in 146 B.C. In the 13th cent. Athens was taken by the Crusaders. It was conquered in 1456 by the Ottoman Turks, who held it until 1833, when it was declared the capital of independent Greece. It is now a major tourist destination.

athlete's foot Form of RINGWORM that affects the feet. In the inflammatory type, the infection may manifest occasional acute episodes in which cracks and blisters develop, mostly between the toes. The dry type is a chronic condi-

A

tion marked by slight redness of the skin and dry scaling; the toenails become thick and brittle.

athletics See TRACK AND FIELD

Athos \ˈä-ˌthôs\, **Mt.** Mountain, N Greece. Reaching a height of 6,670 ft (2,033 m), it is the site of a semiautonomous republic of 20 monasteries and dependencies (*skítes*). St. ATHANASIUS the Athonite founded the first monastery in 963. By 1400 there were 40 monasteries. Long regarded as the holy mountain of the GREEK ORTHODOX CHURCH, it was declared a theocratic republic in 1927. Its churches and libraries house a rich collection of Byzantine art and ancient and medieval manuscripts.

Athyr See HATHOR

Atlanta City (pop., 2000: 416,000; metro. area pop.: 4,112,000), capital of Georgia. Lying in the foothills of the BLUE RIDGE MTNS., Atlanta is Georgia's largest city. In 1837 the site was selected for a railroad terminus; it was named Atlanta in 1845. An important supply depot during the AMERICAN CIVIL WAR, it was burned by Union forces under William T. SHERMAN. Atlanta became the state capital in 1868. Recovering from the war, it began to epitomize the spirit of the "New South." It was the home of M. L. KING and the first major Southern city to elect a black mayor (1970). It is a major trade and transportation center.

Atlanta Campaign Important series of AMERICAN CIVIL WAR battles in Georgia (May–Sept. 1864). Though most of the battles ended in draws, they eventually cut off the main Confederate supply center, Atlanta. Union troops under W. T. SHERMAN forced the city's evacuation of the city (Aug. 31–Sept. 1) and then burned it. His victory assured the reelection of Pres. Abraham LINCOLN later that year.

Atlantic, Battle of the Contest in WORLD WAR II between Britain (and later the U.S.) and Germany for the control of Atlantic sea routes. Initially the Anglo-French coalition controlled the Atlantic, but with the fall of France in 1940, Britain was deprived of French naval support. The U.S. then assisted Britain with the LEND-LEASE program. Early in 1942, Germany began a large-scale submarine offensive against coastal shipping in U.S. waters, and U-BOATS also operated in force along the S. Atlantic ship lanes. After suffering severe losses, the Allies succeeded in tightening their blockade of Axis Europe. By mid-1943 the Allies had recovered control of the sea routes.

Atlantic City City (pop., 2000: 40,000) and resort, SE New Jersey. The resort began to be developed in the mid-19th cent. Amusement piers were constructed, and, in 1870, the world's first beachfront boardwalk. The Miss America Pageant was established there in 1921. After World War II the city began to decline. In 1978 the state legalized gambling in the city, which stimulated a huge influx of money, but much of the surrounding area remained impoverished.

Atlantic Intracoastal Waterway Navigable route, coastal E U.S. Authorized by Congress in 1919, it was originally planned to form a continuous channel from New York City to Brownsville, Texas. Because the link through Florida was never completed, it remains in two separate sections (see GULF INTRACOASTAL WATERWAY). The Atlantic portion consists of rivers, bays, and canals from CAPE COD to Florida Bay, including the Cape Cod Canal and the Chesapeake and Delaware Canal.

Atlantic Monthly, The Journal of literature and opinion, one of the oldest in the U.S. Founded in Boston by Moses Dresser Phillips (1857), it soon became noted for the quality of its fiction and general articles, contributed by such distinguished writers as J. R. LOWELL, R. W. EMERSON, H. W. LONGFELLOW, and O. W. HOLMES. In the 20th cent. it expanded its scope to political affairs, featuring articles by such figures as Theodore ROOSEVELT and Booker T. WASHINGTON. In the 1970s increasing costs nearly closed the magazine; it was purchased in 1980 by Mortimer Zuckerman.

Atlantic Ocean Ocean separating N. and S. America from Europe and Africa. The second-largest of the world's oceans, the Atlantic has an area of 31,830,000 sq mi (82,440,000 sq km). Including the BALTIC, NORTH, BLACK, and MEDITERRANEAN SEAS to the east, and BAFFIN BAY, HUDSON BAY, the Gulf of ST. LAWRENCE, Gulf of MEXICO, and CARIBBEAN SEA to the west, it covers 41,000,000 sq mi (105,000,000 sq km). Its most powerful current is the GULF STREAM.

Atlantis Legendary sunken island in the Atlantic Ocean west of Gibraltar. The main sources for the legend are two of PLATO's dialogues, *Timaeus* and *Critias*. According to Plato, Atlantis had a rich civilization, and its princes made many conquests in the Mediterranean before earthquakes destroyed the island and it was swallowed up by the sea. The legend may have originated with the massive eruption around 1500 B.C. of a volcano on THÍRA.

Atlas In GREEK MYTHOLOGY, the strong man who supported the weight of the heavens on his shoulders. Son of the TITAN Iapetus and brother of PROMETHEUS, according to HESIOD Atlas was one of the Titans who waged war against Zeus, and as punishment he was condemned to hold aloft the heavens.

atlas Collection of maps, usually bound together. The name derives from Gerardus MERCATOR's use of the figure of the Titan ATLAS holding the globe as a frontispiece. Abraham Ortelius's *Epitome of the Theater of the World* (1570) was probably the first modern atlas. Atlases often contain pictures, tabular data, facts about areas, and indexes of place-names keyed to the grids on the maps.

Atlas, Charles *orig.* Angelo Siciliano (1893–1972) U.S. (Italian-born) bodybuilder. He emigrated to the U.S. at age 10. In 1929 he and the advertiser Charles P. Roman launched a course involving isotonic exercises and nutritional maintenance. Their mail-order bodybuilding course became legendary through advertisements in three generations of pulp comic books, the standard ad depicting scenes in which a skinny boy loses his girlfriend to a lifeguard who kicks sand in his face, and regains her after taking the Atlas course.

Atlas Mountains Mountain system, NW and N Africa. It extends some 1,200 mi (2,000 km) from Cape Dra, Morocco, to Cape Bon, Tunisia. It comprises several ranges, including the High Atlas in Morocco, the Maritime or Tell Atlas from Morocco to Tunisia, and the Saharan Atlas in Algeria.

atman \ˈät-mən\ (Sanskrit: "breath" or "self") Basic concept in Hindu philosophy, describing that eternal core of the personality that survives death and transmigrates to a new life or is released from the bonds of existence. Atman became a central philosophical concept in the UPANISHADS. It underlies all aspects of personality, as BRAHMAN underlies the working of the universe. See also SOUL.

atmosphere Gaseous envelope that surrounds the earth. Near the surface it has a well-defined chemical composition (see AIR); in addition to gases, it contains solid and liquid particles in suspension. Scientists divide the atmosphere into five main layers; the TROPOSPHERE (surface to 6–8 mi, or 10–13 km); STRATOSPHERE (4–11 mi, or 6–17 km, to about 30 mi, or 50 km); mesosphere (31–50 mi, or 50–80 km); thermosphere (50–300 mi, or 80–480 km); and exosphere (from 300 mi and gradually dissipating). Most of the atmosphere consists of neutral atoms and molecules, but in the IONOSPHERE a significant fraction is electrically charged. See also OZONE LAYER. See diagram on next page.

atmospheric pressure *or* **barometric pressure** Force per unit area exerted by the air above the surface of the earth. Standard sea-level pressure equals 1 atmosphere (atm), or 29.92 in. (760 mm) of mercury, 14.70 lbs per square in., or 101.35 kilopascals, but pressure varies with elevation and temperature. It is usually measured with a mercury barometer, which indicates the height of a column of mercury that exactly balances the weight of the column of atmosphere above it.

atom Smallest unit into which matter can be divided and still retain the characteristic properties of an ELEMENT. The atom was believed to be indivisible until the early 20th cent., when ELECTRONS and the NUCLEUS were discovered. It is now known that an atom has a positively charged nucleus that makes up more than 99.9% of its MASS but less than a trillionth of its volume. The nucleus is composed of PROTONS and NEUTRONS, each about 2,000 times as massive as an electron. Most of the atom's volume consists of a cloud of electrons, bound to the nucleus by the attraction of opposite charges. In a neutral atom, the protons in the nucleus are balanced by the electrons. An atom that has gained or lost electrons becomes negatively or positively charged and is called an ION. See diagram on next page.

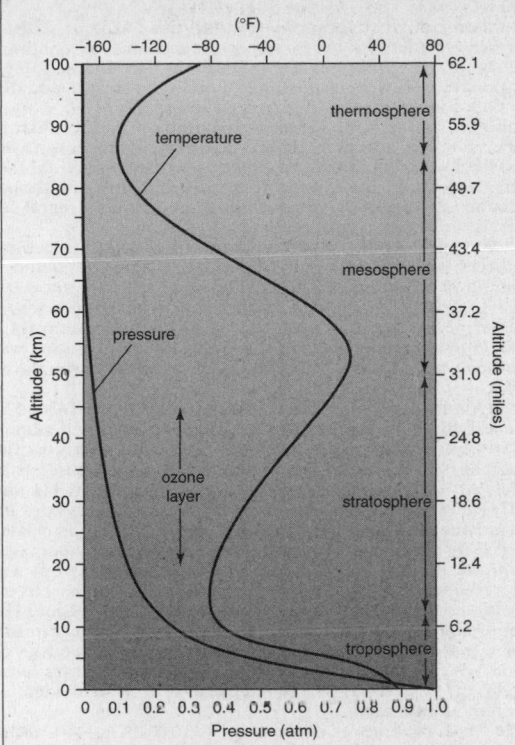

Atmosphere In earth's atmosphere, the limits of the atmospheric layers are approximate and variable, especially with latitude. Most weather occurs within the troposphere. The ozone layer, which absorbs most incoming ultraviolet radiation, forms part of the stratosphere. The thermosphere extends hundreds of miles above earth's surface and is bounded by outer space. Atmospheric pressure drops off steadily with altitude, but temperature rises and falls through successive layers in a more complex manner.

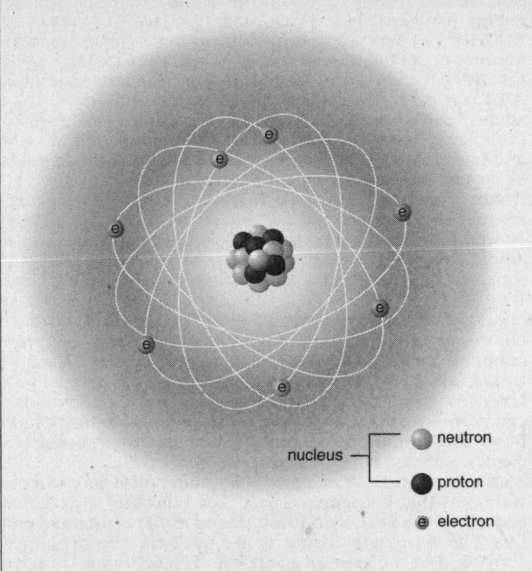

Atom The classical "planetary" model of an atom. The protons and neutrons in the nucleus are circled by electrons in "orbit" around the nucleus. The number of protons determines which element is represented, the number of electrons determines its charge, and the number of neutrons determines which isotope of the element is represented.

atomic bomb Weapon whose great explosive power results from the sudden release of energy upon the splitting, or fission, of the nuclei of such heavy elements as plutonium or uranium (see NUCLEAR FISSION). An atomic bomb containing 2 lbs (1 kg) of uranium-235 will generate a 17-kiloton explosion that creates a huge fireball, a large shock wave, and lethal radioactive FALLOUT. Developed by the MANHATTAN PROJECT during World War II, the first atomic bomb used in warfare was dropped by the U.S. on HIROSHIMA August 6, 1945; a second bomb was dropped on NAGASAKI three days later. In 1949 the Soviet Union tested its first atomic bomb, followed by Britain (1952), France (1960), China (1964), India (1974), Pakistan (1998), and probably Israel. S. Africa has dismantled its own bombs. See also HYDROGEN BOMB, NUCLEAR NONPROLIFERATION TREATY.

atomic number Number of a chemical ELEMENT in the systematic, ordered sequence shown in the PERIODIC TABLE. The elements are arranged in order of increasing number of PROTONS in the NUCLEUS of the ATOM (the same as the number of ELECTRONS in the neutral atom), and that number for each element is its atomic number.

atomic physics Scientific study of the structure of the ATOM, its ENERGY states, and its interaction with other particles and FIELDS. The physical properties of atoms are largely determined by the laws of QUANTUM MECHANICS and QUANTUM ELECTRODYNAMICS. The primary tools for the study of these properties are SPECTROSCOPY, particle collisions (see PARTICLE ACCELERATOR), and statistical models that simulate complex, many-body interactions. A broad field, atomic physics has applications in the study of condensed matter, gases, chemical-reaction mechanisms, atmospheric science, lasers, nuclear physics, and the arrangement of elements in the PERIODIC TABLE.

atomic weapon See NUCLEAR WEAPON

atomic weight Ratio of the average MASS of a chemical ELEMENT's atoms to $^1/_{12}$ the mass of an atom of the carbon-12 ISOTOPE. The original standard of atomic weight, established in the 19th cent., was hydrogen, with a value of 1. From about 1900 until 1961, the reference standard was oxygen, with a value of 16.

Aton *or* **Aten** \'ä-tən, 'a-tən\ In ancient Egyptian religion, a sun god. The pharaoh AKHENATON (r.1353–36 B.C.) declared Aton to be the only god, and in opposition to the Amon-Re priesthood of Thebes, built the city of Akhetaton as the center for Aton's worship. After Akhenaton's death, the old religion was restored.

atonality \ˌā-tō-'na-lə-tē\ Literally, the absence of TONALITY. Originally a derogatory term applied to music of extreme CHROMATICISM, it has become the standard term for 20th-cent. music whose connection with tonality is difficult to hear. Arnold SCHOENBERG and his students Alban BERG and Anton WEBERN are regarded as the principal atonal composers; the SERIALISM of their later work is often distinguished from their earlier "free atonality."

atonement Religious concept in which obstacles to reconciliation with God are removed, usually through sacrifice. In Christianity, atonement is achieved through the death and resurrection of JESUS. In Roman Catholicism, Eastern Orthodoxy, and some Protestant churches, penance is a sacrament that allows for personal atonement (see CONFESSION). In Judaism the annual Day of Atonement, YOM KIPPUR, is the culmination of 10 days centered on repentance.

Atonement, Day of See YOM KIPPUR

ATP *in full* **adenosine triphosphate** \ə-'de-nə-ˌsēn-trī-'fäs-ˌfāt\ Organic compound, substrate in many enzyme-catalyzed reactions (see CATALYSIS) in all CELLS. Because ATP's chemical bonds (see BONDING) store a large amount of chemical energy, it functions as the carrier of chemical energy from energy-yielding oxidation (see OXIDATION-REDUCTION) of food to energy-demanding cellular processes. Sources of ATP and stored energy include FERMENTATION, the TRICARBOXYLIC ACID CYCLE, and cellular respiration. All form ATP from adenosine monophosphate (AMP) or adenosine diphosphate (ADP) and inorganic PHOSPHATE. In the reverse reaction, ATP is broken down to ADP or AMP and phosphate and the energy is used to perform chemical, electrical, or osmotic work for the cell.

Atreus \\'ā-trē-əs\\ In Greek legend, the king of Mycenae. Plagued by a curse on the house of his father, Pelops, Atreus murdered his own son Pleisthenes and was eventually killed by the nephew he had raised as a son. Two more sons, AGAMEMNON and MENELAUS, fought in the Trojan War.

atrial fibrillation \\'ā-trē-əl\\ Irregular rhythm (arrhythmia) of contraction of the atria (upper heart chambers). The most common major CARDIAC ARRHYTHMIA, it may be caused by chest surgery, pulmonary EMBOLISM, severe infection or fever, or heart malformation or disease. If it continues, it can permit formation of blood clots, which can block blood flow to essential organs. Emergency treatment consists of electric shocks (defibrillation).

atrium \\'ā-trē-əm\\ In an ancient Roman house, an open central court that contained a basin for rainwater. It originally contained the hearth and functioned as the center of family life. The term later came to be used for the open front courtyard of a Christian BASILICA. The atrium was revived in the 20th cent. as glass-covered, greenery-filled multistory spaces in shopping centers, office buildings, and large hotels.

atropine \\'a-trə-ˌpēn\\ Anticholinergic drug, a poisonous, crystalline ALKALOID from certain plants, used chiefly in ophthalmology to dilate the pupil or to break up adhesions between the lens and iris. It also dries and relieves hay fever and cold symptoms; relaxes intestinal spasms; is used in treating ENURESIS; inhibits the vagus nerve; and affects the central nervous system. Synthetic substitutes with more specific effects have been developed.

AT&T Corp. *formerly* **American Telephone and Telegraph Co.** U.S. telecommunications corporation. It was established as a subsidiary of Bell Telephone Co. (founded by Alexander Graham BELL in 1877) to build long-distance telephone lines, and later became the parent company of the Bell system. By 1970 it was the world's largest corporation. Antitrust litigation resulted in AT&T's 1984 divestment of its 22 regional telephone companies, which were combined to form seven "Baby Bells": Nynex, Bell Atlantic, Ameritech, BellSouth, Southwestern Bell, US West, and Pacific Telesis. In 1996 AT&T divided into AT&T Corp., Lucent Technologies Inc. (composed of the former WESTERN ELECTRIC and BELL LABORATORIES), and the NCR CORP. (later spun off).

attainder Extinction of civil and political rights after being sentenced, usually for TREASON. A legislative act attainting a person without trial was known as a bill of attainder. The most important consequences of attainder were forfeiture of property and "corruption of blood," meaning that the attainted person was disqualified from inheriting or transmitting property, thus disinheriting his descendants. All forms of attainder except forfeiture following indictment for treason were abolished in the 19th cent. The U.S. Constitution provided that no attainder would affect anyone after the death of the attainted person. The U.S. Supreme Court has also struck down as bills of attainder such things as the test oaths passed after the Civil War to disqualify Confederate sympathizers from certain professions.

Attenborough, Richard (Samuel) *later* **Baron Attenborough** (b.1923) British actor and director. A screen actor from 1942, he appeared in such films as *I'm All Right, Jack* (1959), *The Great Escape* (1963), and *Elizabeth* (1998). As a director he won acclaim for *Oh, What a Lovely War!* (1969) and *Gandhi* (1982, Academy Award). His brother David (later Sir David) (b.1926) joined the BBC in 1952, where he originated the series *Zoo Quest* (1954–64) and later helped produce *The Forsyte Saga, The Ascent of Man*, and *Civilisation*. As an independent producer, he made innovative edu-

cational programs such as *Life on Earth* (1979), *The Living Planet* (1984), and *The Life of Birds* (1998).

attention deficit (hyperactivity) disorder (**ADD** *or* **ADHD**) *formerly* **hyperactivity** Behavioral syndrome in children, whose major symptoms are inattention and distractibility, impulsive behavior, restlessness, inability to sit still, and difficulty concentrating. It occurs in about 5% of all schoolchildren, and is three times more common in boys than in girls. It often adversely affects learning. It appears to be caused by a combination of genetic and environmental factors. Aspects of the syndrome may persist into adulthood. Treatment usually entails counseling and close parental supervision, and may also include medication.

Attica *Greek* **Attiki** \\ˌä-tē-'kē\\ Ancient district, E central Greece. It was bordered by the AEGEAN SEA and included the island of Salamis; its chief cities were ATHENS, PIRAEUS, and ELEUSIS. Originally inhabited by Pelasgians, it was a center of MYCENAEAN culture in the 2nd millennium B.C.; the IONIAN Greeks invaded it around 1000 B.C. Attica was unified under Athens by 700 B.C., traditionally through the efforts of King THESEUS.

Attila \\'a-tᵊl-ə, ə-'ti-lə\\ (d.453) King of the HUNS (434–53). He and his elder brother Bleda coruled an inherited empire that stretched from the Alps and the Baltic nearly to the Caspian Sea. When the Romans failed to pay promised tributes, Attila launched assaults along the Danube in 441 and 443. He murdered his brother in 445 and two years later invaded the Balkan provinces and Greece, a campaign later ended by another peace treaty that exacted heavy damages from the Eastern Romans. He invaded Gaul (451) but was defeated by an alliance of the Romans and Visigoths. His invasion of Italy (452) was ended by famine and plague. His depredations, which seemed to some like divine punishment, earned him the epithet Flagellum Dei ("Scourge of God"). Attila died on his wedding night, possibly murdered by his bride, and was succeeded by his sons, who divided his empire among them.

Attis Mythical consort of the GREAT MOTHER OF THE GODS and vegetation god worshiped in Phrygia and Asia Minor. His worship later spread to the Roman empire. The worship of Attis and the Great Mother included the celebration of mysteries at the beginning of spring.

Attlee, Clement (Richard) *later* Earl Attlee (of Walthamstow) (1883–1967) British prime minister (1945–51). Committed to social reform, he lived for much of the years 1907–22 in a settlement house in London's poor district. Elected to Parliament in 1922, he led the Labour Party (1933–55) and served in the wartime coalition government of Winston CHURCHILL, whom he succeeded as prime minister in 1945. Attlee presided over the establishment of the WELFARE STATE in Britain, the nationalization of major British industries, and the granting of independence to India. He resigned when the Conservatives narrowly won the election in 1951.

attorney, power of Authorization to act as agent or attorney for another. Durable power of attorney becomes effective when the principal becomes unable to manage his or her affairs; general power of attorney authorizes the agent to carry on business for the principal; special power of attorney authorizes the agent to carry out a particular business transaction.

attorney general Chief law-enforcement officer of a state. The office assumed its modern form in the 16th cent. In the U.S., the position dates to the Judiciary Act of 1789. Head of the Department of Justice and a member of the CABINET, the attorney general oversees all the government's law business and acts as the president's legal adviser. Every U.S. state also has an attorney general.

Attucks \\'at-əks\\, **Crispus** (1723?–1770) American patriot and martyr of the BOSTON MASSACRE. Probably a runaway slave of African and Natick Indian ancestry, he may have served on whaling ships. He is the only one of the Massacre's five victims widely remembered.

Atwood, Margaret (Eleanor) (b.1939) Canadian writer. Born in Ottawa, she attended the Univ. of Toronto and Harvard Univ. Her poetry collection *The Circle Game* (1964) celebrates the natural world and condemns materialism. Her novels, several of them best-sellers, are informed by feminism; they include *Surfacing* (1972), *Lady Oracle* (1976), *Bodily Harm* (1981), *The Handmaid's Tale* (1985), *Cat's Eye* (1988), *The Robber Bride* (1993), and *The Blind Assassin* (2000, Booker Prize).

Auckland City (pop., 1997: 372,000; metro. area pop.: 954,000), North Island, New Zealand. It is the country's principal port and largest city. It was the capital from its founding in 1840 until 1865, when WELLINGTON displaced it. It is a major manufacturing and shipping center. A bridge links it with the growing N shore suburbs and with Devonport, New Zealand's chief naval base.

auction Buying and selling of property through open public bidding. Typically, potential purchasers make a succession of increasing bids or offers until the highest (and final) bid is accepted by the auctioneer. At a so-called Dutch auction, by contrast, the seller offers property at successively lower prices until one of his offers is accepted or he withdraws the offered property. Auctions are important in agricultural markets, permitting the rapid sale of perishable goods. Other items often sold at auction include artwork and antiques, secondhand goods, and farms and buildings repossessed by banks or the government. Auction selling is also employed on stock and commodity exchanges.

Auden, W(ystan) H(ugh) (1907–1973) British-U.S. poet and man of letters. He attended Oxford Univ., where he exerted a strong influence on C. DAY-LEWIS, Louis MACNEICE, and Stephen SPENDER. His varied works dealt with intellectual and moral issues of public concern as well as the inner world of fantasy and dream. In the 1930s he became a hero of the left, pointing up the evils of capitalism while also warning against those of totalitarianism. He collaborated with Christopher ISHERWOOD on three verse dramas. Later writing reflects his move to the U.S., his revived Christianity, and his disillusionment with the left, as well as his homosexuality.

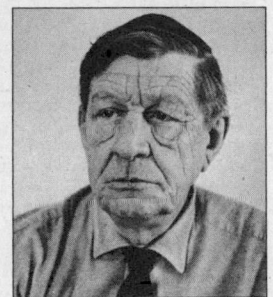
W. H. Auden, 1965

His poetic works include the long poem *The Age of Anxiety* (1947, Pulitzer Prize). With his longtime companion Chester Kallman, he wrote opera librettos, notably *The Rake's Progress* (1951) for Igor STRAVINSKY. After the death of T. S. ELIOT, he was considered the foremost poet writing in English.

audio card See SOUND CARD

audit Examination of financial records and reports of an enterprise by accounting specialists other than those responsible for their preparation. The auditor performs tests to determine whether a firm's statements were prepared in accordance with acceptable accounting principles and fairly present its financial position and operating results. Personal tax audits determine whether people have accurately reported their financial circumstances when filing their taxes. Failing such an audit may result in a fine or criminal prosecution.

auditorium Portion of a theater or hall where an audience sits, as distinct from the stage. It originated in the theaters of ancient Greece, as a semicircular seating area cut into a hillside. Floor levels in a large auditorium may include stalls, private boxes, dress circle, balcony or upper circle, and GALLERY. A sloping floor and converging walls allow for a clear view of the stage and improve acoustics.

Audubon, John James *orig.* Fougère Rabin *or* Jean Rabin *later* Jean-Jacques Fougère Audubon (1785–1851) French-U.S. ornithologist, artist, and known for his drawings and paintings of N. American birds. Born in Haiti, he returned with his father to France, where he studied painting briefly with J.-L. DAVID before moving to the U.S. at 18. From his father's Pennsylvania estate he pursued the first American bird-banding experiments, then concentrated on drawing and studying birds, which took him from Florida to Labrador. His extraordinary four-volume *Birds of America* was published in London in 1827–38, along with the ex-

tensive accompanying text *Ornithological Biography* (5 vols., 1831–39). His multivolume *Viviparous Quadrupeds of North America* (1842–54) was completed by his sons. Though some details are inaccurate, his illustrations are admired as art, and his studies were fundamental to New World ornithology.

Audubon Society, National Organization dedicated to conserving and restoring natural ecosystems, named for J. J. AUDUBON. Founded in 1905, the society has 600,000 members and maintains 100 wildlife sanctuaries and nature centers throughout the U.S. Its high-priority campaigns include preserving wetlands and endangered forests, protecting corridors for migratory birds, and conserving marine wildlife.

auger Tool (or bit) used with a carpenter's brace for drilling holes, usually in wood. It looks like a corkscrew and produces extremely clean holes, almost regardless of how large the bit is. Expansive auger bits have adjustable blades with cutting edges and spurs that can be extended radially to cut large holes. Large augers are used to bore holes in soil for fence posts and telephone poles, or in ice for ice fishing. Horizontal augers as much as 8 ft (2.5 m) in diameter are used in coal mining.

Augsburg \'au̇ks-ˌbu̇rk\ City (pop., 1996 est.: 260,000), BAVARIA, S Germany. Founded as a Roman colony by Caesar AUGUSTUS about 14 B.C., it became an imperial free city in 1276 and joined the Swabian League in 1331. In the 15th–16th cent. the FUGGER and Welser families made the city a major banking and commercial center. It is known for the AUGSBURG CONFESSION (1530), the Peace of AUGSBURG (1555), and the League of Augsburg (from 1686). In 1806 the city became part of Bavaria. Its Fuggerei (1519) is the world's oldest housing settlement for the poor.

Augsburg, Peace of Convention promulgated in 1555 by the Diet of the Holy Roman Empire, which provided the first permanent legal basis for the existence of LUTHERANISM in Germany. The Diet determined that no member of the empire would make war against another on religious grounds. Recognizing only the Roman Catholics and the Lutherans, it stipulated that in each territory of the empire only one denomination was allowed. However, people were allowed to move to states where their faith was adopted. Despite numerous shortcomings, the accord saved the empire from serious internal conflicts for over 50 years.

Augsburg Confession \'au̇ks-ˌbu̇rk\ Basic doctrinal statement of LUTHERANISM. Its principal author was Philipp MELANCHTHON, and it was presented to Emperor CHARLES V at the Diet of Augsburg on June 25, 1530. Its purpose was to defend the Lutherans against misrepresentations of their teachings and to provide a statement of theology that Roman Catholics might accept. It consisted of 28 articles that outlined Lutheran doctrine and listed abuses that had crept into Western Christendom. Translated into English in 1536, it had a major influence on the doctrinal statements of the Anglican and Methodist churches.

Augusta City (pop., 2000: 18,000), capital of Maine. It was established in 1628 by traders from PLYMOUTH as a post on the Kennebec River. Ft. Western was built there in 1754. Incorporated in 1797, the town was renamed the next year for the daughter of an American Revolutionary general. It became the state capital in 1832.

Augustan Age Illustrious period in Latin literary history, about 43 B.C. to A.D. 18. With the preceding period, dominated by CICERO, it forms the Golden Age of Latin literature. Marked by civil peace and prosperity, the age reached its highest expression in polished, sophisticated poetry on patriotism, love, and nature, generally addressed to a patron or to the emperor AUGUSTUS. Writers include VIRGIL, HORACE, LIVY, and OVID. The term is also applied to the "classical" literature of late-17th- and 18th-cent. England.

Augustine (of Hippo), St. (354–430) Roman Catholic theologian. Born in Roman N. Africa, he adopted MANICHAEISM in his youth, but was converted to Christianity by St. AMBROSE, who baptized him in 387. In 396 he became bishop of Hippo (now Annaba, Algeria), a post he held until his death in 430, while the city was under siege by a Vandal army. His best-known works include the *Confessions*, an autobiographical meditation on God's grace, and *The City of God*, on the place of Christianity in history. His *On Christ-*

ian Doctrine and *On the Trinity* are also widely read. His sermons and letters show the influence of Neoplatonism, and his views on predestination influenced later theologians, notably John CALVIN. He was declared a Doctor of the Church in the early Middle Ages.

Augustine of Canterbury \ʾȯ-gəs-ˌtēn, ȯ-ˈgəs-tən\, **St.** (d.604?) First archbishop of Canterbury. A Benedictine prior in Rome, he was chosen by Pope GREGORY I to lead 40 monks as missionaries to England. They arrived in 597 and were welcomed by King ETHELBERT of Kent, who gave them a church in Canterbury. Augustine converted the king and thousands of his subjects and was made bishop of the English. He purified pagan temples, consecrated 12 other bishops, and made Canterbury

St. Augustine Fresco by Sandro Botticelli, 1480

the primary see in England. He tried unsuccessfully to unify his churches with the Celtic churches of N Wales.

Augustinian In the Roman Catholic church, a member of any of the religious orders and congregations whose constitutions are based on the Rule of St. AUGUSTINE. The two main branches of the Augustinians are the Augustinian Hermits and the Augustinian Canons. The former was one of the four great mendicant orders of the Middle Ages, and its members (including Martin LUTHER) were active in European university life and ecclesiastical affairs. The latter became in the 11th cent. the first Roman Catholic order to combine clerical status with full common life. The order declined after the Reformation, but it continues mission, educational, and hospital work.

Augustus, Caesar *or* **Octavian** *orig.* Gaius Octavius *later* Gaius Julius Caesar Octavianus (63 B.C.–A.D. 14) First Roman emperor. Born to a wealthy family, he was named adoptive son and heir of his great-uncle Julius CAESAR at 18. After Caesar's assassination (44 B.C.) he formed the Second TRIUMVIRATE with his chief rivals, LEPIDUS and Mark ANTONY. Battles between the triumvirs ended with his disposing of Lepidus in 32 and Antony at the Battle of ACTIUM in 31 to become sole ruler. The Roman empire is said to begin with his accession. His rule (31 B.C.–A.D. 14) brought changes to every aspect of Roman life and lasting peace and prosperity to the Greco-Roman world. He secured outlying imperial provinces, built roads and public works, established the PAX ROMANA, and fostered the arts. When he died, the empire stretched from Iberia to Cappadocia and from Gaul to Egypt. He was deified after his death.

auk Any of 22 species of diving birds (family Alcidae). Auks are 6–16 in. (15–40 cm) long, with short wings and legs and webbed feet. They occur only in Arctic, subarctic, and temperate regions (with a few species south to Baja California). Auks nest colonially on cliff ledges or in rock crevices or burrows near the sea; many spend the winter far from land. They feed on fish, crustaceans, mollusks, and plankton. See also GREAT AUK.

aulos \ˈȯ-lōs\ Single- or double-reed pipe usually played in pairs, particularly in ancient Greece. The classical pipes were of equal length, each with three or four fingerholes. The principal wind instrument of the ancient Middle East, it existed in Europe up to the early Middle Ages. Its quavering sound, described by PLATO, was classically associated with the rites of DIONYSUS.

Aum Shinrikyo \ˈaùm-shin-ˈrik-yō\ Japanese new religion founded by Shoko Asahara (b.1955 as Chizuo Matsumoto) in 1987. It contains elements of Hinduism and Buddhism and prophesies a series of disasters that will bring an end to this world and inaugurate a new cosmic cycle. In 1995 its members released nerve gas into the Tokyo subway system, killing 12 and injuring 5,000. With adherents once said to number 10,000 in Japan and 20,000 abroad, it has been linked with other violent crimes. Now reduced to about 2,000 members in Japan, the group changed its name to Aleph in 2000.

Aung San \ˈȯŋ-ˈsan\ (1914?–1947) Burmese nationalist leader. He led a students' strike in 1936 and became secretary-general of a nationalist group in 1939. He accepted Japanese aid in raising a Burmese military force, which helped the Japanese in their 1942 invasion, but, doubting that the Japanese would truly deliver Burmese independence, he switched in 1945 to the Allied cause. After the war, he effectively became prime minister, and he negotiated Burmese independence, achieved in 1948. He was assassinated later that year.

Aung San Suu Kyi \ˈȯŋ-ˈsan-ˈsü-ˈchē\ (b.1945) Opposition leader in Myanmar. Daughter of AUNG SAN, she studied in Burma and India and at Oxford Univ. She lived a quiet life until, returning to Myanmar in 1988, she spoke out against the brutality of U NE WIN's military regime and began a nonviolent struggle for democracy and human rights. The 1990 electoral victory of her National League for Democracy (NLD) was ignored by Ne Win's government, and she was held under house arrest 1989–95 and has not been allowed to travel abroad. She was awarded the Nobel Peace Prize in 1991.

Aurangzeb \ˌaù-rəŋ-ˈzeb\ *orig.* Muhi-ud-Din Muhammad (1618–1707) Mughal emperor of India (r.1658–1707). Third son of the emperor SHAH JAHAN, he distinguished himself early with his military and administrative ability. He fought his eldest brother for the right of succession and had several other rival relatives executed. At first he proved a capable Muslim monarch of a mixed Hindu-Muslim empire, disliked for his ruthlessness but respected. From about 1680 his devout religious side came to dominate; he excluded Hindus from public office and destroyed their temples and schools, became embroiled in fruitless warfare with the Marathas in S. India, and executed the Sikh guru Tegh Bahadur (1621?–1675), starting a lengthy Sikh–Muslim feud.

Aurelian \ȯ-ˈrā-lē-ən\ *Latin* Lucius Domitius Aurelianus (A.D. c.215–275) Roman emperor A.D. 270–75. He reunited the empire and restored Roman power in Europe, turning back invaders and quelling revolts, securing provinces in the east and defeating the Germans to the north. He built a new wall around Rome and increased food distribution to the poor, but his monetary and religious reforms failed. While marching to Persia he was slain by a group of officers.

Aurelius, Marcus See MARCUS AURELIUS

Aurgelmir \ˈaùr-gəl-ˌmir\ *or* **Ymir** \ˈi-mir\ In Norse mythology, the first being, a giant created from the drops of water that formed when the ice of Niflheim met the heat of Muspelheim. He was the father of all giants. The gods killed Aurgelmir and put his body into the void, where his flesh became the earth, his blood the seas, his bones mountains, his teeth stones, his skull the sky, and his brains the clouds. His eyelashes (or eyebrows) became the fence around MIDGARD, home of mankind.

Aurignacian culture \ˌȯr-ēn-ˈyā-shən\ STONE-TOOL INDUSTRY and artistic tradition of the Upper PALEOLITHIC PERIOD, named after the village of Aurignac in S France where it was first identified. The Aurignacian period dates to 35,000–15,000 B.C. Its tools included scrapers, burins (for engraving), and blades. Points and awls were fashioned from bones and antlers. Aurignacian art represents the first complete artistic tradition, moving from simple engravings of animal forms on small rocks to finer pieces of carved bone and ivory to clay figurines of pregnant women ("Venus figures"). By the end of the Aurignacian, engravings, reliefs, and paintings appear on the surfaces of limestone caves throughout W Europe, most famously LASCAUX GROTTO.

aurochs \ˈaùr-ˌäks\ *or* **auroch** Extinct wild OX (*Bos primigenius*) of Europe, the species from which CATTLE are probably descended. The aurochs survived in central Poland until 1627. It was black, stood 6 ft (1.8 m) high at the shoulder, and had spreading, forward-curving horns. Attempts have been made to recreate the species. The name has sometimes been wrongly applied to the European BISON.

Aurora Roman goddess of dawn. Her Greek counterpart was Eos. She was the sister of HELIOS, the sun, and SELENE, the moon. By the Titan Astraeus, she became the mother of the winds and of the evening star. In Greek mythology she was also represented as the lover of the hunters Cephalus and ORION.

aurora Luminous phenomenon of the upper atmosphere that occurs primarily at high latitudes. Auroras in the Northern Hemisphere are called aurora borealis, or northern lights; in the Southern Hemisphere, aurora australis, or southern lights. Auroras are caused by the interaction of energetic particles (electrons and protons) with atoms in the upper atmosphere of the earth's magnetic poles. During periods of intense solar activity, auroras occasionally extend to the middle latitudes.

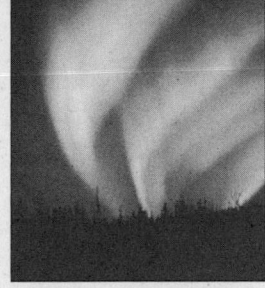

Aurora borealis Multiple arcs, photographed in Alaska

Auschwitz \ˈaúsh-ˌvits\ *or* **Auschwitz-Birkenau** Nazi Germany's largest CONCEN-TRATION CAMP and extermination camp, located in Poland (modern Oswiecim). It consisted of three camps, established in 1940, 1941 (Birkenau), and 1942. Able-bodied Jewish prisoners were sent to a forced-labor camp, while the aged, the weak, and children and their mothers were killed. Some prisoners were also subjected to medical experiments, conducted by Josef MENGELE. An estimated 1 million-2.5 million died at Auschwitz. See also HOLOCAUST.

Ausgleich See COMPROMISE OF 1867

Austen, Jane (1775–1817) English novelist. The daughter of a rector, she lived in the circumscribed world of minor landed gentry and country clergy that she used in her writing. Her earliest works are parodies of sentimental fiction. In her six full-length novels (published anonymously)— *Sense and Sensibility* (1811), *Pride and Prejudice* (1813), *Mansfield Park* (1814), *Emma* (1815), *Persuasion* (1817), and *Northanger Abbey* (published 1817)—she created the COMEDY OF MANNERS of middle-class English life in her time. Her writing is noted for its wit, realism, shrewd sympathy, and brilliant style. Through her treatment of ordinary people in everyday life, she gave the novel its distinctly modern character.

Austerlitz, Battle of (Dec. 2, 1805) First engagement of the War of the Third Coalition (see NAPOLEONIC WARS) and one of NAPOLEON's greatest victories. In the battle, fought near Austerlitz in Moravia (now Slavkov u Brna, Czech Republic), Napoleon's 68,000 troops defeated almost 90,000 Russians and Austrians under Russia's ALEXANDER I and Mikhail KUTUZOV. Also called the Battle of the Three Emperors, Napoleon's resounding victory forced Austria's FRANCIS I to cede Venetia to the French kingdom in Italy, temporarily ending the anti-French alliance.

Austin City (pop., 2000: 656,000), capital of Texas. It was founded in 1835 as the village of Waterloo on the COLORADO RIVER in S central Texas. It was renamed to honor Stephen AUSTIN and made capital of the Republic of Texas in 1839 and of the state in 1845. Home of the Univ. of TEXAS and the Lyndon B. JOHNSON Library, it has expanded as a research and development center for defense and consumer industries.

Austin, Stephen (Fuller) (1793–1836) U.S. colonizer in Texas when it was still part of Mexico. Born in Austinville, Va., he was raised in Missouri Territory and served in its legislature (1814–19). His father conceived a plan to colonize Texas on land obtained from the Mexican government, which Austin continued after his father died (1821), founding a colony of several hundred families on the Brazos River in 1822. He later worked to secure independence for Texas, participating in the Texas revolution, and is considered one of the state's founders. The city of Austin is named for him.

Australia *officially* **Commonwealth of Australia** Smallest continent and sixth-largest country (in area) on earth, lying between the Pacific and Indian oceans. Area: 2,967,909 sq mi (7,686,884 sq km). Population (2000): 19,165,000. Capital: CANBERRA. Most Australians are descendants of Europeans; the largest nonwhite minority is the AUSTRALIAN ABORIGINES. The Asian part of the population has grown as a result of relaxed immigration policy. Language: English (official). Religions: Roman Catholicism, Anglicanism. Currency: Australian dollar. Australia has four major physiographic regions. More than half its land area is the Western Australian Shield, which includes the outcrops of ARNHEM LAND and the Kimberleys in the northwest and the MACDONNELL RANGES in the east. A second region, the Great Artesian Basin, lies east of the shield region. The Eastern Uplands, which includes the GREAT DIVIDING RANGE, is a series of high ridges, plateaus, and basins. The fourth region is the FLINDERS–Mt. Lofty ranges. The country's highest point is Mt. KOSCIUSKO in the AUSTRALIAN ALPS; the lowest, Lake Eyre. Major rivers include the MURRAY RIVER, the Flinders and Swan rivers, and Cooper Creek. There are many islands and reefs along the country's coast, including the GREAT BARRIER REEF, MELVILLE ISLAND, KANGAROO ISLAND, and TASMANIA. Australia is rich in mineral resources, including coal, petroleum, and uranium. A vast diamond deposit was found in WESTERN AUSTRALIA in 1979. The country's economy is basically free-enterprise; its largest components include finance, manufacturing, and trade. Formally a constitutional monarchy, its chief of state is the British monarch, represented by the governor-general. In reality it is a parliamentary state with two legislative houses; its head of government is the prime minister. Australia has long been inhabited by Aborigines, who arrived 40,000–60,000 years ago. Estimates of the population at the time of European settlement in 1788 range from 300,000 to more than 1 million. Widespread European knowledge of Australia began with 17th-cent. explorations. The Dutch landed in 1616 and the British in 1688, but the first large-scale expedition was that of James COOK in 1770, which established Britain's claim to Australia. The first English settlement, at Port Jackson (1788), consisted mainly of convicts and seamen; convicts were to make up a large proportion of the incoming settlers. By 1859 the colonial nuclei of all Australia's states had been formed, but with devastating effects on the Aborigines, whose population declined sharply with the introduction of European diseases and weaponry. Britain granted its colonies limited self-government in the mid-19th cent., and an act federating the colonies into a commonwealth was passed in 1900. Australia fought alongside the British in World War I, notably at GALLIPOLI, and again in World War II, preventing its occupation by the Japanese. It joined the U.S. in the KOREAN and VIETNAM WARS. Since the 1960s the government has sought to deal more fairly with the Aborigines, and a loosening of immigration restrictions has led to a more heterogeneous population. Constitutional links allowing British interference in government were formally abolished in 1968, and Australia has assumed a leading role in Asian and Pacific affairs. During the 1990s, it experienced several debates about giving up its British ties and becoming a republic. See map on following page.

Australian Aborigine \a-bə-ˈri-jə-ˌnē\ Any member of the indigenous race of Australia and Tasmania that arrived 40,000–60,000 years ago. At one time there were as many as 500 groups (tribes) of Aborigines. Hunters and gatherers, groups formed along the male line and centered around a watering place settled by its ancestors. The men were divided into lodges, custodians of the mythology evoked in the DREAMING ritual. The estimated Aboriginal population of 300,000–1,000,000 when European colonization began in the late 18th cent. was devastated by disease and by the bloody 19th-cent. "pacification by force." The government established reserves in the 1920s and '30s; however, Aborigines today number fewer than 260,000. Their traditional culture has been severely modified; all Aborigines have had some contact with modern Australian society, and all are now Australian citizens.

Australian Alps Mountain range, SE Australia. It forms the S end of the GREAT DIVIDING RANGE and the watershed be-

A

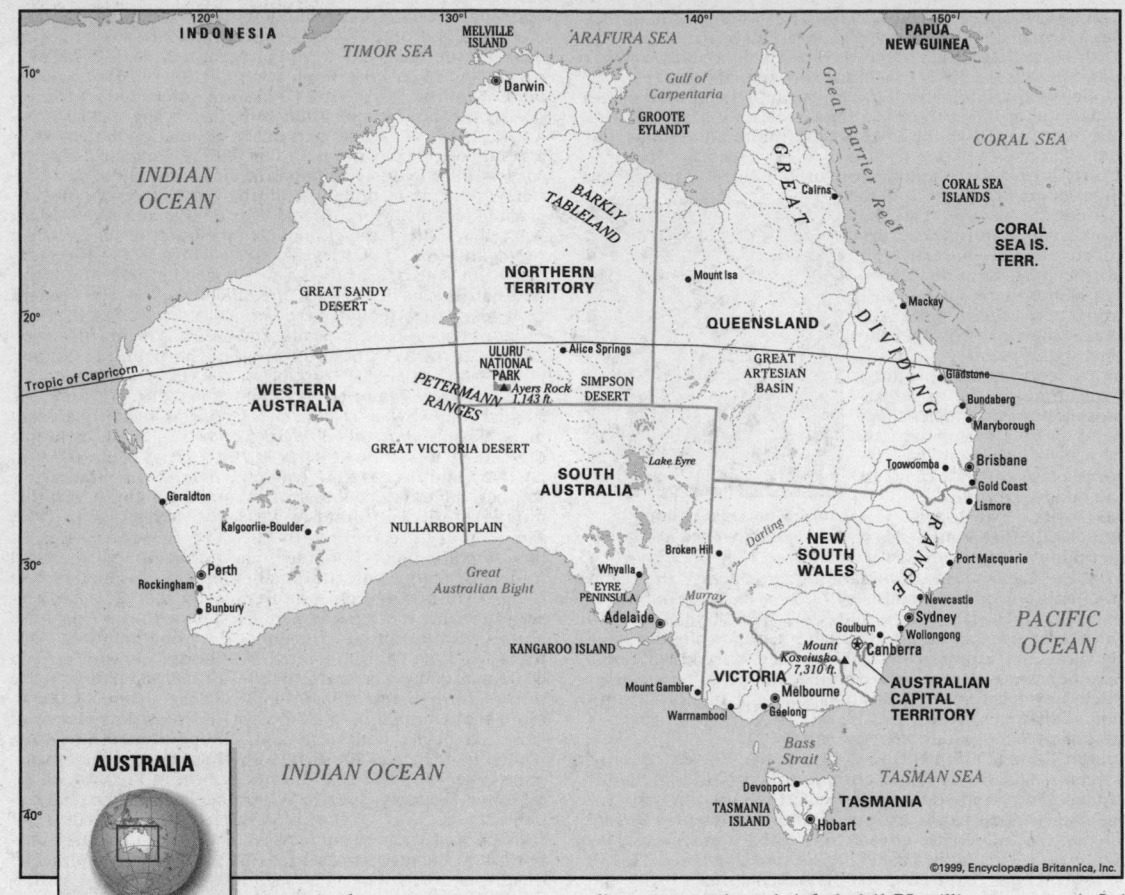

AUSTRALIA

Scale 1: 35,161,000

©1999, Encyclopædia Britannica, Inc.

tween the MURRUMBIDGEE RIVER and the rivers flowing south to the Pacific Ocean. Its highest peak is Mt. KOSCIUSKO.

Australian religion Religion of the AUSTRALIAN ABORIGINES, based in the DREAMING. Religion involved living in agreement with the way of life ordained in the Dreaming. Through dreams and other states of altered consciousness, the living could come into contact with the spiritual realm and gain strength from it; myths, dances, and other rituals bound the human, spiritual, and physical worlds together. A spirit was held to come from the dreaming to animate a fetus, and a person's spiritual heritage was more important than the bond with a parent. Sacred art included ritual objects, sand and cave paintings, and paintings on bark.

Austral Islands Group of islands (pop., 1996: 6,500), S FRENCH POLYNESIA. The southernmost part of French Polynesia (Austral is Latin for "south"), the islands form a chain about 850 mi (1,370 km) long. They were sighted by Capt. James COOK in 1769 and 1777 and were taken over by the French in the late 19th cent.

Australopithecus \ȯ-ˌstrā-lō-ˈpi-thə-kəs\ ("southern ape") Genus of extinct HOMINIDS that lived in S and E Africa from the early Pliocene epoch (beginning c.5.3 million years ago) to the beginning of the Pleistocene (c.1.8 million years ago). It is believed to be ancestral to modern human beings. The australopithecines were distinguished from the APES by their upright posture and bipedal gait. Their brains were small, like those of living apes, but their teeth were more human than apelike. At least five species of australopithecines have been identified: *A. anamensis* (4.2 million years ago), *A. afarensis* (3.75 million years ago), *A. africanus* (3 million–2 million years ago), *A. robustus* (2 million–1 mil-

lion years ago), and *A. boisei* (1.75 million years ago). It is not known which species gave rise to the genus *Homo*, though the evidence suggests it was *A. afarensis*. See also HUMAN EVOLUTION, LUCY, OLDUVAI GORGE.

Austrasia \ȯ-ˈstrā-zhə\ *or* **Ostrasia** \ä-ˈstrā-zhə\ Early medieval European kingdom. During the MEROVINGIAN DYNASTY (6th–8th cent. A.D.), it was the E Frankish kingdom (Neustria was the W kingdom), covering present-day NE France and areas of W and central Germany; its capital was at METZ. In 751 PEPIN III founded the CAROLINGIAN DYNASTY. Austrasia was later consolidated into the HOLY ROMAN EMPIRE by CHARLEMAGNE.

Austria *German* **Österreich** \ˈœ-stər-ˌrīk\ *officially* **Republic of Austria** Nation, S central Europe. Area: 32,375 sq mi (83,851 sq km). Population (2000): 8,091,000. Capital: VIENNA. Language: German. Religion: Roman Catholicism (75%). Currency: euro. Austria can be divided into three regions. The alpine region in the west covers about two-thirds of the country, and includes its highest point, the GROSSGLOCKNER. The Bohemian Forest is a highland region that extends north into the Czech Republic. The lowland region, including the Vienna Basin, lies in the east; it supports mainly agricultural activities. The DANUBE RIVER and its tributaries drain nearly the entire country. Austria has a developed mixed free-market and government-operated economy based on manufacture and commerce; tourism is also important. It is a republic with two legislative houses; its chief of state is the president, and its head of government is the chancellor. Its greatest cultural contribution has been in music (see Joseph HAYDN, W. A. MOZART, Franz SCHUBERT). Major cultural figures in other fields include Oskar KOKOSCHKA, Sigmund FREUD, and Ludwig WITTGENSTEIN. Settlement in Austria goes back some 3,000 years, when Illyrians were probably the main inhabitants. The CELTS in-

AUSTRIA

Scale 1: 8,842,000

©1999, Encyclopædia Britannica, Inc.

vaded around 400 B.C. and established NORICUM. The Romans arrived after 200 B.C. and established the provinces of RAETIA, Noricum, and PANNONIA; prosperity followed and the population became Romanized. With the fall of Rome in the 5th cent. A.D., many tribes invaded, including the SLAVS; they were eventually subdued by CHARLEMAGNE, and the area became ethnically Germanic. The distinct political entity that would become Austria emerged in 976 with Leopold I of Babenberg as margrave. In 1278, Rudolf IV of the HABSBURG DYNASTY (later RUDOLF I of the Holy Roman Empire) conquered the area; Habsburg rule lasted until 1918. While in power, the Habsburgs created a kingdom centered on Austria, Bohemia, and Hungary. The Napoleonic Wars brought about the end of the Holy Roman Empire (1806) and the creation of the Austrian empire. Count von METTERNICH tried to assure Austrian supremacy among Germanic states, but war with Prussia led Austria to divide the empire into the Dual Monarchy of Austria-Hungary. Nationalist sentiment plagued the kingdom, and the assassination of FRANCIS FERDINAND by a Serbian nationalist in 1914 triggered WORLD WAR I, which destroyed the Austrian empire. In the postwar carving up of Austria-Hungary, Austria became an independent republic. It was annexed by Nazi Germany in 1938 (see ANSCHLUSS) and joined the Axis powers in World War II. The republic was restored in 1955 after 10 years of Allied occupation. Austria became a full member of the EUROPEAN UNION in 1995.

Austria-Hungary *or* **Austro-Hungarian Empire** Former monarchy, central Europe. Austria-Hungary at one time included Austria and Hungary, Bohemia, Moravia, Bukovina, Transylvania, Carniola, Küstenland, Dalmatia, Croatia, Fiume, and Galicia. The so-called Dual Monarchy, formed by the COMPROMISE OF 1867, created a king of Hungary in addition to the existing Austrian emperor; though these were the same person, FRANCIS JOSEPH, Hungary was granted considerable autonomy. The monarchy maintained a precarious balance among its many minorities until 1914, when a Serbian nationalist assassinated FRANCIS FERDINAND, precipitating WORLD WAR I. With its defeat in that war and revolutions by the Czechs, Yugoslavs, and Hungarians, the monarchy collapsed in 1918.

Austrian Succession, War of the (1740–48) Group of related wars that took place after the death (1740) of Emperor CHARLES VI. At issue was the right of Charles's daughter MARIA THERESA to inherit the Habsburg lands. The war began when FREDERICK II of Prussia invaded SILESIA in 1740.

His victory prompted other countries to enter the fray. The conflict ended inconclusively in 1748.

Austroasiatic languages Superfamily of about 150 languages spoken by close to 90 million diverse people in S. and S.E. Asia. Today most scholars believe that it is subdivided into two families, MUNDA and MON-KHMER. In prehistoric times Austroasiatic languages most likely extended over a very broad area, including much of SE China. Other than VIETNAMESE and Khmer (in Cambodia), no Austroasiatic language is an official national language.

Austro-German Alliance *or* **Dual Alliance** (1879) Pact between Austria-Hungary and Germany in which the two powers promised each other support in case of attack by Russia. Germany's Otto von BISMARCK saw the alliance as a way to preserve peace, as Russia would not wage war against both empires. The addition of Italy in 1882 made it the Triple Alliance. The agreement remained an important element of both German and Austro-Hungarian foreign policy until 1918.

Austro-Hungarian Empire See AUSTRIA-HUNGARY

Austronesian languages *formerly* **Malayo-Polynesian languages** Family of about 1,200 languages spoken by more than 200 million people in Indonesia, the Philippines, Madagascar, the central and S Pacific island groups, and parts of mainland S.E. Asia and Taiwan. Before European colonial expansion, it had the widest territorial extent of any language family. The Austronesian languages of Taiwan can be separated from the remaining languages, which are divided into Western and Central-Eastern Malayo-Polynesian. Western Malayo-Polynesian includes Javanese, which is spoken by about 76 million people. Eastern Malayo-Polynesian includes Oceanic, the best-defined subgroup of Austronesian, comprising nearly all the languages of POLYNESIA, MICRONESIA, and MELANESIA. Written records in scripts of S.E. Asian provenance (see INDIC WRITING SYSTEMS) survive for several languages, including Old Javanese and Cham.

Austro–Prussian War See SEVEN WEEKS' WAR

auteur theory \ò-'tœr\ Theory that views a film's director as its "author" (French, *auteur*). It originated in France in the 1950s and was promoted by François TRUFFAUT and J.-L. GODARD and the journal *Cahiers du Cinéma*. The director "writes" the film's audio and visual scenario and therefore is considered more responsible for its content than the screenwriter. Supporters maintain that all the most successful films bear the distinctive imprint of their director.

authoritarianism Principle of unqualified submission to authority, as opposed to individual freedom of thought and action. Political power is concentrated in a leader or small elite not constitutionally responsible to those governed. Authoritarian governments usually lack a guiding ideology, tolerate some pluralism in social organization, and exercise their power within relatively predictable limits. See also ABSOLUTISM, DICTATORSHIP, TOTALITARIANISM.

autism Neurobiological disorder that affects physical, social, and language skills. First described in the 1940s, the syndrome usually appears before $2^{1}/_{2}$ years of age. Autistic infants appear indifferent or averse to affection and physical contact. They may be slow in learning to speak and suffer episodes of rage or panic; they may also appear deaf and display an almost hypnotized fascination with certain objects. Autism is often characterized by rhythmic body movements such as rocking or hand-clapping and by an obsession with routines. Autistic individuals may be hypersensitive to some stimuli (e.g., high-pitched sounds) and abnormally slow to react to others (e.g., physical pain). The disorder is three to four times more common in males. It results from abnormalities in the brain structure. "High-functioning" autistic people may have special gifts based on their unusual ability for visual thinking. See also IDIOT SAVANT.

autobiography Biography of oneself narrated by oneself. Little autobiographical literature exists from antiquity; the form takes hold only in the 15th cent. Such works take many forms, including intimate writings not necessarily intended for publication (letters, diaries, journals, and reminiscences). Outstanding examples extend from St. AUGUSTINE's *Confessions* (c.A.D. 400) to Vladimir NABOKOV's *Speak, Memory* (1951).

autoclave Vessel, usually of steel, able to withstand high temperatures and pressures. Autoclaves are used in manufacturing dyes and for other chemical reactions requiring high pressures. In bacteriology and medicine, instruments and culture media are sterilized by superheated steam in an autoclave. In 1679 Denis Papin (1647–c.1712) invented a prototype; still used in cooking, it is now called a pressure cooker.

autoimmune disease Any disease caused by an immune response (see IMMUNITY) against ANTIGENS in the tissues of one's own body. The IMMUNE SYSTEM usually prevents such a response: autoimmune diseases arise when the mechanisms fail and LYMPHOCYTES destroy host tissues. Examples include insulin-dependent DIABETES MELLITUS, systemic LUPUS ERYTHEMATOSUS, PERNICIOUS ANEMIA, and RHEUMATOID ARTHRITIS. Treatment may replace the function of the affected tissue (e.g., insulin therapy for diabetes) or suppress the immune system (see IMMUNOSUPPRESSION). ALLERGIES are another type of autoimmune reaction.

automation Term used to describe a wide variety of systems in which there is a significant substitution of mechanical, electrical, or computerized action for human effort and intelligence. Automation is concerned with performing a process by means of programmed commands combined with automatic feedback control to ensure proper execution of the instructions. The resulting system is capable of operating without human intervention.

automaton \ò-'tä-mə-tən\ Mechanical object, either functional or decorative, that is self-operating. Devices set in motion by water, falling weights, and steam were in use in the 1st cent. A.D. Decorative automatons were made for ecclesiastical use and table ornaments in the Middle Ages and Renaissance. Spectacular fountains and waterworks can be seen in 16th-cent. Italian gardens; elaborate mechanical devices (pictures, snuffboxes) were popular in the 18th–19th cent. The production of expensive automatons virtually ceased by the 20th cent.

automobile Four-wheeled automotive vehicle designed for passenger transportation, commonly propelled by an INTERNAL COMBUSTION ENGINE. The modern automobile consists of about 14,000 parts, divided into several structural and mechanical systems. These include the steel body, containing the passenger and storage space, which sits on the chassis or steel frame; the engine, which powers the car by means of a TRANSMISSION; the steering and braking systems; and the electrical system, which includes a BATTERY, ALTERNATOR, and other devices. Subsystems involve fuel, exhaust, lubrication, cooling, SUSPENSION, and TIRES. Though experimental vehicles were built earlier, not until the 1880s did Gottlieb DAIMLER and Karl BENZ in Germany begin separately to manufacture cars commercially. In the U.S., James and William Packard (1863–1928, 1861–1923) and Ransom Olds (1864–1950) were among the first auto manufacturers, and by 1898 there were 50 U.S. manufacturers. Some early cars operated by steam engine, such as those made by Francis and Freelan STANLEY. The internal combustion engine was used by Henry FORD when he introduced the MODEL T in 1908. In the 1930s European manufacturers began to make small, affordable cars such as the Volkswagen. In the 1950s and '60s, U.S. automakers produced larger cars with more automatic features. In the 1970s and '80s Japanese manufacturers exported their small, reliable, fuel-efficient cars worldwide, and U.S. automakers strove to imitate them, until the trend shifted to the large and inefficient sports utility vehicles in the late 1990s. See also AXLE, BRAKE, BUS, CARBURETOR, ELECTRIC AUTOMOBILE, FUEL INJECTION, MOTORCYCLE, TRUCK.

autonomic nervous system \ˌȯt-ə-'näm-ik\ Part of the NERVOUS SYSTEM that is not under conscious control and that regulates the internal organs. It includes the sympathetic and parasympathetic nervous systems. The first, which connects the internal organs to the brain via spinal nerves, responds to stress by increasing heart rate and blood flow to the muscles and decreasing blood flow to the skin. The second comprises the cranial nerves and lower spinal nerves, which increase digestive secretions and slow the heartbeat. A third division, the enteric nervous system, embedded in the walls of the stomach and intestines, controls digestive movement and secretions. See also HOMEOSTASIS.

autopsy \'ȯ-ˌtäp-sē\ or **necropsy** or **postmortem** Dissection and examination of a dead body to determine cause of death and learn about disease processes. Autopsies have contributed to the development of medicine since at least the Middle Ages. Autopsy is crucial to the accuracy of disease and death statistics, the education of medical students, and the understanding of new and changing diseases.

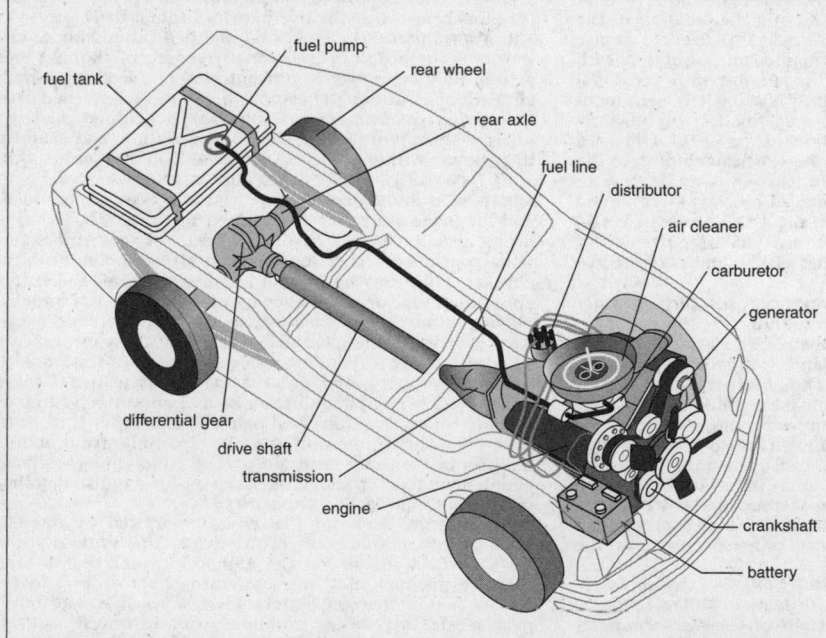

fuel pump
rear wheel
fuel tank
rear axle
fuel line
distributor
air cleaner
carburetor
generator
differential gear
drive shaft
transmission
engine
crankshaft
battery

Automobile A rear-wheel-drive automobile with automatic •transmission. When the key is turned, electricity flows from the battery to the starting motor, which starts the •internal-combustion engine. Power from the engine is converted by the crankshaft to rotary motion, which the transmission receives and sends via the drive shaft to the differential, which transfers power to the driving axles and also allows the outside wheel to turn faster than the inside wheel when turning corners. (In front-wheel-drive cars, the half shaft replaces the drive shaft; it and the differential lie under the hood.) Other important systems include the electric system (incl. the •alternator, •ignition system, and •spark plugs), fuel system, •brake system, cooling system, exhaust system, and support system (see •suspension).

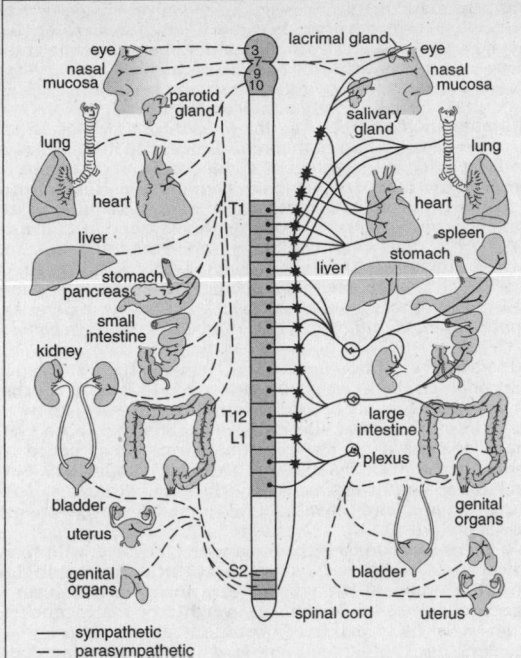

Autonomic nervous system Nervous impulses from the autonomic system begin in motor neurons in the brain or spinal cord. Each motor neuron connects with a second motor neuron outside the central nervous system to carry the impulse to the glands and muscles. These second motor neurons are found in ganglia (masses of neurons), which are interconnected with nerves to form two chains along either side of the spinal cord. Other ganglia form large clusters (plexuses) elsewhere in the body. Preganglionic fibers of the sympathetic division emerge along the thoracic (T) and first three lumbar (L) segments of the spinal cord. Fibers of parasympathetic neurons originating in the brain stem arise from the third, seventh, ninth, and tenth cranial nerves. Other parasympathetic fibers emerge from the second, third, and fourth sacral (S) segments of the spinal cord.

Autry, (Orvon) Gene (1907–1998) U.S. actor and singer. Born on a ranch in Tioga, Texas, he hosted his own radio program from 1931. His first film, *In Old Santa Fe* (1934), launched his career as a cowboy actor. Known as "the Singing Cowboy," he starred in 18 movies, ending with *Alias Jesse James* (1959). His recordings, including "Rudolph the Red-Nosed Reindeer" (1949) and "Frosty the Snowman" (1950), sold millions of copies. He starred in the televised *Gene Autry Show* 1950–54.

Auvergne \ō-'vern\(^y\)\ Region (pop., 1999: 1,310,000), S central France. It was once inhabited by the Arverni, a Gallic people led by VERCINGETORIX and defeated by Julius CAESAR. It was yielded to the VISIGOTHS in A.D. 475, then to the FRANKS under CLOVIS I in 507. It became part of AQUITAINE, and later a countship. It passed to the House of BOURBON in 1416 and to France about 1530.

avalanche Large mass of rock debris or snow that moves rapidly down a mountain slope, sweeping and grinding everything in its path. Avalanches often begin when a mass of material is loosened by spring rains or is partially melted by a warm, dry wind. Vibrations caused by loud noises, such as gunfire or thunder, can also start the mass moving. Avalanche control consists largely of detonating explosives in the upper reaches of avalanche zones, intentionally causing the snow to slide before accumulations become very great.

Avalokitesvara \ˌə-və-ˌlō-ki-'tǎsh-və-rə\ *Chinese* **Guanyin** \'gwän-'yin\ *Japanese* **Kannon** \'kän-'nòn\ BODHISATTVA of infinite compassion and mercy, the most popular of MAHAYANA Buddhist deities. He is the earthly manifestation of the Buddha Amitabha, guarding the world between the departure of the historical BUDDHA, Gautama, and the appearance of the future Buddha, Maitreya. He is the creator of the fourth world, the actual living universe. In China and Japan he is sometimes called a goddess. The most popular deity in Tibet, he is thought to be reincarnated in each DALAI LAMA.

Avalon Island to which Britain's legendary King Arthur (see ARTHURIAN LEGEND) was taken after he was mortally wounded in his last battle. First described by GEOFFREY OF MONMOUTH, it was said to be ruled by MORGAN LE FAY and her eight sisters, all skilled healers. Legend held that when Arthur was healed he would return to rule Britain. Avalon has sometimes been identified with Glastonbury in Somerset.

avatar \'a-və-ˌtär\ In HINDUISM, the incarnation of a deity in human or animal form to counteract an evil in the world. It usually refers to 10 appearances of VISHNU, including an incarnation as the BUDDHA Gautama. The doctrine is set forth in the BHAGAVADGITA by Lord KRISHNA: "Whenever there is a decline of righteousness and rise of unrighteousness then I send forth Myself."

Avebury \'āv-bə-rē\ Village, WILTSHIRE, England, lying partly within one of the largest prehistoric sites in Europe. The site contains vast megalithic remains, including chalk blocks and sandstone pillars placed in circles. Its date and origin are uncertain. Kennet Avenue, a route into the interior of the great circle, linked Avebury with a temple 1 mi (1.6 km) away.

Avedon \'a-və-ˌdän\, **Richard** (b.1923) U.S. photographer. Born in New York City, in 1945 he became a regular contributor to *Harper's Bazaar* and later was closely associated with *Vogue*. He is noted for his celebrity portraits and fashion photographs, which are characterized by strong black-and-white contrast and confrontational poses. His many books include *Observations* (1959; text by Truman CAPOTE), *Nothing Personal* (1964; text by James BALDWIN), and *The Sixties* (1999).

average See MEAN, MEDIAN, AND MODE

Averroës \ə-'ver-ə-ˌwēz\ *Arabic* **Ibn Rushd** \ˌib-ən-'rùsht\ *in full* Abu al-Walid Muhammad ibn Ahmad ibn Muhammad ibn Rushd (1126–1198) Spanish Arabic philosopher. He worked as a judge and physician in Córdoba, Seville, and Morocco. His interpretations of ARISTOTLE (often in reaction against AVICENNA) consisted of three series of commentaries. While mostly faithful to Aristotle's thought, he endowed the Aristotelian "prime mover" with the characteristics of the Plotinian (see PLOTINUS) and Islamic transcendent God, the universal First Cause, and partially synthesized Greek and Arabic philosophical thought.

Avery, Oswald (Theodore) (1877–1955) Canadian-U.S. bacteriologist. Born in Halifax, Nova Scotia, he worked at New York's Rockefeller Institute Hospital. There he discovered transformation, a process by which a change could be introduced into bacteria and passed on to later generations of transformed cells. He and his coworkers reported in 1944 that the substance that caused the transformation was DNA. The discovery opened the door to deciphering the GENETIC CODE.

Avesta \ə-'ves-tə\ *or* **Zend-Avesta** Sacred book of ZOROASTRIANISM. It contains hymns, prayers, and appeals to righteousness ascribed to ZOROASTER. The present text was assembled in the 3rd–7th cent. A.D. It has five parts: the *Gathas*, hymns in what are thought to be Zoroaster's own words; *Visp-rat*, containing homages to spiritual leaders; *Vendidad*, the main source for Zoroastrian law; the *Yashts*, 21 hymns to angels and ancient heroes; and the *Khurda avesta*, composed of minor texts.

aviation Development and operation of heavier-than-air aircraft. In 1783 the balloon became the first aircraft to carry humans (see BALLOONING). Production of a successful GLIDER in 1891 and refinement of the INTERNAL COMBUSTION ENGINE led to the first successful engine-powered AIRPLANE flight by Wilbur and Orville WRIGHT in 1903. World War I accelerated the expansion of aviation, and in the 1920s small airlines began carrying mail and passengers. World War II led to increased aircraft size, speed, and range. In the late 1940s the JET ENGINE made possible the development of commercial airlines throughout the world. See also AIRSHIP, HELICOPTER, SEAPLANE.

Avicenna \ˌa-və-'se-nə\ *Arabic* **Ibn Sina** \'ib-ən-'sē-nä\ *in full* Abu Ali al-Husayn ibn Abd Allah ibn Sina (980–1037) Islamic philosopher and scientist. Born in Bukhara (now in Uzbekistan), he became physician to several sultans and twice served as vizier. His *Canon of Medicine* was long a standard work in the field. He is also known for his great encyclopedia of philosophy, *The Book of Healing (Kitab al-shifa)*. His ideas, especially his interpretations of ARISTOTLE, influenced the medieval European Scholastics.

Avignon \ˌä-vē-'nyöⁿ\ *ancient* Avennio. City (pop., 1999: 86,000), SE France. A Phocaean colony, it was conquered by the Romans, Goths, Burgundians, Ostrogoths, and Franks. It was part of the kingdom of ARLES and briefly a republic (1135–46). Sold to Pope CLEMENT VI in 1348, it was the capital of the papacy (1309–77) and seat of the Avignonese popes during the Western SCHISM. France annexed the city in 1791. Landmarks include the Saint-Bénézet bridge, made famous by the song "Sur le pont d'Avignon."

Avignon papacy Roman Catholic papacy (1309–77), when the popes resided at AVIGNON, France. Elected pope through the machinations of Philip IV of France, CLEMENT V moved the papal capital to Avignon primarily for political reasons. All seven popes of this period were French, as were most of the cardinals, who began to play a stronger role in church government. Church and clergy were reformed, missionary efforts were expanded, and popes tried to settle royal rivalries and establish peace. The heavy French influence damaged the prestige of the papacy, however, and in 1377 Gregory XI returned to Rome. The cardinals elected a new pope to take the Avignon seat, becoming the first ANTIPOPE and beginning the Western SCHISM.

Avignon school School of late Gothic painting associated with the city of Avignon, France. Beginning during the AVIGNON PAPACY, when many Italian artists worked there, the papal palace and secular buildings in nearby towns were decorated with frescoes. By the early 15th cent., Flemish influences had reached the city, consolidating the Italian and N styles. The Avignon Pietà (c.1460), attributed to Enguerrand Charonton, is the masterpiece of the school. The artistic activity at Avignon greatly influenced French painting in the late 15th and 16th cent. See also GOTHIC ART.

avocado Fruit of *Persea americana,* of the LAUREL FAMILY, a tropical and subtropical tree native to the Western Hemisphere. Avocados are variable in shape, size, and color (green to dark purple). The outer skin may be thin, or coarse and woody. The green-yellow flesh has a buttery consistency and a rich, nutty flavor with a high content of unsaturated oil. They provide thiamine, riboflavin, and vitamin A.

avocet \'a-və-ˌset\ Any of several large shorebirds (genus *Recurvirostra*) with boldly contrasting plumage, long bluish legs, and a long black bill upturned at the tip. Avocets inhabit fresh and salt marshes and feed by sweeping the partly open bill in the shallows. They often wade together to corral minnows and crustaceans. The American avocet is about 18 in. (45 cm) long, including the bill.

Avogadro's number Number of units in one MOLE of any substance (defined as its MOLECULAR WEIGHT in grams), equal to 6.0221367×10^{23}. The units may be ELECTRONS, ATOMS, IONS, or MOLECULES, depending on the nature of the substance and the character of the reaction (if any). See also STOICHIOMETRY.

Avon River, Upper River, central England. It flows 96 mi (154 km) into the SEVERN RIVER at Tewkesbury. It is known for its scenic beauty, notably in the Vale of Evesham. Towns along it include STRATFORD, where William SHAKESPEARE was born.

Awakening, Great See GREAT AWAKENING

ax Hand tool used for chopping, splitting, chipping, and piercing. Stone Age hand axes originated in simple stone implements that acquired wooden hafts, or handles, about 30,000 B.C. Copper-bladed axes appeared in Egypt about 4000 B.C. and were followed by axes with blades of bronze and eventually iron. The development of the iron-bladed felling ax in the Middle Ages made possible the vast forest clearances of Europe, N. and S. America, and elsewhere.

axiom In mathematics or logic, an unprovable rule or first principle accepted as true because it is self-evident or particularly useful (e.g., "Nothing can both be and not be at the same time and in the same respect"). The term is often used interchangeably with *postulate*. It should be contrasted with a THEOREM, which requires a rigorous proof.

axiomatic method In LOGIC, the procedure by which an entire science or system of theorems is deduced in accordance with specified rules by logical deduction from certain basic propositions (AXIOMS), which in turn are constructed from a few terms taken as primitive. The oldest examples of axiomatized systems are Aristotle's syllogistic and EUCLIDEAN GEOMETRY. Early in the 20th cent., Bertrand RUSSELL and Alfred North WHITEHEAD attempted to formalize all of mathematics in an axiomatic manner. Attempts to axiomatize the empirical sciences include J. H. Woodger's *The Axiomatic Method in Biology* (1937) and Clark Hull's *Principles of Behavior* (1943).

Axis Powers Coalition headed by Germany, Italy, and Japan that opposed the ALLIED POWERS in World War II. It originated in agreements between Germany and Italy, followed in 1936 by the Rome–Berlin Axis declaration and a German–Japanese pact. The connection was strengthened by the Tripartite Pact signed by all three powers in 1940. Several other countries, including Hungary, Romania, Bulgaria, Croatia, and Slovakia, later joined the original Axis Powers.

axle Pin or shaft on or with which wheels revolve; with fixed wheels, one of the basic simple MACHINES for amplifying FORCE. Combined with the WHEEL, in its earliest form it was probably used for raising weights or water buckets from wells. Its principle of operation can be illustrated in the attachment of large and small GEARS to the same shaft; the tendency of a force applied at the radius on the large gear to turn the shaft is sufficient to overcome a larger force at the radius on the small gear. The mechanical advantage is equal to the ratio of the two forces and also equal to the ratio of the radii of the two gears.

Axum See AKSUM

ayatollah \ˌī-ə-'tō-lə\ In the SHIITE branch of Islam, a high-ranking religious authority regarded by his followers as the most learned person of his age. His legal decisions are accepted as binding by his personal followers and today by the wider community.

Ayckbourn \'āk-ˌborn\, **Alan** (*later* **Sir Alan**) (b.1939) British playwright. He began acting with the Stephen Joseph Co. in Scarborough, Yorkshire, where he also wrote his earliest plays; he was artistic director there from 1970, later winning acclaim in London and New York. He has written over 50 plays, mostly farces and comedies that deal with marital and class conflicts, including *Relatively Speaking* (1967), *Absurd Person Singular* (1972), the trilogy *The Norman Conquests* (1973), *Intimate Exchanges* (1982), and *Communicating Doors* (1995).

Aydid \ī-'dēd\, **Muhammad Farah** (c.1930–1996) Faction leader at the center of the Somalian civil war (1991–95). Following military training in Italy and the U.S.S.R., he served in posts under Mohamed SIAD BARRE (1978–89) before overthrowing him in 1991. After losing the interim presidency he continued warring on rival clans. When U.N. and U.S. troops arrived in Somalia (1992), Aydid ambushed a U.N. contingent and was declared an outlaw. The attempt to capture him led to many deaths, and the foreign troops were withdrawn. He intensified his campaign, but reportedly died of a heart attack after being wounded.

Ayers Rock \'erz\ *or* **Uluru** Rock outcrop, SW Northern Territory, Australia. Located in Uluru National Park, it is 1,100 ft (335 m) high and may be the world's largest monolith. Its arkosic sandstone changes color with the height of the sun. Shallow caves at its base are sacred to several Aboriginal tribes and contain carvings and paintings. In 1985, ownership was officially returned to the Aborigines.

Aymará \ˌī-mə-'rä\ Large S. American Indian group living on the Titicaca plateau of the central Andes in present-day Peru and Bolivia. The Aymará were conquered by the INCAS and the Spanish. Traditional Aymará now herd llamas and alpacas, grow crops, and fish. Numbering 1.5–2 million, they are among the poorest people in the hemisphere.

Ayodhya See AJODHYA

Ayub Khan \ä-'üb-'kän\, **Mohammad** (1907–1974) President of Pakistan (1958–69). An officer in the Indian army 1928–47, he afterward rose through the ranks in the military in newly independent Pakistan. In 1958 Pakistan's Pres. Iskander Mirza abrogated the nation's constitution, and Ayub became chief martial-law administrator. He declared himself president the same year, exiling Mirza. He established close ties to China and in 1965 went to war with India over control of Jammu and Kashmir. The failure to take Kashmir led to riots, and Ayub resigned in 1969.

Ayurveda \ä-yər-,vā-də\ *or* **Ayurvedic medicine** Traditional system of Indian medicine. Its earliest concepts were set out in the portion of the VEDAS known as the Atharvaveda (c.2nd millennium B.C.). Early Ayurvedic texts analyze the human body in terms of earth, water, fire, air, and ether as well as the three bodily humors (wind, bile, and phlegm). To prevent illness, Ayurvedic medicine emphasizes hygiene, exercise, herbal preparations, and yoga. To cure ailments, it relies on herbal medicines, physiotherapy, and diet. It is taught in roughly 100 colleges in India, and it has gained currency in the West as a form of alternative medicine.

azalea Any plant of certain species of the genus *Rhododendron* (HEATH FAMILY), formerly given the generic name *Azalea*. Distinguishing characteristics of RHODODENDRONS and azaleas are not consistent enough to separate them into two genera. Azaleas typically have flowers that are funnel-shaped, somewhat two-lipped, and often fragrant. Cultivated varieties have been bred from species native to the hilly regions of Asia and N. America.

Azerbaijan \,a-zər-bī-'jän\ *officially* **Republic of Azerbaijan** Nation, SW Asia. Area: 33,400 sq mi (86,600 sq km). Population (2000): 8,051,000. Capital: BAKU. The Azerbaijanis

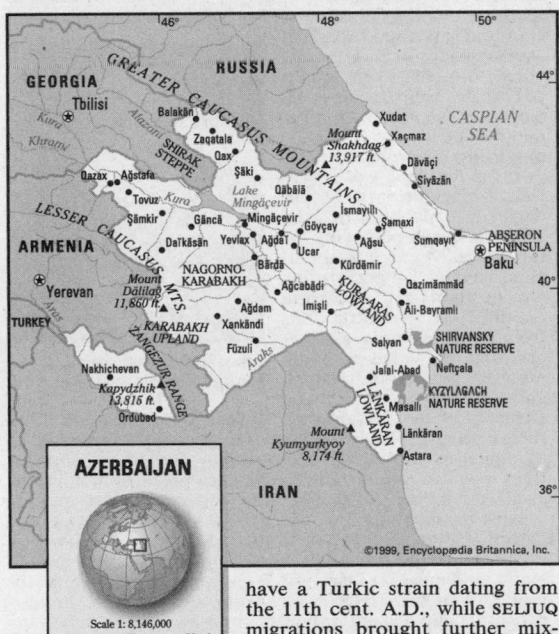

GEORGIA
RUSSIA
Tbilisi
ARMENIA
Yerevan
NAGORNO-KARABAKH
TURKEY
Nakhichevan
IRAN

CASPIAN SEA

Baku

AZERBAIJAN

Scale 1: 8,146,000
0   40   80 mi
0   60   120 km

©1999, Encyclopædia Britannica, Inc.

have a Turkic strain dating from the 11th cent. A.D., while SELJUQ migrations brought further mixtures, including Iranian; Russians are a minority. Languages: Azerbaijani (official), Russian. Religions: Islam, minority Orthodox Christianity. Currency: manat. Azerbaijan is characterized by a variety of landscapes. More than 40% of its territory is lowlands, while areas above 5,000 ft (1,500 m) occupy some 10% of the total area. The central part of the country is a plain through which flow the Kura River and its tributaries, including the Araks, whose upper course forms part of the boundary with Iran. The CASPIAN SEA serves Baku as a trade outlet. Agriculture, petroleum refining, and light manufacturing are economically important. It is a republic with one legislative body; its head of state and government is the president assisted by the prime minister. Azerbaijan adjoins the Iranian region of the same name, and the origin of their respective inhabitants is the same. By the 9th cent. A.D. it had come under Turkish influence, and in ensuing centuries it was fought over by Arabs, Mongols, Turks, and Iranians. Russia acquired what is now independent Azerbaijan in the early 19th cent. After the RUSSIAN REVOLUTION OF 1917, Azerbaijan declared its independence; it was subdued by the Red Army in 1920 and became a Soviet Socialist Republic. It declared independence from the collapsing Soviet Union in 1991. Azerbaijan has two geographic peculiarities. The exclave Naxcivan (Nakhichevan) is separated from the rest of Azerbaijan by Armenian territory. NAGORNO-KARABAKH, which lies within Azerbaijan and is administered by it, has a Christian Armenian majority. Azerbaijan and Armenia went to war over both territories in the 1990s, causing great economic disruption. Though a cease-fire was declared in 1994, the political situation remained unresolved.

Azhar University \'äz-,här\, **al-** Chief center of Islamic and Arabic learning in the world, centered on the al-Azhar Mosque in the medieval quarter of Cairo. It was founded by the Fatimids in 970. The basic program has always focused on Islamic law, theology, and Arabic. Women were first admitted in 1962. Total enrollment is about 90,000.

azimuth See ALTITUDE AND AZIMUTH

Azores \ə-'zōrz\ *Portuguese* **Açores** \ə-'sō-rish\ Archipelago (pop., 1992 est.: 237,000), N Atlantic Ocean, constituting an autonomous region of Portugal. Its capital is Ponta Delgada (on São Miguel). It covers an area of 868 sq mi (2,247 sq km). Subject to earthquakes and volcanic eruptions, the islands lie some 1,000 mi (1,600 km) west of mainland Europe. The uninhabited Azores were reputedly discovered about 1427 by Diogo de Sevilha of Portugal. By 1500, all the islands were inhabited and trade with Portugal was well established. They were subject to Spain 1580–1640, and a famous sea battle between the British and Spanish occurred off Flores in 1591. The Portuguese installed a governor for the whole group in 1766; the islands are given limited autonomy in 1895. Important military bases were set up during World War II; since 1951 the U.S. has maintained a NATO air base on Lajes.

Azov \ə-'zòf, 'ā-,zòf\, **Sea of** Inland sea in Europe between Ukraine and Russia. It is connected to the BLACK SEA by Kerch Strait. About 210 mi (340 km) long and 85 mi (135 km) wide, it occupies 14,500 sq mi (37,600 sq km). With a maximum depth of only about 46 ft (14 m), it is the world's shallowest sea. It is fed by the DON and Kuban rivers; at their entrance, its depth is 3 ft (1 m) or less. In the west lies the Arabat Spit, a 70-mi- (113-km-) long sandbar that separates the Sea of Azov from the Syvash, a system of marshy inlets.

AZT *in full* azidothymidine. Drug that may delay the development of AIDS in patients with HIV and prevent transmission of HIV from infected pregnant women to their fetuses. Since it has a greater effect on the replication of VIRUSES than on body cells, it has fewer side effects than most other AIDS drugs. Its beneficial effects tend to decrease as treatment progresses, so it is now usually given with other drugs.

Aztec Ruins National Monument Archaeological site, NW New Mexico. Located on the Animas River, it was established in 1923. Mistakenly called Aztec by early settlers, the site actually contains the excavated ruins of a 12th-cent. PUEBLO town. It was designated a WORLD HERITAGE SITE in 1987.

Aztecs NAHUATL-speaking people who in the 15th and early 16th cent. ruled a large empire in what is now central and S Mexico. Their empire, which at its height comprised 5–6 million people spread over 80,000 sq mi (200,000 sq km), was made possible by successful intensive cultivation, irrigation, and reclamation of wetlands. The Aztec state was despotic, militaristic, and sharply stratified by class and caste. Aztec religion drew especially on the beliefs of the MAYA. The Aztecs practiced HUMAN SACRIFICE; in a particularly gruesome episode, 20,000–80,000 prisoners were said to have been killed in four days. The empire came to an end when Hernán CORTÉS took the emperor MONTEZUMA II prisoner and conquered TENOCHTITLÁN (present-day Mexico City). See also NAHUA.

B

B-52 *or* **Stratofortress** U.S. long-range heavy BOMBER, designed in 1948 and first flown in 1952. Intended as an atomic-bomb carrier capable of reaching the Soviet Union, it proved highly adaptable and remained in service at the end of the 20th cent. Its wingspan is 185 ft (56 m) and its length more than 160 ft (49 m). Powered by eight JET ENGINES, its maximum speed is 595 mph (960 kph).

Baader-Meinhof Gang \'bä-dər-'mīn-,hōf\ *or* **Red Army Faction** W. German leftist terrorist group formed in 1968, popularly named after its early leaders Andreas Baader (1943–1977) and Ulrike Meinhof (1934–1976). It engaged in terrorist bombings and arson, especially of W. German and U.S. targets in W. Germany. Arrested in 1972, Meinhof eventually hanged herself and Baader apparently also died a suicide. By the mid-1970s the group had turned to international terrorism; two members took part in the 1976 ENTEBBE INCIDENT. After the collapse of communism in E. Germany (1989–90), it was discovered that E. Germany's secret police had provided training and supplies to the gang. The group announced an end to its terrorist campaign in 1992.

Baal \'bäl\ God worshiped in many ancient Middle Eastern communities, especially among Canaanites, for whom he was a fertility deity. In the mythology of CANAAN, he was locked in combat with Mot, the god of death and sterility; depending on the outcome of their struggles, seven-year cycles of fertility or famine would ensue. Baal was also king of gods. The ARAMAEANS used the Babylonian pronunciation Bel; Bel became the Greek Belos, identified with ZEUS. The OLD TESTAMENT often refers to a specific local Baal or multiple Baalim.

Baalbek \'bä-əl-,bek, 'bäl-,bek\ Village, E Lebanon. In ancient times it was a great city. Its identification with the worship of BAAL as a Semitic sun-god gave rise to its Greek name, Heliopolis. It was made a Roman colony by Julius CAESAR. It was administered by Syrian Muslim rulers from A.D. 637 until the 20th cent. After World War I it was made part of Lebanon. It has extensive ruins, including temples of Jupiter, Bacchus, and Venus, and Roman mosaics.

baal shem \bäl-'shäm\ In JUDAISM, a man who worked wonders and cures through secret knowledge of the names of God. The practice dates to the 11th cent. A.D., long before the term was applied to certain rabbis and Kabbalists. They were numerous in 17th- and 18th-cent. E. Europe, where they exorcised demons, inscribed amulets, and performed cures. Because they combined faith healing with use of the KABBALA, they clashed with physicians, rabbis, and followers of the Haskala. See also BAAL SHEM TOV.

Baal Shem Tov \'bäl-'shem-'tòv\ *orig.* Israel ben Eliezer (c.1700–1760) Polish founder of HASIDISM (c.1750). An orphan, he worked in synagogues and yeshivas, and when he retired to the Carpathian Mtns. to engage in mystical speculation he gained a reputation as a BAAL SHEM. From about 1736 he lived in the village of Medzhibozh and devoted himself to spiritual pursuits. He rejected the asceticism of older rabbis and focused on communion with God, service of God in everyday tasks, and rescue of the sparks of divinity that, according to the KABBALA, are trapped in the material world. His discourses during Sabbath meals have been preserved, but no writings.

Baath Party *or* **Bath Party** \'bäth\ Arab political party that advocates formation of a single Arab socialist state. Founded in Damascus by Michel Aflaq and Salah al-Din al-Bitar in 1943, in 1953 it merged with the Syrian Socialist Party to form the Arab Socialist Baath Party. It espoused nonalignment and opposition to imperialism and colonialism. It gained control of Syria in 1963 and of Iraq in 1968. The party also has branches in other Middle Eastern countries. See also PAN-ARABISM.

Bab \'bäb\, **the** *orig.* Mirza Ali Muhammad of Shiraz (1819/20–1850) Iranian religious leader, founder of the Babi religion and one of the central figures of BAHA'I. The son of a merchant, he was influenced by the Shaykhi school of SHIITE Islam. In 1844 he declared himself the Bab (Arabic: "gateway") to the hidden IMAM. Later he would claim to be the imam himself, and finally a divine manifestation. The same year he assembled 18 disciples, who spread the new faith in the various Persian provinces. He had popular support but was opposed by members of the religious class, and he was imprisoned in 1847. In 1848 his followers, the Azali, formally broke with Islam. Mirza was executed by a firing squad at Tabriz in 1850.

Babbage \'bab-ij\, **Charles** (1791–1871) British mathematician and inventor. Educated at Cambridge Univ., he devoted himself from about 1812 to devising machines capable of calculating mathematical tables. In 1823 he obtained government support for the design of a projected machine with a 20-decimal capacity. In the 1830s he developed plans for the so-called analytical engine, capable of performing any arithmetical operation on the basis of instructions from punched cards, a memory unit in which to store numbers, sequential control, and most of the other basic

Charles Babbage Painting by Samuel Lawrence, 1845

elements of the present-day DIGITAL COMPUTER. In 1991 British scientists built Difference Engine No. 2 (accurate to 31 digits) to Babbage's specifications. His other contributions included establishing the modern postal system in England, compiling the first reliable actuarial tables, and inventing the locomotive cowcatcher.

Babbitt, Milton (Byron) (b.1916) U.S. composer. Born in Philadelphia but raised in Mississippi, he studied mathematics and music at Princeton Univ. and later joined its faculty. One of the first U.S. twelve-tone composers, he also became (in his *Three Compositions for Piano*, 1947) perhaps the first composer to write totally serialized music based on ordered structures not only of pitch but of elements such as rhythm and dynamics. Working with RCA's Mark II synthesizer, he was one of the first Americans to write electronically synthesized music. He wrote various works combining live performers and tape; his best-known works include *Composition for Synthesizer* (1961) and *Philomel* (1964).

Babel \'bä-bᵊil\, **Isaak (Emmanuilovich)** (1894–1941) Russian writer. Born Jewish in Ukraine, Babel grew up amid the persecution reflected in his stories. Maxim GORKY encouraged him to travel abroad to expand his horizons. Out of his military experience came the stories in *Red Cavalry*

(1926). His *Odessa Tales* (1931) include realistic and humorous sketches of the Jewish ghetto. Initially well regarded in the Soviet Union, in the late 1930s Babel's writing fell out of official favor; arrested in 1939, he died in a Siberian prison camp. He is considered Russia's greatest writer of short stories after Anton CHEKHOV.

Babel \\'bä-bəl, 'ba-bəl\\, **Tower of** In the Old Testament, a high tower built in Shinar (BABYLONIA). According to GENESIS 11:1–9, the Babylonians wanted to build a tower "with its top in the heavens." Angry at their presumption, God disrupted the enterprise by confusing the languages of the workers so that they could no longer understand each other. The tower was left unfinished and the people dispersed over the face of the earth.

Babism \\'bab-‚iz-əm\\ Religion that developed in Iran around Mirza Ali Muhammad's claim (1844) to be the BAB. Its beliefs are set forth in the *Bayan*. Babism originated as a messianic movement in SHIITE Islam. In 1867 the movement split, with the Azalis remaining faithful to the original teachings of the Bab and those of his successor, Sobh-e Azal. Most Babis accepted the leadership of Sobh-e Azal's half-brother BAHA ULLAH, and under him the BAHA'I faith was developed.

baboon Any of five species of robust MONKEYS (genus *Papio*) of Arabia and sub-Saharan Africa. Baboons have a large head, cheek pouches, and a long, doglike muzzle. They walk on all fours, carrying the tail in a characteristic arch. They weigh 30–90 lbs (14–40 kg) and are about 20–45 in. (50–115 cm) long, excluding the tail. Found mainly in drier savanna and rocky areas, they feed on a variety of plants and animals. Highly intelligent, they travel in large noisy troops. Their enormous canine teeth and powerful limbs make them dangerous opponents.

Babur \\'bä-bər\\ *orig.* Zahir-ud-Din Muhammad (1483–1530) Emperor (1526–30) and founder of the MUGHAL DYNASTY of India. A descendant of GENGHIS KHAN and TIMUR, he tried for 10 years (1494–1504) to gain control of Samarkand, Timur's old capital. After losing his own principality in Fergana, he consoled himself by seizing Kabul (1504). After four failed attempts, he successfully occupied Delhi (1525). Surrounded by enemy states, Babur (Arabic for "Tiger") persuaded his homesick troops to stand their ground, and over the next four years he defeated his foes. His grandson AKBAR consolidated the new empire. Babur was also a gifted poet and a lover of nature who constructed gardens wherever he went. His memoirs, the *Babur-nameh,* have become a world classic of autobiography.

baby boom Generation born in the U.S. between 1946 and 1964. The GREAT DEPRESSION and WORLD WAR II led many couples to delay having children. The war's end, followed by economic prosperity in the 1950s and early 1960s, led to a surge in population. The sheer size of the baby-boom generation (76 million) has magnified its impact on society: when "boomers" were young, the youth culture they defined took center stage; as they age, their consumer patterns dominate the market; and as they retire, their needs are expected to strain public resources.

Babylon Ancient ruined city on the EUPHRATES RIVER, Iraq. It lay about 55 mi (89 km) south of Baghdad. Babylon was one of the most famous cities in antiquity. Probably settled in the 3rd millennium B.C., it came under the Amoritic kings around 2000 B.C. It became the capital of BABYLONIA and the chief city of the Tigris–Euphrates valley (see TIGRIS RIVER). Destroyed by SENNACHERIB in 689 B.C., it was later rebuilt. It attained its greatest glory as capital of the Neo-Babylonian empire under NEBUCHADNEZZAR II (r.605–c.561 B.C.). Taken by ALEXANDER THE GREAT in 331 B.C., it was where he died. Most of the ruins are from the city built by Nebuchadnezzar. The largest city in the world at the time, it contained the great temple of MARDUK with its associated ZIGGURAT, apparently the basis for the story of the Tower of BABEL, and the Hanging Gardens, one of the SEVEN WONDERS OF THE WORLD.

Babylonia Ancient country, EUPHRATES RIVER valley, SW Asia. The area was divided into SUMER (in the southeast) and AKKAD (northwest) when the first Babylonian line of Amorites took power after 2000 B.C., largely because of HAMMURABI (c.1790–1750 B.C.). The Kassites assumed

power around 1595 B.C. and established a dynasty that lasted 400 years. After ELAM conquered Babylonia (c.1157 B.C.), a series of wars established a new Babylonian dynasty whose outstanding member was Nebuchadnezzar I (r.1124?–1103 B.C.). ASSYRIA ruled the area most frequently in the 9th–7th cent. B.C. In the 7th–6th cent. B.C. NEBUCHADNEZZAR II of CHALDEA instituted the last and greatest period of Babylonian supremacy, conquering SYRIA and PALESTINE and rebuilding BABYLON. Conquered in 539 B.C. by the Persian CYRUS THE GREAT, and in 331 B.C. by ALEXANDER THE GREAT, the area was later gradually abandoned.

Babylonian Exile *or* **Babylonian Captivity** Forced detention of Jews in BABYLONIA following its conquest of Judah in 598/7 and 587/6 B.C. The first deportation may have occurred after King Jehoiachin was deposed in 597 B.C. or after NEBUCHADNEZZAR destroyed JERUSALEM in 586. In 538 B.C., the Persian CYRUS THE GREAT conquered Babylonia and allowed the Jews to return to Palestine. Some Jews chose to remain in Babylonia, initiating the Jewish DIASPORA.

Baby Yar \\‚bä-bē-'yär\\ Large ravine near Kiev in Ukraine, the site of a mass grave of more than 100,000 people killed by German Nazi SS squads between 1941 and 1943. Most of the victims were Jews, but some were communist officials and Russian prisoners of war. A symbol of Jewish suffering in the HOLOCAUST, the site came to world attention after the 1961 publication of Yevgeny YEVTUSHENKO's poem *Baby Yar.*

Bacall, Lauren *orig.* Betty Joan Perske (b.1924) U.S. actress. Born in New York City, she worked as a model; her photo on a magazine cover led to her casting in the film *To Have and Have Not* (1944) with Humphrey BOGART, whom she soon married. An instant success, she made three more films with Bogart: *The Big Sleep* (1946), *Dark Passage* (1947), and *Key Largo* (1948). After his death she starred on Broadway in *Cactus Flower* (1965), *Applause* (1970, Tony Award), and *Woman of the Year* (1981, Tony Award).

baccarat Card game in which three hands of two or three cards each are dealt and players may bet either or both hands against the dealer's. In a two-handed version, players may bet on or against the dealer. Players aim for a count of 9. Face (court) cards and 10s are counted as 0. The cards are added to obtain the value, but only the last digit is significant. Thus, in a hand of 6 and 7, the sum is 13, but only the 3 of that number counts. Though a glamorous game that attracts high rollers, baccarat is mostly a game of luck.

Bacchanalia \\‚ba-kə-'näl-yə\\ *or* **Dionysia** In Greco-Roman religion, any of the festivals of the wine god Bacchus (DIONYSUS), which probably originated as fertility rites. The most famous Greek festivals included the Greater Dionysia, the Anthesteria, and the Lesser Dionysia. Bacchanalia were introduced from lower Italy into Rome, where they were at first secret, open only to women, though later they admitted men. In 186 B.C. their reputation as orgies led the Senate to prohibit them throughout Italy, except in special cases.

bacchantes See MAENADS AND BACCHANTES

Bacchus See DIONYSUS

Bach, Carl Philipp Emanuel (1714–1788) German composer. Second son of J. S. BACH, he received a superb musical education from his father. In 1740 he became harpsichordist at the court of FREDERICK II the Great, where he remained for 28 years, after which he moved to Hamburg to take the city's leading musical position. He was the main exponent of the *empfindsamer Stil* ("expressive style"), which emphasized rhapsodic freedom and sentiment. A founder of the Classic style, he is one of the first composers in whose works sonata form becomes clearly evident. He wrote some 200 works for harpsichord, clavichord, and piano, some 50 keyboard concertos, some 20 symphonies, and several oratorios and Passions.

Bach, Johann Christian (1735–1782) German-British composer. Youngest son of J. S. BACH, he studied with his brother C. P. E. BACH before moving to Italy. In 1762 he became composer to the King's Theatre in London, where he would remain the rest of his life, becoming music teacher to the queen, and later the producer of an important series of

concerts (1765–81). He wrote some 50 symphonies, some 35 keyboard concertos, and much chamber music. His melodious and well-formed works were important prototypes of the Classic style and influenced W. A. MOZART.

Bach, Johann Sebastian (1685–1750) German composer. Born in the village of Eisenach to a musical family, from 1700 he held positions as singer and violinist, as organist at the ducal court at Weimar (1708–17), as kapellmeister at the princely court of Cöthen (1717–23), and finally as cantor at the great church of St. Thomas in Leipzig (1723–50). Imbued with the N. German contrapuntal style from early childhood, he encountered the lively Italian style, especially in the works of Antonio VIVALDI, around 1710, and much of his music embodies a superb melding of the two. At St.

Johann Sebastian Bach

Thomas he wrote over 200 church cantatas. His orchestral works include the six Brandenburg Concertos, the four orchestral suites, and many harpsichord concertos, a genre he invented. His great keyboard works include the great didactic set *The Well-Tempered Clavier,* the huge *Art of the Fugue,* the *Goldberg Variations,* numerous suites, and many organ preludes and fugues. His surviving choral works include (in addition to the sacred cantatas) over 30 secular cantatas, two monumental Passions, and the Mass in B Minor. His works, never widely known in his lifetime, went into near-total eclipse after his death, and only in the early 19th cent. were they revived, to enormous acclaim. Perhaps the greatest organist and harpsichordist of his time, today Bach is regarded as the greatest composer of the baroque era, and, by many, as the greatest composer of all time.

Bacharach \\'bak-ə-ˌrak\\, **Burt** (b.1929) U.S. songwriter and pianist. Born in Kansas City, he studied under Darius MILHAUD and Henry COWELL. In the 1950s he wrote pop arrangements and toured with Marlene DIETRICH before beginning his long association with lyricist Hal David (b.1921), which would produce many hits, especially for Dionne Warwick (b.1940), including "Walk On By," "I Say a Little Prayer," and "Do You Know the Way to San Jose?" and the musical *Promises, Promises* (1968).

Bacillariophyta See DIATOM

bacillus \\bə-'si-ləs\\ Any of the rod-shaped, gram-positive bacteria (see GRAM STAIN) of the genus *Bacillus,* widely found in soil and water. The term is sometimes applied to all rodlike bacteria. Bacilli can form SPORES under unfavorable environmental conditions. Resistant to heat, chemicals, and sunlight, these spores remain capable of growing and developing for long periods of time. One type sometimes causes spoilage in canned foods. Another contaminates laboratory cultures and is often found on human skin. Most strains do not cause disease in humans; a notable exception is *B. anthracis,* which causes ANTHRAX. Some bacilli produce useful ANTIBIOTICS.

backbone See VERTEBRAL COLUMN

backgammon Board game played with two dice and counter-pieces (called stones) in which the two players try to be the first to gather their pieces into one corner (home) and then systematically remove them from the board. The board has four sections (tables), each marked with six narrow wedges (points) in two alternating colors. Fifteen white and fifteen black stones represent the two opposing sides. Stones are moved in opposite directions according to the number of points shown on the dice. An ancient game, it dates from 3000 B.C.

backpacking Sport of hiking while carrying clothing, food, and CAMPING equipment in a pack on the back. In the earlier 20th cent., backpacking was primarily a means of getting to wilderness areas inaccessible by car or by day hike. It later became associated with general touring by foot. Types of packs range from the frameless rucksack to the contour

frame pack, with a frame of tubing and often a waistband that transfers most of the pack's weight to the hips.

Bacon, Francis *later* Viscount St. Albans (1561–1626) British statesman and philosopher, father of modern scientific method. Nephew of William CECIL, he studied at Cambridge and Gray's Inn. A supporter of the Earl of ESSEX, he turned against him when Essex was tried for treason. Under JAMES I he rose steadily, becoming successively solicitor general (1607), attorney general (1613), and lord chancellor (1618). Convicted of accepting bribes, he lost his public offices and died deep in debt. As a scientist, he attempted to put natural science on a firm empirical foundation rather than allow it to rest on citations of ancient authorities. His

Francis Bacon Painting by an unknown artist

method was set forth in *Novum Organum* (1620). Philosophically, he was an early empiricist (see EMPIRICISM). His elaborate classification of the sciences inspired the 18th-cent. French Encyclopedists, and his empiricism inspired 19th-cent. British philosophers of science. Other works include *The Advancement of Learning* (1605) and a *History of Henry* VII (1622).

Bacon, Francis (1909–1992) Irish-British painter. Born in Dublin, he settled in London (1929) to begin a career as an interior decorator. With no formal art training, he started painting, drawing, and participating in gallery exhibitions, with little success. In 1944 he achieved instant notoriety with *Three Studies for Figures at the Base of a Crucifixion.* His images depict distorted figures in isolation and despair with nightmarish horror, and his skill in handling paint, smeared with violent color, won the admiration of critics and peers.

Bacon, Roger (c.1220–1292) English scientist and philosopher. Educated at Oxford and the Univ. of Paris, he joined the Franciscan order in 1247. He speculated about lighter-than-air flying machines, microscopes, and telescopes; the term "experimental science" was popularized through his writings. His philosophical thought was Aristotelian; critical of the methods of theologians such as THOMAS AQUINAS, he argued that experimental knowledge of nature would help confirm the Christian faith. He was imprisoned around 1277 by his fellow Franciscans for "suspected novelties."

bacteria Group of microscopic, single-celled organisms that are PROKARYOTES. They may have spherical, rodlike, or spiral shapes. They inhabit virtually all environments. Different types are distinguished in part by the structure of their cell walls (see GRAM STAIN). Many bacteria swim by means of flagella (see FLAGELLUM). The DNA of most bacteria is found in a single circular CHROMOSOME, suspended in the CYTOPLASM. Though some bacteria can cause food poisoning and infectious diseases in humans, most are harmless and many are beneficial. They are used in various industrial processes, especially in the food industry (e.g., the production of yogurt, cheeses, and pickles). See also ARCHAEBACTERIA, COLIFORM BACTERIA, CYANOBACTERIA, DENITRIFYING BACTERIA, EUBACTERIA, NITRIFYING BACTERIA.

bacterial diseases Diseases caused by BACTERIA, ranging from minor skin infections to bubonic PLAGUE, TUBERCULOSIS, and bacterial PNEUMONIA. Improved sanitation, VACCINES, and ANTIBIOTICS have all decreased the mortality rates from bacterial infections, though antibiotic-resistant strains have caused a resurgence in some illnesses. Bacteria cause disease by secreting or excreting TOXINS (as in BOTULISM), by producing toxins internally, which are released when the bacteria disintegrate (as in TYPHOID), or by inducing sensitivity to their antigenic properties (as in tuberculosis). See also CHOLERA, DIPHTHERIA, MENINGITIS, SYPHILIS.

bacteriology Study of BACTERIA. Modern understanding of bacterial forms dates from Ferdinand COHN's classifications. Other researchers, such as Louis PASTEUR, established the connection between bacteria and fermentation and disease. Modern methods of bacteriological technique began in the late 19th cent. Important discoveries came when Pasteur succeeded in immunizing animals against bacterial diseases, which led to the development of IMMUNOLOGY. See also MICROBIOLOGY.

bacteriophage \bak-'tir-ē-ə-ˌfāj\ *or* **phage** Any of a group of usually complex VIRUSES that infect BACTERIA. Discovered in the early 20th cent., bacteriophages were first used unsuccessfully to treat human bacterial diseases; they were abandoned with the advent of ANTIBIOTICS in the 1940s. The rise of drug-resistant bacteria in the 1990s focused renewed attention on their therapeutic potential. Thousands of varieties exist, each of which may infect only one or a few types of bacteria. The core of a bacteriophage's genetic material may be either DNA or RNA. Bacteriophages known as lytic or virulent phages release replicated viral particles by lysing (bursting) the host cell upon infecting it. Other types, known as lysogenic (see LYSOGENY) or temperate, integrate their nucleic acid into the host's chromosome to be replicated during cell division. During this time they are not virulent. The viral genome may later become active, initiating production of viral particles and destruction of the host cell. DNA is the genetic material of phages. They are a favorite research tool of molecular biologists, used in studies of genetic RECOMBINATION, nucleic-acid replication, and protein synthesis.

Bactria Ancient country, SW Asia. It lay between the HINDU KUSH and the AMU DARYA in present-day Afghanistan, Uzbekistan, and Tajikistan. Its capital was Bactra. From the 6th cent. B.C. it was controlled by the ACHAEMENIAN DYNASTY, then (from 323 B.C.) by the SELEUCID DYNASTY. It formed an independent kingdom about 250 B.C. A crossroads for East–West trade as well as for religion and art, it came under Muslim control in the 7th cent. A.D.

Baden \'bäd-ᵊn\ Former German state, S Germany. The name (meaning "baths") refers to the warm mineral springs, particularly in the town of Baden-Baden (pop., 1989: 51,000), valued since Roman times. Baden first became a political unit under the Margrave of Baden in 1112. Subsequently split up many times, the territory was reunited under Margrave Charles Frederick in 1771. Active in the revolutions of 1848–50, it joined the German empire in 1871, and it became part of the Weimar Republic in 1919. The S part became a state of W. Germany in 1949, while the N part was incorporated into the state of Württemberg-Baden. In 1952 the two states merged to form Baden-Württemberg.

Baden-Powell \'bā-dᵊn-'pō-əl\, **Robert (Stephenson Smyth)** *later* **Baron Baden-Powell (of Gilwell)** (1857–1941) British army officer and founder of the Boy Scouts (see SCOUTING). In the S. AFRICAN WAR, he became a national hero in the siege of Mafikeng. Having learned that his military textbook *Aids to Scouting* (1899) was being used to train boys in woodcraft, he wrote *Scouting for Boys* (1908) and that same year established the Boy Scout movement. In 1910, with his sister Agnes and his wife, Olave, he founded the Girl Guides.

badger Any of eight species of stout-bodied carnivores (family Mustelidae) that possess an anal scent gland, powerful jaws, and large, heavy claws on their forefeet. Most species are found in SE Asia; one lives in Europe. Badgers dig to find food and to construct burrows. The American badger *(Taxidea taxus),* the only New World species, lives in W N. America. Badgers feed mostly on small animals, especially rodents. Species may be 13–32 in. (33–81 cm) long, excluding the tail, and may weigh 2–48 lbs (1–22 kg). Badgers can be savage fighters.

Badlands Barren region covering some 2,000 sq mi (5,200 sq km) of SW S. Dakota. It has an extremely rugged landscape created by cloudbursts that have cut deep gullies in poorly cemented bedrock; its extensive fossil deposits have yielded the remains of such animals as the three-toed horse, camel, saber-toothed tiger, and rhinoceros. Badlands National Park (379 sq mi, or 982 sq km) lies mostly between the CHEYENNE and White rivers.

badminton Court or lawn game played with light long-handled rackets and a shuttlecock volleyed over a net. The game is named after the residence of Britain's duke of Beaufort, where it supposedly originated around 1873. Official matches are played indoors to protect the shuttlecock from winds. Play consists entirely of hitting the shuttlecock back and forth without letting it touch the floor or ground. The best-known match is the All-England Championships. It became a full-medal sport at the 1992 Olympics.

Badoglio \bə-'dōl-yō\, **Pietro** (1871–1956) Italian general and politician. He served as chief of the general staff 1919–21 and 1925–28, governed Libya 1928–34, and commanded the Italian forces in Ethiopia 1935–36. In 1940 he resigned as chief of staff in disagreement with Benito MUSSOLINI, and in 1943 he helped organize Mussolini's downfall. As Italy's prime minister (1943–44), Badoglio arranged for an armistice with the Allies.

Baeck \'bek\, **Leo** (1873–1956) Prussian-Polish rabbi, spiritual leader of German Jewry during the Nazi period. After earning a PhD in philosophy, he served as a rabbi in Silesia, Düsseldorf, and Berlin, becoming the leading liberal Jewish religious thinker of his time. *The Essence of Judaism* (1905) and *The Gospel as a Document of Jewish Religious History* (1938) are among his important works. He negotiated with the Nazis to buy time for the German Jews; finally arrested, he was sent to the Theresienstadt concentration camp. Liberated the day before he was to be executed, he settled in England.

Baedeker \'bed-ə-kər\, **Karl** (1801–1859) German publisher. In 1927 Baedeker started a firm at Koblenz that became known for its guidebooks. His aim was to give travelers the practical information they needed to dispense with paid guides. A notable feature was the use of "stars" to indicate places of special interest and reliable hotels. Under his sons the firm expanded to include French and English editions.

Baer \'ber\, **Karl Ernst, Ritter (Knight) von** (1792–1876) Prussian-Estonian embryologist. Studying chick development with Christian Pander (1794–1865), Baer expanded Pander's concept of germ-layer formation to all vertebrates, thereby laying the foundation for comparative EMBRYOLOGY. He emphasized that embryos of one species could resemble embryos of another, and that the younger the embryo the greater the resemblance. He also discovered the mammalian ovum. His *On the Development of Animals* 1828–37) surveyed all existing knowledge on vertebrate development.

Baez \'bī-ez\, **Joan (Chandos)** (b.1941) U.S. folksinger and activist. Born on Staten Island, N.Y., she moved often as a child, receiving little musical training. While still in her teens, her luminous soprano voice brought her to the forefront of the 1960s folk-song revival. An active participant in the protest movements of the 1960s and '70s, Baez made free concert appearances at civil-rights and anti–Vietnam War rallies.

Baffin Bay Large inlet, Atlantic Ocean, between W GREENLAND and E BAFFIN ISLAND. It has an area of 266,000 sq mi (689,000 sq km) and is connected to the Atlantic by DAVIS STRAIT. It was visited by the English captain Robert Bylot in 1615 and named for his navigator, William Baffin (c.1584–1622).

Baffin Island Largest island in Canada and fifth-largest island in the world (183,810 sq mi, or 476,068 sq km), lying between Greenland and the Canadian mainland. Located west of BAFFIN BAY and DAVIS STRAIT, it is part of NUNAVUT. Probably visited by Norsemen in the 11th cent. it was sighted by Martin FROBISHER while seeking a NORTHWEST PASSAGE (1576–78). Largely uninhabited, it is the site of the world's northernmost mines and Auyuittuq National Park (created 1972).

Bagehot \'baj-ət\, **Walter** (1826–1877) English economist, political analyst, and journalist. His early literary essays and economic articles led to his involvement with *The Economist.* As its editor from 1860, he helped make it one of the world's leading business and political journals. His classic *The English Constitution* (1867) describes how the British system of government really operates. His other works include *Physics and Politics* (1872), an early attempt to apply

the concept of evolution to societies, and *Lombard Street* (1873), a study of banking.

Baghdad *or* **Bagdad** City (metro. area pop., 1995: 4,478,000), capital of Iraq. Located on the TIGRIS RIVER, the site has been settled from ancient times. It rose to importance as the capital of the ABBASID DYNASTY from A.D. 762. Under HARUN AL-RASHID it achieved its greatest glory, reflected in the *THOUSAND AND ONE NIGHTS*, as one of the world's largest and richest cities. A center of Islam, it was second only to Constantinople in trade and culture. It began to decline when the capital was moved to Samarra in 809. It was sacked by the Mongols in 1258, taken by TIMUR in 1401, and captured by the Persian SULEYMAN I in 1524. It was a shadow of its former self in 1638, when it was absorbed by the OTTOMAN EMPIRE. In 1921 it became the capital of the kingdom of Iraq. Severely damaged by bombing in the PERSIAN GULF WAR, it has since suffered under trade sanctions.

bagpipes Wind instrument consisting of two or more single- or double-reed pipes whose reeds are vibrated by wind fed by arm pressure on a skin or cloth bag. The bag is inflated either by the mouth or by bellows strapped to the body. Melodies are played on the fingerholes of the melody pipe, or chanter, while the remaining pipes, or drones, sound single notes. Bagpipes existed by about A.D. 100. The early bag was an animal bladder or a nearly whole sheepskin or goatskin. Bagpipes have always been folk instruments.

bagworm moth Any insect of the MOTH family Psychidae, found worldwide, named for the baglike cases the larvae (see LARVA) carry with them. The strong-bodied male has broad, fringed wings with a wingspread averaging 1 in. (25 mm). The wormlike female lacks wings. Bagworm larvae often damage trees, especially evergreens.

Baha'i \bä-ˈhä-ē\ Religion founded in Iran in the mid-19th cent. by BAHA ULLAH. It emerged from BABISM when in 1863 Baha Ullah asserted that he was the messenger of God predicted by the Bab. The writings of the Bab, Baha Ullah, and his son Abd ol-Baha form the sacred literature. Worship consists of readings from scriptures of all religions. Baha'i faith proclaims the essential unity of all religions and the unity of humanity. It is concerned with social ethics and has no priesthood or sacraments. Adherents are expected to pray daily, fast 19 days a year, and keep to a strict ethical code. Baha'i has experienced major growth since the 1960s but has been persecuted in Iran since the fundamentalist revolution of 1979.

Bahamas *officially* **Commonwealth of the Bahamas** Archipelago and nation consisting of about 700 islands and numerous cays, NW edge of the W. INDIES, lying southeast of Florida and north of Cuba. Area: 5,386 sq mi (13,950 sq km). Population (2000): 295,000. Capital: NASSAU (on New Providence Island). The people are a blend of African and European ancestry, the former a legacy of the slave trade. Language: English (official). Religion: Christianity. Currency: Bahamian dollar. Chief among the islands, from north to south, are Grand Bahama, Abaco, Eleuthera, New Providence, Andros, Cat, and Inagua; New Providence has most of the population. All are composed of coraline limestone and lie mostly only a few feet above sea level; the highest point is Mt. Alvernia (206 ft, or 63 m) on Cat Island. There are no rivers. Its market economy is heavily dependent on tourism, for which gambling is a particular attraction, and on international financial services. Most foodstuffs are imported from the U.S.; fish and rum are significant exports. It is a constitutional monarchy with two legislative houses; its chief of state is the British monarch, represented by a governor-general, and the head of government is the prime minister. The islands were inhabited by Lucayan Indians when Christopher COLUMBUS sighted them on Oct. 12, 1492. He is thought to have landed on San Salvador (Watling) Island. The Spaniards made no attempt to settle, but carried out slave raids that depopulated the islands; when English settlers arrived in 1648 from Bermuda, the islands were uninhabited. They became a haunt of pirates and buccaneers, and few of the ensuing settlements prospered. The islands enjoyed some prosperity following the American Revolution, when Loyalists fled the U.S. and established cotton plantations there They were a center for blockade runners during the American Civil War. Not until

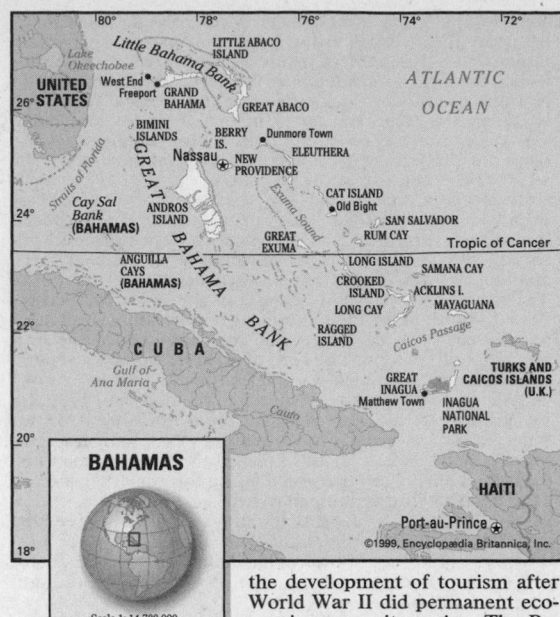

BAHAMAS

Scale 1: 14,788,000
0   60   120 mi
0   90   180 km

©1999, Encyclopædia Britannica, Inc.

the development of tourism after World War II did permanent economic prosperity arrive. The Bahamas was granted internal self-government in 1964, and became independent in 1973.

Baha Ullah \bä-ˈhä-u̇l-ˈlä\ *orig.* Mirza Hoseyn Ali Nuri (1817–1892) Iranian founder of the BAHA'I faith. A Shiite Muslim who allied himself with the BAB, he joined his half-brother Sobh-e Azal in leading the Babi movement after the Bab's execution. In 1867 he declared himself the imam-mahdi foretold by the Bab and sent by God. This pronouncement split BABISM into two factions, with a small group (the Azali) adhering to its original beliefs and a larger group following him into what became the Baha'i faith.

Bahia \bä-ˈē-ä\ State (pop., 1996: 12,541,000), E Brazil. Its capital is SALVADOR. The major river is the SÃO FRANCISCO. The Portuguese first entered the region in 1501. Discovery of gold and gems in the Diamantina Upland attracted settlers in the 18th cent. A state since 1889, Bahia is rich in petroleum, natural gas, lead, copper, chrome, and tin. Its heavy industries include petroleum refining and ironworks. It is also an important agricultural producer.

Bahia See SALVADOR

Bahrain \bä-ˈrān\ *officially* **State of Bahrain** Country, constitutional monarchy, occupying an archipelago consisting of Bahrain Island and about 30 smaller islands, lying along the ARABIAN PENINSULA in the PERSIAN GULF. Area: 255 sq mi (661 sq km). Population (2000): 691,000. Capital: MANAMA. Most of the population is Arabic. Language: Arabic (official). Religion: Islam (official), divided between Sunni and Shiite. Currency: Bahraini dinar. Bahrain Island accounts for seven-eighths of the country's total area and, with the islands of Al Muharraa and Sitra off its NE coast, constitutes the population and economic center of the country. Bahrain Island is 27 mi (43 km) long and 10 mi (16 km) wide, and is connected to Saudi Arabia by a 15-mi (25-km) causeway completed in 1986. The highest elevation is Ad-Dukhan Hill at 440 ft (132 m). The country has a developing mixed state and private-enterprise economy based largely on natural gas and petroleum refining. The chief of state is the emir and head of government is the prime minister. The area has long been an important trading center and is mentioned in Persian, Greek, and Roman references. It was ruled by Arabs from the 7th cent. A.D., but then occupied by the Portuguese 1521–1602. Since 1783 it has been ruled by the Khalifah family, though through a series of treaties its defense remained a British responsibility 1820–1971. After Britain withdrew its forces from the Persian Gulf (1968), Bahrain declared its independence in 1971. It

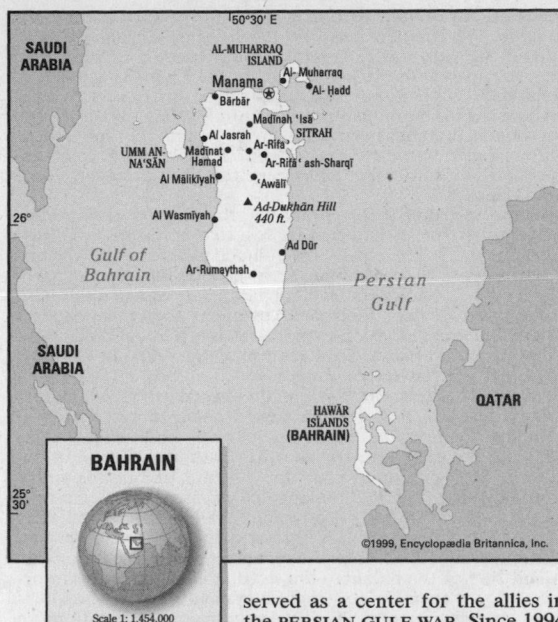

BAHRAIN

Scale 1: 1,454,000

0   6   12 mi
0   8   16 km

©1999, Encyclopædia Britannica, Inc.

served as a center for the allies in the PERSIAN GULF WAR. Since 1994 it has experienced bouts of political unrest mainly by Shiites, who have attempted to get the government to restore the parliament (abolished in 1975).

Baibars I See BAYBARS I

Baikal, Lake *or* **Lake Baykal** \bī-ˈkäl\ Lake, S SIBERIA, Russia in Asia. At 395 mi (636 km) long, with an area of 11,780 sq mi (30,510 sq km), it is the largest freshwater basin in Eurasia. The deepest continental body of water on earth (5,715 ft, or 1,742 m), it contains one-fifth of the fresh water on the earth's surface. Over 300 rivers flow into it. The island of Olkhon is in its center. Plant and animal life are rich and various; more than 1,200 species are unique to the lake and are threatened by growing industrial pollution.

bail Temporary release of a prisoner in exchange for security given to guarantee the prisoner's appearance at a later hearing. It also refers to the actual security given (e.g., cash). Its main use today is to secure the freedom, pending trial, of someone arrested and charged with a criminal offense. The amount of bail is generally set in relation to the gravity of the offense, though other factors, such as the character of the accused and the accused's ability to secure bail, may also be considered. See also BOND.

Bailey, Pearl (Mae) (1918–1990) U.S. singer and entertainer. Born in Newport News, Va., she began her career at 15, appearing in nightclubs and theaters and with jazz bands, including the Count BASIE band. Her first Broadway musical was *St. Louis Woman* in 1946; her first film was *Variety Girl* in 1947. She became known for her lively and earthy style. The most memorable of her Broadway roles, which included Carmen Jones (1954), was as Dolly Levi in an all-black production of *Hello, Dolly!* (1967–69).

Bailly \bà-ˈyē\, **Jean-Sylvain** (1736–1793) French astronomer and politician. Noted for computing an orbit for Halley's Comet (1759), he turned to politics with the outbreak of the French Revolution. He was chosen president of the THIRD ESTATE in May 1789 and the first mayor of Paris in July. He later lost popularity, particularly after his order to disperse a riotous crowd led to the massacre of the Champ de Mars (1791). He retired but was subsequently arrested and guillotined.

Baird, Bil and Cora (1904–1987, 1912–1967) U.S. puppeteers. Born in Grand Island, Neb., Bil (born William Britton) Baird produced his own puppet shows from the mid-1930s. He and Cora Eisenberg (born in New York City) married in 1937 and began to create original puppets, scenery, and music for their shows. They produced television shows in

the 1950s and opened a MARIONETTE theater in New York in 1966. Bil trained such puppeteers as Jim HENSON.

Baird, John L(ogie) (1888–1946) Scottish engineer. Plagued by ill health, he gave up his job as an electric-power engineer in 1922 and devoted himself to television research. In 1926 he became the first person to televise pictures of objects in motion. He demonstrated color television in 1928. The German post office gave him facilities to develop a television service in 1929. Baird was reported to have completed research on stereoscopic television at the time of his death.

Baja California \ˈbä-ˌhä\ *or* **Lower California** Peninsula, NW Mexico. Bounded by the U.S., the Pacific Ocean, and the Gulf of California, it is about 760 mi (1,220 km) long, and has an area of 55,366 sq mi (143,396 sq km). Politically it is divided into the states of BAJA CALIFORNIA and BAJA CALIFORNIA SUR. It has over 2,000 mi (3,200 km) of coastline, with sheltered harbors on both the W coast and the Gulf. The area had been inhabited for 9,000 years when the Spanish arrived in 1533. Jesuit missionaries established permanent settlements in the late 17th cent. The area was separated from what is now California by treaty in 1848 following the MEXICAN WAR.

Baja California State (pop., 2000: 2,487,000), N BAJA CALIFORNIA peninsula, N Mexico. Formerly called Baja California Norte, it covers an area of 27,071 sq mi (70,114 sq. km.). It experienced phenomenal growth beginning in the 1950s, when several foreign companies established factories in the region. Its capital is Mexicali.

Baja California Sur State (pop., 2000: 423,000), S BAJA CALIFORNIA peninsula, N Mexico. With an area of 28,447 sq mi (73,678 sq km), it became a state in 1974. It is sparsely populated. Much cotton has been planted near LA PAZ, the capital, but subsistence agriculture is the norm. Tourism is now alleviating the state's isolation.

Baker, Josephine *orig.* Freda Josephine McDonald (1906–1975) U.S.-French entertainer. Born in St. Louis, Mo., she moved to New York to perform in Harlem nightclubs and on Broadway in *Chocolate Dandies* (1924). She went to Paris in 1925 to dance in *La revue nègre*, and became Paris's most popular music-hall entertainer, receiving star billing at the FOLIES BERGÈRE. In World War II she worked with the Red Cross and entertained FREE FRENCH troops. From 1950 she adopted numerous orphans of all nationalities as "an experiment in brother-

Josephine Baker

hood," returning periodically to the U.S. to advance the cause of civil rights.

Bakersfield City (pop., 2000: 247,000; metro. area: 661,000), S California. Situated in the San Joaquin Valley, it was founded in 1869 by Thomas Baker (1810–1872). Discovery of the Kern River oil fields in 1899 sparked a petroleum boom. The city was quickly rebuilt after a major earthquake in 1952. Nearby vineyards produce about a quarter of the wine made in California.

Baker vs. Carr U.S. Supreme Court case (1962) that forced the Tennessee legislature to reapportion itself on the basis of population, thus ending the traditional overrepresentation of rural areas and establishing that the Court may intervene in apportionment cases. The Court ruled that every citizen's vote should carry equal weight, regardless of the voter's place of residence. Its later ruling in *Reynolds vs. Sims* (1964) required virtually every state legislature to be reapportioned, ultimately causing political power in most states to shift from rural to urban areas.

Bakhtin \bək-ˈtēn\, **Mikhail (Mikhailovich)** (1895–1975) Russian literary theorist. His works offended Soviet authorities, and in 1929 he was exiled from Vitsyebsk to Kazakstan. In *Problems of Dostoevsky's Poetics* (1929), he first advanced theories further developed in *The Dialogic Imagination* (1975). His wide-ranging ideas strongly influenced Western

B

thinking in cultural history, linguistics, literary theory, and aesthetics.

baking Cooking by dry heat, especially in an oven. Baked products include BREAD, cookies, pies, and pastries. Baking ingredients include FLOUR, water, leavening agents (yeast, baking soda, baking powder), shortening (fats and oils), eggs, milk, and sugars. These are mixed to create dough or batter, which is transferred to a pan or sheet and heated. The leavening agent produces gas that becomes trapped in the dough, causing it to rise. Shortening makes doughs more easily workable and the final product tenderer. Eggs are used for color, flavor, and texture. Sugars sweeten and aid FERMENTATION.

baking soda See BICARBONATE OF SODA

Bakongo See KONGO

Bakst \\'bákst\\, **Leon** *orig.* Lev Samuilovich Rosenberg (1866–1924) Russian painter and stage designer. After studies in St. Petersburg and Paris, in 1898 he cofounded the journal *Mir Iskusstva* ("World of Art") with Sergey DIAGHILEV. After designing scenery for the imperial theaters, he began designing sets and costumes for Diaghilev's BALLETS RUSSES in Paris. His bold designs and sumptuous colors, conveying an exotic orientalism, won him international fame. His work revolutionized European stage design and strongly influenced European high fashion.

Baku \\bä-'kü\\ City (pop., 1997 est.: 1,727,000), capital of Azerbaijan. Located at the CASPIAN SEA's best harbor, it dates from the 9th cent. A.D. By the 12th cent. it was capital of the Shirvan shahs. Russia took Baku in 1723, returned it to Persia in 1735, and recaptured it in 1806. The capital of the BOLSHEVIK government in 1917, it became the capital of the new Soviet republic of Azerbaijan in 1920 and of the independent republic in 1991.

bakufu \\bä-'kü-fü\\ (Japanese: "tent government") Military rule of the country by a hereditary SHOGUN, as opposed to rule by the imperial court and the emperor. The Kamakura bakufu (KAMAKURA SHOGUNATE) was established at the end of the 12th cent., the Muromachi bakufu (ASHIKAGA SHOGUNATE) in the early 14th cent., and the Edo bakufu (TOKUGAWA SHOGUNATE) at the beginning of the 17th cent. The last was the most successful, a time of peace and prosperity that lasted over 250 years.

Bakunin \\bə-'kün-yən\\, **Mikhail (Aleksandrovich)** (1814–1876) Russian anarchist and political writer. Active in the REVOLUTIONS OF 1848, he attended the Slav congress in Prague and wrote the manifesto *An Appeal to Slavs* (1848). Arrested for revolutionary intrigues in Germany (1849), he was exiled to Siberia; he escaped in 1861 and continued his militant anarchist teachings. At the FIRST INTERNATIONAL (1872) he engaged in a famous quarrel with Karl MARX, which split the European revolutionary movement.

Balaguer (y Ricardo) \\bä-lä-'ger\\, **Joaquín (Vidella)** (1907–2002) President of the Dominican Republic (1960–62, 1966–78, 1986–96). He held numerous government posts during Gen. Rafael TRUJILLO's 30-year dictatorship. He became president in 1960, but Gen. Trujillo continued to wield actual power until his assassination in 1961. Balaguer's subsequent attempts at liberalization caused his overthrow by the military. Elected president in 1966, he achieved steady economic growth and modest social reforms. He was reelected repeatedly, but his last term was marked by political violence and charges of corruption.

Balakirev \\bə-'lä-kyi-ryif\\, **Mily (Alekseyevich)** (1837–1910) Russian composer. Tutored by Mikhail GLINKA, he himself later became the mentor of César Cui (1835–1918) and Modest MUSSORGSKY. In 1861–62 their group expanded to become the MIGHTY FIVE. In 1862 he cofounded the Free School of Music. After a nervous breakdown in 1871, he adopted a fervent and bigoted form of Orthodoxy. His works include two symphonies, the piano fantasy *Islamey* (1869), and a piano concerto. With his brilliant color and use of folk themes, he was perhaps the most influential proponent of Russian nationalism.

Balaklava \\bə-lə-'klä-və\\, **Battle of** (Oct. 1854) Indecisive military engagement of the CRIMEAN WAR. The Russians sought to capture the British-controlled Black Sea port of Balaklava, and occupied positions on the heights above a nearby valley. To disrupt the Russian troop movements, Lord RAGLAN gave an ambiguous order for Lord CARDI-GAN's Light Brigade to attack. Instead of leading his cavalry against the Russian guns on the heights, Cardigan swept down the valley after the retreating Russian cavalry. The battle ended with the loss of 40% of the Light Brigade.

balalaika \\ˌba-lə-'lī-kə\\ Russian stringed instrument with a triangular body, three strings, and movable frets on its fingerboard. It comes in six sizes, from piccolo to double bass. It developed in the 18th cent. from the dombra. It has been primarily a solo folk instrument for accompanying song and dance.

balance Instrument for comparing the weights of two bodies, usually for scientific purposes, to determine the difference in MASS. The equal-arm balance dates back to the ancient Egyptians, possibly as early as 5000 B.C. By the early 20th cent., it had been developed into an exquisitely precise measuring device. Electronic balances today depend on electrical compensation rather than mechanical deflection. The ultramicrobalance can determine the weight of amounts as small as a few micrograms.

balance of payments Systematic record of all economic transactions during a given period between residents (including the government) of one country and residents (including the governments) of other countries. The transactions are presented in the form of double-entry bookkeeping. The U.S. balance of payments, for example, records how dollars are made available to foreigners through U.S. imports, U.S. tourist spending abroad, foreign lending, and so on. These expenditures are shown on the debit side of the balance. The credit side shows where foreigners put their dollars, including paying for U.S. exports and servicing debts to the U.S. Foreign countries with more dollars than they need to spend on U.S. goods and services may purchase gold or securities; those with fewer dollars may acquire additional dollars by transferring gold, selling holdings in the U.S., and so on. Certain forms of transferring funds (e.g., large outflows of gold) are less desirable as a way of settling foreign debts than others (e.g., transfers of currency acquired through international trade). The INTERNATIONAL MONETARY FUND helps address balance-of-payments issues. See also BALANCE OF TRADE.

balance of power In international relations, an equilibrium of power sufficient to discourage or prevent one nation or party from imposing its will on another. The term came into use at the end of the Napoleonic Wars to denote the power relationships in the European state system. Until World War I, Britain played the role of balancer in a number of shifting alliances. After World War II, a Northern Hemisphere balance of power pitted the U.S. and its allies (see NATO) against the Soviet Union and its satellites (see WARSAW PACT) in a bipolar balance of power backed by the threat of nuclear war. With the Soviet Union's collapse (1991), the U.S. and its NATO allies became the world's paramount military power.

balance of trade Difference in value over a period of time between a nation's imports and exports of goods and services. The balance of trade is part of a larger economic unit, the BALANCE OF PAYMENTS. A nation has a favorable balance of trade, or a trade surplus, if its exports exceed its imports. If imports exceed exports, an unfavorable balance of trade, or a trade deficit, exists. Under MERCANTILISM a favorable balance of trade was a necessity, but in CLASSICAL ECONOMICS it was more important to utilize economic resources fully. The idea of the undesirability of trade deficits has persisted, however, and is often advanced by advocates of PROTECTIONISM.

balance sheet Financial statement that describes the resources under a company's control on a specified date and indicates where they have come from. It consists of three major sections: assets (valuable rights owned by the company), liabilities (funds provided by outside lenders and other creditors), and the owners' equity. On the balance sheet, total assets must always equal total liabilities plus total owners' equity.

Balanchine \\bá-lä°-'shēn\\, **George** *orig.* Georgy (Melitonovich) Balanchivadze (1904–1983) Russian-U.S. choreographer, and cofounder and artistic director of the NEW YORK CITY BALLET (1948–82). After studying at the Imperial Ballet school, he left the Soviet Union in 1925 to join the BALLETS RUSSES, where his choreography of *Apollo* (1928) exemplified the spare neoclassical style that became his trademark. In 1933 Lincoln KIRSTEIN invited "Mr. B." to form the School of American Ballet and its performing group, the American Ballet. The group disbanded in 1941, and Kirstein and Balanchine later founded the Ballet Society, from which emerged the New York City Ballet. Balanchine created over 150 works for the company, including *The Nutcracker* (1954) and *Jewels* (1967), and also choreographed musicals and operas. He collaborated closely with Igor STRAVINSKY, setting over 30 works to the latter's music. Balanchine is widely considered the greatest choreographer of the 20th cent.

Balboa, Vasco Núñez de (1475–1519) Spanish conquistador and explorer. In 1500 he explored the coast of modern Colombia, then settled in Hispaniola. On an expedition to assist a colony in Colombia, in 1511 he helped found Darién, the first stable settlement on the S. American continent. In 1513 he became the first European to see the Pacific Ocean and took possession of it, as the Mar del Sur (South Sea), and adjacent lands for Spain. He became governor of the provinces of Panamá and Coiba but remained subject to a rival, Pedro Arias Dávila (1440?–1531). Charged by Dávila with rebellion and treason, after a farcical trial Balboa was beheaded.

bald eagle Species of sea eagle (*Haliaeetus leucocephalus*) that occurs inland, along rivers and large lakes. Strikingly handsome, it is the only EAGLE solely native to N. America and has been the U.S. national bird since 1782. The adult, about 40 in. (1 m) long, is dark brown with white head and tail, and a wingspan of 6.5 ft (2 m). It nests in lone trees, often on river islands. Though protected in the U.S. since 1940, the eagle population has been depleted by river pollution, pesticides, and loss of nesting sites.

Balder \'bȯl-dər, 'bäl-dər\ In Norse mythology, the just and beautiful son of ODIN and FRIGG. He could be harmed by nothing except mistletoe. Knowing he was invulnerable, the gods amused themselves by throwing things at him. Deceived by LOKI, the blind god Höd hurled mistletoe at Balder and killed him.

baldness *or* **alopecia** \ˌal-ə-'pē-shə\ Lack or loss of HAIR, either permanent (from destruction of hair follicles) or temporary (from short-term follicle damage). Male pattern baldness is inherited and affects up to 40% of men; it is treated by transplanting of follicles from areas where hair still grows and application of drugs (e.g., minoxidil) to the scalp. Temporary hair loss may follow high fever or come from X rays, drugs, malnutrition, or endocrine disorders.

Baldovinetti \ˌbäl-dō-vē-'nät-tē\, **Alesso** (c.1425–1499) Italian artist active in Florence. Little is known of his early training, but his style shows the influence of Fra ANGELICO and DOMENICO VENEZIANO. His masterpiece, *The Nativity* (1460–62), a fresco in the church of the Santissima Annunziata, Florence, and a *Madonna and Child* (1460s) both depict views of the Arno River valley in the background; they are among the earliest European paintings of landscapes.

Baldung \'bäl-dùn\, **Hans** *or* **Hans Baldung Grien** \'grēn\ (1484–1545) German painter and graphic artist. He was assistant to Albrecht DÜRER in Nuremberg and was active in Strasbourg as official painter to the episcopate. He is best known for the high altar of the cathedral at Freiburg, where he lived 1512–17. His paintings are equaled in importance by his drawings, engravings, and woodcuts, frequently depicting the themes of the Dance of Death and Death and the Maiden. In his taste for the gruesome, Baldung is close in style and spirit to Matthias GRÜNEWALD.

Baldwin, James (Arthur) (1924–1987) U.S. writer. He grew up in poverty in Harlem and became a preacher while in his teens. His first novel, *Go Tell It on the Mountain* (1953), regarded as his finest, was followed by the essay

James Baldwin

collections *Notes of a Native Son* (1955) and *Nobody Knows My Name* (1961); the novels *Giovanni's Room* (1956), a story of homosexual life, and *Another Country* (1962); the essay *The Fire Next Time* (1963), prophesying racial violence; and the play *Blues for Mister Charlie* (1964). His eloquence and passion made him for years the country's most prominent black writer.

Baldwin, Roger (Nash) (1884–1981) U.S. civil rights leader. Born in Wellesley, Mass., he taught sociology at Washington Univ. (1906–9) in St. Louis, where he also was secretary of its Civic League. When the U.S. entered World War I, he directed the pacifist American Union Against Militarism, the predecessor of the AMERICAN CIVIL LIBERTIES UNION (ACLU). As the ACLU's director (1920–50) and national chairman (1950–55), he made civil rights, once a leftist cause, a universal one.

Baldwin, Stanley *later* Earl Baldwin (of Bewdley) (1867–1947) British politician. A Conservative Party member of the House of Commons (1908–37), he served as prime minister 1923–24, 1924–29, and 1935–37. He proclaimed a state of emergency in the general strike of 1926 and later secured passage of the antiunion Trade Disputes Act. After 1935 he began to strengthen the British military while showing little public concern about the aggressive policies of Germany and Italy. In 1936 he procured the abdication of EDWARD VIII, whose plan to marry Wallis Simpson Baldwin felt would threaten the prestige of the monarchy.

Baldwin I (1172–1205) First Latin emperor of Constantinople (1204–5). Count of Flanders and Hainaut, he was a leader of the Fourth CRUSADE against the Byzantine Christians and helped capture Constantinople. When crusaders and their Venetian allies seized power, he was made emperor (1204) and recognized by the pope. He created a feudal government on the Western European model, but was later defeated and executed by invading Bulgars.

Baldwin I *known as* **Baldwin of Boulogne** \bu-'lȯn-yə\ (1058?–1118) King of Jerusalem (1100–18). The son of a French count, he joined the First CRUSADE and gained control of Edessa (now in Turkey) in 1098. In 1100 his brother Godfrey died in Jerusalem, and Baldwin was summoned by nobles to succeed him as king of the crusader state. He expanded the kingdom by conquering coastal cities and built an administration that served for 200 years as the basis for Frankish rule in Syria and Palestine.

Baldwin II *known as* **Baldwin of Bourg** \'bürk\ (d.1131) King of Jerusalem (1118–31). A French nobleman, he joined the First CRUSADE and was made count of Edessa by his cousin BALDWIN I in 1100. Captured by Seljuq Turks in 1104, he was ransomed four years later and reclaimed Edessa from the regent by force. He became king of Jerusalem in 1118 on the death of Baldwin I. He later expanded his kingdom and attacked Damascus with the aid of the KNIGHTS OF MALTA and TEMPLARS.

Baldwin II Porphyrogenitus \ˌpȯr-fə-rō-'jen-ət-əs\ ("Born to the purple," thus "of royal birth") (1217–1273) Fifth and last Latin emperor of Constantinople (1228–61). The son of the third Latin emperor, Baldwin succeeded his brother. Invasions by Greeks and Bulgars reduced the empire to the area around Constantinople, and Baldwin's empty treasury obliged him to travel twice to Western Europe to ask for aid. He sold sacred relics to LOUIS IX of France and broke up parts of the imperial palace for firewood. He lost the throne in 1261 when MICHAEL VIII PALAEOLOGUS captured Constantinople and restored Greek rule.

Balearic Islands \ˌba-lē-'ar-ik\ *Spanish* **Islas Baleares** Archipelago, (pop., 1998 est.: 796,000), W Mediterranean Sea, constituting an autonomous community and province, Spain. It occupies an area of 1,936 sq mi (5,014 sq km); its capital is PALMA. The most important islands are MAJORCA, Minorca, and Ibiza. The islands were ruled by CARTHAGE in the 5th cent. B.C., by Rome from about 120 B.C., by the Byzantine empire from A.D. 534, and from the 10th cent. by the UMAYYAD DYNASTY at CÓRDOBA. It was united with the kingdom of ARAGON in 1344. Fought over in the 18th cent. by the Spanish, British, and French, the islands came under Spain in 1802. Their modern economy is fueled by tourism.

baleen whale \bə-'lēn, 'ba-ˌlēn\ Any of about 13 species of CETACEANS in the suborder Mysticeti. Their specialized feeding structure, the baleen, strains PLANKTON and small crustaceans from the water. It consists of two horny plates attached to the roof of the mouth. Each plate (as long as 12 ft, or 3.6 m, in the RIGHT WHALE) is composed of parallel slats with fringes that mat together to form a sieve. Other baleen whales are the BLUE, FIN, gray, HUMPBACK, and sei whales and the rorqual.

Balfour, Arthur James *later* **Earl Balfour (of Whittinge-hame)** (1848–1930) British statesman. The nephew of Lord SALISBURY, Balfour served in Parliament 1874–1911, and succeeded his uncle as prime minister (1902–5). He helped form the ENTENTE CORDIALE (1904). As foreign secretary (1916–19), he wrote the BALFOUR DECLARATION, which expressed official British approval of ZIONISM. He later drafted the Balfour Report (1926), which defined relations between Britain and the dominions expressed in the Statute of WESTMINSTER.

Balfour Declaration (Nov. 2, 1917) Statement issued by the British foreign secretary, A. J. BALFOUR, in a letter to Lionel Walter Rothschild (1868–1937), a leader of British Jewry, that promised the establishment of a homeland for the Jewish people in PALESTINE. The British anticipated gaining control over Palestine after World War I and hoped to win over Jewish public opinion to the side of the Allies. They also hoped that pro-British settlers would help protect the approaches to the SUEZ CANAL.

Bali \\ˈbä-lē, ˈba-lē\\ Island (pop., 1995 est.: 2,900,000), Indonesia. Located in the Lesser Sunda Islands, off the E coast of JAVA, it constitutes, with minor adjacent islands, a province of Indonesia. The island is mountainous; its highest peak is Mt. Agung (10,308 ft, or 3,142 m). Colonized by India in early times, Bali is the remaining stronghold of HINDUISM in the Indonesian archipelago. It came under Dutch rule in the late 19th cent., and became part of Indonesia in 1950. Tourism is increasingly important to its modern economy.

Balinese People of BALI, Indonesia. They differ from other Indonesians in adhering to the Hindu religion, though their culture has been heavily influenced by the Javanese. In Balinese villages each family lives in its own compound, surrounded by earthen or stone walls. Balinese religion fuses Hindu Saivism with Buddhism, ancestor cults, and belief in spirits and magic. Marriage is often limited to members of the same kinship organization.

Balkan Mountains *Bulgarian* **Stara Planina** \\ˈstä-rä-ˌplä-nē-ˈnä\\ Mountain range, E Europe. It extends across central Bulgaria; the highest point is Botev Peak, at 7,793 ft (2,375 m). The range forms the major divide between the DANUBE RIVER in the north and the Maritsa in the south. It is crossed in about 20 places, notably by SHIPKA PASS.

Balkan Peninsula Peninsula, SE Europe. Located between the ADRIATIC SEA, the MEDITERRANEAN SEA, and the AEGEAN and BLACK SEAS, it contains Slovenia, Croatia, Bosnia and Herzegovina, Macedonia, Yugoslavia, Romania, Bulgaria, Albania, Greece, and part of Turkey. Part of the area was incorporated into Roman provinces, including Epirus, Moesia, Pannonia, Thrace, and Dacia. It was subsequently settled by Slavic invaders, Serbs, Croats, Slovenes, and Slavonized Bulgars. It was gradually organized into kingdoms, many of which were overrun by the Ottoman Turks in the 14th–15th cent. The factional strife that occurred there from the early 20th cent., provoking the continual breakups and regroupings of different states, introduced the word *balkanize* into English.

Balkan Wars (1912–13) Two military conflicts that deprived the Ottoman empire of almost all its remaining territory in Europe. In the First Balkan War, the Balkan League (Bulgaria, Serbia, Greece, and Montenegro) defeated the OTTOMAN EMPIRE, which lost Macedonia and Albania. The Second Balkan War broke out after Serbia and Greece quarreled with Bulgaria over the division of their joint conquests in Macedonia. Bulgaria was defeated, and Greece and Serbia divided up most of Macedonia between themselves. The conflicts helped spark World War I.

Balkhash, Lake *or* **Lake Balqash** \\bäl-ˈkäsh\\ Lake, E Kazakstan. It is about 375 mi (600 km) long, with a maximum depth of 85 ft (26 m). Climate affects its size greatly; its area has varied from about 6,000 sq mi (15,500 sq km) to 7,300 sq mi (19,000 sq km) depending on rainfall. It is

frozen from November to March. Damming and industrial pollution have caused severe ecological damage.

Ball, Lucille (Désirée) (1911–1989) U.S. actress and television comedy star. Born in Jamestown, N.Y., she played minor roles in films from 1933. With her bandleader husband, Desi Arnaz (1917–1986), she created the very successful television comedy series *I Love Lucy* (1951–57), the *Lucy-Desi Comedy Hour* (1957–60), and after their divorce in 1960, *The Lucy Show* (1962–68) and *Here's Lucy* (1968–74). With her red hair and rasping voice and a comic persona alternately

Lucille Ball with Desi Arnaz

brassy and feminine, she was the preeminent female star of early television.

ballad Form of narrative folk song. Its distinctive style crystallized in late medieval Europe as part of the oral tradition and has been preserved as a musical and literary form. The oral form has persisted in folk music, and the written, literary ballad evolved from the oral tradition. The folk ballad typically tells a compact tale with deliberate starkness, using devices such as repetition to heighten effects.

ballade \\ba-ˈläd\\ One of several FORMES FIXES in French lyric poetry and song that evolved from the songs of the TROUBADOURS and TROUVÈRES, cultivated especially in the 14th–15th cent. It consists of three stanzas with the same rhyme scheme and identical refrains, and a shortened final dedicatory stanza. The texts were often solemn and formal, containing elaborate symbolism and classical references.

Ballard \\ˈba-lərd\\, **Robert D(uane)** (b.1942) U.S. oceanographer and marine geologist. Born in Wichita, Kan., he became a marine scientist at the Woods Hole (Mass.) Oceanographic Research Institution. He pioneered the use of deep-diving submersibles and participated in the first manned exploration of the MID-ATLANTIC RIDGE. He is best known for his dramatic discovery of the wreck of the *TITANIC* in 1985, and he has gone on to discover the *LUSITANIA* and ships lost in World War II.

ball bearing One of the two types of rolling, or antifriction, BEARINGS (the other is the ROLLER BEARING). Its function is to connect two machine members that move relative to one another so that the frictional resistance to motion is minimal. One of the members is often a rotating shaft and the other a fixed housing. Each ball bearing has three main parts: two grooved, ringlike races and a number of balls. The balls fill the space between the two races and roll with negligible FRICTION in the grooves. The balls may be loosely restrained and separated by means of a retainer or cage.

ballet Theatrical dance in which a formal academic technique (the *danse d'école*) is combined with music, costume, and stage scenery. Developed from court productions of the Renaissance, ballet was renewed under Louis XIV, who established France's Académie Royale de Danse in 1661, where Pierre Beauchamp developed the five ballet positions. Early ballets were often incorporated into opera-ballets by such composers as Jean-Baptiste LULLY. In the 18th cent. Jean-Georges NOVERRE and Gasparo ANGIOLINI separately developed the dramatic ballet (*ballet d'action*) to tell a story through dance steps and mime. Significant developments in the early 19th cent. included pointe work (balance on the extreme tip of the toe) and the emergence of the prima ballerina, exemplified by Marie TAGLIONI and Fanny ELSSLER. In the late 19th and early 20th cent. Russia became the center of ballet production and performance, through such innovators as Sergey DIAGHILEV, Anna PAVLOVA, Vaslav NIJINSKY, Marius PETIPA, and Michel FOKINE; great ballets were composed by P. I. TCHAIKOVSKY and Igor STRAVINSKY. Since then, ballet schools in Great Britain and the U.S. have elevated ballet in those countries to Russia's level and greatly increased its audience.

Ballets Russes \\ba-lā-ˈrües\\ Ballet company founded in Paris in 1909 by Sergey DIAGHILEV. Considered the source of modern ballet, the company employed the most outstanding creative talent of the period. Its choreographers included Michel FOKINE, Léonide MASSINE, and George BALANCHINE, and among its dancers were Tamara KARSAVINA and Vaslav NIJINSKY. Music was commissioned from such composers as Igor STRAVINSKY, Maurice RAVEL, and Claude DEBUSSY, and ballets featured stage designs by Pablo PICASSO, and Henri MATISSE. Among its many influential productions were *The Firebird* (1910), *The Rite of Spring* (1913), and *Parade* (1917). The avant-garde company's great influence lasted well beyond its cessation after Diaghilev's death in 1929.

ballistics Science of propulsion, flight, and impact of projectiles. Internal ballistics deals with propulsion of projectiles, such as within the barrel of a gun; guns and rocket engines convert chemical energy of propellants into KINETIC ENERGY of projectiles. External ballistics deals with projectile flight; the path of a projectile is subject to the forces of gravity (see GRAVITATION), DRAG, and LIFT. Terminal ballistics deals with the impact of projectiles on a target. Wound ballistics deals with the trauma caused by bullets and explosively driven fragments.

ballooning Riding of a balloon in competition or for recreation. Sport ballooning began in the early 20th cent. The balloons used are of lightweight synthetic materials (e.g., polyester coated in aluminized mylar) and are filled with hot air or lighter-than-air gas such as HELIUM or HYDROGEN. In 1783 J.-M. and J.-É. MONTGOLFIER developed a fabric-bag balloon that would rise when filled wth hot air. Balloons provided military observation sites in the 19th cent. and were used in the 20th cent. by Auguste PICCARD and others to gather high-altitude data. Balloon races often involve tasks such as changing elevations or landing on or near a target. The first transatlantic, transcontinental, and transpacific balloon flights were achieved in 1978, 1980, and 1981, respectively. In 1999 Bertrand Piccard and Brian Jones circled the world in a balloon in 19 days. In 2002 the American Steve Fossett circled the globe solo in 13 days.

Ballot Act (1872) British law that introduced the secret ballot for all parliamentary and municipal elections. The secret ballot was also called the Australian ballot, because it was first used in Australian elections (1856). The British law, designed to protect voters from bribery and coercion, was an important achievement of William GLADSTONE's first administration.

ballot initiative See REFERENDUM AND INITIATIVE

ballroom dance European and American social dancing performed by couples. It includes standard dances such as the fox-trot, WALTZ, polka, tango, rumba, CHARLESTON, JITTERBUG, and MERENGUE. Ballroom dance was popularized by Vernon and Irene CASTLE, Fred ASTAIRE, and later Arthur Murray (1895–1991), who established studios throughout the U.S.

balm Any of several fragrant herbs of the MINT family, particularly *Melissa officinalis* (balm gentle, or lemon balm), cultivated in temperate climates for its fragrant leaves, which are used as a scent in perfumes and as a flavoring. The name is also applied to *Monarda didyma* (BERGAMOT, or bee balm), and *Molucella laevis* (Molucca balm, or bells of Ireland), as well as to aromatic substances from species of *Commiphora* (trees and shrubs of the incense-tree family).

Balochis See BALUCHIS
Balochistan See BALUCHISTAN
Balqash, Lake See Lake BALKHASH
balsa Tree (*Ochroma pyramidale,* or *O. lagopus*) of the bombax family (Bombacaceae), native to tropical S. America and noted for its extremely light wood. Because of its buoyancy (about twice that of cork), balsa is well adapted for making floats and life preservers. Its resiliency makes it an excellent shock-absorbing packing material. Its insulating properties make it a good lining material for incubators, refrigerators, and cold-storage rooms. It is also a valuable construction material for transportation containers, airplane passenger compartments, and model airplanes and boats.

balsam Aromatic resinous substance that flows from a plant and is used in medicinal preparations and incense. Balsam of Peru, used in perfumes, is a true balsam, from a lofty leguminous tree, *Myroxylon pereirae,* native to Peru and introduced into Sri Lanka. Balsam of Tolu (Colombia) is used in perfumes and in cough syrups and lozenges; it hardens with age. Canada balsam and Mecca balsam are not true balsams.

Balthus \bál-ˈtüs\ *orig.* Balthazar Klossowski (1908–2001) French painter. Born in Paris to Polish parents, he was considered a child prodigy. Though lacking formal training, he had his first one-man show in 1934. His paintings are characterized by large, mysterious interiors and austere, muted landscapes peopled with isolated, pensive adolescent girls. He served as director of the French Academy in Rome 1961–77. His disturbing and erotic images, including the scandalous *The Guitar Lesson* (1934), and his carefully cultivated persona made him an international cult figure.

Baltic languages Branch of the INDO-EUROPEAN LANGUAGE family whose three attested languages, Lithuanian, Latvian, and Old Prussian, were or are spoken along the E and SE shore and hinterlands of the Baltic Sea. Baltic has certain striking features in common with SLAVIC LANGUAGES, including similarities in the accentuation system for nouns, categories of definiteness in adjectives, and some common vocabulary. However, the deep divisions within Baltic itself make the hypothesis of a common Balto-Slavic protolanguage difficult to defend.

Baltic Sea Sea, N Europe. An arm of the Atlantic Ocean, connecting with the North Sea, it is 1,056 mi (1,699 km) long, covers an area of 163,050 sq mi (422,300 sq km), and has a maximum depth of 1,539 ft (469 m). It receives the VISTULA and ODER RIVERS and many others. It has two large arms, the Gulf of BOTHNIA and the Gulf of Finland. Its waters contain only about one-fourth as much salt as the oceans, and it freezes readily.

Baltic States Republics of Lithuania, Latvia, and Estonia, on the E shore of the BALTIC SEA. The term has sometimes been used to include Finland and Poland. They were created as independent states in 1917 from portions of Russia and Poland. With the aid of German and Allied forces, the Baltic states repelled a BOLSHEVIK invasion in 1919. In 1940 they were occupied by the Soviet Union and incorporated as constituent republics. In 1944 Soviet troops recovered the territory overrun by German forces in 1941. The Baltic states gained independence with the breakup of the Soviet Union in 1991.

Baltimore City (pop., 2000: 651,000), N central Maryland. It is Maryland's largest city and economic hub. Established in 1729, it was named after the Irish barony of Baltimore (seat of the Calvert family, proprietors of the colony of Maryland). It became the first U.S. Roman Catholic diocese in 1789, and in 1827 home to the nation's first railroad operations. In World War I, Baltimore began to develop industrially, and it has since become a major seaport.

Baltimore, David (b.1938) U.S. virologist. Born in New York City, he and Howard Temin (1934–1994) independently discovered an enzyme that synthesizes DNA from RNA, the reverse of the usual process. This enzyme, reverse transcriptase, has become an invaluable tool in recombinant-DNA technology. The research of Baltimore, Temin, and Renato DULBECCO helped illuminate the role of VIRUSES in cancer; the three men shared a Nobel Prize in 1975. He has served as president of Rockefeller Univ. (1990-97) and later of Caltech (from 1997).

Baltimore and Ohio Railroad (B&O) First steam-operated railway in the U.S. to be chartered as a common carrier of freight and passengers (1827). The B&O was established by Baltimore merchants to foster trade with the West. By the 1870s it extended to Chicago and St. Louis. Its long-distance passenger trains were discontinued in 1971, but B&O (now part of CSX Corp.) still runs limited commuter service and hauls freight.

Baluchis \bə-ˈlü-chēz\ *or* **Balochis** \bə-ˈlō-chēz\ Tribes speaking the Baluchi language and inhabiting the province of BALUCHISTAN in Pakistan and neighboring areas of Iran, Afghanistan, and the Punjab (India). Some 70% of the population live in Pakistan, where they number about 4.8 million. Originally from the Iranian plateau, they are mentioned in 10th-cent. Arabic chronicles. Traditional Baluchis are nomads, but settled agricultural existence is becoming

B

more common. They raise camels and other livestock and engage in carpet making and embroidery.

Baluchistan \bə-ˌlü-chi-'stän\ *or* **Balochistan** \bə-ˌlō-chi-'stän\ Province (pop., 1998: 6,511,000), SW Pakistan. Its capital is Quetta (pop., 1998: 560,000). Its landscape includes mountains, barren plains, arid desert, and marshy swamps. It was included in the Bactrian kingdom, then was ruled by Arabs in the 7th–10th cent. A.D. It was ruled by Persia for centuries, except for a brief period under the Mughals (1594–1638). It became a British dependency in 1876, a British province of India in 1887, part of Pakistan in 1947–48, and a separate province in 1970. Wheat, sorghum, and rice are staple crops; industries include cotton and woolen manufacturing.

Balzac \bál-'zak\, **Honoré de** *orig.* Honoré Balssa (1799–1850) French writer. An early attempt at a business career left him with huge debts, and he toiled incessantly thereafter to improve his worsening finances. In 1829 his novels and stories began to achieve some success. In a vast series of some 90 novels and novellas he collectively called *The Human Comedy*, he sought to produce a comprehensive picture of contemporary society. Among his best are *Eugénie Grandet* (1833), *Père Goriot* (1835), *Lost Illusions* (1837–43), *A Harlot High and Low* (1843–47), and *Cousin Bette* (1846).

Honoré de Balzac

His novels are notable for their narrative drive, large casts of vital characters, and an obsessive interest in virtually all spheres of life. His best-known story collection is *Droll Stories* (3 vols., 1832–37). He frequently wrote feverishly for 15 hours at a stretch (his death has been attributed to overwork and excessive coffee). He is considered the major early influence on REALISM, or NATURALISM, in the novel and one of the greatest fiction writers of all time.

Bamako \'bä-mä-ˌkō\ City (pop., 1995 est.: 800,000), capital of Mali. Located in SW Mali on the NIGER RIVER, it became the capital of the former colony of French Sudan in 1908. Now spanning both sides of the river, it has several colleges and most of Mali's industrial enterprises. The city more than tripled in size in the 1960s, largely because of migration from the drought-stricken countryside.

Bambara \bam-'bär-ə\ People of the upper Niger region of Mali. Numbering 3.1 million, the Bambara have their own writing system and are noted for their wood and metal sculpture. In the 17th–18th cent. they developed two empires, one based in Ségou (and including TOMBOUCTOU) and the other in Kaarta.

bamboo Any of the tall, treelike GRASSES found from tropical to mild temperate regions that make up the subfamily Bambusoideae, family Gramineae (Poaceae). Bamboos are giant fast-growing grasses with hollow woody stems. A few species of the genus *Arundinaria* are native to the S U.S. The stems grow in branching clusters from a thick RHIZOME, often forming a dense undergrowth that excludes other plants. All parts of the bamboo are used, for purposes including food, livestock fodder, paper, construction materials, and medicines. Bamboo is also grown as an ornamental.

banana Fruit of the genus *Musa* (family Musaceae), a gigantic herbaceous tropical plant spread by RHIZOMES, and one of the most important food crops of the world. The banana is valued for its flavor, nutritional value, and constant availability. Hundreds of varieties are cultivated. Perhaps the most important species is the common banana, *M. sapientum*. The ripe fruit is high in carbohydrates (mainly sugar), potassium, and vitamins C and A, and low in protein and fat. The U.S. imports more bananas than does any other country. See also PLANTAIN.

Bancroft, George (1800–1891) U.S. historian. Born in Worcester, Mass., he held such political posts as minister to

England (1846–49), Prussia (1867–71), and the German empire (1871–74). The first comprehensive study of the U.S. through the end of the Revolution, his 10-volume *History of the United States* (1834–40, 1852–74) reflected his belief that the U.S. was the closest approximation yet to the perfect state and earned him the name "father of U.S. history."

band Musical ensemble that generally excludes STRINGED INSTRUMENTS. Ensembles of WOODWIND, BRASS, and PERCUSSION INSTRUMENTS originated in 15th-cent. Germany, taking on particularly a military role. In the 15th–18th cent., many European towns had town musicians, or waits, who performed especially for ceremonial occasions in wind bands. In the 18th–19th cent., the English amateur brass band, consisting largely of the many newly developed brass instruments, took on the important nonmilitary function of representing organizations of all kinds. In America, Patrick GILMORE's virtuoso band became famous in the mid-19th cent.; his greatest successor, J. P. SOUSA, bequeathed a repertory of marches that has remained very popular. The "big band" (see SWING) was central to American popular music in the 1930s and '40s. In the rock band, unlike most other bands, stringed instruments (electric guitars and electric bass) are paramount.

Banda, Hastings (Kamuzu) (1902?–1997) First president of Malawi (1963–94). Banda entered politics when white settlers sought the federation of Nyasaland (later Malawi) and the Rhodesias in 1949. In the 1950s he spoke widely against federation and was imprisoned by British colonial officials. In 1963 the federation was dissolved and Banda became prime minister. He concentrated on building infrastructure and increasing agricultural productivity. Named president for life in 1971, he became increasingly autocratic. He was voted out of office in 1994.

Bandama River \bän-'dä-mä\ River, central Ivory Coast. The longest and commercially most important river in the Ivory Coast, it and its tributaries drain half the country's surface area. It flows southward 497 mi (800 km) to enter the Gulf of GUINEA. A major hydroelectric plant is sited at Kossou.

Bandaranaike \ˌbən-də-rə-'nī-kə\, **S(olomon) W(est) R(idgeway) D(ias)** (1899–1959) Statesman and prime minister of Ceylon (present-day Sri Lanka) 1956–59. A prominent member of Ceylon's Western-oriented United National Party, he left it (1951) to found the opposition Sri Lanka Freedom Party. He later formed an alliance of four nationalist-socialist parties which swept elections in 1956 and made him prime minister. Under Bandaranaike, Sinhalese replaced English as the country's official language, and Buddhism (the majority religion) was actively encouraged. He was assassinated in 1959. His widow, Sirimavo Bandaranaike (1916–2000), became the world's first woman prime minister in 1960, serving until 1965, and again in 1970–77. She continued her husband's socialist policies and oversaw adoption of a new constitution proclaiming Sri Lanka a republic (1972). Their daughter, Chandrika Bandaranaike Kumaratunga (b.1945), became president in 1994 (reelected 1999) and named her mother prime minister (1995–2000). Her terms have been marked by continued conflict with the Hindu TAMIL minority.

Bandar Seri Begawan \'bän-där-'ser-ē-be-'gä-wän\ *formerly* **Brunei** Town (pop., 1991: 22,000; metro area pop. 1995 est.: 81,000), capital of Brunei. A trade center and river port, it was heavily damaged during World War II but largely rebuilt. Newer buildings include the largest mosque in E. Asia.

bandicoot Any of about 22 species of MARSUPIALS (family Peramelidae) found in Australia, Tasmania, and New Guinea. Bandicoots are 12–30 in. (30–80 cm) long, including the 4- to 12-in. (10- to 30-cm) tail. They have a stout, coarsehaired body, a tapered muzzle, and hindlimbs longer than their forelimbs. Unlike other marsupials, bandicoots have a placenta. They dig pits to search for insect and plant food. Farmers consider them pests.

band theory In chemistry and physics, a theoretical model describing the states of ELECTRONS in solid materials, which can have energy values only within certain specific ranges, called bands. Ranges of energy between two allowed bands are called forbidden bands. The electrons move from an energy level in one band to another in the same band or in another band. The theory accounts for many of the electrical and thermal properties of solids and forms the basis of the technology of devices such as SEMICONDUCTORS, heating elements, and capacitors (see CAPACITANCE).

Bandung \\'bän-dùn\ City (pop., 1996: 2,429,000), Indonesia. The capital of W. Java province, it was founded by the Dutch in 1810 in the interior of JAVA on a 2,400-ft (730-km) plateau. It is surrounded by beautiful scenery. It is the cultural center for the SUNDANESE, who compose most of W. Java's population and differ in customs and language from their Javanese neighbors.

bandwidth Measurement of the capacity of a communications signal. For digital signals, the bandwidth is the data speed, measured in bits per second (bps). For analog signals, it is the difference between the highest and lowest frequency components, measured in hertz (cycles per second). The human voice, which produces analog sound waves, has a typical bandwidth of three kilohertz between the highest and lowest frequency sounds it can generate.

Banerjea \\'bä-nòr-jē\, **Surendranath** (*later* **Sir Surendranath**) (1848–1925) Indian statesman, one of the founders of modern India. A teacher, he founded a college in Calcutta, which was later named after him. To bring Hindus and Muslims together for political action, for 40 years he put forward a nationalist viewpoint in his newspaper, *The Bengalee.* Twice elected president of the Indian National Congress, he advocated for an Indian constitution on the Canadian model. After serving in two legislative councils (1913–24), he retired to write his autobiography, *A Nation in the Making* (1925).

Banff National Park Park, SW Alberta. Established in 1885 as Canada's first national park, it lies on the E slopes of the ROCKY MTNS. and includes mineral springs, ice fields, and glacial lakes such as Lake Louise. It has been greatly expanded to its present area of 2,564 sq mi (6,641 sq km). Banff is famed for its spectacular beauty.

Bangalore \\'baŋ-gə-,lòr\ City (metro. area pop., 1995: 4,749,000), capital of Karnataka state, S India. It is a cultural meeting place for Kannada-, Telugu-, and Tamil-speaking peoples. Founded in the 17th cent., it became a fief of the Indian ruler Hyder Ali in 1758, but was taken by the British in 1791, then restored in 1881 to the raja of MYSORE (now Karnataka). Today, it is one of India's largest cities and an industrial and educational center.

Banghazi See BENGHAZI

Bangkok *Thai* **KrungThep** \\'krùŋ-'tep\ City (pop., 1999 est.: 5,647,000), capital of Thailand. It is the country's major port and cultural, financial, and educational center. Established as a fort before 1767, it became the capital in 1782. Seized by the Japanese in World War II, it suffered heavy Allied bombing. Since the 1970s it has experienced phenomenal growth. Throughout the city walled Buddhist temples and monasteries are numerous.

Bangladesh *officially* **People's Republic of Bangladesh** Country, S central Asia. Area: 55,126 sq mi (142,776 sq km). Population (2000): 129,194,000. Capital: DHAKA. The vast majority of the population are Bengalis. Language: Bengali (official). Religions: Islam (official; mainly Sunni), Hinduism (over 10%). Currency: taka. Bangladesh is generally flat, its highest point being only 660 ft (200 m). It is characterized by alluvial plains dissected by numerous connecting rivers. The S part consists of the E sector of the Ganges-Brahmaputra Delta. The chief rivers are the GANGES and the BRAHMAPUTRA (here known as the Jamuna), which unite to form the Padma. Though primarily agricultural, the country has been unable to feed itself. The monsoons that occur from May to October produce extreme flooding over much of Bangladesh, often causing severe crop damage and great loss of life; a cyclone in 1991 left 130,000 Bengalis dead, and several in 1997 were extremely disastrous. It is a republic with one legislative house; its chief of state is the president, and its head of government the prime minister. In its early years Bangladesh was known as BENGAL. When the British left the subcontinent in 1947, the area that was E. Bengal became the part of Pakistan called E. Pakistan. Bengali nationalist sentiment increased after the creation of an independent Pakistan. In 1971 violence erupted; some 1 million Bengalis were killed, and millions more fled

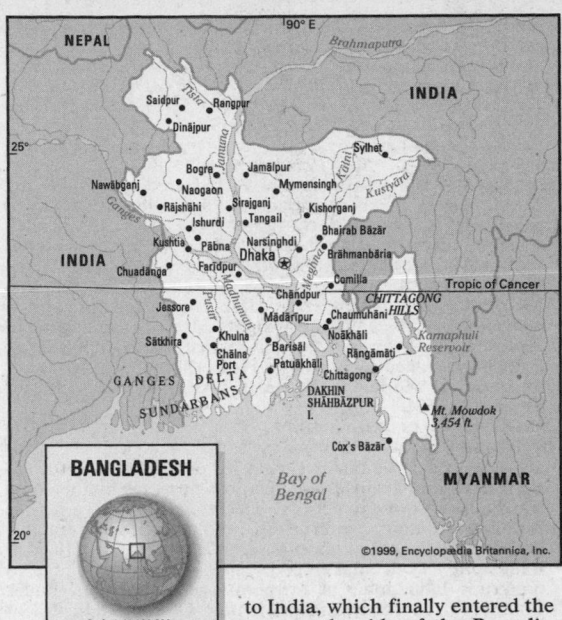

BANGLADESH

Scale 1: 11,181,000

to India, which finally entered the war on the side of the Bengalis, ensuring W. Pakistan's defeat. E. Pakistan became the independent nation of Bangladesh. Little of the devastation caused by the war has been repaired, and political instability, including the assassination of two presidents, has continued.

Bangui \\'bäŋ-gē\ City (pop., 1994: 524,000), capital of the Central African Republic. A major port on the UBANGI RIVER, it is connected by an extended 1,100-mi (1,800-km) river and rail transport system with the Congolese cities of POINTE-NOIRE and BRAZZAVILLE.

Banja Luka \\'bän-yä-'lü-kä\ City (pop., 1997: 160,000), NE Bosnia and Herzegovina. A Turkish military center and seat (1583–1639) of the Bosnian territory governed by a pasha, it was a battlefield between the Austrians and Turks in the 16th–18th cent., and figured in 19th-cent. Bosnian uprisings against Turkey as well as in revolts of the Serbs. It was a center of resistance in Axis-dominated CROATIA during World War II. It became the capital of the autonomous Serbian Republic of Bosnia and Herzegovina in 1992 and was a focus of fighting during the BOSNIAN CONFLICT.

banjo Plucked stringed instrument of African origin. It has a tambourine-like body, four or five strings, and a long fretted neck. The fifth string (if present) acts primarily as a drone. Originally the banjo had only four strings and lacked frets. It was brought by slaves to the U.S., where it was popularized in 19th-cent. MINSTREL SHOWS. It has been an important American folk instrument, especially in BLUEGRASS, and was used in early jazz.

Banjul \\'bän-jül\ *formerly* (*1816–1973*) **Bathurst** Seaport (metro. area pop., 1993: 270,000), capital of Gambia. Located on an island in the Gambia River, it is the country's largest city. Founded by the British in 1816, it became the capital of the British colony of Gambia, and with independence in 1965, the national capital. A transportation center, it has connections to the interior and to Senegal.

bank Institution that deals in MONEY and its substitutes and provides other financial services. Banks accept deposits and make loans and derive a PROFIT from the difference in the interest paid to lenders (depositors) and charged to borrowers, respectively. They also profit from fees charged for services. The three major classes of banks are COMMERCIAL BANKS, INVESTMENT BANKS, and CENTRAL BANKS. See also CREDIT UNION, SAVINGS AND LOAN ASSOCIATION, SAVINGS BANK.

Bankhead, Tallulah (Brockman) (1902–1968) U.S. actress. Born in Huntsville, Ala., to a prominent political family, she made her Broadway debut in 1918 and achieved fame on the London stage in *The Dancer* (1923). Her vivid presence and throaty voice contributed to her singular performances in the hit plays *The Little Foxes* (1939), *The Skin of Our Teeth* (1942), and *Private Lives* (1946). She made such films as Alfred HITCHCOCK's *Lifeboat* (1944), but remained primarily a stage performer; her final appearance was in *The Milk Train Doesn't Stop Here Anymore* (1964).

Bank of the United States Bank chartered in 1791 by the U.S. Congress. It was conceived by Alexander HAMILTON to pay off debts from the AMERICAN REVOLUTION and provide a stable currency. Its establishment, opposed by Thomas JEFFERSON, led to the first U.S. political parties, the FEDERALISTS and the Democratic-Republicans. The national bank restrained private state banks from overexpansion, a restriction opposed by states'-rights advocates, and came to represent privilege and wealth against agrarian populism. Criticism reached its height in Pres. Andrew JACKSON's administration and led to the BANK WAR. The bank's charter expired in 1836.

bank rate See DISCOUNT RATE

bankruptcy Status of a debtor who has been declared by judicial process to be unable to pay his or her debts, or the administration of an insolvent debtor's property by the court for the benefit of the debtor's creditors. Filing by a debtor is called voluntary bankruptcy; involuntary bankruptcy is declared by the court upon petition by a creditor. The U.S. Bankruptcy Code makes four types of relief available to bankrupt individuals or corporations: liquidation (under Chapter 7), reorganization (Chapter 11), debt adjustment for a family farmer (Chapter 12), and debt adjustment for an individual with a regular income (Chapter 13). Municipalities may file under Chapter 9. The court usually determines which debts are to be repaid, the debtor being typically granted a discharge of the rest.

Banks, Joseph (*later* **Sir Joseph**) (1743–1820) British explorer and naturalist. After studying at Oxford, Banks inherited a fortune that allowed him to travel extensively, collecting plant and natural-history specimens. He outfitted and accompanied James COOK's voyage around the world (1768–71). He was the first to suggest the identity of the wheat rust and barberry fungus (1805); he was also the first to show that marsupial mammals are more primitive than placental mammals. He served as president of the Royal Society from 1778 to 1820, and transformed KEW GARDENS into a major botanical institution. His herbarium, one of the most important in existence, and his library are now at the British Museum.

Banks Island Island, Northwest Territories, Canada. The westernmost island in the Canadian ARCTIC ARCHIPELAGO, it lies northwest of VICTORIA ISLAND. About 250 mi (400 km) long, it has an area of 27,038 sq mi (70,028 sq km). First sighted in 1820, it was named for the naturalist Joseph BANKS.

Bank War Controversy in the 1830s over the existence of the BANK OF THE U.S. Pres. Andrew JACKSON objected to the concentration of economic power in the bank's small group of financiers, and the effort to renew the bank's charter became central to the 1832 presidential election. After his reelection Jackson forbade the deposit of government funds in the bank. The bank's president retaliated by calling in loans, which precipitated a credit crisis. Denied renewal of its federal charter, the bank secured a Pennsylvania charter in 1836. Faulty investment decisions forced it to close in 1841.

Banneker, Benjamin (1731–1806) American astronomer and compiler of almanacs. Born a free black in Ellicott's Mills, Md., he owned a farm near Baltimore. He taught himself astronomy and mathematics and began astronomical calculations in 1773, accurately predicting a solar eclipse in 1789. In 1790 he was appointed to the commission that surveyed the site for Washington, D.C. From 1791 to 1802 he published annual almanacs; he sent an early copy to Thomas JEFFERSON to counter a contention that blacks were intellectually inferior.

Banner System Military organization used by the MANCHU tribes of Manchuria (now NE China) to conquer China in the 17th cent. The system was developed by the Manchu leader Nurhachi, who in 1601 organized his warriors into four companies, each known for its banner of a distinguishing color. More Banners (as the companies were known) were soon established, and the Manchus also organized their Chinese and MONGOL captives into similar companies. With these troops the Manchus conquered China and established the QING DYNASTY in 1644. Over time, the Banners' fighting qualities deteriorated; by the late 19th cent. the System was largely ineffective.

Bannister, Roger (Gilbert) (*later* **Sir Roger**) (b.1929) British runner. He attended Oxford Univ. before earning a medical degree. In 1954 he became the first person to complete a mile in less than four minutes (3 minutes 59.4 seconds), a feat widely believed to be impossible. An authority on physiology, he is said to have achieved his speed through scientific training methods.

Bannockburn, Battle of (June 23–24, 1314) Decisive battle in Scottish history, at which the Scots under ROBERT I the Bruce defeated the English under EDWARD II. The Scots were outnumbered three to one by the English soldiers, but they triumphed through masterly use of terrain, forcing the English onto a cramped, marshy battlefield with little room to maneuver. The victory cleared the last English troops from Scotland and secured Scottish independence, establishing Robert I's legitimacy.

Banpo *or* **Pan-p'o** \'bän-'pō\ Site of a NEOLITHIC PERIOD village located on the Wei River in China, dating to the early YANGSHAO CULTURE, 5000–4000 B.C. Some 8,000 stone and bone tools, pottery fragments, and clay figurines have been uncovered. The main cultivated crop was foxtail millet; the diet was supplemented through hunting and gathering. Pigs and dogs were domesticated, and textiles were manufactured.

Banting, Frederick Grant (*later* **Sir Frederick**) (1891–1941) Canadian physician. Born in Alliston, Ontario, he taught at the Univ. of Toronto from 1923. With Charles Best (1899–1978), he was first to obtain a pancreatic extract of INSULIN (1921), which they isolated in the laboratory of J. J. R. MACLEOD in a form effective against diabetes. Banting and Macleod received a 1923 Nobel Prize for the discovery of insulin; Banting voluntarily shared his portion of the prize with Best.

Bantu languages Family of about 500 languages spoken by more than 200 million people in Africa, from roughly below the continent's westward bulge to its S tip. About 35 Bantu languages, including Kongo, Rundi, Rwanda, Gikuyu, Chewa, N. and S. Sotho, Zulu, and Xhosa, have a million or more speakers. The Bantu family belongs to the BENUE-CONGO branch of the NIGER-CONGO LANGUAGE superfamily. The best-known grammatical feature of Bantu languages is their division of nouns into classes (see GENDER) that are marked by prefixes on nouns and that require agreeing prefixes on other parts of speech.

Bantu peoples Speakers of nearly 500 BANTU LANGUAGES, numbering over 200 million, occupying almost the entire S projection of Africa. Included in the highly diverse group are the Bemba, Bena, Chaga, Chewa, Embu, Fang, Ganda, Gusii, Hehe, Herero, HUTU, Kagwe, KIKUYU, Luba, Luhya, Lunda, Makonde, Meru, Nayamwezi, Ndebele, Nkole, Nyakyusa, Nyoro, Pedi, Shona, SOTHO, SWAZI, Tsonga, Tswana, TUTSI, Venda, XHOSA, Yao, Zaramo, and ZULU.

Bantu tribesman, Kenya

banyan Tree (*Ficus benghalensis,* or *F. indica*) of the FIG genus in the MULBERRY FAMILY, native to tropical Asia. Aerial ROOTS decend from its branches to the soil to become new trunks. The banyan reaches a height of up to 100 ft (30 m) and spreads laterally indefinitely. One tree may in time assume the appearance of a very dense thicket as a result of the tangle of roots and trunks.

baobab \'bau̇-ˌbab\ Tree (*Adansonia digitata*) of the bombax family (Bombacaceae), native to Africa. The barrel-like trunk may reach a diameter of 30 ft (9 m) and a height of 60 ft (18 m). The large, gourdlike, woody fruit contains a tasty pulp. A strong fiber from the bark is used for rope and cloth. The trunks are often excavated to serve as water reserves or temporary shelters. A related species, *A. gregorii,* occurs in Australia, where it is called baobab or bottle tree.

Bao Dai \'bau̇-'dī\ *orig.* Nguyen Vinh Thuy (1913–1997) Last reigning emperor of Vietnam (1926–45, 1949–55). Educated in France, he succeeded to a throne that was dominated by the French. He fled the country after the Viet Minh drove the occupying Japanese out (1945), but in 1949 the French invited him to return as sovereign. He did, but accomplished little and retired to France in 1955 when a national referendum called for the country to become a republic.

baptism In Christianity, the SACRAMENT of admission to the church, symbolized by the pouring or sprinkling of water on the head or by immersion in water. In the doctrine originated by St. PAUL, it signifies the wiping away of past SINS and the rebirth of the individual into a new life. Judaism practiced ritual purification by immersion, and JOHN THE BAPTIST baptized JESUS. Baptism was an important ritual in the early church by the 1st cent., and infant baptism appeared by the 3rd cent. Roman Catholic, Orthodox, and most Protestant churches practice infant baptism. The ANABAPTIST reformers insisted on adult baptism; modern BAPTISTS and the DISCIPLES OF CHRIST also practice adult baptism.

Baptist Member of a group of Protestant Christians who hold that only adult believers should be baptized and that it must be done by immersion. Baptist origins in the American colonies can be traced to Roger WILLIAMS, who established a Baptist church in Providence, R.I., in 1639. Baptist growth in the U.S. was spurred by the GREAT AWAKENING in the mid-18th cent. The 1814 General Convention showed divisions among U.S. Baptists over slavery; a formal split occurred when the Southern Baptist Convention was organized in 1845. African-American Baptist churches provided leadership in the 1960s CIVIL RIGHTS MOVEMENT. Baptist belief emphasizes the authority of local congregations in matters of faith and practice; worship is characterized by extemporaneous prayer and hymn-singing as well as by the exposition of scripture in sermons.

Bara \'bar-ə\, **Theda** *orig.* Theodosia Goodman (1885–1955) U.S. film actress. Born in Cincinnati, she had a brief stage career before going to Hollywood. Her first major picture, *A Fool There Was* (1915), was accompanied by publicity billing her as the daughter of an Eastern potentate. Establishing a sultry, exotic persona, she became the prototype of the screen "vamp." She made more than 40 films, but her popularity declined, and she retired in 1926.

Barabbas \bə-'ra-bəs\ In the NEW TESTAMENT, a criminal freed to please the mob before the crucifixion of JESUS. Described as a thief or an insurrectionist, Barabbas is mentioned in all four GOSPELS. Following the custom of setting free one prisoner chosen by popular demand before PASSOVER, Pontius PILATE suggested pardoning Jesus, but the crowd insisted upon the release of Barabbas.

Baraka \bä-'rä-kə\, **(Imamu) Amiri** *orig.* **(Everett) LeRoi Jones** (b.1934) U.S. playwright and black nationalist. He was born in Newark, N.J., and educated at Howard Univ. His first play, *Dutchman* (1964), explored the suppressed hostility of U.S. blacks toward the dominant white culture. *The Slave* and *The Toilet*, also produced in 1964, likewise aroused controversy. He founded the Black Arts Repertory Theater in Harlem, and in 1968 founded a Black Muslim group to promote black culture and political power. He has also written poetry and essays.

Barbados \bar-'bā-dəs\ Island nation, W. Indies. The most easterly of the Caribbean islands, it lies about 270 mi (430 km) northeast of Venezuela. Area: 166 sq mi (430 sq km). Population (2000): 267,000. Capital: BRIDGETOWN. More than 90% of the population is black. Language: English (official). Religion: Christianity. Currency: Barbados dollar. Composed of coral accumulation, Barbados is low and flat except in its N central part; its highest point is Mt. Hillaby, at 1,104 ft (336 m). There is little surface water. It is almost

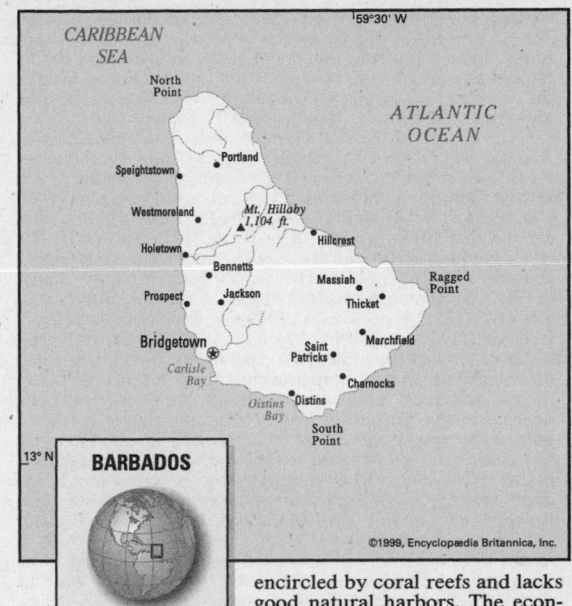

BARBADOS

Scale 1: 737,000

©1999, Encyclopædia Britannica, Inc.

encircled by coral reefs and lacks good natural harbors. The economy is based on tourism and sugar, while the offshore financial sector is growing. It is a constitutional monarchy with two legislative houses; its chief of state is the British monarch, represented by a governor-general, and the head of government is the prime minister. The island was probably inhabited by ARAWAKS who originally came from S. America. Spaniards may have landed by 1518, and by 1536 they had apparently wiped out the Indian population. Barbados was settled by the English in the 1620s. Slaves were brought in to work the sugar plantations, which were especially prosperous in the 17th–18th cent. The British empire abolished slavery in 1834, and all the Barbados slaves were freed by 1838. In 1958 Barbados joined the W. Indies Federation. When the latter dissolved in 1962, Barbados sought independence from Britain; it achieved COMMONWEALTH status in 1966.

Barbara, St. (d.c.A.D. 200) Early Christian martyr and patroness of artillerymen. Her pagan father kept her guarded in a tower to protect her beauty and virginity. When she converted to Christianity he became enraged and took her to the Roman prefect, who ordered her to be tortured and beheaded. Her father performed the execution himself, and on the way home he was killed by lightning. A popular saint during the Middle Ages, she was dropped from the church calendar in 1969.

Barbarossa \ˌbär-bə-'rä-sə\ *orig.* Khidr *later* **Khayr al-Din** (d.1546) Greek-Ottoman pirate and admiral. He and his brother Aruj (or Horuk), sons of a Turk from Lesbos, hated the Spanish and Portuguese for their attacks on N. Africa and took up piracy on the BARBARY COAST in hopes of seizing an African domain for themselves. When Aruj was killed in 1518, Khidr took the title Khayr al-Din. He offered homage to the Ottoman sultan and in return received military aid that enabled him to capture Algiers in 1529, and later all of Tunisia. CHARLES V captured Tunis in 1535, but Khayr al-Din defeated his fleet at the Battle of Preveza (1538), securing the E Mediterranean for the Turks for 33 years. His red beard was the source of the European epithet Barbarossa.

Barbary ape Tailless, terrestrial MACAQUE (*Macaca sylvana*) found in Algeria and Morocco and on the Rock of Gibraltar. It is about 24 in. (60 cm) long and has yellowish brown fur and a naked, pale-pink face. It is the only wild monkey in Europe. According to legend, British dominion over Gibraltar will end when the Barbary ape departs.

Barbary Coast Mediterranean coastal region, N. Africa. It extends from Egypt to the Atlantic Ocean. Conquered by

VANDALS in the 5th cent. A.D., by the Byzantines about A.D. 533, and by Arabs during the 7th cent., the region was eventually divided into the independent Muslim Barbary States (MOROCCO, ALGERIA, TUNISIA, and LIBYA). For centuries the coast was notorious for the pirates who ravaged shipping and collected tribute from leading European states. After the U.S. war with Tripoli (1801–5), the U.S. expedition to Algiers (1815), and the British bombardment of Algiers (1816), the pirates abandoned the exaction of tribute.

Barber, Samuel (1910–1981) U.S. composer. Born in W. Chester, Pa., he studied at the Curtis Institute, where he began a close lifelong association with G. C. MENOTTI. His style, frequently lyrical and neo-Romantic, proved highly attractive to the public. His works include *Dover Beach* (1931), the *Adagio for Strings* (1936), *Knoxville: Summer of 1915* (1947), a piano sonata (1949), a piano concerto (1962, Pulitzer Prize), and the opera *Vanessa* (1957, Pulitzer Prize).

barberry Any of the almost 500 species of thorny evergreen or deciduous shrubs constituting the genus *Berberis*, the largest and most important genus of the family Berberidaceae, in the buttercup order. Most are native to the N temperate zone, particularly Asia. *Berberis* species have yellow wood and yellow flowers. The fruit of several species is made into jellies. Other members of the same family include mayapple *(Podophyllum peltatum)*, a woodland wildflower, and Oregon grape *(Mahonia)*, a genus of broadleaved evergreen shrubs.

barbet \'bär-bət\ Any of about 75 species of tropical birds (family Capitonidae) named for the bristles at the base of their bill. They are big-headed and short-tailed, 3.5–12 in. (9–30 cm) long, and greenish or brownish, with splashes of bright colors or white. Barbets are found throughout Central America to N S. America, in sub-Saharan Africa, and in SE Asia. They sit in treetops when not feeding. They call loudly, jerking the head or tail. Maddeningly vocal species are sometimes called brain-fever birds.

Barbie, Klaus (1913–1991) Nazi leader. As head of the Gestapo in Lyon, France (1942–44), he pursued members of the French RESISTANCE and promoted the torture and execution of thousands of prisoners. After World War II he was seized by U.S. authorities in Germany, who recruited him for counterintelligence work (1947–51) and then moved him and his family to Bolivia. Extradited to France in 1983 to stand trial, "the Butcher of Lyon" remained unrepentant. Held responsible for some 4,000 deaths, he was sentenced to life imprisonment.

barbiturate \bär-'bi-chə-rət\ Any of a class of heterocyclic compounds based on the parent structure, uric acid, and used in medicine. They depress the central NERVOUS SYSTEM. Long-acting **cadmium** Chemical ELEMENT, chemical symbol Cd, atomic number 48. It normally occurs with other metals, especially ZINC, in ORES. A silvery-white metal, cadmium does not corrode under alkaline (see ALKALI) conditions; one of its major uses is in ELECTROPLATING other metals and ALLOYS to protect them. Its compounds (VALENCE 2) are very toxic. They are used as pigments, as phosphors in TELEVISIONS or computer monitors, as pesticides, and in photographic applications and analytical chemistry.

Barbizon school \bär-bə-'zōn\ Group of 19th-cent. French landscape painters. They were part of a larger European movement toward NATURALISM that made a significant contribution to REALISM in landscape painting. Led by Théodore ROUSSEAU and J.-F. MILLET, they attracted a large following of painters who came to live at Barbizon, a village near Paris, including C.-F. DAUBIGNY, Narcisse-Virgile Díaz de la Peña (1806–1876), and Jules Dupré (1811–1889). All emphasized painting out-of-doors directly from nature, using a limited palette, and creating atmosphere or mood in their landscapes.

Barbuda See ANTIGUA AND BARBUDA

Barca, Pedro Calderón de la See Pedro CALDERÓN DE LA BARCA

Barcelona \bär-sə-'lō-nə\ Seaport city (metro. area pop., 1996: 1,509,000), capital of CATALONIA autonomous region, NE Spain. Spain's largest port and second-largest city, it is the country's principal industrial and commercial center. Ruled by the Romans and Visigoths, and taken by the Moors about A.D. 715, it was retaken by the Franks under CHARLEMAGNE in 801 and made capital of the Spanish March (Catalonia). After Catalonia united with ARAGON in 1137, Barcelona flourished as the rival of Italian ports. In the 19th cent. it harbored Catalonian separatist and radical social movements. It was the Loyalist capital in 1937–39 (see SPANISH CIVIL WAR); its capture by Francisco FRANCO brought the collapse of Catalonian resistance and Catalonia's reintegration into Spain. Modern Barcelona is known for its architecture, including buildings by Antoni GAUDÍ, and is a cultural center for the Catalan language.

Barclay de Tolly \bär-'klī-də-'tȯ-lē\, **Mikhail (Bogdanovich)** *later* **Prince Barclay de Tolly** (1761–1818) Russian field marshal prominent in the NAPOLEONIC WARS. Of Scottish descent, in 1812 he commanded one of two Russian armies operating against NAPOLEON. His strategy of avoiding decisive action and retreating into Russia proved unpopular and he was forced to resign. He took part in the invasion of France in 1814, and in 1815 he was commander in chief of the Russian army that invaded France after Napoleon's return from Elba.

bar code Printed series of parallel bars of varying width used for data entry, typically for identifying the object on which the code appears. The width and spacing of the bars represent binary information that can be read by an optical (laser) SCANNER. The coding is used in many different areas of manufacturing and marketing, including inventory control and tracking systems. The bar codes printed on retail merchandise are those of the Universal Product Code (UPC).

Bardeen, John (1908–1991) U.S. physicist. Born in Madison, Wis., he earned a PhD in mathematical physics from Princeton Univ. His work at Bell Telephone Laboratories led to his sharing a 1956 Nobel Prize for the invention of the TRANSISTOR. In 1972 he again shared a Nobel Prize, this time for developing the theory of SUPERCONDUCTIVITY (1957); this theory is the basis for all later theoretical work in superconductivity. Bardeen was also the author of a theory explaining certain properties of SEMICONDUCTORS.

Bardot \bär-'dō\, **Brigitte** (b.1934) French film actress. Discovered by Roger VADIM when she appeared on a magazine cover at 15, she made her film debut in 1952. Vadim crafted her "sex kitten" image for his films *And God Created Woman* (1956) and *The Night Heaven Fell* (1958), which made her an international star. She displayed her acting ability in *Contempt* (1963) and *Viva Maria!* (1965). Since retiring in 1974, she has agitated on behalf of animal rights.

Barenboim \'bar-ən-bȯim\, **Daniel** (b.1942) Israeli (Argentinian-born) pianist and conductor. A prodigy, he made his debut at 8. His family moved to Israel in 1952. As conductor, he led the English Chamber Orchestra (1964–75) and the Orchestre de Paris (1975–89), while pursuing a brilliant career as a pianist. In 1967 he married the cellist Jacqueline Du Pré (1945–1987). In 1991 he became principal conductor of the Chicago Symphony Orchestra. He has been a prominent advocate for peace in the Middle East.

Barents Sea Outlying portion of the ARCTIC OCEAN. Bounded by the Norwegian and NW Russian mainland and the Greenland Sea, it is 800 mi (1,300 km) long and 650 mi (1,050 km) wide. Its maximum depth is 2,000 ft (600 m), in the major Bear Island Trench.

bar graph See HISTOGRAM

Bari \'bä-rē\ *ancient* Barium. Seaport city (pop., 1996: 337,000), and capital of PUGLIA region, SE Italy. Probably inhabited since 1500 B.C., the site became an important Roman port. It was taken from the Moors by the Byzantines in 885. PETER THE HERMIT preached the First Crusade there in 1096. Though razed by the Sicilians in 1156, it burgeoned in the 13th cent. under FREDERICK II. It became an independent duchy in the 14th cent., passed to the Kingdom of NAPLES in 1558, and became part of the Italian kingdom in 1861.

barite \'bar-ıt\ *or* **barytes** \bə-'rī-tēz\ *or* **heavy spar** Most common barium mineral, barium sulfate. It commonly forms as platy crystals (known as crested barite). Barite is abundant in parts of Spain, Germany, and the U.S. Ground barite is used in oil well and gas well drilling muds, as a white pigment, and as an inert material in colored paints.

baritone In vocal music, the voice or register between bass and tenor, the most common category of male voice. Its range is approximately from the A a 10th below middle C to the F above middle C. The term *baritonus* was first employed in 15th-cent. five- and six-voice part music; when four-part settings became standard, the baritone part was dropped. Baritone-range instruments include the baritone saxophone and the baritone horn.

barium \\'bar-ē-əm\\ Chemical ELEMENT, one of the ALKALINE EARTH METALS, chemical symbol Ba, atomic number 56. It is very reactive and in compounds always has VALENCE 2. In nature it is found chiefly as BARITE and witherite (barium carbonate). Barium is used in METALLURGY, and its compounds are used in fireworks, petroleum mining, and radiology and as pigments and reagents. All soluble barium compounds are toxic. Barium sulfate, an extremely insoluble SALT, is the "barium meal" preceding X-RAY examination of the gastrointestinal tract.

bark In woody plants, tissues outside of the vascular cambium. The term is also used more popularly to refer to all tissues outside the WOOD. The inner soft bark is produced by the vascular cambium; it consists of secondary phloem (food-conducting) tissue whose innermost layer transports food from the leaves to the rest of the plant. The layered outer bark contains cork and old, dead phloem.

bark beetle Any member of the BEETLE family Scolytidae, many of which severely damage trees. Bark beetles are cylindrical, brown or black, and usually less than 0.25 in. (6 mm) long. A male and females (as many as 60 females with each male) bore into a tree and form a chamber where each female deposits her eggs. The emerging larvae bore away from the chamber, forming a characteristic series of tunnels, and damage roots, stems, seeds, or fruits. Elm bark beetles transmit DUTCH ELM DISEASE.

Barker, Harley Granville- See Harley GRANVILLE-BARKER

barking deer See MUNTJAC

Barkley, Alben W(illiam) (1877–1956) U.S. vice president (1949–53). Born in Graves Co., Ky., he was elected as a Democrat to the U.S. House of Representatives (1913–27) and the Senate (1927–49), where he served as majority leader 1937–47 and was a leading spokesman for the policies of Pres. Franklin ROOSEVELT. He served as vice president under Pres. Harry TRUMAN (1949–53), then returned to the Senate (1954–56).

Bar Kokhba \\bär-'kòk-bä\\ orig. Simeon bar Kosba (d.A.D. 135) Leader of an unsuccessful Jewish revolt against Roman rule in Palestine. In 131 HADRIAN forbade circumcision and built a temple to Jupiter on the ruins of the Temple of JERUSALEM. The Jews rebelled in 132, led by Simeon bar Kosba. He was called Bar Kokhba ("Son of the Star"), a messianic allusion. His army inflicted heavy casualties, but Hadrian summoned reinforcements and the Romans prevailed. Bar Kokhba was killed at Betar, and the remnant of his army was soon crushed, with total Jewish losses numbering 580,000.

Barlach \\'bär-läk\\, **Ernst** (1870–1938) German sculptor, graphic artist, and writer. He achieved fame in the 1920s and '30s with the execution of several war memorials for the Weimar Republic. An outstanding exponent of German Expressionism, he was also strongly influenced by medieval German wood carving. He also wrote Expressionist plays, which he illustrated with woodcuts and lithographs.

barley CEREAL plant of the genus *Hordeum*, in the family Poaceae (or Gramineae), and its edible grain. Barley is adaptable to a greater range of climate than any other cereal. About half of the world's crop is used as livestock feed, the rest for human food and for malting. Most BEER is made from malted barley, which is also used in distilled beverages. Barley is high in carbohydrates, with moderate quantities of protein, calcium, and phosphorus. Pearl barley, the most popular form in many parts of the world, is often added to soups.

Bar Mitzvah \\bär-'mits-və\\ Jewish ritual celebrating a boy's 13th birthday and his entry into the community of JUDAISM. It usually takes place during a Sabbath service, when the boy reads from the TORAH and may give a discourse on the text. REFORM JUDAISM substituted confirmation of boys and girls after 1810, but many congregations restored the Bar Mitzvah in the 20th cent. A separate ceremony for girls, Bat Mitzvah, has been instituted in Reform and CONSERVATIVE JUDAISM.

Barnabas \\'bär-nə-bəs\\, **St.** orig. Joseph the Levite (fl.1st cent. A.D.) Apostolic Father and early Christian missionary. According to the Acts of the Apostles, he helped found the church in Antioch, calling on St. PAUL to assist him. A conflict eventually separated them, and Barnabas returned to Cyprus, the island of his birth. One legend holds that he was martyred there. His reputed tomb is at Salamis, whose Christian community Paul and Barnabas founded.

barnacle Any of a majority of the 1,000 species of the subclass Cirripedia of marine CRUSTACEANS that, as adults, are covered with a shell made of hard plates and are permanently cemented, head down, to rocks, pilings, ships' hulls, or driftwood, or to the bodies of larger sea creatures, from clams to whales. Barnacles trap food with their cirri, feathery retractable organs that emerge from openings between the shell plates.

Barnacle

Barnard \\'bär-nərd\\, **Christiaan (Neethling)** (1922–2001) S. African surgeon. He showed that intestinal atresia is caused by deficient fetal blood supply, which led to development of a surgical procedure to correct the formerly fatal defect. He introduced open-heart surgery to S. Africa, designed a new artificial heart valve, and did animal HEART TRANSPLANT experiments. In 1967 Barnard's team successfully performed the first human heart transplant, but the patient died 18 days later from pneumonia.

Barnard, Henry (1811–1900) U.S. educator. Born in Hartford, Conn., he helped create a state board of education and the first teachers' institute (1839). With Horace MANN, he undertook to reform the country's common schools, instituting school inspections, textbook reviews, and parent-teacher organizations. As Rhode Island's first commissioner of education (from 1845) he worked to raise teachers' wages, repair buildings, and obtain higher-education appropriations. In 1855 he helped found the *American Journal of Education*. In 1867 he became the first U.S. commissioner of education.

Barnes, Albert C(oombs) (1872–1951) Pharmaceutical manufacturer and art collector. Born in Philadelphia, he obtained a medical degree and in 1902 made a fortune with his new antiseptic Argyrol. In 1905 he built a mansion in Merion, Pa., and began collecting seriously, amassing some 180 paintings by Auguste RENOIR, 66 by Paul CÉZANNE, and 35 by Pablo PICASSO, and an extraordinary collection of 65 works by Henri MATISSE. In 1922 he established the Barnes Foundation. In 1991, after extensive litigation, a controversial ruling overrode his will, resulting in a worldwide traveling exhibition of its paintings and the first color reproductions of them.

Barnett, Ida B. Wells- See I. B. WELLS

barn owl Any of several species of nocturnal BIRDS OF PREY (genus *Tyto*), sometimes called monkey-faced owls because of their heart-shaped facial disk and absence of ear tufts. Barn owls are about 12–16 in. (30–40 cm) long, white to gray or yellowish to brownish orange. Their dark eyes are smaller than those of other OWLS. They hunt mainly small rodents, often on cultivated land, and nest in hollow trees, buildings, towers, and old hawk nests. The common barn owl is found nearly worldwide.

Barnum, P(hineas) T(aylor) (1810–1891) U.S. showman. Born in Bethel, Conn., in 1841 he bought the American Museum in New York City and transformed it into a carnival of live freaks and dramatic curiosities, which he promoted with sensational publicity. He exhibited the midget Tom Thumb with great international success, and brought Jenny

LIND to the U.S. for a profitable concert tour. By the time his museum closed in 1868, he had enticed 82 million visitors there. In 1871 he started a circus and in 1881 joined a rival, James A. Bailey (1847–1906), to form the three-ring Barnum and Bailey's Circus, the "Greatest Show on Earth."

Barocci \bä-ˈròt-chē\, **Federico** (c.1535–1612) Italian painter. He lived in and near Urbino, where he executed altarpieces and devotional paintings in a style characterized by subtle color har-

P. T. Barnum

monies and warmth of feeling. His patrons included the duke of Urbino and Emperor Rudolf II (1552–1612). His famous works include the *Deposition* (1567–69) and the *Madonna del Popolo* (1579). A prolific draftsman, he was one of the first artists to use colored chalks.

Baroja (y Nessi) \bä-ˈrō-hä\, **Pío** (1872–1956) Basque writer. He wrote 11 trilogies dealing with contemporary social problems, including *The Struggle for Life* (1904). His most ambitious project was a long cycle of works about a 19th-cent. insurgent and his era. He wrote almost 100 novels, including *Zalacaín el aventurero* (1909). Because of his anti-Christian views, stubborn nonconformity, and pessimism, he never achieved great popularity. He is considered the foremost Spanish novelist of his time.

barometer Device used to measure ATMOSPHERIC PRESSURE. Because atmospheric pressure changes with distance above or below sea level, a barometer can also be used to measure altitude. In the mercury barometer, atmospheric pressure balances a column of MERCURY (favored because of its density), whose height can be precisely measured. Normal atmospheric pressure is about 14.7 lb per square inch, equivalent to 30 in. (760 mm) of mercury. An aneroid barometer indicates pressure on a dial using a needle that is mechanically linked to a partially evacuated chamber, which responds to pressure changes.

barometric pressure See ATMOSPHERIC PRESSURE

baron Title of nobility, ranking below a VISCOUNT or a COUNT. The wife of a baron is a baroness. In the early Middle Ages the term designated a tenant who held a tenure of barony direct from the king. Gradually, it came to mean a powerful personage. The rights and title may be conferred for military or other honorable service.

Baroque, Late See ROCOCO STYLE

baroque period Era in the arts that originated in Italy in the 17th cent. and flourished elsewhere well into the 18th cent. It embraced painting, sculpture, architecture, the applied arts, and music. The word, derived from a Portuguese term for an irregularly shaped pearl, has long been employed to describe a variety of characteristics, from dramatic and bizarre to overdecorated. The style was embraced by countries absorbed in the COUNTER-REFORMATION; artworks commissioned by the Roman Catholic Church were overtly emotional and sensory. The period's most notable practitioners were Annibale CARRACCI, CARAVAGGIO, and G. L. BERNINI. A spectacular example of the baroque arts is the Palace of VERSAILLES. In music, the baroque era (c.1600–c.1750) introduced such significant genres as OPERA, ORATORIO, CANTATA, SONATA, and CONCERTO, and included such towering composers as Claudio MONTEVERDI, J. S. BACH, and G. F. HANDEL.

Barquisimeto \ˌbär-kē-sē-ˈmä-tō\ City (pop., 2000 est.: 875,000), NW Venezuela. The capital of Lara state, it lies at an altitude of 1,856 ft (566 m). Founded in 1552 as Nueva Segovia, it is one of the country's oldest cities. It was almost destroyed by an earthquake in 1812, and was further damaged in 19th-cent. civil wars. It is a hub of transport and commerce, and the center of an agricultural region.

barracuda Any of about 20 species of predaceous marine fishes (family Sphyraenidae) found in all warm and tropical regions and in some more temperate areas. Swift and pow-

erful, barracudas are slender and have a jutting lower jaw and a large mouth with many large, sharp teeth. They vary in size up to 4–6 ft (1.2–1.8 m) long. They are primarily fish eaters and are themselves popular sport fishes. Bold and inquisitive, they are potentially dangerous to humans when large.

Barranquilla \ˌbä-rän-ˈkē-yä\ City (pop., 1999 est.: 1,226,000), N Colombia. Founded in 1629, it lies 10 mi (16 km) from the mouth of the MAGDALENA RIVER. The clearing of sandbars in the 1930s enabled it to thrive as a Caribbean seaport. It handles goods from the interior and is the terminus of natural-gas pipelines.

Barrault \bä-ˈrō\, **Jean-Louis** (1910–1994) French actor and director. He worked with the COMÉDIE-FRANÇAISE (1940–46) as an actor and director before he and his wife, Madeleine Renaud, formed their own company (1946–58) to perform classics and modern plays that helped revive French theater after World War II. He was director of the Théâtre de France 1959–68. He appeared in over 20 films, notably *The Children of Paradise* (1945).

Barre, Mohamed Siad See Mohamed SIAD BARRE

Barrie, James M(atthew) (*later* **Sir James**) (1860–1937) British playwright and novelist. After moving to London, he wrote *Auld Licht Idylls* (1888) about his native Scotland. His best-selling novel *The Little Minister* (1891) was made into a play in 1897. *Quality Street* (1901) and *The Admirable Crichton* (1902) ran successfully in London. He won great success with his classic children's play *Peter Pan, the Boy Who Wouldn't Grow Up* (1904). His later plays include *What Every Woman Knows* (1908) and *Dear Brutus* (1917).

barrier penetration See TUNNELING

Barrow, Clyde and Bonnie Parker *known as* **Bonnie and Clyde** (1909–1934, 1911–1934) U.S. robbers. Clyde, born in Telico, Texas, had been a robber long before meeting Bonnie (born in Rowena, Texas) in 1930. After Clyde spent time in prison (1930–32), he and Bonnie began their widely reported 21-month criminal spree, robbing gas stations, restaurants, and small-town banks in Texas, Oklahoma, New Mexico, and Missouri and killing a number of people. In 1934 they were betrayed by a friend and shot by police in a roadblock ambush.

Barry, comtesse du See comtesse DU BARRY

Barry, John (1745–1803) U.S. (Irish-born) naval officer. He emigrated to America in 1760 and became a merchant shipmaster. He outfitted the first American fleet in 1776 and as captain of a frigate captured several British ships. He fought the last battle of the AMERICAN REVOLUTION in March 1783 in the Straits of Florida, where he defeated three British ships. Senior captain (from 1794) of the new U.S. Navy, he earned the epithet "Father of the Navy" because he trained many future naval officers.

Barrymore family U.S. theatrical family. Maurice Barrymore (born Herbert Blythe) (1847–1905) made his stage debut in London before moving to New York (1875), where he adopted Barrymore as his stage name and in 1876 married Georgiana Drew (see DREW FAMILY). Their son Lionel (1878–1954) became a leading Broadway actor; he moved to Hollywood in 1926, where he appeared as a character actor in such films as *A Free Soul* (1931, Academy Award), *Grand Hotel* (1932), and 15 "Dr. Kildare" pictures. His sister Ethel (1879–1959) appeared in London and on Broadway to great acclaim. She opened the New York theater named for her in 1928 in *The Kingdom of God* and later starred in *The Corn Is Green* (1940). She appeared in over 30 films, including *None but the Lonely Heart* (1944, Academy Award). Their brother John (1882–1942) was acclaimed on Broadway, especially in *Hamlet* (1922). His films include *Dr. Jekyll and Mr. Hyde* (1920) and *Dinner at Eight* (1933). An alcoholic, he was known for his flamboyant behavior. John's granddaughter Drew Barrymore (b.1975) first won notice at age 7 in *E.T.* (1982).

barter Direct exchange of goods or services without the use of money or any other intervening medium of exchange. Barter is conducted either according to established rates of exchange or by bargaining. It is common in nonliterate societies. See also CURRENCY, GIFT EXCHANGE.

Barth, John *orig.* John Simmons Barth, Jr. (b.1930) U.S. writer. Born in Cambridge, Md., he has made Maryland's eastern shore the locale of much of his writing. His best-known works are the novels *The Floating Opera* (1956), *The End of the Road* (1958), *The Sot-Weed Factor* (1960), *Giles Goat-Boy* (1966), and *The Tidewater Tales* (1987), most of which play with traditional narrative forms, combining philosophical depth with biting satire and boisterous, often bawdy humor.

Barth \\'bärt\\, **Karl** (1886–1968) Swiss theologian. Born in Basel, he studied at the Univs. of Berlin, Tübingen, and Marburg. The tragedy of World War I made him question the liberal theology of his teachers, rooted in post-Enlightenment ideas. His *Epistle to the Romans* (1919) inaugurated a radical turn toward neoorthodoxy in Protestant thought. He was a founder of the Confessing Church, which opposed the Nazi regime. His refusal to take the oath of allegiance to Hitler cost him his professor's chair at Bonn. He spoke at the opening of the World Council of Churches in 1948.

Barthelme \\'bärt-əl-mē\\, **Donald** (1931–1989) U.S. writer. Born in Philadelphia, he worked as a journalist and museum director before his fiction—modernist "collages" marked by experimentation and melancholy gaiety—began to be published. His stories are collected in *Sixty Stories* (1981) and *Forty Stories* (1992); his novels include *Snow White* (1967), *The Dead Father* (1975), *Paradise* (1986), and *The King* (1990). His brother Frederick (b.1943) is also a novelist (*Second Marriage,* 1984) and short-story writer (*Moon Deluxe,* 1983).

Barthes \\'bärt\\, **Roland (Gérard)** (1915–1980) French social and literary critic. His early books (e.g., *Mythologies,* 1957; *On Racine,* 1963) examined the arbitrariness of the constructs of language and applied similar analyses to popular culture, which set off a literary furor, pitting him against more traditional French literary scholars. His later contributions to SEMIOTICS, including the even more radical *S/Z* (1970) and *The Empire of Signs* (1970), his study of Japan, brought his theories wide attention and helped establish STRUCTURALISM as a leading intellectual movement of the 20th cent.

Bartholdi \\bär-'tôl-dē\\, **Frédéric-Auguste** (1834–1904) French sculptor. In 1865 he and several others conceived the idea for a monument to the Franco-American alliance of 1778, which resulted in his design and execution of the STATUE OF LIBERTY (1875–86). His masterpiece is the *Lion of Belfort* (1871–80), carved out of the red sandstone of a hill overlooking Belfort in E France.

Bartholomew, St. (fl.1st cent. A.D.) One of the 12 APOSTLES of JESUS. He is mentioned only briefly in the New Testament. By tradition he was a missionary to Ethiopia, Mesopotamia, and Armenia. He was supposedly martyred at the command of the Armenian king Astyages, who had him flayed and beheaded.

Bartlett, John (1820–1905) U.S. bookseller and editor. Born in Plymouth, Mass., Bartlett owned the Harvard Univ. Bookstore. His best-known work, *Familiar Quotations* (1855), was based largely on a notebook he kept for customers. It was greatly expanded in later editions; the 17th appeared in 2002. He also wrote a concordance to Shakespeare's works (1894), outstanding for the number and fullness of its citations.

Bartok \\'bär-tōk\\, **Bela** (1881–1945) Hungarian composer and ethnomusicologist. In 1904 he set about researching Hungarian folk music, having discovered that the folk-music repertory regarded as Hungarian was in fact largely urban Gypsy music. His fieldwork with Zoltan KODALY formed the basis for all later research in the field, and he published several major studies of Balkan music, while working folk themes and rhythms insistently into his

Bela Bartok Photo by Fritz Reiner

own music. He also toured widely as a virtuoso pianist. He emigrated to the U.S. in 1940, where he was inadequately recognized. His works include the opera *Bluebeard's Castle* (1911), the ballet *The Miraculous Mandarin* (1923), six string quartets (1908–39), the didactic piano set *Mikrokosmos* (1926–39), *Music for Strings, Percussion and Celesta* (1936), *Concerto for Orchestra* (1943), two violin concertos (1908, 1938), and three piano concertos (1926, 1931, 1945). The greatest composer Hungary ever produced, Bartok was one of the giants of 20th-cent. music.

Bartolomé de Cárdenas See Bartolomé BERMEJO

Bartolomeo \\,bär-tō-lō-'mä-ō\\, **Fra** *orig.* Baccio della Porta (1472–1517) Italian painter active in Florence. His early works, such as the *Annunciation* (1497) in Volterra Cathedral, were influenced by PERUGINO and LEONARDO DA VINCI. In 1500 he joined the Dominican order. He painted religious subjects, primarily the Madonna and Child in various settings, with monumental figures grouped in balanced compositions, and became the leading painter in Florence. His brilliant drawings include figure studies and landscape and nature studies.

Barton, Clara (*orig.* Clarissa Harlowe) (1821–1912) U.S. nurse, founder of the American RED CROSS. Born in Oxford, Miss., she initially worked as a schoolteacher. During the Civil War she organized the distribution of supplies for wounded soldiers and set up a bureau of records to help search for missing men, becoming known as the "angel of the battlefield." She later became associated with the International Red Cross and in 1881 founded the American Red Cross, serving as its president until 1904. She lobbied Congress to sign the GENEVA CONVENTION, and wrote the U.S. amendment to the constitution of the Red Cross to provide for relief not only in war but also in natural disasters.

Bartram \\'bär-trəm\\, **John** (1699–1777) U.S. naturalist and explorer, considered the "father of American botany." Born in Darby, Pa., and largely self-educated, he became the botanist for the American colonies to GEORGE III. He was the first N. American experimenter to hybridize flowering plants, and he established a famous botanical garden near Philadelphia. He explored the Alleghenies and the Carolinas and in 1743 was commissioned to explore the wilderness north to Lake Ontario. In 1765–66 he explored extensively in Florida with his son William BARTRAM.

Bartram, William (1739–1823) U.S. naturalist and botanist. Born in Kingsessing, Pa., the son of John BARTRAM, he described the abundant primeval river swamps of the SE U.S. in his *Travels through North and South Carolina, Georgia, East and West Florida* (1791). He was a major precursor of J. J. AUDUBON, and his book was influential among the English and French Romantics.

Baruch \\bə-'rük\\, **Bernard (Mannes)** (1870–1965) U.S. financier. Born in Camden, S.C., he went to work in Wall Street brokerage houses, where he amassed a fortune as a speculator. During World War I he was appointed chairman of the War Industries Board by Pres. Woodrow WILSON, whom he later advised at the Versailles peace conference. In World War II he was an unofficial adviser on economic mobilization to Pres. Franklin ROOSEVELT. Later he was instrumental in setting U.N. policy on the international control of atomic energy.

Barye \\bà-'rē\\, **Antoine-Louis** (1796–1875) French sculptor. He began to sculpt animal forms about 1819, displaying a unique talent for rendering dynamic tension and exact anatomical detail. His most famous works depict wild animals devouring their prey; he also executed groups of domestic animals. His notable bronzes include *Lion Devouring a Gavial Crocodile* (1831) and an equestrian statue of Napoleon at Ajaccio, Corsica (1860–65).

baryon \\'bar-ē-,än\\ Any member of one of two classes of HADRONS. Baryons are heavy SUBATOMIC PARTICLES made up of three QUARKS. They are characterized by a baryon number, B, of 1, and have half-integer spin values. Their antiparticles (see ANTIMATTER), called antibaryons, have a baryon number of –1. Both PROTONS and NEUTRONS are baryons.

Baryshnikov \\bə-'rish-nə-,kóf\\, **Mikhail (Nikolayevich)** (b.1948) Russian-U.S. dancer. He joined the Kirov Ballet as a soloist in 1966, and quickly became popular with Soviet audiences, dancing leading roles created for him in such ballets as *Gorianka* (1968) and *Vestris* (1969). He defected while on tour in Canada in 1974. He danced with the AMERICAN BALLET THEATRE until 1978, winning enormous acclaim, and served as its artistic director 1980–89. In 1990 he cofounded the White Oak Dance Project.

barytes See BARITE

basalt \bə-'sȯlt\ Dark IGNEOUS ROCK that is comparatively rich in iron and magnesium. Some basalts are glassy (have no visible crystals), and many are fine-grained and compact. Basaltic lavas may be spongy or pumice-like. Olivine and augite are the most common minerals in basalts. Basalts may be broadly classified into two main groups. Calc-alkali basalts predominate among the lavas of mountain belts, including the active volcanoes of Mauna Loa and Kilauea. Alkali basalts predominate among the lavas of the ocean basins.

base In chemistry, any substance that in water solution is slippery to the touch, tastes bitter, changes the color of acid-base indicators (e.g., LITMUS paper), reacts with ACIDS to form SALTS, and promotes certain chemical reactions. Examples of bases are the HYDROXIDES of the ALKALI METALS and ALKALINE EARTH METALS and the water solutions of AMMONIA or its derivatives. These produce hydroxide IONS (OH⁻) in water solutions. Broader definitions of bases cover situations in which water is not present. See also ACID-BASE THEORY, ALKALI, NUCLEOPHILE.

baseball Game played with a bat and fist-sized ball between two teams of nine or ten (if a designated hitter is used) players each on a large field having four bases laid out in a square, or diamond, whose outlines mark the course a runner must take to score. Teams alternate positions as batters and fielders, exchanging places when three batters are put out. Batters try to hit a pitched ball out of reach of the fielding team and run a complete circuit around the bases for a run (1 point). The team that scores the most runs in nine innings (times at bat) wins the game. Baseball is traditionally considered the national pastime of the U.S. Once thought to have been invented in 1839 by Abner DOUBLEDAY in Cooperstown, N.Y., it probably actually developed from an 18th-cent. English game called rounders, as modified by A. J. Cartwright (1820–1892). The first professional association, comprising eight teams, was formed in 1871; in 1876 it became the NATIONAL LEAGUE. A rival AMERICAN LEAGUE was founded in 1900, and since 1903 the winning teams of each league have played a postseason WORLD SERIES championship. Canadian teams were admitted to the major

leagues in 1968 and 1976. The separate NEGRO LEAGUES disbanded as black players became integrated into the majors. The regular baseball season extends from early April to early October. A Baseball Hall of Fame is located in Cooperstown.

Basel \'bä-zəl\ *or* **Basle** \'bäl\ *French* **Bâle** \'bäl\ City (pop., 1996: 174,000; metro. area pop.: 404,000), NW Switzerland. It straddles the RHINE at the point where France, Germany, and Switzerland meet. Its university, the first in Switzerland, was founded by Pope Pius II while attending the Council of BASEL (1431–49). In 1501 Basel was admitted into the Swiss Confederation. When Desiderius ERASMUS taught at the university 1521–29, the city became a center of humanism and of the REFORMATION, and it remains primarily German-speaking and Protestant.

Basel, Council of (1431–49) Council of the Roman Catholic Church held in Basel, Switzerland. Addressing the question of papal supremacy and the problem of the HUSSITE heresy, its members renewed the decree *Sacrosancta* (issued by the Council of CONSTANCE), which declared the council's authority greater than the pope's, and voted to receive most Hussites back into the church. In 1437 Pope Eugenius IV transferred the council to Ferrara, but several members remained in Basel as a rump council. Excommunicated by Eugenius, they responded by electing a new pope, Felix V. In 1449 Pope NICHOLAS V obliged Felix to abdicate and ended the rump council.

BASF AG German chemical and plastics manufacturing company. Founded in 1865, BASF was part of the chemical cartel IG FARBEN from 1925 until 1945, when the latter was dissolved by the Allies. Refounded in 1952, BASF today operates in some 30 countries. Its products include oil and natural gas, fertilizers, synthetic fibers, dyes and pigments, inks and printing accessories, electronics, and pharmaceuticals.

Basho \ˌbäsh-'ō\ *or* **Matsuo Basho** \mä-'tsü-ō\ *orig.* Matsuo Munefusa (1644–1694) Japanese poet, greatest practitioner of the HAIKU. Following Zen philosophy, he sought to compress the meaning of the world into the simple pattern of his form, disclosing hidden hopes in small things and showing the interdependence of everything. His *The Narrow Road to the Deep North* (1694), a poetic prose travelogue, is one of the loveliest works of Japanese literature.

BASIC *in full* Beginner's All-purpose Symbolic Instruction Code. Computer PROGRAMMING LANGUAGE developed at Dartmouth College in the mid-1960s. One of the simplest high-level languages, with commands similar to English, it

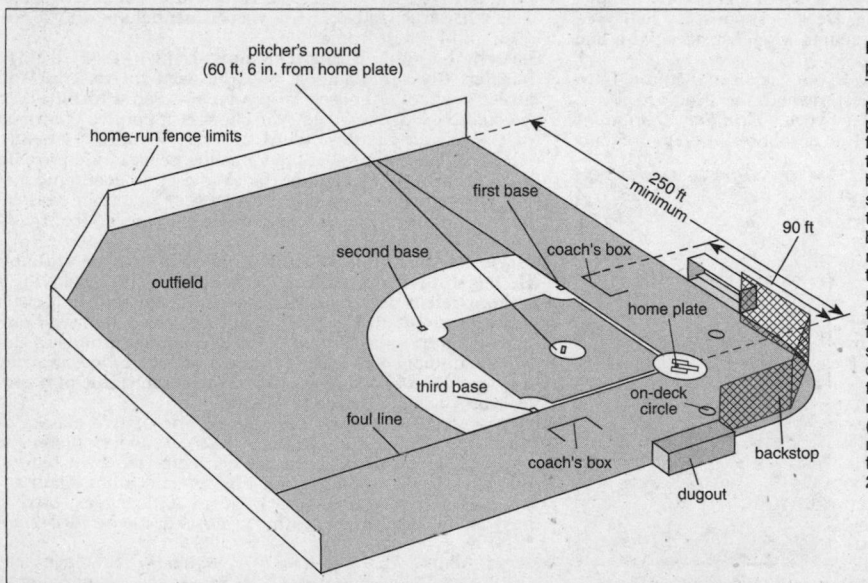

Baseball A typical college or professional baseball field. The batter stands at home plate, the pitcher at the pitcher's mound. When a hit falls outside the foul lines, the batter may not run. Any ball over the fence represents a home run for the batter. Coaches at first and third base tell runners when to run. Players wait to bat in their team's dugout. Home-run fence distances and configurations vary from field to field. Softball is played on a similar field, but with bases closer together (typically 60 ft apart) and the pitcher's mound closer to the plate (40 ft for women, 46 ft for men), and the home-run fence may be as close as 200 ft.

can be learned with relative ease even by schoolchildren and novice programmers. BASIC is popular for use on PERSONAL COMPUTERS.

basic Bessemer process Modification of the BESSEMER PROCESS for converting pig iron into steel. The original Bessemer converter was not effective in removing the PHOSPHORUS from iron made from the high-phosphorus ores common in Britain and Europe. The invention of the basic process by Sidney G. Thomas (1850–1885) and Percy Gilchrist (1851–1935) overcame this problem in 1879 by lining the converter with a basic material such as burned limestone rather than an acid siliceous material, and made it possible for the first time for such high-phosphorus ore to be used for making STEEL.

basic rocks See ACID AND BASIC ROCKS

basidiomycete \bə-ˌsi-dē-ō-ˈmī-ˌsēt\ Any of a large and diverse class of fungi (division Mycota), including jelly and shelf fungi; MUSHROOMS, puffballs, and stinkhorns; and the rusts and smuts. The club-shaped, SPORE-bearing organ (basidium) is borne on a usually large and conspicuous fruiting body. Further classification is determined by method of spore dispersal and qualities of the spores. See also FUNGUS.

Basie \ˈbā-sē\, **Count** (*orig.* William Allen) (1904–1984) U.S. jazz pianist and bandleader, whose band became the most refined exponent of SWING. Born in Red Bank, N.J., Basie was influenced by the Harlem pianists James P. JOHNSON and Fats WALLER, receiving informal tutelage on the organ from the latter. He formed his band in Kansas City in 1936. Its rhythm section, including guitarist Freddie Green, bassist Walter Page, and drummer Jo Jones, quickly became noted for its lightness, precision, and relaxation, as heard on such recordings as "One o'Clock Jump" and "Jumpin' at the Woodside." Basie's piano style became increasingly economical. His soloists included Jimmy RUSHING and Lester YOUNG. Basie's reorganized band of the 1950s placed greater emphasis on ensemble work, and achieved renewed popularity for recordings featuring vocalist Joe Williams, becoming recognized as a jazz institution.

Count Basie, 1969

basil Herb consisting of the dried leaves of *Ocimum basilicum*, an annual herb of the MINT family. The dried large-leaf varieties have a fragrant aroma and a warm, sweet, mildly pungent flavor. The dried leaves of common basil are less fragrant and more pungent in flavor. Basil is widely grown as a kitchen herb.

Basil I \ˈba-zəl\ *known as* **Basil the Macedonian** (c.830–886) Byzantine emperor (867–86). Born into a peasant family in Macedonia, he won employment in official circles in Constantinople and was made chamberlain by the reigning emperor, Michael III. He became co-emperor with Michael in 866 and murdered him the next year. Basil won victories against Muslim forces along the E borders of Asia Minor and asserted control over Slavs in the Balkans. He also formulated the Greek legal code known as the Basilica. In later life Basil showed signs of madness.

Basil II *known as* **Basil Bulgaroctonus** \ˌbùl-gə-ˈräk-tə-nəs\ ("Slayer of the Bulgars") (957?–1025) Byzantine emperor (976–1025). Basil became one of the strongest Byzantine emperors, winning territory in the Balkans, Mesopotamia, Armenia, and Georgia. He was noted for his victory (1014) in the war with Bulgaria, which ended with his blinding all the soldiers in the defeated Bulgarian army. He increased his domestic authority by attacking the landed interests of the military aristocracy and of the church. Because Basil left no able successor, the gains of his rule were soon undone.

basilica Originally, a secular public building in ancient Rome. Typically, a rectangular central hall was flanked by side aisles set off by colonnades, and a raised platform at one or both ends was enclosed by an APSE. Early Christians adopted this design for their churches. In the early Christian basilica, the columns separating the NAVE from the lower side aisles carried either arches or ENTABLATURES, above which rose CLERESTORY walls that supported the roof. The long nave came to be crossed just before the apse by a shorter transept, creating the cross-shaped plan that remains a standard church form. "Basilica" is also a title of honor given to a Catholic or Greek Orthodox church distinguished by its antiquity or its international importance. See also CATHEDRAL.

Basil the Great, St. (c.A.D. 329–379) Early church father. Born into a Christian family in Cappadocia, he studied at Caesarea, Constantinople, and Athens and later established a monastic settlement on his family estate. He opposed ARIANISM, organizing resistance to it after 365. He became bishop of Caesarea in 370. More than 300 of his letters survive; several of his Canonical Epistles have become part of canon law in EASTERN ORTHODOXY.

basketball Court game between two teams of five players each who score by tossing, or shooting, an inflated ball through a raised hoop, or basket, located in their opponent's end of the court. A goal is worth two points, three if shot from outside a specified limit. A free throw worth one point is awarded to any player fouled (through unwar-

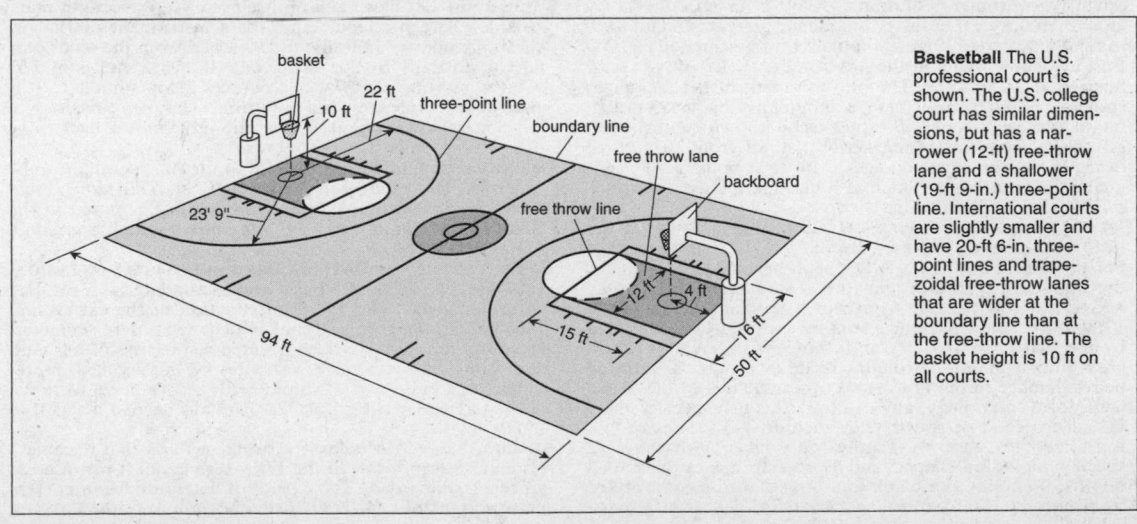

Basketball The U.S. professional court is shown. The U.S. college court has similar dimensions, but has a narrower (12-ft) free-throw lane and a shallower (19-ft 9-in.) three-point line. International courts are slightly smaller and have 20-ft 6-in. three-point lines and trapezoidal free-throw lanes that are wider at the boundary line than at the free-throw line. The basket height is 10 ft on all courts.

ranted physical contact) by another, two free throws if the foul occurs during the act of shooting. Professional games are divided into 12-minute quarters, collegiate games into 20-minute halves. Introduced in 1891 by James NAISMITH in Springfield, Mass., basketball quickly became a popular collegiate sport. The NATIONAL COLLEGIATE ATHLETIC ASSN. (NCAA) postseason tournament (nicknamed "March Madness" for its frenzied and unpredictable play) pits 64 select teams in a series of elimination rounds. Women's collegiate play is similarly organized. A men's professional league was organized in 1898 but did not gain much of a following until 1949, when it was reconstituted as the NATIONAL BASKETBALL ASSN. (NBA). The Women's National Basketball Assn. (WNBA) was organized in 1997. The men's professional basketball season runs from October to April, with postseason matches extending into June. A Basketball Hall of Fame is located in Springfield.

Baskin, Leonard (1922–2000) U.S. sculptor and graphic artist. Born in New Brunswick, N.J., in 1939 he had his first one-man exhibition in New York City, and he later taught for many years at Smith College. He is known for his bleak portrayals of the human figure. His sculptures are dominated by themes of death, vulnerability, and spiritual decay. In his woodcuts he developed a distinctive linear style, depicting figures resembling those in anatomical charts.

Basle See BASEL

Basque \'bask\ *Spanish* Vasco. Member of a people of unknown origin living in Spain and France in the BASQUE COUNTRY. About 850,000 true Basques live in Spain and another 130,000 in France. Physically the Basques are similar to other Western European peoples; the BASQUE LANGUAGE, however, is not Indo-European. The Basques have sought autonomy from Spain since the 19th cent. A national government was proclaimed in the SPANISH CIVIL WAR, which saw the brutal bombing of Guernica (1937). After the war many Basques went into exile as Francisco FRANCO abolished their special privileges. The Basque separatist movement was rekindled after Franco's death. Despite the granting of limited autonomy in 1978, militant separatists, including the terrorist ETA (Basque Homeland and Liberty), continued a campaign for complete independence.

Basque Country *Spanish* **País Vasco** \'pīs-'bäs-kō\ Autonomous community (pop., 1998 est.: 2,098,000) and historical region, N Spain. Bounded by the Bay of BISCAY, it consists of the modern provinces of Vizcaya, Alava, and Guipúzcoa, and has an area of 2,803 sq mi (7,260 sq km); its capital is VITORIA. Inhabited by BASQUES, the area retained virtual autonomy until the 19th cent., when it suffered repression under Alfonso XII. Repression continued under Francisco FRANCO (1939–75). Limited autonomy was granted in 1980, but a campaign of terrorism against the Spanish government continued. Alava is an agricultural region; metallurgical industry is concentrated around BILBAO.

Basque language Language spoken by an estimated 660,000 Basque people living in the BASQUE COUNTRY of N central Spain and SW France. The only remnant of the languages spoken in W. Europe before incursions by INDO-EUROPEAN-speaking peoples, Basque has no known linguistic relatives. Its grammar is markedly distinct from that of all other W. European languages. The first book in the language was printed in 1545, and it has maintained a continuous literary tradition since then.

Basra City (pop., 1987 est.: 407,000), SE Iraq. It lies at the head of the SHATT AL ARAB, about 75 mi (120 km) from the Persian Gulf. Founded in A.D. 638, it became famous under the ABBASID DYNASTY; in the *THOUSAND AND ONE NIGHTS* it was the city from which Sinbad set out. In the 17th–18th cent. it became a trading center. It was occupied by the British in World War I. After World War II, Basra grew into a major petroleum refining center. It suffered heavy damage in the IRAN–IRAQ and PERSIAN GULF WARS.

bass \'bas\ In zoology, any of numerous fish species, many valued for food or sport. They include 400 species of SEA BASS and GROUPER; the family Moronidae, with about 12 species, including striped and European basses; and SUNFISHES, including the black and largemouth basses, prized by fishermen. Many other species are also known as bass,

including the channel bass (a drum) and the calico bass (a CRAPPIE).

bass \'bās\ Lowest musical voice or register. In vocal music, its range is approximately from the second E below middle C to middle C itself. Outside of Russia, the solo bass voice has generally been relegated to certain standard operatic character roles. The lowest-pitched member of most instrumental families is usually called the bass (bass clarinet, DOUBLE BASS, etc.). In Western tonal music, the bass part has usually been the chief determiner of harmonic movement, especially since the appearance of the basso CONTINUO around 1600.

Bassano \bä-'sä-nō\, **Jacopo** *orig.* Jacopo da Ponte (c.1517–1592) Italian painter. He was the most celebrated member of a family of artists from Bassano, near Venice, where he worked for most of his life. He became known for his biblical themes, lush landscapes, and rustic scenes. Four painter sons continued the Bassano workshop tradition: Francesco (1549–1592), Leandro (1557–1622), Giovanni Battista (1553–1613), and Gerolamo (1566–1621).

Basse-Terre \bás-'ter\ Island (pop., 1999: 175,000) and seaport (pop., 1999: 12,000), GUADELOUPE, W. Indies. It is the W part of the French department of Guadeloupe (whose E part is Grande-Terre). Its extremely rugged terrain culminates in the volcanic summit of Mt. Soufrière, at 4,813 ft (1,467 m). The town of Basse-Terre (founded 1643), on the SW coast, is the capital of Guadeloupe.

Basseterre \bás-'ter\ Seaport (pop., 1994 est.: 13,000), St. Kitts Island. It is the chief town of St. Kitts and capital of the federated state of St. Kitts and Nevis. Founded in 1627, it serves as a depot distributing goods to neighboring islands.

basset hound Centuries-old breed of dog developed in France and maintained, chiefly in France and Belgium, as a hunting dog of the aristocracy. It is a slow, deliberate hunter, with a deep voice and a nose exceeded in keenness only by the BLOODHOUND's. Short-legged and heavy-boned, the basset hound has long, dangling ears and a short coat in any combination of black, tan, and white. It stands 12–15 in. (30–38 cm) high and weighs 40–60 lbs (18–27 kg).

Bassi \'bás-ē\, **Agostino** (1773–1856) Pioneer Italian bacteriologist. In 1807 he began investigating the silkworm disease muscardine, which was causing serious economic losses in Italy and France. After 25 years of research, he demonstrated in 1835 that the disease was contagious and was caused by a microscopic parasitic fungus spread by contact and infected food. He theorized that many plant, animal, and human diseases are caused by animal or vegetable parasites, preceding both Louis PASTEUR and Robert KOCH in formulating a germ theory of disease.

basso continuo See CONTINUO

bassoon Large double-reed WOODWIND INSTRUMENT whose bore doubles back on itself (to keep its length manageable). The principal tenor–bass instrument of the orchestral woodwind family, it developed from the older curtal (or dulzian) in the 17th cent. It has a range of $3^1/2$ octaves, starting at B-flat two octaves below middle C. It is an agile instrument with a mild tone. The contrabassoon, a large metal instrument whose tubing doubles back four times, has a range an octave lower.

basswood Any of certain species of LINDEN common to N. America. The name refers especially to *Tilia americana,* found in a vast area of E N. America but centered in the Great Lakes region, and to *T. caroliniana* and *T. georgiana,* found in the SE U.S.

Bastet \'bas-₁tet\ *or* **Bast** *or* **Ubasti** In EGYPTIAN RELIGION, a goddess worshiped first as a lioness and later as a cat. Her nature changed after the domestication of the cat around 1500 B.C. In the Late and Ptolemaic periods, large cemeteries of mummified cats were created at the sites of her cult, and thousands of bronze statuettes of the goddess, represented as a lioness or a woman with a cat's head, were deposited as votive offerings. The Romans carried her cult to Italy.

Bastille \bas-'tēl\ Medieval fortress in Paris that became a symbol of despotism. In the 17th–18th cent., it was used as a French state prison and a place of detention for important persons. On July 14, 1789, at the beginning of the FRENCH

REVOLUTION, an armed mob captured the fortress and released its prisoners, a dramatic action that came to symbolize the end of the ANCIEN RÉGIME. The Bastille was subsequently demolished. Bastille Day (July 14) has been a French national holiday since 1880.

Basutoland See LESOTHO

bat Any member of about 900 species (order Chiroptera) of the only MAMMALS to have evolved true flight. Their wings are greatly elongated fingers joined by a membrane that extends down the side of the body. Most bats use ECHOLOCATION to orient themselves and find prey. Found worldwide, they are particularly abundant in the tropics. Wingspreads vary among species from 6 in. (15 cm) to 5 ft (1.5 m). Nearly all species roost during the day (in caves, caves, burrows, buildings, or trees) and feed at night. Most are INSECTIVORES, consuming enough insects to affect the balance of insect populations. Others feed on fruit, pollen, nectar, or blood (VAMPIRE BATS). Some may live more than 20 years. See also FRUIT BAT.

Bataan Death March \bə-'tan\ (April 1942) Forced march of 70,000 U.S. and Filipino prisoners of war (World War II) captured by the Japanese in the Philippines. From the S end of the Bataan Peninsula, the starving and ill-treated prisoners were force-marched 63 mi (101 km) to a prison camp. Only 54,000 prisoners lived to reach the camp. In 1946 the Japanese commander of the march was convicted by a U.S. military commission and executed.

Batak \bə-'täk\ Several closely related ethnic groups of central Sumatra, Indonesia. Descendants of a powerful Proto-Malayan people who until 1825 lived in relative isolation, they have their own written language. In their traditional religion, ancestors, plants, animals, and inanimate objects are considered to possess souls or spirits; today about a third of the 3.1 million Batak adhere to traditional beliefs, while the rest profess Christianity or Islam.

Bateman, Hester orig. Hester Needham (1708–1794) British silversmith. In 1760, after the death of her husband, John Bateman, she took over the family business. Assisted by her two sons, she executed designs commissioned by other silversmiths. Her shop later became well known for its tableware, such as spoons, sugar bowls, saltcellars, and teapots. Bateman's designs were restrained and graceful, characterized by beaded edges.

Bates College Private liberal-arts college in Lewiston, Me. It was founded in 1855 as an independent academy committed to egalitarian education, including the education of women; it was renamed in 1863 after a benefactor, Benjamin E. Bates. Enrollment is about 1,700.

Bateson, Gregory (1904–1980) British-U.S. anthropologist. Son of William BATESON, he studied at Cambridge Univ. but soon moved to the U.S. His book *Naven* (1936) was a groundbreaking study of cultural symbolism and ritual based on fieldwork in New Guinea. From 1936 to 1950 he was married to Margaret MEAD, with whom he studied the connection between culture and personality, publishing *Balinese Character* in 1942. His later interests included problems of learning and communication among schizophrenics. *Mind and Nature* (1978) synthesized many of his ideas.

Bateson, William (1861–1926) British biologist. In 1900 he realized that the research of Gregor MENDEL explained perfectly the results of his own plant experiments. He was the first to translate Mendel's major work into English. With Reginald C. Punnett (1875-1967), he published the results of a series of breeding experiments that not only extended Mendel's principles to animals but also showed that, contrary to Mendel, certain features were consistently inherited together, a phenomenon that came to be termed linkage. In 1908 he became Britain's first professor of genetics. Gregory BATESON was his son.

Bath City (pop., 1995 est.: 84,000), SW England. It was founded by the Romans, attracted to its hot mineral springs. The Anglo-Saxons arrived in the 6th cent. A.D., followed by the Normans around 1100. It became a center for the cloth trade. When the Roman baths were rediscovered in 1755, Bath had already revived as a spa; its popularity is reflected in the works of Jane AUSTEN, R. B. SHERIDAN, and Tobias SMOLLETT. It was rebuilt and extended in the Palladian style during the 18th cent.

batholith Large body of IGNEOUS ROCK formed beneath the earth's surface by the intrusion and solidification of MAGMA. Batholiths are usually composed of coarse-grained rocks (e.g., granite or quartz diorite), with steep side walls. They may have a surface exposure of 40 sq mi (100 sq km) or more and may be 6–9 mi (10–15 km) thick. A well-known batholith is located in the Sierra Nevada range of California.

Bathory, Stephen See STEPHEN BATHORY

Bath Party See BAATH PARTY

Bathurst See BANJUL

bathyscaphe \'ba-thi-ˌskaf\ Navigable diving vessel developed by Auguste PICCARD, designed to reach great depths in the ocean. The first bathyscaphe was built in 1946–48. A later version, the *Trieste,* was acquired by the U.S. Navy; in 1960 it dived to a record 35,810 ft (10,916 m) in the MARIANA TRENCH. The bathyscaphe consists of two main components: a steel cabin, heavier than water and resistant to sea pressure, and a float, filled with gasoline, which, being lighter than water, provides the necessary lift (replacing cables, which had proven unreliable at great depths).

batik \bə-'tēk\ Method of dyeing textiles, principally cottons, in which patterned areas are covered with wax so that they will not receive color. Multicolored effects are achieved by repeating the dyeing process several times, the initial pattern of wax being boiled off and another design applied before redyeing. Wax was applied with bamboo strips in Indonesia, where the technique originated; a woodblock wax applicator was developed in the 19th cent. Dutch traders imported the cloth and the technique to Europe. Today machines for applying wax in traditional Javanese patterns reproduce the same effects as the hand-dyeing process.

Batista (y Zaldívar) \bä-'tēs-tä\, **Fulgencio** (1901–1973) Soldier, president, and dictator who twice ruled Cuba (1933–44, 1952–59). An army officer, he came to power as a strongman, ruling first through associates. During his first term Batista cultivated the support of the U.S., the army, organized labor, and the civil service, and he achieved gains in education, public works, and the economy as a whole while enriching himself. He lost the 1944 election but returned by way of an army revolt in 1952. His second rule was a corrupt and brutal dictatorship that ended in his overthrow by Fidel CASTRO on January 1, 1959.

Batlle y Ordóñez \'bät-yä-ē-ór-'thōn-yäs\, **José** (1856–1929) President of Uruguay (1903–7, 1911–15). The son of a former president, his narrow victory in the 1903 presidential election led to a brief civil war, but when he held new elections in 1905 he won again, and he was reelected in 1911. He inaugurated labor reforms, limited the profits of foreign-owned businesses, encouraged migration, nationalized and developed public works, and ended the death penalty. He is credited with transforming Uruguay from an unstable dictatorship into a viable democracy and a highly generous welfare state.

Bat Mitzvah See BAR MITZVAH

Baton Rouge \'bat-ᵊn-'rüzh\ City (pop., 2000: 227,000), capital of Louisiana. Located on the Mississippi River, it is the state's second-largest city. Settled by the French in 1719, it was named for a red cypress pole that marked a boundary between Indian tribes. The area was ceded to Britain in 1763, later taken by the Spanish, and ceded to France in 1800. In 1810 the city was annexed to the U.S., and it became the state capital in 1849. It lost its capital status during the AMERICAN CIVIL WAR, but regained it in 1882. It has deepwater port facilities and is an important petroleum refining center. It is home to Louisiana State University.

battered woman syndrome Psychological and behavioral pattern displayed by female victims of domestic violence. Explanations have evolved since the late 1970s from LEARNED HELPLESSNESS to a "cycle of violence" theory and then a form of POST-TRAUMATIC STRESS DISORDER. The term is a legal concept rather than a psychiatric diagnosis, and lacks clearly defined criteria.

battering ram Medieval weapon consisting of a heavy timber with a metal knob or point at the front. Usually suspended by ropes from the roof of a movable shed, the timber was swung back and forth so that it banged against a gate or

wall under siege. The shed's roof was covered with animal skins to protect those inside from bombardment with stones or fiery materials.

battery Any of a class of devices that convert chemical EN-ERGY into electrical energy. A wet cell (e.g., a car battery) contains free liquid ELECTROLYTE; in a dry cell (e.g., a flashlight battery), the electrolyte is held in an absorbent material. Chemicals are arranged so that ELECTRONS released from the battery's negative electrode flow (see ELEC-TRIC CURRENT) through a CIRCUIT outside the battery (in the device powered by it) to the positive electrode. Voltage depends on the chemicals used and the number of cells (in series); current depends on the resistance in the total circuit (including the battery—and thus on electrode size). Multiple batteries may be connected in series, increasing total voltage, or in parallel, increasing total current. Standard dry cells used in flashlights and certain wet cells for marine, mine, highway, and military use are not rechargeable; car batteries, many dry cells used in cordless appliances, and batteries for certain military and aerospace uses may be recharged repeatedly.

battery See ASSAULT AND BATTERY

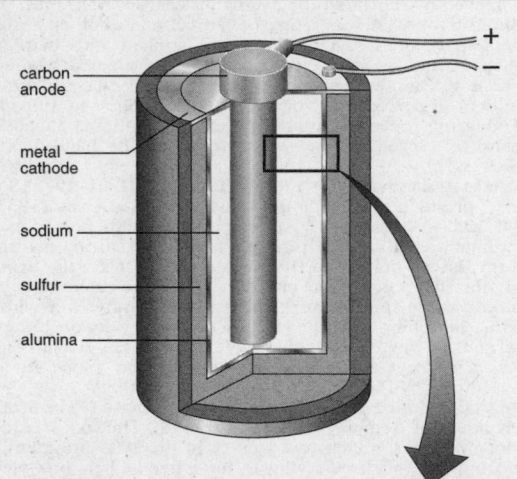

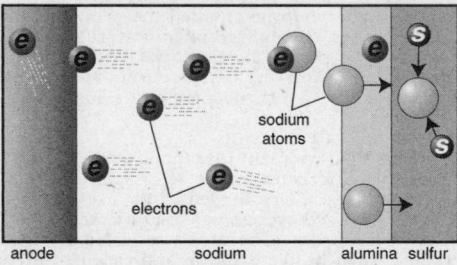

Battery The sodium-sulfur (NaS) battery, still under development, has been used in some electric cars. During discharge, the sodium reacts with the ceramic alumina electrolyte, losing electrons, which travel out the anode to the circuit the battery is powering. The ionic sodium then combines with sulfur, which has acquired electrons from the cathode. The reaction is reversible, so the battery can be recharged. The advantage of this battery over other rechargeables (e.g., lead-acid, nickel-cadmium, or nickel-metal hydride batteries) is that it can provide the same amount of power with a smaller, lighter battery. However, since the chemicals must be heated to a molten state and pure sodium is very reactive, failure of the battery casing or ceramic electrolyte is potentially dangerous.

battlement Parapet (portion above the roof) of the exterior wall of a fortification, consisting of alternating low portions (crenels) and high portions (merlons). Rooftop defenders would shoot from behind the merlons. Medieval battlements were often bracketed out (see CORBEL) to allow dropping of objects on encroachers below.

battleship Capital ship of the world's navies from about 1860 until World War II, when it was superseded by the AIR-CRAFT CARRIER. It combined large size, powerful guns, and heavy armor with impressive speed and cruising radius. The most powerful could hit targets more than 20 mi (30 km) distant and absorb heavy damage while continuing to fight. It originated in early IRONCLAD vessels with mixed sail and steam propulsion, such as the French armored frigate *Gloire* (1859). In 1906 the HMS *Dreadnought* introduced steam-turbine propulsion and an array of ten 12-in. (305-mm) guns. In World War II battleships were used for specialized tasks such as bombarding coastal defenses in AM-PHIBIOUS WARFARE. After the Persian Gulf War, the U.S. decommissioned its last two battleships.

Batu \'bä-tü\ (d.1255?) Grandson of GENGHIS KHAN and founder of the GOLDEN HORDE. In 1235 Batu was elected commander in chief of the W Mongol empire and given responsibility for the invasion of Europe. By 1241 he had conquered Russia, Poland, Bohemia, Hungary, and the Danube valley. Only the death of OGODEI prevented him from invading Western Europe. The Golden Horde in S Russia was ruled by his successors for 200 years.

Baudelaire \bōd-'ler\, **Charles (-Pierre)** (1821–1867) French poet and critic. While a law student, he became addicted to opium and hashish, and contracted the syphilis of which he later died. His early reckless spending on fine clothes and furnishings led to a life dogged by debt. In 1844 a black woman, Jeanne Duval, who would inspire some of his finest poetry, became his mistress. His discovery of the works of E. A. POE in 1852 led to many masterly translations and critical articles. His international reputation rests primarily on the extraordinary poems of *Les fleurs du*

Charles Baudelaire Photo by Étienne Carjat, 1863

mal (1857; *The Flowers of Evil*), which deal with erotic, aesthetic, and social themes in ways that appalled his middle-class readers, and he was convicted of obscenity. The book became perhaps the most influential collection of lyrics of the 19th cent., and he is regarded as the earliest modernist French poet. His *Petits poèmes en prose* (1868) was an innovative experiment in prose poetry. He also wrote provocative essays in art criticism. The years before his death at 46 were darkened by disillusionment, despair, and mounting debt.

Baudot \bō-'dō\, **(Jean Maurice) Émile** (1845–1903) French engineer. In 1874 he patented a telegraph code that by the mid-20th cent. had become the standard telegraphic alphabet. In Baudot's code, each letter is represented by a five-unit combination of current-on or current-off signals providing 32 possibilities (sufficient for the Roman alphabet, punctuation, and control of the machine's mechanical functions). Baudot also invented (1894) a distributor system for simultaneous transmission of several messages on the same telegraphic circuit. The baud, a unit of data transmission speed, is named for him.

Baudouin I \bōd-'waü\ (1930–1993) King of the Belgians (1951–93). The son of King LEOPOLD III, Baudouin lived under house arrest in German-occupied Belgium during World War II. After postwar exile in Switzerland, Baudouin became king on his father's abdication (1951). He helped restore confidence in the monarchy after the stormy reign of his father and became a unifying force in a country divided between Flemish- and French-speaking factions.

Bauhaus \'baú-ˌhaús\ (German: "House of Building") Influential, forward-looking German school of architecture and applied arts (1919–33) founded by Walter GROPIUS with the ideal of integrating art, craftsmanship, and technology. Realizing that mass production had to be the precondition of successful design in the machine age, the Bauhaus designers often achieved a severe but elegant geometric style carried out with great economy of means, though in fact its members' works were richly diverse. Its faculty included Joseph ALBERS, Lyonel FEININGER, Paul KLEE, Vasily KANDINSKY, and Marcel BREUER. The school was based in Weimar until 1925, Dessau through 1932, and Berlin in its final months, under Ludwig MIES VAN DER ROHE. See also INTERNATIONAL STYLE.

Baum \\'bäm\\, **L(yman) Frank** (1856–1919) U.S. writer of children's books. Born in Chittenango, N.Y., a "failure" at 40, he achieved success with his first book, *Father Goose* (1899), and followed it with the even more popular *Wonderful Wizard of Oz* (1900). He wrote 13 more Oz books, gaining a huge readership. The series was continued by Ruth Plumly Thompson after his death.

bauxite Most important ALUMINUM ore, in which aluminum hydroxide or aluminum oxide predominates over such other constituents as iron oxide, silica, and titania. Bauxite has been found in all the continents except Antarctica. Known deposits can supply the world with aluminum for hundreds of years at present production levels.

Bavaria *German* **Bayern** \\'bī-ərn\\ State (pop., 1997 est.: 12,056,000), S Germany. Conquered by the Romans in the 1st cent. B.C., the area was taken by CHARLEMAGNE in 788. It became one of the great duchies of the HOLY ROMAN EMPIRE. Under Maximilian I, Bavaria led the CATHOLIC LEAGUE in the THIRTY YEARS' WAR. It joined the German empire in 1871; its king was overthrown in 1918, and it joined the WEIMAR REPUBLIC in 1919. Adolf HITLER had his first power base there in the 1920s. It became a state of the Federal Republic of Germany in 1949. It has long been Germany's most Roman Catholic area. Its largest cities are MUNICH (its capital), AUGSBURG, and NUREMBERG. Notable regions include the Bavarian ALPS, the BLACK FOREST, and the Bohemian Forest. Bavaria is famous for the beauty of its rolling landscape and the charm of its villages.

Bax, Arnold (Edward Trevor) (*later* **Sir Arnold**) (1883–1953) British composer. Born into a wealthy family, he was free to compose throughout his life and wrote prolifically. His early works frequently evoke Celtic legend. His compositions include seven symphonies, the orchestral works *Spring Fire* (1913), *November Woods* (1917), and *Tintagel* (1919), four piano sonatas, and three string quartets.

bay Any of several small trees with aromatic leaves, especially the sweet bay, or bay laurel (*Laurus nobilis*), source of the bay leaf used in cooking. The bay rum tree, or simply bay (*Pimenta racemosa*), has leaves and twigs that yield oil of bay, which is used in perfumery and in bay rum, a fragrant cosmetic and medicinal liquid.

bay Semicircular or nearly circular concavity of a coastline, usually smaller than a GULF. Bays may range from a few hundred yards to several hundred miles wide. They are usually located where easily eroded rocks, such as clays and sandstones, are bounded by harder, more erosion-resistant formations of igneous rocks, such as granite.

Bayamón \\ˌbī-ä-'mōn\\ Town (pop., 1999 est.: 236,000), NE Puerto Rico, part of the metropolitan area of SAN JUAN. Puerto Rico's first settlement, Caparra, was founded nearby in 1508 by Juan PONCE DE LEÓN. Established as a town in 1772, it is now a manufacturing center and home to Bayamón Central Univ.

Baybars I *or* **Baibars I** \\'bī-bärs\\ (1223–1277) Most eminent MAMLUK sultan. He was sold as a slave after a Mongol invasion in the 1240s and ended up in the service of the Ayyubid sultan of Egypt, who gave him military training. In 1250 his army captured the crusader king LOUIS IX, and he and other Mamluk officers murdered the last Ayyubid sultan. He himself took the throne in 1260. He rebuilt the Syrian fortresses, built up the sultanate's armaments, and seized territory from the crusaders. He harried the Persian Mongols, attacking their Christian allies, and forging an alliance with the Mongols of the GOLDEN HORDE against them. He sent military expeditions into Nubia and Libya and developed extensive diplomatic relations. At home he built canals and the great mosque in Cairo that bears his name, and established efficient postal service between Cairo and Damascus. He died after drinking poison prepared for someone else.

bayberry Any of several aromatic shrubs and small trees of the genus *Myrica* in the bayberry family (Myricaceae), but especially *M. pennsylvanica,* also called candleberry, which has grayish waxy berries that yield the wax used in bayberry candles.

Bayer AG German chemical and pharmaceutical company. Founded in 1863 by Friedrich Bayer (1825–1880), it now operates plants in more than 30 countries. Bayer was the first developer and marketer of ASPIRIN (1899); of Prontosil, the first SULFA DRUG (1935); and of polyurethane (1937). Bayer was part of the chemical cartel IG FARBEN from 1925 to 1945; it was reestablished as an independent company in 1951. Its most noteworthy drug of the 1990s was the antibiotic Cipro.

Bayeux Tapestry \\bä-'yœ\\ Medieval embroidered TAPESTRY depicting the NORMAN CONQUEST. Woven in woolen threads of eight colors on coarse linen, it is 224 ft (68.4 m) long by about 20 in. (50 cm) wide. It consists of 79 consecutive scenes, with Latin inscriptions and decorative borders. It was probably woven within a few years of 1066 and possibly commissioned by Odo, bishop of Bayeux (Normandy), brother of WILLIAM I the Conqueror. The most famous of all pieces of needlework, it now hangs in the Bayeux tapestry museum.

Bayezid II \\ˌbī-ə-'zēd\\ (1448?–1512) Ottoman sultan who consolidated control of the empire begun by his father, MEHMED II. After taking the throne in 1481, he stopped expropriating Muslim religious properties and rejected pro-Europeanism but continued the policy of territorial conquest. He brought Herzegovina under Ottoman control, and strengthened the hold over the Crimea and Anatolia. He fought the SAFAVID DYNASTY in the east, the MAMLUK REGIME in the south, and the Venetians in the west. At home he built extensively and supported jurists, scholars, and poets. He abdicated in favor of his son Selim a month before his death.

Baykal, Lake See Lake BAIKAL

Bayle \\'bel\\, **Pierre** (1647–1706) French philosopher. Educated at a Jesuit school, he converted to Catholicism but later reverted to his original Calvinist faith. His religious views led to his losing two professorships. He believed that philosophical reasoning led to universal SKEPTICISM, but that nature compelled mankind to accept blind faith. His *Historical and Critical Dictionary* (1697) includes quotations, anecdotes, and annotations that cleverly undo whatever orthodox Christian beliefs the articles express, and it was condemned by religious authorities. Bayle's method of subversive criticism was adopted by contributors to Denis DIDEROT's *Encyclopédie.*

Baylis, Lilian (Mary) (1874–1937) British theatrical manager. She assisted her aunt, Emma Cons, in the operation of the Royal Victoria Hall and Coffee Tavern, and on Cons's death in 1912 she converted it into the OLD VIC theater. She made it famous for its Shakespearean productions, staging all of William SHAKESPEARE's plays between 1914 and 1923. In 1931 she took over the derelict Sadler's Wells Theatre and made it a center of opera and ballet.

Bayliss, William Maddock (*later* **Sir William**) (1860–1924) British physiologist. He and Ernest STARLING studied nerve-controlled blood-vessel contraction and dilation and discovered the peristaltic wave. In 1902 they showed that dilute hydrochloric acid mixed with partly digested food activates a chemical in the duodenum that they called secretin. This marked the discovery of HORMONES, a term the men coined. Bayliss also showed how the enzyme trypsin was formed from inactive trypsinogen and measured precisely the time it took to digest protein.

Baylor University Private university in Waco, Texas. It is the world's largest Baptist university and the oldest college (founded 1845) in Texas; it is named for one of its founding missionaries, Judge R. E. B. Baylor. It has schools of business, education, music, medicine, nursing, law, and graduate studies. Total enrollment is about 12,000.

B

Bay of Pigs invasion (Apr. 17, 1961) Abortive invasion of Cuba directed by the CENTRAL INTELLIGENCE AGENCY and carried out by Cuban exiles, intended to spark a rebellion and topple Fidel CASTRO. It began with the bombing of Cuban military bases; two days later a force of about 1,500 landed at sites along the coast, including the Bay of Pigs, and was quickly defeated. The result was a huge propaganda victory for Castro and an embarrassment for the new administration of John F. KENNEDY.

bayonet Short, sharp-edged, sometimes pointed weapon, designed for attachment to the muzzle of a firearm. According to tradition, it was developed in Bayonne, France, early in the 17th cent. and soon spread throughout Europe. The earliest design, the plug bayonet, was inserted into the muzzle of a musket. Later designs, including the socket bayonet invented by Sebastien de VAUBAN (1688), slipped it over the muzzle. Repeating firearms greatly reduced its combat value.

bayou \'bī-ü\ Still or slow-moving section of marshy water, usually a creek, secondary watercourse, or minor river that is a tributary of another river or channel. It may occur in the form of an OXBOW LAKE. Bayous are typical of the Mississippi River DELTA.

Bayreuth \bī-'ròit\ City (pop., 1992 est.: 73,000), E central Germany. It is situated northeast of NUREMBERG. Founded in 1194, it came under the burgrave of Nuremberg in 1248–1398 and the margraves of Brandenburg-Kulmbach in 1603–1769. The margraves patronized the arts and commissioned many baroque buildings. Bayreuth was ceded to Prussia in 1791, captured by NAPOLEON in 1806, and passed to BAVARIA in 1810. Richard WAGNER settled there in 1872 and designed the Festspielhaus, where Wagner festivals have been held since its opening in 1876.

bazooka Shoulder-fired M9A1 rocket launcher adopted by the U.S. Army in World War II. It consisted of a smooth-bore steel tube, originally about 5 ft (1.5 m) long, open at both ends and equipped with a hand grip, shoulder rest, trigger mechanism, and sights. It was called bazooka after a crude horn used by a popular radio comedian. It was developed chiefly for attacking tanks and fortified positions at short range. The U.S. Army replaced it during the Vietnam War with lighter-weight antitank weapons.

BBC *in full* **British Broadcasting Corp.** Publicly financed broadcasting system in Britain. A private company at its founding in 1922, it was replaced by a public corporation under royal charter in 1927. The BBC World Service began in 1932, and by 2000 was broadcasting programs in 42 languages to nearly 200 million people worldwide. BBC television service, a monopoly until 1954, introduced regular color broadcasts in Europe in 1967. The BBC radio monopoly ended in 1972. The BBC today offers five radio networks and two national television channels.

BBS See BULLETIN-BOARD SYSTEM.

B cell One of the two types of LYMPHOCYTES (the others being T CELLS). B cells are involved in so-called humoral IMMUNITY; on encountering a foreign substance (ANTIGEN), the B lymphocyte differentiates into a plasma cell, which secretes immunoglobulin (see ANTIBODY).

BCS theory Comprehensive theory that explains the behavior of superconducting materials. It was developed in 1957 by John BARDEEN, Leon Cooper (b.1930), and J. Robert Schrieffer (b.1931), whose surname initials provide its name. Cooper discovered that ELECTRONS in a superconductor are in pairs (Cooper pairs), and that the motions of all the pairs in a superconductor constitute a system that functions as a single entity. An applied voltage causes all Cooper pairs to move, forming an ELECTRIC CURRENT. When the voltage is removed, the current continues to flow because the pairs encounter no opposition. See also SUPERCONDUCTIVITY.

beach Sediments that accumulate along sea- or lakeshores. One type of beach occurs as a sediment strip bordering a rocky or cliffy coast. A second type is the outer margin of a marine plain. The third type consists of narrow sediment barriers stretching for dozens or even hundreds of miles parallel to the coast; the barriers separate LAGOONS from the open sea and generally are dissected by tidal inlets.

Beach, Amy *orig.* Amy Marcy Cheney *known as* **Mrs. H. H. A. Beach** (1867–1994) U.S. composer and pianist. Born in

Henniker, N.H., to a distinguished family, she was a precociously brilliant musician, and she performed as soloist with major orchestras. As a composer, she was devoted to German Romanticism rather than American themes or sources. Her *Gaelic Symphony* (1894) was the first symphony written by an American woman. Other works include a piano concerto (1899), the opera *Cabildo* (1932), and a piano quintet (1907).

bead Small round object made of wood, shell, bone, seed, nut, metal, stone, glass, or plastic. It is usually pierced for stringing so that it can be worn for decorative or, in some cultures, magical purposes. The earliest Egyptian beads (from c.4000 B.C.) were made of such stones, as lapis lazuli, turquoise, and amethyst and were variously shaped (sphere, cone, animal head). By 3000–2000 B.C., gold beads in tubular shapes were in use. From the Middle Ages to the 18th cent., trade in beads was enormous.

Beadle, George Wells (1903–1989) U.S. geneticist. Born in Wahoo, Neb., he earned his PhD from Cornell Univ. While studying drosophila, he realized that genes must influence heredity chemically, and designed a complex technique to determine the nature of those effects. With Edward TATUM, he found that the total environment of a bread mold could be varied so that researchers could locate and identify mutations relatively easily, concluding that each gene determines the structure of a specific enzyme, which in turn allows a single chemical reaction to proceed. For the "one gene, one enzyme" concept, they shared a 1958 Nobel Prize with Joshua LEDERBERG. He later served as president of the Univ. of Chicago (1960–68).

beagle Breed of small HOUND, popular as both a pet and a hunter. It looks like a small FOXHOUND, with large brown eyes, hanging ears, and a short coat of black, tan, and white. Beagles are solidly built. Two sizes are recognized: those less than 13 in. (33 cm) tall weighing about 18 lbs (8 kg), and those about 15 in. (38 cm) tall weighing about 30 lbs (13.5 kg). Beagles are typically alert and affectionate.

beak *or* **bill** Stiff, projecting oral structure of birds and turtles (both of which lack teeth) and certain other animals (e.g., CEPHALOPODS and some insects, fishes, and mammals). The term bill is preferred for the beak of a bird, composed of upper and lower jaws covered by a horny sheath of skin, with the nostrils on top, usually at the base. The shapes and sizes of bills are adapted for obtaining food, preening, building nests, and other functions.

Beaker culture Culture of the Late NEOLITHIC PERIOD and early BRONZE AGE in N and W Europe, known for its distinctive bell-shaped earthenware beakers decorated with toothed stamps, probably used in rituals of consumption. The people used the bow and arrow as well as copper daggers and spearheads. As they searched for gold and copper, they spread metallurgy into other parts of Europe.

beam In building construction, a horizontal member spanning an opening and carrying a load. The load may be a wall above the opening (see POST-AND-BEAM SYSTEM) or it may be a floor or roof. Beams may be of wood, steel, reinforced or prestressed concrete, plastic, or even brick with steel reinforcement. For weight reduction, metal beams are I-shaped in cross-section. A joist is any of a series of small parallel beams supporting a floor or roof. See also GIRDER.

bean SEED or pod of certain leguminous plants (see LEGUME). The mature seeds of the principal food beans are rich in protein and provide moderate amounts of iron and vitamins B_1 and B_2. Fresh or dried beans are used worldwide for cooking. Varieties differ greatly in size, shape, color, and tenderness of the immature pods. The common string, snap, or green bean (*Phaseolus vulgaris*), of Central and S. American origin, is the dominant edible-podded bean in the U.S., second to the SOYBEAN in importance. Third in importance is the broad, or fava, bean (*Vicia faba*), the principal bean of Europe. The lima bean (*P. limensis*), of Central American origin, is widely consumed in the Americas. The mung bean (*P. aureus*) is native to India and grown extensively in the Orient for food.

Bean, Roy (1825?–1903) U.S. justice of the peace and saloon-keeper. Born in Mason Co., Ky., he left Kentucky in 1847 and moved from town to town, killing at least two men in duels, before settling in Texas. In 1882 he moved to a site on the lower Pecos River that he named for Lillie LANGTRY,

opened a saloon, and dispensed hard, commonsensical, and prankish rulings as an unofficial magistrate, styling himself the "law west of the Pecos."

bear Generally massive, short-legged mammal (family Ursidae), the most recently evolved carnivore, found in Europe, Asia, N. and S. America, and N. Africa. Closely related to the dog and the raccoon, most bears climb with ease and are strong swimmers. Dietary preferences vary among species (POLAR BEARS feed mainly on seals, the spectacled bear on vegetation, etc.). Though they do not truly hibernate, bears often sleep fitfully through much of the winter. They live 15–30 years in the wild, but much longer in captivity. See also BLACK BEAR, BROWN BEAR, SUN BEAR.

Beard, Charles A(ustin) (1874–1948) U.S. historian. Born and reared in Indiana, Beard taught at Columbia Univ. (1904–17) and cofounded New York's New School for Social Research (1919). He is best known for iconoclastic studies of U.S. political institutions, focusing on socioeconomic conflict and change and the intent of the founders. *An Economic Interpretation of the Constitution of the United States* (1913) asserted that the Constitution served the economic interests of the founders. He also wrote *The Economic Origins of Jeffersonian Democracy* (1915) and, with his wife, Mary R. Beard (1876–1958), *The Rise of American Civilization* (1927).

Beard, James (1903–1985) U.S. chef and cookbook author. Born in Portland, Ore., he started a catering business when he could not find work as an actor. In 1945 he became the first chef to demonstrate cooking on network television. Through his Greenwich Village cooking school, he influenced such future chefs as Julia CHILD and Craig Claiborne (1920–2000). Favoring simple dishes, he wrote more than 20 cookbooks, including *James Beard's American Cookery* (1972) and *Beard on Bread* (1973).

Bearden, Romare (Howard) (1914–1988) U.S. painter. Born in Charlotte, N.C., he studied with George GROSZ. After World War II, he attended the Sorbonne and traveled in Europe. During this time he achieved recognition for his complex, semiabstract collages of photographs and painted paper on canvas; aspects of African-American culture, including ritual, music, and family, were his predominant themes. He is regarded as one of the most important African-American artists of the 20th cent.

Beardsley, Aubrey (Vincent) (1872–1898) British illustrator. Though largely self-taught, he quickly became a master of the curvilinear black-and-white ornamental illustration popularized by the ART NOUVEAU movement. In 1893 he illustrated an edition of Thomas MALORY's *Morte Darthur*, and in 1894 achieved notoriety with his erotic illustrations for Oscar WILDE's *Salome*. He became art editor and illustrator of the new quarterly *The Yellow Book* that same year. He died at 25 of tuberculosis.

Aubrey Beardsley, "A Footnote," self-portrait, 1896

Bear Flag Revolt Short-lived rebellion in 1846 by American settlers in California against Mexican authorities. In June a small group captured Sonoma, a settlement north of San Francisco, and declared independence, raising a flag that featured a grizzly bear. Capt. John FRÉMONT was elected to head the "republic." In July U.S. forces occupied San Francisco and Sonoma and claimed California for the U.S.

bearing In machine construction, a connector (usually a support) that permits the connected members to rotate or to move in a straight line relative to one another. Often one of the members is fixed, and the bearing acts as a support for the moving member. Most bearings support rotating shafts against either transverse (radial) or thrust (axial) loads. To minimize FRICTION, the contacting surfaces in a sliding bearing may be separated by a film of oil or gas. In BALL BEARINGS and ROLLER BEARINGS, the surfaces are separated by balls or rollers.

beat In physics, the pulsation resulting from a combination of two waves of slightly different FREQUENCY. Beat frequency is the difference between the frequencies of the combining waves. When the interfering frequencies are in the audible range, the beats are heard as alternating soft and loud pulses. The human ear can detect beats with frequencies up to 10 hertz, or 10 beats per second.

Beatles British musical group that ushered in the climactic phase of rock music. Its members, all born in Liverpool, were Paul MCCARTNEY, John LENNON, George Harrison (1943–2001), and Ringo Starr (b.1940). It began in the pairing of McCartney and Lennon in 1956, joined by Harrison in 1957, along with Stu Sutcliffe (1940–1962) and later Pete Best (b.1941). In 1960 they adopted the name The Beatles. In 1962 they signed a recording contract and replaced Best with Starr. The release in 1962–63 of such direct and energetic songs as "Please Please Me" and "I Want to Hold Your Hand" made them England's most popular rock group, and in 1964 "Beatlemania" struck the U.S. Their long hair and tastes in dress proved influential throughout the world, as did their experimentation with hallucinogenic drugs and Indian mysticism. Guaranteed huge sales, they felt free to experiment with a mix ranging from ballads ("Yesterday") to children's songs ("Yellow Submarine") to songs of social comment ("Eleanor Rigby"). Their public performances ended in 1966. Albums such as *Rubber Soul* (1965) and *Revolver* (1966) set new trends in rock. *Sgt. Pepper's Lonely Hearts Club Band* (1967) was novel for its conception as a dramatic whole, use of electronic music, and character as a studio work unreproducible on stage. They appeared in the films *A Hard Day's Night* (1964) and *Help!* (1965). The group dissolved in 1971.

Beat movement American social and literary movement of the 1950s and '60s, associated with bohemian artists' communities in San Francisco and New York. Alienated from conventional society, the Beats advocated personal release and illumination through heightened consciousness. Beat poets, including Lawrence FERLINGHETTI, Allen GINSBERG, and Gary SNYDER, sought to free poetry from academic refinement, creating verse often chaotic and obscene but also powerful and moving. Jack KEROUAC and William S. BURROUGHS developed a spontaneous, sometimes hallucinatory approach to prose, designed to convey the immediacy of experience. Though it faded by 1970, the movement paved the way for other unorthodox writers.

Beaton, Cecil (Walter Hardy) (*later* **Sir Cecil**) (1904–1980) British photographer and designer. In the 1920s he became staff photographer at *Vanity Fair* and *Vogue*. In his exotic portraits, the sitter is only one element of an overall decorative composition dominated by flamboyant backgrounds. His photographs of the siege of Britain were published in *Winged Squadrons* (1942). He also designed costumes and stage sets, including those for the movies *Gigi* (1958) and *My Fair Lady* (1964).

Beatrix (Wilhelmina Armgard) \bā-ȧ-'trēks\ (b.1938) Queen of the Netherlands. Beatrix went into exile with her family when the Germans invaded the Netherlands in World War II, and she spent the war years in Britain and Canada. In 1965 her betrothal to a German diplomat sparked controversy; they were married in 1966, and the hostility waned with the births of the first male heirs in the House of ORANGE-NASSAU since 1890. Beatrix became queen in 1980 after the abdication of her mother, JULIANA.

Beatty \'bāt-ē\, **(Henry) Warren** *orig.* Henry Warren Beaty (b.1937) U.S. film actor, producer, director, and screenwriter. Born in Richmond, Va., the brother of Shirley MACLAINE, he made his film debut in *Splendor in the Grass* (1961) and later starred in and produced the successful *Bonnie and Clyde* (1967) and *Shampoo* (1975). Often cowriting, directing, or producing his films, he also starred in *Heaven Can Wait* (1978), *Reds* (1981, Academy Award), *Dick Tracy* (1990), *Bugsy* (1991), and *Bulworth* (1998).

Beaubourg Center See POMPIDOU CENTER

Beaufort Sea \'bō-fərt\ Part of the ARCTIC OCEAN northeast of Alaska, northwest of Canada, and west of BANKS ISLAND in the ARCTIC ARCHIPELAGO. Its surface area is about 184,000 sq mi (476,000 sq km), its average depth is 3,239 ft (1,004 m), and its greatest depth is 15,360 ft (4,680 m). It is frozen over almost year-round. The chief settlement is PRUDHOE BAY, Alaska.

Beauharnais \bō-är-'ne\, **Alexandre, vicomte (Viscount) de** (1760–1794) French politician and general. In 1779 he became the first husband of JOSÉPHINE. A prominent figure during the FRENCH REVOLUTION, he presided over the Constituent Assembly in 1791, and was named general in chief of the Army of the Rhine in 1793. He was guillotined during the REIGN OF TERROR, largely because he was a noble.

Beauharnais, Eugène de (1781–1824) French administrator and general. Son of JOSÉPHINE and Alexandre de BEAUHARNAIS, he became a useful military aide to his stepfather, NAPOLEON. In 1804 he received the title of prince. Named Napoleon's viceroy in Italy (1805), he reorganized public finances, built roads, and introduced the French legal system. As commander of the Italian army, in 1814 he held out in Italy against the Austrians and the Neapolitans, but was forced to conclude an armistice.

Beauharnais, (Eugénie-) Hortense de (1783–1837) French-born queen of Holland (1806–10). Daughter of JOSÉPHINE and Alexandre de BEAUHARNAIS, and stepdaughter of NAPOLEON, Hortense married Napoleon's brother, Louis BONAPARTE, who later became king of Holland. The unhappy marriage produced the future NAPOLEON III. When Napoleon was exiled in 1814, Hortense became the center of Bonapartist intrigue; her support of Napoleon during his return led to her banishment from France in 1815.

Beaujolais \ˌbō-zhò-'lä\ Region in N Rhône and NE Loire departments, E central France. It is located east of the MASSIF CENTRAL and west of the SÂONE RIVER. The region is wooded; its highest point is Mt. Saint-Rigaud, at 3,310 ft (1,009 m). East of the mountain are the limestone escarpments of the Côte Beaujolaise, which support a world-famous red wine industry.

Beaumarchais \ˌbō-mär-'shä\, **Pierre-Augustin Caron de** (1732–1799) French playwright. Son of a watchmaker, he invented a clockwork mechanism and became embroiled in lawsuits over its patent; a series of witty pamphlets he wrote in his defense established his reputation as a writer. His comedy *The Barber of Seville* (1772) was kept off the stage for three years because it criticized the aristocracy. His *Marriage of Figaro* (1784) was similarly banned. The plays became famous operas by Gioacchino ROSSINI and W. A. MOZART, respectively. He founded the Société des Auteurs (1777) to enable playwrights to obtain royalty payments. His plays were sometimes said to have sparked the French Revolution.

Beaumont \'bō-ˌmänt\ City (pop., 2000: 109,000), SE Texas. It is connected to the Gulf of Mexico and is a major port of entry. It was founded in 1835. When Spindletop, the first major oil field in Texas, was discovered in 1901, the city grew rapidly. With Port Arthur and Orange, it forms the "Golden Triangle" petrochemical and industrial complex.

Beaumont \'bō-ˌmänt\, **Francis** (1584?–1616) English playwright. He is known chiefly for the 10 very popular plays on which he collaborated with John Fletcher (1579–1625) about 1606–13. These included the tragicomedies *The Maides Tragedy, Phylaster*, and *A King and No King*. Their independent work includes Beaumont's poetry and his parody *The Knight of the Burning Pestle* (1607) and Fletcher's pastoral *The Faithful Shepherdess* (1608). After Beaumont retired in 1613, Fletcher collaborated with other playwrights, possibly including William SHAKESPEARE.

Beauregard \'bō-rə-ˌgärd\, **P(ierre) G(ustave) T(outant)** (1818–1893) U.S. military leader. Born near New Orleans, he served in the Mexican War. In 1861 he resigned his commission and became a general in the Confederate army. He commanded the forces that bombarded Ft. Sumter, S.C., was in command at the battles of BULL RUN and SHILOH, and conducted the defenses of Charleston and Richmond. He was a controversial commander, often questioning orders, and after the war he quarreled with other generals' accounts of his role in the war.

Beauvoir \'bō-ˌvwär\, **Simone (Lucie-Ernestine-Marie-Bertrand) de** (1908–1986) French writer and feminist. At the Sorbonne, she met J.–P. SARTRE, with whom she formed a lifelong intellectual and romantic bond. She is best known for *The Second Sex* (1949), a plea for the abolition of the myth of the "eternal feminine" and a major classic of feminist literature. She also wrote four admired volumes of autobiography (1958–72), philosophical works exploring EXISTENTIALISM, and fiction, notably *The Mandarins* (1954, Prix Goncourt).

Beaux-Arts \bō-'zär\, **École (Nationale Supérieure) des** School of fine arts in Paris. It was founded by the merger in 1793 of the Académie de Peinture et de Sculpture, founded by Charles LE BRUN in 1648, and the Académie d'Architecture, founded in 1671 by Jean-Baptiste COLBERT. The BEAUX-ARTS STYLE in architecture has been particularly influential.

Beaux-Arts style \bō-'zär\ *or* **Second Empire style** *or* **Second Empire Baroque** Architectural style developed at the École des BEAUX-ARTS in Paris. It enjoyed international dominance in the late 19th cent. (see SECOND EMPIRE) and rapidly became an official style for many public buildings. Buildings are typically massive and symmetrical with rooms arranged axially, profuse classicist detail, and often pavilions at the ends and center. Among the most admired is the PARIS OPERA.

beaver Any member of the aquatic rodent family Castoridae (genus *Castor*), well known for its dam-building. Beavers are heavyset and have short legs and large, webbed hind feet. They grow as large as 4 ft (1.3 m) long (including the 1-ft, or 30-cm, tail) and as heavy as 60 lbs (27 kg). Beavers build their dams of sticks, stones, and mud in small rivers, streams, and lakes, often producing sizable ponds. With their powerful jaws and large teeth, they can fell medium-sized trees, whose branches they use in their dams. Family groups share a dome-shaped stick-and-mud lodge built in the water, with tunnel entrances below water level. Their prized pelts stimulated the exploration of W N. America. Old World beavers are now found only in the Elbe and Rhone drainages of Europe.

Beaverbrook (of Beaverbrook and of Cherkley), Baron *orig.* **William Maxwell Aitken** *known as* **Lord Beaverbrook** (1879–1964) Canadian-British politician and newspaper proprietor. He made a fortune in Montreal as a financier, then moved to England, becoming active in Conservative politics. From 1916 he took over or founded newspapers, including the London *Daily Express* and *Evening Standard*. Idiosyncratic and successful as a "press lord," he championed individual enterprise and British imperial interests. He held positions in the British cabinet during both World Wars.

Bebel \'bā-bəl\, **August** (1840–1913) German socialist and writer. A turner by trade, he helped found the Social Democratic Labor Party (later the SOCIAL DEMOCRATIC PARTY) in 1869 and was its most influential and popular leader for more than 40 years. He served in the Reichstag in 1867, 1871–81, and 1883–1913. He spent a total of nearly five years in prison on such charges as "libel of Bismarck." He wrote a number of works, including *Woman and Socialism* (1883).

bebop *or* **bop** JAZZ characterized by harmonic complexity, convoluted melodic lines, and frequent shifting of rhythmic accent. In the mid-1940s, a group of musicians, including Dizzy GILLESPIE, Thelonious MONK, and Charlie PARKER, rejected the conventions of SWING to pioneer a self-consciously artistic extension of improvised jazz, which set new technical standards of velocity and harmonic subtlety. Two genres grew out of bebop in the 1950s: the delicate, dry, understated approach known as cool jazz, and the aggressive, BLUES-tinged earthiness of hard bop.

Beccafumi \ˌbek-ə-'fü-mē\, **Domenico** *orig.* Domenico di Giacomo di Pace *known as* **Mecherino** \ˌmāk-kä-'rē-nō\ (1484–1551) Italian painter and sculptor active in Siena. He adopted the name of his patron, Lorenzo Beccafumi. He is noted for his sense of fantasy and striking effects of light, as in *The Birth of the Virgin* (c.1543). He painted decorations for the Siena town hall (1529–35) and executed designs for the marble pavement of Siena Cathedral. He is considered the outstanding Sienese painter of the Mannerist style.

Beccaria \,bäk-kä-'rē-ə\, **Cesare** (1738–1794) Italian criminologist. He became an international celebrity in 1764 with the publication of *Dei delitti e delle pene* ("Crime and Punishment"), the first systematic statement of principles governing criminal punishment; it argued that effective criminal justice depended more on the certainty of punishment than on its severity. The book greatly influenced criminal-law reform in Western Europe.

Bechet \bə-'shā\, **Sidney** (1897–1959) U.S. saxophonist, one of the first great soloists in jazz. Born in New Orleans, Bechet took up the clarinet at age 6, later switching to the more powerful soprano saxophone. His emergence as a soloist from the New Orleans DIXIELAND tradition established his reputation in the mid-1920s, but his lack of exposure with prominent groups caused his influence on others to be indirect. Bechet moved to France in 1951.

Bechtel \'bek-t∂l\, **Stephen D(avison)** (1900–1989) U.S. construction engineer and president (1936–60) of W. A. Bechtel Co. and its successor, Bechtel Corp. Born in Aurora, Ind., he became a vice president in the family firm of W. A. Bechtel Co. in 1925. In 1937 he and John McCone (1902–1991) formed Bechtel-McCone Corp., a builder of refineries and chemical plants. The companies built ships and made aircraft parts during World War II. After the war, the newly formed Bechtel Corp. became one of the world's largest construction and engineering firms, building pipelines in Canada and the Middle East and power plants worldwide. Bechtel companies helped construct the Hoover Dam, the Alaska oil pipeline, and the city of al-Jubayl in Saudi Arabia.

Bechuanaland See BOTSWANA.

Becker, Boris (Franz) (b.1967) German tennis player. He left school in the 10th grade to concentrate on tennis. In 1985 he became the youngest winner (at 17) of WIMBLEDON's men's singles title and the youngest ever to win a men's Grand Slam tournament, as well as the only unseeded player and the first German ever to win the title. He was victorious at Wimbledon again in 1986 and 1989, and also won singles titles in the 1989 U.S. Open and the 1991 and 1996 Australian Open competitions.

Becker, Gary S(tanley) (b.1930) U.S. economist. Born in Pottsville, Pa., he taught at Columbia Univ. and the Univ. of Chicago, applying the methods of economics to aspects of human behavior previously considered the domain of sociology and demography. In *Human Capital* (1964) and *A Treatise on the Family* (1981), he advanced the theory that rational economic choices, based on self-interest, govern most human activities. He won the Nobel Prize in 1992.

Becket, St. Thomas *or* **Thomas à Becket** (1118?–1170) Archbishop of Canterbury (1162–70). The son of a Norman merchant, he served as chancellor of England (1155–62) under HENRY II. A brilliant administrator, diplomat, and military strategist, he aided the king in increasing royal power. Resistant to the church's increasing autonomy, Henry hoped to reinforce royal control by appointing Becket as archbishop of Canterbury. Becket, however, embraced his new duties devoutly and opposed royal power in the church, and especially the prosecution of clerics. The king issued the Constitutions of CLARENDON (1164) listing royal rights over the church,

St. Thomas Becket From an English psalter, c.1200

and summoned the archbishop to trial. Becket fled to France and remained in exile until 1170, when he returned to Canterbury and was murdered in the cathedral by four of Henry's knights. His tomb became a site of pilgrimage, and he was canonized in 1173.

Beckett, Samuel (Barclay) (1906–1989) Irish playwright. After studying in Ireland and traveling, he settled in Paris in 1937. In the postwar years he wrote, in French, the narrative trilogy *Molloy* (1951), *Malone Dies* (1951), and *The Unnamable* (1953). His play *Waiting for Godot* (1952) was an immediate success in Paris and gained worldwide acclaim when he translated it into English. Marked by minimal plot and action, it typifies the theater of the ABSURD. His later plays, also abstract works with minimal sets that deal with the mystery and despair of human existence in a comic spirit, include *Endgame* (1957), *Krapp's Last Tape* (1958), and *Happy Days* (1961). In 1969 he was awarded the Nobel Prize.

Beckmann \'bek-,män\, **Max** (1884–1950) German Expressionist painter. Trained at the conservative Weimar Academy, in 1903 he moved to Berlin. His experience as a medical orderly in World War I changed his art, which became full of horrifying imagery, with deliberately repulsive colors and erratic forms, combining brutal realism and social commentary. In 1933 the Nazis declared his art "degenerate" and forced him to resign his professorship in Frankfurt; in 1937 he fled to Amsterdam.

Becknell \'bek-n∂l\, **William** (1796?–1865) U.S. trader. Born in Amherst Co., Va., he settled in Missouri and became involved in trade with the Southwest. When the Spanish prohibition on trade with New Mexico was lifted in 1821, he followed the customary route through the Colorado Rocky Mtns. south to Santa Fe, where he sold his goods at great profit. The next year he pioneered a new route, the SANTA FE TRAIL. He later fought for Texas's independence.

Beckwourth, Jim *orig.* James Pierson Beckwith (1798–1867?) U.S. mountain man. Born a slave in Virginia, he was taken by his white father to St. Louis and set free. In 1823–24 he was hired by trading expeditions in the Rocky Mtns. He married a series of Indian women and lived among the Crow for about six years. During the California gold rush (1848) he established a route through the Sierra Nevada. In 1856 a writer he met published many of Beckwourth's stories and recollections.

Becquerel \be-'krel\, **(Antoine-) Henri** (1852–1908) French physicist. The descendant of eminent physicists, he studied phosphorescent materials as well as uranium compounds, and employed photography in his experiments. He is remembered for his discovery of RADIOACTIVITY, which occurred when he found that the element uranium (in a sample of pitchblende) emitted invisible rays that could darken a photographic plate. His 1901 report of a burn caused by a sample of Pierre and Marie CURIE's radium that he carried in his vest pocket led ultimately to the medical use of

Henri Becquerel

radioactive substances. In 1903 he shared a Nobel Prize with the Curies. The unit of radioactivity, the becquerel (Bq), is named for him.

bedbug Any member of some 75 species of nocturnal insects (family Cimicidae) that feed by sucking the blood of humans and other warm-blooded animals. The adult is broad and flat and less than 0.2 in. (4–5 mm) long. Cosmopolitan human parasites, they are found in every kind of dwelling. They digest meals slowly; adults have lived for at least a year without food. The bite is irritating but does not transmit diseases.

Bede, St. *known as* **the Venerable Bede** (672/673–735) Anglo-Saxon historian. Raised in a monastery, he was ordained a priest at 30. He is best known for his *Ecclesiastical History of the English People* (732?), tracing Britain's history from 55 B.C. to A.D. 597, a vital source on the history of the Anglo-Saxon tribes' conversion to Christianity. His method of dating events from Christ's birth (A.D.) came into general use through the popularity of the *History*.

Bedouin \'bed-win\ Arabic-speaking desert nomads of the Middle East. Ethnically, the Bedouin are ARABS. Bedouin social rank is determined by the animals they herd: camel nomads are most prestigious, followed by sheep and goat herders and finally cattle nomads. Traditionally, Bedouin migrated into the desert during the rainy season and returned to cultivated areas during the dry season, but since World War II some national governments have forced them to become more settled. Most, however, retain pride in the nomadic heritage.

bee Any member of some 20,000 INSECT species (superfamily Apoidea, order Hymenoptera), including the familiar BUMBLEBEE. Adults range in size from about 0.08 to 1.6 in. (2 mm–4 cm). Bees are related to WASPS, but rely on flowers for food. Male bees never collect pollen; female bees make and provision the nest and usually have special anatomical structures for carrying pollen. The so-called killer bee, an Africanized subspecies of *Apis mellifera* (see HONEYBEE), reached the U.S. from Mexico around 1990; killer bees react quickly and attack in number.

beech Any of several different types of trees, especially about 10 species of deciduous ornamental and timber trees constituting the genus *Fagus* (family Fagaceae), native to temperate and subtropical regions of the Northern Hemisphere. Beeches are tall, round-headed, and wide-spreading, with smooth, steel-gray bark and toothed, shiny green leaves. The American beech *(F. grandifolia)*, native to E N. America, and the European beech *(F. sylvatica)*, found throughout England and Eurasia, are the most widely known species. Both are economically important timber trees, often planted as ornamentals. Beech wood is durable under water and is valued for indoor use, tool handles, and shipping containers. The nuts yield an edible oil. Beeches are slow-growing but may live to 400 years or more.

Beecham, Thomas *(later* **Sir Thomas)** (1879–1961) British conductor. Born to an aristocratic family and educated at Oxford, he was self-taught as a conductor. Devoted to broadening British musical tastes, he created the Beecham Symphony Orchestra in 1909, and programmed many British premieres of the concert repertoire and operas. In 1932 he founded the London Philharmonic Orchestra, and in 1947 the Royal Philharmonic Orchestra; he also founded opera companies. Though he had significant gaps in his technique, he was an incomparable and beloved interpreter of the music he loved.

Beecher, Catharine (Esther) (1800–1878) U.S. educator who shaped a conservative movement to both elevate and entrench woman's role in the domestic sphere. Born in E. Hampton, N.Y., sister of Harriet Beecher STOWE and Henry Ward BEECHER, she helped found the Hartford Female Seminary (1823) and other organizations devoted to women's education. Her *Treatise on Domestic Economy* (1841) helped standardize domestic practices and reinforce the belief that a woman's proper place was in the home.

Beecher, Henry Ward (1813–1887) U.S. Congregational clergyman. Born in Litchfield, Conn., he was the brother of Harriet Beecher STOWE and Catharine BEECHER. He served as pastor to congregations in Indiana before being called in 1847 to Plymouth Church in Brooklyn, N.Y. A famous orator and one of the most influential preachers of his time, he opposed slavery and supported women's suffrage, Darwin's theory of evolution, and scientific biblical criticism. He gained unfavorable publicity in 1874 when he was tried for adultery, but acquitted.

bee-eater Any of about 25 species of brightly colored birds (family Meropidea) that feed on bees, wasps, and other insects. They are found throughout tropical and subtropical Eurasia, Africa, and Australasia. Bee-eaters range in length from 6 to 14 in. (15–35 cm). Their bill is moderately long, slightly downcurved, and pointed. Their plumage is brilliant green, often with some red, yellow, blue, or purple.

beef Flesh of mature CATTLE, as distinguished from veal, the flesh of calves. The best beef is obtained from steers (castrated males) and heifers (female cows that have not calved). Tenderness and flavor are improved by aging in cold air for about two weeks. The world's primary beef producers and consumers are the U.S., the European Union, Brazil, China, Argentina, and Australia. In the U.S., grades range from prime and choice to utility and canner. Beef provides protein and B vitamins; it also contains saturated fat, which can contribute to heart disease and other health problems.

beekeeping *or* **apiculture** \'ā-pə-ˌkəl-chər\ Care and manipulation of HONEYBEES to enable them to produce and store more honey than they need so that the excess can be collected. Beekeeping is one of the oldest forms of animal husbandry. Early efforts at collecting the honey required destroying the hive; modern beekeepers use an extractor that empties the cells of the honeycomb without damaging them. Maintaining the hive includes protecting the colony against diseases, parasites, and predators.

beer ALCOHOLIC BEVERAGE made usually from malted BARLEY, flavored with HOPS, and brewed by slow FERMENTATION. Known from ancient times, beer was especially common in northern climates too cold for WINE grapes. It is produced with either a bottom-fermenting YEAST, which falls to the bottom of the container after fermentation, or a top-fermenting yeast, which rises to the surface. Lager beers, of German origin, are bottom-fermented and stored at a low temperature for several months; most are light in color, with high carbonation, medium hop flavor, and alcohol content of 3–5% by volume. Top-fermented beers, including ALE, stout, and porter, are characterized by a prominent foamy head and a sharper flavor than lagers; alcohol content is 4–6.5% by volume.

Beerbohm, (Henry) Max(imilian) *(later* **Sir Max)** (1872–1956) English caricaturist and writer. His sophisticated drawings and parodies captured whatever was affected or absurd in his famous contemporaries. His first literary collection (1896) and his first book of drawings, *Caricatures of Twenty-five Gentlemen* (1896), were followed by the fable *The Happy Hypocrite* (1897), the satiric novel *Zuleika Dobson* (1911), and the admired story collection *Seven Men* (1919).

Beer Hall Putsch *or* **Munich Putsch** \'pu̇ch\ (1923) Unsuccessful attempt by Adolf HITLER to start an insurrection against the WEIMAR REPUBLIC. On November 8, Hitler and his men pushed their way into a right-wing political meeting in a Munich beer hall and convinced the leaders to join in carrying the "revolution" to Berlin. The next day, some 3,000 Nazis marched toward the Marienplatz, but were met by police gunfire. Hitler was subsequently sentenced to five years in prison; he only served nine months, time he spent writing *Mein Kampf*.

Beersheba City (pop., 1999 est.: 163,000), S Israel. Historically it marked the extreme S limit of Palestine, hence the biblical phrase "from Dan to Beersheba." It fell to the Arabs in the 7th cent. and to the Turks in the 16th cent. It was a watering place for the nomadic Bedouin tribes of the NEGEV desert. Held by the British from 1917, it was taken by Israel in 1948.

beet Cultivated form of the plant *Beta vulgaris* of the goosefoot family (Chenopodiaceae). Four distinct types are cultivated: the garden beet; the SUGAR BEET, a major source of sugar; the mangel-wurzel, as food for livestock; and the leaf beet, or Swiss CHARD. Beet greens are a source of riboflavin, iron, and vitamins A and C. Beets are grown most extensively in temperate to cool regions or during the cooler seasons.

Beethoven \'bā-ˌtō-vən\, **Ludwig van** (1770–1827) German-Austrian composer. Born in Bonn to a musical family, he was a precociously gifted pianist and violist. After nine years as a court musician in Bonn, he moved to Vienna to study with F. J. HAYDN and remained there the rest of his life. He was soon well known as both a virtuoso and a composer, and he became the first composer to earn a successful living while forsaking employment in the church or court. He uniquely straddled the Classical and Romantic eras. His

Ludwig van Beethoven

astonishing *Eroica Symphony* (1803) was the thunderclap that announced the Romantic century, and it embodies the titanic but rigorously controlled energy that was the hallmark of his style. He infused every instrumental genre that he touched—especially the concerto, symphony, string quartet, and piano sonata—with unprecedented weight and power. His increasing deafness from about 1795 led to near-suicidal depression; from about 1819 he was totally deaf. For his last 15 years he was unrivaled as the world's most famous composer. His works include the celebrated nine symphonies (1800–24), 16 string quartets (1798–1826), 32 piano sonatas (1796–1822), the opera *Fidelio* (1805, rev. 1814), two masses, including the *Missa Solemnis* (1823), five piano concertos, a violin concerto (1806), six piano trios, 10 violin sonatas, and five cello sonatas.

beetle Any of at least 250,000 species of insects constituting the order Coleoptera (the largest order in the animal kingdom), characterized by special forewings, called elytra, which are modified into hardened covers over a second pair of functional wings. Beetles occur in almost all environments. The smallest species are less than 0.04 in. (1 mm) long; the largest can exceed 8 in. (20 cm). Most beetles eat either other animals or plants. Some species destroy crops, timber, and textiles and spread parasitic worms and diseases. Others are valuable predators of insect pests. Some beetles are known by other common names (e.g., borer, chafer, curculio, FIREFLY, WEEVIL). Beetles are preyed on by other insects and by bats, swifts, and frogs.

Begin \be-'gēn *Engl* 'bā-gin\, **Menachem (Wolfovitch)** (1913–1992) Prime minister of Israel 1977–83. Born in Russia, he earned a law degree from the Univ. of Warsaw. During World War II he was imprisoned in Siberia. Released in 1941, he joined the Polish army in exile. He escaped to Palestine, where he became leader of the IRGUN ZVAI LEUMI in 1943. From 1948 to 1977 he led the opposition in the Israeli Knesset, except for three years when he sat in the Government of National Unity (1967–70). He became the LIKUD prime minister in 1977. He shared the 1978 Nobel Peace Prize with Anwar al-SADAT for work leading to the 1979 Israel–Egypt peace treaty. His 1982 invasion of Lebanon turned world opinion against Israel, and he resigned in 1983. See also ARAB–ISRAELI WARS.

begonia \bi-'gōn-yə\ Any of about 1,000 species (genus *Begonia*) of mostly SUCCULENT, tropical or subtropical plants, many with colorful flowers or leaves and used as pot plants or as garden plants. The wax begonia (*B. semperflorens*) is the most popular for use as a summer bedding plant; angel-wing begonias are characterized by their tall stems; hairy begonias have feltlike leaves. Most begonias are tender and intolerant of dry conditions.

Behan \'bē-ən\, **Brendan (Francis)** (1923–1964) Irish author. An alcoholic from age 8 and an anti-English rebel, he was repeatedly arrested. *Borstal Boy* (1958) tells of his time in an English reform school, combining earthy satire and political protest. His explosive first play, *The Quare Fellow* (1954), concerns prison life and capital punishment. His second, *The Hostage* (produced 1958), is considered his masterwork.

behaviorism Highly influential school of thought that dominated psychological theory in the U.S. between the two World Wars. Classical behaviorism focused exclusively on objective evidence of behavior (measured responses to stimuli) and excluded ideas, emotions, and inner mental experience (see CONDITIONING). It emerged in the 1920s and was developed in subsequent decades by Clark HULL and B. F. SKINNER. Through the work of Edward Tolman (1886–1959), strict behaviorist doctrines began to admit such variables as reported mental states and differences in PERCEPTION. A natural outgrowth of behaviorist theory was BEHAVIOR THERAPY.

behavior therapy *or* **behavior modification** Application of principles of LEARNING to the treatment of psychological disorders and the control of behavior. The concept was popularized in the U.S. by theorists of BEHAVIORISM, including B. F. SKINNER. Its techniques are based on operant CONDITIONING, in which desired behaviors are rewarded. There is little or no concern for conscious experience or unconscious processes. Such techniques have been applied to ENURESIS, TICS, PHOBIAS, STUTTERING, and OBSESSIVE-COMPULSIVE DISORDER. Behavior modification more generally refers to the application of reinforcement techniques for shaping individual behavior toward some desired end or for controlling behavior in classrooms or institutional situations. See also PSYCHOTHERAPY.

Behn \'bän, 'ben\, **Aphra** (1640–1689) English dramatist and novelist, the first known Englishwoman to earn her living by writing. Her early life is obscure, but she spent most of it in S. America. She married an English merchant named Behn in 1658. Her novel *Oroonoko* (1688), the story of an enslaved African prince whom she knew in S. America, influenced the development of the English novel. Her first play, *The Forc'd Marriage*, was produced in 1671; her witty comedies, such as the two-part *The Rover* (1677, 1681), were highly successful.

Behrens \'bā-rens\, **Peter** (1868–1940) German architect. In 1907 he was appointed artistic adviser for the large electrical company AEG. His AEG Works turbine factory in Berlin (1909–12), with its sweeping glass CURTAIN WALL, became the most significant building in Germany at that time. Walter GROPIUS, LE CORBUSIER, and Ludwig MIES VAN DER ROHE all worked in his office.

Behrman \'ber-mən\, **S(amuel) N(athaniel)** (1893–1973) U.S. playwright. Born in Worcester, Mass., he won success with his first play, the light comedy *The Second Man* (1927), followed by the popular *Meteor* (1929), *Brief Moment* (1931), and *Biography* (1932). His more serious plays include *Rain from Heaven* (1934) and *No Time for Comedy* (1939). Noted for addressing complex social and moral issues, he wrote over 25 comedies in his 40-year career, and nearly every one was a hit.

Beiderbecke \'bī-dər-ˌbek\, **Bix** (*orig.* Leon) (1903–1931) U.S. jazz cornetist and composer. Born in Davenport, Iowa, Beiderbecke developed a style independent of the influence of Louis ARMSTRONG and became the leading player of the Chicago style of jazz in the 1920s. His interest in the harmonies of composers such as Claude DEBUSSY was reflected in both his playing and his compositions. He worked in the bands of Jean Goldkette and Paul Whiteman. His alcoholism and early death contributed to his status as one of the early romantic legends of jazz.

Beijing \'bā-'jiŋ\ *or* **Peking** \'pē-'kiŋ\ *formerly (1928–49)* **Peiping** \'pā-'piŋ\ City (pop., 1999 est.: 12,570,000), capital of China. It has been settled since ancient times and has been known by various names, including Ch'i, under the ZHOU DYNASTY (1122–255 B.C.), and Khanbalik (or Cambaluc), when it became the royal residence of KUBLAI KHAN in A.D. 1264. It was chosen as the capital in 1421. It suffered heavy damage when it was occupied by European forces in 1860 and 1900 (see BOXER REBELLION). In 1928 the capital was moved to NANJING. Beijing's capital status was restored following the Communist victory in 1949. It is China's cultural and educational center. The old FORBIDDEN CITY contains the former imperial palace. Abutting it is TIANANMEN SQUARE, the world's largest public square. Beijing's 15th-cent. walls were partly demolished in the CULTURAL REVOLUTION.

Beijing Opera (Chinese *jingxi*: "opera of the capital") Traditional Chinese theater, originally devised in 1790. Highly formal and symbolic, it combines orchestral music, speech, song, dance, and acrobatics. The performers enact dramas based on historical epics, legend, and myth. The characters' roles and social ranks are conveyed through elaborate costumes and stylized makeup. It traditionally employed an all-male cast with female impersonators, but has recently admitted female actors. The actor Mei Lanfang brought its influence to the West through his tours in the 1930s.

Beijing University One of the oldest and most important universities in China. It was founded as Capital College in 1898 and became a university in 1911. By 1920 it had become a center for progressive thought. The first disturbances of the CULTURAL REVOLUTION began at Beijing Univ. in 1966; education there ceased between 1966 and 1970. The university has since reasserted its position as China's foremost nontechnical university. It has the largest university library in China. Enrollment is about 13,000.

B

Beirut \bā-ˈrüt\ City (metro. area pop., 1996 est.: 1,900,000), capital of Lebanon. The country's chief port and largest city, it was initially settled by the Phoenicians. It gained prominence under Roman rule in the 1st cent. B.C.. It was captured by the Arabs in A.D. 635. Christian Crusaders held Beirut 1110–1291, after which it was dominated by the Saracens, Druze, and Ottoman Turks. It became the capital of the new state of Lebanon (under French mandate) in 1920, and capital of an independent Lebanon in 1941. It went on to flourish as the chief banking and cultural center of the Middle East. It lost that status during the LEBANESE CIVIL WAR (1975–91), when it suffered heavy damage.

Béjart \bā-ˈzhàr\, **Maurice** *orig.* Maurice Jean Berger (b.1927) French-Belgian dancer, choreographer, and opera director. He danced with various companies before founding his own, Les Ballets de l'Étoile (later Ballet Théâtre de Maurice Béjart), in Paris in 1954. In 1959 it moved to Brussels; renamed the Ballet of the 20th Century, it became one of the world's foremost troupes. Béjart's productions have been noted for reworking tradition in often controversial ways. In 1987 the company moved to Switzerland and took the new name Béjart Ballet Lausanne.

Bekáa Valley \be-ˈkä\ *or* **Al Biqa** \ˌàl-be-ˈkä\ *ancient* Coele-Syria. Valley, Lebanon. Located between the LEBANON and Anti-Lebanon mountain ranges, it is about 80 mi (130 km) long and 10 mi (15 km) wide. It includes BAALBEK, in ancient times a city of great size. In recent decades it has seen continued skirmishes between Syrian and Lebanese and Palestine Liberation Organization forces.

Bel See MARDUK

Belafonte \ˌbel-ə-ˈfän-tā\, **Harry** *orig.* Harold (George) Belafonte, Jr. (b.1927) U.S. singer, actor and producer. He was born in New York City to Caribbean immigrants, and he lived with his mother in Jamaica 1935–40. In the early 1950s he initiated a fad for CALYPSO music with such songs as "Day-O" and "Jamaica Farewell." He starred in several films and later became the first black television producer. In the 1960s and '70s he was a prominent civil-rights activist.

Belarus *or* **Byelarus** \ˌbyä-lə-ˈrüs\ *formerly* **Belorussia** Republic, N central Europe. Area: 80,154 sq mi (207,599 sq km). Population (2000): 9,989,000. Capital: MINSK. The

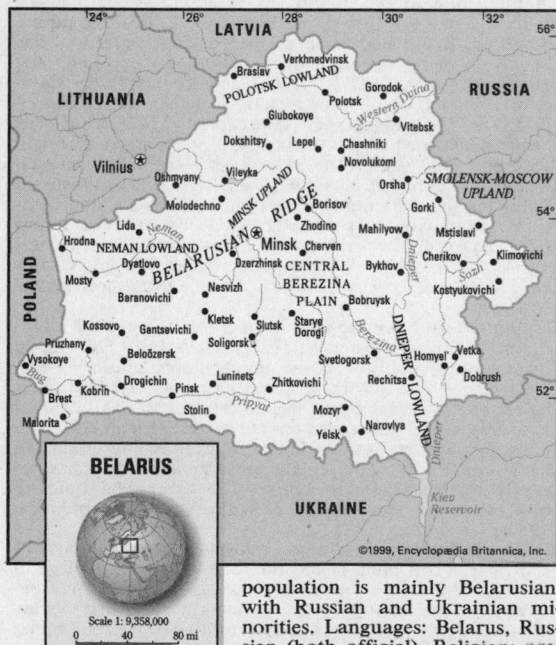

©1999, Encyclopædia Britannica, Inc.

population is mainly Belarusian, with Russian and Ukrainian minorities. Languages: Belarus, Russian (both official). Religion: predominantly Eastern Orthodoxy. Currency: ruble. The N part is crossed by the Western Dvina River; the DNIEPER flows through its E portion; the

south has extensive marshy areas along the PRIPYAT; the upper course of the NEMAN flows in the west; and the BUG forms part of the boundary with Poland in the southwest. The chief settlements, in addition to Minsk, are Homyel, MAHILYOW, and VITSYEBSK. The economy is predominantly agricultural. It is a republic with two legislative houses; its head of state and government is the president. While Belarusians share a distinct identity and language, they never previously enjoyed political sovereignty. The territory that is now Belarus underwent partition and changed hands often; as a result its history is entwined with its neighbors'. In medieval times the region was ruled by Lithuanians and Poles. Following the Third Partition of POLAND it was ruled by Russia. After World War I, the W part was assigned to Poland and the E part became U.S.S.R. territory. After World War II, the Soviets expanded what had been the Belorussian S.S.R. by annexing more of Poland. Much of the area suffered contamination from the CHERNOBYL ACCIDENT in 1986, forcing many to evacuate. Belarus declared its independence in 1991 and later joined the COMMONWEALTH OF INDEPENDENT STATES. Amid increasing political turmoil in the 1990s, it proposed a union with Russia in 1997.

Belasco \bə-ˈlas-kō\, **David** (1853–1931) U.S. theatrical producer and playwright. Born in San Francisco, he became a theater manager in New York in 1880. An independent producer from 1890, he built his own theater in 1906; there he introduced changes in stage lighting, used realistic scenery, and demanded high production standards. He wrote or collaborated on numerous plays, including *Madame Butterfly* (1900) and *The Girl of the Golden West* (1905), which became operas by Giacomo PUCCINI.

Belau See PALAU

Belém \be-ˈlem\ City (pop., 1996: 851,000; metro. area pop: 1,485,000), N Brazil. The capital of Pará state, the port of Belém lies on the Pará River in the vast AMAZON RIVER delta 90 mi (145 km) from the Atlantic Ocean. Established in 1616, it helped consolidate Portuguese supremacy in N Brazil and became the state capital in 1772. It enjoyed prosperity in the late 19th cent. as the main exporting center of the Amazon rubber industry. After the rubber era ended in 1912, it continued to be N Brazil's commercial center and a main port.

Belfast District, seaport, and capital (pop., 1995 est: 297,000) of Northern Ireland. The site was occupied in the Stone and Bronze ages, and the remains of Iron Age forts can still be seen. Belfast's modern history began in the early 17th cent. After the Irish insurrection of 1641, the town grew in economic importance, especially after a large immigration of French HUGUENOTS arrived after the rescinding of the Edict of NANTES (1685) and strengthened the linen trade. It became a center of Irish Protestantism, setting the stage for sectarian conflict in the 19th–20th cent. New conflicts broke out in the 1960s and continued into the 1990s; a provisional peace agreement was reached in 1998.

belfry Bell tower, either freestanding or attached to another structure. More particularly it refers to the room, usually at the top of such a tower, where the bells and their supporting timberwork are hung. The belfry is a prominent feature of Belgian Gothic architecture, especially in Flanders. The term derives from the medieval *berfrei*, a tall wooden structure that could be rolled up to a fortification wall so that the warriors inside could storm the battlements.

Belgian Congo See Democratic Republic of the CONGO

Belgium *French* **Belgique** \bel-ˈzhēk\ *Flemish* **België** \ˈbel-kē-ə\ Kingdom, NW Europe. Area: 11,781 sq mi (30,513 sq km). Population (2000): 10,249,000. Capital: BRUSSELS. The population consists mostly of Flemings and Walloons. The Flemings, more than half the population, speak Flemish and live in the N half of the country; the Walloons, about one-third of the population, speak French and inhabit the S half. Languages: Dutch, French, German (all official). Religion: Roman Catholicism (88%). Currency: euro. Belgium can be divided into several geographic regions. The southeast consists of the forested ARDENNES highland, which extends south of the MEUSE RIVER valley and includes Belgium's highest point, Mt. Botrange (2,277 ft, or 694 m). Middle Belgium is a fertile region crossed by tributaries of

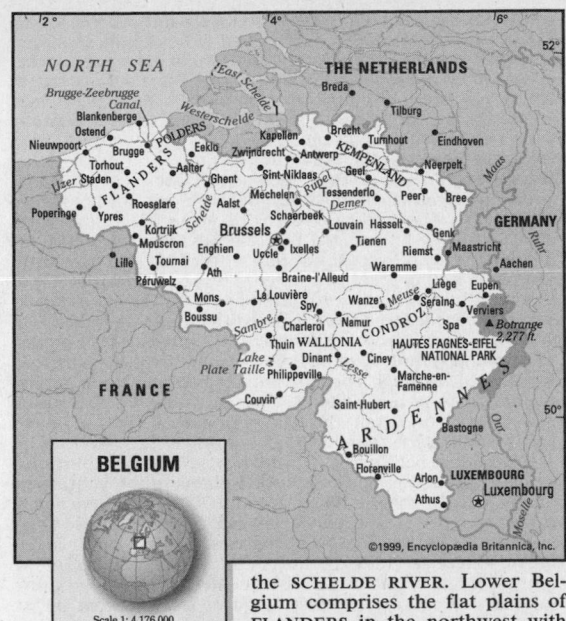

BELGIUM

Scale 1: 4,176,000

the SCHELDE RIVER. Lower Belgium comprises the flat plains of FLANDERS in the northwest with their many canals. Maritime Flanders borders the North Sea and is agriculturally prosperous; the chief North Sea port is Oostende, but ANTWERP, near the mouth of the Schelde, has much greater trade. Belgium has minimal natural resources, so the manufacture of goods from imported raw materials plays a major role in the economy, and the country is highly industrialized. It is a monarchy with a parliament composed of two legislative houses; the chief of state is the monarch, and the head of government is the prime minister. Inhabited in ancient times by the Belgae, a Celtic people, the area was conquered by Julius CAESAR in 57 B.C.; under Caesar AUGUSTUS it became the Roman province of Belgica. Conquered by the Franks, it later broke up into semi-independent territories, including BRABANT and LUXEMBOURG. By the late 15th cent. the territories of the Netherlands, of which the future Belgium was a part, gradually united and passed to the HABSBURGS. In the 16th cent. it was a center for European commerce. The basis of modern Belgium was laid in the S Catholic provinces that split from the N provinces after the Union of Utrecht in 1579. Overrun by the French and incorporated into France in 1801, Belgium was reunited to Holland and with it became the independent kingdom of the Netherlands in 1815. After the revolt of its citizens in 1830, it became the independent kingdom of Belgium. Under LEOPOLD II, it acquired vast lands in Africa. Overrun by the Germans in World Wars I and II, it was the scene of the Battle of the BULGE. Internal discord led to legislation in the 1970s and 1980s that created three nearly autonomous regions in accordance with language distribution: Flemish Flanders, French Wallonia, and bilingual Brussels. In 1993 it became a federation composed of the three regions.

Belgrade *Serbian* **Beograd** \bā-'ò-ˌgräd\ City (pop., 2000: 1,194,000), capital of Yugoslavia. Lying at the juncture of the DANUBE and Sava rivers, it is one of the Balkans' most important commercial centers. Inhabited by Celts in the 4th cent. B.C., it was later taken by the Romans and then destroyed by the Avars. A frontier town of Byzantium, in the 13th cent. it came under the rule of SERBIA. The Ottoman Turks besieged the city in the 15th cent., and SULEYMAN I's forces took it in 1521; it was held by the Turks into the 19th cent. In 1882 it became the capital of Serbia and, after World War I, of the new Kingdom of Serbs, Croats, and Slovenes (renamed Yugoslavia in 1929). It suffered severely under Nazi occupation 1941–44. It was damaged by NATO bombers in the KOSOVO CONFLICT (1999).

Belisarius (c.505–565) Byzantine general. Appointed (c.525) by Emperor JUSTINIAN I to command in the E armies, he defeated the Persians in the Battle of Dara (530). He led expeditions to overthrow the Vandals in N. Africa (533) and regain Sicily and S Italy from the Ostrogoths (535–537), defending Rome 537–538. He was offered a kingship by the Goths, which caused Justinian to recall him in disfavor. Sent again to Rome (544–548) but with inadequate forces, he was replaced by NARSES. Still loyal to Justinian, he was recalled in 559 to repel Hun invaders.

Belize \bə-'lēz\ *Spanish* **Belice** \bā-'lē-sä\ *formerly (1840–1973)* **British Honduras** Country, Central America. It is bounded by Mexico, the Caribbean Sea, and Guatemala. Area: 8,867 sq mi (22,966 sq km). Population (2000): 253,000. Capital: BELMOPAN. Much of the population is racially mixed: Creoles of mixed African and European ancestry, MAYA Indians, Mayan-European mestizos, and Black Caribs. Languages: English (official), Creole, Spanish. Religions: Roman Catholicism, Anglicanism, Pentecostalism, Methodism. Currency: Belize dollar. Belize is a land of mountains, swamps, and tropical jungle. The N half consists of swampy lowlands drained by the Belize and Hondo rivers; the latter forms the boundary with Mexico. The S half is more mountainous and contains the country's highest peak, Victoria (3,681 ft, or 1,122 m). Off the coast lies the world's second-largest barrier reef. Belize is relatively prosperous and has a developing free-market economy with some government participation. It is a constitutional monarchy with two legislative houses; its head of state is the British monarch represented by the governor-general, and the head of government is the prime minister. The area was inhabited by the Maya around 300 B.C.–A.D. 900; the ruins of their ceremonial centers, including Caracol and Xunantunich, can still be seen. The Spanish claimed sovereignty from the 16th

BELIZE

Scale 1: 5,244,000

cent. but never tried to settle Belize, though they regarded as interlopers the British who did. British logwood cutters arrived in the mid-17th cent.; Spanish opposition was finally overcome in 1798. When settlers began to penetrate the interior they met with Indian resistance. In 1862 British Honduras became a crown colony, but an unfulfilled provision of a 1859 British–Guatemalan treaty led Guatemala to claim the territory. The situation had not been resolved when Belize was granted its independence in 1981. A British force, stationed there to ensure the new nation's security, was withdrawn after Guatemala officially recognized the territory's independence in 1991.

Belize City City (pop., 1998: 55,000), Belize. The chief seaport and former capital of Belize, it lies at the mouth of the Belize River, which was a heavily populated trade artery of the MAYA empire. The British settled the area in the 17th cent. The city, only slightly above sea level, has been ravaged by hurricanes, so the capital was moved to BELMOPAN in 1970.

bell Hollow vessel, usually of metal, that produces a ringing sound when struck by an interior clapper or a mallet. In the West, open bells have acquired a standard "tulip" shape; though their vibrational patterns are basically nonharmonic, they can be tuned so that the lower OVERTONES produce a recognizable chord. Bells were first cast, or founded, in the Bronze Age. Bells are particularly important in religious ritual in E. and S. Asia. In Christianity, especially Russian Orthodoxy, bells have also been used ritually. They have tolled the hours from monastery and church steeples, originally to govern monastic routine and later also to fill a similar role for the secular world.

Bell, Alexander Graham (1847–1922) Scottish-U.S. audiologist and inventor. Born in Edinburgh, he moved to the U.S. in 1871 to teach, opening his own school in Boston for training teachers of the deaf (1872). In 1875 he became the first person to transmit intelligible words through electric wire ("Watson, come here, I want you," spoken to his assistant). He patented the telephone the next year, and in 1877 he cofounded Bell Telephone Co. With the proceeds from France's Volta Prize, he founded Volta Laboratory in Washington, D.C., in 1880. His experiments there led to the invention of the audiometer (which measured acuteness of hearing), the Graphophone (an early practical sound recorder),

Alexander Graham Bell

and working wax recording media for the Graphophone. He was chiefly responsible for founding the journal *Science*, and founded the American Assn. to Promote Teaching of Speech to the Deaf (1890).

Bell, (Arthur) Clive (Howard) (1881–1964) British art critic. In 1907 he married Vanessa Stephen, sister of Virginia WOOLF; with Virginia's husband, Leonard Woolf, they formed the core of the BLOOMSBURY GROUP. In *Art* (1914) and *Since Cézanne* (1922), he promoted his theory of "significant form" (the quality that distinguishes works of art from all other objects). His assertion that art appreciation involves an emotional response to purely formal qualities, independent of subject matter, was influential for several decades.

Bella, Ahmed Ben See Ahmed BEN BELLA

belladonna Tall, bushy, herbaceous plant, the deadly nightshade (*Atropa belladonna*) of the NIGHTSHADE FAMILY; also, the crude drug consisting of its dried leaves or roots. The plant is native to Eurasia. It has dull green leaves, violet or greenish flowers, shiny black berries and a large tapering root. Belladonna is highly poisonous and is cultivated for medicinal substances (ALKALOIDS) that are used in sedatives, stimulants, and antispasmodics. Because of toxicity and undesirable side effects, these substances are being replaced by synthetic drugs.

Bellamy \'bel-ə-mē\, **Edward** (1850–1898) U.S. writer. A native of Chicopee Falls, Mass., Bellamy became aware of urban poverty at 18 while studying in Germany. He is known chiefly for his utopian novel *Looking Backward* (1888), which describes the U.S. in the year 2000 as an ideal socialist state featuring cooperation, brotherhood, and industry geared to human need. It sold more than a million copies; a sequel, *Equality* (1897), was less successful.

Bell Burnell, Jocelyn *orig* Susan Jocelyn Bell (b.1943) English astronomer. As a research assistant at Cambridge Univ., she helped construct a large radio telescope and discovered pulsating radio signals that were dubbed PULSARS. These were subsequently determined to be rapidly spinning NEUTRON STARS, providing the first direct evidence for the existence of the latter. The 1974 Nobel Prize was awarded for the discovery of pulsars to Antony Hewish (b.1924), her adviser, and Martin Ryle (1918–1984), sparking a controversy over Bell Burnell's omission.

bell curve See NORMAL DISTRIBUTION

Bellerophon \bə-'ler-ə-fən\ Legendary Greek hero. As a youth in Corinth he tamed and rode the winged horse PEGASUS. The wife of King Proteus of Argos fell in love with him, and when he rejected her, she falsely accused him of attempted rape. Proteus sent him to the king of Lycia with a message asking that he be killed. The king instead ordered him to kill the monster CHIMERA, and with the aid of Pegasus he succeeded and later married the king's daughter.

bellflower Any of about 300 herbaceous plants of the genus *Campanula* (family Campanulaceae) that bear bell-shaped, usually blue flowers. They are native mainly to N temperate regions in both hemispheres. Species native to N Eurasia and E N. America but also grown in gardens are the bluebell (*C. rotundifolia*) and the tall bellflower (*C. americana*). The creeping bellflower (*C. rapunculoides*) is a notorious garden weed. Among the few food plants in the bellflower family, which includes 40 genera and 700 species, are some robust members—especially *Canarina, Clermontia,* and *Centropogon*—that produce edible berries.

Bellini, Vincenzo (1801–1835) Italian composer. Born into a musical family in Sicily, he was educated at the Naples Conservatory. He wrote his first opera at 24, and went on to complete nine more before his death at 33. The most famous are *Il pirata* (1827), *I Capuleti e i Montecchi* (1830), *La sonnambula* (1831), *Norma* (1831), and *I Puritani* (1835). His works, which rely strongly on beautiful vocal melody ("bel canto"), rivaled those of his contemporaries Gioacchino ROSSINI and Gaetano DONIZETTI in popularity.

Bellini family \bāl-'lē-nē\ Family of Italian artists. Jacopo Bellini (c.1400–1470/71) was trained under GENTILE DA FABRIANO, and by about 1440 he had a thriving studio in Venice. More important than his paintings are his two surviving sketchbooks, which total nearly 300 drawings. His son Gentile (c.1429–1507) took over the studio; his most important extant works, *Procession of the Relic of the True Cross* (1496) and *Miracle at the Bridge of San Lorenzo* (1500), depict scenes of contemporary Venetian life. Gentile's brother Giovanni (called Giambellino, c.1430–1516), the greatest artist of the family, transformed Venice into a Renaissance center rivaling Florence and Rome. An early master of oil painting, he was primarily a religious painter but also excelled at portraits, of which *Doge Leonardo Loredan* (c.1501) is his best known. TITIAN and GIORGIONE were probably trained in his workshop. See also VENETIAN SCHOOL.

Bell Laboratories U.S. research and development company, founded 1925. Formerly part of AT&T, it now belongs to Lucent Technologies, Inc., which spun off from AT&T in 1996. Bell Labs has produced thousands of inventions, including the first synchronous-sound MOTION-PICTURE system, the electrical-relay DIGITAL COMPUTER, the TRANSISTOR, the LASER, the SOLAR CELL, UNIX, and the C and C++ programming languages. Several Bell researchers have won Nobel Prizes.

Belloc \'bel-,äk\, **(Joseph–Pierre) Hilaire** (1870–1953) French-British writer. A versatile writer, he is best remembered for his light verse for children and his graceful essays. His works include *The Bad Child's Book of Beasts* (1896), *The Modern Traveller* (1898), *Cautionary Tales* (1907), and several historical works, including a four-volume *History of England* (1925–31).

Bellotto \bel-'lȯt-tō\, **Bernardo** *known as* **Canaletto** (1721–1780) Italian painter of topographical views, known as *vedute* ("view paintings"). He was the nephew of CANALETTO, from whom he took his byname. In 1747 he left Italy to work at various European courts, most notably at Dresden (1747–66) and Warsaw (1767–80). His detailed views of the Polish capital were used as guides to reconstruct the historic sections of the city after their destruction in World War II. His style is distinguishable from his uncle's by its

Dutch characteristics (e.g., cast shadows, massed clouds, somber tone and color).

Bellow, Saul (b.1915) U.S. (Canadian-born) novelist. He was born near Montreal to an immigrant Russian-Jewish family; they moved to Chicago when he was 9. His novels make him representative of the Jewish-American writers whose works became central to American literature after World War II. Dealing with the modern urban dweller, disaffected by society but not destroyed in spirit, they combine cultural sophistication and street wisdom. They include *The Adventures of Augie March* (1953; National Book Award), *Seize the Day* (1956), *Henderson the Rain King* (1959), *Herzog* (1964, National Book Award), *Mr. Sammler's Planet* (1970, National Book Award), and *Humboldt's Gift* (1975, Pulitzer Prize). He won the Nobel Prize in 1976.

bellows Mechanical contrivance for creating a jet of air, consisting usually of a hinged box with flexible sides, which expands to draw in air through an inward-opening valve and contracts to expel the air through a nozzle. Invented in medieval Europe, the bellows was commonly used to speed combustion, as in a blacksmith's or ironworker's FORGE, or to operate reed or pipe ORGANS.

Bellows, George Wesley (1882–1925) U.S. painter and lithographer. Born in Columbus, Ohio, he studied with Robert HENRI and became associated with the ASH CAN SCHOOL. Best known for his boxing scenes, he achieved notoriety with his painting *Stag at Sharkey's* (1909). He was one of the organizers of the ARMORY SHOW. From 1916 he produced a series of some 200 lithographs, including the well-known *Dempsey and Firpo* (1924).

Bell's palsy See PARALYSIS

Belmondo \bel-môⁿ-'dō\, **Jean-Paul** (b.1933) French film actor. He appeared in minor film roles before achieving international fame in J.-L. GODARD's *Breathless* (1960). Though not conventionally handsome, he became the leading antihero of NEW WAVE films, acting in 25 films by 1963, then went on to appear in such international films as *The Thief of Paris* (1967), *Borsalino* (1970), and *Stavisky* (1974).

Belmont family U.S. family prominent in banking and finance, politics, and patronage of the arts. Its founder in the U.S. was the Prussian-born August Belmont (1816–1890), who entered the ROTHSCHILDS' Frankfurt banking house at age 14. In 1837 he moved to New York, where he acted as the Rothschilds' agent and laid the foundation for his own banking house, which became one of the largest in the country. Strongly opposed to slavery, he influenced financiers in England and France in favor of the Union during the Civil War. He introduced Thoroughbred horse racing into the U.S. (see BELMONT STAKES). His son August Belmont, Jr. (1853–1924), took over the banking house and financed the building of New York's subway, while his wife supported the METROPOLITAN OPERA.

Belmont Stakes Oldest of the three U.S. THOROUGHBRED races that constitute the TRIPLE CROWN. It originated in 1867 and is named after August Belmont (see BELMONT FAMILY). The stakes is held in early June at Belmont Park, near Garden City, Long Island; the course is 1.5 mi (2,400 m).

Belmopan \ˌbel-mō-'pän\ City (pop., 1998: 7,000), capital of Belize. It lies in the Belize River valley. After a hurricane did extensive damage to the low-lying former capital, BELIZE CITY, a new site was chosen 50 mi (80 km) inland. Construction began in 1966; Belmopan became the capital in 1970.

Belo Horizonte \'bā-lō-ˌór-ē-'zōn-tē\ City (pop., 1996, city: 2,080,000; metro. area: 3,803,000), E Brazil. Capital of Minas Gerais state, it lies on the W slope of the Serra do Espinhaço, at an elevation of 2,811 ft (857 m). Brazil's first planned city (founded 1897), it follows the radiating pattern of WASHINGTON, D.C., and LA PLATA, Argentina. It is a commercial and industrial center, the hub of a large agricultural region, and home to two universities.

Belorussia See BELARUS

Belsen See BERGEN-BELSEN

Belshazzar \bel-'sha-zər\ (d.c.539 B.C.) Coregent of BABYLON. The Book of DANIEL calls him the son of Nebuchadnezzar, but Babylonian inscriptions suggest that he was the son of King Nabonidus. In the biblical story Belshazzar, as

coregent, holds a last great feast at which he sees a hand writing on a wall the words "mene, mene, tekel, upharsin," which Daniel interprets as a judgment from God foretelling the fall of Babylon. Belshazzar died after Babylon fell to the Persians in 539 B.C.

beluga \bə-'lü-gə\ *or* **hausen** \'haù-zᵊn\ Large species of STURGEON (*Huso huso*, or *Acipenser huso*) that inhabits the Caspian and Black seas and the Sea of Azov. It reaches a length of 25 ft (7.5 m) and a weight of 2,900 lbs (1,300 kg), but its flesh and CAVIAR are less valuable than those of smaller species.

beluga *or* **white whale** Species (*Delphinapterus leucas*) of WHALE found in the Arctic Ocean and adjacent seas, in both deep offshore and coastal waters. A toothed whale with a rounded forehead and no dorsal fin, the beluga is about 13 ft (4 m) long. Born dark blue-gray or blackish, it fades to white or cream at 4–5 years of age. It feeds on fish, cephalopods, and crustaceans and usually lives in groups of five to 10. It has been hunted commercially for its oil, hide, and flesh.

belvedere Roofed architectural structure, freestanding or attached, and open on one or more sides, built in an elevated position to provide a view and capture daylight and fresh air. Used in Italy since the Renaissance, it often assumes the form of a LOGGIA. The term is often used for a GAZEBO on top of a building, especially the glazed viewing room of a Victorian dwelling.

Ben Ali \ben-'ä-lē\, **Zine al-Abidine** (b.1936) President of Tunisia (from 1987). Trained as a soldier, he headed the defense ministry's military intelligence for 10 years (1964–74) before serving as ambassador to Poland and then returning home to hold several domestic government posts, eventually serving as both prime minister and interior minister. In 1987 he replaced Pres. Habib BOURGUIBA, who had been declared medically unfit. He has since been reelected three times.

Benares See VARANASI

Ben Bella, Ahmed (b.1918?) First elected president of Algeria. After a French education, he entered the army, and was decorated by the French during World War II. After the war he took up arms to fight French rule. In 1954 he helped found the National Liberation Front (FLN) and became its political leader. He was imprisoned 1956–62 while the FLN fought to expel the French. After his release, he was elected president (1963). He was deposed in a coup in 1965 and imprisoned until 1980. He spent ten years in exile, returning to Algeria in 1990. See also Houari BOUMÉDIENNE.

Bench, Johnny (Lee) (b.1947) U.S. baseball player. Born in Oklahoma City, he joined the Cincinnati Reds in 1967. In 17 seasons as catcher (1967–83), he helped lead the team to four National League pennants and two World Series victories. He led the league in runs batted in three times (1970, 1972, 1974) and twice in home runs (1970, 1972). He is regarded as one of the greatest defensive catchers ever to play the game.

Benchley, Robert (Charles) (1889–1945) U.S. humorist. Born in Worcester, Mass., he joined the staff of *Life* magazine in 1920. A regular member of the Algonquin Round Table, he was drama critic for the *New Yorker* 1929–40. He acted in 46 short films, including *How to Sleep* (1934, Academy Award). His writing was warmly humorous, his satire sharp but not cruel.

bends See DECOMPRESSION SICKNESS

Benedict, Ruth *orig.* Ruth Fulton (1887–1948) U.S. anthropologist. Born in New York City, she received her PhD under Franz BOAS at Columbia Univ. in 1923 and taught at Columbia from 1930 until her death. In *Patterns of Culture* (1934), her most famous work, she emphasized how small a part of the range of possible human behavior is elaborated or emphasized in any one society, and described how these forms of behavior are integrated into patterns or configurations. In *The Chrysanthemum and the Sword* (1946), she applied her methods to Japanese culture. Her theories had a profound influence on CULTURAL ANTHROPOLOGY.

Benedictine Member of the Order of St. Benedict, the confederated autonomous congregations of monks and lay brothers who follow the Benedictine Rule, created by St. BENEDICT OF NURSIA in the 6th cent. The Rule spread

B

slowly in Italy and Gaul. By the 9th cent. it was nearly universal in N and W Europe, where Benedictine monasteries became repositories of learning, literature, and wealth. The REFORMATION virtually eliminated Benedictines from N Europe, and they declined elsewhere. In the 19th cent. a revival strengthened the order in Europe, especially in France and Germany, and led to the establishment of new congregations worldwide.

Benedict of Nursia, St. (c.A.D. 480–547?) Father of Western MONASTICISM. Born into a prominent family at Nursia in central Italy, he rejected the immoral and profligate life of the rich and became a hermit outside Rome, where he attracted disciples. At his monastery at MONTE CASSINO he formulated the BENEDICTINE Rule, which became standard in monasteries throughout Europe. The Rule includes a vow of obedience, lifelong residence at one monastery, a ban on personal property, and a precisely ordered day consisting of liturgy and prayer, manual work, and spiritual reading.

Benedict XII *orig.* Jacques Fournier (d.1342) Pope (1334–42). A French cardinal and theologian, he became the third pontiff to reign at Avignon (see AVIGNON PAPACY). He devoted himself to the reform of the church and its religious orders; he also tried unsuccessfully to prevent the outbreak of the HUNDRED YEARS' WAR. His bull *Benedictus Deus* (1336) set forth the doctrine of the Beatific Vision as a vision of God granted to the souls of the just immediately after death.

Benedict XIII *orig.* Pedro de Luna (1328?–1423) ANTIPOPE (1394–1423). Named a cardinal in 1375, when the Western SCHISM began in 1378 he supported the antipope Clement VII. Elected pope at Avignon (see AVIGNON PAPACY), he refused French pressure to abdicate and was besieged in the papal palace (1398). Though forced to flee in 1403, he later won back the obedience of France. He refused to yield when deposed by the councils of Pisa (1409) and Constance (1417).

Benedict XIV *orig.* Prospero Lambertini (1675–1758) Pope (1740–58). Nobly born, he received a doctorate in theology and law. As pope he promoted scientific learning; in the Papal States he reduced taxation, encouraged agriculture, and supported free trade. He maintained conciliatory relations with neighboring kingdoms. A lifelong active scholar, he founded several learned societies and laid the groundwork for the Vatican Museum.

benefice \'be-nə-fəs\ System of land tenure used by the Franks in the 8th–10th cent. A Frankish lord leased an estate to a freeman in *beneficium* (Latin: "for the benefit (of the tenant)"), normally until the death of the lord or tenant, though tenants often turned benefices into hereditary holdings. By the 12th cent. benefice referred instead to a church office that carried with it the right of receiving income. A lord or bishop chose a priest, who was granted the benefice in return for the performance of spiritual duties.

beneficiary \ˌbe-nə-'fi-shē-ˌer-ē, ˌbe-nə-'fi-shə-rē\ Person or entity (e.g., a charity or estate) that receives a benefit from something (e.g., a TRUST, life-insurance policy, or CONTRACT). A primary beneficiary receives proceeds from a trust or insurance policy before any other. A contingent beneficiary receives proceeds upon the occurrence of a specified event, such as the death of the primary beneficiary. A direct beneficiary is a third party whom contracting individuals intend to benefit from a contract; an incidental beneficiary benefits without that being the contracting individuals' intention.

Bene-Israel \'ben-ē-ˌiz-rà-'el\ (Hebrew: "Sons of Israel") Jews of India who for centuries lived in Bombay and adjacent regions. Legends state that they arrived as the result of a shipwreck or that they are descended from the 10 lost tribes of ISRAEL. When first discovered by Jews from other lands in the 18th cent., they still practiced circumcision and observed the Sabbath. They speak Marathi and resemble Indians in appearance. Most moved to Israel after 1948 and were accepted as full-fledged Jews in 1964.

Benes \'be-ˌnesh\, **Edvard** (1884–1948) Czechoslovakian statesman. A founder of modern Czechoslovakia, he served as its first foreign minister (1918–35) and president (1935–38). Forced to capitulate to Adolf HITLER's demands over the SUDETENLAND, he resigned. He headed the Czech

government-in-exile in England (1940–45), then reestablished a government in Prague in 1945. Recognizing the need to cooperate with the Soviet Union, he nevertheless refused to sign a new communist constitution and resigned in 1948.

Benét \bə-'nā\, **Stephen Vincent** (1898–1943) U.S. writer. Born in Bethlehem, Pa., he is best known for *John Brown's Body* (1928, Pulitzer Prize), a long narrative poem on the Civil War. *A Book of Americans* (1933), poems written with his wife, brought historical figures to life for schoolchildren. His story "The Devil and Daniel Webster" (1937) was the basis for a play, an opera, and a film.

benevolent despotism See ENLIGHTENED DESPOTISM

Bengal \ben-'gȯl\ Former province, NE British India. It generally corresponds to the area inhabited by speakers of the BENGALI LANGUAGE. In the 8th–12th cent. it was under a Buddhist dynasty, and from 1576 it belonged to the Mughal empire. In the 18th cent. it was dominated by nawabs; they came into conflict with the British, who had established themselves at CALCUTTA in 1690. By 1764 the British had taken possession, and from then on Bengal was the base for British expansion in India. With the end of British rule in 1947, the area was divided. W. Bengal, Bihar, and Orissa became part of India. E. Bengal went to Pakistan; in 1971 it became Bangladesh.

Bengal, Bay of Part of the INDIAN OCEAN. Occupying about 839,000 sq mi (2,172,000 sq km), it is bordered by Sri Lanka, India, Bangladesh, and Myanmar. It is about 1,000 mi (1,600 km) wide, with an average depth of more than 8,500 ft (2,600 m). Many large rivers, including the Godavari, Krishna, Kaveri, Ganges, and Brahmaputra, flow into it. It has long been crossed by Indian and Malaysian traders; Chinese maritime trading dates from the 12th cent. Vasco da GAMA led the first European voyage into the bay in 1498.

Bengali language \ben-'gä-lē\ INDO-ARYAN LANGUAGE spoken principally in Bangladesh and the Indian state of W. Bengal. Bengali has more speakers—close to 190 million—than all but a handful of other languages of the world. Like other Modern Indo-Aryan languages, Bengali has simplified the complex inflectional system of Old Indo-Aryan (see SANSKRIT LANGUAGE). Bengali was the first of the Indian languages to adopt Western secular literary styles, such as fiction and drama.

Benghazi \ben-'gä-zē\ *or* **Banghazi** \bän-'gä-zē\ Coastal city (metro. area pop., 1995: 804,000), NE Libya. It is Libya's second-largest city and was once its capital. Founded by Greeks as Hesperides, it received from PTOLEMY III the additional name Berenice in honor of his wife. It was extensively developed during the Italian occupation of Libya (1912–42). In World War II it suffered considerable damage before being captured by the British in 1942. It is now an administrative and commercial center, and the site of one of the world's largest desalinization plants.

Ben-Gurion \ben-'gúr-ē-ən\, **David** *orig.* David Gruen (1886–1973) First prime minister of Israel. Born in Poland, he emigrated to Ottoman-ruled Palestine in 1906, hoping to fulfill the Zionist aspiration of rebuilding the Jewish state. Expelled at the outbreak of World War I, he traveled to New York, where he married. Following the BALFOUR DECLARATION, he joined the British army's Jewish Legion and returned to the Middle East. In the 1920s and '30s he led several political organizations, including the Jewish Agency, world ZIONISM's highest directing body. On the establishment of the state of Israel, he became prime minister and minister of defense. He succeeded in fusing the underground armies that had fought the British into a national army, which he used successfully against Arab attacks. Unpopular with Britain and the U.S., he found an ally in France during the ALGERIAN WAR and the SUEZ CRISIS. He resigned in 1963. See also ARAB–ISRAELI WARS.

Benigni \bā-'nēn-yē\, **Roberto** (b.1952) Italian film comedian and director. He became popular on Italian television with his wildly mischievous approach to such sensitive topics as God, politics, and sex. He debuted as a film actor in 1977 and as director in 1983. Films such as *Down by Law* (1986) and *Il mostro* (1994) were popular across Europe and in the U.S.; he is best known for his performance in *Life Is Beautiful* (1998, Academy Award).

Benin \bə-ˈnēn\ *officially* **Republic of Benin** *formerly* **Da-homey** Country, W Africa. Area: 43,483 sq mi (112,621 sq km). Population (2000): 6,396,000. Capital: PORTO-NOVO (official), COTONOU (de facto). The FON people and related groups constitute three-fifths of the population; minorities

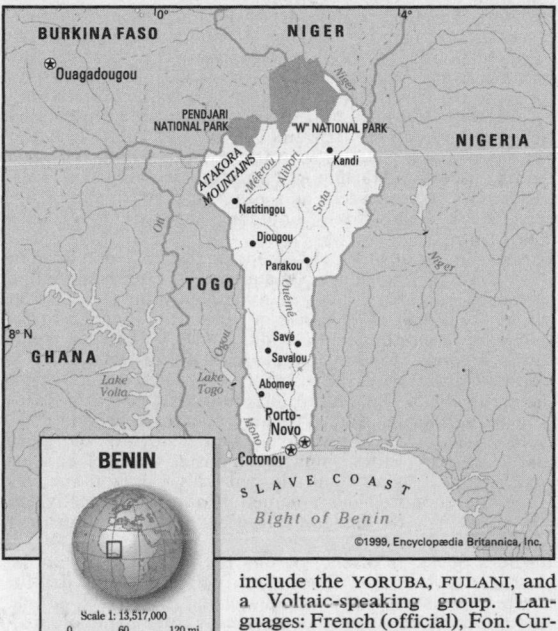

BURKINA FASO
NIGER
Ouagadougou
PENDJARI NATIONAL PARK
"W" NATIONAL PARK
NIGERIA
Kandi
ATAKORA MOUNTAINS
Natitingou
Djougou
Parakou
TOGO
Savé
Savalou
GHANA
Abomey
Porto-Novo
Cotonou
SLAVE COAST
Bight of Benin
©1999, Encyclopædia Britannica, Inc.

BENIN

Scale 1: 13,517,000
0   60   120 mi
0   80   160 km

include the YORUBA, FULANI, and a Voltaic-speaking group. Languages: French (official), Fon. Currency: CFA franc. Religion: traditional religions (two-thirds of the population), Islam and Christianity (one-third). Extending about 420 mi (675 km) inland from the Gulf of GUINEA, the republic consists of a hilly region in the northwest, where the maximum elevation is 2,150 ft (650 km). There are plains in the east and north, and a marshy region in the south, where the coastline extends about 75 mi (120 km). Benin's longest river, the Ouémé, flows into the Porto-Novo Lagoon and is navigable for 125 mi (200 km) of its 280 mi (450 km) length. Benin has a developing, centrally planned economy based largely on agriculture, and is developing its offshore oil field. It is a republic with one legislative house; the head of state and government is the president, assisted by the prime minister. In S Benin, the Dahomey, or Fon, founded the Abomey kingdom in 1625. In the 18th cent. the kingdom expanded to include Allada and Ouidah, where French forts had been established in the 17th cent. In 1857 the French reestablished themselves in the area, and eventually fighting ensued. In 1894 Dahomey became a French protectorate; it was incorporated into the federation of FRENCH W. AFRICA in 1904. It achieved independence in 1960. Dahomey was renaed Benin in 1975. Its chronically weak economy has produced tension between laborers and the government.

Benin, Bight of Bay, N section of Gulf of GUINEA. It extends along the W. African coast about 400 mi (640 km) from Cape St. Paul, Ghana, past Togo and Benin to an outlet of the NIGER RIVER in Nigeria. Major ports include LOMÉ, COTONOU, and LAGOS. It was the scene of extensive slave trading during the 16th–19th cent., and the region of coastal lagoons west of the Niger delta became known as the Slave Coast.

Benin, kingdom of Historic kingdom (13th–19th cent.) of the W African forest region, centered on present-day Benin City in S Nigeria. Under Ewuare the Great in the mid-15th cent., the kingdom traded in ivory, palm oil, pepper, and slaves with the Portuguese and Dutch. From the 18th cent. it was weakened by succession struggles and the end of the slave trade. When the British burned Benin City in 1897, the kingdom was incorporated into British Nigeria.

Benjamin, Judah P(hilip) (1811–1884) British-U.S. politician. Born in St. Croix, he moved with his parents to S. Carolina. From 1832 he built a successful law practice in New Orleans. He was the first Jew elected to the U.S. Senate (1853–61), and was noted for his proslavery speeches. After the South seceded, Jefferson DAVIS appointed him attorney general (1861), secretary of war (1861–62), and secretary of state (1862–65). His unpopular proposal to arm slaves for the Confederate army forced him to flee to England in 1865.

Benjamin \ˈben-yä-ˌmēn, *Engl* ˈben-jə-mən\, **Walter** (1892–1940) German literary critic. Benjamin worked as a critic and translator from 1920 until 1933, when he fled to France. The Nazi takeover of France led him to flee again in 1940; he committed suicide at the Spanish border when his emigration was delayed. Posthumous publications have revealed him to be the leading German literary critic of the early 20th cent., as well as one of the first serious writers about film and photography. His originality is evident in the essays collected in *Illuminations* (1961) and *Reflections* (1979). His writings on art reflect his reading of Karl MARX and his friendships with Bertolt BRECHT and Theodor ADORNO.

Bennett, (Enoch) Arnold (1867–1931) British novelist, playwright, critic, and essayist. He is best known for his highly detailed novels of the "Five Towns"—the Potteries in his native Staffordshire—the setting of *Anna of the Five Towns* (1902), *The Old Wives' Tale* (1908), and the three novels that make up *The Clayhanger Family* (1925). He was also a well-known critic.

Bennett, James Gordon (1795–1872) Scottish-U.S. editor. He came to the U.S. in 1819 and worked on various newspapers before founding the *New York Herald* (1835). His very successful paper introduced many modern methods of news reporting; it published the first Wall Street financial article (1835), sent the first correspondents in Europe (1838), maintained 63 war correspondents during the Civil War, was a leader in using illustrations, and introduced a society department.

Bennett, Michael *orig.* Michael Bennett Difiglia (1943–1987) U.S. dancer, choreographer, and stage musical director. Born in Buffalo, N.Y., he began dancing at 3. He earned fame as choreographer-director of such Broadway musicals as *Promises, Promises* (1968), *Company* (1970), *Follies* (1971), and *Dreamgirls* (1981). His most remarkable musical was *A Chorus Line* (1975, Pulitzer Prize), which he conceived, directed, and choreographed. Bennett personally received eight Tony awards during his career. His early death resulted from AIDS.

Bennett, Richard B(edford) *later* Viscount Bennett (of Mickleham and of Calgary and Hopewell) (1870–1947) Canadian prime minister (1930–35). Born in Hopewell, New Brunswick, he entered the Canadian House of Commons in 1911. He became head of the Conservative Party in 1927 and, having promised relief from the Great Depression, prime minister in 1930. He underestimated the severity of the crisis, and his measures were superficial. He was defeated by the Liberals and Mackenzie KING. In 1939 he retired to England.

Bennett, Tony *orig.* Anthony (Dominick) Benedetto (b.1926) U.S. popular singer. The son of a grocer in Queens, N.Y., his first job was as a singing waiter. In 1949 he joined Pearl Bailey's nightclub revue, and in 1950 Bob HOPE suggested his new name. He had many hits in the 1950s, but his signature song became "I Left My Heart in San Francisco." His style became increasingly jazz-oriented over the years, and in the mid-1990s an appearance on MTV heralded a comeback.

Ben Nevis Highest mountain, British Isles. It is located in the Scottish Highlands; its summit, which reaches 4,406 ft (1,343 m), is a plateau of about 100 acres (40 hectares). Snow lies in some parts all year. It consists of volcanic rocks surmounting ancient schists.

Bennington College Private liberal-arts college in Bennington, Vt. It was founded in 1932 as a women's college; men were first admitted in the late 1960s. It is known for its nontraditional structures and integration of visual and performing arts. It was plagued with financial and tenure problems from the mid-1990s. Enrollment is about 600.

B

Benny, Jack *orig.* Benjamin Kubelsky (1894–1974) U.S. comedian. Born in Chicago, he played the violin in vaudeville from 1912, and later returned as a comedian. He made his film debut in 1927. His weekly *Jack Benny Program* on radio (1932–55) and television (1950–65) won loyal audiences, and he became famous for a unique comic style characterized by subtle verbal inflection, meaningful pauses, serio-comic violin playing, and the stage image of a vain, stingy man.

Bénoué River See BENUE RIVER

bent grass Any of the annual or perennial GRASSES that make up the widely distributed genus *Agrostis,* in the family Gramineae (Poaceae). At least 40 species are found in the U.S.; some are weeds, others forage and TURF plants. They have slender stems and flat blades. Redtop (*A. gigantea*) is a HAY and pasture grass. Creeping bent (*A. stolonifera* variety *palustris*) and colonial bent (*A. tenuis*) are popular lawn grasses also used on golf courses and bowling greens.

Bentham \'ben-thəm\, **Jeremy** (1748–1832) British social and political theorist. Bentham graduated from Oxford at 15. He was an atheist and an exponent of the new laissez-faire economics of Adam SMITH and David RICARDO. The first great champion of UTILITARIANISM, he wrote that government should promote "the greatest happiness." He inspired much reform legislation, especially prison reform, and was a vocal advocate of democracy. Believing society could advance by calculation of pleasure and pain, he tried to compare the relative gratifications of health, wealth, power, friendship, and benevolence, as well as those of "irascible appetite" and "antipathy." He helped found the radical *Westminster Review* (1823). He willed that his clothed skeleton be exhibited permanently at University College London.

Bentley, Richard (1662–1742) British clergyman and classical scholar. He became keeper of the Royal Library in 1694, and master of Trinity College, Cambridge, in 1700. His *Epistola ad Joannem Millium* (1691) displayed his skill in editing ancient metrical texts. In *Dissertation on the Epistles of Phalaris* (1699), he proved the epistles to be fakes. He also published critical texts of classical authors, including HORACE, and made linguistic contributions to the study of ancient Greek.

Benton, Thomas Hart (1782–1858) U.S. politician. Born near Hillsborough, N.C., he moved to St. Louis in 1815 and edited the *St. Louis Enquirer*. Elected to the U.S. Senate in 1820, he became a crusader for the distribution of public lands to settlers, and was soon the Democratic Party's chief spokesman in the Senate. His opposition to the extension of slavery into the West cost him his Senate seat in 1851. His grandnephew was the artist T. H. BENTON.

Benton, Thomas Hart (1889–1975) U.S. painter. Born in Neosho, Mo., he studied in Chicago and Paris, where he came into contact with Synchromism and Cubism. In 1912 he returned to New York, but, failing in his attempts at modernism, he traveled through the rural heartland, sketching people and places. In the 1930s he painted several notable murals, often transposing biblical and classical stories to rural American settings, as in *Susanna and the Elders* (1938). His style, which quickly became influential, is characterized by undulating forms, cartoonlike figures, and brilliant color. He taught at the Art Students League in New York, where Jackson POLLOCK was his best-known student.

Benue-Congo languages \'bā-nwä\ Largest branch of the NIGER-CONGO superfamily of languages. Its major divisions are Defoid, including Yoruba and Itsekiri, with more than 23 million speakers; Edoid, including Edo (see kingdom of BENIN); Nupoid, including Nupe, Ebira, and Gbari; Idomoid, including Idoma; Igboid, including the many dialects of the IGBO people; Cross River, a group of more than 55 languages; and Bantoid. Bantoid, the largest branch, includes over 600 languages, including the BANTU LANGUAGES.

Benue River \'bā-nwä\ *or* **Bénoué River** \bā-'nwä\ River, W Africa. Rising in N Cameroon, the river flows west across E central Nigeria. About 870 mi (1,400 km) long, it is the chief tributary of the NIGER RIVER.

Benz \'bents\, **Karl (Friedrich)** (1844–1929) German mechanical engineer who designed and built the first practical AUTOMOBILE powered by an INTERNAL COMBUSTION ENGINE. The original car, his three-wheeled *Motorwagen,* first ran in 1885. Benz's company produced its first four-wheeled car in 1893 and the first of its series of racing cars in 1899. In 1926 the Benz company merged with the company started by Gottlieb DAIMLER.

benzene Simplest aromatic HYDROCARBON (see AROMATIC COMPOUND), parent substance of a large class. It was discovered in 1825 by Michael FARADAY. The chemical formula is C_6H_6; August Kekulé (1829–1896) was the first to propose the correct structure (1865), a six-membered ring of CARBON atoms, each with one HYDROGEN atom bonded to it (see BONDING). Benzene is a colorless, mobile liquid with a characteristic odor. An excellent solvent, it is also widely used as a starting material for many plastics, dyes, detergents, insecticides, and other industrial chemicals. Benzene is highly toxic, and long exposure may cause LEUKEMIA.

Benzer, Seymour (b.1921) U.S. molecular biologist. Born in New York City, he developed a method for determining the detailed structure of viral genes and coined the term cistron to denote functional subunits of genes. He did much to explain the nature of genetic oddities, called nonsense mutations, in terms of the nucleotide sequence of DNA.

Beowulf \'bā-ə-,wùlf\ Heroic poem considered the highest achievement of Old English literature and the earliest European vernacular EPIC. Probably composed around 700–750, it tells of the Scandinavian hero Beowulf, who gains early fame by vanquishing the monster Grendel and his mother; later, as an aging king, he kills a dragon but dies soon after, honored and lamented. *Beowulf* is poetically and thematically in the Germanic tradition but shows a distinct Christian influence.

Berbers Speakers of the various Berber languages of the MAGHREB, including Tamazight, Tashelhit, and Tarifit. Berber-speakers were the original inhabitants of N. Africa, though many regions succumbed first to Roman colonization and later to the ARAB conquests beginning in the 7th cent. A.D. Berbers gradually accepted Islam, and many switched to Arabic. The Berber languages are still spoken in rural and mountain areas of Morocco and Algeria and by some inhabitants of Tunisia and Libya. Since the 1990s Berber intellectuals have sought to revive interest in the language; an institute for the study of Berber opened in Morocco in 2001. See also ABD AL-KRIM.

Berchtesgaden \'berk-təs-,gäd-³n\ Town (pop., 1992 est.: 8,000), S Germany, in the Bavarian Alps south of SALZBURG. Once part of Austria, it passed to BAVARIA in the early 19th cent. Known as the site of Adolf HITLER's villa retreat before and during World War II., it was destroyed by bombing in 1945, and the villa was leveled in 1952. Mountain climbing and skiing make the area popular.

Berenson \'ber-ən-sən\, **Bernard** (1865–1959) U.S. (Lithuanian-born) art historian. Born in Vilnius, he grew up in Boston and attended Harvard Univ. He lived in Italy most of his life, where he built a reputation as an authority on Italian Renaissance painting. He was adviser to Isabella Stewart Gardner (1840–1924), founder of Boston's Gardner Museum. He bequeathed his villa, I Tatti, near Florence, with its art collection and outstanding library, to Harvard Univ. His books include *The Drawings of the Florentine Painters* (1903, 1938, 1961) and *Italian Painters of the Renaissance* (1952).

Berezina River \bə-'rāz-³n-ə\ River, Belarus. It is 365 mi (587 km) long and flows southeast into the DNIEPER RIVER. On the Berezina near Baryslaw Russian forces inflicted enormous losses on NAPOLEON's retreating army in 1812. In 1941 it was the scene of fierce fighting during the German advance on SMOLENSK.

Berg \'berk\, **Alban (Maria Johannes)** (1885–1935) Austrian composer. Born in Vienna, he was largely self-taught musically until he met Arnold SCHOENBERG at 19 and commenced eight years of study with him. Berg's early late-Romantic tonal works give way to increasing atonality and finally (1925) to twelve-tone composition. His Expressionist opera *Wozzeck* (1922) became the most universally acclaimed post-Romantic opera. His second opera, *Lulu,* remained unfinished at his death at 50, which resulted from septicemia caused by an abscess. His other works include two string quartets, including the *Lyric Suite* (1926); *Three Pieces for Orchestra* (1915); and a violin concerto (1935).

Berg, Paul (b.1926) U.S. biochemist. Born in New York City, he devised methods for splitting DNA molecules and attaching the resulting segments to the DNA of a virus or plasmid, which could then enter bacterial or animal cells. The foreign DNA was incorporated into the host and caused the synthesis of proteins not ordinarily found there. One of the earliest practical results was the development of bacteria that could produce insulin. In 1980 Berg shared a Nobel Prize with Walter Gilbert (b.1932) and Frederick SANGER.

bergamot \'bər-gə-ˌmät\ Any of several N. American perennial plants of the MINT family, also known as bee balm, fragrant balm, and Indian's plume. The leaves are used as an herb to flavor tea and other beverages. *Monarda didyma,* native to the U.S., is made into Oswego tea, a beverage used by the American Indian Oswego tribe and said to be the drink adopted by the 18th-cent. colonists during their boycott of British tea. The pear-shaped fruit of the bergamot orange *(Citrus bergamia),* found chiefly in Calabria, Italy, is valued by the flavoring and perfume industries for the ESSENTIAL OIL extracted from its peel.

Bergen City (metro area pop., 1999: 227,000), SW Norway. It is Norway's second-largest city and most important port. Founded in 1070 by King Olaf III, it was Norway's capital in the 12th–13th cent. In the 14th–16th cent., German HANSEATIC LEAGUE merchants controlled its trade. Repeatedly destroyed by fire, Bergen has been resurrected each time. Its economy is based on fishing and shipbuilding. It was the birthplace of Edvard GRIEG.

Bergen, Edgar *orig.* Edgar John Bergren (1903–1978) U.S. comedian and ventriloquist. As a boy in his native Chicago he developed his skill in ventriloquism. He eventually took his act to radio, where the *Edgar Bergen–Charlie McCarthy Show* (with his caustic and irrepressible dummy Charlie McCarthy) was one of the most popular programs for 20 years (1937–57). His daughter Candice (b.1946), a successful screen actress, achieved her greatest fame in the television series *Murphy Brown* (1988–98).

Bergen-Belsen *or* **Belsen** Nazi CONCENTRATION CAMP near Bergen and Belsen, villages in N central Germany. Established in 1943 as a prisoner-of-war camp and a Jewish transit camp, it eventually held 41,000 prisoners. It contained no gas chambers, but some 37,000 prisoners died there, including Anne FRANK. As the first such camp to be liberated by the Allies (Apr. 15, 1945), it received instant notoriety.

Berger, Victor (Louis) (1860–1929) German-U.S. cofounder of the U.S. Socialist Party. He emigrated to the U.S. in 1878, founded a German-language newspaper (1892), and edited the *Social Democratic Herald* (later *Milwaukee Leader*) 1898–1929. With Eugene DEBS he founded the Social Democratic Party, which became the Socialist Party in 1901. He served in the U.S. House of Representatives (1911–13) as the first Socialist elected to Congress. Elected again in 1918, he was denied his seat after being convicted under the Espionage Act for opposing U.S. participation in World War I. His conviction was overturned, and he again served in the House (1923–29).

Bergerac, Savinien Cyrano de See Savinien CYRANO DE BERGERAC

Bergey \'bər-gē\, **David Hendricks** (1860–1937) U.S. bacteriologist. Born in Skippack, Pa., he became director of biological research for the National Drug Company in Philadelphia. He is best remembered as the primary author of *Bergey's Manual of Determinative Bacteriology,* an invaluable reference for classification, and he researched such varied topics as tuberculosis, food preservatives, and allergic reactions.

Bergman, (Ernst) Ingmar (b.1918) Swedish film writer-director. Son of a Lutheran pastor, he directed his first film in 1945. He won a reputation as one of the world's great filmmakers with *Smiles of a Summer Night* (1955), *The Seventh Seal* (1956), and *Wild Strawberries* (1957). He assembled a group of actors, including Max von SYDOW and Liv ULLMANN, and a cinematographer, Sven NYKVIST, with whom he made powerful films often marked by bleak depictions of human loneliness, including *Through a Glass Darkly* (1961), *Persona* (1966), *Cries and Whispers* (1972), *Scenes from a Marriage* (1973), and *Fanny and Alexander* (1982). Throughout his career Bergman has directed stage productions, usually at Stockholm's Royal Dramatic Theater.

Bergman, Ingrid (1915–1982) Swedish film and stage actress. After appearing in *Intermezzo* in Sweden, she came to the U.S. to act in the English-language version (1939). Her radiance and unaffected charm made her a star in films such as *Casablanca* (1942), *For Whom the Bell Tolls* (1943), *Gaslight* (1944, Academy Award), and Alfred HITCHCOCK's *Spellbound* (1945) and *Notorious* (1946). The scandal caused by her love affair with Roberto ROSSELLINI (1949) kept her off the U.S. screen until *Anastasia* (1956, Academy Award). Her later films include *Indiscreet* (1958), *Cactus Flower* (1969), *Murder on the Orient Express* (1974, Academy Award), and *Autumn Sonata* (1978).

Bergson \berk-'sōⁿ\, **Henri (-Louis)** (1859–1941) French philosopher. His major books include *Time and Free Will* (1889), on the perception of time; *Matter and Memory* (1896), on the MIND-BODY PROBLEM, taking a position opposed to scientific determinism; and *Creative Evolution* (1907), which argued that evolution is driven by *élan vital* ("vital impulse"). He was the first to elaborate a PROCESS PHILOSOPHY, rejecting static values and embracing dynamic values such as motion, change, and evolution. His writing style has been widely admired, and he won the Nobel Prize for Literature in 1927.

Henri Bergson, 1928

Beria \'ber-ē-ə\, **Lavrenty (Pavlovich)** (1899–1953) Soviet politician and director of the secret police. As Communist Party head of the Transcaucasian republics (1932–38), he personally oversaw the political purges initiated by Joseph STALIN (see PURGE TRIALS). He was head of the Soviet secret police 1938–53, and after Stalin's death he became head of the Ministry of Internal Affairs. After attempting to succeed Stalin as sole dictator, he was arrested and executed.

beriberi \ˌber-ē-'ber-ē\ *or* **vitamin B₁ deficiency** Nutritional disorder (its name is from the Sinhalese for "extreme weakness"), with nerve and heart impairment, caused by THIAMINE deficiency. Symptoms include fatigue, digestive problems, and limb numbness and weakness. Vitamin B₁ occurs widely in food but is lost in processing; a well-balanced diet high in unprocessed foods can prevent beriberi. In Western countries, chronic alcoholism is the most common cause.

Bering, Vitus (Jonassen) (1681–1741) Danish-Russian navigator. He joined the fleet of the Russian czar PETER I and in 1724 was appointed leader of an expedition to determine whether Asia and N. America were connected by land. In 1728 he set sail from the Siberian peninsula and passed through the later-named Bering Strait. A second expedition was expanded into Russia's Great Northern Expedition (1733–43), which mapped much of the Arctic coast of Siberia. After exploring the Alaskan coast, he fell ill from scurvy and died after his ship was wrecked. His exploration paved the way for a Russian foothold in N. America.

Bering Sea Body of water, N Pacific Ocean. Enclosed by Alaska, the ALEUTIAN ISLANDS, the KAMCHATKA Peninsula, and E SIBERIA, it covers 885,000 sq mi (2,291,000 sq km). It contains the Aleutians, Nunivak, St. Lawrence, and the PRIBILOF ISLANDS. The sea is connected to the ARCTIC OCEAN by the Bering Strait, which is believed to have been a land bridge during the Ice Age that enabled migration from Asia to N. America. Vitus BERING's explorations of the sea and strait in 1728 and 1741 formed a basis for Russian claims to Alaska.

B

Berio, Luciano (b.1925) Italian composer. He has been an important innovator in electronic music, musical "collage" using borrowed material, and musical "performance pieces." His wife, the singer Cathy Berberian (1925–1983), was his principal collaborator. His best-known works include *Omaggio a Joyce* (1958), *Visage* (1961), *Sinfonia* (1968), *Opera* (1970), and his ongoing series of *Sequenze* (1958–).

Berkeley City (pop., 2000: 103,000), W California, on San Francisco Bay. Founded as Oceanview in 1853, it was selected as a campus site by the College (later Univ.) of CALIFORNIA. The college, named for the philosopher George BERKELEY, opened in 1873.

Berkeley, Busby *orig.* William Berkeley Enos (1895–1976) U.S. film director and choreographer. Born in Los Angeles, he acted and danced in comedies from age 5. After choreographing over 20 Broadway musicals, he was summoned to Hollywood to direct dance numbers for *Whoopee* (1930). His elaborate production numbers and innovative camera techniques in such films as *Gold Diggers of 1933* and *Footlight Parade* (1933) revolutionized the musical. When rising production costs made such extravaganzas unfeasible, he directed less innovative but still popular films such as *The Gang's All Here* (1943).

Berkeley \'bärk-lē\, **George** *known as* **Bishop Berkeley** (1685–1753) Irish bishop, philosopher, and social activist. He worked principally at Trinity College, Dublin (to 1713), and as bishop of Cloyne (1734–52). He is best known for his contention that, for material objects, to be is to be perceived ("Esse est percipi"), but that, even if no human perceives an object, God does, thereby ensuring the continued existence of the physical world. With John LOCKE and David HUME, he was one of the founders of modern EMPIRICISM. His works include *An Essay Towards a New Theory of Vision* (1709), *Treatise Concerning the Principles of Human Knowledge* (1710), and *Three Dialogues between Hylas and Philonous* (1713). In America (1728–31), he advocated educating Indians and blacks; Berkeley, Cal., is named for him.

Berkeley, William (*later* **Sir William**) (1606–1677) British colonial governor of Virginia. As governor (1641–52), he introduced successful programs in crop diversification and manufacturing and promoted peace with the Indians. Reappointed in 1660, he was faced with crop failures and Indian attacks on the frontier. In 1676 Bacon's Rebellion, an expedition against the Indians in defiance of Berkeley's policy of fostering trade, forced Berkeley to fight for control of the colony, which he eventually regained.

Berkshire Hills Segment of the APPALACHIAN MTNS., W Massachusetts. Many summits exceed 2,000 ft (600 m), including Mt. Greylock (3,491 ft, or 1,064 m), the highest point in the state. A continuation of the GREEN MTNS., they include the Hoosac and TACONIC RANGES and are crossed by the APPALACHIAN NATIONAL SCENIC TRAIL. They are home to the Tanglewood music festival (in Lenox).

Berlage \'ber-läk-ə\, **Hendrik Petrus** (1856–1934) Dutch architect. His best-known work is the Amsterdam Stock Exchange (1897–1903), notable for its forthright use of structural steel and traditional Dutch brickwork. Exposed to the work of Louis SULLIVAN and Frank Lloyd WRIGHT in 1911, he later introduced their methods and ideas to Europe. His work was characterized by the honest use of materials based on their fundamental properties and the avoidance of meaningless ornamentation.

Berle \'bərl\, **Milton** *orig.* Milton Berlinger (1908–2002) U.S. comedian. Born in New York City, he appeared in VAUDEVILLE from age 10 and later acted in over 50 silent films. He worked as a nightclub comedian (1939–49), noted for his slapstick routines and facial contortions, and appeared in 19 movies (1937–68), but his greatest success came with the television variety show *Texaco Star Theater* (1948–54), later called *The Milton Berle Show* (1954–56, 1958–59), a show so popular that many people bought television sets just to watch "Uncle Miltie."

Berlin City and state (pop., 1995: 3,470,000), capital of reunified Germany. Founded in the early 13th cent., it was a member of the HANSEATIC LEAGUE in the 14th cent. It became the residence of the HOHENZOLLERNS and the capital of BRANDENBURG. It was successively the capital of PRUSSIA (from 1701), of the German empire (1871–1918), of the WEIMAR REPUBLIC (1919–32), and of the THIRD REICH (1933–45). In World War II much of the city was destroyed by Allied bombing. In 1945 it was divided into four occupation zones: American, British, French, and Soviet. The three Western powers merged their sectors in 1948; the Soviets responded with the BERLIN BLOCKADE. When independent governments were established in E and W Germany in 1949, E. Berlin was made the capital of E. Germany, and W. Berlin, though surrounded by E. Germany, became part of W. Germany. Continuing immigration from E. to W. Berlin prompted the 1961 erection of the BERLIN WALL. The area immediately became the most vivid focal point of the COLD WAR. The dramatic dismantling of the wall in 1989 marked the international upheaval that accompanied the end of the Soviet Union. Berlin became reunified as Germany's official capital in 1991; the transfer of government from BONN was completed in 1999. It is the site of the Univ. of BERLIN, Charlottenburg Palace, the BRANDENBURG GATE, and the Berlin Zoo, and is home to the Berlin Opera and the Berlin Philharmonic Orchestra.

Berlin, Irving *orig.* Israel Baline (1888–1989) U.S. songwriter. He was born to the family of a Russian Jewish cantor that emigrated to New York in 1893. With only two years of schooling, he worked as a street singer and singing waiter. His first published song, "Marie from Sunny Italy," appeared in 1907; a printer's error named him Irving Berlin. Unable to read or write music, he learned and played by ear. In 1911 he wrote the influential hit "Alexander's Ragtime Band." In 1919 he founded his own publishing house. He may have written more than 1,500 songs, including "Oh, How I Hate to Get Up in the Morning," "Always," "Puttin' on the Ritz," and "God Bless America." His 18 film scores include *Top Hat* (1935), *Easter Parade* (1948), and *White Christmas* (1954); *Holiday Inn* (1942) introduced "White Christmas," one of the best-selling songs of all time. His 19 Broadway shows include *Annie Get Your Gun* (1946) and *Call Me Madam* (1950).

Berlin, Isaiah (*later* **Sir Isaiah**) (1909–1997) British (Latvian-born) historian and writer. Berlin taught at Oxford Univ. 1950–67, serving as president of Wolfson College 1966–75 and thereafter teaching at All Souls College. His influential writings on political philosophy include *Karl Marx* (1939), *The Hedgehog and the Fox* (1953), *Historical Inevitability* (1955), *The Age of Enlightenment* (1956), and *Four Essays on Liberty* (1969).

Berlin, University of *or* **Humboldt University of Berlin** Public university in Berlin, founded (as Friedrich Wilhelm Univ.) in 1809–10 by Wilhelm von HUMBOLDT. By the mid-1800s it had attained world renown. Among its faculty were G. W. F. HEGEL, Arthur SCHOPENHAUER, Leopold von RANKE, Hermann von HELMHOLTZ, and Jacob and Wilhelm GRIMM. Under the German Democratic Republic after World War II, it was renamed Humboldt-Universität and given a Marxist-Leninist orientation. Total enrollment is about 23,000.

Berlin blockade and airlift (1948–49) International crisis that arose from an attempt by the Soviet Union to force the Allied powers (U.S., Britain, and France) to abandon their postwar jurisdictions in W. Berlin. The Soviets, regarding the Allied occupation zones as a threat to the E. German economy, blockaded all transportation routes between Berlin and W. Germany. The U.S. and Britain responded by supplying the city with necessities by air transport and airlifting out W. Berlin exports. An Allied embargo on exports from the Eastern bloc forced the Soviets to lift the blockade after 11 months.

Berlin Wall Barrier surrounding W. Berlin (1961–89), a symbol of the COLD WAR's division of E. and W. Germany. It was built in response to the flight of about 2.5 million E. Germans to W. Germany during 1949–61. First erected on the night of August 12–13, 1961, it developed into a system of concrete walls topped with barbed wire and guarded with watchtowers, gun emplacements, and mines. It was opened in the 1989 democratization that swept through Eastern Europe.

Berlioz \'ber-lē-,ōz\, **(Louis-) Hector** (1803–1869) French composer. His *Symphonie fantastique* (1830), written at 27 in the frenzy of an infatuation, had a stormy premiere and became a landmark of the Romantic era. He became a brilliant conductor, with an unsurpassed knowledge of the orchestra. Impulsive and passionate, he was constantly at war with the musical establishment. Though he was the most compelling French musical figure of his time, his idiosyncratic compositional style kept his music out of the repertory until the mid-20th cent. His works include the operas *Benvenuto Cellini* (1837), *Les Troyens* (1858), and *Béatrice et Bénédict* (1862); the program symphonies *Harold in Italy* (1834) and *Romeo and Juliet* (1839); and the choral *Requiem* (1837), *La damnation de Faust* (1846), *Te Deum* (1849), and *L'enfance du Christ* (1854). His orchestration treatise (1843) is the most influential such work ever written.

Berlusconi, Silvio (b.1936) Italian media tycoon and prime minister of Italy (1994, from 2001). After amassing a fortune as a real-estate developer, in 1980 he established Italy's first commercial television network; soon his stations dominated Italian airwaves. He went on to acquire department stores, movie theaters, publishing companies, and a Milan football team. In 1994 he founded the conservative Forza Italia party and was elected prime minister; he soon resigned to face charges of fraud and corruption. Despite his convictions on graft and bribery charges in 1997–98 and criticism of his control of much of the Italian media, he remained the party's leader. Promising tax cuts, he led a coalition to victory in the 2001 elections.

Bermejo \ber-'mä-hō\, **Bartolomé** (c.1440–1495) Spanish painter. He was active in Valencia (1468) and Aragon, and in Barcelona from 1486. His *Pietà* (1490) in Barcelona Cathedral is considered a masterpiece of early Spanish oil painting; the influence of Rogier van der WEYDEN can be seen in the rich detail and color. Bermejo cultivated the Flemish style and was considered the most outstanding painter in Spain before El GRECO.

Bermuda British colony (pop., 2000: 63,000), W Atlantic Ocean. An archipelago of about 300 islands, of which only some 20 are inhabited, it lies about 570 mi (920 km) southeast of Cape HATTERAS, N.C. Its total land area is about 20 sq mi (52 sq km). Its capital is Hamilton, on Bermuda Island. Colonized by the English in 1612, Bermuda became a crown colony in 1684. Its economy is based on tourism and international finance; its per-capita gross national product is among the world's highest.

Bermuda Triangle Triangular area, Atlantic Ocean, whose apexes are usually said to be BERMUDA, MIAMI, Fla., and SAN JUAN, Puerto Rico. It has been the site of numerous disappearances of planes and ships, and discoveries of abandoned vessels. Reports of unexplained occurrences in the region date to the mid-19th cent. Non-supernatural explanations cite the area's violent freak storms, the local turbulence of the GULF STREAM, and the quickly shifting topology of the area's seabed.

Bern City (pop., 1999 est.: 123,000; metro. area pop.: 317,000), capital of Switzerland. Lying on the AARE RIVER, it was founded as a military post in 1191, became a free imperial city in 1218, later an independent state, and in 1353 a member of the Swiss Confederation. It was a scene of disputation in 1528 between Roman Catholics and reformers and later championed Protestant doctrines. It joined the Helvetic Republic and in 1848 was made the capital of Switzerland. It is headquarters of the international postal, railway, and copyright unions.

Bernadette of Lourdes, St. *orig.* Marie-Bernarde Soubirous (1844–1879) French visionary. The daughter of a miller, she had a poverty-stricken childhood and was often ill. In 1858 she had a series of visions of Mary; she defended their authenticity against the doubts of her parents and the clergy. She became a nun in 1866 and remained in seclusion until her death at 35. The grotto at LOURDES became a pilgrimage site; its waters are reputed to have healing powers. Bernadette was canonized in 1933.

Bernadotte (af Wisborg) \ber-nà-'dȯt\, **Folke, Greve (Count)** (1895–1948) Swedish soldier, humanitarian, and diplomat. A nephew of King Gustav V, he headed the Swedish Red Cross in World War II and was credited with saving some 20,000 concentration-camp inmates. Appointed mediator in Palestine by the U.N. Security Council,

he secured a cease-fire between Israel and the Arab states. For proposing that Arab refugees be allowed to return to their homes in what had become Israel, he was assassinated by Jewish extremists.

Bernard \ber-'när\, **Claude** (1813–1878) French physiologist. He discovered the role of the pancreas in digestion, the glycogenic function of the liver in carbohydrate metabolism, and blood-supply regulation by the vasomotor nerves. He helped establish the principles of experimentation in the life sciences, including the need for a hypothesis to be confirmed or refuted. His concept of the internal environment of the organism led to the present understanding of HOMEOSTASIS. Bernard also studied the effects of such poisons as carbon monoxide and curare.

Bernard de Clairvaux \kler-'vō\, **St.** (1090–1153) French CISTERCIAN monk, mystic, and Doctor of the Church. Born into an aristocratic family, he turned away from a literary education for a life of renunciation, entering an austere religious community at Cîteaux in 1112. He established an abbey at Clairvaux, Champagne, in 1115. He was the confidant of five popes and became perhaps the most renowned religious figure in Europe. He opposed the rationalism of Peter ABELARD and defended the cult of the Virgin Mary.

Bernardine See CISTERCIAN

Bernardine of Siena, St. \'bər-nər-dēn\ (1380–1444) Franciscan priest and theologian. A noble orphan, he entered the Observants (1402), a strict branch of the Franciscan order that he later helped to spread throughout Europe. In 1417 he began preaching tours in Italy, seeking to combat the lawlessness and immorality resulting from the Western SCHISM. Through the Council of Florence (1439) he worked to unite the Greek and Roman churches. Numerous miracles are said to have occurred at his tomb.

Bernays, Edward L. (1891–1995) U.S. publicist, the "father of public relations." A nephew of Sigmund FREUD, he was born in Vienna but brought up in New York. His early clients included the U.S. War Department and the Lithuanian government. He took credit for persuading women to smoke in public, writing books favored by the Nazi propagandist Joseph GOEBBELS, and convincing the U.S. to overthrow Guatemala's elected government in 1954. He edited *The Engineering of Consent* (1955), whose title is his often-quoted definition of public relations. He lived to be 103.

Bern Convention *officially* International Convention for the Protection of Literary and Artistic Works. International agreement adopted in Bern, Switzerland, in 1886 (and later modified) to protect COPYRIGHTS on an international basis. Each member country of the Bern Copyright Union grants the authors of other member countries the same rights that its laws grant its own nationals. Protected works include every kind of literary, scientific, and artistic production, including paintings, sculpture, architectural plans, and musical arrangements. Copyright is now protected for 70 years after the creator's death.

Berners-Lee, Tim (b.1955) British physicist. He graduated from Oxford Univ. and in 1980 accepted a fellowship at CERN, a research facility in Geneva. He and his CERN colleagues created a communications protocol called Hyper-Text Transfer Protocol (HTTP) that standardized communication between computer servers and clients. Their text-based Web browser was released to the public in 1991, marking the beginnings of the WORLD WIDE WEB. He declined all opportunities to profit from his valuable innovation. In 1994 he joined MIT's Laboratory for Computer Science as director of the World Wide Web Consortium.

Bernese Alps *German* **Berner Oberland** \bər-nər-'ō-bər-länt\ Segment of the ALPS, Switzerland. Lying north of the RHONE RIVER, the mountains extend east from Martigny-Ville to the valley of the upper AARE RIVER. Many peaks, including the Finsteraarhorn, Jungfrau, and Aletschhorn, rise to more than 12,000 ft (3,660 m). They are crossed by the Lötschberg railway tunnel. Resorts such as Interlaken, Grindelwald, and Gstaad dot the area.

Bernhard \'bern-härt\ (b.1911) Prince of the Netherlands. Born into the German nobility, in 1937 he married the Dutch crown princess JULIANA and took Dutch citizenship. After Germany's invasion of the Netherlands, he took his family to Britain (1940). He served as the Dutch liaison with

the British armed forces, flew with the Royal Air Force (1942–44), and led Dutch troops in the Allied offensive in the Netherlands (1945). During Juliana's reign (1948–80), he served as the Netherlands' goodwill ambassador.

Bernhardt \ber-'när, *Engl* 'bərn-₁härt\, **Sarah** *orig.* Henriette-Rosine Bernard (1844–1923) French actress. The illegitimate child of a courtesan, she joined the Odéon Theatre (1866–72), where she acted in Alexandre DUMAS's *Kean* and Victor HUGO's *Ruy Blas*, charming audiences with her "golden voice." Returning to the Comédie-Française (1872–80), she starred in *Phèdre* to great acclaim in Paris and London. She formed her own company in 1880 and toured the world in *La dame aux camélias*, *Adrienne Lecouvreur*, and in other roles. After an injury to her leg forced its amputation (1915), she strapped on a wooden leg and chose roles she could play largely seated. She was one of the best-known figures in the history of the stage.

Bernini, Gian Lorenzo (1598–1680) Italian architect and artist credited with the invention of baroque sculpture. Among his early sculptures are *Apollo and Daphne* (1622–24). Under Urban VIII, the first of eight popes he was to serve, he created the baldachin over the tomb of St. Peter in Rome. He was appointed architect of ST. PETER'S BASILICA and the Palazzo Barberini in 1629. His works often represent a fusion of architecture and sculpture, as in the Cornaro Chapel, in Santa Maria della Vittoria, Rome, with its celebrated *Ecstasy of St. Teresa* (1645–52). His greatest architectural achievement is the colonnade enclosing the piazza before St. Peter's. His Roman fountains are noted for their architectural composition and detail.

Bernoulli's principle *or* **Bernoulli's theorem** Principle that relates PRESSURE, VELOCITY, and height for a nonviscous FLUID with steady flow. A consequence is that, for horizontal flow, as the speed of a fluid increases, the pressure it exerts decreases. The principle explains the LIFT of an airplane in motion. As the speed of the plane increases, air flows faster over the curved top of the wing than underneath. The upward pressure exerted by the air under the wing is thus greater than the pressure exerted downward above the wing, resulting in a net upward force. A race car's spoiler, shaped like an upside-down wing, produces a net downward force.

Bernstein, Leonard (1918–1990) U.S. conductor, composer, and writer. Born in Lawrence, Mass., he resolved on a music career only after graduating from Harvard Univ. After studying conducting with Fritz Reiner, he became Sergey KOUSSEVITZKY's assistant.

Fame came abruptly when he substituted on short notice at a concert broadcast in 1943. In 1944 he triumphed with his music for Jerome ROBBINS's ballet *Fancy Free* and the hit Broadway show *On the Town*. As principal conductor of the New York Philharmonic (1958–69), he premiered much contemporary music and was instrumental in the Gustav MAHLER revival.

Leonard Bernstein

His best-known composition was the hit musical *West Side Story* (1957); other works include the musicals *Wonderful Town* (1952) and *Candide* (1956), three symphonies, the *Chichester Psalms* (1965), and the theatrical *Mass* (1971). Well known as a television lecturer, he was also a prominent political activist.

Berra \'ber-ə\, **Yogi** (*orig.* Lawrence Peter) (b.1925) U.S. baseball player, manager, and coach. Born in St. Louis, he joined the New York Yankees in 1946 and served as the team's regular catcher from 1949 until 1963. He was named the American League's Most Valuable Player in 1951, 1954, and 1955. He caught in more World Series games (75) than any other catcher, and hit 20 or more home runs a season through 1958. He managed the Yankees in 1964, but was fired and became a coach and manager (1965–75) with the New York Mets. He returned to the Yankees as a coach (1976–82) and later manager (1983–85). He was known for idiosyncratic remarks such as "It ain't over till it's over."

Berrigan, Daniel (Joseph) and Philip (Francis) (b.1921, 1923–2002) U.S. activist priests. Born in Two Harbors, Minn., the brothers both became Catholic priests (Daniel a Jesuit, Philip a Josephite). They soon became involved in campaigns of civil disobedience to oppose racism, nuclear war, and the Vietnam War. They are best known for their Vietnam-era raid of draft-board files in Catonsville, Md., which they destroyed with chicken blood and napalm. Their activism continued, though Philip later left the priesthood. Both wrote numerous books on their work and beliefs; Daniel has written poetry and plays as well.

Berruguete \ber-ü-'gä-tā\, **Pedro** (c.1450–c.1500) Spanish painter. After a sojourn in Italy, he returned to Spain, where he painted numerous altarpieces and also worked as a fresco painter in Toledo Cathedral from 1483. His panel paintings are characterized by luxurious ornament and gold decoration. He was Spain's first great Renaissance painter. His son Alonso (c.1488–1561), a sculptor and painter, worked in Italy (c.1508–16), then returned to Spain. In 1518 he became court painter to CHARLES V, but succeeded primarily as a sculptor. His best-known work is a set of wooden reliefs with highly expressive figures for choir stalls in Toledo Cathedral (1539–43). He is considered the greatest Spanish sculptor of the 16th cent.

Berry \be-'rē\ Historical region and former province, central France. Part of Aquitania Prima under Roman rule, then a Carolingian countship, it fell to the French crown in the 11th cent. When AQUITAINE was acquired by HENRY II of England, Berry was disputed between England and France. For a time it came under Jean de France, duc de Berry, an important patron of the arts. It returned to France in 1601 and remained a province until 1798.

berry Simple, fleshy FRUIT that usually has many seeds (e.g., the GRAPE, TOMATO, or CRANBERRY). The middle and inner layers of the fruit wall often are not distinct from each other. Any small, fleshy fruit is popularly called a berry, especially if it is edible. RASPBERRIES, BLACKBERRIES, and STRAWBERRIES are not true berries, but rather aggregate fruits—fruits that consist of multiple smaller fruits.

Berry, Chuck (*orig.* Charles Edward Anderson) (b.1926) U.S. singer-songwriter, one of the first to shape big-beat blues into rock and roll and to achieve widespread popularity with white audiences. Though first interested in country music, in the early 1950s Berry led a blues trio that played in black nightclubs around his native St. Louis. In 1955 he made his first hit record, "Maybellene," which was soon followed by "Sweet Little Sixteen," "Johnny B. Goode," "Rock and Roll Music," and "Roll Over, Beethoven." In 1959 he began a five-year prison sentence for immoral behavior, and in 1979 he was convicted of income-tax evasion.

Berry \be-'rē\, **Jean de France, duc de** (1340–1416) French nobleman and patron of the arts. Son of King John II of France, he controlled at least one-third of France during the middle period of the HUNDRED YEARS' WAR. Berry worked for peace with England and within France, acting as diplomat and mediator. He invested fortunes in the art treasures that became his monument—paintings, tapestries, jewelry, and illuminated manuscripts that included the famous *Très riches heures du duc de Berry*.

Berryman, John (1914–1972) U.S. poet. Born in McAlester, Okla., he gained a high reputation with *Homage to Mistress Bradstreet* (1956), one of his first experimental poems. His technical daring showed in *77 Dream Songs* (1964, Pulitzer Prize) and *His Toy, His Dream, His Rest* (1968). Later works include *Love & Fame* (1970) and *Recovery* (1973), about his struggle with alcoholism. He is noted for confessional poetry laced with humor. Subject to deep depression, he killed himself by jumping from a bridge.

berserkers *Old Norse* beserkr ("bearskin") In premedieval and medieval Norse and Germanic history, unruly warrior gangs that worshiped ODIN and attached themselves to noble courts as bodyguards and shock troops. They raped and murdered at will in their host communities, and their savagery in battle and animal-skin attire contributed to the WEREWOLF legend.

Bertelsmann AG German media company. Beginning as a religious printer and publisher in 1835, the company grew steadily. By 1998 Bertelsmann AG included more than 300 media companies, with over half its employees in countries other than Germany. Its U.S. acquisitions have included the publishers Bantam Doubleday Dell and RANDOM HOUSE, *Family Circle* and *McCall's* magazines, and RCA. By 2000 the company claimed to be the world's third-largest media conglomerate.

Berthelot \ber-tə-'lō\, (Pierre-Eugène-) Marcellin (1827–1907) French chemist. He did research in ALCOHOLS and CARBOXYLIC ACIDS, the synthesis of HYDROCARBONS, and REACTION RATES, studied the mechanism of explosion, discovered many coal-tar derivatives, and wrote on the history of early chemistry. He pioneered the use of chemical analysis in archaeology. His work helped break down the traditional division between organic and inorganic compounds. He was one of the first to prove that all chemical phenomena depend on physical forces that can be measured.

Bertolucci \ber-tə-'lü-chē\, Bernardo (b.1940) Italian film director. A poet, he entered filmmaking in 1961. His first films, *The Grim Reaper* (1962) and *Before the Revolution* (1964), were followed by the well-received *The Spider's Stratagem* and *The Conformist* (1970). The erotic *Last Tango in Paris* (1972) made him an international sensation. He later directed such films as *1900* (1976), *The Last Emperor* (1987, Academy Award), *Little Buddha* (1994), and *Stealing Beauty* (1996).

beryl \'ber-əl\ Mineral composed of beryllium aluminum silicate, a commercial source of BERYLLIUM. Several varieties are valued as gemstones: AQUAMARINE (pale blue-green); EMERALD (deep green); heliodor (golden yellow); and morganite (pink). Before 1925 beryl was used only as a gemstone, but since then many important uses have been found for beryllium. Most production is a by-product of the mining of feldspar and mica. Brazil is a major producer; others include Zimbabwe, S. Africa, Namibia, and the U.S.

beryllium \bə-'ril-ē-əm\ Chemical ELEMENT, lightest of the ALKALINE EARTH METALS, chemical symbol Be, atomic number 4. It does not occur uncombined in nature but chiefly as the mineral BERYL (emerald and aquamarine are gemstone varieties). Beryllium METAL, particularly in ALLOYS, has many applications. Its compounds (always of VALENCE 2) are generally colorless and sweet-tasting. All soluble beryllium compounds are toxic.

Berzelius \ber-'sā-lē-əs\, Jöns Jacob *later* Baron Berzelius (1779–1848) Swedish chemist. One of the founders of modern chemistry, he made immensely important innovations and discoveries. He introduced basic laboratory equipment that remains in use today; he determined ATOMIC WEIGHTS; he created the modern system of CHEMICAL SYMBOLS; he developed the theory of ELECTROCHEMISTRY; he discovered CERIUM, SELENIUM, and thorium and isolated SILICON, ZIRCONIUM, and TITANIUM; he contributed to the classical techniques of ANALYSIS; and he investigated ISOMERISM and CATALYSIS, both of which he named.

Besant \'be-sənt\, Annie *orig.* Annie Wood (1847–1933) British social reformer. A prominent Fabian socialist, she became an adherent of THEOSOPHY in 1889. She served as international president of the Theosophical Society from 1907, and her writings are considered some of the best expositions of theosophical belief. After emigrating to India, she established the Indian Home Rule League in 1916.

Bessarabia \be-sə-'rā-bē-ə\ Region, E Europe. It is bounded by the Prut and DNIESTER rivers, the BLACK SEA, and the DANUBE RIVER delta. Greek colonies were founded on its Black Sea coast in the 7th cent. B.C., and it was probably part of DACIA in the 2nd cent. A.D. It became part of MOLDAVIA in the 15th cent. and later the Ottoman empire; it remained under Turkish control until the 19th cent. Russia acquired it and half of Moldavia in 1812 and retained control until World War I. A nationalist movement developed, and after the RUSSIAN REVOLUTION OF 1917 Bessarabia voted to unite with Romania. In 1940 the Soviet Union demanded that Romania cede Bessarabia; when Romania complied, the U.S.S.R. set up the Moldavian Soviet Socialist Republic (see MOLDOVA), and incorporated the N region into the Ukrainian S.S.R. Bessarabia remained divided after Ukraine and Moldavia declared independence in 1991.

Bessemer, Henry (*later* Sir Henry) (1813–1898) British inventor and engineer. When he set up his own casting busi-

ness at 17, the only iron-based construction materials were CAST IRON and WROUGHT IRON. So-called steel was made by adding CARBON to pure forms of wrought iron; the resulting material was used almost entirely for cutting tools. During the Crimean War Bessemer worked to devise a stronger cast iron for cannon. The resulting BESSEMER PROCESS enabled the inexpensive production of large, slag-free ingots of steel as workable as any wrought iron. He eventually also discovered how to remove excess oxygen from the iron.

Henry Bessemer Painting by Rudolf Lehmann

Bessemer process Technique for converting pig iron to steel, invented by Henry BESSEMER in England in 1856 and brought to him into commercial production in 1860. Air blown through liquid pig iron in a refractory-lined converter oxidizes the carbon and silicon in the iron. Heat released by the oxidation keeps the metal molten. Robert Mushet (1811–1891) contributed the technique for deoxidizing the converted metal that made the process a success. A. L. Holley (1832–1882) built the first successful Bessemer steel plant in the U.S. in 1865. High-volume production of low-cost steel in Britain and the U.S. by the Bessemer process soon revolutionized building construction and provided steel to replace iron in railroad rails and many other uses. The Bessemer process was eventually superseded by the open-hearth process.

Besson \bes-'ōⁿ\, Jacques (1540–1576) French engineer. His improvements in the LATHE were of great importance in the development of the MACHINE-TOOL industry and of scientific instrumentation. His designs, published in 1569, introduced CAMS and templates to the screw-cutting lathe, thus increasing the operator's control and permitting production of more accurate and intricate work in metal. His description of a more efficient form of WATERWHEEL is considered a prototype of the water TURBINE.

beta-blocker \'bā-tə\ *in full* beta-adrenergic blocking agent. Any of a class of synthetic drugs used to treat diseases and conditions of the sympathetic NERVOUS SYSTEM (see AUTONOMIC NERVOUS SYSTEM). They block receptors in HEART and other smooth MUSCLE cells, which respond to EPINEPHRINE by causing excitation of the sympathetic nervous system. By preventing that excitation, beta-blockers are useful in controlling ANXIETY, HYPERTENSION, and various heart conditions (see HEART DISEASE). They reduce the risk of a second MYOCARDIAL INFARCTION.

beta decay Any of three processes of radioactive disintegration in which a beta particle is spontaneously emitted by an unstable atomic NUCLEUS in order to dissipate excess energy. Beta particles are either ELECTRONS or POSITRONS. The three beta-decay processes are electron emission, positron emission, and electron capture; in all, the positive charge of the original nucleus changes by one unit with no change in mass number. Beta decay is slower than gamma or ALPHA decay, but beta particles can penetrate hundreds of times farther than alpha particles. See also RADIOACTIVITY.

betel \'bē-t³l\ Either of two different plants that are widely used in combination for chewing purposes in S Asia and the E. Indies. The betel nut is the seed of the betel PALM (*Areca catechu*); the betel leaf is from the betel pepper, or pan plant (*Piper betle*), family Piperaceae. For chewing, a small piece of the areca palm's fruit is wrapped in a leaf of the betel pepper, along with a pellet of lime to cause salivation and release the stimulating ALKALOIDS. Chewing results in a heavy flow of red saliva, which may temporarily dye the mouth, lips, and gums orange brown.

Betelgeuse \'bē-t³l-jüs\ (from Arabic *bat al-dshauza*: "the giant's shoulder") Brightest star in the constellation Orion, marking the hunter's E shoulder. About 430 light-years from earth, Betelgeuse is easily identifiable by its brightness, its position in Orion, and its deep reddish color. It is a red SUPERGIANT STAR, one of the largest known; its diameter varies between about 500 and 800 times that of the sun.

Bethe \'bā-tə\, **Hans (Albrecht)** (b.1906) German-U.S. theoretical physicist. He showed how the electric field surrounding an atom in a crystal affects the atom's energy states, work that helped shape QUANTUM MECHANICS and increased understanding of the forces governing the structures of atomic nuclei. He was the first to propose the CARBON CYCLE as a source of energy production in stars (1939). He headed the theoretical physics division of the MANHATTAN PROJECT, but worked in the postwar era to publicize the threat of nuclear warfare. He received the 1967 Nobel Prize for Physics.

Bethel Ancient city, PALESTINE. Now an archaeological site and town (Baytin) located in Israeli-occupied territory, it lies just north of Jerusalem. Important in Old Testament times, it was associated with ABRAHAM and JACOB. After the division of Israel, Bethel was made the chief sanctuary of the N kingdom (Israel).

Bethlehem Town (pop., 1987 est.: 34,000), southwest of JERUSALEM. An ancient town of JUDAEA, it was the early home of King DAVID. Christians regard it as the birthplace of JESUS; the Church of the Nativity, built in the 3rd cent. over a cave identified as the site of the Nativity, is one of the oldest Christian churches extant. Bethlehem was included in the British mandate of Palestine (1923–48); after the ARAB–ISRAELI WAR (1948–49), it was annexed by Jordan in 1950. After the SIX-DAY WAR (1967), it became part of the WEST BANK territory under Israeli administration. It was turned over to Palestine in 1995 under an Israeli–Palestinian self-rule agreement.

Bethlehem Steel Corp. U.S. corporation created in 1904 to consolidate several iron and steel companies. Its principal founder was Charles M. SCHWAB. Based in Bethlehem, Pa. it initially produced primarily coal, iron ore, and steel. It launched more than 1,000 ships in World War II, and made girders for the Empire State Building. It later diversified into plastics, chemicals, and nonferrous ores. The second-largest steel producer in the U.S., it was forced to file for bankruptcy in 2001.

Bethmann Hollweg \'bāt-,män-'hȯl-,vek\, **Theobald von** (1856–1921) German chancellor (1909–17). He was appointed Prussian minister of the interior in 1905 and became German chancellor in 1909. Before World War I, he allowed the militarist factions to dominate the government; in 1914 he supported a "blank check" to Austria-Hungary for measures against Serbia. In 1916 he tried to secure the mediation of the U.S. to end the war, but he also failed to restrict submarine warfare. In 1917 he was forced to resign by angered conservatives.

Bethune \be-'thün\, **Louise Blanchard** orig. Jennie Louise Blanchard (1856–1913) First U.S. professional woman architect. Born in Waterloo, N.Y., she established a firm in Buffalo that designed several hundred buildings in New York State, many in the popular Romanesque Revival style. She was the first woman elected to the American Institute of Architects (1888).

Bethune \bā-'th(y)ün\, **Mary McLeod** orig. Mary Jane McLeod (1875–1955) U.S. educator. Born to former slaves in Mayesville, S.C., in 1904 she founded a school that later became part of Bethune-Cookman College in Daytona Beach, Fla. She was president of the college 1923–42 and 1946–47. A special adviser to Pres. Franklin ROOSEVELT, she directed the Division of Negro Affairs of the National Youth Administration 1936–44.

Bethune \bə-'thün\, **(Henry) Norman** (1890–1939) Canadian surgeon. Born in Gravenhurst, Ontario, he began his medical career with Canadian forces in World War I. During the Spanish Civil War he was a surgeon with the loyalist forces, setting up the first mobile blood-transfusion service. A Communist, he left Canada in 1938 to work with the Chinese army, organizing field hospitals and medical schools, and became a national hero of China.

Betjeman \'bech-ə-mən\, **John** (later **Sir John**) (1906–1984) British poet. His poetry includes *Mount Zion* (1933), *High and Low* (1966), and *A Nip in the Air* (1974), and his prose includes guidebooks to English counties. His nostalgia for the near past and his precise rendering of social nuance just when what he wrote about was vanishing gave him wide appeal. From 1972 until his death he served as poet laureate.

Bettelheim \'be-təl-,hīm\, **Bruno** (1903–1990) Austrian-U.S. psychologist. Trained in Vienna, from 1944 he directed the Univ. of Chicago's Orthogenic School, a laboratory school for disturbed children, and became known especially for his work on autism. He applied psychoanalytic principles to social problems, especially in child rearing. His works include an influential paper on adaptation to extreme stress (1943), *Love Is Not Enough* (1950), *The Informed Heart* (1960), *The Empty Fortress* (1967), *Children of the Dream* (1967), and *The Uses of Enchantment* (1976). His posthumous reputation was clouded by revelations that he had invented his academic credentials and had abused and misdiagnosed children at his school.

Better Business Bureau Any of several U.S. and Canadian organizations formed to protect communities from unfair, misleading, or fraudulent advertising and selling practices. Organized at the local level, Better Business Bureaus set standards for business practices, investigate complaints, and conduct educational campaigns on deceit and fraud in advertising and selling.

Beust \'bȯist\, **Friedrich Ferdinand, Graf (Count) von** (1809–1886) German statesman. A career diplomat in Saxony, he served as its foreign minister 1849–53 and its interior minister 1853–66. Appointed by Saxony's ally and Habsburg emperor FRANCIS JOSEPH as the Austrian minister for foreign affairs (1866) and imperial chancellor (1867–71), Beust negotiated the COMPROMISE OF 1867 and helped restore the Habsburgs' international position.

Beuve, Charles-Augustin Sainte- See C.-A. SAINTE-BEUVE

Beuys \'bȯis\, **Joseph** (1921–1986) German avant-garde sculptor and performance artist. He studied art in Düsseldorf (1947–51) and in 1961 was appointed professor of sculpture at its art academy. In the 1960s he worked with the international group FLUXUS. His most famous and controversial performance was *How to Explain Pictures to a Dead Hare* (1965), in which he walked around an art gallery with his face covered in honey and gold leaf, talking to a dead hare about human and animal consciousness. He succeeded in creating a popular personal mythology and was one of the most influential artists and teachers of the later 20th cent.

Bevan \'bev-ən\, **Aneurin** (1897–1960) British politician. Elected to the House of Commons in 1929, he overcame a speech impediment to become a brilliant orator. As minister of health in Clement ATTLEE's government (1945–51), "Nye" Bevan established the National Health Service. A controversial figure in the Labour Party, he headed its left-wing (Bevanite) group and was the party's leader until 1955.

Beveridge, William (Henry) later Baron Beveridge (of Tuggal) (1879–1963) British economist. He served as director of labor exchanges (1909–16), head of the London School of Economics (1919–37), and master of Univ. College, Oxford (1937–45). Invited by the government to become the architect of the new British WELFARE STATE, he helped shape Britain's social policies and institutions through the Beveridge Report (1942).

Beverly Hills City (pop., 2000: 33,000), SW California. It is surrounded by the city of LOS ANGELES and adjoining HOLLYWOOD. It was established in 1906. The Beverly Hills Hotel was built in 1912. In 1919 Mary PICKFORD and Douglas FAIRBANKS began the fashion among Hollywood celebrities of building lavish homes in Beverly Hills. The city is crossed by the famous Sunset Boulevard, Santa Monica Boulevard, and Rodeo Drive.

Bewick, Thomas (1753–1828) British wood engraver. At 14 he was apprenticed to a metal engraver, with whom he later went into partnership in Newcastle. There he rediscovered the technique of wood engraving and brought to it brilliant innovations, such as the use of parallel lines instead of cross-hatching to achieve a wide range of tones and textures. Some of his finest works are illustrations for books on natural history.

Bhagavadgita \'bä-gə-,väd-'gē-tə\ (Sanskrit: "Song of God") One of the greatest of the Hindu scriptures, constituting part of the *MAHABHARATA*. It is written in the form of a dialogue between the warrior Prince ARJUNA and the charioteer KRISHNA, an incarnation of VISHNU. It was probably composed in the 1st or 2nd cent. A.D. Concerned over the suffering the impending battle will cause, Arjuna hesitates, but Krishna explains that the higher way is the dispassionate discharge of duty without concern for personal triumph. The Bhagavadgita considers the nature of God and ultimate reality and offers the means to transcend the limitations of this world.

Bhagavata \'bä-gə-‚və-tə\ Earliest recorded Hindu sect, representing the beginnings of theistic, devotional worship and modern VAISHNAVISM. The sect originated around the 3rd–2nd cent. B.C. and spread through India. The faith centers on devotion to a personal god, variously called VISHNU, KRISHNA, Hari, or Narayana. The BHAGAVADGITA is the earliest exposition of the Bhagavata system, but its central scripture is the Bhagavata PURANA. The sect was prominent within Vaishnavism until the 11th cent.

bhakti \'bək-tē\ S Asian devotional movement, particularly in HINDUISM, emphasizing the love of a devotee for his or her personal god. Though VISHNU, SHIVA, and Shakti (see SHAKTI) all have cults, bhakti characteristically developed around Vishnu's incarnations as RAMA and KRISHNA. Practices include reciting the god's name, singing hymns, and making pilgrimages. The fervor of S. Indian hymnists in the 7th–10th cent. inspired much poetry and art. Poets such as Mirabai (1450?–1547?) conceived of the relationship between the worshiper and the god in familiar human terms (e.g., as the lover and beloved), while more abstract poets portrayed the divinity as singular and ineffable.

Bhasa \'bä-sə\ (2nd or 3rd cent. A.D.) Indian dramatist. The earliest known dramatist in Sanskrit, he was known only by reputation until the texts of 13 of his dramas were discovered in 1912. Most of his works are on themes of heroism and romantic love borrowed from the *Ramayana* and the *Mahabharata*. He diverged from convention by portraying battles and killings on the stage. His influence is seen in the works of KALIDASA.

bhiksu \'bik-shü\ *Pali* **bhikku** \'bik-ü\ In BUDDHISM, a member of the SANGHA, the ordained order of men established by the Buddha. Originally they were mendicant followers of the Buddha who taught Buddhist ways in return for food. There are more than 200 rules; sexual relations, taking of life, stealing, or boasting of spiritual attainment will lead to expulsion. A bhiksu shaves his head and face, owns a few essential items, and begs daily for his food. THERAVADA Buddhism forbids monks to handle money and perform labor. ZEN Buddhism requires monks to work.

Bhopal Former princely state, central India. Its S boundary is the NARMADA RIVER. It was founded in 1723 by an Afghan chieftain who had served under the Mughal emperor AURANGZEB. It concluded a treaty with the British in 1817. It was the chief state of the Bhopal Agency and the second-largest Muslim principality of the British empire. At India's independence, Bhopal remained a separate Indian province. When it was incorporated into Madhya Pradesh in 1956, BHOPAL city became the state's capital.

Bhopal \bō-'päl\ City (pop., 1991: 1,063,000), capital of Madhya Pradesh state, India. Situated north of NAGPUR, it is a major rail junction. It is the site of India's largest mosque and home to several colleges. In 1984 Bhopal became known for one of the worst industrial accidents in history when tons of toxic gas escaped from a Union Carbide insecticide plant, killing about 3,800 people.

Bhutan \bü-'tän\ *Bhutanese* **Druk-yul** \'drük-'yül\ Kingdom, HIMALAYAS. Area: 16,000 sq mi (41,500 sq km). Population (2001 est.): 2,100,000. Capital: THIMPHU. There are three main ethnic groups: the Buddhist Sharchops (Assamese); the Tibetan Buddhist Bhutia, about three-fifths of the population; and the Hindu Nepalese. Languages: Dzongkha (official), other Tibetan dialects. Religion: Mahayana Buddhism (official). Currency: ngultrum. Its N part lies in the Great Himalayas, with peaks surpassing 24,000 ft (7,300 m) and high valleys lying at 12,000–18,000 ft (3,700–5,500 m). Great Himalayan spurs radiate southward, forming the Lesser Himalayan ranges. Several fertile valleys there, at elevations of 5,000–9,000 ft (1,500–2,700 m), are fairly well

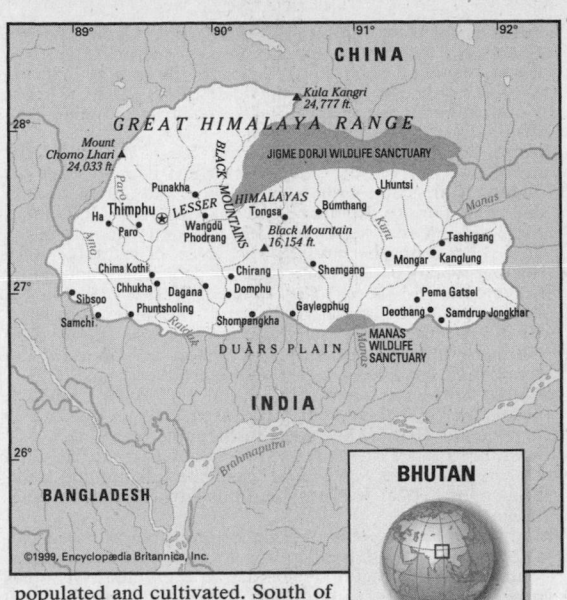

populated and cultivated. South of these mountains lies the Duars Plain, controlling access to the strategic mountain passes; much of it is hot and steamy and covered with dense forest. The Bhutanese economy is mainly agricultural; nearly all exports go to India. It is a constitutional monarchy with one legislative house; its chief of state is the monarch, and its head of government is the chairman of the Council of Ministers. Bhutan's mountains and forests long made it inaccessible to the outside world, and its feudal rulers banned foreigners until well into the 20th cent. It nevertheless became the object of foreign invasions; in 1865 it came under British influence, and in 1910 agreed to be guided by Britain in its foreign affairs. It later became oriented toward British-ruled India, though much of its trade continued to be with Tibet. India took over Britain's role in 1949, and Communist China's 1950 occupation of neighboring Tibet further strengthened Bhutan's ties with India. The apparent Chinese threat made its rulrs aware of the need to modernize, and it has embarked on a program to build roads and hospitals and to create a system of secular education.

Bhutto \'bü-tō\, **Benazir** (b.1953) Pakistani prime minister (1988–90, 1993–96), the first woman leader of a Muslim nation in modern history. After studying at Harvard and Oxford, she led the political opposition to Pres. Mohammad ZIA-UL-HAQ after the 1979 execution of her father, Z. A. BHUTTO. She endured frequent house arrest (1979–84), and was exiled 1984–86. When Zia died in a plane crash in 1988, she became prime minister of a coalition government. She was unable to do much to combat Pakistan's widespread poverty and governmental corruption, and her government was dismissed (1990) on charges of corruption; her second term ended similarly. In 1999 the exiled Bhutto was sentenced in absentia to five years in prison.

Bhutto, Zulfikar Ali (1928–1979) President (1971–73) and prime minister (1973–77) of Pakistan. He served eight years in the government of Mohammad Ayub Khan (1907–1974), then resigned to form the Pakistan People's Party (1967). After the overthrow of the Ayub Khan regime and the Pakistani civil war, Bhutto became president (1971). He nationalized several key industries and taxed landed families. As prime minister, he retained martial law and began a process of Islamization. Bhutto's party won elections in 1977, but the opposition accused him of electoral fraud. Gen. Mohammad ZIA-UL-HAQ seized power and had Bhutto imprisoned and later executed. Benazir BHUTTO is his daughter.

Biafra \bē-'äf-rə\ Former secessionist state, W. Africa. It constituted the former Eastern Region of Nigeria, dominated by the IGBO (Ibo). In the 1960s, the resentment of the HAUSA in the north toward the more prosperous Igbo led to the secession of the Eastern Region as the state of Biafra in 1967. A costly civil war and the death by starvation of about 1 million civilians ended in Biafra's collapse and reincorporation into Nigeria in 1970.

Biafra, Bight of Inlet of the Atlantic Ocean, W. Africa. The innermost bay of the Gulf of GUINEA, it is bounded by Nigeria, Cameroon, Equatorial Guinea, and Gabon, and receives portions of the NIGER and OGOOUÉ rivers. It includes BIOKO island and the ports of MALABO and DOUALA. In the 16th–19th cent. the bay was the scene of extensive slave dealing. Today petroleum is a major economic resource.

Bialystok \byä-ˈwi-stók\ City (pop., 1999 est.: 283,000), NE Poland. Founded in the 14th cent., it was annexed to Prussia 1795–1807, then passed to Russia. It was captured by Germany in both world wars. It is now an important rail junction; it has been a major textile producer since 1863.

Biarritz \byä-ˈrēts\ Town (pop., 1990: 29,000), SW France. It lies on the Gulf of Gascogne (Bay of BISCAY), 11 mi (18 km) from Spain. Biarritz became a fashionable resort after 1854 with the visits of NAPOLEON III and British royalty. Its mild climate and variety of beaches, and the folklore and traditions of the local BASQUES, continue to draw an international clientele.

biathlon Winter sports event combining CROSS-COUNTRY SKIING with rifle sharpshooting. It originated in Scandinavian hunting. It was first included in the Winter Olympics program in 1960. Competitors cover a 20-km (12.5-mi) course, carrying a single-shot rifle and stopping at four points to fire five shots at small targets. Relay and 10-km events were later added.

Bible Sacred scriptures of JUDAISM and CHRISTIANITY. The Jewish scriptures consist of the TORAH (or Pentateuch), the Neviim ("Prophets"), and the Ketuvim ("Writings"), which together constitute what Christians call the OLD TESTAMENT. The Pentateuch and Joshua relate how Israel became a nation and came to possess the Promised Land. The Prophets describe the history of the monarchy and relate the prophets' messages. The Writings include poetry, speculation on good and evil, and history. The Roman Catholic and Eastern Orthodox Bible includes additional Jewish writings called the APOCRYPHA. The NEW TESTAMENT con-

Old Testament: Hebrew Bible

Genesis	Isaiah	Nahum	Song of Songs
Exodus	Jeremiah	Habakkuk	Ruth
Leviticus	Ezekiel	Zephaniah	Lamentations
Numbers	Hosea	Haggai	Ecclesiastes
Deuteronomy	Joel	Zechariah	Esther
Joshua	Amos	Malachi	Daniel
Judges	Obadiah	Psalms	Ezra
1 & 2 Samuel	Jonah	Proverbs	Nehemiah
1 & 2 Kings	Micah	Job	1 & 2 Chronicles

Old Testament: Roman Catholic and Protestant Canons

Catholic	Protestant	Catholic	Protestant
Genesis	Genesis	Wisdom	
Exodus	Exodus	Sirach	
Leviticus	Leviticus	Isaiah	Isaiah
Numbers	Numbers	Jeremiah	Jeremiah
Deuteronomy	Deuteronomy	Lamentations	Lamentations
Joshua	Joshua	Baruch	
Judges	Judges	Ezekiel	Ezekiel
Ruth	Ruth	Daniel	Daniel
1 & 2 Samuel	1 & 2 Samuel	Hosea	Hosea
1 & 2 Kings	1 & 2 Kings	Joel	Joel
1 & 2 Chronicles	1 & 2 Chronicles	Amos	Amos
Ezra	Ezra	Obadiah	Obadiah
Nehemiah	Nehemiah	Jonah	Jonah
Tobit		Micah	Micah
Judith		Nahum	Nahum
Esther	Esther	Habakkuk	Habakkuk
Job	Job	Zephaniah	Zephaniah
Psalms	Psalms	Haggai	Haggai
Proverbs	Proverbs	Zechariah	Zechariah
Ecclesiastes	Ecclesiastes	Malachi	Malachi
Song of Songs	Song of Solomon	1 & 2 Maccabees	

Old Testament: Protestant Apocrypha

1 & 2 Esdras	Additions to Esther	Baruch	Bel and the Dragon
Tobit		Prayer of Azariah	
Judith	Wisdom of Solomon	Susanna	Prayer of Manasses
	Ecclesiasticus		1 & 2 Maccabees

New Testament

Matthew	Romans	Colossians	Hebrews
Mark	1 & 2 Corinthians	1 & 2 Thessalonians	James
Luke	Galatians	1 & 2 Timothy	1 & 2 Peter
John	Ephesians	Titus	1, 2, 3 John
Acts of the Apostles	Philippians	Philemon	Jude
			Revelation

sists of the GOSPELS, which tell of the life, person, and teachings of Jesus; the Acts of the Apostles, which relates the earliest history of Christianity; and the Epistles (Letters), the correspondence of early church leaders (chiefly St. PAUL). The Book of REVELATION foretells the APOCALYPSE.

biblical translation Art and practice of translating the BIBLE. The OLD TESTAMENT was originally written in Hebrew, with scattered passages of Aramaic. It was first translated in its entirety into Aramaic and then, in the 3rd cent. A.D., into Greek. Hebrew scholars created the authoritative Masoretic text (6th–10th cent.) from Aramaic texts, the original Hebrew scrolls having been lost. The NEW TESTAMENT was originally in Greek or Aramaic. St. JEROME's Latin Vulgate (405) was the standard Christian translation for 1,000 years. Martin LUTHER translated the entire Bible into German (1522–34). The first complete English translation appeared in 1382, but it was the King James version (1611) that became the standard for more than three centuries. By the late 20th cent. the entire Bible had been translated into 250 languages.

Bibliothèque Nationale de France \ˌbib-lē-ō-ˈtek-ˌnà-sē-ō-ˈnàl-də-ˈfräⁿs\ Most important library in France and one of the oldest in the world. France's first royal library was established under Charles V (r.1364–80) but later dispersed. Louis XI (r.1461–83) established another; from 1537 it received a copy of every French publication. Moved from Fontainebleau to Paris in the late 16th cent., it opened to the public in 1692 and got its current name in 1795. The collection grew through Revolutionary appropriations and Napoleonic acquisitions. A new facility with a controversial design opened in 1995.

bicameral system System of government in which the LEGISLATURE has two houses. It originated in Britain (see PARLIAMENT) to represent the interests of both the common people and the elite, and to provide a deliberative legislative process. In the U.S., the bicameral system represents a compromise between the claims for equal representation among the states (in the Senate) and equal representation for all its citizens (in the House of Representatives). Each house has powers not held by the other, and measures need the approval of both to become law. Many federal systems of government today have bicameral legislatures, as do all U.S. states but Nebraska. See also CONGRESS OF THE U.S.

bicarbonate of soda *or* **sodium bicarbonate** *or* **baking soda** White, crystalline inorganic compound. It is a weak BASE and dissociates into water and CARBON DIOXIDE gas as it dissolves in the presence of hydrogen ions. In addition to household uses as an antacid, cleaner, and deodorizer, it is used in manufacturing effervescent salts and beverages and baking powder. Industrial uses include production of other sodium salts, treatment of wool and silk, and use in pharmaceuticals, sponge rubber, fire extinguishers, cleaners, lab reagents, mouthwash, and gold and platinum plating.

bichon frise \bē-ˌshōⁿ-frē-ˈzā\ Breed of small dog noted for its fluffy coat and cheerful disposition. Descended from the water SPANIEL, it stands about 9–12 in. (23–30 cm) tall and has a short, blunt muzzle; silky, drooping ears; a puffy, silky, curled coat; and an undercoat. It is mostly white.

bicycle Lightweight, two-wheeled, steerable machine that is propelled by the rider. The wheels are mounted in a metal frame, and the front wheel is held in a movable fork. The

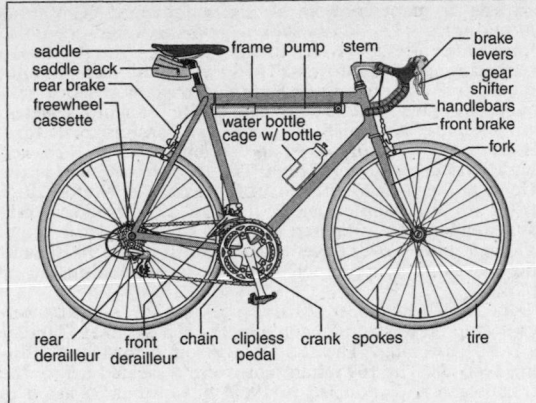

Bicycle Components of a modern touring bicycle.

rider sits on a saddle and steers by handlebars attached to the fork, propelling the bicycle by two pedals attached to cranks that turn a driving sprocket. An endless chain transmits power from the driving sprocket to a back-wheel sprocket. In 1839 the Scottish blacksmith Kirkpatrick Macmillan (1813–1878) built the first bicycle propelled by pedals, cranks, and drive rods. Important innovations were introduced by Pierre and Ernest Michaux in France; by 1865 their company was manufacturing 400 *vélocipèdes* a year. A lighter version produced in England in 1870 (nicknamed the "penny-farthing") featured a large front wheel and small back wheel. By the 1890s the standard bicycle design was established, and with the smooth ride enabled by the new pneumatic tires its popularity exploded. 20th-cent. improvements included lighter frames and improved gears and brakes.

Bidault \bē-ˈdō\, **Georges (-Augustin)** (1899–1983) French statesman. After being imprisoned in Germany (1940), he returned to France (1941) and became head of the French RESISTANCE. After the war he briefly served twice as prime minister (1946, 1949–50) and three times as foreign minister. In 1958 he broke with Charles DE GAULLE and opposed Algerian independence. He advocated terrorism to prevent independence, went underground, and was forced into exile (1962–68).

Biddle, John (1615–1662) Father of English UNITARIANISM. He studied at Oxford Univ. and became master of a free school in Gloucester. In 1644 he wrote *Twelve Arguments Drawn out of Scripture*, denying the deity of the HOLY SPIRIT. For it he was arrested and imprisoned for two years; a second imprisonment followed its publication in 1647. His later writings attacked the doctrine of the Holy TRINITY. Freed from a third imprisonment in 1652, he began to meet for worship with his adherents, who came to be called Unitarians. Oliver CROMWELL exiled him to the Scilly Isles in 1654. He returned in 1658; in 1662 he was again put in prison, where he died.

Biedermeier style \ˈbē-dər-ˌmī-ər\ Style of German and Austrian art, furniture, and decoration (c.1815–48). Gottlieb "Papa" Biedermeier was a fictional cartoon character, the comic symbol of middle-class comfort. The subject matter of the Biedermeier painters was treated sentimentally; Carl Spitzweg (1808–1885) is the best-known. The simplicity and functionality of Biedermeier furniture were derived from the EMPIRE and Directoire styles, but it was characterized by more restrained geometric shapes. The style was revived in the 1960s.

Bielefeld \ˈbē-lə-ˌfelt\ City (pop., 1998 est.: 323,000), NW Germany. The old town was probably founded and chartered in 1214, and the "new town" arose in the late 13th cent. It joined the HANSEATIC LEAGUE in the 14th cent. and passed to BRANDENBURG in 1647. The first mechanized textile mills in Germany were established there in 1851, and it

remains the center of a fabric industry. Heavily damaged in World War II, the city has since been rebuilt.

biennial Any plant that completes its life cycle in two growing seasons. During the first growing season biennials produce roots, stems, and leaves; during the second they produce flowers, fruits, and seeds, and then die. SUGAR BEETS and CARROTS are examples of biennials. See also ANNUAL, PERENNIAL.

Bienville \byaⁿ-ˈvēl\, **Jean-Baptiste Le Moyne de** (1680–1767) Canadian-French explorer, founder of New Orleans. Born in Montreal, he accompanied his brother Pierre d'IBERVILLE on expeditions to the mouth of the Mississippi River. They founded a settlement in 1699, and he later commanded the colony of Louisiana (1701–12, 1717–23). He founded New Orleans in 1718 and made it the colony's capital in 1722. Recalled to France in 1723, he returned as governor of Louisiana 1733–43.

Bierce, Ambrose (Gwinnett) (1842–1914?) U.S. writer. Born in Meigs Co., Ohio, he became a newspaper columnist and editor in San Francisco, specializing in attacks on frauds. Among his short stories (numbering almost 100), the best-known is "An Occurrence at Owl Creek Bridge." His *Devil's Dictionary* (1906) is a volume of caustic definitions. Tired of American life, he went to Mexico in 1913 and vanished, possibly killed in the 1914 siege of Ojinaga.

Bierstadt \ˈbēr-ˌshtät\, **Albert** (1830–1902) U.S. (German-born) painter of the HUDSON RIVER SCHOOL. Having grown up in the U.S., as a young man he traveled through Europe sketching before returning to join a westward-bound expedition in 1859. Specializing in grandiose pictures of vast mountain scenery, he achieved great popularity with his huge panoramic and often fanciful scenes of the West, including *The Rocky Mountains* (1863) and *Mt. Corcoran* (c.1875–77), actually executed in his New York studio.

big bang Model of the origin of the UNIVERSE, which holds that it explosively expanded from a state of extremely high temperature and density 10–15 billion years ago. It assumes that Albert EINSTEIN's general theory of RELATIVITY correctly describes the gravitational interaction of all matter and that one's view of the universe does not depend on direction of observation or on location, allowing calculation of physical conditions in the universe back to a very early time called the Planck time. According to George GAMOW's model, the universe expanded rapidly from a highly compressed state, with a steady decrease in density and temperature. Within seconds, MATTER predominated over ANTIMATTER and certain nuclei formed. It took a million years before ATOMS could form and RADIATION could travel through space unimpeded. The abundances of hydrogen, helium, and lithium and the discovery of COSMIC BACKGROUND RADIATION support the model, which also explains the RED SHIFTS of galaxies.

Big Ben Clock designed by Sir Edmund Beckett (1816–1905), housed in the tower at the E end of Britain's Houses of Parliament. Big Ben is famous for its accuracy and its 13-ton bell. It is named for Sir Benjamin Hall, commissioner of works at the time of its installation in 1859.

Big Bend National Park Preserve, SW Texas. It lies 250 mi (400 km) southeast of EL PASO, and occupies 1,252 sq mi (3,243 sq km). It was established in 1944 and named for the wide bend in the RIO GRANDE along its S edge. It has magnificent mountain and desert scenery; it is home to more than 1,000 species of plants, as well as coyotes, pumas, and roadrunners.

Big Bertha GUN from either of two sets of long-range CANNON produced by the Krupp works (see THYSSEN KRUPP STAHL) in Germany during World War I. The first were 420-mm (16.5-in.) howitzers used by German forces advancing through Belgium in 1914. The second were specially built to bombard Paris in 1918. About 112 ft (34 m) long, they weighed 200 tons (181 metric tons) and were 210 mm (8 in.) or more in caliber. The Paris guns had an unprecedented range of 75 mi (121 km) and bombarded the city for 140 days. They were nicknamed for the Krupp matriarch Bertha von Bohlen.

Big Cypress Swamp Swamp region and national preserve, S Florida. Covering 2,400 sq mi (6,200 sq km), the region merges into the EVERGLADES on the east. It is dominated by

cypress trees, and wildlife is abundant. The SEMINOLE Indians have reservations in the area.

Bigelow, Erastus Brigham (1814–1879) U.S. industrialist. Born in W. Boylston, Mass., at 23 he invented his first LOOM for LACE manufacture, which he followed with looms for weaving figured fabrics, tapestry carpeting, and ingrain carpeting. In 1843 he and his brother Horatio established a gingham mill, around which grew up the town of Clinton, Mass., and he founded the Bigelow carpet mills there several years later. From 1845 to 1851 he developed his greatest invention, a power loom for the manufacture of Brussels and Wilton carpets. He was a cofounder of the MASSACHUSETTS INSTITUTE OF TECHNOLOGY (1861).

Bigfoot *or* **Sasquatch** Large, hairy, humanlike creature that reportedly lives in isolated areas of the NW U.S. and W Canada. Descriptions of Bigfoot, said to be a primate 6–15 ft. (2–4.5 m) in height, are similar to those of the ABOMINABLE SNOWMAN. Footprints have measured up to 24 in (60 cm) in length. Despite many reported sightings, there is still no solid evidence that Bigfoot exists.

bighorn Either of two similar N. American sheep: the Canadian bighorn *(Ovis canadensis)* and the Dall sheep *(O. dalli)*. Bighorn have compact, muscular bodies; short, pointed ears; and very short tails. Both sexes have horns that in the male may curve in a spiral more than 40 in. (1 m) long. Their fur is usually brown with a whitish rump patch. Both species are about 40 in. (1 m) tall at the shoulder; the Canadian bighorn is heavier. They live in remote crags and cliffs of mountainous areas and feed mainly on grasses.

Canadian bighorn sheep *(Ovis canadensis)*

Bighorn Mountains Mountain range, S Montana and N Wyoming. A range of the N ROCKY MTNS. extending 120 mi (193 km), its mountains rise abruptly 4,000–5,000 ft (1,200–1,500 m) above the GREAT PLAINS and Bighorn Basin. The highest is Cloud Peak, at 13,165 ft (4,013 m). Bighorn National Forest covers part of the range. On Medicine Mtn. is the Medicine Wheel, a prehistoric stone-spoked circle 70 ft (20 m) in diameter.

Bighorn River River, Wyoming and Montana. It flows north 336 mi (541 km) into the YELLOWSTONE RIVER in SE Montana. The Little Bighorn joins the main stream at Hardin, Mont. The Bighorn Canyon National Recreation Area stretches along the Montana–Wyoming border. See also Battle of the LITTLE BIGHORN.

Big Stick Policy Policy named by Pres. Theodore ROOSEVELT to describe the assertion of U.S. dominance as a moral imperative. It was taken from an African proverb, "Speak softly and carry a big stick; you will go far." Roosevelt first used it when he asked Congress for money to increase U.S. naval preparedness to support his diplomatic objectives. The press used the phrase to describe Roosevelt's Latin America policy and his domestic policy of regulating monopolies.

Big Sur Scenic region along the Pacific coast of W California. It comprises a ruggedly beautiful stretch of seacoast 100 mi (160 km) long. It extends southward from Carmel to the Hearst Castle at San Simeon. A narrow, mountainous coastal road affords views of the Pacific Ocean and the wilderness areas. The Pfeiffer-Big Sur State Park contains the town of Big Sur; the home of Robinson JEFFERS is a local landmark.

Big Ten Conference *formerly* Western Intercollegiate Conference. U.S. college football league. It was formed in 1896 by seven universities: Chicago, Illinois, Michigan, Minnesota, Northwestern, Purdue, and Wisconsin. Iowa and Indiana were added in 1899, and Ohio State in 1912. Chicago officially withdrew in 1946. Michigan State was added in 1949 and Pennsylvania State in 1990 (bringing the actual total to 11). From 1947 to 2001 it sent a team to every ROSE BOWL. Competition now extends over a variety of sports for both men and women.

big tree *or* **giant sequoia** *or* **Sierra redwood** Coniferous EVERGREEN *(Sequoiadendron giganteum;* see CONIFER) found in scattered groves on the W slopes of the Sierra Nevada range of California. The largest of all trees in bulk, the big tree is distinguished from the coastal REDWOOD *(Sequoia)* by leaves that lie close against the branches, scaleless winter buds, and cones requiring two seasons to mature. Both have a pyramidal shape, reddish-brown furrowed bark, and drooping branches. The largest specimen is the General Sherman tree in SEQUOIA NATIONAL PARK—101.5 ft (31 m) in circumference at its base, 272.4 ft (83 m) tall, and weighing an estimated 6,167 tons (5,593 metric tons). Though some groves have been cut, most of the 70 remaining groves are now protected by state or national forests or parks.

Bikini Atoll with about 20 islets, MARSHALL ISLANDS, MICRONESIA. It was administered by the U.S. from 1947 under a U.N. trusteeship. The U.S. used the atoll for atomic testing 1946–58. The 167 inhabitants were relocated before the tests began and returned in 1969, but evacuated again in 1978 because of high radiation levels. In 1997 the area was pronounced safe. The atoll became part of the Republic of the Marshall Islands in 1979.

Biko \\'bē-kō\\, **Stephen** (1946–1977) S. African political activist. In 1969 he founded the Black Consciousness Movement to raise awareness of APARTHEID oppression. He was "banned" by the S. African government in 1973 and was arrested several times in 1976–77. His death from injuries suffered in police custody made him a martyr for S. African black nationalism. In 1997 five former officers confessed to Biko's murder.

Bilbao \\bil-'bä-,ō, bil-'baù\\ Port city (pop., 1998 est.: 358,000), N Spain. It is located 7 mi (11 km) inland from the Bay of BISCAY. The largest city in the BASQUE COUNTRY, it was chartered in 1300. In the 18th cent. it prospered through trade with Spain's New World colonies. The city was sacked by French troops in the PENINSULAR WAR (1808) and besieged during the Carlist Wars (see CARLISM). It is a center of the metallurgical industries and shipbuilding. Landmarks include the 14th-cent. Cathedral of Santiago and the striking Guggenheim Museum Bilbao.

bildungsroman \\'bil-,dùnz-rō-,män\\ (German: "novel of character development") Class of novel that depicts the moral and psychological development of the main character. It usually ends with the hero's foolish mistakes and painful disappointments behind him and a promising life ahead. It grew out of folk tales in which a dunce goes out into the world to seek adventure. The first example in German, J. W. von GOETHE's *Wilhelm Meister's Apprenticeship* (1795–96), remains a classic.

bile *or* **gall** Greenish-yellow liver secretion passed to the GALLBLADDER and thence into the duodenum for FAT digestion. Bile contains bile acids and salts, CHOLESTEROL, and electrolytes that keep it slightly acidic. In the intestine, products of the acids and salts emulsify fat to prepare it for the action of pancreatic and intestinal fat-splitting enzymes.

bilharziasis See SCHISTOSOMIASIS

bilingualism Ability to speak two languages. It may be acquired early by children in regions where most adults speak two languages. Children may also become bilingual by learning languages in two different social settings; for example, one from their parents and another from their nurses and family servants. A second language can also be acquired in school. Bilingualism can also refer to the use of two languages in teaching. Advocates of bilingual education argue that it speeds learning in all subjects for children who speak a foreign language at home. Detractors counter that it hinders such children from mastering the language of the larger society and limits their later work and educational opportunities.

bill See BEAK

billiards Any of various games played on a cloth-topped, cushion-railed rectangular table by driving small, hard balls against one another or into pockets with a long stick called a cue. Carom, or French billiards, is played with three balls, two white and one red, on a table without pockets. The object is to stroke the white cue ball so that it hits the two object balls in succession, scoring a carom (one point). English billiards is also played with three balls but on a pocketed table; it is scored in various ways. Snooker is another popular British billiards game. The principal billiards game in N. America is pocket billiards, or POOL.

Billings City (pop., 2000: 89,000), S central Montana. Billings was established on the YELLOWSTONE RIVER in 1882 by the Northern Pacific Railway and named for its president. It is now a trading and shipping point for wool, livestock, and agriculture.

Billings, John Shaw (1838–1913) U.S. surgeon and librarian. Born in Switzerland Co., Ind., Billings worked for the U.S. Army 1861–95. He fostered the growth of the surgeon general's library in Washington, D.C., developing what would become the National Library of Medicine. He founded the monthly *Index Medicus* (1879) and published the first *Index Catalogue* (1880–95). He also designed Johns Hopkins Hospital, ran national vital-statistics programs, led the U.S. effort to end yellow fever, and was the first director of the New York Public Library. His organization of U.S. medical institutions was central to modernization of hospital care and maintenance of public health.

Billings, William (1746–1800) American hymn composer, sometimes called the first American composer. Born in Boston, he worked as a tanner and was largely self-taught in music. His *New England Psalm-Singer* (1770) was the first published collection of American music; his other works include *The Singing Master's Assistant* (1778) and *The Continental Harmony* (1794). His robust and primitive style, lacking instrumental parts, has seemed to embody the distinctive virtues of early America.

bill of exchange Short-term negotiable financial instrument consisting of a written order from a seller of goods to a buyer requiring the buyer to pay a certain sum on demand or at a future time. Bills of exchange are often used in international transactions, and the holder of such a bill may redeem it in cash immediately by selling it to a bank at a discount. See also PROMISSORY NOTE.

Bill of Rights (1689) British law, one of the basic instruments of the British constitution. It incorporated the provisions of the Declaration of Rights, which WILLIAM III and MARY II accepted upon taking the throne, and declared illegal various practices of JAMES II. It made the monarchy clearly conditional on the will of PARLIAMENT, and provided freedom from arbitrary government. It also dealt with the succession to the throne.

Bill of Rights First 10 amendments to the U.S. CONSTITUTION, adopted as a single unit in 1791. They are a collection of guarantees of individual rights and of limitations on federal and state governments. The first Congress submitted 12 amendments to the states, 10 of which were ratified. The 1st Amendment guarantees freedom of religion, speech, and the press, and grants the right to petition for redress and to assemble peaceably. The 2nd guarantees the right to keep and bear arms. The 3rd prohibits the quartering of soldiers in private dwellings in peacetime. The 4th protects against unreasonable SEARCH AND SEIZURE. The 5th establishes grand-jury indictment for serious offenses, protects against DOUBLE JEOPARDY in criminal cases, and prohibits compelling a person to testify against himself. The 6th establishes the right of the accused to a speedy trial and an impartial jury, to legal counsel, and to the obtaining of witnesses in his favor. The 7th preserves the right to trial by jury in serious civil suits and prohibits double jeopardy in civil cases. The 8th prohibits excessive bail and cruel and unusual punishment. The 9th states that enumeration of certain rights in the Constitution does not mean the abrogation of rights not mentioned. The 10th reserves to the states and people any powers not delegated to the national government.

Billy the Kid *orig.* William H. Bonney, Jr. *or* Henry McCarty (1859?–1881) U.S. outlaw. Born in New York City, he grew up in New Mexico. His career of lawlessness throughout the Southwest began early, and he had allegedly killed 27 men when he was captured in 1880 by Sheriff Pat GARRETT. Convicted and sentenced to hang, he escaped from jail, killing two deputies, and remained at large until Garrett tracked him down and killed him.

Biloxi \bi-ˈlək-sē, bi-ˈläk-sē\ Peninsular coastal city (pop., 2000: 50,000), SE Mississippi. It grew out of Ft. Louis (established 1719), near the Mississippi valley's first permanent white settlement (1699). It has been under the flags of France, Spain, Britain, the W. Florida Republic, and the Confederacy. Casino gambling has become its chief industry, augmented by seafood processing. Jefferson DAVIS's last home is nearby.

binary code Code used in DIGITAL COMPUTERS, based on a binary number system in which there are only two possible states, off and on, usually symbolized by 0 and 1. In a decimal system each digit position represents a power of 10 (100, 1,000, etc.), but in a binary system each digit position represents a power of 2 (4, 8, 16, etc.). A binary code signal is a series of electrical pulses that represent numbers, characters, and operations to be performed. A device called a clock sends out regular pulses, and components such as TRANSISTORS switch on (1) or off (0) to pass or block the pulses. The four fundamental arithmetic operations (addition, subtraction, multiplication, and division) can all be reduced to combinations of simple Boolean algebraic operations (see BOOLEAN ALGEBRA) on binary numbers.

binary star Pair of stars orbiting a common center of gravity. The distances between them vary widely. Perhaps half of all stars in the Milky Way are binary or multiple stars. Some binaries form a class of VARIABLE STARS (see ECLIPSING VARIABLE STAR), while others are detected only by the motions of a single visible star.

binding energy ENERGY required to separate a particle from a system of particles or to disperse all the particles of a system. Nuclear binding energy is the energy required to separate an atomic NUCLEUS into its constituent PROTONS and NEUTRONS. ELECTRON binding energy, or IONIZATION POTENTIAL, is the energy required to remove an electron from an ATOM, MOLECULE, or ION. The binding energy of a single proton or neutron in a nucleus is about a million times greater than that of a single electron in an atom.

bindweed Any twining plant of the closely related genera *Convolvulus* and *Calystegia* in the MORNING-GLORY FAMILY, producing funnel-shaped flowers. Bellbine, or greater bindweed *(Calystegia sepium),* native in Eurasia and N. America, is a twining perennial that grows from creeping, underground stems and is common in hedges and woods and along roadsides. The weedy, perennial field bindweed *(Convolvulus arvensis),* European but widely naturalized in N. America, twines around crop plants and along roadsides. Rosewood oil comes from certain species of *Convolvulus.*

Binet \bi-ˈnā\, **Alfred** (1857–1911) French psychologist. He served as director of a research laboratory at the Sorbonne 1895–1911. A major figure in the development of experimental psychology in France, he founded *L'Année Psychologique,* the first French journal of psychology, in 1895. He developed experimental techniques to measure reasoning ability; between 1905 and 1911 he and Theodore Simon developed influential scales for the measurement of intelligence of children. His works include *Experimental Study of Intelligence* (1903) and *A Method of Measuring the Development of the Intelligence of Young Children* (1915).

Bingham, George Caleb (1811–1879) U.S. painter and frontier politician. Born in Virginia, he was largely self-taught. He entered politics in Missouri and worked as an itinerant portrait painter before turning to lively scenes of frontier life for inspiration. He is known for his incisive characterizations, clear, golden light, and talent for organizing large, dense compositions. His best-known works include *Fur Traders Descending the Missouri* (1845) and *Jolly Flatboatmen* (1846).

bingo Game of chance played with cards having numbered squares corresponding to numbered balls drawn at random and won by covering five such squares in a row (vertically, horizontally, or diagonally). Cards are purchased and proceeds are placed into a common "pot"; winning cards are awarded a portion of the pot. Wildly popular in the mid-1900s, bingo has since declined, perhaps displaced by LOTTERY operations and legalized gambling.

Binh Dinh Vuong See LE LOI

bin Laden \ˌbin-ˈlä-dən\, **Osama** (b.1957) Terrorist organizer of attacks against the U.S., especially the SEPTEMBER 11 ATTACKS. Born in Saudi Arabia to one of its wealthiest families, bin Laden joined the resistance against the Soviet occupation in Afghanistan and returned home a hero in 1989. Disillusioned with what he saw as corruption in the

B

Saudi government, and opposed to the presence (from 1990) of U.S. troops in Saudi Arabia, he organized the AL-QAEDA terrorist network. Accused of subversion by the Saudi government, he fled to the Sudan (1994), where he organized terrorist training camps until he was expelled (1996). He returned to Afghanistan, where he received protection from its ruling TALIBAN. Several Al-Qaeda attacks on international targets followed. When the U.S. invaded Afghanistan after the SEPTEMBER 11 ATTACKS, he escaped into hiding.

binoculars Optical instrument consisting of two similar TELESCOPES, one for each eye, mounted on a single frame. Each telescope usually has two PRISMS, which reinvert the inverted image provided by the eyepiece of each telescope. Light rays travel along a folded path inside the telescopes, so the instrument has a shorter overall length. The prisms also provide better depth perception at greater distances, by allowing the two objectives (object LENSES) to be set farther apart than the eyepieces.

binomial nomenclature System of naming organisms. Each is given two names, the GENUS (capitalized) and SPECIES (lowercase), both written in italics. For example, the tea rose is *Rosa odorata;* the common horse is *Equus caballus.* The system was developed by Carolus LINNAEUS in the mid-18th cent. By the late 19th cent. the nomenclature of many groups of organisms was confused. International committees in the fields of zoology, botany, bacteriology, and virology have since established rules to clarify the situation. See also TAXONOMY.

binomial theorem In algebra, a formula for expansion of the binomial $(x + y)$ raised to any positive integer power. A simple case is the expansion of $(x + y)^2$, which is $x^2 + 2xy + y^2$. In general, the expression $(x + y)^n$ expands to the sum of terms $n + 1$ in which the power of x decreases from n to 0 while the power of y increases from 0 to n in successive terms.

biochemistry Field of science concerned with chemical substances and processes that occur in plants, animals, and microorganisms. It involves the quantitative determination and structural ANALYSIS of the organic compounds that make up CELLS (PROTEINS, CARBOHYDRATES, and LIPIDS) and of those that play key roles in CHEMICAL REACTIONS vital to life (e.g., NUCLEIC ACIDS, VITAMINS, and HORMONES). Biochemists study the chemical reactions by which proteins are synthesized, food is converted to ENERGY (see METABOLISM), hereditary characteristics are transmitted (see HEREDITY), energy is stored and released, and all biological chemical reactions are catalyzed (see CATALYSIS, ENZYME). Biochemistry uses many techniques of organic, analytical, and PHYSICAL CHEMISTRY, medicine, and physiology.

biodegradability Capacity of a material to decompose by biological action, usually referring to the environmental breakdown of waste by microorganisms. Generally, plant and animal products are biodegradable and mineral substances (e.g., metals, glass, plastics) are not. Presence or absence of oxygen affects biodegradability. Disposal of non-biodegradable waste is a primary source of pollution.

biodiversity Diversity of plant and animal species in an environment. Sometimes habitat diversity (the variety of places where organisms live) and genetic diversity (diversity of genetic information within a species; that is, the number of distinct populations of a species) are also considered types of biodiversity. The estimated 3–30 million species on earth are divided unequally among the world's habitats, with 50–90% of the world's species diversity occurring in tropical regions. The more diverse a habitat, the better chance it has of surviving a change or threat to it. The 1992 Earth Summit resulted in a treaty for the preservation of biodiversity.

bioengineering Application of ENGINEERING principles and equipment to BIOLOGY and MEDICINE. It includes the development and fabrication of life-support systems for underwater and SPACE EXPLORATION, devices for medical treatment (see DIALYSIS, PROSTHESIS), and instruments for monitoring biological processes. Development has been particularly rapid in the area of artificial organs. Bioengineers also develop equipment that enables humans to main-

tain body functions in hostile environments, such as space suits.

biofeedback Information supplied instantaneously about an individual's own physiological processes. Cardiovascular activity, temperature, brain waves, or muscle tension is monitored electronically and returned or "fed back" to the individual through a gauge, a light, or a sound. A type of BEHAVIOR THERAPY, biofeedback training is sometimes used in combination with psychotherapy to help patients understand and change their habitual reactions to stress. Complaints treated through biofeedback include migraine headaches, gastrointestinal problems, high blood pressure, and epileptic seizures.

biography Form of nonfiction whose subject is the life of an individual. The origins of modern biography lie with PLUTARCH's moralizing lives of prominent Greeks and Romans and SUETONIUS' gossipy lives of the Caesars. Few biographies of commoners were written until the 16th cent. The major developments of English biography came in the 18th cent., with such works as James BOSWELL's *Life of Johnson*. Psychoanalysis and impatience with Victorian reticence led in the 20th cent. to highly revealing biographies. See also AUTOBIOGRAPHY.

Bioko \bē-'ō-kō\ *formerly* **Fernando Póo** \fer-'nän-dō-'pō\ Island (pop., 1995 est.: 47,000), Bight of BIAFRA, W. Africa. It lies 100 mi (160 km) northwest of continental Equatorial Guinea, of which it is a part. Bioko became the official name in 1979. Volcanic in origin, with an area of 779 sq mi (2,018 sq km), it rises sharply from the sea; its highest point is Santa Isabel Peak, at 9,869 ft (3,008 m). MALABO, the country's capital, is located on Bioko. The island was visited by the Portuguese explorer Fernão Pó, probably in 1472. Though claimed by Spain after 1778, the first attempt at firm Spanish control came only in 1858.

biological rhythm Periodic biological fluctuation in an organism corresponding to and in response to periodic environmental change, such as day and night, or high and low tide. The internal mechanism that maintains this rhythm even without the apparent environmental stimulus is a "biological clock." Rhythms may have 24-hour (CIRCADIAN RHYTHM), monthly, or annual cycles. See also JET LAG.

biological warfare *or* **germ warfare** Military use of disease-producing agents, such as BACTERIA (including those that cause ANTHRAX and BOTULISM) and VIRUSES, and the means for combating them. A 1925 Geneva protocol prohibited use of biological agents in warfare, and in 1972 more than 70 countries signed the Biological and Toxin Weapons Convention, prohibiting production, stockpiling, or development of biological weapons and requiring destruction of existing stockpiles. One hope was to prevent an agent's escaping from control, as is said to have been the cause of the BLACK DEATH. The British in the French and Indian War, and U.S. Army units in the 19th cent., gave blankets used by SMALLPOX victims to American Indians. In World War I the Germans infected Romanian cavalry horses and U.S. livestock with glanders. The Japanese used biological agents against China in the 1930s. Despite the international ban, several nations are believed to retain stocks of biological-warfare agents.

biology Study of living things and their vital processes. Biology is standardly divided into branches based on the levels of biological organization involved (e.g., molecules, cells, individuals, populations) and on the specific topic under investigation (e.g., structure and function, growth and development). According to this scheme, biology's main subdivisions include morphology, PHYSIOLOGY, TAXONOMY, EMBRYOLOGY, GENETICS, and ECOLOGY. Alternatively, biology can be subdivided into fields especially concerned with one type of living thing; for example, BOTANY (plants), ZOOLOGY (animals), ORNITHOLOGY (birds), entomology (insects), MYCOLOGY (fungi), MICROBIOLOGY (microorganisms), and BACTERIOLOGY (bacteria). See also BIOCHEMISTRY, MOLECULAR BIOLOGY.

bioluminescence \ˌbī-ō-ˌlü-mə-'ne-s°ns\ Emission of light by an organism or biochemical system. It occurs in a wide range of protists and animals, including bacteria and fungi, insects, marine invertebrates, and fish. Luminous species are widely scattered taxonomically, with no clear-cut pattern, though most are marine. It results from a chemical reaction that produces radiant energy very efficiently, giving off very little heat. The essential light-emitting components are usually the organic molecule luciferin and the ENZYME luciferase, which are specific for different organisms. In higher organisms, light production is used to frighten predators and to help members of a species recognize each other. Its functional role in lower organisms such as bacteria, dinoflagellates, and fungi is uncertain.

biome \'bī-ˌōm\ Largest geographic biotic unit, a major community of plants and animals with similar environmental requirements. It is named for the dominant type of vegetation, such as grassland or coniferous forest. Several similar biomes constitute a biome type; for example, the temperate deciduous forest biome type includes the deciduous forest biomes of Asia, Europe, and N. America.

biophysics Discipline concerned with applications of the principles and methods of the physical sciences to biological problems. Biophysics deals with biological functions and interactions that depend on physical agents such as electricity, mechanical force, light, sound, or ionizing radiation, and with interactions between living things and their environment as in locomotion, navigation, and communication. Its subjects include bone, nerve impulses, muscle, and vision as well as organic molecules, using such tools as paper CHROMATOGRAPHY and X-ray CRYSTALLOGRAPHY.

biopsy \'bī-ˌäp-sē\ Procedure in which cells or tissues are removed from a patient and examined by microscope. The sample may be obtained from any organ, by suction through a needle, swabbing, scraping, ENDOSCOPY, or cutting out the entire structure (excision) or part of it (incision) to be tested. Biopsy is a standard step in distinguishing malignant from benign tumors and can provide other useful information.

biosolids Sewage sludge, used as a FERTILIZER. Biosolids must first be stabilized through processing to reduce concentrations of heavy metals and harmful organisms (certain BACTERIA, VIRUSES, and other pathogens). This processing also reduces the volume of material and stabilizes the organic matter in it, thus reducing the potential for odors. Use of biosolids in agriculture has become controversial, critics claiming that even treated sewage may harbor harmful bacteria, viruses, and heavy metals.

biosphere Life-supporting stratum extending from a few miles into the earth's atmosphere to the deep-sea vents of the oceans. The biosphere is a global ECOSYSTEM that can be broken down into regional ecosystems, or BIOMES. Organisms in the biosphere are classified into trophic levels (see FOOD CHAIN) and communities.

biotechnology Application to industry of advances made in the biological sciences. The growth of the field is linked to the development in the 1970s of GENETIC ENGINEERING and the 1980 U.S. Supreme Court decision that "a live human-made microorganism is a patentable matter." Numerous biotechnology firms manufacture genetically engineered substances for a variety of mostly medical, agricultural, and ecological uses.

biotin \'bī-ə-tən\ Organic compound, part of the VITAMIN B COMPLEX, essential for growth and well-being in animals and some microorganisms. Because the bacteria normally present in the LARGE INTESTINE can synthesize biotin, humans do not require it in their diet. Biotin is needed to synthesize FATTY ACIDS and convert AMINO ACIDS to GLUCOSE in the body.

bipolar disorder *or* **manic-depressive psychosis** Mental illness characterized by the alternation of manic and depressive states. DEPRESSION is the more common symptom, and many patients experience only a brief period of overoptimism and mild euphoria during the manic phase. A physiological condition, which seems to be inheritable, it is most commonly treated with LITHIUM carbonate.

Biqa, Al See BEKAA VALLEY

birch Any of about 40 species of short-lived ornamental and timber trees and shrubs of the genus *Betula,* the largest genus of the family Betulaceae, which also contains ALDERS, FILBERTS, *Carpinus* (hornbeam), and the genera *Ostrya* and *Ostryopsis.* Birches are found throughout cool regions of the Northern Hemisphere. Leaves are simple,

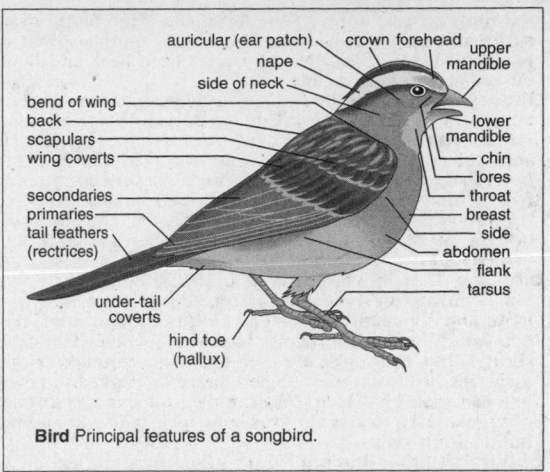

Bird Principal features of a songbird.

serrate, and alternate; male and female flowers are borne on the same plant. The fruit is a small NUT or short-winged samara (dry, winged fruit). Birches produce economically important timber. Oil obtained from birch twigs smells and tastes like wintergreen and is used in tanning Russian leather (see TANNING).

Bird, Larry (Joe) (b.1956) U.S. basketball player. Born in Baden, Ind., the 6-ft 9-in. (2-m 6-cm) Bird was drafted by the Boston Celtics as a forward; he helped lead that team to NBA championships in 1981, 1984, and 1986 and was named the NBA's most valuable player 1984–86. He retired in 1992. Named head coach of the Indiana Pacers in 1997, he immediately took the team to its best record in franchise history. He is considered one of the best all-around players in basketball history.

bird Any member of the warm-blooded VERTEBRATE class Aves, containing about 8,700 living species. FEATHERS distinguish birds from all other animals. They have a four-chambered heart (like MAMMALS), forelimbs modified into WINGS, an egg with a calcium-containing shell, and keen vision. Dietary preferences and NEST structure vary widely. Almost all species incubate their eggs. The big flying birds have evolved skeletons in which part of the bone is replaced by air spaces, reducing their weight. The crop, an enlarged part of the esophagus used for temporary food storage, enables birds to feed while in flight. Humans use birds and their eggs for food, hunt wild birds for sport, and use feathers for decoration and insulation. More than 1,000 extinct species have been identified from fossil remains; the earliest known fossil bird is the ARCHAEOPTERYX.

birding See BIRD-WATCHING

bird-of-paradise Any of about 40 species (family Paradisaeidae) of small to medium-sized forest birds that are rivaled by only a few pheasants and hummingbirds in color and in the bizarre shape of the males' plumage. Courting males perform mating rituals for hours on a perch or in a cleared space on the forest floor. Birds-of-paradise are found in the New Guinea highlands and on nearby islands; some species are found also in Australia.

bird of prey Any bird that pursues other animals for food. Diurnal birds of prey (order Falconiformes, comprising EAGLES, FALCONS, HAWKS, and VULTURES) are also called raptors. Noctur-

King of Saxony's bird-of-paradise (*Pteridophora alberti*)

nal birds of prey (order Strigiformes) are the OWLS. CONDORS and eagles are among the largest and strongest of birds. All birds of prey have a hook-tipped beak and sharp curved claws called talons.

Birdseye, Clarence (1886–1956) U.S. businessman and inventor. Born in New York City, he developed a process for FREEZING foods in small packages suitable for retailing. He achieved rapid freezing by placing packaged food between two refrigerated metal plates. Though his were not the first frozen foods, his highly efficient process largely preserved the original taste of the food. In 1929 his company was bought by Postum, Inc., which later became GENERAL FOODS CORP.

birdsong Certain vocalizations of birds, characteristic of males during the breeding season, for the attraction of a mate and for territorial defense. Birdsong also reinforces pair bonds, and some species have a flight song. Birdcalls, shorter than birdsongs, are used for communication within a species. Birdsong may be hereditary or learned; a newly hatched male chaffinch, for example, can sing a "subsong" but must learn to sing the true song by listening to and imitating adult males.

bird-watching *or* **birding** Observation or identification of wild birds in their natural habitat. Basic equipment includes binoculars, a field guide to aid identification, and a notebook for recording time and place of sightings. The observations compiled by amateurs are often useful to scientists in determining species dispersal, habitat, and migration patterns. Before 1900 most students of birds had to shoot them in order to identify them. Birding's popularity was stimulated particularly by the field guides (beginning in 1934) of R. T. PETERSON.

Birkenau See AUSCHWITZ

Birmingham \'bər-miŋ-,ham\ City (pop., 2000: 246,000), N central Alabama. It is Alabama's largest city. Founded in 1871, it developed as the South's iron and steel center. A barge canal leads south to MOBILE. Birmingham was the scene of civil rights drives by M. L. KING, Jr., in the early 1960s, and in 1963 four black girls were killed in a church bombing; this incident gave major impetus to the CIVIL RIGHTS MOVEMENT.

Birmingham \'bər-miŋ-əm\ City (pop., 1999 est.: 961,000), central England. It lies 100 mi (160 km) northwest of London. Its first charter was granted in 1166. It became a center of the INDUSTRIAL REVOLUTION, counting among its citizens James WATT, Joseph PRIESTLEY, and the typographer John Baskerville (1706–1775). It suffered heavy bombing during World War II. Rebuilt, it remains the chief center of Britain's light and medium industry and the cultural center for a wide area, with two universities.

Birney, (Alfred) Earle (1904–1995) Canadian poet. Born in Calgary, Alberta, he received a PhD from the Univ. of Toronto and published his first poetry collection, *David* (1942), during his time there. After serving in World War II, he wrote *Now Is Time* (1946) and other collections, experimenting with sound poems and exploring concrete poetry. He also wrote two novels, a verse drama, and several radio plays.

Birney, James G(illespie) (1792–1857) U.S. politician and antislavery leader. Born in Danville, Ky., he moved to Alabama and was elected to its legislature in 1819. Active in the state antislavery societies, in 1837 he was elected secretary of the AMERICAN ANTI-SLAVERY SOCIETY. After the group split, he helped lead the moderate faction that became the Liberty Party, and was its presidential candidate in 1840 and 1844.

birth See PARTURITION

birth control Voluntary limiting of human reproduction, using such means as CONTRACEPTION, sexual abstinence, surgical STERILIZATION, and induced ABORTION. The term was coined in 1914–15 by Margaret SANGER. Medically, birth control is often advised when childbirth might endanger the mother's health or substantial risk exists of bearing a severely disabled child. Socially and economically, limitation of reproduction frequently reflects a desire to maintain or improve family living standards.

birthmark Unusual mark or blemish on the skin at birth. They are usually harmless, and many fade in childhood;

those that do not can sometimes be removed by laser surgery or abrasion. See also MOLE.

Biruni \bē-'rü-nē\, **al-** (973–1048) Persian scientist and scholar. Some time after 1017, he went to India and wrote an encyclopedic account of it. Later he settled in Afghanistan, where he was patronized by the GHAZNAVID DYNASTY. Conversant with many languages, he wrote in Arabic, producing works in widely diverse fields. His scientific achievements included accurate calculations of latitude and longitude and explanations of natural springs by the laws of hydrostatics. His best-known works are *India* and *Chronology*.

Biscay, Bay of *or* **Gulf of Gascony** *French* **Golfe de Gascogne** \,gôlf-də-gà-'skòn^y\ *Spanish* **Golfo de Vizcaya** \'gōl-fō-,thä-bēth-'kä-yä\ Inlet of the Atlantic Ocean, bounded by SW France and NW Spain. It has an area of about 86,000 sq mi (223,000 sq km). It is known for its rough seas. It receives the LOIRE, Adour, and GARONNE rivers. Its ports include Brest, NANTES, BORDEAUX, BILBAO, SANTANDER, and Avilés. French coastal resorts include BIARRITZ and Saint-Jean-de-Luz.

Biscayne Bay Inlet of the Atlantic Ocean, SE U.S. Located along SE Florida, it is about 40 mi (64 km) long and 2–10 mi (3–16 km) wide; it forms part of the ATLANTIC INTRACOASTAL WATERWAY. It is bordered by MIAMI on the northwest and the Florida Keys on the east.

Bischof \'bi-shôf\, **Werner** (1916–1954) Swiss photojournalist. In 1942 he began working for the picture magazine *Du*, for which he photographed war-torn France, Germany, and the Netherlands. He died in a car accident while working in Peru. Collections of his photographs include *Japan* (1954), *Incas to Indians* (1956), and *The World of Werner Bischof* (1959).

Bishkek \bish-'kek\ *or* **Pishpek** \pish-'pek\ *formerly* (1926–91) **Frunze** \'frün-zi\ City (pop., 1996: 586,000), capital of Kyrgyzstan. It lies on the Kazakstan border. In 1825 the Uzbek khanate of Kokand (see QUQON) established a fortress on the site; in 1862 it was captured by the Russians. When the Kirgiz (Kyrgyz) Autonomous Soviet Socialist Republic was set up in 1926, the city became its capital and was renamed Frunze after a local Red Army leader. In World War II heavy industries from W Russia were moved there.

bishop In some Christian churches, the chief pastor of a diocese, an area containing several congregations. From the 4th cent. A.D. until the REFORMATION, bishops' powers included the settling of disputes, ordination of clergy, and CONFIRMATION of church members. The Anglican, Roman Catholic, and Eastern Orthodox churches retain the position of bishop and the doctrine of APOSTOLIC SUCCESSION. Some Lutheran and Methodist churches retain bishops but not the principle of apostolic succession; still other churches have abolished the office altogether. In Roman Catholicism, the pope selects bishops; in Anglicanism, the dean and chapter of the cathedral of the diocese elect its bishop; in Methodism a synod chooses the bishop. See also EPISCOPACY.

Bishop, Billy (*orig.* William Avery) (1894–1956) Canadian World War I fighter ace. Born in Owen Sound, Ontario, he served with Canadian forces, and in 1915 transferred to the Royal Flying Corps. While serving in France in 1917, he shot down 72 enemy aircraft, including 25 in one 10-day period. Appointed to the staff of the British Air Ministry, he helped form the Royal Canadian Air Force as a separate brigade.

Bishop, Elizabeth (1911–1979) U.S. poet. Born in Worcester, Mass., she lived with relatives in Nova Scotia after her father died and her mother was institutionalized. In the 1950s and '60s she lived principally in Brazil with her Brazilian female lover. Her first book of poems (1946) was reprinted with additions as *North & South* (1955, Pulitzer Prize). Her works are celebrated for their formal brilliance and close observations of everyday reality, and have elicited notable admiration from other poets. Posthumous publications include *The Collected Prose* (1984) and *One Art* (1994), a fine collection of letters.

Bismarck \'biz-,märk\ City (pop., 2000: 55,000), capital of N. Dakota. It was settled as a MISSOURI RIVER port in the

1830s. In 1873 it was named for Otto von BISMARCK in the hope of attracting German investment. With the discovery of gold in the nearby BLACK HILLS, it became a prospecting center. In 1883 it was made the capital of Dakota Territory, and in 1889 capital of N. Dakota. Today it is the region's business, cultural, and financial center.

Bismarck, Otto (Eduard Leopold) von *later* **Fürst (Prince) von Bismarck** (1815–1898) Prussian statesman who founded the German empire in 1871 and served as its chancellor for 19 years. Born into the Prussian landowning elite, Bismarck held elective and diplomatic posts (1849-62) before becoming prime minister and foreign minister of Prussia (1862–71). Under his leadership Prussia won a war against Denmark in 1864 (see SCHLESWIG–HOLSTEIN QUESTION), the SEVEN WEEKS' WAR (1866), and the FRANCO–PRUSSIAN WAR (1870–71). Through these wars he achieved his goal of political unification of a Prussian-dominated German empire. The "Iron Chancellor" of the empire skillfully preserved the peace in Europe through alliances with Austria-Hungary, Russia, and Italy against France. Domestically, he introduced administrative and economic reforms but sought to preserve the status quo, opposing the SOCIAL DEMOCRATIC PARTY and the Catholic church (see KULTURKAMPF). When Bismarck left office in 1890, the map of Europe had been changed immeasurably. However, the German empire survived him by only 20 years because he had failed to create an internally unified people.

Bismarck Archipelago Island group (pop., 1989 est.: 371,000), W Pacific Ocean. Lying northwest of NEW GUINEA, it has a total area of 19,173 sq mi (49,658 sq km). Its largest components are NEW BRITAIN, New Ireland and the ADMIRALTY ISLANDS. Annexed by Germany in 1884, it was named for Otto von BISMARCK. It was made a mandated territory of Australia in 1920. The group became part of a U.N. Trust Territory after World War II, and part of PAPUA NEW GUINEA in 1975.

bismuth \'biz-məth\ Semimetallic to metallic chemical ELEMENT, chemical symbol Bi, atomic number 83. Hard, brittle, and lustrous, it is gray-white with a reddish tinge. It is often found free in nature and also occurs in compounds and in mixed ORES. Bismuth ALLOYS are used (because of their low melting points) in making metal castings, special solders, automatic sprinkler heads, fuses, and many fire-detection devices. Bismuth phosphomolybdate is a catalyst in the production of fibers and plastics. Salts of bismuth are used in making soothing agents for digestive disorders (especially bismuth subsalicylate), in treating skin infections and injuries, and in lipstick, nail polish, and eye shadow, to which they impart a pearlescent quality.

bison \'bī-s°n, 'bī-z°n\ Species (*Bison bison*) of oxlike BOVID with a convex forehead and a shoulder hump. Its dark-brown, coarse hair is especially long on the head, neck, and shoulders. Both sexes bear heavy, curved horns. A mature bull can stand up to 6.5 ft (2 m) at the shoulder and weigh more than 2,000 lbs (900 kg). The American bison, commonly called BUFFALO, was abundant over most of N. America when Europeans arrived. Hunting drove it nearly to extinction by 1900; today it and the European bison survive only in managed herds.

Bissau \bis-'aù\ Seaport (pop., 1995: 233,000), capital of Guinea-Bissau. Lying on the Gêba River where it flows into the Atlantic Ocean, the port originated in 1687 as a Portuguese fortified post. It has developed into an excellent roadstead for large vessels.

bit *in full* binary digit. Unit of information equivalent to the result of a choice between only two possible alternatives, such as 1 and 0 in the BINARY CODE generally used in DIGITAL COMPUTERS. It is also applied to a unit of MEMORY corresponding to the ability to store the result of a choice between two alternatives. A byte consists of a string of eight consecutive bits and makes up the basic information processing unit of a computer. A byte includes information equivalent to one letter or one symbol (e.g., a comma). The processing and storage capacities of computer hardware are usually given in kilobytes (1,024 bytes), megabytes (1,048,576 bytes), and gigabytes (about 1 billion bytes).

bit-map Method by which a graphic image is defined, including the color of each of its PIXELS (or bits). In effect, a

bit-map is an array of binary data representing the values of pixels in a computer image or display. When a graphic image file is displayed on a computer monitor, the computer reads the bit-map to determine which colors to use to "paint" the screen. In a bit-mapped font, each character is defined as a pattern of dots in a bit-map. See also GIF, JPEG.

bittern Any of 12 species of solitary marsh birds (family Ardeidae), related to HERONS but having a shorter neck and a stouter body. Most bitterns bear a camouflage pattern that enables them to hide by standing upright with bill pointed upward, imitating the reeds and grasses of their habitat. They feed on fish, frogs, crayfish, and other small swamp and marsh animals. Bitterns are found almost worldwide. The largest species grow to 30 in. (75 cm).

bitumen \bə-'tyü-mən\ Mixture of tarlike hydrocarbons derived from PETROLEUM. Black or brown, it varies from viscous to solid; the solid form is usually called ASPHALT. Bitumen occurs in nearly every part of the world and in nearly every geologic stratum.

bituminous coal \bə-'tyü-mə-nəs\ *or* **soft coal** Most abundant form of COAL. It is dark brown to black and has a relatively high heat value. Widely abundant and with the broadest range of commercial uses, it has long been used for steam generation in electric power plants and industrial boiler plants. Certain varieties are also used to make COKE. Burning large quantities of bituminous coal that has a medium to high sulfur content contributes to air pollution and produces ACID RAIN. See also ANTHRACITE.

bivalve Any member of the MOLLUSK class Bivalvia, or Pelecypoda, characterized by having a two-halved (valved) shell. CLAMS, cockles, MUSSELS, OYSTERS, SCALLOPS, and shipworms are bivalves. Most are completely enclosed by the shell, the two valves of which are joined by an elastic ligament, and by two sheets of tissue called the mantle. They feed on PHYTOPLANKTON by pumping water across the gills and trapping food particles that are then moved to the mouth. Bivalves are found in most parts of the ocean.

Biwa \'bē-wä\, **Lake** Lake, central HONSHU, Japan. It is Japan's largest lake, measuring 40 mi (64 km) long and 12

Bivalve Internal structure of a clam. A ligament hinges the shell's two halves (valves) open, and the beating motion of cilia on the gills causes water to enter through the incurrent siphon. As water moves over the gills, oxygen diffuses into the blood, and food particles become trapped in mucus and are moved to the mouth. A pair of adductor muscles can hold the shell tightly closed. A fold of tissue (mantle) encloses the body's organs and releases the material that forms the shell. A large muscular foot allows the clam to creep and burrow. The circulatory system consists of a heart and blood vessels, and kidneys remove wastes from the blood. Deoxygenated blood and wastes are removed in the water that exits through the excurrent siphon.

mi (19 km) wide, with an area of 260 sq mi (673 sq km). Its name refers to the biwa, a lute whose pear shape the lake resembles. Lake Biwa is noted for its pearl culture industry and for its great scenic beauty, long a subject of Japanese poetry and a major tourist attraction.

Bizet \bē-ˈzā\, **Georges** (*orig.* Alexandre-César-Léopold) (1838–1875) French composer. At 17 he wrote a precocious Symphony in C major. Intent on success on the operatic stage, he produced *The Pearl Fishers* (1863), *La jolie fille de Perth* (1866), and *Djamileh* (1871). Disgusted with the frivolity of French light opera, he determined to reform the genre of *opéra comique.* In 1875 his masterpiece, *Carmen,* reached the stage; it quickly won international enthusiasm and was recognized as the supreme example of *opéra comique.* Bizet's death at 37, shortly after its premiere, cut short a remarkable career.

Georges Bizet

Björling \ˈbyœr-liŋ\, **Jussi** (*orig.* Johann Jonaton) (1911–1960) Swedish tenor. He began to sing in public as a child, and toured Europe and the U.S. with his family. Recruited by the Royal Swedish Opera in 1928, he was soon a star performer. He made his Metropolitan Opera debut in 1938 in *La Bohème.* Though not known as an actor, he became a favorite on stage and in recordings for the sheer beauty and musicality of his singing.

Black, Hugo (La Fayette) (1886–1971) U.S. Supreme Court justice (1937–71). Born in Clay Co., Ala., he practiced law from 1906. He served in the U.S. Senate 1927–37, where he was a strong supporter of New Deal legislation. Pres. Franklin ROOSEVELT appointed him to the Supreme Court, where he helped reverse earlier court vetoes of New Deal legislation. In the 1960s he was prominent in the liberal majority that struck down mandatory school prayer and guaranteed the availability of legal counsel to suspected criminals. He became best known for his absolutist belief in the Bill of Rights as a guarantee of civil liberties.

black aesthetic movement *or* **black arts movement** Period of artistic and literary development among black Americans in the 1960s and early '70s. Based on the cultural politics of black nationalism, the movement sought to create art forms capable of expressing the varieties of black experience in the U.S. Leading theorists included Amiri BARAKA and H. L. GATES. Other notable writers included Don L. Lee (b.1942; known as Haki R. Madhubuti), Toni MORRISON, Alice WALKER, and Ntozake Shange (b.1948). The movement also produced notable autobiographies by MALCOLM X (1965), Eldridge Cleaver (1968), and Angela Davis (1974).

Black and Tan Member of a British auxiliary force employed in Ireland against the republicans (1920–21). When Irish nationalist agitation intensified after World War I, many Irish police resigned and were replaced by these temporary English recruits, who dressed in a mixed "black and tan" outfit because of a shortage of uniforms. To thwart the terrorism of the IRISH REPUBLICAN ARMY, the Black and Tans themselves engaged in brutal reprisals.

black bear Forest-dwelling BEAR (*Ursus americanus*) that, despite reductions in population and range, is still the most common N. American bear. The adult ranges from 5 to 6 ft (150–180 cm) in length and weighs 200–600 lbs (90–270 kg). It has various color phases. It eats animals and vegetation and frequently raids campsites to seize anything edible. Though it may be tamed and taught tricks, it often becomes dangerous when mature.

Blackbeard *orig.* **Edward Teach** (d.1718) English pirate. A privateer in the W. Indies, with his 40-gun warship he preyed on shipping off the Virginia and Carolina coasts, sharing his prizes with the governor of the N. Carolina colony in return for protection. He was eventually killed by a British naval force, and his head, with its great black beard, was affixed to the end of his bowsprit. His legendary buried treasure probably never existed.

blackberry Usually prickly, fruit-bearing bush of the genus *Rubus,* in the ROSE family, native chiefly to N temperate regions. The blackberry is abundant in E N. America and on the Pacific coast; in Europe it is common in thickets and hedges. It bears leaves with usually three or five oval, coarsely toothed, stalked leaflets; white, pink, or red flowers in terminal clusters; and black or red-purple aggregate fruits. Blackberries are a fairly good source of iron and vitamin C.

blackbird In the New World, any of several species of songbirds in the family Icteridae; also, an Old World THRUSH (*Turdus merula,* family Turdidae). The best known icterid is the red-winged blackbird (*Agelaius phoeniceus);* it is 8 in. (20 cm) long, and the male's black plumage is set off by red shoulder patches. The Old World blackbird, 10 in. (25 cm) long, is common in woods and gardens throughout temperate Eurasia as well as in Australia and New Zealand. See also GRACKLE.

black codes Laws enacted in the former Confederate states after the AMERICAN CIVIL WAR that restricted the freedom of former slaves. In some states these codes included vagrancy laws that targeted unemployed blacks, apprentice laws that made black orphans and dependents available for hire to whites, and commercial laws that excluded blacks from certain trades and businesses and restricted their ownership of property. Northern reaction to the laws helped produce radical RECONSTRUCTION and creation of the FREEDMEN'S BUREAU. Many provisions of the black codes were reenacted in the JIM CROW LAWS and remained in force until the 1964 CIVIL RIGHTS ACT.

Black Death Widespread outbreak of PLAGUE that ravaged Europe during the 14th cent. The epidemic originated in Asia and was transmitted to Europeans in 1347 when a Turkic army besieging a Genoese trading post in the Crimea catapulted plague-infested corpses into the town. It spread from the Mediterranean ports and ravaged all of Europe 1347–51, with renewed outbreaks until 1400. Whole communities were sometimes destroyed, and much of Europe's economy was devastated. About one-third of its population, or 25 million people, died in the Black Death.

black-figure pottery Type of Greek pottery that originated in Corinth about 700 B.C. The figures were painted in black pigment on the natural red clay ground. Finishing details were then incised into the black pigment, revealing the red ground. The great Attic painters (mid-6th cent. B.C.), most notably Exekias, developed narrative scene decoration and perfected the style. See also RED-FIGURE POTTERY.

blackfly Any member of the insect family Simuliidae, composed of 300 species of DIPTERANS found worldwide. The blackfly has short mouthparts adapted for sucking blood. The females bite and are sometimes abundant enough to kill chickens and even cattle. Some species carry worms capable of causing human disease, including RIVER BLINDNESS. In subarctic regions blackflies may make human habitation impossible.

Blackfoot Group of three ALGONQUIAN-speaking Indian peoples in Alberta and Montana, comprising the Piegan, the Blood, and the Blackfoot proper. They were among the first Algonquians to move westward from timberland to open grassland and, later, among the first to acquire horses and firearms. They were known as the strongest and most aggressive military power on the NW plains, and at the height of their power, in the first half of the 19th cent., held a vast territory extending from N Saskatchewan to SW Montana. For three decades beginning in 1806, the Blackfoot prevented white men from settling in their territory. They signed their first treaty with the U.S. in 1855, after which they were forced into farming and cattle-raising. Today about 25,000 Blackfoot live in Montana and Alberta.

Black Forest *German* **Schwarzwald** \ˈshfärts-ˌvält\ Mountain region, Baden-Württemberg, SW Germany. It extends in a fairly narrow strip about 100 mi (160 km) along the E bank of the upper RHINE RIVER, from the NECKAR to the Swiss border. Its name comes from its dark interior, thickly forested with fir and pine. The setting of many of the GRIMM brothers' fairy tales, it is famed for the beauty and charm of its villages and rolling hills. Visitors are also drawn by its winter sports and by its mineral springs, including Baden-Baden. The forest has suffered serious damage from acid rain.

Black Friday Day (Sept. 24, 1869) when plunging gold prices precipitated a U.S. stock-market PANIC. An attempt by Jay GOULD and James FISK to corner the market in gold depended on preventing the sale of government gold, an arrangement assured through the two men's political influence. When Pres. U. S. GRANT heard of the scheme, he ordered the government to sell $4 million in gold, which caused the price to drop and produced a panic selling of other stocks.

Black Hawk (1767–1838) SAUK Indian leader whose defiance of government orders to vacate villages along the Rock River in Illinois resulted in the brief but tragic Black Hawk War of 1832. Long antagonistic to whites, Black Hawk, who had been driven into Iowa from Illinois in 1831, led his people back across the Mississippi the following year, only to face military opposition and eventual massacre, though he himself survived. The ruthlessness of the war so affected neighboring Indian groups that by 1837 most had fled to the far West, leaving most of the Northwest Territory to white settlers.

Black Hawk Painting by George Catlin, 1832

Black Hills Group of mountains W S. Dakota and NE Wyoming. Occupying about 6,000 sq mi (15,540 sq km), they lie between the CHEYENNE and Belle Fourche rivers and rise to 7,242 ft (2,207 m) at Harney Peak. Their name refers to their dark appearance at a distance. The W SIOUX Indians were guaranteed treaty rights to the region in 1868; however, the discovery of gold in 1874 led to an influx of white miners and to the Black Hills War (1876), including the Battle of the LITTLE BIGHORN. Tourist attractions include the mining town of Deadwood, Mt. RUSHMORE, Wind Cave National Park, and DEVILS TOWER NATIONAL MONUMENT.

black hole Cosmic body with gravity (see GRAVITATION) so intense that nothing, not even LIGHT, can escape. Most are suspected to form when a star more than 10 times the sun's mass dies and collapses. Stars with less mass evolve into WHITE DWARF STARS or NEUTRON STARS. Supermassive black holes may also exist at the centers of QUASARS and many galaxies, causing the energetic activity observed as an ACTIVE GALACTIC NUCLEUS. Stephen HAWKING has theorized the creation of numerous primordial "mini–black holes" during the BIG BANG that lose mass over time and disappear. Details of a black hole's structure are calculated from Albert EINSTEIN's general theory of RELATIVITY: a "singularity" of zero volume and infinite density pulls in all matter and energy that comes within its EVENT HORIZON. Black holes are hard to observe directly, but their enormous gravitational fields draw in nearby matter, which emits X rays as it collides at high speed outside the event horizon. Technically, black holes are still theoretical, but phenomena have been observed that match their predicted behavior.

black humor Humor marked by the use of morbid or grotesque episodes that ridicule human folly. The term became common in the 1960s to describe the work of such novelists as Joseph HELLER, in *Catch–22* (1961); Kurt VONNEGUT, particularly in *Slaughterhouse Five* (1969); and Thomas PYNCHON, in *V* (1963) and *Gravity's Rainbow* (1973). A film exemplar is Stanley KUBRICK's *Dr. Strangelove* (1963). "Black comedy" has been applied to some works in the theater of the ABSURD, especially those of Eugene IONESCO.

blackjack *or* **twenty-one** Card game whose object is to be dealt cards having a higher count than those of the dealer, up to but not exceeding 21. Aces count as 1 or 11, and face cards as 10. Depending on the rules used, bets may be placed before the deal, after each player has been dealt one card facedown, or after each player has received two cards facedown and the dealer has exposed one of his cards.

black lead See GRAPHITE

blackmail See EXTORTION

black market Trading in violation of regulations such as rationing laws, laws against the sale of certain goods, and official rates of currency exchange. Black-market activity is common in wartime, when scarce goods and services are controlled by RATIONING. Black-market foreign-exchange transactions flourish in countries where convertible foreign currency is scarce.

Blackmun, Harry (1908–1999) U.S. jurist. Born in Nashville, Ill., he was resident counsel to the Mayo Clinic (1950–59) before being appointed to the U.S. Court of Appeals. He served on the U.S. SUPREME COURT from 1970 to 1994. Initially perceived as a conservative, Blackmun became progressively more liberal over the years. He wrote the majority decision in *ROE VS. WADE* (1971).

Black Muslims See Nation of ISLAM

Black Panther Party (for Self-Defense) U.S. black revolutionary party founded in 1966 by Huey NEWTON and Bobby Seale (b.1936) in Oakland, Cal., to protect black residents from police brutality. It developed into a Marxist revolutionary group that called for the arming of blacks, release of all black prisoners, and payment of compensation to blacks for centuries of exploitation. By the late 1960s it had over 2,000 members; an early spokesman was Eldridge Cleaver (1935–1998). Conflicts with police involved shootouts in California, New York, and Chicago. By the mid-1970s the group had lost support; it turned to providing neighborhood social services, and soon disbanded.

black pepper *or* **pepper** Perennial, woody climbing vine (*Piper nigrum*) of the family Piperaceae, native to India; also, the SPICE made from its berries. One of the earliest spices known, pepper is probably the most widely used spice in the world today. The plant is cultivated throughout Indonesia and has been introduced into tropical areas elsewhere. It has broad, shiny leaves and dense, slender spikes of small flowers. The small berrylike fruits are called peppercorns. See also PEPPER.

Black Sea Sea between Europe and Asia. Bordered by Ukraine, Russia, Georgia, Turkey, Bulgaria, and Romania, it occupies an area of about 180,000 sq mi (465,000 sq km) and has a maximum depth of 7,250 ft (2,210 m). It is connected with the AEGEAN SEA through the BOSPORUS, the Sea of MARMARA, and the DARDANELLES, and with the Sea of AZOV by Kerch Strait. It receives many large rivers, including the DANUBE. Created when structural upheavals in ASIA MINOR split off the Caspian basin from the Mediterranean Sea, the Black Sea gradually became isolated and its salinity greatly declined. Though long popular for its resorts, it has suffered severe pollution in recent decades.

Blackshirts *Italian* Camicie Nere. Armed squads of Italian Fascists under Benito MUSSOLINI, who wore black shirts as part of their uniform. First organized in 1919, they targeted socialists, communists, republicans, and others; hundreds of people were killed as the squads grew in number. In 1922 Blackshirts from all over Italy participated in the March on ROME. In 1923 they officially became a national militia. With Mussolini's fall in 1943, the Blackshirts fell into disgrace.

Black Sox scandal U.S. baseball scandal, centering on the charge that eight members of the Chicago White Sox had been bribed to lose the 1919 World Series to the Cincinnati Reds. Five admitted their guilt to a grand jury, but their confessions later disappeared. All eight were acquitted in 1921, but commissioner K. M. LANDIS banned them from playing for life.

Blackstone, William (*later* **Sir William**) (1723–1780) British jurist. At Oxford he gave the first university lectures on English COMMON LAW and published a synopsis for students in 1756. His classic *Commentaries on the Laws of England* (1765–69) is the best-known description of the doctrines of English law; it became the basis of university legal education in England and N. America. He also served as a member of Parliament (1761–70), as solicitor general to the queen (from 1763), and as judge of the Court of Common Pleas (1770–80).

Blackwell, Elizabeth (1821–1910) U.S. (British-born) physician. She began her medical education by reading medical books and hiring private instructors. Medical schools rejected her applications until she was accepted at the Geneva Medical (later Hobart) College in 1847. Though ostracized, she graduated at the head of her class in 1849, becoming the first woman doctor in modern times and the first to gain her degree from a U.S. medical school. In 1857, despite much opposition, she established the New York Infirmary, staffed entirely by women, and she later added a full course of medical education for women. She was also a founder of the London School of Medicine for Women.

William Blackstone Painting attributed to Joshua Reynolds

black widow Any member of six known species of SPIDER in the genus *Latrodectus*. They have a venomous bite that is rarely fatal to humans. The female of the most common N. American species is shiny black, usually with a reddish hourglass-shaped design on the underside of the abdomen, and with a body about 1 in. (2.5 cm) long. The black widow preys on insects. The male, about one-fourth the female's size, is often killed and eaten by the female after mating (the source of its name).

bladderwort Any of about 120 widespread species of terrestrial and aquatic CARNIVOROUS PLANTS of the genus *Utricularia* (family Lentibulariaceae). They have small hollow sacs (bladders) that actively capture and digest tiny animals that touch them. Closely related to the bladderworts are the butterworts *(Pinguicula)*, 35 species of land plants that capture insects by means of sticky glands on their leaf surfaces.

Blaine, James G(illespie) (1830–1893) U.S. politician. Born in W. Brownsville, Pa., he moved to Maine in 1854 to become editor of the *Kennebec Journal*, a crusading Republican newspaper. He served in the U.S. House of Representatives 1863–76, becoming speaker in 1868, and in the U.S. Senate 1876–81. As secretary of state in 1881 he took the first steps toward convening an inter-American conference to prevent war in the Americas. He was the Republican presidential nominee in 1884 but lost narrowly to Grover CLEVELAND. He again served as secretary of state (1889–92) and chaired the first Pan-American Conference.

Blair, Tony (*orig.* Anthony Charles Lynton) (b.1953) British politician, prime minister from 1997. Born in Edinburgh, Blair was a lawyer before winning election to the House of Commons in 1983. Entering Labour's shadow cabinet in 1988 at 35, Blair urged the party to move to the political center and deemphasize its traditional advocacy of state socialism. He assumed party leadership in 1994 and revamped its platform. When Labour achieved a landslide victory in the 1997 elections, he became prime minister, Britain's youngest since 1806. He reopened talks on the future of Northern Ireland and in 1998 oversaw the signing of a peace agreement. In 2001 Labour achieved another electoral landslide.

Blais \'ble\, **Marie-Claire** (b.1939) Canadian novelist and poet. Born in Quebec City, she has written entirely in French. In two early, dreamlike novels, *Mad Shadows* (1959) and *Tête blanche* (1960), she staked out her territory, working-class people doomed to unrelieved sorrow and grinding poverty. *A Season in the Life of Emmanuel* (1965) received the Prix Médicis. Later works include *The Manuscripts of Pauline Archange* (1968) and *Deaf to the City* (1979).

Blake, Eubie (*orig.* James Hubert) (1883–1983) U.S. songwriter and pianist. Born in Baltimore, Blake played piano in cafés and brothels as a teenager, and in 1899 he composed his first rag, "Sounds of Africa." *Shuffle Along* (1921), written with lyricist Noble Sissle (1889–1975), introduced Paul ROBESON and Josephine BAKER, and was among the first

musicals written, produced, and directed by blacks. In 1925 Blake cowrote the score to *Blackbirds of 1930*. He achieved his greatest fame when the musical *Eubie* opened on Broadway (1978). In 1981 he was awarded the Medal of Freedom.

Blake, William (1757–1827) English poet and painter. Not formally educated, he was trained as an engraver at the Royal Academy and opened a print shop in London in 1784. He developed an innovative technique for producing colored engravings and published his own "illuminated" books of poetry, including *Songs of Innocence* (1789), *The Marriage of Heaven and Hell* (1793), and *Songs of Experience* (1794). *Jerusalem* (1804–20), his third major epic treating of the fall and redemption of humanity, is his most richly decorated book. His other major works include *The*

William Blake Portrait by John Linnell

Four Zoas (1795–1804) and *Milton* (1804–8). Single-minded and unworldly, he was called mad; he lived on the edge of poverty and died in neglect. His books form one of the most strikingly original and independent bodies of work in the Western cultural tradition. Ignored in his day, he is now regarded as one of the greatest figures of ROMANTICISM.

Blakelock, Ralph (1847–1919) U.S. painter. Born in New York City, he was self-taught as an artist. He developed a highly original style of landscape painting, characterized by luminous moonlit scenes with nocturnal lighting and strangely dappled trees and foliage. Impoverished and neglected by the public, he suffered a breakdown in 1899 and spent the rest of his life in an asylum. During his confinement he achieved some fame, and forgeries of his work became common.

Blakey, Art *later* Abdullah Ibn Buhaina (1919–1990) U.S. jazz drummer. Born in Pittsburgh, Blakey worked with Fletcher HENDERSON and Billy Eckstine's ensembles. His prodigious technique and thunderous attack assured his role as one of the principal drum stylists in modern jazz. With Horace Silver, Blakey formed the Jazz Messengers in 1954, and the group, with its aggressive blues-inflected approach, became the archetypal hard-bop unit. Many band members became celebrated, and the group became one of the most enduring ensembles in modern jazz.

Blanc \'bläⁿ\, **(Jean-Joseph-Charles-) Louis** (1811–1882) French utopian socialist. In 1839 he founded the socialist newspaper *Revue du progrès* and serially published his *Organisation du travail (The Organization of Labor)*, which described his theory of worker-controlled "social workshops" that would gradually take over production until a socialist society came into being. In 1848 he was forced to flee to England after workers unsuccessfully revolted. In exile (1848–70), he wrote a history of the French Revolution.

Blanc \'blank\, **Mel(vin Jerome)** (1908–1989) U.S. entertainer. Born in San Francisco, in 1933 he joined a daily radio program, for which he created several voices to augment the cast. In 1937 he joined the cartoon department of WARNER BROTHERS, and he took part in the development of Looney Tunes and Merrie Melodies, providing the voices of Porky Pig, Daffy Duck, Woody Woodpecker, and Bugs Bunny. In his 50-year career, he supplied the voices for about 3,000 cartoons.

Blanc \'bläⁿ\, **Mont** *Italian* **Monte Bianco** Mountain massif, Europe. Located in the ALPS on the borders of France, Italy, and Switzerland, it is Europe's highest peak, at 15,771 ft (4,807 m). It was first climbed in 1786 by Michel-Gabriel Paccard and Jacques Balmat. The 8-mi (13-km) Mont Blanc Tunnel connects France with Italy. The region has become a major tourist and winter sports center.

Blanda, George (Frederick) (b.1927) U.S. football player. Born in Youngwood, Pa., he played for the Univ. of Kentucky. As a professional quarterback and kicker, he played for the Chicago Bears (1949–58), Houston Oilers (1960–66), and Oakland Raiders (1967–76), setting still-standing records for most seasons played (26), most games played (340), most points scored (2,002), and most points after touchdowns (943).

blank verse Unrhymed verse, particularly iambic pentameter, the preeminent dramatic and narrative verse form in English, as well as in Italian and German. Adapted from Greek and Latin sources, it was introduced in Italy, then in England, where in the 16th cent. William SHAKESPEARE made it the vehicle for his great dramatic poetry. Its potential for grandeur was confirmed with John MILTON's *Paradise Lost* (1667).

Blanqui \blänⁿ-'kē\, **(Louis-) Auguste** (1805–1881) French socialist and revolutionary. A legendary martyr-figure of French radicalism, Blanqui believed that there could be no socialist transformation of society without a temporary dictatorship that would eradicate the old order. His activities, including the formation of various secret societies, caused him to be imprisoned for a total of over 33 years. His disciples, the Blanquists, played an important role in later workers' movements.

Blantyre \blan-'tīr\ City (pop., 1998: 478,000), S Malawi. The largest city in Malawi, it was founded in 1876 as a Church of Scotland mission station and named after David LIVINGSTONE's Scottish birthplace. It attained municipal status in 1895, making it Malawi's oldest municipality. Its colonial trade led to its growth as Malawi's chief commercial center.

Blarney Village (pop., 1995 est.: 3,000), county Cork, Ireland. Situated northwest of CORK, it is famous as the site of Blarney Castle (c.1446). On the S castle wall is the Blarney Stone, which is said to make anyone who kisses it proficient in blarney (smooth, flattering talk).

Blasis \'blä-sēs\, **Carlo** (1803–1878) Italian ballet teacher and writer on the technique, history, and theory of dance. As director of the ballet school at Milan's La Scala from 1837, he trained many of the most brilliant dancers of the 19th cent. One of his many innovations was the technique of spotting (focusing on one spot and snapping one's head around faster than one's body) to prevent dizziness when turning. Many of his teachings still form the basis of classical ballet.

blast furnace Vertical shaft furnace that produces liquid METALS by the reaction of air introduced under pressure into the bottom of the furnace with a mixture of metallic ORE, fuel, and FLUX fed into the top. Blast furnaces are used to produce pig iron from iron ore for subsequent processing into STEEL; they are also employed in processing lead, copper, and other metals. The current of pressurized air maintains rapid combustion. Blast furnaces were used in China as early as 200 B.C., and appeared in Europe in the 13th cent. Modern blast furnaces use COKE fuel and can produce 1,000–10,000 tons (900–9,000 metric tons) of pig iron daily.

Blaue Reiter \ˌblau̇-ə-'rī-tər\, **Der** (German: "The Blue Rider") Organization of Expressionist artists formed in Munich in 1911 by Vasily KANDINSKY and Franz MARC. The name derived from a volume of essays and illustrations they published. Other members included Paul KLEE and August Macke (1887–1914). Influenced by JUGENDSTIL, CUBISM, and FUTURISM but lacking a specific program or philosophy, the group disintegrated at the outbreak of World War I. See also EXPRESSIONISM.

Blavatsky \blə-'vat-skē\, **Helena** *orig.* Helena Petrovna Hahn *known as* **Madame Blavatsky** (1831–1891) Russian spiritualist and writer. After a brief marriage, she studied occultism and spiritualism and traveled widely. In 1873 she became a close companion of Henry Olcott (1832–1907); they and others founded the Theosophical Society (1875; see THEOSOPHY). In 1879 the two went to India and established headquarters at Adyar. Blavatsky claimed psychic powers, but the London Society for Psychical Research in 1885 labeled her a fraud. Her most important work was *The Secret Doctrine* (1888).

bleach Solid or liquid chemical compound used to whiten or remove the natural color of fibers, yarns, paper, and textile fabrics. Sunlight was the chief bleaching agent up to the discovery of CHLORINE in 1774. In textile finishing, the bleaching process is used to produce white cloth, to prepare fabrics for other finishes, or to remove discoloration. Sodium hypochlorite, calcium hypochlorite, and hydrogen PEROXIDE are also commonly used as bleaches.

Bleeding Kansas Period of civil unrest (1854–59) between proslavery and antislavery advocates over control of the new Kansas Territory. Under the doctrine of POPULAR SOVEREIGNTY, antislavery emigrants from the North clashed with armed proslavery groups from Missouri. In 1856 a proslavery raid and burning of a hotel and newspaper in Lawrence were followed by several murders by antislavery radicals under John BROWN. Sporadic battles continued until Kansas was admitted to the Union as a free state in 1861.

Blenheim Palace \'ble-nim\ English residence near Woodstock, Oxfordshire, designed by John VANBRUGH and built (1705–24) by the British Parliament as a gift to John Churchill, duke of MARLBOROUGH. It is regarded as the finest example of baroque architecture in Britain. Henry Wise designed its grounds in the formal style of the Palace of VERSAILLES; Capability BROWN later redesigned them in his natural, pastoral style.

Bligh, William (1754–1817) English admiral. He went to sea at age 7 and was sailing master on Capt. James COOK's final voyage (1776–80). In 1787 he was named to command HMS *BOUNTY*. When its crew mutinied (1789), Bligh and loyal crew members were set adrift; and some two months later they reached Timor. The mutiny made little difference to Bligh's career, though he had another encounter with mutineers while he was governor of New S. Wales, Australia (1805–8). He was unpopular as a commander but was also courageous and a greatly skilled navigator.

blight Any of various plant diseases whose symptoms include sudden and severe yellowing, browning, spotting, withering, or dying. Usually the shoots and other young, rapidly growing tissues of a plant are attacked. Most blights are caused by BACTERIA or fungi (see FUNGUS). Blights are most likely under cool, moist conditions, and most economically important plants are susceptible to one or more of them. Measures taken to fight blight include destroying the infected plant parts; using disease-free seed or stock and resistant varieties; CROP ROTATION; pruning and spacing plants for better air circulation; controlling pests; avoiding overhead watering and working among wet plants; and, where needed, applying FUNGICIDES or ANTIBIOTICS. Maintaining sanitary conditions is the most important measure for stopping the spread of the infestation.

blind fish Any of various species of sightless fishes, among them several unrelated cave-dwelling species. Pale and small, growing to about 4 in. (10 cm) long, they inhabit dark limestone caves of the U.S. All have tactile organs allowing them to feel what they cannot see. Other cave-dwelling fishes tending toward blindness are found in Cuba, Mexico's Yucatán, S. America, and Africa.

blindness Inability to see with one or both eyes. Transient blindness (blackout) can result from vertical acceleration, glomerulonephritis (a kidney disease), or a clot in a blood vessel of the eye. Continuing blindness may arise from injuries or diseases of the eye (e.g., CATARACT, GLAUCOMA), including the RETINA, the optic nerve, or the brain's visual centers. Many infectious, noninfectious, and parasitic systemic diseases can cause blindness. See also MACULAR DEGENERATION.

Bliss, Tasker (Howard) (1853–1930) U.S. general. Born in Lewisburg, Pa., he attended West Point and later was the first commandant of the Army War College (1903–5). As army chief of staff in 1917, he upgraded the army to battle-readiness for World War I and resisted attempts to divide the U.S. force among the various Allied commands. He was a delegate to the Paris Peace Conference and an ardent supporter of U.S. participation in the League of Nations.

blister Rounded SKIN elevation in which fluid fills a separation between layers of skin. The fluid is usually clear; yellowish fluid contains pus, and red fluid contains blood. Blisters often occur on the palms or soles when pressure and friction cause an upper skin layer to move back and forth over the one under it. This type generally heals spontaneously, sometimes leaving a thickened callus. Blisters that occur as symptoms of contact DERMATITIS, viral infection, or AUTOIMMUNE DISEASE can appear anywhere on the body and may leave scars.

blister beetle Any of approximately 2,000 species of BEETLE (family Meloidae) that secrete an irritating substance, cantharidin, used medically to remove warts. In the past, cantharidin was often used for inducing blisters, a common remedy for many ailments, and the dried remains of Spanish fly (*Lytta vesicatoria*) were a major ingredient in so-called love potions. Blister beetles are both helpful and harmful to humans; the larvae eat grasshopper eggs, but the adults destroy crops.

blitzkrieg \'blits-ˌkrēg\ (German: "lightning war") Military tactic used by Germany in WORLD WAR II, designed to create disorganization in enemy forces through the use of surprise, speed, and superiority in matériel or firepower. Used in the successful invasions of Belgium, the Netherlands, and France in 1940, the German blitzkrieg coordinated land and air attacks—using tanks, dive-bombers, and motorized artillery—to paralyze the enemy principally by disabling its communications and coordination capacities.

Bloch \'blȯk\, **Marc (Léopold Benjamin)** (1886–1944) French historian. From 1919 he taught medieval history at Strasbourg, where he cofounded the influential periodical *Annales d'histoire économique et sociale*. He taught at the Sorbonne from 1936. During World War II he joined the French Resistance and was captured and killed. Among his major works are *The Royal Touch* (1924), *French Rural History* (1931), and *Feudal Society* (1939). As founder of the ANNALES SCHOOL, Bloch made an impact on the study of history that is still felt internationally.

blockade Act of war whereby one party blocks entry to or departure from an enemy area, often a coast. Legally, blockades require advance warning to neutral states and impartial application. Penalties for breach of blockade are seizure of ship and cargo and their possible condemnation as lawful prizes. Neutral ships may not be destroyed for blockade running.

Bloemfontein \'blüm-ˌfän-ˌtān\ City (pop., 1991: 127,000), Republic of S. Africa. It was the seat of the British-administered Orange River Sovereignty (1848–54), and later that of Orange Free State, an independent Boer republic formed in 1854. The failure of the Bloemfontein Conference (1899) led to the S. AFRICAN WAR. In the 20th cent. the city became a transportation hub. It is the country's judicial capital.

Blok, Aleksandr (Aleksandrovich) (1880–1921) Russian poet and dramatist. The main representative of Russian Symbolism (see SYMBOLIST MOVEMENT), he later rejected its "sterile bourgeois intellectualism" and embraced the Bolshevik movement. In his musical verse, sound was paramount. His enigmatic ballad *The Twelve* (1918) united the Russian Revolution and Christianity in an apocalyptic vision. In the era of postrevolutionary hardship, he declined into mental and physical illness and died at 40.

Blondin \blȯⁿ-ˈdaⁿ; *Engl* 'blän-dēn\, **Charles** *orig.* Jean-François Gravelet (1824–1897) French tightrope walker. He achieved fame, first in 1859, with his many crossings of Niagara Falls on a tightrope 1,100 ft (335 m) long, 160 ft (48 m) above the water. Each time he used a different variation: blindfolded, in a sack, on stilts, carrying a man on his back, and sitting down midway to cook an omelette. In 1861, at London's Crystal Palace, he turned somersaults on stilts on a rope stretched 170 ft (52 m) from the ground.

blood Circulatory fluid (see CIRCULATION) in multicellular animals. In many species it also carries HORMONES and disease-fighting substances. Blood picks up OXYGEN from the lungs and nutrients from the gastrointestinal tract and carries them to cells throughout the body for METABOLISM. It picks up carbon dioxide and other wastes from those cells and transports them to the lungs and excretory organs. Mammalian blood consists of PLASMA, red and white cells (ERYTHROCYTES and LEUKOCYTES), and PLATELETS (thrombocytes). See also ABO BLOOD-GROUP SYSTEM, ANEMIA, BLOOD PRESSURE, BLOOD TRANSFUSION, BLOOD TYPING, HEMOPHILIA, LEUKEMIA, and RH BLOOD-GROUP SYSTEM.

bloodhound Breed of dog superior to any other in scenting ability. It was known in the Mediterranean area in pre-Christian times. Calm and affectionate, it is often used to track an-

imals and trail persons. A large, strong dog, the bloodhound stands 23–27 in. (58–69 cm) and weighs 80–110 lbs (35–50 kg). It has short hair and long ears, with loose skin that falls into folds and wrinkles around the head and neck. The coat is black-and-tan, red-brown and tan, or tawny.

Bloodless Revolution See GLORIOUS REVOLUTION

blood poisoning See SEPTICEMIA

blood pressure Force originating when the HEART's pumping pushes the BLOOD against the walls of the blood vessels. Usually measured over an arm or leg ARTERY, blood pressure is expressed as two numbers; normal adult blood pressure is about 120/80 mm of mercury. The higher number (systolic) is measured when the heart's ventricles contract and the lower (diastolic) when they relax. See also HYPERTENSION, HYPOTENSION.

blood transfusion Transfer of BLOOD taken from one person into the circulation of another to restore blood volume, increase HEMOGLOBIN levels, or combat SHOCK. Once the blood-group ANTIGENS and ANTIBODIES (see ABO BLOOD-GROUP SYSTEM, RH BLOOD-GROUP SYSTEM) were discovered, BLOOD TYPING of donors and recipients rendered transfusion safe. Undesirable reactions to transfusion are not uncommon.

blood typing Classification of blood by inherited ANTIGENS associated with ERYTHROCYTES (red blood cells), including the ABO BLOOD-GROUP SYSTEM and RH BLOOD-GROUP SYSTEM. Without identification and matching of these factors, BLOOD TRANSFUSION from an incompatible donor may result in destruction of red cells or COAGULATION.

Bloom, Harold (b.1930) U.S. literary critic. Born in New York City, he taught at Yale from 1955. In *The Anxiety of Influence* (1973) and *A Map of Misreading* (1975), he suggested that poets creatively misread the works that most influence and unconsciously threaten them. A series of best-selling books, including *The Western Canon* (1994), has made him the most famous living American critic.

Bloomer, Amelia *orig.* Amelia Jenks (1818–1894) U.S. reformer. Born in Homer, N.Y., she married Dexter Bloomer in 1840. She wrote articles on temperance and women's rights and published the biweekly *Lily* (1849–55). Among her interests was dress reform, and the full trousers that she wore came to be known as bloomers. This publicity attracted large crowds to her lectures in New York, where she often shared the platform with Susan B. ANTHONY.

Bloomfield, Leonard (1887–1949) U.S. linguist. Born in Chicago, he trained in Indo-European languages and taught at the Univ. of Chicago (1927–40) and Yale (1940–49). In *Language* (1933), one of the clearest 20th-cent. presentations of linguistics, he advocated the study of linguistic phenomena in isolation and emphasized the need for objective description. His thinking was influenced by his work on other languages, particularly the ALGONQUIAN family; *The Menomini Language* (1962) is a paragon of linguistic description and American Indian linguistic scholarship.

Bloomsbury group Coterie of English intellectuals and artists who frequently met to discuss aesthetic and philosophical questions at several houses in the Bloomsbury district of London from about 1907 to 1930. Among the group were E. M. FORSTER, Lytton STRACHEY, Clive BELL, the painters Vanessa Bell (1879–1961) and Duncan Grant (1885–1978), J. M. KEYNES, the Fabian writer Leonard Woolf (1880–1969), and Virginia WOOLF.

blowfish See PUFFER

blowfly Any member of the DIPTERAN family Calliphoridae, including the screwworm and the bluebottle, greenbottle, and cluster flies. Metallic blue, green, or bronze, and noisy in flight, blowflies resemble the HOUSEFLY in size and habits. Blowflies were once used to treat gangrene and were used in World War I to clean soldiers' wounds. They may help prevent infection by cleaning away dead flesh, but may also destroy healthy tissue. Some species kill livestock by massive infestation or by carrying diseases such as ANTHRAX, DYSENTERY, and JAUNDICE.

blowgun Long, narrow pipe through which darts or other projectiles are blown. It has been used for hunting by aboriginal peoples in SE Asia, S India, NW S. America, and Central America. Blowguns vary in length from 18 in. to more than 23 ft (45 cm to 7 m) and are often made of cane or bamboo. Darts are usually made of palm-leaf midribs or wood or bamboo splinters. The dart must fit the tube snugly, so that a puff of human breath will cause it to fly from the tube. Against quarry larger than small birds, blow-gun darts require poison.

Blücher \'blü-kər\, **Gebhard von** *later* **Fürst (Prince) von Wahlstatt** \'väl-ˌshtät\ (1742–1819) Prussian military leader. He commanded troops against the French 1793–94 and in the NAPOLEONIC WARS. In 1813 he came out of retirement to defeat the French at Wahlstatt and Leipzig. In 1815 he again commanded Prussian forces in the Battle of WATERLOO, coordinating his army with the allied forces under the duke of WELLINGTON to bring about Napoleon's defeat.

Gebhard von Blücher
Painting by F. C. Gröger, 1817

blue (butterfly) Any member of the widely occurring LEPIDOPTERAN family Lycaenidae. Adults, sometimes known as gossamer-winged butterflies, are small and delicate, with a wingspan of 0.75–1.5 in. (18–38 mm). Blues are rapid fliers, and most species have iridescent wings. Larvae of some species secrete honeydew, a sweet by-product of digestion that attracts ants.

Bluebeard *or* **Gilles de Rais** \zhēl-də-ˈrā\ (1404–1440) Baron and marshal of France renowned for his cruelty. His name was later connected with the story "Bluebeard" by Charles PERRAULT. He fought several battles at the side of JOAN OF ARC and was made marshal of France (1429). Back in Brittany he led a dissipated life and eventually turned to alchemy and satanism. Accused of abducting and murdering more than 140 children, he was tried by ecclesiastical and civil courts. Condemned for heresy, he confessed, repented, and was hanged. The fairy-tale Bluebeard takes a wife, who, curious about the one room of the castle to which he denies her the key, discovers there the skeletons of her predecessors.

bluebell Any plant of the genus *Endymion,* in the LILY FAMILY, native to Eurasia. Bluebell, or wild hyacinth *(E. non-scriptus),* and Spanish bluebell *(E. hispanicus),* bearing clusters of bell-shaped blue flowers, are cultivated as garden ornamentals. Many other plants are commonly known as bluebells, including species of the genera *Campanula, Eustoma, Polemonium,* and *Clematis.* In the U.S. the name bluebell is usually reserved for *Mertensia virginica.*

blueberry Any of several shrubs, native to N. America, of the genus *Vaccinium,* in the HEATH FAMILY. They are prized for their sweet edible fruits, a source of vitamin C and iron. The economically important highbush blueberry *(V. corymbosum),* is cultivated primarily in Maine, New Jersey, SW Michigan, and E N. Carolina.

bluebird Any of three N. American bird species (songbird genus *Sialia*) of the chat-thrush group. The eastern bluebird *(S. sialis),* which is 5.5 in. (14 cm) long, and the western bluebird *(S. mexicana)* are red-breasted forms found east and west of the Rockies, respectively. The mountain bluebird *(S. currucoides),* also found in the West, is all blue. Bluebirds live in open country and woodlands.

bluefish Swift-moving food and game fish *(Pomatomus saltatrix)* found throughout warmer regions of the Atlantic and Indian oceans. It lives in schools and is a voracious predator of smaller fishes. It has a forked tail and a large mouth with strong, pointed teeth. It is blue or greenish and grows to about 4 ft (1.2 m) and 25 lbs (11.5 kg).

bluegrass Any of many slender annual and perennial lawn, pasture, and forage GRASSES of the genus *Poa,* in the family Gramineae (Poaceae). About 250 species are found in temperate and cool climates, more than 50 in the U.S. Kentucky bluegrass *(P. pratensis),* the best-known U.S. species, is a popular lawn and pasture grass in the N states with blue-green leaves. Some species are important W forage grasses. Annual bluegrass *(P. annua),* a small, light-green species, is considered a pest in lawns.

bluegrass In music, a country-and-western style that emerged after World War II, a direct descendant of the string-band music played by such groups as the CARTER FAMILY. Bluegrass was originated by and got its name from Bill MONROE and His Blue Grass Boys. It is distinguished from its predecessors by its more syncopated rhythm, high-pitched tenor (lead) vocals, tight harmonies, driving rhythms, and strong influence of jazz and blues. A very prominent place is given to the banjo, always played in the three-finger style developed by Earl Scruggs (b.1924). Mandolin and fiddle are generally featured, and traditional square-dance tunes, religious songs, and ballads furnish much of the repertory.

Bluegrass region Area of central Kentucky. Containing Kentucky's best agricultural land, it became known for its abundant BLUEGRASS and famous for breeding fine horses; the calcium-rich soil imparts its minerals to the grass and thence into the horses' bones.

blue-green algae See CYANOBACTERIA

blue ground See KIMBERLITE

blue law U.S. statute regulating work, commerce, and amusements on Sundays. The name is said to derive from a list of Sabbath regulations published (on blue paper or in blue wrappers) in New Haven, Conn., in 1781. Throughout colonial New England such laws regulated morals and conduct. Most lapsed after the American Revolution, but some, such as prohibitions against the Sunday sale of alcoholic beverages, remain on the books in some areas.

Blue Nile See NILE RIVER

Blue Ridge (Mountains) Section of the APPALACHIAN MTNS., E U.S. The range extends from NE W. Virginia southwest across Virginia and N. Carolina into Georgia; it is sometimes considered to include a N extension into Maryland, Pennsylvania, and New York. The average elevation is 2,000–4,000 ft (600–1,200 m). The scenic Blue Ridge Parkway, established in 1936, runs 470 mi (756 km) along the crest.

blues Secular musical form incorporating a repeating harmonic structure with melodic emphasis on the flatted or "blue" third and seventh notes of the scale. Its specific origins are not known, but elements of the music of former slaves include the call-and-response pattern and syncopated rhythms of SPIRITUALS and work songs. The codification of its structure as a 12-bar phrase using the chords of the first, fourth, and fifth degrees of the major scale occurred in the early 20th cent. Its origins as a primarily vocal form induced instrumental performers to imitate the human voice with "bent" notes. Lyric stanzas are usually in three lines, the words of the second generally repeating those of the first. The elaboration of the rural blues from Texas and the Mississippi delta established both lyric and instrumental traditions, often featuring speech-like inflection and guitar accompaniment. W. C. HANDY's compositions brought blues elements into popular music. The first blues recordings featured Ma RAINEY and Bessie SMITH in the early 1920s using jazz accompanists. The highly personal interpretations and improvisation of the blues served as the foundation for JAZZ, RHYTHM AND BLUES, and ROCK MUSIC.

blue whale Mottled, blue-gray BALEEN WHALE *(Balaenoptera,* or *Sibbaldus, musculus).* The largest of all animals, the blue whale reaches a maximum length of about 100 ft (30 m) and a maximum weight of 150 tons (136,000 kg). It is found in all oceans. In summer it feeds on KRILL in polar waters, and in winter it moves toward the equator to breed. Once the most important of the commercially hunted baleen whales, it is now critically endangered and is legally protected.

Blum \'blüm\, **Léon** (1872–1950) French politician and writer. A brilliant literary and drama critic, he entered politics in the FRENCH SOCIALIST PARTY. In the Chamber of Deputies (1919–28, 1929–40), he became a leader of the Socialists. The chief architect of an electoral alliance of the left, he became the first Socialist (and the first Jewish) premier of France as head of the POPULAR FRONT govern-

B

ment (1936–37). He introduced such reforms as the 40-hour workweek and collective bargaining. Arrested by the Vichy government in 1940, he was imprisoned until 1945.

Léon Blum

Blunt, Anthony (Frederick) (1907–1983) British art historian and spy. He began his espionage for the Soviet Union after meeting Guy BURGESS at Cambridge Univ. in the 1930s. From 1937 Blunt had a brilliant career as an art historian; his works largely established art history in Britain. In World War II he served in British military intelligence and also gave secret information to the Soviets. In 1945 he was appointed surveyor of the king's (later queen's) pictures, and in 1947 he became director of the prestigious Courtauld Institute. In 1951 he arranged for the escape of Burgess and Donald Maclean (1913–1983) from Britain. In 1964, after the defection of Kim PHILBY, Blunt was questioned and secretly confessed his Soviet connections. When his past was made public in 1979, he was stripped of his knighthood.

Bly, Nellie *orig.* Elizabeth Cochrane (1867–1922) U.S. newspaper writer. Born in Cochrane's Mills, Pa., she started writing feature articles for *The Pittsburgh Dispatch* at 18 on topics like divorce and slum life. For the *New York World,* she feigned insanity to enter an asylum and wrote an exposé that led to needed reforms. In 1889 she circled the globe in about 72 days, 6 hours, beating the fictional record in Jules VERNE's *Around the World in Eighty Days* and making her name a synonym for a female star reporter.

Bly, Robert (Elwood) (b.1926) U.S. poet and translator. Born in Madison, Minn., in 1958 he founded the poetry journal *The Fifties* (later *The Sixties*). He helped found American Writers Against the Vietnam War. His *The Light Around the Body* won the 1968 National Book Award. His best-selling *Iron John* (1990) probed the male psyche, and Bly became the best-known leader of the "men's movement." He has also translated a wide range of poetry.

Blyton \ˈblī-tᵊn\, **Enid (Mary)** (1897–1968) English children's writer. Trained as a teacher, she published her first book, *Child Whispers,* in 1922. Of her more than 600 children's books, probably best known are the series featuring Noddy, the Famous Five, and the Secret Seven. Though often criticized for their stereotyped characters, simple writing, and moralism, her books were widely translated and remained popular long after her death.

BMW *in full* **Bayerische Motoren Werke AG** \ˈbī-er-ish-ə-mō-ˈtŏr-ən-ˈver-kə\ German automaker. Founded in 1929, the company became known for its high-speed motorcycles. During World War II, BMW built the world's first jet airplane engines for the Luftwaffe. After 1969 the company prospered with a line of high-priced sedans engineered like sports cars.

B'nai B'rith \bə-ˈnā-ˈbrith\ (Hebrew: "Sons of the Covenant") Oldest and largest Jewish service organization. Founded in New York City in 1843, it now has chapters worldwide. Its goals include defending human rights, aiding Jewish college students (through the Hillel Foundation), sponsoring educational programs, helping victims of disasters, supporting hospitals, and promoting the welfare of Israel. In 1913 it established the Anti-Defamation League to combat ANTI-SEMITISM.

boa Any of about 60 species of stout-bodied snakes (subfamily Boinae, family Boidae) found in both the Old and New Worlds, mostly in warm regions. Species vary in length from about 8 in. (20 cm) to more than 25 ft (7.5 m). Most are terrestrial or semiaquatic; some live in trees. Most species have blotches and diamonds on their brown, green, or yellowish body. Boas bite their prey, then kill by wrapping their body around the prey and crushing it. Contrary to folklore, boas are not dangerous to humans.

Boadicea See BOUDICCA

boar *or* **wild boar** *or* **wild pig** Any wild member of the PIG species *Sus scrofa,* the ancestor of domestic pigs. It is native to forests ranging from W and N Europe and N. Africa to India, the Andaman Islands, and China and has been introduced to New Zealand and the U.S. It has a bristly coat and stands up to 35 in. (90 cm) tall at the shoulder. Boars are omnivores and are good swimmers. They have sharp tusks and, though normally not aggressive, can be dangerous. The boar has long been a prized game animal.

Board of Trade See Board of TRADE

Boas \ˈbō-ˌaz\, **Franz** (1858–1942) German-U.S. anthropologist. Trained in physics and geography, Boas was part of an early scientific expedition to Baffin Island (1883–84), where he turned to studying ESKIMO culture. From 1896 to 1905 he directed the Jesup N. Pacific Expedition, which investigated the relationships between the aboriginal peoples of Siberia and N. America. His achievements in anthropology are virtually unrivaled. In opposition to the prevailing theory of SOCIOCULTURAL EVOLUTION, Boas argued that all human groups have evolved equally but in different ways. It is largely due to Boas that human differences are now attributed by anthropologists to historic "cultural" rather than genetic factors. Teaching at Columbia Univ. from 1896 until his death, he was the leading organizer of the profession in the U.S. and the mentor of Ruth BENEDICT, Margaret MEAD, and Edward SAPIR. His books include *The Mind of Primitive Man* (1911), *Primitive Art* (1927), and *Race, Language and Culture* (1940).

boat people Refugees fleeing by boat. The term originally referred to the thousands of Vietnamese who fled their country by sea after the fall of S. Vietnam in 1975. Crowded into small vessels, they were prey to pirates, and many suffered dehydration, starvation, and death by drowning. The term was later applied to waves of refugees who attempted to reach the U.S. by boat from Cuba and Haiti.

Bob and Ray U.S. comedian team. Bob (born Robert Brackett) Elliott was born in Boston (1923), Ray (born Raymond Walter) Goulding (1922–1990) in Lowell, Mass. They met while working at a Boston radio station and soon established a program of parodies and satire (1946–51). *The Bob and Ray Show* was nationally syndicated 1951–53, and their comedy sketches were popular in the 1950s and '60s on several networks. They also starred in the Broadway show *The Two and Only* (1970).

bobbin Elongated spool of thread, used in the TEXTILE industry. In modern processes, the spun fibers are wound on bobbins; the weft filling in WEAVING comes off bobbins. Bobbins are essential to the manufacture of bobbin LACE (see LACEMAKING). Early bobbin lace consisted of rows of deep acute-angled points worked from a narrow band. It was much used for ruffs and collars in the 16th–17th cent.

bobcat Bobtailed, long-legged N. American cat (*Felis rufa*) found in forests, deserts, and sometimes suburbs from S Canada to S Mexico. It is a close relative of the LYNX and CARACAL. Bobcats have large paws and tufted ears; are 24–40 in. (60–100 cm) long, excluding the 4–8-in. (10–20-cm) tail; stand 20–24 in. (50–60 cm) at the shoulder; and weigh 15–33 lbs (7–15 kg). The fur is pale brown to reddish with black spots. Bobcats are nocturnal and generally solitary. They feed on small mammals and some birds.

bobolink \ˈbäb-ə-ˌliŋk\ Songbird (*Dolichonyx oryzivorus*) that breeds in N N. America and winters chiefly in central S. America. In the breeding season the 7-in. (18-cm) male bobolink (named for his bubbling song) has a black underside, yellow hindneck, white back and rump, and white patches on the wings; in winter he resembles the brown female.

bobsledding Sport of sliding down a winding ice-covered run on a large metal sled (bobsled) equipped with two pairs of runners, a long seat for two or more (usually four) people, a steering wheel, and a hand brake. It originated in Switzerland in the 1890s, and was included in the first Olympic Winter Games in 1924. The bob run is usually at least 1,500 m (4,920 ft) long, with 15–20 banked turns. Four-man sleds attain speeds approaching 100 mph (160 kph).

bobwhite N. American QUAIL species (*Colinus virginianus*) that exists in about 20 subspecies from S Canada to

Guatemala. It is reddish brown and has a gray tail. Its name is suggestive of its two-note call. It is a popular game bird of the S and central U.S.

Boccaccio \bŏk-'käch-chō\, **Giovanni** (1313–1375) Italian poet and scholar. His early prose works include *The Love Afflicted* (c.1336); *The Book of Theseus* (c.1340) was an ambitious verse epic. He is best known for his *Decameron,* one of the first prose masterpieces in the Italian vernacular, which had enormous influence on literature throughout Europe. Probably composed 1348–53, it unites 100 earthy tales by means of a frame story. With PETRARCH, he prepared the way for Renaissance humanism and through his Italian writings helped give modern literature the same standing as the classics.

Giovanni Boccaccio Fresco by Andrea del Castagno

Boccherini \ˌbä-kə-'rē-nē\, **Luigi (Rodolfo)** (1743–1805) Italian composer. He toured widely in Europe as a cellist before taking positions at the courts of Madrid and Prussia. He wrote some 125 string quintets (more than any other composer), 90 string quartets, 50 string trios, over 25 symphonies, and 11 cello concertos. His music's elegance and charm has ensured its continuing popularity.

boccie *or* **bocci** *or* **bocce** \'bä-chē\ Game of Italian origin played on a long, narrow, packed-clay court enclosed with boarded ends and sides. Each player or team in turn rolls four balls toward a smaller ball. The object is to bring one's ball nearer the small ball than an opponent's ball; one point is awarded for each such roll. The game usually ends at 12 points.

Boccioni \bŏt-'chō-nē\, **Umberto** (1882–1916) Italian painter and sculptor. The most energetic member of the Futurist group (see FUTURISM), he helped publish *Technical Manifesto of the Futurist Painters* (1910), promoting the representation of modern technology, power, time, motion, and speed. His masterpiece of early modern sculpture is *Unique Forms of Continuity in Space* (1913). His painting *The City Rises* (1910) is a dynamic composition of swirling human figures in a fragmented crowd scene.

Böcklin \'bœk-lēn\, **Arnold** (1827–1901) Swiss-Italian painter. He won the patronage of the king of Bavaria with his mural *Pan in the Bulrushes* (1856–58). In 1858–61 he taught in Weimar and executed mythological frescoes for his native Basel. He settled in Italy, painting moody landscapes and sinister allegories that presaged Symbolism. His later style was somber, mystical, and morbid, as in his five versions of *The Isle of the Dead* (1880–86). Though most of his time was spent in Italy, he was the most influential artist in the German-speaking world in the late 19th cent.

Bodensee See Lake CONSTANCE

Bode's law Rule giving the approximate distances of PLANETS from the SUN in ASTRONOMICAL UNITS by adding 4 to each number in the sequence 0, 3, 6, 12, 24, and so on, and dividing the result by 10. First announced in 1766 by Johann Daniel Titius (1729–1796), it was popularized by Johann Elert Bode (1747–1826). All the planets except Neptune orbit at the distances predicted by Bode's law, which also suggested that a planet existed between Mars and Jupiter where the asteroid belt was later discovered.

bodhi \'bō-dē\ (Sanskrit and Pali: "awakening" or "enlightenment") In BUDDHISM, the final enlightenment that ends the cycle of death and rebirth and leads to NIRVANA. This awakening transformed Siddhartha Gautama into the historical BUDDHA. Bodhi is achieved by ridding oneself of false beliefs and the hindrance of passions through the discipline of the EIGHTFOLD PATH.

Bodhidharma \ˌbō-di-'dər-mə\ *Chinese* Damo *Japanese* Daruma (fl.6th cent.) Legendary Indian monk credited with establishing the Chan or ZEN school of BUDDHISM. He is

considered the 28th Indian successor in a direct line from the BUDDHA Gautama. Legend states that he traveled from India to Guang (now Guangzhou), China, where he told the emperor WUDI, who was famous for his good works, that meditation, not good deeds, led to enlightenment. He himself was said to have meditated sitting motionless for nine years.

bodhisattva \ˌbō-di-'sət-və\ Term for the historical BUDDHA Gautama prior to his enlightenment as well as for other individuals destined to become buddhas. In MAHAYANA Buddhism the bodhisattva postpones attainment of NIRVANA in order to alleviate the suffering of others. The number of bodhisattvas is theoretically limitless, and the title has been applied to great scholars, teachers, and Buddhist kings. Celestial bodhisattvas (e.g., AVALOKITESVARA) are considered manifestations of the eternal Buddha and serve as savior figures and objects of personal devotion.

bodhi tree *or* **bo tree** In BUDDHISM, the fig tree under which the BUDDHA sat when he attained enlightenment (BODHI) at Bodh Gaya (near Gaya, India). The tree growing on the site now is believed to be a descendant of the original, planted from a cutting of a tree in Sri Lanka that had been propagated from the original; both trees are sites of pilgrimage.

Bodleian Library \'bŏd-lē-ən\ Library of the Univ. of Oxford and one of the most important reference libraries in Britain. It has particularly rich collections of Oriental manuscripts, English literature, and early printing. Though established earlier, it was not secured by the university until 1410. After a decline, it was restored by Sir Thomas Bodley (1545–1613), a collector of medieval manuscripts, and reopened in 1602. Since 1610 it has been a legal deposit library entitled to free copies of all books printed in Britain.

Bodrum See HALICARNASSUS

bodybuilding Developing of the physique through exercise and diet, often for competitive exhibition. Bodybuilding aims at displaying pronounced muscle tone and exaggerated muscle mass and definition for overall aesthetic effect. WEIGHT TRAINING is the principal form of exercise used; high-protein foods contribute to the diet. The first important international competition was the Mr. Universe contest (1947). It was followed in 1965 by the even more prestigious Mr. Olympia contest. Competition for women began in the 1970s. In 1998 bodybuilding was granted provisional status by the International Olympic Committee. The use of STEROIDS to enhance performance, though generally forbidden, has long been common.

body louse See human LOUSE

Boeing Co. U.S. company and world's largest manufacturer of commercial aircraft. It was founded by William E. Boeing (1881–1956) in 1916. Boeing pioneered in the development of single-wing planes in the 1930s; its B-17 Flying Fortress (1935) and B-29 Superfortress (1942) played prominent roles in World War II. Its postwar B-52 bomber was a mainstay of U.S. strategic forces. In 1954–55 it produced the first U.S. jet airliner, the Boeing 707, the first of a highly successful series of jetliners that would include the 727, 747, 757, and 767. In 1996 it purchased the aerospace and defense electronics businesses of Rockwell International Corp., and in 1997 it acquired the McDonnell Douglas Corp., a purchase that left Boeing without U.S. competitors in commercial airliner production.

Boeotia \bē-'ō-shə\ District and ancient republic, E central Greece. Bounded by ATTICA and the Gulf of Corinth, its chief city was THEBES. The Boeotian League was formed under Theban leadership around 600–550 B.C. Hostile to ATHENS, the League revolted against it about 447 B.C. In the PELOPONNESIAN WAR, Boeotia defeated Athens at Delium in 424 B.C. It dominated Greece until Thebes was destroyed by ALEXANDER THE GREAT about 335 B.C.

Boer See AFRIKANER

Boerhaave \'bür-ˌhä-və\, **Hermann** (1668–1738) Dutch physician. Renowned as a teacher, he is often credited with founding the modern system of teaching medical students at the patient's bedside. His great reputation came partly from his attempts to organize the mass of medical information known at the time, in a series of major texts and encyclopedic works.

Boethius \bō-'ē-thē-əs\ *in full* Anicius Manlius Severinus Boethius (c.480–524) Roman scholar, Christian philosopher, and statesman. He became consul in 510 and later chief minister to the Ostrogothic king THEODORIC. Convicted of treason, he wrote his Neoplatonic *The Consolation of Philosophy* while awaiting execution. The book remained extremely popular and influential through the Middle Ages and later, and his translations of ARISTOTLE and others, with commentaries, became basic texts in medieval SCHOLASTICISM.

Bogart, Humphrey (DeForest) (1899–1957) U.S. actor. Born in New York City, he won success on Broadway as the murderer Duke Mantee in *The Petrified Forest* (1935), a role he reprised on film (1936). He appeared in over 25 films, usually as a gangster, before achieving stardom in *High Sierra* (1941). Often playing a sardonic loner who proves capable of love, he appeared in such films as *The Maltese Falcon* (1941), *Casablanca* (1942), *Treasure of the Sierra Madre* (1948), *Key Largo* (1948), *The African Queen* (1951, Academy Award), and *The Caine Mutiny* (1954) and four films with his fourth wife, Lauren BACALL.

Humphrey Bogart in *Sahara,* 1943

Bogomils \'bä-gə-ˌmilz\ Religious sect that flourished in the Balkans in the 10th–15th cent. Founded by the 10th-cent. Bulgarian priest Bogomil, the sect's beliefs arose from a fusion of dualistic doctrines imported mainly from Asia Minor and a local Slavonic movement to reform the new Bulgarian Orthodox church. Its central teaching was that the visible, material world was created by the devil. The Bogomils denied the doctrine of the incarnation, rejected the Christian conception of matter as a vehicle of grace, and repudiated the Orthodox Church. In the 11th–12th cent. Bogomilism spread through the Byzantine empire. In Bulgaria it remained a powerful force until the late 14th cent. With the Ottoman conquest of SE Europe in the 15th cent., its influence declined.

Bogotá \ˌbō-gō-'tä\ City (pop., 1999: 6,276,000), capital of Colombia. The District Capital area is officially known as Santa Fé de Bogotá. It lies on a plateau east of the ANDES. European settlement began in 1538 when Spanish conquistadores overran Bacatá, the main seat of the Chibcha Indians. It became the capital of NEW GRANADA and a center of Spanish colonial power. It was the scene of revolt against Spanish rule in 1810–11, and Simón BOLÍVAR took the city in 1819, whereupon it became the capital of New Granada (later Republic of Colombia). Today Bogotá is an industrial, commercial, educational, and cultural center.

Boguslawski \ˌbȯ-gü-'släf-skē\, **Wojciech** (1757–1829) Polish actor, director, and playwright. He joined the Polish National Theater as an actor and later became its director (1783–1814). Considered the father of Polish theater, he wrote over 80 plays, including numerous comedies adapted from Western European writers as well as the popular original play *Krakovians and Highlanders* (1794).

Bohemia Former kingdom, central Europe. Settled in the 5th cent. A.D. by the Czechs, it became tributary to CHARLEMAGNE's empire. It was part of the kingdom of MORAVIA in 870, and later a duchy with an important center at PRAGUE. In the 10th cent. it expanded to include parts of SILESIA, Slovakia, and KRAKÓW. From the election of FERDINAND I as king in 1526, it remained under HABSBURG rule until 1918. Following World War I, Bohemia declared independence along with Moravia and Slovakia. It was invaded by Germany in 1939. It became a province of Czechoslovakia (later the Czech Socialist Republic) after World War II, and part of the independent Czech Republic in 1993.

Bohemian language See CZECH LANGUAGE

Böhme \'bœ-mə\, **Jakob** (1575–1624) German mystic. Originally a cobbler, Böhme had a religious experience in 1600 wherein he gained an insight, expounded in *Aurora* (1612), that he thought would help him resolve the tensions of his age. Inspired by PARACELSUS and nature mysticism, in *The Great Mystery* (1623) he explained the Genesis account of creation in Paracelsian terms. In *On the Election of Grace* he expounded the FREE WILL PROBLEM, made acute at the time by the spread of CALVINISM and its doctrine of PREDESTINATION. He had a profound influence on later IDEALISM and ROMANTICISM, and he is regarded as the father of THEOSOPHY.

Bohr \'bȯr\, **Niels (Henrik David)** (1885–1962) Danish physicist. He studied the structure of the atom with J. J. THOMSON and Ernest RUTHERFORD. He was among the first to see the importance of an element's ATOMIC NUMBER and postulated that any atom could exist only in a discrete set of states characterized by definite values of energy. He became the first to apply the quantum theory to atomic and molecular structure, and his concept of the atomic nucleus was a key step in understanding such processes as NUCLEAR FISSION. He directed the Institute for Theoretical Physics in Copenhagen 1920–62. His work won him a Nobel Prize in 1922. Though he contributed to atomic-bomb research in the U.S. during World War II, he later dedicated himself to arms control. Element 107, bohrium, is named in his honor. His son Aage Niels Bohr (b.1922) shared the 1975 Nobel Prize with Ben Mottelson (b.1926) and James Rainwater (1917–1986) for their work on atomic nuclei.

Boigny, Félix Houphouët See Félix HOUPHOUËT-BOIGNY

boil *or* **furuncle** \'fyur-ˌəŋ-kəl\ *or* **furunculosis** Inflamed pus-filled swelling due to STAPHYLOCOCCUS skin infection at a hair follicle. It hurts and feels hard; healing requires discharging the pus. Boils usually occur in hairy areas exposed to friction and maceration, which can introduce staphylococci on the skin into hair follicles. Treatment usually involves keeping the area clean and protected from further infection; antibiotics often help severe cases. See also ABSCESS, STY.

boiler Apparatus for converting a LIQUID to vapor. A boiler consists of a furnace in which fuel is burned, surfaces to transmit heat from the combustion products to the water (or other liquid), and a space where steam (or vapor) can form and collect. A conventional boiler burns a FOSSIL FUEL or waste fuel; a nuclear reactor may instead supply the heat. In a fire-tube boiler, the water surrounds the steel tubes through which hot gases from the furnace flow; easy to install and operate, fire-tube boilers are widely used to heat buildings and to provide power for factories. In a water-tube boiler, the water is inside tubes, with the hot furnace gases circulating outside the tubes; water-tube boilers, which produce more and hotter steam, are used in ships and factories. Large units are found in public-utility power plants, steel mills, paper mills, oil refineries, and chemical plants. See also STEAM ENGINE.

boiling Cooking of food by immersion in water heated to near its BOILING POINT. Boiling is used primarily to cook meats and vegetables. A double boiler, which suspends a pan containing the food above another containing boiling water, is used for scalding and poaching, which heat food to sub-boiling temperatures. At the simmering point, just below boiling, soups, stews, and pot roasts are prepared. Vegetables are often steamed in a rack placed above boiling water.

boiling point TEMPERATURE at which a liquid is converted to vapor (see VAPORIZATION) when heated. At the boiling point, addition of heat results in the transformation of the liquid into its vapor without an increase in temperature. A liquid's boiling point depends on the liquid's characteristics and the applied pressure. Water, at standard atmospheric pressure, or sea level, boils at 212°F (100°C); ethanol boils at about 172°F (78°C). At higher altitudes, boiling points are lower and foods can take longer to cook.

Bois, W. E. B. Du See W. E. B. DU BOIS

Boise \'bȯi-zē\ City (pop., 2000: 185,000), capital of Idaho. The largest city in the state, it lies on the Boise River. Following the 1862 gold rush to the river basin, Boise became the capital of Idaho Territory in 1864, and of the state in 1890. Agricultural expansion and the lumber industry contributed to its rapid growth. Boise is the service center for the Boise National Forest.

Bojangles See Bill ROBINSON

Bok, Edward (William) (1863–1930) U.S. editor. Born to a poor immigrant family in Brooklyn, N.Y., Bok went into book and magazine publishing. As editor of the *Ladies' Home Journal* (1889–1919), he established departments to inform women on diverse subjects and led campaigns for public health and beautification. His refusal of patent-medicine advertising helped lead to the Pure Food and Drug Act (1906). His last years were devoted to civic improvement and world peace. He wrote a notable autobiography, *The Americanization of Edward Bok* (1920, Pulitzer Prize).

Bokassa \bō-ˈkas-ə\, **Eddine Ahmed** (*orig.* **Jean-Bédel**) (1921–1996) President of the Central African Republic (1966–77) and self-proclaimed emperor of the Central African Empire (1977–79). Bokassa joined the French army in 1939 and earned the Croix de Guerre. In 1961 he returned to head the army of the newly independent Central African Republic. Five years later he overthrew its president and in 1977 crowned himself emperor. When he was found to have participated in the massacre of 100 schoolchildren and accused of cannibalism, French paratroops removed him and reestablished the republic. Though sentenced to death in absentia in 1980, he returned in 1986 and was arrested; his death sentence was commuted, and he was freed in 1993.

bok choy *or* **Chinese mustard** *Brassica chinensis,* one of two types of CHINESE CABBAGE. It has glossy dark-green leaves and thick, crisp white stalks in a loose head. Its yellow-flowering center is especially prized. See also BRASSICA, MUSTARD FAMILY.

Bokhara See BUKHARA

Boleyn \bu̇-ˈlin\, **Anne** (1507?–1536) Second wife of HENRY VIII of England. From 1522 Anne lived at Henry's court, and he soon began secret proceedings to rid himself of his first wife, CATHERINE OF ARAGON. For six years Pope CLEMENT VII refused to grant an annulment. In 1533 Henry and Anne were secretly married, and Henry had the archbishop of Canterbury, Thomas CRANMER, annul his previous marriage. Anne gave birth to the future ELIZABETH I, but failed to produce a male heir. In 1536 Henry had her imprisoned on questionable charges of adultery and incest. She was convicted and beheaded.

Bolingbroke \ˈbä-liŋ-ˌbru̇k\, **Viscount** *orig.* Henry Saint John (1678–1751) British politician. He became a prominent Tory in the reign of Queen ANNE, serving as secretary of war (1704–8) and of state (1710–15). He was dismissed from office by GEORGE I and, fearing impeachment because of his intrigues with the JACOBITES, he fled to France. He returned to England in 1725 and waged an influential propaganda campaign in opposition to the Whigs and their leader, Robert WALPOLE. His historical and philosophical works include *The Idea of a Patriot King* (1744, 1749).

Bolívar \bō-ˈlē-vär\, **Simón** (1783–1830) S. American revolutionary and statesman. Son of a Venezuelan aristocrat, Bolívar received a European education. Influenced by European rationalism, he became a prominent political and military leader in Venezuela's independence movement. The revolutionaries overthrew Venezuela's Spanish governor in 1810, but the young republic was defeated in 1814, and Bolívar went into exile. In 1819 he undertook a daring and successful surprise attack on NEW GRANADA (now Colombia, Venezuela, and Ecuador), leading some 2,500 men over routes considered impassable. With the help of Antonio José de SUCRE, he secured the independence of Ecuador in 1822. He completed José de

Simón Bolívar Engraving by C. G. Childs

SAN MARTÍN's revolutionary work in Peru, freeing that country in 1824. On Bolívar's orders, Sucre liberated Upper Peru, now Bolivia (1825). As president of both Colombia (1821–30) and Peru (1823–29), Bolívar oversaw the creation in 1826 of a league of Hispanic-American states, but he proved less successful at ruling countries than at liberating them.

Bolivia *officially* **Republic of Bolivia** Nation, W S. America. Area: 424,162 sq mi (1,098,579 sq km). Population (2000): 8,329,000. Capitals: LA PAZ (administrative), SUCRE (constitutional). The population consists of three principal groups:

©1999, Encyclopædia Britannica, Inc.

Scale 1: 23,517,000

Indians, descendants of the AYMARA and the QUECHUA; Indian-Spanish mestizos; and descendants of the Spanish. Languages: Spanish, Aymara, Quechua (all official). Religions: Roman Catholicism (official), vestiges of pre-Columbian religion. Currency: boliviano. Bolivia may be divided into three major regions. The SW highland area, or ALTIPLANO, where Lake TITICACA is located, extends through SW Bolivia. It is enclosed by the second region, the W and E branches of the ANDES. Much of the E branch is heavily forested terrain, with many deep river valleys; the W branch is a high plateau bordered by volcanoes, including the country's highest peak, Mt. Sajama, at 21,463 ft (6,542 m). The third region is a lowland area that comprises the N and E two-thirds of the country; its rivers include the Guaporé, Mamoré, Beni, and upper PILCOMAYO. Bolivia has a developing mixed economy based on the production of natural gas and agricultural foodstuffs. A republic with two legislative houses, its head of state and government is the president. The Bolivian highlands were the location of the advanced TIAHUANACO culture in the 7th–11th cent., and, with its passing, became the home of the Aymaras, an Indian group conquered by the INCAS in the 15th cent. The Incas were overrun by the invading Spanish under Hernando Pizarro (1475?–1578) in the 1530s. By 1600 Spain had established the cities of Charcas (now Sucre), La Paz, Santa Cruz, and what would become COCHABAMBA, and had begun to exploit the silver wealth of Potosí. Bolivia flourished in the 17th cent., and for a time Potosí was the largest city in the Americas. By the end of the century, the mineral wealth had dried up. Talk of independence began as early as 1809, but not until 1825 were Spanish forces finally defeated. Bolivia shrank in size when it lost Atacama province to Chile at the end of the War of the PACIFIC in 1884, and again in 1939 when it lost most of GRAN CHACO to Paraguay. One of S. America's poorest countries, it was plagued by governmental instability for much of the 20th cent. Economic reforms were introduced in the 1980s and '90s.

Böll \\'bœl\\, **Heinrich (Theodor)** (1917–1985) German writer. He fought on several fronts in World War II, a central experience in forming his antiwar, nonconformist views. His ironic novels of German life during and after the war captured the changing psychology of the German nation. Among his works are *Acquainted with the Night* (1953), *Billiards at Half-Past Nine* (1959), *The Clown* (1963), and *The Lost Honor of Katharina Blum* (1974). He won the Nobel Prize in 1972.

boll weevil \\'bōl-'wē-vəl\\ Small BEETLE *(Anthonomus grandis)* found almost everywhere cotton is cultivated. It is the most serious cotton pest in N. America. Adults vary in size according to how much food they received as larvae, but they average about 0.25 in. (6 mm), including the long, curved snout. Because the larvae and pupae remain inside the cotton bolls, destroying the seeds and surrounding fibers, they cannot be killed with insecticides. The boll weevil destroys an estimated 3–5 million bales of cotton annually.

Bologna \\bō-'lō-nyə\\ City (pop., 1996: 386,000), capital of EMILIA-ROMAGNA region, N Italy. Located north of FLORENCE, it lies at the N foot of the APENNINES. Originally the Etruscan town of Felsina, it became a Roman military colony around 190 B.C. Subject to the Byzantine exarchate of RAVENNA from the 6th cent. A.D., it became a free commune in the 12th cent. Incorporated into the PAPAL STATES in 1506, it was united to the Kingdom of Italy in 1861. The Univ. of BOLOGNA is Europe's oldest university. The city is a road and rail center for traffic between N and S Italy. It is the site of excellent medieval and Renaissance architecture, and is famous for its cuisine.

Bologna, Giovanni da See GIAMBOLOGNA

Bologna, University of Oldest university in Europe, founded in Bologna, Italy, in 1088. It became in the 12th–13th cent. the principal center for studies in civil and canon law, and a model for the organization of universities throughout Europe. Its faculties of medicine and philosophy were formed about 1200. The faculty of science was developed in the 17th cent. In the 18th cent. women were admitted as students and teachers. Total enrollment is about 64,000.

Bolshevik \\'bōl-shə-,vik\\ (Russian: "one of the majority") Member of the wing of the RUSSIAN SOCIAL-DEMOCRATIC WORKERS' PARTY led by Vladimir LENIN. The group arose in 1903 when Lenin's followers insisted that party membership be restricted to professional revolutionaries. Though they joined their rivals, the MENSHEVIKS ("those of the minority"), in the RUSSIAN REVOLUTION OF 1905, the two groups later split, and in 1912 Lenin formed his own party. Its appeal grew among urban workers and soldiers during World War I. The Bolsheviks consolidated power after the RUSSIAN REVOLUTION OF 1917. See also COMMUNIST PARTY, LENINISM.

Bolshoi Theater complex in Moscow where concerts, opera, ballet (see BOLSHOI BALLET) and dramatic works are presented. The institution (whose name means "Large") dates back to 1776, when CATHERINE II licensed a company to give all theatrical performances in Moscow; its scope soon expanded to include opera and dance as well as drama. The original complex was built in 1825; it was rebuilt after a fire in 1853.

Bolshoi Ballet \\bōl-'shȯi\\ Leading ballet company of Russia, noted for elaborate productions of 19th-cent. classical ballets. The company was formed in 1776 and took the name of its home, Moscow's Bolshoi Theater, in 1825. Its influential choreographers included Marius PETIPA, Carlo BLASIS and Alexander Gorsky (1871–1924). Its many successful tours have introduced its outstanding dancers, including Galina ULANOVA and Maya PLISETSKAYA, to audiences worldwide.

Boltzmann \\'bōlts-,män\\, **Ludwig (Eduard)** (1844–1906) Austrian physicist. He was one of the first European scientists to recognize the importance of J. C. MAXWELL's electromagnetic theory. He explained the second law of THERMODYNAMICS by applying the laws of mechanics and the theory of probability to the motions of atoms, and developed

statistical mechanics. His work was widely attacked and misunderstood, but shortly after his death (by suicide) his conclusions were finally supported by discoveries in atomic physics and by recognition that phenomena such as BROWNIAN MOTION could be explained only by statistical mechanics.

Bombay *or* **Mumbai** \\'məm-,bī\\ City (metro. area pop., 2001: 16,368,000), capital of Maharashtra state, W India. Located partly on Bombay Island, it is flanked by Bombay Harbor and the ARABIAN SEA. It is India's principal port on that sea and one of the largest and most densely populated cities in the world. The town was acquired by the Portuguese in 1534 and ceded to the English in 1661. It became the headquarters of the British E. INDIA CO. in 1672, and in 1708 it was made the center of British authority in India. After the opening of the SUEZ CANAL in 1869, Bombay grew to be the largest distributing center in India. It remains India's chief financial and commercial center, its cultural and education center, and headquarters of its huge film industry.

bomber Military aircraft designed to drop bombs on surface targets. Aerial bombardment originated in the Italo–Turkish War (1911). In World War I the Germans used ZEPPELINS as strategic bombers. In the 1930s dive bombers caused great destruction in the Spanish Civil War. World War II saw development of heavy bombers, such as the U.S. B-29, which could carry 20,000 lbs (9,000 kg) of bombs. Bombers were crucial to the Allied victory. During the Cold War, jet-propelled bombers carried nuclear bombs, but from the 1960s strategic bombers began to be replaced by nuclear-armed ballistic MISSILES. Late-20th-cent. efforts to evade sophisticated radar systems culminated in the development of STEALTH bombers, but their enormous cost (and the end of the Cold War) raised questions about their worth.

Bombon, Lake See Lake TAAL

Bon \\'pœn\\ Indigenous religion of Tibet. Its early cult of divine kingship (with kings regarded as manifestations of the sky divinity) was reformulated in TIBETAN BUDDHISM as the reincarnation of LAMAS. Bon's order of oracular priests had their counterparts in Buddhist soothsayers. Though its supremacy ended in the 8th cent., Bon survives in many aspects of Tibetan Buddhism and as a living religion on Tibet's N and E frontiers.

Bon \\'bȯn\\ Popular annual festival in Japan, usually observed July 13–15, in honor of the spirits of deceased family members and of all the dead, who are believed to return to their birthplaces. Memorial stones are cleaned, dances performed, and paper lanterns and fires are lit to welcome the dead and bid them farewell.

Bonaparte, (Marie-Annonciade-) Caroline (1782–1839) Queen of Naples (1808–15). The youngest sister of NAPOLEON, she married Joachim MURAT in 1800. Her ambitious nature was partially responsible for her husband's becoming king of Naples, among other achievements. Murat's shifting allegiances in 1814–15 led to his execution; Caroline then took refuge in Trieste and became comtesse de Lipona.

Bonaparte, Joseph (1768–1844) French lawyer and diplomat. Elder brother of NAPOLEON, he served during Napoleon's reign as king of Naples (1806–8), where he reorganized the judicial, financial, and educational systems, and as king of Spain (1808–13), where his attempts at reform were less successful. After Napoleon's defeat, he lived in the U.S. (1815–32) and later settled in Italy.

Bonaparte, Louis (1778–1846) French soldier. A brother of NAPOLEON, he accompanied Napoleon on the Italian campaign of 1796–97 and was his aide-de-camp in Egypt (1798–99). At Napoleon's insistence, he married Hortense de BEAUHARNAIS in 1802, but the union proved unhappy. Proclaimed king of Holland in 1806, he came in conflict with Napoleon for his unwillingness to join the CONTINENTAL SYSTEM. In 1810 he fled his kingdom and eventually settled in Italy. NAPOLEON III was his son.

Bonaventure \\,bä-nə-'ven-chər\\, **St.** (1217?–1274) Italian FRANCISCAN theologian and cardinal. Born in the Papal States, he recovered from a near-fatal childhood illness through the intercession of St. FRANCIS OF ASSISI. After study at the Univ. of Paris, he entered the Franciscan order in 1244. In 1254 he assumed control of the Franciscan school in Paris. He defended the mendicants against the charge that they defamed the Gospels by begging for alms. He was elected Franciscan minister-general in 1257. In 1273 Pope Gregory X appointed him cardinal of Albano (Italy), and at the Second Council of Lyon he reconciled parish clergy with the mendicant orders.

bond Loan contract issued by governments and corporations, specifying an obligation to return borrowed funds. The issuer promises to pay interest on the debt when due (usually semiannually) at a stipulated percentage of the face value and to redeem the face value of the bond at maturity in legal tender. Bonds usually cover substantial debts (as for airport or toll-road construction) and are issued in more formal fashion than are PROMISSORY NOTES. Government bonds may be backed by taxes, or they may be REVENUE BONDS, backed only by revenue from the supported project (toll roads, etc.). Bonds are rated by independent agencies based on the issuer's creditworthiness; bonds with ratings from AAA to BBB are regarded as suitable for investment. See also JUNK BOND.

bond In law, a formal written agreement by which a person undertakes to perform a certain act (e.g., appearing in court or fulfilling the obligations of a contract). Failure to perform obligates the person to pay a sum of money or forfeit money on deposit. A bond is an incentive to fulfill an obligation; it also provides reassurance that compensation is available if the duty is not fulfilled. See also BAIL.

Bond, (Horace) Julian (b.1940) U.S. politician and civil rights leader. Born in Nashville, Tenn., he attended Morehouse College. In 1960 he helped create the Student Nonviolent Coordinating Committee (SNCC). In 1965 he was elected to the Georgia legislature, but his support of a SNCC statement denouncing U.S. policy in the Vietnam War caused the legislature to deny him his seat. The U.S. Supreme Court ruled his exclusion unconstitutional in 1967, and he served in the legislature (1967–75) and state senate (1975–87). In 1997 he became chairman of the NAACP.

bonding Any of the interactions that account for the association of ATOMS into MOLECULES, IONS, CRYSTALS, METALS, and other stable forms. When atoms' nuclei and ELECTRONS interact, they tend to distribute themselves so that the total energy is lowest; if the energy of a group arrangement is lower than the sum of the components' energies, they bond. The number of bonds an atom can form, its VALENCE, equals the number of electrons it contributes or receives. COVALENT BONDS form molecules: Atoms bond to specific other atoms by sharing an electron pair between them. If the sharing is even, the molecule is not polar; if it is uneven, the molecule is an ELECTRIC DIPOLE. IONIC BONDS are the extreme of uneven sharing: CATIONS give up electrons, ANIONS take them up, and all the ions are held together in a crystal. In crystalline metals, a diffuse electron sharing bonds the atoms (metallic bonding). See also AROMATIC COMPOUND, HYDROGEN BONDING, TRANSITION ELEMENT, VAN DER WAALS FORCES.

Bonds, Barry L(amar) (b.1964) U.S. baseball player. Born in Riverside, Cal., he was a college All-American at Arizona State Univ. A left-handed power hitter and a superb base stealer, he played outfield for the Pittsburgh Pirates (1985–92) and the San Francisco Giants (from 1993). By the end of the 2002 season, he had been named Most Valuable Player an unprecedented five times (1990, 1992, 1993, 2001, 2002) and had earned eight gold glove awards for fielding. In 2001 he hit 73 home runs, breaking Mark MCGWIRE's record of 70.

Bône See ANNABA

bone Rigid CONNECTIVE TISSUE of VERTEBRATES consisting of cells embedded in a hard matrix. Bones serve as the body's supporting framework; provide muscle attachment points for movement; protect the internal organs; house the blood-cell formation system (red BONE MARROW); and hold about 99% of the calcium vital to many body processes. Bone consists of a matrix of crystals of calcium, chiefly the phosphate and carbonate, embedded among COLLAGEN fibers, providing strength and elasticity, and bone cells (less than 5% of its volume). An external layer of compact bone

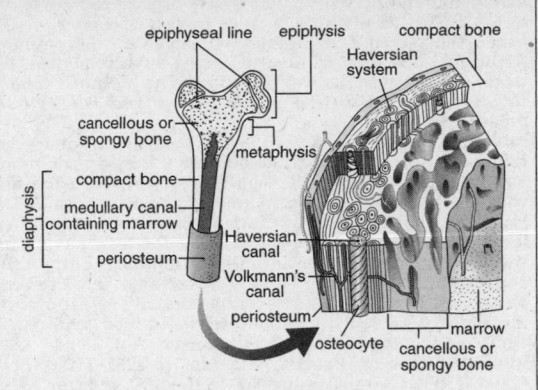

Bone Internal structure of a human long bone, with a magnified cross section of the interior. The periosteum is a connective sheath covering the outer surface of bone. The Haversian system, consisting of inorganic substances arranged in concentric rings around the Haversian canals, provides compact bone with structural support and allows for metabolism of bone cells. Osteocytes (mature bone cells) are found in tiny cavities between the concentric rings. The canals contain capillaries that bring in oxygen and nutrients and remove wastes. Transverse branches are known as Volkmann's canals.

surrounds a central area of spongy bone, except at the marrow cavity. Bone does not grow by cell division; instead, different types of bone cells generate bone matrix, break it down, and maintain it. Bone is remodeled by this process, which strengthens it in areas under greatest stress, permits healing of FRACTURES, and helps regulate calcium levels in body fluid (see CALCIUM DEFICIENCY). The process also causes underutilized bone, as in an immobilized limb, to atrophy. See also RHEUMATOID ARTHRITIS, OSTEOARTHRITIS, RICKETS, OSTEOPOROSIS.

bone marrow *or* **myeloid tissue** Soft, gelatinous tissue that fills BONE cavities. All blood cells except lymphocytes are formed in red marrow, which also takes part in destruction of old ERYTHROCYTES (red blood cells). Yellow bone marrow mainly stores FATS. Because the LEUKOCYTES (white blood cells) produced in bone marrow are involved in immune defenses, marrow transplants can treat some types of IMMUNODEFICIENCY. Radiation and some anticancer drugs can damage marrow and impair IMMUNITY. See also RETICULOENDOTHELIAL SYSTEM.

bongo Large, brightly colored ANTELOPE (*Boocercus*, or *Taurotragus*, *euryceros*) found in dense forests of central Africa. Shy, swift, and elusive, the bongo lives in small groups or in pairs. It stands about 51 in. (1.3 m) at the shoulder and has an erect mane running the length of the back. Both sexes bear heavy, spirally twisted horns. They are reddish brown to dark mahogany with narrow, vertical white stripes on the body.

Bonheur \bä-ˈnər\, **Rosa** (1822–1899) French animal painter. Trained by her father, she began exhibiting regularly at the Paris Salon in 1841. Her unsentimental paintings of lions, tigers, horses, and other animals became very popular; *The Horse Fair* (1853) gained her an international reputation. A colorful personality, she dressed as a man to study horses at the actual Horse Fair in Paris. In 1865 she became the first woman to receive the Grand Cross of the Legion of Honor.

Bonhoeffer \ˈbȯn-ˌhœ-fər\, **Dietrich** (1906–1945) German Lutheran pastor and theologian. From 1931 he lectured in theology at the Univ. of Berlin. He became a leading spokesman for the anti-Nazi Confessing Church and was active in the Resistance movement. He was arrested in 1943. The discovery of documents connecting him with the 1944 attempt on Adolf HITLER's life led to his execution a month

B

before the end of World War II. He argued for a new vision of Christianity that would abolish the division between the sacred and profane and abandon the church's traditional privileges in favor of active involvement in the world's problems. His works include *The Cost of Discipleship* (1937), *Ethics* (1949), and *Letters and Papers from Prison* (1951).

Boniface \\'bä-nə-fəs\\, **St.** (c.675–754) English missionary and reformer. Born in Wessex, he became a Benedictine monk and then a priest. In 718 Pope Gregory II entrusted him with a mission to the pagans east of the Rhine. In 722 at Hesse he founded the first of many Benedictine monasteries. He established four bishoprics in Bavaria, paving the way for its incorporation into the Carolingian Empire. He convened five synods (740–45) to reform the Frankish clergy and Irish missionaries and a council (747) to reform the entire Frankish kingdom. He was killed by Frisians while reading the Bible to recent converts.

Boniface VIII *orig.* Benedict Caetani (c.1235–1303) Pope (1294–1303). Caetani studied law in Bologna and rose to become cardinal-deacon (1281) and pope. In 1296 his attempt to end hostilities between EDWARD I of England and PHILIP IV of France became embroiled in the issue of taxation of clergy without papal consent. Philip and Boniface clashed again in 1301 over control of the clergy when Philip had a French bishop imprisoned. Hearing that Boniface planned to excommunicate Philip, Philip's supporters captured the pope; though rescued two days later, he died shortly thereafter.

Boniface of Querfurt, St. See St. BRUNO OF QUERFURT

Bonifácio, José See J. B. de ANDRADA E SILVA

bonito \\bə-'nē-tō\\ Swift, predacious schooling fishes (genus *Sarda*) of the MACKEREL family (Scombridae). Bonitos, found worldwide, have a striped back and silvery belly and grow to about 30 in. (75 cm) long. Like TUNA, they are streamlined, with a narrow tail base, a forked tail, and a row of small finlets behind the dorsal and anal fins. Bonitos have both commercial and sporting value.

Bonn City (pop., 1998 est.: 304,000), Germany. Located on the RHINE RIVER south of COLOGNE, it was, until 1999, the capital of W. Germany. An old settlement, its name was continued in Castra Bonnensia, a 1st-cent. Roman fortress. By the 9th cent. it had become the Frankish town of Bonnburg. In the 13th cent. it became capital of the Electorate of Cologne. In 1815 Bonn was awarded to PRUSSIA. By the late 19th cent. it was a fashionable residential town. It was bombed heavily in World War II. In 1949 it was chosen as W. Germany's capital. With Germany's reunification in 1990, the national capital was moved to BERLIN. Bonn was the birthplace of Ludwig van BEETHOVEN.

Bonnard \\bȯ-'när\\, **Pierre** (1867–1947) French painter and printmaker. After art study in Paris, in the 1890s he became a leading member of the NABIS group and came under the influence of Art Nouveau and Japanese prints. With his friend Édouard VUILLARD, he developed the intimate domestic interior scene, a genre known as Intimist. He also produced still lifes, self-portraits, seascapes, and large-scale decorative paintings. In 1910 he began a series of luminous landscapes of the Mediterranean region. He was fascinated by perspective, which he employed in such paintings as *The Dining Room* (1913). He was one of the greatest colorists of modern art.

Bonnie and Clyde See Clyde BARROW AND BONNIE PARKER

Bonnie Prince Charlie See C. E. STUART

bonobo \\bə-'nō-bō\\ Species (*Pan paniscus*) of great APE once considered a subspecies of the CHIMPANZEE, which it closely resembles in size, appearance, and way of life. Its range, the lowland rain forests of central Congo (Zaire), is more restricted than that of the chimpanzee, and it has a more slender body and a less protruding face. Bonobos eat mainly fruits but also leaves, seeds, grass, and small animals. They form communities of 50–120 individuals. A striking feature of their social lives is that they engage in sexual activity with great frequency, often as a means of settling quarrels, and with little regard for sex or age.

bonsai (Japanese: "tray planting") Living dwarf tree or trees; also, the art of training and growing them in containers. Bonsai specimens are ordinary trees and shrubs that are

Bonsai pine

dwarfed by a system of pruning and training roots and branches. The art originated in China but has been developed primarily by the Japanese. The direct inspiration for bonsai is in trees that grow in harsh, rocky places and are dwarfed and gnarled throughout their existence. Bonsai may live for a century or more and are handed down from one generation to another as valued family possessions. Bonsai pots, usually earthenware and of variable shape, are carefully chosen to harmonize with the tree. A sizable bonsai industry exists in Japan.

Bonus Army World War I veterans who gathered in Washington, D.C., in summer 1932 to demand payment of their promised bonuses. Over 12,000 veterans and their families camped in tents and shanties near the Capitol, urging support for a bill to force early payment of bonuses already voted by Congress. When the bill was defeated, most of the crowd returned home, but some angry protests caused local authorities to ask Pres. Herbert HOOVER for federal assistance. Army troops led by Gen. Douglas MACARTHUR drove out the protesters and burned their camps. The resulting public outcry was a factor in Hoover's defeat in the 1932 election.

bony fish Any member of the VERTEBRATE class Osteichthyes, including the great majority of living FISHES and all the world's sport and commercial fishes. Also called Pisces, the class excludes jawless fishes (HAGFISHES and LAMPREYS) and cartilaginous fishes (SHARKS, SKATES, and RAYS). There are more than 20,000 species worldwide, all with a skeleton at least partly composed of true bone. Other features include, in most species, a swim bladder, gill covers over the gill chamber, bony platelike scales, a skull with sutures, and external fertilization of eggs.

bony pelvis See PELVIC GIRDLE

booby Any of six or seven species of large tropical seabirds (family Sulidae), named for their presumed lack of intelligence. Two common species are wide-ranging in the Atlantic, Pacific, and Indian oceans, another only in the Pacific. The booby has a long bill, cigar-shaped body, and long, narrow, angular wings. It flies high above the ocean looking for schools of fish and squid. Boobies vary in length from 25 to 35 in. (65–85 cm). They nest in colonies but are territorial.

book Written (or printed) message of considerable length, meant for circulation on any of various light and durable materials. The papyrus roll of ancient Egypt was more nearly the direct ancestor of the modern book than was the clay tablet; examples of both date to around 3000 B.C. Somewhat later, the Chinese independently created an extensive scholarship based on books, many made of wood or bamboo strips bound with cords. Lampblack ink was introduced in China about A.D. 400 and printing from wooden blocks in the 6th cent. The parchment or vellum CODEX (prepared from the skins of animals) superseded the papyrus roll by A.D. 400. By the 15th cent., paper manuscripts were common. Printing spread rapidly in the late 15th cent. Subsequent technical achievements, such as the development of offset printing, improved many aspects of book culture.

bookbinding Joining together of leaves of paper, parchment, or vellum within covers to form a BOOK or CODEX. Early bindings were often splendidly decorated, but the typical artistic bookbinding is of decorated leather and was first produced in the monasteries of Egypt's Coptic Church. Rare books, historical documents, and manuscripts may be bound by hand. The cover (case) of the typical book is now affixed to the leaves by machine.

Booker Prize Prestigious annual British award for full-length novels established in 1968 by the company Booker McConnell. Entries, nominated by publishers, must be written by an English-language author from the United Kingdom, the Commonwealth countries, or Ireland. Sponsored by the Man Group since 2002, the prize is now officially called the Man Booker Prize. In 1992 a Booker Russian Novel Prize was introduced.

bookkeeping Recording of the money values of business transactions. Bookkeeping provides the information from which accounts are prepared but is distinct from ACCOUNTING. Bookkeeping offers information on both the current value, or equity, of an enterprise and on its change in value (due to profit or loss) over a given time period. Managers require such information to examine the results of operations and budget for the future; investors need it to make buy/sell decisions; and credit grantors use it to determine whether to grant a loan. The double-entry method of bookkeeping began in 15th-cent. Italy. The Industrial Revolution stimulated the spread of bookkeeping, and 20th-cent. taxation and government regulations made it a necessity. Though bookkeeping is increasingly computerized, journals and ledgers are still used in the process. The journal contains daily transactions (sales, purchases, etc.); the ledger contains the record of individual accounts. Each month an income statement and a BALANCE SHEET are posted in the ledger.

bookmaking Gambling practice of determining odds and receiving and paying off bets on the outcome of sporting events and other competitions. Horse racing is most closely associated with bookmaking, but boxing, baseball, football, and basketball have also long been of interest to bookmakers ("bookies") and gamblers. Morning-line odds, established by legal bookmakers, are printed in the sports sections of newspapers. Illegal bookmaking operations have often been linked to ORGANIZED CRIME.

Book of Common Prayer See Book of COMMON PRAYER

Book of the Dead Ancient Egyptian collection of mortuary texts made up of spells and charms and placed in tombs to aid the deceased in the next world. It was probably compiled and reedited during the 16th cent. B.C. Later compilations included hymns to RE. Of the many extant copies, none contains all the known chapters.

Boole, George (1815–1864) British mathematician. Though basically self-taught, in 1849 he was appointed professor of mathematics at Queen's College in Ireland. His general symbolic method of logical inference is fully stated in *Laws of Thought* (1854). Boole's two-valued algebra of logic, now called BOOLEAN ALGEBRA, is used in telephone switching and by electronic digital computers.

George Boole

Boolean algebra Symbolic system used for designing logic circuits for DIGITAL COMPUTERS. It is used to represent the truth value of statements, rather than the numeric quantities handled by ordinary algebra. The binary system employed by digital computers uses Boolean algebra, since the only possible truth values, true and false, can be represented by the binary digits 1 and 0. A circuit in computer memory can be open or closed, depending on the value assigned to it, and it is the integrated work of such circuits that gives computers their computing ability. The fundamental operations of Boolean logic, often called Boolean operators, are "and," "or," and "not"; combinations of these make up 13 other Boolean operators.

boomerang Curved throwing stick used chiefly by the aborigines of Australia for hunting and warfare. About 12–30 in. (30–75 cm) long, the returning boomerang varies in shape from a deep curve to almost straight sides of an angle. It is held at one end, above and behind the thrower's shoulder, and swung forward rapidly. The thrower adds spin by flicking the wrist so that the stick will return. Returning boomerangs were used only as playthings, in competition, and to imitate hawks for driving flocks of game birds into nets. The longer, straighter, heavier nonreturning boomerang can kill animals and even humans.

Boone, Daniel (1734?–c.1820) U.S. frontiersman and legendary hero. Born in Berks Co., Pa., he lived on the N. Carolina frontier as a hunter and trapper. He traveled through the CUMBERLAND GAP into E Kentucky (1767, 1769–71) and in 1775 was employed to blaze a permanent trail, called the Wilderness Road. He established the settlement of Boonesboro, which he defended against Indian attack; he was captured by the Shawnee in 1778 but escaped after five months to warn Boonesboro of an impending attack. After losing his Kentucky land claims in the late 1780s, he moved to Missouri Territory. His exploits were featured in a widely read history of Kentucky and in Lord BYRON's epic poem *Don Juan*.

Booth, Edwin (Thomas) (1833–1893) U.S. actor. Born near Bel Air, Md., into a noted theatrical family, he played his first starring roles in 1857. He became famous as Hamlet, appearing in the role for 100 consecutive nights in 1864–65. When his brother J. W. BOOTH assassinated Pres. Abraham LINCOLN, Edwin withdrew from the stage until 1866. His interpretations of Hamlet, Iago, and King Lear won great acclaim in England and Germany. He founded the Players' Club in New York in 1888.

Booth, John Wilkes (1838–1865) U.S. actor and assassin of Pres. Abraham LINCOLN. Born near Bel Air, Md., into a family of famous actors, he achieved success in Shakespearean roles but resented the greater acclaim for his brother, Edwin BOOTH. A fanatical believer in slavery and the South, he made plans with coconspirators to abduct Lincoln; after several failed attempts, he vowed to destroy the president and his cabinet. On April 14, 1865, he shot Lincoln during a performance at Ford's Theater. He broke his leg jumping from the president's box but escaped to a Virginia farm. Tracked down, he refused to surrender and was shot, either by a soldier or by himself.

Booth, William (1829–1912) British religious leader, founder and general (1878–1912) of the SALVATION ARMY. Having undergone a religious conversion at 15, he became a regular preacher of the Methodist New Connection (1852–61) and then an independent revivalist. Aided by his wife, Catherine Mumford Booth (1829–1890), he founded the Christian Mission in 1865, which in 1878 became the Salvation Army. He traveled worldwide to organize branches of the Army. His proposals for remedying social ills received widespread acceptance and the encouragement of EDWARD VII.

Boothia Peninsula Peninsula, Nunavut. Almost an island, it is the northernmost point of the N. American mainland, reaching 71°58′N, and was formerly the location of the N. Magnetic Pole. With an area of 12,483 sq mi (32,330 sq km), it extends into the ARCTIC OCEAN and is separated from BAFFIN ISLAND by the Gulf of Boothia and from Prince of Wales Island by the Franklin Strait. It is sparsely populated.

bootlegging Illegal traffic in liquor in the U.S. The term was probably first used to describe the practice of concealing flasks of illicit liquor in boot tops when going to trade with Indians. It became widely used in the 1920s during PROHIBITION. Early bootleggers smuggled foreign-made liquor into the U.S. from Canada and Mexico and from ships anchored in international waters. Later sources included medicinal whiskey, denatured alcohol, and the manufacture of corn liquor. Bootlegging led to the rise of ORGANIZED CRIME syndicates that controlled operations from the manufacture of liquor to its distribution in restaurants and speakeasies. Today some counties and municipalities continue to ban liquor, and bootlegging is still practiced.

bop See BEBOP

Bophuthatswana \ˌbō-pü-tä-ˈtswä-nä\ Former political entity (pop., 1993 est.: 2,564,000), S. Africa. Consisting of a group of noncontiguous black enclaves, it was established as a "homeland" and granted its independence in 1977, but never internationally recognized. Under the 1993 S. African constitution, Bophuthatswana was reincorporated into S. Africa as parts of Orange Free State (now Free State) and the newly created North-West and Eastern Transvaal (now Mpumalanga) provinces.

Bopp \ˈbóp\, **Franz** (1791–1867) German linguist. He published the first lengthy comparative analysis of INDO-EUROPEAN LANGUAGES, his voluminous *Comparative Grammar* *of Sanskrit, Zend, Latin, Lithuanian, Old Slavic, Gothic, and German* (1833–52). Though the relation of Sanskrit to European languages was known at the time, Bopp was a pioneer in actually isolating common elements in the MORPHOLOGY of Sanskrit and other older Indo-European languages.

Borah, William E(dgar) (1865–1940) U.S. senator (1907–40). Born in Fairfield, Ill., he practiced law in Boise, Idaho. In the Senate he was an isolationist in foreign policy; he wielded great power as chairman of the foreign relations committee from 1924, becoming best known for his role in preventing the U.S. from joining the LEAGUE OF NATIONS. A maverick Republican, he supported many of the New Deal programs to relieve economic hardship.

borax *or* **tincal** \'tiŋ-kəl\ Sodium tetraborate decahydrate, a soft, light, colorless crystalline mineral used as a component of glass and pottery glazes in the ceramics industry, as a solvent for metal-oxide slags in metallurgy, and as a fertilizer additive, a soap supplement, a disinfectant, and a water softener. About 50% of the world's supply comes from S California deserts, including DEATH VALLEY.

Borch, Gerard ter See Gerard TERBORCH

Bordeaux \bȯr-'dō\ City (pop., 1999: 215,000), SW France. Lying on the GARONNE RIVER, Bordeaux has long been noted for its wine production. An important Celtic town, under Roman rule it was capital of Aquitania Secunda. As part of the inheritance of ELEANOR OF AQUITAINE, Bordeaux became English in 1154 on her husband's accession to the English throne as HENRY II. It prospered through trade with the English until it was united to France on the English defeat in the HUNDRED YEARS' WAR (1453). As a GIRONDIN center, it suffered severely in the FRENCH REVOLUTION. During the FRANCO–PRUSSIAN WAR the French government was transferred to Bordeaux, as it was again during World War I. Its university, founded in 1441, educated such figures as MONTESQUIEU.

Borden, Lizzie (Andrew) (1860–1927) U.S. murder suspect. Born in Fall River, Mass., she lived there with her wealthy but parsimonious father and stepmother. On August 4, 1892, Mr. Borden and his wife were discovered dead in their home by Lizzie, brutally mutilated with a sharp instrument. Lizzie was arrested and tried. Evidence against her included her attempt to buy prussic acid the day before the murders. An ax was found in the basement. Acquitted after a widely reported trial, she remained in Fall River until her death, largely ostracized by the community.

Borden, Robert (Laird) (*later* **Sir Robert**) (1854–1937) Prime minister of Canada (1911–20). Born in Nova Scotia, he was elected to the Canadian House of Commons in 1896 and became leader of the Conservative Party in 1901. As prime minister, he implemented conscription in World War I and represented Canada in Britain's imperial war cabinet. He insisted on separate Canadian membership in the League of Nations, which helped transform Canada from a colony to a nation.

border collie Breed of long-haired sheepdog that has been used along the English–Scottish border for about 300 years. Usually black and white, it stands about 20 in. (50 cm) and weighs 30–50 lbs (14–23 kg). It is the most popular working sheepdog in the British Isles.

Bordet \bȯr-'dā\, **Jules (-Jean-Baptiste-Vincent)** (1870–1961) Belgian bacteriologist and immunologist. His research was vital to the foundation of serology, the study of immune reactions in BLOOD and other body fluids. His work with Octave Gengou led to serological tests for many diseases, including typhoid, tuberculosis, and syphilis (the Wassermann test). In 1906 they discovered *Bordetella pertussis,* which causes whooping cough. In 1919 Bordet received a Nobel Prize.

boreal forest See TAIGA

Borg, Björn (Rune) (b.1956) Swedish tennis player. Noted for his powerful serve and two-handed backhand, he became the first man to win the Wimbledon singles championship five successive times (1976–80) since Laurie Doherty (1902–6) and the first to win the French Open four times in a row and six times in all (1974–75, 1978–81). He won a record 41 straight Wimbledon singles matches, and also holds records for consecutive wins in Davis Cup play (33) and at the French Open (28).

Borge \'bȯr-gə\, **Victor** *orig.* Borge Rosenbaum (1909–2000) Danish-U.S. comedian and pianist. He made his concert stage debut in 1922, first appeared in a musical revue in 1934, then began writing and directing shows, developing a style that combined humor with music. He emigrated to the U.S. in 1940. Though he performed with many of the world's leading orchestras, his significant pianistic talent was often overshadowed by his highly popular humor.

Borges \'bȯr-hās\, **Jorge Luis** (1899–1986) Argentine poet, essayist, and short-story writer. From the 1920s on he was afflicted by a growing hereditary blindness. In 1938 a severe head wound seemed to free his deepest creative forces. From 1955 he held the honorary post of director of Argentina's national library. Much of his work is rich in fantasy and metaphorical allegory, including the story collections *Ficciones* (1944), which won him an international following, and *The Aleph* (1949). *Dreamtigers* (1960) and *The Book of Imaginary Beings* (1967) almost erase the distinctions between prose and poetry.

Jorge Luis Borges

Borghese family \bȯr-'gā-sā\ Noble Italian family, originally from Siena, who first gained fame in the 13th cent. as public officials. They moved to Rome in the 16th cent., and after Camillo Borghese became Pope Paul V (1605), the family rose in wealth and fame. Prominent family members included the adopted Scipione Caffarelli (later Borghese) (1576–1633), a cardinal and patron of the arts, and Camillo F. L. Borghese (1775–1832), who married Napoleon's sister Pauline and played an important role in Franco-Italian relations.

Borgia \'bȯr-jä\, **Cesare** *later* **duc (Duke) de Valentinois** \vá-läⁿ-tēn-'wä\ (1475?–1507) Italian military leader. Illegitimate son of the later Pope ALEXANDER VI and brother of Lucrezia BORGIA, he was made archbishop of Valencia (1492) and cardinal (1493). After his brother's murder (1497), he took command of the papal armies, resigned his ecclesiastical offices (1498), and married the sister of the king of Navarre to win French support for a campaign to regain control of the Papal States. With his father, Cesare won a series of military successes in the Papal States (1499–1503), gaining a reputation for ruthlessness; his political astuteness led Niccolò MACHIAVELLI to cite him as an example of the new "Prince." Cesare's gains proved fruitless, however, when his father died (1503) and the new pope, JULIUS II, demanded that he give up his lands. He escaped from prison in Spain and died fighting for Navarre.

Borgia, Lucrezia (1480–1519) Italian noblewoman. The daughter of Pope ALEXANDER VI and sister of Cesare Borgia, she was probably more an instrument for their ambitious projects than an active participant in' their many crimes. Her three marriages into prominent families helped augment the Borgias' power. Her child may have been the issue of an incestuous relationship with her father. After her father's death (1503), she ceased to play a political role, and increasingly turned to religion.

Lucrezia Borgia Fresco by Pinturicchio, 1492–94

Borglum \'bȯr-gləm\, **(John) Gutzon (de la Mothe)** (1867–1941) U.S. sculptor. Born in Bear Lake, Idaho, he studied art in Paris and in 1901 opened a studio in New York. His *Mares of Diomedes* was the first U.S. sculpture purchased by the Metropolitan Museum of Art. He carved the head of Abraham LINCOLN in the U.S. Capitol rotunda. In 1916 he began to sculpt a memorial to the Confederacy on Stone Mtn., Ga., but abandoned the project in 1924; it was completed by others. His most notable project was the Mt. RUSHMORE National Memorial.

Boris I *orig*. Mikhail (d.907) Ruler of Bulgaria (852–89). He resolved to use Christianity to unite his ethnically divided country, and an unsuccessful war with the Byzantines led to his baptism in the Orthodox faith (864). He helped establish the Bulgarian church, and sponsored missionaries to foster Slavic learning and the use of the OLD CHURCH SLAVIC LANGUAGE. He abdicated in 889 to become a monk but returned (893) to drive his reactionary son Vladimir from the throne and install another son, Simeon I, whereupon Boris went back to his monastery. He was later made an Orthodox saint.

Boris Godunov See Boris GODUNOV

Borlaug \'bȯr-ˌlȯg\, **Norman (Ernest)** (b.1914) U.S. agricultural scientist and plant pathologist. Born in Cresco, Iowa, he earned his PhD at the Univ. of Minnesota. As a researcher in Mexico (1944–60), he developed strains of grain that tripled Mexican WHEAT production. Later his dwarf wheats raised harvests in Pakistan and India 60%, ending the food shortages that had plagued the subcontinent in the 1960s. For helping lay the groundwork of the GREEN REVOLUTION, he was awarded the Nobel Peace Prize in 1970. Since 1984 he has taught at Texas A&M Univ.

Bormann \'bȯr-ˌmän\, **Martin** (1900–1945?) German Nazi leader. He served as Rudolf HESS's chief of staff 1933–41, then became one of Adolf HITLER's closest lieutenants. A shadowy but extremely powerful presence, Bormann controlled all legislation, party promotions and appointments, and the personal access of others to Hitler. He disappeared shortly after Hitler's death. Though some reports allege that he escaped to S. America, German authorities have officially declared him dead.

Born, Max (1882–1970) German-British physicist. In 1921 he gave a very precise definition of quantity of HEAT, the most satisfactory mathematical statement of the first law of THERMODYNAMICS. In 1926 he collaborated with his student Werner HEISENBERG to develop the mathematical formulation that would adequately describe Heisenberg's first laws of a new quantum theory. He later showed that the solution of the SCHRÖDINGER EQUATION has a statistical meaning of physical significance. His later work concerned the scattering of atomic particles and calculations dealing with the electronic structures of molecules. In 1954 he shared a Nobel Prize with Walther Bothe (1891–1957).

Borneo Island, MALAY ARCHIPELAGO. It is the third-largest island in the world, measuring 290,320 sq mi (751,929 sq km). The N part includes the Malaysian states of Sabah and Sarawak and the sultanate of Brunei; the S section forms part of Indonesia. Borneo is mountainous and largely covered in dense rain forest; its highest point is Mt. Kinabalu, at 13,455 ft (4,101 m). Its many navigable rivers are the principal lifelines of trade and commerce. It is mentioned in PTOLEMY's *Guide to Geography* (c.A.D. 150); Roman trade beads give evidence of an earlier civilization. Brahman and Buddhist images in the Gupta style indicate the influence of Indians from the 5th cent. In the 16th cent., various Muslim kingdoms were founded, and the Portuguese, followed by the Spanish, set up trading stations. In the early 17th cent. the Dutch broke the Portuguese-Spanish monopoly, but they in turn had to deal with new British interests. After World War II, Sarawak and N. Borneo (later Sabah) became British crown colonies. Dutch Borneo passed to Indonesia in 1949. The British relinquished Sabah and Sarawak to the Malaysian federation in 1963; Brunei became independent in 1984.

Borobudur \ˌbō-rō-bü-'dür\ Buddhist monument in central Java, built around 778–850. Constructed with about 2 million cu ft (57,000 cu m) of gray volcanic stone, it resembles a stepped pyramid, the highest three terraces being circular. Reliefs on its terrace walls represent the ascending stages of enlightenment. The simple and spacious upper terraces carry 72 bell-shaped STUPAS, each containing a statue of the Buddha.

Borobudur

Borodin \ˌbȯr-ə-'dēn\, **Aleksandr (Porfiryevich)** (1833–1887) Russian composer. From 1862 he took lessons from Mikhail BALAKIREV; fired by nationalist sentiment, the two men became the core of the MIGHTY FIVE. A professor of chemistry for much of his life, he left a small compositional output, which includes the orchestral suite *In the Steppes of Central Asia* (1880), two string quartets, and three symphonies, the second of which has remained highly popular. The opera *Prince Igor* was left unfinished after 18 years of intermittent work.

boron Semimetallic chemical ELEMENT, chemical symbol B, atomic number 5. Pure crystalline boron is a black, lustrous, very hard but brittle SEMICONDUCTOR that does not occur naturally. Boron compounds are found as various minerals, including BORAX and the gemstone TOURMALINE. The element is used to harden certain STEELS, and is also used in semiconductors. Its compounds (borates, VALENCE 3) are essential to plant growth and have many uses in soaps, ANTISEPTICS, and eye ointments. Industrially, they are used as herbicides, fire retardants in fabrics, and CATALYSTS in organic reactions, and in ELECTROPLATING and glass and ceramic formulations. Certain exceptionally hard and inert boron compounds are useful as abrasives and reinforcing agents, particularly for high-temperature applications.

Borromeo \ˌbōr-rō-'mä-ō\, **St. Charles** (1538–1584) Archbishop of Milan and leading figure in the COUNTER-REFORMATION. His uncle, Pope Pius IV, appointed him archbishop of Milan in 1560. He was active in directing the Council of TRENT, and he later helped execute its decrees and draw up the Roman catechism in 1566. He gained renown for his heroic behavior during the plague of 1576–78.

Borromini, Francesco *orig*. Francesco Castelli (1599–1667) Italian baroque architect. Though he worked with Gian Lorenzo BERNINI on the famous baldachin in ST. PETER'S BASILICA, the two later became bitter rivals. Borromini's first independent commission was the Roman church and monastery of San Carlo alle Quattro Fontane (1638–41), the dome of which appears to float. His works, composed of flowing concave and convex forms, contain spaces that are irregular ovals and polygons, as at Sant'Ivo della Sapienza (1642–60).

Boru, Brian See BRIAN BORU

Bosch \'bȯsh\, **Hieronymus** *orig*. Jeroen van Aken (c.1450–1516) Netherlandish painter. He was the son and grandson of accomplished painters; his name comes from his native town of 's Hertogenbosch. He enjoyed a successful career and was widely imitated. His paintings blend fantasy and reality in apocalyptic scenes of chaos with half-human, half-animal creatures, devils, and demons interacting with human figures in imaginary architecture and landscapes. His well-known *The Garden of Earthly Delights* depicts the dreams that afflict people who live in a pleasure-seeking world. One of the most original N European artists of the late Middle Ages, he was an outstanding draftsman and one of the first to make drawings as independent works.

Bosch (Gaviño) \'bȯsh\, **Juan** (1909–2001) Scholar, poet, and president of the Dominican Republic (1963). Dismayed by the brutality of the dictator Rafael TRUJILLO, he spent 24 years in exile, but returned after Trujillo's death to build a leftist anticommunist movement. He won the first free presidential elections in 38 years, and undertook reforms to benefit the country's poor, only to be ousted in a military coup. When his supporters revolted in 1965, U.S. Pres. Lyndon B. JOHNSON, claiming that they were communists, sent in troops to suppress the rebellion.

Bose \\'bōs\\, **Subhas Chandra** (1897–1945) Indian revolutionary. Sent by Mohandas GANDHI to organize in Bengal in the 1920s, he was deported and imprisoned several times. He favored industrialization, which put him at odds with Gandhi's economic thought, and though elected president of the INDIAN NATIONAL CONGRESS (1938, 1939), without Gandhi's support he felt bound to resign. He left India in 1941 and carried on his struggle against the British from Nazi Germany and later from S.E. Asia. In 1944 he invaded India from Myanmar with a small army of Indian nationals and Japanese, but was soon forced to retreat. He fled S.E. Asia after the Japanese surrender in 1945 and died of burns from a plane crash.

Bosnia and Herzegovina \\'bäz-nē-ə...,her-tsə-gō-'vē-nə\\ *officially* **Republic of Bosnia and Herzegovina** Country, BALKAN PENINSULA, bounded by modern Yugoslavia and Croatia. Area: 19,904 sq mi (51,750 sq km). Population (2000): 3,836,000 (excludes more than 300,000 refugees in adjacent countries and elsewhere). Capital: SARAJEVO. Major ethnic groups include Bosnian Muslims (about two-fifths

BOSNIA AND HERZEGOVINA

Scale 1: 6,252,000
0   30   60 mi
0   40   80 km

of the population), Serbs (about one-third), and Croats (about one-fifth); they are racially indistinguishable. Language: Serbo-Croatian (official). Religions: Islam, Serbian Orthodoxy, Roman Catholicism. Currency: dinar. The country's relief is largely mountainous, and elevations of more than 6,000 ft (1,800 m) are common; the land drops abruptly southward toward the ADRIATIC SEA; it is drained by the Sava, Drina, and Neretva rivers and their tributaries. Agriculture is a mainstay of the economy; though the area possesses a variety of minerals, it remains one of the poorest regions of the former Yugoslavia. A republic with two legislative houses, its chief of state is the chairman of the tripartite presidency, and the heads of government are the two cochairmen of the Council of Ministers. Habitation long predates the era of Roman rule, when much of the country was included in the province of DALMATIA. SLAV settlement began in the 6th cent. A.D. For the next several centuries, parts of the region fell under the rule of Serbs, Croats, Hungarians, Venetians,

and Byzantines. The Ottoman Turks invaded Bosnia in the 14th cent., and after many battles it became a Turkish province in 1463. Herzegovina, then known as Hum, was taken in 1482. In the 16th–17th cent. the area was an important Turkish outpost, constantly at war with the HABSBURGS and VENICE. During this period much of the native population converted to Islam. Bosnia and Herzegovina was assigned to AUSTRIA–HUNGARY after the RUSSO–TURKISH WAR of 1877–78 and annexed in 1908. Growing Serb nationalism resulted in the 1914 assassination of the Austrian Archduke FRANCIS FERDINAND at Sarajevo by a Bosnian Serb, an event that precipitated World War I. After the war the area was annexed to SERBIA. Following World War II it became a republic of communist Yugoslavia. With the collapse of communist regimes in E Europe, Bosnia and Herzegovina declared its independence in 1992; its Serbian population objected, and conflict ensued among Serbs, Croats, and Muslims (see BOSNIAN CONFLICT). The 1995 peace accord established a loosely federated government roughly divided between a Muslim Croat federation and a Serb republic. In 1996 a NATO peace-keeping force was installed there.

Bosnian conflict (1992–98) Ethnically rooted war in BOSNIA AND HERZEGOVINA. Unrest began with Yugoslavia's breakup in 1990; after a 1992 referendum, the European Community recognized Bosnia's independence. Bosnia's Serbs responded violently, seized 70% of Bosnian territory, besieged Sarajevo, and terrorized Muslims and Croats with mass rapes and summary executions. After bitter fighting between the Bosnian Croats and the Bosnian government, international pressure forced the two factions to sign a cease-fire. Both then concentrated on their common enemy, the Serbs. After rejected peace plans, attacks, and counterattacks, the Western nations imposed a final cease-fire negotiated at Dayton, Ohio, in 1995. After 44 months and more than 200,000 deaths, Bosnia-Herzegovina was to become a single state composed of two autonomous entities. Today it has three de facto monoethnic entities, three separate armies and police forces, and a very weak national government. Political power is concentrated among hardline nationalists.

boson \\'bō-ˌzän\\ SUBATOMIC PARTICLE with integral SPIN that is governed by Bose-Einstein statistics. Bosons include MESONS, nuclei of even mass number, and the particles required to embody the fields of QUANTUM FIELD THEORY. Unlike FERMIONS, there is no limit to the number of bosons that can occupy the same quantum state, a behavior that gives rise to the SUPERFLUIDITY of helium-4.

Bosporus \\'bäs-pə-rəs\\ Strait separating Turkey in Europe from Turkey in Asia. Connecting the Sea of MARMARA with the BLACK SEA, it is 19 mi (31 km) long and 2.8 mi (4.4 km) wide at its widest. Bosporus means "ox ford" and is linked to the legendary figure of Io, who in the form of a heifer crossed the Thracian Bosporus. Because of its strategic importance to Constantinople, which straddled its S end, the Byzantine emperors and Ottoman sultans fortified its shores. With the growing influence of the European powers in the 19th cent., rules were codified governing the transit of vessels. An international commission assumed control of it after World War I; Turkey resumed control in 1936. Two of the world's longest bridges, completed in 1973 and 1988, span the strait.

Boston Seaport city (pop., 2000: 589,000), capital of Massachusetts. Located on Massachusetts Bay, it is the state's largest city. Settled by Gov. John WINTHROP in 1630, it was made the capital of MASSACHUSETTS BAY COLONY in 1632. A locus of events leading to the AMERICAN REVOLUTION, it was the scene of the BOSTON MASSACRE (1770) and BOSTON TEA PARTY (1773). It was the center for the antislavery movement 1830–65. With the INDUSTRIAL REVOLUTION, Boston grew as a manufacturing and textile center. Today financial and high-technology industries are basic to its economy. Numerous institutions of higher education are located there, including BOSTON UNIV. See also CAMBRIDGE.

Boston College Private university in Chestnut Hill, Mass. Founded in 1863, it is affiliated with the Roman Catholic church. It includes schools of education, nursing, management, and law. Enrollment is about 14,000.

Boston Massacre Skirmish on March 5, 1770, between British troops and a crowd in Boston. After provocation by the colonists, British soldiers fired on the mob and killed five men, including Crispus ATTUCKS. The incident was widely publicized as a battle for American liberty, and it contributed to the unpopularity of the British in the years before the AMERICAN REVOLUTION.

Boston Tea Party Incident on December 16, 1773, in which 342 chests of tea were thrown from three British ships into Boston Harbor by American patriots disguised as Indians, led by Samuel ADAMS. The action was taken to prevent the payment of the British-imposed tax on tea and to protest the recently passed TEA ACT. In retaliation, Parliament passed the punitive INTOLERABLE ACTS.

Boston University Private university in Boston. Founded in 1839 (reorganized 1867), it was unusual in banning religious tests for faculty and students and was one of the first American universities to accept black and international students. Today it comprises 15 schools and colleges. Among its archival collections are the papers of Martin Luther KING, Jr., Theodore ROOSEVELT, and Robert FROST. Enrollment is about 30,000.

Boswell, James (1740–1795) Scottish biographer of Samuel JOHNSON. Boswell, a lawyer, met Dr. Johnson in 1763 and visited him often 1772–84, keeping a detailed record of Johnson's conversations. His *Life of Samuel Johnson, LL.D.* (1791) is regarded as the greatest English biography. His *Journal of a Tour to the Hebrides* (1785) describes Johnson's responses to their 1773 trip to Scotland. The publication of Boswell's journals showed that he was also one of history's great diarists.

Bosworth Field, Battle of (Aug. 22, 1485) Final battle in the English Wars of the ROSES. Fought between the forces of King RICHARD III of York and Henry Tudor (later HENRY VII) of Lancaster, the battle occurred when Henry returned from exile, landing with an army at Milford Haven and meeting Richard's forces 12 mi (19 km) west of Leicester. The king's men were defeated and put to flight, and Richard was unhorsed and killed in a bog. The battle established the TUDOR dynasty on the English throne.

botany Branch of BIOLOGY that deals with plants, including the study of the structure, properties, and biochemical processes of all forms of plant life, as well as plant classification, plant diseases, and the interactions of plants with their physical environment. The modern science of botany developed in Europe in the 16th cent., mainly through the work of physicians and herbalists, who began to observe plants seriously to identify those useful in medicine. Today the principal branches of botanical study are morphology, PHYSIOLOGY, ECOLOGY, and systematics (the identification and ranking of all plants). See also FORESTRY, HORTICULTURE.

Botany Bay Inlet of the S. Pacific Ocean, SE Australia. Lying south of SYDNEY off Port Jackson, it is about 6 mi (10 km) at its widest. It was the scene of the first Australian landing by Capt. James COOK in 1770; he named the bay for its great variety of plants. Its shores are now ringed by Sydney's suburbs.

botfly Any member of several DIPTERAN families with bee-like adults and larvae that are parasitic on mammals. Some species are serious pests of horses, cattle, deer, sheep, rabbits, and squirrels, and one species attacks humans. Adults lay many eggs (nits) on the host's body, and the emerging larvae penetrate its skin and later reemerge. In the New World tropics, the botfly's infestation of cattle has led to loss of beef and hides. See also WARBLE FLY.

Botha, P(ieter) W(illem) (b.1916) Prime minister (1978–84) and first state president (1984–89) of S. Africa. Elected to parliament in 1948, Botha served in several subsequent posts before succeeding John VORSTER as prime minister in 1978. Confronting the coming to power of black governments in Mozambique, Angola, and Zimbabwe, an insurgency in S.W. Africa (Namibia), and domestic unrest, he backed antigovernment troops in the bordering states and suppressed rebellion at home. A target of criticism both within and outside his NATIONAL PARTY, Botha fell ill and resigned in 1989.

Bothnia, Gulf of N arm of the BALTIC SEA. Extending between Sweden and Finland, it covers about 45,200 sq mi (117,000 sq km). It is 450 mi (725 km) long and 50–150 mi (80–240 km) wide; its average depth is 965 ft (295 m). Because many rivers drain into it, its salinity is very low; ice cover consequently lasts up to five months of the year.

bo tree See BODHI TREE

Botswana *officially* **Republic of Botswana** *formerly* **Bechuanaland** \ˌbech-'wä-nə-ˌland\ Country, S Africa, bounded by Namibia, Zimbabwe, and S. Africa. Area: 219,916 sq mi (569,582 sq km). Population (2000): 1,576,000. Capital: GABORONE. Less than half the population are ethnic Tswana; other main groups include the Khalagari, Ngwato, Tswapong, Birwa, and Kalanga. Small groups of KHOIKHOI

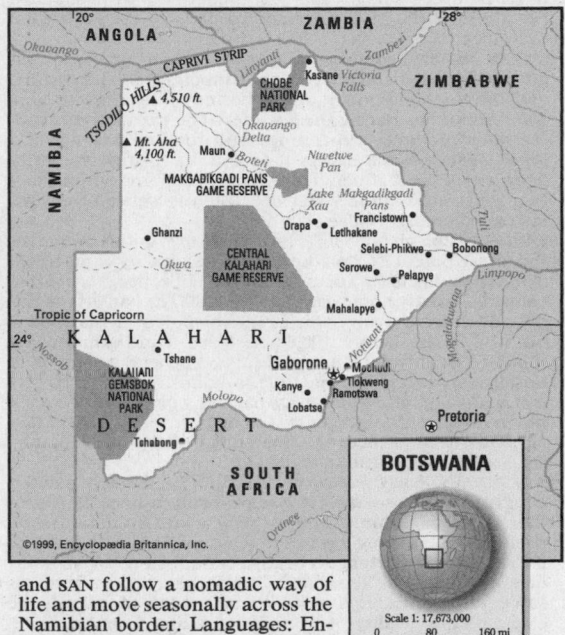

and SAN follow a nomadic way of life and move seasonally across the Namibian border. Languages: English (official), Tswana. Religion: Christian, with a large admixture of traditional African beliefs. Currency: pula. Botswana is essentially a tableland, with a mean elevation of about 3,300 ft (1,000 m). Part of the KALAHARI DESERT is in the southwest and west, while the Okavango Swamp is in the north. The only sources of permanent surface water are the Chobe River, which marks the Namibian boundary; the OKAVANGO RIVER, in the far northwest; and the LIMPOPO RIVER, which marks the S. African boundary in the southeast. The economy is traditionally dependent on livestock raising; the development of diamond mining in the 1980s has increased the country's wealth. It is a republic with one legislative body; its head of state and government is the president. The region's earliest inhabitants were the Khoikhoi and San (Bushmen). Sites were settled as early as A.D. 190 during the southerly migration of Bantu-speaking farmers. Tswana dynasties, which developed in the W TRANSVAAL in the 13th–14th cent., moved into Botswana in the 18th cent. and established several powerful states. European missionaries arrived in the early 19th cent., but it was the discovery of gold in 1867 that excited European interest. In 1885 the area became the British Bechuanaland Protectorate. The next year, the region south of the Molopo River became a crown colony, and it was annexed by the Cape Colony 10 years later. Bechuanaland itself continued as a British protectorate until the 1960s. In 1966 the Republic of Bechuanaland (later, Botswana) was proclaimed an independent member of the British COMMONWEALTH. Independent Botswana tried to maintain a delicate balance between its economic dependence on S. Africa and its relations with the surrounding black countries; the independence of Namibia in 1990 and S. Africa's rejection of apartheid eased tensions.

Botticelli \ˌbät-ə-'chel-ē\, **Sandro** *orig.* Alessandro di Mariano Filipepi (1445–1510) Italian painter active in Florence. He trained with Fra Filippo LIPPI and by 1470 had developed a distinctive style and was established as a master. In 1481 he was among a team of Florentine and Umbrian artists called to Rome to decorate the SISTINE CHAPEL; three of his finest religious frescoes (completed 1482) can be seen there. His mythological paintings are his best-known works. In his outstanding portraits, the figure is placed in front of a landscape. Among his greatest works are the *Primavera, Pallas and the Centaur, Venus and Mars,* and *The Birth of Venus,* all painted about 1477–90. About 75 of his paintings survive, many of them in the Uffizi Gallery. He is one of the most esteemed painters of the Italian Renaissance.

bottom water Lowermost layer of ocean water, distinguished by its characteristic low temperature, high density, and low oxygen content. Most bottom waters are formed near Antarctica during the S winter. The partial freezing of seawater produces salt-free ice and residual brine with a high density, which causes it to sink; it then flows northward along the seafloor. The Arctic Ocean is less important as a source of bottom water because it is isolated by barriers and submarine ridges.

botulism \'bä-chə-ˌli-zəm\ Poisoning by botulin, one of the most potent TOXINS known, produced by *Clostridium botulinum* bacteria (usually from improperly sterilized canned—mostly home-canned—foods). The bacteria multiply and secrete toxin, which remains potent if the food is not well heated before it is eaten. Nausea and vomiting are followed by fatigue, blurry vision, and general weakness. If botulism is recognized in time, administered ANTITOXINS can neutralize it. Respiratory paralysis can cause death if not treated with emergency tracheotomy and respiratory aid. Most victims recover completely if they survive paralysis. See also BIOLOGICAL WARFARE.

Boucher \bü-'shā\, **François** (1703–1770) French painter, engraver, and designer. He was probably trained by his father, a minor painter. For his first major commission he produced 125 engravings of drawings by Antoine WATTEAU. He executed important decorative commissions for Madame de POMPADOUR at Versailles. His playful style and frivolous subject matter exemplify the Rococo style and embody the elegant superficiality of French court life. A principal designer for the royal porcelain factories and director of the Gobelins tapestry factory, in 1765 he became director of the Royal Academy and first painter to LOUIS XV. One of the great artists of the 18th cent., he mastered every branch of decorative and illustrative painting.

Boucicault \'bü-si-ˌkō\, **Dion** *orig.* Dionysius Lardner Boursiquot (1822–1890) Irish-U.S. playwright. He began acting in 1837 and wrote the successful comedy *London Assurance* (1841). In 1853 he moved to New York, where he helped obtain the first copyright law for drama in the U.S. His successful play *The Poor of New York* (1857) was presented elsewhere as, for example, *The Poor of London. The Octoroon* (1859) was a veiled attack on slavery. His popular Irish plays included *The Colleen Bawn* (1860) and *The Shaughraun* (1874).

Boudicca \bü-'dik-ə\ *or* **Boadicea** \ˌbō-əd-ə-'sē-ə\ (d.A.D. 60) Ancient British queen who led a revolt against Roman rule. When her husband, a Roman client king of the Iceni, died in A.D. 60, the Romans annexed his kingdom and mistreated his family and tribesmen. Boudicca raised a rebellion in E. Anglia; according to TACITUS, her forces massacred up to 70,000 Romans and pro-Roman Britons and destroyed the Roman 9th Legion. When the Roman governor rallied his troops and destroyed her huge army, she took poison or died of shock.

Boudin \bü-'daⁿ\, **Eugène** (1824–1898) French landscape painter. Encouraged at an early age by J.-F. MILLET, he became a strong advocate of painting directly from nature. His favorite subjects were beach scenes and seascapes, which show remarkable sensitivity to effects of atmosphere; on the backs of his paintings he recorded the weather, light, and time of day. His works link the careful naturalism of the mid-19th cent. and the brilliant colors and fluid brushwork of Impressionism.

Bougainville \'bü-gən-ˌvil\ Island (pop., 1990 est.: 140,000), Papua New Guinea. The largest of the SOLOMON ISLANDS, it has a land area of about 3,880 sq mi (10,050 sq km). The mountainous island was visited by L.-A. de BOUGAINVILLE in 1768, and it came under German control in the late 19th cent. After World War I it was included in an Australian mandate. After World War II it was made part of a U.N. Trust Territory, and it passed to Papua New Guinea in 1975. Following decades of secessionist activities, an agreement to establish an autonomous provincial government was reached in 2000.

Bougainville \bü-gaⁿ-'vēl\, **Louis-Antoine de** (1729–1811) French navigator. In 1764 he established a colony for France in the Falkland Islands. He led the first French voyage around the world (1766–69), touching Samoa and the New Hebrides, then sailing into waters not previously navigated by any European. He stopped in the Moluccas and in Java before returning to Brittany. His widely read *Voyage Round the World* (1771) helped popularize a belief in the moral worth of man in his natural state. He was secretary to LOUIS XV (1772) and led French ships in support of the American Revolution. The plant genus *Bougainvillea* is named for him.

bougainvillea \ˌbü-gən-'vil-yə, ˌbü-gən-'vē-ə\ Any plant of the genus *Bougainvillea,* containing about 14 species of shrubs, vines, or small trees (family Nyctaginaceae) native to S. America and hardy in warm climates. The woody vines are widely popular; showy cultivated varieties of several species are often grown indoors. The inconspicuous flowers are surrounded by brightly colored papery BRACTS that range from purple to lemon yellow.

Bouguereau \bü-gə-'rō\, **William (-Adolphe)** (1825–1905) French painter. After studies in Paris and Rome (1846–54), he became a successful proponent of academic painting, and was instrumental in the exclusion of the Impressionists from the Salon. Working in a smooth, highly finished style, he painted sentimental religious works, coyly erotic nudes, allegorical scenes, and photographically realistic portraits. In 1876 he was elected to the Academy of Fine Arts. His influence was felt widely, particularly in the U.S.

Boukhara See BUKHARA

Boulanger \bü-läⁿ-'zhā\, **Georges (-Ernest-Jean-Marie)** (1837–1891) French general and politician. He entered the army in 1856 and helped suppress the PARIS COMMUNE (1871). Named minister of war in 1886, he introduced various military reforms. In 1888 he led a short-lived but influential authoritarian movement that threatened to topple the THIRD REPUBLIC. In 1889 he fled Paris. Convicted in absentia for treason, in 1891 he committed suicide.

Boulanger \bü-läⁿ-'zhā\, **Nadia (-Juliette)** (1887–1979) French music teacher and conductor. Having studied composition with Gabriel FAURÉ, she stopped composing in her twenties and devoted herself to conducting, playing the organ, and teaching at the École Normale (1920–39), Paris Conservatoire (from 1946), and especially the American Conservatory at Fontainebleau (from 1921). The most celebrated composition teacher of the 20th cent., her many students included Aaron COPLAND, Darius MILHAUD, Elliott CARTER, and Leonard BERNSTEIN. Her sister, Lili (1893–1918), the first woman composer to win the Prix de Rome (1913), died at 25, having written a remarkable amount of vocal and other music.

Nadia Boulanger

Boulder City (pop., 2000: 95,000), N central Colorado. Located in the ROCKY MTNS. northwest of DENVER, it was settled by miners in 1858 and grew with the arrival of two railroads in 1873. An extensive government-industrial-educational complex has developed in recent decades. It is the site of the Univ. of Colorado.

Boulder Dam See HOOVER DAM

boule \\'bü-lē\\ Deliberative council in the city-states of ancient Greece. It existed in almost all constitutional city-states, especially from the late 6th cent. B.C.. In ATHENS the boule controlled finances, managed the fleet and cavalry, evaluated officials, and received foreign ambassadors. The boule model largely influenced the organization of councils of other cities in the Hellenic period.

Boulez \\bü-'lez\\, **Pierre** (b.1925) French composer and conductor. After studying with Olivier MESSIAEN, he served as music director of the Renaud-Barrault theater company 1946–56. Inspired by the works of Anton WEBERN, he began to experiment with total serialism in 1951. He founded the new-music group Domaine Musical in 1954. He was conductor of the New York Philharmonic 1971–78. He conducted Richard WAGNER's *Ring* at Bayreuth in 1976 and the premiere of the completed version of Alban BERG's *Lulu* in 1979. In 1974 he founded the French national experimental studio IRCAM. His important works include *Le soleil des eaux* (1948), *Le marteau sans maître* (1957), *Pli selon pli* (1962), and three piano sonatas (1946, 1948, 1957). He was the principal figure of the postwar international musical avant-garde.

Boullée \\bü-'lā\\, **Étienne-Louis** (1728–1799) French architect, theorist, and teacher. He opened his own studio by age 19. Through his investigation of the properties of geometric forms, Boullée achieved a pure, modern classicism. In a series of theoretical plans for public monuments, culminating in the design for an immense sphere that would serve as a cenotaph honoring Isaac Newton (1784), he gave imaginary form to his theories.

Boulogne, Jean See GIAMBOLOGNA

Boulton \\'bōlt-ᵊn\\, **Matthew** (1728–1809) British manufacturer and engineer. With James WATT and William Murdock (1754–1839), he established the steam-engine industry by installing pumping engines to drain the Cornish tin mines. Foreseeing great industrial demand for steam power, he urged Watt to make various design improvements. Applying steam power to coining machinery, he made large quantities of coins for the British E. INDIA CO. and also supplied machinery to the Royal Mint.

Boumédienne \\bü-mäd-'yen\\, **Houari** *orig.* Muhammad ben Brahim Boukharouba (1927–1978) Algerian political leader and president (1965–1978). During Algeria's fight for independence, he helped raise an Algerian army in neighboring countries. He deposed Pres. Ahmed BEN BELLA in 1965. His policies in the 1970s created tensions with Morocco and France, but he also negotiated important industrial contracts with Western nations and cultivated close relations with the Soviet bloc, becoming a leading figure in the nonaligned movement.

boundary layer In FLUID MECHANICS, a thin layer of flowing gas or liquid in contact with a surface (e.g., of an airplane wing or the inside of a pipe). The fluid in the boundary layer is subjected to shear FORCES. A range of velocities is established across the boundary layer, from zero (provided the fluid is in contact with the surface) to maximum. Boundary layers are thinner at the leading edge of an aircraft wing and thicker toward the trailing edge. See also DRAG.

Bounty, HMS British transport ship remembered for the MUTINY of its crew on April 28, 1789. Commanded by Capt. William BLIGH, it was sailing from Tahiti to Jamaica when it was seized by the master's mate, Fletcher Christian (1764–1790/93?). The causes have been much debated; Bligh's opponents charged him with tyranny, while Bligh argued that the mutineers had become attached to Tahiti and its women. Bligh and 18 loyal crew members were set adrift in a longboat; after two weeks and some 3,600 mi (5,800 km), they reached Timor. Christian and eight others took the *Bounty* to PITCAIRN ISLAND, where they remained undiscovered until 1808.

bourbon See WHISKEY

Bourbon, Charles-Ferdinand de See duc de BERRY

Bourbon \\bür-'bō\\, *Engl* 'bùr-bən\\, **House of** One of the most important ruling houses of Europe. Its members were descended from Louis I, duc de Bourbon (r.1327–42), grandson of the French king LOUIS IX. Bourbons subsequently ruled in France (1589–1792, 1814–48); in Spain (1700–1868, 1870–73, 1874–1931, and since 1975); and in Naples and Sicily (1735–1861). Among its prominent members were HENRY IV, LOUIS XIII, LOUIS XIV, LOUIS XV, LOUIS XVI, and PHILIP V.

Bourbon Restoration (1814–30) In France, the period that began when NAPOLEON abdicated and the BOURBON monarchs were restored to the throne. The First Restoration (1814–15) occurred when Napoleon fell from power and LOUIS XVIII became king. Louis's reign was interrupted by Napoleon's return (see HUNDRED DAYS), but Napoleon was forced to abdicate again, leading to the Second Restoration. The period was marked by a constitutional monarchy of moderate rule (1816–20), followed by the return to reactionary policies during the reign of Louis's brother, CHARLES X (1824–30). The so-called July Revolution (1830) replaced Charles with LOUIS-PHILIPPE and marked the end of the Bourbon Restoration.

Bourgeois \\bür-'zhwä\\, **Louise** (b.1911) French-U.S. sculptor. Born in Paris, she initially worked as a painter and engraver. In the late 1940s, after moving to New York with her American husband, she turned to sculpture. She achieved recognition with wooden constructions painted uniformly black or white. She has also worked in marble, plaster, latex, and glass. Her abstract works are suggestive of the human figure and express themes of betrayal, anxiety, and loneliness.

bourgeoisie \\,bürzh-,wä-'zē\\ Social order dominated by the property-owning class. In medieval France, it referred to craftsmen who occupied the social tier between rural landlords and the peasantry. With the INDUSTRIAL REVOLUTION, economic relationships began to divide into employer and employee classes; employers (capitalists) came to be termed the bourgeoisie, and workers the proletariat. The term, much employed by 19th-cent. social reformers, is less commonly used today.

Bourguiba \\bür-'gē-bə\\, **Habib (ibn Ali)** (1903–2000) President of Tunisia (1957–87). He studied at the Sorbonne, where he met independence-minded Algerians and Moroccans. After founding a nationalist newspaper, in 1934 he founded the Neo-Destour Party and became central to the Tunisian liberation movement. After imprisoning him three times, the French negotiated independence with him in 1956. In 1957 he became president. During his 30 years in office he kept the army small and devoted much of the budget to education and health. Made president for life in 1975, he had to be removed in 1987 because of ill health. See also Zine BEN ALI.

Bourke-White \\,bərk-'hwīt\\, **Margaret** (1904–1971) U.S. photographer. Born in New York City, she began her professional career as an architectural photographer in 1927. She gained a reputation for originality, and in 1929 was hired by Henry LUCE for his magazine *Fortune*. She covered World War II for *Life* magazine as the first woman photographer to serve with the U.S. armed forces. Collections of her photographs include *You Have Seen Their Faces* (1937), about sharecroppers of the American South.

Bournonville \\'bōr-nōn-,vē-lə\\, **August** (1805–1879) Danish dancer, choreographer, and director of the Royal Danish Ballet for almost 50 years. After studying and performing in Paris and Copenhagen, he became director and choreographer of the Royal Danish Ballet in 1830, where he continued to dance until 1848. Influences absorbed during his European tours blended into his unique style based on bravura dancing and expressive mime, and he built the troupe into one of the world's greatest.

Boutros-Ghali \\'bü-trōs-'gä-lē\\, **Boutros** (b.1922) Sixth secretary-general of the UNITED NATIONS (1992–96). Born into a distinguished Egyptian Coptic family, he was educated at Cairo Univ. and the Univ. of Paris. After teaching at universities around the world, he joined Egypt's foreign ministry in 1977. He became Egypt's deputy prime minister in 1991 and was appointed U.N. secretary-general in 1992, the first Arab and first African to hold the office. He oversaw peacekeeping operations in Bosnia, Somalia, and Rwanda. In 1996 the U.S. blocked his bid for a second term.

Bouts \\'baùts\\, **Dirck** (c.1415–1475) Netherlandish painter. Born in Haarlem, he was active in Louvain, where he was influenced by Rogier van der WEYDEN. His best-known

works are a triptych altarpiece (1464) for the church of St. Peter in Louvain, representing the Last Supper and four Old Testament scenes, and two huge panels representing a scene of secular justice (1470–75) for the Louvain city hall. His treatment of his figures ranges from strong emotion expressed through symbolic gesture to great severity and restraint.

bouzouki \bu̇-ˈzü-kē\ Long-necked lute used in Greek popular music. Developed from a Turkish instrument early in the 20th cent., it has a pear-shaped body and a fretted fingerboard. The modern instrument usually has four courses of strings, which are plucked vigorously with a plectrum.

Boveri \bō-ˈvä-rē\, **Theodor Heinrich** (1862–1915) German cell biologist. Working with roundworm eggs, Boveri proved that chromosomes are separate units within the nucleus of a cell. With Walter SUTTON, he was the first to propose that genes were located on chromosomes. Boveri proved Edouard von Beneden's theory that the ovum (egg) and sperm cell contribute equal numbers of chromosomes to the new cell created during fertilization.

bovid \ˈbō-vid\ Any RUMINANT of the family Bovidae. Bovids have hollow, unbranched, permanently attached horns; they are grazing or browsing animals found in grasslands, scrublands, or deserts. Most species live in large herds. Species range in shoulder height from a 10-in. (25-cm) ANTELOPE to the 6.5-ft (2-m) BISON. Some of the 138 species (including domestic CATTLE, SHEEP, GOATS) are of economic value to humans. Others (such as BIGHORN) are hunted for food, sport, horns, or hides. See also BUFFALO.

Bow \ˈbō\, **Clara** (1905–1965) U.S. film actress. Born in Brooklyn, N.Y., she won a magazine contest that gave her a bit part in a film. Hired by Paramount in 1925, she appeared in *Mantrap* (1926) and *Kid Boots* (1926). After her starring role as a flapper in the successful *It* (1927), Bow was known as "the It girl," with "It" being understood as the appeal of the liberated young woman. She starred in 20 more films (1927–30), but after scandals and nervous breakdowns she retired in 1933.

bow and arrow Weapon consisting of a strip of wood or other flexible material, bent and held in tension by a string. The arrow, a long wooden shaft with a pointed tip, is stabilized in flight by a feathered tail. The arrow is fitted to the string by a notch in the end of the shaft and is drawn back to produce tension in the bow, which propels the arrow when the string is released. Bow construction ranges from wood, bone, and metal to plastic and fiberglass; arrowheads have been made from stone, bone, and metal. The bow was a primary weapon from Egyptian times through the Middle Ages in the Mediterranean world and Europe and even longer in China and Japan. The Huns, Turks, and Mongols excelled in warfare as mounted archers. The Turkish bow, the CROSSBOW, the compound bow, and the English LONGBOW made the arrow a formidable battlefield missile. In many cultures, the bow's importance in warfare has been secondary to its value as a hunting weapon. See also ARCHERY.

Bowditch \ˈbau̇d-ich\, **Nathaniel** (1773–1838) U.S. mathematician and astronomer. Born in Salem, Mass., he was largely self-educated. In 1799 he produced a revised edition of J. H. Moore's *The Practical Navigator*. His *New American Practical Navigator* (1802), the best navigation text of its time, was adopted by the U.S. Department of the Navy. He translated and updated four volumes of Pierre-Simon LAPLACE's *Celestial Mechanics* (1829–39). He discovered the Bowditch curves (describing pendulum motion), which are important in astronomy and physics.

Bowdoin College \ˈbō-dᵊn\ Private liberal-arts college in Brunswick, Me. Founded in 1794, it was named for James Bowdoin (1726–1790), first president of the American Academy of Arts and Sciences. It became coeducational in 1971. Facilities include a coastal studies center and an arctic museum. Its Walker Art Building was designed by Charles MCKIM and Stanford WHITE. Enrollment is about 1,600.

bowel movement See DEFECATION

Bowie \ˈbü-ē\, **Jim** (*orig.* James) (1796?–1836) U.S. soldier. Born in Logan Co., Ky., he lived in Louisiana, where he owned a sugar plantation. In 1828 he settled in Texas, assumed Mexican citizenship, acquired land grants, and married the vice-governor's daughter. In opposition to Mexican legislation to curb the emigration of American settlers, he joined the Texas revolutionary movement. He is remembered for his death leading the forces at the ALAMO. Inventor of the Bowie knife, he became a legendary hero through Western song and ballad.

Jim Bowie Portrait by an unknown artist

Bowles \ˈbōlz\, **Chester (Bliss)** (1901–1986) U.S. advertising executive and diplomat. Born in Springfield, Mass., in 1929 he and William Benton (1900–1973) established the Benton and Bowles advertising company, which became one of the largest in the world. After selling his interest in 1941, Bowles served as director of the Federal Price Administration 1943–46. Elected governor of Connecticut in 1948, he was defeated in 1950 because of his liberal stand on civil rights. He was later ambassador to India (1951–53, 1963–69) and a U.S. Representative (1953–61).

Bowles, Paul (Frederick) (1910–1999) U.S.-Moroccan composer and writer. Born in New York City, he studied composition with Aaron COPLAND and wrote music for over 30 plays and films. He moved to Morocco in the 1940s. He set his best-known novel, *The Sheltering Sky* (1948; film, 1990), in Tangier, and his protagonists are often Westerners bewildered and maimed by contact with traditional cultures. His wife, Jane Bowles (1917–1973), is known for the novel *Two Serious Ladies* (1943) and the play *In the Summer House* (1953).

bowling Game in which a heavy ball is rolled down a long, narrow lane to knock down a group of 10 wooden objects (called pins). Versions have existed since ancient times. Ninepin bowling was brought to the U.S. in the 17th cent. by Dutch settlers. The game grew to enormous popularity in the 20th cent., both as a recreational activity and (since 1958) as a professional sport. Each game is divided into 10 frames, and each player is allowed to deliver up to two balls per frame. If all the pins are knocked down on the first ball, a strike is recorded (10 points). If pins remain standing, and the second ball knocks them down, the player is awarded a spare (10 points). If a strike is thrown in a frame, the number of pins knocked down by the next two balls bowled counts in that frame. After a spare, the score of the next ball counts in its frame. Thus, the maximum point total for a frame is 30. A perfect score is 300, or 12 strikes in a row. Versions of the game include candlepins, duckpins, and skittles.

Bow River \ˈbō\ River, Alberta. Rising in BANFF NATIONAL PARK on the E slopes of the ROCKY MTNS., it flows 315 mi (507 km) southeast through the park and east past CALGARY to unite with the Oldman River and form the S. SASKATCHEWAN RIVER. It is important for power and irrigation.

box In botany, an EVERGREEN shrub or small tree (genus *Buxus*) of the box family (Buxaceae), best known for the ornamental and useful boxwoods. The family comprises seven genera of trees, shrubs, and herbaceous plants, native to N. America, Europe, N. Africa, and Asia. Three species of the genus *Buxus* provide the widely grown boxwood: the common, or English, box (*B. sempervirens*), used for hedges, borders, and TOPIARY figures; the Japanese box (*B. microphylla*); and the tall boxwood tree (*B. balearica*).

Boxer Rebellion Officially supported peasant uprising in 1900 in China that attempted to drive all foreigners from the country. "Boxer" was the English name given to a Chinese secret society that practiced boxing and calisthenic rituals that they believed would make them impervious to bullets. Support for them grew in N China during the late 19th cent., when an impoverished China was forced to grant humiliating concessions to Western powers. In June 1900 an international force was dispatched to stop the Boxer attacks on Westerners. The empress dowager, CIXI, ordered imperial forces to block its advance; the conflict escalated until August, when Beijing was captured and sacked. A treaty protocol required massive reparations to the U.S., Germany, and other foreign powers.

boxing Sport involving attack and defense with the fists. Boxers wear padded gloves and fight bouts of up to 15 three-minute rounds in a square ring. In ancient Greece fighters used leather thongs on their hands and forearms, while in Rome GLADIATORS used metal-studded leather hand coverings *(cesti)* and usually fought to the death. Not until the London Prize Ring rules of 1839 were kicking, gouging, butting, biting, and blows below the belt prohibited. In 1867 the Queensberry rules called for the wearing of gloves. In the late 19th cent. the U.S. became the premier boxing venue, partly because immigrants supplied a constantly renewed pool of boxers. Boxing has been included among the Olympic Games since 1904. Today there are eight traditional weight classes: flyweight, to 112 lbs (51 kg); bantamweight, to 118 lbs (53 kg); featherweight, to 126 lbs (57 kg); lightweight, to 135 lbs (61 kg); welterweight, to 147 lbs (67 kg); middleweight, to 160 lbs (72 kg); light heavyweight, to 175 lbs (79 kg); and heavyweight, over 175 lbs. A bout can be won either by knocking out or felling one's opponent for a count of 10 (a KO) or by delivering the most solid blows and thus amassing the most points. The referee can also stop the fight when one boxer is being badly beaten (a technical knockout, or TKO) or disqualify a fighter for rules violations.

boyars \bō-'yärz\ Upper class of medieval Russian society and state administration. In KIEVAN RUS (10th–12th cent.) the boyars held posts in the army and civil administration and advised the prince through a boyar council. In the 13th–14th cent., they constituted a privileged class of rich landowners in NE Russia. In the 15th–17th cent., the boyars of Muscovy (Moscow) ruled the country along with the grand prince (later the CZAR) and legislated through the boyar council. Their importance declined in the 17th cent., and the title was abolished by PETER I.

boycott Collective and organized ostracism to protest and punish practices considered unfair. The tactic was popularized by Charles Stewart PARNELL to protest high rents and land evictions in Ireland in 1880 by the estate manager Charles C. Boycott (1832–1897). Boycotts are principally used by labor organizations to win improved wages and working conditions or by consumers to pressure companies to change their hiring, labor, environmental, or investment practices. U.S. law distinguishes between primary boycotts (refusal by employees to purchase the goods or services of their employers) and secondary boycotts (pleas to third parties to also shun the target), the latter being illegal in most states.

Boyden, Seth (1788–1870) U.S. inventor. Born in Foxboro, Mass., he worked in Newark, N.J., inventing processes for making patent leather (1819), malleable cast iron (1825), and sheet iron. He also designed a hat-shaping machine, and he manufactured locomotives and stationary steam engines.

Boyer \bwä-'yā\, **Charles** (1897–1978) French-U.S. actor. After his stage debut in Paris in 1920, he became a popular romantic leading man in French theater and film; his rich, accented voice and suave manner made him an international star. His first successful U.S. film, *Private Worlds* (1935), was followed by such films as *Algiers* (1938) and *Gaslight* (1944). He cofounded Four Star Television in 1951 and starred in many of its productions.

Boyle, Kay (1902–1992) U.S. writer. Born in St. Paul, Minn., Boyle moved to Europe in the 1920s and served as a European correspondent for the *New Yorker* 1946–53. Her work is noted for elegance and a consistent leftist stance. Her novels, including *Plagued by the Nightingale* (1931), are less highly regarded than her short stories, including "The White Horses of Vienna," "Keep Your Pity," and "Defeat."

Boyle, Robert (1627–1691) Irish-English chemist and natural philosopher. He settled in Oxford in 1654 and, with his assistant Robert HOOKE, began his pioneering experiments on the properties of GASES, including those expressed in Boyle's law (see GAS LAWS). He demonstrated the physical characteristics of AIR, showing that it is necessary in combustion, respiration, and sound transmission. In *The Sceptical Chymist* (1661) he attacked ARISTOTLE's theory of the four elements (earth, air, fire, and water), espousing a corpuscular view of matter that presaged the modern theory of chemical elements. A founding member of the Royal Society of London, he achieved great renown in his lifetime.

Boy Scouts See SCOUTING

boysenberry Very large BRAMBLE fruit, usually considered a variety of BLACKBERRY *(Rubus ursinus)*. The dark, reddish-black fruit is valued for canning and preserving. It is grown chiefly in the S and SW U.S. and on the Pacific Coast. It was developed in the 1920s by Rudolph Boysen (1895–1950) of Napa, Cal.

BP See BRITISH PETROLEUM CO. PLC

Brabant \'brä-bänt\ Old duchy, NW Europe. In the 9th cent. A.D. it was part of Lotharingia. In the late 12th cent. it became independent; it finally passed to the house of BURGUNDY in 1430. Inherited by the HABSBURGS in 1477, it became a center of culture and commerce (see ANTWERP and BRUSSELS). In 1609 the N section was awarded to the United Provinces, while the S section remained part of Spanish (later Austrian) Netherlands. The N section now forms a Dutch province; the S section became part of Belgium.

bracken *or* **brake** FERN *(Pteridium aquilinum)* with 12 varieties found throughout the world in temperate and tropical regions. It has a perennial black rootstock, which creeps extensively underground and at intervals sends up fronds that may reach a height of 15 ft (5 m) or more. The dead fronds afford cover for game or are harvested for thatching and fodder.

bract Modified, usually small leaflike structure often positioned beneath a flower or INFLORESCENCE. What are often taken to be the petals of flowers are sometimes bracts—for example, the large, colorful bracts of POINSETTIAS or the showy white or pink bracts of DOGWOOD blossoms.

Bradbury, Ray (Douglas) (b.1920) U.S. author. Born in Waukegan, Ill., he is known for highly imaginative science-fiction stories and novels of social criticism, especially of the hazards of runaway technology. *The Martian Chronicles* (1950) is a classic. Other short-story collections include *The Illustrated Man* (1951) and *I Sing the Body Electric!* (1969). His novels include *Fahrenheit 451* (1953; film, 1966), *Dandelion Wine* (1957), and *Something Wicked This Way Comes* (1962).

Braddock, Edward (1695–1755) British army commander in the FRENCH AND INDIAN WAR. He arrived in Virginia in 1755 to command British forces in N. America against the French. On an expedition to attack the French-held Ft. Duquesne (now Pittsburgh, Pa.), his force, which included provincial militiamen such as George WASHINGTON, cut the first road across the Allegheny Mtns. Nearing the fort, his army of over 1,400 men was ambushed and defeated by a group of 254 French and 600 Indians, and he was mortally wounded.

Bradford, William (1590–1657) American governor of the Plymouth Colony. A Puritan Separatist, in 1609 he went to Holland to seek religious freedom. In 1620 he helped organize an expedition of about 100 Pilgrims to the New World. He helped draft the MAYFLOWER COMPACT aboard the group's ship, was unanimously chosen governor of the Plymouth Colony, and served for all but five years from 1621 to 1656. He helped establish and foster the principles of self-government and religious freedom that characterized later American colonial government. His descriptive journal provides a unique historical source for both the voyage and the settlement.

Bradlee, Benjamin C(rowninshield) (b.1921) U.S. newspaper editor. Born in Boston, Bradlee was a reporter for the *Washington Post* before joining *Newsweek* in Paris. Back at the *Post,* he served as its executive editor 1968–91. Under him the *Post* published the PENTAGON PAPERS, broke much of the story surrounding the WATERGATE SCANDAL, and was recognized as one of the most important newspapers in the U.S.

Bradley, Bill (orig. William Warren) (b.1943) U.S. basketball player and politician. Born in Crystal City, Mo., Bradley attended Princeton Univ., where he was named College

Player of the Year in 1964–65. In 1964 he helped the U.S. team win the Olympic gold medal. He studied at Oxford Univ. as a Rhodes scholar, then returned to play with the New York Knicks until 1977, helping them win two NBA championships (1970, 1973). As a prominent U.S. Senator from New Jersey (1979–97), he sought to raise public awareness of race relations and poverty and was a critic of campaign-financing practices. In 1999–2000 he was an unsuccessful candidate for president.

Bradley, Omar N(elson) (1893–1981) U.S. general. Born in Clark, Mo., he graduated from West Point. He directed the army's infantry school at the start of World War II. In 1943 he commanded U.S. forces in the N. AFRICA CAMPAIGN, then led the successful Sicilian invasion. As commander of the 1st Army, he took part in the NORMANDY CAMPAIGN and the liberation of Paris. As commander of the 12th Army Group, the largest U.S. force ever placed under one general, he oversaw European operations until the German surrender. Admired by both officers and men, he was chosen the first chairman of the Joint Chiefs of Staff (1949–53) and promoted to General of the Army (1950).

Bradley, Thomas (1917–1998) Mayor of Los Angeles (1973–93). Born in Calvert, Texas, he grew up in Los Angeles. In 1940 he began a 22-year tenure with the city's police department, earning a law degree. In 1973 he was elected one of the nation's first two black mayors of a major city (with Coleman YOUNG). During five terms as mayor, he helped transform Los Angeles into a bustling business and trading center. He retired in 1992 after riots following the acquittal of police officers in the beating of Rodney King.

Bradshaw, Terry (Paxton) (b.1948) U.S. football quarterback. Born in Shreveport, La., he played for the Pittsburgh Steelers 1970–83, leading the team to a record four SUPER BOWL victories (1975, 1976, 1979, 1980). Bradshaw set two Super Bowl passing records and was twice voted the game's Most Valuable Player. After retiring he pursued a career as a sports broadcaster.

Bradstreet, Anne *orig.* Anne Dudley (1612?–1672) British-American poet, one of the first poets of the American colonies. At 18 she came with other Puritans to Massachusetts Bay. She wrote many of her poems while rearing eight children. Her brother-in-law took her poems to England, where they were published in 1650. Her poetry won critical acceptance in the 20th cent., particularly "Contemplations," a religious sequence first published in the 19th cent. Her prose works include "Meditations," a set of aphorisms.

Brady, Mathew B. (1823–1896) U.S. photographer. Born near Lake George, N.Y., he learned to make daguerreotypes from Samuel MORSE. In 1844 he opened a studio in New York and began photographing famous people. In 1847 he opened a studio in Washington, D.C., and there created, copied, and collected portraits of U.S. presidents. He achieved international fame with *A Gallery of Illustrious Americans* (1850). In 1861 he set out to make a complete record of the Civil War with a staff of more than 20 photographers. He probably photographed the battles of BULL RUN, ANTIETAM, and GETTYSBURG himself.

Bragg, Braxton (1817–1876) U.S. and Confederate army officer. Born in Warrenton, N.C., he graduated from West Point. When N. Carolina seceded, he joined the Confederate army and was promoted to general in 1862. As commander of the Army of Tennessee, he led his troops to victory at the Battle of CHICKAMAUGA. His forces besieged the Union troops at Chattanooga but were eventually routed. He was relieved of his command but appointed military adviser to Jefferson DAVIS.

Bragg law Relation between the spacing of atomic planes in CRYSTALS and the angles of incidence at which the planes produce the most intense reflections of ELECTROMAGNETIC RADIATION and particle waves. The law, first formulated by Lawrence Bragg (1890–1971), is useful for measuring WAVELENGTHS and for determining the lattice spacings of crystals (see CRYSTAL LATTICE), and is the principal way to make precise energy measurements of X RAYS and low-energy GAMMA RAYS.

Brahe \ˈbrä, ˈbrä-hē\, **Tycho** (1546–1601) Danish astronomer. Kidnapped by his wealthy, childless uncle, he was raised at the latter's castle and educated at the Univs. of Copenhagen and Leipzig. He acquired mathematical and astronomical instruments in 1565–70, and on inheriting his father's and uncle's estates built a small observatory. His discovery (1573) of a new star shook faith in the immutable heavens. The new, larger observatory he built (Uraniborg) with the aid of Denmark's King Frederick II became N Europe's center of astronomical study and discovery from which he accurately charted the positions of more than 777 fixed stars. His pupil and assistant Johannes KEPLER used Tycho's observational data to lay the groundwork for Isaac NEWTON's work.

Tycho Brahe Engraving by Hendrik Goltzius, c.1586

Brahma One of three major gods in late Vedic HINDUISM (c.500 B.C.–c.A.D. 500). He was gradually eclipsed by the other two, VISHNU and SHIVA. Brahma was associated with the creator god Prajapati, whose identity he came to assume. All temples of Shiva or Vishnu contain an image of Brahma, but today there is no sect or cult devoted exclusively to him.

Brahman In the UPANISHADS, the eternal, infinite, and omnipresent spiritual source of the finite and changing universe. The schools of VEDANTA differ in interpreting Brahman. In one school, Brahman is the absolute reality onto which humans project their perceptions of differentiation. In another, Brahman is not different from the world it produces. In yet another, the reality people perceive is a glorious manifestation of Brahman, while according to a fourth school both soul and matter are separate from and dependent on Brahman.

Brahman *or* **Brahmin** Any member of the highest of the four VARNAS, or social classes, in Hindu India. Their existence as a priestly CASTE dates to the late Vedic period, and they have long been considered to be more ritually pure than members of other castes. Only Brahmans may perform certain religious tasks, including preservation of the collections of Vedic hymns. The Brahmans dominated Indian scholarship for centuries. They advised the politically powerful warrior caste, and after Indian independence they supplied many heads of state. They still retain traditional privileges, though these are no longer legally sanctioned.

Brahmana \ˈbrä-mə-nə\ Any of a number of discourses on the VEDAS that explain their use in ritual sacrifices and the symbolism of the priests' actions. Dating to 900–600 B.C., they constitute the oldest historical sources for Indian ritual. The discourses include discussions of daily sacrifices, the sacrificial fire and priests' supervision of sacrifices, seasonal and occasional rites, elements of domestic ritual and atonement for mistakes in ritual, and the "going of the cows."

Brahmaputra River \ˌbrä-mə-ˈpü-trə\ River, central and S Asia. From its headsprings in Tibet (as the Zangbo River), it flows across S Tibet to break through the HIMALAYAS in great gorges. It flows southwest through the ASSAM valley and south through Bangladesh. There it merges with the GANGES to form the Ganges-Brahmaputra Delta. About 1,800 mi (2,900 km) long, the river is important for irrigation and transportation. Its identity with the Zangbo was discovered only in 1884–86.

Brahms, Johannes (1833–1897) German-Austrian composer. Born in Hamburg, son of a musician, he became a piano prodigy. In 1853 he met Robert and Clara SCHUMANN; Robert immediately proclaimed him a genius, and Clara became the lifelong object of his affections. In 1863 he moved to Vienna, which would remain his home until his death. He took several positions as choral and orchestral conductor and performed as a soloist. The success of his *German Requiem* (1868) gave him an international reputation; his first symphony (1876) led to even greater fame, and his violin concerto (1878) and second piano concerto (1881) led many to acclaim him the greatest living composer. His music, grounded in the Classical style, was seen as conservative, especially with respect to that of Richard WAGNER and Franz LISZT. His other works include three more symphonies (1877, 1883, 1885), a double concerto (1887), two serenades (1858, 1859), two overtures (1880), much chamber and piano music, and more than 250 lieder.

Braille \\'brāl\\ Universal system of writing and printing for the blind. Louis BRAILLE invented the system in 1824. The system is based on a matrix of six raised dots arranged in two columns of three that are read by passing the fingers lightly over them. The 63 possible combinations stand for letters, numbers, punctuation marks, and common words like *and* and *the*. A Braille code for English was adopted in 1932. Versions also exist for other languages, for mathematical and technical material, and for musical notation. Braille may be handwritten using a stylus, but Braille typewriters and electric embossing machines are more common.

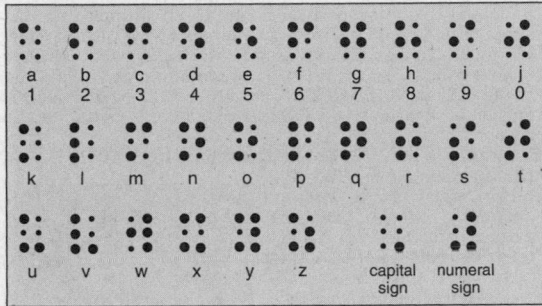

Braille The alphabet and the digits 0–9 in the modern Braille system. Each letter or digit consists of six "cells" that are either embossed or left blank to form a unique pattern. Large dots indicate raised cells; smaller dots indicate cells that are left blank.

Braille \\'brāy\\, **Louis** (1809–1852) French educator who developed the BRAILLE system of printing and writing for the blind. Himself blinded at the age of 3, he went to Paris in 1819 to attend the National Institute for Blind Children, and from 1826 he taught there. His system is a simplified version of one devised by Charles Barbier.

brain Concentration of nerve tissue in the front or upper end of an animal's body that handles sensory information, controls motion, is vital to instinctive acts, and in higher vertebrates is the center of learning. Vertebrate brains consist of the hindbrain, midbrain, and forebrain. The hindbrain comprises the medulla oblongata and the pons, which connects the SPINAL CORD with higher brain levels and transfers information from the CEREBRAL CORTEX to the CEREBELLUM. The midbrain, a major sensory integration center in other vertebrates, serves primarily to link the hindbrain and forebrain in mammals. In the forebrain, the two cerebral hemispheres are connected by a thick bundle of nerve fibers (corpus callosum) and are divided by deep grooves into four lobes (frontal, parietal, temporal, and occipital). The cerebrum, the largest part of the human brain, is involved with its more complex functions.

brain death State of irreversible destruction of the BRAIN. Before the invention of life-support systems, brain death always led quickly to death of the body. Ethical considerations are crucial to defining criteria for brain death (e.g., deep coma with a known cause, absence of any brain-stem functions, and exclusion of hypothermia, drugs, and poison as causes). ELECTROENCEPHALOGRAPHY is useful but not essential in determining brain death. Organ donors must be declared brain-dead before their organs may be removed for transplant.

brain laterality See LATERALITY

brainwashing Systematic effort to destroy an individual's former loyalties and beliefs and to substitute loyalty to a new ideology or power. It has been used by religious cults as well as by radical political groups such as the Chinese

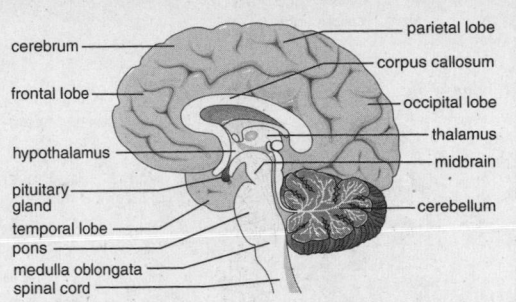

Brain Side view of the brain showing its major structures. The large cerebrum is divided into two halves or hemispheres connected by the corpus callosum, a bundle of nerve fibers. Two grooves divide the hemispheres into four lobes: frontal, temporal, parietal, and occipital. Many nerve cells are found in the convoluted cerebrum's outer surface or cortex, which controls sensory and motor activities. The thalamus relays incoming sensory impulses from the spinal cord to the cortex. The hypothalamus's many functions include control of breathing, blood flow, temperature regulation, and emotions. The pituitary gland is attached to and regulated by the hypothalamus. The midbrain relays signals between the forebrain and hindbrain. The cerebellum, along with the cerebrum, plays a role in voluntary movement as well as balance. The pons serves as a relay point linking the medulla oblongata, midbrain, cerebellum, and cerebrum. The medulla, lying between the pons and the spinal cord and continuous with both, plays a role in essential involuntary regulatory and reflexive responses (incl. breathing, swallowing, and heartbeat) and relays signals between the spinal cord and other brain regions.

Communists in 1949. It usually involves isolation from former associates and sources of information, an exacting regimen calling for absolute obedience and humility, strong social pressures and rewards for cooperation, food and sleep deprivation, and punishments for noncooperation, including social ostracism and criticism, bondage, and torture. Its effects are sometimes reversed through deprogramming, which combines confrontation and intensive psychotherapy.

brake Device for decreasing the speed of a body or stopping its motion. Most brakes act on rotating mechanical elements and absorb KINETIC ENERGY mechanically, hydrodynamically, or electrically. Mechanical brakes are the most common; they dissipate the kinetic energy as heat generated by mechanical FRICTION between a rotating drum or disk and a stationary friction element. A hydrodynamic (fluid) brake has a rotor (rotating element) and a stator (stationary element). Resistance to rotation is created by fluid friction and circulation of the liquid (usually water) from a series of pockets in the rotor to a series of complementary pockets in the stator. See diagram on next page.

brake See BRACKEN

Bramah, Joseph (1748–1814) British engineer and inventor. In 1784 he devised a pick-proof lock, which defied all efforts for 67 years. Since the success of his locks depended on their complexity, mass production required creation of a set of well-designed and precisely engineered machine tools, for which he hired the young Henry MAUDSLAY. Their prototype machines were essential to the founding of the MACHINE-TOOL industry. Bramah's hydraulic press found many industrial uses and led to the development of hydraulic machinery.

Bramante \\brä-'män-tä\\, **Donato** (1444–1514) Italian architect and perspectivist painter. His early architectural works included the church of Santa Maria presso San Satiro (c.1480), in which the choir is painted in perspective to give an illusion of a much larger space. In 1499 he went to Rome, where he spent the rest of his life. His Tempietto was the first masterpiece of the High Renaissance. Under Pope

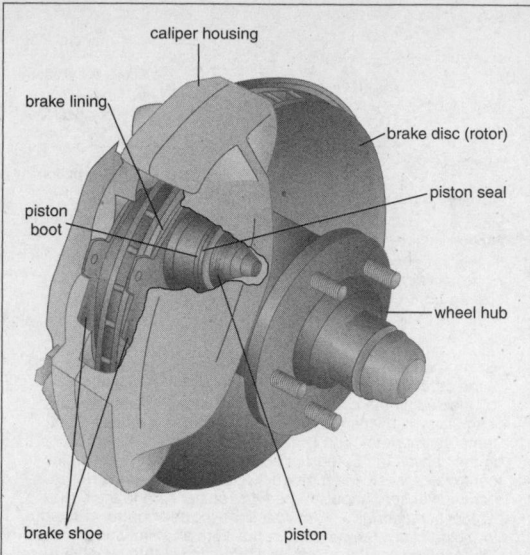

caliper housing

brake lining

brake disc (rotor)

piston boot

piston seal

wheel hub

brake shoe

piston

Brake A disk brake assembly. Wheel rotation is slowed by friction when the hydraulic pistons squeeze the caliper, pressing the brake pads against the spinning disk (rotor), which is bolted to the wheel hub.

JULIUS II, he drew up plans for the immense Belvedere courtyard in the Vatican (begun c.1505) and the vast ST. PETER'S BASILICA (begun 1506), his greatest work. He played an important role in Julius II's plans for rebuilding Rome.

bramble Any plant of the genus *Rubus* (rose family), consisting of usually prickly shrubs, including RASPBERRIES and BLACKBERRIES. Brambles grow wild throughout N. America, as well as in Europe and Asia, and are widely cultivated for their fruits.

Donato Bramante, Tempietto, S. Pietro in Montorio, Rome, 1502

Brân \'bran\ In CELTIC RELIGION, a gigantic deity described in medieval Welsh tales as king of Britain. When Brân was mortally wounded, he asked his companions to cut off his head and keep it with them, telling them it would provide entertainment and allow them to forget their sorrows. Eventually the head was buried on the White Mount in London, where it protected England from invaders until it was finally unearthed.

bran Edible broken seed coat of CEREAL grain, separated from the kernel. In flour processing, it is normally removed from the ground kernels by sifting; whole-grain flours retain the bran. Wheat bran, the most widely processed, contains 16% protein, 11% natural fiber, and 50% carbohydrate. Most bran is coarsely ground for stock feed. In a more refined form, it is used in breakfast cereal, breads, and muffins for its dietary value as roughage.

Branagh \'bra-nə\, **Kenneth (Charles)** (b.1960) British actor, director, and writer. After making his London stage debut in 1981, he joined the ROYAL SHAKESPEARE CO. (1984–87), where he won acclaim in *Hamlet* and *Henry V*. He cofounded the Renaissance Theatre Co. (1987), in which he served as actor, director, and writer. He is best known as the director and star of film versions of *Henry V* (1989), *Much Ado About Nothing* (1993), and *Hamlet* (1996).

Branch Davidians Religious sect founded in 1959 near Waco, Texas, part of an earlier breakaway group from the Seventh-Day Adventists. Under the leadership of David Koresh (*orig.* Vernon W. Howell; 1959–1993), it stockpiled weapons at its compound, where some 130 followers were living by 1993. That year, after a shoot-out in which four federal agents were killed, federal law-enforcement agencies besieged the compound for 51 days. The standoff ended, at the orders of Attorney General Janet Reno, in an assault; sect members set fire to the compound and 82 members died, including several children and Koresh himself. A Congressional investigation, conducted in response to intense controversy, exonerated federal agents in 2000.

Brancusi, Constantin (1876–1957) Romanian-French sculptor. He became adept at carving wooden farm implements as a child and later studied in Bucharest, Munich, and eventually Paris, having walked most of the way from Munich. In 1908 he executed *The Kiss,* his first truly original work. He developed a style of geometrization that became his hallmark, reducing natural forms to an ultimate abstract simplicity. One of his favorite themes was a bird in flight; his most famous treatment was the celebrated polished-bronze *Bird in Space* (1919). Through numerous exhibitions in the U.S. and Europe, he achieved great fame and success, and he is regarded as a pioneer of modern abstract sculpture.

Brandeis \'bran-ˌdīs\, **Louis (Dembitz)** (1856–1941) U.S. jurist. Born in Louisville, Ky., he practiced law in Boston, becoming known as "the people's attorney" for his defense of the constitutionality of several state hours-and-wages laws, his devising of a savings-bank life-insurance plan for working people, and his efforts to strengthen the government's antitrust power. His work influenced passage in 1914 of the Clayton Anti-Trust Act and the Federal Trade Commission Act. He also developed what came to be called the "Brandeis brief," in which economic and sociological data, histori-

Louis Brandeis

cal material, and expert opinion are marshaled to support a legal argument. Appointed to the U.S. Supreme Court (1916), he was noted for his devotion to FREEDOM OF SPEECH. Many of his minority opinions later were accepted by the Court in the New Deal era. His appointment as the first Jewish justice was vigorously opposed by some business interests and anti-Semitic groups. He served until 1939.

Brandeis University \'bran-ˌdīs\ Private university in Waltham, Mass., founded in 1948, the only Jewish-sponsored nonsectarian university in the U.S. It is named for Louis BRANDEIS. Its graduate programs include ancient and modern Jewish thought, history, and culture, as well as social policy, international economics, and biomedical research. Total enrollment is about 4,500.

Brandenburg Historical region and province of PRUSSIA. The earliest Germanic inhabitants were replaced by Slavic Wends, who in turn were overcome in the 12th cent. by Albert the Bear, margrave of Brandenburg. It became one of the seven electorates of the HOLY ROMAN EMPIRE in 1356. Under FREDERICK WILLIAM (the Great Elector, 1640–88), Brandenburg-Prussia grew to be a leading power. It became a province of Prussia in 1815 and was part of united Germany from 1871 until the end of World War II. After the war, the E portion became part of Poland and the W portion part of E. Germany. In 1991 the W part became a German state. Brandenburg city was formerly the residence of Prussia's reigning family.

Brandenburg Gate Monumental gateway in Berlin, the only remaining town gate. Carl G. Langhans (1732–1808), who built the gate (1789–93), modeled it after the propylaeum of the Athenian Acropolis. On top was the "Quadriga of Victory," a statue of a chariot drawn by four horses. Heavily damaged in World War II, the gate was restored in 1957–58. Enclosed by the Berlin Wall 1961–89, the gate was reopened in 1989 with the reunification of E. and W. Berlin.

Brandes \\'bran-dəs\\, **Georg (Morris Cohen)** (1842–1927) Danish critic and scholar. His *Main Currents in 19th-Century Thought* (6 vols., 1872–90) catalyzed the shift from Romanticism to realism in Danish literature. He called on writers to work for progressive ideas and social reform, and championed such writers as Henrik IBSEN and August STRINDBERG. Despite reactionary opposition, he had huge influence throughout Scandinavia. His other critical works include *Men of the Modern Breakthrough* (1883) and *Danish Poets* (1877).

Brando (Jr.), Marlon (b.1924) U.S. actor. Born in Omaha, he won stardom on Broadway as Stanley Kowalski in *A Streetcar Named Desire* (1947). An early member of the ACTORS STUDIO, he brought its Method acting style to his first film, *The Men* (1950). His slurred, mumbling delivery marked his rejection of classical dramatic training, and his passionate performances proved him one of the great actors of his generation. After starring in the screen version of *Streetcar* (1951), he appeared in films such as *Julius Caesar* (1953), *The Wild One* (1954), *On the Waterfront* (1954, Academy Award), *The Godfather* (1972, Academy Award), *Last Tango in Paris* (1972), and *Apocalypse Now* (1979).

Brandt, Bill (*orig.* William) (1904–1983) British photographer. In 1929 he worked in the studio of Man RAY in Paris. He returned to England in 1931 and took up photojournalism, documenting English industrial workers in the 1930s and covering the home front during World War II. He is best known for his photographs of British life, and especially for his unconventional nudes photographed in extremely distorted form, which approach abstract designs.

Brandt, Willy *orig.* Herbert Ernst Karl Frahm (1913–1992) German statesman. As a young Social Democrat, he fled to Norway to avoid arrest by the Nazis in the 1930s. There he assumed the name Willy Brandt and worked as a journalist. Returning to Germany after World War II, he was elected to parliament in 1949 and became mayor of W. Berlin (1957–66), a post in which he achieved world fame. He led a coalition government as chancellor of the Federal Republic of Germany (1969–74). He improved relations with E. Germany, other communist nations in Eastern Europe, and the Soviet Union, and helped strengthen the EUROPEAN ECONOMIC COMMUNITY. He received the Nobel Peace Prize in 1971.

brandy ALCOHOLIC BEVERAGE distilled from WINE or a fermented fruit mash. Most brandies are aged and contain about 50% alcohol by volume. Some are darkened with caramel. They are usually served alone as after-dinner drinks, but are sometimes used in mixed drinks or desserts, or as fuel in flamed dishes such as crêpes suzettes. They are also used to produce LIQUEUR. The finest brandy is usually thought to be French cognac.

Brandywine, Battle of the (Sept. 11, 1777) Battle in the AMERICAN REVOLUTION. The British general William HOWE attempted to remove Pennsylvania from the war by engaging George WASHINGTON's troops on Brandywine Creek, 25 mi (40 km) from Philadelphia. In the end, the British troops occupied the battlefield, but their failure to destroy Washington's army contributed to the later British defeat at the Battle of SARATOGA.

Brant, Joseph (1742–1807) MOHAWK Indian chief and Christian missionary. Brant was converted to the Anglican Church while attending a school for Indians in Connecticut. He fought for the British in the last FRENCH AND INDIAN WAR (1754–63). He led four of the six IROQUOIS nations on the British side in the AMERICAN REVOLUTION, winning several notable battles. After the war Brant was granted land along the Grand River in Ontario, where he ruled peacefully and continued his missionary work.

Brant, Sebastian (1458?–1521) German poet. He served as imperial councillor to Maximilian I. His writings include works on law, religion, politics, and especially morals. His best-known work is *The Ship of Fools* (1494), an allegory telling of fools on a ship bound for a "fool's paradise." The most famous German literary work of the 15th cent., it ridicules the vices of the age.

Braque \\'bräk\\, **Georges** (1882–1963) French painter. He studied painting in Le Havre and Paris. His first important paintings (1905–7) were in the Fauvist style; in 1907 he exhibited at the Salon des Indépendants. Abandoning Fauvism in 1907, with Pablo PICASSO he invented the revolutionary new style known as CUBISM. He painted mostly still lifes featuring geometrical shapes and low-key color harmonies. In 1912 he introduced the collage or *papier collé* (pasted-paper picture) by attaching three pieces of wallpaper to the drawing *Fruit Dish and Glass*. By the 1920s he was a prosperous, well-established modern master. He enjoyed a long and prestigious career, and was honored with worldwide exhibitions. In 1961 he became the first living artist to have his works exhibited in the Louvre.

Brasília City (pop., 1996: 1,692,000), capital of Brazil. It lies on the PARANÁ RIVER. Though the idea of having the country's capital located in the interior was proposed as early as 1789, Brasília's construction began only in 1956. It was designed, to striking effect, by Lúcio Costa (1902–1998) and Oscar NIEMEYER. The government began its move from RIO DE JANEIRO in 1960. Many companies have since built headquarters in Brasília.

Brasov *or* **Brashov** \\brä-'shōv\\ *German* **Kronstadt** \\'krōn-ˌshtät\\ City (pop., 1997 est.: 317,000), Romania. It lies near the center of the country. Founded by Teutonic Knights in 1211, it became the hub for trading in cloth and metalwork throughout much of WALACHIA and MOLDAVIA. The substantial autonomy of its German inhabitants ended in 1876. Brasov is today a center for heavy manufacturing.

brass ALLOY of COPPER and ZINC, important for its hardness and workability. Brass was first used around 1200 B.C. in the Near East. In ancient documents, including the Bible, the term brass is often used to denote BRONZE. The malleability of brass depends on its zinc content; brasses with more than 45% zinc are not workable. Alpha brasses contain less than 40% zinc; beta brasses (40–45% zinc) are less ductile than alpha brasses but stronger. A third group includes brasses with additional elements. The lead brasses are more easily machined; naval and admiralty brasses add tin to improve resistance to corrosion by seawater; and aluminum brasses provide strength and corrosion resistance where the naval brasses may fail.

Brassaï \\brä-'sī\\ *orig.* Gyula Halasz (1899–1984) Hungarian-French photographer. His pseudonym derives from his native city. In 1924 he settled in Paris, where he worked as a journalist and found it necessary to use a camera for his assignments. In the 1930s he became known for his dramatic photographs of Paris nightlife. Books of his photographs, including *Paris After Dark* (1933) and *Pleasures of Paris* (1935), brought him international fame.

brassica Any plant of the large genus *Brassica,* in the MUSTARD FAMILY, containing about 40 species and including the CABBAGES, mustards, and RAPES. The single species *B. oleracea* includes such edible varieties as BROCCOLI, BRUSSELS SPROUTS, cabbage, CAULIFLOWER, KALE, and KOHLRABI. Also included in this genus are the TURNIP, RUTABAGA, and CHINESE CABBAGES.

brass instruments Musical wind instruments, usually made of brass or other metal, in which the vibration of the player's lips against a cup- or funnel-shaped mouthpiece causes an air column to vibrate. The TRUMPET, TROMBONE, FRENCH HORN, TUBA, EUPHONIUM, SOUSAPHONE, CORNET, FLUGELHORN, and BUGLE are brass instruments; the saxophones, though made of brass, are classified as WOODWIND INSTRUMENTS.

Bratislava \\ˌbrä-ti-'slä-və\\ *German* **Pressburg** \\'pres-ˌburk\\ *Hungarian* **Pozsony** \\'pō-ˌzhōnʸ\\ City (pop., 1998: 452,000), capital of Slovakia. Settled by Slavs in the 8th cent., as Pressburg it developed as a trade center and became a free royal town in 1291. The first university in what was then Hungary was founded there in 1467. The city served as the Hungarian capital 1541–1784 and was the seat of the Diet until 1848. The Treaty of Pressburg (1805) was signed here following the Battle of AUSTERLITZ. After World War I, on the formation of Czechoslovakia, it became capital of the province of Slovakia, and it became the national capital on Slovakia's independence in 1992.

Braudel \brō-'del\, **(Paul Achille) Fernand** (1902–1985) French historian. While a prisoner of war, Braudel wrote from memory his thesis on the history of the Mediterranean region in the 16th cent., published as *The Mediterranean and the Mediterranean World in the Age of Phillip II* (1949). With Marc BLOCH and Lucien Febvre, he became a leader of the influential ANNALES SCHOOL. His second major work was *Civilization and Capitalism, 15th–18th Century* (1967, 1979).

Braun \'braůn\, **Eva** (1912–1945) German mistress of Adolf HITLER. A saleswoman in the shop of Hitler's photographer, she became his mistress in the 1930s. He never allowed her to be seen in public with him, and she had no influence on his political life. In April 1945 she joined him in Berlin, against his orders. In recognition of her loyalty, he married her in the Chancellery bunker on April 29. The next day she ended her life at 33 by taking poison; her husband either poisoned or shot himself at her side. Their bodies were burned.

Braun \'braůn\, **Wernher von** (1912–1977) German-U.S. ROCKET engineer. Born into an aristocratic family, in 1936 he became technical director of the new military development facility at Peenemünde, an essential center for the rearmament of Nazi Germany, forbidden by the Versailles accords. Liquid-fueled rocket aircraft and jet-assisted takeoffs were successfully demonstrated there, and the V-2 long-range ballistic missile was developed. By 1944 the sophistication of the rockets and missiles being tested at Peenemünde was many years ahead of that of any other country. When World War II ended, he and his team were immediately set to work on guided missiles by the U.S. Army, and in 1952 he became technical director (later chief) of its ballistic-weapon program. Under his leadership, the Redstone, Jupiter-C, Juno, and Pershing missiles were developed. In 1958 he and his group launched the first U.S. satellite, EXPLORER I. He later led the development of some of the large SATURN space launch vehicles; the engineering success of the Saturn boosters remains unmatched in rocket history.

Braunschweig See BRUNSWICK

Brazil *officially* **Federative Republic of Brazil** Nation, central S. America. Area: 3,284,426 sq mi (8,506,663 sq km). Population (2000): 166,113,000. Capital: BRASÍLIA. Brazil's several ethnic groups have intermixed since the earliest days of its colonial history. Unmixed elements are rare, with those Indians untouched by immigration restricted to the most remote parts of the Amazon Basin. Language: Portuguese (official). Religions: Roman Catholicism, Protestantism, traditional Indian and African beliefs. Currency: real. Brazil may be divided into many regions, but the AMAZON RIVER Basin and the Brazilian Highlands (or Plateau) dominate the landscape. The Highlands, a plateau with an average elevation of 3,300 ft (1,000 m), lies primarily in the southeast, while the Amazon Basin, which lies at elevations of less than 800 ft (250 m), is in the north. The Amazon River, with its more than 1,000 known tributaries, com-

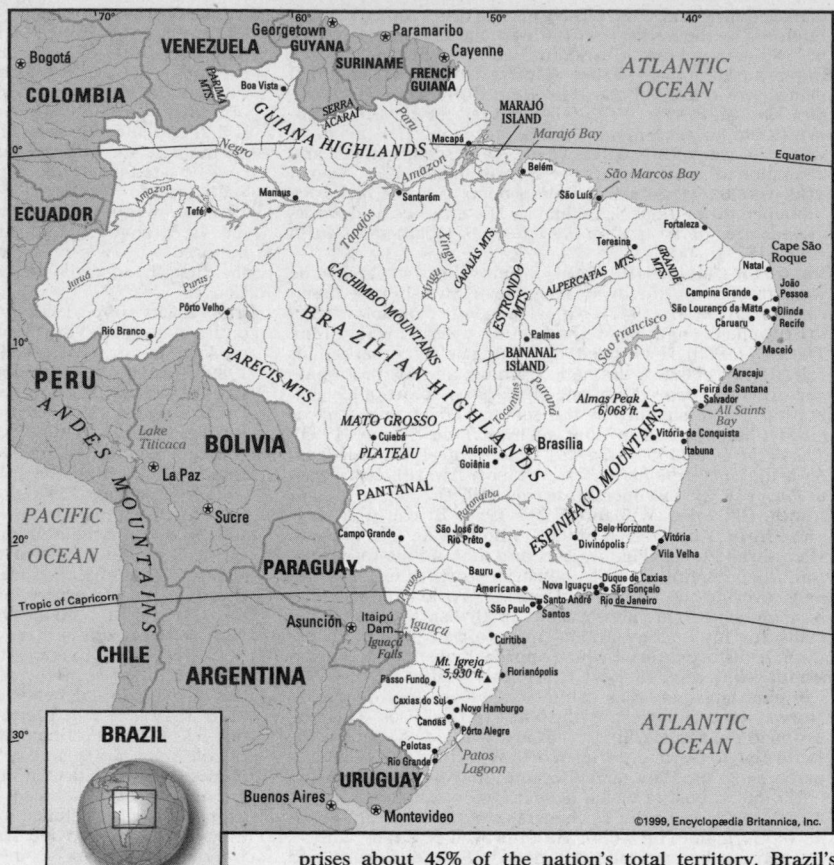

BRAZIL

Scale 1: 43,655,000
0   200   400 mi
0   300   600 km

©1999, Encyclopædia Britannica, Inc.

prises about 45% of the nation's total territory. Brazil's other rivers include the São Francisco, Parnaíba, PARAGUAY, Alto Paraná, and URUGUAY. Except for the islands of Marajó and Caviana at the mouth of the Amazon and Maracá to the north, there are no large islands along the 4,603 mi (7,406 km) of its Atlantic coastline. There are good harbors at BELÉM, Salvador, RIO DE JANEIRO, Santos, and Pôrto Alegre. The country's immense forests are a source of many products, while its savannas support cattle raising. Agriculture is important; its mineral reserves are large. Brazil has a developing market economy based mainly on manufacturing, financial services, and trade. It is a republic with two legislative houses; its chief of state and government is the president. Little is known about Brazil's early indigenous inhabitants. Though the area was theoretically allotted to Portugal by the 1494 Treaty of TORDESILLAS, it was not formally claimed by discovery until P. A. CABRAL accidentally touched land in 1500. It was first settled by the Portuguese in the early 1530s at São Vicente (near modern SÃO PAULO); the French and Dutch created small settlements over the next century. The region was ignored during the Spanish rule of Portugal (1580–1640), but a viceroyalty was established in 1640 and Rio de Janeiro became the capital in 1673. In 1808 Brazil became the refuge and seat of the government of John VI of Portugal when Napoleon invaded Portugal; ultimately the Kingdom of Portugal, Brazil, and Algrave was proclaimed, and John ruled from Brazil 1815–21. On John's return to Portugal, PEDRO I proclaimed Brazilian independence. In 1889 his successor, Pedro II, was deposed, and a constitution mandating a federal republic was adopted. The 20th cent. saw increased immigration and growth in manufacturing along with frequent military coups and suspensions of civil liberties. Construction of a new capital at Brasília, intended to spur development of the country's interior, worsened its inflation rate. After 1979 the military government began a gradual return to democratic practices, and in 1989 the first popular presidential election in 29 years was held. The late 1990s brought a severe economic crisis.

Brazil nut Edible seed of a large S. American tree, *Bertholletia excelsa* (family Lecythidaceae), one of the major commercially traded NUTS in the world. The hard-walled fruit, resembling a large coconut, contains 8–24 hard-shelled nuts (seeds) arranged in it like sections of an orange. Brazil nuts are high in fat and protein. The tree grows wild in stands in the Amazon River basin, reaching heights of 150 ft (45 m) or more.

brazing Process for joining two pieces of METAL by applying heat and adding a filler metal. The filler, which has a lower melting point than the metals to be joined, is either preplaced or fed into the joint as the parts are heated. In brazing parts with small clearances, the filler is able to flow into the joint by CAPILLARITY. The temperature of the molten filler in brazing exceeds 800°F (430°C). In SOLDERING, a related process, the filler metal remains below that temperature. Brazed joints are usually stronger than soldered joints. Most metals can be brazed. Brazed joints are used extensively on rockets, jet engines, and aircraft parts. See also WELDING.

Brazos River \'bra-zəs\ River, central Texas. Formed in N Texas, it flows southeast 840 mi (1,351 km) into the Gulf of MEXICO. The city of WACO is one of the largest on the river. Near its mouth it connects with the GULF INTRACOASTAL WATERWAY. The river valley was a major site of early Anglo-American settlement in Texas. The river's original name was Brazos de Dios ("Arms of God").

Brazza \brä-'zä\, **Pierre (-Paul-François-Camille) Savorgnan de** (1852–1905) French explorer and colonial administrator. Born to Italian nobility in Brazil, he joined the French navy. He explored the Ogooué River in 1875–78 and later the Congo River. He founded the French (Middle) Congo and explored Gabon, as well as BRAZZAVILLE (1883), adding significantly to the French colonial empire. From 1886 to 1897 he governed a colony there.

Brazzaville \'brä-zə-₁vil\ River port (pop., 1992 est.: 938,000), capital of Republic of the Congo. Lying on the north bank of the CONGO RIVER across from KINSHASA, it was founded in 1883 by P. S. de BRAZZA. A base for later claims of France to lands to the northeast, it became the capital of FRENCH EQUATORIAL AFRICA. The river port forms the terminus of the Congo–ocean transport system, with steamer service to the Congo's upper reaches and a railroad to POINTE-NOIRE 245 mi (394 km) west.

bread Baked food product made of FLOUR or meal that is moistened, kneaded into a dough, and often fermented using YEAST. Bread has been made since prehistoric times in various forms using a variety of ingredients and methods. Flat, unleavened bread, made from CORN, BARLEY, MILLET, BUCKWHEAT, WHEAT, or RYE is eaten in the Middle East, Asia, and Africa. Raised bread, common in Europe and the U.S., is usually made of wheat or rye. Both contain the elastic protein gluten, which traps gas from FERMENTATION, helping the bread to rise. Bread is a source of complex CARBOHYDRATES and B vitamins (see VITAMIN B COMPLEX); whole-wheat bread contains more protein, vitamins, minerals, and fiber than white bread. See also BAKING.

breadfruit Tropical fruit of a tree belonging to the MULBERRY FAMILY. *Artocarpus communis* provides a staple food of the S. Pacific. Its brownish-green, roundish ripe fruits have a white fibrous pulp. Cultivated in the Malay Archipelago (where it is thought to be indigenous) since remote antiquity, the breadfruit spread throughout the tropical S. Pacific in prehistoric times. It is high in starch and is seldom eaten raw. In the South Seas cloth is made from the inner bark, the wood is used for canoes and furniture, and glue and caulking material are obtained from the milky juice.

breakbone fever See DENGUE FEVER

breast cancer TUMOR in a breast, usually in women after menopause. Risk factors include family history of breast cancer, prolonged menstruation, late first pregnancy (after age 30), obesity, alcohol use, and some benign tumors. Any lump in the breast needs investigation because it may be cancer. Treatment may begin with MASTECTOMY, followed

by RADIATION THERAPY, CHEMOTHERAPY, or removal of the ovaries or adrenal glands.

breathing See RESPIRATION

Brébeuf \brä-'bœf\, **St. Jean de** (1593–1649) French Jesuit missionary to NEW FRANCE, patron saint of Canada. He arrived in 1625 to work as a missionary among the HURON. Forced out by the English in 1629, he returned to "Huronia" in 1634 to live and work for 15 years. In 1648 the Iroquois began their war against the Huron, and in 1649 they captured Brébeuf and tortured him to death. His writings include historical narratives and a Huron grammar.

breccia \'bre-chə\ Coarse sedimentary rock consisting of angular fragments larger than 0.08 in. (2 mm). Breccia commonly results from landslides or geologic faulting, in which rocks are fractured. It can also be of igneous explosive origin (e.g., volcanic breccia).

Brecht \'brekt\, **Bertolt** (*orig.* Eugen Berthold Friedrich) (1898–1956) German play-wright and poet. His first plays, including *Baal* (1922), were followed by *A Man's a Man* (1926), as well as a considerable body of poetry. With Kurt WEILL he wrote the satirical musicals *The Threepenny Opera* (1928; film, 1931), which gained him a wide audience, and *The Rise and Fall of the City of Mahagonny* (1930), and the dance-drama *The Seven Deadly Sins* (1933). In these years he became a Marxist and developed his theory of "epic theater," which sought to reduce the audience's emotional involvement and thereby ensure its rational

Bertolt Brecht, 1931

grasp of the play's message. With the rise of the Nazis he went into exile, first in Scandinavia (1933–41), then in the U.S., where he wrote such plays as *Mother Courage and Her Children* (1941), *The Good Woman of Sichuan* (1943), and *The Caucasian Chalk Circle* (1948). Harassed for his politics, he returned to E. Germany in 1949, where he established the Berliner Ensemble theater troupe and staged his own plays, including *The Resistible Rise of Arturo Ui* (1957).

Breckinridge, John C(abell) (1821–1875) U.S. vice president (1857–61) and Confederate army officer. Born near Lexington, Ky., he served in the U.S. House of Representatives (1851–55) and in 1856 was elected vice president under James BUCHANAN. In 1860 the Democratic Party split into factions over the slavery issue, and Breckinridge became the Southern wing's nominee for president. After the election of Abraham LINCOLN he worked for compromise, but after the firing on Ft. Sumter he urged Kentucky to secede. As a Confederate general, he took part in the Vicksburg, Wilderness, and Shenandoah Valley campaigns. After the war he fled to England for three years, then returned to Kentucky to resume his law practice.

breeding Application of genetic principles in animal husbandry, agriculture, and horticulture to improve desirable qualities. Ancient agriculturists improved many plants through selective cultivation. Modern plant breeding centers on pollination. Animal breeding consists of choosing the ideal trait (e.g., fine wool, high milk production), selecting the breeding stock, and determining the mating system (e.g., whether mating animals are unrelated, mildly related, or highly inbred).

Brel, Jacques (1929–1978) Belgian-French singer and songwriter. He started singing his songs in public in 1953. Frequently satirical and often implicitly religious, they became hugely popular in Europe. He made a number of films 1967–73. His U.S. reputation was made by the revue *Jacques Brel Is Alive and Well and Living in Paris* (1968).

Bremen City (pop., 1998 est.: 547,000), NW Germany. Located on the WESER RIVER, it was established as a diocese in 787 by CHARLEMAGNE, and was the seat of an archbishopric from 845. In the 10th cent. it became an economic center of N Germany, especially after entering the HANSEATIC LEAGUE in 1358. It joined the GERMAN CONFEDERATION in 1815 and the reconstituted German empire in 1871. After World War II Bremen, with nearby Bremerhaven (pop., 1996 est.: 130,000), became a state of W. Germany and headquarters for many industries.

Brendan, St. (c.A.D. 484–578) Celtic saint and hero of legendary Atlantic voyages. A monk and priest, he was put in charge of the abbey at Ardfert. He later founded monasteries in Ireland and Scotland, notably Clonfert (561). A famous traveler, he voyaged to the Hebrides and perhaps to Wales and Brittany. He was immortalized in *Voyage of Brendan,* an Irish epic that told of his journey to a "Promised Land of Saints."

Brennan, William J(oseph), Jr. (1906–1997) U.S. jurist. Born in Newark, N.J., he rose through the ranks of the New Jersey courts and was named to the U.S. Supreme Court in 1956. He came to be regarded as among the most influential jurists in its history. A liberal constructionist and an articulate defender of the BILL OF RIGHTS, he is perhaps best remembered for his role in a series of obscenity cases, many of which broadened the protection accorded to publishers. In *New York Times Co. vs. Sullivan* (1964), he wrote that even false statements about public officials made without "actual malice" are protected. He also wrote the majority opinion in *BAKER VS. CARR* (1962). He opposed CAPITAL PUNISHMENT and supported abortion rights, AFFIRMATIVE ACTION, and school desegregation. He served until 1990; his decisions numbered more than 1,350.

Brent, Margaret (c.1600–1671?) British-American colonial landowner. She arrived in Maryland in 1638 and obtained a patent for 70 acres, becoming the first woman in the colony to own land; by 1657 she was among its largest landowners. In a border dispute with Virginia in 1646, she organized armed volunteers to support the Maryland colony's governor, Leonard Calvert. On his death in 1647, she became executor of his estate and settled a dispute over back pay for his soldiers that had nearly led to civil war.

Brentano \bren-'tä-nō\, **Clemens** (1778–1842) German poet, novelist, and dramatist. With his brother-in-law Achim von Arnim (1781–1831) he published *Des Knaben Wunderhorn* (1805–8; *The Youth's Magic Horn*), a collection of German folk lyrics (including successful imitations of folk style) that became an important inspiration to lyric poets and composers such as Gustav MAHLER. His fairy-tale collections include *Gockel, Hinkel and Gackeleia* (1838).

Brentano \bren-'tä-nō\, **Franz (Clemens)** (1838–1917) German philosopher. Nephew of Clemens BRENTANO, he was ordained a priest in 1864 but resigned in 1873. To present a systematic psychology that would serve as a science of the soul, he wrote the influential *Psychology from an Empirical Standpoint* (1874). He became the founder of act psychology, or intentionalism, concerned with the mind's "acts" or processes (e.g., perception, judgment, loving, and hating) rather than its contents. He later taught at the Univ. of Vienna and published such works as *The Classification of Psychological Phenomena* (1911).

Brescia \'brä-shä, 'bre-shə\ *ancient* Brixia. City (pop., 1998 est.: 190,000), LOMBARDY region, N Italy. Originally a Celtic stronghold, it was occupied by the Romans around 200 B.C. and became the seat of a Roman colony in 27 B.C. It was devastated by the GOTHS (A.D. 412) and plundered by ATTILA (452). It was a free city 936–1426. It passed to Venice, France, and Austria, then finally Italy in 1860. Its art treasures include works by painters of the 15th- and 16th-cent. Brescia school.

Breslau See WROCLAW

Bresson, Henri Cartier- See Henri CARTIER-BRESSON

Bresson \brə-'sōⁿ\, **Robert** (1901–1999) French film director. He worked as a painter before making his first film in 1934. *Les anges du péché* (1943) established his austere, intellectual style. Noted for his subordination of plot to visual imagery, he also directed *The Diary of a Country Priest* (1950), *A Man Escaped* (1956), *Pickpocket* (1959), and *Balthazar* (1966).

Brétigny \brā-tēn-'yē\, **Treaty of** (1360) Treaty between England and France that ended the first phase of the HUNDRED YEARS' WAR. The treaty was signed after EDWARD

THE BLACK PRINCE defeated and captured John II of France at the Battle of POITIERS (1356). The French ceded extensive territories in NW France to England and agreed to ransom John for 3 million gold crowns, while Edward renounced his claim to the French throne.

Breton \brə-'tōⁿ\, **André** (1896–1966) French writer, critic, and editor. In 1919 he helped found the DADA magazine *Littérature.* Influenced by psychiatry and the SYMBOLIST MOVEMENT, he wrote poetry using the automatic-writing technique. In 1924 he wrote a manifesto for SURREALISM and became its chief promoter. In 1938 he founded the Fédération de l'Art Revolutionnaire Independant with Leon TROTSKY in Mexico. His *Poèmes* appeared in 1948. He also wrote essays, criticism, and novels, including *Nadja* (1928).

Breuer \'broi-ər\, **Marcel (Lajos)** (1902–1981) Hungarian-U.S. architect and designer. He studied and then taught at the BAUHAUS (1920–28), where he invented the famous tubular steel chair (1925). He moved to Cambridge, Mass., in 1937 to teach and practice with Walter GROPIUS. Their synthesis of Bauhaus internationalism with New England wood-frame building greatly influenced U.S. domestic architecture. His commissions include UNESCO's Paris headquarters (1953–58) and the Whitney Museum of American Art (1966).

Brewster, William (1567–1644) British-American Puritan leader of PLYMOUTH Colony. He studied briefly at Cambridge Univ. and became leader of a small Puritan congregation that was forced to emigrate to Holland in 1608, where Brewster printed religious books. In 1620 he joined the first group of Pilgrims aboard the *Mayflower* on the voyage to N. America. At Plymouth, Brewster became the senior elder of the colony, serving as its religious leader and as an adviser to Gov. William BRADFORD.

Breyer \'brī-ər\, **Stephen (Gerald)** (b.1938) U.S. jurist. Born in San Francisco, he taught at Harvard Law School 1967–81. He served as chief counsel (1979–81) to the U.S. Senate Judiciary Committee before being appointed to the First U.S. Court of Appeals (1980); he became chief judge in 1990. He was nominated to the U.S. Supreme Court in 1994 and has usually joined the Court's moderate wing.

Brezhnev \'brezh-ˌnef\, **Leonid (Ilich)** (1906–1982) Soviet leader. An engineer, he directed a technical school in the Ukraine before becoming regional party secretary in 1939. In World War II he rose to major general in the Red Army (1943). In the 1950s he supported Nikita KHRUSHCHEV and became a member of the Politburo. After collaborating in Khrushchev's ouster (1964), Brezhnev emerged as general secretary of the party (1966–82). He developed the Brezhnev Doctrine, which asserted the right of Soviet intervention in such WARSAW PACT countries as Czechoslovakia (1968). In the 1970s he sought normalization of relations with the West and

Leonid Brezhnev

DÉTENTE with the U.S. He was made marshal of the Soviet Union in 1976 and chairman of the Presidium of the Supreme Soviet in 1977, becoming the first to hold the leadership of both the party and the state. He greatly expanded the Soviet Union's military-industrial complex, but deprived the rest of the Soviet economy.

Brian Boru \'brēn-bə-'rü\ (941–1014) High king of Ireland (1002–14). He became king of Munster in 976, won control of the S half of Ireland from the high king in 997, and replaced him in 1002. Leinster and the Norsemen of Dublin united against him in 1013; at the Battle of Clontarf, won by his son Murchad, Brian was killed in his tent by fleeing Norsemen (see VIKINGS). A line of princes, the O'Briens, descended from him.

Briand \brē-ˈäⁿ\, **Aristide** (1862–1932) French statesman. He became secretary-general of the FRENCH SOCIALIST PARTY in 1901 and served in the Chamber of Deputies 1902–32. Between 1909 and 1929 he served 11 times as premier of France, and he held 26 ministerial posts between 1906 and 1932. His achievements included the Pact of Locarno (1925), fixing the boundaries of Western Europe, and the Kellogg-Briand Pact (1928), committing its signers not to use war as an instrument of national policy. He shared the 1926 Nobel Peace Prize with Gustav STRESEMANN.

bribery Crime of giving a benefit (e.g., money) in order to influence the judgment or conduct of a person in a position of trust (e.g., an official or witness). Accepting a bribe also constitutes a crime. Bribery is typically punishable as a FELONY. In any charge of bribery, some element of "corrupt purpose" must be implied or proved; a gift is not a bribe unless it is intended to influence the recipient's official behavior. See also EXTORTION.

Brice, Fanny *orig.* Fannie Borach (1891–1951) U.S. comedian and singer. Born in New York City, she played in vaudeville and burlesque shows, where Florenz ZIEGFELD discovered her in 1910. She became a headliner in his *Follies* with her musical numbers and comedy routines, including satiric sketches of ballet dancers as well as affecting torch songs such as "My Man." The character of Baby Snooks, an incorrigible little girl, became the basis of a popular radio series (1938–51). The musical *Funny Girl* (1964) was based on her life.

brick Small building unit in the form of a rectangular block, first produced in a sun-dried form at least 6,000 years ago. Clay, the basic ingredient, is mined from open pits, formed, and then fired in a kiln to produce strength, hardness, and heat resistance. Brick was used in the ancient Near East, in ancient Rome, and in Western Europe especially for the protection it offered against fire. See also MASONRY, MORTAR.

bridewealth Payment made by the groom or his kin to the kin of the wife in order to ratify the marriage. The practice, common worldwide but perhaps most prevalent in Africa, is part of a long series of exchanges between the two intermarrying families. It represents a pledge that the wife will be well treated, and serves as compensation for her family's loss. Payment may consist of goods or, less frequently, services. See also DOWRY.

bridge Structure that spans horizontally to allow pedestrians and vehicles to cross a void. The simplest bridge is the beam (or girder) bridge, consisting of straight, rigid beams placed across a span. Ancient Roman bridges are famous for their rounded arch form, which permitted spans much longer than those of stone beams. A modification of the arch bridge was the drawbridge, developed during medieval times. The lift bridge, another movable type, can change position to allow clearance for ships and boats. Suspension bridges are capable of spanning great distances; their main support members are massive cables supported by two towers and anchored at each end, and the roadway is supported by vertical cables hung from the main cables. Other bridges include the truss bridge, popular (e.g., for railroad bridges) because it uses a relatively small amount of material to carry large loads, and the cantilever bridge, typically three spans, the outer spans anchored at the shore and the central span resting on the cantilevered arms.

bridge Any of various card games for four players in two partnerships. All 52 cards are dealt face downward. The object is to win tricks, or hands consisting of one card from each player in rotation. The players must, if able, contribute a card of the suit led, and the trick is won by the highest card. Before play begins, a suit may be designated the trump suit, in which case any card in it beats any card of the other suits. In contract bridge, overtricks (i.e., tricks made in excess of the bid) do not count toward game or slam (single-hand) bonuses; in auction bridge, such tricks are scored toward the game.

Bridger, Jim (*orig.* James) (1804–1881) U.S. frontiersman. Born in Richmond, Va., he grew up in Illinois. From 1822 he led fur-trapping expeditions to Utah and Idaho, and was apparently the first white man to visit the Great Salt Lake (1824). In 1843 he established Ft. Bridger, Wyo., as a fur-trading post on the Oregon Trail. After the 1850s, working as a government scout, he became legendary for his knowledge of the territory and its Indian inhabitants.

Bridges, Calvin Blackman (1889–1938) U.S. geneticist. Born in Schuyler Falls, N.Y., he assisted T. H. MORGAN in designing experiments using drosophila that showed that variations in the insect could be traced to observable changes in its genes. These experiments led to the construction of gene maps and proved the CHROMOSOME theory of heredity.

Bridges, Harry (*orig.* Alfred Bryant Renton) (1901–1990) Australian-U.S. labor leader. He arrived in the U.S. as a seaman in 1920, and soon became active in the San Francisco branch of the International Longshoremen's Assn. (ILA). In 1937 he led the Pacific Coast division out of the ILA and reconstituted it as the International Longshoremen's and Warehousemen's Union (ILWU), affiliated with the CIO (see AFL-CIO). His aggressive labor tactics and Communist Party connections led the CIO to expel the ILWU in 1950. He retired as its president in 1977.

Bridget, St. (1303?–1373) Mystic and patron saint of Sweden. She had religious visions from an early age but married and had eight children, including St. Catherine of Sweden (1331/32–1381). On the death of her husband (1344), she retired to a life of prayer. She lived in Rome after 1350, striving to bring the pope back from Avignon. In response to a revelation, she founded a new religious order, the Bridgettines.

Bridgetown Capital (pop., 1990: 6,000) of BARBADOS, W. Indies. Located on Carlisle Bay, it is the island's only port of entry. Founded in 1628, it was originally called Indian

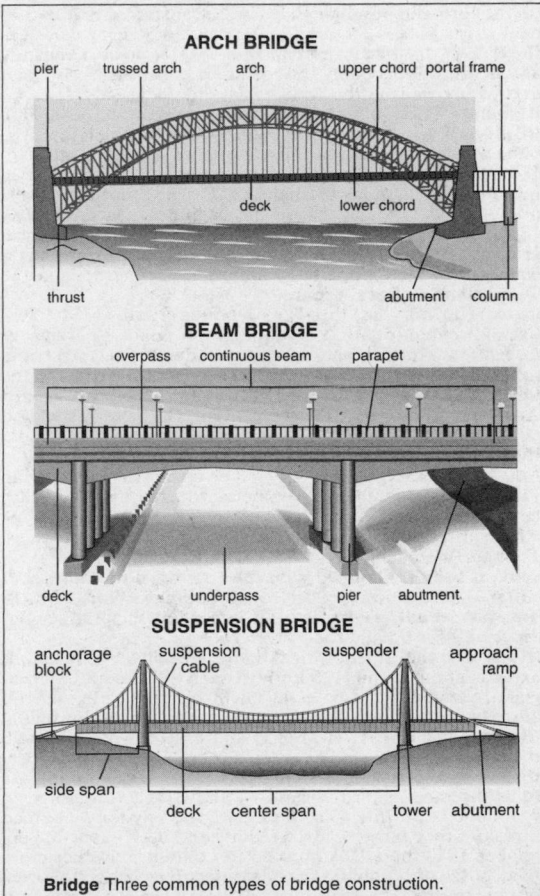

ARCH BRIDGE

pier · trussed arch · arch · upper chord · portal frame

deck · lower chord

thrust · abutment · column

BEAM BRIDGE

overpass · continuous beam · parapet

deck · underpass · pier · abutment

SUSPENSION BRIDGE

anchorage block · suspension cable · suspender · approach ramp

side span

deck · center span · tower · abutment

Bridge Three common types of bridge construction.

Bridge, and later St. Michael's Town. It was ravaged repeatedly by fires, and in 1854 a cholera epidemic killed some 20,000 people. Landmarks include St. Michael's Anglican Cathedral, built of coral rock. Economic mainstays include sugar refining, rum distilling, and tourism.

brier HEATH (*Erica arborea*), also called white heath or tree heath, found in S France and the Mediterranean region. Its roots and knotted stems are used for making briarwood tobacco pipes. Its leaves are needlelike and its flowers almost white. The term brier also applies generally to any plant (as of the genera *Rosa, Rubus,* and *Smilax*) with a woody and thorny or prickly stem.

Brighton Town (pop., 1995 est.: 143,000), S England. Lying on the ENGLISH CHANNEL south of London, it gained popularity in the late 18th cent. when the Prince of Wales (later GEORGE IV) visited and exercised his patronage to improve the town with distinguished Regency style squares. Victorian Brighton grew rapidly with the opening of the railway connecting it to London (1841).

Bright's disease Type of NEPHRITIS without pus formation or edema. The acute stage involves inflammation and back pain, deficient KIDNEY function, swelling, and HYPERTENSION. In the subacute stage, the kidney enlarges, blood does not reach its surface and red blood cells are damaged (leading to anemia), and its tissue breaks down. In the chronic stage, a small, shriveled, scarred kidney cannot function properly, causing UREMIA. Treatment focuses on symptom relief.

Brigit \'bri-jət\ In CELTIC RELIGION, the goddess of poetry, crafts, prophecy, and divination. She was equivalent to the Roman MINERVA and the Greek ATHENA. In Ireland she was worshiped by the *filid,* a poetic and priestly class. Some of the lore surrounding Brigit was transferred to the 5th-cent. Irish abbess St. Brigid. Her feast day, February 1, is the date of the pagan festival Imbolc. Her great monastery at Kildare was probably founded on a pagan sanctuary, and many holy wells in the British Isles are dedicated to her.

Brisbane \'briz-‚bān\ City (pop., 1998 est.: 848,000), QUEENSLAND, Australia. Lying on the N bank of the Brisbane River, the site was first explored by the English in 1823. Founded as a penal colony, in 1824, it was named in honor of Sir Thomas Brisbane (1773–1860), former governor of New S. Wales. Made the capital of Queensland in 1859, it was joined with S. Brisbane in the 1920s to form greater Brisbane. The city is the hub of rail lines and highways and a busy port. It is home to a university and the Queensland Cultural Centre.

Brissot (de Warville) \brē-'sō\, **Jacques-Pierre** (1754–1793) French revolutionary. He founded the popular newspaper *Le Patriote Français* and became a leader of the GIRONDINS (often called Brissotins) in the FRENCH REVOLUTION. In the Legislative Assembly (from 1791) he advocated war against Austria to consolidate the Revolution. He was arrested and guillotined during the REIGN OF TERROR.

Bristol City (pop., 1999 est.: 400,000), SW England, near the BRISTOL CHANNEL. The city received its first charter in 1155. Long a center of commerce, during the 17th–18th cent. it prospered on the triangular slave trade between W. Africa and the W. Indian and American plantation colonies. Though Bristol suffered a decline in trade in the early 19th cent., it soon rebounded with the coming of the railway. It suffered severe destruction from bombing in World War II, but was rebuilt. Today it is an important shipping center, especially for oil and food products.

Bristol Channel Inlet of the Atlantic Ocean, SW England. It extends about 85 mi (135 km) between S Wales and SW England, ranging from 5 to 43 mi (8–69 km) wide, and includes Lundy Island, once a pirate stronghold. Ships bound to or from BRISTOL, SWANSEA, and CARDIFF pass through the channel.

Britain, Battle of (June 1940–Apr. 1941) Series of intense raids directed against Britain by the German air force in WORLD WAR II. Intended to prepare the way for a German invasion, they targeted British ports and RAF bases. In September 1940 the attacks turned to London and other cities in a "blitz" of bombings for 57 consecutive nights, followed by intermittent raids until April 1941. The RAF was outnumbered but succeeded in blocking the German air force through superior tactics, advanced air defenses, and the penetration of German secret codes.

British Broadcasting Corp. See BBC

British Columbia Province (pop., 2000: 4,063,000), W Canada. It is bounded by Yukon Territory, Northwest Territories, Alberta, the Pacific Ocean, and the U.S. (including Alaska); its capital is VICTORIA. The area was inhabited by indigenous peoples, including Coast Salish, Nootka, KWAKIUTL, and HAIDA. It was visited in 1578 by Sir Francis DRAKE and in 1778 by Capt. James COOK, who was searching for the NORTHWEST PASSAGE. Capt. George Vancouver (1758–1798) surveyed the coast (1792–94), and overland expeditions were made by several explorers, including Alexander MACKENZIE, Meriwether LEWIS and William CLARK, and Simon FRASER. The British and Americans contended over VANCOUVER ISLAND for years, until it was recognized as British and made a crown colony in 1849. The mainland became the Colony of British Columbia in 1858; with the colony of Vancouver, it joined Canada in 1871 as the province of British Columbia. The province now has a prosperous economy based on diverse sources, such as logging, mining, agriculture, and shipping.

British East Africa Territory under former British control, Africa. British penetration of the area began at ZANZIBAR in the late 19th cent. In 1888 the British E. Africa Co. established claims in what is now Kenya. British protectorates were established over Zanzibar and Buganda (see UGANDA). In 1919 Britain was awarded Tanganyika as a League of Nations mandate. All achieved political independence in the 1960s.

British empire Worldwide system of dependencies—colonies, protectorates, and other territories—that over a span of three centuries came under the British government. Territorial acquisition began in the early 17th cent. with a group of settlements in N. America and W. Indian, E. Indian, and African trading posts founded by private individuals and trading companies. In the 18th cent. the British took GIBRALTAR, established colonies along the Atlantic seacoast, and began to add territory in India. With its victory in the FRENCH AND INDIAN WAR (1763), it secured Canada and the E Mississippi Valley and gained supremacy in India. From the late 18th cent. it began to build power in Malaya and acquired the Cape of Good Hope, Ceylon (see SRI LANKA), and MALTA. The English settled Australia in 1788, and subsequently New Zealand. ADEN was secured in 1839, and HONG KONG in 1842. Britain went on to control the SUEZ CANAL 1875–1956. In the 19th-cent. European partition of Africa, Britain acquired Nigeria, Egypt, the territories that would become BRITISH E. AFRICA, and part of what would become the Union (later Republic) of S. Africa. After World War I, Britain secured mandates to German E. Africa, part of the Cameroons, part of Togo, German South-West Africa, MESOPOTAMIA, PALESTINE, and part of the German Pacific islands. Prior to 1783, Britain claimed full authority over colonial legislatures; after the U.S. gained independence, Britain gradually evolved a system of self-government for some colonies, as set forth in Lord Durham's report of 1839. Dominion status was given to Canada (1867), Australia (1901), New Zealand (1907), the Union of S. Africa (1910), and the Irish Free State (1921). Britain declared war on Germany in 1914 on behalf of the entire empire; after World War I the dominions signed the peace treaties themselves and joined the LEAGUE OF NATIONS as independent states. In 1931 the Statute of WESTMINSTER recognized them as independent countries "within the British empire," referring to the "British Commonwealth of Nations." After World War II, with "British" no longer officially used, the COMMONWEALTH came to include over 50 countries.

British Guiana See GUYANA

British Honduras See BELIZE

British Library National library of Great Britain, established in 1973. It combines the old BRITISH MUSEUM library, National Central Library, National Lending Library for Science and Technology, and British National Bibliography. The British Museum library, founded in 1753 based on earlier collections and later augmented from royal libraries, had the right to a free copy of all books published in the

United Kingdom. Its collection included a rich series of documents ranging from the 3rd cent. B.C. to modern times.

British Museum Britain's national museum of archaeology and antiquities, established in London in 1753 when the government purchased three large private collections consisting of books, manuscripts, prints, drawings, paintings, medals, coins, and natural curiosities. In 1881 the natural-history collections were transferred to another building to form the Natural History Museum, and in 1973 the library collections were consolidated to form the BRITISH LIBRARY. Among the museum's most famous holdings are the ELGIN MARBLES and the ROSETTA STONE. The department of prints and drawings, opened in 1808, is now one of the world's largest collections.

British North America Act (1867) Act of the British Parliament by which three British colonies—Nova Scotia, New Brunswick, and Canada—were united as "one Dominion under the name of Canada." The act also renamed the regions CANADA EAST and CANADA WEST as the provinces of Quebec and Ontario. It served as Canada's "constitution" until 1982, when it became the basis of the CANADA ACT.

British Petroleum Co. PLC (BP) British petrochemical corporation. Formed in 1909 as the Anglo-Persian Oil Co., Ltd., it became one of the largest oil companies in the world, with oil fields and refineries in Alaska and the North Sea. The British government was for many years BP's largest single stockholder, but by the late 1980s it had turned over the company to private ownership. In 1987 BP consolidated its U.S. interests by acquiring the STANDARD OIL CO. In 1998 it merged with Amoco (formerly Standard Oil of Indiana) to form BP-Amoco. In addition to oil and natural gas, it produces chemicals, plastics, and synthetic fibers.

British Virgin Islands See British VIRGIN ISLANDS

Brittany *French* **Rretagne** \'brə-'tàn^y\ Historical peninsular region, NW France. Known in ancient times as Armorica, it comprised the coastal area between the SEINE and LOIRE rivers. Inhabited by Cymric Celts, it was conquered by Julius CAESAR. Invaded in the 5th cent. A.D. by Britons (Celts from Britain), the extreme NW part was thereafter called Brittany. Subdued by CLOVIS I, it remained a separate state until the 15th cent. It was incorporated into France in 1532 and had province status until the FRENCH REVOLUTION.

Britten, (Edward) Benjamin *later* Baron Britten of Aldeburgh (1913–1976) British composer. At the Royal College of Music he met the tenor Peter Pears (1910–1986), who would become his lifelong companion. His auspicious *Variations on a Theme of Frank Bridge* (1937) was followed by his *Sinfonia da Requiem* (1940) and *Serenade* (1943). In 1945 *Peter Grimes* established him as a leading opera composer. In 1948 he cofounded the Aldeburgh Festival in the small town where he had settled; for the rest of his life his energies would principally be directed toward the festival, for which

Benjamin Britten, 1960

he often conducted and performed as pianist. His operas include *The Rape of Lucretia* (1946), *Albert Herring* (1947), *Billy Budd* (1951), and *The Turn of the Screw* (1954). His vocal works include *A Ceremony of Carols* (1942), *Spring Symphony* (1949), and the acclaimed *War Requiem* (1961). In 1976 he became the first British composer in history to be ennobled, and he is generally regarded as Britain's greatest composer since William BYRD and Henry PURCELL.

Brno \'bər-nō\ *German* **Brünn** \'brēēn\ City (pop., 1998: 385,000), SE Czech Republic. Located southeast of PRAGUE, it lies in an area that shows evidence of prehistoric habitation and traces of Celtic and SLAV settlements in the 5th–6th cent. A.D. German colonization led to city status in 1243. In

various wars it was besieged by the Swedes, Prussians, and French in the 15th–19th cent. Before World War I it was the capital of MORAVIA. The inhabitants, formerly German, are now mainly Czech. Gregor MENDEL worked on his theory of heredity (1865) in the monastery at Brno.

broadband Term describing the RADIATION from a source that produces a broad, continuous SPECTRUM of FREQUENCIES (unlike a LASER, which produces a single frequency or very narrow range of frequencies). A typical broadband-light source that can be used for either emission or absorption SPECTROSCOPY is a metal filament heated to a high temperature, such as a tungsten lightbulb. Sunlight is also broadband radiation. See also BROADBAND TECHNOLOGY.

broadband technology Telecommunications technology that allows communication over a wide band of frequencies, and especially over frequencies divided into several independent channels for the simultaneous transmission of different signals. Broadband systems allow voice, data, and video to be broadcast over the same medium at the same time, or multiple data channels to be broadcast simultaneously.

broadcasting Transmission of sound or images by radio or television. The first U.S. commercial radio station, KDKA of Pittsburgh, began operation in 1920. The number of stations increased rapidly, as did the formation of national radio networks. To avoid radio monopolies, Congress created the FEDERAL COMMUNICATIONS COMMISSION (1927) to oversee broadcast operations. In the 1930s and '40s, the "golden age of radio," radio became the most popular entertainment medium. Television broadcasting began in Germany and Britain in the 1930s. After World War II, the U.S. took the lead, and television soon overshadowed radio. Color television broadcasts began in 1954. By the 1980s, satellite transmission had further expanded the field of broadcasting. See also ABC, BBC, CBS, CNN, NBC, PBS.

broad jump See LONG JUMP

Broadway Theater district in New York City, named for the diagonal avenue in Manhattan where most of the larger theaters are located. Broadway attracted theater producers and impresarios from the mid-19th cent., and by the 1890s the brightly lighted street was called "the Great White Way." By 1925, the height of theatrical activity in New York, about 80 theaters were located on or near Broadway; by 1980 only about 40 remained. In the 1990s the revitalization of the seedy Times Square neighborhood attracted larger audiences, though big musicals continued to supplant more serious works. See also OFF-BROADWAY.

Broca \'brō-kə\, **Paul** (1824–1880) French surgeon. His study of brain lesions contributed significantly to understanding of the origins of APHASIA. Much of Broca's research concerned the comparative study of the skulls of the races of humankind, work that aided the development of modern physical anthropology. His discovery (1861) of the brain's speech center (convolution of Broca) was the first anatomical proof of localization of brain function.

brocade Woven fabric having a raised floral or figured design that is introduced during the weaving process. The design is usually made in a SATIN or twill weave; the background may be twill, satin, or plain weave. The rich, fairly heavy fabric is frequently used for evening dresses, draperies, and upholstery.

broccoli Plant (*Brassica oleracea* 'italica') in the MUSTARD FAMILY. A fast-growing annual plant, it bears dense green clusters of edible flower buds. Native to the E Mediterranean and Asia Minor, it was introduced to the U.S. probably in colonial times. Broccoli thrives in moderate to cool climates. It is one of the most broadly nutritious of all common vegetables. See also BRASSICA.

Brocken Highest point, HARZ MTNS., central Germany. Its granite peak reaches 3,747 ft (1,142 m). When the sun is low, shadows from the peak cast gigantic silhouettes on low-lying clouds or fog below the mountain. This effect, known as the Brocken bow or Brocken specter, has mystical significance in the mountain's folklore. Traditional rites enacted there on WALPURGIS NIGHT became connected with the legend of FAUST.

Brodsky, Joseph *orig.* Iosip Aleksandrovich Brodsky (1940–1996) Russian-U.S. poet. His independence and irregular work record led to a five-year sentence to hard labor. Exiled in 1972, he settled in New York. He was poet laureate of the U.S. 1991–92. His lyric and elegiac poems ponder the universal concerns of life and death. His collections include *A Part of Speech* (1980) and *To Urania* (1988). He was awarded the Nobel Prize in 1987.

Broglie \'broi\, **Louis-Victor (-Pierre-Raymond), duc (Duke) de** (1892–1987) French physicist. Descended from a distinguished family, in his doctoral thesis he described his theory of electron waves, then extended the WAVE-PARTICLE DUALITY theory of light to matter. He is noted both for his discovery of the wave nature of electrons and for his research on quantum theory. Einstein built on de Broglie's idea of "matter-waves"; based on this work, Erwin SCHRÖDINGER constructed the system of wave mechanics. He was awarded a Nobel Prize in 1929.

bromegrass Any of about 100 annual and perennial species of weeds and forage GRASSES that make up the genus *Bromus*, in the family Gramineae (Poaceae). They are found in temperate and cool climates. More than 40 species are found in the U.S.; about half are native grasses. Rescue grass (*B. catharticus*), a forage and pasture grass, and smooth brome (*B. inermis*), a forage plant and soil binder, are the economically important species. Downy brome or cheatgrass (*B. tectorum*), ripgut grass (*B. diandrus*), and foxtail brome (*B. rubens*) have spines that make them dangerous to grazing animals.

bromeliad \brō-'mē-lē-,ad\ Any of the flowering plants of the order Bromeliales, containing a single family, Bromeliaceae, with almost 2,600 species. Most are native to the tropical New World. Bromeliad flowers have three parts like lilies, but with contrasting sepals and petals. Many bromeliads are short-stemmed EPIPHYTES. Many species bear flowers in a long spike, with colored BRACTS below or along the spike. Most have fleshy fruit, but some produce dry pods. SPANISH MOSS and the PINEAPPLE are the major economic products of the family. The leaves of some species contain fibers that are made into rope, fabric, and netting. Some species are cultivated indoors as ornamentals for their colorful flowers and foliage.

bromine \'brō-,mēn\ Nonmetallic chemical ELEMENT, chemical symbol Br, atomic number 35. It is one of the HALOGENS, a deep red, fuming liquid at ordinary temperatures, and does not occur free in nature. It is obtained from seawater and brines or salt beds. Extremely irritating and toxic, bromine is a strong oxidizing agent (see OXIDATION-REDUCTION). Its compounds (VALENCE 1, 3, 5, or 7) have many uses, including as petroleum additives (ethylene dibromide), in photographic emulsions (silver bromide), as sedatives, and in flour (potassium bromate).

bronchitis \brän-'kī-təs\ INFLAMMATION in the bronchi of the LUNGS. Microbes and foreign matter in air stimulate secretion of bronchial mucus, motion of cilia (see CILIUM) to move the foreign material up and out, and coughing; these normal responses can irritate the bronchi and can cause inflammation, particularly if the person has other lung-damaging conditions. A cold, infection, or injury may lead to acute bronchitis; long-term repetitive injury, as from SMOKING, may lead to chronic bronchitis. Untreated acute bronchitis may become chronic bronchitis, in which severe, irreversible damage leaves the lungs open to infection, fibrosis, EMPHYSEMA, PULMONARY HEART DISEASE, and PNEUMONIA. Treatment includes drugs to dilate the bronchi and promote coughing, prevention of infection, and lifestyle adaptations (e.g., quitting smoking).

Brontë family \'brän-tē\ Family of English writers. They were reared by their father, a clergyman, in Haworth on the Yorkshire moors. Charlotte Brontë (1816–1855) served as a governess and,

Charlotte Brontë Drawing by George Richmond, 1850

with her sister Emily, made an unsuccessful attempt to open a school. Charlotte's novel *Jane Eyre* (1847), a powerful story of a woman in conflict with her natural desires and social situation, brought a new truthfulness to Victorian fiction and was an immediate success. It was followed by the novels *Shirley* (1849) and *Villette* (1853). She died at 38. Emily (Jane) Brontë (1818–1848) was perhaps the greatest writer of the three. *Poems by Currer, Ellis and Acton Bell* (1846), published jointly by the sisters, contained 21 of her poems, which reveal poetic genius. Her one novel, *Wuthering Heights* (1847), a highly imaginative story of passion and hatred set on the Yorkshire moors, is now considered one of the finest English novels. Soon after its publication, her health began to fail, and she died at 30. Anne Brontë (1820–1849) wrote two novels, *Agnes Grey* (1847) and *The Tenant of Wildfell Hall* (1848). She died of tuberculosis at 29.

brontosaurus *or* **apatosaurus** \ə-,pa-tə-'sȯr-əs\ Giant herbivorous DINOSAUR (genus *Apatosaurus*), one of the largest land animals of all time. Found in Late Jurassic deposits of N. America and Europe (163–144 million years ago), it weighed as much as 30 tons and was as long as 70 ft (21 m), including the very long neck and tail. Until 1978 the head was depicted as massive and snub-nosed, with spoonlike teeth; scientists now believe brontosaurs had a slender, elongated skull and long, peglike teeth.

Bronx Borough (pop., 2000: 1,285,000), NEW YORK CITY. One of New York's five boroughs, it is connected to MANHATTAN by a dozen bridges and railroad tunnels, and to QUEENS by the Triborough, Bronx-Whitestone, and Throgs Neck bridges. Indians sold it to the Dutch W. India Co. in 1639. The borough was a part of Westchester Co. until 1898. Though it is primarily residential, much of its 80 mi (130 km) of waterfront is used for shipping, warehouses, and industry. It is home to baseball's Yankee Stadium. Its extensive park system includes the BRONX ZOO and the New York Botanical Gardens.

Bronx Zoo *formally* **New York Zoological Park** ZOO in New York City. It opened in 1899 on 265 acres (107 hectares) in the Bronx. In 1941 it added the 4-acre (1.6-hectare) African Plains, which features large groups of animals in natural surroundings. The zoo also includes the World of Darkness (the world's first major exhibit of nocturnal animals, the World of Birds (a huge, indoor free-flight exhibit), the Rare Animal Range (near-extinct species in natural settings), a Children's Zoo, Wild Asia (Asian mammals and birds), and the Congo Gorilla Forest. It supports much research and oversees the Wildlife Survival Center on St. Catherine's Island, Georgia.

bronze ALLOY traditionally composed of COPPER and TIN. Bronze was first made before 3000 B.C. (see BRONZE AGE) and is still widely used, though iron often replaced bronze in tools and weapons after about 1000 B.C. because of its abundance. Bronze is harder than copper, more readily melted, and easier to cast. It is also harder than iron and far more resistant to corrosion. Bell metal (which produces pleasing sounds when struck) is bronze with 20–25% tin content. Statuary bronze, with less than 10% tin and an admixture of zinc and lead, is technically a BRASS. The addition of less than 1% phosphorus improves the hardness and strength of bronze; that formulation is used for pump plungers, valves, and bushings. Manganese bronzes have little or no tin but considerable zinc and up to 4.5% manganese. Aluminum bronzes, containing up to 16% aluminum, are especially strong and corrosion-resistant and are used for pipe fittings, pumps, gears, ship propellers, and turbine blades. Most "copper" coins are actually bronze.

Bronze Age Period of ancient human culture. It followed the PALEOLITHIC and NEOLITHIC PERIODS and preceded the IRON AGE. The Bronze Age was the first period in which metal was used. The date at which the age began varied by region; in Greece and China it began before 3000 B.C., in Britain not until about 1900 B.C. The beginning of the period is sometimes called the Chalcolithic (Copper-Stone) Age, referring to the initial use of pure copper (along with its predecessor, stone). Only in the 2nd millennium B.C. did true BRONZE come to be widely used. The age was marked by increased specialization and the invention of the wheel and the ox-drawn plow. From about 1000 B.C. the ability to heat and forge iron brought the Bronze Age to an end.

Bronzino \brȯn-'dzē-nō\, **Il** *orig.* Agnolo di Cosimo (1503–1572) Italian painter active in Florence. The student and adopted son of Jacopo da PONTORMO, he excelled as a portraitist and was court painter to Cosimo I de' MEDICI for most of his career. His portraits' elegance and decorative qualities embodied the courtly ideal under the Medici dukes. His work influenced European court portraiture for the next century, while his polished, sophisticated religious and mythological paintings epitomized the Mannerist style of his time.

Brook, Peter (Stephen Paul) (*later* **Sir Peter**) (b.1925) British director and producer. As director of the Royal Opera House, COVENT GARDEN (1947–50), he oversaw several new Shakespearean productions that aroused controversy with their innovative approach. Appointed codirector of the ROYAL SHAKESPEARE CO. in 1962, he directed critically acclaimed productions of *King Lear* (1962) and *A Midsummer Night's Dream* (1970). He won international fame with his avant-garde direction of Peter WEISS's *Marat/Sade* (1964). His films include *Lord of the Flies* (1962), *King Lear* (1969), and the six-hour *Mahabharata* (1989).

Brooke, Alan Francis *later* **Viscount Alanbrooke (of Brookeborough)** (1883–1963) British military leader. An expert on gunnery, he began World War II as commander of a corps in France and covered the Dunkirk Evacuation. After serving as commander of the British home forces (1940–41), he was promoted to chief of staff (1941–46). He established good relations with the U.S. forces and exercised a strong influence on Allied strategy. He was promoted to field marshal in 1944.

Brooke, Rupert (1887–1915) English poet. His sonnet sequence *1914* (1915), including the popular "The Soldier," expresses an idealism in the face of death in strong contrast to later poetry from the trenches. His death in World War I contributed to his idealized image in the interwar period.

Brook Farm (Institute of Agriculture and Education) Utopian experiment in communal living in W. Roxbury, Mass. (near Boston), 1841–47, founded by George RIPLEY. The best known of America's 19th-cent. utopian communities, it is remembered for the distinguished figures associated with it, including Charles Dana, Nathaniel HAWTHORNE, Margaret FULLER, Horace GREELEY, J. R. LOWELL, J. G. WHITTIER, and R. W. EMERSON (not all of them actual members), and for the modern educational theory of its excellent school.

Brooklyn Borough (pop., 2000: 2,465,000), NEW YORK CITY. Separated from MANHATTAN by the EAST RIVER, it is bordered to the south by the Atlantic Ocean. Brooklyn is connected to Manhattan by bridges (including the BROOKLYN BRIDGE), a vehicular tunnel, and rapid transit services. Its first settlement was by Dutch farmers in 1636. The Battle of Long Island (1776) was fought in Brooklyn. It became a borough of New York City in 1898. Brooklyn is both residential and industrial, and also handles considerable oceangoing traffic. CONEY ISLAND is located there.

Brooklyn Bridge Suspension bridge built (1869–83) over the East River to link Brooklyn to Manhattan. It was designed by John ROEBLING and his son Washington. A brilliant feat of engineering, the bridge was the first to use steel for cable wire and the first in which explosives were used inside a pneumatic CAISSON during construction. The bridge's main

Brooklyn Bridge

span of 1,595 ft (486 m) was the longest in the world to date. It opened to such fanfare that within 24 hours an estimated quarter-million people crossed over it, using an elevated walkway designed to give pedestrians a dramatic view of the city.

Brooks, Gwendolyn (Elizabeth) (1917–2000) U.S. poet. Born in Topeka, Kan., she was reared in the Chicago slums. With *Annie Allen* (1949), a loosely connected series of poems about growing up in Chicago, she became the first black poet to win the Pulitzer Prize. Her later books include *The Bean Eaters* (1960), *In the Mecca* (1968), *Report from Part One* (1972), *Primer for Blacks* (1980), *Young Poets' Primer* (1981), and *Children Coming Home* (1991).

Brooks, Louise (1906–1985) U.S. film actress. Born in Cherryvale, Kan., she danced in Florenz ZIEGFELD's *Follies* (1925) and soon gained a Hollywood contract. Noted for her magnetic screen presence and dark bobbed hair, she personified the 1920s flapper in the silent films *A Girl in Every Port* (1928) and *Beggars of Life* (1928). In Germany she gave legendary performances in G. W. PABST's *Pandora's Box* (1928) and *Diary of a Lost Girl* (1929). Back in Hollywood (1930), however, she was offered only minor roles, and she retired in 1938.

Brooks, Mel *orig.* Melvin Kaminsky (b.1926) U.S. director, producer, and actor. Born in New York City, he wrote comedy routines for Sid CAESAR's television shows (1949–59), and teamed with Carl Reiner on a series of comedy records. He wrote and directed his first feature film, *The Producers* (1968, Academy Award), which exploded clichés to hilarious effect; he rewrote it as a wildly successful Broadway musical in 2001. He directed, produced, and cowrote (and sometimes acted in) such preposterous film comedies as *Blazing Saddles* (1974), *Young Frankenstein* (1974), *High Anxiety* (1977), *History of the World Part One* (1981), *Spaceballs* (1987), and *Robin Hood: Men in Tights* (1993).

Brooks, Romaine (Goddard) *orig.* Beatrice Romaine Goddard (1874–1970) U.S.-French painter. Born in Rome to wealthy American parents, she studied painting in Italy. After a brief marriage, she moved to Paris in 1905, where she established herself in literary and artistic circles. Her gray-shaded portraits, touched by occasional color, distilled their subjects' personalities to a disturbing degree. *L'Amazone,* Brooks's portrait of her lover Natalie Clifford Barney, is among her finest works.

Brooks, Van Wyck (1886–1963) U.S. literary historian. Born in Plainfield, N.J., he attended Harvard Univ. His *Finders and Makers* series, tracing 19th-cent. American literary history in rich biographical detail and evocative prose, includes *The Flowering of New England, 1815–1865* (1936, Pulitzer Prize); *New England: Indian Summer, 1865–1915* (1940); and *The Confident Years: 1885–1915* (1952).

Brooks Islands See MIDWAY

Brooks Range Mountain range, N Alaska. It extends about 600 mi (1,000 km) from Kotzebue Sound to the Canadian border. Its highest peak is Mt. Isto, at 9,060 ft (2,760 m). Forming the NW end of the ROCKY MTNS., it lies within GATES OF THE ARCTIC NATIONAL PARK. PRUDHOE BAY holds huge reserves of oil.

Brouwer \'brau̇-ər\, **Adriaen** (1605/6–1638) Flemish painter. After studying with Frans HALS, he settled in Antwerp by 1631. His pictures, mostly small and painted on panels, typically depict peasants drinking and brawling in taverns. The coarseness of his subjects was in direct contrast to his delicate technique; his virtuoso brushwork and sparkling tonal values were unsurpassed. Adriaen van OSTADE and David TENIERS were among his many followers.

Browder, Earl (Russell) (1891–1973) U.S. Communist Party leader (1930–44). Born in Wichita, Kan., in 1921 he joined the U.S. Communist Party; he served as its general secretary 1930–44 and was its presidential candidate in 1936 and 1940. In 1944 he was removed from his position for declaring that capitalism and socialism could coexist, and in 1946 he was expelled from the party.

Brown, Capability (*orig.* Lancelot) (1715–1783) British master of naturalistic garden design. He worked for years at Stowe, Buckinghamshire, under William Kent (1685–1748). By 1753 he was the leading "improver of grounds" in En-

B

gland. At BLENHEIM PALACE he almost totally erased the earlier formal scheme. His landscapes consisted of expanses of grass, irregularly shaped bodies of water, and trees placed singly and in clumps. His style opposed that of André LE NÔTRE, designer of the formal VERSAILLES gardens. Brown's nickname arose from his habit of saying that a place had "capabilities."

Brown, Charles Brockden (1771–1810) U.S. writer. Born in Philadelphia, he left the law to become a writer. His gothic novels in American settings began a tradition later adapted by E. A. POE and Nathaniel HAWTHORNE. *Wieland* (1798), his best-known work, shows how easily mental balance is lost when common sense confronts the uncanny. He has been called the "father of the American novel."

Brown, Ford Madox (1821–1893) British painter. While studying in Europe, he came under the influence of the NAZARENES. His use of brilliant color, meticulous handling, and taste for literary subjects had a strong effect on the PRE-RAPHAELITES. His most famous paintings are *The Last of England* (1852–55), a poignant tribute to emigration, and *Work* (1852–63), a Victorian social commentary. In 1861 he became a founding member of William MORRIS's company, for which he designed stained glass and furniture.

Brown, George (1818–1880) Canadian (Scottish-born) journalist and politician. He emigrated to New York in 1837 and moved to Toronto in 1843, where he founded *The Globe* (1844), a reform newspaper. As a member of the Canadian assembly (1857–65), he advocated proportional representation, the confederation of British N. America, and separation of church and state. He was a leader of the CLEAR GRITS movement. In 1873 he was appointed to the Canadian Senate, while continuing to manage his influential newspaper (later *The GLOBE AND MAIL*).

Brown, James (b.1928) U.S. singer and songwriter. Growing up in Georgia during the Depression, Brown sang and danced on street corners for money. He later formed a trio, appearing at small clubs throughout the South. He gradually evolved a highly personal style, combining blues and gospel elements with his own emotionally charged and highly rhythmic delivery. His first hit, "Please, Please, Please" (1956), was followed by other million-selling singles, including "Papa's Got a Brand New Bag"; his distinctive style became known as funk. His checkered personal life was highlighted in 1988 when he received a three-year jail sentence.

Brown, Jim (*orig.* James Nathaniel) (b.1936) U.S. football player, often considered the greatest running back of all time. Born in St. Simons, Ga., in his nine seasons with the Cleveland Browns (1957–65) he set overall rushing and combined yardage records that stood until 1984. He holds the record for highest career rushing average (5.22 yards). He led the NFL in rushing in eight of the nine years he played, a record no one has yet approached. After retiring, Brown became a movie actor.

Brown, John (1800–1859) U.S. abolitionist. Born in Torrington, Conn., he grew up in Ohio. He moved around the country working in various trades, and fathered 20 children. An ardent advocate for overt action to end slavery, he traveled to Kansas in 1855 with his five sons to retaliate against proslavery actions in Lawrence (see BLEEDING KANSAS). In 1858 he proposed to establish a mountain stronghold in Maryland for escaping slaves, to be financed by abolitionists. Hoping that taking the federal arsenal at Harpers Ferry, W.V., would inspire slaves to join his "army of emancipation," in 1859 his small force overpowered the arsenal's guard; after two days it was in turn overpowered by federal forces led by Col. Robert E. LEE. Brown was convicted of treason and hanged. His raid made him a martyr to N abolitionists and heightened sectional animosities that led to the Civil War.

Brown, Joseph (Rogers) (1810–1876) U.S. inventor and manufacturer. Born in Warren, R.I., he perfected and produced a highly accurate linear dividing engine in 1850, and then developed a vernier caliper and also applied vernier methods to the protractor. With Lucian Sharpe he founded the Brown and Sharpe Manufacturing Co. His micrometer caliper appeared in 1867. Perhaps his finest innovation was a universal grinding machine, in which articles were hard-

ened first and then ground, thereby increasing accuracy and eliminating waste.

Brown, Molly *orig.* Margaret Tobin (1867–1932) U.S. social figure. Born in Hannibal, Mo., she followed her brother to Colorado, where she met and married a miner. After he found gold in 1894, they moved to Denver, where she tried unsuccessfully to enter society. Her husband left her, and she traveled to New York and Newport, where her gifts as a raconteur earned her social success. As a passenger on the *Titanic* (1912), she helped command a lifeboat, and was celebrated by the U.S. press as "the Unsinkable Mrs. Brown."

Brown, Robert (1773–1858) Scottish botanist. He studied medicine before entering the British army as an ensign and assistant surgeon (1795). In 1801 he surveyed the coasts of Australia, gathering some 3,900 plant species. He published some of the results of his trip in 1810 in his classic *Prodromus Florae Novae Hollandiae . . .,* laying the foundations of Australian botany and refining prevailing plant classification systems. In 1827 he transferred Joseph BANKS's botanical collection to the British Museum and became keeper of the museum's new botanical department. In 1828 he published his observation of the phenomenon that came to be called BROWNIAN MOTION. In 1831 he noted the existence in plant cells of what he called the NUCLEUS. He was the first to recognize the distinction between GYMNOSPERMS and angiosperms (FLOWERING PLANTS).

Brown, William Wells (1814?–1884) U.S. writer. Born into slavery near Lexington, Ky., he escaped and settled near Boston. He wrote a popular autobiography, *Narrative of William W. Brown, A Fugitive Slave* (1847), and lectured on abolitionism and temperance. *Clotel* (1853), a novel about descendants of Thomas JEFFERSON and a slave, was the first novel ever published by an African-American. His play *The Escape* (1858) is about two slaves who secretly marry.

brown bear Shaggy-haired, characteristically brown species (*Ursus arctos*) of BEAR with numerous races native to Eurasia and to NW N. America. Exceptionally large N. American brown bears are usually called GRIZZLY BEARS. The Siberian brown bear is similar in size to the grizzly. Eurasian brown bears are smaller, usually 48–84 in. (120–210 cm) long and 300–550 lbs (135–250 kg).

brown dwarf Astronomical object intermediate in mass between a PLANET and a STAR. Sometimes described as failed stars, they are believed to form like stars, from interstellar cloud fragments that contract into gravitationally bound objects. However, their mass is too low to produce enough internal heat to trigger NUCLEAR FUSION. They generate some heat and light but cool rapidly and shrink.

Browne, Thomas (*later* **Sir Thomas**) (1605–1682) British physician and author. Practicing medicine and writing were parallel careers. His *Religio Medici* (1642) is a journal of reflections on the mysteries of God, nature, and man. A larger work, commonly known as *Browne's Vulgar Errors* (1646), aimed to correct popular superstitions. He also wrote the beautiful, subtle *Letter to a Friend* (1690).

Brownian motion Any of various physical phenomena in which some quantity is constantly undergoing small, random fluctuations. It was named for Robert BROWN, who in 1827 noticed a "rapid oscillatory motion" of pollen grains suspended in water. He later discovered that similar motions could be seen in smoke or dust particles suspended in air and other FLUIDS. The idea that molecules of a fluid are constantly in motion is a key part of the KINETIC THEORY OF GASES.

Browning, Elizabeth Barrett *orig.* Elizabeth Barrett (1806–1861) British poet. Though a reclusive invalid, she became well known in literary circles for her early volumes of verse (1838, 1844). She met Robert BROWNING in 1845, and after a courtship kept secret from her despotic father, they married and settled in Florence. Her reputation rests chiefly on her *Sonnets from the Portuguese* (1850). Her blank-verse novel *Aurora Leigh* (1857) was a huge popular success.

Browning, Robert (1812–1889) British poet. His early works include the verse drama *Pippa Passes* (1841) and long poems, including *Sordello* (1840). In the years of his marriage (1846–61) to E. B. BROWNING, spent in Italy, he published *Men and Women* (1855), including "Love Among the Ruins," "Fra Lippo Lippi," and "Bishop Blougram's Apology."

Dramatis Personae (1864), including "Rabbi Ben Ezra" and "Caliban upon Setebos," finally won him wide recognition. *The Ring and the Book* (1868–69) is based on a 1698 murder trial in Rome. His use of the dramatic monologue (focused on individual psychology) influenced many modern poets, as did his treatment of a variety of aspects of life in contemporary language.

brown lung disease *or* **byssinosis** \ˌbi-sə-ˈnō-səs\ Respiratory disorder caused by dust from cotton and other fibers, common among textile workers. When inhaled, the dust stimulates HISTAMINE release; air passages constrict, making breathing difficult. Over time the dust accumulates in the lung, producing a typical brown discoloration. Several years of exposure to cotton dust are needed before byssinosis develops. In advanced stages, it causes chronic, irreversible obstructive lung disease. Though cotton is by far the most common cause, flax, hemp, and other organic fibers can also produce byssinosis.

brown recluse spider Venomous species (*Loxosceles reclusa*) of brown SPIDER, most common in the W and S U.S. The brown recluse is light-colored, with a dark violin-shaped design on its back. About 0.25 in. (7 mm) long, it has a leg span of about 1 in. (2.5 cm). It has extended its range into parts of the N U.S. and is often found under stones or in dark corners inside buildings. Its venom destroys the walls of blood vessels near the bite, sometimes causing a skin ulcer; the wound is occasionally fatal.

Brownshirts See SA

Brownsville Affair Racial incident in 1906 involving whites in Brownsville, Texas, and black soldiers stationed at nearby Ft. Brown. On an August night, rifle shots killed one white and wounded another. The mayor accused black soldiers of the crime. Though their white officers stated the soldiers were in their barracks, investigators accepted the mayor's version, and Pres. Theodore ROOSEVELT ordered dishonorable discharges for 167 black soldiers. A 1972 congressional investigation cleared them of guilt.

Brown University Private university in Providence, R.I., a traditional member of the IVY LEAGUE. It was founded in 1764 as Rhode Island College and renamed in 1804 for a benefactor, Nicholas Brown. It became coeducational in 1971 when it merged with Pembroke, a women's college founded in 1891. Research facilities include centers for geological, astronomical, and educational research. Total enrollment is about 7,400.

Brown vs. Board of Education (of Topeka) 1954 case in which the U.S. Supreme Court ruled unanimously that racial SEGREGATION in public schools violated the 14th Amendment to the U.S. Constitution, which says that no state may deny equal protection of the laws to any person within its jurisdiction. The Court declared separate educational facilities to be inherently unequal, thus reversing its 1896 ruling in *PLESSY VS. FERGUSON*. The *Brown* decision was limited to the public schools, but it was believed to imply that segregation is not permissible in other public facilities.

browser SOFTWARE that allows a computer user to find and view information on the INTERNET. The first text-based browser for the WORLD WIDE WEB became available in 1991; Web use expanded rapidly after the release in 1993 of a browser called Mosaic, which had "point-and-click" capability. Web browsers interpret the HTML tags in downloaded documents and display the data according to a set of rules. Netscape Navigator became the dominant Web browser soon after its release in 1994; Microsoft's Internet Explorer was introduced a year later.

Brubeck, Dave (*orig.* David Warren) (b.1920) U.S. jazz pianist and composer. Born in Concord, Cal., Brubeck studied composition with Darius MILHAUD before forming a quartet with saxophonist Paul Desmond in 1951. The recording of Desmond's "Take Five" became the first jazz instrumental to sell over a million copies. Their performances brought many new listeners to jazz, particularly on college campuses during the 1950s and '60s.

Bruce, Blanche K(elso) (1841–1898) U.S. politician. Born in Prince Edward Co., Va., to a slave mother and a white father, he moved to Mississippi during RECONSTRUCTION and served in political positions and purchased a plantation.

Elected to the U.S. Senate (1875–81), he advocated just treatment of blacks and Indians. He later served as register of the U.S. treasury (1881–85, 1895–98).

Bruce, Lenny *orig.* Leonard Alfred Schneider (1925–1966) U.S. comedian. Born in New York City, he began performing stand-up routines in nightclubs in the 1950s, soon developing a style marked by black humor and punctuated with obscenity. As he gained notoriety, he focused his material on criticisms of the social and legal establishments, organized religion, and other controversial subjects. After dying from a drug overdose, he acquired iconic status as a folk hero. His confrontational performance style and uncensored material greatly influenced later stand-up comedians.

Bruch \ˈbrük\, **Max (Karl August)** (1838–1920) German composer. He held many conducting positions and taught at the Berlin Academy. He was known in his lifetime for his choral pieces, including *Odysseus* (1872) and *Das Lied von der Glocke* (1879). Today he is remembered especially for his first violin concerto (1868); his other works include two further violin concertos, three operas, three symphonies, and the *Kol Nidre* (1881).

Brücke \ˈbrǖ-kə\, **Die** (German: "The Bridge") Organization of German Expressionist artists. It was founded in 1905 by four architectural students at the Dresden Technical School, including E. L. KIRCHNER, who were soon joined by other artists. Its name reflects their hope that their work would be a bridge to the art of the future. Strongly influenced by primitive art, German Gothic woodcuts, and the prints of Edvard MUNCH, they produced figure paintings and portraits depicting human suffering and anxiety, as well as still lifes and landscapes characterized by harshly distorted shapes and violent colors. The group disbanded in 1913.

Bruckner \ˈbrük-nər\, **(Joseph) Anton** (1824–1896) Austrian composer. Son of a rural schoolmaster, he was taken into a monastery as a choirboy and there learned to play the organ. Greatly gifted, he became organist at Linz Cathedral in 1855; throughout his career, his orchestrations would be compared to organ sonorities. In 1865 he heard *Tristan und Isolde* in Munich and thereafter idolized Richard WAGNER. In 1868 he was appointed professor at the Vienna Conservatory. He was 60 before he achieved fame with his Symphony No. 7. Socially awkward and eccentric, he was also a deeply devout Christian. His reputation rests on his nine mature symphonies (1866–96), his three masses (1864, 1866, 1868), and his *Te Deum* (1884).

Bruegel \ˈbrȯi-gəl\, **Pieter, the Elder** (c.1525–1569) Greatest Netherlandish painter of the 16th cent. Not much is known of his early life, but in Italy he produced his earliest signed painting, *Landscape with Christ and the Apostles at the Sea of Tiberias* (c.1553). Returning to Flanders in 1555, he achieved some fame with a series of satirical, moralizing prints in the style of Hieronymus BOSCH. He is best known for his paintings of Netherlandish proverbs, seasonal landscapes, realistic views of peasant life and folklore, and biblical events in panoramic scenes. He had many important patrons; most of his paintings were commissioned by collectors. In addition to many drawings and engravings, about 40 authenticated paintings from his enormous output have survived. His sons Peter Brueghel the Younger (1564–1638) and Jan BRUEGHEL the Elder as well as later imitators carried his style into the 18th cent.

Brueghel \ˈbrȯi-gəl\, **Jan, the Elder** (1568–1625) Flemish painter. Son of Pieter BRUEGEL the Elder, early in his career he went to Italy, where he painted under the patronage of Cardinal Federigo Borromeo. After returning to Antwerp in 1596, he enjoyed a highly successful and prestigious career, becoming court painter to the archdukes of Habsburg in 1608. He is known for his small-scale landscapes and exquisite flower paintings, all painted in a miniaturistic style on copper or panel, and his skill at depicting delicate textures. He often collaborated with other artists, including his friend Peter Paul RUBENS.

Brugge \ˈbrǖ-kə, *Engl* ˈbrü-gə\ *or* **Bruges** \ˈbrǖezh\ City (pop., 1997 est.: 116,000), NW Belgium. First mentioned in 7th-cent. records, it was the site of a castle built in the 9th cent. by the first counts of FLANDERS against Norman in-

vaders. It joined the HANSEATIC LEAGUE and was a major marketplace in the 13th cent. As the center of the Flemish cloth industry, it was the commercial hub of N Europe. In the 15th cent. it was home to Jan van EYCK and other painters of the Flemish school (see FLEMISH ART). Its later decline as a port was reversed by canals linking it with the North Sea.

Brugghen, Hendrik ter See Hendrik TERBRUGGHEN

bruise *or* **contusion** Visible bluish or purplish mark beneath the surface of unbroken skin, resulting from the bursting of blood vessels in deeper tissue layers. Usually caused by a blow or pressure, bruises may occur spontaneously in aged persons. The yellowish hue that becomes visible as a bruise heals comes from the formation of bile pigments and the disintegration and gradual absorption of blood.

Brummell, Beau (*orig.* George Bryan) (1778–1840) English dandy. He attended Oxford and became famous for his dress and wit as well as for his friendship with the future GEORGE IV. The leader of English fashion of his time, by 1816 he had exhausted his inherited fortune on gambling and extravagance and his sharp tongue had alienated his patron. He fled to Calais to avoid his creditors. In 1835 his friends rescued him from debtor's prison, but he soon lost all interest in his appearance, and he spent his final years in a charitable asylum.

Brun, Charles Le See Charles LE BRUN

Brundage, Avery (1887–1975) U.S. sports administrator. Born in Detroit, he competed in the 1912 OLYMPIC GAMES, and was U.S. champion in the "all-around" in 1914, 1916, and 1918. After founding a construction company, he served as president of the U.S. Olympic Assn. and Committee 1929–53, and as president of the International Olympic Committee 1952–72. Controversial and domineering, he demanded strict adherence to the rules of amateur competition. He was unable to stop the Games' growth and commercialization, caused partly by worldwide television coverage.

Brundtland \\'brûnt-land\\, **Gro Harlem** *orig.* Gro Harlem (b.1939) First woman prime minister of Norway (1981, 1986–89, 1990–96). Trained as a physician, she worked with various government health services, then served in the Norwegian parliament 1977–97. As leader of the Labor Party group, she became premier three times. In 1998 she was elected director-general of the World Health Organization.

Brunei \\brü-'nī\\ *officially* **State of Brunei Darussalam** \\ˌdär-ə-sə-'läm\\ Independent sultanate, NE BORNEO. The country is divided into two parts, each surrounded by the Malaysian state of Sarawak; they both have coastlines on the S. CHINA SEA and Brunei Bay. Area: 2,226 sq mi (5,765 sq km). Population (2000): 336,000. Capital: BANDAR SERI BEGAWAN. Brunei has a mixture of S.E. Asian ethnic groups: about two-thirds is Malay, one-sixth Chinese, and the remainder indigenous peoples and Indians. Languages: Malay (official); English is widely understood. Religions: Islam (official), Buddhism, Christianity, and animism. Currency: Brunei dollar or ringgit. The narrow N coastal plain gives way to rugged hills in the south. Brunei's W enclave consists of the valleys of the Belait, Tutong, and Brunei rivers; it is mainly hilly, rising more than 1,640 ft (500 m). The E enclave contains the Pandaruan and Temburong river basins, and the country's highest point, Pagan Peak (6,070 ft, or 1,850 m). Much of Brunei is covered by dense tropical rain forest; very little land is arable. Its economy is dominated by production from major oil and natural-gas fields. It has one of the highest per-capita incomes in Asia. It is a monarchy; the head of state and government is the sultan. Brunei traded with China in the 6th cent. A.D. Through allegiance to the Javanese Majapahit kingdom (13th–15th cent.), it came under Hindu influence. In the early 15th cent., with the decline of the Majapahit kingdom, many converted to Islam, and Brunei became an independent sultanate. When Ferdinand MAGELLAN's ships visited in 1521, the sultan of Brunei controlled almost all of Borneo and its neighboring islands. In the late 16h cent., Brunei lost power because of the Portuguese and Dutch activities in the region; they were soon joined by the British. By the 19th cent., the sultanate of Brunei included Sarawak, present-day Brunei, and part of N. Borneo (now part of Sabah). In

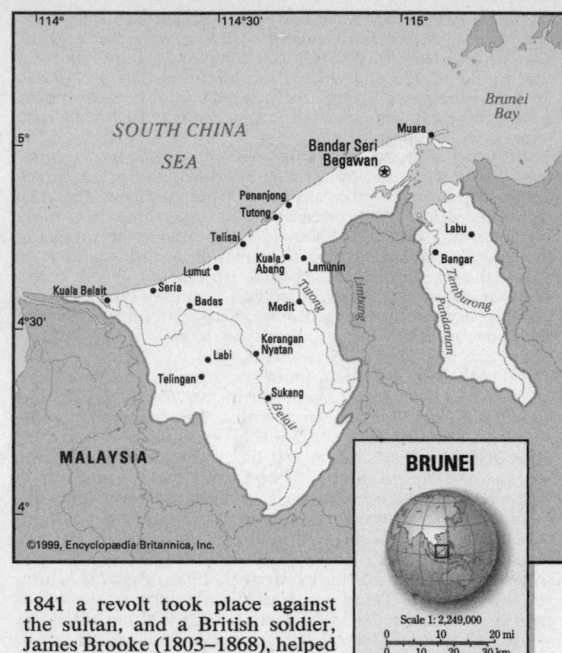

1841 a revolt took place against the sultan, and a British soldier, James Brooke (1803–1868), helped put it down; he was later proclaimed governor. In 1847 the sultanate entered into a treaty with Great Britain, and by 1906 had yielded all administration to a British Resident. Brunei rejected membership in the federation of Malaysia in 1963, negotiated a new treaty with Britain in 1979, and achieved independence in 1984, with membership in the COMMONWEALTH. Today Brunei, emerging from financial crises, is considering ways to diversify the economy and to encourage tourism.

Brunei See BANDAR SERI BEGAWAN

Brunel \\brü-'nel\\, **Isambard Kingdom** (1806–1859) British civil and mechanical engineer. He was the son of Marc BRUNEL. His introduction of the broad-gauge railway made possible high speeds and provided a great stimulus to railroad progress. He built more than 1,000 mi (1,600 km) of railway in Britain, and also oversaw construction of railway lines in Italy, Australia, and India. His use of a compressed-air CAISSON to sink bridge pier foundations was an important innovation. Brunel made outstanding contributions to marine engineering with three steamships—the *Great Western,* the *Great Britain,* and the *Great Eastern*—each the largest in the world at date of launching. The *Great Western* instituted the first regular transatlantic service, and the *Great Eastern* laid the first successful transatlantic cable.

Brunel, Marc (Isambard) (*later* **Sir Marc**) (1769–1849) French-British engineer and inventor. He perfected a method for making ships' blocks (PULLEYS) by mechanical means; the system of 43 machines, run by 10 men, produced blocks superior to those previously handmade by 110 men, and was an early example of completely mechanized production. His tunneling shield (patented 1818) made safe tunneling through waterbearing strata possible. In 1825 operations began for building the Brunel-designed tunnel under the THAMES RIVER, an unprecedented feat completed in 1842.

Brunelleschi \\ˌbrü-nᵊl-'es-kē\\, **Filippo** (1377–1446) Florentine architect and engineer. Trained as a sculptor and goldsmith, he worked out the laws of linear perspective (later codified by Leon Battista ALBERTI). By the early 1420s he was Florence's most prominent architect. His major work, the octagonal dome of the Florence Cathedral (1420–36), was built using machines of his own invention. The Medici family commissioned him to design the (old) sacristy and basilica of San Lorenzo (begun 1421), considered keystones of the early Renaissance; he adhered to the conventional format while adding his own interpretation of antique designs for its elements. His later works foreshadowed the strong profiles and massive grandeur of the work of Alberti and Donato BRAMANTE.

Brunhild *or* **Brunhilda** *or* **Brynhild** Beautiful Amazonlike heroine of ancient Germanic literature. She is known from Old Norse sources and from the German *Nibelungenlied*. She also appears in the operas of Richard WAGNER's *Ring* cycle. She vowed to wed only a man of the most outstanding

Filippo Brunelleschi, Santo Spirito, Florence, begun 1436

qualities who could surpass her in strength. SIEGFRIED wooed her successfully, but when she discovered that he was acting on behalf of another, she exacted vengeance and Siegfried was killed. In some Norse sources, Brunhild is described as a VALKYRIE.

Brüning \'brū̇-niŋ\, **Heinrich** (1885–1970) German politician. Elected to the Reichstag in 1924, he became leader of the Catholic Center Party in 1929. As chancellor of Germany (1930–32) he instituted harsh austerity measures that paralyzed the German economy. He governed by presidential decree, which hastened the drift toward rightist dictatorship and Adolf HITLER's rise to power. Forced to resign, he left Germany in 1934 and taught at Harvard Univ. 1937–52.

Brunn See BRNO

Bruno, Giordano (*orig.* Filippo) (1548–1600) Italian philosopher, astronomer, mathematician, and occultist. Initially a Dominican friar, he was forced out of the order about 1576 because of his freethinking. Traveling Europe as a lecturer, he hypothesized an infinite universe and multiple worlds, conceiving an astronomical theory even more radical than that of COPERNICUS. His theories anticipated elements in modern science and led to his excommunication by both Catholic and Protestant churches. After an eight-year trial by the Inquisition, he was burned at the stake. His ethical ideas have appealed to modern humanistic activists. His most important works are *On the Infinite Universe and Worlds* (1584) and *The Expulsion of the Triumphant Beast* (1584).

Bruno of Querfurt, St. *or* **St. Boniface of Querfurt** \'kfer-ˌfürt\ (974?–1009) Missionary and martyr. After the martyrdom of St. ADALBERT (997), Bruno entered a monastery, taking the name Boniface, and continued Adalbert's work in Christianizing the pagan Prussians. The members of a mission he sent to Poland, including Sts. Benedict and John, were killed en route; Bruno wrote biographies of both saints, as well as an acclaimed biography of Adalbert. As archbishop (1004), he visited the rulers of Germany, Hungary, and Ukraine seeking aid. He was killed on his way to his Prussian mission.

Brunswick *German* **Braunschweig** \'braủn-ˌshfīk\ Former duchy, central Germany. The original duchy of Brunswick-Lüneberg included the lands surrounding the town of Brunswick (founded late 9th cent.). The electorate of Hanover was included in 1692; its rulers established the English royal House of HANOVER. The duchy became part of the German empire in 1871 and a German state after 1919. After World War II the region was incorporated into the state of Lower Saxony. The city of Brunswick (pop., 1996: 252,000) is today an industrial center.

Brusa See BURSA

Brussels *French* **Bruxelles** \brū̇-'sel, brük-'sel\ *Flemish* **Brussel** \'brū̇-səl\ City (pop., 1997 est.: 133,000), capital of Belgium. Part of the Brussels Capital Region (pop., 1998: 953,000), it lies on the Senne River, a tributary of the SCHELDE. It became a holding of the dukes of BRABANT, and in 1530 the capital of the Netherlands, which was then under HABSBURG control. Part of the Kingdom of the Netherlands from 1815, it became a center of Belgian rebel-

lion in 1830 and then the capital of Belgium. An industrial and commercial center, it is the headquarters of both NATO and the EUROPEAN UNION.

Brussels sprout Small CABBAGE-related plant (*Brassica oleracea* 'gemmifera') of the MUSTARD FAMILY, widely grown in Europe and the U.S. The main stem grows to a height of 2–3 ft (60–90 cm) and the buds along the stem develop into small heads (sprouts) similar to tiny heads of cabbage. The plant requires a mild, cool climate and is harmed by hot weather. Highly nutritious, brussels sprouts are a particularly good source of vitamins A and C. See also BRASSICA.

Brutus, Marcus Junius *or* Quintus Caepio Brutus (85–42 B.C.) Roman politician, leader of the conspirators who assassinated Julius CAESAR in 44 B.C. He joined POMPEY's army against Caesar in the civil war (49), but was pardoned by Caesar after Pompey's death. He joined the plot to murder Caesar out of his desire to restore the Roman republic. After Caesar's death, he and Gaius CASSIUS formed an army in Macedonia, but Mark ANTONY and Octavian crushed his army at the Battle of PHILIPPI. Realizing the republican cause was lost, he committed suicide.

Bruyère, Jean de La See Jean de LA BRUYÈRE

Bryan, William Jennings (1860–1925) U.S. lawyer, politician, and orator. Born in Salem, Ill., he practiced law in Nebraska. In the U.S. House of Representatives (1891–95), he became the national leader of the FREE SILVER MOVEMENT. His "Cross of Gold" speech won him the Democratic nomination for president in 1896; he would receive the Democratic nomination twice more, in 1900 and 1908. He founded the *Commoner* newspaper (1901) and lectured widely to audiences who admired the oratorical style of "the Great Commoner." He helped secure the Democratic nomination for Woodrow WILSON in 1912 and served as his secretary of state (1913–15), contributing to world law by espousing arbitration to prevent war. A believer in a literal interpretation of the Bible, he was the chief prosecuting attorney in the SCOPES TRIAL (1925), in which he debated Clarence DARROW; the trial took a heavy toll, and he died soon after it ended.

William Jennings Bryan, c.1908

Bryant, Bear (*orig.* Paul William) (1913–1983) U.S. football coach. Born in Kingsland, Ark., he played blocking end at the Univ. of Alabama (1932–36). As head coach at the Univ. of Kentucky (1946–53), he led his team to a record of 60 games won, 23 lost, and five tied. After coaching at Texas A&M Univ. (1954–57), he returned to Alabama (1957–82). His Alabama coaching record of 323 wins, 85 losses, and 17 ties broke a long-standing record. In all, he took Alabama to 28 bowl games and six national championships.

Bryant, William Cullen (1794–1878) U.S. poet. Born in Cummington, Mass., at 17 he wrote his best-known poem, "Thanatopsis," a meditation on nature and death. Its deism influenced R. W. EMERSON and H. D. THOREAU. From age 21, he spent nearly 10 unhappy years as an attorney. His *Poems* (1821), including "To a Waterfowl," made his name, and in 1825 he moved to New York City, where, as editor of the *Evening Post* (1829–1878), he transformed it into an organ of progressive thought.

Bryce Canyon National Park Park, S Utah. It is not a true canyon but rather a series of natural amphitheaters below which stands an array of limestone and sandstone columns. Its geology is related to that of the GRAND CANYON and

B

ẒION NATIONAL PARK. The park, established in 1928, covers 35,835 acres (14,513 hectares).

Brynhild See BRUNHILD

Bryn Mawr College \'brin-'mȯr\ Private women's liberal-arts college in Bryn Mawr, Pa., near Philadelphia. Though founded in 1885 by a group of Quakers, it has long operated on a nondenominational basis. It has offered PhD programs since its founding, and enjoys academic exchanges with nearby HAVERFORD and SWARTHMORE colleges and the Univ. of PENNSYLVANIA. Enrollment is about 1,700.

bryophyte \'brī-ə-ˌfīt\ Any of the small green, seedless land plants that make up the division Bryophyta, numbering at least 18,000 species and divided into three classes: MOSSES, liverworts, and hornworts. They are distinguished from VASCULAR PLANTS and SEED PLANTS by the production of only one SPORE-containing organ. Found from polar regions to the tropics, they are most abundant in humid environments, though none is marine. Bryophytes are extremely tolerant of dry and freezing conditions. PEAT MOSS is economically important in horticulture and as an energy source. In nature, bryophytes initiate soil formation on barren terrain and maintain soil moisture, and they recycle nutrients in forest vegetation. They are found on rocks, logs, and forest litter.

bryozoan \ˌbrī-ə-'zō-ən\ Aquatic INVERTEBRATE of the phylum Bryozoa ("moss animals"), members (called zooids) of which form colonies. Each zooid is a complete and fully organized animal. Species range in size from a one-zooid "colony" small enough (less than 0.04 in., or 1 mm, long) to live between sand particles to colonies that hang in clumps or chains as much as a 1.6 ft (0.5 m) across. Freshwater bryozoans attach primarily to leaves, stems, and tree roots in shallow water. Marine bryozoans have a wide range of habitats, but are most common just below the tidemarks. Bryozoans feed by capturing plankton with their tentacles.

bubble chamber SUBATOMIC-PARTICLE detector that uses a superheated liquid, which boils into tiny bubbles of vapor around IONS produced along the tracks of particles. As charged particles move through the liquid, they knock electrons from the atoms of the liquid, creating ions. The first bubbles form around these ions. The observable tracks of bubbles trace the path of the charged particles. The bubble chamber allows the observation of many nuclear reactions and was used in the 1960s and '70s to study the behavior of unstable particles of matter.

Buber \'bü-bər\, **Martin** (1878–1965) German Jewish religious philosopher and biblical translator. Brought up in Lemberg (now Lviv, Ukraine), he studied in Vienna, Berlin, Leipzig, and Zurich. Friedrich NIETZSCHE's heroic nihilism led Buber, a nonobservant Jew, to Zionism, but he advocated Jewish-Arab cooperation in Palestine and saw Hasidism as a healing power for the malaise of modern Judaism. Under Nazi pressure, he emigrated to Palestine in 1938. *I and Thou* (1923) expresses Buber's belief that the human encounters God as a distinct being, rather than merging with God in mystical union.

Bubka \'bub-kə\, **Sergey** (b.1963) Ukrainian pole vaulter. He began vaulting at 9 and first cleared 6 m (19 ft 8 in.), long considered impossible, in Paris in 1985. In 1991 he cleared 20 ft (6.1 m), and remains the only pole vaulter to have done so. He won an Olympic gold medal in 1988. In 1994, at Sestriere, Italy, he vaulted a record 6.14 m (20 ft 1³/₄ in.) for his 35th overall record.

buccaneer Any of the British, French, or Dutch sea adventurers who chiefly haunted the Caribbean and the Pacific seaboard of S. America during the later 17th cent., preying on Spanish settlements and shipping. Though inspired by such PRIVATEERS as Francis DRAKE, they were not legitimate privateers, nor were they outlawed as pirates. Usually escaped servants, former soldiers, or loggers, they ran their ships democratically and divided plunder equitably. Stories of their adventures inspired voyages of exploration as well as the tales of Jonathan SWIFT and Daniel DEFOE.

Buchanan \byü-'ka-nən\, **James** (1791–1868) 15th president of the U.S. (1857–61). Born in Mercersburg, Pa., he served in the U.S. House of Representatives (1821–31) and Senate (1834–45). He was secretary of state in Pres. J. K. POLK's cabinet (1845–49) and later minister to Britain

(1853–56). In 1856 he secured the Democratic nomination and election as U.S. president. Though experienced in government and law, he lacked the moral courage to deal effectively with the slavery crisis and equivocated on the question of Kansas's status as a slaveholding state. The ensuing split within his party allowed Abraham LINCOLN to win the election of 1860. He denounced the secession of S. Carolina following the election and sent reinforcements to Ft. Sumter, but failed to respond further to the mounting crisis.

James Buchanan Photo by Mathew Brady

Bucharest \'bü-kə-ˌrest\ *Romanian* **Bucuresti** \ˌbü-kü-'resht'\ City (pop., 1997: 2,027,000), capital of Romania. The rulers of WALACHIA moved there in the 14th cent. VLAD III built its fortress in the 15th cent. to ward off invading Turks; they eventually took it and made it their Ottoman Walachian capital in 1659. The 19th cent. saw the union of Walachia and MOLDAVIA, and Bucharest became the capital of the new Romanian state in 1862. After World War II, it came under communist control. During the 1980s it was the scene of demonstrations against the government of Nicolae CEAUSESCU that resulted in his overthrow and execution.

Buchenwald \'bü-ḵən-ˌvält\ German Nazi concentration camp, established in 1937 near Weimar. Most of its 20,000 prisoners worked as slave laborers in nearby factories. Though there were no gas chambers, many perished through disease, malnutrition, and executions. Inmates were used to test the effects of viral infections and vaccines. The commandant's wife was the infamously sadistic Ilsa Koch (1906?–1967), the "Witch of Buchenwald." See also HOLOCAUST.

Büchner \'büeḵ-nər\, **Georg** (1813–1837) German dramatist. As a medical student, he became involved in revolutionary politics and was forced to flee to Zurich. There he wrote plays marked by vivid imagination and unconventional structure, combining extreme naturalism with visionary power; he is regarded as a forerunner of the Expressionist movement. His first play, *Danton's Death* (1835), was followed by *Leonce and Lena* (1836), a satire on the illusions of Romanticism. His last play, *Woyzeck* (1836), became the basis of a famous opera by Alban BERG. He died of typhoid at 24.

Buchwald \'buk-ˌwȯld\, **Art(hur)** (b.1925) U.S. humorist. Born in Mt. Vernon, N.Y., he moved to Paris in 1948. His popular reviews of the city's nightlife for the *International Herald Tribune* increasingly included offbeat spoofs and candid comments from celebrities. After moving in 1961 to Washington, D.C., he soon became established as one of the sharpest satirists of American politics and modern life. His widely syndicated work won a Pulitzer Prize in 1982.

Buck, Pearl S(ydenstrecker) *orig.* Pearl Sydenstricker (1892–1973) U.S. author. Born in Hillsboro, W.V., she was reared in China by her missionary parents. Her first book to reach a wide audience was *The Good Earth* (1931, Pulitzer Prize), describing the struggles of a Chinese peasant and his slave wife. *Sons* (1932) and *A House Divided* (1935) completed a trilogy. Among her later works are short stories, more novels, and an autobiography. She received the Nobel Prize in 1938.

Buckingham \'bək-iŋ-əm\, **Duke of** *orig.* **George Villiers** (1592–1628) English politician. Charming and handsome, he quickly became a royal favorite of JAMES I and the future CHARLES I. He became lord high admiral in 1619, but his arrogance and abuse of power made him highly unpopular. His erratic foreign policy led to a series of disasters, including failed military expeditions to Spain and France. A bill to impeach him in 1626 prompted Charles to dissolve Parliament. When Buckingham was assassinated, the populace of London rejoiced.

Buckingham Palace London residence of the British sovereign. It takes its name from the house built there early in the 18th cent. for the dukes of Buckingham. VICTORIA was the first sovereign to live there. John NASH began the reconstruction of Buckingham House as a Neoclassical palace in 1821. His garden front remains, but the Mall front was redesigned in 1913 by Sir Aston Webb (1849–1930).

Buckley, William F(rank), Jr. (b.1925) U.S. writer and editor. Born in New York City, in 1955 he founded the journal *National Review* as a forum for his conservative views. His column "On the Right" was syndicated in 1962 and eventually appeared in over 200 newspapers. From 1966 he hosted *Firing Line*, a weekly television interview program in which he often employed his wit and debating talents against ideological opponents. His books include *God and Man at Yale* (1951) and a series of spy novels.

buckminsterfullerene See FULLERENE

buckwheat Either of two species (*Fagopyrum esculentum* and *F. tataricum*) of herbaceous plants and their edible, triangular seeds, used as a CEREAL grain though the plant is not a cereal GRASS. It is particularly adapted to arid, hilly land and cool climates. Because it matures quickly, it can be grown as a late-season crop. It improves conditions for the cultivation of other crops by smothering weeds. Buckwheat is often used as a feed for poultry and other livestock. It is high in carbohydrates. The hulled kernels can be cooked and served much like rice. Buckwheat flour is used to make pancakes.

buckyball See FULLERENE

bud Small growth on the stem of a VASCULAR PLANT that may develop into a flower, leaf, or shoot. In temperate climates, trees form resting buds that are resistant to frost in preparation for winter. Flower buds are modified leaves.

Budapest \'bü-də-ˌpest\ City (pop., 1998: 1,863,000), capital of Hungary. Situated on the DANUBE RIVER, it acquired its name in 1873 when the towns of Buda and Obuda on the river's right bank and Pest on its left bank merged. Inhabited from Neolithic times, Buda was the site of a Roman camp. It was fortified by MATTHIAS I in the 15th cent. and became the capital of Hungary. It was taken and held by the Turks 1541–1686, then retaken by Charles V, duke of Lorraine. In 1848–49 both towns experienced nationalistic revolt, and Pest became the capital of Lajos KOSSUTH's revolutionary government. It became the center of revolt for Hungarian independence in 1918. After World War II, it came under communist control. It was the center of an unsuccessful uprising in 1956 (see HUNGARIAN REVOLUTION). Anticommunist unrest in the 1980s led to the declaration of the Hungarian republic in 1989. Budapest is a vital Hungarian transport center; its economy includes heavy industry and manufactures from telecommunications and electronics.

Buddha \'bü-də\ *orig.* Siddhartha Gautama (fl.c.6th–4th cent. B.C.) Indian spiritual leader and founder of BUDDHISM. The term Buddha (Sanskrit: "Enlightened One") is a title rather than a name, and Buddhists believe that there are an infinite number of past and future buddhas. The historical Buddha, or Buddha Gautama, was born a prince on the India–Nepal border. His sheltered life of luxury was interrupted when he left the palace and encountered an old man, a sick man, and a corpse. Renouncing his princely life, he spent seven years seeking out teachers and trying various ascetic practices, including fasting, to gain enlightenment. Unsatisfied with the results, he meditated beneath the BODHI TREE, where, after temptations by MARA, he realized the FOUR NOBLE TRUTHS and achieved enlightenment. His EIGHTFOLD PATH offered a middle way between self-indulgence and self-mortification and led to the liberation of NIRVANA. The five ascetics who heard this sermon became his first disciples. His mission fulfilled, the Buddha died at Kusinara (present-day Kasia) and escaped the cycle of rebirth.

Buddhism Religion and philosophy founded in NE India in the 5th cent. B.C. based on the teachings of the BUDDHA. One of the major world religions, Buddhism takes as its goal the escape from suffering and the cycle of rebirth and the attainment of NIRVANA, and it emphasizes MEDITATION and the observance of moral precepts. The Buddha adopted

some ideas from the HINDUISM of his time, notably the doctrine of KARMA, but also rejected many of its doctrines and all of its gods. Buddhism's main teachings are summarized in the FOUR NOBLE TRUTHS, of which the fourth is the EIGHTFOLD PATH. Buddhism's two major branches, MAHAYANA and THERAVADA, have developed distinctive practices. Buddhism declined in India after the 3rd cent. B.C. and was nearly extinct there by the 13th cent. It spread south and flourished in Sri Lanka and S.E. Asia, and it also moved through Central Asia and Tibet (see TIBETAN BUDDHISM) to China, Korea, and Japan (see ZEN). Today the various traditions of Buddhism together have about 400 million followers.

Buddhist councils In most Buddhist traditions, two early councils on doctrine and practice. The first, which is probably legendary, was reputedly held within a year of the BUDDHA's death to compile his remembered words, including the SUTRAS and monastic rules. The second, which is accepted as historical, met more than a century later at Vaisali, India, to resolve disputes within the monastic community. THERAVADA Buddhism recognizes a third council, called by ASHOKA around A.D. 247, at which the doctrinal disputes were resolved in its favor, and others continuing up to the mid-20th cent. Other traditions recognize other important councils at which their respective canons were established.

buddleia \'bəd-lē-ə\ *or* **butterfly bush** Any of more than 100 species of plants constituting the genus *Buddleia*, native to tropical and subtropical areas of the world. The genus belongs to the family Buddlejaceae (order Scrophulariales). Most species of *Buddleia* have hairy or scaly leaves and clusters of purple, white, yellow, or orange flowers. Several are cultivated as garden ornamentals.

Budge, (John) Don(ald) (1915–2000) U.S. tennis player. Born in Oakland, Cal., in 1936 he became the first lawn-tennis player to win the Grand Slam (the Australian, French, British, and U.S. singles championships). At Wimbledon in both 1937 and 1938, he won not only the singles but also the men's doubles and mixed doubles. With the U.S. DAVIS CUP team (1935–38), he won 25 of 29 matches. He is noted for having developed the backhand into an offensive stroke.

Buenos Aires \ˌbwā-nəs-'ar-ēz, *Span* ˌbwā-nōs-'ī-rās\ City (pop., 1999 est.: 2,904,000), capital of Argentina. Located on an estuary of the Río de la PLATA about 130 mi (210 km) from the sea, it is nevertheless a major port. First colonized by the Spanish in 1536, it became the seat of the viceroyalty of la Plata in 1776. In 1854 it drew up a separate constitution and began intermittent conflict with the provinces over control of the Argentine government. Upon being made a Federal District and Argentina's capital, it settled with the provinces in 1880, and by World War I it had become a thriving port. It is the country's largest and most influential city.

Buffalo City (pop., 2000: 292,000), W New York. Located at the NE point of Lake ERIE on the NIAGARA RIVER, it is the terminus of the New York State Barge Canal. Settled by American Indians in 1780, the site was a military post in the WAR OF 1812 and was burned by the British. Rebuilt, it became the W terminus of the ERIE CANAL, which brought an economic boom. A major port on the ST. LAWRENCE SEAWAY, it processes much of U.S.–Canadian trade. It is also an educational and medical research center.

buffalo Any member of several BOVID species, including the massive WATER BUFFALO and CAPE BUFFALO. The name is often applied to the American BISON. The anoa (*Anoa depressicornis*) is a tiny, dark-brown buffalo of the dense, mature forests of Sulawesi. A shy animal, it stands 2.5–3 ft (0.75–1 m) at the shoulder and has straight, sharp-tipped horns. A slightly larger species, the tamarau (*A. mindorensis*), inhabits the Philippine island of Mindoro.

Buffalo Bill See W. F. CODY

buffalo soldier Member of black cavalry regiments of the U.S. Army who served in the W U.S. 1867–96. Under the command of white officers, the soldiers' primary charge was controlling Indians in the W frontier (the nickname "buffalo" was given by the Indians); they took part in almost 200 engagements. Noted for their courage and discipline, they had the Army's lowest desertion and court-mar-

tial rates. One of the 10th Cavalry's officers was John PER-SHING, whose nickname Black Jack reflected his advocacy of black troops.

buffer Solution usually containing a weak ACID and its conjugate weak BASE, or a SALT, of such a composition that the PH is held constant within a certain range. An example is a solution containing acetic acid (CH_3COOH) and the acetate ION (CH_3COO^-). Relatively small additions of acid or base will change the concentration of the two species, but their ratio, and hence the pH, will not change much. Different buffers are useful in different pH ranges; they include phosphoric acid, citric acid, and boric acid, each with their salts. Biological fluids such as blood, tears, and semen have natural buffers to maintain them at the pH required for their proper function.

Buffett, Warren (b.1930) U.S. investor. Born in Omaha, he attended Columbia Univ., where he learned to invest in companies selling stock below their intrinsic value. Returning to Omaha, he turned $105,000 of initial investment in his Buffett Partnership (1956–69) into $105 million. Investing under the umbrella of the textile manufacturer Berkshire Hathaway, he is said to be the first person to have made $1 billion in the stock market. His financial reports are read eagerly by stock-market novices and experts alike for their pithy wisdom.

Buffon \byǖ-'fōⁿ\, G(eorges)-L(ouis) Leclerc *later* **comte (Count) de Buffon** (1707–1788) French naturalist. He studied mathematics, medicine, and botany until a duel forced him to cut short his studies. Appointed keeper of the royal botanical garden (Jardin du Roi) in 1739, he was also assigned the cataloging of the royal natural-history collections. His great *Histoire naturelle, generale et particuliere* (1749–1804) was an attempt to account for all known flora and fauna; he published 36 of the proposed 50 volumes before his death.

bug Error in a computer program that prevents it from functioning as designed. Most software companies have a quality-assurance department that looks for bugs while the program is in development (debugging); bugs are also often detected by beta testing (pre-release testing of a product, often by potential consumers). The term originated in a computer context in 1945 when a moth flew into an electrical relay of the Harvard Mark II computer.

bugaku \bü-'gä-kü\ Repertoire of stylized dances of the Japanese imperial court. The dances are divided into two basic forms: those accompanied by music derived from China, with dancers wearing red costumes; and those accompanied by music introduced from Korea, with dancers wearing costumes of blue or green. The dancers wear elaborate masks of painted wood to portray fictional characters.

Bugaku mask, lacquer and painted wood, 14th cent.

Bugatti \bü-'gät-tē\, **Ettore (Arco Isidoro)** (1881–1947) Italian builder of racing and luxury automobiles. His factory at Mosheim, Alsace (founded 1909), produced a highly successful low-powered racer for LE MANS. His luxurious Type 41 ("Golden Bugatti" or "La Royale"), produced in the 1920s, was probably the most meticulously built of all cars; no more than eight were constructed.

bugle Soprano BRASS INSTRUMENT historically used for hunting and military signaling. It developed from an 18th-cent. semicircular German hunting horn, which was reshaped into an oblong double loop. Natural bugles use only five notes in their calls ("Reveille," "Taps," etc.). The keyed bugle, patented in 1810, has six sideholes and keys which give it a complete chromatic scale. In the 1820s valves were added to produce the flugelhorn and, in lower ranges, the baritone, EUPHONIUM, and saxhorns.

Bug River *or* **Western Bug River** \'büg\ River, E central Poland. It flows north along the Poland–Ukraine and Poland–Belarus borders to Brest, and turns west into Poland to the VISTULA RIVER north of WARSAW, running a total of 481 mi (774 km). It was the scene of several World War I battles in 1915. About 200 mi (322 km) of its course formed part of the 1939 Russo–German boundary, and was largely retained after World War II in the U.S.S.R.–Poland boundary.

building code Body of rules that govern and constrain the design, construction, alteration, and repair of buildings. Such codes are based on requirements for the safety, health, and quality of life of building users and neighbors, and vary from city to city. Model codes developed by states, professional societies, and trade associations—including the BOCA (Building Officials and Code Administrators) coda, National Building Code, Uniform Building Code, and Standard Building Code—are typically adopted by local communities, with amendments.

Bujumbura \ˌbü-jəm-'bùr-ə\ *formerly* **Usumbura** City (pop., 1994 est.: 300,000), capital of Burundi. Lying on the N end of Lake TANGANYIKA, it is the country's chief port and largest urban center. Known as Usumbura in the 1890s when it was incorporated into GERMAN E. AFRICA, it was included in a TUTSI kingdom. With Burundi's independence (1962), the city's name was changed to Bujumbura. It specializes in textiles and agricultural products; most of Burundi's foreign trade is shipped from the capital to Tanzania.

Bukhara *or* **Bokhara** *or* **Boukhara** \bȯ-'kä-rä, bü-'kär-ə\ City (pop., 1996: 238,000), W Uzbekistan. Lying east of the AMU DARYA, it was founded in the 1st cent. A.D. and was a major trade center when the Arabs captured it in 710. It became capital of the Samanid realm from BAGHDAD to India and from Bukhara to the PERSIAN GULF. It fell to GENGHIS KHAN in 1220, to TIMUR in 1370, and to the Uzbeks, who in the 16th cent. made it the capital of the khanate of Bukhara. Capital of a Russian protectorate (from 1868) and of a Soviet republic (from 1920), Bukhara became part of the Uzbek S.S.R. in 1924, and of independent Uzbekistan in 1991.

Bukharin \bü-'kär-ən\, **Nikolay (Ivanovich)** (1888–1938) Russian communist leader and economist. After the Bolsheviks seized power, he became the editor of the party newspaper *Pravda* (1917–29). A member of the Politburo and a prominent leader of the Comintern, he also wrote several theoretical economic works. Falsely accused of espionage in the last of the public PURGE TRIALS (1938), he was found guilty and executed.

Bukowski, Charles (1920–1994) U.S. (German-born) writer. His family came to Los Angeles in 1922, and he began publishing short stories in the mid-1940s. His first poetry collection, *Flower, Fist and Bestial Wail*, (1959) and those that followed earned a devoted cult following. His novels include *Post Office* (1971), *Factotum* (1975), and *Hollywood* (1989), about the filming of his screenplay for *Barfly*. His writing, often scurrilous but humorous, reflected his perpetually down-and-out way of life.

Bulawayo \ˌbü-lä-'wä-yō\ City (pop., 1998 est.: 790,000), SW Zimbabwe. The country's second-largest city, it lies 4,400 ft (1,340 m) above sea level. Originally home to the king of the Ndebele, it was occupied in 1893 by the British. It is Zimbabwe's principal industrial center and, as railway headquarters, its main transshipment point for goods to and from S. Africa.

bulb In botany, the resting stage of certain SEED PLANTS, particularly PERENNIAL monocots (see COTYLEDON), consisting of a relatively large, usually globe-shaped, underground BUD with overlapping leaves arising from a short stem. The fleshy leaves function as food reserves that enable a plant to lie dormant during winter or drought and to resume active growth in favorable conditions. There are two main types. One, typified by the ONION, has a thin papery covering protecting its fleshy leaves. The other, the scaly bulb, as seen in true lilies, has naked storage leaves, with no papery covering, making the bulb appear to consist of angular scales. Bulbs enable such ornamentals as NARCISSUS, TULIP, and HYACINTH to flower rapidly in early spring. Other bulb-producing plants bloom in the summer (e.g., lilies) or fall (e.g., the autumn crocus). The solid corms of the CROCUS and GLADIOLUS and the elongated RHIZOMES of some irises are not bulbs.

Bulfinch, Charles (1763–1844) First professional U.S. architect. Born in Boston, he became chiefly a designer of government buildings. As architect of the U.S. CAPITOL 1817–30, he used the plans of Benjamin LATROBE for the wings, but prepared a new design for the ROTUNDA. Most of his works incorporate Classical orders and show a mastery of proportion. His son Thomas (1796–1867) wrote the famous *Bulfinch's Mythology.*

Bulgakov \bùl-'gȧ-kəf\, **Mikhail (Afanasyevich)** (1891–1940) Russian playwright and novelist. He wrote and staged many popular plays in the years 1925–29, some from his own novels, but after 1930 his trenchant criticism of Soviet mores kept him from being published. His works, known for their scathing humor, include the novella *The Heart of a Dog* (written 1925), a satire on pseudoscience, and the dazzling fantasy *The Master and Margarita,* published unexpurgated only in 1973.

Bulgaria *officially* **Republic of Bulgaria** Nation, SE Europe. Area: 42,823 sq mi (110,912 sq km). Population (2000): 8,172,000. Capital: SOFIA. Bulgarians make up about 85% of the population; smaller groups include Turks, Gypsies, and

Macedonians. Languages: Bulgarian (official), regional dialects. Religions: Bulgarian Orthodoxy 36%, Islam 13%. Currency: lev. Three major regions define the landscape. The northernmost is the Danubian Plain, a fertile area occupying a third of the country. Immediately south lie the BALKAN MTNS. (Stara Planina), which rise 3,500–7,800 ft (1,050–2,375 m). In the southwest and south lies the Rhodope Range, with the country's highest point, Musala Peak, at 9,596 ft (2,925 m). Smaller than the three major regions, Bulgaria's Black Sea coast, including its cities of VARNA and Burgas, is a popular E Europe resort area. Its major drainage systems include the Black and AEGEAN seas. It had a planned economy modeled on the Soviet system 1946–89. Since 1991 the noncommunist government has been moving to privatize some sectors of the economy, including agriculture. It is a republic with one legislative body; its chief of state is the president and its head of government, the prime minister. Evidence of human habitation dates from prehistoric times. Thracians were its first recorded inhabitants, dating from about 3500 B.C., and their first state dates from about the 5th cent. B.C.; the area was subdued by the Romans, who divided it

into the provinces of MOESIA and THRACE. In the 7th cent. A.D. the Bulgars took the region to the south of the Danube. The Byzantine empire in 681 formally recognized Bulgar control over the area between the Balkan Mtns. and the Danube. In 1185 Bulgaria fell to the Turks and ultimately lost its independence. At the end of the RUSSO–TURKISH WARS (1877–78), Bulgaria rebelled. The ensuing Treaty of San Stefano was unacceptable to the Great Powers, and the Congress of Berlin (1878) resulted. In 1908 the Bulgarian ruler, Ferdinand, declared Bulgaria's independence from the Ottoman empire. After its involvement in the BALKAN WARS (1912–13, 1913), Bulgaria lost territory. It sided with the Central Powers in World War I and with Germany in World War II. A communist coalition seized power in 1944, and in 1946 a people's republic was declared. With other E European countries in the late 1980s, Bulgaria experienced political unrest; its communist leader resigned in 1989. A new constitution proclaiming a republic was implemented in 1991. The rest of the decade brought economic turmoil.

Bulgarian language S. SLAVIC LANGUAGE spoken by about 9 million people in Bulgaria and enclaves in surrounding countries. Closely related is Macedonian, spoken by 2–2.5 million people in Macedonia and adjacent parts of Albania and Greece. Both languages differ from other major Slavic languages in lacking a case system for nouns and preserving the common Slavic system of verb tenses. Both are direct descendants of OLD CHURCH SLAVIC. Bulgarian became a literary language only in the mid-19th cent.; it was codified on the basis of NE Bulgarian dialects in 1899. Though efforts to create a literary Macedonian were underway before the BALKAN WARS (1912–13), it was not formally recognized as a distinct language until 1944.

Bulge, Battle of the (Dec. 16, 1944–Jan. 16, 1945) In WORLD WAR II, the last German offensive on the Western Front. The "bulge" refers to the wedge that the Germans drove into the Allied lines. In December 1944, Allied forces were caught unprepared by a massive German counterthrust in the wooded Ardennes region of S Belgium, led by Gerd von RUNDSTEDT. Initially successful, it was halted by Allied resistance and reinforcements led by George Patton. The Germans withdrew, but both sides suffered heavy losses.

bulimia \bü-'lē-mē-ə\ Eating disorder, mostly in young females, in which concern with weight and body shape leads to binge eating followed by induced vomiting. Bulimia can have serious medical complications, such as dental decay, stomach rupture, or dehydration, and can be fatal. Since it is associated with depression, anxiety, and low self-esteem, treatment may include psychotherapy. Unlike those with ANOREXIA NERVOSA, most bulimics are of normal weight.

bulldog *or* **English bulldog** Centuries-old breed of dog developed in Britain to fight bulls. Powerful and courageous, the bulldog nearly disappeared when dogfighting was outlawed in 1835. Fanciers of the breed saved it and bred out its ferocity. It is now considered gentle and reliable. It has a large head, folded ears, a short muzzle, a protruding lower jaw, and loose skin that forms wrinkles on the head and face. It stands 13–15 in. (34–38 cm) high and weighs 40–50 lbs (18–23 kg).

bulletin-board system (BBS) Computerized system used to exchange public messages or files. Most are dedicated to a special interest. Any user may "post" his or her own message (so that it appears on the site for all to read). Bulletin boards produce "conversations" between interested participants, who may download or print out messages they desire to keep or pass on to others. See also NEWSGROUP.

bullfighting Spectacle popular in Spain, Portugal, and Latin America, in which MATADORS ceremonially taunt, and usually kill, bulls in an arena. Spectacles with bulls were common in ancient Crete and Rome. In the modern era, Roman amphitheaters were rebuilt for use as bullrings. The corrida, which usually involves six individual fights, begins with a procession. At the beginning of each fight an assistant (banderillero) performs a maneuver to allow the matador to assess the animal's behavior. The matador then performs his capework, drawing the bull as close to him as possible without being gored. Next, horsemen (picadors) jab the bull with lances to weaken its neck and shoulder muscles. The matador then ritually slays the bull using a sword. In the Portuguese version, the bull is fought from horseback and is not killed. Bullfighting has been banned in many countries.

bullfrog Solitary aquatic FROG (*Rana catesbeiana*) named for its loud call. The largest U.S. frog, native to the E states, it has been introduced into the W states and into other countries. Its body is about 8 in. (20 cm) long, and its hindlegs may be 10 in. (25 cm) long. Large adults weigh 1 lb (0.5 kg) or more. Bullfrogs usually live in or near a body of still water.

Bullfighting Manolete executing a natural

Bull Moose Party U.S. dissident political faction that nominated former president Theodore ROOSEVELT for the presidency. Formed in 1911 as the National Republican Progressive League, in opposition to the conservatism of the REPUBLICAN PARTY controlled by Pres. W. H. TAFT, it derived its name from the characteristics of strength and vigor that Roosevelt used to describe himself. In 1912 Roosevelt won 25% of the popular vote, which allowed Woodrow WILSON to win the election. The Republicans were reunited in 1916. See also PROGRESSIVE PARTY.

bull-roarer Flat piece of wood, several inches to a foot in length, fastened at one end to a string, by which it is swung around in the air to produce a whirring or howling sound. It has been observed in diverse indigenous societies. It may symbolize totemic ancestors, or it may be believed to cause or cure sickness, control the weather, or promote fertility in animals and crops.

Bull Run, Battles of Two engagements in the AMERICAN CIVIL WAR fought at a stream near Manassas, Va. The first battle (also called First Manassas) was fought on July 21, 1861, between 37,000 Union troops and 35,000 Confederate troops; the Union assault was beaten back and the army retreated to Washington, D.C. The second battle took place on August 29–30, 1862, between a Confederate force of over 56,000 under Robert E. LEE and a Union army of over 70,000 under John Pope (1822–1892). To prevent the Union force from being joined by the Army of the Potomac, Lee sent troops under Stonewall JACKSON to outflank the Union army. Lee's attack forced the Union troops to withdraw as far as Washington, D.C. Casualties numbered 15,000 for the North and 9,000 for the South. Both battles strengthened the South's resolve and caused the North to review its military leadership and strategy.

bull terrier Breed of dog developed in 19th-cent. England from the BULLDOG and the now-extinct white English TERRIER. The Spanish pointer was later bred into the line to increase its size. The bull terrier was developed as a courageous fighting dog but not an aggressive fight provoker, and it is generally friendly. A muscular dog, it is considered, for its weight, the strongest of all dogs. It stands 19–22 in. (48–56 cm) high and weighs 50–60 lbs (23–27 kg). See also PIT BULL TERRIER.

Bultmann \'bùlt-ˌmän\, **Rudolf (Karl)** (1884–1976) German Protestant theologian. He established his reputation with his analysis of the Gospels in *History of the Synoptic Tradition* (1921). Influenced by his colleague Martin HEIDEGGER, he held that Christian faith should focus less on the historical Jesus and more on the transcendent Christ, and he examined the New Testament in mythical terms. During the Nazi era he supported the anti-Nazi Confessing Church. His postwar books included *Kerygma and Myth* (1953), *History and Eschatology* (1957), and *Jesus Christ and Mythology* (1960).

Bulwer-Lytton, Edward (George Earl) *later* Baron Lytton of Knebworth (1803–1873) British politician, novelist, and poet. His first novel, *Pelham,* was published in 1828. He served in Parliament first as a Liberal (from 1831) and later

as a Tory (from 1852). He won fame for his long historical novels, including *The Last Days of Pompeii* (3 vols., 1834) and *Harold, the Last of the Saxon Kings* (1848). The opening to his 1830 novel *Paul Clifford* ("It was a dark and stormy night . . .") has become a catchphrase.

bumblebee Any member of two genera constituting the insect tribe Bombini (family Apidae, order Hymenoptera), found almost worldwide. Bumblebees are robust and hairy, average about 0.6–1 in. (1.5–2.5 cm) in length, and are usually black with broad yellow or orange bands. *Bombus* species are nest builders, often nesting in the ground. They live in organized groups. *Psithyrus* species are social parasites (see PARASITISM) that lay their eggs in *Bombus* nests.

Bunche \'bənch\, **Ralph (Johnson)** (1904–1971) U.S. diplomat. Born in Detroit, he taught at Howard Univ. from 1928. He collaborated with Gunnar MYRDAL in the study of U.S. race relations *An American Dilemma* (1944). After working in the U.S. war and state departments, in 1947 he became director of the trusteeship department of the U.N. Secretariat. His work in forging a truce between Palestinian Arabs and Jews earned him the 1950 Nobel Peace Prize, the first Nobel Prize won by a black man. As U.N. undersecretary for political affairs, he oversaw U.N. peacekeeping forces around the Suez Canal (1956), in the Congo (1960), and in Cyprus (1964).

bungee jumping \'bən-jē\ Sport in which the jumper falls from a high place with a rubber ("bungee") cord attached both to his or her feet and to the jump site, and, after a period of headfirst free fall, is bounced partway back when the cord rebounds from its maximum stretch. It traces its roots to Pentecost Island, Vanuatu, where divers are tethered to a vine whose length is calculated to allow the jumper to fall until his hair just brushes the ground below. The Oxford Dangerous Sports Club made the first Western bungee jumps, and bungee jumping was first offered commercially in New Zealand in 1988.

Bunin \'bü-nʸin\, **Ivan (Alekseyevich)** (1870–1953) Russian poet and novelist. He made his name as a short-story writer with such masterpieces as the title story of *The Gentleman from San Francisco* (1916). His other works include the novel *Mitya's Love* (1925), the story collection *Dark Avenues* (1943), fictional autobiography, and memoirs. He was the first Russian to win the Nobel Prize for Literature (1933).

Bunker Hill, Battle of Important battle early in the AMERICAN REVOLUTION. Two months after the battles of LEXINGTON AND CONCORD, over 15,000 colonial troops assembled near Boston to stop the British army from occupying several hills around the city. Having fortified Breed's Hill (later Bunker Hill) across the Charles River from Boston, they withstood a cannonade from British ships in Boston Harbor on June 17, 1775, and fought off assaults by 2,300 troops, but were eventually forced to retreat. British casualties (about 1,000) and the colonists' fierce resistance convinced the British that subduing the rebels would be difficult.

Bunsen, Robert (Wilhelm) (1811–1899) German chemist. With Gustav KIRCHHOFF, he observed (c.1859) that each ELEMENT emits LIGHT of a characteristic WAVELENGTH, opening the field of spectrochemical analysis. They discovered several new elements (including HELIUM, CESIUM, and rubidium) by SPECTROSCOPY. He invented the carbon-zinc BATTERY, grease-spot photometer (see PHOTOMETRY), and filter pump. He did not invent the Bunsen burner, but made minor contributions to its development.

Buñuel \ˌbün-yü-'wel\, **Luis** (1900–1983) Spanish film director. At the Univ. of Madrid he met Salvador DALÍ. He went to Paris in 1925 and made the surrealist film *Un chien andalou* (1928) with Dalí, then directed the anticlerical *Golden Age* (1930) and the documentary *Land Without Bread* (1932). After working in Spain and Hollywood, he moved to Mexico, where he directed *Los olvidados* (1950) and *Nazarín* (1958). He returned to Spain to make *Viridiana* (1961), suppressed

Luis Buñuel

there as anticlerical but internationally acclaimed. He attacked conventional morality in such later films as *Belle de jour* (1967), *Tristana* (1970), and *The Discreet Charm of the Bourgeoisie* (1972, Academy Award).

Bunyan, John (1628–1688) English minister and author. Bunyan encountered the seething religious life of various left-wing sects while in Oliver CROMWELL's army. After a period of spiritual crisis, he converted to Puritanism and became a preacher. With the Restoration, he was jailed as a NONCONFORMIST for 12 years, during which he wrote his spiritual autobiography, *Grace Abounding* (1666). He is best known for *The Pilgrim's Progress* (1678–84), a Puritan allegory in the form of a symbolic vision of the character Christian's pilgrimage through life. It was at one time second only to the Bible in popularity among ordinary readers.

Bunyan, Paul Legendary giant lumberjack of the U.S. frontier. A symbol of strength and vitality, he is accompanied by a giant blue ox, Babe. He was credited with creating Puget Sound, digging the Grand Canyon, and building the Black Hills, and was known for his prodigious appetite. Tales of his exploits probably originated in lumber camps, and were first published by James MacGillivray in "The Round River Drive" (1910), which soon led to a national myth.

Buonarroti, Michelangelo See MICHELANGELO

buoyancy See ARCHIMEDES' PRINCIPLE

burakumin \bù-'rä-kù-min\ Japanese minority group that suffers discrimination based on its historical outcaste status. Descendants of those whose occupation involved the taking of life (such as butchers) or the handling of flesh or dead bodies (such as leatherworkers or gravediggers) were stigmatized in the 16th cent. by Buddhist and Shinto beliefs in the polluting nature of these occupations. Though their outcaste status was removed by law in 1871, prejudice remains, and burakumin heritage often stands in the way of marriages and employment opportunities. Burakumin are estimated to number 1–3 million.

Burbank, Luther (1849–1926) U.S. plant breeder. Reared on a farm in Lancaster, Mass., he never obtained a college education. Influenced by Charles DARWIN's writings, he began a plant-breeding career at 21. On the proceeds of his development of the Burbank potato, he set up experimental farms in Santa Rosa, Cal. There he developed more than 800 new and useful strains and varieties of fruits, flowers, vegetables, grains, and grasses, many of which are still commercially important. His laboratory became world-famous, and he helped make plant breeding a modern science.

Burchfield, Charles (Ephraim) (1893–1967) U.S. painter. Born in Ashtabula Harbor, Ohio, he worked initially as a wallpaper designer in Buffalo, N.Y. In the 1920s and '30s he was one of the leading U.S. scene painters; his work was associated with Edward HOPPER in its portrayal of the loneliness and bleakness of small-town life (e.g., *November Evening*, 1934). In the 1940s he abandoned realism for a more personal interpretation of nature, emphasizing its mystery, movement, and color from season to season (e.g., *The Sphinx and the Milky Way*, 1946).

Burckhardt \'bùrk-ˌhärt\, **Jacob (Christopher)** (1818–1897). Swiss historian of art and culture. Having studied art history, he matured into a cultural conservative, preoccupied with reclaiming the past. From 1843 he taught primarily at the Univ. of Basel. He is famous for *The Civilization of the Renaissance in Italy* (1860), which examines daily life in the Renaissance in terms of such phenomena as the modern sense of humor; it became a model for cultural historians. He died while working on a four-volume survey of Greek civilization.

burdock Any plant of the genus *Arctium,* in the COMPOSITE FAMILY, bearing globular flower heads with prickly BRACTS. Native to Europe and Asia, burdock species have naturalized as weeds throughout N. America. Their fruits are round burrs that stick to clothing and fur.

Bureau of Standards *since 1988* **U.S. National Institute of Standards and Technology (NIST)** Agency of the U.S. Department of Commerce responsible for the standardization of weights and measures, timekeeping, and navigation. The agency works closely with the U.S. Naval Observatory and the Bureau International de l'Heure in Paris to ensure global standardized time.

Burger, Warren E(arl) (1907–1995) U.S. jurist. Born in St. Paul, Minn., he was named to the U.S. Court of Appeals for the District of Columbia in 1955, and nominated for chief justice of the U.S. Supreme Court in 1969. Contrary to the expectations of some, he did not try to reverse the tide of activist decisions on civil-rights issues and criminal law made during the tenure of his predecessor, Earl WARREN. The Burger Court upheld the 1966 *MIRANDA VS. ARIZONA* decision, busing as a permissible means of racially desegregating public schools, and the use of racial quotas in the distribution of federal grants and contracts to minorities. Burger voted with the majority in *Roe vs. Wade* (1973). He retired in 1986 and was awarded the Presidential Medal of Freedom in 1988.

Burgess \'bər-jəs\, **Anthony** *orig.* John Anthony Burgess Wilson (1917–1993) English novelist and composer. His experiences in Southeast Asia inspired the trilogy *The Long Day Wanes* (1956–59). *A Clockwork Orange* (1962; film, 1971), his most original work, is a satire on extreme political systems. His other novels, which combine mordant wit, moral seriousness, and verbal dexterity, include *The Wanting Seed* (1962), *Inside Mr. Enderby* (1963), and *Earthly Powers* (1980). In addition to his other extensive writings, he composed over 65 musical works.

Burgess \'bər-jəs\, **Guy (Francis de Moncy)** (1911–1963) British diplomat and Soviet spy. At Cambridge Univ. in the 1930s, he and Donald Maclean (1913–1983) were recruited by Soviet intelligence operatives. Both later supplied information from their positions in the British foreign office. Maclean's post with the British embassy in Washington, D.C., enabled him to pass information about NATO to the Soviets; Burgess also served in Washington. In 1951 they were warned by their colleague Kim PHILBY that an investigation was closing in on Maclean. With the aid of Anthony BLUNT, they fled England, surfacing in Moscow in 1956.

Burgess \'bər-jəs\, **Thornton W(aldo)** (1874–1965) U.S. children's author. Born in Sandwich, Mass., he used his first book, *Old Mother West Wind* (1910), to introduce the animal characters that were to populate his subsequent writings, which included more than 170 books and 15,000 stories for newspaper columns. He promoted conservationism through his "Wildlife Protection Program" and "Radio Nature League."

Burgesses \'bər-jəs-əz\, **House of** Representative assembly in colonial Virginia, the first elective governing body in a British colony. It was a division of the legislature established by the colonial governor at Jamestown in 1619, to which each Virginia settlement was entitled to elect two delegates, or burgesses (citizens of a borough in England).

Burgess Shale \'bər-jəs\ FOSSIL formation containing detailed traces of soft-bodied marine organisms of the middle CAMBRIAN PERIOD about 520 million years ago. Collected from a fossil bed in the Burgess Pass of the Canadian Rockies, it is one of the best preserved fossil formations in the world. Discovered in 1909, it has since yielded over 60,000 specimens.

Burghley, Baron See William CECIL

burglary Crime of breaking into and entering a structure with the intent to commit a FELONY within. Some state statutes specify degrees of burglary based on when and where the crime occurred, the presence of people, and the use (or non-use) of a deadly weapon.

Burgundy *French* **Bourgogne** \bür-'gȯnʸ\ Historical region, France. The name was originally applied to a kingdom in the RHONE valley and W Switzerland founded by the Burgundians, a Germanic people who fled Germany in the 5th cent. Conquered by the MEROVINGIANS around 534, it was incorporated into the Frankish empire. By the Treaty of VERDUN (843), it was included in the Middle Kingdom of Lothair I's HOLY ROMAN EMPIRE. In 933 it became the kingdom of Burgundy; after the 13th cent., it was known as the kingdom of ARLES, while the duchy of Burgundy embraced the NW part of the original kingdom. In 1361 the duchy reverted to the French crown. Given to PHILIP II, by 1477 its lands extended into the LOW COUNTRIES. It was seized by LOUIS XI and annexed to France, and was a province until the FRENCH REVOLUTION. Today the area forms a govern-

mental region with its capital at DIJON. Winemaking is an important part of the economy.

burial Ritual disposal of human remains, often intended to facilitate the deceased's entry into the afterworld. Grave burial dates back at least 125,000 years. Types of grave range from trenches to large burial mounds to great stone tombs such as PYRAMIDS. Caves have also long been used for the dead, as in the case of the ancient Hebrews or the thousands of sepulchral caves (rock temples) of W India and Sri Lanka. Water burial, such as occurred among the Vikings, has also been common. Cremation and the scattering of ashes on water is widely practiced, especially in Asia. Some peoples (American Indian groups, Parsis, etc.) employ exposure to the elements to dispose of their dead. Among many peoples, the first burial is followed by a second, after an interval that often coincides with the duration of bodily decomposition; this reflects a concept of death as slow passage from the society of the living to that of the dead.

Burke, Edmund (1729–1797) British (Irish) orator and political philosopher. Essays he published in 1757–58 gained wide attention, and he was hired to edit a yearly survey of world affairs (1758–88). He entered politics (1765) as secretary to a Whig leader and soon became involved in the controversy over whether Parliament or the monarch controlled the executive, arguing (1770) that GEORGE III's efforts to reassert a more active role violated the constitution's spirit. Elected to Parliament (1774–80), he contended that its members should exercise judgment rather than merely follow their constituents' desires.

Edmund Burke Painting from the studio of Joshua Reynolds, 1771

Though a conservative, he eloquently championed the cause of the American colonists, and he supported the abolition of the international slave trade. He tried unsuccessfully to legislate relief for Ireland and to reform the governance of India. He disapproved of the French Revolution for its anti-aristocratic bloodshed. He is often regarded as the founder of modern CONSERVATISM.

Burkina Faso \bŭr-ˈkē-nə-ˈfä-sō\ *formerly* **Upper Volta** Republic, W. Africa. A landlocked country, it lies south of the SAHARA Desert. Area: 105,869 sq mi (274,201 sq km). Population (2000): 11,946,000. Capital: OUAGADOUGOU. Its two principal ethnic groups are the Voltaic (Gur), and the MOSSI; there are also HAUSA and FULANI. Languages: French (official), Moré, Dyula. Religions: About one-fifth of the population practice traditional religions; another one-fifth are Muslims; a small number are Christian. Currency: CFA franc. Burkina Faso consists of an extensive plateau, characterized by a savanna, grassy in the north and sparsely forested in the south. The plateau is notched by the valleys of the Mouhoun (Black Volta), Nazion (Red Volta), and Nakanbe rivers, which flow south into Ghana. Its economy is largely agricultural. It is a republic with one advisory body and one legislative body; its chief of state is the president and its head of government, the prime minister. Probably in the 14th cent., the Mossi and Gurma peoples established themselves in E and central areas. The Mossi kingdoms of Yatenga and Ouagadougou existed into the early 20th cent. A French protectorate was established over the region 1895–97, and its S boundary was demarcated through an Anglo-French agreement. It was part of the Upper-Senegal-Niger (see MALI) colony, then became a separate colony in 1919. It was constituted an overseas territory within the French Union in 1947, became an autonomous republic within the French Community in 1958, and achieved total independence in 1960. Since then, it has been ruled primarily by the military and has experienced several coups; following one in 1984, the country received its pre-

BURKINA FASO

©1999, Encyclopædia Britannica, Inc.

Scale 1: 14,037,000
0   60   120 mi
0   90   180 km

sent name. A new constitution, adopted in 1991, restored multiparty rule.

burlesque In literature, comic imitation of a serious literary or artistic form. It is generally broader and coarser than PARODY. Early examples include the comedies of ARISTOPHANES. English burlesque is chiefly drama; John GAY's *The Beggar's Opera* (1728) and R. B. SHERIDAN's *The Critic* (1779), for example, are parodies of popular dramatic forms of the period. Victorian burlesque, usually light entertainment with music, was eclipsed by other popular forms, and burlesque eventually came to incorporate striptease acts (see BURLESQUE SHOW).

burlesque show Stage entertainment designed for male amusement. Introduced in the U.S. from England in 1868, it developed as a version of the MINSTREL SHOW, divided into three parts: (1) a series of coarse humorous songs, SLAPSTICK sketches, and comic monologues; (2) the olio, or mixture of variety acts; and (3) chorus numbers and occasionally a takeoff, or burlesque, on politics or a current play. The show ended with an exotic dancer or a boxing match. Such performers as Fanny BRICE, Al JOLSON, and W. C. FIELDS began their careers in burlesque. The addition of the striptease in the 1920s made a star of Gypsy Rose LEE, but censorship and competition from motion pictures soon led to burlesque's decline.

Burlingame, Anson (1820–1870) U.S. diplomat. Born in New Berlin, N.Y., he served in the U.S. House of Representatives (1855–61) and helped found the REPUBLICAN PARTY. As U.S. minister to China (1861–67), he implemented a policy of cooperation with China. In 1867 the Chinese government appointed him imperial envoy to conduct China's international relations. The Burlingame Treaty established reciprocal rights of Chinese and U.S. citizens.

Burma See MYANMAR

Burma Road Former highway, SE Asia. It ran 681 mi (1,096 km) from Lashio (in E Burma, now Myanmar) northeast to Kunming (in Yunnan, China). An extension ran east from Kunming, then north to CHONGQING. Completed in 1939, it functioned as a supply route to the interior of China, carrying war goods. It was seized by the Japanese in 1942. Connected to the STILWELL ROAD from India in 1945, it remains a link in a 2,100-mi (3,400-km) road system from YANGON to Chongqing.

Burmese cat Breed of DOMESTIC CAT, presumably of Asian origin. Compactly built, it has a small, rounded head and wide-set, round, yellow eyes. The short, finely textured, glossy coat darkens as it matures from milk-chocolate to a rich sable brown. The tapered tail may be kinked near the tip.

burn Damage caused to the body by contact with flames, hot substances, some chemicals, radiation (including sunlight), or electricity. Burns are classified by depth and extent of SKIN damage. First-degree burns injure only the epidermis (top layer), with redness, pain, and minimal EDEMA. In a second-degree burn, damage extends into the dermis (inner layer), with redness and blisters. Third-degree burns destroy the entire thickness of the skin; there is no pain, because the skin's pain receptors are destroyed. Secondary SHOCK follows severe burns. Treatment depends on severity; first-degree burns need only first aid; third-degree burns require long-term hospitalization. Depending on the type, extent, and site of the burn, it may be left exposed, covered with a bandage, or excised to remove dead tissue in preparation for skin grafts. Complications of burns include respiratory problems, infection, ulcers in the stomach or duodenum, and, especially in brown skin, thick scarring. Survivors of third-degree burns usually require plastic surgery, long-term physical therapy, and psychotherapy.

Burne-Jones \ˈbərn-ˈjōnz\, **Edward (Coley)** (*later* **Sir Edward**) (1833–1898) British painter, illustrator, and designer. At Oxford he met his future collaborator William MORRIS. In 1856 he became apprenticed to D. G. ROSSETTI. His paintings portray the romantic medieval imagery favored by the PRE-RAPHAELITES. He first achieved great success in 1877 with an exhibition of paintings, including *The Beguiling of Merlin* (1873–77). As a founding member of Morris & Co. (1861), he designed stained glass and tapestry, and executed 87 designs for the great Kelmscott Press edition of *Chaucer* (1896). His revival of the ideal of the artist-craftsman influenced the development of 20th-cent. industrial design.

Burnet \bər-ˈnet\, **(Frank) Macfarlane** (*later* **Sir Macfarlane**) (1899–1985) Australian physician and virologist. He discovered a method for identifying bacteria by the viruses (bacteriophages) that attack them, and shared a 1960 Nobel Prize with Peter MEDAWAR for the discovery of acquired immunological tolerance to tissue transplants.

Burnett, Carol (b.1933) U.S. comedian, actress, and singer. Born in San Antonio, Tex., she made her Broadway debut in *Once upon a Mattress* (1959), then appeared regularly on television, where her gift for parody and her knock-kneed comic grace gained her a wide following. The weekly *Carol Burnett Show* (1966–77) became one of television's most popular programs and won her five Emmy awards.

Burnett, Frances Hodgson *orig.* Frances Eliza Hodgson (1849–1924) British-U.S. playwright and author. She is remembered for *Little Lord Fauntleroy* (1886), a children's novel about an American boy who inherits an English earldom, and *The Secret Garden* (1911), a children's classic. Other works include the novel *Through One Administration* (1883), about political corruption, and the play *A Lady of Quality* (1896).

Burney (d'Arblay), Fanny (*orig.* Frances) (1752–1840) English novelist. Daughter of the music historian Charles Burney (1726–1814), she wrote lively accounts of his social musical evenings. Her *Evelina* (1778), about an unsure young girl's social development, is a landmark novel of manners, and points the way toward Jane AUSTEN. Her later novels include *Cecilia* (1782) and the potboiler *Camilla* (1796).

Burnham, Daniel H(udson) (1846–1912) U.S. architect and city planner. Born in Henderson, N.Y., he pioneered the development of Chicago commercial architecture with his partner, John Wellborn Root (1850–1891). The firm's buildings include Chicago's Rookery (1886), Reliance Building (1890), and Monadnock Building (1891), the last and tallest U.S. masonry skyscraper. As consulting architect for Chicago's World's Columbian Exposition (1893), Burnham favored academic eclecticism, the antithesis of the CHICAGO SCHOOL. The resulting "White City" widely influenced city planning in the U.S. Burnham's plan for Chicago (1907–9) is a classic example of U.S. city planning.

Burns, George *orig.* Nathan Birnbaum (1896–1996) U.S. comedian best known for his collaboration with Gracie Allen (1902–1964). Both were born in New York City and were vaudeville performers from childhood; they married in 1926. They performed on radio in *The George Burns and Gracie Allen Show* (1932–50), with Burns playing the straight man to Allen's malaprop-prone chatterbox, before their show moved to television (1950–58). Burns later acted in such films as *The Sunshine Boys* (1975, Academy Award), *Oh, God!* (1977) and its sequels, and *Going in Style* (1979). Famous for his wry humor and his cigars, he continued performing into his late nineties.

Burns, Ken(neth Lauren) (b.1953) U.S. documentary filmmaker. Born in Brooklyn, N.Y., he founded his own production company in 1975 and made such documentary films as *Brooklyn Bridge* (1981), *The Shakers* (1984), and *The Congress* (1988), all televised on PBS. His acclaimed series *The Civil War* (1990) won numerous awards. His later television documentaries include *Baseball* (1994), *The West* (1996), *Lewis and Clark* (1997), and *Jazz* (2001).

Burns, Robert (1759–1796) National poet of Scotland. Son of a poor farmer, he was unsuccessful at farming himself. Handsome and high-spirited, he engaged in a series of love affairs, some of which produced illegitimate children, and celebrated his lovers in his poems. His *Poems, Chiefly in the Scottish Dialect* (1786) brought acclaim but no financial security. He later began collecting and editing hundreds of traditional airs for James Johnson's *Scots Musical Museum* (1787–1803) and George Thomson's *Select Collection of Original Scottish Airs* (1793–1818); he largely wrote many of them, though he did not claim authorship

Robert Burns Painting by Alexander Nasmyth

or receive payment. Among his best-known songs are "Auld Lang Syne," "Green Grow the Rashes, O," and "A Red, Red Rose." Strongly in sympathy with the common people, he rebelled against orthodox religion and morality. He died at 37 from endocarditis.

Burnside, Ambrose (Everett) (1824–1881) U.S. general in the AMERICAN CIVIL WAR. Born in Liberty, Ind., he graduated from West Point. Promoted to major general in 1862, he replaced George MCCLELLAN as commander of the Army of the Potomac, but was himself soon replaced after the Union loss at the Battle of FREDERICKSBURG. He resigned in 1864 after an error in the Petersburg Campaign resulted in heavy Union losses. He was governor of Rhode Island 1866–69, and a U.S. senator 1875–81. He originated the fashion of side whiskers, later known as "sideburns."

Burnt Njáll See NJÁLS SAGA

Burr, Aaron (1756–1836) U.S. vice president (1801–5). Born in Newark, N.J., he served in the American Revolution on George WASHINGTON's staff until 1779. He had a successful law practice in New York from 1782 and served in the U.S. Senate (1791–97). He ran for president in 1800. The electoral-vote tie between Burr and Thomas JEFFERSON sent the election to the House of Representatives; Jefferson was chosen after Alexander HAMILTON endorsed him, and Burr became vice president. Resentful of Hamilton's action and a later effort to block Burr's nomination for governor of New York in 1804, he challenged Hamilton to a duel following some remarks about Burr's character. He mortally wounded Hamilton and fled to Philadelphia. There he contacted Gen. James WILKINSON, with whom he planned an invasion of Mexico. He was tried for treason in 1807 but acquitted. Still under a cloud, Burr left for Europe, where he tried to interest English and French authorities in his scheme to conquer Florida. In 1812 he returned to New York to resume his law practice.

burro See DONKEY

Burroughs, Edgar Rice (1875–1950) U.S. novelist. Born in Chicago, he initially worked as an advertising copywriter. His *Tarzan of the Apes* (1914) became the first of 25 novels featuring Tarzan, the son of an English nobleman abandoned in Africa and raised by apes. He wrote 43 other novels.

B

Burroughs, John (1837–1921) U.S. naturalist. Born near Roxbury, N.Y., he worked as a teacher, farmer, and U.S. Treasury Department clerk, before moving to a farm in the Hudson River valley. He often traveled and camped out with such friends as John MUIR and Theodore ROOSEVELT. His many books, which helped establish the genre of the nature essay, include *Wake-Robin* (1871), *Birds and Poets* (1877) and *Locusts and Wild Honey* (1879).

Burroughs, William S(eward) (1855–1898) U.S. inventor. Born in Auburn, N.Y., he constructed his first calculating machine in 1885. He patented a more practical model in 1892. This machine was a commercial success, but he died at 43 before he could earn much money from it. In 1905 the Burroughs Adding Machine Co. was organized as successor to the company he had started.

Burroughs, William S(eward) (1914–1997) U.S. novelist. The grandson of W. S. BURROUGHS, he attended Harvard Univ. and later joined the central group of the BEAT MOVEMENT. His experimental novels evoke, in deliberately erratic prose, a nightmarish, sometimes wildly humorous world. His early *Junkie* (1953) frankly describes his experiences as a heroin addict. *The Naked Lunch* (1959; film, 1991), preoccupied with homosexuality and police persecution, vividly satirizes the grotesque world of the addict. His later novels include *The Soft Machine* (1961), *Nova Express* (1964), and *Cities of the Red Night* (1981).

Bursa *formerly* **Brusa** *ancient* Prusa. City (pop., 1996: 1,057,000), NW Turkey. It was founded in the 3rd cent. B.C., near the Mysian Mt. Olympus and the Sea of MARMARA. It flourished under Roman and later Byzantine emperors. After the Crusaders took Constantinople in 1204, it was a seat of Byzantine resistance. The Ottoman empire took it in the early 14th cent. and made it their first great capital. Conquered by TIMUR in the early 15th cent., it was recovered by the Ottomans. Today an agricultural center, it is also noted for its carpets and its many 15th-cent. mosques.

bursitis \bər-ˈsī-təs\ INFLAMMATION of the lubricating sac (bursa) over a JOINT or extension of a joint, or between TENDONS and muscles or bones, caused by infection, injury, ARTHRITIS or GOUT, calcium deposits along a tendon or joint, or repetitive minor irritation (as in "housemaid's knee" and "tennis elbow"). Bursitis in the shoulder is the most common form; it may be so painful that the affected arm cannot be raised. Treatment includes rest, heat, mild exercise, and medication.

Burton, Richard F(rancis) (*later* **Sir Richard**) (1821–1890) British scholar-explorer and Orientalist. Expelled from Oxford, Burton went to India as a subaltern officer; disguised as a Muslim, he wrote detailed reports of merchant bazaars and urban brothels. In Arabia, again disguised, he became the first non-Muslim European to penetrate the forbidden holy cities and recounted his adventures in his classic *Pilgrimage to El-Medinah and Mecca* (1855–56). In 1857–58 he traveled with John Hanning SPEKE in search of the source of the NILE RIVER; stricken with malaria, he turned back after becoming the first European

Richard Burton Painting by Lord Leighton, 1876

to reach Lake TANGANYIKA. His travels produced 43 accounts of such subjects as Mormons, W. African peoples, Brazilian devil cults, Iceland, and Etruscan Bologna. He learned 25 languages; among his 30 volumes of translations were ancient Eastern manuals on the art of love, and he larded his famous *Arabian Nights* translation with ethnological footnotes and daring essays that won him many detractors.

Burton, Richard *orig.* Richard Walter Jenkins, Jr. (1925–1984) British-U.S. actor. He first won success on the stage in *The Lady's Not for Burning* (1949). After his U.S. film debut in *My Cousin Rachel* (1952), he starred in such films as *The Robe* (1953) and *Alexander the Great* (1956). During the filming of *Cleopatra* (1963) he had a highly publicized love affair with Elizabeth TAYLOR, whom he later twice married. Known for his resonant voice and his Welsh mournfulness, he starred again on Broadway in *Camelot* (1960) and an acclaimed *Hamlet* (1964). Among his other films are *Who's Afraid of Virginia Woolf?* (1966) and *Equus* (1977).

Burton, Robert (1577–1640) British scholar and writer. His great *Anatomy of Melancholy* (1621) describes every aspect of melancholy in a lively, elegant, and even humorous style; a mine of classical erudition and curious information, it is an index to the philosophy and psychology of its time. His Latin comedy *Philosophaster* (1606) is a vivacious exposure of charlatanism.

Burton, Tim (b.1958) U.S. film director. Born in Burbank, Cal., he made his first short film in 1982. He directed the hit *Pee-Wee's Big Adventure* (1985), followed by *Beetlejuice* (1988), establishing an original, quirky style, and later the successful *Batman* (1989) and its sequel (1992), *Edward Scissorhands* (1990), *Ed Wood* (1994), *Mars Attacks!* (1996), and *Sleepy Hollow* (1999).

Burundi \bu̇-ˈrün-dē\ *officially* **Republic of Burundi** Country, central Africa. Area: 10,759 sq mi (27,866 sq km). Population (2000): 6,055,000. Capital: BUJUMBURA. The popula-

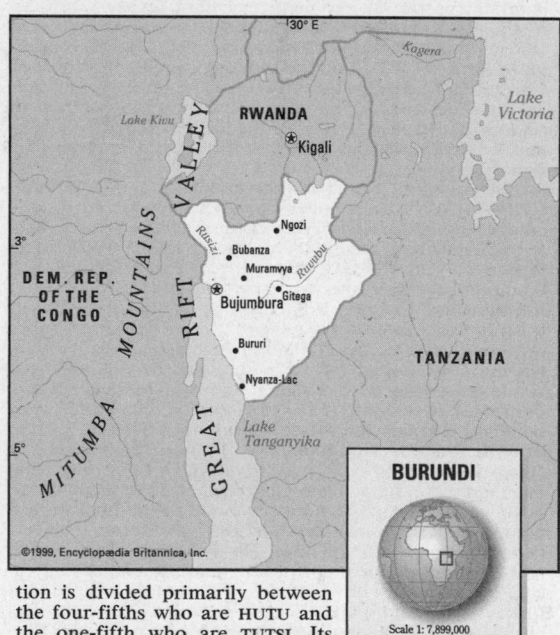

©1999, Encyclopædia Britannica, Inc.

BURUNDI

Scale 1: 7,899,000

tion is divided primarily between the four-fifths who are HUTU and the one-fifth who are TUTSI. Its first inhabitants, the Twa Pygmies, make up about 1% of the population. Languages: Rundi (Kirundi), French (both official); Swahili, English. Religions: Christianity (79%). Currency: Burundi franc. Burundi occupies a high plateau, straddling the divide of the NILE and CONGO (Zaire) rivers. The divide runs north to south, rising to 9,055 ft (2,760 m) at its highest point. The plateau contains the Ruvubu River basin, the southernmost extension of the Nile basin. In the west, the Rusizi River connects Lake Kivu in the north with Lake TANGANYIKA to the south. It has a developing economy, based primarily on agriculture. It is under a military regime. Normally, it has one legislative house, and its head of state and government is the president assisted by two vice presidents. Original settlement by the Twa was followed by Hutu settlement, which occurred gradually and was completed by the 11th cent. The Tutsi arrived 300–400 years later; though a minority, they established the kingdom of Burundi in the 16th cent. In the 19th cent., the area came within the German sphere of influence, but the Tutsi remained in power. Following World War I the Belgians took control of the area, then known as the mandate of Ruanda-Urundi. This was replaced by a U.N. trusteeship after World War II. Colonial-period conditions had intensified Hutu–Tutsi ethnic animosities, and as independence neared, hostilities flared. Independencewas granted in 1962 in the form of a kingdom ruled by the Tutsi. In 1965 the Hutu rebelled but were brutally repressed. The rest of the 20th cent. saw violent clashes between the two groups, leading to over 200,000 deaths amid charges of genocide in the 1990s. The military assumed power in 1996.

bus Device that provides a data path between a computer's CPU and attached devices (keyboard, mouse, disk drives, video cards, etc.). Like a bus that stops at designated stations to pick up or drop off riders, a computer bus receives a data signal from the CPU and drops it off at the appropriate device. Data signals from devices are sent back to the CPU. On a network, a bus provides the data path between the various computers and devices. See also USB.

bus Large motor vehicle designed to carry passengers usually along a fixed route according to a schedule. The first gasoline-powered bus was built in Germany in 1895. The first integral-frame bus was constructed in the early 1920s in the U.S. From the 1930s, DIESEL ENGINES provided greater power to larger buses. With the development of highway systems, transcontinental bus lines became common in N. America. Double-decked buses are used in some European cities; articulated buses pull trailers with flexible joints. Trolley buses, whose electric motors draw power from overhead wires, are now used mostly in European cities.

Bush, George (Herbert Walker) (b.1924) 41st president of the U.S. (1989–93). Born in Milton, Mass., he served in World War II, graduated from Yale Univ., and started an oil business in Texas. He served in the U.S. House of Representatives (1966–70) and as ambassador to the U.N. (1971–72), chief of liaison to China (1974–76), and head of the CIA (1976–77). He served as vice president under Ronald REAGAN (1981–88), whom he succeeded as president. He made no dramatic departures from Reagan's policies. In 1989 he ordered a brief military invasion of Panama, which toppled that country's leader, Gen. Manuel NORIEGA. He helped impose a U.N.-approved embargo against Iraq in 1990 to force its withdrawal from Kuwait. When Iraq refused, he authorized a U.S.-led air offensive that began the PERSIAN GULF WAR. Despite general approval for his foreign policy, an economic recession led to his defeat by William CLINTON in 1992. His son George W. BUSH won the presidency in 2000.

George Bush, 1988

Bush, George W(alker) (b.1946) 43rd president of the U.S. (from 2001). Born in New Haven, Conn., son of George BUSH, he attended Yale Univ. and Harvard Business School. After spending a decade in the oil business with mixed success, he served as managing general partner of the Texas Rangers baseball franchise. In 1994 he was elected governor of Texas; popular for his genial style and support of education reform, he was reelected in 1998. In 1999 he launched his presidential campaign and quickly raised the largest presidential war chest in U.S. history. Despite

George W. Bush

losing the national popular vote to Al GORE, he gained the presidency when a U.S. Supreme Court ruling effectively ended the Florida recount on which hinged an Electoral College majority. As president he pursued a strongly conservative agenda, dominated by a huge tax cut in 2001. After the SEPTEMBER 11 ATTACKS, he initiated the U.S. invasion of Afghanistan and a "war on terrorism."

Bush, Vannevar (1890–1974) U.S. electrical engineer and administrator. Born in Everett, Mass., he taught principally at MIT (1919–38, 1955–71). In the late 1920s and '30s, Bush and his students built several electronic analog computers to solve differential equations. He helped found Raytheon Co., and he served as president of the Carnegie Institute 1939–55. In 1941 he became director of the U.S. Office of Scientific Research and Development, in which capacity he helped organize the MANHATTAN PROJECT, and later he laid the groundwork for the establishment of the National Science Foundation (1950). An information retrieval and annotation system he described became the theoretical prototype of HYPERTEXT.

bushido \'bù-shi-dō\ (Japanese: "Way of the Warrior") Code of conduct of the SAMURAI class of Japan, first formulated in the 17th cent. Its precise content varied over time; along with self-discipline, honor, and austerity, one constant feature was the samurai's obligation to his lord, which superseded even familial ties. This obligation was transferred to the emperor with the MEIJI RESTORATION and was a salient feature of the Japanese national mindset during World War II.

bushmaster Species (*Lachesis muta*) of pit viper, found in scrublands and forests from Costa Rica south to the Amazon River basin. It is normally about 6 ft (1.8 m) long but reportedly may grow to twice this length. It is pinkish or tan, marked with large, dark, diamond-shaped blotches. Its bite is potentially lethal.

Bushmen See SAN

business cycle Periodic fluctuation in the rate of economic activity, as measured by levels of employment, prices, and production. Economists have long debated why periods of prosperity are eventually followed by economic crises (stock-market crashes, bankruptcies, unemployment, etc.). Some have identified recurring eight-to-ten-year (or longer) cycles in market economies. Apart from random shocks such as wars and technological changes, the main influences on economic activity are INVESTMENT and CONSUMPTION. Investment in a new factory leads to consumption because the workers employed to build the factory have wages to spend. Conversely, increases in consumer demand cause new factories to be built to satisfy the demand. Eventually the economy reaches its full capacity, and, with little free capital and no new demand, the process reverses itself and contraction ensues. Natural fluctuations in agricultural markets, psychological factors such as a bandwagon mentality, and changes in the money supply may all cause changes in investment and consumption. Since World War II, government MONETARY POLICY has aimed at moderating the business cycle, preventing the extremes of INFLATION and DEPRESSION.

business finance Raising and managing of funds by business organizations. Typically, senior managers use financial forecasting to develop a long-term plan for the firm, then devise shorter-term budgets to fit within it. When a company plans to expand, it may rely on cash reserves, expected increases in sales, or bank loans and trade credits extended by suppliers. Managers may also decide to raise long-term capital in the form of either debt (BONDS) or equity (STOCK). The value of the company's stock is a constant concern, and managers must decide whether to reinvest PROFITS or to pay DIVIDENDS. When deciding how to deploy corporate assets to increase growth, financial managers must also consider the benefits of mergers and acquisitions, analyzing economies of scale and the ability of businesses to complement each other.

business law *or* **commercial law** *or* **mercantile law** Legal rules and principles bearing on business organizations and commercial matters. It regulates various forms of legal business entities, including sole proprietors, partnerships, and multinational corporations. Nearly all statutory rules governing business organizations are intended to protect

B

creditors or investors. In addition, specific bodies of law regulate commercial transactions, including the sale and carriage of goods, consumer credit agreements, and relations between employers and employees. It is a broad and continually evolving field. See also AGENCY, CORPORATION, INTELLECTUAL PROPERTY, LABOR LAW.

Busoni \bü-'sō-nē\, **Ferruccio (Dante Michelangiolo Benvenuto)** (1866–1924) Italian-German composer and pianist. At 12 he conducted his own *Stabat Mater*. He taught in Helsinki, Moscow, and Boston before settling permanently in Berlin in 1894, where he won fame as a virtuoso pianist. His celebrated opera *Die Brautwahl* (1910) was followed by the operas *Arlecchino* (1916) and *Turandot* (1917), but the posthumously produced *Doktor Faust* is regarded as his masterpiece. Of his many orchestral works, his piano concerto (1904) is most widely performed. His many piano pieces include the *Fantasia contrappuntistica* (1910), six sonatinas (1910–20), and arrangements of many organ works by J. S. BACH.

bustard Any of about 23 species of medium-sized to large game birds in the family Otididae, related to the CRANES and RAILS in the order Gruiformes. Bustards are found in Africa, S Europe, Asia, Australia, and New Guinea. A tall running bird, it has an erect neck placed forward of its long legs. The best-known species is the great bustard *(Otis tarda)*, the largest European land bird; males reach lengths of 4 ft (1.2 m), with 8-ft (2.4-m) wingspreads.

Buthelezi \ˌbüt-ʔl-'ā-zē\, **Mangosuthu G(atsha)** (b.1928) ZULU chief and leader of the INKATHA FREEDOM PARTY. He was elected head of the nonindependent black state of KwaZulu in 1972, and revived Inkatha in 1974 after breaking with the AFRICAN NATIONAL CONGRESS (ANC). Rejecting full independence for KwaZulu, he worked within the white establishment to end APARTHEID. In 1990–94 he engaged in a fierce struggle for leadership with the ANC; thousands were killed in Inkatha–ANC clashes. In 1994 he was appointed minister of home affairs by Nelson MANDELA.

Butler, Nicholas Murray (1862–1947) U.S. educator. Born in Elizabeth, N.J., he received his PhD from Columbia Univ. He was the founding president of what is today Columbia's Teachers College (1886–91). As president of Columbia Univ. itself (1901–45), he led the institution to world renown. A champion of international understanding, he helped establish the Carnegie Endowment for International Peace in 1910 and served as its president 1925–45. In 1931 he shared the Nobel Peace Prize with Jane ADDAMS.

Butler, R(ichard) A(usten) *later* Baron Butler (of Saffron Walden) (1902–1982) British politician. Known as "Rab" Butler, he was elected to Parliament in 1929. As minister of education, he was responsible for the 1944 Education Act, which established free secondary education. After 1945 he helped remold the Conservative Party, serving as its leader 1955–61. He served as chancellor of the exchequer 1951–55, home secretary 1957–62, and foreign secretary 1963–64.

Butler, Samuel (1612–1680) British poet and satirist. As a cleric, he observed cranks and scoundrels like those whose antics he attacked. His mock-heroic poem *Hudibras* (1663–78) skewers the fanaticism, pedantry, and hypocrisy he saw in militant PURITANISM. The most memorable BURLESQUE poem in English, it is the first to successfully satirize ideas rather than personalities.

Butler, Samuel (1835–1902) British novelist, essayist, and critic. Descended from distinguished clergymen, he grappled for years with Christianity and evolution, first embracing, then rejecting Charles DARWIN's theories. His utopian satire *Erewhon* (1872) foreshadowed the end of the Victorian illusion of eternal progress. His autobiographical novel *The Way of All Flesh* (1903) tells, with ruthless wit, of his escape from the suffocating moral atmosphere of his home circle.

butte \'byüt\ (French: "hillock" or "rising ground") Flat-topped isolated hill with steep or precipitous sides, from the bottom of which a slope descends to the plain. Buttes topped by horizontal platforms of hard rock are characteristic of the arid plateau region of the W U.S. A butte is similar to a MESA but generally smaller; both are created by erosional processes.

butter Solid emulsion of FAT globules, water, and salt made by churning CREAM. Butter has long been used as a cooking fat and as a spread. It was traditionally a farm product, but with the advent of the cream separator in the late 19th cent. it began to be mass-produced. It is a high-energy food, containing about 715 calories per 100 grams, with 80–85% butterfat and little protein. Coloring is often added to enhance its natural yellow color (from CAROTENE).

buttercup Any of about 250 species of widely distributed herbaceous flowering plants constituting the genus *Ranunculus* of the family Ranunculaceae. Buttercups are especially common in the woods and fields of the N temperate zone. The turban, or Persian buttercup *(R. asiaticus)*, is the florist's ranunculus. Among the many wild species are the tall meadow buttercup *(R. acris)* and common water crowfoot *(R. aquatilis)*. Their leaves are usually alternate and stalkless and may be simple or much divided. The flowers may be radially symmetrical or irregular. The family includes such flowers as ANEMONE, LARKSPUR, marsh marigold, CLEMATIS, and hepatica (genus *Hepatica*).

butterfly Any of several thousand LEPIDOPTERAN species belonging to about six families and found worldwide. Unlike MOTHS, butterflies are usually bright or strikingly colored and are active during the day. Distinctive features are its club-tipped antennae and its habit of holding its wings vertically over its back when at rest. Representative species (with their families) include the metalmarks (Riodinidae), snout butterflies (Libytheidae), sulphur butterflies (Pieridae), swallowtail (Papilionidae), BLUE (Lycaenidae), and MONARCH (Nymphalidae).

butterfly bush See BUDDLEIA

butterfly effect See CHAOTIC BEHAVIOR

butternut Deciduous NUT-producing tree *(Juglans cinerea)* of the WALNUT family, native to E N. America. Each leaf has 11–17 yellowish-green leaflets that are hairy underneath. The egg-shaped fruit has a sticky, greenish-brown husk. The hard, woody nut bears many ridges and contains a sweet, oily seed. The tree is economically important for its edible nuts and for a yellow or orange dye obtained from the fruit husks. Some substances in the inner bark of the roots are used in medicines.

Buxtehude \ˌbůk-stə-'hü-də\, **Dietrich** (1637?–1707) Danish-German composer. He held two organist positions before being appointed organist at Lübeck's important Marienkirche, where he remained almost 40 years. There he reinstated the tradition of the Abendmusik, an annual series of church concerts. His reputation was such that in 1705 J. S. BACH traveled 200 miles there to hear him play and stayed three months. His surviving works include 130 cantatas, almost 100 works for organ, some 20 keyboard suites, and over 20 chamber sonatas.

buzzard Chiefly British term for any of several BIRDS OF PREY of the HAWK genus *Buteo* (family Accipitridae) and, in N. America, various New World VULTURES, especially the TURKEY VULTURE. In Australia, a large hawk of the genus *Hamirostra* is called a black-breasted buzzard. The buteos, also called buzzard hawks, can usually be distinguished when soaring by their broad wings and expansive rounded tail. Buteos customarily prey on insects, small mammals, and occasionally birds. Species range over much of the New World, Eurasia, and Africa. The red-tailed hawk, the most common N. American buteo, is about 2 ft (60 cm) long.

buzz bomb See V-1 MISSILE

Byblos \'bi-bləs\ *modern* **Jubayl** \jủ-'bāl\ Ancient city, E Mediterranean coast. Located north of modern BEIRUT, it was occupied at least by the NEOLITHIC PERIOD; extensive settlement developed during the 4th millennium B.C. As the chief harbor for the export of cedar to Egypt, it was a great trading center. Papyrus received its early Greek name, *byblos,* from its export to the Aegean through Byblos. Byblos has yielded almost all the known early Phoenician inscriptions, most from the 10th cent. B.C. By that time TYRE had become predominant in Phoenicia.

Bydgoszcz \'bid-ˌgöshch\ City (pop., 1999 est.: 386,000), N Poland. Originally a commercial city of the TEUTONIC ORDER, it received town rights in 1346. It prospered as a grain and timber center until it was devastated in the 17th-cent. Swedish wars. In the 18th cent. the Bydgoszcz Canal, which linked the basins of the VISTULA and ODER rivers, made the city a major inland port. It was under Prussian rule 1772–1919. It was noted for its staunch resistance to the successful Nazi attack of 1939.

Byelarus See BELARUS

bypass surgery See CORONARY BYPASS

Byrd, Richard E(velyn) (1888–1957) U.S. naval officer and polar explorer. Born in Winchester, Va., he worked developing navigational aids for aircraft. In 1926 he and Floyd Bennett claimed to have reached the North Pole by airplane. In 1928 Byrd began his explorations of Antarctica with the first expedition to his "Little America" base, which was followed in 1929 by a flight with three companions over the South Pole, the first such flight. He led subsequent expeditions that discovered and mapped large areas of Antarctica. His several books include *Discovery* (1935) and *Alone* (1938), which chronicled his months spent alone in a camp near the South Pole.

Byrd, William (1543–1623) British composer. He studied under Thomas TALLIS, and was appointed organist of Lincoln Cathedral at 20. In 1572 he became organist of the Chapel Royal jointly with Tallis. In 1575 the two men received from ELIZABETH I the exclusive license for the printing and selling of music in Britain. Though repeatedly prosecuted as a Roman Catholic, Byrd remained in favor with the queen. He apparently taught most of the important composers of the next generation. Britain's finest composer of sacred choral music, Byrd wrote three masses (for three, four, and five voices), some 220 Latin motets, four Anglican services, and some 60 anthems, as well as some 100 harpsichord pieces. He is regarded as the greatest British composer up to his time.

Byron, George (Gordon), Baron *known as* **Lord Byron** (1788–1824) British Romantic poet and satirist. Born with a clubfoot, he unexpectedly inherited his title and estates at 10. He gained notice with *English Bards and Scotch Reviewers* (1809), a satire responding to a review of his first book, *Hours of Idleness* (1807). *Childe Harold's Pilgrimage* (1812–18), a poetic travelogue of his European grand tour expressing melancholy and disillusionment, brought him fame, while his complex personality, dashing good looks, and scandalous love affairs captured the imagination of Europe. Settling near Geneva, he wrote the verse tale *The Prisoner of Chillon* (1816), an indictment

Lord Byron Portrait by Richard Westall, 1813

of tyranny, and *Manfred* (1817), a poetic drama whose hero reflected Byron's own guilt and frustration. His greatest poem, *Don Juan* (1819–24), is an unfinished epic picaresque satire in OTTAVA RIMA. He died of fever while aiding the Greek struggle for independence.

byssinosis See BROWN LUNG DISEASE

byte See BIT

Byzantine architecture \'bi-zən-ˌtēn\ Building style of Constantinople (now Istanbul, formerly ancient Byzantium) after A.D. 330. Byzantine architects were eclectic, at first drawing heavily on Roman temple features. Their combination of the BASILICA and symmetrical central-plan (circular or polygonal) religious structures resulted in the Byzantine Greek-cross-plan church, with a square central mass and four arms of equal length. The most distinctive feature was the domed roof, which was ingeniously designed to rest above a square base. Byzantine structures featured soaring spaces and sumptuous decoration: marble columns and inlay, mosaics on the vaults, inlaid-stone pavements, and gold coffered ceilings. The architecture of Constantinople extended throughout the Christian East and remained in use in Russia after the fall of Constantinople (1453). See also HAGIA SOPHIA.

Byzantine art Art associated with the BYZANTINE EMPIRE. Its characteristic styles were first codified in the 6th cent. and persisted with remarkable homogeneity until the capture of Constantinople in 1453. Almost exclusively religious, it tends to reflect an intensely hierarchical view of the universe. It relies on vigor of line and brilliance of color; individual features are absent, forms are flattened, and perspective is absent. Walls, vaults, and domes were covered in mosaic and fresco in a total fusion of architectural and pictorial expression. The importance of Byzantine art to European religious art was immense; the style was spread by trade and expansion to the Mediterranean basin, E European centers, and especially Russia.

Byzantine empire Empire, SE and S Europe and W Asia. It began as the city of Byzantium, which had grown from an ancient Greek colony founded on the European side of the BOSPORUS. The city was taken in A.D. 330 by CONSTANTINE I, who refounded it as Constantinople. His successor, THEODOSIUS I, divided the empire between his two sons. The fall of Rome in 476 ended the W half of the Roman empire; the E half continued as the Byzantine empire, with Constantinople as its capital. Heir to the civilization of the HELLENISTIC AGE, the E realm was more commercial and more urban. Its greatest emperor, JUSTINIAN (r.527–565), reconquered some of W Europe, built the HAGIA SOPHIA, and issued the basic codification of Roman law. The long controversy over ICONOCLASM within the Eastern Church prepared it for the break with the Roman Church (see SCHISM OF 1054). During the controversy, Arabs and Seljuq Turks increased their power in the area. In the late 11th cent., ALEXIUS I COMNENUS sought help from Venice and the Pope; these allies turned the ensuing CRUSADES into plundering expeditions. In the Fourth Crusade the Venetians took over Constantinople and established a line of Latin emperors. When recaptured by Byzantine exiles in 1261, the empire was little more than a large city-state. In the 14th cent. the Ottoman Turks began to encroach; their extended siege of Constantinople ended in 1453, when the last emperor died fighting on the city walls and the area came under Ottoman control.

Byzantium See ISTANBUL

C

C High-level procedural computer PROGRAMMING LAN-
GUAGE with many low-level features, including the ability
to handle memory addresses and bits. It is highly portable
among platforms and therefore widely used in industry and
among computer professionals. C was developed by Dennis
M. Ritchie (b.1941) of Bell Laboratories in 1972. UNIX is
written almost exclusively in C, and C has been standardized as part of POSIX (Portable Operating System Interface
for UNIX).

C++ \'sē-'pləs-'pləs\ Object-oriented version (see OBJECT-
ORIENTED PROGRAMMING) of the computer PROGRAM-
MING LANGUAGE C. Developed by Bjarne Stroustrup of Bell
Laboratories in the early 1980s, it is traditional C language
with added object-oriented capabilities. C++, along with
JAVA, has become popular for developing commercial soft-
ware packages that incorporate multiple interrelated appli-
cations.

Cabala See KABBALA

cabaret \ˌka-bə-'rā\ Restaurant that serves liquor and offers
light musical entertainment.
The cabaret originated in
France in the 1880s as a small
club that presented amateur
acts and satiric skits. The
first German *Kabarett* was
opened in Berlin about 1900;
it later became a showcase
for the underground works of
such social critics as Berolt
BRECHT and Kurt WEILL, and
a decadent but fertile artistic
milieu. The English cabaret
derived from concerts given
in city taverns in the 18th–
19th cent. and evolved into
the MUSIC HALL. In the U.S.,
the cabaret developed into
the nightclub, where comedians, singers, or musicians performed.

Cabaret "Moulin Rouge-La
Goulue" by Henri de
Toulouse-Lautrec, 1891

cabbage Leafy garden plant
(*Brassica oleracea* 'capitata')
with a globular head of usually green leaves. A member
of the MUSTARD FAMILY, it is
a major VEGETABLE in most countries of the temperate
zone. The term cabbage also refers more generally to a
plant of various horticultural forms developed by long cultivation from the wild, or sea, cabbage (*Brassica oleracea*)
found near the seacoast in England and continental Europe.
The common forms may be classified by the plant parts
used for food: leaves (e.g., KALE, COLLARD, common cabbage, BRUSSELS SPROUT); flowers and flower stalks (e.g.,
BROCCOLI, CAULIFLOWER); and stems (e.g., KOHLRABI).
Cabbages grow best in mild to cool climates and tolerate
frost. They are an excellent source of vitamin C, minerals,
and bulk. See also BRASSICA, CHINESE CABBAGE.

cabbage palmetto See PALMETTO

Cabbala See KABBALA

Cabeza de Vaca \kə-'bā-zə-də-'vä-kə\, **Álvar Núñez** (c.1490–
c.1560) Spanish explorer. He joined an expedition that
reached what is now Tampa Bay, Fla., in 1528. One of only
four survivors of the expedition, he spent eight years in the
Gulf region of modern Texas. His accounts of the legendary
Seven Cities of CÍBOLA probably inspired the extensive explorations of N. America by Hernando DE SOTO and Francisco de CORONADO.

cabinet Body of senior ministers or advisers. An integral
part of parliamentary government in many countries, it
developed from the British Privy Council, when King
CHARLES II and Queen ANNE regularly consulted the
council's leading members to reach decisions before meeting with the unwieldy full council. The modern British
cabinet consists of departmental ministers, drawn from
Parliament by the prime minister. In the U.S., the cabinet
serves as an advisory group to the PRESIDENT and as the
heads of government departments. Members' appointments are subject to Senate approval. The U.S. cabinet includes the secretaries of State, Treasury, Defense, Interior, Agriculture, Commerce, Labor, Health and Human
Services, Housing and Urban Development, Transportation, Education, Energy, and Veterans Affairs and the attorney general.

cable car See STREETCAR

Cable News Network See CNN

cable television System that distributes TELEVISION signals
by means of COAXIAL or FIBER-OPTIC cables. Cable television systems originated in the U.S. in the early 1950s to improve reception in areas where broadcast signals were
weak. In the 1960s they were introduced in cities where reception is sometimes degraded by reflection of signals from
tall buildings. Since the mid-1970s cable systems have offered special services for a monthly fee. Besides providing
high-quality signals, some systems can deliver hundreds of
channels. Cable operators are also involved in the development of video compression, real-time communication for
viewers, and HIGH-DEFINITION TELEVISION.

Cabot, John *orig.* Giovanni Caboto (c.1450–1499?) Italian
navigator and explorer. He became a skilled navigator in
travels for a Venetian mercantile firm. In the 1490s he
moved to Bristol, England, and with support from city merchants, he led an expedition in 1497 to find trade routes to
Asia. After landing in N. America, possibly S Labrador or
Cape Breton Island, he took possession of the land for
HENRY VII. On a second expedition, he probably was lost at
sea. His voyages helped lay the groundwork for the later
British claim to Canada. His son Sebastian (1476?–1557) led
later expeditions for England and Spain.

Cabral, Pedro Álvares (1467?–1520) Portuguese navigator
credited with the discovery of Brazil. A nobleman, Cabral
long enjoyed the favor of MANUEL I of Portugal, who in
1500 sent him and 13 ships westward on the second Portuguese voyage to India, following the route taken by Vasco
da GAMA, to strengthen commercial ties and further Portugal's conquests. On April 22, 1500, he landed on the coast of
what is now Brazil and claimed it for Portugal. The rest of
his journey was beset by misfortune; only four ships returned to Portugal.

Cabrillo \kə-'bri-lō\, **Juan Rodríguez** (d.1543?) Explorer in
the service of Spain and discoverer of California. Possibly
born in Portugal, in 1520 he accompanied Spanish explorers
to Mexico, and was one of the conquerors of present-day
Guatemala. In 1542 he sailed along the California coast, entering San Diego and Monterey bays and landing on several
islands, and apparently died of complications from a broken leg suffered on one such landing.

Cabrini, St. Frances Xavier *known as* **Mother Cabrini** (1850–1917) Italian-U.S. missionary, the first U.S. citizen to be canonized by the Roman Catholic church. She took her vows in 1877 and founded the Missionary Sisters of the Sacred Heart in 1880. In 1889 she was sent to the U.S. to work among Italian immigrants. She lived in New York and Chicago but traveled widely, founding 67 houses of her order. She was canonized in 1946.

cacao \kə-'kaů\ Tropical New World tree (*Theobroma cacao*) of the chocolate family (Sterculiaceae, or Byttneriaceae). Its seeds, after fermentation and roasting, yield cocoa, cocoa butter, and CHOCOLATE. The tree, with large, leathery, oblong leaves, is grown throughout the wet lowland tropics, often in the shade of taller trees. The small, foul-smelling, pinkish flowers are borne directly on the branches and trunk; they are followed by the fruit, or pods, each yielding 20–40 seeds, or cocoa beans.

Caccini \kät-'chē-nē\, **Giulio** or **Giulio Romano** (c.1545–1618) Italian composer and singer. He accompanied his patron, Cosimo I de MEDICI, to Florence in the 1570s; there he became associated with the Camerata, an academy that dedicated much attention to producing an equivalent of ancient Greek drama. His *Euridice* (1600), embodying the Camerata's ideals, was the first opera to be published, and one of the first two surviving operas; the other, also titled *Euridice*, is largely by Jacopo Peri (1561–1633), whose lost *Dafne* (1598) was the first opera of all. Caccini's *Le nuove musiche* (1602), a collection of songs with basso continuo, was of landmark importance in establishing the new monodic style.

cachalot See SPERM WHALE

cache \'kash\ Temporary computer storage used for quick retrieval of data in order to increase processing speed. The cached data can be stored in a reserved area of RAM, a special cache chip that provides faster access than RAM, or on the disk drive. By keeping frequently accessed data in a rapidly accessible place, the computer can respond quickly to requests for those data without having to perform time-consuming searches.

cactus Any of the flowering plants that make up the family Cactaceae, containing about 1,650 species, native through most of N. and S. America. Cacti are SUCCULENT perennials that are well adapted to dry regions. They generally have thick herbaceous or woody stems containing chlorophyll. Leaves usually are absent or greatly reduced; the stem is the site of photosynthesis. Root systems range widely to absorb superficial moisture. Cacti vary greatly in size and appearance, from buttonlike PEYOTE and low clumps of PRICKLY PEAR to the upright columns of barrel cacti and the imposing SAGUARO. Cacti can be distinguished from other succulent plants by the presence of small cushionlike structures (areoles) from which, in almost all species, spines arise, as do flowers, branches, and leaves (when present). Flowers, often large and colorful, are usually solitary. Cacti are widely cultivated as ornamentals. Various species, notably prickly pears and CHOLLAS, are cultivated as food.

CAD/CAM \'kad-ˌkam\ *in full* computer-aided design/computer-aided manufacturing. Integration of design and manufacturing into a system under direct control of DIGITAL COMPUTERS. CAD systems use a computer with terminals featuring video monitors and interactive graphics-input devices to design such things as machine parts, patterns for clothing, or INTEGRATED CIRCUITS. CAM systems use high-performance programmable machine tools and industrial robots (see ROBOTICS). Drawings developed during the design process are converted directly into instructions for the production machines, thus optimizing consistency between design and finished product. These two processes are sometimes grouped as CAE (computer-aided engineering).

caddis fly Any member of about 7,000 species of mothlike aquatic insects (order Trichoptera) found worldwide, usually in freshwater habitats. Caddis flies have long antennae and hairy wings that fold rooflike over the abdomen. They feed primarily on plant juices and flower nectar. Many caddis-fly larvae construct a portable case from grains of sand, bits of shells, and plant debris glued together by a sticky substance they secrete. This case surrounds the larva's abdomen while it matures. Caddis flies clean the water by consuming plant and animal debris and serve as an important food for fish, particularly TROUT.

Cádiz \kə-'diz, *Span* 'kä-thēs\ City (pop., 1998 est.: 143,000), SW Spain. Lying northwest of GIBRALTAR, it is the main seaport of Cádiz province in ANDALUSIA. Founded as Gadir by PHOENICIANS from TYRE about 1100 B.C., it was later ruled by CARTHAGE, Rome, and the VISIGOTHS. It was held by the MOORS from A.D. 711. It was captured in 1262 by Alfonso X of CASTILLA Y LEÓN. It enjoyed great prosperity as a center for Spanish trade with the American colonies in the 16th–18th cent. (see SEVILLE).

Cadmus In GREEK MYTHOLOGY, the brother of EUROPA and founder of THEBES. When ZEUS carried off Europa, Cadmus was sent to find her. The Delphic ORACLE ordered him to end his search, follow a cow, and build a town where it lay down. That town became Thebes. He built the citadel of Thebes with the help of fierce armed men who sprang up where he sowed the teeth of a dragon he had slain. Cadmus was said to have brought the alphabet to Greece.

caduceus \kə-'dü-sē-əs\ Staff carried by HERMES as a symbol of peace. It served as a badge of protection for ancient Greek and Roman heralds and ambassadors. It was originally depicted as a rod or olive branch ending in two shoots and decorated with garlands or ribbons; the garlands later became two snakes and a pair of wings was attached to the staff to represent Hermes' speed. It was adopted as a symbol of physicians because it resembled the staff of ASCLEPIUS.

caecilian \si-'sil-yən\ Any of 155 species of wormlike AMPHIBIANS found in humid regions from Mexico to N Argentina and in Africa, S.E. Asia, and the Seychelles. The elongate, ringed, limbless body is 4–60 in. (10–150 cm) long. Color ranges from blackish to pinkish tan. The tiny eyes are covered by skin and often by bone. A chemosensory tentacle lies between the eye and nostril. Caecilians spend their lives underground and eat worms and insects.

Caedmon \'kad-mən\ (fl.658–680) Earliest Old English Christian poet. According to BEDE, he was a herdsman who received a divine call in a dream to sing of "the beginning of things," and began to utter "verses which he had never heard." He entered a monastery, where he produced sacred poetry from what the learned brethren told him. Only the nine-line original dream hymn is certainly his, but it set the pattern for Anglo-Saxon religious verse.

Caernarvon \kīr-'när-vòn, kär-'när-vòn\ Town (pop., 1995 est.: 10,000), seat of Gwynedd county, Wales. Site of a Roman fort, Segontium, built about A.D. 75, after the Roman withdrawal (c.380–390) it was the seat of local chieftains. After conquering Wales in 1282, EDWARD I transformed the town and built an imposing castle; from 1911 it has been the site of the investiture of the Prince of Wales.

Caesar, (Gaius) Julius (100?–44 B.C.) Celebrated Roman general, statesman, and DICTATOR. A PATRICIAN by birth, he held the prominent posts of QUAESTOR and PRAETOR before becoming governor of Farther Spain 61–60. He formed the First TRIUMVIRATE with POMPEY and Marcus Licinius CRASSUS in 60 and was elected CONSUL in 59 and PROCONSUL in Gaul and Illyria in 58. After conducting the GALLIC WARS, he was instructed by the Senate to lay down his command, Senate conservatives having grown wary of his increasing power. When the Senate

Julius Caesar

would not command Pompey to give up his command simultaneously, Caesar led his forces across the Rubicon River (49) between Gaul and Italy, precipitating the Roman Civil War. Pompey fled from Italy, but was pursued and defeated by Caesar in 48; he then fled to Egypt, where he was murdered. Having followed Pompey to Egypt, Caesar became lover to CLEOPATRA and supported her militarily. Named dictator for life by the Romans, he was in the midst of launching a series of political and social reforms when he was assassinated in the Senate House on the ides of March by conspirators led by CASSIUS and BRUTUS. His writings on the Gallic and Civil wars are considered models of classical historiography.

Caesar, Sid (b.1922) U.S. comedian. Born in Yonkers, N.Y., he began his career as a band musician but switched to comedy. Noted for his pantomime skills and his ability to mimic foreign languages at high speed, he performed comic routines in live television shows and costarred with Imogene Coca (1908–2001) in the popular comedy program *Your Show of Shows* (1950–54), created his own *Caesar's Hour* (1954–57), and later appeared in television specials.

Caesar Augustus See Caesar AUGUSTUS

Caesarea \ˌsē-zə-ˈrē-ə\ *modern* Horbat Qesari \ˈk̇ȯr-bȧt-ˈkä-sä-rē\ Ancient seaport, PALESTINE. Located on the coast of present-day Israel south of HAIFA, it was settled by the PHOENICIANS. Rebuilt in the 1st cent B.C. by HEROD, it was renamed for his patron Caesar AUGUSTUS. The capital of the Roman province of JUDAEA in A.D. 6, it was the site of an early Christian church and often visited by St. PAUL. It was destroyed by BAYBARS I in the 13th cent.

caffeine ALKALOID that has marked physiological effects. It occurs in COFFEE beans, TEA leaves, KOLA NUTS, CACAO, maté, and guarana, and in their products. Its stimulating effect makes it medically useful in treating respiratory depression caused by overdose of BARBITURATES, MORPHINE, or HEROIN. Its positive effects can include improved motor performance, alertness, and sensory activity and decreased fatigue. Excessive caffeine can produce irritability, anxiety, insomnia, and potentially serious symptoms such as heart irregularities and delirium. Much of the caffeine included in over-the-counter cold remedies and painkillers has been removed from decaffeinated coffee and tea.

Cage, John (Milton) (1912–1992) U.S. avant-garde composer and writer. Born in Los Angeles, he studied with Arnold SCHOENBERG and Henry COWELL. From the early 1940s he was closely associated with the choreographer Merce CUNNINGHAM. By 1943 his sonic experiments had marked him as notably original. He soon turned to Zen Buddhism and concluded that all sounds are potentially musical; thenceforth he advocated indeterminism and endeavored to ensure randomness in his works, which often relied on the Taoist *Yi jing (I ching)*. By the 1960s he had expanded into the realm of multimedia. His disparate works include *Bacchanale* for prepared piano (1938), *Imaginary Landscape No. 4* for 12 radios (1951), *Fontana Mix* for tape (1958), and *Roaratorio* (1979). His widely read books include *Silence* (1961), *A Year from Monday* (1967), *Notations* (1969), and *M* (1973). His international influence was far greater than that of any previous American composer.

Cage, Nicolas *orig.* Nicholas Coppola (b.1964) U.S. actor. Born in Long Beach, Cal., a nephew of F. F. COPPOLA, he won fame with his intense performances in such popular films as *Peggy Sue Got Married* (1986), *Raising Arizona* (1987), *Moonstruck* (1987), *Wild at Heart* (1990), and *Leaving Las Vegas* (1995, Academy Award).

Cagliari \ˈkäl-yä-rē\ *ancient* Caralis. City (pop., 1998 est.: 171,000), and capital of SARDINIA region, Italy. Located on the island's S coast, it was founded by the PHOENICIANS. Held successively by Rome, the SARACENS, PISA, Spain, and Austria, it passed to the House of SAVOY in 1718. Its harbor, rebuilt after heavy bombing in World War II, is Sardinia's principal port.

Cagney, James (1899–1986) U.S. actor. Born in New York City, he toured in vaudeville before starring in the successful Broadway musical *Penny Arcade* (1929) and its film version, *Sinner's Holiday* (1930). He played the first of a series of gangster roles in the film *Public Enemy* (1931). As G. M. COHAN in *Yankee Doodle Dandy* (1942, Academy Award) he showed off his dance skills and streetwise charm. Later films include *Mister Roberts* (1955), *Man of a Thousand Faces* (1957), and *Ragtime* (1981).

Caicos Islands See TURKS AND CAICOS ISLANDS

Caillebotte \kȧ-yə-ˈbȯt\, **Gustave** (1848–1894) French painter and art collector. A naval architect born to a wealthy family, he became a prolific painter of contemporary subjects, town and country views, still lifes, and boat-

ing scenes. He was the chief organizer, promoter, and financial backer of the Impressionist exhibitions, and he purchased many Impressionist works. He bequeathed his collection to the state, and in 1897 it formed the basis of the first Impressionist exhibition in a French museum.

caiman \ˈkā-mən\ Any member of several species of Central and S. American reptiles of the ALLIGATOR family. Like the rest of the CROCODILE order, caimans are amphibious, lizardlike carnivores. They live along the edges of rivers and other bodies of water, and reproduce by laying hard-shelled eggs in nests built by the female. The largest species is the black caiman *(Melanosuchus niger)*, a potentially dangerous animal with a maximum length of about 15 ft (4.5 m).

Cain and Abel In the Old Testament, the sons of ADAM AND EVE. According to GENESIS, Cain, the first-born, was a farmer, and his brother Abel was a shepherd. Cain was enraged when God preferred his brother's sacrifice of sheep to his own offering of grain, and he murdered Abel. God sent Cain into exile, but marked him with a sign to signify that he would be avenged if he were killed.

Cairngorm Mountains \ˈkarn-ˌgȯrm\ Mountain range, NE Scotland. It is located in the Highlands between the Spey and Dee river valleys; its highest peak is Ben Macdui, at 4,296 ft (1,309 m) the second-highest (after BEN NEVIS) in the British Isles. Popular for winter sports, it is a chief source of the cairngorm variety of quartz.

Cairo \ˈkī-rō\ *Arabic* Al-Qahirah \ˌäl-ˈkä-hē-rə\ City (pop., 1996: 6,789,000; metro. area pop., 1999 : 10,345,000), capital of Egypt. Located on the NILE RIVER near the site of a Roman city captured by the Arabs in 641, Old Cairo (Al-Fustat) was then built by the Arabs as a military camp. Cairo's newer section (Al-Qahirah) was built by the FATIMID DYNASTY around 968 and was made the capital in 973. From the 13th cent., as the capital of the MAMLUK sultans, it reached its greatest prosperity as a trade and cultural center. In World War II it was a British and U.S. base and the site of two Allied conferences. The ancient metropolis is a blend of old and new, East and West. It is the largest city of the Middle East and of Africa, and the chief cultural center of the Arab world. The Pyramids of GIZA are nearby.

caisson \ˈkä-ˌsän\ In engineering, a type of FOUNDATION most commonly used underwater for a bridge, but sometimes used in building construction. It is a large hollow structure that is sunk down through the earth by workers excavating from inside it; ultimately it becomes a permanent part of the pier. There are three types: the open caisson, open at both top and bottom; the box caisson, closed at the bottom; and the pneumatic caisson, with an airtight chamber to accommodate submerged workers. Caisson columns, typically 2 ft (0.6 m) or more in diameter, may be used as an alternative to bearing piles.

caisson disease See DECOMPRESSION SICKNESS

Cajun Any descendant of French Canadians driven by the British in the 18th cent. from the captured French colony of ACADIA (now Nova Scotia and adjacent areas) who settled in the fertile bayou lands of then-French S Louisiana. Many Cajuns speak a dialect of French. Cajun cuisine, noted for its hot seasoning, and zydeco music have become popular among non-Cajuns.

calabash Tree *(Crescentia cujete)* of the trumpet-creeper family (Bignoniaceae) found in Central and S. America, the W. Indies, and extreme S Florida. It is often grown as an ornamental. It produces large spherical fruits, the hard shells of which are useful as containers when hollowed out. The fruit's shell encloses a whitish pulp and thin, dark brown seeds. The tree bears funnel-shaped, light green and purple-streaked flowers and evergreen leaves.

Calabria \kä-ˈlä-brē-ä\ Autonomous region (pop., 1996 est.: 2,076,000), S Italy. Forming the "toe" of the Italian "boot," it separates the Tyrrhenian and Ionian seas. A mountainous area, it has been subject to earthquakes. Its capital is Catanzaro. Founded as a Greek colony, it was taken by the Romans in the 3rd cent. B.C. and eventually passed to the Byzantines. Conquered by the Normans, it was united to the Kingdom of NAPLES in the 11th cent. A stronghold of Italian republicanism until the RISORGIMENTO, it became part of Italy after the 1860 expedition of Giuseppe GARIBALDI. Long a poor area dependent on farming, it underwent a land reform system in the mid-20th cent. that promoted more diverse profitable crops.

Calais \kȧ-ˈle, ka-ˈlā\ Seaport (pop., 1999: 77,000), N France, on the Strait of DOVER. Fortified by the count of Boulogne in 1224, it was taken by EDWARD III of England (1347), and after 1450 it was the only remaining English possession in France. The 2nd duc de GUISE took Calais from the English in 1558. In WORLD WAR II it was a main objective in the German drive to the sea in 1940. It is an important passenger port and is near the French terminus of the CHANNEL TUNNEL. Calais is famous for its lace and embroideries.

Calamity Jane orig. Martha Jane Cannary (1852?–1903) U.S. frontierswoman. Born in Princeton, Mo., she worked in mining camps, acquiring riding and shooting skills. In 1876 she settled in Deadwood, S.D., site of new gold strikes, and hauled goods and machinery to the outlying camps. There she probably first met Wild Bill HICKOK, often described as her companion. From 1895 she toured with Wild West Shows. Facts about her life were embellished by contemporary feature-magazine writers.

calcedony See CHALCEDONY

calcite \ˈkal-ˌsīt\ Most common form of natural calcium carbonate, a widely distributed mineral known for the great variety of its crystals. It occurs in stalagmites and stalactites and forms the structure of coral reefs. Calcite is the most important mineral in limestones and marbles used in the building, steel, chemical, and glass industries.

calcium Chemical ELEMENT, one of the ALKALINE EARTH METALS, chemical symbol Ca, atomic number 20. The most abundant metallic element in the human body, it is stored in BONES and teeth and has many functions (see CALCIUM DEFICIENCY). It is the fifth most abundant element in the earth's crust but does not occur naturally in the free state. Its compounds (VALENCE 2) include LIMESTONE, CHALK, MARBLE, and DOLOMITE. It occurs in eggshells, pearls, coral, and many marine shells as calcium carbonate, or CALCITE; in APATITE (as calcium phosphate); in GYPSUM (as calcium sulfate); and in many other minerals. Its ALLOY with lead is used as cable sheathing and grids for BATTERIES. Calcite is used as a lime source, filler, neutralizer, and extender; in pure form it is used as an antacid and calcium supplement and in baking powder. Calcium oxide (lime) and hydroxide (slaked lime) are important industrially. Other important compounds are chloride (a drying agent), hypochlorite (a BLEACH), sulfate (gypsum and PLASTER OF PARIS), and phosphate (a plant food and stabilizer for plastics).

calcium deficiency Inadequate supply or METABOLISM of CALCIUM, the main structural element of BONES and teeth (see TOOTH). Its metabolism is regulated by VITAMIN D, PHOSPHORUS, and HORMONES (see PARATHYROID GLAND) and it is pulled from the bones if deficiency develops. Chronic deficiency may cause OSTEOPOROSIS or osteomalacia (softening of bone) and may contribute to HYPERTENSION and colon cancer. Acute calcium deficiency (hypocalcemia), usually the result of a metabolic problem rather than a dietary deficiency, causes numbness, tingling, and painful muscle aches and spasms.

calculator Machine for performing arithmetic operations and certain mathematical functions automatically. Blaise PASCAL devised a digital arithmetic machine in 1642. By the late 19th cent., such machines had become smaller and easier to use, and desktop machines appeared in the early 20th cent. Later, miniature SOLID-STATE DEVICES ushered in calculators that could perform complex mathematical functions and also store data and instructions in memory registers, providing programming capabilities similar to those of small computers.

calculus Field of mathematics that analyzes aspects of change in processes or systems that can be modeled by FUNCTIONS. Through its two primary tools—the DERIVATIVE and the INTEGRAL—it allows precise calculation of rates of change and of the total amount of change in such a system. The derivative and the integral grew out of the idea of a LIMIT, the logical extension of the concept of a function over smaller and smaller intervals. Discovered independently by Isaac NEWTON (see DIFFERENTIAL CALCULUS) and G. W. LEIBNIZ (see INTEGRAL CALCULUS), calculus was

one of the major scientific breakthroughs of the modern era.

Calcutta or **Kolkata** City (metro. area pop., 2001: 13,216,000), NE India. Capital of W. Bengal state, former capital (1772–1912) of British India, and India's second-largest metropolitan area, it was an English trading center in 1690 and the seat of the BENGAL presidency in 1707. Captured by the nawab of Bengal, who in 1756 imprisoned the English there (in a prison later known as the Black Hole), the city was retaken by the British under Robert CLIVE. An extremely busy 19th-cent. commercial center, it declined with the removal of the capital to Delhi in 1912, the partition of the province between India and Pakistan in 1947, and the creation of Bangladesh in 1971. The flood of refugees from these political upheavals added to widespread poverty, which Mother TERESA, among others, tried to combat. Despite its problems, Calcutta remains a major commercial, educational, and cultural center.

Caldecott \ˈkȯl-də-kət\, **Randolph** (1846–1886) British graphic artist and watercolorist. Drawing for such periodicals as *Punch* and *Graphic*, he developed a gently satirical style, and he achieved success with illustrations for Washington IRVING's *Sketch Book* (1875) and *Bracebridge Hall* (1876). He is best known as an illustrator of children's books, including William COWPER's *John Gilpin* (1878). He died at 39 in Florida, where he had gone to improve his frail health. Since 1938 the Caldecott Medal has been awarded annually for the most distinguished U.S. picture book for children.

Calder \ˈkȯl-dər\, **Alexander (Stirling)** (1898–1976) U.S. sculptor. Born in Philadelphia to a family of artists, he studied mechanical engineering, and in 1923 attended the Art Students League, where he was influenced by artists of the ASH CAN SCHOOL. In 1926 he moved to Paris and began making toylike animals and circus figures of wood and wire; from these he developed his famous miniature circus, which led to his later monumental wire sculptures. In the 1930s he became well known also for his portraits, continuous line drawings, and abstract, motor-driven constructions. He is best known as the inventor of the MOBILE. He also constructed nonmovable works known as stabiles, and designed rugs, tapestries, jewelry, and book illustrations.

Calderón de la Barca \ˌkäl-də-ˈrōn-dä-lə-ˈbär-ka\, **Pedro** (1600–1681) Spanish playwright. He abandoned religious studies in 1623 to write plays for the court of PHILIP IV. His secular plays included *The Surgeon of His Honor* (1635), *Life Is a Dream* (1638), and *The Daughter of the Air* (1653). His many plays on religious themes include *The Constant Prince* (1629) and *The Wonder-Working Magician* (1637). He also created 76 one-act religious dramas. Considered the successor to Lope de VEGA, he was noted for his well-constructed plots and his preoccupation with the vanity of human existence.

Caldwell, Erskine (1903–1987) U.S. author. Born in Coweta Co., Ga., he met poor sharecroppers through his father's missionary work. Fame arrived with *Tobacco Road* (1932), a controversial novel of rural squalor; adapted as a play, it ran for over seven years on Broadway. *God's Little Acre* (1933), also a best-seller, portrayed hopelessly poor rural degenerates, mixing violence and sex in grotesque tragicomedy. He also wrote the text for documentary books with photographs by Margaret BOURKE-WHITE, whom he married.

calendar System for dividing time over extended periods, such as DAYS, months, or YEARS, and arranging these divisions in a definite order. Essential for the study of chronology, which uses these divisions to date events, it is also vital for any civilization that needs to measure periods for agricultural or other reasons. The lunation, or period in which the moon completes a cycle of its phases (29^1/$_2$ days), is the basis for the month; most ancient calendars were collections of months. Days and SEASONS, which are a solar phenomena, do not have periods that evenly divide, so ancient calendars employed various means, such as the periodic insertion of an intercalary month, to reconcile the months with the seasons. The GREGORIAN CALENDAR is used almost universally today. See also Jewish CALENDAR, Muslim CALENDAR.

calendar, French republican See FRENCH REPUBLICAN CALENDAR

calendar, Jewish *or* **Hebrew calendar** Religious and (in Israel) civil dating system based on both lunar and solar cycles. In the calendar used today, a day is counted from sunset to sunset, a week comprises 7 days, a month has 29 or 30 days, and a year has 12 lunar months plus approximately 11 days (or 353, 354, or 355 days). In order to bring the calendar in line with the annual solar cycle, a 13th month of 30 days is added seven times in a 19-year cycle. The Jewish calendar in use today was popularly accepted around the 4th cent. C.E. (A.D.) and is based on Biblical calculations placing the creation in 3761 B.C.E. (B.C.).

Month	Days	Month	Days
Tishri (Sept.–Oct.)	30	Nisan (Mar.–Apr.)	30
Heshvan (Oct.–Nov.)	29 or 30	Iyar (Apr.–May)	29
Kislev (Nov.–Dec.)	29 or 30	Sivan (May–June)	30
Tebet (Dec.–Jan.)	29	Tammuz (June–July)	29
Shebat (Jan.–Feb.)	30	Ab (July–Aug.)	30
Adar (Feb.–Mar.)	29 or 30	Elul (Aug.–Sept.)	29

calendar, Muslim *or* **Islamic calendar** Dating system used in the Muslim world and based on a year of 12 months, each month beginning approximately with the new moon. The months are alternately 30 and 29 days long except for the 12th, Dhu al-Hijjah, is 30 days long in 11 years of a 30-year cycle, to keep the calendar in step with the true phases of the moon. Thus the year has either 354 or 355 days. No months are added as in leap years, so the named months do not remain in the same seasons but retrogress through the entire solar, or seasonal, year every $32\frac{1}{2}$ solar years.

Month	Days	Month	Days
Muharram	30	Rajab	30
Safar	29	Shaban	29
Rabi I	30	Ramadan	30
Rabi II	29	Shawwal	29
Jumada I	30	Dhu al-Qadah	30
Jumada II	29	Dhu al-Hijjah	29
		in leap years	30

calendering Process of smoothing and compressing a material (notably PAPER) during production by passing a continuous sheet through a number of pairs of heated rolls. The rolls (calenders), made of hardened steel or steel covered with fiber, typically exert a pressure of 500 lbs per linear in. (89 kg per cm). Coated papers are calendered to obtain a smooth, glossy finish. Calendering is also widely used in the manufacture of TEXTILES, coated fabrics, and plastic sheeting.

Calgary \'kal-gə-rē\ City (metro. area pop., 1996: 822,000), S Alberta, Canada. It was founded in 1875 as a fort on the BOW RIVER. The arrival of the Canadian Pacific Railway in 1883 aided its growth, as did the discovery of nearby oil and gas fields in 1914 and 1947. The annual Calgary Stampede, founded in 1912, is a world-famous rodeo and celebration of the Old West.

Calhoun \kal-'hün\, **John C(aldwell)** (1782–1850) U.S. politician. Born in Abbeville district, S.C., he was elected to the U.S. House of Representatives (1811–17), where as a leader of the WAR HAWKS he introduced the declaration of war against Britain in June 1812. He served as U.S. secretary of war 1817–25. He was elected vice president (under J. Q. ADAMS) in 1824, and again (under Andrew JACKSON) in 1828. A champion of states' rights and slavery, and a supporter of NULLIFICATION, he resigned the vice presidency in 1832 and was elected to the U.S. Senate, where he served 1832–

John C. Calhoun
Daguerreotype by Mathew Brady, c.1849

50, interrupted only by brief service as secretary of state (1844–45). His exuberant defense of slavery as a "positive good" aroused strong anti-Southern feeling in the free states.

Cali \'kä-lē\ City (pop., 1992 est.: 1,624,000), W Colombia. Founded in 1536 far from the coast, it did not develop economically until the 20th cent., when the upper CAUCA RIVER was drained to generate electrical power and prevent flooding. It is a major industrial and service center. In the 1980s and '90s, Cali was a notorious center for cocaine smuggling.

California State (pop., 2000: 33,871,000), W U.S. Lying on the Pacific Ocean, it is the largest state in population and the third-largest in area, extending about 800 mi (1,300 km) north to south and 250 mi (400 km) east to west. The capital is SACRAMENTO. Within 85 mi (137 km) of each other lie Mt. WHITNEY and DEATH VALLEY, the highest and lowest points in the 48 contiguous states. It was inhabited originally by American Indians. The first European coastal expansion took place in 1542–43 when J. R. CABRILLO established a Spanish claim to the area. The first mission was established by Junípero SERRA at SAN DIEGO in 1769. The region remained under Spanish, and after the 1820s, Mexican, control until it was taken by U.S. forces in the MEXICAN WAR, and ceded to the U.S. by the Treaty of GUADALUPE HIDALGO in 1848. Though settlement had begun by the U.S. in 1841, it was greatly accelerated by the 1848 GOLD RUSH. California was admitted to the Union in 1850 as a slavery-free state under the COMPROMISE OF 1850. Its already expanding population grew immensely in the 20th cent. It has the largest economy of any state. It has suffered severe earthquakes, most destructively those of SAN FRANCISCO in 1906 and 1989 and LOS ANGELES in 1994.

California, Gulf of *or* **Sea of Cortés** Gulf separating BAJA CALIFORNIA from the rest of Mexico. Its area is about 59,000 sq mi (153,000 sq km). Some geologists hold that the gulf is structurally part of the Pacific; others claim Baja California is pulling away from the continent as it moves north along the SAN ANDREAS FAULT, allowing the gulf to form.

California, Lower See BAJA CALIFORNIA

California, University of Public university with campuses at Berkeley (main campus), Davis, Irvine, Los Angeles, Riverside, San Diego, San Francisco, Santa Barbara, and Santa Cruz. It is the third-largest university system in the U.S. (total enrollment 152,000). It was established in 1868 in Oakland. In the 1930s research at the Berkeley campus produced the first CYCLOTRON, the isolation of the human polio virus, and the discovery of several new chemical elements. Today Berkeley remains a leader in many academic areas. The San Francisco campus, originally the university's Medical Center (1873), has schools of medicine, nursing, dentistry, and pharmacy. The San Diego campus, founded as a marine station, joined the university in 1912; it includes the Scripps Institution of Oceanography. The Los Angeles branch (UCLA), founded in 1919, includes schools of law, medicine, and engineering. The Santa Barbara campus was granted university status in 1944; the Davis and Riverside campuses were both added in 1959, and those at Santa Cruz and Irvine in 1965. The university operates the Lawrence Livermore National Laboratory and the LOS ALAMOS National Laboratory.

California Institute of Technology *known as* **Caltech** Highly select private university and research institute in Pasadena offering instruction and research in pure and applied science and engineering. Established in 1891, it is today considered one of the world's premier scientific research centers. In 1958 its Jet Propulsion Laboratory, in conjunction with NASA, launched Explorer I, the first U.S. satellite. Facilities include astronomical observatories at Palomar Mtn. and Mt. Wilson, a seismology laboratory, a marine-biology laboratory, and a center for the study of radio astronomy. Total enrollment is about 1,900.

California Institute of the Arts *known as* **Calarts** Private institution of higher learning in Valencia. Created in 1961 it comprises highly regarded schools of art, dance, film and video, music, and theater, and a division of critical studies. All schools award BFA and MFA degrees. Enrollment is about 1,000.

Californian Indians American Indian peoples originally living in and around present-day California. Food varied with the region inhabited (coastal peoples fished, desert peoples hunted and practiced marginal agriculture, etc.), as did style of housing. Shamanism was common to all groups. Californian Indians had a renowned oral literature, and Californian basketwork is considered exquisite. See also NORTHWEST COAST INDIANS, POMO, SHAMAN.

Caligula \kə-'li-gyə-lə\ *officially* Gaius Caesar (Germanicus) (A.D. 12–41) Roman emperor (37–41). Known by his childhood nickname, Caligula ("Little Boots") was declared heir to the throne by TIBERIUS following the suspicious deaths of Caligula's parents and brothers. He suffered a severe illness seven months into his rule and began displaying mental instability, engaging in despotic caprice and cruelty. He executed former supporters, extorted money from the citizens, and made pretensions to divinity. He plundered Gaul in 40 and began planning to invade Britain. Weary of his tyranny, a group of conspirators assassinated him.

caliper Instrument that consists of two adjustable legs or jaws for measuring the dimensions of material parts. Outside calipers measure thicknesses and outside diameters of objects; inside calipers measure hole diameters and distances between surfaces. Hermaphrodite calipers, which have one leg bent inward and one straight leg ending in a sharp point, are used for scribing lines at a specified distance from a flat or curved surface.

caliph \'kā-ləf, 'ka-ləf\ (from Arabic *khalifah*: "deputy, successor") Title given to those who succeeded the prophet Muhammad as ruler of the Muslim world, with all his powers except that of prophecy. Controversy over the selection of the fourth caliph, ALI, split Islam into the SUNNI and SHIITE sects. Ali's rival, al-MUAWIYAH I, established the UMAYYAD DYNASTY, which produced 14 caliphs (661–750). The widely recognized ABBASID DYNASTY (750–945) was associated with 38 caliphs. The FATIMID DYNASTY proclaimed a new caliphate in 920; ABD AL-RAHMAN III announced one in opposition to both the Abbasids and the Fatimids in 928. The MAMLUKS were caliphs from 1258 until the Ottomans took over the title in 1517 (see OTTOMAN EMPIRE). The Turkish republic abolished it in 1924.

calisthenics Systematic rhythmic bodily exercises (e.g., jumping jacks, push-ups), usually performed without apparatus. Calisthenics promote strength, endurance, flexibility, and cardiovascular health. The exercises, initially conceived as primarily for women, arose in the 19th cent. in Germany and Sweden. As their health benefits became known, they became an activity for both sexes.

calla Either of two distinct kinds of plants of the ARUM FAMILY. *Calla palustris* is known as the arum lily, water arum, or wild calla. Several species of *Zantedeschia* are also often called calla lilies. The handsome *C. palustris* occurs widely in wet places in cool, N temperate and subarctic regions. It has heart-shaped leaves, showy white floral leaves, and clusters of brilliant red berries. Its juice is violently poisonous. The most important of the calla lilies, all native to S. Africa, is the common florist's calla (*Z. aethiopica*), a stout herb with a fragrant white spathe and arrow-shaped leaves.

Callaghan \'ka-lə-,han\, **(Leonard) James** (b.1912) British politician. A trade-union official, he entered Parliament in 1945. He served in Labour governments as chancellor of the exchequer (1964–67), home secretary (1967–70), and foreign secretary (1974–76) before becoming prime minister (1976–79). A moderate, he tried to stem the vociferous demands of the trade unions. After a series of paralyzing labor strikes in 1978–79, his government was defeated.

Callaghan \'ka-lə-,han\, **Morley (Edward)** (1903–1990) Canadian novelist and short-story writer. Born in Toronto, he earned a law degree but never practiced. The short stories in *A Native Argosy* (1929) won acclaim. His first novel, *Strange Fugitive* (1928), portrays the destruction of a misfit. Later novels, including *They Shall Inherit the Earth* (1935), emphasize Christian love as an answer to social injustice. *That Summer in Paris* (1963) describes Callaghan's friendship with F. Scott FITZGERALD and Ernest HEMINGWAY. Later works include *A Fine and Private Place* (1975).

Callahan, Harry (Morey) (1912–1999) U.S. photographer. Born in Detroit, he first developed an interest in photography in 1938. In 1941 Ansel ADAMS's photographs inspired him to develop his own style. His subjects included landscapes, cityscapes, and unconventional portraits of his wife and daughter. Best known as a teacher, he was head of the photography department at the Chicago Institute of Design (1949–61) and developed the photography department at RISD (1961–76).

Callao \kä-'yä-ō\ City (pop., 1993: 615,000), chief seaport, Peru. It was founded in 1537 by Francisco PIZARRO on Callao Bay west of LIMA. As the leading shipping point for gold and silver taken by Spanish conquerors from the INCAS, it was frequently assaulted by pirates and Spain's European rivals. It was destroyed by a tidal wave in 1746, then rebuilt. Simón BOLÍVAR landed at Callao in 1823, and in 1826 it was the site of the final Spanish surrender. It suffered heavy earthquake damage in 1940.

Callas \'ka-ləs\, **Maria** *orig.* Cecilia Sophia Anna Maria Kalogeropoulos (1923–1977) U.S. soprano. Born in New York City, she moved to Greece as a teenager and made her debut there in 1939. She became an international star in *La Gioconda* at the 1947 Verona Festival. The conductor Tullio Serafin (1878–1968) convinced her to shift to the bel canto repertoire, in which she became immortal. Her acclaimed roles included Norma, Medea, Lucia di Lammermoor, and Anna Bolena. Though her voice lacked great beauty, her artistic integrity, vivid stage presence, striking features, and fiery temperament made her the most famous opera star in the world.

calligraphy \kə-'lig-rə-fē\ Art of beautiful, stylized, or elegant handwriting or lettering with pen or brush and ink. In the Islamic and Chinese cultures, calligraphy is as highly revered as painting. In Europe in the 14th–16th cent., two scripts developed that influenced all subsequent handwriting and printing: the roman and italic styles. With the invention of modern printing (1450), calligraphy became increasingly bold and ornamental.

Callimachus \kə-'lim-ə-kəs\ (c.305–c.240 B.C.) Greek poet and scholar. He migrated to Egypt, where he worked at the Library of ALEXANDRIA. Of his voluminous writings, only fragments survive. His *Causes* (c.270 B.C.) is a poetical medley of obscure tales explaining the origins of customs, festivals, and names. His *Pinakes* ("Tablets"), in 120 books, is a catalog of the authors whose works were held in the library.

Callisto \kə-'lis-tō\ In GREEK MYTHOLOGY, a nymph and a hunting companion of ARTEMIS. She vowed never to wed but was seduced by ZEUS, who turned her into a she-bear to conceal his infidelity. She was then killed by Artemis during a hunt. In other versions it is Artemis or the jealous HERA who turns her into a bear. After her death Zeus placed her in the heavens as the constellation Ursa Major (Great Bear).

Callot \kä-'lō\, **Jacques** (1592–1635) French etcher, engraver, and draftsman. In 1612, at the court of the MEDICI FAMILY in Florence, he was employed to make pictorial records of pageants and feasts. He had a genius for caricature and the grotesque; his series of etchings *The Miseries of War* (1633) was used as a source by Francisco de GOYA. His output was prodigious; over 1,400 etchings and 2,000 drawings survive. One of the greatest of all etchers, he was also one of the first major artists to practice the graphic arts exclusively.

Calloway, Cab(ell) (1907–1994) U.S. singer and big-band leader who combined audacious showmanship with prodigious vocal range and imagination. Born in Rochester, N.Y., he fronted his first group in 1928; it became the house band at Harlem's Cotton Club, in 1931. An accomplished scat singer, he became most identified with his 1931 hit "Minnie the Moocher." Exposure with his band launched the careers of many important jazz soloists.

calorie Unit of ENERGY or HEAT, about 4.2 joules, the amount of heat needed to raise the temperature of 1 g of water by 1°C. The calorie used by dietitians and food scientists and found on food labels is actually the kilocalorie (also called Calorie by scientists and abbreviated kcal or Cal), or 1,000 calories. It measures the amount of heat energy or metabolic energy contained in the chemical bonds (see BONDING) of a food.

Caltech See CALIFORNIA INSTITUTE OF TECHNOLOGY

calumet \\'kal-yə-ˌmet\\ *or* **sacred pipe** *or* **peace pipe** One of the central ceremonial objects of many American Indian groups. It was considered a microcosm, its parts and its decorative colors and motifs being believed to correspond to the essential parts of the universe. Because of the narcotic effect of the tobacco and the symbolism of the indrawn and ascending smoke, it was employed as a means of communication between the spiritual world and humankind.

Calvary *or* **Golgotha** Hill in JERUSALEM, the site of JESUS' crucifixion. The hill of execution was outside the city walls; its exact location is uncertain, but most scholars specify either the spot now covered by the Church of the Holy Sepulchre or a hillock called Gordon's Calvary north of the Damascus Gate.

Calvert, George, Baron Baltimore (c.1580–1632) English colonialist. He served in the House of Commons from 1621; after he had declared himself a Roman Catholic (1625), he gave up his office as secretary of state. To assure the prosperity of his New World holdings, he took his family to his Newfoundland colony in 1628. When conflict arose over his Catholicism and the climate proved too severe, he petitioned CHARLES I for a land grant in the Chesapeake Bay area. He died before the charter was granted, and his son Cecil became proprietor of the colony of Maryland, whose capital was named for him.

Calvin, John *French* **Jean Cauvin** \\kō-'vaⁿ\\ (1509–1564) French-Swiss Protestant theologian and major figure of the REFORMATION. He studied religion at the Univ. of Paris and law in Orléans and Bourges.

When he returned to Paris in 1531 he became part of a movement that emphasized salvation by grace rather than by works. Government intolerance prompted his move to Basel, Switzerland, where he wrote the first edition of *Institutes of the Christian Religion* (1536). He then went to Geneva to help establish Protestantism in that city. He was expelled by city fathers in 1538 but returned in 1541, when the town council instituted the stern and intolerant church order out-

John Calvin Painting, French school, c.1550

lined in his Ecclesiastical Ordinances. By 1555 Calvin had succeeded in establishing a theocracy in Geneva, where he served as pastor and head of the Genevan Academy and wrote the sermons, biblical commentaries, and letters that form the basis of CALVINISM.

Calvin, Melvin (1911–1997) U.S. biochemist. Born in St. Paul, Minn., he developed a system of using radioactive carbon-14 in his studies of the green alga chlorella. By halting the plant's growth at various stages and measuring tiny amounts of radioactive compounds present, Calvin was able to identify most of the reactions involved in the intermediate steps of PHOTOSYNTHESIS, for which he was awarded a 1961 Nobel Prize. His research also included work in radiation chemistry and processes leading to the origin of life.

Calvinism In PROTESTANTISM, the theology developed and advanced by John CALVIN. It was further developed by his followers and became the foundation of the REFORMED CHURCH and PRESBYTERIANISM. As shaped by Calvin's successor at Geneva, Theodore Beza (1519–1605), Calvinism emphasizes the doctrine of PREDESTINATION, holding that God grants SALVATION only to the chosen, or elect. It views the church as a Christian community in which Christ is head and all members are equal under him, and therefore rejects the episcopal form of church government in favor elected church officers. Calvinism was the basis of theocracies in Geneva and Puritan New England (see PURITANISM).

Calvino \\käl-'vē-nō\\, **Italo** (1923–1985) Italian writer. After early works based on his time with the Italian Resistance in World War II, he turned to fantasy and allegory in the 1950s. *Cosmicomics* (1965) is a collection of whimsical narratives about the creation and evolution of the universe.

The novels *Invisible Cities* (1972), *The Castle of Crossed Destinies* (1973), and *If on a Winter's Night a Traveler* (1979) use playfully innovative structures.

calypso \\kə-'lip-sō\\ Type of folk song originally from Trinidad but sung elsewhere in the Caribbean. The calypso tradition dates to the early 19th cent. The subject of a calypso text, usually witty and satiric, is an event of political or social import. The lyric often incorporates Spanish, Creole, and African phrases, employing newly invented expressions. The exaggeration of local speech patterns is matched by an offbeat rhythm. Favorite accompanying instruments are the shak-shak (maraca), cuatro (a string instrument), tamboo-bamboo (bamboo poles of various lengths struck on the ground), and steel drums.

cam Machine component that either rotates or reciprocates (moves back and forth) to convert rotary to linear motion, or vice versa, in a contacting element (the follower). The shape of the contacting surface of the cam is determined by the motion to be produced and the profile of the follower. Cam-follower mechanisms are particularly useful when a simple motion is to be converted to a more complicated motion that must be accurately timed with respect to the simple motion and may include periods of rest (dwells). Cams are essential elements in MACHINE TOOLS, PRINTING machines, SEWING MACHINES, and textile machinery.

Camagüey \\ˌkä-mä-'gwā\\ City (pop., 1994 est.: 294,000), capital of Camagüey province, Cuba. Founded at the site of the present-day port of Nuevitas, it was moved inland in 1528. It is now Cuba's largest interior city.

Camargo \\kä-mär-'gō\\, **Marie (-Anne de Cupis de)** (1710–1770) French ballerina noted for her technical innovations. She made her Paris Opera debut in 1726, going on to dance in 78 ballets and operas before her retirement in 1751. Admired for her speed and agility, she executed jumping steps previously performed only by male dancers, shortening her skirts and removing the heels from her slippers to do so.

Cambio, Arnolfo di See ARNOLFO DI CAMBIO

Cambodia *or* **Kampuchea** Monarchy, SE Asia. Area: 69,898 sq mi (181,036 sq km). Population (2000): 12,371,000. Capital: PHNOM PENH. The vast majority of the population be-

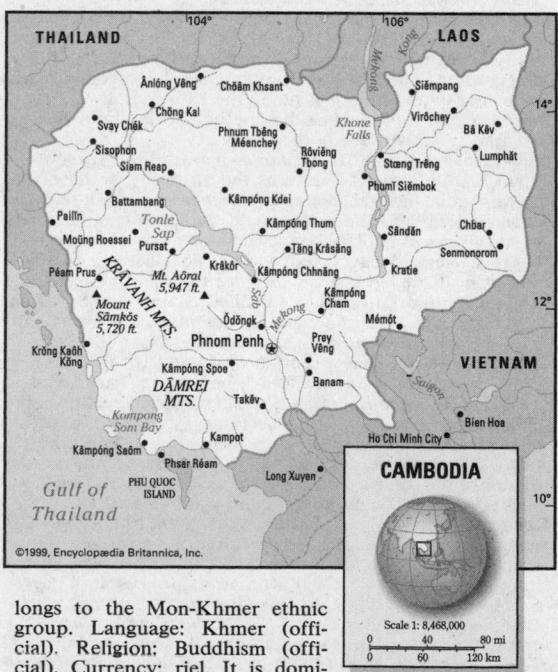

longs to the Mon-Khmer ethnic group. Language: Khmer (official). Religion: Buddhism (official). Currency: riel. It is dominated by large central plains; the Dangrek Mtns. lie along its N border. It lies largely in the basin of the MEKONG RIVER; the large lake TONLE SAP is in its W part. Much of the country is jungle. It is one of the world's poorest countries. Agriculture employs three-fourths of the workforce. It is a constitutional monarchy with one legislative house; its chief of state is the king, and its head of government is the prime minister. In the early Christian era, the area was under Hindu and to a lesser extent Buddhist influence. The KHMER state gradually spread in the early 7th cent., and reached its height under Jayavarman II and his successors in the 9th–12th cent., when it ruled the Mekong Valley and the tributary SHAN states and built ANGKOR. Widespread adoption of Buddhism occurred in the 13th cent., resulting in a script change from SANSKRIT to PALI. From the 13th cent. it was attacked by ANNAM and Siamese city-states and was alternately a province of one or the other. It became a French protectorate in 1863. It was occupied by the Japanese in World War II; it became independent in 1954. Its borders were the scene of fighting in the VIETNAM WAR from 1961, and in 1970 its NE and E areas were occupied by the N. Vietnamese and penetrated by U.S. and S. Vietnamese forces. An indiscriminate U.S. bombing campaign alienated much of the population, enabling the communist KHMER ROUGE under POL POT to seize power in 1975. Their regime of terror resulted in the deaths of over 1 million Cambodians. Vietnam invaded in 1979 and drove the Khmer Rouge into the W hinterlands, but it was unable to effect reconstruction of the country and Cambodian infighting continued. A peace accord was reached by most Cambodian factions under U.N. auspices in 1991, and elections were held in 1993. Civil and military unrest continued. In 1997 King NORODOM SIHANOUK left the country, which was on the verge of civil war, but elections in 1998 led to relative stability.

Cambodian See KHMER.

Cambrian period Earliest time division of the PALEOZOIC ERA. During the Cambrian, 544–505 million years ago, there were widespread seas and probably several scattered landmasses of which the largest was GONDWANA. The average climate was probably warmer than today, with less variation between regions. There were no land plants or animals, but there were marine organisms with either shells or skeletons; TRILOBITES were dominant, and the Cambrian is sometimes called the Age of Trilobites. See table at GEOLOGIC TIME.

Cambridge City (pop., 1994 est.: 113,000), E England. The seat of Cambridgeshire, it lies on the Cam River, a tributary of the OISE, north of London. Two monastic foundations date from the 11th–12th century; the city received its first charter in 1207. It is best known as the site of the Univ. of CAMBRIDGE, noted for its educational excellence and its outstanding architecture.

Cambridge City (pop., 2000: 101,000), NE Massachusetts. Adjacent to Boston, it was founded in 1630. The first American institution of higher learning, HARVARD UNIV., was founded here in 1636. In the 19th cent. it was the home of such literary leaders as H. W. LONGFELLOW, J. R. LOWELL, and O. W. HOLMES. The MASSACHUSETTS INSTITUTE OF TECHNOLOGY moved to Cambridge in 1916.

Cambridge, University of Autonomous institution of higher learning at Cambridge, England. Its beginnings lie in an exodus of scholars from OXFORD UNIV. in 1209; the first college was built in 1284. From 1511 Desiderius ERASMUS did much to inculcate the new learning of the Renaissance at Cambridge. In 1546 Henry VIII founded Trinity College, which remains the largest of Cambridge's 31 colleges. From 1669 Isaac NEWTON taught mathematics, giving this field a unique position there. In 1871 James Clerk MAXWELL accepted the chair of experimental physics, beginning a leadership in physics that would continue into the next century. A host of world-renowned scholars in other fields have also taught at Cambridge. Many of its buildings, including King's College Chapel, are rich in history and tradition. The Fitzwilliam Museum contains noteworthy collections of antiquities. Total enrollment is about 15,000.

Cambridge Platonists \'plā-t°n-ists\ Group of 17th-cent. British philosophic and religious thinkers. Led by Benjamin Whichcote (1609–1683), it included Ralph CUDWORTH and Henry More (1614–1687) at Cambridge and Joseph Glanvill

(1636–1680) at Oxford. Though educated as Puritans, they opposed the Calvinist emphasis on the arbitrariness of divine sovereignty. In their eyes, Thomas HOBBES and the Calvinists erred in assuming that morality consists in obeying the will of a sovereign. Morality, they asserted, is essentially rational, and the good person understands the eternal and immutable nature of goodness.

camel Either of two species of large, hump-backed RUMINANTS (family Camelidae) used as draft and saddle animals in desert regions in Africa and Asia. Adaptations to windblown deserts include double rows of eyelashes, the ability to close the nostrils, and wide-spreading soft feet. The Bactrian camel (*Camelus bactrianus*) is about 7 ft (2 m) tall at the top of the two humps; the Arabian camel (*C. dromedarius*), or dromedary, has one hump and is 7 ft (2 m) high at the shoulder. Camels store fat in their

Bactrian camel (*Camelus bactrianus*)

humps to be used later for sustenance and to manufacture water. They are thus able to go several days without drinking water.

Camelot In ARTHURIAN LEGEND, the seat of King Arthur's court. It has been variously identified with Caerleon in Wales, Queen Camel in Somerset, Camelford in Cornwall, Winchester in Hampshire, and Cadbury Castle in Somerset.

cameo Hard or precious stone, glass, ceramic, or shell carved in relief above the surface. It is the opposite of INTAGLIO. Cameos survive from the early Sumerian period (c.3100 B.C.) to the decline of Roman civilization, and from the Renaissance to the 18th cent. They were carved with mythological scenes and portraits, and many adorned belts, brooches, and bracelets.

camera Device for recording an image of an object on a light-sensitive surface (see PHOTOGRAPHY). It is essentially a light-tight box with an opening (aperture) to admit light focused onto a sensitized film or plate. All cameras have included five crucial components: (1) the camera box, which holds and protects the sensitive film from all light except that entering through the LENS; (2) film, on which the image is recorded; (3) the light control, consisting of an aperture or diaphragm and a shutter, both often adjustable; (4) the lens, which focuses the light rays from the subject onto the film, creating the image; and (5) the viewing system, which may be separate from the lens system or may operate through it by means of a mirror. The camera was developed by Nicéphore NIEPCE and Louis DAGUERRE in the early 19th cent. See also DIGITAL CAMERA.

Cameron, Julia Margaret (1815–1879) British portrait photographer. In 1864, after receiving a camera as a gift, she set up a studio and darkroom and began taking portraits of such friends as Alfred TENNYSON and Charles DARWIN. Her sensitive portraits of women are especially noteworthy. She also made allegorical photographs in imitation of the Pre-Raphaelite paintings. Her work reflects a greater interest in spiritual depth than in technical perfection.

Cameroon *French* **Cameroun** \kảm-'rün\ *officially* **Republic of Cameroon** Republic, W. Africa. Area: 183,591 sq mi (475,501 sq km). Population (2000): 15,422,000. Capital: YAOUNDÉ. The country has more than 200 different ethnic groups, including the Fang (one-fifth of the population), Bamileke (one-fifth), Duala, FULANI, and other smaller groups. Pygmies (locally known as Baguielli and Babinga) live in the S forests. Languages: French and English (official), local languages. Religions: indigenous religions, Christianity, Islam (predominant in the north). Currency: CFA franc. Cameroon has four geographic regions. The S area consists of coastal plains and a densely forested plateau. The central region rises progressively to the north and includes the Adamawa Plateau. In the north a savanna plain slopes downward toward the Lake Chad basin. To the west and north along the Nigerian border the relief is mountain-

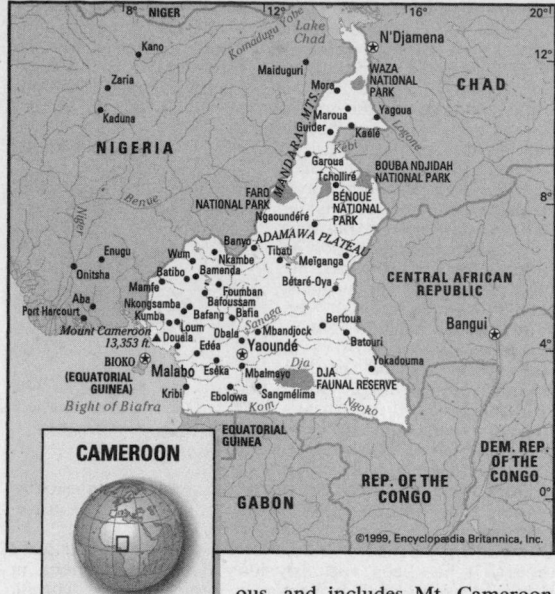

Scale 1: 22,867,000

ous, and includes Mt. Cameroon. Of the main rivers, the Sanaga drains into the Atlantic Ocean, and the BENUE flows westward into the NIGER RIVER basin in Nigeria. Cameroon has a developing market economy based largely on agriculture. It is a republic with one legislative house; its head of state is the president and its head of government, the prime minister. Long inhabited before European colonization, it had BANTU LANGUAGE speakers coming from equatorial Africa to settle in the south. They were followed by Muslim Fulani from the Niger River basin, who settled in the north. Portuguese explorers visited in the late 15th cent. and established a foothold, but they lost control to the Dutch in the 17th cent. In 1884 the Germans took control and extended their protectorate over Cameroon. In World War I joint French-British action forced the Germans to retreat, and after the war the region was divided into French and British administrative zones. After World War II the two areas became U.N. trusteeships. In 1960 the French trust territory became an independent republic. In 1961 the S part of the British trust territory voted for union with the new republic of Cameroon, and the N part for union with Nigeria. In recent decades economic problems have produced unrest in the country.

Camillus \kə-ˈmil-əs\, **Marcus Furius** (d.365 B.C.) Roman soldier and statesman. He allegedly defeated the Gauls after their sack of Rome (c.390), for which he was honored as the city's second founder. Awarded four TRIUMPHS and made DICTATOR five times, he enjoyed his greatest victory in 396 over the Etruscans at Veii. Though a PATRICIAN, he adopted reforms beneficial to the army and the PLEBEIANS (367).

Camisards \ˈkam-ə-ˌzärdz\ Protestant militants in S France who opposed LOUIS XIV's persecution of Protestantism. The armed insurrection began in 1702 in response to Louis's earlier revocation of the Edict of NANTES. The well-organized Camisards, so named for their white shirts (in French dialect, *camisa*), fought successfully and even held royal armies in check. The government burned hundreds of villages and massacred their populations. By 1705 many of the Camisard leaders had been captured and executed.

Camões \kə-ˈmöⁱⁿsh\, **Luís (Vaz) de** (1524/25–1580) Portuguese poet. An impoverished nobleman, he may have spent about 17 years in India. His masterly epic *The Lusiads* (1572) extols glorious deeds in Portuguese history as it recounts Vasco da GAMA's discovery of the sea route to India. His many lyric pieces appeared from 1595 in editions of *Rimas*. He also wrote plays, including the morality play *Filodemo* (1587), and the comedy *The Two Amphitryons*

(1587). No one had more impact on Portuguese and Brazilian literature, and he is Portugal's national poet.

camouflage \ˈka-mə-ˌfläzh\ Art and practice of concealment and visual deception to prevent observation of installations, personnel, equipment, and activities. In World War I, aerial reconnaissance and bombardment required concealment of troops and equipment. By World War II, long-range bombing required that almost everything of military significance be hidden to some degree, using mottled, dull-colored paint patterns, cloth garnishing, netting, and natural foliage.

Luís de Camões Portrait miniature painted in Goa, 1581

Dummies and decoys, including fake cities and airfields, tricked enemy planes into bombing harmless targets. Camouflage was used effectively by Communist guerrilla units in the Vietnam War.

Campania \käm-ˈpä-nyä\ Autonomous region (pop., 1996 est.: 5,763,000), S Italy. Located on the Tyrrhenian Sea, its capital is NAPLES. Occupied successively by Greeks, Etruscans, and Samnites, it became an ally of Rome from about 350 B.C. It is noted for its natural beauty and famous old Roman towns, including CUMAE, POMPEII, Capua, Salernum, and Neapolis (Naples). After the fall of Rome, it was ruled by Gaul, Byzantium, and the Normans, becoming part of the kingdom of Naples in 1282. It was united with Italy in 1861.

campanile \ˌkam-pə-ˈnē-lē\ Italian belltower, originally built beside or attached to a church. The earliest campaniles (7th–10th cent.) were plain round towers with a few small arched openings near the top; the LEANING TOWER OF PISA is an elaborate version of this type. The Venetian form consisted of a tall, square, slim shaft, frequently tapered, with a BELFRY at the top, above which rose the spire, sometimes square as in the famous campanile of ST. MARK'S BASILICA.

campanula See BELLFLOWER

Campbell, Joseph (1904–1987) U.S. writer on comparative mythology. Born in New York City, he explored the common functions of myths in human cultures, examining mythic archetypes in folklore and literature from around the world. His views were popularized through a public-television series in the 1980s. His books include *The Hero with a Thousand Faces* (1949), *The Masks of God* (4 vols., 1959–67), and *The Power of Myth* (1988).

Campbell, Kim (*orig.* Avril Phaedra) (b.1947) Prime minister of Canada (1993). Born in Port Alberni, British Columbia, she was elected in 1988 to the federal parliament as a Progressive Conservative. In Brian MULRONEY's administration, she served as attorney general (1990) and defense minister (1993). On his retirement, she became Canada's first female prime minister in June 1993. Her party was defeated in November, and she resigned as party leader.

Campbell, Mrs. Patrick *orig.* Beatrice Stella Tanner (1865–1940) British actress. She married at age 19 and made her stage debut in 1888, winning fame in *The Second Mrs. Tanqueray* in 1893. She originated the role of Eliza Doolittle in G. B. SHAW's *Pygmalion* (1914), and she and Shaw conducted a famous correspondence for many years. She also achieved great success in Maurice MAETERLINCK's *Pelléas and Mélisande*, Henrik IBSEN's *Ghosts*, and SOPHOCLES' *Electra*.

Camp David Rural retreat of U.S. presidents, N Maryland. The scenic mountainous area was established as "Shangri-La" in 1942 by Pres. Franklin D. ROOSEVELT. In 1953 Dwight EISENHOWER renamed it for his grandson. It has hosted many high-level conferences with foreign heads of state. See also CAMP DAVID ACCORDS.

Camp David Accords (1978) Two agreements reached between Menachem BEGIN of Israel and Anwar al-SADAT of Egypt with the help of Pres. Jimmy CARTER at CAMP DAVID.

One agreement (1979) set the stage for a peace treaty between Egypt and Israel, formally ending 30 years of war. The other agreement created a framework for Palestinian self-rule in the WEST BANK and GAZA STRIP. Israel failed to implement those provisions.

Campeche \käm-ˈpā-chā\ State (pop., 2000 est.: 689,000), SE Mexico. Located on the YUCATÁN PENINSULA, it is bounded by the Gulf of MEXICO, and covers an area of 21,666 sq mi (56,115 sq km); its capital is Campeche. Named after the ancient Mayan province of Kimpech, it comprises much of the W part of the peninsula. Forest products and fishing drive the economy.

camphor Organic compound of the ISOPRENOID family. A white, waxy solid with a penetrating, somewhat musty aroma, it is obtained from the wood of the camphor laurel, or produced synthetically from oil of TURPENTINE. It has long been used in incense and as a medicinal. Modern applications include uses as a plasticizer, moth repellent, or flavoring, in embalming, and in fireworks. Camphorated oil is 20% camphor in olive oil.

Campin \ˈkäm-pin\, **Robert** (c.1375–1444) Flemish painter, probably the painter traditionally known as the Master of Flémalle. He was a master painter in Tournai by 1406; Rogier van der WEYDEN was later one of his students. His principal surviving works are two large panels of an altarpiece once believed to have come from a nonexistent Abbey of Flémalle. The Mérode Altarpiece, formerly regarded as his masterpiece, is now thought to be by a member of his workshop. Despite much uncertainty about his life and work, he was one of the most important and influential Flemish artists of the 15th cent.

camping Recreational activity in which participants live outdoors, often in the wilderness, usually using tents, trailers, or motor homes, but sometimes only a sleeping bag, for shelter. Modern camping originated near the end of the 19th cent. in the U.S. as a rough pastime for hardy lovers of nature. Canoes were the original vehicle; bicycle camping soon followed. Camping was central to the SCOUTING movement. It gained greatly in popularity after World War II, as the number of campgrounds with greater amenities grew. Recent decades have seen its continued growth, to the point of placing a serious strain on the resources of outdoor-recreation areas.

Campylobacter \ˈkam-pi-lō-ˌbak-tər\ Genus of gram-negative (see GRAM STAIN) spiral-shaped BACTERIA infecting mammals. Many species, especially *C. fetus,* cause miscarriage in sheep and cattle. *C. jejuni* is a common cause of FOOD POISONING; perhaps 90% of U.S. chickens are contaminated. Sources also include other meats and unpasteurized milk. See also GASTROENTERITIS.

Camus \kà-ˈmü\, **Albert** (1913–1960) Algerian-French writer. Born into a working-class family in Algiers, he initially worked with a theatrical company. He spent the war years in Paris, and the French Resistance brought him into the circle of J.-P. SARTRE and EXISTENTIALISM. He became a leading literary figure with his enigmatic first novel, *The Stranger* (1942), and the philosophical essay *The Myth of Sisyphus* (1942), an analysis of contemporary nihilism and the concept of the absurd. *The Plague* (1947), his allegorical second novel, and *The Rebel* (1951), a long essay, developed related issues. Other

Albert Camus Photo by Henri Cartier-Bresson

works include the plays *Le malentendu* (1944) and *Caligula* (1944) and the novel *The Fall* (1956). He won the Nobel Prize in 1957. He died at 46 in a car accident.

Canaan \ˈkā-nən\ Ancient name for an area of shifting boundaries but centered on PALESTINE. Coastal Canaanite civilization dates to the Paleolithic era; towns developed in Neolithic times (c.7000–4000 B.C.). The name appears in writings from the 15th cent. B.C. According to the Bible, it was invaded by the Hebrews (JEWS) around 1200 B.C.; however, recent research indicates that the Hebrews may have been indigenous. It was later invaded by the PHILISTINES. In the 10th cent. B.C. the Israelites, under King DAVID, broke the Philistine power, according to the Bible, and Canaan became the Land of Israel, the "Promised Land" of the biblical book of EXODUS.

Canada Nation, N. America. Area: 3,851,808 sq mi (9,976,185 sq km). Population (2000): 30,770,000. Capital: OTTAWA. People of British and French descent compose about half the population; there are significant minorities of German, Italian, Chinese, Ukrainian, Dutch, American Indian, and ESKIMO (Inuit) origin. Languages: English, French (both official). Religions: Roman Catholicism, Protestantism (United Church of Canada, Anglican Church of Canada). Currency: Canadian dollar. Canada may be divided into several physiographic regions. A large interior basin centered on HUDSON BAY and covering nearly four-fifths of the country is composed of the CANADIAN SHIELD, the interior plains, and the Great Lakes–St. Lawrence lowlands. Rimming the basin are highland regions, including the ARCTIC ARCHIPELAGO. Its mountains include the ROCKY MTNS., Coast Mtns., and Laurentian Mtns. Its highest peak is Mt. LOGAN in YUKON TERRITORY. Five of Canada's rivers—the ST. LAWRENCE, MACKENZIE, YUKON, FRASER, and NELSON—rank among the world's 40 largest. In addition to Lakes SUPERIOR and HURON, both shared with the U.S., Canada's GREAT BEAR and GREAT SLAVE lakes are among the world's 11 largest lakes. The country also contains several major islands, including BAFFIN, ELLESMERE, VICTORIA, NEWFOUNDLAND, and Melville, and many small ones. Its border with the U.S., the longest unguarded border in the world, extends 3,987 mi (6,415 km). With a developed market economy that is export-directed and closely linked with that of the U.S., Canada is one of the world's most prosperous nations. It is a parliamentary state with two legislative houses; its chief of state is the British monarch, whose representative is Canada's governor-general, and the head of government is the prime minister. Originally inhabited by American Indians and Inuit, Canada was visited around A.D. 1000 by Scandinavian explorers, whose discovery is confirmed by archaeological evidence from Newfoundland. Fishing expeditions off Newfoundland by the English, French, Spanish, and Portuguese began as early as 1500. The French claim to Canada was made in 1534 when Jacques CARTIER entered the Gulf of ST. LAWRENCE. A small settlement was made in NOVA SCOTIA (Arcadia) in 1605, and by 1608 Samuel de CHAMPLAIN had reached Quebec. Fur trading was the impetus behind the early colonizing efforts. In response to French activity, the English in 1670 formed the HUDSON'S BAY CO. The British–French rivalry for the interior of upper N. America lasted almost a century. The first French loss occurred in 1713 at the conclusion of QUEEN ANNE'S WAR (War of the SPANISH SUCCESSION) when Nova Scotia and Newfoundland were ceded to the British. The SEVEN YEARS' WAR (FRENCH AND INDIAN WAR) resulted in France's expulsion from continental N. America in 1763. After the AMERICAN REVOLUTION the population was augmented by LOYALISTS fleeing the U.S., and the increasing number arriving in Quebec led the British to divide the colony into Upper and Lower Canada

Canadian Prime Ministers

John A. Macdonald	1867–73	Richard Bedford Bennett	1930–35
Alexander Mackenzie	1873–78	W. L. Mackenzie King	1935–48
John A. Macdonald	1878–91	Louis St. Laurent	1948–57
John Abbott	1891–92	John G. Diefenbaker	1957–63
John Thompson	1892–94	Lester B. Pearson	1963–68
Mackenzie Bowell	1894–96	Pierre Elliott Trudeau	1968–79
Charles Tupper	1896	Joseph Clark	1979–80
Wilfred Laurier	1896–1911	Pierre Elliott Trudeau	1980–84
Robert Laird Borden	1911–20	John N. Turner	1984
Arthur Meighen	1920–21	Brian Mulroney	1984–93
W. L. Mackenzie King	1921–26	Kim Campbell	1993
Arthur Meighen	1926	Jean Chrétien	1993–
W. L. Mackenzie King	1926–30		

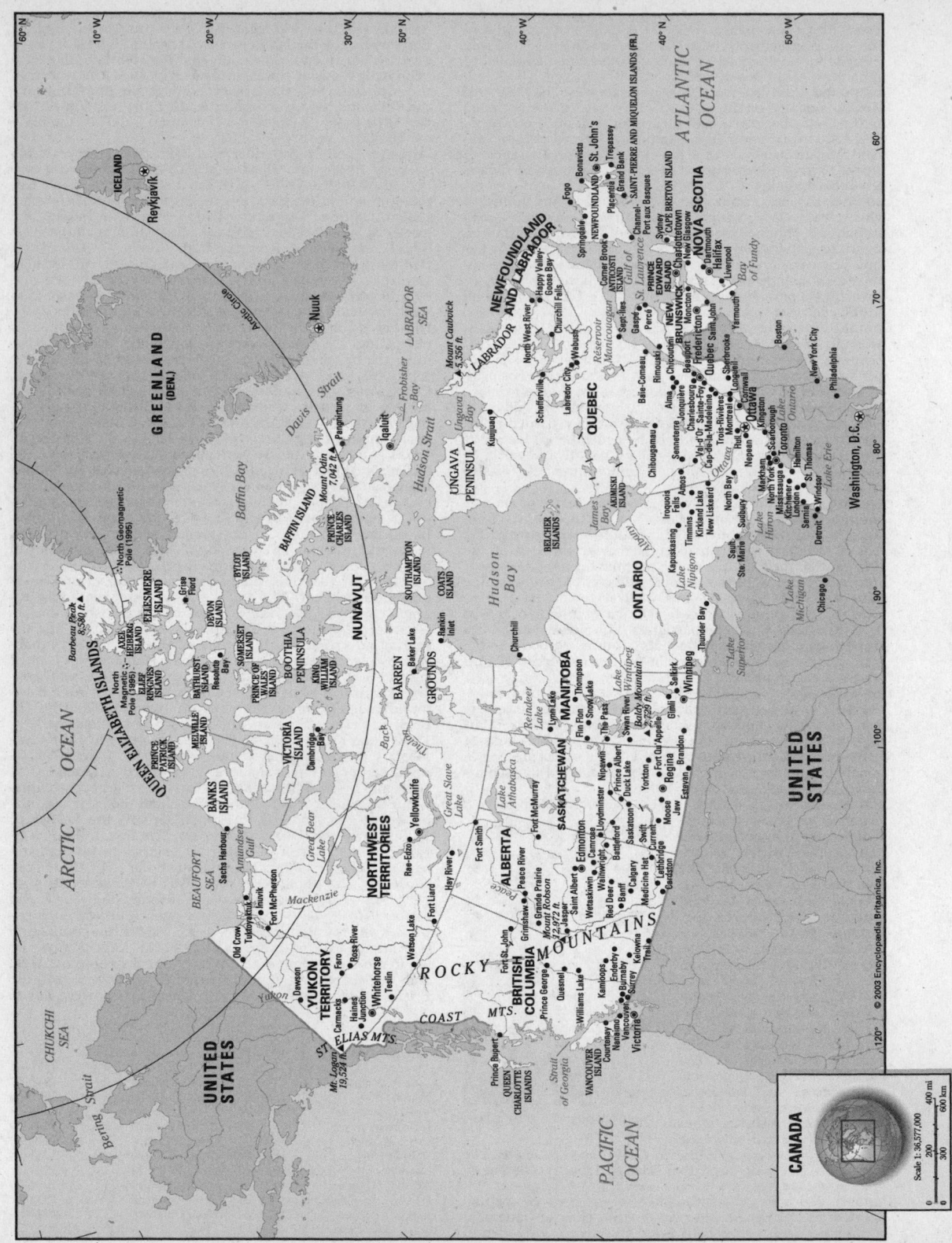

CANADA

Scale 1:36,577,000

0   200   400 mi
0 300   600 km

© 2003 Encyclopædia Britannica, Inc.

in 1791. The British reunited the two provinces in 1841. Canadian expansionism resulted in the confederation movement of the mid-19th cent., and in 1867 the Dominion of Canada, comprising Nova Scotia, New Brunswick, Quebec, and Ontario, came into existence. After confederation, Canada entered a period of westward expansion. The prosperity that accompanied Canada into the 20th cent. was marred by continuing conflict between the English and French communities. Through the Statute of WESTMINSTER (1931), Canada was recognized as an equal partner of Great Britain. With the CANADA ACT of 1982, the British gave Canada total control over its constitution and severed the remaining legal connections between the two countries. French-Canadian unrest continued to be a major concern, with a movement growing for Quebec separatism in the late 20th cent. Referendums for more political autonomy for Quebec were rejected in 1992 and 1995, but the issue remained unresolved.

Canada, Bank of Canadian financial institution established under the Bank of Canada Act (1934). It was founded during the Great Depression to regulate CREDIT and currency. The Bank acts as the Canadian government's fiscal agent and has the sole right to issue paper money.

Canada Act *or* **Constitution Act** Measure formally ending British power to legislate for Canada, approved by the British Parliament on March 25, 1982. The document contains the BRITISH N. AMERICA ACT and was approved by all the Canadian provinces except Quebec, which was denied its claim for a constitutional veto by Canada's Supreme Court.

Canada Day *formerly* **Dominion Day** Annual Canadian holiday. Observed on July 1, it commemorates the formation of the Dominion of Canada on July 1, 1867. With the 1982 passage of the CANADA ACT, its name was officially changed to Canada Day. It is celebrated with parades, fireworks, flag display, and the singing of the national anthem, "O Canada."

Canada East *or* **Lower Canada** Region of Canada now known as QUEBEC. In 1791–1841 it was known as Lower Canada and in 1841–67 as Canada East. Populated mainly by French settlers, it finally agreed to confederation with CANADA WEST in 1867, providing that it would remain a territorial and governmental unit in which French Canadians would have an electoral majority with which to preserve their distinctive identity and cultural traditions.

Canada goose Brown-backed, light-breasted GOOSE (*Branta canadensis*) with black head and neck and white cheeks. Subspecies vary in size, from the 3-lb (1.4-kg) cackling goose to the 20-lb (8-kg) giant Canada goose, which has a wingspread of up to 6.5 ft (2 m). They breed across Canada and Alaska and winter mainly in the S U.S. and Mexico. They are an important game bird. Their almost incessant honking draws attention to their V-formations during migrations. In recent years their population in N. America has greatly increased.

Canada West *or* **Upper Canada** Region of Canada now known as ONTARIO. In 1791–1841 it was called Upper Canada and in 1841–67 Canada West. Though English-speaking, it sought confederation with CANADA EAST in order to achieve effective administration and the construction of intercolonial railways. The unified Dominion of Canada was made official by the BRITISH NORTH AMERICA ACT of 1867.

Canadian Broadcasting Corp. (CBC) Canadian public broadcasting service, created in 1936 to promote Canadian culture and national unity. It offers French- and English-language programs over radio and television networks. Noted for its news and public-affairs programs, it also presents documentaries, dramas, classical music, entertainment, and educational programs as well as sports programs such as its popular weekly National Hockey League broadcasts.

Canadian National Railway Co. Corporation created by the Canadian government in 1918 to operate a number of nationalized railroads as one of Canada's two transcontinental railroad systems. Its passenger services were taken over by VIA Rail Canada in 1978, and the company was privatized in 1995. It bought the Illinois Central Corp. in 1998, thus acquiring a railroad network that links Canada to the Gulf of Mexico.

Canadian Pacific Ltd. Private company known for operating one of Canada's two transcontinental railroad systems. It was created in 1881 to complete a railroad from Montreal to the Pacific. It ceded its passenger services to VIA Rail Canada in 1978. Railroads now account for only a small part of its earnings; in 2001 it reorganized as five independent companies in energy, transportation, and hotel services.

Canadian River River, SW U.S. Flowing across NE New Mexico, it cuts a gorge nearly 1,500 ft (450 m) deep before flowing eastward across Texas to the ARKANSAS RIVER in Oklahoma. It is 906 mi (1,458 km) long. Its course is punctuated by flood-control and irrigation units.

Canadian Shield One of the world's largest CONTINENTAL SHIELDS, centered on Hudson Bay and extending for 3 million sq mi (8 million sq km) over Canada from the Great Lakes to the Canadian Arctic, with small extensions into N Minnesota, Wisconsin, Michigan, and New York. The largest mass of exposed PRECAMBRIAN rock on earth, it is composed of ancient crystalline rocks whose complex structure attests to a long history of uplift and depression, mountain building, and erosion.

canal Artificial waterway built for navigation, crop irrigation, water supply, or drainage. The early Middle Eastern civilizations probably first built canals to supply drinking and irrigation water. The most ambitious navigation canal was a 200-mi (300-km) construction in what is now Iraq. Roman canal systems for military transport extended throughout N Europe and Britain. The most significant canal innovation was the pound lock, developed by the Dutch about 1373. The closed chamber, or pound, of a lock is flooded or drained of water so that a vessel within it is raised or lowered to pass between bodies of water at different elevations. Canals were extremely important in the U.S. before the coming of the railroad. The ERIE CANAL linked the Great Lakes, and another connected the Great Lakes to the Mississippi River. See also GRAND CANAL, PANAMA CANAL, SUEZ CANAL.

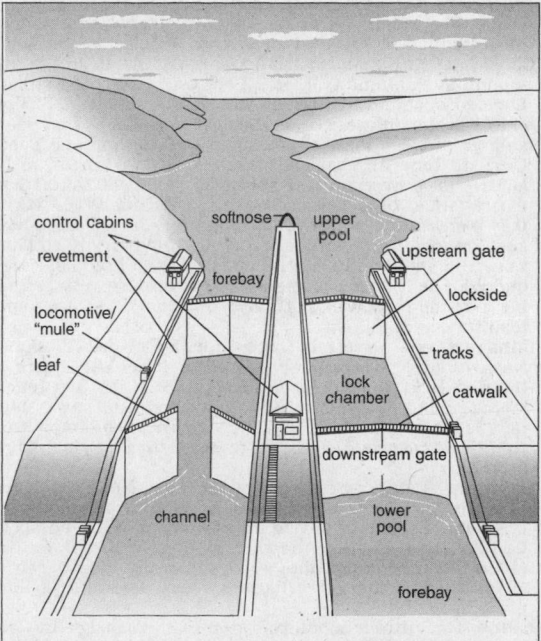

Canal Canal with a basic lock arrangement. Boats traveling upstream pass from the lower to the upper pool through the chamber (or pound) on the left; downstream traffic uses the pound on the right.

Canaletto \ˌka-nᵊl-'e-tō\ *orig.* Giovanni Antonio Canal (1697–1768) Italian painter. Trained in the studio of his father, he worked in Rome (1719–20), painting scenes for operas, until he turned to painting topographical images. After his return to Venice, he produced the picturesque views *(vedute)* that would bring him international fame. His pictures provide dramatic views of Venetian architecture and demonstrate skill in rendering sunlight and shadow. In the 1730s he was kept busy meeting foreign visitors' demand for souvenir views of Venice. He later expanded his output to include imaginative views of Roman ruins, and in 1746 he went to England to paint views of London and the great English country houses. The most famous topographical painter of the 18th cent., he influenced succeeding generations of landscape artists. His nephew, Bernardo BELLOTTO, was also known as Canaletto.

Canal Zone *or* **Panama Canal Zone** Strip of territory, Panama, over which the U.S. exercised jurisdictional rights 1903–79. From 1904 Panama granted to the U.S., in return for annual payments, the sole right to operate and control the PANAMA CANAL, including a strip of land 10 mi (16 km) wide along the canal extending from the Atlantic to the Pacific Ocean and bisecting the Isthmus of Panama. The zone was abolished by treaty in 1979, with the return to Panama of civil control. A joint American–Panamanian commission operated the canal until 2000, when Panama assumed full control.

Canaris \kä-'nä-rəs\, **Wilhelm (Franz)** (1887–1945) German naval officer. Under Adolf HITLER, Canaris became head of military intelligence (Abwehr) in 1935. Believing that the Nazi regime would destroy traditional conservative values and that its foreign ambitions were dangerous, he enlisted some of the anti-Hitler conspirators into the Abwehr and shielded their activities. After the abortive JULY PLOT, he was arrested and executed.

canary Popular cage bird (*Serinus canaria;* in the GOLDFINCH family, Carduelidae) that owes its coloration and sustained vocal powers to 400 years of selective breeding. Well-known breeds include Hartz Mountain, Norwich, and Yorkshire. The average life span of a caged canary is 10–15 years. The canary is native to the Canary, Azores, and Madeira islands. The wild form is mostly greenish brown.

Canary Islands *Spanish* **Islas Canarias** Island group, autonomous community (pop., 1998 est.: 1,630,000), Spain. Located off the NW coast of Africa, the islands lie 823 mi (1,324 km) southwest of the Spanish mainland. They have an area of 2,796 sq mi (7,242 sq km). Their capital is Santa Cruz de Tenerife. Anciently known as the "Fortunate Islands," they were written about by both PLUTARCH and PLINY THE ELDER. Believed to be the W limit of the world, they were visited in the Middle Ages by Arabs, Portuguese, and French. They were taken by Castile (see CASTILLA Y LEÓN) in 1402, and their inhabitants were gradually conquered. The islands became a stop for Spanish vessels trading with the New World. Today agriculture is an economic mainstay, as is tourism.

Canaveral \kə-'na-və-rəl\, **Cape** Cape, E Florida. The site of NASA's John F. Kennedy Space Center, it saw the launch of the first U.S. manned space flight in 1961, the first lunar-landing flight in 1969, and the explosion of the space shuttle *CHALLENGER* in 1986. It was renamed to honor Pres. John F. KENNEDY in 1963 but reverted to its original name in 1973.

Canberra \'kan-ber-ə\ City (pop., 1998 est.: 306,000), capital of Australia. Located on the Molonglo River, it was chosen in 1908 as the site of the capital. An international competition held in 1912 chose the U.S. architect Walter B. Griffin (1876–1937) to design the city, and construction began in 1913. The transfer of Parliament from MELBOURNE took place in 1927.

cancer Uncontrolled multiplication of abnormal cells. Cancerous cells and tissues have abnormal growth rates, shapes and sizes, and functioning. Cancer may progress from a localized TUMOR (confined to the site of origin) to direct extension (spread into nearby tissue or LYMPH NODES) and metastasis (spread to more distant sites via the blood or lymphatic system). This malignant growth pattern distinguishes cancerous tumors from benign ones. Genetic fac-

tors and immune status affect susceptibility. Triggers include hormones, viruses, smoking, diet, and radiation. Cancer can begin in almost any tissue, including blood (see LEUKEMIA) and lymph (see LYMPHOMA). Early diagnosis and treatment increase the chance of cure. Treatment may include CHEMOTHERAPY, surgery, and RADIATION THERAPY. See also BREAST CANCER, CARCINOGEN, KAPOSI'S SARCOMA, LUNG CANCER, SKIN CANCER.

Cancer, Tropic of See TROPIC OF CANCER

Cancún \kan-'kün\ City (pop., 1995: 297,000) and island resort, SE Mexico. The city, at the tip of the YUCATÁN PENINSULA, is a service town for the resort on Cancún Island, connected by a causeway to the city. The area was first described by John Lloyd Stephens in his *Incidents of Travel in Yucatán* (1843). Cancún nonetheless remained a fishing village until in 1970 the area was selected as a suitable site for a resort; today it is Mexico's busiest resort.

Candela \kän-'dā-lə\, **Felix** (1910–1997) Spanish-Mexican engineer and architect. His ferroconcrete structures are distinguished by thin, curved shells that are extremely strong and economical; his imaginative use of paraboloid barrel-vaulting helped dispel mistaken notions of the limits of this material. Works include the expressionistic church of Nuestra Señora de los Milagros in Mexico City (1955), with a hyperbolic paraboloid roof of ferroconcrete only 1.5 in. (3.8 cm) thick.

candida \'kan-də-də\ Any of the parasitic imperfect fungi (see FUNGUS) that make up the genus *Candida,* which resemble YEASTS and occur especially in the mouth, vagina, and intestinal tract. Though usually benign, candidas can become pathogenic, causing diseases including candidiasis and thrush.

Candlemas (Feb. 2) In the Christian church, the celebration of the presentation of the infant JESUS and the post-childbirth purification of MARY in the Temple, in accordance with Jewish law. The festival is first documented in Jerusalem in the late 4th cent.; the custom of observing it with lighted candles dates to at least the mid-5th cent. See also GROUNDHOG DAY.

Candolle \kän-'dòl\, **Augustin (Pyrame de)** (1778–1841) Swiss botanist. In Paris (from 1796) he became an assistant to Georges CUVIER and worked with J.-B. LAMARCK on revising his botanical works. He carried out a botanical and agricultural survey of France (1806–12). In 1813 he published his most important work, *Théorie élémentaire de la botanique,* in which he contended that plant ANATOMY, not PHYSIOLOGY, must be the basis of classification, for which he coined the term TAXONOMY. He introduced the concept of homologous parts for plants (following Cuvier's work on animals). He outlined systematic laws of botanical nomenclature (1818–21) and achieved extensive subdivision of FLOWERING PLANTS; his system supplanted that of Carolus LINNAEUS. He completed seven volumes of a descriptive classification of all known seed plants (from 1824).

Candomblé \ˌkan-dōm-'blä\ Major expression of Afro-Brazilian religion, most prominent in the Brazilian state of Bahia. Its deities, called *orixás,* have personalities (often capricious) and are associated with occupations, colors, days of the week, and natural phenomena. Rituals include the sacrifice of animals, spirit offerings, and dances. See also MACUMBA, VODUN.

Candra Gupta \'kən-drə-'gùp-tə\ *or* **Maurya** (d.297? B.C.) Indian emperor (r.321?–297? B.C.) and founder of the Maurya dynasty (see MAURYAN EMPIRE). An impoverished child sold into slavery, he was eventually purchased by a Brahman politician, who gave him an education in military tactics and the arts. Gathering mercenary soldiers, he overthrew the Nanda dynasty in N India and established his own in modern-day Bihar. On the death of ALEXANDER THE GREAT, he won control of the Punjab (c.322). He expanded his empire west to Persia, south to India's tip, and north to the Himalayas and the Kabul valley. His administration, the first to unify most of India, was patterned on that of the Persian ACHAEMENIAN DYNASTY. He died fasting in sympathy for his people during a time of famine.

candy Sweet SUGAR- or CACAO-based food. The Egyptians made candy from HONEY, fruits, and nuts, since sugar was unknown. With the spread of SUGARCANE cultivation in the

15th cent., the industry began to grow. In the late 18th cent. the first candy manufacturing machinery was produced. To the sweet base are added CHOCOLATE, fruits, nuts, peanuts, eggs, milk, flavors, and colors. Common varieties include hard candy (crystallized sugar), caramels and toffee, jellies, marshmallows, marzipan, cotton candy, and licorice.

Cange, Charles du Fresne, seigneur du See Charles du Fresne, seigneur DU CANGE

canine or **canid** \\'ka-nəd, 'kā-nəd\\ Any domestic or wild DOG or doglike mammal (e.g., WOLF, JACKAL, FOX) in the family Canidae. Canines tend to be slender and long-legged, with a long muzzle, bushy tail, erect pointed ears, and well-developed canine and cheek teeth. They prey on all types of animals; some also eat carrion and vegetable matter. They probably were the first animals to be domesticated. Canines have been hunted for their pelts and slaughtered to prevent their reputed (and sometimes real) destruction of livestock and large game.

Cannae \\'ka-nē\\, **Battle of** (216 B.C.) Major battle in Apulia, SE Italy, during the Second PUNIC WAR. The Romans, with 80,000 men to the Carthaginians' 50,000, were crushed by HANNIBAL's Carthaginians and allied Africans, Gauls, and Spaniards when Hannibal's troops gradually surrounded their foe and annihilated them in a "double envelopment" maneuver. Roman losses exceeded 65,000 men, while the Carthaginians lost only about 6,000.

Cannes \\'kán\\ City (pop., 1990: 69,000), SE France. Located on the Mediterranean Sea southwest of NICE, it was occupied successively by Phocaeans, Celts, and Romans. In the 10th cent. the monks of Lérins built fortifications to guard against Muslim sea raiders. A resort since the 19th cent., the city hosts the CANNES FILM FESTIVAL.

Cannes Film Festival Annual film festival in Cannes, France. First held in 1946 for the recognition of artistic achievement, it became an international marketplace where producers and distributors could exchange ideas, view films, and sign contracts. The concept of international co-production arose at Cannes in the late 1940s. The festival was at times the site of artistic contention as well, as in 1958–59, when advocates and opponents of the French NEW WAVE exchanged diatribes and manifestos.

cannibalism Eating of human flesh by humans. The term derives from the Spanish name (*Caríbales,* or *Caníbales*) for the Carib people, first encountered by Columbus. Reliable firsthand accounts of the practice are rare. Most agree that the consumption of particular portions or organs was a ritual means by which certain qualities of the person eaten might be obtained or by which powers of WITCHCRAFT AND SORCERY might be exercised. Headhunters (see HEADHUNTING) sometimes consumed bits of the bodies or heads of deceased enemies. The AZTECS apparently practiced cannibalism on a large scale as part of the ritual of HUMAN SACRIFICE.

canning Method of preserving food by storing it in sealed containers sterilized by heat. The process was invented in 1809 by Nicolas Appert (c.1750–1841) of France, who used glass bottles. In the 19th cent. tin-coated iron cans with soldered tops, bottoms, and seams were used, but in the early 20th cent. these were improved on. In the later 20th cent. seamless aluminum cans capped with a steel or aluminum lid became common. In modern canning, food is passed under hot water or steam, transferred to a sterile container, sealed inside, and heated to kill any remaining microorganisms. The process preserves most nutrients but often affects consistency and taste.

Canning, George (1770–1827) British politician. As a young man he came under the influence of William PITT, who helped him win a seat in Parliament (1793). Canning served twice as foreign secretary (1807–9, 1822–27); his policies included recognizing the independence of the Spanish-American colonies. He became prime minister in 1827 but died a few months later. He helped the Conservative Party take a more liberal view on many policy questions.

cannon Big GUN, howitzer, or MORTAR, as distinguished from a MUSKET, RIFLE, or other small arms. Huge ARTILLERY first appeared in Europe in the 15th cent. Smoothbored and forged of iron, they weighed 6,000–8,000 lbs (2,800–3,600 kg) and were loaded through the muzzle. They were mounted on wheeled carriages, which were thrown backward when the cannon was fired. Rifled bores and breechloading were adopted in the later 19th cent., and new mechanisms such as the hydraulic buffer absorbed the recoil. Before 1850 ammunition was either cannister, grapeshot, or round, solid cannonballs and black powder, but rifled bores made possible elongated projectiles with a longer range. The SHRAPNEL shell was widely used in the 19th–20th cent.

Cannon, Joseph (Gurney) (1836–1926) U.S. politician. Born in Guilford Co., N.C., he practiced law in Illinois before entering the U.S. House of Representatives (1873–91, 1893–1913, 1915–23). A staunchly conservative Republican, he used his power as speaker (1903–11) in a partisan manner. In 1910 a dissident coalition passed a resolution that made the speaker ineligible to serve on the rules committee, the main source of his power. Personally well liked, he was known as "Uncle Joe."

Cannon, Walter B(radford) (1871–1945) U.S. neurologist and physiologist. Born in Prairie du Chien, Wis., he was the first to use X rays in physiological studies. He also investigated hemorrhagic and traumatic shock during World War I and worked on methods of blood storage. He researched the emergency functions of the sympathetic nervous system and homeostasis. With Philip Bard he developed the Cannon-Bard theory, which proposed that emotional and physiological responses to external situations arise simultaneously and that both prepare the body to act.

canoe Lightweight boat pointed at both ends and propelled by one or more paddles. The earliest canoes had light frames of wood covered by tightly stretched tree bark. The birchbark canoe was first used by the Algonquian Indians in the NE U.S. and Canada, and its use passed westward. Canoes were about 20 ft (6 m) long, though war canoes might extend 100 ft (30 m). The dugout canoe, made from a hollowed-out log, was used by Indians in the SE U.S. and along the Pacific coast, as well as by peoples in Africa and New Zealand. Modern canoes are made of wood, canvas over wood frames, aluminum, and molded plastic or fiberglass.

canon Musical form and compositional technique in which a melody is imitated at a specified time interval by one or more parts, either at the same pitch or at some other pitch. Imitation may occur in augmentation (longer notes), or in diminution (shorter notes); in retrograde order (beginning at its end), mirror inversion (each ascending melodic interval becoming a descending interval, and vice versa), or retrograde mirror inversion; and so on. Canons range from folk rounds such as "Three Blind Mice" to the massively complex canons of J. S. BACH.

canonization Official act of a Christian church declaring a deceased member worthy of veneration and entering his or her name in the canon (authorized list) of SAINTS. The cult of local martyrs was widespread in the early church; in the 13th cent. GREGORY IX formalized church recognition of saints. Responsibility for beatification (declaring a person worthy of limited veneration) was assigned to the ROMAN CURIA under SIXTUS V (r.1585–90). One official gathers evidence in favor of beatification; another (the "devil's advocate") is charged with seeing that the entire truth is made known about the candidate. Canonization requires proof of two miracles subsequent to beatification. The process in the Eastern Orthodox Church is less formal; popular devotion by the faithful serves as the usual basis for sainthood.

canon law Body of laws established within Roman Catholicism, Eastern Orthodoxy, and other churches for church governance. Canon law concerns the constitution of the church, relations between it and other bodies, and matters of internal discipline. The first definitive collection of Roman Catholic canon law was published between 1139 and 1150; it drew on older local collections, councils, Roman law, and church fathers. The enlarged *Corpus juris canonici* ("Corpus of Canon Law") was published in 1500. A commission of cardinals issued the new *Codex juris canonici* ("Code of Canon Law") in 1917 and a revised version (1983) after the Second VATICAN COUNCIL. The Eastern Orthodox, Anglican, Coptic, and Ethiopian Orthodox churches all developed their own canon law.

Canova, Antonio (1757–1822) Italian sculptor. He opened his own studio in Venice by 1775. The figures in his first important sculpture, *Daedalus and Icarus* (1778–79) were so realistic that he was accused of making casts from live models. In 1779 he settled in Rome and became strongly influenced by classical antiquity. Among his most important commissions were the tombs of two popes, Clement XIII and Clement XIV. In 1802 he became court sculptor to NAPOLEON in Paris. In 1816 Pope Pius VII made him marquis of Ischia for arranging the return of Italian art looted by the French. He also painted portraits and re-creations of paintings discovered at POMPEII and HERCULANEUM. The dominant sculptor of his time, Canova was of primary importance in the development of the Neoclassical style.

cantata Work for voice or voices and instruments of the baroque era. From its beginnings in early-17th-cent. Italy, both secular and religious cantatas were written. The earliest were generally for solo voice and minimal instrumental accompaniment. Cantatas soon developed a dramatic character and alternating sections of RECITATIVE and ARIA, paralleling the simultaneous development of OPERA. In Germany the Lutheran cantata almost always involved a chorus. A single chorale (HYMN) often served as the basis for an entire cantata, which might have up to 10 diverse numbers, including duets, recitatives, and choral fugues. The most celebrated are the approximately 200 written by J. S. BACH. After about 1750 the cantata gradually declined.

Canterbury Cathedral town (pop., 1995 est.: 43,000), SE England. The site has been occupied since pre-Roman times; the Roman town was established in A.D. 43. St. AUGUSTINE OF CANTERBURY founded a monastery there in 602, and later a cathedral. The cathedral was the scene of the murder of Archbishop Thomas BECKET in 1170. After his canonization in 1172 it became a pilgrimage shrine; it is the destination of the pilgrims in Geoffrey CHAUCER's *Canterbury Tales*. The town was heavily bombed in World War II, but the cathedral largely escaped damage.

cantilever \\'kan-tə-ˌlē-vər\\ Projecting beam or other horizontal member supported at one or more points but not at both ends. The free, unsupported end is capable of supporting a weight or surface, such as a concrete slab. Any beam built into a wall with a projecting free end forms a cantilever, which may carry a balcony, canopy, roof, or part of a building above. Cantilevering can be used for constructions as simple as bookshelves or as complicated as bridges.

Canton See GUANGZHOU

Cantor \\'kän-tȯr\\ **Georg** (1845–1918) German mathematician, founder of SET THEORY. His work in NUMBER THEORY built on that of C. F. GAUSS. One of his most important discoveries was a way to list the RATIONAL NUMBERS so as to prove them countable. His investigations into such listings led him to the classification of transfinite numbers, which are, informally speaking, degrees of INFINITY. Cantor's work was fundamental to the development of FUNCTIONAL ANALYSIS and TOPOLOGY.

cantus firmus (Latin: "fixed chant") Plainchant of the Catholic church (see GREGORIAN CHANT) used as the basis of counterpoint in musical compositions, starting in the 10th cent. In melismatic ORGANUM, the tones of a plainchant melody were held by one voice (the tenor), while an improvised line was added. The NOTRE-DAME SCHOOL introduced rhythmic patterning of the added voice and the addition of two or three voices. The use of nonliturgical words for the added voice or voices resulted in the independent MOTET. Cantus-firmus technique remained the basis of most composition of the 14th–15th cent. (though the "chant" was now often a secular melody) and remained important in the 16th-cent. MASS.

Canute the Great *Danish* **Knut** \\kə-'nüt\\ (d.1035) Danish king of England (1016–35) and Denmark (1019–35). He helped his father, SWEYN I, invade England in 1013. After Sweyn died (1014), Canute defeated rivals to win the English throne. At first he ruled ruthlessly, killing English opponents and appointing Danes in their places, but within a few years he was granting earldoms to Englishmen. An effective ruler who brought peace and prosperity to England, he also became a strong supporter of the church. With English help he secured the throne of Denmark on his brother's death.

canvas Stout cloth. Canvas has been made from HEMP and FLAX-FAMILY fibers since ancient times for sails. More recently, it has also been made from such fibers as tow, JUTE, and COTTON. Flax canvas is essentially of double warp (see WEAVING), being invariably intended to withstand pressure or rough usage. Articles made from canvas include running shoes, tents, and mailbags. Tarred canvas is used for tarpaulins to cover goods. Artists' canvas for painting is much lighter than sail canvas; the best qualities are made of cream or bleached flax fiber.

canvasback DIVING DUCK (*Aythya valisineria*), one of the most popular game birds. The male weighs about 3 lbs (1.4 kg). During the breeding season he has a red head and neck and a black breast, with white back and sides finely lined in gray. In eclipse (nonbreeding) plumage, he resembles the female, with tan head and gray-brown back. Canvasbacks breed in NW N. America and winter along the coasts from British Columbia and Massachusetts south to central Mexico.

canyon Narrow, deep valley cut by a river through resistant rock and having steep, almost vertical sides. Canyons occur most often in arid or semiarid regions. Some canyons (e.g., the GRAND CANYON) are spectacular natural features.

Canyon de Chelly National Monument \\də-'shā\\ Preserve, NE Arizona. Established in 1931, it occupies 131 sq mi (339 sq km). It includes hundreds of pre-Columbian cliff dwellings, some built in caves on the canyon walls. They represent a broader time span than any other ruins in the Southwest, with many dating from the 11th cent. Modern NAVAJO homes and farms occupy the canyon floor.

Canyonlands National Park Park, SE Utah. Established in 1964, it features water-eroded sandstone spires, canyons, and mesas extending over 527 sq mi (1,366 sq km). Rock walls display Indian petroglyphs. The Needles section contains the Angel and Druid arches, gigantic balanced rock formations.

Cao Cao *or* **Ts'ao Ts'ao** \\'tsaů-'tsaů\\ (A.D. 155–220) Chinese general. He rose to prominence when he suppressed the YELLOW TURBAN rebellion in the last years of the HAN DYNASTY. In the ensuing chaos Cao Cao occupied the strategic N section of China; his domain was known as the kingdom of Wei (see THREE KINGDOMS). He is portrayed as the archetypal unscrupulous villain in the famous 14th-cent. novel *Romance of the Three Kingdoms*. His son, Cao Pei, founded the Wei dynasty (220–265/6).

Cao Dai \\'kaů-'dī\\ Vietnamese religious movement with a strongly nationalist political character. It draws upon ethical precepts from CONFUCIANISM, occult practices from TAOISM, theories of karma and rebirth from BUDDHISM, and hierarchical organization (including a pope) from ROMAN CATHOLICISM. It was established in 1926 after Ngo Van Chieu (1878–1926?), an administrator in Indochina, had a communication from the supreme deity. The movement has long met with resistance from the Vietnamese governments. Today it has some 2 million adherents.

Cao Zhan *or* **Ts'ao Chan** \\'tsaů-'jän\\ (1715?–1763) Chinese novelist. He is the author of *Dream of the Red Chamber* (1791), considered China's greatest novel. Written in the vernacular, it describes in lingering detail the decline of a powerful family and an ill-fated love between cousins. It was completed after his death, probably by Gao E, of whom little is known.

Capa, Robert *orig.* Andrei Friedmann (1913–1954) Hungarian-U.S. photojournalist. He first achieved fame as a war correspondent in the Spanish Civil War (1936). In World War II he covered the fighting in Africa, Sicily, and Italy for *Life* magazine; images of the Normandy invasion are among his most memorable works. In 1947 he founded Magnum Photos with Henri CARTIER-BRESSON and David Seymour. He was killed by a land mine while photographing the French Indochina war for *Life*.

capacitance \\kə-'pa-sə-təns\\ Property of a pair of electric CONDUCTORS separated by a nonconducting material (such as air) that permits storage of electric energy by the separation of ELECTRIC CHARGE, and that is measured by the amount of separated charge that can be stored per unit of electric potential between the conductors (coulombs per volt). If electric charge is transferred between two initially uncharged conductors, they become equally (but oppositely) charged. A potential difference is set up between them and some of the electricity can be stored. The unit of capacitance is coulombs per volt (C/V), or farads (F).

Cape Agulhas See Cape AGULHAS

Cape Breton Island \'bret-°n\ Island, (pop., 1991: 162,000), E part of NOVA SCOTIA. It is 110 mi (175 km) long and up to 75 mi (120 km) wide, with an area of 3,981 sq mi (10,311 sq km). It contains the Bras d'Or salt lakes. Originally called Île Royale as a French colony, it was probably the first land visited by John CABOT on his 1497–98 voyage and was probably named by Basque fishermen from Cap Breton, France. It was ceded to the British in 1763 and joined to Nova Scotia, became a British crown colony in 1784, then rejoined Nova Scotia in 1820. In 1955 it was linked to the mainland by a causeway. Cape Breton Highlands National Park was established in 1936.

Cape buffalo Massive, black, horned BUFFALO *(Syncerus caffer)* formerly found throughout sub-Saharan Africa but now greatly reduced. It inhabits open or scrub-covered plains and open forests. When wounded, it is regarded as one of the most dangerous animals to humans. It stands up to 5 ft (1.5 m) tall at the shoulder, and bulls can weigh almost a ton (about 900 kg). Its heavy horns typically curve downward, then up and inward. A smaller subspecies is found in dense W. African forests.

Cape Canaveral See Cape CANAVERAL

Cape Cod Peninsula, E Massachusetts. Some 65 mi (105 km) long and 1–20 mi (2–32 km) wide, it extends into the Atlantic Ocean in a wide curve. The Cape Cod Canal cutting across its base forms part of the ATLANTIC INTRACOASTAL WATERWAY. Named by an English explorer who took aboard a "great store of codfish" there in 1602, it was the site, near PROVINCETOWN, of the PILGRIMS' landing in 1620. In the 19th cent., Provincetown was an active whaling port. The cape's coastal towns and villages have become densely populated resorts in summer. The cape's N hook was designated the Cape Cod National Seashore in 1961.

Cape Horn See Cape HORN

Capek \'chä-pek\, **Karel** (1890–1938) Czech writer. His "black utopias" show the dangers of technological progress. The cautionary play *R.U.R.: Rossum's Universal Robots* (1920) depicts a society dependent on "robots" (a term he coined). The comic fantasy *The Insect Play* (1921; with his brother Josef) satirizes human greed. *The Makropoulos Affair* (1922) was made into an opera by Leos JANACEK. He also wrote the novel trilogy *Hordubal* (1933), *Meteor* (1934), and *An Ordinary Life* (1934).

Cape Krusenstern National Monument \'krü-zən-,stern\ Preserve, NW Alaska, on the Chukchi Sea. Opened in 1978, it was enlarged in 1980 to 1,031 sq mi (2,670 sq km). Its remarkable archaeological sites illustrate the cultural evolution of the Arctic peoples over some 4,000 years.

Cape of Good Hope See Cape of GOOD HOPE

Capernaum \kə-'pər-nā-əm\ Ancient city, PALESTINE. Located on the NW shore of the Sea of GALILEE, it was the home of JESUS for much of his ministry. His disciples Peter, Andrew, and Matthew were from Capernaum, and he performed many of his miracles there. The long dispute over nearby modern Kefer Nahum's identification with Capernaum was settled in its favor by excavations begun in 1905.

Capet, Hugh See HUGH CAPET

Capetians \kə-'pē-shəns\ *or* **Capets** \'kā-pəts\ Ruling house of France (987–1328), who laid the foundation of the French state. Descended from Robert the Strong (d.866), they included HUGH CAPET (r.987–96), the first Capetian king; PHILIP II AUGUSTUS (r.1180–1223); and LOUIS IX (r.1226–70). Capetians also ruled as dukes of Burgundy and Brittany, emperors of Constantinople, counts of Artois and Provence, kings and queens of Naples, and kings of Hungary and Navarre.

Cape Town *Afrikaans* **Kaapstad** \'käp-,stät\ Seaport city (pop., 1991: 855,000; metro. area pop.: 2,350,000), legislative capital, S. Africa. Long the country's major seaport, it was surpassed in the 1980s by DURBAN. The first settlement at Table Bay, it was established for the Dutch E. INDIA CO. and soon served as a stopover for ships plying the Europe–India route. Under Dutch rule intermittently, it was taken by the British in 1806. It shares capital status with PRETORIA and BLOEMFONTEIN.

Cape Verde \'vərd\ *officially* **Republic of Cape Verde** Island republic, central Atlantic Ocean. Lying 385 mi (620 km) off the W coast of Senegal, it consists of 10 islands and five islets. Area: 1,557 sq mi (4,033 sq km). Population (2000): 401,000. Capital: PRAIA. More than two-thirds of its population is Creole (mulatto); most of the remainder are black

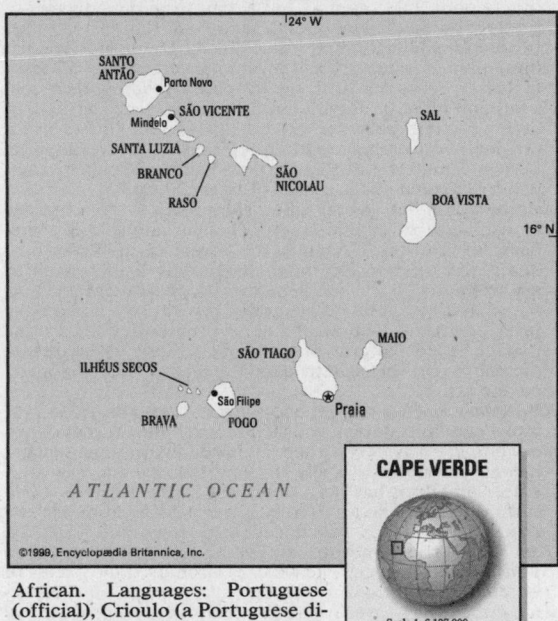

CAPE VERDE
Scale 1: 6,137,000
0 25 50 mi
0 25 50 75 km

©1998, Encyclopædia Britannica, Inc.

African. Languages: Portuguese (official), Crioulo (a Portuguese dialect). Religions: Roman Catholicism (official), Protestantism. Currency: Cape Verde escudo. The mountainous windward islands are craggy and furrowed by erosion; the flat leeward islands are largely plains and lowlands. The islands are volcanic in origin. Fogo Island has an active volcano that erupted in 1951; it is also the location of the highest peak, which rises 9,281 ft (2,829 m). The largest of the other islands are Santo Antão, São Vincente, and São Nicolau. Cape Verde has a developing mixed economy based largely on agriculture, though tourism has been promoted. It is a republic with one legislative house; its chief of state is the president and its head of government, the prime minister. When visited by the Portuguese 1456–60, the islands were uninhabited. In 1460 Diogo Gomes sighted and named Maio and São Tiago, and in 1462 the first settlers landed on São Tiago, founding the city of Ribeira Grande. The city's importance grew with the development of the slave trade, and its wealth attracted pirates so often that it was abandoned after 1712. The prosperity of the Portuguese-controlled islands vanished with the decline of the slave trade in the 19th cent., but later improved because of their position on the great trade routes between Europe, S. America, and S. Africa. In 1951 the colony became an overseas province of Portugal. Many islanders preferred outright independnce, and it was finally granted in 1975. Once associated politically with Guinea-Bissau, Cape Verde split from it in 1981.

capillarity \,ka-pə-'lar-ə-tē\ Rise or fall of liquid in a small passage or tube, caused by the difference in attraction of the liquid molecules to each other and the attraction of the liquid molecules to those of the tube. When a glass tube of small internal diameter is inserted into water, the surface water molecules are attracted to the glass and the water level in the tube rises. The narrower the tube, the higher the water rises. The water is said to "wet" the tube. If a glass tube is inserted into mercury, the level of the liquid in the tube falls. The mercury does not wet the tube. See also SUR-FACE TENSION.

capillary \\'ka-pə-ˌler-ē\ Any of the minute blood vessels that form networks where the arterial and venous CIRCULATION (see ARTERY, VEIN) meet for exchange of oxygen, nutrients, and wastes with body tissues. Capillaries are just large enough for red blood cells to pass through in single file. Their thin walls are semipermeable, allowing small molecules to pass through in both directions.

capital In economics, the stock of resources used to produce other goods. In CLASSICAL ECONOMICS the three factors of production are capital, LABOR, and land. Capital embodies the man-made resources; it is defined to include the buildings, plant, equipment, and inventories created by all three factors. The creation of capital goods requires that consumption must be forgone in favor of saving. The flow of saving becomes a flow of INVESTMENT. Expenditures on education and training are often referred to as investment in human capital. STOCKS and BONDS issued to finance acquisition of capital goods represent financial capital.

capital-gains tax Tax levied on gains realized from the sale or exchange of capital assets. Though capital gains have been taxed in the U.S. since the advent of the federal IN-COME TAX, certain capital gains are only lightly taxed or are exempted from taxation, so as to encourage INVEST-MENT and so stimulate economic growth by encouraging investors to risk their capital in new ventures. Critics argue that distorted patterns of investment result when regular income is converted into capital gains in order to avoid paying tax.

capitalism or **free-market economy** or **free-enterprise system** Economic system in which most of the means of production are privately owned, and production is guided and income distributed largely through the operation of markets. Capitalism has been dominant in the Western world since the end of MERCANTILISM. It was fostered by the RE-FORMATION, which sanctioned hard work and frugality, and by the rise of industry during the INDUSTRIAL REVOLU-TION. Unlike earlier systems, capitalism used the excess of production over consumption to enlarge productive capacity rather than investing it in economically unproductive enterprises, such as cathedrals. The strong national states of the mercantilist era provided the social conditions, such as uniform monetary systems and legal codes, necessary for the rise of capitalism. The ideology of classical capitalism was expressed in Adam SMITH's *Wealth of Nations* (1776), and Smith's free-market theories were widely adopted. In the 20th cent. the GREAT DEPRESSION effectively ended LAISSEZ-FAIRE economics in most countries, but the demise of state-run command economies in Eastern Europe and the former Soviet Union (see COMMUNISM) and the adoption of some free-market principles in China has left capitalism unrivaled.

capital punishment or **death penalty** Penalty of death imposed on a criminal convicted of a serious crime. Though it was formerly prescribed for hundreds of offenses, by the 1970s many countries had eliminated capital punishment. In 1972 the U.S. Supreme Court ruled capital-punishment laws, as then enforced, unconstitutional, but a later ruling found the death penalty per se to be constitutional. Today the U.S. is the only Western industrialized nation that permits capital punishment, though many U.S. states bar it. Advocates maintain that it deters crime and that life imprisonment is not as effective and exposes other prisoners and (in the event of escape or parole) members of society at large to dangerous criminals. Opponents maintain that the death penalty has never been proved to be an effective deterrent, that errors sometimes lead to the execution of innocent persons, and that capital punishment is applied mostly to the poor and members of racial minorities.

Capitol, United States Meeting place of the U.S. Congress. In 1792 a competition for its design was won by William Thornton (1759–1828); his revised FEDERAL-STYLE design of 1795 was executed as the exterior of the wings adjacent to the central ROTUNDA. Benjamin LATROBE, as Surveyor of Public Buildings (1803), followed Thornton's conception of the exterior but used his own interior designs, including his tobacco-leaf and corn-cob capitals. By 1827 Charles

BULFINCH had joined the two wings and built the first dome and the rotunda. Thomas Ustick Walter (1804–1887) later expanded the wings; his cast-iron dome (1855–66) was based on Michelangelo's for ST. PETER'S BASILICA. The marble and sandstone building contains about 540 rooms.

Capitol Reef National Park Park, S Utah. A 20-mi (32-km) buttressed cliff of colored sandstone, it occupies 379 sq mi (982 sq km). Its rock towers resemble coral reefs, while its dome-shaped formations suggest capitol architecture. The cliff walls are covered with pre-Columbian petroglyphs.

Capone, Al(phonse) (1899–1947) U.S. gangster. He joined gangs in his native Brooklyn and earned the nickname "Scarface" after a knife fight. In Chicago he became crime czar (1925), running gambling, prostitution, and bootlegging rackets. He expanded his territory by killing his rivals, most famously in the St. Valentine's Day Massacre, in which members of the gang of Bugs Moran were machine-gunned in a garage on February 14, 1929. In 1931 Capone was convicted for income-tax evasion and sentenced to 11 years in prison. Suffering from paresis, he was released in 1939 and later retired to Florida.

Capote \kə-'pō-tē\, **Truman** orig. Truman Streckfus Persons (1924–1984) U.S. writer. Born in New Orleans, he spent much of his youth in small towns in Louisiana and Alabama. His early "Southern gothic" works include the novels *Other Voices, Other Rooms* (1948) and *The Grass Harp* (1951) and the story collection *A Tree of Night* (1949). He devised a journalistic style for the "nonfiction novel" *In Cold Blood* (1966; film, 1967), about a multiple murder. Other works include the musical *House of Flowers* (1954; with Harold ARLEN), and the novella *Breakfast at Tiffany's* (1958; film, 1961).

Capp, Al orig. Alfred Gerald Caplin (1909–1979) U.S. cartoonist. Born in New Haven, Conn., he studied landscape architecture before turning to cartooning. His comic strip *Li'l Abner* first appeared in the *New York Mirror* in 1934 and was soon being syndicated throughout the country. Set in the backwoods community of Dogpatch, U.S.A., it featured Li'l Abner, a shy, awkward woodsman; Daisy Mae, a persistent maiden; and a host of colorful characters.

Cappadocia \ˌka-pə-'dō-shə\ Ancient district, E Asia Minor. It is a mountainous area located in modern-day central Turkey; its earliest records date from the 6th cent. B.C., when it was a Persian satrapy. Important as a Roman ally and client, it was annexed by TIBERIUS in A.D. 17 and made a Roman province. With its command over strategic passes in the TAURUS MTNS., it went on to become a bulwark of the BYZANTINE EMPIRE until the 11th cent.

Capra, Frank (1897–1991) U.S. (Italian-born) film director. At age 6 he emigrated with his family to the U.S. Working in the film industry, he emerged as a major director with *Platinum Blonde* (1931) and *Lady for a Day* (1933). He won Academy Awards for *It Happened One Night* (1934) and *Mr. Deeds Goes to Town* (1936), portraying naive idealists who triumph over more worldly types, as well as for *You Can't Take It with You* (1938). Other popular films included *Mr. Smith Goes to Washington* (1939), *Lost Horizon* (1937), and *Meet John Doe* (1941). He made the wartime documentary series *Why We Fight*, then won wide audiences with *Arsenic and Old Lace* (1944) and *It's a Wonderful Life* (1946).

Capri \'kä-prē, kə-'prē\ Island, S Italy. Located at the S entrance to the Bay of NAPLES, it has an area of 4 sq mi (10 sq km); its highest point is 1,923 ft (586 m). A favorite resort of Roman emperors, in the Middle Ages it belonged to the abbey of Montecassino and to the republic of AMALFI before passing to the kingdom of NAPLES. Its rocky shores include high cliffs and abound with caves, notably the famous Blue Grotto. Capri is one of Italy's most popular resorts.

Capricorn, Tropic of See TROPIC OF CAPRICORN

capsicum See PEPPER

capuchin (monkey) \'ka-pyə-shən, kə-'pyü-shən\ Any of four species of tropical monkeys (genus *Cebus*) found from Nicaragua to Paraguay. Considered among the most intelligent New World monkeys, capuchins are named for their cap of crown hair, which resembles the cowl of Capuchin monks. These stocky, round-headed monkeys are 12–22 in. (30–55 cm) long, with a hairy, prehensile tail of about the same length. Capuchins live in troops, often in the treetops.

They eat fruit and small animals. Easily trained, they are valued as gentle pets.

Capuchin \'ka-pyə-shən\ Member of the Order of Friars Minor Capuchin, an autonomous branch of the FRANCISCANS. It began in 1525 as an ascetic reform movement led by Matteo da Bascio (c.1495–1552). He and his followers wore robes with pointed hoods (Italian, *cappuccino*), went barefoot, and lived in extreme poverty. The new order was nearly ruined by the defection of its vicar-general, Bernardino Ochino, to Protestantism in 1542, but it later grew quickly, reaching a membership of 17,000 by 1571. It was active in the COUNTER-REFORMATION in keeping the common people loyal to Catholicism. An independent order since 1619, it is known for its missionary and social work.

capybara \kä-pi-'bar-ə\ Either of two species (genus *Hydrochoerus*) of semiaquatic Central and S. American rodents sometimes classified with the CAVY and GUINEA PIG. Capybaras are the largest living rodents, growing as large as 50 in. (1.25 m) long and weighing 110 lbs (50 kg) or more. They are sparsely haired and brownish, with a blunt snout, short legs, small ears, and almost no tail. Capybaras are shy and associate in groups along the banks of lakes and rivers, which they commonly enter to elude predators.

caracal \'kar-ə-ˌkal\ Short-tailed CAT *(Felis caracal)* found in hills, deserts, and plains of Africa, the Middle East, and central and SW Asia. It is sleek and short-haired, with a reddish brown coat and long tufts of black hairs on its pointed ears. Long-legged and short-tailed, it stands 16–18 in. (40–45 cm) and is 26–30 in. (66–76 cm) long, excluding its tail. Generally solitary and nocturnal, it preys on birds and mammals.

Caracalla \ˌkar-ə-'ka-lə\ *officially* Marcus Aurelius Severus Antoninus Augustus *orig.* Septimius Bassianus (A.D. 188–217) Roman emperor (198–217). Until 211 he ruled with his father, Septimius SEVERUS. To assure his undisputed rule, he killed his brother Geta and many of his friends. He built colossal baths in Rome, which still stand. He gave Roman citizenship to all free inhabitants of the empire (212), but showed extreme cruelty toward all who opposed him. He was murdered by the praetorian PREFECT. He is regarded as one of Rome's most bloodthirsty tyrants, and his reign contributed to the empire's decay.

Caracas \kä-'rä-käs, kə-'ra-kəs\ City (pop. 1992: 1,965,000; metro. area pop.: 2,784,000), capital of Venezuela. Its Caribbean port is La Guaira. Lying at an altitude of about 3,000 ft (9,000 m), it is one of the most developed cities in Latin America. Founded in 1567, it was the birthplace of Simón BOLÍVAR (1783), under whose leadership it became the first colony to revolt from Spain (c.1810). Caracas has become the country's center of commerce and culture.

Caramanlis, Constantine See Konstantinos KARAMANLIS

Caravaggio \ˌkar-ə-'vä-jō\ *orig.* Michelangelo Merisi (1571–1610) Italian painter. Born in Caravaggio, he went to Rome in 1590, where he won the patronage of a cardinal. A series of large paintings of the life of St. Matthew (1599–1603) established him as the most renowned and controversial painter in Rome. Breaking with conventional formulas used in depicting saints, he used ordinary people as models and painted them with unforgiving realism. His use of tenebrism, the dramatic illumination of form out of deep shadow, became the outstanding feature of his style and a hallmark of the baroque period. After 1600 he received many commissions, including the monumental *Entombment of Christ* (1602–4) and the controversial *Death of the Virgin* (1601–3). His reputation and income increased despite harsh criticism and a turbulent lifestyle. After killing a man in a brawl in 1606, he fled to Naples, Malta, and Sicily, al-

Caravaggio, "The Deposition of Christ," 1602–4

ways painting. In Naples again, he was attacked and badly wounded at an inn. He died of fever on his way back to Rome, where a papal pardon awaited him. He had an enormous impact on painting throughout Europe; his many followers include José de RIBERA, Hendrik TERBRUGGHEN, Gerrit van HONTHORST, Orazio and Artemisia GENTILESCHI, and Georges de LA TOUR.

caravan Group of merchants, pilgrims, or travelers journeying together, usually for mutual protection, in deserts or other hostile regions. The CAMEL was the most common means of transport. Caravans were a major factor in the growth of settlements along their routes. One caravan trail developed into the SILK ROAD. During the height of caravan travel, which lasted until the 19th cent., a single caravan of Muslim pilgrims journeying from Cairo and Damascus to Mecca might employ as many as 10,000 camels.

caravansary \ˌkar-ə-'van-sə-rē\ *or* **caravanserai** \ˌkar-ə-'van-sə-ˌrī\ Public building used for sheltering caravans and other travelers in the Middle East. The structure is quadrangular in form and enclosed by a massive wall that has small windows near the top and a few narrow air holes near the bottom. The open central court, surrounded by an arcade and storerooms, is usually large enough to contain 300–400 camels.

caraway Dried fruit, commonly called the seed, of *Carum carvi*, a biennial herb of the PARSLEY family. Native to Europe and W Asia, it has been cultivated since ancient times. It is used as a seasoning, and the oil is used to flavor alcoholic beverages and as a medicine.

carbamide See UREA

carbide Inorganic compound, any of a class in which CARBON is combined with a METAL or semimetallic element. The nature of the second element (its position in the PERIODIC TABLE) determines the carbide's type of BONDING and its properties. Calcium carbide is useful as a source of ACETYLENE. Carbides of tungsten, silicon, and boron, called refractory carbides, are extremely hard, remain stable when heated, and have a high melting point and chemical resistance. They are used as abrasives and in cutting tools, as furnace linings, and in other high-temperature applications.

carbohydrate Any member of a very abundant and widespread class of natural organic compounds that includes SUGARS, STARCH, and CELLULOSE. They are classified as MONOSACCHARIDES (simple sugars, e.g., GLUCOSE, FRUCTOSE), disaccharides (2-unit sugars, e.g., SUCROSE, LACTOSE), oligosaccharides (3–10 or so sugars), and POLYSACCHARIDES (large molecules with up to 10,000 monosaccharide units, including cellulose, starch, and GLYCOGEN). Green plants produce carbohydrates by PHOTOSYNTHESIS. In most animals, carbohydrates are the quickly accessible reservoir of energy, and oxidation (see OXIDATION-REDUCTION) of glucose in tissues supplies energy for METABOLISM. Many carbohydrates have the general chemical formula $C_n(H_2O)_n$. The carbon (C) atoms are bonded to hydrogen atoms (–H), hydroxyl groups (–OH; see FUNCTIONAL GROUP), and carbonyl groups (–C=O), whose combinations, order, and geometrical arrangement lead to a large number of ISOMERS with the same chemical formula but different properties. The class is further enlarged because each isomer has various derivatives.

carbon Nonmetallic chemical ELEMENT, chemical symbol C, atomic number 6. The usual stable ISOTOPE is carbon-12; carbon-13, also stable, is 1% of natural carbon. Carbon-14 is the most stable and best known of five radioactive isotopes (see RADIOACTIVITY); it is useful in CARBON-14 DATING and radiolabeling of research compounds. Carbon occurs in three forms: DIAMOND, GRAPHITE, and carbon black (amorphous carbon), including COAL, COKE, and CHARCOAL. Carbon forms more compounds than all other elements combined; several million are known. Each carbon atom forms four bonds (four single bonds, two single and one double bond, two double bonds, or one single and one triple bond) with up to four other atoms. Multitudes of chain, branched, ring, and three-dimensional structures can occur. The study of these carbon compounds and their properties and reactions is organic chemistry (see ORGANIC COMPOUND, HYDROCARBON). With hydrogen, oxygen, nitrogen, and a few other elements, carbon forms the compounds that make up all living things: PROTEINS, CARBOHYDRATES, LIPIDS, and NUCLEIC ACIDS. BIOCHEMISTRY is the study of those compounds. See also CARBONATE, CARBON CYCLE, CARBON DIOXIDE.

carbon-14 dating *or* **radiocarbon dating** Method of determining the age of once-living material, developed by Willard LIBBY in 1947. It depends on the decay of the radioactive isotope carbon-14 to nitrogen. All living plants and animals continually take in carbon, plants in the form of carbon dioxide and animals through the food chain. Some of this carbon is radioactive carbon-14, which slowly decays to the stable isotope nitrogen-14. When an organism dies, the amount of carbon-14 in its tissues decreases at a constant rate; the time since an organism died can be estimated by measuring the amount of radiocarbon in its remains. The method is useful for dating fossils and archaeological specimens from 500 to 50,000 years old. See also DATING.

Carbonari \ˌkär-bə-ˈnä-rē\ (Italian dialect: "Charcoal Burners"). Members of a secret society (the Carbonaria) in early-19th-cent. Italy. Advocating liberal and patriotic ideas, the Carbonari favored constitutional and representative government. They helped lead the unsuccessful revolts of 1820 and 1831 and were gradually absorbed into the YOUNG ITALY movement.

carbonate Any member of two classes of chemical compounds derived from carbonic acid (H_2CO_3) or CARBON DIOXIDE (CO_2). Inorganic carbonates are SALTS of carbonic acid. Shells are calcium carbonate, as is the LIMESTONE they turn into. Many other minerals, including CALCITE, DOLOMITE, and ARAGONITE, consist of or contain carbonates. Sodium carbonate is one of the four most important basic chemical commodities. Organic carbonates are ESTERS of carbonic acid and various ALCOHOL groups (methyl, ethyl, or phenyl). These are liquids used as SOLVENTS and to synthesize plastics and other compounds.

carbonate mineral Any member of a family of minerals that contains the carbonate ion as the basic structural unit. The carbonates are among the most widely distributed minerals in the earth's CRUST; the most common are CALCITE, DOLOMITE, and ARAGONITE. Other relatively common carbonate minerals are siderite, an iron ore, and rhodochrosite, a source of manganese.

carbonation Addition of CARBON DIOXIDE gas to a beverage, imparting sparkle and a tangy taste and preventing spoilage. The liquid is chilled and cascaded down in an enclosure containing carbon dioxide (either dry ice or pressurized liquid) under pressure. Carbonated beverages do not require PASTEURIZATION. The carbonation in sparkling wine comes from FERMENTATION of sugar added to the initial wine.

carbon cycle Circulation of CARBON in the form of the simple ELEMENT and its compounds through nature. The source of carbon in living things is CARBON DIOXIDE. ALGAE and green PLANTS (producers) use CO_2 in PHOTOSYNTHESIS to make CARBOHYDRATES, used in the processes of METABOLISM to make all other compounds in their tissues and those of animals that consume them (HERBIVORES). The carbon may pass through several levels of herbivores and CARNIVORES (consumers). Animals and (at night) plants return the CO_2 to the atmosphere as a byproduct of RESPIRATION. The carbon in animal wastes and the bodies of organisms is released as CO_2 by decay organisms (decomposers). Some carbon has accumulated in the earth's crust in FOSSIL FUELS, LIMESTONE, and CORAL. The carbon of fossil fuels, removed from the cycle in prehistoric times, is being returned in vast quantities as CO_2 via industrial and agricultural processes, some accumulating in the oceans as dissolved CARBONATES and some staying in the atmosphere (see GREENHOUSE EFFECT).

carbon dioxide Inorganic compound, a colorless gas with a faint, sharp odor and a sour taste when dissolved in water, chemical formula CO_2. About 0.03% of air by volume, it is produced when carbon-containing materials burn completely and from FERMENTATION and animal RESPIRATION. Plants use CO_2 in PHOTOSYNTHESIS to make CARBOHYDRATES. In water, it forms a solution of a weak ACID, car-

bonic acid. Its reaction with AMMONIA is the first step in synthesizing UREA. An important industrial material, CO_2 is recovered from sources including flue gases, the process that produces HYDROGEN, and limekilns. It is used as a refrigerant, chemical intermediate, and inert atmosphere; in fire extinguishers, foaming rubber and plastics, carbonated beverages (see CARBONATION), and aerosol sprays; in water treatment, welding, and cloud seeding; and for promoting plant growth in greenhouses. Under pressure it becomes a liquid, the form most used in industry. If the liquid expands, it cools and partially freezes to the solid form, DRY ICE. See also CARBON CYCLE, GREENHOUSE EFFECT.

Carboniferous period Interval of geologic time, 360–286 million years ago, in the PALEOZOIC ERA. The landmasses drew closer together. The supercontinent GONDWANA probably occupied much of the Southern Hemisphere; by the end of the period, present-day N. America, Greenland, and N Europe were also part of Gondwana. Siberia and China (including S.E. Asia) remained individual continents located high in the Northern Hemisphere. Swamp forests became widespread, and enormous coal deposits formed. Amphibians became widespread and diverse, and reptiles appeared and rapidly adapted to many habitats.

carbon monoxide Inorganic compound, a highly toxic, colorless, odorless, flammable gas, chemical formula CO. It is produced when CARBON or carbon-containing fuels do not burn completely to CARBON DIOXIDE, because of insufficient OXYGEN. It is present in the exhaust gases of internal combustion engines and furnaces. CO is toxic because it binds to HEMOGLOBIN much more strongly than oxygen, interfering with transport of oxygen (see HYPOXIA, RESPIRATION). Symptoms of CO poisoning include headache, nausea, fainting, and on to coma, weak pulse, respiratory failure, and death. CO is used industrially as a fuel and in synthesis of numerous organic compounds.

carbon steel ALLOY of IRON and CARBON in which the carbon content may range from less than 0.015% to slightly more than 2%. Adding this tiny amount of carbon produces a material that exhibits great strength, hardness, and other valuable mechanical properties. Carbon steels account for about 90% of the world's STEEL production. They are used extensively for automobile bodies, appliances, machinery, ships, containers, and the structures of buildings.

carboxylic acid \ˌkär-bäk-ˈsi-lik\ Any organic compound with the general chemical formula –COOH in which a carbon (C) atom is bonded to an oxygen (O) atom by a double bond to make a carbonyl group (–C=O; see FUNCTIONAL GROUP) and to a hydroxyl group (–OH) by a single bond (see BONDING). The fourth bond on the carbon links it to a hydrogen (H) atom, a methyl (–CH_3) group (for ACETIC ACID), or another group. In FATTY ACIDS, the fourth group is a HYDROCARBON chain. In aromatic acids (see AROMATIC COMPOUND), it is a ring-structured hydrocarbon. In AMINO ACIDS, it contains a nitrogen atom. Carboxylic acids participate in chemical reactions as ACIDS, usually fairly weak. Many carboxylic acids (acetic acid, CITRIC ACID, LACTIC ACID) are intermediates in METABOLISM and can be found in natural products; others (e.g., SALICYLIC ACID) are used as SOLVENTS and to prepare many chemical compounds. Important carboxylic-acid derivatives include ESTERS, ANHYDRIDES, AMIDES, halides (see HALOGEN), and SALTS (see SOAP).

carburetor \ˈkär-bə-ˌrā-tər\ Device for supplying a spark-ignition ENGINE with a mixture of fuel and air. Carburetors for automobile engines usually contain a storage chamber for liquid fuel, a choke, an idling jet, a main jet, an air-flow restriction, and an accelerator pump. The quantity of fuel in the fuel storage chamber is controlled by a valve actuated by a float. The choke, a butterfly VALVE, adjusts the intake of air. Reduced pressure near the partially closed throttle valve causes the fuel to flow from the idling jet into the intake air. Further opening the throttle valve activates the main fuel jet. Then a venturi-shaped air-flow restriction creates reduced pressure, drawing fuel from the main jet into the air stream at a rate related to the air flow so that a nearly constant fuel-air ratio is obtained. The accelerator pump injects fuel into the inlet air when the throttle is opened suddenly. See also GASOLINE ENGINE, VENTURI TUBE.

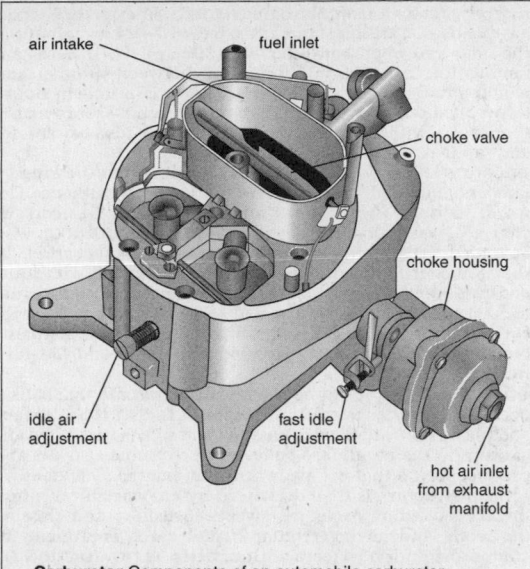

air intake   fuel inlet

choke valve

choke housing

idle air   fast idle
adjustment   adjustment

hot air inlet
from exhaust
manifold

Carburetor Components of an automobile carburetor.

ity to supply the body with blood and lead to HEART FAIL-URE. Severe arrhythmias can trigger ventricular or ATRIAL FIBRILLATION. See also DIGITALIS, ELECTROCARDIOGRA-PHY.

Cardiff City (metro. area pop., 1999: 315,000), capital of Wales. It is located on the BRISTOL CHANNEL in SE Wales. The Romans built a fort there around A.D. 75, but the town itself was only established with the arrival of the Normans in the 11th cent. By the early 20th cent. Cardiff had become the largest coal-exporting port in the world. The coal trade ceased in the 1960s, but the city remains the largest in Wales and its principal commercial center.

Cardigan, Earl of *orig.* James Thomas Brudenell (1797–1868) British general. After entering the army (1824), he purchased promotions to become a lieutenant colonel (1832) and spent his inherited wealth to make his regiment the best dressed in the service (introducing the cardigan jacket). In the CRIMEAN WAR (1853), he was appointed commander of the Light Brigade, which he led in the ill-fated charge at the Battle of BALAKLAVA. Despite the disaster, Cardigan was lionized on his return to England.

Cardin \kàr-'da^n\ **, Pierre** (b.1922) French fashion designer. Initially a tailor at a men's shop, after World War II he joined the Parisian fashion house of Paquin and designed the costumes for Jean COCTEAU's film *Beauty and the Beast* (1945). In the 1950s he opened his own shop, designing gowns for costume balls and ready-to-wear collections for men and women. His men's clothing has influenced other designers, including Bill Blass.

cardinal Member of the Sacred College of Cardinals. Their duties include electing the POPE, acting as his principal counselors, and aiding in governing the Roman Catholic church. Cardinals serve as officers of the ROMAN CURIA, BISHOPS of major dioceses, and papal envoys. Since 769 only cardinals have been eligible to become pope, and since 1059 cardinals have elected the pope. Cardinals are divided into cardinal deacons, cardinal bishops, and cardinal priests. The cardinal priests, the most numerous, are the bishops of important sees around the world. For 400 years, the number of cardinals was limited to 70, but JOHN XXIII removed the limit and there are now more than 100. A red biretta and ring are symbolic of the office.

cardinal *or* **redbird** Songbird (*Cardinalis,* formerly *Richmondena, cardinalis,* family Fringillidae, or Emberizidae) of N. America east of the Rocky Mtns. It is 8 in. (20 cm) long and has a pointed crest. The male is bright red, the female a duller red or olive brown. Pairs of cardinals utter loud, clear whistling notes year-round in gardens and open woodlands. They feed on insects, wild seeds, and fruits.

carding In YARN production, a process of separating individual fibers and causing many of them to lie parallel, and also removing most of the remaining impurities. COTTON, WOOL, waste SILK, and man-made fibers are subjected to carding. Carding produces a thin sheet of uniform thickness that is then condensed to form a thick, continuous, untwisted strand called sliver. Carding may be followed by combing, a process that removes short fibers, leaving a sliver composed entirely of long fibers, all laid parallel, to produce smoother and more lustrous sliver.

cardiology Medical specialty dealing with HEART DISEASES and disorders. After the invention in 1905 of the electrocardiograph, many surgical advances followed (see HEART TRANSPLANT, ARTIFICIAL HEART). Current diagnostic methods include chest percussion (tapping), ELECTROCARDIOGRAPHY, and echocardiography (see ULTRASOUND). Cardiologists provide continuing care of heart patients, doing basic heart-function studies, supervising therapy, including drug therapy, and working closely with heart surgeons.

cardiopulmonary resuscitation (CPR) Emergency procedure to restore breathing and circulation in an unconscious person. A trained rescuer opens the airway and confirms the absence of breathing and PULSE. Resuscitation consists of alternating mouth-to-mouth breathing and repeated pressure on the chest to circulate the blood.

cardiovascular system System of vessels that circulate BLOOD throughout the body, bringing nutrients and oxygen and removing wastes and carbon dioxide. It is essentially a

Carcassonne \,kàr-kà-'sòn\ *ancient* Carcaso. City (pop., 1999: 45,000), SW France. Situated on the Aude River, it was occupied by the IBERIANS in the 5th cent. B.C. Muslims took it in A.D. 728. The English soldier Simon de Montfort captured it about 1209, and in 1247 it was united with the French crown. It was burned by EDWARD THE BLACK PRINCE in 1355. A 13th-cent. church and cathedral survive, as do remains of medieval fortifications.

carcinogen \kär-'si-nə-jən\ Agent that can cause CANCER. Exposure to carcinogens, including certain chemicals, radiation, and certain viruses, can initiate cancer under conditions not completely understood. Some people have a genetic tendency to develop cancer when exposed to specific carcinogens. Repeated local injury or irritation to a part of the body can be carcinogenic. Identifying and eliminating carcinogens in time can reduce the incidence of cancer.

cardamom \'kär-də-məm\ Spice consisting of whole or ground dried fruit, or seeds, of *Elettaria cardamomum,* a perennial herb of the GINGER family. Native to moist forests of S India, the fruit may be collected from wild plants, but most is cultivated. The whole fruit is a green, three-sided oval capsule containing 15–20 dark, hard, angular seeds.

Cárdenas, Bartolomé de See Bartolomé BERMEJO

Cárdenas (del Río) \'kär-d^{ə}n-,äs\, **Lázaro** (1895–1970) President of Mexico (1934–40). Of Indian descent, he joined the armed struggle against Victoriano HUERTA; his faction triumphed, and he was made a general in the Mexican Army in 1920. In 1928 Cárdenas became governor of Michoacán, and in 1934 he became president. He distributed a record amount of land to peasants, organized workers' and peasants' confederations, and nationalized the oil industry and principal railways. He opposed U.S. influence and in later years supported Fidel CASTRO. For many Mexicans he remains the principal symbol of the political left. His son Cuauhtémoc, a leader of the opposition to Mexico's ruling party, is widely believed to have been denied victory in the 1988 presidential elections by fraud; he has since served as mayor of Mexico City.

cardiac arrhythmia \ā-'rith-mē-ə\ Variation from the heartbeat's normal rate or rhythm, caused by problems in the HEART's PACEMAKER or in nerves conducting its signals. Occasional arrhythmias are normal. TACHYCARDIA is a fast regular rhythm; bradycardia is a slow rhythm. Premature beats are extra contractions in normal rhythm. Ongoing arrhythmia in some heart diseases can reduce the heart's abil-

long, closed double circuit—one through the lungs (PUL-MONARY CIRCULATION) and one through the rest of the body (systemic circulation). The HEART pumps blood through the ARTERIES, which branch into smaller arterioles, which feed into microscopic CAPILLARIES. These converge to form small venules, which join to become larger VEINS, generally following the same path as the arteries back to the heart. Cardiovascular diseases include ARTE-RIOSCLEROSIS, congenital and rheumatic heart disease, and vascular inflammation.

Cardozo, Benjamin (Nathan) (1870–1938) U.S. jurist. Born in New York City into a distinguished Jewish family, he was elected to the state supreme court in 1913 and quickly promoted to the Court of Appeals. During his tenure, many thought the quality of the appellate bench exceeded that of the U.S. Supreme Court. A notable legal essayist, he influenced the trend in U.S. appellate judging toward greater involvement in public policy and consequent modernization of legal principles. He served on the U.S. Supreme Court from 1932 to 1938. He wrote the majority opinion upholding the SO-CIAL SECURITY program (1937). In a 1937 case on DOUBLE JEOPARDY, he held that the states were not required to implement all the provisions of the BILL OF RIGHTS, a position that became known as "selective incorporation."

Benjamin Cardozo

Carducci \kär-ˈdü-chē\, **Giosuè** (1835–1907) Italian poet. He taught in Bologna for 40 years, and in later years served as a senator. He opposed the prevailing Romanticism, but his rhetorical tirades provoked resistance to reform. His *New Lyrics* and *The Barbarian Odes* (1887) contain evocations of landscape, memories of childhood, and representations of the glory of ancient Rome. Regarded in his time as Italy's national poet, he won the Nobel Prize in 1906.

Carême \kä-ˈrem\, **Marie-Antoine** (1784–1833) French chef. Born into a poor family, he found work in a pastry shop frequented by C. M. de TALLEYRAND. He served as Talleyrand's chef for 12 years, and later created grandiose dishes for the most splendid households of Europe, including those of the young GEORGE IV and Czar ALEXANDER I. He wrote several classics of *grande cuisine*.

cargo cult Any of the religious movements, chiefly in Melanesia in the late 19th and early 20th cent., based on the observation by local residents of the delivery of exotic supplies by ship and aircraft to colonial officials. The cults exhibited the expectation of a new age of blessing and prosperity to be initiated by the arrival of a special "cargo" of goods from supernatural sources.

Carib \ˈkar-əb\ American Indian people who inhabited the Lesser Antilles and parts of the S. American coast at the time of the Spanish conquest. The Island Carib (now extinct) were a warlike people who reportedly practiced CANNIBALISM (the term derives from their name). Mainland groups lived in the Guianas and south to the Amazon River; they subsisted by hunting and farming and were less aggressive.

Caribbean Sea Arm of the Atlantic Ocean. It covers about 1,049,500 sq mi (2,718,200 sq km) and washes the N coast of S. America, E Central America, and E Mexico. It reaches its greatest known depth, about 25,000 ft (7,500 m), in Cayman Trench, between Cuba and Jamaica. Its generally tropical climate varies, depending on mountain elevations, water currents, and trade winds. The economies of its island countries are greatly dependent on tourism; the region is one of the world's principal winter resort areas. See map on following page.

caribou \ˈkar-ə-ˌbü\ Arctic DEER (*Rangifer tarandus*) of the tundra, taiga, and forests, native to N. America and, until recently, ranging from Scandinavia to E Siberia. Both sexes have antlers. Caribou stand 2.3–4.6 ft (0.7–1.4 m) tall at the shoulder and weigh up to 650 lbs (300 kg). Their herds are famous for their seasonal migration between summer and winter ranges. Their staple winter food is a lichen, popularly called reindeer moss, which they reach by scraping the snow away with their feet. In summer, they also eat grasses and saplings. See also REINDEER.

caricature \ˈkar-i-kə-ˌchur\ Comically distorted drawing or likeness intended to satirize or ridicule its subject. The word, derived from the Italian *caricare* ("to load or charge"), was probably coined by Annibale CARRACCI, who defended the practice as a counterpart to idealization. In the 18th cent., the caricature became connected with journalism and was put to virulent use by political commentators. From the 1880s, illustrated daily newpapers brought caricatures to a wide general public. Important caricaturists include Jacques CALLOT, Honoré DAUMIER, and Gustave DORÉ.

caries \ˈkar-ēz\ *or* **tooth decay** Localized disease that causes decay and cavities in teeth. It begins at the TOOTH's surface and may penetrate the dentin and the pulp cavity. Microorganisms in the mouth are believed to consume SUGARS and produce ACIDS that eat away at tooth enamel. The dentin's protein structure is then destroyed by enzymes. Prevention involves avoiding excessive sweets, brushing and flossing the teeth, and having regular dental care. Treatment includes restoration of teeth with cavities. FLUORIDATION OF WATER can reduce the occurrence of caries by as much as 65%.

carillon \ˈkar-ə-ˌlän\ Musical instrument consisting of at least 23 cast bronze bells tuned in chromatic order. Usually located in a tower, it is played from a keyboard. The carillon originated in Flanders around 1480, and the art of carillon building reached its height in the Netherlands in the 17th cent., when the tuning of the bells became highly refined.

Carissimi \kä-ˈrēs-sē-mē\, **Giacomo** (1605–1674) Italian composer. His approximately 15 oratorios (performed in place of operas during Lent), including *Baltazar, Ezechia, Jephte, Jonas,* and *Judicium extremum,* made him the principal oratorio composer of the mid-17th cent. He also wrote some 150 cantatas and nearly 100 motets.

Carleton, Guy *later* Baron Dorchester (of Dorchester) (1724–1808) British soldier-statesman. In 1759 he was sent to Canada and fought in the Battle of Quebec. As governor (1768–78) of Quebec province, his conciliatory policies toward the French Canadians led to passage of the QUEBEC ACT of 1774. He helped repel the attack on Quebec by American Revolutionary forces in 1775. He was appointed commander of British forces in N. America in 1782 and then governor in chief of British N. America (1786–96).

Carleton College \ˈkär-əl-tən\ Private liberal-arts college in Northfield, Minn., founded in 1866. Small classes, opportunities to participate in faculty research projects, and a high reputation attract a select student body. Enrollment is about 1,700.

Carlism Spanish political movement that originated in the 1820s. Carlists supported the claims of FERDINAND VII's brother Don Carlos (1788–1855) and his descendants to the throne, rejecting the succession of Ferdinand's daughter IS-ABELLA II by invoking the Salic Law, which excluded females from the royal succession. The disputed succession led to several unsuccessful civil rebellions, known as the Carlist Wars (1833–39, 1872–76).

Carlsbad See KARLOVY VARY

Carlsbad Caverns National Park Preserve, SE New Mexico. Established as a national park in 1930, it covers 73 sq mi (189 sq km). Beneath the surface winds a maze of underground chambers; one of the largest caverns ever discovered, the Big Room, is about 2,000 ft (600 m) long and 1,100 ft (330 m) wide, and as much as 255 ft (78 m) high.

Carlyle, Thomas (1795–1881) Scottish historian and essayist. The son of a mason, he was reared a strict Calvinist. An energetic, irritable, fiercely independent idealist, he became a leading moral force in Victorian literature. His humorous essay *Sartor Resartus* (1836) is a fantastic hodgepodge of autobiography and German philosophy. *The French Revolu-*

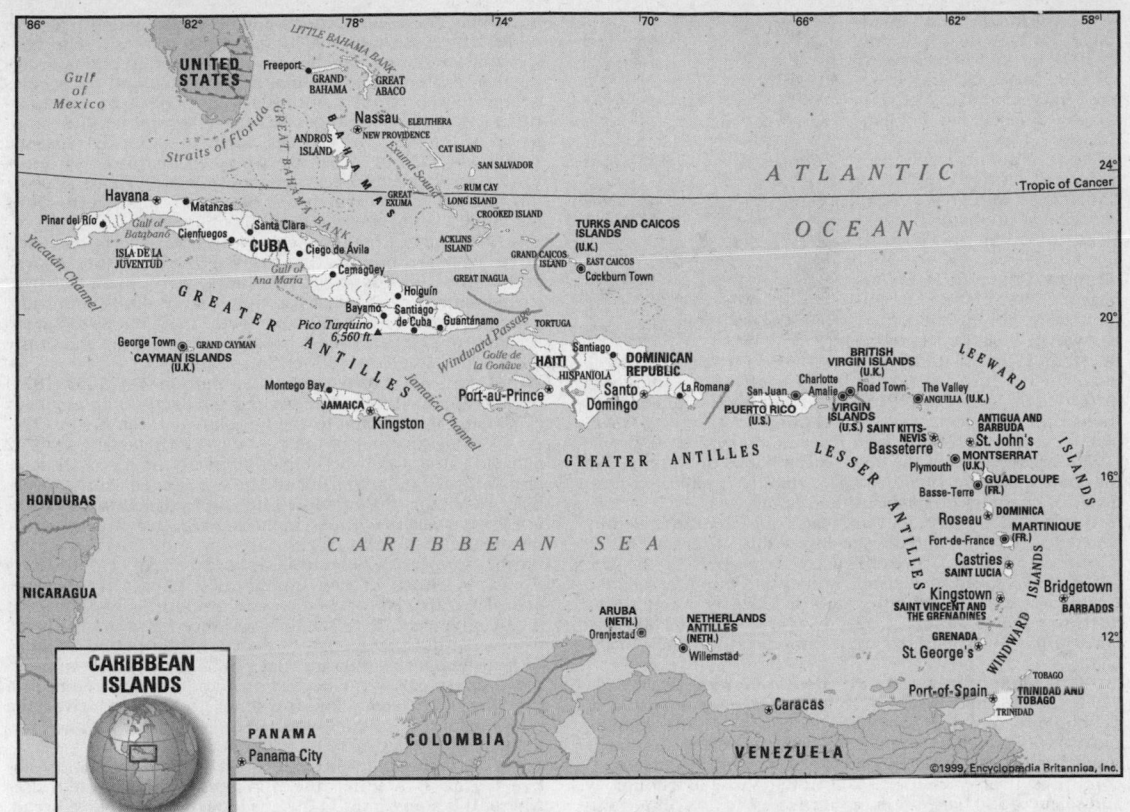

CARIBBEAN ISLANDS

Scale 1: 19,396,000

0   100   200 mi
0   125   250 km

©1999, Encyclopædia Britannica, Inc.

tion (3 vols., 1837), perhaps his best book, has outstanding set pieces and character studies. *On Heroes, Hero-Worship, and the Heroic in History* (1841) showed his reverence for strength and vision, and led to a huge biography of FREDERICK II the Great (6 vols., 1858–65).

Carmelite Mendicant order of the Roman Catholic church. It originated around 1155 on Mt. Carmel in Palestine, where a number of former pilgrims and crusaders began to live as hermits. As Muslim incursions made Palestine increasingly unsafe, the Carmelites scattered to Cyprus, Sicily, France, and England. In England and Western Europe the order transformed itself from a group of hermits into one of mendicant friars. The first institution of Carmelite nuns was founded in 1452. St. TERESA OF ÁVILA and St. JOHN OF THE CROSS reemphasized Carmelite strictness and austerity, establishing Discalced (barefoot) Carmelite orders. The Carmelites suffered greatly during the French Revolution and the Napoleonic era, but they were later restored in Western Europe as well as in the Middle East, Latin America, and the U.S.

Carmichael, Hoagy (*orig.* Hoagland Howard) (1899–1981) U.S. songwriter. Born in Bloomington, Indiana, Carmichael met many jazz musicians while studying law there, including Bix BEIDERBECKE, who recorded his first composition, "Riverboat Shuffle" (1924). The relaxed tunefulness of such later songs as "Georgia on My Mind," "Rockin' Chair," and "Lazy River" made them universally attractive. For Hollywood films he wrote "Two Sleepy People" and "In The Cool Cool Cool of the Evening" (Academy Award). His "Star Dust" is reputedly the most recorded popular song of all time.

Carmona \kär-'mō-nə\, **António Oscar de Fragoso** (1869–1951) Portuguese general and politician. A career officer, he rose to the rank of general by 1922. He took part in the army coup of May 1926 and became premier later that year. He ruled as a virtual dictator before calling for a plebiscite;

elected president, he served from 1928 to 1951, but named Antonio SALAZAR premier in 1932.

Carnap, Rudolf (1891–1970) German-U.S. philosopher. A student of Gottlob FREGE, he was a member of the VIENNA CIRCLE. He fled to the U.S. in 1935, where he taught at the Univs. of Chicago (1936–52) and California (1954–70), contributing to logic, epistemology, the philosophy of language, probability theory, and the philosophy of science. His epistemology systematically analyzes the logic of knowledge. His works include *The Logical Structure of the World* (1928), *The Logical Syntax of Language* (1934), *Introduction to Semantics* (1942), *Meaning and Necessity* (1947), and *The Logical Foundations of Probability* (1950).

carnation Herbaceous plant (*Dianthus caryophyllus*) of the PINK FAMILY, native to the Mediterranean, widely cultivated for its fringe-petaled, often spicy-smelling flowers. The perpetual flowering carnation produces large flowers and blooms almost continuously in the greenhouse; miniature (baby) and spray varieties are also grown for the florist trade. Carnations are among the most popular cut flowers, used in floral arrangements, corsages, and boutonnieres.

Carné \kär-'nā\, **Marcel** (1909–1996) French film director. His first feature, *Jenny* (1936), was followed by *Bizarre, Bizarre* (1937), *Port of Shadows* (1938), and *Daybreak* (1939), works of poetic realism that were the fruit of his collaboration with poet and screenwriter Jacques Prévert, as was his masterpiece, *The Children of Paradise* (1945), which chronicled life in the theater and celebrated the French spirit. His work declined after his breakup with Prévert in 1948.

Carnegie \kär-'ne-gē, 'kär-nə-gē\, **Andrew** (1835–1919) U.S. industrialist and philanthropist. The son of a Scottish weaver, he emigrated to the U.S. in 1848. A job in a telegraph office led to his early career with the PENNSYLVANIA RAILROAD CO., and his canny investments made him wealthy by age 30. In 1872–73 he founded the steelworks near Pittsburgh that became the Carnegie Steel Co. By adopting technological innovations and by increasing efficiency through VERTICAL INTEGRATION, Carnegie built a vast enterprise that dominated the U.S. steel industry. In 1901 he sold his company to J. P. MORGAN, and it became part of U.S. STEEL. Devoting himself to philanthropy, he gave hundreds of millions of dollars to libraries and universities, including CARNEGIE MELLON UNIV., and endowed many foundations, including the Carnegie Corp. of New York.

Andrew Carnegie

Carnegie, Dale orig. Dale Carnegey (1888–1955) U.S. author. Born in Maryville, Mo., he worked as a traveling salesman 1908–12, and began lecturing on public speaking in 1912. After publishing *The Art of Public Speaking* (1915) and other books, he began to focus on the importance of psychology in achieving financial success. His *How to Win Friends and Influence People* (1936) became one of the best-selling books of all time, and the Dale Carnegie Institute subsequently established hundreds of chapters throughout the country.

Carnegie Hall Concert hall in New York City. Endowed by Andrew CARNEGIE and designed by William Burnet Tuthill, it opened in 1891. Threatened by developers in the late 1950s, it was saved by a public outcry and purchased by the city. It was extensively renovated in 1982–86. Admired for its beauty and its superb acoustics, it seats almost 2,800 people and has long been the most famous concert hall in the U.S.

Carnegie Mellon University Private university in Pittsburgh, Pa. It was formed in 1967 from the Carnegie Institute of Technology (created in 1900 through a gift of Andrew CARNEGIE) and the Mellon Institute of Industrial Research (founded in 1913 through a gift of Andrew MELLON). It comprises diverse schools in addition to those of technology and science, and has built a reputation as an arts center. Enrollment is about 7,800.

carnelian \kär-ˈnē-lē-ən\ Translucent, semiprecious variety of CHALCEDONY that owes its reddish color to the incorporation of small amounts of iron oxide. Carnelian was highly valued and used in rings and signets by the Greeks and Romans, some of whose intaglios have retained their high polish. It is mined principally in India, Brazil, and Australia. Its physical properties are those of QUARTZ.

Carniola Region, S Europe. Located northeast of the head of the Adriatic Sea, it is largely mountainous. Its chief town is LJUBLJANA, Slovenia. It was part of the Roman province of PANNONIA. In the 13th cent. it became part of the HOLY ROMAN EMPIRE. A possession of the Austrian HABSBURGS from 1335 to 1849, it was later an Austrian crown land (1849–1918). It was incorporated into Yugoslavia by a 1947 treaty. When Yugoslavia was fragmented in the 1990s, it was included in Slovenia.

carnival Final celebration before the fasting and austerity of LENT in some Roman Catholic regions. The most famous and exuberant carnival is that of Rio de Janeiro, celebrated with masked balls, costumes, and parades; the best-known U.S. celebration is MARDI GRAS. The first day of carnival season varies with local traditions, but carnival usually ends on Shrove Tuesday.

carnivore Any meat-eating animal, but especially any member of the order Carnivora, consisting of 10 families of primarily predatory mammals: Canidae (e.g., DOGS), Ursidae (BEARS), Procyonidae (RACCOONS), Mustelidae (WEASELS), Viverridae (CIVETS), Hyaenidae (HYENAS), Felidae (CATS), Otariidae and Phocidae (SEALS), and Odobenidae (WALRUS). Though most carnivores eat only meat, some rely heavily on vegetation (e.g., the PANDA). The earliest carnivores appeared during the PALEOCENE EPOCH (about 60 million years ago). Carnivores are highly intelligent and therefore comparatively easy to train.

carnivorous plant Any of about 400 diverse species of plants specially adapted for capturing insects and other tiny animals and digesting their nitrogen-rich proteins to obtain nutrients. These adaptations enable such plants to survive under otherwise marginal or hostile conditions. The conspicuous trapping mechanism (a leaf modification) draws the prey's attention to the plant. More than half the species belong to the family Lentibulariaceae, most being BLADDERWORTS. The remainder belong to several families composed of the PITCHER PLANTS, SUNDEWS, and flytraps (see VENUS'S-FLYTRAP). Most are found in damp or wet environments where nitrogenous materials are often scarce or unavailable. Most carnivorous plants are small herbaceous perennials; some become large shrubby vines.

carnosaur Any of the large carnivorous dinosaurs, a branch of THEROPOD dinosaurs that evolved into predators of large herbivorous dinosaurs. Carnosaurs were massive, two-legged animals with small forelimbs, large skulls, and wide, gaping mouths with formidable teeth. TYRANNOSAURS were the largest. The carnosaurs became extinct at the end of the CRETACEOUS PERIOD (65 million years ago).

Carnot \kär-ˈnō\, **Lazare (-Nicolas-Marguerite)** (1753–1823) French administrator. He entered the army as an engineer (1773) and was elected to the Legislative Assembly in 1791. As a leading member of the COMMITTEE OF PUBLIC SAFETY and the DIRECTORY, he helped mobilize the Revolutionary armed forces and matériel, and he was lauded as the "Organizer of Victory." Purged in 1799, he returned to serve NAPOLEON in various offices, including minister of the interior during the HUNDRED DAYS.

Carnot \kär-ˈnō\, **(Nicolas-Léonard-) Sadi** (1796–1832) French scientist, known for describing the Carnot cycle. Son of Lazare CARNOT, he was an army officer most of his life. Convinced that Britain's advanced STEAM ENGINES were a factor in NAPOLEON's defeat, he developed a theory of heat engines predicting that efficiency depends only on the temperature of the hottest and coldest parts and not on the substance (steam or any other fluid) that drives the mechanism. His theory was eventually incorporated into the general theory of THERMODYNAMICS.

carob Leguminous EVERGREEN tree *(Ceratonia siliqua)* native to the E Mediterranean region and cultivated elsewhere. It is sometimes known as locust, or St. John's bread, in the belief that the "locusts" on which JOHN THE BAPTIST fed were carob pods. The tree's red flowers are followed by flat, leathery pods that contain 5–15 hard brown seeds embedded in a sweet, edible pulp that tastes similar to chocolate.

carol Popular religious song, usually joyful, associated with a season such as Christmas. It typically alternates verses with a repeated refrain or burden. The carol originated in medieval England, with texts in English or Latin or both, and was often associated with dancing and processions.

Caroline Islands Archipelago (pop., 1991 est.: 126,000), W Pacific Ocean, south of the Philippines. The islands and their lagoons comprise an area of 3,740 sq mi (9,687 sq km). The group consists of more than 550 islands, including Yap and Palau. Though explored by the Spanish in the 17th cent., they were rarely visited until Germany took them in 1899. Granted to Japan after World War I, they were placed under U.S. trusteeship in 1947. With the exception of Palau, the islands became the Federated States of Micronesia in 1979. Palau became independent in 1994.

Carolingian dynasty Family of Frankish aristocrats that ruled Western Europe 751–887. Pepin I (d.640), the dynasty's founder, came to power as mayor of the palace under the MEROVINGIAN king DAGOBERT I. From this post, his descendants, including CHARLES MARTEL, continued to usurp authority from the Merovingians until 751, when Charles's son PEPIN III deposed Childeric III and formally took the title of King of the Franks. Under Pepin's son CHARLEMAGNE (Carolus Magnus—the source of the dynasty's name), the Carolingian realm was extended over Gaul and into Germany and Italy. On his death his three sons divided the realm, and by 887 Carolingian power had dissipated, though there were resurgences in France (c.895–923, 936–87).

carotene \ˈkar-ə-ˌtēn\ Any of several organic compounds widely distributed in plants and animals. They are PIGMENTS that give orange, yellow, or sometimes red colors to dandelions, apricots, carrots, sweet potatoes, butter, egg yolks, canary feathers, and lobster shells. Carotenes are converted in the body into VITAMIN A. Carotene has an ANTIOXIDANT effect and is therefore used in pharmaceuticals and as a food and feed additive.

Carothers \kə-'rəth-ərz\, **W(allace) H(ume)** (1896–1937) U.S. chemist. Born in Burlington, Iowa, he became director of organic chemical research at Du Pont in 1928, working on polymerization of acetylene and derivatives, leading to the development of neoprene rubber. The theory of linear polymerization was his outstanding achievement; he tested it by synthesizing polymers structurally resembling cellulose and silk, culminating in the production of NYLON, the first synthetic POLYMER fiber to be produced commercially (1938).

carp Hardy, greenish brown fish (*Cyprinus carpio,* family Cyprinidae) native to Asia but introduced into Europe, N. America, and elsewhere. It lives alone or in small schools in quiet, weedy, mud-bottomed ponds, lakes, and rivers. It often stirs up sediment while rooting about for food, adversely affecting many plants and animals. Its average length is about 14 in. (35 cm); some grow to 40 in. (100 cm) and 50 lbs (22 kg). In captivity carp may live more than 40 years.

Carpaccio \kär-'pät-chō\, **Vittore** (c.1460–1525/26) Italian painter active in Venice. Influenced by Gentile BELLINI and ANTONELLO DA MESSINA, in the 1490s he began the first of four cycles of paintings that are his greatest achievement: scenes from the *Life of St. Ursula,* scenes from the *Lives of St. George, St. Jerome, and St. Tryphon* (1502–7), and scenes from the *Life of the Virgin* (c.1500–10) and the *Life of St. Stephen* (1511–20). He was one of the great narrative painters of the VENETIAN SCHOOL.

carpal tunnel syndrome \'kär-pəl\ (CTS) Painful condition of the wrist. The median nerve and the TENDONS that bend the fingers pass through the carpal tunnel, between the wrist (carpal) bones on three sides and a ligament on the fourth. Repetitive finger and wrist movements rub the tendons against the walls of the carpal tunnel and may make the tendons swell, squeezing the nerve. Numbness, tingling, and pain in the wrist and hand may progress to loss of muscle control. CTS is most common in assembly-line workers and computer keyboard users. Treatment may include anti-inflammatory drugs, brace or splint use, and surgery.

Carpathian Mountains \kär-'pā-thē-ən\ Mountain system, E Europe. It extends along the Slovakia–Poland border and southward through Ukraine and E Romania about 900 mi (1,450 km). Its highest peak, Gerlachovka (in Slovakia), rises 8,711 ft (2,655 m). The Little Carpathians and White Carpathians are its SW extensions. The mountains are the source for the VISTULA, DNIESTER, and TISZA rivers.

Carpentaria \ˌkär-pen-'tär-ē-ə\, **Gulf of** Gulf, NE Australia. An inlet of the Arafura Sea, it is bordered by the NORTHERN TERRITORY and by Cape York Peninsula and extends north–south about 480 mi (770 km) and east–west 400 mi (650 km). It was explored by the Dutch 1605–28. It became internationally significant in the late 20th cent. for its bauxite and manganese deposits and its prawn-rich waters.

Carpenter Gothic U.S. domestic architecture style of the 19th cent. The houses executed in this phase of the GOTHIC REVIVAL style display an eclectic and naive use of Gothic decorative motifs, such as turrets, spires, pointed arches, and much decorative gingerbread, made possible by the invention of the scroll saw. Surviving structures are found chiefly in the Northeast and Midwest.

carpet See RUG AND CARPET

carpetbagger Epithet used during the RECONSTRUCTION period (1865–77) to describe a Northerner in the South seeking private gain. The word referred to an unwelcome outsider arriving with nothing more than his belongings packed in a carpetbag. Many carpetbaggers were involved in corrupt financial schemes, but others helped rebuild the economy in the South and participated in educational and social reform.

Carracci family \kä-'rät-chē\ Family of Italian painters. Annibale Carracci (1560–1609) was prominent in the movement against MANNERISM. In the 1580s, with his brother and cousin, he co-founded a teaching academy in Bologna, the Accademia degli Incamminati ("Academy of the Pro-

gressives"). He specialized in fresco painting and monumental religious altarpieces, but was also a pioneer in the development of ideal landscapes, genre subjects, and caricature. The fresco decoration of the Gallery of the Farnese Palace in Rome (1597–1601), depicting the loves of the gods, remains his masterpiece. His brother Agostino (1557–1602) was known primarily as a teacher and engraver; his anatomical studies were used as teaching aids for nearly two centuries. His cousin Lodovico (1555–1619) directed the academy in Bologna after his cousins had gone to Rome, produced works of a passionate and poetic quality, and trained some of the major Bolognese artists of the next generation, including DOMENICHINO and Guido RENI.

Carranza \kär-'rän-sä\, **Venustiano** (1859–1920) First president of the post–Porfirio DÍAZ Mexican Republic (1917–20). The son of a landowner, in 1910 he joined the struggle of Francisco MADERO against Díaz. Because he did little to implement the far-reaching reforms called for in the Constitution of 1917, his presidency was plagued by social unrest and clashes with the more radical Pancho VILLA and Emiliano ZAPATA. His nationalism led him to oppose U.S. intervention, even when he stood to benefit from it. He is held responsible for Zapata's assassination, and was himself murdered while fleeing an armed rebellion. See also MEXICAN REVOLUTION.

Carré, John Le See John LE CARRÉ

Carrel \kə-'rel\, **Alexis** (1873–1944) French surgeon, sociologist, and biologist. He received a 1912 Nobel Prize for developing a way to suture (stitch) blood vessels and laid the groundwork for further studies of blood-vessel and organ transplantation. He also researched preservation of tissues outside the body and the application of the process to surgery, and helped develop the Carrel-Dakin method of flushing wounds with an antiseptic.

Carrier, Willis (Haviland) (1876–1950) U.S. inventor and industrialist. Born in Angola, N.Y., Carrier designed the first system to control temperature and humidity in 1902. His "Rational Psychrometric Formulae," introduced in 1911, initiated scientific AIR-CONDITIONING design. In 1915 he co-founded the Carrier Corp. to manufacture air-conditioning equipment.

Carriera \ˌkä-rē-'ā-rə\, **Rosalba** (1675–1757) Venetian pastel portraitist and miniaturist. She became known for her miniature portraits on snuffboxes and was the first artist to use ivory rather than vellum as a support for miniatures. She achieved spectacular success throughout Europe with her fashionable pastel portraits of notables. On a trip to Paris (1720–21) she painted LOUIS XV as a child, and was elected to the French Royal Academy.

Carroll, Lewis *orig.* Charles Lutwidge Dodgson (1832–1898) British logician, novelist, and photographer. An unmarried deacon, he lectured in mathematics at Oxford. His novel *Alice's Adventures in Wonderland* (1865) is based on stories he told to young friends, especially Alice Liddell. Its sequel, *Through the Looking-Glass* (1871), describes Alice's further adventures. Full of whimsy and sophisticated wit, they became perhaps the most famous and admired children's books in the world. His other works include the nonsense poem *The Hunting of the Snark* (1876) and the children's novel *Sylvie and Bruno* (1889). He was also an important early portrait photographer.

carrot Herbaceous, generally biennial plant (*Daucus carota*) of the PARSLEY family, that produces an edible taproot in the first growing season. Native to central Asia, it is grown extensively in temperate zones. It is a rich source of carotene. Unharvested roots produce large flower stalks in the second season, bearing large compound umbels.

Carson, Johnny (*orig.* John William) (b.1925) U.S. television personality. Born in Corning, Iowa, he worked in radio before hosting several TV quiz shows (1955–62). As the long-standing host of *The Tonight Show* (1962–92), he was noted for his wry monologues, comedy sketches, and genial banter, and the program became a staple for a large and faithful late-night audience.

Carson, Kit (*orig.* Christopher) (1809–1868) U.S. frontiersman, scout, and Indian agent. Born in Madison Co., Ky., he ran away from home at 15 to become a trapper and trader. He served as a guide to John FRÉMONT's explorations of the

Carson

West and guided Gen. Stephen Kearny's expedition to California during the Mexican War, often carrying war dispatches to Washington, D.C. In 1854 he was appointed Indian agent at Taos, N.M. During the Civil War he commanded the 1st New Mexico Volunteers. His contributions to westward expansion made him a folk hero.

Kit Carson

Carson, Rachel (Louise) (1907–1964) U.S. science writer. Born in Springdale, Pa., she had a long career as a marine biologist at the U.S. Fish and Wildlife Service. Her much-praised nature writings include *Under the Sea-Wind* (1941), *The Sea Around Us* (1951, National Book Award), and *The Edge of the Sea* (1955). Her prophetic *Silent Spring* (1962), about the dangers of pesticides in the food chain, became the seminal work of the modern environmental movement, which can be seen to date from its publication.

Carson City City (pop., 2000: 52,000), capital of Nevada. Located east of Lake TAHOE and south of RENO, it was settled in 1858, and later renamed for Kit CARSON. The discovery of silver nearby in 1859 stimulated Carson City's economy. The federal government established a mint there, and it became the state capital in 1864.

Cartagena \ˌkär-tä-ˈhä-nä\ City (pop., 1997 est.: 812,000), Colombia. Located on the NW coast, it is Colombia's principal oil port. Founded in 1533, it became one of Spanish America's chief cities. It was attacked by British forces under Francis DRAKE (1585) but remained under Spanish control until taken by Simón BOLÍVAR (1815). Though soon lost, it was retaken by independence forces in 1821. It gained prominence in the 20th cent. as an oil-processing center.

Cartagena Port city (pop., 1998 est.: 175,000), SE Spain. Founded by the Carthaginians in 227 B.C., it was captured by SCIPIO AFRICANUS THE ELDER in 209 B.C. and made a Roman colony. Sacked by the GOTHS in A.D. 425, it was held by the MOORS from 711 until it was taken by JAMES I of Aragon in 1269. In the 16th cent. PHILIP II made it a great naval port; it remains Spain's chief Mediterranean naval base.

cartel \ˌkär-ˈtel\ Organization of a few independent producers for the purpose of increasing profits (see OLIGOPOLY). This may involve limitation of output, control of price, and allocation of market share. Cartels can be either domestic (e.g., IG FARBEN) or international (e.g., OPEC). Because cartels restrict competition and result in higher prices for consumers, they are outlawed in some countries. The only industry operating in the U.S. with a blanket exemption from the ANTITRUST LAWS is major-league baseball, but several U.S. firms have been given permission to participate in international cartels.

Carter, Elliott *orig.* Elliott Cook Carter, Jr. (b.1908) U.S. composer. Born to a wealthy family, he attended Harvard Univ. and studied in Paris with Nadia BOULANGER. Influenced by Igor STRAVINSKY and Charles IVES, his style evolved into a densely contrapuntal, dissonant, and rhythmically complex texture in which the various instrumental parts frequently suggest conversation and combat. His principal works include *Variations for Orchestra* (1955), a double concerto for piano and harpsichord (1961), a piano concerto (1965), *Concerto for Orchestra* (1969), *Night Fantasies* for piano (1980), and four string quartets (1951, 1959, 1971, 1986), two of which received the Pulitzer Prize. He is often called the greatest American composer of the late 20th cent.

Carter, Jimmy (*orig.* James Earl) (b.1924) 39th president of the U.S. (1977–81). Born in Plains, Ga., he graduated from Annapolis and served in the U.S. Navy until 1953, when he left to manage the family peanut business. Elected governor (1971–75), he opened Georgia's government offices to blacks and women. In 1976 he won the Democratic nomination and the presidency, defeating the sitting president,

Gerald FORD. As president, he helped negotiate a peace treaty between Egypt and Israel, signed a treaty with Panama to make the PANAMA CANAL a neutral zone, and established full diplomatic relations with China. In 1979–80 the IRAN HOSTAGE CRISIS became a major political liability. He responded more forcefully to the Soviet Union's invasion of Afghanistan in 1979. Hampered by high inflation and a recession engineered to tame it, he lost his bid for reelection to

Jimmy Carter, 1979

Ronald REAGAN. He subsequently became involved in numerous international diplomatic negotiations and helped oversee elections in countries with insecure democratic traditions. In 2002 he was awarded the Nobel Peace Prize.

Carteret \ˈkärt-ə-ˌret\ **George** (*later* **Sir George**) (1610?–1680) British colonial proprietor. Noted for his naval exploits and service as lieutenant governor of the Channel Island of Jersey, he became a powerful administrator and legislator. In 1663 he was one of eight original proprietors granted the area of Carolina; in 1664 he received half of New Jersey, named for his birthplace. The other owner sold out to the Quakers in 1674; after his death Carteret's heirs sold his portion to them.

Carter family U.S. singing group, consisting of Alvin Pleasant Carter (1891–1960), his wife Sara (1898–1979), and his sister-in-law Maybelle (1909–1978), that helped popularize Appalachian folk songs. Natives of Virginia, their career began in 1927 in response to an advertisement placed by a talent scout. Over 14 years, with five of their children, they recorded over 300 traditional songs, including "Wabash Cannonball," "It Takes a Worried Man," and "Wildwood Flower." After the original group broke up in 1941, members continued to perform under the Carter family name. The Carter family was the first group admitted to the Country Music Hall of Fame.

Cartesianism Philosophical tradition derived from the philosophy of René DESCARTES. A form of RATIONALISM, Cartesianism also upholds a metaphysical dualism of two finite substances, mind and matter. The essence of mind is thinking; the essence of matter is extension in three dimensions. God is a third, infinite substance, whose essence is necessary existence. God unites minds with bodies to create a fourth, compound substance, homo sapiens. Cartesianism developed different solutions to mind–body dualism (see MIND–BODY PROBLEM). An influential Cartesian theory holds that animals are essentially machines, lacking even the ability to feel pain.

Carthage Ancient city and state, N Africa. Located near modern TUNIS, it was founded by colonists from TYRE, probably in the 8th cent. B.C. It undertook conquests in W Africa, SICILY, and SARDINIA in the 6th cent. B.C. and came to dominate the W Mediterranean. In the 3rd cent. B.C. it fought the PUNIC WARS with Rome. Destroyed by the younger SCIPIO AFRICANUS, it was later the site of a colony founded by Julius CAESAR in 44 B.C.; in 29 B.C. Caesar AUGUSTUS made it the administrative center of the province of Africa. Captured by the VANDALS in 439 and Byzantium in the 6th cent., it was taken by the Arabs in the 7th cent., and was eclipsed by their emphasis on Tunis.

Carthaginian Wars See PUNIC WARS

Carthusian \kär-ˈthü-zhən\ Member of a Roman Catholic monastic order founded by St. Bruno of Cologne (c.1030–1101) in 1084 in the Chartreuse valley of SE France. Carthusians pray, study, eat, and sleep alone but gather for morning mass, vespers, and the night office. They wear hair shirts, abstain from meat, and consume only bread and water on Fridays and fast days. At the motherhouse, or Grande Chartreuse (today in Voiron, Isère), the monks distill the liqueur that bears the house's name.

Cartier \kär-ˈtyā\ **George Étienne** (*later* **Sir George**) (1814–1873) Canadian prime minister jointly with John MACDON-

ALD (1858–62). Born in St. Antoine, Lower Canada (later Canada East, now Quebec), he was appointed provincial secretary (1855) and later attorney general for Canada East (1857). In 1858 he represented Canada East in the alliance with Macdonald, promoting the improvement of Anglo-French relations in Canada. In 1867, despite great opposition, he carried his native province into confederation, and he served in Macdonald's first Confederation cabinet (1867–72).

Cartier \kär-ˈtyā\, **Jacques** (1491–1557) French explorer. He was commissioned by FRANCIS I to explore N. America in the hope of discovering gold, spices, and a passage to Asia. Cartier's explorations of the N. American coast and the St. Lawrence River (1534, 1535, 1541–42) laid the basis for later French claims to Canada.

Cartier-Bresson \kär-tyä-brə-ˈsōⁿ\, **Henri** (b.1908) French photographer. He studied art in Paris and at Cambridge Univ. His interest in photography developed about 1930 when he encountered the works of Eugène ATGET and Man RAY. He is known for spontaneous, sequential images in still photography, a technique inspired by his enthusiasm for filmmaking. He helped establish photojournalism as an art form, and with Robert CAPA and David Seymour founded Magnum Photos (1947). His many collections include *The Decisive Moment* (1952).

cartilage \ˈkär-tᵊl-ij\ Dense CONNECTIVE TISSUE in parts of the human skeleton. A network of COLLAGEN fibers in a firm, gelatinous base, it contains no blood vessels. Different types of cartilage are found at the ends of some bones and in nasal and respiratory structures; in the spinal disks; and in the ear and epiglottis (back of the throat).

Cartland, (Mary) Barbara (Hamilton) (*later* **Dame Barbara**) (1901–2000) English author. Her first novel, *Jigsaw* (1925), was a popular success. Her output grew steadily, and by the 1970s she was averaging 23 books a year, all of which she dictated. Her over 600 books, mostly formulaic romance novels, have sold more than 600 million copies.

cartography \kär-ˈtä-grə-fē\ *or* **mapmaking** Art and science of representing a geographic area graphically, usually by means of a MAP or chart. PTOLEMY's eight-volume *Geography* showed a spherical earth. Medieval European maps followed Ptolemy's guide but placed east at the top of the map. The 14th cent. saw the development of more accurate maps for use in navigation. The first surviving globe dates from 1492. Discovery of the New World led to new techniques in cartography, notably projection of a curved surface onto a flat surface (see Gerardus MERCATOR). Modern cartography uses aerial photography and satellite radar for a degree of accuracy previously unattainable (see GLOBAL POSITIONING SYSTEM). Satellites have also made possible the mapping of features of the moon and of several planets.

cartoon Originally, a full-size drawing used for transferring a design to a painting or tapestry. Cartoons were used from the 15th cent. by fresco painters and stained-glass artists. In the 19th cent. the term acquired its popular meaning of a humorous drawing or parody. Such drawings today convey political commentary, editorial opinion, and social comedy in newspapers and magazines. The greatest early figure is William HOGARTH, in 18th-cent. Britain. In 19th-cent. France, Honoré DAUMIER added text that conveyed his characters' unspoken thoughts. Britain's *Punch* became the foremost 19th-cent. venue for cartoons; in the 20th cent. *The New Yorker* set the American standard. See also CARICATURE, COMIC STRIP.

Cartwright, Edmund (1743–1823) British inventor. On visiting Richard ARKWRIGHT's cotton-spinning mills, he was inspired to construct a power-driven machine for weaving. He invented a power LOOM and set up a weaving and spinning factory in Yorkshire. In 1789 he patented a wool-combing machine. In 1809 the House of Commons voted to reward him for the benefits his loom had conferred on the nation. His other inventions included a rope-making machine and a steam engine that used alcohol instead of water.

Caruso \kə-ˈrü-sō\, **Enrico** (1873–1921) Italian tenor. Born in Naples and apprenticed to a mechanical engineer at 10, at 18 he began to sing in public in his free time. He made his professional debut in 1894, and by 1902 his high notes had

made him an international star. He sang at the Metropolitan Opera 1903–20 in almost 60 roles, becoming the most famous male opera star of his time. His warm, appealing tenor voice of great emotive power made his recordings (which include some of the first vocal recordings ever made) bestsellers for decades after his death at 48.

Enrico Caruso as Radames in *Aïda*

Carver, George Washington (1861?–1943) U.S. agricultural chemist and agronomist. Born a slave near Diamond Grove, Mo., Carver lived until age 10 or 12 on his former owner's plantation. He did not obtain a high-school education until his late twenties; he then obtained bachelor's and master's degrees from Iowa State Agricultural College. In 1896 he joined Booker T. WASHINGTON at the Tuskegee Institute (now TUSKEGEE UNIV.) in Alabama, where he became director of agricultural research. He was soon promoting the planting of PEANUTS and SOYBEANS, legumes that he knew would help restore the fertility of soil depleted from cotton cropping. He worked intensively with the SWEET POTATO and the peanut, ultimately developing hundreds of derivative products from them. His efforts helped liberate the South from its untenable cotton dependency; by 1940 the peanut was the South's second-largest cash crop. During World War II he devised 500 dyes to replace those no longer available from Europe. Though internationally acclaimed, he remained at Tuskegee throughout his life.

Carver, Raymond (Clevie) (1938–1988) U.S. short-story writer and poet. Born in Clatskanie, Ore., he worked at odd jobs before turning to a writing career. His successful short-story collection *Will You Please Be Quiet, Please?* (1976) established his reputation. His stories chronicle the pain-filled lives of the working poor in the Pacific Northwest. His later collections were *What We Talk About When We Talk About Love* (1981), *Cathedral* (1984), and *Where I'm Calling From* (1988). He died of lung cancer at age 50. His "minimalist" style has exerted a strong influence on later writers.

Cary, (Arthur) Joyce (Lunel) (1888–1957) British novelist. Born in Northern Ireland, he served in W. Africa in World War I and began publishing fiction, some set in Africa, including *An American Visitor* (1933) and *Mister Johnson* (1939). *The Horse's Mouth* (1944), his best-known novel, was the third in a trilogy. A second trilogy consisted of *A Prisoner of Grace* (1952), *Except the Lord* (1953), and *Not Honour More* (1955).

caryatid \ˌkar-ē-ˈa-təd\ Supporting column sculpted in the form of a draped female figure. Caryatids first appeared in three small buildings (treasuries) at Delphi (550–530 B.C.). The most celebrated example is the caryatid porch of the Erechtheum (421–406 B.C.), with six figures, on the ACROPOLIS of Athens.

Casablanca Coastal city (metro. area pop., 1994: 2,941,000), W Morocco. Built by the Portuguese on the site of the ancient city of Anfa, in 1515, the new city was occupied by a Moroccan sultan from 1757, then by the French from 1907. Under the French it became Morocco's chief port. In World War II it surrendered to the Allies in 1942, and in 1943 it hosted the Casablanca Conference on global military strategy. Since then, its growth and development have been continuous. The city supplies over half of Morocco's industrial production.

Casa Grande Ruins National Monument \ˈkä-sə-ˈgrän-dä\ Preserve, S Arizona. Established in 1918, it occupies 472 acres (191 hectares). The site's pre-Columbian ruins are dominated by the Casa Grande ("Big House"), a multistory building topped by a watchtower built by Salado Indians in the 14th cent., and the only surviving building of its type.

Casals \kə-'sälz\, **Pablo (Carlos Salvador Defilló)** (*orig.* Pau) (1876–1973) Spanish (Catalan)-U.S. cellist and conductor. Son of an organist, he took up the cello and composition in his teens. Sent by royal sponsors to the Brussels Conservatory in 1895, he was told they could teach him nothing. He performed internationally as soloist, chamber musician, and from the 1920s as a conductor. Refusing to return to Spain after Francisco FRANCO took power, he ultimately made his home in Puerto Rico, renowned as one of the world's most famous musicians.

Casanova \ˌka-sə-'nō-və\, **Giovanni Giacomo** (1725–1798) Italian writer and adventurer. Expelled from a seminary, he launched a dissolute career that took him throughout Europe. In Venice in 1755 he was denounced as a magician and imprisoned; he escaped to Paris, where he mingled with the aristocracy. Fleeing from creditors, he returned to Venice in 1774 to spy for the Venetian inquisitors of state. He spent his late years (1785–98) as librarian to a count in Bohemia. His huge autobiography (12 vols., 1825–38) gives a splendid picture of 18th-cent. Europe and established his reputation as an extraordinary seducer of women.

Casas, Bartolomé de las See Bartolomé de LAS CASAS

Cascade Range Mountain range. W U.S. A continuation of the SIERRA NEVADA, it extends north from LASSEN PEAK in NE California across Oregon and Washington for 700 mi (1,100 km). Its highest elevation is Mt. RAINIER. Some of the summits, including Mt. ST. HELENS, have erupted in the recent past. Its N continuation in British Columbia is known as the Coast Mtns.

Case, Stephen M(aul) (b.1955) U.S. businessman. Born in Hawaii, he graduated from Williams College, then held management positions at Proctor & Gamble, Pizza Hut, and Control Video. In 1985 he cofounded Quantum Computer Services, whose name was changed in 1991 to AMERICA ONLINE. He developed it into the world's leading interactive services company, and helped turn the Internet into a mass medium. In 2001 he oversaw its merger with TIME-WARNER, the largest in history, and later became chairman of AOL Time-Warner. In 2003, after a severe decline in its stock values, he announced his resignation.

Casement, Roger (David) (*later* **Sir Roger**) (1864–1916) British civil servant and Irish rebel. As British consul in Africa (1895–1904) and Brazil (1906–11), he became famous for his reports revealing white traders' cruel exploitation of native labor in the Congo and Peru. Ill health forced his retirement to Ireland (1912), where he joined the Irish nationalists. After World War I broke out, he sought German support for the Irish independence movement. For his additional intrigue in the EASTER RISING, he was convicted of treason and hanged; his execution made him an Irish martyr.

Cash, Johnny (*orig.* John R.) (b.1932) U.S. singer and songwriter. Born in Kingsland, Ark., he learned guitar and began writing songs in the military. Settling in Memphis, he earned regular appearances on "Louisiana Hayride" and the GRAND OLE OPRY with such hits as "Hey, Porter," "Folsom Prison Blues," and "I Walk the Line." By 1957 Cash was acknowledged the top COUNTRY-MUSIC artist. His popularity waned because of health and drug-addiction problems, but in the late 1960s he was rediscovered by a wider audience. In 1968 he married June Carter of the CARTER FAMILY, with whom he had appeared since 1961.

cashew Edible seed or NUT of *Anacardium occidentale,* a tropical and subtropical evergreen shrub or tree in the SUMAC family, native to tropical Central and S. America. The tree also produces wood used for shipping crates, boats, and charcoal, and a GUM similar to gum arabic. A brown oil between the two shells of the nut blisters human skin and is used as a lubricant and an insecticide and in the production of plastics.

cashmere Animal-hair fiber forming the downy undercoat of the Kashmir GOAT. The fibers have diameters finer than those of the best WOOLS. Cashmere fabric is warm and comfortable and has excellent draping qualities and soft texture; it is used mainly for fine coat, dress, and suit fab-

rics and for high-quality knitwear and hosiery. A sweater requires the fleece of four to six goats; an overcoat uses that of 30–40. Because world production is small and gathering and processing are costly, cashmere is a luxury fiber.

Casimir III \'kä-zə-ˌmir\ *Polish* Kazimierz *known as* **Casimir the Great** (1310–1370) King of Poland (1333–70). Son of Wladyslaw I, who revived the Polish kingship, he continued his father's quest to make Poland a power in central Europe. He crafted treaties with Hungary, Bohemia, and the TEUTONIC ORDER, acquired large regions by diplomacy, and arranged dynastic alliances that tied Poland to many royal European families. He codified Teutonic law, gave new towns self-government under the Magdeburg Law, and founded the Univ. of Krakow.

Casimir IV *Polish* Kazimierz *known as* **Casimir Jagiellonian** \ˌyäg-yel-'lō-nē-ən\ (1427–1492) Grand duke of Lithuania (1440–92) and king of Poland (1447–92). Named ruler of Lithuania by the boyars and king of Poland on his brother's death, he sought to preserve the political union between Poland and Lithuania and to recover the lost lands of old Poland. Through his marriage to Elizabeth of Habsburg and dynastic alliances with various European royal houses, he built the JAGIELLON DYNASTY. His effective destruction of the TEUTONIC ORDER (1466) brought Prussia under Polish rule.

casino Building or room used for GAMBLING. The term originally referred to a public hall for music and dancing, but by the later 19th cent. it had come to denote a gaming house, particularly for card and dice games. Today casinos are places where gamblers can risk their money against a common gambler (called the banker or house). One of the oldest is that at Monte Carlo, founded in 1861. Others include those at Cannes and Nice (France), Corfu (Greece), Baden-Baden (Germany), and Las Vegas and Reno. Casino gambling was introduced in Atlantic City, N.J., in 1978, and from the 1980s casinos began appearing on American Indian reservations, which are not subject to state anti-gambling statutes. U.S. casino gambling has expanded vastly as gambling has become legal in more states, particularly as a riverboat operation.

Caspian Sea Inland salt lake between Europe and Asia, bordering Azerbaijan, Russia, Kazakstan, and Iran. With a basin 750 mi (1,200 km) long and 270 mi (434 km) wide and an area of 143,550 sq mi (371,608 sq km), it is the largest inland body of water in the world. It receives many rivers, including the VOLGA and URAL, but has no outlet. In the Middle Ages it formed part of the Mongol–Baltic trade route for goods from Asia. Today it is a source of caviar and oil. Its numerous ports include BAKU in Azerbaijan.

Cass, Lewis (1782–1866) U.S. politician. Born in Exeter, N.H., he served as governor of Michigan Territory 1813–31. As secretary of war (1831–36) under Pres. Andrew JACKSON, he directed the conduct of the Black Hawk and Seminole wars. In the U.S. Senate (1845–48, 1849–57), he supported westward expansion and the Compromise of 1850. As the Democratic presidential nominee in 1848, he lost to Zachary TAYLOR. He later served as secretary of state (1857–60), but resigned when Pres. James BUCHANAN failed to counter the secession of the Southern states.

Cassandra In GREEK MYTHOLOGY, the daughter of King PRIAM of Troy. APOLLO promised her the gift of prophecy if she would grant his desires; she accepted the gift but rebuffed the god, who took revenge by ordaining that no one would believe her prophecies. Her predictions of the fall of Troy and the death of Agamemnon went unheeded. Given as part of the war spoils to Agamemnon, she was murdered with him.

Cassatt \kə-'sat\, **Mary** (1844–1926) U.S. painter active in Paris. Born in Allegheny City, Pa., she spent her early years traveling in Europe with her wealthy family, attended the Pennsylvania Academy of Fine Arts, and later studied in Paris. She became a close friend of Edgar DEGAS, who influenced her style and encouraged her to exhibit with the Impressionists. She portrayed scenes of everyday life, particularly images of mothers and children, and was also skilled at drawing and printmaking. Some of her best works were executed in pastel. Through her social contacts with wealthy private collectors, she influentially promoted IM-PRESSIONISM in the U.S.

cassava \kə-'sä-və\ *or* **manioc** *or* **yuca** Tuberous edible perennial plant (*Manihot esculenta*) of the SPURGE family, from the New World tropics. It is cultivated for its tuberous roots, from which cassava flour, breads, tapioca, a laundry starch, and an alcoholic beverage are derived. Different varieties range from low herbs through many-branched shrubs to slender, unbranched trees.

Cassidy, Butch *orig.* Robert Leroy Parker (1866–1909?) U.S. outlaw. Born in Beaver, Utah, he became a cattle rustler, taking his name from an older outlaw mentor. In 1900 he joined Harry Longabaugh, the Sundance Kid (1870–1909?), nicknamed for a town where he had once been imprisoned. They became the foremost members of the Wild Bunch, a collection of bank and train robbers. The two eluded Pinkerton detectives by escaping to S. America in 1901. They bought a ranch in Argentina but returned to a life of outlawry in 1906. In 1909, trapped by soldiers in Bolivia, Sundance was mortally wounded and Cassidy shot himself. The time, place, and circumstances of their deaths vary widely in different accounts.

Cassini, Gian Domenico (1625–1712) Italian-French astronomer. After his early studies of the sun, he obtained more powerful telescopes and observed the planets. He calculated Jupiter's and Mars's rotational periods and compiled a table of the positions of Jupiter's moons and a large map of earth's moon. In 1683 he concluded that the zodiacal light was of cosmic origin. He discovered four of Saturn's moons: Iapetus (1671), Rhea (1672), Tethys (1684), and Dione (1684). The gap between Saturn's two main rings (Cassini's division) is named for him.

Cassiodorus \,ka-sē-ə-'dōr-əs\, *in full* Flavius Magnus Aurelius Cassiodorus (c.490–c.585) Historian, statesman, and monk who helped preserve Roman culture after the collapse of the Roman empire. He was secretary to THEODORIC and later held other high imperial offices. Soon after 540 he founded a monastery to perpetuate the culture of Rome. He collected pagan and Christian manuscripts and had the monks copy them, establishing a practice continued in later centuries. His own works included the *Chronicon*, a history of mankind to 519.

Cassirer \kä-'sir-ər\, **Ernst** (1874–1945) German philosopher. He taught at the Univs. of Berlin (1905–19) and Hamburg (1919–33) before being forced to flee to Sweden and the U.S. A Neo-Kantian, he believed that human beings have innately determined ways of structuring experiences—myth, language, science—that shape their understanding of themselves and of nature. His most important original work was *The Philosophy of Symbolic Forms* (1923–29).

Cassius (Longinus) \'kash-əs\, **Gaius** (d.42 B.C.) Roman general and administrator. He fought alongside POMPEY against Julius CAESAR, but was reconciled with Caesar after Pompey's defeat. Motivated by jealousy and bitterness, he joined BRUTUS in the successful conspiracy to assassinate Caesar (44 B.C.). With Brutus he raised an army in Macedonia to challenge the Second TRIUMVIRATE. Defeated at the Battle of PHILIPPI by Mark ANTONY, he had his freedmen slay him. He was lamented by Brutus as "the last of the Romans."

cassowary \'ka-sə-,wer-ē\ Any of several species of RATITE (family Casuariidae) of the Australo-Papuan region. Related to the EMU, it can kill humans with slashing blows of its feet, which have long, daggerlike nails on the

Common or Australian cassowary (*Casuarius casuarius*)

innermost toe. It has a black body and a naked blue head protected by a bony helmet. It moves rapidly along narrow tracks in the bush. Cassowaries eat fruits and small animals. The largest species is almost 5 ft (1.5 m) tall.

Castagno \kä-'stä-nyō\, **Andrea del** *orig.* Andrea di Bartolo (1419?–1457) Italian painter active in Florence. Little is known of his early life, and many of his paintings have been lost. In 1447 he began his greatest work, a series of monumental frescoes depicting the Last Supper and Christ's Passion for the convent of Sant' Apollonia. His use of pictorial illusionism and scientific perspective, as well as the powerful, sculptural form of his figures, established him as one of the most influential painters of the 15th cent.

caste Group of people having a specific social rank, defined largely by DESCENT, MARRIAGE, and occupation. Widespread in India, caste is rooted in antiquity. Each caste has its own customs that restrict the occupations and dietary habits of its members and their social contact with other castes. There are about 3,000 castes, or *jatis* ("races"), and more than 25,000 subcastes in India. They are traditionally grouped into four major classes, or VARNAS ("colors"). At the top are the BRAHMANS, followed by the Kshatriyas, VAISHYAS, and Sudras. The UNTOUCHABLES, not formally a caste, rank at the bottom. In the 20th cent., there was increasing upward social mobility and mixing among castes; nevertheless, the caste system has proved adaptable and continues to emerge in new forms.

Castiglione \,käs-tēl-'yō-nā\, **Baldassare** (1478–1529) Italian diplomat, courtier, and writer. A nobleman, he was attached to the courts of Mantua and Urbino and later entered papal service. His *Book of the Courtier* (1528) describes the conduct of the perfect courtier, the qualities of a noble lady, and the ideal relationships between the courtier and his prince. Internationally successful, it became a manual for those aspiring to aristocratic manners.

Castile \ka-'stēl\ *Spanish* **Castilla** \kä-'stē-lyä\ Traditional region, peninsular Spain. Castilian territory was first united under León in the 10th cent. The Spanish part of the kingdom of NAVARRE was annexed by Castile in 1512, thus completing the formation of modern Spain. It remains Spain's center of political and administrative power. See also CASTILLA Y LEÓN, CASTILLA-LA MANCHA.

Castilla-La Mancha \kä-'stē-lyä-lä-'män-chä\ Autonomous community (pop., 1998 est.: 1,716,000) and historic region, central Spain. Established in 1982, it encompasses the provinces of Toledo, Ciudad Real, Cuenca, Guadalajara, and Albacete, and covers an area of 30,591 sq mi (79,231 sq km); its capital is TOLEDO. The watershed of the low-lying Toledo Mtns. bisects the region. Emigration to Madrid has reduced the population; for those who remain, agriculture dominates the economy. See also CASTILE.

Castilla y León \kä-'stē-lyä-ē-lā-'ōn\ Autonomous community (pop., 1998 est.: 2,484,000) and historic region, N Spain. Established in 1983, it encompasses the provinces of Valladolid, Burgos, León, Salamanca, Zamora, Polencia, and Segovia, and covers an area of 36,368 sq mi (94,193 sq km); its capital is VALLADOLID. The Cantabrian Mtns. rise to the north. The population has declined since 1900, with notable emigration to the provincial capitals. The economy is largely agricultural. See also CASTILE.

casting Pouring of molten METAL into a MOLD, where it solidifies into the shape of the mold. The process was well established in the BRONZE AGE, when it was used to form BRONZE pieces now found in museums. It is particularly valuable for the economical production of complex shapes, ranging from mass-produced parts for automobiles to one-of-a-kind production of statues, jewelry, or massive machinery. Most steel and iron castings (see CAST IRON) are poured into silica sand. See also DIE CASTING, FOUNDING, LOST-WAX CASTING.

cast iron ALLOY of IRON that contains 2–4% CARBON, along with SILICON, MANGANESE, and impurities. It is made by reducing iron ORE in a BLAST FURNACE and CASTING the liquid iron into ingots called pigs. Pig iron is remelted, along with scrap and alloying elements, and recast into molds for a variety of products. In the 18th–19th cent., cast iron was a cheaper engineering material than WROUGHT IRON (not requiring intensive refining and hammering). Though it is

more brittle and lacks tensile strength, its load-bearing strength made it the first important structural metal. In the 20th cent., STEEL replaced it as a construction material, but cast iron is still used in automobile engine blocks, agricultural and machine parts, pipes, hollowware, stoves, and furnaces. Though most cast iron is brittle, malleable cast iron (produced by prolonged HEAT TREATING), first made in 18th-cent. France, was developed into an industrial product in the U.S. Cast iron that is ductile as cast was invented in 1948; this now constitutes a major family of metals, widely used for gears, dies, automobile crankshafts, and many other machine parts.

castle Medieval European stronghold, generally the fortified dwelling of the king or lord of a territory. The castle developed rapidly in Western Europe from the 9th cent. The outer wall was surrounded by one or more moats, these being crossed by drawbridges that could be raised from the inner side. The gateway itself was heavily protected and often defended by a barbican, or watchtower. One or more walled courtyards surrounded the DONJON. The age of the medieval castle came to an end with the increasing use of firearms in the 15th–16th cent.

Castle, Vernon and Irene orig. Vernon Blythe and Irene Foote (1887–1918, 1893–1969) British-U.S. husband-and-wife BALLROOM DANCE team. Irene was born in New Rochelle, N.Y. Vernon moved to the U.S. in 1906, and they married in 1911. They gained worldwide popularity for their graceful style, and introduced such dances as the one-step, fox-trot, turkey trot, and hesitation waltz, and popularized several others. Irene is credited with creating the fashion for bobbed hair. Following Vernon's death in an airplane crash, Irene retired from dancing.

Vernon and Irene Castle

Castlereagh, Viscount orig. Robert Stewart (1769–1822) British politician. Born in Ireland, he served in the English Parliament (1794–1805, 1806–22). As chief secretary for Ireland (1798–1801), he singlehandedly forced the Act of UNION through the Irish Parliament. He served as Britain's secretary for war (1805–6, 1807–9) and as secretary for foreign affairs and leader of the House of Commons (1812–22). Considered one of Britain's most distinguished foreign secretaries, he played a leading role in bringing together the Grand Alliance that overthrew NAPOLEON and in forging the peace settlements at the Congress of VIENNA. Beset with paranoia, he eventually committed suicide.

Castor and Pollux See DIOSCURI

castration or **neutering** Removal of the TESTES, stopping most production of TESTOSTERONE and preventing or ending sperm formation and sexual interest and behavior. Livestock and pets are castrated to keep them from reproducing (see STERILIZATION) or to create a more docile animal. In humans, castration has been used for both cultural (see EUNUCH, CASTRATO) and medical (e.g., for testicular cancer) reasons.

castrato \ka-ˈsträ-ˌtō\ Male soprano or alto voice produced as a result of CASTRATION before puberty. The castrato voice was introduced in the Vatican's Sistine Chapel in the 16th cent., when women were still banned from church choirs as well as the stage. It reached its greatest prominence in 17th- and 18th-cent. opera. The illegal and inhumane practice of castration, largely practiced in Italy, could produce a treble voice of extraordinary power, attributable to the lung capacity and physical bulk of the adult male. Their unique tone quality and virtuosic capacities made castrati the rage among opera audiences. The most famous castrati bore the stage names Senesino (d.c.1750), Caffarelli (1710–1783), and FARINELLI.

Castries \kå-ˈstrē, ˈkäs-ˌtrē\ Seaport (pop., 1991: 11,000), capital of ST. LUCIA, W. Indies. Located on the island's NW coast, its fine harbor is St. Lucia's chief port. A fortress on Mt. Fortune (852 ft, or 260 m) overlooks the town.

Castro (Ruz), Fidel (b.1926/27) Political leader of Cuba (from 1959). Son of a sugar planter, he became a lawyer, and was a candidate for Cuba's legislature when Gen. Fulgencio BATISTA overthrew the government in 1952. He organized an unsuccessful rebellion against Batista in 1953, served time in prison, then went to Mexico, where he and others, including Che GUEVARA, continued to plot Batista's overthrow. He led an armed expedition back to Cuba in 1956; the few survivors took refuge in the

Fidel Castro, 1964

mountains, where they gradually organized guerrillas throughout the island. On January 1, 1959, Batista fled the country. Castro nationalized private commerce and industry and took U.S.-owned land and businesses, vastly expanded health services and eliminated illiteracy, and outlawed all political groups but the Communist Party. The U.S. attempted to overthrow him but failed (see BAY OF PIGS), precipitating the CUBAN MISSILE CRISIS. Castro exercised total control of the government and economy, which became increasingly dependent on subsidies from the Soviet Union, whose collapse (1991) devastated Cuba's economy, and Castro has attempted to replace its revenues through tourism.

Castro y Bellvís \ˈkäs-trō-ē-belʸ-ˈvēs\, **Guillén de** (1569–1631) Spanish playwright. Of his 50-odd plays, the best remembered is Las mocedades del Cid ("The Youth of the Cid"; c.1599), on which Pierre CORNEILLE based his Le Cid (1637). He was one of the earliest playwrights to deal with the difficulties of marriage, as in Los mal casados de Valencia ("The Unhappy Marriages of Valencia").

casualty insurance Provision against loss to persons and property, covering legal hazards as well as those of accident and sickness. Major classes include LIABILITY, theft, aviation, WORKERS' COMPENSATION, CREDIT, and title. Liability insurance may cover liability arising from use of an automobile, operation of a business, professional negligence (MALPRACTICE insurance), or property ownership. Credit insurance may cover bad debts from insolvency, death, and disability, loss of savings from bank failure, and loss of export credit due to commercial or political changes.

casuarina \ˌkazh-yə-ˈrē-nə\ Any of the chiefly Australian trees that make up the genus Casuarina (family Casuarinaceae), which have whorls of scalelike leaves and jointed stems resembling HORSETAILS. Several species are valued for their hard, dense, yellowish- to reddish-brown wood, which is strong and reputed to be resistant to termite attack.

CAT See COMPUTED AXIAL TOMOGRAPHY

cat Any member of the most highly specialized CARNIVORE family, Felidae, which consists of the true cats (genera Panthera and Felis) and the CHEETAH (Acinonyx). Cats appeared in the fossil record about 10 million years ago. Cats in the genus Panthera (sometimes Leo) (e.g., TIGER and LION) roar but cannot purr, and their pupils are round. Cats in the genus Felis (e.g., COUGAR) can purr but do not roar; the pupil is usually vertical. Cats have sharp, retractable claws, and their teeth are adapted for stabbing, anchoring, and cutting. They almost always land on their feet when they fall from a height. Most species are nocturnal. Small cats have been domesticated for some 3,500 years (see DOMESTIC CAT). The wild cats include the BOBCAT, CARACAL, JAGUAR, LEOPARD, LYNX, OCELOT, SERVAL, SNOW LEOPARD, and WILDCAT.

catacomb Subterranean cemetery of galleries with recesses for tombs. The term was probably first applied to the cemetery under St. Sebastian's Basilica used for the bodies of Sts. PETER and PAUL in the late 3rd cent. A.D., but it came to refer to all the subterranean cemeteries around Rome. Catacombs in early Christian Rome were the sites of funeral feasts and were also used as hiding places; Pope Sixtus II was supposedly captured and killed (A.D. 258) while hiding in the St. Sebastian's catacomb during the persecution by VALERIAN. Catacombs are also found in Sicily, Egypt, and Lebanon.

Catalhuyuk \chä-ˌtäl-hǖe-ˈyǖek, *Engl* chä-ˌtäl-hü-ˈyük\ Neolithic site, Middle East. Located near KONYA in S Turkey, it was in Neolithic times the center of an advanced culture. The earliest period is tentatively dated to around 6700 B.C. A series of excavated shrines have wall paintings that have been linked with Upper Paleolithic art.

Catalonia Autonomous community (pop., 1998 est.: 6,147,000) and historic region, NE Spain. It encompasses the provinces of Gerona, Barcelona, Tarragona, and Lérida, and covers an area of 12,328 sq mi (31,930 sq km); its capital is BARCELONA. The PYRENEES separate Catalonia from France; the Mediterranean Sea lies to the east. Catalonia was one of Rome's first Spanish possessions. Occupied in the 5th cent. A.D. by the GOTHS, it was taken by the MOORS in 712 and by CHARLEMAGNE in 795. After the unification of Spain (1469), Catalonia lost influence, and by the 17th cent. its conflict of interest with CASTILLA Y LEÓN led to the first of a series of separatist movements. Catalan nationalism became a serious force after 1876. Autonomy won by Catalonia in 1932 was revoked with the 1939 Nationalist victory, and Francisco FRANCO's government repressed Catalan nationalism. Democratic rule after Franco's death again led to autonomy in 1979. Today Catalonia is the richest and most industrialized part of Spain.

catalpa \kə-ˈtal-pə\ Any of 11 species of trees in the genus *Catalpa* (family Bignoniaceae), native to E Asia, E N. America, and the W. Indies. Catalpas have large, attractive leaves and showy white, yellowish, or purplish flowers. The catalpa fruit is a long cylindrical seed pod. The common catalpa, *C. bignonioides*, yields a durable timber and is one of the most widely planted ornamental species.

catalysis \kə-ˈta-lə-səs\ Modification (usually acceleration) of a CHEMICAL REACTION rate (see REACTION RATE) by addition of a CATALYST, which combines with the reactants but is later regenerated so that its amount remains unchanged and the chemical EQUILIBRIUM of the conditions of the reaction is not altered. Catalysts reduce the ACTIVATION ENERGY barrier between reactants and products. When more than one reaction is possible, a catalyst that accelerates only one reaction pathway selectively enhances the creation of its product. Chemisorption (see ADSORPTION), a type of catalysis, often involves BONDING between the catalyst's solid surface and the reactant. To make the accessible surface area as large as possible, such catalysts are finely powdered or highly porous solids. Catalysis is essential to the modern chemical industry. See also ENZYME.

catalyst \ˈka-t°l-əst\ Any substance of which a small proportion notably affects the REACTION RATE of a CHEMICAL REACTION without itself being changed or consumed (see CATALYSIS). One molecule may transform several million reactant molecules a minute. Gaseous, liquid, or solid, catalysts may be inorganic compounds, organic compounds, or complex combinations. They tend to be highly specific, reacting with only one substance or a small set of substances. Substances that alter them or block reactants' access to them may inhibit (poison) them. Most solid catalysts are fine-grained TRANSITION ELEMENTS (metals) or their OXIDES. In a car's CATALYTIC CONVERTER, the PLATINUM catalyst converts unburned HYDROCARBONS and NITROGEN compounds to harmless products. Water, especially salt water, catalyzes oxidation (see OXIDATION-REDUCTION) and CORROSION. ENZYMES are among the most active and selective catalysts known.

catalytic converter In AUTOMOBILES, a component of emission-control systems used to reduce the discharge of noxious gases from the INTERNAL-COMBUSTION ENGINE. It consists of an insulated chamber containing pellets of CATALYST through which the exhaust HYDROCARBONS and CARBON MONOXIDE are converted to water vapor and CARBON DIOXIDE.

catamaran \ˈka-tə-mə-ˌran\ Boat with twin hulls and a deck, based on a raft of two logs bridged by planks used by peo-

ples in Indonesia, Polynesia, and Micronesia. Up to 70 ft (21 m) long, early catamarans were paddled by many men and used for travel, war, and recreation. After the sail was added, voyages as long as 2,000 mi (3,700 km) were made. In the 1870s they sailed so successfully against monohulled boats that they were barred from racing. Engine-powered catamarans achieve speeds of 20 mph (32 kph).

Catania \kä-ˈtä-nyä\ City (pop., 1996: 342,000), SICILY. It was founded by Greeks in 729 B.C. at the foot of Mt. ETNA on the Gulf of Catania. Taken by the Romans in the First PUNIC WAR (263 B.C.), Catania fell successively to the Byzantines, Arabs, and Normans, and suffered devastation by earthquakes especially in 1169 and 1693. In World War II the city was severely damaged by bombing. Rebuilt, it is now Sicily's second-largest city.

catapult Mechanism for forcefully propelling stones, spears, or other projectiles, in use since ancient times. Nearly all artillery catapults operated by a sudden release of tension on wooden beams or twisted cords of horsehair, gut, sinew, or other fibers, though the medieval trebuchet was powered by a counterweight. Modern mechanisms using steam, hydraulic pressure, tension, or other force to launch gliders, aircraft, or missiles are also called catapults.

cataract Opacity of the EYE's crystalline lens. Cataracts in the central visual field are most likely to affect vision. Cataracts may occur in newborns and infants. Diabetes mellitus, prolonged exposure to ultraviolet rays, or trauma can cause them in adults, but they most often occur with age, as the lens gradually loses transparency. A surgical procedure replaces the lens with an artificial one.

catbird Any of several PASSERINE species (family Mimidae) named for their mewing calls, which they use in addition to song. The N. American catbird (*Dumetella carolinensis*) is 9 in. (23 cm) long and gray with a black cap. It is found in gardens and thickets. The black catbird (*Melanoptila glabrirostris*) is found in coastal Yucatán. Three species of bowerbird are also called catbirds.

catechism Manual of religious instruction usually arranged in the form of questions and answers and used to instruct the young, win converts, and testify to the faith. The medieval Christian catechism concentrated on the meaning of faith, hope, and charity. Martin LUTHER's Small Catechism (1529) added discussions of baptism and the EUCHARIST. John CALVIN published a children's catechism in 1542. The Anglican catechism is included in the Book of COMMON PRAYER. The Baltimore Catechism (1885) was the best-known U.S. catechism. In 1992 the Vatican issued a new universal *Catechism of the Catholic Church*.

categorical imperative In Immanuel KANT's moral philosophy, an imperative that presents an action as unconditionally necessary (e.g., "Thou shalt not kill"), as opposed to one that presents an action as necessary only on condition that the agent wills something else (e.g., "Pay your debts on time, if you want a good credit rating"). Kant held that there was only one formally categorical imperative: "Act only according to that maxim by which you can at the same time will that it should become a universal law."

caterpillar LARVA of a BUTTERFLY or MOTH. Caterpillars have a cylindrical body consisting of 13 segments, with three pairs of legs on the thorax and "prolegs" on the abdomen. The head has six eyes on each side, short antennae, and strong jaws. Though not true WORMS, many caterpillars are called worms (e.g., the inchworm and the CUTWORM).

catfish Any of about 2,500 species of scale-less, mostly freshwater, fishes (order Siluriformes) related to CARP and named for their whiskerlike barbels (fleshy feelers). All species have at least one pair of barbels on the upper jaw, and some have a pair on the snout and additional pairs on the chin. Many species possess spines that may be associated with venom glands. They are generally bottom-dwelling scavengers. Species vary from 1.5 in. to 15 ft (4 cm–4.5 m) long and may weigh up to 660 lbs (300 kg). Many small species are popular aquarium fishes; many large species are used for food.

Cathari \ˈka-thə-ˌrī\ *or* **Albigensians** \al-bə-ˈjen-sē-ənz\ Heretical Christian sect that flourished in Western Europe in the 12th–13th cent. The Cathari adhered to the dualist belief that the material world is evil and that humans must re-

nounce the world to free their spirits, which long for communion with God. Jesus was seen as an angel whose human suffering and death were an illusion. By 1200 they had established 11 bishoprics in France and Italy. In an effort to stamp out their HERESY, Pope INNOCENT III declared the bloody ALBIGENSIAN CRUSADE. Persecution through the INQUISITION, sanctioned by St. LOUIS IX, was even more effective, and when the Cathar stronghold of Montségur fell in 1244, most Cathari fled to Italy. The movement disappeared in the 15th cent.

Cathay \ka-'thā\ Former name for China, especially N China. The word is derived from Khitay, the name of a seminomadic people who dominated N China in the 10th–12th cent. The name may have been introduced to Europe by returning Franciscan friars around 1254, but it was Marco POLO's *Travels* 50 years later that put Cathay's image before the European public.

cathedral Church, often large and magnificent, in which a residential bishop has his official seat. Cathedrals are usually embellished versions of early Christian BASILICAS; their construction, on an ever-larger scale, was a major preoccupation throughout Europe in the Middle Ages. Masonry vaulting replaced the earlier timber roofs. Above the arches of the NAVE, and below the CLERESTORY, was the triforium, an arcaded upper story that often contained vaulted tribune GALLERIES open to the nave. The portion containing seats for the choir, usually east of the transept, was called the chancel. Between the chancel and the sanctuary (high altar) was the presbytery, a raised area occupied only by clergy. The chapter house, a popular feature of English cathedrals, was a chamber, typically octagonal, in which business was transacted. Small chapels, including the founder's chantry and the Lady Chapel (dedicated to the Virgin Mary), were often added.

Cather \'ka-thər\, **Willa** *orig.* Willa Sibert (1873–1947) U.S. novelist. Born in Winchester, Va., she moved to Nebraska at 10, returning east 12 years later. *The Troll Garden* (1905) was her first short-story collection. The novels *O Pioneers!* (1913) and *My Ántonia* (1918), often judged her finest, celebrate frontier spirit and courage; *Song of the Lark* (1915) and *Youth and the Bright Medusa* (1920) reflect the struggle of a talent to emerge from small-town provincialism. *One of Ours* (1922, Pulitzer Prize) and *A Lost Lady* (1923) mourn the loss of the pioneer spirit. Pioneers of earlier eras inspired *Death Comes for the Archbishop* (1927) and *Shadows on the Rock* (1931).

Catherine II *Russian* Yekaterina Alekseyevna *orig.* Sophie Friederike Auguste, Prinzessin (Princess) von Anhalt-Zerbst, *known as* **Catherine the Great** (1729–1796) German-born empress of Russia (1762–96). The daughter of an obscure German prince, she was chosen at 14 to be the wife of the future PETER III. Because her neurotic husband was incapable of ruling, the ambitious Catherine saw the possibility of governing Russia herself. After Peter became emperor in 1762, she conspired with her lover, Grigory ORLOV, to force Peter to abdicate (he was murdered soon after) and have herself proclaimed empress. In her 34-year reign, she led Russia into full participation in European political and cultural life. With her ministers she reorganized the administration of the Russian empire and extended its territory, adding the Crimea and much of Poland. Though she had once intended to emancipate the serfs, she instead strengthened the serf system. She had great energy and wide interests, and her personal life was notable for her many lovers, including Grigory POTEMKIN.

Catherine de Médicis \ka-trēn-də-mā-dē-'sēs\ *orig.* Caterina de' Medici (1519–1589) Queen consort of HENRY II (1547–59) and mother of CHARLES IX and HENRY III. One of the MEDICI FAMILY, she married Henry in 1533 and bore him 10 children. She became queen when Henry inherited the crown in 1547 and greatly mourned his accidental death in 1559. After their son Francis (1544–1560) became king, she began a long struggle with members of the extremist GUISE family. After Francis's premature death, she became regent for Charles IX until 1563 and later dominated his reign. She attempted to settle the Wars of RELIGION between Catholics and HUGUENOTS. Traditionally blamed for the ST. BARTHOLOMEW'S DAY Massacre, she did authorize

the assassination of Gustav COLIGNY and his principal followers but apprently not the massacre that followed.

Catherine of Alexandria, St. (fl. early 4th cent. A.D.) Early Christian martyr. According to tradition, she was a learned girl of noble birth who protested the persecution of Christians during the reign of the Roman emperor Maxentius. She converted the emperor's wife but nevertheless was sentenced to be killed with a spiked wheel (the "catherine wheel"); when it broke she was beheaded. One of the most popular saints of the Middle Ages, she was patron of philosophers and scholars. Her historicity is doubtful.

Catherine of Aragon (1485–1536) First wife of HENRY VIII of England. The daughter of FERDINAND V and ISABELLA I, she married Henry in 1509. She gave birth to six children, but only one (later MARY I) survived infancy. Henry's desire for a male heir prompted him in 1527 to appeal to Rome for an annulment, but Pope CLEMENT VII refused, triggering the break that led to the English Reformation. In 1533 Henry had his own archbishop of Canterbury, Thomas CRANMER, annul the marriage.

Catherine of Siena, St. *orig.* Caterina Benincasa (1347–1380) Mystic and patron saint of Italy. She joined the Dominican third order in Siena in 1363 and soon became known for her holiness and severe asceticism. She played a major role in returning the papacy from Avignon to Rome (see AVIGNON PAPACY). Her writings include four treatises on religious mysticism known as *The Dialogue of St. Catherine*.

catheterization \ˌka-thə-tə-rə-'zā-shən\ Threading of a flexible tube (catheter) through a channel in the body to inject drugs or a CONTRAST MEDIUM, measure and record flow and pressures, inspect structures, take samples, diagnose disorders, or clear blockages. A cardiac catheter can also carry pacemaker electrodes. A bladder catheter goes through the urethra into the bladder.

cathode Terminal or ELECTRODE at which electrons enter a system, such as an electrolytic cell or an electron tube. In a BATTERY or other source of DIRECT CURRENT, the cathode is the positive terminal. In a passive load it is the negative terminal. In an electron tube, such as a CATHODE-RAY TUBE, electrons stream off the cathode and travel through the tube toward the ANODE.

cathode ray Stream of ELECTRONS leaving the negative ELECTRODE, or CATHODE, in a discharge tube (an electron tube that contains gas or vapor at low pressure), or emitted by a heated filament in certain electron tubes. Cathode rays cause fluorescent materials to luminesce (see LUMINESCENCE). See also CATHODE-RAY TUBE.

cathode-ray tube (CRT) Vacuum tube that produces images when its phosphorescent surface is struck by electron beams. CRTs can be monochrome (using one electron gun) or color (typically using three electron guns). They come in a variety of display modes, including CGA (Color Graphics Adapter), VGA (Video Graphics Array), XGA (Extended Graphics Array), and the high-definition SVGA (Super Video Graphics Array). See diagram on next page.

Catholic Emancipation Freedom from discrimination granted to the Roman Catholics of Britain and Ireland. After the REFORMATION, Roman Catholics could not purchase land, hold offices or seats in Parliament, or practice their religion without incurring civil penalties. By the late 18th cent., Catholicism no longer seemed so great a social and political danger, and a series of laws, culminating in the Emancipation Act of 1829, eased the restrictions. A major figure in the struggle for full emancipation was Daniel O'CONNELL.

Catholic League (1609–35) Military alliance of the Catholic powers of Germany, designed to stem the growth of Protestantism in Germany. Plans for a league had long been discussed, but the formation of the Protestant Union in 1608 finally caused the Catholics to unite. The League's forces, led by Graf von TILLY, played a key role in the THIRTY YEARS' WAR. The league was abolished by the Peace of Prague (1635).

Catholic Reformation See COUNTER-REFORMATION

Catiline \'kat- əl-ˌīn\ *Latin in full* Lucius Sergius Catilina (108?–62 B.C.) Roman aristocrat turned demagogue who attempted to overthrow the republic. Seeking to be elected

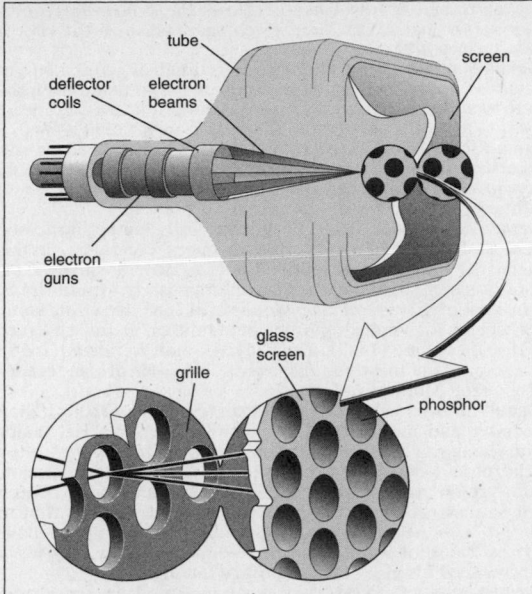

Cathode-ray tube In a color-television tube, three electron guns (one each for red, green, and blue) fire electrons toward the phosphor-coated screen. The electrons are deflected to a specific spot (pixel) on the screen by magnetic fields, induced by the electric coils. To prevent "spillage" to adjacent pixels, a grille or shadow mask is used. When the electrons strike the phosphor screen, the pixel glows. Every pixel is scanned about 30 times per second.

CONSUL and failing twice, he planned a coup, assembling an army outside Rome from his supporters among the alienated and discontented elements of society (63). CICERO, then consul, learned of the conspiracy; he caught and executed a group of the plotters in Rome, and later sent the army to defeat and kill Catiline in N Italy (62).

cation \'kat-ˌī-ən\ ATOM or group of atoms carrying a positive ELECTRIC CHARGE, indicated by a superscript plus sign after the chemical symbol. Cations in a liquid subjected to an ELECTRIC FIELD collect at the negative pole (CATHODE). Examples include SODIUM (Na⁺), CALCIUM (Ca²⁺), and ammonium (NH₄⁺; see AMMONIA). See also ION.

Catlin, George (1796–1872) U.S. painter and author. Born in Wilkes-Barre, Pa., he became a self-taught portrait painter in Philadelphia (1823). Long interested in American Indian life, in 1830 he began a series of visits to various tribes on the Great Plains. He produced some 500 paintings and sketches based on his travels and exhibited them in the U.S. and in Europe, where he lived 1858–70. He published several illustrated books on Native American life. Most of his collection was acquired by the Smithsonian Institution.

catnip *or* **catmint** Aromatic herb (*Nepeta cataria*) of the MINT family. Catnip has spikes of small, purple-dotted flowers. It has been used as a seasoning and as a medicinal tea for colds and fever. Because its mintlike flavor and aroma are particularly exciting to domestic cats, it is often used as a stuffing for cat playthings.

Cato \'kā-tō\, **Marcus Porcius** *known as* **Cato the Censor** *or* **Cato the Elder** (234–149 B.C.) Roman statesman and orator, the first important Latin prose writer. Born of yeoman stock, he fought in the Second PUNIC WAR. His oratorical skills paved the way for his political career. Elected censor (magistrate in charge of censuses, taxes, and the public good) in 184, he tried to combat Greek influence, which he believed undermined Roman morality. He crafted laws against luxury and the financial freedom of women and never ceased to demand the destruction of Carthage. His writings include works on history, medicine, law, military science, and agriculture. His great-grandson Cato the Younger (95–46 B.C.) sought to preserve the republic against Julius CAESAR.

cat's-eye Any of several gemstones that display a luminous band reminiscent of the eye of a cat. Grayish green or greenish quartz cat's-eye is the most common type. The rarer, and more valuable, precious or oriental cat's-eye is a greenish variety of chrysoberyl. The semiprecious crocidolite cat's-eye (African cat's-eye), known as tigereye, has a rich yellow or yellow-brown color. Corundum cat's-eye is an imperfect star sapphire or ruby in which the star is reduced to a luminous zone.

Catskill Mountains Mountain group of the APPALACHIAN MTN. system, SE New York. It is bounded by the MOHAWK and HUDSON rivers. The area has many resorts, and its lakes and reservoirs supply New York City with water. The mountains were made famous through Washington IRVING's stories of Rip Van Winkle, who supposedly took his long nap near the town of Catskill.

Catt, Carrie Chapman *orig.* Carrie Lane (1859–1947) U.S. women's suffrage advocate. Born in Ripon, Wis., she became a high-school principal in Mason City, Iowa, in 1881, and in 1883 one of the nation's first female school superintendents. She married Leo Chapman in 1884. After his death in 1886 she devoted herself to organizing the Iowa Woman Suffrage Assn. (1887–90). After marrying George Catt in 1890, she served as president of the National American Woman Suffrage Assn. (1900–4, 1915–47); from 1920 she reorganized the 2-million-member association as the League of Women Voters to work for progressive legislation.

cattail Any of the tall reedy marsh plants (see REED) that bear brown, furry fruiting spikes and make up the genus *Typha* (family Typhaceae), particularly *T. latifolia,* the long flat leaves of which are used for making mats and chair seats. Cattails are found mainly in temperate and cold regions of the Northern and Southern hemispheres. Important to wildlife, they are also often cultivated ornamentally. The leaves, which swell when wet, are used for caulking cracks in barrels and boats.

cattle Domesticated BOVIDS raised for meat, milk, or hides or for draft purposes. Depending on the breed, mature bulls (fertile males) weigh 1,000–4,000 lbs (450–1,800 kg); cows (fertile females) weigh 800–2,400 lbs (350–1,100 kg). All modern cattle belong to either of two species (*Bos indicus* or *B. taurus*) or a cross of the two. About 277 breeds include those prominent in beef production and DAIRY FARMING. Cattle feed primarily by grazing on pasture, but in modern farming their diet is ordinarily supplemented with prepared animal feeds. See AUROCHS, OX.

Catullus \kə-'təl-əs\, **Gaius Valerius** (84?–54? B.C.) Roman poet. Of 116 extant poems, 25 portray an intense, unhappy affair with a married woman ("Lesbia"); others reflect an affair with a youth, Juventius; still others are outbursts of contempt for personages such as Julius CAESAR. Catullus displayed versatility in varied forms, and his expressions of love and hatred represent perhaps the finest lyric poetry of ancient Rome.

Cauca River \'kaú-kä\ River, W Colombia. It rises in the ANDES and flows northward 838 mi (1,348 km) to join the MAGDALENA RIVER north of Mompós. The Valle del Cauca is important for agriculture and cattle raising. Two-thirds of Colombia's coffee is produced in the adjacent uplands.

Caucasian languages \kó-'kā-zhən\ Group of languages spoken in the Caucasus region that are unrelated to other language families. Caucasian languages, spoken by about 9 million people, are divided into three subgroups: the S. Caucasian, or Kartvelian family; the N.W. Caucasian, or Abkhaz-Adyghe languages; and the N.E. Caucasian, or Nakh-Dagestanian languages. Kartvelian, with over 4.5 million speakers, comprises four relatively closely related languages, including Georgian. N.W. Caucasian languages include Abkhaz and the Circassian dialects. The N.E. Caucasian languages are further divided into two groups, Nakh and Daghestanian. The Nakh languages include Chechen and Ingush, spoken by over a million people mainly in CHECHNYA and Ingushetia. Daghestanian comprises 25–30 languages spoken by some 1.7 million people mainly in N Azerbaijan and Dagestan. In spite of their great diversity, most Caucasian languages have several grammatical and syntactical features in common. Except for Georgian, Caucasian languages with standard written forms employ the CYRILLIC ALPHABET.

Caucasoid See RACE

Caucasus Mountains \'kȯ-kə-səs\ *Russian* **Kavkazskiy Khrebet** \kəf-'kä-skē-ḵryi-'byet\ Mountain range between the BLACK and CASPIAN seas, often considered the SE limit of Europe. It extends about 700 mi (1,125 km) across S Russia, Georgia, Azerbaijan, and Armenia, and is of volcanic origin. Many peaks rise above 15,000 ft (4,575 m); the highest is Mt. ELBRUS. Its resources include considerable water power and valuable petroleum and natural gas reserves.

Cauchy \kō-'shē\ **Augustin-Louis** (1789–1857) French mathematician, pioneer of analysis and GROUP THEORY. He wrote a treatise in 1813 that became the basis of the theory of COMPLEX VARIABLES. He also clarified the theory of CALCULUS by developing the concepts of LIMITS and CONTINUITY, laid the foundations for the mathematical theory of ELASTICITY, and made important contributions to NUMBER THEORY.

caudillo \kaù-'dē-yō\ Latin American military dictator. In the wake of the Latin American independence movement in the early 19th cent., politically unstable conditions and the long experience of armed conflict led to the emergence of charismatic strongmen whose hold on power depended on control of armed followers, patronage, and vigilance. Their legitimacy was always in doubt, and few could withstand the challenges of new leaders from among their own followers and wealthy patrons. See also MACHISMO.

cauliflower Form of CABBAGE (*Brassica oleracea,* Botrytis group) of the MUSTARD FAMILY, consisting of a compact terminal mass of greatly thickened, modified, and partially developed flower structures, on fleshy stalks. This terminal cluster is served as a cooked or raw vegetable and is highly nutritious. See also BRASSICA.

causation Relation that holds between two simultaneous or successive events when the first event (the cause) brings about the other (the effect). David HUME held that the idea of necessary connection that is part of the common conception of causation is subjective. According to Hume, the objective content of an assertion that events of type A cause events of type B is merely that we have found through experience that events of type A are invariably followed by events of type B.

caustic soda SODIUM HYDROXIDE (NaOH), an inorganic compound. The ALKALIES called caustic soda and caustic potash (POTASSIUM hydroxide) are very important industrial chemicals, with uses in the manufacture of soaps, glass, and numerous other products. They have been easily extracted since ancient times by soaking wood ashes in water (see LYE). Most caustic soda today is produced by ELECTROLYSIS.

Cauvery River See KAVERI RIVER

Cavafy \kə-'väf-ē\, **Constantine** *orig.* Konstantinos Petrou Kavafis (1863–1933) Egyptian poet who wrote in Greek. Born to Greek parents in Alexandria, he worked as a civil servant there his entire life. Many of his 200 poems, written in an intimate, realistic, lyrical style, in a strange combination of classical and modern Greek, deal with history, mostly the Hellenistic era; others reflect Cavafy's homosexual life. His poems became popular and influential after his death, and he is now regarded as one of the greatest Greek poets.

Cavalcanti \ˌkä-väl-'kän-tē\, **Guido** (1255?–1300) Italian poet. Born into an influential Florentine family, he studied with the philosopher Brunetto Latini, who had earlier taught DANTE, Cavalcanti's close friend. After Dante, he is considered the greatest 13th-cent. Italian poet. His 50 poems, many addressed to two women and on the theme of love, demonstrate the grace and directness of the *dolce stil nuovo* ("sweet new style").

Cavalier \ˌkav-ə-'lir\ In the ENGLISH CIVIL WARS, the name adopted by CHARLES I's supporters, who contemptuously called their opponents Roundheads (a reference to shorthaired apprentices). The term originally meant a rider or cavalryman. At the RESTORATION, the court party preserved the name Cavalier, which survived until the rise of the term TORY.

Cavalier poets \ˌkav-ə-'lir\ Group of English gentlemen poets who were Cavaliers (supporters of CHARLES I during the ENGLISH CIVIL WARS), including John SUCKLING, Edmund WALLER, Robert HERRICK, Thomas Carew (1594?–1640?), and Richard Lovelace (1618–1657). Accomplished as soldiers, courtiers, and wits, they wrote elegant lyrics, typically on love and dalliance, and sometimes on war, honor, and duty.

Cavalli \kä-'väl-lē\, **(Pier) Francesco** *orig.* Pietro Francesco Caletti-Bruni (1602–1676) Italian opera composer. In his teens he was a singer under Claudio MONTEVERDI at ST. MARK'S BASILICA, Venice. Also an organist, he would rise to the post of *maestro di cappella* there in 1668. He wrote some 30 operas for Venice's public opera houses, including *Egisto* (1643), *Giasone* (1649), *Xerse* (1654), and *Erismena* (1655), becoming the most popular opera composer of the decades following Monteverdi's death.

Cavallini \ˌkä-väl-'lē-nē\, **Pietro** (c.1250–c.1330) Italian painter and mosaicist, active mainly in Rome. His major surviving works are mosaics of *The Life of the Virgin* for the church of Santa Maria in Trastevere (1290s) and fragments of a fresco cycle, including a *Last Judgment,* for the church of Santa Cecilia in Trastevere (c.1293). He was the first to break with the stylizations of Byzantine art; his figures have a real sense of weight and three-dimensionality. His work influenced his great contemporary GIOTTO.

cavalry \'ka-vəl-rē\ Military force mounted on horseback. Cavalry duties included gathering information about the enemy, screening movements of its own army, pursuing a defeated enemy, striking suddenly at detected weak points, turning exposed flanks, and exploiting a penetration or breakthrough. In the late 19th cent., with the introduction of repeating rifles and machine guns, cavalry lost much of its value. By World War I, a cavalry charge against troops with rapid-firing small arms was suicidal. Armored vehicles soon replaced horses, and by the 1950s neither U.S. nor British forces had horse-mounted units. Today's "cavalry" units use helicopters and light armored vehicles in ways analogous to horse cavalry.

cave Naturally formed underground cavity. It often consists of a number of underground chambers or caverns interconnected by smaller passageways. Primary caves, such as lava tubes and coral caves, develop during the time when the host matrix is solidifying or being deposited. The more common secondary caves include solution caves, which form by the chemical dissolution of a soluble host rock that has been weakened by fracturing and erosion; MAMMOTH CAVE and CARLSBAD CAVERNS are examples.

Cavell \'ka-vəl\, **Edith (Louisa)** (1865–1915) English nurse and heroine of World War I. In 1907 she became first matron of a hospital in Brussels, where she greatly improved the standard of nursing. After the German occupation of Belgium (1914), she joined an underground group that helped about 200 Allied soldiers escape to the Netherlands. She was subsequently arrested and executed by the Germans.

Cavendish \'kav-ən-dish\, **Henry** (1731–1810) English physicist and chemist. He discovered the nature and properties of hydrogen, the specific heat of certain sub-

Edith Cavell

stances, and various properties of electricity. He measured the density and mass of the earth by the method now known as the Cavendish experiment. He discovered the composition of air, work that led to the discovery that water is a compound rather than an element, and to the discovery of NITRIC ACID. He anticipated OHM'S LAW, and independently discovered COULOMB'S LAW.

caviar Eggs, or roe, of STURGEON preserved with salt. Most true caviar is produced in Russia and Iran, from fish taken from the Caspian and Black seas. The best grade, beluga, is prepared from large black or gray eggs. Lesser grades are from smaller, denser eggs. In the U.S., the roe of salmon, whitefish, lumpfish, and paddlefish is sometimes sold as caviar.

Cavour \kə-'vùr\, **Camillo Benso, conte (Count) di** (1810–1861) Italian statesman, leading figure of the RISORGIMENTO. Born in Turin, Piedmont, in 1847 he founded the liberal newspaper *Il Risorgimento*, and he helped persuade CHARLES ALBERT to grant a liberal constitution. Elected to Parliament in 1848, Cavour soon became prime minister of Piedmont (1852–59, 1860–61). His exploitation of international rivalries and of revolutionary movements brought about the unification of Italy under the House of SAVOY, with himself as prime minister of the new kingdom (1861).

cavy \'kā-vē\ Any of several species of S. American RODENTS constituting the family Caviidae. Species in the genera *Cavia, Kerodon, Galea,* and *Microcavia* resemble the GUINEA PIG. They are stout, gray or brown, and 10–12 in. (25–30 cm) long, with short ears and legs and no visible tail. The Patagonian and salt desert cavies (*Dolichotis*) are more long-legged and rabbit-like. Cavies are social animals that live in burrows and feed on grass, leaves, and other vegetation.

Patagonian cavy (*Dolichotis patagona***)**

Cawnpore See KANPUR

Caxton, William (1422?–1491) First English printer. Having set up a press in Belgium, he published his translation *The Recuyell of the Historyes of Troye* (1475), the first book printed in English. Back in England, he produced the first dated English book, *Dictes and Sayenges of the Phylosophers* (1477). His output—about 100 items, including books of chivalric romance, morality, and history, and an illustrated encyclopedia—shows that he catered to a general public as well as wealthy patrons.

Cayenne \kī-'en\ Seaport (pop., 1999: 50,000), capital of FRENCH GUIANA. The city was founded by the French in 1643 at the mouth of the Cayenne and Mahury rivers. In the mid-19th cent. it became a center of French penal settlements in Guiana and was known as the "city of the condemned" (see DEVIL'S ISLAND). The prisons were closed in 1945.

Cayley, George (*later* **Sir George**) (1773–1857) British pioneer in AERODYNAMICS. By 1799 he had established the basic configuration of the modern AIRPLANE. He built his first model GLIDER in 1804, and in 1809 he published his groundbreaking aerodynamic research. Further research into the effects of streamlining, stability, and wing design led to his construction of the first full-size glider, which flew briefly in 1853. Cayley also invented the caterpillar TRACTOR (1825).

Cayman Islands British colony (pop., 1990: 25,000), Caribbean Sea. Located about 200 mi (320 km) northwest of Jamaica, it has a total land area of 118 sq mi (306 sq km). Its capital is George Town, on Grand Cayman, the largest island. Discovered by Christopher COLUMBUS in 1503, the islands were ceded to the British in 1670 and settled by the English arriving from Jamaica. They were administered as a dependency of Jamaica until Jamaican independence in 1962; a constitution providing for an elected governor was enacted in 1972. A popular tourist area, it is also a financial center, principally serving as an offshore tax haven for thousands of corporations.

CBS *formerly* **Columbia Broadcasting System** Major U.S. broadcasting network. It began in 1928 as a small radio network directed by William PALEY. By offering programming free to affiliated stations in return for their agreement to broadcast sponsored shows, Paley built the network to 114 stations in 10 years. Such stars as Fred ALLEN, Bing CROSBY, and Kate Smith increased audience ratings into the 1940s. Jack BENNY, Ed SULLIVAN, Lucille BALL, Mary Tyler MOORE, and Walter CRONKITE made CBS the dominant television network into the 1970s. The company diversified into several other fields, but only Columbia Records was successful, and the corporation sold its other divisions in 1985. CBS Inc. merged with WESTINGHOUSE ELECTRIC CORP. in 1995, and with Viacom Inc. in 2000.

CCC See CIVILIAN CONSERVATION CORPS

CCD *in full* **charge-coupled device** SEMICONDUCTOR device in which the electrical charge at the output of one component provides the input to the next. Because they can store electrical charges, CCDs can be used as memory devices, but they are slower than RAMs. CCDs are sensitive to light, and are therefore used as the light-detecting components in video and digital cameras and in optical scanners.

CCNY See CITY UNIV. OF NEW YORK

CD See CERTIFICATE OF DEPOSIT

CD See COMPACT DISC

CDC See CENTERS FOR DISEASE CONTROL AND PREVENTION

CD-ROM *in full* compact disc read-only memory. Type of computer storage medium that is read optically. A CD-ROM drive uses a low-power LASER beam to read data that have been encoded onto an optical disk in the form of tiny pits, then feeds the data to a computer for processing. Because it uses digital data, a CD-ROM can store images and sound in addition to text and is thus used to store music, graphics, and movies (see COMPACT DISC). Unlike conventional magnetic-storage technologies (e.g., HARD DISKS), CD-ROM drives cannot write information. Recordable compact discs (called CD-R) must be written on a CD-R recorder and can be played on any CD-ROM drive. Rewritable discs (CD-RW) can be written, erased, and rewritten numerous times.

Ceausescu \chaù-'shes-kü\, **Nicolae** (1918–1989) Romanian politician. Prominent in the Romanian Communist Party, in 1965 he became its leader. In 1967 he became head of state and in 1974 president of Romania. He charted an independent, nationalistic course, but maintained rigidly repressive controls over internal dissent. His harsh economic policies and grand building projects reduced Romania to near starvation. He was overthrown in a revolution in 1989, and after a hasty trial, he and his wife were executed by firing squad.

Cebu \sā-'bü\ Island (pop., 1990 : 2,646,000) and (with adjacent islets) province, central Philippines. It is 139 mi (224 km) long and about 20 mi (32 km) wide, with an area of 1,707 sq mi (4,421 sq km). Its chief city is CEBU. A mountain chain extends its entire length. Visited by Ferdinand MAGELLAN in 1521, it was occupied by the Spanish in 1565. One of the Philippines' most densely populated islands, it produces coal and copper.

Cebu *officially* **City of Cebu** City (pop., 2000: 662,000), capital of CEBU province, Philippine Islands. The oldest Spanish city in the Philippines, it possesses an excellent harbor, sheltered by Mactan Island. Attracted by Cebu's strategic position, Ferdinand MAGELLAN landed there in 1521 and converted the ruler to Christianity; Magellan was later killed on Mactan Island. It had prominent roles in insurrections against both Spain and the U.S. Heavily damaged in World War II, Cebu is now a cultural and commercial center.

Cech \'chek\, **Thomas (Robert)** (b.1947) U.S. biochemist and molecular biologist. Born in Chicago, in 1982 he became the first to show that an RNA molecule could catalyze a chemical reaction. He and Sidney ALTMAN were awarded a 1989 Nobel Prize for their independent discoveries that RNA, previously thought to be only a messenger of genetic information, can also catalyze cellular chemical reactions essential to life.

Cecil \'se-səl\, **Robert** *later* **Earl of Salisbury** (1563–1612) English statesman. Trained by his father, William CECIL, Robert became acting secretary of state in 1590 and was formally appointed to the post by ELIZABETH I in 1596. He succeeded his father as chief minister in 1598 and guided the peaceful succession of JAMES I, for whom he continued as chief minister and lord treasurer. He negotiated the end of the war with Spain in 1604 and allied England with France.

Cecil (of Chelwood), Viscount *orig.* **(Edgar Algernon) Robert Gascoyne-Cecil** *known as* **Lord Robert Cecil** (1864–

1958) British statesman. Son of the marquess of SALISBURY, he served during World War I as assistant secretary of state for foreign affairs. He was one of the principal draftsmen of the LEAGUE OF NATIONS covenant in 1919 and, as president of the League of Nations Union (1923–45), one of the League's most loyal workers. In 1937 he was awarded the Nobel Peace Prize.

Cecil, William *later* **Baron Burghley** \'bər-lē\ (1520–1598) English statesman, principal adviser to ELIZABETH I and a master of Renaissance statecraft. Having served as cosecretary to EDWARD VI, he was appointed Elizabeth's sole secretary when she became queen in 1558. A dedicated and skillful adviser, Cecil was later appointed lord high treasurer (1572–98). He obtained the trial and execution of MARY, QUEEN OF SCOTS, thus securing the Protestant succession, and his preparations enabled England to survive the Spanish ARMADA, but he failed to induce Elizabeth to marry or to reform her church along more Protestant lines.

Cecilia, St. (fl.2nd–3rd cent. A.D.) Early Christian martyr and patron saint of music. A noble Roman who was married against her will, she eventually effected the conversion of her pagan husband Valerian and his brother. Cecilia's good works infuriated the Roman prefect, who ordered her burned at the stake; when the flames did not harm her, she was beheaded. Valerian and his brother were also martyred.

cedar Any of four species of tall evergreen coniferous trees of the genus *Cedrus,* in the PINE family. These "true" cedars are the Atlas cedar *(C. atlantica),* the Cyprus cedar *(C. brevifolia),* the deodar *(C. deodara),* and the cedar of Lebanon *(C. libani).* Cedarwood is light, soft, resinous, and durable, even when in contact with soil or moisture. Many other conifers known as cedars resemble true cedars in being evergreen and in having aromatic, often red or red-tinged wood that in many cases is decay-resistant and insect-repellent. The giant arborvitae, incense cedar, and some JUNIPERS (red cedar) provide the familiar "cedarwood" of pencils, chests, closet linings, and fence posts.

Cela (Trulock) \'thä-lä\, **Camilo José** (1916–2002) Spanish writer. As a young man he served with Francisco FRANCO's forces in the Spanish Civil War; his writings represent a renunciation of his former sympathies. Primarily novels, short narratives, and travel diaries, they are innovative in form and content. His works helped establish *tremendismo,* a narrative style emphasizing violence and grotesque imagery. His first novel, *The Family of Pascual Duarte* (1942), is his best known; other works include *The Hive* (1951) and the avant-garde *San Camilo, 1936* (1969). He was awarded the Nobel Prize in 1989.

Celan \'tsä-ˌlän\, **Paul** *orig.* Paul Antschel (1920–1970) Romanian poet who wrote in German. When the Nazis overran Romania, Celan, a Jew, was sent to a forced-labor camp; his parents were murdered. He moved to Vienna in 1947. His first two volumes of poetry, *The Sand from the Urns* (1948) and *Poppy and Memory* (1952), established his reputation in W. Germany. He produced seven more volumes of dense, complex verse before taking his own life. His "Todesfuge" is probably the most famous poetic expression of the Holocaust.

Celebes See SULAWESI

Celebes Sea \'se-lə-ˌbēz\ Part of the W Pacific Ocean, bordered by the SULU ARCHIPELAGO, MINDANAO, the Sangihe Islands, SULAWESI, and BORNEO. It occupies about 110,000 sq mi (280,000 sq km). Over half of it is more than 13,000 ft (4,000 m) deep, and its maximum depth is 20,406 ft (6,220 m). Traders and pirates from Borneo and nearby islands ruled the sea until it came under colonial control in the late 19th cent.

celery Herb *(Apium graveolens)* of the PARSLEY family, native to the Mediterranean and the Middle East. The varieties with large, fleshy, succulent, upright leafstalks were developed in the late 18th cent. The tiny fruit, or seed, of the celery resembles the plant itself in taste and aroma and is used as a seasoning.

celestial sphere Apparent surface of the heavens, on which the stars seem to be fixed. Celestial COORDINATE SYSTEMS used to mark the positions of heavenly bodies treat it as a real sphere at an infinite distance from earth. Earth's axis, extended to infinity, touches it at the celestial poles, around which the heavens seem to turn; its intersection with the plane of earth's EQUATOR marks the celestial equator.

celiac disease \'sē-lē-ˌak\ *or* **nontropical sprue** Chronic nutritional disorder of unknown cause. Poor nutrient absorption causes foul, bulky, fatty stools, malnutrition, slow growth, and anemia. It can run in families. Children begin having intermittent intestinal upset, diarrhea, and wasting at 6–21 months. In adults it usually begins after 30, with appetite loss, depression, irritability, and alternating constipation and diarrhea. A high-protein diet low in glutens and saturated fats usually relieves symptoms, suggesting a deficiency of gluten-digesting enzymes.

celibacy \'se-lə-bə-sē\ State of being unmarried, usually in connection with a religious role or practice. It has existed in some form in most world religions. In Hinduism, "holy men" (or women) who have left ordinary secular life to seek final liberation are celibate. Buddhism began as a celibate order, though many sects have given up celibacy. Islam has no institutional celibacy, but individuals may embrace it for personal spiritual advancement. Judaism has prescribed periods of abstinence, but long-term celibacy has not played a large role. The early Christian church tended to regard celibacy as superior to marriage. Since the 12th cent. it has been the rule for Roman Catholic clergy, though clerical celibacy was never adopted by Protestantism.

Céline \sā-'lēn\, **Louis–Ferdinand** *orig.* Louis-Ferdinand Destouches (1894–1961) French writer. Born into poverty, in World War I he suffered wounds and shell shock, with lingering mental and physical effects. From 1924 he practiced medicine. His novel *Journey to the End of Night* (1932) is written in a very innovative vehement, disjointed style. *Death on the Installment Plan* (1936) portrays a bleak world bereft of beauty and decency. He grew ever more conservative, anti-Semitic, and misanthropic. After World War II he fled to Denmark as a suspected Nazi collaborator, but was later exonerated. Later works include the trilogy *Castle to Castle* (1957), *North* (1960), and *Rigadoon* (1969).

cell In biology, the basic unit of which all living things are composed; the smallest structural unit of living matter that is able to function independently. A cell can be a complete organism, as in BACTERIA and PROTOZOANS. In multicellular organisms such as higher plants and animals, groups of specialized cells are organized into tissues and organs. There are two distinct types of cells: prokaryotic cells, found only in bacteria (including CYANOBACTERIA), and eukaryotic cells, composing all other life-forms. Though their structures differ (see PROKARYOTE, EUKARYOTE), their molecular compositions and activities are very similar. The chief molecules in cells are NUCLEIC ACIDS, PROTEINS, and POLYSACCHARIDES. A cell is bounded by a MEMBRANE that enables it to exchange certain materials with its surroundings. In plant cells, a rigid cell wall encloses this membrane. See diagram on following page.

cell division See MEIOSIS, MITOSIS

Cellini \chə-'lē-nē\, **Benvenuto** (1500–1571) Italian sculptor and goldsmith. Early in his career he worked in Rome, producing medallions, vessels, and other objects in precious and semiprecious metals. In 1540 he began his most famous work of this type, a gold saltcellar encrusted with enamel, for FRANCIS I at Fontainebleau. For Cosimo I de' MEDICI he produced large-scale sculpture in the round; the bronze *Perseus* (1545–53) in Florence is his masterpiece. His fame owes much to his autobiography, with its lively account of his tumultuous life and its vivid picture of Renaissance Italy.

cello \'che-ˌlō\ *or* **violoncello** Bowed STRINGED INSTRUMENT, the bass member of the VIOLIN family (its full name means "little violone"—i.e., "little big viol"). Its proportions resemble those of the violin. It is played between the legs, its weight supported by a metal spike that touches the floor. It has four strings, tuned an octave below those of the viola. The cello developed in the early 16th cent. along with the violin and viola. It has been essential to chamber-music ensembles for 250 years. The modern orchestra includes six to 12 cellos.

cell(ular) phone Wireless telephone that permits telecommunication within a defined area that may include hundreds of square miles, using radio waves in the 800–900

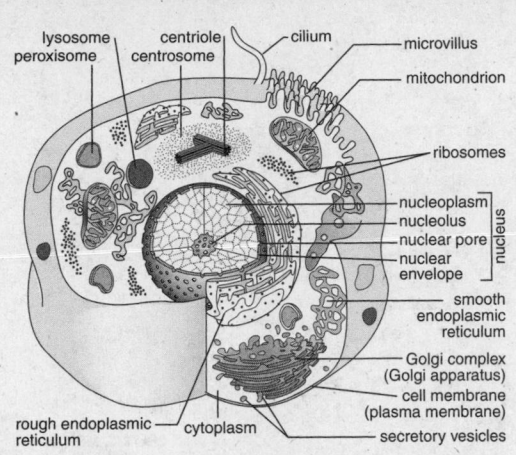

lysosome
peroxisome
centriole
centrosome
cilium
microvillus
mitochondrion
ribosomes
nucleoplasm
nucleolus
nuclear pore
nuclear envelope
} nucleus
smooth endoplasmic reticulum
Golgi complex (Golgi apparatus)
cell membrane (plasma membrane)
secretory vesicles
rough endoplasmic reticulum
cytoplasm

Cell Principal structures of an animal cell. Cytoplasm surrounds the cell's specialized structures, or organelles. Ribosomes, the sites of protein synthesis, are found free in the cytoplasm or attached to the endoplasmic reticulum, through which materials are transported throughout the cell. Energy needed by the cell is released by the mitochondria. The Golgi complex, stacks of flattened sacs, processes and packages materials to be released from the cell in secretory vesicles. Digestive enzymes are contained in lysosomes. Peroxisomes contain enzymes that detoxify dangerous substances. The centrosome contains the centrioles, which play a role in cell division. The microvilli are fingerlike extensions found on certain cells. Cilia, hairlike structures that extend from the surface of many cells, can create movement of surrounding fluid. The nuclear envelope, a double membrane surrounding the nucleus, contains pores that control the movement of substances into and out of the nucleoplasm. Chromatin, a combination of DNA and proteins which coil up into chromosomes, makes up much of the nucleoplasm. The dense nucleolus is the site of ribosome production.

megahertz (MHz) band. To implement a cell-phone system, a geographic area is broken into smaller areas, or cells, usually mapped as uniform hexagrams but in fact overlapping and irregularly shaped. Each cell is equipped with a low-powered radio transmitter and receiver that permit propagation of signals among cell-phone users.

cellulose Complex CARBOHYDRATE (POLYSACCHARIDE) consisting of 1,000–3,000 or more GLUCOSE units in a linear chain structure that can pack into strong fibers. The basic structural component of plant cell walls, cellulose is the most abundant naturally occurring organic compound. Mammals (including humans) cannot digest cellulose, but BACTERIA in the rumens of cattle and other RUMINANTS and PROTOZOANS in the gut of TERMITES can. Soil fungi can also break it down. The most important uses of cellulose are in wood, paper, and fiber products, and as an ethanol and methanol source. Cellulose derivatives are used in plastics, photographic films, rayon fibers, cellophane, coatings, explosives (nitrocellulose), and foods (carboxymethylcellulose).

Celsius \\'sel-sē-əs\\, **Anders** (1701–1744) Swedish astronomer. In 1733 he published a collection of 316 observations of the aurora borealis. In 1744 he built the Uppsala Observatory. He is best known for his invention of the Celsius (often called centigrade) thermometer scale (1742), which set water's freezing point at 0° and its boiling point at 100°.

Celtic languages \\'kel-tik\\ Branch of the INDO-EUROPEAN LANGUAGE family spoken across a broad area of W and central Europe by the CELTS in pre-Roman and Roman times, now confined to small coastal areas of NW Europe. Celtic can be divided into a continental group of languages

(all extinct) and an insular group. The Insular Celtic languages are conventionally divided into Goidelic (IRISH, Manx, and SCOTTISH GAELIC) and Brythonic (WELSH, Cornish, and Breton). English pushed out Cornish at the end of the 18th cent. Manx, spoken on the Isle of Man, expired with the death of the last native speaker in 1974. Enthusiasts have recently tried to revive Manx and Cornish.

Celtic religion Beliefs and practices of the ancient Celts of Gaul and the British Isles. Celtic worship centered on the interplay of the divine element with the natural world. Springs, rivers, and hills were thought to be inhabited by guardian spirits, usually female. Some gods were widely worshiped; lesser deities were associated with particular tribes or places. The most honored god was Lugus, who was skilled in all the arts. Cernunnos was lord of the animals; the goddess of mares and fertility was called Epona, Macha, or Rhiannon. The priests of Celtic religion were the DRUIDS. Oak trees, holly, and mistletoe were considered sacred. The Celts believed in life after death and transmigration of souls. See also BRÂN, BRIGIT.

Celts \\'kelts, 'selts\\ Early Indo-European people who from the 2nd millennium B.C. to the 1st cent. B.C. spread over much of Europe. They were absorbed into the Roman empire as Britons, Gauls, Boii, Galatians, and Celtiberians. Early archaeological evidence (c.700 B.C.) comes from the HALLSTATT site in Austria. By the mid-5th cent. B.C., the LA TÈNE culture emerged along the Rhine and moved into E Europe and the British Isles. Celts sacked Rome around 390 B.C. and raided the whole peninsula, then settled south of the Alps (Cisalpine GAUL) and menaced Rome until they were defeated in 225 B.C. By 58 Julius CAESAR had begun campaigns to annex all of Gaul. Celtic settlement of Britain and Ireland is deduced from archaeological and linguistic evidence. The Celtic social system comprised a warrior aristocracy and freemen farmers; DRUIDS, with magico-religious duties, ranked higher than warriors. They had a mixed farming economy. Their oral literary composition was highly developed, as was their art; they manufactured gold and silver jewelry, swords and scabbards, and shields inlaid with enamel.

Cenis \\sə-'nē\\, **Mont** *Italian* **Monte Cenisio** \\'mòn-tā-chā-'nē-zyō\\ Massif and pass, ALPS. Located in SE France west of TURIN, Italy, the pass was an ancient invasion route and is traversed by a road 24 mi (38 km) long, built by NAPOLEON in 1803–10. The road climbs to Mt. Cenis Pass (elevation 6,834 ft, or 2,083 m). The Mt. Cenis railway tunnel, 8.5 mi (14 km) long, was the first great tunnel through the Alps (opened 1871). The road tunnel, 10 mi (16 km) long, opened in 1980.

Cenozoic era \\sē-nə-'zō-ik\\ Latest of the major eras of earth history, during which the continents assumed their modern configurations and geographic positions and the earth's flora and fauna evolved toward those of the present. The Cenozoic, from the Greek for "recent life," began about 65 million years ago and is divided into two periods, the TERTIARY (65–1.8 million years ago) and the QUATERNARY (1.8 million years ago to the present). See table at GEOLOGIC TIME.

censorship Act of changing or suppressing speech or writing that is condemned as subversive of the common good. Censorship may be preemptive (preventing the publication or broadcast of undesirable information) or punitive (punishing those who publish or broadcast offending material). In Europe, both the Roman Catholic and Protestant churches practiced censorship, as did the absolute monarchies of the 17th–18th cent. Authoritarian governments such as those in China and the former Soviet Union have employed pervasive censorship. In the U.S. in the 20th cent., censorship focused largely on works of literature deemed guilty of OBSCENITY (e.g., James JOYCE's *Ulysses*), though periodic attempts at political censorship also occurred (e.g., the effort to purge school textbooks of possible left-wing content in the 1950s). Recently some have called for censorship of so-called hate speech, language deemed threatening (or sometimes merely offensive) to various subsections of the population. Any censorship is usually opposed by the AMERICAN CIVIL LIBERTIES UNION. See also PENTAGON PAPERS.

centaur \'sen-ₜtȯr\ In GREEK MYTHOLOGY, one of a race of creatures, part horse and part man, living in the mountains of Thessaly and Arcadia. They were best known for their battle with the peaceful Lapiths. Centaurs were known for their drunken and amorous habits, but their king, CHIRON, was notable for being civilized, gentle, and the tutor of heroes.

Centers for Disease Control and Prevention (CDC) Agency of the U.S. Department of HEALTH AND HUMAN SERVICES, headquartered in Atlanta, whose mission is "to promote health and quality of life by preventing and controlling disease, injury, and disability." Part of the Public Health Service, it was founded in 1946 as the Communicable Disease Center to fight malaria and other contagious diseases. As its scope widened, the name was changed. It now subsumes health statistics, infectious diseases, and environmental health; a National Immunization Program; and an Office on Smoking and Health. It consolidates disease control data, health promotion, and PUBLIC-HEALTH programs, and it provides health information to health care professionals and the public, and publications on EPIDEMIOLOGY. Today it is the world's foremost epidemiological center.

centipede Any of about 2,800 species (class Chilopoda) of long, flattened, many-segmented ARTHROPODS having one pair of legs on each segment except the hindmost. At night they prey on other small invertebrates. They move rapidly on 14–177 pairs of legs and have a pair of jawlike, venomous claws just behind the head. The 1-in. (2.5-cm) house centipede of

Centipede *(Scolopendra)*

Europe and N. America is the only species common in dwellings. The largest tropical centipedes may grow as long as 11 in. (28 cm) and can inflict severe bites.

CENTO *in full* **Central Treaty Organization** *originally* Middle East Treaty Organization *or* Baghdad Pact Organization. Mutual-security organization, originally composed of Turkey, Iran, Iraq, Pakistan, and Britain. Formed in 1955, at the urging of the U.S. and Britain, to counter the threat of Soviet expansion into Middle East oil fields, its internal cohesion was never strong. Iraq withdrew after its anti-Soviet monarchy was overthrown in 1959. After the fall of Mohammad Reza Shah PAHLAVI in 1979, Iran withdrew and CENTO was dissolved.

Central African Republic *French* **République Centrafricaine** \ˌrä-pü̇e-'blek-ˌsäⁿ-trä-frē̇'ken\ *formerly* **Ubangi-Shari** \ü̇-ˌbäŋ-gē-'shär-ē\ Republic, central Africa. Area: 240,376 sq mi (622,374 sq km). Population (2000): 3,513,000. Capital: BANGUI. Almost all the inhabitants trace their origin to communities founded in the 18th–19th cent. when various African peoples fled into the interior to escape slave traders. They now form heterogeneous ethnic groups, with the Banda, Baya (Gbaya), Ngbandi, and Azande almost three-quarters of its inhabitants. Languages: French, Sango (both official), Zande. Religions: animism, Christianity. Currency: CFA franc. A landlocked country, it consists of a plateau with an average altitude of about 2,200 ft (670 m). The N half is characterized by savanna and is drained by tributaries of the Chari River. The S half is densely forested. The country has a developing free-enterprise economy of mixed state and private structure; agriculture is its main component. It is a republic with one legislative body; its chief of state is the president and its head of government, the prime minister. Though seemingly inhabited for a long time, the area has yielded few archaeological remains. For several centuries before the arrival of Europeans, the territory was subjected to slave traders. The French explored and claimed central Africa and in 1889 established a post at Bangui. In 1898 they partitioned the colony among commercial concessionaires. United with Chad in 1906 to form the French colony of Ubangi-Shari-Chad, it later became part of FRENCH EQUATORIAL AFRICA. It was separated from Chad in 1920 and became an oversea territory in 1946. An autonomous republic within the French Community in 1958, it achieved independence in 1960. In 1966 the military

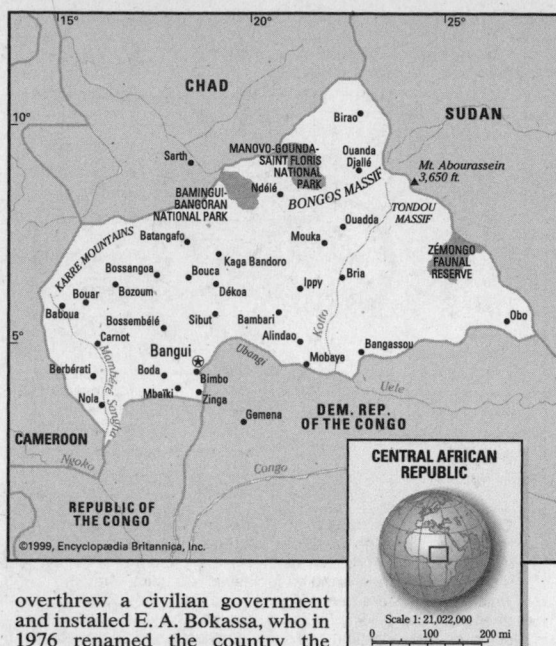

overthrew a civilian government and installed E. A. Bokassa, who in 1976 renamed the country the Central African Empire. He was overthrown in 1979, but the military again seized power in the 1980s. Elections in 1993 led to installation of a civilian government.

Central America S portion of N. America (pop., 1993 est.: 30,610,000). It extends from the S border of Mexico to the NW border of Colombia and from the Pacific Ocean to the Caribbean Sea. It includes Guatemala, Belize, Honduras, El Salvador, Nicaragua, Costa Rica, and Panama. Some geographers also include five states of Mexico: QUINTANA ROO, YUCATAN, CAMPECHE, TABASCO, and CHIAPAS. Area: 202,000 sq mi (523,000 sq km). Two-thirds of the population is of mixed American Indian and Spanish ancestry. Language: Spanish (official), except Belize (English, official); also American Indian languages. Religion: chiefly Roman Catholicism. The region is largely hilly or mountainous, with humid swamps and lowlands extending along both coasts. Tajumulco Volcano, W Guatemala, is the highest point. The region has some 40 volcanoes, many of them active, and it has frequent earthquakes. The volcanic zones have fertile soil and are productive agricultural areas. The area was long inhabited by indigenous peoples, including the MAYA, before the Spanish arrived and conquered the region in the early 16th cent.; they continued to rule for about 300 years. Christopher COLUMBUS skirted the Atlantic coast from Honduras to the Gulf of Darien in 1502; the first European settlement (1510) was on the gulf. Spain organized the region (except Chiapas and Panama) into the captaincy general of Guatemala about 1560. The English arrived in the 17th cent., settling what became British Honduras (Belize). Independence from Spanish rule came in 1821, and in 1823 the United Provinces of Central America was formed (Guatemala, El Salvador, Honduras, Nicaragua, and Costa Rica). British Honduras, still a colony, did not join the federation, and Panama remained part of Colombia. In 1824 the federation adopted a constitution, but in 1838 Costa Rica, Honduras, and Nicaragua seceded, thus effectively terminating the federation. Treaties of amity were drawn up by a Washington conference of Central American states in 1923. The Central American Common Market was established in 1960.

central bank Institution, such as the U.S. FEDERAL RESERVE SYSTEM, charged with regulating the size of a nation's money supply, the availability and cost of CREDIT, and the foreign-exchange value of its CURRENCY. Central banks act as the fiscal agent of the government, issuing notes to be used as legal tender, supervising the operations of the commercial banking system, and implementing MONETARY POLICY. By adjusting the supply of money and credit, they affect interest rates, thereby influencing the economy. Modern central banks regulate the money supply by buying and selling such assets as government securities. They may also raise or lower the DISCOUNT RATE to discourage or encourage borrowing by COMMERCIAL BANKS. By adjusting the minimum cash reserves that banks must hold against their deposit liabilities, central banks contract or expand the money supply (see FRACTIONAL RESERVE SYSTEM) to maintain conditions that support high employment and production and stable domestic prices. Central banks also take part in cooperative international currency arrangements to help stabilize or regulate foreign-exchange rates of participating countries. Central banks have consistently increased their emphasis on the interdependence of monetary and other national economic policies, especially FISCAL POLICIES and debt-management policies.

Central Intelligence Agency (CIA) Principal intelligence and counterintelligence agency of the U.S. Established in 1947 as a successor to the Office of Strategic Services (1942–45), it is limited to activities in foreign countries. Officially a part of the U.S. Defense Department, it prepares analyses for the National Security Council, a presidential advisory group. Though intelligence gathering is its chief occupation, the CIA has also been involved in many covert operations, including the BAY OF PIGS INVASION and support of the Nicaraguan CONTRAS.

central nervous system See NERVOUS SYSTEM

Central Park Public park, NEW YORK CITY. Located in MANHATTAN, it occupies an area of 840 acres (340 hectares). It was designed by F. L. OLMSTED and opened in 1876; it was landscaped to create an impression of wild and varied terrain. It includes footpaths and bicycle paths, athletic fields, boating lakes, and a zoo. Free public concerts and performances are frequent.

Central Powers WORLD WAR I coalition that was defeated by the ALLIED POWERS. Its primary members were the German empire and Austria-Hungary, the "central" European states. The Ottoman empire joined the Central Powers in October 1914, and Bulgaria in 1915.

central processing unit See CPU

Central Treaty Organization See CENTO

Central Valley Valley, California. Located between the SIERRA NEVADA and COAST RANGES, it is over 400 mi (640 km) long and 20–50 mi (30–80 km) wide. The SACRAMENTO and SAN JOAQUIN rivers run through the valley. Generously irrigated, the area now contains some of the richest farmland in the U.S.

centrifugal force \sen-'trif-yə-gəl\ Fictitious force, peculiar to circular motion, that is equal but opposite to the centripetal force that keeps a particle on a circular path (see CENTRIPETAL ACCELERATION). For example, a stone attached to a string and whirling in a horizontal circular path is accelerated toward the center of its path by the tension in the string, the only force acting on the string. However, in a REFERENCE FRAME at rest with the stone, another force—the centrifugal force—must be introduced for NEWTON'S LAWS OF MOTION to apply.

centrifuge \'sen-trə-ˌfyüj\ Machine that applies a sustained CENTRIFUGAL FORCE. Effectively, the centrifuge substitutes a similar, stronger force for that of gravity. Every centrifuge contains a spinning vessel. A revolving object exerts a force away from the center of rotation called the centrifugal force; usually stated as so many "times gravity" or so many "G," it may range from a few G for a home washing machine or an industrial separator to hundreds of thousands of G for centrifuges to separate isotopes of uranium or to purify vaccines.

centripetal acceleration \sen-'trip-ə-təl\ Property of the motion of an object traveling in a circular path. Centripetal describes the FORCE on the object, directed toward the center of the circle, which causes a constant change in the object's direction, thus its ACCELERATION. See also CENTRIFUGAL FORCE.

centroid In geometry, the center of mass of a two-dimensional figure or three-dimensional solid. Thus the centroid of a two-dimensional figure represents the point at which it could be balanced if it were cut out of, for example, sheet metal (see center of GRAVITY). The centroid of a circle or sphere is its center. More generally, the centroid represents the point designated by the mean (see MEAN, MEDIAN, AND MODE) of the coordinates of all the points in a set.

centromere \'sen-trə-ˌmir\ Structure in a CHROMOSOME that holds together the two chromatids. It becomes the point of attachment to the structure that pulls the chromatids to opposite ends of the cell during cell division (MITOSIS). During the middle stage of mitosis, the centromere duplicates and the chromatid pair separates, each chromatid becoming a separate chromosome.

cephalopod \'se-fə-lə-ˌpäd\ Any marine MOLLUSK of the class Cephalopoda (e.g., CUTTLEFISH, NAUTILUS, OCTOPUS, and SQUID), which includes the largest living INVERTEBRATES. Cephalopods are bilaterally symmetrical and typically have a highly developed centralized nervous system. Their heads are armed with tentacles that have rows of round suction disks. Most cephalopods can change skin color to blend in with their surroundings. All swim backward by expelling water forcefully. Most feed on fish, crustaceans, and other mollusks.

Cepheid variable \'sef-ē-əd\ One of a class of VARIABLE STARS whose period of variation is in direct proportion to its luminosity. This relationship, discovered in 1912 by Henrietta Leavitt (1868–1921), has been used to establish the distance of remote star systems. Named for the prototype of this class found in the constellation Cepheus, classical Cepheids have a dependable period-luminosity relationship, with periods from about 1.5 to over 50 days, and are Population I stars (see POPULATIONS I AND II).

Ceram *or* **Seram** \'sā-ˌräm\ Island of the central MOLUCCAS, Indonesia. It has an area of 6,621 sq mi (17,148 sq km). The terrain is mountainous and covered with tropical forests; seismic activity is common. It came under nominal Dutch control around 1650. After World War II it became part of Indonesia.

ceramics Traditionally, objects created from such naturally occurring raw materials as clay minerals and quartz sand, by shaping the material and then hardening it by firing at high temperatures to make the object stronger, harder, and less permeable to fluids. The principal ceramic products are containers, tableware, bricks, and tiles. See also EARTHENWARE, PORCELAIN, POTTERY, STONEWARE, TERRA-COTTA.

Cerberus \'sər-bə-rəs\ In GREEK MYTHOLOGY, the monstrous watchdog of the underworld. He was usually said to have three heads. Heads of snakes grew from his back, and he had a serpent's tail. He devoured anyone who tried to escape HADES' kingdom, and he refused entrance to living humans. One of the labors of HERACLES was to bring Cerberus (temporarily) up to the land of the living.

cereal *or* **grain** Any GRASS yielding starchy seeds suitable for food. The most commonly cultivated cereals are WHEAT, RICE, RYE, OATS, BARLEY, CORN, and SORGHUM. As human food, cereals are usually marketed as ingredients of food products. They also are used as animal feed and industrially in the production of a wide range of substances, such as GLUCOSE, adhesives, oils, and alcohols. Wheat is the world's most widely grown cereal crop; rice is the second. Grains are generally rich in carbohydrates, with moderate amounts of protein. Breads are usually enriched to compensate for any nutritional deficiencies in the cereal used. Though often consumed in the areas where grown, cereal and cereal by-products are also major commodities in international trade.

cereal Prepared foodstuff of CEREAL grain. The first step in making cereal is milling, grinding the grain so that it can be easily processed. Modern automated systems employ steel cylinders; numerous sievings separate the endosperm from the outer coverings and the germ. Cereal products include FLOUR, RICE, meal (coarsely ground and unsifted grain), cornstarch, and PASTA. Breakfast cereals include raw cereals such as rolled oats and farina, shredded cereals (usually whole wheat that is boiled, dried, and cut), flaked cereals (usually corn that is broken down into grits and cooked with syrup before being pressed and toasted), puffed cereals (grains heated in a pressure chamber and then released to

cause expansion), and granular cereals (flour-based cereals made from dough that is cooked and ground). All cereals are high in STARCH.

cerebellum \ser-ə-'bel-əm\ Part of the BRAIN that integrates sensory input from the inner ear and from proprioceptors (see PROPRIOCEPTION) in muscle with nerve impulses from the cerebrum (see CEREBRAL CORTEX), coordinating muscle responses to maintain balance and produce smooth, coordinated movements. It is located below the cerebral hemispheres and behind the upper medulla oblongata and pons. Disorders usually produce neuromuscular disturbances.

cerebral cortex \sə-'rē-brəl, 'ser-ə-brəl\ Layer of gray matter that constitutes the outer layer of the CEREBRUM and is responsible for integrating sensory impulses and for higher intellectual functions. It is divided into lobes, roughly defined by major surface folds. The frontal lobe controls motor activity and speech; the parietal lobe controls touch and position; the temporal lobe handles auditory reception and memory; the occipital lobe holds the brain's major visual-reception area; and the limbic lobe controls smell, taste, and emotional responses.

cerebral palsy Paralysis of voluntary movement on one or both sides of the body from brain damage before or soon after birth. Cases are of two main types: spastic, with spasms contracting the extremities, and often mental retardation and epilepsy; or athetosic, with slow, changing spasms in the face, neck, and extremities, grimacing, and inarticulate speech. Athetosic patients may have normal intelligence but appear retarded.

cerebral seizures See EPILEPSY

cerebrum \sə-'rē-brəm, 'ser-ə-brəm\ Largest part of the human BRAIN. The two cerebral hemispheres consist of an inner core of myelinated nerve fibers (the white matter) and a heavily convoluted outer cortex of gray matter (see CEREBRAL CORTEX). A front-to-back fissure divides the cerebrum's two hemispheres. One is dominant, holding speech and thought centers and determining right- or left-handedness. The other handles more complex perceptions, such as face recognition. Each controls the opposite side of the body. The corpus callosum, a thick band of white matter, connects them, allowing integration of sensory data and responses from both sides of the body. See also HYPOTHALAMUS.

Ceres \'sir-ēz\ In ROMAN RELIGION, the goddess of the growth of food plants, sometimes worshiped with the earth goddess Tellus. Her cult was overlaid by that of DEMETER, who was worshiped in Greece and Sicily. According to tradition, her cult was introduced into Rome in 496 B.C. to check a famine.

Cerf \'sərf\, **Bennett (Alfred)** (1898–1971) U.S. publisher. With Donald Klopfer, in 1925 Cerf acquired the Modern Library imprint, which became a highly profitable series of reprinted classics. In 1927 they began publishing new books as RANDOM HOUSE, of which Cerf was president 1927–65. Known as an opponent of censorship, he published many eminent authors. An inveterate punster and raconteur, he also wrote syndicated newspaper columns and appeared on television's popular *What's My Line?* (1952–68).

cerium \'sir-ē-əm\ Chemical ELEMENT, a RARE EARTH METAL of the LANTHANIDE series, chemical symbol Ce, atomic number 58. It is iron-gray and fairly soft and ductile. Found in many ORES, it is about as abundant as copper. The METAL is used in ALLOYS and other metallurgical applications and (because it oxidizes strongly and rapidly) in illumination, ignition and signaling devices, and propellants. Cerium compounds (VALENCE 3 or 4) are used in the mantles of lanterns, in the ceramic, photographic, and textile industries, and in analytical chemistry.

certificate of deposit (CD) Receipt from a bank acknowledging the deposit of a sum of money. The most common type is for a fixed-term, interest-bearing deposit in a large denomination. It pays higher interest than a savings account, but carries a penalty for early redemption. Introduced in the early 1960s, CDs have become a popular method of saving.

Cervantes (Saavedra) \sər-'vän-₁tēz\, **Miguel de** (1547–1616) Spanish writer, the most celebrated figure in Spanish literature. He served in the Italian infantry, fought the Turks at Lepanto, and was captured and sold into slavery in

Algiers for five years. Back in Spain, his chronic financial problems and tangled affairs led to brief imprisonment. While in a tedious civil-service job, he wrote the pastoral romance *La galatea* (1585) and plays, poetry, and short stories. His great creation *Don Quixote* (1605, 1615), brought immediate literary eminence. It parodies chivalric ROMANCES of the day with the comic adventures of a bemused old would-be knight and with his pragmatic squire, Sancho Panza. Considered the first and one of the greatest of all novels, it has influenced many writers. Cervantes also published a set of comedies and interludes for the stage (1615) and the romance *The Labors of Persiles and Sigismunda* (1617).

cesarean section \si-'zar-ē-ən\ *or* **C-section** Surgical removal of a FETUS from the UTERUS through an abdominal incision at or before full term. It is usually performed when vaginal delivery would endanger the life or health of the mother or the child. Vaginal delivery is often possible in subsequent pregnancies. Cesarean section carries the usual risks of major surgery.

cesium \'sē-zē-əm\ Chemical ELEMENT, one of the ALKALI METALS, chemical symbol Cs, atomic number 55. The first element discovered by SPECTROSCOPY (1860), it is silvery white, liquid at warm room temperature (melting at 83°F, or 28.4°C), and very soft when solid. About half as abundant as lead, it occurs in minute quantities as ORES. It reacts explosively with cold water. It is used as a catalyst and in photoelectric cells, ion propulsion systems, atomic clocks, and PLASMA for thermoelectric conversion. Cesium SALTS have various specialty applications.

Céspedes (y Borja del Castillo) \'säs-pā-₁thäs\, **Carlos Manuel de** (1819–1874) Cuban revolutionary hero. He secretly organized an independence movement, and launched an insurrection in 1868. Thousands flocked to his rebel army, which scored stunning victories. He led a revolutionary government actively seeking annexation by the U.S. He was deposed in 1873 and fled, but was discovered and shot by Spanish troops.

cetacean \si-'tā-shən\ Any of several species of exclusively aquatic placental MAMMALS constituting the order Cetacea. Modern cetaceans are classified into about 70 species of toothed whales (Odontoceti) and 13 species of toothless BALEEN WHALES (Mysticeti). They have a tapered body, no external hind limbs, and a tail ending in a horizontal blade of two lobes, or flukes. Cetaceans must come to the water's surface to breathe through blowholes located on top of their head. See also WHALE.

Ceuta \'thā-ü-tä, 'syü-tä\ *Arabic* **Sebta** \₁seb-tə\ Spanish enclave (pop., 1998 est.: 72,000), N. Africa. A military station and seaport, it constitutes with MELILLA an autonomous community of Spain. The city is at the E end of the Strait of GIBRALTAR, on an isthmus connecting Jebel Musa (one of the PILLARS OF HERCULES) to the mainland. Colonized by Carthaginians, Greeks, and Romans, it was taken by the Portuguese in 1415, and passed to Spain in 1580. In 1995 the Spanish government approved statutes of autonomy for Ceuta.

Ceylon See SRI LANKA

Cézanne \sā-'zän\, **Paul** (1839–1906) French painter. In 1861 he left law school to study art in Paris. He became associated with the Impressionists (see IMPRESSIONISM), and in 1874 and 1877 exhibited with them. Unlike them, he emphasized the structure of objects rather than the vision presented by the light that emanated from them, composing with cubic masses, patches of color, and architectonic lines. From the 1870s he developed a radically new way of simultaneously depicting deep space and flat design; great works of the period include the se-

Paul Cézanne, self-portrait, c.1878–80

ries of monumental landscapes of Mont Ste.-Victoire. He used the same approach in portraiture and everyday scenes, most notably in *Madame Cézanne in a Yellow Armchair* (1890) and *The Card Players* (1890–92). He painted more than 200 still lifes. Public reception of his first one-man exhibition (1895) was cool, but after he exhibited at the Salon des Indépendants (1899, 1901, 1902), the galleries finally began seeking his works. The year after his death, a retrospective exhibit won critical acclaim. His work was a major source of inspiration for the Cubists (see CUBISM). See also IMPRESSIONISM, POSTIMPRESSIONISM.

CFC See CHLOROFLUOROCARBON

Chaadayev \ˌchä-ˌə-ˈdȧ-yəf\, **Pyotr (Yakovlevich)** (1794–1856) Russian writer. His *Lettres philosophiques* (1827–31; "Philosophical Letters") urged a Western path of development for Russia. After a translation of the first letter appeared, it was banned, and Chaadayev was declared insane. He continued to live in Moscow, however, where he was venerated by young Westernizers, whose ideas precipitated the debate between SLAVOPHILES AND WESTERNIZERS.

Chabrier \ˌshä-brē-ˈā\, **(Alexis-) Emmanuel** (1841–1894) French composer. A piano prodigy, he relinquished his government job in 1880 to pursue composition full-time. His opera *Gwendoline* enjoyed several productions in his lifetime, but he never achieved significant success. His other works include nine other operas and operettas, including *Le roi malgré lui* (1887), and the tone poem *España* (1883).

Chabrol \shä-ˈbrȯl\, **Claude** (b.1930) French film director, screenwriter, and producer. After working in 20th Century–Fox's Paris office, he wrote and produced *Bitter Reunion* (1958) and directed *The Cousins* (1959) and *The Good Women* (1960), all representative of the NEW WAVE movement. Among his many other films are *Les biches* (1968), *Le boucher* (1970), *The Story of Women* (1988), and *Madame Bovary* (1991). He admired Alfred HITCHCOCK and used a similar style in several mystery thrillers, including *This Man Must Die* (1969).

Chaco See GRAN CHACO

Chaco Culture National Historical Park National preserve, NW New Mexico. Established as a national monument in 1907 and renamed in 1980, it occupies 53 sq mi (137 sq km) and contains 13 pre-Columbian ruins and over 300 smaller sites representing PUEBLO cultures. The excavated Pueblo Bonito (10th cent.) once contained 800 rooms.

Chaco War \ˈchä-kō\ (1932–35) Costly conflict between Bolivia and Paraguay over possession of the Chaco, a wilderness region thought to contain oil reserves. Bolivia, landlocked since the War of the PACIFIC, was motivated as well by the need to gain access to the Atlantic coast through the Río de la Plata system. The war cost about 100,000 lives. In a treaty, Bolivia was given a corridor to the Paraguay River and a port, but Paraguay gained clear title to most of the disputed region.

Chad *French* **Tchad** \ˈchȧd\ Republic, N central Africa. Area: 495,752 sq mi (1,283,998 sq km). Population (2000): 8,425,000. Capital: N'DJAMENA. The Sara is the largest ethnic group, at about one-quarter of the total population; other groups include the Bagirmi and Bongo, the Lake and Mbum, the Tangale, and the Buduma, Kuri, and Kanemba. Arabs, composed of a multitude of tribes, represent a single ethnic group. Languages: French, Arabic (both official), and more than 100 dialects and languages. Religions: Islam, animism, Roman Catholicism, Protestantism. Currency: CFA franc. The landlocked country's terrain is a shallow basin that rises gradually from 750 ft (228 m) above sea level at Lake Chad. The basin is rimmed by mountains, including the volcanic Tibesti Massif to the north, rising to 11,204 ft (3,415 m) at Mt. Koussi. Its lowest elevation is the Djourab Depression, at 573 ft (175 m). Chad's river network is limited to the Chari and Logone rivers and their tributaries, which flow from the southeast into Lake Chad. It has an agricultural economy. It is a republic with one legislative body; its chief of state is the president and its head of government, the prime minister. Around A.D. 800 the kingdom of Kanem was founded, and by the early 1200s its borders had expanded to form a new kingdom, Kanem-Bornu, in the N regions of the area. Its power peaked in the 16th cent. with its command of the S terminus of the trans-Sahara

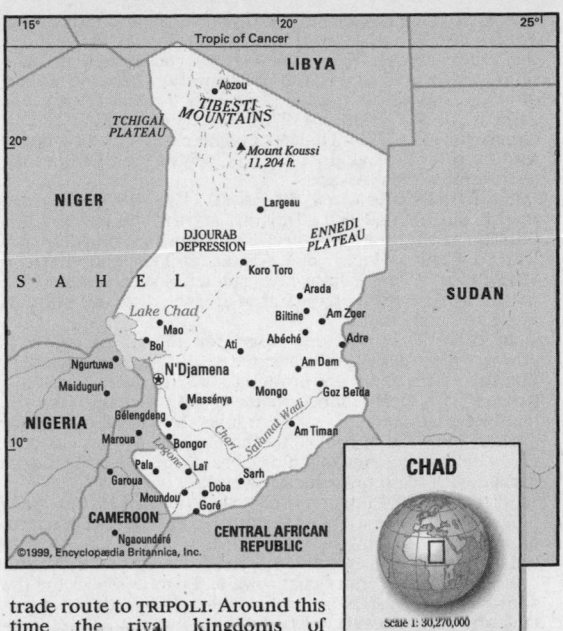

CHAD
Scale 1: 30,270,000
0   150   300 mi
0   200   400 km

©1999, Encyclopædia Britannica, Inc.

trade route to TRIPOLI. Around this time the rival kingdoms of Baguirmi and Wadai evolved in the south. In the years 1883–93 all three kingdoms fell to the Sudanese adventurer Rabih az-Zubayr, who was in turn pushed out by the French in 1891. Extending their power, the French in 1910 made Chad a part of FRENCH EQUATORIAL AFRICA. Chad became a separate colony in 1920 and was made an overseas territory in 1946. The country achieved independence in 1960. This was followed by decades of civil war, and frequent intervention by France and Libya. Chad remains one of the world's poorest nations.

Chagall \shä-ˈgäl\, **Marc** (1887–1985) Belarusan-French painter, printmaker, and designer. After studying painting in St. Petersburg, he moved to Paris in 1910. On a visit home he was caught by the outbreak of World War I and then by the Bolshevik revolution. He was named head of the revolutionary art school in Vitebsk, but in 1923 returned to Paris. There he launched a career in printmaking, producing hundreds of etchings for special editions of books. In 1941 he left for New York, where he designed sets and costumes for Igor STRAVINSKY's ballet *The Firebird*. Returning to France (1948), he produced stained-

Marc Chagall Photo by Arnold Newman, 1956

glass windows and murals for public buildings in Jerusalem, Paris, and the U.S. His distinctive style of fairy-tale fantasy drew principally on Jewish life and folklore.

Chagos Archipelago \ˈchä-gəs\ Island group, central Indian Ocean. Located about 1,000 mi (1,600 km) south of the tip of the Indian subcontinent, it has a total area of 23 sq mi (60 sq km). Acquired by Britain from France in 1814, since 1976 it has been the sole member of the British Indian Ocean Territory. Its chief island, Diego Garcia, was developed as an air and naval refueling station by the U.S. and Great Britain in the mid-20th cent., prompting strong opposition from the region's coastal and island states.

Chaikin \ˈchä-kən\, **Joseph** (b.1935) U.S. stage director, actor, and writer. Born in Brooklyn, N.Y., he joined the Living Theater, winning praise for his performances in *The Connection* (1959) and *Man Is Man* (1962). In 1963 he founded the experimental Open Theater. His celebrated productions, the results of intense collaboration between writer, director, and actors, included *America Hurrah* (1966), *The Serpent* (1969), *Terminal* (1970), *The Mutation Show* (1971), and *Nightwalk* (1973). He later collaborated with Sam SHEPARD on several plays. In 1977 he received the first lifetime-achievement Obie Award.

Chain, Ernst Boris (*later* **Sir Ernst**) (1906–1979) German-British biochemist. With Howard FLOREY he isolated and purified PENICILLIN and performed the first clinical trials with it. Chain, Florey, and Alexander FLEMING shared a 1945 Nobel Prize. Chain also studied snake venoms, the spreading factor (an enzyme that aids the dispersal of fluids in tissue), and insulin.

chain drive Device widely used for the transmission of power where shafts are separated at distances greater than that for which gears are practical. In such cases, sprockets (wheels with teeth shaped to mesh with a chain) take the place of gears and drive one another by means of a chain passing over the sprocket teeth. The chains used in conveyor belts are commonly block chains, in which the blocks engage with teeth on sprocket wheels.

chain mail *or* **mail** Form of body ARMOR worn by European knights and other medieval warriors. Fabric or leather tunics with sewn-on iron rings were worn in late Roman times; medieval armorers interlaced the rings. In the 8th cent., mail was a short coat with a separate sleeve for the sword arm. By the Norman Conquest (1066), the coat was long and fully sleeved; a hood, fitting under a helmet, covered the head and neck. By the 12th cent., mail was fitted to hands, feet, and legs. The addition of plates evolved in the 14th cent. into complete plate armor, displacing mail.

chain reaction Process yielding products that initiate further processes of the same kind. Nuclear chain reactions are a series of NUCLEAR FISSIONS initiated by NEUTRONS produced in a preceding fission. A critical mass, large enough to allow more than one fission-produced neutron to be captured, is necessary for the chain reaction to be self-sustaining. Uncontrolled chain reactions, as in an ATOMIC BOMB, occur when large numbers of neutrons are present and the reactions multiply very quickly. Nuclear reactors control their reactions through the careful distribution of the fissionable material and insertion of neutron-absorbing materials.

Chakkri dynasty Thailand's ruling family. Phraphutthayotfa Chulalok (1737–1809) founded the dynasty under his title Chao Phraya Chakkri (military commander of the Chao Phraya area) and ruled as Rama I (r.1782–1809). He reorganized Siam's defenses to repel numerous Burmese attacks. His descendants have reigned in an unbroken line ever since. Rama III (r.1824–51) increased trade with Europe and negotiated a treaty with the British E. India Co. King MONGKUT (Rama IV; r.1851–68) and King Chulalongkorn (Rama V; r.1868–1910) helped modernize the government along Western lines. King VAJIRAVUDH (Rama VI; r.1910–25) instituted social reforms. Bhumibol Adulyadej (Rama IX; b.1927) has reigned since 1946 as Thailand's ceremonial head of state.

chakra \\'chä-krə\\ In HINDUISM and Tantra, any of 88,000 focal points in the human body where psychic forces and bodily functions can merge and interact. In Hinduism there are seven and in Tantra four major chakras. The most important are the heart chakra, the chakra at the base of the spine, and the chakra at the top of the head.

Chalcedon \\'kal-sə-ˌdän\\, **Council of** (451) Fourth ecumenical council of the Christian Church, held in Chalcedon (modern Kadiköy, Turkey). It approved the creeds of Nicaea (325) and Constantinople (381, later known as the NICENE CREED) and rejected MONOPHYSITISM. The council disciplined clergy and declared Jerusalem and Constantinople patriarchates.

chalcedony *or* **calcedony** \\kal-'se-d°n-ē\\ Very fine-grained variety of QUARTZ. It occurs in a great variety of colors, usually bluish white, gray, yellow, or brown. For centuries, chalcedony has been the stone most used by gem engravers, and many varieties are still cut and polished as ornamental stones.

Chaldea \\kal-'dē-ə\\ Ancient region, on the EUPHRATES RIVER and the PERSIAN GULF. It was originally the S part of BABYLONIA; the name Chaldea has been used (especially in the Bible) for all of Babylonia after it was occupied by the Chaldeans, a Semitic people who established a dynasty about 625 B.C. Under NEBUCHADNEZZAR II the empire expanded, subduing JUDAEA and capturing JERUSALEM. It fell to PERSIA in 539 B.C.

Chalgrin \\shål-'gra^n\\, **Jean-François-Thérèse** (1737–1811) French architect. Trained by Étienne-Louis BOULLÉE, he won the Grand Prix de Rome at 19. His Saint-Philippe-du-Roule, Paris (1764), was influential in reviving the BASILICA plan for European churches; its simplicity of design contrasts starkly with the complex interiors of existing Gothic and Renaissance churches. Chalgrin died before finishing his great ARC DE TRIOMPHE.

Chaliapin \\shə-'lyä-pin\\, **Feodor (Ivanovich)** (1873–1938) Russian singer. Born a peasant, he received little early musical training, but his talent led to work with a touring opera company. His debuts in St. Petersburg (1894) and Moscow (1896) as Boris Godunov, the role he would be most associated with, led to his triumphant 1901 La Scala debut as Mefistofele. His imposing stage presence and fine acting gave him a popularity among male singers second only to that of Enrico CARUSO.

chalk Soft, fine-grained, easily pulverized, white-to-grayish variety of LIMESTONE, composed of the shells of minute marine organisms. The purest varieties contain up to 99% calcium carbonate in the form of CALCITE. Extensive deposits occur in W Europe and in England, notably in the chalk cliffs of Dover and also in the U.S. from S. Dakota to Texas and eastward to Alabama. Chalk is used for making lime and portland cement and as a soil additive. Finely ground and purified chalk is known as whiting and is used as a filler or pigment in a wide variety of materials, including ceramics, plastics, paper, and paints. The chalk used in classrooms is a manufactured substance rather than natural chalk.

Challenger One of the first four U.S. SPACE SHUTTLES. At the launch for its tenth mission in January 1986, faulty O-rings in the seams of its solid rocket booster failed and the booster exploded, destroying the *Challenger* and killing its seven-member crew.

Chamberlain, Joseph (1836–1914) British politician and reformer. In Parliament (1876–1906), he became a leader of the left wing of the Liberal Party. In 1886 in opposition to Irish HOME RULE, he joined other dissident Liberals (Liberal Unionists) to defeat the Liberal government. He used his control of the Liberal Unionists to pressure the subsequent Conservative government to adopt a more progressive social policy. As colonial secretary (1895–1903), he advocated tax reform and a federated empire of self-governing colonies, helping pass the Commonwealth of Australia bill (1900).

Chamberlain, (Arthur) Neville (1869–1940) British prime minister (1937–40). Son of Joseph CHAMBERLAIN, he prospered in the metalworking industry, was elected mayor of Birmingham (1915–16), served in the House of Commons 1918–40, and held Conservative cabinet posts. As prime minister, he sought to prevent the outbreak of war over Adolf HITLER's demand that Czechoslovakia cede the Sudetenland to Germany. In 1938 he and France's Edouard DALADIER granted most of Hitler's demands in the MUNICH AGREEMENT, after which he returned to England a popular hero, speaking of "peace in our time." He repudiated APPEASEMENT after Hitler seized the rest of Czechoslovakia, and when Germany attacked Poland he declared war. He lost support after the failure of a British expedition to Norway and resigned in 1940.

Chamberlain, Wilt(on Norman) (1936–1999) U.S. basketball player, one of the greatest in history. Born in Philadelphia, the 7-ft 1-in. (2-m 16-cm) Chamberlain played center for the Philadelphia Warriors (1959–65), the Philadelphia 76ers (1965–68), and the Los Angeles Lakers (1968–73). In the 1961–62 season he became the first player to score more than 4,000 points in regular-season NBA games. He led the NBA in scoring seven consecutive years (1959–65) and in rebounding 11 times. He is one of only three players to have scored more than 30,000 points in a professional career (31,419), and ranks first in career rebounds (23,924), second in scoring average (30.1), and third in field goals (12,681).

Chamberlain's Men *or* **Lord Chamberlain's Men** English theatrical company, the most important in Elizabethan and Jacobean England. Based at the GLOBE THEATRE 1599–1608, in 1603 it gained royal patronage as the King's Men. William SHAKESPEARE was connected with it for most of his career; it also presented works by Ben JONSON and Francis Beaumont. It ceased to exist when the ENGLISH CIVIL WARS broke out in 1642.

chamber music Music composed for small instrumental ensembles and performed without a conductor. Traditionally performed in a room or reception hall, often solely for the performers' own pleasure, chamber music is now often heard in concert halls. It was long associated with aristocratic households. The duo sonata (usually for violin and CONTINUO) and trio sonata appeared in early-17th-cent. Italy. The STRING QUARTET arose in the 1750s. The serenade, nocturne, and divertimento were Classical genres for varying instrumental forces, often intended to accompany meals and other activities. Standard ensembles include the string trio (violin, viola, cello) and piano trio (piano, violin, cello). Small chamber orchestras are often used for 18th-cent. music and usually require a conductor. See also SONATA.

chamber of commerce *or* **commercial association** Voluntary organization of business firms, public officials, professional people, and public-spirited citizens dedicated to promoting and developing commercial and industrial opportunities in their local area. The International Chamber of Commerce (founded 1920) runs a court of arbitration for settling commercial disputes. National chambers of commerce exist in most industrialized, free-enterprise countries. The first was founded in Paris in 1601; the first U.S. chamber of commerce was that of the state of New York, founded in 1768.

Chambers, Robert and William (1802–1871, 1800–1883) Scottish publishers. Robert, who began business with a bookstall in Edinburgh, wrote historical, literary, and geological works. In 1832 the brothers started *Chambers's Edinburgh Journal*, which led to the establishment of the firm of W. & R. Chambers, Ltd. Their *Chambers's Encyclopaedia* (1859–68) was based on the German *Konversations-Lexikon*. It remains in print today.

Chambers, (David) Whittaker *orig.* Jay Vivian Chambers (1901–1961) U.S. journalist. Born in Philadelphia, he joined the Communist Party in 1923 and worked at various times as an editor at *New Masses, The Daily Worker,* and (after leaving the party in 1938) *Time* magazine. In 1948, before the House Un-American Activities Committee, he named Alger HISS as a fellow member of a 1930s Communist spy ring. Hiss denied the charges and sued Chambers for slander. In the trials that followed, Chambers produced material he claimed Hiss had given him to pass along to Soviet agents. His autobiography, *Witness* (1952), became a bestseller.

chameleon Any member of a group of Old World, primarily tree-dwelling, LIZARDS (family Chamaeleontidae) characterized chiefly by their ability to change body color. Other traits include toes fused into opposite bundles of two and three and a long, slender, extensile tongue. About half of the 89 species are found in Madagascar; the others live mostly in sub-Saharan Africa. Most are 7–10 in. (17–25 cm) long. The bulged eyes move independently. Insects are the main diet, but larger species also eat birds.

chamomile \ˈka-mə-ˌmīl\ Any of the more than 100 species of Eurasian herbs that make up the genus *Anthemis,* in the COMPOSITE FAMILY; also, a similar plant in the genus *Chamaemelum* of the same family. Both genera have yellow or white ray flowers and yellow disk flowers. Several *Anthemis* species are cultivated as ornamentals. The strong-smelling mayweed (*A. cotula*) has been used in medicines and insecticides. Chamomile tea, used as a tonic and an antiseptic, is made from *C. nobile,* or *A. nobilis.*

Chamorro \chä-ˈmȯr-rō\, **Violeta (Barrios de)** (b.1929) President of Nicaragua (1990–96). Born to a wealthy family, she married the publisher of *La Prensa,* a newspaper that op-

posed the Anastasio Somoza dictatorship (see SOMOZA FAMILY). After her husband was assassinated in 1978, she became publisher. When the SANDINISTAS overthrew Somoza, she served briefly on a ruling junta, but her newspaper soon became critical of Daniel ORTEGA and supportive of U.S. policies and the anti-Sandinista CONTRAS. She was elected president in 1990. Her presidency was troubled by continuing deep political divisions and the significant power still held by the Sandinistas.

Champagne \sham-ˈpän\ Historical and cultural region, NE France. It was an important medieval French county, held by the houses of Vernandois, Blois, and NAVARRE. In the 12th and 13th cent., it was the site of six great trade fairs and was a banking center for all Europe. Following the marriage (1284) of Joan of Navarre to the future king PHILIP IV of France, it was united to the crown in 1314. As a frontier region it has been frequently invaded; it was the site of fierce battles in World Wars I and II. The region is famous for its wines.

champagne Sparkling WINE named for the Champagne region of NE France. Champagne is made from only three grapes: pinot and meunier (both black) and chardonnay (white). It is initially fermented in stainless-steel vats. A mixture of wine, sugar, and yeast is added, and a second FERMENTATION in pressure tanks yields carbon dioxide and effervescence. It is chilled, sweetened, bottled, and left to mature. It varies in degree of sweetness, depending on the type.

Champaigne \shäⁿ-ˈpànʸ\, **Philippe de** (1602–1674) Flemish-French painter. Trained in Brussels, he arrived in Paris in 1621. His patrons included LOUIS XIII, MARIE DE MÉDICIS, and Cardinal RICHELIEU, and he became the outstanding French portraitist of the baroque period. A professor at the Royal Academy from 1653, he produced many pieces for the palaces and churches of Paris. His finest work includes two portraits of Richelieu and the austere *Ex-voto: Mother Agnès and Sister Catherine* (1662), commemorating his daughter Catherine's miraculous cure.

Champlain \sham-ˈplän\, **Lake** Lake between Vermont and New York. Extending into Canada about 6 mi (10 km), it is about 125 mi (200 km) long and has an area of 430 sq mi (1,115 sq km). It was visited in 1609 by Samuel de CHAMPLAIN. In 1776 it was the scene of the first British–American naval battle, and in 1814 of a U.S. naval victory over the British. It is a link in the waterway between New York City's harbor and the lower ST. LAWRENCE RIVER.

Champlain, Samuel de (1567–1635) French explorer. He made several expeditions to N. America before founding Quebec in 1608 with 32 colonists, most of whom did not survive the first winter. He promoted the fur trade with the Indians, discovered Lake Champlain (1609), and made other explorations of what are now N New York and the E Great Lakes. English privateers besieged Quebec in 1628 and he was taken prisoner. In 1632 the colony was restored to France, and Champlain returned in 1633.

Champollion \shäⁿ-pȯl-ˈyōⁿ\, **Jean-François** (1790–1832) French scholar who played a major role in deciphering Egyptian HIEROGLYPHS. Champollion was a linguistic prodigy who had immersed himself in Middle Eastern languages in his teens. After study of the ROSETTA STONE and other texts, Champollion demonstrated decisively in *Summary of the Hieroglyphic System of the Ancient Egyptians* (1825) that a phonetic value could be assigned to some hieroglyphs. He became curator of the Louvre's Egyptian collection in 1826.

Champs-Élysées \ˈshäⁿ-zä-lē-ˈzä\ (French: "Elysian Fields") One of the world's most remarkable avenues, stretching 1.17 mi (1.88 km) from the ARC DE TRIOMPHE to the Place de la Concorde, in Paris. The lower part, toward the Place de la Concorde, is surrounded by gardens, museums, theaters, and restaurants. The upper part, toward the Arc de Triomphe, was traditionally a luxury commercial district. Twelve avenues radiate to form a star (*étoile*) at the upper end, centered on the Arc de Triomphe; it was called Place de l'Étoile 1753–1970, then renamed Place Charles de Gaulle.

Chancellorsville, Battle of Assault in May 1863 near Chancellorsville, Va., in the AMERICAN CIVIL WAR that ended in

a Confederate victory. The Union army under Joseph HOOKER attempted to encircle the Confederate army under Robert E. LEE, but was surprised by a flanking force led by Stonewall JACKSON. Three days of fighting resulted in a Union retreat north of the Rappahannock River. The Union army lost over 17,000 men out of 130,000; the Confederate army lost over 12,000, including Jackson, out of 60,000.

Chancery, Court of See EQUITY

Chandigarh \'chən-dē-gər\ City (pop., 1991: 511,000), and union territory (pop., 1994 est.: 725,000), joint capital of Haryana and PUNJAB states, N India. The site was selected to replace the former capital of LAHORE, lost to Pakistan at partition in 1947. The city was laid out in the 1950s by LE CORBUSIER and Indian architects, but the design has since been submerged.

Chandler, Raymond (Thornton) (1888–1959) U.S. writer of detective fiction. Born in Chicago, he worked as an oil-company executive in California before turning to writing. His character Philip Marlowe, a hard-boiled Los Angeles private detective, appears in all seven of his novels, including *The Big Sleep* (1939; film, 1946), *Farewell, My Lovely* (1940; film, 1944), and *The Long Good-Bye* (1953; film, 1973). His screenplays include *Double Indemnity* (1944) and *Strangers on a Train* (1951). Chandler and Dashiell HAMMETT are the classic authors of the hard-boiled genre.

Chandrasekhar \ˌchən-drə-'sā-kär\, **Subrahmanyan** (1910–1995) Indian-U.S. astrophysicist. He determined that following its red-giant phase, a star with a remaining mass over 1.4 times that of the sun (the Chandrasekhar limit) collapses and becomes a neutron star during a supernova explosion. Stellar remnants of more than about three solar masses collapse further to become BLACK HOLES. He shared a 1983 Nobel Prize with William A. Fowler (1911–1995).

Chanel \shȧ-'nel\, **Gabrielle** *known as* **Coco Chanel** (1883–1971) French fashion designer. Little is known of her early life. In 1913 she opened a millinery shop in Deauville, and within five years her innovative designs were attracting wealthy patrons. Stressing simplicity and comfort, she revolutionized the fashion industry for the next 30 years. She popularized turtleneck sweaters, the "little black dress," and the much-copied "Chanel suit." Chanel industries also included perfume laboratories; the financial basis of her empire was Chanel No. 5 perfume, introduced in 1922.

Coco Chanel

Chaney, Lon (*orig.* Alonso) (1883–1930) U.S. film actor. Born in Colorado Springs, Col., to deaf-mute parents, he learned pantomime early. He moved to Hollywood, becoming a star in *The Miracle Man* (1919). Known as "the man of a thousand faces" for his ability to transform himself through makeup, he often played grotesque or dual characters in films directed by Tod Browning, including *The Unholy Three* (1925). His other silent films include *The Hunchback of Notre Dame* (1923), *The Phantom of the Opera* (1925), and *London after Midnight* (1927). His son Lon Chaney, Jr. (1905–1973), appeared in numerous horror films in such repeated roles as the Wolf Man and the Mummy, and notably in *Of Mice and Men* (1939).

Chang Chih-tung See ZHANG ZHIDONG

Changchun *or* **Ch'ang-ch'un** \'chäŋ-'chün\ City (pop., 1999 est.: 2,072,000), capital of Jilin province, NE China. A small village until the late 18th cent., it became important after the completion of the Chinese Eastern Railway (1901). After the Japanese seizure of Manchuria (1931), it became the capital of MANCHUGUO. It grew quickly under Chinese communist rule and became a center for industrial expansion.

Chang River \'chäŋ\ *or* **Yangtze River** \'yäŋ-'tsȧ\ River, China. Rising in the E KUNLUN MTNS. in W China, it flows southeast, then east to the E. CHINA SEA near SHANGHAI. At 3,434 mi (5,525 km) long, it is the world's third-longest river. Navigable for 585 mi (941 km), it becomes harder to navigate above Yichang because of the gorges that occur between CHONGQING, at 650 ft (198 m), and Yichang, at 131 ft (40 m). Several large cities, including SHANGHAI, NANJING, WUHAN, and Chongqing, lie in the river's basin, which is known as the granary of China. The controversial THREE GORGES DAM PROJECT, inaugurated in 1994, will enable freighters to navigate 1,400 mi (2,250 km) inland from the E. China Sea to Chongqing.

Changsha *or* **Ch'ang-sha** \'chäŋ-'shä\ City (pop., 1999 est.: 1,334,000), capital of Hunan province, China. Located on the Xang River in SE central China, it was (according to tradition) formerly enclosed by a wall built in 202 B.C. In A.D. 750–1100 Changsha was an important commercial city, and its population increased greatly. Under the QING DYNASTY, from 1664, it was the capital of Hunan province and a major rice market. Besieged during the TAIPING REBELLION, it was also the scene of major battles in the SINO–JAPANESE WAR. The city is now a major port and a commercial and industrial center.

Chang Tso-lin See ZHANG ZUOLIN

Channel, The See ENGLISH CHANNEL

Channel Islands *or* **Santa Barbara Islands** Chain of islands, S California. Extending 150 mi (240 km) along and 25–90 mi (40–145 km) off the coast, it is divided into the Santa Barbara group (San Miguel, Santa Rosa, Santa Cruz, and Anacapa) and the Santa Catalina group (Santa Barbara, San Nicolas, Santa Catalina, and San Clemente). The largest island is Santa Cruz (98 sq mi, or 254 sq km). Rugged and mountainous, they are frequented by colonies of sea lions, seals, and birds, and are noted for their distinctive plant life (about 830 varieties). The larger islands support sheep and cattle ranches, and Santa Catalina is a noted resort. Most of the group is included in Channel Islands National Park.

Channel Islands Group of islands (pop., 1990 est.: 144,000), United Kingdom. Located in the ENGLISH CHANNEL, the islands cover 75 sq mi (194 sq km). Consisting of the islands of Jersey, Guernsey, Alderney, Sark, and several islets, they are domestically independent of the British government. MENHIRS are evidence of prehistoric occupation. A part of NORMANDY in the 10th cent. A.D., the islands came under the British at the time of the NORMAN CONQUEST in 1066. Two islets were disputed between England and France until 1953, when British sovereignty was confirmed. It was the only British territory occupied by Germany in World War II. The islands are famous for their cattle breeds, including the Jersey and Guernsey.

Channel Tunnel *or* **Eurotunnel** Rail tunnel that runs beneath the English Channel between Folkestone, England, and Sangatte (near Calais), France. The 31-mi (50-km) tunnel, which opened in 1994, consists of three separate tunnels, two for rail traffic and a central tunnel for services and security. Trains, which carry motor vehicles as well as passengers, can travel at speeds up to 100 mph (160 kph).

Channing, William Ellery (1780–1842) U.S. Unitarian clergyman. Born in Newport, R.I., he studied at Harvard Univ. and became in 1803 the pastor of Boston's Federal Street Church. Initially a Congregationalist, he gradually adopted liberal and rationalist views that came to be labeled Unitarian. In 1820 he established a conference of liberal Congregationalist clergy, later reorganized as the American Unitarian Assn. He became a leading figure in New England TRANSCENDENTALISM, and his lectures and essays on slavery, war, and poverty made him highly influential.

chanson de geste \shäⁿ-'sōⁿ-də-'zhest\ Any of several Old French epic poems that form the core of the CHARLEMAGNE legends. More than 80 have survived in 12th–15th-cent. manuscripts. They contain a core of historical truth overlain with legend. Most are anonymous. The *Chanson de Roland* was the formative influence on later chansons de geste, which in turn influenced literature throughout Europe.

Chanson de Roland \shäⁿ-'sōⁿ-də-rȯ-'läⁿ\ *English Song of Roland* Old French epic poem written around 1100, the masterpiece and probably the earliest of the CHANSONS DE GESTE. It deals with the Battle of Roncesvalles (778), a skirmish that is portrayed as a heroic battle against the Saracens. Direct and sober in style, it highlights the clash of recklessly courageous Roland and his prudent friend Oliver, a conflict between divergent ideas of feudal loyalty.

chant See GREGORIAN CHANT

Chantilly lace \shan-'ti-lē\ Lace made at Chantilly, north of Paris. The silk laces that made the town famous date from the 18th cent.; they later included black, white, and blond lace (derived from natural silk). By 1840 machine-made imitations were available. The designs are characterized by naturalistic flowers and ribbons on a spotted background.

Chaos \'kā-,äs\ In Greek cosmology, either the primeval emptiness before things came into being or the abyss of Tartarus, the underworld. In HESIOD's *Theogony*, there was first Chaos, then GAEA and EROS. OVID gave Chaos its modern meaning: the original formless and disordered mass from which the ordered universe is created.

chaos theory \'kā-,äs\ Mathematical theory that describes CHAOTIC BEHAVIOR in a complex system. Applications include the study of turbulent flow in fluids (see TURBULENCE), irregularities in biological systems, population dynamics, chemical reactions, meteorology, transportation dynamics, and many other fields.

chaotic behavior Behavior in a complex system that appears irregular or unpredictable, but is actually determinate. The apparently random, unpredictable behavior in systems governed by complicated deterministic laws is the result of high sensitivity to initial conditions. For example, Edward LORENZ discovered that a simple model of heat CONVECTION exhibits chaotic behavior. In a now-classic example, he suggested that the flapping of a butterfly's wings could eventually result in large-scale changes in the weather.

chaparral \,sha-pə-'ral\ Vegetation composed of broad-leaved evergreen shrubs, bushes, and small trees, often forming dense thickets. Chaparral is found in regions with a Mediterranean climate. The name is applied mainly to the coastal and inland mountain vegetation of SW N. America. Chaparral vegetation becomes extremely dry by late summer. The fires that result are necessary for the germination of many shrub seeds, and they clear away dense ground cover, thus maintaining the growth of shrubs and preventing the spread of trees. New chaparral growth provides good grazing and valuable watershed protection in areas with steep, easily eroded slopes.

chaparral cock See ROADRUNNER

Chaplin, Charlie (*orig.* Charles Spencer) (*later* **Sir Charles**) (1889–1977) British-U.S. actor and director. A vaudeville performer at 8, he was on tour in New York (1913) when Max SENNETT signed him to a film contract. While making his second film, *Kid Auto Races at Venice* (1914), Chaplin developed the costume—baggy pants, derby hat, oversized shoes, and cane—that would define his famous "little tramp" character. He was soon directing his own films, and he became an instant star in *The Tramp* (1915). After cofounding UNITED ARTISTS in 1919, he produced, directed, and starred in such classics as *The Gold Rush* (1925), *City Lights* (1931), *Modern Times* (1936), *The Great Dictator* (1940), *Monsieur Verdoux* (1947), and *Limelight* (1952). Harassed for his leftist political views, he moved to Switzerland in 1952. In 1972 he returned to accept a special Academy Award.

Chapman, Maria Weston *orig.* Maria Weston (1806–1885) U.S. abolitionist. Born in Weymouth, Mass., she helped

Charlie Chaplin as "the Tramp"

found the Boston Female Anti-Slavery Society in 1832. She soon became chief assistant to W. L. GARRISON in the Massachusetts Anti-Slavery Society. In 1839 she published a pamphlet arguing that the divisions among abolitionists stemmed from their disagreements over women's rights.

Chapultepec \chä-'pül-tä-,pek\ Rocky hill, southwest of MEXICO CITY, Mexico. The AZTECS fortified it and built a residence for their rulers in the early 14th cent. In the 1780s the Spanish viceroys constructed a summer palace there, which became the home of the National Military Academy in 1841. The hill was captured by the U.S. (1847) in the MEXICAN WAR. In the 1860s Mexico's emperor MAXIMILIAN rebuilt the castle; it remained the official residence of Mexican presidents until 1940.

charcoal Impure form of CARBON, obtained as a residue when material containing carbon is partially burned. COKE, carbon black, and soot are forms of charcoal. Largely replaced by coke in blast furnaces and by NATURAL GAS as a raw material, charcoal is still used to make black GUNPOWDER and in case-hardening metals. Activated charcoal is a finely powdered, highly porous form whose surface area is hundreds or thousands of square meters per gram. It has many uses as an adsorbent (see ADSORPTION), including for poison treatment, and as a catalyst or catalyst carrier.

Charcot \shär-'kō\, **Jean-Martin** (1825–1893) French medical teacher and clinician. With Guillaume Duchenne (1806–1875) he is considered the founder of modern NEUROLOGY. An extraordinary teacher, he was known for his work with hysteria and hypnosis, which influenced many students, including Sigmund FREUD. He described the symptoms of locomotor ataxia and the disintegration of ligaments and joint surfaces it causes (Charcot's joint), pioneered the linking of brain sites with specific functions.

chard *or* **Swiss chard** Edible BEET (*Beta vulgaris* 'cicla') in which the tender leaves and leafstalks have become greatly developed. They are a good source of vitamins A, B, and C. Chard is popular as a garden vegetable because it is easy to grow, productive, and tolerant of cold and heat. Highly perishable, it is difficult to ship to distant markets.

Chardin \shär-'daⁿ\, **Jean-Baptiste-Siméon** (1699–1779) French painter. In 1728 he was admitted into the Royal Academy of Painting. He became a successful painter of small canvases depicting domestic scenes and objects from everyday middle-class life. In his later years he produced stunning pastel portraits. He was the greatest still-life painter of the 18th cent., well known through engravings of his work. Many 20th-cent. artists were inspired by the abstract qualities of his compositions.

charge-coupled device See CCD

chariot Open two- or four-wheeled vehicle of ancient origin. The chariot probably originated in Mesopotamia about 3000 B.C.; early monuments show heavy vehicles with solid wheels. Two-wheeled horse-drawn versions evolved for speed in battle about 2000 B.C., appearing first in Greece. Chariot racing was popular at the Olympic Games; in Rome it was the main event in the circus games, where two to four horses drew each lightweight chariot in a competition of four or six vehicles; in Byzantium such races became the dominant events of civic life.

charismatic movement See PENTECOSTALISM

Charlemagne \'shär-lə-,mān\ *or* **Carolus Magnus** ("Charles the Great") (742?–814) King of the Franks (768–814) and Holy Roman Emperor (800–14). Son of PEPIN III, he ruled the Frankish kingdom jointly with his brother Carloman until the latter's death in 771. As sole king of the Franks, he began to conquer and Christianize neighboring kingdoms, defeating and becoming king of the Lombards in N Italy (774). His expedition against the Moors in Spain failed (778), but he successfully annexed Bavaria (788). Charlemagne fought against the Saxons for many years, finally defeating and Christianizing them in 804. With the exception of the British Isles, S Italy, and part of Spain, he united in one vast state almost all the Christian lands of Western Europe. His coronation as emperor at Rome on Christmas Day, 800, after restoring Leo III to the papacy, marks the inception of the HOLY ROMAN EMPIRE. He established his capital at Aachen, where he built a magnificent palace and invited many scholars and poets; he codified the laws and

promoted a cultural revival known as the Carolingian renaissance. See also CAROLINGIAN DYNASTY.

Charleroi \shär-lə-'rwä\ City (pop., 1998 est.: 203,000), SW Belgium. Following the Treaty of the Pyrenees (1659), in which Spain was ceded French territory, Spain in 1666 decreed that a new fortress, named for Charles II of Spain, be built at this medieval village site. It was strategically important in the 17th–19th cent. and held variously by France, Spain, Austria, and Holland. The area was the scene of one of the first battles of World War I.

Charles (Philip Arthur George), Prince of Wales (b.1948) Heir apparent to the British throne, son of ELIZABETH II and PHILIP, DUKE OF EDINBURGH. He studied at Cambridge Univ., becoming the first heir to the throne to obtain a university degree (1970), and took a tour of duty with the Royal Navy (1971–76). In 1981 he married Lady Diana Spencer (see DIANA, PRINCESS OF WALES), and they had two sons. Their marriage grew strained amid intense scrutiny from the press and rumors of infidelity; they divorced in 1996. He subsequently began appearing publicly with Camilla Parker Bowles (b.1947). He has been known for his advocacy of excellence in architecture and other causes.

Charles, Ray *orig.* Ray Charles Robinson (b.1930) U.S. pianist, singer, and songwriter. He was born in Georgia, but his family soon moved to Greenville, Fla., where he began his career at age 5 in a neighborhood café. By 7 he had completely lost his sight. He learned to write scores in braille. Orphaned at 15, he left school to play professionally. He recorded "Mess Around" and "It Should've Been Me" in 1952–53, and, combining BLUES and GOSPEL-MUSIC influences, later had hits with "What'd I Say," "Georgia on My Mind," and "Hit the Road, Jack." A country-music album in 1962, marking unusual territory for a black performer, sold over a million copies. He has received 10 Grammy Awards.

Charles I *German* Karl Franz Josef (1887–1922) Emperor of Austria (1916–18) and king of Hungary (as Charles IV), last ruler of the Austro-Hungarian monarchy. After he succeeded FRANCIS JOSEPH in 1916, he made several abortive attempts to take Austria-Hungary out of World War I. He renounced participation in affairs of state in 1918 and was deposed in 1919. After two failed attempts to regain his Hungarian throne in 1921, he was sent into exile in Madeira.

Charles I (1600–1649) King of Great Britain and Ireland (1625–49). Son of JAMES I, he acquired from his father a belief in the divine right of kings. He became king in 1625 and soon after married the Catholic HENRIETTA MARIA. He came into conflict with his first Parliament because of religious issues, his war against Spain, and the general distrust of his adviser the 1st duke of BUCKINGHAM. After dissolving several successive Parliaments, Charles ruled for 11 years without calling a Parliament. In 1639 he went to war against Scotland, and the need to raise money prompted him to summon the so-called Short Parliament and LONG PARLIAMENT. Eventually his authoritarian rule and quarrels with Parliament provoked the ENGLISH CIVIL WARS. After his forces were defeated, the army demanded that he stand trial for treason as "the grand author of our troubles." In 1649 he was convicted and executed, and Oliver CROMWELL proclaimed the Commonwealth.

Charles I *Hungarian* Karoly *known as* **Charles Robert of Anjou** \'an-jü\ (1288–1342) King of Hungary (1301, 1308–42). He claimed the Hungarian throne with papal approval and was crowned in 1301, but his claim was disputed, and he was not recognized as king until 1308. A courtly and pious ruler, Charles restored Hungary to the status of a great power. An alliance with Poland enabled him to defeat the Holy Roman Emperor and the Austrians. He negotiated a pact providing that his eldest son would become king of Poland.

Charles I *known as* **Charles of Anjou** \'an-jü\ (1226–1285) King of Naples and Sicily (1266–85), the first of the ANGEVIN DYNASTY. Count of Anjou and the younger brother of Louis IX of France, Charles allied with the papacy and conquered Naples and Sicily in the 1260s. He created a great but short-lived Mediterranean empire, expanding into the Balkans. In 1282 the Sicilians rebelled against his harsh rule

(see SICILIAN VESPERS) and drove out the Angevins; Charles died while preparing a counteroffensive.

Charles II (1630–1685) King of Great Britain and Ireland (1660–85). Son of CHARLES I, he supported his father in the ENGLISH CIVIL WARS. After his father's execution, he invaded England in 1651 but was defeated at Worcester. He then spent years in exile until conditions favored a return to the monarchy; he was proclaimed king in May 1660 (see RESTORATION). He became known as "the Merry Monarch" for his lifting of Puritan restrictions on entertainment and his own love of pleasure; his best-known mistress was the actress Nell GWYN. By the 1670s the miscarriages of his queen, Catherine of Braganza, had reduced hopes for a legitimate heir (though he left at least 14 illegitimate offspring). He almost lost control of his government when hysteria arose over the so-called POPISH PLOT to replace him with his Catholic brother James (the future JAMES II). Charles's political adaptability and acumen enabled him to steer his country through two wars with the Dutch (see AN-GLO–DUTCH WARS) and the struggle between Anglicans, Catholics, and dissenters that marked his reign.

Charles II *known as* **Charles of Anjou** \'an-jü\ *or* **Charles the Lame** (1254?–1309) King of Naples (1285–1309). He guarded Naples while his father, CHARLES I, launched a campaign to regain Sicily from the Aragonese. After being captured and imprisoned (1284–88), he continued to fight unsuccessfully for Sicily until 1302. He built alliances through the marriages of his children and extended his control over Piedmont, Provence, Hungary, Athens, and Albania.

Charles II *Spanish* **Carlos** (1661–1700) King of Spain (1665–1700), the last monarch of the Spanish HABSBURG DYNASTY. Son of PHILIP IV and Maria Anna of Austria, he was slow-witted and became known as Charles the Mad. After a 10-year regency under the queen mother, his personal government was concerned with resistance to the French imperialism of LOUIS XIV. His death without an heir led to the War of the SPANISH SUCCESSION.

Charles II *known as* **Charles the Bad** (1332–1387) King of Navarre (1349–87). He acquired Normandy from John II of France by threatening an English alliance. Arrested for his treachery in 1356, he escaped a year later and regained Normandy. He pursued shifting alliances in Spain in an effort to expand Navarrese power. CHARLES V voided his claims in France, and the discovery of his plot to poison the French king cost him all of Normandy except Cherbourg.

Charles III *Spanish* **Carlos** (1716–1788) King of Spain (1759–88). Son of PHILIP V and ELIZABETH FARNESE, he was king of Naples (as Charles VII, 1734–59) before becoming king of Spain. He was convinced of his mission to reform Spain and make it once more a first-rate power, but Spain's losses in the SEVEN YEARS' WAR revealed naval and military weakness. He was more successful in strengthening his own empire; during his reign Spain undertook commercial reforms and introduced a modern administrative system. One of the enlightened despots of the 18th cent., he helped lead Spain to a brief cultural and economic revival.

Charles III *known as* **Charles the Fat** (839–888) Frankish king and Holy Roman Emperor (881–87). The great-grandson of CHARLEMAGNE, he inherited the kingdoms of Swabia (876) and Italy (879). Crowned emperor in 881, he gained control of the E. and W. Frankish kingdoms, and by 885 had reunited all of Charlemagne's empire except Provence. Chronically ill, he failed to attack the Saracens and used tribute to buy off VIKING invaders. His nephew Arnulf led an uprising against him in 887, and his fall marked the final disintegration of the empire of Charlemagne.

Charles IV *orig.* Wenceslas *known as* **Charles of Luxembourg** (1316–1378) King of the Germans and of Bohemia (1346–78) and Holy Roman Emperor (1355–78). In 1346 Charles was elected German king and succeeded his father as king of Bohemia. He invaded Italy and won the crown of Lombardy as well as the imperial crown at Rome. Charles enlarged his dynastic power through skillful diplomacy and made Prague the political and cultural center of the empire. He issued the Golden Bull of 1356 and won the right of succession to the German throne for his son Wenceslas.

Charles IV *Spanish* **Carlos** (1748–1819) King of Spain (1788–1808). Son of CHARLES III, he lacked leadership qualities and entrusted the government to his prime minister Manuel de Godoy (1767–1851). After a French invasion in 1794, Spain was reduced to the status of a French satellite. When NAPOLEON again occupied N Spain in 1807, Charles was forced to abdicate (1808) and go into exile.

Charles V *known as* **Charles the Wise** (1338–1380) King of France (1364–80). He raised money to ransom his father, John II, from the English, under the terms of the Treaty of BRÉTIGNY. Crowned king on his father's death in 1364, Charles helped the country recover its losses in the first phase of the HUNDRED YEARS' WAR. When war with England broke out again (1369), he won a series of victories for the French. The plots of his enemy CHARLES II of Navarre prompted him to seize most of Charles's French lands. His support of Pope Clement VII helped cause the Western SCHISM.

Charles V *German* **Karl** (1500–1558) Holy Roman emperor (1519–56) and king of Spain (as Charles I, 1516–56). Grandson of FERDINAND V and ISABELLA I and of Emperor MAXIMILIAN I, he succeeded to his grandfathers' kingdoms on their deaths. Important events of his reign included the Diet of WORMS and the beginning of the REFORMATION; his defeat of FRANCIS I, which assured Spanish supremacy in Italy (see ITALIAN WARS); wars against Süleyman I the Magnificent; the Council of TRENT; and the Peace of AUGSBURG. He struggled to

Charles V Painting by Titian, 1548

hold his vast Spanish and Habsburg empire together against the growing forces of Protestantism, Turkish and French pressure, and even hostility from Pope Adrian VI. In 1556 Charles abdicated his claim to Spain in favor of his son PHILIP II and the title of emperor to his brother FERDINAND I, and in 1557 he retired to a monastery.

Charles VI *known as* **Charles the Well-Beloved** *or* **Charles the Mad** (1368–1422) King of France (1380–1422). Crowned at age 11, he allowed his uncles and advisers to rule France until 1388. He suffered fits of madness from 1392, and royal power waned. The English victory at the Battle of AGINCOURT (1415) obliged Charles to sign the Treaty of Troyes (1420), which provided for the marriage of his daughter to HENRY V of England, who was declared heir to the French throne.

Charles VI *German* **Karl** (1685–1740) Holy Roman emperor (1711–40) and king of Hungary (as Charles III). Son of Emperor LEOPOLD I, he tried unsuccessfully to claim the Spanish throne (see War of the SPANISH SUCCESSION). He conducted a successful war against the Ottoman empire (1716–18) but in a later conflict with Turkey (1736–39) lost most of the territories gained in 1718. He promulgated the PRAGMATIC SANCTION in an attempt to ensure that his daughter MARIA THERESA would succeed him, which led to the War of the AUSTRIAN SUCCESSION.

Charles VII *known as* **Charles the Well-Served** (1403–1461) King of France (1422–61). Despite the treaty signed by his father, CHARLES VI, which excluded his succession, Charles assumed the title of king on his father's death. In 1429, with the aid of JOAN OF ARC, he raised the siege of Orléans. He drove the English from France (1436), and gradually recovered French lands, ending the HUNDRED YEARS' WAR. His financial and military reforms increased the power of the monarchy.

Charles VIII (1470–1498) King of France (1483–98). He abandoned claims to parts of present-day France and Spain, and consolidated French ownership of Brittany, in preparation for an expedition to Italy to assert his inherited right to the kingdom of Naples. This inaugurated inconclusive wars with Italy that lasted more than 50 years (see ITALIAN WARS). Charles was crowned in Naples (1495), but his op-

ponents rallied; he escaped with difficulty and lost his conquests.

Charles IX (1550–1574) King of France (1560–74). Son of CATHERINE DE MÉDICIS, he became king under his mother's regency. Though proclaimed of age in 1563, he remained under his mother's domination. His reign was marked by conflicts between Catholics and HUGUENOTS, and he is remembered for authorizing the SAINT BARTHOLOMEW'S DAY Massacre (1572) at his mother's instigation. He died of tuberculosis at 23.

Charles IX *Swedish* **Karl** (1550–1611) King of Sweden (1604–11). Third son of GUSTAV I VASA, he helped lead a rebellion (1568) that placed his brother on the throne as John III. After the accession (1592) of his devoutly Catholic nephew SIGISMUND III VASA, Charles called the Convention of Uppsala, which demanded that Lutheranism be retained as the national religion. He deposed Sigismund after a civil war, and became the virtual ruler of Sweden (1599–1604). Declared king in 1604, he pursued an aggressive foreign policy that led to war with Poland (1605) and Denmark (the Kalmar War, 1611–13).

Charles X (1757–1836) King of France (1824–30). Grandson of LOUIS XV, he went into exile during the FRENCH REVOLUTION, and became the leader of the ÉMIGRÉ NOBILITY. Returning in 1814, he led the ultraroyalists during the BOURBON RESTORATION. On the death of his brother LOUIS XVIII, Charles became king. His popularity waned as his reign became increasingly reactionary. In 1830 he was forced to abdicate in favor of LOUIS-PHILIPPE. His reign dramatized the failure of the Bourbons to reconcile the tradition of monarchy by divine right with the new democratic spirit.

Charles X Gustav *Swedish* **Karl Gustav** (1622–1660) King of Sweden (1654–60). Nephew of GUSTAV II ADOLF, he failed in his efforts to marry the Swedish queen CHRISTINA, but she named him to succeed her. As king he conducted the First Northern War (1655–60) against a coalition that eventually included Poland, Russia, Brandenburg, the Netherlands, and Denmark, with the aim of establishing a unified northern state. After conquering Poland (1655–56), he won back lands in S Sweden from Denmark by the Treaty of Roskilde (1658).

Charles XI *Swedish* **Karl** (1655–1697) King of Sweden (1660–97). He succeeded his father, CHARLES X GUSTAV, ruling under a regency of aristocrats until he came of age in 1672. The regents drew Sweden into the Dutch War (1672–78), but Charles took control of the armies and won favorable treaty results. Within Sweden, he expanded royal power at the expense of the nobility and established an absolutist monarchy.

Charles XII *Swedish* **Karl** (1682–1718) King of Sweden (1697–1718). Son of CHARLES XI, he became absolute monarch at 15. He defended his country for 18 years in the Second NORTHERN WAR, gradually taking increased responsibility for its armed operations. A disastrous invasion of Russia (1707–9) resulted in the loss of Sweden's status as a great power. A ruler of the early Enlightenment era, he promoted significant domestic reforms. He was killed during an invasion of Norway.

Charles XIV John *Swedish* **Karl Johan** *orig.* Jean-Baptiste Bernadotte (1763–1844) King of Sweden and Norway (1818–44). Born in France, he rose rapidly in the revolutionary army to brigadier general (1794). Named marshal of France in 1804, he supported NAPOLEON in several campaigns (1805–9) but subsequently shifted his allegiance. In 1810 he was invited to become crown prince of Sweden. He helped defeat Napoleon at the Battle of Leipzig (1813), then defeated Denmark (1813), forcing it to transfer Norway to the Swedish crown. On the death of Charles XIII in 1818, he became king of Sweden and Norway. His foreign policy led to a long and favorable period of peace.

Charles Albert *Italian* Carlo Alberto (1798–1849) King of Sardinia-Piedmont (1831–49). A member of the House of SAVOY, he eased the harsh administration of his country and accelerated its economic and social development. The spread of revolutionary ideas forced him to grant a statute for representative government in 1848. After the Austrian occupation of Ferrara, he sought to lead the liberation of

Italy. He went to war against Austria in 1848 and again in 1849, but after his defeats he abdicated in favor of his son, VICTOR EMMANUEL II.

Charles Martel \mär-'tel\ *Latin* Carolus Martellus ("Charles the Hammer") (688?–741) Mayor of the palace of AUSTRASIA (715–41). He was the illegitimate son of Pepin of Herstal, a mayor of the palace who governed parts of the Frankish realm under the weak MEROVINGIAN kings. On his father's death he overcame rivals to reunite and rule the entire Frankish realm. He subdued Neustria (724), attacked Aquitaine, and fought against the Frisians, Saxons, and Bavarians. His victory at the Battle of TOURS/POITIERS (732) stemmed the Muslim invasion, and he controlled Burgundy by 739. His grandson was CHARLEMAGNE.

Charles of Luxembourg See CHARLES IV (H.R.E.)

Charles Robert of Anjou See CHARLES I (HUNGARY)

Charles the Bad See CHARLES II (THE BAD)

Charles the Bold (1433–1477) Duke of BURGUNDY (1467–77). An opponent of LOUIS XI of France, Charles tried to make Burgundy an independent kingdom. He had great success until 1474, casting off French rule, extending Burgundy's possessions, and building a centralized government. Through negotiation, warfare, and purchases he sought to extend his territory as far as the Rhine, but a coalition of Swiss, Austrians, and towns on the upper Rhine resisted him. He suffered defeats by the Swiss in 1476 and was killed in battle near Nancy.

Charles the Fat See CHARLES III (THE FAT)

Charles the Well-Beloved See CHARLES VI (FRANCE)

Charles the Wise See CHARLES V (FRANCE)

Charleston Social jazz dance popular in the 1920s and later, characterized by its toes-in, heels-out twisting steps. Originally a Southern black folk dance, it had parallels in dances of Trinidad, Nigeria, and Ghana. It was popularized in the black musical *Runnin' Wild* in 1923 and took its name from one of the show's songs.

Charleston From the cover of *Life,* designed by John Held, Jr., 1926

Charleston Seaport city (pop., 2000: 96,000), SE S. Carolina. Founded in 1670, during the AMERICAN REVOLUTION it was held by the British 1780–82. It was the chief winter port of the U.S. until the WAR OF 1812. In 1861 the Confederate capture of Ft. Sumter in Charleston Harbor precipitated the AMERICAN CIVIL WAR. It was under siege 1863–65, then evacuated by Gen. William SHERMAN's forces. It was seriously damaged by an earthquake in 1886 and a hurricane in 1989. It is the site of The CITADEL (1842) and the Charleston Museum (1773), the oldest museum in the U.S.

Charleston City (pop., 2000: 53,000), capital of W. Virginia. Situated in the ALLEGHENY MTNS., it was settled around Ft. Lee shortly after the AMERICAN REVOLUTION. Divided in allegiance during the AMERICAN CIVIL WAR, it was occupied by Union troops in 1862. It was named the state capital in 1870. Its capitol building (completed 1932) was designed by Cass GILBERT.

Charlotte City (pop., 2000: 540,000), N. Carolina. The Carolinas' biggest metropolis, it was settled around 1748 and named for Charlotte Sophia of Mecklenburg-Streliz (later the wife of GEORGE III). Until the 1849 GOLD RUSH, it was the center of U.S. gold production. In the American Civil War it was the site of a Confederate naval yard. Presidents Andrew JACKSON and James K. POLK were born nearby. Its industry includes textiles, machinery, and chemical production, and it is the site of several institutions of higher education.

Charlotte *orig.* Charlotte Sophia of Mecklenburg-Strelitz (1744–1818) Queen consort of GEORGE III of England. In 1761 she was selected unseen after the British king asked for a review of all eligible German Protestant princesses. The successful marriage produced 15 children, including

GEORGE IV. After the king was declared insane (1811), Charlotte was given custody of him by Parliament.

Charlotte Amalie \'shär-lət-ə-'mäl-yə\ Seaport city (pop., 1990: 12,000), capital of the island of ST. THOMAS and of the U.S. VIRGIN ISLANDS. It was established as a Danish colony in 1672 and named for the Danish queen. It is the largest city in the Virgin Islands. Two castles, attributed to the pirates BLACKBEARD and Bluebeard, overlook the harbor. Tourism is economically important.

Charlottesville City (pop., 2000: 45,000), central Virginia. Located in the foothills of the BLUE RIDGE Mtns. and settled in the 1730s, it grew as a tobacco-trading center and later was noted as the home of Thomas JEFFERSON and James MONROE. Sites of interest include Jefferson's home, MONTICELLO; Monroe's home, Ash Lawn; and the Univ. of VIRGINIA.

Charlottetown City (pop., 1991: 15,000), capital of PRINCE EDWARD ISLAND. Settled by the French in the 1720s, it was named for the wife of GEORGE III after the island passed to Britain in 1763. It became the capital in 1765. With its excellent harbor, it is the province's commercial center. It is the site of Province House, where in 1864 Canada's unification was first discussed, and the Confederation Center of the Arts.

charm In PARTICLE PHYSICS, the property or internal QUANTUM number that is conserved in strong and electromagnetic interactions, but not in weak interactions (see STRONG FORCE, ELECTROMAGNETIC FORCE, WEAK FORCE). Charmed particles contain at least one charmed QUARK. The first charmed particle was discovered in 1974.

Charolais \,shar-ə-'lā\ Breed of large, light-colored CATTLE developed in France for draft purposes but now kept for beef production and used for crossbreeding. White cattle had long been characteristic of the Charolais region, but the breed was first recognized about 1775. A typical Charolais is massive, horned, and cream-colored or slightly darker. The breed was first imported into the U.S. in 1936.

Charon \'kar-ən\ In GREEK MYTHOLOGY, the son of Erebus (Darkness) and Nyx (Night), whose duty it was to ferry the souls of the dead across the Rivers STYX and Acheron. His payment was the coin placed in the mouth of the corpse before burial.

Charpentier \shär-pän-'tyä\, **Marc-Antoine** (c.1645–1704) French composer. A student of Giacomo CARISSIMI in Rome, he returned to Paris to succeed J.-B. LULLY as music director with MOLIÈRE's acting troupe (later the COMÉDIE-FRANÇAISE), and later held major church posts. Enormously prolific, he was the most important French composer of his generation. He wrote 11 masses, 84 psalm settings, and 207 motets, including some 35 dramatic motets or Latin oratorios, a genre he introduced into France. His works include the oratorio *Judicium Salomonis* (1702), the mass *Assumpta est Maria,* and the operas *Médée* (1693) and *David et Jonathas* (1688).

Charte Constitutionnelle See CHARTER OF 1814

charter Document granting specified rights or functions from the sovereign power of a state to a person, corporation, city, or other unit of local organization. In the MAGNA CARTA, King John granted certain liberties to the English people. Elsewhere in medieval Europe, monarchs issued charters to towns, guilds, and universities, granting them certain privileges and sometimes specifying how they should conduct their internal affairs. Later, charters were granted to overseas trading companies (e.g., the E. INDIA CO.), giving them monopolies in certain areas. Britain's colonies in N. America were established by charter. Today a corporate charter, issued by a governmental body, grants individuals the power to form a corporation, or LIMITED-LIABILITY company. A municipal charter creates a new political subdivision and allows the people within it to organize themselves into a municipal corporation.

chartered company Type of corporation that evolved in the 16th cent. in Europe. Under a charter granted by the state's sovereign authority, the company had certain rights and obligations which usually gave it a trading monopoly in a specific geographic area or for a specific type of trade item. In the 17th cent., chartered companies were established by the English, French, and Dutch governments to assist trade and encourage overseas exploration, especially in the Indies (see E. INDIA CO., Dutch E. INDIA CO., French E. INDIA CO.) and the New World (see HUDSON'S BAY CO.). Some chartered companies were also involved in the settlement of colonists (see LONDON CO., PLYMOUTH CO.).

Charter Oath *or* **Five Articles Oath** Oath issued in 1868 by Japan's MEIJI EMPEROR. One article spurred the creation of a new legislative body. Two articles promised an end to feudal class restrictions and "evil customs of the past," and another stated that all classes should work together to "carry out the plan of government." The last declared that "knowledge shall be sought throughout the world to promote the welfare of the empire." The oath set the progressive tone of the MEIJI PERIOD.

Charter of 1814 *or* **Charte Constitutionnelle** \'shärt-ˌkōⁿ-stē-tǖ-syò-'nel\ French constitution issued by LOUIS XVIII after he became king (see BOURBON RESTORATION). The charter, which remained in effect until 1848, established a constitutional monarchy with a bicameral parliament, guaranteed civil liberties, proclaimed religious toleration, and acknowledged Catholicism as the state religion.

Chartism British working-class movement for parliamentary reform. It was named after the People's Charter, a bill drafted by William Lovett (1800–1877) in 1838 that demanded universal manhood suffrage, equal electoral districts, vote by ballot, annually elected Parliaments, payment of members of Parliament, and abolition of property qualifications for membership. Parliament refused to take action on three Chartist petitions presented to it, and the movement declined after 1848.

Chartres Cathedral \'shärtrᵊ\ Cathedral of Notre–Dame at Chartres, one of the most influential examples of High GOTHIC ARCHITECTURE. The main part of this great cathedral was built between 1194 and 1220. Abandonment of the traditional tribune GALLERIES and the use of a unique type of FLYING BUTTRESS allowed for a larger CLERESTORY. A Renaissance choir screen and 176 stained-glass windows add to its beauty.

Chartres Cathedral

Chase, Salmon P(ortland) (1808–1873) U.S. antislavery leader and sixth chief justice of the U.S. (1864–73). Born in Cornish Township, N.H., he practiced law in Cincinnati from 1830 and defended runaway slaves and white abolitionists. He helped found the FREE SOIL PARTY (1848) and the REPUBLICAN PARTY (1854). He served in the U.S. Senate (1849–55, 1860–61) and was the first Republican governor of Ohio (1855–59). Secretary of the treasury under Pres. Abraham LINCOLN (1861–64), he was appointed chief justice in 1864. He presided over the impeachment trial of Pres. Andrew JOHNSON and tried to protect the rights of blacks from infringement by state action.

Chase, Samuel (1741–1811) U.S. jurist. Born in Princess Anne, Md., he helped lead the Sons of Liberty in violent resistance to the STAMP ACT. He served on the state COMMITTEE OF CORRESPONDENCE (1774), was elected to the CONTINENTAL CONGRESS, and signed the DECLARATION OF INDEPENDENCE. When Alexander HAMILTON exposed his attempt to corner the flour market (1778), Chase retired from Congress, only to return in 1784. Appointed to the U.S. Supreme Court in 1796, Chase upheld the primacy of U.S. treaties over state statutes in *Ware vs. Hylton*. In *Calder vs. Bull* (1798) he contributed to the definition of DUE PROCESS. Chase was impeached for partisan conduct in 1804. His acquittal established the principle that federal judges can be removed only for indictable criminal acts, thus strengthening the independence of the judiciary. Chase served until 1811.

Chase, William Merritt (1849–1916) U.S. painter and teacher. Born in Williamsburg (now Nineveh), Ind., he stud-

ied in New York and Munich. He became the most important U.S. teacher of his generation, first at New York's Art Students League and from 1896 at his own school; among his students were Georgia O'KEEFFE and Charles DEMUTH. He was a prolific painter; his 2,000 paintings include portraits, interiors (e.g., *In the Studio*, 1880–83), figure studies, still lifes, and landscapes characterized by bold, spontaneous brushwork.

Chase Manhattan Corp. U.S. HOLDING COMPANY incorporated in 1969 with the Chase Manhattan Bank as its main subsidiary. The bank was created in 1955 by the merger of the Bank of Manhattan Co. (founded 1799) and the Chase National Bank (founded 1877). Chase Manhattan Corp. exemplifies a movement in U.S. banking to establish holding companies to bring together banks with financial institutions ordinarily excluded by law from the field of banking. In 1996 it merged with Chemical Banking Corp., but kept the Chase Manhattan name.

chat Real-time conversation among computer users in a networked environment such as the INTERNET. After a user types a text message and presses the Enter key, the text immediately appears on the other users' computers, permitting typed conversations. A chat can be private (between two users) or public (where other users can see the messages and participate if they wish). Public chatting is conducted in "chat rooms," Web sites devoted to chat, usually about a specific topic. The thousands of chat rooms now available typically use the IRC (Internet Relay Chat) PROTOCOL, developed in 1988. See also BULLETIN-BOARD SYSTEM.

Chateaubriand \shä-tō-brē-'äⁿ\, **(François-Auguste-) René** *later* **vicomte (viscount) de Chateaubriand** (1768–1848) French author and statesman. A cavalry officer before the Revolution, he refused to join the Royalists and instead sailed to the U.S., where he traveled with fur traders. On Louis XVI's fall he returned to join the Royalist army. *Atala* (1801) drew on his travels in the U.S. *The Genius of Christianity* (1802), asserting Christianity's poetic and artistic appeal as its basic value, influenced Romantic writers and brought him briefly into favor with Napoleon. With the 1814 Restoration he became a major political figure as well as the preeminent French writer of his day. He later wrote his valuable memoirs (6 vols., 1849–50).

Chatham, Earl of See William PITT, THE ELDER

Chattahoochee River \ˌcha-tə-'hü-chē\ River, SE U.S. Rising in NE Georgia, it flows southwest and then south, forming a section of the Alabama–Georgia and Georgia–Florida boundaries, to join the Flint River at Chattahoochee, Fla., after about 436 mi (702 km). Dammed at the Georgia–Florida border, it forms Lake Seminole, below which it is known as the Apalachicola River.

Chattanooga City (pop., 2000: 155,000) and port of entry, SE Tennessee. Lying on the TENNESSEE RIVER, it was established as a trading post in 1815 and developed as a river port. A strategic Confederate communications point in the American Civil War, it was a major objective of the Union armies, with fighting culminating in the battles of CHICKAMAUGA and CHATTANOOGA (1863). The city is the headquarters for the TENNESSEE VALLEY AUTHORITY.

Chattanooga, Battle of (Nov. 23–25, 1863) Decisive engagement in the AMERICAN CIVIL WAR at Chattanooga, Tenn., a vital railroad junction. After the Battle of CHICKAMAUGA, a Confederate army under Benjamin BRAGG besieged a Union force in Chattanooga. To lift the siege, Union troops under U. S. GRANT marched on Bragg's troops at Lookout Mountain and Missionary Ridge and forced the Confederate army to retreat. With this victory, the North was poised to split the South horizontally by marching across Georgia to the sea.

Chatterjee \'chät-ər-jē\, **Bankim Chandra** *orig.* Bankim Chandra Cattopadhyay (1838–1894) Indian novelist. Born in Bengal, he published his first notable Bengali work, *Daughter of the Lord of the Fort*, in 1865. His epoch-making newspaper, *Bangadarsan*, serialized some of his later works. Many saw him as a prophet, and his valiant Hindu heroes aroused national pride. Considered the greatest Bengali novelist, he helped create the Indian school of fiction and established Bengali prose as a literary language.

Chatterton, Thomas (1752–1770) English poet. At 11 he wrote a pastoral poem on an old parchment and passed it off as a 15th-cent. work. Thereafter he created similar works, attributing them to a fictitious monk, Thomas Rowley. In London, he had some success with a comic opera, *The Revenge.* When a potential patron died, he found himself penniless and committed suicide at 17. Considered a precursor of ROMANTICISM, he was praised by S. T. CO-LERIDGE, John KEATS, Lord BYRON, and William WORDS-WORTH.

Chaucer \\'chȯ-sər\\, **Geoffrey** (1342/43–1400) English poet. A courtier, diplomat, and civil servant trusted by three kings, he was a poet only by avocation. In the 1380s he produced mature works including *The Parliament of Fowls,* a dream-vision for St. Valentine's Day about a conference of birds choosing their mates; the tragic verse romance *Troilus and Criseyde*; and the unfinished dream-vision *Legend of Good Women.* His best-known work, the unfinished *Canterbury Tales* (written 1387–1400), employs a pilgrimage to the shrine of Thomas BECKET in Canterbury as a frame for a highly varied set of stories; not only the most famous work in Middle English, it is one of the greatest in English literature. The first great English poet, Chaucer established the S English dialect as England's literary language.

chautauqua movement \\shə-'tȯ-kwə\\ Popular U.S. movement in adult education founded in 1874. It began as a Sunday-school teacher training assembly at Chautauqua Lake, N.Y., but spread to various circuit "chautauquas" and broadened in scope to include general education and popular entertainments. The movement peaked in 1924. Its legacy contributed to the growth of COMMUNITY COLLEGES and CONTINUING EDUCATION programs. See also LYCEUM MOVEMENT.

Chavannes, Pierre Puvis de See Pierre PUVIS DE CHAVANNES
Chávez (y Ramírez) \\'chä-ˌvez\\, **Carlos (Antonio de Padua)** (1899–1978) Mexican composer and conductor. When Mexico's first permanent symphony orchestra was formed in 1928, he became its director; he held the post for 20 years, touring widely and conducting many premieres. As director of the National Conservatory 1928–34, he reformed the curriculum. He was Mexico's most honored musician of the 20th cent.; his works, notable for their rhythmic vitality and orchestral color, include seven numbered symphonies, five ballets, a piano concerto (1940), a violin concerto (1950), and the opera *The Visitors* (1956).

Chavez \\'chä-vās, *Engl* 'chäv-ˌez\\, **Cesar (Estrada)** (1927–1993) U.S. organizer and leader of migrant farm workers. Born into a family of Mexican-American laborers, he spent his early years in a succession of migrant camps. In 1962 he began organizing the largely Hispanic farmworkers of Arizona and California. A charismatic figure, he used strikes and nationwide boycotts to win union recognition and contracts from California grape and lettuce growers. He brought his union into the AFL-CIO, and in 1971 it became the United Farm Workers of America (UFW). During the 1970s, he successfully battled the Teamsters Union for the right to organize field hands.

Chayefsky \\chä-'yef-skē\\, **Paddy** (*orig.* Sidney) (1923–1981) U.S. playwright. Born in New York City, he wrote television plays from 1952, and his work became prominent in early television drama. Known for chronicling the lives of ordinary people, his greatest television and film success was *Marty* (1955, Academy Award). His stage plays include *The Tenth Man* (1959), *Gideon* (1961), and *The Latent Heterosexual* (1968). He returned to screenwriting with *The Hospital* (1971, Academy Award) and *Network* (1976, Academy Award).

chayote \\chī-'yō-tē\\ Tendril-bearing vine (*Sechium edule*) of the GOURD family, native to the New World tropics, where it is widely cultivated for its edible fruits. The vine bears small, white flowers and green or white pear-shaped fruits with furrows. Each fruit contains one seed. The fruits are eaten cooked or raw, and the young root tubers are prepared like potatoes.

Chechnya \\chech-'nyä, 'chech-nyə\\ Subdivision, Russian Federation. Part of the Checheno-Ingush autonomous republic of the former U.S.S.R., it became a republic within Russia in 1992, as did Ingushetia. It is populated mainly by Chechens, a Muslim ethnolinguistic group. Its demand for independence in 1992 led to a devastating Russian invasion in 1993–94. A cease-fire agreement was reached in 1996, but fighting resumed in 1999. The capital, Grozny (pop., 1992 est.: 388,000), a major oil center, has received heavy damage.

check Bill of exchange drawn on a bank and payable on demand. As a written order to pay MONEY, a check may be transferred from one person to another by endorsement. Most checks are paid by the debiting and crediting of bank deposits. There are several special forms of checks. A cashier's check is issued by a bank and has unquestioned acceptability, as does a certified check, which is a depositor's check guaranteed by a bank. Traveler's checks are cashier's checks that must be signed by the payee when they are issued and again when they are cashed; reimbursement is guaranteed if they are lost or stolen.

checkers Board game for two players, each with 12 pieces positioned on (usually) the black squares of a 64-square checkerboard. Play consists of advancing a piece diagonally to an adjoining square, the goal being to jump and thus capture each of an opponent's pieces until all are removed. When a piece reaches the final row, it is crowned with another piece and can begin to move in any direction. Similar games in various cultures date back to antiquity.

cheese Food made from the curd of MILK separated from the whey. When milk sours, it forms a protein-rich gel, or curd, and a lactose-rich fluid, or whey. Adding rennin, an enzyme that acts on the milk's chief protein (casein) aids coagulation. The resulting curd is then cut or broken to release most of the whey. Ripening and curing are affected by moisture content, acidity, presence of microorganisms, and other factors. Cheese is made from the milk of cows, goats, sheep, water buffalo, llamas, yaks, and other animals. Products vary according to fat content of the milk, PASTEURIZATION, and addition of enzymes or cultures of BACTERIA, MOLDS, or YEASTS. Cheese varieties include hard cheeses (e.g., cheddar, Edam, Provolone, Swiss), semisoft cheeses (Gorgonzola, Limburger), and soft cheeses (Camembert, cottage, ricotta). Cheese is a source of protein, fat, minerals (calcium, phosphorus, sulfur, iron), and vitamin A.

cheetah Slender, long-legged CAT (*Acinonyx jubatus*) that lives on open plains of Africa and in the Middle East, where it is all but extinct. The fastest land animal in the world over short distances, it can reach a speed of 60 mph (100 kph). Its claws differ from those of other cats in being only partly retractable and in lacking protective sheaths. Like cats in the genus *Felis,* cheetahs purr rather than roar. The cheetah grows to about 55 in. (140 cm) long, excluding the 29–31-in. (75–80-cm) tail, and weighs 110–130 lbs (50–60 kg). The adult's coarse fur is sandy yellow above, white below, and covered with small black spots.

Cheever, John (1912–1982) U.S. writer. Born in Quincy, Mass., he lived mainly in S Connecticut. In clear, elegant prose, he delineated the drama and sadness of life in comfortable suburban America, often through fantasy and ironic comedy. His collections included *The Enormous Radio* (1953) and *The Stories of John Cheever* (1978, Pulitzer Prize). Among his novels are *The Wapshot Chronicle* (1957), *The Wapshot Scandal* (1964), and *Falconer* (1977). His revealing journals were published in 1991.

Chekhov \\'chek-əf, *Engl* 'chek-ȯf\\, **Anton (Pavlovich)** (1860–1904) Russian playwright and short-story writer. While practicing as a doctor, he had his first full-length play, *Ivanov* (1887), produced, to a disappointing reception. He took up serious themes with such stories as "The Steppe" (1888) and "A Dreary Story" (1889); later stories include "The Black Monk" (1894) and "Peasants" (1897). He converted his second long play, *The Wood Demon* (1889), into the masterpiece *Uncle Vanya* (1897). *The Seagull* (1896) was badly received until its

Anton Chekhov, 1902

successful revival in 1899 by Konstantin STANISLAVSKY and the MOSCOW ART THEATRE. He moved to the Crimea to nurse his eventually fatal tuberculosis, and there he wrote his great last plays, *Three Sisters* (1901) and *The Cherry Orchard* (1904). Chekhov's plays, which take a tragicomic view of provincial life and the passing of the Russian gentry, received international acclaim after being translated; as a short-story writer he is still regarded as virtually unmatched.

Chelyabinsk \chel-'yä-bənsk\ City (pop., 1997: 1,085,000), W Russia. Located 125 mi (200 km) south of YEKATERINBURG on the Trans-Siberian railroad, it is the capital of Chelyabinsk Oblast (pop., 1996 est.: 3,689,000). Founded in 1736, its growth was greatly stimulated by the eastward evacuation of Russian industry in World War II. It is now the principal city of the S Urals industrial region.

chemical dependency See DRUG ADDICTION

chemical element See chemical ELEMENT

chemical engineering Academic discipline and industrial activity concerned with developing processes and designing and operating plants to change materials' physical or chemical states. The field includes research, design, construction, operation, sales, and management activities. Chemical engineers must master CHEMISTRY (including the nature of CHEMICAL REACTIONS, the effects of TEMPERATURE and PRESSURE on EQUILIBRIUM, and the effects of CATALYSTS on REACTION RATES), physics, and mathematics. The engineering aspect, involving fluid flow and HEAT and MASS transfer, is broken down into "unit operations," including VAPORIZATION, DISTILLATION, ABSORPTION, filtration, extraction, crystallization, mixing, drying, and size reduction; each is described mathematically, and its principles apply to any material. Chemical engineers work in the chemical, oil, food, paper, textile, plastics, and nuclear industries and in biotechnology.

chemical equation Method of writing the essential features of a CHEMICAL REACTION using CHEMICAL SYMBOLS. Reactants (present at the start) are on the left, products (present at the end) on the right. A single arrow between them denotes an irreversible reaction, a double arrow a reversible reaction. The law of conservation of MATTER (see CONSERVATION LAW) requires that every ATOM on the left appear on the right (the equation must balance); only their arrangements and combinations change. For example, one OXYGEN MOLECULE combining with two HYDROGEN molecules to form two water molecules is written $2H_2 + O_2 \rightarrow 2H_2O$. See also STOICHIOMETRY.

chemical equilibrium See chemical EQUILIBRIUM

chemical formula Expression of the composition or structure of a chemical COMPOUND. Formulas for MOLECULES use CHEMICAL SYMBOLS with subscript numbers to show the number of ATOMS of each ELEMENT: O_2 for oxygen, O_3 for ozone, CH_4 for methane, C_6H_6 for benzene. Parentheses may enclose ATOMS that act as a group. If the substance does not exist as molecules (see IONIC BOND), empirical formulas show the relative proportions of the constituents (e.g., NaCl for sodium chloride). Structural formulas show bonds (see BONDING) between atoms in a molecule as short lines between symbols. A projection formula also indicates the three-dimensional arrangement of the atoms (see FISCHER PROJECTION, STEREOCHEMISTRY).

chemical reaction In CHEMISTRY, any process in which substances are changed into different ones, with different properties, as distinct from changing position or form (PHASE). Chemical reactions involve the rupture or rearrangement of the bonds holding ATOMS together (see BONDING), never atomic nuclei. The total MASS and number of atoms of all reactants equals those of all products, and ENERGY is almost always consumed or liberated. The speed of reactions varies (see REACTION RATE). Understanding their mechanisms lets chemists alter reaction conditions to optimize the rate or the amount of a given product. Reactions can be syntheses, decompositions, or rearrangements, or additions, eliminations, or substitutions. Examples include OXIDATION-REDUCTION, POLYMERIZATION, HYDROLYSIS, and ACID-BASE reactions.

chemical symbol One- or two-letter notation derived from the names of the chemical ELEMENTS (e.g., S for sulfur, Cl

for chlorine, Zn for zinc). Some hark back to Latin names: Au (aurum) for gold, Pb (plumbum) for lead. Others are named for people or places (einsteinium, Es, for Einstein). John DALTON first used symbols to designate single atoms of elements, and J. J. BERZELIUS gave many of the current names. Chemical formulas of COMPOUNDS are written as combinations of the elements' symbols, with numbers indicating their atomic proportions, using various conventions for ordering and grouping. Thus, sodium chloride is written as NaCl and sulfuric acid as H_2SO_4.

chemical warfare Use of chemical compounds, usually toxic agents, in warfare, and the methods of combating them. In humans, they generally paralyze the nervous system (see NERVE GAS); induce temporary blindness, deafness, nausea, or vomiting; cause severe burns to skin, eyes, or lungs; or stifle respiration. Also included are chemical DEFOLIANTS and HERBICIDES used for military purposes, such as AGENT ORANGE. During World War I the Germans introduced, and the Allies duplicated, a succession of poison gases: CHLORINE, phosgene, and mustard gas. The Allies also developed gas masks for protection. A 1925 Geneva protocol banned chemical warfare, but in World War II the Germans developed highly toxic nerve gases and Italy and Japan used gas against some of their enemies. Chemical weapons were used in the Iran–Iraq War in the 1980s, and Iraq threatened to use them in the Persian Gulf War in 1991. See also BIOLOGICAL WARFARE.

chemistry Science that deals with the properties, composition, and structure of substances (ELEMENTS and COMPOUNDS), the reactions and transformations they undergo, and the ENERGY released or absorbed during those processes. Chemistry is concerned with ATOMS as building blocks (not with the subatomic domain; see QUANTUM MECHANICS), with everything in the material world, and with all living things. Branches of chemistry include inorganic (see INORGANIC COMPOUND), organic (see ORGANIC COMPOUND), physical, and analytical (see ANALYSIS) chemistry; BIOCHEMISTRY; ELECTROCHEMISTRY; and GEOCHEMISTRY. See also CHEMICAL ENGINEERING.

Chemnitz \'kem-nits\ *formerly (1953–90)* **Karl-Marx-Stadt** \ˌkärl-'märks-ˌshtät\ City (pop., 1996: 263,000), E Germany. It lies along the Chemnitz River southeast of Leipzig. It began as a trading place on a salt route to Prague and was chartered in 1143. An industrial center, it was home to Germany's first spinning mill (1800), and the first German locomotive was built there.

chemoreception \ˌkē-mō-ri-'sep-shən\ Sensory process by which organisms respond to external chemical stimuli, by employing specialized cells (chemoreceptors) that convert the stimuli directly or indirectly into nerve impulses. Most mammals possess two classes of chemoreceptors: the receptors involved in smell and located in the epithelium of the nasal cavity, and the receptors involved in TASTE and located in the tongue's taste buds. Aquatic animals and terrestrial species with mucus-secreting skins typically possess chemoreceptors all over the body. For many animals, chemoreception is the most important means of receiving information about their surrounding environment. Chemoreception plays roles in finding appropriate food and in reproductive behavior (see PHEROMONES).

chemotherapy \ˌkē-mō-'ther-ə-pē\ Treatment of diseases, including CANCER, with chemicals. Some cancer drugs interfere with cancer-cell division or enzyme processes. However, they have serious side effects, attacking some healthy cells and reducing resistance to infection. Chemotherapeutic agents include certain STEROIDS and derivatives of plants such as periwinkle (vincristine, vinblastine) and yew (TAXOL).

Chen Duxiu *or* **Ch'en Tu-hsiu** \'chən-'dü-shē-'ü\ (1879–1942) Cofounder of the CHINESE COMMUNIST PARTY. From 1901 he started subversive periodicals that were quickly suppressed by the government. In 1915, after the establishment of the Chinese Republic, he created the monthly *Qingnian zazhi* ("Youth Magazine"), renamed *Xin qingnian* ("New Youth"), in which he proposed that the youth of China rejuvenate the nation intellectually and culturally; HU SHI and MAO ZEDONG were contributors. In 1917 Chen was appointed dean of the School of Letters at Beijing Univ.

Imprisoned briefly for his role in the MAY FOURTH MOVE-MENT, he became a Marxist. With LI DAZHAO he founded the Chinese Communist Party; he is regarded as "China's Lenin." Removed as party leader when the party's alliance with the Nationalists (GUOMINDANG) fell apart (1927), he was imprisoned 1932–37.

Cheney \'chē-nē, 'chā-nē\, **Richard B(ruce)** (b.1941) U.S. politician, vice president of the U.S. (from 2001). Born in Lincoln, Neb., he graduated from the Univ. of Wyoming. A conservative Republican, he served in the U.S. House of Representatives (1979–89) and was U.S. secretary of defense (1989–93) in George BUSH's administration. After serving as head of Halliburton Co. (1995–99), he was elected U.S. vice president on a ticket with George W. BUSH in 2000. His influence in office is believed to have surpassed that of any vice president in U.S. history.

Cheng Ch'eng-kung See ZHENG CHENGGONG

Cheng-chou See ZHENGZHOU

Chengdu or **Ch'eng-tu** \'chəŋ-'dü\ City (pop., 1990: 1,713,000), capital of Sichuan province, China. It lies in the fertile Chengdu plain, the site of one of China's most ancient irrigation systems, watered by the Min River. First set up in the 3rd cent. B.C., the system has survived, and it enables the area to support what has been called the densest agrarian population in the world. Chengdu was the capital of various dynasties, and in the 10th cent. A.D. it was immensely prosperous; its merchants introduced the use of paper money, which spread throughout China. In medieval times it was famous for its brocades and satins. The capital of Sichuan since 1368, it has grown as an administrative and industrial center.

Cheng Ho See ZHENG HE

Chennai See MADRAS

Cherbourg \sher-'bür, *Engl* 'sher-ˌbûrg\ Seaport (pop., 1990: 29,000) and naval station, NW France. Located on the ENGLISH CHANNEL, it was disputed between the French and English in the Middle Ages, taken by the English in 1758, then passed to France and was extensively fortified by LOUIS XVI. Industries include transatlantic shipping and shipbuilding.

Chernobyl accident \chər-'nō-bəl\ Accident at the Chernobyl (Ukraine) nuclear power station in the Soviet Union. On April 25–26, 1986, technicians attempted a poorly designed experiment, causing the chain reaction in the core to go out of control. The reactor's lid was blown off, and a partial meltdown of the core occurred. After Swedish monitoring stations reported abnormally high radiation levels, the Soviet government admitted the disaster. Beyond 32 immediate deaths, several thousand radiation-induced illnesses and cancer deaths were expected in the long term. The incident set off an international outcry over the dangers posed by radioactive emissions.

Chernov \chər-'nóf\, **Viktor (Mikhaylovich)** (1873–1952) Russian revolutionary. Cofounder of the Russian SOCIALIST REVOLUTIONARY PARTY, he wrote the party's platform. He was elected president of the constituent assembly that opened in Petrograd on Jan. 18, 1918, but was dispersed the next day by the Bolsheviks. He emigrated to Paris in 1920 and to the U.S. in 1939, writing (sometimes as Boris Olenin) for anticommunist periodicals.

Cherokee American Indian people who inhabited what is now E Tennessee and the W Carolinas. They possessed stone implements, wove baskets, made pottery, cultivated corn, beans, and squash, and hunted deer, bear, and elk. Wars and treaties in the late 18th cent. severely reduced Cherokee power and landholdings. After 1800 the Cherokee were remarkable for their assimilation of white culture, and most became literate following the development of a syllabary by SEQUOYAH. Beginning around 1835, when gold was discovered on Cherokee land in Georgia, agitation increased for their removal to the West. The ensuing events, culminating in the TRAIL OF TEARS, left many Cherokee dead and most of their descendants (today numbering about 200,000) living in Oklahoma.

cherry Any of various trees of the genus *Prunus*, and their edible fruits. Most are native to and widely grown in the Northern Hemisphere. Sweet-cherry trees (*P. avium*) are large and bear fruit that is generally heart-shaped to nearly globular, varies in color from yellow through red to nearly black, and has a low acid content. Sour-cherry trees (*P. cerasus*) are smaller and bear fruit that is round to oblate, generally dark red, and too acidic to eat fresh. The wood of some cherry species is especially esteemed for the manufacture of fine furniture. Ornamental varieties selected for the beauty of their flowers are a common feature of gardens.

Chersonese \'kər-sə-ˌnēz\ In ancient geography, any of several peninsulas in Europe and Asia (the term means "peninsula"). Tauric Chersonese included the CRIMEA and often the city of Chersonese, near modern SEVASTOPOL. The city, founded by Ionian Greeks in the 6th cent. B.C., later traded widely and flourished under the Romans and Byzantines. Thracian Chersonese constituted the modern GALLIPOLI Peninsula, the site of several cities founded by Aeolians and Ionians in the 7th cent. B.C. Abandoned to DARIUS I in 493 B.C., it was later dominated by Caesar AUGUSTUS.

chert and flint Very fine-grained QUARTZ, a silica mineral with minor impurities. Flint is gray to black and nearly opaque (translucent brown in thin splinters); chert is opaque, dull, and whitish to pale-brown or gray. Chert and flint provided the main source of tools and weapons for STONE AGE people. Flint is used today as an abrasive and grinding agent. Chert is used in road construction and as concrete aggregate. Some chert takes an excellent polish and is used as semiprecious jewelry. See also SILICEOUS ROCK.

cherub In Jewish, Christian, and Islamic literature, a celestial winged being with human, animal, or birdlike characteristics. They are included among the ANGELS, and in the Old Testament they are described as the throne-bearers of God. In Christianity and Islam, they are celestial attendants of God and praise him continually. In art they are often depicted as winged infants. See also SERAPH.

Cherubini \ˌkā-rü-'bē-nē\, **Luigi (Carlo Zanobi Salvadore Maria)** (1760–1842) Italian-French composer. Born into a musical family, the precociously gifted youth had written dozens of works before he was 20, and he produced his first opera that year. In 1788 he settled permanently in Paris. He enjoyed operatic successes in the 1790s, and NAPOLEON expressed his particular admiration. In 1822 he became director of the Paris Conservatoire, where he would remain the rest of his life. Ludwig van BEETHOVEN called Cherubini his greatest contemporary. His nearly 40 operas include *Lodoïska* (1791), *Médée* (1797), and *Les deux journées* (1800). His other important works include a symphony (1815), six string quartets, two requiems, and nine surviving masses.

Chesapeake \'che-sə-ˌpēk\ City (pop., 2000: 199,000), SE Virginia. Located south of NORFOLK, it was formed in 1963. At 341 sq mi (883 sq km), it is one of the largest cities in area in the U.S. The area, encompassing part of DISMAL SWAMP, was once the home of the Chesapeake Indians and was settled by colonists in the 1630s.

Chesapeake Bay Inlet of the Atlantic Ocean, E U.S. With its lower section in Virginia and its upper section in Maryland, it is 193 mi (311 km) long and 3–25 mi (5–40 km) wide and has an area of about 3,230 sq mi (8,365 sq km). It receives many rivers, including the SUSQUEHANNA and POTOMAC. JAMESTOWN, the area's first European settlement, was founded in 1607; a year later, Capt. John SMITH explored and mapped the bay. By the 1970s development of the surrounding area had led to alarming pollution of the bay's formerly rich waters; fishing dropped off sharply. Efforts have since been made to reverse the damage.

Chesnut, Mary *orig.* Mary Boykin Miller (1823–1886) U.S. writer. Born in Pleasant Hill, S.C., she married James Chesnut, Jr., who would play an important role in the Confederacy. She accompanied him on his missions as a staff officer and recorded her observations in her journal. Her *Diary from Dixie*, a perceptive view of Southern life during the Civil War, was first published in 1905.

Chesnutt, Charles (Waddell) (1858–1932) U.S. writer, the first important African–American novelist. He worked as a school principal in N. Carolina, and later as an attorney in Cleveland, writing in his spare time. He published two collections of short stories, a biography of Frederick DOUGLASS, and three novels, including *The Colonel's Dream*

(1905), using familiar scenes of folk life to protest social injustice.

chess Checkerboard game for two players, each of whom moves 16 pieces according to fixed rules across the board and tries to capture or immobilize (checkmate) the opponent's king. The game may have originated in Asia around the 6th cent., and spread into Europe in Byzantine times; its now-standard rules first became generally accepted in the 16th cent. Each opponent, designated black or white, has in his first row a king and queen, two bishops, two knights, and two rooks; in the second row are positioned the pawns. The king moves in any direction, one square at a time. The queen, rook, and bishop can cover all the distance in any direction if not obstructed. The powerful queen has the moves of all the other pieces except the knight. The knight has a peculiar L-shaped movement and may leap over other pieces. The pawn moves only forward. Any piece may capture an enemy piece by landing on its square. In tournament play each player must make a given number of moves

Chess Players begin with their pieces in two rows at opposite ends of the board. Capturing the opponent's king is the object of the game. Each type of playing piece can move in a specific manner. Pawns, the weakest pieces, generally move only straight ahead, one square at a time; they may also move diagonally ahead to capture an opponent's piece, and on reaching the eighth rank may be promoted to any piece except king. Rooks (castles) move only along the ranks or files (side to side, or forward or back), as many spaces as are unoccupied. Knights, the only pieces that can move over an occupied square, make an L-shaped move of two squares in one row and one square in a perpendicular row. (In white's opening move shown here, the knight has moved forward two squares and left one space.) The bishop moves diagonally across any number of unoccupied squares. The powerful queen may move in any direction (along rows or on the diagonal) across any number of unoccupied squares. The king usually may move only one square at a time, in any direction.

in a given period of time. For several decades Russia has produced most of the top players.

Chester *ancient* Deva *or* Devana Castra. City (pop., 1995 est: 120,000), county seat of Cheshire, England. Located on the Dee River south of LIVERPOOL, it is an active port and railroad center. For several centuries after A.D. 60, it was the Roman "camp on the Dee," headquarters of the 20th Legion; Roman walls remain. It was the last place in England to surrender to WILLIAM I the Conqueror (1070). It became an important port in the 13th–14th cent. From about the 14th cent., it was the scene of the presentation of the MYSTERY PLAYS of the Chester Cycle.

Chesterton, G(ilbert) K(eith) (1874–1936) British man of letters. His works of social and literary criticism include *Robert Browning* (1903), *Charles Dickens* (1906), and *The Victorian Age in Literature* (1913). He converted to Roman Catholicism in 1922. His fiction includes *The Napoleon of Notting Hill* (1904), the popular allegorical novel *The Man Who Was Thursday* (1908), and his most successful creation, the series of detective novels featuring the priest-sleuth Father Brown.

chestnut Any of four species of deciduous ornamental and timber trees of the genus *Castanea,* in the BEECH family, native to temperate regions of the Northern Hemisphere, with burrlike fruits that contain two or three edible NUTS. The usually tall trees have furrowed bark and lance-shaped leaves. The majestic American chestnut (*C. dentata*) was almost eliminated by chestnut blight in the early 20th cent. The other three species are the European chestnut (*C. sativa*), the Chinese chestnut (*C. mollissima*), and the Japanese chestnut (*C. crenata*). Their nuts are eaten and exported in large quantities, and varieties of all three are cultivated as ornamentals. The European chestnut produces useful timber as well.

chevalier See KNIGHT

Cheviot Hills \ˈshi-vē-ət\ Range of hills along the England–Scotland border. Extending northeast–southwest by the two countries' boundary, its highest elevation is Cheviot, at 2,676 ft (816 m). Evidence of prehistoric occupation is widespread. Significant areas have become national parks.

chevrotain \ˈshev-rə-ˌtān\ *or* **mouse deer** Any of several species (family Tragulidae) of small, delicately built RUMINANTS of Asia and Africa. Resembling tiny deer, chevrotains stand about 12 in. (30 cm) at the shoulder and seem to walk on their hooftips. Males have small, curved tusks protruding downward from the upper jaw. Shy and solitary, they are active at night. Asiatic chevrotains are found in forests. The water chevrotain of W equatorial Africa inhabits river banks and seeks escape in the water when disturbed.

chewing gum Sweetened product made from chicle or other substances and chewed for its flavor. Tree resins have been chewed as teeth cleaners and breath fresheners since ancient times. The latex of the Central American sapodilla tree (chicle) was first used to mass-produce chewing gum in the 19th cent.; its plasticity, insolubility in water, and ability to hold flavor made it an ideal chewing-gum base. After World War II other gums and synthetic rubbers came to replace chicle.

Cheyenne \shī-ˈan\ City (pop., 2000: 53,000), capital of Wyoming. It is the state's largest city. It became an outfitting point for the BLACK HILLS goldfields to the northeast and a major shipping point for cattle from Texas. Its own grazing lands became famed for their herds and cattle barons. In July it celebrates Frontier Days, which includes one of America's oldest and largest rodeos.

Cheyenne PLAINS INDIAN people who inhabited the regions around the Platte and Arkansas rivers in the 19th cent. Originally farmers, hunters, and gatherers, they became more dependent on buffalo for food after acquiring horses, and they developed a tepee-dwelling, nomadic mode of life. They performed the SUN DANCE and placed heavy emphasis on visions in which an animal spirit adopted the individual and bestowed special powers on him. In the 1870s they participated in various Indian uprisings, joining the SIOUX at LITTLE BIGHORN in 1876. Today there are about 5,000 Cheyenne living in SE Montana and 5,000 Cheyenne-Arapaho in Oklahoma.

Cheyenne River River, N central U.S. Rising in E Wyoming, it flows northeast 527 mi (850 km) to join the MISSOURI RIVER in central S. Dakota. Angostura Dam, part of the Missouri River basin irrigation project, is on the river near Hot Springs, S.D.

Ch'i See QI

ch'i See QI

Chiang Ching-kuo *pinyin* **Jiang Jinguo** \jē-'äŋ-'jiŋ-'gwō\ (1910–1988) Son of CHIANG KAI-SHEK, and his successor as leader of the Republic of China. Elected by the National Assembly to two six-year presidential terms (1978, 1984), he tried to maintain Taiwan's foreign-trade relationships and political independence as other countries established ties with mainland China. Chiang remained opposed to Taiwanese recognition of the Chinese Communist regime and to negotiations for reunification with the mainland.

Chiang Kai-shek \jē-'äŋ-'kī-'shek, *Engl.* chaŋ-kī-'shek\ *pinyin* **Jiang Jieshi** \jē-'äŋ-jē-'esh-'ē\ (1887–1975) Head of the Nationalist government in China (1928–49) and later in Taiwan (1949–75). After military training, in 1918 he joined SUN YAT-SEN, leader of the GUOMINDANG, which was trying to consolidate control over a nation in chaos. Named commander in chief of the revolutionary army (1925), Chiang crushed warlords active in the north (see NORTHERN EXPEDITION). In the 1930s he and WANG JINGWEI vied for control of a new central government with its capital at NANJING. Faced with Japanese

Chiang Kai-shek

aggression in Manchuria and Communist opposition led by MAO ZEDONG in the hinterland, Chiang decided to crush the Communists first. This proved to be a mistake, and Chiang was forced into a temporary alliance with the Communists when war broke out with Japan in 1937. After the war China's civil war resumed, culminating in the Nationalists' flight to Taiwan in 1949, where Chiang ruled, supported by U.S. aid, until his death. His years ruling Taiwan, though dictatorial, oversaw the island's economic development and increasing prosperity. His failure to keep control of mainland China has been attributed to poor morale among his troops and a lack of responsiveness to popular sentiment for deep social and economic changes.

Chian-ning See NANJING

Chiapas \chē-'ä-päs\ State (pop., 2000: 3,920,000), SE Mexico. Bounded by Guatemala and the Pacific Ocean, it covers 28,528 sq mi (73,888 sq km). Its capital is TUXTLA Gutiérrez. Linked with Guatemala in colonial days, Chiapas became a Mexican state in 1824. Inhabited mainly by Indians, Chiapas was the scene of the Zapatista uprising in the 1990s, when impoverished Indians protested the expulsion from their farmlands by large-scale cattle barons. The extraordinary MAYA ruins of PALENQUE are in the NE rain forests.

chiaroscuro \kē-ˌär-ə-'skyu̇r-ō\ (Italian: "light-dark") Contrasting effects of light and shade in a work of art. LEONARDO DA VINCI brought the technique to its full potential, but it is usually associated with such 17th-cent. artists as CARAVAGGIO and REMBRANDT, who used it to outstanding effect.

Chicago City (pop., 2000: 2,896,000), NE Illinois. Located on Lake MICHIGAN, Chicago has extensive port facilities. In the 17th cent. the name was associated with a portage between the Des Plaines and Chicago rivers connecting the ST. LAWRENCE RIVER and the GREAT LAKES with the MISSISSIPPI RIVER. Ft. Dearborn was built in 1803, and the city expanded rapidly after the completion of the Illinois and Michigan Canal (1848), which connected the Chicago and Mississippi rivers, and also became the nation's chief rail center. Rebuilt quickly after a hugely destructive fire in 1871, it was the site of the World's Columbian Exposition in 1893. Birthplace of the steel-frame skyscraper in the late

19th cent., it boasts architecture by Louis SULLIVAN, F. L. WRIGHT, and Ludwig MIES VAN DER ROHE. The first nuclear chain reaction was achieved at the Univ. of CHICAGO in 1942. After World War II the city underwent another building boom. The third-largest U.S. city, it is a major industrial, commercial, and transportation center and is the site of the Chicago Mercantile Exchange, the Chicago Board of Trade, and museums including the Art Institute of Chicago.

Chicago, Judy *orig.* Judy Cohen (b.1939) U.S. multimedia artist. Born in Chicago, she studied at UCLA. Motivated by perceived discrimination in the art world, she developed the concepts of "vaginal iconography" and "central core" imagery. Her most notable work, *The Dinner Party* (1974–79), is a triangular table with place settings for 39 important women represented by ceramic plates with feminine imagery.

Chicago, University of Independent university in Chicago, founded in 1891 with an endowment from John D. ROCKEFELLER. Under Robert M. HUTCHINS (1929–51) it came to be recognized for its broad liberal-arts curriculum. The world's first department of sociology was established there in 1892. In 1942 it was the site of the first controlled self-sustaining nuclear chain reaction, under the direction of Enrico FERMI. Other notable achievements include the development of CARBON-14 DATING and the isolation of PLUTONIUM. Research centers include the Oriental Institute, Yerkes Observatory, the Enrico Fermi Institute, and the Center for Policy Study. The university operates the Argonne National Laboratory. Total enrollment is about 12,000.

Chicago literary renaissance Flourishing of literary activity in Chicago around 1912–25. Its leading writers—Theodore DREISER, Sherwood ANDERSON, E. L. MASTERS, and Carl SANDBURG—realistically depicted city life, condemning the loss of traditional rural values in an increasingly industrialized and materialistic American society. The period also saw The Little Theatre, an outlet for young playwrights; The Little Room, a literary group; magazines including *The Dial*, *Poetry*, and *The Little Review*; and a renewal of journalism as a literary medium.

Chicago Race Riot of 1919 Most severe of about 25 race riots throughout the U.S. in the summer after World War I. Racial friction was intensified by the migration of blacks to the North. In Chicago's South Side, the black population had increased in 10 years from 44,000 to 109,000. The riot was triggered by the stoning death of a black youth swimming in Lake Michigan near a white beach. When police refused to arrest the main suspect, fighting broke out. After 13 days, 38 were dead (23 blacks, 15 whites), 537 injured, and 1,000 black families made homeless.

Chicago school Group of architects and engineers who in the 1890s exploited the twin developments of structural steel framing and the electrified elevator, paving the way for the ubiquitous modern-day skyscraper. Their work earned for Chicago the title "birthplace of modern architecture." Among the school's members were Louis SULLIVAN, Daniel BURNHAM, and John Wellborn Root (1850–1891).

Chichén Itzá \chē-'chen-ēt-'sä\ Ancient ruined Mayan city in Mexico's Yucatán state. Chichén Itzá was founded by MAYAS around the 6th cent. A.D. The city was invaded in the 10th cent.—probably by a Mayan-speaking group under TOLTEC influence—and the invaders constructed another series of buildings, including the famous stepped pyramid known as El Castillo. The site had been largely abandoned when the Spanish arrived in the 16th cent.

chickadee Any of several N. American songbird species in the genus *Parus* (family Paridae), whose name imitates their call notes. They are friendly and easily attracted to feeders. The black-capped chickadee (*P. atricapillus*), is 5 in. (13 cm) long and has a dark cap and bib. Some members of the genus are called tits or titmice.

Chickamauga, Battle of (Sept. 19–20, 1863) Engagement in the AMERICAN CIVIL WAR to control nearby Chattanooga, Tenn. Confederate forces under Benjamin BRAGG and James LONGSTREET attacked Union forces under William ROSECRANS. After two days of fierce battle, most of the

Union army withdrew in disorder, but troops under George THOMAS withstood the assault until he could organize an orderly withdrawal to Chattanooga. Casualties numbering 16,000 Union and 18,000 Confederate troops made this one of the bloodiest battles of the war. The Union prevailed in the subsequent Battle of CHATTANOOGA.

Chickasaw N. American Indian people who formerly inhabited what is now N Mississippi and Alabama. The Chickasaw were a seminomadic people whose dwellings were loosely scattered along rivers rather than clustered in villages. The supreme deity was associated with the sky, sun, and fire. They frequently raided and intermarried with other tribes. In the 1830s they were forcibly removed to Indian Territory (Oklahoma), where today some 20,000 live.

chicken Most widely domesticated poultry species *(Gallus gallus)*, raised worldwide for its meat and eggs. Descended from the wild red jungle fowl of India, chickens have been domesticated for at least 4,000 years. Modern high-volume poultry farms, with rows of cages stacked indoors for control of heat, light, and humidity, began to proliferate in Britain about 1920 and in the U.S. after World War II. Females are raised for meat and eggs; immature males are castrated to become meat birds called capons.

chicken pox or **varicella** \,var-ə-'se-lə\ Contagious VIRAL DISEASE producing itchy blisters. It usually occurs in epidemics among young children, causes a low FEVER, and runs a mild course, leaving patients immune. The virus that causes chicken pox can reactivate years later, causing SHINGLES. Zoster immune globulin (ZIG) can prevent chicken pox in children who are exposed to the virus, and a VACCINE has been developed.

chickpea or **garbanzo** Annual legume *(Cicer arietinum)* widely grown for its nutritious seeds. The bushy 2-ft (60-cm) plants bear pinnate leaves and small white or reddish flowers. The yellow-brown peas are borne one or two to a pod. Chickpeas are an important food plant in India, Africa, and Central and S. America. They are the main ingredient of hummus, a Middle Eastern spread. A kind of meal or flour is also made from chickpeas.

chicory Blue-flowered perennial plant *(Cichorium intybus)* of the COMPOSITE FAMILY. Native to Europe, it was introduced to the U.S. late in the 19th cent. Chicory has a long, fleshy taproot; a rigid, branching, hairy stem; and dandelion-like leaves around the base. Both roots and leaves are edible. The roots are also used as a flavoring in or substitute for coffee.

Ch'ien-lung emperor See QIANLONG EMPEROR

chigger LARVA of some 10,000 MITE species, ranging in length from 0.004 to 0.6 in. (0.1–16 mm). Some are terrestrial; others live in freshwater or salt water. They may be predators, scavengers, or plant feeders, and some are pests of humans. In N. America, the common chigger that attacks humans penetrates clothing and, once attached to the skin, injects a fluid that digests tissue and causes severe itching. After feeding, it drops to the ground and begins to mature.

Chihuahua \chē-'wä-wä\ State (pop., 2000: 3,047,000), N Mexico. The country's largest state, it covers 95,400 sq mi (247,086 sq km) and borders New Mexico and Texas. Its capital is CHIHUAHUA city. It consists largely of an elevated plain sloping toward the RÍO GRANDE. Its W area is broken by the SIERRA MADRE Occidental. Chihuahua's Barranca del Cobre (Copper Canyon) exceeds the GRAND CANYON in scale. The state's chief industries are mining and livestock raising.

Chihuahua Smallest recognized dog breed, named for the Mexican state where it was first noted in the mid-19th cent. It probably derived from the Techichi, a small, mute dog kept by the TOLTECS as long ago as the 9th cent. Typically a feisty-looking, alert dog, sturdier than its small build would suggest, it stands about 5 in. (13 cm) high and weighs 1–6 lbs (0.5–2.7 kg). The coat may be either smooth and glossy or long and soft.

Chihuahua City (pop., 1995: 613,000), capital of CHIHUAHUA state, Mexico. Founded in 1709, it was a prosperous mining center during the colonial era. Now the center of a cattle-raising area, it has many noteworthy buildings, including the superb 18th-cent. Church of San Francisco.

Chikamatsu Monzaemon \chē-'kä-mät-sù-mōn-'zä-ā-mōn\ *orig.* Sugimori Nobumori (1653–1725) Japanese playwright.

He was attached to the Kyoto court before moving to Osaka to be near its bunraku (puppet theater). He wrote over 100 plays, mainly historical romances and domestic tragedies. Most were written for the bunraku, which he raised to artistic heights. His most popular work, *The Battles of Coxinga* (1715), is based on the life of ZHENG CHENGGONG. Also famous is *Double Suicide at Amijima* (1720). He is regarded as the greatest of Japanese dramatists.

Child, Julia *orig.* Julia McWilliams (b.1912) U.S. chef. Born in Pasadena, Cal., she lived in Paris after her marriage in 1945, studying at the Cordon Bleu school of cooking. After cowriting *Mastering the Art of French Cooking* (1961) and moving to Boston, she created the popular PBS cooking series *The French Chef* (1962–73), and later other cooking shows. Through her programs and books, she helped the U.S. public learn to appreciate fine food and wine.

Child, Lydia Maria *orig.* Lydia Maria Francis (1802–1880) U.S. abolitionist. Born in Medford, Mass., she wrote historical novels and a popular manual, *The Frugal Housewife* (1829), and founded the first children's periodical, *Juvenile Miscellany*. After meeting W. L. GARRISON in 1831, she became active in abolitionist work. Her *Appeal in Favor of That Class of Americans Called Africans* (1833) induced many to join the abolitionist cause. She later edited the *National Anti-Slavery Standard* (1841–43).

child abuse Crime of inflicting physical or emotional injury on a child. The term can denote the use of inordinate physical violence or verbal abuse; the failure to furnish proper shelter, nourishment, medical treatment, or emotional support; incest, RAPE, or other instances of sexual molestation; and the making of child PORNOGRAPHY. It can have serious consequences for the victim and is a widespread but underreported phenomenon. At least 500,000 children are physically abused in the U.S. each year; many more are emotionally abused and neglected. In many cases, the abuser suffered abuse as a child.

childbed fever See PUERPERAL FEVER

childbirth See PARTURITION

childhood diseases Illnesses that strike primarily during childhood, including CHICKEN POX, MEASLES, MUMPS, and RUBELLA, and impart long-term IMMUNITY to survivors. They remain a leading cause of mortality in developing countries. Respiratory diseases of childhood include CROUP, WHOOPING COUGH, and RESPIRATORY DISTRESS SYNDROME. See also CONGENITAL DISORDER, PEDIATRICS.

child psychology Study of the psychological processes of children. Data are gathered through observation, interviews, tests, and experimental methods. Principal topics include language acquisition and development, motor skills, personality development, and social, emotional, and intellectual growth. Its major theorists include G. Stanley HALL, Anna FREUD, and Melanie KLEIN, but its most influential figure was Jean PIAGET, who described the various stages of childhood learning and characterized the child's perception of him- or herself and the world at each stage. See also DEVELOPMENTAL PSYCHOLOGY.

Children's Crusade (1212) Religious movement in Europe in which thousands, including many children and young people, set out to take the Holy Land from the Muslims by love instead of by force. According to one version of the events, only partially accurate, the first group of about 30,000 was led by a French shepherd boy who had seen a vision of Jesus; at Marseille they were shipped to slave markets in N. Africa. A German boy led the second group across the Alps; a few survived to reach Rome, where INNOCENT III released them from their vows. Though the movement ended in disaster, it excited religious fervor that helped initiate the Fifth CRUSADE (1217–21).

Childress \'chil-drəs\, **Alice** (1916–1994) U.S. writer. She grew up in Harlem and studied drama with the American Negro Theatre, where she wrote, directed, and starred in her first play, *Florence* (produced 1949). Other plays, some featuring music, include *Trouble in Mind* (produced 1955), *String* (1969), and *Gullah* (1984). Her children's books include *A Hero Ain't Nothing But a Sandwich* (1973).

Chile \'chē-lā, *Engl* 'chi-lē\ *officially* **Republic of Chile** Country, SW S. America, bounded by Peru, Bolivia, Argentina, the DRAKE PASSAGE, and the Pacific Ocean. Area:

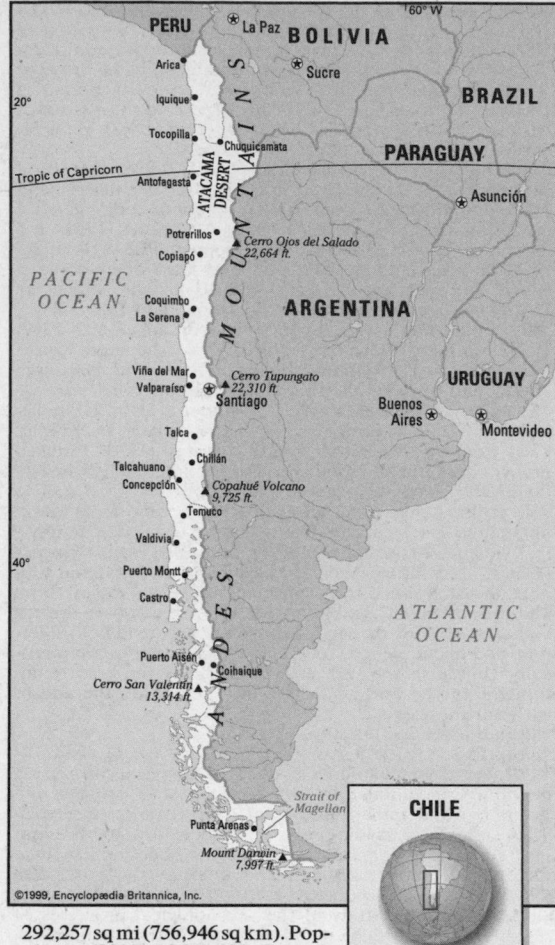

©1999, Encyclopædia Britannica, Inc.

CHILE

Scale 1: 37,206,000

0   150   300 mi

0   200   400 km

292,257 sq mi (756,946 sq km). Population (2000): 15,211,000. Capital: SANTIAGO. The indigenous peoples before Spanish colonization included the Diaguita, Picunche, Mapuche, ARAUCANIANS, Huilliche, Pehunche, and Cunco Indians. Spanish colonists arrived during the 16th–17th cent., followed by BASQUES in the 18th cent. A relatively homogeneous, primarily mestizo population has developed. Language: Spanish (official). Religion: Roman Catholicism. Currency: Chilean peso. Chile is a long narrow country lying between the ANDES and the Pacific Ocean. From north to south, it is 2,650 mi (4,265 km) long, and nowhere more than 221 mi (356 km) wide. The north has an arid plateau, the Atacama Desert, and contains several peaks above 1,900 ft (5,790 m), but most of the highest peaks are on the boundaries with Bolivia and Argentina. Its rivers, including the Bío-Bío, are limited in size. There are many lakes, including the Llanquihue. The extreme S coast is marked by many inlets, islands, and archipelagos; the W half of TIERRA DEL FUEGO and the island on which Cape HORN is located are Chilean, as are small JUAN FERNÁNDEZ ISLANDS and EASTER ISLAND. Chile has a partially developed free-market economy based mainly on mining and manufacturing. It is a republic with two legislative houses; its head of state and government is the president. Originally inhabited by native peoples, the area was invaded by the Spanish in 1536. A settlement begun at Santiago in 1541 was governed under the viceroyalty of PERU, but became a separate captaincy general in 1778. It revolted against Spanish rule in 1810; its independence was finally assured by the victory of José de SAN MARTÍN in 1818, and the area was then governed by Bernardo O'HIGGINS to 1823. In the War of the PACIFIC against Peru and Bolivia, it won the rich nitrate fields on the coast of Bolivia, effectively forcing that country into a landlocked position. Chile remained neutral in World War I; it entered World War II on the side of the Axis, but severed ties with them in 1943. In 1970 Salvador ALLENDE was elected president, becoming the first avowed Marxist to be elected chief of state in Latin America. Following economic upheaval, he was ousted in 1973 in a coup led by Augusto PINOCHET, who harshly suppressed all internal opposition. A national referendum led to elections in 1989 which returned the country to civilian rule.

Chimborazo \ˌchēm-bō-ˈrä-zō\ Mountain peak, Ecuador. The highest peak in the Andean Cordillera Real, at 20,561 ft (6,267 m), it is an active volcano and heavily glaciated. Despite many attempts, the summit was not reached until 1880, by the Briton Edward Whymper (1840–1911).

Chimera \kī-ˈmir-ə\ In GREEK MYTHOLOGY, a fire-breathing female monster, eventually killed by BELLEROPHON. Its foreparts resembled a lion, its middle a goat, and its hindquarters a dragon. The word now often denotes a fantasy or a figment of the imagination.

chimera *or* **chimaera** \kī-ˈmir-ə\ Any of the 28 species of cartilaginous fishes constituting the subclass Holocephali (class Chondrichthyes), found in temperate to cold waters of all oceans. Like SHARKS and RAYS, chimeras have a cartilaginous skeleton, and the males possess external reproductive organs (claspers). Males have a supplemental clasping organ that is unique among fishes. Chimeras have large pectoral and pelvic fins and two dorsal fins, the first preceded by a sharp spine. They range in length from 24 to 80 in. (60–200 cm). They inhabit rivers, estuaries, coastal waters, and open ocean to depths of 8,000 ft (2,500 m) or more. Their liver oil provides a lubricant for guns and fine instruments.

chimpanzee Species (*Pan troglodytes*) of great APE that inhabits the rain forests and woodland savannas of equatorial Africa, the closest living relative to humans. Chimps are 3–5.5 ft (1–1.7 m) tall when standing upright, weigh 55–130 lbs (35–60 kg), and have a brown or black coat and a bare face. They do most of their feeding in the trees, swinging from branch to branch; to move any distance they walk, usually on all fours, on the ground. They are capable of problem solving and can use tools. Chimpanzees are social and live in flexible groups (15–80 members). In captivity they may live up to 50 years. See also BONOBO.

China *officially* **People's Republic of China** *formerly* (*until 1912*) **Chinese Empire** Republic, E Asia. Area: 3,700,000 sq mi (9,583,000 sq km). Population (2000): 1,265,207,000. Capital: BEIJING. The Han, or ethnic Chinese, form more than nine-tenths of the population. Languages: dialects of Han Chinese, most importantly MANDARIN. Religions: Buddhism, Islam, Christianity, Taoism (all legally sanctioned). Currency: renminbi (of which the unit is the yuan). China has several topographic regions. The SW area contains the Plateau of Tibet, which averages over 13,000 ft (4,100 m) above sea level; its central area, averaging more than 16,000 ft (5,000 m), is called "the Roof of the World." Higher yet are the border ranges, the KUNLUN MTNS. to the north and the HIMALAYAS to the south. China's NW region stretches from Afghanistan to the NE Manchurian Plain. The mountains of the TIAN SHAN separate China's two major interior basins, the Tarim Basin (containing the TAKLIMAKAN desert) and the Dzungarian Basin. The Mongolian Plateau contains the southernmost part of the GOBI DESERT. The lowlands of the E region include the Sichuan Basin, which runs along the CHANG (YANGTZE) RIVER. The E region is separated into two parts by the divide between the HUANG (Yellow) and Chang rivers. The Tarim is the major river in the northwest. China's smallest watershed, in the southwest, provides headwaters for the BRAHMAPUTRA, SALWEEN, and IRRAWADDY rivers. Its many other rivers include the XI, AMUR, Songhua, and MEKONG. The discovery of Peking man in 1927 (see ZHOUKOUDIAN) dates the advent of early hominids to the PALEOLITHIC PERIOD. Chinese civilization probably spread from the Huang River valley where it existed around 3000 B.C. The first dynasty for which there is definite historical material is the SHANG (c.17th cent. B.C.);

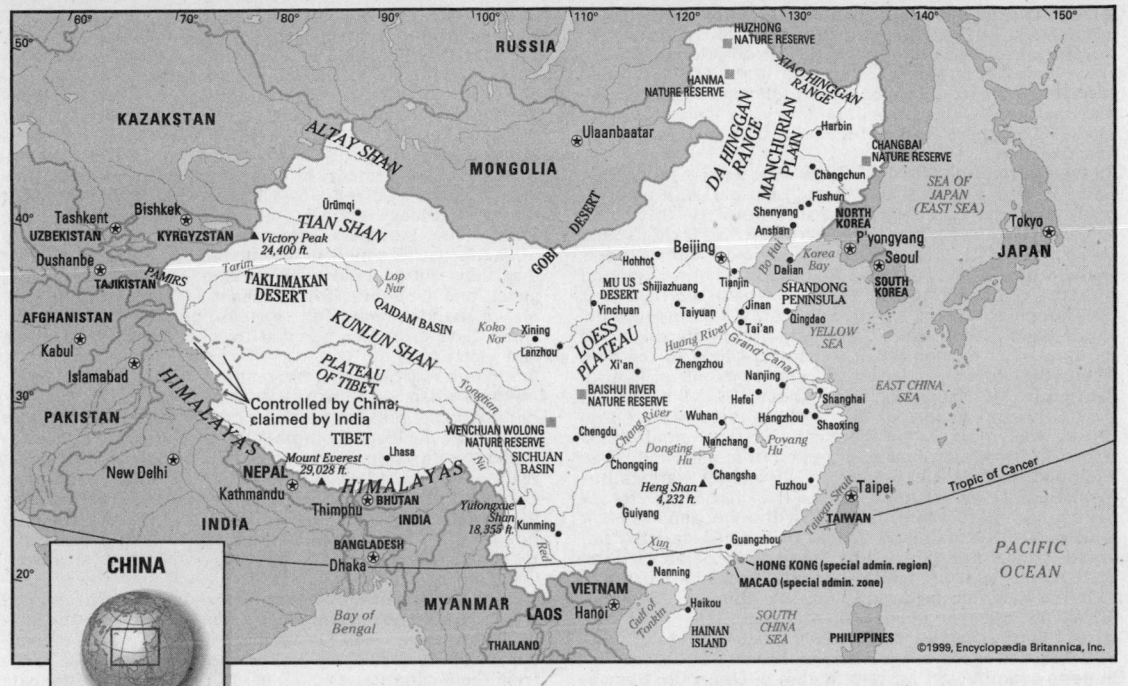

CHINA

Scale 1: 49,053,000

0   200   400 mi

0   300   600 km

©1999, Encyclopædia Britannica, Inc.

it had a writing system and a calendar. A subject people of the Shang defeated them in the 11th cent. B.C. and ruled as the ZHOU DYNASTY until the 3rd cent. B.C. TAOISM and CONFUCIANISM were founded in this era. The area was beset by warring states until in 221 B.C. the QIN (CH'IN) DYNASTY (from whose name China is derived) was established. The HAN DYNASTY assumed the throne in 206 B.C. and ruled until A.D. 220. A time of turbulence followed, and Chinese reunification wasn't achieved until the SUI DYNASTY came to power in 581. The SONG DYNASTY assumed power in 960 and moved its capital to the south because of N invasions. In 1279 they were displaced when Mongol (YUAN DYNASTY) domination began. During this time, Marco POLO visited KUBLAI KHAN. The MING DYNASTY succeeded the Mongols and ruled from 1368 to 1644, cultivating antiforeign feelings to the point that China closed itself off from the rest of the world. Tribes from MANCHURIA overran China in 1644 and established the QING (MANCHU) DYNASTY. Ever-increasing incursions by foreign interests led in the 19th cent. to the OPIUM WARS, the TAIPING REBELLION, and the SINO–JAPANESE WAR, all of which weakened the Manchus. The dynasty fell in 1911 and a republic was proclaimed in 1912 by SUN YAT-SEN. Warlords soon left the republic in shreds. Under Sun's successor, CHIANG KAI-SHEK, some national unification was achieved in the 1920s, but Chiang soon broke with the Communists, who then formed their own armies. Japan invaded N China in 1937; its occupation lasted until 1945 (see MANCHUGUO). The Communists gained support after the LONG MARCH (1934–35), in which MAO ZEDONG emerged as their leader. Upon Japan's surrender at the end of World War II, a fierce civil war began; in 1949 the Nationalists fled to Taiwan and the Communists proclaimed the People's Republic of China. They undertook extensive reforms, but pragmatic policies alternated with periods of revolutionary upheaval, most notably in the GREAT LEAP FORWARD and the CULTURAL REVOLUTION. The chaos of the latter led, after Mao's death in 1976, to a turn to moderation under DENG XIAOPING, who undertook economic reforms and renewed China's ties to the West. It established diplomatic ties with the U.S. in 1979. It suppressed the TIANANMEN SQUARE student demonstration in 1989. The economy has been in transition since the late 1970s as it moved from central planning and state-run industries to a mixture of state-owned and private enterprises in manufacturing and services. The death of Deng in 1997 marked the end of a political era, but power passed peacefully to JIANG ZEMIN. In 1997 HONG KONG reverted to Chinese rule, as did MACAO in 1999. In 2002 China became a full member of the World Trade Organization.

China Sea Part of the Pacific Ocean. Reaching from Japan to the MALAY PENINSULA, it is divided by Taiwan into two sections. The N section is the E. China Sea, which covers 482,300 sq mi (1,249,157 sq km), has a maximum depth of 9,126 ft (2,782 m), and is enclosed by China, S. Korea, and Japan's RYUKYU ISLANDS. The S section is the S. China Sea, which covers 895,400 sq mi (2,319,086 sq km), has a maximum depth of about 15,000 ft (4,600 m), and is enclosed by China, Indochina, the Malay Peninsula, Borneo, and the Philippines.

chinchilla \chin-'chi-lə\ Small S. American RODENT (genus *Chinchilla*, family Chinchillidae) long valued for its extremely fine-textured fur. Chinchillas look like long-tailed, small-eared rabbits. They are about 14 in. (35 cm) long, including the tufted tail. The soft fur is gray with dusky overtones; a black streak runs the length of the tail, above and below. Chinchillas live in loose communities in arid, rocky regions of the Chilean and Bolivian Andes, in burrows or rock crevices. Once hunted almost to extinction, they are still scarce in the wild. They are raised commercially.

Ch'in dynasty See QIN DYNASTY

Chin dynasty See JIN DYNASTY, JUCHEN DYNASTY

Chinese architecture Building styles and methods of China. Though masonry was used for tombs, PAGODAS, and defensive walls (see GREAT WALL), traditional construction is chiefly in timber, and little from ancient times has survived. The basic elements in a Chinese timber building are its platform of stone or tile, post-and-beam frame, system of often elaborate roof-supporting brackets, and heavy tiled roof. Beams are used as tensile elements to define the distinctive curving GABLE shape of the overhanging roof with upturned eaves. Flexibility in overall design is achieved by using multiples of a basic rectilinear unit; these are arranged along a central axis with open, connecting GALLERIES around courtyards. The traditional building system is hierarchical, modular, and highly standardized.

Chinese cabbage Either of two widely cultivated members of the MUSTARD FAMILY, BOK CHOY and *Brassica pekinensis*. The latter vegetable forms a tight head of crinkled light green leaves. It has long been grown in the U.S. as a salad vegetable. All Chinese cabbages are delicate and crisp, qualities that enable them to combine with a wide variety of foods. Kimchi, the Korean pickle, is often made with Chinese cabbage.

Chinese Communist Party (CCP) Political party founded in China in 1921 by CHEN DUXIU and LI DAZHAO. It grew directly from the reform-oriented MAY FOURTH MOVEMENT and was aided by Russian organizers. The CCP held its First Congress in 1921; the Russians also invited many members to the Soviet Union for study and encouraged cooperation with the Chinese Nationalists (see GUOMINDANG). When the Communists were expelled in 1927, CCP fortunes declined rapidly after several failed attempts at uprisings, and the remaining members fled to central China to regroup, where they formed a soviet-style government in Jiangxi. Harried by the Nationalist army under CHIANG KAI-SHEK, the CCP forces undertook the LONG MARCH to N central China, when MAO ZEDONG became the party's undisputed leader. War with the Japanese broke out in 1937 and led to a temporary alliance between the CCP and the Nationalists. In 1947 civil war resumed; the CCP increased its already strong rural base through land redistribution, and in 1949 it took control of mainland China. In the decades that followed, radical moderates led by Mao and moderates led initially by LIU SHAOQI vied for control. After Mao's death in 1976 the party moved steadily toward economic, if not political, liberalization. Today the division of power is constantly shifting among the Politburo, the Politburo's Standing Committee, and the Secretariat. See also LIN BIAO.

Chinese examination system System of competitive examinations for recruiting officials that dominated education from the SONG DYNASTY (960–1279) onward. Candidates faced fierce competition in a series of exams dealing primarily with Confucian texts (see FOUR BOOKS) and conducted on the prefectural, provincial, and national levels. Despite a persistent tendency to emphasize rote learning over original thinking, the exams produced an elite grounded in a common body of teachings and lent credibility to claims of meritocracy. Too inflexible to be capable of modernization, the system was finally abolished in 1905.

Chinese languages *or* **Sinitic languages** Family of languages comprising one of the two branches of SINO-TIBETAN, spoken by about 95% of the inhabitants of China. Linguists regard the major dialect groups of Chinese as distinct languages, though because all Chinese write with a common system of characters (see CHINESE WRITING SYSTEM), traditionally all varieties of Chinese are regarded as dialects. There is a primary division in Chinese languages between the Mandarin dialects—spoken north of the Chang (Yangtze) River and west of Hunan and Guangdong—and a number of other dialect groups concentrated in SE China. Far more people—over 885 million—speak a variety of Mandarin as a first language than any other language in the world. The N Mandarin dialect of Beijing is the basis for Modern Standard Chinese, a spoken norm that serves as a LINGUA FRANCA. Important dialect groups other than Mandarin are Wu, Gan, Xiang, Min, Yue (including Cantonese), and Kejia. The modern Chinese languages are TONE languages, the number of tones varying from four in Modern Standard Chinese to nine in dialects.

Chinese medicine, traditional System of medicine at least 23 centuries old that aims to prevent or heal disease by maintaining or restoring YIN–YANG balance. Detailed questions are asked about a patient's illness and such things as taste, smell, and dreams, but close examination of the pulse, at different sites and times and with varying pressure, is paramount. Of Chinese medicine's numerous remedies, Western medicine has adopted many, including iron (for anemia) and chaulmoogra oil (for leprosy). Chinese medicine used inoculation for smallpox long before Western medicine. Other practices include HYDROTHERAPY, ACUPUNCTURE, and ACUPRESSURE.

Chinese mustard See BOK CHOY

Chinese Nationalists See GUOMINDANG

Chinese New Year See NEW YEAR'S DAY

Chinese writing system System of symbols used to write CHINESE LANGUAGES. Chinese writing is fundamentally logographic: there is an exact correspondence between a single character in the script and a single word or MORPHEME. Each character, no matter how complex, is about the same size. The Chinese script is first found in inscriptions on bone or tortoise shells dating from the SHANG DYNASTY. Shared elements of characters, called radicals, provide a means of classifying Chinese writing. It is thought that an ordinary literate Chinese person can recognize 3,000–4,000 characters. Efforts have been made to reduce in number and simplify the characters, though the fact that they can be read by a speaker of any Chinese language and their link with China's 3,000-year-old culture makes abandonment of the system unlikely. Chinese characters have also been adapted to write Japanese, Korean, and Vietnamese.

Ch'ing dynasty See QING DYNASTY

Chinggis Khan See GENGHIS KHAN

Chinook \shə-ˈnük\ NORTHWEST COAST INDIAN people who lived along the lower Columbia River. They were famous as traders, with connections stretching as far as the Great Plains. They traded dried salmon, canoes, shells, and slaves. Chinook religion focused on salmon rites and guardian spirits, and the POTLATCH was an important social ceremony. Following a smallpox epidemic in the early 19th cent., the remaining Chinook were absorbed into other Northwest Coast groups.

chinook salmon *or* **king salmon** Prized N. Pacific food and sport fish (*Oncorhynchus tshawytscha*) of the SALMON family. The average weight is about 22 lbs (10 kg), but individuals of 50–80 lbs (22–36 kg) are not unusual. They range from the Yukon River to China. In the spring, adults swim as far as 2,000 mi (3,200 km) up the Yukon to spawn and then die. Young salmon enter the sea at one to three years old. They were successfully introduced into Lake Michigan after the virtual elimination of lake trout by sea lampreys.

Ch'in tomb See QIN TOMB

Chios \ˈkī-ˌäs\ *or* **Khíos** \ˈkē- òs\ Island (pop., 1991: 53,000), AEGEAN SEA. Lying 5 mi (8 km) west of Turkey, it constitutes, with some adjacent islands, a department of Greece. Of volcanic origin, it has an area of 325 sq mi (842 sq km). It was noted in antiquity as HOMER's birthplace and the home of a school of sculptors. Though a member of the DELIAN LEAGUE, it revolted several times against Athens. It prospered successively under Rome, VENICE, GENOA, and the Ottoman empire; it passed to Greece after the BALKAN WARS (1912–13).

chip, computer See COMPUTER CHIP, INTEGRATED CIRCUIT

chipmunk Any of 17 species of terrestrial RODENTS in the SQUIRREL family. The eastern chipmunk (*Tamias striatus*), found in E N. America, is 5.5–7.5 in. (14–19 cm) long, excluding a bushy, 3–4-in. (8–10-cm) tail. It is reddish brown with black, brown, and white stripes. The other, smaller species (all in the genus *Eutamia*) are found in W N. America and Central and E Asia. Chipmunks are active burrow dwellers that eat seeds, berries, tender plants, and sometimes flesh. They store seeds underground. Their call is a shrill chirring or chipping sound.

Chippendale, Thomas (1718–1779) English cabinetmaker. Little is known of his life before 1753, when he opened a workshop in London. In 1754 he published *The Gentleman and Cabinet-Maker's Director*, a popular collection of designs illustrating almost every type of domestic furniture. The designs were mostly his improvements on already existing styles. Though much 18th-cent. furniture is attributed to him, few of the attributions are certain.

Chippewa See OJIBWA

Chirac \shē-ˈràk\, **Jacques (René)** (b.1932) President of France (from 1995). In 1967 he was elected to the National Assembly as a Gaullist. He was prime minister 1974–76 then formed a neo-Gaullist Party, Rally for the Republic. As mayor of Paris (1977–95), he continued to build a conservative political base. His campaign for the presidency in 1981 split the conservative vote and allowed François MITTERRAND to win. Mitterrand later appointed Chirac prime minister (1986–88) in an unusual power-sharing arrangement.

Though defeated again in 1988, Chirac won the presidency in 1995.

Chirico \'kē-rē-ˌkō\, **Giorgio de** (1888–1978) Italian (Greek-born) painter. He studied art in Munich and began painting images juxtaposing the fantastic with the commonplace. He moved to Paris in 1911, where he produced ominous scenes of deserted piazzas with classical statues, isolated figures, and oppressive architecture. The element of mystery in his work exerted a great influence on SURREALISM.

Chiron \'kī-ˌrän\ In GREEK MYTHOLOGY, one of the CENTAURS. He lived at the foot of Mt. Pelion in Thessaly and was renowned for his wisdom and medical knowledge. He was the teacher of such heroes as ACHILLES, HERACLES, JASON, and ASCLEPIUS. Accidentally killed by Heracles, he was placed among the stars by Zeus as the constellation Sagittarius.

chiropody See PODIATRY

chiropractic \ˌkī-rə-ˌprak-tik\ System of healing based on the theory that disease results from lack of normal nerve function, often caused by displaced vertebrae putting pressure on nerve roots. Treatment involves manipulations of body structures, primarily the VERTEBRAL COLUMN, and use of other techniques when necessary. The chiropractic method was propounded by Daniel David Palmer (1845–1913). Practitioners are trained at accredited chiropractic colleges.

Chisholm, Shirley *orig.* Shirley Anita St. Hill (b.1924) U.S. politician. Born in Brooklyn, N.Y., she was a schoolteacher before becoming active in local politics. In 1968 she became the first black woman to be elected to the U.S. Congress, where she served until 1983, becoming known as a strong liberal who opposed the Vietnam War and favored full-employment proposals. She cofounded the National Women's Political Caucus and ran for president in 1972.

Chisholm Trail \'chiz-əm\ 19th-cent. route for cattle drives from Texas to Kansas, probably named for the trader Jesse Chisholm (1806?–1868?). The trail ran from south of San Antonio across Oklahoma to Abilene, Kan., where a railhead was established in 1867. Cattle were driven north over the trail to be shipped to markets in the East. After the 1880s the trail's importance declined as other railheads were established.

Chisinau \ˌkē-shē-'nau\ *formerly* (1812–1918, 1940–91) **Kishinev** \'ki-shi-ˌnef\ City (pop., 1996 est.: 655,000), capital of Moldova. Ruled by Moldavia in the 15th cent. and taken by the Ottoman Turks in the 16th cent., it was ceded to Russia in 1812 and controlled by Romania from 1918. It was ceded back to the Soviet Union in 1940 and became the capital of the Moldavian S.S.R. The city is a commercial center.

Chittagong \'chi-tə-ˌgäŋ\ City (pop., 1991: 1,599,000; metro. area pop.: 2,040,000), chief Indian Ocean port, Bangladesh. It is the country's second most important industrial city. Known to Arab sailors by the 10th cent. A.D., it was conquered by Muslims in the 14th cent. and occupied by the governor of BENGAL in the 17th cent. It was ceded to the British E. INDIA CO. in 1760. Damaged in the conflict between India and Pakistan in 1971, its port facilities have been rebuilt.

chivalry \'shi-vəl-rē\ Knightly class of feudal Europe, and especially the gallantry and honor expected of medieval knights. The ideal of courteous knightly conduct developed in the 12th–13th cent. It arose out of feudal obligation (see FEUDALISM) and stressed loyalty and obeisance by a knight to his God, his lord, and his lady. Chivalry was greatly strengthened by the CRUSADES, which led to the founding of the earliest orders of chivalry, the KNIGHTS OF MALTA and the TEMPLARS. In addition to loyalty and honor, the chivalric virtues included valor, piety, courtesy, and chastity. Questions of love and honor were combined in the ethos of COURTLY LOVE. In the 14th–15th cent., chivalry came to be associated increasingly with aristocratic display and public ceremony, particularly in JOUSTING tournaments, rather than with service in the field.

chive Small, hardy perennial plant (*Allium schoenoprasum*) related to the ONION that grows in clumps. Dense, attractive, spherical umbels of bluish or lilac flowers rise above the foliage. Chive leaves may be cut off at ground level and used for seasoning foods.

Chivington Massacre See SAND CREEK MASSACRE

chlamydia \klə-'mi-dē-ə\ Any of the gram-negative (see GRAM STAIN) bacterial parasites of the genus *Chlamydia,* which cause several diseases in humans, including (particularly in newborns) CONJUNCTIVITIS and chlamydial PNEUMONIA. One form causes a variety of sexually transmitted diseases. In men, symptoms are similar to those of GONORRHEA. In women, chlamydial infection ordinarily produces few if any symptoms; however, untreated infections can lead to serious complications. In the 1990s chlamydia was discovered to be the most common sexually transmitted disease in the U.S. The preferred treatment is TETRACYCLINE; other antibiotics are also effective.

Chlamydomonas \ˌkla-mə-'dä-mə-nəs\ Genus of single-celled green ALGAE considered to be primitive life-forms of evolutionary significance. The cell has a spherical cellulose MEMBRANE, an eyespot, and a CHLOROPLAST. Though capable of PHOTOSYNTHESIS, *Chlamydomonas* may also absorb nutrients through the cell surface. It is found in soil, ponds, and ditches polluted by manure. It may color water green. A red-pigmented species turns melting snow red.

chlorella \klə-'re-lə\ Any green ALGAE of the genus *Chlorella,* found in fresh or salt water and in soil. They have a cup-shaped CHLOROPLAST. Because they multiply rapidly and are rich in proteins and in B-complex vitamins, they have been studied as a potential food product for humans both on earth and in space. Chlorella farms, closed systems that provide humans with food, water, and oxygen, have been established in several countries.

chlorine Nonmetallic chemical ELEMENT, chemical symbol Cl, atomic number 17. It is a toxic, corrosive, greenish-yellow GAS. It severely irritates the eyes and respiratory system (and therefore was used as a CHEMICAL-WARFARE agent in World War I). Its best-known VALENCE is 1, as the chloride ION, but it has other valences in hypochlorites, chlorites, chlorates, and perchlorates. Chlorine and its compounds are important industrial materials with myriad uses in the manufacture of other chlorinated compounds, in water purification, in textile industries, in flame retardants, in special BATTERIES, and in food processing. SODIUM CHLORIDE is the most familiar of its compounds. See also BLEACH, HALOGEN.

chlorofluorocarbon (CFC) Any of several organic compounds containing CARBON, FLUORINE, CHLORINE, and HYDROGEN. CFCs are one class of FREONS. Developed in the 1930s, CFCs were widely used because they are non-toxic, nonflammable, and readily evaporated and condensed. However, CFCs released into the atmosphere rise into the stratosphere, where solar radiation breaks them down; the chlorine released reacts with OZONE, depleting the OZONE LAYER. In 1992 most developed countries agreed to end CFC production.

chloroform Clear, colorless, heavy, nonflammable liquid organic compound with a pleasant odor. It was the first substance successfully used as a surgical ANESTHETIC (1847); being somewhat toxic, it has been increasingly displaced by other substances for this purpose. It has some industrial uses, primarily as a solvent.

chlorophyll Any member of one of the most important classes of PIGMENT molecules involved in PHOTOSYNTHESIS. Found in almost all photosynthetic organisms, it consists of a central magnesium atom surrounded by a nitrogen-containing structure called a porphyrin ring, to which is attached a long carbon-hydrogen side chain, known as a phytol chain. Chlorophyll uses energy that it absorbs from light to convert carbon dioxide to carbohydrates. In higher plants it is found in CHLOROPLASTS.

chloroplast Microscopic, ellipsoidal organelle in a green plant cell. It is the site of PHOTOSYNTHESIS. It is distinguished by its green color, caused by the presence of CHLOROPHYLL. It contains disk-shaped structures called thylakoids that make possible the formation of ATP, an energy-rich storage compound. See diagram on next page.

chocolate Food prepared from ground roasted CACAO beans. It is consumed as CANDY, used to make beverages, and added as a flavoring to other foods. It was introduced in Europe by Hernán CORTÉS following his visit to the New World, where he was served a bitter cacao-bean drink. To

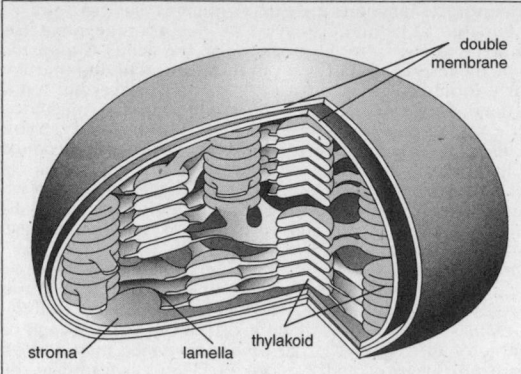

double
membrane

stroma   lamella   thylakoid

Chloroplast The interior contains flattened sacs of photosynthetic membranes (thylakoids) formed by the invagination and fusion of the inner membrane. Thylakoids are usually arranged in stacks (grana) and contain the photosynthetic pigment (chlorophyll). The grana are connected to other stacks by simple membranes (lamellae) within the stroma, the fluid proteinaceous portion containing the enzymes essential for the photosynthetic dark reaction or Calvin cycle.

make chocolate, the kernels of fermented and roasted cacao beans are ground into a paste called chocolate liquor, which may be hardened in molds to form baking (bitter) chocolate. Reducing the cocoa-butter (vegetable-fat) content yields cocoa powder; mixing this with sugar and additional cocoa butter yields sweet (eating) chocolate. The addition of concentrated milk to sweet chocolate produces milk chocolate; white chocolate contains nothing of the cacao except the cocoa butter. Rich in CARBOHYDRATES and FAT and containing small amounts of CAFFEINE, chocolate is an excellent source of quick energy.

Choctaw N. American Indian people that lived in what is now SE Mississippi. The Choctaw were the most skillful of the SE farmers, usually having surplus produce to sell or trade. They fished, gathered nuts and wild fruits, hunted deer and bear, and planted corn, beans, and pumpkins. Their principal religious ceremony was the midsummer Busk (Green Corn) festival. In the 19th cent., pressure by white cotton-growers resulted in 5 million acres being ceded and most Choctaws being removed to Oklahoma. Today Choctaw descendants number about 17,000.

choir Body of singers with more than one voice to a part. For many centuries, church choirs sang only plainsong (see GREGORIAN CHANT). The complexity of early polyphony required solo voices rather than choral performance, but by the 15th cent. polyphony was being performed chorally. The growth of the secular choir (or chorus) coincided with the beginnings of OPERA, which has generally called for professional choruses.

Choiseul \shwä-'zəl\, **Étienne-François, duc (Duke) de** (1719–1785) French foreign minister. After serving as ambassador to the Vatican and Austria, he was named minister of foreign affairs (1758) and soon came to dominate the government of LOUIS XV. In 1761 he concluded a military alliance with Spain (the "Family Compact"), and at the end of the Seven Years' War he negotiated the best terms for a defeated France. He rebuilt France's military strength, but was dismissed in 1770 for advocating war against Britain.

cholera \'kä-lə-rə\ Acute BACTERIAL DISEASE caused by *Vibrio cholerae*, with massive DIARRHEA and severe depletion of body fluids and salts. It often occurs in epidemics, spreading in contaminated water or food. The bacteria secrete a toxin that causes the diarrhea, which along with vomiting leads to DEHYDRATION, with severe muscle cramps and intense thirst. Stupor and coma may precede death by SHOCK. With fluid and salt replacement, the disease passes in two to seven days.

cholesterol Waxy organic compound found in BLOOD and all animal tissues. It is a STEROID, with a four-ringed structure. Cholesterol is essential to life; it is a primary component of cell membranes and a starting or intermediate material from which the body makes BILE acids, other steroid HORMONES, and VITAMIN D. It circulates in the blood in compounds called LIPOPROTEINS, since it is not water-soluble alone. Excess cholesterol in the blood forms deposits in arteries (see ARTERIOSCLEROSIS), which can lead to CORONARY HEART DISEASE. Since the body makes cholesterol from FATS, blood cholesterol cannot be reduced by limiting only the amount of cholesterol in the diet; the amount of fat, especially saturated fat (see SATURATION, FATTY ACID) must also be reduced. See also TRIGLYCERIDE.

choline \'kō-,lēn\ Organic compound, important in METABOLISM as a component of the LIPIDS that make up cell MEMBRANES. It is also important as a source of chemical raw materials for CELLS and in transport of FATS from the LIVER. It is usually classified with the B vitamins (see VITAMIN B COMPLEX) because it resembles them in function and in its distribution in foods. In humans it is interconvertible with certain other compounds, so deficiency does not lead to disease. Choline has various uses in medicine, nutrition, and the processing of foods and feeds.

cholla \'chȯi-yə\ Any CACTUS of the genus *Opuntia*, native to N. and S. America, having needlelike spines partly enclosed in a papery sheath. Chollas vary greatly in size and have small flowers, usually of striking colors. *O. leptocaulis*, the desert Christmas cactus, bears bright red fruits through the winter. Cholla wood, a hollow cylinder with regularly spaced holes, is used for fuel and novelties. Some cholla fruit is edible.

Chomsky, (Avram) Noam (b.1928) U.S. linguist and political activist. Born in Philadelphia, he received his PhD from the Univ. of Pennsylvania. He joined the faculty at MIT in 1955. Through a long series of books and articles beginning with *Syntactic Structures* (1957), Chomsky has gradually developed a theory of universal grammar that would account for all language-specific rules. His work has had two decisive effects. One was to focus new emphasis on SYNTAX. The other was to make theories of language independent of any particular language, so that linguists could develop models of syntax or PHONOLOGY and test them against real-language "facts," rather than generalize from a collection of data. Chomsky has also made a long career of protest against U.S. government foreign policy, from the Vietnam War in the 1960s to the conflict in Afghanistan in 2001, expounding his views in many books and articles.

Ch'ondogyo \'chən-'dȯ-'gyō\ (Korean: "Religion of the Heavenly Way") Korean religion combining elements of Confucianism, Buddhism, Taoism, shamanism, and Roman Catholicism. It espoused equality before Heaven, under its basic principle that "Man and God are one." It was established (as Tonghak) by Ch'oe Che'u (1824–1864) in 1860, but his efforts at social change led to his execution; his successor, Ch'oe Si-hyong (1827–1898), was executed for leading the TONGHAK UPRISING. It received its present name in 1905 when Son Pyong-hi (1861–1922) reorganized the sect. Today it has about 3 million adherents.

Chongqing or **Ch'ung-ch'ing** \'chủn-'chiŋ\ or **Chungking** \'chən-'kiŋ\ City and municipality with provincial status (pop., 1999 est.: 3,193,000), Sichuan province. The leading river port and industrial center of SW China, Chongqing ("Double-Blessed") lies at the confluence of the CHANG (Yangtze) and Jialing rivers. In the 11th cent. B.C., it was a feudal state under the western Chou dynasty. For centuries, its status alternated from being ruled by an empire in N China to being an independent state. It finally came under the MING DYNASTY. It was opened to foreign trade in 1890. It played a large role in the Revolution of 1911. In World War II, it became the GUOMINDANG capital. An important industrial center, it is home to Chongqing Univ. (founded 1929).

Chopin \shō-'paⁿ, *Engl* 'shō-,pan\, **Frédéric (François)** (*orig.* Fryderyk Franciszek) (1810–1849) Polish-French composer and pianist. Born to French parents in Poland, he published his first composition at 7 and began performing in aristocratic salons at 8. A performance in 1830 virtually endowed him with the status of Poland's national composer. He moved to Paris in 1831, and his first Paris concert thrust him into the highest realm of celebrity. He contracted tuberculosis apparently in the 1830s. In 1837 he began a liaison with George SAND; she left him in 1847, and a rapid decline led to his death two years later. Chopin stands not only as Poland's greatest composer but perhaps as the most significant composer in the history of the piano, whose capacities he exhaustively exploited. Apart from two piano concertos (both 1830), virtually all his com-

Frédéric Chopin Portrait by Eugène Delacroix

positions are for solo piano; they include some 60 mazurkas, 27 études, 26 preludes, 21 nocturnes, some 20 waltzes, 16 polonaises, four ballades, four scherzos, and three sonatas.

Chopin \shō-ˈpan\, **Kate** orig. Katherine O'Flaherty (1851–1904) U.S. writer. Born in St. Louis, she moved to Louisiana and began to write after her husband's death. A vivid interpreter of New Orleans culture, she foreshadowed later feminist themes. The best known of her more than 100 short stories is "Désirée's Baby." The Awakening (1899), her acclaimed novel about the sexual and artistic awakening of a young mother, was initially condemned for its frankness.

chord Grouping of three or more musical tones, especially as sounded simultaneously. The tones C–E–G constitute a "C major chord," or "C major triad." Chords may comprise any number of separate tones, and may be highly dissonant (see CONSONANCE AND DISSONANCE). See also HARMONY.

chordate \ˈkôr-ˌdāt\ Any member of the phylum Chordata, which includes the VERTEBRATES as well as the marine invertebrate cephalochordates and tunicates. All chordates, at some time in their life cycle, possess a dorsal supporting rod (notochord), gill slits, and a dorsal nerve cord. Unlike vertebrates, tunicates and cephalochordates lack any kind of brain or skeleton. Chordate bodies consist of a body wall encasing a gut, with a space between called the coelom. The body is usually long and bilaterally symmetrical, with the mouth and sense organs at the front end.

chorea \kə-ˈrē-ə\ Neurological disorder causing irregular, involuntary, purposeless movements, believed to be caused by degeneration of the basal ganglia in the CEREBRAL CORTEX. Sydenham's chorea (St. Vitus' dance) is usually associated with RHEUMATIC FEVER. It usually occurs between ages 5 and 15, more often in girls; typical jerking movements, mostly in the extremities and face, may affect speech and swallowing and range from mild to incapacitating; attacks last several weeks and recur frequently. Senile chorea, a progressive disease resembling Sydenham's chorea, usually occurs late in life. Huntington's chorea is rare, hereditary, and fatal; it usually begins between ages 35 and 50, progressing eventually to totally incapacitating spasms. Mental deterioration begins later and death occurs in 10–20 years.

choreography Art of creating and arranging dances, especially for the BALLET. In the 16th cent., dance masters at the French court arranged their social dances into specific patterns. In the 17th cent., such dances became more complex and were performed as theatrical ballets by trained professionals. In the 18th cent., Jean-Georges NOVERRE and Gasparo ANGIOLINI created the dramatic ballet. This was further developed in 19th-cent. Romantic ballets by Marius PETIPA and others. Radical change in the 20th cent. began with choreographers of the BALLETS RUSSES and continued with George BALANCHINE, Martha GRAHAM, Frederick ASHTON, Jerome ROBBINS, Merce CUNNINGHAM, and Twyla THARP.

chorus Group of actors who performed as an ensemble in Greek drama to describe and comment on the play's action with song, dance, and recitation. Choral performances, which originated in the singing of DITHYRAMBS, dominated

Greek drama until the mid-5th cent. B.C., when AESCHYLUS added a second actor and reduced the chorus from 50 to 12 performers. As the importance of individual actors increased, it gradually disappeared. It was revived in such modern plays as Eugene O'NEILL's Mourning Becomes Electra (1931), and choruses of singers and dancers came to be featured in musical comedies.

Choson dynasty \ˈchō-ˌsòn or **Yi dynasty** (1392–1910) Last and longest-lived of Korea's dynasties. Founded by YI SONG-GYE, it was marked by Chinese cultural influences; NEO-CONFUCIANISM was adopted as the ideology of the state and society. Under the reign of Sejong (1419–50), Korean cultural achievements reached a high point, with the creation of the Korean alphabet (see KOREAN LANGUAGE). After invasions by the Japanese (1592) and MANCHUS (1627), many cultural assets were lost. At the end of the 19th cent. foreign powers once again threatened Korea; it was annexed by Japan in 1910, ending the Choson dynasty's rule.

Chou dynasty See ZHOU DYNASTY

Chou En-lai See ZHOU ENLAI

Chouteau \shü-ˈtō\, **(René) Auguste** (1749–1829) American fur trader and cofounder of ST. LOUIS. Born in New Orleans, he moved to Missouri Territory with his mother and Pierre Laclède Liguest (1724?–1778), with whom he cofounded St. Louis in 1764. The two men built a prosperous fur trade; by 1794 Chouteau had a monopoly on the trade with the Osage, and he helped finance most of the fur-trading companies in Louisiana Territory. He became the unofficial banker to the St. Louis community and its largest landowner.

Chrétien \krā-ˈtyaⁿ\, **(Joseph-Jacques) Jean** (b.1934) Canadian prime minister (from 1993). Born the 18th of 19 children in a working class family in Shawinigan, Quebec, he studied law at Laval Univ. Serving in the Canadian House of Commons 1963–86, he held various posts under Lester PEARSON and Pierre TRUDEAU, including minister of finance (1977), the first French Canadian to hold the office. In 1990 he became leader of the Liberal Party. Advocating a united Canada, he won a landslide victory in 1993 to become prime minister; he won again in 1997 and 2000.

Chrétien de Troyes \krā-ˈtyaⁿ-də-ˈtrwä\ (fl.1165–1180) French poet. He is the author of the five Arthurian ROMANCES Erec, Cligès, Lancelot, Yvain, and Perceval. His vernacular works derived from those of GEOFFREY OF MONMOUTH and combine separate adventures into well-knit stories. Imitated by other French poets, they were translated and adapted frequently as the romance developed. See also ARTHURIAN LEGEND.

Christ, Church of Any of various conservative Protestant churches found mainly in the U.S. Each congregation is autonomous in government, with elders, deacons, and a minister or ministers; there is no national administrative organization. These churches developed from the early-19th-cent. DISCIPLES OF CHRIST movement, which relied on the Bible as the only standard of Christian faith and worship. Controversies split the movement, and the Churches of Christ designated those congregations that opposed organized mission societies and the use of instrumental music in worship.

Christian II (1481–1559) King of Denmark and Norway (1513–23) and of Sweden (1520–23). He succeeded his father, John, king of Denmark and Norway. After defeating the forces of the Swedish regent, he was crowned Sweden's king in 1520. His massacre of Swedish nobles (the Stockholm Bloodbath) helped incite a successful Swedish war for independence, ending the KALMAR UNION in 1523. A revolt in Denmark forced Christian to flee to the Netherlands. After attempting to regain his kingdom, he was arrested in 1532 and spent the rest of his life imprisoned in Danish castles.

Christian IV (1577–1648) King of Denmark and Norway (1588–1648). After two unsuccessful wars against Sweden, he brought disaster to his country by leading it into the THIRTY YEARS' WAR. He was eventually forced to accept the increased power of the nobility, which had long opposed his warlike policies. However, he energetically promoted trade and shipping, was a great builder and founder of cities, left

a national heritage of fine buildings, and was one of the most popular of Danish kings.

Christian X (1870–1947) King of Denmark (1912–47) who symbolized his nation's resistance to the German occupation in World War II. In 1915 he signed a constitution granting equal suffrage to men and women. After the German occupation began in 1940, he rode frequently on horseback through Copenhagen, showing that he had not abandoned his claim to national sovereignty, and he opposed Nazi demands for anti-Jewish legislation. His speech against the occupation forces in 1943 led to his imprisonment until the end of the war.

Christchurch City (pop., 1996: 315,000), South Island, New Zealand. Founded in 1850 as a model Church of England settlement, it was the last and most successful colonizing project inspired by E. G. WAKEFIELD and his New Zealand Co. It is the country's second-largest city; called the "Garden City of the Plains" for its numerous parks and gardens, it is home to Christ's College (founded 1850), the Univ. of Canterbury (1873), and Lincoln Univ. (1990).

Christian Democracy Political movement closely associated with ROMAN CATHOLICISM. It incorporates both traditional church and family values and progressive values such as social welfare. After World War II, a number of Christian Democrat parties appeared in Europe, including the Italian Christian Democratic Party, the French Popular Republican Movement, and the most successful, the German CHRISTIAN DEMOCRATIC UNION. The same period also saw the appearance of Christian Democrat parties in Latin America.

Christian Democratic Union (CDU) German political party advocating regulated economic competition and close cooperation with the U.S. in foreign policy. It held power from the establishment of the W. German republic in 1948 until 1969, and again in 1982–98. In 1990, with Helmut KOHL as chancellor, it oversaw the reunification of Germany. Later it and its coalition partners faced discontent over the economic burden of reunification. Revelations of financial corruption in 1999 severely damaged its reputation. See also Konrad ADENAUER, CHRISTIAN DEMOCRACY.

Christiania See OSLO

Christianity Religion stemming from the teachings of JESUS in the 1st cent. A.D. Its sacred scripture is the BIBLE, particularly the NEW TESTAMENT. Its principal tenets are that Jesus is the son of God (the second person of the Holy TRINITY), that God's love for the world is the essential component of his being, and that Jesus died to redeem humankind. Christianity was originally a movement of Jews who accepted Jesus as the MESSIAH, but the movement quickly became predominantly gentile. The early church was shaped by St. PAUL and other missionaries and theologians; it was persecuted under the Roman empire but recognized by CONSTANTINE I in 313. Christianity has subdivided into numerous sects; the major divisions are ROMAN CATHOLICISM, EASTERN ORTHODOXY, and PROTESTANTISM. Nearly all Christian sects have an ordained clergy, members of which are typically though not universally male. There are now more than 1.7 billion Christians throughout the world.

Christian Science officially **Church of Christ, Scientist** Religious denomination founded in the U.S. in 1879 by Mary Baker EDDY. It subscribes to an omnipotent God and the authority (but not inerrancy) of the Bible, and takes the crucifixion and resurrection of JESUS as essential to human redemption. It departs from traditional Christianity in considering Jesus divine but not a deity and in regarding creation as wholly spiritual. Spiritual cure of disease is a necessary element of redemption from the flesh; most members refuse medical help for disease, and member "practitioners" work full-time as healers. Sunday services are based on readings from the Bible and Eddy's *Science and Health.*

Christian Science Monitor, The Daily newspaper, published Monday through Friday in Boston under CHRISTIAN SCIENCE auspices. Established in 1908 at the urging of M. B. EDDY as a protest against the sensationalism of the popular press, it became one of the most respected U.S. newspapers, famous for its thoughtful treatment of the news. It strictly limits the kinds of advertising it accepts. It maintains its own bureaus to gather news abroad and publishes a weekly world edition.

Christie, Agatha orig. Agatha Mary Clarissa Miller (later **Dame Agatha**) (1890–1976) British detective novelist. Her first novel, *The Mysterious Affair at Styles* (1920), introduced Hercule Poirot, the eccentric Belgian detective who would appear in about 25 novels. The elderly spinster Miss Jane Marple, her other principal detective figure, first appeared in *Murder at the Vicarage* (1930). Most of her approximately 75 novels were best-sellers; translated into many languages, they may have sold over 300 million copies. Her plays include *The Mousetrap* (1952), which set a world record for longest continuous run.

Agatha Christie, 1946

Christina Swedish Kristina (1626–1689) Queen of Sweden (1644–54). The successor to her father, GUSTAV II ADOLF, she was a prime mover in concluding the Peace of WESTPHALIA and ending the THIRTY YEARS' WAR. After 10 years of rule she stunned Europe by abdicating the throne, claiming that she was ill; her real reasons included her secret conversion to Roman Catholicism, proscribed in Sweden. She moved to Rome and later attempted to gain the crowns of Naples and Poland. One of the wittiest and most learned women of her age, she was a lavish patroness of the arts and an influence on European culture.

Christine de Pisan \krēs-ˈtēn-də-pē-ˈzäⁿ\ (1365?–1431?) French writer. Daughter of an astrologer to CHARLES V, she took up writing when she was widowed, producing 10 volumes of graceful verse, much of it in the COURTLY-LOVE tradition. Some works, both poetry and prose, champion women, notably *The Book of the City of Ladies* (1405). *Le Ditié de Jehanne d'*Arc (1429) was inspired by JOAN OF ARC's early victories.

Christmas Christian festival celebrated on December 25, commemorating the birth of JESUS. It was celebrated in Rome by A.D. 336, and the date was probably chosen to coincide with the Roman winter solstice festival and birthday of MITHRA. Gift giving and merrymaking derive from the festival of Saturnalia (Dec. 17); greenery, lights, and gifts to children and the poor were Roman New Year customs. Christmas trees derive from German customs. Christmas today is regarded as a family festival with gifts brought by Santa Claus (see St. NICHOLAS). As an increasingly secular festival, it has come to be celebrated by many non-Christians.

Christo orig. Christo Javacheff (b.1935) Bulgarian-U.S. environmental artist. He moved to Paris in 1958, where he invented *empaquetage,* the wrapping of objects in various materials as art. He began with cans and bottles, and expanded to buildings and landscapes. In 1964 he moved to New York. He is noted for such monumental (but temporary) outdoor projects as *Valley Curtain* (1970–72) in Rifle Gap, Col., and the 24-mile (39-km) *Running Fence* (1972–76) in Marin and Sonoma counties, Cal. In 1995 he wrapped the Berlin Reichstag in metallic silver fabric. Most of his works have been collaborations with his wife, Jeanne-Claude (b.1935).

Christopher, St. (fl.3rd cent. A.D.) Patron saint of travelers. He is said to have been martyred around A.D. 250. In legends, he devoted his life to carrying travelers across a river. One day a small child asked to be transported, and in the middle of the river the child became so heavy that he staggered under the burden. The child revealed that the saint had been carrying Christ and the sins of the world, thus giving rise to Christopher's name (Greek: "Christ-bearer").

chromaticism \krō-ˈma-tə-ˌsi-zəm\ In music, the use of all twelve tones, especially for heightened expressivity. A standard KEY or MODE principally employs seven tones, leaving five tones for discretionary use. Use of all twelve tones in a given piece increased in the 18th and 19th cent. Strictly controlled chromaticism, as in the ornamentation of Frédéric CHOPIN, did not threaten the perception of TONALITY.

However, from the mid-19th cent. on, complaints were increasingly heard that it was difficult to perceive what a given piece's tonal center was, the chromaticism in the works of Richard WAGNER being the most notorious. The virtual breakdown in tonality in the works of advanced composers led to free ATONALITY in the early 20th cent.

chromatography \ˌkrō-mə-ˈtä-grə-fē\ Method first described in 1903 by Mikhail TSVET for separating mixed chemical substances. Tsvet's neglected work, rediscovered in the 1930s, uses the different affinities of substances in a solution in a mobile PHASE (a moving stream of gas or liquid) for adsorbtion onto a stationary phase (a fine-grained solid, a sheet of filtering material, or a thin film of a liquid on a solid surface). Choices of materials for these phases allow enormous versatility for separating substances including biological fluids (e.g., AMINO ACIDS, STEROIDS, CARBOHYDRATES, PIGMENTS), chemical mixtures, and forensic samples. In the original technique, an organic SOLVENT flowed through a column of a powdered solid to separate mixed plant pigments. Among current adaptations are paper chromatography (PC), THIN-LAYER CHROMATOGRAPHY (TLC), liquid chromatography (LC, including high-performance liquid chromatography, or HPLC), and GAS CHROMATOGRAPHY (GC). Some remain laboratory techniques, but some (especially HPLC) can be used on an industrial scale.

chromium Chemical ELEMENT, one of the TRANSITION ELEMENTS, chemical symbol Cr, atomic number 24. A hard, steel-gray METAL that takes a high polish, it is used in ALLOYS (e.g., ferrochromium, steel, stainless steel) to increase strength and corrosion resistance. It usually has VALENCE 2, 3, or 6 and always occurs combined with other elements, especially oxygen. Various colored gemstones (e.g., ruby, emerald, serpentine) owe their color to chromium. Its compounds are used in leather tanning, metal surface treatment and chrome plating, and as catalysts and pigments. Chromium dioxide, strongly magnetic, is used in recording tapes and as a catalyst.

chromodynamics See QUANTUM CHROMODYNAMICS

chromosomal disorder Syndrome caused by CHROMOSOME abnormality. Normally, humans have 23 pairs of chromosomes; any variation causes abnormalities. A chromosome may be duplicated (trisomy) or absent (monosomy); one or more extra full sets of chromosomes can be present; or part of a chromosome may be missing (deletion) or transferred to another (translocation). Resulting disorders include DOWN'S SYNDROME, mental retardation, malformations, abnormal sexual development, malignancies, and sex-chromosome disorders (e.g., KLINEFELTER'S SYNDROME). Chromosomal disorders occur in 0.5% of births; many can now be diagnosed before birth by AMNIOCENTESIS.

chromosome Microscopic, threadlike part of a CELL that carries hereditary information in the form of GENES. The structure and location of chromosomes differentiate prokaryotic from eukaryotic cells (see PROKARYOTE, EUKARYOTE). Every species has a characteristic number of chromosomes; humans have 23 pairs. Except in some viruses, chromosomes consist primarily of DNA. During cell division (see MEIOSIS, MITOSIS), chromosomes are distributed evenly among daughter cells.

chromosphere Layer of the SUN's atmosphere, several thousand miles thick, between the PHOTOSPHERE and the CORONA. The chromosphere (literally "color sphere"), briefly visible as a thin red ring during solar eclipses when the photosphere is obscured by the moon, is observable at other times with special instruments. Its temperature, about 7,000°F (4,000°C) at about 700 mi (1,100 km) above the photosphere, increases with altitude to several hundred thousand degrees. SOLAR FLARES and solar prominences are mainly chromospheric phenomena.

chronic fatigue syndrome (CFS) Sudden debilitating fatigue of unknown cause, usually with mild fever, tender lymph nodes, sore throat, headaches, weakness, muscle and joint pain, and confusion or difficulty in concentrating. To meet the criteria of CFS, the syndrome must be new, with a definite point of onset, and must persist more than six months. Once dismissed as imaginary, CFS has now been recognized by the Centers for Disease Control and Prevention, which estimates that it affects three out of every thou-

sand individuals, mostly women. No diagnostic test yet exists to distinguish it from similar illnesses. No effective treatment has been found, but most patients improve gradually.

chronometer \krə-ˈnä-mə-tər\ Mechanical timekeeping device of great accuracy, particularly one used for determining longitude (see LATITUDE AND LONGITUDE) at sea. Early weight- and pendulum-driven CLOCKS were inaccurate because of friction and temperature changes and could not be used at sea because of the ship's motion. In 1735 John Harrison (1693–1776) constructed the first practical marine timekeeper. Chronometers are suspended to remain horizontal whatever the inclination of the ship. In recent decades, various technologies have displaced the chronometer.

chrysanthemum \kri-ˈsan-thə-ˌməm\ Any of the 100 or so ornamental species that make up the genus *Chrysanthemum*, in the COMPOSITE FAMILY, native primarily to subtropical and temperate areas of the Old World. Cultivated species, often called mums, have large flower heads; those of wild species are much smaller. Most species have aromatic, alternate leaves. Some have both disk and ray flowers in the heads; others lack ray flowers. Pyrethrum, Shasta daisy (hybrid forms of *C. maximum*), florists' chrysanthemum (*C. morifolium*), feverfew (*C. parthenium*), and tansy are popular garden plants. Feverfew and pyrethrum are used in insecticides.

Chrysler Building Office building in New York City (1928–30), designed by William Van Alen (1883–1954). It is the epitome of sleek ART DECO. Its tapering, sunburst-patterned, stainless-steel spire, which reaches 1,048 ft (319 m), remains a striking feature of the Manhattan skyline. Much of its futuristic automotive ornamentation was specified by its owner, Walter P. Chrysler.

Chrysler Corp. U.S. automotive company. Incorporated in 1925 and again in 1986. Founded by Walter P. Chrysler

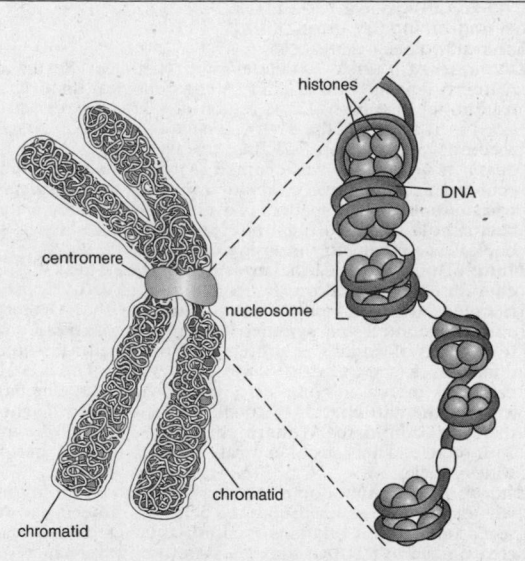

Chromosome Human chromosome with close-up of coiled DNA. Immediately before cell division, DNA, existing as thin uncoiled strands, duplicates to form two daughter strands (chromatids) joined at a centromere. During the first stages of cell division, DNA wraps around binding proteins (histones) to become a highly coiled dense structure recognizable as the rod-shaped chromosome. Following cell division, the DNA uncoils; the uncoiled DNA with its associated proteins is termed chromatin.

(1875–1940), it became the country's second-largest automobile manufacturer, noted for its Plymouth, Dodge, and Chrysler cars. In 1980 it was rescued from bankruptcy by a government bailout organized by Lee IACOCCA. In 1998 it merged with DAIMLER-BENZ to become Daimler Chrysler AG.

Chrysostom \\'kris-əs-təm\\, **St. John** (c.347–407) Early church father. Born in Syria and raised a Christian, he lived as a hermit until his health gave way, after which he was ordained a priest. He earned a reputation as a great preacher. Appointed archbishop of Constantinople in 398, he angered the wealthy with his concern for the poor and criticisms of the misuse of riches. A synod convened in 403 by Theophilus of Alexandria banished him to Armenia. He died en route to a more distant exile on the Black Sea. In 438 his relics were brought to Constantinople, and he was rehabilitated by the church.

Chuang-tzu See ZHUANGZI

chub Any of several freshwater fishes of the CARP family that are commonly caught for bait, sport, and food. Popular species include the European chub (*Leuciscus cephalus*) of Europe and Britain, a voracious predator of insects and other fish, and in N. America, the creek chub, or horned dace (*Semotilus atromaculatus*), and the hornyhead chub (*Nocomis,* or *Hybopsis, biguttata*). These species range in length from 6 in. to 2 ft (15–60 cm). The name is applied to many cyprinids and other, unrelated, fishes.

Chuckchi See SIBERIAN PEOPLES

Chu Hsi See ZHU XI

Chuikov \\'chü-i-ˌkȯf\\, **Vasily (Ivanovich)** (1900–1982) Soviet general. He joined the Red Army at 18. In World War II he commanded the defense at the Battle of STALINGRAD and led the Soviet drive to Berlin. He personally accepted the German surrender of Berlin in 1945. After the war he commanded the Soviet occupation forces in Germany (1949–53).

Chu-ko Liang See ZHUGE LIANG

Ch'ung-ch'ing See CHONGQING

Chungking See CHONGQING

Chunqiu or Ch'un-ch'iu \\'chùn-'chyü\\ (Chinese: "Spring and Autumn Annals") First Chinese chronological history, the traditional history of Lu, a region of China, as revised by CONFUCIUS. One of the FIVE CLASSICS of CONFUCIANISM, it recounts events from 722 B.C. to just before Confucius's death in 479 B.C. It was claimed that records of droughts, eclipses, and so on were intended to warn future rulers of what happens when leaders prove unworthy. Since Confucian scholars were official interpreters of the classics, the book was a means for imposing Confucian ideals.

church Building for Christian worship. The earliest Western churches were based on the Roman BASILICA. In Constantinople, Anatolia, and Eastern Europe, the Orthodox church adopted the symmetrical Greek-cross plan, with four wings of equal size projecting from a central, square, domed area (see BYZANTINE ARCHITECTURE). The late 11th cent. saw increased complexity in CATHEDRALS. The basilica and the hall church (with side aisles equal in height to the nave) dominated Western church design until the mid-20th cent., when architectural experimentation became widespread.

church In Christian doctrine, the religious community as a whole, or an organized body of believers adhering to one sect's teachings. Christians established congregations modeled on the SYNAGOGUE and a system of governance centered on the BISHOP. The SCHISM OF 1054 and the REFORMATION (16th cent.) ended the unity and universality of the Christian Church. St. AUGUSTINE stated that the real church is known only to God, and Martin LUTHER held that the true church was independent of any organization.

Church, Frederic Edwin (1826–1900) U.S. landscape painter. Born in Hartford, Conn., he studied with Thomas COLE and soon became a prominent member of the HUDSON RIVER SCHOOL. He traveled widely, painting spectacular scenery and marvels of nature such as Niagara Falls, volcanoes, icebergs, and the tropical forests of S. America, and achieved fame in the U.S. and Europe.

Churchill, Randolph (Henry Spencer), Lord (1849–1895) British politician. Third son of the 7th duke of Marlbor-

ough, he entered the House of Commons in 1874. In the early 1880s he joined other Conservatives in forming the Fourth Party, which advocated progressive conservatism. In 1886 he became leader of the House of Commons and chancellor of the exchequer, but he resigned after his first budget was rejected. Though he had seemed destined to be prime minister, this miscalculation effectively ended his political career. Winston CHURCHILL was his son.

Churchill, Winston (Leonard Spencer) (*later* **Sir Winston**) (1874–1965) British states-man. Son of Lord Randolph CHURCHILL and the American Jennie Jerome, he had an unhappy childhood. After joining the 4th Hussars in 1895, he saw service as both soldier and journalist, and his dispatches from India and S. Africa, attracted wide attention. Elected to the House of Commons in 1900, he quickly rose to prominence and served as first lord of the admiralty (1911–15), though he later acquired a reputation for erratic judgment. In the years before World War II, his warnings of the threat posed by Adolf HITLER's Germany were repeatedly ignored. When war broke out,

Winston Churchill Photo by Yousuf Karsh, 1941

he was again appointed head of the admiralty. After Neville CHAMBERLAIN resigned, Churchill headed a coalition government as prime minister (1940–45). He committed himself and the nation to all-out war until victory was achieved, and his great eloquence, energy, and indomitable fortitude made him an inspiration to his countrymen, especially in the Battle of BRITAIN. With Franklin ROOSEVELT and Joseph STALIN, he shaped Allied strategy at the 1943 Cairo, Casablanca, and TEHRAN conferences. Though he was the architect of victory, his government was defeated in the 1945 elections. After the war he alerted the West to the expansionist threat of the Soviet Union (see IRON CURTAIN). He led the Conservative Party back into power in 1951 and remained prime minister until 1955, when ill health forced his resignation. For his many writings, including *The Second World War* (6 vols., 1948–53), he was awarded the Nobel Prize for Literature in 1953; his later works include his *History of the English-Speaking Peoples* (4 vols., 1956–58). Knighted in 1953, he later refused the offer of a peerage. In his late years he attained heroic status as one of the titans of the 20th cent.

Churchill Falls *formerly* **Grand Falls** Part of a series of cataracts and rapids on the CHURCHILL RIVER, Newfoundland. The falls drop 245 ft (75 m) and are 200 ft (60 m) wide. Visited in 1839 by John McLean of the HUDSON'S BAY CO., the cataracts were called Grand Falls until 1965, when both falls and river were renamed for Winston CHURCHILL.

Churchill River River, central Canada. Rising in SW Saskatchewan, it flows east across Saskatchewan and N Manitoba and turns northeast into Hudson Bay at Churchill. At 1,000 m (1,609 km) long, it has many rapids and passes through several lakes.

church modes MODES employed for medieval liturgical melodies. The modal system was conceived to codify plainchant (see GREGORIAN CHANT); their names were borrowed from the system used by the ancient Greeks. The modes are distinguished according to the note used as the final (last note) and the emphasis placed on another note, the dominant. The Dorian mode's final is D, the Phrygian's is E, the Lydian's is F, and the Mixolydian's is G. Each of these four original modes had a parallel mode (Hypodorian, Hypophrygian, Hypolydian, and Hypomixolydian) with a lower range. Though they principally employ the tones A–B–C–D–E–F–G, some replace B with B-flat. In the 16th cent., further modes were identified—the Aeolian, on A, and the Ionian, on C.

Church of Christ See Church of CHRIST

Church of England See Church of ENGLAND

Churrigueresque \ˌchür-i-gə-'resk\ Spanish ROCOCO architectural style named after the architect José Churriguera (1665–1725). It featured extravagant ornament and surfaces bristling with broken pediments, undulating cornices, spirals, balustrades, stucco shells, and garlands. In Spanish America, tendencies from Native American and Mudéjar (Spanish-Moorish) art were incorporated.

Chu Teh See ZHU DE

CIA See CENTRAL INTELLIGENCE AGENCY

Ciano \'chä-nō\, **Galeazzo, conte (Count) di Cortellazzo** (1903–1944) Italian politician. A diplomat, he married Benito MUSSOLINI's daughter Edda in 1930. He became minister of foreign affairs (1936) and initiated the Rome–Berlin Axis that helped bring Italy into World War II. After several Axis defeats in 1942, he advocated a separate peace with the Allies. In 1943, Ciano and other leading Fascists forced Mussolini's resignation. Later, on Mussolini's orders, Ciano was tried for treason and executed.

Ciaran of Clonmacnoise \'kir-ən...ˌklan-mək-'nóiz\, **St.** (516?–549?) Irish abbot, one of the founders of monasticism in Ireland. Ciaran was educated with St. COLUMBA at the monastery of Clonard and then lived on the island of Aranmore as a disciple of St. Enda. He traveled to central Ireland and settled with eight companions at Clonmacnoise, where he founded an abbey (548) that later won renown as a center of medieval learning. Ciaran's abbey was so influential that more than half the monasteries in Ireland followed its severely ascetic rule.

Cibber \'sib-ər\, **Colley** (1671–1757) British ACTOR-MANAGER, playwright, and poet. He began his career as an actor in 1690. His *Love's Last Shift* (1696) is considered the first sentimental comedy. Cibber and two other actor-managers, called the "triumvirate," comanaged the DRURY LANE THEATRE 1710–33. He wrote and adapted such plays as *The Non-Juror* (1717) and *The Provok'd Husband* (1728). He was appointed POET LAUREATE in 1730 and retired from acting in 1745.

Cíbola \'sē-bō-lä\, **Seven Cities of** Legendary pueblos of splendor and riches sought by Spanish CONQUISTADORES in N. America during the 16th cent. They were first reported by Álvar CABEZA DE VACA in 1536. Expeditions sent to search for the cities were unsuccessful; one led by F. V. de CORONADO in 1540 located a group of pueblos but failed to find vast treasures.

Ciboney \si-'bō-nä\ Indian people who inhabited the Greater Antilles in the Caribbean Sea. By the time the Spanish arrived in the 16th cent., they had been driven by their more powerful TAINO neighbors to a few isolated locations in present-day Cuba and Haiti. The tool technology of the Cuban Ciboney was based on shell, that of the Haitian Ciboney on stone. Within a century after the first European contact, the Ciboney were extinct.

cicada \sə-'kā-də\ Any insect in the order Homoptera having two pairs of membranous wings, prominent compound eyes, and three simple eyes (ocelli). Most of the 1,500 known species are in the family Cicadidae and are found in tropical deserts, grasslands, and forests. Males produce loud noises by vibrating membranes near the base of the abdomen. Most N. American cicadas produce rhythmical ticks, buzzes, or whines, though the "song" of some species is musical. Periodic cicadas, including the well-known 17-year cicada (often erroneously called the 17-year LOCUST) and 13-year cicada, appear in regular cycles. The larvae (nymphs) burrow into the ground, where they remain for 13 or 17 years, feeding on juices sucked from roots; they then emerge in large numbers to live aboveground as adults for a single week.

Cicero \'si-sə-ˌrō\, **Marcus Tullius** (106–43 B.C.) Roman statesman, lawyer, scholar, and writer. Born to a wealthy family, he was elected consul in 63 B.C. Of his speeches, perhaps the best known are those he made against CATILINE, whose uprising he foiled. He vainly tried to uphold republican principles in the civil wars that destroyed the Roman republic. After the death of Julius CAESAR he delivered his 14 Philippic orations against Mark ANTONY. When the triumvirate of Antony, Octavian (later AUGUSTUS), and Marcus LEPIDUS was formed, he was executed. He is remembered as the greatest Roman orator and the innovator

of what became known as Ciceronian rhetoric, which remained the foremost rhetorical model for many centuries.

cichlid \'si-kləd\ Any of more than 600 primarily freshwater fish species (family Cichlidae), including many popular aquarium species. Cichlids are found in the New World tropics, S Asia, and in great diversity in the major African lakes. They are deep-bodied and have a rounded tail. They usually grow no longer than about 12 in. (30 cm). Cichlids are noted for their complex mating and breeding behavior. Certain species (e.g., TILAPIA), known as mouthbreeders, carry their eggs in the mouth until hatched. See also ANGELFISH.

Cid \'sid\, **the** *Spanish* **El Cid** \'thĕth\ ("the Lord") *orig*. Rodrigo Díaz de Vivar (1043–1099) Castilian military hero. He served Sancho II in his campaign to gain control of León, then shifted to the service of ALFONSO VI. His unauthorized raid on the Moorish kingdom of Toledo (1081) prompted Alfonso to send him into exile. He then entered the service of the Muslim rulers of Saragossa, becoming known as a general who was never defeated in battle. He maneuvered to gain control of the Moorish kingdom of Valencia, finally succeeding in 1094. He is the national hero of Castile, celebrated in a famous 12th-cent. epic poem, the first great work of Spanish literature.

cider Juice of APPLES. Apples are ground into a fine pulp and then pressed. Hard (alcoholic) cider is fermented in vats for up to three months before being filtered and aged in containers (see FERMENTATION). Sweet cider is unfermented and either served directly (as in the U.S.) or mellowed in pressurized tanks first (particularly in Europe). Most cider in the U.S. is now pasteurized. Juice that is pasteurized, treated with a preservative, and filtered is marketed as apple juice.

cigar Cylindrical roll of TOBACCO for smoking, consisting of cut tobacco filler formed in a binder leaf and with a wrapper leaf rolled spirally around the bunch. Wrapper leaf, the most expensive leaf used in cigars, must be strong, elastic, silky in texture, even in color, and pleasant in flavor. Cigars are bigger than CIGARETTES, and the odor and smoke they produce are stronger. Cigars were being smoked by Maya Indians by the 10th cent.; they were reported back to Spain by Christopher COLUMBUS and other explorers.

cigarette Paper-wrapped roll of finely cut TOBACCO for smoking. Cigarette tobacco is usually milder than CIGAR tobacco. The Aztecs and other New World peoples smoked tobacco in hollow reeds or canes, or wrapped in leaves. Early in the 16th cent., beggars in Seville began picking up discarded cigar butts and wrapping them in scraps of paper to smoke, creating the first European cigarettes. In the 19th cent. their use spread throughout Europe. After World War I smoking cigarettes became acceptable for women and consequently increased markedly. In the 1950s and '60s the health hazards associated with smoking (including LUNG CANCER) became widely known, and some countries launched campaigns against smoking. Declines in smoking in those countries have been offset by vastly increased numbers of smokers in developing nations.

Cilicia \sə-'li-shə\ Ancient district, S ASIA MINOR. Located along the Mediterranean coast south of the TAURUS MTNS., in ancient times it controlled the only route from Asia Minor to Syria. Held by the Hittites 14th–13th cent. B.C., the Assyrians 8th cent. B.C., and the Persians 6th–4th cent. B.C., it later came under Macedonian and Seleucid rule. In the 1st cent. B.C. it was a Roman province. Muslim Arabs occupied it 7th–10th cent. A.D., when it was reconquered for Byzantium. Ruled by the Ottoman Turks from 1515, it has belonged to Turkey since 1921.

Cilician Gates See TAURUS MTNS.

cilium \'si-lē-əm\ Short, eyelashlike filament that abounds on tissue cells of most animals. Capable of beating in unison, cilia perform a variety of functions, including providing the means of locomotion for some protozoans, moving mammalian ova (eggs) through oviducts, generating water currents to carry food and oxygen past the gills of clams, and cleaning debris from mammalian respiratory systems. Movement is controlled by the basal body, located just inside the cell surface at the base of the cilium. Beneath the surface of some cells is a network of MICROTUBULES that may coordinate ciliary beating. See also FLAGELLUM.

Cimabue \ˌchē-mə-'bü-ā\ *orig.*
Benciviene di Pepo (c.1240–
1302) Florentine painter.
Documented as a master
painter in Rome in 1272, he
was strongly influenced by
the Greek Byzantine style.
Though a number of works
are attributed to him, the
only one dated is the mosaic
of *St. John the Evangelist*
(1301–2) in Pisa Cathedral.
The outstanding master of
his generation, he began the
movement toward greater realism that culminated in the
Renaissance. His style influenced GIOTTO and DUCCIO.
Cimabue ("Bullheaded") was
a nickname.

Cimabue, "Sta. Trinità
Madonna," c.1290

Cimarosa \ˌchē-mä-'rȯ-zä\,
Domenico (1749–1801) Italian opera composer. Son of a
stonemason, he studied at
the Naples Conservatory. By
the mid-1780s his operas
were internationally known; the most famous was the
comic opera *Il matrimonio segreto* (1792). In addition to
some 75 operas, he wrote several oratorios, over 15 masses,
and some 80 piano sonatas. His reputation as a composer of
Italian opera remained close to that of W. A. MOZART long
after his death.

Cimon \'sī-mən\ (c.510–451? B.C.) Athenian statesman and
general who laid the groundwork for the Athenian empire.
A conservative, he promoted SPARTA and opposed PERI-
CLES. After helping defeat the Persians at the Battle of
SALAMIS (480), he was elected strategus (general and magis-
trate) every year until 461. As commander of the DELIAN
LEAGUE, he cleared the Persians from the E Mediterranean.
In 461 he was accused by Pericles of collaborating with
Macedonia and Sparta and was exiled for 10 years.

Cincinnati City (pop., 2000: 331,000), Ohio. Situated on the
Ohio River across from Kentucky, it was first settled in
1788. A river port after 1811, it grew in importance with the
opening of the Miami and Erie Canal in 1832. It is a major
inland coal port. A cultural center, it has an orchestra and
opera and ballet companies. It is the seat of the Univ. of
Cincinnati (1819).

Cinco de Mayo \'sēŋ-kō-thā-'mī-ō\ (Spanish: "Fifth of May")
Mexican holiday commemorating the Mexican victory over
the French at PUEBLA in 1862. The French army, better
equipped and far larger than the Mexican army, had been
sent by NAPOLEON III to conquer Mexico. The Mexicans, under Gen. Ignacio Zaragoza, defeated the French, who, however, returned the next year to take Puebla. Cinco de Mayo
celebrations often include music, dancing, and parades.

cinder cone *or* **ash cone** Deposit around a volcanic vent,
formed by rock fragments or cinders that accumulate and
gradually build a conical hill with a bowl-shaped crater at
the top. Cinder cones develop from explosive eruptions of
lavas and are often found along the flanks of shield (gently
sloping) volcanoes. Although composed of loose or only
moderately consolidated cinder, many cones are surprisingly long-lasting, because rain falling on them sinks into
the highly permeable cinders instead of running off and
eroding them.

cinéma vérité \'si-nə-mə-ˌver-i-'tā\ (French: "truth cinema")
French film movement of the 1960s that strove for candid
realism by showing people in everyday situations with authentic dialogue. Influenced by DOCUMENTARY filmmaking, the method produced such films as Jean Rouch's
Chronicle of a Summer (1961) and Chris Marker's *Joli Mai*
(1962). In the U.S., where it was also called "direct cinema,"
filmmakers used handheld cameras to record action without narration, as in Frederick Wiseman's *Titicut Follies*
(1967) and the MAYSLES brothers' *Salesman* (1969).

cinnamon Bushy evergreen tree (*Cinnamomum zeylanicum*)
of the LAUREL FAMILY, native to Sri Lanka, India, and

Burma, and cultivated in S. America and the W. Indies for
the spice consisting of its dried inner bark. It was once more
valuable than gold. Today cinnamon is used to flavor various foods, especially in bakery goods. The oil is distilled
from bark fragments for use in food, liqueur, perfume, and
drugs.

circadian rhythm \sər-'kā-dē-ən\ Inherent cycle of approximately 24 hours in length that appears to control or initiate
various biological processes, including sleep, wakefulness,
and digestive and hormonal activity. The natural signal for
the cycle is the change from darkness to light. The controlling mechanism for these cyclic processes within the body is
thought to be the HYPOTHALAMUS.

Circe \'sər-sē\ In Greek legend, a sorceress who, by means of
drugs and incantations, turned humans into lions, wolves,
or swine. ODYSSEUS visited her on his return from the Trojan War, and she changed his companions into swine.
Odysseus himself was protected by an herb given him by
Hermes, and he compelled Circe to restore his companions.
They became lovers, but a year later he resumed his journey homeward.

circle Geometrical curve, one of the CONIC SECTIONS, consisting of the set of all points the same distance (the radius)
from a given point (the center). A line connecting any two
points on a circle is called a chord, and a chord passing
through the center is called a diameter. The distance
around a circle (the circumference) equals the length of a
diameter multiplied by π (see PI). The area of a circle is the
square of the radius multiplied by π. An arc consists of any
part of a circle encompassed by an angle with its vertex at
the center.

circuit *or* **electric circuit** Path that transmits ELECTRIC CUR-
RENT. A circuit includes a BATTERY or a GENERATOR that
gives energy to the charged particles; devices that use current, such as lamps, motors, or electronic computers; and
connecting wires or transmission lines. Circuits can be classified according to whether the current remains whole (series) or divides to flow through several branches simultaneously (parallel). See also ALTERNATING CURRENT, DIRECT
CURRENT, KIRCHHOFF'S CIRCUIT RULES, OHM'S LAW.

circuit, printed See PRINTED CIRCUIT

circulation Process by which nutrients, respiratory gases,
and metabolic products are transported throughout the
body. In humans, BLOOD remains within a closed CARDIO-
VASCULAR SYSTEM composed of the HEART, blood vessels,
and blood. The right and left heart chambers send blood
into separate systemic PULMONARY CIRCULATION. See also
ARTERY, CAPILLARY, VEIN. See diagram on next page.

circumcision Cutting away of all or part of the foreskin
(prepuce) of the PENIS. The practice is known in many cultures. It is performed either shortly after birth (e.g., among
Muslims and Jews), within a few years of birth, or at PU-
BERTY. For Jews it represents the fulfillment of the
covenant between God and Abraham. Evidence regarding
the purported medical benefits of circumcision (e.g., reduced risk of cancer) is inconclusive, and the practice persists mainly for cultural reasons. See also CLITORIDEC-
TOMY.

circumstantial evidence In law, evidence that is drawn not
from direct observation of a fact at issue but from events or
circumstances that surround it. If a witness arrives at a
crime scene seconds after hearing a gunshot to find someone standing over a corpse and holding a smoking pistol,
the evidence is circumstantial, since the person may merely
be a bystander who picked up the weapon after the killer
dropped it. Most criminal convictions are based, at least in
part, on circumstantial evidence that sufficiently links
criminal and crime.

circus Entertainment or spectacle featuring animal acts and
human feats of daring. The modern circus was founded in
England in 1768 by the bareback rider Philip Astley, who
built stands around his performance ring and opened Ast-
ley's Amphitheatre; one of his riders later established the
Royal Circus (1782). The first U.S. circus opened in
Philadelphia in 1793. Horse acts were later joined by wild-
animal acts. After the invention of the flying trapeze by
Jules Léotard (1859), aerial acts were featured. P. T. BAR-
NUM created the three-ring circus (1881) and augmented it

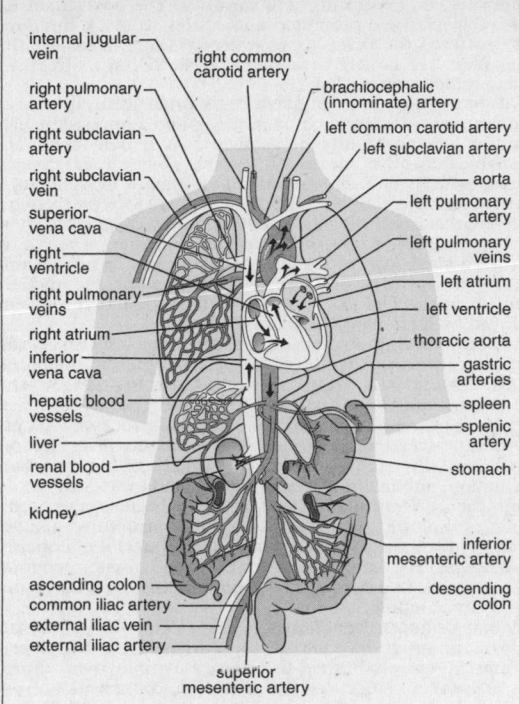

internal jugular vein
right common carotid artery
right pulmonary artery
brachiocephalic (innominate) artery
right subclavian artery
left common carotid artery
right subclavian vein
left subclavian artery
superior vena cava
aorta
right ventricle
left pulmonary artery
right pulmonary veins
left pulmonary veins
right atrium
left atrium
inferior vena cava
left ventricle
hepatic blood vessels
thoracic aorta
liver
gastric arteries
renal blood vessels
spleen
kidney
splenic artery
stomach
inferior mesenteric artery
ascending colon
common iliac artery
descending colon
external iliac vein
external iliac artery
superior mesenteric artery

Circulation Human circulatory system. Oxygen-rich blood is shown in gray, oxygen-poor blood in white. The pulmonary circulation consists of the right ventricle and the exiting pulmonary artery and its branches, the arterioles, capillaries, and venules of the lung, and the pulmonary vein. Unlike the other arteries and veins, the pulmonary arteries carry deoxygenated blood and the pulmonary veins carry oxygenated blood. The aorta arises from the left ventricle. The brachiocephalic artery arises from the aorta and divides into the right common carotid and right subclavian arteries. The left and right common carotids extend on either side of the neck and supply much of the head and neck. The left subclavian artery (arising from the aorta) and the right subclavian artery supply the arms. In the lower abdomen, the aorta divides into the common iliac arteries, which give rise to external and internal branches supplying the legs.

with sideshow performers. Circuses traveled widely, performing in a tent (the Big Top) into the 1950s; today circuses usually perform in permanent buildings.

Cirenaica See CYRENAICA

cirrhosis \sə-'rō-səs\ Degeneration of functioning LIVER cells and their replacement with fibrous CONNECTIVE TISSUE, leading to scarring. The most common cause is alcohol abuse with malnutrition (see ALCOHOLISM). Others include bile duct obstruction, viral infection, toxins, iron or copper accumulation in liver cells, and syphilis. JAUNDICE, EDEMA, and great abdominal swelling are common in all.

Ciskei \'sis-ˌkī\ Former black enclave, S. Africa, bordering the Indian Ocean and S. Africa. In the late 18th cent. the XHOSA peoples living in the area came into conflict with European settlers; the region was incorporated into the Cape Colony by 1900. In 1972 it was declared a self-governing black state; in 1981 it became nominally independent, but was not recognized by the international community. In 1994 it was reincorporated into S. Africa as part of the new Eastern Cape province.

Cistercian \sis-'tər-shən\ or **White Monk** or **Bernardine** Member of a Roman Catholic monastic order founded by St. Robert of Molesme (1098) at Cîteaux (Latin, Cister-

cium), Burgundy, and other BENEDICTINES dissatisfied with their abbey's laxity. St. Stephen Harding organized their rule. Cistercians were severely ascetic. St. BERNARD DE CLAIRVAUX founded 68 abbeys in his lifetime. Discipline declined as the order grew, and Cistercians disappeared from N Europe after the REFORMATION. The order underwent reforms in the 16th–17th cent.; members of the reformed order are popularly known as Trappists after the abbey of La Trapp. Until the 1960s, they slept, ate, and worked in perpetual silence. The original order also survives.

Citadel, The Public military college in Charleston, S.C., founded in 1842. Though it lacks a direct affiliation with the U.S. military, it has long been an important source of trained officers. Citadel cadets fired the shots that began the American Civil War; the college was occupied by federal forces 1865–79. A court decision in 1995 opened its admissions to women. Enrollment is about 3,700.

Citigroup U.S. HOLDING COMPANY formed in 1998 from the merger of Citicorp and Travelers Group, Inc. The $70 billion merger included one of the largest U.S. investment banks, Salomon Smith Barney Inc., and aimed at creating a global retail financial-services business. Citicorp, whose lineage can be traced to the First Bank of the United States, pioneered installation of automated teller machines (ATMs) throughout its branch offices in the 1970s. Before its merger with Travelers, Citicorp was the largest U.S. bank and one of the largest financial companies in the world.

Citizen Genet Affair \zhə-'ne\ Incident precipitated by the French diplomat Edmond C. E. Genet (1763–1834), who was sent to the U.S. in 1793 to gain support for France's war with Britain and Spain. In S. Carolina Genet organized privateers to prey on British commerce and expeditions to attack Spanish and British territories. Pres. George WASHINGTON considered Genet's activities a violation of U.S. neutrality and demanded his recall. Facing the guillotine at home, he was allowed to remain in the U.S.

citizenship Relationship between an individual and a state in which an individual owes allegiance to that state and in turn is entitled to its protection. The right to vote and to hold public office are predicated on citizenship. Its responsibilities include allegiance, payment of taxes, and military service. In ancient Greece, citizenship was granted only to property owners. The Romans granted it to all the empire's free inhabitants in A.D. 212. The concept disappeared in Europe during the feudal era, but was revived in the Renaissance. Citizenship may normally be gained by birth within a certain territory, descent from a citizen parent, marriage to a citizen, or NATURALIZATION.

Citlaltépetl \sē-ˌtläl-'tä-ˌpe-t°l\ or **Orizaba** \ˌō-rē-'sä-bä\ Volcano, S central Mexico. At 18,700 ft (5,700 m), its symmetrical, snowcapped cone is the highest point in Mexico and the third-highest peak in N. America. The volcano has been dormant since 1687.

citric acid Colorless, crystalline organic compound, one of the CARBOXYLIC ACIDS. It is present in almost all plants (especially CITRUS fruits) and in many animal tissues and fluids. It is one of a series of compounds involved in the TRICARBOXYLIC ACID CYCLE. It has a characteristic sharply sour taste and is used in many foods, confections, and soft drinks. Industrially, it is used as a water conditioner, cleaning and polishing agent, and chemical intermediate.

citrine \si-'trēn\ Transparent, coarse-grained variety of QUARTZ. Citrine is a semiprecious gem valued for its yellow to brownish color and its resemblance to the rarer TOPAZ. Citrine is often marketed under various names that confuse it with topaz to inflate its price; it may be distinguished from topaz by its inferior hardness. It occurs mainly in Brazil, Uruguay, the Ural Mtns., Scotland, and N. Carolina.

citron Small evergreen tree or shrub (*Citrus medica*) in the RUE FAMILY, cultivated in Mediterranean countries and the W. Indies. It has irregular, spreading, spiny branches and large, pale green, broadly oblong leaves. The flowers are purple and white or all creamy white. The oval or oblong fruit yields firm pulp, either acidic or sweet, that is used only for by-products. The thick peel can be cured in brine and candied.

citrus Any of the plants that make up the genus *Citrus,* in the RUE FAMILY, that yield pulpy fruits covered with fairly

citrus family

thick skins. The genus includes the LEMON, LIME, sweet and sour ORANGES, TANGERINE, GRAPEFRUIT, CITRON, and shaddock.

citrus family See RUE FAMILY

city Relatively permanent and highly organized center of population, of greater size or importance than a town or village. The first cities appeared in the NEOLITHIC PERIOD, when the development of agricultural techniques assured surplus crop yields large enough to sustain a permanent population. Ancient Greece saw the creation of the CITY-STATE, a form also important in the Roman empire as well as the medieval Italian trading centers of VENICE, GENOA, and FLORENCE. After the Middle Ages, cities came increasingly under the political control of centralized government and served the interests of the nation-state. The INDUSTRIAL REVOLUTION further transformed city life, as factory cities blossomed rapidly in England, NW Europe, and the NE U.S. By the mid-20th cent., 30–60% of a country's population might be living in its major urban centers. Today many cities suffer from lack of adequate housing, sanitation, recreational space, and transportation facilities. Local governments have sought to alleviate these problems through URBAN PLANNING.

city-state Political system consisting of an independent city with SOVEREIGNTY over a fixed surrounding area. The term was coined in the 19th cent. to describe ancient Greek and Phoenician settlements. City-states may have developed when earlier tribal systems broke down and splintered groups established themselves as independent nuclei about 1000–800 B.C.; by the 5th cent. B.C. there were hundreds, with ATHENS, SPARTA, and THEBES among the most important. Strongly independent, they were incapable of forming any lasting union or federation, and eventually fell victim to the Macedonians, the Carthaginians, and the Roman empire. In the 11th cent. the city-state revived in Italy; medieval Italy's city-states, including PISA, FLORENCE, VENICE, and GENOA, prospered from trade with the East, and several survived into the 19th cent. Germany's included HAMBURG, BREMEN, and LÜBECK. The only city-state extant today is VATICAN CITY.

City University of New York (CUNY) Institution created in 1961 to combine New York City's 17 municipally supported colleges. It is the second-largest university system in the U.S. (total enrollment about 200,000). It includes a Graduate Center; City College of New York, Hunter College, Brooklyn College, Queens College, and six other four-year colleges; and seven two-year community colleges. The Mount Sinai School of Medicine is affiliated with CUNY. From 1970 to 1999 a controversial open-admissions policy was observed at some of CUNY's senior colleges.

Ciudad Juárez See Ciudad JUÁREZ

civet \'si-vət\ Any of 15–20 species of long-bodied, short-legged CARNIVORES (family Viverridae) found in Africa, S Europe, and Asia. Catlike in appearance, civets have a thickly furred tail, small ears, and pointed snout. They range in length from 16 to 34 in. (40–85 cm), excluding the 5–26-in. (13–66-cm) tail, and in weight from 3.5 to 24 lbs (1.5–11 kg). Civets mark territories with a greasy, musk-like secretion (called civet) stored in a pouch under the tail; civet is sometimes used in the manufacture of perfumes. Civets feed on small animals and on vegetable matter.

African palm civet (*Nandinia binotata*)

civil defense Nonmilitary actions taken to reduce loss of life and property in case of attack or disaster. Against the threat of aerial attack in World War II, the British government provided its people with gas masks, and most countries trained citizens in fire fighting, rescue, and first aid. Blackouts reduced the lights that could guide enemy pilots; sirens warned of bombing attacks, and citizens took cover in air-raid shelters, basements, and subways. The postwar threat of nuclear attack prompted authorities to mark buildings that offered the best shelter from FALLOUT. By the 1970s the West had largely conceded that surviving a direct nuclear attack was unlikely.

civil disobedience *or* **passive resistance** Refusal to obey government demands or commands and nonresistance to consequent arrest and punishment. As a nonviolent and usually collective means of forcing government concessions, it has been a major tactic of nationalist movements in Africa and India, of the U.S. CIVIL RIGHTS MOVEMENT, and of labor and antiwar movements in many countries. Those who engage in it feel obligated by a higher principle to break a given law. Mohandas GANDHI most clearly formulated the concept of civil disobedience for the modern world; in the U.S., it was most fully articulated and employed by H. D. THOREAU and M. L. KING, Jr.

civil engineering Profession of designing and executing structural works that serve the general public, including BRIDGES, CANALS, DAMS, harbors, LIGHTHOUSES, ROADS, TUNNELS, and WATER-SUPPLY SYSTEMS. The modern field includes power plants, airports, chemical-processing plants, and water-treatment facilities. It involves site investigations and feasibility studies, structural design and analysis, construction, and facilities maintenance, and may draw on design theory from many fields (e.g., hydraulics, thermodynamics, nuclear physics). Research in structural analysis and the technology of materials such as steel and concrete has opened the way for new concepts and greater economy of materials, and structural designs are now rigorously analyzed by computers.

Civilian Conservation Corps (CCC) (1933–42) U.S. unemployment program. One of the earliest NEW DEAL programs, it was established to relieve unemployment during the GREAT DEPRESSION by providing conservation work primarily for young unmarried men. Recruits lived in semi-military work camps and received $30 a month as well as food and medical care. Projects included planting trees, building flood barriers, fighting forest fires, and maintaining forest trails. It employed a total of 3 million men during its existence.

civil law Body of law developed from Roman law and used in continental Europe and most former colonies of European nations, including the province of Quebec and the state of Louisiana. The most significant codifications of modern civil law were the French (NAPOLEONIC CODE, 1804) and the German. The basis of law in civil-law jurisdictions is statute, not custom; civil law is thus to be distinguished from COMMON LAW. In civil law, judges apply principles embodied in statutes, or LAW CODES, rather than turning to case precedent. The term is also used to distinguish the law that applies to private rights from the law that applies to criminal matters. See also CRIMINAL LAW, TORT.

civil liberty In U.S. law, freedom from arbitrary interference in one's pursuits by individuals or by the government as guaranteed by the BILL OF RIGHTS and the 13th, 14th, and 15th Amendments to the U.S. CONSTITUTION. The 13th Amendment prohibits slavery and involuntary servitude; the 14th bars the application of any law that would abridge the "privileges and immunities" of U.S. citizens or deprive any person of "life, liberty, or property . . . without DUE PROCESS of law" or deny any person EQUAL PROTECTION under the law; and the 15th guarantees the right of all U.S. citizens to vote.

Civil Rights Act of 1964 Comprehensive U.S. law intended to end discrimination based on race, color, religion, or national origin. It guarantees equal voting rights (Title I); prohibits segregation or discrimination in places of public accommodation (Title II); bans discrimination, including sex-based discrimination, by trade unions, schools, or employers that are involved in interstate commerce or do business with the federal government (Title VII); calls for the desegregation of public schools (Title IV); and assures nondiscrimination in the distribution of funds under federally assisted programs (Title VI). A 1972 amendment, the Equal Employment Opportunity Act, extended Title VII coverage to state and local governments and increased the authority of the Equal Employment Opportunity Commission, created in 1964 to enforce Title VII provisions. The act was proposed by Pres. John KENNEDY in 1963 and passed into law under Pres. Lyndon JOHNSON.

civil rights movement Movement for racial equality in the U.S. that, through nonviolent protest, broke the pattern of racial segregation in the South. Following the *BROWN VS. BOARD OF EDUCATION* decision (1954), blacks and white supporters attempted to end entrenched segregationist practices. When Rosa PARKS was arrested in 1955 in Montgomery, Ala., a black boycott of the bus system was led by M. L. KING and Ralph ABERNATHY. Using nonviolent methods, the movement spread, and boycotts and sit-ins forced the desegregation of department stores, supermarkets, libraries, and movie theaters. The Deep South remained adamant in its opposition to desegregation, often violently; protesters were attacked and occasionally killed. Their efforts culminated in a march on Washington, D.C., in 1963. Following the assassination of J. F. KENNEDY, Pres. Lyndon JOHNSON persuaded Congress to pass the CIVIL RIGHTS ACT OF 1964, a victory that was followed by the VOTING RIGHTS ACT in 1965. After 1965, militant groups such as the BLACK PANTHER PARTY split off from the movement, and riots in black ghettos and King's assassination caused many supporters to withdraw. Leaders subsequently sought power through elective office and substantive economic and educational gains through AFFIRMATIVE ACTION.

civil service Body of government officials employed in civil occupations that are neither political nor judicial. In well-ordered societies, they are usually recruited and promoted on the basis of a merit-and-seniority system, which may include examinations; elsewhere, corruption and patronage are rampant. They often serve as neutral advisers to elected officials and political appointees, and are charged with the execution of policy. The civil service originated in the earliest known Middle Eastern societies; the modern European civil services date to 17th-cent. Prussia. In the U.S., senior officials change with each new administration; in Europe, regulations minimize favoritism and ensure a wide range of knowledge and skills.

Civil Service Act, Pendleton See PENDLETON CIVIL SERVICE ACT

Civil War See AMERICAN CIVIL WAR

Civil Wars, English See ENGLISH CIVIL WARS

Cixi or **Tz'u-hsi** \'tsə-'shē\ *known as* the **Empress Dowager** (1835–1908) Imperial consort who controlled the Chinese QING DYNASTY for almost 50 years. A low-ranking concubine of the Xianfeng emperor (r.1850–61), Cixi bore his only son in 1856. After the emperor's death, Cixi joined a triumviral regency that governed for her son. During this period the TAIPING REBELLION was put down and the government was briefly revitalized. When Cixi's son died in 1875, Cixi violated the laws of succession and had her adoptive nephew enthroned; she became sole regent in 1884. In 1889 she nominally relinquished control, but returned in 1898 to undo a set of radical reforms and had her nephew imprisoned in his palace. She supported the disastrous BOXER REBELLION. Before she died, she ordered her nephew poisoned.

Cixous \sēk-'züs\, **Hélène** (b.1937) Algerian-French feminist critic, novelist, and playwright. Her essays, in collections such as *The Newly Born Woman* (1975; with Catherine Clément), explore issues of sexual difference and female experience in writing. *The Book of Promethea* (1983) and other works reinterpret myths and the mythic past and analyze Western representations of women. Her novels include *Inside* (1969) and *Reading with Clarice Lispector* (1989).

Clair, René *orig.* René-Lucien Chomette (1898–1981) French film director. He acted in silent films before writing and directing *Paris qui dort* (1923), *Entr'acte* (1924), and the satiric farce *The Italian Straw Hat* (1927), which established his reputation as a leader of the avant-garde. He used sound creatively in early talkies such as *Sous les toits de Paris* (1930) and *À nous la liberté!* (1931). *The Ghost Goes West* (1935), made in England, was an international success. He directed several Hollywood films, including *And Then There Were None* (1945), then returned to France to make *Le silence est d'or* (1947).

clam In general, any BIVALVE mollusk. True clams have equal shells, closed by two opposing muscles, and a powerful burrowing foot. They usually lie buried in the sand in shallow marine waters. Clams draw in and expel water for respiration and feeding. Species range in size from 0.004 in. to 4 ft (0.1 mm–1.2 m) across. Many are edible, including the GEODUCK and quahog.

Clancy, Tom (*orig.* Thomas) (b.1947) U.S. novelist. Born in Baltimore, he worked as an insurance agent. His first novel, the surprise best-seller *The Hunt for Red October* (1984; film, 1990), virtually created the "technothriller" genre, suspenseful novels that rely on extensive knowledge of military technology and espionage. Later successes include *Patriot Games* (1987; film, 1992), *Clear and Present Danger* (1989; film, 1994), and *Sum of All Fears* (1991; film, 2000).

Claremont Colleges Consortium of private colleges in Claremont, Cal. It comprises Pomona College (founded 1887), the Claremont Graduate School (1925), Scripps College (1926), Claremont McKenna College (1946), Harvey Mudd College (1955), and Pitzer College (1963). The campuses are adjacent to one another and many facilities are shared. Total enrollment is about 7,000.

Clarendon, Constitutions of (1164) Sixteen articles issued by King HENRY II defining church–state relations in England. Designed to restrict ecclesiastical privileges and church courts, the constitutions provoked the famous quarrel between Henry and Thomas BECKET. Controversial were the provisions that all revenues from vacant sees and monasteries reverted to the king and that clerics charged with serious crimes were to be tried in secular courts. Becket's martyrdom in 1170 forced Henry to moderate his attack on the clergy, but he did not repudiate the constitutions.

Clarendon, Earl of *orig.* Edward Hyde (1609–1674) English statesman and historian. He became an adviser to CHARLES I, recommending moderate policies, but was unable to prevent the ENGLISH CIVIL WARS. He helped bring about the RESTORATION of CHARLES II, and as lord chancellor (1660–67) he dominated most aspects of the administration. His criticism of the king's immorality eventually destroyed their friendship, and Parliament made him a scapegoat for the inconclusive ANGLO–DUTCH WAR of 1665. Dismissed in 1667, he lived in exile in France, where he completed his *History of the Rebellion and Civil Wars in England*.

Clarendon Code (1661–65) Four acts passed in England during the ministry of the Earl of CLARENDON, designed to cripple the NONCONFORMISTS. The acts forbade municipal office to those not taking the sacraments at a parish church, excluded them from church offices, made meetings for Nonconformist worship illegal, and forbade Nonconformist ministers to live or visit within five miles of any place where they had ministered.

Clare of Assisi, St. (1194–1253) Founder of the order of Poor Clares. Born in Assisi to a noble family, she became devoted to her fellow Assisian St. FRANCIS, who received her vows. She was soon joined by her sister and her mother, as the nucleus of a female community that became its own order, the counterpart of the FRANCISCANS. Still allied with the Franciscans, the Poor Clares are noted for their perfect poverty and their life of penitential prayer led for the good of church and society.

clarinet Single-reed WOODWIND INSTRUMENT. It is a standard member of both orchestras and bands. It has a cylindrical bore and a flared bell, and is usually made of African blackwood (grenadilla). It has a 3 1/2-octave range. It was probably invented by Johann Christoff Denner (1655–1707) in the early 18th cent. The B-flat clarinet is the standard instrument today; the A clarinet often replaces it in sharp keys. Clarinets with the fingering system devised by Theodor Boehm are standard in America, Britain, and France; those employing an older fingering style are used in Germany and Russia. The B-flat bass clarinet is known for its rich timbre. The basset horn is an angled clarinet pitched a 4th lower than the B-flat clarinet; probably invented in Bavaria around 1770, it had largely fallen out of use by 1850.

Clark, Champ (*orig.* James Beauchamp) (1850–1921) U.S. politician. Born near Lawrenceburg, Ky., he moved to Missouri in 1876. A newspaper editor, prosecuting attorney,

and state legislator, he served in the U.S. House of Representatives 1893–95 and 1897–1921. A follower of W. J. BRYAN, he supported agrarian measures. As a member of the House rules committee in 1910, he led the revolt against Joseph CANNON and succeeded him as speaker (1911–19).

Clark, George Rogers (1752–1818) American Revolutionary frontier military leader. Born in Albemarle Co., Va., the brother of William CLARK, he raised troops and defended the region against the British and Indians during the Revolution. He captured settlements along the Mississippi River in the Old Northwest (Illinois), and in 1780 he helped defeat a British attempt to capture St. Louis. Appointed an Indian commissioner, he helped conclude a treaty with the Shawnee.

Clark, Kenneth (Mackenzie) *later* Baron Clark (of Saltwood) (1903–1983) British art historian. He studied at Oxford Univ. and with Bernard BERENSON in Florence. He served as keeper of fine art at Oxford's Ashmolean Museum (1931–34) and director of London's National Gallery (1934–39). He was involved in academic research and public service for most of his life. He published widely and became internationally known in 1969 as the writer and host of the BBC series *Civilisation*, a history of European art.

Clark, Mark (Wayne) (1896–1984) U.S. army officer. Born in Madison Barracks, N.Y., he graduated from West Point and rose to become chief of staff of army ground forces in 1942. He commanded the U.S. landing at Salerno, Italy, in September 1943 and received the government's surrender, then directed the hard-fought campaign to wrest the Italian peninsula from Axis control, taking Rome in June 1944 and N Italy in May 1945. In the Korean War he commanded all U.N. troops 1952–53. After his retirement, he served as president of The Citadel 1954–66.

Clark, William (1770–1838) U.S. explorer and soldier. Born in Caroline Co., Va., the brother of G. R. CLARK, he joined the army and participated in Indian campaigns under Anthony WAYNE. After resigning his commission, he was recruited by his friend Meriwether LEWIS to help lead the LEWIS AND CLARK EXPEDITION (1804–6) to the Pacific coast; he proved an able leader, with valuable wilderness and mapmaking skills. Later, as governor of the Missouri Territory (1813–21), he was known for the effectiveness of his diplomacy with Native Americans.

Clarke, Arthur C(harles) (b.1917) British–Sri Lankan science-fiction writer. He first published stories while in the Royal Air Force and, after earning a degree in physics and mathematics, wrote such novels as the classic *Childhood's End* (1953), and *Earthlight* (1955). He collaborated with Stanley KUBRICK in making *2001: A Space Odyssey* (1968, film and novel). Some of Clarke's ideas have proved remarkably prescient.

class, social Group of people within a society who share the same social and economic status. The most influential early theory of social class was that of Karl MARX, who focused on how one class controls and directs the process of production while other classes are the direct producers and the providers of services to the dominant class. Max WEBER emphasized the importance of political power and social status in maintaining class distinctions. In modern capitalist societies, the upper class is distinguished by the possession of largely inherited wealth (in the U.S., over 30% of all wealth is owned by the top 1% of property owners, and nearly 65% by the top 5%). The working class consists mostly of manual laborers and service-industry workers who earn moderate or low wages. The middle class includes those engaged in technical and professional occupations, supervisors and managers, and such self-employed workers as small-scale shopkeepers, businesspeople, and farmers. There is also often an urban "underclass" of permanently jobless and underemployed workers. See also BOURGEOISIE.

class action In law, an action in which a representative plaintiff sues or a representative defendant is sued on behalf of a class of plaintiffs or defendants who have the same interests in the litigation as their representative and whose rights or liabilities can be better determined as a group than in a series of individual suits. A major recent class-action suit concerned the effects of passive smoking brought against tobacco firms (settled in 1997).

Classical architecture Architecture of ancient Greece and Rome, especially from the 5th cent. B.C. in Greece to the 3rd cent. A.D. in Rome, that emphasized the COLUMN and pediment. Greek architecture was based chiefly on the POST-AND-BEAM SYSTEM, with columns carrying the load. Timber construction was superseded by construction in marble and stone. The column was used as a unit for regulating all temple proportions. The Doric ORDER, probably the earliest, remained the favorite of the Greek mainland and W colonies. The Ionic order developed in E Greece; on the mainland, it was used chiefly for smaller temples and interiors. The greatest Greek architectural achievement was the Athens ACROPOLIS. By the late 5th cent. B.C., the orders were applied to such structures as stoas and theaters. The HELLENISTIC AGE produced more elaborate and richly decorated architecture, with often colossal buildings. Many of the great buildings were secular rather than religious, and the Ionic order and especially the newer Corinthian order were widely used. The Romans contributed two new orders (Tuscan and Composite), though the Corinthian remained by far the most popular. Whereas Greek temples were isolated and almost always faced east–west, Roman temples were oriented with respect to other buildings. Roman columns carried ARCHES as well as ENTABLATURES, permitting greater spatial freedom. The discovery of concrete enormously facilitated construction using the arch, VAULT, and DOME, as in the PANTHEON. Other public buildings included BASILICAS, baths (see THERMAE), AMPHITHEATERS, and TRIUMPHAL ARCHES.

classical economics School of economic thought that originated with Adam SMITH and reached maturity in the works of David RICARDO and J. S. MILL. Its theories were mainly concerned with economic growth. Reacting against MERCANTILISM, classical economics emphasized economic freedom, stressing LAISSEZ-FAIRE and free competition. Many of its fundamental principles were set forth in Smith's *Wealth of Nations* (1776), which argued that a nation's wealth was greatest when its citizens followed their own self-interest. Neoclassical economists showed that the forces of SUPPLY AND DEMAND would ration economic resources to their most effective uses. Smith's ideas were refined by Ricardo, who held that the price of goods produced and sold under competitive conditions tends to be proportionate to the labor costs of producing them. Mill's *Principles of Political Economy* (1848) related the ideas to contemporary social conditions. Among those who have modified classical economics to reach very different conclusions are Karl MARX and J. M. KEYNES.

classicism In the arts, the principles, historical tradition, aesthetic attitudes, or style of the art of ancient Greece and Rome. The term may refer either to work produced in antiquity or to later works inspired by those of antiquity. More broadly, classicism refers to the adherence to virtues regarded as characteristic of classicism or as universally and enduringly valid, including formal elegance and correctness, simplicity, dignity, restraint, order, and proportion. Classicism is often opposed to ROMANTICISM. Periods of classicism in literature, music, and the visual arts have generally coincided.

Classicism and Neoclassicism Art-historical tradition or aesthetic attitudes based on the art of ancient Greece and Rome. "Classicism" refers to the art produced in antiquity or to later art inspired by that of antiquity; "Neoclassicism" refers only to art inspired by that of antiquity. Classicism is traditionally characterized by harmony, clarity, restraint, universality, and idealism. In the visual arts, Classicism has generally denoted a preference for line over color, straight lines over curves, and the general over the particular. The Italian RENAISSANCE was the first period of thorough Classicism after antiquity. Neoclassicism became the dominant aesthetic movement in Europe in the late 18th and early 19th cent., as practiced by Antonio CANOVA and J.-L. DAVID. It bred a reaction that came to be termed ROMANTICISM. Recurring alternations between Classical and non-Classical ideals have characterized Western aesthetics. See also CLASSICAL ARCHITECTURE.

Claudel \klō-ˈdel\, **Camille (-Rosalie)** (1864–1943) French sculptor. The sister of Paul CLAUDEL, by her teens she was a skilled sculptor. In 1882 she met Auguste RODIN. She is best known today as his student, collaborator, model, and mistress. She contributed figures to Rodin's projects, particularly *The Gates of Hell* (1880–1900). She exhibited her own work successfully but also destroyed many pieces. In 1913, still distraught from her break with Rodin in 1898, she was committed to a mental institution, and from 1914 lived in a rest home.

Claudel \klō-ˈdel\, **Paul (-Louis-Charles-Marie)** (1868–1955) French poet, playwright, and diplomat. His brilliant diplomatic career began in 1892, and he eventually served as ambassador to Japan (1921–27) and the U.S. (1927–33). At the same time he pursued a literary career. A Catholic convert, he reached his largest audience through such plays as *Break of Noon* (1906), *Tidings Brought to Mary* (1912), and his masterpiece, *The Satin Slipper* (1929), which explore the struggle between good and evil and the search for salvation. He wrote the librettos for Darius MILHAUD's opera *Christopher Columbus* (1930) and Arthur HONEGGER's oratorio *Joan of Arc* (1938). His best-known poetic work is *Cinq grandes odes* (1910).

Claude Lorrain \ˈklōd-lò-ˈraⁿ\ *orig.* Claude Gellée (c.1600–1682) French painter. Born in the duchy of Lorraine, he trained in Rome with Agostino Tassi and there encountered the work of Nicolas POUSSIN. He became known as the master of the ideal landscape, a view of nature more beautiful and harmonious than nature itself; his landscapes and coastal scenes contain architectural fragments and figures. His reputation is based particularly on his sensitivity to the tonal values of light and atmosphere. By the 1630s he was well known and successful, with illustrious patrons. His work influenced the entire course of European landscape painting. Some 250 paintings and over 1,000 drawings survive.

Claudius *in full* Tiberius Claudius Caesar Augustus Germanicus *orig.* Tiberius Claudius Nero Germanicus (10 B.C.– A.D. 54) Roman emperor (A.D. 41–54). Nephew of TIBERIUS, Claudius became emperor unexpectedly after CALIGULA's murder. Sickly, unattractive, and scholarly, he wrote several histories, none of which survive. He was ruthless toward individual senators and tended to disfavor the upper classes, but catered to the freedmen. The invasion of Britain in 43 was part of his general expansion of frontiers; he also annexed Mauretania in N Africa, Lycia in Asia Minor, and Thrace, and made Judaea a province. He encouraged urbanization, spent lavishly on public works, and extended Roman citizenship throughout the empire. Having executed his scheming third wife in 48, he married his niece AGRIPPINA THE YOUNGER. After pressuring him into naming her son Lucius (later NERO) heir, she may have poisoned Claudius.

Claudius

Clausewitz \ˈklau̇-zə-ˌvits\, **Carl (Philipp Gottlieb) von** (1780–1831) Prussian general and author. He joined the Prussian army at 12 and entered the War College in Berlin in 1801. After serving with distinction in the NAPOLEONIC WARS, he became a general and was appointed director of the War College (1818). His major work on strategy, *On War* (1832–37), emphasized the necessity of a critical approach to strategic problems. He asserted that war is a tool for achieving political aims rather than an end in itself ("merely the continuation of policy by other means"), and argued that defensive warfare is both militarily and politically the stronger position. He also advocated the concept of "total war." *On War* had a profound influence on modern military strategy.

clavichord Early keyboard instrument, an important forerunner of the PIANO. It flourished about 1400–1800, especially in Germany. It is usually rectangular, with the keyboard inset. The strings are struck by metal tangents, rather than plucked as on the HARPSICHORD. The tangent becomes the endpoint of the vibrating string; thus the point where it strikes determines the pitch. Its sound is generally so soft as to be nearly inaudible, and it is thus suited only to solo performance, usually without an audience. The player's touch can produce dynamic variation; variation in finger pressure can even produce vibrato.

clay SOIL particles with diameters less than 0.005 mm; also a material composed essentially of clay particles (see CLAY MINERAL). In soils, clays provide the environment for almost all plant growth. The use of clay in POTTERY making predates recorded human history. As building materials, clay BRICKS (baked and as ADOBE) have been used since the earliest times. Kaolin, or china clay, is required for the finer grades of CERAMIC materials; used for paper coating and filler, it gives the paper a gloss, permitting high-quality reproduction. Earth dams are made impermeable to water by a core of clay, and water loss in canals may be reduced by lining the bottom with clay. The essential raw materials of PORTLAND CEMENT include clays.

Clay, Cassius See Muhammad ALI

Clay, Cassius Marcellus (1810–1903) U.S. abolitionist. Born in Madison Co., Ky., the son of a slaveholder and a relative of Henry CLAY, he was strongly influenced by the ideas of W. L. GARRISON. In 1845 he founded the antislavery publication *True American,* but was forced by opponents to move it to Louisville, where it was renamed *The Examiner.* As U.S. minister to Russia (1861–62, 1863–69), he helped negotiate the ALASKA PURCHASE.

Clay, Henry (1777–1852) U.S. politician. Born in Hanover Co., Va., he practiced law in Virginia and then Kentucky. Serving in the U.S. House of Representatives (1811–14, 1815–21, 1823–25; speaker 1811–14), he urged the U.S. into the WAR OF 1812. He supported a national economic policy of protective tariffs, a national bank, and internal transportation improvements. His support of the MISSOURI COMPROMISE earned him the nickname "The Great Compromiser." Under J. Q. ADAMS he served as secretary of state (1825–29). In the U.S. Senate (1806–7, 1810–11, 1831–42, 1849–52), he supported the compromise tariff of 1833 and later argued strongly for passage of the COMPROMISE OF 1850. He was the Whig Party candidate for president in 1832 and 1844.

clay mineral Any of a group of important hydrous aluminum silicates with a layered structure and microscopic particle size. Clay minerals occur widely in such sedimentary rocks as mudstones and shales, in marine sediments, and in soils. They are used in the petroleum industry (as drilling muds and as catalysts in refining) and in the processing of vegetable and mineral oils (as decolorizing agents).

Clear Grits Political movement in CANADA WEST (now Ontario). It developed in 1849 within the Reform Party in opposition to the province's premier, Robert Baldwin, who advocated reforms that included the use of crown lands to support the Protestant churches. It allegedly took its name from the motto "All sand and no dirt, clear grit all the way through." Its early leaders were Peter Perry and George BROWN. It eventually joined other groups to form the LIBERAL PARTY.

cleavage Tendency of a crystalline substance to split along definite planes. Cleavage surfaces are seldom as flat as crystal faces, but the angles between them are highly characteristic and valuable in identifying a crystalline material. Cleavage is described by its direction (as cubic, prismatic, basal) and by the ease with which it is produced. A perfect cleavage produces smooth, lustrous surfaces.

clef (French: "key") MUSICAL-NOTATION symbol at the beginning of a staff to indicate the PITCH of the notes on the staff. Clefs were originally letters, identifying letter-named pitches, that were affixed to a line on the staff (thus providing a "key" to its identity). Knowing the identity of a single line permitted the musician to identify the other lines and spaces. Clefs were first regularly used in the 12th cent. The Gothic letter forms of G and F evolved into the modern treble and bass clefs; the letter C evolved into the rarer alto, tenor, baritone, and soprano clefs.

cleft palate Fairly common CONGENITAL DISORDER in which a fissure forms in the roof of the mouth. It may affect

only the soft PALATE or extend through the hard palate, so that the nasal cavity opens into the mouth. Cleft lip, a fissure in the lip beneath the nostril, or other abnormalities may accompany it. Cleft palate limits the ability to suck and may lead to malnutrition in infancy and causes speech problems in childhood. Surgical repair is done at about 18 months of age.

Cleisthenes of Athens \\'klīs-thə-ˌnēz\\ (c.570–508? B.C.) Athenian statesman and chief ARCHON (525–524), regarded as the founder of Athenian democracy. He imposed democratic reforms by which the basis of organization was changed from family and clan to locality. The four blood TRIBES were replaced by 10 local tribes, each with representation from city, coast, and hill areas. He based all his reforms on *isonomia* ("equal rights for all").

clematis \\'kle-mə-təs, kli-'ma-təs\\ Any of the more than 200 species of perennial, chiefly climbing shrubs of the genus *Clematis* (BUTTERCUP family), found throughout most of the world. Many species are cultivated for their attractive flowers, either solitary or in large clusters. Common species include old-man's beard (*C. vitalba*), virgin's bower (*C. cirrhosa*), and vine bower (*C. viticella*). The most popular horticultural hybrids are of primarily three species: *C. florida, C. patens,* and *C. jackmanii.*

Clemenceau \\klä-mäⁿ-'sō, *Engl* ˌkle-mən-'sō\\, **Georges** (1841–1929) French statesman and journalist. A doctor before turning to politics, he served in the Chamber of Deputies 1876–93, becoming a leader of the radical republican bloc. He founded several newspapers and came to be ranked among the foremost political writers of his time. His support for Alfred DREYFUS brought him into favor, and he served in the Senate 1902–20 and as premier 1906–9. During World War I, at 76, he became premier again (1917–20), and his steadfast pursuit of the war won him the title "Father of Victory." He also helped frame the postwar Treaty of VERSAILLES, endeavoring to reconcile French interests with those of Britain and the U.S.

Clemens, (William) Roger (b.1962) U.S. baseball player. Born in Dayton, Ohio, he has played for the Boston Red Sox (1984–96), Toronto Blue Jays (1997–1998), and New York Yankees (from 1999). In 1986 he became the first pitcher to strike out 20 batters in a single (nine-inning) game. He won the Cy Young Award for best pitcher an unprecedented six times (1986, 1987, 1991, 1997, 1998, 2001).

Clemente \\klə-'men-tā\\, **Roberto** (1934–1972) U.S. baseball player. Born in San Juan, Puerto Rico, he joined the Pittsburgh Pirates in 1955. He led the National League in hitting in 1961, 1964, 1965, and 1967. He was also known for his fielding, throwing, and base-stealing. His career was cut short when he died in the crash of an airplane loaded with relief supplies he had collected for Nicaraguan earthquake victims.

Roberto Clemente

Clementi, Muzio (1752–1832) British (Italian-born) composer, publisher, and manufacturer. Brought to England at 13 by a wealthy English traveler who had heard his organ playing, he was set to solitary music studies for seven years on a country estate. His keyboard playing and early sonatas thereafter gained him renown in London, and he later toured extensively. In 1798 he restarted a successful music-publishing and piano-manufacturing firm. His influential piano pieces include over 100 piano sonatas and *Gradus ad Parnassum* (3 vols., 1817–26), a popular pedagogical set of 100 diverse piano pieces.

Clement of Alexandria, St. *Latin* Titus Flavius Clemens (c.A.D. 150–215) Christian apologist and missionary. Born in Athens, he was converted to Christianity by Pantaenus, a former Stoic who preceded him as head of the catechetical school at Alexandria. Clement believed that Greek philosophy, like the Jewish Law of Moses, was a preparatory discipline leading to the truth. He asserted that men lived first as citizens of heaven and second as earthly citizens. Persecution by the emperor Severus in 201–2 obliged him to leave Alexandria for Jerusalem. He was revered as a saint in the Latin church until 1586, when doubts about his orthodoxy led to his removal from the list of Roman saints.

Clement V *orig.* Bertrand de Got (c.1260–1314) Pope (1305–14), the first to reside at Avignon, France. He became archbishop of Bordeaux in 1299 and was elected pope six years later. By creating a majority of French CARDINALS, he ensured the election of a line of French popes. In 1309 he moved the seat of the papacy to Avignon, primarily for political reasons (see AVIGNON PAPACY). PHILIP IV of France forced him to restrict the church's role in secular affairs and to dissolve the TEMPLARS. Clement's decretals, the *Clementinae*, were a notable contribution to canon law.

Clement VI *orig.* Pierre Roger (1291?–1352) Pope (1342–52). The archbishop of Sens and Rouen, he was made cardinal in 1338 and pope at Avignon four years later (see AVIGNON PAPACY). He launched a crusade against Smyrna in 1344, ending the piracy of the Ottoman Turks. He also restored papal authority in the Italian region of Romagna. In exchange for his protection, JOAN I of Naples sold him Avignon, where he enlarged the papal palace and fostered art and scholarship.

Clement VII *orig.* Giulio de' Medici (1478–1534) Pope (1523–34). The illegitimate son of Giuliano de' Medici, he was raised by his uncle Lorenzo de' MEDICI. In 1513 he was made archbishop of Florence and cardinal by his cousin Pope LEO X. He commissioned art from RAPHAEL and MICHELANGELO. A weak and vacillating political figure, Clement allied with France in 1527, which led to Emperor CHARLES V's sack of Rome. Clement's indecisiveness complicated HENRY VIII's request for an annulment of his marriage to Catherine of Aragon.

Cleomenes I \\klē-'ä-mə-ˌnēz\\ (d.491 B.C.) Spartan king (519–491). He ruled jointly with Demaratus. In 510 he expelled the tyrant Hippias (d.490 B.C.) from Athens, then supported the oligarchic party against the democratic CLEISTHENES and refused to help Athens combat Persia. His policies did much to solidify Sparta's position as the leading power in the Peloponnese. He bribed the oracle at DELPHI to depose Demaratus, but was discovered and fled. Though reinstated, he went insane and committed suicide.

Cleon (d.422 B.C.) Athenian politician. The first prominent representative of the merchant class in Athenian politics, he became leader of Athens in 429 B.C. after the death of his enemy PERICLES. Cleon advocated an offensive strategy in the PELOPONNESIAN WAR; he reached the summit of his fame when he captured the Spartan island of Sphacteria. He was killed by the Spartans while trying to retake Thrace.

Cleopatra (VII) (69–30 B.C.) Egyptian queen (of Macedonian descent), last ruler of the Ptolemaic dynasty in Egypt. Daughter of Ptolemy XII (112?–51 B.C.), she ruled with her two brother-husbands, Ptolemy XIII (51–47) and Ptolemy XIV (47–44), both of whom she had killed, and with her son, Ptolemy XV or Caesarion (44–30). She claimed the latter was fathered by Julius CAESAR, who had become her lover after entering Egypt in 48 B.C. in pursuit of POMPEY. She married Mark ANTONY (36), Caesar's heir apparent, incurring the wrath of Octavian (later AUGUSTUS), whose sister Antony had earlier wed. At a

Cleopatra Bas-relief, c.69–30 B.C.

magnificent celebration in Alexandria, Antony bestowed Roman lands on his foreign wife and family. Octavian declared war on Cleopatra and Antony and defeated their joint forces at the Battle of ACTIUM (31). Antony committed suicide and, after a failed attempt to beguile Octavian, so too did Cleopatra, possibly by means of an asp.

clepsydra See WATER CLOCK

clerestory \'klir-ˌstȯr-ē\ Windowed wall of a room that rises higher than the surrounding roofs to light the interior space. In large buildings, where internal walls are far from the outermost walls, the clerestory provides daylight to spaces that otherwise would be dark. This device was most highly developed in Romanesque and Gothic cathedrals. As the NAVE rose much higher than the roofs of the side aisles, its walls could be pierced by a row of windows near the ceiling.

Clergy Reserves Lands set aside for the Church of England in Canada. Established by the CONSTITUTIONAL ACT of 1791, they amounted to one-seventh of all land grants. They became controversial after 1815, as some Protestant denominations demanded equal reserves and most argued that the lands should serve general public purposes independent of religion. An imperial act of 1827 allowed for the sale of one-fourth of the reserved land. The reserves were finally secularized in 1854.

Cleveland City (pop., 2000: 478,000), NE Ohio. Located on the S shore of Lake ERIE, it is Ohio's second-largest city. Initially the site of French and Indian trading posts, it expanded following the opening of the ERIE CANAL and the arrival of the railroad in 1851. The AMERICAN CIVIL WAR provided the stimulus for iron and steel processing and oil refining, and John D. ROCKEFELLER founded Standard Oil there. Over 400 medical and industrial research centers and numerous educational institutions are in the area. The Rock and Roll Hall of Fame and Museum opened in 1995.

Cleveland, (Stephen) Grover (1837–1908) 22nd and 24th president of the U.S. (1885–89, 1893–97). Born in Caldwell, N.J., he practiced law in Buffalo, N.Y., from 1859, eventually becoming mayor (1881–82). As governor of New York (1883–85), he earned the hostility of TAMMANY HALL with his independence, but in 1884 he won the Democratic nomination for president. The first Democratic president since 1856, he supported civil-service reform and opposed high protective tariffs, which became an issue in the 1888 election, when he was nar-

Grover Cleveland

rowly defeated by Benjamin HARRISON. In 1892 he was reelected by a huge popular plurality. In 1893 he attributed the U.S.'s severe economic depression to the Sherman Silver Purchase Act of 1890 and urged repeal. The economic unrest resulted in the PULLMAN STRIKE in 1894. By 1896 supporters of the FREE SILVER MOVEMENT controlled the Democratic Party, which nominated W. J. BRYAN instead of Cleveland for president. He retired to New Jersey, where he lectured at Princeton Univ.

Cliburn \'klī-ˌbərn\, **Van** *orig.* Harvey Lavan Cliburn, Jr. (b.1934) U.S. pianist. Born in Shreveport, La., he was taught piano by his mother and at the Juilliard School, and made his debut with the New York Philharmonic. In 1958 he became a national sensation as the first American to win the Tchaikovsky Competition in Moscow. In 1962 he established the Van Cliburn International Piano Competition in Fort Worth, Texas.

click In phonetics, a suction sound made in the mouth. Click sounds occur in various African languages and are often used as interjections in other languages—for example, the sound of disapproval represented in English by "tsk, tsk." Clicks are a regular part of the consonant system in the KHOISAN LANGUAGES and in BANTU LANGUAGES such as Xhosa and Zulu.

client-server architecture Architecture of a computer NETWORK in which many clients (remote processors) request and receive service from a centralized SERVER (host computer). Ideally, clients need not be aware of the specifics of the system that is providing the service. Today clients are often situated at WORKSTATIONS or on PERSONAL COMPUTERS, while servers are located elsewhere on the network,

usually on more powerful machines. This computing model is especially effective when clients and the server each have distinct tasks that they routinely perform. Many clients can access the server's information simultaneously, and, at the same time, a client computer can perform other tasks, such as sending e-mail. Because both client and server computers are considered intelligent devices, the client-server model is completely different from the old "mainframe" model, which utilized a centralized mainframe computer that performed all the tasks for its associated "dumb" terminals.

cliff dwelling Prehistoric, usually multistoried house of the ancestors of present-day PUEBLO INDIANS, built from around 1000 along the sides or under the overhangs of cliffs. The use of hand-hewn stone building blocks and ADOBE mortar in these dwellings was unexcelled. Rooms on upper levels could be entered either by doorways from adjoining rooms or by ladders through holes in the ceilings; ground-floor rooms were entered through the ceiling. Cliff dwellings were probably built as a defense against invading tribes. All were deserted by the end of the 13th cent. Many ruins remain, including notable ones at CANYON DE CHELLY NATIONAL MONUMENT and MESA VERDE NATIONAL PARK.

Clift, (Edward) Montgomery (1920–1966) U.S. actor. Born in Omaha, he acted on Broadway and was a founding member of the ACTORS STUDIO. He became a star in *Red River* (1948). Noted for his serious, sensitive roles, he portrayed troubled characters in such films as *A Place in the Sun* (1951), *From Here to Eternity* (1953), and *The Young Lions* (1958). Scarred by a car crash in 1956, he became addicted to drugs and alcohol and died of a heart attack at 45.

climate Condition of the ATMOSPHERE at a particular location over a period of time (generally 30 years). Climate is the sum of such atmospheric elements as solar radiation, temperature, humidity, clouds and precipitation, atmospheric pressure, and wind. It may include not only the atmosphere but also the HYDROSPHERE, LITHOSPHERE, BIOSPHERE, and such extraterrestrial factors as the sun. See also WEATHER.

climatic adaptation, human Genetic adaptation of human beings to different environmental conditions, such as extreme cold, humid heat, desert conditions, and high altitudes. Extreme cold favors short, round bodies with short arms and legs, flat faces with fat pads over the sinuses, narrow noses, and a heavy layer of body fat. These adaptations provide minimum surface area in relation to body mass for minimum heat loss. In conditions of humid heat, body heat must instead be dissipated; selection favors tall and thin bodies with dark skin to protect against harmful solar radiation. The desert-adapted person must compensate for water loss through sweating. A thin but not tall body minimizes both water needs and water loss. Adaptation to night cold, often part of a desert environment, provides increased metabolic activity to warm the body during sleep. High altitudes demand, in addition to cold adaptation, adaptation for low air pressure and the consequent low oxygen, usually by an increase in lung tissue.

climatology Science concerned with CLIMATE. Climatology treats the same atmospheric processes as METEOROLOGY, but it also seeks to identify slower-acting influences and longer-term changes, including the circulation of the oceans, the concentrations of atmospheric gases, and variations in the intensity of solar radiation.

Cline, Patsy (1932–1963) U.S. singer, the first female country singer to cross over into pop. Born in Tennessee, she began recording in the mid-1950s, and won first place on Arthur Godfrey's television show with "Walking After Midnight" (1957). In 1960 she joined the GRAND OLE OPRY. After recovering from injuries sustained in a car crash, she returned in 1962 with such hits as "I Fall to Pieces" and "Crazy." She was killed in an airplane crash at 30.

clinical psychology Branch of psychology concerned with the diagnosis and treatment of mental disorders. Clinical psychologists evaluate patients through interviews, observation, and psychological tests, make diagnoses, and assign treatments. Most hold an academic degree (PhD or PsyD) rather than a medical degree (MD) and cannot prescribe medications. Most work in hospitals or clinics or in private practice, often in tandem with psychiatrists and social

workers, treating mentally or physically disabled patients, prison inmates, drug and alcohol abusers, and geriatric patients, among others. See also SOCIAL WORK.

Clinton, DeWitt (1769–1828) U.S. politician. Born in Little Britain, N.Y., a nephew of George CLINTON, he served as state senator, mayor of New York City (1803–15 except for two annual terms), lieutenant governor (1811–13), and governor (1817–23, 1825–28). He proposed the idea of a canal across New York state, and oversaw the ERIE CANAL project (1816–25), which assured the development of New York City as the major port of trade with the Midwest.

Clinton, George (1739–1812) U.S. politician and vice president (1805–12). Born in Little Britain, N.Y., he served in the French and Indian War. He was a leading member of the New York assembly (1768–75) and a delegate to the Continental Congress (1775). As governor of New York (1777–95, 1801–4) he was a forceful leader and able administrator. A supporter of Thomas JEFFERSON, he was twice elected vice president (with Jefferson and James MADISON); he died in office.

Clinton, Henry (*later* **Sir Henry**) (1730?–1795) British commander in chief during the American Revolution. Commissioned in the British army in 1751, he went to N. America in 1775 as second in command to William HOWE. He commanded British troops to victories in New York, then succeeded Howe in 1778. His offensive in the Carolinas in 1780 effected the fall of Charleston. On his return to New York, he left Charles CORNWALLIS in charge of subsequent operations that ultimately resulted in the British surrender. He resigned in 1781 and returned to England, where he found himself blamed for the defeat.

Clinton, Hillary Rodham *orig.* Hillary Diane Rodham (b.1947) U.S. lawyer, first lady, and politician. Born in Chicago, she attended Wellesley College and Yale law school. She began her professional life in Arkansas focusing on family law and children's rights. In 1975 she married her classmate William CLINTON, and she became first lady of Arkansas on his election as governor in 1979. When her husband became U.S. president (1993), she wielded power and influence almost unprecedented for a first lady. As head of the Task Force on National Health Care Reform, she proposed the first national health-care program in the U.S., but saw the initiative defeated. In 2000 she was elected to the U.S. Senate from New York.

Clinton, William J(efferson) *orig.* William Jefferson Blythe III *known as* **Bill Clinton** (b.1946) 42nd president of the U.S. (1993–2001). Born in Hope, Ark., after his father's death, he was adopted by his stepfather, Roger Clinton. He attended Georgetown Univ., Oxford Univ. (as a Rhodes Scholar), and Yale law school, then taught at the Univ. of Arkansas law school. As governor (1979–81, 1983–92), he reformed Arkansas's educational system. He won the Democratic presidential nomination in 1992 after withstanding charges of personal impropriety, and defeated the incumbent, George BUSH. As president, he obtained approval of the N. AMERICAN FREE TRADE AGREEMENT in 1993. He and his wife, H. R. CLINTON, strongly advocated their plan to overhaul the U.S. health-care system, but Congress rejected it. In 1994 the Democrats lost control of Congress for the first time since 1954. Clinton responded by offering a deficit-reduction plan while opposing efforts to slow government spending on social programs. He defeated Robert DOLE to win reelection in 1996. In 1997 he helped broker a peace agreement in N. Ireland. He faced renewed charges of personal impropriety (see LEWINSKY AFFAIR); he denied the charges before a grand jury, but ultimately acknowledged "improper relations." In 1998 he became the second president in history to be impeached.

William Clinton

Charged with perjury and obstruction of justice, he was acquitted at his Senate trial in 1999. His two terms saw sustained economic growth and successive budget surpluses, the first in three decades.

cliometrics \ˌklī-ə-ˈme-triks\ Application of economic theory and statistical analysis to the study of history, developed by Robert W. Fogel (b.1926) and Douglass C. North (b.1920), who were awarded the Nobel Prize for Economics in 1993. In *Time on the Cross* (1974), Fogel used statistical analysis to examine the politics and profitability of American slavery. North studied the link between a market economy and legal and social institutions such as property rights in such works as *Structure and Change in Economic History* (1981). See also ECONOMETRICS.

clipper ship Classic sailing ship of the 19th cent., renowned for its beauty, grace, and speed. The true clipper evolved first in the U.S. around 1833 and later in Britain. It was a long, slim, graceful vessel with a projecting bow, a streamlined hull, and a huge spread of sail on three tall masts. Clippers carried tea from China and goldminers to California. Famous clippers included the American *Flying Cloud* and the British *Cutty Sark*. Though much faster than the early steamships, they were eventually outrun by improved steamships and largely disappeared in the 1870s.

clitoridectomy *or* **female circumcision** *or* **female genital mutilation** Ritual surgical procedure ranging from drawing blood, to removing the clitoris alone, to infibulation or Pharaonic circumcision—removing the external genitals, joining the sides and leaving a small opening. Now often illegal, it dates to ancient times and purports to guard virginity and reduce female sexual desire in traditional societies in many parts of the less-developed world. Infibulation is usually done by a midwife, often in unhygienic conditions. It may lead to severe bleeding, infection, exquisite pain, and death; urination and sexual intercourse can be painful and menstrual blood may be retained. Women are reinfibulated after childbirth.

Clive, Robert *later* **Baron Clive (of Plassey)** (1725–1774) British soldier and colonial administrator. In 1743 he was sent to Madras for the E. INDIA CO., where hostilities between it and the French E. INDIA CO. soon allowed him to demonstrate his military skills. He was sent back to India (1755–60), where his victory over the nawab of Bengal at Plassey made him the virtual master of Bengal. His first government, though tainted by corruption and duplicity, was a tour de force of generalship and statecraft. He returned to India as governor and commander in chief of Bengal (1765–67); his reorganizing of the colony, including his fight against corruption, helped establish Britain's power in India. He himself was attacked by Parliament on charges of corruption; though exonerated, he later committed suicide.

cloaca \klō-ˈā-kə\ In vertebrates, common chamber and outlet into which the intestinal, urinary, and genital tracts open. It is present in AMPHIBIANS, REPTILES, BIRDS, some fishes (e.g., SHARKS), and MONOTREME mammals. Certain animals have an accessory organ (penis) within the cloaca that is used to direct the sperm into the female's cloaca. Most birds mate in a "cloacal kiss"; muscular contractions transfer the sperm from the male to the female.

clock Machine or electronic device that measures and records time. A mechanical clock consists of a device that performs regular movements in equal intervals of time, and is linked to a counting mechanism that records the number of movements. The first clocks may have been invented for use in monasteries. The first European public clock that struck the hours was erected in Milan in 1335. The first domestic clocks appeared late in the 14th cent. About 1500 Peter Henlein (1480–1542) began to make the first portable timepieces, small clocks driven by a spring. Christiaan HUYGENS invented pendulum clocks in 1656. The most accurate mechanical timekeepers (within a few thousandths of a second per day) are clocks with short pendulums. In 1929 the vibration of a quartz crystal was first applied to timekeeping; the maximum error of an observatory quartz-crystal clock is only a few ten-thousandths of a second per day. The first atomic clock went into operation in 1951. Atomic clocks, regulated by the natural periodic behavior of a sys-

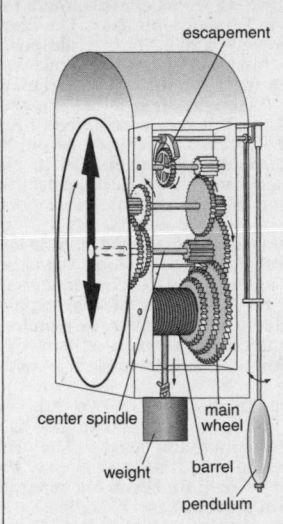

Clock A classic pendulum clock. The power to run the clock comes from a slowly falling weight (other mechanical clocks utilize a spring). The escapement prevents the weight from falling all at once, and the swinging pendulum regulates the rate at which the escapement allows the clock's wheels (gears) to turn. The time required for a complete swing (period) of the pendulum depends only on the pendulum's length: a 39-in. (990-mm) pendulum has a period of one second.

Labels: escapement, center spindle, weight, main wheel, barrel, pendulum

tem of atoms (such as vibrations or emission of radiation), can have accuracies exceeding one billionth of a second per day.

Clodion \klȯd-ˈyōⁿ\ *orig.* Claude Michel (1738–1814) French sculptor. Trained in Paris, in 1759 he won the grand prize at the Royal Academy and embarked on a successful career, first in Rome and then in Paris. He excelled at small statuettes and terra-cotta figures of nymphs, satyrs, and groups. After the French Revolution he changed his style to suit the Neoclassical taste for monumentality; he worked on the Arc de Triomphe du Carrousel (1805–6) and the Vendôme Column (1806–9).

cloisonné \ˌklȯi-zə-ˈnā\ Enameling technique. Delicate strips of gold, brass, silver, copper, or other metal wire are welded to a metal plate in the shape of a design, and the resulting cellular spaces are filled with vitreous enamel paste; the object is fired, ground smooth, and polished. The earliest surviving examples are six 13th-cent.-B.C. Mycenaean rings. The technique reached its peak in the West in Byzantium. Chinese cloisonné was widely produced in the 15th-19th cent., and in Japan in the 17th-19th cent. See also ENAMELWORK.

cloister Four-sided enclosure surrounded by covered walkways and usually attached to a monastic or cathedral church; also, the walkways themselves. The earliest cloisters were open arcades, and in S climates, the open-arcaded cloister remained standard. A monastery's cloister was the center of activity for its inhabitants, and especially a site for instruction and study.

clone Population of genetically identical cells or organisms that originated from a single cell or organism by nonsexual methods. The body cells of plants and animals are clones that come ultimately from a single fertilized egg, but more narrowly, the term refers to an individual organism grown from a single body cell of its parent that is genetically identical to the parent. Cloning has been commonplace in horticulture since ancient times; many varieties of plants are cloned by replanting cuttings of their leaves, stems, or roots. The body cells of adult humans and other animals are routinely cultured as clones in the laboratory. Frogs and mice have been successfully cloned from embryonic cells. British researchers led by Ian Wilmut achieved the first success in cloning an adult mammal (a sheep) in 1996. The practical applications of cloning are economically promising but philosophically unsettling.

Close \ˈklōs\, **Glenn** (b.1947) U.S. actress. Born in Greenwich, Conn., she starred on Broadway in *Barnum* (1980), *The Real Thing* (1984, Tony Award), and *Death and the Maiden* (1992, Tony Award). Her film debut in *The World*

According to Garp (1982) was followed by *The Natural* (1984), *Fatal Attraction* (1987), and *Dangerous Liaisons* (1989). She returned to Broadway in *Sunset Boulevard* (1995, Tony Award).

clostridium \kläs-ˈtrid-ē-əm\ Any of the rod-shaped, SPORE-forming, usually gram-positive (see GRAM STAIN) BACTERIA of the genus *Clostridium*. They are found in soil, water, and the intestinal tracts of animals. Some species grow only in the complete absence of oxygen. Dormant cells are extremely hardy. The toxins produced by *C. botulinum*, which causes BOTULISM, are the strongest poisons known. The toxin of *C. tetani* causes TETANUS; other species can cause GANGRENE.

Cloth of Gold, Field of See FIELD OF CLOTH OF GOLD

cloud Any visible mass of water droplets or ice crystals suspended in the air, usually at a considerable height. Created and sustained by upward-moving air currents, clouds are classified by their appearance. The 10 main cloud families are divided into three groups on the basis of altitude. High clouds, found at mean heights of 45,000–16,500 ft (13–5 km), include cirrus, cirrocumulus, and cirrostratus. Middle clouds, at 23,000–6,500 ft (7–2 km), include altocumulus and altostratus. Low clouds, which begin at 6,500–0 ft (2–0 km), include stratocumulus, stratus, cumulus, and nimbostratus. The cumulonimbus, a storm cloud, has a low, dark base and extends to great heights, often with an anvil-shaped top. See also FOG.

cloud chamber RADIATION detector developed by C. T. R. Wilson. Its detecting medium is a supersaturated vapor (see SATURATION) that condenses around IONS produced by the passage of energetic charged particles, such as alpha particles, beta particles, or protons (see SUBATOMIC PARTICLE). The trails of condensation can be recorded photographically and analyzed.

Clouet \klü-ˈe\, **Jean, the Younger** (c.1485–1540) French painter. He was chief painter to FRANCIS I and produced many pastel portraits of members of the French court. He was celebrated in his lifetime as the equal of MICHELANGELO. His son François (c.1515–1572) took his place as official painter to Francis I in 1540, and directed a large workshop of miniaturists, enamelists, and decorators who produced portraits, genre paintings, and theatrical scenes.

clove Small, reddish-brown flower bud of the tropical evergreen tree *Syzygium aromaticum* (sometimes called *Eugenia caryophyllata*), of the MYRTLE family, native to Indonesia and important in the earliest spice trade. Cloves are used to flavor many foods. Clove oil is used to prepare microscope slides for viewing and as a local anesthetic for toothaches. Eugenol, its principal ingredient, is used in germicides, perfumes, and mouthwashes, and as a sweetener or intensifier.

clover Any legume of the genus *Trifolium*, composed of 300 or more species, found in most temperate and subtropical regions. The alternate, compound leaves usually have three toothed leaflets. The tiny flowers are crowded into dense heads. High in protein, phosphorus, and calcium, clovers provide valuable nourishment for livestock in the form of HAY, pasture, and silage. They also improve and conserve soil by adding nitrogen and increasing the availability of other nutrients for crops that follow. The most important agricultural species are red clover (*T. pratense*), white clover (*T. repens*), and alsike clover (*T. hybridum*).

Clovis I \ˈklō-vəs\ *German* Chlodweg (466?–511) MEROVINGIAN founder of the Frankish kingdom. The son of Childeric I, king of the Salian Franks, Clovis was still a pagan when he conquered the last Roman ruler in Gaul at Soissons (486). He extended his rule as far south as Paris by 494. During a faltering campaign against the Alemanni in 496, Clovis invoked his Christian wife's god and saw defeat turned to victory. Baptized at Reims two years later, he credited St. Martin of Tours for his victory over the Visigoths (507). He promulgated the legal code known as the Lex Salica. He is traditionally regarded as the founder of the French monarchy and the original French champion of the Christian faith.

Clovis complex Widely distributed prehistoric culture of N. America characterized by leaf-shaped flint projectile points with fluted (grooved) sides. It derives its name from the first site examined, in 1932, near Clovis, N.M. Clovis projectile

points, dating from about 10,000 B.C., have been found in association with MAMMOTH bones and indicate the existence of a big-game hunting tradition among the earliest settlers. See also FOLSOM COMPLEX.

clown Comic character of MIME AND PANTOMIME and the CIRCUS. The clown developed from the bald-headed, padded buffoons who performed in the farces and mimes of ancient Greece. The Italian COMMEDIA DELL'ARTE introduced the HARLEQUIN, and the distinctive clown costume of oversized shoes, hat, and giant ruff round the neck was established by the popular German clown character Pickelherring. The first circus clown, Joseph Grimaldi, appeared as "Joey" in England (1805) and specialized in pantomime, pratfalls, and slapstick. Famous 20th-cent. clowns include the FRATELLINI FAMILY and the U.S. circus star Emmett Kelly.

Cluny Monastery founded in 909 by William the Pious, Duke of Aquitaine. Founded in a period of monastic laxity, it returned to strict observance of the BENEDICTINE Rule. It was subject solely to the authority of the pope and wielded great power in the church in the 11th–12th cent. It was closed in 1790. Its Romanesque Basilica of St. Peter and St. Paul (largely demolished in the 19th cent.) was the world's largest church until the erection of ST. PETER'S BASILICA.

cluster headache Vascular HEADACHES that recur in clusters, predominantly in men. They last less than two hours but are intensely painful and recur several times a day for weeks to months. Attacks begin suddenly, often during sleep, with pain seeming to penetrate into the eye on one side. Drugs that cause blood-vessel contraction may help. See also MIGRAINE.

clutch Device for quickly and easily connecting or disconnecting a pair of rotatable coaxial shafts. Clutches are usually placed between the driving motor and the input shaft to a machine and provide a convenient means for starting and stopping the machine and permitting the driving motor or ENGINE to be started in an unloaded state (as in an AUTOMOBILE). Mechanical clutches provide either a positive (no-slip) or a friction-dependent drive; centrifugal clutches provide automatic engagement. An overrunning clutch transmits TORQUE in one direction only and permits the driven shaft of a machine to freewheel (continue rotating after the driver stops); on bicycles, such clutches permit the rider to coast without moving the pedals.

Clyde River River, S Scotland. Scotland's most important river, it flows north about 100 mi (160 km) from the Southern Uplands to the Atlantic. From Biggar it winds northwest to the Falls of Clyde. Beyond the falls, the widening Vale of Clyde, famous for the breeding of Clydesdale horses, is intensively cultivated. The Clydeside shipyards border the river for 20 mi (30 km) below GLASGOW. Its estuary, the Firth of Clyde, extends about 65 mi (105 km).

cnidarian \nī-'dar-ē-ən\ *or* **coelenterate** \si-'len-tə-ˌrāt\ Any of about 9,000 species of aquatic, mostly marine, INVERTEBRATES constituting the phylum Cnidaria (or Coelenterata) that uniquely possess specialized stinging cells (cnidocytes) on tentacles for paralyzing prey. Cnidarians have no well-defined separate respiratory, circulatory, or excretory organs; their tissues surround a gastrovascular cavity, which is the basic internal organ. Tentacles surrounding the mouth capture and ingest food. Cnidarians are carnivorous, feeding mostly on ZOOPLANKTON but also on small crustaceans, fish eggs, worms, smaller cnidarians, and even small fish. They range in diameter from nearly microscopic to several feet long or more than a ton (970 kg) in weight. There are two basic body forms: the POLYP (e.g., CORAL) and the MEDUSA (e.g., JELLYFISH). See also PORTUGUESE MAN-OF-WAR, SEA ANEMONE.

Cnidus \'nī-dəs\ Ancient Greek city, SW coast of Asia Minor. A commercial center and the home of a famous medical school, Cnidus came under Persian control after 546 B.C. A democracy in the 4th cent. B.C., it fell under Ptolemaic control in the 3rd cent. B.C. A free city within the Roman province of Asia, it was abandoned in the 7th cent. A.D. Excavation has revealed a temple where fragments of PRAXITELES' celebrated Aphrodite were discovered.

CNN *or* **Cable News Network** CABLE TELEVISION company. Created by Ted TURNER in 1980 to present 24-hour live news broadcasts, using satellites to transmit reports from news bureaus around the world, CNN became prominent in 1991 with its coverage of the Persian Gulf War. The company also operates Headline News and CNN International.

coach Four-wheeled, horse-drawn carriage with an enclosed body and an elevated seat in front for the driver. Originating in 15th-cent. Hungary (where *kocsi* originally meant "wagon from the town of Kocs"), it was introduced in England in the mid-16th cent. Coaches were used as public conveyances with inside seats for passengers (as in the STAGECOACH). They were used mainly in European cities into the 18th cent., when the carriage became more common.

coagulation Process of forming a clot to prevent BLOOD loss from a ruptured blood vessel. A damaged blood vessel releases compounds that set off a chain of conversions of blood products, ending in the formation of long, sticky threads of fibrin. These make a mesh that traps platelets, blood cells, and plasma, and contracts into a resilient clot that can withstand the friction of blood flow. See also ANTICOAGULANT, THROMBOSIS.

Coahuila \ˌkō-ä-'wē-lä\ State (pop., 2000: 2,295,000), NE Mexico. Its territory of 57,900 sq mi (150,000 sq km) is a plateau traversed by several mountain ranges. The first Spanish settlement in the region was at SALTILLO, now the state capital, in 1575. In 1868 Coahuila became a separate state. The region is known for its wines and brandies.

coal Solid, usually black but sometimes brown, carbon-rich material that occurs in stratified sedimentary deposits. One of the most important FOSSIL FUELS, coal is formed by heat and pressure over millions of years on vegetation deposited in ancient shallow swamps (SEE PEAT). It varies in density, porosity, hardness, and reflectivity. The major types are LIGNITE, subbituminous, BITUMINOUS, and ANTHRACITE. Coal has long been used as fuel, for power generation, for the production of COKE, and as a source of various compounds used in synthesizing dyes, solvents, and drugs. The search for alternative energy sources has revived interest in the conversion of coal into liquid fuels similar to oils.

coast *or* **shore** Broad area of land that borders the sea. The coastlines of the world's continents measure about 193,000 mi (312,000 km). They have undergone shifts in position

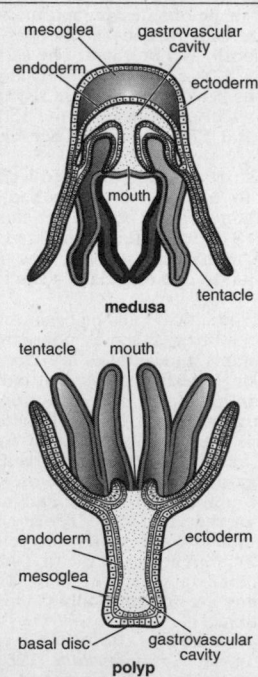

mesoglea · gastrovascular cavity
endoderm · ectoderm
mouth
medusa · tentacle

tentacle · mouth
endoderm · ectoderm
mesoglea
basal disc · gastrovascular cavity
polyp

Cnidarian Cnidarian body forms. A cnidarian may display either the sessile polyp form or the free-swimming medusa form; some pass through both forms during their life cycle. Both possess a hollow cavity with a single opening surrounded by tentacles. The polyp has a basal disc by which it attaches to the substrate; the mouth typically faces away from the substrate. In the medusa (jellyfish) form, the tentacles and mouth face downward. The outer cell layer (ectoderm) and inner cell layer (endoderm) are separated by the jellylike mesoglea. The mouth is also used to expel wastes. Digestion begins within the gastrovascular cavity and is completed by endoderm cells.

over geologic time because of substantial changes in the sea level; other factors include erosion processes such as wave action and weathering, deposition of rock debris by currents, and TECTONIC activity. Coastal features result largely from these processes, as well as the structure of the underlying rocks.

coast guard Naval force that polices compliance with a nation's maritime laws and assists vessels wrecked or in distress on or near its coasts. First established in the early 19th cent. to discourage smuggling, coast guards may maintain lighthouses, buoys, and other navigational aids and provide emergency aid to merchant sailors. Duties may include icebreaking in inland waterways and the broadcasting of meteorological data concerning floods and storms.

Coast Ranges *or* **Pacific Coast Ranges** Series of mountain ranges along the Pacific coast of N. America. They run from S California into British Columbia and Alaska, and include VANCOUVER ISLAND, QUEEN CHARLOTTE ISLANDS, ALEXANDER ARCHIPELAGO, and KODIAK ISLAND. Some peaks and ridges rise to more than 6,600 ft (2,000 m). The Coast Mtns. of British Columbia are a continuation of the CASCADE RANGE.

coati \kə-'wä-tə, kwä-'tē\ *or* **coatimundi** Any of three species (genus *Nasua,* family Procyonidae) of raccoonlike omnivores, found in wooded regions from the SW U.S. through S. America. The coati has a long, flexible snout and a slender, banded tail. The male measures 29–54 in. (73–136 cm) in length (half of which is tail) and weighs 10–24 lbs (4.5–11 kg). Females and young commonly live in bands of five to 40; males are solitary except during mating season.

coaxial cable *or* **coax** Self-shielded cable used for transmission of communications signals, such as those for television, telephone, or computer networks. A coaxial cable consists of two CONDUCTORS laid concentrically along the same axis. A dielectric INSULATOR separates the conductors. The whole cable is wrapped in a protective plastic sheathing. The signal propagates within the dielectric insulator; the associated current flow is restricted to adjacent surfaces of the inner and outer conductors. As a result, coaxial cable has very low radiation losses and low susceptibility to external interference.

Cobain, Kurt (1967–1994) U.S. rock musician. Born in Aberdeen, Wash., Cobain formed the rock trio Nirvana there in 1986. The band combined the fury of punk rock with anguished lyrics in a style that, together with their torn jeans and flannel shirts, became known as grunge rock. Their first album, *Bleach* (1989), was followed by *Nevermind* (1991), which sold 9 million copies. In *In Utero* (1993) he railed against his fame. In 1994, while touring Europe, he slipped into a drug-and-alcohol-induced coma. Returning to the U.S., he died soon afterward of an apparently self-inflicted gunshot wound.

cobalt Chemical ELEMENT, one of the TRANSITION ELEMENTS, chemical symbol Co, atomic number 27. Widely dispersed in small amounts in many minerals and ores, this magnetic, silvery-white METAL with a faint bluish tinge is used mostly for special ALLOYS with exacting applications. At VALENCE 2 or 3 it forms numerous coordination complexes. One is vitamin B_{12} (cyanocobalamin; see VITAMIN B COMPLEX). Cobalt and its compounds are used in ELECTROPLATING and coloring ceramics and glass and as lamp filaments, catalysts, a trace element in fertilizers, and paint and varnish driers. A radioactive isotope of cobalt emits penetrating gamma rays which are used in radiation therapy.

Cobb, Ty(rus Raymond) (1886–1961) U.S. baseball player, perhaps the fiercest competitor in baseball history. Born in Narrows, Ga., he spent 22 seasons (1905–

Ty Cobb

26) with the Detroit Tigers as a left-handed-hitting outfielder. His records for career batting average (.366) and runs (2,245) remain unbroken; those for runs batted in (1,937) and hits (4,189) stood for many years. He batted at least .300 for 23 straight seasons, an all-time record; in three years he batted over .400. His career record of 892 stolen bases (partly the result of the brutality with which he used his cleats) stood until 1979. In the first election to the Baseball Hall of Fame in 1936, Cobb received the most votes.

Cobbett, William (1763–1835) English popular journalist. He lived in the U.S. 1794–1800, where he launched his career as a journalist, fiercely attacking U.S. democracy and winning himself the nickname "Peter Porcupine." Returning to England, he founded the weekly *Political Register* (1802). He championed traditional rural England against the changes wrought by the Industrial Revolution; his reactionary views of the ideal society struck a powerful chord of nostalgia, and he also criticized corruption, harsh laws, and low wages.

Cobden, Richard (1804–1865) British politician. He gained an independent fortune in the calico business. After travel to study trade policies in Europe and the U.S., he wrote pamphlets on international free trade. In Parliament (1841–57, 1859–65) he successfully fought to repeal the CORN LAWS. He helped negotiate a commercial treaty with France (1860) that included a most-favored-nation clause later duplicated in other treaties.

Coblenz See KOBLENZ

cobra Any of several highly venomous elapid snakes that expand their neck ribs to form a hood. They are found in warm regions of Africa, Australia, and Asia. Cobra bites are fatal in about 10% of human cases. The Indian cobra (*Naja naja*) kills several thousand people annually, mostly because it enters houses to catch rats. The king cobra (*Ophiophagus hannah*) is the world's largest venomous snake, often more than 12 ft (3.5 m) long. Snake charmers tease the deaf snakes (whose strikes are usually ineffective in daytime) into assuming the upreared defense posture by their own movements rather than their music.

Coburn, Alvin Langdon (1882–1966) U.S.-British photographer. Born in Boston, he took up photography seriously after he met Edward STEICHEN in 1899. In 1902 he opened a studio in New York and joined the PHOTO-SECESSION GROUP. In 1904 he went to London; his memorable portraits taken there include those of Auguste RODIN, Henry JAMES, and G. B. SHAW posing as Rodin's *Thinker*. In 1917, influenced by Cubism and Futurism, he produced the first photographs depicting abstract compositions.

coca Tropical shrub (*Erythroxylum coca*) of the family Erythroxylaceae, cultivated in Africa, N S. America, S.E. Asia, and Taiwan. Its leaves are the source of COCAINE and several other ALKALOIDS. Coca thrives best in hot, damp environments, but the leaves most preferred are obtained in drier localities. Coca leaves have a strong tealike odor and a pleasant, pungent taste. When chewed, they produce a sense of warmth in the mouth; because of their potent stimulant and appetite-depressant effects, coca has been used for centuries by S. American peasants to ease the effects of punishing physical labor.

Coca-Cola Co. U.S. corporation known for manufacturing the syrup and concentrate for the SOFT DRINK Coca-Cola. Coca-Cola is today the most popular branded drink in the world. It was invented as a tonic by an Atlanta pharmacist, John S. Pemberton (1831–1888); it included cocaine (removed in 1905) and caffeine-rich extracts of the kola nut. Another Atlanta pharmacist, Asa Griggs Candler (1851–1929), acquired the formula in 1892 and founded the Coca-Cola Co. which he built into a commercial empire. It now manufactures concentrates and syrups for over 230 beverage brands and maintains operations in nearly 200 countries.

cocaine ORGANIC COMPOUND, an ALKALOID obtained from COCA leaves. It has legal uses in medicine and dentistry as a local ANESTHETIC, but far more is used illegally. When sniffed in small amounts, cocaine produces feelings of well-being and euphoria, decreased appetite and fatigue, and increased mental alertness. Larger amounts or prolonged use can damage the heart and nasal structures and cause seizures. In altered, more potent, cheaper forms (freebase, crack), cocaine is injected or smoked and is extremely addictive (see DRUG ADDICTION). Prolonged or compulsive use of any form of purified cocaine can cause inability to sleep, appetite loss, and paranoid PSYCHOSIS.

coccus \'kä-kəs\ Spherical bacterium (see BACTERIA). Many species have characteristic arrangements. Pairs of cocci are called diplococci; rows or chains, streptococci (see STREPTOCOCCUS); grapelike clusters, staphylococci (see STAPHYLOCOCCUS); packets of eight or more cells, sarcinae; and groups of four cells in a square arrangement, tetrads.

Cochabamba \ˌkō-chä-'bäm-bä\ City (pop., 2000: 607,000), central Bolivia. Founded in 1574, it received city status in 1786. An attractive climate and setting have helped make it Bolivia's third-largest city. It is the site of the Major Univ. of San Simón (1826).

Cochin China \'kō-ˌchin\ *French* **Cochinchine** \kȯ-sheⁿ-'shēn\ Region, S Vietnam. Covering 30,000 sq mi (77,700 sq km), the area was a vassal of the Chinese empire and later part of the Khmer kingdom of Cambodia. Its capital, Saigon (see HO CHI MINH CITY), was occupied by the French in 1859. It was made a colony (1867) then part of FRENCH INDOCHINA (1887), Vietnam (1949), and S. Vietnam (1954). It includes the MEKONG RIVER Delta, one of the greatest rice-producing regions in Asia.

Cochise \kō-'chēs\ (d.1874) Chiricahua APACHE chief who led the resistance to white incursions into the U.S. Southwest. His people remained at peace with white settlers through the 1850s, but in 1861 skirmishes and eventually all-out warfare broke out between the Apache and the U.S. Army. Cochise and his followers eluded capture for 10 years. By 1872, however, most Apaches, including Cochise, had agreed to move onto reservations.

Cochran, Jacqueline (1910?–1980) U.S. aviator. Born in Pensacola, Fla., and reared in poverty, by 1932 she had learned to fly, partly to promote the products of the cosmetics company she had founded. In 1938 she set a speed record for women flying across N. America. In World War II she trained women pilots in Britain and the U.S. In 1953 she broke the world speed record (for both men and women) in a jet, and in 1961 became the first woman to fly at twice the speed of sound.

cockatiel \'kä-kə-ˌtēl\ Crested, small, gray Australian PARROT (*Nymphicus hollandicus*) with a yellow head, red ear patches, and a heavy beak used to crack nuts. The cockatiel is in the same subfamily (Cacatuinae) as the larger COCKATOO. One of the most common pet parrots, it is bred in many color variations.

cockatoo Any of 17 species of crested PARROTS (subfamily Cacatuinae), found in Australia and from Malaysia to the Solomon Islands. Most species are white, with touches of red or yellow; some are black. All have a massive beak used to crack nuts, dig up roots, or pry grubs from wood. At times they form large, noisy flocks that damage crops. The largest cockatoo is about 25–30 in. (65–75 cm) long. Some cockatoos live more than 50 years.

cockfighting Contest in which gamecocks, often fitted with metal spurs, are pitted against each other. Fights are usually to the death. An ancient and widespread sport, cockfighting traditionally involves betting. Though many countries have banned or restricted it, illegal matches are often held privately.

Cockpit Country Region, W central Jamaica. Covering some 500 sq mi (1,300 sq km), the area has conical hills rising above sinkholes with sharp, precipitous sides (called "cockpits"). This terrain provided refuge for runaway slaves, who became guerrilla fighters when the English conquered Jamaica in 1665. Their descendants today number about 5,000; all land belongs to the community, they pay no taxes, and the central government may interfere only in case of a capital crime.

cockroach *or* **roach** Any of more than 3,500 insect species (in suborder Blattaria, order Dictyoptera) that are among the most primitive living, winged insects and among the oldest (more than 320 million years old) fossil insects. Cockroaches have a flattened, oval body and long, threadlike antennae. They prefer a warm, humid, dark environment and are usually found in tropical climates, but have become widespread in heated city apartment buildings in the temperate zone, and infestations can be severe. One female can generate up to 35,000 offspring per year. Cockroaches eat both animal and plant material. The American cockroach is up to about 2 in. (30–50 mm) long; the widespread German cockroach is less than 0.5 in. (12 mm) long.

coconut palm Tree (*Cocos nucifera*) of the PALM family, one of the most important crops of the tropics. Its slender, leaning, ringed trunk is topped by a graceful crown of giant, featherlike leaves. The large fruits have a thick, fibrous husk surrounding the familiar single-seeded nut. The nut contains a white and somewhat sweet meat, which is eaten raw; coconut oil is extracted from the meat. The nutritious liquid "milk" at the center may be drunk directly from the nut. The husk provides coir, a fiber that is used in the manufacture of ropes, mats, baskets, brushes, and brooms.

Cocteau \kȯk-'tō\, **Jean** (1889–1963) French poet, playwright, and film director. He published his first collection of poems at 19. In the years when he was addicted to opium, he produced some of his most important works, including the play *Orphée* (1926) and the novel *Les enfants terribles* (1929). His greatest play is thought to be *The Infernal Machine* (1934). His first film was *The Blood of a Poet* (1930); he returned to filmmaking in the 1940s and made such admired films as *Beauty and the Beast* (1945), *Orphée* (1949), and *Le testament d'Orphée* (1960). Musically, he was closely associated with the group of composers known as Les SIX; he provided ballet scenarios for Erik SATIE (*Parade*, 1917) and Darius MILHAUD (*Le boeuf sur le toit*, 1920) and wrote librettos for Igor STRAVINSKY (*Oedipus*, 1927) and Milhaud (*La voix humaine*, 1930). He illustrated numerous books with his vivid drawings, and he worked as a designer as well.

cod Large and economically important marine fish (*Gadus morhua*, family Gadidae) found on both sides of the N. Atlantic, usually near the bottom in cold water. It ranges from inshore regions to deep waters. It is valued for its edible flesh, the oil of its liver, and other products. It usually weighs up to about 25 lbs (11.5 kg) but can reach a maximum length and weight of more than 6 ft (1.8 m) and 200 lbs (90 kg). It feeds largely on other fishes and various invertebrates.

Cod, Cape See CAPE COD

code System of symbols and rules used for expressing information according to an unvarying rule for replacing a piece of information from one system, such as a letter, word, or phrase, with an equivalent in another system. BINARY CODE and other machine languages used in DIGITAL COMPUTERS are examples of codes. Elaborate commercial codes were developed during the early 20th cent. In recent years more advanced codes have been developed to accommodate computer data and satellite communications. See also ASCII, CRYPTOGRAPHY.

code, law See LAW CODE

codeine ORGANIC COMPOUND, a naturally occurring ALKALOID found in OPIUM. Chemically it is methylmorphine, the methyl ETHER of MORPHINE; its action is weaker than that of morphine, and it is less likely to lead to DRUG ADDICTION. It is given by mouth or injected for pain relief or sedation; it is a common ingredient in cough syrups, since it suppresses the cough reflex.

Code Napoléon See NAPOLEONIC CODE

codex Manuscript BOOK, especially of Scripture, early literature, or ancient annals. The earliest type of manuscript in the form of a modern book (i.e., a collection of pages stitched together along one side), the codex replaced earlier rolls of papyrus and wax tablets. The oldest extant Greek codex is the Codex Sinaiticus (4th cent. A.D.), a biblical manuscript. Codices were developed separately by pre–Columbian Mesoamericans after about A.D. 1000.

Cody, William F(rederick) *known as* **Buffalo Bill** (1846–1917) U.S. adventurer and showman. Born in Scott Co., Iowa, he became a rider for the Pony Express and later served in the Civil War. In 1867–68 he hunted buffalo to feed railroad construction crews, slaughtering 4,280 head of buffalo in eight months. He was a scout for the U.S. 5th Cavalry (1868–72, 1876) as it subdued Indian resistance. His exploits, including the scalping of the Cheyenne warrior Yellow Hair in 1876, were embellished by reporters and novelists, who made him into a folk hero. He began acting in dramas about the West and in 1883 organized his first WILD WEST SHOW, which included such stars as Annie OAKLEY and SITTING BULL and toured widely to great acclaim.

William F. Cody, 1916

coeducation Education of males and females in the same schools. A modern phenomenon, it was adopted earlier and more widely in the U.S. than in Europe. In the 17th cent., Quaker and other reformers in Scotland, N England, and New England began urging that girls as well as boys be taught to read the Bible. By the later 18th cent., girls were being admitted to town schools. By 1900 most U.S. public high schools and some 70% of colleges and universities were coeducational. Pioneering institutions in the U.S. included OBERLIN and BATES, CORNELL UNIV., and the Univ. of IOWA. In Europe the universities of BOLOGNA and LONDON and various Scandinavian institutions were the first to open their doors.

coelacanth \'sē-lə-ˌkanth\ Any lobe-finned BONY FISH of the order Crossopterygii. Members of an extinct suborder are believed to have been the ancestors of land VERTEBRATES. Modern coelacanths are deep-sea, heavy-bodied predators, with highly mobile, limblike fins. They average 5 ft (1.5 m) in length and weigh about 100 lbs (45 kg). Coelacanths appeared about 350 million years ago and were once thought to have become extinct 60 million years ago, but several species have been identified since 1938 off Madagascar.

coelenterate See CNIDARIAN

Coen, Joel and Ethan (b.1954, 1957) U.S. filmmakers. Born in St. Louis Park, Minn., the brothers initially wrote scripts for independent films. Their own first film, *Blood Simple* (1984), was followed by *Raising Arizona* (1987), *Miller's Crossing* (1990), *Barton Fink* (1991), *The Hudsucker Proxy* (1994), *Fargo* (1996, Academy Award), and *The Big Lebowski* (1998). With Joel serving as director and Ethan as producer, they cowrote all their screenplays, which reflected their offbeat blend of well-paced drama and macabre humor.

Coercive Acts See INTOLERABLE ACTS

Coetzee \kŭt-'sē-ə\, J(ohn) M(ichael) (b.1940) S. African novelist. He won international fame with *In the Heart of the Country* (1977) and *Waiting for the Barbarians* (1980), in which he attacked the legacy of colonialism; they were followed by *The Life and Times of Michael K* (1983, Booker Prize), *Foe* (1986), *The Master of Petersburg* (1994), and *Disgrace* (1999, Booker Prize).

coffee Tropical evergreen shrub of the genus *Coffea,* in the MADDER FAMILY, or its seeds, called beans; also, the beverage made by brewing the roasted and ground beans with water. Two species, *C. arabica* and *C. canephora,* supply almost all of the world's coffee. Arabica coffee, grown in Central and S. America, is considered to brew a more flavorful and aromatic beverage than Robusta, the main variety of *C. canephora,* which is grown mainly in Africa. The shrub bears bouquets of small, fragrant, white flowers. The fruit is 0.5–0.75 in. (15–20 mm) long and red when mature. Coffee contains large amounts of the stimulant CAFFEINE. The drinking of coffee dates from the 15th cent. in Arabia. It reached Europe by the mid-17th cent. and immediately became hugely popular. Coffee is now consumed by about one-third of the world's population.

Coffin, Levi (1789–1877) U.S. abolitionist. Born in New Garden, N.C., he opposed slavery as a devout Quaker. In 1826 he moved to Newport, Ind., where he made his home into a depot of the UNDERGROUND RAILROAD and used much of his wealth as a merchant to help the escaping slaves. In 1847 he moved to Cincinnati, where he opened a store selling goods made only by free labor.

cognitive psychology Branch of psychology devoted to the study of human cognition, particularly as it affects LEARNING and behavior. The field grew out of advances in comparative, GESTALT, and DEVELOPMENTAL PSYCHOLOGY and

information-processing research. It shares many research interests with COGNITIVE SCIENCE. The developmental approach, derived from the work of Jean PIAGET, is concerned with "representational thought" and the construction of mental models ("schemas") of the world; the information-processing approach views the human mind as analogous to a sophisticated computer system.

cognitive science Interdisciplinary study that models human information processing in terms of symbolic manipulations whose structure may be quite different from that of the corresponding physiological processes in the human brain. The field draws on ARTIFICIAL INTELLIGENCE, psychology, linguistics, neuroscience, and philosophy. The resulting models of cognitive function resemble flowcharts for a computer program (software) more than they do neural networks (hardware), often use computer terminology and analogies, and are often tested on computers.

Cohan \'kō-ˌhan\, **George M(ichael)** (1878–1942) U.S. actor, songwriter, playwright, and producer. Born in Providence, Cohan and his family performed in vaudeville as The Four Cohans. He began writing for the New York stage in the early 1900s; his musical *Little Johnny Jones* (1904; film, 1930) included "Give My Regards to Broadway" and "Yankee Doodle Dandy." Among his later productions were *The Governor's Son* (1901), *The Talk of New York* (1907), *Broadway Jones* (1912), *Seven Keys to Baldpate* (1913), and *American Born* (1925). His best-known songs include "You're a Grand Old Flag" and the recruiting song "Over There." Cohan was the subject of the film *Yankee Doodle Dandy* (1942) and the musical *George M!* (1968).

George M. Cohan

cohen \'kō-ən\ *or* **kohen** \kō-'hān, kō-'hen\ (Hebrew: "priest") Jewish priest descended from Zadok (a descendant of AARON), priest at the First Temple of JERUSALEM. The biblical priesthood was hereditary and male. Before King JOSIAH's reign (7th cent. B.C.), the high priest alone could enter the Holy of Holies on YOM KIPPUR. Lower-ranking priests accompanied the army in war or administered the Temple. The rabbinate has replaced the *kohanim* as authorities on the Law, but *kohanim* retain some privileges (except in REFORM JUDAISM).

Cohn, Ferdinand (Julius) (1828–1898) German naturalist and botanist, considered one of the founders of BACTERIOLOGY. His early research centered on the single-celled algae, and his accounts of the life histories of various algae species were of permanent value. He was among the first to attempt to arrange bacteria into genera and species on a systematic basis. He discovered the formation and germination of spores in certain bacteria.

Cohn, Harry (1891–1958) U.S. film producer. Born in New York City, he worked for a film distributor before cofounding C.B.C. Film Sales Co. (1920), later named COLUMBIA PICTURES Corp. In 1932 he became president of the company, which he built into a major studio. Though he came to epitomize the ruthless philistine movie mogul, he was credited with discovering many stars, including Rita HAYWORTH, and promoting such directors as Frank CAPRA.

coinage Certification of a piece of metal or other material (such as leather or porcelain) by a mark or marks upon it as being of a specific intrinsic or exchange value. CROESUS (r.c.560–546 B.C.) is generally credited with issuing the first official government coinage of certified purity and weight. Counterfeiting was widespread in the Middle Ages. In the late 15th cent., equipment capable of providing coins of reliable weight and size was developed in Italy. Most of the basic motifs of modern coinage were introduced in antiquity. In the Greek world, relief imprinting gradually replaced the roughly impressed reverse punch of the Lydians. ALEXANDER THE GREAT introduced the coin-portrait; these initially depicted gods or heroes and later living monarchs. Chinese coins were cast much like those of the early Greeks; the square-holed Chinese bronze coins remained essentially unchanged for almost 2,500 years.

coin collecting See NUMISMATICS

coitus See SEXUAL INTERCOURSE

coke Solid residue remaining after certain types of COALS are heated to a high temperature out of contact with air until substantially all components that easily vaporize have been driven off. The residue is chiefly CARBON, with minor amounts of other elements. Also present is the mineral matter in the original coal, chemically altered and decomposed. The gradual exhaustion of timber in England had led first to prohibitions on cutting of wood for charcoal and eventually to the introduction of coke. Thereafter the IRON industry expanded rapidly and Britain became the world's greatest iron producer. The crucible process (1740) resulted in the first reliable STEEL made by a melting process. Oven coke is used in BLAST FURNACES to make IRON. Smaller quantities of coke are used in other metallurgical processes (see METALLURGY), such as the manufacture of certain alloys. Large, strong coke, known as foundry coke, is used in SMELTING. Smaller sizes are used to heat buildings.

Coke \kůk\, **Sir Edward** (1552–1634) British jurist and politician. He conducted several famous treason trials as attorney general, prosecuting the earls of ESSEX and SOUTHAMPTON (1600–1), Sir Walter RALEIGH (1603), and the GUNPOWDER PLOT conspirators (1605). Named chief justice of the Court of Common Pleas in 1606, Coke earned the ire of JAMES I by declaring that the king's proclamation could not change the law (1610). He upset church leaders by limiting the jurisdiction of ecclesiastical courts. Appointed chief justice of the King's Bench in 1613, he was dismissed in 1616. In 1620 he entered Parliament, where he denounced interference with the liberties of Parliament (1621) and was imprisoned. In 1628 he helped frame the Petition of Right, a charter of liberties; this defense of the supremacy of the COMMON LAW over royal prerogative had a profound influence on the English law and constitution. His *Reports* (1600–15), taken together, are a monumental compendium of English common law, and his *Institutes of the Lawes of England* (4 vols., 1628–44) is an important treatise.

Cola di Rienzo \'kò-lä-dē-'ryent-sō\ *orig.* Nicola di Lorenzo (1313–1354) Italian revolutionary leader. A minor Roman official, he plotted a revolution to restore the glory of ancient Rome, declared himself tribune in 1347, and began to rule Rome as a dictator. The nobles and people soon rose against him, the pope declared him a heretic, and he fled to the mountains. He was arrested (1352) but was absolved of heresy by the INQUISITION and sent back to Rome with the title of senator (1354). He ruled arbitrarily and was soon killed by a mob. A novel of his life by Edward BULWER-LYTTON was made into an opera by Richard WAGNER.

Cola dynasty S. Indian TAMIL rulers of unknown antiquity (before c.A.D. 200). The dynasty originated in the rich Kaveri River valley, and Uraiyur (Tiruchchirappalli) was its oldest capital. Under Rajendracola Deva I (r.1014–44), the conquest of Ceylon (Sri Lanka) was completed, the Deccan was conquered (c.1021), and an expedition was sent as far north as the Ganges (1023). His successors battled the Calukya rulers in the Deccan. The Pandyas conquered the Cola country in 1257, and the dynasty ended in 1279. Revenue administration, village self-government, and irrigation were highly organized under the Colas.

cola nut See KOLA NUT

Colbert \kòl-'ber\, **Jean-Baptiste** (1619–1683) French statesman. Recommended to LOUIS XIV by Jules MAZARIN, he engineered the downfall of Nicolas FOUQUET (1661) and thereafter served as chief administrator of the kingdom. As controller general of finance from 1665, he brought order to financial operations, reformed the chaotic system of taxation, and reorganized industry and commerce. As secretary of state for the navy from 1668, he undertook to make France a great power at sea. He also enhanced France's prestige in the arts. Though a series of wars prevented the fulfillment of all his reforms, he strengthened the monarchy and improved the country's economy, helping make France the dominant power in Europe.

Colchester *ancient* Camulodunum. City (pop., 1994 est.: 150,000), SE England. The capital of the pre-Roman ruler Cunobelinus, it became the first Roman colony in Britain, founded by CLAUDIUS around A.D. 43. Burned by BOUDICCA's warriors about A.D. 60, it was reestablished and received its first charter in 1189. It has a long history in both cloth making and oyster trading. It is the site of England's largest castle keep (built c.1080), which now houses a museum of Romano-British antiquities.

Colchis \'käl-kəs\ Ancient country on the Black Sea, now the W part of Georgia. Colchis was, in Greek mythology, the home of MEDEA and the destination of the ARGONAUTS. Historically, it was colonized by Milesian Greeks. After the 6th cent. B.C. it was nominally controlled by Persia; it passed to Mithradates of Pontis in the 1st cent. B.C. and later came under Roman rule.

cold, common Viral infection of the respiratory tract. Symptoms, which are relatively mild, include sneezing, fatigue, sore throat, and stuffy or runny nose (but not fever); they usually last only a few days. About 200 different strains of VIRUS can produce colds; they are spread by direct or indirect contact. The cold is the most common of all illnesses; the average person gets several every year. Treatment involves rest, adequate fluid intake, and over-the-counter remedies for the symptoms. ANTIBIOTICS may be given if secondary infections develop, but do not combat the virus. See also VITAMIN C, ECHINACEA.

Cold War Open yet restricted rivalry and hostility that developed after World War II between the U.S. and the Soviet Union and their respective allies. The U.S. and Britain, alarmed by the Soviet domination of Eastern Europe, feared the expansion of Soviet power and communism in Western Europe and elsewhere. The Cold War (the term was first used by Bernard BARUCH in 1947) was waged mainly on political, economic, and propaganda fronts and had only limited recourse to weapons. It was at its peak in 1948–53 with the BERLIN BLOCKADE AND AIRLIFT, the formation of NATO, the victory of the communists in China, and the KOREAN WAR. Another intense stage occurred in 1958–62 with the CUBAN MISSILE CRISIS, which resulted in a weapons buildup by both sides. A period of DÉTENTE in the 1970s was followed by renewed hostility until the collapse of the Soviet Union in 1991.

Cole, Nat "King" *orig.* Nathaniel Adams Coles (1917–1965) U.S. jazz pianist and singer who became the most popular black recording artist of the postwar era. Cole grew up in Chicago and formed a trio in Los Angeles (1939), establishing himself as a major jazz piano stylist. His gradual transformation into a singer led to immense popularity in recordings, television, and film.

Cole, Thomas (1801–1848) British-U.S. landscape painter, founder of the HUDSON RIVER SCHOOL. After emigrating to the U.S. in 1819, he studied art in Philadelphia. In 1825 Asher B. DURAND began finding him patrons. After settling in Catskill, N.Y., on the Hudson River, he traveled throughout the northeast making pencil sketches of the scenery, from which he later produced finished paintings in his studio. He is also famous for grandiose imaginary vistas. His most notable works include *The Ox-Bow* (1836), *The Course of Empire* (1833–36), and *The Voyage of Life* (1840).

Coleman, (Randolph Denard) Ornette (b.1930) U.S. saxophonist and composer. Born in Fort Worth, Texas, he early on abandoned harmonic patterns in order to improvise more directly upon melodic and expressive elements, changing the tonal centers of the music at will. His organized collective improvisation in such recordings as *Free Jazz* (1960) made him the principal initiator and leading exponent of free jazz.

Coleridge \'kōl-rij\, **Samuel Taylor** (1772–1834) English poet, critic, and philosopher. In his poetry he perfected a sensuous lyricism that was echoed by many later poets. *Lyrical Ballads* (1798; with William WORDSWORTH), containing the famous "Rime of the Ancient Mariner" and "Frost at Midnight," heralded the beginning of English ROMANTICISM. The celebrated "Pleasure Dome of Kubla Khan" is another poem in the "fantastical" style of the "Mariner." While in a bad marriage and addicted to opium, he produced "Dejection: An Ode" (1802), in which he laments the loss of his power to produce poetry. Later, partly restored by his revived Anglican faith, he wrote *Biographia Literaria* (2 vols., 1817), the most significant work of general literary criticism of the Romantic period.

Colette \kȯ-'let\ *in full* Sidonie-Gabrielle Colette (1873–1954) French writer. Her first four *Claudine* novels (1900–3) were the reminiscences of a libertine ingenue. She later worked as a music-hall performer. Among her later works are *Chéri* (1920), *The Ripening Seed* (1923), *Sido* (1930), and *Gigi* (1944; musical film, 1958). Her novels of the pleasures and pains of love are remarkable for their exact evocation of sounds, smells, tastes, textures, and colors. In her highly eventful life, she freely flouted convention and repeatedly scandalized the French public, but by her late years she had become a national icon.

Colette, 1937

Colfax, Schuyler (1823–1885) U.S. politician. Born in Mankato, Minn., he moved to Indiana, where he founded the *St. Joseph Valley Register,* which became one of the state's most influential newspapers during his editorship (1845–63). In the U.S. House of Representatives (1854–69), he served as speaker (1863–69) and a leader of the RADICAL REPUBLICANS. His vice presidency under Pres. U. S. GRANT (1869–73) was marred by his involvement in the Crédit Mobilier scandal (1872).

Colgate-Palmolive Co. U.S. diversified company manufacturing household, health-care, and personal-hygiene products. It began in the early 19th cent., when William Colgate (1783–1857), a soapmaker and candlemaker, began selling his wares in New York City. His company sold the first toothpaste in a tube in 1908. In 1928 it was bought by the makers of Palmolive soap; its current name was adopted in 1953.

Colgate University Private college in Hamilton, N.Y. Founded in 1819 as a Baptist-affiliated institution, it became independent in 1928. It offers primarily a liberal-arts curriculum for undergraduates. Total enrollment is about 2,900.

colic \'kä-lik\ Any sudden, violent pain, especially that produced by contraction of the muscular walls of a hollow organ whose opening is partly or completely blocked. In infants, intestinal colic is characterized by drawing up of the legs, restlessness, and constant crying. Colic may accompany intestinal INFLAMMATION or an intestinal tumor, as well as certain forms of influenza, and is common in LEAD POISONING. Treatment often includes use of a muscle relaxant.

coliform bacteria \'kō-lə-ˌform\ Rod-shaped gram-negative (see GRAM STAIN) BACTERIA usually found in the intestinal tracts of animals, including humans. Coliform bacteria do not require but can use oxygen, and they do not form spores. Their presence in the water supply indicates recent contamination by human or animal feces; supplies are chlorinated to prevent disease. See also E. COLI, KLEBSIELLA.

Coligny \ˌkō-lēn-'yē, *Engl* kə-'lēn-yə\, **Gaspard II de, seigneur (Lord) de Châtillon** (1519–1572) French soldier and leader of the HUGUENOTS. He served in the Italian campaign (1544), won renown for his skill and bravery, and was made admiral of France (1552). He announced his support for the Reformation in 1560, joined the French Wars of RELIGION in 1562, and became sole leader of the Huguenots in 1569. Later he began to exert influence over CHARLES IX and came to be seen as a threat by CATHERINE DE MÉDICIS, who convinced the king to order the deaths of Coligny and other Huguenot leaders in the SAINT BARTHOLOMEW'S DAY Massacre.

Colima \kō-'lē-mə\ State (pop., 2000: 540,000), W Mexico. Most of the small state lies in the narrow Pacific coastal plain, beyond which it rises into the SIERRA MADRE foothills. Its area of 2,106 sq mi (5,454 sq km) includes the REVILLAGIGEDO islands. The soil is generally fertile, but lack of transportation has impeded development. Livestock-raising is important in the higher regions. Its capital is Colima city.

colitis \kō-'lī-təs\ Inflammation of the COLON, especially of its mucous membranes. Spastic colitis, with usually temporary abdominal pain and diarrhea, may account for 50% of all digestive-tract illnesses. In ulcerative colitis, the inflamed membranes develop patches of tiny ulcers; the DIARRHEA contains blood and mucus. It often becomes chronic, with sustained FEVER and weight loss; complications and death may result. If treatment with sulfasalazine or steroids does not control it, part or all of the colon may need to be removed.

collage \kə-'läzh\ (from French, *coller:* "to glue") Pictorial technique of applying printed or found materials (e.g., newspaper, fabric, wallpaper) to a flat surface, often in combination with painting. It was first given serious attention as an art technique by Pablo PICASSO and Georges BRAQUE in 1912–13. Many other 20th-cent. artists produced collages, including Juan GRIS, Henri MATISSE, Joseph CORNELL, and Max ERNST. It was used as a major form of POP ART, especially by Robert RAUSCHENBERG.

collagen \'kä-lə-jən\ Any of a class of organic compounds, the most abundant PROTEINS in animals, occurring in TENDONS, LIGAMENTS, dentin (see TOOTH), CARTILAGE, and other CONNECTIVE TISSUES. Their molecules share a triple-helix configuration. Collagens occur as whitish, inelastic fibers of great TENSILE STRENGTH and low solubility in water. Glue made from collagen in animal hides and skins is a widely used adhesive. Specially treated forms of collagen are used in medicine and surgery, in prostheses, and as sausage casings. Collagen is converted to GELATIN by boiling it in water.

collard Headless form of CABBAGE (*Brassica oleracea* 'acephala') with the same botanical name as KALE but with leaves that are much broader and are not frilled. The leaves are highly nutritious, rich in minerals and in vitamins A and C.

collective bargaining Process of negotiation between representatives of workers (usually labor-union officials) and management to determine conditions of employment. The agreement reached may cover not only wages but hiring practices, layoffs, promotions, working conditions and hours, and benefits. Collective bargaining developed in England at the end of the 18th cent. Agreements reached through collective bargaining are now common in the U.S. and Europe; they are less often found in developing countries with large pools of surplus labor. See also LABOR UNION, STRIKE.

collective farm *Russian* kolkhoz. In the former Soviet Union, a cooperative agricultural enterprise operated on state-owned land. Under the policy of collectivization, pursued most intensively by Joseph STALIN in 1929–33, peasants were forced to give up their individual farms and join large collective farms. They objected violently and in many cases slaughtered their livestock and destroyed their equipment before joining. By 1936 almost all the peasantry had been collectivized, though millions had also been deported to prison camps. With the breakup of the Soviet Union in 1990–91, the collective farms began to be privatized.

college Institution that offers postsecondary education. The term has various meanings. In Roman law a *collegium* was a body of persons associated for a common function. The name was used by many medieval institutions, including GUILDS. In most UNIVERSITIES of the later Middle Ages, *collegium* meant an endowed residence hall for university students. The colleges kept libraries and scientific instruments and offered salaries to tutors who could prepare students to be examined for DEGREES. In England, secondary schools such as ETON are sometimes called colleges. Canada also has collegiate schools. In the U.S., college may refer to a four-year institution offering a bachelor's degree, or to a two-year junior or COMMUNITY COLLEGE offering an associate's degree. The four-year college, usually emphasizing a liberal-arts or general education, may be an independent private institution or an undergraduate division of a university.

collider See PARTICLE ACCELERATOR

collie Breed of working dog developed in Britain, probably by the 18th cent. The rough-coated variety was originally used to guard and herd sheep; the smooth-coated variety was used to drive livestock to market. Both have a tapering head, almond-shaped eyes, and erect ears. They stand 22–26 in. (56–66 cm) high and weigh 50–75 lbs (23–34 kg). See also BORDER COLLIE.

Collie

Collingwood, R(obin) G(eorge) (1889–1943) British historian and philosopher. Teaching at Oxford Univ. (1912–41), he became a leading authority on the archaeology and history of Roman Britain. Believing that "the chief business of 20th-cent. philosophy is to reckon with 20th-cent. history," he maintained in his most influential work, *The Idea of History* (1946), that historical thinking requires explanation as part of any description, and that the philosopher must articulate and justify historical methodology.

Collins, Michael (1890–1922) Irish national leader. After fighting in the Easter Rising, he was elected as a member of Sinn Féin to the Irish assembly (1918), and became the Irish republic's first minister of home affairs. He was general of the volunteers and director of intelligence of the IRISH REPUBLICAN ARMY in the Anglo–Irish War (1919-21). He signed the controversial Anglo–Irish Treaty, which gave Ireland dominion status, and he and Arthur GRIFFITH became leaders of the provisional government. When civil war broke out, Collins commanded the government forces fighting the anti-treaty republicans, and on Griffith's death he became head of the government. Ten days later he was killed in an ambush at 31.

Collins, (William) Wilkie (1824–1889) English novelist. For two works, he is remembered as one of the first and best writers of English mystery novels. *The Woman in White* (1860), inspired by an actual criminal case, made him famous. *The Moonstone* (1868), one of the first English detective novels, introduced features that became conventions in the genre. Among his other books are *No Name* (1862) and *Armadale* (1866).

colloid \ˈkä-ˌlȯid\ Substance consisting of particles substantially larger than ATOMS and ordinary MOLECULES (10^{-7}–10^{-3} cm), dispersed in a continuous phase. Both the disperse phase and the continuous phase may be solid, liquid, or gas; examples include suspensions, AEROSOLS, smokes, EMULSIONS, gels, sols, pastes, and foams. DYES, DETERGENTS, POLYMERS, PROTEINS, and many other important substances exhibit colloidal behavior.

colobus monkey \ˈkä-lə-bəs\ Any of 10 species of long-tailed African OLD WORLD MONKEY in the genus *Colobus* (family Cercopithecidae). They are diurnal, generally gregarious vegetarians, and make long leaps from tree to tree. The four species of black-and-white colobus are 22–24 in. (55–60 cm) long, excluding the long (30–32-in., or 77–82-cm) tail. The five species of red colobus are brown or black with red markings and are 18–24 in. (46–60 cm) long. The olive colobus has short, olive-colored fur. Several races of red colobus are endangered.

Cologne \kə-ˈlōn\ *German* **Köln** \ˈkœln\ City (pop., 1998 est.: 964,000), W Germany. Located on the RHINE RIVER, it is one of Europe's key inland ports. Settled by Romans in the 1st cent. B.C., its commercial importance grew out of its location on the major European trade routes. In the Middle Ages it also became an ecclesiastical center and an important center of art and learning. Despite almost complete destruction in World War II, the city retains some buildings and monuments of all periods. Its famous cathedral is the largest Gothic church in N Europe. The city remains a banking center. Wine and textile manufacturing are prominent, as is the making of eau de cologne. It is famous for its pre-Lenten carnival.

Colombia *officially* **Republic of Colombia** Country, S. America. Area: 440,800 sq mi (1,141,700 sq km). Population

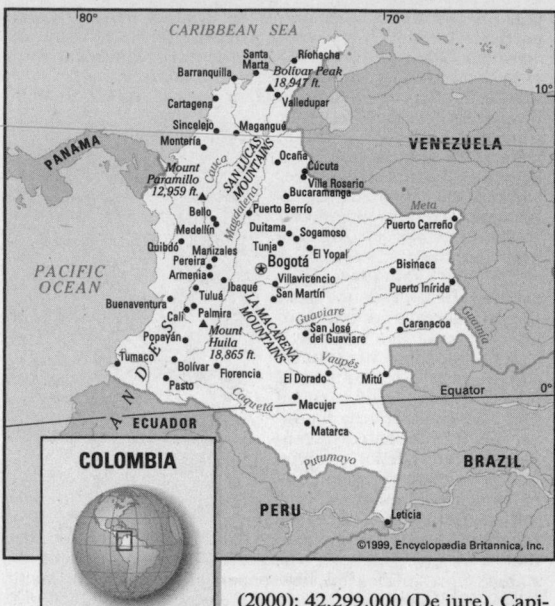

COLOMBIA

Scale 1: 26,728,000
0 — 100 — 200 mi
0 — 100 — 200 — 300 km

©1999, Encyclopædia Britannica, Inc.

(2000): 42,299,000 (De jure). Capital: BOGOTÁ. Over half the population is mestizo, followed by Europeans (about 20%), mulattoes (15%), and blacks and Indians (some 400 tribes). Language: Spanish (official). Religion: Roman Catholicism. Currency: peso. Lying at the NW corner of the continent, it is dominated by the Colombian ANDES. To the southeast lie vast lowlands, drained by the ORINOCO and AMAZON rivers. Colombia's economy is based primarily on agriculture and manufacturing, with coffee the principal cash crop. Marijuana and coca are grown illicitly on a major scale and are a seriously disruptive factor in the country. Rich in minerals, Colombia is the world's largest producer of emeralds and S. America's third-largest producer of gold. It is a multiparty republic with two legislative houses; its head of state and government is the president. Its earliest known inhabitants were Chibchan-speaking Indians. The Spanish arrived around 1500 and by 1538 had defeated them and made the area subject to the viceroyalty of Peru. After 1740 authority was transferred to the newly created viceroyalty of NEW GRANADA. Parts of Colombia threw off Spanish jurisdiction in 1810, and full independence came after Spain's defeat by Simón BOLÍVAR in 1819. An orderly government was established, but civil war in 1840 checked development. Conflict between liberals and conservatives led to continued violence that culminated in the War of a Thousand Days (1899–1903). Years of relative peace followed, but hostility erupted again in 1948; the two parties agreed in 1958 to a scheme for alternating governments. In the late 1970s Columbia became a center for marijuana and cocaine production. Drug-related violence became widespread. Leftist guerrilla groups, formed in the 1960s, simultaneously began seizing territory. About 2 million Colombians left the country during 1997–2000 because of violence and high unemployment.

Colombo \kə-ˈləm-bō\ City (pop., 1997: 800,000), administrative capital of Sri Lanka. Situated on the W coast of the island, it is a major port with one of the largest artificial harbors in the world. Settled in the 8th cent. by Arab traders, it was occupied by the Portuguese in 1517, the Dutch in 1656, and the English in 1796, and became capital in 1815. Western influence diminished after Sri Lanka gained its independence in 1948. Its manufacturing industries produce machinery and process food products.

colon \ˈkō-lən\ Segment that makes up most of the LARGE INTESTINE. Though the two terms are often used interchangeably, the colon technically excludes the cecum (a pouch at the beginning of the large intestine), RECTUM, and anal canal. It runs up the right side of the abdomen, across it, and down the left side. It has no digestive function but lubricates waste products, absorbs remaining fluids and salts, and stores waste products until EXCRETION. Problems involving the colon include COLITIS, constipation and DIARRHEA, gas discomfort, megacolon (enlarged colon), and cancer.

colonialism Control by one power over a dependent area or people. Its purposes include economic exploitation of the colony's natural resources and creation of new markets for the colonizer. From 1500 to 1900 Europe colonized all of N. and S. America and Australia, most of Africa, and much of Asia by sending settlers to populate the land or by taking control of governments. The first colonies were established in the Western Hemisphere by the Spanish and Portuguese in the 15th–16th cent. The Dutch colonized Indonesia in the 16th cent., and Britain colonized N. America and India in the 17th–18th cent., and later Australia and New Zealand. Colonization of Africa only began in earnest in the 1880s, but by 1900 virtually the entire continent was controlled by Europe. The colonial era ended gradually after World War II; the only territories still governed as colonies today are small islands. See also DECOLONIZATION.

colony In antiquity, any of the new settlements established in conquered territory by the Greeks (8th–6th cent. B.C.), ALEXANDER THE GREAT (4th cent. B.C.), and the Romans (4th cent. B.C.–2nd cent. A.D.). Greek colonies extended to Italy, Sicily, Spain, the E Mediterranean (including Egypt), and the Black Sea. Alexander pushed even farther into Central Asia, SW Asia, and Egypt. Roman colonization covered much of the same area and regions south to Africa, west to Spain, and north to Britain and Germany. Reasons for colonizing included expansion of trade, acquisition of raw materials, resolution of political unrest or overpopulation, and craving for land and rewards. Ancient colonization spread Hellenic and Roman culture to the far reaches of the empires, often assimilating local populations, some of whom acquired citizenship in the mother state.

color Aspect of any object that may be described in terms of hue, brightness, and saturation. It is associated with the visible WAVELENGTHS of ELECTROMAGNETIC RADIATION, which stimulate the sensor cells of the eye. Red LIGHT has the longest wavelengths, blue the shortest, and other colors such as orange, yellow, and green are in between. Hue refers to dominant wavelengths. Brightness refers to the intensity or degree of shading. Saturation pertains to purity, or the amount of white light mixed with a hue. The colors red, green, and blue, known as primary colors, can be combined in varying proportions to produce all other colors of light.

Colorado State (pop., 2000: 4,301,000), W central U.S. Covering 104,247 sq mi (269,864 sq km), its capital is DENVER. Lying astride the ROCKY MTNS., the state has three physiographic regions: the plains, a semiarid segment of E Colorado; the Colorado Piedmont in the central part of the state, where most of the population lives; and the S Rocky Mtns. and mesas of W Colorado. Its large urban population has grown faster than the national average. Its original inhabitants were PLAINS and Great Basin Indians, including the ARAPAHO, CHEYENNE, and UTE. The area was claimed by Spain in 1706 but later passed in large part to France. E Colorado was part of the LOUISIANA PURCHASE in 1803; the remainder stayed in Spanish and, after independence, in Mexican hands until 1848. Gold was discovered in 1859 and touched off a population boom. Organized as the territory of Colorado in 1861, it achieved U.S. statehood in 1876. Agriculture, cattle production, and mining, as well as manufacturing, are important to the economy. Government military installations and service industries have become prominent, and tourism (see ASPEN, BOULDER, VAIL) is a major source of the state's income.

Colorado River River, W Texas. It flows southeast 862 mi (1,387 km) past AUSTIN and across the coastal plain to enter Matagorda Bay. The river, the largest entirely within Texas, is the site of flood-control, power, irrigation, and recreational projects.

Colorado River River, N. America. Rising in the ROCKY MTNS. of Colorado, it flows west and south 1,450 mi (2,330 km) to empty into the Gulf of CALIFORNIA in NW Mexico. It drains a vast sector of the N. American continent. No other river in the world has cut so many deep trenches, of which the GRAND CANYON is the most spectacular. More than 20 dams, including HOOVER DAM, have been built on it and its tributaries.

Colorado Springs City (pop., 2000: 360,000), central Colorado. It was founded in 1871 on a mesa near PIKES PEAK. Growth followed the Cripple Creek gold strikes in the 1890s. Military installations propelled development: it is home to the N. American Aerospace Defense Command (NORAD), the U.S. Space Command, Ft. Carson, and the U.S. AIR FORCE ACADEMY, along with 20 other colleges and universities. The Garden of the Gods, a natural park with red sandstone monoliths, is one of many scenic attractions.

color blindness Inability to distinguish one or more colors. The human RETINA contains three types of cone cells; absence of one or more types causes color blindness to red, green, and/or blue. Color blindness is a sex-linked recessive trait (see RECESSIVENESS) 20 times more common in men than in women.

colorimetry \ˌkə-lə-ˈri-mə-trē\ Measurement of the intensity of ELECTROMAGNETIC RADIATION in the visible SPECTRUM transmitted through a solution or transparent solid. It is used to identify and determine the concentrations of substances that absorb LIGHT of a specific wavelength or color. A PHOTOCELL is often used to measure the amount of light transmitted through a glass tube containing the solution to be analyzed; the result is compared with results from a similar tube containing solvent alone. Most ELEMENTS and many COMPOUNDS, in appropriately treated samples, may be identified by colorimetry or SPECTROPHOTOMETRY, a closely related technique.

color printing Specialized PRINTING technique using colored INKS and modified presses. Juxtaposition of colors is achieved by submitting each sheet to successive impressions by typeforms each of which prints only on areas designed to carry a single color and inked only in that color. Three colors of ink can reconstitute the visual effect of all the range of colors by combining them appropriately. Standard color printing, called four-color printing, employs magenta, yellow, cyan (blue), and black inks.

Colosseum Flavian Amphitheater in Rome, erected around A.D. 70–82 under VESPASIAN and TITUS. The later name Colosseum referred to its immense size and capacity, holding nearly 50,000 people. Unlike earlier amphitheaters, which were nearly all dug into hillsides, it is a freestanding oval colonnaded structure of stone and concrete. It was the scene of combats between gladiators, contests of men with animals, and even mock naval engagements.

Colosseum, Rome, c.A.D. 72–80

Colossus of Rhodes See Colossus of RHODES

colostomy \kə-ˈläs-tə-mē\ Surgical formation of an artificial anus by making an opening from the COLON through the abdominal wall. It may be done to decompress an obstructed colon, to allow EXCRETION when part of the colon must be removed, or to permit healing of the colon. Colostomy may be temporary or permanent. A sigmoid colostomy, the most common type of permanent colostomy, requires no appliances (though a light pouch is sometimes worn for reassurance). See also OSTOMY.

Colt, Samuel (1814–1862) U.S. inventor. Born in Hartford, Conn., in his teens he conceived the idea for his first REVOLVER, later patented (1835–36). Colt's six-shooters were slow to sell; his company failed in 1842, and he started a telegraph business using the first underwater cable. Soldiers' favorable reports led to an order for 1,000 pistols during the Mexican War, and Colt resumed manufacture. With Eli Whitney Jr., he advanced the development of interchangeable parts and the ASSEMBLY LINE. His firm produced the revolvers most widely used in the American Civil War and in the settlement of the West, including the famous Colt .45.

Coltrane, John (William) (1926–1967) U.S. saxophonist and composer, the most influential JAZZ musician of the 1960s. Born in Hamlet, N.C., he moved to Philadelphia as a youth. Associations with Miles DAVIS and Thelonious MONK in the 1950s established his place in the vanguard of modern jazz, and his quartet of the early 1960s is one of the outstanding groups in jazz history. His style encompassed Davis's modal jazz, the complex chord structures of his own compositions, and ultimately the extremes of timbre, dynamics, and register associated with free jazz.

Columba, St. *or* **Colum** *or* **Columcille** \ˈkəl-əm-ˌkil\ (521?–597) Irish abbot and missionary. Ordained about 551, he founded two famous monasteries in Ireland before taking 12 disciples to the Scottish island of Iona (c.563). There they built a church and monastery that served as a base for the conversion of the Scottish PICTS, and thereby Scotland, to Christianity.

Columban, St. (543?–615) Irish abbot and missionary. One of the greatest missionaries of the Celtic church, he initiated a revival of spirituality on the European continent. He left Ireland about 590 with 12 monks and settled in the Vosges Mtns. in Gaul, building two monasteries. For his criticism of the sins of the Burgundian court, he was forced out of France into Switzerland, where he preached to the Alemanni. He later settled in Italy and founded the monastery of Bobbio (c.612).

Columbia City (pop., 2000: 116,000), capital of S. Carolina. Located in the center of the state, it dates from 1786. During the AMERICAN CIVIL WAR, it was the seat of many Confederate agencies; in 1865 it was occupied by Union troops and virtually destroyed by fire. Rebuilt, it developed a diversified economy based on government, industry, and agriculture. Cotton, peaches, and tobacco are important crops in the surrounding area. It is the seat of the Univ. of S. Carolina.

Columbia SPACE SHUTTLE that exploded in 2003. After 16 days in orbit, the shuttle blew up at high altitude over E Texas on February 1, scattering debris over a wide area. The seven crew members included two women and the first Israeli to participate in space flight. The first space shuttle orbiter, *Columbia* was initially launched in 1981 and had made 28 flights. See also *CHALLENGER*.

Columbia Broadcasting System See CBS

Columbia Pictures Entertainment, Inc. Major U.S. film studio. It originated in 1920 when Jack and Harry COHN formed a company with Joe Brandt to produce short films and low-budget westerns. It became Columbia Pictures in 1924. Harry Cohn, president from 1932, was the driving force behind its success. The studio produced the 1930s films of Frank CAPRA and many other successful films, including *All the King's Men* (1949), *From Here to Eternity* (1953), *The Caine Mutiny* (1954), *Lawrence of Arabia* (1962), *Five Easy Pieces* (1970), *Close Encounters of the Third Kind* (1977), *Tootsie* (1982), and *The Last Emperor* (1987). After Columbia was purchased by the COCA-COLA CO. in 1982, it helped launch Tri-Star Pictures. The two studios merged in 1987 as Columbia Pictures Entertainment, which was bought by SONY CORP. in 1989.

Columbia River River, SW Canada and NW U.S. Rising in the Canadian Rockies, it flows through Washington state and Oregon to the Pacific Ocean, with a total length of 1,240 mi (2,000 km). It was a major transportation artery until the coming of the railroads. Development of the river began in the 1930s with the Grand Coulee and Bonneville dams, and within 50 years the entire river within the U.S. had been converted into a series of "stair steps" by 11 dams. Its many hydroelectric plants are basic to power generation in the Pacific Northwest.

Columbia University Private university in New York City, a traditional member of the IVY LEAGUE. Founded in 1754 as King's College, it was renamed Columbia College when it reopened in 1784 after the American Revolution. It became Columbia Univ. in 1912. Neighboring Barnard College, founded in 1889 and part of Columbia since 1900, remains a women's liberal-arts school. From the outset Columbia offered atypical subjects such as nature study, commerce, history, and government. It has strong graduate programs in the arts and sciences and several notable research institutes. Among its professional schools are those of medicine, law, education, engineering, journalism, business, public health, social work, and international and public affairs. Total enrollment is about 20,000 (with affiliates, 27,000).

columbine Any of approximately 70 species of perennial herbaceous plants constituting the genus *Aquilegia,* in the BUTTERCUP family, native to Europe and N. America. They are distinctive for their brightly colored, five-petaled flowers with long, backward-extending spurs. *A. caerulea* and *A. chysantha* are native to the Rocky Mtns. The widely found wild columbine of N. America (*A. canadensis*) bears red flowers with touches of yellow. Many garden hybrids are cultivated for their showy flowers.

Columbus City (pop., 2000: 179,000), W Georgia. Located on the CHATTAHOOCHEE RIVER, it was founded in 1827 and by 1840 had become a leading inland cotton port. During the AMERICAN CIVIL WAR it was a major supply city for the Confederacy. It has become one of the South's largest textile centers. It is home to the Confederate Naval Museum. Ft. Benning (established 1918) is nearby.

Columbus City (pop., 2000: 711,000), capital of Ohio. The city was planned in 1812, and the state government moved there in 1816. The arrival of roads, canals, and rail in the mid-19th cent. led to significant growth, and by 1900 Columbus had emerged as an important transportation and commercial center. Ohio's largest city, its economy is supported by industry, governmental agencies, and numerous educational and research institutions, including OHIO STATE UNIV.

Columbus, Christopher *Spanish* Cristóbal Colón (1451–1506) Spanish navigator and explorer. Born in Genoa, Italy, to a Spanish couple, he began his career in the Portuguese marine. In 1492 he obtained the sponsorship of the Spanish monarchs FERDINAND V and ISABELLA I for an attempt to reach Asia by sailing westward. He set sail in August 1492 with three ships—the *Santa María*, the *Niña*, and the *Pinta*—and sighted land (in the present-day Bahamas) on October 12. Named viceroy of the Indies, he made a second voyage (1493–96) with 17 ships, and founded La Isabela (in modern Dominican Republic), the first European town in the New World. This voyage also began Spain's effort to promote Christian evangelization. On his third voyage (1498–1500), he reached S. America. Reports of his poor administration led to his being replaced as viceroy and returned to Spain in chains. On his fourth voyage (1502–4), he returned to S. America and sailed along the coasts of modern Honduras and Panama. Unable to gain reinstatement of his honors, he died in relative poverty and neglect. His character has long been seen as mixed; an intrepid and brilliant navigator, he has also been decried for his vanity, greed, and harsh treatment of native peoples.

Christopher Columbus
Painting by Sebastiano del Piombo, 1519

Columcille See St. COLUMBA

column In architecture, a vertical element, usually a slender shaft, that provides structural support by carrying axial loads in compression. Columns may be exposed or hidden in walls; they may be constructed of precast concrete, masonry, stone, or wood or of steel wide-flange, pipe, or tubular sections; they may be plain, fluted, or sculpted, with or without a capital and base. See also ORDER.

coma Complete lack of consciousness, usually associated with cerebral injury. Simple CONCUSSIONS cause short losses of consciousness. Coma from lack of oxygen may last several weeks and is often fatal. Coma caused by STROKE can be sudden; that caused by metabolic abnormalities (as in diabetes mellitus) or cerebral tumors comes on gradually. Treatment depends on the cause.

Comanche \kə-ˈman-chē\ Nomadic N. American Indian group that roved the S Great Plains in the 18th and 19th cent. Their staple food was buffalo meat, and their highly skilled horsemen set the pattern of equestrian nomadism on the Plains. In 1864 Col. Kit CARSON led U.S. forces in an unsuccessful campaign against them. Treaties were signed in 1865 and 1867, but the federal government failed to keep whites off the land promised to them, which led to violent conflicts. Today about 4,000 Comanche live in and around Lawton, Okla.

Comaneci \ˌkō-mə-ˈnē-chē\, **Nadia** (b.1961) Romanian-U.S. gymnast. She entered her first international competition in 1972 and won three gold medals. In the 1976 Olympic Games, the first in which a perfect score of 10 was ever awarded in a gymnastic event, she received an astounding seven perfect scores and won the gold medals for the balance beam, uneven parallel bars, and all-around competitions. In the 1980 Olympics she won gold medals for the beam and the floor exercises.

combination See PERMUTATIONS AND COMBINATIONS

combine harvester Farm machine used to harvest wheat and often other cereals. The mechanical ancestor of today's large combines was Cyrus MCCORMICK's reaper, introduced in 1831. Threshing machines were powered first by men or animals, often using treadmills, later by STEAM ENGINES and INTERNAL-COMBUSTION ENGINES. The modern combine harvester, originally introduced in California around 1875, came into wide use in the U.S. in the 1920s and '30s. The combine cuts the standing grain, threshes out the grain from the straw and chaff, cleans the grain, and empties it into bags or grain-storage facilities. Whereas in 1829 harvesting an acre of wheat required 14 man-hours, the modern combine requires less than 30 minutes.

comb jelly See CTENOPHORE

Comden, Betty *orig.* Elizabeth Cohen (b.1919) U.S. musical-comedy writer and lyricist. Born in Brooklyn, N.Y., Comden formed a nightclub act in 1938 with Adolph Green (1915–2002), Judy Holliday (1922–1965), and others. In 1944 Comden and Green wrote the book and lyrics for Leonard BERNSTEIN's *On the Town.* They later collaborated with Jule STYNE on such musicals as *Peter Pan* (1954), *Bells Are Ringing* (1956), and *Hallelujah, Baby!* (1967, Tony Award). Their lyrics for *Wonderful Town* (1953), *Applause* (1970), and *On the 20th Century* (1978) won them three more Tonys. Their screenplays include *Singin' in the Rain* (1952). "Just in Time" and "The Party's Over" are two of their best-known songs.

Comédie-Française \kō-mā-ˈdē-frä-ˈsez\ National theater of France. The world's longest-established national theater, it was founded in 1680 by the merger of two Paris theatrical companies, one of which had worked under MOLIÈRE. The French Revolution divided the company's loyalties, and the revolution's supporters moved to the theater's present home in 1791. Under its rules of organization, established by NAPOLEON in 1812, its members share responsibilities and profits. Its illustrious actors have included Sarah BERNHARDT and J.-L. BARRAULT. Known for productions of the French classics, it also performs contemporary plays.

comedy Genre of dramatic literature that deals with the light and amusing, or with the serious and profound in a light, familiar, or satirical manner. Comedy can be traced to revels associated with worship in Greece in the 5th cent. B.C. In the late Middle Ages, the term was used to mean simply a story with a happy ending (e.g., Dante's *Divine Comedy*), the same meaning it has in novels of the last three centuries (e.g., the fiction of Jane AUSTEN). See also TRAGEDY.

comedy of manners Witty, ironic form of drama that satirizes the manners and fashions of a particular social class or set. It is concerned with the ability or inability of certain characters to meet social standards, which are often exacting but morally trivial. The plot, usually concerning an illicit love affair or other scandalous matter, is subordinate to the play's witty dialogue and pungent commentary on human foibles. Its notable exponents include William CONGREVE, Oscar WILDE, and Noël COWARD.

Comenius \kə-ˈmē-nē-əs\, **John Amos** *Czech* Jan Amos Komensky (1592–1670) Czech educational reformer and religious leader. He favored the learning of Latin to facilitate the study of European culture, and his *Janua Linguarum*

Reserata (1631), a textbook in both Latin and Czech, revolutionized Latin teaching and was translated into 16 languages. He also produced one of the first illustrated schoolbooks, *Orbis Sensualium Pictus* (1658).

comet Any of a class of small objects orbiting the sun that develop diffuse gaseous envelopes and often long glowing tails when near the sun, identified by their composition, hazy appearance, and elongated orbits. Many originate in the OORT CLOUD or the KUIPER BELT. Other bodies' gravity can alter their orbits to bring them close to the sun. Short-period comets return within 200 years, others in thousands of years or never. Comets usually consist of a small, irregular nucleus ("dirty snowball"), with dust and other materials frozen in water mixed with volatile compounds. Near the sun, heat melts its surface, releasing these materials to form a cloud (coma) around its core; this may later be pushed away from the sun by its radiation and the SOLAR WIND, forming tails that scatter sunlight. METEOR SHOWERS occur when earth passes through dust left by a comet's passage.

comfrey \ˈkəm-frē\ Any herb of the Eurasian genus *Symphytum* (borage family). Best known is the medicinal common comfrey *(S. officinale),* used to treat wounds and as a source of a GUM used to treat wool. Organic farmers use it to deter slugs and as a green manure. Common comfrey is about 3 ft (90 cm) tall, with winged, hairy stems and coiled sprays of bell-like blue, purplish, or yellow flowers.

comic book Bound collection of COMIC STRIPS, usually in chronological sequence, typically telling a single story or a series of different stories. The first true comic books were marketed in 1933 as giveaway advertising premiums. By 1935 reprints of newspaper strips and books with original stories were selling in large quantities. During World War II comics dealing with war and crime found many readers among soldiers stationed abroad, and in the 1950s comic books were blamed for juvenile delinquency. In the 1960s comic books satirizing the cultural underworld became popular, especially among college students. Today comic "zines" represent a thriving subculture.

comic strip Series of drawings that read as a narrative, arranged together on the page of a newspaper, magazine, or book. In 1897 Rudolph DIRKS's *Katzenjammer Kids,* in the *New York Journal,* featured the first humorous strips containing words presumably spoken by the characters. Soon speeches in balloons appeared in other CARTOONS, arranged in a series to form a strip. The comic strip arrived at its maturity in 1907 with Bud Fisher's *Mutt and Jeff.* Important later comic-strip artists include George HERRIMAN, Al CAPP, Walt KELLY, Charles SCHULZ, and Garry TRUDEAU.

Cominform *in full* **Communist Information Bureau** Agency of international communism founded under Soviet auspices in 1947. Its original members were the Communist parties of the Soviet Union, Bulgaria, Czechoslovakia, Hungary, Poland, Romania, Yugoslavia, France, and Italy, but Yugoslavia was expelled in 1948. Its activities consisted mainly of publishing propaganda to encourage international communist solidarity. It was dissolved in 1956.

Comintern *or* **Communist International** *or* **Third International** Association of national communist parties founded in 1919 by Vladimir LENIN to undermine efforts to revive the SECOND INTERNATIONAL. To join, parties were required to model their structure on the Soviet pattern and to expel moderate socialists and pacifists. Though its stated purpose was the promotion of world revolution, it functioned chiefly as an organ of Soviet control over the international communist movement. In 1943 Joseph STALIN dissolved the Comintern to allay fears of communist subversion among his World War II allies.

Comitia Centuriata \kə-ˈmish-ə-ˌsen-ˌtûr-ē-ˈä-tə\ Ancient Roman military assembly, instituted around 450 B.C. It decided on war and peace, passed laws, elected CONSULS and other officials, and considered appeals of capital convictions. Unlike the older patrician Comitia Curiata, it included PLEBEIANS as well as PATRICIANS. The votes of the wealthier groups outweighed those of the poorer.

commedia dell'arte \kōm-ˈmäd-yä-del-ˈlär-tä\ Italian theatrical form that flourished throughout Europe in the 16th–18th cent. The characters, many portrayed by actors wear-

Commedia dell'arte Engraving by Jacques Callot, 1632

ing masks (including the witty gentleman's valet HARLE-QUIN, the simpleminded servant Pierrot, and the maidservant Columbina) were derived from the exaggeration of regional or stock fictional types. The style emphasized improvisation within a framework of stock situations. It was acted by professional companies using vernacular dialects and plenty of comic action. Outside Italy, it had its greatest success in France as the Comédie-Italienne; in England, it was adapted in the harlequinade and the PUNCH-and-Judy show. See also ANDREINI FAMILY.

Commerce, U.S. Department of (DOC) Federal executive division responsible for programs and policies relating to international trade, national economic growth, and technological advancement. Established in 1913, it administers the Bureau of the Census, National Oceanic and Atmospheric Administration, Patent and Trademark Office, and U.S. Travel and Tourism Administration.

commercial bank Bank that makes loans to businesses, consumers, and nonbusiness institutions. Early commercial banks were limited to accepting deposits of money or valuables for safekeeping and verifying coinage or exchanging one jurisdiction's coins for another's. By the 17th cent. most essentials of modern banking, including foreign exchange, the payment of INTEREST, and the granting of loans, were in place. It became common for individuals and firms to exchange funds through bankers with a written draft, the precursor to the modern CHECK. Because a commercial bank is required to hold only a fraction of its deposits as cash reserves (see FRACTIONAL RESERVE SYSTEM), it can use some of the money to extend loans. Commercial banks also offer savings accounts, safe-deposit boxes, and trust services. See also BANK, CENTRAL BANK, INVESTMENT BANK, SAVINGS BANK.

commercial law See BUSINESS LAW

Commercial Revolution Great increase in commerce in Europe that began in the late Middle Ages. It received stimulus from the voyages of exploration undertaken by England, Spain, and other nations to Africa, Asia, and the New World. Its features included a surge in overseas trade, the appearance of the CHARTERED COMPANY, acceptance of the principles of MERCANTILISM, the creation of a money economy, and such new institutions as the state bank and the bourse. The Commercial Revolution helped set the stage for the INDUSTRIAL REVOLUTION.

Committee of Public Safety Political body of the FRENCH REVOLUTION that controlled France during the REIGN OF TERROR. Set up in April 1793 to defend France against foreign and domestic enemies, it was first dominated by Georges DANTON and his followers; they were soon replaced by the radical JACOBINS, including Maximilien de ROBESPIERRE. Harsh measures were taken against alleged enemies of the Revolution, the economy was placed on a wartime basis, and mass conscription was undertaken. After the downfall of Robespierre in 1794, it declined in importance.

Committees of Correspondence Groups appointed by the legislatures of all 13 American colonies to provide a means of intercolonial communication. The first was formed by Samuel ADAMS in Boston (1772), and within three months

80 others were formed in Massachusetts. In 1773 Virginia organized a committee with 11 members, including Thomas JEFFERSON and Patrick HENRY. The committees were instrumental in promoting colonial unity and in summoning the First CONTINENTAL CONGRESS in 1774.

Commodus *in full* Caesar Marcus Aurelius Commodus Antoninus Augustus *orig.* Lucius Aelius Aurelius Commodus (A.D. 161–192) Roman emperor (A.D. 177–92). He ruled with his father, MARCUS AURELIUS, until the latter's death in 180; recalled from the frontier, he plunged into a life of dissipation in Rome. After his sister tried to have him killed (182), he executed the senators involved and began ruling capriciously. His brutality stirred unrest that ended years of Roman stability and prosperity. He renamed Rome Colonia Commodiana (Colony of Commodus) and performed as a gladiator, claiming he was Hercules. His mistress and advisers had him strangled, ending the Antonine dynasty.

common cold See common COLD

Commoner, Barry (b.1917) U.S. biologist and educator. Born in Brooklyn, N.Y., he taught at Washington Univ. and Queens College. His warnings, since the 1950s, of the environmental threats posed by nuclear weapons, pesticides, and ineffective waste management in such works as his classic *Science and Survival* (1966) made him one of the foremost environmentalist spokesmen of his time.

common law Body of law based on custom and general principles and that, embodied in case law, serves as precedent or is applied to situations not covered by statute. When a court decides and reports its decision concerning a particular case, the case becomes part of the body of law and can be used in later cases involving similar matters. Common law has been administered in the courts of England since the Middle Ages; it is also found in the U.S. and in most of the British Commonwealth. It is distinguished from CIVIL LAW.

common-lead dating See URANIUM-THORIUM-LEAD DATING

Common Market See EUROPEAN ECONOMIC COMMUNITY

Common Prayer, Book of Liturgical book used by the churches of the Anglican Communion. First authorized for the Church of England in 1549, it went through several versions. The Church of ENGLAND and the Protestant EPISCOPAL CHURCH in the U.S. adopted a liturgy in contemporary language in the 1970s.

common rorqual See FIN WHALE

Commons, House of Popularly elected lower house of the bicameral British PARLIAMENT. With the power to levy taxes and allocate expenditures, it is Britain's chief legislative authority. It originated in the late 13th cent., when property owners (commoners rather than nobility) first gained the right to commit their constituents to the payment of taxes and present their grievances to the king. It was the less powerful house until 1911, when the Reform Bill gave it the power to override the House of LORDS. The party with the greatest representation in the Commons forms the government. In 2002 there were 659 members, elected from single-member districts.

Commonwealth *or* **Commonwealth of Nations** Free association of sovereign states consisting of Britain and many of its former dependencies (see BRITISH EMPIRE) who have chosen to maintain ties of friendship and cooperation. It was established in 1931 by the Statute of WESTMINSTER as the British Commonwealth of Nations. Later its name was changed (1946) and it was redefined to include independent nations. The British monarch serves as its symbolic head, and meetings of the more than 50 Commonwealth heads of government take place every two years.

Commonwealth

Member	Date Joined or Rejoined	Member	Date Joined or Rejoined
Antigua/Barbuda	1981	Nauru	1968
Australia	1931	New Zealand	1931
Bahamas	1973	Nigeria	1960–95†
Bangladesh	1972		1999
Barbados	1966	Pakistan	1947–72*
Belize	1981		1989–99†
Botswana	1966	Papua New Guinea	1975
Brunei	1984	St. Kitts-Nevis	1983

Commonwealth (cont.)

Member	Date Joined or Rejoined	Member	Date Joined or Rejoined
Cameroon	1995	St. Lucia	1979
Canada	1931	St. Vincent and	
Cyprus	1961	the Grenadines	1979
Dominica	1978	Samoa	1962
Fiji	1970–1987*	Seychelles	1976
	1997	Sierra Leone	1961
Gambia	1965	Singapore	1965
Ghana	1957	Solomon Islands	1978
Grenada	1974	South Africa	1931–61*
Guyana	1966		1994
India	1947	Sri Lanka	1948
Jamaica	1962	Swaziland	1968
Kenya	1963	Tanzania	1961
Kiribati	1979	Tonga	1970
Lesotho	1966	Trinidad/Tobago	1962
Malawi	1964	Tuvalu	1978
Malaysia	1963	Uganda	1962
Maldives	1982	United Kingdom	1931
Malta	1964	Vanuatu	1980
Mauritius	1968	Zambia	1964
Mozambique	1995	Zimbabwe	1980–
Nambia	1990		2002†

* withdrew   † suspended from councils

Commonwealth Games Sports competition for Commonwealth countries, founded in 1891. It includes athletics (TRACK AND FIELD), GYMNASTICS, bowls, and SWIMMING events for both men and women, and BOXING, CYCLING, shooting, WEIGHT LIFTING, and WRESTLING for men only. ROWING, BADMINTON, and FENCING have also occasionally been included.

Commonwealth of Independent States (CIS) Free association of sovereign states formed in 1991, comprising Russia and 11 other former Soviet republics (Ukraine, Belarus, Kazakhstan, Kyrgyzstan, Tajikistan, Turkmenistan, Uzbekistan, Armenia, Azerbaijan, Georgia, and Moldova). The CIS coordinates its members' policies regarding their economies, foreign relations, defense, immigration policies, environmental protection, and law enforcement.

commune \ˌkäm-ˌyün, kə-ˈmyün\ Group of people who hold property in common and live according to principles endorsed by the group. The UTOPIAN SOCIALISM of Robert OWEN and others led to experimental communities in 19th-cent. Britain and the U.S., including BROOK FARM and the ONEIDA COMMUNITY. B. F. SKINNER's *Walden Two* (1948) inspired many American attempts at communal living, especially in the 1960s and '70s. See also COLLECTIVE FARM, KIBBUTZ.

commune \ˈkäm-ˌyün, kə-ˈmyün\ In medieval Europe, a town that acquired self-governing municipal institutions. Most such towns were defined by an oath binding its citizens to mutual protection and assistance. The group became an association able to own property, make agreements, exercise jurisdiction over members, and exercise governmental powers. Communes were particularly strong in N and central Italy, where the lack of a powerful central government allowed them to develop into independent city-states.

Commune of Paris See PARIS COMMUNE

communications satellite Earth-orbiting system capable of receiving a signal and relaying it back to the ground. Communications satellites have been a significant part of domestic and global communications since the 1970s. Typically they move in orbits about 22,300 mi (35,900 km) above the earth and operate at frequencies between 4 and 6 gigahertz (GHz).

communism Political theory advocating community ownership of all property, the benefits of which are to be shared by all according to the needs of each. The theory was principally the work of Karl MARX and Friedrich ENGELS. Their *Communist Manifesto* (1848) further specified a "dictatorship of the proletariat," a transitional stage Marx called SOCIALISM; communism was the final stage in which not only class division but even the organized state would be transcended (see MARXISM). That distinction was soon lost, and

"communist" began to apply to a specific party (see COMMUNIST PARTY). Vladimir LENIN maintained that the proletariat needed professional revolutionaries to guide it (see LENINISM). STALINISM was synonymous to many with TOTALITARIANISM. MAO ZEDONG mobilized peasants rather than an urban proletariat in China's Communist revolution (see MAOISM). EUROCOMMUNISM lost most of its following with the collapse of the Soviet Union (1991). See also DIALECTICAL MATERIALISM.

Communism Peak *formerly* **Stalin Peak** *or* **Garmo Peak** Peak, W PAMIRS, NE Tajikistan. Located in the Academy of Sciences Range, it rises to 24,590 ft (7,495 m), and is the highest point in Tajikistan and in the system. It was first climbed by a Russian team in 1933.

Communist Information Bureau See COMINFORM

Communist International See COMINTERN

Communist Party Political party organized to implement COMMUNISM. Russia was the first country in which communists came to power (1917). In 1918 the BOLSHEVIK party was renamed the All-Russian (later All-Union) Communist Party, to distinguish it from the socialists who had supported capitalist governments in World War I. Its basic unit was the workers' council (SOVIET), above which were district, city, regional, and republic committees. At the top was the party congress, which met only every few years; the delegates elected the members of the Central Committee, who in turn elected the members of the POLITBURO. The Soviet Union dominated communist parties worldwide through World War II. Yugoslavia challenged that hegemony in 1948, and China in the 1950s (see CHINESE COMMUNIST PARTY). Communist parties have survived the demise of the Soviet Union (1991), but with reduced political influence. The Cuban and N. Korean parties remain in control.

Communist Party of the Soviet Union (CPSU) Major political party of Russia and the Soviet Union from the RUSSIAN REVOLUTION OF 1917 to 1991. It arose from the BOLSHEVIK wing of the RUSSIAN SOCIAL-DEMOCRATIC WORKERS' PARTY and soon dominated the Soviet Union's political, economic, social, and cultural life. The constitution and other legal documents that supposedly regulated the government were actually subordinate to the CPSU. Mikhail GORBACHEV's efforts to reform the country's economy and political structure weakened the party, and in 1990 it voted to surrender its monopoly of power. The Soviet Union's dissolution in 1991 marked the party's formal demise.

community center See SETTLEMENT HOUSE

community college *or* **junior college** Educational institution that provides up to two years of COLLEGE-level academic instruction as well as technical and vocational training. Roots of the community college may be traced to the CHAUTAUQUA MOVEMENT and other adult-education programs created after the American Civil War. The first junior college opened in Joliet, Ill., in 1901. Usually publicly sup-

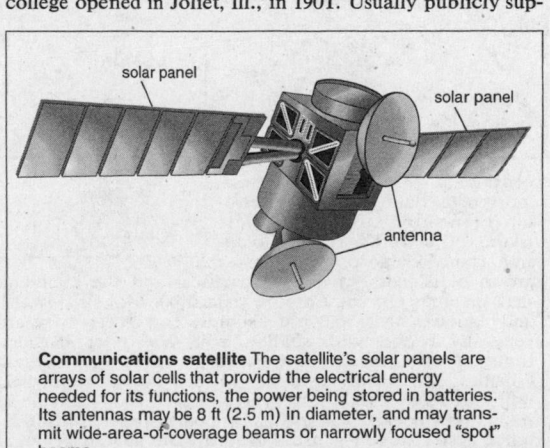

Communications satellite The satellite's solar panels are arrays of solar cells that provide the electrical energy needed for its functions, the power being stored in batteries. Its antennas may be 8 ft (2.5 m) in diameter, and may transmit wide-area-of-coverage beams or narrowly focused "spot" beams.

ported, community colleges offer a variety of flexible, often nontraditional programs. They have pioneered in offering part-time study, evening sessions, instruction by television, and weekend workshops. Students rarely live on campus. Graduates ordinarily earn an associate's degree; they may transfer to a four-year college or enter the workforce. See also CONTINUING EDUCATION.

commutative law Two closely related laws of number operations. In symbols, they are stated: $a + b = b + a$ and $ab = ba$. Stated in words: Quantities to be added or multiplied can be combined in any order. More generally, if two procedures give the same result when carried out in arbitrary order, they are commutative. See also ASSOCIATIVE LAW, DISTRIBUTIVE LAW.

Commynes \kò-'mēn\, **Philippe de** (1447?–1511) French statesman and chronicler. Brought up in the Burgundian court, he was counselor to CHARLES THE BOLD (1467–72) and then to Charles's former enemy LOUIS XI. He was implicated in the "Mad War" between Anne of Beaujeu, regent of France, and the duc d'Orleans (later LOUIS XII). Restored to favor in 1489, he later helped formulate Louis's Italian policy. His *Mémoires* (1524) reveal much about the era.

Como, Lake *ancient* Lacus Larius. Lake, LOMBARDY, N Italy. It lies at an elevation of 653 ft (199 m), surrounded by limestone and granite mountains. It is 29 mi (47 km) long and up to 2.5 mi (4 km) wide, with a maximum depth of 1,358 ft (414 m). Famous for its natural beauty, its shores have many resorts.

Comoros \'kä-mə-ˌrōz\ *officially* **Federal Islamic Republic of the Comoros** Islamic republic off the E coast of Africa. Area: 863 sq mi (2,235 sq km). Population (2000): 578,000. Capital: MORONI. The people are a mixture of Malay immigrants, Arab traders, and peoples from Madagascar and

Mitsamiouli
GRANDE COMORE ISLAND
Mbeni
INDIAN OCEAN
Moroni
Mount Karthala
7,746 ft.
Foumbouni
Dembéni
Point Sud
144° E
12° S
ANJOUAN ISLAND
Mutsamudu
Sima
Domoni
Hoani
Fomboni
Moya
MOHÉLI ISLAND
Niouachoua
M'Ramandi
Mozambique Channel
©1999, Encyclopædia Britannica, Inc.

COMOROS
Scale 1: 2,406,000
0 10 20 mi
0 15 30 km

continental Africa. Languages: Comorian (a Bantu language), Arabic, French (all official). Religion: Islam (official). Currency: Comorian franc. Comoros comprises a group of islands between Madagascar and the mainland that includes Grande Comore (Njazidja), Mohéli (Mwali), and Anjouan (Nzwani) but excludes MAYOTTE. They are generally rocky, with shallow soils and poor harbors, though Mohéli, the smallest, has fertile valleys and forested hillsides. Mt. Karthala, an active volcano, is the highest point, at 7,746 ft (2,361 m). The climate is tropical. One of the world's poorest nations, its economy is based on subsistence agriculture. The usual head of state and government is the president. Known to European navigators since the 16th cent., the dominant influence on the islands was then

and for long afterward Arab. In 1843 France officially took possession of Mayotte and in 1886 placed the other three islands under protection. Subordinated to Madagascar in 1914, the Comoros became an overseas territory of France in 1947. In 1961 they were granted autonomy. In 1974 majorities on three of the islands voted for independence, which was granted in 1975. The following decade saw several coup attempts, culminating in the assassination of the president in 1989. French intervention permitted multiparty elections in 1990, but the country remained in a state of chronic instability. In 1999 the army took control of the government.

compact disc (CD) Molded plastic disc containing digital data that is scanned by a laser beam for the reproduction of recorded sound or other information. Introduced in 1982, the audio CD has become the dominant format for high-fidelity recorded music. Digital audio data can be converted to analog form to reproduce the original audio signal (see DIGITAL-TO-ANALOG CONVERSION). Coinvented by Philips Electronics and Sony Corp. in 1980, the compact disc has expanded into other storage-and-distribution uses, notably for computers (CD-ROM) and entertainment systems (DVD). An audio CD can store just over an hour of music. A CD-ROM can contain up to 680 megabytes of computer data. A DVD, the same size as traditional CDs, is able to store up to 17 gigabytes of data.

Companions of the Prophet *Arabic* Sahaba *or* Ashab. Followers of MUHAMMAD who had personal contact with him. They are the most important sources of HADITH. SUNNI Muslims regard the first four CALIPHS (among the ten Companions to whom Muhammad promised paradise) as the most important. SHIITE Muslims disregard the Companions.

compass In NAVIGATION or SURVEYING, the chief device for direction-finding on the earth's surface. Compasses may operate on magnetic or gyroscopic (see GYROSCOPE) principles or by determining the direction of the sun or a star. The oldest type is the magnetic compass. Magnetic compasses work as they do because earth itself acts as a MAGNET with a north–south field (see GEOMAGNETIC FIELD) that causes freely moving magnets to align themselves with the field.

compiler Computer SOFTWARE that translates (compiles) source code written in a high-level language into a set of MACHINE-LANGUAGE instructions that can be understood by a computer. Compilers are very large programs, with error-checking and other abilities. Some compilers translate high-level language into an intermediate ASSEMBLY LANGUAGE, which is then translated (assembled) into machine code. Other compilers generate machine language directly.

complementary medicine See ALTERNATIVE MEDICINE

complex number Any number consisting of both REAL NUMBERS and IMAGINARY NUMBERS. It has the form $a + bi$, where a and b are real numbers and $i = \sqrt{-1}$; a is called the real part and bi the imaginary part. Because a or b can equal 0, any real or imaginary number is also a complex number. Invented so that certain ALGEBRAIC EQUATIONS such as $x^2 + 1 = 0$ would have solutions, the complex numbers form an algebraic field; they obey the COMMUTATIVE LAW and the ASSOCIATIVE LAW in much the same way real numbers do (see FIELD THEORY).

complex variable In mathematics, a VARIABLE that can take on the value of a COMPLEX NUMBER. In basic algebra, the variables x and y generally stand for values of real numbers. The algebra of complex numbers (complex analysis) uses the complex variable z to represent a number of the form $a + bi$. The modulus of z is its ABSOLUTE VALUE. A complex variable may be graphed as a VECTOR from the origin to the point (a,b) in a rectangular COORDINATE SYSTEM, its modulus corresponding to the vector's length.

composite (material) Solid material that results when two or more different substances are combined (physically, not chemically) to create a new substance whose properties are superior in a specific application to those of the original components. The term specifically refers to a structural material within which a fibrous material is embedded. Glass-fiber-reinforced plastic is the best-known composite. Because of their stiffness, lightness, and heat resistance, composites are the materials of choice in numerous structural, reinforcing, and high-performance applications.

composite family Family Compositae, one of the largest plant families (also known as Asteraceae, DAISY family, and ASTER family), which contains more than 1,100 genera and almost 20,000 species of herbaceous plants, shrubs, and trees, found throughout the world. Composites tend to grow in sunlit places in temperate and subtropical regions. The family includes many garden ornamentals, including asters, CHRYSANTHEMUMS, COSMOS, DAHLIAS, MARIGOLDS, and ZINNIAS. Some genera include weeds such as DANDE-LION, RAGWEED, and THISTLE. ARTICHOKE, ECHINACEA, ENDIVE, SAFFLOWER, LETTUCE, and SUNFLOWER are important for the products derived from them. Flower heads in this family are composed of many small flowers (florets) surrounded by BRACTS. Disk florets form the center of each head; ray florets extend out like petals from the center. Some species have flowers with only disk or only ray florets.

compost Mass of rotted organic matter made from decomposed plant materials or from waste-plant residues. It is used in agriculture and gardening generally to improve soil structure rather than as a fertilizer, because it is low in plant nutrients. Composts commonly contain about 2% nitrogen, 0.5–1% phosphorus, and about 2% potassium. Lime and nitrogen fertilizers and manure may be added to speed decomposition.

compound Any substance composed of identical MOLE-CULES consisting of ATOMS of two or more ELEMENTS. Millions are known, each unique, with unique properties. Most common materials are mixtures of compounds. Pure compounds can be obtained by physical separation methods, such as precipitation and DISTILLATION. Compounds can be broken down into their constituents to various degrees or changed into new compounds by CHEMICAL REACTIONS. Atoms always combine into molecules in fixed proportions, distinguishing compounds from SOLUTIONS and other mechanical mixtures. Compounds are often classified as INOR-GANIC and ORGANIC COMPOUNDS. Compounds may also be classified by whether they have IONIC or COVALENT bonds.

compressed air AIR reduced in volume and held under PRESSURE. FORCE from compressed air is used to operate numerous tools and instruments, including rock drills, train brake systems, riveters, forging presses, paint sprayers, and atomizers. Bellows have been used since the Early Bronze age to provide air for smelting and forging. The 20th cent. witnessed a large increase in the use of compressed-air devices. The introduction of jet engines stimulated the use and improvement of centrifugal and axial-flow compressors. Digital-logic pneumatic-control components can be used in power and control systems.

compressor Machine for increasing the pressure of a GAS by mechanically decreasing its volume. Air is the most frequently compressed gas, but natural gas, oxygen, and nitrogen are also frequently compressed. Positive-displacement compressors are usually of the reciprocating piston type (see PISTON AND CYLINDER), useful for supplying small amounts of a gas at relatively high pressures. Centrifugal compressors are particularly suited for compressing large volumes of gas to moderate pressures. Axial compressors are used for jet aircraft engines and gas turbines.

Compromise of 1850 Series of measures passed by the U.S. Congress to settle slavery issues and avert SECESSION. The crisis arose in late 1849 when the territory of California asked to be admitted to the Union with a constitution prohibiting slavery. The problem was complicated by the unresolved question of slavery's extension into other areas ceded by Mexico in 1848. Sen. Henry CLAY offered a series of measures that admitted California as a free state, left the question of slavery in the new territories to be settled by the local residents, and provided for the enforced return of runaway slaves. Support from Daniel WEBSTER and Stephen DOUGLAS helped ensure passage of the compromise, which averted secession for another decade but sowed seeds of discord.

Compromise of 1867 or **Ausgleich** \ˈaus̩-ˌglīk\ Compact that established the dual monarchy of AUSTRIA-HUNGARY. The kingdom of Hungary desired equal status with the Austrian empire, which was weakened by its defeat in the Austro–Prussian War of 1866. The Austrian emperor FRANCIS

JOSEPH gave Hungary full internal autonomy, and in return it agreed that the empire should still be a single great state for purposes of war and foreign affairs.

Compton-Burnett, Ivy (*later* **Dame Ivy**) (1884–1967) British novelist. With her novel *Pastors and Masters* (1925) she introduced the style—employing extensive clipped, precise dialogue —that made her name. Her novels often dealt with struggles for power: *Men and Wives* (1931) featured a tyrannical mother, *A House and Its Head* (1935) a tyrannical father.

Compton effect Change in WAVELENGTH of X RAYS and other energetic forms of ELECTROMAGNETIC RADIATION when they collide with ELECTRONS. It is a principal way in which radiant energy is absorbed by matter, and is caused by the transfer of energy from PHOTONS to electrons. When photons collide with electrons, they transfer some of their energy and momentum to the electrons, which then recoil. New photons of less energy and momentum, and hence longer wavelength, are produced. The effect demonstrates the nature of the photon as a true particle with both energy and momentum. Its discovery in 1922 by Arthur H. Compton (1892–1962) was essential to establishing the WAVE-PAR-TICLE DUALITY of electromagnetic radiation.

computed axial tomography (CAT) \tə-ˈmäg-rə-fē\ *or* **computed tomography (CT)** DIAGNOSTIC-IMAGING method using a low-dose X-RAY beam that crosses the body in a single plane at many different angles. This major advance in imaging technology became generally available in the early 1970s. Detectors record the strength of the exiting X rays; this information is then processed by computer to produce a detailed two-dimensional cross-sectional image of the body. A series of such images in parallel planes or around an axis can show the location of abnormalities (especially tumors and other masses) more precisely than can conventional X-ray images.

computer, analog See ANALOG COMPUTER

computer Programmable machine that can store, retrieve, and process data. Today's computers have at least one CPU and a BUS. Auxiliary data storage is usually provided by an on-board HARD DISK and may be supplemented by other media such as FLOPPY DISKS or CD-ROMS. Peripheral equipment includes input devices (e.g., keyboard, MOUSE) and output devices (e.g., monitor, PRINTER), as well as the circuitry and cabling that connect all the components. First-generation computers, developed mostly in the U.S. after World War II, used VACUUM TUBES and were enormous. The second generation, introduced around 1960, used TRANSISTORS and were the first successful commercial computers. Third-generation computers (late 1960s) were characterized by miniaturization of components and use of INTEGRATED CIRCUITS. The MICROPROCESSOR chip, first introduced in 1974, defines fourth-generation computers. The fifth generation emphasizes ARTIFICIAL INTELLIGENCE and logic programming languages. Early machines were ANALOG COMPUTERS, but most today are DIGITAL COMPUTERS. In the last 50 years computers have changed the way people live and work, and their development has made the information age possible. See diagram on next page.

computer, digital See DIGITAL COMPUTER

computer animation Form of animated graphics that has replaced "stop-motion" ANIMATION of scale-model puppets or drawings. Computers can be used in every step of sophisticated animation—for example, to automate the movement of the rostrum camera or to supply the in-between drawings for full animation. When a three-dimensional figure is digitized, the computer can generate and display a sequence of images that seem to move or rotate the object through space. Hence computer animation can simulate highly complex motion for medical and other scientific researchers.

computer chip *or* **chip** Small wafer of SEMICONDUCTOR material embedded with integrated circuitry (see INTEGRATED CIRCUIT). Chips comprise the processing and memory units of the modern DIGITAL COMPUTER (see MICROPROCESSOR, RAM). Chip making is extremely precise and is usually done in a "clean room," since even microscopic contamination could render the chip defective. Computer chips have grown smaller and more powerful at a steady rate for decades.

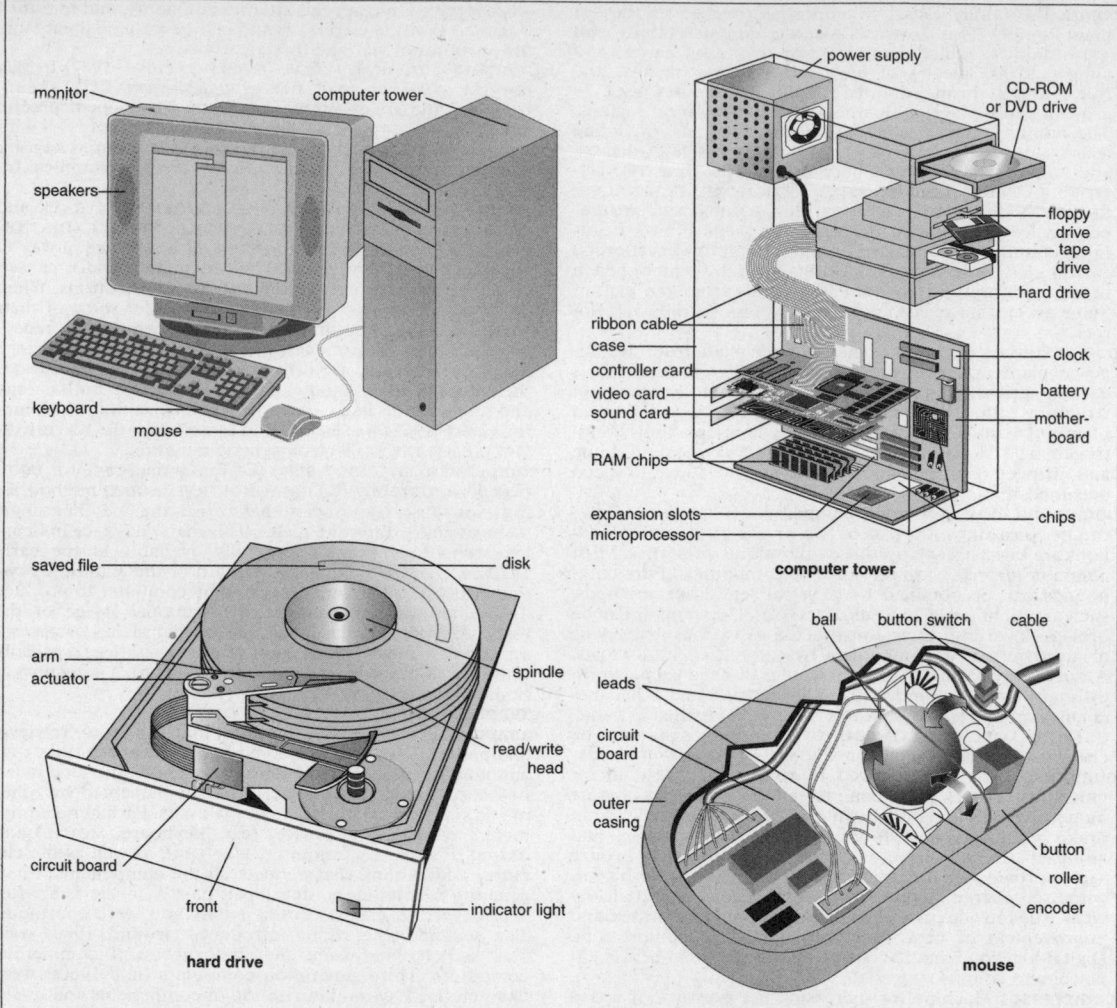

monitor
computer tower
speakers
keyboard
mouse

power supply
CD-ROM or DVD drive
floppy drive
tape drive
hard drive
clock
battery
motherboard
chips
ribbon cable
case
controller card
video card
sound card
RAM chips
expansion slots
microprocessor

computer tower

saved file
disk
arm
actuator
spindle
read/write head
circuit board
front
indicator light

hard drive

ball
button switch
cable
leads
circuit board
outer casing
button
roller
encoder

mouse

Computer A typical personal computer system consists of the computer itself, a video monitor, a keyboard, a mouse, and speakers. Other peripheral devices may include a printer, scanner, camera, microphone, or external storage device. Chips and circuit boards ("cards") are plugged into the motherboard. Other components, such as disk drives, are housed in the computer case and controlled by a card called a controller. The microprocessor directs the computer's activity via the motherboard and processes data with its millions of transistors. Data and programs in use are stored in the RAM chips. The floppy and hard drives store data not in immediate use on magnetic disks. Optical disks, such as CD-ROMs and DVDs, may store data as well. Some circuit boards are dedicated to specific functions; the sound card, for example, generates sounds and music. Additional boards, such as a modem, may be added by inserting them into an expansion slot, a row of electrical connectors that the board is plugged into. The power supply converts standard AC power into the voltages and currents required to operate the computer's components. A battery retains clock and configuration data when the AC power is turned off. The hard drive, the primary storage medium, usually contains several rigid disks attached to a spindle that spins them thousands of times a minute. The disks are accessed by read/write heads attached to the ends of moving arms; the positions of the head arms are controlled by the head actuator. The heads, under the control of a circuit board, read data by detecting the orientation of magnetic particles on the disks, and write new data to the disks by rearranging the magnetic particles, using a tiny electromagnet. The mouse is an input device used to position a pointer on the computer's screen and to make on-screen selections. When the user moves the mouse, a rubber ball turns, causing two rollers, corresponding to horizontal and vertical motion on the screen, to turn. The rollers are attached to wheels with electrical contacts (encoders), which sense the direction and amount of motion and send corresponding signals to the computer. On-screen selections are made by pressing one of the mouse's buttons, which closes an electrical switch, sending a signal to the computer.

computer graphics Use of computers to produce visual images, or the images so produced. Creating computer graphics requires a DIGITAL COMPUTER to store and manipulate images, a display screen, input/output devices, and specialized SOFTWARE that enables the computer to draw, color, and manipulate images. The field has widespread use in business, scientific research, and entertainment. Computer SIMULATION using graphically displayed quantities permits scientific study and testing of such phenomena as nuclear and chemical reactions, gravitational interactions, and physiological systems.

computer network See computer NETWORK

computer printer See computer PRINTER

computer program See computer PROGRAM

computer science Study of computers, their design, and their uses for computation, data processing, and systems control, including design and development of computer HARDWARE and SOFTWARE, and programming. The field encompasses theory, mathematical activities such as design and analysis of algorithms, and performance studies of systems and their components. Because computer systems are often too large and complicated for failure or success of a design to be easily predicted, experimentation is built into the development cycle.

computer virus Computer program designed to copy itself into other programs, with the intention of causing mischief or damage. On execution, it copies the viral code into any number of other programs and files stored in the computer, or via e-mail onto other computers. The corrupted programs may continue to perform their intended functions while also executing the virus's instructions, thus further propagating it. A harmless virus may simply cause a cryptic message to appear on the monitor; a more damaging virus can destroy valuable data. Antivirus software detects and removes viruses from a computer, but the software must be updated frequently for protection against new viruses.

computing, quantum See QUANTUM COMPUTING

Comstock, Anthony (1844–1915) U.S. reformer. Born in New Canaan, Conn., he began early to agitate against abortion and pornography. He lobbied successfully for the enactment (1873) of a severe federal statute outlawing the transportation of obscene matter in the mails (the Comstock Law). That same year he founded the Society for the Suppression of Vice. As a special agent of the U.S. Post Office (1873–1915), he conducted spectacular raids on publishers and vendors. His books include *Traps for the Young* (1883).

Comte \\'kōⁿt\\, **(Isidore-) Auguste (-Marie-François-Xavier)** (1798–1857) French philosopher, founder of SOCIOLOGY and of POSITIVISM. A disciple of Henri de SAINT-SIMON, he taught at the École Polytechnique (1832–42) but gave free lectures to workingmen. He named the science of sociology and established its conceptual basis, believing that social phenomena could be reduced to laws just as natural phenomena could. His ideas influenced such figures as J. S. MILL (who supported him financially for many years), Émile DURKHEIM, and Herbert SPENCER. His most important works are *Cours de philosophie positive* (6 vols., 1830–42) and *Système de politique positive* (4 vols., 1851–54).

Auguste Comte Drawing by Tony Toullion, 19th cent.

Conakry \\'kä-nə-ˌkrē, kó-nä-'krē\\ Capital (pop., 1993: 1,090,000), largest city, and chief Atlantic port of Guinea. Located on Tombo Island and the Kaloum Peninsula, it was founded by the French in 1884. It became the capital successively of the protectorate of Rivières du Sud (1891), the colony of French Guinea (1893), and independent Guinea (1958). The city was industrialized in the 1950s with the development of iron mining and bauxite production. It is the seat of the Univ. of Conakry (founded 1962).

Conan Doyle, Arthur See A. C. DOYLE

Conant \\'kō-nənt\\, **James B(ryant)** (1893–1978) U.S. educator and scientist, president of HARVARD UNIV. (1933–53). Educated at Harvard, he taught chemistry there until he was elected its president. He led the university to diversify its student body, and he was chiefly responsible for instituting the SAT nationwide. During World War II he was a central figure in organizing American science and developing the atomic bomb. In 1953 he was appointed U.S. high commissioner for W. Germany, and in 1955 ambassador. His publications include books on science and on educational policy.

concentration camp Internment center established by a government to confine political prisoners or members of national or minority groups for reasons of state security, exploitation, or punishment. Nations that have used such camps include Britain during the S. AFRICAN WAR, the Soviet Union (see GULAG), the U.S. (see MANZANAR RELOCATION CENTER), and Japan. "Reeducation camps," sometimes extremely brutal, were widely used by the communists in China during the CULTURAL REVOLUTION and in Cambodia under the KHMER ROUGE. Most notorious are the death camps of Nazi Germany, including AUSCHWITZ, BERGEN-BELSEN, BUCHENWALD, DACHAU, and TREBLINKA.

Concepción \\ˌkȯn-sep-'syón\\ City (pop., 1999: 362,000), capital of Bío-Bío region, S central Chile. Chile's second-largest city, it was founded in 1550 on the Pacific coast, and was shortly afterward burned twice by ARAUCANIAN Indians. Struck by numerous earthquakes and two tsunamis, in 1754 it was moved inland up the Bío-Bío River. Despite frequent earthquakes, it has become a major commercial and industrial center, manufacturing textiles, food products, and steel.

conceptual art Any of various art forms in which the idea for a work of art is considered more important than the finished product. In the 1960s and '70s it became a major international movement; its leading exponents were Sol LeWitt (b.1928) and Joseph Kosuth (b.1945). Its adherents radically redefined art objects, materials, and techniques, and began questioning the very existence and use of art, claiming that the "true" work of art is not a physical object but rather consists of "concepts" or "ideas." Typical conceptual works include photographs, graphs, and image-text combinations that are intentionally made visually uninteresting in order to divert attention to the "ideas" they express. One example is Kosuth's *One and Three Chairs* (1965), which combines a real chair, a photograph of a chair, and a dictionary definition of "chair." Conceptual art was fundamental to much of the art produced in the late 20th cent.

concerto \\kən-'cher-tō\\ Musical composition for solo instrument and orchestra. The solo concerto grew out of the older CONCERTO GROSSO. Giuseppe Torelli's violin concertos of 1698 are the first known solo concertos. Antonio VIVALDI, the first important concerto composer, wrote over 350 solo concertos, mostly for violin. From the Classical period on, most concertos have been written for piano (W. A. MOZART wrote 27 piano concertos), followed in popularity by the violin. From the outset the concerto has been a three-movement form, with fast tempos in the outer movements and a slow central movement. It has generally been intended to display the soloist's virtuosity, particularly in the often improvised cadenzas near the ends of the outer movements. 19th- and 20th-cent. concertos were usually conceived as a kind of dramatic struggle between soloist and orchestra.

concerto grosso Principal orchestral form of the baroque era, characterized by contrast between a small group of soloists and a larger orchestra. The small group (concertino) usually consisted of two violins and CONTINUO, the instruments of the older trio sonata. The larger group (ripieno) generally consisted of stringed instruments with continuo. Alessandro Stradella wrote the first known concerto grosso around 1675. Arcangelo CORELLI's set of 12 (c.1680–90), J. S. BACH's six Brandenburg Concertos (c.1720), and G. F. HANDEL's 12 Op. 6 concertos (c.1740) are the most celebrated examples. From 1750 it was eclipsed by the solo CONCERTO.

conch \\'käŋk, 'känch\\ Marine SNAIL whose shell has a broadly triangular outer whorl and a wide lip. True conchs (family Strombidae) feed on fine plant matter in warm waters. The queen conch *(Strombus gigas)*, found from Florida to Brazil, has an ornamental shell with a distinctive large pink opening. The clam-eating fulgur conchs (family Melongenidae) include the channeled conch *(Busycon canaliculatum)* and the lightning conch *(B. contrarium)*, both about 7 in. (18 cm) long and common on the U.S. Atlantic coast. See also WHELK.

Conciliar Movement \\kən-'si-lē-ər\\ (1409–49) In Roman Catholicism, an effort to strengthen the authority of church

councils over that of the papacy. Originally aimed at ending the Western SCHISM, the movement emerged as a force at the Council of Pisa (1409), which elected a third pope in an unsuccessful attempt at compromise. A second council, the Council of CONSTANCE (1414–18), ended the schism by voiding all papal offices and electing a new pope. Participants hoped to play an ongoing role in the church, but the popes continued to seek supremacy, and the Council of BASEL (1431–49) ended fruitlessly.

conclave In the Roman Catholic church, the assembly of CARDINALS gathered to elect a new POPE, and the system of strict seclusion to which they are submitted. From 1059 the election became the responsibility of the cardinals. The system of meeting in closed conclave began in the 13th cent. but was not codified until 1904, by Pius X. Today election requires a majority of two-thirds plus one. Voting by secret ballot takes place twice a day; ballots are burned after each vote. Until the needed majority is obtained, they are burned with wet straw to make black smoke; white smoke issuing from the Vatican Palace indicates that the vote has resulted in election of a new pope.

Concord Town (pop., 2000: 17,000), E Massachusetts. Founded in 1635, it was the first inland Puritan settlement. In 1775 the British were marching to seize its storehouse of military supplies when they were checked by MINUTEMEN (see Battles of LEXINGTON AND CONCORD). In the 19th cent., it was a noted cultural center and the home of R. W. EMERSON, H. D. THOREAU, Nathaniel HAWTHORNE, and L. M. ALCOTT. Walden Pond, where Thoreau lived and wrote, is nearby.

Concord City (pop., 2000: 40,000), capital of New Hampshire. It lies along the Merrimack River above MANCHESTER. Incorporated in 1733 by Massachusetts as Rumford, it was determined in 1762 to belong to New Hampshire. Renamed Concord, it was made the capital in 1808. Quarrying of Concord granite has continued since its early years.

Concord, Battle of See Battles of LEXINGTON AND CONCORD

Concorde First supersonic, passenger-carrying, commercial airplane. Built jointly by British and French manufacturers, it entered regular service in 1976. Its maximum cruising speed is 1,354 mph (2,179 kph), more than twice the speed of sound; the London–New York flight takes less than four hours.

concrete Artificial stone made of a mixture of cement (a fine powder of lime and other minerals), aggregate (hard material), and water. Its immense compressive strength, adaptability to virtually any form, and fire-resistance have made it one of the most common building materials in the world. The usual binder today is PORTLAND CEMENT. The aggregate is usually sand and gravel. Additives called admixtures may be used to accelerate the curing (hardening) process in low-temperature conditions. Others can slow shrinkage and increase strength. See also PRESTRESSED CONCRETE, REINFORCED CONCRETE.

concussion Period of nervous-function impairment that results from relatively mild brain injury, often with no bleeding, in the CEREBRAL CORTEX. It causes brief unconsciousness, followed by mental confusion and physical difficulties. These effects usually clear up within hours, but in some cases disturbance of consciousness continues, and there may be residual symptoms. Some level of AMNESIA often accompanies concussion.

Condé \kōⁿ-ˈdā\, **Louis II de Bourbon, 4th prince de** known as **the Great Condé** (1621–1686) French military leader. He distinguished himself in the Thirty Years' War, and in 1649 he helped suppress the first FRONDE uprising. After being arrested by Cardinal Mazarin in 1650, he rebelled and led the second Fronde; defeated, he fled (1652) to fight for Spain. Pardoned in 1659, he again became one of LOUIS XIV's greatest generals, winning numerous battles in Spain, Germany, and Flanders. He was a man of great courage and independence of mind; broadly cultivated, he counted MOLIÈRE and Jean RACINE among his friends.

condensation Formation of a liquid or solid from its vapor, usually onto a surface that is cooler than the adjacent gas. A substance condenses when the PRESSURE exerted by its vapor exceeds the vapor pressure of its liquid or solid phase at the temperature of the surface where the condensation is

to occur. The process causes the release of thermal energy (see HEAT). Condensation occurs on a glass of cold water on a warm, humid day, and also accounts for the formation of dew, fog, rain, snow, and clouds.

condenser Device for reducing a gas or vapor to a liquid. Condensers are used in power plants to condense exhaust steam from TURBINES and in REFRIGERATION plants to condense refrigerant vapors, such as AMMONIA and FREONS. The petroleum and chemical industries use condensers for hydrocarbons and other chemical vapors. In DISTILLATION, a condenser transforms vapor to liquid. All condensers work by removing heat from the gas or vapor. In some, the gas passes through a long tube of heat-conductive metal, such as copper, and heat escapes into the surrounding air. Large industrial condensers use water or some other liquid to remove the heat.

conditioning Process in which the frequency or predictability of a behavioral response is increased through reinforcement (i.e., a stimulus or a reward for the desired response). Classical, or respondent, conditioning, involving stimulus substitution, is based on the work of Ivan PAVLOV, who conditioned dogs by ringing a bell each time the aroma of food was presented. Eventually the dogs salivated when the bell rang, even if no food odor was present; salivation was thus the conditioned response. In instrumental, or operant, conditioning, a spontaneous (operant) behavior is either rewarded (reinforced) or punished. When rewarded, a behavior increases in frequency; when punished, it decreases. Operant conditioning was studied in detail by B. F. SKINNER.

condominium In modern property law, individual ownership of one dwelling unit within a multidwelling building. Unit owners have undivided ownership interest in the land and those portions of the building shared in common. In the U.S., this type of cooperative ownership has been popular in crowded urban areas.

condor Either of two species of large New World VULTURE. Two of the largest flying birds, each is about 50 in. (130 cm) long and weighs about 20 lbs (10 kg). Both feed on dead animals. The Andean condor (*Vultur gryphus*), which ranges from the Pacific coast of S. America to the high Andes, has slightly longer wings (10 ft, or 3 m) and is black with a white ruff and bare pinkish head, neck, and crop. The California condor (*Gymnogyps californianus*) is nearly black, with white wing linings, bare yellow head, and red neck and crop. It was narrowly saved from extinction in the 1980s.

Condorcet \kōⁿ-dȯr-ˈse\, **marquis de** orig. Marie-Jean-Antoine-Nicolas de Caritat (1743–1794) French philosopher and revolutionary. He showed early promise as a mathematician and was a protégé of Jean d'ALEMBERT. In 1777 he became secretary of the Academy of Sciences. In sympathy with the French Revolution, he was elected to the Legislative Assembly (1791–92), where he called for a republic. His opposition to the arrest of the moderate GIRONDINS led to his being outlawed (1792). While in hiding he wrote his famous *Sketch for a Historical Picture of the Progress of the Human Mind*, proposing the continuous progress of humanity to an ultimate perfection. He was captured and subsequently found dead in prison.

conducting Art of leading a group of musical performers. Before about 1800, the first violinist or the keyboard player usually gave the few necessary conducting signals. The growing size of ensembles and growing complexity of the music in the 19th cent., including its varying tempos and heightened expressiveness, made it necessary for a person to coordinate and interpret the music for the group. The first conductors, including Felix MENDELSSOHN, Hector BERLIOZ, and Richard WAGNER, were composers themselves. By the end of the 19th cent., conducting had become a specialty and the great conductors had become musical stars.

conduction See THERMAL CONDUCTION

conductor Any of various substances that allow the flow of ELECTRIC CURRENT or thermal energy (see HEAT). A conductor is a poor INSULATOR because it has a low RESISTANCE to such flow. Electrical conductors, usually metallic, are used to conduct electric current, as in the metal wires of an electric CIRCUIT. Thermal conductors include materials such as metal and glass.

cone or **strobilus** \strō-'bī-ləs, 'strō-bə-ləs\ In botany, a mass of scales or bracts, containing the reproductive organs of certain non-flowering plants. A distinguishing feature of PINES and other CONIFERS, the cone is roughly analogous to the FLOWER of other plants. Cones (strobili) are also found on club mosses and HORSETAILS.

Conestoga wagon Horse-drawn covered freight wagon. It originated in the 18th cent. in the Conestoga Creek region of Pennsylvania. It had a flat body and low sides; with its floor curved up at each end to prevent freight from shifting, it was well suited for travel over early American roads. As later adapted by westward-traveling pioneers, with its tall white canvas top it resembled a sailing ship from a distance, which earned it the name "prairie schooner."

Conestoga wagon

Coney Island Amusement area, S BROOKLYN, New York, on the Atlantic Ocean. Formerly an island, after its creek silted up it became part of LONG ISLAND. Its first pavilion and bathhouse were erected in 1844, and its popularity grew with the coming of the subway in 1920. It has a 3.5-mi (5.6-km) boardwalk; its amusement park, known for its Cyclone rollercoaster, formerly included freak shows, burlesque houses, and a parachute jump. It is also the site of the New York Aquarium.

Confederate States of America or **Confederacy** Government of the 11 Southern states that seceded from the Union in 1860–61 until its defeat in the AMERICAN CIVIL WAR in 1865. In the months following Abraham LINCOLN's election as president in 1860, seven states of the Deep South (Alabama, Florida, Georgia, Louisiana, Mississippi, S. Carolina, and Texas) seceded. After the attack on FORT SUMTER in April 1861, Arkansas, N. Carolina, Tennessee, and Virginia joined them. The government was directed by Jefferson DAVIS as president. Its principal goals were the preservation of states' rights and the institution of slavery. It counted on the influence of KING COTTON to exert financial and diplomatic pressure on the Union from sympathetic European governments. Battlefield victories in 1861–62 gave the Confederacy the moral strength to continue fighting, but from 1863 dwindling finances and battlefield reverses led to its defeat and dissolution.

Confederation, Articles of See ARTICLES OF CONFEDERATION

confession In the Judeo-Christian tradition, acknowledgment of sinfulness, in public or private, regarded as necessary for divine forgiveness. In Judaism, YOM KIPPUR is a day of prayer, fasting, and confession. The early Christian Church followed JOHN THE BAPTIST's practice of confession before BAPTISM, but soon instituted confession and penance for the forgiveness of sins committed after baptism. The Roman Catholic and Eastern Orthodox churches consider penance a SACRAMENT.

configuration In chemistry, the arrangement in space of the ATOMS in a MOLECULE. It is especially important in organic chemistry (see ORGANIC COMPOUND), because each CARBON atom is at the center of a tetrahedron, with four bonds (see BONDING), one to each corner; if three or all four atoms bonded to the carbon are different, the molecule can assume two different mirror-image (see OPTICAL ACTIVITY, ISOMER) forms. Configuration also applies to some inorganic compounds. Electron configuration is used to describe the number of electrons in the various shells of an atom, which defines its chemical reactivity and the type of bonding it participates in.

confirmation Christian rite in which believers reaffirm the faith into which they were baptized as infants or young children. The rite did not exist in the early church, whose members joined as adults. As BAPTISM of infants became common, some means of ascertaining their knowledge and commitment as young adults became necessary, and a period of instruction, followed by examination and confirma-

tion, was introduced. In Roman Catholicism confirmation became a SACRAMENT; the rite is also used in the Anglican and Lutheran churches.

Confucianism Scholarly tradition and way of life propagated by CONFUCIUS in the 6th–5th cent. B.C. and followed by the Chinese for more than two millennia. Though not organized as a religion, it has deeply influenced E. Asian spiritual and political life in a comparable manner. The core idea is *ren* ("humaneness"), signifying excellent character in accord with *li* (ritual norms), *zhong* (loyalty to one's true nature), *shu* (reciprocity), and *xiao* (filial piety). Together these constitute DE (virtue). Confucianism did not become influential until the 2nd cent. B.C., when it was recognized as the Han state cult. More than TAOISM and BUDDHISM, Confucian ethics have had the strongest influence on the moral fabric of Chinese society. A revival of Confucian thought in the 11th cent. resulted in NEO-CONFUCIANISM, a major influence in Korea during the CHOSON dynasty and in Japan during the EDO PERIOD. See also FIVE CLASSICS, MENCIUS.

Confucius Chinese **Kongfuzi** or **K'ung-fu-tzu** \'kùŋ-'fü-'dzə\ (551–479 B.C.) Ancient Chinese philosopher and political theorist. Born into a poor family, he educated himself in the six arts—ritual, music, archery, charioteering, calligraphy, and arithmetic—along with history and poetry, and began a brilliant teaching career in his thirties. Confucius saw education as a process of constant self-improvement, with the primary function of training noblemen *(junzi)*. He saw public service as the natural consequence of education and sought to revitalize all of China's social institutions. He served in government posts, eventually becoming minister of justice in Lu, but his policies attracted little interest. After a 12-year self-imposed exile, he returned to Lu at 67 to teach and write. His life and thoughts are recorded in the *LUNYU (Analects).* See also CONFUCIANISM.

congenital disorder Structural abnormality, functional problem (e.g., CYSTIC FIBROSIS, PHENYLKETONURIA), or disease present at birth. Almost all are due to genetic factors (inherited or spontaneous MUTATIONS, CHROMOSOMAL DISORDERS), environmental influences during pregnancy (RUBELLA or other maternal factors, exposure to toxins or radiation), or both. The most sensitive period is the first eight weeks after conception, as the human EMBRYO is being formed. Some inherited disorders result from simple Mendelian DOMINANCE or RECESSIVENESS. Others may involve multiple genes. At least 30 significant defects probably occur per thousand births. Incidence of specific defects varies widely in different racial groups. See also DOWN'S SYNDROME, NEURAL TUBE DEFECT.

conger eel Any of about 100 species of marine EEL (family Congridae) with no scales, a large head, large gill slits, a wide mouth, and strong teeth. Found in all oceans, sometimes in deep water, they may grow about 6 ft (1.8 m) long. Conger eels are carnivores. Many species, such as the European conger *(Conger conger),* are valued as food. The American conger, or sea eel *(C. oceanicus),* is a fierce game fish.

congestive heart failure HEART failure resulting in symptoms that are distant from the heart, related mainly to salt and water retention in the tissues. It may vary from the most minimal symptoms to sudden pulmonary EDEMA or a rapidly lethal shocklike state (see SHOCK). Chronic states of varying severity may last years. Symptoms tend to worsen as the body's attempts to compensate for the condition create a vicious circle. The patient has trouble breathing, at first during exertion and later even at rest. Fluid accumulates at the lowest point of the body. Blood pools in the veins because the heart pumps too weakly to return it.

conglomerate \kən-'glä-mə-rət\ In petrology, lithified sedimentary rock consisting of rounded fragments larger than 0.08 in. (2 mm) in diameter. It is commonly contrasted with BRECCIA. Conglomerates are usually subdivided by size into pebble (fine), cobble (medium), and boulder (coarse).

Congo, Democratic Republic of the formerly (1971–97) **Republic of Zaire** (1960–71) **Congo** (1908–60) **Belgian Congo** (1885–1908) **Congo Free State** Republic, central Africa. Area: 905,356 sq mi (2,344,872 sq km). Population (2000): 51,965,000. Capital: KINSHASA. Bantu-speakers, including the Mongo, KONGO, and Luba, form a majority of the coun-

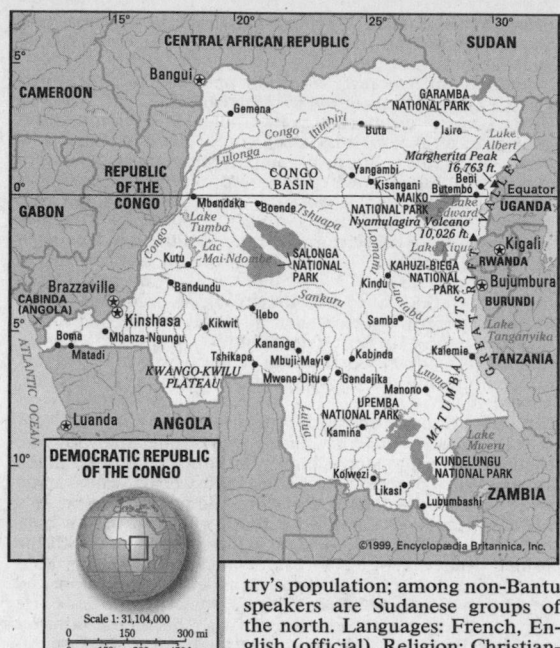

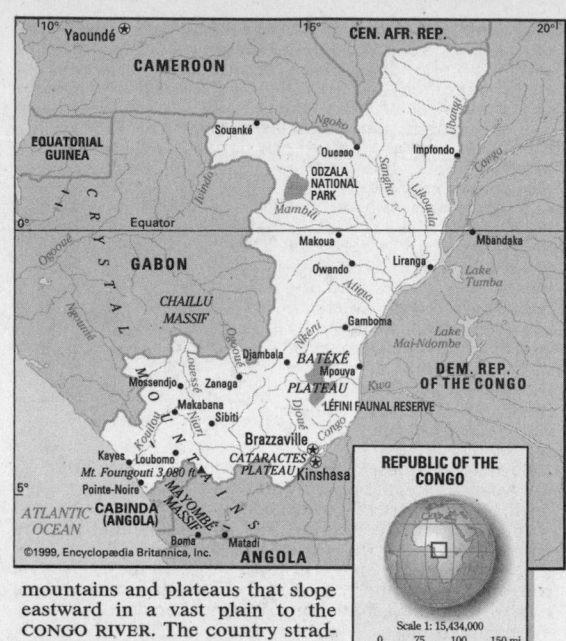

try's population; among non-Bantu speakers are Sudanese groups of the north. Languages: French, English (official). Religion: Christianity. Currency: Congolese franc. The Democratic Republic of the Congo, with the third-largest land-area in Africa, occupies the heart of the CONGO RIVER basin, from which high plateaus rise in every direction. At its narrow strip of Atlantic coast the Congo empties into the sea. The country straddles the equator; its climate is humid and tropical. It is one of the poorest countries in the world; its economy is based on mining and agriculture. Export crops include coffee, palm products, tea, cocoa, and cotton; mining products include copper, cobalt, and industrial diamonds. It is ruled by a military regime; the head of state is the president, which office was taken by the regime's leader in the late 1990s. Prior to European colonization, several native kingdoms had emerged in the region, including the 16th-cent. Luba kingdom and the Kuba federation, which reached its peak in the 18th cent. European development began late in the 19th cent. when King LEOPOLD II of Belgium financed H. M. STANLEY's exploration of the Congo River. The 1884–85 Berlin W. Africa Conference recognized the Congo Free State with Leopold as its sovereign. The growing demand for rubber helped finance the exploitation of the Congo, but abuses against native peoples outraged Western nations and forced Leopold to grant the Free State a colonial charter as the Belgian Congo (1908). Independence was granted in 1960, and the country's name was changed to Zaire. The post-independence period was marked by unrest, culminating in a military coup that brought Gen. MOBUTU SESE SEKO to power in 1965. Mismanagement, corruption, and increasing violence devastated the infrastructure and economy. Mobutu was deposed in 1997 by Laurent KABILA, who restored the country's name to Congo. Instability in neighboring countries and desire for Congo's mineral wealth led to military involvement by numerous African countries. Kabila was assassinated in 2001 and succeeded by his son, who signed a comprehensive peace accord in 2002.

Congo, Republic of the *formerly* **Middle Congo** Republic, W central Africa. Area: 132,047 sq mi (342,000 sq km). Population (2000): 2,831,000. Capital: BRAZZAVILLE. Nearly half of the population belongs to one of the KONGO tribes. The Teki are less numerous, as are the Ubangi people. Language: French (official), various Bantu languages. Religions: Christianity, traditional religions. Currency: CFA franc. A narrow coastal plain edges the Congo's 100-mi (160-km) stretch of Atlantic coastline, rising into low mountains and plateaus that slope eastward in a vast plain to the CONGO RIVER. The country straddles the equator; rain forests cover nearly two-thirds of the country, and wildlife is abundant. The Congo has a centrally planned, developing economy. Mining products, crude petroleum and natural gas, account for more than 90% of the country's exports. A 1997 transitional constitution vested executive power in the president and legislative power in a national transitional council. In precolonial days the area was home to several thriving kingdoms, including the KONGO, which had its beginnings in the 1st millennium A.D. The SLAVE TRADE began in the 15th cent. with the arrival of the Portuguese; it supported the local kingdoms and dominated the area until its suppression in the 19th cent. The French arrived in the mid-19th cent. and established treaties with two of the kingdoms, placing them under French protection prior to becoming part of the colony of French Congo. In 1910 it was renamed FRENCH EQUATORIAL AFRICA and the area of the Congo became known as Middle (Moyen) Congo. In 1946 Middle Congo became a French overseas territory and in 1958 voted to become an autonomous republic within the French Community. Full independence came two years later. The area has suffered from political instability since independence. Congo's first president was ousted in 1963. A Marxist party, the Congolese Labor Party, gained strength, and in 1968 another coup, led by Major Marien Ngouabi, created the People's Republic of the Congo. Ngouabi was assassinated in 1977. A series of military rulers followed, at first militantly socialist but later oriented toward social democracy. Fighting between local militias in 1997 badly disrupted the economy; a peace accord was signed in 1999.

Congo Free State See Democratic Republic of the CONGO

Congo River *or* **Zaire River** \zä-ⁱir\ River, W central Africa. Rising in Zambia as the Chambeshi and flowing 2,900 mi (4,700 km) through the Democratic Republic of the Congo to the Atlantic Ocean, it is the second-longest river in Africa. It flows through three regions: the upper Congo, with lakes, waterfalls, and rapids; the middle Congo, with seven cataracts known as Boyoma (Stanley) Falls; and the lower Congo, whose two branches form a vast lake area called the Malebo (Stanley) Pool.

Congregationalism Movement that arose among English Protestant Christian churches in the late 16th and early 17th cent. It developed as one branch of PURITANISM and emphasized the right and duty of each congregation to govern itself independent of higher human authority. Its greatest influence and numbers were in the U.S., where Puritans first established it at Plymouth Colony. The GREAT AWAK-ENING led U.S. Congregationalism away from its Calvinist roots. Many churches defected to UNITARIANISM. In general, Congregationalists eschew creeds and emphasize preaching over sacraments, accepting only BAPTISM and the EUCHARIST. Most U.S. Congregationalists are now part of the United Church of Christ.

Congress, Library of Library of the U.S., the largest of what may be considered national libraries. Founded in Washington, D.C., in 1800, it was housed in the Capitol until the building was burned by British troops in 1814; it moved to permanent quarters in 1897. It is outstanding among the learned institutions of the world, with magnificent collections of books, manuscripts, music, prints, and maps. It contains some 18 million books and more than 54 million manuscripts.

Congress of the United States Legislature of the U.S., established under the CONSTITUTION OF THE U.S. (1789) and separated structurally from the executive and judiciary. It consists of the Senate and the House of Representatives. Representation in the Senate is fixed at two senators per state. In the House, representation is proportional to each state's population; total membership is restricted (since 1912) to 435 members. Congressional business is processed by committees: bills are debated in committees in both houses, and reconciliation of the two resulting versions takes place in a conference committee. A presidential veto can be overridden by a two-thirds majority in each house. Congress's constitutional powers include the setting and collecting of taxes, borrowing money on credit, regulating commerce, coining money, declaring war, and raising and supporting armies. All finance-related legislation must originate in the House; the Senate must approve presidential nominations, ratify treaties, and adjudicate impeachments. See also BICAMERAL SYSTEM.

Congress Party See INDIAN NATIONAL CONGRESS

Congreve, William (1670–1729) English dramatist. He was a young protégé of John DRYDEN when his first major play, *The Old Bachelour* (1693), met with great success. Later came *The Double-Dealer* (1693), *Love for Love* (1695) and *The Way of the World* (1700), his masterpiece. Congreve shaped the English COMEDY OF MANNERS with his brilliant comic dialogue, satirical portrayal of fashionable society, uproarious bawdiness, and ironic scrutiny of the affectations of his age. See also RESTORATION LITERATURE.

conic section Any two-dimensional curve traced by the intersection of a right circular cone with a plane. If the plane is perpendicular to the cone's axis, the resulting curve is a CIRCLE. Intersections at other angles result in ELLIPSES, PARABOLAS, and HYPERBOLAS. The conic sections are studied in EUCLIDEAN GEOMETRY and in ANALYTIC GEOMETRY. They have useful applications to optics, antenna design, structural engineering, and architecture.

conifer Any member of the order Coniferales, woody plants that bear their SEEDS and POLLEN on separate, CONE-shaped structures. They constitute the largest division of GYMNOSPERMS, with more than 550 species. Most are evergreen trees and shrubs. They grow throughout the world (except in Antarctica) and prefer temperate climate zones. Conifers include the PINES, JUNIPERS, SPRUCES, HEMLOCKS, FIRS, LARCHES, YEWS, CYPRESSES, bald cypresses *(Taxodium)*, DOUGLAS FIRS, arborvitaes *(Thuja)*, and related groups. Conifers supply SOFTWOOD timber as well as pulpwood for paper. The wood is also used as fuel and in manufacturing. The trees are the source of RESINS, volatile oils, TURPENTINE, tars, and pharmaceuticals. Conifer leaves generally have a reduced surface area to minimize water loss. Especially in the pines, firs, and spruces, the leaves are long and stiff and are commonly called needles. Cypresses, CEDARS, and others have smaller, scalelike leaves. Conifers were the dominant type of vegetation just before the advent of angiosperms (see FLOWERING PLANT).

conjoined twins See SIAMESE TWINS

conjunctivitis Inflammation of the lining of the eyelids and the front of the white of the EYE. It may be caused by infection ("pink eye"), chemical burn, physical injury, or allergy. Often the cornea is also inflamed. Infectious causes include several viruses and bacteria, including those that cause trachoma and GONORRHEA, both of which can lead to blindness.

conjuring Art of entertaining by giving the illusion of performing impossible feats. The conjurer is an actor who employs psychology, manual dexterity, and mechanical aids. The form was established by the medieval era, when traveling conjurers performed at fairs and in the homes of the nobility. In the 19th–20th cent., conjuring was performed on stage by such magicians as J.-E. ROBERT-HOUDIN, Harry HOUDINI, and Harry Blackstone. In the late 20th cent. such magicians as Doug Henning and David Copperfield performed colorful spectacles on television, while the postmodern team Penn and Teller emphasized irony and illusion.

Conkling, Roscoe (1829–1888) U.S. politician. Born in Albany, N.Y., he served in the U.S. House of Representatives (1859–65) and Senate (1867–81), where he became a leader of the Radical Republicans and advocated severe Reconstruction measures. Resisting efforts by Pres. Rutherford B. HAYES to achieve civil-service reform, he retained control of New York patronage. In 1881 he resigned from the Senate in a patronage dispute with Pres. James GARFIELD.

Connecticut State (pop., 2000: 3,405,000), NE U.S. The southernmost of the NEW ENGLAND states, it borders LONG ISLAND SOUND and covers 5,018 sq mi (12,997 sq km). Its capital is HARTFORD. The original inhabitants were ALGONQUIAN-speaking Indians. The area was colonized by English Puritans from the MASSACHUSETTS BAY COLONY during the 1630s. One of the original states of the Union, it was the fifth to ratify the U.S. Constitution. It was an agricultural region until the early 19th cent., when textile factories were established, and by 1850 employment in manufacturing exceeded agriculture; the state remains a manufacturing center. NEW HAVEN, home of YALE UNIV., is one of New England's largest ports, while Stamford is the headquarters for some of the U.S.'s largest corporations. New London is home to the U.S. Coast Guard Academy. Highways and railways traverse Connecticut and serve the densely settled coastal and CONNECTICUT RIVER valley regions. The state abounds with historical sites and memorials, and there are numerous state forests and state parks.

Connecticut River River, NEW ENGLAND, NE U.S. Rising in N New Hampshire, it flows south for 407 mi (655 km) to empty into LONG ISLAND SOUND. It forms the entire boundary between Vermont and New Hampshire. The longest river in New England, it is extensively developed for hydroelectric power.

connective tissue Tissue in the body that maintains the form of the body and its organs and provides cohesion and internal support, including BONE, LIGAMENTS, TENDONS, CARTILAGE, ADIPOSE TISSUE, and aponeuroses. Its major components are different kinds of cells and extracellular fibers and the ground substance, which varies in consistency from thin gel to rigid structure. Connective-tissue diseases are either genetic disorders (e.g., MARFAN'S SYNDROME) or acquired inflammatory or immune-system diseases (e.g., RHEUMATOID ARTHRITIS, OSTEOARTHRITIS, systemic LUPUS ERYTHEMATOSUS, and RHEUMATIC FEVER).

Connelly, Marc(us Cook) (1890–1980) U.S. playwright, screenwriter, and director. Born in McKeesport, Pa., he covered theatrical news in Pittsburgh and New York. He collaborated with G. S. KAUFMAN on *Dulcy* (1921), which they followed with the comedies *To the Ladies* (1922) and *Beggar on Horseback* (1924) and the librettos for *Helen of Troy, New York* (1923), and *Be Yourself* (1924). Connelly went on to write *Green Pastures* (1930, Pulitzer Prize; film, 1936). His screenplays include *Captains Courageous* (1937).

Connery, Sean (*orig.* Thomas) (*later* **Sir Sean**) (b.1930) Scottish actor. He made his London stage debut in the chorus of *South Pacific* (1951). After minor roles, he starred as James Bond in the film version of Ian FLEMING's *Dr. No* (1962) and six other Bond films. A compelling character actor as well as a perennial sex symbol, he has acted in films such as *The Man Who Would Be King* (1975), *The Name of the Rose* (1986), *The Untouchables* (1987, Academy Award), and *The Russia House* (1990).

Connolly, Maureen (Catherine) (1934–1969) U.S. tennis player. Born in San Diego, she became the youngest winner

of the National Girl's Tournament at age 14. In 1953 she became the first woman to win the Grand Slam (the Wimbledon, U.S., Australian, and French singles competitions). Her career was ended in 1954 by a horseback-riding accident.

Connor, Ralph orig. Charles William Gordon (1860–1937) Canadian novelist. He served as a missionary to mining and lumber camps; this experience and memories of his childhood in Glengarry, Ontario, provided material for his novels, including *The Sky Pilot* (1899), which, combining adventure with religious messages and wholesome sentiment, made him the best-selling Canadian novelist of the early 20th cent. His best books are considered to be *The Man from Glengarry* (1901) and *Glengarry School Days* (1902).

Connors, Jimmy (orig. James Scott) (b.1952) U.S. tennis champion. Born in E. St. Louis, Ill., in 1974 he won three Grand Slam tournaments (U.S., Australian, and Wimbledon) but was barred from the French Open because he had joined World TeamTennis. He won the U.S. singles titles in 1976, 1978, 1982, and 1983. His temper tantrums ushered in an era of such displays on the championship circuit.

conquistador \kän-'kēs-tə-ˌdòr\ Any of the adventurers who took part in the Spanish conquest of the Americas in the 16th cent. Under Hernán CORTÉS, 500 men and 16 horses conquered Mexico's AZTEC empire. A force under Pedro de Alvarado went on to subdue Guatemala. Francisco PIZARRO defeated the INCAS in Peru with 180 men and 37 horses; his companion Diego de ALMAGRO led an expedition to Chile. Though renowned for their bravery, the conquistadors remain notorious for their avarice and the destruction they wrought on native populations and civilizations.

Conrad, Joseph orig. Józef Teodor Konrad Korzeniowski (1857–1924) Polish-British writer. His father was a Polish patriot who was exiled to N Russia, and Conrad was an orphan by 12. In 1878 he joined the British merchant navy, where he pursued a career for most of the next 15 years; his naval experiences would provide the material for most of his novels. Though he knew little English before he was 20, he became one of the master English stylists. He is noted for tales in rich prose of dangerous life at sea and in exotic places, settings he used to reveal his real concern, his deeply pessimistic vision of the human struggle. Such novels as *The Nigger of the "Narcissus"* (1897), *Lord Jim* (1900), *Nostromo* (1904), *The Secret Agent* (1907), and *Under Western Eyes* (1911) are regarded as masterpieces. He also published seven story collections; the novella "Heart of Darkness" (1902) is his most famous shorter work. Conrad's influence on later novelists has been profound.

Conrad II (c.990–1039) German king (1024–39) and Holy Roman Emperor (1027–39). After Conrad was crowned king of Germany in 1024, a rebellion of German nobles and princes of Lombardy collapsed (1025), and he was made successively king of Italy (1026) and emperor (1027). He instituted legislative reforms, issuing a new set of feudal constitutions for Lombardy. His son Henry (later Henry III) became his chief counselor. Conrad defeated Poland (1028), regaining lands lost earlier. He inherited Burgundy (1034) and resolved dissensions among the great princes in Italy (1038).

Conrad III (1093–1152) German king (1138–52), the first of the HOHENSTAUFEN DYNASTY. Nephew of Emperor Henry V of Germany, he revolted when he was passed over as heir by the electors, and he was crowned antiking at Nuremberg (1127) and king of Italy (1128). He fought the German king Lothair II 1132–35, then submitted and was pardoned. He became king when Lothair died, quelling resistance in Bavaria and Saxony. Conrad joined the Second CRUSADE (1147) and visited Constantinople (1148), where he cemented an alliance with MANUEL I COMNENUS. Unable to visit Rome, he never received the imperial crown.

Conrail in full **Consolidated Rail Corp.** U.S. railroad company created by the federal government in 1973 to take over six bankrupt NE railroads. Conrail began operations in 1976 with major portions of the Erie Lackawanna, Lehigh & Hudson River, Lehigh Valley, Penn Central, and Reading railroads and the Central Railroad Co. of New Jersey. Conrail's network carries freight traffic over 15 states. Its pas-

senger traffic was turned over to AMTRAK and regional authorities in 1983. Its stock was first offered to the public in 1987.

conscientious objector One who opposes participation in military service on the basis of religious, philosophical, or political belief. A feature of Western society since the beginning of the Christian era, conscientious objection developed as a doctrine of the MENNONITES (16th cent.), the Society of FRIENDS (17th cent.), and others. Exemptions may be unconditional, conditioned on alternative civilian service, or limited to combat duty. See also PACIFISM.

consciousness Quality or state of being aware. As applied to the lower animals, consciousness refers to the capacity for sensation and, usually, simple volition. In higher animals, this capacity may include thinking and EMOTION. In human beings, consciousness is understood to include "meta-awareness," an awareness that one is aware. The term is contrasted with UNCONSCIOUS processes. Levels of consciousness (e.g., attention vs. SLEEP) are correlated with patterns of electrical activity in the brain (brain waves).

conscription or **draft** Compulsory enrollment for service in a country's armed forces. It has existed at least since the Egyptian Old Kingdom in the 27th cent. B.C. It usually takes the form of selective service rather than universal conscription. The U.S. established a draft in the American Civil War but did not use it again until 1917. Like Britain, the U.S. abandoned conscription at the end of World War I but reverted to it when World War II threatened. The U.S. retained the draft 1948–73.

conservation Planned management of a natural resource or of a particular ECOSYSTEM to prevent exploitation, pollution, destruction, or neglect and to ensure its future usability. Living resources are renewable; minerals and fossil fuels are nonrenewable. In the West, conservation dates to 17th-cent. efforts to protect European forests in the face of increasing demands for fuel and building materials. NATIONAL PARKS, first established in the 19th cent., were dedicated to preserving uncultivated land as a safe haven to wildlife and to protect watershed areas and help ensure a clean water supply. Legislation, treaties, and regulations aim to balance the need for development with the need to conserve the environment.

conservation law or **law of conservation** In physics, the principle that certain quantities within an isolated system do not change over time. When a substance in an isolated system changes PHASE, the total amount of MASS does not change. When ENERGY is changed from one form to another in an isolated system, the total amount of energy does not change. When a transfer of MOMENTUM occurs in an isolated system, the total amount of momentum is conserved. The same is true for ELECTRIC CHARGE in a system: charge lost by one particle is gained by another. Conservation laws make it possible to predict the macroscopic behavior of a system without having to consider the microscopic details of a physical process or chemical reaction.

conservation of energy See conservation of ENERGY

conservatism Political attitude or ideology denoting a preference for institutions and practices that have evolved historically and are thus manifestations of continuity and stability. It was first expressed in the modern era through the works of Edmund BURKE in reaction to the FRENCH REVOLUTION, which he believed tarnished its ideals by its excesses. Conservatives believe that the implementation of change should be minimal and gradual. Their perspective tends to be right of center, appreciative of history, and more realistic than idealistic. See also CHRISTIAN DEMOCRACY, LIBERALISM, REPUBLICAN PARTY.

Conservative Judaism Form of Judaism that mediates between REFORM JUDAISM and ORTHODOX JUDAISM. Founded in 19th-cent. Germany as the Historical School, it arose among German-Jewish theologians who advocated change but found Reform positions extreme, wishing to maintain a stricter observance of Jewish law (e.g., dietary laws) and belief in the coming of the MESSIAH. The founding in 1886 of the Jewish Theological Seminary of America (New York) led to its development as a religious movement.

Conservative Party (Canada) See PROGRESSIVE-CONSERVATIVE PARTY OF CANADA

Conservative Party *officially* National Union of Conservative and Unionist Associations. British political party. Its principles include promotion of private property and enterprise, a strong military and foreign policy, and traditional cultural values and institutions. It is the heir of the old TORY Party, whose members began forming "conservative associations" after electoral rights were extended to the middle class in 1832. The modern party (whose members are often known as Tories) divides into a traditionalist, communitarian wing and a libertarian, individualist wing. Its membership is heavily dependent on the landowning and middle classes, but its electoral base has extended at times to incorporate about one-third of the working class. Since World War I, it and the LABOUR PARTY have dominated British politics.

conservatory In architecture, a mostly glass structure, frequently attached to and directly entered from a dwelling, in which plants are protected and displayed. Unlike the GREENHOUSE, an informal structure situated in the working area of a garden, the conservatory became a popular 19th-cent. decorative architectural feature proclaiming the status of its owner. The most outstanding example is Joseph Paxton's CRYSTAL PALACE.

conservatory School devoted to musical training. Originating in the 16th-cent. name for Italian orphanages, which often gave their charges musical training, the term gradually came to apply to music schools. They typically offer instruction to people of all ages, but the primary focus is on students aged 10–25. Important U.S. conservatories include the Curtis Institute (Philadelphia), Eastman School (Rochester, N.Y.), JUILLIARD SCHOOL, Manhattan School (New York), and New England Conservatory (Boston).

consonance and dissonance Perceived qualities of musical CHORDS and INTERVALS. Consonance is often described as relative "stability," dissonance as "instability." In musical contexts, certain intervals seem to call for motion by one of the tones to "resolve" perceived dissonance. The most consonant intervals are the unison and octave; the next most consonant interval is the perfect 5th. Consonance tends to reflect the early intervals of the OVERTONE series (including the major and minor 3rds and the perfect 4th), but many musical factors can affect the perception of consonance and dissonance.

consonant Any speech sound made by moving mouth parts, or closing or narrowing the vocal tract completely or partially; also, any letter or symbol representing such a sound. Consonants are usually classified according to place of articulation (e.g., palate, teeth, lips); manner of articulation, as in stops (complete closure of the oral passage), fricatives (forcing of breath through a constricted passage), and trills (vibration of a mouth part); and presence or absence of voicing, nasalization, and other features.

conspiracy Agreement between two or more persons to commit an unlawful act or to accomplish a lawful end by unlawful means. Individual conspirators need not even know of the existence or the identity of all other conspirators. In a chain conspiracy the parties act separately and successively (as in distributing narcotics). A civil conspiracy is not prosecuted as a crime but forms the grounds for a lawsuit. In ANTITRUST LAW, conspiracies in restraint of trade (e.g., price fixing) are rigorously prosecuted.

Constable, John (1776–1837) British painter. He began his career in 1799 on entering the Royal Academy Schools in London. Inspired by the English countryside, in 1813–14 he filled two sketchbooks with over 200 landscape drawings. His most significant achievement was the production of many small oil sketches, painted directly from nature, depicting the atmospheric effects of changing light and moving clouds, unique at the time they were painted. In 1830 a series of mezzotints were published from his paintings. He is ranked with J. M. W. TURNER as one of the greatest 19th-cent. British landscape painters.

Constance (1154–1198) Queen of Sicily (1194–98) and Holy Roman empress-consort (1191–97). The daughter of King ROGER II of Sicily, she married the future emperor Henry VI in 1186 and was later crowned with him in Rome. Her marriage gave the HOHENSTAUFEN DYNASTY a claim to the Sicilian throne, which she asserted against the opposition of her nephew TANCRED. When Henry died (1197), she had her son FREDERICK II crowned king.

Constance, Council of (1414–18) Sixteenth ecumenical council of the Roman Catholic church. It was convened to deal with three competing popes, examine the writings of Jan HUS and John WYCLIFFE, and reform the Church. Two of the three contending popes were deposed; the third abdicated, and in 1417 the council selected a new pope, Martin V. The Council condemned propositions of Hus and Wycliffe, and Hus was burned at the stake by secular authorities.

Constance, Lake *German* **Bodensee** \'bŏd-ᵊn-ˌzā\ *ancient* Lacus Brigantinus. Lake, bordering Switzerland, Germany, and Austria. At an elevation of 1,299 ft (396 m), it has an area of 209 sq mi (541 sq km) and an average depth of 295 ft (90 m). It forms part of the RHINE RIVER, and by the Middle Ages was a major traffic center. Bordering alpine scenery makes the lakeshore an attractive resort area. Remains of NEOLITHIC lake dwellings are found in the area.

Constans II Pogonatus \'kän-ˌstanz...ˌpō-gə-'nāt-əs\ (630–668) Byzantine emperor (641–68). His reign saw the loss of Byzantium's S and E provinces to the Arabs. Muslim Arabs took Egypt (642), invaded Armenia (647), and defeated Constans at sea in 655. A civil war among Arabs prevented them from attacking Constantinople, and he secured a nonaggression treaty with Syria (659). Within the empire he tried to force unity on the church, forbidding debate on divisive theological questions. He aroused public outrage by ordering the murder of his own brother (660). He left Constantinople (663) and settled in Sicily, where he was assassinated.

Constanta \kŏn-'stänt-sə\ *Turkish* **Kustenja** \ˌkᵜe-sten-'yä\ *ancient* Constantiana *or* Tomis. City (pop., 1997: 344,000), chief seaport, Romania. The area was first settled by the Greeks at Tomis in the 7th cent. B.C. Romans annexed the region in the 1st cent. B.C.; OVID was exiled there in A.D. 9–17. In the 4th cent. A.D., Tomis was reconstructed by CONSTANTINE the Great as Constantiana. It declined following the Turkish conquest in the early 15th cent. Its modern development dates from its return to Romania in 1878.

Constantine \'kän-stən-ˌtēn\ *ancient* Cirta. City (pop., 1998: 462,000), NE Algeria. A natural fortress built on a rocky height above the Rhumel River, by the 3rd cent. B.C. it was one of NUMIDIA's most important towns, and it thrived under Micipsa in the 2nd cent. B.C. Ruined in subsequent wars, it was restored in A.D. 313 and renamed for its patron, CONSTANTINE I the Great. Overrun by the Arabs in the 7th cent. and later by the Turks, it was captured by the French in 1837. It was an important Allied campaign base in World War II. The city retains its medieval walls. Today it is an agricultural market for the region.

Constantine, Donation of See DONATION OF CONSTANTINE

Constantine I *known as* **Constantine the Great** *officially* Flavius Valerius Constantinus (after A.D. 280?–337) First Roman emperor to profess Christianity. The eldest son of the emperor Constantius I Chlorus (d.306), he was passed over as successor to the throne but fought to become emperor. Victory at the Milvian Bridge outside Rome (312) made him emperor in the West; according to legend, a cross and the words *in hoc signo vinces* ("By this sign thou shalt conquer") appeared to him there and he forthwith adopted Christianity. In 313 he issued, with LICINIUS, the Edict of Milan, granting tolerance to Christians; he also gave land for churches and granted the church special privileges. He opposed DONATISM and ARIANISM, and convoked the important Council of Nicaea. After defeating and executing Licinius, he gained control of

Constantine I

the East and became sole emperor. He moved the capital from Rome to the site of Byzantium, which he renamed Constantinople (324). In 326 he had his wife and eldest son killed for reasons that remain obscure. Under his patronage, Christianity began its growth into a world religion.

Constantine I *Greek* Constantinos (1868–1923) King of Greece (1913–17, 1920–22). Educated in Germany, he was commander in chief of Greek forces in the BALKAN WARS. He succeeded his father, George I, in 1913, but his pro-German attitude during World War I caused the Allies and his Greek opponents to depose him in 1917. He was restored to the throne in 1920, but after a catastrophic war in Anatolia he abdicated in favor of his son, George II, in 1922.

Constantine II *Greek* Constantinos (b.1940) King of Greece (1964–74). He succeeded his father, Paul I, in 1964. After a military coup in 1967, he and his family fled to Rome. In 1973 the military regime proclaimed a republic and abolished the monarchy. In 1974 a civilian referendum officially ended the monarchy.

Constantine V Copronymus \kə-'prän-ə-məs\ (718–775) Byzantine emperor (741–75). The son of LEO III, he ruled with his father from 720. He spent his life defeating Arab and Bulgar threats to the empire and was unable to prevent the Lombards from taking Ravenna (751), thus ending Byzantine influence in N and central Italy. A strong iconoclast (see ICONOCLASM), he persecuted monks who disagreed with his position.

Constantine VII Porphyrogenitus \ˌpȯr-fə-rō-'jen-ət-əs\ (905–959) Byzantine emperor (913–59). His father-in-law, Romanus I Lecapenus, was crowned co-emperor with him in 920 and soon became the primary ruler. Shut out of government, the young emperor devoted himself to scholarship; his writings include works on the Slavic and Turkic peoples and on Byzantine ceremonies. In 944 the sons of Romanus, impatient for power, had their father deported, and the ensuing public outcry emboldened Constantine to banish them in 945; he then ruled alone until his death.

Constantine XI Palaeologus \ˌpā-lē-'ä-lə-gəs\ (1404–1453) Last Byzantine emperor (1449–53). He became emperor when his brother John VIII Palaeologus died childless, but he faced a losing battle against the Ottoman Turks, who were directing all their resources toward the capture of Constantinople. He acknowledged the obedience of the Greek church to Rome in order to secure help from the West, but in vain. He was killed fighting at the walls of Constantinople as the Turks broke through.

Constantine IX Monomachus \mō-'nä-mə-kəs\ (c.980–1055) Byzantine emperor (1042–55). He gained the imperial throne by marrying the empress ZOE. An opponent of the great military leaders, he neglected imperial defenses, instead spending extravagantly on luxuries and magnificent buildings. Rebellions broke out at home and abroad, and Byzantine lands were threatened by invaders. Constantine tried to ally with the papacy to save S Italy from the Normans, but growing differences between Rome and Constantinople resulted in the SCHISM OF 1054.

Constantinople See ISTANBUL

Constantinople, Council of (A.D. 381) Second ecumenical council of the Christian church. It promulgated the NICENE CREED and declared finally the Trinitarian doctrine of the equality of Father, Son, and HOLY SPIRIT. Only Eastern bishops were summoned to the Council, but the Greeks claimed that it was ecumenical. The Second Council of Constantinople, called in 553 by JUSTINIAN I, lent support to the notion that Christ's nature was entirely divine, despite his human incarnation. The Third Council, held in 680, condemned the Monothelites, who claimed that Christ had a single will despite his two natures. The Fourth Council, held in 869–70, resulted in the excommunication of St. PHOTIUS and increased the animosity between the Eastern and Western churches.

constellation Any of certain groupings of STARS imagined to look like objects, mythological figures, or creatures. They are useful for locating certain stars. A constellation's stars are often designated by its name and Greek letters in order of brightness. Of 88 named constellations in Western astronomy, about half retain the names PTOLEMY gave 48 of them in his *Almagest*. See also ZODIAC.

constitution Set of doctrines and practices that form the fundamental organizing principle of a political state. It may be written (e.g., the CONSTITUTION OF THE U.S.) or partly written and uncodified (e.g., Britain's constitution). Its provisions usually specify how the government is to be organized, what rights it shall have, and what rights shall be retained by the people. Modern constitutional ideas developed during the ENLIGHTENMENT, when such philosophers as Thomas HOBBES, Jean-Jacques ROUSSEAU, and John LOCKE proposed that constitutional governments should be stable, adaptable, accountable, and open, should represent the governed, and should divide power according to its purpose.

Constitution, USS *known as* **Old Ironsides** One of the first frigates built for the U.S. Navy. Launched in 1797, it carried more than 50 guns and a crew of 450. It was the successful flagship of the Tripolitan War (1801–5), and in the WAR OF 1812 it vanquished the British frigate *Guerrière*. It was condemned as unseaworthy in 1828, but O. W. HOLMES's poem "Old Ironsides" sparked a public preservation campaign. Restored in 1927–31, it is now berthed in Boston, sails on special occasions, and is open to the public.

Constitution Act See CANADA ACT (1982)

Constitutional Act or **Canada Bill** (1791) British law repealing certain portions of the QUEBEC ACT of 1774. The new act provided a more democratic constitution, establishing an elected legislature for each province and a governor and an executive council appointed by the crown. Bills could originate in the legislature, but they could be disallowed by the crown.

Constitutional Convention (May–Sept. 1787) Assembly that drafted the CONSTITUTION OF THE U.S. All states but Rhode Island sent delegates in response to a call by the ANNAPOLIS CONVENTION for a meeting in Philadelphia to amend the ARTICLES OF CONFEDERATION. The delegates decided to replace the Articles with a document that strengthened the federal government. An important issue was the apportioning of legislative representation. Two plans were presented: the Virginia plan, favored by the large states, apportioned representatives by population or wealth; the New Jersey plan provided for equal representation for each state. A compromise established the bicameral Congress to ensure both equal and proportional representation. The document was approved on September 17 and sent to the states for ratification.

Constitutional Democratic Party or **Kadet** Russian political party advocating a constitutional monarchy like Britain's. It was founded in October 1905 by the Union of Liberation and other liberals associated with the ZEMSTVOS. Its members, called Kadets, dominated the first DUMA in 1906 but were less successful thereafter. After 1917, the party was outlawed.

constitutional monarchy System of government in which a monarch (see MONARCHY) has agreed to share power with a constitutionally organized government. The monarch may remain the de facto head of state or may be a purely ceremonial head. Britain became a constitutional monarchy under the Whigs; other constitutional monarchies include Belgium, Cambodia, Jordan, the Netherlands, Norway, Spain, Sweden, and Thailand.

Constitution of the United States Fundamental law of the U.S. federal system of government and a landmark document of the Western world. It is the oldest written national constitution in operation, completed in 1787 at a convention of 55 delegates who met in Philadelphia, ostensibly to amend the ARTICLES OF CONFEDERATION. Because ratification in many states hinged on the promised addition of a BILL OF RIGHTS, the Constitution was not fully certified until 1791. The Constitution's separation of the legislative, executive, and judicial branches of government, the checks and balances of each branch against the other, and the explicit guarantees of individual liberty were all designed to strike a balance between authority and liberty. Article I vests all legislative powers in the CONGRESS. Article II vests executive power in the PRESIDENT. Article III places judicial power in the hands of the courts. Article IV deals, in part, with relations among the states and with the privileges of the citizens, Article V with amendment procedure, and

Article VI with public debts and the supremacy of the Constitution. Article VII gives ratification terms. The 10th Amendment restricted the national government's powers to those expressly listed in the Constitution; the states, unless otherwise restricted, possess all the remaining (or "residual") powers of government. Twenty-seven amendments have been added to the Constitution since 1789. In addition to the Bill of Rights, these include the 13th (1865), abolishing slavery; the 14th (1868), requiring DUE PROCESS and EQUAL PROTECTION under the law; the 15th (1870), guaranteeing the right to vote regardless of race; and the 19th (1920), instituting women's suffrage. See also CIVIL LIBERTY, EQUAL RIGHTS AMENDMENT, FREEDOM OF SPEECH, JUDICIARY, STATES' RIGHTS.

Constitutions of Clarendon See Constitutions of CLARENDON

Constructivism Russian movement in art and architecture, initiated in 1914 by the abstract geometric constructions of Vladimir TATLIN. In 1920 Tatlin was joined by Antoine Pevsner and Naum GABO. Their *Realist Manifesto,* which directed their followers to "construct art," gave the movement its name. The group, soon joined by Aleksandr RODCHENKO and El LISSITZKY, produced abstract works reflecting modern machinery and technology, using plastic, glass, and other industrial materials. They spread the movement's ideals throughout Europe and to the U.S. after Soviet opposition dispersed the group.

Constructivism "Column" by Naum Gabo, 1923

consul In the ROMAN REPUBLIC, either of two annually elected chief magistrates. The consuls had sacred rights and near-absolute authority. They were nominated by the Senate and elected by the popular assembly. As heads of state, they commanded the army, presided over the Senate and assemblies and acted on their decrees, and handled foreign affairs. At the end of his one-year term, a consul was generally appointed to serve as governor of a province. The office continued in weaker form under the empire.

Consulate (1799–1804) French government established after the overthrow of the DIRECTORY. Its executive branch consisted of three consuls, but the First Consul, NAPOLEON, wielded all real power, while the other two, E.-J. SIEYÈS and Pierre-Roger Ducos (1747–1816), were figureheads. The executive branch was given the power to draft new laws, the legislative branch became little more than a rubber stamp, and elections became an elaborate charade. Napoleon abolished the Consulate when he declared himself emperor.

consumerism Movement or policies aimed at regulating the products, services, methods, and standards of manufacturers, sellers, and advertisers in the interests of the buyer. Such regulation may be institutional, statutory, or embodied in an industry-wide voluntary code. Governments often establish formal regulatory agencies to ensure CONSUMER PROTECTION (in the U.S., e.g., the FEDERAL TRADE COMMISSION and the FOOD AND DRUG ADMINISTRATION). Early consumer-protection laws were created to prevent sale of tainted food and harmful drugs. The U.S. consumer protection movement grew in the 1960s and '70s as consumer activists led by Ralph NADER lobbied for laws setting safety standards for automobiles, toys, and numerous household products. Consumer advocates have also won passage of "truth-in-advertising" laws. The International Organization of Consumers Unions (IOCU) provides global consumer advocacy.

consumer price index Measure of living costs based on changes in retail prices. Consumer PRICE INDEXES are widely used to measure changes in the cost of maintaining a given STANDARD OF LIVING. The goods and services commonly purchased by the population covered are priced periodically, and their prices are combined in proportion to their relative importance. This set of prices is compared with the initial set of prices collected in the base year to determine the percentage increase or decrease. The population covered may be restricted to wage and salary earners or to city dwellers, and special indexes may be used for special population groups (e.g., retirees).

consumer protection Legal framework promoting customer safety and education and providing protection from hazardous or substandard products and from fraud. In the U.S., the FEDERAL TRADE COMMISSION (established 1914) and the FOOD AND DRUG ADMINISTRATION (established 1927) help ensure consumer protection. Regulations address manufacture and design, advertising, labeling, and sales methods. The U.N.'s Guidelines for Consumer Protection provide a framework and a benchmark for governments (particularly of less developed countries) to establish a legal basis for consumer protection. See also CONSUMERISM.

consumption In economics, the final using up of goods and services. The term excludes the use of intermediate products in the production of other goods (e.g., the purchase of buildings and machinery by a business). Economists use statistical information to trace trends in consumption, seeking to map consumer demand for goods and services. In CLASSICAL ECONOMICS, consumers are assumed to be rational and to allocate expenditures in such a way as to maximize total satisfaction from all purchases. Incomes and PRICES are seen as consumption's two major determinants. Critics of the model point out that there are many exceptions to rational consumer behavior.

consumption See TUBERCULOSIS

contact lens Thin artificial lens worn on the surface of the EYE to correct refractive defects of vision. Early glass contact lenses, invented in 1887, were uncomfortable and could not be worn long. Modern plastic lenses, made to measurements taken by optical instruments, come in several types. Hard lenses are better for ASTIGMATISM but have a limited wearing time. Soft lenses are more comfortable, and some can be worn for several weeks.

containment Strategic U.S. foreign policy of the late 1940s and early 1950s designed to check the expansionist policy of the Soviet Union. It was conceived by George KENNAN soon after World War II, when the U.S. provided military and economic aid to Greece and Turkey to counter Soviet influence there.

contempt In law, willful disobedience to or open disrespect of a court, judge, or legislative body. An act of disobedience to a court order may be treated as either criminal or civil contempt. An act or language that consists solely of an affront to a court or interferes with the conduct of its business constitutes criminal contempt; such contempt carries sanctions designed to punish as well as to coerce compliance. In the U.S., a congressional committee can compel the attendance of witnesses. Any witness failing to appear or otherwise obstructing the committee in the course of exercising its powers may be in contempt. See also PERJURY.

continent One of seven large continuous masses of land: Asia, Africa, N. America, Antarctica, Europe, and Australia (listed in order of size). Europe and Asia are sometimes considered a single continent, Eurasia. More than two-thirds of the world's continental land area lies north of the equator. See also CONTINENTAL DRIFT.

Continental Congress Body of delegates that acted for the American colonies and states during and after the AMERICAN REVOLUTION. The First Continental Congress, meeting in Philadelphia in Sept. 1774, was called by the colonial COMMITTEES OF CORRESPONDENCE. The delegates adopted a declaration of personal rights, denounced taxation without representation, petitioned the British crown for a redress of grievances, and called for a boycott of British goods. The Second Continental Congress, meeting in May 1775, appointed George WASHINGTON commander in chief of the army. It later approved the DECLARATION OF INDEPENDENCE (1776) and prepared the ARTICLES OF CONFEDERATION (1781).

Continental Divide Most notable watershed of the N. American continent. The mountains comprising it extend generally north–south, thus dividing the continent's principal drainage into waters flowing eastward (e.g., into HUDSON BAY in Canada or the MISSISSIPPI RIVER in the U.S.) and waters flowing westward (into the Pacific Ocean). Most of the divide runs along the crest of the ROCKY MTNS. Its central point is Colorado, where it has many peaks above 13,000 ft (3,962 m). It continues southward into Mexico, roughly paralleling the SIERRA MADRE, and into Central America.

continental drift Large-scale movements of CONTINENTS over geologic time. In 1912 Alfred WEGENER postulated that a single supercontinent, which he called PANGAEA, fragmented late in the TRIASSIC PERIOD (248–208 million years ago) and the parts began to move away from one another. He pointed to the similarity of rock strata in the Americas and Africa as evidence. Wegener's ideas were widely rejected until they were combined with the SEAFLOOR SPREADING hypothesis in the 1960s. The modern theory states that the Americas were joined with Europe and Africa until about 190 million years ago, when they split apart along the MID-ATLANTIC RIDGE. Subsequent tectonic plate movements brought the continents to their present positions.

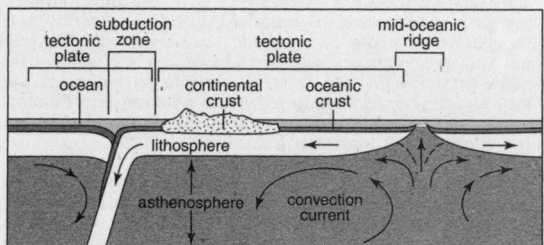

Continental drift The continents are embedded in tectonic plates. As new lithosphere is created at one plate margin and subducted at another, the plate, and with it the continent, moves over the underlying mantle. The "drift" of continents amounts to only inches per year, but over hundreds of millions of years this alters their relative positions by thousands of miles.

Continental philosophy Collective term for the many distinct traditions, methods, and styles that shaped 20th-cent. European philosophy. It is usually contrasted with Anglo-American philosophy, or ANALYTIC PHILOSOPHY, and includes PHENOMENOLOGY and EXISTENTIALISM. Thinkers such as Martin HEIDEGGER, Jean-Paul SARTRE, and Maurice MERLEAU-PONTY combine elements of both.

continental shelf Broad, relatively shallow submarine platform that forms a border to a continent, typically extending from the coast to depths of 330–660 ft (100–200 m). Its average width is about 40 mi (65 km). Almost everywhere it is a continuation of the continental landmass: narrow, rough, and steep off mountainous coasts but broad and comparatively level offshore from plains. Usually covered with a layer of sand and silty muds, the surface features small hills that alternate with shallow depressions. In a few cases, steep-walled V-shaped submarine canyons cut deeply into both the shelf and the CONTINENTAL SLOPE below.

continental shield Any of the large stable areas of low relief (little variation in elevations) in the earth's CRUST that are composed of PRECAMBRIAN crystalline rocks. Always more than 570 million years, some rocks are as old as 2–3 billion years. Continental shields occur on each of the continents.

continental slope Usually steep slope from a CONTINENTAL SHELF to the beginning of the ocean basins at depths of 330–10,500 ft (100–3,200 m). The world's combined continental slope is about 200,000 mi (300,000 km) long. The slope is most gradual off stable coasts without major rivers and is steepest off coasts with young mountain ranges. The dominant sediments of continental slopes are muds; there are smaller amounts of sediments of sand or gravel.

Continental System In the NAPOLEONIC WARS, the blockade designed by NAPOLEON to paralyze Britain's commerce.

In the decrees of Berlin (1806) and Milan (1807), France ordered neutrals and French allies not to trade with the British. England responded with a counterblockade, which led indirectly to the WAR OF 1812. Because of England's naval superiority, the contest proved disastrous to Napoleon.

continuing education *or* **adult education** Any form of learning provided for adults. In the U.S., the Univ. of WISCONSIN was the first academic institution to offer such programs (1904). Empire College of the State Univ. of NEW YORK was the first to be devoted exclusively to adult learning (1969). Continuing education encompasses independent study; broadcast, videotape, on-line, and correspondence courses; group discussion and study circles; conferences, seminars, and workshops; and full- or part-time classroom study. Remedial programs, and topics ranging from auto repair to retirement planning to computer skills are common. See also CHAUTAUQUA MOVEMENT.

continuity In mathematics, a property of FUNCTIONS and their GRAPHS. A continuous function is one whose graph has no breaks, gaps, or jumps. It is defined using the concept of a LIMIT. Specifically, a function is said to be continuous at a value x if the limit of the function exists there and is equal to the function's value at that point. When this condition holds true for all REAL NUMBER values of x in an interval, the result is a graph that can be drawn over that interval without lifting the pencil. Such functions are crucial to the theory of CALCULUS.

continuo *or* **basso continuo** In baroque music, a special subgroup of an instrumental ensemble. It consists of two instruments reading the same part: a bass instrument, such as a CELLO, and a chordal instrument, most often a HARPSICHORD. Its appearance in the early 17th cent. reflected the radically new musical texture of accompanied melody that was especially typical of the new vocal genre of OPERA. The continuo came to be employed in virtually all ensemble music of the baroque era. See also FIGURED BASS.

contraception Birth control by prevention of conception or impregnation. The most common method is STERILIZATION. The most effective temporary methods are nearly 99% effective if used consistently and correctly. Many methods carry health risks; barrier devices and avoidance of SEXUAL INTERCOURSE during the most fertile period are safest. Hormonal contraceptives use ESTROGEN and/or PROGESTERONE to inhibit ovulation. The "morning-after pill" (high-dose hormones) is effective even after intercourse. The most serious side effect of oral contraceptives is the risk of blood-clotting disorders. Intrauterine devices (IUDs) are placed inside the UTERUS and appear to cause a mild endometrial inflammation that either inhibits fertilization or prevents a fertilized egg from implanting. Barrier devices, such as condoms, diaphragms, cervical caps, female condoms (vaginal pouches), and vaginal sponges,

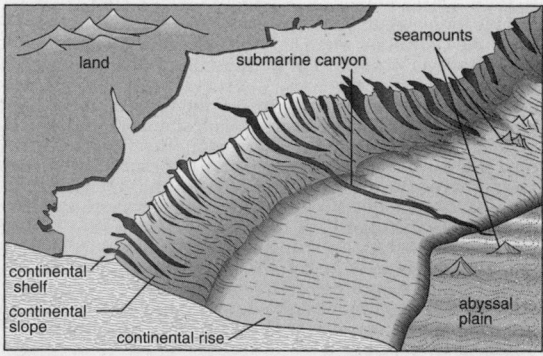

Continental shelf The broad, gentle pitch of the continental shelf gives way to the relatively steep continental slope. The more gradual transition to the abyssal plain is a sediment-filled region called the continental rise. The continental shelf, slope, and rise are collectively called the continental margin. Depth is exaggerated here for effect.

prevent SPERM from entering the uterus. Condoms also prevent SEXUALLY TRANSMITTED DISEASES. Used with spermicides, condoms are nearly 100% effective. Fertility awareness techniques involve keeping track of the menstrual cycle (the so-called "rhythm method"; see MENSTRUATION) to avoid intercourse around the time of ovulation. Experimental forms of birth control include an oral contraceptive for men.

contract Agreement between two or more parties that creates in each party a duty to do something (e.g., provide goods at a certain price according to a specified schedule), and may also create the duty not to do something (e.g., divulge an employer's trade secrets to third parties). Failure to honor a contract allows the other party to bring an action for DAMAGES in a court of law. All contracts must be entered into both willingly and freely. A contract also must have a lawful objective.

contralto See ALTO

contras Counterrevolutionary force that sought to overthrow Nicaragua's SANDINISTA government. The original contras had been National Guardsmen during the regime of Anastasio Somoza. The U.S. played a key role in training and funding the group, whose terrorist tactics were widely decried. In 1984 the U.S. Congress banned military aid to the contras; the Ronald REAGAN administration's efforts to circumvent the ban led to the IRAN–CONTRA AFFAIR. A regional peace was negotiated by Oscar ARIAS, and in 1990 Pres. Violeta CHAMORRO negotiated the contras' demobilization.

contrast medium Substance comparatively opaque to X RAYS, which allows a body structure that does not normally contrast with its background to be seen clearly on the film. Common contrast media include BARIUM sulfate and iodized organic compounds. They are given by the route that introduces them into the structure to be examined—swallowed or as an enema, inhaled, or injected. Serious reactions to contrast media are not infrequent. See also DIAGNOSTIC IMAGING.

contredanse See COUNTRY DANCE

convection Process by which HEAT is transferred by movement of a heated FLUID such as air or water. Most fluids expand when heated, becoming less dense and more buoyant, and so rising. The heated molecules eventually cool, become more dense, and sink. This sets up convection currents that account for the uniform heating of the air in a room or water in a kettle. Air convection can be forced by a fan, and water convection by a pump. Atmospheric convection currents can be set up by local heating effects such as solar radiation or contact with cold surfaces.

Convention, National See NATIONAL CONVENTION

convention, political See POLITICAL CONVENTION

convergence Mathematical property of INFINITE SERIES, INTEGRALS on unbounded regions, and certain sequences of numbers. An infinite series is convergent if the sum of its terms is finite. The series $1/2 + 1/4 + 1/8 + 1/16 + 1/32 + \ldots$ sums to 1 and thus is convergent. An integral calculated over an interval of infinite width describes a region that is unbounded in at least one direction. If such an integral converges, the unbounded region has finite area. A sequence of numbers converges to a particular number when the difference between successive terms becomes arbitrarily small. The sequence 0.9, 0.99, 0.999, etc., converges to 1.

conveyor belt One of various devices that provide mechanized movement of material, as in a FACTORY. Conveyor belts are used in industry, on large farms, in warehousing and freight-handling, and in movement of raw materials. Belt conveyors of fabric, rubber, plastic, leather, or metal are driven by a power-operated roll mounted underneath or at one end. The belt forms a continuous loop and is supported either on rollers (for heavy loads) or on a metal slider pan (if loads are light enough to prevent frictional drag on the belt).

convolvulus See BINDWEED

convulsive disorder See EPILEPSY

Conway, Thomas (1735–c.1800) Irish-French officer in the American Revolution. Sent by France to aid the Revolutionary army, he fought at the Brandywine and Germantown, then was promoted to major general by Congress,

against George WASHINGTON's advice. He advocated that Washington be replaced by Horatio GATES; his "plot," called the Conway Cabal, was exposed, and he was forced to resign.

Cook, James *known as* **Captain Cook** (1728–1779) British explorer. In 1763–67 he surveyed the St. Lawrence River and the coast of Newfoundland. In 1768-71 he led the first scientific expedition to the Pacific; sailing on the HMS *Endeavour,* he found and charted all of New Zealand and explored the E coast of Australia. That voyage collected much scientific material and was notable for Cook's successful prevention of scurvy among crew members. He was then sent with two ships to make the first circumnavigation and penetration into the Antarctic; on that expedition (1772-75), one of the greatest of all sailing-ship voyages, he successfully completed the first west-east circumnavigation in high latitudes. On a third voyage (1776–79) in search of a Northwest Passage around Canada and Alaska, he was killed by Polynesian natives on Hawaii.

Cook, Mt. See MOUNT COOK NATIONAL PARK

Cook, Thomas (1808–1892) British innovator of the conducted tour. A Baptist missionary, in 1841 he arranged for a special train to be run to a temperance meeting; this was probably the first publicly advertised excursion train in England. He began to arrange excursions on a regular basis, and in 1856 he led his first grand tour of Europe. With his son, John Mason Cook (1834–1899), he founded the Thomas Cook & Son travel agency.

Cooke, (Alfred) Alistair (b.1908) British-U.S. journalist and commentator. From the late 1930s he has provided lively and insightful interpretations of American culture and history to British audiences in newspapers and radio broadcasts. His weekly radio program *Letter from America* began in 1946 and has run for more than half a century. His television programs include *Omnibus* (1956–61) and the series *America* (1972–73), and he hosted *Masterpiece Theatre* for many years.

cookie Information put on a Web user's hard disk by a visited WEB SITE that is retrievable whenever the user returns to that site. Cookies are used to store registration data, to customize information for visitors to a Web site, to track which sites a user has visited, and to keep track of the products a user wishes to order on-line. Early cookies could retrieve data from other parts of the user's hard disk; current versions prevent this and permit a site to have access only to cookies written by that site.

Cook Islands Island group (pop., 1990 est.: 17,000), S Pacific. Located 2,000 mi (3,000 km) northeast of New Zealand, the fifteen islands are scattered from north to south over 900 mi (1,450 km) of ocean. All of the seven N Cooks are true atolls; most of the S eight islands have volcanic interiors. They were probably settled by Polynesians from TONGA and SAMOA before A.D. 1100. Capt. James COOK explored them during the 1770s. A British protectorate as of 1888, they were annexed by New Zealand in 1901. Self-government in association with New Zealand was achieved in 1965.

Coolidge, (John) Calvin (1872–1933) 30th president of the U.S. (1923–29). Born in Plymouth, Vt., he practiced law in Massachusetts before becoming governor (1918–20). He gained national attention by calling out the state guard during the Boston police strike in 1919. In 1920 "Silent Cal" ran for vice president on Warren HARDING's winning ticket; when Harding died in 1923, Coolidge became president. He restored confidence in an administration discredited by scandals and won the presidential election in 1924, defeating Robert LA FOLLETTE. His presidency was marked by apparent prosperity; Congress instituted tax reductions that favored capital. Coolidge declined to run for a second term. His conservative policies of domestic

Calvin Coolidge

and international inaction have come to symbolize the era between World War I and the GREAT DEPRESSION.

Coomassie See KUMASI

coon cat See MAINE COON CAT

Cooper, Gary (*orig.* Frank James) (1901–1961) U.S. film actor. Born in Helena, Mont., from 1924 he acted in low-budget westerns before becoming a star with *The Virginian* (1929). Lanky and handsome, he played the strong, soft-spoken man of action in such films as *A Farewell to Arms* (1932), *Mr. Deeds Goes to Town* (1936), *Beau Geste* (1939), *Sergeant York* (1941, Academy Award), *For Whom the Bell Tolls* (1943), *The Fountainhead* (1949), and *Friendly Persuasion* (1956). His performance in *High Noon* (1952, Academy Award) is considered his finest.

Cooper, James Fenimore (1789–1851) U.S. writer, the nation's first major novelist. He grew up in the primitive settlement of Cooperstown, N.Y., founded by his father. *The Spy* (1821), set during the American Revolution, brought him fame. His best-known novels, the series *The Leatherstocking Tales,* feature the frontier adventures of the wilderness scout Natty Bumppo and include *The Pioneers* (1823), *The Last of the Mohicans* (1826), *The Prairie* (1827), *The Pathfinder* (1840), and *The Deerslayer* (1841). He also wrote popular sea novels, notably *The Pilot* (1823), and a history of the U.S. Navy (1839).

Cooper, Peter (1791–1883) U.S. inventor. Born in New York City, Cooper became involved with the Canton Iron Works, built to supply the BALTIMORE AND OHIO RAILROAD CO., for which he devised and built the diminutive but powerful *Tom Thumb* locomotive. His factory at Trenton, N.J., produced the first structural-iron beams for buildings. He supported the Atlantic-cable project of Cyrus Field (1819–1892), and became president of the N. American Telegraph Co. His inventions include a washing machine, and a compressed-air engine for ferry boats. A social idealist, he founded the COOPER UNION in 1859.

cooperative Organization owned by and operated for the benefit of those using its services. Cooperatives have been successful in the processing and marketing of farm products, the purchasing of equipment and raw materials, and the wholesaling, retailing, electric power, credit and banking, and housing industries. The modern consumer cooperative stems from Britain's Rochdale Society of Equitable Pioneers (1844). In the U.S., agricultural marketing cooperatives developed in rural areas in the 19th cent., and consumer and housing cooperatives have spread in metropolitan areas in recent years. See also CREDIT UNION.

Cooper Union (for the Advancement of Science and Art) Tuition-free undergraduate college located in New York City. It was endowed in 1859 by Peter COOPER, and its financial resources were later increased by the Hewitt and Carnegie families. Instruction is open to any student able to pass an entry exam. It comprises schools of art, architecture, engineering, and humanities and social sciences. Many national social-welfare agencies were founded at Cooper Union. Its library was the city's first free public reading room. Enrollment is about 1,000.

coordinate geometry See ANALYTIC GEOMETRY

coordinate system Arrangement of reference lines or curves used to identify the location of points in space. In two dimensions, the most common system is the Cartesian (after René DESCARTES) system. Points are designated by their distance along a horizontal (x) and vertical (y) axis from a reference point, the origin, designated (0,0). Cartesian coordinates also can be used for three (or more) dimensions. A polar coordinate system, which locates a point by its direction relative to a reference direction and its distance from the origin, is used in radar or sonar tracking and is the basis of navigation systems.

coordinate system, spherical See SPHERICAL COORDINATE SYSTEM

coot Any of 10 species of ducklike waterbirds (genus *Fulica*) in the RAIL family. Coots are found worldwide in larger inland waters and streams, where they swim and bob for food, mostly plants, seeds, mollusks, and worms. Their toes are fringed by a lobed membrane that helps them swim and walk over marshes. The short conical beak is topped by a flattened, fleshy shield. The European and

N. American coots are about 18 in. (45 cm) long and weigh 2 lbs (900 g).

cootie See human LOUSE

Copacabana \ˌkō-pə-kə-ˈba-nə\ SE district of RIO DE JANEIRO, Brazil. It is a popular resort area, famous for its magnificent 2.5-mi (4-km) curved beach along the entrance to Guanabara Bay. Hotels, nightclubs, and restaurants line the waterfront.

Copán \kō-ˈpän\ Ruined ancient MAYA city, Honduras. It lies near the Guatemalan border on the Copán River. An important center of Mayan art and astronomy from the 5th cent. A.D., by the 8th cent. it may have been home to as many as 20,000 people. The site consists of stone temples, two large pyramids, several stairways and plazas, and a ball court, with notable friezes on the buildings. The Maya had completely abandoned the site by about 1200.

Cope, Edward Drinker (1840–1897) U.S. paleontologist. Born in Philadelphia, he discovered about 1,000 species of extinct vertebrates in the W U.S., and developed the evolutionary histories of the horse and of mammalian teeth. His theory of kinetogenesis, stating that the natural movements of animals aided in the alteration and development of moving parts, led him to support J.-B. LAMARCK's theory of evolution. He engaged in a bitter, long-running feud with O. C. MARSH and produced 1,200 books and papers.

Copenhagen \ˌkō-pən-ˈhā-gən, ˈkō-pən-ˌhä-gən\ *Danish* **København** \ˌkœ-bən-ˈhaùn\ Capital and largest city (pop., 1999 est.: 491,000), Denmark. It was a village site by the early 10th cent. A.D.; in 1167 Bishop Absalon fortified the town. In 1445 it became the capital and the residence of the royal family. Its palaces include Amalienborg, home to the Danish monarchs, and Christiansborg, now housing Parliament. Tivoli amusement park (built 1843) is a popular attraction. A leading cultural and educational center, its oldest university was founded in 1479. Historically a trade and shipping hub, it has also become an industrial city and a shipbuilding center.

copepod \ˈkō-pə-ˌpäd\ Any of the 10,000 known species of CRUSTACEANS in the subclass Copepoda. Copepods are widely distributed and serve as food for many species of fish. Most species are free-living, found from the sea's surface to great depths. Some live in freshwater or in damp vegetation; others are parasites. Most species are 0.02–0.08 in. (0.5–2 mm) long. The largest species, a parasite of the FIN WHALE, grows to a length of about 13 in. (32 cm). Nonparasitic forms feed on microscopic plants or animals. Members of the genus *Cyclops* (order Cyclopoida) are called water fleas.

Copernican system \kə-ˈpər-ni-kən\ *or* **Copernican principle** Model of the SOLAR SYSTEM centered on the sun, with the PLANETS revolving around it, formulated by Nicolaus COPERNICUS in the mid-16th cent. Having the sun at the center explained the apparent motion of planets relative to the fixed stars and was truer than PTOLEMY's earth-centered system. The Copernican system led to belief in a much larger universe (because, if the earth revolved around the sun, the stars would have to be very distant not to appear to alter their position); more broadly, it is invoked against any theory that would give the solar system a special place in the universe. Dethronement of earth from the center of the universe challenged the entire system of ancient authority and required a complete change in the philosophical conception of the universe.

Copernicus \kə-ˈpər-ni-kəs\, **Nicolaus** *Polish* Mikołaj Kopernik (1473–1543) Polish astronomer. After mastering all the knowledge of the day in mathematics, astronomy, medicine, and theology, he published *On the Revolutions of the Celestial Spheres* (1543), a landmark of Western thought (see COPERNICAN SYSTEM). Copernicus had conceived of his revolutionary model, which explained the motion of the planets, decades earlier. However, because it raised new problems, required verification of old observations, and had to be presented in a way that would not provoke the religious authorities, he delayed publication until he was on his deathbed. His idea that earth had a daily rotation around its own axis and a yearly revolution around a stationary sun had far-reaching implications for the rise of modern science. Only with Johannes KEPLER was Copernicus's model fully transformed into a new philosophy about the fundamental structure of the universe.

copier See PHOTOCOPIER

Copland \'kō-plənd\, **Aaron** (1900–1990) U.S. composer. Born to immigrant parents in Brooklyn, N.Y., he studied with Nadia BOULANGER at Fontainebleau. Though cosmopolitan in his tastes, he adopted notably American traits in his music, especially after 1930. He cofounded the American Composers Alliance, and for over 20 years he headed the Berkshire Music Center's faculty. Famously public–spirited and generous, he came to be unofficially regarded as the

Aaron Copland

U.S.'s national composer. He is best known for his ballets, including *Billy the Kid* (1938), *Rodeo* (1942), and *Appalachian Spring* (1944, Pulitzer Prize). His film scores include *Of Mice and Men* (1939), *Our Town* (1940), and *The Heiress* (1948). His orchestral works include a piano concerto (1926), *El Salón México* (1936), *A Lincoln Portrait* (1942), and three symphonies.

Copley, John Singleton (1738–1815) U.S. painter. An accomplished draftsman before age 20, he flourished as a portrait artist in his native Boston. He was famous for his *portraits d'apparat*, portrayals of his subjects with the objects associated with them in their daily lives or professions. In 1775 he settled in London and turned to the more fashionable history painting. His first important English work, *Watson and the Shark* (1778), depicts one of the great themes of Romanticism, the struggle against nature. He is considered the finest artist of colonial America.

copper Chemical ELEMENT, one of the TRANSITION ELEMENTS, chemical symbol Cu, atomic number 29. Sometimes found in the free state in nature, it is a reddish METAL, very ductile and an unusually good conductor of electricity and heat. Most copper is used by the electrical industries; the remainder is combined with other metals to form ALLOYS (e.g., BRASS, BRONZE, nearly all coinage metals). In compounds copper usually has VALENCE 1 (cuprous) or 2 (cupric). Copper compounds have a variety of uses, including as pigments, decolorizing agents, catalysts, wood preservatives, mordants, disinfectants, feed additives, pesticides, germicides, and soil additives. Copper is a necessary trace element in the diet and essential to plant growth.

Copper Age First part of the BRONZE AGE. Its beginning is sometimes called the Chalcolithic (Copper-Stone) Age, referring to the initial use of pure COPPER along with stone. By 3500 B.C., a rapidly developing copper metallurgy, with cast tools and weapons, was a factor leading to urbanization in Mesopotamia. By 3000 B.C. the use of copper had extended into the Mediterranean area and was beginning to infiltrate the Neolithic cultures of Europe. The Copper Age began in India around 3100 B.C., in S. America around 1200 B.C., and in Africa around 600 B.C.

Copperhead Term used during the AMERICAN CIVIL WAR to describe a Northerner who opposed the war policy and favored a negotiated settlement with the South. The term referred to the copperhead snake that strikes without warning. Most Copperheads (or Peace Democrats) were from the Midwest, where agrarian interests distrusted the growing federal power. Though the movement was unable to influence the conduct of the war, Republicans used the Copperhead label to discredit the Democratic Party.

copperhead Any of several unrelated species of snake named for their reddish head color. The N. American copperhead *(Agkistrodon contortrix)*, also called highland moccasin, is a pit viper of swampy, rocky, and wooded regions of the central and E U.S. It is usually less than 3 ft (1 m) long with reddish brown, often hourglass-shaped crossbands on its back. Its bite is rarely fatal to humans. The Australian copperhead is an elapid, and the Indian copperhead is a rat snake.

Coppola \'kō-pə-lə\, **Francis Ford** (b.1939) U.S. film maker. Born in Detroit, he worked under Roger CORMAN before scoring his first success with *You're a Big Boy Now* (1967). He wrote or cowrote screenplays for several films, including *Patton* (1970, Academy Award). He won acclaim for writing and directing the Mafia epic *The Godfather* (1972, Academy Awards for best picture and screenplay). His other films include *The Conversation* (1974), *The Godfather, Part II* (1974, Academy Awards for best director, picture, and screenplay), and the extraordinary *Apocalypse Now* (1979). Perhaps the most celebrated American director of the 1970s, he has failed to sustain his reputation in his many later films.

Coptic Orthodox Church Principal Christian church in Egypt. Until the 19th cent. it was called simply the Egyptian Church. It agrees doctrinally with EASTERN ORTHODOXY except that it holds that Jesus has a purely divine nature and never became human, a belief the Council of CHALCEDON rejected (see MONOPHYSITISM) in A.D. 451. Church government is democratic, and the patriarch, who resides in Cairo, is elected. The church is in communion with the Ethiopian, Armenian, and Syrian Jacobite churches.

copulation See SEXUAL INTERCOURSE

copyright Exclusive right to reproduce, publish, or sell an original work of authorship. It protects from unauthorized copying any published or unpublished work that is fixed in a tangible medium (e.g., a book, musical score, blueprint, or building). It does not protect matters such as an idea, process, or system. Protection in the U.S. generally extends for the life of the creator plus 70 years after his or her death. Works made for hire after 1977 may be protected for a maximum of 95 years from the date of publication. In 1989 the U.S. joined the BERN CONVENTION, an agreement that governs international copyright. See also INTELLECTUAL PROPERTY, PATENT, TRADEMARK.

coral Any of about 2,300 species of marine CNIDARIANS in the class Anthozoa that are characterized by stonelike, horny, or leathery skeletons (external or internal). The skeletons are also called coral. Corals are found in warm seas worldwide. The body is of the POLYP type. Stony corals, the most familiar and widely distributed forms, are both colonial and solitary. Atolls and CORAL REEFS, composed of stony coral, grow at an average rate of 0.2–1.1 in. (0.5–2.8 cm) per year.

coral reef Ridge formed in shallow ocean areas from the external skeletons of CORALS. The skeleton consists of calcium carbonate, or limestone. A coral reef may grow into a permanent coral island, or it may take one of four principal forms. Fringing reefs consist of a flat reef area around a nonreef island. Barrier reefs may lie a mile or more offshore, separated from the landmass by a LAGOON or channel. Atolls are circular reefs without a central landmass. Patch reefs have irregular tablelike or pinnacle features.

Coral Sea Part of the SW Pacific Ocean. It is located between QUEENSLAND, Australia, on the west and VANUATU and NEW CALEDONIA on the east, and bordered on the north by PAPUA NEW GUINEA and the SOLOMON ISLANDS. Occupying 1,849,800 sq mi (4,791,000 sq km), it was named for its many coral formations, including the GREAT BARRIER REEF. During World War II it was the scene of a strategic U.S. naval and air victory over the Japanese (1942).

coral snake Any of about 65 species of strongly patterned burrowing elapids (family Elapidae). True forms are limited to the New World, chiefly the tropics, but similar forms occur in Asia and Africa. The venom of some can kill humans. More than 50 species in the largest genus, *Micrurus,* range from the S U.S. to Argentina. They are ringed with red, black, and yellow or white. The eastern coral snake, or harlequin snake *(Micrurus fulvius),* of N. Carolina and Missouri to NE Mexico is about 30 in. (76 cm) long and has wide bands of red and black separated by yellow. "Red touching yellow, dangerous fellow" distinguishes it from similar-looking harmless species.

corbel \'kȯr-bəl\ Block or brick partially embedded in a wall, with one end projecting out from the face. The weight of added masonry above keeps the block from falling out of the wall. Corbeling often occurs over several courses, with

each block or brick overhanging the one below so as to resemble a set of inverted steps; continuous corbeling is seen in the corbeled arch. Corbeling was used extensively before the development of true ARCHES and VAULTS.

Corbusier, Le See LE CORBUSIER

Corday (d'Armont) \kȯr-'dē\, **(Marie-Anne-) Charlotte** (1768–1793) French patriot.

Charlotte Corday Engraving after a portrait by J.-J. Hauer

A noblewoman from Caen, she moved to Paris to work for the GIRONDIN cause in the FRENCH REVOLUTION. Horrified by the REIGN OF TERROR, she sought an interview with J.-P. MARAT. On July 13, 1793, she stabbed him through the heart while he was in his bath. Arrested on the spot, she was convicted and guillotined.

Cordeliers \kȯr-dəl-'yā, *Engl* ‚kȯr-də-'lērz\, **Club of the** *officially* Society of the Friends of the Rights of Man and of the Citizen. Club founded in 1790 in the FRENCH REVOLUTION to prevent "infractions of the rights of man." Popularly named for its original meeting place at the nationalized monastery of the Cordeliers (Franciscans), the club became a political force under J.-P. MARAT and Georges DANTON. Led later by Jacques HÉBERT and other radicals, it fell into oblivion after Hébert's execution in 1794.

Córdoba \'kȯr-thō-bä\ City (pop., 1999: 1,275,000), the second-largest in Argentina. Founded in 1573, its location between the coast and the interior settlements favored its early development. In 1599 Jesuits settled in the city and founded the country's first university (1613). Córdoba's growth was stimulated by the completion of rail connections in 1869 and the San Roque Dam in 1866, providing irrigation and hydroelectric power.

Córdoba *or* **Cordova** \'kȯr-də-və\ *ancient* Corduba. City (pop., 1998 est.: 309,000), capital of Córdoba province, S Spain. Lying on the banks of the GUADALQUIVIR RIVER, it probably had Carthaginian origins. Occupied by the Romans in 152 B.C., it became, under Caesar AUGUSTUS, the capital of the Roman province of Baetica. It was captured by the Muslims in 711. Abd al-Rahman I, of the UMAYYAD family, made it his capital in 756 and founded the Great Mosque of Córdoba, which still stands. By the 10th cent. it was the largest city in Europe, filled with palaces and mosques. It fell to the Castilian king Ferdinand III in 1236 and became part of Christian Spain.

Cordobés \‚kȯr-thō-'bäs\, **El** *orig.* Manuel Benítez Pérez (b.1936?) Spanish bullfighter. He grew up an illiterate orphan in Córdoba (his nickname means "The Córdovan"), began his career in 1959, and became a full matador in 1963. In the month of August 1965 alone, he killed a record 64 bulls. The crudity of his technique was offset by his exceptional reflexes and courage; handsome and flamboyant, he became the most highly paid torero in history.

core Central part of the earth that extends downward from about 1,800 mi (2,900 km) beneath the surface. It consists largely of an iron-rich metallic alloy and is thought to have a two-part structure: an outer fluid region and a solid, extremely dense inner region that measures only about 1,500 mi (2,400 km) across. The alloy composition is deduced from the chemistry of iron meteorites that presumably came from the breakup of a planetary body that also had an iron core. See also CRUST, MANTLE.

Corelli, Arcangelo (1653–1713) Italian composer and violinist. He settled in Rome, where he became widely known as a violinist, director, and teacher, his many students including Francesco Geminiani (1687–1762) and Pietro Locatelli (1695–1764). As the first composer whose fame was based exclusively on his nonvocal music, his reputation rests on four sets of 12 trio sonatas each, a set of 12 solo sonatas, and a set of 12 concerti grossi. Long after his death, his works were widely studied and imitated for their classic poise and serenity. In his music the ideal of full-blown TONALITY first becomes securely established.

Corfu \kȯr-'fü\ *Greek* **Kérkyra** \'ker-kē-rä\ One of the IONIAN ISLANDS, NW Greece. With adjacent small islands it forms the Corfu department (pop., 1995 est.: 108,000) of Greece. It was settled by the Corinthians around 734 B.C.; the first naval battle of Greek history was fought between Corfu and CORINTH about 664 B.C. Around 435 B.C. it sought the aid of ATHENS against Corinth, precipitating the PELOPONNESIAN WAR. Taken by Rome in 229 B.C., it later passed to the Byzantines, then to the Normans. It was ruled by Venice 1386–1797, and by the British 1815–64. Now a popular tourist spot, it also produces olive oil, figs, oranges, lemons, and wine.

Corinth \'kȯr-ənth\ *Greek* **Kórinthos** \'kȯr-ēn-thȯs\ Ancient city of the PELOPONNESE, Greece. Occupied from before 3000 B.C., the site was developed as a commercial center in the 8th cent. B.C. but was outstripped by ATHENS in the late 6th cent. B.C. Occupied in 338 B.C. by PHILIP II, it was destroyed in 146 B.C. by Rome. In 44 B.C. Julius CAESAR reestablished Corinth as a Roman colony; St. PAUL addressed letters to its Christian community. Its ruins are near the modern city of Corinth (pop., 1991: 29,000).

Corinth, League of Alliance established at CORINTH in 337 B.C. It comprised the ancient Greek states except SPARTA, and was led by PHILIP II of Macedonia. Its major act was to condemn the Thebans to slavery and distribute their lands among other states following revolts in 336 and 335. It was disbanded after the death of ALEXANDER THE GREAT (323).

Coriolanus \‚kȯr-ē-ə-'lā-nəs\, **Gnaeus Marcius** Legendary Roman hero. He is said to have lived in the late 6th and early 5th cent. B.C., and to have owed his surname to his courage at the siege of Corioli (493 B.C.) in the war against the Volsci. For trying to have the office of TRIBUNE abolished during a famine in Rome, he was sent into exile. Taking refuge with the King of the Volsci, he led the Volscian army against Rome, but turned back in response to pleas from his family.

Coriolis force \‚kȯr-ē-'ō-ləs\ Apparent FORCE that must be included if NEWTON'S LAWS OF MOTION are to be used in a rotating system. First described by Gustave-Gaspard Coriolis (1792–1843) in 1835, the force acts to the right of the direction of body MOTION for counterclockwise rotation and to the left for clockwise rotation. On earth, an object that moves along a north–south path will be apparently deflected to the right in the Northern Hemisphere and to the left in the Southern Hemisphere. The Coriolis effect is important in METEOROLOGY, OCEANOGRAPHY, BALLISTICS, and ASTROPHYSICS.

Cork Seaport city (pop., 1995 est.: 173,000), SW Ireland. The seat of county Cork, it was founded as a monastery in the 7th cent.; often raided, it was eventually settled by the Danes. It passed to HENRY II of England in 1172. The city was taken by Oliver CROMWELL in 1649 and by the duke of MARLBOROUGH in 1690. It was heavily damaged in 1920 during the Irish uprising against England. Its industries include brewing and distilling.

cork Outer bark of the evergreen cork oak (*Quercus suber*), native to the Mediterranean. Cork is obtained from the new outer sheath of bark that forms after the original rough outer bark has been removed. This outer sheath can be stripped repeatedly without hurting the tree. Cork is unique because it is made of air-filled, watertight cells that are a remarkably effective insulating medium. Though specialized plastics and other artificial substances have replaced cork in some of its former uses, it has retained its traditional importance as a stopper for wine bottles.

Corman, Roger (William) (b.1926) U.S. film director and producer. Born in Detroit, he directed his first films, *Five Guns West* and *Apache Woman,* in 1955, and by 1960 was a prolific maker of low-budget "exploitation" films. His film versions of stories by E. A. POE, including *The House of Usher* (1960) and *The Masque of the Red Death* (1964), won him a cult following as a master of the macabre. Among his other films are *The Little Shop of Horrors* (1960), *The Wild Angels* (1966), *The Trip* (1967), *Bloody Mama* (1970), and *I Never Promised You a Rose Garden* (1977).

cormorant \\'kȯr-mə-rənt\\ Any of the 26–30 species of water birds, constituting the family Phalacrocoracidae, that dive for fish. In the Orient and elsewhere, these glossy black underwater swimmers have been tamed for fishing. Their guano is valued as a fertilizer. Cormorants live on seacoasts, lakes, and some rivers, nesting on cliffs or in bushes or trees. They have a long, hook-tipped bill, patches of bare skin on the face, and a small throat pouch (gular sac). The common, or great, cormorant *(Phalacrocorax carbo)* grows up to 40 in. (100 cm) long and breeds throughout much of the world.

corn *or* **maize** CEREAL plant *(Zea mays)* of the family Gramineae (Poaceae), originating in the New World. American Indians taught colonists to grow corn, including some varieties of yellow corn that are still popular as food, as well as the ornamental varieties called Indian corn. The tall, annual grass has a stout stem and large narrow leaves with wavy margins. Corn is used as livestock feed, as human food, and as raw material in industry. It is inferior to other cereals in nutritional value. Inedible parts of the plant are used in industry—stalks for paper and wallboard; husks for filling material; cobs for fuel, to make charcoal, and in the preparation of industrial solvents. Corn is one of the most widely distributed of the world's food plants; it is exceeded in acreage planted only by WHEAT and is the most important crop in the U.S.

Corn Belt Traditional area, midwestern U.S. Roughly covering W Ohio, Indiana, Illinois, Iowa, S Minnesota, E S. Dakota, Missouri, E Nebraska, and E Kansas, it is a region in which corn and soybeans are the dominant crops. Despite the name, the region is agriculturally diverse, raising various feed-grains and livestock.

Corneille \\kȯr-'nā\\, **Pierre** (1606–1684) French poet and playwright. A king's counselor in Rouen (1628–50), he wrote his first comedy, *Mélite* (performed 1629), before he was 20. He responded to the call for a new approach to classical verse tragedy by writing *Médée* (1635) and then *Le Cid* (1637), an instant success that established him as the creator of French classical tragedy; the play is regarded as the most significant in the history of French drama. His next tragedies, *Horace* (1641), *Cinna* (1643), and *Polyeucte* (1643), have

Pierre Corneille Painting attributed to Charles Le Brun, 1647

joined *Le Cid* as Corneille's "classical tetralogy." He returned to comedy with the classic *Le menteur* (1644). From 1660 he wrote one play a year, ending with the tragedy *Suréna* (1674).

cornelian See CARNELIAN

Cornell, Joseph (1903–1972) U.S. sculptor. Born in Nyack, N.Y., he had no formal artistic training. In the 1930s and '40s, he was associated with the Surrealists in New York (see SURREALISM). He was an originator of the assemblage; his most distinctive works were "boxes," usually with glass fronts, containing objects and pieces of collage arranged in elegant but enigmatic compositions. Recurrent motifs include astronomy, music, birds, seashells, glamour photographs, and souvenirs of travel.

Cornell University Comprehensive research university in Ithaca, N.Y., a traditional member of the IVY LEAGUE. It is both publicly and privately supported. Founded in 1868 as a land-grant university under the MORRILL ACT, it was also privately endowed by Ezra Cornell (1807–1874), a founder of Western Union. It was the first U.S. university to admit women, and the first to be divided into colleges offering different degrees. Agricultural science has long been important at Cornell; today the life sciences, business management, engineering, the social sciences, and the humanities are equally strong. Total enrollment is about 19,000.

cornet Valved BRASS INSTRUMENT. Like the TRUMPET, it has three valves, but its bore is somewhat more conical. It is a transposing instrument, usually in B-flat. Its range parallels

that of the trumpet. Its agility made it a very popular solo instrument; it often displaced the trumpet in 19th-cent. orchestras, and it preceded the trumpet in modern dance and jazz bands. The two instruments have since become very similar, and the cornet's popularity has waned as a result.

Corn Laws Regulations governing the import and export of grain (called corn by the English) in Britain. Known as early as the 12th cent., they became politically important in the 1790s–1830s, during the grain shortage caused by Britain's growing population, bad harvests, and the blockades imposed in the Napoleonic Wars. After efforts by Richard COBDEN and the reformist Anti–Corn Law League, the laws were repealed in 1846.

Cornplanter *or* **John O'Bail** (1732?–1836) American Indian leader. Born to a white trader and a Seneca mother, he fought for the British in the American Revolution, leading attacks in W New York and Pennsylvania. He later helped negotiate treaties that ceded large tracts of Indian land to the U.S. He earned the enmity of his tribe after advocating Indian nonresistance to white expansion.

corn sugar See GLUCOSE

Cornwall County (pop. 1998 est.: 490,000), SW England. Located on a peninsula jutting into the Atlantic Ocean and terminating in LAND'S END, it is the most remote of English counties. Tin, mined in Cornwall for at least 3,000 years, attracted prehistoric settlers who left stone relics. Since 1337 the manors of Cornwall have belonged to the English sovereign's eldest son, who acts as duke of Cornwall. Since 1974 the county has included the Isles of SCILLY. S Cornwall is a popular tourist area.

Cornwallis, Charles *later* **Marquess Cornwallis** (1738–1805) British general and statesman. In 1780 he became British commander in the American South and defeated Horatio GATES at Camden, S.C. He then marched into Virginia and encamped at YORKTOWN; trapped and besieged there, he was forced to surrender, a defeat that marked the end of the AMERICAN REVOLUTION. Despite his defeat, he retained esteem in England. As governor-general of India (1786–93, 1805), he introduced major reforms; the Cornwallis Code (1793) established a tradition of incorruptible British civil servants. In the third Mysore War he defeated Tippu Sultan in 1792. As viceroy of Ireland (1798–1801), he supported the parliamentary union of Britain and Ireland.

corona \\kə-'rō-nə\\ Outermost region of the SUN's (or any STAR's) atmosphere, consisting of PLASMA. It has a temperature of about 3,600,000°F (2,000,000°C) and a very low density. Extending more than 8 million mi (13 million km) from the PHOTOSPHERE, it continually varies in size and shape with the sun's MAGNETIC FIELD. Its expanding gases form the SOLAR WIND. Normally overwhelmed by the brilliance of the solar surface, the corona is visible to the unaided eye during a total ECLIPSE.

Solar corona at minimum sunspot activity

Coronado, Francisco Vázquez de (1510–1554) Spanish explorer of the N. American Southwest. Appointed governor of Nueva Galicia in W central Mexico, Coronado was sent north to locate and capture the legendary Seven Golden Cities of CÍBOLA, reported to be fabulously wealthy. He was disillusioned to discover instead the ZUNI pueblos of New Mexico and a seminomadic Indian tribe in Kansas. Though the treasure eluded him, his explorers were the first Europeans to view the Grand Canyon, and he extended Spanish territory over huge areas of N. America.

coronary bypass Surgical treatment for CORONARY HEART DISEASE to relieve ANGINA PECTORIS and prevent MYOCARDIAL INFARCTION. One or more blood vessels—usually an artery in the chest or a vein from the leg—are transplanted to create new paths for blood to flow from the AORTA to the heart muscle, bypassing the obstructed coronary arteries.

coronary heart disease *or* **ischemic heart disease** \\is-'kē-mik\\ Progressive reduction of blood supply to the heart muscle due to narrowing or blocking of a coronary artery (see ARTERIOSCLEROSIS). Short-term oxygen deprivation can cause ANGINA PECTORIS. Long-term, severe oxygen depletion causes MYOCARDIAL INFARCTION (heart attack). CORONARY BYPASS or ANGIOPLASTY is needed if medication and diet do not help.

coroner Public official whose principal duty is to inquire into any death that appears to be unnatural. In the U.S., the office is elective or appointive, depending on the jurisdiction. Coroners often possess both legal and medical qualifications, but the office is sometimes filled by laypeople, including undertakers, sheriffs, and justices of the peace. In many states the office has been replaced by that of the medical examiner, who is usually a licensed pathologist.

Corot \kȯ-ˈrō\, **(Jean-Baptiste-) Camille** (1796–1875) French landscape painter. Unsuited to the family business, at 25 he was given a small allowance to pursue art training in Paris. He traveled frequently and painted topographical landscapes, but preferred making small oil sketches and drawings from nature; from these he produced large finished paintings for exhibition. By the 1850s he had achieved critical success and a large income, and he was generous to less successful artists. His naturalistic oil sketches are now more highly regarded than his finished paintings. A master of tonal gradation and soft edges, he prepared the way for the Impressionist landscape painters and had an important influence on Claude MONET, Camille PISSARRO, and Berthe MORISOT.

corporal punishment Infliction of physical pain upon a person's body as punishment for a crime or infraction. Such penalties include beating, branding, mutilation, blinding, and the use of the stock and pillory. The term also denotes the physical disciplining of children in the schools and at home. Today corporal punishment has been almost entirely replaced in the West by imprisonment or other nonviolent penalties. Several international conventions on HUMAN RIGHTS prohibit it. Beatings and other corporeal punishments continue to be administered in the prison systems of many countries. Whipping and even amputation remain prescribed punishments in some Middle Eastern and Asian societies. Corporal punishment of schoolchildren is still sanctioned in many states.

corporation Specific legal form of organization of persons and material resources, chartered by the state, for the purpose of conducting business. As contrasted with the other two major forms of business ownership, the sole proprietorship and the PARTNERSHIP, the corporation has several characteristics that make it a more flexible instrument for large-scale economic activity. Chief among these are LIMITED LIABILITY, transferability of shares (rights in the enterprise may be transferred readily from one investor to another without constituting legal reorganization), juridical personality (the corporation itself as a fictive "person" has legal standing and may thus sue or be sued, make contracts, and hold property), and indefinite duration (the life of the corporation may extend beyond the participation of any of its founders). Its owners are the shareholders, who purchase with their investment a share in the proceeds of the enterprise and who are nominally entitled to a measure of control over its financial management. Today salaried managers exercise strong control over the corporation and its assets.

Corporation for Public Broadcasting See PBS

Corpus Christi City (pop., 2000: 277,000) and port, S Texas. Founded in 1838 as a trading post, it was the scene of MEXICAN WAR operations. The arrival of the railroad in 1881 stimulated a land boom. The exploitation of gas (1923), development of a deepwater port (1926), and discovery of the Saxtet oil field (1939) laid the city's economic foundation. Resort facilities are found on nearby PADRE ISLAND.

Correggio \kə-ˈre-jō\ *orig.* Antonio Allegri (c.1489–1534) Italian painter. Born in Correggio, he was influenced by LEONARDO DA VINCI, MICHELANGELO, and RAPHAEL. By 1518 he was in Parma, the scene of his greatest activity. His first large-scale commission there was the ceiling decoration of the Camera di San Paolo (c.1518–19). His fresco in the dome of Parma Cathedral (c.1525–30) features the dramatic illusionistic style that influenced dome painting in the

baroque period. His use of bold foreshortening, his brilliant, highly original approach to color and light, and the exquisite grace of his figures established him as one of the most inventive artists of the High Renaissance.

Correll, Charles See Freeman GOSDEN AND CHARLES CORRELL

Correns \ˈkȯr-ens\, **Carl Erich** (1864–1933) German geneticist. In the same year as Erich TSCHERMAK VON SEYSENEGG and Hugo DE VRIES (1900), he independently rediscovered Gregor MENDEL's paper outlining the principles of heredity. He conducted research with garden peas, from which he drew the same conclusions Mendel had. He helped provide the overwhelming body of evidence in support of Mendel's thesis, and developed a theory of a physical coupling of genetic factors to account for the consistent inheritance of certain traits together. See also William BATESON.

Correspondence, Committees of See COMMITTEES OF CORRESPONDENCE

corrosion Wearing away due to CHEMICAL REACTIONS, mainly oxidation (see OXIDATION-REDUCTION, OXIDE). It occurs whenever a gas or liquid chemically attacks an exposed surface, often a metal, and is accelerated by warm temperatures and by ACIDS and SALTS. Normally, corrosion products (e.g., rust, patina) stay on the surface and protect it. Removing these deposits reexposes the surface, and corrosion continues. Some materials resist corrosion naturally; others can be treated to protect them.

corruption Improper and usually unlawful conduct intended to secure a benefit for oneself or another. Its forms include BRIBERY, EXTORTION, and the misuse of inside information. It exists where there is community indifference or a lack of enforcement policies. In a culture of ritualized gift giving, the line between acceptable and unacceptable gifts is often hard to draw.

corset Article of clothing worn to shape or constrict the torso. It dates to about 2000 B.C., when it was worn as an outer garment by men as well as women in Minoan Crete. In the 16th–17th cent. it was worn to flatten the chest, and was reinforced with wood; after 1660 it was shaped to accentuate the breasts. In the 19th cent. the corset, now reinforced with whalebone or metal, changed with the style of dresses. Abandoned in the 1920s, when straight clothes came into fashion, it was replaced in the 1930s by the elastic brassiere and girdle.

Corsica \ˈkȯr-si-kə\ *French* **Corse** Island (pop., 1991 est.: 251,000), in the Mediterranean Sea. It is a territorial collective of France, and the fourth-largest island in the Mediterranean. Evidence of human habitation dates from at least the 3rd millennium B.C.; the island's recorded history begins around 560 B.C., when Greeks from Asia Minor founded a town there. It later became a prosperous Roman colony. It was granted to PISA in the 11th cent., and later ruled mainly by GENOA. In 1768 it became a province of France. It was the birthplace of NAPOLEON. The island's economic life is based on tourism and agriculture.

Cort, Henry (1740–1800) British inventor and industrialist. In 1783 he obtained a patent for producing iron bars quickly and economically in a rolling mill with grooved rolls. In 1784 he patented his puddling process for converting pig iron into WROUGHT IRON in a reverberatory furnace. His two inventions led to the quadrupling of Britain's iron production in the next 20 years.

Cortázar \kȯr-ˈtä-sär\, **Julio** (1914–1984) Argentine-French writer. His first story collection, *Bestiario* (1951; "Bestiary"), was published the year he moved to Paris. His masterpiece, *Hopscotch* (1963), is an open-ended novel, or ANTINOVEL, in which the reader is invited to rearrange the chapters. One of his stories became the basis for the film *Blowup* (1966).

Cortes \ˈkȯr-tās\ Representative assembly of the medieval Iberian kingdoms. The Cortes developed when elected representatives of the free municipalities acquired the right to take part in the affairs of the Curia Regis ("king's court"). They were admitted because the crown was short of funds and lacked the right to raise taxes without the consent of the municipalities. Cortes were established in the 13th cent. in León, Castile, Catalonia, Aragon, Valencia, and Navarre.

Today the term refers to the national legislatures of Spain and Portugal.

Cortés \kȯr-ˈtez\, **Hernán** *later* Marqués del Valle de Oaxaca (1485–1547) Spanish CON-QUISTADOR who won Mexico for Spain. He joined Diego Velázquez de Cuéllar (1465–1524) in the conquest of Cuba (1511). In 1519, with 508 men and 16 horses, he burned his ships on Mexico's SE coast, to commit himself to its conquest. After gaining thousands of Indian allies who resented AZTEC domination, he forged ahead to TENOCHTITLÁN, the Aztec capital. The emperor MONTEZUMA II, believing Cortés to be the god QUETZALCÓATL, welcomed him, but was taken prisoner. Hearing that a Spanish force from Cuba was coming to relieve him of command, Cortés left Te-

Hernán Cortés Painting by an unknown artist, 1530

nochtitlán under the command of a captain and set out to defeat the Spanish force. He returned to find the city had revolted and was forced to retreat, but returned in 1521 to conquer the city and with it the empire. The absolute ruler of a huge territory, he retired after a disastrous expedition in 1524 to the Honduran jungles.

Cortés, Sea of See Gulf of CALIFORNIA

cortisone STEROID HORMONE produced by the cortex of the ADRENAL GLAND. It participates in the regulation of the conversion of PROTEINS to CARBOHYDRATES, and to some extent it regulates salt METABOLISM. Introduced medically in 1948 for its anti-inflammatory effect to treat ARTHRITIS, it has been largely replaced by related compounds that do not produce its undesired side effects. See also CUSHING'S SYNDROME.

Cortona, Luca da See Luca SIGNORELLI

Cortona, Pietro da See PIETRO DA CORTONA

corundum \kə-ˈrən-dəm\ Aluminum oxide mineral that is, after diamond, the hardest known natural substance. Gem varieties are SAPPHIRE and RUBY; mixtures with iron oxides and other minerals are called emery. Corundum is widespread, although large deposits are rare; rich deposits occur in India, Russia, Zimbabwe, and S. Africa. In addition to being a precious gem, corundum is used as an abrasive for grinding optical glass and for polishing metals. For most industrial applications, however, it has been replaced by synthetic materials such as alumina.

Corybant \ˈkȯr-ə-ˌbant\ In Oriental and Greco-Roman mythology, any of the wild, half-demonic beings who were attendants of the GREAT MOTHER OF THE GODS. They were distinctly Asian in origin, and their rites were orgiastic. Their wild dance was credited with healing mental disorder.

Cosby, Bill (*orig.* William Henry) (b.1937) U.S. television actor and producer. Born in Philadelphia, he initially worked as a comedian in New York nightclubs. In the series *I Spy* (1965–68) he became the first black actor to star in a dramatic role on network television. He later frequently appeared on the children's program *Sesame Street*. His succession of "Cosby" shows (1969–73, 1984–92, 1994, 1996–), whose broad cross-cultural appeal rests on his relaxed, winning charm and an avoidance of racial stereotypes, has made him one of the most durable and popular stars in the history of television.

Cosgrave, William Thomas (1880–1965) Irish statesman, first president (1922–32) of the Irish Free State. A veteran of the 1916 Easter Rising, as president he restored settled government in Ireland. He continued in office despite various crises until Eamon DE VALERA's victory in 1932. In 1944 he resigned as head of the United Ireland Party (FINE GAEL). His son Liam (b.1920) served as prime minister 1973–77.

Cosimo, Piero di See PIERO DI COSIMO

Cosimo the Elder See Cosimo de' MEDICI

cosine See TRIGONOMETRIC FUNCTION

cosines, law of Generalization of the PYTHAGOREAN THEOREM relating the lengths of the sides of any triangle. If a, b, and c are the lengths of the sides and C is the angle opposite side c, then $c^2 = a^2 + b^2 - 2ab\cos C$.

cosmetics Preparations applied to the body for beautifying, preserving, or altering the appearance or for cleansing, coloring, conditioning, or protecting the skin, hair, nails, lips, eyes, or teeth. The earliest known cosmetics were in use in Egypt in the 4th millennium B.C. Cosmetics were in wide use in the Roman Empire, but disappeared from much of Europe with the fall of the Roman Empire (5th cent. A.D.) and did not reappear until crusaders returned from the Middle East with cosmetics and PERFUMES. By the 18th cent. they had come into use by nearly all social classes. Modern cosmetics include skin-care preparations; foundation, face powder and rouge (blusher); eye makeup; lipstick; shampoo; hair curling and straightening preparations; hair colors, dyes, and bleaches; and nail polish.

cosmic background radiation ELECTROMAGNETIC RADIATION, mostly in the MICROWAVE range, believed to be the highly red-shifted residual effect (see RED SHIFT) of the BIG BANG. Discovered by accident in 1964 by Robert W. WILSON and Arno PENZIAS, its presence supports the big-bang theory.

cosmic ray High-speed particle (NUCLEUS or ELECTRON) that travels through the GALAXY. Collisions of primary cosmic rays with nuclei in earth's ATMOSPHERE create secondaries. Because lower-energy primaries are strongly influenced by the interplanetary magnetic field and earth's magnetic field, most of those detected near earth have very high energy. Although some originate from the sun, satellite observations indicate that most cosmic rays come from the galaxy's disk. The highest-energy ones are probably extragalactic. Details remain unclear, but apparently expanding shock waves from supernovas can accelerate particles. Short-lived SUBATOMIC PARTICLES were discovered through cosmic-ray collisions, leading to the rise of PARTICLE PHYSICS. PARTICLE ACCELERATORS have been used since the 1950s, but even the most powerful cannot impart energy anywhere near that of the highest-energy cosmic rays.

cosmogony See CREATION MYTH

cosmological constant Term reluctantly added by Albert EINSTEIN to his equations of general RELATIVITY in order to obtain a solution to the equations that described a static universe, as he believed it to be at the time. The constant has the effect of a repulsive force that acts against the gravitational attraction of matter in the universe. When Einstein heard of the evidence that the universe is expanding, he called the introduction of the cosmological constant the "biggest blunder" of his life.

cosmology Field of study that brings together the natural sciences, especially ASTRONOMY and PHYSICS, to try to understand the UNIVERSE as a unified whole. The first great age of scientific cosmology began in Greece in the 6th cent. B.C., when the Pythagoreans introduced the concept of a spherical earth and hypothesized that the heavenly bodies moved according to natural laws. Their thought culminated in the Ptolemaic model (see PTOLEMY) (2nd cent. A.D.). The introduction of the COPERNICAN SYSTEM in the 16th cent. ushered in the second great age. The third began in the early 20th cent., with the elucidation of special and then general RELATIVITY by Albert EINSTEIN. The basic assumptions of modern cosmology are that the universe is, on the average, homogeneous in space and that the laws of physics are the same everywhere.

cosmonaut See ASTRONAUT

cosmos \ˈkäz-məs\ Any of the garden plants that make up the genus *Cosmos* (COMPOSITE FAMILY), containing about 20 species native to the tropical New World. Flowers are borne along long flower stalks or together in an open cluster. The disk flowers are red or yellow; the ray flowers are usually white, pink, or red. Most annual ornamental varieties have been developed from the common garden cosmos (*C. bipinnatus*).

Cossacks Peoples dwelling in the N hinterlands of the Black and Caspian seas. The term (from the Turkic *kazak*, "free person") originally referred to semi-independent Tatar

groups; later it was also applied to peasants who had fled from serfdom. The Cossacks had a tradition of independence and received privileges from the Russian government in return for military services, often on the Russian frontier. Attempts in the 17th–18th cent. to reduce their privileges caused revolts, led by Stenka RAZIN and Yemelyan PUGACHOV, and the Cossacks gradually lost their autonomous status.

cost Monetary value of goods and services that producers and consumers purchase. In a basic economic sense, cost is the measure of the alternative opportunities forgone in the choice of one good or activity over others. For consumers, cost describes the PRICE paid for goods and services. For producers, cost relates to the value of production inputs and the level of output. Total cost refers to all the expenses incurred in reaching a particular level of output. A portion of the total cost known as fixed cost (e.g., the costs of building rental or of heavy machinery) does not vary with the quantity produced. Variable costs, like the costs of labor or raw materials, change with the level of output. Economic decisions are based on marginal cost, the additional cost of an incremental unit of production or consumption.

Costa-Gavras \ˌkōs-tə-ˈgav-rəs\, **Constantine** orig. Konstantinos Gavras (b.1933) Greek-French film director. He left Greece to study in Paris, where he became an assistant to several filmmakers. He directed his first film, *The Sleeping Car Murders,* in 1966. His drama of political assassination, *Z* (1968, Academy Award), brought him international fame. He later directed such political thrillers as *The Confession* (1970), *State of Siege* (1972), and *Missing* (1982, Academy Award).

Costa Rica officially **República de Costa Rica** Country, Central America. Area: 19,730 sq mi (51,100 sq km). Population (2000): 3,644,000. Capital: SAN JOSÉ. Most of the people are of Spanish ancestry, with Indian and black admix-

COSTA RICA

Scale 1: 5,424,000

©1999, Encyclopædia Britannica, Inc.

tures. Language: Spanish (official). Religion: Roman Catholicism (official). Currency: colón. Costa Rica's narrow Pacific coast rises abruptly into central highlands and a volcanic mountain chain that forms the backbone of the country, descending gradually to the Caribbean coastal plain. With a climate ranging from temperate to tropical, it contains a wide variety of plants and animals that include both N. and S. American species. It has a developing market economy largely based on coffee and banana exports. Other cash crops include beef, sugar, and cocoa. It is a multiparty republic with one legislative house; the head of state and government is the president. Christopher COLUMBUS landed

in Costa Rica in 1502 in an area inhabited by a number of small, independent Indian tribes. These peoples were not easily dominated, and it took almost 60 years for the Spaniards to establish a permanent settlement. Ignored by the Spanish crown because of its lack of mineral wealth, the colony grew slowly. Coffee exports and the construction of a rail line improved its economy in the 19th cent. It joined the short-lived Mexican empire in 1821, was a member of the United Provinces of Central America 1823–38, and adopted a constitution in 1871. In 1890 Costa Ricans held what is considered to be the first free and honest election in Central America, beginning a tradition of democracy for which Costa Rica is renowned. A new constitution in 1948 abolished the national army. In 1987 then-president Oscar ARIAS SÁNCHEZ was awarded the Nobel Peace Prize. Costa Rica suffered severe damage from a hurricane in 1996.

cost-benefit analysis In planning and budgeting, the attempt to measure the overall benefits of a proposed project in monetary terms and compare them with its costs. Proposed in 1844 by Jules Dupuit (1804–1866), the procedure was not seriously applied until the 1936 U.S. Flood Control Act, which required that the benefits of flood-control projects exceed their costs. A wide range of variables must be considered because the value of the benefits may be indirect or projected far into the future.

Costello, Lou See ABBOTT AND COSTELLO

Costner, Kevin (b.1955) U.S. film actor and director. Born in Los Angeles, he first gained a starring role in *The Untouchables* (1987) as Eliot Ness. After further success in *Bull Durham* (1988) and *Field of Dreams* (1989), he formed his own production company. In 1990 he produced, directed, and acted in *Dances with Wolves* (Academy Awards for best director and picture). Among his later films were *JFK* (1991), *Waterworld* (1995), and *The Postman* (1997).

cost of living Monetary cost of maintaining a particular standard of living, usually measured by calculating the average cost of a number of goods and services. Measurement of the cost of a minimum standard of living is essential in determining relief payments, social-insurance benefits, and MINIMUM WAGES, and in comparing the costs of maintaining similar living standards in different areas. The cost of living is customarily measured by a PRICE INDEX such as the CONSUMER PRICE INDEX. See also SOCIAL INSURANCE.

Côte d'Azur \ˌkōt-dá-ˈzŪr\ Region bordering the Mediterranean Sea, SE France. Encompassing the French RIVIERA between Menton and CANNES, it is noted for its scenery, and is a major tourist center. See also NICE, MONACO.

Côte d'Ivoire See IVORY COAST

Cotonou \ˌkō-tō-ˈnü\ Port city (pop., 1994 est.: 750,000), de facto capital of Benin. Situated along the Gulf of GUINEA, it is the starting point of the Benin–Niger Railway and the site of deepwater port facilities. The economic hub of Benin and its largest urban center, it is home to the National Univ. of Benin (1970).

Cotopaxi \ˌkō-tō-ˈpäk-sē\ Volcanic peak in the ANDES, central Ecuador. Rising to 19,347 ft (5,897 m), it is the world's highest continuously active volcano. Its almost perfectly symmetrical cone is often hidden by clouds that are lit at night by the crater's fires. With a long record of violent eruption, it has seldom remained quiet for more than 15 years.

cotton Seed-hair fiber of various plants of the genus *Gossypium,* in the MALLOW FAMILY, native to most subtropical countries. The shrubby plants produce creamy-white flowers, followed by small green seedpods (cotton bolls), which contain the seeds. Fibers growing from the outer skin of the seeds become tightly packed within the boll, which bursts open at maturity to reveal soft masses of the white fibers. Cotton is harvested when the bolls open. One of the world's leading agricultural crops, cotton is plentiful and economically produced, making cotton products relatively inexpensive. Cotton fabrics can be extremely durable and are comfortable to wear. Nonwoven cotton, made by fusing or bonding the fibers, is useful for making disposable products including paper towels and medical products.

Cotton, John (1585–1652) British-American Puritan leader. He served as a vicar in Lincolnshire 1612–33. After being charged with Nonconformism, he sailed for New England.

As "teacher" of the First Church of Boston (1633–52), he became an influential leader of the Massachusetts Bay Colony. He wrote a widely used children's catechism and defended Puritan orthodoxy in such books as *The Way of the Churches of Christ in New England* (1645). He opposed freedom of conscience, favoring a national theocratic society. His daughter married Increase MATHER.

Cotton, King See KING COTTON

Cotton, Robert Bruce (*later* **Sir Robert**) (1571–1631) English antiquarian. From about 1585 Cotton collected ancient records, manuscripts, books, and coins. His acquisition of public documents aroused misgivings, and after he wrote several works criticizing policies of CHARLES I, his library was sealed in 1629. His heirs regained possession of the library, and his great-grandson presented it to the nation in 1700. The Cottonian Library's historical documents formed the basis of the manuscript collection of the BRITISH MUSEUM.

Cotton Belt Agricultural region of the SE U.S. where cotton is the main cash crop. Once confined to the pre–Civil War South, today it extends primarily through N. and S. Carolina, Georgia, Alabama, Mississippi, W Tennessee, E Arkansas, Louisiana, E Texas, and S Oklahoma.

cotton gin Machine for cleaning COTTON of its seeds. The design that became standard was invented in the U.S. by Eli WHITNEY in 1793. The mechanization of spinning in England had created a greatly expanded market for U.S. cotton, but production was bottlenecked by the manual removal of the seeds from the raw fiber. The cotton gin pulled the cotton

Cotton gin Replica of Eli Whitney's 1793 machine

through a set of wire teeth mounted on a revolving cylinder, the fiber passing through narrow slots in an iron breastwork too small to permit passage of the seed. Its simplicity caused it to be widely copied. It is credited with making cot-

ton virtually the only crop of the U.S. South and so institutionalizing slavery.

cottonmouth moccasin See WATER MOCCASIN

cottonwood Any of several fast-growing trees of N. America, of the genus *Populus*, in the WILLOW family, with triangular, toothed leaves and cottony seeds. The dangling leaves clatter in the wind. Species include eastern cottonwood (*P. deltoides*), Carolina poplar (*P. angulata*), Eurasian black poplar (*P. nigra*), and Alamo or Fremont cottonwood (*P. fremontii*), the tallest of the group. See also POPLAR.

cotyledon \kä-tə-ˈlē-dᵊn\ Seed leaf within the embryo of a seed that provides energy and nutrients for the developing seedling. After the first true leaves have formed, they wither and fall off. FLOWERING PLANTS with a single cotyledon are grouped as monocots, or monocotyledonous plants; embryos with two cotyledons are dicots, or dicotyledonous plants. Unlike flowering plants, GYMNOSPERMS usually have several cotyledons.

Coubertin \kü-ber-ˈtaⁿ\, **Pierre, baron de** (1863–1937) French educator, primarily responsible for the revival of the OLYMPIC GAMES in 1894. He was one of the first advocates of physical education in France. His drive to restart the Olympics after 1,500 years was partly inspired by the excavation of the ancient Olympic site. He served as the second president (1896–1925) of the International Olympic Committee.

Coué \ˈkwä\, **Émile** (1857–1926) French psychologist. A pharmacist, he studied hypnosis, then opened a free clinic at Nancy in 1910 and developed his own method of psychotherapy based on autosuggestion, "Couéism", which most famously required constant repetition of the formula "Every day, and in every way, I am becoming better and better."

cougar *or* **puma** \ˈpü-mə, ˈpyü-mə\ *or* **mountain lion** *or* **panther** Species (*Felis concolor*) of large graceful CAT that occurs from British Columbia to Patagonia in mountains, deserts, and jungles. In many regions, the species is now restricted to wilderness areas. Cougars range from pale buff to reddish brown. The adult weighs from 75 to more than

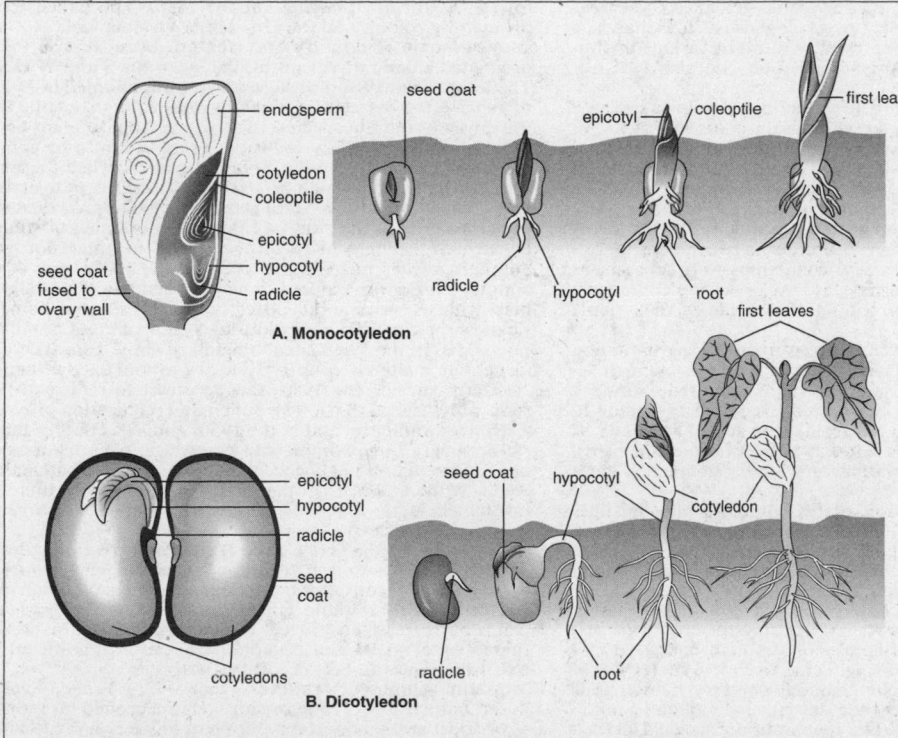

Cotyledon A. Monocotyledon (internal structures of a corn seed with stages of germination). Nutrients are stored in the cotyledon and endosperm tissue. The radicle and hypocotyl (region between the cotyledon and radicle) give rise to the roots. The epicotyl (region above the cotyledon) gives rise to the stem and leaves and is covered by a protective sheath (coleoptile). B. Dicotyledon (internal structures of a bean seed with stages of germination). All nutrients are stored in the enlarged cotyledons. The radicle gives rise to the roots, the hypocotyl to the lower stem, the epicotyl to the leaves and upper stem.

220 lbs (35–100 kg). A male may be about 9 ft (3 m) long, one-third of which is tail, and stand 24–30 in. (60–75 cm) tall at the shoulder. Since it occasionally kills livestock, it has been intensively hunted by farmers and basically exterminated from the E U.S. It is valuable for preventing overpopulation of prey animals (mostly deer, in N. America). It rarely attacks humans.

Coughlin \\'käg-lən\\, **Charles E(dward)** *known as* **Father Coughlin** (1891–1975) Canadian-U.S. clergyman. Born in Hamilton, Ontario, he was ordained a Catholic priest and became pastor of a Michigan church. In 1930 he began radio broadcasts of his sermons, into which he gradually injected reactionary political views and anti-Semitic rhetoric, attracting the first mass audience in broadcast history. He attacked Herbert HOOVER and Franklin ROOSEVELT; Wall Street and Communism were other targets of his magazine, *Social Justice,* which was banned from the mails. In 1942 the Church ordered Coughlin to stop broadcasting.

Coulomb \\kü-'lōⁿ, *Engl* 'kü-,läm\\, **Charles-Augustin de** (1736–1806) French physicist. To investigate Joseph PRIESTLEY's law of electrical repulsions, he invented a sensitive instrument to measure the electrical forces involved. He is best known for formulating COULOMB'S LAW. He also did research on friction of machinery, on windmills, and on the elasticity of metal and silk fibers. The coulomb, a unit of electric charge, was named in his honor.

Coulomb's law Law formulated by C.-A. de COULOMB that describes the electric force between charged objects. It states that (1) like charges repel each other and unlike charges attract each other, (2) the attraction or repulsion acts along the line between the two charges, (3) the size of the force varies inversely as the square of the distance between the two charges, and (4) the size of the force is proportional to the value of each charge.

counseling Professional guidance through use of such psychological methods as collecting case-history data, personal interviews, and testing of interests and aptitudes. The counselor suggests opportunities to fulfill personal needs and aspirations, usually attempting to clarify the client's own thinking rather than to solve his or her problems. Professional counselors (such as educational guidance and career counselors) and counseling psychologists (such as marriage and bereavement counselors) are found in various institutional settings and in private practice. See also PSYCHOTHERAPY.

count *or* **earl** European title of nobility, ranking below a MARQUESS or (in countries without marquesses) a DUKE. In England, the title of earl is the equivalent of count and ranks above a VISCOUNT. The wife of a count or earl is a countess. The Roman *comes* (count) was originally a household companion of the emperor; under the Franks he was a local commander and judge. The counts were later incorporated into the feudal structure, some becoming subordinate to dukes, though a few countships were as great as duchies. As royal authority was reasserted, the counts lost their political authority, though they retained their noble privileges.

counterfeiting Crime of making an unauthorized imitation of a genuine article, typically money, with the intent to deceive or defraud. Because of the value conferred on money and the high level of technical skill required to imitate it, counterfeiting is singled out from other acts of FORGERY. It is generally punished as a FELONY. Software, credit cards, designer clothing, and watches are among nonmoney items commonly counterfeited.

counterpoint Combination of two or more melodic lines (also called polyphony); also, the technique of controlling the relationship between simultaneous lines. The first recorded use of two melodic lines simultaneously was in 9th-cent. treatises showing examples of ORGANUM. The desire to ensure pleasant consonances and avoid unpleasant dissonances when improvising (see CONSONANCE AND DISSONANCE) called for principles of simultaneous vocal motion (voice leading), and rules came to govern such types of relative motion as parallel motion, contrary motion (one voice moving up, the other down), and oblique motion (only one voice moving). The systematic pedagogical method known as species counterpoint was developed in the 18th

cent. by Johann Joseph Fux (1660–1741). The "vertical" aspect of counterpoint came to be studied as HARMONY, especially from the 18th cent. Though harmony and counterpoint are intimately intertwined, most medieval and Renaissance music is felt to be essentially polyphonic or contrapuntal—that is, to consist of a combination of relatively independent and integral melodic lines. In the baroque era, with the invention of FIGURED BASS and the CONTINUO, the balance began to shift toward a harmonic orientation.

Counter-Reformation *or* **Catholic Reformation** In ROMAN CATHOLICISM, efforts in the 16th and early 17th cent. to oppose the Protestant REFORMATION and reform the Catholic Church. In response to criticism of the worldliness and corruption of the clergy, PAUL III (r.1534–49) convened the important Council of TRENT (1545–63), which reacted to Protestant teachings on faith, grace, and the sacraments and attempted to reform training for the priesthood. The Roman INQUISITION was established in 1542 to control HERESY within Catholic territories, and the JESUITS undertook educational work aimed at conversion or reconversion. Emperors CHARLES V and PHILIP II took military action against Protestant growth. Other important reformers included Sts. Charles BORROMEO, Philip NERI, JOHN OF THE CROSS, TERESA OF ÁVILA, FRANCIS DE SALES, and VINCENT DE PAUL.

countertenor Adult male alto voice, either natural or falsetto. Like the CASTRATO tradition, the countertenor developed as a result of the prohibition on women taking part in church choirs. Since the falsetto voice lacks power, it was little used in opera. The countertenor tradition was preserved in the English cathedral choir. Today it is again being widely cultivated internationally, primarily for Renaissance and Baroque music.

country dance *or* **contredanse** \\'kän-trə-,dans\\ Type of social dance for couples that became popular in the 17th cent. Derived from English folk dance, it is performed in one of three forms: circular or round; "longways," with rows of couples facing each other; and geometric, in squares or triangles. The main source of its steps and songs is John Playford's *The English Dancing Master* (1650). The dance was brought by colonists to the U.S. as the Virginia reel.

country music *or* **country and western** Musical style that originated among whites in rural areas of the S and W U.S. The term "country and western music" was adopted in 1949 to replace the derogatory "hillbilly music." Its roots lie in the music of the European settlers of the Appalachians and other areas. In the early 1920s the genre began to be commercially recorded; Fiddlin' John Carson recorded its first hit. Radio programs such as Nashville's GRAND OLE OPRY and Chicago's "National Barn Dance" fueled its growth, and such musicians as the CARTER FAMILY and Jimmie RODGERS began performing and recording. With the migration of Southern whites to industrial cities in the 1930s and '40s, country music was exposed to new influences; its nostalgic bias, with its lyrics about poverty, heartbreak, and homesickness, held special appeal during a time of great population shifts. In the 1930s such "singing cowboy" film stars as Gene Autry altered country lyrics to produce a synthetic "western" music. The 1940s saw an effort to return to its root values (see BLUEGRASS), but commercialization proved a stronger influence, and in the 1950s and '60s country music became a huge commercial enterprise. Country music has become increasingly acceptable to national urban audiences. While embracing other styles, it has kept an unmistakable character as one of the few truly indigenous American musical styles.

coup d'état \\,kü-dā-'tä\\ *or* **coup** (French: "stroke of state") Sudden overthrow, often violent, of an existing government by a group of conspirators. Coups are most common in countries with unstable governments. Their success depends on surprise and speed. Coups rarely alter a nation's fundamental social and economic policies or significantly redistribute power. See also REVOLUTION.

Couperin \\küp-'raⁿ\\, **François** (1668–1733) French composer, harpsichordist, and organist. He succeeded his father as organist at the important church of St. Gervais at 17 and kept the post for some 50 years. He was later also appointed organist and harpsichordist at the court of LOUIS XIV. He is best known for four books of harpsichord pieces containing some 220 elegant, vivacious, and richly ornamented works (*Pièces de clavecin*, 1713–30). His other works include a collection of organ works, much sacred vocal music, and several sets of chamber music. His *Art of Playing the Harpsichord* (1716) is the most valuable instrumental treatise of its time. He was the foremost French composer of his generation.

Courbet \kür-'bä\, **Gustave** (1819–1877) French painter. His early works were controversial but received wide acclaim. His images of everyday life, characterized by a powerful naturalism and boldly portrayed (see REALISM), cast him as a revolutionary socialist. His audacity and disrespect for authority were notorious. In 1855, refused by the jury of the Paris Universal Exposition, he opened a pavilion for his own work, calling it Le Pavillon du Réalisme. Proficient in all genres, Courbet immortalized the French countryside. In 1865 his series depicting storms at sea astounded the art world and opened the way for IMPRESSIONISM.

coureur de bois \kü-'rœr-də-'bwä\ (French: "wood-runner") French-Canadian fur trader of the late 17th and early 18th cent. Most of the coureurs de bois traded illicitly (i.e., without the license required by the Quebec government). Though they defied the colonial authorities, they ultimately benefited them by exploring the frontier, developing the fur trade, and helping ally Indians with the French and against the English (see FRENCH AND INDIAN WAR).

court In architecture, an outdoor area surrounded by buildings or walls. Courts have existed in all civilizations from the earliest recorded times. The small garden court (ATRIUM) of a Roman house was the center of domestic activity. In medieval Europe the court was a feature of all major residential buildings, as the CLOISTER of a monastery, ward of a CASTLE, and quadrangle of a college. A courtyard is often a utilitarian court (as for stables).

court Official assembly with judicial authority to hear and determine disputes in particular cases. In the U.S., each state has its own comprehensive system of courts, usually consisting of a superior (appellate) court, trial courts of general jurisdiction, and specialized courts (e.g., PROBATE courts). The U.S. also has a system of federal courts, established to adjudicate distinctively national questions and cases not appropriately tried in state courts. At the apex of the national system is the U.S. SUPREME COURT. The secondary level consists of the U.S. COURTS OF APPEALS. U.S. DISTRICT COURTS form the tertiary level. Crimes committed by military figures may be tried in a COURT-MARTIAL, and in the past ecclesiastical courts also had broad jurisdiction. See also INTERNATIONAL COURT OF JUSTICE, JUDICIARY.

Court, Margaret Smith *orig.* **Margaret Smith** (b.1942) Australian tennis player. She dominated women's tennis in the 1960s, winning 62 Grand Slam titles between 1960 and 1975, more than any other person. In 1970 she became the second woman to win the Grand Slam (the Wimbledon, U.S., Australian, and French singles titles). In 1963, with Kenneth Fletcher, she won the Grand Slam in doubles.

courtly love Late-medieval code that prescribed the highly conventionalized behavior and emotions of aristocratic ladies and their lovers. It was the theme of an extensive literature that began with late-11th-cent. TROUBADOUR poetry in France and swiftly pervaded Europe. The courtly lover faithfully served and worshiped his lady-saint. Courtly love was invariably adulterous, given that upper-class marriage at the time was usually the result of economic interest or the seal of a power alliance. Its literary sources are believed to be found in Arabic literature; the growing religious cult of MARY was another influence. Examples of works inspired by the ideal are PETRARCH's sonnets to Laura, and DANTE's *Divine Comedy*. See also CHIVALRY.

court-martial Military court for hearing charges brought against members of the armed forces or others within its jurisdiction; also, the legal proceeding of such a court. Courts-martial are generally convened as ad hoc courts to try cases referred by some high military authority. The convening officer chooses officers, and sometimes enlisted personnel, from his or her command to sit on the court, determine guilt or innocence, and hand down sentences. See also MILITARY LAW.

Courts of Appeals, U.S. See UNITED STATES COURTS OF APPEALS

Cousteau \kü-'stō\, **Jacques-Yves** (1910–1997) French ocean explorer. A navy officer, he coinvented the Aqua-Lung (see SCUBA DIVING), and founded the later-named Center of Advanced Marine Studies in Marseille. Beginning in 1950 he traveled the world in research vessels named *Calypso*. He invented a process for using television underwater, and hosted an internationally successful television series (1968–76). In his later years he issued increasingly dire warnings about human destruction of the oceans. His many popular books include *The Silent World* (1953) and *The Living Sea* (1963); his films include *The Golden Fish* (1960, Academy Award).

Cousy \'kü-zē\, **Bob** (*orig.* Robert Joseph) (b.1928) U.S. basketball player and coach. Born in New York City, he joined the Boston Celtics in 1950. One of the game's great ball-handling guards and playmakers, he led the NBA in assists from 1953 to 1960. He coached at Boston College 1963–69, but returned to the professional game as coach of the Cincinnati Royals 1969–73.

covalent bond \'kō-'vā-lənt\ Force holding ATOMS in a MOLECULE together as a specific, separate entity (as opposed to, e.g., colloidal aggregates; see BONDING). In covalent bonds, one or more pairs of valence ELECTRONS are shared between two atoms to give each the stability found in a NOBLE GAS. In single bonds (e.g., H–H in H_2), one electron pair is shared; in double bonds (e.g., O=O in O_2 or $H_2C=CH_2$ in ethylene), two; in triple bonds (e.g., HC≡CH in acetylene), three. In coordinate covalent bonds, additional electron pairs are shared with another atom, usually forming a group, like SULFATE or PHOSPHATE. The number of bonds and the atoms participating in each (including any additional paired electrons) give molecules their CONFIGURATION; the slight negative and positive charges at the opposite ends of a covalent bond are the reason most molecules have some polarity (see ELECTROPHILE, NUCLEOPHILE). Carbon in organic compounds has four single bonds, each pointing to one vertex of a tetrahedron; making certain molecules exist in mirror images (see OPTICAL ACTIVITY). The configurations of ENZYMES and their substrates, determined by their covalent bonds (particularly the peptide bonds) and hydrogen bonds, are crucial to the reactions they participate in, which are fundamental to all life. See also IONIC BOND.

covenant \'kə-və-,nant\ In the OLD TESTAMENT, an agreement or treaty among peoples or nations, but most memorably God's promises to humankind (e.g., the promise to ABRAHAM that his descendants would inherit the land of Israel). God's revelation of the law to MOSES created a pact between God and Israel (the Sinai covenant). In Christianity, JESUS' death established a new covenant between God and humanity. Islam holds that the Last Covenant was between God and MUHAMMAD.

Covenanters Scottish Presbyterians of the 17th cent. who made convenants in which they pledged to maintain specific forms of worship and church government. After the signing of the National Covenant of 1638, the Scottish Assembly abolished governance by bishops (EPISCOPACY). In the Bishops' Wars of 1639–40 the Scots fought against England to maintain their religious liberty. The expenses of these wars were a factor in the ENGLISH CIVIL WAR. Cromwell's settlement failed to satisfy the Covenanters, but their situation worsened considerably once CHARLES II came to the throne in 1660. Episcopacy was brought back, and the Covenanters endured severe persecutions. Not until the GLORIOUS REVOLUTION of 1688 was PRESBYTERIANISM reestablished in Scotland.

Covent Garden \'kə-vənt\ Square in London, now the site of the Royal Opera House, home of the British national opera and ballet companies. The land around the site was once a convent garden. The original Covent Garden playhouse, called the Theatre Royal, was built in 1732 and served for performances of plays, pantomimes, and opera. Twice destroyed by fire and rebuilt, the theater became the Royal Opera Co. in 1888. The square was also the site of a fruit, flower, and vegetable market from 1670 to 1974.

Coventry City (pop., 1999 est.: 294,000), central England. It was the home of Lady GODIVA, who, with her husband, founded a Benedictine abbey there in 1043. It was probably the site of the Coventry MYSTERY PLAYS in the 15th–16th cent. During World War II, heavy bombing by the Germans left the town severely damaged. The spire of the 15th-cent. St. Michael's Cathedral and its ruined nave stand beside the new cathedral built in 1962.

cover crop Fast-growing crop, such as RYE, BUCKWHEAT, cowpea, or VETCH, planted to prevent soil EROSION, increase nutrients in the soil, and provide organic matter. Cover crops are grown either in the season during which cash crops are not grown or between the rows of some crops (e.g., fruit trees).

Coverdale, Miles (1488?–1569) English bishop who issued the first printed English Bible. Ordained in 1514, he later adopted Lutheran beliefs. By 1528 he was preaching against graven images and the mass. He lived abroad 1528–34 to escape persecution, and while in Antwerp he translated the entire Bible into English; his Bible was published in 1535. He returned to England and edited the Great Bible (1539), but was soon forced to flee by the religious policies of HENRY VIII. After Henry's death he became bishop at Exeter in 1551. Under the Catholic MARY I, he lost his office.

Coward, Noël (Peirce) (later **Sir Noël**) (1899–1973) British playwright, actor, and songwriter. An actor from age 12, he wrote light comedies between engagements, but it was a serious drama, *The Vortex* (1924), that established his reputation. His classic comedies *Hay Fever* (1925), *Private Lives* (1930), *Design for Living* (1933), *Present Laughter* (1939), and *Blithe Spirit* (1941) presented sophisticated characters in a worldly milieu. His most popular musical play was *Bitter Sweet* (1929). He wrote the poignant film *Brief Encounter* (1945), and he acted in the film versions of many of his plays. He also wrote short stories, novels, and numerous songs, including "Mad Dogs and Englishmen."

cowbird Any of six or seven PASSERINE species in the family Icteridae that are parasitic egg layers. Cowbirds lay their eggs in the nests of other birds, usually one to each host nest. Young cowbirds displace competing nestlings or take over their food. Cowbirds forage on the ground, often associating with cattle in order to catch insects stirred up by the cows' hooves. The male of most species is a uniform glossy black, the female grayish brown.

cowboy Horseman skilled at handling cattle in the U.S. West. From about 1820, cowboys were employed in small numbers on Texas ranches, where they had learned the skills of the Mexican *vaquero*. After the Civil War, their numbers rapidly multiplied as cattle raising became a lucrative industry. Cowboys rounded up and branded the cattle, kept watch over the herd, and drove those ready for market to railroad towns. The open range was gradually transformed into farms, and by 1890 cowboys had been forced to settle on ranches. The romance of their image lived on in folklore, movies, and television.

Cowell, Henry (Dixon) (1897–1965) U.S. avant-garde composer. Born in Menlo Park, Cal., he began early to experiment with such techniques as tone clusters and direct manipulation of piano strings. Five tours of Europe as composer-pianist (1923–33) brought him notoriety. Immensely prolific, he wrote nearly 1,000 pieces, includng 19 completed symphonies, hundreds of piano works, and many ballets. In 1927 he founded the journal *New Music*. His book *New Musical Resources* (1930) presented his compositional ideas.

Cowley, Abraham (1618–1667) British poet and essayist. He was a fellow at Cambridge Univ., but was ejected for his political opinions during the English Civil Wars; he joined the queen's court, performing Royalist missions until 1656. In his poetic works—which include *The Mistress* (1647, 1656), the unfinished epic *Davideis* (1656), and *Pindarique Odes* (1656)—he used grossly elaborate, fanciful language that was more decorative than expressive. In his retirement he wrote sober, reflective essays.

Cowley, Malcolm (1898–1989) U.S. literary critic and social historian. Born in Belsano, Pa., he served as literary editor of the *New Republic* (1929–44) and took part in many Depression-era literary and political battles, usually on the leftist side. He revived the reputation of William FAULKNER with *The Portable Faulkner* (1946). His books include *Exile's Return* (1934) and *The Literary Situation* (1954).

Cowper \ˈkü-pər\, **William** (1731–1800) British poet. Throughout his life he was plagued by recurring mental instability and religious doubt. *Olney Hymns* (1779; with John Newton), a book of devotional verse, includes hymns that are still favorites in England. His long discursive poem *The Task* (1785) was an immediate success. He is considered one of the best letter writers in English. His work, often about everyday rural life, brought a new directness and humanitarianism to 18th-cent. nature poetry, foreshadowing ROMANTICISM.

cowrie Any of several marine SNAILS (genus *Cypraea*) found chiefly in coastal waters of the Indian and Pacific oceans. Its humped, thick shell is beautifully colored (often speckled) and glossy. That of the 4-in. (10-cm) golden cowrie was traditionally worn by royalty on Pacific Islands. The money cowrie, a 1-in. (2.5-cm) yellow species, has served as currency in Africa and elsewhere.

Cox, James M(iddleton) (1870–1957) U.S. politician. Born in Jacksonburg, Ohio, he worked as a reporter before buying the *Dayton News* (1898) and *Springfield Daily News* (1903). A supporter of Woodrow WILSON, he served as governor of Ohio (1913–15, 1917–21), where he introduced workers' compensation and the minimum wage. He won the Democratic presidential nomination in 1920, but was crushed by W. G. HARDING in a Republican landslide.

coyote \kī-ˈō-tē, ˈkī-ˌōt\ Species (*Canis latrans*) of wild DOG found from Alaska to Costa Rica. It weighs about 30–50 lbs (9–23 kg) and is about 3–4 ft (1–1.3 m) long, including its 12–16-in. (30–40-cm) tail. Its legs are reddish, and its tail is bushy and black-tipped. The coyote feeds mainly on rodents and hares. Though persecuted by humans because of its potential (generally overstated) to prey on domestic or game animals, it has adapted well to human-dominated environments, including urban areas. A coyote-dog cross is called a coydog.

coypu See NUTRIA

CPR See CARDIOPULMONARY RESUSCITATION

CPU *in full* **central processing unit** Principal component of a DIGITAL COMPUTER, composed of a control unit, an instruction-decoding unit, and an arithmetic-logic unit. The control unit integrates computer operations. It selects instructions from the main memory and sends them to the instruction-decoding unit, which interprets them so as to activate functions of the system at appropriate moments. Input data are transferred via the main memory to the arithmetic-logic unit for processing (i.e., addition, subtraction, multiplication, division, and logic operations). Larger computers may have two or more CPUs (or "processors," because each is no longer a "central" unit).

crab Any of 4,500 species of short-tailed DECAPOD, found in all oceans, in freshwater, and on land. Its carapace (upper body shield) is usually broad, and its first pair of legs is modified into pincers. Most crabs live in the sea and breathe through gills, which in land crabs are modified to serve as lungs. They walk or crawl, generally with a sideways gait; some are good swimmers. Crabs are omnivorous scavengers, but many are predatory and some are herbivorous. The largest known CRUSTACEAN is the giant crab of Japan (13 ft, or 4 m, from claw tip to claw tip), a spider crab; other species are less than an inch long. Well-known crabs include the HERMIT CRAB, blue crab, DUNGENESS CRAB, fiddler crab, and king crab.

Crabbe \ˈkrab\, **George** (1754–1832) English poet. Reared in an impoverished seacoast village, Crabbe initially became a surgeon. In 1780 he left for London, where his poem *The Village* (1783) brought him fame. *The Newspaper* followed in 1785, but he did not publish again until 1807. In "The Parish Register," he used the register of births, deaths, and marriages to depict the life of a rural community. Considered the last of the Augustan poets, he wrote in heroic couplets. His story of the isolated and violent Peter Grimes in *The Borough* (1810) became the basis of a famous opera by Benjamin BRITTEN.

crabgrass Any of about 300 species of GRASSES in the genus *Digitaria*, especially *D. sanguinalis* and *D. ischaemum* (smooth crabgrass). *D. sanguinalis* has long hairs covering its leaves and five or six spikelets; *d. ischaemum* has no hair and only two or three spikelets. Both are natives of Europe that became widely naturalized as weeds in N. America and are very troublesome in lawns and fields. Arizona cottontop (*D. californica*) is a useful forage grass in the American Southwest.

crab louse See human LOUSE

Crab Nebula Bright NEBULA in the constellation Taurus, about 5,000 light-years from earth. Roughly five to 10 light-years across, it is the remnant of a SUPERNOVA recorded by Chinese and other astronomers in 1054 that was visible in daylight for 23 days and at night for almost 2 years. Identified as a nebula about 1731, it was named (for its shape) in the mid-19th cent. Still expanding at a rate of about 700 mi/second (1,100 km/second), the Crab is unusual in that it emits RADIATION over the entire ELECTROMAGNETIC SPECTRUM.

crack (cocaine) Potent form of COCAINE. First produced in the mid-1970s, it is obtained by treating the hydrochloride of cocaine with ammonia or sodium bicarbonate to create small chips. When smoked, it produces an intense and very short-lived euphoria that is extremely addicting (see DRUG ADDICTION). Probably the form of cocaine most detrimental to mental and physical health, it has been blamed for numerous social ills, especially in poor urban neighborhoods.

Cracow See KRAKOW

cramp Painful, involuntary, sustained contraction of muscle in limbs or some internal organs. Causes may be neurological, reflex, or psychological. Common muscle cramps include swimmer's cramp from overexertion in cold water, heat cramps from loss of salt in sweat, leg cramps, and occupational (e.g., writer's) cramp. Menstrual cramps are uterine muscle contractions before or during MENSTRUATION.

Cranach \'krä-ˌnäk\, **Lucas, the Elder** orig. Lucas Müller (1472–1553) German painter and printmaker. He took his name from Kronach, the town of his birth. In Vienna (c.1501–4) he painted some notable portraits and landscapes. As court painter in Wittenberg (1505–50), he achieved great success and wealth painting portraits, mythological subjects, and religious altarpieces. A friend of Martin LUTHER, he became known as the chief pictorial propagandist of the Protestant cause. He produced numerous engravings and over 100 woodcuts, notably for the first German edition of the New Testament (1522). His style was perpetuated by his son, Lucas the Younger (1515–1586).

cranberry Fruit of any of several small creeping or trailing plants of the genus *Vaccinium* (HEATH FAMILY), related to the BLUEBERRY. The northern cranberry (*V. oxycoccus*) is found in marshy land in N N. America and Asia and in N and central Europe. Its crimson berries have an acid taste. The American cranberry (*V. macrocarpon*), found wild in most of the NE U.S. and cultivated in several N states, is more robust than *V. oxycoccus*, with larger, variably colored berries. Cranberries are used in drinks, sauces, jellies, and baked goods.

crane Any of a diverse group of machines that lift and move heavy objects. Cranes differ from hoists, elevators, and other devices intended for vertical lifting, and from conveyors, which continuously lift or carry bulk materials such as grain or coal. They range in type and function from the largest derrick cranes to small, mobile truck cranes. Most derrick cranes can lift 5–250 tons (4.5–230 metric tons). Floating cranes, built on barges for constructing bridges or salvaging sunken objects, may be able to lift 3,000 tons (2,700 metric tons). Small truck cranes are mounted on heavy, modified trucks; they make up in mobility and ease of transport what they lack in hoisting capacity.

crane Any of 15 species (family Gruidae) of tall wading birds that resemble HERONS but are usually larger and have a partly naked head, a heavier bill, more-compact plumage, and an elevated hind toe. In flight, the long neck stretches out in front and the stiltlike legs trail behind. Cranes are

found worldwide except in S. America. Many populations are endangered. Two well-known species are the WHOOPING CRANE and the SANDHILL CRANE.

Crowned crane (*Balearica pavonina*)

Crane, (Harold) Hart (1899–1932) U.S. poet. Born in Garrettsville, Ohio, he moved to New York. *White Buildings* (1926), his first book, includes "For the Marriage of Faustus and Helen." In his most noted work, the long and difficult poem *The Bridge* (1930), he attempts to create an epic myth of the American experience, celebrating the richness of modern life with visionary intensity. Alcoholic and despondent, he committed suicide at 32 by jumping overboard from a ship in the Caribbean.

Crane, Stephen (1871–1900) U.S. novelist and short-story writer. Born in Newark, N.J., he produced a milestone of literary naturalism in his first novel, *Maggie: A Girl of the Streets* (1893), a sympathetic study of a slum girl's descent into prostitution. He achieved international fame with his masterwork, *The Red Badge of Courage* (1895), about a young Civil War soldier, and with his first book of poems, *The Black Riders* (1895). While traveling as a war correspondent, his ship sank, resulting in his great story "The Open Boat" (1898). His story collections include *The Little Regiment* (1896), *The Monster* (1899), and *Whilomville Stories* (1900). He died at 28 of tuberculosis.

Crane, Walter (1845–1915) English illustrator and designer. The son of a portrait painter, he was inspired by the ideas of the PRE-RAPHAELITES and John RUSKIN. He achieved international popularity designing Art Nouveau textiles and wallpapers, but is chiefly known for his illustrations of children's books. In 1894 he worked with William MORRIS on *The Story of the Glittering Plain*, a book printed in the style of 16th-cent. woodcuts. In 1888 he cofounded the Arts and Crafts Exhibition Society (see ARTS AND CRAFTS MOVEMENT).

crane flower See BIRD-OF-PARADISE

crane fly Harmless, slow-flying DIPTERAN (family Tipulidae) usually found around water or abundant vegetation. It ranges in size from tiny to slightly over 1 in. (2.5 cm) long. Larvae of the range crane fly (*Tipula simplex*) are called leatherjackets because of their tough brown skin. In N latitudes a wingless crane-fly species is found on snow.

craniosynostosis \ˌkrā-nē-ō-ˌsin-ˌäs-'tō-səs\ or **craniostosis** \ˌkrā-nē-ō-'stō-səs\ Cranial deformity produced when the bones of the SKULL fuse too early. Pressure from the growing brain normally causes the skull bones to grow along the seams (cranial sutures) between them. If all the sutures fuse early, the head remains abnormally small, which can cause mental retardation or blindness. If only one or some fuse early, the skull becomes deformed. Surgery in the first two years minimizes these complications.

crank In MECHANICS, an arm secured at right angles to a shaft with which it can rotate or oscillate. Next to the wheel, the crank is the most important motion-transmitting device, because, with the connecting rod, it provides means for converting linear to rotary motion, and vice versa. The crank is said to have appeared in China in the 1st cent. A.D. The first mechanical connecting rods were reportedly used on a treadle-operated machine in 1430. About this time, FLYWHEELS were added to the rotating members to carry the members over the "dead" positions when the rod and the crank arm are lined up with each other.

Cranmer, Thomas (1489–1556) First Protestant archbishop of Canterbury. He was ordained in 1523. In 1533 HENRY VIII appointed him archbishop of Canterbury, putting him in a position to help overthrow papal supremacy in En-

gland. He annulled Henry's marriage to CATHERINE OF ARAGON, supported his marriage to Anne BOLEYN, and later helped him divorce her. After Henry's death in 1547, he became an influential adviser to EDWARD VI, moving England firmly in a Protestant direction. He wrote the Forty-two Articles, from which the Thirty-nine Articles of Anglican belief were derived. When the anti-Protestant MARY I became queen, Cranmer was convicted of heresy and burned.

crannog \'kra-ˌnȯg, kra-'nōg\ In Scotland and Ireland, an artificially constructed site for a house or settlement, usually on an islet or in the shallows of a lake. Made of timber or stone, crannogs date from the Late BRONZE AGE into the Middle Ages. Usually fortified by stockades, they were among the latest prehistoric strongholds. See also LAKE DWELLINGS.

crappie Either of two deep-bodied freshwater N. American fish species (family Centrarchidae) that are prized by sport fishermen. Native to the E U.S. but introduced elsewhere, crappies may reach a length of about 12 in. (30 cm) and a weight of about 4 lbs (2 kg). The white crappie *(Pomoxis annularis)* generally inhabits warm, silty lakes and rivers. The black crappie, or calico bass *(P. nigromaculatus),* typically lives in clear lakes and streams.

Crash of 1929 See STOCK MARKET CRASH OF 1929

Crassus, Lucius Licinius (140–91 B.C.) Roman lawyer and politician. He is regarded, with Marcus Antonius (143–87), as one of the greatest Latin orators before CICERO. Made CONSUL in 95, he cosponsored a law that provided for the prosecution of anyone falsely claiming Roman citizenship, which led to the revolt of Rome's Italian allies in 90–88.

Crassus, Marcus Licinius (c.115–53 B.C.) Roman financier and politician. He sided with SULLA against MARIUS in the civil war of 83–82 B.C. and came into conflict with POMPEY. In 72–71 he put down SPARTACUS' slave rebellion. In 70 Crassus and Pompey were elected co-consuls. In 60 Crassus, Julius CAESAR, and Pompey formed the first TRIUMVIRATE. As governor of Syria (54) he invaded PARTHIA; his death at the Battle of Carrhae led to civil war between Caesar and Pompey.

crater Circular depression in the surface of a planetary body. Most craters are the result of impacts of METEORITES or of volcanic explosions. METEORITE CRATERS are more common on the moon and Mars than on the earth. Craters made by exploding volcanoes (e.g., Crater Lake, Ore.) are more common on the earth than on the moon, Mars, or Jupiter's moon Io, where they have also been identified.

Crater Lake Lake, CASCADE RANGE, SW Oregon. The intensely blue lake is in a huge volcanic caldera, whose crater is 6 mi (10 km) in diameter and 1,932 ft (589 m) deep. It is the remnant of a mountain destroyed in an eruption more than 6,000 years ago. Crater Lake National Park covers 250 sq mi (647 sq km).

Crawford, Joan *orig.* Lucille Lesueur (1906?–1977) U.S. film actress. Born in San Antonio, Tex., she was a dancer in a Broadway chorus line when she won her first Hollywood contract. After portraying flappers in such films as *Our Dancing Daughters* (1928), she played girls out for the main chance in *Grand Hotel* (1932) and *The Women* (1939). With her dark eyebrows, padded shoulders, and hysterical intensity, she reinvented herself as a suffering heroine in *Mildred Pierce* (1945, Academy Award) and in psychological melodramas including *Possessed* (1947) and *Sudden Fear* (1952). Her later films included *What Ever Happened to Baby Jane?* (1962).

Craxi \'kräk-sē\, **Bettino** (*orig.* Benedetto) (1934–2000) Italy's first Socialist prime minister (1983–87). Elected to the Chamber of Deputies in 1968, he rose to become the Socialist Party's general secretary in 1976. He united the faction-ridden party and committed it to moderate policies. As prime minister, he pursued anti-inflationary fiscal policies and steered a pro-U.S. course in foreign affairs. In 1993 multiple charges of political corruption forced Craxi, who denied the allegations, to resign as party leader. He moved to Tunisia, and was twice sentenced in absentia to prison terms.

Cray, Seymour R(oger) (1925–1996) U.S. electronics engineer. Born in Chippewa Falls, Wis., he worked in the 1950s on the UNIVAC I, a landmark first-generation digital computer that was the first commercially available computer. He led the design of the world's first transistor-based computer (the CDC 1604). In 1972 he founded Cray Research, Inc., and there built the most powerful computers in the world, using his innovative design of multiprocessors. The Cray-2 (1985) could perform 1.2 billion calculations per second, an incredible pace in its day.

crayfish *or* **crawfish** *or* **crawdad** Any of more than 500 species of DECAPOD closely related to the LOBSTER. Nearly all live in freshwater. They have a joined head and thorax (midsection) and a segmented body. The head has a sharp snout, and the eyes are on movable stalks. The exoskeleton is tough, and the front pair of legs have large pincers. Crayfish are usually about 3 in. (7.5 cm) long but range from 1 to 16 in. (2.5–40 cm) long.

Crazy Horse (1843?–1877) Oglala SIOUX Indian chief. Refusing to abide by an 1868 treaty granting the Sioux a large reservation in the Black Hills, Crazy Horse led his warriors in continued raids against enemy tribes as well as whites. In 1876 he joined with CHEYENNE forces in a surprise attack against Gen. George Crook in S Montana, forcing Crook's withdrawal. He then united with Chief SITTING BULL for the Battle of the LITTLE BIGHORN, where he helped annihilate Col. G. A. CUSTER's troops. In 1877, his tribe weakened by cold and hunger, Crazy Horse surrendered to Crook; he was later killed in a scuffle with soldiers.

cream Fat part of MILK that rises to the surface naturally if unhomogenized milk is allowed to stand. In the dairy industry, cream is separated mechanically. Cream is graded by percentage of fat content. In the U.S., half-and-half, a mixture of milk and cream, contains 10.5–18% butterfat; light cream, commonly served with coffee, contains no less than 18%; heavy cream (including whipped and sour cream) contains about 35%. See also ICE CREAM.

creation myth *or* **cosmogony** \käz-'mä-gə-nē\ Symbolic narrative of the creation and organization of the world. Not all creation myths include a creator, though a supreme creator deity is very common. Myths in which the world emerges gradually emphasize the latent power of the earth. In other creation myths, the world is the offspring of primordial parents, derives from a cosmic egg, or is brought up from primordial waters. Humans may be placed on earth by a god or rise from its depths or from a cultic rock or tree. There are often three stages of creation: that of primordial beings or gods, that of semidivine human ancestors, and that of humans. Creation myths explain or validate basic beliefs, patterns of life, and culture.

creation science *or* **creationism** Theory that matter, the various forms of life, and the world were created by God out of nothing. Creationism grew as a result of the advancement of the theory of EVOLUTION after the 1859 publication of Charles DARWIN's *On the Origin of Species*. Within two decades, most of the scientific community had accepted some form of organic evolution, but many religious leaders feared that the theory would result in a loss of faith. The most famous case in which the issue was argued was the SCOPES TRIAL (1925).

creativity Ability to produce something new or original through imaginative skill, whether a new solution to a problem, a new method or device, or a new artistic object or form. The term generally refers to a richness of ideas and originality of thinking. Highly creative people tend to have a strong interest in the challenges posed by apparent disorder, contradiction, and imbalance, and often possess an exceptionally deep, broad, and flexible awareness of themselves. Studies also show that INTELLIGENCE has little correlation with creativity.

Crécy \krā-'sē\, **Battle of** (Aug. 26, 1346) English victory in the first phase of the HUNDRED YEARS' WAR against the French. At Crécy-en-Ponthieu, EDWARD III of England defeated PHILIP VI of France, even though the English forces were greatly outnumbered. The English gained the advantage because their archers were armed with LONGBOWS and because of their strong defensive position.

credit Transaction between two parties in which one (the creditor or lender) supplies money, goods, services, or securities in return for a promised future payment by the other (the debtor or borrower). Such transactions normally include the payment of INTEREST. Credit may be extended to finance business activities, agricultural operations, consumer expenditures, or government projects. Large sums are usually extended through specialized financial institutions such as COMMERCIAL BANKS or through government lending programs.

credit bureau Organization that provides information to merchants or other businesses concerning the creditworthiness of their customers. Credit bureaus may be private enterprises or may be operated cooperatively by local merchants. Users pay a fee and receive information from various sources, including businesses that have granted the customer credit, public records, newspapers, the customer's employment record, and direct investigation.

credit card Small card that authorizes the person named on it to charge goods or services to his or her account. It differs from a debit card, which permits automatic deductions from a bank account. Credit-card use originated in the U.S. in the 1920s; early credit cards were issued by various firms for use at their outlets only. The first universal credit card, usable at a variety of establishments, was issued by Diners' Club in 1950. Bank cards such as MasterCard and Visa allow customers to pay only a portion of their bill; INTEREST accrues on the unpaid balance. Credit-card companies get revenue from annual fees and interest paid by cardholders and from fees paid by participating merchants. The huge increase in U.S. credit-card use in recent decades has led to unprecedented levels of consumer debt.

credit union Credit COOPERATIVE formed by a group of people with some common bond who, in effect, save their money together and make low-cost loans to each other. The loans are usually short-term consumer loans, mainly for automobiles, household needs, medical debts, and emergencies. Credit unions are particularly important in less developed countries, where they may be their members' only source of credit. The first cooperative societies providing CREDIT were founded in Germany and Italy in the mid-19th cent.; the first N. American credit unions were founded by Alphonse Desjardins in Lévis, Quebec (1900), and Manchester, N.H. (1909). The Credit Union National Assn. (CUNA) was established in 1934 and became a worldwide association in 1958.

Cree One of the major ALGONQUIAN-speaking Indian peoples of Canada, formerly occupying an immense area from W Quebec to E Alberta. They acquired firearms and engaged in the fur trade with Europeans beginning in the 17th cent. There were two major divisions: the Woodland Cree, whose culture was essentially an EASTERN WOODLANDS type, and the Plains Cree, bison hunters of the N Great Plains. Today over 100,000 Cree live in scattered communities in Canada.

creed Officially authorized, usually brief statement of the essential articles of faith of a religious community, often used in public worship or initiation rites. Creeds are most numerous in Western traditions. In Islam, the *shahada* declares that only God is God and MUHAMMAD is his prophet. In Judaism, early creeds are preserved in Hebrew scripture, and later creeds include Moses MAIMONIDES' Thirteen Principles of Faith. In Christianity, the NICENE CREED (A.D. 381) excluded Arianism; the Apostles' Creed (8th cent.) was based on earlier baptismal creeds. Buddhism, Zoroastrianism, and modern movements of Hinduism also possess creeds.

Creek N. American Indian people that originally occupied much of the Georgia and Alabama flatlands. There were two major divisions: the Muskogee (or Upper Creeks), and the Hitchiti and Alabama (or Lower Creeks). They cultivated corn, beans, and squash. Each Creek town had a plaza or community square, often with a temple, around which were built the rectangular houses. Religious observances included the midsummer Busk (Green Corn) ceremony. The Creek War against the U.S. (1813–14) ended with the defeated Creeks ceding 23 million acres and being forcibly removed to Indian Territory (Oklahoma). Today about 50,000 Creeks live in Oklahoma.

creep Slow change in the dimensions of a material from prolonged stress. Most common METALS exhibit creep behavior. In the creep test, loads below those that ordinarily cause plastic flow or fracture are applied to the material, and the deformation over a period of time (creep strain) under constant load is measured, usually with an extensometer or strain gauge. Time to failure is also measured against stress. Mathematical techniques are available for extrapolating creep behavior; thus, designers can use thousand-hour test data, for example, to predict ten-thousand-hour behavior.

cremation Disposing of a corpse by burning. In the ancient world cremation took place on an open pyre. It was practiced by the Greeks (who considered it suitable for heroes and war dead) and the Romans (among whom it became a status symbol). In India the custom is very ancient. Early Christianity opposed cremation and it became rare in Europe after A.D. 1000. It reemerged in the late 19th cent., and was eventually accepted by both Protestants and Roman Catholics. Today most bodies in some European countries are cremated; it has remained less popular in the U.S. In modern cremation, the body is placed in a chamber and subjected to intense heat that reduces it to ash; the ashes may be scattered or buried or kept in an urn.

Creole In the 16th–18th cent., a person born in Spanish America of Spanish parents, as distinguished from one born in Spain but residing in America. Under Spanish colonial rule Creoles suffered from discrimination; it was consequently Creoles who led the 19th-cent. revolutions against Spain. Today Creole has widely varying meanings. In Louisiana it can mean either French-speaking white descendants of early French and Spanish settlers, or mixed-race people who speak a form of French and Spanish. In Latin America it may denote a local-born person of pure Spanish extraction or a member of the urban Europeanized classes as opposed to rural Indians. In the West Indies it refers to all people, regardless of ancestry, who are part of the Caribbean culture. CREOLE is also a term for a PIDGIN language.

creole Any PIDGIN language that has become established as the native language of a speech community. A creole usually arises when speakers of one language become dominant over speakers of another. A modified form of the dominant group's language (pidgin), used for communication between the two groups, may eventually become the native language of the less powerful community. Examples include Sea Island Creole (formerly Gullah, derived from English), spoken in S. Carolina's Sea Islands, and Haitian Creole (derived from French).

cress Any of several plants of the MUSTARD FAMILY whose spicy young basal leaves are used in salads and as seasonings and garnishes. WATERCRESS is the most popular of the edible cresses. Common garden cress, or peppergrass (*Lepidium sativum*), is widely grown, especially in its curl-leaved form, and used as a garnish.

Cressent \kres-ˈän\, **Charles** (1685–1768) French cabinetmaker. In 1715 he became official cabinetmaker to Philippe II, duc d'Orléans. From 1719 he received important commissions from French aristocrats, including Madame de POMPADOUR. His early works were in the LOUIS XIV STYLE, but later pieces (c.1730–50) were lighter and more curvilinear. The leading proponent of the graceful Régence style, he introduced marquetries of colored wood and ormolu to case decoration.

Creston, Paul *orig.* Giuseppe Guttivergi (1906–1985) U.S. composer. Born to poor immigrant parents in New York City, he was largely self-taught in music. His numerous works, many of which achieved wide performance, are highly rhythmical and tonally accessible. They include six symphonies, a requiem and three masses, and several concertos.

Cretaceous period \kri-ˈtā-shəs\ Interval of geologic time, 144–65 million years ago, in the MESOZOIC ERA. In the seas, marine invertebrates flourished and bony fishes evolved. On land, flowering plants arose, and insects, bees in particular, began their thriving partnership with them. Mammals and birds remained inconspicuous, while the reptiles continued their dominance. The DINOSAURS reached the peak of their evolution during this period but suddenly became extinct at its end. See table at GEOLOGIC TIME.

Crete *Greek* **Kríti** \'krē-tē\ *ancient* Creta. Island (pop., 1991: 537,000), E Mediterranean Sea. An administrative region of Greece, it is 152 mi (245 km) long and from 7.5 to 35 mi (12 to 56 km) wide. It was home to the MINOANS from about 3000 B.C., and was known for its palaces at KNOSSOS, Phaestus, and Mallia; the civilization reached its peak in the 16th cent. B.C. A major earthquake about 1450 marked the end of the Minoan era. In 67 B.C. Rome annexed Crete; in A.D. 395 it passed to Byzantium. In 1204 Crusaders sold the island to Venice: it fell to the Ottoman Turks in 1669 after one of history's longest sieges. Taken by Greece in 1898, it was autonomous until its union with Greece in 1913. Crete is a leading producer of olives, olive oil, and grapes, and a popular tourist destination.

cretinism \'krē-tᵊn-ˌi-zəm\ Endocrine disorder resulting from thyroid hormone deficiency (hypothyroidism) during fetal or early postnatal life. In the fetus, thyroid deficiency causes profound deviations from normal physical and physiological development. Visible signs of cretinism change as the child grows but generally include thick skin, sluggish movements, enlarged tongue, and broad, flat facial features. Intelligence is well below average. See also THYROID GLAND.

Creutzfeldt-Jakob disease \'krȯits-ˌfelt-'yä-ˌkōb\ *or* **CJD** Rare fatal degenerative disease of the central nervous system. It is a spreadable disease that destroys brain tissue, making it spongy and causing progressive loss of mental functioning and motor control. Patients usually die within a year. There is no known cure. The disease is caused by a PRION that builds up in neurons. Inherited or random mutation accounts for 99% of cases. See also MAD COW DISEASE

crevasse \kri-'vas\ Fissure or crack in a GLACIER resulting from stress produced by movement. Crevasses range up to 65 ft (20 m) wide, 150 ft (45 m) deep, and several hundred yards long. Crevasses may be bridged by snow and become hidden, and they may close up as the glacier moves.

cribbage Card game, usually for two players, in which each tries to form various counting combinations of cards, the score being kept by moving pegs on a narrow rectangular board. Each player receives six cards. (There is also a five-card variant, as well as four-hand and three-hand variants.) The game usually ends at 121 (twice around the board plus one). Invented by the 17th-cent. English poet John SUCKLING, cribbage is a popular pastime in Britain and the U.S.

crib death See SUDDEN INFANT DEATH SYNDROME

Crick, Francis (Harry Compton) (b.1916) British biophysicist. He worked with James WATSON, Maurice WILKINS, and Rosalind FRANKLIN to construct a molecular model of DNA consistent with its known physical and chemical properties, work for which the three men shared a 1962 Nobel Prize. Crick also discovered that each group of three bases (a codon) on a single DNA strand designates the position of a specific amino acid on the backbone of a protein molecule, and he helped determine which codons code for each amino acid.

cricket Game played with a ball and bat by two sides of 11 players each on a field centering on two wickets, each defended by a batsman. A bowler throws the ball (with a straight-arm overhand delivery), attempting to hit the wicket, which is one of several ways the batsman may be put out. Runs are scored each time the batsmen exchange positions without being put out. Cricket was first definitively recorded in England in the late 16th cent, and the first set of rules was written in 1744. During England's colonial history, it was exported around the world. Cricket matches are divided into innings consisting of one turn at bat (approximately 10 batters) for each team; depending on pregame agreement, a match may consist of either one or two innings.

Cricket W. G. Grace (right) batting in an 1890s match

cricket Any of the approximately 2,400 species of leaping insects (family Gryllidae) known for the musical chirping of the male. Crickets vary in length from around 0.1 to 2 in. (3–50 mm) and have thin antennae, hind legs modified for jumping, and two abdominal sensory appendages (cerci). Two long, membranous hind wings are used in flying. Male crickets chirp by rubbing a scraper located on one forewing along a row of 50–250 teeth on the opposite forewing. Their songs include a calling song, a courtship or mating song, and a fighting chirp.

crime Act, usually deemed socially harmful or dangerous, that is prohibited by public law and that carries a specific punishment (e.g., incarceration or a fine). A crime generally consists of both conduct (the *actus reus*) and a concurrent state of mind (the *mens rea*). Criminal acts include ARSON, ASSAULT AND BATTERY, BRIBERY, BURGLARY, CHILD ABUSE, COUNTERFEITING, EMBEZZLEMENT, EXTORTION, FORGERY, FRAUD, HIJACKING, HOMICIDE, KIDNAPPING, PERJURY, PIRACY, RAPE, SEDITION, SMUGGLING, TREASON, THEFT, and USURY. See also ARREST, CONSPIRACY, CRIMINAL LAW, FELONY AND MISDEMEANOR, INDICTMENT, statute of LIMITATIONS, SELF-INCRIMINATION, WAR CRIME.

Crimea \krī-'mē-ə\ administrative subdivision (pop., 1998 est.: 2,157,000), S UKRAINE, coextensive with the Crimean Peninsula, which extends into the BLACK SEA. It covers 10,400 sq mi (27,000 sq km); its capital is Simferopol. Settled by Greeks in the 6th cent. B.C., it became the kingdom of the Cimmerian Bosporus (5th cent. B.C.). Later subject to Rome, it was subsequently invaded repeatedly. Russia annexed Crimea in 1783. It was the scene of the CRIMEAN WAR (1853–56). In 1921 it became an autonomous republic of the Russian S.S.R. It was occupied by the Nazis 1941–44. The area became an oblast of Ukraine in 1954. After Ukraine became independent in 1991, Crimea obtained partial autonomy.

Crimean War (Oct. 1853–Feb. 1856) War fought mainly in the CRIMEA between the Russians and an alliance consisting mainly of the Ottoman empire, Britain, and France. It arose from the conflict of great powers in the Middle East and was directly caused by Russian demands to protect the Orthodox subjects of the Ottoman sultan. The war was commanded poorly by both sides; battles were fought at the Alma River, BALAKLAVA, and Inkerman, before the besieged SEVASTOPOL was taken by the allies. Disease accounted for many of the approximately 250,000 men lost by each side. After Austria threatened to join the allies, Russia accepted peace terms. The war did not settle the relations of the powers in Eastern Europe, but it did alert ALEXANDER II to the need to modernize Russia.

criminal law Body of law that defines criminal offenses, regulates the apprehension, charging, and trial of suspected offenders, and fixes punishment for convicted persons. Criminal offenses are those construed as being against the state. Substantive criminal law defines crimes, and PROCEDURAL LAW establishes procedure for the prosecution of crime. Today's substantive criminal law originated for the most part in COMMON LAW, which was later codified in federal and state statutes.

Crispi \'krēs-pē\, **Francesco** (1819–1901) Italian politician. A Sicilian, he was exiled for his revolutionary activities. He became an associate of Giuseppe MAZZINI and encouraged Giuseppe GARIBALDI to conquer Sicily in 1860. He served in the new Italian parliament (1861–96). As premier (1887–91, 1893–96), he instituted liberal reforms but became increasingly repressive. He embarked on a disastrous foreign policy, organizing Eritrea as a colony and attempting colonial expansion in Africa; he was forced to resign after the Italian defeat at the Battle of Adowa.

critical care unit See INTENSIVE CARE UNIT

critical point In science, the set of conditions under which a liquid and its vapor become identical. The conditions are the critical TEMPERATURE, the critical PRESSURE, and the critical DENSITY. If a closed vessel is filled with a pure substance, partly liquid and partly vapor, and the average density equals the critical density, the critical conditions can be achieved.

critical theory Neo-Marxian social philosophy associated with the work of the FRANKFURT SCHOOL. Drawing particularly on the thought of Karl MARX and Sigmund FREUD, it maintains that a primary goal of philosophy is to promote emancipation by helping overcome dominating or oppressive relationships in society. Critical theorists caution against the faith in scientific rationality that accompanied modernization, and maintain that scientific efficiency must not be taken as an end in itself. Since the 1970s, critical theory has become immensely influential internationally, especially in the study of the social sciences, history, and literature.

Crittenden Compromise Series of compromises in 1860–61 intended to forestall the AMERICAN CIVIL WAR. Kentucky Sen. John Crittenden proposed constitutional amendments that would extend provisions of the MISSOURI COMPROMISE to the W territories, indemnify owners of fugitive slaves, allow a form of popular sovereignty in the territories, and protect slavery in the District of Columbia. The plan was rejected by president-elect Abraham LINCOLN and narrowly defeated.

Croatia \krō-ʹā-shə\ *officially* **Republic of Croatia** *Serbo–Croatian* **Hrvatska** \hər-ʹvät-skä\ Country, W central Balkans. Area: 21,829 sq mi (56,538 sq km). Population

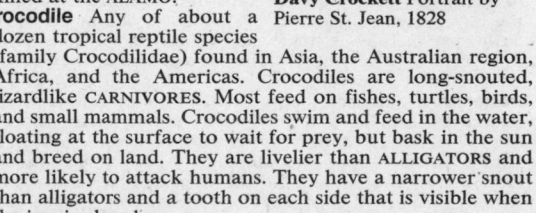

CROATIA

Scale 1: 7,071,000

0   30   60 mi
0   30   60   90 km

©1999, Encyclopædia Britannica, Inc.

(2000): 4,282,000. Capital: ZAGREB. The people are mainly Croats, with a large Serb minority. Language: Croatian (official). Religions: Roman Catholicism (Croats), Serbian Orthodoxy (Serbs). Currency: kuna. Croatia includes the traditional regions of DALMATIA, Istria, and Croatia-Slavonia. Istria and Dalmatia, in the southwest, cover the rugged Adriatic coast. The northwest, known as the central mountain belt, contains part of the Dinaric Alps. The northeast is a fertile agricultural area; cattle breeding is also important. The central mountain belt is known for fruit, and the farms of Istria and Dalmatia produce grapes and olives. The most important industries are food processing, winemaking, textiles, chemicals, and petroleum and natural gas. It is a republic with a two-chambered legislature, its head of state is the president, and the head of government is the prime minister. The Croats, a S Slavic people, arrived in the 7th cent. A.D., and in the 8th cent. came under CHARLEMAGNE. They converted to Christianity soon afterward and formed a kingdom in the 10th cent. Coming under Hungarian control in the 11th cent., it remained an independent kingdom, while the union lasted some eight centuries. Most of Croatia was taken by the Turks in 1526; the rest voted to accept Austrian rule. In 1867 it became part of the Austro-Hungarian empire, with Dalmatia and Istria ruled by VIENNA

and Croatia-Slavonia a Hungarian crown land. In 1918, after the defeat of AUSTRIA-HUNGARY in World War I, it joined other south Slav territories to form the Kingdom of Serbs, Croats, and Slovenes, renamed YUGOSLAVIA in 1929. In World War II, an independent state of Croatia was established by Germany and Italy, embracing Croatia-Slavonia, part of Dalmatia, and Bosnia and Herzegovina; after the war Croatia was rejoined to Yugoslavia as a people's republic. It declared its independence in 1991, sparking insurrections by Croatian Serbs, who carved out autonomous regions with Serbian-led Yugoslav army help; Croatia had taken back most of these regions by 1995. With some stability returning, Croatia's economy began to revive in the late 1990s.

Croce \ʹkrō-chä\, **Benedetto** (1866–1952) Italian patriot, aesthetician, critic, and cultural historian. He founded and edited (1903–37) *La Critica,* an influential journal of cultural criticism. A passionate anti-Fascist, he helped revive liberal institutions in the years following World War II, including the Liberal Party, which he led 1943–52. In 1947 he founded the Italian Institute for Historical Studies.

Crockett, Davy (*orig.* David) (1786–1836) U.S. frontiersman and politician. Born in E Tennessee, he fought in the Creek War (1813–15). A popular local figure, he was elected to the U.S. House of Representatives (1827–31, 1833–35). Attempting to offset Andrew JACKSON, the Whig Party promoted him as a "coonskin" politician and sent him on a speaking tour of the East. The many stories in books and newspapers led to the legend of an eccentric but shrewd "b'ar hunter" and Indian fighter. In 1835 he went to Texas to join the war against Mexico and was killed at the ALAMO.

Davy Crockett Portrait by Pierre St. Jean, 1828

crocodile Any of about a dozen tropical reptile species (family Crocodilidae) found in Asia, the Australian region, Africa, and the Americas. Crocodiles are long-snouted, lizardlike CARNIVORES. Most feed on fishes, turtles, birds, and small mammals. Crocodiles swim and feed in the water, floating at the surface to wait for prey, but bask in the sun and breed on land. They are livelier than ALLIGATORS and more likely to attack humans. They have a narrower snout than alligators and a tooth on each side that is visible when the jaw is closed.

crocus Any of about 75 species of low-growing plants, with corms, that make up the genus *Crocus* (IRIS FAMILY), native to the Alps, S Europe, and the Mediterranean and widely grown for their cuplike blooms in early spring or fall. The spring-flowering sorts have a floral tube so long that the ovary is belowground, sheltered from climatic changes. SAFFRON comes from *C. sativus* of W Asia. Dutch yellow crocus *(C. flavus)* and *C. biflorus* are popular spring-flowering species.

Croesus \ʹkrē-səs\ (d.546? B.C.) Last king of LYDIA, famous for his great wealth. He succeeded his father as king around 560 B.C., and after completing the conquest of mainland Ionia he faced the rising threat of the Persians under CYRUS THE GREAT. He forged an alliance with Babylon, Egypt, and Sparta to combat the Persians, but the campaign was inconclusive, and he returned to his capital at SARDIS. The Persians stormed Sardis in 546 and conquered Lydia.

Cro-Magnon \krō-ʹmag-nən, krō-ʹman-yən\ Population of anatomically modern *HOMO SAPIENS* dating from the Upper PALEOLITHIC PERIOD (c.35,000–10,000 B.C.). First discovered in 1868 at the Cro-Magnon cave in S France, Cro-Magnon was relatively more robust and powerful than contemporary humans, with a somewhat larger brain capacity. The Cro-Magnons are generally associated with the AURIGNACIAN CULTURE. They probably lived in caves or primitive huts and lean-tos, moving only when necessary to

find new hunting. It is difficult to determine how long the Cro-Magnons lasted and what happened to them; presumably they were gradually absorbed into later European populations.

Cromer, Earl of *orig.* **Evelyn Baring** (1841–1917) British administrator in Egypt. After serving as an army officer (1858–72) and as private secretary to the viceroy of India, in 1877 he went to Egypt to help resolve Egypt's financial problems. As British agent and consul general (1883-1907), he instituted a form of government known as the Veiled Protectorate, whereby he ruled the Egyptian khedives (governors). Cromer's parsimony and encouragement of agricultural projects increased Egypt's prosperity, and he profoundly influenced its development as a modern state.

Cromwell, Oliver (1599–1658) English soldier and statesman, lord protector of the republican Commonwealth of England, Scotland, and Ireland (1653–58). He served in Parliament 1628–29, and from 1640 in the LONG PARLIAMENT. When differences between CHARLES I and Parliament erupted into the ENGLISH CIVIL WARS, Cromwell became a general on the Parliamentary side, winning many notable victories, including the Battle of MARSTON MOOR. He was among those who brought the king to trial and signed his death warrant. After the British Isles were named the Commonwealth (1649), he served as the first chairman of the Council of State. In the next few years he fought against the Royalists; when CHARLES II invaded England, Cromwell destroyed his army at Worcester (1651). As lord protector (1653–58), Cromwell raised his country's status once more to that of a leading European power. Though a devout Calvinist, he pursued policies of religious toleration. He refused the title of king, offered to him by Parliament in 1657. He was succeeded (1658–59) by his son Richard Cromwell (1626–1712).

Cromwell, Thomas *later* **Earl of Essex** (1485?–1540) English politician and principal adviser (1532–40) to HENRY VIII. He was a confidential adviser to Thomas WOLSEY before entering Henry's service in 1530. He was chiefly responsible for establishing the REFORMATION in England, for the dissolution of the monasteries, and for strengthening the royal administration. He eventually came into complete control of the government, though he pretended to act on the king's authority. In 1539 he made the mistake of inducing Henry to marry ANNE OF CLEVES. He was arrested for heresy and treason and executed.

Cronenberg \'krō-nən-ˌbərg\, **David** (b.1943) Canadian film maker. Born in Toronto, he began making horror films in the 1970s. After *Scanners* (1981) and *Videodrome* (1982), he won a wider horror-film audience with *The Dead Zone* (1983), *The Fly* (1986), and *Dead Ringers* (1988). Later films included *Naked Lunch* (1991), *M. Butterfly* (1993), and *Crash* (1996).

Cronin, A(rchibald) J(oseph) (1896–1981) Scottish novelist. Trained as a surgeon, his work in coal mining communities influenced his later writings. His books combine sentimentality with social criticism. His first novel, *Hatter's Castle* (1931; film, 1941), was an immediate success. His classic *The Stars Look Down* (1935; film, 1939) chronicles social injustice in a mining community. Other works include *The Citadel* (1937; film, 1938), *The Keys of the Kingdom* (1942; film, 1944), and *A Thing of Beauty* (1956).

Cronkite, Walter (Leland, Jr.) (b.1916) U.S. journalist and television newscaster. Born in St. Joseph, Mo., he worked for United Press (1939–48) and served as a war correspondent in Europe (1942–45). He joined CBS in 1950 and became managing editor and anchor of the widely watched *CBS Evening News* (1962–81). He hosted numerous special reports, notably on the assassination of Pres. John KENNEDY and the 1969 moon landing. His reassuring, avuncular manner made him one of the most beloved figures in the U.S.

Cronus *or* **Cronos** *or* **Kronos** In GREEK RELIGION, a male agricultural deity. He was the youngest of the 12 TITANS borne by URANUS and GAEA, and his castration of his father separated heaven from earth. With his sister and consort RHEA, he fathered HESTIA, DEMETER, HERA, HADES, and POSEIDON, all of whom he swallowed because he had been warned that he would be overthrown by his own child. Rhea hid his son ZEUS, who later forced Cronus to disgorge the others and then vanquished him. He was identified with the Roman god SATURN.

Cronyn \'krō-nən\, **Hume and Jessica Tandy** (b.1911, 1909–1994) U.S. actors. Cronyn, born in London, Ontario, made his Broadway debut in 1934, was a successful character actor in many plays, including *Hamlet* (1964, Tony Award), and directed such plays as *Hilda Crane* (1950) and *The Egghead* (1957). Tandy, born in London, England, made her Broadway debut in 1930. She was the original Blanche Du Bois in *A Streetcar Named Desire* (1947, Tony Award). She and Cronyn married in 1942 and acted together in such successful plays as *The Fourposter* (1951), *A Delicate Balance* (1966), *The Gin Game* (1977), and *Foxfire* (1982); the last two earned Tony awards for Tandy. Cronyn's many films included *Lifeboat* (1944) and *Sunrise at Campobello* (1960), and Tandy's included *Driving Miss Daisy* (1989, Academy Award).

crop duster Aircraft used for dusting or spraying large acreages with PESTICIDES. Aerial spraying and dusting permit coverage of large areas at the moment when application of pesticide is most effective and avoid the need for wheeled vehicles that might damage crops. Today ultra-low-volume applicators distribute concentrated pesticides in extremely small amounts.

crop rotation Successive cultivation of different crops in a specified order on the same fields. A typical scheme selects rotation crops from three classifications: cultivated row crops (e.g., corn, potatoes), close-growing grains (oats, wheat), and sod-forming, or rest, crops (clover). Most cropping systems include deep-rooting LEGUMES. In addition to the many beneficial effects on soils and crops, well-planned crop rotations make the farm a more effective year-round enterprise by providing more efficient handling of labor, power, and equipment, reduction in weather and market risks, and improved ability to meet livestock requirements.

croquet \krō-'kā\ Game in which players using mallets drive wooden balls through a series of wickets, or hoops, set out on a lawn. The object is to be the first to complete the course by passing through all the wickets and hitting a goal peg. Croquet evolved from the 13th-cent. French game pall-mall.

Crosby, Bing (*orig.* Harry Lillis) (1903–1977) U.S. singer and actor. Born in Tacoma, Wash., Crosby began to sing and play drums while studying law. As a singer with the Paul Whiteman orchestra in 1927, his mellow "crooning" style and casual stage manner proved highly popular. He appeared in the early sound film *King of Jazz* (1931), and later had his own radio program. By the late 1930s his records had sold millions of copies. His "White Christmas" and "Silent Night" are among the most popular recordings of all time. His film career included the seven *Road* film comedies

Bing Crosby

with Bob HOPE, *Going My Way* (1944, Academy Award), *The Bells of St. Mary's* (1945), and *White Christmas* (1954). Over 300 million of his records may have been sold, a total surpassed only by Elvis PRESLEY among solo artists.

cross Principal symbol of CHRISTIANITY, recalling the CRUCIFIXION of JESUS. There are four basic iconogaphic representations: the *crux quadrata*, or Greek cross, with four equal arms; the *crux immissa*, or Latin cross, with a base stem longer than the other arms; the *crux commissa* (St. Anthony's cross), resembling the Greek letter tau (T); and the *crux decussata* (St. Andrew's cross), resembling the Roman numeral 10 (X). Tradition holds that the *crux immissa* was used for Christ's crucifixion. Displaying the cross was not common before CONSTANTINE I abolished crucifixion in the 4th cent. A crucifix shows Christ's figure on a cross and is typical of Roman Catholicism and Eastern Orthodoxy.

Greek	Latin	St. Anthony's	St. Andrew's	Celtic
Patriarchal	Papal	Maltese	Russian	Jerusalem

Cross Several traditional types of crosses.

crossbow Leading missile weapon of the Middle Ages, consisting of a short bow mounted crosswise on a stock, with a groove to guide an arrow or dart and a trigger to release it. First used in antiquity, it was an important advance in warfare. Its metal bow could propel an arrow with enough velocity to pierce CHAIN MAIL and gave it a range of up to 1,000 ft (300 m). Powerful and versatile, it remained in use even after the introduction of the LONGBOW and firearms, until the 15th cent.

cross-country skiing Skiing in open country over rolling, hilly terrain. It originated in Scandinavia as a means of travel as well as recreation. The skis used are longer, narrower, and lighter than those used in downhill skiing, and bindings allow more heel movement. The standard lengths of races range from 10 to 50 km (6.2–31 mi) for men and 5 to 30 km (3.1–18.6 mi) for women. It has long been an Olympic sport.

cross-fertilization Fusion of male and female sex cells from different individuals of a species. Cross-fertilization is necessary in animal and plant species that have male and female organs on separate individuals. Methods of cross-fertilization are diverse in animals. Among most species that breed in water, both sexes shed their sex cells into the water, where FERTILIZATION takes place. Among land breeders, fertilization is internal, with the sperm being introduced into the body of the female. By recombining genetic material from two parents, cross-fertilization maintains a greater range of variability for NATURAL SELECTION to act on, thereby increasing the capacity of a species to adapt to environmental change.

crossword puzzle Puzzle in which words are filled into a pattern of numbered squares in answer to correspondingly numbered clues and in such a way that words can be read across and down. The first crosswords, intended primarily for children, appeared in England in the 19th cent. In the U.S., the puzzle developed into a popular adult pastime. By 1923, crosswords were being published in most of the leading U.S. newspapers. Today crosswords are found in almost every country and language.

croup \'krüp\ Acute throat INFLAMMATION and spasms in young children, with harsh cough, hoarseness, and difficulty breathing. Causes include infection, allergy, and physical irritation of the LARYNX. Viral croup of infants can usually be treated at home with a cool mist vaporizer. Bacterial croup rapidly causes severe breathing and swallowing difficulty, requiring antibiotics and insertion of a breathing tube.

Crow PLAINS INDIAN people that occupied the area around the Yellowstone River in N Wyoming and S Montana. Much of Crow life revolved around the buffalo and the horse, and the Crow were prominent as middleman traders. Crow religious life emphasized the supernatural vision, induced by fasting and isolation. The Crow continually suffered losses from wars with the BLACKFOOT and SIOUX and sided with the whites in the Indian wars of the 1860s and '70s. In 1868 they accepted a reservation carved from former tribal lands in S Montana. Today they number about 6,500.

crow Any of more than 20 species of black songbirds in the genus *Corvus* (family Corvidae) that are smaller than most RAVENS and less heavily billed. Found in N. America and Eurasia, they eat grain, berries, insects, carrion, and the eggs of other birds. Crows may damage grain crops, but they also eat many economically harmful insects. At times crows roost together in the tens of thousands. After the ravens, the crows are considered the most intelligent of all birds, and pet crows can be taught to imitate speech.

crowfoot See BUTTERCUP

crown vetch VETCH (*Coronilla varia*), native to the Mediterranean but widely grown in temperate areas as a ground cover. It has fernlike leaves and clusters of white to pink flowers. The sturdy roots bind the soil of steep slopes and roadside embankments. Crown vetch draws nitrogen from the air, trapping it in the roots, and thus improves soil fertility. It dies back to the crown each fall in cold areas, resuming growth in spring.

crucifixion Method of CAPITAL PUNISHMENT among the Persians, Seleucids, Jews, Carthaginians, and Romans from about the 6th cent. B.C. to the 4th cent. A.D. The hands of the condemned man were tied or nailed to a crossbeam, which was attached to a tall upright, and his feet bound or nailed to the upright. Death was by heart failure or asphyxiation. Political or religious agitators and those without civil rights were crucified. Its overwhelming association today is with JESUS. Crucifixion was abolished by CONSTANTINE I in A.D. 337 after his conversion to Christianity. See also STIGMATA.

crude oil See PETROLEUM

cruelty, theater of Theory, advanced by Antonin ARTAUD in *The Theatre and Its Double* (1938), that the theater's function was to rid audiences of the repressive effects of civilization and liberate their instinctual energy. He proposed to do so by shocking them with mythic spectacles that would include groans, screams, pulsating lights, and oversized stage puppets. His ideas influenced such avant-garde movements as the theater of the ABSURD.

Cruikshank, George (1792–1878) English illustrator and caricaturist. His series of political caricatures for *The Scourge* (1811–16) established him as the leading political cartoonist of his generation, and he continued to satirize the policies of the Tories and Whigs until about 1825. In the 1820s and '30s he produced book illustrations, notably for Charles DICKENS's *Oliver Twist* (1838). He later embraced the cause of temperance with his series *The Bottle* (1847) and *The Drunkard's Children* (1848).

Cruise, Tom orig. Thomas Cruise Mapother IV (b.1962) U.S. actor. Born in Syracuse, N.Y., he made his screen debut in 1981 and rose to stardom in *Taps* (1981), *Risky Business* (1983), and *Top Gun* (1986). He received acclaim for his dramatic roles in *The Color of Money* (1986), *Rain Man* (1988), and *Born on the Fourth of July* (1989). His later films include *A Few Good Men* (1992), *The Firm* (1993), *Jerry Maguire* (1996), and Stanley KUBRICK's *Eyes Wide Shut* (1999).

cruise missile Type of low-flying strategic guided missile developed by the U.S. and the Soviet Union in the 1960s and '70s. Powered by JET ENGINES, cruise missiles may carry either a nuclear or a conventional warhead. Launched from ships, submarines, airplanes or the ground, they are designed to hug the ground so as to minimize detection by RADAR.

Crumb, George (Henry) (b.1929) U.S. composer. Born in Charleston, W.V., from 1965 he taught at the Univ. of Pennsylvania. His style is known for its unusual and hauntingly evocative timbres. *Echoes of Time and the River* (1967, Pulitzer Prize) and *Ancient Voices of Children* (1970) brought him wide fame. His other works include *Madrigals, Books I–IV* (1965–70), *Night of the Four Moons* (1969), and *Black Angels* (1970).

Crusade, Children's See CHILDREN'S CRUSADE

crusader states Former territories on the Palestine coast taken by the Christian army during the first of the CRUSADES. The states were established as the kingdom of Jerusalem (1099–1187), the principality of Antioch (1098–1268), the county of Edessa (1098–1144), and the county of Tripoli (1109–1289). Threats to the states led the pope to call for future crusades.

Crusades Series of military expeditions by European Christians (the name derives from the Latin word for "cross")

against Muslim powers between 1095 and 1291, aimed at gaining control of Jerusalem. In response to a plea for help from Byzantines and Eastern Christians living under Muslim rule, Pope URBAN II called on Western nobles to aid the East. The result of his preaching and that of others, including PETER THE HERMIT, was the First Crusade (1095–99). Led by many important nobles of the period, the crusaders helped the Byzantines repel the Seljuq Turks and regain W Anatolia, parts of Armenia and Syria, and Jerusalem (1099). The resultant foundation of Western principalities (see CRUSADER STATES) formed the basis of the crusading movement, which focused on protecting the lands won. The Second Crusade (1147–49) ended in failure, and by 1187 most of the principalities had been lost. Jerusalem's fall to SALADIN prompted the Third Crusade (1189–92), during which RICHARD I the Lionheart and PHILIP II of France captured Cyprus and Acre but failed to reach Jerusalem. The Fourth Crusade (1202–4), directed against Egypt, was instead diverted to Constantinople, where crusaders set up the Latin empire of Constantinople. Enthusiasm remained high and spawned the so-called CHILDREN'S CRUSADE of 1212. The Fifth Crusade (1217–21) failed to capture Egypt and ended with a truce. The Sixth Crusade (1227–29) was led by the emperor FREDERICK II, who negotiated the surrender of Jerusalem with the Egyptian sultan; however, the city later fell to the Turks (1244). The Seventh Crusade (1248–50), led by LOUIS IX of France, aimed at the conquest of Egypt and the liberation of Palestine. Despite careful planning, the Westerners were badly defeated. Louis planned the abortive Eighth Crusade (1270), but he and much of his army died of disease shortly after landing in Tunis. The fall of Acre in 1291 and the loss of outposts on the mainland ended the era of the Crusades.

crust Outermost solid part of the earth, essentially composed of IGNEOUS and METAMORPHIC ROCK types. In continental regions, the crust is chiefly granitic rock, whereas the composition of the ocean floor is mainly BASALT and GABBRO. On average, the crust extends 22 mi (35 km) downward from the surface to the underlying MANTLE, from which it is separated by the MOHO. The crust and top layer of the mantle together form the LITHOSPHERE.

crustacean \krəs-'tā-shən\ Any member of nearly 39,000 ARTHROPOD species (subphylum Crustacea) worldwide, distinguished by having two pairs of antenna-like appendages in front of the mouth and other paired appendages near the mouth that act like jaws. Most species are marine, including SHRIMP and BARNACLES. Some, including CRAYFISH, live in freshwater habitats; others (e.g., sand fleas, land CRABS, and sow bugs) live in moist terrestrial environments. The typical adult body has a series of segments (somites) either fused or linked to each other by flexible areas that form movable joints. Many species (including COPEPODS and KRILL) are the chief diet of larger organisms. See also DECAPOD.

Cruz \krüs\, **Celia** (b.1924?) Cuban-U.S. singer. Having decided on a singing career after winning a talent show, in the early 1950s she became lead singer with the popular orchestra La Sonora Matancera, often headlining at the Tropicana nightclub. After Cuba's 1959 revolution the orchestra moved to Mexico, and later to the U.S. In the 1960s she released over 20 albums in the U.S., including seven with Tito PUENTE; she has since recorded dozens more. Her many awards include the National Medal of Arts (1994).

cryogenics \ˌkrī-ə-'je-niks\ Study and use of low-temperature phenomena. The cryogenic temperature range is from –238°F (–150°C) to ABSOLUTE ZERO. At low temperatures, matter has unusual properties; gases can be liquefied, and metals lose electrical RESISTANCE (see SUPERCONDUCTIVITY). Cryogenics dates from 1877, when oxygen was first liquefied (at –297°F, or –183°C); superconductivity was discovered in 1911. Applications of cryogenics include the storage and transport of liquefied gases, food preservation, cryosurgery, rocket fuels, and superconducting ELECTROMAGNETS.

crypt Subterranean chamber, usually under a church floor. The CATACOMBS of the early Christians were known as *cryptae,* and when churches came to be built over the tombs of saints and martyrs, subterranean chapels were built

around the actual tomb. As early as the reign of CONSTANTINE I (A.D. 306–37), the crypt was considered a normal part of a church. Later its size was increased; the crypt of Canterbury Cathedral is an elaborate underground church with its own APSE.

Crypt, Canterbury Cathedral, England, 12th cent.

cryptographic key See cryptographic KEY

cryptography \krip-'tä-grə-fē\ Encoding and decoding of messages in order to render them unintelligible to all but the intended receiver. Cryptography may also refer to the art of cryptanalysis, by which cryptographic codes are broken. The principles of cryptography are today applied particularly to the encryption of banking, government, and commercial communications. See also DATA ENCRYPTION.

cryptomonad \ˌkrip-tō-'mō-ˌnad\ Any small organism with two flagella that is considered both a PROTOZOAN and an alga (see ALGAE). Occurring in both fresh and salt water, cryptomonads contain pigments found only in red algae and CYANOBACTERIA. They sometimes live harmlessly within other organisms. Some species conduct PHOTOSYNTHESIS; others lack pigment-containing structures and consume organic matter.

crystal Any solid material whose ATOMS are arranged in a definite pattern and whose surface regularity reflects its internal symmetry. Each of a crystal's millions of individual structural units (unit cells) contains all the substance's atoms, molecules, or ions in the same proportions as in its chemical formula (see FORMULA WEIGHT). The cells are repeated in all directions to form a geometric pattern, manifested by the number and orientation of external planes (crystal faces). Crystals are classified into seven crystallographic systems based on their symmetry. Crystals are generally formed when a liquid solidifies or a vapor or a liquid SOLUTION can no longer retain dissolved material, which is precipitated (see PRECIPITATION). METALS, ALLOYS, MINERALS, and SEMICONDUCTORS are all crystalline, at least microscopically. (A noncrystalline solid is "amorphous.") See also LIQUID CRYSTAL.

crystal lattice Three-dimensional configuration of points connected by lines used to describe the orderly arrangement of ATOMS in a CRYSTAL. Each point represents one or more atoms in the actual crystal. The lattice is divided into a number of identical blocks or cells that are repeated in all directions to form a geometric pattern. Lattices are classified into seven groups according to their dominant symmetries. See also CRYSTALLOGRAPHY, SOLID-STATE PHYSICS.

crystalline rock Any rock composed entirely of crystallized minerals. Intrusive igneous rocks (see INTRUSIVE ROCK) are nearly always crystalline. Metamorphic rocks are always completely crystalline and are termed crystalline SCHISTS or GNEISSES. Sedimentary rocks can also be crystalline, such as crystalline limestones that precipitate directly from solution.

crystallography \ˌkris-tə-'läg-rə-fē\ Branch of science that deals with discerning the arrangement and bonding of atoms in crystalline solids and with the geometric structure of CRYSTAL LATTICES. Classically, the optical properties of CRYSTALS were of value in mineralogy and chemistry for the identification of substances. Modern crystallography is largely based on the analysis of the DIFFRACTION of X RAYS, by which chemists are able to determine the internal structures and bonding arrangements of minerals and molecules, including the structures of large complex molecules such as proteins and DNA.

Crystal Night See KRISTALLNACHT

Crystal Palace Giant glass-and-iron exhibition hall in Hyde Park, London, that housed the Great Exhibition of 1851. It was taken down and rebuilt at Sydenham Hill, where it survived until 1936. Designed by Sir Joseph Paxton (1801–1865), it was a remarkable assembly of prefabricated parts. Its intricate network of slender iron rods sustaining walls of clear glass set a standard for later international exhibitions, likewise housed in glass CONSERVATORIES.

C-section See CESAREAN SECTION

ctenophore \'te-nə-ˌfōr\ *or* **comb jelly** Any of nearly 90 species (phylum Ctenophora) of marine invertebrates with vertical ciliary combs over their bodies. Ctenophores are sometimes mistaken for JELLYFISH. The body is round or spherical, with tentacles to capture food; the combs beat to provide locomotion. Most species are small (up to 0.1 in., or 3 mm, in diameter), but at least one grows larger than 3 ft (1 m). Ctenophores live in almost all ocean regions, floating freely in the water. All comb jellies except one parasitic species are carnivores.

Ctesibius of Alexandria See KTESIBIOS OF ALEXANDRIA

Ctesiphon \'te-sə-ˌfän\ Ancient ruined city, Iraq. Located on the TIGRIS RIVER, southeast of modern BAGHDAD, it was first a Greek army camp. Destroyed by the Romans in the 1st cent. A.D., it was resettled by the Sasanian empire in the 3rd cent. The Arabs conquered the city in A.D. 637, but abandoned it by 763. The site is famous for the remains of a gigantic vaulted hall, the Taq Kisra, which has one of the largest single-span brick arches in the world.

Cuauhtémoc \kwaù-'te-ˌmōk\ *or* **Guatimozin** \ˌgwät-ə-'mōt-sən\ (c.1495–1522) Last AZTEC emperor, nephew and son-in-law of MONTEZUMA II. He became emperor on the death of Montezuma's successor in 1520, while Hernán CORTÉS was marching for the second time on TENOCHTITLÁN, the Aztec capital. He defended the city during a terrible four-month siege that ended in his defeat. Pressed to reveal where Aztec treasure was hidden, his stoicism under torture became legendary. Later Cortés, hearing of a plot against the Spaniards, had him hanged.

Cuba *officially* **Republic of Cuba** Socialist republic, W. Indies. Located 90 mi (145 km) south of Florida, it includes the island of Cuba and surrounding small islands. Area: 42,804 sq mi (110,861 sq km). Population (2000): 11,148,000. Capital: HAVANA. The population is about one-third mulatto

(black-Spanish) or black and about two-thirds white, mostly of Spanish descent. Language: Spanish (official). Religions: Roman Catholicism, Santería (both formerly discouraged). Currency: Cuban peso, U.S. dollar. The main island of Cuba is 746 mi (1,200 km) long and 25–125 mi (40–200 km) wide. About one-quarter is mountainous, with Pico Turquino at 6,476 ft (1,974 m) the highest peak; the remainder is extensive plains and basins. The climate is semitropical. Cuba was the first communist republic in the Western Hemisphere. It has a centrally planned economy that depends on the export of sugar and, to a much lesser extent, tobacco and nickel. Its cigars are considered the world's best. It is a republic with one legislative house, its head of state and government is the president. Several Indian groups, including the CIBONEY and the ARAWAK, inhabited Cuba at the time of the first Spanish contact. Christopher COLUMBUS claimed the island for Spain in 1492, and the Spanish conquest began in 1511, when the settlement of Baracoa was founded. The native Indians were eradicated over the succeeding centuries, and African slaves, from the 18th cent. until slavery was abolished in 1886, were imported to work the sugar plantations. Cuba revolted unsuccessfully against Spain in the Ten Years' War (1868–78); a second war of independence began in 1895. In 1898 the U.S. entered the war (see SPANISH–AMERICAN WAR); Spain relinquished its claim to Cuba, which was occupied by the U.S. for three years before gaining its independence in 1902. The U.S. invested heavily in the Cuban sugar industry in the first half of the 20th cent., and this, combined with tourism and gambling, caused the economy to prosper. Inequalities in the distribution of wealth persisted, however, as did political corruption. In 1958–59 the communist revolutionary Fidel CASTRO overthrew its longtime dictator Fulgencio BATISTA and established a socialist state aligned with the Soviet Union, abolishing capitalism and nationalizing foreign-owned enterprises. Relations with the U.S. deteriorated, reaching a low point with the 1961 BAY OF PIGS INVASION and the 1962 CUBAN MISSILE CRISIS. In 1980 about 125,000 Cubans, including many officially labeled "undesirables," were shipped to the U.S. in the so-called Mariel Boat Lift. When communism collapsed in the U.S.S.R., Cuba lost important financial backing and its economy suffered greatly. The latter gradually improved in the 1990s with the encouragement of tourism, though diplomatic relations with the U.S. were not resumed.

Cubango River See OKAVANGO RIVER

Cuban missile crisis (1962) Major confrontation between the U.S. and the Soviet Union over the presence of Soviet nuclear missiles in Cuba. In October 1962 a U.S. spy plane detected a ballistic missile on a launching site in Cuba. Pres. John F. KENNEDY ordered a naval blockade, and for several days the U.S. and the Soviet Union hovered on the brink of war. Nikita KHRUSHCHEV finally agreed to remove the missiles in return for a secret commitment to withdraw U.S. missiles from Turkey and never to invade Cuba. See also Fidel CASTRO.

Cubism Movement in the visual arts created by Pablo PICASSO and Georges BRAQUE in Paris between 1907 and 1914. They were later joined by Juan GRIS, Fernand LÉGER, Robert DELAUNAY, and others. The name derives from a review that described Braque's work as images composed of cubes. The style was inspired by African sculpture and the later paintings of Paul CÉZANNE. A major source of ABSTRACT ART, it emphasized the flat, two-dimensional, fragmented surface of the picture plane, rejecting perspective and modeling in favor of geometrical forms. Picasso's *Demoiselles d'Avignon* (1907) signaled the new style, which also strongly influenced 20th-cent. sculpture and architecture.

Cú Chulainn *or* **Cuchulain** \kü-'kəl-ən\ In ancient Irish Gaelic literature, a powerful warrior and the central character in the ULSTER CYCLE. The son of the god Lugus, he was the greatest of the warriors loyal to King Conchobar. He had 14 fingers, 14 toes, and 14 eye pupils. He defended Ulster single-handed at 17 against the forces of Medb, queen of Connaught.

cuckoo Any of some 60 species of tree-dwelling birds (family Cuculidae) and numerous terrestrial species found worldwide but most diverse in the Old World tropics. Species range from 6.5 to 36 in. (16–90 cm) long. Most are drab gray, but a few are brightly colored or iridescent. Aside from the European cuckoo's familiar two-note call, cuckoos are best known for their habit of brood PARASITISM (see COWBIRD); their eggs resemble those of the host species, and the adult cuckoo removes one or more host eggs to ensure that the substitution is indetectable.

cucumber Creeping plant *(Cucumis sativus)* of the GOURD family, probably originating in N India and widely culti-

©1999, Encyclopædia Britannica, Inc.

CUBA

Scale 1: 18,754,000

vated for its oblong fruit. It is a tender annual with a trailing stem, branched tendrils, and hairy leaves with pointed lobes. Its food value is low, but its delicate flavor makes it popular for salads and relishes.

Cudworth, Ralph (1617–1688) English theologian and philosopher. Reared as a Puritan, he eventually adopted Nonconformist views and became a leader of the CAMBRIDGE PLATONISTS. In ethics, his outstanding work is *A Treatise Concerning Eternal and Immutable Morality* (1731), which stresses the natural good or evil inherent in an event or act, as against Puritan Calvinism, René DESCARTES's theology, and Thomas HOBBES's reduction of morality to civil obedience.

Cuéllar, Javier Pérez de See Javier PÉREZ DE CUÉLLAR

Cuernavaca \ˌkwer-nə-ˈvä-kə\ City (pop., 1995: 311,000), capital of MORELOS state, S central Mexico. Originally known as Cuauhnáhuac, about 1521 it was taken by Hernán CORTÉS and is the site of his palace, now the Morelos State House, which is decorated with murals by Diego RIVERA. Nearby are pre-Columbian ruins. A favorite retreat of the emperor MAXIMILIAN, the area is still popular with tourists. It is home to the Univ. of Morelos (established 1953).

Cukierman, Yizhak See Itzhak ZUCKERMAN

Cukor \ˈkyü-kər\, **George (Dewey)** (1899–1983) U.S. film director. Born in New York City, he directed plays on Broadway before going to Hollywood in 1929. His first film, *Tarnished Lady* (1931), was followed by the acclaimed *Little Women* (1933), *David Copperfield* (1935), *Camille* (1937), *The Philadelphia Story* (1940), *Gaslight* (1944), and *Born Yesterday* (1950). He directed several comedies starring Katharine HEPBURN and Spencer TRACY, including *Pat and Mike* (1952). He was noted for his skill in working with actors, particularly women. Among his other memorable films are *A Star Is Born* (1954) and *My Fair Lady* (1964, Academy Award).

Cullen, Countee *orig.* Countee Porter (1903–1946) U.S. poet of the HARLEM RENAISSANCE. Reared in New York City, he was unofficially adopted at 15 by Rev. F. A. Cullen and received an MA from Harvard. His first collection of poems, *Color* (1925), received critical acclaim while he was still in college. *Copper Sun* (1927) was criticized by blacks for not giving race the attention it had in *Color*. He taught in the city's public schools from 1934 until his death.

cultivar \ˈkəl-tə-ˌvär\ Any variety of a plant originating through cloning or hybridization (see CLONE, HYBRID) and not occurring naturally. In asexually propagated plants, a cultivar is a clone considered valuable enough to have its own name; in sexually propagated plants, a cultivar is a pure line (for self-pollinated plants) or, for cross-pollinated plants, a population that is genetically distinguishable.

cultural anthropology Branch of ANTHROPOLOGY that deals with the study of CULTURE and that uses the methods, concepts, and data of ARCHAEOLOGY, FOLKLORE, LINGUISTICS, and related fields to describe and analyze the diverse peoples of the world. Until the mid-20th cent. it mainly studied small-scale (or "primitive"), non-Western societies. Today its field extends to all forms of human association, from village communities to corporate cultures to urban gangs. Two key perspectives used are those of holism, or understanding society as a complex interactive whole, and cultural relativism, or the appreciation of cultural phenomena within their own context. Areas of study traditionally include social structure, law, politics, religion, magic, art, and technology.

Cultural Revolution *officially* **Great Proletarian Cultural Revolution** (1966–76) Upheaval launched by MAO ZEDONG to renew the spirit of the Chinese revolution. Fearing urban social stratification and contamination by capitalist ideas and believing that programs instituted to correct for the failed GREAT LEAP FORWARD showed a lack of commitment to the revolution, he organized China's urban youths into groups called the RED GUARDS, encouraging them to attack all traditional values and "bourgeois things." They soon splintered into zealous rival groups, and in 1968 Mao sent millions of them to the rural hinterland, bringing some order to the cities. Within the government, his associates fought with more moderate elements, many of whom, including LIU SHAOQI and LIN BIAO, were purged and died.

From 1973 politics shifted between the Maoist GANG OF FOUR and the moderates headed by ZHOU ENLAI and DENG XIAOPING; Mao's death (1976) ended the Cultural Revolution. By that time, nearly three million party members and countless wrongfully purged citizens awaited reinstatement, and more than a million may have died. The post-Mao repudiation of the Cultural Revolution disillusioned many in China.

cultural studies Interdisciplinary field concerned with the role of social institutions in the shaping of CULTURE. Among its central concerns are the place of RACE (or ethnicity), CLASS, and gender in the production of cultural knowledge. It has had broad influence in SOCIOLOGY, ANTHROPOLOGY, HISTORIOGRAPHY, LITERARY CRITICISM, and PHILOSOPHY.

culture Integrated pattern of human knowledge, belief, and behavior that depends on humankind's capacity for learning and transmitting knowledge to succeeding generations. Culture consists of language, ideas, beliefs, customs, taboos, codes, institutions, tools, techniques, works of art, rituals, ceremonies, and symbols. Culture has played a crucial role in HUMAN EVOLUTION, allowing human beings to adapt the environment to their own purposes rather than depend solely on NATURAL SELECTION to achieve adaptive success. Every human society has its own particular culture. An individual's attitudes, values, ideals, and beliefs are greatly influenced by the culture in which he or she lives. Culture change takes place as a result of ecological, socioeconomic, political, religious, or other fundamental changes affecting a society. See also SOCIOCULTURAL EVOLUTION.

Cumae \ˈkyü-mē\ Ancient city west of Naples. Probably the oldest Greek mainland colony in the west, it was home to the Cumaean SIBYL, whose cavern still exists. Founded about 750 B.C. by Greeks but taken by the Samnites in the 5th cent. B.C., it was subjugated by Rome in 338 B.C. It was destroyed in A.D. 1205. Remains of fortifications and graves from all these periods have been found throughout the area.

Cumberland Gap National Historical Park National historical park, Tennessee. Created in 1940 to preserve the Cumberland Gap, a natural pass through the Cumberland Plateau, it includes the Wilderness Road, blazed by Daniel BOONE, which became the main artery that opened the Northwest Territory. The park covers 32 sq mi (83 sq km).

Cumberland Plateau Tableland that forms the W section of the APPALACHIAN MTNS. and a part of the Allegheny Plateau. It extends southwest for 450 mi (725 km) from S W. Virginia to NE Alabama, averages 50 mi (80 km) in width, and is 2,000–4,145 ft (600–1,263 m) high. The highest portion is a narrow ridge about 140 mi (225 km) long in E Kentucky and NE Tennessee; the name Cumberland Mtns. is applied to this area, which includes the CUMBERLAND GAP NATIONAL HISTORICAL PARK.

Cumberland River River, Kentucky and Tennessee. It rises in SE Kentucky and flows west, looping through N Tennessee before returning north to join the OHIO RIVER after a course of 687 mi (1,106 km). A series of lakes on the Cumberland were developed as part of the TENNESSEE VALLEY AUTHORITY system. Wolf Creek Dam (1952) created Lake Cumberland.

Cumberland Sound Inlet of DAVIS STRAIT, Nunavut. Indenting the SE coast of BAFFIN ISLAND, it is 170 mi (270 km) long and 100 mi (160 km) wide. John Davis (1550?–1605), an English navigator, sailed into the sound in 1585 in search of the NORTHWEST PASSAGE. By the late 19th cent. the area was noted for whaling.

Cumbria County (pop. 1998 est.: 492,000), NW England. Extending along the IRISH SEA coast, it includes the famous LAKE DISTRICT. Human occupation dates from the NEOLITHIC PERIOD. The Romans constructed roads, forts, and the great complex of HADRIAN'S WALL. After the mid-10th cent., N Cumbria alternated between Scottish and English rule until taken by the English in 1157. Lead, silver, and iron ore have been mined in the area since the 12th cent.

Cummings, E(dward) E(stlin) (1894–1962) U.S. poet and painter. Born in Cambridge, Mass., his experience in World War I of being held in a detention camp gave rise to his first prose book, *The Enormous Room* (1922). His first book of poems, *Tulips and Chimneys* (1923), was followed by 11 more. His poetry, rooted in New England traditions of dissent and self-reliance, attracted attention for its lack of capitalization, eccentric punctuation and phrasing, and often childlike playfulness, which won it a wide readership.

Cunard \kyù-'närd\, **Samuel** (*later* **Sir Samuel**) (1787–1865) Canadian-British shipowner. Born in Halifax, Nova Scotia, he became prosperous in commerce. Planning to establish mail service between England and N. America, he went to England and in 1839 cofounded the British and N. American Royal Mail Steam Packet Co., known as the Cunard Line. In 1840, four Cunard liners began the first regular service across the Atlantic.

cuneiform writing \kyù-'nē-ə-ˌfôrm\ System of writing employed for a number of ancient SW Asian languages. The main writing material for cuneiform texts was a damp clay tablet, into which the scribe would press a wedge-shaped stroke with a reed stylus. A configuration of such impressions constituted a character, or sign. A single cuneiform sign could be a logogram (an arbitrary representation of a word) or a syllabogram (a representation of the sound of a syllable). The first language to be written in cuneiform was Sumerian (see SUMER). AKKADIAN began to be written in cuneiform c.2350 B.C. Later the script was adapted to other SW Asian languages. Cuneiform was slowly displaced in the first millennium B.C. by the rise of ARAMAIC, written in a Phoenician ALPHABET script. Knowledge of the cuneiform signs was lost until the mid-19th cent., when European scholars deciphered them.

original pictograph	pictograph in position of later cuneiform	early Babylonian	Assyrian	original or derived meaning
				bird
				fish
				sun, day
				to plow, to till

Cuneiform Examples illustrating the evolution of cuneiform writing.

Cunningham, Glenn (1909–1988) U.S. runner. Born in Atlanta, Kan., he was badly burned when he was 7 and not expected to walk again. With intensive therapy and application, he was running competitively by high school. He was the fastest miler in the Amateur Athletic Union in 1933 and 1935–38, and in 1934 he set a world record (4:06.7).

Cunningham, Imogen (1883–1976) U.S. photographer. Born in Portland, Ore., she began taking pictures in 1901, opened a portrait studio in Seattle in 1910, and soon established a national reputation. Encouraged by Edward WESTON, she exhibited her plant photographs in San Francisco, where she would work for the remainder of her career. In her later years she taught at the San Francisco Art Institute.

Cunningham, Merce (b.1919) U.S. avant-garde dancer and choreographer. Born in Centralia, Wash., he joined Martha GRAHAM's company in 1939. As an independent choreographer in 1945–52,

Merce Cunningham, 1970

he began his long collaboration with the composer John CAGE. In 1952 he formed his own company, developing his interest in isolated movement and "choreography by chance." His *Suite by Chance* (1952) was the first dance performed to an electronic score.

CUNY See CITY UNIV. OF NEW YORK

Cupid Ancient Roman god of love in all its varieties, identified with the Greek EROS. Cupid was the son of MERCURY and VENUS. He was represented as a winged infant or a beautiful youth who carried a bow and quiver of arrows, and whose wounds inspired love or passion. Though generally beneficent, he could be mischievous in his matchmaking.

Curaçao \ˌkùr-ə-'sō, ˌkyùr-ə-'saù\ Largest island (pop., 1994 est.: 147,000) of the NETHERLANDS ANTILLES, off the coast of Venezuela. WILLEMSTAD is its chief town, with the best natural harbor in the W. Indies. It was settled by the Spanish in 1527; Portuguese Jews soon established the oldest continuously inhabited Jewish community in the Western Hemisphere. The Dutch West India Co. gained control of the island in 1634; it was awarded to the Netherlands by the 1815 Treaty of Paris. Internal self-government was granted in 1954. Products include oranges, Curaçao liqueur, and aloes.

curare \kyù-'rär-ē\ Organic compound, an ALKALOID that occurs in various tropical American plants and causes PARALYSIS. Crude preparations have long been used by native people as an arrow poison. A purified form is used in ANESTHESIOLOGY to prevent any movement of patients during surgery. It has other medical uses as a relaxant and diagnostic aid.

curia \'kyùr-ē-ə\ In European medieval history, a court, or group of persons who attended a ruler at any given time for social, political, or judicial purposes. The ruler and curia made policy decisions (as on war, treaties, finances, church relations), and under a powerful ruler the curia often became active as a court of law. In England, the Curia Regis (King's Court), which began at the time of the Norman Conquest (1066), was the germ from which the higher courts of law, the Privy Council, and the Cabinet were to spring. See also ROMAN CURIA.

Curia, Roman See ROMAN CURIA

Curie, Frédéric Joliot- See Frédéric JOLIOT-CURIE

Curie \kyùr-'ē\ **Marie** *orig.* Maria Sklodowska (1867–1934) Polish-French physical chemist. Seeking for RADIOACTIVITY, recently discovered by Henri BECQUEREL in uranium, in other matter, she found it in thorium. In 1895 she married fellow physicist Pierre Curie (1859–1906). Together they discovered the elements polonium and RADIUM, and they distinguished alpha, beta, and gamma radiation. For their work on radioactivity (a term she coined), the Curies shared a 1903 Nobel Prize with Becquerel. After Pierre's death, Marie assumed his professorship and became the first woman to teach at the Sorbonne. In 1911 she won a Nobel Prize for discovering polonium and isolating pure radium, becoming the first

Marie Curie

person to win two Nobel Prizes. She died of leukemia caused by her long exposure to radioactivity. See also Frédéric JOLIOT-CURIE.

Curitiba \ˌkùr-ə-'tē-bə\ City (pop., 1996: 1,476,000), capital of Paraná state, S Brazil. It lies about 3,050 ft (930 m) above sea level in the Brazilian Highlands near the headwaters of the IGUAZÚ RIVER. Founded in 1654 as a gold-mining camp, it became the state capital in 1854. European immigration was followed by the arrival of Syrians and Japanese. Its cathedral (1894) was inspired by that of BARCELONA.

curlew Any of eight species (genus *Numenius*) of shorebirds having a sickle-shaped bill that curves downward at the tip, a streaked, gray or brown body, and a long neck and legs. Curlews breed inland in temperate and subarctic regions of the Northern Hemisphere and migrate far south. They eat insects and seeds during migration but feed on worms and fiddler crabs while wintering on marshes and coastal mudflats. The eastern curlew is the largest species (24 in., or 60 cm, long).

Curley, James Michael (1874–1958) U.S. politician. Born in Boston, he served in the U.S. House of Representatives (1911–14, 1943–47). As mayor (1914–18, 1922–26, 1930–34, 1947–50), he colorfully dominated Boston politics for 50 years. He owed much of his success to serving the needs of Irish immigrants in exchange for votes, spending large sums on job-rich public-works projects that nearly bankrupted Boston, and continued to do so as governor of Massachusetts (1935–37). His last mayoral term included a five-month jail term for mail fraud before Pres. Harry TRUMAN pardoned him.

curling Game in which two teams of four players each slide an ellipsoidal stone by means of a gooseneck handle over a 138-ft (42-m) stretch of ice toward a target circle (the house). Stones average 40 lbs (18.1 kg) and may not weigh more than 44 lbs (20 kg). Team members use brooms to sweep the ice ahead of the oncoming stone to facilitate a longer slide. Curling originated in Scotland in the 16th cent. Curling became an Olympic sport in 1992.

Curling Players sweeping as a teammate's stone nears the house

currant Any shrub of at least 100 species in the genus *Ribes,* in the GOOSEBERRY family, native to temperate climates of the Northern Hemisphere and W S. America. The Rocky Mtns. are especially rich in species. The red or black berries are used chiefly in jams and jellies. Currants are extremely high in vitamin C and also supply calcium, phosphorus, and iron. The name currant is also given to a seedless raisin frequently used in cooking.

currency In industrialized nations, the portion of the national money supply (consisting of banknotes and government-issued paper money and coins) that does not require endorsement to serve as a medium of exchange. Since the abandonment of the GOLD STANDARD, governments have not been obligated to repay the holders of currency in any form of precious metal. Consequently, the volume of currency has been determined solely by the actions of the government or CENTRAL BANK.

current, density See DENSITY CURRENT

current, electric See ELECTRIC CURRENT

Currier and Ives U.S. lithographers. Nathaniel Currier (1813–1888), born in Roxbury, Mass., set up in business in New York City in 1835. He hired the New York-born James Merritt Ives (1824–1895) as a bookkeeper and made him his partner in 1857. Currier & Ives met and greatly increased the public demand for graphic images by publishing fine-quality, black-and-white and hand-colored lithographs (see LITHOGRAPHY) depicting disasters, political satire, views of city life, outdoor country scenes, and sentimental domestic scenes. Between 1840 and 1890 they published more than 7,000 titles. The firm continued under their sons until 1907.

curry (from Tamil *kari,* "sauce") Food, dish, or sauce in Asian cuisine seasoned with a mixture of pungent spices such as turmeric, cumin, and cayenne pepper. Some curry spices are known for their antiseptic and preservative properties. Curries have been a part of S and SE Asian cookery since antiquity. The curries of S India, Thailand, and Myanmar are the most pungent, often containing hot chilies.

curtain wall Nonbearing wall of glass, metal, or masonry attached to a building's exterior structural frame. After World War II, low energy costs propelled the concept of the tall building as a glass prism, an idea originally put forth by LE CORBUSIER and Ludwig MIES VAN DER ROHE in the 1920s. The U.N.'s Secretariat Building (1949), with its green-tinted glass walls, helped set a worldwide standard for skyscrapers.

Curtis, Charles Gordon (1860–1953) U.S. inventor. Born in Boston, he became an associate of Thomas EDISON. He patented the Curtis steam TURBINE in 1896. Its principles are still used in large naval vessels; General Electric Co. has used it worldwide in its power installations. Curtis is also credited with inventing the first U.S. gas turbine and helped develop propulsion mechanisms for naval torpedoes.

Curtis, Cyrus (Herman Kotzschmar) (1850–1933) U.S. publisher. Born in Portland, Me., he began publishing a local weekly there. After moving to Boston and then Philadelphia, he founded *The Tribune and Farmer,* (1879) from which he formed the *Ladies' Home Journal.* In 1890 he organized the Curtis Publishing Co. Later acquisitions included *The Saturday Evening Post* (1897); *The Country Gentleman* (1911); the *Philadelphia Public Ledger* (1913); and the *Philadelphia Inquirer* (1930). His daughter founded the Curtis Institute of Music (1924).

Curtiss, Glenn (Hammond) (1878–1930) U.S. aviation pioneer. Born in Hammondsport, N.Y., he initially built engines for motorcycles. In 1908 he flew an experimental plane to win the first public U.S. flight of 1 km (0.6 mi). In 1911 he built the first practical SEAPLANE and was awarded the first contract to build airplanes for the U.S. Navy. His factories later supplied planes to Britain and Russia as well. His best-known plane was the JN-4, or "Jenny," a trainer widely used in World War I and later by barnstormers.

Curtiz, Michael \kər-'tēz, 'kùr-tis\ *orig.* Mihaly Kertesz (1888–1962) Hungarian-U.S. film director. He directed films in Hungary and elsewhere in Europe before he was invited to Hollywood by Warner Brothers in 1926. He directed more than 100 Warner Brothers films, including adventure movies with Errol FLYNN such as *Captain Blood* (1935), *The Adventures of Robin Hood* (1938), and *The Sea Hawk* (1940). His many other notable films include *Yankee Doodle Dandy* (1942), the hugely successful *Casablanca* (1942, Academy Award), and *White Christmas* (1954).

curve In mathematics, an abstract term used to describe the path of a continuously moving point (see CONTINUITY). Such a path is usually generated by an equation. The word can also apply to a straight line or to a series of line segments linked end to end. A closed curve is a path that repeats itself, and thus encloses one or more regions (e.g., CIRCLES, ELLIPSES, and POLYGONS). Open curves such as PARABOLAS, HYPERBOLAS, and spirals have infinite length.

Curzon (of Kedleston) \'kər-zᵊn\, **Marquess** *orig.* George Nathaniel Curzon *known as* Lord Curzon (1859–1925) British viceroy of India (1898–1905). Son of a baron, he entered Parliament in 1886. A world tour left him with an infatuation for Asia, and in 1891 he became undersecretary of state for India. Named viceroy of India (1898), he reduced taxes and ordered immediate punishment of any Briton who ill-treated Indian nationals. He presided over the unpopular Partition of Bengal and resigned after a clash with Lord KITCHENER. He later served in the cabinets of H. H. ASQUITH and David LLOYD GEORGE.

Cush *or* **Kush** Ancient country, NUBIA region of the NILE RIVER valley. In the 2nd millennium B.C. it was subject to Egypt. In the 8th cent. B.C. its King Piankhi invaded and conquered Egypt. It was ruled from 716 B.C. by Piankhi's brother Shabaka, who also invaded Egypt, and set up the 25th dynasty; he subsequently made MEMPHIS his capital. In the early 6th cent. B.C. the Cushite kingdom's capital was transferred to Meroë, where the Cushites ruled for another 900 years.

Cushing \'kùsh-iŋ\, **Harvey Williams** (1869–1939) U.S. surgeon. Born in Cleveland, he became known as the leading neurosurgeon of the early 20th cent., developing many procedures still basic to BRAIN SURGERY and greatly reducing its mortality rate. The leading expert in the diagnosis and treatment of intracranial tumors, he was also the first to ascribe to pituitary-gland malfunction what is now known as Cushing's disease (see CUSHING'S SYNDROME). His biography of Sir William Osler (1925) won a Pulitzer Prize.

Cushing's syndrome Metabolic disorder named for Harvey CUSHING, caused by adrenal-cortex overactivity, usually due to other diseases. If caused by a PITUITARY-GLAND tumor, it is called Cushing's disease. Symptoms include obesity of the trunk and face ("moon face"), muscle wasting, high blood pressure, easy bruising, osteoporosis, diabetes mellitus, and fat between the shoulders ("buffalo hump"). Excess glucocorticoid HORMONES, whether produced by the ADRENAL GLAND or given as drugs, cause the symptoms, which are treated by surgery, radiation, cortisol-blocking drugs, or ending of steroid treatment.

Cushman, Charlotte (Saunders) (1816–1876) U.S. actress. She made her opera debut in her native Boston at 19, but her singing voice soon failed and she turned to the stage. In 1837 she first played her most popular role, Meg Merrilies in *Guy Mannering,* and became the first native-born U.S. star. From 1842 she managed a theater in Philadelphia, where she starred with William MACREADY in *Macbeth.* Noted for her powerful emotional reach, she also took on such male roles as Romeo and Hamlet.

Custer, George Armstrong (1839–1876) U.S. cavalry officer. Born in New Rumley, Ohio, he graduated from West Point and at 23 became a brigadier general. His pursuit of Confederate troops under Gen. Robert E. LEE in retreat from Richmond hastened Lee's surrender in 1865. In 1874 he led U.S. troops in search of gold in the BLACK HILLS, a sacred Indian hunting ground; the resulting gold rush led to hostile encounters with the Indians. In 1876 Custer commanded one of two columns advancing on Indians camped near Montana's Little Bighorn River; his rash attack in the Battle of the LITTLE BIGHORN ended in disaster.

George Armstrong Custer

customs duty See TARIFF

customs union Trade agreement by which a group of countries charges a common set of TARIFFS to the rest of the world while allowing free trade among themselves. It is intermediate between free-trade zones, which allow mutual FREE TRADE but lack a common tariff system, and common markets, which utilize common tariffs and allow free movement of resources including capital and labor between members. Well-known customs unions include the Zollverein, a 19th-cent. organization of German states, and the European Economic Community, which passed through a customs-union stage on the path to fuller economic integration. See also EUROPEAN COMMUNITY, N. AMERICAN FREE TRADE AGREEMENT, WORLD TRADE ORGANIZATION.

cuttlefish Any of about 100 species of marine CEPHALOPODS in the order Sepioidea, characterized by an internal shell called the cuttlebone. Species range between 1 and 35 in. (2.5–90 cm) in length. All have large heads surrounded by eight arms and two longer tentacles used to capture prey. The arms and the tips of the tentacles bear suction cups. Notable for their apparent intelligence, cuttlefish can change color rapidly for protective camouflage or emit clouds of ink to hinder an attacker. They inhabit tropical or temperate coastal waters.

cutworm LARVA of certain species of owlet MOTHS (family Noctuidae). It is a serious pest of tobacco and other crops. Some species attack such plants as corn, grasses, tomatoes, and beans at night, severing roots and stems near ground level. Other species live underground and feed on plant roots.

Cuvier \kū̄-'vyā\, **Georges (-Léopold-Chrétien-Frédéric-Dagobert)** *later* **Baron Cuvier** (1769–1832) French zoologist who established the sciences of comparative ANATOMY and PALEONTOLOGY. As a staff member at the Museum of Natural History in Paris, he published his "correlation of parts" theory (1817), in which every animal organ is functionally related to all its other organs and an animal's func-

tions and habits determine its anatomic form. Cuvier's classification of animals into four discrete groups was a significant advance over the system of Carolus LINNAEUS. He applied his functional concept to the study of fossils, and his work put paleontology on a firm empirical foundation. As Napoleon's inspector of public instruction, he helped establish France's provincial universities, and he also served as chancellor of the Univ. of Paris.

Cuyahoga River \ˌkī-ə-'hȯ-gə, ˌkī-ə-'hō-gə\ River, NE Ohio. It flows past AKRON, where it drops into a deep valley and turns north, emptying into Lake ERIE at CLEVELAND. It is navigable for lake freighters for only about 5 mi (8 km) of its total length of about 80 mi (130 km). It was at one time so severely polluted that it caught fire; by the late 1970s, antipollution measures had substantially improved its condition.

Cuyp \'kœip\, **Aelbert Jacobsz(oon)** (1620–1691) Most famous member of a family of Dutch landscape painters. Trained by his father, Jacob Gerritsz Cuyp (1594–after 1651), he lived most of his life in his native Dordrecht, painting animals and birds, portraits, and most notably river scenes and landscapes with cattle and figures bathed in a subtle glow of light and atmosphere. Many of his surviving paintings are signed but few are dated.

Cuzco \'kü-skō\ City (pop., 1998 est.: 278,000), S central Peru. It is located high in the ANDES at an elevation of 11,152 ft (3,399 m). Founded in the 11th cent., it was once the capital of the vast INCA empire and was known as the "City of the Sun." Francisco PIZARRO captured the city in 1533. It suffered major earthquake damage in 1950. Nearby ruins include an ancient Inca fortress, MACHU PICCHU, and the Temple of the Sun. Its cathedral (1654) and university (1692) date from the colonial era.

cyanide \'sī-ə-ˌnīd\ Any compound containing the combining group of chemical formula –CN. Ionic (see ION, IONIC BOND) and organic cyanide compounds differ in chemical properties, but both are toxic, especially the ionic ones. Cyanide poisoning is extremely rapid, and an ANTIDOTE must be given promptly. Cyanides occur naturally in certain seeds (e.g., apple seeds, wild cherry pits). Cyanides, including hydrogen cyanide (HCN, or hydrocyanic acid), are used industrially in the production of synthetic rubber and other plastics as well as in electroplating, case-hardening of iron and steel, fumigation, and concentration of ORES.

cyanobacteria \ˌsī-ə-ˌnō-bak-'tir-ē-ə\ *or* **blue-green algae** Any of a large group of prokaryotic, mostly photosynthetic organisms. Though classified as BACTERIA, they resemble the eukaryotic ALGAE in many ways, including some physical characteristics and ecological niches. They contain certain pigments, which, with their chlorophyll, often give them a blue-green color, though many species are actually green, brown, yellow, black, or red. They are common in soil and in both salt and fresh water, and can grow over a wide range of temperatures. They are often among the first species to colonize bare rock and soil. Some are capable of NITROGEN FIXATION; others can produce free oxygen as a by-product of PHOTOSYNTHESIS. They may reproduce explosively in nitrogen-polluted waters, forming dense concentrations called blooms, usually colored an opaque green. Cyanobacteria played a large role in raising the level of free oxygen in the atmosphere of early earth.

Cybele See GREAT MOTHER OF THE GODS

cybernetics Science of regulation and control in animals (including humans), organizations, and machines when they are viewed as self-governing systems consisting of parts and their organization. It was conceived by Norbert WIENER, who coined the term in 1948. Cybernetics views communication and control in all self-contained complex systems as analogous. It differs from the empirical sciences (physics, biology, etc.) in not being interested in material form but in organization, pattern, and communication. Because of the increasing sophistication of computers and the efforts to make them behave in humanlike ways, cybernetics today is closely allied with ARTIFICIAL INTELLIGENCE and ROBOTICS.

Cyclades \'sī-klə-ˌdēz\ *Greek* **Kikládhes** \kē-'klä-thēs\ Group of about 220 islands, S Aegean Sea. They cover a land area of 976 sq mi (2,528 sq km), and constitute the Cyclades de-

partment (pop., 1991: 94,000) of Greece. Their name refers to the ancient tradition that they formed a circle around the sacred island of DELOS. The chief islands include Andros, NAXOS, Melos, and THÍRA. They were the center of a Bronze Age culture, the Cycladic, noted for its white marble idols, and later belonged to the MYCENAEAN culture in the 2nd millennium B.C. Colonized by Ionians in the 10th–9th cent. B.C., they later were successively held by Persians, Athenians, Ptolemaic Egypt, Macedonia, and Venice. They fell to the Turks in 1566, and became part of Greece in 1829. The economy is now based on tourism and exports.

cycling Use of the BICYCLE in competitive sport or in recreation. The classic professional races are held mainly in Europe; the first was held in Paris in 1868. There are basically two types of race: road races and track races. The first U.S. cycling competition, a six-day race, was held in 1891. Six-day racing was reintroduced to Europe as a two-man team event in the 20th cent., but it has largely died out in the U.S. The first TOUR DE FRANCE, the premier race, was held in 1903.

cyclone Any large system of winds that rotates about a center of low atmospheric pressure in a counterclockwise direction north of the equator and in a clockwise direction south of it. Anticyclones rotate in the opposite directions. Cyclones occur chiefly in the midlatitudes, often over the oceans. Cyclones that form in the tropics are smaller but more violent (see TROPICAL CYCLONE).

Cyclops \'sī-ˌkläps\ In GREEK MYTHOLOGY, any of several one-eyed giants. In the *Odyssey*, the Cyclopes were cannibals who lived in a faraway land. ODYSSEUS was captured by the cyclops POLYPHEMUS. According to HESIOD, there were three Cyclopes, who forged thunderbolts for ZEUS. In a later tradition, they assisted HEPHAESTUS in this task. Apollo destroyed them after one of their thunderbolts killed ASCLEPIUS.

cyclotron \'sī-klə-ˌträn\ PARTICLE ACCELERATOR that accelerates charged atomic or SUBATOMIC PARTICLES in a constant MAGNETIC FIELD. It consists of two hollow semicircular ELECTRODES, called dees, in a large evacuated cylindrical box. An alternating ELECTRIC FIELD between the dees continuously accelerates the particles from one dee to the other, while the magnetic field guides them in a circular path. A cyclotron can accelerate protons to energies of up to 25 million electron volts.

Cydones \sī-'dō-nēz\, **Demetrius** (1324?–1398?) Byzantine humanist scholar, statesman, and theologian. After studying under a Greek scholar, he made Greek translations of AUGUSTINE and THOMAS AQUINAS. He was twice prime minister of the Byzantine empire (1369–83, 1391–96). An academy of Greek culture that he established in Venice in 1390 diffused Greek thought throughout Italy, stimulating the Italian Renaissance. A convert to Latin Catholicism, he worked unsuccessfully for East–West Christian unity. He is considered the most brilliant Byzantine writer of the 14th cent.

Cygnus A \'sig-nəs\ Brightest cosmic source of radio waves in the sky, lying in the constellation Cygnus, about 700 million light-years from earth. It was once thought to be two galaxies colliding, but this would not account for its immense energy output. Instead, it may be a relatively nearby QUASAR whose central source is obscured by a surrounding dust cloud. See also ACTIVE GALACTIC NUCLEUS.

cylinder See PISTON AND CYLINDER

cymbal Percussion instrument consisting of a circular metal plate that is struck with a drumstick or two such plates that are struck together. Cymbals are of great antiquity (dating back to at least 1200 B.C.) and universality. They reached Europe by the 13th cent. A.D. They were uncommon in Western orchestras until the late 18th cent. Though Asian cymbals are often flat, Middle Eastern and Western cymbals usually have a central concave dome, or boss, so that only the edges touch when they are clashed. In popular music, a cymbal suspended on a sticklike stand may be brushed or struck, and horizontal "hi-hat" cymbals are clashed lightly by use of a pedal mechanism.

Cynewulf *or* **Kynewulf** 'kin-ə-ˌwùlf\ *or* **Cynwulf** \'kin-ˌwùlf\ (fl.8th or 9th cent. A.D.) Anglo-Saxon poet. He is the author of four Old English poems from late-10th-cent. manu-

scripts: *Elene*, about St. Helena; *The Fates of the Apostles*, on the mission and death of each Apostle; *The Ascension*, part of a trilogy by different authors; and *Juliana*, a life of St. Juliana. Nothing is known of the poet outside of the text.

Cynics \'si-niks\ Greek philosophical sect that flourished from the 4th cent. B.C. to the 6th cent. A.D. Antisthenes (c.445–365 B.C.), a disciple of SOCRATES, is considered its founder, but DIOGENES OF SINOPE was its paradigm. Named principally for their meeting place, the Cynosarges, the Cynics considered virtue—including a life of poverty and self-sufficiency and the suppression of desires—to be the sole good. They were known for their unconventional manners and way of life. The Cynics influenced the development of STOICISM.

cypress Any of about 20 species of ornamental and timber evergreen CONIFERS constituting the genus *Cupressus* of the family Cupressaceae, which includes more than 130 species found throughout the world. The leaves are usually paired or in threes and are small and scalelike. The *Cupressus, Thuja*, and *Juniperus* (JUNIPER) genera are especially important as timber sources or ornamentals. They also contain useful oils, resins, and tannins.

Cyprian \'sip-rē-ən\, **St.** *Latin* Thascius Caecilius Cyprianus (c.A.D. 200–258) Early Christian theologian and church father. Born in Carthage, he converted to Christianity around A.D. 246. Within two years he was elected bishop of Carthage, and in 250 he went into hiding to escape the Decian persecution. The following year he returned; bishops in council supported his assertions that the church could remit the sin of apostasy and that bishops in council had final disciplinary authority. Cyprian asserted that the people and their bishop constituted the church, that there was no "bishop of bishops" in Rome. He was martyred under Valerian.

Cyprus *officially* **Republic of Cyprus** *Greek* **Kypros** \'kē-prós\ *Turkish* **Kibris** \'kē-bris\ Island nation, NE Mediterranean Sea. Area: 3,572 sq mi (9,251 sq km). Population (2000): 865,000 (whole island). Capital: NICOSIA (Lefkosia).

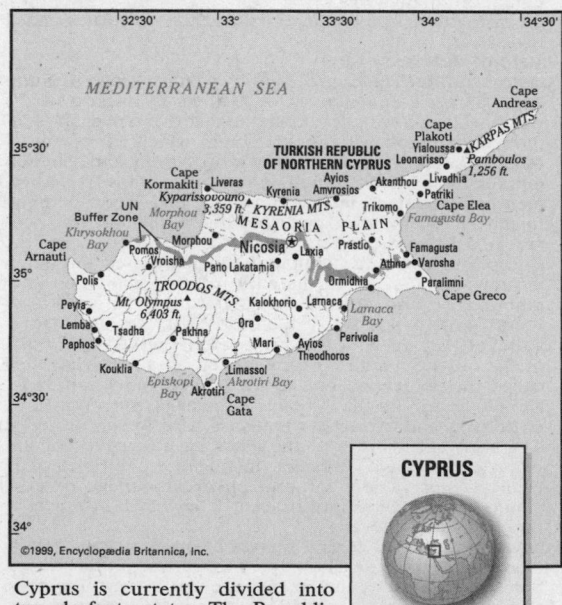

©1999, Encyclopædia Britannica, Inc.

Cyprus is currently divided into two de facto states. The Republic of Cyprus, the internationally recognized government, occupies the S two-thirds of the island. Its population (2000: 673,000) is predominantly Greek. Language: Greek (official). Religion: Eastern Orthodoxy. Currency: Cyprus pound. The Turkish Republic of Northern Cyprus occupies the N third of the country. Its population (2000: 192,000) is overwhelmingly Turkish. Language: Turkish (official), English. Religion: Islam. Currency: Turkish lira. The third-largest island in the Mediterranean, Cyprus lies about 40 mi (65 km) south of Turkey. It is largely mountainous, with a fertile heartland and coastal plains. Mt. Olympus is its highest peak, at 6,401 ft (1,951 m). The climate is Mediterranean. Cyprus has a free-enterprise economy based mainly on trade and manufacturing, and it ranks high in the world in merchant shipping. The internationally recognized government is a multiparty republic with a unicameral legislature; its head of state and government is the president. Cyprus was inhabited by the early NEOLITHIC PERIOD; by the late BRONZE AGE it had been visited and settled by MYCENAEANS and Achaeans, who introduced Greek culture and language, and it became a trading center. By 800 B.C. PHOENICIANS had begun to settle there. Ruled over the centuries by the Assyrian, Persian, and Ptolemaic empires, it was annexed by Rome in 58 B.C. It was part of the Byzantine empire in the 4th–11th cent. A.D. It was conquered by RICHARD I in 1191. A part of the Venetian empire from 1489, it was taken by Ottoman Turks in 1573. In 1878 the British assumed control, and Cyprus became a British crown colony in 1924. It gained independence in 1960. Conflict between Greek and Turkish Cypriots led to the establishment of a U.N. peacekeeping mission in 1964. In 1974, fearing a movement to unite Cyprus with Greece, Turkish soldiers occupied the N third of the country and Turkish Cypriots established a functioning government, which obtained recognition only from Turkey. Conflict has continued to the present, and the U.N. peacekeeping mission has remained in place. Reunification talks have remained deadlocked.

Cyrano de Bergerac \'sir-ə-ˌnō-də-ˌber-zhə-'räk\, **Savinien** (1619–1655) French dramatist. A soldier until 1641, he wrote plays and fantastical works, combining science-fantasy and political satire, that inspired such later writers as Jonathan SWIFT. He became the basis of many romantic legends, including Edmond ROSTAND's play *Cyrano de Bergerac* (1897), in which he is portrayed as a gallant but shy lover, with a remarkably large nose (which in fact he had).

Cyrenaica *or* **Cirenaica** \ˌsir-ə-'nā-ə-kə\ NE region of present-day Libya. It was colonized by the Greeks (c.631 B.C.), and later the Romans (67 B.C.). Arab armies conquered it in A.D. 642, as did the Ottomans in the 15th cent. Italy colonized it in the early 20th cent., but Italian forces were expelled during World War II. In 1963 it was incorporated into Libya.

Cyrene \sī-'rē-nē\ Ancient city, N Africa. It was founded around 630 B.C. by a group of emigrants from the island of THÍRA. Under the aegis of Ptolemaic Egypt (from 323 B.C.), Cyrene became one of the great intellectual centers of the classical world, boasting such scholars as ERATOSTHENES and Aristippus, founder of the Cyrenaics. It declined under the Romans, and with the Arab conquest of A.D. 642 it ceased to exist. Excavations have uncovered impressive ruins.

Cyril and Methodius \'sir-əl...mi-'thō-dē-əs\, **Sts.** (827?–869; c.825–884) Christian missionaries. Born in Macedonia, the brothers began missionary work among the Slavs of Moravia in 863. Gifted scholars and linguists, they translated the Holy Scriptures into the language later known as OLD CHURCH SLAVIC and are credited with inventing the CYRILLIC ALPHABET. In 868 they traveled to Rome to defend the use of a Slavic liturgy. When Cyril died, Methodius returned to Moravia as an archbishop. Known as the "apostles to the Slavs," the two brothers influenced the religious and cultural development of all Slavic peoples.

Cyrillic alphabet \sə-'ril-ik\ ALPHABET used for Russian, Serbian (see SERBIAN AND CROATIAN LANGUAGE), BULGARIAN and Macedonian, Belarusian, UKRAINIAN, and many non-Slavic languages of the former Soviet Union, as well as Khalka Mongolian (see MONGOLIAN LANGUAGES). The Cyrillic alphabet is derived from 9th-cent. Greek uncial capital letters, with the non-Greek letters probably taken from an alphabet in which (along with Cyrillic) OLD CHURCH SLAVIC was written. Many scholars believe that followers of Sts. CYRIL AND METHODIUS developed Cyrillic in the S Balkans around the end of the 9th cent. The 44 original Cyrillic letters were reduced in number for vernacular languages, and some wholly original letters were introduced for non-Slavic languages. See table at RUSSIAN LANGUAGE.

Cyril of Alexandria, St. (c.A.D. 375–444) Christian theologian and bishop. He became bishop of Alexandria in 412. Zealously orthodox, he closed the churches of the Novatians, a heterodox sect, and expelled the Jews from Alexandria. He clashed with NESTORIUS over the nature of JESUS; Cyril emphasized the unity of Jesus' divine and human natures notably at the Council of Ephesus (431) while Nestorius emphasized their distinctness. Eventually Nestorius was declared a heretic and a compromise on Christ's nature restored peace to the church (433).

Cyrus the Great *or* **Cyrus II** (c.585–529? B.C.) Conqueror and founder of the ACHAEMENIAN DYNASTY. He came to power by overthrowing his grandfather, the king of the Medes. The empire he developed was thenceforth centered on Persia and included Media, Ionia, Lydia, Mesopotamia, Syria, and Palestine. Cyrus conquered by diplomacy as well as by force. The subject of a rich legend in Persia and Greece, he was called the father of his people. He appears in the Bible as the liberator of the Jews held captive in Babylon. He died battling nomads in Central Asia. His legacy is the founding not only of an empire but of a culture and civilization that continued to expand after his death and lasted for two centuries. He exerted a strong influence on the Greeks and ALEXANDER THE GREAT. He has long been revered by Persians almost as a religious figure.

cyst \'sist\ Enclosed sac within body tissues. It has a distinct MEMBRANE and generally contains liquid. Most cysts are benign, but several kinds may be malignant or precancerous. Benign cysts often press on nearby organs and require removal. They can contain natural secretions, abnormal breakdown products, or bacteria, larval parasites, and microbial products. Some organs, including the kidney, liver, and breast, can become filled with cysts as a result of cystic diseases that may be dangerous or may hide more serious diseases. See also TUMOR.

cystic fibrosis \'sis-tik-fī-'brō-səs\, **(CF)** *or* **mucoviscidosis** \ˌmyü-kō-ˌvis-ə-'dō-səs\ Inherited metabolic disorder characterized by production of thick, sticky mucus. It is recessive (see RECESSIVENESS) and the most common inherited disorder (about 1 per 2,000 live births) in those of European ancestry. Concentrated mucous secretions in the lungs plug the bronchi, making breathing difficult, promoting infections, and producing chronic cough, recurrent pneumonia, and progressive loss of lung function, the usual cause of death. Treatment includes enzyme supplements, a diet high in calories, protein, and fat, vigorous physical therapy, and antibiotics. Affected persons once seldom survived beyond childhood; now more than half reach adulthood.

cystitis \sis-'tī-təs\ INFLAMMATION of the urinary bladder (see URINARY SYSTEM). Infections with bacteria, viruses, fungi, or parasites usually spread from nearby sites. Symptoms include burning pain during and right after urination, unusually urgent or frequent urination, and lower back pain. Women are more susceptible to cystitis, most resulting from *E. coli* bacteria from the rectum. Recurrent or persistent infection can lead to chronic cystitis, with bladder-wall thickening. Diagnosis is made by finding bacteria or other organisms in the (normally sterile) urine. It is treated with drugs or surgery.

cytochrome \'sī-tə-ˌkrōm\ Any of a group of cell PROTEINS that serve a vital function in the transfer of energy within cells. Their protein component is linked to a nonprotein, iron-bearing component (a heme group), which can undergo the reversible OXIDATION-REDUCTION reactions that yield energy for the cell. At least 30 different cytochromes have been identified.

cytology \sī-'tä-lə-jē\ Study of CELLS. Its earliest phase began with Robert HOOKE's microscopic investigations of cork in 1665, during which he introduced the term "cell." M. J. SCHLEIDEN (in 1838) and Theodor SCHWANN (1839) were among the first to state clearly that cells are the fundamental units of both plants and animals. In 1892 Oscar Hertwig (1849–1922) suggested that processes at the organism's level are reflections of cellular processes, thus establishing cytology as a separate branch of biology. See also PHYSIOLOGY.

cytomegalovirus (CMV) Any of several VIRUSES in the herpes family. Most prevalent in crowded, poor communities, it is transmitted by sexual contact or infected body fluids but is not highly contagious and rarely causes serious illness in healthy adults; however, it can lead to serious consequences, including blindness, in those with depressed immune systems. In newborns, CMV is the most common congenital infection and a major cause of congenital deafness; it may also induce retardation and blindness. There is no effective treatment.

cytoplasm \\'sī-tə-ˌpla-zəm\\ Portion of a eukaryotic CELL (see EUKARYOTE) outside the NUCLEUS. The cytoplasm contains all the organelles except the nucleus itself, including the mitochondria (see MITOCHONDRION), CHLOROPLASTS, ENDOPLASMIC RETICULUM, Golgi apparatus (which packages large molecules for transport), LYSOSOMES, and peroxisomes. The cytoplasm also contains the CYTOSKELETON and the cytosol (the fluid mass that surrounds the various organelles). See also VACUOLE.

cytosine \\'sī-tə-ˌsēn\\ Organic compound of the PYRIMIDINE family, consisting of a single ring, containing both nitrogen and carbon atoms, and an amino group. It occurs in combined form in NUCLEIC ACIDS and several coenzymes. In DNA its complementary base is GUANINE. It or its corresponding NUCLEOSIDE or NUCLEOTIDE is made from DNA by HYDROLYSIS.

cytoskeleton \\'sī-tə-ˌske-lə-tᵊn\\ System of microscopic filaments or fibers, present in the CYTOPLASM of eukaryotic cells (see EUKARYOTE), that organizes other cell components, maintains cell shape, and is responsible for cell locomotion and for movement of the organelles within it. Three major types of filaments make up the cytoskeleton: actin filaments, MICROTUBULES, and intermediate filaments. Actin filaments occur as constantly changing bundles of parallel fibers, playing a role in cell shape, movement, adhesion, and division. Intermediate filaments are very stable structures that form the cell's true skeleton.

czar *or* **tsar** \\'zär, '(t)sär\\ Byzantine or Russian emperor. The title, derived from "caesar," was used in the Middle Ages to refer to a supreme ruler, particularly the Byzantine emperor. With the fall of the Byzantine empire in 1453, the Russian Orthodox clergy considered the Russian monarch a possible new supreme head of Orthodox Christianity. IVAN IV was the first to be crowned czar, in 1547. Though theoretically wielding absolute power, he and his successors were actually limited by the power of the church, the BOYAR council, and legal codes. In 1721 PETER I changed his title to "emperor of all Russia," but he and his successors continued to be popularly called czars.

Czech language *formerly* **Bohemian language** W. SLAVIC LANGUAGE spoken by close to 12 million people in the historical regions of Bohemia, Moravia, and SW Silesia, all now in the Czech Republic. The earliest Old Czech texts date from the late 13th cent. The Czech spelling system, which adds diacritics to letters of the LATIN ALPHABET to denote consonants that did not exist in Latin and to mark vowel length, was introduced in the early 15th cent. The system was later adopted by other Slavic languages using the Latin alphabet, including Slovak, Slovene, and Croatian (see SERBIAN AND CROATIAN LANGUAGE). There is a wide gulf between Standard Czech, the literary language, and Common Czech, the spoken language.

Czech Republic *Czech* **Ceská Republika** \\'ches-kä-rä-'pùb-li-kə\\ *formerly (1918–92), with Slovakia,* **Czechoslovakia** Republic, central Europe. Area: 30,450 sq mi (78,864 sq km). Population (2000): 10,273,000. Capital: PRAGUE. Czechs make up nine-tenths of the population; Slovaks are the

CZECH REPUBLIC

Scale 1: 6,810,000

©1999, Encyclopædia Britannica, Inc.

largest minority. Language: Czech (official). Religion: Roman Catholicism, Protestantism. Currency: koruna. The landlocked Czech Republic is dominated by the Bohemian Massif, a ring of mountains rising to 3,000 ft (900 m) to encircle the Bohemian Plateau. The MORAVA RIVER valley, known as the Moravian Corridor, separates the Bohemian Massif from the CARPATHIAN MTNS. Woodlands are a characteristic feature of the Czech landscape; most regions have a moderate oceanic climate. The economy has been privatized since the collapse of communism and is now largely market-oriented. It is a multiparty republic with two legislative houses; its head of state is the president, and the head of government is the prime minister. Until 1918, the history of what is now the Czech Republic was largely that of BOHEMIA. In that year the independent republic of Czechoslovakia was born through the union of Bohemia and MORAVIA with SLOVAKIA. Czechoslovakia came under the domination of the Soviet Union after World War II, and from 1948 it was ruled by a Communist government. Its growing political liberalization was suppressed by a Soviet invasion in 1968 (see PRAGUE SPRING). After Communist rule collapsed in 1989–90, separatist sentiments emerged among the Slovaks, and in 1992 the Czechs and Slovaks agreed to break up their federated state. On Jan. 1, 1993, the Czechoslovakian republic was peacefully dissolved and replaced by two new countries, the Czech Republic and Slovakia, with the region of Moravia remaining in the former. In 1999 it joined NATO, and it has pursued membership talks with the EUROPEAN UNION.

Czerny \\'cher-nē\\, **Karl** (1791–1857) Austrian composer, teacher, and pianist. He made his piano debut at 9 and began study with Ludwig van BEETHOVEN at 10. A brilliant pianist, he later became a famous piano teacher; his students included Franz LISZT. Though his compositions include six symphonies, six piano concertos, and 11 piano sonatas, he is known today almost exclusively for his hundreds of piano exercises and études.

D

dabbling duck Any of about 43 species (tribe Anatini; including 38 species in genus *Anas*) of DUCKS found worldwide, chiefly on inland waters and in temperate regions of the Northern Hemisphere. Strongly migratory, dabbling ducks include some of the world's finest game birds: the black duck, the gadwall, the garganey, the MALLARD, the pintail (perhaps the world's most abundant waterfowl), the shoveler, the TEALS, and the wigeons. They feed mainly on water plants, which they obtain by tipping-up in shallows, and infrequently by diving. They have a flat, broad bill, float high in the water, and are swift fliers.

Dabbling duck Common, or northern, pintail *(Anas acuta)*

Dacca See DHAKA

Dachau \'dä-ˌkaủ\ First Nazi CONCENTRATION CAMP in Germany, established in 1933. The model for all other ss-organized camps, in World War II it was supplemented by about 150 branches in S Germany and Austria, which were collectively called Dachau. It was the first camp at which laboratories were set up to perform medical experiments on inmates. Such experiments and the harsh living conditions made Dachau one of the most notorious camps, though it was not designed as an extermination camp.

dachshund \'däks-ˌhủnd, 'däk-sənt\ Dog breed of HOUND and TERRIER ancestry developed in Germany to pursue BADGERS (German, *Dachs*) into their burrows. It is a long-bodied, lively dog with a deep chest, short legs, tapering muzzle, and long ears. It is bred in three coat types (smooth, long, and wiry). The standard dachshund stands about 7–10 in. (18–25 cm) high and weighs 16–32 lbs (7–14.5 kg); the miniature is shorter and weighs less than 9 lbs (4 kg).

Dacia \'dā-shə\ Ancient country, central Europe. Roughly equivalent to modern Romania, it is known for its rich silver, iron, and gold mines. The region was made a Roman province in A.D. 107 after two centuries of hostilities. It was abandoned to the Goths in 270 and ultimately divided into WALACHIA and MOLDAVIA.

Dada \'dä-ˌdä\ Nihilistic movement in the arts that originated in Zurich in 1916 and flourished in New York, Berlin, and Paris in the early 20th cent. The name, French for "hobbyhorse," selected by a chance procedure, was adopted by a group of artists, including Jean ARP, Marcel DUCHAMP, Man RAY, and Francis PICABIA, to symbolize their emphasis on the illogical and absurd, growing out of disgust with bourgeois values and despair over World War I. The archetypal Dada forms of expression were the nonsense poem and the READY-MADE. Its highly influential creative techniques of accident and chance were sustained in SURREALISM, ABSTRACT EXPRESSIONISM, CONCEPTUAL ART, and POP ART.

Daddi \'däd-dē\, **Bernardo** (fl.c.1320–1348) Italian painter. A leading painter in Florence after the death of his teacher, GIOTTO, he specialized in devotional panels and altarpieces. His works include a triptych for the Church of Ognissanti (1328) and the polyptych *Crucifixion with Eight Saints* (1348). His influential style, a fusion of Giotto's seriousness and the lightness of Sienese art, featured smiling Madonnas and abundant flowers and draperies.

daddy longlegs *or* **harvestman** Any of the 3,400 ARACHNID species constituting the order Opiliones. Daddy longlegs differ from SPIDERS in having extremely long, thin legs and a spherical or oval body that is not divided in two. The fragile legs may be 20 times the body length. Adults have a pair of glands that secrete a foul-smelling fluid. Daddy longlegs are very widely distributed in temperate regions and in the tropics. They feed on insects, mites, spiders, carrion, and vegetable matter.

Daedalus \'de-də-ləs, 'dē-də-ləs\ In GREEK MYTHOLOGY, the architect who built for King MINOS of Crete the Labyrinth in which the MINOTAUR was kept. Later the king imprisoned Daedalus, who then made wings for himself and his son Icarus so they could fly to freedom. Despite his father's warnings, Icarus flew too close to the sun; the wax holding the feathers to his wings melted, and he fell into the sea and drowned.

daemon See DEMON

daffodil Bulb-forming flowering plant *(Narcissus pseudonarcissus)*, native to N Europe and widely cultivated. It grows to about 16 in. (40 cm) and has five or six leaves about 12 in. (30 cm) long that grow from the bulb. The stem bears one large yellow trumpet-shaped blossom. The daffodil's popularity has resulted in the production of many varieties differing mainly in color.

da Gama, Vasco See Vasco da GAMA

Dagobert I \'dag-ə-ˌbərt\ (605–639) Last Frankish king of the MEROVINGIAN DYNASTY to rule a politically united realm. He became king of AUSTRASIA in 623 and of all the Franks in 629. He secured a treaty with the Byzantine emperor, defeated the Gascons and Bretons, and campaigned against the Slavs in the east. He moved his capital to Paris, then made his son king of Austrasia in 634. Dagobert also revised Frankish law, patronized the arts, and founded the great abbey of St.-Denis.

Daguerre \dà-'ger\, **Louis (-Jacques-Mandé)** (1787–1851) French inventor. Initially a scene painter for the opera, in 1822 he opened the Diorama, an exhibition of views with effects induced by changes in lighting. In 1826 Nicéphore NIEPCE learned of Daguerre's experiments in obtaining permanent pictures by the action of sunlight, and the two became partners in the development of Niepce's heliographic process. After Niepce's death in 1833, Daguerre discovered that exposing an iodized silver plate in a camera would create a lasting image if the latent image on the plate was developed and fixed. In 1839 a description of his DAGUERRE-OTYPE process was announced at the Academy of Sciences.

daguerreotype \də-'ge-rō-ˌtīp\ First successful form of PHOTOGRAPHY. It is named for Louis DAGUERRE, who invented the technique in collaboration with Nicéphore NIEPCE. They found that if a copper plate coated with silver iodide was exposed to light in a CAMERA, then fumed with mercury vapor and fixed (made permanent) by a solution of common salt, a permanent image would be formed. The first daguerreotype image was produced in 1837. Many daguerreotypes, especially portraits, were made in the mid-19th cent.; the technique was gradually replaced by the wet collodion process, introduced in 1851.

Dahl \'däl\, **Roald** (1916–1990) British writer. A fighter pilot during World War II, he began his writing career with combat adventure stories, which were published by the *Saturday Evening Post*. The short-story collection *Someone Like You* (1953) was a best-seller; his later stories often include bizarre or supernatural elements. His popular children's books *James and the Giant Peach* (1961) and *Charlie and the Chocolate Factory* (1964) were made into films.

dahlia \'dal-yə\ Any of the 12–20 species of tuberous-rooted herbaceous plants that make up the genus *Dahlia*, in the COMPOSITE FAMILY, native to higher elevations of Mexico and Central America. The leaves of most are segmented and toothed or cut. About six species have been bred for cultivation as ornamental flowers, such as the common garden dahlia (*D. bipinnata*). *Dahlia* flowers may be white, yellow, red, or purple.

Dahomey See BENIN

Dahomey kingdom W African kingdom that flourished in the 18th–19th cent. in what is now central Benin. Initially called Abomey, it was renamed Dahomey after conquering the neighboring kingdoms of Allada (1724) and Whydah (1727). It thrived on the slave trade with Europe, reaching its high point under Gezu (1818–1858), under whom it became independent of the OYO EMPIRE. Society was rigidly stratified. The nation was organized for war, both to increase its territory and to take captives for the slave market, and women served as soldiers along with men. With the end of the slave trade in the 1840s came an economic decline. In 1892 Dahomey was defeated by a French expedition and became part of the French colony of the same name.

Dahshur \dä-'shür\ Ancient pyramid site near MEMPHIS, Egypt, on the W bank of the Nile. Two of its pyramids date from the 4th dynasty and were built by Snefru (r.2575–2551 B.C.); the smaller is believed to be the first true pyramid. The three remaining pyramids belong to the 12th dynasty (1938–1756 B.C.). Nearby tombs have yielded a remarkable collection of jewelry and personal accoutrements.

Dahshur Blunted pyramid of King Snefru

Daigo, Go- See GO-DAIGO

Daimler \'dīm-lər\, **Gottlieb (Wilhelm)** (1834–1900) German automotive inventor. He cofounded an engine-building company in 1882, patented one of the first successful INTERNAL COMBUSTION ENGINES in 1885, and built the first prototype MOTORCYCLE. Further innovations culminated in 1889 in a commercially feasible four-wheeled automobile. In 1890 the Daimler company was founded at Cannstadt, and in 1899 it produced the first Mercedes car. In 1926 it merged with the company founded by Karl BENZ. See also DAIMLER-BENZ AG.

Daimler-Benz AG \'dīm-lər-'benz\ German manufacturer. It was formed in 1926 by the merger of the pioneering auto companies founded by Gottlieb DAIMLER and Karl BENZ. The Mercedes-Benz luxury car, first produced by Daimler in 1901, remained the basis of Daimler-Benz's success. The company also made heavy-duty trucks, buses, and jet and motor-vehicle engines. In 1998 it merged with CHRYSLER CORP. to form Daimler Chrysler AG.

daimyo \'dī-mē-ˌō\ Powerful feudal landholding magnates in Japan (c.10th–19th cent.). The term was originally applied to military lords who gained territorial control over the various private estates into which the country had been divided; later, in the 14th–15th cent., daimyo acted as military governors for the ASHIKAGA SHOGUNATE. As the nation descended into internecine war, daimyo tended to hold small but consolidated domains; gradually, through constant battles, fewer and fewer daimyo came to hold more and more territory. When TOKUGAWA IEYASU completed unification of Japan in 1603, roughly 200 daimyo had been brought under the TOKUGAWA SHOGUNATE; they acted as local rulers in most of the country. After the MEIJI RESTORATION, the daimyo were converted into a pensioned nobility residing in Tokyo.

Dainan See T'AI-NAN

Dairen See DALIAN

dairy farming Form of animal husbandry that uses mammals, primarily cows, to produce MILK and products processed from it. Though CATTLE, GOATS, and SHEEP have

been kept for milking since the earliest historical times, modern dairy farming resulted from recent advances: the factory system for processing; sterile storage; refrigeration, fast vehicles, and paved roads; and pasteurization and the enforcement of food-safety laws. Outstanding dairy breeds include the Holstein, Guernsey, Jersey, Ayrshire, and Brown Swiss.

daisy Any of several species of garden plants in the COMPOSITE FAMILY, especially the oxeye daisy (*Chrysanthemum leucanthemum*) and the English, or true, daisy (*Bellis perennis*). Both are native to Europe but have become naturalized in the U.S. Daisies have a flower composed of 15–30 white ray flowers surrounding a bright yellow disk flower. The cultivated Shasta daisy (*C. maximum*) resembles the oxeye daisy but has larger flower heads.

Dakar \dä-'kär, 'da-ˌkär\ City (pop. 1994: 785,000; metro. area pop.: 1,869,000), capital of Senegal. It is one of the chief seaports on the W African coast. Founded by the French in 1857, its development was spurred by the opening in 1885 of W Africa's first railway. In 1902 it became capital of FRENCH W. AFRICA, and in 1960 of Senegal. Dakar is one of tropical Africa's leading industrial and service centers.

Dakota See SIOUX

Daladier \dä-läd-'ye\, **Édouard** (1884–1970) French politician. A member of the Radical Party, he served in several different cabinets, and formed short-lived governments in 1933 and 1934. As premier (1938–40), he sought to avoid war by signing the MUNICH AGREEMENT. Arrested after France fell (1940), he was imprisoned by the Germans until 1945, then returned to the Chamber of Deputies (1946–58).

Dalai Lama \ˌdä-lī-'lä-mə\ Head of the dominant DGE-LUGS-PA order of TIBETAN BUDDHISM. The first of the line was Dge-'dun-grub-pa (1391–1475), founder of a monastery in central Tibet. His successors were regarded as his reincarnations and, like himself, manifestations of the BODHISATTVA AVALOKITESVARA. The second head of the order established its base near Lhasa, and the third received the title Dalai ("Ocean") from Altan Khan. The Dalai Lama held temporal and spiritual power in Tibet after the Chinese were expelled in 1912. The 14th Dalai Lama, Bstan-'dzin-rgya-mtsho (b.1935), was enthroned in 1940 but fled to India in 1959 with 100,000 followers after a failed revolt against the Chinese, who had occupied Tibet since 1950. A revered figure worldwide, he was awarded the 1989 Nobel Peace Prize in recognition of his nonviolent campaign to end Chinese domination of Tibet.

d'Alembert, Jean Le R. See Jean Le R. d'ALEMBERT

Daley, Richard J(oseph) (1902–1976) U.S. politician, mayor of Chicago (1955–76). A lawyer in his native Chicago, Daley served as state director of revenue (1948–50) and clerk of Cook Co. (1950–55) before being elected mayor. He pushed urban renewal and highway construction and a sweeping reform of the police department, but was criticized for his reluctance to check racial segregation in housing and public schools, and for measures taken against demonstrators at the 1968 Democratic National Convention. His tight control of city politics through job patronage won him his reputation as "the last of the big-city bosses." His son Richard M. Daley (b.1942) was elected mayor in 1989.

Dalhousie \dal-'haù-zē\, **Marquess of** *orig.* James Andrew Broun Ramsay (1812–1860) British governor-general of India (1847–56). As president of the Board of Trade, he gained a reputation for administrative efficiency. As governor-general of India, he acquired territory by both peaceful and military means. Though he created the map of modern India through his controversial annexations of independent provinces, his greatest achievement was the molding of these provinces into a modern centralized state. He developed a modern communication and transportation system and instituted social reforms. The INDIAN MUTINY (1857) followed his departure.

Dalí (y Domenech) \'dä-lē, *Span* dä-'lē\, **Salvador (Felipe Jacinto)** (1904–1989) Spanish painter and designer. He studied in Spain before moving to Paris, where, in the late 1920s, after reading Sigmund FREUD's writings on subconscious imagery, he joined the Surrealists (see SURREALISM). His paintings depict a dream world in which commonplace objects, painted with meticulous realism, are juxtaposed or deformed in bizarre ways. In his most famous painting, *The Persistence of Memory* (1931), limp watches melt in an eerie landscape. With Luis BUÑUEL he made the Surrealist films *Un chien andalou* (1928) and *L'age d'or* (1930). Expelled from the Surrealist movement when he adopted a more academic style, he later designed stage sets, jewelry, and book illustrations. His highly accessible art—and the publicity attracted by the eccentric flamboyance he cultivated, especially while living in the U.S. (1940–55)—made him extremely wealthy.

Dalian *or* **Ta-lien** \'dä-'lyen\ *or* **Lüda** *or* **Lü-ta** \'lǖe-'dä\ *or* **Dairen** \'dī-'ren\ City (pop., 1999 est.: 2,000,000) and leading port of NE China. Leased to Russia in 1898, it was made a free port and terminus of the TRANS-SIBERIAN RAILROAD (1899). The Japanese occupied it 1904–6. Soviet troops captured the city in 1945, but it remained under Chinese sovereignty; Soviet troops withdrew in 1955. Industries include fishing, shipbuilding, and oil refining.

Dallapiccola \ˌdäl-lä-pēk-'kō-lä\, **Luigi** (1904–1975) Italian composer. Influenced by the music of Claude DEBUSSY and Arnold SCHOENBERG, he became the leading Italian twelve-tone composer. His cantata *Canti di prigionia* (1941) was inspired by the experience of fascism, as was his opera *Il prigioniero* (1948). Other important works include the operas *Volo di notte* (1939), *Job* (1950), and *Ulisse* (1968) and the piano set *Quaderno musicale di Annalibera* (1952).

Dallas City (pop., 2000: 1,188,000), N Texas. Located on the Trinity River, it was first settled in 1841. While cotton fed the town's growth, the discovery in 1930 of the great E. Texas oil field made the city a major petroleum center. It saw spectacular growth after World War II, when several aircraft-manufacturing firms located in the area, along with electronics and automobile-assembly plants and more than 100 insurance companies. It is the Southwest's leading financial center, as well as a transportation hub and home to Southern Methodist Univ. It is known for its cultural activities; the Dallas Theater Center is the only theater designed by F. L. WRIGHT.

Dalmatia \dal-'mä-shə\ *Serbo-Croatian* **Dalmacija** \ˌdäl-'mät-sē-yä\ Region of Croatia consisting of a coastal strip and islands along the Adriatic Sea. Its scenic beauty has made tourism a major economic factor; DUBROVNIK and SPLIT are Mediterranean tourist attractions. Occupied by Illyrians from about 1000 B.C., it was colonized by Greeks from the 4th cent. B.C. and later controlled by Rome. Under Venetian rule in 1420, it passed to Austria after the fall of NAPOLEON. Most of Dalmatia came under Yugoslavia in 1920; it passed to Yugoslavia in 1947 as part of the Croatian republic.

dalmatian Breed of dog named after Dalmatia, its first definite home. It has served as a guard dog, war dog, fire-department mascot, hunter, shepherd, and performer, but became best known as a coach or carriage dog, escorting and guarding horse-drawn vehicles. Sleek and short-haired, it is distinguished by its dark-spotted white coat. It stands 19–23 in. (48–60 cm) high and weighs 50–55 lbs (23–25 kg), and is generally even-tempered and friendly.

Dalriada \ˌdal-rē-'ä-də\ Ancient kingdom, NE Ireland. Known from the 5th cent. A.D., it included the N part of the present Co. Antrim in Northern Ireland and part of the Inner HEBRIDES ISLANDS and Argyll in Scotland. Earlier, Argyll had received N Irish people known as Scoti, and had become an Irish (i.e. "Scottish") area. In the late 5th cent. the rulers of Irish Dalriada expanded into Scottish Dalriada. In the mid-9th cent. the PICTS were brought under Dalriadic rule, and the area was thereafter known as Scotland.

Dalton, John (1766–1844) British chemist and physicist. His work on GASES led him to state Dalton's law (see GAS LAWS). He devised a system of CHEMICAL SYMBOLS, as-

John Dalton Engraving after a portrait by William Allen, 1814

certained the relative weights of atoms, and arranged them into a table. His masterpiece of synthesis was the atomic theory—the theory that each element is composed of tiny, indestructible particles called ATOMS that are all alike and have the same ATOMIC WEIGHT—which elevated chemistry to a quantitative science. He was also the first to describe color blindness (1794), and his lifelong meteorological journal contains over 200,000 observations.

Dalton brothers U.S. outlaws. Probably born in Cass Co., Mo., they had become horse thieves by 1889 and soon were robbing trains and banks. In 1892 Bob, Grat, and Emmett Dalton and two other gang members rode into Coffeyville, Kan., to rob its banks; they were recognized, and vigilante citizens killed all but Emmett, who was sent to prison for 14 years. Bill Dalton had returned to Oklahoma before the raid; he later formed his own gang, and was shot by lawmen in 1894 while playing with his daughter.

dam Barrier built across a river to conserve water for human consumption, irrigation, flood control, or electric-power generation. The earliest recorded dam is believed to be a masonry structure 49 ft (15 m) high built across the Nile River in Egypt about 2900 B.C. Modern dams are generally built of earth fill, rock fill, masonry, or monolithic concrete. Earth-fill (or embankment) dams, such as Egypt's ASWAN HIGH DAM, are usually used across broad rivers to retain water; in profile, they form a broad-based triangle. Concrete dams may take various forms. The gravity dam uses its own dead weight to resist the horizontal force of the water. Concrete-buttress dams reduce material in the wall itself by using support buttresses around the outside base. An arch dam, such as HOOVER DAM, is built in a convex arch facing the reservoir, and owes its strength essentially to its shape.

damages In law, the money awarded to a party in a civil suit as reparation for the loss or injury for which another is liable. The theory of an award of damages is that injured parties should be placed in the position they would have been in if the injury had not occurred, so far as this can be accomplished with a monetary award. More than one type of damages (e.g., direct, incidental, and punitive) may be awarded for a single injury.

Damascus \də-'mas-kəs\ *Arabic* **Dimashq** \di-'mäshk\ *French* **Damas** \dä-'mäs\ Largest city (pop., 1994: 1,550,000) and capital of Syria. Believed to be the world's oldest continuously inhabited city, it has evidence of occupation from the 4th millennium B.C. The first written reference to it is in Egyptian tablets of the 15th cent. B.C., and biblical sources refer to it as the capital of the ARAMAEANS. It changed hands repeatedly over the centuries: its rulers included Assyria, Babylon, Persia, Greece, Rome, and Byzantium. It fell to the Arabs in 635; it flourished as the UMAYYAD capital, and the remains of their Great Mosque still stand. Taken by the Turks in 1516, it remained in the Ottoman empire for some 400 years. It was occupied by France in 1920 and finally regained its independence, with Syria, in 1946. Today the city is a flourishing trading center, with many educational and scientific institutions.

d'Amboise \däⁿ-'bwäz\, **Jacques** *orig.* Jacques Joseph Ahearn (b.1934) U.S. dancer of the NEW YORK CITY BALLET (1949–84), noted for his athletic interpretations of classical roles. Born in Dedham, Mass., he joined the troupe at 15 and created leading roles in such ballets as *Western Symphony* and *Who Cares?*, becoming one of the first American male ballet stars. He later founded the National Dance Institute to bring dance teaching into the public schools.

Damien \'dä-mē-ən\, **Father** *orig.* Joseph de Veuster (1840–1889) Belgian priest. He joined the Society of the Sacred Hearts of Jesus and Mary in 1858. He went as a missionary to the Sandwich (Hawaiian) Islands in 1863 and was ordained there in 1864. In 1873 he volunteered to take charge of the leper colony on Molokai Island, dramatically improving living conditions and building two orphanages. He contracted leprosy himself in 1884 and died at Molokai five years later.

Damocles \'dam-ə-ˌklēz\ (fl.4th cent. B.C.) Member of the court of DIONYSIUS I the Elder at Syracuse in Sicily. Legend holds that after Damocles spoke extravagantly of Dionysius' happiness, the sovereign invited Damocles to a ban-

DE

quet and seated him beneath a sword suspended by a thread to demonstrate the precarious fortunes of men who hold power.

Dampier, William (1651–1715) English buccaneer and explorer. In his early years he engaged in piracy, chiefly along the W coast of S. America and in the Pacific. In 1699–1701 he explored the coasts of Australia, New Guinea, and New Britain for the British Admiralty. He later led a privateering expedition to the South Seas (1703–7). He was a keen observer of natural phenomena; one of his ship's logs contains the earliest known European description of a typhoon.

damselfly Any of numerous insect species in the suborder Zygoptera (order Odonata) having eyes that project to each side and wings on a stalk. When at rest, the damselfly holds its narrow, net-veined wings vertically rather than horizontally, unlike the DRAGONFLY. Like dragonflies, damselflies have male copulatory organs at the front part of the abdomen and commonly fly in pairs during mating.

Dana, James D(wight) (1813–1895) U.S. geologist and naturalist. Born in Utica, N.Y., he joined a U.S. exploring expedition to the South Seas (1838–42), acting as a geologist and zoologist. His contributions to the *American Journal of Science* from 1840 stimulated U.S. geological inquiry. His research into the formation of the earth's continents and oceans led him to believe in the progressive evolution of the earth's physical features. During his lifetime, and largely under his leadership, U.S. geology grew from a collection and classification of unrelated facts into a mature science.

Dana \'dā-nə\, **Richard Henry** (1815–1882) U.S. writer and lawyer. Born in Cambridge, Mass., he left Harvard College and shipped out as a common sailor; upon returning he became a lawyer. He is remembered for his autobiographical *Two Years Before the Mast* (1840), which revealed the abuses endured by sailors. *The Seaman's Friend* (1841) became the authoritative guide to seamen's legal rights and duties.

Danaë \'da-nə-ˌē\ In Greek legend, the daughter of Acrisius, king of Argos. Her father confined her in a tower after an oracle warned that she would bear a son who would slay him. ZEUS visited her in the form of a shower of gold, and she gave birth to PERSEUS. Mother and child were then placed in a wooden box and cast into the sea, but they drifted to safety. Perseus grew up and became the hero who slew the MEDUSA.

Da Nang *formerly* **Tourane** Seaport city (pop., 1992 est.: 383,000), central Vietnam. It was first ceded to France in 1787. It increased in importance after the partition of Vietnam in 1954, and during the VIETNAM WAR it was the site of a U.S. military base. Its port has an excellent deepwater harbor; its manufactures include textiles and machinery.

dance Form of expression that uses bodily movements that are rhythmic, patterned (or sometimes improvised), and usually accompanied by music. One of the oldest art forms, dance is found in every culture and is performed for purposes ranging from the ceremonial, liturgical, and magical to the theatrical, social, and simply aesthetic. Primitive dances often evolved into FOLK DANCES, which became stylized in the social dances of the European courts. BALLET developed from the court dances and became refined by innovations in CHOREOGRAPHY and technique. In the 20th cent., MODERN DANCE introduced new modes of expressive movement. See also BALLROOM DANCE, COUNTRY DANCE, HULA, JITTERBUG, MERENGUE, MINUET, MORRIS DANCE, POLKA, SQUARE DANCE, SWORD DANCE, TANGO, TAP DANCE, WALTZ.

dance notation Written recording of dance movements. The earliest notation, in the late 15th cent., consisted of letter-symbols. Several attempts were made in later centuries to describe dance steps, but no unified system combined both rhythm and steps until the 1920s, when Rudolf Laban (1879–1958) devised his system of Labanotation. In the 1950s, the competing system of Benesh notation, or "choreology," devised by Rudolf and Joan Benesh, came into use.

dance of death *or* **danse macabre** \ˈdäⁿs-má-ˈkȧ-brᵊ\ *or* **skeleton dance** Medieval allegorical concept of the all-conquering and equalizing power of death. It is a literary or pictorial representation of a procession or dance of both living and dead figures, the living arranged in order of their rank, from pope and emperor to child, clerk, and hermit, and the dead leading them to the grave.

dandelion Any of the weedy perennial herbaceous plants that make up the genus *Taraxacum,* in the COMPOSITE FAMILY, native to Eurasia but widespread in temperate N. America. The most familiar species, *T. officinale,* has a rosette of leaves at its base; a deep taproot; a smooth, hollow stem; and a solitary yellow flower head composed only of ray flowers that produces a ball-shaped cluster of small, tufted, one-seeded fruits that are borne away in the wind. The young leaves are edible; the roots can be used as a coffee substitute.

Dandolo \ˈdän-dō-lō\, **Enrico** (1107?–1205) DOGE of the republic of VENICE (1192–1205). After a career as a Venetian diplomat, he was elected doge at age 85. He instituted reforms, revising the penal code and publishing the first Venetian civil code. He also revised the coinage and sought to promote trade with the East. In 1199 he fought a victorious war against the Pisans. He was prominent in the Fourth CRUSADE, offering ships and supplies and helping lead (while in his nineties) the conquest of Constantinople, which resulted in considerable territorial gains by Venice.

dandruff Skin disorder of the scalp, a mild form of DERMATITIS. The scalp, which normally sheds its dead outer skin cells continuously, starts to shed them intermittently, causing a scaly buildup before shedding and noticeable flakes of skin on shedding. Dandruff is common and not contagious and often goes away spontaneously; special shampoos can control it.

Danegeld \ˈdän-ˌgeld\ Tax levied in Anglo-Saxon England to buy off Danish invaders during the reign of ETHELRED II (978–1016). The term continued to be used to refer to taxes collected by the Anglo-Norman kings in the 11th and 12th cent.

Daniel (c.6th cent. B.C.) One of the OLD TESTAMENT PROPHETS, the central figure in the Book of Daniel. The first six chapters tell of Daniel's adventures in BABYLON, including the stories of Daniel's delivery from the lion's den, the Jews in the fiery furnace, and the writing on the wall at BELSHAZZAR's feast. The rest of the book offers apocalyptic visions of the end of history and the last judgment. The book is thought to have been written in the 2nd cent. B.C. during the persecutions of the Jews under ANTIOCHUS IV EPIPHANES.

Daniel Romanovich \rə-ˈmän-ə-ˌvich\ *known as* **Daniel of Galicia** (1201–1264) Russian ruler of GALICIA and Volhynia. He inherited the two principalities (located in present-day Poland and Ukraine) at age 4, but pretenders to the succession kept him from ruling. He finally gained control over Volhynia in 1221 and Galicia in 1238. Forced to acknowledge the rule of the khan, he led a rebellion against the MONGOLS (1256) and drove them out of Volhynia, but another Mongol force subdued the principality in 1260.

Danilova \də-ˈnē-lə-və\, **Alexandra (Dionisyevna)** (1903–1997) Russian-U.S. dancer and teacher, instrumental in bringing Russian repertoires to the U.S. A soloist at the MARIINSKY THEATER, in 1924 she joined the BALLETS RUSSES. From 1938 to 1952 she danced with the Ballet

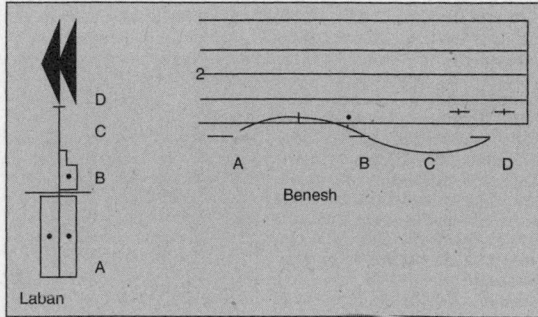

Dance notation Comparison of the Laban and Benesh systems. (A) Stand with the feet together. (B) Step forward on the right foot (count 1). (C) Spring into the air. (D) Land to the left, feet together, knees bent (count 2).

Russe de Monte Carlo, touring worldwide as its prima ballerina and creating leading roles in such works as *Swan Lake* and *Coppélia*. She retired in 1957, and taught full-time at the School of American Ballet 1964–89.

D'Annunzio \dän-ˈnünt-sē-ō\, **Gabriele** (1863–1938) Italian writer and military hero. His prodigious output includes *The Triumph of Death* (1894), his best-known novel; *Alcyone* (1904), considered his greatest poetic work; and the powerful play *The Daughter of Jorio* (1904). His works are marked by egocentrism, fluent and melodious style, and an overriding emphasis on sensual gratification. He urged Italy's entry into World War I, in which he distinguished himself militarily.

Alexandra Danilova in *Swan Lake*

In 1919 he set himself up as dictator of the port city Fiume in defiance of the Treaty of Versailles; he was forced to step down in 1920. He later became an ardent fascist. His eloquence, daring, political leadership, extravagant spending, and scandalous amours made him one of the most striking personalities of his day.

danse macabre See DANCE OF DEATH

Dante Alighieri \ˈdän-tā-ˌa-lə-ˈgyer-ē\ (1265–1321) Italian poet. A native of Florence of noble ancestry, he was exiled (1302) from the city for political reasons. His life was given direction by his spiritual love for Beatrice Portinari (d.1290). *La Vita Nuova* (1293?) celebrates Beatrice in verse. In his difficult years of exile, he wrote the verse collection *The Banquet* (c.1304–7); *De vulgari eloquentia* (1304–7; "Concerning Vernacular Eloquence"), the first theoretical discussion of the Italian literary language; and *On Monarchy* (1313?), a major treatise on political philosophy. He is best known for the monumental epic poem *The Divine Comedy* (written c.1310–14), a profoundly Christian vision of human temporal and eternal destiny. It is an allegory of universal human destiny in

Dante "Dante and His Work" by Domenico di Michelino, 1465

the form of a pilgrim's journey through hell and purgatory, guided by VIRGIL, then to Paradise, guided by Beatrice. By writing it in Italian rather than Latin, Dante almost single-handedly made Italian a literary language, and he stands as one of the towering figures of European literature.

Danton \däⁿ-ˈtoⁿ\, **Georges (-Jacques)** (1759–1794) French revolutionary leader. A lawyer before the FRENCH REVOLUTION, he cofounded the Club of the CORDELIERS (1790) and frequently made impassioned speeches before both it and the JACOBIN CLUB. Elected minister of justice in 1792, he became a member of the first COMMITTEE OF PUBLIC SAFETY in April 1793. Effectively the head of government for three months, he pursued a policy of compromise and negotiation. When he was not reelected to the Committee, he became leader of the moderate Indulgents. His opposition to the REIGN OF TERROR led to his own death at the guillotine.

Danube River \ˈdan-ˌyüb\ *German* **Donau** \ˈdō-ˌnaủ\ *Slovak* **Dunaj** \dü-ˈnī\ *Serbo-Croatian and Bulgarian* **Dunav** \ˈdü-

näv\ *Romanian* **Dunarea** \ˈdü-nər-ˌyä\ *Russian* **Dunay** \dü-ˈnī\ River, central Europe. The second-longest European river (after the VOLGA), it rises in Germany's BLACK FOREST and flows about 1,770 mi (2,850 km) to the Black Sea, passing along or through Germany, Austria, Slovakia, Hungary, Croatia, Yugoslavia, Bulgaria, Romania, and Moldova. It has been an important highway from antiquity. The lower Danube is a major avenue for freight transport, and the upper Danube is an important source of hydroelectricity. A regulatory body of the nations on its banks was established in 1948. A major hydroelectric and navigation complex was built in the 1970s at Iron Gate Gorge in Romania. A canal linking Kelheim on it and Bamberg on the MAIN RIVER, allowing traffic to flow between the North and Black seas, was completed in 1992.

Danzig See GDANSK

dao See TAO

Daode jing See TAO-TE CHING

Daoism See TAOISM

Daphne \ˈdaf-nē\ In GREEK MYTHOLOGY, the personification of the laurel tree. The beautiful daughter of a river god, Daphne rejected every lover. When APOLLO pursued her, she prayed to GAEA or to her father to save her, whereupon she was transformed into a laurel. Apollo took its leaves to weave garlands that were thenceforth awarded to prize-winning poets.

Da Ponte \dä-ˈpōn-tā\, **Lorenzo** *orig*. Emmanuele Conegliano (1749–1838) Italian poet and librettist. He took priestly orders in 1768, while teaching literature and publishing poetry. At odds with the authorities for his progressive views, he was expelled from the Venetian republic in 1779 for adultery. As court poet for Vienna's Italian theater, he wrote over 40 opera librettos, including the masterpieces *The Marriage of Figaro* (1786), *Don Giovanni* (1787), and *Così fan tutte* (1790) for W. A. MOZART. He settled in New York in 1805, taught at Columbia College, wrote his colorful memoirs, and helped establish Italian opera in the city.

Dapsang See K2

DAR See DAUGHTERS OF THE AMERICAN REVOLUTION

Dardanelles \ˌdär-d^ən-ˈelz\ *ancient* **Hellespont** \ˈhe-lə-ˌspänt\ Narrow strait between the peninsula of Gallipoli in Europe and the mainland of Turkey in Asia. Some 38 mi (61 km) long, and 0.75–4 mi (1–6 km) wide, it links the Aegean Sea with the Sea of Marmara. In 480 B.C. XERXES I crossed the strait to invade Greece, as did ALEXANDER THE GREAT in 334 B.C. on his expedition against Persia. Held by the Byzantine empire and later the Ottoman Turks, it is of great strategic and economic importance as the gateway from the Black Sea to the Mediterranean. See also GALLIPOLI.

Dardanelles Campaign *or* **Gallipoli Campaign** \gə-ˈli-pə-lē\ (1915–16) Unsuccessful British-led operation against Turkey in WORLD WAR I. In response to a Russian appeal to relieve pressure against its troops, Britain agreed to a naval action against Turkey at the DARDANELLES strait. When bombardment alone failed, British and Australian and New Zealand (Anzac) troops landed on the GALLIPOLI peninsula in April 1915, where they met strong resistance from Turkish forces under M. K. ATATURK. After six months of standoff, the campaign was halted and allied troops were skillfully withdrawn under difficult conditions. Allied casualties numbered about 250,000. The failed campaign prompted the resignation of Winston CHURCHILL as first lord of the admiralty.

Dare, Virginia (b.1587) First child born in America to English parents. Her parents were among the 120 settlers who landed at ROANOKE ISLAND, Va., in 1587. Her grandfather, John WHITE, was the colony's governor; he left to collect supplies in England nine days after her birth. A relief expedition that finally reached the colony in 1590 found only the word "croatoan" carved on a post; Virginia had vanished along with all the other colonists.

Dar es Salaam \ˌdär-ˌes-sä-ˈläm\ Capital, largest city (pop., 1994: 1,606,000), and major port of Tanzania. Founded in 1862 by the sultan of ZANZIBAR, it came under the German E. Africa Co. in 1887. It served as the capital of GERMAN E. AFRICA (1891–1916), of Tanganyika (1961–64), and subsequently of Tanzania. Its harbor is the major outlet for Tanzania's exports.

DE

Darío \dä-'rē-ō\, **Rubén** *orig.* Félix Rubén García Sarmiento (1867–1916) Nicaraguan poet, journalist, and diplomat. The diverse collection *Azul* (1888), written in an innovative simple, direct style, is his first major work. As a diplomat in Buenos Aires (from 1893), he became the center of the new MODERNISMO movement. His *Profane Hymns* (1896) was influenced by the French Symbolists. *Songs of Life and Hope* (1905) represents the culmination of his technical experimentation and artistic resourcefulness. In addition to his poetry, he wrote about 100 short stories. Poor and rundown, he died of pneumonia at 49.

Darius I \da-'rī-əs\ *known as* **Darius the Great** (550–486 B.C.) King of Persia (522–486 B.C.). He was the son of Hystaspes, satrap (provincial governor) of PARTHIA. Much of what is known of him is through his own inscriptions. He took the throne by force and continued the conquests of his predecessors, subduing THRACE, MACEDONIA, some Aegean islands, and land stretching to the Indus Valley. He twice tried and failed to conquer Greece. Among the greatest of the ACHAEMENIAN DYNASTY, he was noted for his administrative genius and his building projects, especially those at PERSEPOLIS.

Darjeeling *or* **Darjiling** Town (metro. area pop., 1991: 73,000), NE India. It was purchased in 1835 from the raja of Sikkim and was developed as a sanatorium for British troops. Located at an average elevation of 7,500 ft (2,300 m), it is the summer headquarters of the Bengal government. Its economy is based primarily on plantation-grown tea.

dark matter Nonluminous MATTER hypothesized to exist because the mass of the visible matter in the universe cannot account for observed gravitational effects. Believed to exist in large quantities, it enters into many theories of the origin and structure of the universe and into models of GRAVITATION and other fundamental forces. Numerous candidates for dark matter have been proposed, but none has yet been detected.

Darlan \där-'läⁿ\, **(Jean-Louis-Xavier-) François** (1881–1942) French admiral. Navy commander in chief until France's defeat by Germany in World War II, he entered Philippe PÉTAIN's government as vice premier and foreign minister (1941–42), then became commander in chief of all VICHY FRANCE's military forces. In 1942 he concluded an armistice with the Allies in Algiers, then was killed by an anti-Vichy assassin.

Darrow \'dar-ō\, **Clarence (Seward)** (1857–1938) U.S. lawyer and orator. Born near Kinsman, Ohio, he moved to Chicago in 1887 and immediately joined the effort to free anarchists charged in the HAYMARKET RIOT. General attorney for the Chicago and North Western Railway, he left the railroad to defend Eugene DEBS in the PULLMAN STRIKE (1894), which established his reputation as a union and criminal lawyer. He represented striking Pennsylvania coal miners, drawing attention to the use of child labor (1902–3); secured

Clarence Darrow, 1924

the acquittal of William HAYWOOD in the assassination of the governor of Idaho (1907); saved Richard Loeb and Nathan Leopold from a death sentence for the murder of 14-year-old Robert Franks (1924); and won acquittal for a black family that had fought a mob trying to expel it from its home in a white Detroit neighborhood (1925–26). Perhaps his most famous case was the SCOPES TRIAL (1925).

darshan *or* **darsan** \'dər-shən, 'där-shən\ In Hindu worship, the beholding of an auspicious deity, person, or object. The experience is often conceived to be reciprocal and results in a blessing of the viewer. In *rathayatra*s (car festivals), images are carried through the streets to allow viewing by those who formerly would not have been allowed in the temple. In Indian philosophy, darshan also refers to a philosophical system (e.g., VEDANTA).

Dart, Raymond A(rthur) (1893–1988) Australian-S. African physical anthropologist and paleontologist. In 1924, when Asia was still believed to have been the cradle of humankind, Dart's discovery of the so-called Taung skull near the Kalahari Desert substantiated Charles DARWIN's prediction that such ancestral HOMINID forms would be found in Africa. Dart made the skull the type-specimen of a new genus and species, *AUSTRALOPITHECUS africanus*. He taught at the Univ. of Witwatersrand from 1923 to 1958.

darter Any of about 100 species of small, slender freshwater fishes (family Percidae), native to E N. America. Darters live near the bottom of clear streams, darting about when feeding or when disturbed. They often are brightly colored. Most species are 2–3 in. (5–7 cm) long, but some grow to 9 in. (23 cm). Some species lay their eggs and abandon them; the males of other species establish a nest and guard the eggs until hatched.

Dartmouth College \'därt-məth\ Private institution of higher learning in Hanover, N.H., a member of the IVY LEAGUE. It is consistently ranked as one of the best liberal-arts colleges in the U.S. It was founded in 1769 by Rev. Eleazar Wheelock (1711–1779) for the education of "youth of the Indian Tribes . . . English Youth and others." The original charter was approved by George III. Women were first admitted in 1972. Enrollment is about 5,300. See also DARTMOUTH COLLEGE case.

Dartmouth College case *formally* **Trustees of Dartmouth College vs. Woodward** Case in which the U.S. Supreme Court held (1819) that the charter of DARTMOUTH COLLEGE, granted in 1769 by George III, was a contract and as such could not be impaired by the New Hampshire legislature, which had tried to alter its terms regarding the board of trustees. The decision was far-reaching in its application to business charters, protecting businesses and CORPORATIONS from much government regulation. Daniel WEBSTER argued Dartmouth's case.

darts Indoor target game played by throwing feathered darts at a circular board with numbered spaces. The board, usually made of cork, bristle, or elmwood, is divided into 20 sectors valued at points from 1 to 20. Six concentric rings determine scoring. The official throwing distance in most countries is 7 ft 9¹/₄ in. (2.37 m). In Britain, darts is normally played in pubs.

Darwin *formerly* **Palmerston** Seaport (pop., 1995 est.: 82,000), capital of NORTHERN TERRITORY, Australia. Lying on the Timor Sea, it has one of Australia's best harbors. The port was settled in 1869. Darwin is a supply and shipping center for N Australia. It was bombed by the Japanese in 1942, then extensively rebuilt. A cyclone in 1974 damaged or destroyed nearly all of the city; again rebuilt, it is now one of Australia's most modern cities.

Darwin, Charles (Robert) (1809–1882) British naturalist. The grandson of Erasmus DARWIN and Josiah WEDGWOOD, he studied medicine at Edinburgh Univ. and biology at Cambridge. He was recommended as naturalist on HMS *Beagle,* which was bound on a long scientific survey expedition to S. America and the South Seas (1831–36). His zoological and geological discoveries on the voyage resulted in numerous important publications, and formed the basis of his theories of EVOLUTION. He saw NATURAL SELECTION as the mechanism by which advantageous VARIATIONS were passed on to later genera-

Charles Darwin Photo by J. M. Cameron, 1868

tions and less advantageous traits gradually disappeared. He worked on his theory for 20 years before publishing a paper in 1858 with Alfred Russel WALLACE. His famous *On the Origin of Species by Means of Natural Selection* (1859) was immediately in great demand and his intensely controversial theory was accepted quickly in most scientific circles; most opposition came from religious leaders. Though Darwin's ideas were modified by later developments in genetics and molecular biology, his work remains central to modern evolutionary theory. His many other important works included *Variation in Animals and Plants Under Domestication* (1868) and *The Descent of Man . . .* (1871). See also DARWINISM.

Darwin, Erasmus (1731–1802) British physician, grandfather of Charles DARWIN and Francis GALTON. In *Zoonomia or the Laws of Organic Life* (1794–96), he advanced a theory of evolution similar to that of Jean-Baptiste de LAMARCK, suggesting that species modified themselves by adapting to their environment in an intentional way. His conclusions, drawn from simple observation, were rejected by the more sophisticated 19th-cent. scientists, including his grandson Charles.

Darwinism Theory of the mechanism of EVOLUTION proposed by Charles DARWIN as an explanation of organic change. Evolution is brought about by the interplay of three principles: VARIATION (present in all forms of life), HEREDITY (the force that transmits similar organic form from one generation to another), and the struggle for existence (which determines the variations that will be advantageous in a given environment, thus altering the species through selective reproduction). Current knowledge of the genetic basis of inheritance has contributed to scientists' understanding of the mechanisms behind Darwin's ideas, in a theory known as neo-Darwinism.

da Sangallo the Younger \dä-sän-'gäl-lō\, **Antonio (Giamberti)** (1483–1546) Italian architect. Nephew of the architects Giuliano da Sangallo (1445?–1516) and Antonio da Sangallo the Elder (1455–1535), he worked for decades on ST. PETER'S BASILICA, first as Donato BRAMANTE's assistant and after 1520 as chief architect. His imposing Palazzo Farnese in Rome (1534–46) exercised immense influence well into the 19th cent.

da Silva, Luis Inácio Lula (b.1945) President of Brazil (from 2003). A factory worker from age 14, he became a trade union leader (1975) and founded the Workers Party, Brazil's only socialist party, in 1980. He ran for president three times unsuccessfully before winning in a landslide in 2002. The election of Lula (as he is known) was hailed as a vote to increase social services and to improve the lot of the poor.

database Collection of data or information organized for rapid search and retrieval, especially by a computer. Databases are structured to facilitate storage and manipulation of data using various data-processing operations. A database consists of a file or set of files broken down into records, each of which consists of one or more fields, the basic units of data storage. Users retrieve information primarily through queries. Using keywords and sorting commands, users can rapidly search, rearrange, group, and select information to retrieve or create reports on groups of data according to the rules of the DATABASE MANAGEMENT SYSTEM being used.

database, relational See RELATIONAL DATABASE

database management system (DBMS) System for search and retrieval of information from a DATABASE. The DBMS determines how data are stored and retrieved. It must address problems such as security, accuracy, consistency among different records, response time, and memory requirements. Ever-higher processing speeds are required for efficient database management. Relational DBMSs, in which data are organized into a series of tables ("relations") that are easily reorganized, are the most widely used today.

data encryption Process of disguising information as "ciphertext," or data that will be unintelligible to an unauthorized person. Decryption is the process of converting ciphertext back into its original format. Computers encrypt data by applying an ALGORITHM to a block of data. A personal key known only to the message's transmitter and intended receiver is used to control the encryption. A key 16 characters long selected at random from 256 ASCII characters could take far longer than the 15-billion-year age of the universe to decode, assuming the perpetrator attempted 100 million different key combinations per second. Symmetric encryption requires the same key for both encryption and decryption. Asymmetric encryption requires two different keys.

data mining Type of database analysis that attempts to discover useful patterns or relationships in a group of data. The analysis uses advanced statistical methods and sometimes employs ARTIFICIAL INTELLIGENCE or NEURAL-NETWORK techniques. A major goal of data mining is to discover previously unknown relationships among the data. Businesses can use these new relationships to develop new advertising campaigns or make predictions about how well a product will sell.

data transmission Sending and receiving data via cables (e.g., telephone lines or FIBER OPTICS) or wireless relay systems. The high frequencies associated with data transmission suffer a loss of amplitude and transmission speed over telephone lines. Data signals must therefore be translated into a format compatible with the signals used in telephone lines. Digital computers use a MODEM to send and receive digital electronic data over telephone lines. Specialized data-transmission links carry signals at frequencies higher than those used by the public telephone network. See also BROADBAND TECHNOLOGY, DSL, FAX, ISDN, RADIO, TELETYPE, WIRELESS COMMUNICATIONS.

Date Line See INTERNATIONAL DATE LINE

date palm Tree (*Phoenix dactylifera*) of the PALM family, found in the Canary Islands and N Africa, the Middle East, Pakistan, India, and California. The trunk, strongly marked with the pruned stubs of old leaf bases, ends in a crown of long, graceful, shining, pinnate leaves. The fruit, called the date, is a usually oblong brown BERRY. Dates have long been an important food in desert regions, supplying syrup, alcohol, vinegar, and a strong liquor. Other parts of the tree are used for timber, furniture, basketry, fuel, rope, and packing material. The seeds are sometimes used as stock feed. The leaves are used for the celebration of Palm Sunday (among Christians) and the Feast of Tabernacles (among Jews). Date sugar is obtained from the sap of the closely related *P. sylvestris*.

dating In geology and archaeology, the process of determining an object's or event's place within a chronological scheme. Scientists may use either relative dating, in which items are sequenced on the basis of stratigraphic clues (see STRATIGRAPHY) or a presumed evolution in form or structure, or absolute dating, in which items are assigned a date independent of context. See also CARBON-14 DATING, DENDROCHRONOLOGY, FISSION-TRACK DATING, HELIUM DATING, LEAD-210 DATING, POTASSIUM-ARGON DATING, RUBIDIUM-STRONTIUM DATING, URANIUM-234–URANIUM-238 DATING, URANIUM-THORIUM-LEAD DATING.

Daubigny \dō-bēn-'yē\, **Charles-François** (1817–1878) French landscape painter of the BARBIZON SCHOOL. Trained by his father, he began by painting historical and religious works but soon turned to landscapes, painting rivers, beaches, and canals from a boat. His images were notable for their accurate depiction of natural light. He is considered the link between mid-19th-cent. naturalism and Impressionism.

Daudet \dō-'de\, **Alphonse** (1840–1897) French short-story writer and novelist. He wrote his first novel at 14. He later joined the army, but fled the terrors of the PARIS COMMUNE of 1871. His health was long undermined by poverty and by the venereal disease that eventually cost him his life. He is remembered for his humorous, sentimental portrayals of the life and characters of S France, inspired by his experiences at many social levels. His many works include the story collection *Monday Tales* (1873), the play *L'Arlésienne* (1872), the novels *The Nabob* (1877) and *Sappho* (1884), and several volumes of memoirs.

Daughters of the American Revolution (DAR) U.S. patriotic society for direct descendants of those who aided the cause of independence. Organized in 1890 and chartered by Congress in 1895, it stresses the study of U.S. history and preservation of Americana, provides scholarships and loans, supports schools for underprivileged youth and for Americanization training, sponsors prizes, and publishes manuals. It was long known for its conservatism; its refusal in 1939 to let Marian ANDERSON perform at Washington's Constitution Hall led to her famous concert at the Lincoln Memorial.

Daumier \dōm-'yā\, **Honoré (-Victorin)** (1808–1879) French painter, sculptor, and caricaturist. From age 13 he worked for a bailiff in a law court and later as a clerk in a bookstore, where he observed people of different social classes. In 1829, after studying lithography, he began contributing cartoons and drawings satirizing 19th-cent. French politics and society to periodicals, and came to enjoy a wide reputation. He produced over 4,000 lithographs and 4,000 illustrative drawings. His paintings, documenting contemporary life and manners, were executed in a vigorous, sketchy style. In sculpture he specialized in caricature heads and figures. See also REALISM.

Davao \'dä-ˌvaủ\ City (pop., 2000: 1,147,000), SE Mindanao Island, Philippines. An international port and the leading commercial center in the region, it developed as a Japanese colony. Razed during World War II, the rebuilt city is a blend of Spanish, American, and Moorish influences. It is one of the world's largest cities in area, covering 854 sq mi (2,212 sq km). It is the site of the Univ. of Mindanao (1946).

Davenant \'dav-ə-nənt\, **William** *or* **William D'Avenant** (*later* **Sir William**) (1606–1668) British poet, playwright, and theater manager. Early works include the comedy *The Witts* (licensed 1634) and a volume of poems, *Madagascar* (1638). He was made poet laureate in 1638. Involved in intrigues during the English Civil Wars, he was imprisoned at the Tower of London, where he worked on his verse epic *Gondibert* (1651). Later he made the first attempt to revive English drama (banned under Oliver CROMWELL) and brought the first opera to the English public stage.

David (d.c.962 B.C.) Second of the Israelite kings (r.c.1000–c.962 B.C.). David was an aide at the court of SAUL until the monarch's jealousy forced him into outlawry. He became king of Israel on Saul's death. He captured Jerusalem from the Jebusites and made it his capital, defeated the PHILISTINES, and gained control of many bordering kingdoms. He faced several revolts, including one by his third son, ABSALOM. He unified all Israel into one kingdom and made Jerusalem its center. Though the kingdom split under David's son and successor, SOLOMON, religious unity endured, and the house of David symbolized the bond between God and Israel. The word MESSIAH comes from *hameshiach,* the title of kings of the line of David.

David \'dä-vət\, **Gerard** (c.1460–1523) Netherlandish painter. He worked mainly in Bruges, where he became the city's leading painter after the death of Hans MEMLING. Most of his works are altarpieces featuring traditional religious themes, but his best-known paintings, *The Judgment of Cambyses* and *The Flaying of Sisamnes* (1498), deal with the theme of justice. His works are among the earliest Flemish paintings to feature such Italian Renaissance devices as putti (male child angels) and garlands.

David \dä-'vēd\, **Jacques-Louis** (1748–1825) French painter. At 18 he entered the Royal Academy of Painting and Sculpture. In 1775 he went to Rome and became a proponent of the Neoclassical style (see CLASSICISM AND NEOCLASSICISM). In Paris he soon prospered as a painter of historical events and classical themes. He became the unchallenged painter of the French Revolution, and later was appointed official portraitist to NAPOLEON. A founding member of the new Institut de France, which replaced the Royal Academy, he produced commemorative medals and other revolutionary propaganda. Among his masterpieces is *The Death of Marat* (1793). The principal exponent of Neoclassicism,

Jacques-Louis David, self-portrait, 1794

he had a pervasive influence on European art; his pupils included A.-J. GROS and J.-A.-D. INGRES.

David, Star of *Hebrew* Magen David ("Shield of David"). Jewish symbol composed of two overlaid equilateral triangles that form a six-pointed star. It appears on synagogues, tombstones, and the flag of Israel. An ancient sign not much used by Jews before the Middle Ages, it was popularized by Kabbalists for protection against evil spirits. Its use became widespread in the 17th cent.; though it has neither biblical nor Talmudic authority, it became a nearly universal emblem of Judaism in the 19th cent.

David I (1082?–1153) King of the Scots (1124–53). Crowned king of Scotland on the death of his brother Alexander I, he created a rudimentary central administration, issued the first Scottish royal coinage, and admitted into Scotland an influential Norman aristocracy. David also reorganized Scottish Christianity to conform with European and English usages and founded many religious communities. Having obtained lands in central England through marriage, he won title to Northumberland from the future HENRY II in 1149.

David II (1324–1371) King of the Scots from 1329. In keeping with an Anglo-Scottish peace treaty, he was married at age 4 to the sister of EDWARD III of England. He went into exile in France in 1334 after Edward supported a rival for the throne; David returned in 1341 and carried out raids against the English, who captured him in 1346. He was released in 1357 on the promise of ransom, and his offer to trade the Scottish throne for forgiveness of the ransom money was repudiated in Scotland. His reign was marked by a decline in the prestige of the monarchy.

Davies, Peter Maxwell (*later* **Sir Peter**) (b.1934) British composer. He cofounded the contemporary ensemble The Fires of London and wrote many of his works for the group. Since 1970 he has lived in the remote Orkney Islands. He has written many musical theater works, and has conducted orchestras worldwide. His most famous compositions are *Eight Songs for a Mad King* (1969) and *An Orkney Wedding, with Sunrise* (1985); his other works include the operas *Taverner* (1968) and *The Martyrdom of St. Magnus* (1976) and seven symphonies.

Davies, (William) Robertson (1913–1995) Canadian novelist and playwright. Born in Thamesville, Ontario, he is best known for three trilogies: the *Deptford Trilogy* consists of *Fifth Business* (1970), *The Manticore* (1972), and *World of Wonders* (1975), novels examining the intersecting lives of three men from a small Canadian town; the *Salterton Trilogy*, three comedies of manners set in a provincial university town; and the so-called Cornish trilogy—*The Rebel Angels* (1981), *What's Bred in the Bone* (1985), and *The Lyre of Orpheus* (1988).

da Vinci, Leonardo See LEONARDO DA VINCI

Davis, Angela Y(vonne) (b.1944) U.S. political activist. Born in Birmingham, Ala., she became a doctoral candidate at the Univ. of California. Because of her Marxist political views, her college teaching position was not renewed. She was arrested in 1970 for complicity in the abortive courtroom escape led by the so-called Soledad Brothers, in which four people, including the trial judge, were killed. An all-white jury acquitted her.

Davis, Benjamin O(liver), Jr. (1912–2002) U.S. pilot and the first black general in the U.S. Air Force. Born in Washington, D.C., son of the first black brigadier general in U.S. history, he organized the first all-black air unit and in 1943 organized and commanded the TUSKEGEE AIRMEN, flying 60 combat missions. In 1948 he helped plan the desegregation of the Air Force, and he later commanded a fighter wing in the Korean War.

Davis, Bette (*orig.* Ruth Elizabeth) (1908–1989) U.S. film actress. Born in Lowell, Mass., she went to Hollywood in 1931, and established her reputation with *Of Human Bondage* (1934) and *Dangerous* (1935, Academy Award). Known for her intense characterizations of strong women, she gave electrifying performances in such films as *The Petrified Forest* (1936), *Jezebel* (1938, Academy Award), *Dark Victory* (1939), *The Little Foxes* (1941), *Now, Voyager* (1942), *All About Eve* (1950), and *The Virgin Queen* (1955). Later films include *What Ever Happened to Baby Jane?* (1962).

Davis, Jefferson (1808–1889) U.S. political leader, president of the CONFEDERATE STATES OF AMERICA (1861–65). Born in Christian Co., Ky., he graduated from West Point, served in the army, and later became a planter in Mississippi. In the MEXICAN WAR, he distinguished himself at the Battle of

Buena Vista. A national hero, he served in the U.S. Senate (1847–51, 1857–61) and as Pres. Franklin PIERCE's secretary of war (1853–57). He advocated states' rights while trying to discourage secession, but after Mississippi seceded in 1861 he was chosen president of the Confederacy. He conducted the South's war effort in the face of a lack of manpower, supplies, and money, and hampered by discord from radicals within his administration. On Lee's surrender, he fled Richmond, hoping to continue the fight until he could secure better terms from the North. Captured and indicted for treason, he was released in poor health in 1867. He retired to Mississippi; his citizenship was restored posthumously in 1978.

Davis, Miles (Dewey) (1926–1991) U.S. trumpeter and bandleader. Born in Alton, Ill., Davis briefly studied at the Juilliard School. He worked with Charlie PARKER 1946–48. His early efforts as a bandleader resulted in recordings known as "Birth of the Cool" (1949), in which a relaxed aesthetic replaced the freneticism of BEBOP and launched the "cool jazz" school of the 1950s. From 1955 Davis's groups framed his own spare, lyrical approach in contrast to the dense complexity of saxophonists such as John COLTRANE. His brooding tone, logically paced improvisations, and use of the Harmon mute were widely imitated. The 1959 album *Kind of Blue* was a pioneering example of modal harmonic jazz. His music became more aggressive during the 1960s, and his use of electric instruments on *Bitches Brew* (1969) gave rise to the jazz-rock fusion of the 1970s.

Davis, Stuart (1894–1964) U.S. abstract painter. Born in Philadelphia, he studied in New York with Robert HENRI (1909–12), associated with the ASH CAN SCHOOL, and exhibited in the ARMORY SHOW. A visit to Paris in 1928–29 inspired his own version of Cubism; he began rearranging natural forms from everyday life into flat posterlike patterns with sharp outlines and contrasting colors (the dissonant colors and repetitive rhythms reflecting his interest in jazz), in a style that eventually led to totally abstract patterns.

Davis Cup Trophy awarded to the winning team of an international lawn-tennis tournament for men. It was donated in 1900 by Dwight F. Davis for a competition between teams from the U.S. and Britain. Since then, the tournament has become truly international, and more than 100 nations have participated.

Davis Strait Strait, N Atlantic Ocean. Lying between SE BAFFIN ISLAND and SW GREENLAND, it separates BAFFIN BAY to the north from the Labrador Sea to the south, and forms part of the NORTHWEST PASSAGE. It was explored in 1585 by the English navigator John Davis (1550?–1605). The Greenland Current carries warm water northward, while the cold Labrador Current transports icebergs southward along Baffin Island's E shore.

Davos \dä-ˈvōs\ Commune (pop., 1990: 12,000), E Switzerland. It consists of two villages in a valley of the ALPS. Settled in the 13th cent., it became the capital of the League of Ten Jurisdictions or Courts in 1436, and was ruled by Austria 1477–1649. After the 1860s it became a fashionable health resort, and in the 20th cent. a center for winter sports. Since 1971 it has been the site of the World Economic Forum.

Davout \dà-ˈvü\, **Louis-Nicolas** (1770–1823) French general in the NAPOLEONIC WARS. Despite his noble origins, in 1790 he led his regiment in a pro-Revolutionary revolt. He accompanied NAPOLEON to Egypt (1798–99). As a corps commander, he had a significant impact on the victories at AUSTERLITZ (1805), Auerstedt (1806), and Wagram (1809). Created a duke (1808) and prince (1809) by Napoleon, Davout served as minister of war during the HUNDRED DAYS.

Davy, Humphry (*later* **Sir Humphry**) (1778–1829) English chemist. By his early 20s his work on gases had established his reputation. His discovery of the anesthetic effect of NITROUS OXIDE was a major contribution to surgery. Davy was the first to apply chemical principles systematically to farming. He was the first to isolate POTASSIUM, SODIUM, BARIUM, STRONTIUM, MAGNESIUM, and CALCIUM; he also discovered BORON and studied CHLORINE and IODINE extensively. He analyzed many pigments, and proved that DI-

AMOND is a form of CARBON. He was one of the greatest exponents of the SCIENTIFIC METHOD. His research on mine explosions and flame and his invention of the safety lamp brought him great prestige, and in 1820 he was made president of the Royal Society.

daw See JACKDAW

Dawes, Charles G(ates) (1865–1951) U.S. politician. Born in Marietta, Ohio, he became a lawyer and financier in Chicago. In World War I he headed supply procurement for the American Expeditionary Force in France. In 1923 he chaired the Allied Reparations Commission and arranged the Dawes Plan to reorganize Germany's reparations, for which he shared the 1925 Nobel Peace Prize. He served as vice president (1925–29) under Calvin COOLIDGE.

Dawes General Allotment Act (1887) U.S. land-distribution law proposed by Massachusetts Sen. Henry L. Dawes (1816–1903) as a way to make farmers of the American Indians. Grants of 80–160 acres were offered to each Indian head of household. The unintended result was a weakened tribal structure, the inability of many nomadic Indians to adjust to an agrarian existence, and a reservation life of poverty, disease, and despondency. A provision made available for public sale any "surplus" reservation land, and whites had acquired two-thirds of the Indian land by 1932.

dawn redwood Coniferous, nonevergreen tree (*Metasequoia glyptostroboides*), the only living species of the genus *Metasequoia*, of the family Taxodiaceae, native to remote valleys of central China. Both branchlets and leaves grow out in pairs from points along the stem. The bright-green, feathery leaves turn reddish brown in autumn. At least 100 million years old, the tree was thought to be extinct until living specimens were discovered in the 1940s; since then, seeds and cuttings have been planted throughout the world.

day Time required for a celestial body to turn once on its axis; especially, the period of the earth's rotation. The apparent solar day is the time between two successive transits

Days

Day	Derivation
Sunday	from Old English translation of Latin *solis dies* ("sun's day")
Monday	from Old English translation of Latin *lunae dies* ("moon's day")
Tuesday	from Old English *tīwesdæg* ("Tyr's day")*
Wednesday	from Old English *wōdnesdæg* ("Woden's day")*
Thursday	from Old English *thursdæg* ("Thor's day")*
Friday	from Old English *frigedæg* ("Frigg's day")*
Saturday	from Old English translation of Latin *Saturni dies* ("Saturn's day")

*In translating the Latin names, the Germanic peoples sometimes substituted the names of their own gods. Thus, *Martis dies* ("Mars's day") became *tīwesdæg* ("Tyr's day"), *Mercurii dies* ("Mercury's day") became *wōdnesdæg* ("Woden's day"), and *Veneris dies* ("Venus' day") became *frigedæg* ("Frigg's day").

Months

Month	Derivation
January (31 days)	from the Roman republican calendar month Januarius, named for Janus, god of beginnings
February (28, 29 in leap year)	from the Roman month Februarius, named for Februa, the festival of purification held on the 15th
March (31)	from the Roman month Martius, named for Mars
April (30)	from the Roman month Aprilis, perhaps derived from the Greek Aphrodite (the month being sacred to her Roman equivalent, Venus), or from Latin *aperire*, "to open," for the unfolding of buds and blossoms
May (31)	from the Roman month Maius, probably named for the goddess Maia
June (30)	from the Roman month Junius, probably named for Juno
July (31)	from the Roman month Julius (formerly Quintilis), named for Julius Caesar in 44 BC
August (31)	from the Roman month Augustus (formerly Sextilis), named for Augustus in 8 BC
September (30)	seventh month of the early Roman republican calendar, from Latin *septem*, "seven"
October (31)	eighth month of the republican calendar, from Latin *octo*, "eight"
November (30)	ninth month of the republican calendar, from Latin *novem*, "nine"
December (31)	tenth month of the republican calendar, from Latin *decem*, "ten"

of the sun over the same meridian. Because the orbital motion of the earth makes the sun seem to move slightly eastward each day relative to the stars, the solar day is about four minutes longer than the sidereal day (see SIDEREAL PERIOD).

Day, Doris *orig.* Doris von Kappelhoff (b.1924) U.S. singer and film actress. Born in Cincinnati, she worked as a band vocalist in the 1940s and went on to great success as a solo recording artist, also starring in such film musicals as *Calamity Jane* (1953), *Young at Heart* (1955), and *The Pajama Game* (1957). Playing a sunny, wholesome girl-next-door, she embodied the idealized American woman of the 1950s. She played dramatic roles in *Love Me or Leave Me* (1955) and *The Man Who Knew Too Much* (1956) before starring in bedroom comedies such as *Pillow Talk* (1959) and *That Touch of Mink* (1962).

Day, Dorothy (1897–1980) U.S. journalist and social reformer. Born in Brooklyn, she initially worked for the radical journals *The Call* and *The Masses*. In 1927 she broke her ties with radicalism and converted to Roman Catholicism. After writing for the liberal Catholic journal *Commonweal*, in 1933 she and Peter Maurin (1877–1949) cofounded *The Catholic Worker*. She sought to aid the poor by establishing urban houses of hospitality as part of the Catholic Worker movement. Though her outspoken pacifist views were criticized by Catholic conservatives, she influenced many Catholic liberals.

Dayan \dī-ˈän\, **Moshe** (1915–1981) Israeli soldier and statesman. Born on Israel's first KIBBUTZ of Russian parents, he became a guerrilla fighter against Arab raiders. Later he joined the HAGANA. He lost an eye fighting the Vichy French in Syria during World War II. He was army chief of staff during the SUEZ CRISIS (1956) and later agriculture minister (1959–64). He was defense minister (1967–74) during the SIX-DAY WAR, which brought him widespread adulation. He joined the opposition LIKUD as foreign minister in 1977 and helped broker the 1978 CAMP DAVID ACCORDS. See also ARAB–ISRAELI WARS.

Day-Lewis, C(ecil) (1904–1972) Irish-British poet. Day-Lewis became part of a circle of left-wing poets centered on W. H. AUDEN in the 1930s, though he later turned to an individual lyricism expressed in traditional forms. His works include translations of VIRGIL's *Georgics* (1940), *Aeneid* (1952), and *Eclogues* (1963), and the verse collections *The Room* (1965) and *The Whispering Roots* (1970). He wrote detective novels under the pseudonym Nicholas Blake. He became poet laureate of England in 1968. He was the father of the actor Daniel Day-Lewis (b.1957).

daylight saving time System for uniformly advancing clocks, especially in summer, so as to extend daylight hours. In the Northern Hemisphere, clocks are usually set one hour ahead of STANDARD TIME in late March or in April and are set back in late September or in October. In the U.S. and Canada, daylight saving time begins on the first Sunday in April and ends on the last Sunday in October.

day lily Any plant of the genus *Hemerocallis*, in the LILY FAMILY, consisting of about 15 species of PERENNIAL herbaceous plants distributed from central Europe to E Asia. Members have long-stalked clusters of yellow to red funnel- or bell-shaped flowers that are each short-lived (hence "day" lily). The narrow, sword-shaped leaves are grouped at the base of the plant. Some species are cultivated as ornamentals or for their edible flowers and buds.

Dayton City (pop., 2000: 166,000), SW Ohio. Settled on the Miami River in 1796, it developed as a river port. The 1829 opening of the Miami and Erie Canal between Dayton and CINCINNATI, and the arrival in 1851 of the railroad, stimulated its industrial growth. It was home to Wilbur and Orville WRIGHT. It is the site of Wright-Patterson Air Force Base (established 1946) and the Air Force Institute of Technology (1947).

Daytona Beach Coastal city (pop., 2000: 65,000), NE Florida. Founded in 1870, in 1926 it absorbed the cities of Seabreeze and Daytona. The Ormond-Daytona beach of hard, white sand has been used for automobile speed trials since 1903. The city is known for the Daytona International Speedway.

DC See DIRECT CURRENT

D-Day See NORMANDY CAMPAIGN

DDT *in full* dichlorodiphenyltrichloroethane. Synthetic INSECTICIDE. In 1939 its toxicity in a wide variety of insects was discovered (by Paul Hermann Müller, who was awarded a Nobel Prize) and effectively used against many disease vectors. By the 1960s, many species of insects had developed populations resistant to DDT; meanwhile, DDT was accumulating along the FOOD CHAIN and having toxic effects on birds and fishes. It and similar chemicals were found to have severely reduced the populations of certain birds, including the bald eagle; its use is now tightly controlled in the U.S.

de *or* **te** \ˈde\ (Chinese: "virtue".) In TAOISM, the potentiality of TAO that is present in all things; in CONFUCIANISM, the virtue of internal goodness and propriety. In both systems, it is regarded as the life or moral principle. Personal de flourishes when one abandons ambition and the spirit of contention for a life of naturalness, leading to an awareness of the underlying unity that permeates the universe.

tion. De Vries discovered and named mutation.

DEA See DRUG ENFORCEMENT ADMINISTRATION

Dead Sea *Arabic* **Bahret Lut** \ˈbä-ret-ˈlüt\ *ancient* Lacus Asphaltites. Landlocked salt lake between Israel and Jordan. The lowest body of water on the earth, it averages about 1,312 ft (400 m) below sea level. At 50 mi (80 km) long and up to 11 mi (18 km) wide, its N half belongs to Jordan, while its S half is divided between Jordan and Israel. After the 1967 ARAB–ISRAELI WAR, however, the Israeli army remained in occupation of the entire W shore. It has been associated with biblical history since the time of ABRAHAM.

Dead Sea Scrolls Caches of ancient, mostly Hebrew, manuscripts found at several sites on the NW shore of the DEAD SEA (1947–56). The writings date from between the 3rd cent. B.C. and the 2nd cent. A.D. and total 800–900 manuscripts in 15,000 fragments. Those deposited in 11 caves near the ruins of QUMRAN probably belonged to an ESSENE sectarian community. The community rejected the rest of the Jewish people and saw the world as sharply divided between good and evil. They cultivated a communal life of ritual purity. The Dead Sea Scrolls as a whole represent a wider spectrum of Jewish belief and may have been the contents of libraries from Jerusalem hidden during the war of A.D. 66–73.

deafness Partial or total inability to hear. In conduction deafness, the passage of sound vibrations through the EAR is interrupted. The obstacle may be earwax, a ruptured eardrum, or stapes fixation, which prevents the stapes bone from transmitting sound vibrations to the INNER EAR. In nerve deafness, a defect in the sensory cells of the INNER EAR (e.g., injury by excessive noise) or in the vestibulocochlear nerve prevents the transmission of sound impulses to the brain. See also HEARING AID, SIGN LANGUAGE.

Deák \ˈde-äk\, **Ferenc** (1803–1876) Hungarian politician. A leader of the reform movement for the political emancipation of Hungary, he was appointed minister of justice in 1848 and was the principal author of the reforming "April laws." In the 1860s he put forth Hungary's conditions for reconciliation with Austria in terms that led to the COMPROMISE OF 1867, establishing the dual monarchy of Austria-Hungary.

Dean, Dizzy (*orig.* Jay Hanna) (1911–1974) U.S. baseball pitcher. Born in Lucas, Ark., he did not finish elementary school. He joined the St. Louis Cardinals in 1932, and in five seasons with them led the National League four times in complete games and four times in strikeouts. In 1937 he teamed with his brother Paul ("Daffy") to win the World Series; he won 30 games and lost seven that year, and remains the league's last 30-game winner. He developed arm trouble the same year and never fully regained his form. He was known for his colorful personality, which, after his retirement at 30, served him well as a broadcaster.

Dean, James (Byron) (1931–1955) U.S. film actor. Born in Marion, Ind., he acted on Broadway, where his role in *The Immoralist* (1954) led to a brilliant though brief movie career. He first starred in *East of Eden* (1955). As a misunderstood teenager in *Rebel Without a Cause* (1955) he personified the confused and restless youth of the 1950s. He played a nonconformist ranch hand in his last film, *Giant* (1956).

His death at 24 in an automobile crash before its release contributed to his idolization as a cult figure.

Dearborn City (pop., 2000: 97,000), SE Michigan. Settled in 1795, it originated as a stagecoach stop between DETROIT and CHICAGO. It is the birthplace of Henry FORD and the headquarters of the FORD MOTOR CO. Industrial development began with the building of the Ford assembly plant in 1917.

death penalty See CAPITAL PUNISHMENT

James Dean in *Giant*, 1956

Death Valley Valley, SE California. The lowest, hottest, driest portion of N. America, it is about 140 mi (225 km) long and from 5 to 15 mi (8–24 km) wide. A small pool on the Amargosa River, Badwater, at 282 ft (86 m) below sea level is the lowest point in N. America. Declared a national monument in 1933, it was made a national park in 1994; the park covers 3,336,000 acres (2,351,000 hectares) and extends into Nevada.

DeBakey \də-ˈbā-kē\, **Michael (Ellis)** (b.1908) U.S. surgeon. Born in Lake Charles, La., he devised the "roller pump," to be used in heart-lung machines. His work with the U.S. Surgeon General's office led to the development of mobile army surgical hospitals (MASH units). He also developed an efficient method of grafting frozen blood vessels to correct aortic ANEURYSMS and pioneered the use of plastic tubing instead of grafts. He was the first to perform a successful CORONARY BYPASS, and the first to insert a mechanical device into the chest to assist the heart.

De Beers Consolidated Mines World's largest producer and distributor of diamonds. Diamonds were first discovered in S Africa in the mid-1860s on the de Beer farm. Two diamond mines dug there were at one time the world's most productive. Cecil RHODES bought a claim to the De Beers mine in 1871, and eventually bought claims to most of S Africa's diamond mines. To keep prices high and demand steady, he formed the Diamond Syndicate in the 1890s; as the Central Selling Organization (a De Beers subsidiary), it now controls nearly 80% of the world diamond trade.

Deborah (c.1150–c.1050 B.C.) Prophetess and political leader of ancient Israel. Her story is told in the Old Testament's Book of Judges. With her general, Barak, she is credited with defeating the Canaanite armies led by Sisera. The Israelite victory over the Canaanites was celebrated in the Song of Deborah (Judges 5), possibly the earliest portion of the Bible.

Debs, Eugene V(ictor) (1855–1926) U.S. labor organizer. Debs was born in Terre Haute, Ind., and left home at 14 to work in the railroad shops. He became president of the American Railway Union in 1893. His role in the PULLMAN STRIKE led to a six-month prison term in 1895. He helped found the U.S. Socialist Party in 1898, and ran as its presidential candidate five times (1900–20). In 1905 he helped found the INDUSTRIAL WORKERS OF THE WORLD. Debs was charged with sedition in 1918 after denouncing the 1917 Espionage Act; he conducted his last presidential campaign from prison.

Debussy \ˌde-byü-ˈsē\, **(Achille-) Claude** (1862–1918) French composer. Born into near-poverty, he showed an early gift for the piano. Influenced by the Symbolist poets and Impressionist painters, he was early led toward a compositional style of great originality, shunning the strictures of traditional counterpoint and harmony to achieve new effects of great subtlety through unusual voice leading and timbral colors to evoke pictorial images and moods. He is regarded as the founder of musical IMPRESSIONISM. His works significantly weakened the hold of traditional tonal harmony, and his effect on such composers as Maurice RAVEL, Igor STRAVINSKY, Bela BARTOK, and Pierre BOULEZ have made him the most influential French composer of the last three centuries. His works include the opera *Pelléas et Mélisande* (1902); the orchestral works *Prelude to The After-*

noon of a Faun (1894), *Nocturnes* (1899), *La mer* (1905), and *Images* (1912); the piano sets *Estampes* (1903), *Images* (1905, 1907), *Children's Corner* (1908), *24 Préludes* (1910, 1913), and *12 Études* (1915); and many songs.

Decadents Group of poets of the end of the 19th cent., including some French Symbolists (see SYMBOLIST MOVEMENT), notably Stéphane MALLARMÉ and Paul VERLAINE, and the later generation of England's Aesthetic movement (see AESTHETICISM), notably Oscar WILDE. Many nonpoets, including the artist Aubrey BEARDS-

Claude Debussy Painting by Marcel Baschet, 1884

LEY, are also often associated with the Decadents. The Decadents emphasized art for art's sake, seeing it as autonomous and opposed to nature and to the materialistic preoccupations of industrialized society, and therefore stressed the bizarre, incongruous, and artificial in both their work and their lives.

decapod Any of more than 8,000 species (order Decapoda) of CRUSTACEANS having five pairs of legs attached to the thorax. The shrimplike species, which can be as small as 0.5 in. (12 mm), have a slender body with well-developed fantail and, often, long, slender legs. The crablike types, whose claw span can measure 13 ft (4 m), have a flattened body and, frequently, stout short legs and a reduced tail fan. Decapods are commercially valuable throughout the world. Some species (e.g., fiddler and HERMIT CRABS) are adapted to terrestrial environments. See also CRAB, CRAYFISH, LOBSTER, SHRIMP.

Decapolis \di-ˈka-pə-lis\ League of 10 ancient Greek cities, including DAMASCUS, in E PALESTINE. It was formed after the Roman conquest in 63 B.C. for mutual protection against their Semitic neighbors. The name also denotes the roughly contiguous territory formed by these cities, all but one of which lay east of the JORDAN RIVER. The league survived until the 2nd cent. A.D.

decathlon Composite athletic contest that consists of ten different track-and-field competitions: the 100-, 400-, and 1,500-m runs, the 110-m high hurdles, the JAVELIN and DISCUS throws, SHOT PUT, POLE VAULT, HIGH JUMP, and LONG JUMP. It is a two-day Olympic event. Decathletes are often regarded as the finest all-around athletes in the world.

Decatur \di-ˈkā-tər\, **Stephen** (1779–1820) U.S. naval officer. Born in Sinepuxent, Md., in the Tripolitan War he led a daring 1804 expedition into the harbor of Tripoli to burn a captured U.S. ship. In the War of 1812 he captured the British ship *Macedonian*. In 1815 he commanded a squadron in the Mediterranean that forced a peace with the Barbary Coast states on U.S. terms. At a banquet on his return he gave a toast that included the words "Our country, right or wrong." He was killed in a duel.

Deccan Peninsula of India south of the NARMADA RIVER. In a more restricted sense, it is the tableland between the Narmada and Krishna rivers. Its average elevation is about 2,000 feet (600 m). Its principal rivers, the GODAVARI, Krishna, and KAVERI, flow from the W. GHATS eastward to the Bay of BENGAL. Its early inhabitants were not reached by the 2nd millennium B.C. Aryan invasion. Ruled by MAURYAN (4th–2nd cent. B.C.) and GUPTA (4th–6th cent. A.D.) dynasties, it became an independent Muslim kingdom in 1347. Later split up into five Muslim sultanates, Deccan was largely conquered by the MUGHAL DYNASTY in the 17th cent. In the 18th cent. it was the scene of rivalry between the British and French, and subsequently of the British struggle against the Maratha confederacy.

Decembrist revolt (Dec. 1825) Unsuccessful uprising by Russian revolutionaries. Following the death of ALEXANDER I, a group of liberal citizens and military officers staged a rebellion to prevent the accession of NICHOLAS I. The poorly organized revolt was easily suppressed. Afterwards

289 Decembrists were tried; five were executed, and the rest were imprisoned or banished. Their martyrdom inspired later generations of Russian dissidents.

decibel (dB) Unit for measuring the relative intensities of sounds or the relative amounts of acoustic or electric power. Because the decibel scale is a logarithmic one, a sound with an intensity that is twice that of a reference sound corresponds to an increase of a little more than 3 dB. In common practice, the reference point of 0 dB is set at the intensity of the least perceptible sound, the threshold of hearing. On such a scale, a 10-dB sound is 10 times the intensity of the reference sound, a 20-dB sound is 100 times the reference intensity, and so on.

Nonlinear (Decibel) and Linear (Intensity) Scales

Decibels	Intensity*	Type of sound
130	10	artillery fire at close proximity (threshold of pain)
120	1	amplified rock music; near jet engine
110	10^{-1}	loud orchestral music, in audience
100	10^{-2}	electric saw
90	10^{-3}	bus or truck interior
80	10^{-4}	automobile interior
70	10^{-5}	average street noise; loud telephone bell
60	10^{-6}	normal conversation; business office
50	10^{-7}	restaurant; private office
40	10^{-8}	quiet room in home
30	10^{-9}	quiet lecture hall; bedroom
20	10^{-10}	radio, television, or recording studio
10	10^{-11}	soundproof room
0	10^{-12}	threshold of hearing

*In watts per square meter.

deciduous tree Broad-leaved tree that sheds all its leaves during one season. Deciduous forests occur naturally in temperate climates with a winter season and year-round precipitation in E N. America, W Eurasia, and NE Asia. OAKS, BEECHES, BIRCHES, CHESTNUTS, ASPENS, ELMS, MAPLES, and BASSWOODS (or LINDENS) are the dominant trees in these deciduous forests. Other plants that shed their leaves seasonally may also be called deciduous. See also CONIFER, EVERGREEN.

decision theory In STATISTICS and related subfields of philosophy, the theory and method of formulating and solving general decision problems. Such a problem is specified by a set of possible states of the environment or possible initial conditions; a set of available experiments and a set of possible outcomes for each experiment, giving information about the state of affairs preparatory to making a decision; a set of available acts depending on the experiment's outcomes; and a set of possible consequences of the acts, in which each possible act assigns to each possible initial state some particular consequence. The problem is dealt with by assessing probabilities of consequences, and by assigning a utility function to the set of consequences. See also COST–BENEFIT ANALYSIS, GAME THEORY.

Declaration of Independence (July 4, 1776) Document approved by the CONTINENTAL CONGRESS that announced the separation of 13 N. American British colonies from Britain. The ongoing AMERICAN REVOLUTION gradually convinced the colonists that separation from Britain was essential. At the Continental Congress on June 7, R. H. LEE of Virginia offered a resolution for independence. The congress appointed Thomas JEFFERSON, John ADAMS, Benjamin FRANKLIN, Roger SHERMAN, and Robert LIVINGSTON to draft a declaration. Jefferson was persuaded to write the draft, which was presented with few changes on June 28. It began with a declaration of individual rights and then listed the acts of tyranny by GEORGE III as justification for seeking independence. After debate and changes to accommodate regional interests, including deletion of a condemnation of slavery, it was approved on July 4 as "The Unanimous Declaration of the Thirteen United States of America." It was printed and read aloud to a crowd outside, then engrossed (written in script) on parchment and signed by the 56 delegates.

Declaration of the Rights of Man and of the Citizen Manifesto adopted by France's National Assembly in 1789, which contained the principles that inspired the FRENCH

REVOLUTION. One of the basic charters of human liberties, it declared that "all men are born free and equal in rights," specified as the rights of liberty, private property, the inviolability of the person, and resistance to oppression. It also established the principle of equality before the law and the freedoms of religion and speech.

decolonization Process by which colonies become independent of the colonizing country. Decolonization was gradual and peaceful for some British colonies largely settled by expatriates, but violent for others, where native rebellions were energized by nationalism. The postwar European nations generally lacked the wealth and political capacity necessary to suppress faraway revolts and lacked the support of the new superpowers, the U.S. and the Soviet Union. The U.S. relinquished the Philippines in 1946. Britain left India in 1947, Palestine in 1948, and Egypt in 1956; it withdrew from Africa in the 1950s and '60s, from various island protectorates in the 1970s and '80s, and from Hong Kong in 1997. The French left Vietnam in 1954 and N. Africa by 1962. Portugal gave up its African colonies in the 1970s.

decompression chamber See HYPERBARIC CHAMBER

decompression sickness *or* **bends** *or* **caisson disease** Harmful effects of rapid change from a higher- to a lower-pressure environment. Small amounts of the gases in air are dissolved in body tissues. When pilots of unpressurized aircraft go to high altitudes, or when divers breathing compressed air return to the surface, some gases come out of solution. Rising slowly allows the gases to enter the bloodstream and be taken to the lungs and exhaled; with a quicker ascent, the gases (mostly nitrogen) form bubbles in the tissues. In the nervous system, they can cause paralysis, convulsions, and motor and sensory problems; in the joints, severe pain and restricted mobility (the bends); in the respiratory system, coughing and difficulty breathing. Severe cases include SHOCK. See also HYPERBARIC CHAMBER.

deconstruction Method of literary criticism that assumes that language refers only to itself rather than to a reality outside the text and that asserts multiple conflicting interpretations of a text. From this view, the "meaning" of a text may bear little relation to the author's conscious intentions. Deconstruction was initiated by Jacques DERRIDA in the 1960s and has become an important part of POSTMODERNISM, especially in POSTSTRUCTURALISM and textual analysis.

Decoration Day See MEMORIAL DAY

deduction In LOGIC, a type of inference distinguished by the fact that if the premises of the inference are all true, then the conclusion must also be true. This does not imply that all the premises or the conclusion of any deduction must in fact be true. See also INDUCTION.

deed See ESCROW

Deep Blue Computer chess-playing system designed by IBM. In 1996 Deep Blue made history by defeating the world champion, Garry KASPAROV. In the 1997 rematch, it won the deciding sixth game in only nineteen moves; its victory marked the first time a current world champion had lost a match to a computer under tournament conditions. In its final configuration, Deep Blue used 256 processors working in tandem to evaluate 200 million chess positions per second, as opposed to the three positions per second that Kasparov can evaluate.

deep-sea trench *or* **oceanic trench** Any long, narrow, steep-sided depression in the ocean bottom in which maximum oceanic depths (24,000–36,000 ft, or 7,000–11,000 m) occur. The deepest is the MARIANA TRENCH. Most trenches occur at SUBDUCTION ZONES, where one tectonic plate is thrust under another.

deep-sea vent Hydrothermal (hot-water) vent formed on the ocean floor when seawater circulates through hot volcanic rocks, often located where new oceanic crust is being formed. The hot solution emerging into cold seawater precipitates mineral deposits that are rich in iron, copper, zinc, and other metals. Outflow of these heated waters probably accounts for 20% of the earth's heat loss. Exotic biological communities are now known to exist around the vents, depending not on photosynthesis but on chemosynthesis by sulfur-fixing bacteria.

deer Any of the RUMINANTS in the family Cervidae, which have two large and two small hooves on each foot and antlers on the males of most species and on the females of some species. Deer live mainly in forests but may be found in deserts, tundra, and swamps and on high mountainsides. They are native to Europe, Asia, N. America, S. America, and N Africa and have been introduced widely elsewhere. Females are usually called does, and males bucks. Deer range in shoulder height from the 12-in. (30-cm) pudu (genus *Pudu*) to the 6.5-ft (2-m) MOOSE. They shed their antlers each year, and new ones grow in. Deer feed on grass, twigs, bark, and shoots. They are hunted for their meat, hides, and antlers. See also CARIBOU, ELK, MULE DEER, MUNTJAC, WHITE-TAILED DEER.

Deere, John (1804–1886) U.S. inventor and manufacturer of agricultural implements. Born in Rutland, Vt., he worked as a blacksmith before moving to Illinois. There he found that wood-and-cast-iron plows, used in the E U.S. from the 1820s, were unsuited to the heavy, sticky prairie soils. By 1838 he had sold three plows of his design, and by 1857 10,000. In 1868 Deere & Co. was incorporated, and it gradually began making cultivators and other farm machinery.

deer mouse *or* **white-footed mouse** Any of about 60 species (genus *Peromyscus,* family Cricetidae) of small, delicate RODENTS that are active at night and are found in habitats from Alaska to S. America. Deer mice are 3–6.5 in. (8–17 cm) long (excluding the long tail) and have large eyes, soft fur, and relatively large ears. They eat plant and animal matter and nest in burrows or trees. Clean, easily cared for, and prolific, they are often used as laboratory animals.

defamation In law, issuance of false statements about a person that injure the reputation of or deter others from associating with that person. Libel and slander are the legal subcategories of defamation. Libel is defamation in print, pictures, or any other visual symbols. Slander is defamation by oral communication. The defense in defamation cases often takes the form of seeking to establish the truth of the statements in question.

defecation \ˌdef-ə-ˈkā-shən\ *or* **bowel movement** Elimination of FECES. PERISTALSIS moves feces through the COLON to the RECTUM, where they stimulate the urge to defecate. The rectum shortens, pushing the feces into the anal canal, where internal and external sphincters allow them to be passed or retained. Long delay of defecation causes constipation and hardened feces. See also DIARRHEA, INCONTINENCE.

Defense, U.S. Department of Federal executive division responsible for ensuring U.S. national security and supervising U.S. military forces. Based in the PENTAGON, it includes the Joint Chiefs of Staff, the departments of the U.S. ARMY, U.S. NAVY, and U.S. AIR FORCE, and numerous defense agencies and allied services. It was formed in 1947 by an act of Congress (amended 1949) combining the War and Navy Departments.

defense mechanism In psychoanalytic theory, an often unconscious mental process that makes possible compromise solutions to personal problems or conflicts by concealing from oneself internal drives or feelings that threaten to lower self-esteem or provoke ANXIETY. The term was first used by Sigmund FREUD in 1894. The major defense mechanisms are REPRESSION, the process by which unacceptable desires are excluded from consciousness; reaction formation, an emotional response opposite to what one really feels; projection, the attribution of one's own ideas, feelings, or attitudes (especially blame or guilt) to others; regression, reversion to an earlier mental or behavioral level; denial, the refusal to accept a painful fact; rationalization, the substitution of rational and creditable motives for the true (but threatening) ones; and sublimation, the diversion of an instinctual desire from its primitive form to a more socially or culturally acceptable form. See also EGO, NEUROSIS, PSYCHOANALYSIS.

deficit financing In government, the practice of spending more money than is received as revenue, the difference being made up by borrowing or minting new funds. The term usually refers to a conscious attempt to stimulate the economy by lowering tax rates or increasing expenditures. Critics denounce it as shortsighted. Advocates argue that it can be used successfully in response to a RECESSION or DEPRESSION, proposing that the ideal of an annually balanced budget should give way to that of a budget balanced over the span of a BUSINESS CYCLE. See also NATIONAL DEBT.

definition In philosophy, the specification of the meaning of an expression relative to a language. Lexical definition specifies the meaning of an expression by stating it in terms of other expressions whose meaning is assumed to be known (e.g., a ewe is a female sheep). Ostensive definition specifies the meaning of an expression by pointing to examples of things to which the expression applies (e.g., green is the color of grass, limes, and emeralds). Stipulative definition assigns a new meaning to an expression (or a meaning to a new expression).

deflation Contraction in the volume of available money or CREDIT that results in a general decline in prices. Attempts are sometimes made to bring on deflation in order to combat INFLATION and slow the economy. Deflation is characteristic of DEPRESSIONS and RECESSIONS.

Defoe \di-ˈfō\, **Daniel** *orig.* Daniel Foe (1660–1731) British novelist, pamphleteer, and journalist. A well-educated London merchant, he became an acute economic theorist and began to write eloquent, witty, often audacious tracts on public affairs. A satire he published resulted in his being imprisoned in 1703. In 1704–13 he wrote practically single-handedly the periodical *Review,* a serious and forceful paper that influenced later essay periodicals. Late in life he turned to fiction. He achieved literary immortality with the novel *Robinson Crusoe* (1719). He is also remembered for the vivid, picaresque *Moll Flanders* (1722); the nonfictional *Journal of the Plague Year* (1722), on the GREAT PLAGUE OF LONDON in 1664–65; and *Roxana* (1724), a prototype of the modern novel.

defoliant Chemical dust or spray applied to plants to cause their leaves to drop off prematurely. Defoliants sometimes are applied to crop plants such as COTTON to facilitate harvesting. They have also been used in warfare to eliminate enemy food crops and potential areas of concealment. See also AGENT ORANGE.

De Forest, Lee (1873–1961) U.S. inventor. Born in Council Bluffs, Iowa, he had invented many gadgets by age 13. After earning a PhD from Yale Univ., he founded the De Forest Wireless Telegraph Co. (1902) and gave public demonstrations of wireless telegraphy, including a live performance by Enrico CARUSO in 1910. He developed a sound-on-film optical-recording system called Phonofilm and demonstrated it in theaters (1923–27); the film industry soon converted to talking pictures using a

Lee De Forest, 1907

similar process. A poor businessman and a poorer judge of people, he was twice defrauded by his business partners. He sold his patents at low prices to such firms as American Telephone & Telegraph Co., which profited highly from their commercial development. He was widely honored as the father of radio and the grandfather of television.

deforestation Process of clearing forests. Rates of deforestation are particularly high in the tropics, where poor soil quality has led to the practice of routine clear-cutting to create new crop land. Deforestation can lead to EROSION, drought, loss of biodiversity through extinction of plant and animal species, and increased atmospheric carbon dioxide. Many nations have undertaken afforestation or reforestation projects to reverse its effects or to increase available timber. See also GREENHOUSE EFFECT.

Degas \də-ˈgä\, **(Hilaire-Germain-) Edgar** (1834–1917) French painter, graphic artist, and sculptor. The son of a wealthy banker, he spent much time in Italy copying the old masters and became a skilled draftsman, producing history paintings and portraits. In the 1860s he was introduced to IMPRESSIONISM by Édouard MANET and turned for his subject matter to the city life of Paris, particularly the ballet, theater, circus, racetrack, and cafés. Influenced by Japanese prints and the new medium of photography, he created figure groups seen informally and in movement, similar in effect to snapshots (e.g., *Place de la Concorde*). His fascination with the ballet and the racetrack sprang from his interest in picturing people absorbed in the practiced movements of their occupations. He worked often in pastel, his favorite medium, producing series of bathers, ballerinas, and horse races. From about 1880 he modeled wax figures, which were cast in bronze after his death.

De Gasperi \dā-gäs-'pā-rē\, **Alcide** (1881–1954) Italian prime minister (1945–53). Born in the S Tirol, he served in the Austrian parliament 1911–19, and sought the annexation of his region to Italy. He later served in the Italian parliament (1921–27) as a founder of the ITALIAN POPULAR PARTY. In World War II he was active in the resistance. He returned to Italian politics as head of the newly formed Christian Democratic Party. As prime minister (1945–53), he enacted a new constitution, instituted land reform, oversaw Italy's postwar economic reconstruction, and led Italy into NATO.

de Gaulle, Charles (-André-Marie-Joseph) (1890–1970) French soldier and president of France (1958–69). He joined the army in 1913 and fought with distinction in World War I. In 1940 he was promoted to brigadier general; after the fall of France, he left for England and started the FREE FRENCH movement. He moved to Algiers in 1943 and became president of the French Committee of National Liberation. After the liberation of Paris, he headed two provisional governments, then resigned in 1946. He actively opposed the FOURTH REPUBLIC before retiring from public life in 1953. When an insurrection in Algeria threatened to bring civil war to France, he returned in 1958 as prime minister with powers to reform the constitution. That same year he was elected president of the new FIFTH REPUBLIC. He ended the ALGERIAN WAR and transformed France's African territories into 12 independent states. He withdrew France from NATO, and his policy of neutrality during the Vietnam War was seen by many as anti-Americanism. He sought détente with Iron Curtain countries and traveled widely to form a bond with French-speaking countries. After the civil unrest of May 1968 by students and workers, he was defeated in a referendum on constitutional amendments and resigned in 1969.

Charles de Gaulle, 1967

degenerative joint disease See OSTEOARTHRITIS

degree, academic Title conferred by a COLLEGE or UNIVERSITY to indicate completion of a course of study or extent of academic achievement. In medieval Europe, there were only two degrees: master (a scholar of arts and grammar) and doctor (a scholar of philosophy, theology, medicine, or law). The baccalaureate, or bachelor's degree, was originally simply a stage toward mastership. Today in Anglo-American countries the Bachelor of Arts degree (BA or AB) or Bachelor of Science (BS) is awarded after four years of college study, the Master of Arts (MA) or Master of Science (MS) after about two additional years, and the Doctor of Philosophy (PhD) after several years of postbaccalaureate study and research. The Associate of Arts degree (AA) is now awarded by U.S. COMMUNITY COLLEGES. Common professional degrees are the Doctor of Jurisprudence (JD) and the Doctor of Medicine (MD). In France the *licence* is conferred on completion of three or four years of university study, the *maîtrise* on the passing of advanced examinations, and the *doctorat* on completion of several years of advanced academic studies. In Germany the doctorate is the only degree granted, though diploma examinations are offered to students who forgo the doctoral requirements.

De Havilland, Geoffrey (*later* Sir Geoffrey) (1882–1965) British aircraft designer and manufacturer. In 1910 he built and flew an airplane with a 50-horsepower engine. He formed his own company in 1920 and built the commercially successful two-seater Moth. In World War II the twin-engined Mosquito was the company's most successful product. After the war he pioneered the manufacture of jet-propelled airplanes with his Comet passenger jet.

de Havilland \də-'ha-və-lənd\, **Olivia (Mary)** (b.1916) U.S. film actress. Born in Tokyo to British parents, she was raised in California. After playing the delicate heroine opposite Errol FLYNN in such swashbucklers as *Captain Blood* (1935) and *The Adventures of Robin Hood* (1938), she revealed dramatic depth in *Gone with the Wind* (1939), *To Each His Own* (1946, Academy Award), *The Snake Pit* (1948), and *The Heiress* (1949, Academy Award). Her victory in a landmark lawsuit against WARNER BROTHERS (1945) limited actors' contracts to seven years. Her sister Joan Fontaine (b.1917) also had a notable screen career, appearing in such films as *Rebecca* (1940) and *Suspicion* (1941, Academy Award).

dehydration Method of preserving food in which moisture is removed to inhibit the growth of microorganisms and reduce bulk. It is an ancient practice, used by prehistoric peoples in sun-drying seeds, by N. American Indians in sun-drying meat, and by the Japanese in drying fish and rice. It was used to prepare troop rations in World War II, and campers and relief agencies also discovered its advantages. Commercial dehydration equipment includes tunnel dryers, kilns, and vacuum dryers. A combination of dehydration and freezing is used in the process of freeze-drying, whereby solid food remains frozen while its liquid escapes as vapor.

dehydration Loss of WATER, almost always along with SALT, from the body, caused by restricted water intake or excessive water loss. Early symptoms of water deprivation are thirst, decreased saliva, and impaired swallowing. Later, tissues shrink, including the skin and eyes. Mild FEVER rises as PLASMA volume and cardiac output decrease, and PERSPIRATION decreases or stops. URINE output falls, and the KIDNEYS cannot filter wastes from the blood. Irreversible SHOCK can occur at this point. The cause of dehydration is treated first; then water and electrolytes are given.

deinonychus \dī-'nä-ni-kəs\ Any of a genus (*Deinonychus*) of THEROPOD DINOSAURS that flourished during the Early CRETACEOUS PERIOD (144–98 million years ago). Deinonychus walked and ran on two legs, yet its killing devices, large sickle-like talons, required it to stand on one foot while slashing at its prey with the other. Its long, outstretched tail was enclosed in bundles of bony rods, making it very rigid. About 8–13 ft (2.4–4 m) long and weighing 100–150 lbs (45–68 kg), it had a large brain and was evidently a fast, agile predator.

Deism Belief in God based on reason rather than revelation or the teaching of any specific religion. A form of natural religion, Deism originated in England in the early 17th cent. as a rejection of orthodox Christianity. Deists asserted that reason could find evidence of God in nature and that God had created the world and then left it to operate under his laws. By the late 18th cent. Deism was the dominant religious attitude among Europe's educated classes; it was accepted by many upper-class Americans of the same era, including the first three U.S. presidents.

de Klerk \də-'klerk\, **F(rederik) W(illem)** (b.1936) President of S. Africa (1989–94) who ended the APARTHEID system and negotiated a transition to majority rule. Replacing P. W. BOTHA as NATIONAL PARTY leader and president, de Klerk released political prisoners, including Nelson MANDELA, and lifted the ban on the AFRICAN NATIONAL CONGRESS. He and Mandela jointly received the 1993 Nobel Peace Prize. Following all-race elections in 1994, Mandela became president and de Klerk second deputy president. He retired in 1997.

de Kooning, Willem (1904–1997) Dutch-U.S. painter. He studied art in Rotterdam and entered the U.S. as a stowaway in 1926. Settling in Hoboken, N.J., he supported himself as a house painter before moving to New York City, where he came under the influence of Arshile GORKY. He worked for the WPA FEDERAL ART PROJECT 1935–37. In the

1930s and '40s his work was both figurative and abstract; the two tendencies eventually fused, and in the 1940s he became one of the leading exponents of ABSTRACT EXPRESSIONISM, and particularly of ACTION PAINTING. Among his best-known works is a series of deliberately vulgar images of women done with roughly applied pigment and raw colors (e.g., *Woman I*, 1950–52; *Woman and Bicycle,* 1953).

Delacroix \de-lə-ˈkrwä\, **(Ferdinand-) Eugène (-Victor)** (1798–1863) French painter. As a young man he was strongly influenced by his fellow student Théodore GERICAULT and by the English landscape painters, but he painted mostly historical events and scenes from literature. In 1822 he exhibited *Dante and Virgil in Hell,* a landmark in French 19th-cent. Romanticism. After his success at the Paris Salon, he was commissioned to decorate government buildings and became one of the most distinguished mural painters in the history of French art. In 1830 he painted *Liberty Leading the People* to commemorate the July Revolution that brought LOUIS-PHILIPPE to the French throne. On a trip to Morocco in 1832 he acquired a wealth of visual imagery on which he would draw throughout his life. His output was enormous; after his death, more than 9,000 works were found in his Paris studio (now a museum). His use of color influenced the development of IMPRESSIONISM.

Delany, Martin R(obison) (1812–1885) U.S. abolitionist. Born in Charles Town, Va., he worked in Pittsburgh as a doctor's assistant. In the 1840s he founded a newspaper, *Mystery,* to publicize grievances of blacks and copublished the *North Star* (1846–49) with Frederick DOUGLASS. One of the first blacks admitted to Harvard Medical School, he later practiced in Pittsburgh. He moved to Canada in 1856, but returned early in the Civil War to recruit for the 54th Massachusetts Volunteers. He was made a major, the first black to receive a regular army commission.

Delany, Samuel R. *in full* Samuel Ray Delany, Jr. (b.1942) U.S. science-fiction novelist and critic. Born in New York City into a distinguished black family, he published his first novel in 1962. His highly imaginative works address racial and social issues, sexuality, heroic quests, and the nature of language. *Dhalgren* (1975), his most controversial novel, tells of a young bisexual man searching for identity in a large, decaying city. Other works include the novels *Babel-17* (1966), *The Einstein Intersection* (1967), *Triton* (1976), and *Stars in My Pocket Like Grains of Sand* (1984).

Delaunay \də-lō-ˈnā\, **Robert** (1885–1941) French painter. He spent his early career as a stage designer. In 1909–11 his color experiments culminated in a series of paintings of the Eiffel Tower, which combined fragmented Cubist forms with dynamic movement and vibrant color. The introduction of bright color to Cubism, which came to be known as Orphism, distinguished his work from that of the more orthodox Cubist painters. With his wife, the Ukrainian-born painter and textile designer Sonia Terk Delaunay (1885–1979), he painted abstract mural decorations for the 1937 Paris Exposition.

De Laurentiis \dä-laů-ˈren-tēs, *Engl* ˌdē-lȯr-ˈen-shəs\, **Dino** (b.1919) Italian-U.S. film producer. He produced his first film at 20 and scored his first hit with *Bitter Rice* (1948). In partnership with Carlo Ponti (b.1910), he produced such admired films as Federico FELLINI's *La strada* (1954, Academy Award) and *The Nights of Cabiria* (1956, Academy Award). In the early 1960s he built a studio, Dinocittà, where he made several unsuccessful epics; he was forced to sell it in the early 1970s. He then moved to the U.S., where he produced such films as *Serpico* (1973), *Ragtime* (1981), and *Crimes of the Heart* (1986). A string of failures forced him into bankruptcy, but he recovered and continued producing films into his eighties.

Delaware State (pop., 2000: 783,000), middle Atlantic region, U.S. Covering 2,057 sq mi (5,328 sq km), its capital is DOVER. Originally inhabited by ALGONQUIAN tribes, Delaware's first permanent white settlement was by Swedes at Fort Christina, now WILMINGTON, in 1638. In 1655 New Sweden was taken by the Dutch of New Amsterdam and in 1664 by the English. Delaware was thereafter a part of New York until 1682, when it was ceded to William PENN. It was governed by Pennsylvania until 1776, although it was granted its own assembly in 1704. The first state to ratify the U.S. Constitution in 1787, it is the nation's second-smallest state but one of its most densely populated. Chemical manufacturing is the major industry, followed by food processing. Delaware's most important transportation artery is the Chesapeake and Delaware Canal, deepened for ocean shipping, which shortens the water route between PHILADELPHIA and BALTIMORE.

Delaware *or* **Lenni Lenape** \le-nē-ˈle-nə-pē\ Confederation of ALGONQUIAN-speaking N. American Indians who occupied the Atlantic seaboard from what is now S Delaware to W Long Island, especially the Delaware River Valley. They depended primarily on agriculture, but also hunted and fished. The Delaware were the Indians most friendly to William PENN; they were rewarded by the infamous Walking Purchase, a treaty that deprived them of their own lands and forced them to settle on lands assigned to the Iroquois. After 1690 they drifted westward. They sided with the French in the FRENCH AND INDIAN WAR (1754–63) and helped defeat the British general Edward Braddock. In 1867 most of the remaining Delaware were removed to Oklahoma. Today they number about 10,000.

Delaware Bay Inlet of the Atlantic Ocean. With the Delaware River, it forms the New Jersey–Delaware state border. Bordered by marshy lowlands, the bay is an important link in the ATLANTIC INTRACOASTAL WATERWAY.

De La Warr \ˈde-lə-ˌwȯr\, **Baron** *or* **Baron Delaware** *orig.* Thomas West (1577–1618) English founder of Virginia. After serving under the Earl of Essex in the Netherlands and Ireland, he became a member of the Virginia Co. and was appointed governor in 1610. He and 150 settlers arrived at Jamestown as another group was abandoning the colony. He established two forts on the James River and rebuilt Jamestown. The state of Delaware is named for him.

Delbrück \ˈdel-ˌbru̇k\, **Max** (1906–1981) German-U.S. biologist. In 1939 he discovered a one-step process for growing bacteriophages that, after an hour of inactivity, would induce a phage to multiply to produce several hundred thousands of progeny. In 1946 he and A. D. Hershey (1908–1997) independently discovered that the genetic material of different kinds of viruses can combine to create new types of viruses, a process previously believed to be limited to higher, sexually reproducing forms of life. In 1969 he shared a Nobel Prize with Hershey and Salvador LURIA.

Delcassé \del-kä-ˈsā\, **Théophile** (1852–1923) French politician. A journalist, he was elected to the Chamber of Deputies in 1885. As foreign minister in six successive governments (1898–1905), he reached agreement with the British that led to the ENTENTE CORDIALE. Considered the principal architect of the new system of European alliances formed before World War I, he also paved the way for the Anglo–Russian agreement of 1907.

De Leon, Daniel (1852–1914) U.S. (Dutch-born) socialist. Born in Curaçao, he arrived in the U.S. in 1874. He joined the Socialist Labor Party in 1890 and soon became one of its leaders. Finding the labor union leadership insufficiently radical, he led a faction that seceded from the Knights of Labor in 1895, and in 1905 he helped found the INDUSTRIAL WORKERS OF THE WORLD (IWW). In 1908 his leadership was rejected by extremists who favored more violent forms of political activity.

Delft City (pop., 1995 est.: 93,000), SW Netherlands. Founded in 1075 and chartered in 1246, it was a trade center in the 16th–17th cent., famous for its delftware pottery. It was the birthplace of Johannes VERMEER (1632). Landmarks include a Gothic church, a Renaissance-style town hall, and a 17th-cent. armory.

Delhi sultanate Principal Muslim sultanate in N. India, 13th–16th cent. Its creation owed much to the campaigns of Muhammad of Ghur between 1175 and 1206. During the reign of Sultan Iltutmish (1211–36), a permanent capital was established at Delhi and political ties with Ghur were severed. Under the Khalji dynasty, the sultanate was an imperial power 1290–1320. Shattered by TIMUR's invasion (1398–99), it somewhat recovered under the Lodi (Afghan) dynasty (1451–1526). It fell again to BABUR (1526), then finally was subsumed into AKBAR's Mughal empire (1556).

Delian League \ˈdē-lē-ən\ Confederacy of ancient Greek states led by Athens and based on the island of DELOS.

DE

Founded in 478 B.C. to combat Persia, its members included Aegean states and islands. It achieved a major victory in 467–466 when its fleet drove out Persian garrisons on the S Anatolian coast. After 454 its leaders moved the treasury to Athens for safekeeping, used it to rebuild the city's temples, and treated the league as the Athenian empire. After defeating Athens in battle in 405, Sparta disbanded the league in 404. Fear of Sparta helped revive the league in the early 4th cent., but it weakened as Sparta declined and was crushed by PHILIP II at the Battle of Chaeronea (338).

Delibes \də-ˈlēb\, **(Clément Philibert) Léo** (1836–1891) French composer. He worked as a church organist and as chorus master at the Paris Opera. Though he composed almost 30 operas, operettas, and ballets, as well as many choral pieces, he is remembered today for three works: the ballets *Coppélia* (1870) and *Sylvia* (1876) and the opera *Lakmé* (1883).

DeLillo \de-ˈlil-ō\, **Don** (b.1936) U.S. novelist. Born in the Bronx, N.Y., he worked in advertising before beginning to write seriously. His postmodernist works portray the unrest and alienation of an America cosseted by material excess and stupefied by empty mass culture and politics. *Ratner's Star* (1976) displayed a baroque comic sense and verbal facility. His vision later turned darker and his characters more willful in their destructiveness and ignorance, as in *The Names* (1982), *White Noise* (1985), *Libra* (1988), *Mao II* (1991), and *Underworld* (1997).

delirium Mental disturbance with disorientation and confused thinking. The patient is drowsy, restless, and fearful of imaginary disasters, sometimes with hallucinations. Delirium usually results from a disorder affecting the brain (e.g., fever, intoxication, head trauma). Alcoholic delirium results not from excessive alcohol consumption alone but from exhaustion, malnutrition (particularly lack of THIAMINE), and DEHYDRATION.

delirium tremens (DTs) \di-ˈlir-ē-əm-ˈtrē-menz\ DELIRIUM seen in severe cases of alcohol withdrawal (see ALCOHOLISM) complicated by exhaustion, lack of food, and dehydration. The whole body trembles, sometimes with seizures, disorientation, and hallucinations. It lasts 3–10 days, with a reported death rate of 1–20%. Hallucinations may develop independently and may last days to weeks.

Delius \ˈdē-lē-əs\, **Frederick (Theodore Albert)** (1862–1934) British-French composer. Born to German parents in England, he studied music in Germany and later moved to France, eventually settling in a village near Paris. After World War I he gradually succumbed to paralysis and blindness, the consequence of syphilis. His works include the operas *A Village Romeo and Juliet* (1901) and *Fennimore and Gerda* (1910); the tone poems *Brigg Fair* (1907) and *On Hearing the First Cuckoo in Spring* (1912); and the choral works *Appalachia* (1903) and *A Mass of Life* (1908).

delivery See PARTURITION

dell'Abbate, Niccolo See Niccolo dell'ABBATE

Della Robbia family \ˌdäl-lä-ˈrôb-yə\ Family of Italian artists active in Florence. The first works of Luca Della Robbia (1399/1400–1482) were reliefs sculptured in marble, most notably those in Florence Cathedral (1432–37). He is remembered mainly for his development of glazed terra-cotta as a medium for sculpture, as in his roundels of the Apostles (c.1444) in Filippo BRUNELLESCHI's Pazzi Chapel in Santa Croce. In time the Della Robbia studio became a potters' workshop-industry, famous especially for its renderings of the Madonna and Child in white enamel on a blue ground. Luca's nephew Andrea (1435–1525) assumed control of the workshop about 1470. Trained as a marble sculptor, his best-known works are ten roundels of infants on the facade of Florence's Foundling Hospital (c.1487). Andrea's son Giovanni (1469–1529) took control of the family workshop after his father's death. His early works, notably a lavabo in Santa Maria Novella (1497), were collaborations with his father.

Delos \ˈdē-ˌläs\ *Greek* **Dhílos** \ˈthē-ˌlós\ Island, Greece. One of the smallest of the CYCLADES, it was an ancient center of religious, political, and commercial life in the Aegean. It was the legendary birthplace of APOLLO and ARTEMIS. The DELIAN LEAGUE was established there in 478 B.C., following the PERSIAN WARS. Made a free port by Rome in 166 B.C., it was a flourishing commercial center and slave market. Its ruins have been extensively excavated.

Delphi \ˈdel-ˌfī\ Site of the ancient temple and ORACLE of APOLLO in Greece. Located on the slopes of Mt. PARNASSUS, it was the center of the world in ancient Greek religion. According to legend, the oracle was originally sacred to GAEA, and Apollo acquired it by slaying her child, the serpent Python. From 582 B.C. Delphi was the site of the PYTHIAN GAMES.

delphinium See LARKSPUR

delta Low-lying plain composed of stream-borne sediments deposited by a river at its mouth. Sands, silts, and clays deposited by floodwaters are extremely productive agriculturally, and major civilizations flourished in the deltaic plains of the Nile and Tigris-Euphrates rivers. Geologists have discovered that much of the world's petroleum resources are found in ancient deltaic rocks. Deltas vary widely in size, though many are triangular (the shape of the Greek letter delta).

de Man \də-ˈmän\, **Paul** (1919–1983) Belgian-U.S. literary critic. He emigrated to the U.S. in 1947 and in 1970 joined the faculty at Yale. His groundbreaking *Blindness and Insight* (1971) made Yale the American center for deconstructive literary criticism (see DECONSTRUCTION). His other works include *Allegories of Reading* (1979) and *Aesthetic Ideology* (1988). His reputation was undermined with the posthumous revelation of his wartime writings for the pro-Nazi Belgian newspaper *Le Soir*.

deme \ˈdēm\ (Greek, *demos*) In ancient Greece, a country district or village, as distinct from a POLIS. In CLEISTHENES' democratic reforms (508–507 B.C.), the demes of Attica (the area around Athens) gained a voice in local and state government. The Attic demes had their own police powers, cults, and officials. Males became registered members of the deme at 18. Each deme sent representatives to the Athenian BOULE in proportion to its size. The term continued to be applied to local districts in Hellenistic and Roman times.

dementia \di-ˈmen-shə\ Chronic, usually progressive, deterioration of intellectual functions. Most common in the elderly, it usually begins with short-term memory loss, once thought normal but now known to result from ALZHEIMER'S DISEASE. Other common causes are Pick's disease and cerebral ARTERIOSCLEROSIS. Treatable causes include hypothyroidism (see THYROID GLAND), other metabolic diseases, and some malignant tumors. Treatment may arrest dementia's progress but usually does not reverse it. See also SENILE DEMENTIA.

dementia See SENILE DEMENTIA

Demeter \di-ˈmē-tər\ In Greek religion, a consort of ZEUS and the goddess of agriculture, especially grain. Though not an Olympian deity, she is probably an ancient goddess. In the story of PERSEPHONE, her lack of attention to the harvest causes a famine. Demeter was also sometimes worshiped as a divinity of the Underworld and as a goddess of health, birth, and marriage.

de Mille \də-ˈmil\, **Agnes (George)** (1905–1993) U.S. dancer and choreographer who expanded the innovative use of American themes. Born in New York City, she graduated from UCLA and soon was touring the U.S. with her own mime-dance concerts (1929–40). She choreographed works for Ballet (later AMERICAN BALLET) THEATRE; in *Rodeo* (1942) she used TAP DANCE for the first time in a ballet. She choreographed many Broadway musicals, including *Oklahoma!* (1943), *Carousel* (1945), and *Brigadoon* (1947).

DeMille \də-ˈmil\, **Cecil B(lount)** (1881–1959) U.S. film director and producer. Born in Ashfield, Mass., he made his Broadway acting debut in 1900. In 1913 he joined Jesse Lasky (1880–1958) and Samuel GOLDWYN to form the forerunner of PARAMOUNT COMMUNICATIONS. Their first venture, *The Squaw Man* (1914), was the first full-length feature film produced in Hollywood. He made numerous comedies before creating such biblical spectacles as *The Ten Commandments* (1923, remade 1956) and *The King of Kings* (1927), becoming known for his taste for huge casts and extravagant sets. Among his 70 other films are *Samson and*

Delilah (1949) and *The Greatest Show on Earth* (1952, Academy Award).

Deming, W(illiam) Edwards (1900–1993) U.S. advocate of quality control in industrial production. Born in Sioux City, Iowa, he received his PhD in mathematical physics from Yale Univ., and he subsequently taught at NYU for 46 years. From the 1930s he worked with statistical analysis to achieve better industrial quality control. In 1950 he was invited to Japan to teach executives and engineers. His ideas, which centered on tallying product defects, analyzing and addressing their causes, and recording the effects of the changes on subsequent quality, eventually helped Japanese products dominate markets worldwide. Deming's ideas were taken up by U.S. corporations in the 1980s, particularly under the rubric of Total Quality Management.

Demiurge \ˈde-mē-ərj\ Subordinate god who shapes and arranges the physical world. PLATO identified the Demiurge as the force that fashioned the world from the preexisting materials of chaos. In early GNOSTICISM, the Demiurge is regarded as an inferior, evil deity who created the imperfect, material world and who opposed the supreme God of goodness.

democracy Philosophy of government in which supreme power is vested in the people and exercised by them directly or indirectly through representation. In a direct democracy, the public participates directly in government (as in some ancient Greek city-states and some New England TOWN MEETINGS). Representative democracy arose from ideas and institutions developed in medieval Europe, during the Enlightenment, and in the American and French Revolutions. Today democracy has come to imply universal suffrage, competition for office, freedom of speech and the press, and the rule of law.

Democratic Party One of the two major political parties in the U.S., historically the party of labor, minorities, and progressive reformers. In the 1790s a group of Thomas JEFFERSON's supporters called themselves "Democratic Republicans" or "Jeffersonian Republicans" to show their belief in the principle of popular government. The party adopted its present name in the 1830s during the presidency of Andrew JACKSON. Democrats won nearly every presidential election in the years 1836–60, but the issue of slavery split the party; the Northern Democrats advocated POPULAR SOVEREIGNTY in the new territories, while the Southern Democrats called for protection of slavery. As a result, in 1860 the new antislavery REPUBLICAN PARTY won its first national victory under Abraham LINCOLN. From 1861 to 1913 the only Democratic president was Grover CLEVELAND; in these years the party was basically conservative and agrarian-oriented. It returned to power under Woodrow WILSON, instituting greater federal regulation of banking and industry, but the Republicans' frank embrace of big business drew voters amid the prosperity of the 1920s. Democrats became dominant again in 1932, electing Franklin ROOSEVELT. A coalition of urban workers, small farmers, liberals, and others sustained Democrats in office until 1953, and the party regained the presidency with the 1960 election of J. F. KENNEDY.

Democratic Party of the Left *formerly (1921–91)* **Italian Communist Party** Major Italian political party. Founded in 1921 by dissidents of the Italian Socialist Party's left wing, it was outlawed with other political parties by the Fascists in 1926. After World War II it joined in coalition governments and was consistently successful at the polls. In 1956, after revelation of Joseph STALIN's crimes, Palmiro TOGLIATTI tried to dissociate it from the Soviet Union. Enrico Berlinguer, as party leader 1972–84, became a leading proponent of EUROCOMMUNISM. In 1991, to broaden its base, it adopted its current name. It became Italy's second-largest political party and Western Europe's largest communist party.

Democratic Republic of the Congo See Democratic Republic of the CONGO

Democritus \di-ˈmä-krə-təs\ (c.460–370 B.C.) Greek philosopher. He was apparently the first to describe invisible "atoms" as the basis of all matter. His atoms—indestructible, indivisible, incompressible, and uniform, differing only in size, shape, and motion—anticipated with surprising accuracy those discovered by 20th-cent. scientists. For his amusement at human foibles, he has been called "the Laughing Philosopher."

demon *or* **daemon** \ˈdē-mən\ In religions worldwide, any of various evil spirits that mediate between the supernatural and human realms. To the Greeks a *daimon* was a divine or semidivine power that determined a person's fate. ZOROASTRIANISM had a hierarchy of demons. In Judaism demons inhabited desert wastes, ruins, and graves and inflicted disorders on humankind. Christianity placed Satan or Beelzebub at the head of the ranks of demons, and Islam designated Iblis or Satan as the leader of a host of evil jinn. Hindu demons, called *asura*s, oppose the gods. Buddhist demons are tempters who prevent the achievement of nirvana.

Demosthenes \di-ˈmäs-thə-ˌnēz\ (384–322 B.C.) Athenian statesman known as the greatest orator of ancient Greece. According to PLUTARCH, he was a stutterer who improved his speech by practicing with pebbles in his mouth. His talents were recognized early, and powerful clients engaged him as a speechwriter. Throughout his life he espoused democratic principles. He roused Athens against PHILIP II by his great *Philippics,* and later against Philip's son ALEXANDER THE GREAT. In so doing he incurred the enmity of AESCHINES. He succeeded in having Aeschines ostracized (330), but was himself later exiled (324).

Dempsey, Jack (*orig.* William Harrison) (1895–1983) U.S. boxer. Born in Manassa, Col., he worked in the copper mines and started fighting in 1914 as Kid Blackie. After an impressive number of first-round knockouts, he defeated the heavyweight titleholder, Jess Willard, in three rounds. He held the title until his defeat by Gene TUNNEY in 1926 in a 10-round decision. In the next year's rematch, in the famous "Long Count" bout, Dempsey would not go to a neutral corner after knocking Tunney down, allowing the champion extra time to recover and win the fight. The "Manassa Mauler" was a ferocious fighter who kept continuously on the offensive. He retired in 1940 and became a successful restaurateur. In 84 fights he compiled a record of 62 wins, 51 by knockout.

Jack Dempsey

Demuth \də-ˈmüth\, **Charles** (1883–1935) U.S. painter. Born in Lancaster, Pa., he studied in Philadelphia and later in Europe. On his return, he helped channel modern European movements into American art. Best known as an exponent of PRECISIONISM, he executed an outstanding watercolor series of flowers, circuses, and café scenes. Later he incorporated advertisements and billboard lettering into hard-edged, abstract cityscapes such as *Buildings, Lancaster* (1930). His so-called "poster portraits" include *I Saw the Figure 5 in Gold* (1928), a symbolic portrait of W. C. WILLIAMS.

Denali See Mt. MCKINLEY

Denali National Park \də-ˈnä-lē\ Preserve, S central Alaska. Established in 1980, it comprises the former Mt. McKinley National Park (1917) and Denali National Monument (1978). Highlights include Mt. MCKINLEY, the large glaciers of the ALASKA RANGE, and abundant wildlife. The park's total area is 5,000,000 acres (2,025,000 hectares).

Dench, Judi(th Olivia) (*later* **Dame Judi**) (b.1934) British actress. She made her stage debut in 1957 in *Hamlet,* and Shakespearean works became her specialty. She starred in the London premiere of *Cabaret* in 1968. Among her many other notable credits were the 1981–84 TV series "A Fine Romance" and the films *84 Charing Cross Road* (1986), *Mrs. Brown* (1997)—in which she starred as Queen Victoria—and *Shakespeare in Love* (1998, Academy Award).

dendrochronology \ˌden-drō-krə-ˈnä-lə-jē\ Method of scientific DATING based on the analysis of tree rings. Because the width of annular tree rings varies with climatic conditions, laboratory analysis of timber core samples allows scientists to reconstruct the conditions that existed when a tree's rings developed. By taking thousands of samples from different sites and different strata within a particular region, researchers can build a comprehensive historical sequence. Such master chronologies are used by archaeologists, climatologists, and others.

Deneuve \də-ˈnœv\, **Catherine** *orig.* Catherine Dorléac (b.1943) French film actress. She appeared in films from age 13 and won fame with her role in *The Umbrellas of Cherbourg* (1964). Her cool blond beauty and skillful performances in Roman POLANSKI's *Repulsion* (1965) and Luis BUÑUEL's *Belle de jour* (1967) and *Tristana* (1970) made her an international star. Her numerous other films include *The Last Metro* (1980) and *Indochine* (1992).

dengue \ˈdeŋ-gē\ *or* **breakbone fever** Acute, infectious, mosquito-borne HEMORRHAGIC FEVER, temporarily disabling but rarely fatal. Symptoms include extreme joint pain and stiffness, intense pain behind the eyes, a return of fever after brief pause, and a characteristic rash. The dengue VIRUS is usually carried by the *Aedes aegypti* mosquito, which also carries YELLOW FEVER. There are four strains of virus; infection with one does not confer immunity to the others. Treatment focuses on relieving symptoms. Prevention relies on mosquito control.

Deng Xiaoping *or* **Teng Hsiao-p'ing** \ˈdəŋ-ˈshaů-ˈpiŋ\ (1904–1997) Chinese Communist leader. General secretary of the CHINESE COMMUNIST PARTY (CCP) from 1956, he fell from favor during the CULTURAL REVOLUTION but was rehabilitated in 1973 under the sponsorship of ZHOU ENLAI. Though seen as a likely successor to Zhou as premier, Deng was again ousted, this time by the GANG OF FOUR, when Zhou died in 1976. When MAO ZEDONG died later that year, the ensuing power struggle resulted in the arrest of the Gang of Four and Deng's second rehabilitation. His reform program, which encompassed virtually all aspects of China's political, economic, and social life, abandoned many orthodox communist doctrines and introduced free-enterprise elements into the economy. Deng's harsh treatment of student protesters in TIANANMEN SQUARE in 1989 tarnished the image of a man who had transformed China into a major world force.

Denikin \dyi-ˈnyē-kyin\, **Anton (Ivanovich)** (1872–1947) Russian general. He was a lieutenant-general in the imperial Russian army in World War I. After the Russian Revolution of 1917, he fled south and assumed command of the anti-Bolshevik ("White") forces in the RUSSIAN CIVIL WAR. In 1919 he launched a major offensive toward Moscow, but his forces were defeated at Orel. Forced to retreat, he turned over his command to Pyotr WRANGEL (1920), then fled Russia and later settled in France (1925–45).

denim Durable twill-woven fabric with colored (usually blue) warp (lengthwise) and white filling (crosswise) threads, also sometimes woven in colored stripes. Denim is usually all-COTTON, though it is sometimes made of a cotton-synthetic mixture. Decades of use in the clothing industry, especially in overalls and trousers worn for heavy labor, have demonstrated denim's durability, a quality that, along with its comfort, made denim jeans extremely popular for leisure wear.

De Niro \də-ˈnir-ō\, **Robert** (b.1943) U.S. film actor. Born in New York City, he followed his acclaimed performance in *Bang the Drum Slowly* (1973) with *Mean Streets* (1973) and other films directed by Martin SCORSESE, including *Taxi Driver* (1976), *Raging Bull* (1980, Academy Award), and *GoodFellas* (1990). Noted for his intensely committed performances, he also starred in *The Godfather, Part II* (1974, Academy Award), *The Deer Hunter* (1978), and *Wag the Dog* (1997). He directed his first film, *A Bronx Tale,* in 1993.

Denis, Ruth Saint See Ruth SAINT DENIS

Denis \də-ˈnē, *Engl* ˈde-nəs\, **St.** *or* **St. Denys** (d.A.D. 258?) Patron saint of France and first bishop of Paris. Probably born in Rome, he was sent to convert the people of Gaul during the reign of Decius. He may have been martyred during VALERIAN's persecutions. A 9th-cent. legend says that he was beheaded on Montmartre and that his decapitated body carried his head to the area northeast of Paris where the Benedictine abbey of St. Denis was founded.

denitrifying bacteria Microorganisms whose action results in the conversion of NITRATES to gaseous NITROGEN or nitrous or nitric oxide. Many common BACTERIA of soil and other environments can denitrify. Without denitrification, earth's nitrogen supply would eventually accumulate in the oceans, since nitrates are highly soluble. See also NITRIFYING BACTERIA.

Denmark *officially* **Kingdom of Denmark** *Danish* **Danmark** \ˈdàn-ˌmärk\ Constitutional monarchy, N central Europe. Area: 16,639 sq mi (43,094 sq km). Its territory includes GREENLAND and the FAEROE ISLANDS, which are self-governing dependencies. Population (2000): 5,339,000. Capital: COPENHAGEN. The majority of the population is Nordic.

Language: Danish (official). Religion: Evangelical Lutheranism (official). Currency: Danish krone. Lying between the North and Baltic seas, it occupies the JUTLAND peninsula and an archipelago to its east. The two largest islands, Zealand, (SJÆLLAND) and Fyn, together make up more than one-fourth of the country's total land area. With a 4,500-mi (7,300-km) coastline, Denmark has a generally temperate and often wet climate. It has a mixed economy based on services and manufacturing and boasts one of the world's oldest and largest social-welfare systems. Its standard of living is among the highest in the world. Its chief of state is the Danish monarch, while the head of government is the prime minister. Inhabited from 100,000 B.C., it was settled by Danes, a Scandinavian branch of the Teutons, about the 6th cent. A.D. During the VIKING period the Danes expanded their territory, and by the 11th cent. the united Danish kingdom included parts of what are now Germany, Sweden, England, and Norway. Scandinavia was united under Danish rule from 1397 until 1523, when Sweden became independent; a series of debilitating wars with Sweden in the 17th cent. resulted in the Treaty of Copenhagen (1660), which established the modern Scandinavian frontiers. Denmark gained and lost various other territories, including Norway, in the 19th and 20th cent.; it went through three constitutions between 1849 and 1915 and was occupied by Nazi Germany in 1940–45. A founding member of NATO (1949), Denmark adopted its current constitution in 1953. It became a member of the EUROPEAN UNION in 1973, and modified its membership during the 1990s. The island of Zealand, on which Copenhagen stands, was connected to the central island of Funen by a rail tunnel and bridge in 1997, ending more than 100 years of ferry service.

Dennison, Aaron Lufkin (1812–1895) U.S. watch manufacturer. Born in Freeport, Me., he applied the methods used at the SPRINGFIELD ARMORY to the technical difficulties of machine production of small parts, set up a factory in Waltham, Mass., in 1850, and began to produce the first inexpensive factory-made watches with interchangeable parts. His introduction of machinery into the manufacture of paper products resulted in the founding of the Dennison Manufacturing Co.

density MASS of a unit volume of a material substance. It is calculated by dividing an object's mass by its volume. In the INTERNATIONAL SYSTEM OF UNITS, and depending on the units of measurement used, density can be expressed in grams per cubic centimeter (g/cm^3) or kilograms per cubic meter (kg/m^3). See also SPECIFIC GRAVITY.

density current Any current in either a liquid or a gas that is kept in motion by the force of gravity acting on small differences in density. Density currents flow along ocean and lake bottoms, because the water entering is colder, saltier, or contains more suspended sediment than the surrounding water. Density currents are a factor in WATER POLLUTION, as the industrial discharge of large amounts of polluted or heated water can generate harmful density currents.

dentistry Profession concerned with the teeth (see TOOTH) and MOUTH. It includes repair or removal of decayed teeth (see CARIES), straightening and adjustment of teeth for proper occlusion, and design, manufacture, and fitting of false teeth and other prosthetic devices. X RAYS are used to show conditions not visible on examination. Decay that reaches a tooth's root risks infection of the nerve and requires root-canal surgery. Teeth that must be extracted are replaced by crowns for single teeth and full or partial dentures for more.

Denver City (pop., 2000: 554,000), capital of Colorado. Just east of the ROCKY MTNS., its elevation of 5,280 ft (1,609 m) gives it the nickname "Mile High City." An early stopping place for Indians and trappers, it was settled in the 1859 gold rush and became the capital in 1867. The 1870s and '80s saw a silver boom that ended in 1893, but new gold discoveries helped prevent a major decline. Modern Denver, a transportation, industrial, and commercial hub, has one of the nation's largest livestock markets and is a major center for winter sports. Its branch of the U.S. Mint (opened 1906) produces about 75% of U.S. coinage and is the nation's second-largest gold depository.

De Palma \də-ˈpäl-mə\, **Brian (Russell)** (b.1940) U.S. film director. Born in Newark, N.J., he made his first feature-length film in 1964. The commercial success of *Carrie* (1976) established him as a director of graphic horror-suspense films. After openly imitating the work of Alfred HITCHCOCK, he found his own style in *Dressed to Kill* (1980), *Blow Out* (1981), and *Body Double* (1984). Later films include *The Untouchables* (1987), *Casualties of War* (1989), and *Carlito's Way* (1993).

Depardieu \də-pär-ˈdyœ\, **Gérard** (b.1948) French film actor. After his performance in *Going Places* (1974) brought him a major role in Bernardo BERTOLUCCI's *1900* (1976), he became French cinema's top male star in the 1980s, also making films elsewhere in Europe and in the U.S. Noted for a screen image that combines sensitivity with masculine strength, he delivered compelling performances in *The Last Metro* (1980), *The Return of Martin Guerre* (1981), *Jean de Florette* (1986), *Manon of the Spring* (1986), and *Cyrano de Bergerac* (1990).

department store Retail establishment that sells a wide variety of goods. These usually include ready-to-wear apparel and accessories, yard goods, household wares, furniture, and electrical appliances and accessories, backed by merchandising, advertising, service, accounting, and budgetary control activities. The Bon Marché in Paris, which began as a small shop in the early 19th cent., is often considered the first department store. The first U.S. department-store chains—J. C. Penney and SEARS, ROEBUCK AND CO.—date to the 1920s.

dependency In international relations, a weak state dominated by or under the jurisdiction of a more powerful state but not formally annexed by it. Examples include AMERICAN SAMOA (U.S.) and GREENLAND (Denmark). The dominant state may control certain of its affairs, such as defense, foreign relations, and internal security, and allow it autonomy in domestic affairs such as education, health, and infrastructure development.

depletion allowance In tax law, the deductions from gross income allowed investors in exhaustible mineral deposits (including oil or gas) for the depletion of the deposits. They are intended as an incentive to stimulate investment in this high-risk industry, though critics argue that mineral deposits are valuable enough to justify high levels of investment without incentives. See also DEPRECIATION.

depreciation Accounting charge for the decline in value of an asset spread over its economic life. Depreciation includes deterioration from use, age, and exposure to the elements, as well as decline in value caused by obsolescence, but not losses caused by fire, accident, or disaster. Depreciation is often used in assessing the value of property (e.g., buildings, machinery) or other assets of limited life (e.g., a leasehold or copyright) for tax purposes. See also DEPLETION ALLOWANCE, INVESTMENT CREDIT.

depression In economics, a major downswing in the BUSINESS CYCLE characterized by sharply reduced industrial production, widespread unemployment, a serious decline in construction, and great reductions in international trade. Unlike RECESSIONS, which may be limited to a single country, severe depressions such as the GREAT DEPRESSION encompass many nations.

depression Neurotic or psychotic disorder marked by sadness, inactivity, difficulty in thinking and concentration, a significant increase or decrease in appetite and time spent sleeping, dejection and hopelessness, and sometimes suicidal tendencies. Probably the most common psychiatric complaint, its course is extremely variable from person to person; it may be fleeting or permanent, mild or severe. Depression is more common in women than in men. The rates of incidence increase with age in men, while the peak for women is between the ages of 35 and 45. Its causes can be both psychosocial (e.g., the loss of a loved one) and biochemical (chiefly, reduced quantities of the monoamines NOREPINEPHRINE and SEROTONIN). Treatment is usually a combination of PSYCHOTHERAPY and drug therapy (see ANTIDEPRESSANT). See also BIPOLAR DISORDER.

Depression of 1929 See GREAT DEPRESSION

depth charge *or* **depth bomb** Weapon used to attack submerged submarines. Developed by the British in World War I, it consisted of a canister filled with explosives and dropped off a ship near a submerged submarine. Its explosive shock waves would loosen the submarine's joints and damage its instruments, forcing it to the surface, where naval gunfire could sink it. Modern depth charges can be fired as far as 2,000 yards (1,800 m) from a ship or launched from aircraft. Atomic depth charges have a nuclear warhead and a vastly increased killing radius.

De Quincey, Thomas (1785–1859) English essayist and critic. While a student at Oxford he first took opium medicinally. His lifelong addiction inspired his best-known work, *Confessions of an English Opium-Eater* (1822), whose highly poetic and imaginative prose made it an enduring masterpiece. As a critic he is best known for the essay "On the Knocking at the Gate in *Macbeth*" (1823).

Derain \də-ˈraü\, **André** (1880–1954) French painter. He developed his early style in association with his friends Maurice de VLAMINCK and Henri MATISSE; the three were the principal exponents of FAUVISM. Derain's landscapes and figure studies featured brilliant colors, broken brush strokes, and impulsive lines. By the 1920s, however, he had turned to a Neoclassical style. He produced numerous book illustrations and designs for stage sets, notably for Sergey DIAGHILEV's BALLETS RUSSES.

Derby \ˈdär-bē\, **Earl of** *orig.* Edward (George Geoffrey Smith) Stanley (1799–1869) British statesman. He entered Parliament in 1820, and eventually became leader of the Conservative Party (1846–68) and prime minister (1852, 1858, and 1866–68). Legislation adopted during his tenure included the transfer of India's administration from the E. INDIA CO. to the crown and the Reform Bill of 1867, extending the note to workingmen. He was one of England's greatest parliamentary orators.

derivative In mathematics, a fundamental concept of DIFFERENTIAL CALCULUS representing the instantaneous rate of change of a FUNCTION. The first derivative of a function is a function whose values can be interpreted as SLOPES of TANGENT LINES to the graph of the original function at a given point. The process of finding a derivative is called DIFFERENTIATION.

derivatives Financial contracts whose value is derived from another asset, which can include stocks, bonds, currencies, interest rates, commodities, and related indexes. Purchasers of derivatives are essentially wagering on the future performance of that asset. Derivatives include such widely accepted products as FUTURES and options. After well-publicized derivative-related losses in 1994 involving Orange Co., Cal., and the collapse of the London-based merchant bank Barings PLC in 1995, securities regulators from 16 countries agreed on measures to improve control of derivatives.

dermatitis *or* **eczema** \ig-ˈzē-mə, ˈeg-zə-mə\ INFLAMMATION of the SKIN, usually itchy, with redness, swelling, and blistering. Causes and patterns vary. Contact dermatitis appears at the site of contact with an irritating substance or allergen. Atopic dermatitis, with patches of dry skin, occurs in young people with genetic hypersensitivities. Stasis dermatitis affects the ankles and lower legs because of chronic poor blood flow. Seborrheic dermatitis appears as scaly skin, most often on the scalp (DANDRUFF) and areas rich in SEBACEOUS GLANDS. Neurodermatitis is apparently caused by repeated scratching of an itchy skin area.

dermatology Medical specialty dealing with diseases of the SKIN. Dermatology deals with DERMATITIS, fungal diseases, skin cancers, PSORIASIS, and life-threatening skin diseases such as pemphigus, SCLERODERMA, and LUPUS ERYTHEMATOSUS.

dermestid (beetle) \dər-ˈmes-təd\ Any member of about 700 species (family Dermestidae) of widely distributed BEETLES that are household pests. Usually brown or black, some are brightly colored or patterned, and they vary in shape from elongated to oval. Dermestids range from 0.05 to 0.5 in. (1–12 mm) long and are covered with hairs or scales that easily flake off. The wormlike larvae feed on furs, skins, feathers, horn, and hair; some feed on cheese and dried meats or on carpets, rugs, furniture, and clothing. Two are museum pests that have destroyed collections of stuffed animals. Dermestid larvae are sometimes used to clean the soft tissue attached to animal skeletons.

Dermot Macmurrough \ˈdər-mət-mək-ˈmər-ō\ *Irish* Diarmaid Macmurchada (d.1171) Irish king of Leinster (1126–71). He faced a number of rivals in claiming the throne of his father, Enna, and he asserted his authority by killing or blinding 17 rebel chieftains (1141). He abducted another Irish king's wife in 1153, beginning a bitter feud in which he was driven from Ireland (1166). He returned with the backing of Anglo-Norman lords, and in 1170 they captured Dublin. Dermot's appeal for Norman help in settling an internal dispute thus proved instrumental in the Norman conquest of Ireland.

Derrida \de-rē-ˈdä\, **Jacques** (b.1930) French (Algerian-born) philosopher. His critique of Western philosophy encompasses literature, linguistics, and psychoanalysis. His thought is based on his disapproval of the search for an ultimate metaphysical certainty or source of meaning. Instead, he offers DECONSTRUCTION, a way of reading philosophic texts intended to reveal underlying suppositions and assumptions through a close analysis of language. His works on deconstructive theory and method include *Speech and Phenomena* (1967), *Writing and Difference* (1967), and *Of Grammatology* (1967).

Derry *or* **Londonderry** Seaport (pop., 1995 est.: 77,000) and district seat of Derry, Northern Ireland. St. COLUMBA established a monastery there in the 6th cent., but the settlement was repeatedly destroyed by Norse invaders. In 1600 an English force seized Derry; JAMES I of England granted it to the citizens of London, who brought in Protestant settlers, and it was renamed Londonderry. Growth of the modern city dates from the 1850s, when linen shirt making became important. It was the site of terrorist violence in the late 20th cent. Its name was officially changed to Derry in 1984.

Dershowitz, Alan (Morton) (b.1938) U.S. lawyer. Born in New York City, he joined the Harvard Law School faculty at age 25. Known as a civil-liberties and criminal lawyer, he has defended such clients as Claus von Bulow and O. J. SIMPSON. He writes a widely syndicated newspaper column, and his many books include *Reasonable Doubts* (1966) and *The Best Defense* (1982).

dervish In Islam, a member of a Sufi fraternity. These mystics stress emotional aspects of devotion through ecstatic trances, dancing, and whirling. Wandering or mendicant dervishes (fakirs) are often regarded as holy men who possess miraculous powers. Dervishes are viewed as unorthodox and extreme by most Muslims. See also SUFISM.

Desai \ˈdä-ˌsī, de-ˈsī\, **Anita** *orig.* Anita Mazumdar (b.1937) Indian novelist. Considered India's premier imagist writer, she excels in evoking character and mood through visual images. Her works include *Fire on the Mountain* (1977), *Clear Light of Day* (1980), *Baumgartner's Bombay* (1988), and the popular children's book *The Village by the Sea* (1982).

desalination *or* **desalting** Removal of dissolved salts from SEAWATER, highly mineralized GROUNDWATERS, and municipal wastewaters. Desalination makes such waters fit for human consumption, irrigation, and industrial applications. DISTILLATION is the most widely used desalination process; freezing and thawing, electrodialysis, and reverse osmosis are also used. All are energy-intensive and therefore expensive. Currently, more than 2 billion gallons (8 million cu m) of fresh water are produced each day by several thousand desalination plants throughout the world, the largest plants being in the Arabian Peninsula.

Descartes \dā-ˈkärt\, **René** (1596–1650) French mathematician, scientist, and philosopher, considered the father of modern philosophy. Born near Tours, he traveled widely for years before settling in Holland in 1628, where he would remain until 1649. Descartes's ambition was to introduce into philosophy the rigor and clarity of mathematics. In his *Discourse on Method* (1637) and *Meditations on First Philosophy* (1641), he began by methodically doubting knowledge based on authority, the senses, and reason, in the hope of arriving in the end at something indubitable. This he reached in his famous "Cogito ergo sum" ("I think, therefore I am").

René Descartes Painting by Frans Hals

His task was to deduce from this a series of other propositions, and thus to produce a philosophical system as indisputable as Euclid's geometry. In his dualistic system, he distinguished radically between mind, whose essence is thinking, and matter, whose essence is extension in three dimensions. His metaphysics is rationalistic (see RATIONALISM), but his physics and physiology are empiricistic (see EMPIRICISM) and mechanistic. As a mathematician, he founded ANALYTIC GEOMETRY and reformed algebraic notation.

descent System of acknowledged social parentage whereby a person may claim kinship ties with another. Descent is of practical importance as a means for individuals to assert rights, duties, privileges, or status. It has special influence when rights to succession, INHERITANCE, or residence follow kinship lines. One method of limiting the recognition of kinship is to emphasize the relationship through one parent only; patrilineal systems emphasize relationships through the father, while matrilineal systems stress relationships through the mother. Cognatic systems, in which neither line predominates, tend to characterize the more industrialized countries, where individual rights and duties are increasingly defined institutionally or legally.

desert Large, extremely dry area of land with fairly sparse vegetation and a mean annual precipitation of less than 10 in. (250 mm). Deserts occur in circumpolar areas as well as the more familiar hot, arid regions. Desert terrain may consist of rugged mountains, high plateaus, or plains; many occupy broad mountain-rimmed basins. Surface materials include bare bedrock, plains of gravel and boulders, and vast tracts of shifting sand. Wind-blown sands, commonly thought to be typical of deserts, make up only about 2% of N. American deserts, 10% of the Sahara, and 30% of the Arabian Desert.

desertification Spread of a desert environment caused by climatic changes, human influence, or both. Climatic factors include periods of severe drought and long-term climatic changes toward dryness. Human factors include removal of vegetation (which can lead to unnaturally high EROSION), excessive cultivation, and the exhaustion of water supplies. Desertification It is characterized by a declining GROUNDWATER table, salt accumulation in topsoil and water, a decrease in surface water, increasing erosion, and the disappearance of native vegetation.

De Sica \də-'sē-kə\, **Vittorio** (1901–1974) Italian film director and actor. He joined an acting company in 1923 and soon became a matinee idol, appearing on screen as a leading man in a series of light comedies. He directed his first film in 1940 and, working with screenwriter Cesare Zavattini, made a major contribution to the Neorealism of the postwar Italian cinema with *Shoeshine* (1946, Academy Award) and *The Bicycle Thief* (1948, Academy Award). His later films include *Umberto D* (1952), *Two Women* (1961), *Yesterday, Today, and Tomorrow* (1963, Academy Award), and *The Garden of the Finzi-Continis* (1971, Academy Award).

Desiderio da Settignano \dä-sē-'der-yō-dä-ˌsät-tēn-'yä-nō\ (c.1430–1464) Italian sculptor. Born into a family of stonemasons, he based his style on DONATELLO's work, and his skill as a marble cutter established him as a master of bas-relief. His delicate, original technique was best expressed in portrait busts of women and children. His most important public work was the richly detailed tomb of Carlo Marsuppini in the church of Santa Croce.

designer drug Synthetic version of a controlled NARCOTIC substance. Designer DRUGS are manufactured with a molecular structure slightly different from that of a related controlled substance in order to create a drug not specifically listed by law-enforcement organizations as illicit. Because they are made in clandestine laboratories, often by amateurs, such drugs can be dangerous. One of the best-known is MDMA, a variation of methamphetamine that is known as "ecstasy." Non-narcotic synthetic chemical compounds designed to combat disease have also been called designer drugs.

desktop publishing (DTP) Use of a personal computer to perform publishing tasks. DTP allows an individual to combine text, tables, and images in a document that can be output on a printer or a phototypesetter. A typical DTP system includes a personal computer, a high-resolution printer, and input devices such as an optical SCANNER. Text and graphic elements are commonly created or manipulated with several separate software programs and then combined with a page-makeup program.

Des Moines \di-'moin\ City (pop., 2000: 198,000), capital of Iowa. Located at the juncture of the Raccoon and DES MOINES rivers, Ft. Des Moines was established in 1843 to protect the Sauk and Fox Indians. The area was opened to white settlers in 1845. It became the capital in 1857. The state's largest city, it is a communications hub and a manufacturing, governmental, and publishing center (especially for farm journals). It is the site of Drake Univ. (1881) and home to the huge KRNT Theatre.

Des Moines River River, SW Minnesota into Iowa. Rising near Pipestone, it flows 525 mi (845 km) southeast to join the Mississippi River near Keokuk, Iowa. From the late 1830s until the end of the AMERICAN CIVIL WAR, it was the main commercial artery for central Iowa. Although none survive, 80 grain mills were built (1840–90) along its banks.

Desmoulins \dā-mü-'laⁿ\, **(Lucie-Simplice-) Camille (-Benoist)** (1760–1794) French journalist influential in the French Revolution. A lawyer, he emerged as an inspiring orator when the Revolution began, inciting the storming of the Bastille. In his pamphlets and newspapers he campaigned for the establishment of a republic. Elected to the National Convention, he joined the MONTAGNARDS against the GIRONDINS. Later he and Georges DANTON became leaders of the moderate Indulgents. After attacking the REIGN OF TERROR, he was guillotined.

de Soto \thä-'sō-tō, *Engl* di-'sō-tō\, **Hernando** (1496?–1542) Spanish explorer and conquistador. In 1514 he joined an expedition to the W. Indies, and in Panama he made his mark as a slave trader and explorer. He joined Francisco PIZARRO on an expedition to conquer Peru in 1532, returning to Spain in 1536 with great wealth. Commissioned by Spain to conquer what is now Florida, he departed in 1538 in command of 10 ships and 700 men. He explored the extensive region that was to become the SE U.S. and discovered the Mississippi River. He died of fever in Louisiana and was buried in the Mississippi.

Hernando de Soto

despotism, enlightened See ENLIGHTENED DESPOTISM

des Prez, Josquin See JOSQUIN DES PREZ

Dessalines \ˌdä-sə-'lēn\, **Jean-Jacques** (1758?–1806) Emperor of Haiti who drove out the French in 1804. He joined a slave rebellion in 1791 and became a lieutenant of TOUSSAINT-LOUVERTURE, but submitted to the French expedition that deposed Toussaint in 1802. NAPOLEON's decision to reintroduce slavery led Dessalines and others to rebel, and with British help they expelled the French. In 1805 Dessalines proclaimed himself emperor. He made it illegal for whites to own property and killed thousands; he also discriminated against mulattoes. He was killed during a mulatto revolt.

De Stijl See De STIJL

destroyer Fast naval vessel used to protect other ships. In the 1890s destroyers protected BATTLESHIPS from TORPEDO boats. By World War I destroyers often scouted for the enemy, beat back its destroyers with CANNON fire, then launched torpedoes against its battleships and cruisers. When the SUBMARINE became the main torpedo-launching vessel, destroyers armed with DEPTH CHARGES protected convoys and battle fleets against submarine attack. In World War II, with the addition of RADAR and ANTIAIRCRAFT guns, its escort role included air defense. Modern destroyers, with a crew of about 300, carry surface-to-air and antiship missiles and often submarine-hunting helicopters.

detached retina Separation of most layers of the RETINA of the eye from the choroid, the pigmented middle layer of the eyeball. With age, small tears can develop in the retina, and the vitreous humor inside the eyeball leaks behind the retina. Disease or accidents can also cause retinal detachment. It usually develops slowly, without pain. Floating black spots and flashes of light appear in the affected eye, and vision becomes increasingly blurred. Prompt treatment prevents permanent blindness. Draining the fluid behind the retina and applying heat, a laser beam, or extreme cold seals the tears and prevents future detaching.

detective story Type of popular literature dealing with the step-by-step investigation and solution of a crime, usually murder. The first detective story was E. A. POE's "The Murders in the Rue Morgue" (1841). The genre soon expanded to novel length. Sherlock Holmes, the first fictional detective to become a household name, first appeared in A. C. DOYLE's *A Study in Scarlet* (1887). The 1930s was the golden age of the detective novel, exemplified by the books of Dashiell HAMMETT. The introduction of mass-produced paperback books in the late 1930s made detective stories readily accessible to a wide public, and well-known fictional detectives were created by such writers as Agatha CHRISTIE, Raymond CHANDLER, and Georges SIMENON.

détente \dā-'tänt\ Period of the easing of COLD WAR tensions between the U.S. and the Soviet Union from 1967 to 1979. The era was a time of increased trade and cooperation and the signing of the SALT treaties. Relations cooled again with the Soviet invasion of Afghanistan.

detergent Any of various surfactants (substances that reduce SURFACE TENSION) used to dislodge dirt from soiled surfaces and retain it in suspension, allowing it to be rinsed away. The term usually refers to synthetic substances and excludes SOAPS. The characteristic features of any detergent are a hydrophilic (soluble) end and a hydrophobic (insoluble) end. Besides those used in water to wash dishes and laundry, detergents that function in other SOLVENTS are used in lubricating oils, gasolines, and dry-cleaning solvents to prevent or remove unwanted deposits.

determinant In LINEAR ALGEBRA, a numerical value associated with a MATRIX having the same number of rows as columns. It is particularly useful in solving SYSTEMS OF (LINEAR) EQUATIONS and in the study of VECTORS. Determinants of large matrices involve complicated arithmetic combinations of the terms and are usually solved using a calculator or computer.

determinism Theory that all events, including human decisions, are completely determined by previously existing causes. The traditional FREE WILL PROBLEM arises from the question, Is moral responsibility consistent with the truth of determinism? Pierre-Simon LAPLACE framed its classical formulation in the 18th cent. For Laplace, the present state of the universe is the effect of its previous state and the cause of the state that follows it, and the future would be completely knowable if every aspect of the present were known.

Detroit City (pop., 2000: 951,000), largest in Michigan. Located on the Detroit River, and founded by the French in 1701, it became a trading center for the GREAT LAKES region. It fell to the British during the FRENCH AND INDIAN WAR. The capital of Michigan 1805–47, it grew as a shipping and flour-milling center. In the 20th cent. it became the automobile capital of the world with the help of Henry FORD. Its industrial growth attracted migrants, including large numbers of Southern blacks. The decline in the area's automotive industry brought economic hardship in the late 20th cent. Wayne State Univ. (1868) is the city's oldest college.

deus ex machina \'dā-əs-₁eks-'ma-ki-nə, ₁dā-əs-₁eks-mə-'shē-nə\ Stage device in Greek and Roman drama in which a god appeared in the sky by means of a crane (Greek, *mechane*) to resolve the plot of a play. The term now denotes something that appears suddenly and unexpectedly and provides an artificial solution to an apparently insoluble difficulty.

deuterium \dü-'tir-ē-əm\ *or* **heavy hydrogen** ISOTOPE of HYDROGEN, chemical symbol ^2H or D, atomic number 1 (but ATOMIC WEIGHT approximately 2). Harold UREY won a Nobel Prize for its discovery and isolation. Its nucleus contains one PROTON and one NEUTRON. A stable substance found as about 0.015% of ordinary hydrogen, deuterium can be purified by DISTILLATION of hydrogen or by ELECTROLYSIS of WATER. It enters into all the same chemical reactions as ordinary hydrogen. NUCLEAR FUSION of deuterium or deuterium and TRITIUM releases enormous amounts of ENERGY (see NUCLEAR WEAPONS). Deuterium is useful as a tracer in research into reaction mechanisms and biochemical pathways. See also HEAVY WATER.

deuterium oxide See HEAVY WATER

de Valera \₁dev-ə-'ler-ə\, **Eamon** (*orig.* Edward) (1882–1975) Irish (U.S.-born) politician. Born in New York City to a Spanish father and an Irish mother, at age 2 he was sent to live in Ireland. He helped lead the rebels in the EASTER RISING, and was elected president of SINN FÉIN in 1918. Repudiating the treaty that formed the Irish Free State (1921), he supported the republican resistance in the ensuing civil war. In 1924 he founded FIANNA FÁIL, which won the 1932 elections. As prime minister (1932–48), he made his country a "sovereign" state, renamed Ireland, or Éire. After serving again as prime minister (1951–54, 1957–59), he became president of Ireland (1959–73).

de Valois \də-val-'wä\, **Ninette** (*later* **Dame Ninette**) *orig.* Edris Stannus (1898–2000) British dancer, choreographer, and founder of the precursor to the ROYAL BALLET. A professional dancer from age 16, she joined the BALLETS RUSSES as a soloist in 1923. She founded the Academy of Choreographic Art in 1926 to teach movement to actors. She founded and directed the Vic-Wells Ballet (1931) and its successors, the Sadler's Wells Ballet and the Royal Ballet, which she directed until 1963.

developmental psychology Branch of PSYCHOLOGY concerned with changes in cognitive, motivational, psychophysiological, and social functioning throughout the life span. In the late 19th and early 20th cent., developmental psychologists focused on CHILD PSYCHOLOGY. In the 1950s they became interested in the relationship between child rearing and adult personality. Today they study psychological development over the entire life span.

development bank National or regional financial institution designed to provide medium- and long-term capital for productive investment, usually accompanied by technical assistance. Some development banks are government-owned, while others are private. Many operate under the auspices of the WORLD BANK, including the Inter-American Development Bank, the Asian Development Bank, and the African Development Bank.

Devi \'dā-vē\ Term used to designate a goddess in HINDUISM. It is sometimes used as an honorific title for women. In the 5th–6th cent., Hindu texts first began to identify Devi as the Great Goddess and the embodiment of matter, energy, and illusion. Her many aspects include the beautiful but menacing DURGA, the destructive KALI, and the sexually powerful Shakti (see SHAKTI).

devil Spirit or power of evil. Though sometimes used to refer to DEMONS, the term more often designates the prince of evil spirits. In Judaism, Christianity, and Islam, he is viewed as a fallen ANGEL who tried to usurp the position of God. In the Bible the devil is known as Satan, Beelzebub, and LUCIFER; in the Quran he is called Iblis. In Christianity he tempts humans to SIN; in Islam he tempts the unfaithful but not the true believer.

devilfish See MANTA RAY

devil ray See MANTA RAY

Devil's Island *French* **Île du Diable** \₁ēl-dǖ-'dyȧbl°\ Rocky islet off the coast of FRENCH GUIANA. It is a narrow strip of land 3,900 ft (1,200 m) long and 1,320 ft (400 m) wide. Part of a penal settlement since 1852, it housed the convicts' leper colony until the islands were made a maximum-security area. It shared the notoriety for cruelty of the mainland French Guiana penal colony. Spies and political prisoners, including Alfred DREYFUS, were held there. It closed in 1946.

Devils Tower National Monument National preserve, NE Wyoming. The first U.S. national monument (1906), it includes 1,347 acres (545 hectares) and features a natural rock tower, the remnant of a volcanic intrusion exposed by erosion. The tower has a flat top and is 865 ft (263 m) high.

Devon \'de-vən\ County, SW England. It adjoins CORNWALL and has coasts on the BRISTOL CHANNEL and ENGLISH CHANNEL. EXETER is its county seat. Its area includes the moorlands of Dartmoor, inhabited from prehistoric times, a popular tourist area. Devonshire clotted cream is still produced.

Devonian period \di-'vō-nē-ən\ Interval of geologic time, 410–360 million years ago, in the PALEOZOIC ERA. A giant continent was situated in the Southern Hemisphere (see GONDWANA). Siberia was separated from Europe by a broad ocean, and N. America and Europe were joined. Many types of primitive marine and freshwater fish proliferated, and the period is sometimes called the Age of Fishes. Ferns and primitive GYMNOSPERMS diversified and created the first forests. See table at GEOLOGIC TIME.

Devrient \dəv-rē-'aⁿ, dev-'rēnt\, **Ludwig** (1784–1832) German actor. At the Dessau court theater he developed his talent for character parts. After his Berlin debut in *The Robbers* (1814), he played Falstaff, Shylock, King Lear, and Richard III and was acclaimed the greatest German actor of the Romantic period. His nephew Karl August Devrient (1797–1872) acted in Hanover (1839–72), where he was popular in plays by Shakespeare, Goethe, and Schiller. Karl's brother Eduard (1801–1877) was first an opera singer, then an actor and director in Dresden (1844–52) and Karlsruhe (1852–70), where he directed German classics and retranslated Shakespeare's plays. Karl's other brother, Emil (1803–1872), acted with the Dresden court theater (1831–68); his greatest successes were as Hamlet and as Goethe's Tasso. Eduard's son Otto (1838–1894) worked as a director in Weimar from 1873, produced his own version of Goethe's *Faust* (1876), and wrote several tragedies. Karl's son Max (1857–1929) acted with the famed Vienna Burgtheater from 1882.

de Vries \də-'vrēs\, **Hugo (Marie)** (1848–1935) Dutch botanist and geneticist. He taught at Amsterdam Univ. 1878–1918, where he introduced the experimental study of organic EVOLUTION. His rediscovery in 1900 (simultaneously with Carl Erich CORRENS and Erich TSCHERMAK VON SEYSENEGG) of Gregor MENDEL's principles of HEREDITY and his own theory of biological MUTATION made possible the universal acceptance and active investigation of Charles DARWIN's theory of organic evolution. De Vries discovered and named mutation.

dew Moisture condensed at night onto the surfaces of exposed objects. Dew forms on clear nights, when exposed surfaces lose heat by radiation and become colder than the air. The cold surface cools the air in its vicinity, and, if the air is humid enough, it may cool below its dew point, the temperature at which water vapor condenses out of the air onto the surface. See also FROST.

Dewar \'d(y)ü-ər\, **James** (*later* **Sir James**) (1842–1923) British chemist and physicist. He built a machine for producing liquid oxygen in quantity. His double-walled, vacuum-insulated Dewar flask for storing liquefied gases became essential in low-temperature scientific work; its principle is used in the Thermos bottle. Dewar was the first to liquefy and solidify hydrogen, and his discovery that cooled charcoal can help create high vacuums was useful in atomic physics.

Dewey, George (1837–1917) U.S. naval commander. Born in Montpelier, Vt., he served with Union naval forces in the Civil War. In 1897 he commanded the U.S. Asiatic squadron. When the SPANISH–AMERICAN WAR began, he sailed from Hong Kong to the Philippines; he decisively defeated the Spanish fleet at the Battle of MANILA BAY (1898), opening fire with the command "You may fire when you are ready, Gridley." In 1899 Congress created for him the rank of admiral of the navy.

Dewey, John (1859–1952) U.S. philosopher and educator who was one of the founders of PRAGMATISM, a pioneer in functional psychology, and a leader of the progressive movement in U.S. education. Educated at Johns Hopkins Univ., he taught 10 years at the Univ. of Michigan before moving to the Univ. of Chicago. Influenced by G. Stanley HALL and William JAMES, he developed a theory of knowledge that conceived of ideas as tools for the solution of problems encountered in the environment. Believing the experimental methods of science provided the most promising approach to social and ethical problems, he applied this view to studies of

John Dewey

democracy and liberalism. His writings on education, notably *The School and Society* (1899) and *The Child and the Curriculum* (1902), emphasized the interests of the child and the use of the classroom to cultivate the interplay between thought and experience. At Chicago he created laboratory schools to test his theories. His work in psychology focused on the total organism. In 1904 Dewey joined the Columbia Univ. faculty. In 1925 he produced his magnum opus, *Experience and Nature*.

Dewey, Melvil(le Louis Kossuth) (1851–1931) U.S. librarian. Born in Adams Center, N.Y., in 1876 he published *A Classification and Subject Index for Cataloguing and Arranging the Books and Pamphlets of a Library*, in which he outlined the DEWEY DECIMAL CLASSIFICATION system. He was one of the founders of the American Library Assn. and of *Library Journal* (both 1876). He also set up the School of Library Economy, the first U.S. institution for training librarians, and established the system of traveling libraries.

Dewey, Thomas E(dmund) (1902–1971) U.S. attorney and politician. Born in Owosso, Mich., he was elected district attorney in New York in 1937. His successful prosecution of organized crime led to three terms as governor of New York (1943–55), in which he pursued a policy of political and fiscal moderation. He received the Republican presidential nomination in 1944 and again in 1948, when he was widely predicted to defeat the incumbent, Harry TRUMAN, but failed to capture the vote of farmers and labor. Dewey retired from politics in 1955 but continued to advise Republican administrations.

Dewey Decimal Classification *or* **Dewey Decimal System** System for organizing the contents of a library based on the division of all knowledge into 10 groups, with each group assigned 100 numbers. Subdivisions eventually extend into decimal numbers; for example, the history of England is placed at 942, the history of the Stuart period at 942.06, and the history of the English Commonwealth at 942.063. The system was first formulated in 1873 by Melvil DEWEY. The Library of Congress classification system has largely replaced the Dewey system in recent decades.

dextrose See GLUCOSE

Dge-lugs-pa *or* **Gelukpa** \'gä-lük-bä\ Yellow Hat sect of TIBETAN BUDDHISM, the chief religion in Tibet since the 17th cent. It was founded by Tsong-kha-pa (1357–1419), whose reforms included strict monastic discipline and celibacy. The head of Lhasa's chief monastery received the title of DALAI LAMA from Altan Khan in 1578. With his aid the Dge-lugs-pa triumphed over the Karma-pa, or Red Hat, sect. The Dge-lugs-pa ruled Tibet until the Chinese Communist takeover (1950); many of its members, including the Dalai Lama, remain in exile.

Dhaka *or* **Dacca** \'da-kə, 'dä-kə\ City (pop., 1991: 3,839,000; metro. area pop. 1991: 6,105,000), capital of Bangladesh. It can be traced to the 1st millennium A.D., but it did not rise to prominence until the 17th cent., when it served as the MUGHAL capital of BENGAL province. It came under British control in 1765. It was the capital of E. Bengal province in 1947 and of E. Pakistan in 1956, it suffered heavy damage during the war of independence in 1971. Dhaka is the country's leading industrial center. Its buildings include temples, churches, and some 700 mosques dating back to the 15th cent.

dharma In HINDUISM, the religious and moral law governing individual and group conduct. It is treated in the Dharma Sutras, the oldest collection of Hindu laws, and in the compilations of law and custom called the *Dharma Sastra*s. In BUDDHISM, dharma is the universal truth common to all individuals at all times. In JAINISM, dharma signifies moral virtue as well as the eternal life force.

diabetes mellitus \'mel-ət-əs\ Disorder of insufficient production of or reduced sensitivity to INSULIN. Blood sugar levels increase, and excess sugar is excreted in the urine. Symptoms include increased urine output, thirst, weight loss, and weakness. Type I, or insulin-dependent diabetes mellitus (IDDM), formerly known as juvenile-onset diabetes, an AUTOIMMUNE DISEASE in which no insulin is produced, must be treated by insulin injections. Type II, or non-insulin-dependent diabetes mellitus (NIDDM), formerly adult-onset diabetes, in which tissues do not respond to insulin, is linked to heredity and obesity and may be controllable by diet. Careful attention to content and timing of meals, with periodic checking of blood sugar, may manage diabetes. If not, injected or oral insulin is necessary. Complications, including heart disease, diabetic retinopathy (a leading cause of blindness), kidney disease, and nerve disorders, especially in the legs and feet, account for most deaths. Reversible diabetes may occur as a complication of pregnancy. See also GLUCOSE TOLERANCE TEST, PANCREAS.

DE

Diaghilev \dē-'ä-gə-ˌlef\, **Sergey (Pavlovich)** (1872–1929) Russian impresario, founder-director of the BALLETS RUSSES. After studying law, he cofounded and edited (1899–1904) the avant-garde magazine *Mir Iskusstva* ("World of Art"). He then left Russia for Paris to present productions of Russian ballet and opera, and in 1909 he established the Ballets Russes, in which he achieved a stunning synthesis of dance, art, and music. A tyrannical and mercurial personality, he led the company until his death. Diaghilev's massive influence was felt throughout the 20th-cent. arts.

Sergey Diaghilev, c.1916

diagnosis Identification of a disease or disorder. Diagnosis requires a medical history (including family history), a physical examination, and usually tests and diagnostic procedures (e.g., DIAGNOSTIC IMAGING). A list of possible causes—the differential diagnosis—is developed and then narrowed down by further tests that eliminate or support specific possibilities.

diagnostic imaging *or* **medical imaging** Use of ELECTROMAGNETIC RADIATION to produce images of internal body structures for diagnosis. X RAYS have been used since 1895. Denser tissues, such as bones, absorb more X rays and show as lighter areas on X-ray film. A CONTRAST MEDIUM can be used to highlight soft tissues in still X-ray pictures, or can be followed on X-ray motion-picture films. See also ANGIOGRAPHY, COMPUTED AXIAL TOMOGRAPHY, MAGNETIC RESONANCE IMAGING, NUCLEAR MEDICINE, POSITRON EMISSION TOMOGRAPHY, ULTRASOUND.

dialect Variety of a language spoken by a group of people and having features of vocabulary, grammar, and/or pronunciation that distinguish it from other varieties of the same language. Dialects develop as a result of geographic, social, political, or economic barriers between groups of people who speak the same language. When dialects diverge to the point that they are mutually incomprehensible, they become separate languages. This was the case with Latin, whose dialects evolved into the different ROMANCE LANGUAGES.

dialectical materialism Philosophical approach expressed through the writings of Karl MARX and Friedrich ENGELS, the official philosophy of COMMUNISM. Its central tenet, borrowed from HEGELIANISM, is that all historical growth, change, and development results from the struggle of opposites. The class struggle between the capitalist and landowning classes, on the one hand, and the proletariat and peasantry, on the other, creates the dynamic of history. The laws of historical dialectics are seen to be so powerful that individual leaders are of little historical consequence. Originally a social, economic, and political concept, the principle was extended in the 20th cent. to the scientific realm as well, with damaging effects on Soviet science. Marx and Engels stated their philosophical views mainly in the course of polemics and brief historical studies; there is no systematic exposition of dialectical materialism.

dialysis \dī-'a-lə-səs\ *or* **hemodialysis** \ˌhē-mō-dī-'a-lə-səs\ Process of removing blood from a patient with KIDNEY FAILURE, purifying it with a hemodialyzer (artificial kidney), and returning it to the bloodstream. Many substances (including UREA and inorganic SALTS) in the blood pass through a porous membrane in the machine; particles such as blood cells and PROTEINS are too large to pass.

diamagnetism Kind of MAGNETISM characteristic of materials that line up at right angles to a MAGNETIC FIELD and are repelled by it. In most materials, the magnetic fields of the ELECTRONS balance each other and add up to zero. However, the interaction of the field with the electrons in a diamagnetic material induces an internal field in the opposite direction in that material, which can then be weakly repelled by magnets. Examples of diamagnetic substances include bismuth, antimony, sodium chloride, gold, and mercury.

diamond Mineral composed of pure CARBON, the hardest naturally occurring substance known and a valuable gemstone. Diamonds are formed deep in the earth by tremendous pressures and temperatures over long periods of time. Diamonds vary from colorless to black and may be transparent, translucent, or opaque. Most gem diamonds are transparent and colorless or nearly so; colorless or pale blue stones are most valued, but most gem diamonds are tinged with yellow. Because of their extreme hardness, diamonds have important industrial applications. Most industrial diamonds are gray or brown and are translucent or opaque. The diamond is the birthstone for April.

Diamond Necklace, Affair of the (1785) Scandal at the court of LOUIS XVI. The Countess de La Motte schemed to acquire a valuable necklace by duping Cardinal de Rohan into believing that MARIE-ANTOINETTE wanted to obtain it surreptitiously and that he could gain favor by facilitating its purchase. When the scheme came to light, Louis XVI had the cardinal arrested. Though he was acquitted, the arbitrary treatment of the cardinal discredited the monarchy on the eve of the FRENCH REVOLUTION.

Diamond Sutra *in full* Diamond-Cutter Perfection of Wisdom Sutra. Wisdom text of MAHAYANA Buddhism. Composed around A.D. 300, it takes the form of a dialogue between the BUDDHA Gautama and a questioning disciple. The work emphasizes the transitory nature of the material world and suggests that spiritual fulfillment can be attained only by transcending ephemeral phenomena and abandoning rationalism.

Diana Roman goddess of nature, animals, and the hunt. As a fertility deity, she was invoked for aid in conception and childbirth. Her Greek counterpart is ARTEMIS. In her cult in Rome she was considered the protector of the lower classes.

Diana, Princess of Wales *orig.* Lady Diana Frances Spencer (1961–1997) Consort (1981–96) of CHARLES, PRINCE OF WALES. Daughter of Viscount Althorp (later Earl Spencer), she married Charles in 1981 in a globally televised ceremony. They had two sons, Princes William (1982) and Henry (1984). Her beauty and popularity attracted intense press attention. The marriage gradually broke down; Charles and Diana separated in 1992 and were divorced in 1996. She continued her activities on behalf of numerous charities. In 1997 she was killed in a car crash in Paris, along with her companion, Emad Mohamed (Dodi) al-Fayed (1955–1997), and their driver. Her death produced a massive outpouring of grief.

Diane de Poitiers \dē-'än-də-pwä-'tyā\ *later* duchesse de Valentinois (1499–1566) Mistress of HENRY II of France. Diane came to the French court as a lady-in-waiting, where Henry, 20 years her junior, fell violently in love with her. After the death of her husband, Diane became Henry's mistress (c.1536). Throughout his reign (1547–59) she was queen of France in all but name, while the real queen, CATHERINE DE MÉDICIS, lived in comparative obscurity. Beautiful and cultivated, Diane was a patron of poets and artists.

Dianetics See Church of SCIENTOLOGY

dianthus See PINK FAMILY

diaphragm \'dī-ə-ˌfram\ Dome-shaped muscular and membranous structure between the THORACIC and ABDOMINAL cavities. The principal muscle used in RESPIRATION, it is also important in coughing, vomiting, excretion, and other expulsive functions. The AORTA passes behind the diaphragm; the inferior VENA CAVA and ESOPHAGUS pass through it. See also HERNIA, HICCUP.

Diarmaid Macmurchada See DERMOT MACMURROUGH

diarrhea \ˌdī-ə-'rē-ə\ Abnormally fast passage of waste material through the large intestine, resulting in frequent DEFECATION with loose FECES and sometimes cramps. Causes can include CHOLERA, DYSENTERY, highly seasoned foods or high alcohol intake, poisons (including FOOD POISONING), drug side effects, GRAVES' DISEASE, and psychoneurosis. Mild cases of diarrhea are treated with bismuth subsalicylate (trade name Pepto-Bismol); extreme cases are treated with fluid and electrolyte replacement until the disease passes. Traveler's diarrhea affects up to half of people who travel to developing countries; prevention includes taking bismuth subsalicylate tablets, and consuming only canned, peeled, or piping hot foods and beverages. Severe cases require ANTIBIOTICS. Severe MALNUTRITION coupled with diarrhea is responsible for millions of deaths annually in underdeveloped countries.

Dias \ˈdē-əsh\, **Bartolomeu** or **Bartholomew Diaz** \ˈdē-äs\ (c.1450–1500) Portuguese explorer. Given command of an expedition to ascertain the S limit of Africa, he set sail in 1487. He became the first European to round the Cape of Good Hope (1488); his voyage opened the sea route to Asia via the Atlantic and Indian oceans. He later commanded a ship in an expedition under Pedro CABRAL, and participated in the discovery of Brazil.

Diaspora \dī-ˈas-pə-rə, dē-ˈas-pə-rə\, **Jewish** All Jewish communities outside Israel. The first Diaspora (Greek: "dispersion") was the BABYLONIAN EXILE of 586 B.C. The largest Diaspora flourished in Alexandria, where, in the 1st cent. B.C., Jews represented 40% of the population. Diaspora Jews far outnumbered Jews in PALESTINE even before Jerusalem was destroyed in A.D. 70. Today, of the estimated 14 million Jews worldwide, some 5 million live in Israel, 6 million in the U.S., and 2.2 million in Russia and other republics of the former Soviet Union.

diathermy \ˈdī-ə-ˌthər-mē\ Use of high-frequency electric current for deep heating of tissues in physical therapy. Shortwave, ULTRASOUND, and MICROWAVE diathermy act at different depths for different purposes. Low heat eases muscle pain. Higher degrees of diathermy destroy tissue; this is useful in surgery, particularly on the eye or nerves, to coagulate, limit bleeding, and seal off traumatized tissues.

diatom \ˈdī-ə-ˌtäm\ Tiny planktonic (see PLANKTON), unicellular or colonial ALGAE of the phylum Bacillariophyta (about 16,000 species), found floating in all the waters of the earth. The intricate markings of the silicified cell wall are useful in testing the resolving power of microscopes. The beautiful symmetry and design of diatoms justify their title "jewels of the sea." Diatoms serve directly or indirectly as food for many animals. Diatomaceous earth, composed of fossil diatoms, is used in filters, insulation, abrasives, paints, and varnishes, and as an insecticide.

Diatom (highly magnified)

diatomaceous earth \ˌdī-ə-tə-ˈmā-shəs\ or **kieselguhr** \ˈkē-zəl-ˌgùr\ Light-colored, porous, and friable sedimentary rock composed of DIATOM remains. It is used in industrial filtration applications; as a filler or extender in paper, paint, detergent, and other products; in insulation for high-temperature devices; and as a sound insulator. The oldest and best-known commercial use is as a very mild abrasive in metal polishes and toothpaste. Large deposits occur in the NW U.S., Denmark, France, Russia, and Algeria.

Díaz \ˈdē-ˌäs\, **Porfirio** (1830–1915) Soldier and president of Mexico (1877–80, 1884–1911). When peace was restored to Mexico under Benito JUÁREZ, Díaz resigned his military command, but he soon became dissatisfied with the government. After leading two revolts, he was elected president in 1877. He bolstered the economy through foreign investment, while suppressing opposition, rigging elections, and abusing patronage. He was overthrown in the MEXICAN REVOLUTION. See also Francisco MADERO.

dice Set of small cubes (each called a die) marked on each face with from one to six spots and used in GAMBLING and in various social games by being shaken and thrown down to come to rest at random on a flat surface. The combined number of the spots on the topmost surface of the tossed dice decides, according to the rules of the game being played, whether the thrower (or "shooter") wins, loses, or continues to throw. In numerous board games dice determine the player's moves. Dice, which may be traced back to prehistory, were in many cultures magical devices used to divine the future.

Dickens, Charles (John Huffam) (1812–1870) British novelist, generally considered the greatest of the Victorian period. He was born in Portsmouth. When his father, a clerk, was thrown into debtors prison, Charles was withdrawn from school and forced to work in a factory. His fiction career began with short pieces reprinted as *Sketches by "Boz"* (1836). The comic novel *The Pickwick Papers* (1837) made him the most popular English author of his time. *Oliver Twist* (1838), *Nicholas Nickleby* (1839), and *The Old Curiosity Shop* (1841) followed. After a

Charles Dickens

trip to America, he wrote *A Christmas Carol* (1843) in a few weeks, followed by *Martin Chuzzlewit* (1844). He expressed uneasiness about the evils of Victorian industrial society in works such as *David Copperfield* (1850), *Bleak House* (1853), *Hard Times* (1854), *Great Expectations* (1861), and *Our Mutual Friend* (1865). Dickens's works are characterized by attacks on social evils and inadequate institutions, an encyclopedic knowledge of London, pathos, a vein of the macabre, a pervasive spirit of benevolence and geniality, inexhaustible powers of character creation, an acute ear for characteristic speech, and a highly individual prose style.

Dickey, James (Lafayette) (1923–1997) U.S. poet, novelist, and critic. Born in Atlanta, he published his poetry in such volumes as *Into the Stone* (1960), *Drowning with Others* (1962), *Helmets* (1964), *Buckdancer's Choice* (1965), and *The Zodiac* (1976), combining themes of nature mysticism, religion, and history. He became widely known with his powerful novel *Deliverance* (1970; film, 1972).

Dickinson, Emily (Elizabeth) (1830–1886) U.S. poet. Born in Amherst, Mass., she was educated at Amherst Academy and Mount Holyoke Female Seminary. She subsequently spent virtually all her life in her family home in Amherst. The subjects of her deceptively simple lyrics, whose depth and intensity contrast with the apparent quiet of her life, include love, death, and nature. Her numerous letters are sometimes equal in artistry to her poems. By 1870 she was dressing only in white and declining to see most visitors, and she never again left the boundaries of the property. Of her 1,775 poems, only seven were published during her lifetime. After posthumous publications, her reputation and readership grew. Her complete works were published in 1955, and she has since become universally regarded as one of the two or three greatest American poets.

Dickinson, John (1732–1808) American statesman. Born in Talbot Co., Md., he wrote an open letter to colonists that influenced opinion against the TOWNSHEND ACTS (1767). A delegate to the Continental Congress, he helped draft the ARTICLES OF CONFEDERATION. As a Delaware delegate to the CONSTITUTIONAL CONVENTION, he signed the U.S. Constitution and urged its adoption in a series of letters signed "Fabius." He is sometimes called the "penman of the Revolution."

dicot See COTYLEDON, FLOWERING PLANT

dictator In the ROMAN REPUBLIC, a temporary magistrate with extraordinary powers. Nominated in times of crisis by a consul, the dictator's term was six months or the duration of the crisis, and he had authority over all other magistrates. By 300 B.C. his powers were limited; no dictators were chosen after 202. The dictatorships of SULLA and Julius CAESAR were a new form with almost unlimited powers. Caesar became dictator for life just before his assassination; afterward the office was abolished.

dictatorship Form of government in which one person or an OLIGARCHY possesses absolute power. Modern dictators usually use force or fraud to gain power and then keep it through intimidation, terror, suppression of civil liberties, and control of the mass media. In 20th-cent. Latin America, nationalist leaders often achieved power through the military and attempted either to maintain the privileged elite or to institute far-reaching social reform, depending on their class sympathies. In Europe's communist and fascist dictatorships, a charismatic leader of a mass party used an official ideology to maintain his regime, and terror and propaganda to suppress opposition. In post-colonial Africa and Asia, dictators have often retained power by establishing one-party rule after a military takeover.

dictionary Reference work that lists words, usually in alphabetic order, and gives their meanings and often other information such as pronunciations, etymologies, and variant spellings. The earliest dictionaries, such as those created by Greeks of the 1st cent. A.D., emphasized explaining changes that had occurred in the meanings of words over time. The close juxtaposition of languages in Europe led to the appearance of many bilingual and multilingual dictionaries from the early Middle Ages. The first purely English dictionary was Robert Cawdrey's *A Table Alphabetical* (1604), treating some 3,000 words. In 1746–47 Samuel JOHNSON undertook the most ambitious English dictionary to that time, a list of 43,500 words. Noah WEBSTER's dictionary of Americanisms in the early 19th cent. sprang from a recognition of the changes and variations within language. The immense *Oxford English Dictionary* was begun in the late 19th cent. Modern lexicographers (dictionary makers) describe current and past language but rarely prescribe its use.

Diderot \dēd-'rō\, **Denis** (1713–1784) French man of letters and philosopher. From 1745 to 1772 he served as chief editor of the 35-volume *Encyclopédie*, a principal work of the ENLIGHTENMENT. He composed such influential works as *Letter on the Deaf and Dumb* (1751), which studies the function of language, and *Thoughts on the Interpretation of Nature* (1754), acclaimed as the method of philosophical inquiry of the 18th cent. The first great art critic, he was especially admired posthumously for his *Essay on Painting* (written 1765). His novels include *Rameau's Nephew* (finished 1774).

Didion, Joan (b.1934) U.S. novelist and essayist. Her writing explores disorder and personal and social unrest. Her first novel, *Run River,* was published in 1963; later novels include *Play It As It Lays* (1970), *A Book of Common Prayer* (1977), and *Democracy* (1984). Her essay collections include *Slouching Towards Bethlehem* (1968) and *The White Album* (1979).

Dido \'dī-dō\ In Greek legend, the founder of CARTHAGE. She fled to N. Africa after the murder of her husband and bought land from a local chieftain, but killed herself rather than marry him. VIRGIL adapted the story; in his *Aeneid,* Dido welcomes AENEAS to Carthage, becomes his lover, and kills herself when he abandons her.

Didrikson, Babe See B. D. ZAHARIAS

die Tool or device for imparting a desired shape, form, or finish to a material. Examples include a perforated block through which METAL or PLASTIC is drawn or extruded, the hardened steel forms for producing the patterns on coins and medals by pressure, and the hollow molds into which metal or plastic is forced. The early techniques of Honoré Blanc in France (from 1780) were adopted and enlarged in the U.S. by Eli WHITNEY and others, who used templates (tool-guiding patterns) and fixtures—the antecedents of today's tools and dies—to mass-produce firearms for the U.S. Army. Today the demand for dies used in metal forming, DIE CASTING, and plastic molding is filled by tool- and die-making shops.

Diebenkorn \'dē-bən-ˌkȯrn\, **Richard** (1922–1993) U.S. painter. While teaching at the Calif. School of Fine Arts (1947–50), he developed an abstract style under the influence of such painters as Clyfford STILL and Mark ROTHKO. Turning to an expressionistic figurative style in the mid-1950s, he produced accomplished figure drawings, still lifes, and landscapes. Throughout his career he alternated between figuration and abstraction. His best-known works are the *Ocean Park* series, begun in the 1960s, comprising over 140 large abstract paintings that retain allusions to landscape.

Die Brücke See Die BRÜCKE

die casting Forming metal objects by injecting molten metal under pressure into DIES or MOLDS. An early and important

use was in the Linotype typesetting machine (1884), but the mass-production automobile assembly line gave die casting its real impetus. Great precision is possible, and products range from tiny parts for sewing machines to aluminum engine-block castings.

Diefenbaker \'dē-fən-ˌbā-kər\, **John G(eorge)** (1895–1979) Prime minister of Canada (1957–63). Born in Grey Co., Ontario, he was elected to the Canadian House of Commons in 1940. He became leader of the Progressive Conservative Party (1956–67) and was named prime minister in 1957. He became chancellor of the Univ. of Saskatchewan in 1969.

die making See TOOL AND DIE MAKING

Diemen \'dē-mən\, **Anthony van** (1593–1645) Dutch colonial administrator. As governor-general of the Dutch E. INDIA CO. settlements (1636–45), he enabled the Dutch to gain a monopoly of the spice trade in the Moluccas, conquer cinnamon-producing areas in Ceylon, seize the key Portuguese stronghold of Malacca, and capture Formosa (Taiwan). By 1645 he had established the Dutch as the paramount power in the E. Indies. Van Diemen also initiated the exploring expeditions of Abel TASMAN.

Dien Bien Phu \'dyen-'byen-'fü\, **Battle of** (1953–54) Decisive engagement in the first of the INDOCHINA WARS. The French fought the VIET MINH for control of a small mountain outpost near Laos. The French occupied the outpost, but the Vietnamese cut all the roads into it, leaving the French to rely on air supplies. Gen. VO NGUYEN GIAP then attacked the base with heavy artillery and a force of 40,000 men; the base fell despite heavy U.S. aid to the French. Most of the 10,000 French taken prisoner died in captivity, and the French soon abandoned Indochina.

Dieppe \'dyep, dē-'ep\ Town (pop., 1995 est.: 38,000) and seaport, N France, on the ENGLISH CHANNEL. French kings, realizing its strategic importance, granted it numerous privileges. In 1668 almost 10,000 of its people died during a plague, and in 1694 it was largely destroyed by the English and Dutch fleets. In World War II it was the site of an unsuccessful Allied commando landing (1942). Its port's shallowness hinders modern shipping.

Dies \'dīz\, **Martin, Jr.** (1901–1972) U.S. politician. Born in Colorado, Texas, he served as a U.S. Representative 1931–45 and 1953–59. In 1938 he was named chairman of the HOUSE UN-AMERICAN ACTIVITIES COMMITTEE; popularly known as the Dies Committee, it pursued alleged subversives in New Deal agencies and labor unions. Conservatives applauded its exposure of supposed subversives, and liberals decried Dies's tactics of smearing reputations with unproved charges.

Diesel, Rudolf (Christian Karl) (1858–1913) German thermal engineer. In the 1890s he invented the INTERNAL-COMBUSTION ENGINE that bears his name, producing a series of increasingly successful models of the DIESEL ENGINE that culminated in his demonstration in 1897 of a 25-horsepower, one-cylinder engine.

diesel engine INTERNAL-COMBUSTION ENGINE in which air is compressed to a temperature sufficiently high to ignite fuel injected into the cylinder, where combustion and expansion activate a piston (see PISTON AND CYLINDER). It converts the chemical energy stored in the fuel into mechanical energy, which can be used to power large trucks, locomotives, ships, small electric-power generators, and some automobiles. Unlike other internal-combustion engines, it has no IGNITION SYSTEM. Diesel fuel is low-grade and comparatively unrefined. Compared to other internal-combustion engines, diesel engines are expensive and heavy and produce more air pollution, noise, and vibration.

dietary fiber See dietary FIBER

Diet of Worms See Diet of WORMS

Dietrich \'dē-trik̲, *Engl* 'dē-trik\, **Marlene** (*orig.* Maria Magdalene) (1901–1992) German-U.S. film actress and singer. Initially a stage actress, she became an international star as a destructive cabaret singer in Josef von STERNBERG's *The Blue Angel* (1930). Sternberg brought her to Hollywood, where they made many films together, including *Morocco* (1930), *Shanghai Express* (1932), and *The Devil Is a Woman* (1935), which established her aura of glamorous sophistication and languid sensuality. During World War II she made over 500 appearances before Allied troops. She also starred in such films as *Destry Rides Again* (1939), *A Foreign Affair* (1948), and *Touch of Evil* (1958). She toured widely as a nightclub performer into the 1960s, singing trademark songs such as "Falling in Love Again."

Marlene Dietrich

Diez \ˈdēts\, **Friedrich Christian** (1794–1876) German linguist, regarded as the founder of Romance philology. He applied the methodology of comparative linguistics pioneered by Jakob GRIMM and Franz BOPP to the ROMANCE LANGUAGES. In his *Grammar of the Romance Languages* (1836–44) and *Etymological Dictionary of the Romance Languages* (1853), he demonstrated the relationship of "Vulgar" or Spoken LATIN to Classical Latin and the Romance languages' evolution from Spoken Latin into their modern form.

differential In CALCULUS, an expression based on the DERIVATIVE of a FUNCTION, useful for approximating certain values of the function. The differential of an independent VARIABLE x, written dx, is an infinitesimal change in its value. The differential of the function $f(x) = y$, written dy (or $df(x)dx$), represents the change in the value of the function brought about by the infinitesimal change in the variable x denoted by dx. The RATIO of the differential of x to that of $f(x)$ equals the derivative of the function at x.

differential calculus Branch of mathematical analysis, devised by Isaac NEWTON and G. W. LEIBNIZ, and concerned with the problem of finding the rate of change of a FUNCTION with respect to the variable on which it depends. Thus it involves calculating DERIVATIVES and using them to solve problems involving nonconstant rates of change.

differential equation Mathematical statement that contains one or more DERIVATIVES. It states a relationship involving the rates of change of continuously changing quantities modeled by FUNCTIONS. Differential equations are very common in physics, engineering, and all fields involving quantitative study of change. They are used whenever a rate of change is known but the process giving rise to it is not. The solution of a differential equation is generally a function whose derivatives satisfy the equation. See also DIFFERENTIATION.

differential gear GEAR arrangement that transmits power from the engine to a pair of driving WHEELS, dividing the force equally between them but permitting them to follow paths of different lengths, as when turning a corner or traversing an uneven road. When turning a corner the outside wheel has farther to go and would turn faster than the inner wheel if unrestrained. The automobile differential was invented in 1827 for use on steam-driven vehicles.

differentiation Mathematical process of finding the DERIVATIVE of a FUNCTION. Defined abstractly as a process involving LIMITS, in practice it may be done using algebraic manipulations that rely on three basic formulas and four rules of operation. The derivation and exploration of the formulas and rules is the subject of DIFFERENTIAL CALCULUS. See also INTEGRATION.

diffraction Spreading of WAVES around obstacles. It occurs with water waves, SOUND, electromagnetic waves (see ELECTROMAGNETIC RADIATION), and small moving particles such as ATOMS, NEUTRONS, and ELECTRONS, which show wavelike properties. When a beam of light falls on the edge of an object, it is bent slightly by the contact and causes a blur at the edge of the shadow of the object.

diffusion Process by which there is a net flow of matter from a region of high concentration to one of low concentration. It occurs more rapidly in fluids than in solids. Diffusion can be observed by adding a few drops of food coloring to a glass of water. Any scent quickly permeates a room because of random motion of the vapor molecules.

digestion Process of dissolving and chemically converting food for absorption by cells. In the mouth, food is chewed, mixed with SALIVA, which begins to break down starches, and kneaded by the tongue for swallowing. In the stomach, food mixes with ACID and ENZYMES, which further break it down. The mixture enters the DUODENUM, where BILE from the liver breaks up FAT globules, and enzymes from the pancreas and intestinal glands act on CARBOHYDRATES, PROTEINS, and fats. Breakdown products are absorbed by the bloodstream. Indigestible substances, such as FIBER, pass into the large intestine, where water and ions are reabsorbed and FECES held for EXCRETION. See also METABOLISM, PERISTALSIS.

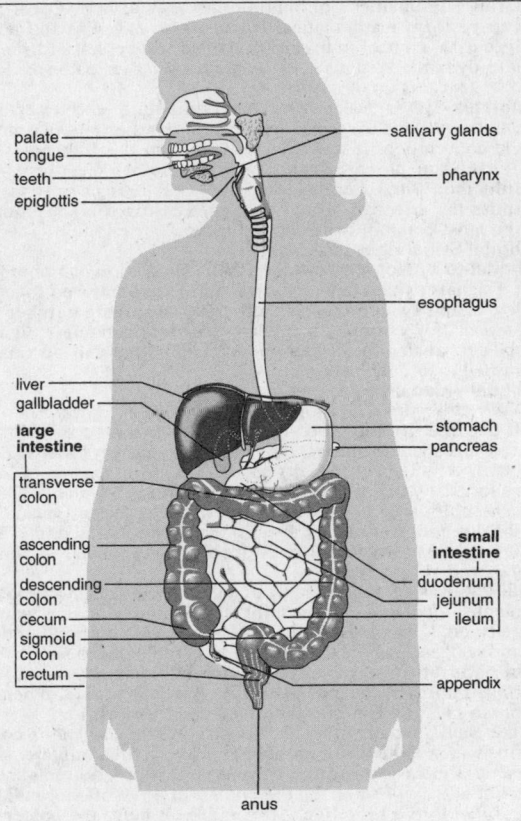

palate
tongue
teeth
epiglottis
salivary glands
pharynx
esophagus
liver
gallbladder
large intestine
transverse colon
ascending colon
descending colon
cecum
sigmoid colon
rectum
stomach
pancreas
small intestine
duodenum
jejunum
ileum
appendix
anus

Digestion Food taken in by the mouth is moistened and lubricated with saliva secreted by the salivary glands. Enzymes in the saliva begin the breakdown of starches. Movement of the palate against the back of the pharynx helps keep food from entering the nasal cavity. The epiglottis, a flap of tissue, prevents food from entering the larynx from the pharynx during swallowing. Muscles in the esophagus wall contract in waves to move the food to the stomach. A mixture of substances secreted by the stomach (incl. enzymes, hydrochloric acid, and mucus) assist in the breakdown of food. Partly digested food passes into the small intestine, where larger molecules are broken down into sugars, amino acids, and fatty acids. The pancreas secretes digestive enzymes into the duodenum. The liver secretes bile salts that make insoluble fats entering the small intestine water-soluble and vulnerable to enzymatic action. Excess bile salts are stored in the gallbladder. Small molecules are absorbed into the bloodstream through the jejunum and ileum. The large intestine (colon) serves primarily to compact and store undigestible material, which moves into the cecum from the ileum, and muscular contractions move the feces into the rectum to be expelled from the anus.

DE

digestive tract See ALIMENTARY CANAL

digital camera CAMERA that captures images electronically rather than on film. The image is captured by an array of charge-coupled devices (CCDs), stored in the camera's memory or a special diskette, and transferred to a computer for modification, long-term storage, or printing. Since the technology produces a graphics file, the image can be readily edited using suitable software. Models designed and priced for the mass consumer market first became available in 1996. They appeal particularly to users who want to send pictures over the Internet or to modify their photographs.

digital computer COMPUTER capable of solving problems by processing information expressed as numbers. By manipulating combinations of binary digits (see BINARY CODE), it can perform mathematical calculations, organize and analyze data, control industrial and other processes, and simulate dynamic systems such as global weather patterns. See also ANALOG COMPUTER.

digitalis \ˌdi-jə-ˈta-ləs\ Organic compound derived from FOXGLOVE and used as a drug that strengthens HEART muscle contraction. It was first prescribed in the 18th cent. Its active principles are STEROIDS. Their dosage must be carefully monitored, because the lethal dose may be only three times the effective dose. Digitoxin and digoxin are among the most commonly prescribed forms.

Digital Subscriber Line See DSL

digital-to-analog conversion (DAC) Process by which digital signals (which have a binary state) are converted to analog signals (which theoretically have an infinite number of states). For example, a modem converts computer digital data to analog audio-frequency signals that can be transmitted over telephone lines.

digital video disk See DVD

Dijon \dē-ˈzhōⁿ\ City (pop., 1999: 149,000), E central France. It became the capital of the duchy of BURGUNDY in 1015 and prospered under the VALOIS dynasty (1364–1477). LOUIS XI annexed the city in the late 15th cent. It is surrounded by eight forts; historic buildings include a 13th-cent. church and 14th-cent. town hall (the former palace of the dukes of Burgundy). Its university was founded in 1722. It is best known for its food products (e.g., mustard, vinegar, and gingerbread).

dik-dik Any of four species of delicate African ANTELOPE (genus *Madoqua*), named for the sound it makes when alarmed. It stands 12–16 in. (30–40 cm) high at the shoulder and weighs 7–11 lbs (3–5 kg). It has an elongated snout. An upright tuft on the crown may partially conceal the short, ringed horns of the male. Dik-diks live in dry areas of dense brush in S and E Africa, and feed chiefly on shrubs.

dike Bank, usually of earth, constructed to control or confine water. Dikes were purely defensive at first, but later became a means to acquire polders, tracts of land reclaimed from a body of water by the construction of offshore dikes parallel to the shoreline. After a dike is built, the polder is drained by opening gates at low tide or pumping out the water over the dike. The most notable example of polder construction is adjacent to Holland's IJSSELMEER (Zuider Zee) barrier dam. If the Netherlands were to lose the protection of its dikes, its most densely populated portion would be inundated.

Dili City (pop., 1999 est.: 65,000), capital of East Timor. It lies on the N coast of Timor Island and is the country's chief port and commercial center. In 1999 much of the city was destroyed when Indonesian forces rioted following a pro-independence referendum.

dill Annual or biennial herb (*Anethum graveolens*) of the PARSLEY family, or its dried seeds, used to season foods. Native to Mediterranean countries and SE Europe, dill is now widely cultivated in Europe, India, and N. America. The entire plant is aromatic.

Dillinger \ˈdil-ən-jər\, **John** (**Herbert**) (1903?–1934) U.S. bank robber. Born in Indianapolis, he was arrested in 1924 in the holdup of a grocery and sentenced to prison, where he learned the craft of bank robbery. Paroled in 1933, he soon led his gang in five bank robberies in Indiana and Ohio. Again captured, he escaped and returned to bank robbery until his recapture. In 1934 he used a wooden pistol to escape from an Indiana prison. His bank robberies continued

until he was killed in an ambush involving the FBI, Indiana police, and a friend and brothel madam (the "lady in red"), who drew him to Chicago's Biograph Theater.

DiMaggio \də-ˈmä-zhē-ˌō, di-ˈma-jē-ˌō\, **Joe** (*orig.* Joseph Paul) (1914–1999) U.S. baseball star. Born in Martinez, Cal., he played for the New York Yankees from 1936 until his retirement in 1951. He played center field with such languid grace that some inattentive fans thought he was lazy. Known as "Joltin' Joe" or "the Yankee Clipper," he achieved a career batting average of .325. In 1941 he accomplished one of the most remarkable of all major-league records by hitting safely in 56 consecutive games. DiMaggio helped the

Joe DiMaggio

Yankees win nine World Series titles. His brothers Vincent and Dominic also played in the major leagues. His second wife (for nine months in 1954) was Marilyn MONROE.

dimension In mathematics, a number indicating the fewest coordinates necessary to identify a point in a geometric space; more generally, a number indicating a measurement of length. One-dimensional space can be represented by a numbered line, on which a single number identifies a point. In two-dimensional space, two numbers identify a point (see COORDINATE SYSTEM). Three numbers suffice in three-dimensional space, and so on.

dimethyl ketone See ACETONE

Dinesen \ˈdē-nə-sən\, **Isak** *orig.* Karen Christence Dinesen *later* Baroness Blixen-Finecke (1885–1962) Danish writer. She married her cousin, a baron, and they moved to Kenya; *Out of Africa* (1937; film, 1985), a memoir of her years on their coffee plantation (1914–31), reveals an almost mystical love of Africa and its people. Her finely crafted stories, set in the past and pervaded with an aura of supernaturalism, appeared in such collections as *Seven Gothic Tales* (1934) and *Winter's Tales* (1942).

Ding Ling *or* **Ting Ling** \ˈdiŋ-ˈliŋ\ *orig.* Jiang Weizhi (1904–1986) Chinese writer. She wrote three short-story collections before publishing the proletarian-oriented *Flood* (1931), which was acclaimed as a model of SOCIALIST REALISM. She later expressed dissatisfaction with the Communist Party, for which she was imprisoned for five years during the CULTURAL REVOLUTION. Her later works include critical essays and fiction, some published in *I Myself Am a Woman* (1989).

dingo Australian wild dog (*Canis dingo*), apparently introduced from Asia 5,000–8,000 years ago. It has short, soft fur, a bushy tail, and erect, pointed ears. It is about 4 ft (1.2 m) long, including the 12-in. (30-cm) tail, and stands about 24 in. (60 cm) high. Dingoes hunt alone or in small groups. They formerly preyed on kangaroos but now feed mainly on rabbits and sometimes livestock. They contributed, through competition for resources, to the extermination of the Tasmanian wolf and TASMANIAN DEVIL on the Australian mainland.

Dinka Cattle-herding people of the Nile basin in S Sudan. Numbering about 3 million, they live in independent groups of 1,000–30,000 led by priest-chiefs. In recent years they have warred with government troops in a struggle for greater autonomy. See also NILOTES.

dinoflagellate \ˌdī-nō-ˈfla-jə-lət\ Any of numerous one-celled, aquatic organisms that have two dissimilar flagella and characteristics of both ALGAE and PROTOZOANS. Most are microscopic and marine. The group is an important component of PHYTOPLANKTON in all but the colder seas, and an important link in the food chain. Dinoflagellate populations may reach 60 million organisms per liter of water. Such rapid growths, called blooms, result in the RED TIDES that discolor the sea and poison fish and other marine animals.

dinosaur Any of the extinct REPTILES that were the dominant land animals during most of the MESOZOIC ERA (248–

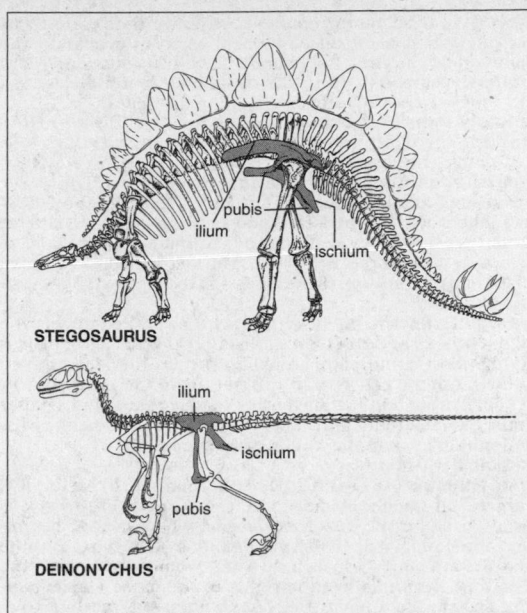

STEGOSAURUS

ilium
pubis
ischium

DEINONYCHUS

ilium
ischium
pubis

Dinosaur Skeletons of an ornithischian dinosaur (stegosaurus) and a saurischian dinosaur (deinonychus). The skeleton of stegosaurus shows a pelvic arrangement resembling that of birds, with a long ilium and a pubis having a short blade anteriorly which extends backward into a long thin process lying below and parallel to the ischium. The pelvic girdle of deinonychus shows the triangular outline formed by the ischium, pubis, and ilium characteristic of the saurischians.

65 million years ago). Various species appeared at different times. Many were carnivores, but several were herbivores. Dinosaurs are classified as either ORNITHISCHIANS or SAURISCHIANS, based on PELVIC GIRDLE structure. Most had a long tail, which they held straight out, apparently to maintain balance. Some were probably warm-blooded. Dinosaur fossils have been found on every continent. Most types of dinosaur flourished until late in the CRETACEOUS PERIOD (65 million years ago), then disappeared within the next million years. Two theories are that mountain-building cycles altered habitat and changed climate, or that an asteroid hit the earth, producing dust clouds that blocked sunlight for several years. Birds are thought by many to be descendants of the dinosaurs. See also CARNOSAUR.

Dinosaur National Monument National preserve, NW Colorado and NE Utah. It was set aside in 1915 to preserve rich fossil beds that include dinosaur remains. It now covers 330 sq mi (855 sq km). It protects the canyons of the Green and Yampa rivers, which contain highly colored geologic formations.

Diocletian \ˌdī-ə-ˈklē-shən\ *Latin* Gaius Aurelius Valerius Diocletianus *orig.* Diocles (A.D. 245–316) Roman emperor (284–305) who restored efficient government after the near-anarchy of the 3rd cent. Though brought to power by the army, Diocletian sought to remove the military from politics. He established a tetrarchy (four-ruler system) to spread his influence and combat rebellions throughout the empire. Proclaiming himself and his corulers as gods, he added the trappings of a theocracy to the reign. His fiscal, administrative, and military reorganization laid the foundation for the BYZANTINE EMPIRE in the east and briefly strengthened the fading empire in the west. In 303–4 he issued four edicts decreeing the last great persecution of Christians. He abdicated in 305.

diode Electronic device that has two ELECTRODES (ANODE and CATHODE). An applied voltage can cause electrons to flow only in one direction, from the cathode to the anode, and then back to the cathode through an external circuit. Diodes are used especially as rectifiers—which change ALTERNATING CURRENT into DIRECT CURRENT—and to vary the amplitude of a signal in proportion to the voltage in a circuit, as in a radio or television receiver. The most familiar diodes are VACUUM TUBES and SEMICONDUCTOR diodes. Semiconductor diodes consist of two electrodes and a P-N JUNCTION. Such diodes form the basis for more complex semiconductor devices (including TRANSISTORS). Semiconductor diodes include LIGHT-EMITTING DIODES and laser diodes; the latter emit LASER light, useful for telecommunications via FIBER OPTICS and for reading COMPACT DISCS.

Diogenes of Sinope \dī-ˈäj-ə-ˌnēz...sə-ˈnō-pē\ (d.c.320 B.C.) Greek philosopher, principal member of the CYNICS. He conveyed the Cynic philosophy by personal example rather than any system of thought. He strove to destroy social conventions (including family life) as a way of returning to a "natural" life. To this end he lived as a vagabond pauper and advocated shamelessness (performing harmless unconventional actions), outspokenness, and training in austerity.

Diomedes \ˌdī-ə-ˈmē-ˌdēz\ Greek hero in the TROJAN WAR. His exploits included wounding the goddess APHRODITE, killing Rhesus and his Thracian followers, and stealing the Trojan Palladium (Troy's sacred image of ATHENA). Aphrodite punished him by making his wife unfaithful to him, and he returned home to find his claim to the throne of ARGOS disputed. He then sailed to Italy and founded the colony of Argyripa (later Arpi).

Dionysia See BACCHANALIA

Dionysius I *or* **Dionysius the Elder** (c.430–367 B.C.) Tyrant of SYRACUSE (405–367). A brutal military despot, he held Carthaginian expansion on Sicily in check and became the chief power in Greek Italy. Syracuse's economy depended on war, and under Dionysius great advances were made in the technology of large-scale artillery and the manufacture of munitions. His disastrous third campaign against the Carthaginians resulted in the ceding of money and territory; he died during the next Carthaginian conflict.

Dionysus \ˌdī-ə-ˈnī-səs\ Greek god of vegetation and fruitfulness, known especially as the god of wine and ecstasy. His Roman equivalent was Bacchus. His worship was introduced into Greece from Asia Minor, and he became one of the most important of all the Greek gods. A son of ZEUS and (according to the standard tradition) SEMELE, he was brought up by the MAENADS. The first creator of wine, he traveled widely teaching the winemaking art, with a following of satyrs, sileni (see SATYR AND SILENUS), and NYMPHS. He had the gift of prophecy, and his principal oracle was at Thrace. Festivities called Dionysia or (among the Romans) BACCHANALIA were held in his honor; in their earlier years they were wild, ecstatic occasions. Dionysus originally appeared in art as a bearded man, but later more often as a slim youth. The DITHYRAMB, a choral hymn in his honor, is often seen as the basis of Western drama.

Dior \ˈdyȯr, *Engl* dē-ˈȯr, ˈdē-ȯr\, **Christian** (1905–1957) French fashion designer. After illustrating fashions for a weekly periodical, in 1942 he joined the house of the Parisian designer Lucien Lelong. In 1947 he introduced his revolutionary "New Look," which featured small shoulders and long, full skirts, a dramatic change from the World War II style of padded shoulders and short skirts. In the 1950s the "sack" or "H" line became his characteristic silhouette. His extraordinary success was instrumental in commercializing Parisian fashion on a worldwide scale.

Christian Dior, 1957

Dioscuri \ˌdī-əs-ˈkyúr-ī, dī-ˈäs-kyə-ˌrī\ *or* **Castor and Pollux** Twin gods of ancient Greece. They aided shipwrecked sailors and granted favorable winds. Castor was mortal and

DE

Pollux was immortal; when Castor was killed, Pollux disowned his immortality to join his brother. Zeus later changed them into the constellation Gemini.

dioxin \dī-'äk-sən\ AROMATIC COMPOUND, any of a group of contaminants produced in making herbicides (e.g., AGENT ORANGE), disinfectants, and other agents. Dioxins have two benzene rings connected by a pair of oxygen atoms; when substituents on the rings are chlorine atoms, the molecules are particularly toxic. They are extremely stable chemically; they do not dissolve in water but do in oils (and thus accumulate in body fat). Their human toxicity is disputed and the subject of continuing research.

diphtheria \dif-'thir-ē-ə\ Acute infectious BACTERIAL DISEASE caused by *Corynebacterium diphtheriae.* A thick membrane develops that adheres to throat tissues and sometimes blocks the TRACHEA. The bacteria produce a TOXIN that causes other symptoms, including FEVER, chills, sore throat, and lesions in heart muscle and peripheral nerve tissue that may cause death from heart failure and paralysis. Diphtheria is treated with an ANTITOXIN that produces long-term IMMUNITY, and a VACCINE can prevent it.

diplodocus \də-'plä-də-kəs\ Any member of a dinosaur genus (*Diplodocus*) found as fossils in Late Jurassic rocks of N. America. A relative of *Apatosaurus* (see BRONTOSAURUS), diplodocus was one of the longest land animals that ever lived; the longest known was 87.5 ft (about 27 m) long. It had a long neck and extremely small brain and skull. Most species weighed about 30 tons, and some as much as 80 tons. Diplodocus may have spent much time in water, but could move freely on land. It apparently fed on soft vegetation.

diplomacy Art of conducting relationships for gain without conflict; the chief instrument of FOREIGN POLICY. Its methods include secret negotiation by accredited envoys (though political leaders also negotiate) and international agreements and laws. Its use predates recorded history. Safeguarding the state's independence, security, and integrity is of prime importance; preserving the widest possible freedom of action for the state is nearly as important. Beyond that, diplomacy seeks maximum national advantage without using force and preferably without causing resentment.

diplopia See DOUBLE VISION

dipole See ELECTRIC DIPOLE

Di Prima \di-'prē-mə\, **Diane** (b.1934) U.S. poet. Born in New York City, she became one of the few women to attain prominence in the BEAT MOVEMENT. In 1961 she cofounded *Floating Bear,* a monthly featuring notable Beat writers. Her collections include *The New Handbook of Heaven* (1963), *Earthsong* (1968), *Loba* (1978), and *Pieces of a Song* (1990). She also founded two publishing houses that specialized in young poets.

dipteran \'dip-tə-rən\ Any member of the more than 85,000 species in the insect order Diptera (the two-winged, or "true," flies), characterized by the use of only one pair of wings for flight and the reduction of the second pair of wings to knobs used for balance. Dipterans live in all habitats worldwide, including the subarctic and high mountains. They range in size from about 0.05 in. (1 mm) long (MIDGES) to 3 in. (8 cm) long (robber flies). Many species are annoying bloodsuckers, and several (e.g., HOUSEFLY, MOSQUITO, sand fly, TSETSE FLY) are vectors of disease. Other species cause great damage to agricultural crops. See also BLOWFLY, CRANE FLY, FRUIT FLY, GNAT, HORSEFLY.

Dirac \di-'rak\, **Paul A(drien) M(aurice)** (1902–1984) English mathematician and theoretical physicist. His first major contribution, in 1925–26, was a general and logically simple form of QUANTUM MECHANICS. Around the same time, he developed ideas of Enrico FERMI which led to Fermi-Dirac statistics. He then applied Albert EINSTEIN's special theory of relativity to the quantum mechanics of the electron, and showed that the electron must have spin of 1/2. His theory also revealed new states later identified with the positron. He shared a 1933 Nobel Prize with Erwin SCHRÖDINGER.

direct current (DC) Flow of ELECTRIC CHARGE that does not change direction. Direct current is produced by BATTERIES, FUEL CELLS, rectifiers, and GENERATORS with commutators. Direct current was supplanted by ALTERNATING CUR-

RENT (AC) for common commercial power in the late 1880s because it was then uneconomical to transform it to the high voltages needed for long-distance transmission. Techniques developed in the 1960s overcame the obstacles, and DC is now transmitted over very long distances.

Directory *French* **Directoire** \dē-rek-'twär\ (1795–99) Government set up at the end of the FRENCH REVOLUTION. Legislative power was placed in the Council of Five Hundred and the Council of Ancients, while executive power was placed in a five-member Directory. Though the Directors inherited the centralized powers of the COMMITTEE OF PUBLIC SAFETY, they had no funds to finance their projects or courts to enforce their will. Marked by administrative chaos and corruption, the regime was overthrown by NAPOLEON in 1799.

dire wolf Extinct WOLF (*Canis dirus*) that existed during the PLEISTOCENE EPOCH (1.8 million–10,000 years ago), probably the most common mammalian species found preserved in the LA BREA TAR PITS. It differed from the modern wolf in being larger and having a more massive skull and smaller brain. Skeletal remains have been found in Florida, the Mississippi Valley, and the Valley of Mexico.

dirigible See AIRSHIP

Dirks, Rudolph (1877–1968) U.S. (German-born) cartoonist. Largely self-taught, he moved to New York at 17 to work as a staff artist for the *New York Journal*, where in 1897 he created the comic strip *The Katzenjammer Kids*, virtually the first strip to employ speech. In 1912, when he moved to the *New York World,* he lost the rights to the name Katzenjammer and started a new strip, *The Captain and the Kids*, featuring the same "kids." His strip was continued by his son after his death.

Dirksen \'dərk-sən\, **Everett McKinley** (1896–1969) U.S. politician. Born in Pekin, Ill., he served in the U.S. House of Representatives 1932–48, where he remained an isolationist until the U.S. entered World War II. He later served in the U.S. Senate (1950–69), becoming minority leader in 1959. He was noted for his oratorical style. Though a conservative, he helped secure passage of the Nuclear Test Ban Treaty, the Civil Rights Act, and the Voting Rights Act.

dirty sandstone See GRAYWACKE

disarmament Reduction in armaments by one or more nations. It may be imposed by a war's victors on the defeated (as happened after Germany's defeat in World War I). Bilateral disarmament agreements may apply to a specific area. The term is most commonly used for multilateral reduction and limitation agreements, particularly in the context of nuclear weapons. See also ARMS CONTROL.

Disciples of Christ Group of U.S. Protestant churches that originated in the frontier revivals of the early 19th cent. Movements founded by Thomas and Alexander Campbell (1763–1854, 1788–1866) and Barton W. Stone (1772–1844) merged in 1832 and took the name Disciples of Christ. The new denomination grew rapidly. Although its goal was to unite all Protestants on the basis of NEW TESTAMENT practices, the movement itself split into the more conservative Churches of Christ (which rejects any innovation without New Testament precedent) and the Christian Church (Disciples of Christ). Other conservative congregations separated from the latter in the 1920s, establishing their own N. American Christian Convention in 1927. In 1985 the Disciples of Christ entered into an ecumenical partnership with the United Church of Christ.

disco Style of dance music that arose in the mid-1970s, characterized by hypnotic rhythm, repetitive lyrics, and electronically produced sounds. It evolved largely in New York underground nightclubs, in which disc jockeys would play dance records for hours without interruption, synchronizing the beats so as to make a seamless change between records. Artists such as Donna Summer, Chic, and the Bee Gees had many hits in the genre. Its powerful influence, especially its sequenced electronic beats, continues to affect much of pop music.

discount rate *or* **bank rate** Interest rate charged by a CENTRAL BANK for loans of reserve funds to COMMERCIAL BANKS and other financial intermediaries. It is one important indicator of the condition of MONETARY POLICY in an economy. Because raising or lowering the discount rate alters the rates that commercial banks charge on loans, it is used as a tool to combat RECESSION and INFLATION.

discovery In law, pretrial procedures providing for the exchange of information between the parties involved. Discovery may be made through interrogatories, written questions sent from one side to the other, or through depositions, whereby a witness is sworn and, in the presence of attorneys for both sides, is subjected to questions. Other forms of discovery include an order of production and inspection, which compels the opposing party to produce relevant documents or other evidence, and requests for medical examination if a party's mental or physical condition is at issue.

discus throw Sport of hurling for distance a disk-shaped object known as a discus. About 220 mm (8³/₄ in.) in diameter and thicker in the center than at the perimeter, it must weigh at least 2 kg (4 lbs 6¹/₂ oz) for men's events, 1 kg (2 lbs 3¹/₄ oz) for women's. It is thrown by means of a whirling movement made by the athlete within a circle 2.5 m (8 ft 2¹/₂ in.) in diameter. Part of the PENTATHLON since antiquity, today the sport is also an Olympic event in its own right.

disk, hard See HARD DISK

diskette See FLOPPY DISK

disk flower See COMPOSITE FAMILY

dislocation Displacement of the bones of a JOINT. It disrupts the LIGAMENTS, MUSCLES, and capsule (encasing membrane) holding the joint in place. The joint, painful and tender, appears misshapen and swollen, with discoloration of the overlying skin. The bones must be returned to their normal position (reduction) and the joint kept immobile until healed. Recurrent and congenital dislocations usually require surgery.

Dismal Swamp *or* **Great Dismal Swamp** Heavily wooded marshy region, SE Virginia and NE N. Carolina. About 30 mi (48 km) long and 10 mi (16 km) wide, it is home to many rare birds and poisonous snakes. Noted for its fishing and hunting, it is crossed by the Dismal Swamp Canal, part of the ATLANTIC INTRACOASTAL WATERWAY.

Disney, Walt(er Elias) (1901–1966) U.S. film producer and cartoonist. Born in Chicago, in the 1920s he joined with Ub Iwerks (1901–1971) to create animated commercials and cartoons. He later moved to Hollywood, enlisted his brother Roy as his business manager, and persuaded Iwerks to join them. Together they created Mickey Mouse, and starred him in the first animated film with sound, *Steamboat Willie* (1928). The brothers formed Walt Disney Productions (later the DISNEY CO.) in 1929. Mickey Mouse's instant popularity led them to invent such other characters as Donald Duck, Pluto, and Goofy and to make several short cartoon films, including *The Three Little Pigs* (1933). Their first full-length animated film, *Snow White and the Seven Dwarfs* (1937), was followed by such classics as *Pinocchio* (1940), *Fantasia* (1940), *Dumbo* (1941), *Cinderella* (1950), and *Peter Pan* (1953). Disney also produced other films, including *Mary Poppins* (1964), and television shows. He created the plans for DISNEYLAND AND DISNEY WORLD.

Walt Disney

Disney Co. U.S. entertainment corporation. Founded by Walt DISNEY and his brother Roy as Walt Disney Productions in 1929 to incorporate their cartoon ANIMATION studio, it expanded in the 1950s to make nature documentaries, live-action films, and television programs. It expanded further with the opening of Disneyland (1955) and Walt Disney World (1971) (see DISNEYLAND AND DISNEY WORLD). It declined after Disney's death in 1966 but was revitalized under new management in the 1980s, producing such films as *The Little Mermaid* (1989) and *Toy Story* (1995), the first full-length computer-animated film. The films *Beauty and the Beast* (1991) and *The Lion King* (1994) were recreated as

Broadway musicals. In 1996 it acquired the ABC television network to become the world's largest media and entertainment corporation.

Disneyland and Disney World Two theme parks built by the Walt Disney Co. (see DISNEY CO.). Disneyland, an interactive, family-oriented fantasy environment that opened in Anaheim, Cal., in 1955, was Walt DISNEY's response to typical amusement parks, which entertained children but not their parents. Its architecture is a blend of futurism and nostalgic 19th-cent. reproductions, and it has different sections devoted to specific themes. The much larger Walt Disney World opened near Orlando, Fla., in 1971, with Epcot Center (an idealized city), Disney-MGM Studios, and the Magic Kingdom and Animal Kingdom theme parks. It was the first amusement park to incorporate hotels and sports facilities into its master plan.

dispersion Any phenomenon associated with the propagation of individual waves at speeds that depend on their WAVELENGTHS. Wavelength determines the speed at which a wave travels through a medium. This variation in speed causes RADIATION to separate into components that have different FREQUENCIES and wavelengths. For example, when a beam of white light is sent through a glass prism, REFRACTION disperses it into an array of its component colors of light.

Disraeli \diz-'rā-lē\, **Benjamin** *later* Earl of Beaconsfield (1804–1881) British politician, author, and prime minister (1868, 1874–80). Of Italian-Jewish descent, he was baptized a Christian as a child. He first made his mark as a writer with *Vivian Grey* (1826–27); later novels included *Coningsby* (1844) and *Sybil* (1845). Elected to Parliament in 1837, he made a series of brilliant speeches against Robert PEEL and became leader of the Conservatives. He served as chancellor of the exchequer (1852, 1858–59, 1865–68) and pushed through the Reform Bill of 1867, extending the vote to workingmen. He was prime minister briefly in 1868, then returned in his second ministry (1874–80) to promote social reform. An advocate of a strong foreign policy, he secured a triumph for imperial prestige with his large acquisition of Suez Canal Co. shares. A trusted friend of Queen VICTORIA, he introduced a bill conferring on her the title Empress of India.

dissociative identity disorder See MULTIPLE PERSONALITY DISORDER

dissonance See CONSONANCE AND DISSONANCE

distemper Viral disease in two forms, canine and feline. Canine distemper is acute and highly contagious, affecting dogs, foxes, wolves, mink, raccoons, and ferrets. Most untreated cases are fatal. Infected animals are best treated with serum globulins and antibiotics. Feline distemper causes a severe drop in the number of the infected cat's white blood cells. It rarely lasts more than a week, but the mortality rate is high. Vaccines offer effective immunity for both forms.

distillation VAPORIZATION of a LIQUID and subsequent CONDENSATION of the resultant GAS back to liquid form. It is used to separate liquids from nonvolatile solids or solutes (e.g., ALCOHOLIC BEVERAGES from the fermented materials, water from other components of seawater) or to separate two or more liquids with different BOILING POINTS (e.g., gasoline, kerosene, and lubricating oil from crude oil). Many variations have been devised for industrial applications. See diagram on next page.

distilled liquor ALCOHOLIC BEVERAGE (such as BRANDY, WHISKEY, RUM, or arrack) obtained by distillation from WINE or other fermented fruit juice or brewed GRAINS. The essential ingredient is usually a sugar or a starch that can be easily converted into a sugar. The distillation process is based on the different boiling points of water (212°F, 100°C) and alcohol (173°F, 78.5°C). The alcohol vapors that arise while the fermented liquid boils are trapped and recondensed to create a concentrated alcoholic liquid. The resultant distillate is matured, often for several years, before it is packaged and sold. See also GIN, LIQUEUR, VODKA.

distribution See FREQUENCY DISTRIBUTION, NORMAL DISTRIBUTION

distributive law One of the laws relating to number operations. In symbols, it is stated: $a(b + c) = ab + bc$. It can

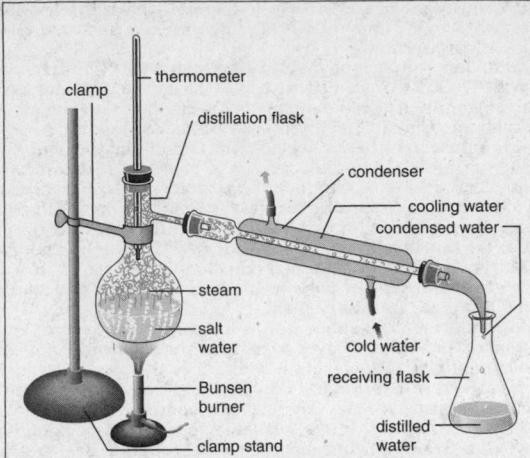

clamp

thermometer

distillation flask

condenser

cooling water

condensed water

steam

salt water

cold water

receiving flask

Bunsen burner

distilled water

clamp stand

Distillation A laboratory distillation apparatus, demonstrating desalinization of water. In the distillation flask, salt water is boiled to produce water vapor, while the salt remains in the liquid solution. The vapor is forced out the top of the flask and into the condenser, which consists of a glass tube, within a larger tube. Cooling water flows through the outer section, the vapor in the inner section cools and condenses, and the (purified) liquid water flows down to the receiving flask.

also be stated in words: The result of first adding several numbers and then multiplying the sum by some number is the same as first multiplying each separately by the number and then adding the products. See also ASSOCIATIVE LAW, COMMUTATIVE LAW.

District Court, U.S. See UNITED STATES DISTRICT COURT

District of Columbia Federal district of the U.S. Coextensive with the city of WASHINGTON, D.C., it is bounded by Maryland and Virginia. The site was chosen by Pres. George WASHINGTON. Originally 100 sq mi (259 sq km), the territory was authorized by Congress in 1790; it now occupies 69 sq mi (179 sq km). It was the seat of the federal government by 1800. Part of the district (Alexandria, Va.) was retroceded to Virginia in 1847. The territorial government was replaced in 1874 by a commission appointed by the President. Residents were granted suffrage in national elections in 1961. The mayor-council form of government was established in 1967; the mayor and councilors became elected officials in 1973.

dithyramb \'dith-i-,ram(b)\ Choric poem, chant, or hymn of ancient Greece sung by revelers at the festival in honor of DIONYSUS. The form originated about the 7th cent. B.C. with improvised songs of banqueters; it was a recognized literary genre by the end of the 6th cent. B.C. Dithyrambs were composed by ARION and PINDAR, among others. By around 450 B.C. the poems had become increasingly pompous and the form was declining.

Dittersdorf \'dit-ərs-,dörf\, **Carl Ditters von** *orig.* Carl Ditters (1739–1799) Austrian composer. A violin prodigy, he served as kapellmeister at the court of the Prince-Bishop of Breslau 1770–95. Extremely prolific, he wrote some 120 symphonies and about 40 concertos (many for violin). Most important are some 40 stage works, particularly his singspiels, including *Doctor und Apotheker* (1786) and *Die Liebe im Narrenhause* (1787).

diuretic \,dī-yủr-'e-tik\ Any drug that increases the flow of URINE. Diuretics promote removal of excess water, salts, poisons, and metabolic wastes to help relieve EDEMA, KIDNEY FAILURE, or GLAUCOMA. Diuretics that allow the body to retain POTASSIUM are used for patients with HYPERTENSION or CONGESTIVE HEART FAILURE.

Divali *or* **Diwali** \də-'wä-lē, də-'vä-lē\ In HINDUISM, a five-day religious festival in autumn. It honors LAKSHMI, goddess of wealth, or, in Bengal, the goddess KALI. Earthen-

ware lamps are lit and placed on the parapets of houses and temples or set adrift on rivers and streams. The fourth day of the festival marks the start of a new year, a time of gift-giving and socializing. Divali is celebrated by Jains and Sikhs as well.

diver See LOON

divergence In mathematics, a differential operator applied to a three-dimensional vector-valued FUNCTION. The result is a function that describes a rate of change. The divergence of a vector **v** is given by

$$\text{div } \mathbf{v} = \frac{\partial \mathbf{v}_1}{\partial x} + \frac{\partial \mathbf{v}_2}{\partial y} + \frac{\partial \mathbf{v}_3}{\partial z}$$

in which $\mathbf{v}_1$, $\mathbf{v}_2$, and $\mathbf{v}_3$ are the vector components of **v**, typically a velocity field of fluid flow.

diverticulum \,dī-vər-'ti-kyə-ləm\ Small pouch or sac formed in the wall of a major organ, usually the ESOPHAGUS, SMALL INTESTINE, or LARGE INTESTINE. In the latter, feces pushed into a pouch can make it bulge out from the colon wall, a symptomless condition known as diverticulosis. In the more serious condition called diverticulitis, those sacs become inflamed, causing pain and cramps, chills, and sometimes fever. Mild cases need only bed rest, antibiotics, an enema, and a bland diet. Severe cases can cause PERITONITIS. Rupture may require COLOSTOMY. Meckel's diverticulum, a congenital malformation, may require surgical removal.

dividend Individual share of earnings distributed among stockholders of a corporation or company in proportion to their holdings. Dividends may be distributed either as cash or as additional shares of STOCK. Preferred stockholders receive a preferential dividend; common stockholders get a portion of what remains after payment of the dividends on preferred stock.

divination Practice of discerning the hidden significance of events and foretelling the future. Divination is found in all societies, though methods vary. In the West, psychics claim innate ability to predict the future, and HOROSCOPES, palm reading, and TAROT cards are popular methods of divination. Other methods include interpreting dreams, discovering OMENS, reading animal entrails, casting lots, and consulting ORACLES. PROPHETS, SHAMANS, and magicians are typical practitioners. See also ASTROLOGY.

Divine, Father *orig.* George Baker (1877?–1965) U.S. religious leader. Born near Savannah, Ga., he began preaching around 1900 in the South and later in Baltimore as "The Messenger." He settled in New York in 1915 and adopted the name Major J. Devine (later Father Divine). In 1919 he established his first communal settlement. His predominantly black following expanded rapidly, and his settlements ("heavens") eventually numbered about 170. He taught his followers (many of whom believed him to be God) to renounce personal property; his moral code included celibacy and a ban on alcohol and tobacco.

divine kingship Religious-political concept that views a ruler as an incarnation or agent of the sacred. In some non-literate societies, members view their rulers or chiefs as inheritors of the community's own magical power. The ruler is usually responsible for influencing the weather and the land's fertility to ensure the harvest necessary for survival. In other societies, particularly those of ancient China, the Middle East, and S. America, the ruler was identified with a particular god or as a god himself; in Japan, Peru (Incas), Mesopotamia, and the Greco-Roman world, the ruler was regarded as the son of a god. In both these cases, the ruler protected the community from enemies and generally fed and cared for its members.

diving Sport of plunging into water, usually headfirst and often following one or more acrobatic maneuvers (such as flexing or somersaulting). A competitive sport since the late 19th cent., it became part of the Olympic Games in 1904. Dives are performed from a firm platform 5 or 10 m (16.4 or 32.8 ft) above the water, or from an elastic springboard 1 or 3 m (3.3 or 9.8 ft) above the water. Olympic contests use the 10-m platform and 3-m springboard. Contestants are required to do certain dives, as well as dives of their own choice. Judges score each dive, and the total score is multiplied by the dive's degree of difficulty.

diving duck Any DUCK that obtains its food by diving to the bottom in deep water rather than by dabbling in shallows (see DABBLING DUCK). Diving ducks prefer marine environments. Bay ducks (tribe Aythyini, family Anatidae), including CANVASBACK, redhead, SCAUP, and allied species, are usually found in estuaries and tidal lagoons. Sea ducks (20 species in tribes Mergini and Somateriini) include the bufflehead, eiders, goldeneye, MERGANSERS, oldsquaw, and scoters.

division of labor Specialization in the production process. Complex jobs can usually be less expensively completed by a large number of people each performing a small number of specialized tasks than by one person attempting to complete the entire job. Since specialization reduces costs, consumer prices should also fall. Division of labor is the basic principle underlying the ASSEMBLY LINE in mass production.

divorce Dissolution of a valid MARRIAGE, usually freeing the parties to remarry. In contexts in which religious authority is still strong and the religion holds that marriage is indissoluble (e.g., ROMAN CATHOLICISM, HINDUISM), divorce may be difficult and rare. In the U.S., nearly half of all marriages end in divorce, on such common grounds as drug or alcohol addiction, adultery, cruelty, and desertion.

Diwali See DIVALI

Dix, Dorothea (Lynde) (1802–1887) U.S. reformer. Born in Hampden, Mass. (now in Maine), she opened a school for girls in Boston in 1821. In 1841 she began teaching Sunday school in a jail, where she found the mentally ill imprisoned with criminals. After a tour of mental institutions, in 1843 she reported their deplorable conditions to the Massachusetts legislature. She soon expanded her campaign to other states; through her work, special mental hospitals were built in 15 states and in Canada.

Dix, Otto (1891–1969) German painter. He experimented with Impressionism and Dada before arriving at Expressionism with a nightmarish personal vision of contemporary social reality (see NEUE SACHLICHKEIT), depicting the horrors of war and the depravities of a decadent society. Appointed professor at the Dresden Academy in 1926 and elected to the Prussian Academy in 1931, his antimilitary works incensed the Nazi regime and he was dismissed from his academic posts in 1933. His later work was marked by religious mysticism.

Dixiecrats *or* **States' Rights Democrats** Right-wing Democratic splinter group in the 1948 election. Organized by Southerners who objected to the Democrats' civil rights program, the Dixiecrats met in Birmingham, Ala., and nominated Gov. Strom THURMOND of S. Carolina for president. He received over 1 million votes in the 1948 election and carried four states.

Dixieland *or* **New Orleans jazz** JAZZ played by a small ensemble featuring collective and solo improvisation. The earliest jazz ensembles grew out of the RAGTIME and brass bands of New Orleans. In groups such as those led by King OLIVER and Jelly Roll MORTON, the trumpet or cornet plays the melody, with clarinet and trombone providing accompaniment. The alternation of soloists with ensemble refrains combines with a distinctive two-beat rhythm to give the music its character, often a joyous cacophony at fast tempos or slow, mournful dirges. Dixieland groups usually include banjo, tuba, and drums.

Dixon, Joseph (1799–1869) U.S. inventor and manufacturer. Born in Marblehead, Mass., he began his pioneering industrial use of GRAPHITE in 1827 with the manufacture of lead pencils, stove polish, and lubricants. Finding that graphite crucibles withstood high temperatures, he secured patents on graphite crucibles for making steel and pottery, and established a crucible steelworks in Jersey City in 1850. He also devised a technique for printing banknotes in color to prevent counterfeiting.

Djakarta See JAKARTA

Djibouti \ji-'bü-tē\ *officially* **Republic of Djibouti** *formerly (1885–1967)* **French Somaliland** *(1967–77)* **French Territory of the Afars and Issas** \ä-'fär...ē-'sä, ä-'färz...ē-'säz\ Republic, E Africa, on the Gulf of ADEN at the entrance to the RED SEA. Area: 8,880 sq mi (22,999 sq km). Population (2000): 451,000. Capital: DJIBOUTI. Over half of the people

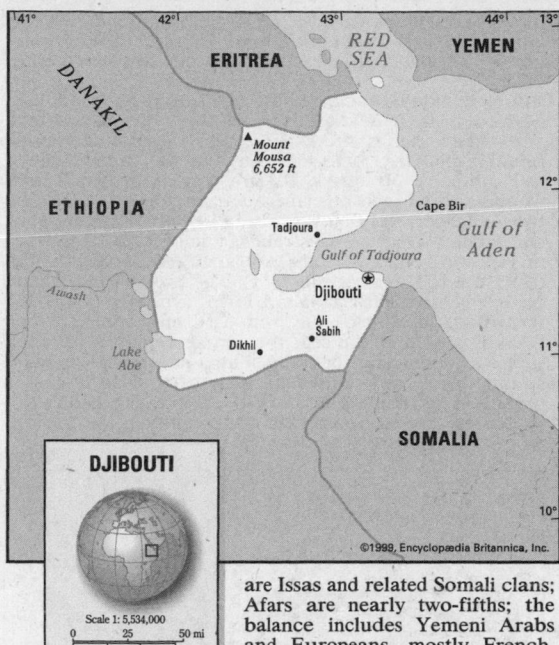

DJIBOUTI
Scale 1: 5,534,000
0   25   50 mi
0   25   50   75 km
©1999, Encyclopædia Britannica, Inc.

are Issas and related Somali clans; Afars are nearly two-fifths; the balance includes Yemeni Arabs and Europeans, mostly French. Languages: French, Arabic (both official). Religion: Sunnite Islam. Currency: Djibouti franc. Djibouti is divided into three principal regions: the coastal plain; the volcanic plateaus in the country's south and center; and the mountain ranges in the north, reaching 6,654 ft (2,028 m) at Mt. Mousâ. The land is primarily desert: hot, dry, and desolate; less than 1% is arable. Djibouti has a developing market economy that is almost entirely based on trade and commercial services, centering around Djibouti city. The country is a republic with one legislative house; its head of state and government is the president. Settled around the 3rd cent. B.C. by the Arab ancestors of the Afars, it was later populated by Somali Issas. In A.D. 825, Islam was brought to the area by missionaries. Arabs controlled the trade in this region until the 16th cent.; it became the French protectorate of French Somaliland in 1888. In 1946 it became a French overseas territory, and in 1977 gained its independence. In the late 20th cent., the country received refugees from the Ethiopian–Somali war, and from civil conflicts in Eritrea. In the 1990s it suffered from political unrest.

Djibouti Port city (pop., 1995 est.: 383,000) and capital of Djibouti. Located on the Gulf of Tadjoura in the Gulf of ADEN, it was founded by the French in 1888, and made the capital of French Somaliland in 1892. Linked by rail to ADDIS ABABA in 1917, it was made a free port in 1949. The economic life of both the city and the nation depends on the city's use as a transshipment point, especially between Ethiopia and the RED SEA trade. The city grew as drought and war during the 1980s and early '90s brought many refugees from Somalia and Ethiopia.

Djilas \'ji-läs\, **Milovan** (1911–1995) Yugoslav politician and writer. He joined the Yugoslav Communist Party's central committee in 1938 and its politburo in 1940. In World War II he played a major role in the partisan resistance to the Germans. In 1953 he became president of the Federal People's Assembly, but his criticism of the party led to his ouster by TITO. He was arrested several times after his influential books criticizing communism, including *The New Class* (1957), were published in the West.

Dmitry, False *or* **Pseudo-Demetrius** Any of three pretenders to the Muscovite throne who claimed to be IVAN IV's murdered child Dmitry. The first False Dmitry challenged Boris GODUNOV's right to the throne and was proclaimed czar in 1605. In 1606 he was murdered by Vasily Shuysky, who succeeded him (see Time of TROUBLES). A second pretender gained a large following before being killed in 1610. A third False Dmitry appeared in 1611, gaining the allegiance of the COSSACKS, but was executed in 1612.

DNA *or* **deoxyribonucleic acid** \dē-ˈäk-si-ˌrī-bō-nyü-ˈklē-ik, dē-ˈäk-si-ˌrī-bō-nyü-ˈklā-ik\ One of two types of NUCLEIC ACID (the other is RNA); a complex organic compound found in all living CELLS and many VIRUSES. It is the chemical substance of GENES. Its structure, with two strands wound around each other in a double helix to resemble a twisted ladder, was first described (1953) by Francis CRICK and James WATSON. Each strand is a long chain (POLYMER) of repeating NUCLEOTIDES: ADENINE (A), GUANINE (G), CYTOSINE (C), and THYMINE (T). The two strands contain complementary information: A forms hydrogen bonds (see HYDROGEN BONDING) only with T; C only with G. When DNA is copied in the cell, the strands separate and each serves as a template for assembling a new complementary strand; this is the key to stable HEREDITY. DNA in cells is organized into dense protein-DNA complexes called CHROMOSOMES. See also GENETIC ENGINEERING, MUTATION, NUCLEUS, PLASMID.

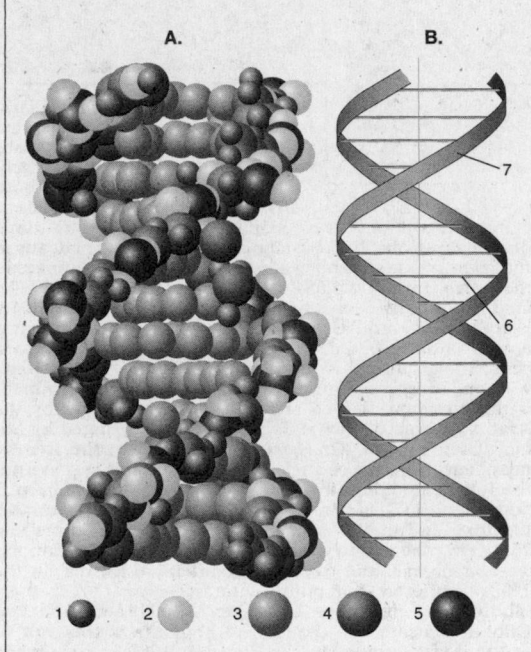

A.   B.

1   2   3   4   5

DNA DNA double helix. A. Molecular model of DNA. The molecules include (1) hydrogen, (2) oxygen (3) carbon and nitrogen in the linked nitrogenous bases, (4) carbon in the sugar deoxyribose, and (5) phosphorus. B. Schematic representation of DNA. The twisted ladder shape consists of (6) nitrogenous base pairs joined by hydrogen bonds, on (7) a sugar-phosphate backbone.

DNA fingerprinting Method developed by Alec Jeffreys (b.1950) in 1984 for isolating and making images of sequences of DNA. The DNA from a sample of cells (e.g., skin, blood, or hair) is extracted, purified, and cut by ENZYMES; the resulting fragments of varying lengths undergo procedures that permit them to be analyzed. The pattern of fragments is unique for each individual. DNA fingerprinting is used to help solve crimes and determine paternity; it is also used to locate gene segments that cause genetic diseases, and to produce biological drugs from genetically altered cells. See also GENETIC ENGINEERING, HUMAN GENOME PROJECT.

Dnieper River \ˈnē-pər\ *Russian* **Dnepr** \də-ˈnyeprᵊ\ *ancient* Borysthenes. River, E central Europe. One of the longest rivers in Europe, it rises west of MOSCOW and flows south through Belarus and Ukraine into the Black Sea, a course of 1,420 mi (2,285 km). More than 300 hydroelectric plants operate in the Dnieper basin; its huge dams have created a series of reservoirs. Navigable for about 1,042 mi (1,677 km), it is an important shipping artery for E Europe.

Dniester River \ˈnē-stər\ *Russian* **Dnestr** \də-ˈnyestrᵊ\ *ancient* Tyras. River, S central Europe. Rising on the N side of the CARPATHIAN MTNS., it flows south and east for 840 mi (1,352 km) to the Black Sea. The second-longest river in Ukraine and the main water artery of Moldova, it is navigable for 750 mi (1,200 km).

Dnipropetrovsk \də-ˌnye-prə-pē-ˈtrófsk\ *formerly (1783–1926)* **Ekaterinoslav** \i-ˌkä-ti-ˈrē-nə-ˌsläf\ City (pop., 1998 est.: 1,122,000), S central Ukraine. Located on the DNIEPER RIVER, it was founded in 1783. It grew after the railroad arrived in the 1880s. A railway junction and center of the wheat trade, it is one of the largest industrial cities of Ukraine, with a huge iron and steel industry.

Doberman pinscher \ˈdō-bər-mən-ˈpin-chər\ Breed of working dog developed in Germany by Louis Dobermann (1834–1894), a dog-pound keeper. This sleek, agile, powerful dog stands 24–28 in. (60–70 cm) high and weighs 60–90 lbs (27–40 kg). It has a short, smooth coat. Dobermans have a reputation for fearlessness, alertness, loyalty, and intelligence. They have been used in police and military work, as watchdogs, and as guide dogs for the blind.

Doberman pinscher

dobsonfly Any insect of the family Corydalidae with four net-veined wings, found in N. and S. America, Asia, Australia, and Africa. The species *Corydalus cornutus* has a wingspread of about 5 in. (13 cm), and the male has very large jaws (mandibles) of about 1 in. (2.5 cm) or more. Larvae live in streams; they are ferocious predators on other aquatic insects and small invertebrates and can inflict painful bites on humans. They are eaten by fish, especially bass, and are used as bait by fishermen.

Dobzhansky \dəb-ˈzhan-skē\, **Theodosius** *orig.* Feodosy Grigorevich Dobrzhansky (1900–1975) Ukrainian-U.S. geneticist and evolutionist. He laid the groundwork for a theory combining Darwinian evolution and Mendelian genetics by changing the then commonly held view that natural selection produced something close to ideal results and that changes would be rare and slow and not apparent over one life span. He observed extensive genetic variability in wild populations of drosophila, and found that in a given population some genes would regularly change in abundance with the seasons of the year.

Doctorow \ˈdäk-tə-ˌrō\, **E(dgar) L(aurence)** (b.1931) U.S. novelist. Born in New York City, he initially worked as an editor. His best-selling novels have often focused on the working class and the dispossessed of earlier decades in America. *The Book of Daniel* (1971) concerned the Rosenberg spy case. *Ragtime* (1975; film, 1981) incorporates actual figures of early-20th-cent. America. *Loon Lake* (1980), *World's Fair* (1985), and *Billy Bathgate* (1989; film, 1991) examine the Great Depression and its aftermath.

Doctors Without Borders *French* **Médecins Sans Frontières** \mäd-ˈsaⁿ-säⁿ-frōⁿ-ˈtyer\ Independent international medical relief agency. Established by a group of French physicians in 1971, it aids victims of armed conflict, epidemics, and disasters, and others who lack health care due to geographic remoteness or ethnic marginalization. In front-line hospitals, refugee camps, disaster sites, towns, and villages, teams provide primary health care, perform surgery, rehabilitate hospitals, and train local medical staff. The organization depends on volunteer health professionals (over 2,000 annually). It received the 1999 Nobel Peace Prize.

documentary Film that interprets factual material for educational or entertainment purposes. Robert Flaherty's *Nanook of the North* (1922) is considered the prototype of the genre. John Grierson's *Drifters* (1929) and Pare Lorentz's *The Plow That Broke the Plains* (1936), influenced documentary filmmaking in the 1930s, as did Leni RIEFENSTAHL's aesthetically powerful documentaries. In World War II propaganda documentaries included, in the U.S., Frank CAPRA's series *Why We Fight* (1942–45), and in Britain, *London Can Take It* (1940) and *Desert Victory* (1943). The popularity of documentaries on television in the 1960s and '70s led to such television miniseries as Ken BURNS's *Civil War* (1990). See also CINÉMA VÉRITÉ.

documentary theater See theater of FACT

dodder Any of the leafless, twining, parasitic vines that make up the genus *Cuscuta* (family Cuscutaceae), containing more than 150 species found throughout temperate and tropical regions. The stringlike stems may be yellow, orange, pink, or brown. Dodders contain no CHLOROPHYLL, instead absorbing water and food through rootlike organs called haustoria that penetrate the tissue of a host plant and may kill it. Dodder can do great damage to crops of CLOVER, ALFALFA, FLAX, HOPS, and BEANS.

Dodge, Mary Mapes *orig.* Mary Elizabeth Mapes (1831–1905) U.S. author. Born in New York City, she began writing children's stories when she was suddenly widowed. Her *Irvington Stories* (1864) was followed by *Hans Brinker; or, The Silver Skates* (1865), which became a children's classic. In 1873 she was named editor of the new children's magazine *St. Nicholas*; its success stemmed from her high standards, which attracted such writers as Mark TWAIN, L. M. ALCOTT, and Rudyard KIPLING.

dodo Extinct flightless bird *(Raphus cucullatus)* of Mauritius, first seen by Portuguese sailors about 1507. Humans and their animals exterminated the dodo by 1681. It weighed about 50 lbs (23 kg) and had blue-gray plumage, a big head, a 9-in. (23-cm) blackish bill with a reddish hooked tip, small useless wings, stout yellow legs, and a tuft of curly feathers high on its rear end. The Réunion solitaire *(R. solitarius),* also driven to extinction, may have been a white version of the dodo.

Dodoma \dō-'dō-mä\ City (pop., 1988: 204,000), Tanzania. Designated the national capital since 1974, it awaits complete transfer of official functions from DAR ES SALAAM, the current capital. It is located in a sparsely populated agricultural region at an elevation of 3,720 ft (1,135 m).

Doe, Samuel K(anyon) (1950/51–1990) Liberian soldier and head of state (1980–90). Doe led a coup in 1980 that overthrew and killed Pres. William Tolbert (1913–1980). He suspended Liberia's constitution until 1984, and in 1985 won a presidential election widely denounced as fraudulent. His regime was considered corrupt and brutal. In the civil war that broke out in 1989 Doe was captured and killed.

Doenitz, Karl See Karl DÖNITZ

Doesburg \'düs-ˌbʉrg\, **Theo van** *orig.* Christian Emil Maries Kupper (1883–1931) Dutch painter, decorator, and art theorist. In 1900 he began painting under the influence of Postimpressionism and Fauvism. After meeting Piet MONDRIAN in 1915, he turned to geometric abstraction. He was instrumental in founding the De STIJL group. His advocacy of the geometric style was well received at the BAUHAUS, where he influenced LE CORBUSIER, Walter GROPIUS, and Ludwig MIES VAN DER ROHE. In 1926 he wrote his manifesto, *De Stijl*, and in 1930 moved to Paris, where his studio became the focus of the movement.

dog Any member of the CANINE genus *Canis,* particularly the domestic species, *Canis familiaris.* Domestic dogs seem to have descended from the WOLF or a wolflike ancestor. Dogs were apparently the first animals to be domesticated. Humans have developed myriad breeds that vary widely in size (from the tiny CHIHUAHUA to the huge mastiff), physical form (e.g., the short-legged DACHSHUND and the flat-faced BULLDOG), coat texture and length (e.g., the sleek DOBERMAN PINSCHER and the long-haired AFGHAN HOUND), and behavioral patterns (e.g., sporting dogs, TOY DOGS, and WORKING DOGS). The American Kennel Club recognizes almost 150 breeds; other clubs recognize many more.

dogbane family Family Apocynaceae, of the GENTIAN order, with about 1,000 member species of trees, shrubs, woody vines, and herbaceous plants, found mostly in the tropics and subtropics. Dogbanes have milky, often poisonous juice and usually clustered, showy flowers. Garden ornamentals include PERIWINKLE, OLEANDER, and crepe jasmine *(Tabernaemontana coronaria).* Arrow poisons are obtained from many dogbanes, and the poisonous ALKALOIDS of some species are used in medicines.

doge \'dōj\ (Venetian Italian: "duke") Highest official of the republic of VENICE in the 8th–18th cent. The doge was chosen from among the ruling families of Venice and held office for life. He held extensive power, as evidenced by the rule of Enrico DANDOLO (r.1192–1205), though from the 12th cent. the aristocracy placed limits on the doge's authority. Under Francesco Foscari (r.1423–57), Venice undertook the first conquests of the Italian mainland. The last doge was deposed when NAPOLEON conquered N Italy in 1797.

dogfish Any of several species of small SHARK. The spiny dogfish *(Squalus acanthias,* family Squalidae) has a sharp spine in front of each of its two dorsal fins. It is abundant along N Atlantic and Pacific coasts. It is gray with white spots, about 2–4 ft (60–120 cm) long, and often found in schools. It often steals bait and damages fishing nets. Other well-known species are the spotted dogfishes (family Scyliorhinidae), which are sold as food, and the smooth hound or smooth dogfish *(Mustelus canis,* family Triakidae), common on the U.S. Atlantic coast.

Dogon \'dō-ˌgän\ People of the central plateau region of Mali. Numbering about 350,000, the agricultural Dogon are known for their fine wood sculptures, metalwork, and leatherwork, but principally for their elaborate mud buildings, often on cliff faces.

dogsled racing Sport of racing sleds pulled by dogs over snow-covered cross-country courses. It developed from a traditional Eskimo method of transportation. Modern sleds are usually of wood (ash) construction, with leather lashings and steel- or aluminum-covered runners. Sled dogs are usually Eskimo dogs, SIBERIAN HUSKIES, SAMOYEDS, or ALASKAN MALAMUTES; teams typically consist of 4–10 dogs. The course is usually 12–30 mi (19–48 km) long, though some, including the IDITAROD, are considerably longer.

Dog Star See SIRIUS

dogwood Shrubs, trees, and herbaceous plants of the genus *Cornus,* in the dogwood family (Cornaceae), found in temperate and warm temperate zones and on tropical mountains. Some members, such as the flowering dogwood *(Cornus florida),* are chiefly ornamental; others yield wood for furniture. In the flowering dogwoods, colored bracts surround the cluster of small true flowers.

Doha \'dō-hə\ *Arabic* **ad-Dawhah** \ˌäd-'daü-hə\ City (pop., 1993 est.: 339,000), capital of Qatar. Located on the E coast of the Qatar Peninsula, it contains about three-fifths of Qatar's population. Long a center of pirate activity in the PERSIAN GULF, Doha was a small village when it became the capital of newly independent Qatar in 1971. The city has been thoroughly modernized, and its deepwater port, built in the 1970s, accommodates oceangoing vessels.

Dole, Robert J(oseph) (b.1923) U.S. politician. Born in Russell, Kan., he was wounded during World War II, losing the use of his right arm. He earned a law degree before serving in the U.S. House of Representatives (1961–69) and Senate (1969–96). He was Pres. Gerald FORD's running mate in 1976. He became Senate majority leader in 1984 and minority leader in 1987. In 1996 he received the Republican presidential nomination but was defeated by William CLINTON. His wife, Elizabeth Hanford Dole (b.1936), was elected to the Senate in 2002.

Dole, Sanford B(allard) (1844–1926) Hawaiian politician. Born in Honolulu to U.S. missionaries, he served in Hawaii's legislature (1884–87) and on its supreme court (1887–93). He led the committee formed by local sugar interests that overthrew Queen LILIUOKALANI and sought annexation by the U.S., then served as the first president of the Republic of Hawaii 1894–1900. After annexation, he served as governor of the Territory of Hawaii (1900–3) and later as federal district judge (1903–15).

DE

Dolin, Anton (*later* **Sir Anton**) *orig.* Sydney F. P. C. Healey-Kay (1904–1983) British dancer and choreographer. In 1921 he joined the BALLETS RUSSES, where he created leading roles as a soloist. In the 1930s and '40s, he helped form several ballet companies; in 1949 he and his partner Alicia MARKOVA founded the forerunner of London's Festival Ballet, of which he was artistic director and premier dancer until 1961. He choreographed such works as *Capriccioso* (1940), *The Romantic Age* (1942), and *Variations for Four* (1957).

doline See SINKHOLE.

doll Small-scale figure of a human being, used especially as a child's plaything. The doll is perhaps humankind's oldest toy, though some ancient dolls may have served religious or magical functions. Dolls were buried in children's graves in Egypt, Greece, and Rome. In Europe, dolls have been commercially manufactured since the 16th cent. Doll heads were made of wood, terra-cotta, alabaster, and wax. In about 1820, glazed porcelain (Dresden) doll heads and unglazed bisque (ceramic) heads became popular. These were supplanted in the 20th cent. by molded plastic. In Japan, dolls are traditionally festival figures; in India, elaborately dressed dolls were given to child brides by both Hindus and Muslims. Today dolls are often collected as antiques.

Dollar Diplomacy U.S. foreign policy created by Pres. W. H. TAFT to ensure financial stability in a region in exchange for favorable treatment of U.S. commercial interests. The policy was carried out in Central America (1909) and China (1910) by Taft's secretary of state, Philander Knox. Pres. Woodrow WILSON repudiated the policy in 1913. The term has become a disparaging reference to the manipulation of foreign affairs for economic ends.

Dollfuss \'dȯl-ˌfu̇s\, **Engelbert** (1892–1934) Austrian politician. He rose rapidly in Austrian politics to become chancellor in 1932. Opposed to the Nazis, he welcomed Benito MUSSOLINI as an ally, converting Austria virtually into an Italian satellite state. In 1933 he abolished the parliament and in 1934 he issued a new constitution establishing a Fascist dictatorship. Germany soon incited the Austrian Nazis to civil war, and Dollfuss was assassinated in a raid on the chancellery.

Dollond \'däl-ənd\, **John and George** (1706–1761, 1774–1852) British optical scientists. John developed an achromatic (non-color-distorting) refracting TELESCOPE and a practical heliometer (a telescope that measures the sun's diameter and the angles between celestial bodies). His grandson George invented various precision instruments used in astronomy, geodesy, and navigation. His micrometer made of rock crystal was used by astronomers; his atmospheric recorder simultaneously measured and recorded on paper tape temperature, atmospheric pressure, wind speed and direction, evaporation, and electrical phenomena.

dolmen \'dȯl-mən\ Prehistoric monument usually consisting of several large stone slabs set edgewise in the earth to support a flat stone roof, all covered by a mound of earth that in most cases has weathered away. Designed as a burial chamber, the structure is typical of the NEOLITHIC PERIOD in Europe. See also MEGALITH, MENHIR.

dolomite Type of LIMESTONE, the carbonate fraction of which is dominated by the mineral dolomite, calcium magnesium carbonate. The CARBONATE MINERAL dolomite occurs in marbles, talc schists, and other magnesium-rich metamorphic rocks. It is most common as a rock-forming mineral in carbonate rocks.

Dolomites \'dō-lə-ˌmīts\ *Italian* **Alpi Dolomitiche** \'äl-pē-dō-lō-'mē-tē-kē\ Mountain group, N Italian Alps. Including a number of impressive peaks, 18 of which rise to more than 10,000 ft (3,050 m), the range and its characteristic rock are named for the geologist Dieudonné Dolomieu (1750–1801), who made the first scientific study of the region. The mountains are formed of light-colored dolomitic limestone, which erosion has carved into grotesque shapes. The range is popular with tourists and mountain-climbers.

dolphin Either of two types of animals: aquatic mammals or oceanic fishes. Mammalian dolphins are small toothed whales, usually with a beaklike snout. The common dolphin (*Delphinus delphis*) and the bottlenose dolphin (*Tursiops*

truncatus), both of the family Delphinidae, are found widely in warm temperate seas. Most of the 32 delphinid species are about 3–13 ft (1–4 m) long. River dolphins (family Platanistidae; four species) live mainly in freshwater in S. America and Asia. The family Stenidae (eight species), or long-snouted dolphins, inhabit tropical rivers and oceans. One of the two fish species, *Coryphaena hippuras* (family Coryphaenidae), also called mahimahi and dorado, is a popular food and sport fish of tropical and temperate waters worldwide. The pompano dolphin (*C. equiselis*) is similar. See also KILLER WHALE.

Domagk \'dō-ˌmäk\, **Gerhard** (1895–1964) German bacteriologist and pathologist. He noticed the antibacterial action of a dye, Prontosil red, against streptococcal infection in mice. Found to be effective in humans, Prontosil became the first sulfonamide drug. Awarded a Nobel Prize in 1939, Domagk was unable to accept it until 1947 because of Nazi policy. He also was active in research on tuberculosis and cancer.

domain name Address of a computer, organization, or other entity on a network such as the INTERNET. Domain names are typically in a three-level "server.organization.type" format. The top level denotes the type of organization, such as "com" (for commercial sites) or "edu" (for educational sites); the second level includes the name of the organization (e.g., "m-w.com" for Merriam-Webster); and the third level identifies a specific host server, such as the "www" (WORLD WIDE WEB) host server for "m-w.com". A domain name is ultimately mapped to an IP (Internet Protocol) address. A domain name must be unique on the Internet, and must be assigned by an accredited registrar. See also URL.

dome In architecture, a hemispherical structure evolved from the ARCH, forming a ceiling or roof. Domes first appeared on small round huts and tombs in the ancient Mid-

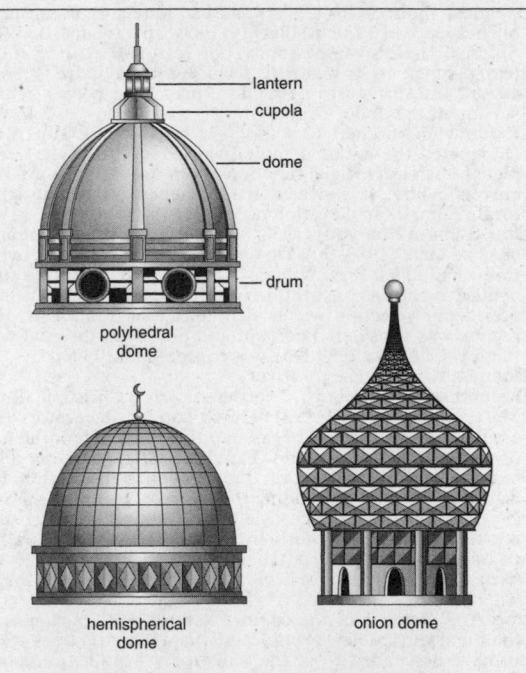

Dome A dome is traditionally supported primarily by a cylindrical or polygonal drum; it may be surmounted by a cupola, which may have a lantern to admit light. The classic hemispherical dome has a circular base and semicircular section; the polyhedral dome has segments resting on a polyhedral base and meeting at the top; the onion dome rests on a circular base and has an ogee section.

dle East, India, and the Mediterranean. The Romans introduced the large-scale masonry hemisphere. The earliest monumental examples (see PANTHEON) required heavy supporting walls. Byzantine architects invented a technique for raising domes on piers, and setting the hemisphere on a cubic base. Bulbous or pointed domes were widely used in Islamic architecture. The design spread to Russia, where it gained great popularity in the form of the onion dome. The modern geodesic dome, developed by R. Buckminster FULLER, is fabricated of lightweight triangular framing that distributes stresses within the structure itself.

Domenichino \ˌdō-mä-nē-ˈkē-nō\ *orig.* Domenico Zampieri (1581–1641) Italian painter. He trained in the academy of the CARRACCI FAMILY in Bologna and worked under them in the decoration of the Farnese Palace in Rome. His easel paintings were noted for their idyllic mood and subdued color, a radical departure from the monumental classicism of his frescoes. He became Rome's leading painter and had a succession of major decorative commissions. He was an outstanding draftsman and portraitist; his paintings were regarded as second only to those of RAPHAEL into the 18th cent.

Domenico Veneziano \dō-ˈmä-nē-kō-və-ˌnet-sē-ˈä-nō\ (fl.1438–1461) Italian painter. Born in Venice, he was active mainly in Florence. Two signed works survive: fresco fragments of the Virgin and Child from a street tabernacle (1430s) and the extraordinary St. Lucy Altarpiece (c.1445), his most successful experiment in rendering outdoor light. He used color and texture as the basis of perspective and composition; his influence can be seen in the work of Alesso BALDOVINETTI.

Dome of the Rock *or* **Mosque of Omar** Oldest existing Islamic monument. It is located on Temple Mount, previously the site of the Temple of JERUSALEM. The rock over which it was built in the 7th cent. is sacred to both Muslims and Jews. In Islam it is the site from which MUHAMMAD ascended into heaven. In Judaism it is the site where ABRAHAM prepared to sacrifice Isaac. The octagonal building has richly decorated walls and a gold-overlaid dome mounted above a circle of piers and columns.

Domesday Book \ˈdümz-ˌdā, ˈdōmz-ˌdā\ (1086) Original record or summary of WILLIAM I the Conqueror's survey of England. A remarkable administrative feat, the survey was carried out, against popular resentment, by panels of commissioners who compiled accounts of the estates of the king and his tenants. Originally called "the description of England," the name Domesday Book (a reference to doomsday, when people face a final accounting of their lives) was later popularly attached to it. It now serves as the starting point for the history of most English towns and villages.

domestication Process of hereditary reorganization of wild animals and plants into forms more accommodating to the interests of people. The fundamental distinction of domesticated animals and plants from their wild ancestors is that they are created to meet specific human needs and are adapted to the conditions of continuous care people maintain for them. Animals have been domesticated for food (e.g., CATTLE, CHICKENS, PIGS), clothing (e.g., SHEEP, silkworms, transportation and labor (e.g., CAMELS, DONKEYS, HORSES), and pleasure (e.g., CATS, DOGS). See also BREEDING, SELECTION.

domestic cat *or* **house cat** Domesticated CARNIVORE *(Felis catus)* with characteristics of the larger wild CATS but differences in coat and size. Breeds are either shorthaired (e.g., SIAMESE) or longhaired (e.g., Persian). Males may reach lengths of 28 in. (70 cm), and females are usually about 20 in. (50 cm); weights generally vary from 6 to 10 lbs (2.5–4.5 kg). Nonpedigreed cats may weigh up to 28 lbs (13 kg). The most closely related wild species are the N. African wildcats (including *Felix lybica)*; they were being domesticated in ancient Egypt to protect grain supplies from rodents by 1500 B.C. The Cat Fanciers' Assn. now recognizes 40 breeds.

domestic service Employment of hired workers for housecleaning, cooking, child care, gardening, and personal service. In ancient Greece and Rome, domestic service was performed almost exclusively by slaves. In medieval Europe, serfs provided much of the labor force. Indentured servants were widely used in colonial America, as were black slaves in the pre–Civil War South. In Victorian England, many middle- and upper-class households hired domestic servants; the royalty and gentry often employed huge staffs with an elaborate hierarchy. Domestic service has declined in the U.S. and Europe since the early 1920s because of the leveling of social classes, greater job opportunities for women, and the spread of labor-saving household devices.

domestic system *or* **putting-out system** Production system widespread in 17th-cent. Europe in which merchant-employers "put out" materials to rural home workers, who then returned finished products for payment. It differed from the handicraft system in that home workers neither bought materials nor sold products. It undermined the urban GUILDS and brought the first widespread industrial employment of women and children. The system was generally superseded by employment in FACTORIES but remains widespread in India and China.

dominance In GENETICS, the greater influence by one of a pair of GENES (ALLELES) that affect the same inherited trait. If a pea plant that has one allele for tallness and one for shortness is the same height as one that has two alleles for tallness, the tallness allele is said to be completely dominant. If the plant is shorter than one with two tallness alleles but still taller than one with two shortness alleles, the tallness allele is said to be partially or incompletely dominant. See also RECESSIVENESS.

Domingo, Plácido (b.1941) Spanish tenor and conductor. Born in Madrid, he moved with his parents, both zarzuela singers, to Mexico in 1949. He studied voice, piano, and conducting, making his debut as a baritone. After developing his tenor range, he made his U.S. debut with Joan SUTHERLAND, spent three years in Tel Aviv, and debuted with the Metropolitan Opera in 1966. Acclaimed for his great musicality and impressive voice, he has a repertoire of some 80 roles.

Dominic, St. *orig.* Domingo de Guzmán (c.1170–1221) Founder of the Order of Friars Preachers, or DOMINICANS. Born in Spain, he encountered the Albigensian heresy (see CATHARI) on a visit to S France in 1203 and determined to fight it. He gathered a group of preachers willing to travel the roads barefoot and in poverty, and in 1206 he founded a convent of nuns converted from heresy. Dominic and St. FRANCIS OF ASSISI became good friends. In 1216 he received sanction for his order from Pope HONORIUS III. He established schools of theology near the Univs. of Paris and Bologna.

Dominica \ˌdä-mə-ˈnē-kə\ *officially* **Commonwealth of Dominica** Island republic of the Lesser ANTILLES in the Caribbean Sea, between the French islands of GUADELOUPE and MARTINIQUE. Area: 289 sq mi (749 sq km). Population (2000): 76,000. Capital: ROSEAU. The majority of the people are of African or mixed African and European descent. Languages: English (official), French patois. Religion: mainly Roman Catholicism. Currency: Eastern Caribbean dollar. A mountainous island, it is broken midway by a plain drained by the Layou River. It has a warm tropical climate with heavy rainfall. Among the poorest of the Caribbean nations, its main crop is bananas. A developing tourist trade was helped by the establishment in 1975 of Morne Trois Pitons National Park, a unique tropical mountain wilderness, but the country was ravaged by hurricanes in 1979 and 1980. With financial help from Britain, it is trying to protect its coastline. It is a republic with one legislative house; its chief of state is the president, and its head of government is the prime minister. At the time of Christopher COLUMBUS's arrival in 1493, it was inhabited by the CARIBS. With its steep coastal cliffs and inaccessible mountains, it was one of the last islands to be explored by Europeans, and the Caribs remained in possession until the 18th cent.; it was then settled by the French and ultimately taken by Britain in 1783. Subsequent hostilities between the settlers and the native inhabitants resulted in the Caribs' near extinction. Incorporated with the LEEWARD ISLANDS in 1833 and with the WINDWARD ISLADS in 1940, it became a member of the West Indies Federation in 1958. Dominica became independent in 1978. See also WEST INDIES.

Dominican Member of the Order of Friars Preachers, a Roman Catholic preaching and teaching order founded by St.

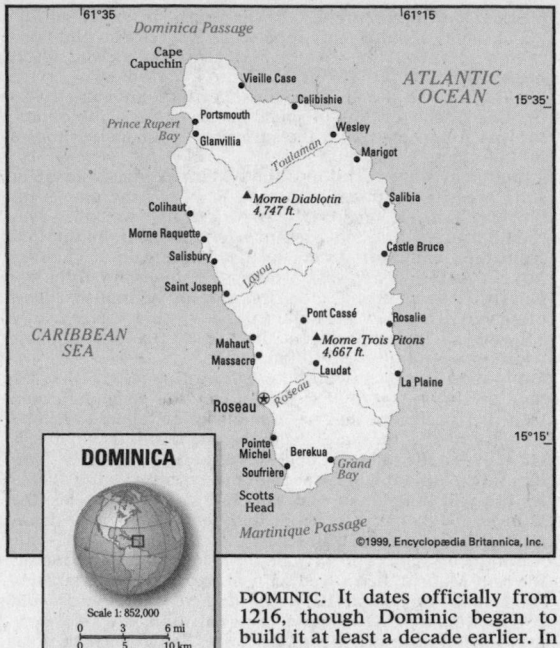

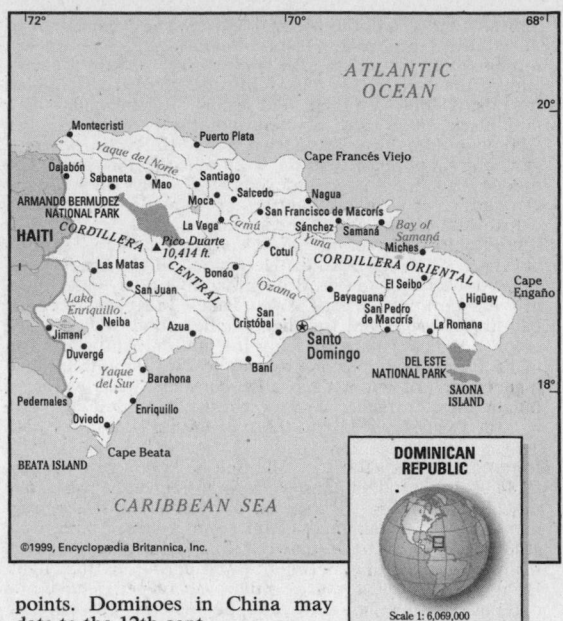

DOMINIC. It dates officially from 1216, though Dominic began to build it at least a decade earlier. In contrast with earlier orders, the Dominicans were not organized in autonomous monastic houses, but joined the order at large. Dominican preachers spoke out against the CATHARI, the MOORS, and the Jews and were among the first missionaries under the Spanish and Portuguese explorers. Dominicans were put in charge of the INQUISITION when it was founded. Perhaps their most famous member was St. THOMAS AQUINAS.

Dominican Republic Republic of the WEST INDIES, occupying the E two-thirds of the island of HISPANIOLA, which it shares with Haiti. Area: 18,657 sq mi (48,322 sq km). Population (2000): 8,443,000. Capital: SANTO DOMINGO. The majority of the people are of mixed European and African ancestry. Language: Spanish (official). Religion: mainly Roman Catholicism. Currency: Dominican peso. The country is generally mountainous, with ranges and hills running from northwest to southeast. The Central Highlands reach a height of 10,417 ft (3,175 m). The highest point in the West Indies. The Cibao Valley in the north is noted for its fertility; the W part of the country is generally dry with large stretches of desert. One of the poorest countries of the Caribbean, it has a mixed economy heavily dependent on the production and export of sugar. It is a republic with two legislative houses; its head of state and government is the president. The Dominican Republic was originally part of the Spanish colony of Hispaniola. In 1697 the W third of the island, which later became Haiti, was ceded to France; the remainder of the island passed to France in 1795. The E two-thirds of the island was returned to Spain in 1809, and the colony declared its independence in 1821. Within a matter of weeks it was overrun by Haitian troops and occupied until 1844. Since then the country has been under the rule of a succession of dictators, except for short interludes of democratic government, and the U.S. has frequently been involved in its affairs. The termination of the dictatorship of Rafael TRUJILLO in 1961 led to civil war in 1965, and U.S. military intervention. The country suffered from severe hurricanes in 1979 and 1998.

dominoes Game of several variations played with a set of flat rectangular blocks (dominoes) whose faces are divided into two equal parts that are blank or bear from one to six dots arranged as on DICE faces. The usual set consists of 28 pieces. The principle in nearly all modern dominoes games is to match one end of a piece to another that is identically or reciprocally numbered. The game may be set at 50 or 100 points. Dominoes in China may date to the 12th cent.

Domitian \də-'mish-ən\ *Latin* Caesar Domitianus Augustus *orig.* Titus Flavius Domitianus (A.D. 51–96) Roman emperor (81–96). The son of VESPASIAN, he succeeded his brother TITUS, whom he probably had killed. Though his administration was egalitarian and based on precedent, his laws were severe. Defeats in Britain and Germany undid his successes. From 89 he became crueler, imposing a reign of terror over prominent senators and confiscating his victims' property to cover imperial expenses. The group that killed him included his wife and possibly his successor, NERVA.

Donahue, Phil (b.1935) U.S. television personality. Born in Cleveland, he worked at a Dayton radio station (1959–67) before hosting *The Phil Donahue Show* on television (1967–74). With his syndicated talk show *Donahue*, he pioneered the noncelebrity talk show, in which a topical social issue was discussed by a panel of guests affected by it. His show won some 20 Emmy awards. The format he introduced gradually degenerated into spectacles known as "tabloid TV."

Donaldson \, Walter (1893–1947) U.S. songwriter. A native of Brooklyn, he began as a music publisher's pianist, and would later establish his own music publishing company. After his first Broadway success with "My Mammy" (1918), he continued writing for Broadway revues for more than 25 years, composing such songs as "My Blue Heaven," "Yes Sir! That's My Baby," and "Makin' Whoopee." He also wrote for many films, including *The Great Ziegfeld* (1936) and *Saratoga* (1937).

Donatello \,dō-nä-'tel-lō, *Engl* ,dä-nə-'te-lō\ *orig.* Donato di Niccolò (c.1386–1466) Italian sculptor. He learned stone carving from the sculptors of the Florence Cathedral (c.1400), and joined the workshop of Lorenzo GHIBERTI (1404–7). With his marble statues of St. Mark (1411–13) and St. George (c.1415) for the church of Or San Michele in Florence, he revolutionized the concept of sculpture; not since antiquity had the human body been rendered with such naturalism and emotional impact. He invented his own style of bas-relief with his marble panel

Donatello, bronze equestrian statue of Gattamelata, 1447–53

St. George Killing the Dragon (c.1417). His bronze sculpture *David* was the first large-scale, free-standing nude statue of the Renaissance. In Florence he worked for the MEDICI FAMILY (1433–43), producing sculptural decoration for the sacristy of San Lorenzo, and in Padua (1450s) for the church of Sant'Antonio. The greatest sculptor of the 15th cent., he influenced painters as well as sculptors, and was a founder of the Renaissance style.

Donation of Constantine Document concerning the supposed grant by CONSTANTINE I to Pope Sylvester I (314–35) and later popes of temporal power over Rome and the Western empire. The gift was said to have been motivated by Constantine's gratitude to Sylvester for miraculously healing his leprosy and converting him to Christianity. Proved in the 15th cent. to be a forgery, the document was already questioned by OTTO III but was often cited in the 11th–15th cent. to support papal claims in the struggle between church and state.

Donation of Pepin (754) Promise made by the Frankish king PEPIN III to win for Pope Stephen II lands in Italy conquered by the Lombards. In 756 it was written into a document that became the basis of papal rule over central Italy, which lasted until the 19th cent. Pepin made the donation to repay the pope for his support in deposing the MEROVINGIANS. Pepin won territory from the Lombard king in two military campaigns (754, 756) and gave it to the papacy.

Donatism \'dō-nə-ˌti-zəm, 'dä-nə-ˌti-zəm\ Schismatic Christian movement in N. Africa in the 4th cent. It arose out of the debate over the status of church leaders who had cooperated with Roman officials during persecutions of Christians. Its leader, Donatus (d.c.A.D. 355), denied the validity of priestly duties performed by such leaders, on the ground that they were not in a state of grace. The debate came to a head in 311, when Caecilian was consecrated bishop of Carthage by a lapsed bishop. The Donatists declared the election invalid, but CONSTANTINE I decided in favor of Caecilian, and the Donatists broke with the church. Donatism survived in N. Africa until the advent of Islam (7th cent.).

Donbas See DONETS BASIN

Donen \'dō-nən\, **Stanley** (b.1924) U.S. film director and choreographer. Born in Columbia, S.C., he danced in the stage chorus of *Pal Joey* (1940), where he met Gene KELLY. He and Kelly choreographed *Best Foot Forward* (1941; film, 1943) and other musicals, and codirected *On the Town* (1949) and the acclaimed *Singin' in the Rain* (1952). Donen later directed and produced such films as *Seven Brides for Seven Brothers* (1954), *Funny Face* (1957), *Damn Yankees* (1958), and *Two for the Road* (1967).

Donets Basin \də-'nyets, *Engl* də-'nets\ *or* **Donbas** \'dän-ˌbas\ Large mining and industrial region, SE Ukraine and SW Russia. Notable for its coal and iron reserves, the exploited area of the coalfield covers nearly 9,000 sq mi (23,300 sq km) south of the DONETS RIVER. By 1913 the Donets Basin was producing 87% of Russian coal. An ironworks was set up in 1872 in DONETSK; by 1913 it was making 74% of all Russian pig iron. The area today is the largest producing area of iron and steel in Ukraine and one of the world's major heavy-industrial complexes.

Donetsk \də-'nyetsk\ *formerly (1924–61)* **Stalino** \'stä-lyi-nō\ City (pop., 1998: 1,065,000), SE Ukraine. In 1872 an ironworks was founded there to produce rails for the growing Russian rail network. With the rich deposits of the DONETS BASIN, both coal mining and steelmaking developed rapidly. Heavy destruction in World War II led to postwar modernization and growth. Modern Donetsk is one of Ukraine's largest metallurgical centers.

Donets River River, SW Russia and E Ukraine. Rising in the Central Russian Upland, it winds south and east for some 650 mi (1,050 km) to join the DON RIVER below Konstantinovsk. It flows along the N DONETS BASIN industrial region, which uses it for heavy shipping and also causes severe pollution problems. A canal connects the DNIEPER to the Donets. Six weirs make navigation possible upstream to the city of DONETSK.

Dongbei See MANCHURIA

Dong Son culture \'dȯŋ-'sȯn\ Prehistoric culture of Indochina that developed in the 1st millennium B.C. Excava-

tions at the site of Dong Son in N Vietnam revealed bronze objects, iron, pottery, and Chinese artifacts. The Dong Son, a seafaring people who traded throughout S.E. Asia, made the Red River delta area a great rice-growing region. Dong Son culture, transformed by Chinese and Indian influence, became the basis of the general civilization of Indochina. Its homeland was taken over by China in A.D. 43.

Dönitz \'dœ-nits, *Engl* 'dər-nəts\, **Karl** *or* **Karl Doenitz** (1891–1980) German admiral. He oversaw the illegal creation of the German U-BOAT fleet in the 1930s, and as its commander conducted the Battle of the ATLANTIC in World War II. Commander in chief of the navy 1943–45, he succeeded Adolf HITLER as Germany's leader in the last few days of the war and executed Germany's surrender. Convicted of war crimes at the Nuremberg Trials, he served 10 years in prison.

Donizetti \ˌdō-nēd-'zā-tē, *Engl* ˌdä-nə-'ze-tē\, **Gaetano (Domenico Maria)** (1797–1848) Italian opera composer. He was tutored and guided by the opera composer Simone Mayr (1763–1845). The premiere of *Anna Bolena* in 1830 made his name internationally. Later successes included *L'elisir d'amore* (1832), *Lucrezia Borgia* (1833), *Lucia di Lammermoor* (1835), *Roberto Devereux* (1837), *La fille du régiment* (1840), *Linda di Chamonix* (1842), and *Don Pasquale* (1843). Enormously prolific, he could produce an entire opera in weeks. He completed almost 70 operas, as well as over 150 sacred works and hundreds of songs. Donizetti, Gioacchino ROSSINI, and Vincenzo BELLINI were the foremost Italian opera composers of the early 19th cent. and the principal masters of the bel canto style.

donjon \'dän-jən\ *or* **keep** Most heavily fortified area of a medieval castle, usually a tower, to which the occupants could retire during a siege. It contained a well, quarters, offices, and service rooms. One side often overlooked the bailey (grounds between encircling walls); the other commanded the field and approaches to the castle.

Don Juan Fictional character famous as a heartless womanizer but also noted for his charm and courage. In Spanish legend, he seduced a young girl of noble family and killed her father. Coming across a stone effigy of the father in a cemetery, he invited it home to dine with him. The ghost of the father arrived for dinner as the harbinger of Don Juan's death. Don Juan's first literary appearance was in TIRSO DE MOLINA's tragedy *The Seducer of Seville* (1630). He was also central to works by W. A. MOZART, MOLIÈRE, G. B. SHAW, and Lord BYRON.

donkey *or* **burro** Descendant of the African wild ASS that has been used as a beast of burden since 4000 B.C. The average donkey stands about 40 in. (100 cm) high at the shoulder, but breeds range from 24 to 66 in. (60–170 cm). The mane is short and upright, and the tail has long hairs only at the end. The very long ears are dark at the base and tip. Donkeys are surefooted and can carry heavy loads over rough terrain. See also MULE.

Donne \'dən\, **John** (1572–1631) English poet. Born into a Roman Catholic family, he entered Oxford Univ. at 12. He later converted to Anglicanism; ordained in 1615, he became a preacher of great power and eloquence and was installed as dean of St. Paul's Cathedral in 1621. The greatest of the English Metaphysical poets (see METAPHYSICAL POETRY), he is noted for his love lyrics, religious verse and treatises, and sermons. His secular poetry, most written early in his career, is direct, intense, brilliantly witty, and daringly imaginative. Later his tone darkened with works such as the *Anniversaries* (1611–12), two long poems meditating on the decay of the world. His 19 famous "Holy Sonnets" (written 1607–13) were published posthumously. Among his prose works, many as dramatic and intimate as his poetry, the most enduring is *Devotions upon Emergent Occasions* (1624).

Donner party Group of U.S. pioneers stranded en route to California. In late 1846, 87 immigrants led by George and Jacob Donner were trapped by heavy snow in the Sierra Nevada. Fifteen of the group set out to find help. When the others' food ran out, they resorted to eating those already dead. The 47 survivors were rescued in Feb. 1847. Donner Lake and Donner Pass, Cal., are named for them.

Donostia-San Sebastian See SAN SEBASTIAN

Don River \'dȯn\ *Tatar* **Duṇa** \'dü-nə\ *ancient* Tanais. River, SW Russia. Rising south of MOSCOW, it flows south for 1,162 mi (1,870 km) to enter the Sea of AZOV. The Tsimlyansk Reservoir dominates its lower course. Most of its basin is rich farmland and timberland. A major shipping artery, it is navigable (in the spring) as far as 990 mi (1,584 km) from the Sea of Azov.

Doolittle, Hilda *known as* **H.D.** (1886–1961) U.S. poet. Born in Bethlehem, Pa., she moved to Europe in 1911. One of the first Imagists (see IMAGISM), she wrote clear, impersonal, sensuous verse that combined classical themes with modernist techniques. Her later work was looser and more passionate. Her collections include *Sea Garden* (1916), *Hymen* (1921), and *Red Roses for Bronze* (1929). She was also acclaimed for her translations, verse drama, and prose works.

Doolittle, Jimmy (*orig.* James Harold) (1896–1993) U.S. general. Born in Alameda, Cal., he enlisted in the army in World War I and became an aviator. After the war he earned a PhD in engineering, remaining in the Army Air Corps as a test pilot until 1930. During World War II he led a daring bombing raid on Tokyo (1942), for which he received the Congressional Medal of Honor. He commanded air operations on many fronts, including attacks on Germany in 1944–45. He received the Presidential Medal of Freedom in 1989.

door Movable barrier installed in the entry of a room or building to restrict access or provide visual privacy. Early doors were hides or textiles. With monumental architecture came pivoting doors of rigid materials; important chambers often had stone or bronze doors. Pompeiian doors looked much like modern wooden doors. The typical Western medieval door was of vertical planks backed with horizontal or diagonal bracing. In the 20th cent., a single, hollow-core panel door became most common. Other types include the revolving door, folding door, sliding door (inspired by the Japanese SHOJI), rolling door, and Dutch door (divided so that the lower or upper part can be opened separately).

dopa *or* **L-dopa** *or* **levodopa** ORGANIC COMPOUND from which the body makes DOPAMINE, a NEUROTRANSMITTER deficient in persons with PARKINSONISM. Large daily doses of dopa can lessen the effects of the disease. However, it becomes less effective over time and causes abnormal involuntary movements.

dopamine \'dō-pə-ˌmēn\ ORGANIC COMPOUND widely distributed in the central NERVOUS SYSTEM from which EPINEPHRINE and NOREPINEPHRINE are formed. It is a NEUROTRANSMITTER essential to control of motion; it also acts as a HORMONE. Degeneration of certain dopamine-producing brain cells results in PARKINSONISM.

Doppler effect Apparent difference between the FREQUENCY at which WAVES—including light, sound, and radio waves—leave a source and that at which they reach an observer. The effect, first described by Christian Doppler (1803–1853), is caused by the relative motion of the observer and the wave source. It can be observed by listening to the blowing horn or siren of a vehicle, whose pitch rises as the vehicle approaches and falls as it recedes. It is used in RADAR and to calculate the speed of stars.

Doré \dȯ-'rā\, **Gustave (-Paul)** (1832–1883) French printmaker. In Paris he began producing lithographic caricatures for a weekly journal and several albums of lithographs (1847–54). He achieved fame with his wood-engraved book illustrations, including editions of DANTE's *Inferno* (1861) and the Bible (1866). His vivid work is characterized by images of the bizarre. Employing over 40 block cutters, he produced more than 90 illustrated books.

Doren, Carl and Mark Van See Carl and Mark Van DOREN

Doria \'dȯr-yä\, **Andrea** (1466–1560) Genoese statesman and admiral. A soldier of fortune, in 1522 he entered the service of FRANCIS

Andrea Doria Portrait by Sebastiano del Piombo

I, who was fighting Emperor CHARLES V in Italy. Doria later transferred his services to Charles and in 1528 drove the French out of Genoa. As the new ruler of Genoa, he reorganized its government into an effective and stable oligarchy. He commanded several naval expeditions against the Turks, and helped Charles V extend his domination over the Italian peninsula. Though greedy and authoritarian, Doria was also a fearless and brilliant commander.

Dorians Major division of the ancient Greeks. Coming from the north and northwest, they conquered the PELOPONNESE around 1100–1000 B.C., overran the remnants of the MYCENAEAN and MINOAN civilizations, and ushered in a dark age that lasted almost three centuries, until the rise of the Greek city-states. To Greek culture they gave the Doric order of architecture, the tragic choral lyric, and a militarized aristocratic government.

Dorset County (pop. 1998 est.: 387,000), SW England. It is located on the ENGLISH CHANNEL. Prehistoric peoples left abundant monuments of Neolithic, Bronze, and Iron Age dates, including Maiden Castle, a huge earthworks. The area became part of the W. Saxon kingdom. As Wessex it appears in the writings of Thomas HARDY.

Dorsey, Thomas A(ndrew) (1899–1993) U.S. songwriter, singer, and pianist, the "Father of GOSPEL MUSIC." Born in Villa Rica, Ga., to a revivalist preacher, Dorsey played piano in secular "hokum" music (sometimes in brothels) as "Georgia Tom." In 1926 he moved to Chicago and began touring with Ma RAINEY. From 1929 on, his increasing spiritual concerns led him to create many gospel standards (he had coined the term "gospel music" in the early 1920s), including "Precious Lord, Take My Hand," "Peace in the Valley," and "If We Ever Needed the Lord Before." Many were introduced by Mahalia JACKSON. He founded and directed the National Convention of Gospel Choirs and Choruses.

Dorsey, Tommy (*orig.* Thomas) (1905–1956) U.S. trombonist and leader of one of the most popular SWING bands. Born in Shenandoah, Pa., Dorsey led the Dorsey Brothers Orchestra from 1934 with his brother, saxophonist and clarinetist Jimmy Dorsey (1904–1957); they later separated to lead their own groups. Tommy's band combined smooth ballad performances with up-tempo jazz arrangements featuring such musicians as Frank SINATRA and arranger Sy Oliver. His own seamless phrasing and sweet tone influenced singers and brass players alike.

Dortmund \'dȯrt-ˌmu̇nt\ *ancient* Throtmannia. City (pop., 1996 est.: 599,000), N. Rhine-Westphalia, W Germany. It became a free imperial city in 1220 and later joined the HANSEATIC LEAGUE. A prosperous trading center, it declined after the THIRTY YEARS' WAR. The development of coal and iron-ore mining and the completion of the Dortmund–Ems Canal in 1899 stimulated its regrowth. Largely destroyed in World War II, it was extensively rebuilt. It is a major industrial center of the RUHR RIVER area.

Dos Passos \däs-'pa-sǝs\, **John (Roderigo)** (1896–1970) U.S. writer. Born in Chicago, he saw wartime service as an ambulance driver. His later work as a journalist led him to see the U.S. as "two nations," one for the rich and one for the poor. His reputation as social historian, radical critic of American life, and major novelist of the postwar "lost generation" rests primarily on his powerful trilogy *U.S.A.*, comprising *The 42nd Parallel* (1930), *1919* (1932), and *The Big Money* (1936).

Dostoyevsky \däs-tǝ-'yef-skē\, **Fyodor (Mikhaylovich)** (1821–1881) Russian novelist. Born in Moscow to a middle-class family, he was arrested in 1849 for belonging to a radical discussion group; sentenced to be shot, he was reprieved at the last moment and spent four years at hard labor in Siberia, where he developed epilepsy and experienced a deepening of his religious faith. Later he published and wrote for several periodicals while producing his best novels. His novels are concerned especially with faith, suffering, and the meaning of life; they are famous for their psychological insight and their near-prophetic treatment of issues in philosophy and politics. Best known are the novella *Notes from the Underground* (1864) and the great novels *Crime and Punishment* (1866), *The Idiot* (1869), *The Possessed* (1872), and *The Brothers Karamazov* (1880), his masterpiece, which focuses on the problem of evil, the nature of freedom, and the characters' craving for some kind of faith. His works had a profound influence on 20th-cent. literature.

Dou \\'daú\\, **Gerrit** (1613–1675) Dutch painter active in Leiden. He studied with REMBRANDT (1628–31), adopting his teacher's subject matter, careful draftsmanship, and dramatic treatment of light and shadow. When Rembrandt left Leiden, Dou developed his own style, painting smooth, meticulously detailed small-scale domestic interiors and portraits. He used the "frame within a frame" device of surrounding his figures by a window or curtain, and excelled at scenes lit by candlelight.

Douala \\dü-'ä-lä\\ City (pop., 1992 est.: 1,200,000), chief port of Cameroon, on the Bight of BIAFRA. Cameroon's largest city, it is one of central Africa's major industrial centers, and its deepwater port handles most of the country's overseas trade. It is home to a variety of commercial, agricultural, and industrial schools.

double bass Lowest-pitched of the modern STRINGED INSTRUMENTS. It varies in size, up to 80 in (200 cm) tall. Its shape also varies; its shoulders usually slope more than those of the violin, reflecting its status as a hybrid of the VIOL and VIOLIN families. It normally has four strings; the orchestral instrument often has a lower fifth string (more often, an extension is added to the fourth string), and the jazz instrument has a higher fifth string. Its range is an octave below the CELLO's. It is normally bowed in orchestral music and plucked in jazz. In rock bands, the electric bass is used instead.

Double bass

Doubleday, Abner (1819–1893) U.S. Army officer, once thought to be the inventor of BASEBALL. Born in Ballston Spa, N.Y., he served as a major general in the American Civil War; he gave the first order to fire at Fort Sumter, and later fought in other major battles. In 1907 a commission concluded that Doubleday formulated the essential rules of baseball in 1839 at Cooperstown, N.Y., leading to the choice of Cooperstown as the site of the Baseball Hall of Fame. It was later proved that Doubleday was not in Cooperstown in 1839.

double jeopardy In law, the prosecution of a person for an offense for which he or she has already been prosecuted. The 5th Amendment to the U.S. CONSTITUTION bars second prosecutions after acquittal or conviction and prohibits multiple convictions for the same offense. Thus a person cannot be guilty of both murder and manslaughter for the same homicide, nor can a person be retried for the same crime after the case has been resolved. See also DUE PROCESS.

double vision or **diplopia** Perception of two images of an object. Normally, the brain fuses slightly different images from each eye by matching corresponding points on each RETINA. When an eye muscle is paralyzed, the image falls at a different point and the images do not correspond. Double vision may be an early symptom of BOTULISM or MYASTHENIA GRAVIS and occurs in other infections, head injuries, and nerve or muscle disorders.

Douglas, James (*later* **Sir James**) (1803–1877) Canadian statesman. Born in Demerara, British Guiana, he joined the HUDSON'S BAY CO. in 1821 and was soon directing its operations west of the Rocky Mtns. As governor of Vancouver (1851–64) when gold was discovered on the Fraser River in 1858, he extended his authority to the mainland to preserve Britain's Pacific foothold. When Britain created the colony of British Columbia, Douglas was appointed governor (1858–64).

Douglas, Kirk *orig.* Issur Danielovitch *later* Isadore Demskey (b.1916) U.S. film actor and producer. Born in Amsterdam, N.Y., he emerged as a major star in *Champion* (1949). Despite sensitive performances in *The Glass Menagerie* (1950) and *Paths of Glory* (1957), he became identified with the forceful roles he played in such films as *The Bad and the Beautiful* (1952), *Lust for Life* (1956), *Gunfight at the O.K. Corral* (1957), *Spartacus* (1960), and *Seven Days in May* (1964). His son Michael (b.1944) has given notable performances in such films as *Fatal Attraction* (1987), *Wall Street* (1987, Academy Award), and *Basic Instinct* (1992).

Douglas, Stephen A(rnold) (1813–1861) U.S. politician. Born in Brandon, Vt., he sat on the Illinois supreme court before serving in the U.S. House of Representatives (1843–47) and Senate (1847–61). Strongly supporting the Union, he developed the policy of POPULAR SOVEREIGNTY and influenced passage of the KANSAS-NEBRASKA ACT. Short and heavyset, he was dubbed "the Little Giant" for his oratorical skill. Abraham LINCOLN's challenge to him for his Senate seat led to the LINCOLN–DOUGLAS DEBATES. The Democrats nominated Douglas for president in 1860, but a splinter group of Southerners nominated John BRECKINRIDGE, which divided the vote and gave the presidency to Lincoln. On a mission for Lincoln to gain support among the border states and in the Northwest, he died of typhoid.

Douglas, Tommy (*orig.* Thomas Clement) (1904–1986) Canadian (Scottish-born) politician. His family emigrated to Winnipeg in 1919. Ordained a minister, he became active in the socialist Co-operative Commonwealth Federation. As premier of Saskatchewan (1944–61), he led Canada's first socialist government. He established socialized medicine in the province, and the rest of Canada soon adopted it. He resigned to become leader of the New Democratic Party (1961–71).

Douglas, William O(rville) (1898–1980) U.S. jurist and public official. Born in Maine, Minn., he served as chairman of the SECURITIES AND EXCHANGE COMMISSION (1937–39), where he engineered the reorganization of the nation's STOCK EXCHANGES, instituted measures for the protection of small investors, and began government regulation of the sale of SECURITIES. He was appointed to the U.S. Supreme Court in 1939 and served until 1975. He wrote the opinions in many complicated financial cases, but became most famous for his pronouncements on CIVIL LIBERTIES. He rejected government limitations on FREEDOM OF SPEECH and was an outspoken defender of an unfettered press. He also strove to uphold the rights of the accused. He wrote numerous books on history, politics, foreign relations, and conservation, including *Of Men and Mountains* (1950) and *A Wilderness Bill of Rights* (1965).

Douglas fir Any of about six species of coniferous evergreen timber trees (see CONIFER) that make up the genus *Pseudotsuga*, in the PINE family, native to W N. America and E Asia. Spirally arranged yellow- or blue-green needles grow directly from the branch. The N. American tree commonly called Douglas fir is *P. menziesii* (sometimes *P. douglasii*), which may grow to 250 ft (75 m) tall and 8 ft (2.4 m) in diameter. One of the best timber trees in N. America, it is also a popular ornamental and Christmas tree.

Douglas-Home \\'dəg-ləs-'hyüm\\, **Sir Alec** (*orig.* Alexander Frederick) *later* Baron Home (of the Hirsel of Coldstream) (1903–1995) British statesman. A member of Parliament from 1931, he served as minister of state for Scotland (1951–55), leader of the House of Lords (1957–60), and foreign secretary (1960–63) before succeeding Harold MACMILLAN as prime minister in 1963, relinquishing his hereditary titles. He antagonized Conservatives by opposing price-fixing, but gained U.S. approval for his anti-Communism. Defeated in 1964, he again served as foreign secretary 1970–1974.

Douglass, Frederick *orig.* Frederick Augustus Washington Bailey (1817–1895) U.S. abolitionist. Born in Tuckahoe, Md., to a slave mother and a white father, he worked as a house servant in Baltimore, where he learned to read, and as a plantation slave. In 1838 he fled to New York, then to New Bedford, Mass., changing his name to elude slave hunters. His elo-

Frederick Douglass

quence at an 1841 antislavery convention gave him a new career as an agent for the Massachusetts Anti-Slavery Society. In 1845 he wrote his autobiography, now regarded as a classic. He lectured in England and Ireland (1845–47), then founded the antislavery *North Star,* which he published until 1860 in Rochester, N.Y. In 1851 he split with the radical W. L. GARRISON and allied with the moderates led by James BIRNEY. In the Civil War he was a consultant to Pres. Abraham LINCOLN. During RECONSTRUCTION he fought for full civil rights for freedmen and supported women's rights.

dove Any of certain birds of the PIGEON family (Columbidae). The names pigeon and dove are often used interchangeably. Though "dove" usually refers to the smaller, long-tailed members of the pigeon family, the common street pigeon is frequently called the rock dove. The common names do not necessarily reflect accurate biological relationships.

Dove, Rita (Frances) (b.1952) U.S. writer. Born in Akron, Ohio, she began publishing her poetry in 1977. Her poems and short stories focus on the particulars of family life and personal struggle, addressing the larger dimensions of the African-American experience primarily by indirection. Her poetry collections include *Museum* (1983), *Thomas and Beulah* (1986, Pulitzer Prize), and *Mother Love* (1995). She was poet laureate of the U.S. 1993–95.

Dover ancient Dubris Portus. Town (pop., 1995 est.: 34,000; metro. area pop. 1995 est.: 104,000) and seaport on the Strait of DOVER, SE England. A pre-Roman settlement existed on the site, and in the 4th cent. A.D. it was guarded by a Saxon fort. Dover Castle was besieged by rebellious barons in 1216. The town was held by Parliamentarians in the ENGLISH CIVIL WARS. It was a naval base in World War I and was bombed by Germans in World War II. Famous for the white chalk cliffs rising above it, Dover is a leading passenger port.

Dover City (pop., 2000: 32,000), capital of Delaware, on the St. Jones River. Laid out in 1717 by order of William PENN, it became the capital in 1777. Its many colonial buildings include the Old State House (rebuilt 1787–92). The modern city is a farm trade center.

Dover, Strait of French **Pas de Calais** \ˌpäd-kȧ-ˈlā\ ancient Fretum Gallicum. Channel separating SE England from NW France. Connecting the ENGLISH CHANNEL with the NORTH SEA, it is about 20 mi (32 km) wide at its narrowest point. Lined on the British side with the famous White Cliffs, composed of soft chalk, it is one of the world's busiest seaways. It was the scene of several historic naval battles, including the repulse by the English of the Spanish ARMADA in 1588. Allied troops in the DUNKIRK EVACUATION crossed to Dover in 1940. The strait is the site of the CHANNEL TUNNEL.

Dow, Herbert H(enry) (1866–1930) U.S. (Canadian-born) inventor and manufacturer. Born in Belleville, Ontario, he attended college in Cleveland. He developed and patented electrolytic methods (the Dow process) for extracting BROMINE from brines. In 1895 he founded the Dow Chemical Co. to electrolyze brine for CHLORINE, used in insecticides. He was the first U.S. producer of IODINE (which he also extracted from brine). His company eventually became one of the world's leading chemical manufacturers.

Dow Jones average STOCK price average computed by Dow Jones & Co. Founded in 1882 by Charles H. Dow (1851–1902) and Edward D. Jones (1856–1920), the company has published the *Wall Street Journal* since 1889. It began computing a daily industrials average in 1897. Today it publishes averages based on 20 transportation stocks, 15 utility stocks, and 30 selected industrial stocks, as well as a composite average of all three; the industrial-stocks average is closely followed by investors. See also STOCK EXCHANGE.

Dowland, John (1563–1626) English composer. Educated at Oxford, he was refused a court position in 1594 and, believing his adoptive Catholicism had been the cause, he left for the continent, where he took a position at the Danish court. In 1612 he was finally appointed lutenist to the English court. He left about 80 works for solo lute and some 80 lute songs, including "Flow my tears" and "Weep you no more, sad fountains." His *Lachrimae* is a collection for viol-and-lute ensemble.

Downing, Andrew Jackson (1815–1852) U.S. horticulturist, landscape gardener, and architect. Born in Newburgh, N.Y., he collaborated with the British architect Calvert Vaux (1824–1895) on estates in New York's Hudson River valley and on Long Island. The foremost U.S. landscape designer of his day, Downing was commissioned in 1851 to lay out the grounds for the Capitol, White House, and Smithsonian Institution. Though his plans were interrupted by his accidental death at 36, his books became standard works, and his influence on American conceptions of the middle-class home were far-reaching.

Down's syndrome *or* **Down syndrome** *or* **trisomy 21** \ˈtrī-ˌsō-mē\ CONGENITAL DISORDER caused by an extra CHROMOSOME on the chromosome 21 pair. Those with the syndrome may have broad, flat faces; up-slanted eyes, (whence its former name, mongolism); mental retardation; and heart and/or kidney malformations. Many persons with Down's syndrome can live and work independently or in a sheltered environment, but they age prematurely and have a short (55-year) life expectancy. Older mothers are more likely to bear a Down's syndrome child; it can be detected by AMNIOCENTESIS.

dowry \ˈdaů-rē\ Property that a wife or a wife's family gives to her husband upon MARRIAGE. The dowry has a long history in Europe, India, Africa, and other parts of the world. Some of its basic functions are to protect the wife against ill treatment by her husband, since a dowry can be a conditional gift; to provide the wife with support in case of her husband's death; and to compensate the groom's kin for their payment of BRIDEWEALTH. In Europe, the dowry has served to build the power and wealth of great families and often played a role in the politics of grand alliance through marriage. It began to disappear in the 19th cent., as industrialization grew.

dowsing \ˈdaů-ziŋ\ Occult practice used for finding water, minerals, or other hidden substances. A dowser generally holds the two prongs of a Y-shaped piece of hazel, rowan, or willow wood. If the rod quivers violently or points downward, some buried substance has been located. First practiced in medieval Europe, dowsing is most often used to find water but may also be used to find buried treasure, archaeological remains, or even dead bodies.

Doyle, Arthur Conan (*later* **Sir Arthur**) (1859–1930) British writer. Born in Edinburgh, he was knighted for his medical work in the second S. AFRICAN WAR, but he is best known for his fictional detective Sherlock Holmes, who first appeared in the novel *A Study in Scarlet* (1887) and returned in numerous stories. Tiring of Holmes, he devised his death in 1893, only to be forced by public demand to restore him to life. The Holmes novels include *The Hound of the Baskervilles* (1902) and *The Valley of Fear* (1915). Doyle's other novels include *The White Company* (1890) and *The Lost World* (1912).

Arthur Conan Doyle Portrait by H. L. Gates, 1927

Drabble, Margaret (b.1939) British novelist. She acted briefly before committing herself to writing. Her novels include *A Summer Bird-cage* (1962), *The Realms of Gold* (1975), and *The Gates of Ivory* (1991). She has also written literary biographies and has edited the *Oxford Companion to English Literature* (1985).

dracaena \drə-ˈsē-nə\ Any of about 50–80 species of ornamental foliage plants that make up the genus *Dracaena,* in the AGAVE FAMILY, native primarily to the Old World tropics. Most have short stalks and narrow, sword-shaped leaves. The small flowers are red, yellow, or green. *D. sanderiana* and *D. fragrans* are often grown as houseplants.

Draco \ˈdrā-kō\ *or* **Dracon** (7th cent. B.C.) Athenian lawgiver. Almost nothing is known of his life. His harsh legal code (621 B.C.) punished most crimes, even trivial ones, with death. SOLON repealed Draco's code, retaining only the homicide statutes.

draft See BILL OF EXCHANGE

draft See CONSCRIPTION

Draft Riot of 1863 Four days of violence in New York City to protest the inequities of AMERICAN CIVIL WAR conscription. The law permitted draftees to buy their way out of army service for $300, a sum relatively few men could afford. When the drawing of names began on July 11, mobs of foreign-born workers surged into the streets, burning buildings and assaulting blacks, who they had feared would take their jobs. About 100 people (mostly rioters) died.

drag FORCE exerted by a fluid stream on any obstacle in its path or felt by an object moving through a fluid. Its magnitude and how it may be reduced are important to designers of moving vehicles, ships, suspension bridges, cooling towers, and other structures. Drag forces are conventionally described by a drag coefficient, which can be used to predict the drag forces experienced by other bodies in other fluids at other velocities. Engineers use this principle of dynamic similarity when they apply results obtained with a model structure to predict the behavior of other structures. See also FRICTION.

dragon Legendary monster usually depicted as a huge, batwinged, fire-breathing lizard or snake with a barbed tail. The dragon symbolized evil in the ancient Middle East. The Greeks and Romans sometimes represented dragons as evil creatures and sometimes as beneficent powers acquainted with the secrets of the earth. In Christianity the dragon symbolized sin and paganism. In the Far East the dragon was a beneficent creature, wingless but regarded as a power of the air. In China it served as the emblem of the royal family.

dragonfly Any member of the insect suborder Anisoptera (order Odonata), characterized by four large, membranous, many-veined wings that, when at rest, are held horizontally rather than vertically (see DAMSELFLY). Dragonflies are agile and have bulging eyes that often occupy most of the head and a wingspan of about 6 in. (16 cm). The dragonfly is one of the fastest-flying and most predaceous insects; in 30 minutes it can eat its own weight in food. Male and female often fly in tandem during sperm transfer.

drag racing Form of motor racing in which two contestants race side by side from a standing start over a straight quarter-mile strip of pavement. There are three main classes of vehicle: (1) the Top Fuel Eliminator (called a "rail" or "slingshot"), a lightweight, long-chassied vehicle with wide rear tires that is fueled by a special mixture, such as methanol and nitromethane; (2) the "funny car," a high-performance copy of a late-model production car that uses special fuel; and (3) the standard production car, a modified version of a gasoline-powered production car. Drag racing is most popular in the U.S.

Drake, Francis (*later* **Sir Francis**) (c.1540–1596) English admiral and explorer. He went to sea at 13, gained a reputation as an outstanding seaman, and became wealthy through raids against Spanish colonies. In 1577 he was commissioned by ELIZABETH I to lead an expedition to S. America and beyond. He set sail with five ships, but ultimately only his flagship, the *Golden Hind,* made its way through the Strait of Magellan up the coast of S. and N. America. He anchored off modern San Francisco, claiming the area for Elizabeth. He sailed westward to the Philippines and around the Cape of Good Hope, and returned in 1580 laden with treasure, the first captain ever to sail his own ship around the world. Appointed vice admiral (1588), he played a crucial role in defeating the Spanish ARMADA and became England's hero, achieving a popularity unequaled until Horatio NELSON's. On his last voyage, to the W. Indies, he succumbed to fever and was buried at sea.

Francis Drake Painting by an unknown artist

Drake equation *or* **Green Bank equation** Equation claimed to yield the number of technically advanced civilizations in the MILKY WAY GALAXY as a function of several factors, largely developed by Frank D. Drake (b.1930) in 1961 at a SETI conference in Green Bank, W.V. Of all the stars that form in the galaxy, only some will have life-supporting planets, of which only some will generate life capable of high technology that avoids technological destruction. Because all these numbers are poorly known, results vary from zero to millions. Recent data supporting the existence of a limited "habitable zone" in both planetary systems and galaxies reduce the likelihood of intelligent life on other planets.

Drake Passage Strait, connecting the Atlantic and Pacific oceans between TIERRA DEL FUEGO and the S. SHETLAND ISLANDS. About 100 mi (660 km) north of the Antarctic Peninsula, it is 600 mi (1,000 km) wide. An important trade route in the 19th and early 20th cent., its stormy seas and icy conditions made the rounding of Cape HORN a difficult journey.

Drau River See DRAVA RIVER

Drava River \\'drä-və\\ *German* **Drau** \\'draủ\\ River, S central Europe. It rises in the Carnic Alps and flows east through Austria, where it forms the long Drautal valley. Flowing southeast through Slovenia and on to N Croatia, where it forms part of the Croatian–Hungarian border and enters the DANUBE RIVER, it is 447 mi (719 km) long. Its valley was the chief passage through which invaders historically penetrated the alpine countries.

Dravidian languages \\drə-'vi-dē-ən\\ Family of more than 25 languages indigenous to and spoken principally in S Asia by more than 210 million people. The four major Dravidian languages of S India—TELUGU, TAMIL, Kannada, and MALAYALAM—have independent scripts and long documented histories; they account for most Dravidian-speakers. All have borrowed liberally from SANSKRIT. The Dravidian family, with no demonstrated relationship to other language families, is assumed to have covered a much more extensive area of S. Asia prior to the spread of INDO-ARYAN and was the source of loanwords into early Indo-Aryan dialects.

Dreadnought, HMS British BATTLESHIP launched in 1906 that set the pattern of the warships of the world's navies for the next 35 years. It carried only big guns because recent improvements in naval gunnery had made preparation for short-range battle unnecessary. Powered by steam turbines, it sailed at a record top speed of 21 knots. It displaced 18,000 tons (16,300 metric tons), was 526 ft (160 m) long, and carried a crew of about 800. By World War I it was nearly outclassed by faster "superdreadnoughts" with bigger guns. It was broken up for scrap in 1923.

dream Series of thoughts, images, or emotions occurring during SLEEP, particularly rapid-eye-movement (REM) sleep. Dreams range from the ordinary and realistic to the fantastic and surreal. Humans have always attached great importance to dreams, which have been variously viewed as windows to the sacred, the past and the future, or the world of the dead. Dreams have provided creative solutions to intellectual and emotional problems and have furnished artistic inspiration. The most famous theory of the significance of dreams is the psychoanalytic model of Sigmund FREUD, in which desires ordinarily repressed because they represent forbidden impulses are given expression in dreams, often in disguised (i.e., symbolic) form.

Dreaming, the *or* **Dream-Time** In the religion of the AUSTRALIAN ABORIGINES, the mythological time of the creation, when the environment was shaped and humanized by mythic beings who took animal or human form or changed their form at will. In Aboriginal belief, those beings continue to exist, though they may have traveled beyond the lands of the people who sing about them or have metamorphosed into natural features such as rocky outcrops or waterholes. See also AUSTRALIAN RELIGION.

Dred Scott decision *formally* **(Dred) Scott vs. Sandford** 1857 ruling of the U.S. Supreme Court that made slavery legal in all territories. Scott was a slave whose master had taken him in 1834 from a slave state (Missouri) to a free state and free territory, then back to Missouri. Scott sued

for his freedom in Missouri in 1846, saying his residence in free areas made him free. Roger B. TANEY declared that Scott was not entitled to rights as a U.S. citizen (and, in fact, had "no rights which any white man was bound to respect"), and went on to declare the MISSOURI COMPROMISE unconstitutional because Congress had no power to prohibit slavery in the territories (see STATES' RIGHTS). The decision fed the sectional strife that led to war in 1861.

Dreiser \\'drī-zər\\, **Theodore (Herman Albert)** (1871–1945) U.S. novelist. Born in Terre Haute, Ind., he worked as a journalist in Chicago and as a magazine editor and publisher in New York. His first novel, *Sister Carrie* (1900), about a young kept woman who goes unpunished for her transgressions, was denounced as scandalous. His subsequent novels would confirm his reputation as the outstanding American practitioner of NATURALISM. They include *Jennie Gerhardt* (1911); a trilogy consisting of *The Financier* (1912), *The Titan* (1914), and *The Stoic* (published 1947); *The Genius* (1915); and its sequel, *The Bulwark* (published 1946). *An American Tragedy* (1925) made him a hero among social reformers.

Dresden City (pop., 1996 est.: 469,000), E Germany, situated on the ELBE RIVER. It was the residence of the margraves of Meissen in the early 13th cent. The Dresden china industry was moved to Meissen in 1710 (see MEISSEN PORCELAIN). NAPOLEON I made the town a center of military operations and won his last great battle there in 1813. Dresden was occupied by Prussia in 1866. In World War II, it was severely damaged in the firestorm caused by ferocious Allied bombing raids in 1945, which resulted in 35,000–130,000 deaths. Several of its historic buildings have been restored or reconstructed. It is known for its cultural institutions.

Drew family U.S. theatrical family. Louisa Lane (later Louisa Lane Drew; 1820–1897) began her stage career at 8 in Philadelphia, where her widowed mother had brought her from England. Her many successful parts included Lady Teazle, Mrs. Malaprop, and such "breeches" roles as Shakespeare's Romeo and Mark Antony. In 1850 she married the Irish comic actor John Drew (1827–1862), who comanaged the Arch Street Theatre in Philadelphia. She managed the theater from 1861, directing the renamed Mrs. John Drew's Arch Street Theatre company with notable success. Their son John Drew, Jr. (1853–1927) made his debut (1873) with his mother's company, then joined other companies, and was noted for his roles in Shakespearean comedy, society drama, and light comedies. Their daughter Georgiana Emma Drew (1856–1893) made her acting debut with her mother's company (1872) and in 1876 married Maurice Barrymore (see BARRYMORE FAMILY).

Drexel, St. Katherine (1858–1955) U.S. missionary. Born in Philadelphia, she inherited a vast fortune, which she used to fund her charitable enterprises. She built several mission schools for American Indians, and in 1887 Pope Leo XIII asked her to become a missionary. In 1891 she founded the Blessed Sacrament Sisters for Indians and Colored People (now Sisters of the Blessed Sacrament), a congregation of missionary nuns. She also founded Xavier Univ. in New Orleans (1915). She was canonized in 2000.

Dreyer \\'drī-ər\\, **Carl Theodor** (1889–1968) Danish film director. He worked in the film industry as a scriptwriter and editor. His first film as a director was *The President* (1919); his most famous silent film was *The Passion of Joan of Arc* (1928). Considered the most important figure in Danish cinema, he created a new directorial style based on extensive close-ups and authentic settings. His other films include *Vampire* (1932), the celebrated *Day of Wrath* (1943), *The Word* (1955), and *Gertrud* (1964).

Dreyfus \\dre-'fṻs, *Engl* 'drī-fəs, 'drā-fəs\\, **Alfred** (1859–1935) French army officer. Son of a Jewish textile manufacturer, he entered the army and rose to the rank of captain (1889). Assigned to the war ministry, in 1894 he was accused of selling military secrets to Germany. He was convicted and sentenced to life imprisonment on Devil's Island. The legal proceedings were highly irregular, but public opinion and the French press, led by its virulently anti-Semitic section, welcomed the verdict. Doubts began to grow with evidence that C. F. Esterhazy (1847–1923) was the true traitor. Protest gained momentum after Émile

ZOLA's open letter "J'accuse" accused the army of covering up its errors in making the case. After a new court-martial (1899) again found Dreyfus guilty, he was pardoned by the president of the republic, and in 1906 a civilian court cleared Dreyfus. Formally reinstated and decorated with the Legion of Honor, he later served in World War I. The "Dreyfus Affair" resulted in the separation of church and state in 1905 and brought the political left to power.

Alfred Dreyfus, before 1894

drill Tool to make holes, usually by revolving. Drills, gimlets, and AUGERS have cutting edges that detach material to leave a hole. Drilling usually requires high speed and low TORQUE, with little material being removed during each revolution of the tool. The earliest (perhaps BRONZE AGE) drill points had sharp edges that ultimately developed into arrow shapes with two distinct cutting edges. This shape remained popular until the late 19th cent., when factory-made, spiral-fluted twist drills became available at reasonable cost to displace the blacksmith-made articles. Rotating drill bits containing diamonds or other hard materials are used for drilling rock.

drill Large, short-tailed MONKEY (*Mandrillus leucophaeus*, family Cercopithecidae), formerly found from Nigeria to Cameroon, now restricted to remote forest regions of Cameroon. Like the related MANDRILL, the drill is stout-bodied and has vividly colored buttocks. The male is about 32 in. (82 cm) long and has a black face. Its lower lip is bright red, the hairs around the ears are yellowish white, and the rest of the fur is olive-brown. An omnivore, it is mainly terrestrial, gregarious, and powerful.

driver Computer program that acts as an intermediary between the OPERATING SYSTEM and a device such as a disk drive, video card, printer, or keyboard. The driver contains a detailed knowledge of the device, including its set of specialized commands. The presence of a separate driver program frees the operating system from having to understand the details of every device; instead, the operating system issues general commands to the driver, which in turn translates them into specific instructions for the device, or vice versa.

drop forging Process of shaping metal and increasing its strength. In most FORGING, an upper DIE is forced against a heated workpiece positioned on a stationary lower die. If the upper die or hammer is dropped, the process is known as drop forging. To increase the force of the blow, power is sometimes applied to augment gravity.

drosophila \\drō-'sä-fə-lə\\ Any member of about 1,000 species in the DIPTERAN genus *Drosophila*, commonly known as vinegar flies but also called FRUIT FLIES. Some species, particularly *D. melanogaster*, are used extensively in laboratory experiments on genetics and evolution because they are easy to raise and have a short life cycle (less than two weeks at room temperature). More data have been collected concerning the genetics of drosophila than for any other animal.

Drottningholm Palace \\'drùt-niŋ-ˌhȯlm\\ Palace, formerly the Swedish royal family's summer residence, near Stockholm. It was designed by Nicodemus Tessin (1615–1681) and built 1662–86. It shows French Baroque influences in its plan, gardens, and interior, but it also has Italian Classical elements and is capped by a Nordic *sateri* roof. A theater attached to it, built in the 1760s, is now a theatrical museum.

drought Lack or insufficiency of rain for an extended period that severely disturbs the HYDROLOGIC CYCLE in an area. Droughts involve water shortages, crop damage, and depletion of groundwater and soil moisture. Drought is the most serious hazard to agriculture in nearly every part of the world. Efforts have been made to control it by seeding clouds to induce rainfall, with only limited success.

drug Any chemical agent that affects the function of living things. Some, including ANTIBIOTICS, STIMULANTS, TRANQUILIZERS, ANTIDEPRESSANTS, ANALGESICS, NARCOTICS, and HORMONES, have generalized effects. Others, including LAXATIVES, heart stimulants, ANTICOAGULANTS, DIURETICS, and ANTIHISTAMINES, act on specific systems. Medicinal drugs may protect against attacking organisms, substitute for a missing or defective substance in the body, or interrupt an abnormal process. A drug must bind with receptors in or on cells and cannot work if the receptors are absent or its CONFIGURATION does not fit theirs. Drugs may be given by mouth, by injection, by inhalation, rectally, or through the skin. The modern drug era began when antibiotics were discovered in 1928. Drugs must be not only effective but safe; side effects can range from minor to dangerous. Many illegal drugs also have medical uses (see COCAINE, HEROIN, DRUG ADDICTION). See also DRUG RESISTANCE, PHARMACOLOGY, PHARMACY.

drug addiction *or* **chemical dependency** Physical and/or psychological dependency on a psychoactive (mind-altering) substance, defined as continued use despite knowing that the substance causes harm. Physical dependency results when the body builds up a tolerance to a drug, needing increasing doses to achieve the desired effects and to prevent withdrawal symptoms. The most common addictions are to alcohol (see ALCOHOLISM), BARBITURATES, TRANQUILIZERS, AMPHETAMINES, NICOTINE, and CAFFEINE. Initial treatment (detoxification) should be conducted with medical supervision. Individual and group psychotherapy are critical elements. See also ALCOHOLICS ANONYMOUS.

Drug Enforcement Administration (DEA) Agency of the U.S. Department of JUSTICE charged with enforcing laws that cover trafficking in controlled substances. Established in 1973, the DEA works to control the cultivation, production, smuggling, and distribution of illicit drugs. Most of its efforts are directed against international smuggling organizations.

drug resistance Property of a disease-causing organism that allows it to withstand DRUG therapy. In any population of infectious agents, some have a MUTATION that helps them resist the action of a drug. The drug then kills more of the nonresistant microbes, leaving the mutants without competition to multiply into a resistant strain. This situation is more likely if the drug is not taken properly (e.g., a course of ANTIBIOTICS not completed, anti-HIV drug doses missed) or not prescribed properly (e.g., an antibiotic given for a viral disease). The overprescription of antibiotics in humans and the addition of antibiotics to animal feed have accelerated the evolution of resistant strains.

Druid Member of a learned class of priests, teachers, and judges among the ancient Celtic peoples. The Druids instructed young men, oversaw sacrifices, judged quarrels, and decreed penalties. They studied ancient verse, natural philosophy, astronomy, and religious lore. They sometimes practiced human sacrifice to cure gravely ill people or protect warriors in battle. The Druids were suppressed in Gaul and Britain by the Romans. They lost their priestly functions in Ireland after the coming of Christianity. See also CELTIC RELIGION.

drum Musical instrument whose sound is produced by the vibration of a stretched membrane. Drums are usually either cylindrical or bowl-shaped. The drum is a universal instrument and very ancient; a drum dating to 6000 B.C. has been found in Moravia. Drums have been important ritually in cultures worldwide. Drums may have a definite pitch or be unpitched; those of Africa, S. and S.E. Asia, and the Middle East are mostly pitched, whereas Western drums are more often unpitched. Drumming has attained its highest degree of development in Africa and India. The side drum, or snare drum, has coiled wires or gut strings strung across the lower head, which vibrate against it when the upper head is struck. The powerful bass drum is used especially in marching bands. The pitched TIMPANI are the standard orchestral drums. The drum set used in popular music normally includes a snare drum, tom-toms, and a pedal-operated bass drum.

Drury Lane Theatre Oldest English theater still in use. Built in London by Thomas Killigrew for his acting company as the Theatre Royal (1663), it burned in 1672 and was rebuilt in 1674 with Christopher WREN as architect. It prospered under such actor-managers as Colley CIBBER (1710–33), David GARRICK (1747–76), and R. B. SHERIDAN (1776–88). Burned in 1809 and rebuilt in 1812 with over 2,000 seats, it declined in popularity from the 1840s, but revived in the 1880s with melodramas and spectacles. More recently it has played host to many U.S. musicals.

Druze *or* **Druse** \'drüz\ Highly secretive Middle Eastern religious sect. It originated in Egypt in 1017 and is named for one of its founders, Muhammad al-Darazi (d.1019/20). Strictly monotheistic and based in ISLAM, Druze beliefs include an eclectic mixture of elements from other Middle Eastern religions. The Druze believe in the divinity of the sixth caliph of the FATIMID DYNASTY of Egypt, and expect him to return someday to inaugurate a golden age. They do not permit converts or intermarriage. Their religious system is kept secret from the outside world. Today they number about one million, mostly in Syria and Lebanon.

dryad \'drī-əd, 'drī-ˌad\ *or* **hamadryad** In GREEK MYTHOLOGY, tree NYMPHS. Dryads were originally the spirits of oak trees, but the name was later applied to all tree nymphs. They resembled beautiful young women, and it was believed that they lived only as long as the trees they inhabited.

dry cleaning System of cleaning textiles with chemical SOLVENTS instead of water. The chemicals, often halides or organohalogens (compounds that contain HALOGEN atoms bonded to carbon atoms), dissolve dirt and grease from fabrics. Carbon tetrachloride was once widely used, but its adverse health effects have cut back its use; more stable and less toxic organic halogen compounds are now preferred, particularly tetrachloroethylene.

Dryden, John (1631–1700) British poet, dramatist, and literary critic. His poetry celebrating the Restoration so pleased Charles II that he was named poet laureate (1668–88) and, two years later, royal historiographer. Many of his nearly 30 comedies, tragedies, and dramatic operas—including *Marriage à-la-Mode* (1672), *Aureng-Zebe* (1675), and *All for Love* (1677)—were outstandingly successful. His *Of Dramatick Poesie* (1668) was the first substantial piece of modern dramatic criticism. Turning away from drama, he became England's greatest verse satirist, producing the masterpieces *Absalom and Achitophel* (1681) and *Mac Flecknoe* (1682). He also produced extensive translations of Latin poetry, including VIRGIL's *Aeneid*.

John Dryden Painting by Godfrey Kneller

dry ice CARBON DIOXIDE in SOLID form. It is a dense, snow-like substance that passes directly from solid to vapor at −109.3°F (−78.5°C). It is used chiefly to keep foods, vaccines, and other perishable products cold during shipping or storage.

dry lake See PLAYA

dry rot Symptom of fungal disease in plants (see FUNGUS), characterized by firm spongy to leathery or hard decay of the stem (branch), trunk, root, rhizome, corm, bulb, or fruit. The fungus consumes the CELLULOSE of wood, leaving a soft skeleton that is readily reduced to powder.

Dry Tortugas National Park \tȯr-'tü-gəz\ Park located on the Dry Tortugas islands, SW Florida, west of Key West. Established in 1935 as Ft. Jefferson National Park, it occupies an area of about 64,700 acres (26,200 hectares). The park includes the remains of fortifications built in 1846.

DSL *in full* **Digital Subscriber Line** Broadband digital communications connection that operates over standard copper telephone wires. It requires a DSL MODEM, which splits transmissions into two frequency bands: the lower frequencies for voice (ordinary telephone calls) and the upper band for digital data, especially for connection to the INTERNET. Data can be transferred via DSL at much higher rates than with ordinary dial-up modem service; the range of DSL signals, however, is very small. Connections can be made only within a few miles of the nearest transmitting station. ADSL (Asymmetric DSL) is a popular type of DSL in which most of the bandwidth of the connection is devoted to downloading data from the network to the user. In HDSL (High bit-rate DSL) and SDSL (Symmetric DSL) the upstream and downstream rates are the same. Still faster types are under development.

Dual Alliance See AUSTRO–GERMAN ALLIANCE

Dual Monarchy See AUSTRIA-HUNGARY

du Barry \dē-bȧ-'rē\, **comtesse (Countess)** *orig.* (Marie-) Jeanne Bécu *known as* **Madame du Barry** (1743–1793) French mistress of LOUIS XV. Originally the mistress of Jean du Barry, who introduced her into Parisian high society, she joined Louis XV's court in 1769 after a nominal marriage to Jean's noble brother qualified her as Louis's official royal mistress. She supported unpopular factions and contributed to the decline of the prestige of the crown. After Louis's death (1774), she was banished from court. In the French Revolution she was condemned as a counterrevolutionary and guillotined.

Dubayy *or* **Dubai** \dü-'bī\ Constituent emirate (pop., 1999 est.: 858,000), United Arab Emirates. It is surrounded by the emirates of ABU DHABI and Ash-Shariqah, and it has 45 mi (72 km) of coastline on the PERSIAN GULF. Occupying 1,510 sq mi (3,900 sq km), it is the second most populous and second largest state of the federation. Its capital is Dubayy city (pop., 1995: 669,000). Settled in 1799 by people from Abu Dhabi, Dubayy became a locally powerful state in the early 19th cent., and until the 1930s it was known for its pearl exports. It has since been enriched by oil wealth. Dubayy city is now a financial center.

Dubcek \'düb-,chek\, **Alexander** (1921–1992) Czech politician. In World War II he joined the underground resistance to Nazi occupation. After the war he rose in Communist Party ranks, and in 1968 he replaced Antonin Novotny (1904–1975) as head of the party. He introduced liberal reforms in the brief PRAGUE SPRING period, which ended when the Soviet Union invaded Czechoslovakia. Demoted to lesser posts, he was expelled from the party in 1970. In 1989, after the party had given up its monopoly on power, he was elected speaker of the Czech parliament.

Dublin *ancient* Eblana. City (pop., 1997 est.: 480,000), capital of Ireland. On the River LIFFEY, it was settled by Vikings in the 9th cent. A.D. It was taken by the Irish in the 11th cent. Under English control in the 12th cent., it was given a charter by HENRY II, establishing it as a seat of government. It prospered in the 18th cent. as a center of the cloth trade. In the 19th–20th cent. it was the site of bloody nationalist violence, including the 1867 FENIAN MOVEMENT and the 1916 EASTER RISING. It is the country's chief port, center of finance and commerce, and seat of culture. Educational and cultural institutions include the Univ. of DUBLIN and the National Library and National Museum; Leinster House (1748) is the seat of the Irish parliament.

Dublin, University of *or* **Trinity College** Oldest university in Ireland, founded in 1591 by Elizabeth I and endowed by the city of Dublin. Trinity was intended to be the first of many constituent colleges of the university, but no others were established and the two names became interchangeable. The full benefits of the university (including degrees) were for many years limited to Anglicans, but in 1873 all religious requirements were eliminated. The library contains many illuminated manuscripts, including the *Book of Kells*. Total enrollment is about 12,000.

Dublin Bay prawn See SCAMPI

Du Bois \dü-'bȯis\, **W(illiam) E(dward) B(urghardt)** (1868–1963) U.S. sociologist and black-rights leader. Born in Great Barrington, Mass., he received a PhD from Harvard Univ. After studying the social situation of U.S. blacks, he concluded that change could be attained only through agitation and protest, a view that clashed with that of Booker T.

WASHINGTON. His famous book *The Souls of Black Folk* appeared in 1903. In 1905 Du Bois founded the Niagara Movement, the forerunner of the NAACP. He served as editor of the NAACP's magazine, *Crisis* (1910–34). He taught at Atlanta Univ. and wrote several more important books. Moving leftward politically, he became disillusioned with the U.S., and in 1961 he joined the Communist Party and moved to Ghana.

Dubos \dü-'bōz\, **René (Jules)** (1901–1982) French-U.S. microbiologist and environmentalist. He pioneered in isolating antibacterial substances from soil microorganisms, discovering major antibiotics. He researched and wrote on antibiotics, acquired immunity, tuberculosis, and bacteria native to the gastrointestinal tract. He later wrote about the relationship of humans to the natural environment; *So Human an Animal* (1968) won the Pulitzer Prize.

Dubrovnik \'dü-,brȯv-nik\ Port city (pop., 1991: 56,000), Croatia. It is situated on the S Adriatic coast southwest of SARAJEVO. Founded in the 7th cent. by Roman refugees, it later came under Byzantine rule. It was under Venetian control 1205–1358, but remained largely independent and became a mercantile power. It was known as a center of Slavic literature and art in the 15th–17th cent. It was passed to Austria in 1815 and to Yugoslavia in 1918. It was bombed by the Serbs in 1991–92 during Croatia's struggle for independence. The old city is enclosed by medieval city walls.

Dubuffet \dü-bü-'fe\, **Jean (-Philippe-Arthur)** (1901–1985) French painter and sculptor. He studied painting in Paris, but in 1929 began making a living as a wine merchant. When he returned to art full-time (c.1942), he became a leading artist in Paris and proponent of art brut ("raw art"). He executed crude images incised into rough impasto surfaces made of such materials as plaster, gravel, and ashes bound with varnish and glue, and sculptural works made of junk materials; their unfinished appearance provoked public outrage. In his later years he produced large fiberglass sculptures for public spaces.

du Cange \'kä[n]zh\, **Charles du Fresne, seigneur (Lord)** (1610–1688) French linguist. Du Cange's most important works, *A Glossary for Writers of Middle and Low Latin* (1678) and *A Glossary for Writers of Middle and Low Greek* (1688), relied on his vast knowledge of history, law, archaeology, and geography. His historical approach and effort to distinguish these languages' medieval vocabularies from their classical counterparts inspired later scholars to examine the development of language historically. Frequently reedited, his dictionaries retained their usefulness through the 20th cent.

Duccio (di Buoninsegna) \'düt-chō\ (fl.c.1278–1318/19) Italian painter. Little is known of his life, but two documented works survive, the Rucellai Madonna for the Florentine church of Santa Maria Novella (1285) and the famous *Maestà* altarpiece for Siena Cathedral (1308–11); both represent landmarks in Italian painting. His style reflected the influence of CIMABUE and Byzantine art, though he introduced a warmth of human feeling comparable to that of GIOTTO in Florentine painting. He was the leading painter in Siena, a vital artistic center in the Middle Ages.

Duchamp \dü-'shä[n]\, **Marcel** (1887–1968) French artist. In 1904 he arrived in Paris and earned his living by drawing cartoons for comic magazines. In 1913 he caused a sensation at the ARMORY SHOW with his painting *Nude Descending a Staircase, No. 2* (1912), combining the principles of Cubism and Futurism. He then abandoned conventional media and, with Francis PICABIA, became the

Marcel Duchamp, "Nude Descending a Staircase, No. 2," 1912

leader of the New York DADA movement. He invented the READY-MADE, notably a urinal titled *Fountain* (1917), and snubbed the traditional values of art, living by the conviction that life is meaningless and absurd. He greatly influenced the Surrealists, and his attitude toward art and society led to POP ART and other modern and postmodern movements. A legend in his lifetime, he is considered one of the leading spirits of 20th-cent. art.

duck Any of various relatively small, short-necked, large-billed WATERFOWL (several genera in subfamily Anatinae, family Anatidae). The legs of true ducks (Anatinae) are placed rearward (as are those of SWANS), resulting in a waddling gait. Most true ducks differ from swans and true geese (see GOOSE) in that male ducks molt twice annually, females lay large clutches of smooth-shelled eggs, and both sexes have overlapping scales on the skin of the leg and exhibit some differences between sexes in plumage and in call. True ducks may be grouped as perching ducks, DABBLING DUCKS, and DIVING DUCKS. The whistling duck species, also called tree ducks, are not true ducks.

duckbill See PLATYPUS

duck hawk See PEREGRINE FALCON

ductility Capacity of a material to deform permanently (e.g., stretch, bend, or spread) in response to stress. Most common STEELS, for example, are quite ductile and hence can accommodate local stress concentrations. Brittle materials, such as glass, cannot accommodate concentrations of stress because they lack ductility, and therefore fracture easily. When a material specimen is stressed, it deforms elastically (see ELASTICITY) at first; above a certain deformation, called the elastic limit, deformation becomes permanent.

Dudley, Robert See Earl of LEICESTER

duel Formal combat with weapons fought between two persons in the presence of witnesses. Intended to settle a quarrel or point of honor, it represented an alternative to the usual process of justice. The judicial duel, in which two parties met in a duel by order of a judge, was prevalent in medieval Europe; it was believed that the righteous would emerge victorious. Duels of honor were private encounters over real or imagined slights or insults. Duels (later fought with pistols) remained frequent in France until the late 19th cent. and in Germany until World War I. The most famous U.S. duel was that between Alexander HAMILTON and Aaron BURR (1804). See also ORDEAL.

due process Legal proceedings carried out fairly and in accord with established rules and principles (called also procedural due process). Substantive due process refers to a requirement that laws and regulations be related to a legitimate government interest (e.g., crime prevention) and not contain provisions that result in unfair or arbitrary treatment. The 5th Amendment to the U.S. CONSTITUTION states that "no person shall . . . be deprived of life, liberty, or property, without due process of law." This right was extended to the states by the 14th Amendment (1868). The boundaries of due process are the subject of endless judicial interpretation. Fundamental to procedural due process are adequate notice before the government can deprive one of life, liberty, or property, and the opportunity to be heard and defend one's rights. Substantive due process limits the government's power to enact laws that affect one's life, liberty, or property rights.

Dufay \dü-ˈfē\, **Guillaume** (c.1400–1474) Franco-Flemish composer, principal composer of the Burgundian school. As a boy he sang in the choir of Cambrai Cathedral. Ordained a priest, in 1428 he joined the papal singers in Rome. He returned to Cambrai around 1440 to supervise the cathedral's music. Many musicians came to learn under him, and he enjoyed renown as the greatest living composer. His surviving works, which employ a richly harmonic texture, include some 90 chansons, 13 isorhythmic motets, and at least six complete masses, including such early cantus-firmus masses as *Missa L'homme armé* and *Missa Se la face ay pale*.

Du Fu *or* **Tu Fu** \ˈdü-ˈfü\ (712–770) Chinese poet, often considered the greatest of all time. His early poetry, which celebrates the natural world and bemoans the passage of time, garnered him renown. He suffered periods of extreme personal hardship, and as he matured his verse began to ex-

press profound compassion for humanity. An expert in all the poetic genres of his day, he is renowned for his superb classicism and skill in prosody, though many of the subtleties of his art do not survive translation.

Dufy \dü-ēs-ˈfē\, **Raoul** (1877–1953) French painter and designer. He studied in Paris (1900) and experimented with IMPRESSIONISM, then with Fauvism (1905). He developed a distinctive style characterized by rapid drawing on backgrounds of bright, decorative color; his subjects included such recreational scenes as horse races, parades, and concerts. He also designed textiles and made numerous book illustrations. His highly accessible works did much to popularize modern art.

dugong \ˈdü-ˌgän\ Large marine mammal (*Dugong dugon*, the sole living member of the family Dugongidae) that lives in shallow coastal waters from the Red Sea and E Africa to the Philippines, New Guinea, and N Australia. It is 7–11 ft (2.2–3.4 m) long and usually weighs 500–800 lbs (230–360 kg). Its round, tapered body ends in a flipper with paired, pointed, horizontal branches. The forelimbs

Dugong (Dugong dugon)

are rounded flippers; there are no hind limbs. The head blends into the body. Once heavily hunted, they are now protected throughout most of their range. See also MANATEE.

duiker \ˈdī-kər\ Any of about 14 species of small, shy ANTELOPE. They live in most of Africa but are rarely seen by humans. The gray, or bush, duiker (*Sylvicapra grimmia*) has long legs and lives in regions with bush or grass cover. It stands 22–26 in. (57–67 cm) tall at the shoulder. Only males have horns, which are straight and spiky. Forest duikers (about 13 species, genus *Cephalophus*) are short-legged, hunchbacked animals that stand 14–18 in. (36–46 cm) tall. Both sexes have horns.

Duisburg \ˈdü-ēs-ˌbùrk, *Engl* ˈdüz-bərg\ City (pop., 1996: 533,000), N. Rhine-Westphalia state, W Germany. It lies at the junction of the RHINE and RUHR rivers and is connected with the North Sea ports by the Rhine–Herne Canal. A Roman camp, by A.D. 740 it was a seat of the Frankish kings. It passed to Cleves in 1290 and to BRANDENBURG in 1614. It suffered in the THIRTY YEARS' WAR, then revived as a university town 1655–1818. It is now one of the world's largest inland ports.

Dukakis \dü-ˈkä-kis\, **Michael S(tanley)** (b.1933) U.S. politician. Born in Brookline, Mass., he attended law school at Harvard and served in the state legislature (1963–71). Elected governor for three terms (1975–79, 1983–91), he coped with a budgetary crisis, restoring the state's fiscal health. As the Democratic presidential nominee in 1988, he lost to George BUSH.

Dukas \dü-ˈkäs\, **Paul (Abraham)** (1865–1935) French composer. Perfectionism led him to destroy much of his work. His fame rests almost entirely on the tone poem *The Sorcerer's Apprentice* (1897); his other works include the opera *Ariane et Barbe-bleue* (1906), the ballet *La péri* (1912), and a symphony in C (1896).

duke European title of nobility, the highest rank below a prince or king except in countries having such titles as archduke or grand duke. The wife of a duke is a duchess. The Romans gave the title *dux* to high military commanders with territorial responsibilities. It was later used in France and Germany for rulers of very large areas. In some European countries a duke was a sovereign prince who ruled an independent duchy. In Britain, where there were no ducal titles until 1337, it is a hereditary title.

Duke, James B(uchanan) (1856–1925) U.S. tobacco magnate and philanthropist. Born in Durham, N.C., in 1890 he became president of the American Tobacco Co., which controlled the entire U.S. tobacco industry until it was broken up under antitrust laws in 1911 into several companies that would become the principal U.S. cigarette makers. He oversaw the family's contributions to Trinity College in Durham, which was renamed DUKE UNIV.

DE

Duke, Vernon *orig.* Vladimir (Aleksandrovich) Dukelsky (1903–1969) Russian-U.S. composer. He fled Russia at 16, settling in Constantinople. He composed classical works in Europe, including *Zéphyr et Flore* (1925) for the BALLETS RUSSES, but moved permanently to the U.S. in 1929. His songs for shows (including *Walk a Little Faster*, 1932) and movies (including *Cabin in the Sky*, 1943, and *Sadie Thompson*, 1944) include "April in Paris," "Taking a Chance on Love," and "Banjo Eyes."

Duke University Private university in Durham, N.C. It was created in 1924 through an endowment from James B. DUKE, though the original college (Trinity) traces its roots to the mid-19th cent. Besides an undergraduate liberal-arts college, the university includes schools of graduate studies, engineering, law, business, divinity, medicine, nursing, and environmental studies. Total enrollment is about 12,000.

Dulbecco \dəl-'be-kō\, **Renato** (b.1914) Italian-U.S. virologist. With Marguerite Vogt he pioneered the culturing of animal viruses and investigated how certain viruses gain control of the cells they infect. They showed that polyoma virus inserts its DNA into the DNA of the host cell, and that the cell is then transformed into a cancer cell, reproducing the viral DNA along with its own and producing more cancer cells. Dulbecco suggested that human cancers could be caused by similar reproduction of foreign DNA fragments. He shared a 1975 Nobel Prize with two former students, Howard Temin (1934–1994) and David BALTIMORE.

dulcimer *or* **hammered dulcimer** ZITHER whose strings are beaten with small hammers. Its soundbox is flat and usually trapezoidal; each pair of strings produces a single note, and the pairs slope upward alternately left and right to facilitate rapid playing. The Hungarian cimbalom, much used in Gypsy orchestras, has legs and a damper pedal. The Appalachian dulcimer is a narrow zither with a fretted fingerboard and three to five strings, which are stopped with one hand and plucked with a plectrum.

DuLhut \dū-'lūt\, **Daniel Greysolon, Sieur** (1639?–1710) French soldier and explorer. He made two voyages to New France before 1674 and returned to Montreal in 1675. He negotiated fur-trade agreements with Indian tribes, rescued Louis HENNEPIN from the Sioux, and is credited with establishing French control over the land north and west of Lake Superior. Duluth, Minn., is named for him.

Dulles \'də-ləs\, **Allen W(elsh)** (1893–1969) U.S. diplomat. Born in Watertown, N.Y., he held diplomatic posts before practicing law with his brother, J. F. DULLES. In World War II he served in the Office of Strategic Services. When the CENTRAL INTELLIGENCE AGENCY was established in 1951, he became its deputy director. As director (1953–61) he oversaw its early successes, but the U-2 INCIDENT (1960) and BAY OF PIGS INVASION (1961) led to his resignation.

Dulles, John Foster (1888–1959) U.S. diplomat. Born in Washington, D.C., he was counsel to the American Peace Commission at Versailles. He helped prepare the charter of the U.N. and was a delegate to its General Assembly (1946–49). He negotiated the complex Japanese peace treaty (1949–51). As secretary of state under Pres. Dwight EISENHOWER (1953–59), he advocated active opposition to Soviet actions and developed the EISENHOWER DOCTRINE. His critics considered him an inflexible practitioner of "brinkmanship"; later assessments credit his firmness in checking Communist expansion.

Duluth \də-'lüth\ City (pop., 2000: 87,000) and inland port, NE Minnesota, on Lake SUPERIOR. Its harbor is the W terminus of the ST. LAWRENCE SEAWAY. Through it are shipped iron ore, coal, grain, and oil. The site was named after Daniel DULHUT. It was incorporated as a city in 1870.

Duma *Russian* Gosudarstvennaya Duma ("State Assembly") Elected legislative body that, with the State Council, constituted the imperial Russian legislature 1906–17. It had only limited power to control spending and initiate legislation, and the four Dumas that convened (1906, 1907, 1907–12, 1912–17) rarely enjoyed the cooperation of the ministers or the emperor, who retained the right to rule by decree when the Duma was not in session. In the Soviet era, SOVIETS were the basic unit of government. After the fall of the Soviet Union (1991), a new constitution (1993) established a Russian parliament composed of a Federation Council (in which all 89 of Russia's republics and regions have equal representation) and a revived Duma, with 450 members elected through proportional representation on a party basis and through single-member constituencies.

Dumas \dū-'mä\, **Alexandre** *known as* **Dumas** *père* (1802–1870) French playwright and novelist. His first success was as a writer of melodramatic plays, including *Napoléon Bonaparte* (1831) and *Antony* (1831). His immensely popular historical novels include *The Three Musketeers* (1844), a romance about four swashbuckling heroes in the age of Cardinal RICHELIEU, and *The Count of Monte Cristo* (1844–45). His illegitimate son Alexandre Dumas (1824–1895), called Dumas *fils*, is best known for his play *La Dame aux Camélias* (1848), the basis of Giuseppe VERDI's opera *La Traviata*.

Alexandre Dumas *père*

du Maurier \dù-'mȯr-ē-ˌā\, **Daphne** (*later* **Dame Daphne**) (1907–1989) British novelist and playwright. She is best known for the gothic suspense novel *Rebecca* (1938), one of many successful tales set on the wild coast of Cornwall. Her other novels include *Jamaica Inn* (1936), *Frenchman's Creek* (1942), and *My Cousin Rachel* (1951). Her story "The Birds," like *Jamaica Inn* and *Rebecca,* was filmed by Alfred HITCHCOCK.

du Maurier, George (Louis Palmella Busson) (1834–1896) British caricaturist and novelist. His drawings for *Punch*, *Once a Week,* and *The Leisure Hour* were acute commentaries on the Victorian scene. His highly successful novel *Trilby* (1894), about an artist's model who falls under the spell of the musician Svengali, has entered popular mythology. His other novels were *Peter Ibbetson* (1891) and *The Martian* (1897).

Dumont d'Urville \dū-mōⁿ-dūr-'vēl\, **Jules (-Sébastien-César)** (1790–1842) French navigator. His exploration of the S. Pacific (1826–29) resulted in extensive revision of charts of South Sea waters and redesignation of island groups into Melanesia, Micronesia, Polynesia, and Malaysia. He set sail for Antarctica in 1837; though unable to penetrate the pack ice, his expedition surveyed the Straits of Magellan, discovered Joinville Island, and sighted the Adélie Coast (named after Dumont's wife).

Dunant \dū-'näⁿ\, **(Jean-) Henri** (1828–1910) Swiss humanitarian. An eyewitness to the Battle of Solferino (1859), he organized emergency aid for the Austrian and French wounded. In 1862 he proposed the formation of voluntary relief services in all countries and an international agreement covering the war wounded. In 1864 he founded the RED CROSS, and the GENEVA CONVENTION came into being. He continued to promote interest in prisoners of war and other humanitarian causes. In 1901 he shared with Frédéric Passy (1822–1912) the first Nobel Peace Prize.

Dunbar, Paul Laurence (1872–1906) U.S. author. Born in Dayton, Ohio, the son of former slaves, he was one of the first black writers to attain national prominence. He wrote for a largely white readership, using black dialect and depicting the pre–Civil War South in pastoral, idyllic tones. His verse collections include *Oak and Ivy* (1893), *Majors and Minors* (1895), and *Lyrics of Lowly Life* (1896). He also published four short-story collections and four novels, including *The Sport of the Gods* (1902).

Duncan, David Douglas (b.1916) U.S. photojournalist. He joined the staff of *Life* magazine in 1946 and covered the Korean War (1950); his photographs depicting the life of the ordinary soldier were published in *This Is War!* (1951). Resuming his freelance life, in 1956 he met Pablo PICASSO, with whom he became fast friends; his photographic essays on Picasso's works include *The Private World of Pablo Picasso* (1958) and *Picasso's Picassos* (1961).

Duncan, Isadora (*orig.* Angela) (1877–1927) U.S. interpretive dancer. Born in San Francisco, she soon rejected the conventions of classical ballet and based her technique on natural rhythms and movement inspired by ancient Greece, dancing barefoot in a tunic without tights. In 1898 she moved to Europe, where she gave recitals to great acclaim throughout her life, earning notoriety for her liberated unconventionality, and founded several dance schools. She was killed when her long scarf caught in the spokes of a car's wheel. Her emphasis on "free dance" made her a precursor of MODERN DANCE, and she inspired a range of avant-garde artists.

Duncan I (d.1040) King of the Scots (1034–40). The grandson of King MALCOLM II, his accession to the throne violated the system in which kingship alternated between two branches of the royal family. He was challenged by his cousin Macbeth, Mormaor (subking) of Moray, who may have had a stronger claim to the throne. Macbeth killed Duncan in battle in 1040.

Dundee \ˌdən-ˈdē\ City (pop., 1998 est.: 146,000), Scotland. An important seaport, it is situated on the Firth of Tay, a NORTH SEA inlet. Earliest mention of the town dates from the late 12th cent., and over the next several centuries it saw repeated sackings by the English. Among surviving buildings, the City Churches are a focal point in the modern city. The Univ. of Dundee was founded in 1881.

dung beetle Any member of one subfamily (Scarabaeinae) of SCARAB BEETLE, which shapes manure into a ball (sometimes as large as an apple) with its scooperlike head and paddle-shaped antennae. They vary from 0.2 to more than 1 in. (5–30 mm) long. In early summer it buries itself and the ball and feeds on it. Later the female deposits eggs in dung balls on which the larvae will feed. They can eat more than their own weight in 24 hours.

Dungeness crab \ˈdən-jə-nəs\ Edible CRAB (*Cancer magister*) found along the Pacific coast from Alaska to lower California, one of the coast's largest and most important commercial crabs. The male is 7–9 in. (18–23 cm) wide and 4–5 in. (10–13 cm) long. It lives on sandy bottoms below the high-tide mark. Closely related N. American species are the rock crab of the Atlantic coast, the Jonah crab in coastal waters from New England to Canada, and the red and Pacific rock crabs, both in Pacific coastal waters. All are edible.

Dunham, Katherine (b.1910) U.S. dancer, choreographer, and anthropologist. Born in Chicago, in 1940 she formed the U.S.'s first all–black dance company, for which she choreographed revues (including *Tropics* and *Le jazz hot*) based on her anthropological research in the Caribbean. She later received a PhD in anthropology from the Univ. of Chicago. Her dance school in New York (1945–55) trained many important black dancers. She also choreographed Broadway stage productions, operas, and movies.

Katherine Dunham in *Tropical Revue*, 1945–46

Dunkirk Evacuation (1940) In WORLD WAR II, the evacuation of British and other Allied troops, cut off by the Germans, from the French seaport of Dunkirk (Dunkerque) to England. Naval vessels and hundreds of civilian boats were used in the 10-day evacuation. About 198,000 British and 140,000 French and Belgian troops were saved. Its success was due to fighter cover by the RAF and (unintentionally) to Adolf HITLER's order halting the advance of German armored forces into Dunkirk.

Dunmore's War, Lord See LORD DUNMORE'S WAR

Dunne, Finley Peter (1867–1936) U.S. journalist and humorist. Born in Chicago of Irish immigrants, Dunne began contributing Irish-dialect sketches to Chicago newspapers in 1892, in which his character Martin Dooley commented on current events in a rich Irish brogue. Mr. Dooley soon became a force for clear thinking and tolerance in public affairs. Many of Dunne's more than 700 dialect essays were republished in such collections as *Mr. Dooley in Peace and War* (1898).

Duns Scotus \ˌdənz-ˈskō-təs\, **John** (1266?–1308) Medieval Scottish philosopher and scholastic theologian. He taught first at Oxford and later at the Univ. of Paris, from which he was briefly exiled for supporting Pope BONIFACE VIII in his quarrel with King PHILIP IV. In 1307 he became professor of theology at Cologne, perhaps to escape charges of heresy over his defense of the IMMACULATE CONCEPTION. His two major works, *Ordinatio* and *Quaestiones quodlibetales,* were unfinished at his death.

Dunstable \ˈdən-stə-bəl\, **John** (c.1390–1453) English composer. Little is known of his life. After his death he came to be credited with the achievements of all his English contemporaries. He left at least 50 compositions, all for three and four voices and almost all sacred. Their full triadic harmony and frequent parallel motion in the voices represented an important innovation that influenced such composers as Guillaume DUFAY, softening the austerity of 14th-cent. polyphony.

duodenum \ˌdü-ə-ˈdē-nəm, dù-ˈä-dᵊn-əm\ First and shortest (9–11 in., or 23–28 cm) segment of the SMALL INTESTINE. It curves down and then up from the pylorus of the stomach. Ducts from the pancreas and gallbladder bring in bicarbonate to neutralize stomach acid, pancreatic enzymes to further digestion, and bile salts to break up fats (see DIGESTION). Nutrient absorption begins in the lower duodenum, which has a mucous lining. Exposure to stomach acid makes the upper duodenum susceptible to PEPTIC ULCERS.

Du Pont Co. *in full* **E.I. du Pont de Nemours & Co.** \nə-ˈmür\ U.S. manufacturer. Founded near Wilmington, Del., in 1802 by a French immigrant, Éleuthère Irénée du Pont de Nemours (1771–1834), son of the eminent economist Pierre-Samuel du Pont de Nemours (1739–1817), the company originally manufactured gunpowder and other explosives. In the early 20th cent. it diversified its product line, partly through extensive acquisitions. It developed nitrocellulose plastics in 1915 and synthetic rubber in 1931, and later developed the fibers nylon, Orlon, Dacron, Kevlar, and Lycra, as well as Mylar film and Teflon resin. Run by the du Pont family until World War II, today it is a diverse conglomerate with major electronics, automotive, and pharmaceutical branches.

Durand \dù-ˈrand\, **Asher B(rown)** (1796–1886) U.S. painter and engraver. Born in Jefferson Village, N.J., he had established his reputation as an engraver by 1823 with his print of John TRUMBULL's *Declaration of Independence* and his portraits of prominent contemporaries. He later devoted himself to landscape painting, becoming a founder of the HUDSON RIVER SCHOOL and one of the earliest U.S. artists to work directly from nature. He cofounded the National Academy of Design (1826), and served as its president 1845–61.

Durango \dù-ˈraŋ-gō\ State (pop., 2000: 1,445,000), N central Mexico. The W portion of the state's 47,560 sq mi (123,181 sq km) territory lies within the mineral-laden Sierra Madre Occidental; semiarid plains, used for ranching, comprise the E portion. The Río Nazas, the largest river in the state, supports commercial agriculture, including the Laguna cotton district near DURANGO city, the state's capital. First explored by Europeans in 1562, Durango shared the colonial history of CHIHUAHUA; the two became separate states in 1823.

Durango *officially* **Victoria de Durango** City (pop., 1995: 397,000) capital of DURANGO state, N central Mexico. It lies in a valley of the SIERRA MADRE, 6,197 ft (1,889 m) above sea level. Nearby is the Cerro del Mercado, one of the world's largest iron ore deposits. First settled in 1556, Durango was the capital of Nueva Vizcaya, which included Durango and CHIHUAHUA until 1823. The city, long known as a health resort, is an important commercial and mining center.

Durant \dù-ˈrant\, **Will(iam James)** and **Ariel** *orig.* Ada Kaufman (1885–1981, 1898–1981) U.S. writers. Will was born in N. Adams, Mass., Ariel in Prosurov, Russia. After the great success of Will's *Story of Philosophy* (1926), they cowrote the 11-volume *The Story of Civilization* (1935–75), including *Rousseau and Revolution* (1967, Pulitzer Prize).

Durant, William C(rapo) (1861–1947) U.S. industrialist, founder of GENERAL MOTORS CORP. Born in Boston, he es-

DE

tablished a carriage company in 1886. He joined the Buick Motor Car Co. (founded by David Buick in 1902) in 1903–4 and quickly revived it. He brought together several automotive manufacturers to form the General Motors Co. in 1908, but lost control of it two years later. In 1911, with Louis Chevrolet (1878–1941), he founded the Chevrolet Motor Co., which acquired General Motors in 1915. As president of General Motors Corp. until 1920, he presided over its steady expansion.

Durante \də-'ran-tē\, **Jimmy** (*orig.* James Francis) (1893–1980) U.S. comedian. Born in New York City, in the 1920s he teamed with Lou Clayton and Eddie Jackson to star in vaudeville and nightclubs. After his film debut in *Roadhouse Nights* (1930), he brightened many films and musicals with his gravelly voice, malapropisms, and warmhearted buffoonery. Nicknamed the "Schnozzola" for his large nose, he is remembered for ending his radio and TV programs with the line "Goodnight, Mrs. Calabash, wherever you are."

Duras \dǖ-'ràs\, **Marguerite** *orig.* Marguerite Donnadieu (1914–1996) French (Indochina-born) writer. Indochina was the setting for Duras's first successful novel, *The Sea Wall* (1950), after which her writing grew increasingly minimal and abstract. Among her major novels are *The Afternoon of Monsieur Andesmas* (1962), *L'Amour* (1971), and the semiautobiographical *The Lover* (1984, Prix Goncourt; film, 1992). Highly prolific, she was also acclaimed for her screenplays of *Hiroshima mon amour* (1959) and *India Song* (1975).

Durban City (pop., 1991: 716,000; metro. area pop.: 1,137,000) and chief seaport, S. Africa. Located on Natal Bay of the Indian Ocean, it was the site of a European trading settlement from 1824 and was named Port Natal by the traders. Land was ceded to them by the Zulu king SHAKA. Durban was founded in 1835 on the site of Port Natal. In the 1840s the Boers clashed with the British over control of Durban. One of the world's major commercial ports, it is the headquarters of S. Africa's sugar industry and a center of diverse manufacturing and tourism.

Dürer \'dǖr-ər, *Engl* 'dùr-ər\, **Albrecht** (1471–1528) German painter and printmaker. Apprenticed at 15 to a painter in his native Nuremberg, he opened his own workshop around 1494 and began producing woodcuts and copper engravings. His extensive travels took him twice to Italy; its artistic influence can be seen in such engravings as *The Four Witches* (c.1497) and *Adam and Eve* (1504). He became known for his penetrating half-length portraits and self-portraits. In 1506, in Venice, he completed his great altarpiece *The Feast of the Rose Garlands* in the church of San Bartolommeo. Later important graphic works include

Albrecht Dürer, "Self-portrait in Furred Coat," 1500

his famous *Passion* and *Small Passion* series (1507–13) and his greatest engravings: *St. Jerome in His Study, Melencolia I,* and *The Knight, Death, and the Devil* (1513–14). Back in Nuremberg he worked for Emperor MAXIMILIAN I (1512–19). By now internationally famous, in 1518 he became a devoted follower of Martin LUTHER. His finest painting is the *Four Apostles* of 1526. He was the greatest Renaissance artist in N Europe and had many pupils and imitators.

Durga In Hinduism, one form of the goddess DEVI or Shakti (see SHAKTI), and the wife of SHIVA. She was created out of flames that issued from the mouths of BRAHMA, VISHNU, Shiva, and other gods, who created her to slay the buffalo-demon Mahisasura, whom they were unable to overcome. She is usually depicted riding a lion or tiger, each of her multiple arms bearing a weapon.

Durham *Saxon* Dunholme. City and county seat (metro. area pop., 1995 est.: 85,000), N England. Fortified by

WILLIAM I the Conqueror, it became a seat of the feudal prince-bishops of Durham. Medieval Durham was a place of pilgrimage, holding the remains of St. Cuthbert in its cathedral (begun in 1093). Its bishops helped establish the city as an educational center. It is home to the Univ. of Durham.

Durham, Earl of *orig.* John George Lambton (1792–1840) British colonial administrator in Canada. He served in the cabinet of Charles GREY (1830–33), and in 1838 was appointed governor-general of Canada. He appointed a new executive council to placate the rebellious French Canadians of Lower Canada (later Quebec). Criticized in England for his action, he resigned. He later issued the influential Durham Report, which advocated the union of Lower Canada and Upper Canada and the expansion of self-government.

Durkheim \dǖr-'kem\, **Émile** (1858–1917) French social scientist, the founder of the French school of SOCIOLOGY. In *The Division of Labor in Society* (1893) and *Suicide* (1897), he described how ethical and social structures were endangered by industrialization, during which the division of labor produced alienation among workers and increasing prosperity generated greed and passions that threatened the equilibrium of society. He drew attention to anomie, or social disconnectedness, and studied suicide as a decision to renounce life. He came to regard education and religion as the most potent means of reforming humanity and molding new social institutions. In *Elementary Forms of the Religious Life* (1915) he viewed religion as expressing the collective conscience of a society and producing social solidarity. Durkheim also wrote influential works on sociological method. He taught at the Universities of Bordeaux (1887–1902) and Paris (1902–17).

Durocher \dù-'rō-shər\, **Leo (Ernest)** (1905–1991) U.S. baseball player and manager. Born in W. Springfield, Mass., he played for various teams 1928–38, distinguishing himself by his sharp fielding at shortstop. He gained notoriety as the cheeky, contentious manager of the Brooklyn Dodgers (1939–46, 1948); he was suspended from managing for the entire 1947 season for "conduct detrimental to baseball." He managed the New York Giants 1948–55, left to become a commentator, but later coached the Los Angeles Dodgers (1961–64) and managed the Chicago Cubs (1966–72) and the Houston Astros (1972–73).

Durrani, Ahmad Shah See AHMAD SHAH DURRANI

Durrell \'də-rəl\, **Lawrence (George)** (1912–1990) British (Indian-born) writer. He spent most of his life in Mediterranean countries, often in diplomatic posts. He is best known for his *Alexandria Quartet,* composed of the novels *Justine* (1957), *Balthazar* (1958), *Mountolive* (1958), and *Clea* (1960). His poetry and his nonfiction books about locales, including *Prospero's Cell* (1945) and *Bitter Lemons* (1957), are often considered his best works.

Dürrenmatt \'duer-ən-ˌmät\, **Friedrich** (1921–1990) Swiss playwright. His plays, showing the influence of Bertolt BRECHT as well as the theater of the ABSURD, were central to the post-1945 revival of the German theater. In his first play, *Es steht geschrieben* ("All as It Is Written"; 1947), and his next two plays, *The Marriage of Mr. Mississippi* (1952) and *An Angel Comes to Babylon* (1953), he took comic liberties with historical facts to present parables about modern life. His play *The Visit* (1956) and the modern morality play *The Physicists* (1962) earned him international acclaim.

Duryea \'dùr-ˌyā\, **Charles E(dgar) and J(ames) Frank** (1861–1938, 1869–1967) U.S. automotive inventors. Born near Canton, Ill., Charles worked as a bicycle mechanic before designing a gasoline-powered automobile, and in 1893 he and his brother Frank constructed the first U.S. automobile, which they drove successfully on the streets of Springfield, Mass. In Chicago in 1895, Frank drove an improved model to win the first U.S. auto race. In 1896 their company manufactured the first commercially produced U.S. automobiles; 13 cars were sold before the company failed. Frank later developed the Stevens-Duryea limousine, which was produced into the 1920s.

Dusan, Stefan See STEFAN DUSAN

Duse \'dü-zā\, **Eleonora** (1858–1924) Italian actress. She acted in several French plays to great acclaim from 1878

and toured with her own company in Europe and the U.S. after 1885. She fell in love with Gabriele D'ANNUNZIO in the 1890s and acted in several plays he wrote for her, notably *Francesca da Rimini*. The most fluent and expressive actress of her day, she was especially noted for her roles in Henrik IBSEN's plays. She retired in 1909 but returned to the stage in 1921 and was touring the U.S. when she died.

Eleonora Duse

Dushanbe \'dyü-ˌshäm-bə, ˌdyü-shäm-'bä\ *formerly* (*1929–61*) **Stalinabad** \ˌstä-lyi-nə-'bäd\ City (pop., 1994 est.: 524,000), capital of Tajikistan. It was built in the Soviet period on the site of Dyushambe, part of the khanate of BUKHARA; it suffered severely in the fighting during the Soviet takeover in 1920. In 1924 it became the capital of the new Tajik Autonomous S.S.R., and rapid growth followed. An important transport junction, it accounts for much of the republic's industrial output.

Düsseldorf \'düe-səl-ˌdȯrf\ City (pop., 1998 est.: 571,000), capital of N. Rhine-Westphalia state, W Germany. Located on the RHINE RIVER, it is the principal city of the industrial Rhine-Ruhr area. Chartered in 1288, it suffered in the THIRTY YEARS' WAR and the War of the SPANISH SUCCESSION. It was transferred to Prussia in 1815 and grew rapidly with the establishment of iron and steel industries in the 1870s. It was heavily damaged in World War II. It is the site of the first German skyscraper, the Wilhelm-Marx-Haus (1924). It was the birthplace of Heinrich HEINE.

Dust Bowl Section of the U.S. GREAT PLAINS that extended over SE Colorado, SW Kansas, the panhandles of Texas and Oklahoma, and NE New Mexico. After World War I the area's grasslands were converted to agricultural fields, and overcultivation added to the effect of a severe drought in the early 1930s, when heavy winds blew the loose topsoil in "black blizzards" that blocked out the sun and piled the dusty dirt in drifts. Thousands of families left the region for California and elsewhere. The planting of windbreaks and grassland enabled the area to recover by the early 1940s.

Dutch East India Co. See Dutch EAST INDIA CO.

Dutch East Indies See INDONESIA

Dutch elm disease Widespread disease that kills ELMS, caused by the FUNGUS *Ceratocystis ulmi*. It was first identified in the U.S. in 1930, and an eradication campaign could not stop its spread wherever the American elm (*Ulmus americana*) grew. The leaves on one or more branches of a stricken tree suddenly wilt, turn dull green to yellow or brown, curl, and may drop early. The fungus can spread up to 50 ft (15 m) from diseased to healthy trees by natural root grafts. Overland, the fungus normally is spread by BARK BEETLES. Control involves exclusion of the beetles, usually by use of an insecticidal spray applied to the tree.

Dutch Guiana See SURINAME

Dutch language W. GERMANIC LANGUAGE spoken by more than 20 million people in the Netherlands, N Belgium, Suriname, and the Netherlands Antilles. Dutch and Flemish (spoken in Belgium) are actually regarded as the same language, called Nederlands in both the Netherlands and Belgium, where efforts have been made to unify spelling and literary usage. Many Dutch-speakers command both a local dialect and Standard Dutch, based on the speech of the major urban centers of N. and S. Holland.

Dutch Reformed Church See REFORMED CHURCH

Dutch Republic *officially* **Republic of the United Netherlands** Former state (1581–1795), about the size of the modern kingdom of the Netherlands. It consisted of the seven N Netherlands provinces that formed the Union of Utrecht in 1579 and declared independence from Spain in 1581 (finally achieved in 1648). In the 17th cent. the Dutch Republic developed into a world colonial empire far out of proportion to its resources, emerging as a center of international finance and a cultural capital of Europe. Later eclipsed by England, in 1795 the republic collapsed under the impact of a Dutch democratic revolution and invading French armies.

Dutch Wars See ANGLO–DUTCH WARS

Duvalier \dü-'val-yä\, **François** *known as* **Papa Doc** (1907–1971) President of Haiti (1957–71). He received his MD in 1934, and held government positions until Pres. Dumarsais Estimé was overthrown by Paul Magloire in 1950. Duvalier led the opposition to Magloire, and became president soon after Magloire's resignation in 1956. He reduced the size of the military and organized the Tontons Macoutes ("Bogeymen"), a private force that terrorized and assassinated alleged foes of his regime. He also played on the culture of VODUN to intimidate the opposition. He declared himself

François Duvalier, 1963

president for life in 1964. His regime's corruption and despotism isolated Haiti, the poorest country in the hemisphere, from the rest of the world. His 19-year-old son, Jean-Claude (b.1951), succeeded him. Continued abuses under "Baby Doc" led to social unrest which forced him to flee to France in 1986.

DVD *in full* **digital versatile disk** Type of optical disk that uses a low-power LASER to read digitized (binary) data encoded onto the disk in the form of tiny pits. A DVD can store any kind of data, including movies, music, and text. DVDs are available in single- and double-sided versions, with one or two layers of information per side. A double-sided, dual-layer version can store about 30 times as much information as a standard CD. Containing far more information than video tape, DVDs produce sharper images and higher-fidelity sound. DVDs are made in a ROM (read-only memory) format as well as in recordable (DVD-R) formats. Though DVD players can usually read CDs, CD players cannot read DVDs. DVDs are expected eventually to replace video cassettes and CDs.

Dvorak \'vȯr-ˌzhäk, də-'vȯr-ˌzhäk\, **Antonin (Leopold)** (1841–1904) Bohemian (Czech) composer. Son of a rural innkeeper and butcher, he was permitted to attend organ school in Prague in 1857. He played viola in a theater orchestra, and eventually found employment that left him ample time for composition. Assisted by Johannes BRAHMS, by 1880 his fame had spread throughout Europe. He served as director of New York's new National Conservatory of Music 1892–95, which resulted in his "New World" Symphony (1893). His music, which frequently draws on folk tunes, is seen as an expression of Czech nationalism. Highly prolific, he is known for his nine symphonies, concertos for piano, violin, and cello, 14 string quartets, *Slavonic Dances* (1878, 1886) for piano, the choral *Stabat Mater* (1877), and 13 operas, including *Rusalka* (1900).

dwarfism Growth retardation resulting in abnormally short adult stature, caused by a variety of hereditary and metabolic disorders. Pituitary dwarfism is caused by insufficient GROWTH HORMONE. Several hereditary dwarfisms occur; intelligence is normal in most forms of dwarfism, but some kinds, such as CRETINISM, include mental retardation. Dwarfism may also result from inadequate nutrition in early life (see RICKETS).

dwarf star Any star of average or low luminosity, mass, and size, including WHITE DWARF STARS and red dwarf stars. Most main-sequence stars (see HERTZSPRUNG-RUSSELL DIAGRAM), including the SUN, are dwarf stars. Colors ranging from blue to red correspond to temperatures from over 17,500°F (10,000°C) to a few thousand degrees.

dybbuk \'di-bək\ In Jewish folklore, a disembodied human spirit that must wander restlessly, burdened by former sins, until it inhabits the body of a living person. Belief in such spirits was common in Eastern Europe in the 16th–17th cent. Individuals thought to be possessed by a dybbuk were taken to a BAAL SHEM, who would carry out a rite of EXORCISM. The folklorist S. Ansky depicted such a spirit in his classic Yiddish drama *The Dybbuk* (c.1916).

Dyck, Anthony Van See Anthony VAN DYCK

dye Any of a class of complex organic compounds that are intensely colored, used to color textiles, leather, paper, and other materials. Major dyes known to the ancients came from plants or from the shells of mollusks; today most dyes are made from coal tar and PETROCHEMICALS. The chemical structure of dyes is relatively easy to modify, so many new colors and types of dyes have been synthesized. Dye molecules are deposited from solution onto materials in such a way that they cannot be removed by the original solvent. Fiber-reactive dyes form a COVALENT BOND with the fiber. Other dyes require previous application of a mordant, an inorganic material that causes the dye to precipitate as an insoluble salt, or vat dyeing, in which a soluble colorless compound is absorbed by the fibers, then oxidized (see OXIDATION-REDUCTION) to the insoluble colored compound.

Dylan \'dil-ən\, **Bob** *orig.* Robert Zimmerman (b.1941) U.S. singer and songwriter. He grew up in Duluth and Hibbing, Minn., adopted the first name of Dylan THOMAS, and traveled around the U.S. in imitation of Woody GUTHRIE. In the early 1960s he began releasing albums that brought him admiring attention. His songs "Blowin' in the Wind" and "The Times They Are a-Changin'" became civil-rights anthems, and "Mr. Tambourine Man" was interpreted as a paean to hallucinogenic drugs. In 1965 he adopted electrically amplified instruments and the rhythms of rock and roll in a major departure. The landmark albums *Highway 61 Revisited* (1965) and *Blonde on Blonde* (1966) established him as a leading figure in rock, bringing him to the pinnacle of his popularity. After a motorcycle accident in 1966, he released several albums that, with their muted, reflective tone and COUNTRY-MUSIC elements, again surprised his public. His many later albums have included *Blood on the Tracks* (1975) and *Time out of Mind* (1997). He is perhaps the most admired and influential American songwriter of his time.

dynamics Branch of MECHANICS that deals with the MOTION of objects in relation to FORCE, MASS, MOMENTUM, and ENERGY. Its foundations were laid by GALILEO, who derived the law of motion for falling bodies and was the first to recognize that all changes of velocity of a body are the result of forces. Isaac NEWTON formulated this observation in his second law of motion (see NEWTON'S LAWS OF MOTION).

dynamite Blasting EXPLOSIVE, patented in 1867 by Alfred NOBEL. Dynamite is based on NITROGLYCERIN but is much safer to handle than nitroglycerin alone. By mixing the nitroglycerin with kieselguhr, a porous silica-containing earth, Nobel produced an essentially dry and granular solid

that was resistant to shock but readily explodable by heat or sudden impact. Later, wood pulp was substituted as the absorbent, and sodium nitrate was added as an oxidizing agent to increase the strength of the explosive.

dysentery \'di-sᵊn-ₜter-ē\ Infectious intestinal disorder with INFLAMMATION, abdominal pain and straining, and DIARRHEA, often containing blood and mucus. Dysentery is spread in food or water contaminated by feces. Bacillary dysentery (shigellosis), caused by *Shigella* bacteria, may be mild or may be sudden, severe, and fatal. Fluid loss causes DEHYDRATION. It is treated with antibiotics, fluid replacement, and sometimes blood transfusion. Amoebic (or amebic) dysentery, caused by *Entamoeba histolytica,* has two forms, one much like bacillary dysentery and the other chronic and intermittent. It is treated with drugs that kill the amoebae.

dyslexia \dis-ˈlek-sē-ə\ Chronic neurological disorder causing inability or great difficulty in learning to read or spell, despite normal intelligence. Symptoms, including very poor reading skills, reversed word and letter sequences, and illegible handwriting, usually become evident in the early school years. With early recognition and specialized teaching, most dyslexics can learn to read. Anomalies have recently been found in reading-related pathways in the brains of dyslexic persons.

dysmenorrhea \ˌdis-ₘme-nə-ˈrē-ə\ Pain or cramps before or during MENSTRUATION. In primary dysmenorrhea, severity varies widely. Irritability, fatigue, backache, or nausea may also occur. It is due to excess PROSTAGLANDINS, which contract the UTERUS, causing cramps. ANALGESICS that block prostaglandin formation (e.g., ACETAMINOPHEN, NSAIDs) decrease its severity. Secondary dysmenorrhea is caused by other disorders, including genital obstructions, pelvic inflammation, infection, polyps, or tumors.

Dyson \'dī-sən\, **Freeman (John)** (b.1923) English-U.S. physicist and educator. At Princeton's Institute for Advanced Study (from 1953), he has done extensive research into QUANTUM theory, but is perhaps best known for his speculative work on human colonization of the solar system and beyond, and for his researches into modes of searching for intelligent extraterrestrial life. He has written many books for a general audience.

dysphasia See APHASIA

dysphemia See STUTTERING

dysplasia \dis-ˈplā-zhə\ Abnormal formation of a bodily structure or tissue, usually bone, that may occur in any part of the body. In the most common human type, epiphyseal dysplasia, the ends of children's bones (epiphyses) grow and harden very slowly; DWARFISM often results (sometimes only in the legs), and degenerative joint disease usually develops by middle age. Large dogs bred for narrow hips may have hip dysplasia.

Dyushambe See DUSHANBE

Ea \ˈā-ä\ In Mesopotamian religion, the god of water. He formed a triad of deities with ANU and Bel. Originally a local deity in the city of Eridu, he evolved into the lord of the fresh waters beneath the earth, the god of ritual purification, and a patron of sorcery and incantations. His half-fish, half-goat Sumerian counterpart Enki was the origin of the astrological figure of Capricorn.

eagle Any of many large, heavy-beaked, big-footed BIRDS OF PREY belonging to the family Accipitridae. Generally larger than HAWKS, they may resemble VULTURES in build and flight characteristics, but they have a fully feathered (often crested) head and strong feet equipped with great curved talons. Most species subsist mainly on live prey, which they generally capture on the ground. They mate for life. They nest in inaccessible places and use the same nest each year. Species vary from 24 in. to 3.3 ft (60 cm–1 m) long. The sea eagles include the BALD EAGLE. See also GOLDEN EAGLE.

Eakins \ˈā-kənz\, **Thomas** (1844–1916) U.S. painter. After art training at the École des Beaux-Arts in Paris (1866–70), he spent most of his life in his native Philadelphia. He reinforced his study of the live model at the Pennsylvania Academy of Fine Arts by studying anatomy at a medical college. *The Gross Clinic* (1875), depicting a surgical operation, was too realistic for his contemporaries but is now seen as his masterpiece. In 1876 he began teaching at the Pennsylvania Academy, but was forced to resign in 1886 for working with nude models in mixed classes. In addition to numerous portraits, he painted boating and other outdoor scenes that reflect his fascination with the human body in motion. He was the outstanding U.S. painter of the 19th cent.

Eames \ˈēmz, ˈāmz\, **Charles and Ray** (1907–1978, 1916–1988) U.S. designers. Born in St. Louis, Charles was trained as an architect; Ray (born Ray Kaiser), a native of Sacramento, studied painting with Hans HOFMANN (1933–39). After marrying in 1941, they moved to California, where they designed movie sets and researched the uses of plywood for furniture. In 1946 an exhibit at the Museum of Modern Art resulted in the mass production of their molded plywood chairs, and their furniture soon became known for its beauty, comfort, and elegance. After 1955 they made educational films, notably *Powers of Ten* (1969).

Charles and Ray Eames, molded plywood chair, 1946

ear Organ of HEARING and balance. The outer ear directs sound vibrations through the auditory canal to the eardrum, which transmits sound vibrations to the middle ear. There a chain of three tiny bones conducts the vibrations to the INNER EAR. Fluid inside the cochlea of the inner ear stimulates sensory hairs, which initiate the nerve impulses that travel to the brain. The inner ear is also an organ of balance: dizziness is felt when fluid inside the inner ear's semicircular canals continues to move and stimulate sensory hairs after the body has come to rest. The eustachian tube connects the middle ear with the nasal passages; that

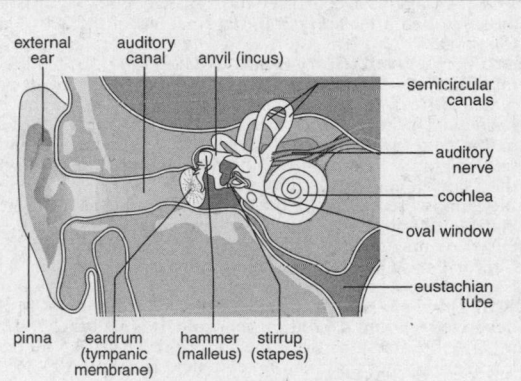

Ear The cartilaginous pinna and auditory canal direct sound waves to the middle ear. The eardrum, stretched across the end of the canal, vibrates as sound waves reach it. Vibrations are transmitted via three small bones (hammer, anvil, stirrup) to the membranous oval window that links the middle ear to the inner ear. The cochlea is a coiled, fluid-filled tube lined with sensory hairs. Vibrations in the oval window cause movement of the cochlear fluid, stimulating the hairs to initiate impulses which travel along a branch of the auditory nerve to the brain. The eustachian tube, running from the middle ear to the nasopharynx, equalizes pressure between the middle and outer ear. The fluid-filled semicircular canals play a role in balance, as hairs in the canals respond to movement-induced changes in the fluid by initiating impulses that travel to the brain.

connection allows colds to spread from the nasal passages to the middle ear, especially in infants and small children. See also DEAFNESS, OTITIS.

Earhart \ˈer-ˌhärt\, **Amelia (Mary)** (1897–1937) U.S. aviator. Born in Atchison, Kans., she was a social worker in Boston before becoming, in 1928, the first woman to cross the Atlantic in a plane, though as a passenger. In 1932 she accomplished the flight alone, becoming the first woman and the second person to do so. In 1935 she became the first person to fly solo from Hawaii to California. In 1937 she set out with a navigator, Fred Noonan, to fly around the world; they had completed over two-thirds of the distance when her plane disappeared without a trace in the central Pacific Ocean. Speculation about her fate has continued to the present.

earl See COUNT

Amelia Earhart

Early, Jubal A(nderson) (1816–1894) U.S. and Confederate military leader. Born in Franklin Co., Va., he graduated from West Point and served in the Mexican War. He opposed secession but supported Virginia when it joined the Confederacy. He fought at BULL RUN and in Virginia. In 1864 he led his forces down the Shenandoah Valley and threatened Washington, D.C., but was defeated by Union troops under Philip SHERIDAN. Relieved of command, he fled to Mexico and then Canada, returning in 1869.

Earnhardt, (Ralph) Dale (1951–2001) U.S. stock-car racer. Born in Kannopolis, N.C., he followed his father into NASCAR racing in 1975. He won his first Winston Cup title in 1980 and won six more (1986–87, 1990–91, 1993–94), before winning the sport's premier event, the Daytona 500, in 1998. An aggressive driver who relished bumps and spin-outs, he died after a crash in the final lap of the 2001 Daytona 500.

Earp \\'ərp\\, Wyatt (Berry Stapp) (1848–1929) U.S. frontiersman. Born in Monmouth, Ill., he worked in the 1870s as a police officer in Wichita and Dodge City, where he befriended Doc HOLLIDAY and Bat MASTERSON. By 1881 he had moved to TOMBSTONE, Ariz., living as a gambler and a saloon guard. There he and his four brothers feuded with the Clanton gang; in a shootout at the O.K. Corral, three of the gang were killed. In 1882 Morgan Earp was murdered, and Wyatt and others killed two suspects in retaliation. Accused of murder, he fled to Colorado and later settled in California. A posthumous biography (1931), written with Earp's collaboration, portrayed him as a fearless lawman.

earth Third PLANET in distance outward from the SUN. Believed to be about 4.6 billion years old, it is about 92,960,000 mi (149,573,000 km) from the sun, orbiting at 18.5 mi (29.8 km) per second, making one complete revolution in 365.25 days and rotating on its axis, once every 23 hours 56 minutes 4 seconds. The fifth-largest planet of the SOLAR SYSTEM, it has an equatorial circumference of 24,902 mi (40,076 km). Its total surface area is roughly 197,000,000 sq mi (509,600,000 sq km), of which about 29% is land. Earth's atmosphere consists chiefly of nitrogen and oxygen. Its only MOON orbits the planet at a distance of about 238,870 mi (384,400 km). The earth's surface is subdivided into seven CONTINENTS, surrounded by the so-called World OCEAN.

earth-crossing asteroid *or* **Apollo asteroid** ASTEROID whose path crosses earth's orbit. Some astronomers have mounted a full-scale search for such asteroids, partly to calculate whether they may collide with earth, in hopes of deflecting them. More than 400 are now cataloged. About 150 are larger than 0.6 mi (1 km) across; collisions of such asteroids with earth are believed to occur a few times every million years, producing an explosion with the force of several hydrogen bombs, possibly resulting in a disturbance in the world's climate or catastrophic tidal waves. The extinction of the dinosaurs may have been triggered by the impact just north of the Yucatán Peninsula of an asteroid or COMET of this size.

earthenware POTTERY that has been fired at low heat and is slightly more porous and coarser than STONEWARE and PORCELAIN. For practical and decorative purposes, it is usually glazed. The earliest known pottery, a soft earthenware excavated at a Neolithic settlement in Turkey, is about 9,000 years old. Earthenware is still widely used for cooking, freezing, and serving.

earthquake Sudden disturbance within the earth manifested at the surface by a shaking of the ground caused by SEISMIC WAVES. Most major earthquakes can be explained in terms of FAULTS and PLATE TECTONICS. Earthquake magnitude is usually expressed in terms of the RICHTER SCALE. Earthquake intensity is a qualitative measure (e.g., "barely felt" or "catastrophic destruction") of damage to terrain and structures at any given location. In general, a quake's intensity decreases with distance from its epicenter, the point directly above the source (or focus) of an earthquake. See also SEISMOLOGY.

earthshine Sunlight reflected from earth, especially that reflected onto the dark side of the MOON. For a few days before and after each new moon, this doubly reflected earthshine makes the whole moon visible, producing the effect of "the new moon holding the old moon in her arms."

earthworm Any of more than 1,800 species of terrestrial WORMS in the ANNELID class Oligochaeta (in particular, members of the genus *Lumbricus*). The most common U.S. species, *L. terrestris,* grows to about 10 in. (25 cm), but an Australian species can grow as long as 11 ft (3.3 m). The segmented body is tapered at both ends. Earthworms eat decaying organisms and, in the process, ingest soil, sand, and pebbles, aerating the soil, promoting drainage, and improving the soil's nutrient content for plants.

earwig Any of about 1,100 insect species (order Dermaptera) characterized by large membranous hind wings that lie hidden under short, leathery forewings. Species vary from 0.2 to 2 in. (5–50 mm) long, and all are flat, slender, and dark, with a shiny outer covering and simple biting mouthparts. Earwigs have a pair of horny, forceps-like tail filaments, or pincers (cerci), at the back end of the abdomen that may function in defense, capturing prey, or fighting courtship battles.

easement In Anglo-American property law, an interest in land owned by another that entitles its holder to a specific limited use or enjoyment, such as the right to cross the land or have a view over it continue unobstructed. It may be created expressly by a written deed of grant conveying the specific usage right, or it may be created by implication, as when an owner divides property into two parcels in such a way that an already existing, obvious, and continuous use of one parcel (e.g., for access) is necessary for the reasonable enjoyment of the other. Numerous kinds of easements have been important in Anglo-American law. See also REAL AND PERSONAL PROPERTY.

East African Rift System See GREAT RIFT VALLEY

East Anglia Traditional region of England. Consisting of the counties of Norfolk and SUFFOLK and parts of Cam-

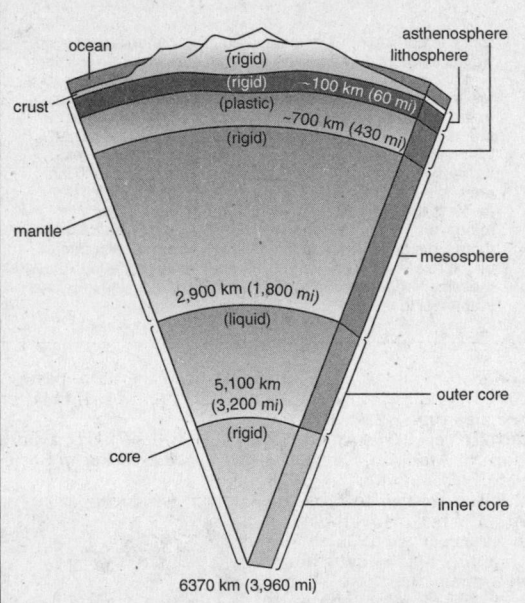

ocean
asthenosphere
lithosphere
(rigid)
(rigid) ~100 km (60 mi)
crust
(plastic)
~700 km (430 mi)
(rigid)
mantle
mesosphere
2,900 km (1,800 mi)
(liquid)
5,100 km (3,200 mi)
outer core
(rigid)
core
inner core
6370 km (3,960 mi)

Earth The earth's layers may be identified in two distinct ways. In chemical terms, the rock has three basic layers (left): the crust consists of granitic and basaltic rock, the mantle of silicate materials, and the core primarily of nickel and iron. In terms of physical properties, the earth has five principal layers (right): the lithosphere is a rigid outer layer, the asthenosphere is a thin layer of plastically deforming material that flows under stress, the mesosphere is a rigid layer that extends down to the core, the outer core is a viscous liquid in which the earth's magnetic field is believed to originate, and the inner core is solid. The layers are not drawn to scale.

bridgeshire and ESSEX, its traditional center is the city of NORWICH. The easternmost area in England, it has been settled for thousands of years; Colchester is the oldest recorded town in England. E. Anglia was one of the kingdoms of Anglo-Saxon England and was later ruled by Danes in the 9th cent. Along the coast are many important fishing ports and holiday resorts.

East China Sea See CHINA SEA

Easter Major Christian festival celebrating the resurrection of JESUS on the third day after his CRUCIFIXION. In Western churches it falls on a Sunday between March 22 and April 25, depending on the date of the first full moon after the spring equinox. In the Eastern Orthodox calendar it often falls later. Easterends the long period of penance called LENT. The word is probably derived from Eostre, a Germanic goddess of spring; some of its folk customs (e.g., the decoration of eggs as symbols of new life) may have originated with ancient pagan spring festivals.

Easter Island *Spanish* **Isla de Pascua** *native* **Rapa Nui** \'rä-pä-'nü-ē\ Island (pop., 1989 est.: 3,000), E Pacific Ocean. Located 2,200 mi (3,600 km) west of Chile, it has an area of 63 sq mi (163 sq km). Initially inhabited around A.D. 400 by Polynesians from the MARQUESAS, it has long been famous for its monolithic stone statues in human form. They are 10–40 ft (3–12 m) high and some weigh more than 50 tons. They were probably erected about 1000–1600 A.D. Annexed by Chile in 1888, the island has been declared a WORLD HERITAGE SITE.

Easter Island Sculptures cut from volcanic rock

Eastern Air Lines, Inc. Former U.S. airline that served primarily the E U.S. It was founded in 1928 as Pitcairn Aviation, Inc. Under its colorful presidents Eddie RICKENBACKER and astronaut Frank Borman (b.1928), it flourished for several decades, but financial reverses led to its sale to Texas Air Corp. in 1986 and liquidation in 1991.

Eastern Catholic Church See EASTERN RITE CHURCH

Eastern Orthodoxy *officially* **Orthodox Catholic Church** One of the three major branches of CHRISTIANITY. Its adherents live mostly in Greece, Russia, the Balkans, Ukraine, and the Middle East. Its titular head is the ecumenical patriarch of Constantinople (Istanbul), but its many territorial churches (including the huge RUSSIAN ORTHODOX CHURCH and the GREEK ORTHODOX CHURCH) are governed autonomously. The separation of the Eastern churches from the Western branch began with the division of the Roman empire under CONSTANTINE I. The SCHISM OF 1054 marked the formal break. Doctrinally, Eastern Orthodoxy differs from ROMAN CATHOLICISM in not accepting the primacy of the POPE and in not believing that the HOLY SPIRIT proceeds from both the Father (God) and the Son (Jesus). Today Eastern Orthodoxy has more than 200 million adherents worldwide.

Eastern Rite Church *or* **Eastern Catholic Church** Any of several Eastern Christian churches that trace their origins to ethnic or national Eastern churches but are united with the Roman Catholic church (see ROMAN CATHOLICISM). Most of these churches rejoined Rome in the 16th cent. or later. Eastern Rite churches acknowledge the authority of the POPE but retain their own ancient liturgies, rites, and customs more typical of EASTERN ORTHODOXY, such as allowing priests to marry. The Eastern Rite includes the Ukrainian Orthodox church, the MARONITE CHURCH, and some Armenians, Ruthenians, and Melchites (in Syria). Today Eastern Catholics number more than 12 million.

Eastern Woodlands Indians American Indians of the largely wooded area stretching east from the Mississippi River Valley to the Atlantic coastline and extending north into Canada and south into what are now Illinois and N. Carolina. Individual groups included the Abenaki, Woodland CREE, DELAWARE, FOX, HURON, Illinois, IROQUOIS, MAHICAN, Menominee, Miami, MICMAC, MOHAWK, MOHEGAN, MONTAGNAIS AND NASKAPI, OJIBWA, ONEIDA, Ottawa, PEQUOT, POWHATAN, SAUK, SENECA, Tuscarora, and WINNEBAGO.

Easter Rising *or* **Easter Rebellion** (1916) Republican insurrection in Ireland against the British. On Easter Monday, some 1,560 Irish Volunteers and 200 members of the Irish Citizen Army seized the General Post Office and other strategic points in Dublin. After five days of fighting, British troops put down the rebellion, and 15 of its leaders were tried and executed. Though the uprising itself had been unpopular with most of the Irish, the executions caused revulsion and heralded the end of British power in Ireland.

East India Co. *or* **English East India Co.** English CHARTERED COMPANY formed for trade with E. and S.E. Asia and India, incorporated in 1600. It began as a monopolistic trading body; trade in spices broadened to include cotton, silk, and other goods. Becoming involved in politics, it acted as the chief agent of British imperialism in India in the 18th–19th cent., exercising substantial power over much of the subcontinent. Its activities in China in the 19th cent. served as a catalyst for the expansion of British influence there and led to the first OPIUM WAR (1839–42). Its autonomy diminished after two acts of Parliament (1773, 1774) established a regulatory board responsible to Parliament. It ceased to exist as a legal entity in 1873.

East India Co., Dutch Trading company founded by the Dutch in 1602 to protect their trade in the Indian Ocean. The Dutch government granted it a trade monopoly in the waters between the Cape of Good Hope and the Straits of Magellan. Under forceful governors-general, including Anthony van DIEMEN, it was able to defeat the British fleet and largely displace the Portuguese in the E. Indies. It prospered through the 17th cent. but then began to decline; it was dissolved in 1799.

East India Co., French Trading company founded in 1664 to oversee French commerce with India, E. Africa, and the E. Indies. In competition with the already-established Dutch E. INDIA CO., it mounted expensive expeditions that were often harassed by the Dutch. It also suffered in the French economic crash of 1720, and by 1740 the value of its trade with India was half that of the English E. INDIA CO. It languished until its disappearance in the FRENCH REVOLUTION.

Eastman, George (1854–1932) U.S. inventor and manufacturer. Born in Waterville, N.Y., Eastman in 1880 perfected a process for making dry plates for photography. In 1889 he introduced transparent film, and in 1892 he reorganized his Rochester (N.Y.) company as the EASTMAN KODAK CO. The introduction of the first Kodak camera helped promote large-scale amateur photography, and by 1927 Eastman Kodak had a virtual monopoly of the U.S. photographic industry. The Univ. of Rochester named its Eastman School of Music in acknowledgment of his bequests.

Eastman Kodak Co. U.S. manufacturer of film, cameras, and photographic supplies. It was incorporated in Rochester, N.Y., in 1901 as the successor to a business founded in 1880 by George EASTMAN, whose innovations included the perfection of a process for making dry plates, roll film (1884), and the Kodak camera (1888), the first camera simple and portable enough to appeal to large numbers of amateur photographers. Its later innovations included the first home-movie equipment, the easy-to-use Kodachrome color slide film, the cartridge-loaded Instamatic cameras, and the highly automatic Disc cameras.

East Pacific Rise Submarine mountain range on the floor of the S. Pacific Ocean, roughly paralleling the W coast of S. America. The main portion lies about 2,000 mi (3,200 km) off the coast, and rises about 6,000–9,000 ft (1,800–2,700 m) above the surrounding seafloor. It has a generally smooth surface, and drops sharply away at the sides; it is composed largely of basic igneous crust, overlain or abutted by flat-lying sediments.

DE

East Prussia *German* **Ostpreussen** \'òst-ˌpròis-ᵊn\ Historical region and former Prussian province, east of POMERANIA. Part of the kingdom of PRUSSIA, in the 19th cent. it was a stronghold of Prussian Junkers, a military aristocracy. It was the scene of successful resistance against the Russians in World War I. Following the war it was separated from the rest of Germany by the POLISH CORRIDOR (1919); it was reunited with the Reich by the German conquest of Poland in 1939. In 1945 it was divided between the Soviet Union and Poland.

East River Navigable tidal strait linking Upper New York Bay with LONG ISLAND SOUND in NEW YORK CITY. It separates MANHATTAN and the BRONX from BROOKLYN and QUEENS. About 16 mi (26 km) long, it connects with the HUDSON RIVER.

East Timor *or* **Timor Timur** Country occupying the E half of the island of TIMOR, the nearby islands of Atauro (Kambing) and Jaco, and the enclave of Ambeno surrounding the town of Pante Makasar on Timor's NW coast, S.E. Asia.

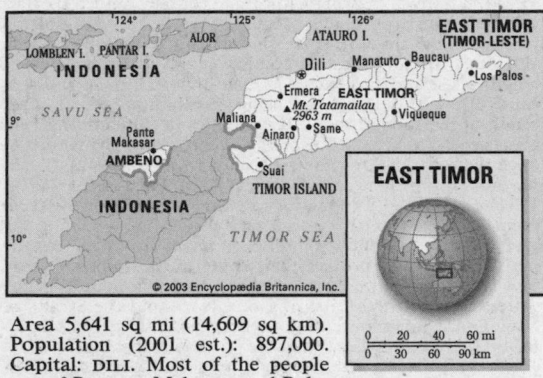

Area 5,641 sq mi (14,609 sq km). Population (2001 est.): 897,000. Capital: DILI. Most of the people are of Papuan, Malayan, and Polynesian origin. Languages: Tetum, Portuguese. Religion: predominantly Christian. Currency: U.S. dollar. E. Timor is rugged, with mountains rising to 9,700 ft (2,960 m). It has a dry tropical climate and moderate rainfall. Wildlife includes monkeys, deer, and crocodiles. Agriculture is the mainstay of the economy; products include copra,, hides, coffee, and coconut, as well as pearls and sandalwood. Soap, perfumes, and processed food are produced. The Portuguese first settled on Timor in 1520; the Dutch took the W portion of the island in 1613. The Dutch and Portuguese fought for supremacy; Portuguese sovereignty over the E half took full effect only in 1914. E. Timor province remained Portuguese until 1975, when the Fretilin political party declared its independence. Indonesia invaded and in 1976 formally annexed it. Tens of thousands died resisting the annexation or from famine and disease. In response to international pressure, Indonesia authorized a referendum on independence in 1999, and subsequently rescinded its annexation; the transfer of power was accompanied by widespread violence. The territory achieved full status as a sovereign state in 2002.

East–West Schism See SCHISM OF 1054

Eastwood, Clint(on) (b.1930) U.S. film actor and director. Born in San Francisco, he won attention in the television series *Rawhide* (1959–66) before his roles in three of Sergio LEONE's "spaghetti westerns" (1964–66) made him an international star. He returned to the U.S. for the hugely successful *Dirty Harry* (1971), the first of a series of action films in which he played laconic and dangerous heroes. He combined directing with acting in such films as *Play Misty for Me* (1971), *Pale Rider* (1985), *Unforgiven* (1992, Academy Award), *A Perfect World* (1993), and *The Bridges of Madison County* (1995). His interest in jazz led him to direct and produce *Bird* (1988), about Charlie PARKER.

eating disorders Abnormal eating patterns, including ANOREXIA NERVOSA, BULIMIA, compulsive overeating, and pica (appetite for nonfood substances). These disorders, which usually have a psychological component, may lead to underweight, OBESITY, or MALNUTRITION.

Eaton, Cyrus S(tephen) (1883–1979) Canadian-U.S. industrialist and philanthropist. Born in Pugwash, Nova Scotia, he built several electric-power plants in W Canada and soon diversified into other utilities, banking, and steel in the U.S. In 1930 he merged several steel companies to form Republic Steel, the third-largest U.S. steel company. An active advocate of nuclear disarmament and improved Soviet-U.S. relations, he helped inaugurate the PUGWASH CONFERENCES in 1957.

Ebb, Fred See John KANDER

Ebert \'ā-bert\, **Friedrich** (1871–1925) German politician. A trade unionist, he became chairman of the German SOCIAL DEMOCRATIC PARTY in 1913. Under his leadership, it gained increasing influence. After revolution broke out in 1918, he formed a coalition government, and in 1919 he was elected the first president of the WEIMAR REPUBLIC. Facing threats to the new government, he waged a civil war against Socialists and Communists and suppressed the reactionary Kapp Putsch. His authority was weakened in 1923 by the crisis over the RUHR OCCUPATION and his party's withdrawal from the governing coalition.

Ebla *modern* **Tell Mardikh** \'tel-'mär-dik\ Ancient city, NW Syria. Located south of ALEPPO, it dominated N Syria, Lebanon, and parts of N MESOPOTAMIA around 2600–2240 B.C. and enjoyed trade with states as far away as Egypt, Iran, and Sumer. The city's archives, dating to the 3rd millennium B.C., were discovered virtually intact in 1975 excavations.

Ebola \ē-'bō-lə\ VIRUS responsible for a severe and often fatal HEMORRHAGIC FEVER in primates, including humans. Initial symptoms are fever, severe headaches and muscle aches, and loss of appetite; blood clots and hemorrhaging appear within days, followed by nausea, vomiting, and diarrhea. Death occurs in 8–17 days; fatality rates range from 50% to 90%. There is no known treatment. It is named for the Ebola River in N Congo (Zaire), where it first emerged in 1976. How it attacks cells is unknown. It can be transmitted through contact with bodily fluids; unsanitary conditions and lack of adequate medical supplies have been factors in its spread.

ebony Wood of several species of trees of the genus *Diospyros* (family Ebenaceae), found widely in the tropics. The best is very heavy, almost black, and from heartwood only and is used for cabinetwork and inlaying, piano keys, knife handles, and turned articles. The best Indian and Ceylon ebony is produced by *D. ebenum*. Jamaica, American, or green ebony comes from *Brya ebenus*, a leguminous tree or shrub.

Ebro River \'ā-ˌbrō\ *ancient* Iberus. River, NE Spain. It rises in the Cantabrian Mtns. and flows for 565 mi (910 km) southeasterly to the Mediterranean Sea, between BARCELONA and VALENCIA. The second-longest Spanish river, it has the greatest discharge of any Spanish river, and its drainage basin is Spain's largest.

EB virus See EPSTEIN-BARR VIRUS

Eça de Queirós \'ē-sà-də-'kā-ˌrüsh\, **José Maria de** (1845–1900) Portuguese novelist. He began a career in law but turned to writing; later he held diplomatic posts. He was associated with the Generation of '70, a group of intellectuals committed to social and artistic reform. His novels, in which he introduced naturalism and realism to Portuguese fiction, include *The Sin of Father Amaro* (1876), *Cousin Bazilio* (1878), and his masterpiece, *The Maias* (1888). He is often considered his country's greatest novelist.

ecclesia \ə-'klē-zē-ə\ In ancient Greece, the assembly of citizens in a CITY-STATE. The Athenian ecclesia already existed in the 7th cent.; under SOLON it consisted of all male citizens of age 18 and over. It controlled policy, including the right to hear appeals in the public court, elect ARCHONS, and confer special privileges. Ecclesias existed in most Greek city-states through Roman times, though their powers faded under the empire.

echidna \i-'kid-nə\ *or* **spiny anteater** Either of two species of egg-laying mammals (MONOTREME family Tachyglossidae). Echidnas are stocky and virtually tailless. They have strong-clawed feet and spines on the upper part of the brownish body. The snout is narrow, and the tongue long and sticky for feeding on termites and ants. New Guinea echidnas are 18–31 in. (45–78 cm) long and piglike; echidnas of Australia and Tasmania are 14–21 in. (35–53 cm) long. See also ANTEATER, PANGOLIN.

echinacea \ˌe-ki-ˈnā-shə, ˌe-ki-ˈnā-sē-ə\ Any member of the coneflower genus *Echinacea* (COMPOSITE FAMILY). Commonly called the purple coneflower, echinacea is used as a border plant. The leaves and roots are used in herbal remedies to boost the immune system and in the treatment of colds and flu.

echinoderm \i-ˈkī-nə-ˌdərm\ Any of various marine INVERTEBRATES (phylum Echinodermata) characterized by a hard spiny covering, a calcite skeleton, and five-rayed radial body symmetry. About 6,000 existing species are grouped in six classes: feather stars and sea lilies (Crinoidea), STARFISHES (Asteroidea), brittle stars and basket stars (Ophiuroidea), SEA URCHINS (Echinoidea), sea daisies (Concentricycloidea), and SEA CUCUMBERS (Holothurioidea). Echinoderms are found throughout all the oceans. Most species have numerous tube feet modified for locomotion, respiration, tunneling, sensory perception, feeding, and grasping. Movement of water through a water vascular system controls extension and retraction of the tube feet.

Echo In GREEK MYTHOLOGY, a mountain NYMPH transformed into a disembodied voice. According to OVID, HERA punished Echo for her chattering by depriving her of independent speech, rendering her able only to repeat the last words spoken by another. When NARCISSUS failed to requite her love, she faded away into a voice only.

echolocation \ˌe-kō-lō-ˈkā-shən\ Physiological process for locating objects (such as prey) by emitting sound waves that are reflected back by the objects. Echolocation is used by an animal to avoid obstacles, find food, and interact socially. Most BATS employ echolocation, as do most, if not all, toothed whales, a few SHREWS, and two kinds of birds (oilbirds and certain cave swiftlets). Echolocation pulses consist of short bursts of sound at frequencies ranging from about 1,000 Hz in birds to at least 200,000 Hz in whales.

Eck, Johann *orig.* Johann Maier (1486–1543) German Roman Catholic theologian. Ordained in 1508, he taught theology at the Univ. of Ingolstadt. Initially friendly with Martin LUTHER, Eck assailed Luther's NINETY-FIVE THESES as heretical. LEO X commissioned Eck to publish and enforce the papal bull condemning the Theses. Eck's *Enchiridion Against the Lutherans* (1525), summarizing contested Catholic beliefs, Protestant objections to them, and Catholic answers to the objections, became the best-known Catholic polemical handbook of the 16th cent.

Eckhart, Meister (*orig.* **Johannes**) (c.1260–1327/28?) German theologian and mystic. He studied theology at Cologne and Paris and became a popular preacher and teacher. His mystical writings examined the relationship between God and humanity; he pictured the soul achieving complete union with God and posited something (Godhead) beyond God. He took up a professorship in Cologne in his 60th year; shortly thereafter he was charged with heresy. He died before he could rebut a second charge.

eclampsia See PREECLAMPSIA AND ECLAMPSIA

eclipse Complete or partial obscuring of one celestial body by another as seen from a third when they are aligned. The eclipsing body can come between an observer and a luminous source, as when the moon comes between earth and the sun (solar eclipse), or between the luminous source and the eclipsed object, which is darkened by its shadow, as when earth comes between the moon and the sun (lunar eclipse). In a total eclipse, the object is in the central umbra, where no direct sunlight penetrates, and in a partial eclipse, it is in the penumbra, reached by light from part of the sun's disk. Records of eclipses date back to the earliest civilizations, some of which (e.g., Babylonian, Maya, Chinese) learned to predict eclipses accurately. Solar eclipses visible from different parts of earth occur two to five times a year; one total solar eclipse occurs in most years. When earth is closest to the sun and the moon farthest from earth, the moon's shadow may fall entirely within the sun's disk, with a ring of the disk visible around it (annular eclipse). Total solar eclipses allow studies of the CHROMOSPHERE and CORONA. Lunar eclipses occur as often as solar eclipses; during total lunar eclipses, the moon may appear deep red from sunlight refracted through earth's atmosphere.

eclipsing variable star *or* **eclipsing binary** BINARY STAR in an orbit whose plane passes through or very near earth, from which one star is seen to pass periodically before the other and diminish its light through an ECLIPSE. The star Algol, in the constellation Perseus, was the first such star recognized (1782); several thousand are now known. Comparing eclipse duration to orbital period yields the stars' sizes. See also VARIABLE STAR.

ecliptic \i-ˈklip-tik\ Apparent path of the SUN among the constellations over a year, or projection on the CELESTIAL SPHERE of earth's orbit around the sun, which intersects the plane of the celestial equator at the vernal and autumnal EQUINOXES. The constellations of the ZODIAC lie along the ecliptic.

eclogue \ˈek-ˌlog, ˈek-ˌläg\ Short, usually pastoral, poem in the form of a dialogue or soliloquy. The eclogue as a pastoral form first appeared in the idylls of THEOCRITUS, was adopted by VIRGIL, and was revived in the Renaissance by DANTE, PETRARCH, and BOCCACCIO. Edmund SPENSER's *Shepheardes Calender*, a series of 12 eclogues, was the first outstanding pastoral poem in English. 18th-cent. English poets used the eclogue for ironic verse on nonpastoral subjects. See also PASTORAL.

Eco \ˈā-kō, *Engl* ˈe-kō\, **Umberto** (b.1932) Italian critic and novelist. In *The Open Work* (1962), he suggested that some literature and modern music is fundamentally ambiguous and invites the audience to participate in the interpretive and creative process. Later critical works include *A Theory of Semiotics* (1976) and *The Limits of Interpretation* (1991). His novels include the erudite but best-selling murder mystery *The Name of the Rose* (1980; film, 1986), *Foucault's Pendulum* (1988), and *The Island of the Day Before* (1995).

E. coli \ˈkō-ˌlī\ *in full* **Escherichia coli** \ˌesh-ə-ˈri-kē-ə-ˈkō-ˌlī\ Species of BACTERIA that inhabits the stomach and intestines. *E. coli* can be transmitted by water, milk, food, or flies and other insects. Mutations can lead to strains that cause diarrhea. Therapy consists largely of fluid replacement, though specific drugs sometimes help. The illness is usually self-limiting, with no long-lasting effects. However, one dangerous strain causes bloody diarrhea, kidney fail-

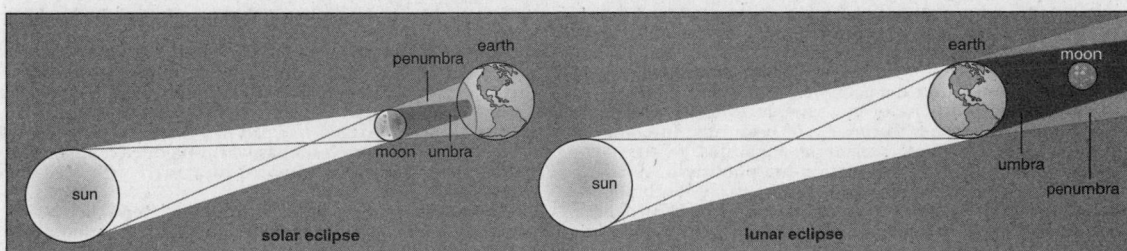

Eclipse A solar eclipse occurs when the moon passes between the earth and the sun. Observers in the moon's penumbral shadow see a partial blocking of the sun; those in the umbra see the sun completely covered by the moon. A lunar eclipse occurs when the moon passes into the earth's shadow. In the penumbra, the moon may appear dimmed; when it enters the umbra, the full moon becomes quite dark and may take on a reddish tinge.

ure, and death in extreme cases. Pasteurization, cooking, proper storage, and washing reduce likelihood of infection.

ecology Study of the relationships between organisms and their environment. Physiological ecology focuses on the relationships between individual organisms and the physical and chemical features of their environment. Behavioral ecologists study the behaviors of organisms as they react to their environment. Population ecology, including population GENETICS, studies processes that affect the distribution and abundance of animal and plant populations. Community ecology studies how communities of plant and animal populations function and are organized. Paleoecology studies the ecology of FOSSIL organisms. Applied ecology applies ecological principles to the management of populations of crops and animals. Theoretical ecologists provide simulations of particular practical problems and develop models of general ecological relevance.

econometrics Statistical and mathematical analysis of economic relationships. Econometrics creates equations to describe phenomena such as the relationship between changes in price and demand. Econometricians estimate production functions and cost functions for firms, supply-and-demand functions for industries, income distribution in an economy, macroeconomic models and models of the monetary sector for policy makers, and business cycles and growth for forecasting. Their findings help both private businesses and the government make decisions and set MONETARY and FISCAL POLICY.

Economic Cooperation and Development, Organization for See ORGANIZATION FOR ECONOMIC COOPERATION AND DEVELOPMENT

economic development Process whereby simple, low-income national economies dependent on agriculture or resource extraction are transformed into modern industrial and diversified economies. Economic development projects have typically involved large capital investments in infrastructure (roads, irrigation networks, etc.), industry, education, and financial institutions. More recently, the realization that creating capital-intensive industrial sectors provides only limited employment and can disrupt the rest of the economy has led to smaller-scale economic development programs that aim to utilize the specific resources and natural advantages of developing countries and to avoid disruption of their social and economic structures.

economic forecasting Prediction of future economic activity and developments. Economic forecasts, which range from a few weeks to many years, are widely used in business and government to help formulate policy and strategy. Macroeconomic forecasts predict the course of the aggregate economy and concentrate on variables such as interest rates, the rate of inflation, and the rate of unemployment. Forecasts of private consumption and investment, government expenditures, and net exports help those responsible for fiscal policy (e.g., by predicting the likely economic effects of a proposed change in tax policy). Microeconomic forecasts project the effects of change at the level of an industry or a firm, based on assumptions about the aggregate economy. See also ECONOMETRICS, MACROECONOMICS, MICROECONOMICS.

economic indicator Statistic used to measure the state of general economic activity or to predict it in the future. A leading indicator is one that tends to turn up or down before the general economy does (e.g., building permits, common stock prices, and business inventories). Coincident indicators move in line with the economy; lagging indicators change direction after the economy does.

economic planning Use of government to make economic decisions with respect to the use of resources. In communist countries with a state planning apparatus, LAND, CAPITAL, and the means of production are publicly owned and centrally allocated, and the government makes both microeconomic decisions (what goods and services to produce, the quantities to produce, the prices to charge, the wages to pay, etc.) and macroeconomic decisions (the rate of investment, the extent of foreign trade, etc.). In most industrialized countries, few key economic sectors are publicly owned, and governments influence their economies indirectly through monetary and fiscal policies. Japan is the most notable example of economic planning in a capitalist framework; government and industry cooperate closely in planning patterns of capital investment, research and development, and export strategies.

economics Social science that analyzes the consequences of choices made concerning scarce productive resources. Economics is the study of how individuals and societies choose to employ those resources: what goods and services will be produced, how they will be produced, and how they will be distributed among the members of society. Economics is customarily divided into MICROECONOMICS (which focuses on individual consumers, firms, and industries) and MACROECONOMICS (which focuses particularly on the rate of economic growth, the inflation rate, and the rate of unemployment). Specialized areas include agricultural economics, ECONOMIC DEVELOPMENT, environmental economics, industrial organization, international trade, LABOR ECONOMICS, money supply and banking, public finance, urban economics, and WELFARE ECONOMICS. Mathematical economics and ECONOMETRICS provide tools used by all economists. Economics overlaps with many other disciplines, notably history, MATHEMATICS, POLITICAL SCIENCE, and SOCIOLOGY.

Economist, The British weekly magazine of news and opinion, founded in 1843, generally regarded as one of the world's preeminent journals of its kind. Despite its name, it gives wide-ranging coverage of general news and particularly of international political developments and prospects bearing on the world's economy. Its editorial position is centrist.

ecosystem \\'ē-kō-ˌsis-təm\\ Complex of living organisms, their physical environment, and all their interrelationships in a particular unit of space. An ecosystem's abiotic (nonbiological) constituents include minerals, climate, soil, water, sunlight, and all other nonliving elements; its biotic constituents consist of all its living members. Two major forces link these constituents: the flow of energy and the cycling of nutrients. Energy (originally from the sun) and organic matter are passed along an ecosystem's FOOD CHAIN. The study of ecosystems is now instrumental in assessing and controlling the environmental effects of agricultural development and industrialization. See also BIOME.

Ecstasy Synthetic AMPHETAMINE analogue. A euphoria-inducing stimulant and HALLUCINOGEN, it was developed in 1913 as an appetite suppressant and was used from the 1970s as a psychotherapeutic drug. By increasing the brain's production of SEROTONIN and DOPAMINE, it gives users feelings of increased energy and happiness; harmful effects can include increased blood pressure, confusion, depression, and paranoia. In the 1980s, parties and dances that featured Ecstasy use ("raves") became popular. Despite its 1985 ban in the U.S. and abroad, the drug remains popular in youth subcultures.

ectopic pregnancy \\ek-'tä-pik\\ *or* **extrauterine pregnancy** Condition in which a fertilized egg is implanted outside the UTERUS (see FERTILIZATION). Early on, it may resemble a normal PREGNANCY. Later, most patients have pain as the growing embryo stretches the structure it is attached to. Rupture may cause life-threatening bleeding. A tubal pregnancy occurs in a fallopian tube. In an ovarian pregnancy, the egg is fertilized before it leaves the OVARY. Implantation elsewhere in the abdomen produces an abdominal pregnancy.

ectotherm \\'ek-tə-ˌthərm\\ Any so-called cold-blooded animal; that is, any animal whose regulation of body temperature depends on external sources, such as sunlight or a heated rock surface. The ectotherms include the FISHES, AMPHIBIANS, REPTILES, and INVERTEBRATES. Ectotherms do not require as much fuel as warm-blooded animals (ENDOTHERMS), but most cannot deal as well with cold surroundings.

Ecuador *officially* **Republic of Ecuador** Republic, NW S. America. Area: 109,480 sq mi (283,560 sq km), including the GALÁPAGOS ISLANDS. Population (2000): 12,646,000. Capital: QUITO. The people are about 50% Indian (mostly QUECHUA) and 40% mestizo (Indian-Spanish). Language: Spanish (official). Religion: predominantly Roman Catholicism. Currency: U.S. dollar. Its Pacific coastal lowlands rise

Map: Ecuador

PACIFIC OCEAN

COLOMBIA

Ancón de Sardinas Bay
San Lorenzo
Valdez
Esmeraldas
Muisne
Tulcán
San Gabriel
COTACHI-CAYAPAS ECOLOGICAL RESERVE
CHONGÓN MTS.
Ibarra
Otavalo
CAYAMBE-COCA ECOLOGICAL RESERVE
Equator
Santo Domingo de los Colorados
Quito
Cayambe Volcano 18,996 ft.
Cotopaxi Volcano 19,347 ft.
Aguarico
Napo
Puerto Francisco de Orellana
YASUNI NATIONAL PARK
Manta
Portoviejo
Quevedo
Latacunga
Ambato
Tena
Napo
PLATA I.
Balzar
Babahoyo
Chimborazo Volcano 20,701 ft.
Riobamba
Puyo
EASTERN REGION
Jipijapa
Sangay Volcano 17,159 ft.
SANGAY NATIONAL PARK
Guayaquil
Macas
Tigre
Salinas
Santa Elena Point
SANTA ELENA PENINSULA
PUNÁ I.
Azogues
Naranjal
Cuenca
Girón
General Leonidas Plaza Gutiérrez
CORDILLERA DE CUTUCÚ
Ecuador repudiates the entire eastern boundary established by the Rio Protocol of 1942.
Gulf of Guayaquil
Machala
Jubones
Pasaje
Huaquillas
Piñas
Yantzaza
PERU
Macará
Zamora
CORDILLERA DEL CÓNDOR
Santiago
Sullana

©1999, Encyclopædia Britannica, Inc.

ECUADOR

Scale 1: 10,610,000
0   50   100 mi
0   80   160 km

to the peaks and highlands of the ANDES, which give way to the Ecuadorian portion of the tropical AMAZON basin in the east. The Andes rise dramatically in two north-to-south chains separated by high valleys. The highest peak is CHIMBORAZO; COTOPAXI, the world's highest active volcano, is nearby. The country lies in an active earthquake zone. Almost half is forested, with tropical rain forests in the east. Straddling the equator, it experiences climate variations from tropical in the lowlands to temperate in the highlands. It has a developing economy based primarily on trade, followed by manufacturing and agriculture. Principal exports include crude petroleum, shrimp, bananas, coffee, and cacao. It is a republic with one legislative house; its head of state and government is the president. Ecuador was conquered by the INCAS in A.D. 1450 and came under Spanish control in 1534. Under the Spaniards it was a part of the viceroyalty of Peru until 1740, when it became a part of the viceroyalty of NEW GRANADA. It gained its independence from Spain in 1822 as part of the republic of Gran Colombia, and in 1830 became a sovereign state. A succession of authoritarian governments ruled into the mid-20th cent., and economic hardship and social unrest prompted the military to take a strong role. Border disputes led Peru to invade Ecuador in 1941; the dispute flared up again in the 1980s. The economy, booming in the 1970s with petroleum profits, was depressed in the 1980s by reduced oil prices and earthquake damage. A new constitution was adopted in 1979. In the 1990s social unrest caused political instability and several changes of heads of state.

ecumenism \e-ˈkyü-mə-ˌni-zəm, ˈe-kyü-mə-ˌni-zəm\ Movement toward unity or cooperation among the Christian churches. The first major step in the direction of ecumenism was the International Missionary Conference of 1910, a gathering of Protestants. Several Protestant denominations inaugurated a Life and Work Conference in 1925 (on social and practical problems) and a Faith and Order Conference (on church doctrine and governance) in 1927. After World War II the WORLD COUNCIL OF CHURCHES was established; the International Missionary Conference joined it in 1961. The Roman Catholic church has also shown strong interest in improving interchurch relations since the Second VATICAN COUNCIL (1962–65). The more conservative or fundamentalist Protestant denominations have generally refrained from involvement.

eczema See DERMATITIS.

Edda Body of ancient Icelandic literature. Contained in two 13th-cent. books, it is the fullest source for modern knowl-

edge of Germanic mythology. The *Prose Edda* (or *Younger Edda*; c.1222) is a handbook on poetics by SNORRI STURLUSON that includes tales from Norse mythology. The *Poetic Edda* (*Elder Edda*; c.1250–1300) is a collection of mythological and heroic poems of unknown authorship composed around 800–1100, the oldest surviving antecedents of the *Nibelungenlied* legends.

Eddington, Arthur (Stanley) (*later* Sir Arthur) (1882–1944) British astronomer, physicist, and mathematician. At Cambridge Univ. he won every mathematical honor and became director of its observatory in 1914. Religious and pacifistic, he declared that the world's meaning could not be discovered by science. His studies included stellar structure, subatomic sources of stellar energy, white dwarf stars, and diffuse matter in interstellar space. He believed that unifying quantum theory and general relativity would permit the calculation of certain universal constants.

Eddy, Mary Baker *orig.* Mary Morse Baker (1821–1910) U.S. religious leader, founder of CHRISTIAN SCIENCE. Born near Concord, N.H., she married in 1843; her husband died the following year, and she married again in 1853. She suffered from ill health for much of her life. In 1866 she suffered a severe fall and lost hope for recovery, only to be healed by reading the New Testament. She considered that moment her discovery of Christian Science and spent several years evolving her system. In 1875 she published *Science and Health*, which her followers regarded as divinely inspired. Having divorced in 1873, in 1877 she

Mary Baker Eddy

married one of her followers, Asa G. Eddy (d.1882). The First Church of Christ, Scientist was organized in 1879. Eddy also founded three periodicals, notably the *Christian Science Monitor* (1908).

edelweiss \ˈā-dᵊl-ˌvīs, ˈā-dᵊl-ˌwīs\ Perennial plant (*Leontopodium alpinum*) of the COMPOSITE FAMILY, native to alpine areas of Europe and S. America. It has 2–10 yellow flower heads in a dense cluster. Below it, 6–9 lance-shaped, woolly, white leaves are arranged in the form of a star. Most varieties are ornamentals.

edema \i-ˈdē-mə\ Abnormal accumulation of watery fluid in the spaces between CONNECTIVE-TISSUE cells, usually a symptom of diseases of the kidneys, heart, veins, or lymphatic system. Treatment must usually focus on the underlying cause. Edema may be local (e.g., HIVES from allergies), or generalized (also called dropsy), sometimes involving body cavities as well as tissues.

Eden, (Robert) Anthony *later* Earl of Avon (1897–1977) British politician. Elected to the House of Commons in 1923, he became foreign secretary in 1935 but resigned in 1938 to protest Neville CHAMBERLAIN's policy of appeasement. He held the post again 1940–45 and 1951–55, and helped settle the Anglo–Iranian oil dispute and arranged an armistice in Indochina. Succeeding Winston CHURCHILL as prime minister in 1955, he attempted to ease international tension by welcoming Nikita KHRUSHCHEV to Britain. His fall began when he supported an Anglo-French intervention in the SUEZ CRISIS. He resigned in 1957.

Ederle \ˈed-ər-lē\, **Gertrude (Caroline)** (b.1906) U.S. swimmer, the first woman to swim the English Channel. Born in New York City, in 1924 she shared an Olympic gold medal (400-m relay). In 1926 she swam the 35-mi (56-km) Channel in 14 hours 31 minutes, breaking the men's record by 1 hour 59 minutes. Her record was broken only in 1950, by Florence Chadwick (13 hours 20 minutes).

Edessa \i-ˈde-sə\ Chief city (pop., 1991: 18,000), Macedonia, Greece. Located on a steep bluff above the valley of the Loudhiás River, it is a prominent trading and agricultural center. Fought over by the Bulgarians, Byzantines, and

Serbs, Edessa was taken by the Turks in the 15th cent. In 1912 it passed to Greece.

Edgar the Aetheling \'ath-ə-liŋ\ (d.c.1125) Anglo-Saxon prince. He was proposed as king of England after the Battle of HASTINGS (1066) but instead served the Norman kings WILLIAM I the Conqueror and WILLIAM II. Rebellions in favor of the aetheling (prince) continued in England until 1069. Edgar led the Norman conquest of Apulia in S Italy (1086) but was deprived of his Norman lands by William II in 1091. In 1097, on William's orders, he overthrew Donald Bane, a Scottish king hostile to the Normans.

Edgeworth, Maria (1767–1849) British-Irish writer. From age 15 she assisted her father in managing his estate, gaining a knowledge of rural economy and the Irish peasantry. Her early children's stories, published as *The Parent's Assistant* (1796), feature the first convincing child characters since Shakespeare. *Castle Rackrent* (1800), her first novel, revealed her gift for social observation and authentic dialogue. Other notable works are *Belinda* (1801) and the six-volume *Tales of Fashionable Life* (1809–12), including the novel *The Absentee*.

Edgeworth-Kuiper belt See KUIPER BELT

Edinburgh \'e-d°n-ˌbər-ə\ City (pop., 1998 est.: 450,000) capital of Scotland. Located in SE Scotland, the original burgh, now known as Old Town, arose in the 11th cent. A.D., around Edinburgh Castle, the royal residence of Malcolm III MacDuncan. In 1329 ROBERT I the Bruce granted Edinburgh a town charter; it became the capital of the Scottish kingdom in 1437. The city was destroyed in 1544 in the border wars with England; its characteristic use of stone architecture began with this rebuilding. Edinburgh was home to such luminaries as David HUME, Adam SMITH, Robert BURNS, and Walter SCOTT. It was the birthplace of the *ENCYCLOPÆDIA BRITANNICA* (1768) and the *Edinburgh Review* (1802). It is the center of Scottish culture and education, and is home to the Univ. of EDINBURGH, National Library, National Gallery, Royal Scottish Museum, and the new Scots national parliament.

Edinburgh, University of Private university in Edinburgh, Scotland. Founded under Presbyterian auspices in 1583, it achieved university status around 1621 after a school of divinity was added. Graduates include Sir Walter SCOTT, John Stuart MILL, Thomas CARLYLE, Charles DARWIN, Robert Louis STEVENSON, and Alexander Graham BELL. Current enrollment is about 18,000.

Edinburgh Festival International festival of the arts, with emphasis on music and drama. Founded in 1947, it is held for three weeks each summer. Its theatrical offerings include plays by major international companies; plays premiered include T. S. ELIOT's *The Cocktail Party* (1949) and Thornton WILDER's *The Matchmaker* (1954). Musically, it offers concerts, recitals, and operas by international companies, orchestras, and soloists. The adjunct Edinburgh Fringe, the largest arts festival in the world, attracts amateur theater groups and has launched such works as *Beyond the Fringe* (1960) and Tom STOPPARD's *Rosencrantz and Guildenstern Are Dead* (1966).

Edison, Thomas Alva (1847–1931) U.S. inventor. Born in Milan, Ohio, he had very little formal schooling. He set up a laboratory in his father's basement at age 10. He worked

Thomas Edison and his phonograph, photo by Mathew Brady, 1878

as a telegrapher (1862–68) before deciding to pursue invention and entrepreneurship. He was strongly motivated to overcome his handicap of partial deafness. For Western Union he developed a machine capable of sending four telegraph messages down one wire, only to sell the invention to Western Union's rival, Jay GOULD, for more than $100,000. He created the world's first industrial-research laboratory, in Menlo Park, N.J. There he invented the carbon-button transmitter (1877), still used in telephone speakers and microphones today; the phonograph (1877); and the incandescent lightbulb (1879). In 1882 he supervised the installation of the world's first permanent commercial central power system, in lower Manhattan. In 1884 he built a new laboratory in W. Orange, N.J. Its first major endeavor was the commercialization of the phonograph, which A. G. BELL had improved on since Edison's initial invention. At the new laboratory Edison and his team also developed an early movie camera, an instrument for viewing moving pictures, and the alkaline storage battery. Edison continued to work into his 80s. Singly or jointly, he held a world-record 1,093 patents. He always invented with the object of devising something new that he could manufacture. More than any other person, he laid the basis for the technological revolution of the modern electric world.

Edmonton City (pop., 1996: 616,000), capital of Alberta. It began as a series of fur-trading posts built from 1795. With the arrival of the railway and settlers in the late 19th cent., Edmonton began to prosper economically, and in 1905 it became the capital of the new province of Alberta. The 1947 discovery of petroleum in the area greatly stimulated the city's growth. It is the distribution center of NW Canada and home to the Univ. of Alberta (1906).

Edom \'ē-dəm\ Ancient country, south of the DEAD SEA. The Edomites probably occupied the area around the 13th cent. B.C. Though closely related to the Israelites, they were in frequent conflict and were probably subject to the Israelite kingdom (11th–10th cent. B.C.). Located on the trade route between Arabia and the Mediterranean, Edom was known for its copper industry. The Edomites later migrated to S JUDAEA.

Edo period \'ed-ō\ (1603–1867) Cultural period of Japanese history corresponding to the political period of governance by the TOKUGAWA SHOGUNATE. Edo (present-day Tokyo), chosen as Japan's new capital, became the site of a thriving urban culture. In literature, the Edo period saw BASHO's development of the HAIKU and the virtuoso comic linked-verse compositions and humorous novels of Ihara Saikaku (1642–1693); in theater, both KABUKI (with live actors) and bunraku (with puppets) entertained the townsmen. The development of multicolored printing techniques made it possible for ordinary people to obtain woodblock prints (see UKIYO-E). In scholarship, National Learning called attention to Japan's most ancient poetry and oldest written histories. Dutch Learning, the study of Europe and its sciences, became popular, as did NEO-CONFUCIANISM. See also GENROKU PERIOD.

education Learning that takes place in schools or schoollike environments (formal education) or in the world at large; the transmission of the values and accumulated knowledge of a society. In primitive cultures there is little formal education. In more complex societies, the school and teacher become necessary. The philosophy and content of formal education, its duration, and who receives it have varied widely. Some philosophers (e.g., John LOCKE) have seen individuals as blank slates onto which knowledge can be written; others (e.g., Jean-Jacques ROUSSEAU) have seen the innate human state as desirable in itself and therefore to be tampered with as little as possible, a view often taken in ALTERNATIVE EDUCATION. See also ELEMENTARY EDUCATION, HIGHER EDUCATION, KINDERGARTEN, PROGRESSIVE EDUCATION, PUBLIC SCHOOL, SPECIAL EDUCATION.

Education, U.S. Department of Federal executive division responsible for carrying out government education programs. Established in 1980 by Jimmy CARTER, it seeks to ensure access to education and to improve the quality of education nationwide.

educational psychology Branch of psychology concerned with the learning processes and psychological issues associated with the teaching and training of students. The educational psychologist studies cognitive development, aptitude and learning measurement, the creative process, and motivational forces that influence student–teacher dynamics. Two early leaders in the field were G. Stanley HALL and Edward L. Thorndike (1874–1949).

Edward I *known as* **Edward Longshanks** (1239–1307) King of England (1272–1307). The eldest son of HENRY III, he supported his father in a civil war with the barons, contributing to Henry's defeat at the battle of Lewes (1264) but later winning out over the rebels. Edward's reign was a time of rising national consciousness, in which he strengthened the crown against the feudal nobility. He fostered the development of Parliament and played an important role in defining English common law. He conquered Wales (1277), but his conquest of Scotland (1296), including the defeat of William WALLACE, was undone by later revolts. He died on a campaign against ROBERT I, who had proclaimed himself king of Scotland the previous year.

Edward II *known as* **Edward of Caernarvon** \kär-ˈnä-vən\ (1284–1327) King of England (1307–27). The son of Edward I, he angered the barons by ennobling his favorite, Piers Gaveston; the barons drew up the Ordinances (1311) to limit the king's power over finances and appointments, and executed the arrogant Gaveston (1312). The English defeat by ROBERT I at the Battle of BANNOCKBURN (1314) ensured Scottish independence and left Edward at the mercy of powerful barons, notably Thomas of Lancaster. He defeated and executed Lancaster in 1322 and revoked the Ordinances. His queen, Isabella, helped her lover Roger de Mortimer and other dissatisfied nobles depose Edward in favor of his son, EDWARD III. Edward II was imprisoned and probably murdered.

Edward III *known as* **Edward of Windsor** (1312–1377) King of England (1327–77). His mother, Isabella of France, helped depose his father, EDWARD II, and crowned the 15-year-old Edward in his place. Isabella and her lover Roger de Mortimer governed in Edward's name for four years and persuaded him to grant the Scots their independence (1328). After having Mortimer executed in 1330, Edward asserted his right to the French crown and began the HUNDRED YEARS' WAR. He defeated the French at the Battle of CRÉCY (1346) and captured Calais (1347), though lack of funds forced him to sign a truce. The Scots surrendered to Edward in 1356, and his son EDWARD THE BLACK PRINCE won a major victory for the English at the Battle of POITIERS. In 1360 Edward gave up his claim to the French crown in return for Aquitaine. The war later resumed when CHARLES V repudiated the Treaty of Calais; Edward lost Aquitaine, and he signed a new truce in 1375. In his later years he fell under the influence of his greedy mistress Alice Perrers and his son JOHN OF GAUNT.

Edward IV (1442–1483) King of England (1461–70, 1471–83). His father, a Yorkist claimant to the throne, was killed in 1461, and Edward was crowned, thanks largely to his cousin the earl of WARWICK. This alliance did not last, and Edward was deposed and fled in 1470. He returned (1471) to become a leading participant in the Wars of the ROSES, killing Warwick and nearly all the Lancastrian leaders. After murdering HENRY VI and repelling an attack on London, Edward remained secure as king. He invaded France unsuccessfully, but made an excellent financial settlement. His administrative achievements made his reign a time of prosperity and success. His two sons were probably murdered in the Tower of London, and his eldest daughter married HENRY VII.

Edward VI (1537–1553) King of England and Ireland (1547–53). Son of HENRY VIII and Jane SEYMOUR, he succeeded to the throne after Henry's death. During the young king's reign, power was wielded by the duke of SOMERSET and the duke of NORTHUMBERLAND. Facing death from tuberculosis, Edward was persuaded to exclude his half sisters (later MARY I and ELIZABETH I), from the succession in favor of Northumberland's daughter-in-law, Lady Jane GREY.

Edward VII *orig.* Albert Edward (1841–1910) King of the United Kingdom (1901–10). Son of Queen VICTORIA, he was noted for his interest in racing and yachting. For his sometimes scandalous personal behavior, he was excluded by Victoria from most affairs of state until he was over 50 years old. His reign helped restore luster to the monarchy after her long seclusion as a widow. Immensely popular, he helped pave the way for the ENTENTE CORDIALE with his state visit to Paris in 1903.

Edward VIII (1894–1972) King of the United Kingdom (1936). Son of GEORGE V, he made extensive goodwill tours of the British empire and became very popular with the English people. In 1930 he became friends with Wallis Simpson and her husband and by 1934 had fallen in love with her. In January 1936 he succeeded to the throne. Unable to gain acceptance for their proposed marriage, he abdicated in December, becoming the only British sovereign to resign voluntarily. He was created duke of Windsor and in 1937 married Simpson, who became the duchess of WINDSOR. After 1945 the couple lived in Paris. Not until 1967 were they invited to attend an official public ceremony with the royal family.

Edward VIII The Duke and Duchess of Windsor, photo by Cecil Beaton, 1937

Edward, Lake Lake, E Africa. One of the great lakes of the W GREAT RIFT VALLEY, it lies on the border of Congo (Zaire) and Uganda and is 48 mi (77 km) long and 26 mi (42 km) wide. It empties north through the Semliki River to Lake ALBERT. The lake abounds in fish; wildlife about its shores is protected within Virunga and Queen Elizabeth National Parks. It was named by H. M. STANLEY in 1888–89.

Edwards, Jonathan (1703–1758) U.S. theologian. Born in E. Windsor, Conn., and educated at Yale, in 1727 he became a pastor at his grandfather's church in Northampton, Mass. His sermons gave rise to a revival in the Connecticut River Valley in 1734, and in the 1740s he was also influential in the GREAT AWAKENING. In 1750 he was dismissed from the Northampton church over a disagreement over communion, and he became pastor in Stockbridge in 1751. He died shortly after accepting the presidency of the College of New Jersey (now Princeton Univ.). A staunch Calvinist, he emphasized original sin and predestination. His sermon "Sinners in the Hands of an Angry God" vividly evokes the torments of hell.

Edwards, Robert See Patrick STEPTOE AND ROBERT EDWARDS

Edward the Black Prince (1330–1376) Prince of Wales (1343–76). Son of EDWARD III, he apparently received his sobriquet because he wore black armor. He was one of the outstanding commanders of the HUNDRED YEARS' WAR, winning a major victory at Poitiers in 1356. He was prince of Aquitaine 1362–72, but his rule there was a failure. He returned sick and broken to England and formally surrendered his principality to his father. His son became RICHARD II.

Edward the Confessor, St. (1003?–1066) King of England (1042–66). The son of ETHELRED II, he was exiled to Normandy (1016–41) while the Danes held England. For the early years of his reign the real master of England was Godwine, earl of Wessex. Edward outlawed Godwine in 1051 and appointed Normans to high positions in government, thus preparing the way for the NORMAN CONQUEST. Godwine's son Harold (later HAROLD II) dominated England after 1053. Edward named Harold as his successor on his deathbed, but the duke of Normandy (the future WILLIAM I) invaded England to claim the crown earlier promised him. Though an ineffectual monarch, Edward was famous for his piety, which earned him the epithet "the Confessor."

eel Any of more than 500 fish species (order Anguilliformes) that are slender, elongated, and usually scaleless, with long dorsal and anal fins that are continuous around the tail tip. Eels are found in all seas. Freshwater eels are active, predaceous fish with small embedded scales; they grow to maturity in freshwater and return to the sea, where they spawn and die. Freshwater eels, considered valuable food fish, include species ranging from 4 in. (10 cm) to about 12 ft (3.5 m) long. See also MORAY.

DE

efficiency *or* **mechanical efficiency** In MECHANICS, the measure of the effectiveness with which a system performs. It is stated as the ratio of a system's WORK output to its work input. The efficiency of a real system is always less than 1 because of FRICTION between moving parts. A machine with an efficiency of 0.8 returns 80% of the work input as work output; the remaining 20% is used to overcome friction.

eft See NEWT

egg In biology, the female sex cell, or gamete (Latin term *ovum*). The egg or ovum, like the male gamete (SPERM), bears only a single (haploid) set of CHROMOSOMES; when female and male gametes unite during FERTILIZATION, the double (diploid) set of chromosomes is restored. In humans, the ovum matures inside one of the OVARY's follicles and is released when the follicle ruptures (ovulation). The ovum passes into the fallopian (uterine) tube, and will degenerate if not fertilized within about 24 hours. In animals, the amount of nutritive material (yolk) deposited in an egg depends on the length of time before the developing animal can feed itself or, in the case of mammals, begins to receive nourishment from the maternal circulation. Most animal eggs are enclosed by one or more membranes. Insect eggs are covered by a thick, hard outer membrane, and amphibian eggs are surrounded by a jellylike layer. The hard-shelled reproductive body produced by a bird or reptile is also called an egg.

eggplant Tender perennial plant *(Solanum melongena)* of the NIGHTSHADE FAMILY, usually grown as an annual for its fleshy fruit. It has an erect, bushy stem; large ovate, slightly lobed leaves; and pendant, violet, solitary flowers. The fruit (technically a BERRY) is large, glossy, and egg-shaped, varying in color from dark purple to red, yellowish, or white. It is a staple in cuisines of the Mediterranean region.

Eginhard See EINHARD

Eglevsky \ig-ˈlyef-skəi\, **André** (1917–1977) U.S. (Russian-born) ballet dancer and teacher. He left Russia as a child and studied in Paris, becoming a lead dancer with the Ballet Russe de Monte Carlo at 14. He moved to the U.S. in 1937. He danced with a number of companies before joining the NEW YORK CITY BALLET (1951–58), where he created leading roles in several of George BALANCHINE's ballets. In 1961 he established the Eglevsky Ballet.

ego (Latin: "I") In psychoanalytic theory, the portion of the psyche experienced as the "self" or "I." It is the part that remembers, evaluates, plans, and in other ways is responsive to and acts in the surrounding physical and social world. According to Sigmund FREUD, it coexists with the ID (the unconscious, instinctual portion of the psyche) and the SUPEREGO (the portion representing the conscience, or the internalization of societal norms). It serves to integrate the PERSONALITY and the body with the memory, imagination, and behavior, and it mediates between the id and the superego by building up various defense mechanisms.

egoism In ETHICS, the principle that we should each act so as to promote our own interests. The great advantage of such a position is that it avoids any possible conflict between morality and self-interest; if it is rational for us to pursue our own interest, the rationality of morality is equally clear. Psychological egoism, by contrast, is a generalization about human motivation, namely, that everyone always acts so as to promote his or her own interests.

egret \ˈē-grət\ Any of several species (mainly in the genus *Egretta*) of wading birds in the same family (Ardeidae) as HERONS and BITTERNS. Egrets live in marshes, lakes, humid forests, and other wetland environments worldwide. They catch and eat small fishes, amphibians, reptiles, mammals, and crustaceans. They nest in trees and bushes or on the ground. Most are white and develop long plumes for the breeding season. The value of plumes as ornamental objects once drove egrets to near-extinction.

Egypt *officially* **Arab Republic of Egypt** *formerly* **United Arab Republic** *Arabic* **Misr** \ˈmisr\ *ancient* Aegyptus. Republic, NE Africa. Area: 386,900 sq mi (1,002,070 sq km). Population (2000): 65,871,000. Capital: CAIRO. The people are mainly a homogeneous mix of Hamitic and Semitic lineages. Language: Arabic (official). Religion: Islam (official); minority, Coptic Christianity. Currency: Egyptian pound. Egypt occupies a crossroads between Africa, Europe, and

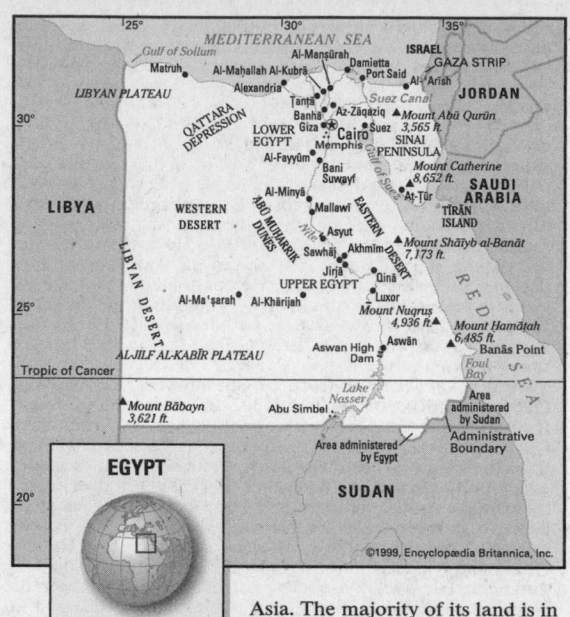

Scale 1: 21,787,000

©1999, Encyclopædia Britannica, Inc.

Asia. The majority of its land is in the arid Western and ARABIAN DESERTS, separated by the country's dominant feature, the NILE RIVER. The Nile forms a flat-bottomed valley, generally 5–10 mi (8–16 km) wide, that fans out into the densely populated delta lowlands north of Cairo. The Nile valley (Lower Egypt) and delta (Upper Egypt), along with scattered oases, support all of Egypt's agriculture and have more than 99% of its population. It has a developing, mainly socialist but partly free-enterprise economy, based primarily on industry, including petroleum production, and agriculture. It is a republic with one legislative house; its chief of state is the president, while the head of government is the prime minister. It is one of the world's oldest continuous civilizations. In about 3000 B.C., Upper and Lower Egypt were united, beginning a period of cultural achievement and a line of native rulers that lasted nearly 3,000 years. Egypt's ancient history is divided into the Old, Middle, and New Kingdoms, spanning 31 dynasties and lasting to 332 B.C. The PYRAMIDS date from the Old Kingdom; the cult of OSIRIS and the refinement of sculpture from the Middle Kingdom; the era of empire and the EXODUS of the Jews from the New Kingdom. An Assyrian invasion occurred in the 7th cent. B.C., and the Persian Achaemenids established a dynasty in 525 B.C. The invasion by ALEXANDER THE GREAT in 332 B.C. inaugurated the Macedonian Ptolemaic period, and the ascendancy of ALEXANDRIA. The Romans held Egypt from 30 B.C. to A.D. 395; later it was placed under the control of Constantinople. CONSTANTINE I's granting of tolerance in 313 to the Christians began the development of a formal Egyptian (COPTIC ORTHODOX) church. Egypt came under Arab control in 642, and ultimately was transformed into an Arabic-speaking state, with ISLAM as the dominant religion. Held by the UMAYYAD and ABBASID dynasties, in 969 it became the center of the FATIMID DYNASTY. In 1250, the Mamluks established a dynasty that lasted until 1517 (see MAMLUK REGIME), when Egypt fell to the Ottoman Turks. An economic decline ensued, and with it a decline in Egyptian culture. Egypt became a British protectorate in 1914 and received nominal independence in 1922, when a constitutional monarchy was established. A coup overthrew the monarchy in 1952, with G. A. NASSER taking power. Following three wars with Israel (see ARAB–ISRAELI WARS), Egypt, under Nasser's successor, Anwar al-SADAT, ultimately played a leading role in Middle East peace talks. Sadat was succeeded by Hosni MUBARAK, who followed Sadat's peace initiatives, and in 1982 regained Egyptian sovereignty (lost in 1967) over the SINAI peninsula. Although Egypt took part in the coalition against Iraq during the PERSIAN GULF WAR (1991), it later began peace overtures with countries in the region, including Iraq.

Egyptian architecture Houses, palaces, temples, tombs, and other buildings of ancient Egypt. Most Egyptian towns were situated on the floodplain and have been lost, but many religious structures built on higher ground have survived. Mud brick and wood were the standard domestic building materials, but from the Old Kingdom (c.2575–c.2130 B.C.) on, stone was used for tombs and temples. Egyptian masons used stone to reproduce the forms of wood and brick buildings. Mastabas (rectangular structures with sloping walls) and step pyramids were used for tomb superstructures, but the most characteristic form of the Old Kingdom was the true PYRAMID. The finest example is the Great Pyramid of Khufu (Cheops) at GIZA. For nonroyal burials, simple chapel rooms with stelae (see STELE) were located at some distance from the royal burial compounds. In the New Kingdom (1539–1075 B.C.), royal tombs were cut into the face of cliffs to discourage looting; elaborate complexes of tombs and mortuary temples were built in the Valley of the Kings at THEBES. Imposing remains of great stone cult temples (for worship of the gods) can be seen at LUXOR, KARNAK, ABYDOS, and ABU SIMBEL.

Egyptian art Ancient sculptures, paintings, and decorative crafts produced in the dynastic periods of the 3rd–1st millennia B.C. in the Nile Valley. Much of what has survived is associated with ancient tombs. The course of art in Egypt paralleled the country's political history and is divided into three periods: Old Kingdom (c.2700–c.2150 B.C.), Middle Kingdom (c.2000–c.1670 B.C.), and New Kingdom (c.1550–c.1070 B.C.). The Old Kingdom's stone tombs and temples were decorated with vigorous and brightly painted reliefs illustrating the daily life of the people. Rules for portraying the human figure

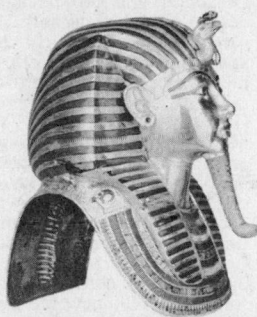

Egyptian art Gold funerary mask of Tutankhamen, c.1323 B.C.

were established, specifying proportions, postures, and placement of details, often linked to the subjects' social standing. The Middle Kingdom was notable for its expressive portrait sculptures of kings and its excellent relief sculptures and painting. The New Kingdom brought a magnificent flowering of the arts; great granite statues and wall reliefs glorified rulers and gods, painting became an independent art, and the decorative crafts reached new peaks, the treasure of TUTANKHAMEN's tomb typifying the variety of luxury items created.

Egyptian language Extinct AFROASIATIC LANGUAGE of the Nile valley. Its very long history comprises five periods: Old Egyptian (3000–2000 B.C.), known from epitaphs and some religious inscriptions called the Pyramid Texts; Middle Egyptian (2000–1300 B.C.), the classical literary language; Late Egyptian (1300–700 B.C.), known mainly from manuscripts; Demotic (700 B.C.–A.D. 500), used in the periods of foreign dominance, and differing from Late Egyptian chiefly in its graphic system; and Coptic (A.D. 300–1500), the language of Christian Egypt, gradually pushed out by Arabic from the 9th cent. on but still partly preserved in the liturgy of the COPTIC ORTHODOX CHURCH. Egyptian was originally written in HIEROGLYPHS, out of which evolved hieratic, a cursive rendering of hieroglyphs, and demotic, a further simplification. Coptic was written in a modified form of the Greek alphabet, with seven signs added from the demotic.

Egyptian religion Polytheistic belief system of ancient Egypt from the 4th millennium B.C. to the first centuries A.D. Local deities that sprang up along the Nile Valley were synthesized into national deities and cults after political unification around 2925 B.C. The gods were not all-powerful or all-knowing, but were immeasurably greater than humans. Their characteristics overlapped, especially among the leading deities. HORUS was the god-king who ruled the universe; he represented the earthly Egyptian king. Other major divinities included RE, PTAH, ATON, ISIS, and OSIRIS. The concept of Ma'at ("order") was fundamental: the king maintained Ma'at both on a societal and cosmic level. Belief in and preoccupation with the afterlife permeated Egyptian religion, as the surviving tombs and PYRAMIDS attest. See also BOOK OF THE DEAD.

Ehrenberg \'er-ən-ˌberk\, **Christian Gottfried** (1795–1876) German biologist, explorer, and founder of micropaleontology (the study of fossil microorganisms). The only survivor of a scientific expedition to the Middle East (1820–25), he identified and classified land and marine plants, animals, and microorganisms collected on that and other expeditions. He proved that fungi come from spores and demonstrated the sexual reproduction of molds and mushrooms. He was the first to study coral in detail, and he identified planktonic microorganisms as the cause of phosphorescence in the sea. He advanced the view that all animals, including the tiniest, possess complete organ systems.

Ehrlich \'ər-lik\, **Paul** (1854–1915) German medical scientist. After early work on distribution of foreign substances in the body and on cell nutrition, he found uses for staining agents in diagnosis (including that of tuberculosis) and treatment. He also researched typhoid, fever medications, and eye diseases. Ehrlich developed a method of stimulating production of ANTITOXINS by injecting increasing amounts of toxin into animals. He and Élie METCHNIKOFF received a 1908 Nobel Prize. With Sahachiro Hata (1837–1938), he developed Salvarsan, the first effective syphilis treatment.

Ehrlich \'ər-lik\, **Paul R(alph)** (b.1932) U.S. biologist. Born in Philadelphia, he taught at Stanford Univ. from 1959. Though much of his research was done in entomology, his overriding concern became unchecked population growth. His most influential work was *The Population Bomb* (1968).

Eichendorff \'ī-kən-ˌdorf\, **Joseph, Freiherr (Baron) von** (1788–1857) German poet and novelist. Born to the nobility, he and his family lost their castle in the Napoleonic Wars. His most important prose work, *Memoirs of a Good-for-Nothing* (1826), is considered a high point of Romantic fiction. In the 1830s he wrote poetry that achieved the popularity of folk songs and inspired such composers as Robert SCHUMANN, Felix MENDELSSOHN, Johannes BRAHMS, and Richard STRAUSS.

Eichmann \'īk-ˌmän\, **(Karl) Adolf** (1906–1962) German Nazi official. In 1932 he joined the Nazi Party and became a member of the SS. In World War II he organized the identification, assembly, and transportation of Jews to Auschwitz and other death camps. In 1945 he was captured but escaped and eventually settled in Argentina. In 1960 he was arrested near Buenos Aires and taken to Israel, where he was tried as a war criminal, with huge worldwide publicity, and hanged.

Eider River \'ī-dər\ River, Schleswig-Holstein state, N Germany. It rises east of Rendsburg and flows west for 117 mi (188 km) to the North Sea. It formed the N limit of the Roman empire from the reign of CHARLEMAGNE (768–814), was the boundary of the HOLY ROMAN EMPIRE from 1027, and formed the internal frontier between Schleswig and Holstein.

Eiffel Tower \'ī-fəl\ Parisian landmark built for the Centennial Exposition of 1889. Conceived by the bridge engineer Gustave Eiffel (1832–1923), the 984-ft (300-m) tower of open-lattice wrought iron was a technological masterpiece and (until 1930) the world's tallest building. Making use of advanced knowledge of the behavior of metal arch and TRUSS forms under loading, the structure presaged a revolution in civil engineering and architectural design.

Eight, The Group of U.S. painters who reacted against the traditions of the National Academy of Design. In 1908 Robert HENRI, Everett Shinn (1876–1953), John SLOAN, Arthur B. Davies (1862–1928), Ernest Lawson (1873–1939), Maurice PRENDERGAST, George Luks (1867–1933), and William GLACKENS (later joined by George BELLOWS) exhibited together in New York City. Saloons, tenements, pool halls, and slums were among their favorite subjects, and their style was rough and realistic. They were soon absorbed into the ASH CAN SCHOOL.

Eightfold Path Buddhist doctrine, stated by the BUDDHA in his first sermon near Varanasi, India. It is regarded as the way to deal with the problems named in the FOUR NOBLE TRUTHS. The path consists of right understanding (faith in the Buddhist view of existence), right thought (the resolve to practice the faith), right speech (no falsehoods, slander, or abuse), right action (no taking of life, stealing, or improper sexual behavior), right livelihood (no occupations contrary to Buddhist principles), right effort (development of good mental states), right mindfulness (awareness of body, feelings, and thought), and right concentration (meditation). It is also called the Middle Path, because it steers a course between sensuality and asceticism. Following the Path leads to escape from suffering and attainment of NIRVANA.

Eijkman \ˈīk-ˌmän, ˈāk-ˌmän\, **Christiaan** (1858–1930) Dutch physician and pathologist. Having noticed a resemblance between a nerve disorder in his laboratory chickens and that seen in beriberi, he eventually showed that the cause was their diet of white (THIAMINE-deficient) rather than brown rice. His work led to the discovery of VITAMINS and earned him a 1929 Nobel Prize, shared with Frederick HOPKINS.

Eindhoven \ˈīnt-ˌhō-vən\ Commune (pop., 1999 est.: 199,000), S Netherlands. Situated southeast of ROTTERDAM, it was chartered in 1232. After 1900 it developed from a small village into one of the largest industrial centers of the Netherlands, and in 1920 it annexed five adjoining municipalities. The city is the headquarters of PHILIPS ELECTRONICS NV.

Einstein, Albert (1879–1955) German-Swiss-U.S. scientist. Born to a Jewish family in Ulm, he grew up in Munich. He became an examiner at the Swiss patent office in 1902 and began producing original theoretical work that laid many of the foundations for 20th-cent. physics. He received his doctorate in 1905, the same year he won international fame with three articles: one on BROWNIAN MOTION, demonstrating the existence of molecules; one on the PHOTOELECTRIC EFFECT, in which he demonstrated the particle nature of light; and one on his special theory of RELATIVITY, which

Albert Einstein

included his formulation of the equivalence of mass and energy ($E = mc^2$). In 1915 he published his general theory of relativity, which was confirmed experimentally during a solar eclipse in 1919. He received a Nobel Prize in 1921 for his work on the photoelectric effect, his work on relativity still being controversial. He made important contributions to QUANTUM FIELD THEORY, and for decades he sought to discover the mathematical relationship between ELECTROMAGNETISM and GRAVITATION, which he believed would be a first step toward formulating a UNIFIED FIELD THEORY, but it eluded him. His theories of relativity and gravitation represented a profound advance over Newtonian physics and revolutionized scientific and philosophical inquiry. When Adolf HITLER came to power he moved to Princeton, N.J., where he joined the Institute for Advanced Study. Though a longtime pacifist, he was instrumental in persuading Pres. Franklin Roosevelt in 1939 to initiate the MANHATTAN PROJECT for the production of an atomic bomb, a technology his own theories greatly furthered. The most eminent scientist in the world in the postwar years, he became a strong advocate for nuclear disarmament.

Einstein's mass-energy relation Relationship between MASS *(m)* and ENERGY *(E)* in Albert EINSTEIN's special theory of RELATIVITY, expressed $E = mc^2$, where c equals 186,000 mi/second (300,000 km/second), the speed of LIGHT. Whereas mass and energy were viewed as distinct in earlier physical

theories, in special relativity a body's mass can be converted into energy in accordance with the formula. Such a release of energy decreases the body's mass (see CONSERVATION LAW).

Eisenhower \ˈī-zən-ˌhaù-ər\, **Dwight D(avid)** (1890–1969) 34th president of the U.S. (1953–61). Born in Denison, Texas, he graduated from West Point (1915). In World War II Gen. George MARSHALL chose him to command U.S. forces in Europe (1942). After planning the invasions of N. Africa, Sicily, and Italy, he was appointed supreme commander of Allied forces (1943). He planned the NORMANDY CAMPAIGN (1944) and the conduct of the war in Europe until the German surrender (1945). He was promoted to five-star general (1944) and was named army chief of staff in 1945. He

Dwight D. Eisenhower, 1952

served as president of Columbia Univ. from 1948 until being appointed supreme commander of NATO in 1951. Both Democrats and Republicans courted Eisenhower as a presidential candidate; in both 1952 and 1956, as the Republican candidate, he decisively defeated Adlai STEVENSON. His achievements included efforts to contain Communism with the EISENHOWER DOCTRINE. He sent federal troops to Little Rock, Ark., to enforce integration of a city high school (1957). When the Soviet Union launched Sputnik I (1957), he was criticized for failing to develop the U.S. space program and responded by creating NASA (1958).

Eisenhower Doctrine U.S. foreign-policy pronouncement by Pres. Dwight EISENHOWER (1957) that promised military and economic aid to anti-Communist governments, at a time when Communist countries were providing arms to Egypt and offering strong support to Arab states. Developed by J. F. DULLES to contain expansion of the Soviet sphere of influence, the doctrine continued pledges made under the TRUMAN DOCTRINE.

Eisenstaedt \ˈī-zən-ˌstat\, **Alfred** (1898–1995) German-U.S. photojournalist. He became a professional photographer in Berlin in 1929, and his work appeared in many European picture magazines. In 1935 he emigrated to New York, where he became one of the first four photographers hired by *Life* (1936). He would contribute more than 2,500 picture stories and 90 cover photos to the magazine, including outstanding portraits of kings, dictators, film stars, and ordinary people. Collections of his work include *Witness of Our Time* (1966) and *The Eye of Eisenstaedt* (1969).

Eisenstein \ˈī-zən-ˌstīn\, **Sergey (Mikhaylovich)** (1898–1948) Russian film director. He began his career at a workers' theater in Moscow in 1920, then turned to filmmaking. In *Strike* (1924) he introduced his influential concept of film MONTAGE, adding startling and often discordant images to the main action to create the maximum psychological impact. He further developed the style in *The Battleship Potemkin* (1925), sometimes called the greatest film of all time. Among his other films are *October (Ten Days that Shook the World;* 1928) and *The General Line* (1929). After a frustrating period in Hollywood and Mexico (1930–33), he returned to Russia and made two more classics, *Alexander Nevsky* (1938) and *Ivan the Terrible* (2 parts, 1945–46).

eisteddfod \ī-ˈsteth-ˌvòd, ā-ˈsteth-ˌvòd\ Formal assembly of Welsh bards and minstrels that originated in the traditions of medieval court bards. Early eisteddfods were competitions of musicians (especially harpists) and poets. The assembly at Carmarthen in 1451 authoritatively established the arrangement of the strict meters of Welsh poetry. The modern annual National Eisteddfod includes awards for music, prose, drama, and art, but the investiture of the winning poet remains its high point.

ejido \ā-ˈhē-thō\ In Mexico, village lands held in the traditional Indian system of land tenure, blessed by Mexican law in the 1920s, that combines communal ownership with individual use. The ejido consists of cultivated land, pastureland, other uncultivated lands, and the *fundo legal,* or town site. The cultivated land is generally apportioned in family holdings, which cannot be sold but can be passed down to heirs. Ejidos taken from the Indians on the 18th cent. were restored by the 1917 constitution. In 1992 the Carlos SALINAS government revoked the ban on the sale of ejido land.

Ekaterinoslav See DNIPROPETROVSK

Ekron \'e-ˌkrän\ Ancient Canaanite and PHILISTINE city. It was one of the five cities of the Philistine pentapolis, in what is now central Israel. Though allocated to JUDAH after the Israelite conquest, it was a Philistine stronghold in DAVID's time; it was later associated with the worship of the deity Baalzebub. Taken by Egyptians (c.918 B.C.), it was tributary to ASSYRIA in the 7th cent. B.C.

El Aaiún \ä-'yün\ *or* **Laâyoune** \lä-'yün\ Town (pop., 1982: 94,000), NW Africa. The capital (1940–76) of the overseas Spanish province of WESTERN SAHARA and since 1976 of the Laâyoune province of Morocco (not internationally recognized), it lies in the N part of Western Sahara, 8 mi (13 km) inland from the Atlantic Ocean. It was developed by Spain in 1938.

Elagabalus \ˌe-lə-'ga-bə-ləs\ *or* **Heliogabalus** \ˌhe-lē-ō-'ga-bə-ləs\ *officially* Caesar Marcus Aurelius Antoninus Augustus *orig.* Varius Avitus Bassianus (A.D. 204–222) Roman emperor (218–22). Passed off as CARACALLA's illegitimate son, he became emperor with the support of the army. He identified himself with the Syrian god BAAL and imposed Baal worship on the empire. His execution of dissidents, promotion of favorites, and homosexual orgies outraged the Romans. After he named his cousin Alexander heir and then changed his mind, the Praetorian Guards murdered him and made Alexander emperor.

El Alamein \ˌa-lə-'mān\, **Battles of** Two battles in Egypt in WORLD WAR II. German forces under Erwin ROMMEL began a drive eastward along the N. African coast in early 1942. Though initially checked by the British, they reached El Alamein on June 30. The first engagement ended in mid-July with Rommel on the defensive. In October British forces under Bernard MONTGOMERY began a devastating attack from El Alamein, routing Rommel's vastly outnumbered forces. By November 6 the British had driven him back into Libya.

Elam \'ē-ləm\ Ancient country, SW modern-day Iran. It was located at the head of the Persian Gulf east of BABYLONIA; its capital was Susa. It was closely tied culturally to MESOPOTAMIA, and was in conflict with the Sumerians (see SUMER) and Akkadians (see AKKAD) from around 3000 B.C. In the 13th cent. B.C., it became a dominant power; it included most of Mesopotamia east of the TIGRIS RIVER and reached almost to PERSEPOLIS. This domination ended when Nebuchadnezzar I of Babylon (r.1124–1103 B.C.) captured Susa.

eland \'ē-lənd\ Either of two species of easily tamed, oxlike ANTELOPE (genus *Taurotragus*) found in herds on the plains or in lightly wooded areas of central and S Africa. The largest of the antelope, they may stand up to 6 ft (1.8 m) tall at the shoulder and weigh as much as 2,200 lbs (1,000 kg). They have a short dark mane, a dewlap, and long horns twisted in a tight spiral.

elasticity Ability of a deformed material body to return to its original shape and size when the forces causing deformation are removed. Most solids show some elastic behavior, but there is usually a limit—the material's "elastic limit," which depends on its internal structure—to the force from which recovery is possible. Stresses beyond its elastic limit cause the material to yield, or flow, and the result is permanent deformation or breakage. Thus, steel can be extended only about 1% of its length, whereas rubber can be extended about 1,000%.

Elba Island (pop., 1991: 29,000) off the W coast of Italy, in the Tyrrhenian Sea. Occupying an area of 86 sq mi (223 sq km), it is the largest island of the Tuscan Archipelago. France obtained Elba from Rome in 1802. When NAPOLEON abdicated in 1814, he was exiled to Elba, but returned to France the next year to begin the HUNDRED DAYS. Thereafter Elba was restored to TUSCANY.

Elbe River \'el-bə\ *Czech* **Labe** \'lä-be\ *ancient* Albis. River, central Europe. One of the continent's major waterways, it rises on the Czech–Polish border, flows southwest across Bohemia and northwest across Germany, and empties into the North Sea north of HAMBURG. From 1945 to 1990 it formed part of the boundary between E. and W. Germany. It is 724 mi (1,165 km) long, and connected by canals with the BALTIC SEA, the Havel River and BERLIN, the RUHR RIVER industrial region, and the RHINE RIVER. It is navigable for 1,000-ton barges as far upstream as PRAGUE through the VLTAVA RIVER.

Elbrus \el-'brüs\, **Mt.** Peak, CAUCASUS MTNS., SW Russia. The highest peak in the Caucasus and in Europe, it is an extinct volcano with twin cones reaching 18,510 ft (5,642 m) and 18,356 ft (5,595 m) high. Covering 53 sq mi (138 sq km) of Elbrus are 22 glaciers. It is a major center for mountaineering and tourism.

Elburz Mountains \el-'bùrz\ Mountain range, N Iran. It is 560 mi (900 km) long and extends along the S shore of the CASPIAN SEA. It includes Iran's highest peak, Mt. Damavand, at 18,934 ft (5771 m) high. The forests of the Elburz cover more than 8 million acres (3 million hectares). The Hyrcanian tigers for which they were famous are now very rare.

El Cid See The CID

elder Any of about 20–30 species, mainly shrubs and small trees, that make up the genus *Sambucus*, in the HONEYSUCKLE FAMILY. Most are native to forested temperate or subtropical areas. Their berries (elderberries) provide food for wildlife and are used for wines, jellies, pies, and folk medicines. Elders have divided leaves and flat, roundish clusters of tiny, yellowish-white, saucer-shaped flowers. The American elder *(S. canadensis)* is the most important species horticulturally.

El Dorado (Spanish: "The Golden") Legendary golden city sought by Spanish explorers in the New World. Its king was said to have been covered with gold dust so many times that he was permanently gilded. Many Spanish and English expeditions were sent to find it. In 1540 F. V. de CORONADO ventured as far north as Kansas seeking the Seven Golden Cities of CÍBOLA. Walter RALEIGH led a search expedition up the Orinoco River in 1595.

Eldridge, (David) Roy (1911–1989) U.S. trumpeter, one of the most vital and creative jazz musicians of the SWING era. Born in Pittsburgh, he was influenced by saxophonists such as Coleman HAWKINS and developed a fast, nimble technique matched with harmonic sophistication. He was featured with the big bands of Gene Krupa and Artie Shaw in the 1940s. The dominant voice on his instrument in the swing style, he exerted a strong influence on BEBOP musicians.

Eleanor of Aquitaine (1122?–1204) Queen consort of Louis VII of France (1137–52) and HENRY II of England (1152–1204), the most powerful woman of 12th-cent. Europe. Beautiful, capricious, and strong-willed, she accompanied Louis on the Second CRUSADE (1147–49), and her conduct aroused his jealousy. The marriage was annulled (1152), and she married Henry Plantagenet, soon to be Henry II; the marriage united England, Normandy, and W France under his rule. Her court at Poitiers became a center of culture, fostering the poetry of the TROUBADOURS. She may have spurred her sons RICHARD I the Lionheart and JOHN Lackland to revolt against Henry (1173); when the rebellion failed she was captured and confined until his death (1189). She was active in government during the reign of Richard I, ruling during his crusade to the Holy Land and ransoming him from Austria. After John became king (1199), she saved Anjou and Aquitaine for John against French threats, then retired to a monastery.

Eleanor of Castile (1246–1290) Queen consort of EDWARD I of England. Daughter of the king of Castile, she brought Edward title to Gascony on their marriage in 1254. She joined Edward on a crusade to the Holy Land (1270–73), and legend says she saved his life by sucking poison from a dagger wound. On her death, Edward erected Eleanor Crosses at each place where her coffin rested en route to London.

Eleatics \ˌel-ē-'a-tiks\ School of philosophy that flourished in the 5th cent. B.C. One of the principal schools of PRE-SO-

D
E

CRATICS, it took its name from the Greek colony of Elea (Velia) in S Italy. It is distinguished by its radical monism—i.e., its doctrine of the One, according to which all that exists is a static and undifferentiated Being as such. Thus, all differentiation, motion, and change must be illusory. Its literary sources are fragments: 19 from PARMENIDES, four from his pupil ZENO OF ELEA, and 10 from another pupil, Melissus (fl.5th cent. B.C.).

elector *German* Kurfürst. Prince of the HOLY ROMAN EMPIRE who had a right to participate in electing the German emperor. Beginning about 1273, and with the confirmation of the Golden Bull of 1356, there were seven electors: the archbishops of Trier, Mainz, and Cologne; the duke of Saxony; the count palatine of the Rhine; the margrave of Brandenburg; and the king of Bohemia. Other electorates were created much later, but by the 17th cent. the office had become meaningless because the HABSBURG DYNASTY produced the de facto emperors.

electoral college Constitutionally mandated process for electing the U.S. PRESIDENT and vice president. Each state appoints as many electors as it has senators and representatives in CONGRESS. A winner-take-all rule operates in every state but Maine and Nebraska. The loser of the national popular vote has been elected by means of an electoral-college victory three times (Rutherford B. HAYES, Benjamin HARRISON, George W. BUSH). Though pledged to vote for their state's winners, electors are not required to do so. Victory requires 270 of the 538 votes.

Electoral Commission (1877) Commission created to resolve the disputed 1876 presidential election between Republican Rutherford B. HAYES and Democrat Samuel TILDEN. Tilden had won the popular vote and was only one electoral vote short of victory, but the Republicans contested the tallies in four states, charging fraud. Congress appointed a 15-member commission, evenly divided except for one justice, Joseph P. Bradley, a Republican considered nonpartisan; Republicans pressured him, and the tally went to Hayes.

Electra In Greek legend, the daughter of AGAMEMNON and Clytemnestra. When Clytemnestra and her lover murdered Agamemnon, Electra saved her young brother ORESTES by sending him away. Orestes later returned, and Electra helped him kill them both. The story is treated in plays by AESCHYLUS, SOPHOCLES, and EURIPIDES.

Electra complex See OEDIPUS COMPLEX

electrical engineering Branch of ENGINEERING concerned with the practical applications of ELECTRICITY in all its forms, including those of ELECTRONICS. Electrical engineering deals with electric light and POWER systems and apparatuses; electronics engineering deals with wire and RADIO communication, the stored-program electronic COMPUTER, RADAR, and automatic control systems. The first practical application of electricity was the TELEGRAPH, in 1837. Electrical engineering emerged as a discipline in 1864 when James Clerk MAXWELL summarized the basic laws of electricity in mathematical form and predicted that radiation of electromagnetic energy would occur in a form that later became known as radio waves. The need for electrical engineers was not felt until the invention of the TELEPHONE (1876) and the INCANDESCENT LAMP (1878).

electric automobile Battery-powered motor vehicle. Originating in the 1880s, electric cars were used for private passenger, truck, and bus transportation in cities, where their low speeds and limited battery range were not drawbacks, and the cars became popular for their quietness and low maintenance costs. Until 1920 they were competitive with gasoline-fueled cars; they became less so after the electric self-starter made gasoline-powered cars more attractive and MASS PRODUCTION lowered their prices. Renewed interest in electric cars beginning in the 1970s, spurred by concern about pollution and foreign oil dependency, led to improvements in speed and range. Recent laws, particularly in California, have mandated commercial production. Hybrid cars employing both electric and internal combustion engines have recently become commercially available. Experimental vehicles have used solar FUEL CELLS.

electric charge Quantity of ELECTRICITY that flows in ELECTRIC CURRENTS or that accumulates on the surfaces of dissimilar nonmetallic substances that are rubbed together briskly. It occurs in discrete natural units, equal to the charge of an ELECTRON or PROTON. It cannot be created or destroyed (see CONSERVATION LAW). Charge can be positive or negative; one positive charge can combine with one negative charge, and the result is a net charge of zero. Two objects of the same charge repel each other, and two objects with opposite charge attract each other. The unit of charge is the coulomb.

electric circuit See CIRCUIT

electric current Movement of ELECTRIC CHARGE carriers. In a wire, electric current is a flow of ELECTRONS and is a measure of the quantity of electrical charge passing any point of the wire per unit time. Current in gases and liquids generally consists of a flow of positive IONS in one direction together with a flow of negative ions in the opposite direction. In ALTERNATING CURRENT (AC) the motion of the charges is periodically reversed; in DIRECT CURRENT (DC) it is not. A common unit of current is the ampere, a flow of one coulomb of charge per second.

electric dipole \'di-pōl\ Pair of equal and opposite ELECTRIC CHARGES, the centers of which do not coincide. An ATOM in which the center of the negative cloud of ELECTRONS has been shifted slightly away from the NUCLEUS by an external ELECTRIC FIELD is an induced electric dipole. A water molecule, in which two hydrogen atoms stick out of one side of an oxygen atom, is a permanent electric dipole; the oxygen side is always slightly negative, the hydrogen side slightly positive.

electric discharge lamp *or* **vapor lamp** Lighting device consisting of a transparent container within which a gas is energized by an applied voltage and made to glow. After practical generators were devised in the 19th cent., many experimenters applied electric power to tubes of gas. From about 1900, electric discharge lamps were in use in Europe and the U.S. Fluorescent, neon, mercury, sodium, and metal-halide lamps are of the electric discharge variety.

electric eel Eel-shaped S. American fish (*Electrophorus electricus*) capable of producing an electric shock strong enough to stun a human. The electric eel (not a true EEL) is a sluggish inhabitant of slow freshwater. Long, cylindrical, scaleless, and gray-brown, it can reach a length of 9 ft (2.75 m) and a weight of 50 lbs (22 kg). The tail region contains the electric organs. The shock (up to 650 volts discharged at will) is used mainly to immobilize fish and other prey.

electric eye See PHOTOCELL

electric field Region around an ELECTRIC CHARGE in which an electric FORCE is exerted on another charge. An electric field has both magnitude and direction and can be represented by lines of force, or field lines, that start on positive charges and terminate on negative charges. The electric field is stronger where the field lines are close together than where they are farther apart. The value of the electric field has dimensions of force per unit charge and is measured in units of newtons per coulomb.

electricity Phenomenon associated with stationary or moving ELECTRIC CHARGES. Effects due to stationary charges, or static electricity, were the first electrical phenomena to be studied. Not until the early 19th cent. were static electricity and ELECTRIC CURRENT shown to be aspects of the same phenomenon. The discovery of the ELECTRON, which carries a charge designated as negative, showed that the various manifestations of electricity are the result of the accumulation or motion of numbers of electrons. The invention of the incandescent lightbulb (1879) and the construction of the first central power station (1881) by Thomas EDISON led to the rapid introduction of electric power. See also J. C. MAXWELL.

electric ray Any of the aquatic RAYS (families Torpedinidae, Narkidae, and Temeridae) that produce an electrical shock. They are found worldwide in warm and temperate seas, mostly in shallow water. Slow-moving bottom-dwellers, they feed on fishes and invertebrates. They range in length from less than 1 ft (30 cm) to about 6 ft (1.8 m). They are soft and smooth-skinned, with a circular or nearly circular body disk formed by the head and pectoral fins. They are harmless unless touched or stepped on, in which case the shock from the electric organs may reach 220 volts, strong enough to fell a human adult.

electric shock Physical effect of an ELECTRIC CURRENT that enters the body, ranging from a minor static-electricity discharge to a power-line accident or lightning strike. The effects depend on the current (not the voltage), and the worst damage occurs along its path from the entry to the exit point. Causes of immediate death are ventricular fibrillation and paralysis of the brain's breathing center or of the heart. CARDIOPULMONARY RESUSCITATION is the best first aid.

electrification, rural See RURAL ELECTRIFICATION

electroacoustic music Music in which the sounds are produced or modified by electronic components. In the late 1940s, magnetic tape began to be used, especially in France, to modify natural sounds (playing them backward, at different speeds, etc.), creating the genre known as musique concrète. By the early 1950s, composers were employing conglomerations of OSCILLATORS, filters, and other equipment to produce entirely new sounds. The development of voltage-controlled oscillators and filters led to the first SYNTHESIZERS in the 1950s. No longer relying on tape editing, electroacoustic music could now be created in real time. Since the late 1970s, personal computers have been used to control the synthesizers. Digital sampling—the use of actual recorded sounds corresponding to every pitch, activated generally by a keyboard—has largely replaced the use of oscillators as a sound source.

electrocardiography \i-ˌlek-trō-ˌkärd-ē-ˈäg-rə-fē\ Method of tracing the ELECTRIC CURRENT of a heartbeat to provide information on the HEART. Electrocardiograms (ECGs) are made by applying ELECTRODES, usually to the arms, legs, and chest wall, attached to an electrocardiograph, which records the heart current. Deviations from a patient's norm point to a possible heart disorder and its site.

electrochemistry Branch of CHEMISTRY concerned with the relation between ELECTRICITY and chemical change. Many spontaneous CHEMICAL REACTIONS liberate electrical ENERGY, and some of these reactions are used in BATTERIES and fuel cells to produce electric power. Conversely, electric current can bring about many reactions that do not occur spontaneously. ELECTROLYSIS is an electrochemical process. Electrochemistry is important for METALLURGY and the study of CORROSION. See also OXIDATION-REDUCTION.

electroconvulsive therapy See SHOCK THERAPY

electrocution Method of execution or accidental death in which one receives a heavy charge of electric current. A condemned person is shackled into a wired chair, and ELECTRODES are fastened to the head and one leg so that the current will flow through the body. One electrical shock may not be enough to kill the person; if a doctor does not confirm the death, several shocks may be applied. The electric chair was first used in 1890.

electrode Electric CONDUCTOR, usually metal, used as one of two terminals to conduct ELECTRIC CURRENT through a conducting medium. A simple voltaic cell, or BATTERY, consists of two electrodes immersed in an electrolytic solution (see ELECTROLYTE).

electrodynamics, quantum See QUANTUM ELECTRODYNAMICS

electroencephalography \i-ˌlek-trō-in-ˌsef-ə-ˈläg-rə-fē\ Procedure for recording electrical activity in the brain. Pairs of ELECTRODES on the scalp transmit signals to an electroencephalograph, which records them as peaks and troughs on a tracing called an electroencephalogram (EEG). Different wave patterns on the EEG are associated with normal and abnormal waking and sleeping states. They help diagnose conditions such as tumors, infections, and epilepsy.

electrolysis \i-ˌlek-ˈträ-lə-səs\ Process in which ELECTRIC CURRENT passed through a substance causes a chemical change, usually the gaining or losing of ELECTRONS (see OXIDATION-REDUCTION). It is carried out in an electrolytic cell consisting of separated positive and negative ELECTRODES immersed in an ELECTROLYTE SOLUTION containing IONS. Electric current enters through the CATHODE; positively charged CATIONS travel to it and combine with electrons. Negatively charged ANIONS give up electrons at

the ANODE. Both thus become neutral molecules. Electrolysis is used extensively in METALLURGY to extract or purify METALS from ORES or compounds and to deposit them from solution (ELECTROPLATING).

electrolyte Substance that conducts ELECTRIC CURRENT as a result of dissociation of its molecules into positively and negatively charged particles called IONS. The most familiar electrolytes are ACIDS, BASES, and SALTS, which ionize when dissolved in SOLVENTS such as water or alcohol. Many salts, including SODIUM CHLORIDE, behave as electrolytes when melted in the absence of solvent, since they have IONIC BONDS.

electromagnet Device consisting of a core of magnetic material such as iron, surrounded by a coil through which an ELECTRIC CURRENT is passed to magnetize the core. When the current is stopped, the core is no longer magnetized. Electromagnets are particularly useful wherever controllable magnets are required, as in devices in which the MAGNETIC FIELD is to be varied, reversed, or switched on and off. Devices that utilize electromagnets include scrap-yard lifts, particle accelerators, telephone receivers, loudspeakers, and televisions.

electromagnetic force One of the four known basic FORCES in the universe. Electromagnetism is responsible for interactions between charged particles that occur because of their charge, and for the emission and absorption of PHOTONS (ELECTROMAGNETIC RADIATION). The phenomena of ELECTRICITY and MAGNETISM are consequences of this force. The physical description of electromagnetism has been combined with QUANTUM MECHANICS into the theory of QUANTUM ELECTRODYNAMICS. The electromagnetic force is about 10^{36} times as strong as the gravitational force (see GRAVITATION), but much weaker than the WEAK FORCE and STRONG FORCE.

electromagnetic induction Induction of an ELECTROMOTIVE FORCE in a CIRCUIT by varying the magnetic flux linked with the circuit. The phenomenon was first investigated in 1830–31 by Joseph HENRY and Michael FARADAY, who discovered that when the MAGNETIC FIELD around an electromagnet varied, an ELECTRIC CURRENT could be detected in a separate nearby CONDUCTOR. A current can also be induced by constantly moving a permanent magnet in and out of a coil of wire, or by constantly moving a conductor near a stationary permanent magnet.

electromagnetic radiation Energy propagated through free space or through a material medium in the form of waves of any type in the ELECTROMAGNETIC SPECTRUM. Electromagnetic radiation exhibits wavelike properties such as REFLECTION, REFRACTION, DIFFRACTION, and INTERFERENCE, but also exhibits particlelike properties in that its energy occurs in discrete packets, or quanta (see QUANTUM).

electromagnetic spectrum Total range of FREQUENCIES or WAVELENGTHS of ELECTROMAGNETIC RADIATION. The

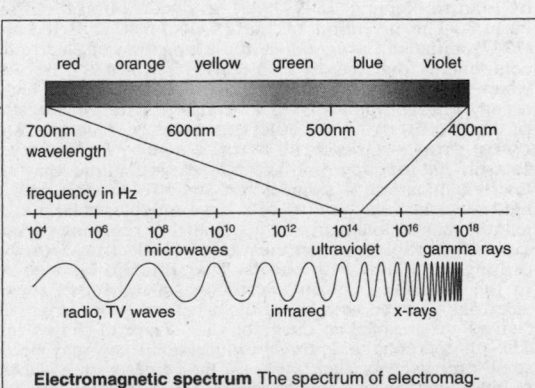

Electromagnetic spectrum The spectrum of electromagnetic waves ranges from low-frequency radio waves to high-frequency gamma rays. Only a small portion of the spectrum, representing wavelengths of roughly 400–700 nanometers, is visible to the human eye.

spectrum ranges from waves of long wavelength (low frequency) to those of short wavelength (high frequency); it includes, in order of increasing frequency (or decreasing wavelength): long-wave RADIO WAVES, MICROWAVES, INFRARED RADIATION, visible LIGHT, ULTRAVIOLET RADIATION, X RAYS, and GAMMA RAYS. In a VACUUM, all waves of the electromagnetic spectrum travel at the same speed, 299,792,458 m/s (186,282 miles/second).

electromagnetism Branch of physics that deals with the relationship between ELECTRICITY and MAGNETISM. Their merger into one concept is tied to three landmark historical events. The accidental discovery in 1820 by Hans Christian Ørsted (1777–1851) that MAGNETIC FIELDS are produced by ELECTRIC CURRENTS spurred efforts to prove that magnetic fields can induce currents. Michael FARADAY showed in 1831 that a changing magnetic field can induce a current in a circuit. J. C. MAXWELL predicted that a changing electric field has an associated magnetic field. Electromagnetic technology led to the development of electric power and modern communications.

electromotive force Energy per unit ELECTRIC CHARGE that is imparted by an energy source, such as an electric GENERATOR or a BATTERY. The WORK done on a unit of electric charge or the energy gained by the unit charge is the electromotive force *emf* (or *E*) and is characteristic of any energy source capable of driving electric charge around a circuit. A common unit of electromotive force is the volt *V*, a unit equal to the difference in electric potential between two points in a conductor carrying a current of one ampere and dissipating one watt of power between the two points.

electromyography \i-,lek-trō-mī-'äg-rə-fē\ Process of graphically recording the electrical activity of MUSCLE, which normally generates an electric current only when contracting or when its nerve is stimulated. Electrical impulses are recorded as an electromyogram (EMG), which can show whether muscle weakness or wasting is due to nerve impairment (as in AMYOTROPHIC LATERAL SCLEROSIS and POLIOMYELITIS) or muscle impairment or disease (myopathy).

electron Lightest electrically charged SUBATOMIC PARTICLE known. It carries a negative charge (see ELECTRIC CHARGE), the basic charge of ELECTRICITY. An electron has a small mass, less than 0.1% the mass of an ATOM. Under normal circumstances, electrons move about the NUCLEUS of an atom in ORBITALS that form an electron cloud. The first subatomic particle discovered, the electron was identified in 1897 by J. J. THOMSON.

electronic mail See E-MAIL

electronics Branch of physics that deals with the emission, behavior, and effects of ELECTRONS and with electronic devices. The beginnings of electronics were experiments with ELECTRICITY. In the 1880s Thomas EDISON and others observed the flow of current between elements in an evacuated glass tube. A two-electrode VACUUM TUBE constructed by John A. Fleming (1849–1945) produced a useful output current. The invention of the TRANSISTOR at Bell Labs (1947) initiated a progressive miniaturization of electronic components that led to high-density MICROPROCESSORS, which in turn led to tremendous advances in computer technology and computer-based automated systems. See also DIGITAL COMPUTER, INTEGRATED CIRCUIT, LASER, SEMICONDUCTOR, SOLID-STATE DEVICE, SUPERCONDUCTIVITY.

electron microscopy \mī-'kräs-kə-pē\ Technique that allows examination of samples too small to be seen with a light MICROSCOPE. ELECTRONS have much smaller wavelengths than visible light and hence higher resolving power. To be observable, samples must be made electron-dense by coating or staining with metals. Two different kinds exist. In the scanning electron microscope, a moving beam of electrons scanned across an object is focused by magnetic "lenses" to produce an image of the surface of the object. The photographs look three-dimensional; they may be of small organisms or their parts, of molecules such as DNA, or even of large individual atoms (e.g., uranium). In the transmission electron microscope, the beam passes through a very thin, carefully prepared sample to visualize the interior structure of such samples as cells and tissues.

electrophile ATOM or MOLECULE that in a CHEMICAL REACTION seeks an atom or molecule containing an ELECTRON

pair available for BONDING or the negative end of a polar molecule (see COVALENT BOND, ELECTRIC DIPOLE). In the Lewis electron theory (see ACID-BASE THEORY), electrophiles are by definition Lewis acids. Examples include the hydronium ion (H_3O^+) and the HALOGEN molecules (F_2, Cl_2, Br_2, and I_2). See also ACID, NUCLEOPHILE.

electrophoresis \i-,lek-trə-fə-'rē-səs\ Movement of electrically charged particles in a fluid under the influence of an ELECTRIC FIELD. The particles migrate toward the ELECTRODE of the opposite ELECTRIC CHARGE, often on a gel-coated slab or plate, sometimes in a fluid flowing down a paper. Originated about 1930 as a technique for ANALYSIS, electrophoresis is used to analyze and separate COLLOIDS (e.g., PROTEINS) or deposit coatings.

electroplating Process of coating with METAL by means of an ELECTRIC CURRENT. Plating metal may be transferred to conductive surfaces (e.g., metals) or to nonconductive surfaces (e.g., plastics, wood, leather) if a conductive coating has been applied. Usually the current deposits a given amount of metal on the CATHODE (workpiece), and the ANODE (source of metal) dissolves to the same extent, maintaining a fairly uniform solution. SILVER plating is used on tableware, electrical contacts, and engine bearings; GOLD plating is used on jewelry; ZINC coatings prevent the corrosion of steel; and NICKEL and CHROMIUM plate are used on automobiles and household appliances.

electroweak theory Theory that describes both the ELECTROMAGNETIC FORCE and the WEAK FORCE. Though the forces appear to be different, they are actually different facets of a more fundamental force. This landmark theory, formulated by Sheldon Glashow (b.1932), Steven Weinberg (b.1933), and Abdus Salam (b.1926), won its authors a 1979 Nobel Prize. It was validated in the 1980s with the discovery of the W PARTICLE and Z PARTICLE, which it had predicted. See also STANDARD MODEL, UNIFIED FIELD THEORY.

electrum Natural or artificial ALLOY of GOLD with at least 20% SILVER. Most natural electrum also contains copper, iron, palladium, and bismuth. The color varies from white-gold to brassy, depending on the percentages of its constituents. The first Western coinage consisted of irregular ingots of electrum bearing the stamp of King Gyges of Lydia (7th cent. B.C.).

elegy \'e-lə-jē\ Meditative lyric poem. The classical elegy was any poem written in elegiac meter (alternating lines of dactylic hexameter and pentameter). Today the term may refer to this meter rather than to content, but in English literature since the 16th cent. it has meant a lament in any meter. A distinct variety with a formal pattern is the pastoral elegy, such as John MILTON's "Lycidas" (1638). Poets of the 18th-cent. Graveyard School, including Thomas GRAY, reflected on death and immortality in elegies.

element, chemical One of the 115 currently known kinds of substances that constitute all MATTER at and above the level of ATOMS, the smallest unit of any element. All atoms of an element are identical in nuclear charge (number of PROTONS) and number of ELECTRONS (see ATOMIC NUMBER), but their MASS (ATOMIC WEIGHT) may differ if they have different numbers of NEUTRONS (see ISOTOPE). Each element has a one- or two-letter CHEMICAL SYMBOL. Elements combine to form a wide variety of COMPOUNDS. All elements with atomic numbers greater than 83 (bismuth), and some isotopes of lighter elements, are unstable and radioactive (see RADIOACTIVITY). The transuranium elements, with atomic numbers greater than 92 (see URANIUM), artificially created by bombardment of other elements with neutrons or other heavy particles, have been discovered since 1940. The most common elements (by weight) in the earth's crust are oxygen, 49%; silicon, 26%; aluminum, 8%; and iron, 5%. Of the known elements, 11 (hydrogen, nitrogen, oxygen, fluorine, chlorine, and the six noble gases) are GASES, two (bromine and mercury) are LIQUIDS (two more, cesium and gallium, melt at about or just above room temperature), and the rest are SOLID under ordinary conditions. See also PERIODIC TABLE.

elementary education *or* **primary education** Traditionally, the first stage of formal education, beginning at age 5–7 and ending at age 11–13. Elementary education is often preceded by some form of PRESCHOOL. It usually includes mid-

PERIODIC TABLE OF THE ELEMENTS

IA								VIII						IIIA	IVA	VA	VIA	VIIA	Zero
1 H	IIA																	1 H	2 He
3 Li	4 Be													5 B	6 C	7 N	8 O	9 F	10 Ne
11 Na	12 Mg	IIIB	IVB	VB	VIB	VIIB				IB	IIB			13 Al	14 Si	15 P	16 S	17 Cl	18 Ar
19 K	20 Ca	21 Sc	22 Ti	23 V	24 Cr	25 Mn	26 Fe	27 Co	28 Ni	29 Cu	30 Zn			31 Ga	32 Ge	33 As	34 Se	35 Br	36 Kr
37 Rb	38 Sr	39 Y	40 Zr	41 Nb	42 Mo	43 Tc	44 Ru	45 Rh	46 Pd	47 Ag	48 Cd			49 In	50 Sn	51 Sb	52 Te	53 I	54 Xe
55 Cs	56 Ba	57 La	72 Hf	73 Ta	74 W	75 Re	76 Os	77 Ir	78 Pt	79 Au	80 Hg			81 Tl	82 Pb	83 Bi	84 Po	85 At	86 Rn
87 Fr	88 Ra	89 Ac	104 Rf	105 Db	106 Sg	107 Bh	108 Hs	109 Mt	110	111	112			114		116		118	

Lanthanide Series	58 Ce	59 Pr	60 Nd	61 Pm	62 Sm	63 Eu	64 Gd	65 Tb	66 Dy	67 Ho	68 Er	69 Tm	70 Yb	71 Lu
Actinide Series	90 Th	91 Pa	92 U	93 Np	94 Pu	95 Am	96 Cm	97 Bk	98 Cf	99 Es	100 Fm	101 Md	102 No	103 Lr

Chemical elements The periodic table arranges the elements into groups (vertically) of elements sharing common physical and chemical characteristics, and into periods (horizontally) of sequentially increasing atomic number and electron-shell configuration. The elements are listed in the accompanying table by their full names. Elements 110, 111, 112, and 114 have been created experimentally but have not yet been named.

Chemical Elements

Element	Symbol	Atomic no.	Atomic weight*	Element	Symbol	Atomic no.	Atomic weight*
actinium	Ac	89	227.028	hydrogen	H	1	1.0079
aluminum	Al	13	26.9815	indium	In	49	114.82
americium	Am	95	(243)	iodine	I	53	126.9045
antimony	Sb	51	121.76	iridium	Ir	77	192.217
argon	Ar	18	39.948	iron	Fe	26	55.845
arsenic	As	33	74.9216	krypton	Kr	36	83.80
astatine	At	85	(210)	lanthanum	La	57	138.9055
barium	Ba	56	137.33	lawrencium	Lr	103	(262)
berkelium	Bk	97	(247)	lead	Pb	82	207.2
beryllium	Be	4	9.0122	lithium	Li	3	6.941
bismuth	Bi	83	208.9804	lutetium	Lu	71	174.967
bohrium	Bh	107	(264)	magnesium	Mg	12	24.305
boron	B	5	10.81	manganese	Mn	25	54.938
bromine	Br	35	79.904	meitnerium	Mt	109	(268)
cadmium	Cd	48	112.41	mendelevium	Md	101	(258)
calcium	Ca	20	40.078	mercury	Hg	80	200.59
californium	Cf	98	(251)	molybdenum	Mo	42	95.94
carbon	C	6	12.011	neodymium	Nd	60	144.24
cerium	Ce	58	140.116	neon	Ne	10	20.180
cesium	Cs	55	132.9054	neptunium	Np	93	(237)
chlorine	Cl	17	35.453	nickel	Ni	28	58.6934
chromium	Cr	24	51.996	niobium	Nb	41	92.9064
cobalt	Co	27	58.9332	nitrogen	N	7	14.0067
copper	Cu	29	63.546	nobelium	No	102	(259)
curium	Cm	96	(247)	osmium	Os	76	190.23
dubnium	Db	105	(262)	oxygen	O	8	15.9994
dysprosium	Dy	66	162.50	palladium	Pd	46	106.42
einsteinium	Es	99	(252)	phosphorus	P	15	30.9737
erbium	Er	68	167.26	platinum	Pt	78	195.078
europium	Eu	63	151.96	plutonium	Pu	94	(244)
fermium	Fm	100	(257)	polonium	Po	84	(209)
fluorine	F	9	18.9984	potassium	K	19	39.0983
francium	Fr	87	(223)	praseodymium	Pr	59	140.9077
gadolinium	Gd	64	157.25	promethium	Pm	61	(145)
gallium	Ga	31	69.72	protactinium	Pa	91	(231)
germanium	Ge	32	72.64	radium	Ra	88	(226)
gold	Au	79	196.9665	radon	Rn	86	(222)
hafnium	Hf	72	178.499	rhenium	Re	75	186.207
hassium	Hs	108	(277)	rhodium	Rh	45	102.9055
helium	He	2	4.0026	rubidium	Rb	37	85.4678
holmium	Ho	67	164.9303	ruthenium	Ru	44	101.07

Chemical Elements

Element	Symbol	Atomic no.	Atomic weight*	Element	Symbol	Atomic no.	Atomic weight*
rutherfordium	Rf	104	(261)	thallium	Tl	81	204.383
samarium	Sm	62	150.36	thorium	Th	90	232.0381
scandium	Sc	21	44.9559	thulium	Tm	69	168.9342
seaborgium	Sg	106	(266)	tin	Sn	50	118.71
selenium	Se	34	78.96	titanium	Ti	22	47.867
silicon	Si	14	28.0855	tungsten (wolfram)	W	74	183.84
silver	Ag	47	107.868	uranium	U	92	(238)
sodium	Na	11	22.9898	vanadium	V	23	50.9415
strontium	Sr	38	87.62	xenon	Xe	54	131.29
sulfur	S	16	32.07	ytterbium	Yb	70	173.04
tantalum	Ta	73	180.9479	yttrium	Y	39	88.9059
technetium	Tc	43	(98)	zinc	Zn	30	65.39
tellurium	Te	52	127.60	zirconium	Zr	40	91.224
terbium	Tb	65	158.9253				

*Weights are based on the naturally occuring isotope compositions and scaled to $^{12}C = 12$. For elements lacking stable isotopes, the mass number of the most stable nuclide is shown in parentheses.

dle school, or junior high school (ages 11–13), though this is sometimes regarded as part of SECONDARY EDUCATION. Nearly all nations are committed to some form of elementary education, though in many developing countries most children drop out of school before the fifth grade. The elementary curriculum usually emphasizes reading and writing, arithmetic, and basic social studies and science.

elementary particle See SUBATOMIC PARTICLE.

elephant Either of two large UNGULATE species in the order Proboscidea (family Elephantidae) with long trunks, tusks, massive legs, large ears, and huge heads. The trunk is used for breathing, drinking, and reaching for food. The African elephant *(Loxodonta africana),* of sub-Saharan Africa, is the largest living land animal, weighing up to 16,500 lbs (7,500 kg) and standing 10–13 ft (3–4 m) tall at the shoulder. The Indian elephant *(Elephas maximus),* of the Indian subcontinent and SE Asia, weighs about 12,000 lbs (5,500 kg) and stands about 10 ft (3 m) tall. Both live in habitats ranging from thick jungle to savanna, in small family groups or bachelor herds. Elephants migrate seasonally. They may eat more than 500 lbs (225 kg) of vegetation daily. The Indian elephant is considered endangered and the African elephant threatened.

Elephant Man *orig.* **Joseph (Carey) Merrick** (1862–1890) Englishman disfigured by a disease that caused overgrowths over his skin and bone surfaces. His head was 3 ft (.9 m) around, with large bags of skin hanging from it, the jaw so deformed he could not speak clearly. One arm and his legs were badly deformed. He escaped from a workhouse at 21 to join a freak show, where a London physician discovered him and admitted him to London Hospital. He died at 27 of accidental suffocation. His disease was probably the very rare Proteus syndrome. A successful play and film were based on Merrick's life.

elephant seal Either of the two largest pinniped species: the N elephant seal *(Mirounga angustirostris),* of coastal islands off California and Baja California, or the S elephant seal *(M. leonina),* of sub-Antarctic regions. Both are gregarious earless SEALS. The male has an inflatable, trunklike snout. Males reach a length of about 20 ft (6.5 m) and a weight of about 7,800 lbs (3,530 kg) and are much larger than the females. Elephant seals feed on fish and squid or other CEPHALO-PODS. During the breeding season, bulls fight to establish territories and to acquire harems of up to 40 cows.

Elephant seal bull *(Mirounga)*

El Escorial \ˌes-kȯr-ˈyäl\ Palace-monastery northwest of Madrid, built in 1563–67 for PHILIP II. It is the burial place of Spanish sovereigns and one of the largest religious establishments in the world. It was conceived by Juan Bautista de Toledo (1530–1567) and completed by Juan de Herrera (c.1530–1597). Its plan is a giant rectangle, with a domed church at the center flanked by the palace, monastery, college, library, cloisters, and courts. The massive granite walls, relieved only by unadorned windows and Doric pilasters, produced an austerity beyond anything the Italian Renaissance ever envisaged.

Eleusinian Mysteries \ˌel-yù-ˈsi-nē-ən\ Most famous MYSTERY RELIGION of ancient Greece. It was based on the story of DEMETER, whose daughter PERSEPHONE was kidnapped by HADES. While searching for Persephone, Demeter stopped at ELEUSIS, revealed her identity to the royal family, and taught the natives her rites. The Greater Mysteries, celebrated in autumn, included a procession from Athens to the temple at Eleusis, a ritual bath in the sea, three days of fasting, and, finally, completion of secret rites.

Eleusis \i-ˈlü-səs\ *Greek* **Elevsís** \ˌe-lef-ˈsēs\ Town, with ruins of an ancient city, E Greece. Famous as the site of the ELEUSINIAN MYSTERIES, it is about 14 mi (23 km) west of Athens. It was independent until the 7th cent. B.C., when Athens annexed the city and made the Eleusinian Mysteries a major Athenian religious festival. The Gothic leader ALARIC I destroyed Eleusis in A.D. 395. It is now a suburb of Athens. Some excavated ruins date back 3,000 years.

elevator Car that moves in a vertical shaft to carry passengers or freight between the levels of a multistory building. The use of mechanical lifting platforms dates to Roman times. Steam and hydraulic elevators came into use in the 19th cent. Most modern elevators are electrically propelled through cables and pulleys with the aid of a counterweight, though hydraulic elevators are still used in low buildings. The introduction of an automatic safety device by Elisha Otis (1811–1861) in 1853 made the passenger elevator possible. By opening the way to higher buildings, the elevator played a decisive role in shaping the modern city.

Elgar, Edward (William) *(later* **Sir Edward)** (1857–1934) British composer. His *Enigma Variations* (1899) brought him fame, and for the rest of his life he was a great national figure, regarded as having inaugurated the "English musical renaissance," a revival of British composition after the long lackluster era since the 18th cent. His works include the five *Pomp and Circumstance Marches* (1901–7), two symphonies (1908, 1911), concertos for violin (1910) and cello (1919), and the oratorio *The Dream of Gerontius* (1900).

Elgin \ˈel-gən\, **Earl of** *orig.* James Bruce (1811–1863) British governor-general of Canada (1847–54). Elgin implemented the policy of responsible, or cabinet, government recommended by Lord DURHAM. He supported the Rebellion Losses Act (1849), which compensated Canadians for losses during the 1837 rebellion in Lower Canada, a stand criticized by Tories in England and French-Canadian rioters in Montreal. He negotiated the Reciprocity Treaty (1854) between the Canadian colonies and the U.S.

Elgin Marbles \ˈel-gən\ Collection of ancient Greek marble sculptures and architectural fragments in the BRITISH MUSEUM. They were removed from the PARTHENON in Athens and other buildings by Thomas Bruce, Lord Elgin (1766–1841), ambassador to the Ottoman Empire, and shipped to England 1802–11. Elgin claimed he was saving the works from destruction by the Turks, who then controlled Greece, and who gave him permission to remove "any pieces of stone" bearing figures or inscriptions. Amid mounting criticism, he sold them to the British crown in 1816. The Greek government continues to demand their return.

El Greco See El GRECO

Eliade \\el-ē-'ä-dā\\, **Mircea** (1907–1986) Romanian-U.S. historian of religion. He studied Sanskrit and Indian philosophy at the Univ. of Calcutta. In 1945 he moved to Paris to teach at the Sorbonne, and from 1956 he taught at the Univ. of Chicago. For Eliade, religious experiences were manifestations of the sacred in the world, and his work traced the forms they have taken in different times and places. His books include *The Myth of the Eternal Return* (1949) and *A History of Religious Ideas* (3 vols., 1978–85); he edited the 16-volume *Encyclopedia of Religion.*

Elijah \\i-'lī-jə\\ *or* **Elias** *Hebrew* Eliyyahu (9th cent. B.C.) Hebrew PROPHET. The Bible relates that he denounced foreign cults and defeated 450 prophets of BAAL. This earned him the enmity of King AHAB and his consort, JEZEBEL, who forced him to flee into the wilderness. Later he was taken up into heaven in a whirlwind; ELISHA was his successor. His insistence that only the God of Israel is entitled to the name of divinity expresses a fully conscious monotheism.

Elijah ben Solomon (1720–1797) Lithuanian scholar and Jewish leader. He traveled extensively before settling in Vilna, Lithuania, the cultural center of E European Jewry. A recluse devoted to study and prayer, he nevertheless became famous and revered in the Jewish community. His scholarly interests included biblical exegesis, Talmudic studies, folk medicine, grammar, and philosophy. He opposed HASIDISM and its claims to miracles, visions, and spiritual ecstasy, calling instead for the intellectual love of God.

Elion \\'e-lē-ən\\, **Gertrude (Belle)** (1918–1999) U.S. pharmacologist. Born in New York City, in 1944 she became George H. HITCHINGS's assistant at Burroughs Wellcome, and they developed drugs for leukemia, autoimmune disorders, urinary-tract infections, gout, malaria, and viral herpes using innovative research methods. They examined the biochemistry of normal human cells and of disease-causing agents and used the results to formulate drugs that could kill or inhibit reproduction of a particular pathogen but leave host cells unharmed. In 1988 they shared a Nobel Prize with Sir James Black (b.1924).

Eliot, Charles William (1834–1926) U.S. educator. Born in Boston, he studied at HARVARD UNIV. and taught mathematics and chemistry there and at MIT. Named president of Harvard in 1869, he set about a program of fundamental reforms. He demanded a place for the sciences in liberal education, and he instituted the elective system for undergraduates; the graduate school of arts and sciences was created (1890), Radcliffe College established (1894), and the university became an institution of world renown. His reforms had widespread influence in American higher education. After resigning in 1909, he edited the 50-volume *Harvard Classics* (1909–10) and devoted himself to public service.

Eliot, George *orig.* Mary Ann Evans *later* Marian Evans (1819–1880) British novelist. She was raised with a strong evangelical piety, but broke with religious orthodoxy in

Elgin marbles Lapith fighting a centaur

her twenties. She worked as a translator, critic, and editor before turning to fiction. Adopting a masculine pseudonym to evade prejudice against women, she first brought out *Scenes of Clerical Life* (1858). This was followed by such classic works as *Adam Bede* (1859), *The Mill on the Floss* (1860), *Silas Marner* (1861), *Felix Holt, the Radical* (1866), and *Daniel Deronda* (1876). Her masterpiece, *Middlemarch* (1871–72), provides a thorough study of every class of provincial society. The method of psychological analysis she developed would become characteristic of modern fiction.

Eliot, John (1604–1690) English Puritan missionary to the Indians of Massachusetts Bay Colony. He emigrated to Boston in 1631 and became pastor of a church in nearby Roxbury. He soon began a mission to the Indians that inspired the creation in 1649 of the first genuine missionary society. His translation of the Bible into the Algonquian language was the first Bible printed in N. America.

Eliot, T(homas) S(tearns) (1888–1965) U.S.-British poet, playwright, and critic. Born in St. Louis, he moved to England in 1914, where he would work as an editor from the early 1920s until his death. His first important poem, and the first modernist masterpiece in English, was the radically experimental "Love Song of J. Alfred Prufrock" (1915). *The Waste Land* (1922), which expresses with startling power the disillusionment of the postwar years, made his international reputation. His first critical volume, *The Sacred Wood* (1920), introduced concepts much discussed in later critical theory. His conversion to Anglicanism in 1927 shaped all his subsequent works. His last great work was *Four Quartets* (1936–42). Influential later essays include *The Idea of a Christian Society* (1939) and *Notes Towards the Definition of Culture* (1948). His play *Murder in the Cathedral* (1935) is a verse treatment of Thomas BECKET's martyrdom. From the 1920s on he was the most influential English-language modernist poet. After winning the Nobel Prize in 1948, he achieved public adulation unequaled by any other 20th-cent. poet.

Elis \\'ē-lis\\ *modern* **Ilía** \\ēl-'yä\\ Ancient Greek region and city-state, NW PELOPONNESE, Greece. Bounded by Achaea, ARCADIA, Messenia, and the Ionian Sea, the region was known for its horse breeding and was the site of the OLYMPIC GAMES. As an ally of Athens in the PELOPONNESIAN WAR, Elis lost much of its territory. Later, by emphasizing the sanctity of the games, it regained some land and some independence after the Roman occupation (146 B.C.). The modern-day locality contains the archaeological site of OLYMPIA.

Elisabethville See LUBUMBASHI

Elisha \\i-'lī-shə\\ (9th cent. B.C.) Hebrew prophet, the successor of ELIJAH. He instigated a revolt against the ruling house of Israel, the dynasty of Omri, that resulted in the death of the king and his family. Elisha's story is told in the Old Testament books of I and II Kings.

Elizabeth (1837–1898) Empress consort of Austria (1854–98) and queen of Hungary (1867–98). Regarded as the most beautiful princess in Europe, she married her cousin, Emperor FRANCIS JOSEPH, in 1854. She was popular with her subjects but offended Viennese high society by her impatience with court etiquette. The Hungarians admired her for her support of the COMPROMISE OF 1867. She was assassinated by an Italian anarchist.

Elizabeth *Russian* Yelizaveta Petrovna (1709–1761) Empress of Russia (1741–61). Daughter of PETER I, she was proclaimed empress after deposing IVAN VI and his mother. She encouraged the development of education and art and left most state affairs to her advisers and favorites. Her reign was characterized by court intrigues and a deteriorating financial situation; however, Russia's prestige as a major European power grew. Russia adhered to a pro-Austrian, anti-Prussian foreign policy, annexed a portion of S Finland after a war with Sweden, improved its relations with Britain, and fought Prussia in the SEVEN YEARS' WAR.

Elizabeth I (1533–1603) Queen of England (1558–1603). Daughter of HENRY VIII and Anne BOLEYN, she was a precocious child and received the rigorous education normally reserved for male heirs. Her situation was precarious during the reigns of her half brother EDWARD VI and her half sister

George Eliot Drawing by F. W. Burton, 1865

DE

MARY I. Her accession to the throne on Mary's death was greeted with public jubilation. She assembled such experienced advisers as William CECIL and Francis WALSINGHAM but zealously retained her power to make final decisions. Important events of her reign included the restoration of England to Protestantism, the execution of MARY, QUEEN OF SCOTS, and the defeat of the Spanish ARMADA. She lived under constant threat of conspiracies by Catholics. She became known as the Virgin Queen, wedded to her kingdom; many important suitors came forward, but she remained single. She had a suitor, the 2nd earl of ESSEX, executed in 1601 for treason. Though her later years saw an economic decline and disastrous military efforts to subdue the Irish, her reign had already seen England's emergence as a world power. Highly intelligent and strong-willed, Elizabeth inspired ardent expressions of loyalty, and her reign saw a brilliant flourishing in the arts (see ELIZABETHAN LITERATURE).

Elizabeth II *orig.* Elizabeth Alexandra Mary (b.1926) Queen of the United Kingdom from 1952. She became heir presumptive when her father became king as GEORGE VI. In 1947 she married her distant cousin PHILIP, DUKE OF EDINBURGH; their four children include CHARLES, PRINCE OF WALES. She has made numerous visits to Commonwealth countries and paid state visits to other countries worldwide. Aware of the modern role of the monarchy, she has favored simplicity in court life and taken an informed interest in government business. In the 1990s the monarchy was troubled by the highly publicized marital difficulties of two of her children.

Elizabeth II, 1985

Elizabethan literature \i-ˌli-zə-ˈbē-thən\ Body of works written during the reign of ELIZABETH I (1558–1603). Probably the most splendid age in the history of English literature, it saw a flowering of poetry and drama and inspired a wide variety of illustrious prose. It encompasses the work of Edmund SPENSER, Christopher MARLOWE, William SHAKESPEARE, and others.

Elizabeth Farnese \fär-ˈnā-zā\ *Spanish* **Isabella Farnese** (1692–1766) Queen consort of PHILIP V of Spain. She became Philip's second wife in 1714 and quickly established ascendancy over her weak husband. Because his two older sons were in line to succeed him, she sought to secure Italian possessions for her own children, including CHARLES III, which embroiled Spain in wars for three decades. However, she chose able ministers, who introduced beneficial reforms and improved Spain's economy. After Philip's death in 1746, she ceased to exert influence.

elk Any of several species of large DEER in the genus *Cervus*, notably the red deer of Europe, the Kashmir stag, and the Himalayan shou, as well as the N. American deer more correctly called WAPITI. The creature called elk in Europe (*Alces alces*) is known in N. America as MOOSE.

Ellesmere Island \ˈelz-ˌmēr\ Island, Nunavut, Canada. The largest of the QUEEN ELIZABETH ISLANDS, it is roughly 300 mi (500 km) wide by 500 mi (800 km) long. It is the most rugged island in the ARCTIC ARCHIPELAGO, with towering mountains and vast ice fields. Cape Columbia is the most northerly point of Canada. Ellesmere Island National Park Reserve was established in 1986.

Ellice Islands See TUVALU

Ellington, Duke (*orig.* Edward Kennedy) (1899–1974) U.S. pianist, bandleader, arranger, and composer, and a dominant figure in American music. Ellington formed his band in 1924 in his native Washington, D.C.; by 1927 it was performing regularly at the Cotton Club in Harlem. Until the end of his life Ellington's band would enjoy the highest professional and artistic reputation in jazz. Many of his players

spent most of their careers with the band, including saxophonists Johnny Hodges and Harry Carney, bassist Jimmy Blanton, and trumpeters Bubber Miley and Cootie Williams. Billy STRAYHORN was his frequent collaborator. Ellington composed a massive body of work, including music for dancing, popular songs, large-scale concert works, musical theater, and film scores. His best-known compositions include "Mood Indigo," "Satin Doll," "Don't Get Around Much Anymore," and "Sophisticated Lady."

ellipse Closed curve, one of the CONIC SECTIONS of ANALYTIC GEOMETRY, consisting of all points whose distances from each of two fixed points (foci) add up to the same value. The midpoint between the foci is the center. One property of an ellipse is that the reflection off its boundary of a line from one focus will pass through the other. In an elliptical room, a person whispering at one focus is easily heard by someone at the other.

Ellis, (Henry) Havelock (1859–1939) British sexuality researcher. A medical doctor, he gave up his practice to devote himself to scientific and literary work. His major work, the seven-volume *Studies in the Psychology of Sex* (1897–1928), was a comprehensive, groundbreaking encyclopedia of human sexual biology, behavior, and attitudes whose topics included homosexuality, masturbation, and the physiology of sexual behavior. Sale of the first volume led to a trial when the salesman was arrested on obscenity charges; the later volumes had to be published in the U.S. and were legally available only to the medical profession until 1935.

Ellis Island Island, Upper New York Bay, SE New York. It lies southwest of MANHATTAN island and has an area of about 27 acres (11 hectares). It served as the nation's major immigration station 1892–1943. It became part of the STATUE OF LIBERTY NATIONAL MONUMENT in 1965; its restored main hall is the site of the Ellis Island Immigration Museum (opened 1990).

Ellison, Ralph (Waldo) (1914–1994) U.S. writer. Born in Oklahoma City, he won eminence for his novel *Invisible Man* (1952). Narrated by a nameless young black man, it reflects bitterly on American race relations; it is regarded as one of the greatest American novels of the century. He later published two essay collections. An edition of his unfinished second novel was published by his literary executor with the title *Juneteenth* in 1999.

Ellsworth, Oliver (1745–1807) U.S. politician, diplomat, and jurist. Born in Windsor, Conn., he served in the CONTINENTAL CONGRESS (1777–83) and coauthored the Connecticut Compromise (1787), which resolved the issue of representation in Congress. In 1789 he became one of Connecticut's first U.S. senators. He was the chief author of the Judiciary Act (1789), which established the federal court system. He was appointed chief justice of the U.S. Supreme Court in 1796; ill health forced his resignation in 1800.

elm Any of about 18 species of forest and ornamental shade trees that make up the genus *Ulmus* (family Ulmaceae), native mostly to N temperate areas. The flowers, which lack petals, appear before the doubly toothed leaves and are borne in clusters. Seeds are borne in a samara (dry, winged fruit). Many species, including the lordly American elm (*U. americana*), are susceptible to DUTCH ELM DISEASE. Elm wood is important for boats and farm buildings because it is durable in water; it is also used for furniture.

El Niño In oceanography and climatology, the appearance, every few years, of unusually warm surface waters of the Pacific Ocean along the tropical W coast of S. America. It affects fishing, agriculture, and local weather from Ecuador to Chile and can cause climatic anomalies in Asia and N. America. The name (Spanish for "the Christ Child") was originally used to describe the annual flow of warm equatorial waters southward around Christmastime. Peruvian scientists later noted that every few years more intense changes lasting for a year or more were associated with high rainfall along the normally arid coast. The more unusual episodes gained world attention in the late 20th cent. See also LA NIÑA.

El Paso City (pop., 2000: 563,000), W Texas. Located on the RIO GRANDE river opposite Ciudad JUÁREZ, Mexico, it is the largest of the U.S.–Mexican border cities. The area was the site of several missions from the 16th cent. It became U.S. territory in 1848, when an army post was erected; the town was laid out in 1859. It grew slowly until 1881, when four railways arrived; in a decade its population increased more than tenfold. Spanish language and culture distinguish the modern city. A commercial and financial center, it is the site of Ft. Bliss (home of the U.S. Army Air Defense Center); the White Sands Missile Range is nearby.

El Salvador *officially* **Republic of El Salvador** Republic in CENTRAL AMERICA. Area: 8,260 sq mi (21,393 sq km). Population (2000): 6,123,000. Capital: SAN SALVADOR. The majority of the people are mestizo (mixed European and Indian), with small numbers of Indians (mostly Pipil), and

90° 88°

GUATEMALA

HONDURAS

MONTECRISTO NATIONAL PARK

Mount El Pital 8,954 ft.

Chingo Volcano 5,852 ft.

Lake Coatepeque

Santa Ana

Chalatenango

14° N

Chalchuapa

Santa Ana Volcano 7,755 ft.

Ilobasco

Sonsonate

Izalco

Lake Ilopango

Cojutepeque

Sensuntepeque

Nueva San Salvador

San Vicente

San Francisco

Acajutla

San Salvador

San Miguel Volcano 6,957 ft.

San Miguel

Zacatecoluca

Usulután

EL JOCOTAL WILDLIFE REFUGE

La Unión

PACIFIC OCEAN

Gulf of Fonseca

NICARAGUA

Point Cosigüina

EL SALVADOR

©1999, Encyclopædia Britannica, Inc.

Scale 1: 3,810,000
0   25 mi
0 20 40 km

people of European descent. Language: Spanish (official). Religion: Roman Catholicism 78%; Protestantism 17%. Currency: Salvadoran colón. The smallest but most densely populated Central American country, it is crossed by two volcanic mountain ranges, with a narrow coastal region and high central plains in the southern region. The climate ranges from hot and wet in the lowlands to cooler and wetter in the highlands. Cloud forests predominate at the highest elevations. El Salvador has a developing economy; coffee, sugarcane, and cotton are the major export crops. It is a republic with one legislative house; its chief of state and head of government is the president. The Spanish arrived in the area in 1524 and subjugated the Pipil Indian kingdom of Cuzcatlán by 1539. The country was divided into two districts, San Salvador and Sonsonate, both attached to Guatemala. When independence came in 1821, San Salvador was incorporated into the Mexican empire; upon its collapse in 1823, Sonsonate and San Salvador combined to form the new state of El Salvador within the United Provinces of Central America. From its founding, it experienced a high degree of political turmoil. It was ruled by military-backed dictatorships, sometimes elected in tainted elections, from 1931 until the 1980s. The 1980s saw widespread political violence; most notorious was the work of the right-wing "death squads." An accord in 1992 brought an uneasy truce.

Elsevier family See ELZEVIR FAMILY

Elsheimer \'els-ˌhī-mər\, **Adam** (1578–1610) German painter and printmaker. After study in Frankfurt, he went to Rome in 1600 and began producing images of Italian classical subjects, nocturnal scenes, and landscapes. He frequently depicted illumination by firelight, candlelight, and moonlight. His *Flight into Egypt* (1609) was the first painting to depict the constellations accurately. Important in the devel-

opment of 17th-cent. landscape painting, he greatly influenced Dutch, Italian, and French artists.

Elssler, Fanny (1810–1884) Austrian ballerina who introduced character dance into ballet. She toured in Europe before making her Paris Opera debut in 1834. Her warm, spirited style, contrasting with the cool academic style of the then-reigning Marie TAGLIONI, made her an immediate success. During 1840–42 Elssler toured the U.S., earning adulation and large sums of money. She returned to Europe to tour until her retirement to Vienna in 1851.

Éluard \ā-lüē-'àr\, **Paul** *orig.* Eugène Grindel (1895–1952) French poet. In 1919 he met André BRETON and Louis ARAGON, with whom he founded the movement they would call SURREALISM. His subsequent poetry—including *Capitale de la douleur* (1926), *La rose publique* (1934), and *Les yeux fertiles* (1936)—is considered the best to have come out of the movement. After the Spanish Civil War he abandoned Surrealist experimentation. During World War II his poems of suffering and brotherhood were circulated secretly and strengthened the morale of the Resistance.

eluviation Removal of dissolved or suspended material from a layer or layers of the soil by the movement of water when rainfall exceeds evaporation. Often referred to as leaching, the process of eluviation influences soil composition.

Elway, John (Albert) (b.1960) U.S. football player. Born in Port Angeles, Wash., he played professional baseball briefly before joining the Denver Broncos in 1983. One of only three quarterbacks to have passed for more than 45,000 yards, he holds the record for victories by a starting quarterback (148), and ranks second for pass attempts (7,250), pass completions (4,123), and total yardage (51,475). He is famous for his many fourth-quarter game-winning or game-tying touchdown drives. He retired in 1999 after leading the Broncos to a second consecutive Super Bowl victory.

Elysium \i-'li-zhē-əm, i-'li-zē-əm\ *or* **Elysian Fields** Ancient Greek paradise reserved for heroes to whom the gods granted immortality. HOMER described it as a land of perfect happiness at the end of the earth. From the time of PINDAR (c.500 B.C.) on, Elysium was imagined as a dwelling place for those who had lived a righteous life.

Elytis \e-'lē-ˌtēs\, **Odysseus** *orig.* Odysseus Alepoudhelis (1911–1996) Greek poet. His early verse, influenced by French Surrealism, reveals his love of the Greek landscape and the Aegean Sea. During World War II he joined the antifascist resistance and became something of a bard among young Greeks. One of his best-known poems is *The Axion Esti* (1959); later works include *The Sovereign Sun* (1971). He won the Nobel Prize in 1979.

Elzevir family *or* **Elsevier family** \'el-zə-ˌvir\ Family of Dutch booksellers, publishers, and printers, 15 members of which were in business between 1587 and 1681. They were best known for their books or editions of the Greek New Testament and the classics. Their work enjoyed an almost legendary reputation for excellence of typography and design.

e-mail *in full* electronic mail. Messages and other data exchanged between individuals using COMPUTERS in a network. An e-mail system allows computer users to send text and other forms of data to other users. It developed from large organizations using an internal messaging system. The mass provision of e-mail addresses for private individuals by INTERNET SERVICE PROVIDERS led to the development of e-mail as a system to supplement or replace communication by letter. By 2002, some 30 billion e-mail messages were being sent daily.

Emancipation, Edict of (1861) Manifesto issued by ALEXANDER II that freed the serfs of the Russian empire. Defeat in the CRIMEAN WAR, change in public opinion, and violent peasant revolts convinced Alexander of the need for reform. The final edict was a compromise that granted personal liberties to the serfs, but the process by which they were to acquire land was slow, complex, and expensive. Though it failed to create a class of peasant proprietors, its psychological impact was immense.

Emancipation Proclamation (1863) Edict issued by Pres. Abraham LINCOLN that freed the slaves of the Confederacy. On taking office, Lincoln was concerned with preserving the Union and wanted only to prevent slavery from ex-

DE

panding into the W territories; but after the South seceded, there was no political reason to tolerate slavery. In Sept. 1862 he called on the seceded states to return to the Union or have their slaves declared free. He issued the proclamation on Jan. 1, 1863. It had no power in the Confederacy but provided moral inspiration for the North and permitted recruitment of blacks for the Union army; by 1865 nearly 180,000 had enlisted. The 13th Amendment to the Constitution, ratified in 1865, officially abolished slavery.

embargo Detention of merchant vessels or other property to prevent their movement to a foreign territory. A civil embargo is the detention of national vessels in home ports; a hostile embargo is the detention of the ships or property of a foreign state. The term is also used to mean a legal prohibition on commerce. When employed as a political tool by an international organization, an embargo's effectiveness requires cooperation from nonmembers as well as members of the organization.

Embargo Act Legislation by the U.S. Congress in Dec. 1807 that closed U.S. ports to all exports and restricted imports from Britain. The act was Pres. Thomas JEFFERSON's response to British and French interference with neutral U.S. merchant ships during the NAPOLEONIC WARS. It had little effect in Europe, but it imposed an unpopular restriction on New England merchants and exporters (see HARTFORD CONVENTION). The embargo was lifted in 1809, but continued British interference led to the WAR OF 1812.

Embden-Meyerhof-Parnas pathway See GLYCOLYSIS

embezzlement Crime of fraudulently appropriating property entrusted to one's care. It occurs when a person gains possession of goods lawfully and then misappropriates them, in contrast to larceny, the taking of goods from another without the latter's consent. The most widely adopted embezzlement statutes cover custodians of public funds. Many laws subject public servants to severe penalties, even if funds are lost through improper administration. See also FRAUD, THEFT.

embolism \'em-bə-ˌli-zəm\ Obstruction of blood flow by an embolus—a substance (e.g., a blood clot, a fat globule, or a gas bubble) not normally present in the bloodstream. Obstruction of an artery to the brain may cause STROKE. Pulmonary embolism (in the pulmonary artery or a branch) causes difficulty breathing, chest pain, and death of a section of lung tissue. Embolism in a coronary artery can cause MYOCARDIAL INFARCTION. See also THROMBOSIS.

embroidery Art of decorating textiles with needle and thread. The earliest surviving examples are Scythian (c.5th–3rd cent. B.C.). Notable Chinese examples are the imperial silk robes of the Qing dynasty (1644–1911/12). Islamic embroideries (16th–17th cent.) show stylized geometric patterns based on animal and plant shapes. N European embroidery was mostly ecclesiastical until the Renaissance. European skills prevailed in N. America in the 17th–18th cent. The Native Americans embroidered skins and bark with dyed porcupine quills and later beads. The BAYEUX TAPESTRY is the most famous surviving piece of needlework.

embryo \'em-brē-ˌō\ Early stage of development of an organism in the EGG or the UTERUS, during which its essential form and its organs and tissues develop. In humans, the embryo stage lasts for seven or eight weeks after conception; after that it is called a FETUS. During the second week following fertilization, cell differentiation and migration result in the formation of three tissue types, which develop into different organ systems: the ectoderm becomes the skin and nervous system; the mesoderm becomes connective tissues, the circulatory system, muscles, and bones; and the endoderm becomes the lining of the digestive system, lungs, and urinary system. By about the fourth week, the head and trunk can be distinguished and the brain, spinal cord, and internal organs begin to develop. By the fifth week, limbs begin to appear and the embryo is about .33 in. (.8 cm) long. By the end of eight weeks, the embryo has grown to about 1 in. (2.5 cm) long and all subsequent change is limited primarily to growth and specialization of existing structures. Any CONGENITAL DISORDERS begin in those early weeks. See also PREGNANCY.

embryology Study of the formation and development of an EMBRYO and FETUS. Before widespread use of the microscope, embryology was based on descriptive and comparative studies. From the time of Aristotle it was debated whether the embryo was a preformed, miniature individual or an undifferentiated form that gradually became specialized. The latter theory was proved in 1827 when K. E. von BAER discovered the mammalian ovum (EGG). The German anatomist Wilhelm Roux (1850–1924), noted for his pioneering studies on frog eggs, became the founder of experimental embryology.

emerald Grass-green variety of BERYL that is highly valued as a gemstone. Its physical properties are those of beryl. The color that gives this gem its value is due to the presence of small amounts of chromium. The most important production of fine quality gem material is from Colombia; emeralds are also mined in Russia, Australia, S. Africa, and Zimbabwe. Synthetic emeralds are identical to natural crystals and may rival them in color and beauty. The emerald is the birthstone for May.

Emerson, Ralph Waldo (1803–1882) U.S. poet, essayist, and lecturer. Born in Boston, he was ordained a Unitarian minister in 1829, but his questioning led him to resign the ministry three years later. He formulated his philosophy in *Nature* (1836); the book helped initiate New England TRANSCENDENTALISM, of which he soon became the leading exponent. In 1834 he moved to Concord, Mass., the home of his friend H. D. THOREAU. His lectures on the proper role of the scholar and the waning of the Christian tradition caused controversy. In 1840, with Margaret FULLER, he helped launch the Transcendentalist journal

Ralph Waldo Emerson Lithograph by Leopold Grozelier, 1859

The Dial. He became internationally famous with his *Essays* (1841, 1844), including "Self-Reliance." *The Conduct of Life* (1860) is his most mature work. His *Poems* (1847) and *May-Day* (1867) established his reputation as a major poet.

émigré nobility \ˌā-mē-'grā, *Engl* 'e-mi-ˌgrā\ Members of the French nobility who fled France during the FRENCH REVOLUTION. In exile, mainly in England, the émigrés plotted against the Revolutionary government. In response, Revolutionary leaders decreed that those émigrés who did not return by 1792 were liable to death as traitors, and their property was confiscated. NAPOLEON granted most of them amnesty in 1802; they were an important force in the BOURBON RESTORATION.

Emilia-Romagna \ā-'mēl-yä-rō-'män-yä\ Autonomous region (pop., 1996 est.: 3,924,000), N Italy. Located on the Adriatic Sea, the area includes the PO RIVER to the north and the APENNINES to the west and south. BOLOGNA is the chief city and regional capital. It became part of the kingdom of Italy in 1861; the present political region was created in 1948. The fertile Emilian Plain in the north makes Emilia-Romagna one of the leading agricultural regions of Italy.

Emin Pasha \e-'mēn-pä-'shä\, **Mehmed** *orig.* Eduard Schnitzer (1840–1892) German physician, explorer, and administrator. Schnitzer adopted a Turkish name while serving as a medical officer in the Ottoman government. In 1876 he joined Gen. Charles GORDON's forces at Khartoum. In 1878 he was appointed governor of Sudan's Equatoria province. During the MAHDIST MOVEMENT uprising, the Egyptian government abandoned the Sudan (1884); Emin was rescued by Henry Morton STANLEY in 1888. He was killed by Arab slave-traders. His papers and collections contributed vastly to the knowledge of African geography, natural history, ethnology, and languages.

emir \i-'mir\ In the Muslim Middle East, a military commander, governor of a province, or high military official. The first leader to call himself emir was the second CALIPH, UMAR IBN AL-KHATTAB. The title was used by all his successors until the abolition of the caliphate in 1924. In the 10th cent. the commander of the caliph's armies at Baghdad held the title. It was later adopted by the rulers of independent states in central Asia.

Emmett, Daniel Decatur (1815–1904) U.S. showman and songwriter. Born in Ohio, he joined the army at 17 as a fifer. In 1843 in New York he helped organize the Virginia Minstrels, one of the earliest MINSTREL-SHOW troupes. He is credited with writing "Dixie" (1859), a minstrel "walk-around" that became the Confederacy's unofficial national anthem. His other songs include "Old Dan Tucker" and "Blue-Tail Fly."

Emmy awards Annual awards for outstanding achievement in U.S. television. Its name is taken from the nickname "immy" for the image orthicon, a television camera tube. The Emmys are presented by the National Academy of Television Arts and Sciences, founded in 1946, for numerous categories of programs and individuals.

Emory University Private university in Atlanta, Ga. It was chartered as a college in 1836 under Methodist auspices; in 1915 it merged with a school of medicine to become a university. It comprises two undergraduate colleges (one four-year and one two-year) and numerous graduate and professional schools. Research facilities include the Carter Presidential Center, the Yerkes Primate Center, and a cancer center. Total enrollment is about 11,000.

emotion Affective aspect of CONSCIOUSNESS. The emotions represent a synthesis of subjective experience, expressive behavior, and neurochemical activity. As part of the human evolutionary legacy, they may serve adaptive ends by adding to general awareness and the facilitation of social communication. Some nonhuman animals are also considered to possess emotions, as first described by Charles DARWIN in 1872. William JAMES and Carl Georg Lange (1834–1900) independently proposed that emotion was a perception of internal physiological reactions to external stimuli. Walter CANNON proposed the thalamus as a possible source of the emotions. Later researchers have focused on the brain stem structure known as the reticular formation, which integrates brain activity. Cognitive psychologists have emphasized the role of comparison, matching, appraisal, memory, and attribution in the forming of emotions. All modern theorists agree that emotions influence what people perceive, learn, and remember, and play an important part in personality development. Many emotions are universal, but their specific content and manner of expression vary considerably by culture.

Empedocles \em-ˈped-ə-ˌklēz\ (c.490–430 B.C.) Greek philosopher, statesman, poet, and physiologist. He held that all matter was composed of four elements: fire, air, water, and earth. Like HERACLEITUS, he believed that two forces, love and strife, interact to unite and separate the four substances. He declared that salvation requires abstention from the flesh of animals, whose souls may once have inhabited human bodies.

emperor Title of the sovereigns of the ancient Roman empire and various later rulers. Caesar AUGUSTUS was the first Roman emperor. Byzantine emperors ruled at Constantinople until 1453. CHARLEMAGNE became the first of the Western emperors (later Holy Roman emperors) in 800. After Otto I became emperor in 962, only German kings held the title. Monarchs who ruled multiple kingdoms (e.g., ALFONSO VI, who ruled Léon and Castile) sometimes took the title. NAPOLEON's assumption of the title, as a putative successor of Charlemagne, was a direct threat to the HABSBURG DYNASTY. Queen VICTORIA took the title empress of India. Non-European peoples whose rulers have been called emperor include the Chinese, Japanese, Mughals, Incas, and Aztecs.

emphysema \ˌem-fə-ˈzē-mə, ˌem-fə-ˈsē-mə\ *or* **pulmonary emphysema** Abnormal distension of the lungs with air, usually associated with cigarette SMOKING and chronic BRONCHITIS. Elastic tissue degenerates, severely interfering with exhalation. Capillary walls disappear, leaving lung tissue dry and pale. The walls of the pulmonary alveoli (see PULMONARY ALVEOLUS) break down, so the lung fills with pools of air. Symptoms include severe breathlessness, weight loss, bluish skin, chest tightness, and wheezing. Emphysema is irreversible, and may lead to death. See also PULMONARY HEART DISEASE.

Empire State Building Steel-framed 102-story building in New York City designed by Shreve, Lamb & Harmon Associates and completed in 1931. At a height of 1,250 ft (381 m), it surpassed the CHRYSLER BUILDING to become the highest structure in the world (until 1954). It is notable for its use of the SETBACK.

Empire style \ˈäm-ˌpir, ˈem-ˌpīr\ Style of furniture and interior decoration that flourished in France during the First Empire (1804–14). Responding to the desire of NAPOLEON for a style inspired by imperial Rome, the architects Charles Percier (1764–1838) and Pierre Fontaine (1762–1853) decorated his state rooms with classical styles of furniture and ornamental motifs, supplemented by sphinxes and palm leaves to commemorate his Egyptian campaigns. The style influenced the arts (J.-L. DAVID, Antonio CANOVA) and fashion and spread quickly throughout Europe.

empiricism Pair of closely related philosophical doctrines, one pertaining to concepts and the other to beliefs. The doctrine concerning concepts is that concepts (e.g., "gravity") can be understood only if they are connected with experience (e.g., weight, unsupported objects falling). The doctrine concerning beliefs (e.g., that gravity bends space) holds that they depend ultimately on experience for their justification (e.g., light passing near the sun appears to deviate from a straight path). Neither doctrine implies the other. Several empiricists have admitted that there are A PRIORI propositions but denied that there are a priori concepts. Few have denied the existence of a priori propositions while maintaining the existence of a priori concepts. John LOCKE, George BERKELEY, and David HUME are classical representatives of empiricism.

Empson, William (*later* Sir William) (1906–1984) British poet and critic. His *Seven Types of Ambiguity* (1930), which suggests that uncertainty or overlap of meanings in the use of a word can be an enrichment of poetry rather than a fault, had an immense influence on 20th-cent. criticism; its close examination of poetic texts helped lay the foundation for NEW CRITICISM. His verse, influenced by John DONNE, is elliptical, difficult, and pessimistic.

Ems River *ancient* Amisia. River, NW Germany. It rises in N. Rhine-Westphalia and flows west and northwest 230 mi (371 km) to the North Sea. Canals built 1892–99 connect it with the Dortmund–Ems Canal and the Ruhr River industrial district; it carries heavy traffic.

emu \ˈē-ˌmyü\ RATITE of Australia. After the OSTRICH, the emu is the largest living bird. It stands more than 5 ft (1.5 m) tall and often weighs more than 100 lbs (45 kg). The common emu (*Dromaius*, or *Dromiceius, novaehollandiae*, family Dromaiidae) has a stout body and long legs. Emus can run up to 30 mph (50 kph); if cornered, they kick with their large feet. They mate for life and forage in small flocks for fruits and insects but sometimes damage crops. See also CASSOWARY.

emulsion Mixture of two or more liquids in which one is dispersed in the other as microscopic or ultramicroscopic droplets (see COLLOID). Emulsions are stabilized by agents (emulsifiers) that form films at the droplets' surface or impart mechanical stability. Less stable emulsions separate spontaneously into two liquid layers; more stable ones can be destroyed by inactivating the emulsifier, by freezing, or by heating. Many familiar and industrial products are oil-in-water (o/w) or water-in-oil (w/o) emulsions: milk (o/w), butter (w/o), latex paints (o/w), floor and glass waxes (o/w), and many cosmetic and personal-care preparations and medications (either type).

enamelwork Metal objects decorated with an opaque glaze fused to the surface by intense heat. The resulting surface is hard and durable, and can be brilliantly colorful. Objects most suitable for enamelwork are delicate, small (e.g., jewelry, snuffboxes, scent bottles, watches), and made of copper, brass, bronze, or gold. Enamelwork was produced as early as the 13th cent. B.C., reached its peak in the Byzantine empire, and flourished in medieval and Renaissance Europe. In the early 20th cent., Carl FABERGÉ produced highly prized objects. See also CLOISONNÉ.

encephalitis \in-ˌse-fə-ˈlī-təs\ INFLAMMATION of the BRAIN, most often due to infection, usually with a virus. One type (including MULTIPLE SCLEROSIS) attacks the myelin sheath that insulates nerve fibers rather than the neurons themselves. In most cases, symptoms include FEVER, headache, lethargy, and coma. Characteristic neurological signs include uncoordinated, involuntary movements and localized weakness. Treatment usually aims to relieve the symptoms and ensure quiet rest. Various symptoms may remain after recovery.

enclosure movement Division or consolidation of communal lands in Western Europe into the individually owned farm plots of modern times. Before enclosure, farmland was under the control of individual cultivators only during the growing season; otherwise it was used by the community mostly for the grazing of livestock. In England the movement for enclosure began in the 12th cent. and proceeded rapidly from 1450 to 1640; the process was virtually complete by the late 19th cent. In the rest of Europe, enclosure made little progress until the 19th cent. Common rights over arable land have now been largely eliminated.

encomienda \en-ˌkō-mē-ˈen-də\ In colonial Spanish America, a system by which the Spanish crown defined the status of the Indian population. An encomienda consisted of a grant of a specified number of Indians living in a particular area. The receiver could exact tribute from the Indians and was required to protect them and instruct them in the Christian faith. The *encomenderos* effectively gained control of Indian lands. Though the original intent was to reduce the abuses of forced labor, in practice it became a form of enslavement.

encryption, data See DATA ENCRYPTION

Encyclopædia Britannica Oldest and largest English-language general encyclopedia. Its three-volume first edition was published in 1768–71 in Edinburgh, Scotland. In subsequent editions it grew in size and reputation. The most famous edition was the 11th (1910–11), which, with contributions from more than 1,500 experts of world reputation, was the first to divide the traditionally lengthy treatises into more particularized articles. The current edition, the 15th, embodied a new structure, dividing the major articles from the shorter ones. It now also appears in CD-ROM and online versions. Since the 1940s it has been published in Chicago.

encyclopedia Reference work that contains information on all branches of knowledge or that treats a particular branch of knowledge comprehensively. It is self-contained and explains subjects in greater detail than a DICTIONARY and is designed to be easy to consult and to be readily understood by the layperson. Though generally written in the form of many separate articles, encyclopedias vary greatly in format and content. The prototype of modern encyclopedias is usually acknowledged to be Ephraim Chambers's *Cyclopaedia* (1728), and the first modern encyclopedia was the French *Encyclopédie* (1751–65). See also *Encyclopædia Britannica*.

Encyclopédie \äⁿ-ˌsē-klȯ-pā-ˈdē\ French encyclopedia created by the PHILOSOPHES, a principal work of the ENLIGHTENMENT. Under the full title *Encyclopédie, ou dictionnaire raisonné des sciences, des arts et des métiers* ("Encyclopedia, or Classified Dictionary of Sciences, Arts, and Trades"), it was inspired by the success of Ephraim Chambers's British *Cyclopaedia* (1728). Under the direction of Denis DIDEROT, initially aided by Jean d'ALEMBERT, 17 volumes were published between 1751 and 1765; other volumes were added later for a total of 35. Though opposed by conservatives and subjected to censorship, the *Encyclopédie* attracted articles from such important thinkers as J.-J. ROUSSEAU and VOLTAIRE, who were called "Encyclopedists." In its skepticism, emphasis on scientific determinism, and criticism of contemporary legal, judicial, and clerical institutions, the work had widespread influence as an expression of progressive thought.

endangered species Any species of plant or animal threatened with EXTINCTION. The Species Survival Commission of the International Union for Conservation of Nature and Natural Resources (IUCN) publishes information online about endangered species worldwide as the *Red List of Threatened Species*. The U.S. Fish and Wildlife Service is responsible for the CONSERVATION and management of fish and wildlife, including endangered species, and their habitats. Its list now consists of about 1,200 domestic species of endangered or threatened animals and plants, and some 200 recovery programs are in effect.

endive \ˈen-ˌdīv, ˌän-ˈdēv\ Edible annual leafy plant (*Cichorium endivia*) of the COMPOSITE FAMILY. It has been culti-

vated in Europe since the 16th cent. Its many varieties form two groups, the curly-leaved, or narrow-leaved, endive *(crispa),* and the Batavian, or broad-leaved, endive *(latifolia).* The former is used mostly for salads, the latter for cooking.

endocarditis \ˌen-dō-kär-ˈdī-təs\ INFLAMMATION of the heart lining, in association with a noninfectious disease (e.g., systemic LUPUS ERYTHEMATOSUS) or caused by INFECTION. Severe bacterial infection causes an acute form with fever, sweating, chills, joint pain and swelling, and EMBOLISMS. Subacute endocarditis usually comes from bacteria that do not ordinarily cause disease. Bacterial endocarditis is usually treated with long-term antibiotics.

endocrine system \ˈen-də-krən\ Group of ductless GLANDS that secrete HORMONES. The major endocrine glands are the HYPOTHALAMUS, PITUITARY, THYROID, islets of LANGERHANS, ADRENALS, PARATHYROIDS, OVARIES, and TESTES. Secretion is regulated either by regulators in a gland that detect high or low levels of a chemical and inhibit or stimulate secretion, or by a complex mechanism involving the hypothalamus and the pituitary. TUMORS that produce hormones can throw off this balance. Diseases of the endocrine system result from over- or underproduction of a hormone or an abnormal response to a hormone. See also ENDOCRINOLOGY.

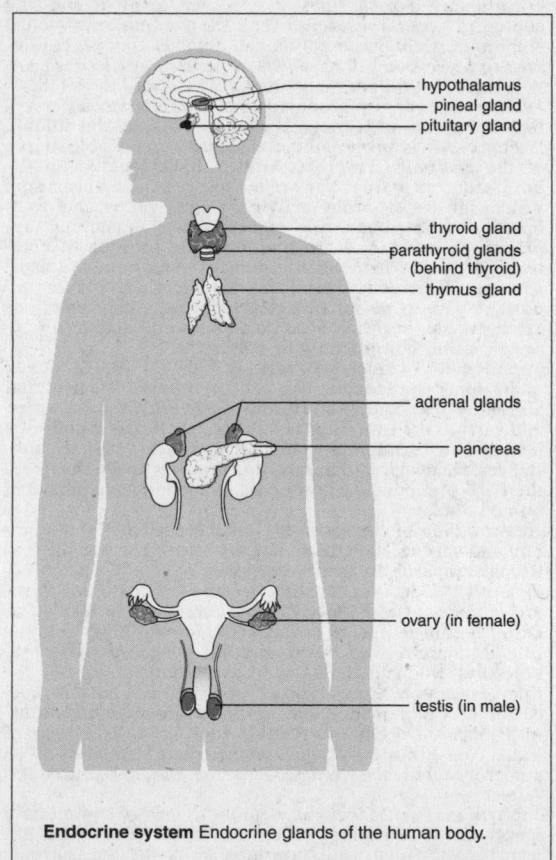

hypothalamus
pineal gland
pituitary gland

thyroid gland
parathyroid glands (behind thyroid)
thymus gland

adrenal glands

pancreas

ovary (in female)

testis (in male)

Endocrine system Endocrine glands of the human body.

endocrinology \ˌen-də-kri-ˈnäl-ə-jē\ Medical discipline dealing with regulation of body functions by HORMONES and other biochemicals and treatment of ENDOCRINE-SYSTEM imbalances. Endocrine therapy is based on replacing deficient hormones with purified extracts. Nuclear technology has led to new treatments; use of radioactive iodine for hyperthyroidism greatly reduced the need for THYROID-GLAND surgery. The detection of minute amounts of hormone with radioimmunoassays (see RADIOLOGY) permits early diagnosis and treatment of endocrine disorders. See also GLAND.

endometriosis \ˌen-dō-ˌmē-trē-ˈō-səs\ Disorder of the female reproductive system in which endometrium (uterine lining) grows in an abnormal location because some endometrial fragments become embedded in the abdominal cavity rather than exiting the UTERUS via the vagina (during MENSTRUATION). Symptoms include pain, heavy menstrual flow, blood in the urine, and infertility. Diagnosis is best made by LAPAROSCOPY. Treatment includes surgery and hormones to suppress ovulation for six to nine months.

endoplasmic reticulum \ˌen-də-ˈplaz-mik-rə-ˈtik-yə-ləm\ (ER) Highly intricate membrane system within the CYTOPLASM of a eukaryotic cell (see EUKARYOTE), important in the synthesis of proteins and lipids. The ER usually makes up more than half the MEMBRANE of the cell and is continuous with the outer membrane of the nuclear envelope (see NUCLEUS). There are two distinct regions of ER: rough ER, or RER, and smooth ER (SER).

endorphin \en-ˈdȯr-fən\ Any of a group of PROTEINS occurring in the brain, with pain-relieving properties typical of OPIUM and related opiates. Discovered in the 1970s, they include enkephalin, beta-endorphin, and dynorphin. Endorphins are released in response to PAIN or sustained exertion (causing "runner's high"). They are also believed to have a role in appetite control, release of PITUITARY SEX HORMONES, and SHOCK. They are apparently connected with "pleasure centers" in the brain, and they seem to be activated by ACUPUNCTURE. Knowledge of their behavior has implications for treating addictions and chronic pain.

endoscopy \en-ˈdäs-kə-pē\ Examination of the body's interior through an instrument inserted into a natural opening or an incision. Endoscopes can examine the esophagus, bronchi, stomach, and rectum and lower colon. With FIBER OPTICS, much more maneuverable instruments can reach formerly inaccessible sites, while causing much less discomfort. Attachments can take tissue samples, excise polyps and small tumors, and remove foreign objects. See also LAPAROSCOPY.

endotherm So-called warm-blooded animals; that is, those that maintain a constant body temperature independent of the environment. The endotherms include the BIRDS and MAMMALS. If heat loss exceeds heat generation, metabolism increases to make up the loss or the animal shivers to raise its body temperature. If heat generation exceeds heat loss, mechanisms such as panting or perspiring increase heat loss. Unlike ECTOTHERMS, endotherms can be active and survive at quite low external temperatures, but require high quantities of "fuel" (i.e., food).

energy Capacity for doing WORK. Energy exists in various forms—including KINETIC, POTENTIAL, thermal, chemical, electrical (see ELECTRICITY), and NUCLEAR—and can be converted from one form to another. For example, batteries convert chemical energy to electrical energy. Though energy may be converted from one form to another, it may not be created or destroyed; that is, total energy in a closed system remains constant (see CONSERVATION LAW). All forms of energy are associated with MOTION, whether of macroscopic objects, molecules, atoms, or subatomic particles. HEAT and work involve the transfer of energy. See also ACTIVATION ENERGY, BINDING ENERGY, MECHANICAL ENERGY, THERMODYNAMICS.

energy, conservation of Principle of physics according to which the ENERGY of interacting bodies or particles in a closed system remains constant though it may take different forms (e.g. KINETIC ENERGY, POTENTIAL ENERGY, thermal energy, or energy in an ELECTRIC CURRENT or stored in an ELECTRIC or MAGNETIC field or in chemical bonds). With the advent of RELATIVITY physics in 1905, MASS was recognized as equivalent to energy.

Energy, U.S. Department of (DOE) Federal executive division responsible for administering national energy policy. Established in 1977, it promotes energy efficiency and the use of renewable energy, oversees nuclear-energy resources, oversees waste management and cleanup activities at inactive facilities, and develops policies and regulations concerning the use of natural gas, coal, and electric energy.

Its regional power administrations transmit electric power produced at federal hydroelectric projects.

Engels \ˈeŋ-əls\, **Friedrich** (1820–1895) German Socialist philosopher. Son of a factory owner, he eventually became a successful businessman himself, never allowing his criticism of capitalist ways to interfere with the profitable operations of his firm. As a young man he became persuaded that the logical consequence of HEGELIANISM and dialectic was communism. In 1844 he published *The Condition of the Working Class in England*. With Karl MARX, whom he first met in Cologne, he formed a partnership to promote the socialist movement. After persuading the second Communist Congress to adopt their views, the two men were authorized to draft the *Communist Manifesto* (1848). After Marx's death (1883), Engels served as the foremost authority on MARXISM and edited volumes 2 and 3 of Marx's *Das Kapital*.

engine MACHINE that can convert any of various forms of ENERGY into mechanical POWER or MOTION. The STEAM ENGINES developed during the INDUSTRIAL REVOLUTION to power stationary machinery were modified in the 19th cent. to propel locomotives and ships, and were joined later by steam turbines. INTERNAL-COMBUSTION ENGINES were developed by Nikolaus OTTO and Rudolf DIESEL in the late 19th cent. Gas turbines and ROCKET engines came into use in the later 20th cent. See also DIESEL ENGINE, GASOLINE ENGINE, JET ENGINE, ROTARY ENGINE.

engineering Professional art of applying science to the optimum conversion of the resources of nature to the uses of humankind. Engineering is based principally on physics, chemistry, and mathematics and their extensions into MATERIALS SCIENCE, solid and fluid MECHANICS, THERMODYNAMICS, transfer and rate processes, and systems analysis. A great body of special knowledge is associated with engineering; preparation for professional practice involves extensive training. Engineers employ two types of natural resources, materials and ENERGY. Materials acquire uses that reflect their properties: strength, ease of fabrication, lightness, or durability; ability to insulate or conduct; and chemical, electrical, or acoustical properties. Energy sources include fossil fuels (coal, petroleum, gas), wind, sunlight, falling water, and nuclear fission. See also CIVIL ENGINEERING, CHEMICAL ENGINEERING, GENETIC ENGINEERING, MECHANICAL ENGINEERING.

England, Church of English national church and the mother church of the Anglican Communion. Christianity was brought to England in the 2nd cent. and was reestablished after the mission of St. AUGUSTINE OF CANTERBURY in 597. Medieval conflicts between church and state culminated in HENRY VIII's break with ROMAN CATHOLICISM. When the pope refused to annul Henry's marriage to CATHERINE OF ARAGON, the king issued the Act of Supremacy (1534), which declared the English monarch to be head of the Church of England. Under Henry's successor, EDWARD VI, more Protestant reforms were instituted. After a five-year Catholic reaction under MARY I, ELIZABETH I ascended the throne (1558), and reestablished the church. The Book of Common Prayer (1549) and the Thirty-nine Articles (1571) became the standards for liturgy and doctrine. The rise of PURITANISM in the 17th cent. led to the ENGLISH CIVIL WARS and the suppression of the Church of England, which was reestablished in 1660. It has maintained an episcopal form of government, and its leader is the archbishop of Canterbury. In 1992 it voted to ordain women as priests. In the U.S., the Protestant EPISCOPAL CHURCH is descended from and remains associated with the Church of England.

England *Latin* **Anglia** S part (pop., 1998 est.: 49,493,000) of the island of Great Britain, excluding Wales. It is the largest unit of the United Kingdom of Great Britain and Northern Ireland. Despite the political, economic, and cultural legacy that has perpetuated its name, England enjoys no separate political status within the United Kingdom. It is a land of low hills and plateaus, with a 2,000-mi (3,200-km) coastline. A substantial upland, the PENNINES, divides N England; the CHEVIOT HILLS define the Scottish border. In the southwest lie the Cotswold Hills and the plateau regions of Exmoor and Dartmoor; in the southeast lie the Downs, and in the south the Salisbury Plain. England's 50,363-sq-mi (130,439-sq-km) area is divided into eight traditional geographic regions. The South East, centered on LONDON, is economically dominant, and contains an extensive range of manufacturing and science-based industry and commercial endeavors. The W. Midlands, in W central England, is a diversified manufacturing region centered on BIRMINGHAM; it also includes STRATFORD-UPON-AVON. The E. Midlands, in E central England, is also a manufacturing region and contains coalfields and some of England's best farmland. E. ANGLIA, the easternmost part of England, is mainly an agricultural region, but high-technology industries have developed there. MANCHESTER and LIVERPOOL are the chief cities of the North West, where textile manufacturing is gradually giving way to engineering industries. The Humberside region lies to the east and is noted for textiles and steel making; it also has chemical and engineering industries and extensive farmland. The North region extends north to the Scottish border; it includes the celebrated LAKE DISTRICT, as well as coalfields and shipyards. The South West region, which includes CORNWALL, has a growing tourist industry. England is especially noted for its long and rich literary tradition, as well as for its architecture, painting, theaters, museums, and universities (see Univ. of OXFORD, Univ. of CAMBRIDGE).

English Channel *or* **The Channel** *French* **La Manche** \là-'mäüsh\ Strait between S England and N France. It connects the Atlantic Ocean with the North Sea through the Strait of DOVER. The French name ("The Sleeve") refers to its shape, which gradually narrows from west to east. Historically both a route for and a barrier to invaders of Britain, it is today one of the world's busiest sea routes for oil tankers and ore carriers. The CHANNEL TUNNEL now provides a rail route between Paris and London.

English Civil Wars (1642–51) Armed conflict in the British Isles between Parliamentarians and supporters of the monarchy (Royalists). Tension between CHARLES I and the House of Commons had been building for some time, and after his unsuccessful attempt to arrest five members of Parliament, both sides prepared for war. The first phase (1642–46) was initially characterized by inconclusive encounters, but victories by Parliamentarian forces under Oliver CROMWELL at MARSTON MOOR and Naseby (see NEW MODEL ARMY) turned the tide. In 1646 the Royalist forces were disbanded. In 1647 Charles negotiated with a Scottish group for assistance, starting the second phase of the wars. A series of Royalist rebellions and a Scottish invasion (1648) were defeated, and Charles was executed in 1649. The fighting continued, and Royalist forces under CHARLES II invaded England in 1651. Parliamentary forces defeated them at Worcester and Charles fled abroad, effectively ending the civil wars.

English East India Co. See EAST INDIA CO.

English horn Large OBOE pitched a 5th below the ordinary oboe. It has a bent metal crook to hold the double reed, and a bulbous bell. It is a transposing instrument in F. "Neither English nor a horn," it has remained a basically orchestral instrument since its first appearance around 1750.

English language W. GERMANIC language widely spoken on six continents. The primary language of the U.S., Britain, Canada, Australia, Ireland, New Zealand, and various Caribbean and Pacific island nations, it is also an official language of India, the Philippines, and many sub-Saharan African countries. It is the second most widely spoken native language in the world, the mother tongue of more than 350 million people, the most widely taught foreign language, and the international language of science and business. English relies mainly on word order to indicate relationships between words (see SYNTAX). Written in the LATIN ALPHABET, it is most closely related to Frisian, GERMAN, and DUTCH. Its history began when Jutes, Angles, and SAXONS from Germany and Denmark migrated to Britain in the 5th–6th cent. The NORMAN CONQUEST of 1066 brought many French words into English. Greek and Latin words began to enter in the 15th cent. English easily borrows words from other languages and has coined many new words to reflect advances in technology.

English sparrow See HOUSE SPARROW

engraving Any of various processes of cutting a design into a plate or block of metal or wood. Cut by a burin on a copper, zinc, aluminum, or magnesium plate, the design is printed with a roller press from ink rubbed into the incised grooves. Wood engraving derives from the WOODCUT, but boxwood cut with the engraver's burin produces a finer, more detailed image. By contrast with engraving from metal plates, the printing of wood engravings is done from the surface; the parts that are not to be printed are cut away. See also ETCHING.

ENIAC \'ē-nē-ˌak, 'en-ē-ˌak\ *in full* Electronic Numerical Integrator and Computer. Early electronic DIGITAL COMPUTER built in the U.S. in 1945 by J. Presper Eckert (1919–1995) and John Mauchly (1907–1980). Weighing 30 tons and filling an entire room, it used some 18,000 VACUUM TUBES, 70,000 resistors, and 10,000 capacitors. In December 1945 it solved its first problem, calculations for the HYDROGEN BOMB. It was later used to prepare artillery-shell trajectory tables and perform other military and scientific calculations.

enlightened despotism *or* **benevolent despotism** In the 18th cent., a form of government in which absolute monarchs pursued reforms inspired by the ENLIGHTENMENT. Among the most prominent enlightened despots were FREDERICK II the Great, PETER I the Great, CATHERINE II the Great, MARIA THERESA, JOSEPH II, and LEOPOLD II. They typically instituted administrative reform, religious toleration, and economic development but did not propose reforms that would undermine their sovereignty.

Enlightenment European intellectual movement of the 17th–18th cent. in which ideas concerning God, reason, nature, and man were blended into a worldview that inspired revolutionary developments in art, philosophy, and politics. Central to Enlightenment thought were the use and celebration of reason; received authority, whether in science or religion, was to be subject to the investigation of unfettered minds. In the sciences and mathematics, the logics of induction and deduction made possible the creation of a sweeping new cosmology. The search for a rational religion led to DEISM; the more radical products were SKEPTICISM, ATHEISM, and materialism. The Enlightenment produced modern secularized theories of psychology and ethics by men such as John LOCKE and Thomas HOBBES. Locke, Jeremy BENTHAM, J.-J. ROUSSEAU, MONTESQUIEU, VOLTAIRE, and Thomas JEFFERSON all contributed to the outline of a form of social organization higher than the authoritarian state, based on natural rights. One of the Enlightenment's enduring legacies is the belief that human history is a record of general progress.

Enron Corp. U.S. energy company. Formed in 1985 from a merger of Houston Natural Gas and InterNorth of Omaha, it soon expanded to provide natural gas and power services throughout the U.S. and abroad. Noted for its aggressive trading and marketing methods, it was ranked as the U.S.'s seventh-largest corporation by 2001, when it was charged with overstating its earnings, having hidden its debt through a network of partnerships. Its ensuing bankruptcy was the largest in U.S. history; its chief officers were indicted, and thousands of employees lost their jobs and savings in stocks. The Arthur Andersen accounting firm, implicated in the scandal, also soon collapsed.

Ensor \'en-sȯr\, **James (Sidney)** *later* Baron Ensor (1860–1949) Belgian painter and printmaker. In 1883 he joined a group of Symbolist artists and began depicting skeletons, phantoms, masks, and other images of grotesque fantasy as social commentary. His *Entry of Christ into Brussels* (1888), painted in smeared, garish colors, provoked outrage. Continuing negative criticism drove him into cynical reclusion. The exhibition of *Entry of Christ* in 1929 led to his being ennobled by King Albert. He was a formative influence on EXPRESSIONISM.

entablature Assemblage of horizontal moldings and bands supported by the columns of Classical buildings. The lowest band, or architrave, originally took the form of a beam running from support to support; the central band, or frieze, is an unmolded strip with or without ornament; the top band, or cornice, is constructed from a series of moldings that project from the edge of the frieze. Most entablatures correspond to the Doric, Ionic, or Corinthian ORDER.

entamoeba \ˌen-tə-'mē-bə\ Any PROTOZOAN of the genus *Entamoeba,* most of which are parasites in the intestines of vertebrates, including humans. *E. histolytica* causes human amebic DYSENTERY. Infection of the large intestine with *E. histolytica* often causes no symptoms; however, diarrhea, abdominal pain, and fever may result from invasion and ulceration of intestinal walls. Cysts of *E. histolytica* are transmitted through food and water, often by fly and cockroach droppings.

Entebbe incident \en-'te-bē\ (July 3–4, 1976) Israeli rescue of 103 hostages from a French airliner hijacked by members of the PALESTINE LIBERATION ORGANIZATION and flown to Entebbe, Uganda, where they were permitted to remain by Pres. Idi AMIN. The hijackers demanded that Israel release 53 imprisoned PLO members. In a brilliantly executed raid by Israeli soldiers, seven hijackers, one soldier, and three hostages were killed.

Entente Cordiale \än-'tänt-kȯrd-'yȧl\ (French: "Cordial Understanding") (1904) Anglo-French agreement that settled numerous colonial disputes. It granted freedom of action to Britain in Egypt and to France in Morocco. The agreement was upsetting to Germany, which had benefited from Franco–British antagonism, and led to Anglo-French diplomatic cooperation against Germany before World War I and later.

enthalpy \'en-thəl-pē\ Sum of the internal energy E and the product of the PRESSURE P and volume V of a thermodynamic system (see THERMODYNAMICS). So, enthalpy $H = E + PV$. According to the law of conservation of energy (see CONSERVATION LAW), the change in internal energy is equal to the HEAT transferred to the system minus the WORK done by the system.

entropy \'en-trə-pē\ Measure of a system's ENERGY that is unavailable for WORK, or of the degree of a system's disorder. The concept, first proposed in 1850 by Rudolf Clausius (1822–1888), is sometimes presented as the second law of THERMODYNAMICS, which states that entropy increases during irreversible processes such as spontaneous mixing of hot and cold gases, uncontrolled expansion of a gas into a vacuum, and combustion of fuel. In popular, nontechnical use, entropy is regarded as a measure of the chaos or randomness of a system.

enuresis \ˌen-yu̇-'rē-səs\ Repeated URINATION into bedding or clothing, usually at night, in a normal child old enough to have completed toilet training. Stressful life events, poor toilet training, and chronic social disadvantage increase its likelihood. It usually resolves with time. Treatment includes family education, reassurance, and behavior therapy. An alarm to wake the child when urination begins has proved highly effective. Drug treatment is sometimes effective.

Enver Pasa \en-'ver-pä-'shä\ (1881–1922) Turkish soldier and politician. One of the YOUNG TURKS who deposed the Ottoman sultan ABDULHAMID II in 1908, he was later army chief of staff in the Second Balkan War (1913), and minister of war during World War I. He unsuccessfully sought Soviet help to overthrow M. K. ATATURK (1920). The Soviets permitted him to help organize the Turkic and Muslim Central Asian republics, but he joined rebels against the Soviet Union and was killed fighting the Red Army.

environmentalism Advocacy of the preservation or improvement of the natural environment, especially the social movement to control environmental pollution. Other specific goals of environmentalism include control of human population growth, conservation of natural resources, and restriction of the negative effects of modern technology. Influential U.S. and British environmentalists have included T. R. MALTHUS, John MUIR, Rachel CARSON, Barry COMMONER, Paul EHRLICH, and E. O. WILSON.

Environmental Protection Agency (EPA) U.S. government agency that sets and enforces national pollution-control standards. It was established by Pres. Richard NIXON (1970) to supersede a welter of confusing and ineffective state environmental laws. Its early accomplishments include banning use of DDT (1972), setting deadlines for the removal of lead from gasoline (1973), establishing health standards for drinking water (1974), and monitoring fuel efficiency in automobiles (1975).

enzyme Substance that acts as a CATALYST in living organisms, regulating the REACTION RATE at which life's CHEMI-CAL REACTIONS proceed without being altered in the process. Enzymes reduce the ACTIVATION ENERGY needed to start these reactions. Because they are not consumed, only tiny amounts are needed. Enzymes catalyze all aspects of cell metabolism, including the digestion of food, the conservation and transformation of chemical energy, and the construction of cellular materials and components. Almost all enzymes are PROTEINS; many contain a cofactor, either an organic compound (e.g., a VITAMIN) or an inorganic ION (e.g., iron, zinc). The enzyme-cofactor combination assumes an active CONFIGURATION, usually including an active site for the substance (substrate) involved in the reaction to fit into. Many enzymes are specific to one substrate. If a competing molecule blocks the active site or changes its shape, the enzyme's activity is inhibited. If the configuration is destroyed, its activity is lost. Most enzyme names end in "-ase." FERMENTATION of wine, leavening of bread, curdling of milk into cheese, and brewing of beer all are enzymatic reactions. Uses in medicine include killing disease-causing microorganisms, promoting wound healing, and diagnosing certain diseases.

Eocene epoch \'ē-ə-ˌsēn\ Interval of geologic time, 55–34 million years ago, in the TERTIARY PERIOD. The name, from the Greek *eos* ("dawn"), refers to the dawn of recent life; during the Eocene, all the major divisions, or orders, of modern mammals appeared, as well as many essentially modern bird orders. Climates were warm and humid; temperate and subtropical forests were widespread. See table at GEOLOGIC TIME.

Eolie, Isole See LIPARI ISLANDS

eon Longest span of geologic history. Geologic eons include the the PHANEROZOIC, (dating from the present back to 544 million years ago), the PROTEROZOIC, and the ARCHEAN, preceded by the pre-geologic HADEAN EON. Less formally, eon refers to a span of one billion years. See table at GEOLOGIC TIME.

EPA See ENVIRONMENTAL PROTECTION AGENCY

Epaminondas \i-ˌpam-ə-'nän-dəs\ (c.410–362 B.C.) Theban statesman, tactician, and leader. After defeating the Spartans at Leuctra in 371, he made Thebes the most powerful state in Greece. In 370–369 he freed the Messenian HELOTS from Spartan enslavement. In 362, at the head of a large allied force, he defeated Sparta, Athens, and their allies at MANTINEA, but was mortally wounded.

ephemeris \i-'fe-mə-rəs\ Table of the positions of celestial bodies at regular intervals, often with supplementary data. Constructed as early as the 4th cent. B.C. and still essential to astronomers and navigators, ephemerides are now calculated, with heavy computing and careful checking, from mathematical descriptions of bodies' observed motion. Various national ephemerides are published; the best, the U.S. ephemeris, first published in 1852, is now published as *The Astronomical Almanac.*

Ephesus \'e-fə-səs\ Ancient Ionian Greek city whose ruins lie near the modern village of Selcuk in W Turkey. It was the site of the Temple of ARTEMIS. One of the 12 Ionian Cities, it was involved in the PERSIAN and PELOPONNESIAN wars. It was taken by ALEXANDER THE GREAT about 334 B.C. and prospered throughout the HELLENISTIC AGE. It passed to Rome in 133 B.C.; under Caesar AUGUSTUS it became the capital of the Roman province of Asia. It was an early seat of Christianity, visited by St. PAUL, and the recipient of the Epistle to the Ephesians. The Goths destroyed the city and temple in A.D. 262.

epic Long narrative poem in an elevated style that celebrates heroic achievement and treats themes of historical, national, religious, or legendary significance. The poems of HOMER are usually regarded as the first important epics and the main source of epic conventions in Western Europe. These conventions include the centrality of a HERO, sometimes semidivine; an extensive, perhaps cosmic, setting; heroic battle; extended journeying; and the involvement of supernatural beings.

Epictetus \ˌep-ik-'tēt-əs\ (c.A.D. 55–c.135) Greek philosopher associated with STOICISM. His teachings were transmitted by his pupil Arrian (d.c.A.D. 180) in two works, the *Discourses* and the *Encheiridion.* True education, Epictetus believed, consists in recognizing that the only thing that belongs to an individual fully is his will. Humans are not responsible for the ideas that come to their consciousness, but they are wholly responsible for how they react to them.

Epicureanism \ˌe-pi-kyu̇-ˈrē-ə-ˌni-zəm, ˌe-pi-ˈkyu̇r-ē-ə-ˌni-zəm\ Philosophy taught by EPICURUS. Since antiquity the term has been used as a synonym for hedonism, the doctrine that pleasure or happiness is the only intrinsic good. Popularly, Epicureanism thus means devotion to pleasure, comfort, and high living, with a certain elegance of style, though these meanings are only loosely related to Epicurus' actual teachings.

Epicurus \ˌe-pi-ˈkyu̇-rəs\ (341–270 B.C.) Greek philosopher. His school in Athens, the Garden, competed with PLATO's Academy and ARISTOTLE's Lyceum. Several fundamental concepts characterize his philosophy. In physics, these are atomism, a mechanical model of causality, limited by the idea of a spontaneous motion, or "swerve," of the atoms, which interrupts the necessary effect of a cause; the infinity of the universe and the equilibrium of all forces that circularly enclose its phenomena; and the existence of gods, conceived as completely extraneous to happenings in the world. In ethics, he identifies good with pleasure, and the supreme good and ultimate end with the absence of pain. See also EPICUREANISM.

Epicurus Bronze bust from a Greek original, c.280–270 B.C.

Epidaurus \ˌe-pi-ˈdȯr-əs\ Town, ancient Greece. An important commercial center in the NE PELOPONNESE, it was famed for its 4th-cent.-B.C. temple of ASCLEPIUS. Excavations have uncovered that temple and other buildings. Inscriptions record divine medical cures.

epidemiology \ˌe-pə-ˌdē-mē-ˈä-lə-ˌjē\ Study of disease distribution in populations and the factors that determine it, chiefly through STATISTICS. Descriptive epidemiology surveys a population to see what segments (e.g., age, sex, ethnic group, occupation) are affected by a disorder, follows its incidence or mortality over time and in different locations, and helps identify syndromes or suggest associations with risk factors. Analytic epidemiology tests the conclusions of descriptive surveys or laboratory observations. Epidemiologic data on diseases is used to find those at high risk, identify causes and take preventive measures, and plan new health services.

epigram Short poem treating concisely, pointedly, and often satirically a single thought and often ending with a witticism or ingenious turn of thought. By extension, the term applies to a terse, sage, or witty saying. Writers of Latin epigrams included CATULLUS and MARTIAL. Later masters of the epigram have included Ben JONSON, VOLTAIRE, Alexander POPE, Oscar WILDE, and G. B. SHAW.

epilepsy *or* **cerebral seizures** *or* **convulsive disorder** Sudden, recurrent disturbances in mental function, consciousness, sensory activity, or body movements, caused by paroxysmal malfunction of neurons in the CEREBRAL CORTEX. Not a specific disease but a complex of symptoms, epilepsy includes generalized (grand mal) seizures, absence (petit mal) seizures (momentary lapses of awareness), and focal seizures (localized movements and sensations). Neurologists classify cases by clinical pattern, site of origin (often located by ELECTROENCEPHALOGRAPHY), and cause. Treatable causes include some brain tumors, infections, metabolic and endocrine-system abnormalities, and trauma. Seizures may be controlled by anticonvulsant drugs.

epinephrine \ˌe-pə-ˈne-frən\ *or* **adrenaline** \ə-ˈdre-nᵊl-ən\ One of two similar HORMONES (the other being NOREPINEPHRINE) secreted by the ADRENAL GLANDS, as well as at some nerve endings (see NEURON), where they serve as NEUROTRANSMITTERS. They increase the rate and force of heart contractions, increasing blood output and raising BLOOD PRESSURE. Epinephrine also stimulates breakdown of GLYCOGEN to GLUCOSE in the liver, raising blood glucose levels, and both hormones increase the level of circulating free FATTY ACIDS. All these effects ready the body for action in times of stress or danger requiring increased alertness or exertion. Epinephrine is used in medical situations including cardiac arrest, ASTHMA, and acute allergic attack (see ALLERGY).

Epiphany Christian festival celebrated on January 6. One of the oldest Christian holy days, it originated in the Eastern church and was adopted in the Western church by the 4th cent. Its eve is called Twelfth Night. It commemorates the first manifestation of JESUS to the Gentiles, as represented by the MAGI. Epiphany also celebrates the (much later) baptism of Jesus by JOHN THE BAPTIST and Jesus' first miracle, performed at Cana.

epiphyte *or* **air plant** Any plant that grows upon or is attached to another plant or object merely for physical support. Epiphytes are found mostly in the tropics. Lacking attachment to the ground, they obtain water and minerals from rain and from debris on the supporting plants. ORCHIDS, FERNS, and members of the PINEAPPLE family are common tropical epiphytes. LICHENS, MOSSES, liverworts, and ALGAE are epiphytes of temperate regions.

Epirus \i-ˈpī-rəs\ Ancient country, NW Greece. It was bounded by ILLYRIA, MACEDONIA, THESSALY, AETOLIA, Acarnania, and the Ionian Sea. In the NEOLITHIC PERIOD it was populated by Greek-speaking peoples from the SW Balkans who may have been among the founders of MYCENAE. It was the launching area of the DORIAN invasions (1100–1000 B.C.) into Greece. The area became a Roman province in the 2nd cent. B.C., and later a part of the BYZANTINE EMPIRE. An independent state in A.D. 1204, it was taken in 1430 by the Ottoman Turks. It is now divided between Greece and Albania.

episcopacy \i-ˈpis-kə-pə-sē\ System of church government by BISHOPS. It existed as early as the 2nd cent. A.D., when bishops were chosen to oversee preaching and worship within a specific region, now called a diocese. Only bishops can ordain priests, perform the rite of CONFIRMATION, and consecrate other bishops. Some Protestant churches abandoned episcopacy during the REFORMATION, but it was retained by the Roman Catholic, Eastern Orthodox, Anglican, and Swedish Lutheran churches, among others. See also APOSTOLIC SUCCESSION.

Episcopal Church, Protestant Descendant of the Church of ENGLAND in the U.S. With the American Revolution, the Church of England was disestablished in the U.S. (1789), and American Anglicans renamed it the Protestant Episcopal Church. The church accepts a modified version of the Thirty-nine Articles of the Church of England. The General Convention is the highest ecclesiastical authority, and it is headed by a presiding bishop, which it elects. The church accepted the ordination of women in 1976.

epistemology Study of the origin, nature, and limits of human knowledge. One major issue is whether all knowledge is derived from experience. EMPIRICISM affirms this view for all nonanalytic propositions; RATIONALISM rejects it. Related issues include whether beliefs that cannot be verified or falsified by experience can be considered knowledge. Philosophers have long disputed whether knowledge is a type of belief. PLATO characterized knowledge as justified true belief, and most modern epistemological discussions start from that point.

epistolary novel \i-ˈpis-tə-ˌler-ē, ˌe-pi-ˈstȯl-ə-rē\ NOVEL in the form of a series of letters written by one or more of the characters. It allows the author to present the characters' thoughts without interference, convey events with dramatic immediacy, and present events from several points of view. It was one of the first novelistic forms to be developed. Distinguished epistolary works include Samuel RICHARDSON's *Pamela* (1740) and Tobias SMOLLETT's *Humphry Clinker* (1771). Its reliance on subjective points of view makes it the forerunner of the modern psychological novel.

epoch Unit of geologic time during which a rock series is deposited, a subdivision of a geologic PERIOD. The use of the term is usually restricted to divisions of the TERTIARY and QUATERNARY PERIODS.

epoxy \i-'päk-sē\ Any of a class of thermosetting POLYMERS, polyethers built up from MONOMERS with an ETHER group that takes the form of a three-membered epoxide ring. The familiar two-part epoxy adhesives consist of a RESIN with epoxide rings at the ends of its MOLECULES and a curing agent containing AMINES or ANHYDRIDES. When mixed and cured, these react to yield a complex network. Stable, tough, and resistant to corrosive chemicals, epoxies are excellent adhesives and useful surface coatings.

Epstein \'ep-ˌstīn\, **Jacob** (*later* **Sir Jacob**) (1880–1959) U.S.-British sculptor. Born in New York City, he studied in Paris and settled in England in 1905. His 18 figures known as the Strand Statues (1907–8) provoked outrage by their nudity, as did his nude angel on the tomb of Oscar WILDE (1912). Affiliated with VORTICISM, he developed a style characterized by simple forms and calm surfaces in pieces carved from stone or modeled in plaster, such as *The Rock Drill* (1913–14). He is best known for religious and allegorical figures carved in colossal blocks of stone, and for bronze portrait busts of celebrities. His monumental bronzes included *St. Michael and the Devil* (1958) for Coventry Cathedral.

Epstein-Barr virus \ˌep-ˌstīn-'bär\ *or* **EB virus (EBV)** Herpesvirus, named for two of its discoverers. The VIRUS infects only salivary-gland cells and one type of white blood cell. Saliva is the only bodily fluid that has been proved to contain infectious EBV particles. In less-developed nations, infection with EBV without symptoms occurs in almost all children under 5. When EBV infection occurs in the teen or early adult years, the usual response is infectious MONONUCLEOSIS. Other, rarer disorders have also been linked with Epstein-Barr virus, including certain cancers. There are no specific treatments for any form of EBV infection, and no vaccines have been developed.

equal protection Guarantee under the 14th Amendment to the U.S. CONSTITUTION that a state must treat an individual or class of individuals the same as it treats other individuals or classes in like circumstances. Until the 1960s it was applied sparingly, and primarily to cases involving discrimination against blacks, but the U.S. Supreme Court under Earl WARREN dramatically transformed the concept, applying it to cases involving welfare benefits, exclusionary ZONING, municipal services, and school financing. Under Warren BURGER, the Court extended it to cases involving sex discrimination and ALIENS. Under William REHNQUIST, it was applied to cases involving homosexual rights and discrimination against persons with disabilities.

Equal Rights Amendment (ERA) Unratified amendment to the U.S. CONSTITUTION designed to invalidate many state and federal laws that discriminated against women. Its central tenet was that sex should not be a determining factor in establishing the legal rights of individuals. It was first introduced in Congress in 1923; finally approved by the U.S. Senate in 1972, it was subsequently ratified by only 30 of the 50 state legislatures. Critics claimed it would cause women to lose privileges and protections, such as exemption from compulsory military service; supporters, led by the NATIONAL ORGANIZATION FOR WOMEN, argued that discriminatory laws left many women in a state of economic dependency.

equation Statement of equality between two expressions consisting of VARIABLES and/or NUMBERS. In essence, equations are questions, and the development of mathematics has been driven by attempts to find answers to those questions in a systematic way. Equations vary in complexity from simple ALGEBRAIC EQUATIONS to DIFFERENTIAL EQUATIONS, exponential equations, and integral equations. They are used to express many of the laws of PHYSICS. See also SYSTEM OF EQUATIONS.

equation, algebraic See ALGEBRAIC EQUATION

equation, quadratic See QUADRATIC EQUATION

equation of motion See equation of MOTION

equations, system of See SYSTEM OF EQUATIONS

equator Great circle around the earth that is everywhere equidistant from the geographic poles and lies in a plane perpendicular to the earth's axis. This geographic, or terres-trial, equator divides the earth into the Northern and Southern Hemispheres. In astronomy, the celestial equator is the great circle in which the plane of the terrestrial equator intersects the CELESTIAL SPHERE. When the sun lies in its plane, day and night are everywhere of equal length (see EQUINOX). See also LATITUDE AND LONGITUDE.

Equatorial Africa See FRENCH EQUATORIAL AFRICA

Equatorial Guinea *officially* **Republic of Equatorial Guinea** *formerly* **Spanish Guinea** Republic on the W coast of equatorial Africa, partly on the mainland, and including BIOKO Island. Area: 10,831 sq mi (28,051 sq km). Population (2000):

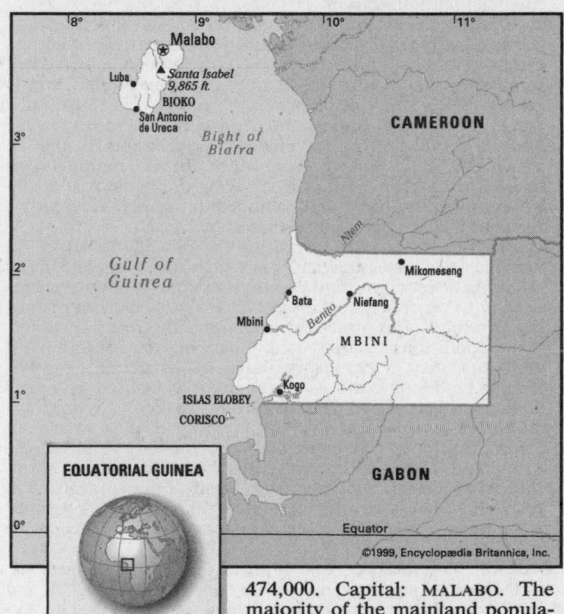

EQUATORIAL GUINEA

Scale 1: 6,500,000
0 20 40 mi
0 30 60 km

©1999, Encyclopædia Britannica, Inc.

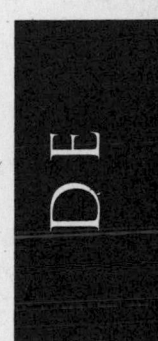

474,000. Capital: MALABO. The majority of the mainland population are Bantu-speaking Fang people, with a minority of other Bantu-speaking tribes (see BANTU LANGUAGES). The majority on Bioko are the Bubi, descendants of Bantu migrants from the mainland. Languages: Spanish, French (both official); pidgin English is commonly spoken. Religion: Roman Catholicism 93%; the Bubi retain their traditional religion. Currency: CFA franc. Bordered by Cameroon and Gabon, Equatorial Guinea's mainland region, Río Muni (Mbini), is separated by the Bight of BIAFRA from the island area of Bioko to the northwest. The mainland has a coastal plain some 12 mi (20 km) wide, with a long stretch of beach, low cliffs to the south, and hills and plateaus to the east. The Benito River divides the region. The island of Bioko consists of three extinct volcanic cones and has several crater lakes and rich lava soils. Dense tropical rain forest prevails throughout the mainland and includes valuable hardwoods. Animal life has been decimated by overhunting. Cacao, timber, and coffee are the only exports. Equatorial Guinea is a republic with one legislative house; its chief of state is the president, and the head of government is the prime minister. The first inhabitants of the mainland region appear to have been PYGMIES. The now-prominent Fang and Bubi reached the mainland region in the 17th-cent. Bantu migrations. Equatorial Guinea was ceded by the Portuguese to the Spanish in the late 18th cent.; it was frequented by slave traders, as well as by British, German, Dutch, and French merchants. Bioko was administered by British authorities (1827–58) before the official takeover by the Spanish. The mainland (Río Muni) was not effectively occupied by the Spanish until 1926. Independence was declared in 1968, followed by a reign of terror and economic chaos under the dictatorial president Macías Nguema, who was overthrown by a military coup in 1979 and later executed. A new constitution was adopted in 1982, but political unrest persisted.

New discoveries in the Gulf of Guinea fueled an oil boom beginning in 2000.

eques \\'e-ˌkwes, 'ē-ˌkwēz\\ (Latin: "horseman") In ancient Rome, a knight. In early Rome, the equites (in full, *equites equo publico,* "horsemen with mounts provided at public expense") were of the senatorial class. They were the most influential members of the COMITIA CENTURIATA. By the early 4th cent. B.C., non-senators could be equites, providing their own horses. AUGUSTUS reorganized them as a military class, removing them from politics. They were later permitted civil careers, and became particularly involved in financial administration.

equilibrium Condition in which the net FORCE acting on a particle is zero. A body in equilibrium experiences no ACCELERATION and, unless disturbed by an outside force, will remain in equilibrium indefinitely. A stable equilibrium is one in which small displacements from that state produce forces that tend to oppose the displacement and return the body to equilibrium. An unstable equilibrium is one in which the least departures produce forces tending to increase the displacement. A brick lying on the floor is in stable equilibrium, but a ball balanced on an edge is in unstable equilibrium. See also MECHANICS.

equilibrium, chemical Condition in the course of a reversible CHEMICAL REACTION in which no net change in the amounts of reactants and products occurs: Products are reverting to reactants at the same rate as reactants are forming products. For practical purposes, the reaction under those conditions is completed. Changing the conditions of TEMPERATURE or PRESSURE changes the reaction's equilibrium; a high temperature or pressure may be used to "push" a reaction that at ordinary conditions makes little product.

equine \\'ē-ˌkwīn, 'e-ˌkwīn\\ Any member of the UNGULATE family Equidae, which includes the modern HORSES, ZEBRAS, and ASSES, all in the genus *Equus,* as well as more than 60 species known only from fossils. Equines descended from the dawn horse (eohippus). Wild horses were smaller than their domesticated descendants. See also PRZEWALSKI'S HORSE.

equinox \\'ē-kwə-ˌnäks, 'e-kwə-ˌnäks\\ Either of two moments in the year when the sun is exactly above the EQUATOR and day and night are of equal length all over the earth. The vernal equinox, when spring begins in the Northern Hemisphere, occurs about March 21, when the sun moves north across the celestial equator. The autumnal equinox falls about September 23, as the sun crosses the celestial equator going south. See also SOLSTICE.

equinoxes, precession of the Motion of the points where the sun crosses the celestial equator, caused by precession of earth's axis. HIPPARCHUS noticed a consistent shift in the stars' positions from earlier measures, indicating that the earth, not the stars, was moving. This precession, caused by the gravity of the sun and the moon acting on earth's equatorial bulge, makes the N and S celestial poles (see CELESTIAL SPHERE) trace out circles on the sky over a cycle of almost 26,000 years and affects the celestial equator, changing its points of intersection (equinoxes) with the ECLIPTIC.

equistetum See HORSETAIL

equity Justice according to fairness, especially as distinguished from mechanical application of rules under COMMON LAW. Courts of equity (also called chancery courts) arose in England in the 14th cent. in response to the increasingly strict rules of proof and other requirements of the courts of law. Equity provided remedies not available under the old WRIT system. The equity courts eventually established their own precedents, rules, and doctrines and began to rival the law courts in power. The two systems were united in 1873. Courts of equity also developed early in U.S. history, but by the early 20th cent. most jurisdictions had combined them with courts of law into a single system. Modern courts apply both legal and equitable principles and offer both legal and equitable relief.

equivalence relation In mathematics, a generalization of the idea of equality between elements of a SET. All equivalence relations (e.g., that symbolized by the equals sign) obey three conditions: reflexivity (every element is in the relation to itself), symmetry (element A has the same relation to element B that B has to A), and transitivity (see TRANSITIVE LAW). Congruence of triangles is an equivalence relation in geometry.

ERA See EQUAL RIGHTS AMENDMENT

era Long span of geologic time, which divides an EON. Three eras are recognized: PALEOZOIC, MESOZOIC, and CENOZOIC. Because of the difficulties involved in establishing accurate chronologies, PRECAMBRIAN TIME, or the earliest era, is classified independently. An era is composed of one or more geologic PERIODS.

Era of Good Feelings See Era of GOOD FEELINGS

Erasmus \\i-'raz-məs\\, **Desiderius** (1469–1536) Dutch humanist, considered the greatest European scholar of the 16th cent. Ordained a priest in 1492, he studied at the Univ. of Paris and traveled throughout Europe, coming under the influence of Thomas MORE. The book that first made him famous was the *Adagia* (1500, 1508), an annotated collection of Greek and Latin proverbs. He became noted for his editions of classical authors, Church Fathers, and the New Testament as well as for his own works, including *Handbook of a Christian Knight* (1503) and *Praise of Folly* (1509). Using the methods of Italian humanists, he helped lay the groundwork for the

Erasmus Painting by Hans Holbein the Younger, 1523

historical-critical study of the past. By criticizing ecclesiastical abuses, he encouraged reform, which found expression both in the Protestant REFORMATION and in the Catholic COUNTER-REFORMATION. Under pressure to attack Martin LUTHER, he took an independent stance, rejecting both Luther's doctrine of predestination and the powers claimed for the papacy.

Eratosthenes of Cyrene \\ˌer-ə-'täs-thə-ˌnēz\\ (276?–194? B.C.) Greek scientific writer, astronomer, and poet. He settled in Alexandria around 255 B.C. and became director of its great library. He was the first to calculate the earth's circumference. He also accurately measured the tilt of earth's axis, compiled a star catalog, worked out a calendar with leap years, and tried to fix the dates of literary and political events since the siege of Troy.

Erdős \\'er-dȯsh\\, **Paul** (1913–1996) Hungarian mathematician. He proved a classic theorem of NUMBER THEORY (1933), founded the study of probabilistic number theory with Aurel Wintner and Mark Kac, and with Atle Selberg gave an astounding elementary proof of the prime number theorem (1949). Famously eccentric, he traveled almost constantly for his last 40 years, collaborating with hundreds of mathematicians on numerous problems.

Erech \\'ē-ˌrek\\ *or* **Uruk** \\'ü-ˌrük\\ Ancient city of MESOPOTAMIA. Located northwest of UR on the EUPHRATES RIVER, it was one of the greatest cities of SUMER. Its brickwork walls were supposedly built by GILGAMESH. Excavations have traced successive cities from the prehistoric Ubaid period (c.5000 B.C.) down to Parthian times (126 B.C.–A.D. 224), when around 70 B.C. learned scribes were still using CUNEIFORM WRITING.

eremite See HERMIT

Eretria \\e-'rē-trē-ə\\ Ancient Greek town, on the island of EUBOEA. Jointly with its neighbor Khalkís, it founded CUMAE in Italy around 750 B.C., the first of the Greek colonies in the west. Subsequent rivalry with Khalkís culminated in war. In 499–498 B.C. Eretrian triremes sailed to support the Ionian revolt against PERSIA, for which act DARIUS I destroyed the city (490 B.C.) and deported the population. Extensive ruins mark the site.

Erfurt \\'er-ˌfu̇rt\\ City (pop., 1996 est.: 211,000), central Germany. St. BONIFACE founded a bishopric there in A.D. 742, and by 805 it was an important center on the Frankish empire's E border. Granted municipal rights about 1250, it joined the HANSEATIC LEAGUE in the 15th cent. It formed part of Prussian SAXONY 1802–1945. It is dominated by its 12th-cent. cathedral; other buildings include the monastery where Martin LUTHER was a monk (1505–8).

ergot \\'er-gət, 'er-ˌgät\ Disease of CEREAL GRASSES, especially RYE, caused by the FUNGUS *Claviceps purpurea*. Ergot is the source of drugs used to control postpartum hemorrhage and to treat migraine headaches. Lysergic acid, from which LSD is synthesized, comes from ergot. Overdoses of ergot-derived medications or eating flour milled from ergot-infected rye can cause ergotism (also called St. Anthony's Fire) in humans and livestock; symptoms may include convulsions, miscarriages in females, and dry gangrene, and may result in death.

Erhard \\'er-ˌhärt\, **Ludwig** (1897–1977) German economist and politician. As economics minister (1949–63), he was the chief architect of W. Germany's remarkable postwar economic recovery; his "social market system" was based on free-market capitalism but included special provisions for housing, farming, and social programs. In 1963 he succeeded Konrad ADENAUER as chancellor. His government was troubled by an economic downturn, and he was forced to resign in 1966.

Erickson, Arthur (Charles) (b.1924) Canadian architect. Born in Vancouver, he first earned wide recognition with his plan for Simon Fraser Univ. (1963–65), designed with Geoffrey Massey, which included an enormous skylit indoor plaza. Robson Square, Vancouver (1978–79), a large civic center, incorporates waterfalls, a roof garden, plazas, and stairs with integrated ramps. Other works include UBC's Museum of Anthropology (1976) and the Canadian Embassy in Washington, D.C. (1989).

Ericsson, John (1803–1889) Swedish-U.S. naval engineer and inventor. He moved to England in 1826, where he constructed a steam locomotive (1829) and later devised a caloric engine and patented a screw propeller. He emigrated to the U.S in 1839. During the Civil War he proposed, designed, and built a novel warship, the *Monitor*. Its battle with the *Merrimack* led the government to place an order for many more such vessels. Wholly steam-powered and with a screw propeller and an armored revolving turret, it set a new pattern for U.S. warships.

Eric the Red See ERIK THE RED

Erie City (pop., 2000: 103,000), NW Pennsylvania. Named for the Erie Indians, it was the site of a French fort (1753) on Lake ERIE. The site was acquired by the U.S. in 1795. Nearby naval shipyards built most of the fleet that defeated the British at the Battle of Lake Erie (1813) in the WAR OF 1812. Economic development began with the opening (1844) of the Erie and Pittsburgh Canal. Pennsylvania's only port on the ST. LAWRENCE SEAWAY, it is a shipping point for lumber, coal, and petroleum.

Erie, Lake Lake, in U.S. and Canada. One of the five GREAT LAKES, it lies between Lakes HURON and ONTARIO, forming part of the U.S.–Canada boundary. It is 240 mi (388 km) long and has a maximum width of 57 mi (92 km), with a surface area of 9,910 sq mi (22,666 sq km). The Detroit River carries inflow from Lake Huron, and the lake discharges through the NIAGARA RIVER. It is an important link in the ST. LAWRENCE SEAWAY; its ports handle steel, iron ore, coal, and grain. The area was once inhabited by Erie Indians; by the 17th cent. the Iroquois had displaced them. It was the site of the Battle of Lake Erie in the WAR OF 1812.

Erie Canal Historic waterway, New York. It stretches from BUFFALO on Lake ERIE to ALBANY on the HUDSON RIVER. Commissioned by Gov. DeWitt CLINTON, it opened in 1825. It connected the GREAT LAKES with NEW YORK CITY and contributed greatly to the settlement of the Midwest, allowing for the transport of people and supplies. Enlarged several times, the canal is 340 mi (547 km) long, 150 ft (46 m) wide, and 12 ft (4 m) deep. Now used mainly for pleasure boating, it is part of the New York State Canal System.

Erigena \ə-'rē-ge-nə\, **John Scotus** *Latin* Johannes Scotus Eriugena (c.A.D. 810–877?) Irish-born theologian, translator, and commentator. In his philosophical system, which came to be known as Scotism, he attempted to integrate Greek philosophy and NEOPLATONISM with Christian belief. *On Predestination* (851) and *On the Division of Nature*

(862–66) were both condemned by church authorities. His Latin translations of major works of Greek PATRISTIC LITERATURE made them accessible to Western thinkers. Remembered for the nonconformity of his thought, he is said to have been stabbed to death by his students with their pens for attempting to make them think.

Erikson, Erik H(omburger) (1902–1994) German-U.S. psychoanalyst. Trained in Vienna by Anna FREUD, he came to the U.S. in 1933, where he practiced child psychoanalysis in Boston. In 1938 he began to study cultural influences on psychological development, working with American Indian children. He held that personality development takes place through a series of identity crises that must be overcome and internalized in preparation for the next developmental stage; he posited eight such stages. His other concerns included the interactions of psychology with history, politics, and culture. He held teaching positions at Harvard, Yale, and UC–Berkeley. His works include *Childhood and Society* (1950), *Young Man Luther* (1958), and *Gandhi's Truth* (1969).

Eriksson, Leif See LEIF ERIKSSON THE LUCKY

Erik the Red *orig.* Erik Thorvaldson (late 10th cent.) Founder of the first European settlement on Greenland (c.986) and father of LEIF ERIKSSON THE LUCKY. A native of Norway, Erik grew up in Iceland; exiled for manslaughter around 980, he set sail and landed on Greenland. With 350 colonists he founded a colony that numbered about 1,000 settlers by 1000 A.D. In 1002 the colony was ravaged by sickness, and it gradually died out. Erik's story is told in the Icelandic *Eiriks saga*.

Eris \\'er-is\ Ancient Greek personification of strife. Her Roman counterpart was Discordia. She was best known for her role in starting the TROJAN WAR, when she threw a golden apple inscribed "for the most beautiful" in among the guests at a wedding. HERA, ATHENA, and APHRODITE each claimed it, and ZEUS assigned the task of judging to the Trojan PARIS. He awarded the apple to Aphrodite, who in turn helped him carry off the beautiful HELEN, an act that triggered war.

Eritrea \ˌer-ə-'trē-ə, ˌer-ə-'trā-ə,\ *officially* **State of Eritrea** *Tigrinya* **Ertra** Country, E Africa. It extends for about 600

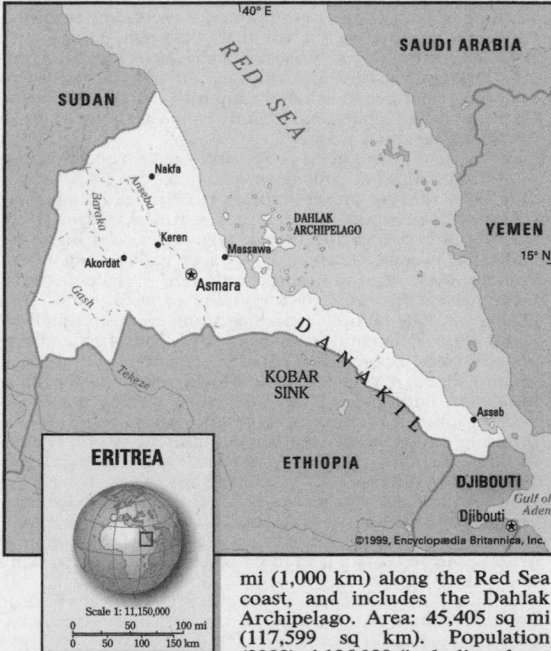

ERITREA
Scale 1: 11,150,000
0   50   100 mi
0   50   100 150 km

©1999, Encyclopædia Britannica, Inc.

mi (1,000 km) along the Red Sea coast, and includes the Dahlak Archipelago. Area: 45,405 sq mi (117,599 sq km). Population (2000): 4,136,000 (including about 350,000 refugees from The Sudan). Capital: ASMARA. There is no official religion or language. The varied population is about half Tigrinya-speaking (see TIGRAY) Christians, with a large minority of

Muslims and diverse other peoples. Arabic, English, and Italian are also spoken. Currency: Nakfa. Eritrea's land varies from temperate central highlands to coastal desert plain, with savanna and open woodlands in the W lowlands. Its economy is based on livestock herding and subsistence agriculture. Industry, based in Asmara, includes food products, textiles, and leather goods; exports include salt, hides, cement, and gum arabic. Eritrea's form of government is a transitional regime with one interim legislative body; the head of state and government is the president. As the site of the main ports of the Aksumite empire, it was linked to the beginnings of the Ethiopian kingdom, but it retained much of its independence until it came under Ottoman rule in the 16th cent. In the 17th–19th cent., control of the territory was disputed among Ethiopia, the Ottomans, the kingdom of Tigray, Egypt, and Italy; it became an Italian colony in 1890. Eritrea was used as the main base for the Italian invasions of Ethiopia (1896 and 1935–36), and in 1936 became part of Italian E. Africa. It was captured by the British in 1941, federated to Ethiopia in 1952, and made a province of Ethiopia in 1962. Thirty years of guerrilla warfare by Eritrean secessionist groups ensued. A provisional Eritrean government was established in 1991 after the overthrow of the Ethiopian government, and independence came in 1993. A new constitution was ratified in 1997. A border war with Ethiopia that began in 1998 ended in an Ethiopian victory in 2000.

Erivan See YEREVAN

ermine \'ǝr-mǝn\ Any of several WEASEL species (genus *Mustela,* family Mustelidae) whose white winter coat is the ermine of the fur trade. Ermines are found in N N. America, Eurasia, and N. Africa in thickets, woodland, and semi-timbered areas. Species are 5–12 in. (13–29 cm) long (excluding the 2–5-in., or 5–12-cm, tail) and weigh less than 11 oz (0.3 kg). Voracious carnivores, ermines feed on small mammals, birds, eggs, and frogs. The ermine used in the Middle Ages for royal robes was from a species called stoat (*M. erminea*).

Ernst, Max \'ernst, 'ǝrnst\ (1891–1976) German-French painter and sculptor. After serving in World War I, he became the leader of the DADA movement in Cologne (1919), working in collage and photomontage. In 1922 he settled in Paris and was among the founders of SURREALISM. After 1934 the irrational and whimsical imagery seen in his paintings appeared also in his sculpture. In 1941 he moved to New York and began collaborating with Marcel DUCHAMP. He returned to France in 1953 and continued to produce lyrical and abstract works.

Eros \'er-ˌäs, 'ir-ˌäs\ Greek god of love. HESIOD declared him one of the primeval gods born of CHAOS, but he was later said to be the son of APHRODITE. His Roman counterpart was CUPID. Eros was depicted as a beautiful winged youth carrying a bow and a quiver of arrows. In later literature and art he became increasingly younger, ending as an infant.

erosion Removal and transportation of surface material from the earth's crust by the action of wind, water, and glacial ice. The complementary actions of erosion and deposition or sedimentation alter existing landforms and create new ones. Erosion will often occur after rock has been altered through WEATHERING. Moving water is the most important natural agent of erosion, mainly by sea waves and the abrasive action of sand and pebbles, and by the scouring action of the sediment-containing rivers. Glacial erosion occurs as the ice, embedded with debris, moves slowly over the ground. Wind plays a key role in arid regions as blowing sand breaks down rock and dislodges surface sand from unprotected sand dunes. Human intervention, as by the removal of natural vegetation for farming or grazing purposes, can lead to or accelerate erosion by wind and water.

error In applied mathematics, the difference between a value and an estimate of that value. In STATISTICS, a common example is the difference between the mean age of a given group of people (see MEAN, MEDIAN, AND MODE) and that of a sample drawn from the group. In NUMERICAL ANALYSIS, an example of round-off error is the difference between the true value of PI and commonly substituted expressions like 22/7 or 3.14159. Truncation error results from using only the first few terms of an infinite series. Relative error is the ratio of the size of an error to the size of the quantity measured.

Erskine \'ǝr-skǝn\, **Thomas** *later* Baron Erskine (of Restormel) (1750–1823) Scottish lawyer. He made important contributions to the protection of personal liberties. His defense of politicians and reformers on charges of treason and related offenses checked repressive measures taken by the British government in the aftermath of the French Revolution. He contributed to the law of criminal responsibility by defending, on the novel ground of insanity, a would-be assassin of GEORGE III. He served in Parliament (1783–84, 1790–1806), and was lord chancellor (1806–7) in William Grenville's "ministry of all talents." In 1820 he defended Queen Caroline, whom GEORGE IV had brought to trial before the House of Lords for adultery in order to deprive her of her rights and title.

Erté \'er-'tä\ *orig.* Romain de Tirtoff (1892–1990) Russian-French fashion illustrator and designer. In 1912 he left his native St. Petersburg for Paris, where he worked for Paul POIRET. From 1916 to 1937 he published elegant, highly stylized illustrations depicting models in mannered poses against Art Deco interiors in *Harper's Bazaar.* He also designed theatrical scenery and costumes for the Folies Bergère (1919–30), and for U.S. revues, notably the *Ziegfeld Follies.* His designs continue to be widely reproduced.

Erté, black-and-white satin afternoon dress

Erving, Julius (Winfield) \'ǝr-viŋ\ (b.1950) U.S. basketball star. Born in Roosevelt, N.Y., at 6 ft 7 in. (2 m), "Doctor J" played forward for the Virginia Squires (1971–73) of the ABA, the New York Nets (1973–76), and the Philadelphia 76ers (1977–87), and was known for his fast breaks, balletic leaps, and climactic slam dunks. He is one of only three professional players whose career point totals exceeded 30,000 (with 30,026).

erythrocyte \i-'rith-rǝ-ˌsīt\ *or* **red blood cell** *or* **red corpuscle** BLOOD cell that carries oxygen and carbon dioxide for exchange with other tissues. HEMOGLOBIN gives the cell—and whole blood—its color. Red cells are small, round, flexible, and concave on both sides, and lack a NUCLEUS. They are formed in BONE MARROW and stored in the SPLEEN. Mature cells live 100–120 days. Adult human blood has about 5.2 million per cu mm. Some conditions change their shape (e.g., PERNICIOUS ANEMIA, SICKLE-CELL ANEMIA) or number (e.g., ANEMIA).

escalator Moving staircase used as transportation between floors or levels in stores, airports, subways, and other mass pedestrian areas. The name was first applied to a moving stairway shown at the Paris Exposition of 1900. Modern escalators are electrically powered, driven by chain and sprocket, and held in place by two tracks. As the treads approach a landing, they pass through a comb device.

escape velocity Minimum speed allowing a body to escape from a gravitational center of attraction. It decreases with altitude and equals the square root of 2 (about 1.414) times the speed needed to orbit at the same altitude. Escape velocity is about 6.96 mi/second (11.20 km/second) at earth's surface and about one-third of this at the moon's surface.

eschatology \ˌes-kǝ-'tä-lǝ-jē\ Theological doctrine of the "last things," or the end of the world. Judaism, Christianity, and Islam have historical eschatologies. Old Testament eschatology sees the catastrophes that beset the people of Israel as due to their disobedience to the laws and will of God, and holds that conformity to God's will will result in renewal and the fulfillment of God's purpose. In Christianity, the end times are thought to have begun with the life and ministry of Jesus. MILLENNIALISM focuses especially on Christ's second coming and the reign of the righteous on earth. In SHIITE Islam, the MAHDI, or restorer of the faith, will come to inaugurate the last judgment.

Escher \'e-shər\ **M(aurits) C(ornelis)** (1898–1972) Dutch graphic artist. After studies in Haarlem, he traveled and sketched throughout Europe. From the 1940s he became well known for prints in which he used realistic detail to achieve bizarre optical illusions, such as staircases that appear to lead both up and down from the same level and unexpected metamorphoses of mundane objects. His works were of interest to

M. C. Escher, "Encounter," 1944

mathematicians, cognitive psychologists, and the general public, and were widely reproduced especially in the 1960s and '70s.

Escoffier \es-kȯf-'yā\, **(Georges-) Auguste** (1846–1935) French chef known for his innovations in fine cooking. He earned a worldwide reputation as director of the kitchens at hotels in Monte Carlo and London. He helped reform *grande cuisine* by simplifying and refining it and making its preparation more efficient. He wrote *Guide culinaire* (1903), *Ma cuisine* (1934), and other classic works. He is often called the greatest chef of all time.

Escorial, El See EL ESCORIAL

escrow \'es-ˌkrō\ Instrument, such as a deed, money, or PROPERTY, that constitutes evidence of obligations between two or more parties and is held by a third party. It is delivered by the third party only upon fulfillment of some condition. In commercial usage, this condition is most often the performance of an act (e.g., payment) by the party who is to receive the instrument. Escrow is also used in family transactions (e.g., when a death in the family results in an instrument being delivered to another family member).

Esdraelon \ˌez-drə-'ē-lən\, **Plain of** *Hebrew* **Emeq Yizreel** \'e-mek-ˌyēz-rä-'el\ Plain, N Israel. About 25 mi (40 km) long, it divides the hilly areas of GALILEE in the north and SAMARIA in the south. Part of the ancient passage between Egypt and the FERTILE CRESCENT, it was an avenue of commerce and a scene of conflict from remotest antiquity. At the northwest is the site of ancient MEGIDDO. Since 1920 the land has been reclaimed, and dozens of settlements have been built.

Esfahan \ˌes-fä-'hän\ *or* **Isfahan** \ˌis-fä-'hän\ City (pop., 1996: 1,266,000), W central Iran. A major city of the SELJUQ DYNASTY (11th–13th cent. A.D.) and of the SAFAVID DYNASTY of Iran (16th–18th cent.), it began a golden age in 1598 when Shah ABBAS I made it his capital and rebuilt it into one of the 17th cent.'s largest cities. At its center he created the immense Meydan-i-Shah, a great rectangular garden enclosing the noted Masjid-i-Shah (Royal Mosque). In 1722 Afghanis took the city, and it went into decline. It is now a major textile center.

Eskimo *or* **Inuit** \'i-nú-wət\ Group of peoples who, with the closely related ALEUT, constitute the native population of the Arctic and subarctic regions of Greenland, Alaska, Canada, and far E Siberia. The name Eskimo, first applied by Europeans, is favored by Arctic peoples in Alaska, while those in Canada and Greenland prefer Inuit. The Eskimo are of Asian origin, like the AMERICAN INDIANS, but are distinguishable from the latter by their CLIMATIC ADAPTATIONS, B blood type, and languages. Traditional Eskimo culture was totally adapted to an extremely cold, snow- and ice-bound environment. Harpoons and one-person kayaks or larger umiaks were used for hunting on the sea. Clothing was fashioned of caribou furs and sealskins. Snow-block IGLOOS or semisubterranean sod and stone houses were used in winter, while in summer animal-skin tents were erected. Dogsleds were the basic means of land transport. Religion centered on the unseen world of spirits. Today snowmobiles have replaced dogsleds, and rifles harpoons. Many Eskimo have abandoned their nomadic hunting pursuits and moved into N towns and cities. There are about 43,000 Eskimo in Alaska, 21,000 in Canada, 51,000 in Greenland and Denmark, and 1,600 in Siberia.

esophagus \i-'sä-fə-gəs\ Muscular tube that conveys food by PERISTALSIS from the PHARYNX to the STOMACH. Both ends have sphincters (muscular constrictions), which relax to let food through and close to keep it from backing up. Disorders include ulceration and bleeding, heartburn from stomach acid, failure of a sphincter to open, and muscle spasms.

ESP See EXTRASENSORY PERCEPTION

Español, Pedro See Pedro BERRUGUETE

Esperanto \ˌes-pə-'rän-tō\ Artificial language created in 1887 by Lazarus Ludwig Zamenhof (1859–1917), a Polish oculist, as an international second language. Zamenhof's *Fundamento de Esperanto* (1905) outlines its basic principles. All words, derived from roots commonly found in the European languages, are spelled as pronounced, and grammar is simple and regular. Nouns have no gender and end in *-o*, and there is only one definite article, *la*. Verbs are regular and have only one form for each tense or mood. Estimates of the number of Esperanto-speakers range from 100,000 to several million.

espionage \'es-pē-ə-ˌnäzh\ Process of obtaining military, political, commercial, or other secret information by means of spies, secret agents, or illegal monitoring devices. It is sometimes distinguished from the broader category of intelligence gathering by its aggressive nature and its illegality.

essay Analytic, interpretative, or critical literary composition, usually dealing with its subject from a limited and often personal point of view. Flexible and versatile, the essay was perfected by Michel de MONTAIGNE. The essay has been the vehicle of literary and social criticism in some countries, while in others it became semipolitical, earnestly nationalistic, and often polemical, playful, or bitter.

Essen City (pop., 1996: 612,000), N. Rhine-Westphalia state, W Germany. Located on the RUHR RIVER, it is the site of the most extensive iron- and steelworks in Europe. It was originally the seat of a convent (founded 852), whose 15th-cent. cathedral still stands. It became a city in the 10th cent. and passed to Prussia in 1802. The development of ironworks, steelworks, and coal mines stimulated growth in the 19th cent. Largely destroyed in World War II, it has since been thoroughly rebuilt.

Essene \i-'sēn, 'e-sēn\ Member of a Jewish monastic sect active in Palestine from the 2nd cent. B.C. to the 1st cent. A.D. The Essenes strictly observed the laws of MOSES and the Sabbath and held their property in common. They avoided temple worship in Jerusalem and supported themselves by manual labor. They usually excluded women. It is likely that the DEAD SEA SCROLLS were composed, copied, or collected by the Essenes.

essential oil Any of a class of highly volatile (readily evaporating) organic compounds found in plants and usually named for them (e.g., rose oil, peppermint oil). They have been known and traded since ancient times. Many contain ISOPRENOIDS. Some have one predominant component, but most have dozens or hundreds. Trace components impart the characteristic odor, which synthetic or blended oils can rarely duplicate. Essential oils have three primary commercial uses: as odorants (in perfumes, soaps, detergents); as flavors (in baked goods, candies, soft drinks); and as pharmaceuticals, in dental products and many medicines (see AROMATHERAPY).

Essex County (pop. 1998 est.: 1,294,000), E England. It extends along the North Sea coastline between the THAMES RIVER and Stour River estuaries. It was a Roman center until the 5th-cent. Saxon invasions, and an Anglo-Saxon kingdom of the Heptarchy with its center at London. It came under Danish control in the 9th cent. and was later reconquered by WESSEX. The modern county now takes much of London's overflow. Though much of the country is still farmed, it is also the site of petroleum installations and of a nuclear power plant.

Essex, 2nd Earl of *orig.* **Robert Devereux** (1567–1601) English soldier and courtier. As a young man he became the aging ELIZABETH I's favorite, though their relationship was stormy. In 1596 he commanded English forces in the sack of Cádiz. Sent to Ireland as lord lieutenant, he fought an unsuccessful campaign against Irish rebels and concluded an unfavorable truce; Elizabeth deprived him of his offices in 1600. In 1601 he attempted to raise a revolt against Elizabeth; he was captured, tried by his former mentor Francis BACON, and beheaded.

2nd Earl of Essex Painting after Marcus Gheeraerts the Younger

Estates General *or* **States General** *French* États-Généraux. In pre-Revolutionary France, the representative assembly of the three "estates" or orders of the realm: the clergy, the nobility, and the THIRD ESTATE, which represented the majority of the people. It met at irregular intervals from the 14th cent. on but was of limited effectiveness because the monarchy usually dealt with local Estates instead. The last meeting of the Estates General was at the start of the FRENCH REVOLUTION in 1789, when the deputies of the Third Estate led in founding the NATIONAL ASSEMBLY.

estate tax Levy on the value of property changing hands at the death of the owner, fixed mainly by reference to its total value. Estate tax is generally applied only to estates evaluated above a set amount and is applied at graduated rates. An estate tax was first instituted in the U.S. in 1898 to help finance the Spanish–American War; it was repealed in 1902 but permanently reimposed in 1916, initially to help finance mobilization for World War I.

Este family \'es-tā\ Princely family prominent in medieval and Renaissance Italy. Its founder was the margrave Alberto Azzo II (d.1097). The family first gained prominence as leaders of the Guelphs in the wars between the GUELPHS AND GHIBELLINES. Members of the family ruled in Ferrara in the 13th–16th cent. ending with Alfonso II (1533–1597), the fifth and last duke of Ferrara. The family also ruled in Modena and Reggio from the late Middle Ages to the late 18th cent. In addition to their political prominence, members of the family also were important promoters of art and culture.

ester Any of a class of organic compounds that can react with water (see HYDROLYSIS) to produce an ALCOHOL and an organic or inorganic ACID. They are formed by the reverse process, esterification: Acid reacts with alcohol to form an ester and water. Hydrolysis of esters in the presence of an ALKALI (saponification) is used to make SOAPS from FATS and OILS. Many carboxylic acid esters are colorless, volatile liquids with pleasant odors; they give flavor and fragrance to fruits and flowers and are used as synthetic flavors and fragrances. Others are used as SOLVENTS for lacquers, paints, and varnishes. Certain POLYMERS are esters, including Lucite and Dacron. Esters of alcohols and inorganic acids include nitrate esters (e.g., NITROGLYCERIN), which are explosive; phosphate esters, including such biologically important compounds as NUCLEIC ACIDS; and others used as flame retardants, solvents, plasticizers, gasoline and oil additives, and insecticides.

Esterhazy family \'es-tər-ˌhà-zē\ Aristocratic MAGYAR family that produced numerous Hungarian diplomats, army officers, and patrons of the arts. By the 18th cent. the Esterhazys were the largest landowners in Hungary and wealthier than the Habsburg emperors, whom they supported. The great Esterhazy palace was built at Eisenstadt, where F. J. HAYDN spent most of his career as music director. The family's various members held important governmental, ecclesiastical, diplomatic, and military posts in Hungary well into the 20th cent.

Esther OLD TESTAMENT heroine of the Book of Esther. She was the Jewish wife of the Persian king Ahasuerus (XERXES I). She and her cousin MORDECAI persuaded the king to cancel an order for the extermination of Jews in his realm, plotted by the king's chief minister, Haman. Instead, Haman was hanged on the gallows he had built for Mordecai, and the Jews were permitted to destroy their enemies. The Jewish festival of PURIM celebrates this event.

Estienne \ā-ˈtyen\, **Henri II** (1528–1598) French scholar-printer. He traveled Europe studying ancient manuscripts and visiting scholars before returning to his father's Geneva printing firm to publish the first printed editions of several Greek texts. His edition of HERODOTUS (1566) included a controversial apologia in which he bitterly satirized his own age. His voluminous output included a 13-volume edition of PLUTARCH and a five-volume Greek dictionary (both 1572). New editions of the dictionary, his greatest work, were printed into the 19th cent.

estimation In mathematics, use of a FUNCTION or formula to derive a solution or make a prediction. In STATISTICS it connotes the careful selection and testing of a function called an estimator. In CALCULUS, it usually refers to an initial guess for a solution to an equation, which is refined by a process that generates closer estimates. The difference between the estimate and the exact value is the ERROR.

Estonia *officially* **Republic of Estonia** *Estonian* **Eesti** \'ā-stē\ Country, NE Europe. It consists of a mainland area and some 1,500 islands and islets in the Baltic Sea. Area: 17,413 sq mi (45,100 sq km). Population (2000): 1,435,000. Capital: TALLINN. Estonians are nearly two-thirds of the population.

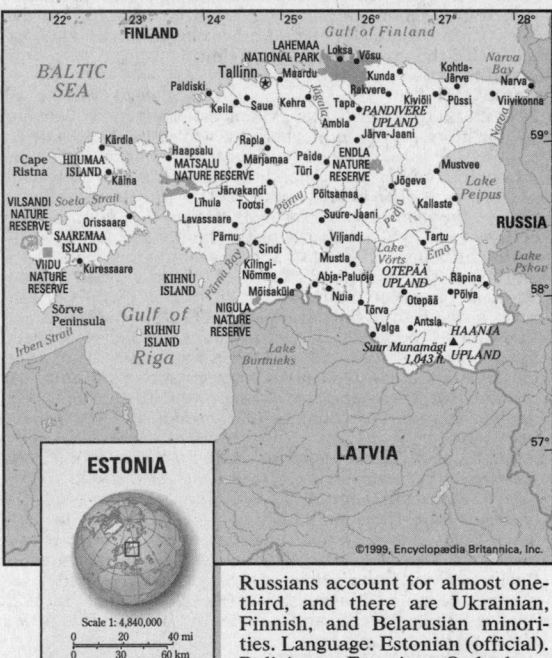

©1999, Encyclopædia Britannica, Inc.

ESTONIA

Scale 1: 4,840,000
0   20   40 mi
0   30   60 km

Russians account for almost one-third, and there are Ukrainian, Finnish, and Belarusian minorities. Language: Estonian (official). Religions: Estonian Orthodoxy, Evangelical Lutheranism, Methodism. Currency: kroon. The land is low and hilly, with numerous lakes and forests and many rivers. It has a cool-temperate and humid climate. The economy is mainly industrial, producing shale oil, machinery, fabricated metal products, and building materials. It is noted for its textiles, and woodworking is a traditional and important industry. It is a republic with one legislative body; the chief of state is the president, while the head of government is the prime minister. It was invaded by Vikings in the 9th cent. A.D. and later by Danes, Swedes, and Russians, but the Estonians were able to withstand the assaults until the Danes took control in 1219. In 1346 the Danes sold their sovereignty to the TEUTONIC ORDER, which was then in possession of LIVONIA (S Estonia and Latvia). In the mid-16th cent., Estonia was once again divided, with N Estonia capitulating to Sweden, and Poland gaining Livonia, which it surrendered to Sweden in 1629. Russia acquired Livonia and Estonia in

1721. Nearly a century later, serfdom was abolished, and from 1881 Estonia underwent intensive Russification. In 1918 Estonia obtained independence from Russia, which lasted until the Soviet Union occupied the country in 1940 and forcibly incorporated it into the U.S.S.R. Germany held the region (1941–44) during World War II, but the Soviet regime was restored in 1944, after which Estonia's economy was collectivized and integrated into that of the Soviet Union. In 1991, along with other parts of the former U.S.S.R., it proclaimed its independence, and subsequently held elections. Estonia continued negotiations with Russia to settle their common border.

estrogen \'es-trə-jən\ Organic compound, any of a class of SEX HORMONES that primarily influence the female REPRODUCTIVE SYSTEM's development, maturation, and function. The three major estrogens—estradiol, estrone, and estriol—are produced mainly by the OVARIES and PLACENTA; the ADRENAL GLANDS and the TESTES secrete smaller amounts. They influence the structural differences between female and male bodies. In experimental animals, loss of estrogens diminishes mating desires and other behavioral patterns.

estrus Period in the sexual cycle of female MAMMALS, except the higher PRIMATES, during which they are in heat (ready to accept a male for mating). Some animals (e.g., DOGS) have only one heat during a breeding season; others (e.g., GROUND SQUIRRELS) come into heat repeatedly during the breeding season until impregnated. During estrus the female secretes PHEROMONES that signal her receptivity.

estuary \'es-chə-ˌwer-ē\ Partly enclosed coastal body of water in which river water is mixed with seawater. An estuary is thus defined by salinity rather than geography. Some of the oldest continuous civilizations have flourished in estuarine environments (e.g., the Tigris and Euphrates rivers, the Nile delta, and the lower Huang River valley). Cities such as London (Thames River), New York (Hudson River), and Montreal (St. Lawrence River) developed on estuaries.

etching Method of engraving in which lines or textures are incised by acid into a metal plate, usually copper. The image produced has a spontaneity of line that comes from drawing directly on the plate. The first etchings date from the early 16th cent., but the basic principle had been used earlier for the decoration of armor. Among its pioneers were Albrecht DÜRER and PARMIGIANINO; the greatest of all etchers was REMBRANDT. In the 20th cent., etching was popular for book illustration. See also AQUATINT, ENGRAVING.

ethanol \'e-thə-ˌnȯl\ or **ethyl alcohol** or **grain alcohol** Organic compound, most important of the ALCOHOLS. Produced by FERMENTATION, it is the intoxicating ingredient in ALCOHOLIC BEVERAGES. In the U.S., ethanol for industrial purposes is made by chemical synthesis, purified by DISTILLATION, and, to avoid the tax on ethyl alcohol for drinking, made unfit to drink by adding METHANOL, CAMPHOR, BENZENE, or KEROSENE. Ethanol has many uses as a solvent, raw material, antifreeze, antiseptic, and gasoline additive and substitute. It is toxic, depressing the central NERVOUS SYSTEM, and addictive to some persons (see ALCOHOLISM). Moderate amounts depress the inhibitory activities of the brain, and so appear stimulatory, but larger amounts seriously impair coordination and judgment, and excessive consumption can cause COMA and death. Taking ethanol in combination with BARBITURATES or related drugs is especially dangerous.

Ethelbert I or **Aethelberht I** (d.616) King of Kent (560–616). He married the Christian Bertha, daughter of the king of Paris, and when AUGUSTINE OF CANTERBURY and other missionaries arrived in Kent in 597, he welcomed them. Though baptized by Augustine along with thousands of his subjects, he did not try to establish Christianity by decree. He produced the first written laws in Anglo-Saxon.

Ethelred II or **Aethelred Unraed** known as **Ethelred the Unready** (968?–1016) King of the English (978–1013, 1014–16). An ineffectual ruler, he failed to mount an organized defense against the Danish invasions (from 980); his massacre of Danish settlers (1002) provoked further attacks. When SWEYN I was accepted as king in England in 1013,

Ethelred fled to Normandy. He returned to the throne on the death of Sweyn in 1014, but on his death he was succeeded by the Dane CANUTE THE GREAT. His epithet "Unraed" means "evil counsel," and has been translated incorrectly as "the Unready."

ether \'ē-thər\ Any of a class of organic compounds whose molecular structure has an oxygen atom between two carbon atoms, with the general chemical formula R_1OR_2. Ethers resemble ALCOHOLS but generally are less dense, less soluble in water, more volatile, and more inert. They are used in chemical processing, for extraction and separation of chemicals, and as solvents. They are also used in medicine and pharmacology. "Ether" often refers to ethyl ether ($C_2H_5OC_2H_5$), best known as an anesthetic but also used as a solvent, extractant, and reaction medium.

Etherege \'eth-rij\, **George** later (**Sir George**) (c.1635–1692?) English playwright, creator of the Restoration comedy of manners. His Love in a Tub (1664), an immediate success, introduced realistic scenes of lively comedy and life of the day. He also wrote She Wou'd if She Cou'd (1668) and the popular The Man of Mode (1676). His style of comedy was adopted by later playwrights and persisted into modern times. See also RESTORATION LITERATURE.

Ethernet Telecommunications networking PROTOCOL introduced by Xerox Corp. in 1979. It was developed as an inexpensive way of sending information quickly between office machines in a single room or building, but it rapidly became a standard computer interconnection method. The original specification required COAXIAL CABLE, but costs have been reduced through the employment of simple paired wires. See also computer NETWORK.

ethical relativism Philosophical view that what is right or wrong and good or bad is not absolute but variable and relative, depending on the person, circumstances, or social situation. Rather than claiming that rightness or wrongness depends on the circumstances or on the social conditioning of those involved, it claims (in one common form) that what is truly right depends solely on what the individual or the society thinks is right. Because what people think will vary with time and place, what is right will also vary. If, however, changing and even conflicting moral principles are equally valid, there is apparently no objective way of justifying any principle as valid for all people and all societies.

ethics Branch of philosophy concerned with ultimate value and the standards by which human actions can be judged right or wrong. Ethics may be subdivided into normative ethics, metaethics, and applied ethics. Normative ethics seeks to set norms or standards for conduct; a crucial question is whether actions are to be judged solely on the basis of their consequences. Theories that do so have traditionally been known as TELEOLOGICAL ETHICS, or consequentialism, while those that judge actions by their intrinsic moral quality have been called deontological ethics. Metaethics is concerned with the analysis of the logical and semantic aspects of moral language; major theories include naturalism, nonnaturalism (or intuitionism), emotivism, and prescriptivism. Applied ethics is the application of normative ethical theories to practical moral problems (e.g., abortion, suicide).

Ethiopia \ˌē-thē-'ō-pē-ə\ officially **Federal Democratic Republic of Ethiopia** formerly **Abyssinia** Country, E Africa. It is situated on the Horn of Africa, the continent's easternmost projection. Area: 437,794 sq mi (1,133,882 sq km). Population (2000): 64,117,000. Capital: ADDIS ABABA. The people are about one-third AMHARA and one-third OROMO, with the balance mostly Tigray, Afar, Somali, Saho, and Agew. Languages: Amharic, Oromo. Religions: Ethiopian Orthodoxy, 50%; Islam, 33%; Protestantism, 10%. Currency: birr. The landlocked country is mountainous in the north, with lowlands to the east and west. The central Ethiopian Plateau is split by the GREAT RIFT VALLEY, which divides the E and W highlands. The climate is temperate in the highlands, which are mainly savanna, and hot in the arid lowlands. Excessive lumbering has led to severe erosion; this, along with periodic droughts, has led to food shortages. The country's once abundant wildlife has been decimated; many species are endangered. Ethiopia is one of the

DE

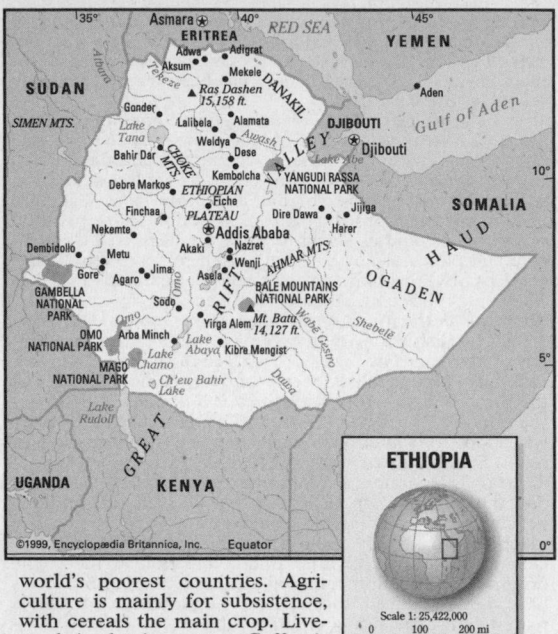

ETHIOPIA

Scale 1: 25,422,000
0 100 200 mi
0 200 400 km

©1999, Encyclopædia Britannica, Inc.   Equator

world's poorest countries. Agriculture is mainly for subsistence, with cereals the main crop. Livestock is also important. Coffee is the main export, followed by hides and skins. A new republic was established in 1995: it has two legislative houses; the chief of state is the president, and the head of government is the prime minister. Ethiopia, the Biblical land of CUSH, was inhabited from earliest antiquity, and was once under ancient Egyptian rule. Geez-speaking agriculturalists established the kingdom of Daamat in the 2nd millennium B.C. After 300 B.C. they were superseded by the kingdom of AKSUM, whose king Menile I, according to legend, was the son of King SOLOMON and the Queen of Sheba. Christianity was introduced in the 4th cent. A.D. and became widespread. Ethiopia's prosperous Mediterranean trade was cut off by the Muslim Arabs in the 7th–8th cent. and the area's interests were directed eastward. Contact with Europe resumed in the late 15th cent. with the arrival of the Portuguese. Modern Ethiopia began with the reign of TEWODROS II, who began the consolidation of the country. In the wake of European encroachment, the coastal region was made an Italian colony in 1890, but under Emperor MENILEK II, the Italians were defeated and ousted in 1896. Ethiopia prospered under his rule, and his modernization programs were continued by emperor HAILE SELASSIE in the 1930s. In 1936 Italy again gained control of the country, and held it as part of Italian Africa until 1941, when it was liberated by the British. Ethiopia incorporated ERITREA in 1952. In 1974 Haile Selassie was deposed and a Marxist government, plagued by civil wars and famine, controlled the country until 1991. In 1993 Eritrea gained its independence, but border conflicts with it and neighboring Somalia continued in the 1990s.

ethnocentrism Tendency to interpret or evaluate other cultures in terms of one's own. Generally considered a human universal, ethnocentrism is evident in the widespread practice in the West, especially in previous centuries, of labeling non-Western peoples as "savages" or "barbarians" simply because their societies differed from those of the West. The opposite of ethnocentrism is cultural relativism, the understanding of cultural phenomena within the context in which they occur.

ethnomusicology Scholarly study of music as an aspect of culture. Taking an anthropological approach, it has tended to focus on non-Western music, particularly music of oral traditions. The field's origins lie in the late 19th cent. with the work of such scholars as F.-J. Fétis (1784–1871), and much work was motivated by the search for musical universals, under the assumption that prehistory could be studied through research into "primitive" cultures of the present. Recognizing that traditional societies were quickly disappearing, it soon put its highest priority on collection (by field recording) and transcription. A number of classification schemes for comparative analysis of different musics have been proposed.

ethology \ē-'thä-lə-jē\ Study of animal behavior, a combination of laboratory and field science, with strong ties to other disciplines (e.g., neuroanatomy, ECOLOGY, EVOLUTION). The modern science of ethology is considered to have arisen as a discrete discipline with the work in the 1920s of Nikolaas TINBERGEN and Konrad LORENZ. Focused on the behavioral process, ethologists often study one type of behavior (e.g., aggression) in various unrelated animals.

ethyl alcohol See ETHANOL

ethylene Simplest HYDROCARBON containing a double bond (see BONDING), a colorless, flammable gas with a sweetish taste and odor. The highest-volume PETROCHEMICAL, it occurs in PETROLEUM and NATURAL GAS but is usually produced by heating higher hydrocarbons. Ethylene is polymerized to POLYETHYLENE. It reacts with numerous other chemicals to produce ETHANOL, solvents, gasoline additives, ANTIFREEZE, detergents, and various plastics. In plants, ethylene is a hormone that inhibits growth and promotes leaf fall and fruit ripening.

ethylene glycol \'e-thə-,lēn-'glī-,kól\ Simplest member of the GLYCOL family. It is a colorless, oily liquid with a mild odor and sweet taste. Widely used as an ANTIFREEZE in automobile cooling systems, it is also used in many other chemical processes. It and some of its derivatives are fairly toxic.

ethyne See ACETYLENE

Etna, Mt. Active volcano, E coast of Sicily. The highest active volcano in Europe, its elevation is over 10,000 ft (3,200 m); its circumference is about 93 mi (150 km). It has erupted repeatedly over the centuries, most violently in 1669, when the lava flow submerged part of CATANIA. Activity was almost continuous in the decade following 1971; in 1983 an eruption lasted four months.

Eton College \'ē-tən\ Largest public school (independent secondary school) in England and one of the most prestigious. It is located in Eton, Berkshire. It was founded by Henry VI in 1440–41. Boys enter Eton about age 13. Most come from England's wealthiest families, though 70 scholarships are awarded on the basis of competitive examination. Total enrollment is about 1,000.

Etosha National Park \ē-'tō-shə\ National reserve, N Namibia. Covering some 8,598 sq mi (22,269 sq km), it centers on the Etosha Pan, a vast expanse of salt with lone salt springs, used by animals as salt licks. It has one of the largest accumulations of big-game species in the world, including lion, elephant, rhinoceros, eland, zebra, and springbok.

Etruria \i-'trùr-ē-ə\ Ancient country, central Italy. It covered the region that now constitutes TUSCANY and part of UMBRIA. It was inhabited by the ETRUSCANS, who established a civilization by the 7th cent. B.C. Their chief confederation reached its height in the 6th cent. B.C., extending into N and S Italy, but its cities were gradually absorbed by Rome during the 3rd cent. B.C.

Etruscans Ancient people of ETRURIA, whose urban civilization reached its height in the 6th cent. B.C. By the 7th cent. they had incorporated all of TUSCANY into their territory, and in the 6th cent. they became rulers of Rome. The Etruscans gave the city its first public works, including walls and a sewer system. By the end of the 6th cent., pressure from other peoples in the region had weakened Etruria; the Romans expelled their dynasty in 509 B.C. They left a rich cultural heritage, including art that featured wall frescoes and realistic tomb portraits. Many features of the culture were adopted by the Romans.

eubacteria \,yü-bak-'tir-ē-ə\ Group consisting of the true BACTERIA, one of two major groups of the PROKARYOTES. The other is the ARCHAEBACTERIA, which are as different from eubacteria as either is from EUKARYOTES. Virtually all the familiar bacteria that cause diseases (e.g., E. coli, STAPHYLOCOCCUS and SALMONELLA strains, MYCOBACTERIA) or are important in food, agriculture, biotechnology, and other industrial activity (e.g., *Lactobacillus*, NITRIFY-ING and DENITRIFYING BACTERIA and STREPTOMYCES strains) are eubacteria.

Euboea \yü-'bē-ə\ *Greek* **Évvoia** \'e-vē-ä\ Island, Aegean Sea. One of the largest in Greece, it is about 110 mi (180 km) long and 4–30 mi (6–48 km) wide. The island, mainly mountainous, includes the fertile plain of the Lílas River, in antiquity a famous horse-breeding region. It is connected with BOEOTIA by a bridge built by the Chalcidians. Its main cities of Khalkís and ERETRIA were involved in the PERSIAN and PELOPONNESIAN wars. Conquered by the Turks in 1470, it passed to Greece in 1830.

eucalyptus \‚yü-kə-'lip-təs\ Any of the more than 500 species of mostly very large trees in the genus *Eucalyptus,* in the MYRTLE family, native to Australia, New Zealand, Tasmania, and nearby islands. Many species are grown throughout temperate regions of the world. The leaf glands of many species, especially *E. salicifolia* and *E. globulus,* contain a medicinal aromatic oil known as eucalyptus oil. Eucalyptus wood is used extensively in Australia as fuel, and the timber is commonly used in buildings and fencing. The bark of many species is used in papermaking and tanning.

Eucharist \'yü-kə-rəst\ *or* **Holy Communion** *or* **Lord's Supper** Christian rite commemorating the Last Supper of JESUS with his disciples. On the night before his death, Jesus consecrated bread and wine and gave them to his disciples, saying "this is my body" and "this is my blood." A central rite of Christian worship, the Eucharist involves consecration of bread and wine by the clergy and their consumption by worshipers. In Roman Catholicism the Eucharist is a SACRAMENT, and the bread and wine are thought to become the actual body and blood of Jesus. Anglicans and Lutherans also emphasize the divine presence in the Eucharist, while other Protestant denominations regard it as largely symbolic.

Euclid \'yü-kləd\ (fl.c.300 B.C.) Greek mathematician of antiquity, known primarily for his highly influential treatise on geometry, the *Elements.* He founded a school in Alexandria during the reign of PTOLEMY I. The *Elements,* based on the works of earlier mathematicians, is a brilliant synthesis of old and new. It has been a major influence on rational thought and a model for many philosophical treatises, and has set a standard for logical thinking and methods of proof in the sciences. The starting point not just of EUCLIDEAN GEOMETRY but of an approach to reasoning, it is sometimes said to be the most translated, published, and studied work after the Bible.

Euclidean geometry Study of points, lines, angles, surfaces, and solids based on EUCLID's AXIOMS. Its chief importance lies in the highly influential systematic method Euclid used to develop and present them. From 10 axioms and postulates, Euclid deduced 465 theorems, or propositions, concerning aspects of plane and solid geometric figures. This work was long held to constitute an accurate description of the physical world and to provide a sufficient basis for understanding it. During the 19th cent., rejection of some of Euclid's postulates resulted in two NON-EUCLIDEAN GEOMETRIES that proved just as valid and consistent. See also EUCLIDEAN SPACE.

Euclidean space In geometry, a two- or three-dimensional space in which the axioms and postulates of EUCLIDEAN GEOMETRY apply; also, a space in any finite number of dimensions, in which points are designated by coordinates (one for each dimension) and the distance between two points is given by a distance formula. The only conception of physical space for over 2,000 years, it remains the most compelling and useful way of modeling the world as it is experienced.

Eudocia Macrembolitissa \yü-'dō-shə-‚mak-rəm-‚bä-lə-'ti-sə\ (1021–1096) Byzantine empress, called the wisest woman of her time. As the wife of Constantine X Ducas, she became regent for her three sons after his death (1067). To fend off the Seljuq Turks, she married a Cappadocian general, making him emperor; after his capture at the Battle of Manzikert (1071), Eudocia and her son Michael deposed him and ruled jointly. Michael soon succeeded to the throne, and Eudocia entered a convent.

Eugene City (pop., 2000: 138,000), W Oregon. Located on the Willamette River, it was settled by Eugene Skinner in 1846, and grew as an agricultural and lumber center with the arrival of the railroad in 1870. It is the site of the Univ. of Oregon and is a tourist center for outdoor rereation.

Eugene of Savoy *orig.* François-Eugène, prince de Savoie-Carignan (1663–1736) French-Austrian general. He found his ambitions severely restrained by LOUIS XIV, prompting him to leave France (c. 1683) and enter the service of Emperor LEOPOLD I. He later served Joseph I and CHARLES VI. He quickly distinguished himself in battle and became imperial field marshal at 29. He fought notably against France in the War of the GRAND ALLIANCE and the War of the SPANISH SUCCESSION; with his friend the duke of MARLBOROUGH, he won the important victory at Blenheim (1704) and ousted the French from Italy. In 1718 he won a great triumph over the Turks, taking the city of Belgrade. He later served as governor in the Austrian Netherlands (1714–24). An outstanding strategist and an inspired leader, he was regarded as one of the greatest soldiers of his generation.

eugenics \yü-'je-niks\ Study of human improvement by genetic means. The first thorough exposition of eugenics was made by Francis GALTON, who in *Hereditary Genius* (1869) proposed that a system of arranged marriages between men of distinction and women of wealth would eventually produce a gifted race. The American Eugenics Society, founded in 1926, supported Galton's theories. U.S. eugenicists also supported restriction on immigration from nations with "inferior" stock and argued for the sterilization of insane, retarded, and epileptic citizens. Sterilization laws were passed in more than half the states. The assumptions of eugenicists were discredited after the German Nazis used eugenics to support the extermination of Jews, blacks, and homosexuals.

Eugénie \‚œ-zhä-'nē\ *orig.* Eugénia María de Montijo de Guzmán (1826–1920) Wife of NAPOLEON III and empress of France (1853–70). Daughter of a Spanish noble, she married Napoleon III in 1853, and came to have an important influence on his foreign policy. She favored a strong papacy, and she encouraged opposition to a Prussian candidate for the Spanish throne in the controversy that precipitated the FRANCO–PRUSSIAN WAR. After the French defeat, she joined her family in exile in England.

eukaryote \yü-'kar-ē-‚ōt\ Any organism composed of one or more CELLS, each of which contains a clearly defined NUCLEUS enclosed by a membrane. Intracellular organelles include mitochondria (see MITOCHONDRION), CHLOROPLASTS, a Golgi apparatus (which packages large molecules for transport), an ENDOPLASMIC RETICULUM, and LYSOSOMES. All organisms except BACTERIA are eukaryotes; bacteria are PROKARYOTES.

Eulenspiegel \'òil-ən-‚shpē-gəl\, **Till** German peasant trickster of folk and literary tales. The historical Till is said to have died in 1350; anecdotes associated with his name were printed from the early 16th cent. and widely translated. In the tales the stupid yet cunning peasant demonstrates his superiority to the narrow, dishonest, condescending townsman, as well as to the clergy and nobility.

Euler \'òi-lər\, **Leonhard** (1707–1783) Swiss mathematician. Working in St. Petersburg (1727–41), he developed the theory of trigonometric and logarithmic FUNCTIONS and advanced mathematics generally. At the Berlin Academy (1741–66), he developed the concept of function in mathematical analysis and discovered the imaginary logarithms of negative numbers. Throughout his life he was interested in NUMBER THEORY. In addition to inspiring the use of arithmetic terms in writing mathematics and physics, Euler introduced many symbols that became standard, including e for the base of the natural LOGARITHM; a, b, and c for the sides of a triangle and A, B, and C for the opposite angles; $f(x)$ for a function; π for the ratio of the circumference to the diameter of a circle; and i for $\sqrt{-1}$. Much of his work was done after he was blinded in 1766 and returned to Russia.

Eumenes II \'yü-mə-‚nēz\ (d.160/159 B.C.) King of PERGAMUM (197–c.160 B.C.). He helped defeat ANTIOCHUS III, thus enlarging his realm. He brought his kingdom to its height and made it a great center of Greek culture, and is credited in particular with constructing nearly all the public buildings and sculpture on the Pergamum acropolis. He was suspected of disloyalty in the Roman struggle against PERSEUS; Rome subsequently withdrew its support, and Eumenes' power and the glory of Pergamum declined.

eunuch \ˈyü-nək\ Castrated human male. From remote antiquity on, eunuchs were employed in the Middle East and China as guards and servants in harems or other women's quarters, and as chamberlains to kings. Many of the patriarchs of Constantinople during Byzantine times were eunuchs. Eunuch advisers as a class only disappeared with the end of the Ottoman empire in the 19th cent. See also CASTRATO.

euonymus \yu̇-ˈä-nə-məs\ Any of about 170 species of shrubs, woody climbers, and small trees that make up the genus *Euonymus* (family Celastraceae), native to temperate Asia, N. America, and Europe, including many popular landscape ornamental shrubs and ground covers. The winged spindle tree *(E. alata)*, also called burning bush, is a handsome shrub with corky winged stems.

euphonium \yu̇-ˈfō-nē-əm\ *or* **tenor tuba** Large valved BRASS INSTRUMENT, the leading lower-pitched instrument in military bands. Developed in Germany around 1840, it has four valves and a wide conical bore resembling the tuba's. Its range is an octave below the trumpet and cornet. It is played either vertically or with the bell facing forward. The very similar baritone is distinguished only by its narrower bore. Both are essential members of bands of all kinds, and are often given significant solo roles.

euphorbia See SPURGE

Euphrates River \yu̇-ˈfrā-tēz\ *Turkish* **Firat Nehri** \fə-ˈrät-ne-ˈrē\ *Arabic* **Al-Furat** \ˌal-fú-ˈrät\ River, W Asia. The largest river in W Asia, it rises in Turkey, flows southeast across Syria and Iraq to unite with the TIGRIS, and continues, as SHATT AL ARAB, to the PERSIAN GULF. In all, it is 2,235 mi (3,596 km) long. Its valley was heavily irrigated in ancient times, and many great cities lined its banks. With the Tigris, it defined the area known as MESOPOTAMIA.

Euripides \yu̇-ˈri-pə-ˌdēz\ (484?–406 B.C.) Greek playwright. With AESCHYLUS and SOPHOCLES, he was one of Athens' three great tragic dramatists. An associate of ANAXAGORAS, he expressed his questions about Greek religion in his plays. Repeatedly chosen to compete in the dramatic festival of Dionysus, he won his first victory in 441 B.C. Of his 92 plays, about 19 survive, including *Medea* (431 B.C.), *Hippolytus* (428), *Electra* (418), *The Trojan Women* (415), *Ion* (413), *Iphigenia at Aulis* (406), and *The Bacchae* (406). Many include prologues and rely on a DEUS EX MACHINA. Unlike Aeschylus and Sophocles, Euripides made his characters' tragic fates stem almost entirely from their own flawed natures and uncontrolled passions.

euro Unit of exchange adopted in 1999 that represents the combined currencies of 12 nations of the EUROPEAN UNION, including the German deutsche mark, the French franc, and the Italian lira. The new currency is intended to strengthen Europe as an economic power, increase international trade, simplify monetary transactions, and lead to pricing equality throughout Europe. It became the single currency of a unified Western European economy in 2002. A few EU members, notably Britain, have withheld commitment to the euro.

Eurocommunism Trend among European communist parties toward independence from Soviet COMMUNIST PARTY doctrine in the 1970s and '80s. Rejecting the Soviet doctrine of one monolithic world communist movement, it advocated instead that each country's communist party base its policies on the traditions and needs of its own country. With Mikhail GORBACHEV's encouragement, all communist parties took independent courses in the late 1980s; most declined after the breakup of the Soviet Union.

Europa \yu̇-ˈrō-pə\ In GREEK MYTHOLOGY, the daughter either of Phoenix or of Agenor, king of Phoenicia. Her beauty inspired the love of ZEUS, who approached her in the form of a white bull and carried her off across the sea to Crete. She bore Zeus three sons, one of whom grew up to become King MINOS of Crete. On Crete she was worshiped under the name Hellotis. The continent of EUROPE is named for her.

Europe Second smallest continent on earth. It is bordered by the Arctic Ocean, the Atlantic Ocean, and the Mediterranean, Black, and Caspian seas. The continent's E boundary runs along the URAL MTNS. and the URAL RIVER. Indented by bays, fjords, and seas, Europe's irregular coastline is about 24,000 mi (38,000 km) long. Area: 4,000,000 sq mi (10,400,000 sq km). Population (1997 est.): 542,578,000. The greater part of Europe combines low elevations with low relief. The highest points are in the mountain systems crossing the S part of the continent, including the PYRENEES, ALPS, APENNINES, and CARPATHIAN and BALKAN MTNS. A well-watered continent with many rivers, it has few sizable lakes. Glaciers cover about 44,800 sq mi (116,000 sq km). Roughly one-third of Europe is arable, and about half of that land is devoted to cereals, principally wheat and barley. One-third is forested. It was the first of the world's regions to develop a modern economy based on commercial agriculture and industry, and it maintains average per capita income among the world's highest. The people of Europe constitute about one-seventh of the world's population, and the vast majority belong to the European (or Caucasoid) geographic race. Most of its approximately 60 native languages belong to the ROMANCE, GERMANIC, or SLAVIC languages. Europe's population is overwhelmingly Christian. Modern humans supplanted the scanty NEANDERTHAL population in Europe about 40,000 years ago, and by 2000 B.C. the general population groups that would become the historical peoples and nations of Europe were in place. The Greek civilizations were the earliest in Europe, and they laid the foundation for European civilization. By the mid-2nd cent. B.C. the Greeks had come under Roman control, and the vast Roman empire brought to the conquered parts of Europe the civilization the Greeks had begun. It was through the Romans that Christianity penetrated into Europe. The Roman empire in the west finally collapsed in the 5th cent. A.D., leading to an extensive breakdown of classical civilization, not to be revived until the RENAISSANCE in the 15th–16th cent., which began the modern European traditions of science, exploration, and discovery. The Protestant REFORMATION of the 16th cent. ended the dominance of the Roman church over W and N Europe, and the ENLIGHTENMENT of the 17th–18th cent. stressed the primacy of reason. In the late 18th cent., Enlightenment ideals helped spur the FRENCH REVOLUTION, which spearheaded the movement toward democracy and equality. The late 18th cent. also marked the beginning of the INDUSTRIAL REVOLUTION, which led to Europe's dominance over much of the world for the next century. In the early 20th cent. World War I led to the effective end of monarchy in Europe and created a host of new nations in central and E Europe. World War II marked the passing of world power from the states of W Europe and saw the rise of communism in E Europe, with the Soviet Union and its satellites sharply dividing the continent. In the late 20th cent., with the collapse of communism in the U.S.S.R., many of its member states became independent and E. and W. Germany were reunified. See also EUROPEAN UNION, NATO.

European Community (EC) Organization formed in 1967 with the merger of the EUROPEAN ECONOMIC COMMUNITY (EEC), European Coal and Steel Community, and European Atomic Energy Community. The merger created a single Commission of the European Community and a single Council of Ministers. Other executive, legislative, and judicial bodies were also collected under its umbrella. In 1993 the EC became the basis for the EUROPEAN UNION, and the EEC was renamed the European Community.

European Court of Justice Judicial branch of the EUROPEAN UNION (EU), established in 1958 to ensure the observance of international agreements negotiated by predecessor organizations of the EU. It reviews the legality of the acts of the EU executive bodies and rules on cases of civil law between member states or private parties. It can invalidate the laws of EU members when their laws conflict with EU law. Its 15 judges and eight advocates-general are appointed by the member governments. See also INTERNATIONAL COURT OF JUSTICE.

European Economic Community (EEC) *later* **European Community (EC)** *known as* **the Common Market** Economic

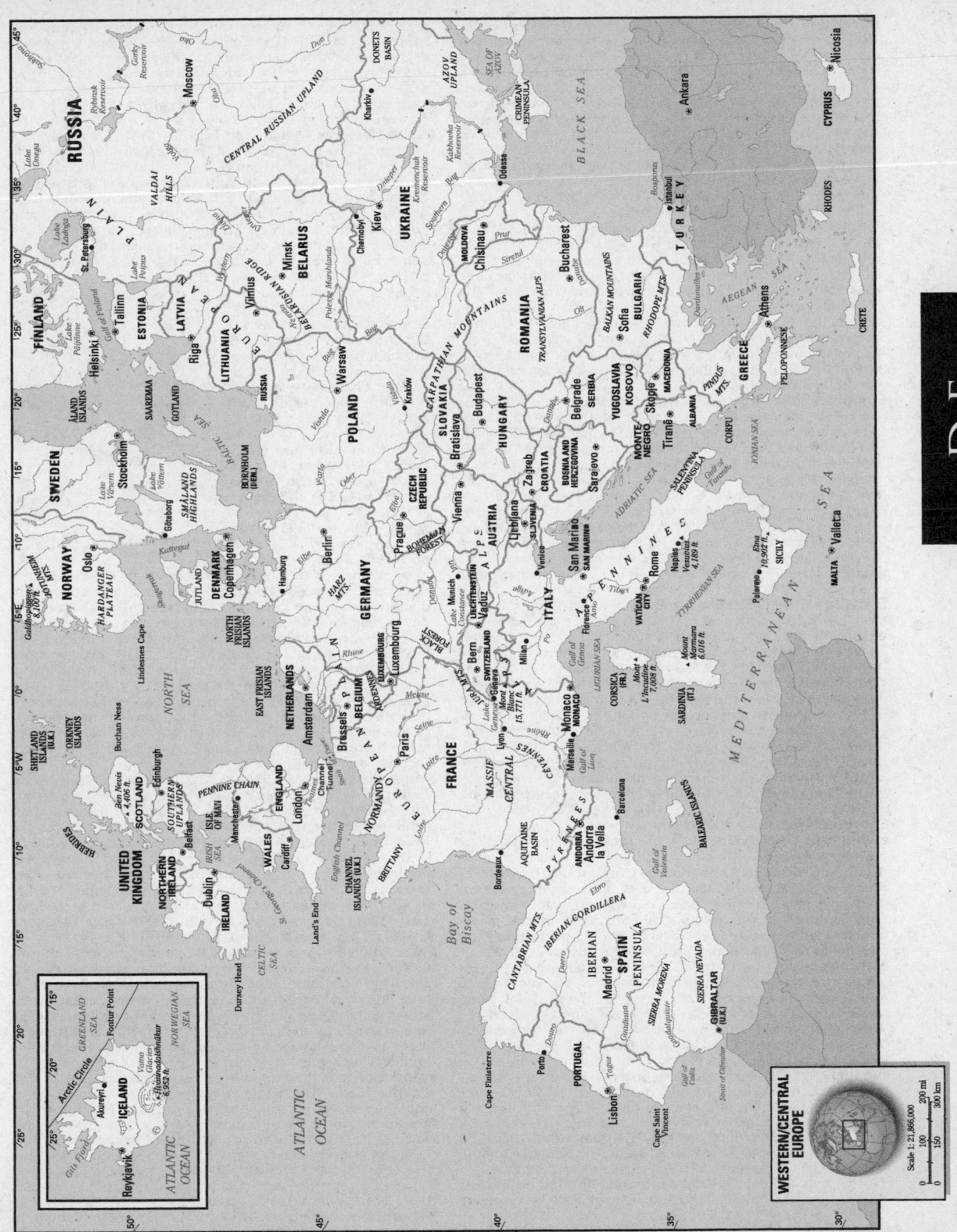

WESTERN/CENTRAL EUROPE

Scale 1:21,866,000

| 0 | 100 | 200 mi |

0 150 300 km

association of European countries. It was established in 1957 to develop the economies of the member states into one large common market and build a political union of the states of Western Europe. The EEC also sought to establish a single commercial policy toward nonmember countries, to coordinate transportation systems, agricultural policies, and general economic policies, and to remove measures restricting free competition. Its liberalized trade policies greatly increased trade and economic prosperity in Western Europe. In 1967 its governing bodies were merged into the EUROPEAN COMMUNITY. In 1993 the EEC was renamed the European Community (EC); it is now the principal organization within the EUROPEAN UNION.

European Parliament Legislative assembly of the EUROPEAN UNION (EU), established in 1958. Elected by direct universal suffrage, its members are apportioned according to the member nations' populations, and currently number over 500. A president and 14 vice presidents are elected for 30-month terms. The EU Council of Ministers, which represents the member states, consults the parliament, which is empowered to discuss whatever matters it wishes. Though its powers were expanded with passage of the MAASTRICHT TREATY (1993), the parliament remains subordinate to the Council of Ministers.

European Space Agency (ESA) *French* Agence Spatiale Européenne. Western European space and space-technology research organization based in Paris, founded in 1975 when the European Launcher Development Organization (ELDO) and the European Space Research Organization (ESRO) merged. Its members are Austria, Belgium, Britain, Denmark, Finland, France, Germany, Ireland, Italy, the Netherlands, Norway, Portugal, Spain, Sweden, and Switzerland. The ESA developed Ariane, a three-stage launch vehicle, and a launch facility in French Guiana. It has launched weather satellites (Meteosat); the Giotto probe, which examined Halley's Comet; and Hipparcos, which measured the parallaxes of over 100,000 stars.

European Union (EU) Organization of most of the states of Western Europe, formed in 1993 to oversee the economic and political integration of these states. It was created by the MAASTRICHT TREATY and ratified by all members of the EUROPEAN COMMUNITY (EC), out of which the EU developed. The successful EC had made its members more receptive to greater integration and provided a framework for unified action in security and foreign policy. In its major goal to create a common monetary system, the EU established the EURO, which replaced national currencies in 2002. By then the EU had 15 members and was preparing for the accessism of 13 more. The EU's principal institutions are the European Community, the Council of Ministers, the EUROPEAN PARLIAMENT, and the EUROPEAN COURT OF JUSTICE.

Eurotunnel See CHANNEL TUNNEL.

euthanasia \ˌyü-thə-ˈnā-zhə\ *or* **mercy killing** Painless killing of a person with a painful, incurable disease or incapacitating disorder. Most legal systems consider it murder, but a physician may lawfully decide not to prolong life or may give drugs to relieve pain even when they may shorten life. Associations promoting legal euthanasia exist in many countries. The ability of medical technology to prolong life has led to difficult ethical questions. See also LIVING WILL.

eutrophication \yü-ˌtrō-fə-ˈkā-shən\ Gradual increase in the concentration of PHOSPHORUS, NITROGEN, and other plant nutrients in an aging aquatic ecosystem such as a lake, from material that enters mainly through runoff that carries debris. Algal blooms often develop on the surface, preventing the light penetration and oxygen absorption necessary for underwater life. See also WATER POLLUTION.

evangelicalism \ˌe-ˌvan-ˈje-li-kə-ˌli-zəm\ Protestant movement that stresses conversion experiences, the Bible as the only basis for faith, and evangelism at home and abroad. The 18th-cent. religious revival referred to as the evangelical revival included PIETISM in Europe, METHODISM in Britain, and the GREAT AWAKENING in America. In London in 1846, the Evangelical Alliance was organized by evangelical Christians from several denominations and countries. In the U.S., the National Assn. of Evangelicals was formed in 1942. See also PENTECOSTALISM.

Evans, Arthur (John) (*later* **Sir Arthur**) (1851–1941) British archaeologist. Son of the archaeologist Sir John Evans (1823–1908), he served as a curator at Oxford's Ashmolean Museum (1884–1908). Beginning in 1899 he devoted several decades to excavating the ruins of the ancient city of KNOSSOS in Crete, uncovering evidence of a sophisticated BRONZE AGE civilization that he named MINOAN. His work, one of archaeology's major achievements, was recounted in *The Palace of Minos* (4 vols., 1921–36).

Evans, Bill (*orig.* William John) (1929–1980) U.S. pianist and composer. Born in Plainfield, N.J., Evans was classically trained. His subtle harmonies and lyrical melodic sensitivity were particularly well suited to modal improvisation, demonstrated on the landmark Miles DAVIS recording *Kind of Blue* (1959). As leader of his own trio, Evans established near-telepathic communication with his fellow musicians, creating music of rare depth and introspection.

Evans, Edith (Mary) (*later* **Dame Edith**) (1888–1976) British actress. She made her stage debut in 1912 and joined the OLD VIC company in 1925. One of the finest actresses of the 20th cent., she appeared in London and on Broadway in plays by William SHAKESPEARE, G. B. SHAW, and Noël COWARD. She played Lady Bracknell in Oscar WILDE's *The Importance of Being Earnest* on stage and screen (1952). Her other films include *The Chalk Garden* (1964) and *The Whisperers* (1967).

Edith Evans as Mrs. Ross in *The Whisperers,* 1967

Evans, Oliver (1755–1819) U.S. inventor. Born in Newport, Del., Evans began early to apply himself to industrial problems. In 1784 he built a flour mill, for which he created the first continuous production line in any industry: all movement was automatic, power being supplied by waterwheels, and grain was passed by conveyors and chutes through the stages of milling and refining to emerge as finished flour. His high-pressure STEAM ENGINE (patented 1790) shares credit for the invention often given solely to Richard TREVITHICK. His Amphibious Digger (1805), a steam-engine scow that could run on both land and water, was the first powered road vehicle to operate in the U.S. His Mars Iron Works (founded 1806) made more than 100 steam engines for processing cotton, tobacco, and paper.

Evans, Walker (1903–1975) U.S. photographer. Born in St. Louis, he was influenced by the photographs of Eugène ATGET. In 1934 his images of New England architecture were exhibited in the first one-man photographic show at the Museum of Modern Art. From 1935 he photographed rural victims of the Great Depression for the Farm Security Administration; these images were published in *American Photographs* (1938). With James AGEE he documented the life of Alabama sharecroppers in *Let Us Now Praise Famous Men* (1941). He was later an editor of *Fortune* magazine (1945–65) and a professor at Yale Univ. (1965–74).

evaporation Process by which liquid water enters the atmosphere as water vapor. Evaporation, mostly from the sea and from vegetation, replenishes the humidity of the air. It is an important part of the exchange of energy in the earth-atmosphere system that produces weather and climate. The rate of evaporation depends on the temperature difference between the evaporating surface and the air, the relative humidity, and wind.

evaporator Industrial apparatus for converting LIQUID into GAS or vapor. The single-effect evaporator consists of a container or surface and a heating unit; the multiple-effect evaporator, used in industrial and steam heating plants, uses the vapor produced in one unit to heat a succeeding unit. Some evaporators are used to concentrate a solution by vaporizing and eliminating water (e.g., in a concentration plant for sugar and syrup). In purification processes such as DESALINATION, evaporators convert the water to vapor (later condensed), leaving mineral residues behind. In a REFRIGERATION system, the cooling is produced as the rapid evaporation of the liquid refrigerant absorbs heat.

Evenki See SIBERIAN PEOPLES

event horizon Boundary marking the limits of a BLACK HOLE, at which the ESCAPE VELOCITY is equal to the speed of LIGHT. Since general RELATIVITY states that nothing can go faster than this speed, nothing inside the event horizon, whether it enters from outside or is generated within it, can ever escape or be observed from outside it, including light. Particles may, however, be radiated from just outside the event horizon. A nonrotating black hole has a spherical event horizon at a distance defined by the SCHWARZSCHILD RADIUS. Rotating black holes have distorted, nonspherical event horizons. The event horizon is not a material surface but a mathematically defined boundary, so nothing prevents matter or radiation from entering a black hole, only from exiting one.

Everest, Mt. *Tibetan* **Chomolungma** \ˌchō-mō-ˈlün̈-mə\ Peak on the crest of the HIMALAYAS, in Asia. The highest point on earth, with a summit at 29,035 ft (8,850 m), it lies on the border between Nepal and Tibet. The summit was finally reached by Edmund HILLARY of New Zealand and TENZING NORGAY of Nepal in 1953. In dispute is whether English explorer George Mallory (1886–1924) had reached the peak in 1924 and was descending it when he died.

Everglades Subtropical saw-grass marsh region, S Florida. Covering about 4,000 sq mi (10,000 sq km) of S Florida, the area has water moving slowly through it from the lip of Lake OKEECHOBEE to mangrove swamps bordering the Gulf of MEXICO. Everglades National Park, established in 1934, encompasses the SW portion, covering 2,354 sq mi (6,097 sq km). The largest subtropical wilderness left in the continental U.S., it provides an environment for myriad birds, alligators, snakes, and turtles. A large portion of the glades has been reclaimed by drainage canals.

evergreen Any plant that retains its leaves through the winter and into the following summer. Many tropical species of broad-leaved FLOWERING PLANTS are evergreen, but in cold-temperate and Arctic areas, most evergreens are CONIFERS. The leaves of evergreens usually are thicker and more leathery than those of DECIDUOUS TREES and often are needle-like or scalelike in cone-bearing trees. A leaf (or needle) may last for two years or longer and may fall during any season.

Evers \ˈe-vərz\, **Medgar (Wiley)** (1925–1963) U.S. civil rights activist. Born in Decatur, Miss., he organized local affiliates of the NAACP and in 1954 became its first field secretary in Mississippi. He traveled throughout the state recruiting members and organizing boycotts. In June 1963 Evers was shot and killed in an ambush outside his home. A white segregationist, charged but set free after two trials in 1964 resulted in hung juries, was convicted after a third trial in 1994. Evers's widow, Myrlie Evers-Williams, later headed the NAACP (1995–98).

Evert, Chris(tine Marie) *formerly* **Chris Evert Lloyd** (b.1954) U.S. tennis player. Born in Fort Lauderdale, Fla., she repeatedly won the U.S. Open women's singles (1975–78, 1980, 1982), the Wimbledon singles (1974, 1976, 1981), the French Open singles (1974, 1975, 1979, 1980, 1983, 1985, 1986), and the Australian Open singles (1982, 1984), for a total of 18 Grand Slam titles.

evidence In law, something (e.g., testimony; documents, or physical objects) presented at a judicial or administrative proceeding for the purpose of establishing the truth or falsity of an allegation of fact. To preserve legal DUE PROCESS and to prevent the jury from being misled, an extensive body of evidentiary rules has sprung up. In the U.S., all federal and many state courts adhere to the *Federal Rules of Evidence,* which covers such elements as admissibility, relevance, competency of witnesses, confessions, and expert testimony. Most evidence received at trial is in the form of verbal statements of witnesses, who are subject to questioning by attorneys from both sides. Two important categories of evidence are direct evidence, offered by a witness with firsthand knowledge of a factual matter, and CIRCUMSTANTIAL EVIDENCE. See also EXCLUSIONARY RULE.

evil eye Superstition holding that a glance can cause injury or death to those on whom it falls. The belief was found in ancient Greece and Rome as well as in folk cultures around the world, and it has persisted into modern times. The evil eye is often thought to stem from envy and malice toward prosperity and beauty, and thus in many cultures ·unguarded praise of one's possessions or children is thought to invite misfortune. Safeguards include amulets, charms, and sacred texts.

Evita See Eva PERÓN

evolution Biological theory that animals and plants have their origin in other types and that the distinguishable differences are due to modifications in successive generations. In 1858 Charles DARWIN and Alfred Russel WALLACE published a paper on evolution that revolutionized all later biological study. The heart of Darwinian evolution is the mechanism of NATURAL SELECTION. In 1937 Theodosius DOBZHANSKY applied Mendelian GENETICS (see Gregor MENDEL) to Darwinian theory. Part of the proof of evolution is in the fossil record, which shows a succession of gradually changing forms leading up to those known today. Structural similarities and similarities in embryonic development also point to common ancestry. Molecular biology (especially the study of genes and proteins) provides the most detailed evidence of evolutionary change. Though the theory of evolution is accepted by nearly the entire scientific community, it has sparked much controversy; most objections have come from religious leaders and thinkers (see CREATION SCIENCE). See also BREEDING, HUMAN EVOLUTION, PHYLOGENY, SOCIOCULTURAL EVOLUTION, SPECIATION.

Ewald \ˈā-vəlt\, **Johannes** (1743–1781) Danish poet and dramatist. With *The Death of Balder* (1774), he became the first Danish poet to use themes from Scandinavian myth and saga. Of his dramatic works, only the operetta *Fiskerne* (1779; "The Fishermen") is still performed. He is especially known for his great personal odes and for songs such as "King Christian Stood by the Lofty Mast," used as a national anthem, and "Lille Gunver," the first Danish romance. His memoirs (published 1804) are his greatest prose work.

Ewe \ˈā-wā\ Peoples of SE Ghana, S Benin, and S Togo. The Ewe, who number about 3.5 million, never formed a single centralized state. Most are farmers; some coastal Ewe fish. Spinning, weaving, pottery making, and blacksmithing are important crafts. Many have been converted to Christianity.

excavation In ARCHAEOLOGY, the exposure, recording, and recovery of buried material remains. The process begins with site location, followed by careful surveying and mapping, site sampling, and development of an excavation plan. The actual digging consists of the removal of surplus dirt and the painstaking examination, through observation, sifting, and other means, of remaining soil, artifacts, and context. Common tools include the trowel, penknife, and brush. The excavation of a site may last decades or be a short-term emergency salvage operation (as when a site is threatened by new construction).

exchange, bill of See BILL OF EXCHANGE

exchange rate Price of one country's money in relation to another's. Exchange rates may be fixed or flexible. An exchange rate is fixed when two countries agree to maintain a fixed rate through the use of MONETARY POLICY. Historically, the most famous fixed exchange-rate system was the GOLD STANDARD. An exchange rate is flexible, or "floating," when two countries agree to let international market forces determine the rate through SUPPLY AND DEMAND. The rate will fluctuate with a country's exports and imports. Most world trade currently takes place with flexible exchange rates that fluctuate within relatively fixed limits.

Exchequer \iks-ˈche-kər, ˈeks-ˌche-kər\ English government department of public revenue. Established by HENRY I in the 12th cent., its name refers to the checkered cloth on which the reckoning of revenues took place. Originally, the lower Exchequer was an office for the receipt and payment of money, while the upper Exchequer was a court sitting twice a year to regulate accounts. The English judicial system grew out of the upper Exchequer, and the lower Exchequer became the Treasury. "Exchequer" is still the unofficial name of the Treasury in Britain.

exclusionary rule In U.S. law, the principle that evidence seized by police in violation of constitutional protection from unreasonable SEARCH AND SEIZURE may not be used against a criminal defendant at trial. The U.S. Supreme

DE

Court first established the validity of the rule in *Weeks vs. U.S.* (1914); in *U.S. vs. Leon* (1984), the Court allowed an exception, holding that evidence obtained "in good faith" with a search warrant later ruled invalid is admissible.

excommunication Form of censure by which a member of a religious body is excluded from the congregation of believers and from the rites of the church. In Christianity, it is a punishment for grave offenses such as HERESY. In Roman Catholicism, an excommunicated person is barred from receiving the SACRAMENTS and from burial in consecrated ground. The offender may be absolved by a priest and received back into the church after confessing his or her SIN and doing penance for it. In Protestant denominations, other terms may be attached to essentially the same censure.

excretion Bodily process for disposing of undigested food waste products and by-products of METABOLISM, regulating water content, and maintaining acid-base balance. It refers to both URINATION and DEFECATION and to the processes that take place in the digestive and URINARY systems, as the KIDNEY and LIVER filter wastes, toxins, and drugs from the blood and food reaches the last stage of digestion. Ammonia from PROTEIN digestion is converted to UREA to be excreted in URINE.

exegesis \ˌek-sə-ˈjē-səs, ˈek-sə-ˌjē-səs\ Scholarly interpretation of religious texts, using linguistic, historical, and other methods. In Judaism and Christianity, it has been used extensively in the study of the BIBLE. Textual criticism tries to establish the accuracy of biblical texts. Philological criticism pursues the goal of faithful translation. Literary criticism classifies texts according to style and attempts to establish authorship, date, and audience. Tradition criticism seeks the sources of biblical materials. Still other types of exegesis include redaction criticism, form criticism, and historical criticism.

Exeter \ˈek-sə-tər\ *ancient* Isca Dumnoniorum. City (pop., 1991: 101,000), seat of DEVON, England. Located on the River Exe about 10 mi (16 km) above the English Channel, it commands an important river crossing. It was home to an early British tribe, the Dumnonii, for whom the Romans later named the town. The main town in SW England during the Middle Ages, it was subjected to a number of sieges. ALFRED the Great twice held it against the Danes (877 and c.894); they finally took the city in 1003 but lost it in 1068 to WILLIAM I the Conqueror. Exeter's Norman cathedral was consecrated in 1133.

existentialism Philosophical movement oriented toward the analysis of human existence and the centrality of human choice. Existentialism's chief energies are thus devoted to questions about ONTOLOGY and decision. It traces its roots to the writings of Søren KIERKEGAARD and Friedrich NIETZSCHE. As a philosophy of human existence, existentialism found its best 20th-cent. exponent in Karl JASPERS; as a philosophy of human decision, its foremost representative was Jean-Paul SARTRE. Sartre finds the essence of human existence in freedom—in the duty of self-determination and the freedom of choice—and therefore confronts humanity's perverse attempts to deny its own responsibility and flee from the truth of its inescapable freedom.

Exodus Second book of the OLD TESTAMENT. The title refers to the departure of the Israelites from Egypt under MOSES in the 13th cent. B.C. The book begins with the story of the Israelites' enslavement in Egypt and God's call to Moses to become a prophet. It tells of their escape and of their 40 years of wandering in the Sinai desert. It also recounts how God made a COVENANT with Israel at Mt. SINAI, handing down the TEN COMMANDMENTS. In Exodus God establishes his reliability as Israel's protector and savior, and lays claim to its loyalty and obedience.

exophthalmic goiter See GRAVES' DISEASE

exorcism In Christianity, a ceremony used to drive DEMONS out of a person they have possessed. Jesus healed people tormented by evil spirits, casting them out with a word. By the 3rd cent. this task was assigned to a specially trained class of lower clergy. Rituals for exorcism of people and places also exist in many other traditions.

expanding universe Current understanding of the state of the universe, based on the finding that all GALAXIES are moving away from each other. General RELATIVITY theory and detection of RED SHIFT of other galaxies proved in the 1920s that all galaxies are receding. The universe may either expand indefinitely (open) or eventually collapse (close) into an extremely dense state, as it began, according to the BIG-BANG model.

experimentalism See INSTRUMENTALISM

experimental psychology Branch or type of psychology that employs empirical principles and procedures in the study of psychological phenomena. The experimental psychologist conducts tests under controlled conditions to discover an unknown effect or law, examine or establish a hypothesis, or illustrate a known law. The areas of study that rely most heavily on the experimental method include those of sensation and PERCEPTION, LEARNING and MEMORY, MOTIVATION, and physiological psychology.

Explorer Any of the largest series (1958–75) of unmanned U.S. spacecraft. Explorer 1, the first satellite sent into orbit by the U.S., discovered the innermost VAN ALLEN RADIATION BELT. Explorer 38 (1968) studied galactic radio sources and low frequencies in space, and Explorer 53 (1975) explored X-ray sources within and beyond the Milky Way.

explosive Any substance or device that can produce a volume of rapidly expanding GAS in an extremely brief period. Mechanical explosives, depending on a physical reaction (e.g., overloading a container with compressed air) are little used except in mining. Chemical explosives are of two types: detonating (high) explosives (e.g., TNT, DYNAMITE) have extremely rapid decomposition and development of high pressure; deflagrating (low) explosives (e.g., black powder, smokeless powder) merely burn fast and produce relatively low pressure. Modern high explosives use mixtures of ammonium nitrate and fuel oil or water gels (along with TNT and other fuels). See also NUCLEAR WEAPON.

exponential function In mathematics, a FUNCTION in which a constant base is raised to a VARIABLE power. Exponential functions are used to model changes in population size, in the spread of diseases, in the growth of investments, and in the decline typified by radioactive decay. The essence of exponential growth, and a characteristic of all exponential growth functions, is that they double in size (or halve) over regular intervals.

Export-Import Bank of the United States (EXIMBANK) One of the principal U.S. government agencies in international finance. Since 1934 it has helped finance U.S. exports, principally by lending money to foreign buyers of U.S. goods and services through credits to foreign banks and governments in connection with development projects. See also DEVELOPMENT BANK.

Expressionism Artistic style in which the artist depicts not objective reality but the subjective emotions that objects or events arouse. This aim is accomplished through distortion and exaggeration of shape and the vivid or violent application of color. Its roots are found in the works of Vincent VAN GOGH, Edvard MUNCH, and James ENSOR. In 1905 the movement took hold with the German group Die BRÜCKE; their works influenced such artists as Georges ROUAULT, Chaim SOUTINE, Max BECKMANN, Käthe KOLLWITZ, and Ernst BARLACH. The BLAUE REITER group was also considered Expressionist. Expressionism was the dominant style in Germany after World War I; postwar Expressionists included George GROSZ and Otto DIX. Its emotional qualities were adopted by other 20th-cent. art movements (see ABSTRACT EXPRESSIONISM).

extinction (of species) Dying out or termination of a species. It occurs when a species can no longer reproduce at replacement levels. Most past extinctions are thought to have resulted from environmental changes to which the doomed species could not adapt; or adapted so thoroughly as to become a new species. Humans, through hunting, collecting, and habitat destruction, have become the principal factor in plant and animal extinctions.

extortion Unlawful exaction of money or property through intimidation or undue exercise of authority. It may include threats of physical harm, criminal prosecution, or public exposure. Some forms of threat, especially those made in writing, are occasionally singled out for separate statutory treatment as blackmail. See also BRIBERY.

extradition Process by which one state, at the request of another, returns a person for trial for a crime punishable by the laws of the requesting state and committed outside the state of refuge. Extradition is regulated within countries by extradition acts and between countries by treaties. Most countries decline to surrender their own nationals, and most recognize the right of political ASYLUM, but countries are otherwise usually willing to cooperate in bringing criminals to justice.

extrasensory perception (ESP) Awareness of information about something (such as a person or event) not gained through the SENSES and not deducible from previous experience. Classic forms of ESP include telepathy, clairvoyance, and precognition. Though it remains unverified scientifically, belief in the phenomenon remains widespread, and people who claim to possess ESP are sometimes employed by investigative search teams. See also PARAPSYCHOLOGY.

extrasolar planets See PLANETS OF OTHER STARS

extrauterine pregnancy See ECTOPIC PREGNANCY

extreme sports Untraditional sports characterized by high speed or high risk. Organized sports include aggressive in-line skating, wakeboarding, and street luge, which hold championship competitions. Such sports as mountain-bike downhill racing, snowboarding, and skateboarding, previously considered extreme sports, have been included in recent OLYMPIC GAMES. Less organized activities include ice climbing, glacier skiing, canyoning, and free climbing.

extrovert See INTROVERT AND EXTROVERT

extrusion Process in which metal or other material is forced through a series of DIES to create desired shapes. Many CERAMICS are manufactured by extrusion. In a commercial screw-type extruder, a screw auger continuously forces the plastic feed material through an orifice or die to produce cylindrical rods and pipes, rectangular solid and hollow bars, and long plates. In metalworking, extrusion converts a billet of metal into a length of uniform cross-section by forcing the billet through the orifice of a die; formed sheet aluminum for opaque curtain-wall panels and window frames is easily extruded.

extrusive rock Any IGNEOUS ROCK derived from MAGMA that is poured out or ejected at the earth's surface. Extrusive rocks are usually distinguished from INTRUSIVE ROCKS on the basis of their texture and mineral composition. Lava flows and fragmented volcanic material are extrusive; they are commonly glassy (e.g., obsidian) or finely crystalline (e.g., basalts and felsites).

Exupéry, Antoine de Saint- See Antoine de SAINT-EXUPÉRY

Exxon Mobil Corp. Multinational corporation concentrated in petroleum products. Exxon Corp. was founded as Standard Oil Co. (New Jersey) in 1882 by the Standard Oil Trust. It was soon a multinational company, with holdings on four continents. In 1899 it became the holding company for all companies previously grouped in the trust, though it was forced to divest many of its subsidiaries in 1911. Its trade name Esso, introduced in 1926, was changed to Exxon in 1972. Mobil traces its roots to Vacuum Oil Co. (1866) and Standard Oil Co. of New York, or Socony (1882). The two merged in 1931; the new company took the name Socony Mobil in 1955 and Mobil in 1966. Exxon and Mobil merged in 1999 to become, by some measures, the world's largest corporation. Exxon Mobil's investments and operations extend beyond petroleum and natural gas to coal, nuclear fields, chemicals, and ores, and it operates pipelines and a huge fleet of tankers and other ships.

Eyck \ˈīk\, **Jan van** (c.1395–1441) Flemish painter. He is recorded in 1422 as a master painter and from 1425 was employed by PHILIP III the Good, duke of Burgundy. Securely attributed paintings survive only from the last decade of his career. He produced portraits and religious subjects that are unmatched for their technical brilliance, intellectual complexity, and richness of symbolism. His masterpiece is the *Adoration of the Lamb* (1432), known as the Ghent Altarpiece, which he painted with his brother Hubert (c.1370–1426). He is commonly regarded as the greatest N European artist of the 15th cent.

eye Organ that receives light and visual images. Non-image forming, or direction, eyes are found among many inver-

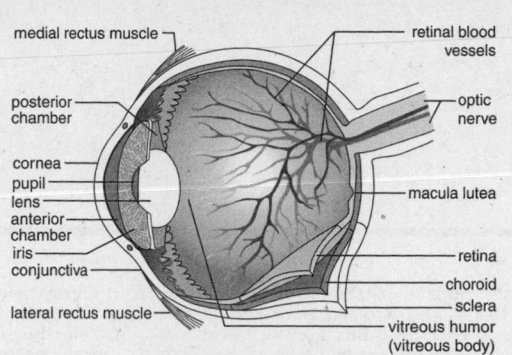

Eye Structure of the human eye. The outer portion consists of the white protective sclera and transparent cornea, through which light enters. The middle layer includes the blood-supplying choroid and pigmented iris. Light passing into the interior through the pupil is regulated by muscles that control the pupil's size. The retina comprises the third layer and contains receptor cells (rods and cones) that transform light waves into nervous impulses. The lens lying directly behind the iris focuses light onto the retina. The macula lutea, in the center of the retina, is a region of high visual acuity and color discrimination. Nerve fibers pass out through the optic nerve to the brain's visual center. The eye's anterior and posterior chambers contain a watery fluid that nourishes the cornea and lens. The vitreous humor helps maintain the eye's shape. A thin layer of mucous membrane (conjunctiva) protects the eye's exposed surface. External muscles, incl. the medial rectus and lateral rectus muscles, connect and move the eye in its socket.

tebrates; image-forming eyes are found in certain mollusks, most arthropods, and nearly all vertebrates. Arthropods have compound eyes; they see a multiple image that is partially integrated in the brain. Lower vertebrates such as fish have eyes on either side of the head, producing two separate fields of vision. In predatory birds and mammals, evolutionary changes in the placement of the eyes permitted a larger overlap of the two visual fields, resulting in the higher mammals in a line of direct sight. The human eye is roughly spherical. Light passes through its transparent front and stimulates receptor cells on the RETINA, which send impulses through the optic nerve to the brain. Vision disorders include near- and farsightedness and ASTIGMATISM, COLOR BLINDNESS, and night blindness. Other eye disorders (including DETACHED RETINA and GLAUCOMA) can impair vision or cause BLINDNESS. See also OPHTHALMOLOGY, PHOTORECEPTION.

Ezekiel \i-ˈzēk-yəl\ (fl.6th cent. B.C.) Priest and PROPHET of ancient Israel, the subject and partial author of the Old Testament Book of Ezekiel. He began to prophesy to the Jews in Palestine around 592 B.C., pronouncing God's judgment on a sinful nation. He witnessed the conquest of Jerusalem by BABYLON, but offered a promise of Israel's restoration in his famous vision of a valley of dry bones that revive and assemble themselves.

Ezhov, Nikolay See Nikolay YEZHOV

Ezra (fl.5th–4th cent. B.C.) Jewish religious leader and reformer. He restored the Jewish community after its exile in BABYLON, persuading the people of JUDAH to return to a strict observance of Mosaic law. He served as a commissioner of the Persian government, which was tolerant of other religions. For creating a Jewish community based on Law, which could exist without political statehood, he is often considered the founder of modern JUDAISM. His story is told in the books of Ezra and NEHEMIAH.

Eye labels: medial rectus muscle, posterior chamber, cornea, pupil, lens, anterior chamber, iris, conjunctiva, lateral rectus muscle, retinal blood vessels, optic nerve, macula lutea, retina, choroid, sclera, vitreous humor (vitreous body)

DE

F

Fabergé \fà-ber-'zhā\, **(Peter) Carl** (*orig.* Karl Gustavovich) (1846–1920) Russian goldsmith, jeweler, and designer. He took over his father's jewelry business in St. Petersburg in 1870. The objects he designed quickly won him the patronage of European and Russian royalty. Specializing in gold, silver, malachite, jade, lapis lazuli, and gemstones, he manufactured not only conventional jewelry but objects of fantasy. He became most famous for his jeweled Easter eggs for ALEXANDER III and NICHOLAS II. His workshops were shut down after the 1917 revolution, and he died in exile.

Fabian Society \'fā-bē-ən\ Socialist society founded in 1883–84 to establish a democratic socialist state in Britain. The name derived from the Roman general Fabius Maximus Cunctator, whose elusive tactics in avoiding pitched battles led to victory over stronger forces. Fabians believed in evolutionary socialism rather than revolution, and used lectures, research, and publishing to educate the public. Important early members included G. B. SHAW and Sidney and Beatrice WEBB. They helped organize a separate party that became the LABOUR PARTY in 1906.

fable Narration intended to enforce a useful truth, especially one in which animals or inanimate objects speak and act like human beings. Unlike a folktale, it has a moral that is woven into the story and often stated at the end. The Western fable tradition began with tales ascribed to AESOP. It flourished in the Middle Ages and reached a high point in 17th-cent. France in the works of Jean de LA FONTAINE. Fables also have ancient roots in India, China, and Japan.

Fabriano, Gentile da See GENTILE DA FABRIANO

Fabricius (ab Aquapendente) \fə-'brish-əs\, **Hieronymus** *Italian* Girolamo Fabrici (1537–1619) Italian surgeon and anatomist, student and successor of Gabriel FALLOPIUS at the Univ. of Padua. In 1603 he gave the first clear description of the valves of the veins. His *De formato foetu* (1600) contained the first detailed description of the placenta and opened the field of comparative embryology. He was the first to perceive the larynx as a vocal organ and to demonstrate that the pupil of the eye changes size. He was the teacher of William HARVEY.

Fabritius \fà-'brēt-sē-ūes\, **Carel** (1622–1654) Dutch painter. He studied with REMBRANDT in the early 1640s, then settled in Delft. His earliest known work, *The Raising of Lazarus* (c.1645), was strongly influenced by Rembrandt, but he soon developed a personal style marked by cool color harmonies, subtle lighting effects, and illusionistic perspective. His portraits and his genre and narrative paintings influenced Pieter de HOOCH and Jan VERMEER. Most of his paintings were destroyed by the explosion of the Delft powder magazine, which killed him as well.

factor In multiplication, one of two or more numerical or algebraic components of a product. A whole number's factors are the whole numbers that divide evenly into it (e.g., 1, 2, 3, 4, 6, and 12 are factors of 12). To factor a counting number means to break it down into its PRIME NUMBER factors. To factor a POLYNOMIAL is to find its prime polynomial factors. According to thc fundamental theorem of arithmetic, the prime factorization of any number or polynomial is unique.

factorial For any whole number, the product of all the counting numbers up to and including itself. It is indicated with an exclamation point: 4! (read "four factorial") is $1 \times 2 \times 3 \times 4 = 24$. Factorials are particularly useful in calculating the number of ways an event can occur, for example, the number of possible orders of finish in a race. See also PERMUTATIONS AND COMBINATIONS.

factory Structure in which work is organized to meet the need for production on a large scale usually with power-driven machinery. In the 17th–18th cent., the DOMESTIC SYSTEM of work in Europe began giving way to larger units of production, and capital became available for industrial investment. The movement of population from country to city also contributed to change in work methods. MASS PRODUCTION, which transformed the organization of work, came about by the development of the MACHINE-TOOL industry, With precision equipment, large numbers of identical parts could be produced at low cost and with a small workforce. The ASSEMBLY LINE was first widely used in the U.S. meat-packing industry; Henry FORD designed an automobile assembly line in 1913, and by 1914 chassis assembly time had fallen by almost 90%. See also AMERICAN SYSTEM OF MANUFACTURE.

fact–value distinction In philosophy, the ontological distinction between what is (facts) and what ought to be (values). David HUME provided its classical formulation in his dictum that it is impossible to derive an "ought" from an "is."

Fadhlallah \fäd-'ləl-lə\, **Ayatollah Sayyid Muhammad Hussayn** (b.1935) Shiite cleric and spiritual leader of HIZBULLAH. Born in Iraq of Lebanese parents, he moved to Lebanon in 1966 and became a leading religious authority. Fadhlallah's eloquence led many to believe that he was Hizbullah's leader, but both he and the party deny this, while acknowledging his strong spiritual influence. In 1985 it was widely reported that he was the target of an aborted U.S.-Saudi car-bomb assassination.

Faeroe Islands *or* **Faroe Islands** \'far-ō\ Group of islands (pop., 1994 est.: 45,000) north of the British Isles, a self-governing region within Denmark. There are 17 inhabited islands and many islets and reefs, with a total area of 540 sq mi (1,399 sq km). The islands are high and rugged, deeply indented with fjords. The economy is based on fishing and sheep-raising. First settled by Irish monks (c.700), the islands were colonized by the Vikings (c.800) and later were ruled by Norway; in 1380 they passed to Denmark. They received self-government in 1948.

Fahrenheit, Daniel (Gabriel) (1686–1736) German-Dutch physicist and instrument maker. He is best known for inventing a successful alcohol thermometer (1709) and mercury thermometer (1714) and for developing the Fahrenheit temperature scale, setting zero at the FREEZING POINT of an equal mixture of ice and salt. He discovered that water can remain liquid below its freezing point and that the BOILING POINT of liquids varies with atmospheric pressure.

faience \fā-'äns, fī-'äⁿs\ Tin-glazed EARTHENWARE made in France, Germany, Spain, and Scandinavia, similar to the Italian Faenza majolica, for which it was named. The term is also applied to glazed earthenware made in ancient Egypt, where it was used for beads, amulets, jewelry, and small animal and human figures, most notably the blue-glazed hippopotamus figures of the Middle Kingdom (c.2000–c.1670 B.C.).

fair Temporary market where buyers and sellers gather to transact business. Fairs are held at regular intervals, generally at the same location and time of year. An important form of commerce before the INDUSTRIAL REVOLUTION, fairs solved the problem of distribution and made possible the demonstration of arts and crafts and the sale and BARTER of goods. In the Roman Empire and medieval Europe, they were held at major caravan-route intersections and near religious festivals. The rules of the fair eventually became the basis of European business law. Fairs began to die out as cities grew larger and transportation networks became more extensive, though some continued as religious festivals or recreational events. Agricultural fairs are still held in the U.S. and Europe. The TRADE FAIR, in which exhibitors from one industry display their goods, gained popularity in the 20th cent.

Fairbanks City (pop., 2000: 30,000), E central Alaska. Founded in 1902 after a gold strike, it is the N terminus of the Alaska Highway and the railroad, and the main supply center for the N Alaskan oil business (see TRANS-ALASKA PIPELINE). Nearby are Ft. Wainwright, Eielson Air Force Base, and the Univ. of Alaska, Fairbanks (1917). It is the site of the annual 800-mi (1,290-km) Yukon Marathon boat race and the N. American Championship Sled Dog Races.

Fairbanks, Douglas *orig.* Douglas Elton Ulman (1883–1939) U.S. film actor. Born in Denver, he was a Broadway star by 1910, noted for his exuberance and physical agility. He made his film debut in *The Lamb* (1915). As co-founder of UNITED ARTISTS (1919), he produced and starred in such films as *The Mark of Zorro* (1920), *Robin Hood* (1922), and *The Thief of Baghdad* (1924), earning the title "King of Hollywood." His 15-year marriage to Mary PICKFORD ended in 1935. His son by his first wife, Douglas Fairbanks, Jr. (1909–2000), was a debonair leading man in U.S. and British films, including *Catherine the Great*

Douglas Fairbanks in *The Black Pirate*, 1926

(1934), *The Prisoner of Zenda* (1937), and *State Secret* (1950).

Fairfax (of Cameron), Thomas, Baron (1612–1671) English general. During the ENGLISH CIVIL WARS, his tactical skill and courage helped bring about many Parliamentary victories. As commander in chief of the NEW MODEL ARMY, he defeated CHARLES I at the Battle of Naseby. He refused to serve on the commission that condemned Charles to death, and resigned to protest the proposed invasion of Scotland. In 1658 he helped George MONCK restore Parliamentary rule in the face of army opposition.

fair-trade law In the U.S., any law allowing manufacturers of brand-name or trademarked goods to fix the actual or minimum resale prices of these goods. Fair-trade laws were passed by many states during the GREAT DEPRESSION to protect independent retailers from price-cutting by large chain stores, but most were later repealed. Critics argued that such laws restricted competition; the complexity of post–World War II marketing channels also made enforcement impracticable. In 1975 the few that remained were repealed by Congress.

Fairweather, Mt. Mountain, British Columbia. It is located on the Alaska border in the ST. ELIAS MTNS., at the SW end of GLACIER BAY NATIONAL PARK. The highest peak in the province, it reaches 15,299 ft (4,663 m). It was named by Capt. James COOK in 1778 while navigating the bay in "fair weather."

fairy In folklore, any of a race of supernatural beings who have magic powers and sometimes meddle in human affairs. Some have been described as of human size, while others are only a few inches high. The term was first used in medieval Europe. Fairy lore is especially common in Ireland, Cornwall, Wales, and Scotland. The fairies of the past were powerful and sometimes dangerous beings who could be friendly, mischievous, or cruel, depending on their whim. Fairies were thought to be beautiful, to live much longer than human beings, and to lack souls. They sometimes carried off human infants and left changelings as substitutes,

and occasionally they took human lovers. See also LEPRECHAUN.

fairy tale Simple narrative dealing with supernatural beings (such as fairies, magicians, ogres, or dragons) that is typically of folk origin and written or told for the amusement of children, or a more sophisticated narrative containing supernatural or obviously improbable events, scenes, and personages and often having a whimsical, satirical, or moralistic character. The term embraces popular folktales such as "Cinderella" and "Puss in Boots," as well as art fairy tales of later invention, such as those by H. C. ANDERSEN.

Faisal I \ˈfī-səl\ (1885–1933) Arab statesman and king of Iraq (1921–33). Son of Husayn ibn Ali, he helped his father plot Arab nationalist rebellion against the OTTOMAN EMPIRE during World War I. In 1918 an Arab military force occupied Damascus, and Faisal was declared king of Syria. When France invaded Syria (1920), Faisal went into exile in London. The British sponsored him as king of Iraq, in anticipation of Iraqi independence; he was crowned in 1921, and Iraq became independent in 1932.

Faisalabad \ˈfī-sə-lə-ˌbad\ *formerly (until 1979)* **Lyallpur** \ˈlīl-ˌpủr\ City (pop., 1998: 1,977,000) and district, PUNJAB province, Pakistan. Founded in 1890, it became headquarters of the Lower Chenab colony and in 1898 was incorporated as a municipality. Its industries produce chemicals and synthetics, textiles, and food products.

faith healing Curing of an illness or disability by recourse to divine power, without the use of traditional medicine. A healer may act as intermediary. Certain places are also believed to effect cures among believers. In ancient Greece, temples honoring ASCLEPIUS were built near springs with healing waters. In Christianity, support for faith healing is based on the miraculous cures wrought by Jesus. CHRISTIAN SCIENCE is noted for faith healing, and it is also practiced in a more dramatic way in PENTECOSTALISM.

Falange \fä-ˈlän-hä, *Engl* ˈfā-lanj\ (Spanish: "Phalanx") Extreme nationalist political group in Spain. Founded in 1933 by José Primo de Rivera (1903-1936) and influenced by Italian FASCISM, the Falange gained popularity in opposition to the POPULAR FRONT government of 1936. Gen. Francisco FRANCO merged the group with other right-wing factions in 1937 and became its chief; 150,000 Falangists served in Franco's armed forces in the SPANISH CIVIL WAR. After their victory, the Falange's fascism was subordinated to the Franco regime's conservative values. The Falange was abolished in 1977.

Falasha \fə-ˈlä-shə\ Jewish Ethiopians. The Falasha call themselves House of Israel and claim descent from Menilek I, son of King SOLOMON and the Queen of SHEBA. Probably descended from local Agew peoples converted by Jews in S Arabia, they remained faithful to Judaism after the Ethiopian kingdom was converted to Christianity in the 4th cent. A.D. Though ignorant of the TALMUD, members adhered strictly to the Mosaic law and observed some festivals of Judaism. In 1975 the Israeli rabbinate affirmed that Falashas were Jews, and from 1980 to 1992 some 45,000 Falasha emigrated to Israel.

falcon Any of nearly 60 species of diurnal BIRDS OF PREY in the family Falconidae, characterized by long, pointed wings and swift, powerful flight. The name is sometimes restricted to the more than 35 species of true falcons, genus *Falco*. Species range from 6 to 24 in. (15–60 cm) long. Females of the genus *Falco* are preferred for FALCONRY. Falcons, found worldwide, commonly nest in treeholes or on cliff ledges. Some species capture birds, others live on hares, mice, lizards, and insects. See also GYRFALCON, HAWK, KESTREL, PEREGRINE FALCON.

Falconet \fȧl-kȯ-ˈne\, **Étienne-Maurice** (1716–1791) French sculptor. After studies in Paris, he developed an intimate, delicate style. Through Madame de POMPADOUR's influence, he became director of the Sèvres porcelain factory (1757–66). From 1766 to 1778 he worked in Russia; his masterpiece was the colossal equestrian statue of PETER I the Great in St. Petersburg (made famous as *The Bronze Horseman* by Aleksandr PUSHKIN). He is best known for adapting the classical style of the French baroque period to the Rococo ideal.

falconry Sport of employing FALCONS or other HAWKS in hunting game. Falconry has been practiced in the Middle East at least since the 8th cent. B.C. It flourished among the privileged classes in Europe in the Middle Ages but waned after the advent of the shotgun and the enclosure of open lands in the 17th cent. The bird most commonly used is the PEREGRINE FALCON, though the goshawk and sparrow hawk have also been used. Birds are caught wild or raised from birth. Training involves selective use of a leather hood and leg thongs to keep the animal under control while familiarizing it with its new environment. Once the bird has brought down its prey, it returns to the hawker or is collected at the kill site.

Falkland Islands *Spanish* **Islas Malvinas** \'ēs-ˌläs-mäl-'bē-näs\ British self-governing colony (pop., 1993 est.: 2,000), about 300 mi (480 km) northeast of the S tip of S. America. It is made up of two main islands, E. Falkland and W. Falkland, and about 200 smaller islands; they cover some 4,700 sq mi (12,200 sq km). The capital is Stanley, on E. Falkland. The population is English-speaking and of British descent. The economy is based on sheep-raising. The French settled E. Falkland in 1764, and the British settled W. Falkland in 1765. In 1770 the Spanish purchased the French settlement. In 1820 Argentina proclaimed its sovereignty over the Falklands, but the British took them back in 1833. Argentina invaded in 1982, and the British repulsed them (see FALKLAND ISLANDS WAR).

Falkland Islands War *or* **Malvinas War** (1982) Brief undeclared war between Argentina and Britain over the FALKLAND ISLANDS, which both countries had long claimed. In 1982, giving up on protracted negotiations with Britain, Argentina invaded the islands with some 10,000 troops. Margaret THATCHER dispatched a naval task force, and in three months Britain had reoccupied the islands. Britain lost about 250 men, Argentina about 700. Argentina's defeat discredited its military government and helped restore civilian rule in 1983.

Fall, Albert B(acon) (1861–1944) U.S. secretary of the interior (1921–23). Born in Frankfort, Ky., he practiced law in New Mexico before serving in the U.S. Senate (1913–21). An investigation after he left the Interior Department revealed that he had accepted a bribe in return for government oil-reserve leases in the TEAPOT DOME SCANDAL. Convicted in 1929, he was imprisoned for nine months.

Falla \'fä-yə\, **Manuel de** (1876–1946) Spanish composer. He studied with Felipe Pedrell and conceived a powerful musical nationalism. His first major work was the opera *La vida breve* (1905). The intensely Spanish ballet *El amor brujo* (1915) gained him further acclaim. His other works include *Nights in the Gardens of Spain* (1915), *The Three-Cornered Hat* (1919), the puppet opera *El retablo de maese Pedro* (1923), a harpsichord concerto (1926), and the huge unfinished oratorio *L'Atlántida*. He is regarded as the greatest Spanish composer of recent centuries.

fallacy, formal and informal In philosophy, reasoning that fails to establish its conclusion because of deficiencies in wording or form. Fallacies have traditionally been divided into formal and informal classes. Formal fallacies are deductively invalid arguments that typically commit an easily recognizable logical error. Informal fallacies can be divided into material and verbal fallacies. The material fallacies are also known as fallacies of presumption, because the premises "presume" too much, either avoiding the issue in view, or covertly assuming the conclusion, as in "begging the question," which occurs when the premises presume the very conclusion that is to be proved. Verbal fallacies, or fallacies of ambiguity, arise when the conclusion is achieved through an improper use of words.

Fallen Timbers, Battle of (Aug. 20, 1794) Decisive victory of Gen. Anthony WAYNE over the NW Indian Confederation, securing white settlement of former Indian territory, mainly in Ohio. Wayne led over 1,000 soldiers to confront the 2,000 Indians, who had gathered behind a protective tangle of fallen trees along the Maumee River (near modern Toledo). The Indians, abandoned by their British allies, fled in disarray. A treaty in 1795 ceded Indian lands to the U.S. and ended British influence in the area.

Fallopius \fə-'lō-pē-əs\, **Gabriel** *Italian* Gabriello Fallopio (1523–1562) Italian anatomist. He discovered the fallopian tubes, which connect the ovaries to the uterus, and several major nerves of the head and face, and he described the semicircular canals in the ear. He and Andreas VESALIUS overturned many of GALEN's principles, a development essential to Renaissance medicine.

fallout Descent of radioactive materials from the atmosphere. Atmospheric radioactivity may arise naturally from COSMIC RAYS, or from nuclear explosions and atomic reactor operations. Exploded NUCLEAR WEAPONS produce local, tropospheric, and stratospheric fallout. The first, intense but relatively short-lived, occurs as larger radioactive particles are deposited near the explosion site. Tropospheric fallout occurs when the finer particles enter the TROPOSPHERE, and it spreads over a larger area in the month after the explosion. Stratospheric fallout, made of fine particles in the STRATOSPHERE, may continue years after the explosion, with worldwide distribution. Only long-lived isotopes such as CESIUM-137 and STRONTIUM-90 are deposited as stratospheric fallout.

Falun Gong \'fä-ˌlùn-'gón\ *or* **Falun Dafa** \'dä-fä\ China-based social movement combining healthful exercises with meditation for the purpose of "moving to higher levels." It was founded in 1992 by Li Hongzhi (b.1952), a former grain-bureau clerk. He originally registered it as a form of the natural-healing discipline qigong, but increasingly stressed its spiritual (rather than health-related) emphasis. It claims a worldwide following of 100 million, with 70 million in China; Chinese authorities claim it has only 20 million members. The movement has been regarded as a threat by the Chinese government, which started arresting its followers in 1999.

Falwell \'fól-ˌwel\, **Jerry L.** (b.1933) Protestant fundamentalist evangelist. Born in Lynchburg, Va., he studied engineering before turning to religion. He founded Thomas Road Baptist Church in 1956 and later founded Liberty Baptist College. Using his "Old-Time Gospel Hour" television show, in 1979 he organized the Moral Majority to encourage his followers to become involved in politics. He is known for his sometimes extreme conservatism.

family Basic social unit consisting of persons united by ties of MARRIAGE (affinity), "blood" (consanguinity), or adoption and usually representing a single household. The essence of the family group is the parent-child relationship, whose outlines nevertheless vary widely among cultures. The nuclear family consists of the marital pair and their offspring living in a separate dwelling. While some scholars believe this to be the oldest form, others point to the inconclusive prehistorical record and the widespread existence of other forms such as the polygynous family (a husband, two or more cowives, and their offspring) and the extended family (parents, married children, and their offspring). The family provides for the rearing and socialization of children, the care of the aged, sick, or disabled, the legitimation of procreation, and the regulation of sexual conduct.

family practice *or* **family medicine** *or* **general practice** Field of MEDICINE that stresses comprehensive primary health care, emphasizing the family unit. Practitioners must be familiar to some degree with medical specialties and, especially in HEALTH MAINTENANCE ORGANIZATIONS, are now often gatekeepers who refer patients to specialists when necessary. Once virtually the only kind of medicine, family practice has been defined as a separate field only since increasing specialization in medicine led to a shortage of practitioners.

family sagas See ICELANDERS' SAGAS

famine Extreme and protracted shortage of food, resulting in widespread hunger and a substantial increase in the death rate. Causes of famine may be natural or human. Natural causes include drought, flooding, unfavorable weather conditions, plant disease, and insect infestation. The chief human cause is war; others include overpopulation, bad distribution systems, and high food prices. In the 20th cent. severe famines have occurred in China (1928–29, 5–10 million dead; 1959–60, several million), Russia (1921–22, 1.25–5 million; 1932–34, 5 million), India (1943–

44, 1.5 million), Cambodia (1975–79, 1 million), and sub-Saharan Africa.

fan Rigid or folding hand-held device used for cooling, air circulation, or ceremony. Early Egyptian fans were of the rigid type, with a handle or stick attached to a rigid leaf or to feathers. In China, the folding fan came into fashion during the Ming dynasty (1368–1644); many great Chinese painters devoted their talents to fan decoration. Portuguese traders in the 15th cent. brought fans to Europe. Through the 19th cent. in the West, fan decoration and size varied with European fashion.

Fanfani \fän-'fä-nē\, **Amintore** (1908–1999) Italian politician. He became secretary-general of the Christian Democratic Party (1954) after serving briefly as premier. With his party's victory in 1958, he again became premier (1958–59) and stressed social reforms; he then returned as premier (1960–63). He gained Italy's election to the U.N. Security Council (1958) and served as president of the U.N. General Assembly in 1965. He again served as premier in 1982–83 and 1987.

Fang Lizhi \'fäŋ-'lē-'jē\ (b.1936) Chinese astrophysicist and dissident. Expelled from the CHINESE COMMUNIST PARTY in 1957 for decrying the Marxist position on physics, he later taught at Beijing's Univ. of Science and Technology (Keda). In 1966–69 he was sent to a communal farm to be "reeducated." Appointed a vice president of one branch of Keda in 1985, he began work on reforming educational policy. He helped provoke the 1989 student demonstrations in TIANANMEN SQUARE, and in 1990 was allowed to leave China. He has taught at the Univ. of Arizona.

fantasy Mental images or imaginary narratives that distort or entirely depart from reality. Primary fantasies arise spontaneously from the UNCONSCIOUS, while secondary fantasies are consciously summoned and pursued. Sigmund FREUD saw fantasy as a vehicle for the expression of repressed desires (see REPRESSION). Fantasy is important in the lives of children and is a vital element in play. In adult life it is crucial to creative thinking and the making of art.

Fantin-Latour \fäⁿ-taⁿ-là-'tür\, **(Ignace-) Henri (-Jean-Théodore)** (1836–1904) French painter and printmaker. Son of a portrait painter, he was a traditionalist best known for his portraits and still lifes with flowers. His portrait groups, reminiscent of 17th-cent. Dutch guild portraits, depict literary and artistic persons of the time; his flower paintings were especially popular in England. His later years were devoted to lithography.

Faraday, Michael (1791–1867) English physicist and chemist. He went to work as an assistant to Humphry DAVY, from whom he learned chemistry. He discovered a number of new organic compounds, including benzene, and was the first to liquefy a "permanent" gas. His major contributions were in the fields of ELECTRICITY and MAGNETISM. He was the first to report induction of an electric current from a magnetic field. He invented the first electric motor and dynamo, demonstrated the relation between electricity and chemical bonding, discovered the effect of magnetism on light, and discovered and named DIAMAGNETISM. He also provided the experimental, and much of the theoretical, foundation on which J. C. MAXWELL built his electromagnetic field theory.

Farah, Nuruddin (b.1945) Somali writer, Somalia's first novelist and first English-language author. His first published novel, *From a Crooked Rib* (1970), describes a woman's determination to maintain her dignity in a sexist society. His other works include a trilogy—*Sweet and Sour Milk* (1979), *Sardines* (1981), and *Close Sesame* (1983)—about life under an African dictatorship. The political nature of his fiction forced him into exile in 1972.

farce Light dramatic composition that uses highly improbable situations, stereotyped characters, violent horseplay, and broad humor. Farce is generally regarded as inferior to COMEDY in its crude characterizations and implausible plots, but it has remained popular since ancient times.

Fargo City (pop., 2000: 90,000), E N. Dakota. The state's largest city, it is located on the Red River of the North. It was founded in 1871 and named for William G. Fargo (1818–1881) of WELLS FARGO & CO. The development of

wheat-growing consolidated the city's role as a transportation, marketing, and distribution center. N. Dakota State Univ. (1890) is a noted center of agricultural research. Nearby meat-packing plants and stockyards rank among the nation's largest.

Farinelli *orig.* Carlo Broschi (1705–1782) Italian castrato soprano. After being castrated, he became a student of the composer Nicola Porpora (1686–1768), making his debut in 1720. Renowned for his vocal power and amazing agility, he moved to London in 1734, where he became the greatest opera star of his time. In 1747 he abandoned the public stage for the court of PHILIP V in Madrid, where his singing revived the ailing monarch. Farinelli took over the court's musical establishment and engaged in extravagant projects until his retirement in 1759.

Farmer, Fannie (Merritt) (1857–1915) U.S. cookery expert. Born in Boston, she became director of the Boston Cooking School in 1894, and in 1896 published *The Boston Cooking-School Cook Book*. The first cookbook to standardize the methods and measurements of recipes, it became one of the best-selling cookbooks of all time. In 1902 she established Miss Farmer's School of Cookery for housewives.

Farnese \fär-'nā-sā\, **Alessandro** *later* duca (Duke) di Parma e Piacenza (1545–1592) Italian general and diplomat. He was educated at the court of Madrid, where he had been sent to prove his father's loyalty to the Habsburgs. In 1578 PHILIP II of Spain appointed him governor-general of the Netherlands. His great achievement was the restoration of Spanish rule in the S provinces and perpetuation of Roman Catholicism there. He succeeded by astute statesmanship and military operations against the alliance of rebellious Protestant provinces led by WILLIAM I the Silent.

Farnese, Elizabeth See ELIZABETH FARNESE

Farnese family Italian family that ruled the duchy of Parma and Piacenza from 1545 to 1731. The family became noted for its statesmen and soldiers. In 1545 Pope PAUL III, a Farnese, detached Parma and Piacenza from the papal dominions and made them into duchies. The first duke was his illegitimate son, Pier Luigi Farnese (1503–1547), whose son Ottavio (1542–1586) made Parma the capital and consolidated the family's power. The 3rd duke, Alessandro FARNESE, was Spain's regent of the Netherlands. His son and grandson left heavy financial and diplomatic debts by inconclusive military campaigns in the THIRTY YEARS' WAR. In 1649 Pope Innocent X seized the fief; the duchy survived precariously. Francesco Farnese (1678–1727) married his niece ELIZABETH FARNESE to PHILIP V of Spain (1714). In 1731 the duchy passed to Elizabeth's son, the future CHARLES III.

Farnsworth, Philo T(aylor) (1906–1971) U.S. engineer and inventor. Born in Beaver, Utah, as a teenager he began developing the early technology required for TELEVISION, and in 1927 he successfully transmitted an image composed of 60 horizontal lines. He formed Farnsworth Television in 1929 and invented numerous devices related to television, including equipment for converting an optical image into an electrical signal; amplifier, cathode-ray, and vacuum tubes; and electrical scanners and photoelectric materials.

Faroe Islands See FAEROE ISLANDS

Farouk I \fə-'rük\ *Arabic* Faruq Al-Awwal (1920–1965) King of Egypt (1936–52). Son of King Fuad I (1868–1936), he ascended the throne in 1936. Farouk's administration was hampered by internal rivalries. His alienation of the military, especially after its loss to Israel (1948), led to his own downfall. In 1952 a coup led by G. A. NASSER forced him to abdicate. In 1953 Egypt became a republic.

Farquhar \'fär-kər, 'fär-kwər\, **George** (1678–1707) Irish playwright. His early experience as an actor in Dublin was the source of the originality of dialogue and stage sense that gave his work its great comic power. His popular plays included *Love and a Bottle* (1699), but his real contribution to English drama came with *The Recruiting Officer* (1706) and particularly *The Beaux' Stratagem* (1707), in which he introduced a verbal vigor and love of character reminiscent of Elizabethan dramatists.

Farragut \'far-ə-gət\, **David G(lasgow)** (1801–1870) U.S. naval officer. Born near Knoxville, Tenn., he served in the

FG

War of 1812 and received his first command in 1824. During the Civil War, he commanded the Union blockade of the W Gulf of Mexico; in the Battle of New Orleans (1862) he captured the port through which the Confederacy received much of its war supplies. In 1864 he successfully attacked in the Battle of Mobile Bay, leading his ships across a blockade of mines, or torpedoes, with the order "Damn the torpedoes, full speed ahead!" He became a full admiral in 1866.

David Farragut

Farrakhan \ˈfär-ə-ˌkän\, **Louis** *orig.* Louis Eugene Walcott (b.1933) U.S. religious leader. Born in New York City, he joined the Black Muslims in 1955, and for a time he assisted MALCOLM X in Boston. After the latter converted to SUNNI Islam, the two became enemies. Farrakhan has repeatedly denied involvement in Malcolm's assassination. When W. Deen Muhammad, Elijah MUHAMMAD's successor as leader of the Nation of ISLAM, gradually began integrating the organization into the orthodox Muslim community, Farrakhan broke away and formed his own organization, also called Nation of Islam (1978). A strong proponent of black self-help and unity, he is known for his forceful speeches marked by calls for racial separatism as well as by anti-Semitism and conspiracy theories.

Farrell \ˈfar-əl\, **James T(homas)** (1904–1979) U.S. novelist and short-story writer. A native of Chicago, he is known for his realistic portraits of the city's lower-middle-class Irish population. His well-known *Studs Lonigan* trilogy—*Young Lonigan* (1932), *The Young Manhood of Studs Lonigan* (1934), and *Judgment Day* (1935)—traces the self-destruction of a spiritually crippled young man. He later planned a cycle of 25 novels, of which he completed 10. *The Face of Time* (1953) is among his best novels. He also produced 17 short-story collections.

Farrell, Suzanne *orig.* Roberta Sue Ficker (b.1945) U.S. ballet dancer. Born in Cincinnati, she joined the NEW YORK CITY BALLET at 16, becoming a soloist at 18. She danced many roles created for her by George BALANCHINE in ballets such as *Meditation, Don Quixote,* and *Slaughter on Tenth Avenue.* After several years as principal dancer with Maurice BÉJART's Ballet of the 20th Century (1970–75), she returned to the City Ballet as principal dancer, continuing to create leading roles until she retired in 1989 and joined the faculty of the School of American Ballet.

Farsi language See PERSIAN LANGUAGE

fascism \ˈfa-ˌshi-zəm\ Philosophy of government that stresses the primacy and glory of the state, unquestioning obedience to its leader, subordination of the individual will to the state's authority, and harsh suppression of dissent. Martial virtues are celebrated, while liberal democratic values are denigrated. 20th-cent. fascism arose partly out of fear of the rising power of the lower classes and differed from contemporary communism by its protection of the corporate and landowning powers and preservation of a class system. The fascist governments that ruled Italy (1922–43), Germany (1933–45), and Spain (1939–75) were led by charismatic politicians (Benito MUSSOLINI, Adolf HITLER, Francisco FRANCO), who represented to their publics the strength that could rescue their nation from chaotic political and economic conditions. See also TOTALITARIANISM.

Fashoda Incident \fə-ˈshō-də\ (Sept. 18, 1898) Climax, at Fashoda (now Kodok), Egyptian Sudan, of a series of territorial disputes between Britain and France. Britain had sought to extend its empire from Cairo to the Cape of Good Hope, while France had sought to extend its own from Dakar to the Sudan. A French force was the first to arrive at a strategically located fort at Fashoda, soon followed by a British force under Lord KITCHENER. After a tense standoff the French withdrew, but they continued to press claims to other posts in the region. In March 1899 the French and British agreed that the watershed of the Nile and the Congo rivers should mark the frontier between their spheres of influence.

Fassbinder \ˈfäs-ˌbin-dər\, **Rainer Werner** (1946–1982) German film director. A member of the avant-garde theater movement in Munich, he helped form the Antitheater (1967). His first full-length film (1969) was soon followed by 40 others, including *The Bitter Tears of Petra von Kant* (1972), *The Marriage of Maria Braun* (1979), the 15-hour *Berlin Alexanderplatz* (1980), *Lola* (1981), and *Veronika Voss* (1982). A leader of the German New Wave, he helped revitalize German cinema. Defiantly homosexual and provocative, he died from a drug overdose at 36.

fasting Abstaining from food, usually for religious or ethical reasons. In ancient religions fasting prepared worshipers or priests to approach deities, to pursue a vision, to demonstrate penance for sins, or to assuage an angered deity. All the major world religions include fasting among their practices. Judaism has several fast days, notably YOM KIPPUR. The 40-day Christian LENT includes the traditional fast days of Ash Wednesday and Good Friday. In Islam the month of RAMADAN is a period of total abstention from food from dawn to dusk. Hunger strikes (using fasting as a political protest) have been employed by, among others, 19th-cent. female suffragists, Mohandas GANDHI, and late-20th-cent. Irish nationalists. Moderate fasting is also sometimes practiced for its claimed health benefits.

fat Any organic compound of plant or animal origin that is not volatile, does not dissolve in water, and is oily or greasy. Chemically, fats from animals and from vegetables (OILS) are identical, consisting mainly of TRIGLYCERIDES; the differences are in the melting temperature and physical state (solid or liquid) of each, which depends on the SATURATION of the fatty acids and the length of the carbon chain. Natural fats such as corn oil have small amounts of compounds besides triglycerides, including PHOSPHOLIPIDS, plant STEROIDS, tocopherols (VITAMIN E), VITAMIN A, WAXES, carotenoids, and many others. Fats in foods come from ripe seeds and fruits (corn, peanuts, olives, avocados) and from animal sources (meat, eggs, milk). They contain more than twice as much energy (CALORIES) per unit of weight as PROTEINS and CARBOHYDRATES. DIGESTION of fats in foods, often partial, is done by ENZYMES called lipases. The breakdown products are absorbed from the intestines into the blood, which carries microscopic fat droplets reconstituted from digested fats or synthesized in cells to sites of storage or use. Fats are readily broken down, primarily into glycerol and fatty acids, by HYDROLYSIS, a first step for many of their numerous industrial uses. See also LIPID.

Fatah \ˈfät-ᵊh, *Engl* ˈfä-tä\ Inverted acronym of Harakat al-Tahrir al-Watani al-Filastini (Palestine National Liberation Movement), which also means "opening" in Arabic. It was founded by Yasir ARAFAT and Khalil al-Wazir in the late 1950s to free Palestine from Israeli control. It eventually became the biggest group within the PALESTINE LIBERATION ORGANIZATION and attacked Israeli interests worldwide. It has moved its headquarters several times under pressure from sympathizers and foes alike. It gave up terrorism in 1993 when Arafat agreed to enter into talks with Israel.

Fates In Greek and Roman mythology, the three goddesses who determined human destiny. They were usually depicted as old women: Clotho spun the thread of human life, Lachesis dispensed it, and Atropos cut the thread. They determined the length of each person's life as well as its share of suffering. Their Roman names were Nona, Decuma, and Morta.

Father's Day See MOTHER'S DAY AND FATHER'S DAY

fatigue In engineering, manifestation of progressive fracture in a solid under cyclic loading, as in the case of a metal strip that ruptures after repeated bending back and forth (see METAL FATIGUE). Fatigue fracture begins with one or several cracks that spread in the course of repeated application of forces until complete rupture suddenly occurs. See also DUCTILITY.

Fatima *or* **Fatimah** \ˈfa-tə-mə\ (c.605–633) Daughter of MUHAMMAD and the object of veneration in SHIITE Islam. In 622 she emigrated with her father from Mecca to Medina, where she married her cousin ALI. Their sons Hasan and al-HUSAYN IBN ALI are considered by Shiites Muhammad's rightful inheritors. Fatima cared for her father in his last illness (632). She clashed with his successor, ABU BAKR, over property and died a year later. Later tradition added to the majesty of her life, and the FATIMID DYNASTY derived its name from hers.

Fátima \\'fa-tə-mə\\ Village in central Portugal, site of a shrine dedicated to the Virgin MARY. In 1917 three peasant children reported visions of a woman who identified herself as the Lady of the Rosary. On October 13, a crowd of about 70,000 witnessed an amazing solar phenomenon following one such vision. The first national pilgrimage to the site occurred in 1927. Construction of a basilica started in 1928. Many miraculous cures have since been reported at Fátima.

Fatimid dynasty \\'fa-tə-məd\\ (909–1171) Muslim political dynasty of N. Africa and the Middle East. Its members traced their descent from Fatima, the daughter of Muhammad. They opposed the Sunni ABBASID caliphate, which they were determined to overthrow. From Yemen they expanded into N. Africa and Sicily, and in 909 they proclaimed the new dynasty. The first four Fatimid caliphs ruled from Tunisia, but the conquest of Egypt in 969 occasioned the building of a new capital, Cairo. At its height, the dynasty controlled Mecca and Medina, Syria, Palestine, and Africa's Red Sea coast. In 1057–59 the Fatimid caliph was briefly proclaimed in Baghdad, the Abbasid capital, but Fatimid fortunes declined thereafter. Foreign attacks and factionalism in the armed forces weakened the caliphate, and the rise of the ASSASSINS sealed its fate. See also SALADIN.

fatty acid Organic compound that is an important component of LIPIDS in plants, animals, and microorganisms. Fatty acids are CARBOXYLIC ACIDS with a long HYDROCARBON chain, usually straight, as the fourth substituent group on the carboxyl (–COOH) group (see FUNCTIONAL GROUP) that makes the molecule an acid. If the carbon-to-carbon bonds (see BONDING) in that chain are all single, the fatty acid is saturated; artificial SATURATION is called HYDROGENATION. A fatty acid with one double bond is monounsaturated; one with more is polyunsaturated. Most unsaturated fats are liquid at room temperature, so food manufacturers hydrogenate them to make them solid (see MARGARINE). A high level of saturated fatty acids in the diet raises blood CHOLESTEROL levels. Fatty acids in nature are always combined, usually with GLYCEROL as TRIGLYCERIDES in FATS. Most animals, including mammals, cannot synthesize some unsaturated "essential" fatty acids; humans need linoleic, linolenic, and arachidonic acids in their diet.

fatty tissue See ADIPOSE TISSUE

Faulhaber \\'faùl-ˌhä-bər\\, **Michael von** (1869–1952) German religious leader. Ordained in 1892, he rose to become Munich's archbishop (1917) and a cardinal (1921). In 1923 he contributed to the failure of Adolf HITLER's BEER HALL PUTSCH. His famous sermons later published as *Judaism, Christianity, and Germany* (1934) emphasized the Jewish background of Christianity and asserted that Christian values were fundamental to German culture. Despite attempts on his life, he vigorously criticized Nazism until the collapse of the Third Reich.

Faulkner \\'fòk-nər\\, **William** orig. William Cuthbert Falkner (1897–1962) U.S. writer. Born in New Albany, Miss., he dropped out of high school. He is best known for his cycle of works set in fictional Yoknapatawpha Co., which becomes an emblem of the American South and its tragic history. His first major novel, *The Sound and the Fury* (1929), was marked by radical technical experimentation, including stream of consciousness. Other works include *As I Lay Dying* (1930), *Light in August* (1932), *Absalom, Absalom!* (1936), *The Hamlet* (1940), and *Go Down, Moses* (1942), which contains the story "The Bear." He won the Nobel Prize in 1949. His *Collected Stories* (1950) won the National Book Award. He was among the most influential writers of the 20th cent.

fault In geology, a fracture in the earth's crust, where forces cause the rocks on the opposite sides of the fracture to be displaced relative to each other. Faults range in length from a few inches to hundreds of miles, and displacement may also range from less than an inch to hundreds of miles along the fracture surface (the fault plane). Almost all EARTH-QUAKES are caused by rapid movement along faults. Faults are common throughout the world. A well-known example is the San Andreas Fault near the W coast of the U.S.

faunal succession, law of Observation that taxonomic groups of animals follow each other in time in a predictable manner. Sequences of successive strata and their corresponding fauna have been matched to form a composite picture detailing the history of the earth. Faunal succession is the fundamental tool of STRATIGRAPHY and the basis for the geologic time scale. Floral (plant) succession is also an important tool.

Faunus \\'fò-nəs\\ Ancient Italian rural deity, the Roman counterpart of the Greek god PAN. He was depicted as half-man, half-goat, like a satyr. Originally a god who bestowed fertility on fields and flocks, he ended as a woodland deity.

Faure \\'fòr\\, **(François-) Félix** (1841–1899) President of the French THIRD REPUBLIC (1895–99). A successful industrialist, he served in several cabinet posts, then was elected president of France in an unexpected victory that was a rebuff to the political left. He opposed reopening the case of Alfred DREYFUS, which encouraged agitation from both left and right. He died suddenly, and his funeral was the scene of a confrontation between pro- and anti-Dreyfus groups.

Fauré \\fò-'rā\\, **Gabriel (Urbain)** (1845–1924) French composer. Born into the minor aristocracy, he enrolled at age 9 in a Paris music school, where he studied with Camille SAINT-SAËNS and remained 11 years. He held the prestigious organist positions in Paris, and in 1896 he also became professor of composition at the Paris Conservatoire, where he taught such students as Maurice RAVEL. He served as its director 1905–20. In 1909 he accepted the presidency of the Société Musicale Indépendante, a group of dissident young composers. His works include the opera *Pénélope* (1913), the orchestral suite

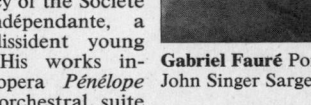

Gabriel Fauré Portrait by John Singer Sargent

Pelléas et Mélisande (1898), a famous *Requiem* (1900), and many beautiful songs.

Faust \\'faùst\\ Legendary German necromancer or astrologer who sold his soul to the devil for knowledge and power. There was a historical Faust (perhaps two; both died around 1540), who traveled widely performing magic, referred to the devil as his crony, and had a wide reputation for evil. The *Faustbuch* (1587), a collection of tales purportedly by Faust, told of such reputed wizards as MERLIN and ALBERTUS MAGNUS. Magic manuals bearing Faust's name did a brisk business; the classic *Magia naturalis et innaturalis* was known to J. W. von GOETHE, who, like Gotthold LESSING, saw Faust's pursuit of knowledge as noble; in Goethe's great *Faust* the hero is redeemed.

Fauvism \\'fō-ˌvi-zəm\\ Style of painting that flourished in France about 1898–1908, characterized by the use of intensely vivid color and turbulent emotionalism. The dominant figure of the group was Henri MATISSE; others were André DERAIN, Maurice de VLAMINCK, Georges BRAQUE, and Georges ROUAULT. The name derives from the judgment of a critic who visited their first exhibit in Paris (1905) and referred to them disparagingly as "les fauves" ("wild beasts"). Fauvism was a transitional phase for most of the artists, who by 1908, having renewed their interest in Paul CÉZANNE's vision of structure, abandoned Fauvism for CUBISM.

favela \\fə-'ve-lə\\ In Brazil, a slum or shantytown. A favela gets its start when squatters occupy vacant land at the edge of a city and construct shanties of salvaged or stolen materials. Communities form over time, often developing an array of social and religious organizations and forming associations to obtain such services as running water and electricity. Crowding, unsanitary conditions, poor nutrition, pollution, and disease are common in the poorer favelas.

Fawkes, Guy (1570–1606) English conspirator. A zealous convert to Roman Catholicism, Fawkes joined the Spanish army in the Netherlands in 1593 and became noted for his military skill. In 1604 he was enlisted by the Catholic leaders of a plot to blow up the Parliament building. When details of the GUNPOWDER PLOT were discovered, Fawkes was arrested, tortured to reveal his accomplices, tried, and executed. November 5 is celebrated as Guy Fawkes Day with fireworks and the burning of Fawkes's effigy.

fax *in full* facsimile. Device for the transmission and reproduction of documents by digitized signals sent over telephone lines. Fax machines scan printed text and graphics and convert the image into a digital code: 1 for dark areas, 0 for white areas. The code is transmitted through the telephone network to similar devices, where the documents are reproduced. Though the concepts for fax technology were developed in the 19th cent., widespread use did not occur until the 1970s, when MODEMS became common.

FBI See FEDERAL BUREAU OF INVESTIGATION

FCC See FEDERAL COMMUNICATIONS COMMISSION

FDA See FOOD AND DRUG ADMINISTRATION

FDIC See FEDERAL DEPOSIT INSURANCE CORP.

feather Component structure of the outer covering and flight surfaces of all modern birds. Unique to birds, feathers apparently evolved from the scales of birds' reptilian ancestors. Feathers are variously specialized for insulation, flight, formation of body contours, display, and sensory reception. Feathers are arranged in symmetrical tracts alternating with areas of bare skin, which may contain the small, soft feathers called down. A typical feather consists of a central shaft (rachis), with serial paired branches (barbs) forming a flattened, usually curved surface—the vane. The barbs possess further branches, the barbules, which attach to one another by hooks, stiffening the vane.

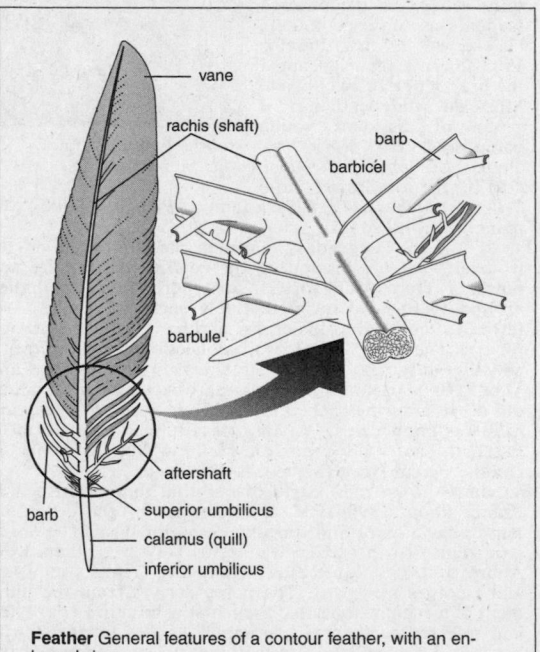

Feather General features of a contour feather, with an enlarged view.

February Revolution (1848) Rioting in France that led to the overthrow of the JULY MONARCHY and precipitated the REVOLUTIONS OF 1848. A flowering of socialist thought, urban workers' discontent, a major recession in 1846–47, and the increasing arbitrariness of the rule of King LOUIS-PHILIPPE led to an opposition campaign that brought crowds of students and workers into the streets. The king tried to appease the demonstrators, but when an army unit killed 40 of them he abdicated rather than face civil war.

feces \'fē-ˌsēz\ *or* **excrement** *or* **stools** Solid bodily waste discharged from the COLON through the anus during DEFECATION. Normal feces are 75% water. The rest is about 30% dead BACTERIA, 30% indigestible food matter, 10–20% CHOLESTEROL and other FATS, 10–20% inorganic substances, and 2–3% PROTEIN. The color and odor are produced by bacterial action. Many disorders produce constipation or DIARRHEA. Bleeding in the stomach or intestines may show up as dark red to black stools. High fat content usually indicates disease of the pancreas or small intestine. Many diseases are spread by contamination of food with feces of infected persons.

Federal Bureau of Investigation (FBI) Largest investigative agency of the U.S. government, founded in 1908. J. Edgar HOOVER was named its director in 1924 and served for 48 years. Since 1968 its director, who reports to the attorney general, has been appointed by the president for a 10-year term. Part of the U.S. Justice Department, the FBI has 6,000–7,000 special agents. Its responsibilities include investigating violations of federal criminal law, collecting evidence in civil cases to which the U.S. is a party, and providing internal security.

Federal Communications Commission (FCC) Independent U.S. agency. Established in 1934, it regulates interstate and foreign communications by radio, television, wire, satellite, and cable. Its standards and regulations apply only to the technical aspects, including frequency and equipment, of communication systems, not broadcast content (apart from certain rules covering obscenity and slander).

Federal Deposit Insurance Corp. (FDIC) Independent U.S. government corporation created in 1933 to insure bank deposits against loss in the event of a bank failure and to regulate certain banking practices. It insures bank deposits in eligible banks up to $100,000 for each deposit. All members of the FEDERAL RESERVE SYSTEM are required to insure their deposits with the FDIC, and almost all COMMERCIAL BANKS in the U.S. choose to do so.

federalism Political system that binds a group of states into a larger, noncentralized, superior state while allowing its constituent members to maintain their own political identities. Common to all successful federal systems are a written constitution or basic law stipulating the distribution of powers, diffusion of power among the constituent elements, and territorial divisions to ensure neutrality and equality in the representation of various groups and interests. Changes require the consent of those affected. Successful federal systems also have a sense of common nationality and direct lines of communication between the citizens and all the governments that serve them.

Federalist, The Eighty-five essays on the proposed U.S. CONSTITUTION and the nature of republican government, published in 1787–88 by Alexander HAMILTON, James MADISON, and John JAY in an effort to persuade New York State voters to support ratification. Most first appeared serially in newspapers; all were signed "Publius." They presented a masterly exposition of the federal system and the means of attaining the ideals of justice, general welfare, and rights of individuals.

Federalist Party Early U.S. political party that advocated a strong central government. "Federalist" was first used in 1787 to describe supporters of the U.S. CONSTITUTION, with its emphasis on a federal union. By the 1790s other policies defined the party, including Alexander HAMILTON's fiscal program, creation of a central bank, a tariff system, favorable treatment for U.S. shipping, John JAY's treaty with Britain, and neutrality in foreign affairs. It elected John ADAMS as president in 1796 but was unable to organize effectively after 1801. It lost favor for its opposition to the EMBARGO ACT and the WAR OF 1812; an internal split by the New England faction (see HARTFORD CONVENTION) further weakened the party. By the 1820s most of its original principles had been adopted by the opposition Democratic Party, and the Federalist Party disappeared.

Federal Reserve System U.S. CENTRAL BANK system consisting of 12 Federal Reserve districts with a Reserve bank in each district. The system is supervised by a board of governors in Washington, D.C., and various advisory councils. As a result of the Federal Reserve Act of 1913, all NATIONAL BANKS are required to join the system; state banks may join if they meet membership qualifications. The Federal Reserve is responsible for MONETARY POLICY. The original act set requirements for the U.S. FRACTIONAL RESERVE SYSTEM; it allowed each district bank to determine its DISCOUNT RATE. The modern Federal Reserve resulted from the Federal Reserve Act of 1935, which allowed the board to determine reserve requirements within defined limits. It became responsible for approving the discount rates of the district banks. Most importantly, the act created the Federal Reserve Open Market Committee to conduct operations in financial markets that increase or decrease the amount of reserves in the system. If the Federal Reserve wants to ease monetary policy, it will use open-market operations and increase the amount of reserves through the purchase of financial assets. To tighten monetary policy, it may sell financial assets.

Federal style Neoclassical style of American architecture and interior design that flourished 1785–1820 (later in governmental buildings) and was influenced by the GEORGIAN STYLE and the work of James and Robert ADAM. Inspired by the Roman republic, which the new nation believed it resembled, it was associated with Thomas JEFFERSON and Benjamin LATROBE and featured shallow arches, slender proportions, delicate decoration, entrances framed by columns and pediments, and fanlights over doors.

Federal Trade Commission (FTC) Independent U.S. agency charged with preventing unfair or deceptive trade practices. It regulates advertising, marketing, and consumer credit practices, and also prevents antitrust agreements. Though it has no authority to punish violators, it can monitor compliance with trade laws, conduct legal investigations, file civil suits in U.S. district courts, and ensure that court orders are followed.

Feiffer, Jules (b.1929) U.S. cartoonist and dramatist. He became famous for "Feiffer," a satirical strip whose verbal elements are usually monologues in which the speaker exposes his or her own insecurities. His drawings, syndicated from 1959, are collected in books beginning with *Sick, Sick, Sick* (1958). In 1986 he received a Pulitzer Prize. His other works include plays, novels, screenplays, and children's books.

Feininger \ˈfī-niŋ-ər\, **Andreas (Bernhard Lyonel)** (1906–1999) French-U.S. photographer and writer. Son of Lyonel FEININGER, he graduated from the BAUHAUS in 1925. He moved to Sweden in 1933 and specialized in architectural and industrial photography. In 1939 he settled in New York, where he worked for *Life* magazine 1943–62. Among his many books are *The Complete Photographer* (1966) and the collection *The World Through My Eyes* (1964).

Feininger \ˈfī-niŋ-ər\, **Lyonel (Charles Adrian)** (1871–1956) U.S.-German painter. Born in New York City, he went to Germany in 1887 to study. Around 1910, under the influence of Cubism, he developed a unique style, using prismatic interpenetrating planes of color to depict architectural and marine subjects. An influential teacher at the BAUHAUS (1919–33), he is noted for introducing compositional discipline and lyrical color to German Expressionism. After the Nazis came to power, he returned to the U.S.

feldspar Any of a group of aluminosilicate (containing aluminum and silicon) minerals that also contains calcium, sodium, or potassium. Feldspars are the most common minerals in the earth's CRUST and are the major component in nearly all IGNEOUS ROCKS. They also are common in metamorphic and some sedimentary rocks. Their complex chemical and structural properties make them useful for interpreting the origins of rocks. See also PLAGIOCLASE.

Fellini, Federico (1920–1993) Italian film director. After collaborating with Roberto ROSSELLINI on the screenplays for *Open City* (1945) and *Paisan* (1946), he undertook his first solo venture in 1952. He won international acclaim with *La strada* (1954, Academy Award), *The Nights of Cabiria* (1957, Academy Award), and *La dolce vita* (1960). He continued his distinctive autobiographical style of filmmaking—a kind of poetic surrealism that displayed a sympathetic fascination with the bizarre—in *8 1/2* (1963, Academy Award),

Federico Fellini, 1965

but turned to gaudy spectacle in *Juliet of the Spirits* (1965) and *Fellini Satyricon* (1969). The best of his later films was *Amarcord* (1973, Academy Award). He received a special Academy Award for lifetime achievement in 1992.

felony and misdemeanor In Anglo-American law, two categories of criminal offense. A crime is classed as one or the other according to its seriousness. In U.S. law, a felony is typically defined as a crime punishable by a term of imprisonment of not less than one year. Misdemeanors are often defined as offenses punishable only by fines or by short terms of imprisonment in local jails.

female circumcision See CLITORIDECTOMY

feminism Social movement that seeks equal rights for women. Widespread concern for women's rights dates from the ENLIGHTENMENT; its first important expression was Mary WOLLSTONECRAFT's *A Vindication of the Rights of Woman* (1792). The 1848 SENECA FALLS CONVENTION called for full legal equality with men, including in education and compensation, and the WOMEN'S SUFFRAGE MOVEMENT began to gather momentum. From America the movement spread to Europe. U.S. women gained the right to vote by constitutional amendment in 1920, but their participation in the workplace remained limited. Milestones in the rise of modern feminism included Simone de BEAUVOIR's *The Second Sex* (1949) and Betty FRIEDAN's *The Feminine Mystique* (1963) and the founding in 1966 of the NATIONAL ORGANIZATION FOR WOMEN. See also EQUAL RIGHTS AMENDMENT, WOMEN'S LIBERATION MOVEMENT.

fencing Sport involving attack and defense with a light sword, specifically a foil, épée, or saber that has a covered point. In the 14th cent. swordplay became important both in war and in the European gentleman's daily life, and by the 15th cent. guilds of fencing masters had formed. Strokes that were originally jealously guarded secrets eventually became orthodox fencing moves. By the later 17th cent., various rules and conventions had been imposed. Hits are made with the point only, except in saber matches, and, in matches using épées, are restricted to certain areas of the body. Defense is effected by the blade. Each valid hit scores one or more points, depending on which part of the body is struck. Men's fencing was included in the first modern Olympic Games in 1896, women's in the 1924 games.

Fénelon \fān-ˈlōⁿ\, **François (de Salignac de La Mothe-)** (1651–1715) French archbishop, theologian, and man of letters. His *The Education of Young Gentlewomen* (1687) supported liberal education and argued against coercing Protestants to convert. As tutor to a grandson of Louis XIV, he composed his famous novel *Les aventures de Télémaque* (1699); he was banished from court for its political content. He was similarly condemned by the church for his leanings toward Quietism, which emphasized spiritual passivity. His liberal views on politics and education exerted a lasting influence on French culture.

feng shui \ˈfəŋ-ˈshwā\ Ancient Chinese method of aligning the human and social world with the forces of the cosmos, including QI and YIN-YANG. Diviners determine the exact cosmic forces affecting a site, appropriate sites being chosen particularly in relation to bodies of water and mountains. Feng shui, especially as it affects interior design, has recently become popular in the West.

Fenian cycle \ˈfē-nē-ən\ *or* **Fionn cycle** \ˈfin\ *or* **Ossianic cycle** Irish tales and ballads centering on the deeds of the legendary Finn MacCumhaill (MacCool) and his war band, the Fianna Éireann. An elite volunteer corps of warriors and huntsmen skilled in poetry, the Fianna flourished in the 3rd cent. Fenian lore attained its greatest popularity around 1200, when its outstanding story, *The Colloquy of the Old Men,* was written down. The cycle, a vital part of Irish folklore, contains many beloved folktales.

FG

Fenian movement Irish nationalist society active chiefly in Ireland and the U.S. in the 1860s. The name derived from the Fianna Éireann, legendary warriors led by FINN MAC-CUMHAILL. Plans for a rising against British rule in Ireland miscarried, but in the U.S. Fenians staged abortive raids into British Canada and caused friction between the U.S. and British governments. The Irish wing, sometimes called the Irish Republican Brotherhood, continued after Fenianism died out in the 1870s (see SINN FÉIN).

fennel Perennial or biennial aromatic herb (*Foeniculum vulgare*) of the PARSLEY family, native to S Europe and Asia Minor and widely cultivated. The blanched shoots are eaten as a vegetable. The oblong oval seeds smell and taste like ANISE. The seeds and extracted oil are used for scenting soaps and perfumes and for flavoring candies, liqueurs, medicines, and foods.

Ferber, Edna (1885–1968) U.S. writer. Born in Kalamazoo, Mich., she collected her early stories in *Emma McChesney & Co.* (1915) and other volumes. She won acclaim for such best-selling novels as *So Big* (1924, Pulitzer Prize), *Show Boat* (1926)—which, with music by Jerome KERN, became a seminal work of the American musical theater—and *Giant* (1952; film, 1956), which offer a compassionate, lively portrait of middle-class Midwestern America.

fer-de-lance \'fer-dᵊl-'ants\ (French: "spearhead") Extremely venomous pit viper (genus *Bothrops*), found in diverse tropical American habitats. It has a broad, triangular head and is marked by a series of black-edged diamonds. It is about 4–7 ft (1.2–2 m) long. Its bite can be fatal to humans. The name is sometimes applied to all members of the genus *Bothrops* and to an Asian genus, *Trimeresurus*.

Ferdinand (1793–1875) Emperor of Austria (1835–48). He was the eldest son of Emperor FRANCIS II, who insisted that Ferdinand be the heir, despite Ferdinand's feeblemindedness. He was crowned king of Hungary in 1830 and became emperor of Austria in 1835. Government affairs were controlled by a body of counselors, led by the chancellor, Klemens von METTERNICH. In the REVOLUTIONS OF 1848 hostility was directed against his counselors, and Ferdinand abdicated in favor of his nephew, FRANCIS JOSEPH.

Ferdinand I (1503–1564) Holy Roman emperor (1558–64). The brother of Emperor CHARLES V, he was Charles's deputy in the Habsburg German lands (1522–58). In 1526 he took possession of Bohemia without difficulty, but he faced rival claimants in Hungary and fought periodically against the Ottoman empire. He helped Charles defeat the Protestant Schmalkaldic League, and later signed the Peace of AUGSBURG (1555), ending the era of religious strife in Germany. Elected emperor after Charles's abdication, Ferdinand centralized the imperial administration.

Ferdinand I (1751–1825) King of the Two SICILIES (1816–25). He became king of Naples in 1759, as Ferdinand IV, when his father ascended the Spanish throne as CHARLES III. A weak ruler, he was greatly influenced by his wife, Maria Carolina of Austria (1752–1814). When the French invaded Naples, he fled to Sicily (1798–99, 1806–16). He returned to Naples in 1816 as king of the united kingdom of the Two Sicilies. His despotic rule led to an uprising in 1820 and he was forced to grant a constitution. With Austria's aid, he overthrew the constitutional government in 1821.

Ferdinand II (Aragon) See FERDINAND V (CASTILE)

Ferdinand II (1578–1637) Holy Roman emperor (1619–37), king of Bohemia (1617–19, 1620–27), and king of Hungary (1618–25). A year after he was recognized by the Bohemian Diet as king, they deposed him and elected Frederick V, an event that sparked the THIRTY YEARS' WAR. After annihilating the rebel army in 1620, he forcibly Catholicized Bohemia and suppressed Protestantism throughout his lands. He maintained much of his power through the victories of Albrecht von WALLENSTEIN, but later concluded a compromise peace with the Protestant princes (1635). He was a leading champion of the COUNTER-REFORMATION.

Ferdinand III (1608–1657) Holy Roman emperor (1637–57), king of Hungary (1625–57) and king of Bohemia (1627–57). Denied command of the Habsburg armies in the THIRTY YEARS' WAR, Ferdinand conspired to overthrow Gen. Albrecht von WALLENSTEIN, whom he replaced as commander (1634–35). As emperor, he refused to allow religious freedom in his own domains, but he compromised with Europe's Protestant powers and agreed to the Peace of WESTPHALIA, ending 30 years of religious strife.

Ferdinand V *known as* **Ferdinand the Catholic** (1452–1516) King of Castile from 1474 (joint sovereign with ISABELLA I until 1504), king of Aragon (as Ferdinand II) from 1479, king of Sicily (as Ferdinand II, 1468–1516), and king of Naples (as Ferdinand III, 1503–16). The son of John II of Aragon (1398–1479), Ferdinand married Isabella of Castile in 1469, and fought to impose his authority over the nobles in the two kingdoms. They banned all religions other than Roman Catholicism, leading to the Spanish INQUISITION (1478) and the expulsion of the Jews (1492). Conquest of Granada in 1492 made it possible to support Christopher COLUMBUS's voyages. Ferdinand furthered his expansionary policies in the Mediterranean and in Africa. After the conquest of Naples in 1503, during the ITALIAN WARS, Spain rivaled France as the most powerful state in Europe. By uniting the Spanish kingdoms, Ferdinand began Spain's entry into the modern period of imperial expansion.

Ferdinand VI *Spanish* Fernando (1713–1759) King of Spain (1746–59). Son of PHILIP V and his first wife, he was kept out of politics by his father's second wife, ELIZABETH FARNESE. During his own reign, he tried to avoid conflicts while relying on his father's minister to bring about reforms. Ferdinand and his beloved wife, Maria Bárbara, were patrons of the arts and learning. He was succeeded by CHARLES III.

Ferdinand VII *Spanish* Fernando (1784–1833) King of Spain (1808, 1813–33). He became king briefly in 1808 after the French invasion of Spain, but NAPOLEON soon replaced him with Joseph BONAPARTE, and held Ferdinand in France. The Spanish populace rose against the French invaders in the name of Ferdinand; in 1812 independent Spaniards adopted a liberal constitution, which Ferdinand overthrew on his return as king in 1813. His reign saw the loss of most of Spain's possessions in the Americas. He abolished the Salic Law, excluding females from succession, to allow his daughter, the future ISABELLA II, to succeed him, instead of his brother, Don Carlos, which caused the rise of CARLISM.

Ferdinand the Catholic See FERDINAND V (CASTILE)

Ferdowsi \fər-'daù-sē\ *or* **Firdusi** *or* **Firdousi** \fər-'dü-sē\ *orig.* Abu ol-Qasem Mansur (935?–1020/26?) Persian poet. He gave the final and enduring form to the Persian national epic, the *Shah-nameh*, or *Book of Kings* (completed c.1010). Modern Iranians regard the poem's nearly 60,000 couplets as a sonorous, majestic evocation of a glorious past. He reportedly worked on it for 35 years to earn a dowry for his only daughter.

Ferenczi \'fer-ənt-sē\, **Sándor** (1873–1933) Hungarian psychoanalyst. He met Sigmund FREUD in 1908 and became a member of Freud's inner circle, the Vienna Psychoanalytic Society. He founded the Hungarian Psychoanalytic Society in 1913 and began teaching psychoanalysis at the Univ. of Budapest in 1919. He diverged from classic psychoanalytic practice in arguing that recovery of traumatic memories was not essential to modify neurotic behavior, and urging that therapists create a loving, permissive atmosphere. His works include *The Development of Psychoanalysis* (with Otto Rank; 1924).

Fergana Valley *or* **Fergana Basin** \ˌfir-gə-'nä\ Enormous valley between the TIAN SHAN and Gissar and Alay mountain systems, mainly in E Uzbekistan and partly in Tajikistan and Kyrgyzstan. It has an area of 8,500 sq mi (22,000 sq km). Densely populated, it is a major producer of cotton, fruit, and raw silk. Its mineral deposits include coal, oil, and mercury. It was conquered by the Arabs (8th cent. A.D.), GENGHIS KHAN (13th cent.), and TIMUR (14th cent.). The khans of Kokand (see QUQON) ruled it from the late 18th cent. until it was taken by Russia in 1876.

Ferlinghetti \ˌfer-liŋ-'ge-tē\, **Lawrence (Monsanto)** *orig.* Lawrence Ferling (b.1919) U.S. poet. Born in Yonkers, N.Y., he was a founder of the BEAT MOVEMENT in San Francisco in the mid-1950s. His City Lights bookstore was an early gathering place of the Beats; its publishing arm was the first to print the Beats' poetry. His own poetry—lucid, witty, and composed to be read aloud—became popular in coffeehouses and on college campuses, especially the widely popular *A Coney Island of the Mind* (1958).

Fermat \fer-'mä\, **Pierre de** (1601–1665) French mathematician. Of Basque origin, Fermat was a jurist by profession. A contemporary of René DESCARTES, he discovered independently the basic principles of ANALYTIC GEOMETRY, but because his work was published after his death, the field became known as Cartesian geometry. He found equations for TANGENT LINES to curves through processes equivalent to DIFFERENTIATION and INTEGRATION and was coauthor (with Blaise PASCAL) of PROBABILITY THEORY. His work in NUMBER THEORY, especially divisibility, led to some of its most important theorems. He seldom demonstrated his results, which led to a centuries-long quest to prove a famous conjecture Fermat claimed was easily shown (see FERMAT'S LAST THEOREM).

Fermat's last theorem Statement that there are no natural numbers x, y, and z such that $x^n + y^n = z^n$, in which n is a natural number greater than 2. About this, Pierre de FERMAT in 1637 jotted the note "I have discovered a truly remarkable proof but this margin is too small to contain it." Mathematicians were long unable either to prove or disprove the general statement, though it has been proved for many specific values of n. In 1994 Andrew Wiles (b.1953) and Richard Taylor (b.1962) announced a proof.

fermentation Process that allows RESPIRATION to occur in the absence of oxygen. GLYCOLYSIS, the breakdown of glucose, is a form of fermentation. Alcoholic fermentation occurs when yeast cells convert carbohydrate sources to ETHANOL and carbon dioxide. Fermentation reactions are common in muscle cells, yeasts, some bacteria, and plants. See also BEER, WINE.

Fermi, Enrico (1901–1954) Italian-U.S. physicist. He began the work, later fully developed by Paul DIRAC, that led to Fermi-Dirac statistics. He developed a theory of BETA DECAY that applies to other reactions through the WEAK FORCE, which was not improved until 1957, when the weak force was found not to conserve PARITY. He discovered neutron-induced RADIOACTIVITY, for which he was awarded a 1938 Nobel Prize. Moving to the U.S., he became one of the chief architects of practical nuclear physics. He was a member of the MANHATTAN PROJECT, and in 1942 directed the first controlled nuclear CHAIN REACTION. Element number 100, fermium, was named in his honor.

fermion Any of a group of SUBATOMIC PARTICLES having odd half-integral SPIN (1/2, 3/2). Fermions are named for the Fermi-Dirac statistics that describe their behavior. They include particles in the class of LEPTONS, BARYONS, and nuclei of odd mass number (e.g., tritium, helium-3, uranium-233). They obey the PAULI EXCLUSION PRINCIPLE. Fermions are produced and undergo annihilation in particle-antiparticle pairs. See also BOSON.

fern Any of about 10,000–12,000 species (division Filicophyta) of nonflowering VASCULAR PLANTS that have true roots, stems, and complex leaves and reproduce by SPORES. Ferns appeared over 350 million years ago. They come in a wide variety of sizes and shapes. Many are small, fragile plants; others are treelike. The life cycle is characterized by an ALTERNATION OF GENERATIONS between the mature, fronded form (the SPOROPHYTE) familiar in greenhouses and gardens, and the form that strongly resembles a MOSS or liverwort (the GAMETOPHYTE). Ferns are popular houseplants.

Fernando Póo See BIOKO

Ferrara \fer-'rä-rä\ City (pop., 1998 est.: 133,000), N Italy. Situated near the PO RIVER, it was captured from RAVENNA by the Lombards in A.D. 753. It became a cultural center and the seat of a principality, but declined after its incorporation into the PAPAL STATES in 1598. The site of an Austrian garrison from 1832, it became part of the kingdom of Italy in 1861. Sites of interest include a 12th-cent. cathedral, a 14th-cent. moated castle, and the Univ. of Ferrara (founded 1391).

Ferraro, Geraldine (Anne) (b.1935) U.S. politician. Born in Newburgh, N.Y., she was assistant U.S. district attorney (1974–78), before serving in the U.S. House of Representatives (1978–84). In 1984 she became the first woman nominated for vice president by a major political party when she

was chosen for the Democratic ticket by Walter MONDALE. Investigations of her husband's finances undermined the campaign. In 1992 and 1998 she ran unsuccessfully for the U.S. Senate.

ferret Either of two species in the CARNIVORE family Mustelidae. The common ferret (*Mustela putorius furo*) is a domesticated form of the European polecat. Its average length is 20 in. (50 cm), including the 5-in. (13-cm) tail, and it weighs about 2 lbs (1 kg). It was originally domesticated for hunting mice, rats, and rabbits; today ferrets are commonly kept as pets. The black-footed ferret (*M. nigripes*), of

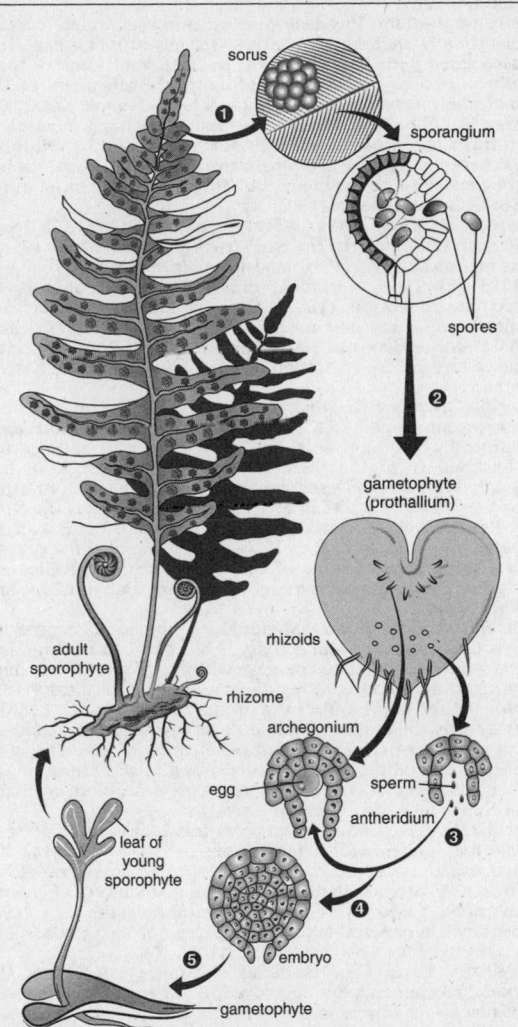

Fern The life cycle of the fern. (1) Clusters (sori) of sporangia (spore cases) grow on the undersurface of mature fern leaves. (2) Released from its spore case, the haploid spore is carried to the ground, where it germinates into a tiny, usually heart-shaped, gametophyte (gamete-producing structure), anchored to the ground by rhizoids (rootlike projections). (3) Under moist conditions, mature sperm are released from the antheridia and swim to the egg-producing archegonia that have formed on the gametophyte's lower surface. (4) When fertilization occurs, a zygote forms and develops into an embryo within the archegonium. (5) The embryo eventually grows larger than the gametophyte and becomes a sporophyte.

FG

the N. American plains, is an endangered species, owing to the loss of its main source of food, the PRAIRIE DOG.

ferrimagnetism Type of permanent MAGNETISM that occurs in solids, in which the MAGNETIC FIELDS associated with individual atoms spontaneously align themselves, some parallel (as in FERROMAGNETISM), and others antiparallel. The materials are less magnetic than ferromagnets, as the antiparallel atoms dilute the magnetic effect. Ferrimagnetism occurs mainly in magnetic oxides known as ferrites. Above a temperature called the Curie point, the alignment is disrupted and ferrimagnetism is destroyed, but it is restored upon cooling.

ferromagnetism Physical phenomenon in which certain electrically uncharged materials strongly attract others. It is associated with IRON, COBALT, NICKEL, and some of their alloys or compounds. It is caused by the alignment of the material's ATOMS, each of which acts as a simple ELECTROMAGNET. The tiny magnets spontaneously align themselves in the same direction, so their MAGNETIC FIELDS reinforce each other. Above a temperature called the Curie point, they cease to be magnetic, but they resume upon cooling. See also FERRIMAGNETISM.

Ferry \fe-'rē\, **Jules (-François-Camille)** (1832–1893) French politician. In the early THIRD REPUBLIC, he served as mayor of Paris (1870) and premier of France (1880–81, 1883–85). His government established free, compulsory, secular education (1882) through enacting anticlerical measures. Ferry extended France's colonial territories in Asia and Africa, but public anger over colonial expenditures forced his resignation. He was assassinated by a madman.

Fertile Crescent Region, MIDDLE EAST. The term describes a crescent-shaped area of fertile land, probably more agriculturally productive in antiquity than it is today, that stretched from the SE coast of the Mediterranean Sea around the Syrian Desert north of the ARABIAN PENINSULA to the PERSIAN GULF; in general, it often includes the NILE valley as well. Sedentary agricultural settlements can be dated to about 8000 B.C. It was the scene of the struggles and migrations of some of the earliest known peoples, including Sumerians, Assyrians, Akkadians, Babylonians, and Phoenicians.

fertility Ability of an individual or couple to reproduce through normal sexual activity. About 80% of healthy, fertile women are able to conceive within one year if they have SEXUAL INTERCOURSE regularly without CONTRACEPTION. Normal fertility requires the production of enough healthy SPERM by the male and viable EGGS by the female, successful passage of the sperm and penetration of a healthy egg, and implantation of the fertilized egg in the lining of the UTERUS (see REPRODUCTIVE SYSTEM). A problem with any of these steps can cause INFERTILITY.

fertilization Reproductive process in which a male sex cell (SPERM) unites with a female sex cell (EGG). During the process, the chromosomes of the egg and sperm merge to form a zygote, which divides to form an EMBRYO. Once one sperm has fused with the egg cell membrane, the outer layer becomes impenetrable to other sperm. See also CROSS-FERTILIZATION, IN VITRO FERTILIZATION.

fertilizer Natural or artificial substance containing the chemical elements that improve growth and productiveness of plants. Fertilizers enhance the natural fertility of the soil or replace the chemical elements taken from the soil by previous crops. The use of MANURE and COMPOSTS as fertilizers is probably almost as old as agriculture. Modern chemical fertilizers include one or more of the three elements most important in plant nutrition: NITROGEN, PHOSPHORUS, and POTASSIUM.

Fès \'fes\ *or* **Fez** \'fez\ *Arabic* **Fas** \'fas\ City (pop., 1994: 510,000), N Morocco. The oldest of Morocco's four imperial cities, it was founded on opposite banks of the Wadi Fès by IDRIS I about 789 and Idris II about 809. The two parts were united by the ALMORAVIDS in the 11th cent. Fès reached its zenith as a center of learning and commerce in the mid-14th cent. and has kept its religious primacy. The site of the oldest mosque in N Africa, it is also the seat of an Islamic university founded in 859. Until the late 19th cent. it was the only place where the fez hat was made.

fetal alcohol syndrome (FAS) Various CONGENITAL DISORDERS in a newborn caused by heavy drinking of alcohol by the mother around conception or during pregnancy. The main symptoms are retarded growth, central-NERVOUS-SYSTEM abnormalities, and certain face and head abnormalities. The child may be mentally retarded. Behavioral problems (e.g., poor concentration, impulsiveness) are sometimes the only obvious symptoms. Even moderate alcohol consumption during pregnancy may cause mild symptoms.

fetish Object believed to have magical power to protect or aid its owner, and by extension, an object regarded with superstitious or extravagant trust or reverence. In the 18th cent. it was applied to W. African amulets; it has also been used for various items in American Indian religion. In psychology, a fetish is an object that substitutes for a person as the focus of sexual desire.

fetus \'fēt-əs\ Unborn young of any vertebrate, particularly mammals, after it has acquired its basic form. In humans, this stage begins about eight weeks after conception (see EMBRYO), and is marked by increased growth and full de-

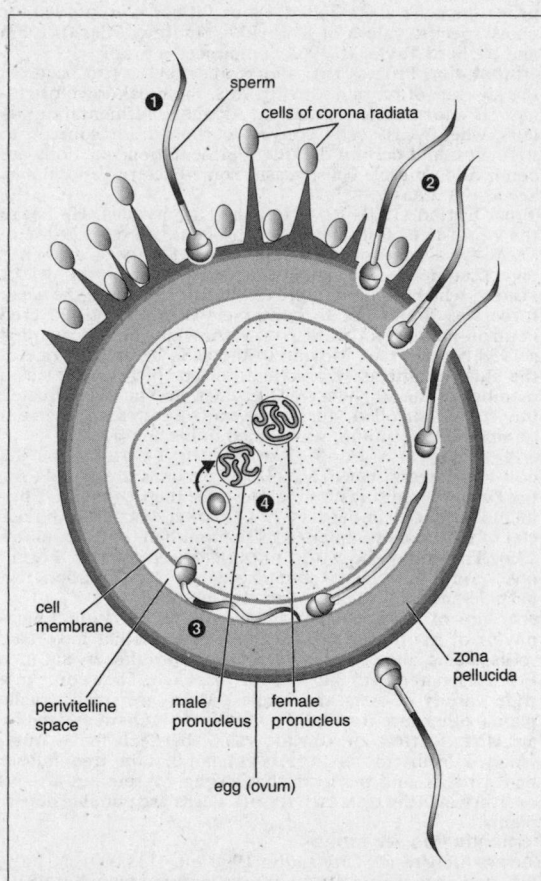

Fertilization Fertilization of a human egg. (1) The sperm release enzymes that help disperse the corona radiata and bind to the zona pellucida. (2) The outer sperm head layer is sloughed off, exposing enzymes that digest a path through the zona pellucida. (3) The sperm fuses with the egg cell membrane, causing the zona pellucida to become impenetrable to other sperm. (4) The tail separates from the sperm head, and the male pronucleus enlarges and travels to the female pronucleus in the center of the cell. Chromosomes merge to form a fertilized egg.

velopment of the organ systems, climaxing in birth (see PREGNANCY, PARTURITION). By the end of the third month, the arms and legs begin to move. After four months the fetus is about 5.3 in. (135 mm) long and weighs about 6 oz (170 g). During the fifth month, downy hairs (lanugo) cover the body and the skin becomes less transparent. Fat is deposited under the skin during the eighth month, when the fetus typically weighs about 5 lbs (2.2 kg). A full-term fetus is about 266 days old.

feudalism Social system of rights and duties based on land tenure and personal relationships that prevailed in Europe in the 9th–14th cent. It originated with the early Frankish kingdom (8th cent.), and spread into N Italy, Spain, Germany, and the Slavic lands. It reached Britain in 1066, and the CRUSADES took it to the Near East. Under the feudal system, kings granted FIEFS to their vassals—lords who, in return for protection, pledged their loyalty and armed forces to the king's use. These vassals in turn granted fiefs to their own vassals, and so on. The ranks of European nobility generally corresponded to the level of vassalage, the number of armed KNIGHTS they commanded, and the amount of land they owned. Feudalism went hand in hand with MANORIALISM. Being based on personal loyalty, feudalism tended to fragment public authority. With the growing power of the European monarchies and increasing national integration, feudalism was greatly weakened by the end of the 14th cent., though it remained important in Germany and especially Russia into the 19th cent. Feudalism was the predominant social system in Japan in the 12th–19th cent. (see DAIMYO, HAN, SHOGUN).

Feuillants \fœ-'yäⁿ\, **Club of the** Political club in the FRENCH REVOLUTION, which met in the former monastery of the Feuillants. It was founded in 1791 by deputies who left the JACOBIN CLUB in opposition to a petition to replace the king. The conservative Feuillants feared that the Revolution would lead to destruction of the monarchy and private property. The club represented a substantial group in the Legislative Assembly, but it disappeared in 1792 with the overthrow of the monarchy.

fever or **pyrexia** \pī-'rek-sē-ə\ Abnormally high body temperature. It most often occurs with INFECTION. Normal core body temperature, measured orally, does not exceed 99°F (37.2°C). Up to 105°F (40.6°C), fever is best treated with ASPIRIN, ACETAMINOPHEN, or other antipyretic drugs. At 108°F (42.2°C) or more, it can lead to convulsions and death. In treatment, it is important to know the underlying cause. Fever appears to be a defense against infectious disease, stimulating LEUKOCYTES and increasing ANTIBODY production and perhaps killing or inhibiting BACTERIA and VIRUSES.

Feydeau \fā-'dō\, **Georges (-Léon-Jules-Marie)** (1862–1921) French playwright. An actor and director, he wrote 39 plays, taking the farce to new heights on the French stage. His plots often depended on farfetched cases of mistaken identity, and he used complicated mechanical props and elaborate stage settings. His plays, including *The Girl from Maxim's* (1899) and *A Flea in Her Ear* (1907), have remained in the repertoire of the COMÉDIE-FRANÇAISE.

Feynman \'fīn-mən\, **Richard P(hillips)** (1918–1988) U.S. physicist. Born in New York City, during World War II he worked on the MANHATTAN PROJECT. The Feynman diagram, for representing the interactions of elementary particles, was one of the many problem-solving tools he invented. With Julian Schwinger (b.1918) and Shinichiro Tomonaga (1906–1979), he shared a 1965 Nobel Prize for his brilliant work on QUANTUM ELECTRODYNAMICS. He was principally responsible for identifying the cause of the 1986 *CHALLENGER* disaster. Famed for his wit, he also wrote best-selling books on science. His work, which tied together all the varied phenomena at work in light, radio, electricity, and magnetism, altered the way scientists understand the nature of waves and particles.

Fez See FÈS

Fianna Fáil \'fē-ə-nə-'fȯil\ (Irish: "Warriors of Ireland") Political party in Ireland; also called, loosely, the Republican Party. It was founded in 1926 by those opposed to the treaty with Britain that in 1921 brought about the Irish Free State. Organized and led by Eamon DE VALERA, it remained the principal governing party 1932–73, but from 1961 it did so with the aid of other parties. It returned to power in later coalition governments. Its main opposition has been from FINE GAEL.

Fiat SpA International holding company and major Italian manufacturer of automobiles, trucks, and industrial vehicles. It is the world's sixth-largest automaker. In 1899 Giovanni Agnelli (1866–1945) founded the firm that was incorporated as Fiat in 1906; he led it until his death. His grandson Giovanni Agnelli (1921–2003) became chairman in 1966. In 1986 Fiat acquired Alfa Romeo SpA. Among its automotive names are Ferrari and Lancia.

Fibber McGee and Molly See Jim and Marian JORDAN

fiber, dietary Food material not digestible by the human small intestine and only partially digestible by the large intestine. Fiber is beneficial in the diet because it relieves and prevents constipation, may reduce the risk of colon cancer, and reduces plasma CHOLESTEROL levels and therefore the risk of heart disease. The typical American diet is deficient in fiber; doctors urge increased consumption. Whole grains, vegetables, nuts, and fruits are all good sources.

fiberglass or **glass fiber** Fibrous form of GLASS, developed in the 1930s. Liquid glass issues in fine streams through hundreds of fine nozzles, and the solidifying streams are gathered into a single strand. Strands can be twisted into yarns, woven into fabrics, or chopped into short pieces. Glass filaments and yarns add strength and electrical resistivity to molded plastic products. Glass fabrics are used as electrical insulators and as reinforcing belts in tires. Discontinuous fibers are formed into wools, mats, or boards, commonly used in buildings, appliances, and plumbing.

fiber optics Thin transparent fibers of glass or plastic that transmit data as light through their length by internal reflections. Fiber-optic technology is used in long-distance TELEPHONE lines and to link computers in LOCAL AREA NETWORKS, with digitized light pulses replacing the electric current used for the signal in copper wires. TELECOMMUNICATION using fiber optics is usually conducted with infrared light. Fiber optics uses visible light to transmit images directly, in various technical devices such as those developed for ENDOSCOPY.

Fibonacci sequence \ˌfi-bə-'nä-chē\ In mathematics, a sequence of numbers with surprisingly useful applications in botany and other natural sciences. Beginning with two 1's, each new term is generated as the sum of the previous two: 1, 1, 2, 3, 5, 8, 13, ... Leonardo of Pisa (c.1170–after 1240), also known as Fibonacci, discovered the sequence. The number of petals in most types of flowers, and numbers involved in branching and seed-formation patterns, come from the Fibonacci sequence. The ratio of any two successive terms approaches the value of the GOLDEN RATIO as the terms become large.

fibrillation See ATRIAL FIBRILLATION

fibrocystic disease \ˌfī-brə-'sis-tik\ Either of two unrelated diseases, one affecting the breast and the other affecting the pancreas (see CYSTIC FIBROSIS). In fibrocystic disease of the breast, noncancerous CYSTS often swell and become tender before the menstrual period. Women with the disease are more likely to develop BREAST CANCER. Diagnosis requires differentiating between the several types of fibrocystic disease and cancer.

fibromyalgia \ˌfī-brō-ˌmī-'al-jə\ Rheumatic disorder affecting soft tissues. Characterized by pain, tenderness, and stiffness of muscles, ligaments, and tendons, it is often accompanied by varying degrees of fatigue. Digestive symptoms and headaches are also common, as is depression or anxiety. No cause has been found, although stress and poor sleep can aggravate the disorder, which may affect up to 5% of the population, principally women. The syndrome was not formally recognized until the 1980s.

Fichte \'fik-tə\, **Johann Gottlieb** (1762–1814) German philosopher and patriot. Fichte's *Science of Knowledge* (1794), incited by Immanuel KANT's *Critique of Practical Reason* (1788), was his most original and characteristic work. To demonstrate that PRACTICAL REASON is really the root of reason in its entirety, the absolute ground of all knowledge as well as of humanity altogether, he based his system on a supreme sovereign principle, the ego. He attempted to rally

FG

German nationalists against Napoleon in his famous patriotic *Addresses to the German Nation* (1807–8). He is regarded as one of the great transcendental idealists.

Ficino \fē-ē-'chē-nō\, **Marsilio** (1433–1499) Italian philosopher, theologian, and linguist. His translations and commentaries on the writings of classical Greek authors generated the Florentine Platonist Renaissance. In conceiving the universe as a hierarchy of substances, he was strongly influenced by NEOPLATONISM and medieval views. The CAMBRIDGE PLATONISTS and related movements in France and Italy reflect Ficino's original Platonist revival. Of his own writings, *Platonic Theology* (1482) and the *Book on the Christian Religion* (1474) are most significant.

Johann Gottlieb Fichte After a painting by H. A. Daehling

Fides \'fī-dēz\ Roman goddess of good faith and honesty, who oversaw the integrity of the Romans. She was closely associated with JUPITER. In the later Roman period she was called Fides Publica ("Public Faith") and was considered the guardian of state documents, which were placed in her temple (built 254 B.C.) for safekeeping.

fiduciary \fə-'dü-shē-,er-ē\ In law, one in a position of authority whom the law obligates to act solely on behalf of the person he or she represents (as when managing money or property) and in good faith. Examples are agents, executors, trustees, GUARDIANS, and officers of CORPORATIONS. Unlike people in an ordinary business relationship, fiduciaries may not seek personal benefit from their transactions with those they represent.

Fiedler \'fēd-lər\, **Arthur** (1894–1979) U.S. conductor. Born in Boston, he joined the Boston Symphony Orchestra in 1915. In the 1920s he began conducting and recording with his own Boston Sinfonietta. In 1929 he organized a series of open-air concerts, which eventually became an institution, the Boston Pops. Thereafter his name was inextricably linked with the Pops, which achieved enormous success under him.

fief \'fēf\ In European FEUDALISM, a vassal's source of income, granted to him by his lord in exchange for his services. The fief usually consisted of land and the labor of peasants who were bound to cultivate it. The income it provided supported the vassal, who fought for his lord as a knight.

field In physics, a region in which each point is affected by a FORCE. Objects fall to the ground because they are affected by the force of earth's gravitational field (see GRAVITATION). A pin, placed in the MAGNETIC FIELD surrounding a magnet, is pulled toward the magnet, and two like magnetic poles repel each other when one is placed in the other's magnetic field. An ELECTRIC FIELD surrounds an ELECTRIC CHARGE. The strength of a field, or the forces in a particular region, can be represented by field lines; the closer the lines, the stronger the forces in that part of the field.

Field, Marshall (1834–1906) U.S. DEPARTMENT STORE owner. Born near Conway, Mass., he became an errand boy for a dry-goods store. In 1856 he was hired by a Chicago mercantile house, in which he later attained full partnership. In 1867 he and a partner took control of a merchandising firm; in 1888 it became Marshall Field and Co. Field's elegant store emphasized customer service, stressing liberal credit, the one-price system, and the privilege of returning merchandise. His was the first to have a restaurant for shoppers.

Field, Stephen J(ohnson) (1816–1899) U.S. jurist. Born in Haddam, Conn., he was appointed to the U.S. Supreme Court in 1863 and served until 1897. He became chief architect of the constitutional approach that largely exempted U.S. industry from government regulation after the American Civil War, basing his interpretation principally on the 14th Amendment (1868), which had been passed as a

civil-rights measure. Field's stance toward industry would be maintained by the Court until the 1930s.

field hockey Game played between two teams of 11 players each on a turfed field 100 yards (91.4 m) by 60 yards (55 m) in size. The object is to direct a ball into the opponent's goal with a curve-ended hockey stick. Field hockey began to be played in English schools in the late 19th cent., and the British Army introduced it into India and the Far East. By 1928 it had become India's national game. Men's hockey has been included in the Olympic Games since 1908, women's since 1980. In the U.S. it became particularly popular at women's schools, colleges, and clubs.

Fielding, Henry (1707–1754) British novelist and playwright. In his 25 early plays, he was essentially a satirist of political corruption; because of his sharp commentary he was eventually effectively banished from the theater, whereupon he took up law. In 1748 he was appointed a magistrate, in which role he established a new tradition of justice and suppression of crime in London. His entertaining and original novel *Joseph Andrews* (1742) was followed by *Tom Jones* (1749), his most popular work, noted for its great comic gusto, vast gallery of characters, and contrasted scenes of high- and lowlife. The more sober *Amelia* (1751) anticipates the Victorian domestic novel. In these works he helped develop the English novel as a planned, realistic narrative genre surveying contemporary society.

field mouse *or* **wood mouse** In general, any MOUSE that normally lives in fields; more strictly, any of about seven species of small, long-tailed mice in the genus *Apodemus* (family Muridae), found in fields, woodlands, and mountain meadows in Eurasia. They are grayish or light or reddish brown and are 2–5 in. (6–12 cm) long excluding the tail. They generally live in burrows and build nests of grass and other plants. They eat seeds, roots, and other plant material.

Field of Cloth of Gold Setting for meetings between HENRY VIII of England and FRANCIS I of France in June 1520, near Calais, France. Splendid temporary palaces were erected, and jousts and other entertainments were held, but the political results were negligible. In July Henry met Emperor CHARLES V, Francis's rival, near Calais, and they agreed to make no new alliances with France for two years.

Fields, Dorothy (1904–1974) U.S. lyricist and librettist. Born in Allenhurst, N.J., to a well-known theater family, Fields taught drama and wrote poetry, and later wrote songs for Broadway and Cotton Club revues with Jimmy McHugh (1896–1969), including "I Can't Give You Anything But Love" and "On the Sunny Side of the Street." With Jerome KERN, she later wrote songs for Hollywood, including "The Way You Look Tonight," and she wrote the book or lyrics for many Broadway musicals, including *Annie Get Your Gun* (1946) and *Sweet Charity* (1966).

Fields, W. C. *orig.* Claude William Dukenfield (1880–1946) U.S. actor and screenwriter. Born in Philadelphia, he was a vaudeville headliner as a juggler and appeared for seven seasons (1915–21) in the *Ziegfeld Follies*. His first major film role was in *Sally of the Sawdust* (1925). He emerged as a top film comedian only after the advent of sound pictures, when audiences could hear his distinctive raspy voice. His screen personality—an unlovable but hilarious con man and hater of children and dogs—was largely his own. Fields wrote and improvised the action for most of his films, which included such comedies as *My Little Chickadee* (1940), *The Bank Dick* (1940), and *Never Give a Sucker an Even Break* (1941).

field theory In mathematics, a branch of higher algebra dealing with a special type of system that consists of a set of objects (e.g., numbers) and two combining operations (e.g., addition and multiplication). The most commonly encountered fields are the RATIONAL NUMBERS, the REAL NUMBERS, and the COMPLEX NUMBERS, along with ordinary addition and multiplication. The investigation of polynomial equations and their solutions led to the discovery of field theory. See also GROUP THEORY.

Fiennes \'fīnz\, **Ralph (Nathaniel)** (b.1962) British actor. He joined the Royal Shakespeare Co. in 1989. His television performance in *A Dangerous Man: Lawrence after Arabia* (1991) led to the role of a Nazi commandant in the film *Schindler's List* (1993). His later films include *Quiz Show*

(1994), *The English Patient* (1996), and *Oscar and Lucinda* (1997). He also appeared on Broadway in *Hamlet* (1995, Tony Award).

Fiesole, Mino da See MINO DA FIESOLE

Fifth Republic Government of France from 1959 to the present. Under the constitution, crafted mainly by Charles DE GAULLE, executive power was increased at the expense of the National Assembly. In 1962 de Gaulle pushed through an amendment that provided for direct popular election of the president, and in 1965 he became the first French president elected by popular vote since 1848. He was succeeded by Georges POMPIDOU (1969–74), Valery GISCARD D'ESTAING (1974–81), François MITTERRAND (1981–95), and Jacques CHIRAC (from 1995).

fig Any plant of the genus *Ficus,* in the MULBERRY FAMILY. Yielding the well-known figs of commerce, *F. carica* is native to an area from Asiatic Turkey to N India, but natural seedlings grow in most Mediterranean countries, where figs are used extensively, both fresh and dried. Hundreds of different varieties are grown in various parts of the world. The fig was one of the first fruit trees to come under cultivation. Its fruit contains significant amounts of calcium, potassium, phosphorus, and iron.

fighter aircraft Aircraft designed for destroying enemy aircraft in combat. Developed in World War I, they engaged in aerial combat, shot down enemy bombers, and conducted tactical missions. Most were biplanes with wooden frames and cloth skins, equipped with light machine guns synchronized to fire through the propeller. World War II saw the development of all-metal monoplanes with speeds of 450 mph (725 kph); famous fighters included the Focke-Wulf 190, the P-47 and P-51, and the Zero. Jet aircraft appeared at the end of the war, and jet fighters such as the U.S. Sabre and the Soviet MiG saw service in the Korean War and later conflicts.

fighting fish See SIAMESE FIGHTING FISH

Figueres (Ferrer) \fē-'ger-ās\, **José** (1906–1990) Costa Rican statesman and president (1948–49, 1953–58, 1970–74). An opponent of the right-wing regime of Rafael Ángel Calderón, in 1948 he led an uprising to force Calderón to yield the presidency to the democratically elected Otilio Ulate. A junta dominated by Figueres wrote a new constitution that abolished the army and gave women the right to vote. Figueres himself was elected president by a landslide in 1953; a moderate socialist, he adopted a pro-U.S. policy and outlawed the Communist Party. Returned to power in 1970, he is given much credit for Costa Rica's enduring stability and democracy.

figured bass Style of music notation used for the CONTINUO part in baroque music. It consists of a bass line notated in the standard way, but with numerals below the staff (e.g., 6, 6/4, 7) representing INTERVALS to be played above the bass tone by the keyboard player. They began to appear around 1600, and by mid-century had been adopted universally. Figured bass, which permitted very rapid notation by the composer, became highly important as the conceptual underpinning of composition in the 17th–18th cent. Vestiges can still be found in the chord symbols of popular music.

figurehead Ornamental symbol or figure placed on a prominent part of a ship, usually at the bow. It could be a religious symbol, a national emblem, or a figure symbolizing the ship's name. The custom of decorating a ship probably began in ancient Egypt or India. As early as 1000 B.C., the stem- and sternposts were carved and painted to distinguish one ship from another. The Vikings built ships with high bows and a projecting stem bearing a menacing figurehead. Figureheads remained popular until after World War I.

figure of speech Form of expression used to convey meaning or heighten effect, often by comparing or identifying one thing with another that has a meaning or connotation familiar to the reader or listener. Common figures of speech include SIMILE, METAPHOR, personification, hyperbole, IRONY, alliteration, onomatopoeia, and puns.

figure skating Sport in which ice skaters, singly or in pairs, perform various jumps, spins, and dance movements. The figure skate blade has a special serrated toe pick. Until 1991, competition included a compulsory section in which prescribed figures were traced. Figure-skating events have long been part of the Olympics. Competition for individuals includes two free-skating programs: a shorter, technical program that must incorporate a number of prescribed elements or maneuvers; and a long program that has no mandatory requirements. Jumps fall into two main groups: the edge jumps, which take off from one foot; and the toe jumps, which are assisted by a vault off the toe pick of the other foot. Jumps are further classified as single, double, and so on. Additional pair moves, involving a man and a woman skating together, include lifts, pair spins, and throw jumps. Figure-skating programs are judged on both technical merit and artistic impression.

Fiji *officially* **Republic of Fiji** *Fijian* **Viti** Nation and archipelago, S. Pacific Ocean. It lies east of Vanuatu and southwest of Samoa. Area: 7,055 sq mi (18,272 sq km). Population (2000): 819,000. Capital: SUVA. The majority of Fijians are of mixed Melanesian-Polynesian stock. Languages: English, Fijian, Hindustani (all official). Religions: Christianity, Hinduism (among the large Asian-Indian minority), Islam. Currency: Fiji dollar. It lies 1,300 mi (2,100 km) north of New Zealand, and includes some 540 islets and 300 islands, of which about 100 are inhabited. The main islands are Viti Levu and Vanua Levu. It also includes, since 1881, Rotuma, an island located about 400 mi (640 km) to the northwest. The two large Fiji islands are mountainous and volcanic in origin, rising abruptly from densely populated coasts to forested central mountains. The smaller islands are formed mostly of coral reefs. The coastal deltas of the principal rivers contain most of Fiji's fertile arable land. It has a tropical oceanic climate. It has a market economy based largely on agriculture (particularly sugar production), tourism, and light industries; significant quantities of gold, silver, and limestone are mined. It is a republic with an interim government since 2000; its chief of state is the president, while the head of government is the prime minister. Archaeological evidence shows that the islands were occupied in the late 2nd millennium B.C. and had developed pottery by about 1300 B.C. The first European sighting was by the Dutch in the 16th cent.; in 1774 the islands were visited by Capt. James COOK, who found a mixed Melanesian-Polynesian population with a complex society. Traders and the first missionaries arrived in 1835. In 1857 a British consul was appointed, and in 1874 Fiji was proclaimed a crown colony. It became independent as a member of the COMMONWEALTH in 1970, and was declared a republic in 1987 following a military coup. Elections in 1992 restored civilian rule. A new constitution was approved in 1997. A coup in May 2000 was put down two months later. See also map at OCEANIA.

filbert *or* **hazel(nut)** Any of about 15 species of deciduous trees and shrubs that make up the genus *Corylus,* in the BIRCH family, native to the N temperate zone; also, their edible NUTS, produced by two Eurasian trees, the European filbert *(C. avellana)* and the giant filbert *(C. maxima),* and by hybrids of these species. An oil from *C. avellana* is used in food products, perfumes, and soaps; the tree yields a soft, reddish-white timber that is useful for small articles such as tool handles and walking sticks.

file transfer protocol See FTP

filibuster Tactic of delaying action on a bill by talking long enough to wear down the majority in order to win concessions or force withdrawal of the bill. Normally employed by a group or individual who cannot muster enough votes to defeat a bill by vote, filibustering is possible in the U.S. Senate because Senate rules allow unlimited debate on a bill. Calling for a vote to limit debate (cloture)—which requires 60 votes in the Senate—or holding around-the-clock sessions to tire the speakers are measures used to defeat filibusters.

Fillmore, Millard (1800–1874) 13th president of the U.S. (1850–53). Born into poverty in Locke, N.Y., he became an indentured apprentice at 15. He studied law with a local judge and began to practice in Buffalo in 1823. He joined the WHIG PARTY and was soon a leader of its N wing; he served in the U.S. House of Representatives (1833–35, 1837–43). In 1848 the Whigs nominated Fillmore as vice president, and he was elected with Zachary TAYLOR. He became president on Taylor's death in 1850. Though he ab-

FG

horred slavery, he insisted on federal enforcement of the FUGITIVE SLAVE ACT. His stand, which alienated the North, led to his defeat by Winfield SCOTT at the Whigs' nominating convention in 1852 and effectively led to the death of the party. An early champion of U.S. trade expansion in the Pacific, in 1853 he sent Matthew PERRY with a U.S. fleet to Japan, forcing its isolationist government to enter into trade and diplomatic relations. In 1856 he was nominated for president by the KNOW-NOTHING PARTY.

Millard Fillmore

film See MOTION PICTURE

film noir \\'nwär\\ (French: "black film") Film genre that offers dark or fatalistic interpretations of reality. The term is applied to U.S. films of the late 1940s and early '50s that portrayed a seamy or criminal underworld and cynical characters, often shot at night or in shadowy interiors. The genre includes such films as John HUSTON's *The Maltese Falcon* (1941), Alfred HITCHCOCK's *Spellbound* (1945), and Billy WILDER's *Double Indemnity* (1944). Later examples include Roman POLANSKI's *Chinatown* (1974) and Stephen Frears's *The Grifters* (1990).

finance Raising funds or capital for any kind of expenditure. It is the process of channeling funds from savers and investors (whose funds could earn interest or dividends if put to productive use) to consumers, businesses, and governments (who need funds to make purchases or conduct their operations) in the form of credit, loans, or invested capital through agencies including COMMERCIAL BANKS, SAVINGS AND LOAN ASSOCIATIONS, CREDIT UNIONS, and investment companies. Finance can be divided into three broad areas: BUSINESS FINANCE, personal finance, and public finance. All three involve generating budgets and managing funds for the optimum results.

finance company Institution that supplies credit for consumer purchases. Finance companies purchase unpaid customer accounts at a discount from merchants and collect payments due from customers. They also grant small loans directly to consumers at a relatively high rate of interest.

finback whale See FIN WHALE

finch Any of several hundred species of small, conical-billed, seed-eating songbirds (in several families), including the bunting, CANARY, CARDINAL, chaffinch, crossbill, GOLD-FINCH, grass finch, GROSBEAK, SPARROW, and weaver. Finches are small, compact birds 3–10 in. (10–27 cm) long. Many are brightly colored, often with shades of red and yellow. Found throughout the temperate areas of the Northern Hemisphere and S. America and in parts of Africa, finches are among the dominant birds in many areas. They are often kept as singing cage birds.

Fine Gael \\'fē-nə-'gāl\\ (Irish: "Gaelic Nation") Major political party in Ireland, also known as United Ireland Party. It was founded in 1933 by several groups, including the Cumann na nGaedheal, which had been formed by W. T. COSGRAVE and others who accepted the Anglo-Irish treaty of 1921. It held power briefly in 1948, but FIANNA FÁIL dominated Irish politics until 1973. Since then the two parties have vied for power, with Fine Gael coalition governments in power in 1973–77, 1982–87, and 1994–97.

Finger Lakes Group of narrow, glacial lakes, W New York state. They lie in north-to-south valleys between SYRACUSE and Geneseo. The region, noted for its scenery, has many resorts and produces fruits (especially grapes) and vegetables. Seneca Lake is the largest in the group.

fingerprinting Act of taking an impression of a person's fingerprint. Because every person's fingerprints are unique, fingerprinting is used as a method of identification, especially in police investigations. The FEDERAL BUREAU OF INVESTIGATION maintains a fingerprint file on more than 90 million people; fingerprints retrieved from a crime scene

may be compared with those on file to identify suspects. DNA analysis, which examines regions of DNA unique to each person, is sometimes called DNA FINGERPRINTING.

Finland *officially* **Republic of Finland** *Finnish* **Suomi** \\'swô-mē\\ Country, N Europe. Area: 130,559 sq mi (338,145 sq km). Population (2000): 5,178,000. Capital: HELSINKI. The

FINLAND
Scale 1: 18,656,000
©1999, Encyclopædia Britannica, Inc.

majority of the people are Finns; there is a small Sami (Lapp) population in LAPLAND. Languages: Finnish, Swedish; the Sami speak a Finno-Ugric language. Religion: Evangelical Lutheranism. Currency: euro. Finland is about 725 mi (1,165 km) long and 340 mi (550 km) at its widest; a third of the country is north of the Arctic Circle. Heavily forested, it contains thousands of lakes, numerous rivers, and extensive areas of marshland. Except for a small highland region in the extreme northwest, the country is a lowland less than 600 ft (180 m) above sea level. The south has relatively mild weather; the north has severe and prolonged winters and short summers. Finland has a developed free-market economy combined with state ownership of a few key industries. It is among the wealthiest countries in Europe and in the world. Lumbering is a major industry, and manufacturing is highly developed; service industries are also notable. It is a republic with one legislative house; its chief of state is the president, and the head of government is the prime minister. Human habitation in Finland dates back to at least 7200 B.C. and included the ancestors of the present-day Sami. The ancestors of the present-day Finns came from the S shore of the Gulf of Finland in the 1st millennium B.C. The area was gradually Christianized from the 11th cent. From the 12th cent. Sweden and Russia contested for supremacy in Finland, until in 1323 Sweden ruled most of the country. Russia was ceded part of Finnish territory in 1721; in 1808 ALEXANDER I of Russia invaded Finland, which in 1809 was formally ceded to Russia. The subsequent period saw the growth of Finnish nationalism. Russia's losses in World War I and the RUSSIAN REVOLUTION OF 1917 set the stage for Finland's independence in 1917. It was defeated by the Soviet Union in the Russo–Finnish War (1939–40) but then sided with Nazi Germany against the Soviets during World War II and regained the territory it had lost. Facing defeat again by the advancing Soviets in 1944, it reached a peace agreement with the U.S.S.R., ceding territory and paying reparations. Finland's economy recovered after World War II. It joined the EUROPEAN UNION in 1995.

Finney, Albert (b.1936) British actor. Established as a Shakespearean actor in the late 1950s, in 1960 he won praise as a working-class rebel in the play *Billy Liar* and the film *Saturday Night and Sunday Morning.* He starred in *Luther* on Broadway and became an international star in the film *Tom Jones* (1963). He later starred in *Night Must Fall* (1964), *Two for the Road* (1967), *The Dresser* (1983), and *Under the Volcano* (1984).

Finnish language FINNO-UGRIC LANGUAGE of Finland, spoken by close to 6 million people worldwide. Finnish was an unwritten language until the 16th cent., when Mikael Agricola (1509–1557) produced an alphabet book (1543) and a translation of the New Testament (1548); he is regarded as the founder of the Finnish literary language. Finnish was accorded official status in 1809, when Finland entered the Russian empire after six centuries of Swedish domination. The publication in 1835 of the national folk epic, the *Kalevala,* encouraged the movement to forge a common national language encompassing all dialect areas.

Finn MacCumhaill *or* **Finn MacCool** \'fin-mə-'kül\ Hero of the Irish Gaelic tales and ballads of the FENIAN CYCLE. He was chief of a band of warriors, the Fianna Éireann, who were skilled in poetry, hunting, and warfare. Finn's band was defeated in the Battle of Gabhra (A.D. 268), which Finn's son Oisín survived.

Finno-Ugric languages \'yü-grik\ Branch of the URALIC LANGUAGE family spoken by about 25 million people in NE Europe, N Asia, and N. America. More than 20 million speak FINNISH or HUNGARIAN. The Ugric subbranch comprises Hungarian and Ob-Ugrian. The latter consists of two language complexes of W Siberia with fewer than 15,000 speakers. The Finnic branch comprises the Sami (Saami, Lappish) languages, the Baltic Finnic (Fennic) languages, Mordvin, Mari, and the Permic languages. Sami is spoken by some 20,000 people in N Scandinavia and adjacent Russia. The Baltic Finnic languages include Finnish and Estonian (with 1.1 million speakers worldwide). Mordvin (Mordva) is spoken by 1.1 million people in central European Russia. Mari (Cheremis) has about 600,000 speakers in central Russia. The Permic (Permian) languages, spoken in NE European Russia, have nearly one million speakers. Finno-Ugric languages written in Russia use variants of the CYRILLIC ALPHABET, while those outside Russia use the LATIN ALPHABET.

fin whale *or* **finback whale** *or* **razorback whale** *or* **common rorqual** \'ror-kwəl\ Swift, slender-bodied BALEEN WHALE (*Balaenoptera physalus*) named for the ridge on its back. It is 60–80 ft (18–24 m) long, with a triangular dorsal fin, short baleen, and several dozen grooves along its throat and chest. It is found in oceans worldwide, in groups of a few to several hundred. It lives in polar waters in summer, feeding on crustaceans and small fishes, and moves to warmer waters in winter to breed. Commercially valuable, it has been overhunted and is now listed as an endangered species.

Fionn cycle See FENIAN CYCLE

fiord See FJORD

fir Properly, any of about 40 species of trees that make up the genus *Abies,* in the PINE family. Many other evergreen CONIFERS (e.g., DOUGLAS FIR, HEMLOCK fir) are also commonly called firs. True firs are native to N. and Central America, Europe, Asia, and N Africa. Their needlelike leaves grow directly from the branch and have bases, shaped like suction cups, that leave conspicuous circular scars when the leaves fall. N. America boasts 10 native species of fir, found chiefly from the Rocky Mtns. westward. Their wood is generally inferior to that of pine or SPRUCE but is used for lumber and pulpwood. The balsam fir (*A. balsamea*) is a popular ornamental and Christmas tree.

Firdusi See FERDOWSI

fire Rapid burning of combustible material, producing heat and usually accompanied by flame. For eons, LIGHTNING was the only source of fire. The earliest controlled use of fire seems to date to around 1,420,000 years ago, but not until about 7000 B.C. did Neolithic humans acquire reliable firemaking techniques. Fire was used initially for warmth, light, and cooking; later it was used in fire drives in hunting and warfare, and for clearing forests of underbrush to facilitate hunting. The first agriculturalists used fire to clear fields and produce ash for fertilizer; such "slash-and-burn"

cultivation is still used widely today. Fire also came to be used for firing pottery and for smelting bronze (c.3000 B.C.) and later iron (c.1000 B.C.).

fire ant Any of a genus (*Solenopsis*) of red or yellowish ANTS, several species of which are common in N. America. They can inflict a severe sting. The semipermanent nest consists of a loose mound with open craters for ventilation. The workers are notorious for damaging planted grain and attacking poultry.

firefly *or* **lightning bug** Any of the nocturnal luminous BEETLES of the family Lampyridae, consisting of about 1,900 species that inhabit tropical and temperate regions (including the common GLOWWORM). Adult fireflies are 0.2–1 in. (5–25 mm) long and have light-producing organs on the underside of the abdomen. Some do not eat; others feed on pollen and nectar. Most fireflies produce short, rhythmic flashes in a pattern that is characteristic of the species and an important mating signal.

Fire Island Elongated sandspit, off the S shore of LONG ISLAND, New York state. Measuring 32 mi (51 km) long and 0.5 mi (1 km) at its widest, its name refers to fires that were built there as signals to ships during the WAR OF 1812. Now a popular summer resort, it is connected to Long Island by two bridges and by ferry. Fire Island includes a state park and a national seashore area.

fireplace Opening made in the base of a chimney to hold an open fire. The opening is framed, usually ornamentally, by a mantel (or mantelpiece). A medieval development that replaced the open central hearth for heating and cooking, early fireplaces were made of stone; later, brick came into use. In 1624 Louis Savot developed a fireplace in which cool air was drawn in through passages under the hearth and hot air was discharged into the room through a grille.

fireproofing Use of fire-resistant materials in a building to prevent structural collapse and allow safe exit of occupants in case of fire. The fire-resistive ratings of various materials are established by laboratory tests and usually specified in terms of hours a material or assembly can be expected to withstand exposure to fire. Building codes require fire-resistant construction (e.g., using concrete block) for exits, flame-spread ratings of carpeting and wall coverings, and use of such inherently fire-resistant materials as reinforced concrete and heavy timber.

Firestone, Harvey S(amuel) (1868–1938) U.S. industrialist. Born in Columbiana, Ohio, he established a retail carriage-tire business in 1896. In 1904 he began manufacturing automobile tires. Sales to FORD MOTOR CO. helped put Firestone Tire and Rubber Co. at the top of the U.S. tire industry. Firestone promoted the use of trucks for hauling freight and lobbied for the construction of vast highway systems. His son succeeded him in 1932.

fire walking Religious ceremony that involves walking across hot coals, red-hot stones, or burning wood. It has been practiced in such parts of the world as ancient Greece, India, China, Tahiti, Bulgaria, and Spain. It usually involves striding across a layer of embers, but sometimes devotees walk through a blazing log fire. Reasons for fire walking include purification and as an ordeal to prove innocence. Devotees believe that only those who lack faith will be burned, and many fire walkers do escape without injury.

firewall Security system that controls the flow of data from one computer or NETWORK to another. Firewalls protect the resources of a private network from access by an external user, especially via the Internet. Users inside the private network may also be prevented from accessing external computers. To accomplish this, all communications are routed through a "proxy server" that determines whether a message or file will be allowed to enter or exit the private network.

fireworks EXPLOSIVES or combustibles used for display. Of ancient Chinese origin, fireworks evidently developed out of military rockets and explosive missiles, and accompanied the spread of military explosives westward to Europe. In force-and-spark compositions, potassium nitrate, sulfur, and ground charcoal are used; additional ingredients produce various types of sparks. In flame compositions, such as the stars that shoot out of rockets, potassium nitrate, salts of antimony, and sulfur may be used; for colored fire, a metal salt determines the color. Rockets are lifted by recoil from the jet of fire thrown out by the burning composition.

First International *officially* International Working Men's Association. Federation of workers' groups, founded in 1864 by British and French trade-union leaders. Its structure was highly centralized, based on local groups that were integrated into national federations. A clash between Karl MARX's centralized socialism and Mikhail BAKUNIN's anarchism in 1872 caused the International to split, and it was dissolved in 1876. Though it was feared as a formidable power, its membership was never more than 20,000 and it served mainly as a unifying force for labor in Europe.

FIS See ISLAMIC SALVATION FRONT

fiscal policy Measures employed by governments to stabilize the economy, specifically by adjusting the levels and allocations of taxes and government expenditures. When the economy is sluggish, the government may cut taxes to encourage spending and CONSUMPTION. An increase in public-works spending may likewise pump cash into the economy. Conversely, a decrease in government spending or an increase in taxes tends to cause the economy to contract. Fiscal policy is often used in tandem with MONETARY POLICY. Until the 1930s, fiscal policy aimed at maintaining a balanced budget; since then it has been used "countercyclically," as recommended by J. M. KEYNES, to offset the cycle of expansion and contraction in the economy. Fiscal policy is more effective at stimulating than cooling an economy, partly because spending cuts and tax increases are unpopular. See also BUSINESS CYCLE.

Fischer, Bobby (*orig.* Robert James) (b.1943) U.S. chess master, the youngest grand master in history. Born in Chicago, he became a grand master at 15. In 1972 Fischer defeated Boris SPASSKY to become the first U.S. player to hold the title of Chess Champion of the World. Intense and deeply eccentric, he frequently condemned the Soviet Union for godlessness, and was deprived of his title in 1975 after refusing to meet his Soviet challenger, Anatoly KARPOV. He returned to the game to win a private rematch with Spassky in Yugoslavia in 1992; the game violated U.S. sanctions against Yugoslavia, and Fischer has remained abroad since.

Fischer, Emil (Hermann) (1852–1919) German organic chemist. He determined the structures of uric acid, CAFFEINE, and related compounds, showing that all are derivatives of a single compound he named PURINE. This led him to study PROTEIN structure. He determined the molecular structures of GLUCOSE, FRUCTOSE, and many other SUGARS, verifying his results by synthesizing each. His researches into the sugars were of unparalleled importance to organic chemistry; he won the second Nobel Prize for Chemistry (1902). His investigations of FERMENTATION laid the foundations of ENZYME chemistry.

Fischer-Dieskau \'fi-shər-ˈdēs-ˌkaú\, **Dietrich** (b.1925) German baritone and conductor. Born in Berlin, he had his first extensive performance experience as a prisoner of war in Italy, and he made his debut in 1947. One of the most remarkable singers of his time, he was equally successful in opera and lied. He recorded most of the standard art-song repertoire, as well as numerous unusual and contemporary works.

Fischer projection Method of representing the three-dimensional structures of MOLECULES devised by Emil FISCHER. By convention, horizontal lines represent bonds projecting toward the viewer, and vertical lines represent bonds on the side away from the viewer. Fischer projections are a convenient way to depict chiral molecules (see OPTICAL ACTIVITY). They are most often used to depict ISOMERS of SUGARS. See also CHEMICAL FORMULA.

fish Any of various cold-blooded freshwater and saltwater VERTEBRATES. Living species range from the primitive LAMPREYS and HAGFISHES through the cartilaginous SHARKS, SKATES, and RAYS to the abundant and diverse BONY FISHES. Species range in length from 0.4 in. to more than 60 ft (10 mm–20 m). Most species that inhabit surface or midwater regions are streamlined or are flattened side to side; most bottom-dwellers are flattened top to bottom. Tropical species are often brightly colored. Most species

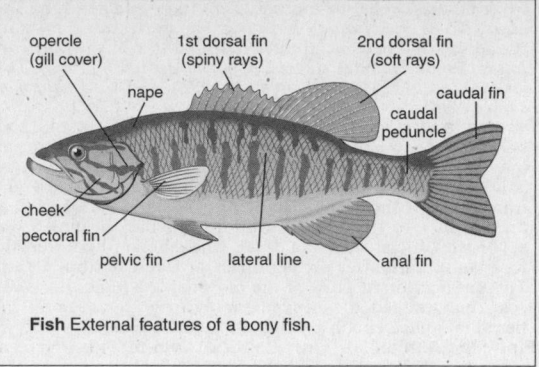

Fish External features of a bony fish.

have paired fins and skin covered with either bony or tooth-like scales. Fish generally respire through gills. Most bony fishes have a swim bladder, a gas-filled organ used to adjust swimming depth. Most species lay eggs. Fishes first appeared more than 450 million years ago.

Fish, Hamilton (1808–1893) U.S. secretary of state (1869–77). Born in New York City, he served as governor (1849–50) and U.S. senator (1851–57). As secretary of state in Ulysses S. GRANT's administration, he skillfully promoted peaceful arbitration of explosive international situations, producing agreements with Britain in several disputes. He helped draft the Treaty of Washington (1871), which provided for international arbitration. As a respected member of Grant's cabinet, he worked to counter graft, improper appointments, and violations of blacks' civil liberties.

fish duck See MERGANSER

fisher Rare N. American CARNIVORE (*Martes pennanti,* family Mustelidae) of N forests. Related to the WEASEL and similarly shaped, it has a bushy tail and tapered muzzle. The adult is usually 20–25 in. (50–63 cm) long, excluding the 13–17-in. (33–43-cm) tail, and weighs 3–15 lbs (1.4–6.8 kg). It hunts on the ground and in trees, attacking rodents and other animals. It has been trapped for its valuable fur. See also MARTEN.

Fisher, Frederick (John) (1878–1941) U.S. automobile-body manufacturer. Born in Sandusky, Ohio, he worked for his father, a carriage maker, before moving to Detroit in 1902. From 1908 to 1916 he and his five brothers formed several companies building bodies for cars. When merged in 1916 as Fisher Body Corp., they were producing almost 400,000 bodies a year. In 1926 it became a division of General Motors.

Fisher, R(onald) A(ylmer) (*later* **Sir Ronald**) (1890–1962) British statistician and geneticist. To avoid unintentional bias in selection of materials used in experiments, he introduced the principle of randomization. It states that before an experimental effect can be attributed to a given cause or treatment, the experiment must be repeated on control units of the material, and all material used in experiments must be selected at random from the whole population. He also developed the concept of the analysis of variance, a statistical procedure used to design experiments that answer several questions at once.

fish hawk See OSPREY

fishing *or* **sport fishing** Sport of catching fish, freshwater or saltwater, typically with rod, line, and hook. Fishing is as old as the human ability to use tools to capture prey. The first significant modern innovations, including use of a reel, a rod with line guides, and a hook with an offset point, came in the 17th and 18th cent. Horsehair was originally used as line; today nylon and other synthetics are used. Wood and bamboo rods yielded to rods of fiberglass and other synthetics. In fly fishing (freshwater), a fly-like hook is repeatedly cast upon the water surface to attract biting fish; in bait fishing (fresh- and saltwater), live or artificial bait is set or drawn below the surface; in big-game fishing (saltwater), heavy-duty tackle is used to land large marine species from a motorized boat.

fishing industry Taking, processing, and marketing of fish and other seafood from oceans, rivers, and lakes. Fishing is one of the primary forms of food production; it probably predates farming. The fishing industry employs more than 5 million people worldwide. The major countries engaged in marine fishing are Japan, China, the U.S., Chile, Peru, India, S. Korea, Thailand, and the countries of N Europe. The aquatic life harvested is processed into food for human consumption, animal feeds, fertilizers, and ingredients for use in other commercial commodities.

Fisk, James (1834–1872) U.S. financier. Born in Bennington, Vt., he joined Daniel Drew (1797–1879) and Jay GOULD against Cornelius VANDERBILT in the "Erie War" (1967–68), in which the three tried to seize control of the Erie Railroad Co. by issuing fraudulent stock. Their attempt to corner the gold market by inflating the price led to the panic of 1869. Known as "the Barnum of Wall Street," Fisk produced theatrical shows and dallied with showgirls; he was fatally shot by an associate at age 37 after quarreling over business matters and a mistress.

Fisk University Private, historically black university in Nashville, Tenn. Founded in 1865, it is affiliated with the United Church of Christ. It offers master's programs in several fields. The Fisk Jubilee Singers (from 1871) introduced black spirituals to a large white audience. Enrollment is about 1,000.

fission-track dating Method of determining the age of a mineral that utilizes the damage done by the spontaneous fission of uranium-238 (see URANIUM). The fission tracks are made visible by preferential leaching (removal of material by solution) of the host substance, which allows the etched fission-track pits to be counted under a microscope. When compared against another population of tracks, related to the uranium concentration of the mineral, the ratio of naturally produced to induced fission tracks is a measure of the age of the sample. See also DATING.

fitnah \\'fit-nə\\ (Arabic: "trial" or "test") In Islam, trials or temptations that test the unity of the Muslim community. There were four in early Islam. The first (656–661), the murder of the caliph Uthman, resulted in the schism between the SUNNIS and the SHIITES. The second (680–715) was a continuation of the struggle between claimants to the caliphate. The third (744–50) resulted in the ascendancy of the ABBASIDS. The fourth (833–48) was a conflict over the nature of the QURAN. See also ALI, HUSAYN IBN ALI, AL-MUAWIYAH I.

FitzGerald, Edward (1809–1883) British writer. He is best known for *The Rubáiyát of Omar Khayyám* (1859), a free adaptation from OMAR KHAYYAM's verses that is itself a classic of English literature. Many of its images, such as "A jug of wine, a loaf of bread, and thou" and "The moving finger writes, and, having writ, moves on" have passed into common currency.

Fitzgerald, Ella (1917–1996) U.S. singer. Born in Newport News, Va., Fitzgerald won an amateur contest at Harlem's Apollo Theater in 1934 and became the star of Chick Webb's big band in 1935. Her association with manager and impresario Norman Granz from the late 1940s led to a famous series of "Songbook" recordings, each featuring the work of a single popular-song composer. One of the greatest scat singers in jazz, her clear, girlish voice and virtuosity made her one of the best-selling vocal recording artists in history.

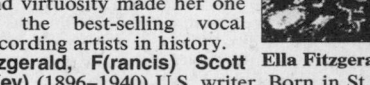
Ella Fitzgerald

Fitzgerald, F(rancis) Scott (Key) (1896–1940) U.S. writer. Born in St. Paul, Minn., he attended Princeton Univ., but dropped out with bad grades. His works, including the early novels *This Side of Paradise* (1920) and *The Beautiful and Damned* (1922), capture the Jazz Age's vulgarity and dazzling promise. His brilliant *The Great Gatsby* (1925), a story of American wealth and cor-

ruption, was eventually acclaimed one of the century's greatest novels. In 1920 he married Zelda Sayre (1900–1948), and in 1924 they joined the expatriate community on the French Riviera, the setting of *Tender Is the Night* (1934). His fame and prosperity proved disorienting and he became seriously alcoholic. After a mental breakdown in 1932, Zelda spent most of her remaining years in a sanitarium. In 1937 Scott moved to Hollywood to write film scripts; the experience inspired the unfinished *The Last Tycoon* (1941).

Five, The See MIGHTY FIVE

Five Articles Oath See CHARTER OATH

Five Classics Chinese Wujing. Ancient Chinese books associated with CONFUCIUS. For more than 2,000 years they were invoked as authorities on Chinese society, government, literature, and religion. Chinese students usually studied the shorter FOUR BOOKS before attempting the Five Classics, which consist of the *YI JING* ("Classic of Changes"), the *Classic of History*, the *Classic of Poetry*, the *Collection of Rituals*, and the *CHUNQIU* ("Spring and Autumn Annals"). Until the early 20th cent., proficiency in the texts was required for any scholar applying for a post in the vast government bureaucracy.

Five Dynasties Period in Chinese history betweeen the fall of the TANG DYNASTY (907) and the founding of the SONG DYNASTY (960), when five would-be dynasties (the Hou Liang, Hou Tang, Hou Jin, Hou Han, and Hou Zhou) followed one another in quick succession in N China. Though unstable politically, it was a period of cultural accomplishment. Printing with wooden blocks was fully developed, enabling the first complete printing of the Confucian Classics in 953. The form of lyric poetry called *ci (tz'u)* flourished, and flower painting became a branch of nonreligious painting.

Five Pecks of Rice Taoist-inspired popular movement that occurred near the end of China's HAN DYNASTY (206 B.C.–A.D. 220) and greatly weakened the government. It became a prototype of the religiously inspired popular rebellions that were to erupt periodically in China throughout its history. Its founder, Zhang Daoling (34?–156?), was originally a faith healer, and the movement's name came from the five pecks of rice that clients paid him for their cure or as dues to the cult. Later, during a time of poverty and misery, Zhang's grandson Zhang Lu set up an independent theocratic state that encompassed present-day Sichuan province; in 215 he surrendered to CAO CAO. See also TAOISM.

Five-Year Plans Method of planning economic growth over limited periods, through the use of quotas. In the Soviet Union, the first Five-Year Plan (1928–32), implemented by Joseph STALIN, concentrated on developing heavy industry and collectivizing agriculture, causing a drastic fall in consumer goods. During the second plan (1933–37), collectivization led to terrible famines that caused the deaths of millions. The third (1938–42) emphasized the production of armaments. The fourth (1946–53) again stressed heavy industry and military buildup. In China, the first Five-Year Plan (1953–57) stressed rapid industrial development, with Soviet assistance; it proved highly successful. The second plan began in 1958, but the GREAT LEAP FORWARD, with its conflicting goals, led to failure and the withdrawal of Soviet aid in 1960.

fjord *or* **fiord** \\fē-'ȯrd\\ Long, narrow arm of the sea, often extending well inland, that results from marine inundation of a glaciated valley. Many fjords are remarkably deep; (see SOGNE FJORD); it is assumed that huge glaciers eroded the bottoms of the valleys far below sea level. After the glaciers melted, the waters of the sea invaded the valleys.

flag Piece of cloth or similar material displaying the insignia of a community, an armed service, an office, or an individual. It is usually oblong and attached by one edge to a staff or halyard. Originally used in warfare, it was a sign of leadership, serving as identification of friend or foe. The flag was invented in ancient India or China. In Europe, where national flags first appeared in the Middle Ages, they became accepted symbols of nations, kings, organizations, cities, and guilds.

flagellants \\'fla-jə-lənts\\ Medieval religious sects that included public beatings with whips as part of their discipline and devotional practice. Arising in N Italy, they had become widespread by about 1260. Groups marched through European towns, whipping each other to atone for their sins and calling on the populace to repent. They gained many new members while the BLACK DEATH was ravaging Europe. Though periodically suppressed by the authorities, flagellant sects had sporadic resurgences into the 16th cent.

flagellum \flə-'jel-əm\ Hairlike structure that acts mainly as an organelle of movement in the cells of many living organisms, including some PROTOZOANS and the sex cells of ALGAE, fungi (see FUNGUS), MOSSES, and SLIME MOLDS. Flagellar motion causes water currents necessary for respiration and circulation in SPONGES and CNIDARIANS. Most motile BACTERIA move by means of flagella. The flagella in PROKARYOTES differ from those in EUKARYOTES. See also CILIUM.

Flagler, Henry M(orrison) (1830–1913) U.S. financier. Born in Hopewell, N.Y., he joined John D. ROCKEFELLER, Sr., in founding what in 1870 became the STANDARD OIL CO. He was hugely influential in the development of Florida as a vacation center, organizing and extending the Florida East Coast Railway, dredging Miami's harbor, and building a chain of luxury hotels.

Flagstad \'fläg-stä, *Engl* 'flag-,stad\, **Kirsten (Marie)** (1895–1962) Norwegian soprano. She made her operatic debut in 1913. In 1934 she was invited to sing Sieglinde in *Die Walküre* and Gutrune in *Götterdämmerung* at Bayreuth. Recognized as the greatest Wagnerian soprano of her generation, she toured widely until 1941, returning to Norway to be with her husband, a member of Vidkun QUISLING's government. Though cleared of charges of collaboration with the Germans, her later U.S. appearances were controversial.

flake tool STONE AGE devices, usually flint (see CHERT AND FLINT), shaped by flaking off small particles or by breaking off a large flake to use as a tool. Prehistoric humans preferred flint and similar siliceous stones because of the ease with which they could be chipped and for their sharp cutting edges. They also used SANDSTONES, QUARTZITES, QUARTZ, OBSIDIAN, and volcanic rocks. Stone tools were chipped by striking a block of flint with a hammer of stone, wood, or bone or by striking the block itself on the edge of a fixed stone. Pressure flaking consists of applying pressure by means of a pointed stick or bone to detach small flakes. See also STONE-TOOL INDUSTRY.

flamen \'flā-mən\ One of 15 priests in ancient Rome, each devoted to the service of a specific god. The most important were those who served JUPITER, MARS, and QUIRINUS. They offered daily sacrifices and led strictly regulated lives. Their wives assisted them. In imperial times a group of *flamines* were devoted to the worship of deified emperors.

flamenco \flə-'meŋ-kō\ Music and dance of the Andalusian GYPSIES, or Flamencos, which developed from the 14th cent. onward. Its essence is *cante,* or song, often accompanied by guitar music and improvised dance. It falls into three categories: *jondo,* or *grande* ("profound," or "grand"), intensely sad and dealing with themes of death, anguish, or religion; *intermedio,* less profound, but also moving, often with an oriental cast; and *chico* ("small"), with subjects of love, gaiety, and the countryside. Essential is the *duende,* or possession of the performer by the emotion of the music or dance. Performances are often accompanied by *jaleo*—intricate hand clapping, finger snapping, and shouts.

flamethrower Military assault weapon that projects a stream of blazing oil or gasoline. It consists of one or more fuel tanks, a cylinder of compressed gas to supply the propelling force, and a hose with a trigger-nozzle that ignites and sprays the fuel. Portable flamethrowers are carried by ground troops; larger units may be installed on tank turrets. Flamethrowers were used in World Wars I and II and later wars. They are often used in dense underbrush and against fortified positions at close range.

flamingo Any of four species of tall wading birds constituting the family Phoenicopteridae. The plumage is mainly pink. Flamingos have webbed feet, a slender body, a long thin neck, large wings, and a short tail. They are about 3–5 ft (90–150 cm) tall. Flamingos flock by the hundreds (sometimes by the millions) in flight formations and wading

groups. They tramp the shallows, stirring up tiny mollusks and crustaceans, which they eat. They populate Atlantic and Gulf coasts of tropical and subtropical N. America and in S. America, Africa, S Europe, Asia, and India.

Flaminius \flə-'min-ē-əs\, **Gaius** (d.217 B.C.) Roman political leader. As TRIBUNE (232) he supported Roman expansion in N Italy; his land bill gave land to Roman PLEBEIANS and gained him great popularity, but the Gallic invasion of 225 was said to have been caused by the bill's passage. He was elected CONSUL in 223 and 217. As censor (220) he built the Circus Flaminius in Rome and the Via Flaminia to Ariminum (Rimini). He died fighting HANNIBAL in the Second PUNIC WAR.

Flanders *Flemish* **Vlaanderen** \'vlän-də-rən\ Medieval principality extending along the coast of the LOW COUNTRIES. Its lands are now divided among France, Belgium, and the Netherlands. Its strategic location between the Mediterranean Sea and the Scandinavian and Baltic countries fostered its growth as a commercial center. It passed to BURGUNDY in 1384 and then to the Austrian HABSBURGS in 1477. It remained part of the Netherlands under Spanish rule in the 17th cent. It was the scene of intense fighting during both World Wars. Limited autonomy was granted to Belgian Flanders in the 1980s, and it became one of the three regions in the new federation of Belgium in 1993.

flat See PLAYA

flatfish Any of about 600 species (order Pleuronectiformes) of oval-shaped, flattened BONY FISHES (e.g., FLOUNDER, turbot), found from tropical to cold waters. Most are marine and live along the continental shelf, but some enter or live permanently in freshwater. Flatfishes are carnivorous bottom-dwellers that habitually rest on one side, often partly buried. Some can also change color to blend with their surroundings. Both eyes are on one side of the head. Species vary from 4 in. (10 cm) to 7 ft (2 m) long, and some (e.g., the Atlantic HALIBUT) may weigh as much as 720 lbs (325 kg). Many species are highly valued as food. See also PLAICE, SOLE.

Flathead N. American Indian people who inhabited what is now W Montana. Salish was the native name of the tribe, but Flathead is now customary; they themselves did not practice head-flattening, but some of their slaves came from tribes that did. The Flatheads were PLATEAU INDIANS, but like the PLAINS INDIANS they acquired horses and went on bison hunts. The Plains TEPEE was their usual dwelling. Western Flatheads used bark canoes, and for all groups fishing was important. Religious belief centered on guardian spirits, with whom one communicated in visions. Since 1872 the Flatheads have resided primarily on a reservation north of Missoula, Mont. Today they number about 4,000.

Flatt, Lester (1914–1979) U.S. BLUEGRASS guitarist and singer. Born in Overton Co., Tenn., he began performing with his wife Gladys in the late 1930s. In 1945 he joined Bill MONROE's Blue Grass Boys. There he met the banjoist Earl Scruggs (b.1924), a native of Flint Hill, N.C., who had perfected a picking technique involving the thumb and first two fingers of the right hand that came to be called the "Scruggs style." In 1948 the two men left to form Flatt and Scruggs and the Foggy Mountain Boys. They made dozens of records and hosted their own syndicated radio and TV shows. Scruggs's original instrumental compositions, including "Foggy Mountain Breakdown," were especially popular. In 1969 Scruggs joined his sons in the Earl Scruggs Revue.

flatworm *or* **platyhelminth** Any of a phylum (Platyhelminthes) of soft-bodied, usually much-flattened WORMS, including both free-living and parasitic species. Flatworms live in marine, freshwater, and terrestrial habitats worldwide. They range in length from a fraction of a millimeter to 50 ft (15 m) and are of three main types: turbellarians (including the PLANARIAN), trematodes (see FLUKE), and cestodes (see TAPEWORM). Flatworms lack respiratory, skeletal, and circulatory systems and a body cavity.

Flaubert \flō-'ber\, **Gustave** (1821–1880) French novelist. His masterpiece, *Madame Bovary* (1857), a sharply realistic portrayal of provincial bourgeois boredom and adultery, led to his trial for immorality. His other novels include the exotic *Salammbô* (1862), set in ancient Carthage; *A Senti-*

mental Education (1869), a classic bildungsroman; and *The Temptation of Saint Anthony* (1874), notable for its depiction of spiritual torment. *Trois Contes* (1877) contains three novellas. His collected letters are considered perhaps the finest such collection of all time. He is regarded as the foremost exponent of French REALISM.

Flavian dynasty \\'flā-vē-ən\\ (A.D. 69–96) Ancient Roman imperial dynasty of VESPASIAN and his sons TITUS and DOMITIAN, members of the Flavia gens, or clan. Vespasian sought to give the office of emperor permanent form by making Caesarism (dictatorship) hereditary by natural descent or adoption. Worship of the deified caesars (subemperors) became the symbol of imperial continuity and legitimacy.

flax family Family Linaceae (order Linales), composed of about 14 genera of herbaceous plants and shrubs found throughout the world. The genus *Linum* includes flax, perhaps the most important member of the family, grown for LINEN fiber and linseed oil and as a garden ornamental.

Flaxman, John (1755–1826) British sculptor, illustrator, and designer. After 1775 he worked for Josiah WEDGWOOD, producing designs based on classical antiquity; he directed the Wedgwood studio in Rome (1787–94). His book illustrations for the *Iliad* (1793), *Odyssey* (1795), and *Divine Comedy* (1807) became very well known. The leading Neoclassical artist in England, he became the Royal Academy's first professor of sculpture (1810), known for his monuments with large groups of free-standing figures.

flea Any member of 1,600 species and subspecies of small, wingless, bloodsucking (parasitic) INSECTS (order Siphonaptera), found from the Arctic Circle to the Arabian deserts. Though domestic cats and dogs are well-known hosts, rodents are the mammals most commonly afflicted by fleas. The adult flea is 0.04–0.4 in. (1–10 mm) long and lives from a few weeks to more than a year.

Flea *(Ctenocephalides)*

Powerful leg muscles allow it to jump distances up to 200 times its body length. Flea infestations have had enormous consequences; fleas were the chief carriers of the bubonic PLAGUE.

Fleischer, Max and Dave (1883–1972, 1894–1979) U.S. animators. Max was born in Vienna, Dave in New York City. The brothers worked as newspaper cartoonists before founding their own studio in 1921 to make animated cartoons. They produced early sound-on-film animations, and later created the popular cartoon series *Betty Boop* (1931–39) and *Popeye the Sailor* (1929–42), and the feature-length cartoon *Gulliver's Travels* (1939).

Fleming, Alexander (*later* **Sir Alexander**) (1881–1955) Scottish bacteriologist. While serving in the Royal Army Medical Corps in World War I, he conducted research on antibacterial substances that would be nontoxic to humans. In 1928 he inadvertently discovered PENICILLIN when he noticed that a mold contaminating a bacterial culture was inhibiting the bacteria's growth. He shared a 1945 Nobel Prize with Ernst CHAIN and Howard FLOREY.

Fleming, Ian (Lancaster) (1908–1964) British suspense novelist. He worked as a Moscow journalist, banker and stockbroker, naval intelligence officer, and newspaper manager before publishing *Casino Royale* (1953), the first of 12 novels featuring James Bond, the stylish, high-living secret-service agent 007, one of the most successful heroes of 20th-cent. fiction. Packed with violent action and sex, all 12 books became popular movies.

Fleming, Peggy (Gale) (b.1948) U.S. figure skater. Born in San Jose, Cal., she won the first of five consecutive Senior Ladies' championships when she was 15. She won the N. American title competition in 1967, won the world championship three consecutive years (1966–68), and won a gold medal in the 1968 Olympics.

Flemish art Art of the 15th to early 17th cent. in Flanders. The dukes of BURGUNDY established a powerful Flemish-Burgundian political alliance that lasted from 1363 to 1482.

PHILIP III the Good moved the Burgundian capital from Dijon to Bruges and in 1425 hired Jan van EYCK as his painter. The next generation of artists, including Rogier van der WEYDEN, Hugo van der GOES, Hans MEMLING, and Gerard DAVID, built on van Eyck's heritage and began looking to Italy for inspiration. In the 16th cent., Pieter BRUEGEL, under the influence of Hieronymus BOSCH, depicted peasant life with an eye for the grotesque. The great master of the 17th cent., Peter Paul RUBENS, demonstrated unrivaled skill in oil painting; his style epitomized the Flemish baroque period.

Fletcher, John See Francis BEAUMONT

Flexner, Abraham (1866–1959) U.S. educator. Born in Louisville, Ky., he was asked by the Carnegie Foundation to evaluate the 155 U.S. and Canadian medical colleges, and his report (1910) had a sensational impact; many of the colleges he severely criticized closed, and others revised their policies and curricula. Flexner thereafter channeled over half a billion dollars from the Rockefeller Foundation into improving U.S. medical education. In 1930 he founded the Institute for Advanced Study in Princeton, N.J., to which he brought some of the world's outstanding scientists.

flicker Any of six species of New World WOODPECKER (genus *Colaptes*) noted for spending much time on the ground eating ants. The sticky saliva of the flicker is alkaline, perhaps to counteract the formic acid that ants secrete. Most flickers have a white rump, black breast band, and varied head markings, and most are about 13 in. (33 cm) long.

flight recorder Instrument that records the performance and condition of an aircraft in flight. Regulatory agencies require these devices on commercial aircraft to make possible the analysis of crashes or other unusual occurrences. They are housed in heavy steel within layers of insulation, protecting them against impacts and fires. The recording tape is also protected against inadvertent erasure and contact with seawater. It records airspeed, altitude, heading, vertical acceleration, and aircraft pitch; a separate device records voice communication within the aircraft and by radio. Both recorders are carried in the tail of the aircraft.

Flinders, Matthew (1774–1814) British navigator. In two expeditions (1795–99, 1801–3) he circumnavigated Australia and Tasmania, charting their coasts and waters. His *Voyage to Terra Australis* (1814) recounted his adventures. Flinders PETRIE was his grandson.

Flinders Ranges Mountain region, S. Australia. It extends some 250 mi (400 km) north from Gulf Saint Vincent. Beyond Peterborough to the northeast, the highland region continues as the Mt. Lofty Ranges. Its high point is St. Mary Peak at 3,825 ft (1,166 m). The ranges feature scenic landscapes and include two national parks.

Flint City (pop., 2000: 125,000), E Michigan. The city was laid out in 1836 and became a fur-trading and agricultural center. Abundant timber led to the development in 1886 of the Durant-Dort Carriage Co.; by 1900 it was producing over 100,000 horse-drawn vehicles a year. Several companies became suppliers for what would become the GENERAL MOTORS CORP. By the 1950s, the city was second only to DETROIT in U.S. automobile manufacturing. The closing of G.M. plants in the 1980s and '90s left Flint with a shrinking economy.

flint See CHERT AND FLINT

flood High-water stage in which water overflows its banks onto normally dry land, such as a river inundating its floodplain. Uncontrollable floods likely to cause considerable damage commonly result from excessive rainfall in a brief period. Flood control includes improving channels, constructing protective levees, and implementing soil and forest conservation to absorb runoff from storms.

floor Rigid building assembly that divides space horizontally into stories and forms the bottom of a room. It may consist of joist-supported wood planks or panels, decking or panels supported by wood or steel beams, a slab of stone or concrete on the ground, or a reinforced-concrete slab carried by concrete beams and columns. The floor assembly must support its own dead load plus the live load of occupants, activities, and furnishings. The horizontal supports—and the vertical supports into which they frame—must be suffi-

FG

ciently large and spaced closely enough to prevent sagging of the assembly.

floppy disk *or* **diskette** Magnetic storage medium used with COMPUTERS. Floppy disks are made of flexible plastic coated with a magnetic material, enclosed in a hard plastic case. They are typically 3.5 in. (9 cm) in diameter. Data are arranged on their surfaces in concentric tracks. When a disk is inserted into a computer, a small electromagnet writes each binary digit (1 or 0) onto the disk by magnetizing a tiny spot on the disk in different directions, or reads digits by detecting the magnetization direction of the spots. With the increasing use of e-mail attachments to transfer files from computer to computer, the use of floppy disks has waned, though they are still used to keep second (backup) copies of valuable files.

Flora Roman goddess of flowering plants. Her cult was supposedly introduced into Rome during its earliest years. Her temple stood near Rome's Circus Maximus, and her festival, the Floralia, was instituted in 238 B.C.

Florence *Italian* **Firenze** \fē-'rent-sā\ City (pop., 2000 est.: 377,000), capital of TUSCANY region, central Italy. Built on both sides of the ARNO RIVER, the city has been a republic, a seat of the duchy of Tuscany, and a capital (1865–71) of Italy. A Roman military colony in the 1st cent. B.C., it was controlled in turn by the Goths, Byzantines, and Lombards. A leading city of Tuscany by the late 12th cent., it was ruled after 1434 by the powerful MEDICI FAMILY. It became a republic under SAVONAROLA, after whose downfall the Medici were restored as dukes of Florence (1531). Florence's vernacular became the Italian language, and from the 14th to the 16th cent. Florence was among the greatest cities of Europe. Over time, many notables flourished there, including LEONARDO DA VINCI, MICHELANGELO, BRUNELLESCHI, DANTE, MACHIAVELLI, and GALILEO. Its buildings, including the Baptistery of St. John, the Gothic Duomo, and the UFFIZI GALLERY, are works of art themselves. Among its palaces and parks are the Pitti Palace and its Boboli gardens. Its university was founded in 1321. Florence's economy is based primarily on tourism.

Florey, Howard (Walter) *later* **Baron Florey** (1898–1968) Australian pathologist. He purified lysozyme, a bacteria-destroying enzyme found in tears and saliva, and characterized the substances it acted on. He surveyed other naturally occurring antibacterial substances, concentrating on PENICILLIN, which, with Ernst CHAIN, he isolated and purified for general clinical use. The two demonstrated penicillin's curative properties in human studies and developed methods for producing it in quantity. In 1945 he shared a Nobel Prize with Chain and Alexander FLEMING.

floriculture Branch of ornamental HORTICULTURE concerned with growing and marketing flowers and ornamental plants, as well as with flower arrangement. Floriculture is largely thought of as a GREENHOUSE industry, although many flowers are cultivated outdoors. Both the production of bedding plants and the production of cuttings to be grown in greenhouses or for indoor use (foliage plants) are usually considered part of floriculture. See also NURSERY.

Florida State (pop., 2000: 15,982,000), SE U.S. It comprises a peninsula and adjoining mainland areas, and covers 58,664 sq mi (151,940 sq km); its capital is TALLAHASSEE. Indian groups entered Florida from the north as early as 10,000 years ago. It was explored by Juan PONCE DE LEÓN around 1513, and in 1565 Spaniards founded ST. AUGUSTINE. Florida became a British possession in 1763 after the FRENCH AND INDIAN WAR. The area reverted to Spanish control after the AMERICAN REVOLUTION (1783) but was used by the British as a base of operations during the WAR OF 1812. Andrew JACKSON's capture of Pensacola during that war led to the cession of Florida to the U.S. in 1819. A war with the SEMINOLE Indians followed (see SEMINOLE WARS). Florida became a state in 1845. It seceded from the Union in 1861, then was readmitted in 1868. In the late 20th cent., it became one of the fastest growing states in the U.S. It produces about 75% of the nation's citrus fruits, and is second only to California in vegetable production. Tourism is a leading industry, with DISNEY WORLD a major attraction. Electronics manufacture is important, and the aerospace industry, centered on the Kennedy Space Center (see

Cape CANAVERAL), employs many thousands of people. The state, and especially the city of MIAMI, with its large Cuban population, plays a major economic role in the Caribbean region. Among its many recreational areas is EVERGLADES National Park.

flotation *or* **froth flotation** Most widely used process for extracting many MINERALS from their ORES. It separates and concentrates ores by altering their surfaces so that they are either repelled or attracted by water. Unwetted particles, which adhere to air that is bubbled through the water, will float in the froth, while wetted particles will sink. The process was developed to remove very fine mineral particles that formerly had gone to waste in gravity concentration plants. With its use to concentrate copper, lead, and zinc minerals, many complex ore mixtures formerly of little value have become major sources of certain metals.

flounder Any of about 300 species of FLATFISHES (order Pleuronectiformes). When born the flounder is bilaterally symmetrical, with an eye on each side, and it swims near the sea's surface. After a few days, it begins to lean to one side, and the eye on that side migrates to what eventually becomes the top side. As an adult, the flounder lives on the bottom, with the eyed side on top. Several species are important food fishes.

flour Finely ground meal of CEREAL grain, usually WHEAT, used as a basic ingredient in BAKING. In the production of refined flour, milling is used to separate the starchy endosperm from the other parts of the kernel. In the production of whole-wheat flour, all parts of the kernel are used. Following milling, the particles of endosperm (called semolina) are ground to flour and often bleached. Flour grades are based on the residual amount of branny particles. When flour is mixed with water to make dough, its protein content is converted to gluten, an elastic substance that is capable of retaining gas, thus causing the baked product to expand, or rise.

flower Reproductive portion of any FLOWERING PLANT (angiosperm). Popularly, the term applies especially when part or all of the reproductive structure is distinctive in color and form. Flowers vary widely in color, size, form, and anatomical arrangement. In some plants, individual flowers are very small and are borne in a cluster (INFLORESCENCE). Each flower bears the essential organs of reproduction (STAMENS and PISTILS) and usually accessory organs (sepals and petals); the latter may serve both to attract pollinating insects (see POLLINATION) and to protect the essential organs. Flower parts are arrayed usually in whorls, but sometimes spirally. Four distinct whorls are common: the outer calyx (sepals), the corolla (petals), the androecium (stamens), and, in the center, the gynoecium (pistils). The sepals often resemble reduced leaves; the petals are usually colorful and showy. POLLEN is produced in the stamens. A pollen-receptive stigma rests atop each pistil. The pistil encloses an ovary that contains the ovules, or potential SEEDS. After fertilization, the ovary enlarges to form the FRUIT. Flowers have been symbols of beauty in most civilizations, and flower giving is among the most popular of social amenities.

flowering plant Any of the more than 250,000 species of angiosperms (division Magnoliophyta) having roots, stems, leaves, and well-developed conductive tissues. They are often differentiated from GYMNOSPERMS by their production of seeds within a closed chamber (the ovary) within the flower, but this distinction is not always clear-cut. The division is composed of two classes: monocots and dicots (see COTYLEDON). Monocots have flower parts in threes, and usually prominent parallel veins in the leaves. Dicots have flower parts in fours or fives, a net-veined pattern in the leaves, and a cambium, which causes secondary growth of stems. Flowering plants account for more than 300 families growing on every continent, including Antarctica. Most reproduce sexually by seeds via the specialized reproductive organs that are present in all flowers.

flow meter Device that measures the velocity of a GAS or LIQUID. It has applications in medicine, chemical engineering, aeronautics, and meteorology. Examples include PITOT TUBES and VENTURI TUBES. Ultrasonic flow meters, in which reflecting ultrasound off a flowing liquid leads to a

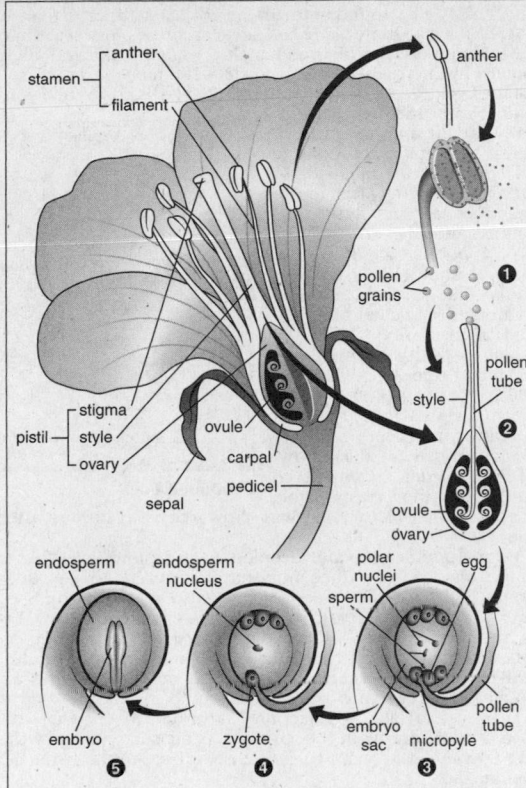

Flowering plant The life cycle of a flowering plant. (1) A pollen grain is released from the anther and settles on the stigma. (2) A pollen tube forms and grows through the style toward the ovule opening (micropyle). (3)Two of the nuclei (polar nuclei) in the ovule's embryo sac migrate to the center to form a single cell. Three cells migrate to the micropyle, and one enlarges to become the egg. Two sperm that have formed from mitotic division of the pollen grain's generative cell enter the embryo sac through the micropyle. (4) One sperm fuses with the egg, resulting in a fertilized egg (zygote), which develops into an embryo. The second sperm fuses with the two polar nuclei to form a triploid nucleus (containing three sets of chromosomes). (5) This nucleus divides to form a tissue (endosperm) that provides nutrients for the developing embryo.

Doppler shift (see DOPPLER EFFECT) that is calibrated to provide the flow rate of the liquid, have important industrial applications and have also been used to measure arterial blood flow.

flu See INFLUENZA

flugelhorn Valved BUGLE. It has three valves and a wider bore than the CORNET and is usually pitched in B-flat. Invented in Austria in the 1830s, it has long been part of European military bands; today it is also used in jazz and popular music.

fluid Any LIQUID or GAS that cannot sustain a shearing force when at rest and that undergoes a continuous change in shape when subjected to such a stress. Compressed fluids exert an outward PRESSURE on the walls of their containers. A perfect fluid lacks VISCOSITY, but real fluids do not.

fluid mechanics Study of the effects of forces and energy on LIQUIDS and GASES. One branch of the field, HYDROSTATICS, deals with fluids at rest; the other, fluid dynamics, deals with fluids in motion and with the motion of bodies through fluids. The subject has numerous applications in fields varying from aeronautics and marine engineering to the study of blood flow and the dynamics of swimming.

fluke *or* **trematode** Any member of almost 6,000 species of parasitic FLATWORMS. Flukes are found worldwide and range in size from about 0.2 to 4 in. (5–100 mm) long. They most commonly parasitize fish, frogs, and turtles, but also humans, domestic animals, and invertebrates such as mollusks and crustaceans. They include external parasites (ectoparasites), internal parasites (endoparasites), and semi-external parasites (those that attach to the lining of the mouth, to gills, or to the cloaca). Fluke infestations may cause illness (e.g., SCHISTOSOMIASIS) or death in humans.

fluorescence Emission of ELECTROMAGNETIC RADIATION, usually visible light, caused by excitation of ATOMS in a material, which then reemit within about 10^{-8} seconds. The initial excitation is usually caused by absorption of energy from incident radiation or particles, such as X rays or electrons. Because reemission occurs so quickly, the fluorescence ceases as soon as the exciting source is removed, unlike PHOSPHORESCENCE. A fluorescent lightbulb is coated on the inside with a powder and contains a gas; electricity causes the gas to emit ultraviolet radiation, which then stimulates the tube coating to emit light. The pixels of a television or computer screen fluoresce when electrons from an electron gun strike them. The addition of a fluorescing agent to detergents causes fabrics to appear whiter in sunlight. X-ray fluorescence is used to analyze minerals.

fluorescent lamp Type of ELECTRIC DISCHARGE LAMP consisting of a glass tube filled with a mixture of argon and mercury vapor. Electricity causes the vapor to produce ultraviolet radiation that, in turn, excites a phosphor coating inside the tube, causing it to fluoresce (see FLUORESCENCE). Fluorescent lamps are cooler and more efficient than INCANDESCENT LAMPS.

fluoridation of water Addition of fluoride compounds (see FLUORINE) to water (at one part per million) to reduce dental CARIES. Fluoridation decreases the number of decayed, missing, and filled teeth in children (which increases if fluoridation is stopped), but it has provoked controversy in some places. Excess fluoride may cause tooth mottling (a problem of appearance only) and, in higher doses, bone abnormalities. Fluoridation also helps prevent RICKETS and helps THYROID GLAND function.

fluorine \'flur-,ēn, 'flor-,ēn\ Nonmetallic chemical ELEMENT, chemical symbol F, atomic number 9. The lightest HALOGEN, it is the most reactive element, forming compounds with all others except the lighter NOBLE GASES. Its only VALENCE is 1. A toxic pale yellow GAS with a pungent odor, it can be produced only by ELECTROLYSIS under special conditions. Its chief source is FLUORITE; it also occurs in cryolite, fluorapatite, seawater, bones, and teeth. Hydrogen fluoride (HF) is a raw material for many other fluorides. Its water solution, hydrofluoric acid, is used to clean metals and polish, etch, or frost glass. Other fluorides are useful CATALYSTS and raw materials. Fluorocarbons are HYDROCARBONS in which some hydrogens have been replaced by fluorines; examples include FREONS and TEFLON. See also FLUORIDATION OF WATER.

fluorite *or* **fluorspar** Common halide mineral, calcium fluoride, the principal fluorine mineral. Fluorite occurs most commonly as a vein mineral and is often associated with lead and silver ores. It is widespread in China, S. Africa, Mongolia, France, Mexico, Russia, and the central U.S. Fluorite is used in the manufacture of steel, aluminum fluoride, and aluminum, and also in glassmaking, in the production of hydrofluoric acid, and in the refining of lead and antimony.

Flushing N section, QUEENS, New York City. It was settled in 1645 by English nonconformists, and became a center for Quakers (see Society of FRIENDS). It was absorbed by Queens in 1898. Flushing Meadow-Corona Park was the site of the 1939–40 and 1964–65 New York world's fairs. Flushing is the scene of the U.S. Open tennis championships and home to Shea Stadium.

flute WOODWIND INSTRUMENT whose sound is produced by blowing against a sharp edge. The transverse flute of Western music is a tubular instrument held sideways to the right, which appeared in Greece and Etruria by the 2nd cent. B.C.

By the 16th cent. a family of boxwood flutes, with fingerholes but no keys, was in use in Europe. Keys began to be added in the late 17th cent. Theodor Boehm's 19th-cent. innovations resulted in the modern flute, which permits thorough expressive control and great agility. The cylindrical tube may be made of wood or, more often, a precious metal or alloy. The flute family includes the piccolo (pitched an octave higher) and the alto flute.

flux In METALLURGY, any substance introduced in the SMELTING of ores to promote fluidity and to remove objectionable impurities in the form of slag. LIMESTONE is commonly used in smelting IRON ores. Other materials used as fluxes are silica, dolomite, lime, borax, and fluorite. In SOLDERING, the flux removes oxide films, promotes wetting, and prevents reoxidation of the surfaces during heating. Rosin is widely used when electronic equipment is soldered; in other applications, a water solution of zinc chloride and ammonium chloride may be used.

Fluxus \'flək-səs\ International avant-garde group of artists founded in Germany by the American artist George Maciunas (1931–1978) in 1962. Its members included Joseph BEUYS, John CAGE, Yves KLEIN, and Yoko Ono (b.1933). Opposed to tradition and professionalism in the arts, the group shifted the emphasis from what an artist makes to the artist's personality, actions, and opinions. Throughout the 1960s and '70s they staged "action" events, engaged in politics and public speaking, and produced sculptural works featuring unconventional materials. Influential in Europe, the group's work aroused much controversy.

flying buttress Masonry structure typically consisting of an inclined bar carried on a half arch that extends ("flies") from the upper part of a wall to a pier some distance away and carries the thrust of a roof or vault. A pinnacle (vertical ornament) often crowns the pier, adding weight and enhancing stability. The design evolved in the Gothic era, increasing the supporting power of the buttress and enabling the creation of the high-ceilinged churches typical of GOTHIC ARCHITECTURE.

flying fish Any of about 40 species of warm-water oceanic fishes (family Exocoetidae) noted for their ability to "fly." All species are less than 18 in. (45 cm) long and have winglike, rigid fins. Two-winged species have only the pectoral fins enlarged; four-winged species have both the pectoral and the pelvic fins enlarged. Rather than flying, they actually glide. Some can travel as much as 600 ft (180 m) in a single glide, and compound glides may cover 1,300 ft (400 m). Flight is primarily a means for escaping predators.

flying squirrel Any member of two distinct groups of RODENTS that make gliding leaps using membranes connecting their forelegs and hind legs on each side. N. American and Eurasian flying squirrels, in the SQUIRREL family (Sciuridae), are slender, long-limbed forest dwellers with soft fur and large eyes. They are 3–24 in. (8–60 cm) long, excluding the often-flattened tail. They seldom descend to the ground. They can glide 200 ft (60 m) or more from one tree to another. The scaly-tailed flying squirrels of Africa (family Anomaluridae) have rows of scales on their tufted tail that help them climb and cling to trees.

Flynn, Errol (Leslie Thomson) (1909–1959) Australian-U.S. film actor. After acting in Australia and England, in 1935 he went to Hollywood, and became an instant success as the swashbuckling hero of *Captain Blood*. He continued to play dashing heroes in such films as *The Charge of the Light Brigade* (1936), *The Adventures of Robin Hood* (1938), *The Sea Hawk* (1940), and *Gentleman Jim* (1942). After a period marred by scandal, he returned to acclaim in *The Sun Also Rises* (1957).

flytrap See VENUS'S-FLYTRAP

flywheel Heavy wheel attached to a rotating shaft to smooth out delivery of power from a motor to a machine. Its inertia opposes and moderates fluctuations in the speed of the engine and stores the excess energy for intermittent use. In automobile engines, the flywheel smooths out the pulses of energy provided by the combustion in the cylinders and provides energy for the compression stroke of the pistons.

FM *in full* frequency modulation. Variation of the frequency of a RADIO WAVE in accordance with variations in the audio signal being sent. Developed by Edwin ARMSTRONG in the early 1930s, FM is less susceptible to outside interference

and noise (e.g., thunderstorms, nearby machinery) than is AM. FM is also better able to transmit sounds in stereo than AM. Commercial FM broadcasting stations transmit their signals in the frequency range of 88–108 megahertz (MHz).

Foch \'fȯsh, *Engl* 'fäsh\, **Ferdinand** (1851–1929) French general. From 1885 he periodically taught military strategy at the war college, becoming its commandant in 1908. In WORLD WAR I, after commanding at the Battles of YPRES and the SOMME, he was appointed chief of the general staff (1917), adviser to the Allied armies, and then commander in chief of all Allied armies (May 1918), in which capacity he prevailed in the battle of wills with Erich LUDENDORFF. When Germany was forced to ask for an armistice, the conditions were dictated by now-Marshal Foch. Considered the leader most responsible

Ferdinand Foch

for the Allied victory, he was showered with honors after the war.

fog CLOUD of small water droplets near ground level that is dense enough to reduce horizontal visibility to less than about 3,000 ft (1,000 m). Fog may also refer to clouds of smoke particles (SMOG). When visibility is more than 3,000 ft, the phenomenon is termed mist or haze, depending on whether it is caused by water drops or by solid particles. Most fogs occur when the surface is colder than the air above. Fogs can also occur when cold air moves over a warm, wet surface and becomes saturated by the evaporation of moisture from the surface. As air currents carry the fog upward, it appears to rise as steam or smoke from the wet surface.

Fokine \fȯ-'kēn\, **Michel** (*orig.* Mikhail Mikhaylovich) (1880–1942) Russian-U.S. dancer and choreographer. He debuted in St. Petersburg with the MARIINSKY THEATER at 18. Following his creation of *The Dying Swan* for Anna PAVLOVA in 1905, he was in demand as a choreographer. Sergey DIAGHILEV engaged him at the BALLETS RUSSES in 1909, where he produced such unified creations as *The Firebird* (1910), *Petrushka* (1911), and *Daphnis and Chloe* (1912). He moved to New York in 1923, and choreographed over 60 works for companies in the U.S. and Europe.

Fokker, Anthony (*orig.* Anton Herman Gerard) (1890–1939) Dutch-U.S. aircraft designer and manufacturer. He built his first plane in 1910 and in 1912 established a small aircraft factory near Berlin. In World War I he produced over 40 types of airplanes for Germany, having originally offered his designs to both sides. He also developed a gear system that allowed a machine gun to fire through a spinning propeller's field. In 1922 he moved to the U.S. and opened an aircraft factory, where he produced numerous commercial aircraft.

folate See FOLIC ACID

fold In geology, a bend in the stratified rocks of the earth's CRUST. Stratified rocks were originally formed from sediments that were deposited in flat, horizontal sheets, but in some places the strata have warped. The warping may be so gentle that the bend is barely perceptible, or it may be so pronounced that the strata of the two flanks are parallel. Folds vary widely in size; the tops of large folds are commonly eroded away.

foliation In geology, a planar arrangement of features in any rock type, but particularly the alignment of mineral grains of a METAMORPHIC ROCK along straight or wavy planes. Foliation commonly occurs parallel to original bedding, and is shown prominently by sheety minerals, such as mica or chlorite.

folic acid \'fō-lik\ *or* **folate** Organic compound essential to animal growth and health. Part of the VITAMIN B COMPLEX, folic acid is necessary for synthesis of NUCLEIC ACIDS and formation of the oxygen-carrying component of red blood cells. To prevent NEURAL TUBE DEFECTS in babies, it should ideally be taken by the mother starting at least a month before conception. Dietary folate sources include leafy and dark green vegetables, citrus fruits, cereals, beans, poultry, and egg yolks. Low intake leads to folic-acid-deficiency ANEMIA.

Folies Bergère \fȯ-ˈlē-ber-ˈzher\ MUSIC HALL AND VARIETY THEATER in Paris. It opened in 1869, presenting operettas and pantomimes; its shows later included vaudeville sketches, acrobats, ballets, and magicians. After the vogue of nudity appeared in music halls (1894), its sensational displays of women in scanty but opulent costumes overshadowed its other performances. Under Paul Derval (1918–1966), the Folies became one of Paris's major tourist attractions. Each show requires about 10 months of preparation, 40 sets, and 1,000 costumes.

folk dance Dance that has developed without a choreographer and reflects the traditional life of the common people of a country or region. The term, coined in the 18th cent., is sometimes used to distinguish between dances of the people and those of the aristocracy. Many courtly and formal dances of the 16th–20th cent., including the MINUET and WALTZ, often developed from folk dances. See also COUNTRY DANCE, HULA, MORRIS DANCE, SQUARE DANCE, SWORD DANCE.

folklore Oral literature and popular tradition preserved among a people. Its subject matter includes fairy tales, ballads, epics, folk plays, proverbs, and riddles as well as music, dance, and traditional arts and crafts. Studies of folklore began in the early 19th cent. and first focused on rural peasants and others believed to be untouched by modern ways. The aim was to trace archaic customs and beliefs. In Germany Jacob and Wilhelm GRIMM published their classic collection of fairy tales in 1812. James FRAZER's *The Golden Bough* (1890) reflects the use of folklore as a tool to reconstruct ancient beliefs and rituals. The catalog of motifs of folktales and myths developed by Antti Aarne and Stith Thompson (1910, rev. 1961) encouraged comparisons of variants of the same tale or other item from different regions and times. After World War II folklorists studied urban as well as rural people.

folk music Music held to be typical of a nation or ethnic group, known to all segments of its society, and preserved usually by oral tradition. Knowledge of its history and development is largely conjectural, since musical notation of folk songs is rare in historical records. As Christianity expanded in medieval Europe, attempts were made to suppress folk music because of its association with heathen rites and customs. During the Renaissance, new humanistic attitudes encouraged acceptance of folk music, and composers made extensive use of the music; folk tunes were often used as raw material for motets and masses, and Protestant hymns borrowed from folk music. In the 19th cent., folk songs came to be considered a "national treasure," on a par with cultivated poetry and song, and became a means of promoting nationalistic ideologies. Since the 1890s, folk music has been collected and preserved by mechanical recordings. Publications and recordings have promoted wide interest, making possible the revival of folk music where traditional folk life and folklore are moribund. After World War II, archives of field recordings were developed throughout the world. The influence of such singer-songwriters as Woody GUTHRIE, Pete SEEGER, and Bob DYLAN expanded the genre to include original music that largely retains the form and simplicity of traditional compositions.

folly In architecture, an eccentric structure erected to enhance a romantic landscape. Follies were particularly in vogue in England in the 18th and early 19th cent. They might resemble medieval towers, ruined castles overgrown with vines, or crumbling Classical temples complete with fallen columns. In the U.S., the term has been applied to ornate gazebos and other extravagant or whimsical buildings.

Folsom complex Prehistoric culture of N. America on the E side of the Rocky Mtns. that is characterized by flint projectile points having a concave base with side projections and a longitudinal groove on each face. The complex, first identified at Folsom, N.M., also included a variety of scrapers, knives, and blades. It is generally dated to 8000–9000 B.C. and, like the earlier CLOVIS COMPLEX, is considered to be part of a Paleo-Indian big-game hunting tradition.

Fon \ˈfän\ People of S Benin and adjacent parts of Togo. Numbering about 2 million, the Fon are farmers, ironworkers, sculptors, weavers, and potters. The social unit is the polygynous family, each woman and her children occupying a house within a compound. The kingdom of DAHOMEY was peopled principally by Fon.

Fonda, Henry (Jaynes) (1905–1982) U.S. actor. Born in Grand Island, Neb., he achieved success on Broadway in *The Farmer Takes a Wife* (1934), and in the film version (1935). He portrayed a thoughtful man of integrity in such films as *Young Mr. Lincoln* (1939), *The Grapes of Wrath* (1940), and *The Ox-Bow Incident* (1943). He also made such comedies as *The Lady Eve* (1941) and dramas such as *Twelve Angry Men* (1957) and *Advise and Consent* (1961). He returned to the stage in *Mister Roberts* (1948, Tony Award; film, 1955). His last film, *On Golden Pond* (1981, Academy Award), also starred his daughter Jane FONDA. His son Peter (b.1939) achieved fame in *Easy Rider* (1969), which he also cowrote and produced.

Fonda, Jane (Seymour) (b.1937). U.S. film actress. Born in New York City, the daughter of Henry FONDA, she made her film debut in *Tall Story* (1960). After playing comic roles in such films as *Cat Ballou* (1965) and *Barefoot in the Park* (1967), she appeared as a sex kitten in then-husband Roger VADIM's futuristic *Barbarella* (1968). She then plunged into leftist political activity, marrying the activist Tom Hayden and loudly condemning the Vietnam War. Later films included *Klute* (1971, Academy Award) and *Coming Home* (1978, Academy Award). She made a series of hugely popular exercise books and videotapes. After marrying Ted TURNER in 1991, she retired from the screen.

font *or* **typeface** *or* **type family** Set of type (alphanumeric characters used for printing), all of one coherent style. Be-

A B G P a b g p
Bodoni roman

A B G P a b g p
Bodoni regular italic

A B G P a b g p
Bodoni bold

A B G P a b g p
Bodoni bold italic

A B G P
Bodoni small caps

A B G P a b g p
Bodoni poster

— descender
— serif
— ascender
Bodoni, serif typeface

Typefaces are designed to include space above and below so that the descenders of one line do not touch the ascenders of the next.

leading
x-height
baseline
Helvetica, sans-serif typeface

Font The term *font* commonly refers to a type family such as Bodoni or Helvetica, which includes the entire alphabet in various weights (regular, bold, extra bold, etc.) and styles (roman, italics, or display type such as Bodoni Poster). Type can be set in capitals ("caps"), lowercase, or small caps. The x-height of a font (the height of a lowercase letter that has no ascender or descender) will vary from typeface to typeface. The space between lines of type is referred to as "leading"—a term that dates back to a time when spacing was added with strips of lead. The specification of the example above is indicated as 10/11, or 10-point type with 11 points from baseline to baseline.

FG

fore the advent of computers, fonts were expressed in cast metal that was used as a template for printing. Fonts are now stored as digitized images that can be modified for printing on electronic printers or phototypesetters. Fonts typically include the normal typeface (roman) as well as italic, bold, and bold italic versions. See also TYPESETTING, TYPOGRAPHY.

Fontaine, Jean de La See Jean de LA FONTAINE

Fontainebleau \fōⁿ-ten-ˈblō\ Château in N France, near the town of Fontainebleau. One of the largest structures built by the kings of France, it was originally a medieval hunting lodge, but was rebuilt (from 1528) under FRANCIS I. Its numerous renovations show the transition from early Renaissance to Mannerist (Late Renaissance) styles. The château is a succession of five courts of different shapes.

Fontainebleau, school of French and foreign artists associated with the court at FONTAINEBLEAU in the 16th cent. In 1528 FRANCIS I began to rebuild the palace and hired Rosso Fiorentino and Francesco PRIMATICCIO to produce the mural decoration, stuccowork, and sculptural reliefs; also among the Italian artists was Benvenuto CELLINI. The Italian masters successfully adapted their own styles to the French taste and, assisted by French and Flemish artists, produced a distinctive style of Mannerism. The innovation of stucco ornament in combination with mural painting had great influence on French art of the time.

Fontane \fôn-ˈtä-nə\, **Theodor** (1819–1898) German writer. His *Before the Storm* (1878) is considered a masterpiece of historical fiction. *Effi Briest* (1895), known for its superb characterizations and skillful portrayal of his native Brandenburg, is one of his several sympathetic treatments of women in circumscribed domestic lives. He is considered the first master of modern German REALISM.

Fontanne, Lynn See Alfred LUNT AND LYNN FONTANNE

Fonteyn \fän-ˈtān\, **Margot** (*later* **Dame Margot**) *orig.* Margaret Hookham (1919–1991) British ballerina. She debuted with the Vic-Wells (later ROYAL) BALLET in 1934 and soon became its leading dancer, creating many roles in works by Frederick ASHTON. In the 1960s she won worldwide acclaim for her appearances with Rudolf NUREYEV in such ballets as *Swan Lake*, *Raymonda*, and *Le corsaire*. She is considered one of the greatest dancers of the 20th cent.

Margot Fonteyn in *Ondine*

Food and Drug Administration (FDA) Agency of the U.S. Department of HEALTH AND HUMAN SERVICES. Established in 1927, it inspects, tests, approves, and sets safety standards for foods and food additives, drugs, chemicals, cosmetics, and household and medical devices. It can prevent untested products from being sold, and take legal action to halt the sale of products that present health or safety risks. Its authority is limited to interstate commerce.

food chain Sequence of transfer of matter and energy from organism to organism in the form of food. PLANTS and other photosynthetic organisms (such as PHYTOPLANKTON), which convert solar energy to food, are the primary food source. In a predator chain, a plant-eating animal is eaten by a larger animal. In a parasite chain (see PARASITISM), a smaller organism consumes part of a larger host and may itself be parasitized by even smaller organisms. In a saprophytic chain, microorganisms live on dead organic matter. Because energy, in the form of heat, is lost at each step, or trophic level, chains do not normally encompass more than four or five trophic levels.

food poisoning Acute gastrointestinal illness from eating foods containing TOXINS, whether natural POISONS in plants and animals, chemical contaminants, or toxic products of microorganisms. Most cases are due to bacteria (including SALMONELLA and STAPHYLOCOCCUS) and their tox-

ins (including BOTULISM). Normally harmless bacteria, such as *E. coli*, may develop harmful strains. Chemical poisons include heavy metals (see MERCURY POISONING). Food additives may have a long-term cumulative toxic effect. See also MUSHROOM POISONING.

fool *or* **jester** Comic entertainer whose madness or imbecility, real or pretended, made him a source of amusement and gave him license to abuse and poke fun at even his most exalted patrons. Professional fools flourished in diverse societies from ancient Egyptian times until the 18th cent. Often deformed, dwarfed, or crippled, fools were kept for luck as well as amusement, in the belief that deformity can avert the evil eye and that abusive raillery can transfer ill luck from the abused to the abuser.

fool's gold See PYRITE

foot Any of numerous lineal measures (commonly 9.8–13.4 in., or 25–34 cm) based on the length of the human foot and used exclusively in English-speaking countries. In most countries and in all scientific applications, the foot has been superseded by the METER. In the U.S. the definition of the foot as exactly 30.48 cm took effect in 1959. See also INTERNATIONAL SYSTEM OF UNITS.

foot End part of the leg, consisting of the heel, arch, and toes, on which a person stands. Its major function is locomotion. The human foot cannot grasp and is adapted for running and striding. Its arched structure helps it support the body's weight. See also PODIATRY.

foot, metrical Basic unit of verse meter, consisting of any of various fixed combinations or groups of stressed and unstressed (or long and short) syllables. The prevailing kind and number of feet determines the meter of a poem. The most common feet in English verse are the iamb, an unstressed followed by a stressed syllable; the trochee, a stressed followed by an unstressed syllable; the anapest, two unstressed syllables followed by a stressed syllable; and the dactyl, a stressed syllable followed by two unstressed syllables. See also PROSODY.

foot-and-mouth disease (FMD) *or* **hoof-and-mouth disease** *or* **aftosa** Highly contagious VIRAL DISEASE of cloven-footed mammals (including cattle), spread by inhalation and ingestion. The animal stops eating because blisters on mouth tissues become raw and painful; udders and hooves also blister. Endemic in many places, FMD can cause 50% mortality in severe epidemics. Survivors experience weight loss, reduced milk flow, and other ill effects. No effective treatment exists; vaccines control epidemics but have not eliminated them. Since the virus can persist, quarantine, slaughter, incineration, and decontamination must be rigorous. In early 2001 a major outbreak occurred in the United Kingdom, followed shortly by outbreaks in The Netherlands and France.

football In the U.S., a game played between two teams of 11 players each on a field having two goalposts at each end, whose object is to get an oblong ball, in possession of one side at a time, over a goal line or between goalposts by running, passing, or kicking. A team must advance the ball 10 yards in four attempts (called downs), in order to continue to have the ball for another four downs. A run or completed pass over the goal line (touchdown) counts as six points. A kick through the goalposts (field goal) counts as three points. A post-touchdown goal kick counts as one point; two points are awarded if the ball is run or passed over the goal line. U.S. football evolved in the 19th cent. from RUGBY and SOCCER. In 1873 the first collegiate rules were standardized and the IVY LEAGUE was formed. Collegiate football grew into one of the most popular U.S. sports. In 1998 a point plan was implemented for picking the country's top two teams, which would meet in a championship game. Professional football began in the 1890s but did not become a major sport until after World War II. The NATIONAL FOOTBALL LEAGUE was formed in 1922; in 1966 it subsumed the rival American Football League (created in 1959). The NFL is now divided into an American and a National conference; their winners compete in the SUPER BOWL. See diagram on following page.

Foote, (Albert) Horton (b.1916) U.S. dramatist. Born in Wharton, Texas, he is best known for *The Trip to Bountiful* (1953; film, 1985) and a series of plays about rural Texas, in-

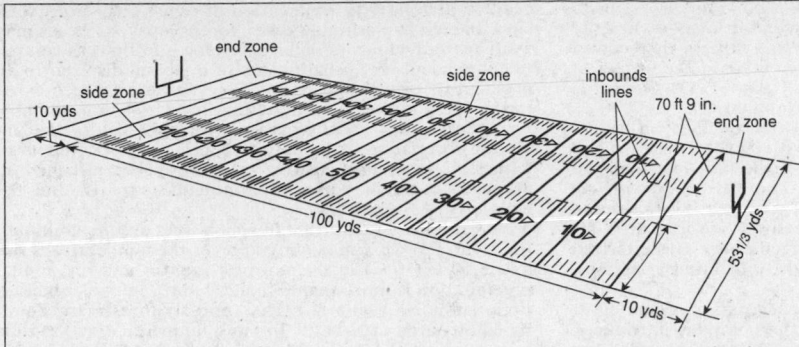

end zone   **side zone**   **inbounds lines**   **70 ft 9 in.**   **end zone**

side zone

10 yds

100 yds   **53⅓ yds**

10 yds

Football A professional Amer. football field. The standard college field is nearly identical but has a wider inbounds zone. Whenever the ball is downed in a side zone, it is put in play on the next down at the nearest inbounds line. The line marking the end zone (within which the ball may be caught) is the goal line.

cluding *The Widow Claire, Valentine's Day*, and *1918* (1974–77). His screenplays include *To Kill a Mockingbird* (1962, Academy Award) and *Tender Mercies* (1983, Academy Award). His quietly insightful play *The Young Man from Atlanta* (1994) won the Pulitzer Prize.

Forbes family U.S. publishing family. Bertie Charles Forbes (1880–1954) was born in Scotland and emigrated to the U.S. in 1904. He founded the business and finance magazine *Forbes*, in 1916. His son, the colorful Malcolm S. Forbes (1919–1990), was born in New York. He was decorated for his service in World War II, and later turned the failing publication into a success. On his death, his son Malcolm S. ("Steve") Forbes, Jr. (b.1947), took over the magazine, assisted by his three brothers. He ran unsuccessfully for president in 1996 and 2000.

Forbidden City Imperial Palace complex in Beijing, containing hundreds of buildings and some 9,000 rooms. It served the emperors of China from 1421 to 1911. No commoner or foreigner was allowed to enter it without special permission. The moated palaces, with their throne halls and courtyards, golden tiled roofs and red pillars, are surrounded by high walls with a tower on each corner. North of the front gate, a great courtyard lies beyond five marble bridges. Farther north, raised on a marble terrace, is the massive, double-tiered Hall of Supreme Harmony, one of the largest wooden structures in China. Today the palaces are public museums.

force Action that tends to maintain or alter the position of a body or to distort it. It is a VECTOR quantity, having both magnitude and direction. Force is commonly explained in terms of NEWTON'S LAWS OF MOTION. Force is measured in newtons (N); a force of 1 N will accelerate a mass of one kilogram at a rate of one meter per second per second. See also CENTRIFUGAL FORCE, CORIOLIS FORCE, ELECTROMAGNETIC FORCE, MAGNETIC FORCE, MECHANICS, STRONG FORCE, WEAK FORCE.

Ford, Ford Madox *or* **Ford Madox Hueffer** \\'hwəf-ər\\ *orig.* Ford Hermann Hueffer (1873–1939) English novelist, editor, and critic. He collaborated with Joseph CONRAD on *The Inheritors* (1901) and *Romance* (1903). As the founder of the *English Review* (1908), he generously encouraged younger writers. He was gassed and shell-shocked in World War I. Of more than 70 published works, the best known are *The Good Soldier* (1915), a novel about the demise of aristocratic England; and the tetralogy *Parade's End* (1924–28), which explores the breakdown of Edwardian culture and the emergence of new values.

Ford, Gerald R. *in full* Gerald Rudolph Ford, Jr. *orig.* Leslie Lynch King, Jr. (b.1913) 38th president of the U.S. (1974–77). Born in Omaha, Neb., he took the name of his stepfather. Educated at the Univ.

Gerald R. Ford

of Michigan and Yale law school, he served in the U.S. House of Representative 1948–73, becoming minority leader in 1965. After Spiro AGNEW resigned as vice president in 1973, Richard NIXON nominated Ford to the post. When the WATERGATE SCANDAL forced Nixon's departure, Ford became the first president who had not been elected to either the vice presidency or the presidency. A month later he pardoned Nixon; to counter widespread outrage, he voluntarily appeared before a House subcommittee to explain his action. Ford's relations with the Democratic Congress were typified by his more than 50 vetoes, of which more than 40 were sustained. In the final days of the Vietnam War in 1975, he ordered an airlift of 237,000 anti-Communist Vietnamese, most of whom came to the U.S. Reaction against Watergate contributed to his defeat by Jimmy CARTER in 1976.

Ford, Harrison (b.1942) U.S. film actor. Born in Chicago, he achieved stardom in George LUCAS's hit *Star Wars* (1977) and its sequels, *The Empire Strikes Back* (1980) and *Return of the Jedi* (1983). He also starred in the adventure film *Raiders of the Lost Ark* (1981) and its sequels (1984, 1989). He played dramatic roles in *Witness* (1985), *Patriot Games* (1992), *Clear and Present Danger* (1994), and *Air Force One* (1997). His rugged good looks and wry charm made him one of the most popular actors of his time.

Ford, Henry (1863–1947) U.S. industrialist and pioneer automobile manufacturer. Born in Wayne Co., Mich., he worked his way up from machinist's apprentice (at age 15) to chief engineer at the Edison Co. in Detroit. He built his first experimental car in 1896. In 1903, with several partners, he formed the FORD MOTOR CO. In 1908 he designed the MODEL T; demand became so great that Ford developed new MASS-PRODUCTION methods, including the first moving ASSEMBLY LINE in 1913. He developed the Model A in 1928 to replace the Model T, and in 1932 he introduced the V-8 engine. He observed an eight-hour workday and

Henry Ford, 1933

paid his workers far above the average, holding that well-paid laborers become the consumers that industrialists require, but strenuously opposed labor unions. As the first to make car ownership affordable to large numbers of Americans, he exerted a vast and permanent influence on American life.

Ford, John *orig.* Sean Aloysius O'Feeney (1895–1973) U.S. film director. Born in Cape Elizabeth, Me., he became a director of early westerns, achieving success with *The Iron Horse* (1924). His distinctive style united action and colorful characterization and reflected his sense of history and his skill in the creation of mood, shown in such westerns as *Stagecoach* (1939), *My Darling Clementine* (1946), *She Wore*

FG

a Yellow Ribbon (1949), and *The Man Who Shot Liberty Valance* (1962), and in such historical dramas as *Mary of Scotland* (1936) and *Young Mr. Lincoln* (1939). He received Academy Awards for *The Informer* (1935), *The Grapes of Wrath* (1940), *How Green Was My Valley* (1941), *The Quiet Man* (1952), and two wartime documentaries.

Ford, John (1586–1639?) British dramatist. Early in his career he wrote collaboratively with several other playwrights, but his reputation rests on the first four plays he wrote alone: *The Broken Heart*; *The Lover's Melancholy* (1628); *Perkin Warbeck;* and *'Tis Pity She's a Whore*, an eloquently sympathetic story of incestuous lovers that is his best-known work. His revenge tragedies are characterized by scenes of austere beauty, insight into human passions, and poetic diction of a high order.

Ford Motor Co. U.S. automotive corporation. Founded in Detroit in 1903 by Henry FORD, the company introduced the hugely successful MODEL T in 1908 and by 1923 was producing more than half of all U.S. automotive vehicles. Through the Lincoln Motor Co. (acquired in 1922), Ford produced luxury Lincolns and Continentals. After years of declining sales, the Model T was succeeded by the Model A in 1927; other companies such as General Motors took the opportunity to make serious inroads into Ford's dominance. Henry's son Edsel served as president 1919–43. In 1938 the Mercury was introduced. Henry's grandson Henry Ford II led the company 1945–79, reviving its fortunes considerably. Its stock was first publicly traded in 1956. Ford acquired the British Jaguar firm in 1989–90. In 2001, the founder's great-grandson William Clay Ford, Jr. (b.1957) was named CEO.

foreclosure Legal proceeding by which a borrower's rights to a mortgaged property may be extinguished if the borrower fails to live up to the obligations agreed to in the loan contract. The lender may then declare the entire debt due and owing and may seek to satisfy it by foreclosing. Foreclosure is commonly by a court-decreed sale of the property to the highest bidder, who is often the lender. See also MORTGAGE.

Foreign Legion *French* Légion Étrangère. French military corps consisting originally of foreigners but now including many Frenchmen. Founded in 1831 as a highly disciplined professional army to help control French colonies in Africa, it has since been in almost continuous combat, in such places as the Crimea, Mexico, Syria, and Indochina. The new volunteer swears to serve not France but the legion; after serving five years with good conduct, foreign-born soldiers are eligible for French citizenship. Since it keeps a volunteer's past secret, it has been romanticized as a haven for those seeking new identities, including criminals, but most legionnaires are professional soldiers who enjoy combat.

foreign policy Underlying direction of the activities and relationships of one state in its interactions with other states. Development of foreign policy is influenced by domestic considerations, the policies or behavior of other states, or a plan to advance a specific geopolitical design. DIPLOMACY is the tool of foreign policy, and war, alliances, and international trade may all be manifestations of it.

Foreman, George (b.1949) U.S. boxer. Born in Marshall, Texas, he won the Olympic gold medal in 1968. His first world heavyweight title victory was his second-round knockout of Joe Frazier in 1973. He had won all 40 of his professional bouts, many by knockout, before he fell in eight rounds to Muhammad ALI in 1974 in the famous "Rumble in the Jungle" in Kinshasa, Zaire. He retired in 1978, but began a remarkable comeback in 1987 at age 38; he regained the title in ten rounds against Michael Moorer in 1994 to become, at 45, the oldest titleholder ever. He has been an ordained minister since 1977.

forensic medicine Science of applying medical knowledge to legal questions. Its primary tool is AUTOPSY, to identify the dead or determine cause of death. Forensic psychiatry determines the mental health of an individual about to stand trial. Forensic genetics allows paternity to be determined and can identify blood or other tissue samples as coming from a particular person (see DNA FINGERPRINTING). Forensic TOXICOLOGY is concerned with such topics as intentional poisonings and drug use.

forensic psychology Application of psychology to legal issues. In civil and criminal cases, forensic psychologists may evaluate individuals to determine such questions as competency to stand trial, relationship of a mental disorder to an accident or crime, and potential for future dangerous behavior. In addition to conducting interviews and administering tests, they usually gather a forensic history that includes hospital records, police reports, and statements of witnesses. In a child-custody case, a psychologist may be asked to evaluate home environments, parents, and the character of the child.

forest Complex ECOSYSTEM in which trees are the dominant life form. Forests can occur wherever the temperatures rise above 50°F (10°C) in the warmest months and the annual precipitation is more than 8 in. (200 mm). In cool, high-latitude subpolar regions, TAIGA (boreal) forests are dominated by hardy CONIFERS. In more temperate high-latitude climates, mixed forests of both conifers and broad-leaved DECIDUOUS TREES predominate. Broad-leaved deciduous forests develop in midlatitude climates. In humid equatorial climates, tropical RAIN FORESTS develop where the heavy rainfall supports broadleaf EVERGREENS. Forests are among the most complex ecosystems in the world, with extensive vertical layering. Conifer forests have the simplest structure: a tree layer, a shrub layer that is spotty or sometimes absent, and a ground layer covered with LICHENS, MOSSES, and liverworts. Deciduous forests are more complex (the tree canopy is divided into an upper and lower story), and rain-forest canopies are divided into at least three layers. Many forest animals are adapted for vertical movement through the environment. Because food other than ground plants is scarce, many ground-dwelling animals use forests only for shelter. The forest is nature's most efficient ecosystem, with a high rate of PHOTOSYNTHESIS affecting both plant and animal systems in complex organic relationships.

Forest, Lee De See Lee DE FOREST

Forester, C(ecil) S(cott) (1899–1966) British novelist and journalist. He is best known as the creator of the naval officer Horatio Hornblower, whose rise from midshipman to admiral and peer during the Napoleonic Wars is told in 12 novels published 1937–67. Many of his novels were adapted to movies, including *The African Queen* (1935).

forestry Management of forested land (see FOREST), together with associated waters and wasteland, primarily for harvesting timber but also for CONSERVATION and recreation purposes. Forestry is built around the principle of multiple-use land management, though the main objective is to maintain a continuous supply of timber through carefully planned harvest and replacement. The forest manager is also responsible for the application of other land controls, including the protection of wildlife and protection of the forest from weeds, insects, plant diseases, EROSION, and fire. The planned management of forests originated in early medieval Europe. In the 19th cent. private forestry schools were established in Europe; and in 1891 the U.S. government authorized its first reserves of forested land. In the 20th cent. many nations undertook reforestation or afforestation programs.

forge Open furnace for heating METAL ORE and metal for working and forming, or a workshop containing forge hearths and related equipment. From earliest times, smiths heated IRON in forges and formed it by hammering on an anvil. A BELLOWS operated by an assistant or by a foot treadle, and later by a waterwheel or animal power, provided the forced draft for raising the temperature of the fire. Modern forges have mechanically powered bellows or rotary blowers.

forgery In law, the making of a false writing with the intent to defraud. "Writing" need not be handwriting: the law of forgery also covers printing, engraving, and keyboarding. COUNTERFEITING is usually regarded as a specific type of forgery. Checks, negotiable instruments, contracts, wills, and deeds are examples of documents that may be forged. Evidence may also be forged.

forget-me-not Any of about 50 species of plants that make up the genus *Myosotis,* in the borage family, native to temperate Eurasia and N. America and to mountains of the Old

World tropics. Some are favored as garden plants for their clusters of pink flowers which mature to blue.

forging In METALLURGY, the process of shaping METAL and increasing its strength by hammering or pressing. In most forging an upper DIE is forced against a heated workpiece positioned on a stationary lower die. To increase the force of the blow, power is sometimes applied to augment gravity. The number of blows struck is carefully gauged by the operator to give maximum effect with minimum wear on the die. Forging presses employ hydraulic or mechanical pressure instead of blows; the most powerful are capable of up to 50,000 tons of pressure. See also DROP FORGING.

form In the philosophy of PLATO and SOCRATES, an intelligible essence that exists separately from the material world yet is central in its intelligible structure. There was, as Plato put it, a "place accessible to the intelligence," the realm of forms, which has a hierarchical order, the highest level being that of the form of the good. Whereas the physical world, perceived with the senses, is in constant flux and knowledge derived from it is restricted and variable, the realm of forms, apprehensible only by the mind, is eternal and changeless. There are forms of such things as human, stone, shape, color, beauty, and justice, of which the things of this world are only imperfect copies.

formaldehyde \fȯr-'mal-də-ˌhīd\ *or* **methanal** \'me-thə-ˌnal\ Simplest ALDEHYDE. Formaldehyde (37%) in water solution (formalin) is used as a preservative, embalming agent, and disinfectant. Large amounts of formaldehyde are used in the manufacture of various familiar PLASTICS: Bakelite (the first plastic) is the trademark name for formaldehyde and PHENOL POLYMER; Formica is the trademark name for formaldehyde and UREA polymer. Because formaldehyde reacts with PROTEINS, it is used in the tanning industry and for treating various vegetable proteins to render them fibrous.

Formalism *or* **Russian Formalism** Russian school of literary criticism that flourished 1914–28. Making use of the linguistic theories of Ferdinand de SAUSSURE, Formalists were concerned with what technical devices make a literary text literary, apart from its psychological, sociological, biographical, and historical elements. The movement was condemned by the Soviet authorities in 1929 for its lack of political perspective. Later it became influential in the West, notably in NEW CRITICISM and STRUCTURALISM.

formalism See NEW CRITICISM

formal system In LOGIC, a formal language together with a deductive apparatus by which some well-formed formulas can be derived from others. Each formal system has a formal language composed of primitive symbols that figure in certain rules of formation (statements concerning the expressions allowable in the system) and a set of THEOREMS developed by inference from a set of AXIOMS. The primitive symbols are undefined and all other symbols are defined in terms of them, using the AXIOMATIC METHOD. In EUCLIDEAN GEOMETRY, for example, such concepts as "point," "line," and "lies on" are usually posited as primitive terms. From the primitive symbols, certain formulas are defined as well as formed, some of which are listed as axioms; and rules are stated for inferring one formula as a conclusion from one or more other formulas.

Forman, Milos (b.1932) Czech-U.S. film director. After success with the ironic comedies *Loves of a Blonde* (1965) and *The Fireman's Ball* (1967), he moved to the U.S. and applied his light touch to the generation gap in *Taking Off* (1971), then triumphed with *One Flew Over the Cuckoo's Nest* (1975, Academy Award). He directed successful screen adaptations of the musical *Hair* (1979) and *Ragtime* (1981); his later films include *Amadeus* (1984, Academy Award) and *The People vs. Larry Flynt* (1996).

formes fixes \'fȯrm-'fēks\ Principal forms of music and poetry in 14th- and 15th-cent. France. Three forms predominated. The rondeau followed the pattern *ABaAabAB*. (*A* (*a*) and *B* (*b*) represent repeated musical phrases; capital letters indicate repetition of text in a refrain, while lowercase letters indicate new text.) The ballade employed the pattern *aabC*. The virelai used the pattern *AbbaA*. Composers who employed the forms included the TROUVÈRE Adam de la Halle (b.c.1250), Guillaume de MACHAUT, and Guillaume DUFAY.

Formosa See TAIWAN
Formosa Strait See TAIWAN STRAIT
formula weight Sum of the ATOMIC WEIGHTS of all ATOMS in a chemical formula. The term is generally applied to a substance that consists of ions (see IONIC BOND) rather than individual molecules (and thus does not have a MOLECULAR WEIGHT). Such a substance's chemical formula describes the simplest ratio of the number of atoms of the constituent ELEMENTS. See also STOICHIOMETRY.

formwork Mold used to form concrete into structural shapes (beams, columns, slabs, shells) for building. Formwork can be of timber, steel, plastic, or fiberglass. Important for highrise construction is slipforming, whereby a vertical concrete element is continuously cast using a short section of formwork that is repeatedly disassembled and moved upward as each section is finished or that moves slowly and continuously as concrete is being placed.

Forster, E(dward) M(organ) (1879–1970) British writer. His early works include *The Longest Journey* (1907), *A Room with a View* (1908), and his first major success, *Howard's End* (1910), novels that show acute observation of middle-class life and its values. From around 1907 he was a member of the informal BLOOMSBURY GROUP. After periods in India and Alexandria, he wrote his finest novel, *A Passage to India* (1924), examining the failure of human understanding between ethnic and social groups under British rule, His *Aspects of the Novel* (1927) is a classic discussion of aesthetics and the creative process.

E. M. Forster

forsythia \fȯr-'si-thē-ə\ Any of the seven species of ornamental shrubs that make up the genus *Forsythia,* in the OLIVE family, native to E Europe and E. Asia. In some species the yellow flowers borne along the stems appear before the leaves in early spring. Common forsythia (*F. intermedia*) has arching stems to about 20 ft (6 m) and bright yellow flowers.

Fortas, Abe (1910–1982) U.S. jurist. Born in Memphis, he cofounded a major Washington, D.C. law firm in 1946, and represented some of the largest U.S. corporations. In 1963 he successfully argued the case of *Gideon vs. Wainwright,* which established the right of the accused to counsel in criminal trials, regardless of ability to pay. Nominated to the U.S. Supreme Court in 1965, he failed to win Senate approval to become chief justice in 1968, and he resigned in 1969 following a threat of impeachment over securities dealings.

Fort-de-France \ˌfȯr-də-'fräⁿs\ City (pop., 1999: 94,000), capital of MARTINIQUE, West Indies. Located on the island's W coast, it was formerly called Fort-Royal, and has been Martinique's capital since 1680. Until 1918, when its commercial growth began, its swamps made it notorious for yellow fever. It is the French West Indies' largest town, chief port, and busiest commercial center and has long sheltered the French fleet in the West Indies. Sugarcane, cacao, and rum are exported.

Fortescue \'fȯrt-ə-ˌskyü\, **John** (*later* **Sir John**) (c.1385–1479?) English jurist. As chief justice of the King's Bench from 1442, he was the first to state the basic principle that it is better that the guilty escape than that the innocent be punished. He fled to Scotland after HENRY VI's defeat in 1461. Hoping for a restoration of the House of LANCASTER, he educated Prince Edward in France, and he wrote for Edward's instruction *In Praise of the Laws of England* (c.1470), the first book about law written for the layperson.

Forth River, S central Scotland. It flows east for 116 mi (187 km) from the slopes of Ben Lomond to enter the Firth of Forth, a long estuary on the North Sea. The river has a short highland section and a longer lowland section; the latter, called the Links of Forth, was the site of the Battle of BANNOCKBURN (1314).

FG

Fort Knox U.S. military reservation, N Kentucky, southwest of Louisville. Established in 1918, it became a permanent military post in 1932. The U.S. Gold Bullion Depository was built there in 1936 to hold the bulk of the nation's gold. Since 1940 it has been the U.S. Army Armor Headquarters and the site of associated training schools.

Fort-Lamy See N'DJAMENA

Fort Lauderdale City (pop., 2000: 152,000), SE Florida. It is located on the Atlantic Ocean, 25 mi (45 km) north of MI-AMI. A fort built in 1838 gave its name to the town, established in 1895 and later developed as a shipping center and residential resort. The ATLANTIC INTRACOASTAL WATER-WAY is connected to the city's deepwater port, Port Everglades. The city is interlaced with recreational waterways and has extensive boating facilities.

Fort McHenry Military fort and national monument, BALTI-MORE. During the WAR OF 1812, the British bombarded it in 1814 but failed to capture the city it defended. F. S. KEY witnessed the battle while being held aboard a British ship, and wrote "The Star-Spangled Banner." The fort was used as a federal prison during the AMERICAN CIVIL WAR, then served as a military post. It was named a national monument in 1939.

FORTRAN Computer PROGRAMMING LANGUAGE developed for numerical analysis by John Backus (b.1924) and others at IBM in 1957. For many years it was the most widely used high-level language for scientific and engineering computations, and it is still the language of choice for numerical analysis. It has been revised several times and now includes capabilities for handling structured data, recursions (procedures that call themselves), and other features.

Fort Stanwix, Treaties of (1768, 1784) Agreements by which the IROQUOIS CONFEDERACY ceded land in what is now W Pennsylvania, Kentucky, W. Virginia, and New York, opening vast tracts to white settlement. In 1768 about 3,400 Iroquois gathered at Ft. Stanwix (now Rome), N.Y., to sign a new treaty with the British that replaced the PROCLAMA-TION OF 1763. Weakened by the frontier campaign against them during the American Revolution, the Iroquois were persuaded in 1784 to sign a second treaty (also called the Treaty with the Six Nations), ceding more land.

Fort Sumter National Monument National preserve, CHARLESTON, S.C. Construction of the fort was still in progress when it became the site of the first engagement of the AMERICAN CIVIL WAR, Apr. 12, 1861. The national monument, established in 1948, also includes Ft. Moultrie, site of an American victory against the British (June 28, 1776) in the AMERICAN REVOLUTION, when the fort was called Ft. Sullivan.

Fort Wayne City (pop., 2000: 205,000), NE Indiana. Once the chief town of the Miami Indians, it was the site of a French trading post in the late 17th cent. It was taken by the English (1760) and then by Indians under PONTIAC (1763). A log stockade built in 1794 by Gen. Anthony WAYNE gave the town its name. The Wabash and Erie Canal sparked industrial growth in the 1830s. Fort Wayne now manufactures a range of machinery, including automotive and electrical equipment. Johnny APPLESEED is buried there.

Fort Worth City (pop., 2000: 534,000), N Texas, part of the Dallas–Fort Worth urban complex. Founded in 1849 to repel COMANCHE raids, it was a stopover point for cattle drives on the CHISHOLM TRAIL. It became a cattle-shipping boomtown after the railroad arrived in 1876. Oil finds brought the petroleum-refining industry in 1920, and in 1949 aircraft manufacturing began there, expanded now to include aerospace and electronic equipment.

forum In ancient Roman cities, a centrally located open area surrounded by public buildings and colonnades that served as a multipurpose public gathering place. The forum was an adaptation of the Greek AGORA and ACROPOLIS. In the Roman republic, the *forum Romanum* (the flat space between the Palatine and Capitoline hills) was the site of public meetings, law courts, and gladiatorial games and was lined with shops and open-air markets. Under the Roman empire, it held many of Rome's most imposing temples, basilicas, and monuments. New forums were devoted to judicial or administrative affairs or to trade. Trajan's Forum (2nd cent. A.D.), with its harmonious complex of buildings and court-

yards and its tiers of shops, influenced many subsequent town planners.

Foscolo \ˈfȯs-kō-lō\, **Ugo** orig. Niccolò Foscolo (1778–1827) Italian poet and novelist. His works articulated the feelings of many Italians during the turbulent epoch of the French Revolution, the Napoleonic Wars, and the restoration of Austrian rule. His popular novel *The Last Letters of Jacopo Ortis* (1802) bitterly denounced Napoleon's cession of Venetia to Austria. Among his poems are the patriotic "Dei sepolcri" (1807) and the acclaimed but unfinished *Le grazie*.

Fosse \ˈfȯs-ē\, **Bob** (orig. Robert Louis) (1927–1987) U.S. choreographer and director. Born in Chicago, Fosse began dancing professionally at 13. He won his first Tony award for choreographing the musical *The Pajama Game* (1954) and went on to win six more for such hit shows as *Damn Yankees* (1955) and *Sweet Charity* (1966)—both starring his wife, Gwen Verdon (1925–2000)—as well as *Pippin* (1973) and *Dancin'* (1978). His films included *Cabaret* (1972, Academy Award) and *All That Jazz* (1979).

Fossey, Dian (1932–1985) U.S. zoologist. Born in San Francisco, in 1963 she met Louis LEAKEY, who persuaded her to study the mountain gorilla in Rwanda's Virunga Mtns., where she patiently gathered detailed knowledge of gorilla habits, communication, and social structure. She earned a PhD in 1974 and taught at Cornell Univ. while remaining involved with her Karisoke Research Center in Africa (established in 1967). She recounted her observations in *Gorillas in the Mist* (1983; film, 1988). The drastic measures she took to protect the Virunga gorillas from poachers and farmers apparently led to her being murdered at her campsite.

fossil Remnant, impression, or trace of an animal or plant of a past geologic age that has been preserved in the earth's CRUST. Data from fossils (the fossil record) are the primary source of information about the history of life on the earth. Only a small fraction of ancient organisms are preserved as fossils, and usually only organisms that have a solid skeleton or shell. Unaltered hard parts, such as the shells of clams, are relatively common in sedimentary rocks. The embedding of insects in amber and the preservation of mammoths in ice are rare but striking examples of the fossil preservation of soft tissues. Traces of organisms may also occur as tracks, trails, or even borings.

fossil fuel Any material of biologic origin occurring within the earth's crust that can be used as a source of energy. Fossil fuels include COAL, PETROLEUM, and SHALE OIL. They all contain carbon and were formed as a result of geologic processes acting on the remains of (mostly) plants and animals that lived and died hundreds of millions of years ago. All fossil fuels can be burned to provide heat. They supply nearly 90% of all the energy used by industrially developed nations. Being nonrenewable, all fossil fuels are being steadily depleted.

Foster, Jodie (orig. Alicia Christian) (b.1962) U.S. film actress and director. Born in Los Angeles, she was a professional actress by age 3 and played child roles in family films. She earned praise as a teenage prostitute in *Taxi Driver* (1976). As an adult she won acclaim in such films as *The Accused* (1988, Academy Award) and *The Silence of the Lambs* (1991, Academy Award). She turned to directing with *Little Man Tate* (1991) and *Home for the Holidays* (1995).

Foster, Stephen (Collins) (1826–1864) U.S. songwriter. Born in Lawrenceville, Penn., Foster began writing songs as a child. His musical influences came in part from black church services he attended with the family's servant. In 1848 "Oh! Susanna" became an international hit. He was commissioned to write songs for Edwin P. Christy's minstrel show; his "Old Folks at Home" became one of the most popular songs of the century. In 1857, drinking heavily and in financial difficulties, he sold all rights to his future songs to his publishers for about $1,900. He died penniless at 37 from a fall in a Bowery hotel. He left about 200 songs, including "Camptown Races," "My Old Kentucky Home," and "Jeanie with the Light Brown Hair," and is regarded as the greatest American songwriter of the 19th cent.

Foster, William Z(ebulon) (1881–1961) U.S. labor organizer. Born in Taunton, Mass., he came to national prominence as an AFL leader in the steel strike of 1919. In 1921 the Soviet

Communists chose him as a leader of the U.S. Communist Party, and he ran as its presidential candidate in 1924, 1928, and 1932 on a platform that envisioned a workers' republic. Ill health forced his resignation in 1932. Soviet dissatisfaction with his successor, Earl BROWDER, brought him back as chairman (1945–56) until he fell from favor.

Foucault \fü-ˈkō\, **Jean (-Bernard-Léon)** (1819–1868) French physicist. In 1850 he measured the speed of light with extreme accuracy. He invented the FOUCAULT PENDULUM and also a simple but extremely accurate method of testing telescope mirrors for surface defects.

Foucault \fü-ˈkō\, **Michel (Paul)** (1926–1984) French structuralist philosopher and historian. He examined the codes by which societies operate, especially the "principles of exclusion" (such as the distinctions between the sane and the insane) by which a society defines itself, and theorized that, by surveying social attitudes in relation to institutions such as asylums, hospitals, and prisons, one can examine the development and omnipresence of power. His books, including *Madness and Civilization* (1961), *The Order of Things* (1966), *Discipline and Punish* (1975), and *History of Sexuality* (3 vols., 1976–84), made him one of the most influential intellectuals of his time.

Foucault pendulum \fü-ˈkō\ Large PENDULUM that is free to swing in any direction. As it swings, the earth rotates beneath it, so its perpendicular plane of swing rotates in relation to the earth's surface. Devised by Jean FOUCAULT in 1851, it provided the first laboratory demonstration that the earth spins on its axis. A Foucault pendulum always rotates clockwise in the Northern Hemisphere and counterclockwise in the Southern Hemisphere (a consequence of the CORIOLIS FORCE); at the equator, it does not rotate.

Fouché \fü-ˈshā\, **Joseph** *later* duc (Duke) d'Otrante (1758?–1820) French police organizer. In the French Revolution, he was sent on missions to the provinces to ensure their loyalty, and in Lyon he ordered the massacre of rebels. Minister of police from 1799, he supported NAPOLEON's coup and subsequently organized the secret police. Having intrigued against Napoleon from 1807, he was dismissed in 1809, but was brought back several times to undertake missions for Napoleon. He was minister of police during the HUNDRED DAYS, but was ultimately exiled in 1816.

foundation Part of a structural system that supports and anchors the superstructure of a building and transmits its loads directly to the earth. To prevent damage from repeated freeze-thaw cycles, the bottom of the foundation must be below the frost line. The foundations of low-rise residential buildings are nearly all supported on spread footings, wide bases (usually of concrete) that support walls or piers and distribute the load over a greater area. A concrete grade beam supported by isolated footings, piers, or piles may be placed at ground level, especially in a building without a basement, to support the exterior wall. Spread footings are also used—in greatly enlarged form—for high-rise buildings. Other systems for supporting heavy loads include piles, concrete CAISSON columns, and building directly on exposed rock.

foundation Nongovernmental, nonprofit organization, with assets provided by donors and income expended for socially useful purposes. Foundations can be traced back to ancient Greece. The late 19th cent. first saw the establishment of large foundations with broad purposes and great freedom of action, usually originating in the fortunes of wealthy industrialists. Notable examples include the SMITHSONIAN INSTITUTION (1846), the Carnegie Corp. of New York (1911), the Rockefeller Foundation (1913), and the Ford Foundation (1936), the third-largest in the world.

founder principle In genetics, the principle whereby a daughter or migrant population may differ in genetic composition from its parent population because the founders of the daughter population were not a representative sample of the parent population. For example, if only blue-eyed inhabitants of a town whose residents included brown-eyed people decided to found a new town, their descendants would all be blue-eyed. See also GENETIC DRIFT.

founding Process of pouring molten metal into a MOLD. When the metal solidifies, the result is a CASTING, a metal object conforming to that shape. Multitudinous metal objects are molded at some point during their manufacture. Modern foundries are characterized by a high degree of mechanization, automation, and robotics; microprocessors accurately control the automated systems. Advances in chemical binders have resulted in stronger molds and cores and in more accurate castings. Accuracy and purity are increased in vacuum conditions.

fountain Artificially produced jet of water, and the structure from which it rises. Fountains have been an important feature of landscape design from ancient times. They reached their peak in the Renaissance and baroque era, with designs in which sculpture became prominent (e.g., Rome's Trevi Fountain). Supplying water through conduits to multiple fountains, as at the Palace of VERSAILLES, was an important feat. In Muslim countries, fountains for drinking and for ablutions are of great importance, ranging from the simple spout and basin enclosed in a graceful niche to richly decorated pavilions.

Fouquet \fü-ˈke\, **Jean** (c.1420–1481) French painter. A trip to Rome in the 1440s exposed him to Italian Renaissance art, which influenced his N European style. His most famous works were produced for Charles VII's secretary, Étienne Chevalier, and include a large *Book of Hours* with some 60 full-page miniatures and a diptych from Notre-Dame at Melun (c.1450). In 1475 he became royal painter to LOUIS XI. He broadened the range of miniature painting to include vast panoramas of architecture and landscape and made brilliant use of aerial perspective and color tonality. He was the preeminent French painter of the 15th cent.

Fouquet \fü-ˈke\, **Nicolas** (1615–1680) French finance minister (1653–61). A wealthy supporter of Cardinal MAZARIN and LOUIS XIV's government during the FRONDE, in 1653 he was appointed superintendent of finance. After Mazarin's death (1661), J.-B. COLBERT sought to succeed Fouquet by destroying his reputation with the king. Fouquet was arrested for embezzlement, while Colbert suppressed papers that would have absolved him. In 1664 he was imprisoned in the fortress of Pignerol, where he died.

Four Books *Chinese* Sishu. Ancient Confucian texts used as the basis of study for civil-service examinations (see CHINESE EXAMINATION SYSTEM) in China 1313–1905. They served as an introduction to CONFUCIANISM and were traditionally studied before the more difficult FIVE CLASSICS. The texts are *Da xue* ("Great Learning"); *Zhong yong* ("Doctrine of the Mean"); the *Analects* (see *LUNYU*), deemed the most reliable source of Confucius's teachings; and *MENCIUS*.

Fourdrinier machine \ˌför-drə-ˈnir\ Machine for producing PAPER, paperboard, and other fiberboards. A moving endless belt of wire or plastic screen receives a mixture of pulp and water and allows excess water to drain off, forming a continuous sheet for further drying by suction, pressure, and heat. CALENDERING smooths and finishes the surface. The first machine to produce a continuous web (roll), the Fourdrinier machine was patented in France in 1799 by Louis Robert and later improved in England by Henry (1766–1854) and Sealy (d.1847) Fourdrinier. With further improvements, it is still in use today.

Four Freedoms Essential social and political objectives described by Pres. Franklin ROOSEVELT in his State of the Union message in January 1941: freedom of speech, freedom of religion, freedom from want, and freedom from fear of physical aggression (through a "worldwide reduction in armaments"). In August 1941 he and Winston CHURCHILL included the four freedoms in the Atlantic Charter.

Four Horsemen Name given by the sportswriter Grantland Rice to the backfield of the Univ. of NOTRE DAME's undefeated football team of 1924: Harry Stuhldreher, Don Miller, Jim Crowley, and Elmer Layden. The team, coached by Knut ROCKNE, lost only two of 30 games in the years 1922–24.

Fourier \für-ˈyā, *Engl* ˈfür-ē-ˌā\, **(François-Marie-) Charles** (1772–1837) French social theorist. He advocated a reconstruction of society based on communal associations of producers that he felt would distribute wealth more equitably than under capitalism, contributing both to a cooperative lifestyle and to individual self-fulfillment. Cooperative set-

FG

tlements based on Fourierism were started in France and the U.S., including BROOK FARM.

Fourier \\'fur̄-ē-ˌā\, (Jean-Baptiste-) **Joseph** *later* **Baron Fourier** (1768–1830) French mathematician and Egyptologist. While an engineer on Napoleon's Egyptian expedition, he conducted (1798–1801) anthropological investigations and wrote the preface to the monumental *Description de l'Égypte,* whose publication he oversaw (1809–28). In mathematics, he is primarily known for his work in heat conduction (1807–22), for his use of the Fourier series to solve DIFFERENTIAL EQUATIONS, and for the related concept of the Fourier transform.

Joseph Fourier Lithograph by Jules Boilly, 1823

Fourneyron \fur̄-ne-'rōⁿ\, **Benoît** (1802–1867) French inventor of the water TURBINE. His large turbine was capable of 2,300 revolutions per minute, 80% EFFICIENCY, and 60 horsepower, with a wheel 1 ft (30 cm) in diameter weighing 40 lbs (18 kg). Besides its more obvious advantages over the WATERWHEEL, it could be installed horizontally with a vertical shaft. Immediately successful, it powered industry in continental Europe and the U.S., notably the New England textile industry. In 1895 Fourneyron turbines were installed at Niagara Falls to generate electric power.

Four Noble Truths Statement of the basic doctrines of BUDDHISM. The truths are (1) existence is suffering; (2) desire, or thirst, is its cause; (3) the cessation of suffering is possible; and (4) the way to accomplish this is to follow the EIGHTFOLD PATH. Though differently interpreted, these four truths are recognized by virtually all Buddhist schools.

Fourteen Points Outline of proposals by Pres. Woodrow WILSON for a post–World War I peace settlement, given in an address in January 1918. The emphasis on "open covenants of peace, openly arrived at" was proposed to change the usual method of secret diplomacy practiced in Europe. Other points outlined territorial adjustments following the war. The last point called for "a general association of nations," which presaged the LEAGUE OF NATIONS.

Fourth of July See INDEPENDENCE DAY

Fourth Republic Government of the French Republic from 1946–58. The postwar provisional president Charles DE GAULLE resigned in 1946, expecting that public support would bring him back to power with a mandate to impose his constitutional ideas. Instead, the constituent assembly chose the Socialist Félix Gouin. The new constitution was narrowly approved in 1946. The structure of the Fourth Republic was remarkably like that of the THIRD REPUBLIC. The lower house of parliament, renamed the National Assembly, was the locus of power. Shaky coalition cabinets succeeded one another, and the lack of a clear-cut majority hampered coherent action. Political leaders included Georges BIDAULT, Pierre Mendès-France, René PLEVEN, and Robert SCHUMAN.

Fowler, H(enry) W(atson) (1858–1933) English writer. With his brother, he wrote *The King's English* (1906) and *The Concise Oxford Dictionary of Current English* (1911). His major work was *A Dictionary of Modern English Usage* (1926), an alphabetical listing of points of grammar, syntax, style, pronunciation, and punctuation, whose depth, style, and humor have made it a classic.

Fowles, John (Robert) (b.1926) British novelist. His richly allusive and descriptive works combine psychological probings—chiefly of sex and love—with an interest in the social and philosophical context of human behavior. His novels include *The Collector* (1963; film, 1965), about a shy man who kidnaps a girl in a hapless search for love, *The Magus* (1966; film, 1968), and *The French Lieutenant's Woman* (1969; film, 1981), his most famous work, set in Victorian England.

Fox Native American people who traditionally lived in what is now NE Wisconsin. They cultivated corn, beans, and squash and hunted bison on the prairies. Religious life centered on the Grand Medicine Society, whose members enlisted supernatural aid to heal the sick and ensure success in warfare. In the 18th cent. the Fox joined with the SAUK to war against the French and English. Though unconquered, they retreated south to Illinois and later west to Iowa. In 1832 BLACK HAWK led a group of Fox and Sauk in an unsuccessful attempt to return to their Illinois lands. Today most Fox (numbering about 1,500) live in Iowa.

fox Any of various CANINES resembling small to medium-sized, bushy-tailed dogs. Foxes have long fur, pointed ears, relatively short legs, and a narrow snout. They have often been hunted for sport or fur. The name specifically refers to about 10 species of true foxes (genus *Vulpes*), especially the red fox. See also ARCTIC FOX.

Fox, Charles James (1749–1806) British politician. He entered Parliament in 1768 and became leader of the Whigs; he used his brilliant oratorical skills to strongly oppose Britain's policy toward the American colonies. Though almost always in the political opposition, he conducted a vendetta against George III and later William PITT. He served as Britain's first foreign secretary (1782, 1783, 1806). He steered through Parliament a resolution to end the slave trade, and in 1792 an act that restored to juries their right to decide what constituted libel.

Fox, George (1624–1691) English preacher and founder of the Society of FRIENDS, or Quakers. The son of a weaver, he left home at 18 in search of religious experience. Probably beginning as a Puritan, he came to regard personal experience as the true source of authority, placing God-given "inward light," or inspiration, above creeds and Scripture. He traveled the countryside preaching to small groups and establishing congregations. The Society of Friends arose in the 1650s. The Quakers' denunciation of ministers and public officials and their refusal to pay tithes or take oaths led to persecution, and Fox was imprisoned eight times between 1649 and 1673. His *Journal* gives an account of his life and of the rise of Quakerism.

Fox (Quesada), Vicente (b.1942) President of Mexico (from 2000). After graduating from the Ibero-American Univ., he worked for Coca-Cola's Mexican subsidiary, becoming its chief executive (1975–79). He turned to politics in the 1980s, joining the National Action Party (PAN), and was elected governor of Guanajuato state in 1995. Pledging to end government corruption and improve the economy, he won the presidential election in 2000, ending 71 years of rule by the INSTITUTIONAL REVOLUTIONARY PARTY (PRI).

Fox Broadcasting Co. U.S. television broadcasting company. Founded in 1986 by Rupert MURDOCH, it began with 79 affiliated stations that reached 80% of U.S. homes, then gradually expanded to become available across the U.S. Concentrating on shows that appealed to affluent young viewers, it added programming divisions for children, sports, and news in the 1990s.

foxglove Any of 20–30 species of herbaceous plants of the genus *Digitalis,* in the SNAPDRAGON FAMILY, especially *D. purpurea.* Native to Europe, the Mediterranean region, and the Canary Islands, foxgloves typically have a tall stem capped by a one-sided cluster of pendulous, bell-shaped, purple, yellow, or white flowers, often marked with spots within. *D. purpurea* is cultivated as the source of the heart-stimulating drug DIGITALIS.

foxhound Either of two breeds of dogs traditionally kept in packs for FOX HUNTING. The English foxhound stands 21–25 in. (53–64 cm) high and weighs 60–70 lbs (27–32 kg). It has a short coat, usually of black, tan, and white. The American foxhound is more

Foxglove (*Digitalis*)

lightly built. It is the oldest breed of sporting dog in the U.S., developed from English foxhounds beginning in 1650. Both breeds display strength, speed, and versatility; they are rarely kept as house pets.

fox hunting Chase of a fox by horsemen with a pack of hounds. In England, home of the sport, it dates from at least the 15th cent. Modern fox hunting became popular among the upper classes in the 19th cent. A hunt is led by a master; the dogs (usually 15–20 matched pairs) are controlled by the huntsman. The hunt may take place on any grounds (woodlands, heath, or fields) where a fox is suspected to be. The riders, in distinctive red uniforms, meet at a host's house, and the hounds are sent off to search out the fox; when it is found, the hunt begins. The fox is chased until it either escapes or is cornered and killed. From a peak in popularity before World War I, the sport has declined because of the decreasing number of large estates and growing popular opposition; in 2002 it was banned in Scotland.

Foyt, A(nthony) J(oseph), Jr. (b.1935) U.S. automobile racing driver. Born in Houston, he began racing at 17. The first four-time winner of the Indianapolis 500 (1961, 1964, 1967, 1977), he is the only driver to have won the Indy 500, the Daytona 500, and the Le Mans Grand Prix. He was national champion stock-car driver in 1968, 1978, and 1979.

fractal geometry In mathematics, the study of complex shapes with the property of self-similarity. A self-similar object's component parts resemble the whole, so that each part, and each of *its* parts, when magnified, looks roughly like the whole object (examples include snowflakes and tree bark). The term *fractal* was coined by Benoit MANDELBROT in 1975. Fractals can describe irregularly shaped objects or spatially nonuniform phenomena that cannot be described by EUCLIDEAN GEOMETRY. Fractal simulations have been used to plot the distributions of galactic clusters and to generate lifelike images of complicated, irregular natural objects, including rugged terrains and branching patterns. See also CHAOS THEORY.

fraction In arithmetic, a number expressed as a quotient, in which a numerator is divided by a denominator. In a simple fraction, both are INTEGERS. A complex fraction has a fraction in the numerator or denominator. In a proper fraction, the numerator is less than the denominator. If the numerator is greater, it is called an improper fraction. Any fraction can be written in decimal form by dividing the numerator by the denominator. The result may end at some point, or one or more digits may repeat without end.

fractional reserve system Banking system followed by all modern banks, in which less than 100% of bank deposits are held in the bank. The vast majority of the deposits are invested in loans and securities to earn income for the bank, and interest paid on deposits comes from this income. A bank needs a reserve because, on a given day, the amount of money it takes in may be less than what it must pay out. In the U.S., reserve requirements are established both by the FEDERAL RESERVE SYSTEM and by state banking authorities. When an individual bank needs more reserves, it can call in loans, sell financial assets, or borrow them either from the Federal Reserve at the DISCOUNT RATE or from other banks at what is known as the Federal funds rate.

fracture Break in a BONE, caused by sudden or repeated stress. It causes pain, tenderness, and inability to use the part with the fracture. The site appears deformed, swollen, and discolored, and the bone moves in abnormal ways. It must be protected from weight bearing and movement between the broken ends while it heals. Complications include failure to heal, healing in the wrong position, and loss of function despite good healing. See also OSTEOPOROSIS.

fracture zone, submarine See SUBMARINE FRACTURE ZONE

Fragonard \frä-gȯ-'när\, **Jean-Honoré** (1732–1806) French painter. He studied with François BOUCHER in Paris and subsequently won a Prix de Rome; while in Italy (1756–61) he executed many sketches of the countryside, especially the gardens at the Villa d'Este. In 1765 his large historical painting *Coresus Sacrifices Himself to Save Callirhoë* won him election to the French Royal Academy. He soon abandoned this style to concentrate on landscapes, portraits, and the decorative, semierotic outdoor party scenes for which he became famous (e.g., *The Swing*, c.1766). After 1767 he worked primarily for private patrons. His close associations with royalty made his work unacceptable during the French Revolution, and he lost patrons and his livelihood. His works, with those of Boucher, epitomize the Rococo period.

frambesia See YAWS

Frame, Janet *in full* Janet Paterson Frame Clutha (b.1924) New Zealand novelist, short-story writer, and poet. Her first book was the story collection *The Lagoon* (1951). Several times committed to mental institutions, she narrowly escaped undergoing a frontal lobotomy. Her novel *Owls Do Cry* (1957) investigates sanity and madness. Her many other novels, several of which draw on Maori legends, include *Scented Gardens for the Blind* (1963) and *The Carpathians* (1988). Her memoirs include *An Angel at My Table* (1984).

framed structure *or* **frame structure** Structure supported mainly by a skeleton, or frame, of wood, steel, or reinforced concrete rather than by load-bearing walls. Rigid frames have fixed joints that help resist lateral forces; other frames require diagonal bracing or shear walls and diaphragms for lateral stability. Heavy timber framing was the most common type of construction in E Asia and N Europe from prehistoric times to the mid-19th cent. It was supplanted by the balloon frame and the platform frame (see LIGHT-FRAME CONSTRUCTION). The strength of steel framing made possible buildings with longer spans. Concrete frames impart

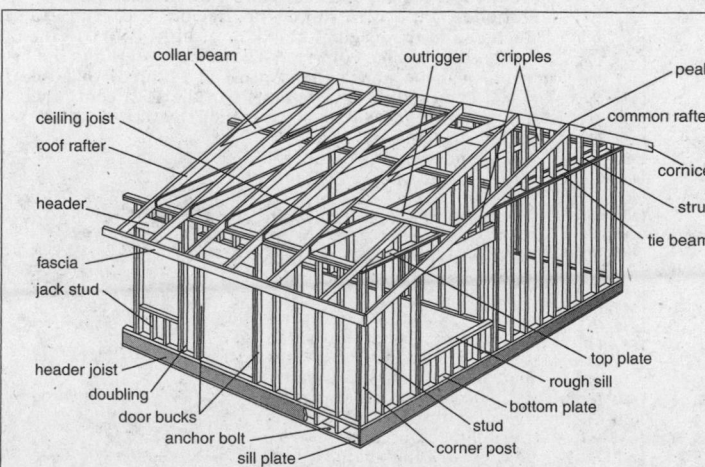

collar beam · outrigger · cripples · peak · ceiling joist · common rafter · roof rafter · cornice · header · strut · tie beam · fascia · jack stud · header joist · doubling · door bucks · anchor bolt · sill plate · corner post · stud · bottom plate · rough sill · top plate

Framed structure Frame of a simple wooden frame house. The frame's most important elements are the studs (uprights to which sheathing, paneling, or laths are fastened), joists (small horizontal timbers that support a floor or ceiling), and rafters (parallel beams that support a roof). The frame is usually built from 2″ × 4″ pieces of lumber ("two-by-fours"); heavier lumber is used for joists and other supporting timbers. Framed structures traditionally were constructed individually at each house site; today framing is usually mass-produced in sections and assembled on site. The lightweight wood-frame structure remains popular today in residential construction.

FG

greater rigidity and continuity; such advances as the shear wall and slipforming have made concrete a serious competitor with steel in high-rise structures.

frame of reference See REFERENCE FRAME

France *officially* **French Republic** *French* **République Française** \rä-pǖ-'blēk-fräⁿ-'sez\ Republic, W Europe. It includes the principality of MONACO, and the island of CORSICA. Area: 210,026 sq mi (543,965 sq km). Population

FRANCE

Scale 1: 18,620,000
0   80   160 mi
0   80   160   240 km

(2000): 58,835,000. Capital: PARIS. The people are mainly French. Language: French (official). Religions: Roman Catholicism (three-fourths), Islam, Protestantism. Currency: euro. It has extensive plains, rivers, and a number of mountain ranges, including the PYRENEES and the ALPS. France's climate is generally moderate. About three-fifths of the land is suitable for agriculture, and forests, largely unexploited, cover about one-fourth of the area. France has a developed, mixed economy with a preponderance of small

firms. Its chief of state is the president, while the head of government is the prime minister; the legislature consists of two houses. It is one of the major economic powers of the world and was a founding member of the European Community (see EUROPEAN UNION). Culturally, France has enjoyed a significant role in the world from the early Middle Ages. Archaeological excavations in France indicate continuous settlement from Paleolithic times. Around 1200 B.C. the Gauls migrated into the area and in 600 B.C. Ionian Greeks established several settlements, including one at MARSEILLE. Julius CAESAR completed the Roman conquest of Gaul in 50 B.C. During the 6th cent. A.D., the Salian FRANKS ruled; by the 8th cent. power had passed to the CAROLINGIANS, the greatest of whom was CHARLEMAGNE. The HUNDRED YEARS' WAR (1337–1453) resulted in the return to France of land that had been held by the British; by the end of the 15th cent., France approximated its modern boundaries. The 16th cent. was marked by the Wars of RELIGION between Protestants (HUGUENOTS) and Roman Catholics. HENRY IV's Edict of NANTES (1598) granted substantial religious toleration, but this was revoked in 1685 by LOUIS XIV, who helped to raise monarchical absolutism to new heights. In 1789 the FRENCH REVOLUTION proclaimed the rights of the individual and destroyed the ANCIEN REGIME. NAPOLEON ruled from 1799 to 1814, after which a limited monarchy was restored until 1871, when the THIRD REPUBLIC was created. World War I (1914–18) ravaged the N part of France. After Nazi Germany's invasion during World War II, the collaborationist VICHY FRANCE regime governed. Liberated by Allied and Free French forces in 1944, France restored parliamentary democracy under the FOURTH REPUBLIC. A costly war in Indochina (see INDOCHINA WARS) and rising nationalism in French colonies during the 1950s overwhelmed the Fourth Republic. The FIFTH REPUBLIC was established in 1958 under Charles DE GAULLE, who presided over the dissolution of most of France's overseas colonies (see ALGERIAN WAR, FRENCH EQUATORIAL AFRICA, FRENCH W. AFRICA). In 1981 France elected its first Socialist president, François MITTERRAND. During the 1990s the French government, balancing right- and left-wing forces, moved toward solidifying European unity.

France \'fräⁿs\, **Anatole** *orig.* Jacques-Anatole-François Thibault (1844–1924) French novelist and critic. His ironic and urbane skepticism appeared in his early novels, including *Le crime de Sylvestre Bonnard* (1881). Later he introduced both bitter satire and humanitarian concerns into many works, such as the tetralogy *L'histoire contemporaine* (1897–1901). He was an influential supporter of Alfred DREYFUS. The comedy *Crainquebille* (1903) proclaims the hostility toward the bourgeois order that led him to embrace socialism. He won the Nobel Prize in 1921.

Francesca, Piero della See PIERO DELLA FRANCESCA

Franche-Comté \fräⁿsh-kôⁿ-'tā\ Region, E central France. Included in the original kingdom of BURGUNDY in the 5th cent. A.D., and part of the HOLY ROMAN EMPIRE in the 11th cent., it came under the control of Philip II the Bold in 1384. It passed to MAXIMILIAN I in the 15th cent., then to the Spanish HABSBURGS. Occupied by LOUIS IX, it was ceded to him by Spain in 1678, and was a province of France until the 1789 Revolution.

Francis I *French* **François** \fräⁿ-'swä\ (1494–1547) King of France (1515–47). Son-in-law of LOUIS XII, Francis succeeded to the throne in 1515. In the ITALIAN WARS, he recovered the Duchy of Milan (1516). He was a Renaissance patron of the arts, a humanist, and a popular king who traveled throughout France, curtailing abuses by nobles and providing games and processions for the people. When CHARLES V was elected

Francis I Portrait after a drawing by Jean Clouet

French Monarchs

Carolingian dynasty		Philip III	1270–85
Charlemagne	768–814	Philip IV	1285–1314
Louis I	840–43	Louis X	1314–16
Charles II	843–77	John I	1316
Louis II	877–79	Philip V	1316–22
Louis III	879–82	Charles IV	1322–28
Carloman	879–84	*Valois dynasty*	
Charles (III)	884–87	Philip VI	1328–50
Robertian (Capetian) dynasty		John II	1350–64
Eudes	888–98	Charles V	1364–80
Carolingian dynasty		Charles VI	1380–1422
Charles III	893/98–923	Charles VII	1422–61
Robertian (Capetian) dynasty		Louis XI	1461–83
Robert I	922–23	Charles VIII	1483–98
Rudolf	923–36	*Valois dynasty (Orléans branch)*	
Carolingian dynasty		Louis XII	1498–1515
Louis IV	936–54	*Valois dynasty (Angoulême branch)*	
Lothair	954–86	Francis I	1515–47
Louis V	986–87	Henry II	1547–59
Capetian dynasty		Francis II	1559–60
Hugh Capet	987–96	Charles IX	1560–74
Robert II	996–1031	Henry III	1574–89
Henry I	1031–60	*House of Bourbon*	
Philip I	1060–1108	Henry IV	1589–1610
Louis VI	1108–37	Louis XIII	1610–43
Louis VII	1137–80	Louis XIV	1643–1715
Philip II	1180–1223	Louis XV	1715–74
Louis VIII	1223–26	Louis XVI	1774–92
Louis IX (St. Louis)	1226–70	Louis (XVII)	1793–95

emperor, his lands encircled France. Francis vainly sought an alliance with HENRY VIII, then waged a series of wars with Charles from 1521. Taken captive in 1525, he refused to accede to Charles's exorbitant demands; a treaty was concluded in 1526. The war with Charles resumed in 1536, and one of Francis's last diplomatic achievements was an alliance with the Turks against the emperor.

Francis I *German* **Franz** (1708–1765) Holy Roman emperor (1745–65). The son of the duke of Lorraine, in 1736 he married MARIA THERESA, heiress to Emperor CHARLES VI, who agreed to the marriage on the condition that Francis cede Lorraine to STANISLAW I. He served with Maria Theresa as coregent (1740–45), and was elected emperor during the War of the AUSTRIAN SUCCESSION. He was overshadowed by his wife during his rule.

Francis II *German* **Franz** (1768–1835) Last Holy Roman emperor (1792–1806), and emperor of Austria as Francis I (1804–35). He succeeded his father, LEOPOLD II, in 1792. Twice defeated by France, he elevated Austria to an empire (1804) soon after NAPOLEON made himself emperor of France. Napoleon dictated the dissolution of the Holy Roman Empire, and Francis abdicated in 1806. Though forced by reasons of state to marry his daughter MARIE-LOUISE to Napoleon in 1810, Francis helped destroy Napoleon's power in battles in 1813–14. After the Congress of VIENNA (1815), he supported his chief minister, Klemens von METTERNICH, in instituting a conservative and restrictive political system in Germany and Europe.

Francis II *Italian* **Francesco** \frän-'chä-skō\ (1836–1894) King of the Two SICILIES (1859–60). He succeeded his father, Ferdinand II, in 1859 and rejected proposals by Count CAVOUR that he join in the war against Austria and grant liberal reforms. Alarmed by the invasion of Sicily by Giuseppe GARIBALDI in 1860, Francis capitulated to the liberals in his kingdom, granting freedom of the press and promising new elections, but it was too late to save the monarchy. The Bourbon forces were defeated by Garibaldi and Francis was deposed by a plebiscite.

Franciscan Member of a Christian religious order founded in 1209 by St. FRANCIS OF ASSISI. The Franciscans actually consist of three orders. The first comprises priests and lay brothers who have sworn to a life of prayer, preaching, and penance. The second (founded 1212) consists of cloistered nuns known as the Poor Clares. The third consists of religious members and laypersons who observe Franciscan principles in teaching, charity, and social service. The friars, who owned no property, wandered and preached among the people, helping the poor and sick. Their impact was immense; within 10 years they numbered 5,000. After the death of St. Francis in 1226, the order was divided by conflicts over the vow of poverty. Though continuing dissent led to divisions of the order into the 19th cent., the Franciscans remain the largest Roman Catholic religious order.

Francis de Sales, St. (1567–1622) Roman Catholic bishop of Geneva and Doctor of the Church. He was consecrated bishop of Geneva in 1602. In 1610, with St. Jane Frances de Chantal, he founded the Visitation of Holy Mary (the Visitation Nuns), a teaching order. His *Introduction to a Devout Life* (1609) argued that spiritual perfection is possible for ordinary individuals busy with worldly affairs. Pius XI named him patron saint of writers.

Francis Ferdinand *German* **Franz Ferdinand** (1863–1914) Archduke of Austria, whose assassination was the immediate cause of WORLD WAR I. Nephew of Emperor FRANCIS JOSEPH, he became heir apparent in 1896. He exerted influence in military matters from 1906 and became inspector general of the army in 1913. While on an official visit in Sarajevo in June 1914, he and his wife were assassinated by a Serb nationalist. In July, Austria declared war against Serbia, precipitating World War I.

Francis Joseph *German* **Franz Josef** (1830–1916) Emperor of Austria (1848–1916) and king of Hungary (1867–1916). He became emperor after the abdication of his uncle, FERDINAND I, and soon achieved a powerful position for Austria. His harsh, absolutist rule produced a strong central government but also led to rioting and an assassination attempt. Following Austria's defeat by Prussia in the SEVEN WEEKS' WAR (1866), he responded to Hungarian national

unrest by accepting the COMPROMISE OF 1867. He later formed the Triple Alliance (1882) with Prussian-led Germany and Italy. In 1898 his wife was assassinated, and in 1889 his son and heir apparent RUDOLF died in a suicide love pact. In 1914 his ultimatum to Serbia following the murder of FRANCIS FERDINAND led Austria and Germany into WORLD WAR I.

Francis of Assisi, St. *orig.* Francesco di Pietro di Bernardone (1181/82–1226) Italian saint and founder of the FRANCISCAN religious order. Born into a wealthy family, he experienced a conversion in his early twenties. He sold his property, gave the proceeds to the church, and began a life of poverty and devoutness. He soon attracted followers, and in 1209 INNOCENT III gave approval for the Franciscan order. The Rule of St. Francis stressed the need to imitate the life of Jesus. Francis viewed all nature as a mirror of God and called all creatures his brothers and sisters. In 1212 he allowed formation of an order for women, called the Poor Clares. In 1219 he went to Egypt, preached to the sultan, and visited the holy places of Jerusalem. In 1224 he became the first person to receive the STIGMATA. His influence helped restore popular faith in the church.

Franck \'fräŋk\, **César (Auguste)** (1822–1890) Belgian-French composer. A piano prodigy, he arrived in Paris at 14 to study at the Paris Conservatoire. In 1858 he became organist at the large church of Ste. Clotilde, where he would remain the rest of his life. In 1872 he also became professor of organ at the Conservatoire. His compositions, which tend to be serious, German-influenced, and often religious, include the famous Symphony in D (1888), the oratorio *Les béatitudes* (1879), a piano quintet (1879), a violin sonata (1886), and many works for organ and piano.

Franco \'fräŋ-kō, *Engl* 'fraŋ-kō\, **Francisco** *in full* Francisco Paulino Hermenegildo Teódulo Franco Bahamonde (1892–1975) Spanish general and head of the government of Spain (1939–75). A career army officer, he became army chief of staff in 1935. He joined the insurgents in the SPANISH CIVIL WAR and was named caudillo (head) of the Nationalist forces (1936). In 1937 he reorganized the fascist FALANGE party as the regime's political movement. Though in sympathy with the AXIS POWERS in WORLD WAR II, Spain remained formally neutral, but after the war Franco was ostracized as the "last surviving Fascist dictator." Relations with other nations improved during the COLD WAR, as Franco became a leading anticommunist statesman, his domestic policies moderated, and Spain made great economic progress. Having overseen a referendum in 1947 that made the Spanish state a monarchy, in 1969 he designated Prince JUAN CARLOS as his successor.

Franconia *German* **Franken** Former duchy, S central Germany. A medieval duchy, after A.D. 843 it was the German part of the former CAROLINGIAN empire. After the Carolingian line died out, its duke became the first elected German king as Conrad I. The name Franconia was abolished in 1806, but revived in 1837 by the kingdom of BAVARIA in its subdivisions. It is part of present-day Bavaria state.

Franco–Prussian War *or* **Franco–German War** (1870–71) War in which a coalition of German states led by Prussia defeated France. The immediate cause was the candidacy of Prince Leopold of Hohenzollern-Sigmaringen for the Spanish throne, which raised the possibility of a combination of Prussia and Spain against France. When France tried to block Leopold's candidacy, the Prussian chancellor Otto von BISMARCK published a document insulting the French government to provoke it into declaring war (July 1870). German troops under Gen. Helmuth von MOLTKE, superior in numbers and organization, scored repeated victories. After NAPOLEON III surrendered at the Battle of Sedan (Sept. 2), French resistance was carried on by a new government, which deposed the emperor and established the THIRD REPUBLIC. Paris surrendered, but while treaty negotiations were going on, an insurrection by radicals created the short-lived PARIS COMMUNE. A harsh peace treaty was implemented: Germany annexed Alsace and half of Lorraine, and France was occupied until a large indemnity was paid. WILLIAM I was proclaimed German emperor in 1871. The peace was an unstable one, marked by France's determination to recover Alsace-Lorraine and Germany's mounting imperialism. Their mutual animosity was a driving force that led to WORLD WAR I.

Frank \'fräŋk, *Engl* 'fraŋk\, **Anne(lies Marie)** (1929–1945) German diarist. She was a young Jewish girl who kept a record of the two years her family spent in hiding in Amsterdam to escape Nazi persecution. Discovered in 1944, the family was transported to concentration camps; Anne died of typhus at Bergen-Belsen. Friends found the diary, which her father published as *The Diary of a Young Girl* (1947). Precocious in style and insight, it is a classic of war literature.

Frank, Robert (b.1924) Swiss-U.S. photographer. In the 1940s he worked as a fashion photographer for *Harper's Bazaar* in Paris. He abandoned fashion work in 1947 to travel in the U.S. and S. America and explore the use of the 35-mm camera. His collection *The Americans* (1959), with its gritty, discordant images of 1950s America, had enormous influence and established him as a major figure. His short film *Pull My Daisy* (1959), a collaboration with Jack KEROUAC, became an underground classic.

Frankenthaler, Helen (b.1928) U.S. painter. She studied with Rufino TAMAYO at Bennington College, then returned to her native New York City and joined the Abstract Expressionists. Influenced by Jackson POLLOCK and Arshile GORKY, she developed a style featuring abstract color combinations within large expanses of bare canvas. She perfected the color stain technique, producing diaphanous color by thinning the oils and letting them soak into the unprimed canvas. Though abstract, many of her lyrical paintings (e.g., *Ocean Desert*, 1975) evoke landscapes. Her work influenced the color-field painters Morris LOUIS and Kenneth NOLAND.

Frankfort \'fraŋk-fərt\ City (pop., 2000: 27,000), capital of Kentucky. Located on the Kentucky River, it was founded in 1786 and has been the capital since statehood (1792). Twice it was burned, and twice the larger LOUISVILLE and LEXINGTON tried to become the state capital. Frankfort was retained because of its central location. Part of the BLUEGRASS REGION, it produces tobacco, corn, and Thoroughbred horses.

Frankfurt (am Main) City (pop. 1996: 648,000), W Germany. Located on the MAIN RIVER, it served as a royal residence of the CAROLINGIANS from the 9th cent. through the Middle Ages. It was a free imperial city 1372–1806 and after 1815, and the capital of Germany 1816–66. It was annexed by Prussia in 1866. Its Old Town, once the largest surviving medieval city in Germany, was mostly destroyed in World War II; its red sandstone cathedral, dedicated in 1239, survives. International trade fairs have been held in Frankfurt since 1240; the modern-era annual book, automobile, and computer fairs are popular. Frankfurt produces the high-quality sausages known as frankfurters. It was the birthplace of J. W. von GOETHE.

Frankfurter, Felix (1882–1965) U.S. (Austrian-born) jurist. He emigrated to the U.S. at 12 and graduated from Harvard Law School, where he later taught (1914–39). Secretary of war 1911–13, he advised Woodrow WILSON at the PARIS PEACE CONFERENCE (1919) and counseled Franklin D. ROOSEVELT on NEW DEAL legislation (1933–39). He promoted ZIONISM in the U.S. and helped found the AMERICAN CIVIL LIBERTIES UNION. On the U.S. Supreme Court (1939–62) he became a leading exponent of judicial restraint, holding that judges should adhere closely to precedent and largely disregard their personal opinions; his opinions evince a hands-off attitude toward legislative action and a concern with the integrity of government, sometimes at the expense of individual liberties.

Frankfurt school Group of influential thinkers associated with the Institut für Sozialforschung (Institute for Social Research), founded in Frankfurt in 1923 by Felix J. Weil, Carl Grünberg, Max Horkheimer, and Friedrich Pollock. Closed by the Nazis, it reopened in 1949. Though its founders were neo-Marxians, there is no doctrine common to all those associated with it. Important Frankfurt-school thinkers, influenced by G. W. F. HEGEL, Immanuel KANT, Karl MARX, Wilhelm Dilthey, Friedrich NIETZSCHE, and Sigmund FREUD, include Theodor ADORNO, Walter BENJAMIN, Herbert MARCUSE, and Jürgen Habermas. See also CRITICAL THEORY.

frankincense Fragrant GUM RESIN obtained from trees of the genus *Boswellia* (family Burseraceae), particularly several varieties found in Somalia, Yemen, and Oman. It was used in ancient times in religious rites and in embalming and was one of the gifts of the magi to the infant Jesus. It is used today in incense and fumigants and as a fixative in perfumes.

Franklin, Aretha (b.1942) U.S. popular singer. Her family moved from Memphis to Detroit when she was 2. Her father, C. L. Franklin, was a well-known revivalist preacher, and she made her first gospel recording at 12. At first she performed only on the gospel and "chitlin" circuits, but in 1967 her powerful and fervent voice took the country by storm in a string of soul hits including "I Never Loved a Man," "Respect," "Chain of Fools," "Think," and "Natural Woman." Her later albums include *Amazing Grace* (1972), *Sparkle* (1976), and *Who's Zoomin' Who* (1985). She was the first woman inducted into the Rock and Roll Hall of Fame (1987).

Franklin, Benjamin (1706–1790) American statesman and scientist. Born in Boston, he was apprenticed at 12 to his brother, a printer. In 1723 he moved to Philadelphia, where he founded the *Pennsylvania Gazette* (1730–48) and wrote *Poor Richard's Almanack* (1732–57), whose proverbs and aphorisms emphasized prudence, industry, and honesty. He became prosperous and promoted public services in Philadelphia, including a library, fire department, hospital, and insurance company, and an academy that became the Univ. of PENNSYLVANIA. His inventions included the Franklin stove and bifocal spectacles,

Benjamin Franklin Portrait by J.-S. Duplessis, c.1784

and his experiments led to the invention of the lightning rod. He served as a member of the colonial legislature (1736–51), and represented the colony in England in a dispute over land and taxes (1757–62). His initial belief in a unified colonial government under British rule gradually changed over the issue of taxation. He helped secure repeal of the STAMP ACT. A member of the committee to draft the DECLARATION OF INDEPENDENCE, in 1776 he went to France to seek aid for the AMERICAN REVOLUTION. Lionized by the French, he negotiated loans and military support for the Revolution (1778). In 1781 he helped negotiate a preliminary peace treaty with Britain. As a member of the 1787 Constitutional Convention, he was instrumental in achieving adoption of the U.S. CONSTITUTION. He is regarded as one of the most extraordinary public servants in U.S. history.

Franklin, Rosalind (Elsie) (1920–1958) British biologist. She produced the excellent X-ray diffraction pictures that allowed James WATSON and Francis CRICK to deduce that the three-dimensional form of DNA was a double helix. In studies of the tobacco mosaic virus, she helped show that its RNA is located in its protein rather than in its central cavity, and that this RNA is a single-stranded helix. Her death from cancer at age 37 probably cost her a share of the 1962 Nobel Prize awarded to Watson, Crick, and Maurice WILKINS.

Franks Germanic-speaking people who invaded the W Roman empire in the 5th cent. A.D. They lived east of the Rhine in the 3rd cent., but gained control of N Gaul by 494 and S Gaul by 507; the conversion of their leader, CLOVIS I, to Christianity helped unite them as a people. They established one of the most powerful kingdoms of the early Middle Ages, ruling lands in present-day France (to which they gave their name), Belgium, and W Germany. The MEROVINGIAN DYNASTY to which Clovis belonged was succeeded by the CAROLINGIAN DYNASTY, whose most notable ruler was CHARLEMAGNE. The Frankish kingdom disintegrated in the 10th cent.

Franz Josef See FRANCIS JOSEPH

Franz Josef Land *Russian* **Zemlya Frantsa Iosifa** \zim-'lyä-'frånts-sə-'yô-sə-fə\ Archipelago, NE BARENTS SEA. Consisting of about 190 islands, it is the northernmost territory of Russia, and the most northerly land of the Eastern Hemisphere. With a land area of about 8,000 sq mi (20,720 sq km), the islands are 85% ice-covered. The Soviet Union annexed the islands in 1926.

Fraser, Simon (1776–1862) Canadian (U.S.-born) explorer and fur trader. Born in Bennington, N.Y., he moved to Canada in 1784. He was made a partner in the NORTH WEST CO. in 1801. In 1805 he set out to search for more suitable trade routes for the fur company. He discovered a river (later FRASER RIVER) that he mistook for the Columbia River, only realizing his error after having followed its course for over a year. He was arrested in 1817 for his alleged participation in the SEVEN OAKS MASSACRE but acquitted.

Fraser River \'frā-zər, 'frā-zhər\ River, S central British Columbia. Rising in the ROCKY MTNS. near Yellowhead Pass, it flows nearly to the U.S. border, then turns west in a spectacular canyon to empty into the Strait of Georgia south of VANCOUVER; it is 850 mi (1368 km) long. The Cariboo gold rush (1858) took place in the Fraser River basin.

Fratellini family \ˌfra-tə-'lē-nē\ European circus family best known for the Fratellini Brothers clown trio—Paul (1877–1940), François (1879–1951), and Albert (1886–1961). For their unique triple act, Albert designed makeup (high black brows, exaggerated mouth, and bulbous red nose) that influenced many later clowns. The brothers toured in Europe and Russia before joining the Cirque Medrano in Paris, where they were widely admired for their wit and charm. Many of their children became successful clowns, notably Paul's son Victor (1901–1979) and granddaughter Annie (b.1932).

fraternity and sorority In the U.S., student organizations for social or scholastic activities, fraternities being for men and sororities for women. They are usually residential houses, and are often important centers of campus life, though they have earned a reputation for rowdiness. Certain honorary societies, such as Phi Beta Kappa, are also called fraternities. See also SECRET SOCIETY.

fraud In law, the deliberate misrepresentation of fact for the purpose of depriving someone of a valuable possession or legal right. Any omission or concealment that is injurious to another or that allows a person to take unconscionable advantage of another may constitute criminal fraud. The most common type is the obtaining of property by giving a check for which there are insufficient funds in the signer's account. Another is the assumption of someone else's or a fictitious identity with the intent to deceive. Also important are mail and wire fraud. A TORT action based on fraud is sometimes referred to as an action of deceit.

Frazer, James George (*later* **Sir James**) (1854–1941) British anthropologist. Frazer attended Cambridge Univ., where he became a professor and remained the rest of his life. In his seminal work *The Golden Bough* (1890; enlarged to 12 vols., 1911–15), Frazer examined the evolution of modes of thought from the magical to the religious and, finally, to the scientific. His synthesis of the new science of CULTURAL ANTHROPOLOGY with traditional humanistic concerns and his lively descriptions of exotic cultural beliefs and practices had a wide influence among men of letters.

Frederick I *German* Friedrich *known as* **Frederick Barbarossa** ("Redbeard") (1123?–1190) German king and Holy Roman Emperor (1152–90). He signed the Treaty of Constance (1153), which promised him the imperial crown in return for his allegiance to the papacy. He launched six military campaigns against N Italy, conquering Milan (1158) but later meeting opposition from the LOMBARD LEAGUE. Excommunicated in 1160, in the Peace of Venice (1177) he acknowledged ALEXANDER III as the true pope, and a treaty with the Lombards was confirmed in 1183. Frederick strengthened the feudal system and curbed the power of the princes by creating a stronger imperial administration. He set out on the Third CRUSADE in 1189 but drowned while crossing a river in Turkey.

Frederick I *German* **Friedrich** \'frē-ˌdrik\ (1657–1713) King of Prussia (1701–13). In 1688 he succeeded his father, FREDERICK WILLIAM, as elector of Brandenburg (as Frederick III). In European politics, Frederick allied himself with Austria, England, and Holland against France. Austria and Prussia signed a secret treaty that permitted Frederick to crown himself king of Prussia, which was obliged to support Austria militarily. Prussia's diverse HOHENZOLLERN lands were turned into provinces, and Frederick freed the new kingdom from imperial control and increased its revenues.

Frederick II *German* Friedrich (1194–1250) King of Sicily (1197–1250), German king (1212–50) and Holy Roman Emperor (1220–50). The grandson of FREDERICK I Barbarossa, he became king of Sicily at age 3 but did not gain control over the strife-ridden country until 1212. Though the planned union of Sicily and Germany alarmed the pope (1220), Frederick negotiated a compromise and was crowned emperor. A delay in departing for the Sixth CRUSADE brought excommunication (1227), later revoked. By 1229 Frederick was king of Jerusalem. On his return he quelled a rebellion in Germany led by his son Henry, who had allied with the LOMBARD LEAGUE. Seeing Frederick as a growing threat to papal authority, GREGORY IX excommunicated him again in 1239; the emperor responded by invading the PAPAL STATES. By the time of his death Frederick had lost much of central Italy, and his support in Germany was uncertain.

Frederick II *German* Friedrich *known as* **Frederick the Great** (1712–1786) King of Prussia (1740–86). The son of FREDERICK WILLIAM I, he suffered an unhappy early life, subject to his father's capricious bullying. On his father's death (1740), the intellectual and artistic Frederick became king and asserted his leadership. He seized parts of Silesia during the War of the AUSTRIAN SUCCESSION, invaded Saxony in 1756, and marched into Bohemia. In the SEVEN YEARS' WAR (1756–63), he and PETER III signed a Russo-Prussian peace treaty that lasted until 1780. The First Partition of POLAND in 1772 led to enormous territorial gains. Austro–Prussian rivalry led to the War of the Bavarian Succession (1778–79), a diplomatic victory for Frederick. Under his leadership Prussia became one of the great states of Europe, with vastly expanded territories and impressive military strength. At home, Frederick espoused the ideas of ENLIGHTENED DESPOTISM and instituted numerous economic, civil, and social reforms.

Frederick III *German* Friedrich (1415–1493) Holy Roman emperor (1452–93) and king of Germany (as Frederick IV) from 1440. He united the Austrian holdings of two rival branches of the HABSBURG DYNASTY (partitioned in 1379), helping lay the foundations for its greatness in European affairs. By marrying his son Maximilian (later MAXIMILIAN I) to Mary, daughter of CHARLES THE BOLD, he obtained a large part of Burgundy and made the Austrians a European power.

Frederick Barbarossa See FREDERICK I (HOLY ROMAN EMPIRE)

Fredericksburg, Battle of (Dec. 13, 1862) Engagement of the AMERICAN CIVIL WAR at Fredericksburg, Va., that resulted in a decisive Confederate victory. Over 120,000 Union troops under Ambrose BURNSIDE were met by an entrenched Confederate force of 78,000 under Robert E. LEE. The Union attack failed with over 12,500 casualties, compared with 5,000 for the Confederates. Burnside was relieved of his command, and the victory restored Confederate morale lost after the defeat at ANTIETAM.

Frederick the Great See FREDERICK II

Frederick William *German* **Friedrich Wilhelm** *known as* **the Great Elector** (1620–1688) Elector of Brandenburg (1640–88). At his accession to the electorship, Brandenburg was ravaged by the THIRTY YEARS' WAR. He maintained neutrality between the warring Swedes and Habsburgs, started to build a standing army, and added to his territories with the Peace of WESTPHALIA (1648). In the First Northern War (1655–60) he gained sovereignty over Prussia. In the complex power struggles in Europe, he shifted allegiance by always joining with the weaker party, hoping to maintain the balance of power. He issued the Edict of Potsdam in 1685, granting asylum to Huguenots expelled from France. When he died, he left a centralized political administration, sound finances, and an efficient army.

Frederick William I *German* **Friedrich Wilhelm** (1688–1740) King of Prussia (1713–40). The son of FREDERICK I, he received valuable military experience in the War of the SPANISH SUCCESSION. As emperor, he built up the army into a strong military presence on the Continent, instituted economic and financial reforms, centralized his administration, encouraged industry and manufacture, and mandated compulsory primary education (1717). He was succeeded by his son, FREDERICK II the Great.

Frederick William II *German* **Friedrich Wilhelm** (1744–1797) King of Prussia (1786–97). He succeeded his uncle FREDERICK II the Great. Prussia expanded under his rule, adding territories in the Partitions of POLAND and acquiring additional German lands. He entered into an Austro-Prussian alliance, chiefly in opposition to the French Revolution, but signed a separate treaty with France in 1795 after defeat in the FRENCH REVOLUTIONARY WARS. Cultural activities, especially music, flourished in his reign.

Frederick William III *German* **Friedrich Wilhelm** (1770–1840) King of Prussia (1797–1840). He pursued a policy of neutrality in the early years of the NAPOLEONIC WARS, then joined the third coalition against France in 1806 and suffered crushing defeat at Jena and Auerstedt. Convinced of the need to make decisive changes, he allowed his chief ministers, K. A. von HARDENBERG and Karl von STEIN, to make domestic reforms, though the state remained absolutist. The Congress of VIENNA confirmed Prussia's acquisition of Westphalia and much of Saxony, but the last 25 years of the king's reign brought a decline in Prussia's fortunes.

Fredericton City (pop., 1995 est.: 49,000), capital of New Brunswick. Originally the site of a French fort (1692), Fredericton was laid out as the provincial capital in 1785. After 1825 Fredericton became a British garrison town, and its reconstructed military compound is a federal historic site. Now primarily an administrative and educational center, it is the seat of the Univ. of New Brunswick.

free association See ASSOCIATION

Freed, Arthur *orig.* Arthur Grossman (1894–1973) U.S. film producer and lyricist. Born in Charleston, S.C., he was hired by MGM in 1929 to write lyrics for musicals, and over the next decade he produced such hits as "Singin' in the Rain," "Temptation," and "You Are My Lucky Star." As a producer, he was largely responsible for the high quality of MGM's musicals of the 1940s and '50s, including *Meet Me in St. Louis* (1944), *Easter Parade* (1948), *An American in Paris* (1951, Academy Award), *Singin' in the Rain* (1952), *Gigi* (1958, Academy Award), and *Bells Are Ringing* (1960).

Freedmen's Bureau (1865–72) U.S. agency established during RECONSTRUCTION to help freed black Americans in their transition to freedom. Directed by Oliver HOWARD, it built hospitals and provided medical assistance to over 1 million freed blacks, built over 1,000 black schools, and helped found black colleges and teacher-training institutes, but had little success in safeguarding civil rights and promoting land redistribution. Congress responded to pressure from white Southerners by terminating the bureau.

freedom of speech Right, as stated in the 1st and 14th Amendments to the U.S. CONSTITUTION, to express information, ideas, and opinions free of government restrictions based on content. It may be restricted if it poses a "clear and present danger," a risk or threat to safety or other public interests that is serious and imminent (hence the prohibitions against falsely setting off a fire alarm or inciting others to violence). Many cases involving freedom of speech and of the press have also concerned DEFAMATION, OBSCENITY, and prior restraint (see PENTAGON PAPERS). See also CENSORSHIP.

free energy Measure of the total combined ENERGIES derived from HEATS of transformation, disorder, and other forms of internal energy (e.g., electrostatic charges). A system will change spontaneously to achieve a lower total free energy. Thus, free energy is the driving force toward equilibrium conditions. The change in free energy between an initial and a final state is useful in evaluating certain ther-modynamic processes and can be used to judge whether transformations will occur spontaneously.

free-enterprise system See CAPITALISM

free fall In mechanics, the state of a body that moves freely in any manner in the presence of gravity. A body in free fall, like the planets in the sun's gravitational field, follows an orbit such that the sum of gravitational and inertial forces equals zero. See also GRAVITATION, NEWTON'S LAWS OF MOTION.

Free French French movement to continue warfare against Germany after France's 1940 defeat in WORLD WAR II. Led by Charles DE GAULLE from London, the Free French Forces gained power in 1942 with the growing RESISTANCE movement in France and the defection of many VICHY FRANCE troops stationed in NW Africa. After a power struggle with Henri Giraud, French commander in chief in N. Africa, by 1944 de Gaulle controlled the entire French war effort. The 300,000 Free French forces took part in the invasions of S France and Normandy and were the first Allied troops to enter Paris.

free-market economy See CAPITALISM

Freemasonry Teachings and practices of the fraternal order of Free and Accepted Masons, the largest worldwide SECRET SOCIETY. Originating with the GUILDS of medieval stonemasons, the organization became an honorary society in the 17th and 18th cent., adopting the rites and trappings of ancient religious orders and chivalric brotherhoods. The first association of lodges was founded in England in 1717, and Freemasonry soon spread through the British Empire. Freemasons took an active role in the American Revolution and later in U.S. politics. Membership is extended only to adult males willing to express belief in a Supreme Being and the immortality of the soul. In Latin countries, the lodges have often attracted freethinkers and anticlerical types; in Anglo-Saxon nations, membership has mostly been drawn from white Protestants.

free radical *or* **radical** MOLECULE containing at least one unpaired ELECTRON. Most molecules contain even numbers of electrons, and their COVALENT BONDS normally consist of shared electron pairs. Cleavage of such bonds produces two free radicals, each with an unpaired electron (in addition to any paired electrons). They may be electrically charged or neutral and are highly reactive and usually short-lived. They combine with one another or with atoms that have unpaired electrons. In reactions with intact molecules, they abstract a part to complete their own electronic structure, generating new radicals, which go on to react with other molecules. Such chain reactions are particularly important in decomposition at high temperatures and in POLYMERIZATION. In the body, oxidized (see OXIDATION-REDUCTION) free radicals can damage tissues. ANTIOXIDANT nutrients (e.g., VITAMIN C and VITAMIN E, SELENIUM) may reduce these effects. Heat, ULTRAVIOLET RADIATION, and ionizing radiation (see RADIATION INJURY) all generate free radicals.

Free Silver Movement U.S. political movement that advocated unlimited coinage of silver. Proponents included owners of W silver mines, farmers who wanted higher crop prices, and debtors who believed an expanded currency would allow them easier payment. An 1878 law required the U.S. Treasury to purchase millions of dollars in silver and coin it. In 1890 Congress again increased silver purchases, and free silver was an objective of the POPULIST MOVEMENT in the 1892 election. In 1893 the amount of gold in the treasury dropped sharply, precipitating a panic, and Congress repealed the act of 1890. In 1896 the Democrats nominated W. J. BRYAN for president and backed free silver. The Republican William MCKINLEY narrowly won; in 1900 a Republican Congress enacted the Gold Standard Act.

Free Soil Party Minor but influential political party that opposed extension of slavery into the W territories. In 1846 proponents of the WILMOT PROVISO and other antislavery factions formed a party; in 1848 it nominated former Pres. Martin VAN BUREN for president. Though Van Buren lost, many party supporters were elected to the U.S. House of Representatives. By 1854 the party was absorbed into the REPUBLICAN PARTY.

Free State See ORANGE FREE STATE

Freetown Capital (pop., 1985: 470,000) and largest city of Sierra Leone. It has the best harbor in W Africa. It was founded in 1787 by an English abolitionist, Granville Sharp (1735–1813), as a haven for freed African slaves from England. Later, more freed slaves from Nova Scotia and runaway slaves from Jamaica settled there. Their descendants, known as Creoles, are now outnumbered by Mende and Temne immigrants from the interior. In 1821 Freetown became the seat of government for Britain's W. African possessions; it became the nation's capital in 1961.

free trade Policy in which a government does not discriminate against imports or interfere with exports. A free-trade policy does not mean that the government abandons all control and taxation of imports and exports, but rather that it avoids hindering international trade with TARIFF barriers, currency restrictions, and import QUOTAS. Free-trade theory is based on Adam SMITH's argument that the division of labor among countries leads to specialization, greater efficiency, and higher production, all best fostered, Smith believed, by allowing nations to make and sell whatever products can compete in an international market.

free verse Poetry organized according to the cadences of speech and image patterns rather than a regular metrical scheme. Its rhythms are based on patterned elements such as sounds, words, phrases, sentences, and paragraphs, rather than on the traditional units of metrical feet (see metrical FOOT). It became current in English poetics in the early 20th cent. See also PROSODY.

free will problem Problem arising from the apparent inconsistency between causal DETERMINISM in nature and the human power or capacity to choose among alternatives or act freely in certain situations. Free will is generally considered a necessary presupposition of moral responsibility, while determinism has (at least until the advent of QUANTUM MECHANICS) been regarded as a necessary presupposition of natural science. Arguments for free will are based on the subjective experience of freedom, on sentiments of guilt, on revealed religion, and on the supposition of responsibility for personal actions that underlies the concepts of law, reward, punishment, and incentive. In theology, free will must be reconciled with such issues as God's foreknowledge.

freezing Method of preserving food in which low temperatures (0°F, −18°C, or lower) are used to inhibit the growth of microorganisms. Used for centuries in cold regions, it was not until the advent of mechanical REFRIGERATION in the mid-19th cent. that the process was commercialized. In the 20th cent., quick (or flash) freezing was developed by Clarence BIRDSEYE. Except for beef and venison, which benefit from aging, meat is frozen right after slaughter. Fruits and vegetables are often frozen in a syrup or vacuum-sealed to exclude air and prevent spoilage.

freezing point Temperature at which a LIQUID becomes a SOLID. The addition of some solids can lower the freezing point of a liquid, as when salt is used to melt ice on frozen surfaces. For pure substances, the freezing point is the same as the MELTING POINT. In mixtures and certain organic compounds, the early solid formation changes the composition of the remaining liquid, usually steadily lowering its freezing point. The freezing point of pure water at standard atmospheric pressure is 32°F (0°C). To change a liquid at its freezing point to a solid at the same temperature, the heat of fusion (see LATENT HEAT) must be removed.

Frege \'frā-gə\, (Friedrich Ludwig) Gottlob (1848–1925) German mathematician and logician, founder of modern mathematical LOGIC. He taught at the Univ. of Jena 1871–1917. In his *Begriffsschrift* (1879), he first presented a modern system of mathematical logic. In discovering the fundamental ideas that have made possible the modern development of logic, and devising the notation of quantifiers and variables, Frege invented an entire discipline. His contributions to the philosophy of language include a highly influential theory of the distinction between sense and reference.

Frei (Montalva) \'frā\, Eduardo (1911–1982) Chilean politician and president (1964–70). A center-left candidate, he offered a moderate program of agrarian reform, economic stabilization, "Chileanization" of U.S.-owned copper interests, and a more equitable distribution of wealth. Though he raised expectations of major change and made marked progress in education for the poor, most of his reform efforts failed, and his administration was plagued by inflation and labor unrest. His son Eduardo Frei Ruiz-Tagle (b.1942) served as president 1994–2000. See also Salvador ALLENDE.

Freiburg (im Breisgau) \'frī-ˌbùrk\ City (pop., 1998 est.: 200,000), SW Germany, on the W slopes of the BLACK FOREST. Chartered in 1120, it was ruled by the HABSBURGS 1368–1806, then passed to BADEN. It was heavily bombed by the Allies during World War II. Since rebuilt, it is now the cultural and economic center of the Black Forest region. The Univ. of Freiburg was founded in 1457.

Fremont City (pop., 2000: 203,000), California. It is located on the SE shore of San Francisco Bay. The site of Mission San José de Guadalupe (founded 1797), the city was formed in 1956 through the amalgamation of five communities. Freeway connections stimulated residential and industrial growth as part of the San Francisco Bay development.

Frémont \'frē-ˌmänt\, John C(harles) (1813–1890) U.S. explorer. Born in Savannah, Ga., in 1838 he helped Jean-Nicolas Nicollet (1786–1843) survey and map the upper Mississippi and Missouri rivers. He later led government survey expeditions to map much of the area between the Mississippi River valley and the Pacific Ocean. In 1845, on an expedition to California, he supported the BEAR FLAG REVOLT. In the Mexican War he helped conquer California, and was appointed its military governor. In a dispute with Gen. Stephen Kearny, he was arrested and court-martialed; he later resigned. He became wealthy in the gold rush and was elected one of California's first U.S. senators (1850–51). He was the Republican Party's unsuccessful presidential candidate in 1856. In the 1870s he embarked on railroad ventures and lost his fortune. He served as governor of Arizona Territory 1878–83.

French, Daniel Chester (1850–1931) U.S. sculptor. Born in Exeter, N.H., he produced his first important commission for the town of Concord, Mass.—the famous statue of *The Minute Man* (1874). The leading American turn-of-the-century sculptor, he was best-known for the seated marble figure of Abraham LINCOLN in the Lincoln Memorial, dedicated in 1922. His other notable public monuments include the equestrian statues of Ulysses S. GRANT in Philadelphia (1898) and George WASHINGTON in Paris (1900).

French and Indian War N. American phase of a war between France and Britain to control colonial territory (1754–63). The war's more complex European phase was the SEVEN YEARS' WAR. Earlier phases of the quest for overseas mastery were KING WILLIAM'S WAR (1689–97), QUEEN ANNE'S WAR (1702–13), and KING GEORGE'S WAR (1744–48). The final N. American dispute was over whether the upper Ohio River valley was a part of the British or the French empire. Though British settlers were the majority, French exploration, trade, and Indian alliances predominated. In 1754 the French ousted a British force at Ft. Necessity, Pa. In 1758 Britain increased aid to its troops and won victories at Louisbourg, Ft. Frontenac, and Ft. Duquesne (Pittsburgh). The final British victory at the Battle of QUEBEC (1759) led to the fall of NEW FRANCE (1760). In the Treaty of PARIS (1763) France ceded its N. American territory to Britain.

French Communist Party French branch of the international communist movement. It was founded in 1920 but did not gain significant influence until it affiliated with Léon BLUM's Popular Front coalition government in 1936. In 1945–68 it won almost 25% of the vote in each election and had a large representation in the National Assembly. In the early 1980s it allied with the Socialist Party. It has since lost many of its traditional working-class supporters.

French Congo See FRENCH EQUATORIAL AFRICA

French East India Co. See French EAST INDIA CO.

French Equatorial Africa *formerly* **French Congo** Former federation of French possessions, W central Africa. It was in existence from 1910 to 1959; its capital was BRAZZAVILLE. With independence in 1960, the former territory of Ubangi-Shari became the Central African Republic and the Republic of Chad; the Middle Congo became the Republic of the Congo; and Gabon became the Republic of Gabon.

FG

French Guiana \gē-'a-nə, gē-'ä-nə\ *French* **Guyane Française** \gwē-'yȧn-fräⁿ-'sez\ Overseas department (pop., 2000: 165,000) of France, NE coast of S. America. It has an area of 33,399 sq mi (86,504 sq km) and is bounded by Brazil, Suriname, and the Atlantic Ocean. The capital is CAYENNE. Most of French Guiana is low-lying, with mountains in the south and a swampy coastal plain. French Guiana's population is mostly Creole. The principal languages are French (official) and Creole; more than 80% of the people are Roman Catholic. The territory was awarded to France in 1667, and the inhabitants were made French citizens after 1877. By 1852 the French were using the territory as a penal colony; the prison on DEVIL'S ISLAND was especially notorious. It became a department of France in 1946; the penal colonies were closed by 1953.

French Guinea See GUINEA

French horn Valved circular horn with a wide bell. It is normally a transposing instrument in F. It has a wide bore and three (sometimes four) rotary valves; its conical mouthpiece produces a mellow tone. Horns long relied on separable crooks—circular lengths of tubing that could be attached and removed rapidly—for music modulating to new keys. The modern horn has built-in crooks in F and B-flat that can be selected rapidly by means of a thumb valve. The symphony orchestra usually includes four horns. Though difficult to play, its tone is widely admired.

French Indochina Former name (until 1950) for the E part of INDOCHINA peninsula, SE Asia. The area, corresponding approximately to the old empire of ANNAM, had been united under French rule by 1898. During World War II it was occupied by Japan, and in 1945 it was made the autonomous state of Vietnam. After the Japanese surrender, the VIET MINH under HO CHI MINH proclaimed the Democratic Republic of Vietnam. Laos and Cambodia were reoccupied by the French. The First INDOCHINA WAR soon erupted. In 1949–50 the French ratified treaties recognizing Vietnam, Laos, and Cambodia as independent states within the French Union. Fighting continued until 1954, when the area achieved true independence after the Geneva Conference.

French language ROMANCE LANGUAGE spoken as a first language by about 72 million people in France, Belgium, Switzerland, Canada, and many former French colonies. French is an official language of more than 25 countries. Its earliest written materials date from the 9th cent. Numerous regional DIALECTS were eventually pushed aside by Francien, the dialect of Paris, adopted as the standard language in the mid-16th cent. French grammar has been greatly simplified from Latin. Nouns do not have cases, and masculine and feminine gender are marked only in the article and adjective. The verb is conjugated for three persons and for singular and plural; though spelled differently, several of these forms are pronounced identically. See also OCCITAN LANGUAGE.

French Polynesia *French* **Polynésie Française** \pȯ-lē-nȧ-'zē-fräⁿ-'sez\ *formerly* **French Oceania** \ˌō-shē-'a-nē-ə\ French overseas territory (pop., 2000: 234,000), in the S Pacific. It comprises 130 islands in five archipelagoes: the SOCIETY ISLANDS, the Tuamotu Archipelago, the Gambier Islands, the MARQUESAS ISLANDS, and the AUSTRAL ISLANDS. TAHITI is the site of the capital, PAPEETE. While the islands cover an area of some 1,550 sq mi (4,000 sq km), more than two-thirds of the population lives on Tahiti. The islands became French protectorates in the 1840s, and in the 1880s the French colony of Oceania was established. It became an overseas territory of France after World War II.

French republican calendar Dating system adopted in 1793 during the FRENCH REVOLUTION that sought to impose a rational scheme that avoided Christian associations. The 12 months each contained three *décades* of 10 days each; the year ended with five (six for leap year) supplementary days. The year began with the autumnal equinox (Sept. 22, 1792) as 1 Vendémiaire, year I. The other autumn months, Brumaire and Frimaire, were followed by Nivôse, Pluviôse, Ventôse, Germinal, Floréal, Prairial, Messidor, Thermidor, and Fructidor (all named for natural phenomena). On Jan. 1, 1806, the Gregorian calendar was reestablished.

French Revolution Movement that shook France between 1787 and 1799 and ended the ANCIEN RÉGIME. Causes included a large underfed population, loss of peasant support for the feudal system, an expanding bourgeoisie excluded from political power, and a fiscal crisis worsened by participation in the AMERICAN REVOLUTION. The efforts of the regime in 1787 to increase taxes levied on the privileged classes initiated a crisis. In response, LOUIS XVI convened the ESTATES-GENERAL in 1789. The king grudgingly concurred in the formation of the NATIONAL ASSEMBLY, but rumors of an "aristocratic conspiracy" led Parisians to seize the BASTILLE on July 14. The assembly drafted a new constitution that introduced the DECLARATION OF THE RIGHTS OF MAN AND OF THE CITIZEN, proclaiming liberty, equality, and fraternity. The Assembly nationalized church lands to pay off the public debt and reorganized the church. The king tried to flee the country, but was apprehended. Newly nationalistic, France declared war on Austria and Prussia in 1792, beginning the FRENCH REVOLUTIONARY WARS. Revolutionaries imprisoned the royal family and massacred nobles and clergy at the Tuileries in 1792. A new assembly, the NATIONAL CONVENTION, abolished the monarchy and established the First Republic in September 1792. Louis XVI was judged and executed for treason on Jan. 21, 1793. The MONTAGNARDS seized power and adopted radical policies that provoked violent reactions, including the Wars of the VENDÉE. Opposition was broken by the REIGN OF TERROR. Military victories in 1794 brought a change in the public mood, and Maximilien ROBESPIERRE was overthrown (see THERMIDORIAN REACTION). Royalists tried to seize power in Paris but were crushed by NAPOLEON in 1795. A new constitution placed executive power in a DIRECTORY, but the war and schisms in the Directory led to disputes that were settled by coups d'état (1799) in which Napoleon declared himself leader of France. See also COMMITTEE OF PUBLIC SAFETY, Georges DANTON, J.-P. MARAT, MARIE-ANTOINETTE, Louis de SAINT-JUST, E.-J. SIEYÈS.

French Revolutionary Wars (1792–99) Series of wars undertaken to defend and then to spread the ideas of the FRENCH REVOLUTION. In 1791 Austria and Prussia called on European rulers to assist LOUIS XVI in reestablishing power. France declared war in 1792 and soon occupied Belgium. The First Coalition (Prussia, Spain, the United Provinces, and Britain) was formed against France in 1793, and in response the French declared a levy on all Frenchmen, creating a massive army. By 1795 France had defeated the allies; Prussia signed a peace treaty, and the Netherlands became the French-influenced Batavian Republic. NAPOLEON took command of the Italian campaign and in 1797 forced Austria to recognize the French-organized republics in N Italy. He then sailed to Egypt to conquer the Ottoman empire, but was defeated by Britain in the Battle of the NILE (1798). Other French forces established republican regimes in Rome, Switzerland (the Helvetic Republic), and Italy (the Parthenopean Republic). The Second Coalition, comprising Britain, Russia, the Ottoman empire, Naples, Portugal, and Austria, was short-lived. By 1799 the danger of foreign intervention was over, but conflict continued in the NAPOLEONIC WARS.

French Socialist Party *in full (1905–69)* French Section of the Workers' International (SFIO). Political party founded in 1905 that supported far-reaching nationalization of the economy. Led by Jean JAURÈS, the party grew quickly, though it suffered a setback with the separation of the left wing into the FRENCH COMMUNIST PARTY (1920). In the 1930s it was central to Léon BLUM's Popular Front government. It participated in the wartime RESISTANCE and emerged after the war as France's second-largest party. In the 1960s it declined. Renamed the Socialist Party in 1969, it was revived by François MITTERRAND, but lost its dominant position in the 1990s.

French Somaliland See DJIBOUTI

French West Africa Former federation of French dependencies, W Africa. It consisted of what are now the independent republics of BENIN, BURKINA FASO, GUINEA, IVORY COAST, MALI, MAURITANIA, NIGER, and SENEGAL. The capital was at DAKAR. The federation was established in 1895 and dissolved 1958–59.

Freneau \fre-'nō\, **Philip (Morin)** (1752–1832) American poet, essayist, and editor. After the outbreak of the revolution he began to write anti-British satire. After two years in the Caribbean, where he wrote such poems as "The Beauties of Santa Cruz" and "The House of Night," he became an active participant in the war. He was captured and imprisoned by the British, an experience he bitterly recounted in the poem *The British Prison-Ship* (1781).

Freon Trademark name for any of several organic compounds containing FLUORINE (fluorocarbons) and sometimes CHLORINE (CHLOROFLUOROCARBONS, or CFCs). Nonflammable, nontoxic, and noncorrosive, they have conveniently low boiling points, which makes them useful as refrigerants. By the mid-1970s, they were in wide use in refrigeration and air conditioning systems, as blowing agents for plastic foams, as fire-extinguishing agents, and in aerosol sprays. Their decomposition in the stratosphere destroys OZONE there (see OZONE LAYER), so most of their uses have been banned.

frequency Number of waves that pass a fixed point per unit time; also, the number of cycles or VIBRATIONS undergone in unit time by a body in periodic motion. Frequency f is the reciprocal of the time T taken to complete one cycle (the period), or $1/T$. The frequency with which earth rotates is once per 24 hours. Frequency is usually expressed in units called hertz (Hz) or cycles per second. The musical PITCH A above middle C (the A string of a violin) has been widely standardized as 440 Hz.

frequency distribution In STATISTICS, a GRAPH or data set organized to show the frequency of occurrence of each possible outcome of a repeatable event observed many times. Simple examples are election returns and test scores listed by percentile. A frequency distribution can be graphed as a HISTOGRAM or pie chart. For large data sets, the stepped graph of a histogram is often approximated by the smooth curve of a distribution function. The famed bell curve or NORMAL DISTRIBUTION is the graph of one such function. Frequency distributions are particularly useful in summarizing large data sets and assigning probabilities.

frequency modulation See FM

Frescobaldi \ˌfres-kə-ˈbäl-dē\, **Girolamo** (1583–1643) Italian composer and organist. In 1608 he became organist at St. Peter's, where he would remain the rest of his life. He was celebrated for both his playing and his diverse and ingenious compositions, including toccatas, ricercars, and canzonas for organ and harpsichord, sacred vocal works, and secular songs. His most famous work is *Fiori musicali* (1635), a large collection of organ music for the mass.

fresco painting Method of wall painting in which water-based pigments are applied to wet, freshly laid lime plaster. The dry-powder colors, when mixed with water, penetrate the surface and become a permanent part of the wall. In *fresco secco*, or "dry" fresco, paint is applied to dry plaster. Early Minoan, Greek, and Roman wall paintings were frescoes. The Italian Renaissance was the greatest period of fresco painting, as seen in the works of CIMABUE, GIOTTO, MASACCIO, Fra ANGELICO, and CORREGGIO. MICHELANGELO's frescoes in the Sistine Chapel and RAPHAEL's in the Vatican are the most famous of all. By the 18th cent., fresco had been largely replaced by oil painting. In the early 20th cent. it was revived by Diego RIVERA and others.

Fresco painting "The Creation of Adam" by Michelangelo, 1508–12

Fresno \ˈfrez-nō\ City (pop., 2000: 427,000), central California. Located in the SAN JOAQUIN RIVER valley, it was settled in 1872 as a station on the Central Pacific Railroad, and be-

came an agricultural community in the 1880s. A marketing and shipping center, it processes cotton, grain, fruits, wines, and dairy products. It is a gateway to resort areas of the SIERRA NEVADAS.

Freud \ˈfróid\, **Anna** (1895–1982) Austrian-British psychiatrist, founder of the field of child psychiatry. Daughter of Sigmund FREUD, she pioneered in developing psychoanalytic theory and practice. In *The Ego and Defense Mechanisms* (1936), she called repression the principal human defense mechanism, giving a strong, new impetus to the role of ego in psychology. She coauthored three books on the effects of war on children. Her thought is summarized in *Normality and Pathology in Childhood* (1968).

Freud, Lucian (b.1922) British (German-born) painter. Grandson of Sigmund FREUD, he moved with his family to London when he was 10. He is known for somber, realistic figure paintings that represent his subjects' raw physical characteristics and inner tensions; his coarse style makes no attempt to idealize its usually nude subjects. Internationally influential in reviving a representational style, in 1993 he was awarded the Order of Merit.

Freud, Sigmund (1856–1939) Austrian neuropsychologist, founder of PSYCHOANALYSIS, and one of the major intellectual figures of the 20th cent. Trained as a neurologist, Freud went to Paris in 1885 to study with J.-M. CHARCOT, whose work on hysteria led Freud to conclude that mental disorders might be caused purely by psychological factors. Returning to Vienna (1886), Freud collaborated with the physician Josef Breuer (1842–1925) in further studies on hysteria, developing such key psychoanalytic concepts as free

Sigmund Freud, 1921

association, the unconscious, resistance (later defense mechanisms), and neurosis. In 1899 he published *The Interpretation of Dreams*, which proposed that dreams are the disguised expression of unconscious wishes. In his controversial *Three Essays on the Theory of Sexuality* (1905), he delineated the complicated stages of psychosexual development (oral, anal, and phallic) and the formation of the Oedipus complex. During World War I, he wrote papers on the workings of the id, ego, and superego. Freud eventually applied his insights to such diverse phenomena as jokes, ethnographic data, religion and mythology, and modern civilization. Works of note include *Totem and Taboo* (1913), *Beyond the Pleasure Principle* (1920), *The Future of an Illusion* (1927), and *Civilization and Its Discontents* (1930). Despite the relentless challenges mounted against virtually all of his ideas, Freud has remained one of the most influential figures in contemporary thought.

Freyja \ˈfrā-yə\ Most important Norse goddess, one of a group of fertility deities called VANIR. She was the goddess of battle and death as well as love and fertility. Half the heroes slain in battle went to her domain, Folkvangr, the other half to ODIN's VALHALLA. She taught a powerful magic to the AESIR, probably involving sexuality.

Freyr \ˈfrār\ or **Frey** \ˈfrā\ Norse god of peace, fertility, rain, and sun, one of a group of fertility deities called VANIR. In pre-Christian Sweden, he was considered the progenitor of the royal line. The best-known story about him told of his love and lust for the giantess Gerd, who was wooed and won for him by his servant. His worship was believed to bring good weather and great wealth.

Frick, Henry Clay (1849–1919) U.S. industrialist. Born in W. Overton, Pa., he began building and operating coke ovens in 1870. From 1889 he was chairman of Carnegie Steel Co., the world's largest manufacturer of steel and coke. He was shot and stabbed in the violent steel strike of 1892 in Homestead, Pa. He was instrumental in forming the U.S. STEEL CORP. in 1901. A noted art collector and philanthropist, he bequeathed the Frick Collection to New York City. See also Andrew CARNEGIE.

friction FORCE that resists sliding or rolling of one solid object over another. Some friction helps us, such as the traction used to walk without slipping. Much friction, though, is undesirable opposition to motion, such as between moving parts of machines. For example, about 20% of the WORK done by an automobile engine is needed to overcome friction between moving parts. Friction is a result of attractive forces between the contact regions of two bodies, and the amount of friction is almost independent of the area of contact.

Friedan, Betty \fri-'dan\ *orig.* Betty Naomi Goldstein (b.1921) U.S. feminist. Born in Peoria, Ill., she attended Smith College before marrying and having children. Her dissatisfaction with her role as housewife prompted her to write *The Feminine Mystique* (1963), which sparked the modern American feminist movement. In 1966 she cofounded the NATIONAL ORGANIZATION FOR WOMEN.

Friedman \'frēd-mən\, **Milton** (b.1912) U.S. conservative economist. Born in Brooklyn, N.Y., he joined the faculty of the Univ. of Chicago in 1946 and became the leading U.S. advocate of MONETARISM. He oversaw the economic transition in Chile after the overthrow of Salvador ALLENDE. In the 1980s his ideas were taken up by Pres. Ronald REAGAN and Britain's Margaret THATCHER. His many books include *Capitalism and Freedom* (1962) and *Free to Choose* (1980), with Rose Friedman, and *A Monetary History of the United States, 1867–1960* (1963) and *Monetary Trends of the United States and the United Kingdom* (1981), with Anna Schwartz. He received the Nobel Prize in 1976.

Friedrich \'frē-drik\, **Caspar David** (1774–1840) German painter. After 1798 he settled in Dresden and began his career as a topographical draftsman. His first important oil painting, *The Cross in the Mountains* (1807–8), achieves an overwhelming sense of isolation. In 1824 he was appointed professor at the Dresden Academy. His vast, mysterious landscapes and seascapes, proclaiming human helplessness against the forces of nature, did much to establish the sublime as a primary focus of the Romantic movement.

Friel \'frēl\, **Brian** (b.1929) Irish dramatist and short-story writer. Born in Northern Ireland, he taught school before settling in Co. Donegal, Ireland. His first dramatic success was *Philadelphia, Here I Come!* (1963). He wrote about the troubles in Northern Ireland in such plays as *The Freedom of the City* (1973) and *Making History* (1988). Such plays as *Translations* (1980) and *Dancing at Lughnasa* (1990, Tony Award; film, 1998) deal with family relationships and their connection to language, customs, and the land. His short-story collections include *The Diviner* (1983).

Friendly, Fred W. *orig.* Ferdinand Friendly Wachenheimer (1915–1998) U.S. broadcast producer and journalist. Born in New York City, he joined CBS and in the 1950s collaborated with E. R. MURROW to produce the radio news series *Hear It Now* and the television series *See It Now*. Friendly also produced *CBS Reports* (1961–71) and many special programs. He served as president of CBS News (1964–66), then taught journalism at Columbia Univ. An outspoken critic of the quality of most TV programming, he helped establish the PBS network.

friendly society Mutual-aid organization formed by individuals to protect members against debts incurred through illness, death, or old age. Friendly societies arose in 17th- and 18th-cent. Europe and became most numerous in the 19th cent. They trace their roots to the medieval GUILDS. In attempting to define the magnitude of the risk against which they guarded and to determine how much members should contribute to meet that risk, friendly societies used what is now the basic principle of INSURANCE.

Friends, Society of *known as* **Quakers** Protestant denomination that arose in England in the mid-17th cent. The movement began with radical English Puritans called Seekers. They took their faith from itinerant preachers such as George FOX, who emphasized "inward light," or inward apprehension of God, as the source of religious authority. Quaker meetings are characterized by patient silence in which members wait for inspiration to speak. The movement grew rapidly after 1650 (when a judge gave them their name because "we bid them tremble at the word of God"), but its members were often persecuted for rejecting the state church and refusing to pay tithes or swear oaths. Some emigrated to America, where they found toleration in Rhode Island and in the Quaker colony of Pennsylvania (see William PENN). Other characteristics of the Quakers were plain speech and dress, pacifism, and opposition to slavery. The group also emphasizes philanthropy, especially aid to refugees and famine victims; Quaker service groups won the 1947 Nobel Peace Prize.

frieze \'frēz\ Any long, narrow, horizontal panel used for decorative purposes around the walls of a room or exterior walls of a building. In Greco-Roman architecture it is a horizontal band, often decorated with relief sculpture, between the architrave and cornice of a building. The most famous decorative frieze is on the outer wall of the PARTHENON in Athens.

frigate bird *or* **man-o'-war bird** Any member of five species of large seabirds constituting the family Fregatidae, found worldwide along tropical and semitropical coasts. Frigate birds have extremely long, slender wings, which span up to about 8 ft (2.3 m), and long, deeply forked tails. Most adult males are all black; most females are marked with white below. The long hooked bill is used to attack and rob other seabirds of their fish. The courting male's throat pouch becomes bright red and greatly inflated. Perhaps the most aerial of all birds except the SWIFTS, frigate birds land only to sleep or tend the nest.

Great frigate bird (*Fregata minor*)

Frigg \'frig\ *or* **Friia** \'frē-ə\ Norse goddess, the wife of ODIN and mother of BALDER. She was considered the patron of marriage and fertility. Some Icelandic stories depict her as a devoted mother, while others stress her loose morals. One version of Frigg's name survives in the word Friday.

Friml \'fri-məl\, **(Charles) Rudolf** (1879–1972) Czech-U.S. composer. Born in Prague, he studied under Antonin DVORAK, and he emigrated to the U.S. in 1906. In 1912 he composed the highly successful operetta *The Firefly* (with Otto Harbach). The next major success of his approximately 30 operettas, *Rose Marie* (1924), was followed by *The Vagabond King* (1925) and *The Three Musketeers* (1928), among the last operettas to enjoy popular success.

fringe benefit Any nonwage payment or benefit granted to employees by employers. Examples include PENSION plans, PROFIT-SHARING programs, vacation pay, and company-paid life, HEALTH, and UNEMPLOYMENT INSURANCE. They are not usually taxed. If the cost of fringe benefits were paid directly as wages, the worker would pay taxes on this amount and therefore have less to spend when purchasing equivalent benefits independently.

Frisch \'frish\, **Karl von** (1886–1982) Austrian-born zoologist and pioneer of behavioral physiology. He found that bees communicate the distance and direction of a food supply to other members of the colony by two types of rhythmic movement. In 1949 he established that bees, through their perception of polarized light, use the sun as a compass even when it is not visible. He also established that fish can hear and distinguish colors. He shared a 1973 Nobel Prize with Konrad LORENZ and Nikolaas TINBERGEN.

Frisch, Max (Rudolf) (1911–1991) Swiss dramatist and novelist. He is noted for his Expressionist depictions of the moral dilemmas of 20th-cent. life. His early drama *Santa Cruz* (1947) established the central theme of his subsequent works: the predicament of the complicated, skeptical individual in modern society. Other plays include *The Chinese Wall* (1947), and *Andorra* (1961). Among his novels are *I'm Not Stiller* (1954), *Homo Faber* (1957), and *Man in the Holocene* (1979).

Frisian Islands \'fri-zhən\ Chain of islands, North Sea. They extend 3–20 mi (5–32 km) along the Dutch and German coasts and Denmark's JUTLAND peninsula. The W. Frisian Islands are owned by the Netherlands, the E. Frisian Islands by Germany, and the N. Frisian Islands by Germany and

Denmark. The Dutch and German governments have spent large sums to protect the islands' seaward coasts and reclaim the land for farming. Beaches and resorts attract many tourists.

Friuli-Venezia Giulia \frē-'ü-lē-vā-'net-sē-ä-'jül-yä\ Autonomous region (pop., 1996 est.: 1,189,000), NE Italy. It borders on Austria, Slovenia, and the Adriatic Sea; its capital is TRIESTE. It was divided after the barbarian invasions into a coastal part, dominated by the Byzantines, and an inland zone, ruled by the dukes of Friuli and the counts of Gorizia. From the 15th cent. it was controlled by Austria and Venice, and after 1815 it came under HABSBURG rule. Divided after World War II between Yugoslavia and the free territory of Trieste, the region was restored to Italy in 1954. It suffered a severe earthquake in 1976. It is known for its ham and dairy products.

Frobisher, Martin (*later* **Sir Martin**) (1535?–1594) English explorer. Searching for a Northwest Passage to the Pacific Ocean, he crossed the Atlantic in 1576 and reached Labrador and Baffin Island. Returning with reports of possible gold mines, he obtained royal backing for further expeditions in 1577 and 1578 but brought back nothing of value. In 1585 he sailed as vice admiral of Francis DRAKE's expedition to the W. Indies, and in 1588 was prominent in the campaign against the Spanish ARMADA.

Frobisher Bay \'frō-bi-shər\ Inlet of the N. Atlantic Ocean. Extending northwest from the SE tip of BAFFIN ISLAND, Canada, it is about 150 mi (240 km) long and 20–40 mi (32–64 km) wide. It was visited in 1576 by Martin FROBISHER. The town of IQALUIT at the head of the bay is the capital of NUNAVUT.

Frobisher Bay See IQALUIT.

Froebel \'frœ-bəl\, **Friedrich (Wilhelm August)** (1782–1852) German educator. Influenced by the theories of J. H. PESTALOZZI, he founded a school in 1837 that he called the KINDERGARTEN, or "garden of children." He believed in "self-activity" and play as essential factors in child education, the teacher's role being not to drill or indoctrinate but rather to encourage self-expression through play. He greatly influenced PRESCHOOL EDUCATION, including the ideas of John DEWEY.

frog Any of various tailless AMPHIBIANS in the order Anura. The name may be limited to the family Ranidae (true frogs); more broadly, it distinguishes smooth-skinned, leaping anurans from squat, warty, hopping ones (TOADS). Frogs generally have protruding eyes, strong webbed hind feet, and smooth moist skin. Most are aquatic, but some live on land. They range in length from 0.4 to 12 in. (10 mm–30 cm). Though frogs have poisonous skin glands, they rely on camouflage for protection. Most eat insects, but several also eat other frogs, rodents, and reptiles. They usually breed in freshwater, where their eggs hatch into tadpoles. Since 1989 researchers have become increasingly alarmed by striking declines in frog populations worldwide, suspected to be linked to climatic factors or a fungal disease.

Froissart \frwä-'sär\, **Jean** (1333?–1400/01) French court historian and poet. As a scholar Froissart traveled widely. His *Chronicles*, a firsthand narrative covering the HUNDRED YEARS' WAR from 1325 to 1400, is the most important and detailed document of feudal times and the best contemporary exposition of chivalric and courtly ideals. He also wrote ballades, rondeaux, and allegorical poetry celebrating COURTLY LOVE.

Fromm, Erich (1900–1980) German-U.S. psychoanalyst and social philosopher. A disciple of Sigmund FREUD, Fromm joined the FRANKFURT SCHOOL in the 1920s and left Nazi Germany for the U.S in 1933. Taking issue with Freud, he argued that psychoanalytic principles could be applied to cure cultural ills. He taught at the National Univ. of Mexico (1951–67) and NYU (from 1962). His popular books included *Escape from Freedom* (1941), *The Sane Society* (1955), and *The Crisis of Psychoanalysis* (1970); *The Art of Loving* (1956) became a durable best-seller.

Fronde \'frōⁿd\, **the** (1648–53) Civil wars in France during the minority of LOUIS XIV. The Fronde (named for the "sling" of a game played in the streets of Paris in defiance of authorities) tried to check the growing power of royal government, but its failure paved the way for the absolutism of Louis's reign. The first phase, the Fronde of the Parlement (1648–49), sought to place constitutional limits on the queen regent, ANNE OF AUSTRIA, and her chief minister, Jules MAZARIN. Uprisings forced the government to concede to the Parlement's demands. The more serious second phase, the Fronde of the Princes (1650–53), sprang from aristocratic opposition to Mazarin. When the prince de CONDÉ was arrested, his supporters joined the Parisian party (the Old Fronde) in successfully calling for Condé's release and Mazarin's resignation. Condé lost his position when Anne joined with the Old Fronde against him; after losses in battle, he fled. The king entered Paris in triumph in 1652, followed by Mazarin in 1653.

front In meteorology, the boundary between two air masses of different density and temperature. It is frequently accompanied by low barometric pressure, marked changes in wind direction and relative humidity, and considerable cloudiness and precipitation.

Frontenac \frōⁿ-tə-'nȧk\, **comte (Count) (de Palluau et) de** *orig.* Louis de Buade (1622–1698) French governor of New France (1672–82, 1689–98). Despite a record of misgovernment, he encouraged exploration that led to the expansion of the French empire in Canada. He established fur-trading posts that brought him into conflict with the Montreal fur traders, but he later expanded the posts west. When the IROQUOIS CONFEDERACY turned against the French, the colony was left defenseless. LOUIS XIV recalled Frontenac in 1682; reappointed when the FRENCH AND INDIAN WAR started (1689), he distinguished himself by repulsing British attacks on Quebec.

frost Atmospheric moisture that crystallizes directly on the ground and on exposed objects. Frost crystals, sometimes called hoarfrost, form when water vapor passes into the ice-crystal phase without going through the intermediate liquid phase. Frost forms under conditions that would form DEW if the temperature were above freezing. In agriculture, frost refers to the freezing of the water in plant cells, which causes the cells to burst and thereby destroys the plant.

Frost, Robert (Lee) (1874–1963) U.S. poet. He was born in San Francisco, but his family soon moved to New England. He published his first collections, *A Boy's Will* (1913) and *North of Boston* (1914), while living in England. At the outbreak of war he returned to New England to farm and to pursue a distinguished college teaching career. He acutely observed the details of rural life and endowed them with universal meaning, using colloquial language and symbols taken from common life to express both the pastoral ideals and the dark complexities of New England life. His collections include *Mountain Interval* (1916), *New Hampshire* (1923; Pulitzer Prize), *West-Running Brook* (1928), *Collected Poems* (1930; Pulitzer Prize), *A Further Range* (1936; Pulitzer Prize), and *A Witness Tree* (1942; Pulitzer Prize). He was unique among American poets of the 20th cent. in simultaneously achieving wide popularity and deep critical admiration.

Robert Frost, 1954

frostbite Freezing of living tissue, when it loses enough heat in below-freezing weather for ice to form. High winds, wet skin, tight clothes, and alcohol use increase the risk of frostbite. Cell damage, tissue dehydration, and oxygen depletion caused by freezing and thawing can lead to blood-cell disruption, clotting in capillaries, and GANGRENE. The toes, fingers, ears, and nose are usually affected first, becoming cold, hard, white, or bloodless. The lack of pain is dangerous. Core temperature should be brought to near normal before rapid thawing in warm (under 115°F, or 46°C) water. The outlook is best when freezing is short-term, thawing is by rapid rewarming, and large blisters extending to the end of the part develop early. Tissue that is refrozen after thawing must almost always be amputated. See also HYPOTHERMIA.

froth flotation See FLOTATION

fructose \\'frək-ˌtōs, 'frük-ˌtōs\\ *or* **levulose** \\'lev-yə-ˌlōs\\ *or* **fruit sugar** Organic compound, one of the simple SUGARS (MONOSACCHARIDES). It occurs in fruits, honey, syrups (especially corn syrup), and certain vegetables, usually along with its ISOMER, GLUCOSE. Fructose and glucose are the components of the disaccharide SUCROSE (table sugar). The sweetest of the common sugars, fructose is used in foods and medicines.

fruit In its strict botanical sense, the fleshy or dry ripened ovary (enlarged portion of the PISTIL) of a FLOWERING PLANT, enclosing the seed or seeds. APRICOTS, BANANAS, and GRAPES, as well as BEAN pods, CORN grains, TOMATOES, and (in their shells) acorns and ALMONDS are all technically fruits. Popularly, the term is restricted to the ripened ovaries that are sweet and either succulent or pulpy. The principal botanical purpose of the fruit is to protect and spread the seed. There are two broad categories of fruit: fleshy and dry. Fleshy fruits include BERRIES, such as tomatoes, oranges, and cherries, which consist entirely of succulent tissue; aggregate fruits, including BLACKBERRIES and STRAWBERRIES, which form from a single flower with many PISTILS; and multiple fruits, such as PINEAPPLES and mulberries, which develop from the mature ovaries of an entire INFLORESCENCE. Dry fruits include the LEGUMES, CEREAL grains, and NUTS. Fruits are important sources of dietary fiber and vitamins (especially vitamin C).

fruit bat Any of numerous tropical Old World BATS in the family Pteropodidae. Most species rely on vision rather than ECHOLOCATION. Most roost in trees, though some inhabit caves, rocks, or buildings. Some are red or yellow, and some are striped or spotted. They eat fruit or flowers. The smallest species, the long-tongued fruit bats, reach a length of about 2.5 in. (6–7 cm) and a wingspan of about 10 in. (25 cm). The same family contains the largest of all bats, the flying foxes, which attain wingspans of 5 ft (1.5 m).

fruit fly Any DIPTERAN species of two families: large fruit flies (Trypetidae) and small fruit flies, or vinegar flies (family Drosophilidae; see DROSOPHILA). The larvae feed on fruit or other vegetation. Many species attack cultivated fruits, sometimes causing significant economic loss. Some species are leaf miners, which ingest leaf tissue; others burrow in plant stems. Well-known fruit-fly pests include the MEDITERRANEAN FRUIT FLY and the apple maggot of the U.S., the Mexican and Oriental fruit flies, and the olive fruit fly of the Mediterranean.

fruit sugar See FRUCTOSE

Frunze See BISHKEK

Frunze \\'frün-zyə\\, **Mikhail (Vasilyevich)** (1885–1925) Soviet army officer. An active revolutionary from 1905, he became an outstanding commander in the RUSSIAN CIVIL WAR. With the support of Joseph STALIN, Frunze replaced Leon TROTSKY as commissar for war in 1925. His "unitary military doctrine" asserted that the RED ARMY should be trained in offensive action to carry out the task of promoting world revolution. He introduced peacetime compulsory military service and standardized military formations.

Frye, (Herman) Northrop (1912–1991) Canadian literary critic. Born in Sherbrooke, Quebec, he taught at the Univ. of Toronto. In *Anatomy of Criticism* (1957), his most influential work, he analyzed various modes of literary criticism and stressed the recurring importance of archetypal symbols in literature. His other influential works include *Fearful Symmetry: A Study of William Blake* (1947) and *The Great Code: The Bible and Literature* (1982).

FTP *in full* file transfer protocol. INTERNET PROTOCOL that allows a computer to send files to or receive files from another computer. Like many Internet resources, FTP works by means of a CLIENT-SERVER ARCHITECTURE. On the FTP server, a program called a daemon allows the user to download and upload files. FTP was one of the most popular methods of exchanging information over the Internet before HTTP.

Fuchs \\'füks\\, **(Emil) Klaus (Julius)** (1911–1988) German physicist and spy. He joined the German Communist Party in 1930 but fled the Nazis in 1933. He settled in Britain, earned a doctorate and worked on the ATOMIC BOMB in Britain and the U.S. In 1943 he began passing scientific secrets to the Soviet Union, which accelerated Soviet development of the bomb. His activities were detected in 1950 and he was imprisoned until 1959, when he moved to E. Germany, becoming deputy director of the Central Institute for Nuclear Research.

fuchsia \\'fyü-shə\\ Any of about 100 species of flowering shrubs and trees in the genus *Fuchsia* (family Onagraceae), native to tropical and subtropical regions of Central and S. America and to New Zealand and Tahiti. Several species are grown in gardens, pots, and greenhouses. Fuchsias are valued for their showy pendulous flowers, tubular to bell-shaped, in shades of red and purple to white.

fuel cell Device that converts chemical energy of a fuel directly into ELECTRICITY (see ELECTROCHEMISTRY). Fuel cells are intrinsically more efficient than most other energy-conversion devices. Electrolytic chemical reactions cause ELECTRONS to be released on one ELECTRODE and flow through an external circuit to a second electrode. Whereas in BATTERIES the electrodes are the source of the active ingredients, in fuel cells the gas or liquid fuel (often hydrogen, methyl alcohol, or hydrazine) is supplied continuously to one electrode and oxygen or air to the other from an external source. So, as long as fuel and oxidant are supplied, the fuel cell will not run down or require recharging. Usable in place of virtually any other source of electricity, it is especially being developed for use in ELECTRIC AUTOMOBILES, in the hope of achieving enormous reductions in pollution.

fuel injection In an INTERNAL-COMBUSTION ENGINE, introduction of fuel into the cylinders by a pump rather than by the suction created by the movement of the pistons (see PISTON AND CYLINDER). On DIESEL ENGINES, which lack SPARK PLUGS, the heat created by compressing air in the cylinders ignites the fuel, which has been pumped in as a spray. In engines with spark ignition, fuel-injection pumps are often used instead of conventional CARBURETORS. Fuel injection distributes the fuel more evenly to the cylinders than does a carburetor, enhancing power and reducing emissions. In pistonless engines with continuous combustion, such as gas TURBINES and liquid-fueled ROCKETS, fuel-injection systems are necessary.

Fuentes \\fü-'en-tās\\, **Carlos** (b.1928) Mexican writer and diplomat. While working as a diplomat he began publishing his experimental novels. His first, *Where the Air Is Clear* (1958), a bitter indictment of Mexican society, won him national prestige. *The Death of Artemio Cruz* (1962), about the final hours of an unscrupulous former revolutionary, made his international reputation. Among his later novels are *Terra Nostra* (1975) and *The Old Gringo* (1985). *The Buried Mirror* (1992) is a long essay on Hispanic cultures. He received the Cervantes Prize in 1987.

Fugard \\fü-'gärd\\, **Athol (Harold Lannigan)** (b.1932) S. African playwright, director, and actor. His play *The Blood Knot* (1961), a penetrating analysis of apartheid, established his international reputation. He resumed the theme in *Hello and Goodbye* (1965) and *Boesman and Lena* (1969; film, 1973, with Fugard as Boesman). He experimented with an imagist approach in such plays as *Orestes* (1971), then returned to more traditionally structured plays. His "*Master Harold*" . . . *and the Boys* (1982), *The Road to Mecca* (1984), and *A Lesson from Aloes* (1989) were acclaimed in London and New York.

Fugger family \\'fü-gər\\ German mercantile and banking dynasty that dominated European business in the 15th–16th cent. The family traced its origins to Hans (Johannes) Fugger (1348–1409), a weaver in Augsburg. Under his grandsons Ulrich (1441–1510), Georg (1453–1506), and especially Jakob (1459–1525), the company became established in international trade, including the lucrative spice and slave trades, and built a fortune in mining. Their loans to kings and emperors and involvement with the sale of papal INDULGENCES made the family highly influential and earned the criticism of Martin LUTHER. It declined after the 16th cent.

Fugitive Slave Acts U.S. laws of 1793 and 1850 (repealed in 1864) that provided for the seizure and return of runaway slaves. Northern opposition led to enactment of state personal-liberty laws that entitled slaves to a jury trial and as early as 1810 prompted individuals to aid the UNDERGROUND RAILROAD. The second statute, part of the COMPROMISE OF 1850, imposed penalties on federal marshals who refused to enforce the law and on individuals who helped slaves to escape; fugitives were not permitted a jury trial. Its severity led to increased interest in the abolition movement, and additional personal-liberty laws were enacted by N states to thwart the act.

fugue \\'fyüg\\ Musical composition characterized by systematic imitation of one or more themes in COUNTERPOINT. The fugue emerged gradually from the imitative polyphony of the 13th cent. Fugues vary greatly in their actual form. The principal theme (subject) is imitated—i.e., repeated successively in similar form at different pitch levels by different parts or voices—in the so-called exposition. The countersubject is the continuation of the subject that accompanies the subject theme's subsequent entries in the other voices. Episodes using modified themes often separate the subject's entries. J. S. BACH's keyboard fugues are the most famous of all. The works of Bach and G. F. HANDEL inspired many later composers, who commonly included fugues in the final movements of symphonies, string quartets, and sonatas.

Fuji, Mt. *Japanese* **Fujisan** Mountain, central Japan. The highest mountain in Japan, it rises to 12,388 ft (3,776 m) near the Pacific coast in central HONSHU. Mt. Fuji, with its graceful volcanic cone (dormant since 1707), has become famous internationally. It is considered a sacred symbol of Japan, and thousands of Japanese climb to the shrine on its peak every summer.

Fujimori \\ˌfü-jē-ˈmô-rē\\, **Alberto (Kenyo)** (b. 1938) President of Peru (1990–2000). Principal of Agrarian National Univ. 1984–89, he entered politics in 1989 by founding the political party Cambio 90. He won a surprise victory in the 1990 presidential election, and implemented extreme austerity measures that successfully dealt with Peru's severe inflation and indebtedness. In 1992 he dissolved the National Congress and took other steps to consolidate his power. With the capture of the leader of the SHINING PATH guerrillas, he curtailed a decade-long violent insurrection. He was reelected in 1995 and asserted victory, despite charges of fraud, in 2000, but scandal involving his secret-police chief forced him to flee to Japan.

Fujiwara family \\'fu-jē-'wä-rä\\ Dynastic family that dominated Japanese court government in the 9th–12th cent. The Fujiwara acted as regents for child emperors and later created the post of *kampaku*, or chancellor, essentially a regent for an adult emperor. Fujiwara Michinaga (966–1028) married three daughters to emperors and a fourth to an heir apparent; his ascendancy marked the height of the HEIAN PERIOD. The family's power at court waned after Michinaga and was eliminated in the 12th cent.

Fukuoka \\ˌfü-kü-ˈō-kä\\ City (pop., 1995: 1,285,000) and port, Japan. It incorporates the former city of Hakata and is located across Tsushima Strait from S. Korea. It was the scene of attempted invasions by KUBLAI KHAN in the 13th cent. It is the site of Kyushu Univ. (1911). Hakata *ningyo*, elaborately costumed ceramic figurines found in most Japanese homes, are made there.

Fulani \\'fü-ˌlä-nē\\ Primarily Muslim people, numbering about 18 million, found in many parts of W Africa, from Lake Chad west to the Atlantic coast. In the 1790s the Fulani priest USMÁN DAN FODIO led a holy war (JIHAD) that created a large empire. Its decay in the 19th cent. aided the establishment of British rule over N Nigeria. Many Fulani of N Nigeria have adopted the HAUSA LANGUAGE and culture and established themselves as an urban aristocracy.

Fulbright, J(ames) William (1905–1995) U.S. politician. Born in Sumner, Mo., he earned degrees from the Univ. of Arkansas and Oxford Univ.; he returned to the Univ. of Arkansas to teach law, and served as its president 1939–41. As a U.S. representative (1943–45) he introduced a resolution favoring U.S. participation in what would become the U.N. As a U.S. senator (1945–75), he initiated the FULBRIGHT SCHOLARSHIP program. As chairman of the foreign-relations committee (1959–74), he presided over influ-

ential televised hearings in 1966 on the VIETNAM WAR and became a leading advocate for ending the bombing of N. Vietnam and opening peace talks. In 1974 he lost his bid for reelection.

Fulbright scholarship Educational grant under an international exchange program conceived by Sen. J. William FULBRIGHT and instituted by the Fulbright Act of 1946 and the Fulbright-Hays Act of 1961. Most participants are graduate students, but teachers and researchers may also qualify. The program is administered by the U.S. Dept. of State.

Fuller, J(ohn) F(rederick) C(harles) (1878–1966) British military theoretician and historian, chief of staff of the British tank corps in World War I. He planned the surprise attack of 381 tanks at the Battle of Cambrai (Nov. 20, 1917), the first massed tank assault in history. After the war he crusaded for the mechanization of the British army. His focus on the armored offensive met with resistance, but he was largely vindicated by World War II. His works include *Tanks in the Great War* (1920), *Machine Warfare* (1942), and *A Military History of the Western World* (1954–56).

Fuller, Loie *orig.* Marie Louise Fuller (1862–1928) U.S. pioneer of MODERN DANCE. Born in Fullersburg, Ill., she began acting at age 4. From 1892 in Paris she gained attention with her "serpentine dance," in which she used yards of flowing silk illuminated by theatrical lighting. She added a "fire dance" (dancing on an illuminated pane of glass) and other acts, attracting critical and public adulation, especially in Europe.

Fuller, (Sarah) Margaret (1810–1850) U.S. critic, teacher, and woman of letters. Born in Cambridgeport, Mass., she became a close friend of Ralph Waldo EMERSON, and was the founding editor of the Transcendentalist magazine *The Dial* (1840–42) (see TRANSCENDENTALISM). Her *Summer on the Lakes, in 1843* (1844) was followed by *Woman in the Nineteenth Century* (1845), a plea for women's political, intellectual, and spiritual fulfillment. She traveled to Europe in 1846 as a correspondent, and married a revolutionary marquis; forced into exile, they perished in a shipwreck while returning to the U.S.

Margaret Fuller Engraving by R. Babson and J. Andrews, c.1860

Fuller, Melville (Weston) (1833–1910) U.S. jurist. Born in Augusta, Me., he built up a major legal practice in Chicago. Appointed chief justice of the U.S. Supreme Court in 1888 by Pres. Grover CLEVELAND, he would remain on the Court until his death. He served on the Hague Court of International Arbitration 1900–10.

Fuller, R(ichard) Buckminster (1895–1983) U.S. inventor, futurist, and architect. Born in Milton, Mass., he was expelled twice from Harvard Univ. Failure in a prefab construction business led him to search for design patterns that would most efficiently use the earth's resources for humanity's greatest good. His innovations included the inexpensive, lightweight, factory-assembled Dymaxion House and the energy-efficient, omnidirectional Dymaxion Car. In his vectorial system of geometry ("Energetic-Synergetic geometry") the basic unit is the tetrahedron, which, when combined with octahedrons, forms the most economic space-filling structures, which led Fuller to invent the important geodesic DOME (1947).

fullerene Any of a class of closed, hollow compounds discovered in 1985, forms of CARBON whose MOLECULES have 12 pentagonal and differing numbers of hexagonal faces. The best known, C_{60} (buckminsterfullerene, or "buckyballs," named for Buckminster FULLER), has the shape of a soccer ball. The molecules are exceptionally stable. Certain other molecules can become trapped in the hollow interior, a unique and exciting feature.

Fulton, Robert (1765–1815) U.S. inventor and engineer. Born in Pennsylvania, he studied painting with Benjamin

WEST in London but soon turned to engineering, designing a system of inland waterways. He failed to interest the French and British governments in his prototypes of submarines and torpedoes. In 1801 he was commissioned by Robert LIVINGSTON to build a steamboat, and in 1807 Fulton's *Clermont* made the journey up the Hudson from New York to Albany in one-third of the usual sailing time. It became the first commercially successful steamboat in the U.S. He later designed the world's first steam warship (1812).

fumarole \ˈfyü-mə-ˌrōl\ Vent from which volcanic vapors issue. Fumaroles, like GEYSERS, are caused by HOT SPRINGS, which disperse groundwater heated by MAGMA. As magma begins to solidify, the gases in it, mostly water vapor, become concentrated by the pressure of the remaining liquid; the liquid is forced into cracks in the surrounding rock, and a fumarole forms if a crack extends to the surface.

Funafuti \ˌfü-nä-ˈfü-tē\ Coral atoll (pop., 1995 est.: 4,000), location of Fongafale, capital of Tuvalu, W central Pacific Ocean. It comprises some 30 islets, which encircle a lagoon that affords good anchorage. A U.S. military base was established there in 1943; the U.S. dropped its claim to the atoll in 1983.

Funchal \fün-ˈshäl\ City (pop., 1991: 126,000) and capital of the autonomous region of MADEIRA, Portugal. Lying on the S coast of Madeira island in the N. Atlantic, it was founded in 1421 by the Portuguese navigator João Gonçalves Zarco. The city attracts many tourists.

function In mathematics, an expression, rule, or law that defines a relationship between one VARIABLE (the independent variable) and another (the dependent variable), which changes along with it. Most functions are numerical; that is, a numerical input value is associated with a single numerical output value. The formula $A = \pi r^2$, for example, assigns to each positive real number r the area A of a circle with a radius of that length. The symbols $f(x)$ and $g(x)$ are typically used for functions of the independent variable x. A multivariable function such as $w = f(x,y)$ is a rule for deriving a single numerical value from more than one input value. Periodic functions (e.g., the TRIGONOMETRIC FUNCTIONS) repeat values over fixed intervals. See also EXPONENTIAL FUNCTION, INVERSE FUNCTION.

functional analysis Branch of mathematical analysis dealing with functionals, or FUNCTIONS of functions. It emerged as a distinct field in the 20th cent., when it was realized that diverse mathematical processes exhibit very similar properties. A functional, like a function, is a relationship between objects, but the objects may be numbers, vectors, or functions. Groupings of such objects are called spaces. DIFFERENTIATION is an example of a functional because it defines a relationship between a function and another function (its derivative). INTEGRATION is also a functional.

functional group In MOLECULES, any of numerous combinations of ATOMS that undergo characteristic CHEMICAL REACTIONS. Organic compounds are often classified according to their functional groups. Common functional groups include hydroxyl (–OH), in ALCOHOLS and PHENOLS; carboxyl (–COOH), in CARBOXYLIC ACIDS; carbonyl (–C=O), in ALDEHYDES, KETONES, AMIDES, CARBOXYLIC ACIDS, and ESTERS; and nitro (–NO$_2$) and amino (–NH$_2$), in certain organic nitrogen compounds.

Functionalism In architecture, the doctrine that a building's form should be determined by practical considerations of use, material, and structure, and not by a preconceived picture in the designer's mind. It is closely associated with the modernist architecture of the second quarter of the 20th cent. The fight for an "honest" form of expression by Louis SULLIVAN, LE CORBUSIER, and others resulted from changes in building techniques, new types of buildings required, and discontent with the prevailing historical revivalism.

functionalism In the social sciences, a theory that stresses the interdependence of the patterns and institutions of a society and their interaction in maintaining cultural and social unity. In sociology, functionalism emerged from the work of Émile DURKHEIM, who viewed society as a kind of "organism" that carried with it certain "needs" that must be fulfilled. Similar views were adopted in anthropology by

A. R. RADCLIFFE-BROWN and by Bronislaw MALINOWSKI, who looked at culture as the expression of the totality of individual and collective achievement, where "every custom, material object, idea and belief fulfills some vital function." The U.S. sociologist Talcott Parsons (1902–1979) analyzed large-scale societies, focusing on problems of social order, integration, and equilibrium. Later writers argued that functionalism was too rigid to account for the breadth, depth, and contingencies of social life and ignored the role of history in shaping society.

fundamentalism, Christian Conservative Protestant movement that arose out of 19th-cent. MILLENNIALISM in the U.S. It emphasized as fundamental the literal truth of the Bible and the imminent physical Second Coming of Jesus. It spread in the 1880s and '90s among Protestants dismayed by labor unrest, Catholic immigration, and biblical criticism. Displeasure over the teaching of EVOLUTION and over biblical criticism gave fundamentalism momentum in the 1920s. In the 1930s and '40s, many fundamentalist Bible institutes and colleges were established, and fundamentalist groups within some Baptist and Presbyterian denominations broke away to form new churches. In the later 20th cent., fundamentalists made use of television as a medium for evangelizing and became vocal in politics. See also EVANGELICALISM, PENTECOSTALISM.

fundamentalism, Islamic Conservative religious movement that seeks a return to Islamic values and Islamic law (see SHARIA) in the face of Western modernism. Though popularly associated in the West with terrorist groups such as AL-QAEDA, only a few Islamic fundamentalists are terrorists. Iran and Saudi Arabia are Islamic fundamentalist states, as was Afghanistan under the TALIBAN. Islamic fundamentalist movements have varying degrees of support in N. Africa, Pakistan, Bangladesh, and Muslim S.E. Asia, but Islamic fundamentalism represents a minority viewpoint within world Islam. See also WAHHABI.

Fundy, Bay of Inlet of the Atlantic Ocean, SE Canada. Located between the provinces of New Brunswick and Nova Scotia, it extends 94 mi (151 km) inland, and is 32 mi (52 km) wide at its entrance. It is noted for its fast-running tides, which may produce rises as great as 70 ft (20 m), the highest in the world. It is noted also for the spectacular rock formations and forests of its shorelines.

fungicide Any TOXIN used to kill or inhibit growth of fungi (see FUNGUS) that cause economic damage to crop or ornamental plants (including rusts in cereals, blight in potatoes, mildew in fruits) or endanger the health of domestic animals or humans. COPPER compounds, especially copper sulfate, and SULFUR (Bordeaux mixture) have long been used for this purpose, but now synthetic organic compounds are commonly used. Plants produce many antifungal substances.

fungus Any of about 50,000 species of the kingdom Fungi, or Mycota, including YEASTS, rusts, smuts, MOLDS, MUSHROOMS, and MILDEWS. Though sometimes classified as plants, they lack CHLOROPHYLL and the organized plant structures of stems, roots, and leaves. Fungi contribute to the disintegration of organic matter that results in the release of carbon, oxygen, nitrogen, and phosphorus from dead plants and animals into the soil or the atmosphere. They can be found in the water, soil, air, plants, and animals of all regions of the world that have sufficient moisture to enable them to grow. Essential to many household and industrial processes, fungi are also used in the production of ENZYMES, organic acids, VITAMINS, and ANTIBIOTICS. They also can destroy crops, cause such diseases as ATHLETE'S FOOT, and ruin clothing and food with mildew and rot. The body of a typical fungus consists of a mycelium through which CYTOPLASM flows. The mycelium generally reproduces by forming SPORES, often in special fruiting bodies that are the visible part of the fungus. The soil provides an ideal habitat for many species. Lacking chlorophyll, fungi are unable to carry out PHOTOSYNTHESIS and must obtain their carbohydrates by secreting enzymes onto the surface on which they are growing to digest the food, which they absorb through the mycelium. Saprophytic fungi live off dead organisms. Parasitic fungi invade living organisms, often causing disease and death (see PARASITISM). Fungi establish symbiotic relationships with ALGAE (forming LICHENS), plants (forming mycorrhizae), and certain insects.

Furies *Greek* Erinyes. Group of Greco-Roman goddesses of vengeance. The Furies lived in the underworld and ascended to earth to pursue the wicked. Those who feared to speak their name often called them by euphemisms such as Eumenides ("Kind Ones"). According to HESIOD, they were daughters of GAEA, the earth goddess. EURIPIDES was the first to speak of them as three in number.

Furtwängler \\'fürt-ˌveŋ-lər\\, **(Gustav Heinrich Ernst Martin) Wilhelm** (1886–1954) German conductor and composer. He made his conducting debut in 1906. His revised *Te Deum* (1910) established him as a composer, and in 1917 a guest-conducting job in Berlin earned the phrase "Furtwängler miracle." From 1922 he led the Leipzig Gewandhaus and Berlin Philharmonic orchestras, becoming especially renowned in the music of Ludwig van BEETHOVEN and Richard WAGNER. Though criticized for staying in Germany during the Nazi era, he was no friend of the regime, continuing to program modern music and helping Jewish musicians escape.

furuncle See BOIL

fuse Safety device that protects electric CIRCUITS from the effects of excessive ELECTRIC CURRENTS. A fuse commonly consists of a current-conducting strip or wire of easily fusible metal; whenever the circuit is made to carry a current larger than intended, the strip melts to interrupt it.

Fuseli \\'fyü-ˈzel-ē\\, **Henry** *orig.* Johann Heinrich Füssli (1741–1825) Swiss-British painter. He left his native Zurich for London in 1764. Encouraged by Sir Joshua REYNOLDS, he lived in Italy 1770–78; on his return, his works exhibited at the Royal Academy, such as *The Nightmare* (1781), secured his reputation. His subject matter was chiefly literary and his images portrayed macabre fantasies and the grotesque.

futhark See RUNIC WRITING

futures Commercial contracts calling for the purchase or sale of specified quantities of a good at specified future dates. The good in question may be grain, livestock, precious metals, or financial instruments such as TREASURY BILLS. Up until delivery, the price is subject to speculation. Futures contracts originated with agricultural commodities; for example, American grain farmers were able to sell their harvest in advance on the Chicago Board of Trade, a commodity exchange.

Futurism Early-20th-cent. art movement, centered in Italy, that celebrated the dynamism, speed, and power of the machine and the vitality and restlessness of modern life. The term was coined by F. T. MARINETTI, who in 1909 published a manifesto glorifying the new technology of the automobile. In 1910 Umberto BOCCIONI and others published a manifesto on painting. They adopted the Cubist technique of depicting several views of an object simultaneously with fragmented planes and outlines. Their preferred subjects were speeding vehicles and urban crowds. With Boccioni, the most prominent Futurist artists were his teacher, Giacomo Balla (1871–1958), and Gino Severini (1883–1966). Boccioni's death in 1916 and World War I brought an end to the movement, which had a strong influence in postrevolutionary Russia and on DADA.

Futurism Literary, artistic, and political movement begun in Italy about 1909 and marked especially by violent rejection of tradition and an effort to give formal expression to the dynamic energy and movement of mechanical processes. Russian and Italian Futurist poets discarded logical sentence construction and frequently presented an incoherent story of words used for their sound alone. Futurist writers and artists include F. T. MARINETTI, Umberto BOCCIONI, and Vladimir MAYAKOVSKY. The movement's influence had ceased to be felt by 1930.

Fuzuli \\fü-zü-ˈlē\\, **Mehmed bin Suleyman** (c.1480–1556) Turkish poet. Considered the greatest figure in classical Turkish literature, he composed poems with equal facility and elegance in Turkish, Persian, and Arabic. His works transcended the highly formalized Islamic literary aesthetic and influenced many poets up to the 19th cent. His most famous poems include his rendition of the Muslim classic *Leyla ve Mecnun*. His two poetry anthologies, one in Azerbaijani Turkish and one in Persian, contain his most lyrical verses.

fuzzy logic LOGIC based on the concept of fuzzy sets, in which membership is expressed in varying probabilities or degrees of truth—that is, as a continuum of values ranging from 0 (does not occur) to 1 (definitely occurs). As additional data are gathered, many fuzzy-logic systems are able to adjust the probability values assigned to different parameters. Because some such systems appear able to learn from their mistakes, they are often considered a crude form of ARTIFICIAL INTELLIGENCE. Advanced clothes-washing machines use fuzzy-logic systems to detect and adapt to patterns of water movement, increasing efficiency and reducing water consumption. Other products using fuzzy logic include camcorders, microwave ovens, and dishwashers. Other applications include self-regulating industrial controls and computerized speech- and handwriting-recognition programs.

FG

G

gabbro Any of several medium- or coarse-grained rocks that consist primarily of PLAGIOCLASE and PYROXENE. Gabbros are found widely on the earth and on the moon. Its direct economic value is minor, but it is valued for the nickel, chromium, and platinum minerals that occur almost exclusively in association with it. Magnetite (iron) and ilmenite (titanium) are also found in gabbroic complexes.

Gabin \gȧ-'baⁿ\, **Jean** *orig.* Jean-Alexis Moncorgé (1904–1976) French film actor. He began as a performer at the Folies Bergère (1923). After his film debut in 1931, he earned acclaim in *Maria Chapdelaine* (1934), *Pépé le moko* (1937), *Grand Illusion* (1937), *The Human Beast* (1938), and *Daybreak* (1939), often portraying the silent, tough antihero surviving in a world of social outcasts. He later appeared in several films as Inspector Maigret.

gable Triangular section formed by a roof with two slopes, extending from the eaves to the ridge where the two slopes meet. If the gable end projects above the roof level to form a parapet, the edge is often trimmed to form an ornamental silhouette, as in Dutch town houses of the 16th–17th cent. In Asia, gables often feature projecting roof tiles and grotesque sculptures of animals.

Gable, (William) Clark (1901–1960) U.S. film actor. Born in Cadiz, Ohio, he debuted on Broadway in 1928 and went to Hollywood in 1930. There he triumphed in *It Happened One Night* (1934, Academy Award). With his sardonic virility and lighthearted charm, he became known as "the King." Among his 70-odd films are *Mutiny on the Bounty* (1935), *San Francisco* (1936), *Saratoga* (1937), and, most memorably, *Gone with the Wind* (1939). After the death of his third wife, Carole LOMBARD, he served heroically as a bomber pilot in World War II. He later starred in such films as *The Hucksters* (1947), *Mogambo* (1953), and *The Misfits* (1961).

Gabo \'gä-bō\, **Naum** *orig.* Naum Pevsner (1890–1977) Russian-U.S. sculptor. He studied at the Univ. of Munich, and in 1913 he was introduced to avant-garde art in Paris by his brother, Antoine Pevsner (1886–1962). In 1920 the brothers returned to Russia and issued the *Realist Manifesto*, setting forth the principles of European CONSTRUCTIVISM. Gabo produced abstract works of such unorthodox materials as glass, plastic, and wire to achieve a sense of movement. He settled in the U.S. in 1946 and taught at Harvard's architecture school. He was one of the earliest artists to experiment with KINETIC SCULPTURE.

Gabon \gȧ-'bōⁿ\ *officially* **Gabonese Republic** Country, central Africa. Area: 103,347 sq mi (267,667 sq km). Population (2000): 1,208,000. Capital: LIBREVILLE. Gabon has more than 40 ethnic groups: the Fang make up a majority and live N of the OGOOUÉ RIVER; the largest groups south of the river are the Punu, Sira, and Nzebi. Languages: French (official); indigenous languages. Religion: Christianity, primarily Roman Catholicism. Currency: CFA franc. Gabon straddles the equator on the W coast of Africa. It has a narrow coastal plain and becomes hilly in the south and north. The basin of its chief river, the Ogooué, covers most of the country; about three-fourths is equatorial rain forest, which supports numerous plant and animal species. Gabon has reserves of manganese that are among the largest in the world; it also has huge deposits of high-grade iron ore. Gabon has a mixed, developing economy based largely on the exploitation of these mineral and timber resources. Its head of state is the president, and the head of government is the prime minister; the parliament consists of two houses.

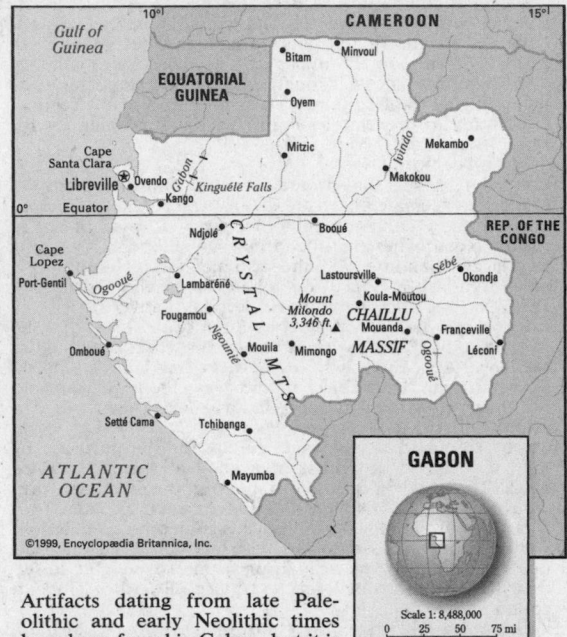

GABON

©1999, Encyclopædia Britannica, Inc.

Scale 1: 8,488,000
0   25   50   75 mi
0   50   100 km

Artifacts dating from late Paleolithic and early Neolithic times have been found in Gabon, but it is not known when the BANTU speakers who established Gabon's ethnic composition arrived. PYGMIES were probably the original inhabitants. The Fang arrived in the late 18th cent. and were followed by the Portuguese and by French, Dutch, and English traders. The SLAVE TRADE dominated commerce in the 18th and much of the 19th cent. The French then took control, and Gabon was administered (1843–86) with FRENCH WEST AFRICA. In 1886 the colony of French Congo was established to include both Gabon and the Congo; in 1910 Gabon became a separate colony within FRENCH EQUATORIAL AFRICA. An overseas territory of France from 1946, it became an autonomous republic within the French Community in 1958 and declared its independence in 1960. Rule by a sole political party was established in the 1960s, but discontent with it led to riots in Libreville in 1989. Legalization of opposition parties led to new elections in 1990. Peace negotiations with neighboring Chad rebels were successfully concluded in 2002.

Gaborone \ˌgä-bō-'rō-nā\ *formerly (until 1969)* **Gaberones** \ˌgä-bə-'rō-nəs\ City (pop., 1997: 183,000), capital of Botswana. It is located in SE Botswana, near the border with S. Africa. It is the seat of the Univ. of Botswana (1976) and also has a national museum and art gallery (1968).

Gabriel In the Bible, one of the archangels. In the Old Testament he explained DANIEL's visions, and in the New Testament he revealed to Zechariah the coming birth of JOHN THE BAPTIST and told MARY that she was to be the mother of JESUS. In Christian tradition it is believed that he will blow the trumpet on Judgment Day. In the Quran, he is known as JIBRIL.

Gabriel *or* **Gabriel Prosser** (1775?–1800) American slave who planned the first slave rebellion in U.S. history. Born near Richmond, Va., he grew up as the slave of Thomas H. Prosser. In 1800 he planned a slave insurrection to create an independent slave state in Virginia with himself as king. Intending to attack Richmond, he assembled 1,000 slaves outside the city on August 30, but a violent rainstorm washed out bridges and scattered the rebels. Before they could reassemble, Gov. James MONROE ordered out the state militia. Gabriel and 34 others were arrested, tried, and hanged.

Gabrieli \ˌgä-brē-'e-lē\, **Andrea and Giovanni** (d.1586, c.1555–1612) Italian composers. Andrea was born in Venice and in 1566 became an organist at ST. MARK'S BASILICA, where he remained the rest of his life. He wrote over 200 madrigals and much other secular vocal music. His sacred vocal works, which number over 150, include many splendid settings for church festivals employing separated choirs (*cori spezzati*). His nephew and student Giovanni joined him as organist at St. Mark's in 1584. He too wrote numerous festive works for separated choirs and instrumental groups. His best-known works today are his works for wind instruments (canzonas, ricercars, sonatas, toccatas, etc.), which employ dramatic dynamic and spatial effects.

Gaddi \'gäd-dē\, **Taddeo** (c.1300–1366) Italian painter active in Florence. He was a student of GIOTTO. His best-known works are frescoes in the church of Santa Croce in Florence. He directed a flourishing workshop for three decades, producing pictures in the style of Giotto but featuring more vivid picturesque effects with narrative detail. His son Agnolo (c.1350–1396) was an influential and prolific artist who likewise produced a notable series of frescoes for Santa Croce, *The Legend of the True Cross* (c.1388–93). His concentration on design and the elegance of his pale colors influenced the style of late Gothic art.

Gaddis, William (Thomas) (1922–1998) U.S. novelist. Born in New York City, he is known for his long experimental novels characterized by complex and allusive plotting and language and a dark (if often humorous) view of contemporary American society. His first, *The Recognitions* (1955), was only belatedly recognized as a masterpiece. Discouraged by its reception, he published nothing more until *JR* (1975, National Book Award), which depicts greed, hypocrisy, and banality in business. His later novels include *A Frolic of His Own* (1994, National Book Award).

Gadsden Purchase (1853) U.S. purchase of land in Mexico. Following the MEXICAN WAR (1848), advocates of a S transcontinental railroad endorsed the purchase of 30,000 sq mi (78,000 sq km) of N Mexican territory, now S Arizona and S New Mexico. Negotiated by James Gadsden, U.S. minister to Mexico, for $10 million, the acquisition fixed the borders of the later 48 contiguous states.

Gaea \'jē-ə\ Greek goddess of the earth. She was both mother and wife to URANUS, or Heaven, as well as mother of CRONUS, a TITAN. According to HESIOD, she was the mother of all 12 Titans, as well as of the FURIES and the Cyclopes (see CYCLOPS). She may have originated as a mother goddess worshiped in pre-Hellenic Greece.

Gaelic See IRISH LANGUAGE, SCOTTISH GAELIC LANGUAGE

Gaelic revival Resurgence of interest in Irish language, literature, history, and folklore inspired by the growing Irish nationalism of the early 19th cent. With the 17th-cent. English conquest of Ireland, Irish almost disappeared as a literary language. By the mid-19th cent., translations of ancient heroic tales had led to the popularity of poets who wrote in patterns echoing ancient bardic verse. The revival laid the groundwork for the IRISH LITERARY RENAISSANCE. See also BARD.

gagaku \gä-'gä-kü\ Traditional court and religious music of Japan. It first appeared as an import from Korea in the 5th cent. A.D. and became established at court by the 8th cent., and it continues to be performed at Shinto ceremonies. Gagaku employs transverse flute (*ryuteki*), double-reed pipe (*hichiriki*), mouth organ (*sho*), gong (*shoko*), drums, and stringed instruments including the *biwa* and KOTO. It may accompany dance (BUGAKU) or be played independently (*kangen*).

Gagarin \gə-'gär-ən\, **Yury (Alekseyevich)** (1934–1968) Soviet cosmonaut, first human to travel into space. His 1961 flight on Vostok 1, which orbited earth once in 1 hour and 29 minutes, brought him worldwide fame. Gagarin never went into space again, but trained other cosmonauts. He was killed at 34 when his jet crashed during a training flight.

Gaia hypothesis \'gī-ə\ Model of the earth in which its living and nonliving parts are viewed as a complex interacting system that can be thought of as a single organism. Developed about 1972 largely by British chemist James E. Lovelock and U.S. biologist Lynn Margulis, the Gaia hypothesis (named for the Greek earth goddess) postulates that all living things have a regulatory effect on earth's environment that promotes life overall. The theory is highly controversial.

Gainsborough, Thomas (1727–1788) British painter. At 13 he left his native Suffolk to study in London. By around 1750, back in Suffolk, he had established a reputation in portraiture and landscape painting. He painted landscapes for pleasure; portraiture was his profession. In 1759 he moved to the fashionable spa of Bath, and in 1768 he became a founding member of the Royal Academy of Art. He developed an elegant, formal portrait style inspired by Anthony VAN DYCK, seen in such portraits as his famous *Blue Boy* (1770). In 1774 he moved to London and became a favorite of the royal family. His love of landscape came from studying 17th-cent. Dutch artists, evident in *The Watering Place* (1777). His prodigious output also included many seascapes, pastoral subjects, and children. Among the great portrait painters of the era, he alone devoted serious attention to landscapes.

Gajah Mada \'gä-jä-'mä-dä\ (d.1364) Prime minister of the Majapahit empire (13th–16th cent.) and a national hero in Indonesia. Born a commoner, Gajah Mada rose to power under King Jayanagara (1309–1328), whom he later had killed when the latter took his wife. During the reigns of Jayanagara's daughter Tribhuvana (r.1328–50) and grandson Hayam Wuruk (r.1350–89), Gajah Mada was the most powerful figure in Majapahit, conquering territories that may have included the entire Indonesian archipelago and part of Malaysia. A law book that had great significance in Javanese history was compiled under his instructions, and he was the patron of the principal poet of the era, Prapancha (fl.14th cent.).

galactic cluster See OPEN CLUSTER

galactic halo Nearly spherical volume of thinly scattered stars, GLOBULAR CLUSTERS, and tenuous gas surrounding spiral GALAXIES. It may extend far beyond the disk and contain most of the galaxy's mass. The MILKY WAY GALAXY's halo is thought to be 10,000 light-years across and may be mainly DARK MATTER.

galactic nucleus See ACTIVE GALACTIC NUCLEUS

Galahad \'gal-ə-ˌhad\ In ARTHURIAN LEGEND, the pure knight who achieved a vision of God through the Holy Grail. The illegitimate son of LANCELOT, he alone was worthy to sit in the Siege Perilous at the Round Table, reserved for the one destined to succeed in the quest for the GRAIL. Unlike his father, Galahad was chaste and filled with spiritual fervor. By finding the grail he healed the Fisher King and brought fertility back to the land. See also PERCEVAL.

Galápagos Islands \gə-'lä-pə-gəs\ *Spanish* **Archipiélago de Colón** \ˌär-chē-'pyä-lä-gō-thä-kō-'lōn\ Island group, E Pacific Ocean. A province (pop., 2000 est.: 17,000) of Ecuador, the Galápagos are a group of 19 islands lying on the equator 600 mi (1,000 km) west of the mainland, scattered over 23,000 sq mi (59,500 sq km) of ocean. They became internationally famous after being visited in 1835 by Charles DARWIN; their unusual fauna, including the giant TORTOISE (Spanish, *galápago*), contributed to his ideas on natural selection. Ecuador made the Galápagos a wildlife sanctuary in 1935, and a national park in 1968.

Galati \gä-'läts, gä-'lät-sē\ *German* **Galatz** \'gä-ˌläts\ City (pop., 1997 est.: 331,000), SE Romania. Located at the confluence of the DANUBE and Siret rivers, it was occupied by the Turks from the early 16th cent. until 1829. During World War II, retreating German troops devastated the town and reduced the population, substantially Jewish, to less than half. Extensively rebuilt, it is one of Romania's chief ports and the site of its largest shipyard.

FG

Galatia \gə-'lā-shə\ Ancient district, central ASIA MINOR. It was occupied early in the 3rd cent. B.C. by Celtic tribes (Galatae) who were then overpowered by the SELEUCID king ANTIOCHUS I SOTER in 275 B.C. Passing successively under the rule of PERGAMUM and PONTUS, Galatia became a Roman protectorate in 85 B.C. By the 2nd cent. A.D., the region had become absorbed into the Hellenistic civilization.

galaxy Any of the billions of systems of STARS and interstellar matter that make up the UNIVERSE. Size, composition, and structure vary, but nearly all occur in clusters of a few to as many as 10,000. Each has millions to trillions of stars; in many, as in the MILKY WAY GALAXY, nebulae (see NEBULA) can be detected. Roughly 70% of the bright galaxies in the sky are spiral galaxies, with a central disk and spiral arms containing most of the galaxy's interstellar gas and dust, where stars can form. A large, round bulge surrounds the center (nucleus). Outside this and the disk is a GALACTIC HALO. Elliptical galaxies vary greatly in size and have a spherical or spheroidal shape. Dwarf ellipticals (with a few million stars) are by far the most common kind of galaxy, though none is conspicuous in the sky. Irregular galaxies, like the MAGELLANIC CLOUDS, are relatively rare. Radio galaxies are very strong sources of RADIO WAVES. Seyfert galaxies, with extremely bright nuclei, often emit radio waves and may be related to QUASARS.

Galba \'gal-bə, 'gȯl-bə\ *in full* Servius Galba Caesar Augustus *orig.* Servius Sulpicius Galba (3 B.C.–A.D. 69) Roman emperor (68–69). A member of the Senate, he became CONSUL in 33 and was made governor of Nearer Spain in 60. He led a rebellion in 68 against NERO, who committed suicide. After being accepted as emperor, Galba executed many important Romans, including some responsible for his accession. His seven-month administration was priggish and cruel, his advisers allegedly corrupt. When he chose a successor unacceptable to the PRAETORIAN GUARD, they killed him and his chosen heir.

Galbraith \'gal-ˌbrāth\, **John Kenneth** (b.1908) Canadian-U.S. economist and public servant. Born in Iona Station, Ontario, he held important government posts during the New Deal and World War II. A professor at Harvard Univ. (1949–75), he was an adviser to Pres. John KENNEDY and ambassador to India (1961–63). His influentially liberal writings, praised for their literary merit, examine the strengths and weaknesses of U.S. CAPITALISM and consumerism. *The Affluent Society* (1958) called for less emphasis on production and more attention to public services.

Galdós, Benito Pérez See Benito PÉREZ GALDÓS

Galen \'gā-lən\ *Latin* Galenus (A.D. 129–c.200) Greek physician, writer, and philosopher. He became chief physician to the gladiators in A.D. 157, and later physician to COMMODUS. Based on animal experiments, he described cranial nerves and heart valves and showed that arteries carry blood, not air. However, in extending his findings to human anatomy he was often in error. Following Hippocratic concepts (see HIPPOCRATES), he believed in three connected body systems—brain and nerves for sensation and thought, heart and arteries for life energy, and liver and veins for nutrition and growth—and four humors (body fluids)—blood, yellow bile, black bile, and phlegm—that needed to be in balance. He wrote about 300 works, of which about 150 survive. His influence spread to the Byzantine empire, Arabia, and then Western Europe. In the 16th cent., new anatomical investigations caused the overthrow of his ideas when Andreas VESALIUS found anatomical errors and William HARVEY correctly explained blood circulation.

galena \gə-'lē-nə\ *or* **lead glance** Gray lead sulfide, the chief ore mineral of LEAD. One of the most widely distributed sulfide minerals, it occurs in many types of deposits; in the U.S., it is mined principally in the Mississippi River valley. Galena often contains silver and so is often mined for that metal as well as for lead. It also frequently occurs in close association with antimony, copper, and zinc.

Galerius \gə-'lir-ē-əs\ *in full* Gaius Galerius Valerius Maximianus (d.A.D. 311) Roman emperor (305–11). As caesar (subemperor) and a victorious commander, he apparently induced DIOCLETIAN to begin the persecution of Christians.

In 305 Galerius became augustus (senior emperor) of the East and briefly made himself supreme ruler. He imposed a harsh poll tax on the urban population and kept up the ruthless oppression of Christians. He fell ill in 311; fearing the Christian God was taking vengeance, he issued an edict of tolerance.

Galicia \gə-'li-shə\ *Polish* **Halicz** \'häl-ich\ *Russian* **Galitsiya** \gə-'lēt-sē-yə\ Historic region, E Europe. Covering 30,645 sq mi (79,371 sq km), it included the N slopes of the CARPATHIAN MTNS. and the valleys of the upper VISTULA, DNIESTER, BUG, and Seret rivers. In 1349 the Polish king CASIMIR III annexed Galicia. When Poland was partitioned, beginning in 1772, the territory passed to Austria. Restored to Poland after World War I, E Galicia was taken by the Soviet Union in World War II and united to the Ukrainian S.S.R. After the war, E Galicia remained part of the U.S.S.R. (after 1991, part of Ukraine), while W Galicia was attached to Poland.

Galicia \gə-'lē-shə\ *ancient* Gallaecia. Autonomous community (pop., 1998 est.: 2,724,000) and ancient kingdom, NW Spain. Its name is derived from the Celtic Gallaeci, conquered by the Romans around 137 B.C. Taken by the VISIGOTHS in A.D. 585, the area next passed to the Moors, then to the kingdom of Asturias in the 8th–9th cent. It lost much of its autonomy after the unification of CASTILE and Aragon in 1479. The region was made an autonomous community in 1981; its capital is SANTIAGO DE COMPOSTELA. Agriculture, forestry, and fishing dominate the economy.

Galilean satellite \ˌga-lə-'lē-ən, ˌga-lə-'lā-ən\ Any of the four large moons of JUPITER discovered by GALILEO in 1610. Io is the most volcanically active body in the solar system. Europa may have a liquid ocean under its frozen surface. Ganymede (largest moon in the solar system) and Callisto are larger than Pluto and Mercury.

Galilee *Hebrew* Ha-Galil. Northernmost region of biblical and modern Israel. It contains two of the four holy cities of Judaism, TIBERIAS and Zefat. It was the boyhood home of JESUS and the setting for much of his ministry. It became the center of Jewish scholarship after the destruction of Jerusalem (A.D. 70). In the modern era, the first wave of Jewish immigrants settled there (1882); the first KIBBUTZ, Deganya, was established in 1909 on the Sea of GALILEE.

Galilee, Sea of *or* **Lake Tiberias** Freshwater lake, N Israel. It is 13 mi (21 km) long and 7 mi (11 km) wide; it lies about 700 ft (212 m) below sea level, and receives most of its inflow from the JORDAN RIVER. Archaeological finds dating to some 500,000 years ago are among the oldest in the Middle East. In the 1st cent. A.D., the region was the scene of many episodes in the life of JESUS. Today the lake provides irrigation for agriculture. Modern health resorts have grown up and the baths at TIBERIAS are winter resort attractions.

Galileo \ˌga-lə-'lē-ō, ˌga-lə-'lā-ō\ *in full* **Galileo Galilei** (1564–1642) Italian mathematician, astronomer, and physicist. Inventing the hydrostatic balance (c.1586) made him famous. His 1589 treatise on the center of gravity in solids won him the post of mathematics lecturer at the Univ. of Pisa. He disproved the Aristotelian idea that bodies of different weights fall at different speeds; he also proposed the law of uniform acceleration for falling bodies and showed that a thrown object's path is a parabola. The first to use a TELESCOPE

Galileo Painting by J. Sustermans, c.1637

to study the skies, he discovered (1609–10) that the moon's surface was irregular, that the Milky Way consisted of stars, and that Jupiter had moons (see GALILEAN SATELLITE). In 1611 he spoke persuasively for the COPERNICAN SYSTEM, which put him at odds with Aristotelian professors and led to Copernicanism's being declared false (1616) by the Church. Permitted to write about the Copernican system if he discussed it noncommittally, he wrote his masterpiece,

Dialogue Concerning the Two Chief World Systems (1632). It enraged the Jesuits, and the INQUISITION found Galileo guilty of heresy and forced him to recant. He spent the rest of his life under house arrest, continuing to write and conduct research even after going blind in 1637.

Galileo NASA mission to study JUPITER and its GALILEAN SATELLITES with an orbiter and an atmospheric probe, launched in 1989. Its high-gain antenna failed, so its wealth of valuable data was transmitted back to earth very slowly en route. On arrival in 1995, the probe, released into Jupiter's clouds, discovered large thunderstorms. The orbiter found evidence of volcanoes on Io hotter than earth's and of a liquid ocean below Europa's icy surface, a magnetic field around Ganymede, and evidence of a possible subsurface ocean on Callisto.

gall Abnormal, localized outgrowth or swelling of plant tissue caused by infection from bacteria, fungi, viruses, or nematodes, or by irritation by insects and mites. The common plant disease crown gall is caused by the bacterium *Agrobacterium tumefaciens.*

gall See BILE

Gall, Franz Joseph (1758–1828) German anatomist and physiologist, founder of PHRENOLOGY. Convinced that mental functions reside in specific brain areas and determine behavior, he assumed that the skull surface reflected development of these areas. Paul BROCA proved the first concept, but the second was invalidated (the skull's thickness varies, so its shape does not reflect the brain's). Gall was the first to identify gray matter with active tissue (nerves) and white matter with conducting tissue.

Galla See OROMO

Gallatin \\'ga-lə-t³n\\, (Abraham Alfonse) Albert (1761–1849) U.S. (Swiss-born) secretary of the treasury (1801–14). At 19 he emigrated to Pennsylvania, where he became successful in business and finance. In the U.S. House of Representatives (1795–1801), he set up the forerunner of the ways and means committee. As secretary of the treasury he reduced the national debt by $23 million. He negotiated the treaty ending the War of 1812. Minister to France (1816–23) and to Britain (1826–27), he became the president of the National (later Gallatin) Bank in New York City (1831–39).

Gallaudet \\ˌgal-ə-'det\\, Thomas Hopkins (1787–1851) U.S. philanthropist. Born in Philadelphia, he graduated from Yale College and in 1816 established the first free American school for the deaf at Hartford, Conn. For over 50 years it would remain the main American training center for instructors of the deaf. GALLAUDET UNIV. is named in his honor.

Gallaudet University \\ˌgal-ə-'det\\ Private university for deaf and hard-of-hearing students in Washington, D.C. It has its roots in a school for deaf and blind children founded in 1856 by Amos Kendall and headed 1857–1910 by Edward M. Gallaudet, son of Thomas GALLAUDET. It consists of a college of arts and sciences and additional schools. Total enrollment is about 2,000.

gallbladder Muscular membranous sac under the LIVER that stores and concentrates BILE. Pear-shaped and expandable, it holds about 1.7 fluid oz (50 ml). The gallbladder contracts to discharge bile through the bile duct into the DUODENUM. Disorders include GALLSTONES and inflammation. Its surgical removal produces no serious side effects.

Gallé \\gȧ-'lā\\, **Émile** (1846–1904) French glass and furniture designer. From 1867 he worked in his father's faience and furniture factory in Nancy. His deeply colored opaque pieces, layered and carved or etched with plant motifs, were a great success at the Paris Exhibitions of 1878 and 1889. He used such special effects as metallic foil and air bubbles to produce what he called "marquetry of glass." His furniture designs featured floral inlay and carving; some incorporated inlaid quotations. A proponent of the Art Nouveau style, he collaborated with many colleagues.

gallery In architecture, a long, covered space open on one side, such as a PORTICO or a colonnade. It may be recessed into a wall or elevated on columns or CORBELS. Within an interior, a gallery may be a platform or upper floor projecting from a wall with seating for spectators. In a church NAVE, the long, narrow platforms supported by colonnades are called tribune galleries. In a theater, the gallery is the highest balcony. Galleries appeared in Renaissance houses as long, narrow rooms used as promenades and to exhibit art. The modern art gallery is their descendant.

galley Large seagoing vessel propelled primarily by oars. The Egyptians and Cretans used sail-equipped galleys for war and commerce. About 700 B.C. the Phoenicians apparently launched the bireme, with its two banks of oars. The Greeks first built the TRIREME around 500 B.C. War galleys would cruise in columns, usually several abreast, and would engage the enemy as a phalanx, again abreast. A galley could also confront the enemy with its bow, which was equipped with a ram, grappling irons, and missile-hurling devices. Its maneuverability maintained its military importance into the 16th cent. See also LONGSHIP.

Gallia Narbonensis See NARBONENSIS

Gallic Wars (58–50 B.C.) Campaigns in which Julius CAESAR conquered GAUL. Clad in a bloodred cloak, he led his troops to victories throughout the province, relying on superior strategy, tactics, discipline, and military engineering. Having driven back the Helvetii, subdued the Belgic tribes, and reconquered the Veneti (56), he crossed the Rhine River to raid Germany (55), and crossed the Channel to raid Britain (55, 54). His major triumph was the defeat of VERCINGETORIX in 52. He described the campaigns in *De bello Gallico* ("On the Gallic War").

Gallienus \\ˌgal-ē-'ē-nəs\\, **Publius Licinius Egnatius** (A.D. 218?–268) Roman emperor who ruled jointly with his father, VALERIAN (253–60), then alone (260–68). He took charge of the W frontiers, winning a series of battles against the Goths and others. When the Persians devastated the East and his father died in captivity, he was left with only Italy and the Balkans. He was killed while trying to put down a Goth insurgency. His reforms as emperor included the transfer of army command to professional equestrian officers, expansion of the cavalry, and an intellectual renaissance at Rome, discernible in its art and literature.

gallinule \\'ga-lə-ˌnül\\ Any of several species of marsh birds (family Rallidae). Gallinules are about 12–18 in. (30–45 cm) long, with a compressed body like those of the related RAILS and COOTS. They have a fleshy plate on the forehead and long, thin toes that enable them to run over floating vegetation. Many species have brightly colored areas of plumage or skin. They are noisy, inquisitive, and less secretive than most rails. They build a bulky nest of rushes on or near the water.

Gallipoli \\gə-'li-pə-lē\\ *Turkish* **Gelibolu** \\ˌge-lē-bȯ-'lü\\ *ancient* Callipolis. Seaport and town (pop., 1990: 18,000), European Turkey. It lies at the entrance to the Sea of MARMARA, southwest of ISTANBUL. First colonized by the Greeks, it was the site of an important Byzantine fortress. It became the first Ottoman conquest in Europe (c.1356) and was used as a naval base. Much of the town was destroyed in World War I during the DARDANELLES CAMPAIGN. Historic sites include tombs of Thracian kings.

Gallipoli Campaign See DARDANELLES CAMPAIGN

gallstone Mass of crystallized substances that forms in the GALLBLADDER. The most common type occurs when the liver secretes BILE with too much CHOLESTEROL to stay in solution. In the gallbladder, stones may cause INFLAMMATION or produce no symptoms. A stone obstructing the bile duct causes severe pain. Gallstones usually must be removed with the gallbladder by LAPAROSCOPY or broken up with ULTRASOUND. In some cases a stone can be treated by giving the patient bile salts, which help redissolve cholesterol.

Gallup, George (Horace) (1901–1984) U.S. public-opinion statistician. Born in Jefferson, Iowa, he taught journalism until 1932, when an advertising firm hired him to conduct public-opinion surveys for its clients. He became a pioneer in the scientific sampling of public opinion, and his Gallup Poll, as well as other public-opinion polls, gained credibility after forecasting Franklin ROOSEVELT's 1936 presidential victory. Gallup founded the American Institute of Public Opinion (1935) and the Audience Research Institute (1939).

Galsworthy \\'gȯlz-ˌwər-thē\\, **John** (1867–1933) English novelist and playwright. He gave up a law career to become a writer, and many of his works have legal themes. He published several works before *The Forsyte Saga* (1906-22), the

FG

family chronicle by which he is chiefly remembered. He continued the Forsyte story in three further novels collected in *A Modern Comedy* (1929). His naturalistic plays usually examine a controversial ethical or social problem; they include *The Silver Box* (1906) and *Loyalties* (1922). He won the Nobel Prize in 1932.

Galton, Francis (*later* **Sir Francis**) (1822–1911) British explorer, anthropologist, and eugenicist. Galton, a cousin of Charles DARWIN, studied medicine at Cambridge Univ. but never took a degree. As a young man he traveled widely in Europe and Africa, making useful contributions in zoology and geography. He was among the first to recognize the implications of Darwin's theory of evolution, eventually coining the word EUGENICS to denote the science of planned human betterment through selective mating. He also wrote important works on human intelligence, fingerprinting, applied statistics, twins, blood transfusions, criminality, meteorology, and measurement.

Francis Galton Painting by G. Graef, 1882

Galvani \gäl-'vä-nē\, **Luigi** (1737–1798) Italian physician and physicist. His early research focused on comparative anatomy, including the structure of kidney tubules and the middle ear. His interest in electricity was inspired by the fact that dead frogs underwent convulsions when attached to an iron fence to dry. He experimented with muscular stimulation by electrical means, using an electrostatic machine and a Leyden jar; animal electricity was henceforth his major field of investigation.

galvanizing Protection of IRON or STEEL against exposure to the atmosphere and consequent rusting by application of a ZINC coating. Properly applied, galvanizing may protect from atmospheric CORROSION for 15–30 years or more. If the coating is damaged, the iron or steel continues to be protected by sacrificial corrosion, atmospheric oxidation that spares the iron and affects the zinc (as long as it lasts).

galvanometer \gal-və-'nä-mə-tər\ Instrument for measuring small ELECTRIC CURRENTS. A common galvanometer consists of a light coil of wire suspended from a metallic ribbon between the poles of a permanent magnet. As current passes through the coil, the MAGNETIC FIELD it produces reacts with the magnetic field of the permanent magnet, producing a TORQUE. The torque causes the coil to rotate, moving an attached needle or mirror. The current flowing in the coil is measured by the movement of the needle or by the deflection of a beam of light reflected from the mirror.

Galveston City (pop., 2000: 60,000) and port of entry, SE Texas. Located at the NE end of Galveston Island in the Gulf of Mexico, it was the pirate Jean LAFFITE's headquarters (1817–21). During the Texas revolt against Mexico (1835–36), it briefly served as the capital. During the AMERICAN CIVIL WAR it was an important Confederate supply port. The city has suffered from several hurricanes in the 20th cent. but remains a major deepwater port.

Gálvez \'gäl-₁ves\, **José** *later* marqués (Marquess) de la Sonora (1720–1787) Spanish colonial administrator. As inspector general in New Spain (Mexico) 1765–71, he reorganized the tax system, formed a government tobacco monopoly, and occupied Upper California. As minister of the Indies (from 1775), he worked to expand commerce. He introduced the intendancy system in 1786. Gálvez is considered Spain's greatest colonial administrator.

Galway \'gȯl-₁wā\ County (pop., 1995 est.: 179,000), W Ireland. With an area of 2,293 sq mi (5,939 sq km), it lies on the Atlantic Ocean. Its seat is the town of Galway (pop., 1995 est.: 51,000). Still largely agricultural, Galway has the largest Gaelic-speaking population of any Irish county.

Gama, Vasco da *later* conde (Count) da Vidigueira (c.1460–1524) Portuguese navigator. On his first voyage to India

(1497–99), he traveled around the Cape of Good Hope with four ships. In 1502 MANUEL I sent a fleet of 20 ships led by da Gama to establish Portuguese supremacy in India; da Gama forced allegiance along the way from local rulers and attacked Arab shipping. After various battles, he secured obedience to Portuguese rule and returned home. Appointed Portuguese viceroy in India, he died shortly after arriving in Goa. His voyages opened the sea route from Western Europe to the East.

Vasco da Gama Painting, Portuguese school, early 16th cent.

Gambetta \₁gäⁿ-bə-'tä, *Engl* gam-'be-tə\, **Léon** (1838–1882) French statesman who helped found the THIRD REPUBLIC. He became famous as a lawyer defending republican critics of the SECOND EMPIRE. He helped direct the defense of France during the FRANCO–PRUSSIAN WAR. He used his persuasive skill to push for ratification of the Constitutional Laws of 1875, which became the basis of the new parliamentary republic. As president of the Chamber of Deputies (1879–81) and premier (1881–82), he continued his advocacy of democratic ideals.

Gambia *officially* **Republic of the Gambia** Republic, W Africa. Constituting an enclave in Senegal, it lies along the Gambia River stretching inland 295 mi (475 km) from the Atlantic Ocean. Area: 4,127 sq mi (10,689 sq km). Population (2000): 1,367,000. Capital: BANJUL. About two-fifths of

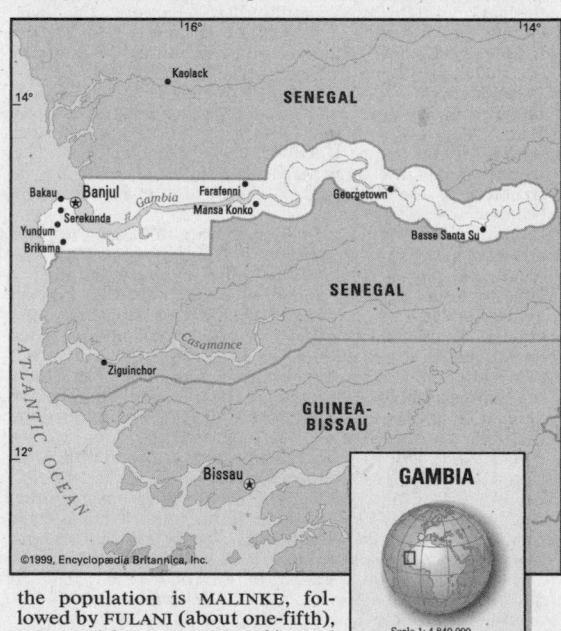

©1999, Encyclopædia Britannica, Inc.

the population is MALINKE, followed by FULANI (about one-fifth), WOLOF (about one-seventh), and other groups. Language: English (official). Religion: Islam. Monetary unit: dalasi. Gambia is generally hilly and the climate subtropical, with savanna in the uplands and swamps in low-lying areas. It has a developing market economy based largely on the production and export of peanuts, though only about one-sixth of the country is arable. The river serves as a major transportation artery. Tourism is an important source of revenue. It is a republic with one legislative body; its head of state and government is the president. Beginning around the 13th cent. A.D., the Wolof, Malinke, and Fulani peoples settled in different parts of what is now Gambia and established villages and then kingdoms in the region. European exploration began when the Portuguese sighted the Gambia River in 1455. In the 17th cent., when Britain and France both settled in the area, the British Ft. James, on an island about 20 mi (32 km) from the river's mouth, was an important collection point for the SLAVE TRADE. In 1783 the Treaty of Versailles reserved the Gambia River for Britain. After the British abolished slavery in 1807, they built a fort at the mouth of the river to block the continuing slave trade. In 1889 Gambia's boundaries were agreed upon by Britain and France; the British declared a protectorate over the area in 1894. Independence was proclaimed in 1965, and Gambia became a republic within the Commonwealth in 1970. It formed a limited confederation with Senegal in 1982, which was dissolved in 1989. The political turmoil of the 1990s continued in the new century.

gambling Betting or staking of something of value on the outcome of a game or event. Commonly associated with gambling are HORSE RACING, BOXING, numerous PLAYING-CARD and DICE games, COCKFIGHTING, JAI ALAI, and recreational BILLIARDS and DARTS. BINGO and LOTTERY also represent forms of gambling. Probability in gambling is usually expressed in terms of "odds against winning." Casino gambling is now legal in many states, and lotteries are employed by many states to raise revenues. See also BOOK-MAKING.

gamelan \'ga-mə-ˌlan\ Indigenous orchestra of Java and Bali, and more generally of Indonesia and Malaysia, usually consisting largely of gongs, xylophones, and xylophone-like metallophones. Gamelan polyphony is complex and many-voiced. The melody is taken by the voice, flute, or rebab (a bowed stringed instrument); under it, the other instruments provide rhythmic paraphrases of the melody, producing a shimmering, variegated texture. The gamelan has influenced Western composers from Claude DEBUSSY to Philip GLASS.

game show *or* **quiz show** Radio or television show designed to test the knowledge or luck of contestants or experts. Among the shows popular on U.S. radio were *Dr. I.Q.* (1939–49), *Information, Please* (1938–48), and *The Quiz Kids* (1940–53). The genre was adopted by television and cash awards were increased. To increase their shows' popularity, some producers began feeding answers to contestants chosen to win; an accusation of unfair practices on *Twenty-one* (1958) led to a government investigation and the quick demise of the big-money shows. The game show later regained popularity in formats with lower stakes and easier questions, as on *The Price Is Right, Jeopardy!,* and *Wheel of Fortune.*

game theory Branch of applied mathematics devised to analyze certain situations in which there is an interplay between parties that may have similar, opposed, or mixed interests. Game theory was developed by John VON NEUMANN and Oscar Morgenstern in their book *The Theory of Games and Economic Behavior* (1944). In a typical game, decision-making "players," who each have their own goals, try to outsmart one another by anticipating the others' decisions; the game is finally resolved as a consequence of these decisions. See also DECISION THEORY.

gametophyte \gə-ˈmē-tə-ˌfīt\ In certain plants, the sexual phase (or an individual representing the phase) in the ALTERNATION OF GENERATIONS. The alternate, nonsexual phase is the SPOROPHYTE. In the gametophyte phase, male and female organs develop and produce eggs and sperm (gametes), which unite in fertilization. The fertilized egg (zygote) develops into the sporophyte, which produces numerous single-celled SPORES, which in turn develop directly into new gametes.

gamma globulin \'gläb-yə-lən\ Subgroup of the GLOBULINS. In humans and many other mammals, most ANTIBODIES are in the gamma globulin fraction of blood. A human gamma globulin preparation may be administered (by injection) to persons lacking IMMUNITY, either generally or to a particular disease.

gamma ray Penetrating very short-wavelength ELECTROMAGNETIC RADIATION, similar to an X ray but of higher energy, that is emitted spontaneously by some radioactive substances (see RADIOACTIVITY). Gamma radiation also originates in the decay of certain SUBATOMIC PARTICLES, and in particle-antiparticle annihilation. Gamma rays can initiate NUCLEAR FISSION, can be absorbed by ejection of an electron (see PHOTOELECTRIC EFFECT), and can be scattered by free electrons (see COMPTON EFFECT).

gamma-ray astronomy Study of astronomical objects that emit GAMMA RAYS. Gamma-ray telescopes are designed to study high-energy astrophysical systems, including stellar CORONAS, WHITE DWARF STARS, NEUTRON STARS, BLACK HOLES, SUPERNOVA remnants, clusters of galaxies, and diffuse gamma-ray COSMIC BACKGROUND RADIATION. Puzzling gamma-ray bursts detected in the early 1960s have an even distribution (unlike that of stars in this galaxy), making their origin likely to be extragalactic. In the early 1970s the first gamma-ray observatory satellite detected a bright gamma-ray source with no obvious optical counterpart. Detection of periodic X-ray and gamma-ray emission in 1992 suggested that it is a PULSAR, the nearest known.

Gamow \'ga-ˌmȯf\, **George** *orig.* Georgy Antonovich Gamov (1904–1968) Russian-U.S. nuclear physicist and cosmologist. His quantum theory of radioactivity gave the first successful explanation of the behavior of radioactive elements. His "liquid drop" model of atomic nuclei was the basis for modern theories of nuclear fission and fusion. He came to the U.S. in 1934 and worked with Edward TELLER on beta decay (1936) and a theory of the structures of red giant stars (1942). In the 1950s he pursued biochemistry; his theories of genetic-code structure were later proved true. He also wrote popular works on subjects such as relativity and cosmology.

Gance \'gäⁿs\, **Abel** *orig.* Eugène Alexandre Péréthon (1889–1981) French film director. He worked in the cinema from 1909, finally winning acclaim with *Mater dolorosa* (1917) and *Tenth Symphony* (1918). His *J'accuse* (1918) and *The Wheel* (1923) were critically hailed. In his masterpiece, *Napoléon* (1927), he used experimental techniques to emphasize cinematic movement; battle sequences were projected on a triple screen to produce a three-dimensional effect, and the film pioneered in the use of stereophonic sound. A triumph in Europe, it fared badly in a harshly cut version in the U.S. but was finally released in its original glory in 1981.

Gandhi \'gän-dē\, **Indira** *orig.* Indira Priyadarshini Nehru (1917–1984) Prime minister of India (1966–77, 1980–84). The only child of Jawaharlal NEHRU, she studied in India and at Oxford Univ. In 1942 she married Feroze Gandhi (d.1960), a fellow member of the INDIAN NATIONAL CONGRESS. In 1966 she became leader of the Congress Party and, consequently, prime minister. She instituted major reforms, including a strict population-control program. In 1971 she mobilized Indian forces against Pakistan in the cause of E. Bengal's secession (now Bangladesh). She oversaw the incorporation of Sikkim in 1974. Convicted in 1975 of violating election laws, she declared a state of emergency, jailing opponents and limiting personal freedoms. Defeated in the following election, she returned to power in 1980. In 1984, in response to Sikh separatist violence, she ordered an army attack on their GOLDEN TEMPLE, which resulted in over 450 Sikh deaths. She was shot and killed by her own Sikh bodyguards in revenge.

Gandhi, Mohandas K(aramchand) *known as* **Mahatma Gandhi** (1869–1948) Preeminent leader of Indian nationalism and prophet of nonviolence in the 20th cent. Gandhi grew up in a home steeped in religion, and he took for granted *ahimsa* (noninjury to all living beings) and religious tolerance. He studied law in England and joined an Indian firm in S. Africa. There he became an effective advocate for Indian rights, and in 1906 he first put into action SATYAGRAHA, his technique of nonviolent resistance. He returned to India in 1914, and soon became the leader of a nationwide struggle for Indian home rule. He refashioned the INDIAN NATIONAL CONGRESS into an effective political instrument of Indian nationalism and undertook major campaigns of nonviolent resistance in 1920–22, 1930–34 (including his momentous march to the sea to collect salt to protest a government monopoly), and 1940–42. In the 1930s

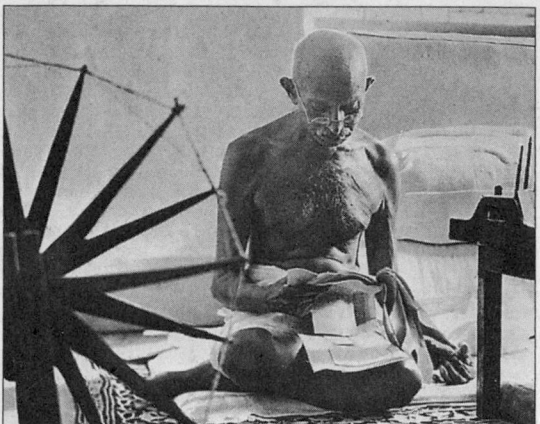

Mohandas K. Gandhi, 1946

he also campaigned against discrimination against India's untouchable class and concentrated on educating rural India and promoting cottage industry. In 1947 the country was partitioned into India and Pakistan, a great disappointment to Gandhi, who had long worked for Hindu-Muslim unity. In September 1947 he ended rioting in Calcutta by fasting. In January 1948 he was shot down by a young Hindu fanatic. Gandhi won the affection and loyalty of millions and became known to all as the Mahatma, or great soul.

Gandhi, Rajiv (Ratna) (1944–1991) Indian politician, prime minister of India (1984–89). Son of Indira GANDHI, he became an airline pilot. He entered politics after the death of his brother Sanjay in 1980. Sworn in as prime minister the day his mother was assassinated, he led the Congress (I) Party to a landslide victory in elections that year. He strove to reform the government bureaucracy and liberalize the country's economy, but his attempts to discourage separatist movements failed. He resigned in 1989 but remained leader of the party. He was assassinated in 1991 while running for reelection. His widow, Sonia (b.1947), was elected head of the Congress (I) Party in 1998.

Ganesha *or* **Ganesa** \gə-'nā-shə\ Elephant-headed Hindu god, the son of SHIVA and Parvati. He is also revered in Jainism, and he is important in the art and mythology of Buddhist Asia. As the remover of obstacles, Ganesha is invoked when beginning worship or starting any new venture. He was popular with Indian nationalists, who saw British colonialism as an obstacle to be removed. The patron of letters and learning, he is the legendary scribe who wrote down the *MAHABHARATA*.

Ganga dynasty \'gäŋ-gə\ Either of two distinct but remotely related Indian dynasties. The Western Gangas ruled in Mysore state about 250–1004. They encouraged scholarly work, built some remarkable temples, and encouraged cross-peninsular trade. The Eastern Gangas ruled KALINGA 1028–1435. They were great patrons of religion and the arts; the temples of the Ganga period rank among the masterpieces of Hindu architecture.

Ganges River \'gan-ˌjēz\ *Hindi* **Ganga** \'gəŋ-gə\ River, N India. It is held sacred by followers of HINDUISM. On its 1,560-mi (2,510-km) course, it flows southeast through the Indian states of Bihar and W. Bengal. In Bangladesh it is joined by the BRAHMAPUTRA and Meghna rivers. Their combined waters empty into the Bay of BENGAL and form a delta 200 mi (320 km) wide. Its plain is one of the most fertile and densely populated regions in the world.

Gangetic Plain \gan-'je-tik\ *or* **Indo-Gangetic Plain** Fertile region in north-central India stretching westward from the BRAHMAPUTRA River valley and the Ganges Delta to the INDUS RIVER valley. It contains the subcontinent's richest and most densely populated areas. It is largely made up of alluvial soil, deposited by the Ganges, Brahmaputra, and Indus rivers. The E part of the plain has summer rainfall so heavy that vast areas become swamps or shallow lakes.

ganglion \'gaŋ-glē-ən\ In vertebrates, an aggregate of nerve-cell bodies outside the central NERVOUS SYSTEM (CNS). The two types of spinal ganglion contain the nerve-cell bodies of the nerve fibers that carry impulses toward the CNS (afferent NEURONS in dorsal root ganglia) or away from it (efferent neurons in ventral root ganglia).

Gang of Four Powerful members of a radical political elite convicted for implementing the harsh policies of MAO ZEDONG during the CULTURAL REVOLUTION. The four were Wang Hongwen, Zhang Chunqiao, Yao Wenyuan, and Mao's wife, JIANG QING. Manipulating the youthful RED GUARDS, the Gang of Four controlled areas of education policy and party policies regarding intellectuals. They maintained their power until Mao's death in 1976, when they were imprisoned; they stood trial in 1980–81.

gangrene Localized soft-tissue death from prolonged blood-supply blockage. It can occur in ARTERIOSCLEROSIS, DIABETES MELLITUS, or decubitus ULCER, and after severe BURNS or FROSTBITE. In dry gangrene, gradual blood-supply decrease turns the part discolored and cold, then dark and dry. Treatment requires improving blood flow. Moist gangrene comes from a sudden blood-supply cutoff. Bacterial infection causes swelling, discoloration, and then a foul smell. Along with antibiotics, tissue removal may be needed to prevent spread, which can be fatal. A highly virulent form, gas gangrene, is named for gas bubbles under the skin produced by a highly lethal toxin from CLOSTRIDIUM bacteria.

Gangtok \'gəŋ-ˌtók\ Town (pop., 1991: 25,000), capital of SIKKIM state, NE India. At an elevation of 5,600 ft (1,700 m), it was the governmental seat of the kingdom of Sikkim until the monarchy was abolished (1975), an important point on the India–Tibet trade route until the border with Tibet was closed (1962). The former royal palace and chapel are located there; the noted Buddhist monastery of Rumtek is nearby.

Ganioda'yo See HANDSOME LAKE

gannet Any of three oceanic bird species (family Sulidae) closely related to the BOOBY. Gannets are found in the N. Atlantic, where they are the largest seabirds, and in temperate waters around Africa and Australia. Adults are mainly white with black-tipped wing feathers. They have a tapered beak and pointed tail. They dive with half-closed wings to catch fish and squid. Expert fliers, they spend most of their lives over water. They nest in dense colonies on cliffs. The largest species is the 40-in. (100-cm) northern gannet.

Gannett Co., Inc. U.S. newspaper group. It originated with Frank Ernest Gannett (1876–1957) in 1906 and was incorporated in 1923. It promoted innovative technology with the teletypesetter, shortwave radio, and telephoto network. In 1982 it began publishing *USA Today*, the first national general-interest newspaper in the U.S. Today it owns about 100 daily papers, with a total circulation of about 6 million, mostly in small and medium-sized cities. Its larger papers include the *Des Moines Register* and the *Detroit Evening News*. It also owns about 20 television stations.

Ganymede *Latin* Catamitus. In Greek legend, a boy of unusual beauty who was carried off by ZEUS disguised as an eagle and made cupbearer to the gods. Other versions of the legend trace his abduction to other gods or to King MINOS of Crete.

GAO See GENERAL ACCOUNTING OFFICE

gar Any of several large N. or Central American fishes (genus *Lepisosteus*) dating back to the EOCENE EPOCH. Gars are found chiefly basking at the surface in sluggish freshwater and commonly breathe atmospheric air. Their jaws and face form a sharp-toothed beak, and their body is encased in an armor of diamond-shaped, thick scales. They are highly voracious predators, with long rows of needlelike teeth. The alligator gar of the S U.S. attains a length of about 10 ft (3 m) and is one of the largest freshwater fishes.

Garand \gə-'rand, 'gar-ənd\, **John C(antius)** (1888–1974) U.S. (Canadian-born) firearms engineer. Born in St. Rémi, Quebec, he moved with his family to Connecticut in 1898. From 1919 he worked at the SPRINGFIELD ARMORY; after 17 years, he devised a gas-operated weapon of .30-in. caliber that was 43 in. (109 cm) long yet weighed only 9.5 lbs (4.3 kg). Adopted in 1936, the M1 became the world's first standard-issue autoloading infantry rifle; it gave U.S. troops in World War II and the Korean War such an advantage in firepower that George PATTON called it "the greatest battle implement ever devised." More than 5 million M1s were manufactured.

garbanzo See CHICKPEA

Garbo, Greta *orig.* Greta Louisa Gustafsson (1905–1990) Swedish-U.S. film star. She was discovered by the Swedish film director Mauritz Stiller, who cast her in *The Story of Gösta Berling* (1924) and became her mentor and coach. They were hired by MGM in 1925, and Garbo's beauty and magnetic personality made her an instant star in her first U.S. film, *The Torrent* (1926). Aloof, enigmatic, yet passionate, she mesmerized audiences in such films as *Love* (1927), *Anna Christie* (1930), *Grand Hotel* (1932), *Anna Karenina* (1935), *Camille* (1937), and *Ninotchka* (1939). Her reclusive life after her sudden retirement at age 36 added to her mystique.

Greta Garbo in *Camille*, 1936

García Lorca \gär-'thē-ä-'lȯr-kä\, **Federico** (1898–1936) Spanish poet and dramatist. He was an established experimental poet when he became famous for *The Gypsy Ballads* (1928), a verse collection lyrically combining his musical, poetical, and spiritual impulses; as in many of his later works, its themes and images were drawn from folk traditions. Of his many poems of death, *Lament for the Death of a Bullfighter* (1935) is his greatest poem. His dramatic trilogy consisting of *Blood Wedding* (1933), *Yerma* (1934), and *The House of Bernarda Alba* (1936) is the best known of his masterpieces. He was shot without trial by fascists in the SPANISH CIVIL WAR at 38.

García Márquez \gär-'sē-ä-'mär-käs\, **Gabriel (José)** (b.1928) Colombian-Mexican writer. He worked many years as a journalist, screenwriter, and publicist. His enormously admired and influential novel *One Hundred Years of Solitude* (1967), became the principal vehicle for the style known as MAGIC REALISM. Later novels include *The Autumn of the Patriarch* (1975), *Love in the Time of Cholera* (1985), and *The General in His Labyrinth* (1989). His collections of short stories and novellas include *No One Writes to the Colonel* (1968) and *Leaf Storm* (1955). He received the Nobel Prize in 1982.

Gabriel García Márquez, 1982

Gard, Roger Martin du See Roger MARTIN DU GARD

Garda, Lake *ancient* Lacus Benacus. Lake, N Italy. Largest of the Italian lakes, it is 34 mi (54 km) long and 2–11 mi (3–18 km) wide, with a shoreline of 78 mi (125 km). It is fed by the Sarca River, while the Mincio flows out toward the PO RIVER. The lake is encircled by the Gardesana scenic route, opened in 1931, and is sheltered by the ALPS to the north, which promotes a temperate Mediterranean climate. It is a popular resort area.

garden Plot of ground where plants are cultivated. The earliest surviving detailed garden plan is Egyptian and dates from about 1400 B.C.; it shows tree-lined avenues and rectangular ponds. Hellenistic and Byzantine gardens were conspicuously luxurious in their display of precious materials. Islamic gardens made use of water, often in pools and fed by narrow canals. In Renaissance Europe, gardens reflected confidence in human ability to impose order on the external world; Italian gardens emphasized the unity of house and garden. French 17th- and 18th-cent. gardens were rigidly symmetrical. In 18th-cent. England, "natural" gardens were developed that made use of irregular, nonsymmetrical layouts. Chinese and Japanese gardens have generally harmonized with the natural landscape, and have employed rocks gathered from great distances as a universal decorative feature. Later developments include the abstract garden, which might feature only sand and rocks, and miniature gardens made in trays (see BONSAI).

garden city Ideal planned community as envisioned by the British town planner Ebenezer Howard (1850–1928). It was to combine the amenities of urban and rural life. At the center would be a garden ringed with a civic and cultural complex, a park, housing, and industry, the whole surrounded by an agricultural green belt. Traffic would move along radial avenues and ring roads. The first garden city was built at Letchworth, England, in 1903. Imitators have often ignored Howard's stipulation that the town be a self-contained, true mixed-use community.

Garden Grove City (pop., 2000: 165,000), SW California. Located south of ANAHEIM, it is the site of the Crystal Cathedral, a church sheathed in 10,000 panes of glass, designed by Philip JOHNSON.

gardenia Any of the approximately 200 species of ornamental shrubs and trees in the genus *Gardenia,* in the MADDER FAMILY, native to tropical and subtropical Africa and Asia. Gardenias have white or yellow tubular flowers, evergreen leaves, and large, berrylike fruits. Cape jasmine (*G. jasminoides),* native to China, is the fragrant species sold by florists.

Gardner, Alexander (1821–1882) Scottish-U.S. photographer. In 1856 he emigrated from Scotland and was hired by Mathew BRADY as a portrait photographer. In 1861 he began to assist Brady in making a photographic record of the Civil War. Brady refused to give him public credit, so in 1863 he opened his own portrait studio and continued photographing the war on his own. From 1867, he chronicled the building of the Union Pacific Railroad.

Gardner, Erle Stanley (1889–1970) U.S. detective novelist. Born in Malden, Mass., he became a trial lawyer and began writing pulp fiction, basing the courtroom scenes and brilliant legal maneuvers on his own tactics. He gave up the law following the success in 1933 of his first novels featuring the lawyer-detective Perry Mason, *The Case of the Velvet Claws* and *The Case of the Sulky Girl*, and 80 Perry Mason novels followed. He also wrote two other series of detective stories, one under the pseudonym A. A. Fair.

Garfield, James A(bram) (1831–1881) 20th president of the U.S. (1881). Born in Orange, Ohio, he taught at and headed an academy that became Hiram College. In the Civil War he led the 42nd Ohio Volunteers and fought at Shiloh and Chickamauga. He resigned as a major general to serve in the U.S. House of Representatives (1863–80). A RADICAL REPUBLICAN during Reconstruction, he was the House Republican leader from 1876. At the 1880 Republican nominating convention, the delegates deadlocked; on the 36th

James A. Garfield, 1880

ballot Garfield was nominated in a compromise, with C. A. ARTHUR as vice president, and he won the presidency by a narrow margin. His brief term, less than 150 days, was marked by a dispute with Sen. Roscoe CONKLING over patronage. On July 2 he was shot at Washington's railroad station by Charles J. Guiteau, an Arthur supporter. He died on Sept. 19 after 11 weeks of public debate over the ambiguous constitutional conditions for presidential succession (later clarified by the 20th and 25th Amendments).

gargoyle Carved spout that drains water from a rooftop gutter. The Gothic gargoyle was usually a grotesque bird or animal sitting on the back of a cornice and projecting forward several feet. The term is often applied to any grotesque or fantastic beast, such as the chimeras that decorate NOTRE-DAME DE PARIS.

Garibaldi \ˌgar-ə-ˈbȯl-dē\, **Giuseppe** (1807–1882) Italian patriot and soldier of the RISORGIMENTO. He came under the influence of Giuseppe MAZZINI in 1834, took part in a failed republican revolution in Piedmont, and escaped to France. In exile in S. America (1836–48), he learned guerrilla warfare tactics during liberation attempts in Brazil and Uruguay. He returned to Italy in 1848 with his small band of "Red Shirts" and fought in Milan against Austria and in Rome against the French. His bold retreat through central Italy made him a well-known figure. In 1859 he led an army in N Italy against Austria. In 1860, with no government backing, he raised an army of about 1,000 men and attacked Sicily; by the end of his campaign, he commanded 30,000 men, with whom he seized Naples. He handed all of S Italy over to VICTOR EMMANUEL II and hailed him as the first king of a united Italy. With secret support from Victor Emmanuel, he led unsuccessful campaigns into the Papal States in 1862 and 1867.

Garland, Judy *orig.* Frances Gumm (1922–1969) U.S. singer and film actress. Born into a vaudeville family in Grand Rapids, Minn., she made her stage debut at 3 and toured with her sisters until her debut in a short film, *Every Sunday* (1936). She was a hit in *Broadway Melody of 1938* and starred as a wholesome girlfriend in nine films with Mickey ROONEY. She became an international star as Dorothy in *The Wizard of Oz* (1939). Among her other musical hits are *Meet Me in St. Louis* (1944), *Easter Parade* (1948), and *Summer Stock* (1950). Her sweet but power-

Judy Garland

ful voice and emotional range made her legendary as a concert performer. After record-breaking engagements at the London Palladium and New York's Palace Theatre, she returned to the screen in triumph in *A Star Is Born* (1954). Her life was troubled by broken marriages and reliance on drugs, which led to her early death. Her daughter Liza Minnelli (see Vincent MINNELLI) followed her to the musical stage.

garlic Bulbous perennial plant (*Allium sativum*) of the LILY FAMILY, native to central Asia and growing wild in Italy and S France. A classic ingredient in many national cuisines, garlic has a powerful, onionlike aroma and pungent taste. Since ancient and medieval times it has been prized for its medicinal properties; it was formerly carried as a charm against vampires and other evils. Garlic bulbs are used sliced or crushed to flavor sauces, stews, and salad dressings. The membranous skin of the garlic bulb encloses up to 20 edible cloves.

Garmo Peak See COMMUNISM PEAK

Garner, John Nance (1868–1967) U.S. politician. Born in Red River Co., Texas, he served in the U.S. House of Representatives (1903–33), becoming speaker in 1931. Adept at backstage maneuvering, he supported the graduated income tax and the Federal Reserve System. Elected vice president under Franklin ROOSEVELT in 1932 and 1936, he was a conservative within the New Deal administration, and he broke with Roosevelt in his second term over the effort to pack (enlarge) the U.S. Supreme Court.

garnet Any of a group of common SILICATE MINERALS with identical crystal structure but highly variable chemical composition. Garnets are most often found in metamorphic rocks; they may be colorless, black, or many shades of red and green. They are used as abrasives for fine sanding and polishing of wood, leather, glass, metals, and plastics, as sandblasting agents, and in nonskid surface coatings. Garnet is the birthstone for January. Garnets are mined in New York, Maine, and Idaho in the U.S., the world's leading producer.

Garnier \gȧrn-ˈyā\, **Francis** (*orig.* Marie-Joseph-François) (1839–1873) French naval officer and explorer. He joined

the navy and participated in the French advance into S Vietnam in 1861. He promoted the exploration of the Mekong River and took part in the first European expedition to enter Yunnan from the south (1866–68). His *Voyage of exploration in Indo-China, 1866–68* (1873) is a valuable account of the countries through which he passed. Summoned to Saigon in 1873 to rein in unauthorized trading with China, he instead tried to seize territory for France in N Vietnam and was killed in the attempt.

Garnier \gȧrn-ˈyā\, **Tony** (1869–1948) French architect. The son of Charles Garnier (see PARIS OPERA), he held the position of architect of Lyon 1905–19. He is known chiefly for his Cité Industrielle, a farsighted plan for an industrial city. Most striking is his depiction of simplified REINFORCED-CONCRETE forms. The most important work in Lyon to emerge from his Cité Industrielle was the large stockyard complex of 1908–24.

Garonne River \gȧ-ˈrȯn\ *ancient* Garumna. River, SW France. The most important river of SW France, it is 357 mi (575 km) long. Formed by two glacial headstreams in the central Spanish PYRENEES, it flows north through mountain passes and descends to flow east across France. It continues to TOULOUSE and to BORDEAUX, then unites with the Dordogne to form the vast Gironde Estuary.

Garrett, Pat(rick Floyd) (1850–1908) U.S. lawman. Born in Chambers Co., Ala., he worked as a cowboy until 1879, when he settled in Lincoln Co., N.M., and became sheriff. In 1881 he tracked down and shot the escaped BILLY THE KID. He was fatally shot in a dispute over a ranch lease, but suspicion lingered that he was executed by an enemy from his days as sheriff.

Garrick, David (1717–1779) British actor, producer, and playwright. Winning fame with his debut as Richard III in 1741, he played diverse roles in such plays as *King Lear, Hamlet,* and Ben JONSON's *The Alchemist;* he was acclaimed for his naturalistic style and came to be regarded as one of England's greatest actors. As ACTOR-MANAGER of the DRURY LANE THEATRE (1747–76) he reformed theatrical stage practices, replaced many Restoration adaptations of Shakespeare with his own versions, and made it London's most prosperous theater. He wrote over 20 plays.

Garrison, William Lloyd (1805–1879) U.S. journalist and abolitionist. Born in Newburyport, Mass., he joined the abolitionist movement at 25 and edited several local newspapers dedicated to moral reform. In 1831 he founded *The Liberator,* which became the most radical of the antislavery journals. In 1833 he helped found the AMERICAN ANTI-SLAVERY SOCIETY. Following a split within the society, partly over women's participation (which he favored), he became president of the smaller society (1840–65). As his influence waned, his radicalism increased; through *The Liberator* he hailed John BROWN's raid. In the Civil War he forswore pacifism to support Pres. Abraham LINCOLN and welcomed the Emancipation Proclamation. In 1865 he retired but continued to press for women's suffrage, temperance, and free trade.

Garter, (The Most Noble) Order of the English order of knighthood founded by EDWARD III in 1348, the highest British honor. According to legend, Edward was dancing with the Countess of Salisbury when one of her garters dropped to the floor. As bystanders snickered, Edward gallantly picked it up and put it on his own leg, admonishing the courtiers in French with what is now the order's motto, "Honi soit qui mal y pense" ("Shame to him who thinks evil of it"). Its core membership consists of the British sovereign and the prince of Wales with 25 "knight companions."

garter snake Any of more than a dozen species of snakes (genus *Thamnophis,* family Colubridae) with a pattern resembling a garter: longitudinal yellow or red stripes, with checkered blotches between. Types without stripes are called grass snakes. Found in gardens and vacant lots, garters are among the most common snakes from Canada to Central America. They are small (usually less than 24 in., or 60 cm, long) and harmless, but may strike if provoked.

Garvey, Marcus (Moziah) (1887–1940) Jamaican-U.S. black-nationalist leader. In 1914 he founded the Universal Negro Improvement Assn.; after moving to the U.S. in 1916, he established branches in New York's Harlem and other ghettos in the North. By 1919 the rising "Black Moses" claimed a following of about 2 million. His newspaper, *Negro World* (1919–33), advocated an independent black economy, and he established black-run businesses, including the Black Star shipping line. In 1920 he convened an international convention to unify blacks and encourage trade with Africa. His influence declined rapidly when he was indicted in 1922 for mail fraud. After two years in prison, he was deported (1927). His movement, the first important black-nationalist movement in the U.S., soon died out.

Marcus Garvey, 1922

Gary City (pop., 2000: 102,000), NW Indiana. Located at the S end of Lake MICHIGAN, it was laid out by the U.S. STEEL CORP. in 1906 and named for Elbert H. GARY. A port city lying midway between major iron ore and coal deposits, Gary prospered until a decline in the steel industry in the 1980s led to plant closings.

Gary, Elbert H(enry) (1846–1927) U.S. businessman, chief organizer of the U.S. STEEL CORP. Born near Wheaton, Ill., he became an authority on corporate law. In 1898 he was named president of Federal Steel Co. When Federal became part of U.S. Steel Corp. in 1901, Gary was elected chairman of the board. As chief executive officer for 26 years, he presided over its growth. He promoted profit sharing, higher wages, and better working conditions, but was a firm opponent of unions. GARY, Ind., named in his honor, was laid out in 1906 by U.S. Steel.

gas One of the three fundamental states of MATTER, in which matter has no definite shape, is very fluid, and has a density about 0.1% that of LIQUIDS. Gas is very compressible, and expands indefinitely to fill any container. A small change in temperature or pressure produces a substantial change in its volume; these relationships are expressed as equations in the GAS LAWS. The term gas can also mean GASOLINE, NATURAL GAS, or the anesthetic NITROUS OXIDE. See also KINETIC THEORY OF GASES, SOLID.

gas chromatography (GC) Type of CHROMATOGRAPHY with a GAS mixture as the mobile phase. In a packed column, the packing or solid support (held in a tube) serves as the stationary phase (vapor-phase chromatography, or VPC) or is coated with a liquid stationary phase (gas-liquid chromatography, or GLC). The sample of gas or volatile liquid to be analyzed is injected into the inlet; its components move through with a carrier gas at rates influenced by their degree of interaction with the stationary phase. The gas stream from the column's end passes through a detector, where its properties are compared with those of known reference substances. GC is used to measure air pollutants, ESSENTIAL OILS, gases or alcohol in blood, and composition of industrial process streams.

Gascony \'gas-kə-nē\ *French* **Gascogne** \gȧ-'skȯnʸ\ *ancient* Vasconia. Historical region, SW France. It consisted of the N foothills of the PYRENEES, and extended east from the BASQUE COUNTRY along the France–Spain border to TOULOUSE on the upper GARONNE RIVER. The Roman province of Novempopulana, it was taken successively by the Visigoths, the Franks, the Basques, or Vascones, and the Frankish kings. In 1052 it was conquered by AQUITAINE, and in the 12th cent. it passed to the PLANTAGENET kings of England. In the HUNDRED YEARS' WAR, it retained English allegiance until the French reconquest in the mid-15th cent.

Gascony, Gulf of See Bay of BISCAY

Gaskell \'gas-kəl\, **Elizabeth** *orig.* Elizabeth Cleghorn Stevenson *known as* **Mrs. Gaskell** (1810–1865) British writer. *Cranford* (1853), her most popular novel, and the unfinished *Wives and Daughters* (1864–66), perhaps her best, are about the lives of country villagers. *Mary Barton* (1848), *Ruth* (1853), and *North and South* (1855) examine social problems of the urban working class. She also wrote the first biography of her friend Charlotte BRONTË (1857).

gas laws Laws that relate the PRESSURE, volume, and TEMPERATURE of a GAS. Boyle's law—named for Robert BOYLE—states that, at constant temperature, the pressure P of a gas varies inversely with its volume V. Charles's law—named for J.-A.-C. Charles (1746–1823)—states that, at constant pressure, the volume V of a gas is directly proportional to its absolute (Kelvin) temperature T. These can be combined to form a single generalization of the behavior of gases, $PV = nRT$, where n is the number of gram-moles of a gas and R is called the universal gas constant. Though this law describes the behavior of an IDEAL GAS, it closely approximates the behavior of many real gases. See also Joseph GAY-LUSSAC.

gasoline *British* **petrol** Mixture of volatile, flammable HYDROCARBONS derived from PETROLEUM, used as fuel for INTERNAL-COMBUSTION ENGINES (also as a solvent for OILS and FATS). Gasoline became the preferred automobile fuel because it releases so much ENERGY when burned, it mixes readily with air in a CARBURETOR, and initially was cheap due to a large supply. Costs have now increased greatly except where subsidized. A gasoline's octane number indicates its ability to resist knocking (which means combustion is too rapid) and can be altered by changing the proportions of certain components. LEAD, once added to reduce knocking, has been banned as toxic. Other additives include DETERGENTS, ANTIFREEZES, and ANTIOXIDANTS. Since the mid-20th cent. gasoline fumes have been a major component of urban AIR POLLUTION. Efforts to reduce dependence on gasoline, which is a nonrenewable resource, include use of "gasohol," a 90:10 mix of gasoline and ETHANOL, and the development of ELECTRIC AUTOMOBILES.

gasoline engine Most widely used form of INTERNAL-COMBUSTION ENGINE. Gasoline engines vary significantly in size, weight, and arrangement of components. The principal type is the reciprocating-piston engine. In four-stroke engines, each cycle requires four strokes of the piston—intake, compression, power (expansion), and exhaust—and two revolutions of the crankshaft. In a two-stroke cycle, the compression and power strokes of the four-stroke cycle are carried out without the inlet and exhaust strokes, in one upstroke and one downstroke of the piston and one revolution of the crankshaft. The size, weight, and cost of the engine per horsepower are therefore less, and two-stroke-cycle engines are used in motorcycles and smaller machines (e.g., lawnmowers).

Gasparini, Angelo See Gasparo ANGIOLINI

Gaspé Peninsula \gȧ-'spā\ Peninsula, SE Quebec. It extends 150 mi (240 km) into the Gulf of ST. LAWRENCE, lying south of the ST. LAWRENCE RIVER and north of New Brunswick. Much of the region is within conservation areas. Famous for its scenery, it is also noted for hunting and fishing.

Gasperi, Alcide De See Alcide DE GASPERI

gastroenteritis \ˌga-strō-ˌen-tə-'rī-təs\ Acute infectious syndrome of the stomach lining and intestines. Symptoms include DIARRHEA, VOMITING, and abdominal CRAMPS. Severity varies from transient diarrhea to life-threatening DEHYDRATION. Many microorganisms produce it, either by secreting TOXINS or by invading the gut walls. Forms of gastroenteritis include FOOD POISONING, CHOLERA, and traveler's diarrhea. Treatment includes antibiotics or simply supportive care.

gastroenterology \ˌga-strō-ˌen-tə-'rä-lə-jē\ Medical specialty dealing with DIGESTION and the digestive system. Lavage (washing out the stomach) and ENDOSCOPY were developed in the 19th cent., and ENDOSCOPY and X RAYS with a CONTRAST MEDIUM were first used to visualize the stomach and digestive organs in the 1890s. Gastroenterologists diagnose and treat disorders of the stomach, intestines, liver, and pancreas, including ULCERS, TUMORS, inflammatory diseases (including COLITIS and ILEITIS), and rectal disorders.

gastropod Any member of the class Gastropoda, the largest group of MOLLUSKS, including about 65,000 species. Gastropods, which include the SNAILS, CONCHS, WHELKS, LIMPETS, PERIWINKLES, ABALONES, SLUGS, and sea slugs (see NUDIBRANCH), are found worldwide, in marine, freshwater, and terrestrial environments. Gastropods typically have a large foot, a single coiled shell, and a head that bears eyes and tentacles. However, some forms lack shells and

FG

others have shells with two halves, like BIVALVES. Most feed by using a radula, a ribbon of small horny teeth. They may be herbivores, carnivores, predators, parasites, or filter feeders of plankton and detritus.

Gates, Bill *orig.* William Henry Gates III (b.1955) U.S. computer programmer and businessman. Born in Seattle, Gates as a teenager helped form a group who computerized their high school's payroll system and founded a company that sold traffic-counting systems. At 19 he dropped out of Harvard Univ. and cofounded MICROSOFT CORP. with Paul G. Allen (b.1954). Microsoft began its domination of the microcomputer industry when Gates licensed the operating system MS-DOS to IBM in 1981. He then began developing application software such as spreadsheets and word-processing programs. In 1990 Microsoft introduced Windows 3.0, which quickly became the most popular operating system worldwide. A billionaire at 31, Gates is today the wealthiest person in the world. In 1999 he and his wife created the largest charitable foundation in the U.S.

Gates, Henry Louis, Jr. (b.1950) U.S. critic and scholar. Born in Keyser, W.V., he has chaired Harvard Univ.'s esteemed department of Afro-American Studies for many years. In such works as *Figures in Black* (1987) and *The Signifying Monkey* (1988) he linked African and African-American literary histories; his other books include *Thirteen Ways of Looking at a Black Man* (1998). He has edited many anthologies, including the *Norton Anthology of African American Writers* (1997), and has restored and edited many lost works by black writers. He wrote the television series *Wonders of the African World* (1999).

Gates, Horatio (1728?–1806) British-American general. He served in the British army during the French and Indian War. In 1772 he emigrated to Virginia, where he sided with colonial interests. He was made adjutant general of the Continental Army (1775) and succeeded Gen. Philip Schuyler in New York (1777). Assisted by Benedict ARNOLD, he forced the surrender of the British forces at the Battle of SARATOGA (1777). Supporters, including Thomas CONWAY, sought to have Gates replace George WASHINGTON, but the plan failed. In 1780 Gates was transferred to the South, where he attempted to oust the British forces under Charles CORNWALLIS but was defeated at the battle of Camden, S.C. He retired to Virginia, and freed his slaves in 1790.

Gates of the Arctic National Park National preserve, N Alaska. Its area of 11,756 sq mi (30,448 sq km) is entirely north of the ARCTIC CIRCLE. It is a tundra wilderness including wild rivers and known for arctic caribou, grizzly bears, moose, and wolves. It includes a portion of the Central BROOKS RANGE.

Gatling gun First reliable MACHINE GUN, invented by Richard J. Gatling (1818–1903) during the American Civil War. Gatling assembled 10 barrels rotated by a hand crank, each of which was loaded and fired once during a complete rotation. The barrels were loaded by gravity and the action of the cartridge container, and the spent cartridge cases were ejected. Without equal in its era, it could fire 3,000 rounds per minute. It became obsolete in the 1880s when the invention of smokeless powder led to development of a truly automatic machine gun.

Gatun Lake \gä-'tün\ *Spanish* **Lago Gatún** \'lä-gō-gä-'tün\ Lake, Panama. Constituting part of the PANAMA CANAL system, its area is 166 sq mi (430 sq km). Its dam (completed 1912) and spillway serve to hold sufficient water for use in the canal's locks during dry spells. Guacha Island, a wildlife sanctuary, lies in the center of the lake.

gaucho Any of the nomadic and colorful horsemen of the Argentine and Uruguayan PAMPAS, who remain folk heros famed for hardiness and lawlessness. Gauchos flourished from the mid-18th to the mid-19th cent. At first they rounded up the herds of horses and cattle that roamed freely on the vast grasslands east of the Andes. Later they fought in the armies that defeated the Spanish colonial regime, and then for the CAUDILLOS who jockeyed for power. Gaucho literature became an important part of the Argentine cultural tradition.

Gaudí (i Cornet) \'gaù-thē\, **Antoni** *Spanish* Antonio Gaudí y Cornet (1852–1926) Spanish (Catalan) architect. Initially conservative, his work after 1902 eluded all convention. His "equilibrated" structures, able to stand on their own without bracing, employed piers and columns that tilt to transmit diagonal forces and thin-shell, laminated-tile vaults. Works such as the Park Güell (1900–14), Casa Milá (1905–10), and Casa Batlló (1904–6) feature undulating surfaces and polychrome decoration. His extraordinary Church of the Holy Family (Sagrada Familia) became a complex forest of flowing forms and exuberant detail, with spiral-shaped piers, vaults, towers, and a hyperbolic paraboloid roof.

gauge \'gāj\ Device used to determine whether a dimension is larger or smaller than a reference standard. A snap gauge, for example, is formed like the letter C, with outer "go" and inner "not go" jaws, and is used to check diameters, lengths, and thicknesses. Screw-thread pitch gauges have triangular serrations spaced to correspond with various pitches, or numbers of threads per inch or per centimeter. Deviation-type or dial gauges indicate the amount by which an object deviates from the standard.

Gauguin \gō-'gaⁿ\, **(Eugène-Henri-) Paul** (1848–1903) French painter. Born in Paris, he spent his childhood in Lima, Peru. From about 1872 he was a successful stockbroker in Paris. Inspired by IMPRESSIONISM, he started painting, and throughout the 1880s he exhibited with the Impressionists. In 1883 he lost his job; disillusioned with bourgeois materialism, in 1886 he moved to Pont-Aven, Brittany, where he became the focus of a group of artists who emulated his style. A meeting with Vincent VAN GOGH (1886) and a trip to Martinique (1887) changed his life; he broke with Impressionism and in 1891 moved to Tahiti. His works became open protests against materialism and allegories of life unspoiled by civilization. He was an influential innovator; FAUVISM owed much to

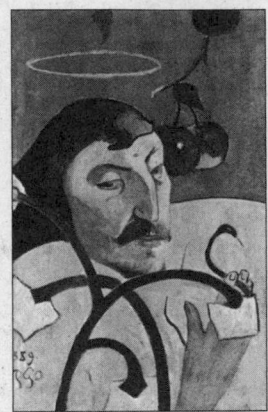
Paul Gauguin, self-portrait, 1889

his use of color, he inspired Pablo PICASSO, and his primitivism and stylistic simplifications led to an appreciation of African art and the development of CUBISM. See also POSTIMPRESSIONISM.

Gauhati \gaù-'hä-tē\ *or* **Guwahati** \ˌgü-wə-'hä-tē\ Town (pop., 1991: 584,000), W ASSAM state, NE India. Located on the BRAHMAPUTRA River, it was the capital of a Hindu kingdom around A.D. 400. It became the seat of the Ahom governor of Lower Assam in 1681. It was ceded to the British in 1826 and was the administrative seat for Assam until 1874. Gauhati is now an important river port and Assam's main commercial center. Nearby temples are Hindu pilgrimage sites.

Gaul *Latin* **Gallia** Ancient country, Europe, located generally south and west of the RHINE, west of the ALPS, and north of the PYRENEES. The Gauls of the PO RIVER harried Rome from around 400 B.C.; by 181 B.C. Rome had subjugated and colonized that area of N Italy they called Cisalpine Gaul. Over the next century, Rome conquered Transalpine Gaul including most of modern France and Belgium and parts of Switzerland, Germany, and the Netherlands. Julius CAESAR completed the conquest of Gaul (see GALLIC WARS) in 58–50 B.C.; Lugdunum (LYON) became the capital. By A.D. 260 it had become a center of unrest; by the 6th cent., Rome had given up all its Gallic territories.

Gaulle, Charles de See Charles DE GAULLE

Gauss \'gaùs\, **Carl Friedrich** (*orig.* Johann Friedrich Carl) (1777–1855) German mathematician, astronomer, and physicist. A prodigy of astounding depth, by his early teens he had already performed astonishing proofs. He published over 150 works and made such important contributions as the fundamental theorem of algebra, the least squares method, Gauss-Jordan elimination (for solving MATRIX equations), and the bell curve (see NORMAL DISTRIBUTION). After he died, many important unpublished papers were found. His development of NON-EUCLIDEAN GEOMETRY went unnoticed for decades. Gauss also pioneered the application of mathematics to gravitation, electricity, and magnetism, and developed the fields of potential theory and real analysis. With ARCHIMEDES and NEWTON, he is one of the greatest mathematicians of all time.

Gaussian distribution See NORMAL DISTRIBUTION

Gautier \gō-'tyā\, **Théophile** (1811–1872) French poet, novelist, critic, and journalist. He insisted on the sovereignty of the beautiful in such works as the novel *Mademoiselle de Maupin* (1835). He developed a poetic technique for recording his exact impressions of works of art, as in the formally perfect poems of *Émaux et camées* (1852). Travel inspired some of his best poetry, in *España* (1845), and finest prose, in *Voyage en Espagne* (1845). His works inspired such poets as Charles BAUDELAIRE, and his prodigious and varied output influenced literary sensibilities for decades.

Gawain \gə-'wān, 'gä-₁wān\ Knight of King Arthur's Round Table. He appears in early ARTHURIAN LEGEND as a model of perfection; in later romances, his character is flawed. In the 14th-cent. Middle English poem *Sir Gawain and the Green Knight*, he accepts a challenge from a mysterious Green Knight, who offers to let Gawain chop off his head if he can return the blow a year later. Gawain decapitates him, and the Knight picks up his head and leaves the court. After passing through a series of temptations on his journey to find the knight, Gawain meets him and suffers only a small wound, his neck protected by a magical green sash.

Gay, John (1685–1732) British poet and dramatist. From an ancient but impoverished Devonshire family, Gay was apprenticed to a silk mercer in London but was released early. He soon cofounded the journal *The British Apollo*. His poetry collections included *Rural Sports* (1713), *Trivia* (1716), and *Fables* (1727, 1738). Of his many plays, he is best known for the ballad opera *The Beggar's Opera* (1728), with music by J. C. Pepusch (1667–1752), a cynical tale of thieves and highwaymen intended to mirror the moral degradation of society; its success made it a landmark in music-theater history.

Gaye, Marvin *orig.* Marvin Pentz Gay (1939–1984) U.S. singer and songwriter. Born in Washington, D.C., son of a Pentecostal minister, he learned music in church. At Motown Records he played drums on early Smokey ROBINSON hits. His own hits (from 1962) climaxed in "I Heard It Through the Grapevine," and he also paired with female singers, including Tammi Terrell (1946–1970). With *What's Goin' On?* (1971) his songs became more socially conscious. Troubled in his personal relationships and finances, he was shot to death by his father in a quarrel.

Gay-Lussac \'gā-lə-'sak, gel-ē̄-'säk\, **Joseph (-Louis)** (1778–1850) French chemist and physicist. He showed that all gases expand by the same fraction of their volume for a given temperature increase; this led to the devising of a new temperature scale whose profound significance in THERMODYNAMICS was later established by Lord KELVIN. Taking measurements from a balloon at over 20,000 ft (6,000 m), he concluded that earth's magnetic intensity and atmospheric composition were constant to that altitude. With Alexander von HUMBOLDT, he determined the proportions of hydrogen and oxygen in water.

Gaza Strip *Arabic* **Qita Ghazzah** \kē-'tä-'gä-zə\ *Hebrew* **Rezuat azza** \re-zü-'ät-'äz-ə\ Territory, SE Mediterranean Sea coast. Occupying 140 sq mi (363 sq km) northeast of the SINAI Peninsula, it includes the town of Gaza (pop., 1988 est.: 57,000). The town, long a prosperous trading center, is first mentioned in the 15th cent. B.C. It was ruled by the Ottoman Turks from the 16th cent. After World War I the strip became part of the British mandate of PALESTINE. In 1948 the first ARAB–ISRAELI WAR broke out; the prevailing Egyptian forces made Gaza town their headquarters in Palestine. The occupied area was later reduced to territory 25 mi (40 km) long and became known as the Gaza Strip. In the SIX-DAY WAR (June 1967) it was retaken by Israel. Large numbers of Gaza's Palestinian Arab refugees live in extreme poverty. In 1987, rioting in Gaza marked the birth of the INTIFADA. Continued unrest led, in 1994, to an accord between Israel and the PALESTINE LIBERATION ORGANIZATION granting self-rule to the Gaza Strip. Bomb attacks, gunship raids, and reprisals have persisted.

gazel See GHAZEL

gazelle Any of numerous species of graceful ANTELOPE (genus *Gazella*) found on open plains and semideserts from Mongolia to Africa. Gazelles are 2–3 ft (60–90 cm) high at the shoulder. They range in herds that usually contain five to 10 individuals but may include several hundred. Many have a horizontal dark band along each side. Their horns are short to medium in length, with numerous raised rings, and are variously shaped, but all are slightly upturned at the ends. Some species are considered endangered.

Gdansk \gə-'dänsk\ *German* **Danzig** \'dänt-sik\ City (pop., 1999: 459,000), N Poland. Located at the mouth of the VISTULA RIVER on the Baltic Sea, it was the capital of the dukes of POMERANIA in the 13th cent. It was taken by the TEUTONIC ORDER in 1308; in 1466 CASIMIR IV regained the territory for Poland. From 1793 it was controlled mainly by Prussia; following World War I, it was a free city governed by Poland. In 1938 Adolf HITLER demanded that Gdansk be given back to Germany; when Poland refused, he attacked in 1939, precipitating WORLD WAR II. The greatly damaged city was returned to Poland in 1945. The independent labor union SOLIDARITY was founded there in 1980.

GDP See GROSS DOMESTIC PRODUCT

GE See GENERAL ELECTRIC CO.

gear Machine component consisting of a toothed wheel attached to a rotating shaft. Gears operate in pairs, the teeth of one engaging the teeth of a second, to transmit and modify rotary MOTION and TORQUE. To transmit motion smoothly, the contacting surfaces of gear teeth must be carefully shaped to a specific profile. If the smaller of a gear pair, often known as the pinion, is on the driving shaft, the pair acts to reduce speed and to amplify torque; if it is on the driven shaft, the pair acts to increase speed and reduce torque.

gecko Any of about 750 species of harmless but noisy LIZARDS in the family Gekkonidae: small, usually nocturnal reptiles that have a short, stout body, a large head, and weak limbs often equipped with suction-padded digits. The pads contain tiny hairlike projections with microscopic hooks that cling to small surface irregularities, allowing geckos to climb absolutely smooth and vertical surfaces and even to run across ceilings. Most are 1–6 in. (3–15 cm) long, including the tail. They live in warm areas worldwide. When kept as pets in houses or apartments, they are allowed to run free and eat insects.

Diurnal gecko (Phelsuma)

Geertz \'gərts\, **Clifford (James)** (b.1926) U.S. cultural anthropologist. He stresses the importance of SYMBOLS and interpretation in human social life. Culture, according to Geertz, is "a system of inherited conceptions expressed in symbolic forms" that serve to impose meaning on the world and make it understandable. Geertz's influential writings include *The Religion of Java* (1960), *The Interpretation of Cultures* (1973), *Local Knowledge* (1983), and *Works and Lives* (1988). He taught at the Univ. of Chicago 1960–70 and has been a fellow at the Institute for Advanced Study. See also CULTURAL ANTHROPOLOGY.

Gehrig \'ger-ig\, **(Henry) Lou(is)** (1903–1941) U.S. baseball player. Born in New York City, he attended Columbia Univ. before joining the New York Yankees. From 1925 to 1939, "the Iron Horse" played first base in 2,130 consecutive games, a record not broken until 1995. In 1932 he became the first player to hit four home runs in a single game. In two seasons (1934, 1936) he hit 49 home runs. He left baseball with a career batting average of .340 and 493 home runs. His 1,990 runs batted in place him third in history. In 1939 it was learned that he was dying of AMYOTROPHIC LATERAL SCLEROSIS, which came to be known as Lou Gehrig's disease.

Gehry \\'ger-ē\\, **Frank (Owen)** (b.1929) Canadian-U.S architect. Born in Toronto, he studied at USC and Harvard Univ. His use of inexpensive materials (chain-link fencing, plywood, corrugated steel) gave many of his early buildings an unfinished, whimsical air. His structures often use unconventional or distorted shapes and have a sculptural or fragmented, collage-like quality. Of particular note is his Guggenheim Museum in Bilbao, Spain (1997), a shimmering pile of sharply twisting, curving shapes surfaced in titanium. Gehry won the Pritzker Architecture Prize in 1989.

Geiger counter *or* **Geiger-Müller counter** Device used for detecting and counting individual particles of RADIATION. Invented by Hans Geiger (1882–1945), the device is a gas-filled metal tube with a wire through its axis and a high voltage applied to the wire. Particles entering the tube create a large avalanche of IONIZATION in the gas, which then discharges, creating a brief electric pulse. The tube produces the same output pulse for virtually every charged particle that passes through the gas and so is useful for detecting individual particles.

Geisel \\'gī-zəl\\, **Theodor Seuss** *known as* **Dr. Seuss** (1904–1991) U.S. writer and illustrator. Born in Springfield, Mass., he did doctoral work at Oxford then began working in 1927 as a freelance cartoonist, illustrator, and writer. Under his pseudonym, Geisel began creating immensely popular children's books peopled with outlandish invented creatures and brimming with nonsense words. *And to Think That I Saw It on Mulberry Street* (1937) was followed by the hugely successful *Horton Hatches the Egg* (1940), *The Cat in the Hat* (1957), *Green Eggs and Ham* (1960), and other perennial favorites that made him the best-selling children's author in the world.

geisha \\'gā-shə\\ Member of a professional class of women in Japan whose traditional occupation is to entertain men. A geisha must be adept at making conversation, singing, dancing, and playing the samisen (a lutelike instrument). The geisha system is thought to have emerged in the 17th cent. to provide a class of well-trained entertainers set apart from courtesans and prostitutes: though geisha sometimes had sexual relationships with their clients, they were supposed to entertain primarily through their accomplishments. The numbers of geisha have declined from some 80,000 in the 1920s to a few thousand at present, almost all confined to Tokyo and Kyoto, where they are patronized by wealthy businessmen and influential politicians.

gelatin \\'je-lə-tᵊn\\ Animal PROTEIN that forms a gel, used primarily in food products. Derived from COLLAGEN, it is extracted by boiling animal skin and bones. Immersed in a liquid, it takes up moisture and swells. It is used to make such foods as molded desserts, soups, candies, and aspics and to stabilize such emulsion and foam food products as ice cream and marshmallows. It is also used in various pharmaceutical products.

Gell-Mann \\'gel-ˌmän\\, **Murray** (b.1929) U.S. physicist. Born in New York City, he taught at Caltech from 1955. In 1953 he introduced the concept of "strangeness," a QUANTUM property that accounted for decay patterns of certain MESONS. In 1961 he and Yuval Ne'eman (b.1925) proposed a scheme (the "Eightfold Way") that grouped mesons and BARYONS into multiplets of 1, 8, 10, or 27 members on the basis of various properties. He speculated that it was possible to explain certain properties of known particles in terms of even more fundamental particles, which he called QUARKS. He was awarded a 1969 Nobel Prize.

Gelukpa See DGE-LUGS-PA

Gempei War \\'gem-ˌpā\\ (1180–85) Final struggle between two Japanese warrior clans, the Minamoto (Genji) and the Taira (Heike), for supremacy in Japan, resulting in the Minamoto's victory and the establishment of the KAMAKURA SHOGUNATE. Stories of the rise and fall of the two families

have a popularity in Japan akin to that of the ARTHURIAN LEGEND in English-speaking countries.

Gemsbok National Park \\'gemz-ˌbȯk\\ National preserve, SW Botswana, bordering S. Africa's Kalahari Gemsbok National Park. It was established as a game reserve in 1932 to protect animal populations that cross between the two countries. Its wildlife includes gemsbok, gnu (wildebeest), and springbok.

gemstone Any of various minerals prized for beauty, durability, and rarity. A few noncrystalline materials of organic origin (e.g., pearl, red coral, and amber) also are classified as gemstones. Of the more than 3,500 identified natural minerals, fewer than 100 are used as gemstones; the most important include BERYL, CORUNDUM, DIAMOND, GARNET, JADE, OPAL, QUARTZ, TOPAZ, TOURMALINE, TURQUOISE, and ZIRCON. In virtually all cases, the minerals have to be cut and polished for use in jewelry.

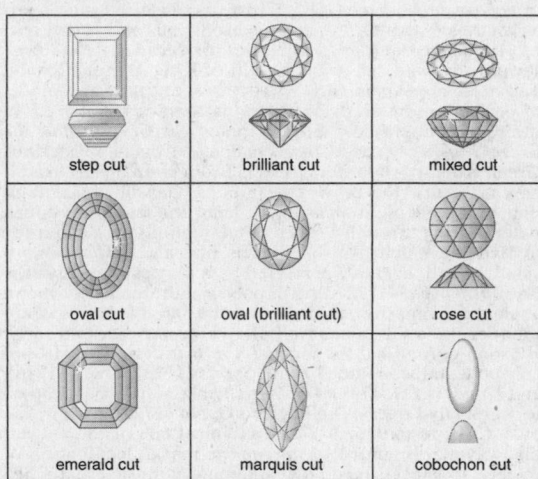

step cut	brilliant cut	mixed cut
oval cut	oval (brilliant cut)	rose cut
emerald cut	marquis cut	cobochon cut

Gemstone Several traditional gemstone cuts.

gender In language, a grammatical category for distinctions of sex or animateness. Gender marking may be natural, with linguistic markers of gender corresponding to real-world gender, or purely grammatical. In languages with grammatical gender, nouns are divided into sets. Membership of a noun in a set may be expressed by its form and/or by the forms of other parts of speech controlled by the noun. Closely related to gender systems in language are class systems, as in BANTU LANGUAGES, in which nouns are divided into numerous categories for things such as plants, animals, and tools.

gene Unit of HEREDITY that occupies a fixed position on a CHROMOSOME. Genes achieve their effects by directing PROTEIN synthesis. They are composed of DNA, except in some viruses that contain RNA instead. The sequence of nitrogenous bases along a strand of DNA determines the GENETIC CODE. Experiments have shown that many of the genes within a cell are inactive much or even all of the time, but they can be switched on and off. MUTATIONS occur when the number or order of bases in a gene is disrupted. See also GENETIC ENGINEERING, GENETICS, HARDY-WEINBERG LAW, HUMAN GENOME PROJECT.

genealogy Study of family origins and history. Originally concerned with tracing royal, aristocratic, or clerical lines, genealogy has broadened its scope over the centuries, and many ordinary people now pursue it as a hobby. In preliterate cultures genealogical information was transmitted orally, usually as a list of names; later generations recorded this information. Divine origins were often ascribed to kings and heroes. Modern genealogists use artifacts, including ancient records, coins, deeds, tapestries, paintings, and monuments, to help them in their work.

General Accounting Office (GAO) U.S. legislative agency. Established in 1921, it audits and evaluates government programs and activities to ensure effective receipt and disbursement of public funds. As the investigative arm of Congress, it performs reviews requested by committee chairs and ranking minority members, as well as those required by law or initiated by the GAO itself.

General Dynamics Corp. Major U.S. defense contractor. Its forerunner, the Electric Boat Co., was founded in 1899 and built the *Holland*, the first submarine purchased by the U.S. Navy. After World War II it diversified into military aircraft, armored vehicles, and tankers. It took its present name in 1952. In 1954 it launched the *Nautilus*, the first nuclear-powered submarine; it later produced the Trident submarines. A $12 billion family of companies, it also manufactures commercial ships, business aircraft, and surveillance systems.

General Electric Co. (GE) Major U.S. corporation and one of the largest companies in the world. Its products include electrical and electronic equipment, plastics, aircraft engines, and medical imaging equipment, and financial services. The company was incorporated in 1892, acquiring all the assets of the Edison General Electric Co. The company established a research laboratory in 1900, and many of its later products, including various home appliances, were developed by in-house scientists. In 1986 GE purchased the RCA CORP., including its television network, NBC.

General Foods Corp. Former U.S. manufacturer of packaged grocery and meat products. It was incorporated in 1922, having developed from the earlier Postum Cereal Co. founded by C. W. POST. It soon began acquiring other companies and products: Jell-O Co. (1925), Minute Tapioca Co. (1926), Log Cabin (1927), Maxwell House (1928), Birdseye (1929), Sanka coffee (1932), Kool-Aid (1953), Oscar Mayer (1981), and Entenmann's bakery products (1982), among others. In 1985 it was bought by Philip Morris Cos. (later Altria).

General Mills, Inc. Leading U.S. producer of packaged foods, especially flour, breakfast cereals, snacks, and prepared mixes. General Mills was incorporated in 1928 to acquire Washburn Crosby Co. and four other milling companies. The company introduced Wheaties and Cheerios breakfast cereals, Gold Medal flour, and Bisquick baking mix, as well as the Betty Crocker line of products. It diversified into other industries in the 1960s, but by the 1990s had refocused on consumer foods. In 2001 it acquired Pillsbury.

General Motors Corp. (GM) U.S. corporation, the world's largest automotive manufacturer for most of the 20th cent. It was founded in 1908 by William C. DURANT, and it soon included the makers of Buick, Oldsmobile, Cadillac, and Oakland (later Pontiac) autos. GM merged with the Chevrolet auto company in 1918. By 1929 GM had passed FORD MOTOR CO. to become the leading U.S. auto manufacturer. GM bought Electronic Data Systems Corp. in 1984, and Hughes Aircraft Co. in 1986. Faced with severe competition from Japanese imports, in 1984 it founded a new division, Saturn.

general practice See FAMILY PRACTICE

generator Machine that converts mechanical ENERGY to ELECTRICITY for transmission and distribution over power lines to customers. Generators also produce the electric power required for automobiles, aircraft, ships, and trains. The mechanical power for an electric generator is usually obtained from a rotating shaft and is equal to the shaft TORQUE multiplied by the rotational, or angular, velocity (speed). The mechanical power may come from various sources: TURBINES powered by water, wind, steam, or gas; GASOLINE ENGINES; or DIESEL ENGINES.

Genesee River \ˌje-nə-ˈsē, ˈje-nə-ˌsē\ River, Pennsylvania and New York. It flows north from Pennsylvania to enter Lake ONTARIO after 158 mi (254 km). Midway, it flows into a 25-mi (40-km) gorge with sides rising at times 800 ft (245 m); called the "Grand Canyon of the East," it is the focal point of Letchworth State Park.

Genesis \ˈje-nə-səs\ First book of the BIBLE. Genesis provides the creation story for Judaism and Christianity and begins the history of the Israelite people. It includes the stories of ADAM AND EVE, CAIN AND ABEL, NOAH, the Tower of BABEL, and God's COVENANT with ABRAHAM, ISAAC, and JACOB, concluding with the story of Jacob's son JOSEPH. It is traditionally ascribed to MOSES, but modern scholarship

has identified at least three literary strains in it, dating from 950 B.C. to the 5th cent. B.C. and incorporating material from much earlier. It is one of the five books of the Pentateuch (see TORAH).

Genet, Citizen Edmond See CITIZEN GENET AFFAIR

Genet \zhə-ˈnä\, **Jean** (1910–1986) French novelist and dramatist. An illegitimate child abandoned by his mother, he began to write while imprisoned for burglary. His first novel, *Our Lady of the Flowers* (1944), portrays an underworld of thugs, pimps, and hustlers. *The Thief's Journal* (1949) recounts his life as a tramp, pickpocket, and prostitute. He became a leading figure in avant-garde theater with such plays as *The Maids* (1947) and *The Blacks* (1958), stylized Expressionist dramas designed to shock and implicate an audience by revealing its hypocrisy and complicity in an exploitative social order.

gene therapy *or* **gene transfer therapy** Introduction of a normal GENE into an individual in whom that gene is not functioning, either into those tissue cells that normally express the gene (curing that individual only) or into an early embryonic cell (curing the individual and all future offspring). Prerequisites for each procedure include finding the best delivery system (often a VIRUS) for the gene, demonstrating that the transferred gene can express itself in the host cell, and establishing that the procedure is safe. Diseases for which gene-therapy research is advanced include cystic fibrosis, Huntington's disease, and familial hypercholesterolemia; research continues on other applications. Some aspects of gene therapy, including genetic manipulation and selection, research on embryonic tissue, and experimentation on human subjects, raise questions of ethics.

FG

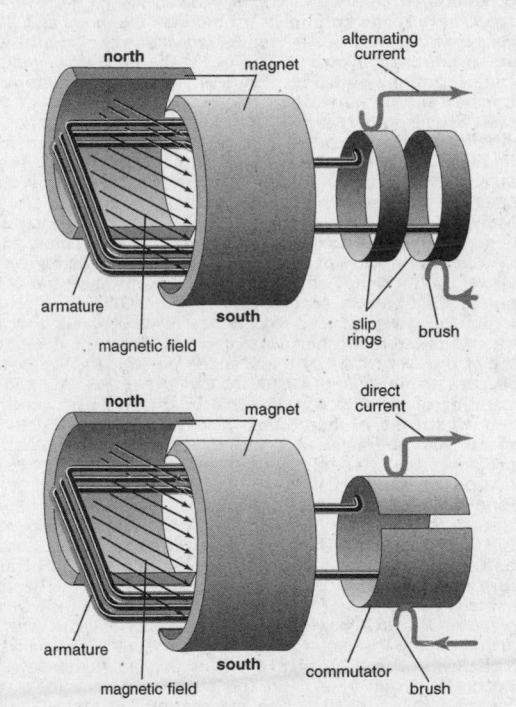

Generator A basic generator consists of a loop or coil of wire (armature) rotating in a magnetic field. The magnetic field causes a current to flow in the (moving) wire, via induction. Either alternating or direct current may be generated, depending on whether the ends of the looped wire are attached to a set of slip rings (top: AC) or to a commutator (bottom: DC).

genetic code Sequence of NUCLEOTIDES in DNA and RNA that determines the AMINO-ACID sequence of PROTEINS. A messenger RNA molecule synthesized from the DNA directs the synthesis of the protein. Three adjacent nucleotides constitute a unit known as a codon; each codon codes for a single amino acid. There are 64 possible codons, 61 of which (many are duplications) specify the 20 amino acids that make up proteins; the others are "stop signs." The genetic code has been found to vary slightly in certain organisms and in the mitochondria of some eukaryotes.

genetic drift Change in the pool of GENES of a small population that takes place strictly by chance. Genetic drift can result in genetic traits being lost from a population or becoming widespread in a population without respect to the survival or reproductive value of the gene pairs (ALLELES) involved. A random statistical effect, genetic drift can occur only in small, isolated populations in which the gene pool is small enough that chance events can change its makeup substantially. See also FOUNDER PRINCIPLE.

genetic engineering Artificial manipulation, modification, and RECOMBINATION of DNA or other NUCLEIC-ACID molecules in order to modify an organism or population of organisms. The term initially meant any of a wide range of techniques; it now denotes the narrower field of recombinant-DNA technology, or gene cloning, in which DNA molecules from two or more sources are combined, either within cells or in test tubes, and then inserted into host organisms in which they are able to reproduce. With such techniques, bacteria have been created that can synthesize human insulin, human interferon, human growth hormone, a hepatitis-B vaccine, and other medically useful substances. Recombinant-DNA techniques, combined with production of antibodies via the POLYMERASE CHAIN REACTION, have made an impact on medical diagnosis and cancer research. Genetically engineered plants can fix nitrogen and produce their own pesticides. At the same time, genetic engineering may introduce such adverse genetic manipulations as antibiotic-resistant bacteria or new strains of disease. See also BIOTECHNOLOGY, MOLECULAR BIOLOGY.

genetics Study of HEREDITY in general and of GENES in particular. Modern genetics began with the work of Gregor MENDEL, who formulated the basic laws of heredity. Walter SUTTON proposed that CHROMOSOMES were the site of Mendel's hereditary factors. T. H. MORGAN provided evidence that genes occur on CHROMOSOMES and that adjacent genes on the same chromosome form linkage groups. Oswald AVERY showed that DNA is the chromosome component that carries genetic information. DNA's molecular structure was deduced by James WATSON and Francis CRICK. These and other developments led to the deciphering of the GENETIC CODE and made possible the RECOMBINATION techniques of GENETIC ENGINEERING. An understanding of genetics is useful for the diagnosis, prevention, and treatment of hereditary diseases, the BREEDING of plants and animals, and the development of industrial processes that use microorganisms. See also EVOLUTION, HARDY-WEINBERG LAW.

Geneva \jə-'nē-və\ *French* **Genève** \zhə-'nev\ *German* **Genf** \'genf\ *Italian* **Ginevra** \jē-'nä-vrä\ City (pop., 1999 est.: 172,000), SW Switzerland. It lies at the tip of Lake GENEVA on the RHONE RIVER. In the 16th cent. John CALVIN transformed Geneva into a theocratic state and the intellectual center of Protestant Europe. In the 18th cent., as the birthplace of J.-J. ROUSSEAU and the sanctuary of VOLTAIRE, it attracted the elite of the ENLIGHTENMENT. It joined the Swiss Confederation in 1814. It was the site of the GENEVA CONVENTION in 1864, and the LEAGUE OF NATIONS was founded there in 1919. An international center of commerce and finance, it is the headquarters of the International RED CROSS (1864) and the European branch of the UNITED NATIONS.

Geneva, Lake *French* **Lac Léman** \'läk-lä-'män\ *German* **Genfersee** \'gen-fər-,zā\ Lake, between SW Switzerland and SE France. The RHONE RIVER enters at the E end and leaves at the W end through the city of GENEVA. Lying at an elevation of 1,220 ft (372 m), it is 45 mi (72 km) long, with an average width of 5 mi (8 km). The water is subject to fluctua-

tions of level known as seiches, in which the lake's mass rhythmically swings from shore to shore.

Geneva, University of Institution of higher learning in Geneva. It was founded by John CALVIN and Théodor de Bèze (1519–1605) in 1559 as Schola Genevensis (later called the Academy), a theological seminary. Today many foreign students are attracted by its reputation in international studies and botany; the Institut Jean-Jacques Rousseau is a renowned school of education. Total enrollment is about 14,000.

Geneva Conventions International agreements (1864, 1906, 1929, 1949) signed in Geneva that established the humanitarian principles by which the signatory nations are to treat an enemy's military and civilian nationals in wartime. The first was initiated by Henri DUNANT; it established that medical facilities were not to be war targets, that hospitals should treat all wounded impartially, that civilians aiding the wounded should be protected, and that the RED CROSS symbol should serve to identify those covered by the agreement. Later conventions stated that prisoners of war should be treated humanely and that prison camps should be open to inspection by neutral countries. Two 1977 amendments extended protection to guerrilla combatants; the U.S. did not sign them. Public opinion and disapprobation are the only sanctions that can be applied to violators.

Genghis Khan \'gen-gəs-'kän, 'jen-gəs-'kän\ *or* **Chinggis Khan** \'chiŋ-gəz-'kän\ *orig.* Temujin (c.1160–1227) Mongolian warrior-ruler. The leader of a destitute clan, Temujin fought various rival clans and formed a MONGOL confederacy, which in 1206 acknowledged him as Genghis Khan ("Universal Ruler"). Leading the united Mongols, he moved out beyond the steppe, adapting his method of warfare, moving from dependence on pure cavalry to the use of sieges, catapults, and other techniques to capture and destroy cities. In less than 10 years he took over N China; he then overwhelmed Muslim-controlled Central Asia while his generals raided Iran and Russia. He is infamous for his slaughter of whole cities and destruction of fields and irrigation systems, but admired for his military brilliance and ability to learn. He died on a military campaign, and the empire, one of the greatest of all time, was divided among his sons, including OGODEI, and grandsons.

genie See JINNI

genius Person of extraordinary intellectual power. The genius displays originality, CREATIVITY, and the ability to think and work in areas not previously explored. Though geniuses usually leave their mark in a particular field, their general INTELLIGENCE is also exceptionally high. Genius appears to be a function of both hereditary and environmental factors.

Genoa \'je-nō-ə\ *Italian* **Genova** \'je-nō-və\ *ancient* Genua. City (pop., 1998 est.: 647,000) and seaport, NW Italy. Capital of LIGURIA region, it is the center of the Italian RIVIERA. Flourishing under the Romans, it went on to become a chief Mediterranean commercial city (12th–13th cent.), rivaled only by VENICE. It declined in the 14th–15th cent., after it lost a century-long struggle with Venice for control of the LEVANT. Taken by NAPOLEON in the early 19th cent., it later regained its independence and prospered, especially after Italian unification. Birthplace of Christopher COLUMBUS, Genoa is still noted for its maritime tradition, with shipbuilding its major industry. Its university was founded in 1471.

genocide \'je-nə-,sīd\ Deliberate and systematic destruction of a racial, religious, political, or ethnic group. The term was coined after the Nazi era (1933–45) to define a legal concept describing a premeditated effort to destroy a population (see HOLOCAUST). In 1946 the U.N. General Assembly declared genocide a punishable crime, whether committed by an individual, group, or government, even against one's own people, in either peacetime or wartime. Suspects may be tried by a court in the country where the act was committed or by an international court.

genotype \'jē-nə-,tīp\ Genetic makeup of an organism. The genotype determines the hereditary potentials and limitations of an individual. Among organisms that reproduce sexually (see MEIOSIS), an individual's genotype comprises the entire unique complex of GENES inherited from both parents. See also PHENOTYPE, VARIATION.

genre painting \'zhän-rə\ Painting of scenes from everyday life, of ordinary people at work or play, depicted in a realistic manner. Originally a derogatory term, it is now popularly used to describe works by 17th-cent. Dutch and Flemish painters such as Jan STEEN, Gerard TERBORCH, Adriaen van OSTADE, and Jan VERMEER, and later masters such as J.-B.-S. CHARDIN in France, Pietro LONGHI in Italy, and G. C. BINGHAM in the U.S.

Genroku period \,gen-'rō-,kü\ (1688–1704) Period in Japanese history characterized by a flourishing of the culture of the non-samurai city dweller. Ostentatious displays of wealth were prohibited, but the affluent townsmen of Kyoto, Osaka, and Edo (Tokyo) spent time and money in the pleasure quarters, districts where theaters, brothels, and teahouses were located; this "floating (i.e., fleeting) world," or *ukiyo,* was commemorated in brightly colored woodblock prints (see UKIYO-E). The Genroku period set the standards for an urban culture that continued throughout the EDO PERIOD.

gentian family \'jen-shən\ Family Gentianaceae (order Gentianales), composed of some 1,100 species of annual and perennial herbaceous plants native mostly to N temperate regions. The four or five united petals that make up the flower overlap and are twisted in the bud. Some species are used in herbal remedies and in the making of dyes. Others (genus *Gentiana*) are cultivated as garden ornamentals. Gentians occur widely in moist meadows and woods.

Gentile \jen-'tē-lā\, **Giovanni** (1875–1944) Italian philosopher sometimes called the "philosopher of Fascism." He and Benedetto CROCE edited the journal *La Critica* (1903–22), and he served in education posts in Benito MUSSOLINI's government. His philosophy of "actual idealism," strongly influenced by G. W. F. HEGEL, denied the existence of individual minds. He planned and edited the *Enciclopedia Italiana* (1936) and wrote prolifically on education and philosophy. After Mussolini's fall in 1943, he supported the Fascist republic established by the Germans at Salò; he was killed by anti-Fascists.

Gentile da Fabriano \jen-'tē-lä-dä-,fäb-rē-'ä-nō\ *orig.* Gentile di Niccolò di Massio (c.1385–1427) Italian painter. In 1409 he was commissioned to decorate the Doges' Palace in Venice with historical frescoes, now lost. Another fresco cycle, also destroyed, was in the church of St. John Lateran in Rome. His major surviving painting is the celebrated Strozzi Altarpiece (1423), featuring *The Adoration of the Magi.* Its combination of naturalism and rich ornamentation influenced Fra ANGELICO and Benozzo GOZZOLI and established Gentile as a proponent of the International Gothic style.

Gentileschi \,jän-tē-'les-kē\, **Artemisia** (1593–1652/53) Italian painter. The daughter of Orazio GENTILESCHI, she studied with him and with the landscape painter Agostino Tassi. Her earliest known work is *Susanna and the Elders* (1610). In 1616 she joined the Academy of Design in Florence and became one of the greatest of CARAVAGGIO's followers and the most violent, arguably as a result of her rape by Tassi and the trial at which she was forced under torture to give evidence against him. She favored such subjects as Judith beheading Holofernes and other images of heroic women. She was the first woman artist to attain an international reputation.

Gentileschi, Orazio *orig.* Orazio Lomi (1562–1639) Italian painter. He went to Rome about 1576–78 and painted frescoes in various churches (c.1590–1600). His later paintings reveal the influence of CARAVAGGIO's strong chiaroscuro and contemporary figure types. Invited to England by CHARLES I in 1626, he remained there as court painter the rest of his life. Artemisia GENTILESCHI was his daughter.

genus Biological classification that ranks below family and above SPECIES, consisting of related species or a single species. For example, the species of roses collectively form the genus *Rosa,* and those of horses, donkeys, and zebras form the genus *Equus.* The genus name, capitalized and usually italicized, is the first word of a scientific name in the system of BINOMIAL NOMENCLATURE.

geochemistry Scientific discipline dealing with the relative abundance, distribution, and migration of the earth's chemical elements. Historically, geochemistry was concerned primarily with defining elemental abundances in minerals and rocks. Modern geochemical research also studies the continual recycling of the earth's constituent materials through geologic processes, the cyclic flow of elements between living and nonliving systems, and certain areas of COSMOLOGY.

geochronology DATING and interpretation of geologic events in the history of the earth. The classical technique of geochronology was STRATIGRAPHY. Since the mid-20th cent., radiometric dating has provided absolute age data to supplement the relative dates obtained from the fossil record (see CARBON-14 DATING).

geode Hollow mineral body found in limestones and some shales, commonly a slightly flattened globe 1–12 in. (2.5–30 cm) in diameter and containing a CHALCEDONY layer surrounding an inner lining of crystals. The hollow interior often is nearly filled with inward-projecting crystals, new layers growing on top of old. The crystals are often of quartz.

geoduck \'gü-ē-,dək\ Marine BIVALVE (*Panopea generosa*) that inhabits the intertidal zone of the Pacific coast from S Alaska to Baja California. It is the largest known burrowing bivalve, with a shell about 7–9 in. (18–23 cm) long and siphons that extend up to about 4 ft (1.3 m). It may weigh as much as 8 lbs (3.6 kg). Though highly prized for food, it lives in deep burrows and is difficult to dig out.

Geoffrey of Monmouth \'män-məth\ (d.1155) Medieval British chronicler. His mostly fictional *History of the Kings of Britain* (c.1135–39) traced the descent of British princes from the Trojans; it brought the figure of Arthur (see ARTHURIAN LEGEND) into European literature and introduced the enchanter MERLIN, whose story he related in the *Vita Merlini* (c.1148–51?). The *History* was one of the most popular books of the Middle Ages and had an enormous influence on later chroniclers.

geography Science of the earth's surface, which describes and analyzes the spatial variations in its physical, biological, and human phenomena, their interrelationships, and their significant regional patterns. Once associated entirely with mapping and the exploration of the earth, the field today is wide-ranging, and geographers use methods and techniques drawn from numerous disciplines. Subfields of geography include physical, human, and regional geography.

geologic oceanography See MARINE GEOLOGY

geologic time Interval of time occupied by the earth's geologic history, extending from about 3.8 billion years ago (corresponding to the age of the oldest known rocks) to the present day. It is, in effect, the part of the earth's history that is recorded in rock strata. The geologic time scale is classified in nested intervals distinguished by characteristic geologic and biologic features. From longest to shortest duration, the intervals are EON, ERA, PERIOD, and EPOCH. See table on following page.

geology Scientific study of the earth, including its composition, structure, physical properties, and history. Subdisciplines study the chemical makeup of the earth, including its minerals (MINERALOGY) and rocks (PETROLOGY); the structure of the earth (structural geology) and volcanic phenomena (VOLCANOLOGY); landforms and the processes that produce them (GEOMORPHOLOGY and GLACIOLOGY); geologic history, including fossils (PALEONTOLOGY), the development of sedimentary strata (STRATIGRAPHY), and the evolution of planetary bodies (astrogeology); and economic geology with such branches as mining geology and petroleum geology. Fields closely allied to geology are GEOPHYSICS and GEOCHEMISTRY.

geomagnetic field Magnetic field associated with the earth. It is essentially dipolar (i.e., it has a N and S magnetic pole) on the earth's surface; away from the surface, the field becomes distorted. It is explained by means of dynamo theories, whereby a source of energy in the earth's CORE causes a self-sustaining magnetic field, and fluid motion in the core involves the movement of conducting material within an existing magnetic field, thus creating a current and a self-enforcing field.

F G

Geologic Time

Eons	Eras	Periods and systems	Epochs and series	Beginning of interval*	Biological forms
Phanerozoic	Cenozoic	Quaternary	Holocene	0.01	
			Pleistocene	1.8	Earliest humans
		Tertiary	Pliocene	5	
			Miocene	24	Earliest hominids
			Oligocene	34	
			Eocene	55	Earliest grasses
			Paleocene	65	Earliest large mammals
	Cretaceous-Tertiary boundary (65 million years ago): extinction of dinosaurs				
	Mesozoic	Cretaceous	Upper	98	
			Lower	144	Earliest flowering plants; dinosaurs in ascendancy
		Jurassic		208	Earliest birds and mammals
		Triassic		248	Age of Dinosaurs begins
	Paleozoic	Permian		286	
		Carboniferous			
		Pennsylvanian		320	Earliest reptiles
		Mississippian		360	Earliest winged insects
		Devonian		410	Earliest amphibians and bony fish
		Silurian		438	Earliest land plants and insects
		Ordovician		505	Earliest corals
		Cambrian		544	Earliest fishes
Proterozoic	Precambrian			2,500	Earliest colonial algae and soft-bodied invertebrates
Archean				3,800	Earliest surviving microfossils of primitive single-celled organisms
Hadean				4,600	No surviving fossils

*In millions of years before the present

geomagnetic reversal Alternation of the earth's magnetic polarity. The earth's internal magnetic field reverses, on average, about every 300,000 to 1 million years. This reversal is very sudden on a geologic time scale, apparently taking about 5,000 years. The time between reversals is highly variable, from less than 40,000 years to as long as 35 million years. A long interval of one polarity may be followed by a short interval of opposite polarity. See also POLAR WANDERING.

geometry See ANALYTIC GEOMETRY, EUCLIDEAN GEOMETRY, FRACTAL GEOMETRY, NON-EUCLIDEAN GEOMETRY

geomorphology Scientific discipline that describes and classifies the earth's topographic features. Some systems of classifying landforms group topographic features primarily according to the processes that shaped or modified them. Others consider additional factors (e.g., character of the surface rocks and climatic variations) and include the developmental stage of landforms as an aspect of their evolution.

geophysics Major branch of earth science that applies the principles and methods of physics to the study of the earth. This includes such geologic phenomena as the temperature distribution of the earth's interior; the source, configuration, and variations of the GEOMAGNETIC FIELD; and the large-scale features of the terrestrial CRUST. Modern geophysical research also examines phenomena of the outer parts of the earth's atmosphere and even the physical properties of other planets.

George, St. (fl.c.3rd cent.) Early Christian martyr and patron saint of England. His historicity is uncertain, but from the 6th cent. he was the subject of legends as a warrior-saint. He was said to have rescued a Libyan king's daughter from a dragon, which he killed in return for a promise that the king's subjects would be baptized. In art, he often wears knight's armor ornamented with a scarlet cross.

George I *orig.* George Louis *German* Georg Ludwig (1660–1727) First king of England (1714–27) from the House of HANOVER. He succeeded his father as the elector of Hanover (1698). As a great-grandson of JAMES I of England and under the Act of SETTLEMENT, George succeeded to the English throne in 1714. He formed a Whig ministry and left internal politics to his ministers, including Robert WALPOLE. He was unpopular because of his German manner and German mistresses, but he strengthened Britain's position by forming an alliance with France.

George I *Greek* Georgios *orig.* Prins Vilhelm af Danmark (Prince William of Denmark) (1845–1913) King of Greece. Son of Christian IX of Denmark, he was nominated to the Greek throne by Britain, France, and Russia after the Greek king, Otto, was deposed, and ascended the throne in 1863. He oversaw the incorporation of territory in Thessaly and Epirus into Greece as well as the annexation of Crete. In the unrest caused by the BALKAN WARS, he was assassinated at Salonika.

George II *orig.* George Augustus *German* Georg August (1683–1760) King of Great Britain and elector of Hanover (1727–60). Succeeding his father, GEORGE I, he retained Robert WALPOLE as his key minister until 1742. His new minister, John Carteret (1690–1763), brought England into the War of the AUSTRIAN SUCCESSION, where George fought courageously at Dettingen (1743), the last time a British king appeared on the battlefield. The parliament and ministers forced Carteret's resignation (1744) and the appointment of William PITT. George gradually lost interest in politics.

George III *orig.* George William Frederick (1738–1820) King of Great Britain and Ireland (1760–1820) and elector (1760–1814) and king (1814–20) of Hanover. The grandson of GEORGE II, he ascended the throne during the SEVEN YEARS' WAR. England was in financial distress caused by the war, and George supported attempts to raise funds through taxation of the American colonies, which led to the AMERICAN REVOLUTION. With Lord NORTH, his prime minister, he was blamed for prolonging the war and losing the colonies. He reasserted his power when North and C. J. FOX planned to take control of the E. INDIA CO.; he forced them to resign (1782) and reaffirmed his control through a new "patriotic" prime minister, William PITT the Younger. George supported him until fears of uprisings in France and Ireland caused Pitt to propose political emancipation of the Roman Catholics. George's vehement opposition led to Pitt's resignation in 1801. In 1811 George's ill health and a return of the madness that had afflicted him for short periods earlier in his life caused Parliament to enact the regency of his son, the future GEORGE IV.

George IV *orig.* George Augustus Frederick (1762–1830) King of the United Kingdom (1820–30) and king of Hanover (1820–30). The son of GEORGE III, he earned his father's ill will by his extravagances and dissolute habits. In 1811 George became regent for his father, who had been declared insane. Retaining his father's ministers rather than appointing his Whig friends, he saw Britain and her allies triumph over Napoleon in 1815. A patron of the architect John NASH, he sponsored the restoration of WINDSOR CASTLE.

George V *orig.* George Frederick Ernest Albert (1865–1936) King of the United Kingdom (1910–36). He succeeded his father, EDWARD VII. Respect for the new king increased during World War I, and he visited the front in France several times. After the war he faced serious industrial unrest, which was dealt with by his new prime minister, Stanley BALDWIN. After the collapse of the pound and the subsequent financial crisis in 1931, he persuaded Ramsay MACDONALD to remain in office and form a national coalition government.

George VI *orig.* Albert Frederick Arthur George (1895–1952) King of the United Kingdom (1936–52). The second son of GEORGE V, he was proclaimed king following the abdication of his brother, EDWARD VIII. He was an important symbolic leader during World War II, supporting Winston CHURCHILL and visiting his armies on several battlefronts. In 1949 he was formally recognized as head of the COMMONWEALTH. He earned the respect of his people by scrupulously observing the responsibilities of a

George VI

constitutional monarch. He was succeeded by his daughter, ELIZABETH II.

George, David Lloyd See David LLOYD GEORGE

George, Henry (1839–1897) U.S. land reformer and economist. Born in Philadelphia, in 1858 he went to California, where he worked for newspapers (briefly founding his own) and took part in Democratic party politics. In his influential *Progress and Poverty* (1879), he proposed that the state tax away all economic rent—the income from the use of the bare land, but not from improvements—and abolish all other taxes. George envisaged that the income from this "single tax" would be large enough to allow significant expansion of public works.

George, Lake Lake, NE New York. It is 32 mi (51 km) long and 1–4 mi (1.6–6.4 km) wide, and is connected to Lake CHAMPLAIN through a series of waterfalls. Noted for its scenic beauty, it is a popular resort area. Memorialized in J. F. COOPER's novels as Lake Horicon, it was the scene of numerous battles during the FRENCH AND INDIAN WAR and the AMERICAN REVOLUTION.

George \gā-'ȯr-gə\, **Stefan** (1868–1933) German poet. George traveled widely, becoming associated with Stéphane MALLARMÉ and the SYMBOLIST MOVEMENT in Paris and the Pre-Raphaelites in London. Returning to Germany, he edited the journal *Blätter für die Kunst* 1892–1919 and became the center of the "George Circle," a close-knit aesthetic band of young poets. His collections include *Hymnen* (1890), *Der siebente Ring* (1907), and *Der Stern des Bundes* (1914). A supporter of "pure poetry," he opposed not only the debasement of the language but also materialism and naturalism. Though politically conservative, he turned down Nazi offers of money and honors, preferring exile.

Georges Bank Submerged sandbank in the Atlantic Ocean, east of Massachusetts. It has long been an important fishing ground, but known for dangerous crosscurrents and fog. In 1994 it was closed to commercial fishing to replenish depleted stock; portions were reopened in 1999.

George's War, King See KING GEORGE'S WAR

Georgetown Largest city (pop., 1999 est.: 275,000) and capital of Guyana. The nation's chief port, it lies on the Atlantic Ocean at the mouth of the Demerara River. It was founded by the British in 1781. Taken by the Dutch in 1784, it was renamed Stabroek. The British regained control in 1812. Lying below sea level at high tide, it is protected by a dike. It is home to a notable botanical garden. The Univ. of Guyana was founded in 1963.

Georgetown University Private university in Washington, D.C. Founded in 1789, it was the first Roman Catholic (Jesuit) college in the U.S., but has always been open to people of all faiths. Many graduates have served in government positions. Facilities include a seismological observatory, the Woodstock Theological Center, and various medical research centers. Total enrollment is about 13,000.

George Washington University, The Private university in Washington, D.C. It was chartered in 1821, the original impetus for a university in the capital having come from George WASHINGTON. It has schools of international affairs, law, medicine and health sciences, business and public management, engineering, and education, as well as research institutes. Total enrollment is about 19,000.

Georgia State (pop., 2000: 8,186,000), SE U.S. One of the original, and the last, of the 13 English colonies, it covers 58,910 sq mi (152,577 sq km) and is the largest state east of the Mississippi River; its capital is ATLANTA. The area was inhabited by the CREEK and CHEROKEE Indians when Spanish missions arrived in the 16th cent. English settlement began in 1733 at SAVANNAH when James OGLETHORPE established a refuge for debtors. European settlement accelerated after the AMERICAN REVOLUTION, and the last of the Indians were forcibly removed in the 1830s. Georgia seceded from the Union in 1861, and the AMERICAN CIVIL WAR was particularly hard on the state. It was the last former Confederate state to be readmitted to the Union in 1870. Its landscape sweeps from the BLUE RIDGE Mtns. in the north to the OKEFENOKEE SWAMP (which it shares with Florida) on the south. For most of the 19th cent. it was the capital of the cotton empire of the South; in the 20th cent. industry predominated. The state's population grew throughout the 20th cent., with Atlanta especially attracting national corporations.

Georgia *officially* **Republic of Georgia** *Georgian* **Sakartvelo** \sä-'kärt-ve-.lō\ Republic, SW Asia. In the Caucasus Mtns., on the SE shores of the Black Sea, it includes the autonomous republics of Abkhazia and Adzharia. Area: 26,831 sq

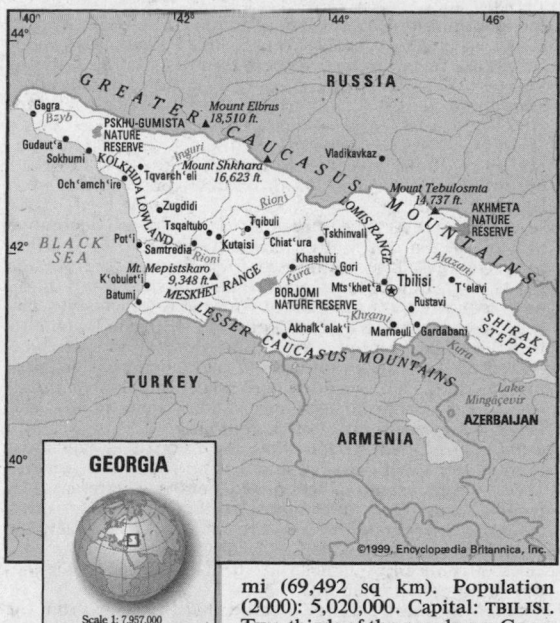

©1999, Encyclopædia Britannica, Inc.

mi (69,492 sq km). Population (2000): 5,020,000. Capital: TBILISI. Two-thirds of the people are Georgian (Karttvelebi); minorities include Armenians, Russians, and Azerbaijanis. Language: Georgian (official). Religion: Georgian Orthodoxy. Currency: lari. Most of Georgia is mountainous; many peaks rise higher than 15,000 ft (4,600 m). The Caucasus protect it against cold air from the north, and the climate is mainly subtropical. Fertile lowlands lie near the shores of the Black Sea. It has a well-developed industrial base, noted for hydroelectric power, coal and steel, machinery production, and textiles. Agricultural land is in short supply and difficult to farm; crops include tea, citrus fruits, wine grapes, sugar beets, and tobacco. It is a republic with one legislative body; its head of state and government is the president. Ancient Georgia was the site of the kingdoms of Iberia and COLCHIS, whose fabled wealth was known to the ancient Greeks. The area was part of the Roman empire by 65 B.C., and became Christian in A.D. 337. For the next three centuries it was involved in the conflicts between the Byzantine and Persian empires; after 654 it was controlled by Arab caliphs, who established an emirate in Tbilisi. It was controlled by the Armenian Bagratids from the 8th to the 12th cent., and the zenith of Georgia's power was reached in the reign of Queen Tamara, whose realm stretched from Azerbaijan to Circassia, forming a pan-Caucasian empire. Invasions by Mongols and Turks in the 13th–14th cent. disintegrated the kingdom, and the fall of Constantinople (now ISTANBUL) to the Ottoman Turks in 1453 isolated it from W Christendom. The next three centuries saw repeated invasions by the Armenians, Turks, and Persians. Georgia sought Russian protection in 1783, and in 1801 was annexed to Russia. After the RUSSIAN REVOLUTION OF 1917, the area was briefly independent; in 1921 a Soviet regime was installed, and in 1936 Georgia became the Georgian S.S.R., a full member of the Soviet Union. In 1990 a noncommunist coalition came to power in the first free elections ever held in Soviet Georgia, and in 1991, Georgia declared independence. In the 1990s, while Pres. Eduard SHEVARDNADZE tried to steer a middle course, internal dissension resulted in conflicts with the Abkhaz Republic. Political instability has continued, and relations with Russia remain tense.

Georgia Institute of Technology Public institution of higher learning in Atlanta, founded in 1885. It consists of colleges of architecture, computing, engineering, sciences, and public policy and administration, and is home to many research-and-development centers. Total enrollment is about 13,000.

Georgian poetry Body of lyrical poetry produced in Britain in the early 20th cent. Desiring to make new poetry more accessible to the public, Rupert BROOKE and Sir Edward Marsh (1872–1953) produced five anthology volumes— containing works by Robert GRAVES, Walker de la Mare (1873–1956), and others—called *Georgian Poetry* (1912–22). "Georgian" was meant to suggest the opening of a new poetic age with the accession in 1910 of GEORGE V; however, much of the Georgians' work was conventional and even backward-looking.

Georgian style Architecture, interior design, and decorative arts of Britain during the reigns (1714–1830) of the first four Georges. It encompassed Palladianism (see Andrea PALLADIO), turned to an austere Neoclassicism, moved on to GOTHIC REVIVAL, and ended with the Regency style. The era is said to mark the summit of house design in Britain. Its legacy can be seen in the city squares of uniform, symmetrical brick London townhouses with Classical pilasters, pedimented doors and windows, and graceful moldings. Interiors integrated harmonious proportions, quiet colors, and Roman-derived stucco ornamentation.

geosyncline Linear trough of the earth's crust, in which vast amounts of sediment accumulate. The filling of a geosyncline with thousands of feet of sediment is accompanied by folding, crumpling, and faulting of the deposits. Intrusion of crystalline igneous rock and regional uplift complete the transformation into a belt of folded mountains. The concept, introduced by James Hall in 1843, is basic to the theory of mountain building.

geothermal energy Power obtained by using heat from the earth's interior. Most geothermal resources are in regions of active VOLCANISM, including hot springs, geysers, and fumaroles. The ancient Romans used hot springs to heat baths and homes, and similar uses are still found in Iceland, Turkey, and Japan. Geothermal energy's greatest potential lies in the generation of electricity; its first such use was in Italy in 1904. Today geothermal power plants operate in New Zealand, Japan, Iceland, Mexico, the U.S., and elsewhere.

Gerald of Wales See GIRALDUS CAMBRENSIS

geranium Any of the approximately 300 species of perennial herbaceous plants or shrubs that make up the genus *Geranium* (family Geraniaceae), native mostly to subtropical S Africa. They are among the most popular bedding and greenhouse plants. The closely related genus *Pelargonium* contains some 280 species also commonly called geraniums.

Some geraniums are grown as basket plants indoors and out; they are also used as ground covers in warm areas. Some species have fragrant leaves. Geranium oil smells like roses and is used chiefly in perfumes, soaps, and ointments.

gerbil \\'jər-bəl\\ Any of almost 100 species of burrowing mouselike RODENTS (in the family Cricetidae) found in Africa and Asia. Gerbils have large eyes and ears and soft, brown or grayish fur. Most are 4–6 in. (10–15 cm) long, excluding the long, hairy tail. Many species have long hind legs used for leaping. One species (*Meriones unguiculatus*) is a popular pet. Members of one African genus (*Tatera*) are possible carriers of bubonic PLAGUE.

geriatrics See GERONTOLOGY AND GERIATRICS

Géricault \\zhā-ri-'kō\\, (Jean-Louis-André-) Théodore (1791–1824) French painter. Under Pierre Guérin (1774–1833) and Carle Vernet (1758–1835), he developed great skill in figure construction and composition and at capturing animal movement. He was inspired by the contemporary subject matter of A.-J. GROS. The macabre subject matter and political overtones of his huge *Raft of the Medusa* (1818–19) aroused great controversy. In 1820–21 he went to England and produced a large body of lithographs, watercolors, and oils of jockeys and horses. An avid horseman, he died at 32 after a riding accident. His work had enormous influence, most notably on Eugène DELACROIX and on the development of Romantic art in France.

Germain \\zher-'maⁿ\\, **Thomas** (1674–1748) French silversmith. In 1691 he was apprenticed to a silversmith in Rome. Back in France, he worked on church commissions, such as a silver-gilt monstrance for Notre-Dame de Paris (1716). In 1723 LOUIS XV appointed him a royal goldsmith. His other patrons included the Portuguese court; his workshop produced some 3,000 silver objects for the palace at Lisbon over a 40-year period. Though some of his pieces are simple and elegant, he is best known for elaborate objects in Rococo style.

German Confederation (1815–66) Organization of the states of central Europe. Established by the Congress of VIENNA to replace the destroyed HOLY ROMAN EMPIRE, it was a loose political association of 39 German states. Delegates met in a federal diet, dominated by Austria. Amid a growing call for reform and economic integration, Klemens von METTERNICH persuaded the confederation to pass the repressive Carlsbad Decrees (1819); in the 1830s he led the federal Diet in passing additional measures to crush liberalism and nationalism. The REVOLUTIONS OF 1848 undermined the confederation; it was dissolved with the Austro–Prussian War (1866).

German East Africa Former dependency of imperial Germany, corresponding to present-day Rwanda and Burundi, continental Tanzania, and a small section of Mozambique. In 1891 the German imperial government took over administration of the area. During World War I it was occupied by the British, who received a mandate to administer most of it (Tanganyika Territory) by the Treaty of VERSAILLES (1919). A smaller portion (Ruanda-Urundi) was entrusted to Belgium.

Germanic languages \\jər-'ma-nik\\ Branch of the INDO-EUROPEAN LANGUAGE family. It is divided into W. Germanic, including ENGLISH, GERMAN, Frisian, DUTCH, AFRIKAANS, and YIDDISH; N. Germanic, including Danish, SWEDISH, Icelandic, NORWEGIAN, and Faeroese (the language of the Faeroe Islands); and E. Germanic, now extinct, comprising Gothic and the languages of the Vandals, Burgundians, and a few other tribes. The Gothic Bible of A.D. 350 is the earliest extensive Germanic text. The W. Germanic languages developed around the North Sea and in overseas areas colonized by their speakers. The N. Germanic, or Scandinavian, languages, were carried as far west as Greenland and as far east as Russia by the Vikings.

Germanic religion Beliefs, rituals, and mythology of the pre-Christian Germanic peoples, in a geographic area extending from the Black Sea across central Europe and Scandinavia to Iceland and Greenland. The religion died out in central Europe with the conversion to Christianity (4th cent.) but continued in Scandinavia until the 10th cent. The Old Norse literature of medieval Iceland recounts the lore of the Germanic gods. The earth was held to have been created out of a cosmic void or, in another account, from the body of a primeval giant, AURGELMIR. There were two sets of gods in the Germanic pantheon, the warlike AESIR and the agricultural VANIR. Religious rites were conducted in the open or in groves and forests; animal and human sacrifice was practiced. RAGNAROK is the Germanic doomsday.

Germanicus Caesar \jər-'ma-ni-kəs\ (15 B.C.–A.D. 19) Nephew and adopted son of TIBERIUS, brother of CLAUDIUS, and father of CALIGULA and AGRIPPINA THE YOUNGER. A successful and popular general, he stifled a rebellion in the West on the death of AUGUSTUS (A.D. 14). Though urged to take imperial power, he deferred to Tiberius. In the East he came into conflict with Gnaeus Calpurnius Piso, governor of Syria. His death may have been due to poisoning ordered by Piso, though Tiberius was also suspected. Only his premature death prevented Germanicus from becoming emperor.

germanium Chemical ELEMENT, discovered in 1886, chemical symbol Ge, atomic number 32, with physical properties similar to SILICON, used especially in SEMICONDUCTOR devices. It remains of primary importance in the manufacture of TRANSISTORS and of components for other devices such as rectifiers and photocells. It is also used as a component of alloys, in phosphors for fluorescent lamps, and in the glasses of certain optical components, such as camera and microscope lenses.

German language Official language of Germany and Austria and an official language of Switzerland, used by over 100 million speakers. It belongs to the W. Germanic group of the GERMANIC LANGUAGES. German has four noun cases and three genders. Its many DIALECTS belong to either the High German (Hochdeutsch) or Low German (Plattdeutsch) groups. Modern High German, spoken in the central and S highlands of Germany, Austria, and Switzerland, is now standard written German used in administration, higher education, literature, and the mass media.

German measles See RUBELLA

German National People's Party (DNVP) (1919–33) Radical right-wing political party active during the WEIMAR REPUBLIC. Hostile to the republic, it supported the restoration of the monarchy and a united Germany. During a controversy (1929–30) over paying war reparations to the Allies, it allied with the NAZI PARTY in favor of stopping payments. In 1933 it joined a coalition that supported Adolf HITLER as chancellor; soon afterward, all German political parties except the Nazis were dissolved.

German shepherd or **Alsatian** Breed of WORKING DOG developed in Germany. A strongly built, long-bodied dog, it stands 23–25 in. (58–64 cm) high and weighs 75–95 lbs (34–43 kg). Its coarse coat is often gray and black or black and tan. Noted for intelligence, alertness, and loyalty, it is used as a guide for the blind, as a watchdog, and in police and military work.

German–Soviet Nonaggression Pact (1939) Agreement stipulating mutual nonaggression between the Soviet Union and Germany. In the pact, the two states pledged publicly not to attack each other; its secret provisions divided Poland between them and gave the Soviet Union control of Latvia, Lithuania, Estonia, and Finland. The Soviets also hoped to buy time to build up their forces in the face of German expansionism; Germany wished to proceed with its invasion of Poland and the countries to its west without worrying about the Red Army. News of the pact shocked the world. Nine days later, Germany began WORLD WAR II. The agreement was voided when Germany attacked the Soviet Union in 1941.

Germany officially **Federal Republic of Germany** German **Deutschland** \'dȯich-ˌlänt\ Republic, N central Europe. Area: 137,828 sq mi (356,974 sq km). Population (2000): 82,225,000. Capital: BERLIN. The majority of the people are German. Language: German (official). Religions: Lutheranism, Roman Catholicism. Currency: euro. The land is generally flat in the north and hilly in the northeast and central region, rising to the Bavarian Alps in the south. The RHINE RIVER basin dominates the central and W part of the country, while other important rivers are the ELBE, DANUBE, and ODER. It has a developed free-market economy largely based on services and manufacturing; it is one of the richest

countries in the world. Exports include motor vehicles and iron and steel products. The chief of state is the president, while the head of government is the chancellor. Federal power is centered in the bicameral Parliament. Germanic tribes entered Germany around the 2nd cent. B.C., displacing the Celts. The Romans failed to conquer the region, which only became a political entity with the division of the CAROLINGIAN empire in the 9th cent. A.D. The monarchy's control was weak, and power increasingly devolved upon the nobility, organized in feudal states. The monarchy was restored under Saxon rule in the 10th cent., and the HOLY ROMAN EMPIRE, centering on Germany and N Italy, was revived. Continuing conflict between the Holy Roman emperors and the Roman Catholic popes undermined the empire, and its dissolution was accelerated by Martin LUTHER's revolt in 1517, which divided Germny, and ultimately Europe, into Protestant and Catholic camps, culminating in the THIRTY YEARS' WAR (1618–48). Germany's population and borders were greatly reduced, and its numerous feudal princes gained virtually full sovereignty. In 1862 Otto von BISMARCK came to power in PRUSSIA, and over the next decade reunited Germany in the German empire. It was dissolved in 1918, after the German defeat in World War I. Germany was stripped of much of its territory and all of its colonies. The postwar government, the WEIMAR REPUBLIC, was replaced in 1934 by Adolf HITLER's Third Reich, dominated by the NAZI PARTY. Hitler's fanatical policies plunged the world into World War II. Following its defeat, Germany was divided by the Allied Powers into four zones of occupation. Disagreement with the Soviet Union over their reunification led to the creation in 1949 of the Federal Republic of Germany (W. GERMANY) and the German Democratic Republic (E. GERMANY). Berlin, the former capital, remained divided. W. Germany became a prosperous parliamentary democracy, E. Germany a one-party state under Soviet control. The E. German people overthrew the communist government in 1989 in a peaceful revolution, and Germany was reunited in 1990. After the initial euphoria over unity, during which the former W. Germany sought to incorporate the former E. Germany both politically and economically, the wealthier W. Germans experienced a large financial drain. However, it moved toward political and economic integration through its membership in the EUROPEAN UNION.

Germany, East officially **German Democratic Republic** Former republic (1945–90), N central Europe. It is now the E portion of the Federal Republic of Germany. In 1945, occupied Germany was divided into U.S., British, French, and

Soviet zones. In 1949 the U.S., British, and French zones were combined as W. GERMANY, while the Soviet zone formed E. Germany as a Communist state. The BERLIN WALL was constructed at its border with W. BERLIN in 1961 to stem the flight of its citizens to the West. The Communist government was dismantled in 1989–90, and the country merged with W. Germany in October 1990.

Germany, West *officially* **Federal Republic of Germany** Former republic (1949–90), W central Europe. It consisted of the W two-thirds of what is now the Federal Republic of Germany. It was formed in 1949 when the U.S., British, and French zones of occupation in Germany were united, while the Soviet zone became E. GERMANY. It united with SAARLAND in 1957, and joined the U.N. in 1973. It was reunited with E. Germany in October 1990.

germinal mutation See MUTATION

germination Sprouting of a SEED, SPORE, or other reproductive body, usually after a period of dormancy. Absorption of water, passage of time, chilling, warming, oxygen availability, and light exposure may all operate in initiating the germination process.

germ-plasm theory Concept of the physical basis of HEREDITY expressed by August Weismann (1834–1914). It claimed that germ plasm, which Weismann believed to be independent from all other cells of the body, was the essential element of germ cells (EGGS and SPERM) and was the hereditary material passed down the generations. Though its details have been altered, its idea of the stability of hereditary material is the basis of the modern understanding of physical inheritance.

germ theory Theory that certain diseases are caused by invasion of the body by microorganisms. Louis PASTEUR showed that organisms in the air cause FERMENTATION and spoil food; Joseph LISTER was first to use an ANTISEPTIC to exclude germs in the air to prevent infection; and Robert KOCH first linked a specific organism with a disease (ANTHRAX). The full implications of germ theory for medical practice were not immediately apparent after it was proven; surgeons operated without masks or head coverings as late as the 1890s.

germ warfare See BIOLOGICAL WARFARE

Gérôme \zhā-ˈrōm\, **Jean-Léon** (1824–1904) French painter and sculptor. He painted many melodramatic and often erotic historical and mythological compositions. His best-known works are Oriental scenes, inspired by several visits to Egypt. In his later years he produced mostly sculpture. He exerted much influence as a teacher at the École des Beaux-Arts; his pupils included Odilon REDON and Thomas EAKINS. A staunch defender of the academic tradition, he tried in 1893 to block the government's acceptance of the Impressionist works bequeathed by Gustave CAILLEBOTTE.

Geronimo \jə-ˈrä-nə-ˌmō\ (1829–1909) Chiricahua APACHE leader. In the 1870s Geronimo led a revolt of 4,000 Apaches who had been forcibly removed by U.S. authorities to a barren reservation in E central Arizona. Years of turmoil and bloodshed followed; Geronimo finally surrendered in 1884, only to escape with a band of followers. On a false promise of safe return to Arizona, Geronimo was arrested (1886) and put to hard labor, then placed on a reservation at Ft. Sill, Okla.; there he dictated his autobiography, *Geronimo: His Own Story*.

gerontology and geriatrics \ˌjer-ən-ˈtäl-ə-jē...ˌjer-ē-ˈa-triks\ Scientific and medical disciplines, respectively, concerned with all aspects of health and disease in the elderly and with the normal AGING process. Gerontology is concerned primarily with the changes that occur between maturity and death and with the factors that influence these changes, addressing the social and economic effects of an aging population and the physiological and psychological aspects of aging. Geriatrics deals with prevention and treatment of diseases once assumed to be inevitable in old people (e.g., ALZHEIMER'S DISEASE).

Gerry \ˈger-ē\, **Elbridge** (1744–1814) U.S. statesman. Born in Marblehead, Mass., he was an early advocate for independence and signed the Declaration of Independence. He served in the U.S. House of Representatives 1789–93, and in 1797 was sent to France, becoming involved in the XYZ AFFAIR. While he was governor of Massachusetts (1810–11),

his party's majority in the state legislature redrew the district lines to favor themselves, a practice that became known as GERRYMANDERING. In 1812 he was elected vice president on the ticket with James MADISON.

gerrymandering \ˈjer-ē-ˌman-driŋ\ Drawing of electoral district lines to give one political party unfair advantage by concentrating its opponents' votes in too few districts. The practice is named after Massachusetts Gov. Elbridge GERRY, who submitted a state-senate redistricting plan that favored the Democratic-Republican Party. Some of Gerry's new districts were necessarily odd-shaped; one district's outline, seen to resemble a salamander, gave rise to the scornful term gerrymander. The practice has persisted to the present day, and redistricting battles in the state legislatures have often had to be decided by the courts.

Gershwin, George *orig.* Jacob Gershvin (1898–1937) U.S. composer. Born in E. New York to Russian-Jewish immigrants, he worked as a song plugger in his teens. In 1918 his "Swanee" achieved extraordinary success. His first complete score was *La, La Lucille* (1919). His hugely successful orchestral work *Rhapsody in Blue* (1924) was followed by his first major Broadway success, *Lady, Be Good!* (1924), a collaboration with his brother Ira (1896–1983). They soon established themselves as one of the great teams in Broadway history; their shows included *Oh, Kay!* (1926), *Strike Up the Band* (1927), *Funny Face* (1927), *Girl Crazy* (1930), and the satire *Of Thee I Sing* (1931), the first musical to win a Pulitzer Prize. His most ambitious work was the "folk opera" *Porgy and Bess* (1935). His classical compositions include a piano concerto (1925) and the tone poem *An American in Paris* (1928). Gershwin died at 38 of a brain tumor.

Gestalt psychology \gə-ˈstält, ge-ˈshtält\ 20th-cent. school of psychology that provided the basis for the modern study of PERCEPTION. Its precepts, in reaction against the atomism of previous theories, emphasized that the whole of anything is different from the sum of its parts: organisms tend to perceive entire Gestalts (German for "pattern") rather than bits and pieces. The school emerged in Austria and Germany at the end of the 19th cent. and gained impetus through the works of Max Wertheimer (1880–1943), Wolfgang KÖHLER, Kurt Koffka (1886–1941), and Kurt Lewin (1890–1947). A form of PSYCHOTHERAPY only loosely related to Gestalt principles and influenced by EXISTENTIALISM and PHENOMENOLOGY was developed by Frederick (Fritz) Perls (1893–1970) in the 1940s. Gestalt therapy directs the client toward appreciating the form, meaning, and value of his or her perceptions and actions.

Gestapo \gə-ˈstä-pō\ *in full* Geheime Staatspolizei (German: "Secret State Police") Political police of Nazi Germany. It was created by Hermann GÖRING in 1933 from the political and espionage units of the Prussian police and by Heinrich HIMMLER from the police of the remaining German states. Himmler was given command in 1934. As part of the SS, the Gestapo operated without civil restraints. Thousands of Jews, leftists, intellectuals, trade unionists, political clergy, and homosexuals disappeared into concentration camps after being arrested by the Gestapo. In World War II it suppressed partisan activities in the occupied territories.

Gesta Romanorum \ˌjes-tə-ˌrō-mə-ˈnō-rəm\ (Latin: "Deeds of the Romans") Latin collection of anecdotes and tales, probably compiled in early-14th-cent. England. Very popular in its time, it became a source for much later literature, including works by Geoffrey CHAUCER and William SHAKESPEARE. It contains stories from classical history and legend and from various Oriental and European sources, all unified by their moral purpose and realistic detail. It may have been intended as a manual for preachers.

Gesualdo \jā-ˈswäl-dō\, **Carlo, principe (Prince) of Venosa** (1561?–1613) Italian composer. Nobly born, he was a passionate musical dilettante. In 1590 he had his wife and her lover (a duke) murdered, which earned him great notoriety but no punishment. He later married the duke of Ferrara's niece. His deepening melancholia was reflected in his music, which included some 125 madrigals and about 75 sacred vocal works. Their extreme chromaticism and abrupt changes in tempo and dynamics would have no rival until the 20th cent., when his works were rediscovered.

Gethsemane \geth-'se-mə-nē\ Garden outside JERUSALEM on the Mount of OLIVES. It is where JESUS is said to have prayed after the Last Supper and where he was arrested by Roman soldiers. The name comes from the Hebrew term for "oil press." Armenian, Greek, Latin, and Russian churches have accepted an olive grove on the W slope of the Mt. of Olives as the garden site.

Getty, J(ean) Paul (1892–1976) U.S. oil billionaire, reputed to be the richest man in the world at his death. Born in Minneapolis, the son of an oil millionaire, he began buying and selling oil leases in Oklahoma in 1913. He acquired Pacific Western Oil Corp. in 1932 and other acquisitions followed. He renamed his oil concern Getty Oil Co. in 1956. His most lucrative venture was a 60-year oil concession in Saudi Arabia. His holdings eventually encompassed some 200 enterprises. A zealous art collector, he founded the J. Paul GETTY MUSEUM near Malibu, Cal., in 1953.

Getty Museum, J. Paul Museum established by J. Paul GETTY to house his large collection of artworks. In 1974 they were moved from his ranch house in Malibu, Cal. to a new building in Malibu, a lavish re-creation of a Roman villa uncovered at Herculaneum. On Getty's death the museum became the most richly endowed in the world. It now is housed in the Getty Center, a striking six-building complex in Los Angeles designed by Richard MEIER, which opened in 1997. Its collections include European paintings, sculpture, drawings, and decorative arts to 1900, illuminated manuscripts, and photographs. Greek and Roman antiquities remain in the Malibu villa.

Gettysburg, Battle of (July 1–3, 1863) Major engagement in the AMERICAN CIVIL WAR at Gettysburg, Pa., regarded as the war's turning point. After defeating Union forces at CHANCELLORSVILLE, Robert E. LEE decided to invade the North with 75,000 troops. Learning that the Union's Army of the Potomac had a new commander, George MEADE, he led his own troops to Gettysburg, a strategic crossroads. On the decisive third day of battle, Lee sent 15,000 troops to assault Cemetery Ridge, held by 10,000 Union troops. A Confederate spearhead broke through the Union artillery defense but was stopped by a fierce Union counterattack on three sides. At night under cover of a heavy rain on July 4, Lee led his troops back to Virginia; Meade was later criticized for not pursuing him. Losses totaled about 23,000 casualties among 88,000 Union troops and over 20,000 among 75,000 Confederates.

Gettysburg Address (Nov. 19, 1863) Speech by Pres. Abraham LINCOLN at the dedication of a cemetery at Gettysburg, Pa., for those killed at the Battle of GETTYSBURG. Following a two-hour address by the renowned orator Edward Everett (1794–1865), Lincoln's brief speech, honoring the Union dead and the principles of democracy and equality they died for, lasted two minutes. Soon recognized as an extraordinary piece of prose poetry, it remains the most famous speech ever delivered in the U.S.

Getz, Stan(ley) (1927–1991) U.S. jazz saxophonist. Born in Philadelphia, Getz became known for his light tone and ethereal approach while one of the "Four Brothers" of Woody HERMAN's Second Herd (1947–49). He dominated popularity polls on his instrument in the cool jazz of the 1950s, and his incorporation of Brazilian bossa-nova music in the early 1960s brought him even wider success.

geyser \'gī-zər\ (Icelandic *geysir*, "to rush forth") Any HOT SPRING that discharges jets of steam and water intermittently. It is produced by the heating of underground waters that have come into contact with, or are very close to, MAGMA. Geyser discharges as high as 1,600 ft (500 m) have been recorded, but 150 ft (50 m) is much more common (e.g., Old Faithful in Yellowstone National Park).

Ghana \'gä-nə\ *officially* **Republic of Ghana** *formerly* **Gold Coast** Republic, W Africa. Area: 92,098 sq mi (238,533 sq km). Population (2000): 19,534,000. Capital: ACCRA. Ghana is home to some 75 different tribes; the most numerous are the Akan, followed by the Mole-Dagbani (MOSSI). Language: English (official). Religions: Christianity (both Protestantism and Roman Catholicism) and indigenous religions. Currency: cedi. The land is generally flat, dominated by the VOLTA RIVER basin. The north is characterized by grassland plains; the south is heavily forested. The S coastal

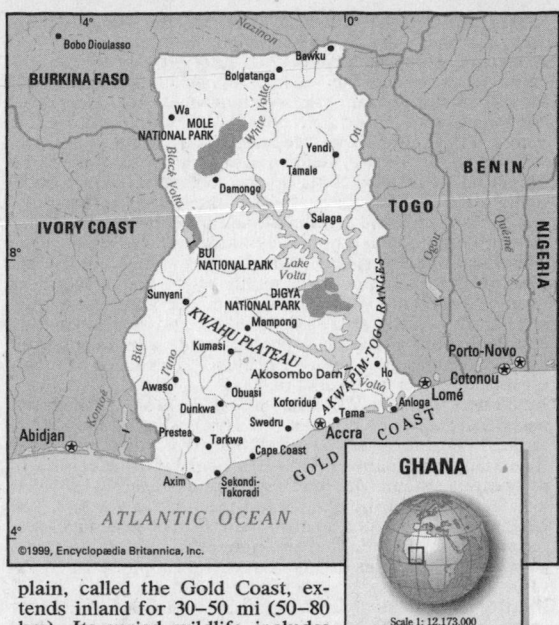

©1999, Encyclopædia Britannica, Inc.

plain, called the Gold Coast, extends inland for 30–50 mi (50–80 km). Its varied wildlife includes lion, leopard, and elephant. It has a developing mixed economy based largely on agriculture and mining. Cacao is the mainstay of the economy; mineral exports include gold and diamonds. It is a republic with one legislative house; its head of state and government is the president. The modern state of Ghana is named after the ancient GHANA EMPIRE that flourished until the 13th cent. A.D. in the W Sudan, about 500 mi (800 km) northwest of the modern state. The Akan peoples then founded their first states in modern Ghana. Gold-seeking Mande traders arrived by the 14th cent. and HAUSA merchants by the 16th cent. During the 15th cent. the Mande founded the states of Dagomba and Mamprussi in the N half of the region. The ASHANTI, an Akan people, originated in the central forest region and formed a strongly centralized empire that was at its height in the 18th–19th cent. European exploration of the region began early in the 15th cent., when the Portuguese landed on the Gold Coast; they latr established a settlement at Elmina as headquarters for the SLAVE TRADE. By the mid-18th cent. the Gold Coast was dominated by numerous forts controlled by Dutch, British, and Danish merchants. Britain made the Gold Coast a crown colony in 1874, and British protectorates over the Ashanti and the N territories were established in 1901. In 1957, under Kwame NKRUMAH, the Gold Coast became the independent state of Ghana. Since independence, numerous political coups have occurred; those of Jerry RAWLINGS (1979, 1981) led to a stable democratic government.

Ghana empire First of the great medieval trading empires of W Africa (7th–13th cent.), located in what is now SE Mauritania and Mali. Its inhabitants acted as intermediaries between Arab and BERBER salt traders to the north and gold and ivory producers to the south. As the empire grew richer it extended its reach, incorporating gold-producing S lands and cities to the north. The king exacted tribute from subject tribes. Ghana began to decline with the rise of the Muslim ALMORAVIDS; ABU BAKR seized the Ghanaian capital of Kumbi in 1076, the empire's subject peoples began to break away, and in 1240 the empire's remains were incorporated into the Sundiata empire of Mali.

Ghats \'gȯts\, **Eastern and Western** Two mountain ranges forming the edges of the DECCAN plateau in S India. The Eastern Ghats extend about 500 mi (800 km) along the SE and E coast; their average elevation is about 2,000 ft (600 m). The Western Ghats run 800 mi (1,290 km) along the SW and W coast; their elevations range from 3,000 ft (900 m) to

FG

5,000 ft (1,500 m). Wiith heavy rainfall, the Western Ghats comprise peninsular India's principal watershed.

Ghazan \gä-'zän\, **Mahmud** (1271–1304) Best-known subordinate KHAN to rule the MONGOL dynasty in Persia. In 1284 his father, the Persian ruler Arghun, made him viceroy of NE Persia. In 1295 he converted from Buddhism to Islam before taking the throne. He successfully fought the MAMLUK REGIME in Syria, defeating their army at Homs. The Mamluks reoccupied Syria on his departure, and he eventually died leaving Damascus in their hands. He spoke many languages and commissioned a history of the Mongols and others with whom they had come in contact.

ghazel *or* **ghazal** *or* **gazel** \'gaz-el, *Arabic* 'gà-zál\ In Islamic literature, a lyric poem, generally short and graceful in form and typically dealing with love. The genre developed in late-7th-cent. Arabia. The poems begin with a rhymed couplet whose rhyme is repeated in all subsequent even lines, while the odd lines are unrhymed. It reached its greatest refinement in the works of HAFEZ.

Ghaznavid dynasty \'gœz-nə-vəd\ (977–1186) Turkish dynasty that ruled in Khorasan (NE Iran), Afghanistan, and N India. It was founded by Sebuktigin (r.977–97), a former slave. His son Mahmud (998–1030) enlarged the empire to its greatest extent. Mahmud's grandson Masud I (1031–41) lost the W half of the empire to the SELJUQ DYNASTY. The Ghaznavids continued to rule their E provinces until suffering defeat in 1186. They are noted for their architecture, government, theories of governance, and support for literature.

Ghent \'gent\ *Flemish* **Gent** \'kent\ *French* **Gand** \'gäⁿ\ City (pop., 1998: 224,000), capital of E. Flanders province, NW Belgium. One of the chief towns of medieval FLANDERS, it was by the 13th cent. one of the largest towns in N Europe. Its prosperity was based on its manufacture of luxury cloths, which were famous throughout Europe. It began to decline in the late 16th cent. but revived with the introduction of cotton-spinning machinery to become the center of the Belgian textiles industry. Belgium's second-largest port, it is also a horticultural center.

Ghent, Pacification of (1576) Declaration by which the N and S provinces of the LOW COUNTRIES united in revolt against the Spanish Habsburgs. As the first major expression of the Netherlands' national consciousness, it called for the expulsion of Spanish troops and an end to the persecution of Calvinists. The Spanish governor soon resumed hostilities, however, and religious differences caused a split in 1579 between the Calvinist north (Union of Utrecht) and the Catholic south (Union of Arras).

Gheorghiu-Dej \'gyór-gyü-'dā\, **Gheorghe** (1901–1965) Romanian politician. He became head of the Communist Party in 1944. As prime minister (1952–55), he gradually adopted policies that served Romania's national interests. As president of the State Council (1961–65), he pursued a program of industrialization, despite the objections of other Sovietbloc countries that wanted Romania to remain agricultural. He further demonstrated Romania's independence by forming cordial relations with noncommunist nations and with China.

Gherardo delle Notte See Gerrit van HONTHORST

ghetto Street or quarter of a city set apart as a legally enforced residence area for Jews. The name comes from an island (the site of a foundry, or *ghetto*) where Venetian Jews were required to live. Forced segregation of Jews spread throughout Europe in the 14th–15th cent. Ghettos were customarily enclosed with walls and gates and kept locked at night and during Christian festivals. Ghettos were abolished in Western Europe in the 19th cent.; those revived by the NAZI PARTY (see WARSAW GHETTO UPRISING) were overcrowded holding places preliminary to extermination. More recently, the term ghetto has been applied to impoverished urban areas exclusively settled by a minority group and perpetuated by economic and social pressures.

Ghibellines See GUELPHS AND GHIBELLINES

Ghiberti \gē-'ber-tē\, **Lorenzo** (c.1378–1455) Italian sculptor. Trained as a goldsmith and painter, in 1402 he won a competition to make a pair of bronze doors for the Baptistery of Florence Cathedral, defeating Filippo BRUNELLESCHI. The honor brought him immediate fame. Work on the doors lasted from 1403 to 1424. In 1425 he was asked to make a second pair, known as the Gates of Paradise, which he completed in 1452. The reliefs on the first doors are the major sculptural works of the International Gothic style in Italy; those on the second are among the finest examples of Italian Renaissance art. His other commissions included three bronze statues for Or San Michele (1413–29). He directed a large workshop with many assistants, including DONATELLO and Paolo UCCELLO. His treatise on art includes the earliest surviving autobiography of an artist.

Ghirlandaio \,gir-lən-'dä-yō\, **Domenico** *orig.* Domenico di Tommaso Bigordi (1449–1494) Italian painter. In 1481–82 he painted several frescoes, including the *Calling of Sts. Peter and Andrew,* in the Vatican's Sistine Chapel. His greatest fresco cycle, in Santa Maria Novella in Florence (1485–90), depicts scenes from the lives of the Virgin and St. John the Baptist in contemporary dress against detailed patrician interiors. It has become a major source of current knowledge on the furnishings of a late-15th-cent. Florentine palace. With his two brothers he directed one of the most prosperous workshops in Florence. His finest portrait is *The Old Man and His Grandson* (c.1480–90).

ghost Soul or specter of a deceased person. Belief in ghosts has been common worldwide since ancient times. Ghosts are believed to inhabit the netherworld and to be capable of returning to the world of the living, appearing as living beings or in a nebulous likeness of the deceased. They are thought to be especially likely to haunt places or people connected with some strong emotion of their past life, such as fear, remorse, or the terror of a violent death.

Ghost Dance 19th-cent. cult that arose in 1889, when the PAIUTE prophet-dreamer Wovoka (1858–1932) announced the imminent return of the dead (hence "ghost"), the ousting of the whites, and the restoration of Indian lands and way of life, all of which would be hastened by dances and songs revealed in Wovoka's spiritual visions. The Ghost Dance spread rapidly; it coincided with the SIOUX outbreak of 1890, which culminated in the massacre at WOUNDED KNEE. The cult soon became obsolete.

Giacometti \,jä-kə-'me-tē\, **Alberto** (1901–1966) Swiss sculptor and painter. He studied art in Geneva and Paris, and developed a style related to the Cubist sculpture of Alexander ARCHIPENKO and Jacques LIPCHITZ, partly inspired by African and Oceanic art. By the 1940s he had developed his signature style, producing thin, attenuated sculptures of solitary, skeletal figures and heads. He became well known, especially in the U.S., through two exhibitions in New York (1948, 1950) and an essay on his art by Jean-Paul SARTRE. His work evokes a sense of existential tragedy. In 1963 he designed the stage set for Samuel BECKETT's *Waiting for Godot.*

Alberto Giacometti Photo by Yousuf Karsh, 1965

Giambologna \,jäm-bō-'lōn-yä\ (1529–1608) Flemish-Italian sculptor. He went to Rome in 1550, where his style was influenced by Hellenistic sculpture and the works of MICHELANGELO, and settled in Florence in 1552. He produced many of his most important works for the MEDICI FAMILY, but it was the *Fountain of Neptune* (1563–66) in Bologna that made him famous. His bronze equestrian statue of Cosimo I de' MEDICI (1587–93), the first of its kind made in Florence, became a pattern for similar statues all over Europe. His garden sculptures, notably for Florence's Boboli Gardens, enjoyed great popularity. He was the outstanding sculptor of Italian MANNERISM.

Giannini \,jē-ə-'nē-nē\, **A(madeo) P(eter)** (1870–1949) U.S. banker. Born in San Jose, Cal., the son of Italian immigrants, he began working in the family wholesale produce business at 13. In 1904 he and five partners founded the

Bank of Italy in San Francisco. Their bank was unusual in making loans to small farmers and businessmen and actively soliciting customers. In 1909 he began buying other California banks, creating the first statewide branch-banking system in the U.S. Acquiring a second network of branch banks, he merged the two in 1930 under the name Bank of America National Trust and Savings Assn. By the time of his death, Bank of America had more than 500 branch banks.

giant See GIGANTISM

giant sequoia See BIG TREE

giant star Star with a large radius for its mass and temperature; this yields a large radiating area, so such stars are bright. They include SUPERGIANT STARS, red giants (low temperatures, very bright), and subgiants (slightly reduced radii and brightness). Some are hundreds of thousands of times brighter than the sun. With masses 10–30 times that of the sun and volumes millions of times greater, giants and supergiants are low-density stars.

Giap, Vo Nguyen See VO NGUYEN GIAP

Giardia lamblia \jē-'är-dē-ə-'lam-blē-ə\ *or G. intestinalis* Single-celled PROTOZOAN parasite. Pear- or beet-shaped, the cells have two nuclei and eight flagella, and attach to the intestinal mucous membrane with a sucking organ. They cause the disease giardiasis, with diarrhea, pain, and distension of the stomach. Generally spread by ingesting traces of human feces containing the parasite, giardiasis is common wherever there is contamination of water in lakes, rivers, and reservoirs, and is a major cause of diarrhea worldwide. Beaver feces are often responsible for giardiasis among campers who take water from lakes and rivers.

gibbon \'gi-bən\ Any of about six species (genus *Hylobates*) of lesser APES (family Hylobatidae), found in Indo-Malayan forests. Gibbons use their long arms to swing from branch to branch. They walk erect on the ground, live in small groups, and feed principally on shoots and fruits. They have long hair and are about 16–26 in. (40–65 cm) long. They have large canine teeth, and their voices are noted for their volume, musical quality, and carrying power.

Gibbon \'gi-bən\, **Edward** (1737–1794) British historian. On a trip to Rome he was inspired to write the history of the city. His *Decline and Fall of the Roman Empire* (6 vols., 1776–88) is a continuous narrative from the 2nd cent. A.D. to the fall of Constantinople in 1453. Though Gibbon's conclusions have been modified by later scholars, his acumen, historical perspective, and superb literary style have given his work its lasting reputation as the greatest historical work ever written in English.

Gibbs, J(osiah) Willard (1839–1903) U.S. theoretical physicist and chemist. Born in New Haven, Conn., he began his career in engineering but turned to theory, analyzing the EQUILIBRIUM of James WATT's steam-engine governor. His major works were on fluid THERMODYNAMICS and the equilibrium of heterogeneous substances, and he developed statistical mechanics. Gibbs was the first to expound with mathematical rigor the "relation between chemical, electrical, and thermal energy and capacity for work." Though little appreciated during his lifetime, his application of thermodynamic theory to chemical reactions converted much of physical chemistry from an empirical to a deductive science, and he is regarded as one of the greatest scientists of the 19th cent.

Gibbs, William Francis (1886–1967) U.S. naval architect. Born in Philadelphia, during World War I he and his brother Frederick H. Gibbs designed ships for the U.S. government; after the war they reconditioned the *Leviathan*. Gibbs's design for the *Malolo* (1927), with its watertight compartments and other safety features, became an industry standard. In 1940 he designed a cargo ship suitable for mass production; using prefabrication techniques, he reduced production time from up to four years to as little as four days, an innovation of enormous value in World War II. His passenger liner *United States* (1952) set speed records in transatlantic service.

Gibeon \'gi-bē-ən\ Ancient city of CANAAN, lying northwest of JERUSALEM at modern Al-Jib. According to the Bible, its inhabitants made an alliance with the Israelite leader JOSHUA at the time of the conquest of Canaan but were in-stead made slaves. Excavations in 1956 revealed that the site had been occupied in the Late Bronze Age just before Joshua's conquest of Canaan.

GI Bill (of Rights) *or* **Servicemen's Readjustment Act** (1944) U.S. legislation that provided benefits to World War II veterans. Through the Veterans Administration (VA), the bill provided grants for school and college tuition, low-interest mortgage and small-business loans, job training, hiring privileges, and unemployment payments. Later legislation extended the benefits to all who had served in the armed forces.

Gibraltar \jə-'brȯl-tər\ British colony (pop., 1995 est.: 31,000), Mediterranean coast in S Spain. The site of a British air and naval base that guards the Strait of GIBRALTAR, it occupies a narrow peninsula 3 mi (5 km) long and 3/4 mi (1.2 km) wide, known as the Rock. It appears from the east as a series of sheer, inaccessible cliffs, which makes it strategically important. The Moors held Gibraltar from 711 to 1501, when it was annexed by Spain. Captured by the British in 1704, it became a British crown colony in 1830. It remains the center of a sovereignty dispute between Spain and England.

Gibraltar

Gibraltar, Strait of *ancient* Fretum Herculeum. Channel, connecting the Mediterranean Sea with the Atlantic Ocean. Lying between southernmost Spain and northwesternmost Africa, it is 36 mi (58 km) long and narrows to 8 mi (13 km). At the strait's E extreme stand the PILLARS OF HERCULES. It has long been of great strategic and economic importance.

Gibran \ji-'brän\, **Khalil** *orig.* Jubran Khalil Jubran (1883–1931) U.S. (Lebanese-born) philosophical essayist, novelist, poet, and artist. He emigrated with his parents to the U.S. in 1895. His effusively lyrical works, written in both Arabic and English, express his deeply religious and mystical nature. *The Prophet* (1923), a book of poetic essays, achieved cult status among American youth for several generations. His other English works include *The Madman* (1918) and *Jesus, the Son of Man* (1928).

Gibson, Althea (b.1927) U.S. tennis player. Born in Silver, S.C., she moved to New York City when she was 3. The first black to win the French (1956) and Wimbledon and U.S. singles championships (1957–58), she also won the U.S. mixed doubles, Australian women's doubles (both 1957), and U.S. professional women's title (1960), for a total of 11 Grand Slam events. She was voted Female Athlete of the Year by the Associated Press in 1957 and 1958, the first black to receive that honor.

Gibson, Bob (*orig.* Robert) (b.1935) U.S. baseball pitcher. Born in Omaha, as a pitcher for the St. Louis Cardinals (1961–75) he won seven of nine World Series games and in 1968 had an earned run average of 1.12 (fourth all-time) and 13 shutouts (tied for second all-time). His 3,117 strikeouts made him the first pitcher to exceed 3,000 since the 1920s.

Gibson, Charles Dana (1867–1944) U.S. illustrator. Born in Roxbury, Mass., he studied at New York's Art Students League and began to contribute drawings to magazines. His

F G

"Gibson girl" drawings, relying on his wife as a model, defined the U.S. ideal of spirited feminine beauty at the turn of the century, and his refined pen-and-ink style was widely imitated. *Collier's* reportedly paid him the unprecendented sum of $50,000 to produce a double-page illustration every week for a year.

Gibson, Josh(ua) (1911–1947) U.S. baseball player. Born in Buena Vista, Ga., he played as an outstanding catcher for the Pittsburgh Crawfords (1927–29, 1932–36) and the Homestead (Pa.) Grays (1930–31, 1937–46). He is believed to have led the NEGRO LEAGUES in home runs for 10 consecutive seasons and to have had a career batting average of .347. Often called "the black Babe Ruth," he died at 35 of a stroke three months before the major leagues admitted their first black ballplayer. He was elected to the Baseball Hall of Fame in 1972.

Gibson, Mel (Columcille) (b.1956) Australian (U.S.-born) film actor and director. He won a following in the futuristic action film *Mad Max* (1979), and its sequels *Road Warrior* (1981) and *Beyond Thunderdome* (1985). He won international acclaim for his roles in *Gallipoli* (1981), *The Year of Living Dangerously* (1983), and *The Bounty* (1984), played a tough cop in *Lethal Weapon* (1987) and its sequels (1989, 1992, 1998), and directed and starred in *The Man Without a Face* (1993) and *Braveheart* (1995, Academy Awards for best picture and director).

Gibson, William (Ford) (b.1948) U.S.-Canadian science-fiction writer. Born in Conway, S.C., he published his first novel, *Neuromancer*, in 1984 and emerged as a leading exponent of cyberpunk, a school of science fiction whose works are characterized by countercultural antiheroes trapped in a dehumanized, high-tech future. His concept of "cyberspace," a computer-simulated reality, is a major contribution to the genre. His later books include *Count Zero* (1986), *Mona Lisa Overdrive* (1988), and *Virtual Light* (1993).

Gide \'zhēd\, **André (-Paul-Guillaume)** (1869–1951) French writer. His great creative period began with the novellas *The Immoralist* (1902) and *Strait Is the Gate* (1909). In 1908 he cofounded *La Nouvelle Revue Française*, the literary review that would unite progressive French writers for 30 years. The autobiographical *If It Die . . .* (1924) is among the great works of confessional literature. *Corydon* (1924), a defense of homosexuality, was violently attacked. *The Counterfeiters* (1926) is his most complex novel. He become a champion of society's rejects and outcasts, and was for a

André Gide Painting by P. A. Laurens, 1924

time attracted to communism; with the outbreak of World War II he gained a greater appreciation for tradition. He received the Nobel Prize in 1947.

Gideon Judge and hero of ancient Israel, whose deeds are described in the Old Testament Book of Judges. The book contains two versions of Gideon's story. In one account, he led his tribe in a victorious campaign against the Midianites, then fell into idolatry; in another version, he replaced worship of the local deity, BAAL, with that of Yahweh (the God of Israel), and the power of Yahweh enabled his tribe to destroy the Midianites.

Gielgud \'gil-ˌgu̇d, 'gēl-ˌgu̇d\, **(Arthur) John** (*later* **Sir John**) (1904–2000) British actor and director. He joined the OLD VIC company in 1929, becoming widely acclaimed for such Shakespearean roles as Hamlet and Richard II, and also excelling in such plays as *The School for Scandal, The Importance of Being Earnest, The Seagull,* and *Tiny Alice.* He directed several repertory seasons in the 1940s and toured the world with the solo recital *Ages of Man* (1958–59). He appeared in many films in Britain and the U.S. from 1924, including *Arthur* (1981, Academy Award) and *Prospero's Books* (1991). For almost 70 years he was regarded as one of the finest actors in the English language.

GIF \'gif\ *in full* Graphics Interchange Format. Standard computer file format for graphic images. GIF files use data compression to reduce the file size. The original format was developed by CompuServe in 1987. The current version supports animated GIFs (graphic images that move). GIF and JPEG are the most commonly used graphics formats on the INTERNET.

gift exchange Transfer of goods or services that is part of expected social behavior. First studied by Marcel MAUSS, the gift-exchange cycle entails obligations to give, receive, and return, each phase being surrounded with sanctions and calculations involving prestige and the maintenance of social relations. Some SACRIFICES may be viewed as gifts to supernatural powers from which a return in the form of aid or approval is expected. See also POTLATCH.

gigantism Excessive growth, resulting from heredity, diet, or growth regulation disorder. ANDROGEN deficiency causes long bones to continue growing after they would normally stop. Overproduction of GROWTH HORMONE—usually due to a tumor—causes pituitary gigantism. Height may reach 8 ft (240 cm), with normal proportions. Greater susceptibility to infection, injury, and metabolic disorders shortens the life span. Surgery or radiation can be employed to curtail further growth.

Gila monster One of the only two species (both in the family Helodermatidae) of venomous LIZARDS, named for the Gila River basin and found in the SW U.S. and N Mexico. The Gila monster *(Heloderma suspectum)* grows to about 20 in. (50 cm) long, is stout-bodied with black and pink blotches or bands, and has beadlike scales. During warm weather, it feeds on small mammals, birds, and eggs and stores fat in the tail and abdomen for the winter. It is sluggish but has a strong bite, though it is rarely fatal to humans. The other venomous species is the Mexican beaded lizard *(H. horridum)*.

Gilbert, Cass (1859–1934) U.S. architect. Born in Zanesville, Ohio, he became known for his 60-story Woolworth Building (1910–13) in New York, with its Gothic detail in terra-cotta over a steel frame; a model of tall commercial building design, it was for years the tallest building in the world. Other works include the U.S. Supreme Court Building (completed 1935) and the campuses of the Univs. of Minnesota and Texas.

Gilbert, Humphrey (*later* **Sir Humphrey**) (1539?–1583) English soldier and navigator. The half brother of Walter RALEIGH, he proposed in his *Discourse* (1566) a voyage in search of the NORTHWEST PASSAGE. Queen ELIZABETH I instead sent him to Ireland (1567–70), where he ruthlessly suppressed an uprising. In 1578 he set out with seven ships, intending to colonize N. America, but through his poor leadership some ships returned and others turned to piracy. He sailed again in 1583, this time arriving in Newfoundland, which he claimed for the queen.

Gilbert, W(illiam) S(chwenck) (*later* **Sir William**) (1836–1911) British librettist. His early ambition was for a legal career, but in 1861 he began to publish comic ballads, signed "Bab." In 1870 he met Arthur SULLIVAN, and they soon produced the light opera *Thespis* (1871), which was followed by *Trial by Jury* (1875) and four productions staged by Richard D'Oyly Carte (1844–1901): *The Sorcerer* (1877), *H.M.S. Pinafore* (1878), *The Pirates of Penzance* (1879), and *Patience* (1881). Carte built the Savoy Theatre in 1881 for productions of the partners' work, which included *Iolanthe* (1882), *Princess Ida* (1884), *The Mikado* (1885), *The Yeomen of the Guard* (1888), and *The Gondoliers* (1889). Mounting tensions between Gilbert and Sullivan led to a break, but they reunited in 1893 for two more operas. Gilbert's lyrics include some of the finest comic verse ever written in English.

Gilbert Islands Group of 16 coral atolls (pop., 1990: 67,000), part of the island nation of Kiribati, W Pacific Ocean. The largest of the islands is TARAWA. In 1892 they became a British protectorate. In 1916 they became part of the Gilbert and Ellice Islands Crown Colony. They were occupied by Japanese forces 1941–43 and saw heavy fighting. Made a separate territory in 1976, they became part of Kiribati in 1979.

Gilead \'gi-lē-əd\ Area of ancient Palestine, east of the JORDAN RIVER. Now NW Jordan, it was bounded in the north by the Yarmuk River and in the southwest by what were known then as the plains of Moab. The name first appears in the biblical account of the last meeting of Jacob and Laban. The scene of the battle between Gideon and the Midianites, it was also the home of the prophet ELIJAH.

Gilgamesh \\'gil-gə-‚mesh, gil-'gä-məsh\\ Hero of the ancient AKKADIAN-LANGUAGE *Epic of Gilgamesh.* The great literary work of ancient MESOPOTAMIA, the epic is known principally from 12 incomplete tablets discovered at NINEVEH in the library of ASHURBANIPAL. The character Gilgamesh is probably based on the Gilgamesh who ruled Uruk in the 3rd millennium B.C. The epic presents him as a great warrior and builder, who rejects the marriage proposal of the goddess ISHTAR. With the aid of his friend and companion Enkidu, he kills the divine bull that Ishtar sends to destroy him. Enkidu's death prompts Gilgamesh to try to learn how to escape death. The epic ends with the return of the spirit of Enkidu, who gives a dismal report on the underworld.

Gilles de Rais See BLUEBEARD

Gillespie, Dizzy (*orig.* John Birks) (1917–1993) U.S. jazz trumpeter, composer, and bandleader. Born in Cheraw, S.C., Gillespie played with the big bands of Cab CALLOWAY, Earl HINES, and Billy Eckstine before leading small groups in the mid-1940s. He pioneered BEBOP with Charlie PARKER and Thelonious MONK. Bringing this approach to his big band in the late 1940s, Gillespie popularized the use of Afro-Cuban rhythms in jazz. His virtuosity and comic wit (and puffed cheeks and upturned trumpet bell) made him one of the most charismatic and influential musicians in jazz.

Dizzy Gillespie, 1955

Gilman, Charlotte (Anna) Perkins (Stetson) (1860–1935) U.S. feminist writer. Born in Hartford, Conn., she gained worldwide fame as a lecturer on women, ethics, labor, and society. In *Women and Economics* (1898), she proposed that women's sexual and maternal roles had been overemphasized and that only economic independence could bring true freedom. Her other works include the celebrated short story "The Yellow Wallpaper" (1899) and her autobiography, *The Living of Charlotte Perkins Gilman* (1935).

Gilmore, Patrick (Sarsfield) (1829–1892) Irish-U.S. bandmaster. He emigrated to the U.S. at 19. In 1859 he took over the Boston Brigade Band (later known as Gilmore's Band). A flamboyant showman, Gilmore organized extravaganza performances in 1869 and 1872 with more than 10,000 instrumentalists. From 1872 until his death he led the New York 22nd Regiment Band. His innovations reduced the heavy reliance on brass instruments in favor of the higher proportion of reeds characteristic of modern concert bands.

Gil Robles (y Quiñones) \\kēl-'rō-blās\\, **José María** (1898–1980) Spanish politician. In 1931 he formed the Catholic party Acción Popular, which became the main component of the right-wing coalition CEDA, a powerful bloc in the Spanish Second Republic after 1933. In 1936 he led an alliance of conservative parties in the Cortes. Marked for assassination by the right for his nonviolence when the SPANISH CIVIL WAR broke out, he fled into exile in Portugal (1936–53, 1962–64). He later worked to establish a Christian Democratic party in Spain.

gin Colorless DISTILLED LIQUOR made from grain and flavored with JUNIPER berries and aromatics (such as ANISE and CARAWAY seeds). Its origin is attributed to a 17th-cent. Dutch medical researcher, Franciscus Sylvius. The two principal types are a malty-flavored and full-bodied Netherlands type (35% alcohol) and a dry, purified type favored in Britain and the U.S. (40–47% alcohol). Dry gin is served either unmixed or in cocktails. Dutch gins are usually served unmixed or with water.

ginger Herbaceous perennial plant (*Zingiber officinale*; family Zingiberaceae), probably native to SE Asia, or its aromatic, pungent RHIZOME, which is used as a spice, flavoring, food, and medicine. The spice is used to flavor breads, sauces, curry dishes, confections, pickles, and ginger ale. The fresh rhizome, green ginger, is used in cooking. The leafy stems of the plant bear flowers in dense, conelike spikes.

ginkgo Tree (*Ginkgo biloba,* family Ginkgoaceae) that is the only living representative of the gymnosperm order Ginkgoales. Native to China, it has existed for some 250 million years and is often termed a living fossil. It has long been planted in Chinese and Japanese temple gardens and is now valued in many parts of the world as an attractive, fungus- and insect-resistant ornamental tree. It tolerates cold weather and, unlike most gymnosperms, can survive the adverse atmospheric conditions of urban areas. The light-colored wood, soft and weak, has little economic value. The leaves are fan-shaped and leathery. The silvery nut, when roasted, is considered a delicacy. Studies have suggested that *Ginkgo biloba* supplements can enhance memory function in the elderly and delay the onset of Alzheimer's disease.

Ginsberg, Allen (Irwin) (1926–1997) U.S. poet. Born in Newark, N.J., he attended Columbia Univ. His epic poem *Howl* (1956), a denunciation of the failings of American society, became the most famous poem of the BEAT MOVEMENT; in it and later works, he celebrated the pleasures of psychotropic drugs, footloose wandering, and homosexuality. *Kaddish* (1961) is a long confessional poem about his mother's insanity and suicide. His collections include *Reality Sandwiches* (1963) and *The Fall of America* (1972). His life was one of ceaseless travel, poetry readings, and left-wing political activity, and he was an influential guru of the American youth counterculture in the 1960s and '70s.

Ginsburg, Ruth Bader *orig.* Ruth Joan Bader (b.1933) U.S. jurist. Born in New York City, she graduated at the top of her class at Columbia Law School in 1959, but was turned down for numerous jobs because of her sex. She taught at Columbia 1972–80, where she became the first tenured female professor. For the AMERICAN CIVIL LIBERTIES UNION, she argued six landmark cases on gender equality before the U.S. Supreme Court. In 1980 she was appointed to the U.S. Court of Appeals, and in 1993 she ascended to the Supreme Court as its second female justice in history.

ginseng \\'jin-'seŋ\\ Either of two herbs of the family Araliaceae or their roots. *Panax quinquefolium,* the N. American ginseng, is native from Quebec and Manitoba southward to the Gulf of Mexico. Asian ginseng (*P. schinseng*) is native to Manchuria and Korea and cultivated elsewhere. Its root has long been regarded by the Chinese as a panacea for illness; taken as a drug or brewed as tea, its purported effects include improved mental performance, ability to learn, and memory and sensory awareness.

G. intestinalis See GIARDIA LAMBLIA

Giolitti \\jō-'lēt-tē\\, **Giovanni** (1842–1928) Italian politician and five-time prime minister. His distinctive political technique (*giolittisma*) emphasized personal deals rather than party loyalty, as well as electoral corruption. As prime minister (1892–93), he instituted reforms but became enveloped in a bank scandal. In his next two terms (1903–5, 1906–9), he displayed a calm attitude toward widespread strikes. In his fourth ministry (1911–14) he oversaw the ITALO–TURKISH WAR, then opposed Italy's entrance into World War I. In his final term (1920–21), he undertook Italy's reconstruction. He tolerated the early Fascists but in 1924 withdrew his support.

Giordano \\jōr-'dä-nō\\, **Luca** (1634–1705) Italian painter. He was inspired by the work of Paolo VERONESE and PIETRO DA CORTONA, whose influence is most evident in his huge ceiling fresco in the gallery of the Medici-Riccardi Palace (1682–85/86), Florence. In 1692 he went to Spain as court painter to CHARLES II; his frescoes in EL ESCORIAL are considered his best works of the period. In 1702 he returned to Naples, where he completed his last great work, the ceiling of the Treasury Chapel of the Certosa di San Martino (1704). Most of his enormous oil and fresco output depicted religious or mythological themes.

Giorgione \\jòr-'jō-nē\\ *orig.* Giorgio Barbarelli (c.1477–1510) Italian painter active in Venice. Nothing is known of his early life, but he probably studied with Giovanni BELLINI. His major public commission was the execution of frescoes on the exterior of the German Exchange (since destroyed). Of the few paintings attributed to Giorgione, two were completed by other artists after his death, one by TITIAN. Though the attribution, dating, and interpretation of his paintings are controversial, it is clear that he was a pioneer in the technique of oil painting on canvas and a master of creating mood and mystery, as epitomized in *The Tempest* (c.1505), a milestone in Renaissance landscape painting. See also VENETIAN SCHOOL.

Giotto (di Bondone) \\'jót-tō\\ (c.1267–1337) First of the great Italian painters. He decorated chapels and churches in Assisi, Rome, Padua, Florence, and Naples with frescoes and panel paintings. His works in Rome include the heavily restored mosaic of *Christ Walking on the Water* over the entrance to St. Peter's Basilica. In Padua, the Arena Chapel contains frescoes of the Last Judgment and scenes from the lives of the Virgin Mary and Christ. He later executed frescoes in four chapels in the church of Santa Croce in Florence, two of which survive. Appointed surveyor of Florence Cathedral in 1334, he designed its campanile. His most important extant panel painting is *The Madonna in Glory* (c.1305–10). He achieved great fame in his lifetime. For breaking with the impersonal stylizations of Byzantine art and introducing new ideals of naturalism and humanity, three-dimensional space and three-dimensional form, he is considered the father of European painting. His students and followers, included Taddeo GADDI, Andrea ORCAGNA, and Pietro and Ambrogio LORENZETTI.

Giotto, from the fresco "Lamentation," c.1305–6

Giovanni da Bologna See GIAMBOLOGNA

Giovanni di Paolo (di Grazia) \\jō-'vän-nē-dē-'paù-lō\\ (c.1399–1482) Italian painter active in Siena. He produced his most characteristic works from the 1440s, notably the monumental altarpiece *The Presentation of Christ in the Temple* (1447–49), 12 scenes from the life of St. John the Baptist, and a Madonna (1463) altarpiece in Pienza Cathedral. His tormented spirituality and expressionistic style were little appreciated until the 20th cent.

Gippsland \\'gips-,land\\ Region, SE Victoria, Australia, west of MELBOURNE. It has an area of 13,600 sq mi (35,200 sq km). Fertile and well watered, Gippsland is the focus of the state's dairy industry; petroleum and natural gas are tapped in Bass Strait. The SE area has coastal resorts and the Lakes National Park. The first settlers were attracted by gold finds in the 1850s; farmers arrived after the completion of a rail line in 1887.

giraffe RUMINANT (*Giraffa cameleopardalis*, family Giraffidae), the tallest of all mammals, reaching 18 ft (5.5 m) or more. It has extremely long legs and neck, a short body, a tufted tail, and two to four short, skin-covered horns. The back slopes downward to the hindquarters. The coat is pale buff, with reddish brown spots. It feeds primarily on ACACIA leaves. It lives in herds in open country and is native to most of sub-Saharan Africa. Giraffes are still numerous in E Africa, where they are protected. The only other member of the family is the OKAPI.

Giraldus Cambrensis \\jə-'ról-dəs-kam-'bren-səs\\ *or* **Gerald of Wales** (1146?–1223?) Historian and archdeacon of Brecknock, Wales (1175–1204). Educated in Paris, he returned to Wales and struggled unsuccessfully to become bishop of St. David's, hoping to make the see independent of Canterbury. He advised HENRY II and Henry's son JOHN on Welsh and Irish issues. His accounts of life in the late 12th cent. have proved valuable to historians.

Girard \\zhē-'ràr, *Engl* jə-'rärd\\, **Stephen** (1750–1831) French-U.S. financier and philanthropist. A sailor at 14, by 1774 he was involved in American coastal trade with the W. Indies. After settling in Philadelphia during the American Revolution, he developed an efficient, worldwide trading fleet and amassed a fortune. In 1812 he bought out the First BANK OF THE U.S., renaming it the Bank of Stephen Girard. During the War of 1812 he purchased government bonds, which by 1814 constituted 95% of the U.S.'s war loan. He bequeathed his fortune to social-welfare institutions.

Girardon \\zhē-ràr-'dōⁿ\\, **François** (1628–1715) French sculptor. In 1666 he received his most famous commission, the *Apollo Tended by the Nymphs,* for the Grotto of Thetis at VERSAILLES. Of his other works at Versailles, the most notable are *The Bath of the Nymphs* (1668–70) and *The Rape of Persephone* (1677–79). Works in Paris include the tomb of Cardinal RICHELIEU in the church of the Sorbonne (1675–94). Though influenced by the work of G.-L. BERNINI, his own style was more restrained.

Giraudoux \\zhē-rō-'dü\\, **(Hyppolyte-) Jean** (1882–1944) French novelist, essayist, and playwright. He made the diplomatic service his career, while becoming known as an avant-garde writer with early poetic novels such as *Suzanne et le Pacifique* (1921). He created an impressionistic form of drama by emphasizing dialogue and style rather than realism. His most famous works are *Tiger at the Gates* (1935), about the Trojan War, and *The Madwoman of Chaillot* (1946).

girder In building construction, a large main supporting BEAM, commonly of steel or REINFORCED CONCRETE, that carries a heavy transverse (crosswise) load. In a floor system, beams and joists transfer their loads to the girders, which in turn frame into the columns.

Girondin \\jə-'rän-din\\ *or* **Girondist** Moderate republican member in the Legislative Assembly during the FRENCH REVOLUTION. Many members were originally from the department of Gironde; as followers of J.-P. BRISSOT, they were initially called Brissotins. In 1792 the NATIONAL CONVENTION was divided between them and the more radical MONTAGNARDS; in 1793 they were driven out and many were guillotined in the REIGN OF TERROR.

Giscard d'Estaing \\zhis-kär-des-'taⁿ\\, **Valéry** (b.1926) French president of the Fifth Republic (1974–81), Elected to the National Assembly in 1956, he served as finance minister under Charles DE GAULLE (1962–66) and Georges POMPIDOU (1969–74). In 1974 he became president after defeating François MITTERRAND and helped strengthen the EUROPEAN ECONOMIC COMMUNITY. In 1981 he was defeated in another runoff election with Mitterrand.

Gish, Lillian (Diana) (1893–1993) U.S. actress. Born in Springfield, Ohio, she acted on the stage from age 5, often with her sister, Dorothy (1898–1968). Their screen careers began when D. W. GRIFFITH featured them in *An Unseen Enemy* (1912). Lillian won international fame in *The Birth of a Nation* (1915) and starred as the luminous heroine of such other Griffith films as *Broken Blossoms* (1919), *Way Down East* (1920), and *Orphans of the Storm* (1921). After the films *La Bohème* and *The Scarlet Letter* (both 1926), Lillian returned to the stage in such plays as *Uncle Vanya* (1930), *Hamlet* (with John GIELGUD, 1936), *Life with Father* (1940), and *The Trip to Bountiful* (1953). Returning to the screen, she was acclaimed in *The Night of the Hunter* (1955), *A Wedding* (1978), and *The Whales of August* (1987).

Gislebertus \\,gēz-lə-'ber-tùs\\ (fl.c.1120–1140) French sculptor. His most notable works are at the Romanesque cathedral at Autun: a tympanum sculpture depicting the Last Judgment, a masterpiece of expressionistic carving; a large-scale reclining nude Eve; and some 60 carved capitals and doorways illustrating biblical scenes. His highly imaginative work had a lasting effect on the development of French GOTHIC ART.

Gissing, George (Robert) (1857–1903) British novelist. After a brilliant academic career, he experienced the life of near poverty and constant drudgery that he described in *New Grub Street* (3 vols., 1891), his best-known work, and *The Private Papers of Henry Ryecroft* (1903). He wrote a cycle of 22 novels, which included *Born in Exile* (1892) and *The Odd Women* (1893). His realistic novels of lower-middle-class life are noted for their acute perception of women's social position and psychology.

Giulio Romano \\'jü-lē-ō-rō-'mä-nō\\ *orig.* Giulio Pippi (1499?–1546) Italian painter and architect. Apprenticed to RAPHAEL in Rome, on his master's death he became his principal heir and artistic executor, completing several of Raphael's important Vatican frescoes. From 1524 he lived at the Gonzaga court in Mantua, where he developed a personal, anticlassical style. His most important commission, the Palazzo del Te (begun 1526), was one of the first Mannerist buildings to deliberately flout the tenets of Classical architecture. His work presaged the illusionistic ceiling painting of the baroque period.

Giza \'gē-zə\ or **Al-Jizah** \ál-'jē-zə\ City (pop., 1996: 2,222,000), Upper Egypt. Located on the W bank of the Nile, it is a suburb of CAIRO. A noted entertainment district, it is also the center of Egypt's motion-picture industry. West of the city lie the Great Sphinx and the three great PYRAMIDS of the PHARAOHS.

glacial age See ICE AGE

glacier Large mass of perennial ice that forms on land and moves forward under its own weight. The term ice sheet describes a glacier that covers an extensive tract of relatively level land and flows from the center outward. Glaciers occur where snowfall in winter exceeds melting in summer, conditions that prevail only in high mountain areas and polar regions. Glaciers occupy about 11% of the earth's land surface but hold roughly 75% of its fresh water; 99% of glacier ice lies in Antarctica and Greenland.

Glacier Bay Narrow inlet of the Pacific Ocean, SE Alaska coast. About 60 mi (97 km) long, it contains 16 active glaciers. The bay has fjordlike inlets and many largely treeless islands, used as rookeries by thousands of seabirds. It is the focus of GLACIER BAY NATIONAL PARK.

Glacier Bay National Park National park, SE Alaska. Located on the Gulf of ALASKA, it covers 3,225,284 acres (1,305,226 hectares). It includes GLACIER BAY, part of Mt. FAIRWEATHER, and the U.S. portion of the Alsek River. Among its notable features are great tidewater glaciers, one of which, Muir Glacier, rises 265 ft (81 m) above the water and is nearly 2 mi (3 km) wide. The park's wildlife includes brown and black bears, mountain goats, whales, seals, and eagles.

Glacier National Park National preserve, British Columbia. Lying amidst the Selkirk Mtns., within the N bend of the COLUMBIA RIVER, it was established in 1886; it occupies 521 sq mi (1,349 sq km). Snowcapped peaks flanked by ice fields and glaciers form an alpine panorama; features include the Illecillewaet Glacier and the Nakimu Caves.

Glacier National Park National preserve, NW Montana. Set in the state's ROCKY MTNS. wilderness, it adjoins Canada's Waterton Lakes National Park. Established in 1910, it encompasses 1,013,572 acres (410,178 hectares). The park, with its active glaciers, straddles the CONTINENTAL DIVIDE.

glaciology \glā-shē-'ä-lə-jē\ Scientific discipline concerned with all aspects of ice on landmasses. It studies the structure and properties of GLACIER ice, its formation and distribution, the dynamics of ice flow, and the interactions of ice accumulations with climate. Glaciological research is conducted by radar sounding, boreholes, lateral tunnels, and remote sensing from satellites.

Glackens, William (James) (1870–1938) U.S. painter. Born in Philadelphia, he worked initially as a newspaper illustrator. In 1891 he met Robert HENRI, and he subsequently became a member of The EIGHT and the ASH CAN SCHOOL. He favored colorful street scenes of urban middle-class life (e.g., *Hammerstein's Roof Garden*, 1902), heavily influenced by Impressionism. His drawings (e.g., *Seated Woman*, 1902) reveal an elegant style not seen in his paintings. In 1913 he helped organize and exhibited in the ARMORY SHOW.

gladiator (Latin: "swordsman") Combatant in ancient Rome who engaged in fights to the death as a spectator sport. Gladiators originally performed at ETRUSCAN funerals, the intent being to give the dead man armed attendants in the next world. At Rome gladiator matches, sometimes involving hundreds of combatants, were wildly popular from 264 B.C. After a few victories a gladiator could be freed. Most were slaves or criminals, but a talented or handsome one could become a favorite of society; since they often served as bodyguards, they occasionally became politically important. With the coming of Christianity the games began to fall into disfavor, but they may have continued into the 6th cent.

gladiolus \gla-dē-'ō-ləs\ Any of about 300 species of flowering plants of the genus *Gladiolus,* in the IRIS FAMILY, native to Europe, Africa, and the Mediterranean and widely cultivated for cut flowers. The flowering spike, which springs from a corm, reaches 2–3 ft (60–90 cm) in height and has many funnel-shaped flowers on one side of the stem. Culti-

vated gladioli, which come in all colors, have been developed mostly from S and E African species.

Gladstone, William E(wart) (1809–1898) British prime minister (1868–74, 1880–85, 1886, 1892–94). He entered Parliament in 1833 as a Tory, and served as chancellor of the exchequer (1852–55, 1859–66) before converting to liberalism and becoming Liberal Party leader in 1866. In his first term as prime minister (1868–74), he oversaw national education reform and voting reform (see BALLOT ACT). In his second term, he secured passage of the voting Reform Bill of 1884. His failure to rescue C. G. GORDON in Khartoum (1885) caused his government's defeat. In 1886 he used Irish HOME RULE to regain control of Parliament, but when his Home Rule Bill was rejected

William E. Gladstone

he resigned. He devoted the next six years to trying to convince the electorate to grant Home Rule to Ireland. Liberals won a majority again in 1892, and in his fourth cabinet he piloted through another Home Rule Bill, but it was soundly rejected by the House of Lords.

Glåma River \'glô-mə\ River, E Norway. The longest river in SCANDINAVIA, it rises near the Swedish–Norwegian border. It flows generally south to enter Oslo Fjord at Fredrikstad, after a course of 380 mi (610 km). A major source of hydroelectric power, it is navigable up to Sarpsborg.

gland Collection of cells or tissue that removes specific substances from the blood, alters or concentrates them, and then either releases them for use by the body or eliminates them. Endocrine, or ductless, glands (e.g., PITUITARY, THYROID, ADRENAL) discharge HORMONES into the bloodstream directly rather than through ducts (see ENDOCRINE SYSTEM). Exocrine glands (e.g., digestive, MAMMARY, SALIVARY, SWEAT) discharge their products through ducts.

glandular fever See infectious MONONUCLEOSIS

Glasgow \'glas-gō\ City (pop., 1999 est.: 619,000), W Scotland. The largest city in Scotland, it is on the River CLYDE, 20 mi (32 km) from its mouth on the Atlantic coast. St. Kentigern (St. Mungo) established a religious community there about 550 A.D. Made a royal burgh in 1450, it prospered in the 18th cent., when tobacco, sugar, and rum from the Americas made fortunes for Glasgow merchants. Its economy wavered as the tobacco trade was cut off by the AMERICAN REVOLUTION, and the cotton industry by the AMERICAN CIVIL WAR. With the INDUSTRIAL REVOLUTION came coal mining, iron founding, and, especially, shipbuilding. A notable education center, Glasgow today has many cultural amenities.

Glasgow, Ellen (Anderson Gholson) (1873–1945) U.S. novelist. Born in Richmond, Va., she lived the life of a Southern belle. With *Virginia* (1913), she completed a five-novel series (begun 1900) depicting the state's social history. She was past 50 when she gained critical notice for *Barren Ground* (1925). *The Sheltered Life* (1932) is part of a trilogy of ironic novels of manners. Later works include the novel *In This Our Life* (1941, Pulitzer Prize). Her realistic depiction of Virginia life helped direct Southern literature away from sentimentality and nostalgia.

glasnost \'gläs-ˌnōst, 'glas-ˌnōst\ (Russian: "openness") Soviet policy of open discussion of political and social issues. Instituted by Mikhail GORBACHEV in the late 1980s, it began the democratization of the Soviet Union. It also permitted criticism of government officials and allowed the media freer dissemination of news and information. See also PERESTROIKA.

glass Solid material, typically a mix of inorganic compounds, usually transparent or translucent, hard, brittle, and impervious to the natural elements. It is made by cooling molten ingredients fast enough so no visible crystals form. A poor conductor of heat and electricity, glass takes on colors when certain metal OXIDES are included in the mix. Most glass breaks easily. Everyday glass ("soda-lime" or "soda-lime-silica") is made of silica (silicon dioxide), soda (sodium carbonate), and LIMESTONE (calcium carbonate), with magnesia (magnesium oxide) for sheet glass or alumina (aluminum oxide) for bottle glass. Fused silica is an excellent glass but expensive because of pure silica's very high melting point. Borosilicate glass (Pyrex) is used for cookware and laboratory glassware because it expands very little when heated. Even more specialized glasses include optical, photosensitive, metallic, and fiber-optic. Since glass has no sharp melting point, most types can be shaped while hot by many techniques, mostly blowing or molding. See also OBSIDIAN, VOLCANIC GLASS.

Glass, Philip (b.1937) U.S. composer. Born in Baltimore, he studied with Nadia BOULANGER in Paris, but his later studies in India produced a radical shift in his style. He became the leading exponent of musical "minimalism," employing insistently repeated notes and chords, subtly shifting timbres, and blocklike harmonic progressions. He achieved fame with the opera *Einstein on the Beach* (1976), and has since written about 20 more operas, including *Satyagraha* (1980) and *Akhnaten* (1984); some 50 film scores; and such other works as *Glassworks* (1981) and *Songs from Liquid Days* (1986). His appeal to fans of popular music has made him perhaps the world's most famous living composer.

glass, decorative See LUSTERED GLASS, STAINED GLASS, VENETIAN GLASS, WATERFORD GLASS

glass fiber See FIBERGLASS

glaucoma \glau̇-'kō-mə, glȯ-'kō-mə\ Disease caused by increased pressure in the EYE as a result of blockage of the flow of fluid (aqueous humor) at the outer edge of the iris. This pressure is transmitted to the optic nerve head and the RETINA. Chronic glaucoma can be treated with drugs. Permanent relief requires surgery to provide an outlet for the fluid. Untreated glaucoma causes vision impairment or blindness.

Glaucus \'glȯ-kəs\ Name of several figures in GREEK MYTHOLOGY. One Glaucus was the young son of King MINOS; he fell into a jar of honey and died, but was restored to life with a magic herb. Glaucus Pontius was a fisherman and diver who ate a magic plant and became divine. Glaucus, son of SISYPHUS and father of BELLEROPHON, fed his horses human flesh and was torn to pieces by them. Another Glaucus was a grandson of Bellerophon, who assisted King Priam in the TROJAN WAR.

Glazunov \'gla-zə-ˌnȯf\, **Alexander (Konstantinovich)** (1865–1936) Russian composer. A prodigy, he achieved success with his Symphony No. 1 at 16. He became director of the St. Petersburg Conservatory in 1905. Though honored by the government after the revolution, from 1928 he lived largely abroad. His works, generally conservative and Romantic, include the ballets *Raymonda* (1897) and *The Seasons* (1899), eight symphonies, four concertos, and many orchestral tone poems and suites.

Gleason, Jackie (*orig.* Herbert John) (1916–1987) U.S. comedian and actor. Born in Brooklyn, N.Y., he began performing in carnivals and nightclubs. He achieved success in the television comedy series *Cavalcade of Stars* (1950–52), *The Jackie Gleason Show* (1952–59, 1961–70), and *The Honeymooners* (1955–56). He starred on Broadway in *Take Me Along* (1959, Tony Award), and on screen in *The Hustler* (1961) and *Smokey and the Bandit* (1977) and its sequels (1980, 1983).

Glendale City (pop., 2000: 195,000), SW California. Located north of Los Angeles, it was part of Rancho San Rafael (1784), the first Spanish land grant in California. It was laid out in 1886. The city's Forest Lawn Memorial Park is known for its elaborate statuary.

Glendale City (pop., 2000: 218,000), S central Arizona. Located in the Salt River valley, west of PHOENIX, it was founded in 1892, and is a regional trading center for fruits, vegetables, and cotton, as well as antiques. It is one of the fastest growing cities in the U.S.

Glendower \glen-'dau̇-ər\, **Owen** *Welsh* Owain Glyndwr (1354?–1416?) Self-proclaimed prince of Wales. Educated in England, he returned to Wales and touched off an uprising against HENRY IV (under whom he had previously fought) in N Wales in 1400. Soon in control of most of Wales, he set up a Welsh parliament. In 1403 his alliance with English nobles was crushed at Shrewsbury; his strongholds at Aberystwyth and Harlech fell to the future HENRY V in 1408–9. Active as a guerrilla warrior as late as 1412, he led the last major Welsh attempts to throw off English rule.

Glenn, John H(erschel), Jr. (b.1921) U.S. astronaut and senator. Born in Cambridge, Ohio, he was an outstanding Marine Corps pilot in World War II and the Korean War. The oldest of the seven astronauts selected in 1959 for the Mercury project, he was a backup pilot for Alan B. SHEPARD and Virgil I. Grissom (1926–1967). Glenn made the first orbital flight in 1962 with three orbits in his space capsule, *Friendship 7*. He left the space program in 1964 and ran for U.S. Senator from Ohio, serving 1975–99. In 1998, at 77, he made his second spaceflight (on the space shuttle *Discovery*).

glider Nonpowered heavier-than-air craft capable of sustained flight. Early experimenters included George CAYLEY, who built the first man-carrying glider in 1853, and Otto Lilienthal (1848–1896), who introduced tail stabilizers on his first practical man-carrying craft in 1891. Improvements by Octave Chanute (1832–1910) in 1896 enabled Wilbur and Orville WRIGHT to perfect the control needed for developing their powered airplane in 1903. The slender-winged glider was launched by being towed behind an airplane or a car. Used in World War II to carry troops, today gliders are mainly used for recreation. See also HANG GLIDING.

gliding See SOARING

Glinka, Mikhail (Ivanovich) (1804–1857) Russian composer. In 1836 his first opera, *A Life for the Czar,* immediately earned him the reputation of Russia's leading composer. Elements of Russian folk music were heard even more clearly in *Ruslan and Ludmila* (1842) and the orchestral work *Kamarinskaya* (1848). The influence of these works on later Russian composers was huge, and Glinka is regarded as the father of the Russian national school.

globalization Process of worldwide economic integration. Factors that have contributed to globalization include increasingly sophisticated communications and transportation technologies and services, mass migration and the movement of peoples, transnational industrial combinations and commercial groupings, and international agreements that reduce the cost of doing business abroad. Globalization offers huge potential profits to companies and nations, but has been complicated by widely differing expectations, standards of living, cultures and values, and legal systems as well as unexpected global cause-and-effect linkages. See also FREE TRADE.

Global Positioning System (GPS) Precise, satellite-based navigation and location system developed for U.S. military use but available to the general public. GPS is a fleet of 24 communications satellites that transmit signals globally around the clock. With a GPS receiver one can quickly and accurately determine the latitude, longitude, and in most cases the altitude of a point on or above the earth's surface. A single GPS receiver can find its own position in seconds to an accuracy of 10 meters; greater accuracy can be achieved with military-specification receivers. This capability has reduced the cost of acquiring spatial data for making maps while increasing accuracy. Other applications include measuring the movement of polar ice sheets, or finding the best auto route between given points.

global warming Potential increase in average global atmospheric temperatures resulting from enhancement of the GREENHOUSE EFFECT by AIR POLLUTION. Many scientists predict that temperatures will increase by as much as 9°F (5°C) by the mid-21st cent. Such global warming would cause the polar ice caps and mountain glaciers to melt rapidly, raising the levels of coastal waters, and would produce new patterns and extremes of drought and rainfall, seriously disrupting food production in certain regions. The 1992 Earth Summit and a follow-up 1997 U.N. conference attempted to address the issue, but they were hindered by conflicting national economic agendas and disputes between rich and poor nations over the cost and consequences of reducing emissions of greenhouse gases.

Globe and Mail, The Daily newspaper published in Toronto, the most prestigious and influential journal in Canada. It was formed in 1936 when George McCullagh bought and merged two competing papers, the liberal *Globe* (founded 1844) and the conservative *Mail and Empire* (founded 1872 as *The Mail*). Canada's newspaper of record, it is especially strong in international news coverage.

Globe Theatre London theater in which the plays of William SHAKESPEARE were performed after 1599. It was built by the actor Richard Burbage (1567?–1619) and his brother Cuthbert. The wooden theater, built in the shape of an O with no roof over the central area, was destroyed by fire in 1613, rebuilt in 1614, and finally pulled down in 1644. Reconstructed near its original site, it reopened in 1996.

globular cluster Any large group of Population II (see POPULATIONS I AND II) stars closely packed in a symmetrical, near-spherical form. About 100 have been identified in the MILKY WAY GALAXY. Globular clusters, with 10,000–1 million stars, can be several hundred light-years across. Most are too far from the solar system to see with the unaided eye, but Omega Centauri and a few others appear as hazy patches of light. See also OPEN CLUSTERS.

globulin \\'gläb-yə-lən\\ Any of a major class of PROTEINS insoluble in pure water and soluble in dilute salt SOLUTIONS. Globulins are found in many plants, especially cereals. Globulins in animal fluids include ENZYMES, ANTIBODIES (the GAMMA GLOBULINS), LIPOPROTEINS, complement components, transport proteins, and various types of fibrous and contractile proteins.

glockenspiel \\'glä-kən-ˌspēl, 'glä-kən-ˌshpēl\\ Percussion instrument consisting of a set of tuned steel bars, arranged like a piano keyboard, which are struck with hammers. Another form of the instrument employs an actual keyboard. The bell lyre, held vertically, is the portable form of glockenspiel used in marching bands.

Glorious Revolution *or* **Bloodless Revolution** *or* **Revolution of 1688** In English history, the events of 1688–89 that resulted in the deposition of JAMES II and the accession of his daughter MARY II and her husband WILLIAM III. James's Roman Catholicism and the prospect of a Catholic heir to the throne brought discontent to a head, and seven eminent Englishmen invited the Protestant William of Orange to bring an army to redress the nation's grievances. James's supporters turned against him and he fled to France. The Convention Parliament asked William and Mary to rule jointly and set out the BILL OF RIGHTS.

Gloucester \\'gläs-tər\\ *ancient* Glevum. City (pop., 1995 est.: 107,000), SW England. The seat of GLOUCESTERSHIRE, it lies on the River SEVERN, and is linked by ship canal to docks in the Severn estuary. It was founded as the Roman colony of Glevum in A.D. 96–98. An abbey was founded there in 681; the town later became the capital of the Anglo-Saxon kingdom of MERCIA. Incorporated in 1483, it continued to flourish as a trading center.

Gloucestershire \\'gläs-tər-ˌshir\\ County (pop., 1998 est.: 557,000), W England. It is located at the head of the SEVERN RIVER estuary on the Welsh border; GLOUCESTER is the county seat. Prehistoric peoples were active in the area; later, the Romans had military camps within the county. The Saxons subsequently occupied the area. Throughout the Middle Ages Gloucestershire was a battlefield, reflected in the imposing Norman defensive castles built on the Welsh frontier. The charming Cotswold Hills area is an important sheep-farming region; most of its E half is scenic, with a large area given to Dean National Forest Park.

glowworm Any crawling, luminous insect that emits light either continuously or in prolonged glows rather than in the brief flashes characteristic of most FIREFLIES. Glowworms include larvae and adult (often wingless) females of fireflies and certain other BEETLE species and larvae of certain GNAT species. The many differences in the bioluminescent organs suggest that the light-producing ability of the various species evolved independently.

gloxinia \\gläk-'si-nē-ə\\ Any of the 20 plant species that make up the genus *Sinningia*, in the gesneriad family, native to Brazil, especially *S. speciosa*, an ornamental pot plant. Gloxinias produce large, erect bell-shaped flowers in rich, velvety colors, usually violet or purple.

Gluck \\'glůk\\, **Christoph Willibald** *later* Ritter (Knight) von Gluck (1714–1787) German opera composer. Son of a

forester, he ran away to study music in Prague. He traveled widely, writing operas for various cities, before settling in Vienna in 1750, where he would remain—except for an interlude in Paris (1773–79)—the rest of his life. In 1762 he wrote his famous opera *Orfeo ed Euridice,* in which he achieved a simplified dramatic style that decisively broke with the static and calcified Italian style. His preface to *Alceste* (1767) laid out the musico-dramatic principles of his "reform opera." In Paris he won acclaim for *Iphigénie en Aulide* (1774), *Armide* (1777), and *Iphigénie en Tauride* (1779). In all he wrote more than 40 operas. He also wrote five ballets, of which *Don Juan* (1761) was one of the first successful *ballets d'action.*

glucose *or* **dextrose** *or* **grape sugar** *or* **corn sugar** Organic compound, a simple SUGAR (MONOSACCHARIDE). The product of PHOTOSYNTHESIS in plants, it is found in fruits and honey. The major circulating free sugar in blood, it is the source of energy in cell function and a major participant in METABOLISM. Control of its level and metabolism is of great importance (see INSULIN). Glucose is used in foods, medicine, brewing, and wine making and as the source of various other organic chemicals. See also CELLULOSE, GLYCOGEN, POLYSACCHARIDE, STARCH, SUCROSE.

glucose tolerance test Test of ability to metabolize GLUCOSE. It helps diagnose DIABETES MELLITUS, HYPOGLYCEMIA, and other impairments of glucose metabolism. The subject drinks a solution high in glucose, and blood and urine samples are taken after a half hour, one, two, and three hours. Normally, blood glucose peaks within an hour and returns to normal within two and a half hours.

glue Adhesive substance resembling GELATIN, extracted from animal tissue, particularly hides and bones, or from fish, casein (milk PROTEIN), or vegetables. Glue was used as early as 3000 B.C. in wooden-furniture construction in Egypt. Synthetic RESIN adhesives such as the EPOXIES are replacing glue for many uses, but glue is still widely used in woodworking and in industrial processes.

glutamic acid \\glü-'ta-mik\\ One of the nonessential AMINO ACIDS, closely related to glutamine. The two constitute a substantial fraction of the amino acids in many PROTEINS (10–20% in many and up to 45% in some plant proteins). An important metabolic intermediate as well as a neurotransmitter, glutamic acid is used in medicine and biochemical research. Its sodium salt is monosodium glutamate (MSG).

gluten Mixture of PROTEINS not readily soluble in water that occurs in wheat and most other CEREAL grains. Its presence in flour makes production of leavened baked goods (see BAKING) possible because the chainlike gluten molecules form an elastic network that traps CARBON DIOXIDE gas and expands with it. Doughs can range from soft and extensible to tough and elastic, depending on gluten composition. Persons with an ALLERGY to gluten can often eat RICE or spelt products.

glycerol \\'gli-sə-ˌrȯl\\ *or* **glycerin** Clear, colorless, viscous, sweet-tasting liquid organic compound of the ALCOHOL family. With three hydroxyl (–OH) groups, it can form three types of ESTERS (monoglycerides, diglycerides, and TRIGLYCERIDES). Mono- and diglycerides are common food additives. FATS and OILS are triglycerides. Glycerol has thousands of uses, including as an emulsifier, softening agent, plasticizer, and stabilizer in baked goods, ice cream, and tobacco; in skin lotions, mouthwashes, and cough medicines; as a protective medium for freezing red blood cells, sperm, corneas, and other tissues; in printing inks, paints, coatings, and ANTIFREEZE mixtures; as a nutrient in FERMENTATION, and as a raw material for NITROGLYCERIN.

glyceryl trinitrate See NITROGLYCERIN

glycogen \\'glī-kə-jən\\ Principal storage CARBOHYDRATE of animals, occurring primarily in the liver and resting muscles. It is also found in various bacteria, fungi, and yeasts. Glycogen is a branched POLYSACCHARIDE, a long chain of GLUCOSE units, into which it is broken down when energy is needed.

glycol \\'glī-ˌkȯl\\ Any of a class of organic compounds of the ALCOHOL family in which two hydroxyl groups (–OH; see FUNCTIONAL GROUP) are attached to different carbon atoms. The term is often used for the simplest of the class, ETHYLENE GLYCOL. Propylene glycol, much like ethylene

glycolysis

glycol but not toxic, is used extensively in foods, cosmetics, and oral hygiene products as a solvent, preservative, and moisture-retaining agent. Other important glycols are used as raw materials for plastics and other chemicals, and as an insect repellent.

glycolysis \glī-'kä-lə-səs\ *or* **glycolytic pathway** *or* **Embden-Meyerhof-Parnas pathway** \'em-dən-'mī-ər-ˌhôf-'pär-nəs\ Sequence of 10 CHEMICAL REACTIONS taking place in most cells that breaks down GLUCOSE, releasing energy that is then captured and stored in ATP. One molecule of glucose (plus coenzymes and inorganic PHOSPHATE) makes two molecules of pyruvate (or pyruvic acid) and two molecules of ATP. The pyruvate enters into the TRICARBOXYLIC ACID CYCLE if enough OXYGEN is present or is fermented into LACTIC ACID or ETHANOL if not. Thus, glycolysis produces both ATP for cellular energy requirements and building blocks for synthesis of other cellular products.

GM See GENERAL MOTORS CORP.

gnat Any member of several species of small DIPTERANS, most of which bite or annoy humans. MIDGES are also sometimes called gnats. In N. America the name is also applied to the BLACKFLY, FRUIT FLY, and other small flies.

Gneisenau \'gnī-zə-ˌnau\, **August (Wilhelm Anton), Graf (Count) Neidhardt von** (1760–1831) Prussian field marshal. He helped remold the mercenary Prussian army shattered by NAPOLEON (1806) into an instrument of modern warfare, introducing universal military service. In 1811–12 he traveled on secret missions to negotiate a new war against Napoleon. As chief of staff to Gebhard von BLÜCHER he planned Prussian, and sometimes Russian, strategy. Gneisenau's insistence on the decisive battle and relentless pursuit proved successful at the Battle of WATERLOO.

gneiss \'nīs\ Medium- to coarse-grained METAMORPHIC ROCK with district parallel, somewhat irregular banding that has little tendency to split along planes. The principal rock over extensive metamorphic terrains, gneiss contains quartz and feldspar.

Gnosticism \'näs-tə-ˌsi-zəm\ Religious and philosophical movement popular in the Roman world in the 2nd–3rd cent. A.D. The term, coined in the 17th cent. from the Greek *gnosis* ("knowledge"), was applied liberally to ancient Christian heretical sects, especially those described by their orthodox contemporaries as radically dualistic and world-denying, and who sought salvation through esoteric revelation and mystical spirituality. Research has replaced that view of Gnosticism with several groupings. One group, represented by the well-known *Gospel of Thomas*, emphasized the teachings of JESUS, rather than his death and resurrection, as the key to salvation. Other texts previously considered Gnostic are now assigned to such traditions as Hermeticism (see HERMETIC WRITINGS), Mandaeanism (which still survives in Iraq and SW Iran), and MANICHAEISM. The texts of the Sethians are perhaps the most "Gnostic"; they describe one supreme, good God and the creation, by a junior heavenly being (Sophia), of an arrogant creature who then claims to be God. That creature withholds from humanity moral knowledge and eternal life, but Sophia plants the divine spirit within people to save them. Male and female saviors (including Jesus) were sent to instruct humanity about the true God and humanity's own divine nature.

gnu \'nü\ *or* **wildebeest** Either of two species of African ANTELOPE (genus *Connochaetes*). The gnu stands higher at the shoulder than at the rump, reaching a shoulder height of 3–4 ft (1–1.3 m). The S African form, the white-tailed gnu, or black wildebeest, has a black mane and flowing white tail. Today it exists only in national parks and preserves. The brindled gnu, or blue wildebeest, is reasonably abundant over much of central and SE Africa. It is silvery gray with dark vertical bands on the sides and has a black mane, tail, and face. Both sexes of both species have horns. Gnu live in often large, constantly moving herds and graze on the grasses and scrub of open plains.

Go Japanese game played between two players who alternately place black and white stones on a board checkered by 19 vertical and 19 horizontal lines. The players attempt to conquer territory by surrounding vacant areas or capture stones by surrounding them. Go originated in either India or China as early as 2356 B.C. and was brought to Japan around A.D. 500.

Goa \'gō-ə\ State (pop., 1994 est.: 1,235,000), India. Located on the W coast, it has a 62-mi (100-km) coastline on the Arabian Sea and includes the offshore island of Goa. The capital is PANAJI. Ruled by Hindu dynasties until 1472, it came under the Portuguese in 1510, and Old Goa became the capital of Portuguese India. After attaining independence in 1947, India demanded that Portugal cede Goa. Indian troops finally occupied Goa in 1961; it was incorporated into India in 1962 and became a state in 1987. It is predominantly agricultural; its distinctive architecture and fine beaches make it a popular tourist resort.

goat Any hollow-horned RUMINANT in the BOVID genus *Capra*. Goats have a lighter build and straighter hair than SHEEP; their horns arch backward, and the tail is short. Males usually have a beard. Wild goats include the IBEX and markhor. Domesticated goats are descended from the pasang. In China, Great Britain, Europe, and N. America, the domestic goat produces MILK that is used for cheese. Some breeds, notably the Angora and cashmere, are raised for their WOOL; young goats are the source of kid leather.

goatsucker See NIGHTJAR.

Gobelin family \gȯ-'blaⁿ\ French dyers and clothmakers. In the late 15th cent., the brothers Jean (d.1476) and Philibert Gobelin discovered a scarlet dye and opened a dyeing factory near Paris, which flourished until the late 16th cent. In 1601 HENRY IV brought in Flemish weavers to produce tapestries. In 1662 LOUIS XIV reorganized the factory and appointed Charles LE BRUN director; it produced tapestry and upholstery furnishings for the royal palaces until 1694. By the 18th cent. only tapestries were manufactured. Since 1826 it has manufactured carpets and tapestries.

Gobi Desert \'gō-bē\ Desert, central Asia. One of the great desert and semidesert regions of the world, the Gobi stretches across large areas of Mongolia and China. It occupies an arc of land 1,000 mi (1,609 km) long and 300–600 mi (500–1,000 km) wide, with an estimated area of 500,000 sq mi (1,300,000 sq km). Much of the Gobi is not sand but bare rock.

Gobind Singh \gō-'bin-də-'siŋ-gə, 'gō-ˌbind-'siŋ\ *orig.* Gobind Rai (1666–1708) Sikh GURU. He was 9 when his father, Guru Tegh Bahadur (1621?–1675), was executed, and he became the 10th and last GURU of SIKHISM. He is credited with putting the ADI GRANTH into its final form and with founding (1699) the Khalsa, the egalitarian community that gave Sikhism its political and religious definition. He was continually at war with local Hindu chiefs and the Mughal authorities, who together forced the Sikhs from their base at Anandpur in 1704. After the death of AURANGZEB, he supported the claim of the future emperor, Bahadur Shah (1643–1712), to the throne. He was assassinated before he could persuade Bahadur to allow the Sikhs' return to Anandpur.

goby Any of more than 800 species of carnivorous fishes (suborder Gobioidei, order Perciformes) especially abundant in the tropics. Most species are small bottom-dwellers. About 700 species are typically elongated, sometimes scaleless, fishes found along shores and among reefs in tropical and temperate seas. They have two dorsal fins and a rounded tail, and are often brightly colored. Most adults are no longer than 4 in. (10 cm).

God Deity or Supreme Being. Each of the major monotheistic world religions worships a Supreme Being, the sole god of the universe, the maker of all things, omniscient and all-powerful. God is also good. In ancient Israel God was named Yahweh. The God of the Hebrew Bible also became the God of Christianity. In Islam the term is ALLAH. See also MONOTHEISM.

Go-Daigo \'gō-dī-'gō\ (1288–1339) Emperor of Japan (1318–39). When Go-Daigo came to the throne in 1318, political authority was divided between the emperor and the KAMAKURA SHOGUNATE, though neither had real power, their positions being controlled by powerful families (see HOJO FAMILY). Go-Daigo sought to hold the reins of government himself; but he alienated Ashikaga Takauji (see ASHIKAGA FAMILY), whose support had been crucial to his victory, by neglecting to appoint him SHOGUN. When Takauji rebelled and elevated another member of the imperial family to the throne. Go-Daigo fled south with his court; the period of Northern and Southern Courts *(nanboku cho)* that followed lasted until 1392.

god and goddess Generic terms for the many deities of ancient and modern polytheistic religions. There may be deities of earthly and celestial phenomena as well as deities related to human values, pastimes, and institutions, including love, marriage, hunting, war, and the arts. They are often immortal and always more powerful than humans, though they are often described in human terms, with all the flaws and emotions of humans. See also POLYTHEISM.

Godard \gȯ-'där\, **Jean-Luc** (b.1930) French film director. He wrote film criticism for the influential journal *Cahiers du cinéma* before making his first feature film, the improvisatory and original *Breathless* (1960), which established him as an apostle of the NEW WAVE. He continued to explore new techniques in such films as *My Life to Live* (1962), *Pierrot le fou* (1965), *Alphaville* (1965), and *Weekend* (1968). He returned to themes of more universal concern with *Every Man for Himself* (1979) and *Passion* (1982), but shocked audiences and the Vatican with *Hail Mary!* (1985).

Godavari River \gō-'dä-və-rē\ River, central India. It rises in the Western GHATS, flows east across the DECCAN Plateau, along the Maharashtra–Andhra Pradesh border, and crosses Andhra Pradesh to flow into the Bay of BENGAL. Its total length is about 910 mi (1,465 km). An irrigation-canal system has made its delta area one of the richest rice-growing areas of India. The Godavari is sacred to the Hindus.

Goddard, Robert H(utchings) (1882–1945) U.S. inventor, regarded as the father of modern rocketry. Born in Worcester, Mass., he taught at Clark Univ. for most of his career. His experiments with ROCKETS began in 1908, when he proved that thrust and consequent propulsion can take place in a vacuum. He was the first to develop a rocket motor using liquid fuels (tested in 1926) and the first to explore mathematically ratios of energy and thrust per weight of liquid oxygen and liquid hydrogen. In 1935 he first shot a liquid-fueled rocket faster than the speed of sound. He patented the first practical automatic steering apparatus for rockets, developed step rockets designed to gain great altitudes, and developed the first rocket-fuel pumps and self-cooling rocket motors. Much of his work anticipated that of Wernher von BRAUN, but was ignored by the U.S. government until after his death.

Goddard family New England cabinetmakers. Of English ancestry, the Goddards intermarried with the Townsend family, equally famous cabinetmakers. John Goddard (1723–1785) moved in the 1740s from Massachusetts to Newport, R.I., where by the 1760s he had become Newport's leading cabinetmaker, producing simple adaptations in the Queen Anne style. He originated the blockfront, a distinctive front for desks, secretaries, and cabinets, decorated with his characteristic carved shell ornaments. Some 20 Goddard and Townsend craftsmen of four generations are known.

Gödel \'gœ̄-dəl, *Engl* 'gə(r)-dəl\, **Kurt** (1906–1978) Austrian-U.S. mathematician and logician. He produced his groundbreaking proof (see GÖDEL'S THEOREM) in the early 1930s. He emigrated to the U.S. in 1940 and taught at the Institute for Advanced Study at Princeton. There, his close friendship with Albert EINSTEIN led him into the field of general relativity theory, and to solutions of some of Einstein's equations.

Gödel's theorem Principle of the foundations of mathematics. It states the impossibility of defining a complete system of AXIOMS that is also consistent (does not give rise to contradictions). Any formal system (e.g., a computer program or a set of mathematical rules and axioms) powerful enough to generate meaningful statements can generate statements that are true but that cannot be proven or derived within the system. As a consequence, mathematics cannot be placed on an entirely rigorous basis. Stated by Kurt GÖDEL in 1931, it immediately had major consequences for philosophy (particularly logic) and other areas. Its ramifications continue to be debated.

Godey's Lady's Book \'gō-dēz\ Monthly magazine for women (1830–98), one of the most successful and influential periodicals in 19th-cent. America. Founded in 1830 in Philadelphia by Louis Antoine Godey (1804–1878), it became an important arbiter of fashion and etiquette. It also published works by such writers as R. W. EMERSON, H. W. LONGFELLOW, and Nathaniel HAWTHORNE. It was edited first by Godey and then by S. J. HALE.

Godfrey, Arthur (Morton) (1903–1983) U.S. radio and television entertainer. Born in New York City, his relaxed manner and affable banter as a radio host won him such a wide following that he had two daily shows and a weekly show on CBS in the 1940s. His variety show, transferred to television (1948–60), launched the careers of numerous popular entertainers.

Godfrey of Saint-Victor (1125?–1194) French monk, philosopher, theologian, and poet. After 20 years in a monastery, he moved to a rural priory, where he wrote his principal work, *Microcosmus*, an attempt to systematize history and knowledge into a rational structure. It asserts that mankind is a microcosm containing the material and spiritual elements of reality. In his other notable work, *Fons philosophiae* (c.1176; "The Fount of Philosophy"), he proposed a classification of learning. His writings are considered prime examples of 12th-cent. humanism.

Godiva \gə-'dī-və\, **Lady** (fl.c.1040–1080) Anglo-Saxon gentlewoman famous for her legendary ride while nude through Coventry, England. She was the wife of Leofric, earl of Mercia (d.1057), with whom she founded a monastery at Coventry. There is no evidence connecting the rider with the historical Godiva. According to the legend, Leofric, exasperated over Godiva's ceaseless imploring that he reduce Coventry's heavy taxes, declared he would do so if she rode naked through the marketplace. She did so, her long hair covering most of her body. A later chronicle asserts that Godiva required the townsmen to remain indoors at the time fixed for her ride; Peeping Tom, a citizen who looked out his window, was struck blind or dead.

Godthab See NUUK

Godunov \'gō-də-n-ˌȯf\, **Boris (Fyodorovich)** (1551?–1605) Czar of Russia (1598–1605). After serving in the court of IVAN IV, he was named guardian to Ivan's dim-witted son Fyodor I (1557-1598) and became the virtual ruler of Russia from 1584. When Fyodor's little brother Dmitry died mysteriously in 1791, Godunov was suspected of murder. When Fyodor died, an assembly of clergy and gentry elected Godunov czar. A capable ruler, he instituted many reforms, but continuing BOYAR opposition and a famine (1601–3) eroded his popularity. The False DMITRY led an army into Russia, and on Boris's sudden death the country lapsed into the Time of TROUBLES.

Godwin, William (1756–1836) British writer. A former Presbyterian minister, his *Enquiry Concerning Political Justice* (1793), condemning the institution of marriage, among other things, captivated S. T. COLERIDGE, William WORDSWORTH, and P. B. SHELLEY (who was to become his son-in-law). *The Adventures of Caleb Williams* (1794) was his masterpiece. He married Mary WOLLSTONECRAFT in 1797.

Goebbels \'gœ-bəls, *Engl* 'gə(r)-bəlz\, **(Paul) Joseph** (1897–1945) German Nazi leader. After earning a doctorate from Heidelberg Univ., he joined the NAZI PARTY and was appointed district leader in Berlin by Adolf HITLER in 1926. A gifted speaker, Goebbels also edited the party's journal and began to create the Führer myth around Hitler, instituting the party demonstrations that helped convert the masses to Nazism. He controlled the national propaganda machinery during World War II, raising hopes on the home front. He was named chancellor in Hitler's will. One day after Hitler's death, Goebbels and his wife killed themselves and their six children.

Goering, Hermann See Hermann GÖRING

Goes \'güs\, **Hugo van der** (c.1440–1482) Flemish painter. In 1467 he became a master in the painters' guild in Ghent, and he received numerous commissions from the town (processional banners, heraldic shields, etc.) through 1475. That year, at the height of his career, he entered a monastery near Brussels as a lay brother, though he continued to paint and travel. A mental breakdown in 1481 led to a suicide attempt, and he died the following year. His masterpiece and only documented work is the Portinari Altarpiece (c.1473–78); an outstanding early example of N realism, it shows an emotional intensity unprecedented in Flemish art.

Goethals \ˈgō-thəlz\, **George Washington** (1858–1928) U.S. Army officer and engineer. Born in Brooklyn, N.Y., he graduated from West Point, then served in the Army Corps of Engineers. Appointed by Pres. Theodore ROOSEVELT to build the PANAMA CANAL, he solved complex engineering problems while supervising 30,000 workers from many nations; the esprit de corps he engendered became legendary. He was appointed the Canal Zone's first governor (1914–17). In World War I, he directed procurement for and the movement of U.S. troops at home and abroad.

Goethe \ˈgœ̄-tə, *Engl* ˈgə(r)-tə\, **Johann Wolfgang von** (1749–1832) German poet, novelist, playwright, and natural philosopher. In 1773 he provided the STURM UND DRANG movement with its first major drama, *Götz von Berlichingen*, and in 1774 with its first novel, *The Sorrows of Young Werther*, in which he created the prototype of the Romantic hero. In 1775 he joined the ducal court at Weimar, where he would remain the rest of his life; his presence would establish Weimar as a literary and intellectual center. His poetry includes lyrics in praise of natural beauty and ballads that echo folk themes. Many early works were inspired by a series of passionate loves.

Johann Wolfgang von Goethe Painting by J. K. Stieler, 1828

Classical Greek and Romantic culture influenced his plays, including *Iphigenie auf Tauris* (1787) and *Torquato Tasso* (1790), and the poems in *Roman Elegies* (1795). From 1794, his friendship with Friedrich SCHILLER became the most important of his life. *Wilhelm Meister's Apprenticeship* (1795–96) is often called the first BILDUNGSROMAN. His masterpiece, the drama *Faust* (Part I, 1808; Part II, 1832), concerns the struggle of the soul for knowledge, power, happiness, and salvation. The greatest figure of German Romanticism, he is regarded as a giant of world literature.

Gogh, Vincent van See Vincent VAN GOGH

Gogol \ˈgō-ˌgól\, **Nikolay (Vasilyevich)** (1809–1852) Russian writer. Born in Ukraine, he achieved literary success with *Evenings on a Farm near Dikanka* (1831–32). His pessimism is revealed in such stories as "Taras Bulba" (1835) and "Diary of a Madman" (1835). His farcical drama *The Government Inspector* (1836) lampooned a corrupt government bureaucracy. He laid the foundations of 19th-cent. Russian realism with his masterpiece, the novel *Dead Souls* (1842), a satire about serfdom and bureaucratic inequities, and his story "The Overcoat" (1842). His collected stories (1842) received great acclaim. Having come under the influence of a fanatical priest, he burned the manuscript of the second volume of *Dead Souls*; he died a few days later at 42, on the verge of madness.

goiter Enlargement of the THYROID GLAND, causing a prominent swelling at the throat. The thyroid can grow to 50 times normal weight, interfere with breathing and swallowing, and cause a choking feeling. Simple (endemic) goiter is due to low IODINE intake and resulting inadequate thyroid hormone synthesis. Advanced cases are treated with thyroid hormone or surgical removal. The cause of sporadic goiter, in which iodine intake is adequate, remains a mystery. An enlarged thyroid may have normally functioning tissue or may produce too much hormone (hyperthyroidism). See also GRAVES' DISEASE, IODINE DEFICIENCY.

Golan Heights \ˈgō-ˌlän\ *Arabic* **Al-Jawlan** \äl-ˌjaù-ˈlän\ Hilly area (pop., 1988 est.: 24,000), SW Syria. It overlooks the upper JORDAN RIVER valley; its maximum elevation is 7,297 ft (2,224 m). It was held by Syria from 1941 to 1967, when it came under Israeli occupation after the SIX-DAY WAR. After the ARAB–ISRAELI WAR of 1973, a U.N. buffer zone was established in the heights. In 1981 Israel unilaterally annexed the part that it held. In 2000 Syria and Israel began talks to resolve the situation.

Golconda \gäl-ˈkän-də\ Fortress and ruined city, Andhra Pradesh state, S India. Located west of modern HYDERABAD, it was the capital (1512–1687) of one of the five Muslim sultanates of the DECCAN. It was conquered in 1687 by AURANGZEB and annexed to the MUGHAL empire. Historically, Golconda was famous for its diamonds, mined in the nearby hills.

gold Chemical ELEMENT, one of the TRANSITION ELEMENTS, chemical symbol Au, atomic number 79. It is a dense, lustrous, yellow, malleable precious METAL, so durable that it is virtually indestructible, often found uncombined in nature. Jewelry and other decorative objects have been crafted from gold for thousands of years. It has been used for coins, to back paper currencies, and as a reserve asset. Gold is widely distributed in all IGNEOUS ROCKS, usually pure but in low concentrations; its recovery from ores and deposits has been a major preoccupation since ancient times. Pure gold is too soft for prolonged handling; it is usually used in ALLOYS with SILVER, COPPER, and other metals. Gold is used in electrical contacts and circuits, as a reflective layer in space applications and on building windows, and in filling and replacing teeth. Dental alloys are about 75% gold, 10% silver. In jewelry, its purity is expressed in 24ths, or karats: 24-karat is pure, 12-karat is 50% gold, etc. Its compounds (VALENCE 1 or 3) are used mainly in plating and other decorative processes; a soluble chloride compound has been used to treat RHEUMATOID ARTHRITIS.

Goldberg, Rube (*orig.* Reuben Lucius) (1883–1970) U.S. cartoonist. Trained in engineering, he worked as a sportswriter and cartoonist for San Francisco newspapers (1904–7), then joined the *New York Evening Mail* (1907–21), where he created three long-running comic strips and the cartoon character Professor Lucifer Gorgonzola Butts, an inventor of contraptions that did simple tasks in hilariously roundabout ways. From 1938 to 1964, he did editorial cartooning for the *New York Sun*, among other publications, winning a 1948 Pulitzer Prize.

Gold Coast Section of the coast of the Gulf of GUINEA, W Africa. Extending approximately from Axim, Ghana, to the VOLTA RIVER, it was so called because it was an important source of gold. It was an area of intense colonial rivalry from the 17th cent. Acquired by the British in the 19th cent. and named the Gold Coast colony, the area achieved independence as part of Ghana in 1960.

Gold Coast See GHANA

golden eagle Dark-brown EAGLE (*Aquila chrysaetos*) with golden nape feathers, fully feathered legs, large yellow feet, and large talons. Its wingspread reaches almost 8 ft (2.3 m). It ranges from central Mexico (where it is the national bird) along the Pacific coast and through the Rocky Mtns. to Alaska (with small numbers from Newfoundland to N. Carolina) and across Russia to S China and Japan. The species is protected in the U.S.

Golden eagle (*Aquila chrysaetos*)

Golden Gate Bridge Suspension bridge spanning the Golden Gate, San Francisco. From its completion in 1937 until 1964, it had the world's longest main span, 4,200 ft (1,280 m). It remains incomparable in its magnificence. Its construction, supervised by Joseph B. Strauss (1870–1938), involved many difficulties: rapidly running tides, frequent storms and fogs, and the problem of blasting rock under deep water to plant earthquake-resistant foundations.

Golden Horde Russian designation for the W part of the MONGOL empire around 1235–1425. The name is traditionally said to derive from the golden tent of BATU, a grandson of GENGHIS KHAN, who expanded the domain of the Golden Horde in a series of brilliant campaigns. At its peak, its territory included most of European Russia. The outbreak of the BLACK DEATH in 1347 marked the beginning of its disintegration; in the 15th cent. it broke into several smaller khanates.

golden ratio *or* **golden rectangle** *or* **golden section** Numerical proportion considered to be an aesthetic ideal in classical design. It refers to the ratio of the base to the height of a rectangle or to the division of a line segment into two in such a way that the ratio of the shorter part to the longer is equal to that of the longer to the whole (about 1.61803:1). The ratio appears widely in nature (e.g., in crystals, sunflower florets, and mollusk shells) as well as in works of art.

goldenrod Any of the approximately 100 species of weedy, usually perennial herbaceous plants that make up the genus *Solidago,* in the COMPOSITE FAMILY. Most are native to N. America; a few grow in Europe and Asia. They have toothed leaves and clustered yellow flower heads composed of both disk and ray flowers. They are found almost everywhere in E N. America and are a prominent feature of autumn from the Great Plains east to the Atlantic. Unlike ragweed, which blooms at the same time, they are not a cause of HAY FEVER.

goldenseal PERENNIAL medicinal herb *(Hydrastis canadensis)* of the BUTTERCUP family, native to woods of the E U.S. The plant has a single greenish-white flower, the sepals of which fall as they open, followed by a cluster of small red berries. Goldenseal is grown commercially for the yellow rootstocks, which yield hydrastine, an ALKALOID. Used medicinally by American Indians, it is now a popular herbal supplement taken for minor pain and infections.

Golden Temple *Punjabi* Darbar Sahib *or* Harimandir. Chief house of worship for the Sikhs of India (see SIKHISM) and their most important pilgrimage site, located in the city of Amritsar in Punjab state. Founded by Guru Ramdas (1574–1581) and completed by Guru ARJAN in 1604, the temple welcomes all creeds and castes. Though destroyed in the 1760s by Afghan invaders, it was rebuilt and in the early 19th cent. acquired its marble walls and gold-plated copper domes. In a 1984 confrontation with Sikh separatists, government troops attacked and seriously damaged the complex, but it has since been restored.

goldfinch Any of several species (genus *Carduelis,* family Carduelidae) of songbirds with a short notched tail, much yellow in the plumage, and a bill more pointed than that of most FINCHES. They live in flocks, feeding on weeds. Various species live in W Eurasia, N. and S. America, and New Zealand and Australia. They are typically 4–5.5 in. (10–14 cm) long. The male of the American goldfinch (or wild canary), found across N. America, is bright yellow, with black cap, wings, and tail.

goldfish Ornamental aquarium and pond fish *(Carassius auratus)* of the CARP family, native to E. Asia. It was domesticated by the Chinese at least as early as the Song dynasty (960–1279). Selective breeding has produced more than 125 breeds, including the common, pet-shop comet and the veiltail, with a three-lobed, flowing tail. Usually gold or orange, they feed on plants and small animals, and, in captivity, on small crustaceans and other foods. They have become naturalized in many parts of the E U.S.

Golding, William (Gerald) *(later* **Sir William)** (1911–1993) British novelist. His first and best-known novel was *Lord of the Flies* (1954), about a group of boys isolated on an island who revert to savagery. Later works, several of which are likewise parables that show the thinness of the veneer of civilization, include *Pincher Martin* (1956), *Free Fall* (1959), *Darkness Visible* (1979), and *Rites of Passage* (1980, Booker Prize). He won the Nobel Prize in 1983.

Goldman, Emma (1869–1940) U.S. (Lithuanian-born) anarchist. She emigrated in 1885 to the U.S., where she met the Russian anarchist Alexander Berkman (1870–1936). For an assassination attempt on H. C. FRICK, Berkman was imprisoned 1892–1906, during which they corresponded regularly. Goldman lectured on anarchism and was jailed in 1893 for inciting a riot in New York. She founded and

edited (1906–17) the anarchist magazine *Mother Earth.* In 1917 she and Berkman were convicted of obstructing the military draft. On her release in 1919, she was deported to Russia. She moved to England in 1921, and later to Canada and Spain, continuing to lecture throughout Europe.

Goldmark, Peter Carl (1906–1977) Hungarian-U.S. engineer. He emigrated to the U.S. in 1933. From 1936 to 1972 he worked at Columbia Broadcasting System Laboratories. In 1940 he demonstrated the first commercial color-television system; based on a rotating three-color disk, his system found wide application in closed-circuit television for industry, medical institutions, and schools. In 1948 he introduced the long-playing (LP) phonograph record, which revolutionized the recording industry. In 1950 he developed the scanning system that would allow U.S. spacecraft to relay photographs from the moon to earth.

Goldoni, Carlo (1707–1793) Italian playwright. He practiced law but preferred to write plays, beginning with *Belisario* (1734). He renovated the COMMEDIA DELL'ARTE form by introducing realistic characters, tightly constructed plots, and spontaneity in such plays as *Pamela* (1750), based on Samuel RICHARDSON's novel. His comedy of manners *La locandiera* (1753) is still performed (as *Mine Hostess*). When rivals ridiculed his innovations, he took his realistic comedy to Paris, where he directed the Comédie-Italienne and wrote many plays in French. He later rewrote them for Italian audiences, and *Il vantaglio* (1763, *The Fan*) became one of his greatest successes.

gold reserve Fund of gold bullion or coin held by a government or bank. In the past, COMMERCIAL BANKS received deposits subject to repayment in gold on demand and issued notes redeemable in gold on demand. Most gold reserves eventually shifted to CENTRAL BANKS, which took over the function of issuing paper money. In the 1930s, many governments required their central banks to turn over their gold holdings to the national treasuries. In the U.S., the Gold Reserve Act of 1934 required Federal Reserve banks to turn over all gold bullion or coin to the U.S. Treasury, which placed most of the reserves at FORT KNOX.

gold rush Rapid influx of fortune seekers to the site of newly discovered gold deposits. The first major gold strike occurred in California in 1848, when a carpenter building a sawmill for John SUTTER found gold. Within a year about 80,000 "forty-niners" had flocked to the California gold fields, and 250,000 had arrived by 1853. Some mining camps grew into permanent settlements, which propelled the new state's economy. Smaller gold rushes occurred in Colorado (1859, 1892), Nevada (1859), Idaho (1861), Montana (1863), S. Dakota (1876), Arizona (1877), and Alaska (1898) and resulted in settlement of many areas; where gold veins proved small, the settlements became ghost towns. Major gold rushes also occurred in Australia (1851), S. Africa (1886), and Canada (1896; see KLONDIKE GOLD RUSH).

Goldsmith, Oliver (1730–1774) Irish-British essayist, poet, novelist, and dramatist. After studying medicine, he settled in London and began writing essays, some of which were collected in *The Citizen of the World* (1762). In 1764 he became an original member of Samuel JOHNSON's famous Club. He won a reputation as a poet with *The Traveller* (1764), confirmed by his famous pastoral elegy *The Deserted Village* (1770). *The Vicar of Wakefield* (1766) revealed his skill as a novelist. The charming farce *She Stoops to Conquer* (1773) was his most effective play. He is noted for his exceptionally graceful, lively style.

Oliver Goldsmith Painting from the studio of Joshua Reynolds, 1770

gold standard Monetary system in which the standard unit of CURRENCY is a fixed quantity of GOLD or is freely convertible into gold at a fixed price. The gold standard was first adopted in Britain in 1821 then in Germany, France, and the U.S. in the 1870s. It ended with the outbreak of World War I in 1914; when it was reestablished in 1928, most nations adopted a gold-exchange standard, supplementing their gold reserves with currencies convertible into gold at a stable rate of exchange. Though the gold-exchange standard collapsed again during the Great Depression, the U.S. set a minimum dollar price for gold, which allowed for the restoration of an international gold standard after World War II. In 1971 dwindling gold reserves and an unfavorable BALANCE OF PAYMENTS led the U.S. to suspend the free convertibility of dollars into gold, ending the gold standard. See also EXCHANGE RATE, SILVER STANDARD.

Goldwater, Barry M(orris) (1909–1998) U.S. senator. Born in Phoenix, Ariz., he headed the family department-store business from 1937, and served as an Air Force pilot (1941–45). In his initial years as senator (1953–64), he established himself as a strong conservative, calling for a harsh stance toward the Soviet Union, opposing arms-control negotiations, and charging the Democrats with quasi-socialism. His 1964 presidential bid against Pres. Lyndon JOHNSON was doomed by the charge that his extremist views might prompt war with the Soviets, and Johnson won a landslide victory. He returned to the Senate (1969–87); his views moderated, and he became a symbol of high-minded conservatism.

Goldwyn, Samuel *orig.* Schmuel Gelbfisz *later* Samuel Goldfish (1879–1974) U.S. film producer. He emigrated from Poland to New York (1896), where he became a top glove salesman. In 1913 he formed a film company with his brother-in-law, Jesse L. Lasky (1880–1958), and C. B. DE MILLE. In 1917 he and Edgar Selwyn established Goldwyn Pictures Corp. When that company merged into MGM (1924), he gained total control and emerged as a great showman, employing top screenwriters, directors, and actors to produce films of high quality, including *Wuthering Heights* (1939), *The Little Foxes* (1941), *The Best Years of Our Lives* (1946), and *Porgy and Bess* (1959).

golem \'gō-ləm\ In Jewish folklore, an image that comes to life. In medieval tales, wise men brought clay effigies to life by means of magic. Golems began as perfect servants, whose only fault lay in fulfilling their master's commands too literally or mechanically. Later golems were imagined as protectors of the Jews in times of persecution, but also had a frightening aspect.

golf Game in which a player using special clubs attempts to sink a small, dimpled ball with as few strokes as possible into each of the nine or 18 successive holes on an outdoor course. A hole includes (1) a teeing area, from which the ball is initially driven toward the actual hole, or cup; (2) a fairway, a long, closely mowed, and often angled lane; (3) a putting green, a smooth grassy area containing the hole; and (4) often one or more natural or artificial hazards. Each hole has associated with it a par, or score standard, usually from par 3 to par 5. Golf developed in Scotland from the 15th cent.; the courses were originally fields that sheep had clipped short in their characteristic grazing style. Golf balls, originally made of wood, are now made of hard rubber. Clubs are known by the traditional names of "irons" (primarily for mid-range to short shots) and "woods" (primarily for longer shots); today most irons are made of stainless steel, and the heads of woods are usually steel or titanium. The principal men's tournaments include the U.S. Open, the MASTERS, the British Open, and the PGA championship. See also RYDER CUP.

Golf Joyce Wethered, champion British golfer of the 1930s

Golgotha See CALVARY

goliard \'gōl-yərd, 'gō-lə-ˌärd\ Any of the wandering students and clerics in medieval England, France, and Germany remembered for their satirical verses and poems in praise of debauchery and against the church and pope. They described themselves as followers of the legendary Bishop Golias. From 1227 on, the church gradually revoked their clerical privileges. *Carmina Burana* is a collection of 13th-cent. Latin goliard poems and songs; some were set in a famous cantata by Carl ORFF (1937). In the 14th cent. the term came to mean JONGLEUR, or minstrel.

Golitsyn, Vasily (Vasilyevich), Prince (1643–1714) Russian statesman. After commanding in the Ukraine, he served in the court of Fyodor III (r.1676-82) and reorganized the Russian army. When SOPHIA became regent in 1682, she appointed her lover Golitsyn head of the foreign office and chief adviser. He negotiated an alliance with Poland (1686), but failed in his two campaigns against the Ottoman Turks (1687, 1689). He also concluded a treaty with China that gained recognition for Russia as an equal state. In 1689 he was exiled after a coup placed PETER I on the throne.

Goltzius \'gȯlt-sē-ʉes\, **Hendrik** (1558–1617) Dutch printmaker. He set up his own copperplate engraving business in Haarlem and became the leading master of Dutch Mannerist engraving. His early works included reproductions of prints by Albrecht DÜRER and LUCAS VAN LEYDEN. Among his best-known original prints are an engraving of the *Farnese Hercules* (c.1592), the chiaroscuro woodcut *Hercules Killing Cacus* (1588), and the series *Roman Heroes* (1586). His miniature portrait drawings are outstanding, and his landscape drawings anticipate the great 17th-cent. landscapes.

Gómez \'gō-mäs\, **Juan Vicente** (1857?–1935) Dictator of Venezuela (1908–35). He rose to power by joining a private army that captured Caracas and the government. In 1908 he seized control from his former commander; thereafter he ruled either as president or through puppet governments until his death. Under Gómez, Venezuela achieved a measure of independence and economic progress, but he controlled the nation through force and terror while vastly enriching himself.

Gomorrah See SODOM AND GOMORRAH

Gompers, Samuel (1850–1924) U.S. (British-born) labor leader. In 1863 he emigrated to New York, where he became a cigar maker and a union organizer. Opposed to radicalism, Gompers argued that unions should avoid political involvement and focus on economic goals, bringing about change through strikes and boycotts. He stressed the primacy of the national organization over local and international affiliations, as well as the need for written contracts. In 1886 he led the national organization of cigar makers out of the KNIGHTS OF LABOR to form the American Federation of Labor (AFL), which he served as president 1886–1924 (except 1895). See also AFL-CIO.

Gomulka \'gō-'mùl-kə\, **Wladyslaw** (1905–1982) Leader of the Polish Communist Party (1956–70). In 1926 he joined the underground Communist Party and became a union organizer; after World War II he rose through the party ranks quickly. Though ruthless in eliminating opposition to communist rule, he publicly opposed some Soviet policies and was accused of "nationalist deviation" by Joseph STALIN in 1948 and arrested in 1951. He was rehabilitated in 1956 and elected party first secretary. At first universally supported, in 1970 he was ousted along with other top leaders following workers' riots over food prices.

Gonçalves Dias \gȯⁿ-'säl-vish-'dē-ȧsh\, **Antônio** (1823–1864) Brazilian poet. His songs, collected in *First Poems* (1847), *More Poems* (1848), and *Last Poems* (1851), continually celebrated the New World, with exuberance and longing, as a tropical paradise. His "Song of Exile" (1843) is known to every Brazilian schoolchild, and he is regarded as the national poet of Brazil.

Goncourt \gȯⁿ-'kür\, **Edmond (-Louis-Antoine Huot de) and Jules (-Alfred Huot de)** (1822–1896, 1830–1870) French writers. They produced a series of social histories (from 1854) as well as a body of art criticism. The most lasting of their meticulously detailed naturalistic novels is *Germinie Lacerteux* (1864). Their published journals (kept 1851–96) represent a monumental history of social and literary life in 19th-cent. Paris. By his will Edmond established the Académie Goncourt, which annually awards the Prix Goncourt, France's preeminent literary prize.

Gondwana *or* **Gondwanaland** Hypothetical former supercontinent in the Southern Hemisphere that included modern S. America, Africa, India, Australia, and Antarctica. Alfred WEGENER in 1912 envisioned a single great landmass, PANGAEA, which supposedly began to separate late in the TRIASSIC PERIOD. See also CONTINENTAL DRIFT, LAURASIA.

Góngora (y Argote) \'gȯn-gō-rä\, **Luis de** (1561–1627) Spanish poet. Very influential in his era, he developed the difficult, complex poetic style that became known as *gongorismo;* it provoked scorn from many of his contemporaries and was so exaggerated by less gifted imitators that his reputation suffered until the 20th cent. *Soledades* (1613; "Solitudes") is perhaps his most outstanding work in the style. His lighter poetry achieved greater popular success.

gonorrhea \ˌgä-nə-'rē-ə\ SEXUALLY TRANSMITTED DISEASE with genitourinary INFLAMMATION, caused by the bacterium *Neisseria gonorrhoeae* (gonococcus). Symptoms in men include burning on urination, discharge of pus, and, with deeper infection, frequent urination, sometimes with blood. Women may have no symptoms, or mild vaginal discharge and burning. It may cause sterility in both sexes but is rarely fatal. Gonorrhea is common worldwide. PENICILLIN, generally a successful treatment, reduced its incidence, but resistant strains are increasingly found. Penicillin may mask coexisting SYPHILIS (since the dose to cure gonorrhea does not cure syphilis).

Gonzaga dynasty \gȯn-'dzä-gä\ Italian dynasty that ruled Mantua 1328–1707. Its history began with Luigi I (or Lodovico; 1267–1360), who gained control of Mantua in 1328. Its rulers, many noted as military and political leaders and patrons of the arts, included Giovan Francesco II (d.1444), founder of the first school based on humanistic principles (1423); and Federigo II (d.1540), captain general of the papal forces, who was made duke of Mantua in 1530. Mantua was annexed by Austria in 1708.

Goodall, Jane (b.1934) British ethologist. At Louis LEAKEY's suggestion she began studying CHIMPANZEES, earning a PhD from Cambridge Univ. She remained at the research center she founded in Gombe, Tanzania, until 1975. Her observations established, among other things, that chimpanzees are omnivorous rather than vegetarian, can make and use tools, and have highly developed social behaviors. Her widely read writings include *In the Shadow of Man* (1971) and *The Chimpanzees of Gombe* (1986).

Good Feelings, Era of (1815–25) Period of U.S. national unity and complacency. A Boston newspaper coined the term in 1817 to describe a nation free from the influence of European political and military events. The good feelings were stimulated by two events of 1816, during James MADISON's presidency: enactment of the first U.S. protective tariff, and establishment of the second national bank. The presidency of James MONROE (1817–25) was marked by the dominance of the Democratic-Republican Party and the decline of the FEDERALIST PARTY.

Good Friday Friday before EASTER, commemorating the CRUCIFIXION of JESUS. As early as the 2nd cent. it was kept by Christians as a day of penance and fasting. The Eastern Orthodox and Roman Catholic churches have special liturgies for the day, and Protestant churches also hold special services on Good Friday.

Good Hope, Cape of Rocky promontory, SW coast, S. Africa. It was sighted by Bartolomeu DIAS in 1488. Known for stormy weather and rough seas, the cape lies at the convergence of warm currents from the Indian Ocean and cool currents from Antarctic waters. It was the site of the first Dutch settlement (1652) at Table Bay (later Cape Town harbor).

Goodman, Benny (*orig.* Benjamin David) (1909–1986) U.S. jazz clarinetist and leader of the most popular band of the SWING era. Born in Chicago, Goodman formed a big band in 1934. Its sensational broadcast from Los Angeles's Palomar Ballroom in 1935 is seen as the beginning of the swing era. Goodman's band featured trumpeter Harry JAMES and drummer Gene Krupa. Goodman's small group was among

the first racially integrated ensembles known to a wide public. His virtuosity and immense popularity earned him the sobriquet "King of Swing."

Good Neighbor Policy Popular name for the policy toward Latin America pursued by Pres. Franklin ROOSEVELT in the 1930s. In a departure from its traditional practice, the U.S. repudiated its assumed right to intervene unilaterally in Latin American affairs and withdrew its Marines from Haiti. U.S. anticommunist policies after World War II led to renewed distrust between N. and Latin America and an end to non-interventionism.

Goodyear, Charles (1800–1860) U.S. inventor of VULCANIZATION. Born in New Haven, Conn., he became interested in treating RUBBER so that it would lose its adhesive quality and not melt; he discovered vulcanization in 1839 when he accidentally dropped a rubber-sulfur mixture onto a hot stove. He patented the process in 1844, but had to fight numerous patent infringements in the U.S. and Europe. He never profited from his discovery and died in debt. The Goodyear Tire and Rubber Co. (founded 1898) honors his name.

gooney See ALBATROSS

goose Any large, heavy-bodied WATERFOWL (family Anatidae) of the genera *Anser* (so-called gray geese) and *Branta* (so-called black geese), all found in the Northern Hemisphere. Geese are less fully aquatic than DUCKS and SWANS, and their legs are farther forward, allowing them to walk readily. Males (called ganders) are usually larger than females. Both sexes utter loud honking or gabbling cries while on the wing or when danger appears. Geese pair for life. Flocks traveling in V-formation migrate between their breeding grounds and wintering grounds far south. See also CANADA GOOSE, GREYLAG.

gooseberry Hardy fruit bush of the Northern Hemisphere, often placed in the genus *Ribes* with the CURRANT in the family Saxifragaceae. The spiny bushes bear clusters of greenish to greenish-pink flowers. The tart, oval berries may be prickly, hairy, or smooth. They are eaten ripe and often made into jellies, preserves, pies and other desserts, or wine.

GOP See REPUBLICAN PARTY

gopher *or* **pocket gopher** Any of about 40 species (family Geomyidae) of stocky RODENTS found in N. and Central America. Gophers range in length from 5 to 18 in. (13–45 cm), including a short tail. They have chisel-like front teeth, strong claws on their forefeet, and fur-lined pouches on each side of the mouth. Gophers live alone in extensive, shallow underground burrows marked by a series of mounds on the surface. They feed on the underground parts of plants, which they collect in their pouches as they tunnel along.

Gorbachev \ˌgȯr-bə-'chȯf, 'gȯr-bə-ˌchef\, **Mikhail (Sergeyevich)** (b.1931) Last president of the Soviet Union (1990–91). After earning a law degree, he rose through the ranks to become general secretary of the COMMUNIST PARTY OF THE SOVIET UNION (1985–91). His extraordinary reform policies of GLASNOST and PERESTROIKA were resisted by party bureaucrats; to reduce their power, Gorbachev changed the Soviet constitution in 1988 to allow multicandidate elections and removed the monopoly power of the party in 1990. In 1989–90 he supported the new democratically elected governments of Eastern Europe. In 1990 he was awarded the Nobel Peace Prize. Russia's economic and political problems led to a 1991 coup attempt by hard-liners. In alliance with Russia's president Boris YELTSIN, Gorbachev quit the Communist Party, disbanded its Central Committee, and shifted political powers to the Soviet Union's constituent republics. Events out-

Mikhail Gorbachev, 1985

FG

paced him, and the various republics formed the COM-MONWEALTH OF INDEPENDENT STATES under Yeltsin's leadership. On Dec. 25, 1991, Gorbachev resigned the presidency of the Soviet Union, which ceased to exist that same day.

Gordimer, Nadine (b.1923) S. African writer. The daughter of Jewish immigrants, her later works include *The Conservationist* (1974, Booker Prize), *Burger's Daughter* (1979), A *Sport of Nature* (1987), *None to Accompany Me* (1994), and *The House Gun* (1998). Her works, written in a clear, controlled, unsentimental style, often concern exile and alienation. She was a strong opponent of her country's apartheid policy, and concerns about black-white relations are frequently expressed in her fiction. She received the Nobel Prize in 1991.

Gordium Ancient city, capital of PHRYGIA, in what is now NW Turkey. Excavations revealed early BRONZE AGE and HITTITE settlements, but the city achieved its greatest prominence as the flourishing capital of Phrygia in the 9th–8th cent. B.C. According to legend, it was founded by the peasant Gordius, who contrived the knot later cut by ALEXANDER THE GREAT. Gordium remained the political center of Phrygia until the Cimmerians overran it in the early 7th cent. B.C.

Gordon, Charles George (1833–1885) British general who became a national hero for his exploits in China and his ill-fated defense of KHARTOUM. He distinguished himself in the CRIMEAN WAR (1853–56), and volunteered for the second OPIUM WAR (1856–60). In 1862 he helped defend Shanghai during the TAIPING REBELLION. In 1873 the Egyptian ruler Isma'il Pasha appointed Gordon governor of Equatoria in S Sudan (1874–76) and governor-general of the Sudan (1874–80), where he crushed rebellions and suppressed the slave trade. He was sent to the Sudan again in 1884 to evacuate Anglo-Egyptian forces from Khartoum, which was threatened by MAHDIST MOVEMENT insurgents. The city was soon besieged and remained isolated for several months until it finally succumbed (Jan. 26, 1885). Gordon was killed in the action.

Gordon, George, Lord (1751–1793) English agitator. Son of the duke of Gordon, he entered Parliament in 1774. In 1779 he organized the extremist Protestant Association to secure repeal of the Catholic Relief Act (1778). In 1780 he led a mob to Parliament to present a petition against the act. The ensuing weeklong riot caused great property damage and nearly 500 casualties. Gordon was charged with, but not convicted of, high treason. Convicted of libeling the queen of France in 1787, he was imprisoned in Newgate, where he died.

Gordy, Berry, Jr. See MOTOWN

Gore, Al *in full* Albert Arnold Gore, Jr. (b.1948) U.S. politician. Born in Washington, D.C., son of the future senator Albert Gore, he graduated from Harvard Univ. and served in the Vietnam War as a military reporter (1969–71). He later worked as a reporter in Nashville (1971–76) while attending divinity school and then law school at Vanderbilt Univ. He served in the U.S. House of Representatives (1977–85) and Senate (1985–93). A moderate Democrat, he was elected vice president in 1992 on William CLINTON's ticket; they were reelected in 1996. As the Democratic presidential nominee in 2000, he surpassed George W. BUSH in the popular vote but lost the electoral vote when the U.S. Supreme Court ended a recount in the decisive state of Florida.

Goren, Charles H(enry) (1901–1991) U.S. contract BRIDGE authority. Born in Philadelphia, he learned bridge while a law student at McGill Univ. His innovative system of point-count bidding and repeated successes in tournaments made him one of the world's most famous and influential players. His several popular books include *Goren's Bridge Complete* (1963).

Gorey, Edward (St. John) (1925–2000) U.S. writer, illustrator, and designer. Born in Chicago, he published his first children's book, *The Doubtful Guest,* in 1957. In this and such later books as *The Hapless Child* (1961) and *The Gashlycrumb Tinies* (1962), his arch nonsense verse and mock-Victorian prose accompany pen-and-ink drawings of beady-eyed, blank-faced individuals in Edwardian costume whose

dignified demeanor is undercut by silly, often macabre events.

Gorgas \'gȯr-gəs\, **William (Crawford)** (1854–1920) U.S. Army surgeon. Born in Mobile, Ala., he took charge of sanitation measures in Havana with the army's medical corps in 1898; conducting experiments on mosquito transmission of YELLOW FEVER, he effectively eliminated it from the area. Sent to Panama in 1904, he eradicated yellow fever from the Canal Zone and brought MALARIA under control, removing the chief obstacles to building the PANAMA CANAL.

Gorgon One of three monsters in GREEK MYTHOLOGY, the most famous of which was MEDUSA. Classical art depicts them as winged females with snakes for hair.

gorilla Largest of the great APES. A stocky, powerful forest dweller native to equatorial Africa, the gorilla (*Gorilla gorilla*) has black skin and hair, large nostrils, and prominent brow ridges. Adults have long, powerful arms; short, stocky legs; an extremely thick, strong chest; and a protruding abdomen. Males, about twice as heavy as females, may reach a height of about 5.5 ft (1.7 m) and a weight of 300–600 lbs (135–275 kg). Gorillas are mainly terrestrial, walking about on all four limbs. They live in stable family groups of six to 20, led by one or two silverbacked males. They eat leaves, stalks, and shoots. They are unaggressive and even shy unless provoked. Calmer and more persistent than chimpanzees, gorillas are highly intelligent and capable of problem solving. Hunted for its meat, and with its habitat disappearing, the gorilla is an endangered species.

Göring \'gœ-riŋ\, **Hermann** *or* **Hermann Goering** (1893–1946) German Nazi leader. In 1922 he joined the NAZI PARTY and was given command of the SA. After the BEER HALL PUTSCH, he escaped to Austria, then returned in 1927. Chosen president of the Reichstag (1932), his power mounted after Adolf HITLER was named chancellor. As Hitler's most loyal supporter, Göring held numerous posts and established the GESTAPO. He also became head of the German air force (Luftwaffe). After it failed to win the Battle of BRITAIN, he lost face and semiretired to his country estate, where he displayed the vast art collection he had confiscated from Jews in occupied countries. Condemned to death at the NUREMBERG TRIALS, he committed suicide by taking a poison capsule.

Gorki See NIZHNIY NOVGOROD

Gorky, Arshile *orig.* Vosdanik Adoian (1904–1948) Armenian-U.S. painter. In 1920 he emigrated to the U.S., and he studied and then taught at New York's Grand Central School of Art (1926–31). He sought to assimilate the aesthetic visions of Paul CÉZANNE, Joan MIRÓ, and Pablo PICASSO until he encountered the Surrealists, when he developed his own style of abstraction with biomorphic forms suggesting plants or human viscera floating over a background of melting colors. After suffering a studio fire that destroyed many of his paintings, a crippling car accident, cancer, and abandonment by his wife, he hanged himself. He is the most important direct link between SURREALISM and ABSTRACT EXPRESSIONISM.

Gorky, Maxim *orig.* Aleksey Maksimovich Peshkov (1868–1936) Russian writer. After a childhood of poverty, he became a wandering tramp. His early works offered sympathetic portrayals of the social dregs of Russia; they include the successful play *The Lower Depths* (1902). For his revolutionary activity, he spent the years 1906–13 in exile. His works include the autobiographical trilogy *My Childhood* (1913–14), *In the World* (1915–16), and *My Universities* (1923). Though initially an open critic of Vladimir LENIN, after 1919 he cooperated with Lenin's government. He soon became the undisputed leader of Soviet writers and helped establish SOCIALIST REALISM. He died suddenly while under medical treatment, possibly killed on Joseph Stalin's orders

Maxim Gorky

Gortyn \'gȯr-ˌtīn\ Ancient city, CRETE. It shared or disputed control of post-Minoan Crete with KNOSSOS until the Roman annexation in the 1st cent. B.C., when it became the administrative capital of the Roman province of Crete and Cyrenaica. The great civic law code of Gortyn, discovered in its ruins in the 19th cent., is the most extensive account of Greek law before the Hellenistic Age.

Gosden, Freeman F(isher) and Charles J. Correll (1899–1982, 1890–1972) U.S. comedians. Gosden (born in Richmond, Va.) and Correll (born in Peoria, Ill.) performed comedy routines in traveling variety shows before creating two black characters, Sam and Henry, for a Chicago radio show (1926–28). In 1929 they devised a larger cast of characters for a new nightly radio program, *Amos 'n' Andy,* thus creating the first situation comedy. As Amos the cab driver and his sidekick Andy, they anchored radio's most popular program in the 1930s, which ensured the success of radio broadcasting as a form of mass entertainment. Their show ended in 1954, criticized as offensive to blacks.

goshawk \'gäs-ˌhȯk\ Any of the more powerful accipiters (HAWKS in the genus *Accipiter*), primarily short-winged, forest-dwelling bird catchers. Best known is the northern goshawk, which reaches about 2 ft (60 cm) in length with a 4.3-ft (1.3-m) wingspread and has finely barred gray plumage. Long used for FALCONRY, it takes game as large as foxes and grouse. It lives in temperate to N forests throughout the Northern Hemisphere. Several other species are found in the Southern Hemisphere.

Gospel Any of the four NEW TESTAMENT books narrating the life and death of JESUS. The Gospels of MATTHEW, MARK, LUKE, and JOHN make up about half its total text. The first three are often called the Synoptic Gospels, because they give similar accounts of the ministry of Jesus.

gospel music Form of black American music derived from 19th-cent. Pentecostal church services and from spiritual and BLUES singing. Following the scriptural direction "Let everything that breathes praise the Lord," Pentecostal churches began welcoming timbrels, pianos, banjos, and even brass instruments into their services by the 1920s. Choirs often featured the extremes of female vocal range in antiphonal counterpoint with the preacher's sermon. Other forms of gospel music have included the singing and guitar playing of itinerant street preachers, and harmonizing male quartets, whose acts included dance routines and stylized costumes. Its principal figures included Thomas A. DORSEY, the blind wandering preacher Rev. Gary Davis (1896–1972); Sister Rosetta Tharpe (1915–1973), who took gospel into nightclubs and theaters in the 1930s; and Mahalia JACKSON. Gospel music was a significant influence on RHYTHM AND BLUES and SOUL MUSIC.

Gossart \'gȯs-ärt\, **Jan** or **Jan Gossaert** *known as* **Mabuse** \mä-'büe-zə\ (c.1478–1532) Flemish painter. After a stay in Italy in 1508–9, he turned from the ornate style of the Antwerp school to the High Renaissance style. *Neptune and Amphitrite* (1516) reflects his attempt to assimilate the art of classical antiquity and the Italian Renaissance. Despite his efforts, he retained the jewellike technique and careful observation of traditional Early Netherlandish art. He was among the first to introduce the Italian Renaissance style into the Low Countries.

Gosse \'gȯs\, **Edmund** (*later* **Sir Edmund**) (1849–1928) British literary historian and critic. He wrote the literary histories *18th Century Literature* (1889) and *Modern English Literature* (1897), as well as biographies of Thomas GRAY, John DONNE, Henrik IBSEN and others, and introduced many works by continental European writers to English readers. His autobiography, *Father and Son* (1907), has been much admired.

Göteborg \'yœ-tä-ˌbȯrʸ\ or **Gothenburg** \'gäth-ᵊn-ˌbərg\ City (pop., 1999: 459,000), SW Sweden. The country's chief seaport and second-largest city, it lies along the Göta River estuary above the KATTEGAT. Founded in 1603, it was destroyed in the Kalmar War with Denmark (1611–13), but was refounded in 1619. Many early inhabitants were Dutch, who built urban canals and laid out the city center. A prosperous period began with the completion of the Göta Canal (1832) and the start of a transoceanic shipping service.

Gothic, Carpenter See CARPENTER GOTHIC

Gothic architecture Architectural style in Europe from the mid-12th cent. to the 16th cent., particularly a style of masonry building characterized by cavernous spaces with the expanse of walls broken up by overlaid TRACERY. In the 12th–13th cent., feats of engineering permitted increasingly gigantic buildings. Solutions to the problem of building a very tall structure while maximizing natural light were the rib VAULT, FLYING BUTTRESS, and pointed (Gothic) arch. Stained glass rendered startling sun-dappled interior effects. One of the earliest buildings to combine these elements into a coherent style was the abbey of Saint-Denis, Paris (c.1135–44). The High Gothic years (c.1250–1300), heralded by CHARTRES CATHEDRAL, were dominated by France and the RAYONNANT STYLE. Britain, Germany, and Spain produced variations of this style, while Italian Gothic used brick and marble rather than stone. Late Gothic (15th-cent.) architecture included the British PERPENDICULAR STYLE and the French and Spanish Flamboyant style, but reached its heights in Germany's vaulted hall churches.

Gothic art Architecture, sculpture, and painting that flourished in Europe in the Middle Ages. It evolved from ROMANESQUE ART and lasted from the mid-12th to the 16th cent. Its loftiest form of expression is architecture (see GOTHIC ARCHITECTURE). Sculpture was closely tied to architecture and often used to decorate the exteriors of religious buildings. Painting evolved from stiff, two-dimensional forms to more natural ones. Religious and secular subjects were depicted in illuminated manuscripts. Panel and wall painting evolved into the Renaissance style in Italy in the 15th cent., and in the early 16th cent. elsewhere in Europe.

gothic novel European Romantic, pseudo-medieval fiction with a prevailing atmosphere of mystery and terror. Such novels were often set in castles or monasteries equipped with subterranean passages, dark battlements, and hidden panels, and had plots involving ghosts, madness, outrage, superstition, and revenge. Horace WALPOLE's *Castle of Otranto* (1765) initiated the vogue, which peaked in the 1790s. Ann RADCLIFFE's *The Mysteries of Udolpho* (1794) and *The Italian* (1797) are among the finest examples. Gothic traits appear in the works of many major writers, and persist today in thousands of paperback romances.

Gothic Revival Architectural movement (c.1730–c.1930) associated with Romanticism. The first nostalgic imitation of GOTHIC ARCHITECTURE appeared in the 18th cent., when scores of houses with castle-style battlements were built in England, but only toward the mid-19th cent. did a true Gothic Revival develop, as architects began to create original works based on underlying Gothic principles. French architects, particularly E.-E. VIOLLET-LE-DUC, were the first to apply the Gothic skeleton structure to modern ends. Gothic-style churches and collegiate buildings continued to be constructed in Britain and the U.S. well into the 20th cent.

Goths Germanic people whose two branches, the OSTROGOTHS and the VISIGOTHS, harassed the Roman empire for centuries. Legend holds that they originated in S Scandinavia, crossed to the S shore of the Baltic Sea, then migrated to the Black Sea in the 2nd cent. A.D. They raided the Roman provinces in Asia Minor and the Balkan peninsula in the 3rd cent. and drove the Romans out of the province of Dacia.

Gotland Island (pop., 1999 est.: 58,000), SE Sweden. Located in the Baltic Sea, it covers 1,159 sq mi (3,001 sq km). A trading center since the BRONZE AGE, Gotland became part of Sweden in the 9th cent. By the 12th cent. its traders dominated the routes between Russia and W Europe. German merchants brought it into the HANSEATIC LEAGUE. Gotland was at the height of its prosperity when it was taken by the Danish in 1361. It was finally returned to Sweden in 1645. The island's modern economy centers on agriculture, fishing, and tourism.

Gottfried von Strassburg \'gȯt-ˌfrēt-fȯn-'shträs-ˌbůrk\ (fl.c.1210) German poet, one of the greatest of the Middle Ages. His courtly epic *Tristan und Isolde* (c.1210) is based on an Anglo-Norman version of the story, which came from Celtic legend. Though unfinished, it is one of the most perfect creations of the medieval courtly spirit, distinguished by its refined and elevated tone and its skillful technique.

FG

Göttingen \\'gȫ-tiŋ-ən\\, **University of** *German* Georg-August-Universität zu Göttingen. Eminent European university, founded in 1737 in Göttingen, Germany. It was one of the first and most influential secular universities. In the late 18th cent. it was the center of the Göttinger Hain, a circle of poets who were forerunners of German Romanticism. Its Mathematical Institute was headed at various times by Carl Friedrich GAUSS, Bernhard RIEMANN, and David HILBERT. Its physics faculty has included Max BORN, Werner HEISENBERG, and Max von LAUE. Current enrollment is about 27,000.

Gottschalk \\'gät-ˌshȯk\\, **Louis Moreau** (1829–1869) U.S. composer and pianist. Born in New Orleans, he was exposed early to the colorful life of the city's Caribbean and Latin American population. Sent to France at 13 to study music, he quickly became known throughout Europe as a piano virtuoso and a composer of exotic piano works. He returned in 1853 and toured widely throughout the New World. He is remembered for his over 200 piano pieces, including *Bamboula, Le bananier, Le banjo, L'Union,* and *The Dying Poet.* Gottschalk was the first international musical star produced by the U.S.

gouache \\'gwäsh\\ Opaque watercolor. Also known as poster paint, it differs from transparent WATERCOLOR in that the pigments are bound by liquid glue, which is used as a thinner. Gouache paints dry to a matte finish and, if desired, without visible brush marks. The suede finish and crisp lines characteristic of many Indian and Islamic miniature paintings is produced by this medium; it is used in Western screen and fan decoration and was used by modern artists such as Georges ROUAULT and Paul KLEE.

Gould \\'güld\\, **Chester** (1900–1985) U.S. cartoonist. Born in Pawnee, Okla., he studied cartooning through a correspondence school. From 1931 his "Dick Tracy" action comic strip became the first popular cops-and-robbers series. Drawn with hard outlines and accurate in the details of crime and criminal investigation, the widely syndicated strip featured a clean-cut detective with a jutting jaw, and a gallery of grotesquely caricatured criminals. Gould retired from the strip in 1977.

Gould \\'güld\\, **Glenn (Herbert)** (1932–1982) Canadian pianist. Born in Toronto, he planned to concentrate on composing, but the acclaim that greeted his first recording of J. S. BACH's *Goldberg Variations* (1955) led to an international career as a pianist. His interpretations of Bach set a new standard with their technical brilliance and subtle intelligence. Famously eccentric, he often wore gloves while playing and was intensely hypochondriac. Never happy performing, in 1964 he left the concert stage forever for the recording studio. He later composed highly individual musical radio "documentaries."

Gould \\'güld\\, **Jay** (*orig.* Jason) (1836–1892) U.S. railroad executive, speculator, and unscrupulous robber baron. Born in Roxbury, N.Y., he first worked as a surveyor. By 1859 he was speculating in the stocks of small railways. In 1867 he became a director of the Erie Railroad and joined with James FISK to keep Cornelius VANDERBILT from buying control of it. He bribed New York legislators to legalize the sale of watered stock. He and Fisk joined with W. M. TWEED to profit from further stock manipulations. In 1869 they attempted to corner the gold market, causing the BLACK FRIDAY panic. In 1872 public outcry forced Gould to cede control of the Erie. He controlled the Union Pacific by 1874, then sold it to amass a huge rail system southwest of St. Louis. He gained control of Western Union (1881), the New York *World* (1879), and the Manhattan Elevated Railroad (1886), and remained ruthless to the end.

Gould, Stephen Jay (1941–2002) U.S. paleontologist and evolutionary biologist. Born in New York City, he joined the faculty of Harvard Univ. in 1967. With Niles Eldredge (b.1943), he developed the controversial theory of punctuated equilibrium (1972), a revision of DARWINISM proposing that the creation of new species occurs in rapid bursts. He was widely known as a popularizing writer, especially in *Natural History* magazine; his numerous books include *The Panda's Thumb* (1980), *The Mismeasure of Man* (1981), and *The Structure of Evolutionary Theory* (2002).

Gounod \\gü-'nō\\, **Charles (François)** (1818–1893) French composer. He studied music at the Paris Conservatoire, but also studied for the priesthood and worked as an organist, and he remained torn between the theater and the church. His reputation largely rests on his opera *Faust* (1859). Of his 15 other operas, *Roméo et Juliette* (1867) is the best known. Other works include 17 masses, over 150 songs, and two symphonies.

gourami \\gü-'rä-mē\\ Any of several of the freshwater, tropical labyrinth fishes (order Perciformes), especially *Osphronemus goramy,* an E. Indian fish caught or raised for food. Compact and oval, with a long ray extending from each pelvic fin, it weighs up to 20 lbs (9 kg). Other gouramis, several popular in home aquariums, are Asian members of different genera and families: the giant gourami (*Colisa fasciata*), blue-green and reddish brown, and 5 in. (12 cm) long; the dwarf gourami (*C. lalia*), 2.5 in. (6 cm) long, brightly striped in red and blue; and the kissing gourami (*Helostoma temmincki*), greenish or pinkish white, noted for its "kissing."

gourd Any of the approximately 700 species of annual food and ornamental herbaceous plants that make up the family Cucurbitaceae (order Violales), including MELONS, SQUASHES, and PUMPKINS. Most species trail or climb by tendrils. Economically important food gourds include pumpkin, CUCUMBER, WATERMELON, CHAYOTE, and squash. Gourds are generally low in nutrients; one exception is winter squash. The hard shells of many gourds have made them useful as containers and utensils. Colorful and oddly shaped gourds are picked for ornamental use.

Gourmont \\gür-'mōⁿ\\, **Rémy de** (1858–1915) French novelist, poet, and playwright. He worked 10 years at the national library; his dismissal resulted from an allegedly unpatriotic article in the *Mercure de France,* a journal he had cofounded. He played a major role in disseminating the aesthetic doctrines of the SYMBOLIST MOVEMENT. His 50 published volumes are mainly collections of essays. His novels include *Very Woman* (1890) and *The Dream of a Woman* (1899).

gout Hereditary metabolic disorder in which excess uric-acid salts, normally excreted in urine, are deposited as needle-sharp crystals in joints, causing attacks of severe INFLAMMATION. The most common site is the base of the big toe. Gout is far more common in men, usually beginning in middle age. Attacks cause extreme tenderness and pain, and often subside in a week or two. Drugs are used to treat acute attacks and inhibit uric-acid synthesis.

government Political system by which a body of people is administered and regulated. Different levels of government typically have different responsibilities. The level closest to those governed is local government. Regional governments comprise a grouping of communities. National governments nominally control all the territory within internationally recognized borders and have responsibilities not shared by their subnational counterparts. Most governments exercise executive, legislative (see LEGISLATURE), and judicial (see JUDICIARY) powers. Political forms at the national level determine the powers exercised at the subnational levels. See also DEMOCRACY, FASCISM, MONARCHY, OLIGARCHY, THEOCRACY, TOTALITARIANISM.

government budget Forecast of governmental expenditures and revenues for the following fiscal year. In modern industrial economies, the budget is the key instrument for the execution of government economic policies. Because views about priorities in spending differ widely, government budgets are the focus of competing political interests. In the U.S. the federal budget is prepared by the president's Office of Management and Budget. The U.S. Congress influences its preparation through negotiations with the president and detailed consideration upon its official submission to Congress.

governor Device that automatically maintains the rotary speed of an engine regardless of the load. A typical governor regulates an engine's speed by varying the rate at which fuel or working fluid is furnished to it. Nearly all governors work by CENTRIFUGAL FORCE and consist of a pair of masses rotating about a spindle driven by the engine and kept from flying outward, usually by springs. With an increase in speed, the controlling force of the springs is overcome and the masses move outward, opening valves supplying the engine with its working fluid or fuel. Modern governors are used to regulate the flow of gasoline to IN-TERNAL-COMBUSTION ENGINES and the flow of steam, water, or gas to various types of TURBINES. See also FLY-WHEEL.

Gower \'gaù-ər, 'gòr\, **John** (1330?–1408) English poet. His works, in the tradition of COURTLY LOVE and moral allegory, strongly influenced other poets of his day. *Vox clamantis* (1385?), his major Latin poem, owes much to OVID. His greatest work in English is the *Confessio Amantis* (begun c.1386), a long collection of exemplary tales of love.

Goya (y Lucientes), Francisco (José) de (1746–1828) Spanish painter and printmaker. He came to maturity in 1775 with the first of some 60 cartoons for the royal tapestry factory. In 1786 he was appointed painter to CHARLES III. By 1799, under the patronage of CHARLES IV, he had become the most successful artist in Spain; his famous *The Family of Charles IV* was painted at this time (1800). Though he welcomed his honors and success, the record he left of his patrons and their society is ruthlessly penetrating. The eroticism of his famous *Naked Maja* and *Clothed Maja* (c.1800–5)

Francisco de Goya, self-portrait, c.1798

caused him to be summoned before the Inquisition in 1815. After an illness left him permanently deaf in the 1790s, his work took on an exaggerated realism. His 80 satirical *Caprices* (publ. 1799) represent an outstanding achievement in the history of printmaking. When Napoleon invaded Spain (1808–15), Goya produced the 82-etching series *The Disasters of War* (1810–20). He settled in Bordeaux, France, in 1824, resigned as court painter in 1826, and began working in lithography. Exceptionally prolific and versatile, he completed some 500 oil paintings and murals, 300 etchings and lithographs, hundreds of drawings, and more than 200 portraits. His work profoundly influenced 19th-cent. European art.

Goyen \'küi-ə, *Engl* 'gòi-ən\, **Jan Josephs(zoon) van** (1596–1656) Dutch painter and etcher. Confining himself primarily to the scenery of Holland, he painted on wood panels; intricate detail and subtle atmospheric effects characterize his work. He excelled at capturing the moods of sky and water, Dutch cities (e.g., *View of Leiden*, 1643), and lowland winter scenes. A prolific draftsman, he also executed many landscape etchings. With Salomon van Ruysdael, he was the outstanding master of tonal landscape painting in 17th-cent. Holland.

Gozzoli \gòt-'tsò-lē\, **Benozzo** *orig.* Benozzo di Lese (c.1420–1497) Italian Renaissance painter. Early in his career he assisted Lorenzo GHIBERTI in Florence and Fra ANGELICO in Rome and Orvieto. His reputation today rests on the breathtaking fresco cycle *The Journey of the Magi* (1459–61) in the chapel of Florence's Medici-Riccardi Palace. His work as a whole, which included several altarpieces and a series of 25 frescoes of Old Testament scenes for the Camposanto in Pisa (1468–84), was undistinguished.

GPS See GLOBAL POSITIONING SYSTEM

Graaff, Robert Van de See Robert VAN DE GRAAFF

Gracchus \'gra-kəs\, **Gaius Sempronius** (154?–121 B.C.) Roman TRIBUNE (123–122 B.C.) He joined the outcry over the murder of his brother, Tiberius Gracchus (133 B.C.), and helped implement the latter's agrarian law. He passed reforms aimed at curbing the corruption of the nobility. His attempts to extend citizenship to Rome's Italian allies and more freedom to plebeians were unpopular. His policies were seen by extreme conservatives as an attempt to destroy the aristocracy. He committed suicide while under siege on the Aventine Hill.

Grace One of a group of Greek goddesses who personified charm and beauty. Originally fertility goddesses, they were frequently associated with APHRODITE. Their number varied in different legends, but often there were three.

grace In Christian theology, the unmerited gift of divine favor, which brings about SALVATION. The concept has given rise to debate over the nature of human depravity and the extent to which individuals may contribute to their own salvation through free will. The question of whether grace may be given as a reward for good works or for faith alone was important in the Protestant REFORMATION. There has also been controversy over the means of grace: Roman Catholics, Eastern Orthodox, and some Protestants believe that it is conferred through the SACRAMENTS, while other Protestants (e.g., Baptists) hold that grace results from personal faith alone. See also ORIGINAL SIN.

grackle Any of several songbird species (in the family Icteridae) having iridescent black plumage and a long tail. Grackles use their stout, pointed bill to snap up insects, dig grubs, and kill small vertebrates, including fishes and baby birds. The common grackle (*Quiscalus quiscula*) of N. America is about 12 in. (30 cm) long. The males of two *Cassidus* species (boat-tailed and great-tailed grackles) have a long, deeply keeled tail. See also BLACKBIRD, MYNAH.

Graf, Steffi (*orig.* Stephanie Maria) (b.1969) German tennis player. At 13 she became the second-youngest player ever to earn an international ranking. In 1988 she won all four Grand Slam events (French, Australian, U.S., and Wimbledon) and an Olympic gold medal. Sidetracked by knee surgery in 1997, she played her way back to the top, winning the French Open in 1999, her final season, for her 22nd Grand Slam title.

graft In horticulture, the act of placing a portion of one plant (called a bud or scion) into or on a stem, root, or branch of another (called the stock) in such a way that a union forms and the partners continue to grow. Grafting is used to repair injured trees, retain varietal characteristics, adapt varieties to adverse soil or climatic conditions, ensure pollination, produce multifruited or multiflowered plants, and propagate certain species (such as hybrid roses) that can be propagated in no other way. In theory, any two plants that are closely related botanically and that have a continuous cambium can be grafted. Grafts between species of the same genus are often successful and between genera occasionally so.

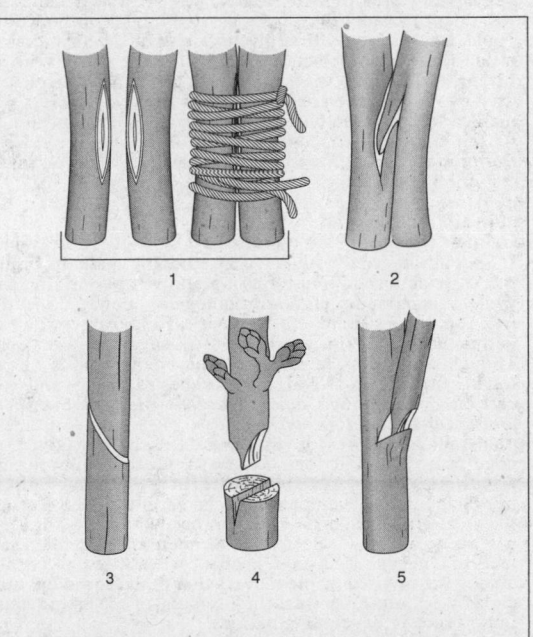
Graft Some methods of grafting. (1) simple splice graft, showing cut surfaces of stock and scion and the cut surfaces joined and bound, (2) tongued graft, (3) whip graft, (4) cleft graft, (5) side cleft graft.

FG

Graham, Billy *orig.* William Franklin Graham, Jr. (b.1918) U.S. Christian evangelist. Born in Charlotte, N.C., son of a dairy farmer, he underwent a conversion experience at 16 during a revival. He was ordained a Southern Baptist clergyman in 1939. He won numerous converts with his tent revivals and radio broadcasts, and by 1950 he had become fundamentalism's leading spokesman. He led a series of widely televised international revival crusades and became spiritual adviser to a series of U.S. presidents.

Graham, Katharine *orig.* Katharine Meyer (1917–2001) U.S. publisher. Born in New York City, the daughter of Eugene Meyer (1875–1959), owner of *The Washington Post* (1933–46), she married Philip Graham, who later became the *Post*'s publisher. In 1963 she succeeded him as head of the Washington Post Co. (which had purchased *Newsweek* in 1961). Under her leadership the *Post* became one of the nation's most powerful newspapers, particularly with its coverage of the Watergate Scandal. Her best-selling autobiography is *Personal History* (1997, Pulitzer Prize).

Graham, Martha (1894–1991) U.S. dancer, teacher, choreographer, and foremost exponent of MODERN DANCE. Born in Pittsburgh, she trained from 1916 under Ted SHAWN. In New York she founded her own school in 1927 and a performing company in 1929. She choreographed over 160 works, creating unique "dance plays." Many are based on American themes, including *Appalachian Spring* (1944); other works include *Primitive Mysteries* (1931), *El Penitente* (1940), *Letter to the World* (1940), and *Phaedra* (1962). She collaborated for many years with Louis Horst (1884–1964), her musical director, and Isamu NOGUCHI, who designed many of her sets. She retired from dancing in 1970 but continued to teach and choreograph. Her technique became the first significant alternative to classical BALLET, and her influence extended worldwide.

Grahame, Kenneth \ˈgrā-əm, ˈgram\ (1859–1932) British writer of children's books. He wrote articles and stories that he collected in such books as *The Golden Age* (1895) and *Dream Days* (1898). He is best known for his classic *The Wind in the Willows* (1908), whose animal characters—principally Mole, Rat, Badger, and Toad—captivatingly combine human traits with authentic animal habits.

grail *or* **Holy Grail** In ARTHURIAN LEGEND, a sacred cup that was the object of a mystical quest by knights of the Round Table. The grail was first given Christian significance as a mysterious, holy object by CHRÉTIEN DE TROYES in the 12th cent. The grail was sometimes said to be the same cup used by JESUS at the Last Supper and later by Joseph of Arimathea to catch the blood flowing from the wounds of Jesus on the cross. According to Thomas MALORY's *Morte Darthur*, Sir GALAHAD found the grail and achieved mystical union with God.

grain See CEREAL

grain alcohol See ETHANOL

Grainger, (George) Percy (Aldridge) (1882–1961) Australian-U.S. composer and pianist. After studying music in Frankfurt, he established himself as a piano virtuoso in England, while also pursuing ethnomusicological interest, collecting folk tunes in England and Denmark. He moved to the U.S. permanently in 1914, teaching in Chicago and New York. Though an inveterate musical experimenter, he is known for his tuneful short works for orchestra, piano, and concert band, including *Country Gardens, Molly on the Shore, Mock Morris,* and *Lincolnshire Posy.*

grain mill Structure for grinding CEREAL. WATERWHEELS were first exploited for such tasks. Geared mills turning grindstones (see GEAR) were used in the Roman Empire, but their fullest development occurred in medieval Europe; the great grain mill near Arles, France, with its 16 7-ft (2-m) cascaded overshot wheels and wooden gearing, may have met the needs of 80,000 people. WINDMILLS were also among the original prime movers that replaced animal muscle as a source of power; they remain of major industrial importance in developing nations.

gram Unit of MASS or WEIGHT used especially in the centimeter-gram-second (CGS) system of measurement. One gram is equal to 0.001 kg, about 0.035 oz, or 15.43 grains. The gram is very nearly equal to the mass of 1 cc of pure water at its maximum density. The gram of FORCE is equal to the weight of a gram of mass under standard gravity. See also METRIC SYSTEM.

grammar Rules of a language governing its PHONOLOGY, MORPHOLOGY, SYNTAX, and SEMANTICS. The first Europeans to write grammar texts were the Greeks of the 1st cent. B.C. The Romans applied the Greek grammatical system to Latin. The works of the Latin grammarians were widely used to teach grammar in medieval Europe. By 1700, grammars of 61 vernacular languages had been printed. These were mainly used for teaching and to reform or standardize language. In the 19th–20th cent., linguists began studying languages to trace their evolution rather than to prescribe correct usage. Descriptive linguists studied spoken language by collecting and analyzing samples. Transformational grammarians examined the underlying structure of language. The older approach to grammar as a body of rules needed to speak and write correctly is still the basis of primary and secondary teaching.

Grammy Awards Annual awards given by the Recording Academy (National Academy of Recording Arts and Sciences). The first Grammies were given in 1958. The awards, which reflect the votes of the Academy's large membership of musicians, producers, and other music professionals, have since expanded considerably to reflect the variety of musical taste and production; today awards are given in dozens of categories.

Grampians, the Mountain range, W Victoria, Australia. It is noted for deep gorges, weathered rock formations, and wildflowers. The highest peak, Mt. William, rises to 3,827 ft (1,166 m). The range was named after the Grampian of Scotland.

Gramsci \ˈgräm-shē\, **Antonio** (1891–1937) Italian politician. He joined the Italian Socialist Party in 1914; in 1921 he left to found the Italian Communist Party. In 1924 he became head of the party and was elected to the national legislature. The party was outlawed by the fascist government in 1926, and Gramsci was arrested and imprisoned for 11 years; in poor health, he was released to die at 46. His influential *Letters from Prison* (1947) outlines a version of communism less dogmatic than Soviet communism.

gram stain Staining technique for the initial identification of BACTERIA, devised in 1884 by Hans Christian Gram (1853–1938). The stain reveals fundamental differences in the biochemical and structural properties of a living cell. A slide containing a smear of bacteria is treated with a purple dye; the slide is then dipped in an iodine solution, followed by an organic solvent (such as alcohol) that can dissolve the dye. Gram-positive bacteria remain purple because they have thick cell walls that the solvent cannot easily penetrate; gram-negative bacteria lose their color because their thin cell walls allow the solvent to penetrate and remove the dye.

Granada \grä-ˈnä-thä\ City (pop., 1998 est.: 241,000), ANDALUSIA, S Spain. Settled in the 5th cent. B.C., as the seat of the Moorish kingdom of Granada it was the final stronghold of the MOORS in Spain, until 1492. Nearby is the ALHAMBRA. The city has fine Renaissance, baroque, and neoclassical architecture and is a major tourist center. It has been the see of an archbishop since 1493; the Univ. of Granada was founded in 1526.

Granados (y Campiña) \grä-ˈnä-thōs\, **Enrique** (1867–1916) Spanish composer. He studied composition with Felipe Pedrell, concertized as a pianist, and from 1901 taught at the music school he founded in Barcelona. He wrote four zarzuelas, including *María del Carmen* (1898), and two "poemas" (also stage works), but his fame rests on the piano suite *Goyescas* (1911). Returning from the New York premiere of his opera of the same name, Granados's ship was torpedoed by a German submarine.

Gran Chaco \grän-ˈchä-kō\ *Spanish* **Chaco** *or* **El Chaco** Plain, S central S. America. An arid lowland, it is bounded by the ANDES, the PARAGUAY and PARANÁ rivers, a marshy area in Bolivia, and the Río Salado in Argentina. Its area is about 280,000 sq mi (725,000 sq km). The region's main part, in the fork of the Paraguay and PILCOMAYO rivers, was fought over by Bolivia and Paraguay in the 1932–35 CHACO WAR. By a 1938 treaty, a larger E part went to Paraguay and a smaller W part to Bolivia. Chaco's wildlife is abundant, including at least 60 species of snake.

Grand Alliance, War of the (1689–97) War of LOUIS XIV of France against an alliance led by Britain and Austria. Underlying the war was the rivalry between the BOURBON and HABSBURG dynasties. Louis launched a campaign in the 1680s to position the Bourbons for future succession to the Spanish throne. To oppose him, the Habsburg emperor LEOPOLD I formed the League of Augsburg. The league proved ineffective, but in 1689–90 Britain, the Netherlands, Brandenburg, Saxony, Bavaria, and Spain, alarmed at Louis's successes, joined with Leopold to form the Grand Alliance. As war broke out in Europe and in overseas colonies, including America (see KING WILLIAM'S WAR), Louis found his military inadequately prepared, and France suffered heavy naval losses. In 1695 Louis started secret peace negotiations, which culminated in the Treaty of Rijswijk (1697). The underlying Habsburg–Bourbon and English–French conflicts resurfaced four years later in the War of the SPANISH SUCCESSION.

Grand Banks Portion of N. American continental shelf, in the Atlantic Ocean. Lying southeast and south of NEWFOUNDLAND, it is a noted international fishing ground and extends 350 mi (560 km) north–south and 420 mi (675 km) east–west. The cold LABRADOR CURRENT and the warm GULF STREAM meet in its vicinity, causing heavy fogs. The banks were first reported in 1498 by John CABOT.

Grand Canal Series of waterways in N China that link Hangzhou with Beijing, at 1,085 mi (1,747 km) the world's longest man-made waterway. It was built to transport surplus grain from the agriculturally rich Chang (Yangtze) and Huai river valleys to feed the capital cities and large standing armies in the north. The oldest portion, in the south, may date from the 4th cent. B.C. It continues to be used today for barge shipping and irrigation.

Grand Canyon Gorge cut by the COLORADO RIVER, NW Arizona. Noted for its rock formations and coloration, it varies from 0.1 to 18 mi (0.2–29 km) wide, and extends about 277 mi (446 km) from N Arizona to Grand Wash Cliffs, near the Nevada border. The deepest section, 56 mi (90 km) long, is within Grand Canyon National Park, which stretches from Lake Powell to Lake MEAD. The canyon is in places more than a mile deep. The national park, now containing 1,904 sq mi (4,931 sq km), was created in 1919.

Grand Central Station Railroad terminal in New York City designed and built (1903–13) by Reed & Stem in collaboration with Warren & Wetmore. The concourse, with its 125-ft (43-m) ceiling vault painted with constellations, was one of the largest enclosed spaces of its time. A gem of BEAUX-ARTS STYLE, its symmetrical main facade features a large clock and sculptures of an American eagle and Roman deities.

Grand Coulee Dam Dam on the COLUMBIA RIVER in NE Washington. Built in 1942, it rises 550 feet (168 m) above bedrock and is 5,223 feet (1,592 m) wide. The dam creates a reservoir, Franklin D. Roosevelt Lake, that has a storage capacity of about 9,562,000 acre-feet (11,795,000,000 cubic m). The largest and most complex of a series of dams on the Columbia River, it provides irrigation, assists in flood control, and furnishes hydroelectric power.

Grande, Rio See RIO GRANDE

grande école \grän-dā-ˈkȯl\ (French: "great school") Any of several preeminent specialized institutions of higher learning in France. The École Normale Supérieure serves mainly to prepare future university and *lycée* (senior secondary-school) teachers. The École Normale d'Administration trains the highest ranks of civil servants. The renowned Collège de France offers lectures by eminent scholars; it does not grant degrees or certificates. The École Polytechnique trains technicians for the army. Other grandes écoles include institutes for advanced study in social science, architecture, and the arts.

Grand Falls See CHURCHILL FALLS

grandfather clause Statute enacted by seven Southern U.S. states (1895–1910) to deny suffrage to black men. It exempted descendants of men who voted before 1867 from meeting new literacy and property requirements. Since most black men could not vote until 1870, this clause effectively excluded them from voting. The U.S. Supreme Court declared the clause unconstitutional in 1915.

grand jury Jury that examines accusations against persons charged with crime and, if the evidence warrants it, makes formal charges on which the accused are later tried. It does not decide guilt or innocence, only whether there is "probable cause" to believe that a person has committed a crime, and it issues or elects not to issue an indictment. Public officials (prosecutors and police) provide information and summon witnesses for the jury. The proceedings are usually secret. Some U.S. states have abolished the grand jury and authorize indictments by prosecutors.

Grandma Moses See Grandma MOSES

Grand Ole Opry COUNTRY-MUSIC radio show in Nashville, Tenn. Founded in 1925 by George Dewey Hay, the show was originally known as the "WSM Barn Dance." Its music developed from Dave Macon's ballads, the string bands, cowboy music, and western swing of the 1930s, and later the traditional music characterized by the career of Roy ACUFF. After World War II, the honky-tonk style of Ernest Tubb and later Hank WILLIAMS, and the bluegrass of Bill MONROE all became Opry staples. In 1941 the Opry became a live stage show. In 1974 it moved to the Opryland amusement park and entertainment center. The Opry initiated and promoted the creation of Nashville as the center of country music.

Grand Prix racing \ˈgräⁿ-ˈprē\ Automobile racing in which formula cars (open-wheel, open-cockpit, rear-engine vehicles) are run on closed highways or other courses somewhat simulating road conditions. The cars used (known as Formula One cars) are generally smaller than those used in speedway races. Grand Prix racing began in 1906 and today comprises more than 15 major international events.

Grand Rapids City (pop., 2000: 197,800), W Michigan. Located on the Grand River, it was founded in 1826 as a trading post. Lumber from nearby forests soon fueled a woodworking industry. After Grand Rapids furniture was shown at the Philadelphia Centennial in 1876, the city became known as the furniture capital of America. After World War I, metal-based manufacturing exceeded its furniture industry. It was the boyhood home of Pres. Gerald FORD.

Grand River See NEOSHO RIVER

Grand Staircase–Escalante National Monument National preserve, S Utah. Established in 1996, it covers a vast area of 1.7 million acres (.7 million hectares). Its W section has cliffs and plateaus, and its E section has canyons along the Escalante River. A natural rock "staircase" climbs 5,000 ft (1,500 m) to the rim of Bryce Canyon. Dinosaur tracks have been found there. The area was once inhabited by the ANASAZI people.

Grand Teton National Park \ˈtē-ˌtän\ National preserve, NW Wyoming. Established in 1929, it now covers 484 sq mi (1,254 sq km). The spectacular snow-covered peaks of its TETON RANGE rise 7,000 ft (2,000 m) above the nearby SNAKE RIVER valley. The fertile valley of Jackson Hole is home to buffalo, moose, and pronghorns.

Grand Traverse Bay \ˈtra-vərs\ NE arm of Lake MICHIGAN, indenting NW Michigan. The Leelanau Peninsula forms its W boundary. The bay is noted for its year-round fishing, and the area is an important summer-resort region.

grand unified theory (GUT) Theory that attempts to unify the electroweak force (see ELECTROWEAK THEORY) with the STRONG FORCE. The unification of all four fundamental interactions is sometimes called UNIFIED FIELD THEORY. So far, no successful GUTs have been devised. See also STANDARD MODEL.

Grange, Red (*orig.* Harold) (1903–1991) U.S. football player. Born in Forksville, Pa., he had an outstanding collegiate career at the Univ. of Illinois, where in 1924 he ran for five touchdowns in a single game. In 1925 he

Red Grange, 1920s

joined the Chicago Bears, where his exploits earned him the nickname "the Galloping Ghost" and stimulated public interest in professional football. After a knee injury in 1927, he was never again a dangerous runner. He retired in 1934 and subsequently worked as a sportscaster.

Granger movement \\'grän-jər\ Coalition of U.S. farmers, mainly in the Midwest, that fought monopolistic grain-transport practices in the 1870s. In 1867 the Patrons of Husbandry was organized to bring farmers together to learn new farming methods. By the mid-1870s almost every state had at least one branch, or Grange, and membership passed 800,000. The Grangers influenced some states to prohibit price-fixing by railroads and grain-storage facilities. Outgrowths included the GREENBACK and POPULIST MOVEMENTS. The Grangers dropped to about 100,000 members by 1880; they rebounded in the early 20th cent., but again declined.

Granit \grä-'nēt\, **Ragnar Arthur** (1900–1991) Finnish-Swedish physiologist. His "dominator-modulator" theory states that in addition to the RETINA's three kinds of cone cells, which respond to different colors, certain optic-nerve fibers respond either to the whole spectrum (dominators) or to specific colors (modulators). He also proved that light inhibits as well as stimulates optic-nerve impulses. He shared a 1967 Nobel Prize.

granite Coarse- or medium-grained INTRUSIVE ROCK that is rich in QUARTZ and FELDSPAR. One of the most common rocks of the earth's CRUST, it is formed by the cooling of MAGMA. Granite was once used extensively as paving blocks and building stone, but today its principal uses are as roadway curbing, veneer for building faces, and tombstones. Granite characteristically forms irregular masses, ranging from less than 5 mi (8 km) in maximum dimension to BATHOLITHS that are often hundreds of square miles in area.

Grant, Cary *orig.* Archibald Alexander Leach (1904–1986) British-U.S. film actor. Initially part of an acrobatic comedy troupe, he made his film debut in *This Is the Night* (1932) and earned stardom with Mae WEST in *She Done Him Wrong* (1933). His debonair charm and stunning good looks made him a longtime popular star in such sophisticated comedies as *Topper* (1937), *Bringing Up Baby* (1938), *His Girl Friday* (1940), and *The Philadelphia Story* (1941). He also starred in Alfred HITCHCOCK's thrillers *Suspicion* (1941), *Notorious* (1946), *To Catch a Thief* (1955), and *North by Northwest* (1959).

Grant, Ulysses S. (*orig.* Hiram Ulysses) (1822–1885) U.S. general and 18th president of the U.S. (1869–77). Born in Point Pleasant, Ohio, he served in the Mexican War under Zachary TAYLOR; he resigned his commission in 1854 and worked unsuccessfully at farming in Missouri and at his family's leather business in Illinois. When the AMERICAN CIVIL WAR began (1861), he was appointed brigadier general; his 1862 attack on Ft. Donelson, Tenn., produced the first major Union victory. He drove off a Confederate attack at SHILOH but was criticized for

Ulysses S. Grant

heavy Union losses. He devised the campaign to take the stronghold of VICKSBURG, Miss., in 1863, cutting the Confederacy in half from east to west. Following his victory at CHATTANOOGA in 1864, he was appointed commander of the Union army. While William T. SHERMAN made his famous march across Georgia, Grant attacked Robert E. LEE's forces in Virginia, bringing the war to an end in 1865. Grant's administrative ability and innovative strategies were largely responsible for the Union victory. His successful Republican presidential campaign made him, at 46, the youngest man yet elected president. His two terms were marred by political scandal involving members of his cabinet, including the Crédit Mobilier scandal and the WHISKEY

RING operation. He was more successful in foreign affairs, in which he was aided by his secretary of state, Hamilton FISH. He supported amnesty for Confederate leaders and protection for black civil rights. In 1881 he moved to New York; when a partner defrauded his son's investment firm, the family was impoverished. His memoirs were published by his friend Mark TWAIN.

Granville-Barker, Harley (1877–1946) British producer, playwright, and critic. An actor from age 15, he directed his own first play, *The Marrying of Ann Leete*, in 1901. As comanager of the Court Theatre (1904–7) he produced many of G.B. SHAW's early plays as well as plays by Henrik IBSEN and others. He influenced 20th-cent. theater with his naturalistic stagings of Shakespeare's plays, which emphasized continuous action on an open stage and rapid, lightly stressed speech. He later moved to Paris and wrote his classic *Prefaces to Shakespeare* (1927–46).

grape Any of the 60 plant species that make up the genus *Vitis* (family Vitaceae), native to the N temperate zone, including varieties that may be eaten as fruit, dried to produce raisins, or crushed to make grape juice or WINE. *V. vinifera* is the species most commonly used in wine making; innumerable varieties have been developed. The grape is usually a woody vine, climbing by means of tendrils. Botanically, the fruit is a BERRY. Grapes contain such minerals as calcium and phosphorus and are a source of vitamin A as well as glucose and fructose.

grapefruit Tree (*Citrus paradisi*) of the RUE FAMILY and its edible fruit. It probably originated in Jamaica. The dark, shiny green foliage is very dense. The large, white flowers are borne singly or in clusters. The fruit is 4–6 in. (100–150 mm) in diameter, about twice as large as a medium-sized orange. The mildly acidic pulp—light yellowish, pink, or red and juicy—is an excellent source of vitamin C.

grape sugar See GLUCOSE

graph Visual representation of a data set or a mathematical EQUATION, INEQUALITY, or FUNCTION to show relationships or tendencies. Though HISTOGRAMS and pie charts are also graphs, the term usually applies to point plots on a COORDINATE SYSTEM. For example, a graph of the relationship between real numbers and their squares matches each real number on a horizontal axis with its square on a vertical axis, generating a PARABOLA. A graph of an inequality is usually a shaded region on one side of a curve, whose shape depends not only on the equation or inequality but on the coordinate system chosen.

graphical user interface (GUI) Computer display format that allows the user to select commands, call up files, start programs, and do other routine tasks by using a MOUSE or touch screen rather than typing in text commands. The first GUI in a PERSONAL COMPUTER appeared in Apple Computer's Lisa, introduced in 1983; it became the basis of Apple's extremely successful Macintosh (1984). In 1985 Microsoft Corp. introduced Windows, a GUI that gave MS-DOS-based computers many of the same capabilities as the Macintosh. GUIs are also used in BROWSERS and application programs.

graphic art Traditional category of fine arts, including any form of visual artistic expression (e.g., PAINTING, drawing, PHOTOGRAPHY, PRINTMAKING), usually produced on flat surfaces. It often includes TYPOGRAPHY, but also encompasses plans and patterns for the decorative arts, interiors, engineering, and architecture.

graphite *or* **plumbago** \ˌpləm-'bā-gō\ *or* **black lead** Mineral form of CARBON. It is dark gray to black, and very soft. Its layered structure, with rings of six ATOMS arranged in horizontal sheets, gives it its slippery quality. It occurs in nature and is used (mixed with clay) as the "lead" in pencils as well as in lubricants, crucibles, polishes, arc lamps, batteries, brushes for electric motors, and nuclear-reactor cores.

grass Any of many low, green, nonwoody plants that make up the families Gramineae (Poaceae), Cyperaceae (SEDGES), and Juncaceae (RUSHES). Only the 8,000–10,000 species in the family Gramineae are true grasses. They are economically the most important of all flowering plants because of their nutritious grains (see CEREAL) and soil-forming function. Grasses provide forage for grazing animals, shelter for wildlife, and construction materials, furniture, utensils, and food for humans. Some species are grown as garden ornamentals, cultivated as TURF, or planted for erosion control. Most have round stems that are hollow between the joints, bladelike leaves, and extensively branching fibrous root systems.

Grass \'gräs\, **Günter (Wilhelm)** (b.1927) German novelist, poet, and playwright. Born in Danzig (now Gdansk, Poland), Grass passed through the Hitler Youth movement, was drafted at 16, and became a prisoner of war. His first novel, *The Tin Drum* (1959), brought him worldwide fame, and he became the literary spokesman for the generation that grew up in the Nazi era. It was followed by *Cat and Mouse* (1961) and *Dog Years* (1963); the three novels form a trilogy set in Danzig. His other works, all politically topical, include *The Flounder* (1977);

Günter Grass

Headbirths (1980); *A Broad Field* (1995), controversial for its opposition to German reunification; and *My Century* (1999). He received the Nobel Prize in 1999.

grasshopper Any of the leaping insects of the family Acrididae (short-horned grasshoppers) or Tettigoniidae (long-horned grasshoppers), both in the order Orthoptera. Grasshoppers are most common in tropical forests, semiarid regions, and grasslands. Colors range from green to olive or brown. Grasshoppers eat plant material and may damage crops. Some species are more than 4 in. (11 cm) long. The male can produce a buzzing sound by rubbing its wings and legs together. Grasshoppers are a favorite food of many birds, frogs, and snakes. See also KATYDID, LOCUST.

Grateful Dead U.S. rock group, formed in San Francisco in the mid-1960s by Jerry Garcia (1942–1995) on guitar, Phil Lesh (b.1940) on bass, Ron "Pigpen" McKernan (1945–1973) on keyboards, Bob Weir (b.1947) on guitar, and Bill Kreutzmann (b.1946) on drums. It emerged from the Haight-Ashbury psychedelic-drug-and-music scene. Though they regularly released albums, their focus was on live music; their concerts featured Garcia's marathon four-hour musical meanderings to an entourage of "Deadheads," nomadic fans who followed the band in spirited makeshift communities. In the late 1980s, the Grateful Dead was the most successful touring band in the world. They stopped touring after Garcia died of a heart attack at a drug rehabilitation center.

Gratian \'grā-shən\ *Latin in full* Flavius Gratianus Augustus (359–383) Roman emperor (367–83). He originally shared the office with his father, VALENTINIAN I (364–75), and his uncle, Valens (364–78). He later shared authority with his 4-year-old half brother, who was supported by the army. On his uncle's death he became ruler of the Eastern Empire, and summoned THEODOSIUS I to share power with him. Influenced by St. AMBROSE, Gratian was the first Roman ruler to omit the words *pontifex maximus* ("supreme priest") from his title. He was murdered opposing the usurper Magnus Maximus.

gravel Aggregate of rounded rock fragments coarser than sand (i.e., more than 0.08 in., or 2 mm, in diameter). Gravel beds in some places contain heavy metallic ore minerals, such as cassiterite (a major source of tin), or native metals, such as gold, in nuggets or flakes. Deposits accumulate in parts of stream channels or on beaches where the water moves too rapidly to permit sand to remain. In many regions gravel terraces (or raised beaches) extend great distances inland, indicating that the sea at one time stood higher than it does today. Gravels are widely used building materials.

Graves, Michael (b.1934) U.S. architect. Born in Indianapolis, in 1962 he began a long teaching career at Princeton Univ. In the late 1970s he rejected orthodox modernism and began seeking a richer, postmodernist vocabulary. The hulking masses of the Portland Building in Portland, Ore. (1980), and the Humana Building in Louisville, Ky. (1982), display his personal, Cubistic rendering of such classical elements as colonnades and loggias. Though considered somewhat awkward, these and his later buildings (e.g., Indianapolis Art Center, 1996) have been acclaimed for their ironic interpretation of traditional forms.

Graves, Robert (von Ranke) (1895–1985) British-Spanish man of letters. His first three volumes of poetry were published during World War I, in which he was severely wounded; they include some of the finest English love poems of the century. In 1926 he began a 13-year relationship with the American poet Laura Riding (1901–1991), with whom he collaborated as a publisher and writer. The most famous of his more than 120 books are the war memoir *Good-bye to All That* (1929); the historical novel *I, Claudius* (1934; televised in 1976); and the erudite, controversial study in mythology *The White Goddess* (1948).

Graves, Robert James (1796–1853) Irish physician. In 1821 he set up the Park Street School of Medicine, where he gave his advanced students responsibility for patients (under supervision) and lectured in English, not Latin. He introduced timing of the pulse by watch and giving patients with fevers nourishment instead of withholding it. He was a leader of the Irish (Dublin) school of diagnosis, which stressed observation of patients, and was one of the first to fully describe exophthalmic goiter (GRAVES' DISEASE).

Graves' disease *or* **toxic diffuse goiter** *or* **exophthalmic goiter** \,ek-säf-'thal-mik\ Most common type of hyperthyroidism (oversecretion of thyroid hormone), usually with GOITER and eyeball protrusion. Symptoms include increased cardiac output, rapid heartbeat, and possibly heart failure. Graves' disease is considered an AUTOIMMUNE DISEASE. It can sometimes be controlled by drugs; severe cases require partial or total removal of the THYROID GLAND.

gravitation Universal FORCE of attraction that acts between all bodies that have MASS. Though it is the weakest of the four known forces (see ELECTROMAGNETIC FORCE, STRONG FORCE, WEAK FORCE), it shapes the structure and evolution of the entire universe. The laws of gravity determine the trajectories of bodies in the solar system and the MOTION of objects on earth. Isaac NEWTON was the first to develop a quantitative theory of gravitation, holding that the force of attraction between two bodies is proportional to the product of their masses and inversely proportional to the square of the distance between them. Albert EINSTEIN proposed a new concept of gravitation involving the four-dimensional continuum of SPACE-TIME, which is curved by the presence of matter, and showed that a body accelerating uniformly is indistinguishable from one that is stationary in a gravitational field.

gravitational radius See SCHWARZSCHILD RADIUS

gravity, center of Imaginary point where the total WEIGHT of a material body may be thought to be concentrated. A body's center of gravity may coincide with its geometric center (see CENTROID), especially if the body is symmetric and composed of homogeneous material. In asymmetric, unhomogeneous, or hollow objects, the center of gravity may be at some distance from the geometric center, or even at a point in space external to the object, such as between the legs of a chair.

gravure printing \grə-'vyur\ PRINTING processes used for catalogs, magazines, newspaper supplements, cartons, floor and wall coverings, textiles, and plastics. Karl Klic (1841–1926) made photogravure a practical commercial process in 1878. An image is etched in the copper surface of the printing cylinder, as pits or wells of different depths. In rotogravure printing, the cylinder rotates through a trough filled with fast-drying ink. A thin steel doctor blade removes the ink from the surface. The cylinder comes in contact with the paper, which draws the ink out of the wells. Because of the various depths of the wells, a full range of tonal values can be printed. In COLOR PRINTING, a separate cylinder is prepared for each color. See also LETTERPRESS PRINTING, OFFSET PRINTING.

Gray, Asa (1810–1888) U.S. botanist. Born in Sauquoit, N.Y., he studied medicine and spent his spare time studying plant specimens. He collaborated with John Torrey (1796–

F G

1873) on *Flora of North America* (1838–43) and in 1842 joined the faculty at Harvard Univ., where he taught until 1873. He was largely responsible for the unification of the taxonomic knowledge of the N. American flora; his most widely used book, commonly called *Gray's Manual* (1848), remains a standard work. He was the chief early American supporter of the theories of Charles DARWIN.

Gray, Thomas (1716–1771) British poet. He wrote poems of wistful melancholy filled with truisms phrased in striking, quotable lines. Though his output was small, he became the dominant poetic figure in his day. He is remembered especially for *An Elegy Written in a Country Church Yard* (1751), the greatest work of the English "graveyard school."

grayhound See GREYHOUND

graywacke \'grā-ˌwak\ *or* **dirty sandstone** Sedimentary rock composed of sand-sized grains in a fine-grained clay matrix. The sand-sized grains frequently include pyroxenes, amphiboles, feldspars, and quartz). The clay matrix may constitute up to 50% of the volume; it tends to bind the grains strongly and form a relatively hard rock.

Graz \'gräts\ City (pop., 1999: 240,000), capital of Styria state, SE Austria. The country's second-largest city, it grew from a fortress settlement and received town rights about 1240 A.D. It became the center of Steiermark (Styria) during the Middle Ages, and was the residence of the Leopoldine HABSBURGS after 1379. Its fortifications, built in the 15th–16th cent., successfully withstood numerous sieges by Hungarians and Turks. Johannes KEPLER taught at its university, founded in 1585. A rail and industrial center, Graz has an active trade in agricultural products.

Great Atlantic & Pacific Tea Co. (A&P) U.S. corporation operating one of the largest supermarket chains in the U.S. The Great American Tea Co. was founded in New York in 1859 as a direct-mail operation to trade in tea from the cargoes of clipper ships. The first retail stores were incorporated in 1869 under the name Great Atlantic & Pacific Tea Co. By 1925 it was the largest U.S. grocery chain, and in 1936 A&P opened its first supermarket. By 1969 it was the largest supermarket chain in the U.S., but it declined thereafter; in 1979 it was bought by the German supermarket giant Tengelmann.

great auk Flightless seabird (*Pinguinus impennis*) extinct since 1844. Great auks bred in colonies on rocky islands off N. Atlantic coasts; fossil remains have been found as far south as Florida, Spain, and Italy. Their bodies were about 30 in. (75 cm) long; the wings, used for swimming underwater, were less than 6 in. (15 cm) long. They stood erect on land. Great auks were hunted to extinction for food and bait. About 80 specimens are preserved in museums. See also AUK.

Great auk (*Pinguinus impennis*)

Great Awakening Religious revival in British N. America from 1720 into the 1740s. It was part of a movement, known as PIETISM or Quietism on the European continent and evangelicalism in England, that swept Western Europe in the late 17th and early 18th cent. In N. America the Great Awakening had a strong Calvinist element (see CALVINISM). Revivalist preachers emphasized the need for sinners to fear punishment and to hope for the unearned gift of GRACE from God. George Whitefield (1714–1770) was one of the most popular, preaching to huge crowds throughout the colonies in 1739–40. Jonathan EDWARDS was the movement's most important theologian. Another revival, known as the Second Great Awakening, occurred in New England and Kentucky in the 1790s.

Great Barrier Reef Long stretch of CORAL REEF, off the NE coast of QUEENSLAND, Australia. The largest deposit of CORAL in the world, it extends for more than 1,250 mi (2,000 km) along the Australian coast and has an area of 80,000 sq mi (207,000 sq km). In addition to 350 species of coral, marine life includes anemones, lobsters, crayfish, and crabs. Encrusting red ALGAE form the purplish red algal rim that is one of the reef's characteristic features.

Great Basin National Park National preserve, E Nevada. A national park since 1986, it has an area of 121 sq mi (313 sq km) and consists of the S part of the Snake Mtns., a chain that rises abruptly from the desert floor to reach a height of 13,063 ft (3,982 m) at Wheeler Peak. It includes Lehman Caves, a group of limestone caverns.

Great Bear Lake Lake, Northwest Territories. Lying astride the Arctic Circle, it was visited before 1800 by NORTH WEST CO. traders. It is roughly 200 mi (320 km) long and 25–110 mi (40–175 km) wide and has a maximum depth of 1,356 ft (413 m). It is the largest lake entirely within Canada and the fourth-largest in N. America. The lake's waters abound with fish, including speckled trout.

Great Britain *or* **Britain** Kingdom, W Europe. Comprising ENGLAND, SCOTLAND, and WALES, the kingdom, which entirely occupies the largest island in Europe, covers 88,150 sq mi (228,300 sq km). With Northern IRELAND, it constitutes the UNITED KINGDOM of Great Britain and Northern Ireland.

Great Dane Breed of WORKING DOG developed at least 400 years ago in Germany, where it was used for BOAR hunting. Any association with Denmark is unclear. Tallest of the working breeds, it stands 28–32 in. (71–81 cm) tall and weighs 120–150 lbs (54–68 kg). It has a massive, square-jawed head, a short coat, and elegant body lines. It is typically swift and alert and is noted for courage, friendliness, and dependability.

Great Depression *or* **Depression of 1929** Longest and most severe economic depression ever experienced by the Western world. It began in the U.S. with the STOCK MARKET CRASH OF 1929 and lasted until about 1939. By late 1932 stock values had dropped to about 20% of their previous value, and by 1933 11,000 of the U.S.'s 25,000 banks had failed. This led to much-reduced levels of demand and production, resulting in high unemployment (by 1932, 25–30%). The U.S. financial collapse led to collapses of other economies, especially those of Germany and Britain. To protect domestic production, nations imposed tariffs and quotas, and international trade fell sharply. The Great Depression contributed to political upheaval. It led to the election of Franklin ROOSEVELT in the U.S. and major changes in the U.S. economy brought about by his NEW DEAL. It directly contributed to Adolf HITLER's rise to power in Germany and to political extremism in other countries. Before the Great Depression, governments relied on impersonal market forces to achieve economic correction; afterward, government action came to assume a principal role in ensuring economic stability.

Great Dismal Swamp See DISMAL SWAMP

Great Dividing Range Entire extent of mountain ranges roughly paralleling the coast of E Australia. Beginning in the north on Cape York Peninsula, they extend south to become the AUSTRALIAN ALPS, near the New S. Wales–Victoria border. Bending west in Victoria, they end in the GRAMPIANS; a S spur emerges from Bass Strait to form the central uplands of TASMANIA. The range stretches for 2,300 mi (3,700 km). The region is important for agriculture, lumbering, and mining.

Great Fire of London (Sept. 2–5, 1666) Worst fire in London's history. It destroyed most of the civic buildings, ST. PAUL'S CATHEDRAL, 87 parish churches, and about 13,000 houses. It began accidentally at the house of the king's baker in Pudding Lane near London Bridge, and a violent east wind encouraged the flames. On the fourth day houses were blown up by gunpowder to master the fire. The Thames River swarmed with vessels filled with people trying to save their goods.

Great Lakes Chain of lakes, central N. America. Comprising Lakes SUPERIOR, MICHIGAN, HURON, ERIE, and ONTARIO, they form a natural boundary between the U.S. and Canada. They cover an area of about 94,850 sq mi (245,660 sq km), and constitute the largest freshwater surface in the world. They are connected to form a single waterway that discharges down the ST. LAWRENCE RIVER into the Atlantic

Ocean. With the ST. LAWRENCE SEAWAY they form a 2,000-mi (3,200-km) shipping lane that carries oceangoing traffic as far west as DULUTH, Minn. Large quantities of iron ore, coal, grain, and manufactured goods are moved between lake ports and shipped overseas. Pollution and other factors have reduced the once-thriving fishing industry.

Great Leap Forward Failed industrialization campaign undertaken by the Chinese Communists 1958–60. MAO ZEDONG hoped to develop labor-intensive methods of industrialization that would emphasize manpower rather than expensive heavy machinery. Instead of large new factories, he proposed developing backyard steel furnaces in every village. Rural people were organized into communes where agricultural and political decisions emphasized ideological purity rather than expertise. The program was implemented so hastily and zealously that many errors occurred; these were exacerbated by a series of natural disasters and the withdrawal of Soviet technical personnel. China's agriculture was so disrupted that about 20 million people died of starvation from 1958 to 1962. By early 1960 the government had begun to return private plots to peasants and emphasize expertise again.

Great Mother of the Gods *or* **Cybele** \'si-bə-lē\ Deity of the ancient Mediterranean world. Her cult originated in Phrygia in Asia Minor and spread to the Greek world, where she was identified with RHEA. It reached Rome by the 3rd cent. B.C. and became a major cult during the empire. Known by a variety of local names, Cybele was venerated as the universal mother of gods, humans, and animals. Her lover was the fertility god ATTIS.

Great Northern Railway Co. U.S. railroad founded by James J. Hill (1838–1916) in 1890. Hill bought the St. Paul and Pacific Railroad in 1878 and extended it north to Canada and west to the Pacific coast, encouraging thousands of homesteaders to settle along its tracks. Together with J. P. MORGAN of the Northern Pacific Railway Co., Hill bought control of the Chicago, Burlington & Quincy Railroad in 1901 and set up a HOLDING COMPANY to control the three railroads. In 1904 the U.S. Supreme Court ordered it dissolved, but the Burlington continued under control of the Great Northern and the Northern Pacific. In 1970 the three were merged under the name Burlington Northern, Inc.

Great Northern War See Second NORTHERN WAR

Great Plague of London (1664–66) Epidemic of plague that ravaged London, killing over 75,000 of a population of 460,000. As early as 1625, 40,000 Londoners had died of the plague, but this was the worst and the last of the epidemics. The greatest devastation was in the city's outskirts in areas where the poor were densely crowded. The disease spread throughout the country. The plague's decline was attributed to various causes, including the GREAT FIRE OF LONDON.

Great Plains Continental slope of central N. America. It stretches from the RIO GRANDE in the south to the MACKENZIE RIVER delta along the Arctic Ocean in the north, and from the Interior Lowlands and the Canadian Shield in the east to the ROCKY MTNS. in the west. The plains embrace parts of ten U.S. states and four Canadian provinces, covering about 1,125,000 sq mi (2,912,000 sq km). A high plateau of semiarid grassland, these prairie regions produce most of the wheat grown in each country and are also important cattle- and sheep-herding areas.

Great Proletarian Cultural Revolution See CULTURAL REVOLUTION

Great Red Spot Storm on JUPITER that moves in longitude but remains at about latitude 23° south. Discovered in 1665 by G. D. CASSINI, it is a high-pressure center about 8,700 mi (14,000 km) north to south, roughly the diameter of earth, and twice as wide. Its brick-red to brownish color may blend into the coloring of other cloud belts; it tends to change over a period of years.

Great Rift Valley *or* **Rift Valley** *or* **East African Rift System** Rift system (see RIFT VALLEY), extending from Jordan south to Mozambique. It is some 4,000 mi (6,400 km) long and averages 30–40 mi (50–65 km) wide. The rift has been forming for some 30 million years, as Africa and the Arabian Peninsula separate. Its main branch, the Eastern Rift Valley, is occupied in the north by the JORDAN RIVER, the DEAD SEA, and the Gulf of AQABA. It continues south along the RED SEA to several lakes in Kenya, and on to the Indian Ocean near Beira, Mozambique. Its W branch, the Western Rift Valley, extends north from the N end of Lake MALAWI in an arc that includes Lakes Rukwa, TANGANYIKA, Kivu, EDWARD, and ALBERT.

Great St. Bernard Pass *ancient* Mons Jovis. Pass in the ALPS. At 8,100 ft (2,469 m), it lies on the Italian–Swiss border and connects Valais, Switzerland, with Aosta, Italy. Historically the most important transalpine route, it was often used by pilgrims to Rome and later by medieval armies. In 1800 it was crossed by NAPOLEON and his 40,000 troops. A famous hospice on the pass, founded by St. Bernard of Menthon in the 11th cent., is still kept by Augustinian monks who, with their ST. BERNARD dogs, provide services to travelers. Open only five months a year, it has been partly superseded by a tunnel beneath the pass.

Great Salt Lake Lake, N Utah. It is the largest inland body of salt water in the W Hemisphere and one of the most saline in the world. It fluctuates greatly in size; its surface area has varied from about 2,400 sq mi (6,200 sq km) in 1873 and the mid-1980s to about 950 sq mi (2,460 sq km) in 1963. Surrounded by stretches of sand, salt land, and marsh, the shallow lake remains isolated, though in recent years it has become important as a source of minerals, a tourist area, and a wildlife preserve.

Great Schism See Western SCHISM

great sea otter See SEA OTTER

Great Slave Lake Lake, S central Northwest Territories. Named for the Slave Indians, it is fed by several rivers, including the Slave, and drained by the MACKENZIE RIVER. The lake, with an area of 11,031 sq mi (28,570 sq km), is the fifth largest in N. America, with a maximum depth of more than 2,000 ft (600 m). While supporting a fishing industry, the lake is an integral part of the Mackenzie River waterway.

Great Smoky Mountains W range of the APPALACHIAN MTNS. It extends along the N. Carolina–Tennessee boundary and blends into the BLUE RIDGE Mtns. to the east. The highest part lies within the GREAT SMOKY MTNS. NATIONAL PARK and includes Clingmans Dome, which at 6,643 ft (2,025 m) is the highest peak. Covered by forests, it was originally the domain of the CHEROKEE. A popular resort area, it includes part of the APPALACHIAN NATIONAL SCENIC TRAIL, and the Blue Ridge Parkway.

Great Smoky Mountains National Park National preserve, E Tennessee and W N. Carolina. It is 20 mi (32 km) wide and extends southwest for 54 mi (87 km) from the Pigeon River to the Little Tennessee River. Established in 1934 to preserve the U.S.'s last remaining sizable area of southern primeval hardwood forest, it covers 520,269 acres (210,553 hectares) and contains some of the highest peaks in the APPALACHIAN MTNS. Lower elevations have mountain laurel, rhododendron, and azaleas. It was designated a WORLD HERITAGE SITE in 1983.

Great Society Slogan used in 1965 by Pres. Lyndon JOHNSON to identify his legislative program of national reform. In his first State of the Union address, Johnson described his vision of a "Great Society" that would include a "war on poverty" and federal support for education, medical care for the elderly, and legal protection for blacks deprived of voting rights by state regulations. Congress enacted almost all his programs, the largest number of legislative programs since the NEW DEAL. See also CIVIL RIGHTS ACT OF 1964, MEDICARE AND MEDICAID.

Great Trek Emigration of 12,000–14,000 AFRIKANERS from Cape Colony, S. Africa, between 1835 and the early 1840s, in rebellion against British policies and in search of fresh pasturelands. The trek, regarded by Afrikaners as the origin of the S. African nation, enabled the settlers to penetrate Natal and the Highveld and carry white settlement north to the Limpopo River.

Great Victoria Desert Arid region, WESTERN AUSTRALIA and S. Australia. Lying between Gibson Desert on the north and Nullarbor Plain on the south, it extends east from Kalgoorlie almost to the Stuart Range. Much of its E end is occupied by aboriginal reserves. A vast expanse of sand hills, it is crossed by the Laverton–Warburton Mission Track, which links the mission station in the Warburton Range with Laverton, 350 mi (560 km) southwest. There are several national parks and reserves in the area.

Great Wall (of China) *Chinese* **Wanli Changcheng** \'wän-'lē-'chäŋ-'cheŋ\ Defensive wall, N China. Perhaps the largest building-construction project ever carried out, it runs (with all its branches) at least 4,000 mi (6,400 km) east to west. Parts of the fortification date from the 4th cent. B.C. In 214 B.C. SHI HUANGDI connected existing defensive walls into a single system fortified by watchtowers. Originally constructed partly of masonry and earth, it was faced with brick in its E portion. It was rebuilt in later times, especially in the 15th–16th cent. The basic wall is about 30 ft (9 m) high, and the towers rise to about 40 ft (12 m). It was designated a WORLD HERITAGE SITE in 1987.

great white shark *or* **white shark** Large, aggressive SHARK (*Carcharodon carcharias,* family Isuridae), considered the species most dangerous to humans. It is found in tropical and temperate regions of all oceans and is noted for its voracious appetite. It is powerfully built, with a crescent-shaped tail and large, saw-edged, triangular teeth. It may reach a length of about 35 ft (11 m) and is generally gray or bluish, shading suddenly into a whitish belly. Though widely feared, it rarely kills humans and is itself probably endangered.

Great Zimbabwe See ZIMBABWE

grebe Any of about 18 species of diving birds (family Podicipedidae) found in most tropical and temperate areas and often in subarctic regions. Grebes have a pointed bill, short narrow wings, and a vestigial tail. The position of their legs, set at the rear of the body, makes walking awkward. Courting or rival males perform elaborate aquatic dances in pairs. Species range from about 8 to 29 in. (21–73 cm) long.

Greco, El (Spanish: "The Greek") *orig.* Domenikos Theotokopoulos (c.1541–1614) Cretan-Spanish painter, the first great master of Spanish painting. He was in Venice until 1566–70 and may have studied in TITIAN's workshop. His first commission in Spain (1577) was for church altarpieces in Toledo (1577–79); the paintings *The Assumption of the Virgin* and *The Trinity* show the influence of Titian and MICHELANGELO. Their elongated human figures became his signature style. His masterpiece, *The Burial of the Count of Orgaz* (1586–88), portrays a supernatural, semiabstract vision of heaven above, filled with tall, phantomlike figures, and a normal view of earth below. After 1590 his output was prodigious. His major commissions included the complete altar complex for the Hospital de la Caridad at Illescas (1603–5), for which he also worked as architect and sculptor. He excelled as a portraitist. Two landscapes survive, notably his *View of Toledo* (c.1610).

Greco–Persian Wars See PERSIAN WARS

Greco-Roman wrestling Style of WRESTLING in which the legs are prohibited from being used to obtain a fall and in which no holds may be taken below the waist. It originated in France in the early 19th cent., in imitation of classical Greek and Roman representations of the sport. Until the acceptance of freestyle wrestling in the late 20th cent., it was the style practiced exclusively in Olympic and international amateur competition.

Greco–Turkish Wars (1897, 1921–22) Two military conflicts between the Greeks and the Turks. The first, or Thirty Days' War, took place after an 1896 rebellion on Turkish-ruled Crete between Christian residents and their Muslim rulers. Greek troops occupied the island in 1897, but the European powers imposed a blockade to prevent assistance to the island. After the Greeks were defeated in Thessaly, a peace treaty forced the Greeks to withdraw; Turkish troops also left Crete, which had been made an international protectorate and was later (1913) ceded to Greece. The second war occurred when the Greeks attempted to claim territories assigned to them after World War I. In 1921 Greek forces launched an offensive in Anatolia against nationalist Turks, but were driven out by M. K. ATATURK; a revised treaty (1923) returned the disputed territories to Turkey.

Greece *officially* **Hellenic Republic** *Greek* **Ellás** \e-'läs\ *ancient* Hellas. Country, BALKAN PENINSULA, S Europe. Area: 50,949 sq mi (131,957 sq km). Population (2000): 10,562,000. Capital: ATHENS. The people are mainly ethnic Greek. Lan-

GREECE

Scale 1: 11,646,000

0   50   100 mi
0   80   160 km

©1999, Encyclopædia Britannica, Inc.

guage: Greek (official). Religion: Greek Orthodoxy (official). Currency: euro. The land, with its 2,000-odd islands and 2,500-mi (4,000-km) coastline, is intimately linked with the sea. It is mountainous, with less than a fourth in lowland, much of this as coastal plains along the Aegean or mountain valleys and small plains near river mouths. The country's interior is dominated by the Pindus Mtns., which extend from Albania on Greece's NW border into the PELOPONNESE. Mt. OLYMPUS is the country's highest peak. Among its islands are the AEGEAN and IONIAN groups and CRETE. Greece has a Mediterranean climate. It has an advanced developing, mainly private-enterprise economy based on agriculture, manufacturing, and tourism. It is a multiparty republic with one legislative house; the chief of state is the president, and the head of government is the prime minister. The earliest urban society in Greece was the palace-centered MINOAN civilization, which reached its height on Crete about 2000 B.C. It was succeeded by the mainland MYCENAEAN civilization, which arose about 1600 B.C. following a wave of Indo-European invasions. Around 1200 B.C. a second wave of invasions destroyed the BRONZE AGE cultures, and a dark age followed, known mostly through the epics of HOMER. At the end of this time, classical Greece began to emerge (c.750 B.C.) as a collection of independent city-states, including SPARTA in the Peloponnese and ATHENS in Attica. The civilization reached its zenith after repelling the Persians at the beginning of the 5th cent. B.C. (see PERSIAN WARS) and began to decline after the civil strife of the PELOPONNESIAN WAR at the century's end. In 338 B.C. the Greek city-states were taken over by PHILIP II of Macedon, and Greek culture was spread by Philip's son ALEXANDER THE GREAT throughout his empire. The Romans, themselves heavily influenced by Greek culture, conquered the Greek states in the 2nd cent. B.C. After the fall of Rome, Greece remained part of the BYZANTINE EMPIRE until the mid-15th cent., when it became part of the expanding OTTOMAN EMPIRE; it gained its independence in 1832. It was occupied by Nazi Germany during World War II. Civil war followed and lasted until 1949, when communist forces were defeated. A military junta ruled the country from 1967 to 1974, when democracy was restored and a referendum declared an end to the Greek monarchy. In 1981 Greece joined the European Community (see EUROPEAN UNION), the first E European country to do so. The 1990s upheavals in the Balkans strained Greece's relations with some neighboring states, including the former Yugoslav entity newly formed into the Republic of Macedonia.

Greek alphabet Writing system developed in Greece about 1000 B.C., the ancestor of all modern European ALPHABETS. Derived from the N. Semitic alphabet via that of the PHOENICIANS, it modified an all-consonant alphabet to represent vowels. Letters for sounds not found in Greek became the Greek letters *alpha, epsilon, iota, omicron,* and *upsilon,* representing the vowels *a, e, i, o,* and *u.* In 403 B.C. Athens officially adopted the Ionic version of the alphabet, which became standard. It had 24 letters, all capitals—ideal for monuments; various scripts better suited to handwriting were later derived from it.

Letters	English Spelling	Names	Letters	English Spelling	Names
A α	a	alpha	N ν	n	nu
B, β	b	beta	Ξ ξ	x	xi
Γ γ	g	gamma	O o	o	omicron
Δ δ	d	delta	Π π	p	pi
E ε	e	epsilon	P ρ	r, rh	rho
Z ζ	z	zeta	Σ σ, ς	s	sigma
H η	ē	eta	T τ	t	tau
Θ θ	th	theta	Υ υ	y, u	upsilon
I ι	i	iota	Φ φ	ph	phi
K κ	k	kappa	X χ	ch	chi
Λ λ	l	lambda	Ψ ψ	ps	psi
M μ	m	mu	Ω ω	ō	omega

Greek alphabet The modern Greek alphabet, with English sound equivalents.

Greek Civil War (1944–45, 1946–49). Two-stage conflict during which Greek communists tried to gain control of Greece. The two principal Greek guerrilla forces that had resisted Nazi Germany's occupation—the communist-controlled National Liberation Front–National Popular Liberation Army and the royalist Greek Democratic National Army—were brought together by the British (1944) in an uneasy coalition. Because the communist guerrillas refused to disband their forces, a bitter civil war broke out in late 1944 that was put down by British forces. After elections boycotted by the communists, the Greek king was restored to his throne. In 1946 a full-scale guerrilla war was reopened by the communists. The U.S. government took over the defense of Greece, creating the TRUMAN DOCTRINE as justification. After fierce skirmishes in the mountains, in 1949 the communists announced the end of open hostilities. An estimated 50,000 Greeks died in the conflict, which left a legacy of bitterness.

Greek fire Any of several flammable mixtures used in ancient and medieval warfare, particularly a petroleum-based mixture invented by the Byzantine Greeks in the 7th cent. Thrown in pots or discharged from tubes, it apparently caught fire spontaneously, and water could not put it out. Greek fire launched from tubes mounted on ship prows wreaked havoc on the Arab fleet attacking Constantinople in 673. Its effectiveness was a prime reason for the long survival of the Byzantine Empire. The recipe was so secret that its precise composition remains unknown.

Greek Independence, War of (1821–32) Rebellion of Greeks within the OTTOMAN EMPIRE. The revolt began in 1821 under the leadership of Alexandros Ypsilanti (1792–1828). He was soon defeated, but in the meantime other rebels in Greece and on several islands gained control of the Pelo-

ponnese and declared Greek independence (1822). Repeated invasions and internal rivalries prevented the Greeks from extending their control. In 1826, with Egyptian reinforcements, the Turks successfully invaded the Peloponnese, but the intervention of the European powers saved the Greek cause. A settlement in 1830 declared Greece an independent monarchical state; it was recognized by the Turks in 1832.

Greek language INDO-EUROPEAN LANGUAGE spoken mostly in Greece. Its history can be divided into four phases: Ancient Greek, Koine, Byzantine Greek, and Modern Greek. Ancient Greek included the Attic dialect, which was the language of Greek classical literature. The second phase, Koine (Hellenistic Greek), arose during Alexander the Great's reign in the 4th cent. B.C. and spread throughout the Hellenized world. Purists who rejected Koine as a corruption successfully advocated adoption of the Classical language for all writing. Thus, the written form, Byzantine Greek (5th–15th cent. A.D.), stayed rooted in the Attic tradition. Modern Greek, dating from the 15th cent., has many local dialects. Standard Modern Greek, Greece's official language, is largely based on a form called demotic (used in popular speech).

Greek mythology Oral and literary traditions of the ancient Greeks concerning their gods and heroes and the nature and history of the cosmos. They are known today primarily from the classic works of HOMER, HESIOD, OVID, and the dramatists AESCHYLUS, SOPHOCLES, and EURIPIDES. The myths deal with the creation of the gods and the world, the struggle among the gods for supremacy, the gods' love affairs and quarrels, and the effects of their adventures and powers on the mortal world. The great stories of Greek mythology and legend include those of the TROJAN WAR, the voyage of ODYSSEUS, JASON's search for the Golden Fleece, the exploits of HERACLES, the adventures of THESEUS, and the tragedy of OEDIPUS. See also GREEK RELIGION.

Greek Orthodox Church Independent Eastern Orthodox church of Greece. The term is sometimes used erroneously for EASTERN ORTHODOXY in general. Since its independence from the patriarch of Constantinople (1833), it has been governed by 67 metropolitan bishops, presided over by an archbishop.

Greek religion Beliefs, rituals, and mythology of the ancient Greeks. Though the worship of the sky god ZEUS began as early as the 2nd millennium B.C., Greek religion in the established sense began around 750 B.C. and lasted for over a thousand years, extending its influence throughout the Mediterranean world and beyond. The Greek gods controlled various natural and social forces (e.g., POSEIDON the sea, HERA marriage). Different deities were worshiped in different localities, but HOMER's epics helped create a unified religion, in which the major gods were believed to live

Greek Gods and Goddesses

Aeolus	god of the winds	Helios	god of the sun
Aphrodite	goddess of love, beauty, and procreation	Hephaestus	god of fire and metalworking
		Hera	queen of heaven, goddess of marriage and women
Apollo	god of sunlight, prophecy, music, and poetry		
		Hermes	messenger god and god of commerce
Ares	god of war		
Artemis	goddess of the moon, hunting, and fertility	Hestia	goddess of the hearth
		Iris	goddess of the rainbow, messenger of the gods
Athena	goddess of wisdom		
Boreas	god of the north wind		
Cybele	goddess of fertility and the mountains	Morpheus	god of dreams
		Nemesis	goddess of vengeance
Demeter	goddess of fruit, crops, and vegetation	Nike	goddess of victory
		Pan	god of pastures, forests, and herds
Dionysus	god of wine		
Eos	goddess of the dawn	Persephone	goddess of the underworld
Eros	god of love		
Gaea	goddess of the earth	Poseidon	god of the sea
Hades	god of the underworld	Rhea	mother of the gods
Hebe	goddess of youth	Selene	goddess of the moon
Hecate	goddess of magic, ghosts, and witchcraft	Uranus	god of the sky
		Zeus	lord of heaven

on Mt. OLYMPUS under the rule of Zeus. The Greeks also worshiped gods of the countryside: PAN, NYMPHS, naiads, DRYADS, NEREIDS, and satyrs (see SATYR AND SILENUS), along with the FURIES and the FATES. Heroes from the past were also venerated. Animal sacrifices were of great importance; other cultic activities included prayers, libations, processions, athletic contests, and divination through ORACLES. Death was seen as a hateful state; the dead lived in the realm of HADES, and only heroes enjoyed ELYSIUM. Great wrongdoers suffered in TARTARUS. MYSTERY RELIGIONS emerged to satisfy the desire for personal guidance, salvation, and immortality. Greek religion lost its last great advocate with the death of JULIAN in A.D. 363. See also GREEK MYTHOLOGY.

Greek Revival Architectural style, based on 5th-cent.-B.C. Greek temples, which spread throughout Europe and the U.S. in the early 19th cent. Architects often tacked majestic facades with Grecian columns onto existing buildings; banks and institutions became imitation Doric temples, and Greek Revival houses often sport large PORTICOES made up of heavy PILASTERS and reinterpreted pediments. The British Museum (1847), utilizing the Greek Ionic ORDER on a massive scale, is the most powerful English example of the style. See also NEOCLASSICAL ARCHITECTURE.

Greeley, Horace (1811–1872) U.S. newspaper editor and political leader. Born in Amherst, N.H., he moved to New York City, where he edited a literary magazine and weeklies for the Whig Party. In 1841 he founded the highly influential *New York Tribune,* a daily paper dedicated to reforms, economic progress, and the elevation of the masses. He became known especially for his articulation of the North's antislavery sentiments in the 1850s. His unrealized lifelong ambitions for public office culminated in 1872 in an unsuccessful run for president.

Horace Greeley Watercolor by Thomas Nast, 1872

Green, Adolph See Betty COMDEN

Green, Hetty *orig.* Henrietta Howland Robinson (1835–1916) U.S. financier, reputedly the wealthiest U.S. woman of her time. She was born in New Bedford, Mass. In 1865 her father and aunt both died, leaving her an estate valued at $10 million. By shrewd management she increased it to more than $100 million at her death.

Green, William (1873–1952) U.S. labor leader, president of the American Federation of Labor (AFL). Born in Coshocton, Ohio, he was a coal miner from age 16 and worked his way up to become president of the AFL in 1924, a post he kept until his death. The formation in 1935 of the Committee for Industrial Organization (CIO), headed by John L. LEWIS, led to bitter public disputes, ending in the expulsion of the CIO from the AFL in 1936. See also AFL-CIO, LABOR UNION.

Greenaway, Kate (*orig.* Catherine) (1846–1901) British children's-book illustrator. She studied art in London, and in 1868 began to exhibit drawings, contribute illustrations to magazines, and de-

Kate Greenaway, illustration for *Marigold Garden,* 1885

sign Christmas and Valentine cards. Her first book, *Under the Window* (1878), was followed by *The Birthday Book* (1880), *Mother Goose* (1881), and many others that were enormously successful and strongly affected contemporary fashions. Her yearly almanacs (1888–97) also became very popular.

Greenback movement (1868–88) Campaign mainly by U.S. farmers to maintain or increase the amount of paper money in circulation. To finance the AMERICAN CIVIL WAR the U.S. government issued paper money not backed by gold and printed in green ink, called greenbacks. After the war, farmers and others who wanted to maintain high prices opposed calls for an end to greenbacks. The depression after the panic of 1873 intensified the demand for more greenbacks or unlimited silver coinage (see FREE SILVER MOVEMENT). The Resumption Act (1875) provided for redemption of greenbacks in gold; the newly formed Greenback-Labor Party sought its repeal. In 1878 it elected 14 members of Congress, but support waned after 1884.

Green Bank equation See DRAKE EQUATION

Green Bay City (pop., 1996 est.: 102,000), NE Wisconsin. Located on the Fox River at Green Bay, on Lake MICHIGAN, it was the site of French trading posts from 1634 until the WAR OF 1812. With the opening of the ERIE CANAL, it developed as a lumbering and agricultural center and a major shipping port. The city is famous for its professional football team, the Green Bay Packers (founded in 1919).

Green Berets \bə-ˈrāz\ *or* **Special Forces** Elite unit of the U.S. Army specializing in counterinsurgency. The Green Berets (whose berets can be colors other than green) came into being in 1952. They were active in the Vietnam War, and they have been sent to areas of conflict around the world to assist governments supported by the U.S. to employ guerrilla warfare tactics against insurgents.

Greenberg, Clement (1909–1994) U.S. art critic. After graduating from Syracuse Univ., he returned to his native New York City and began writing for such publications as *Partisan Review* and *The Nation,* promoting an approach to looking at art that became known as "Greenberg formalism." The chief arbiter of art in the U.S. in the 1940s and '50s, he was a champion of ABSTRACT EXPRESSIONISM and of its leading exponent, Jackson POLLOCK. He also promoted the work of many others, including Helen FRANKENTHALER, Mark ROTHKO, and David SMITH. He disavowed such later movements as POP ART and wrote little after the 1960s.

Greenberg, Hank (*orig.* Henry Benjamin) (1911–1986) U.S. baseball player. Born in the Bronx, N.Y., he began his career at first base with the Detroit Tigers in 1933. He twice helped the Tigers win the World Series (1935, 1940) and was named the American League's Most Valuable Player both years. In 1938 he hit 58 home runs. He often encountered prejudice on the field, but his refusal to play on Jewish holidays won him praise. He served four years in the military in World War II, and retired in 1948. He was general manager of the Cleveland Indians until 1957 and of the Chicago White Sox 1959–63. The first Jewish star player in the major leagues, he was elected to the Baseball Hall of Fame in 1956.

Greenberg, Joseph H(arold) (1915–2001) U.S. anthropologist and linguist. Born in Brooklyn, N.Y., he received his PhD from Northwestern Univ. He developed an approach he termed "mass" or "multilateral" comparison, which involved looking for phonetic resemblances among words in many languages simultaneously. His 1963 classification of AFRICAN LANGUAGES into four families (AFROASIATIC, NIGER-CONGO, NILO-SAHARAN, and KHOISAN) was widely accepted. However, his 1987 classification of all AMERICAN INDIAN LANGUAGES into just two families, Amerind and Na-Dene (see ATHABASKAN LANGUAGES), was generally rejected.

Greene, Charles Sumner and Henry Mather (1868–1957, 1870–1954) U.S. architects. Born in Brighton, Ohio, the Greene brothers established a partnership in Pasadena, Cal., in 1894. In the years 1904–11, they pioneered the influential California bungalow, a single-storied house with a low-pitched roof. Their bungalows feature wide, low volumes, balconies and verandas to meld indoor and outdoor space, and frank utilization of wood members (sticks), exquisitely worked and extending gracefully beyond the edges of the spreading GABLES.

Greene, (Henry) Graham (1904–1991) British author. Beginning around 1930, he worked as a freelance journalist for several decades, during which he traveled widely. *Stamboul Train* (1932; also titled *Orient Express*; film, 1934) was the first of his "entertainments," thrillers with considerable moral complexity and depth; others included *The Confidential Agent* (1939; film, 1945) and *The Third Man* (1949; film, 1949). His finest novels—*Brighton Rock* (1938; film, 1948), *The Power and the Glory* (1940; film, 1962), *The Heart of the Matter* (1948; film, 1954), and *The End of the Affair* (1951; film, 1999)—all have distinctly religious themes. Third-world nations on the brink of political upheaval were the settings of several of his novels, including *The Quiet American* (1955; film, 1957) and *Our Man in Havana* (1958; film, 1959).

Greene, Nathanael (1742–1786) American Revolutionary general. Born in Potowomut, R.I., he served as commander of the colonial militia (1775), then led troops in the Continental Army at Boston and New York, and in the battles at Trenton, Brandywine, and Germantown. At age 36 he succeeded Gen. Horatio GATES as commander in chief of the S army (1778), and his strategy so weakened the British troops that Gen. Charles CORNWALLIS abandoned plans to conquer N. Carolina (1781). By late June Greene had forced the British back to Charleston.

greenhouse Building designed for the protection of tender or out-of-season plants against excessive cold or heat. It is usually a glass- or plastic-enclosed structure with a framing of aluminum, galvanized steel, or such woods as redwood, cedar, or cypress. It is heated partly by the sun and partly by artificial means. This controlled environment can be adapted to the needs of particular plants.

greenhouse effect Warming of the earth's surface and lower atmosphere that tends to intensify with an increase in atmospheric CARBON DIOXIDE and certain other gases. Visible light from the sun heats the earth's surface. Part of this energy is reradiated in the form of long-wave INFRARED RADIATION, much of which is absorbed by molecules of carbon dioxide and water vapor in the atmosphere and reradiated back toward the surface as more heat. This process is analogous to the glass panes of a greenhouse that transmit sunlight but hold in heat. The trapping of infrared radiation causes the earth's surface and lower atmosphere to warm more than they otherwise would, making the surface habitable. The increase in atmospheric carbon dioxide caused by widespread combustion of FOSSIL FUELS may intensify the greenhouse effect and cause long-term climatic changes. Increases in such trace gases as CHLOROFLUORO-CARBONS, NITROUS OXIDE, and METHANE may aggravate greenhouse conditions. It is estimated that since the begin-

ning of the INDUSTRIAL REVOLUTION atmospheric carbon dioxide has increased 30% and methane has doubled. Today the U.S. is responsible for about one-quarter of all human-produced greenhouse-gas emissions. See also GLOBAL WARMING.

Greenland *Danish* **Grønland** \ˈgrœn-ˌlän\ *Greenlandic* **Kalaallit Nunaat** \kä-ˈlät-lēt-nû-ˈnät\ Island (pop., 2000: 56,000), NE N. America. The world's largest island (excluding Australia), it covers 840,000 sq mi (2,175,600 sq km). It

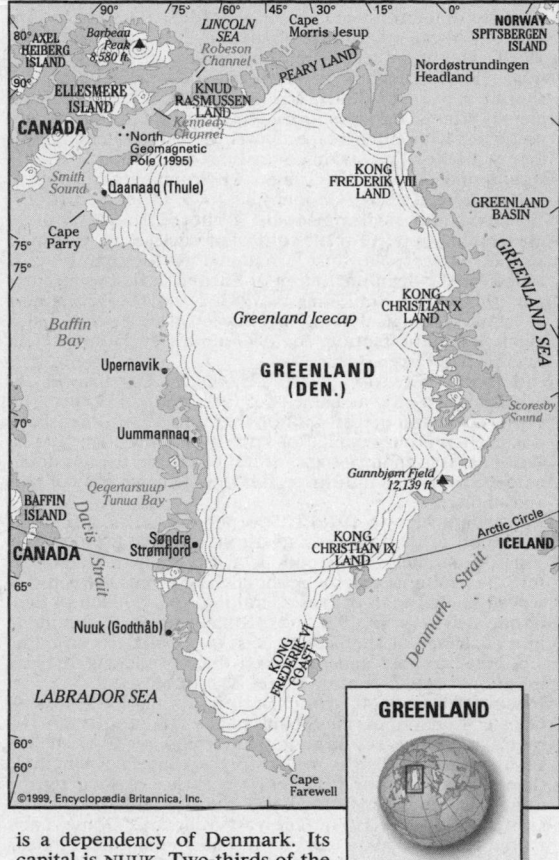

is a dependency of Denmark. Its capital is NUUK. Two-thirds of the island lies within the Arctic Circle; it is dominated by the massive GREENLAND ICE SHEET. More than four-fifths of the population are native Greenlanders, principally of Inuit (see ESKIMO) descent. The Inuit probably crossed to NW Greenland from N. America, along the islands of the Canadian Arctic, from 4000 B.C. to A.D. 1000. The Norwegian ERIK THE RED visited Greenland in 982; his son, LEIF ERIKSSON THE LUCKY, introduced Christianity in the 11th cent. Greenland came under joint Danish-Norwegian rule in the late 14th cent. The Norse settlements disappeared, but Greenland was recolonized by Denmark in 1721. It became part of the kingdom of Denmark in 1953, and home rule was established in 1979.

Greenland Ice Sheet Single ice cap, GREENLAND. Covering about 80% of the island of Greenland, it is the largest ice mass in the Northern Hemisphere, second worldwide only to the Antarctic. It extends 1,570 mi (2,530 km) north to south, and has a maximum width of 680 mi (1,094 km) near its N margin; its average thickness is about 5,000 ft (1,500 m). The ice sheet rises to two domes; the N dome, reaching more than 10,000 ft (3,000 m), is its thickest and coldest point.

Green Mountains Part of the APPALACHIAN MTNS. system. It extends for 250 mi (400 km) through the center of Vermont,

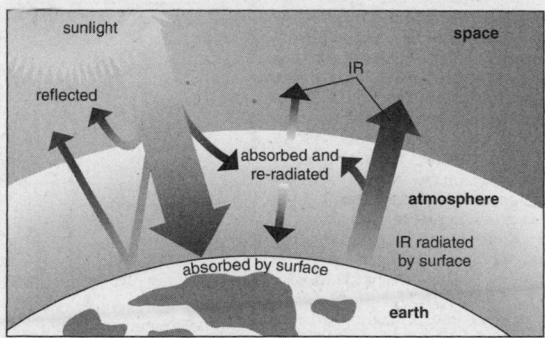

Greenhouse effect Some incoming sunlight is reflected by the earth's atmosphere and surface, but most is absorbed by the surface, which is warmed. Infrared (IR) radiation is then emitted from the surface. Some IR radiation escapes to space, but some is absorbed by the atmosphere's greenhouse gases (especially carbon dioxide, water, and methane) and reradiated in all directions, some to space and some back toward the surface, where it further warms the surface and lower atmosphere.

and has a maximum width of 30 mi (50 km). The highest peak is Mt. Mansfield, at 4,393 ft (1,339 m). Known for their skiing facilities, the mountains are traversed by the Long Trail (part of the APPALACHIAN NATIONAL SCENIC TRAIL). Green Mtns. National Forest covers 214,000 acres (86,600 hectares).

green revolution Great increase in production of food grains (especially WHEAT and RICE) that resulted in large part from the introduction into developing countries of new, high-yielding varieties, beginning in the mid-20th cent. Its early dramatic successes were in Mexico and in the Indian subcontinent, where millions of lives may have been saved. The new varieties require large amounts of irrigation, chemical fertilizers, and pesticides, raising concerns about cost, sustainability, and potentially harmful environmental effects. Farmers unable to afford the fertilizers and pesticides have often reaped lower yields with these grains than with the older strains. See also Norman BORLAUG.

Greens, the *German* die Grünen. Environmentalist political party founded in W. Germany in 1979. Composed of 250 ecological and environmentalist groups, it sought to organize public support for the control of nuclear energy and of air and water pollution. A national party from 1980, it called for the demilitarization of Europe. It first won representation in the Bundestag in 1983. It experienced almost constant ideological tensions between its left wing and a more pragmatic faction. By 1990 almost every country in Europe had Green parties.

Greensboro City (pop., 2001: 223,000), N. Carolina. Established in 1808, it was named for Gen. Nathanael GREENE. Toward the end of the AMERICAN CIVIL WAR, Greensboro was the temporary capital of both the Confederacy and N. Carolina. It is an important insurance center; textiles dominate its diversified industries. It is the site of several colleges and universities.

Greenspan, Alan (b.1926) U.S. economist and chairman of the board of the FEDERAL RESERVE SYSTEM. Born in New York, he studied the saxophone at the Juilliard School before becoming a private economic consultant. Greenspan served as chairman of Pres. Gerald FORD's Council of Economic Advisers. In 1987 Pres. Ronald REAGAN appointed him chairman of the Federal Reserve Board, a position he continued to hold under the next three presidents, fighting inflation through controlling the DISCOUNT RATE.

Greenwich \'gre-nich, 'gri-nij\ Borough (pop., 1991: 201,000), Greater London, on the S bank of the THAMES RIVER. The meridian that passes through the borough serves as the basis for standard time as well as for reckonings of longitude throughout the world. Greenwich Park, enclosed by the duke of Gloucester in 1423, was the site of the Royal Observatory (1675–c.1958). The vast Millennial Dome, completed 1998, was used to usher in millennium celebrations.

Greenwich Mean Time (GMT) Former name for mean solar time of the longitude (0°) of the former Royal Observatory at Greenwich, England, or Greenwich meridian. GMT was used to avoid potentially confusing references to local time systems (zones). In accord with tradition, 0000 GMT (denoting the start of a solar day) occurred at noon. In 1925 the system was changed so that the day (like the civil day) began at midnight. Some confusion resulted, and in 1928 the International Astronomical Union changed the designation to UNIVERSAL TIME. The term GMT is still used for some purposes (including navigation) in English-speaking countries.

Greenwich Village Residential section, Lower MANHATTAN, NEW YORK CITY. A village settlement during colonial times, it became, after 1910, a rendezvous for writers, artists, students, bohemians, and intellectuals. The quaintness of its old townhouses led to rising rents in the 1980s and 1990s. Washington Square, in its center, is dominated by Washington Arch and NEW YORK UNIV.

Gregorian calendar Solar dating system now in general use. It was proclaimed in 1582 by Pope GREGORY XIII as a reform of the Julian calendar, whose solar year comprised 365¼ days. A slight inaccuracy in the measurement of the solar year caused the calendar dates of the seasons to regress almost one day per century; by Pope Gregory's time, they were 10 days out of sync with the seasons. In 1582, to bring the vernal equinox (and thus Easter) back to its proper date, 10 days were dropped (Oct. 5 became Oct. 15). The Gregorian calendar differs from the Julian only in that no century year is a leap year unless it is exactly divisible by 400 (e.g., 1600, 2000). A further refinement, the designation of years evenly divisible by 4,000 as common (not leap) years, will keep the calendar accurate to within one day in 20,000 years.

Gregorian chant Liturgical music of the Roman Catholic church consisting of unaccompanied melody sung in unison to Latin words. It is named for Pope GREGORY I the Great, who may have contributed to its collection and codification. Of the five bodies of medieval Latin liturgical music, it is the dominant repertoire, and the name is often used to include them all. It apparently derived principally from Jewish cantillation. Chant has traditionally been performed at the MASS and daily monastic prayer services. The melodies are classified as belonging to one or another of the eight CHURCH MODES. Chant rhythm is not strictly metrical, and its notation does not indicate rhythm. Since the Second VATICAN COUNCIL, the performance of chant has diminished greatly. See also CANTUS FIRMUS.

Gregory, Augusta *orig.* Isabella Augusta Persse *known as* **Lady Gregory** (1852–1932) Irish playwright. Important in the IRISH LITERARY RENAISSANCE, with W. B. YEATS she helped found the ABBEY THEATRE. She wrote many dialect comedies based on Irish peasant life, including those collected in *Seven Short Plays* (1909). She also translated plays by Molière and others into an Anglo-Irish dialect called Kiltartan, and translated and arranged Irish sagas into continuous narratives, published as *Cuchulain of Muirthemne* (1902) and *Gods and Fighting Men* (1904).

Gregory I, St. *known as* **Gregory the Great** (c.540–604) Pope (590–604) and doctor (teacher) of the church. After attaining the office of prefect, Rome's highest civil office (c.572–574), he felt called to the religious life. He built several monasteries and served as a papal representative before being elected pope in 590. He became the architect of the medieval papacy. He strove to curb corruption by centralizing the papal administration. In 598 he won temporary peace with the Lombards. Eager to convert pagan peoples, Gregory sent AUGUSTINE OF CANTERBURY on a mission to England (596). Under Gregory, Gothic Arian Spain became reconciled with Rome. He laid the basis for the PAPAL STATES. He was a strong opponent of slavery, and he extended tolerance to Jews and heathens. He wrote the *Pastoral Rule,* a guide for church government. His extensive recodification of the liturgy and chant led to his name being given to GREGORIAN CHANT. He is remembered as perhaps the greatest of all the medieval popes.

Gregory VII, St. *orig.* Hildebrand (c.1020–1085) Pope (1073–85). One of the great medieval reformers, Gregory attacked simony and clerical marriage and insisted that his papal legates had authority over local bishops. He is remembered chiefly for his conflict with Emperor HENRY IV in the INVESTITURE CONTROVERSY. Gregory's excommunication of the emperor gave rise to a bitter quarrel that ended with Henry begging forgiveness in a memorable scene in the snow at Canossa, Italy, in 1077. A renewed quarrel led Gregory to excommunicate him again in 1080, and Henry's forces

Gregory VII laying a ban of excommunication on the clergy, 12th cent.

took Rome in 1084. Gregory was rescued by ROBERT GUISCARD but forced to withdraw to Salerno, where he died.

Gregory IX *orig.* Ugo di Segni (c.1170–1241) Pope (1227–41). A defender of papal authority, in 1227 he excommunicated FREDERICK II when the emperor delayed in keeping his pledge to lead a crusade. Gregory ordered an attack on the kingdom of Sicily in the emperor's absence, but his forces were defeated. In 1234 he published the Decretals, a code of canon law that remained fundamental to Catholicism until World War I. To attack heresy, he founded the papal IN-QUISITION. Frederick's invasion of Sardinia, a papal fief, led Gregory to renew his excommunication (1239).

Gregory XIII *orig.* Ugo Buoncompagni (1502–1585) Pope (1572–85) who promulgated the GREGORIAN CALENDAR. He taught at the Univ. of Bologna, attended the Council of TRENT, and was elected pope in 1572. A promoter of the COUNTER-REFORMATION, he compiled the *Index librorum prohibitorum* and founded several Jesuit colleges and seminaries. Aided by an astronomer and a mathematician, he corrected the errors in the Julian calendar and issued the Gregorian calendar (1582), which was later adopted worldwide.

Gregory of Tours \'tůr\, **St.** *orig.* Georgius Florentius (538/ 539–594/595) Frankish bishop and writer. Born into an aristocratic family that had supplied several bishops of what is today central France, Gregory succeeded his cousin as bishop of Tours in 573. The complicated political situation involved him in numerous political events. His fame rests on his *History of the Franks,* a chief source for knowledge of the 6th-cent. Franco-Roman kingdom. His other writings, including *Lives of the Fathers,* afford unique evidence of life in Merovingian France.

Gregory the Great See St. GREGORY I

Grenada \grə-'nā-də\ Self-governing state, WINDWARD IS-LANDS, W. Indies. Area: 133 sq mi (344 sq km). Population (2000): 102,000. Capital: SAINT GEORGE'S. Blacks, mulattoes, and E. Indians make up most of the population. Language: English (official). Religion: Roman Catholicism. Currency: Eastern Caribbean dollar. Grenada is the most

GRENADA
Scale 1: 1,100,000
0   8 mi
0   6   12 km

southerly of the Windward Islands, lying about 100 mi (160 km) north of Venezuela; its territory includes the S GRENADINES. Volcanic in origin, it is dominated by a thickly forested mountain ridge rising to 2,757 ft (840 m) at Mt. St. Catherine. The S coast is indented with beaches and natural harbors. Its tropical maritime climate supports rich vegetation. Often called the Isle of Spice, it is known for its nutmeg, cinnamon, and vanilla, as well as cocoa. It has a developing market economy dependent on agricultural exports and tourism. The chief of state is the British sovereign, represented by the governor-general; the head of government is the prime minister. The warlike CARIB Indians dominated Grenada when Christopher COLUMBUS sighted the island in 1498 and named it Concepción; they ruled it for the next 150 years. In 1672 it became subject to the French crown and re-

mained so until 1762, when British forces captured it. In 1833 the island's black slaves were freed. Grenada was the headquarters of the government of the British Windward Islands 1885–1958 and a member of the W. Indies Federation 1958–62. It became a self-governing state in association with Britain in 1967 and gained its independence in 1974. In 1979 a left-wing government took control in a bloodless coup. Relations with its U.S.-oriented Latin-American neighbors became strained as Grenada leaned toward Cuba and the Soviet bloc. In order to counteract this trend, the U.S. invaded the island in 1983; democratic self-government was reestablished in 1984.

grenade Small explosive, chemical, or gas bomb used at short range. Invented in the 15th cent., it became so important that 17th-cent. European armies had specially trained grenade throwers, or grenadiers. After about 1750 grenades were largely abandoned due to the increasing range and accuracy of firearms. Their effectiveness in World War I TRENCH WARFARE made them a standard part of combat equipment. Most common is the explosive grenade, with a core of high explosive in an iron jacket and a fuse that detonates it either on impact or after a brief delay. Chemical and gas grenades generally burn rather than explode.

Grenadines \ˌgre-nə-'dēnz\, **The** Chain of about 600 islands and islets, SE Lesser ANTILLES, W. INDIES. The islands span over 60 mi (100 km) at the E end of the Caribbean Sea. The N Grenadines are administratively part of ST. VINCENT AND THE GRENADINES, while the S islands are a dependency of GRENADA. Rainfall is low, and few of the islands are inhabited.

Grenoble \grə-'nóblə, *Engl* grə-'nō-bəl\ City (pop., 1999: 153,000), SE France. It lies along the Isère River, which divides the city into two parts. It is the former capital of the Dauphiné province. It was a center of the French RESIS-TANCE during World War II. Sites of interest include a 13th-cent. cathedral, the 15th-cent. Palais de Justice, and the Univ. of Grenoble (founded 1339).

Grettis saga Latest of the ICELANDERS' SAGAS, written around 1320. It tells of the brave and wellborn Grettir, who at 14 kills a man and is outlawed. He spends his years of exile performing brave deeds. Returning to Iceland, he saves the people from a ghost that is ravaging the countryside, which in dying curses him. Outlawed again, he is finally overwhelmed with the aid of witchcraft. The saga's distinction rests on its hero's complex character and its skillful incorporation of folklore motifs.

Gretzky, Wayne (Douglas) (b.1961) Canadian ice-hockey player, considered the greatest in the history of the game. Born in Brantford, Ontario, he was the youngest player and leading scorer in Junior League Cup competition in 1977. As center and captain for the Edmonton Oilers (1979–88), he led his team to four Stanley Cup victories. He was traded successively to the Los Angeles Kings (1988), the St. Louis Blues (1996), and the New York Rangers (1996), with whom he ended his career in 1999, by which time he held 61 National Hockey League records. He holds the all-time NHL records for goals (894), assists (1,963), and points (2,857). He is the only player to have been named most valuable player eight consecutive seasons (1979–87). His modesty and courtesy in an often brutal sport brought him respect as a model of sportsmanship.

Greuze \'grœz, *Engl* 'grə(r)z\, **Jean-Baptiste** (1725–1805) French painter. His first exhibited painting, *The Father Reading the Bible to His Children,* won him immediate success at the Salon of 1755. Throughout the 1760s he won acclaim with such sentimental genre paintings as *The Village Betrothal* (1761) and *Prodigal Son* (c.1765). When a large historical work he submitted to the Royal Academy was rejected, he refused to exhibit anywhere but his own studio for 30 years, earning a living with morality pictures and images of young women in innocent disarray, but in time his popularity waned. His drawings and portraits display great technical gifts.

Grévy \grā-'vē\, **(François-Paul-) Jules** (1807–1891) French president (1879–87) in the THIRD REPUBLIC. Leader of the liberal opposition in the legislature, he became president of the National Assembly (1871–73) and of the Chamber of Deputies (1876). As France's president he sought to minimize presidential powers, preferring a strong legislature. He resisted nationalist demands for revenge against Germany after the FRANCO—PRUSSIAN WAR and opposed colonial expansion.

Grew, Nehemiah (1641–1712) British botanist. His writings noted the existence of cells and coined such terms as radicle (for the embryonic root). His highly significant *Anatomy of Plants* (1682) contained the first thorough account of plant anatomy; its many excellent wood engravings represented the three-dimensional, microscopic structure of plant tissue. He discovered that the stamen (with its pollen) is the male sex organ and the pistil corresponds to the female sex organ. He is considered a founder of the science of plant anatomy.

Grey, 2nd Earl *orig.* Charles Grey (1764-1845) British politician and prime minister (1830–34). Grey entered Parliament in 1786 and soon became prominent among the aristocratic Whigs, led by C. J. FOX, in opposition to William PITT's conservative government. In 1806–7 Grey served as foreign secretary and leader of the Whigs. Having lost his posts, from 1815 to 1830 he was more patron than leader of the divided Whig opposition. In 1830 he became prime minister with popular backing for parliamentary reform. After considerable debate and conflict, he won adoption of the REFORM BILL OF 1832.

Grey, Lady Jane (1537–1554) Titular queen of England for nine days in 1553. The great-granddaughter of HENRY VII, she was married in May 1553 to the son of the duke of NORTHUMBERLAND. Northumberland persuaded the dying EDWARD VI to name as successor the Protestant Lady Jane; she was proclaimed queen on July 10. On July 19 Edward's Catholic half sister Mary Tudor (MARY I) was proclaimed queen after Lady Jane gladly relinquished the crown. She and her husband were committed to the Tower of London. Their death sentence was initially suspended, but her father's participation in Wyatt's rebellion against Mary sealed her fate, and she was beheaded.

Lady Jane Grey Panel attributed to Master John, c.1545

Grey, Zane *orig.* Pearl Grey (1872–1939) U.S. novelist. Born in Zanesville, Ohio, he began his career as a dentist. He first visited the American West in 1906. His first novel set there, *The Heritage of the Desert* (1910), achieved success, and his second, *Riders of the Purple Sage* (1912), became the most popular of all his novels. With these books he helped created a new literary genre, the WESTERN. His later westerns number more than 80. In 1918 he formed his own film production company. He remains one of the best-selling authors of all time.

greyhound *or* **grayhound** Fastest dog, one of the oldest breeds (dating from about 3000 B.C. in Egypt), and long symbolic of the aristocracy. It has a narrow head, long neck, deep chest, long, muscular hindquarters, and a short, smooth coat. It stands 25–27 in. (64–69 cm) high and weighs 60–70 lbs (27–32 kg). Streamlined and slender, it can reach a speed of about 45 mph (72 kph). Greyhounds may be used to hunt hares, deer, or foxes. They are frequently raced for sport.

Greyhound Lines, Inc. U.S. corporation that has provided the major intercity bus transportation in the U.S. and Canada. It was founded in 1926 as Motor Transit Management. Backed by the railroads, the company soon had a network of lines spreading across the country. It adopted its current name in 1930. By 1933 Greyhound's routes covered 40,000 mi (65,000 km). In the early 1980s deregulation led Greyhound to drop many local bus lines. In 1999 it was purchased by Canada's Laidlaw Inc.

greylag Most common Eurasian representative (*Anser anser*) of the so-called gray GOOSE, and ancestor of all Occidental domestic geese. It nests in temperate regions. It is pale gray with pink legs; the bill is pink in the eastern race and orange in the western race.

Grieg \'grig\, **Edvard (Hagerup)** (1843–1907) Norwegian composer. He studied music in Leipzig and later with Niels Gade in Copenhagen, where he became inspired with the ideal of a Norwegian national music. His incidental music to Henrik IBSEN's *Peer Gynt* (1875), which the playwright invited him to write, became, with his piano concerto (1868), his most popular work. His other works include *Symphonic Dances* (1897), *Lyric Suite* (1904), over 150 songs, and many works for piano, including 66 *Lyric Pieces* (1867–1901). By the end of his life he was a national institution, and he is still regarded as Norway's greatest composer.

Edvard Grieg

Grien, Hans Baldung See Hans BALDUNG

Griffes \'grif-əs\, **Charles T(omlinson)** (1884–1920) U.S. composer. Born in Elmira, N.Y., he studied music in Berlin, then taught at a boys' school in Tarrytown, N.Y., for the rest of his short life. His mature style combined Impressionism and orientalism. His principal works are for piano, though some were later orchestrated: *The Pleasure-Dome of Kubla Khan* (1912), a piano sonata (c.1912), and *Roman Sketches* (including "The White Peacock") (1915).

Griffith, Arthur (1872–1922) Irish nationalist, principal founder of SINN FÉIN. As a young man he edited political newspapers and urged passive resistance to British rule. He did not participate in the EASTER RISING (1916), but was jailed with other Sinn Féin members. In 1918 the Irish members of the House of Commons declared a republic and chose Eamon DE VALERA as president and Griffith as vice president. In 1921 Griffith led the Irish delegation to the self-government treaty conference and accepted partition, embodied in the Anglo—Irish Treaty. In 1922 de Valera resigned and Griffith was elected president. Exhausted from overwork, he died soon after.

Griffith, D(avid) W(ark) (1875–1948) U.S. film director. Born in Floydsfork, Ky., he initially sold film scenarios to the Biograph Co., which then hired him as a director (1908–13). In over 400 films for Biograph he developed filmmaking as an art form with such techniques as the close-up, the scenic long shot, and crosscutting, and helped to create the fadeout, fade-in, and soft-focus shots. He introduced such future stars as Mary PICKFORD and Lillian GISH. His epic dramas *The Birth of a Nation* (1915) and *Intolerance* (1916) greatly influenced later filmmakers. After cofounding UNITED ARTISTS CORP., he directed *Broken Blossoms* (1919), *Way Down East* (1920), and *Orphans of the Storm* (1921). His last films were *Abraham Lincoln* (1930) and *The Struggle* (1931). He is regarded as one of the seminal figures in the history of motion pictures.

Griffith Joyner, (Delorez) Florence *orig.* Delorez Florence Griffith (1959–1998) U.S. sprinter. Born in Los Angeles, she started running at 7 and attended UCLA. At the 1984 Olympics she won a silver medal in the 200-m race and became a celebrity with her long, decorated fingernails and eye-catching racing suits. In 1987 she married Al Joyner, an Olympic gold medalist and brother of Jackie JOYNER-KERSEE. At the 1988 Olympic trials, she set a world record in the 100-m sprint (10.49 sec); at the games themselves, "FloJo" captured three gold medals (in the 100-m, 200-m, and 4 x 100-m relay). Her world-record time in the 200 m (21.34 sec) and her earlier 100-m record still stood at the time of her death, attributed to a brain seizure.

Grillparzer \'gril-ˌpärt-sər\, **Franz** (1791–1872) Austrian dramatist. His early tragedies include *The Ancestress* (1817), *Sappho* (1818), and the pessimistic *The Golden Fleece*

(1821). *King Ottocar, His Rise and Fall* (1825), a story based on Napoleon's life, met censorship difficulties. *The Waves of Sea and Love* (1831) is often considered his greatest tragedy; another masterpiece is *A Dream Is Life* (1834), an Austrian *Faust*. His tragedies were belatedly recognized as the greatest works of the Austrian stage.

Grimké \'grim-kē\, **Sarah (Moore) and Angelina (Emily)** (1792–1873, 1805–1879) U.S. antislavery and women's-rights advocates. The sisters were born in Charleston, S.C., to a wealthy slaveholding family but developed an early dislike of slavery. In the mid-1820s they became Quakers and moved to the North. From 1835 they wrote letters and pamphlets urging Southern women to use moral force against slavery. They lectured throughout New England as the first female agents of the AMERICAN ANTI-SLAVERY SOCIETY, enlisting women in the cause and becoming pioneers in the women's-rights movement. In 1838 Angelina married Theodore WELD, and the sisters collaborated with him.

Grimm, Jacob (Ludwig Carl) and Wilhelm (Carl) (1785–1863, 1786–1859) German folklorists and philologists. They are most famous for *Kinder- und Hausmärchen* (1812–15), known in English as *Grimm's Fairy Tales*, a collection of 200 tales taken mostly from oral sources, which helped establish the science of folklore. Together and separately, they also produced many other scholarly studies and editions, including Jacob's *German Mythology* (1835), a highly influential study of pre-Christian German faith and superstition, and his *Deutsche Gram-*

Jacob and Wilhelm Grimm
Oil portrait by Elisabeth Jerichau-Baumann, 1855

matik (1819–37), in which he elaborates the important principle of historical linguistics now known as Grimm's law. In the 1840s the brothers began work on the *Deutsches Wörterbuch*, a vast historical dictionary of the German language that required several generations to complete and remains the standard work of its kind.

grinding machine MACHINE TOOL that uses a rotating abrasive grinding wheel to change the shape or dimensions of a hard, usually metallic, workpiece. Grinding is the most accurate of all the basic machining processes. All grinding machines use a wheel made from one of the manufactured ABRASIVES, silicon carbide or aluminum oxide. To grind a cylindrical form, the workpiece rotates as it is fed against the grinding wheel. To grind an internal surface, a small wheel moves inside the hollow of the workpiece, which is gripped in a rotating chuck.

Grinnell College \gri-'nel\ Private liberal-arts college in Grinnell, Iowa. It was the first college established west of the Mississippi River (1846) and the first U.S. college to establish a political-science department (1883). Total enrollment is about 1,300.

grippe See INFLUENZA

Gris \'grēs\, **Juan** *orig.* José Victoriano González Pérez (1887–1927) Spanish painter active in Paris. After studying engineering in Madrid, in 1906 he moved to Paris and began producing drawings in the Art Nouveau style. He became involved with the Cubist artists, notably Pablo PICASSO, and soon developed his own version of Synthetic CUBISM, a style more severe and classical than that of other Cubists. His technique included the use of paper collage.

grisaille \grē-'zī, grə-'zäl\ Painting technique by which an image is executed entirely in shades of gray and usually modeled to produce the illusion of sculpture or relief. It was used especially by 15th-cent. Flemish painters (e.g., Jan van EYCK's Ghent Altarpiece, 1432) and in the late 18th cent. to imitate classical sculpture in wall and ceiling decoration. In the 16th cent., grisaille enamels were developed in Limoges, France; the technique achieves a dramatic effect of light and shade.

grizzly bear Large N. American BROWN BEAR whose forms, including the Alaskan brown BEARS, are usually considered

races or subspecies of a single species (*Ursus arctos*). The more than 80 forms once ranged over open regions of W N. America from Mexico to Alaska, but their numbers have dwindled. They may grow to about 8 ft (2.5 m) long and weigh 900 lbs (400 kg). One variety, the Kodiak bear, is the largest living land carnivore, reaching lengths of more than 10 ft (3 m) and a weight of 1,700 lbs (750 kg). Grizzlies feed on game, fish, and berries. They have been known to attack humans.

Gromyko \grə-'mē-kō\, **Andrey (Andreyevich)** (1909–1989) Soviet foreign minister (1957–85). Though never strongly identified with any political faction, he served dependably as a skilled emissary and spokesman. He was ambassador to the U.S. 1943–46 and Soviet representative to the U.N. Security Council 1946–48. In 1957 he began his long tenure as foreign minister and became renowned for his negotiating skills. In 1985 he became president of the Supreme Soviet.

Gropius \'grō-pē-əs\, **Walter (Adolph)** (1883–1969) German-U.S. architect. He joined the office of Peter BEHRENS in 1907, and in 1919 he became director of the Staatliches Bauhaus Weimar. He designed a new school building and housing for the BAUHAUS when it moved to Dessau (1925). With its dynamic INTERNATIONAL STYLE composition, asymmetrical plan, smooth white walls set with horizontal windows, and flat roof, it became a monument of the modernist movement. At the Bauhaus and later as chair (1938–52) of Harvard Univ.'s architecture department, he established a new prototype of design education, ending the 200-year supremacy of the French École des BEAUX-ARTS. In his view, all design requires systematic study of the particular needs and problems involved, taking into account modern construction techniques without reference to previous forms or styles.

Gros \'grō\, **Antoine-Jean** (1771–1835) French Romantic painter. Trained by his father and later by J.-L. DAVID in Paris, in the 1790s he accompanied NAPOLEON on his campaigns as his official battle painter. The dramatic power of such paintings as *Napoleon Visiting the Pesthouse at Jaffa* (1804) influenced Théodore GÉRICAULT and Eugène DELACROIX. When David went into exile after Napoleon's defeat, Gros took over his studio and tried to work in the Neoclassical style. His best works after 1815 were portraits. Haunted by a sense of failure, he drowned himself in the Seine.

grosbeak \'grōs-ˌbĕk\ Any of several songbird species in the family Fringillidae that have an exceptionally large, conical bill. Species are found in N. America (e.g., rose-breasted, black-headed, blue, and evening grosbeaks) and N Eurasia (pine grosbeak). See also CARDINAL.

Evening grosbeak
(*Hesperiphona vespertina*)

Gross, Samuel D(avid) (1805–1884) U.S. surgeon, teacher of medicine, and author. Born in Easton, Pa., in 1839 he published his *Elements of Pathological Anatomy*, a pioneering effort that organized knowledge on the subject in English. His *System of Surgery* (2 vols., 1859) had a profound effect on surgical thought worldwide. His *Manual of Military Surgery* (1861) was written at the government's request. He also invented many surgical tools. He was memorably portrayed in Thomas EAKINS's masterpiece "The Gross Clinic."

gross domestic product (GDP) Total market value of the goods and services produced by a nation's economy during a specific period, usually a year. It is defined to include all final goods and services—that is, those that are produced by the economic resources located in that nation regardless of their ownership, and are not resold in any form. GDP differs from gross national product (GNP), which is defined to include all final goods and services produced by resources owned by that nation's residents, whether located in the nation or elsewhere.

Grosseteste \'grōs-ˌtest\, **Robert** (c.1175–1253) English bishop and scholar. He introduced Latin translations of Greek and Arabic writings in philosophy and science to Europe. After serving as chancellor of the Univ. of Oxford (c.1215–21), he served as first lecturer in theology to the Franciscans. As bishop of Lincoln from 1235, he promoted belief in the importance of the cure of souls, a centralized, hierarchical church, and the superiority of the church over the state.

Grossglockner \'grōs-ˌglók-nər\ Highest mountain in Austria. It reaches an elevation of 12,457 ft (3,797 m) and was first climbed in 1800. Its Pasterze Glacier is 5 mi (8 km) long and 3 mi (5 km) wide. The mountain offers winter sports, mountain climbing, and beautiful scenery.

Grosz \'grōs\, **George** (*orig.* Georg) (1893–1959) German-U.S. painter and illustrator. After studying art in Dresden and Berlin, he began selling caricatures to magazines. During World War I he served in the German army; discharged as unfit in 1917, he moved to Berlin and developed a graphic style that combined a highly expressive use of line with ferocious social satire in his depictions of war and depravity. He was a prominent member of the DADA group in Berlin. His *Face of the Ruling Class* (1921) and *Ecce Homo* (1922), collections of drawings featuring greedy capitalists and social decadence, earned him an international reputation. In 1932 he emigrated to the U.S., where he taught at New York's Art Students League while continuing to produce magazine cartoons, nudes, and landscapes.

grotesque In architecture and decorative art, a mural or sculptural decoration combining animal, human, and plant forms. The word derives from the Italian *grottesco*, in reference to the grottolike underground rooms *(grotte)* where such ornaments were found during the excavation of Roman buildings about 1500. A fashion for the grotesque in 16th-cent. Italy quickly spread to the rest of Europe; it was used most frequently in fresco decoration until the 19th cent.

Grotius \'grō-shē-əs\, **Hugo** *orig.* Huigh de Groot (1583–1645) Dutch jurist, humanist, and poet. Born in Delft, he studied law in France and became the official historiographer of Holland; he wrote the history of the Dutch revolt against Spain. He became attorney general of Holland in 1607. Imprisoned in 1618 when his patron was executed, he escaped to Paris in 1621 (by hiding in a trunk of books) and returned ten years later, having achieved great international prestige. His legal works advance the idea that nations are bound by NATURAL LAW; his masterpiece, *De Jure Belli ac Pacis* (1625; "On the Law of War and Peace"), one of the first great contributions to modern INTERNATIONAL LAW, prescribes rules for the conduct of war. He also published many translations and works of classical scholarship.

Grotowski \grò-'tóv-skē\, **Jerzy** (1933–1999) Polish stage director. He joined the Polish Laboratory Theatre of Wroclaw in 1959 and directed its U.S. debut with *Akropolis* (1969), followed by *Undertaking Mountain* (1977) and *Undertaking Earth* (1977–78). An avant-garde theorist, he sought to create dramatic tension by setting up emotional confrontations between audience and actors. His book *Towards a Poor Theater* (1968) emphasized the centrality of the actor and advocated minimal stage sets. He strongly influenced U.S. experimental theater movements.

groundhog See WOODCHUCK

Groundhog Day (Feb. 2) In the U.S., the day that the groundhog predicts whether spring will be coming soon. depending on whether he sees his shadow (indicating six more weeks of winter) or not (indicating spring is imminent). The tradition stems from English beliefs about seeing shadows on CANDLEMAS (also Feb. 2).

ground squirrel Any of numerous short-legged, terrestrial RODENTS of the SQUIRREL family (Sciuridae), found in N. America, Africa, Europe, and Asia. The name is often wrongly applied to CHIPMUNKS. Ground squirrels belong to the genera *Ammospermophilus, Xerus, Atlantoxerus,* and *Spermophilus.* They live in burrows. They are primarily herbivores. Many collect food in their cheek pouches, then store it. Those in cold areas may hibernate in winter; those

in dry areas may become dormant in summer. Species range from about 7 to 20 in. (17–52 cm) in length, including the tail.

groundwater *or* **subsurface water** Water that occurs below the surface of the earth, where it occupies spaces in soils or geologic strata. Most groundwater comes from precipitation that percolates into the earth. Typically, 10–20% of precipitation eventually enters AQUIFERS. Most groundwater is free of pathogenic organisms, and purification is not necessary. Groundwater supplies are not seriously affected by short droughts and are available in many areas that do not have dependable surface water supplies.

groundwater table See WATER TABLE

grouper Any of numerous species of fishes (family Serranidae) widely distributed in warm seas, especially members of the genera *Epinephelus* and *Mycteroperca.* Groupers are characteristically large-mouthed, heavy-bodied fishes. Some species grow larger than 6 ft (about 2 m) long and 500 lbs (225 kg). They are prime food fishes and provide sport for anglers and spearfishermen. A few species carry a toxic substance in their flesh and can cause poisoning when consumed. See also SEA BASS.

group theory In modern algebra, a system consisting of a set of elements and an operation for combining the elements, which together satisfy certain AXIOMS. These require that the combination of any two elements produces another element of the group, that the group obey the ASSOCIATIVE LAW, that it contain an identity element (which, combined with any other element, leaves the latter unchanged), and that each element have an inverse (which combines with an element to produce the identity element). If the group also satisfies the COMMUTATIVE LAW, it is called an abelian group. The set of integers under addition, where the identity element is 0 and the inverse is the negative of a positive number or vice versa, is an abelian group. See also FIELD THEORY.

group therapy Form of PSYCHOTHERAPY in which several patients or clients discuss their personal problems, usually in the presence of a therapist or counselor. In one approach, the aim is to raise members' awareness and morale and combat feelings of isolation; an outstanding example is ALCOHOLICS ANONYMOUS. The other principal approach fosters uninhibited self-revelation; members are helped to more successful behavior through mutual examination of their reactions to people in their lives, including one another.

grouse Any of various game birds in the family Tetraonidae (order Galliformes), including the PRAIRIE CHICKEN and PTARMIGAN, or the sandgrouse (order Columbiformes). The best-known Old World species is the black grouse *(Lyrurus tetrix).* Grouse are noted for the male's communal courtship dances. The best-known N. American species is the ruffed grouse *(Bonasa umbellus)*; the male has a neck ruff of erectile black feathers, and beats its wings loudly to proclaim its territory.

growth hormone (GH) *or* **human growth hormone (HGH)** *or* **somatotropin** \sō-ˌma-tə-'trō-pən\ PEPTIDE HORMONE secreted by the anterior lobe of the PITUITARY GLAND. It promotes growth of bone and other body tissues. Excessive production causes GIGANTISM or other malformations; deficient production results in DWARFISM, dramatically relieved if GH is given before puberty. GENETIC ENGINEERING techniques now permit large-scale production of adequate amounts of GH for that purpose.

Gruen, Victor (1903–1980) Austrian-U.S. architect and city planner. Trained in Vienna, he moved in 1938 to the U.S., where he established Victor Gruen Associates, comprising professionals from engineering, architecture, and planning. The firm produced the master plan for Tehran, and Gruen served as planning consultant for cities worldwide. He is best known as a pioneer of regional shopping centers and of the renewal of city core areas.

Grünewald \'grǖ-nə-ˌvält, *Engl* 'grü-nə-ˌwóld\, **Matthias** *orig.* Mathis Gothardt Neithardt (c.1475/80–1528) German painter. By 1509 he was court painter to the archbishop of Mainz and had established a successful career, concentrating on religious themes. Around 1511 he added two wings to Albrecht DÜRER's *Assumption of the Virgin* altarpiece. In 1515 he completed his most important commission, the wings of the Isenheim Altarpiece in the Antonite monastery in S Alsace (now in the museum in Colmar, France). Considered his masterpiece, it features distorted figures, extreme emotional intensity, brooding color, and draperies that expand and contract in accordion pleats, a hallmark of his style. About 10 paintings and 35 drawings survive. His painterly achievement remains one of the most striking in the history of N European art.

Guadalajara \ˌgwä-d^ᵊl-ə-'hä-rə\ City (pop., 1995: 1,633,000), capital of JALISCO state, Mexico. Mexico's second-largest city, it lies at an altitude of 5,141 ft (1,567 m). It was founded by the Spanish in 1531. In 1810 it was occupied briefly by Miguel HIDALGO. Since 1940 it has become a major industrial producer, while retaining a rich agricultural trade. The governor's palace, begun in 1743, is a noted example of Spanish Mexican architecture. Guadalajara is the site of two universities.

Guadalcanal \ˌgwä-d^ᵊl-kə-'nal\ Island, SOLOMON ISLANDS, SW Pacific Ocean. The largest in the island group, it has an area of 2,047 sq mi (5,302 sq km). The economy is based mainly on fishing and agriculture; gold-mining began in the 1990s. It was annexed in 1893 by the British as part of the Solomon Islands protectorate. During World War II it was the scene of a bloody six-month battle (1942–43), which resulted in the U.S. capture of a vital Japanese airbase. Several naval battles were also fought in the area. The national capital, HONIARA, lies on the N coast.

Guadalquivir River \ˌgwä-d^ᵊl-ki-'vir\ *Arabic* **Wadi al-Kabir** \'wä-dē-ˌál-kə-'bir\ *ancient* Baetis. River, S Spain. Rising in the mountains of Jaén province, it flows west 408 mi (657 km) to empty into the Gulf of Cádiz. Spain's second-longest river, it has one of the most varied natural environments in Europe, containing representatives of half of Europe's plant species and nearly all those of N. Africa.

Guadalupe Hidalgo \ˌgwä-d^ᵊl-'ü-pä-ē-'thäl-gō\, **Treaty of** (Feb. 2, 1848) Treaty between the U.S. and Mexico that ended the MEXICAN WAR. It drew the U.S.–Mexico boundary at the Rio Grande and the Gila River. For $15 million the U.S. received more than 525,000 sq mi (1.36 million sq km) of land. By leaving Mexicans unsure of their country's future and reopening the question of the expansion of slavery in the vast territory ceded to the U.S., it was a factor in the civil wars that followed in both countries.

Guadalupe Mountains National Park \ˌgwä-də-'lü-pä\ National park, W Texas, east of EL PASO. Established in 1972, it occupies 86,416 acres (34,998 hectares). It is centered around two peaks: Guadalupe Peak (8,751 ft, or 2,667 m), and El Capitan (8,078 ft, or 2,462 m). The park is of great geological interest, with a major PERMIAN limestone fossil reef.

Guadeloupe \'gwä-də-ˌlüp, ˌgwä-də-'lüp\ Overseas department of France (pop., 1996: 427,000), E W. INDIES. Consisting of the islands of Basse-Terre and Grande-Terre and several smaller islands, its land area is 687 sq mi (1,780 sq km); the capital is BASSE-TERRE. Forests and tree crops such as coffee abound on the mountains of Basse-Terre, while sugarcane is cultivated on Grande-Terre. After battles with the Carib Indians, the islands came under French control by 1674. The British occupied Guadeloupe for short periods in the 18th–19th cent. In 1946 it was made a department of France. Tourism has benefited the economy in recent decades.

Guainía, Río See RÍO NEGRO

Guam \'gwäm\ Island (pop., 2000: 154,000), largest and southernmost of the MARIANA ISLANDS, Micronesia. Guam is an unincorporated U.S. territory with an area of 209 sq mi (541 sq km). Its capital is Agana. The native people are the Chamorro, of Malayo-Indonesian stock mixed with Spanish, Filipino, and Mexican. Possibly visited by Ferdinand MAGELLAN in 1521, Guam was formally claimed by Spain in 1565 and remained Spanish for two centuries. It was ceded to the U.S. after the SPANISH–AMERICAN WAR in 1898. Occupied by the Japanese 1941–44, it subsequently became a major U.S. air and naval base. In 1950 it was made a U.S. territory and placed under the Department of the Interior.

Guanajuato \ˌgwä-nä-'hwä-tō\ State (pop., 2000: 4,656,000), central Mexico. It lies on the interior plateau at an average elevation of about 6,000 ft (1,800 m) and has an area totaling 11,773 sq mi (30,491 sq km); the capital is GUANAJUATO city. The north is mountainous, while the south, consisting of fertile plains, is largely devoted to agriculture. The first Spanish settlement was at San Miguel de Allende (1542). The principal industry is mining (silver, gold, tin, lead, and opals).

Guanajuato City (pop., 1990: 114,000), capital of GUANAJUATO state, Mexico. It lies 6,725 ft (2,050 m) above sea level. Founded in 1554, it is an outstanding example of the Spanish colonial city. One of the greatest silver-mining centers of the 16th cent., the city manifested its wealth in its richly endowed churches. In 1810 it was the first major city to fall to the independence leader Miguel HIDALGO. It is the site of the Univ. of Guanajuato (1945).

Guangzhou *or* **Kuang-chou** \'gwäŋ-'jō\ *English* **Canton** City (pop., 1999 est.: 3,306,000), China. Located on the Zhu River about 80 mi (130 km) from the sea, it is one of China's largest cities and S China's chief port. Part of the Chinese empire in the 3rd cent. B.C., it became an important city under the MING DYNASTY. The first Chinese seaport opened to foreigners, it was regularly visited by Arab and Hindu traders, and later by the Portuguese, the English, the French, and the Dutch. Its resistance to the English opium trade led to war (1839–42), and it was occupied by the British and French in 1856–61. In the 19th cent. it was the seat of Nationalist ideas promoted by the GUOMINDANG. Occupied by the Japanese 1938–45, it was taken by the Chinese communists in 1949. Its industrial growth expanded, and it was designated as one of several economic investment areas for foreigners in 1984.

Guan Hanqing *or* **Kuan Han-ch'ing** \'gwän-'hän-'chiŋ\ (1241?–1320?) Chinese dramatist, often considered the greatest in Chinese classical theater. He belonged to a writers' guild that provided plays for performing groups, and his plays often dealt with everyday events and portrayed women of low social standing with sympathy. Of his 60 plays, 14 survive, including *Injustice Suffered by Doue, Butterfly Dream,* and *Saving a Prostitute.*

guanine \'gwä-ˌnēn\ Organic compound of the PURINE family, consisting of two rings and an amino group. It occurs in combined form in many important biological molecules, particularly NUCLEIC ACIDS, and free or combined in various natural sources, including guano, sugar beets, yeast, and fish scales. In DNA its complementary base is CYTOSINE. It or its corresponding NUCLEOSIDE or NUCLEOTIDE may be prepared from nucleic acids by HYDROLYSIS.

Guantánamo Bay Inlet of the Caribbean Sea, SE Cuba. It is one of the largest bays in the world: its harbor is about 6 mi (9 km) wide and 12 mi (19 km) long. Its strategic value was proved during U.S. landings in the SPANISH–AMERICAN WAR. A U.S. naval base was established there by treaty in 1903; since 1959, the Cuban government has periodically threatened to seize the base.

Guanyin See AVALOKITESVARA

Guaraní \ˌgwär-ə-'nē\ S. American Indian group that inhabited E Paraguay and adjacent areas of Brazil and Argentina. Aboriginal Guaraní were warlike and took captives to be sacrificed (and allegedly eaten). Their slash-and-burn agriculture required them to move their settlements every few years. Only a few true Guaraní communities remain, but Paraguay still claims a strong Guaraní heritage, and most of the million peasants living along the Paraguay River near Asunción speak a version of the Guaraní language.

Guardi \'gwär-dē\, **Francesco** (1712–1793) Italian landscape painter. He and his two brothers collaborated in a flourishing studio-workshop in Venice. By the 1750s he was producing *vedute* (view paintings) of Venice. His many romantic impressions of the city never achieved the popularity of CANALETTO's *vedute,* and his work came to be appreciated only after the rise of Impressionism.

guardian In law, one who has, or is legally appointed to, the care and management of another, usually a minor. A natural guardian is a guardian by natural relationship (usually the father or mother). A guardian may be appointed by the court when it decides that a child needs one (usually when the parents have died or disappeared).

Guardian, The Influential newspaper published in London and Manchester. Founded in 1821 as the weekly *Manchester Guardian,* it became a daily in 1855; 100 years later "Manchester" was dropped from the name, as it had become a national daily with an international reputation. The paper has always taken an independent liberal stance in its editorials and maintained great breadth and depth of news coverage.

Guare \\'gwar\\, **John** (b.1938) U.S. dramatist. Born in New York City, in 1971 he earned critical acclaim for *The House of Blue Leaves. Two Gentlemen of Verona* (1972; with Mel Shapiro), a rock-musical version of William SHAKESPEARE's comedy, won him a Tony Award. His later works include *Six Degrees of Separation* (1990; film, 1993) and *Four Baboons Adoring the Sun* (1992). His screenplays include *Atlantic City* (1981).

Guarini \\gwä-'rē-nē\\, **(Giovanni) Battista** (1538–1612) Italian poet. In 1567 he entered the service of Alfonso II, Duke of Ferrara. In 1579 he replaced his friend Torquato TASSO as court poet. With Tasso, he is credited with developing the genre of PASTORAL drama. Guarini retired in 1582 and wrote *Il pastor fido* (1590; "The Faithful Shepherd"), a pastoral tragicomedy that became one of the most famous works of the age.

Guarneri \\gwär-'ner-ē\\, **Andrea** (1626–1698) Italian musical-instrument maker. He apprenticed with the great Nicola Amati 1641–54. Setting up his own shop in Cremona, he made violas and cellos as well as violins. His son Giuseppe (1666–1740?) inherited the Cremona business from his father in 1698. During his lifetime his name was obscured by Antonio STRADIVARI's fame, but his violins and cellos are today highly prized. Giuseppe's son Bartolomeo (1698–1744), called Guarneri del Gèsu, was one of the finest instrument makers in history.

Guatemala \\ˌgwä-tə-'mä-lə\\ *officially* **Republic of Guatemala** Country, CENTRAL AMERICA. Area: 42,042 sq mi (108,889 sq km). Population (2000): 11,385,000. Capital: GUATEMALA. Mayan Indians are about 55% of the popula-

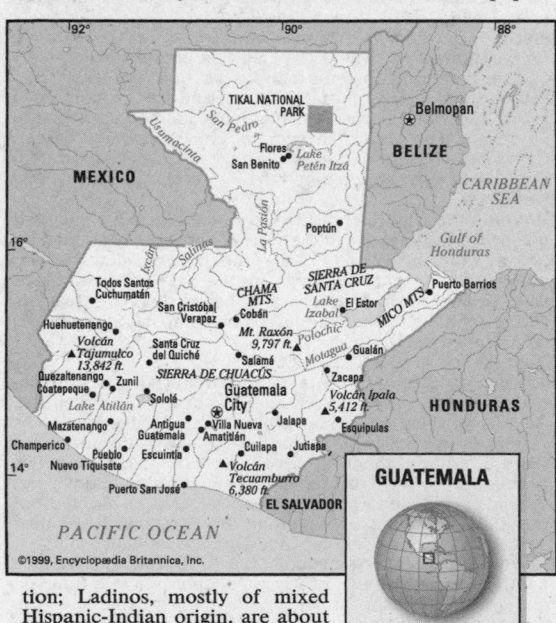

GUATEMALA

Scale 1: 7,482,000

©1999, Encyclopædia Britannica, Inc.

tion; Ladinos, mostly of mixed Hispanic-Indian origin, are about 42%. Language: Spanish (official). Religion: Roman Catholicism. Currency: quetzal. Guatemala has extensive lowlands in the Petén portion of the YUCATÁN PENINSULA and the Caribbean coastal region in the north. Mountains make up about half the total area and cut across the country's midsection. The N tropical rain forests of the Petén are rich in fine woods and rubber. It has a developing market economy based

largely on agriculture, and is Central America's leading coffee producer. It is a republic with one legislative body; its head of state and government is the president. From simple farming villages dating to 2500 B.C., the MAYA of Guatemala and the Yucatán developed an impressive civilization. Its heart was the N Petén, where the oldest Mayan stone pillars and the ceremonial center of TIKAL are found. Mayan civilization declined after A.D. 900, and the Spanish began the subjugation of their descendants in 1523. Independence from Spain was declared by the Central American colonies in Guatemala City in 1821, and Guatemala was incorporated into the Mexican empire until its collapse in 1823. In 1839 Guatemala became an independent republic under the first of a series of dictators who held power almost continuously for the next century. In 1945 a liberal-democratic coalition came to power and instituted sweeping reforms. Attempts to expropriate land belonging to U.S. business interests prompted the U.S. government in 1954 to sponsor an invasion. In the following years Guatemala's social revolution came to an end and most of the reforms were reversed. Chronic political instability and violence henceforth marked Guatemalan politics; most of the 200,000 deaths that resulted were blamed on government forces. In the 1990s it established diplomatic relations with Belize but continued to claim most of its territory. It continued to experience violence as guerrillas sought to seize power. A peace treaty was signed in 1996, and the country started slowly to recover from its civil war.

Guatemala *or* **Guatemala City** City (metro. area pop., 1995 est.: 1,167,000), capital of Guatemala. The largest city in CENTRAL AMERICA, it lies in the central highlands at an elevation of 4,897 ft (1,493 m). Founded in 1776, it served as capital of the province of Central America under the Mexican empire of Agustín de ITURBIDE, and later of the Republic of Guatemala. It is the country's political, social, cultural, and economic center and the site of the San Carlos Univ. of Guatemala (1676); its museums include the National Archaeological Museum. The modern city was severely damaged by earthquakes in 1917–18 and 1976.

guava Any of many trees and shrubs of the genus *Psidium* (MYRTLE family), native to the New World tropics. The two important species are common guava (*P. guajava*) and cattley, or strawberry, guava (*P. littorale*). Guavas are processed into jams, jellies, and preserves. Fresh guavas are rich in vitamins A, B, and C; they are eaten raw or sliced and are served as desserts.

Guayaquil \\ˌgwī-ä-'kēl\\ *in full* **Santiago de Guayaquil** Largest city (pop., 2000: 2,118,000) and chief port, Ecuador. It is situated on the Guayas River, 45 mi (72 km) from the Pacific Ocean. Founded by the Spanish at its present site in 1537, in 1822 it was the scene of a historic conference between Simón BOLÍVAR and José de SAN MARTÍN, after which Bolívar emerged as sole leader of the S. American liberation movement. It has become a major Pacific port and is the site of three universities.

Gudbrandsdalen \\'gùd-ˌbräns-ˌdä-lən\\ Valley, S central Norway. About 140 mi (225 km) long, it was the scene of severe fighting in World War II, in which the Norwegians and British attempted to hold off a German invasion. It is the setting for Henrik IBSEN's play *Peer Gynt.*

Guderian \\gü-'dä-rē-än\\, **Heinz (Wilhelm)** (1888–1954) German general. His book *Attention! Tanks!* (1937) incorporated theories by J. F. C. FULLER and Charles DE GAULLE. As a principal architect of armored warfare and the BLITZKRIEG, he contributed decisively to Germany's victories early in World War II. In 1943, as inspector general of armored troops, he simplified and accelerated tank production. After the JULY PLOT against Adolf HITLER, he became acting chief of staff (1944–45).

Guelphs and Ghibellines \\'gwelfs...'gi-bə-ˌlēnz\\ Opposing factions in German and Italian politics during the Middle Ages. The terms Guelph (from the German Welf dynasty) and Ghibelline (from Waiblingen, the castle of the Welfs' HOHENSTAUFEN opponents) first acquired significance in Italy when the emperor FREDERICK I Barbarossa tried to assert imperial authority over N Italy and was opposed by Pope ALEXANDER III. The split between the Guelphs, who sided with the papacy, and the Ghibellines, who were sympathetic to the Holy Roman emperors, contributed to chronic strife in the cities of N Italy in the 13th–14th cent., reflected in DANTE's *Divine Comedy*.

Guercino \gwär-'chē-nō\, **Il** (Italian: "The Squinter") *orig.* Giovanni Francesco Barbieri (1591–1666) Italian painter. Strongly influenced by the Bolognese school, he was called to Rome in 1621 by Pope Gregory XV and, among other commissions, decorated the Villa Ludovisi; the ceiling fresco *Aurora* is painted to appear as if there were no ceiling, so that Aurora's chariot is seen to float directly over the building. He returned to his native town of Cento in 1623. In 1642, on the death of Guido RENI, he moved to Bologna and was its leading painter until his death. He had a profound impact on 17th-cent. baroque decoration.

Guernsey \'gərn-zē\ Second-largest of the CHANNEL ISLANDS (pop., 1995 est.: 59,000). Situated in the ENGLISH CHANNEL just west of NORMANDY, it has an area of 24 sq mi (62 sq km). With other islets, it forms the bailiwick of Guernsey. The island was known as Sarnia to the Romans. It was home to Victor HUGO 1855–70. The Guernsey breed of cattle originated there.

Guerrero \gär-'rā-rō\ State (pop., 2000: 3,075,000), SW Mexico. Its 24,819-sq-mi (64,281-sq-km) territory, except for its narrow Pacific coastal plain, lies entirely within the Sierra Madre del Sur, the valleys of which are fertile but difficult to access. Its capital is Chilpancingo, but its best-known cities are ACAPULCO and Taxco, a preserved colonial town. It derives its income from agriculture, mining, and tourism.

guerrilla \gə-'ri-lə\ Member of an irregular military force fighting small-scale, limited actions, in support of an overall political-military strategy, against conventional military forces. Guerrilla tactics involve constantly shifting attacks, sabotage, and TERRORISM. The word was first used of Spanish-Portuguese irregulars who drove the French from the Iberian Peninsula in the early 19th cent. Guerrillas seek to harass the enemy until they gain the strength to win or to pressure the enemy to seek peace. SUNZI (4th cent. B.C.) laid down the rules of guerrilla tactics.

Guest, Edgar (Albert) (1881–1959) U.S. (British-born) writer. He became an office boy for the *Detroit Free Press*, and later a reporter and writer of daily sentimental rhymes. His first book, *A Heap o' Livin'* (1916), became a best-seller and was followed by similar collections of optimistic verse on such subjects as home, mother, and the virtue of hard work.

Guevara \ge-'vär-ə\, **Che** *orig.* Ernesto Guevara de la Serna (1928–1967) Guerrilla tactician and prominent figure in Fidel CASTRO's revolution in Cuba (1956–59). After training as a doctor in his native Argentina, he traveled widely in Latin America. The overthrow of Guatemala's Pres. Jacobo ARBENZ persuaded him that the U.S. would always oppose leftist governments and that only revolution would end the poverty of the masses. In Mexico he met Castro and joined his cause. After the Cuban revolution he held key posts as one of Castro's most trusted aides; handsome and charismatic, he served as one of the revolution's most effective

Che Guevara

voices. He left Cuba in 1965 to organize guerrilla fighters in Congo and later Bolivia. Captured and shot by the Bolivian army, he won fame and the status of a martyred hero among leftists worldwide.

Guggenheim \'gü-gən-ˌhīm\, **Meyer and Daniel** (1828–1905, 1856–1930) U.S. industrialists, father and son. Born in Switzerland, Meyer emigrated to the U.S. in 1847 and built an import firm specializing in Swiss embroideries. His investments in two Colorado copper mines in the 1880s were the foundation of extensive mining interests. His seven sons, especially Daniel, built a large organization of smelting and refining operations. In 1901 the Guggenheims merged their holdings with the American Smelting and Refining Co. Daniel directed this trust until 1919 and acquired mines throughout the world. Philanthropies include the John Simon Guggenheim Memorial Foundation (1925) to award fellowships to artists and scholars studying abroad, and the Solomon R. Guggenheim Foundation (1937), which oversees New York's GUGGENHEIM MUSEUM and the Guggenheim Collection in Venice, founded by Meyer's granddaughter Peggy (1898–1979).

Guggenheim Museum \'gü-gən-ˌhīm\ Museum in New York City housing the Solomon R. Guggenheim collection of modern art. An example of the "organic architecture" of Frank Lloyd WRIGHT, the radically innovative building (constructed 1956–59) spirals upward and outward in a smooth coil of massive, unadorned white concrete. The exhibition space, a six-story-high spiral ramp encircling an open center volume, has been criticized for upstaging the artwork displayed.

GUI See GRAPHICAL USER INTERFACE

Guianas \gē-'ä-nəz, gī-'a-nəz\, **the** Region, N S. America. Located on the Atlantic and Caribbean coasts, it lies between the ORINOCO, NEGRO, and AMAZON rivers, and covers about 181,000 sq mi (468,800 sq km). It consists of Guyana (formerly British Guiana), Suriname (formerly Dutch Guiana), and FRENCH GUIANA. Most of it is covered by dense forests; settlements are largely confined to the coast and river valleys. The Dutch founded settlements around 1580, and the French and English in the early 17th cent.

guild Association of craftsmen or merchants formed for mutual aid and advancement of their professional interests. Guilds flourished in Europe between the 11th and 16th cent. Merchant guilds included all the merchants of a particular town or city; craft guilds included all the craftsmen in a particular branch of industry (e.g., weavers, painters, goldsmiths). They established trade monopolies, set standards for quality of goods, maintained stable prices, and influenced local governments to further the interests of the guild. Craft guilds also established hierarchies of craftsmen based on level of training (e.g., masters, journeymen, and apprentices).

guillemot \'gi-lə-ˌmät\ Any of three species of black-and-white seabirds (genus *Cepphus,* family Alcidae). All are deep divers that feed at the bottom. The best-known species, the black guillemot, breeds around the Arctic Circle and winters south to the British Isles and Maine; it is about 14 in. (35 cm) long. The pigeon guillemot breeds along both coasts of the N. Pacific; the spectacled guillemot breeds from Japan to the Kuril Islands. In British usage, the name also refers to birds called murres in the U.S.

guillotine \ˌgē-ə-'tēn, 'gi-lə-ˌtēn\ Instrument for inflicting capital punishment by decapitation. A minimal wooden structure, it supported a heavy blade that, when released, slid down in vertical guides to sever the victim's head. It was introduced in the FRENCH REVOLUTION, though similar devices had been used in other European countries, often for executing criminals of noble birth. A French physician and member of the National Assembly, Joseph-Ignace Guillotin (1738–1814), led in passing a law (1792) requiring all sentences of death to be carried out "by means of a machine," so that execution by relatively painless decapitation would no longer be confined to nobles. The last execution by guillotine in France took place in 1977.

Guin, Ursula Le See Ursula LE GUIN

Guinea \'gi-nē\ *officially* **Republic of Guinea** *formerly* **French Guinea** Country, W Africa. Area: 94,926 sq mi (245,857 sq km). Population (2000): 7,466,000 (including 600,000 refuges from Liberia and Sierra Leone). Capital: CONAKRY. The FULANI people are in the majority, followed by the MALINKE and many other groups. Language: French (official). Religion: Islam. Currency: Guinean franc. Facing the Atlantic Ocean to the west, Guinea has four topographical regions. Lower Guinea comprises the coast and coastal plain, which are sandy and interspersed with lagoons and mangrove swamps. To the east the Fouta Djallon highlands rise sharply from the coastal plain to elevations above 3,000 ft (900 m); W Africa's three major rivers—the NIGER, SÉNÉGAL, and Gambia—originate there. Upper Guinea comprises the Niger Plains. The Forest Region, an isolated

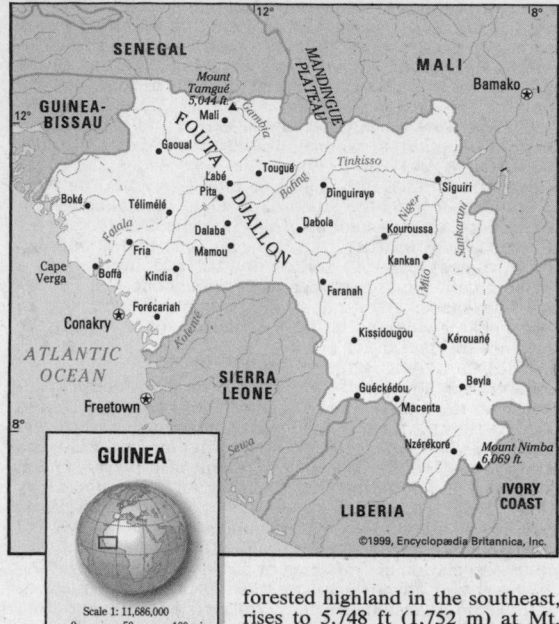

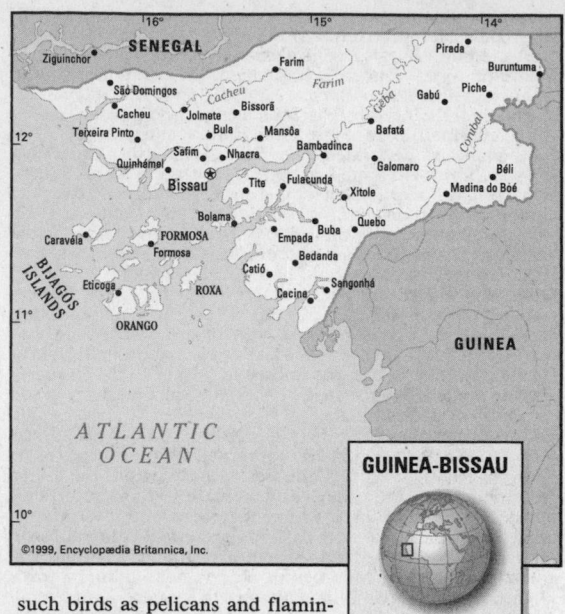

forested highland in the southeast, rises to 5,748 ft (1,752 m) at Mt. Nimba, the country's highest peak. Most of the country has a humid tropical climate, while more than two-fifths is covered by tropical rain forest. Export crops include rice, bananas, and coffee. Guinea is the world's second-largest producer of bauxite. Its developing, mixed economy is based on agriculture, mining, and trade. It is a multiparty republic with one legislative house; the head of state and government is the president, assisted by the prime minister. Around A.D. 900, successive migrations of the Susu swept down from the desert and pushed the original inhabitants, the Baga, to the Atlantic coast. Small kingdoms of the Susu rose in importance in the 13th cent. and later extended their rule to the coast. In the mid-15th cent. the Portuguese visited the coast and developed a slave trade. In the 16th cent. the Fulani established domination over the Fouta Djallon region; they ruled into the 19th cent. In the early 19th cent. the French arrived, and in 1849 proclaimed the coastal region a French protectorate. In 1895 French Guinea became part of the federation of FRENCH WEST AFRICA. In 1946 it was made an overseas territory of France, and in 1958 achieved independence. Following a military coup in 1984, Guinea began implementing Westernized government systems. A new constitution was adopted in 1991, and the first multiparty elections were held in 1993. During the 1990s, Guinea received several hundred thousand war refugees from neighboring Liberia and Sierra Leone.

Guinea, Gulf of Great inlet of the Atlantic Ocean, W central African coast. It includes the Bights of BENIN and BIAFRA. Its natural resources include offshore oil deposits and metal ore deposits. Its coastline forms part of the W edge of the African tectonic plate and corresponds remarkably to the continental margin of S. America from Brazil to the Guianas, a confirmation of the theory of CONTINENTAL DRIFT.

Guinea-Bissau \'gi-nē-bi-'saủ\ *officially* **Republic of Guinea-Bissau** *formerly (until 1974)* **Portuguese Guinea** Country, W Africa. Its territory includes the Bijagós Archipelago, off the Atlantic coast to the southwest. Area: 13,948 sq mi (36,125 sq km). Population (2000): 1,286,000. Capital: BISSAU. The four major ethnic groups are the Balanta Brassa, FULANI, MALINKE, and Mandyako. Language: Portuguese (official); each tribe speaks its own vernacular. Religion: Islam; traditional beliefs. Currency: CFA franc. Most of the country consists of low, marshy terrain and flat plateau. The climate is generally hot and tropical. Much of the country's wildlife is aquatic; crocodiles, snakes, and

such birds as pelicans and flamingos abound. It has a developing, primarily agricultural economy; cashews and peanuts are the main cash crops. It is a multiparty republic with one legislative house, its chief of state is the president, and the head of government is the prime minister. More than 1,000 years ago the coast of Guinea-Bissau was occupied by iron-using agriculturists. They grew irrigated and dry rice and were also the major suppliers of marine salt to the W Sudan. At about the same time, it came under the influence of the MALI EMPIRE and became a tributary kingdom known as Gabú. After 1546 Gabú was virtually autonomous; vestiges of the kingdom lasted until 1867. The earliest overseas contacts came in the 15th cent. with the Portuguese, who imported slaves from the Guinea area to the offshore CAPE VERDE Islands. Portuguese control of Guinea-Bissau was marginal despite their claims to sovereignty there. The end of the slave trade forced he Portuguese inland in search of new profits. Their subjugation of the interior was slow and sometimes violent; it was not effectively achieved until 1915, though sporadic resistance continued until 1936. Guerrilla warfare in the 1960s led to the country's independence in 1974, but political turmoil continued and the government was overthrown by a military coup in 1980. A new constitution was adopted in 1984, and the first multiparty elections were held in 1994. A destructive civil war in 1998 was followed by a military coup in 1999, then national elections and a peaceful transfer of power in 2000.

guinea fowl Any of a family (Numididae) of African birds, sometimes placed in the family Phasianidae. One species *(Numida meleagris)* is widely domesticated for its flesh and, because it gabbles loudly at the least alarm, as a "watchdog" on farms. Wild forms of this species are known as helmet guinea fowl because of their large bony crest. About 20 in. (50 cm) long, in its typical form it has a bare face, brown eyes, red and blue wattles at the bill, white-spotted black plumage, and a hunched posture. It lives in flocks and feeds on seed tubers and some insects.

guinea pig Domesticated species *(Cavia porcellus)* of S. American CAVY (family Caviidae). It resembles most other cavies in being stout, short-legged, and about 10 in. (25 cm) long. It has small ears and no external tail. Coat color and hair length vary. It feeds largely on grass and other green plants. Domesticated in pre-Incan times, it was introduced into Europe in the early 16th cent. It is a popular pet and a valuable research animal.

Guinevere See ARTHURIAN LEGEND

Guinness (de Cuffe) \\'gi-nəs\\, **Alec** (*later* **Sir Alec**) (1914–2000) British actor. After his stage debut in 1934, he joined the OLD VIC company (1936) and starred in classic works. A versatile actor, he won praise in New York in Shakespearean roles and in T. S. ELIOT's *The Cocktail Party* (1946). His many films include comedies such as *Kind Hearts and Coronets* (1949), *The Lavender Hill Mob* (1951), and *Our Man in Havana* (1959) as well as dramas such as *The Bridge on the River Kwai* (1957, Academy Award) and *Tunes of Glory* (1960). He won a new generation of fans in three *Star Wars* films (1977, 1980, 1983).

Guiscard, Robert See ROBERT GUISCARD

Guise, 2nd duc (Duke) de *orig.* **François de Lorraine** (1519–1563) French soldier, greatest member of the House of GUISE. He fought in FRANCIS I's army and was badly wounded at the siege of Boulogne (1545), earning him the nickname "the Scarred." He scored other victories against the English and the Spanish. On the accession of Francis II (1559), Guise became grand master of the royal household. The BOURBONS' conspiracy to overthrow the Guises was ruthlessly suppressed (1560). When CATHERINE DE MÉDICIS became regent (1560), she supported religious toleration for the HUGUENOT movement as against the Guises and Catholic dominance. The first of the resultant Wars of RELIGION again showed Guise to be an outstanding soldier. He was assassinated by a Huguenot in 1563.

Guise, 3rd duc (Duke) de *orig.* **Henri I de Lorraine** (1550–1588) French leader of the Catholic party during the French Wars of RELIGION. When CATHERINE DE MÉDICIS turned to the Guises in 1572 for help in removing the Huguenot Gaspar de COLIGNY, Henri helped plan the SAINT BARTHOLOMEW'S DAY Massacre. Fearing Guise's growing popularity, HENRY III made peace with the Huguenots in 1576, and Guise angrily countered by forming the Holy League. Guise's victory in the War of the Three Henrys (1588) forced Henry to surrender to the League's demands, and Guise was appointed lieutenant general of France. Soon afterward, the king's bodyguard stabbed Guise to death.

Guise \\'gēz\\, **House of** Noble French Roman Catholic family prominent in 16th-cent. French politics. Claude de Lorraine (1496–1550) was created the 1st duc (duke) de Guise in 1527 for his service to FRANCIS I in the defense of France. Claude's sons François, 2nd duc de GUISE, and Charles, cardinal de Lorraine (1524–1574), gained great power during the reign of Francis II. Supported by Spain and the papacy, their persecution of the HUGUENOTS led to transfer of power to the House of BOURBON. The Guise-led massacre of a Huguenot congregation at Vassy precipitated the Wars of RELIGION, in which Henri I, 3rd duc de GUISE, was a prominent leader. Charles de Lorraine, 4th duc de Guise (1571–1640), lived through the rapid decline of the family's power, which Henri II, 5th duc de Guise (1614–1664), tried unsuccessfully to revive.

guitar Plucked STRINGED INSTRUMENT. It normally has six strings, a fretted fingerboard, and a soundbox with a pronounced waist. It probably originated in Spain in the early 16th cent. By 1800 it was being strung with six single strings; 19th-cent. innovations gave it its modern form. Always primarily an amateur's instrument, it remains an important folk instrument in many countries. The 12-string guitar is strung in six double courses. The Hawaiian or steel guitar is held horizontally and the strings are stopped by the pressure of a metal bar, producing a sweet glissando tone. Electric pickups were attached to the acoustic guitar in the 1920s, and electroacoustic guitars were soon being produced. In the 1940s Les PAUL invented the solid-body guitar; lacking a soundbox, it transmits only the string vibrations. With its long-sustained notes, affinity for strong amplification, and capacity for producing wailing melodic lines as well as harshly percussive rhythms, it soon became the principal instrument of Western popular music.

Guiyang \\'gwē-'yäŋ\\ *or* **Kuei-yang** \\'gwā-'yäŋ\\ City (pop., 1999 est.: 1,320,000), capital of Guizhou province, S China, south of CHONGQING. The SUI (581–618) and TANG (618–907) dynasties established outposts there, but the city developed only after the MONGOL invasion in 1279. Under the MING (1368–1644) and QING (1644–1911) dynasties, Guiyang became the seat of a prefecture. The SINO–JAPANESE WAR spurred its growth.

Gulag \\'gü-ˌläg\\ System of Soviet labor camps and prisons that from the 1920s to the mid-1950s confined millions of political prisoners and criminals. The term (from the Russian words for Chief Administration of Corrective Labor Camps) was largely unknown in the West until the 1973 publication of Aleksandr SOLZHENITSYN's *Gulag Archipelago*. The Gulag consisted of hundreds of camps, under the control of the secret police, where prisoners felled timber, worked in the mines, or labored on construction projects. At least 10% died each year from harsh working conditions and summary executions. The Gulag reached its height in the years of collectivization of Soviet agriculture (1929–32) and during Joseph STALIN's purges (1936–38), shrinking only after Stalin's death in 1953. An estimated 15–30 million Russians died in the camps.

gulf Any large coastal indentation, similar to a BAY but larger. Most existing gulfs were formed or greatly extended by the rise in sea level after the last ice age. Some resulted from warping, folding, or downfaulting of the earth's crust. Most gulfs are connected with the sea by one or more straits. Gulfs may differ from the adjoining sea in water properties and sedimentation.

Gulf Intracoastal Waterway System of inland waterways along the U.S. coast of the Gulf of MEXICO. It extends 1,100 mi (1,770 km) from Apalachee Bay, Fla., to Brownsville, Texas. It includes MOBILE BAY and Mississippi Sound, passes through NEW ORLEANS, and takes in the Sabine-Neches Waterway and the ship canal at HOUSTON. With the ATLANTIC INTRACOASTAL WATERWAY, it forms the 3,000-mi (4,800-km) Intracoastal Waterway.

Gulf of Tonkin Resolution (Aug. 5, 1964) Resolution by the U.S. Congress authorizing Pres. Lyndon JOHNSON to use "all necessary measures" to repel attacks against U.S. forces in Vietnam, drafted in response to the alleged shelling of two U.S. ships by N. Vietnam in the Gulf of Tonkin. Later information disputed the severity of the attack. The resolution was cited as authorization for the expansion of the VIETNAM WAR; many came to see it as a blank check, and it was repealed in 1970.

Gulf Oil Corp. Major U.S. petroleum company. Gulf Oil began with an oil gusher near Beaumont, Texas, in 1901. The oil well was developed by the Pittsburgh Mellon family (see Andrew W. MELLON). Gulf acquired the world's first drive-in filling station, in Pittsburgh in 1913. By 1923 the Gulf refinery in Port Arthur, Texas, was the largest in the world. Gulf Oil continued to develop oil fields in Texas, Oklahoma, and Louisiana, as well as in Mexico and Venezuela. In 1984 it was bought by Chevron, another oil company.

Gulf Stream Warm ocean current, part of a general clockwise-rotating system of currents in the N. Atlantic. Its warming effect on the climates of adjacent land areas causes the winter air over the ocean west of Norway to be more than 40°F (22°C) warmer than the average for that latitude; winters in SW England are also very mild because of the Gulf Stream. Regions of the Gulf Stream, such as the GRAND BANKS, have been among the most productive commercial fishing grounds in the world.

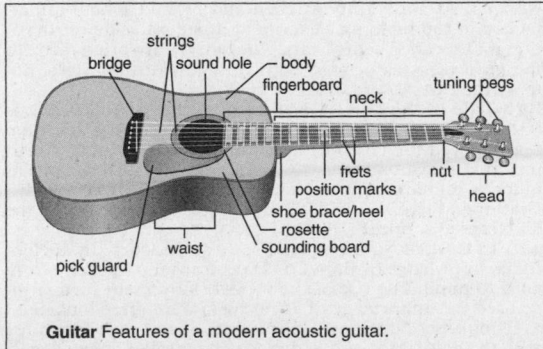

strings
bridge   sound hole   body
fingerboard   neck   tuning pegs
frets   nut
position marks   head
shoe brace/heel
rosette
pick guard   waist   sounding board

Guitar Features of a modern acoustic guitar.

F G

gull Any of more than 40 species of heavily built, web-footed seabirds (family Laridae) that are most abundant in temperate to arctic regions of the Northern Hemisphere. Adults are mainly gray or white. The bill is strong and slightly hooked. Wingspreads range from 24 to 63 in. (0.6–1.6 m). Gulls feed on insects, mollusks, crustaceans, worms, grubs, fish, and garbage. Some large gulls prey on the eggs and young of other birds, including their own kind. See also HERRING GULL.

gum In botany, an adhesive substance of vegetable origin, mostly obtained as exudate from the bark of trees or shrubs belonging to the PEA family. Gum arabic (from a species of ACACIA) is used in lithography. Gum tragacanth (from several shrubs in the genus *Astragalus*) is used in pill manufacture and as an emulsifier in processed foods. Some plant gums are used in cosmetics.

gum *or* **gingiva** \'jin-jə-və, jin-'jī-və\ Mucous MEMBRANE attached to and surrounding the necks of the teeth and the bone of the jaw. Fibers of the ligament that holds the teeth in their sockets enter the gum and hold it tightly against the teeth. Healthy gums have limited sensitivity to pain, temperature, and pressure. Changes in color or abnormal sensitivity are early signs of gingivitis, in which pockets form between the gum and teeth and become infected, with inflammation, bleeding, and, in severe cases, loss of teeth.

gum, chewing See CHEWING GUM

gum tree See TUPELO

gun Weapon consisting essentially of a metal tube from which a missile is shot by the force of exploding GUNPOWDER or some other propellant. The term is often limited today to the so-called big guns, CANNON larger than a howitzer or MORTAR. It may also refer to military small arms such as the RIFLE, MACHINE GUN, and PISTOL, as well as to nonmilitary firearms such as the SHOTGUN. Guns were not developed until the Europeans acquired gunpowder in the 13th cent. The earliest guns (c.1327) resembled old-fashioned soda bottles; they apparently were fired by applying a red-hot wire to a touchhole drilled through the top. Separating the barrel and the powder chamber resulted in breechloaders, which were used in naval swivel guns and fortress wallpieces well into the 17th cent. Small arms, as opposed to hand cannon, did not exist until the matchlock of the 15th cent.

gunpowder Any of several mixtures used as propelling charges and blasting agents. The first such EXPLOSIVE was black powder, a mixture of SALTPETER (potassium nitrate), sulfur, and charcoal, originating in 9th-cent. China. The recipe was refined and finally set in the 14th cent.; black powder is still widely used for ignition charges, primers, fuses, blank charges in military ammunition, and fireworks. In the 1860s a form of nitrocellulose known as guncotton came into use as an ingredient of gunpowder. In the 1880s Paul Vieille (1854–1934) used nitrocellulose to create smokeless gunpowder; modern gunpowder consists of nitrocellulose alone or in combination with NITROGLYCERIN.

Gunpowder Plot (1605) Conspiracy by English Roman Catholic zealots to blow up Parliament and kill JAMES I. Angered by James's refusal to grant more religious toleration to Catholics, a group of conspirators recruited Guy FAWKES to their plot. One conspirator warned his brother-in-law Lord Monteagle not to attend Parliament on the appointed day (Nov. 5, 1605), and Monteagle alerted the government. Fawkes was arrested in a cellar under the building, where he had concealed 20 barrels of gunpowder. The conspirators were tried and executed. The plot bitterly intensified Protestant suspicions of Catholics.

Gunther, John (1901–1970) U.S. writer. Born in Chicago, he worked as a journalist in London (1924–36) before publishing *Inside Europe* (1936), the first of his highly successful books describing and interpreting various regions of the world, including *Inside Asia* (1939), *Inside Africa* (1955), *Inside Russia Today* (1958), and *Inside S. America* (1967). He was also a war correspondent and radio commentator.

Guomindang *or* **Kuomintang** \'gwō-'min-'dän\ *or* **Nationalist Party** Political party that governed mainland China 1928–49 and subsequently ruled Taiwan. Founded in 1912 by Song Jiaoren (1882–1913) and led by SUN YAT-SEN, it evolved from a revolutionary league working to overthrow the QING DYNASTY into a political party. In the early 1920s it received guidance from the Soviet Union; until 1927 it collaborated with the CHINESE COMMUNIST PARTY. Sun's program, which stressed nationalism, democracy, and people's livelihood, was ineffectively implemented by his successor, CHIANG KAI-SHEK, who became increasingly conservative and dictatorial. In 1949 the Nationalists were driven from the mainland to Taiwan by the Communists. There they maintained a monopoly on political power until 1989, when the first legal opposition party won seats in the legislature.

Guo Moruo \'gwȯ-'mȯ-'rwȯ\ *or* **Kuo Mo-jo** \'gwȯ-'mȯ-'jȯ\ *orig.* Guo Kaizhen (1892–1978) Chinese scholar and writer. After producing a popular translation of J. W. von GOETHE's *Sorrows of Young Werther* (1922), he wrote prolifically in every genre, including poetry, fiction, plays, autobiography, translations of Western works, and historical and philosophical treatises, including a monumental study of ancient inscriptions. A Marxist, his work was banned by the Guomindang. Following the 1949 revolution, he was named to the highest official literary positions, and later to the presidency of the Chinese Academy of Sciences.

guppy Colorful, freshwater, live-bearing topminnows (*Lebistes reticulatus* and *Poecilia reticulata*) popular in home aquariums. Guppies are hardy and energetic. The male, smaller and much more brightly colored than the female, grows to about 1.5 in. (4 cm). Guppies have been bred in various ornate strains characterized by color or pattern and by shape and size of the tail and dorsal fins.

Gupta dynasty \'gup-tə\ (4th–6th cent.) Rulers of an empire in N and parts of central and W India. The dynasty was founded by Candra Gupta I (r.320–c.330). He was succeeded by his son, Samudra Gupta (r.330–c.380), who soon controlled most of the Ganges River valley and the N Deccan. He exterminated nine monarchs and subjugated 12 others in his campaigns. His son Candra Gupta II (r.380–c.415) continued to expand the empire; his reign is associated mainly with cultural achievements. From about 470, Gupta emperors faced invasions by the Hunas, and by the mid-6th cent. the dynasty had ended. The Gupta period is noted for the flourishing of Sanskrit literature (see KALIDASA), its sophisticated metal coins, its advanced mathematics, which made use of decimal notation and zero, and its astronomical advances.

Gurdjieff \gər-'jēf\, **George (Ivanovitch)** *orig.* George S. Georgiades (1872?–1949) Armenian mystic and philosopher. He apparently traveled in the Middle East, Africa, and Central Asia as a young man. In 1919 he founded the Institute for the Harmonious Development of Man at Tiflis (now Tbilisi), Georgia. In 1922 he reestablished the institute at Fontainebleau, France; there he and his followers engaged in philosophical dialogue, ritual exercises, and dance. Gurdjieff believed that ordinary living was akin to sleep and that spiritual discipline made possible heightened levels of vitality and awareness. The institute closed in 1933, but Gurdjieff continued to teach in Paris until his death.

gurdwara \gür-'dwä-rä\ Sikh place of worship. Each houses a copy of the ADI GRANTH and serves as a meeting place for worship. A community kitchen and often a school are attached to the building. A room at home set aside for devotion is also called a gurdwara. Pilgrimages are often made to the gurdwaras associated with the Sikh GURUS' lives, notably the GOLDEN TEMPLE.

Guru Title of the first 10 leaders of SIKHISM. The first was NANAK, who before his death (1539) began the tradition that allowed the Guru to name his successor. Later Gurus included AMAR DAS and ARJAN. In time the Guru became as much a military as a spiritual leader. GOBIND SINGH discontinued the office in 1708 and vested its authority in the Sikh sacred scripture, the ADI GRANTH.

guru In HINDUISM, a personal spiritual teacher. In ancient India, knowledge of the VEDAS was transmitted orally from guru to pupil. The rise of the BHAKTI movement further increased the importance of gurus, who were often looked on as living embodiments of spiritual truth and were identified with the deity. Men or women may be gurus, though generally only men have established lineages.

Gustafson \ˌgəs-'taf-sən\, **Ralph (Barker)** (1909–1995) Canadian poet. A native of Quebec, Gustafson attended Oxford Univ. His work shows a development from traditional form and manner to an elliptical style reflecting the influence of Anglo-Saxon verse and the metrical experiments of G. M. HOPKINS. His fine later works include *Rivers Among Rocks* (1960), *Conflicts of Spring* (1981), and *Shadows in the Grass* (1991). He also published collections of short stories.

Gustav I Vasa *orig.* Gustav Eriksson Vasa (1496?–1560) King of Sweden (1523–60). In the rebellion against CHRISTIAN II of Denmark, who controlled most of Sweden, Gustav became leader of the rebels (1520), secured crucial aid from the rich free city of Lübeck to establish Sweden's independence, and in 1523 was elected king. He imposed heavy taxes to pay his debts to Lübeck and to strengthen royal authority. He hoped to seize the Roman Catholic church's wealth, and he pushed Sweden toward becoming a Protestant (Lutheran) country. An autocratic ruler, he built a strong monarchy and an efficient administration.

Gustav II Adolf *Latin* **Gustavus Adolphus** (1594–1632) King of Sweden (1611–32) who made Sweden a major European power. The son of CHARLES IX, Gustav ended the war with Denmark in 1613 and ended the war with Russia in 1617. With his trusted chancellor, Axel OXENSTIERNA, Gustav introduced major reforms, establishing an efficient central administration and improving education. Resuming the war with SIGISMUND III VASA in 1621, he obtained much of Polish Livonia (Latvia and Estonia). He saw his Polish campaigns as part of the struggle of PROTESTANTISM against the COUNTER-REFORMATION. He entered the THIRTY YEARS' WAR in 1630 to secure the Swedish state and church from danger. An outstanding military tactician, he led an army of unusual quality, and his position was strengthened by alliances with France, Brandenburg, and Saxony. Success in the Battle of Breitenfeld let him sweep through central Germany and claim large territories, particularly Pomerania (1631). At Lützen in 1632, the Swedes defeated Austria, but Gustav was killed in battle.

Gustav III (1746–1792) King of Sweden (1771–92). The son of King Adolf Frederick (1710–1771), he succeeded to a weakened Swedish throne. In 1772 he established a new constitution that increased the crown's power and introduced numerous enlightened reforms. He waged an unpopular war on Russia (1788–90), and when some Swedish officers mutinied, he again augmented royal authority in a new constitution (1789). The Swedish nobility remained opposed to him and had him assassinated. A patron of the arts and a playwright, Gustav's reign was known as the Swedish enlightenment.

Gustav IV Adolf (1778–1837) King of Sweden (1800–1809). Son of the assassinated GUSTAV III, he came to the throne in 1792 under the regency of his uncle Charles, duke of Södermanland (later Charles XIII). In 1805 Gustav brought Sweden into the European coalition against NAPOLEON. Russia joined with France in 1807, leading to a Russian attack on Finland. Denmark-Norway also declared war on Sweden, causing the loss of additional territory. In 1809 Gustav was overthrown in a coup and left Sweden for exile, settling in Switzerland.

Gutenberg \'gü-t⁼n-ˌbərg\, **Johannes (Gensfleisch zur Laden zum)** (c.1395–1468) German inventor of a method of PRINTING from movable type. Born in Mainz, he was experimenting with printing by 1438. He obtained backing in 1450 from the financier Johann Fust (c.1400–1466); Fust's impatience led to Gutenberg's loss of his establishment to Fust in 1455. Gutenberg's masterpiece, and the first book ever printed from movable type, is the "Forty-Two-Line" Bible, completed no later than 1455. A magnificent Psalter was published in 1457, after the loss of his press. His invention's unique elements included a mold, with which type could be cast precisely and in large quantities; a type-metal alloy; a new press, derived from those used in winemaking and papermaking; and an oil-based printing ink. None of these features existed in Chinese or Korean printing, in the existing European technique of stamping letters on various surfaces, or in woodblock printing. Gutenberg's invention, seminal to the course of Western civilization, remained the source of the basic elements of typesetting for 500 years.

Guthrie, (William) Tyrone (*later* **Sir Tyrone**) (1900–1971) British theater director and producer. He served as director of the Shakespeare Repertory Company (1933–45), which performed at the OLD VIC and Sadler's Wells theaters. Noted for his original approach to Shakespeare, he also directed such operas as *Peter Grimes* (1946) and *Carmen* (1949) and his own play, *Top of the Ladder* (1950). He helped found and direct the STRATFORD FESTIVAL (1953–57), strongly influencing the development of Canadian theater, and the Minneapolis (later Tyrone Guthrie) Theatre (1961–63).

Guthrie, Woody (*orig.* Woodrow Wilson) (1912–1967) U.S. singer and songwriter. Born in Okemah, Okla., Guthrie left home at 15 to travel the country by freight train. With his guitar and harmonica he sang in the hobo and migrant camps of the Great Depression, later becoming a musical spokesman for labor and populist sentiment. He wrote over 1,000 songs, including "So Long (It's Been Good to Know Yuh)," "Hard Traveling," and "Union Maid." In New York he joined Pete SEEGER in the activist Almanac Singers. His "This Land Is Your Land" became an unofficial national anthem. His son Arlo (b.1947) also achieved success as a songwriter and singer.

Guwahati See GAUHATI

Guyana \gī-'ä-nə\ *officially* **Co-operative Republic of Guyana** *formerly (until 1966)* **British Guiana** Republic, NE S. America. Area: 83,044 sq mi (215,083 sq km). Population (2000): 792,000. Capital: GEORGETOWN. The people are about half E. Indian, with a large black (Afro-Guyanese)

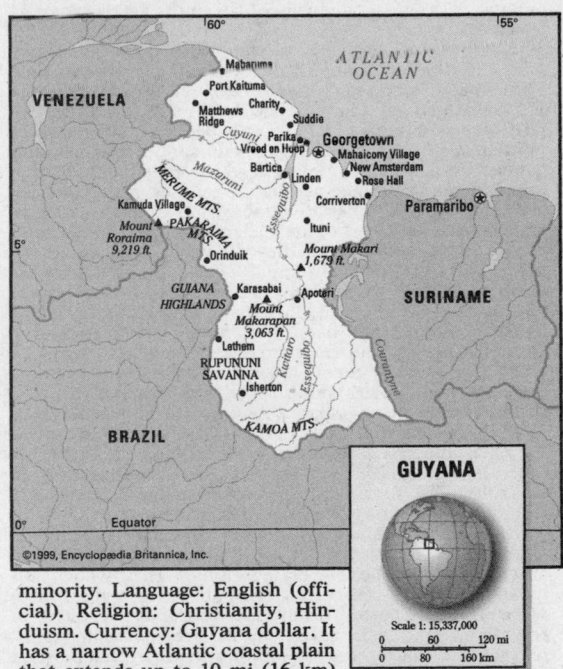

GUYANA

Scale 1: 15,337,000

©1999, Encyclopædia Britannica, Inc.

minority. Language: English (official). Religion: Christianity, Hinduism. Currency: Guyana dollar. It has a narrow Atlantic coastal plain that extends up to 10 mi (16 km) inland and includes reclaimed land protected by sea walls and canals. The tropical forest zone begins some 40 mi (64 km) inland and covers more than 80% of the country. The Pacaraima Mtns. in the west provide headwaters for the Essequibo River. It has a developing market economy with both public and private ownership. Major exports are sugar, rice, bauxite and aluminum. It is a multiparty republic with one legislative house; its head of state and government is the president. It was colonized by the Dutch in the 17th cent.; during the NAPOLEONIC WARS the British occupied the territory and afterward purchased the colonies of Demerara, Berbice, and Essequibo, united in 1831 as British Guiana. The slave trade was abolished in 1807, but emancipation of the 100,000 slaves in the colonies was not complete until 1838. From the

FG

1840s, E. Indian and Chinese indentured servants were brought to work the plantations; by 1917 almost 240,000 E. Indians had migrated to British Guiana. It was made a crown colony in 1928 and granted home rule in 1953. Political parties began to emerge, developing on racial lines as the People's Progressive Party (largely E. Indian) and the People's National Congress (largely black). The PNC formed a coalition government and led the country into independence as Guyana in 1966. In 1970 Guyana bcame a republic within the COMMONWEALTH; in 1980 it adopted a new constitution. Venezuela has long claimed land west of the Essequibo River, and the U.N. has continued to arbitrate the issue.

Gwalior \'gwä-lē-ˌȯr\ City (pop., 1991: 691,000), N central India. It is built around a walled fortress on a cliff 300 ft (90 m) above the plain. First known around A.D. 525, it was under Hindu rule until 1232 and then changed hands several times between Muslims and Hindus until 1751; thereafter it remained a Maratha stronghold. The fortress contains outstanding examples of Hindu architecture, including reservoirs, palaces, temples, and a mosque. Just below its walls are 15th-cent. rock-cut Jain statues nearly 60 ft (18 m) high.

Gwyn, Nell (*orig.* Eleanor) (1650–1687) British actress. She was selling oranges at the DRURY LANE THEATRE when she became the mistress of its leading actor, Charles Hart, who trained her for the stage. The leading comedienne of the King's Company (1666–69), "pretty, witty Nell" was in demand as a speaker of impudent prologues and epilogues. She became the mistress of CHARLES II (1669–85) and was popular with the public for her high spirits and frank recklessness.

gymnasium In Germany, a state-maintained secondary school that prepares pupils for higher academic education. This type of nine-year school originated in Strasbourg in 1537. The usual graduation age is 19 or 20. Secondary or postprimary education is also provided by middle schools (*Mittelschulen*), teachers colleges, and commercial schools.

gymnastics Competitive sport in which individuals perform optional and prescribed acrobatic exercises, mostly on special apparatus, in order to demonstrate strength, balance, and body control. Part of the ancient Olympic Games, gymnastics in its modern form was virtually reinvented in the modern era by Friedrich Jahn (1778–1852). The sport became part of the revived Olympics in 1896; women's gymnastics was instituted in 1936. Men's events include the horizontal bar, parallel bars, side horse (pommel horse), VAULTING, rings, and floor exercises. Women's events include the balance beam, uneven parallel bars, vaulting, floor exercises, and rhythmic sportive gymnastics.

gymnosperm \'jim-nə-ˌspərm\ Any woody plant that reproduces by means of a seed (or ovule) in direct contact with the environment, as opposed to an angiosperm, or FLOWERING PLANT, whose seeds are enclosed by mature ovaries, or fruits. The four surviving gymnosperm divisions are Coniferophyta (CONIFERS, the most widespread), Cycadophyta (cycads), Ginkgophyta (GINKGOS), and Gnetophyta. Gymnosperms occur on all continents except Antarctica, and especially in the temperate latitudes. Their wood is often called SOFTWOOD to differentiate it from the HARDWOOD of angiosperms. Gymnosperms also are a source of essential oils used in soaps, air fresheners, disinfectants, pharmaceuticals, cosmetics, and perfumes; of tannin, used for curing leather; and of TURPENTINES. Gymnosperms were a major component in the vegetation that was compressed over millions of years into COAL. Most are EVERGREENS. They produce male and female reproductive cells in separate male and female strobili (see CONE).

gynecology See OBSTETRICS AND GYNECOLOGY

Gypsies *or* **Rom** People originating in N India but now living worldwide, principally in Europe. Most Gypsies speak ROMANY in addition to the local language. It is thought that Gypsy groups left India in repeated migrations, reaching Western Europe by the 15th cent. In the 20th cent. they spread to N. and S. America and Australia. Population estimates today run from 2 to 3 million. How many Gypsies remain nomadic is unclear, but those that migrate do so at least seasonally along patterned routes that ignore national boundaries. Gypsies pursue occupations compatible with a nomadic life. In the past they were often livestock traders, tinkers, fortune-tellers, and entertainers; today they are often car mechanics and workers in traveling circuses and amusement parks. Bands of 10–100 families elect chieftains for life, but their title is not heritable. Women are organized as a group within the band and represented by a senior woman. Gypsies have often been persecuted and harassed; the Nazis killed about 400,000 Gypsies in extermination camps. Modern Gypsy culture faces erosion from urban influences.

gypsum \'jip-səm\ Common sulfate mineral, hydrated calcium sulfate, of great commercial importance. The U.S., Canada, France, Italy, and Britain are among the leading producers. Crude gypsum is used as a fluxing agent, soil conditioner, and filler in paper and textiles. Most of the total production is calcined (heated) for use as plaster of paris and as building materials in plaster, board products, and tiles and blocks.

gypsy moth Species (*Lymantria dispar*) of tussock moth, a serious pest of trees. The European strain was introduced into E N. America about 1869. The heavy-bodied, weak-flying female is white with black zigzag markings. The smaller, darker male is a stronger flier. The voracious larvae can completely defoliate deciduous trees within weeks. The larger Asian gypsy moth (wingspan of about 3.5 in., or 90 mm) is even more threatening, and the larvae eat the leaves of both conifers and deciduous trees. It was introduced into NW N. America in 1991. Sprayed insecticides remain the most effective means of control.

Gypsy Rose Lee See G. R. LEE

gyrfalcon \'jər-ˌfal-kən\ Arctic BIRD OF PREY (*Falco rusticolus*), the largest FALCON. It may reach 2 ft (60 cm) in length. It breeds in the North Pole region but is sometimes seen at lower latitudes when food is scarce. It varies from pure white with black speckling to dark gray with barring. It hunts for hares, rodents, and birds of the tundra and seacoast. In traditional FALCONRY, the gyrfalcon was the bird of kings.

Gyrfalcon (*Falco rusticolus*)

gyroscope \'jī-rə-ˌskōp\ Device consisting of a rapidly spinning wheel set in a framework that permits it to tilt freely in any direction, or to rotate about any axis. The MOMENTUM of such a wheel causes it to retain its attitude when the framework is tilted (see CONSERVATION LAW). Because of this ability, gyroscopes are used in compasses, automatic pilots on ships and aircraft, and inertial guidance systems.

H

Haakon IV Haakonsson \'hä-kȯn...'hä-kȯns-ˌsȯn\ *known as* **Haakon the Old** (1204–1263) King of Norway (1217–63). After he became king his mother answered doubts about his paternity by passing through an ordeal of hot irons. He made a commercial treaty with England (1217), the earliest such treaty by either nation, and with the N German trading city of Lübeck (1250). He consolidated the monarchy's power and established Norwegian sovereignty over Iceland and Greenland (1261–62). He was a noted patron of the arts, and his reign began the "golden age" in medieval Norwegian history.

Haakon VII \'hȯ-kən\ (1872–1957) King of Norway (1905–57). Born Prince Carl of Denmark, he was offered the Norwegian crown after the restoration of the country's independence in 1905. Receiving approval by a plebiscite, he took the Old Norse name of Haakon. In World War II he fled to England after the German invasion of Norway (1940), and his refusal to abdicate inspired the Norwegians to resist the occupation.

Haarlem City (pop., 1999 est.: 148,000), W Netherlands. It was chartered in 1245, and incorporated in the United Netherlands in 1577. Its prosperity peaked in the 17th cent., when it was a refuge for HUGUENOTS and also an artistic center. An industrial city now, it is also the center for a tulip-growing region. Sites of interest include the 13th-cent. town hall and the 14th-cent. Great Church.

Habakkuk \hə-'bak-ək, 'hab-ə-ˌkük\ (6th or 7th cent. B.C.) One of the 12 Minor Prophets of the OLD TESTAMENT, traditional author of the Book of Habakkuk. (His prophecy is part of a larger book, The Twelve, in the Jewish canon.) He denounced the sins of Judah, identifying their enemies the Chaldeans (Babylonians) as instruments of God's punishment, but predicted the triumph of righteousness.

habeas corpus \'hā-bē-əs-'kȯr-pəs\ In COMMON LAW, any of several WRITS issued to bring a party before a court. The most important is used to correct violations of personal liberty by directing judicial inquiry into the legality of a detention. Common grounds for relief include a conviction based on illegally obtained evidence, a denial of effective assistance of counsel, or a conviction by a jury that was improperly selected or impaneled. The writ may be used in civil matters to challenge a person's custody of a child or the institutionalization of a person declared incompetent.

Haber-Bosch process \'hä-bər-'bȯsh\ *or* **Haber ammonia process** *or* **synthetic ammonia process** First economically feasible method of directly synthesizing AMMONIA from HYDROGEN gas and atmospheric NITROGEN. It was developed about 1909, prompted by rapidly increasing demand for nitrogen fertilizer. It was the first industrial process to use high pressure (200–400 atmospheres) for a chemical reaction. Still the cheapest means of industrial NITROGEN FIXATION, it is a basic process of the chemical industry.

habitat Place where an organism or a community of organisms lives, including all living and nonliving factors or conditions of the surrounding environment. A host organism inhabited by parasites is as much a habitat as a grove of trees or a small pond. "Microhabitat" refers to the conditions and organisms in the immediate vicinity of a plant or animal.

Habsburg dynasty \'haps-ˌbərg\ *or* **Hapsburg dynasty** Royal German family, one of the chief dynasties of Europe from the 15th to the 20th cent. As dukes, archdukes, and emperors, the Habsburgs ruled Austria from 1282 until 1918. They also controlled Hungary and Bohemia (1526–1918) and ruled Spain and the Spanish empire for almost two centuries (1504–6, 1516–1700). One of the earliest Habsburgs to rise to great power was RUDOLF I, who became German king in 1273. Frederick IV, the Habsburg king of Germany, was crowned Holy Roman Emperor as FREDERICK III in 1452, and Habsburgs continued to hold that title until 1806. Frederick's son MAXIMILIAN I acquired the Netherlands, Luxembourg, and Burgundy through marriage. The zenith of Habsburg power came in the 16th cent. under CHARLES V. See also HOLY ROMAN EMPIRE.

hacienda \ˌ(h)ä-sē-'en-də\ In Latin America, a large landed estate. The hacienda originated in the colonial period. Laborers, ordinarily Indians, were theoretically free wage earners, but in practice their employers, who controlled the local governments, were able to bind them to the land through perpetual indebtedness. By the 19th cent., half of Mexico's rural population was entangled in the peonage system. Many haciendas were broken up by the MEXICAN REVOLUTION. Haciendas are known as *estancias* in Argentina and *fazendas* in Brazil.

Hackman, Gene (*orig.* Eugene Alden) (b.1930) U.S. film actor. Born in San Bernardino, Cal., he made his film debut in *Lilith* (1964). Praised for his performances in *Bonnie and Clyde* (1967) and *I Never Sang for My Father* (1970), he attained star status in *The French Connection* (1971, Academy Award). Noted for his portrayals of ordinary men, he won further acclaim for *The Conversation* (1974), *Mississippi Burning* (1988), *Unforgiven* (1992, Academy Award), and *Heist* (2001).

haddock Valuable N. American food fish (*Melanogrammus aeglefinus,* family Gadidae). A bottom-dweller that feeds on invertebrates and fishes, it resembles the COD, but has a dark (rather than light) lateral line and a dark spot on each shoulder. It is gray or brownish above, paler below. It grows to about 3 ft (90 cm) long and 25 lbs (11 kg).

Hadean eon \'hä-dē-ən\ Eon of pre-geologic history. It dates from about 4.6 billion to 3.8 billion years ago and spans the time between the formation of the solar system and the formation of the first rocks on the earth. See table at GEOLOGIC TIME.

Hades \'hā-ˌdēz\ Greek god of the underworld. He was also known as Pluto; his Roman equivalent was Dis. Hades was the brother of ZEUS and POSEIDON. His queen was PERSEPHONE, the daughter of DEMETER, whom he spirited away to the underworld. Stern and pitiless, he presided over the trial and punishment of the wicked after death. His name became a synonym for Hell.

Hadith \hä-'dēth\ In ISLAM, the oral traditions attributed to the Prophet MUHAMMAD, his family, and the COMPANIONS OF THE PROPHET. Hadith is a major source of religious law and moral guidance. It consists of two parts: the oral law itself and the Isnad, or chain of authorities who passed it down to posterity.

Hadrian \'hā-drē-ən\ *Latin* Caesar Traianus Hadrianus Augustus *orig.* Publius Aelius Hadrianus (A.D. 76–138) Roman emperor (117–38). He was adopted and named successor just before the death of his uncle, TRAJAN. He quickly executed his senatorial opponents and abandoned Trajan's conquests in Armenia and Mesopotamia. He traveled widely, and many of his accomplishments were related to his visits abroad. He quelled disturbances in the provinces and began construction of HADRIAN'S WALL. An admirer of Greek civilization, he completed the temple of Zeus in Athens and created a federation of Greek cities. He launched a building program at Delphi and was initiated into the ELEUSINIAN MYSTERIES. After his young companion Antinoüs drowned in the Nile (130), he erected statues of the boy throughout the realm, and cults sprang up widely.

Hadrian

Hadrianopolis, Battle of See Battle of ADRIANOPLE

Hadrian's Villa HADRIAN'S country residence, built (c.A.D. 125–34) at Tivoli near Rome. A sumptuous imperial complex with parks and gardens on a grand scale, it included baths, libraries, sculpture gardens, theaters, alfresco dining areas, pavilions, and private suites. The buildings, which covered about 7 sq mi (18 sq km), were reproductions of celebrated structures the emperor had seen in his travels. Significant portions have survived.

Hadrian's Wall Continuous Roman defensive barrier, begun by HADRIAN in A.D. 122, that guarded the NW frontier of the province of Britain from barbarian (particularly Celtic) invaders. It extended 73 mi (118 km) from coast to coast. It had towers, gates, and forts at regular intervals; a ditch fronted it and an earthwork ran behind it. It remained in use until around 410. Portions remain visible today.

hadron \'ha-ˌdrän\ Any of the SUBATOMIC PARTICLES that are built from QUARKS and thus interact via the STRONG FORCE. The hadrons fall into two groups: MESONS and BARYONS. Except for PROTONS and NEUTRONS, which are bound in nuclei, all hadrons have short lives and are produced in high-energy collisions of subatomic particles. All hadrons are subject to GRAVITATION; charged hadrons are subject to ELECTROMAGNETIC FORCES. Some hadrons break up by way of the WEAK FORCE (as in radioactive decay); others decay via the strong and electromagnetic forces.

Haeckel \'he-kəl\, **Ernst (Heinrich Philipp August)** (1834–1919) German zoologist and evolutionist. His work concentrated on diverse marine invertebrates. Influenced by Charles DARWIN, Haeckel saw evolution as the basis for an explanation of all nature. He attempted to create the first genealogical tree of the entire animal kingdom. He proposed that each species illustrates its evolutionary history in its embryological development ("Ontogeny recapitulates phylogeny"). Through his theories of the evolution of humans (some of them wrong), he brought attention to important biological questions. Through his numerous books, he was an influential popularizer of evolutionary theory.

haematite See HEMATITE

Haemophilus \hē-'mä-fə-ləs\ Genus of tiny rod-shaped BACTERIA. All are strict parasites occurring in the respiratory tracts of warm-blooded animals, including humans, and in certain cold-blooded animals. They are gram-negative (see GRAM STAIN), do not move, and require a growth factor found in blood. One species causes chancroid, a sexually transmitted disease. Another causes secondary infection in persons with influenza.

Ha-erh-pin See HARBIN

Hafez \'kȯ-fez\ or **Hafiz** \'kȯ-fiz\ orig. Mohammad Shams al-Din (1325/26–1389/90) Persian poet. The recipient of a traditional religious education, he served as court poet to several rulers. He perfected the GHAZEL as a verse form of 6–15 couplets linked by unity of subject and symbolism rather than by a logical sequence of ideas. His poems are notable for their simple, often colloquial, musical language and his unaffected use of homely images and proverbial expressions. His most famous work is the *Divan*.

Hafsid dynasty \'haf-səd\ BERBER dynasty of the 13th–16th cent. founded by the ALMOHAD governor Abu Zakariyya Yahya in N central Africa about 1229. His son Mustansir

(r.1249–77) enlarged the empire to its peak of power and prestige. It had trade relations with Italian, Spanish, and Provençal communities despite running pirate operations in the Mediterranean. Dynastic struggles after 1452 weakened the Hafsids, allowing Arabs to take over. The Turks incorporated their land into a province in 1574.

Hagana \hä-gä-'nä\ Zionist military organization (1920–48). It fought off the attacks of Palestinian Arabs on Jewish settlements, and effectively defended them despite being outlawed by the British authorities. It turned to terrorism after World War II when the British refused to permit unlimited Jewish immigration to Palestine. In 1947 it clashed openly with British and Arab forces. With the creation of Israel in 1948, the Hagana became its national army.

Hagen, Walter (Charles) (1892–1969) U.S. golfer. Born in Rochester, N.Y., he won numerous important championships from the mid-1910s to the late 1920s and captained the U.S. Ryder Cup team 1927–37. A colorful, self-confident man, he insisted that professional golfers be treated as gentlemen (not always previously the case). Among his well-known remarks is the observation that, in life, one should take the time to "stop and smell the roses."

hagfish Any of about 30 species of primitive jawless fishes in two families of the class Agnatha. Hagfishes are eel-like, scaleless, and soft-skinned. Species grow to 16–32 in. (40–80 cm) long. They have a cartilaginous skeleton. The mouth is a slitlike, sucking opening with horny teeth. Found in cold seawater, to depths of over 4,000 ft (1,200 m), they habitually lie buried in burrows on soft bottoms. They eat invertebrates and dead or crippled fishes, and may bore their way into the bodies of fish caught on lines or in nets and eat the fish from the inside. They secrete extraordinary amounts of slime when handled. See also LAMPREY.

Haggadah or **Haggada** \ˌhä-gä-'dä, hə-'gä-də\ In Judaism, the text that guides the performance of ritual acts and prayers at the SEDER dinner celebrating PASSOVER. The Haggadah retells the story of EXODUS, offering commentaries and supplying answers to the traditional questions asked by children at the beginning of the Seder. More broadly, Haggadah can refer to the part of rabbinical literature not concerned with the law.

Haggai \'hag-ē-ˌī, 'hag-ˌī\ (fl.6th cent. B.C.) One of the 12 Minor Prophets of the OLD TESTAMENT, traditional author of the Book of Haggai. (His prophecy is part of a larger book, The Twelve, in the Jewish canon.) He returned to Israel when the Babylonian Exile ended and helped mobilize the Jewish community to rebuild the Temple of JERUSALEM. His book consists of four prophecies delivered in 521 B.C.

Haggard, H(enry) Rider (later **Sir Rider**) (1856–1925) British novelist. After holding posts in S. Africa (1875–81), he began writing stories set in Africa. Of his 34 colorful adventure novels, the best-known is *King Solomon's Mines* (1885); others include *She* (1887), *Allan Quatermain* (1887), *Cleopatra* (1889), and *Ayesha* (1905). Also a farmer, he wrote *A Farmer's Year* (1899) and *Rural England* (2 vols., 1902).

Hagia Sophia \'hä-gē-ə-sō-'fē-ə, ˌhä-jē-ə-sō-'fē-ə\ (Greek: "Holy Wisdom") Church in Istanbul, later a mosque and now a museum. It is the masterpiece of BYZANTINE ARCHITECTURE. Designed under JUSTINIAN I by Anthemius of Tralles and Isidorus of Miletus, the original building was completed in less than six years (A.D. 532–37). It combined a longitudinal BASILICA and a centralized building with a huge main dome (rebuilt 563). Great marble piers rise up to support the dome. Light from windows above the galleries and at the base of the dome obscures the supports, giving the impression that the canopy floats on air.

hagiography \ˌha-gē-'ä-grə-fē, ˌhä-jē-'ä-grə-fē\ Literature describing the lives of the saints. Christian hagiography includes accounts of saints' martyrdom and of the miracles connected with their relics, tombs, icons, or statues. Hagiographies were being written as early as the 2nd cent. and were widely popular during the Middle Ages.

Hague \'häg\, **The** Dutch **'s-Gravenhage** \ˌskräv-ə°n-'hä-kə\ or **Den Haag** \den-'häk\ City (pop., 1999 est.: 440,000), seat of government of the Netherlands. Located 4 mi (6 km) from the North Sea, it is the nation's administrative, judicial, and legislative capital, though nearby AMSTERDAM is the official capital. The principal residence of the counts of Holland (1248) became the seat of the Dutch government in 1585. The city grew rapidly in the 19th and 20th cent. A center of international law and corporate administration, most of its businesses are engaged in trade, banking, and insurance. The U.N. INTERNATIONAL COURT OF JUSTICE is housed in the Peace Palace (1913). The city is filled with notable architecture.

Hague Conventions International agreements signed at The Hague (1899, 1907). The first conference, requested by Russia, discussed rules to limit warfare and attempted arms limitations; 26 countries approved several proposed conventions, including prohibition of the use of asphyxiating gases (not renewed in 1907) and creation of a Permanent Court of Arbitration. The 1907 meeting, called by Theodore ROOSEVELT, was attended by 44 countries and also had arms limitation as a goal, which again went unmet. The conferences influenced creation of the LEAGUE OF NATIONS and the UNITED NATIONS.

Hahn, Otto (1879–1968) German physical chemist. With Lise MEITNER he discovered several radioelements. In 1938, with Meitner and Fritz Strassmann (1902–1980), he found the first chemical evidence of NUCLEAR-FISSION products, created when they bombarded uranium with neutrons. For his discovery of nuclear fission, Hahn was awarded a 1944 Nobel Prize. He later spoke out strongly against further development of nuclear weapons.

Hahnemann \'hä-nə-mən\, **(Christian Friedrich) Samuel** (1755–1843) German physician, founder of HOMEOPATHY. Struck by the similarity of the symptoms quinine produced in the healthy body to those of the disorders it cured, he theorized that "likes are cured by likes" and proposed that substances used this way are most effective in small doses. His chief works were *Organon of Rational Medicine* (1810) and *Pure Pharmacology* (6 vols., 1811).

Haida \'hī-də\ NORTHWEST COAST INDIAN people of the Queen Charlotte Islands, British Columbia, and S Prince of Wales Island, Alaska. There were two major tribal divisions, or moieties; each consisted of lineages that owned rights to land, had their own chiefs, waged war, and held ceremonies such as POTLATCHES. Haida economy was based on fishing and hunting. The Haida are known for their craftsmanship and their art, which includes TOTEM POLES. Today they number about 3,500.

Haidarabad See HYDERABAD

Haifa \'hī-fə\ *ancient* Sycaminum. City (pop., 1999 est.: 265,000) and chief port, NW Israel. Located on the Bay of Haifa overlooking the Mediterranean Sea, it is first mentioned in the TALMUD (c.1st–4th cent. A.D.). Conquered in 1100 by the Crusaders, it was taken by NAPOLEON in 1799. Occupied by British forces in 1918, it became part of mandated PALESTINE. It came under Israeli control in 1948, during the first ARAB–ISRAELI WAR. Modern Haifa is a tourist resort, commercial center, and world headquarters of the BAHA'I movement.

Haig, Douglas *later* Earl Haig (1861–1928) British general in World War I. A career army officer, in 1915 he became commander in chief of British forces. Advocating a strategy of attrition, he was criticized for the enormous British losses at the SOMME (1916) and YPRES (1917). He was promoted to field marshal in 1916. In 1918 he secured the appointment of Ferdinand FOCH as commander of Allied forces. After helping stop the last German offensive, Haig led the victorious Allied assault in August 1918.

haiku \'hī-ˌkü\ Unrhymed Japanese poetic form consisting of 17 syllables arranged in three lines containing five, seven, and five syllables, respectively. Haiku expresses much and suggests more in the fewest possible words. The form gained distinction in the 17th cent., when BASHO elevated it to a highly refined art. It remains Japan's most popular poetic form.

hail Precipitation of balls or pieces of ice with a diameter of 0.2–4 in. (5 mm–10 cm). Small hail (also called sleet) has a diameter of less than 0.2 in. Destructive to buildings and crops, large hail may also be dangerous to animals. Hailstones 6 in. (15 cm) in diameter have fallen during storms in the U.S. Midwest. Hailstorms usually last around 15 min-

utes and ordinarily occur in the afternoon; they may accompany thunderstorms.

Haile Mariam, Mengistu See MENGISTU HAILE MARIAM

Haile Selassie \'hī-lē-sə-'las-ē\ *orig.* Tafari Makonnen (1892–1975) Emperor of Ethiopia (1930–74) and messiah of the RASTAFARIANS. Tafari was a son of a chief adviser to MENILEK II. After Menilek's daughter, Zauditu, became empress (1917), Ras (Prince) Tafari, who had married Menilek's great-granddaughter, was named regent and heir apparent to the throne. When Zauditu died (1930), Tafari became emperor, took the name of Haile Selassie ("Might of the Trinity"), and pursued a policy of modernization. He brought Ethiopia into the League of Nations and the U.N. and made Addis Ababa the center for the ORGANIZATION OF AFRICAN UNITY (OAU). Though popular among the majority Christian population, he was deposed in 1974 by MENGISTU HAILE MARIAM and apparently killed by his captors.

Hail Mary *Latin* **Ave Maria** Principal Roman Catholic prayer addressed to the Virgin MARY. It begins with the words of the Archangel GABRIEL and Mary's cousin Elizabeth in the Gospel of Luke: "Hail Mary, full of grace, the Lord is with thee. Blessed art thou among women and blessed is the fruit of thy womb, Jesus." A closing petition, "Holy Mary, Mother of God, pray for us sinners, now and at the hour of our death," came into general use later.

Haiphong \'hī-'fȯṅ\ Seaport city (pop., 1992 est.: 783,000), N Vietnam. Lying on the RED RIVER delta, off the Gulf of TONKIN, it is the nation's third-largest city and serves as the port of the capital, HANOI, 60 mi (97 km) to the west. A leading industrial center, it sustained heavy damage from U.S. bombing during the VIETNAM WAR.

hair Threadlike outgrowths of the SKIN. Babies shed a layer of downy, slender hairs (lanugo) before or just after birth. Fine, short, unpigmented hairs (vellus) then grow. At puberty, terminal hair, longer, coarser, and more pigmented, develops in the armpits, crotch, sometimes on parts of the trunk and limbs, and, in males, on the face. Scalp hair, eyebrows, and eyelashes are different types. The number of scalp hairs, which grow about 0.5 in. (13 mm) per month, averages 100,000–150,000. The hair shaft (above the skin) is dead tissue, composed of KERATIN. Only a few growing cells at the base of the root are alive. Vellus lasts about four months, scalp hairs three to five years.

Haiti \'hā-tē\ *officially* **Republic of Haiti** Republic, W. INDIES. It occupies the W third of the island of HISPANIOLA, with the Dominican Republic to the east. Area: 10,695 sq mi (27,700 sq km). Population (2000 est.): 6,868,000. Capital: PORT-AU-PRINCE. About 95% of the population is black, 5% mulatto. Language: Haitian Creole and French (both official). Religion: Roman Catholicism; vodun. Currency: gourde. Most of its land is mountainous, with about two-fifths above 1,600 ft (490 m). The mountain ranges alternate with fertile but overpopulated lowlands. Its climate is tropical, modified by the mountains, and subject to periodic droughts and hurricanes. Its longest river is the Artibonite. The poorest country in the Americas, it has a developing market economy based in large part on agriculture and light industries; coffee is the main cash crop. It is a multiparty republic with two legislative houses; the chief of state is the president, and the head of government is the prime minister. Its early history is that of HISPANIOLA. Haiti gained its independence when the former slaves of the island, led by TOUSSAINT-LOUVERTURE in the 1790s, and J.-J. DESSALINES in 1804, rebelled against French rule. The new republic encompassed the entire island of Hispaniola, but the E portion was restored to Spain in 1809. It was reunited under Haitian Pres. Jean-Pierre Boyer (1818–43); after his overthrow the E portion revolted and formed the Dominican Republic. Haiti's government was marked by instability, with frequent coups and assassinations. It was occupied by the U.S. 1915–34. In 1957 François DUVALIER came to power as president for life. Despite an economic decline and continued internal discord, Duvalier ruled as dictator until his death in 1971. He was succeeded by his son, Jean-Claude ("Baby Doc") Duvalier, who was forced into exile in 1986. Haiti's first free presidential elections, held in 1990, were won by J.-B. ARISTIDE. He was deposed by a military

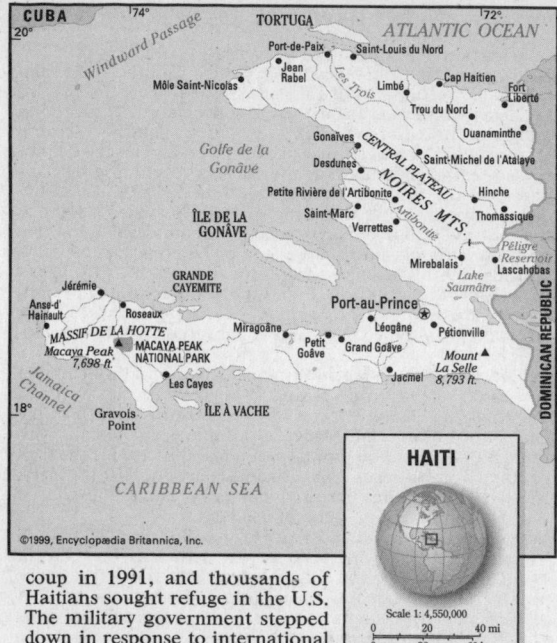

Scale 1: 4,550,000

HAITI

©1999, Encyclopædia Britannica, Inc.

coup in 1991, and thousands of Haitians sought refuge in the U.S. The military government stepped down in response to international pressure, and in 1994 Aristide returned from exile and resumed the presidency. Civil unrest remained widespread and a U.N. peacekeeping force was stationed there.

hajj \'häj\ In ISLAM, the pilgrimage to MECCA required of all Muslims at least once in their lifetime, provided they are physically and financially able. It is one of the Five Pillars of ISLAM. By tradition the pilgrimage is undertaken between the seventh and twelfth days of the last month of the Islamic year. Among the rituals required of pilgrims is walking seven times around the KAABA shrine and sacrificing an animal in honor of ABRAHAM's near-sacrifice of Isaac.

Hakluyt \'hak-₁lüt\, **Richard** (1552?–1616) British geographer. A clergyman and the first professor of modern geography at Oxford Univ., he became acquainted with the most important sea captains and merchants of England, and took on the role of publicist for explorers. In Paris (1583) as chaplain to the English ambassador, he also served as an intelligence officer, collecting information on the Canadian fur trade and on other overseas enterprises. His *Principall Navigations, Voiages and Discoveries of the English Nation* (1589) described the early English voyages to N. America.

Halab See ALEPPO

Halakhah *or* **Halakha** \,hä-lä-'k̲ä, hä-'lä-k̲ə\ In Judaism, all laws and ordinances evolved since biblical times to regulate worship and Jewish daily life. In contrast to the laws written in the TORAH, the Halakhah represents an oral tradition. They were first written down in the 1st–3rd cent. A.D. in the compilation called the MISHNA, which became the foundation of the TALMUD.

Halas \'ha-ləs\, **George Stanley** (1895–1983) U.S. coach and team owner. Born in Chicago, he briefly played baseball for the New York Yankees. In 1920 he founded the Chicago Bears football team, and he served as its coach for most of the next 50 years (1920–30, 1933–43, 1946–55, 1958–67). Under his coaching the Bears won seven league championships and four divisional titles. He retained ownership of the Bears until his death. He helped found the NATIONAL FOOTBALL LEAGUE.

Haldane \'hól-₁dän\, **J(ohn) B(urdon) S(anderson)** (1892–1964) British geneticist. Son of J. S. HALDANE, he began studying science as his father's assistant at age 8. Haldane, R. A. FISHER, and Sewall WRIGHT, in separate mathematical arguments, related Charles DARWIN's evolutionary theory and Gregor MENDEL's laws of heredity. Haldane also con-

tributed to the theory of enzyme action and to studies in human physiology.

Haldane, John Scott (1860–1936) British physiologist and philosopher. He developed procedures for studying the physiology of breathing and of the blood, and devices for measuring hemoglobin and for analyzing blood gas and mixtures of gases. He discovered that breathing is regulated by the amount of carbon dioxide in the blood. He studied the effects of low air pressure, investigated the action of gases in mine suffocations and explosions, and developed a staged decompression method for ascent from deep-sea dives. He was the father of J. B. S. HALDANE.

Hale, George E(llery) (1868–1938) U.S. astronomer. Born in Chicago, he organized the Kenwood Observatory there in 1888. In 1892 he began organizing the Yerkes Observatory at the Univ. of Chicago; he built its 40-in. (1-m) refracting telescope, still the largest of its type. He established the *Astrophysical Journal* in 1895. In 1904 he organized the Mount Wilson Observatory, where he built powerful solar apparatus and the huge 60-in. (1.5-m) and 100-in. (2.5-m) reflecting telescopes. In 1928 he began work on a 200-in. (5-m) reflecting telescope at Caltech's Palomar Observatory; completed in 1948, it was named for him. He is also known for discovering magnetic fields in sunspots.

Hale, Matthew (*later* **Sir Matthew**) (1609–1676) British legal scholar. He defended Royalists during the ENGLISH CIVIL WARS (1642–51), and he played a major role in reforming the legal system and promoting CHARLES II's restoration. He later became chief baron of the exchequer (1660) and chief justice of the King's Bench (1671–76). One of the greatest scholars of the history of English COMMON LAW, he is best known for his *History of the Pleas of the Crown* (published 1736).

Hale, Nathan (1755–1776) American Revolutionary officer. Born in Coventry, Conn., he joined a Connecticut regiment in 1775. Made a captain in 1776, he helped capture a British provision sloop on Long Island. Volunteering for spy duty, he penetrated British lines but was captured and hanged without trial at 21. His last words reportedly were, "I only regret that I have but one life to lose for my country."

Hale, Sarah Josepha *orig.* Sarah Josepha Buell (1788–1879) U.S. writer and editor. Born in Newport, N.H., Hale turned to writing in 1822 as a widow trying to support her family. She edited *Godey's Lady's Book* (1837–77); as the first female magazine editor, she shaped many of the attitudes and ideas of women of the period. She is also remembered for her verse "Mary Had a Little Lamb" (1830).

Haleakala National Park \,hä-lä-ä-kä-'lä\ National park, E Maui Island, Hawaii. It occupies an area of 28,655 acres (11,597 hectares). Its central feature is Haleakala Crater, the world's largest dormant volcanic crater, more than 2,500 ft (762 m) deep and about 20 mi (32 km) in circumference. The crater floor, covering more than 19 sq mi (49 sq km), has areas of forest, desert, and meadow. It is the site of Science City, a research-observatory complex.

Hale-Bopp, Comet COMET discovered in 1994 by amateur astronomers Alan Hale and Thomas Bopp beyond JUPITER's orbit, farther than any detected before by amateurs. Its nucleus was estimated to be about 25 mi (40 km) across, far larger than most comets. At its closest to the sun in April 1997, it was one of the intrinsically brightest comets in several centuries, though not the brightest as seen from earth. The comet triggered a mass suicide by the Heaven's Gate religious cult, whose leader said they would be reincarnated in a spacecraft in the comet's wake.

Haley, Alex(ander Murray Palmer) (1921–1992) U.S. writer. Born in Ithaca, N.Y., he served in the Coast Guard (1939–59) and later became a journalist. With MALCOLM X he cowrote the best-selling *Autobiography of Malcolm X* (1965; film, 1992). His greatest success was *Roots* (1976, special Pulitzer Prize), a partly fictional history of seven generations of his ancestors beginning with their enslavement. Adapted for television, it became one of the most popular television shows ever and spurred great interest in genealogy.

halftone process In PRINTING, a technique of breaking up an image into dots to permit reproduction of the full tone range of a photograph or artwork. It is traditionally done by placing a glass screen printed with a tight grid of lines over the plate being exposed. The grid breaks up the image into hundreds of tiny dots, each of which is read by the camera as either black or white—or, in the case of color art, as either a single printing color or white. The resulting image, called a halftone, is then rephotographed for printing. Screens are made with a varying number of lines per inch, depending on the printing paper.

halibut Any of various FLATFISHES, especially the Atlantic and Pacific halibuts (genus *Hippoglossus,* family Pleuronectidae), both of which have eyes and color on the right side. The Atlantic halibut is the largest flatfish; it may reach a length of about 7 ft (2 m) and a weight of 720 lbs (325 kg). The smaller and slimmer Pacific halibut is found on both sides of the N. Pacific. Other edible halibut include the Greenland halibut and the California halibut (family Bothidae).

Halicarnassus \ˌha-lə-kär-ˈna-səs\ *modern* **Bodrum** \bō-ˈdrům\ Ancient Greek city, Asia Minor. Situated on a peninsula in the Aegean Sea, it became the capital of Caria (c.370 B.C.) under Mausolus, who built a great wall, public buildings, and a secret dockyard and canal. His widow erected (c.350 B.C.) the Mausoleum, one of the SEVEN WONDERS OF THE WORLD; its remains are now in the BRITISH MUSEUM. Halicarnassus was the birthplace of HERODOTUS. The ruins of the castle of the Knights of St. John (c.A.D. 1400) dominate the ancient site.

Halifax City (pop., 1996: 113,000), capital of Nova Scotia. Sited on an inlet of the Atlantic Ocean, it was settled by the British in 1749 as a counterbalance to French holdings at CAPE BRETON ISLAND. During World Wars I and II, Halifax was Canada's most important naval base. A munitions-ship explosion in 1917 killed nearly 2,000 people. Its port is one of the busiest in Canada. Its educational institutions include Dalhousie Univ. (1818); historic buildings include St. Paul's Church (1750), Canada's oldest Protestant church.

halite \ˈha-ˌlīt, ˈhā-ˌlīt\ Naturally occurring SODIUM CHLORIDE, common or rock salt. Halite occurs on all continents, in beds that range from a few feet to more than 1,000 ft (300 m) in thickness. Formed by the evaporation of saline water in partially enclosed basins, it is associated with beds of limestone, dolomite, and shale. Halite is found in large deposits in New York and in Russia, France, India, and Canada.

Hall, Charles Martin (1863–1914) U.S. chemist. Born in Thompson, Ohio, in 1885 he discovered the method of producing ALUMINUM by ELECTROLYSIS (simultaneously with Paul Héroult), an innovation that brought the metal into wide commercial use. Supported by the Mellon family, he formed the Pittsburgh Reduction Co. (later ALCOA). In 1895 the company became the first customer for Niagara Falls' new power plant.

Hall, G(ranville) Stanley (1844–1924) U.S. psychologist. Born in Ashfield, Mass., he earned the first psychology PhD in America (Harvard, 1878). He helped establish Clark Univ. (1888) and worked there to shape experimental psychology into a science. Regarded as the founder of child psychology and educational psychology, he also did much to assimilate the ideas of Charles DARWIN and Sigmund FREUD into American psychology. He founded several journals, including the *American Journal of Psychology,* and helped found the American Psychological Assn., of which he was the first president.

Hall, James (1811–1898) U.S. geologist and paleontologist. Born in Hingham, Mass., he became state geologist for the Geological Survey of New York in 1836; his studies culminated in the massive *Geology of New York* (part 4, 1843), a classic in American geology that introduced the geosynclinal theory of mountain building (see GEOSYNCLINE). He directed the state's Museum of Natural History 1871–98. His major later work was the huge *Paleontology of New York* (13 vols., 1847–94).

Hall, Peter (Reginald Frederick) (*later* **Sir Peter**) (b.1930) British director. As director of London's Arts Theatre (1955–56) he staged London premieres of important continental plays. Especially renowned for his Shakespearean productions, he served as managing director of the Royal Shakespeare Co. 1962–68, and continued to direct plays for

it long afterward. He succeeded Laurence OLIVIER as managing director of London's National Theatre (1973–88), then formed his own theatrical production company. He has also directed the Covent Garden Opera and many operas at Glyndebourne, as well as several films.

Hall, Radclyffe *orig.* Marguerite Radclyffe-Hall (1880–1943) English writer. Hall began her literary career by writing verses, which eventually were collected into five volumes. She won prizes for her novel *Adam's Breed* (1926), a plea for animal rights. Her groundbreaking *The Well of Loneliness* (1928), one of the first lesbian novels in English, was judged obscene and banned in Britain. Most of her five other novels express her strong Christian beliefs.

Halle (an der Saale) \ˈhä-lə\ City (pop., 1998 est.: 268,000), E central Germany. Early settlements (c.1000–400 B.C.) centered around the local salt deposits. Halle and its valuable saltworks were granted to the archbishopric of Magdeburg in A.D. 968. It was a member of the HANSEATIC LEAGUE 1281–1478. It is an important rail junction and a principal commercial and industrial center. It was the birthplace of G. F. HANDEL.

Halley \ˈha-lē, ˈhā-lē\, **Edmond** (1656–1742) English astronomer and mathematician. In 1676 he set sail for the S. Atlantic to compile an accurate star catalog for the Southern Hemisphere, recording the positions of 341 stars. He met Isaac NEWTON at Cambridge and had a prominent role in the development of NEWTON'S LAW OF GRAVITATION. Halley edited Newton's *Principia Mathematica,* bringing it to print in 1687. He produced the first meteorological chart (1686, showing the prevailing winds in the oceans) and magnetic charts of the Atlantic and Pacific (1701). He described the parabolic orbits of 24 comets observed 1337–1698 and showed that three must have been the same comet (see HALLEY'S COMET).

Halley's Comet First COMET whose return was predicted, proving that at least some comets are members of the SOLAR SYSTEM. Edmond HALLEY showed in 1705 that comets seen in 1531, 1607, and 1682 were one comet and predicted its return in 1758. It was later identified with the large, bright comet seen during the NORMAN CONQUEST (shown in the BAYEUX TAPESTRY) and in other sightings about 76 years apart, the first in 240 B.C. The only easily seen comet that returns in one lifetime, most recently in 1985–86, it is roughly 9 mi (15 km) across.

Halley's Comet, 1986

Halloween Holiday observed on October 31, the eve of ALL SAINTS' DAY. Its pagan origins can be traced to the Celtic festival of Samhain, celebrated in ancient England and Ireland to mark the beginning of the Celtic new year. The souls of the dead were supposed to revisit their homes on Samhain eve, and witches, goblins, black cats, and ghosts were said to roam abroad. The pagan observances influenced the Christian festival of All Hallows' Eve, celebrated on the same date. The holiday was gradually secularized and was introduced into the U.S. by the late 19th cent. Today it is celebrated by children in costume who gather candy by ringing doorbells and calling out "trick or treat," "trick" referring to the pranks and vandalism that are also part of the Halloween tradition.

Hallstatt \ˈhäl-ˌshtät, *Engl* ˈhȯl-ˌstat\ Site in upper Austria where objects characteristic of the Early IRON AGE (from c.1100 B.C.) were first identified. More than 2,000 graves lay near a salt mine that preserved implements, parts of clothing, and bodies of miners. Hallstatt art in general is geometric and symmetrical, with a tendency toward the extravagant.

HIJ

hallucination Perception of objects, sounds, or sensations having no demonstrable reality, usually arising from a disorder of the nervous system or in response to certain drugs (see HALLUCINOGEN). Like DREAMS, they derive their content from perceptions known to MEMORY, though these can be greatly transformed. Hallucinations can result when attention collapses from intense arousal due to extreme anxiety, fatigue, or excitement. They figure prominently in SCHIZOPHRENIA.

hallucinogen \hə-'lü-s°n-ə-jən\ Substance that produces psychological effects normally associated only with DREAMS, SCHIZOPHRENIA, or religious visions. It produces changes in perception, thought, and feeling. Those that have aroused the most controversy include LSD, MESCALINE, psilocybin (from certain mushrooms), and bufotenine (from the skin of toads); some would add MARIJUANA. The mode of action is still unclear; NEUROTRANSMITTERS may be affected.

halogen \'ha-lə-jən\ Any of the five nonmetallic ELEMENTS with similar chemical properties: FLUORINE, CHLORINE, BROMINE, IODINE, and astatine (At). They occur next to the rightmost column of the PERIODIC TABLE as usually arranged. All are highly reactive oxidizing agents (see OXIDATION-REDUCTION) with VALENCE 1. They combine readily with most metals and nonmetals to form a variety of compounds and never occur uncombined in nature. Astatine occurs naturally in minute amounts as an intermediate decay product; it has no stable nonradioactive ISOTOPE. Halogen SALTS with metals (halides) are very stable; sodium chloride is the most familiar. Halogen compunds coating fluorescent lamps phosphoresce to produce light in response to electric discharges inside the lamp (see ELECTRIC DISCHARGE LAMP).

halogen lamp *or* **tungsten-halogen lamp** INCANDESCENT LAMP with a quartz bulb and a gas filling that includes a HALOGEN. It gives brilliant light from a compact unit. The halogen combines with the tungsten evaporated from the hot filament to form a compound that is attracted back to the filament, thus extending the filament's life. First used in the late 1960s in motion-picture production, halogen lamps are now also used in automobile headlights, underwater photography, and residential lighting.

Hals \'hälz, 'häls\, **Frans** (1581/85–1666) Dutch portrait painter. He spent his life in Haarlem, where he was registered as a master artist in 1610. His group portraits, notably the monumental *Banquet of Officers of the Civic Guard of St. George* (1616), were painted with a technique close to Impressionism in its looseness, unique in Dutch art at the time. He introduced a jovial spirit that revolutionized portraiture; his subjects exude joie de vivre, with an occasional hint of sadness. After 1650 he portrayed elderly people; these portraits, such as *The Women Regents of the Almshouse at Haarlem* (1664), are his masterpieces. His work greatly influenced Édouard MANET and Vincent VAN GOGH.

Frans Hals, "The Merry Toper," c.1628–30

Halsey \'hól-sē, 'hól-zē\, **William F(rederick), Jr.** *known as* **Bull Halsey** (1882–1959) U.S. admiral. Born in Elizabeth, N.J., he became a naval aviator and was promoted to vice admiral in 1940. After the Japanese attacked Pearl Harbor, his fleet, the only U.S. naval presence in the Pacific for months, carried out surprise attacks in the Marshall and Gilbert islands. A leading exponent of carrier-based aircraft, he became famous for his daring and imaginative tactics. As commander of the S. Pacific naval forces, he was instrumental in the victory at GUADALCANAL. In 1944 he became commander of the 3rd Fleet, leading his carrier task force in brilliant air strikes. He was responsible for finding and destroying the Japanese fleet at the Battle of Leyte Gulf.

Halsted, William S(tewart) (1852–1922) U.S. pioneer of scientific SURGERY. Born in New York City, in 1881 he discovered that blood could be aerated and reinfused. He developed conduction anesthesia (1885) by experimenting with injecting cocaine into his own nerve trunks. At Johns Hopkins Univ. he established the first surgical school in the U.S. and created hospital surgical residencies. He ntroduced the use of thin rubber gloves in surgery, and he emphasized homeostasis during surgery, gentleness in handling living tissue, and precise realignment of severed tissues.

ham Cut of meat consisting of the thigh of a hog preserved through salting, smoking, or drying. In addition to preserving the meat, this gives it additional flavor. Produced throughout the Old World except by observant Muslims and Jews, ham became a favored food on the farms of N. America. The distinctive qualities of hams of various regions of the world result from unique combinations of hog-raising and meat-processing technologies. Virginia hams, for example, are cut from razorback hogs fed on peanuts and peaches, and smoked over apple- and hickory-wood fires. Ham is a compact source of high-grade animal protein, thiamine, and iron.

hamadryad See DRYAD

Hamas \hà-'màs\ *officially* Harakat-al-Muqawima al-Islamiyya (Islamic Resistance Movement). Militant movement dedicated to the destruction of Israel and the creation of a Palestinian Islamic state. It was founded in 1988 by Sheikh Ahmad Yasin, and its leadership comes from the MUSLIM BROTHERHOOD. Hamas takes the position that Palestine cannot be surrendered to non-Muslims, and opposes the 1993 peace agreement between the PALESTINE LIBERATION ORGANIZATION and Israel.

Hamburg \'häm-,bùrg, *Engl* 'ham-,bərg\ City (pop., 1998 est.: 1,704,000), constituting a state, N Germany. Located on the ELBE RIVER, it is Germany's largest port. It grew around a 9th-cent. castle. Treaties with LÜBECK in the mid-13th cent. led to the formation of the HANSEATIC LEAGUE, of which it was a leader. It became a member of the GERMAN CONFEDERATION as a free city in 1815. In 1943 Allied firebombing killed some 55,000 people and devastated the city. The birthplace of Felix MENDELSSOHN and Johannes BRAHMS and home to the Hamburg Opera, it has enjoyed a distinguished musical history. It is Germany's foremost industrial city.

Hamhung \'häm-,hùŋ\ City (pop., 1987 est.: 701,000), E central N. Korea. The chief city of NE Korea during the CHOSON dynasty (1392–1910), it developed as a modern industrial city in the 1920s. During the KOREAN WAR, most industrial plants in the area were destroyed by U.S. bombing raids, but they were later rebuilt.

Hamilton City (pop., 1996: 322,000), SE Ontario. Located at the W end of Lake ONTARIO, it was settled by British loyalists fleeing the AMERICAN REVOLUTION. The opening of the Burlington Canal (1830), linking the harbor to Lake Ontario, led to development as an important port and rail center. It is now one of Canada's leading industrial centers, a financial hub, and the site of McMaster Univ. and one of Canada's largest open-air markets.

Hamilton, Alexander (1755?–1804) U.S. statesman. Born on Nevis in the Leeward Islands, he arrived in New Jersey in 1772. In the American Revolution he joined the Continental Army and showed conspicuous bravery at the Battle of Trenton. He served as aide-de-camp to Gen. George WASHINGTON (1777–81) and, fluent in French, became a liaison with French commanders. At the Continental Congress, he argued for a strong central government. With James MADISON and John JAY, he wrote articles for *The FEDERALIST* that explained the new Constitution and helped win its

Alexander Hamilton Painting by John Trumbull

ratification. Appointed the first secretary of the treasury (1789), he established national fiscal policies that strengthened the national government and helped institute the BANK OF THE U.S. He caused a rift in the FEDERALIST PARTY, which he had helped form, by opposing its nomination of John ADAMS for president in 1796. In 1800 he tried to prevent Adams's reelection, circulating a private attack which Aaron BURR, long at odds with Hamilton, obtained and published. When Jefferson and Burr both defeated Adams but received equal electoral votes, Hamilton helped persuade the Federalists in Congress to choose Jefferson. In 1804 he opposed Burr's candidacy for governor of New York. This affront, coupled with alleged remarks questioning Burr's character, led Burr to challenge Hamilton to a duel, in which Hamilton was mortally wounded.

Hamilton, Edith (1867–1963) U.S. (German-born) scholar and educator. After graduating from Bryn Mawr, she was invited to head its preparatory school when she was 29. Preferring classical studies to school administration, she retired to write such popular historical works as *The Greek Way* (1930) and *The Roman Way* (1932). Her *Mythology* (1943) was studied by millions as a textbook.

Hamilton, Emma, Lady *orig.* Amy Lyon (1761?–1815) English mistress of Horatio NELSON. She became the mistress, and in 1791 the wife, of Sir William Hamilton (1730–1803), British envoy to Naples. A beautiful woman frequently painted by George ROMNEY, she became Nelson's mistress in 1798 and gave birth to their daughter, Horatia, in 1801. She later squandered the money both men left her, was imprisoned for debt (1813–14), and died in poverty.

Hamito-Semitic languages See AFROASIATIC LANGUAGES

Hammarskjöld \'ha-mər-ˌshəld\, **Dag (Hjalmar Agne Carl)** (1905–1961) Second secretary-general of the UNITED NATIONS (1953–61). Son of a prime minister of Sweden and chairman of the Nobel Prize Foundation, Hammarskjöld studied law and economics and taught at the Univ. of Stockholm (1933–36) before serving in the finance ministry and the foreign ministry, where he became chair of the Swedish delegation to the U.N. (1952). Appointed secretary-general in 1953, and reappointed in 1957, he dealt with the SUEZ CRISIS, conflict in Lebanon and Jordan, and civil strife following the creation of the Republic of the Congo (1960). He died in a plane crash on a mission to Africa. He was posthumously awarded the Nobel Peace Prize (1961). His journals, published as *Markings* (1963), reveal a man of deep religious convictions.

Hammer, Armand (1898–1990) U.S. industrialist and philanthropist. Born in New York City, Hammer made his first million dollars in pharmaceuticals before earning his medical degree from Columbia Univ. He went to Soviet Russia in 1921 to provide medical aid to famine victims and was persuaded by Vladimir LENIN to remain. His ventures were eventually bought out by the Soviets, and in 1930 he returned to the U.S. laden with artworks formerly owned by the ROMANOV DYNASTY. He increased his fortune through whiskey, cattle, and broadcasting interests, and later founded and headed the Occidental Petroleum Corp. (1957–90). He was a longtime advocate of broadening U.S.-Soviet trade ties. The Armand Hammer Museum in Los Angeles houses his art collection.

hammered dulcimer See DULCIMER

Hammerfest \'hä-mər-ˌfest\ Northernmost town in Europe (pop., 1990 est.: 7,000), on the island of Kvaløya, NW Norway. Chartered in 1789, it was largely destroyed by fire in 1891. Germans occupied the town 1940–44. Despite its latitude, its harbor is ice-free year-round because of the warming N. Atlantic Current. The sun shines continuously May 17–July 29; there is no sunlight from Nov. 21 to Jan. 21. Tourism and fish-oil processing are important economically.

hammerhead shark Any of the swift, powerful SHARKS in the family Sphyrnidae, having a broad, flattened, hammershaped head, with eyes and nostrils at the ends of the sidewise projections. In warm and temperate waters of all oceans, they feed on fish, stingrays, skates, and other sharks. Three species seem particularly dangerous to humans: the great hammerhead (growing to 15 ft, or 4.5 m, or more), the scalloped hammerhead, and the smooth hammerhead. All are grayish and found throughout the tropics.

Hammerstein \'ha-mər-ˌstīn, 'ha-mər-ˌstēn\, **Oscar, II** (1895–1960) U.S. lyricist and producer. Born in New York City, he studied law at Columbia Univ. before beginning his theater career. Among his early musicals are *Rose Marie* (1924; with Rudolf FRIML), *The Desert Song* (1925; with Sigmund ROMBERG), and the Jerome KERN musicals *Sunny* (1925) and *Show Boat* (1927). In the early 1940s he began a collaboration with Richard RODGERS; the two soon became the preeminent figures in the American musical theater, creating *Oklahoma!* (1943; Pulitzer Prize), *Carousel* (1945), *State Fair* (1945), *Allegro* (1948), *South Pacific* (1949; Pulitzer Prize), *The King and I* (1951), *Me and Juliet* (1953), *Flower Drum Song* (1958), and *The Sound of Music* (1959).

hammer throw Athletic event in which a 16-lb (7.26-kg) metal ball attached to a spring steel handle is thrown for distance. The thrower makes three full, quick turns of the body before flinging the weight. The sport developed centuries ago in the British Isles; it has been an Olympic sport since 1900.

Hammett, (Samuel) Dashiell (1894–1961) U.S. detective novelist. Born in St. Mary's Co., Md., he left school at 13. He spent eight years as a private detective before beginning to publish fiction in pulp magazines. His first novels were *Red Harvest* (1929) and *The Dain Curse* (1929). *The Maltese Falcon* (1930; film, 1941) introduced Sam Spade, the prototype of the hard-boiled detective. *The Thin Man* (1934), featuring the witty detective couple Nick and Nora Charles, spawned a popular series of movies. Nora was based on Lillian HELLMAN, with whom Hammett had a romantic alliance from 1930 until his death. For refusing to answer questions about his Communist Party affiliations, he served a prison sentence in the 1950s.

Hammurabi \ˌha-mə-'rä-bē\ (d.c.1750 B.C.) Sixth and best-known Babylonian ruler of the Amorite dynasty. His desire to control the Euphrates led him to conquer the cities of Uruk (ERECH) and Isin in 1787 B.C.; he then turned to the northwest and the east in 1784. Twenty years of peace followed, and then 14 years of almost continuous warfare that resulted in a unified MESOPOTAMIA. He used control of water and waterways to defeat his enemies. He also engaged in building and restoring temples and infrastructure. His laws, collected in the Code of HAMMURABI, demonstrate his desire to be a just ruler.

Hammurabi, Code of Most complete and perfect extant collection of Babylonian laws, developed during the reign of HAMMURABI. It consists of 282 of his legal decisions, inscribed on a stela in the temple of MARDUK. Despite a few references to family solidarity, trial by ordeal, and the *lex talionis* (an eye for an eye), it represents an advance over tribal custom in that it recognizes no blood feud, private retribution, or marriage by capture. Most of the code is preserved in the Louvre Museum in Paris.

Hampshire \'hamp-ˌshir\ County (pop., 1998 est.: 1,238,000), S central England. It lies on the English Channel; WINCHESTER is the county seat. It was settled in the Bronze Age. Towns developed at Silchester and Winchester during the Roman occupation. Though attacked by Norsemen, during the Middle Ages it was comparatively peaceful and came to be known for its woolens. PORTSMOUTH and Gosport form one of Britain's principal naval centers, while SOUTHAMPTON is a major passenger port.

Hampton City (pop., 2000: 146,000), SE Virginia. Located on CHESAPEAKE BAY and the N shore of HAMPTON ROADS, it forms part of a metropolitan complex that includes NEWPORT NEWS, NORFOLK, VIRGINIA BEACH, CHESAPEAKE, and PORTSMOUTH. Permanent settlement dates from 1610–11, making it the nation's oldest continuously settled community of English origin. It was burned by its Confederate residents in 1861 to prevent Union occupancy; it was rebuilt after the AMERICAN CIVIL WAR. Hampton Univ. (1868) was established there by the FREEDMEN'S BUREAU to educate former slaves.

Hampton, Lionel (1909–2002) U.S. jazz vibraphonist, drummer, and bandleader. Born in Louisville, Ky., he made his first vibraphone recording, accompanying Louis ARMSTRONG, in 1930. He became well known as a member of Benny GOODMAN's small groups (1936–40) before forming his own big band. With its rhythmic drive and excitement,

the band highlighted his virtuosic playing and extroverted showmanship and became a direct progenitor of RHYTHM AND BLUES.

Hampton, Wade (1818–1902) U.S. military leader. Born in Charleston, S.C., in the Civil War he organized and led "Hampton's Legion" of S. Carolina troops, fighting at Bull Run and Gettysburg under J. E. B. STUART. After Stuart died, he was promoted to major general and led the cavalry (1864). After the war he opposed the policies of Reconstruction, and as governor of S. Carolina (1876–79) led the fight to restore white supremacy. He served in the U.S. Senate 1879–91.

Hampton Roads Channel through which three rivers flow into CHESAPEAKE BAY. About 4 mi (6 km) wide and 40 ft (12 m) deep, it has been important militarily since colonial days. In 1862 it was the scene of the Battle of the MONITOR AND MERRIMACK. NEWPORT NEWS, NORFOLK, and PORTSMOUTH constitute the Port of Hampton Roads, one of the busiest U.S. seaports.

hamster Any of various stout Old World RODENTS (in the subfamily Cricetidae) with a short tail, soft fur, and long cheek pouches for carrying food. Hamsters are nocturnal and generally live in burrows; they feed on fruits, grain, and vegetables, though some species also eat insects and other small animals. The common hamster of Europe and W Asia is 8–12 in. (20–30 cm) long, without the 1–2.5-in. (3–6-cm) tail. The smaller golden hamster of Syria is a popular pet and is widely used as a laboratory animal.

Hamsun \\'häm-ˌsùn\\, **Knut** *orig.* Knut Pedersen (1859–1952) Norwegian novelist, dramatist, and poet. Of peasant origin, he had almost no formal education. His semiautobiographical first novel, *Hunger* (1890), about a starving young writer, revealed his impulsive, lyrical style. He established himself as a leader of the Neoromantic revolt against SOCIAL REALISM with works such as *Mysteries* (1892), *Pan* (1894), and *Victoria* (1898). Many of his novels express a message of fierce individualism and back-to-nature philosophy. He won the Nobel Prize in 1920. His antipathy to modern Western culture led to his support for the Nazi occupation of Norway.

Hancock, John (1737–1793) American Revolutionary leader. Born in Braintree, Mass., he entered the family mercantile business in Boston in 1754. His identification with the patriot cause dated from the STAMP ACT. He chaired the Boston town committee formed after the BOSTON MASSACRE. He became president of the provincial congress (1774–75), and he and Samuel ADAMS led the Massachusetts Patriots. In 1775 both were forced to flee from British troops sent to arrest them for treason. Hancock was a member of the Continental Congress 1775–80, serving as its president 1775–77; the bold flourish with which he signed the DECLARATION OF INDEPENDENCE has made his name synonymous with "signature." He twice served as governor of Massachusetts (1780–85, 1787–93).

Hand, (Billings) Learned (1872–1961) U.S. jurist. Born in Albany, N.Y., he was appointed a federal district judge in 1909. In 1924 he was elevated to the U.S. Circuit Court of Appeals, on which he served as chief judge from 1939 to 1951. His 52-year tenure on the federal bench represents a record. Several of his decisions, including in the Alcoa antitrust case (1945) and a 1950 case involving communist-conspiracy charges, are considered landmarks. Though he never reached the U.S. Supreme Court, his reputation surpasses that of all but a few who have sat there.

handball Game played in a three- or four-walled court or against a single wall by two or four players who use their hands to strike a small rubber ball, attempting to place it beyond the reach of their opponents. The game runs to 21 points. Handball games were played in ancient Rome and later (as PELOTA) in Spain and France. Modern handball developed in Ireland. Widely played among Irish immigrants in New York, it eventually spread around the continent. It is a forerunner of modern JAI ALAI.

Handel, George Frideric *orig.* Georg Friederich Händel (1685–1759) German-British composer. Born in Halle, he studied organ, violin, and composition. Moving to Hamburg in 1703, he had his first opera produced there in 1705. In Florence and Rome, patronized by cardinals and nobil-

ity, he wrote oratorios, cantatas, and more operas. Before beginning work for the elector at Hanover (1710), he visited London, where his opera *Rinaldo* (1711) immediately made his name; forsaking Hanover, he remained in England the rest of his life. In 1714 the German elector became GEORGE I of England, and the king became one of his patrons. Handel became director of the new Royal Academy of Music, an opera house. When the public taste shifted away from Italian opera, he revised his oratorio *Esther* for a public performance in 1732, the first public oratorio performance in England. Its success was followed by many more oratorios, including his

George Frideric Handel
Painting after Thomas Hudson, 1756

great *Messiah* (1741). Handel's posthumous reputation grew to mammoth proportions and dominated English music for more than a century. He wrote about 45 Italian operas, including *Giulio Cesare* (1723), *Orlando* (1733), and *Alcina* (1735). His oratorios include *Israel in Egypt* (1739) and *Jephtha* (1752). His orchestral works include the famous *Water Music* (1717) and *Royal Fireworks Music* (1749), 18 concerti grossi, and 17 organ concertos.

handicap In sports and games, a method of offsetting the varying abilities or characteristics of competitors in order to equalize their chances of winning. In horse racing, a track official may assign weights to horses according to their speed in previous performances. In golf, a poorer player may reduce his score by a few strokes.

Handke \\'hänt-kə\\, **Peter** (b.1942) Austrian writer. His unconventional plays include *Offending the Audience* (1966), in which actors analyze the nature of theater and alternately insult the audience and praise its "performance." His novels, mostly ultraobjective, deadpan accounts of characters in extreme states of mind, include *The Goalie's Anxiety at the Penalty Kick* (1970) and *The Left-Handed Woman* (1976). A dominant theme is the deadening effects and underlying irrationality of ordinary language, everyday reality, and rational order.

Handsome Lake *or* **Ganioda'yo** \\ˌgän-yō-'dī-yō\\ (1735?–1815) Seneca Indian chief. Born in Ganawaugus, N.Y., he led a somewhat dissolute life before becoming seriously ill in 1799; on recovering, he reported a vision from the Great Spirit. He developed a religion he called Gai'wiio (Good Message) that combined elements of Christianity and Indian beliefs, and preached abstention from adultery, drunkenness, laziness, and witchcraft. The religion revitalized the demoralized Iroquois.

Handy, W(illiam) C(hristopher) (1873–1958) U.S. composer, cornetist, and bandleader known for integrating BLUES elements into RAGTIME, changing the course of popular music. Born in Florence, Ala., Handy worked with several bands and became active as a music publisher in Memphis (1908) and later New York (1918). Handy's compositions, including "St. Louis Blues," "Beale Street Blues," and "Memphis Blues," became hits in the 1920s, helping to codify the blues as a framework within which to improvise.

Han dynasty \\'hän\\ (206 B.C.–A.D. 220) Second great Chinese dynasty. In contrast to the preceding QIN DYNASTY, the Han, founded by LIU BANG, was a period of cultural flowering. A great early history, the *Shiji*, was composed, and the *fu*, a poetic form that became the norm for creative writing, began to flourish. The Yuefu, or Music Bureau, collected and recorded not only ceremonial chants but also folk songs and ballads. Lacquerware reached a level of great mastery, and silk was woven for export trade. Buddhism entered China during the Han. Paper was invented, time was measured with water clocks and sundials, and calendars were published. So thoroughly did the Han dynasty establish what was thereafter considered Chinese culture that the Chinese word for Chinese people is Han.

Hanfeizi \ˈhan-ˈfā-ˈtsə\ *or* **Han-fei-tzu** \ˈhan-ˈfā-ˈdzü\ (d.233 B.C.) Greatest of China's legalist philosophers. His works are collected in the *Hanfeizi,* presumably compiled after his death. In 55 sections, it presents a synthesis of legal theories up to his time. To Hanfeizi it was axiomatic that political institutions must change with changing historical circumstances and must be adapted to the prevailing pattern of human behavior, which is determined not by moral sentiments but by economic conditions. The ruler should not try to make people good but only to restrain them from doing evil.

Han Gaozu See LIU BANG

hang gliding Use of a kitelike GLIDER by a harnessed rider in gliding down usually from a cliff or hill. The hang glider was developed as a flexible-wing parachute by NASA officials in the 1960s, but soon was redesigned as a glider for recreational and competitive sport. World championships have been held and records kept since 1976.

Hangzhou *or* **Hang-chou** \ˈhäŋ-jō\ *or* **Hangchow** \ˈhaŋ-ˈchaù\ City (pop., 1999 est.: 1,346,000), capital of Zhejiang province, China. It lies on Zhejiang Bay and is the S terminus of the GRAND CANAL. Its buildings and gardens are renowned, and some of China's most famous monasteries are located nearby. Its importance as a port decreased as the bay silted up, but it remained a commercial center, and was opened to foreign trade in 1896. In addition to its cultural importance, it is also the center for an industrial area.

Han Kao-tsu See LIU BANG

Hanks, Tom (*orig.* Thomas J.) (b.1956) U.S. film actor. Born in Concord, Cal., he became a film star in the comedies *Splash* (1984) and *Big* (1988). After winning praise for *A League of Their Own* (1992) and *Sleepless in Seattle* (1993), he proved himself an accomplished dramatic actor in *Philadelphia* (1993, Academy Award), *Forrest Gump* (1994, Academy Award), *Apollo 13* (1995) and *Saving Private Ryan* (1998). He made his debut as director and screenwriter with *That Thing You Do* (1996).

Hanna, Mark (*orig.* Marcus Alonzo) (1837–1904) U.S. political kingmaker. Born in New Lisbon, Ohio, he became a businessman in Cleveland, with interests in banking, coal and iron, transportation, and publishing. Convinced that business success depended on the Republican Party, in 1892 he helped William MCKINLEY secure the Ohio governorship. His corporate fund-raising for McKinley's successful 1896 presidential campaign allowed Republicans to spend an unprecedented $3.5 million and cemented the alliance between big business and the party. He served in the U.S. Senate 1897–1904.

Hanna, William (Denby) (1910–2001) U.S. animator known for his collaborative productions with Joseph Barbera (b.1911). Hanna was born in Melrose, N.M., Barbera in New York City. At MGM they collaborated to create the Tom and Jerry cartoon characters, producing (1940–57) over 200 *Tom and Jerry* cartoon films, seven of which won Academy Awards. They founded Hanna-Barbera Productions in 1957 and collaborated on such popular television cartoon series as *The Flintstones, The Jetsons, Yogi Bear, Huckleberry Hound,* and *Scooby Doo.*

Hannibal (247–183? B.C.) Carthaginian general, one of the great military leaders of antiquity. Son of the Carthaginian general Hamilcar Barca (d.229/228 B.C.), he was sworn to eternal enmity with Rome. He conquered Spain, then crossed the Ebro River into Roman territory; thus began the Second PUNIC WAR (218–201 B.C.). He marched over the Alps into Italy; encumbered by elephants and horses, he was beset by Gallic tribes, harsh winter weather, and defection of his Spanish troops. In 216 he won the Battle of CANNAE. In 203 he left for N Africa to help Carthage fend off SCIPIO AFRICANUS THE ELDER's forces. He lost decisively to Scipio's ally Masinissa (c. 240–148 B.C.) at the Battle of Zama, but escaped. He headed the Carthaginian government (c.202–195); forced to flee, he sought refuge with ANTIOCHUS III, whose fleet he commanded against Rome, with disastrous results. After the Battle of Magnesia (190) the Romans demanded he be handed over; he eluded them until, seeing no escape, he took poison.

Hanoi \ha-ˈnȯi\ City (pop., 1992 est.: 1,074,000), capital of Vietnam. Located in N Vietnam on the RED RIVER, it became the capital of Vietnam's Ly dynasty in 1010. It was the main capital of Vietnam until 1802, when the NGUYEN DYNASTY transferred the capital south to HUE. In 1902 it was made the capital of FRENCH INDOCHINA. It became the capital of N. Vietnam after the French defeat in 1954. During the VIETNAM WAR, many of its monuments and palaces were destroyed by U.S. bombing. As the capital of a united Vietnam since 1975, it has been rebuilt, its industrial base has grown, and tourism is regaining importance.

Hanover \ˈha-ˌnō-vər\ *German* **Hannover** \hä-ˈnō-fər\ City (pop., 1998 est.: 520,000), NW Germany. It joined the HANSEATIC LEAGUE in 1386. From 1495 it belonged to the Welf Dynasty (later the House of HANOVER). It was capital of the kingdom of Hanover (1815–66), then was annexed by Prussia. It became the capital of Lower Saxony in 1946. It suffered destruction in World War II but was rebuilt.

Hanover, House of British royal house of German origin. It was descended from George Louis, elector of Hanover, who succeeded to the British crown as GEORGE I in 1714, as determined by the Act of SETTLEMENT. The dynasty also provided the monarchs GEORGE II, GEORGE III, GEORGE IV, WILLIAM IV, and VICTORIA. It was succeeded in 1901 by the House of Saxe-Coburg-Gotha, renamed in 1917 the House of WINDSOR.

Hansberry, Lorraine (1930–1965) U.S. playwright. She was born in Chicago, and her childhood experiences in a black family in a hostile white neighborhood lent power to her first play, *A Raisin in the Sun* (1959; film, 1961). The first play by a black woman produced on Broadway, it won high critical praise. Her next play was *The Sign in Sidney Brustein's Window* (1964). Her promising career was cut short by her death from cancer.

Hanseatic League \ˌhan-sē-ˈa-tik\ *or* **Hansa** (from German *Hanse,* "association") Organization founded by N German towns and merchant communities to protect their trading interests. Dominating commercial activity in N Europe from the 13th to the 15th cent., it protected transport of goods by quelling pirates and fostered safe navigation by building lighthouses. Most important, it controlled trade by winning commercial privileges and monopolies and by establishing trading bases overseas. In extreme cases its members resorted to warfare, as when they raised an armed force that defeated the Danes in 1368 and confirmed the league's supremacy in the Baltic Sea. Over 150 towns were at some point associated with the league, including BREMEN, HAMBURG, and LÜBECK.

Hansen's disease See LEPROSY

Hanson, Howard (Harold) (1896–1981) U.S. composer, conductor, and educator. Born in Wahoo, Neb., he studied in Italy with Ottorino RESPIGHI. He became director of the Eastman School of Music (1924) and remained there 40 years, building the school into a world-renowned institution. His best-known works are his seven symphonies—including the second ("Romantic") and fourth ("Requiem"; Pulitzer Prize)—and his opera *Merry Mount* (1934).

hantavirus Genus of VIRUSES that cause PNEUMONIA and HEMORRHAGIC FEVERS. Carried by rodents, they spread to humans directly or by inhalation. An outbreak in the 1990s in the SW U.S. caused an often fatal, flulike illness in previously healthy adults. The culprit was a hantavirus type carried by mice and not previously associated with human illness in the U.S.

Hanukkah \ˈhä-nə-kə, ˈkä-nə-kə\ In Judaism, a holiday celebrating the rededication of the Second Temple of JERUSALEM in 164 B.C., after its desecration three years earlier. The MACCABEES recaptured Jerusalem and reconsecrated the Temple after leading a successful revolt against Syrian rule. The lighting of the MENORAH recalls the story that a one-day supply of oil burned miraculously in the Temple for eight days until new oil could be obtained. Hanukkah is celebrated for eight days in December, during which the ceremonial candles are lit and children play games and receive gifts. The holiday has become more lavishly celebrated because it falls near CHRISTMAS.

Hanuman \ˈhə-nù-ˌmän, ˌhə-nù-ˈmän\ Monkey god of Hindu mythology, a central figure in the *RAMAYANA.* He was a

HIJ

guardian spirit whose great heroic exploit was recovering RAMA's wife, SITA, from captivity by the demon RAVANA. Hanuman also flew to the Himalayas and carried back a mountain of medicinal herbs to cure Rama's grievously wounded brother Laksmana. He is revered for his strength and his faithfulness.

Han Yu *or* **Han Yü** \'hän-'yūe\ (768–824) Chinese poet and prose writer, the first proponent of NEO-CONFUCIANISM. While serving in several high government posts, he attacked Taoism and Buddhism and sought to restore Confucianism to its former status. He revived interest in the writings of MENCIUS and other neglected Confucian classics. His own works were written in a notably simple style, and he became known as the Prince of Letters.

Hapsburg dynasty See HABSBURG DYNASTY

hara-kiri See SEPPUKU

Harald III Sigurdsson *known as* **Harald Hardraade** \'hòr-,rò-də\ *or* **Harald the Ruthless** (1015–1066) King of Norway (1045–66). He fought against the Danes in 1030, then fled the country, taking service in the Russian and Byzantine armies. He returned in 1045 to take the throne, then struggled unsuccessfully to conquer Denmark (1045–62). He expanded Norway's possessions in the Orkney, Shetland, and Hebrides islands, and he attempted to conquer England in 1066 but was defeated and killed at Stamford Bridge.

Harare \hä-'rä-rā\ *formerly* **Salisbury** \'sòlz-bə-rē\ City (pop., 1999 est.: 1,686,000), capital of Zimbabwe. Founded as Salisbury by the British in 1890, it was the capital, successively, of the colony of Southern Rhodesia, the Federation of Rhodesia and Nyasaland (1953–63), and RHODESIA (1965–79). When Zimbabwe won independence (1980), it was renamed Harare. The center of Zimbabwe's industry and commerce, it is a cultural and educational nucleus and the site of the Univ. of Zimbabwe (1957). Important gold mines lie nearby.

Harbin \'här-bən, här-'bin\ *or* **Ha-erh-pin** \'hä-'ər-'bin\ City (pop., 1999 est.: 2,586,000), NE China. Located in the center of MANCHURIA, it grew with the arrival of the Chinese Eastern Railway, built by the Russians in the late 19th cent. A Russian military base during the RUSSO–JAPANESE WAR, it was a haven for Russian refugees after the RUSSIAN REVOLUTION OF 1917, and had the largest Russian population of any city outside the Soviet Union. Chinese Communist forces took the city in 1946 and from it directed their conquest of Manchuria. Since 1949 it has become the chief industrial base of NE China.

harbor seal Nonmigratory, earless SEAL (*Phoca vitulina*) found throughout the Northern Hemisphere. The adult male may reach a length of about 6 ft (1.8 m) and a weight of almost 300 lbs (130 kg); the female is smaller. Found along coastlines and in a few freshwater lakes in Canada and Alaska, the harbor seal is a gregarious animal that feeds on fish, squid, and crustaceans. Its populations have declined in recent years.

Harburg, E(dgar) Y(ipsel) *orig.* Isidore Hochberg (1898–1981) U.S. lyricist, producer, and director. Born in New York City, Harburg attended CCNY with his friend Ira Gershwin. When his business went bankrupt in 1929, he devoted himself to writing songs for Broadway, including "Brother, Can You Spare a Dime?" From 1935 Harburg and Harold ARLEN wrote songs for many films, including *The Wizard of Oz* (1939). Blacklisted for his political views, Harburg returned to Broadway to write musicals, notably *Finian's Rainbow* (1947; with Burton Lane).

Hardanger Fjord \här-'dän-ər-,fyòrd\ Fjord, SW Norway. The country's second-largest fjord, it extends inland 70 mi (113 km) from the North Sea. It has a maximum depth of 2,922 ft (891 m). Waterfalls pour from the surrounding mountains, which rise to about 5,000 ft (1,500 m). Frequented by tourists, the area has many branch fjords.

hard coal See ANTHRACITE

hard disk Magnetic storage medium for a MICROCOMPUTER. Hard disks are flat, circular plates made of aluminum or glass and coated with a magnetic material, capable of storing up to several gigabytes (billions of bytes) of information. A small electromagnet writes a binary digit (1 or 0) by magnetizing tiny spots on the spinning disk in different directions and reads digits by detecting the magnetization of the spots. A computer's hard drive is a device consisting of several hard disks, read/write heads, a drive motor to spin the disks, and circuitry, all sealed in a metal case to protect the disks.

Hardee, William J(oseph) (1815–1873) U.S. military leader. Born near Savannah, Ga., in 1855 he wrote *Rifle and Light Infantry Tactics,* a popular manual later used by both sides in the Civil War. When Georgia seceded in 1861, he assumed command of Confederate forces in NE Arkansas, demonstrating his military skills at the battles of Shiloh and Chattanooga. As commander of the military department of S. Carolina, Georgia, and Florida, he attempted to halt William T. SHERMAN's march across Georgia.

Harden, Arthur (*later* **Sir Arthur**) (1865–1940) British biochemist. His extensive studies of sugar FERMENTATION advanced knowledge of metabolic processes in all living forms. In 1929 he shared a Nobel Prize with Hans von Euler-Chelpin. He also did pioneering studies of bacterial ENZYMES and METABOLISM.

Hardenberg \'här-dən-,berk\, **Karl August, Fürst (Prince) von** (1750–1822) Prussian statesman. During the NAPOLEONIC WARS, he served Prussia's FREDERICK WILLIAM III as foreign minister 1804–6. He was forced to withdraw from political life, at NAPOLEON's behest, after Prussia's collapse in the war of 1806–7 against France. When Prussia could not pay war indemnities in 1810, Napoleon agreed to Hardenberg's reinstatement and he became prime minister with full powers. He continued the domestic reforms introduced by Karl von STEIN and liberalized financial, economic, and agricultural policies. He formed an alliance with Russia in 1813, and later represented Prussia at the Congress of VIENNA.

hardening Increase in HARDNESS of a METAL induced, deliberately or accidentally, by hammering, rolling, drawing, or other physical processes. The first few deformations imposed by such treatment weaken the metal, but because of the crystalline structure of metal its strength increases with continued deformations. Crystals slip against each other; but the more such slips are multiplied, the more they tend to place obstacles in the way of further slippage, as the various dislocation lines crisscross each other. See also HEAT TREATING, TEMPERING.

hardening of the arteries See ARTERIOSCLEROSIS

Harding, Warren G(amaliel) (1865–1923) 29th president of the U.S. (1921–23). Born in Corsica, Ohio, he became a newspaper publisher in Marion, where he was allied with the Republican Party's political machine. As U.S. senator (1915–21), he supported conservative policies. At the deadlocked 1920 Republican presidential convention, he was chosen in a compromise. Pledging a "return to normalcy" after World War I, he defeated James COX with over 60% of the popular vote, the largest margin to that time. On his recommendation, Congress established a budget system for the federal government, passed a high protective tariff, revised wartime taxes, and restricted immigration. His ill-advised cabinet and patronage appointments, including Albert FALL, led to the TEAPOT DOME SCANDAL and characterized his administration as corrupt. While in Alaska, he received word of the corruption about to be exposed and headed back. He arrived in San Francisco in bad health and died there on Aug. 2 under unclear circumstances. He was succeeded by Calvin COOLIDGE.

Warren G. Harding

hardness Resistance of a MINERAL to scratching, described relative to the MOHS HARDNESS scale. Hardness is an important diagnostic property in mineral identification. There is a general link between hardness and chemical composition (via CRYSTAL structure); thus, most hydrous minerals, halides, carbonates, sulfates, phosphates, and sulfides are relatively soft, and most anhydrous oxides and silicates are hard. See also HARDENING.

hardness scale See MOHS HARDNESS

hardpan Cemented or compacted and often clayey layer in soil that cannot be penetrated by roots. Lime, gypsum, iron, and other minerals may be carried up to the surface by capillary action and deposited to form a natural concrete. Special equipment may be used to chisel away hardpan so that crop plants can grow.

hardware Computer machinery and equipment, including memory, cabling, power supply, peripheral devices, and circuit boards. Computer operation requires both hardware and SOFTWARE. Hardware design specifies a computer's capability; software instructs the computer on what to do. The advent of MICROPROCESSORS in the late 1970s led to much smaller and cheaper hardware assemblies. Today's PERSONAL COMPUTERS are as powerful as the early MAIN-FRAMES, while mainframes are now smaller and have vastly more computing power than the early models.

hard water Water that contains mineral salts of calcium and magnesium, principally as bicarbonates, chlorides, and sulfates, and sometimes iron. Hardness caused by calcium bicarbonate is known as temporary; hardness from the other salts is called permanent. Water is softened on a large scale by adding lime to precipitate the calcium as carbonate and the magnesium as hydroxide, and then sodium carbonate is added to remove the remaining calcium salts. Home water softeners make use of the ion exchange properties of ZEOLITE minerals.

hardwood Timber obtained from broad-leaved, flower-bearing trees. Hardwood trees are usually DECIDUOUS TREES. The term applied originally to such hard European woods as beech and oak but also includes some of the softest of woods.

Hardy, Oliver See LAUREL AND HARDY

Hardy, Thomas (1840–1928) British novelist and poet. Son of a country stonemason and builder, he set many of his novels in the imaginary county of Wessex. *Far from the Madding Crowd* (1874) was his first success; later works include *The Return of the Native* (1878), *The Mayor of Casterbridge* (1886), *Tess of the D'Urbervilles* (1891), and *Jude the Obscure* (1895), all expressing his stoical pessimism and his sense of the inevitable tragedy of life. Their continuing popularity owes much to their richly varied style and their combination of romantic plots with convincingly presented characters. Hardy's works became increasingly at odds with Victorian morality, and public indignation at *Jude* so disgusted him that he wrote no more novels. He returned to poetry with *Wessex Poems* (1898); *The Dynasts* (1910) is a huge poetic drama of the Napoleonic Wars.

Thomas Hardy

Hardy-Weinberg law Equation that describes genetic balance within a population. It may be stated as follows: In a large, random-mating population, the proportion of dominant and recessive GENES (see DOMINANCE, RECESSIVENESS) tends to remain constant through generations unless outside forces act to change it. Forces that can disturb this natural balance are SELECTION, MUTATION, gene flow, and NATURAL SELECTION. The equation is used to calculate the probability of human matings that may result in defective offspring, and to determine whether the number of harmful mutations in a population is increasing as a result of radiation, medical techniques, or fallout.

hare Bounding mammal (in the family Leporidae) whose young, unlike those of RABBITS, are born fully haired, with open eyes, and sufficiently advanced to hop about a few minutes after birth. The common hare *(Lepus europaeus)* is native to central and S Europe, the Middle East, and Africa; introduced into Australia, it has become a pest there. In N. America the jackrabbit and SNOWSHOE HARE are widespread. Hares have well-developed hind legs, and the ears are usually longer than the head. Species vary in length from 16 to 28 in. (40–70 cm), without the short tail. Hares in N latitudes are white in winter. Hares are primarily herbivorous.

Hare Krishna movement \ˈhär-ē-ˈkrish-nə\ *officially* **International Society for Krishna Consciousness (ISKCON)** Conemporary Hindu religious movement. It was founded in the U.S. by A.C. Bhaktivedanta Swami (1896–1977) in 1966 and claims a lineage of spiritual masters reaching back to a 16th-cent. incarnation of KRISHNA. Hare Krishna was popular among Western young people of the 1960s and '70s counterculture, who often appeared in public places dressed in saffron robes, chanting, dancing, and asking for contributions. The communes in which many members live are governed by an international commission. The movement has endured several schisms.

harem In Muslim countries, that part of a house set apart for women. Harems existed in the pre-Islamic Middle East and in the courts of pre-Islamic Assyria, Persia, and Egypt. Large harems for wives and concubines were common in wealthy Arab households into the 20th cent.; the great harem of the Turkish sultans (15th–20th cent.) contained several hundred women, guarded by eunuchs. By the later 20th cent., the full harem system existed only among conservative Arabs. The harem also existed in the courts of China and Japan as well as in India and S.E. Asia.

Hargreaves, James *or* **James Hargraves** (c.1725–1778) British inventor of the SPINNING JENNY. A poor, uneducated spinner and weaver, he is said to have conceived the idea when he observed a SPINNING WHEEL accidentally overturned; as the spindle continued to revolve while upright, he reasoned that many spindles could be so turned, and went on to construct the first machine (patented 1770) with which one person could spin several threads at once.

Haring, Keith (1958–1990) U.S. painter and draftsman. Born in Reading, Pa., he studied at New York's School of Visual Arts. Inspired by graffiti, cartoons, and comic strips, he drew clandestinely at night on subway-station walls around the city, using signs, abstract symbols, and human and animal figures writhing and wriggling in a spaceless, airless design. In the 1980s he exhibited internationally, achieving great commercial success. His early death resulted from AIDS.

Harlan, John Marshall (1833–1911) U.S. jurist. Born in Boyle Co., Ky., he served on the U.S. Supreme Court from 1877 to 1911 and became one of the most forceful dissenters in its history. His best-known dissents, such as those in *Plessy vs. Ferguson* (1896) and the Civil-Rights Cases (1883), favored the rights of blacks. He also issued famous dissents in favor of the federal income tax (1895) and opposing monopolies in cases arising under the Sherman Antitrust Act of 1890. His grandson John Marshall Harlan (1899–1971) also served on the Supreme Court (1955–71).

Harlem District occupying part of N MANHATTAN Island, NEW YORK CITY. It lies north of CENTRAL PARK, with its business district centered on 125th Street. Founded by Peter STUYVESANT in 1658, during the AMERICAN REVOLUTION it was the site of the Battle of Harlem Heights (Sept. 16, 1776). A fashionable residential district in the 19th cent., it was populated mostly by blacks by World War I, and in the 1920s it was the center of the HARLEM RENAISSANCE.

Harlem Globetrotters All-black professional U.S. basketball team. The Globetrotters play exhibition games all over the world, displaying spectacular ball handling and humorous antics. Their usual opposition is another traveling team, the Washington Generals, which is never allowed to win. The team was organized in 1927 by Abe Saperstein.

Harlem Renaissance *or* **New Negro Movement** Period of outstanding literary vigor centered in New York's black ghetto of HARLEM in the 1920s. Its leading figures included J. W. JOHNSON, Claude MCKAY, Countee CULLEN, Langston HUGHES, and Z. N. HURSTON. The movement, which coincided with the great creative and commercial growth of jazz, led black American literature away from conventional

HIJ

imitations and toward sophisticated explorations of black life and culture.

harlequin \'här-li-k(w)ən\ Principal stock character of the Úa wily, unscrupulous comic servant, and by the 17th cent. he was a faithful valet involved in amorous exploits. His costume of peasant clothes covered with colored patches developed into a tight-fitting costume decorated with bright triangles and diamond shapes. He carried a *batte* or slapstick and wore a black half-mask. In England the harlequin was the principal character of the slapstick form called the harlequinade.

Harlequin "Seated Harlequin" by Pablo Picasso, 1923

Harley, Robert *later* Earl of Oxford (1661–1724) English politician. He was speaker of the House of Commons 1701–5, and secretary of state 1704–8. A favorite of Queen ANNE, he became chancellor of the exchequer and head of the Tory ministry in 1710. He secured favorable terms for Britain at the Peace of UTRECHT (1713). He was exiled from power by the Hanoverian succession and imprisoned (1715–17).

Harlow, Jean *orig.* Harlean Carpenter (1911–1937) U.S. film actress. Born in Kansas City, Mo., she had her first success in *Hell's Angels* (1930). With her plantinum-blonde hair and flashy vulgarity, she became a sex symbol in *The Public Enemy* and *Platinum Blonde* (1931). She was revealed as an able actress with a flair for comedy in such films as *Dinner at Eight* (1933), *China Seas* (1935), *Libeled Lady* (1936), and *Saratoga* (1937). After surviving two divorces, the suicide of her second husband, and public scandal, she died of uremic poisoning at 26.

harmonic See OVERTONE

harmonica *or* **mouth organ** Small rectangular wind instrument consisting of free metal reeds set in slots in a wooden frame and blown through two parallel rows of wind channels. Successive notes of the scale are obtained by alternately blowing and sucking; the tongue covers channels not required. In chromatic models, a finger-operated stop selects either of two sets of reeds tuned a semitone apart. The harmonica was invented by Friedrich Buschmann of Berlin in 1821 (also inventor of the ACCORDION).

harmonium *or* **reed organ** Keyboard instrument in which wind from a foot-operated bellows causes metal reeds to vibrate. Pitch is determined by the size of the reed; there are no pipes. Separate sets of reed produce different tone colors, the sound quality being determined by the size and shape of the tone chamber surrounding each reed. The harmonium developed in the 19th cent. and was a very popular church and household instrument into the 1930s.

harmony Combination and relation of simultaneous musical notes, and the science of the structure, relation, and progression of individual harmonies in a piece of music. Harmony has always existed as the "vertical" aspect of older music that is primarily contrapuntal; the rules of COUNTERPOINT are intended to control CONSONANCE AND DISSONANCE, which are fundamental aspects of harmony. However, the sense of harmony as dominating the individual contrapuntal lines followed on the invention of FIGURED BASS around 1600. The most influential theory of harmony, that of J.-P. RAMEAU, employed the symbols of figured bass. See also CHORD, KEY, TONALITY.

Harmsworth, Alfred See Viscount NORTHCLIFFE

harness racing Sport of racing STANDARDBRED horses harnessed to lightweight, two-wheeled, bodiless (seat-only) vehicles known as sulkies. Its origins date to ancient CHARIOT races. Today two types of horse are used, trotters and pacers. The former employ a gait in which the legs move in diagonal pairs, the latter a gait in which the legs move in lateral pairs. Since the establishment of PARI-MUTUEL racing under lights in the 1940s, the sport has grown tremendously in popularity.

Harnett, William (Michael) (1848–1892) U.S. (Irish-born) still-life painter. Brought to Philadelphia as a child and trained as an engraver, he developed outstanding skill in TROMPE L'OEIL painting. His best-known works include *After the Hunt* (1885), *The Old Violin* (1886), and *The Faithful Colt* (1890). His work, popular with the public, was generally dismissed by critics.

Harold I *known as* **Harold Harefoot** (d.1040) King of England (1035–40). The illegitimate son of CANUTE THE GREAT, he served as regent of England for his half brother Hardecanute, king of Denmark. In 1036 he murdered the royal claimant, Alfred the Aetheling, and proclaimed himself king. He fended off Welsh and Scottish invaders and was succeeded by Hardecanute.

Harold II *known as* **Harold Godwineson** (c.1020–1066) King of England (1066). The son of the powerful Godwine, earl of Wessex, he inherited his father's earldom in 1053. When EDWARD THE CONFESSOR died in 1066, Harold's supporters chose him as king. He was opposed by King HARALD III of Norway, whom he defeated that year at Stamford Bridge near York. He then marched south to meet William, duke of Normandy, and was killed at the Battle of HASTINGS.

Harold III (Norway) See HARALD III SIGURDSSON

harp Plucked STRINGED INSTRUMENT in which the resonator is perpendicular to the plane of the strings. Harps are roughly triangular. In early harps and many folk harps, the strings are strung between the resonating "body" and the "neck." Such harps lack the forepillar or column—forming the third side of the triangle—that characterizes frame harps; the column permits high string tension and higher-pitched tuning. Small, primitive harps date back to at least 3000 B.C.; in Europe they became particularly important in Celtic societies. The large modern orchestral harp emerged in the 18th cent. It has 47 strings and a range of almost seven octaves. It plays the entire chromatic scale by means of seven pedals, each of which can alter the pitch of a note by two semitones. Its massive resonator permits considerable volume of tone.

Harper brothers U.S. printers and publishers. The two oldest brothers, James (1795–1869) and John (1797–1875), established J. & J. Harper in 1817; two siblings joined later. The company began publishing periodicals in 1850 with *Harper's New Monthly Magazine* (see *Harper's Magazine*), which was followed by *Harper's Weekly* (1857) and *Harper's Bazaar* (1867). In 1900 the business passed out of family hands, though the name survives in two magazines and the book publisher HarperCollins.

Harpers Ferry National Historical Park National preserve, W. Virginia, in the BLUE RIDGE MTNS. at the point where W. Virginia, Virginia, and Maryland converge. A historical park since 1963, it covers 1,909 acres (772 hectares). It is spectacularly located at the confluence of the Shenandoah and POTOMAC rivers. It is the site of the 1859 raid by abolitionist John BROWN, a harbinger of the AMERICAN CIVIL WAR, and of several battles during the war.

Harper's Magazine One of the oldest and most prestigious literary and opinion journals in the U.S. Founded in 1850 as *Harper's New Monthly* by the HARPER BROTHERS, it was a leader in publishing works by illustrious British and U.S. authors. By 1865 it had become the most successful periodical in the U.S. In the 1920s its format changed to that of a forum on public affairs, balanced with short stories.

harp seal Migratory earless SEAL (*Pagophilus groenlandicus,* sometimes *Phoca groenlandica)* of the N. Atlantic and Arctic oceans. Adults are light grayish or yellowish, with brown or black on the head. They are about 6 ft (1.8 m) long and 400 lbs (180 kg). Strong swimmers, they feed on fish and crustaceans and spend much of the year at sea. They breed near Newfoundland and in the Greenland and White seas. Until two weeks old, the pups bear a fluffy white coat highly valued by the fur trade; public indignation over hunting methods (including clubbing) has led to increased regulation.

harpsichord Keyboard instrument whose strings are set in vibration by a plucking mechanism. The latter consists of plectra mounted on vertical wooden jacks that are activated by the keys. It often has two parallel keyboards (or manuals) and generally has two or more sets of strings; these permit the simultaneous sounding of pitches an octave higher or lower than the note struck as well as alternative tone colors (produced by plectra of different material plucking the strings at different points). The notes' loudness is not affected by the power with which the keys are struck, and there is no way to sustain a note after the key is released. Primitive harpsichords existed by the mid-15th cent. In the 17th–18th cent. it became a very important solo, accompanimental, and ensemble instrument. From about 1750 the pianoforte began to displace it, and by 1820 it had largely vanished. It was revived in the 20th cent. by scholars, performers, and builders.

Harpy In Greek and Roman mythology, a bird of prey with a woman's face. Often depicted on tombs, Harpies may originally have been conceived of as ghosts. In early Greek literature they were wind spirits and were not represented as ugly or repellent. In the legend of JASON and the Argonauts, however, the Harpies were hideous, foul-smelling creatures sent to punish King Phineus of Thrace; they were frightened away by the sons of Boreas.

harrier Any of about 11 species of HAWKS (subfamily Circinae; family Accipitridae) that are plain-looking, long-legged, long-tailed, and slender. Harriers cruise low over meadows and marshes looking for mice, snakes, frogs, small birds, and insects. They are about 20 in. (50 cm) long and have face feathers that form a facial disk. Best known is the marsh hawk *(Circus cyaneus),* commonly called hen harrier in Britain. Other common species are found in Africa, S. America, Europe, and Asia.

Harriman, Edward H(enry) (1848–1909) U.S. financier and railroad magnate. Born in Hempstead, N.Y., he worked as a stockbroker before going into railroad management. In 1898 he organized a syndicate to acquire the UNION PACIFIC RAILROAD CO., which he led from bankruptcy to prosperity. Using unpopular business methods, he acquired several other lines, notably the Southern Pacific. His 1901 contest with James J. Hill for control of the Northern Pacific led to one of Wall Street's most serious financial crises. The railway trust he formed with J. P. MORGAN was dissolved by the U.S. Supreme Court in 1904.

Harriman, W(illiam) Averell (1891–1986) U.S. diplomat. Born in New York City, the son of Edward HARRIMAN, he worked for the Union Pacific Railroad Co. from 1915, serving as board chairman 1932–46. Pres. Franklin ROOSEVELT sent him to Britain in 1941 to expedite lend-lease aid, and he later served as ambassador to the Soviet Union (1943–46) and Britain (1946), secretary of commerce (1947–48), and special U.S. representative to supervise the MARSHALL PLAN (1948–50). He served as governor of New York 1954–58. Under Pres. John F. KENNEDY, he helped negotiate the Nuclear Test Ban Treaty. Under Pres. Lyndon JOHNSON, Harriman led the U.S. delegation to the Paris peace talks with N. Vietnam (1968–69).

Harris, Joel Chandler (1848–1908) U.S. writer. Born in Eatonton, Ga., he became famous in his day as a newspaper humorist. He created a vogue for a distinct type of dialect literature with "Tar-Baby" (1879) and later stories that drew on folklore and featured the character Uncle Remus, a wise, genial old black man who weaves his philosophy of life into tales about Brer Rabbit, Brer Fox, and other animals.

Harris, Julie (Ann) (b.1925) U.S. actress. Born in Grosse Pointe Park, Mich., she made her stage debut in 1945 and won acclaim in *The Member of the Wedding* (1950; film, 1952). On Broadway she received Tony awards for *I Am a Camera* (1952), *The Lark* (1956), *Forty Carats* (1969), *The Last of Mrs. Lincoln* (1973), and *The Belle of Amherst* (1977). She played memorable roles in such films as *East of Eden* (1955), *Requiem for a Heavyweight* (1962), and *Harper* (1966), and in many television plays, winning Emmy awards for *Little Moon of Alban* (1959) and *Victoria Regina* (1962).

Harris, Roy (*orig.* LeRoy Ellsworth) (1898–1979) U.S. composer. Born near Chandler, Okla., he farmed and did odd jobs to support his music studies. In the 1920s he studied with Arthur Farwell (1872–1952) and Nadia BOULANGER. Of his 12 completed symphonies, the third (1937) is the best

known. His music, while unmistakably modern, has roots in folk song and is often somber and plainspoken.

Harris, Townsend (1804–1878) U.S. diplomat. Born in Sandy Hill, N.Y., he became president of New York City's board of education and helped found the Free Academy (later CCNY). In 1847 he embarked on trading voyages in the Pacific and Indian oceans. In 1856 he was appointed consul general to Japan; he was unwelcome at first, but his perseverance eventually produced a commercial treaty in 1858 that opened Japanese ports to U.S. trade.

Harrisburg City (pop., 2000: 53,000), capital of Pennsylvania. Located in SE Pennsylvania on the SUSQUEHANNA RIVER, the site was first established around 1718 as a trading post and ferry service by John Harris (1673–1748). It was made the state capital in 1812. In 1839 it was the scene of the first national WHIG PARTY convention. After completion of the PENNSYLVANIA RAILROAD's main line from Harrisburg to PITTSBURGH in 1847, it developed as a transportation center. The state capitol, with a dome patterned after St. Peter's in Rome, was completed in 1906.

Harrison, Benjamin (1833–1901) 23rd president of the U.S. (1889–93). Born in N. Bend, Ohio, the grandson of W. H. HARRISON, he served in the Union army in the Civil War, rising to brigadier general. He served in the U.S. Senate 1881–87. Nominated for president by the Republicans, he defeated the incumbent, Grover CLEVELAND, even though Cleveland won the popular vote. Harrison's domestic policy was marked by passage of the SHERMAN ANTITRUST ACT. His foreign policy expanded U.S. influence abroad; his secretary of state,

Benjamin Harrison

James BLAINE, presided at the conference that led to the establishment of the Pan-American Union and negotiated a treaty with Britain in the Bering Sea dispute (1891). Defeated for reelection by Cleveland in 1892, he returned to Indianapolis to practice law. In 1898–99 he represented Venezuela in its boundary dispute with Britain.

Harrison, Rex (*orig.* Reginald Carey) (*later* **Sir Rex**) (1908–1990) British actor. He made his debut in films and on the London stage in 1930, later appearing in such successful plays as *French Without Tears* (1936). A suave leading man in such films as *Blithe Spirit* (1945) and *Notorious Gentleman* (1945), he made his U.S. film debut in *Anna and the King of Siam* (1946). His most famous role, as Prof. Henry Higgins in *My Fair Lady* (1956, Tony Award), won him equal acclaim in its film version (1964, Academy Award).

Harrison, William Henry (1773–1841) Ninth president of the U.S. (1841). Born in Charles City Co., Va., he served in the army under Anthony WAYNE. As governor of the new Indiana Territory (1800–12), he negotiated treaties with the Indians that ceded millions of acres of additional land to the U.S. When TECUMSEH organized an uprising in 1811, Harrison led a U.S. force to defeat the Indians at the Battle of TIPPECANOE. In the WAR OF 1812 he defeated the British and their Indian allies at the Battle of the THAMES in Ontario. After the war he moved to Ohio, where he be-

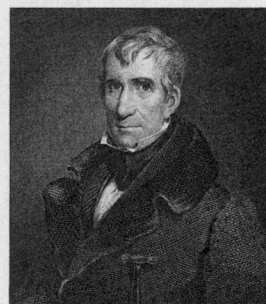

William Henry Harrison

came prominent in the WHIG PARTY. He served in the U.S. House of Representatives (1816–19) and Senate (1825–28). As the Whig candidate in the 1836 presidential election, he lost narrowly. In 1840 he and his running mate, John TYLER, won with a slogan emphasizing Harrison's frontier triumph: "Tippecanoe and Tyler too." The 68-year-old Harrison delivered his inaugural speech without a hat or over-coat in a cold drizzle, contracted pneumonia, and died one month later.

Harrods \'har-ədz\ Renowned London DEPARTMENT STORE. It was founded by a miller, Henry Charles Harrod, as a gro-cery store in 1849. The store expanded in the late 1800s, and many new departments were added. Known for its zealous customer service, it is considered the best department store in Britain. In 1985 it was bought by Mohammed al-Fayed (b.1933).

Harrow School Educational institution in Harrow, Greater London, founded by John Lyon (d.1592). ELIZABETH I granted the school's charter in 1571, and the first building was opened in 1611. It has long been renowned as one of the two or three greatest English public (i.e., independent) schools; its graduates include Richard Brinsley SHERIDAN, Lord BYRON, Robert PEEL, and Winston CHURCHILL.

Hart, Basil Liddell See Basil LIDDELL HART

Hart, Lorenz (Milton) (1895–1943) U.S. lyricist. Born in New York City, he initially worked as a translator of German. In 1918 he met Richard RODGERS at Columbia Univ. Their many Broadway hits would include *The Garrick Gaieties* (1925), *A Connecticut Yankee* (1927), *The Boys from Syra-cuse* (1938), and *Pal Joey* (1940). Their often difficult 25-year collaboration yielded nearly 1,000 songs, including "Blue Moon," "My Funny Valentine," "The Lady Is a Tramp," and "Bewitched, Bothered, and Bewildered."

Hart, Moss (1904–1961) U.S. playwright and director. Born in New York City, he collaborated with G. S. KAUFMAN on the popular comedies *Once in a Lifetime* (1930; film, 1933), *You Can't Take It with You* (1936, Pulitzer Prize; film, 1938), and *The Man Who Came to Dinner* (1939; film, 1942). Hart later wrote and directed such plays as *Lady in the Dark* (1941; film, 1944) and *Winged Victory* (1943; film, 1944), and directed the long-running musicals *My Fair Lady* (1956, Tony Award) and *Camelot* (1960). Among his screenplays are *Gentleman's Agreement* (1947) and *A Star Is Born* (1954). He wrote a best-selling autobiography, *Act One* (1959).

Hart, William S(urrey) (1870–1946) U.S. actor. Born in New-burgh, N.Y., he made his stage debut in 1889 and portrayed western heroes in the plays *The Squaw Man* (1905), *The Vir-ginian* (1907), and *The Trail of the Lonesome Pine* (1912). In Hollywood his stern, taciturn performances made him a star and the first cowboy hero. Among his numerous films, many of which he wrote and directed, were *The Passing of Two-Gun Hicks* (1914–15), *The Square-Deal Man* (1917), and *Wild Bill Hickok* (1923).

Harte, Bret *orig.* Francis Brett Harte (1836–1902) U.S. writer. Born in Albany, N.Y., he briefly experienced camp life in California mining country before becoming a news-paper and periodical editor and writer. His works, which helped create the local-color school in American fiction, in-clude the short stories "The Luck of Roaring Camp" (1868) and "The Outcasts of Poker Flat" (1869), the poem "The Heathen Chinee" (1870), and the play *Ah Sin* (1877; with Mark TWAIN). In an era when the West was a popular sub-ject, they made him internationally famous.

hartebeest \'här-tə-ˌbēst\ Either of two species of swift, slender ANTELOPE (genus *Alcelaphus*) found in herds on open plains and scrublands of sub-Saharan Africa. They of-ten mingle with herds of other antelope or ZEBRAS. Harte-beests stand about 4 ft (1.2 m) tall at the shoulder, and the back slopes downward from heavy forequarters to narrow hindquarters. The long face is accentuated by ringed, lyre-shaped horns united at the base.

Hartford City (pop., 2000: 121,000), capital of Connecticut. Lying on the CONNECTICUT RIVER, it was settled by Dutch traders in the 1630s. The Fundamental Orders of Connecti-cut, which later served as a model for the U.S. CONSTITU-TION, were adopted (1639) in Hartford. The city's insurance industry, its major business, dates from 1794. Its statehouse (1796) was designed by Charles BULFINCH. The birthplace of J. P. MORGAN, it was the home of H. B. STOWE and Mark TWAIN.

Hartford Convention (Dec. 5, 1814–Jan. 5, 1815) Secret meeting of New England FEDERALIST PARTY delegates who opposed the WAR OF 1812. It adopted a strong states'-rights position in opposition to the mercantile policies of Pres.

James MADISON and measures that prohibited trade with Britain and France. News of the peace treaty (Dec. 24, 1814) discredited the nascent secessionist movement and weakened Federalist influence.

Hartley, Marsden (1877–1943) U.S. painter. Born in Lewis-ton, Me., he attended the Cleveland School of Art, then set-tled in New York. From 1900 he spent most summers in Maine, painting landscapes. In 1913 he exhibited at the AR-MORY SHOW. His early style of painting abstracts with strongly outlined forms and brilliant colors evolved into a personal interpretation of Expressionism, most evident in his bold and brooding Maine landscapes. He produced a dramatic series of pastels and oil paintings of New Mexico (1918–20), and in 1932 a notable series of the volcano Popocatépetl in Mexico.

Harun al-Rashid \hä-ˈrün-äl-rä-ˈshēd\ (c.765–809) Fifth AB-BASID caliph, who ruled the Arabian empire from Baghdad at its peak of size and wealth (786–809). His father was the third caliph. He succeeded to the caliphate after the myste-rious death of his brother, the fourth caliph. Despite local-ized rebellions, Harun's reign created vast wealth for the caliphate, as described in the *Thousand and One Nights*. He divided the empire for inheritance by two of his sons, thereby acknowledging a split between Persian and Arab in-terests.

Harvard University Oldest institution of higher learning in the U.S. (founded 1636) and perhaps the most prestigious. Harvard College was named for a Puritan minister, John Harvard (1607–1638), who left the school, in Cambridge, Mass., his books and half of his estate. Its schools of divin-ity, law, and medicine were established in the early 19th cent. Charles William ELIOT, during his long tenure as pres-ident (1869–1909), made Harvard an institution with na-tional influence. Harvard has educated seven U.S. presi-dents, many Supreme Court justices, cabinet officers, congressional leaders, and dozens of major literary and in-tellectual figures. Its undergraduate school, Harvard Col-lege, contains about one-third of the total student body. Radcliffe College (1879) was a coordinate undergraduate women's college; in 1999 it was absorbed by Harvard. Har-vard Univ. also has graduate or professional schools of medicine, law, business, divinity, education, government, dentistry, architecture and landscape design, and public health. Its Widener Library is one of the greatest libraries in the world. Total enrollment is about 18,000.

harvester See COMBINE HARVESTER

harvestman See DADDY LONGLEGS

Harvey, William (1578–1657) English physician. He became one of JAMES I's physicians around 1618, and continued as a king's physician for CHARLES I. Harvey's elucidation of blood CIRCULATION overturned the work of GALEN and ad-vanced that of Andreas VESALIUS and Hieronymus FABRI-CIUS. His *Anatomical Exercise Concerning the Motion of the Heart and Blood in Animals* (1628) recorded his findings. It clarified the function of HEART valves, proved that blood did not pass through the septum in the heart, explained the purpose of valves in the veins and of the pulmonary circu-lation, showed that blood is pumped from the atria into the ventricles and then into the rest of the circulatory system, and proved that the pulse reflected heart contractions.

Harz Mountains \'härts\ Mountain range, central Germany. Lying between the WESER and ELBE rivers, it is 60 mi (100 km) long and about 20 mi (32 km) wide. The NW and high-est portion is known as the Oberharz; the SE part is the Un-terharz. The highest peak is Mt. BROCKEN. The range was intensively mined in the 10th–16th cent. Its most important modern industry is tourism.

Hasanlu \'hä-sən-ˌlü\ Archaelogical site, NW Iran. Excava-tions have revealed the area's prehistory, especially the late 2nd and early 1st millennia B.C. It was inhabited from about 2100 to about 825 B.C., but the richest period, often called Mannaean, dates to the 10th–9th cent. B.C. It was crowned by a high citadel surrounded by a fortification wall.

hashish \ha-ˈshēsh\ Hallucinogenic drug preparation de-rived from RESIN from the flowers of HEMP plants. MARI-JUANA, a product of the same plant, is far less potent. Hashish is smoked or eaten. The active ingredient, tetrahy-drocannabinol (THC), makes up 10–15% of hashish.

Hasidism \'hä-sə-ˌdi-zəm\ Pietistic and mystical movement in JUDAISM that originated in 18th-cent. Poland. It was a reaction against rigid legalism and Talmudic learning in favor of a joyful form of worship that served as a spiritual outlet for the common people. The BAAL SHEM TOV taught that God was immanent in all things and that piety was more important than scholarship. Dov Baer founded the first Hasidic community about 1710, and countless small communities soon sprang up in Poland, Russia, Lithuania, and Palestine. Though excommunicated from ORTHODOX JUDAISM in 1772, the community continued to flourish. By the 19th cent. Hasidism had become ultraconservative. Huge numbers of followers died in the HOLOCAUST, but survivors established themselves in Israel and the U.S. The Lubavitcher sect, based in Brooklyn, N.Y., numbers about 200,000.

Hassam \'has-əm\, **(Frederick) Childe** (1859–1935) U.S. painter and printmaker. Born in Boston, he studied there and in Paris before settling in New York. City life was his favorite subject; paintings such as *Washington Arch, Spring* (1890) are characterized by clear, luminous atmosphere and brilliant color. He also produced some 400 etchings and lithographs. From 1898 to 1918 he exhibited together with a group of New York and Boston painters known as The Ten, who became the foremost proponents of U.S. IMPRESSIONISM.

Hassan II \'hä-sàn, *Engl* ha-'sän\ *orig.* Mawlay Hassan Muhammad ibn Yusuf (1929–1999) King of Morocco (1961–99). On his succession he introduced a new constitution providing for a popularly elected legislature, but exercised authoritarian rule throughout much of his reign. He claimed the former Spanish Sahara, which Algeria also claimed; Morocco's annexation of it led to ongoing hostilities. In 1986 he became the second Arab leader to meet publicly with an Israeli leader. He condemned the 1990 invasion of Kuwait by Iraq. Under his leadership Morocco achieved political stability and some economic and social development, though human rights remained an issue.

Hassuna \ha-'sü-nə\ Archaeological site, N Iraq. An ancient Mesopotamian town located south of MOSUL, it was excavated in 1943–44, and was found to represent an advanced village culture. Six layers of houses were uncovered, each progressively more substantial. Vessels and pottery dating to around 5600–5350 B.C. were discovered. Similar wares found elsewhere in the Middle East show that by the 6th millennium B.C. an extensive trade network existed in the region.

Hastings, Battle of (Oct. 14, 1066) Battle that ended in the defeat of HAROLD II of England by William, duke of Normandy, and established the NORMANS as rulers of England. On his deathbed EDWARD THE CONFESSOR had supposedly granted the English throne to Harold, despite an earlier promise to make William his heir. William crossed to England from Normandy with a skilled army of 4,000–7,000 men. Harold met the Norman invaders at Hastings with an army of 7,000 men, many of whom were untrained peasants. The English were defeated after a day-long battle in which Harold was killed, and the Norman duke was soon crowned WILLIAM I. See also NORMAN CONQUEST.

Hastings, Warren (1732–1818) British colonial administrator in India. A member of the English E. INDIA CO. council in Bengal (1761–64) and Madras (1769), he became governor of Bengal (1772–74), moved the central government to Calcutta, and remodeled the justice system. In 1774 he acquired the new title of governor-general, with responsibilities for supervising other British settlements in India. He sought to counter the instability created by the fall of the Mughal empire and maintain peaceful relations with neighboring states, but was drawn into the MARATHA WARS. This disrupted the company's trade and antagonized opinion in England, as did several dubious ventures Hastings entered into to raise extra funds. In 1785, leaving an India at peace, he retired to England. In 1786 Edmund BURKE introduced an impeachment process against him on charges of corruption; after a long trial (1788–95), Hastings was acquitted.

hat Head covering of any of various styles, used for warmth, fashion, or religious or ceremonial purposes, when it often symbolizes office or rank. Through the Middle Ages men wore hats in the form of caps or hoods and women wore veils, hoods, or head draperies. The silk top hat originated in Florence around 1760. The derby (bowler) was introduced in 1850. The cloth cap with visor was for decades the international standard for workingmen and boys. Women's hats went through periods of astonishing ostentation up to World War I. In the East, colorful turbans are the traditional headgear; in E and S Mediterranean countries, men wear the fez; in Asia, the Chinese devised the simple coolie hat and the Japanese the elaborate cap-shaped *kammuri*. In Latin America and the SW U.S., the broadbrimmed sombrero is still popular. Since about 1960 the wearing of hats has greatly declined in Western industrialized countries.

Hatfields and McCoys Two families of the Appalachian Mtns. who engaged in a backwoods feud in the late 19th cent. The large families lived on opposite sides of a border stream, the Hatfields in W. Virginia and the McCoys in Kentucky. The feud may have originated in opposing allegiances in the Civil War. In 1882 the first murder of a Hatfield was followed by the murder of three McCoys. Retaliatory raids and murders continued with little interference from local police. In 1888 a posse of McCoys led by a deputy sheriff captured nine Hatfields and took them to Kentucky to stand trial. W. Virginia officials charged them with kidnapping. The U.S. Supreme Court eventually ruled in favor of Kentucky. Flare-ups gradually abated by the 1920s.

Hathor \'hä-tòr\ *or* **Athyr** \'ä-'thir\ In ancient EGYPTIAN RELIGION, the goddess of the sky, women, fertility, and love. Her principal animal form was a cow, and she was strongly associated with motherhood. Her worship was linked at Heliopolis with that of RE and in Upper Egypt with that of HORUS. In the NECROPOLIS at Thebes she was the patroness of the dead.

Hatshepsut \hat-'shep-süt\ Queen of Egypt (c.1472–1458 B.C.). She first acted as regent for her stepson, THUTMOSE III, but soon ordered herself crowned as pharaoh. She attained unprecedented power, adopting the titles and regalia of a pharaoh, complete with a false beard. She devoted much of the profit from expanded trade and tribute to an extensive building program, most notably to a splendid temple at Dayr al-Bahri. Whether she died naturally or was deposed and killed is uncertain.

Hatteras \'ha-tə-rəs\, **Cape** Long, narrow, curved sandbar forming a promontory on Hatteras Island, N. Carolina. It extends 70 mi (113 km) along the OUTER BANKS between the Atlantic Ocean and PAMLICO SOUND. Much of it is included in Cape Hatteras National Seashore. It is the site of the tallest lighthouse in the U.S., 208 ft (63 m) high.

Hauptmann \'haùpt-ˌmän\, **Gerhart (Johann Robert)** (1862–1946) German playwright and poet. His first play, the starkly realistic *Before Dawn* (1889), made him famous and signaled the end of the highly stylized German drama. His naturalistic plays on themes of social reality and proletarian tragedy, including *The Weavers* (1892), *The Beaver Coat* (1893), and *Drayman Henschel* (1898), made him the most prominent German playwright of his era. He was awarded the Nobel Prize in 1912. In his novels, poems, and later plays, he abandoned naturalism for mystical religiosity.

Gerhart Hauptmann Etching by Hermann Struck, 1904

Hausa \'haù-sə\ People of NW Nigeria and S Niger who speak the HAUSA LANGUAGE. The Hausa, numbering 30 million, are the largest ethnic group in the area. In the mid-14th cent. a confederation of Hausa states was formed, influenced by the spread of Islam from the MALI EMPIRE. The head of an emirate is surrounded by titled officeholders who hold villages as fiefs, from which their agents collect taxes. The economy has traditionally rested on agriculture, craftwork, and trade. Hausa society is highly hierarchical; social rank is expressed in an elaborate etiquette. See also FULANI.

Hausa language \\'haú-sə, 'haú-zə\\ Chadic language of W. Africa (see AFROASIATIC LANGUAGES), with some 30 million first-language speakers in N Nigeria and S Niger. Hausa is also a LINGUA FRANCA across a broad area of the African Sahel and savanna region. In common with most or all other Chadic languages, Hausa is tonal (see TONE), has two grammatical GENDERS, and has the customary word order subject-verb-object. Hausa is now customarily written in the LATIN ALPHABET, though writing in an adaptation of the ARABIC ALPHABET continues in Koranic schools.

hausen See BELUGA

Haussmann \\ōs-'mȧn\\, **Georges-Eugène** *later* **Baron Haussmann** (1809–1891) French administrator and city planner. As prefect of the Seine department (1853–70), he inaugurated a wide-reaching and influential program of municipal improvements in Paris, including a new water supply and sewage system, creation of wide avenues through Paris's mass of small streets, landscape gardening of the Bois de Boulogne, and construction of the PARIS OPERA and Les Halles market.

Havana *Spanish* **La Habana** \\,lä-ä-'bä-nä\\ City (pop., 1995 est.: 2,241,000), capital of Cuba. The largest city in the Caribbean, it is Cuba's chief port, and has one of the best harbors in the Western Hemisphere. Founded by the Spanish in 1515 and made the capital of Cuba in 1592, it was Spain's chief naval station in the New World. The destruction of the U.S. battleship *Maine* in the harbor in 1898 was the immediate cause of the SPANISH–AMERICAN WAR. Before 1959, when Fidel CASTRO came to power, Havana was a haven for U.S. tourists, offering gambling and showy nightlife. It contains many buildings reflecting Spanish colonial style, including the cathedral (1704) and Morro Castle. Central Havana is now a WORLD HERITAGE SITE.

Havel \\'hä-vəl\\, **Vaclav** (b.1936) Czech playwright and first president of the Czech Republic (1993–2003). He worked in a Prague theater from 1959 and became resident playwright by 1968. His satirical plays, including *The Memorandum* (1965), explore the moral compromises made by those living under totalitarianism. They were banned by the communist authorities, and Havel was imprisoned 1979–83. In 1989 he became a leader in the Civic Forum, a coalition of groups pressing for democratic reforms. The Communist Party capitulated (in the bloodless "Velvet Revolution") and formed a coalition government with the Civic Forum, and Havel was elected president in 1989. In 1993 he was elected president of the new Czech Republic.

Havelok (the Dane) \\'ha-və-,läk\\ Middle English metrical ROMANCE of some 3,000 lines, written around 1300. Of the literature produced after the Norman Conquest, it offers the first view of ordinary life. It tells the story of the English princess Goldeboru and the orphaned Danish prince Havelok, who defeats a usurper to become king of Denmark and part of England.

Haverford College Private liberal-arts college in Haverford, Pa., near Philadelphia. Founded by Quakers in 1833 as a men's college, it became coeducational in 1980. Consistently ranked as one of the top U.S. colleges, it maintains cooperative programs with BRYN MAWR and SWARTHMORE colleges and the Univ. of PENNSYLVANIA. Enrollment is about 1,200.

Havre, Le See LE HAVRE

Hawaii *formerly* **Sandwich Islands** State (pop., 2000: 1,211,000), U.S., comprising a group of islands in the central Pacific Ocean that covers 6,471 sq mi (16,760 sq km). Its capital is HONOLULU. Located 2,397 mi (3,857 km) west of San Francisco, the state's major islands are, from west to east, Niihau, Kauai, OAHU, Molokai, Lanai, Kahoolawe, Maui, and HAWAII; there are over 120 islets. The state's active volcanoes include MAUNA LOA and KILAUEA. People of at least part-Hawaiian descent constitute about one-eighth of Hawaii's total population, followed by those of Japanese ancestry, who constitute one-fourth. The majority of the state's residents live on Oahu. The original Hawaiians were of Polynesian origin and came from the MARQUESAS ISLANDS around A.D. 400. Capt. James COOK visited the islands in 1778, and called them the Sandwich Islands. In 1796 KAMEHAMEHA I united the group under his rule. American whalers began to stop there; they were followed in 1820 by New England missionaries, and Western influences changed the islands. While Kamehameha III in 1851 placed Hawaii under U.S. protection, a coup later fomented by U.S. sugar interests resulted in the monarchy's overthrow and the establishment of a Republic of Hawaii (1893). In 1898 the new republic and the U.S. agreed on annexation, and in 1900 Hawaii became a U.S. territory. The bombing of PEARL HARBOR by the Japanese in 1941 led to U.S. involvement in WORLD WAR II, and Hawaii became a major naval station. Hawaii became the 50th state in 1959. Its largest industry is tourism. It is also a world astronomy center, with telescopes atop MAUNA KEA.

Hawaii Volcanic island, part of the state of Hawaii. It lies south of Maui; Hilo (pop., 2000: 40,000) is its main town. Known as the Big Island, it is the largest in area, at 4,028 sq mi (10,433 sq km), and southeasternmost of the Hawaiian Island group. KILAUEA, the world's most active volcano, is located there in HAWAII VOLCANOES NATIONAL PARK. The island has other volcanic peaks, including MAUNA KEA. Sugar, tourism, cattle, orchids, and coffee are the basis of the economy.

Hawaiians Aboriginal people of Hawaii, descendants of Polynesians who migrated to Hawaii from the Marquesas Islands (c.400) and from Tahiti (c.900). Without metals, pottery, or beasts of burden, Hawaiians made implements of stone, wood, shell, teeth, and bone. They had a highly developed oral culture and possessed percussion, string, and wind instruments. Their basic unit of land, the *ahupuaa*, usually extended from the seashore to the mountaintop, providing the occupants with the means to grow and gather all they needed. Hawaiians had four principal gods. After the arrival of Christian missionaries in 1820, some of the more repressive laws and taboos were abolished, but the native population was devastated by Western diseases. Numbering about 300,000 in 1778, full-blooded Hawaiians today number fewer than 10,000.

Hawaii Volcanoes National Park National preserve, SE shore of HAWAII island. Established in 1916, it occupies an area of 358 sq mi (927 sq km) and includes the active volcanoes MAUNA LOA and KILAUEA. Other highlights are Kau Desert, an area of lava formations near Kilauea, and a tree-fern forest.

hawk Any of many small to medium-sized diurnal BIRDS OF PREY, particularly those in the genus *Accipiter*. The term is often applied to other birds in the Accipitridae family (including BUZZARDS, HARRIERS, and KITES) and sometimes to certain FALCONS. Hawks usually eat small mammals, reptiles, and insects but occasionally kill birds. Hawks are found nearly worldwide. Most nest in trees. True hawks (accipiters) can be distinguished in flight by their long tails and short, rounded wings. They are exemplified by the 12-in. (30-cm) sharp-shinned hawk (*A. striatus*), gray above with fine rusty barring below, found throughout the New World. See also GOSHAWK, SPARROW HAWK.

Hawking, Stephen W(illiam) (b.1942) English theoretical physicist. He has worked primarily on general RELATIVITY and particularly the physics of BLACK HOLES. In 1971 he suggested that after the big bang, numerous "mini–black holes" formed with as much as 1 billion tons of mass in the size of a proton, that are uniquely subject to the laws both of relativity, due to their immense mass and gravity, and of QUANTUM MECHANICS, due to their minute size. In 1974 he proposed that black holes "evaporate" by what is now known as Hawking radiation; his work greatly spurred efforts to theoretically delineate their properties and showed how these relate to the laws of classical thermodynamics and quantum mechanics. Hawking's achievements, despite near-total paralysis from amyotrophic lateral sclerosis, have earned him extraordinary honors. His books include the best-selling *A Brief History of Time* (1988).

Hawkins, Coleman (Randolph) (1904–1969) U.S. musician, the first important tenor-saxophone soloist in jazz. Born in St. Joseph, Mo., Hawkins came to prominence as a member of Fletcher HENDERSON's big band (1924–34), with which he developed the smooth legato phrasing and robust tone that set the technical standard for all tenor players. He worked in Europe 1934–39, and soon after his return recorded "Body and Soul," one of the masterpieces of improvised jazz.

Hawkins, John (*later* **Sir John**) (1532–1595) English naval commander. A relative of Francis DRAKE, he became a merchant in the African trade and the first English slave trader (1562). A Spanish fleet attacked him on his third slave-trading voyage (1567–69), with Drake, beginning the quarrel between England and Spain that led to war in 1585. As treasurer (1577) and controller (1589) of the navy, he rebuilt older ships and helped design the faster ships that withstood the Spanish ARMADA. He later devised the naval blockade to intercept Spanish treasure ships. He is considered the chief architect of the Elizabethan navy.

hawk moth *or* **sphinx moth** Any MOTH of the LEPIDOPTERAN family Sphingidae. These stout-bodied moths have long, narrow forewings and shorter hind wings, with wingspans ranging from 2 to 8 in. (5–20 cm). Many species pollinate flowers while sucking nectar; the proboscis of some species is up to 13 in. (33 cm) long. The larvae, which are smooth and have a dorsal "horn," are called hornworms; larvae of two N. American species attack tomato, tobacco, and potato crops.

Hawks, Howard (Winchester) (1896–1977) U.S. film director. Born in Goshen, Ind., he wrote screenplays in Hollywood before making his first major film, *A Girl in Every Port* (1928). A master technician and storyteller, he directed over 40 films (many of which he also produced and wrote) in a variety of genres: adventure (*The Dawn Patrol*, 1930), crime (*Scarface*, 1932), comedy (*Bringing Up Baby*, 1938), war (*Sergeant York*, 1941), musicals (*Gentlemen Prefer Blondes*, 1953), film-noir thrillers (*The Big Sleep*, 1946), science fiction (*The Thing*, 1951), and westerns (*Red River*, 1948; *Rio Bravo*, 1959).

hawthorn Any of various thorny shrubs or small trees of the genus *Crataegus*, in the ROSE family, native to the N temperate zone. Many species are native to N. America. The simple leaves are usually toothed or lobed. Hawthorns bear white or pink flowers, usually in clusters, and small apple-like fruits. Many cultivated varieties are grown as ornamentals.

Hawthorne, Nathaniel (1804–1864) U.S. novelist and short-story writer. Descended from Puritans of Salem, Mass., he was imbued with a deep moral earnestness. "My Kinsman, Major Molineux" (1832), "Roger Malvin's Burial" (1832), and "Young Goodman Brown" (1835) rank among his greatest tales. His story collections include *Twice-Told Tales* (1837) and *Mosses from an Old Manse* (1846). He is best known for the novels *The Scarlet Letter* (1850), a story of adultery set in colonial New England, and *The House of the Seven Gables* (1851), the story of a family that lives under a curse for generations. A skilled literary craftsman and a master of allegory and symbolism, he ranks among the greatest American fiction writers.

hay In agriculture, dried GRASSES and other foliage used as animal feed. Typical hay crops are timothy, ALFALFA, and CLOVER. Usually the material is cut in the field while still green and then either dried in the field or mechanically dried by forced hot air. Balers compress hay into tightly packed rectangular or cylindrical bales. Loose hay may also be "vacuumed" off the field and then blown into stacks in a barn or other storage facility. Properly cured hay with 20% or less moisture can be stored for months.

Hay, John (Milton) (1838–1905) U.S. diplomat and writer. Born in Salem, Ind., he studied law in Springfield, Ill., where he met Abraham LINCOLN. He served as Pres. Lincoln's secretary (1861–65), held diplomatic posts in Europe (1865–70), wrote editorials for the *New York Tribune* (1870–75), and coauthored a 10-volume biography of Lincoln (1890). As secretary of state (1898–1905), he helped negotiate the end of the SPANISH–AMERICAN WAR, supported the decision to retain the Philippines for the U.S., promulgated the OPEN DOOR POLICY, and negotiated treaties to give the U.S. exclusive rights to build the Panama Canal.

Haydarabad See HYDERABAD

Haydn \'hī-dᵊn\, **Franz Joseph** (1732–1809) Austrian composer. He was recruited at 8 to the choir at St. Stephen's

Church, Vienna, where he learned violin and keyboard. Later supporting himself by teaching and playing violin, he worked for the composer Nicola Porpora (1686–1768) in exchange for lessons. Gaining entrée to high society, in 1761 he became head of the musical establishment at the great but remote palace of the ESTERHÁZY FAMILY, which would support him for most of his career. In this position of artistic isolation but with excellent resources, Haydn felt free to experiment and was forced to become original. By his late years he was recognized as the greatest living composer. He composed important works in almost every genre, and his elegant and ingratiating works balance wit and seriousness, custom and innovation. The first great symphonist, he composed 108 symphonies, including the 12 great "London symphonies" (1791–95). He virtually invented the string quartet, and his 68 quartets remain the foundation of the quartet literature. His choral works include 15 masses and the oratorios *The Creation* (1798) and *The Seasons* (1801). The principal shaper of the Classical style, he exerted major influence on his friend W. A. MOZART and his student Ludwig van BEETHOVEN.

Hayek \'hī-ak\, **Friedrich (August) von** (1899–1992) Austrian-British economist. He moved to London in 1931 and held positions at the Univ. of London, the London School of Economics, and later the Univ. of Chicago (1950–62). He opposed the theories of J. M. KEYNES and criticized government intervention in the free market as destructive of individual values and ultimately ineffective against inflation, unemployment, and recession. His books include *The Road to Serfdom* (1944), *The Constitution of Liberty* (1960), and *The Political Order of a Free People* (1979). His views have been highly influential among conservatives, including Margaret THATCHER. In 1974 he shared the Nobel Prize with Gunnar MYRDAL.

Hayes (Brown), Helen (1900–1993) U.S. actress. Born in Washington, D.C., she made her Broadway debut at age 9. She went on to star in such Broadway productions as *Caesar and Cleopatra* (1925), *What Every Woman Knows* (1926), and *The Animal Kingdom* (1932), becoming known as "First Lady of the American Theater." Memorable in *Mary of Scotland* (1933–34) and *Victoria Regina* (1935–39), she also starred in revivals of *The Skin of Our Teeth* (1955), *The Glass Menagerie* (1956), and *Long Day's Journey into Night* (1971). She acted in numerous radio and television plays, and won Academy Awards for her films *The Sin of Madelon Claudet* (1931) and *Airport* (1970), as well as three Tony awards and the Presidential Medal of Freedom.

Hayes, Rutherford B(irchard) (1822–1893) 19th president of the U.S. (1877–81). Born in Delaware, Ohio, he practiced law in Cincinnati, representing defendants in several fugitive-slave cases. After fighting in the Union army, he served in the U.S. House of Representatives (1865–67). As governor of Ohio (1868–72, 1875–76), he advocated a sound currency backed by gold. In 1876 he won the Republican nomination for president. His opponent, Samuel TILDEN, won a larger popular vote in the election, but Hayes's managers contested the electoral vote, and a special ELECTORAL COMMISSION

Rutherford B. Hayes

awarded the election to Hayes. As part of a secret compromise, he withdrew the remaining federal troops from the South, ending RECONSTRUCTION, and promised not to interfere with elections there, ensuring the return of white supremacy. He introduced civil-service reform based on merit, incurring a dispute with Roscoe CONKLING and the conservative "stalwart" Republicans. Declining to run for a second term, he retired to work for humanitarian causes.

hay fever Seasonal sneezing, nasal congestion, and tearing and itching of the eyes caused by ALLERGY to the POLLEN of certain plants, chiefly those pollinated by the wind (e.g.,

HIJ

RAGWEED in N. America). ANTIHISTAMINES provide temporary relief; long-range treatment involves desensitization. Unless properly treated, about one-third of patients with hay fever develop ASTHMA.

Haymarket Riot (May 4, 1886) Violent confrontation between police and labor protesters in Chicago. Radical unionists had called a mass meeting in Haymarket Square to protest police brutality in a strike action. A bomb was thrown into the crowd, killing seven policemen. Police and workers fired on each other. Public demand for action led to the arrest of eight anarchists. Convicted of conspiracy to murder, they were sentenced to death; four were executed, one committed suicide, and three were pardoned in 1893 by Gov. J. P. ALTGELD.

Hays Office *formally* Motion Picture Producers and Distributors of America. U.S. organization that promulgated a moral code for films. In 1922, after a number of scandals involving Hollywood personalities, film-industry leaders formed the organization to counteract the threat of government censorship. Under Will H. Hays (1879–1954), it inserted morals clauses into actors' contracts, and in 1930 developed a Production Code that detailed what was morally acceptable on the screen. The code was supplanted in 1966 by a voluntary rating system.

Haywood, William D(udley) (1869–1928) U.S. labor leader. Born in Salt Lake City, he became a miner at 15. In 1905 he helped found the INDUSTRIAL WORKERS OF THE WORLD. Acquitted in 1907 on a charge of involvement in the murder of Idaho's antilabor former governor, Frank Steunenberg (1861–1905), "Big Bill" Haywood became a spokesman for the Socialist Party, which later forced him out for advocating violence. In 1917 he was convicted of sedition for his opposition to World War I and sentenced to 20 years in prison; in 1921, while free on bail, he fled to Russia.

Hayworth, Rita *orig.* Margarita Carmen Cansino (1918–1987) U.S. film actress. Born in Brooklyn, N.Y., she played bit parts in films from 1935. She cultivated a sophisticated glamour in *Only Angels Have Wings* (1939), *Strawberry Blonde* (1941), and *Blood and Sand* (1941). The musicals *You'll Never Get Rich* (1941) and *Cover Girl* (1944) made her a favorite pinup of U.S. GIs. Her worldly, erotic role in *Gilda* (1946) confirmed her status as Hollywood's "love goddess." Her later films included *The Lady from Shanghai* (1948), *Pal Joey* (1957), and *Separate Tables* (1958). She suffered from Alzheimer's disease for the last 15 years of her life.

hazel See FILBERT

Hazlitt, William (1778–1830) British essayist. He studied for the ministry, but to remedy his poverty he became instead a prolific critic, essayist, and lecturer. He began contributing to journals, notably Leigh HUNT's Examiner, and to essay collections, notably *The Round Table* (1817). His lecture courses were published as *On the English Poets* (1818) and *On the English Comic Writers* (1819). Many of his most brilliant essays appeared in his two most famous books, *Table Talk* (1821) and *The Plain Speaker* (1826).

H.D. See Hilda DOOLITTLE

Head, Bessie *orig.* Bessie Amelia Emery (1937–1986) S. African-Botswanan writer. Born of an illegal union between a white mother and a black father, she suffered rejection and alienation from an early age. She described the contradictions and shortcomings of pre- and postcolonial African society in morally didactic novels and stories, including *When Rain Clouds Gather* (1969), *Maru* (1971), *A Question of Power* (1973), and *Serowe, Village of the Rainwind* (1981).

headache Pain in the upper portion of the head. Episodic tension headaches are the most common, usually causing mild to moderate pain on both sides. They result from sustained contraction of face and neck muscles, often due to fatigue, stress, or frustration. Headaches are treated with ASPIRIN, ACETAMINOPHEN, or other NSAIDS. Chronic daily headaches are similar but more frequent. They usually have a psychological cause and respond to certain antidepressants. Headaches may also be caused by distension of arteries at the base of the brain, from fever, hangover, high blood pressure, MENINGITIS, hemorrhagic STROKE, or TUMOR. See also CLUSTER HEADACHE, MIGRAINE.

Heade \'hēd\, **Martin Johnson** (1819–1904) U.S. painter. Born in Lumberville, Pa., he studied in Europe, then returned to take up portrait and landscape painting. An avid naturalist, he traveled in S. and Central America and the Caribbean (1863–70), where he produced luminous, meticulously detailed images of the tropical forests and landscapes (e.g., *Orchids and Hummingbird*, c.1865). The New England coast also inspired notable paintings (e.g., *Salt Marshes, Newport, R.I.*, c.1863). He was a leading exponent of LUMINISM.

headhunting Practice of removing, displaying, and in some cases preserving human heads. Headhunting often arises from a belief in a more or less material soul matter that resides in the head. The headhunter seeks to transfer this soul matter to himself and his community. Headhunting is thus sometimes found with CANNIBALISM or HUMAN SACRIFICE. It has been practiced worldwide and may go back to Paleolithic times. Among the MAORI, the heads of enemies were dried and preserved so that tattoo marks and facial features were recognizable. In S. America, the skulls were removed and the skin packed with hot sand to create a shrunken head.

head louse See human LOUSE

Health and Human Services, U.S. Department of Federal executive division responsible for carrying out government programs and policies relating to human health, welfare, and income security. It was established in 1980 when responsibility for education was removed from the Department of Health, Education and Welfare.

health insurance System for the advance payment of medical expenses through contributions or taxes paid into a common fund as specified in an insurance policy or law. The key elements are advance payment, pooling of funds, and eligibility for benefits on the basis of contributions or employment without an income or assets test. Health insurance may apply to a limited or comprehensive range of medical services and may provide for full or partial payment of the costs of specific services. Private health insurance is organized and administered by an insurance company or other private agency; public health insurance is run by the government (see SOCIAL INSURANCE). Both are to be distinguished from socialized medicine and government medical-care programs, in which doctors are employed directly or indirectly by the government, which also owns the health-care facilities. See also INSURANCE.

health maintenance organization (HMO) Public or private organization providing medical care to subscribers on the basis of a prepaid contract for a fixed fee. In the prepaid group-practice model, physicians are organized into a group practice with one insuring agency. A medical care foundation, or individual practice association, usually involves multiple insurance companies and reimburses members of a loose network of individual physicians from subscribers' prepaid fees. HMOs have become controversial because some limit care by refusing to pay for tests or treatment against their own doctors' advice.

Heaney \'hē-nē\, **Seamus (Justin)** (b.1939) Irish poet. Appalled by the violence in his native Northern Ireland, he moved to the Republic of Ireland in 1972. In recent years he has taught at Harvard, Oxford, and Cambridge. His works, rooted in Northern Irish rural life, evoke historical events and draw on Irish myth, but also reflect the land's recent troubled decades. His collections include *Death of a Naturalist* (1966), *North* (1975), *The Haw Lantern* (1987), and *The Spirit Level* (1996). He received the Nobel Prize in 1995.

hearing *or* **audition** *or* **sound reception** Physiological process of perceiving SOUND. Hearing entails transforming sound vibrations into nerve impulses, which travel to the brain and are interpreted as sounds. Only ARTHROPODS and VERTEBRATES are capable of sound reception. Hearing enables animals to sense danger, locate food, find mates, and communicate (see ANIMAL COMMUNICATION). All vertebrates have two ears, often with an inner chamber housing auditory hair cells (papillae) and an outer eardrum that receives and transmits sound vibrations. Sound reception in mammals is well developed and often highly specialized, as in bats and dolphins, which use ECHOLOCATION, and whales and elephants, which can hear mating calls from tens or even hundreds of miles away. The human EAR can detect frequencies of 20–20,000 hertz (Hz); it is most sensitive at 1,000–3,000 Hz. Hearing may be impaired by disease, injury, or old age; some disorders, including DEAFNESS, may be congenital.

hearing aid Device that increases the loudness of sounds in the user's EAR. Its principal components are a microphone, an amplifier, and an earphone. Hearing aids are increasingly smaller and less conspicuous. Different types, with widely differing characteristics, may amplify different components of speech sounds for maximum comprehension by each wearer and vary the amplification automatically with the input.

Hearn, (Patricio) Lafcadio (Tessima Carlos) *Japanese* Koizumi Yakumo (1850–1904) Irish-U.S.-Japanese writer, translator, and teacher. He emigrated to the U.S. at 19 and worked as a reporter and translator. In 1890 he traveled to Japan, where he soon became a teacher, took a Japanese wife and name, and became a Japanese subject. Articles and books about Japan's customs, religion, and literature followed, including *Glimpses of Unfamiliar Japan* (1894), *In Ghostly Japan* (1899), and *A Japanese Miscellany* (1901). It was Hearn who, perhaps more than any other single person, introduced the broad culture of Japan to the West.

Hearst \'hərst\, **William Randolph** (1863–1951) U.S. newspaper publisher. Born in San Francisco, Hearst in 1887 took over the struggling *San Francisco Examiner,* which he remade into a successful blend of investigative reporting and lurid sensationalism. After buying the *New York Morning Journal* in 1895, he fought fierce circulation wars with other papers and helped bring about the era of YELLOW JOURNALISM, employing circulation-boosting strategems that profoundly influenced U.S. journalism. Distorted reportage in Hearst papers fanned public sentiment that led to the SPANISH-AMERICAN WAR. He served in Congress (1903–7). At the peak of his fortune in 1935 he owned 28 major newspapers, 18 magazines, radio stations, movie companies, and news services. Extravagance and the Depression weakened him financially, and by 1940 he had lost control of his empire.

heart Organ that pumps blood throughout the body (see CIRCULATION). The human heart is a four-chambered double pump with right and left sides separated by a septum and subdivided on both sides into an atrium above and a ventricle below. The right heart receives venous blood from the venae cavae (see VENA CAVA) and propels it into the PULMONARY CIRCULATION. The left heart takes in blood from the pulmonary veins and sends it into the systemic circulation. Electrical signals from a natural PACEMAKER cause the heart muscle to contract. Valves in the heart keep blood flowing in one direction. Their snapping shut after each contraction causes the sounds heard as the heartbeat. See also CARDIOVASCULAR SYSTEM, HEART DISEASE.

heart attack See MYOCARDIAL INFARCTION

heart disease Any disorder of the heart, including CORONARY HEART DISEASE, heart malformation, and PULMONARY HEART DISEASE, as well as rheumatic heart disease (see RHEUMATIC FEVER), hypertensive heart disease (see HYPERTENSION), inflammation of the heart muscle (myocarditis) or of its inner or outer membrane (ENDOCARDITIS, pericarditis), and heart valve disease. Abnormalities of the heart's natural PACEMAKER or of the nerves that conduct its impulses cause CARDIAC ARRHYTHMIAS. Some CONNECTIVE-TISSUE or AUTOIMMUNE DISEASES diseases can affect the heart. See also HEART FAILURE.

heart failure Inability of one or both sides of the HEART to pump enough blood for the body. Causes include PULMONARY HEART DISEASE, HYPERTENSION, and coronary atherosclerosis (see ARTERIOSCLEROSIS). Left-sided heart failure produces shortness of breath and abnormally high pressure in the pulmonary veins. Right-sided failure produces abnormally high pressure in the systemic veins, liver enlargement, and accumulation of fluid in the legs. A person with failure of both ventricles has an enlarged heart and a three-beat heartbeat. Treatment includes rest, DIGITALIS, restricted SODIUM intake, and elimination of the underlying cause. See also CONGESTIVE HEART FAILURE.

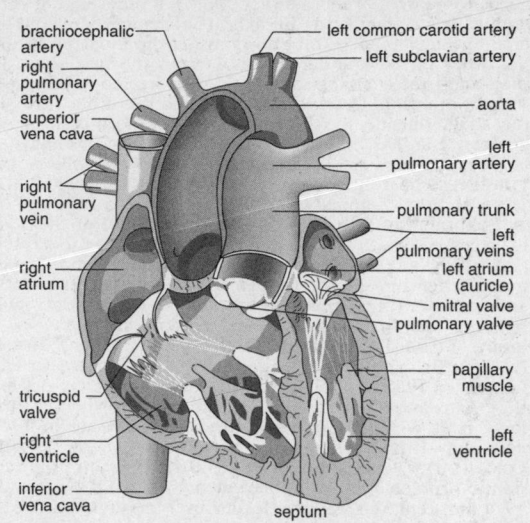

Heart Structure of the human heart. Oxygen-rich blood from the lungs enters the heart through the pulmonary veins, passing into the left atrium and on to the left ventricle. Contraction of the muscles of the left ventricle forces blood into the aorta. The mitral valve prevents blood from moving back into the left atrium during contraction. Various arteries branch off from the aorta to supply blood to all parts of the body. Oxygen-poor blood draining from the body into the superior vena cava and inferior vena cava flows to the right atrium, through the tricuspid valve, and into the right ventricle. As the right ventricle contracts, oxygen-poor blood passes through the pulmonary valve into the pulmonary arteries and on to the lungs to receive oxygen.

heart transplant Procedure to remove a diseased HEART and replace it with a healthy one from a legally dead donor. The first TRANSPLANT was performed in 1967 by Christiaan BARNARD. The diseased heart is removed (except for the natural PACEMAKER), and the new heart is put in place and connected to the recipient's blood vessels. Patients and donors are matched for tissue type, but IMMUNOSUPPRESSION must also be induced.

heartworm Species (*Dirofilaria immitis*) of filarial worm that parasitizes mammals, especially dogs. Up to 500 adult heartworms, which can grow to 6–12 in. (15–30 cm) long, live in the dog's heart, and the microfilariae (embryonic larvae) pass into the blood. Mosquitoes transfer infested blood from dog to dog. Blood flow to the lungs, kidneys, and liver is restricted; by the time visible symptoms (chronic cough, labored breathing, listlessness, heart failure) develop, it may be too late for treatment. Preventive medicines and treatments exist.

heat ENERGY transferred from one body to another as the result of a difference in TEMPERATURE. Heat flows from a hotter body to a colder body when the two bodies are brought together. This transfer of energy usually results in an increase in the temperature of the colder body and a decrease in that of the hotter body. A substance may absorb heat without an increase in temperature as it changes from one PHASE to another—that is, when it melts or boils.

heat capacity Ratio of HEAT absorbed by a material to the change in TEMPERATURE. It is usually expressed as calories per degree in terms of the amount of the material being considered. Heat capacities are measured with a calorimeter and are important as a means of determining the ENTROPIES of materials.

heat exchanger Device that transfers HEAT from a hot to a cold FLUID. In many engineering applications, one fluid needs to be heated and another cooled, a requirement economically accomplished by a heat exchanger. In double-pipe exchangers, one fluid flows inside the inner pipe, and the other in the annular space between the two pipes. In shell-and-tube exchangers, many tubes are mounted inside a shell; one fluid flows in the tubes and the other flows in the shell, outside the tubes. Boilers, evaporators, super-heaters, condensers, and coolers are all heat exchangers. Heat exchangers are used extensively in power plants, gas TURBINES, heating and AIR CONDITIONING, REFRIGERATION, and the chemical industry.

heat exhaustion *or* **heat prostration** Response of the body to excessive heat. The body temperature rises moderately and heavy PERSPIRATION persists. It results from inadequate water and salt intake and can lead to DEHYDRATION and collapse. It may progress to HEATSTROKE if not treated by lying down in a cool place and drinking fluids.

Heath, Edward (Richard George) (*later* **Sir Edward**) (b.1916) British prime minister (1970–74). Elected to Parliament in 1950, after 1964 he led the Conservative opposition. As prime minister, he faced the crisis in Northern Ireland, over which he imposed direct British rule in 1972, and won British entry into the EUROPEAN ECONOMIC COMMUNITY. Unable to cope with Britain's mounting economic problems, he was succeeded by Harold WILSON in 1974 and replaced as party leader by Margaret THATCHER in 1975.

heather Low evergreen shrub (*Calluna vulgaris*) of the HEATH FAMILY, widespread in W Europe and Asia, N. America, and Greenland. It is the chief vegetation on many wastelands. *C. vulgaris* is distinguished from true heaths, which are sometimes loosely called heather, by the lobes of its calyx (see FLOWER), which conceal the petals; in true heaths the petals cover the calyx. Heather has purple stems, close-leaved green shoots, and feathery spikes of bell-shaped flowers.

heath family Family Ericaceae, made up mostly of widely distributed shrubs and small trees, including AZALEAS, RHODODENDRONS, MOUNTAIN LAUREL, BLUEBERRIES, and the low EVERGREEN shrubs of the genus *Erica*. A large percentage of the family's approximately 110 genera and 4,000 species are cultivated. They are often evergreen species that thrive on open, barren land with usually acid and poorly drained soils. See also HEATHER.

heating Process of raising the temperature of an enclosed space. Heat can be delivered by CONVECTION, RADIATION, and THERMAL CONDUCTION. Most cultures have relied on direct heating methods such as FIREPLACES and stoves. Central heating, employed by the ancient Romans and revived in the 19th cent., is a method of indirect heating: heat is produced away from the occupants and then conveyed to them. In warm-air heating, air heated by a furnace rises through ducts and grilles to rooms above. In hot-water systems, a pump circulates water from a boiler through a system of pipes to radiators or convectors in rooms. In steam systems (no longer widely used), steam is generated in the boiler and led to radiators through pipes. In electric heating systems, electric current is usually converted to heat by resistors that emit radiant energy. See also RADIANT HEATING, SOLAR HEATING.

heat pump Device for transferring HEAT from a substance or space to another at a higher TEMPERATURE. A compressor delivers vaporized refrigerant to a condenser in the space to be heated. There, cooler air condenses the refrigerant and itself becomes heated. The liquid refrigerant enters a throttle valve and expands, coming out as a liquid-vapor mixture at a lower temperature and pressure. It enters an evaporator, where the liquid is evaporated by contact with the warmer space. The vapor then passes to the compressor and the cycle is repeated. A heat pump is a reversible system and is commonly used both to heat and to cool buildings. See also REFRIGERATION.

heatstroke Debility caused by prolonged exposure to heat and humidity, called sunstroke when caused by direct sunlight. Body temperature is 106–110°F (41–43°C) or higher. PERSPIRATION almost stops, leading to the rapid temperature rise, collapse, and coma. Cooling with ice-water baths or packs, with massage to promote circulation, is urgent to

save the victim's life but not always successful. See also HEAT EXHAUSTION.

heat treating Changing the properties of METALS (including IRON, STEEL, and ALUMINUM) by processes involving heating. It is used to harden metals that have different crystal structures at low and high temperatures. The metal is heated and then quenched (cooled rapidly) to retain the high-temperature constituent. TEMPERING may then be used to attain the desired hardness. Heating followed by ANNEALING is used to soften metals.

heaven Dwelling place of God or the gods and the abode of the blessed dead. The term also refers to the celestial sphere, the place of the sun, moon, planets, and stars and the source of light, which symbolizes good. In later Judaism and Christianity, heaven is contrasted with HELL, the place of punishment for the wicked. Islam has a similar belief. In Chinese religion, heaven is equated with the divine will.

Heaviside \'he-vē-ˌsīd\, **Oliver** (1850–1925) English physicist. In 1902 he predicted the presence of the IONOSPHERE. Heaviside's work on telephone theory made long-distance service practical. In his *Electromagnetic Theory*

Heaven "The Angel Shows John the Heavenly Jerusalem," c.1020

(1893–1912), he postulated that an electric charge would increase in mass as its velocity increased, anticipating one aspect of Albert EINSTEIN's special theory of relativity.

heavy hydrogen See DEUTERIUM

heavy spar See BARITE

heavy water *or* **deuterium oxide** \dü-'tir-ē-əm\ Water composed of two DEUTERIUM atoms and one OXYGEN atom, chemical formula D_2O. Ordinary water from most natural sources contains about 0.015% deuterium oxide; this can be enriched or purified by DISTILLATION, ELECTROLYSIS, or chemical processing. Heavy water is used as a moderator in NUCLEAR POWER plants, and is also used in research as an isotopic tracer for chemical reactions and biochemical pathways. Water with TRITIUM (T_2O) rather than deuterium may also be called heavy water.

Hebe \'hē-bē\ Greek goddess of youth, daughter of ZEUS and HERA. She served as cupbearer to the gods, and when HERACLES ascended into heaven after his painful death, she became his bride.

Hébert \ā-'ber\, **Jacques (-René)** *known as* **Père Duchesne** \per-dǖē-'shen\ (1757–1794) French Revolutionary leader. He wrote political satires under his pen name, and his newspaper, *Le père Duchesne,* was widely read. He became influential in the Club of the CORDELIERS and with his followers, called Hébertists, helped overthrow the monarchy in 1792. He had the Cathedral of Notre-Dame and 2,000 other churches converted to the worship of Reason. As spokesman for the SANSCULOTTES, he helped institute the REIGN OF TERROR. By 1794 he was regarded as a dangerous extremist, and the Committee of Public Safety had him guillotined.

Hebrew alphabet Script used to write the HEBREW LANGUAGE and a number of other languages used as vernaculars by Jews, including Ladino and YIDDISH. The 22-letter ALPHABET in use today differs only slightly from the script adapted by Jewish scribes in the early centuries B.C. from the square script used to write Imperial ARAMAIC. Hebrew is written from right to left, and the letter shapes—at least originally—represented only consonants. Later certain of the consonants were utilized to denote vowels in certain positions, and by about A.D. 600 a system of diacritics, or "points," was used to show all vowels in the text of the Bible. See table on following page.

Hebrew language NW SEMITIC LANGUAGE that is both a sacred language of Judaism and a modern vernacular in the state of Israel. Like ARAMAIC, to which it is closely related,

Hebrew has a documented history of nearly 3,000 years. The earliest fully attested stage of the language is Biblical Hebrew, dating from about 500–200 B.C. Post-Biblical Hebrew, variously termed Rabbinic or Mishnaic Hebrew (see MISHNA), has an early period when Hebrew was still probably widely spoken, and a later period when Aramaic became the everyday speech of Jews in SW Asia. The 6th and 7th cent. marked a transition to Medieval Hebrew. The resurrection of Hebrew as a vernacular is closely linked with ZIONISM. Contemporary Israeli Hebrew is spoken by about 5 million people. See also HEBREW ALPHABET.

Hebrew University of Jerusalem Independent university in Jerusalem, founded in 1925. The foremost university in Israel, it attracts many Jewish students from abroad; Arab students also attend. Its faculties include humanities, science, social science, law, medicine, social work, pharmacy, applied science and technology, and library science. Total enrollment is about 23,000.

Hebrides \'he-brə-ˌdēz\ *or* **Western Isles** *ancient* Ebudae. Group of islands (pop., 1991: 31,000), west of Scotland. They are separated into two groups, the Outer Hebrides and the Inner Hebrides, divided by the Little Minch Strait. Only a few of the more than 40 islands are inhabited. The original inhabitants were Celts. Norse raids, which led to Norse rule, began after the 8th cent. and lasted until 1266, when the islands were ceded to Scotland. Their economy centers on farming, fishing, and weaving, the latter noted especially for Harris tweed.

Hebron \'he-brän\ *Arabic* **Al-Khalil** \ˌàl-kà-'lēl\ City (pop., 1995 est.: 117,000), southwest of JERUSALEM. It is a sacred city of JUDAISM and ISLAM as the home of ABRAHAM. According to the Bible, King DAVID made Hebron his capital briefly in the 10th cent. B.C. Muslims generally ruled the city from A.D. 635 until after World War I. It was part of Palestine from 1923 until its annexation by Jordan in 1948. Captured by Israel during the SIX-DAY WAR (1967), it became part of the WEST BANK territory under Israeli administration.

Hecate \'he-kə-tē\ Greek goddess of magic and spells. She probably originated in Asia Minor. HESIOD represented her as the bestower of wealth and the blessings of daily life. Pillars called Hecataea were erected at doorways and crossroads to ward off evil spirits. She was sometimes depicted as three bodies back to back, so that she could look in all directions at a crossroads.

Hecht \'hekt\, **Ben** (1894–1964) U.S. writer. Born in New York City, he worked for Chicago newspapers 1910–22, perfecting a type of human-interest sketch that was widely emulated. Later, with Charles MACARTHUR, he wrote the successful plays *The Front Page* (1928), about the newspaper world; *Twentieth Century* (1932); and *Ladies and Gentlemen* (1939). His film scripts, often written with MacArthur, include *Gunga Din* (1938), *Wuthering Heights* (1939), *Spellbound* (1945), and *Notorious* (1946).

Hector In Greek legend, the eldest son of PRIAM and HECUBA and the chief Trojan warrior. In HOMER's *Iliad* he is notable not only for his military prowess but also for his nobility of character. He was killed by ACHILLES and dragged naked around the walls of Troy after he slew Achilles' friend Patroclus.

Hecuba \'he-kyə-bə\ In Greek legend, the wife of the Trojan king PRIAM and mother of HECTOR. At the end of the TROJAN WAR she was taken prisoner. According to EURIPIDES, she blinded King Polymestor of Thrace and killed his sons because he failed to protect her youngest son, Polydorus, from death. Her grave beside the Hellespont became a landmark for ships.

hedgehog Any of 14 species of insectivores in the family Erinaceidae. The nine species of spiny hedgehogs have short spines on the back, a round body, small head, and little or no tail. Species range from 4 to 17 in. (10–44 cm) long. Spiny hedgehogs are native to Britain, N Africa, and Asia. The five species of gymnure, or hairy hedgehog, are Asian. They have coarse guard hairs but no spines and are extremely malodorous. The common gymnure may be 18 in. (46 cm) long and have a 12-in. (30-cm) tail. See also PORCUPINE.

hedging In commodities, securities, and foreign-exchange markets, a method of reducing RISK of loss from price fluctuation. It consists of the purchase or sale of equal quantities of the same or very similar commodities in two markets at the same time, with the expectation that a future price change in one market will be offset by an opposite change in the other market. For example, a grain-elevator operator may buy a ton of wheat and at the same time sell a FUTURES contract for a ton of wheat; when the wheat is sold, he buys back the futures contract. If the grain price has dropped, he can buy back the futures contract for less than he sold it for; his profit from doing so will be offset by his loss on the grain. See also STOCK OPTION.

Hegel \'hā-gəl\, **Georg Wilhelm Friedrich** (1770–1831) German philosopher. He served as headmaster of the gymnasium at Nuremberg (1808–16), then taught principally at the Univ. of Berlin (1818–31). His work, following on that of Immanuel KANT, Johann Gottlieb FICHTE, and Friedrich Schelling, marks the pinnacle of post-Kantian German IDEALISM. Inspired by Christian insights and grounded in his vast fund of knowledge, Hegel found a place for everything—logical, natural, human, and divine—in a dialectical scheme that repeatedly swung from

G. W. F. Hegel

thesis to antithesis and back again to a higher and richer synthesis. His panoramic system engaged philosophy in the consideration of all the problems of history and culture, while depriving all the implicated elements of their autonomy, reducing them to symbolic manifestations of the Absolute Spirit's quest for and conquest of its own self. His principal works are *Phenomenology of Mind* (1807), *Encyclopedia of the Philosophical Sciences* (1817), and *Philosophy of Right* (1821). HEGELIANISM has been as fertile in the reactions it precipitated—in Søren KIERKEGAARD, Karl MARX, G. E. MOORE, and the VIENNA CIRCLE—as in its positive impact. Hegel is regarded as the last of the great philosophical system builders.

Hegelianism \hi-'gā-lē-ə-ˌni-zəm\ Diversified philosophical movement that developed out of G. W. F. HEGEL's system of thought. Four phases can be distinguished. The first consists of the tri-part Hegelian school in Germany 1827–50.

Letters	English Spelling	Names	Letters	English Spelling	Names
א	–	aleph	מ [ם]	m	mem
בּ ב	b, v	beth	נ [ן]	n	nun
גּ ג	g, gh	gimel	ס	s	samekh
דּ ד	d, dh	daleth	ע	–	ayin
ה	h	he	פּ פ [ף]	p, f	pe or phe
ו	w, v or vav	waw or vav	צ [ץ]	ts	sadhe
ז	z	zayin	ק	q	qoph
ח	h	heth	ר	r	resh
ט	t	teth	שׂ שׁ	s, sh	sin or shin
י	y	yod	תּ ת	t, th	taw or tav
כּ כ [ך]	k, kh	kaph			
ל	l	lamed			

Hebrew alphabet The modern Hebrew alphabet, with English sound equivalents.

The right, or "Old Hegelians," stressed evangelical orthodoxy and conservative political policies. The left, or "Young Hegelians," interpreted Hegel's identification of the rational with the real in a revolutionary sense. The center focused on the Hegelian system in its genesis and significance. In the second or Neo-Hegelian phase (1850–1904), the works of the center predominated. After Wilhelm Dilthey discovered unpublished papers from Hegel's youth in the early 20th cent., a third phase, the Hegel renaissance, arose to reconstruct the genesis of Hegel's thought. The fourth stage, after World War II, promoted the value of Hegel for MARXISM.

Hegira or **Hejira** \hi-ˈjī-rə, ˈhe-jə-rə\ (Arabic *Hijra,* "flight") Flight of MUHAMMAD from MECCA to MEDINA in A.D. 622 in order to escape persecution and found a community of believers. The date represents the beginning of ISLAM and the starting point for the Muslim calendar; years are now denoted by the initials A.H. (Latin, *Anno Hegirae:* "in the year of the Hegira").

Heian period \ˈhā-ˈän\ (794–1185) Period of Japanese history named for the capital city of Heian-kyo (Kyoto). It is known mainly for the flourishing culture of the court aristocracy, which devoted itself to the pursuit of aesthetic refinement through poetry and calligraphy. MURASAKI SHIKIBU's contemporaneous novel *The Tale of Genji* depicts that life. Aesthetics were also emphasized by the Shingon Buddhist sect. Pietism gained popularity in the late Heian, leading to the founding of the Pure Land Buddhist sect. Politically, the FUJIWARA FAMILY and later other civilians dominated until 1156, when warriors were called in to settle a political dispute and never left; the Taira military clan ruled until 1185.

Heidegger \ˈhī-di-gər\, **Martin** (1889–1976) German philosopher. He taught at the Univs. of Marburg (1923–27) and Freiburg (1927–44). In 1927 he published his magnum opus, *Sein und Zeit (Being and Time),* which strongly influenced Jean-Paul SARTRE and other existentialists, and became known as the leading atheistic existentialist. To raise the question of the meaning of being afresh in a meaningful way, he conducted an analysis of *Dasein* ("being there"— i.e., being human), employing the method of PHENOMENOLOGY. In the early 1930s his thought experienced a *Kehre* ("turning around"), which some have seen as an abandonment of the problem of *Being and Time,* and he became involved in the cultural politics of the Third Reich. His work has been fundamental for Jacques DERRIDA and other DECONSTRUCTION theorists.

Heidelberg \ˈhīd-ᵊl-ˌbərk\ City (pop., 1998 est.: 139,000), SW Germany, on the NECKAR RIVER. It was the capital of the Rhenish PALATINATE and the residence of the electoral counts Palatine until 1720. A center of German CALVINISM in the 16th cent., it was devastated during the THIRTY YEARS' WAR (1622) and by the French in 1689 and 1693. It is the site of the 13th-cent. Heidelberg Castle, a major tourist attraction, and of the Univ. of HEIDELBERG (1386), the oldest in Germany.

Heidelberg, University of *German* Ruprecht-Karl-Universität Heidelberg. Autonomous university at Heidelberg, Germany. It was founded by the Cistercian order in 1386 and modeled on the Univ. of PARIS. After a decline in the 17th–18th cent., it regained its prestige, becoming a center of sciences, law, and philosophy, and its lively student life became the subject of many Romantic stories. Current enrollment is about 28,000.

Heifetz \ˈhī-fəts\, **Jascha** (1901–1987) Russian-U.S. violinist. A prodigy, he performed Felix MENDELSSOHN's concerto brilliantly at age 8. From 1909 to 1914 he studied in St. Petersburg with Leopold Auer (1845–1930). He emigrated to the U.S. in 1917, where for many years he performed in a trio with Arthur RUBINSTEIN and Gregor Piatigorsky (1903–1976). Despite an aloof stage manner, Heifetz had impeccable technique and musical flair, and he became perhaps the world's most famous violinist.

Heilong River See AMUR RIVER

Heimlich maneuver \ˈhīm-lik\ Emergency procedure for dislodging a foreign body from a choking victim's throat, devised by the U.S. surgeon Henry J. Heimlich (b.1920). It is used only when the airway is totally obstructed, as shown by inability to speak or breathe. The rescuer reaches around the victim from behind, grasps one fist in the other just below the victim's rib cage, and makes several upward thrusts into the victim's belly. This expels the foreign object with air from the victim's own lungs. An unconscious victim is laid faceup and the thrusts are given by a kneeling or squatting rescuer.

Heine \ˈhī-nə\, **(Christian Johann) Heinrich** *orig.* Harry Heine (1797–1856) German-French poet. Born of Jewish parents, he established his international literary reputation with *The Book of Songs* (1827), a collection of bittersweet love poems. His prose *Pictures of Travel* (4 vols., 1826–31) was widely imitated. After 1831 he lived in Paris. His articles and studies on social and political matters, many critical of German conservatism, were censored in Germany, and German spies watched him in Paris. His third verse collection, *Romanzero* (1851), is notably bleak but has been greatly admired. He is regarded as one of Germany's greatest lyric poets, and many of his poems were set as songs by such composers as Franz SCHUBERT, Robert SCHUMANN, and Johannes BRAHMS.

Heinlein \ˈhīn-līn\, **Robert A(nson)** (1907–1988) U.S. science-fiction writer. Born in Butler, Mo., he pursued graduate study in physics and mathematics, and began his writing career in the pulp magazine *Astounding Science Fiction* in the 1930s. The novel *Stranger in a Strange Land* (1961), his best-known work, attracted a large cult following. His other books include *Starship Troopers* (1959), *The Moon Is a Harsh Mistress* (1966), and *I Will Fear No Evil* (1970). He won an unprecedented four Hugo Awards, and his sophisticated works did much to develop the genre.

heir One who inherits or is entitled to succeed to the possession of property after the death of its owner. In most jurisdictions, statutes of descent determine transfer of title to property if no WILL names the recipient. One may be either heir apparent or heir presumptive during the lifetime of the property holder. An heir apparent's right to an inheritance cannot be voided or undone except by exclusion under a valid will. An heir presumptive's right to inherit may be defeated by the birth of a nearer relative. See also PRIMOGENITURE.

Heisei emperor See AKIHITO

Heisei period \ˈhā-ˈsā\ Japanese reign period that began in 1989 when AKIHITO became emperor. The Heisei period has been marked by turbulent politics (with nine prime ministers in its first nine years), an economic slowdown, and crises in the financial world. A devastating earthquake in KOBE and AUM SHINRIKYO's nerve-gas attack (both in 1995) have contributed to the dark picture of the period to date. Positive events include the wedding of the crown prince and the hosting of the 1998 Winter Olympics in Nagano.

Heisenberg \ˈhī-zᵊn-bərg\, **Werner (Karl)** (1901–1976) German physicist. In 1925 he solved the problem of how to account for the stationary discrete energy states of an anharmonic oscillator, a solution that launched the development of QUANTUM MECHANICS. In 1927 he published his famous UNCERTAINTY PRINCIPLE. He also made important contributions to the theories of the hydrodynamics of turbulence, the atomic nucleus, ferromagnetism, cosmic rays, and subatomic particles. He was awarded a Nobel Prize in 1932. He led Nazi Germany's short-lived project to build an atomic bomb.

Heisenberg uncertainty principle See UNCERTAINTY PRINCIPLE

Heisman Trophy Cup awarded annually to the outstanding college football player in the U.S., as determined by a poll of sportswriters. Instituted in 1935 by New York's Downtown Athletic Club, it was named for its first athletic director, the player-coach John Heisman (1869–1936).

Hejaz \he-ˈjaz\ *Arabic* **Al-Hijaz** \ˌäl-hē-ˈjäz\ Region of W Saudi Arabia. It occupies an area of 134,600 sq mi (348,000 sq km) along the N Red Sea coast. In the 7th cent. A.D. its cities of MECCA and MEDINA saw the birth of ISLAM, and they remain (with JERUSALEM) Islam's holiest cities. In 1258 it fell to the Egyptians and in 1517 to the Turks. In 1916 Sharif HUSAYN IBN ALI proclaimed himself king of Hejaz. Abdulaziz IBN SAUD assumed the title in 1926, and in 1932 united Hejaz, Nejd, and other districts to form the Kingdom of Saudi Arabia.

Hel In Norse mythology, the realm of the dead and, later, the goddess of the dead. Her kingdom, Niflheim, was divided into several sections. Murderers, perjurers, and adulterers suffered torment in a castle filled with serpents' venom, while the dragon Nidhogg sucked their blood. Those who fell in battle went instead to VALHALLA.

Helen In GREEK MYTHOLOGY, the most beautiful woman in the world and the indirect cause of the TROJAN WAR. A daughter of ZEUS, Helen was the wife of MENELAUS. When PARIS, son of King PRIAM of Troy, was asked to decide which goddess was the most beautiful, he chose APHRODITE, who rewarded him by helping him seduce Helen. Paris carried her off to Troy, and the Greeks sent a military force to pursue them. At the war's end, with Paris dead, Helen returned to Sparta with Menelaus.

Helena \'he-lə-nə\ City (pop., 2000: 25,000), capital of Montana. Located near the Missouri River in W central Montana, it was settled after gold was discovered there in 1864. It became capital of the territory in 1875 and of the state in 1889. Helena is an agricultural and livestock trade center.

Helena, St. (A.D. 248?–328?) Mother of CONSTANTINE I. The wife of Constantius I Chlorus (d.306) before he became caesar (subemperor), she bore Constantine before being renounced for political reasons. She became a Christian under her son's influence. Implicated in the execution of her daughter-in-law (326), she made a pilgrimage to the Holy Land and had churches built on the sites of the Ascension and the Nativity. She was reputed to have found Christ's cross.

Helga, St. See St. OLGA

helicon See SOUSAPHONE

Helicon, Mt. Mountain, E central Greece, part of the Helicon range, a continuation of the higher Parnassus range. Located near the Gulf of Corinth, it is 5,738 ft (1,749 m) high. It was celebrated by the ancient Greeks as the home of the MUSES.

helicopter Aircraft with one or more power-driven horizontal propellers or rotors that enable it to take off and land vertically, move in any direction, or remain stationary in the air. One of the earliest ideas for flying, it appeared in China and Renaissance Europe as a toy and in LEONARDO DA VINCI's designs. The Frenchman Paul Cornu made the first manned flight in 1907. Igor SIKORSKY produced the first successful prototype in 1939, which was followed by rapid development in the U.S. and Europe. Widely used in the Korean and Vietnam wars to move and rescue troops, it is now used for civilian rescue work and various commercial purposes.

Heliogabalus See ELAGABALUS

Heliopolis \ˌhē-lē-'ä-pə-ləs\ *biblical* On. Ancient holy city, Egypt. The city, now mainly ruins lying northeast of CAIRO, was the seat of worship of the sun god RE. Its great temple was second in size only to that of Amon at THEBES, and its priesthood wielded great influence. The city's surviving monument is the obelisk of Sesostris I, the oldest in existence. Two obelisks erected there by THUTMOSE III and known as Cleopatra's Needles now stand in London and New York City.

Helios \'hē-lē-ˌös\ Sun god of ancient Greece. He drove his chariot from east to west across the sky each day and sailed across the ocean each night in a huge cup. He was later displaced by APOLLO. The Romans worshiped him as SOL.

helium Chemical ELEMENT, chemical symbol He, atomic number 2. A NOBLE GAS, it is colorless, odorless, tasteless, completely unreactive, and nontoxic. First found by SPECTROSCOPY of the sun's atmosphere in 1868, it is the second most abundant and second-lightest element in the universe (after hydrogen). Helium makes up a tiny proportion of the atmosphere but up to 7% of NATURAL GAS. It is the product of radioactive decay (see RADIOACTIVITY) and is used in HELIUM DATING. It is used as an inert gas in welding, rocket propulsion, balloon flight, HYPERBARIC CHAMBERS, deepsea diving, GAS CHROMATOGRAPHY, luminous signs, and CRYOGENICS. Liquid helium is a "quantum fluid" (see FLUID MECHANICS), with unique properties, including SUPERFLUIDITY, SUPERCONDUCTIVITY, and near-zero VISCOSITY.

helium dating Method of DATING that depends on the production of helium during the decay of radioactive isotopes of uranium and thorium. Because of this decay, the helium content of any rock capable of retaining helium will increase during its lifetime, and the proportion becomes a measure of geologic time. Fossils may also be dated by helium dating. The relatively large amount of helium in rocks may make it possible to extend helium dating to rocks and minerals as young as a few tens of thousands of years old.

hell Abode of evildoers after death, or the state of existence of souls damned to punishment after death. Most ancient religions included the concept of a place that divided the good from the evil or the living from the dead. The view that hell is the final dwelling place of the damned is held by Zoroastrianism, Judaism, Christianity, and Islam. The Jewish concept of Gehenna as an infernal region of punishment for the wicked was the basis for the Christian hell, a fiery place of punishment for those who die without repenting of their sins. In Hinduism hell is only one stage in the career of the soul as it passes through the phases of reincarnation. In Buddhism hell has usually been associated either with punishment or purgatory. In Jainism, hell is a purgatory.

Hellenistic Age In the E Mediterranean and the Middle East, the period between the death of ALEXANDER THE GREAT (323 B.C.) and the conquest of Egypt by Rome (30 B.C.). Alexander and his successors established Greek monarchies that controlled the area from Greece to Afghanistan. The Macedonian Antigonid kingdom, the Middle Eastern SELEUCID kingdom, and the Egyptian Ptolemaic kingdom spread Greek culture, mixed Greek and non-Greek populations, and fused Greek and Oriental elements. They produced effective bureaucracies and a common, creative culture based at ALEXANDRIA. A

Hellenistic Age "Laocoön"

great flowering of the arts, literature, and science occurred particularly in the period 280–160. The decline of the Hellenic states occurred as Rome gained strength and turned the kingdoms and their allies into Roman provinces. Egypt was the last to fall, after having been drawn into the civil war between Mark ANTONY and Octavian (AUGUSTUS).

Heller, Joseph (1923–1999) U.S. writer. Born in Brooklyn, N.Y., Heller flew 60 combat missions as a bombardier in World War II. His satirical novel *Catch-22* (1961), based on his wartime experiences, was one of the most significant works of postwar protest literature and a huge critical and popular success. His later novels include *Something Happened* (1974), *Good as Gold* (1979), and *Closing Time* (1994).

Hellespont See DARDANELLES

Hellman, Lillian (Florence) (1905–1984) U.S. playwright. Born in New Orleans, she had her first major success with *The Children's Hour* (1934), a play about two schoolteachers accused of lesbianism. She examined family infighting in her hit *The Little Foxes* (1939) and political injustice in *Watch on the Rhine* (1941). All were made into successful films. Called before the House Un-American Activities Committee in 1952, she refused to testify. She adapted VOLTAIRE's *Candide* for a musical version by Leonard BERNSTEIN (1956). Her *Toys in the Attic* (1960) was also filmed. She wrote several memoirs and edited the works of her longtime companion, Dashiell HAMMETT.

Hells Canyon Gorge of the SNAKE RIVER. Part of the Idaho–Oregon boundary, it is 125 mi (200 km) long and for 40 mi (64 km) is more than a mile deep. A maximum depth of 7,900 ft (2,400 m) makes it the deepest gorge in N. America. Hells Canyon was designated a national recreation area in 1975.

Helmholtz \'helm-ˌhōlts\, **Hermann (Ludwig Ferdinand) von** (1821–1894) German scientist. After training in medicine, he taught physiology and later physics at several German universities. His interests continually shifted to new disciplines, in which he applied his earlier insights to every

problem he examined. He made fundamental contributions to physiology, optics, electrodynamics, mathematics, acoustics (discovering the OVERTONE series), and meteorology, but is best known for his statement (1847) of the law of conservation of ENERGY. He invented several measurement instruments, including the myograph, ophthalmoscope, and ophthalmometer. He described body heat and energy, nerve conduction, and the physiology of the eye. His mathematical analysis of vortices in fluids (1858) was a tour de force.

helots \'he-ləts\ Native peoples of Laconia and Messenia conquered and controlled by SPARTA. They were state-owned serfs or slaves who worked the land to feed and clothe the Spartan population, whom they vastly outnumbered. The Spartans lived in constant fear of a helot revolt, and annually declared war on them to legally keep them in place by force. During wartime helots attended their masters on campaigns, serving as troops and as rowers in the fleet. The Messenian helots were liberated around 370 B.C., those in Laconia not until the 2nd cent. B.C.

Helpmann, Robert (Murray) (*later* **Sir Robert**) (1909–1986) Australian dancer, choreographer, actor, and director. In 1933 he went to London to study; at the Vic-Wells (later ROYAL) BALLET, he became a regular partner of Margot FONTEYN. His own ballets included *Hamlet* (1942) and *Adam Zero* (1946). He danced in the films *The Red Shoes* and *Tales of Hoffmann,* acted in many Shakespeare plays, and also directed several plays. He was artistic codirector of the Australian Ballet 1965–76.

Helsinki *Swedish* **Helsingfors** City (pop,, (2000 est.: 551,000), capital of Finland. Located in S Finland on a peninsula with natural harbors, it is the country's leading seaport. Often called the "white city of the north" because many of its buildings are made of a local light-colored granite, it moved to its present site in 1640. Under the Russian czar ALEXANDER I (from 1808), it became the capital of the grand duchy of Finland in 1812. In 1917 Finland declared independence from Russia, and a brief but bloody civil war ensued in the capital. In subsequent decades it developed into an important trade center.

Helsinki Accords Agreement signed in Helsinki, Finland, in 1975 to reduce tension between the Soviet and Western blocs by securing their common acceptance of the post–World War II status quo in Europe, including Germany's division. The nonbinding accords, signed by all the countries of Europe (except Albania) as well as the U.S. and Canada, were sought by the Soviet Union to gain recognition of its postwar hegemony in Eastern Europe. In return, the U.S. and its Western European allies pressed for respect for human rights and economic and scientific cooperation. Follow-up meetings in Belgrade (1977–78), Madrid (1980–83), and Ottawa (1985) saw strong criticism of Soviet human-rights abuses. A 1990 conference in Paris formally ended the COLD WAR and recognized German reunification.

hematite *or* **haematite** \'hē-mə-ˌtīt\ Heavy and relatively hard oxide mineral that constitutes the most important IRON ore. Much hematite (from the Greek word meaning "blood," for its red color) occurs in a soft, fine-grained, earthy form called red ocher or ruddle. Red ocher is used as a paint pigment; a purified form, rouge, is used to polish plate glass. The world's largest production comes from W Australia.

hematology \ˌhē-mə-ˈtä-lə-jē\ Branch of medicine concerned with the nature, function, and diseases of the BLOOD. It covers the cellular and serum composition of blood, the COAGULATION process, blood-cell formation, HEMOGLOBIN synthesis, and disorders of all these. Marcello MALPIGHI, was the first to examine red blood cells (ERYTHROCYTES). William Hewson (1739–1774) examined the lymphatic system and blood clotting. In the 19th cent., the bone marrow was recognized as the site of blood-cell formation and diseases of the blood such as ANEMIA and LEUKEMIA were identified. In the early 20th cent., the ABO BLOOD-GROUP SYSTEM was discovered and the role of nutrition in blood formation was studied. Hemoglobin synthesis and the role of PLATELETS in blood coagulation have been the focus of later research.

Hemingway, Ernest (Miller) (1899–1961) U.S. writer. Born in Oak Park, Ill., he began work as a journalist after high school; he was wounded while serving as an ambulance driver in World War I. He later became part of a famous group of expatriate writers in Paris, and soon embarked on an adventuresome life of travel that would be reflected in his work. His story collection *In Our Time* (1925) was followed by the novel *The Sun Also Rises* (1926). Later novels included *A Farewell to Arms* (1929) and *To Have and Have Not* (1937). He worked as a correspondent during the Spanish Civil War, which resulted in the novel *For Whom the Bell Tolls* (1940). Other short-story collections include *Men Without Women* (1927) and *Winner*

Ernest Hemingway Photo by Yousuf Karsh, 1959

Take Nothing (1933). He lived primarily in Cuba from around 1940, the locale of his novella *The Old Man and the Sea* (1952, Pulitzer Prize). He was awarded the Nobel Prize in 1954. The succinct and concentrated prose style of his early works strongly influenced many British and American writers for decades.

hemispheric asymmetry See LATERALITY

hemlock Any of 10 species of coniferous evergreen trees that make up the genus *Tsuga,* in the PINE family, native to N. America and central and E Asia. Some are important timber trees, and many are popular ornamentals. Hemlocks are tall and pyramidal with purplish or reddish-brown bark, slender horizontal or drooping branches, and short, blunt needles. See also POISON HEMLOCK.

hemodialysis See DIALYSIS

hemoglobin \'hē-mə-ˌglō-bən\ PROTEIN in the blood of many animals (in vertebrates it is in red blood cells) that transports OXYGEN from the lungs to the tissues and CARBON DIOXIDE back. It is bright red when combined with oxygen, and purple-blue when not. Abnormal hemoglobins (see SICKLE-CELL ANEMIA) can be used to trace past human migrations and to study genetic relationships among populations.

hemophilia \ˌhē-mə-ˈfi-lē-ə\ Hereditary bleeding disorder caused by deficiency of a COAGULATION factor. Most types are transmitted by sex-linked heredity; a rarer type has dominant inheritance and occurs in females as well as males. Spontaneous bleeding may occur. Even trivial injury can cause life-threatening blood loss. Drugs can be given to stop bleeding. Heavy blood loss requires blood transfusions. See diagram at HEREDITY.

hemorrhage \'he-mə-rij\ Escape of blood from blood vessels into surrounding tissue. Normally, COAGULATION closes the injured vessel and stops the bleeding. Uncontrolled hemorrhage can result from ANTICOAGULANT therapy, HEMOPHILIA, or severe blood-vessel damage, leading to excessive blood loss and SHOCK.

hemorrhagic fever \ˌhe-mə-ˈra-jik\ Disease with high FEVER, HEMORRHAGE of internal organs and in small spots in the skin, HYPOTENSION and SHOCK, and sometimes neurologic effects. It is caused by several kinds of virus (including EBOLA, DENGUE, and HANTAVIRUS), some carried by ticks or mosquitoes and some apparently by animals.

hemorrhoid \'he-mə-ˌroid\ *or* **pile** Mass formed by distension of the network of veins supplying the anal canal. It may develop from infection or increased abdominal pressure (as in pregnancy or heavy lifting). Mild hemorrhoids may require only ointments, laxatives, and baths. If clotting, bleeding, or pain occurs, surgical removal may be needed.

hemp Annual herbaceous plant (*Cannabis sativa,* family Cannabaceae); also its fiber. It is often separated into two species, of which one (*C. sativa*) is tall and loosely branched and one (*C. indica*) is low-growing and densely branched. Hemp originated in Central Asia and is now cultivated widely in the N temperate zone. It is grown primarily for its strong and durable fiber, which is used for ropes and for artificial sponges and such coarse fabrics as sacking (burlap) and canvas. It is also cultivated to yield the drugs MARIJUANA and HASHISH.

Henderson, Fletcher (Hamilton) (1897–1952) U.S. pianist, arranger, and leader of one of the most influential big bands in jazz. Born in Cuthbert, Ga., Henderson formed a dance band in New York in 1923. The band soon distinguished itself by engaging Louis ARMSTRONG as principal soloist and using arrangements by Henderson and Don Redman (1900–1964) that codified the roles of the sections within the ensemble to replace the old collective improvisation. Nearly all big bands subsequently followed their example. He was forced to dissolve his band several times, but his arrangements played a key role in the success of Benny GOODMAN.

Hendrix, Jimi (*orig.* James Marshall) (1942–1970) U.S. rock guitarist. Born in Seattle of mixed black-Cherokee ancestry, he taught himself to play the guitar, which he held upside down. After serving as an army paratrooper and touring as a backup musician, in 1966 he moved to London and formed a trio, The Jimi Hendrix Experience. His sensational appearance at the Monterey Pop Festival in 1967 and the success that year of the album *Are You Experienced?* lifted him to instant stardom, and his subsequent albums were among the most influential of the 1960s. He died at 27 of an apparently accidental drug overdose.

Henie \'he-nē\, **Sonja** (1912–1969) Norwegian-U.S. figure skater. Born in Kristiania, she was trained in ballet. She won the world amateur championship for women 10 consecutive years (1927–36) and won three Olympic gold medals (1928, 1932, 1936). With her dancer's training, she was largely responsible for converting a predictable series of colorless exercises into a spectacular and popular exhibition. She achieved further renown as a movie actress.

Hennepin \ˌe-nə-'paⁿ, *Engl* 'he-nə-pən\, **Louis** (1626–1701?) French missionary and explorer. A Franciscan, he traveled to Canada in 1675 and with R.-R. LA SALLE explored the Great Lakes region, founding Ft. Crèvecoeur (near Peoria, Ill.) in 1680. Hennepin and others explored the upper Mississippi River and were captured by Sioux Indians and taken to a site he named the Falls of St. Anthony (later Minneapolis); after four months they were rescued by Daniel DULHUT. Hennepin returned to France in 1682 and wrote an account of his journeys.

Henri \'hen-rē\, **Robert** *orig.* Robert Henry Cozad (1865–1929) U.S. painter. Born in Cincinnati, he studied in Philadelphia and Paris and taught art in Philadelphia. After settling in New York in 1900, he became the leader of The EIGHT. As a portrait painter he demonstrated facile brushwork, lively colors, and an ability to catch fleeting gestures and expressions. At New York's Art Students League (1915–28), he became one of the most influential art teachers in the U.S. and a powerful force in turning young artists away from academicism and toward the rich subject matter of modern city life. His belief in the artist as a social force led to the formation of the ASH CAN SCHOOL.

Henri I de Lorraine See 3rd duc de GUISE

Henrietta Maria *French* Henriette-Marie (1609–1669) French-born English queen, wife of CHARLES I (from 1625) and mother of CHARLES II and JAMES II. The daughter of HENRY IV of France and MARIE DE MÉDICIS, she was no stranger to political intrigue. By openly practicing Roman Catholicism at court, she alienated many of Charles's subjects. During the ENGLISH CIVIL WARS, her efforts to enlist support for Charles from the Pope, the French, and the Dutch infuriated many Englishmen. Deterioration of the Royalist position caused her to flee to France in 1644, and she never again saw her husband.

Henry, Joseph (1797–1878) U.S. physicist. Born in Albany, N.Y., he aided Samuel MORSE in developing the telegraph. He discovered several important principles of ELECTRICITY, including self-induction. He observed electromagnetic induction a year before Michael FARADAY announced its discovery. He made improvements to electromagnets, discovered the laws on which the transformer is based, investigated electric discharge, and demonstrated that sunspots radiate less heat than the general solar surface. In 1846 he became the first director of the Smithsonian Institution, and his work led to creation of the U.S. Weather Bureau. The standard unit of electrical inductance, the henry, was named in his honor.

Henry, O. *orig.* William Sydney Porter (1862–1910) U.S. short-story writer. Born in Greensboro, N.C., he wrote for newspapers and later worked as a bank teller in Texas, where he was convicted of embezzlement; he began writing stories in prison as O. Henry. He moved to New York, where his many tales depicting the lives of ordinary New Yorkers, and often using coincidence and surprise endings, became highly popular. His collections include *Cabbages and Kings* (1904), *The Four Million* (1906), *The Trimmed Lamp* (1907), and *Whirligigs* (1910).

Henry, Patrick (1736–1799) American Revolutionary leader. Born in Studley, Va., he became a lawyer, renowned for his oratorical skill. In the Virginia House of BURGESSES, he opposed the STAMP ACT and was a leader in the radical opposition to the British. He was a founding member of the COMMITTEES OF CORRESPONDENCE and a delegate to the Continental Congress. In 1775 at a Virginia assembly he made his famous defense of liberty, "Give me liberty or give me death." He helped draft the state's first constitution and served twice as governor (1776–79, 1784–86). In 1788 he opposed ratification of the U.S. Constitution, which he felt did not secure individual liberties, and was instrumental in the adoption of the BILL OF RIGHTS.

Henry I *known as* **Henry Beauclerc** \'bō-klɛr\ ("Good Scholar") (1069–1135) King of England (1100–35). The youngest son of WILLIAM I, he became king on the death of WILLIAM II. His eldest brother, Robert Curthose (ROBERT II), returned from the First CRUSADE to claim the English throne in 1101. Henry placated him by giving him Normandy, but Robert ruled it badly, and in 1106 Henry seized Normandy and imprisoned his brother. Henry quarreled with ANSELM OF CANTERBURY over the issue of investiture (see INVESTITURE CONTROVERSY), but they were reconciled in 1107.

Henry II *known as* **Henry of Anjou** \'an-jü\ *or* **Henry Plantagenet** \plan-'ta-jə-nət\, (1133–1189) King of England (1154–89). The son of MATILDA and grandson of HENRY I, he inherited Normandy and Anjou and added vast territories in France by marrying ELEANOR OF AQUITAINE (1152). He invaded England and in settlement of the war King STEPHEN named Henry as heir (1153). As king, Henry extended his holdings in N England and W France, strengthened royal administration, and reformed the court system. His attempt to assert royal authority at the expense of the church (see Constitutions of CLARENDON) led to a quarrel with the archbishop of Canterbury, his former close friend Thomas BECKET, which ended with Becket's murder and Henry's subsequent penance at Canterbury (1174). His reign was plagued by family disputes, especially struggles for precedence among his sons, including RICHARD I the Lionheart and JOHN Lackland, who allied with PHILIP II of France to drive Henry from the throne in 1189.

Henry II *French* **Henri** \äⁿ-'rē\ *orig.* duc (Duke) d'Orléans (1519–1559) King of France (1547–59). The rebellious son of FRANCIS I, he continued many of his father's policies, but he raised the Catholic House of GUISE to favor and vigorously suppressed Protestantism within his kingdom. He continued his father's warfare against Emperor CHARLES V until 1559, when he signed the Treaty of Cateau-Cambrésis. The treaty was to be cemented by the marriage of Henry's daughter to PHILIP II of Spain; during the festivities he was hit in the head by a lance, and died from the wound.

Henry III (1207–1272) King of England (1216–72). He inherited the throne at age 9 but did not begin to rule until French-backed rebels were expelled (1234). He alienated the barons by his indifference to tradition and was forced to accept the Provisions of OXFORD (1258), which he renounced in 1261. His former favorite Simon de MONTFORT led a rebellion in 1264, defeating and capturing the king. Henry's son Edward (later EDWARD I) turned the tables a year later, and Henry, weak and senile, allowed Edward to take charge of the government.

Henry III *French* **Henri** *orig.* duc (Duke) d'Anjou (1551–1589) King of France (1574–89). Son of HENRY II and CATHERINE

HIJ

DE MÉDICIS, he commanded the royal army against the HUGUENOTS in the Wars of RELIGION. Succeeding his brother CHARLES IX, he made concessions to the Huguenots, causing the Roman Catholics to form the Holy League. When the Protestant Henry of Navarre (later HENRY IV) became heir to the throne, Henry III tried to placate the Holy League, but he was forced by a mob to flee Paris. In 1588 he had the Catholic leaders Henry, 3rd duc de GUISE, and Cardinal Louis II de Lorraine assassinated. In 1589 Henry was himself assassinated by a fanatical Jacobin friar.

Henry IV *orig.* Henry Bolingbroke (1366–1413). King of England (1399–1413). Son of JOHN OF GAUNT, he initially supported RICHARD II against the duke of Gloucester. Banished in 1398, he invaded England in 1399 and usurped the crown. Henry consolidated his power in the face of repeated uprisings of powerful nobles. However, he failed to subdue the Welsh under Owen GLENDOWER, was defeated by the Scots, and was unable to overcome the fiscal and administrative weaknesses that contributed to the eventual downfall of the House of LANCASTER.

Henry IV *or* **Henry of Navarre** *French* Henri de Navarre (1553–1610) King of France (1589–1610) and king of Navarre (as Henry III, 1572–89), one of the most popular figures in French history. Brought up as a Protestant, he fought in the Wars of RELIGION. His marriage to MARGARET OF VALOIS in 1572 provided the opportunity for the ST. BARTHOLOMEW'S DAY Massacre six days later. Henry was held at the French court 1572–76, then escaped to join the forces against HENRY III. He became king after Henry III was assassinated in 1589, but was forced to fight the Holy League for nine years to secure his kingdom. He converted to Catholicism to remove all pretext for resistance to his rule and entered Paris amid cheers in 1594. The Edict of NANTES in 1598 ended 40 years of civil war. With the aid of his ministers, including the duc de SULLY, Henry brought order and new prosperity to France. His earlier marriage was annulled and in 1600 he married MARIE DE MÉDICIS. In 1610 he was assassinated by a fanatical Roman Catholic.

Henry IV *German* Heinrich (1050–1106) German king (1054–1106) and Holy Roman Emperor (1084–1105/6). He inherited the throne at age 6 (although not crowned until 1084); his unworldly mother was regent until 1062, and Henry gained control of the government in 1065. He engaged in a long struggle with Pope GREGORY VII on the issue of lay investiture (see INVESTITURE CONTROVERSY); Gregory excommunicated him in 1077 and absolved his subjects of their oaths of loyalty. Seeking absolution, Henry was forced to cross the Alps in winter and, according to tradition, stand barefoot in the snow three days before the castle at Canossa where the pope was staying before the latter would rescind his order. The German princes deserted Henry (1077) and elected Rudolf as king. Excommunicated again (1080), Henry responded by conquering Rome (1084) and installing a new pope. In his last years his sons Conrad and Henry led rebellions against his rule.

Henry V (1387–1422) King of England (1413–22). The eldest son of Henry IV, he fought Welsh rebels (1403–8). As king he harshly suppressed a LOLLARD uprising (1414) and a Yorkist conspiracy (1415). He claimed extensive lands in France and launched an invasion (1415); his stunning victory at the Battle of AGINCOURT made England one of the greatest powers in Europe. His continuing victories forced the French to sign the Treaty of Troyes (1420), naming Henry heir to the French throne and regent of France. He married Catherine, daughter of the French king, but died of camp fever before he could return home.

Henry VI (1421–1471) King of England (1422–61, 1470–71). Son of HENRY V, he grew up a pious and studious recluse, who suffered episodes of mental instability. England's political affairs were dominated by the rivalries of the Houses of LANCASTER and YORK, and Henry's incapacity for government became one of the causes of the Wars of the ROSES. In 1461 a Yorkist was proclaimed EDWARD IV. After leading a rising, Henry was captured and imprisoned (1465-70). After a quarrel in the York faction, he was restored to the throne in 1470. Edward fled, but soon returned to regain the throne. Henry was murdered in the Tower of London soon afterward.

Henry VII *or* **Henry Tudor** (1457–1509) King of England (1485–1509) and founder of the TUDOR dynasty. As earl of Richmond and a kinsman in the House of LANCASTER, he fled to Brittany after the triumph of the Yorkist forces in 1471. He later returned, rallied the opponents of RICHARD III, and defeated him at the Battle of BOSWORTH FIELD (1485). Crowned king, he married Elizabeth of York and ended the Wars of the ROSES. He made peace with France (1492), the Netherlands (1496), and Scotland (1499) and used his children's marriages to build European alliances. His commercial treaties and promotion of trade made England wealthy and powerful. He was succeeded by his son HENRY VIII.

Henry VIII (1491–1547) King of England (1509–47). Son of HENRY VII, he married his brother's widow, CATHERINE OF ARAGON (the mother of MARY I), soon after his accession in 1509. His first chief minister, Thomas WOLSEY, exercised nearly complete control over policy 1515–27. In 1527 Henry pursued a divorce from Catherine to marry Anne BOLEYN, but Pope CLEMENT VII denied him an annulment. Wolsey, unable to help Henry, was ousted. The new minister, Thomas CROMWELL, in 1532 decided that the English Church should separate from Rome, allowing Henry to marry Anne in 1533. A new archbishop, Thomas CRANMER, declared the first marriage annulled. A daughter, the future ELIZABETH I, was born soon after. Becoming head of the Church of ENGLAND represented Henry's major achievement. His power was greatly enlarged, especially by gaining the wealth of the monasteries and by new clerical taxes, but his reputation as a man of learning became buried under his enduring fame as a man of blood. Many, including Thomas MORE, were killed for refusing to accept the new order. The king grew tired of Anne, and in 1536 had her executed for adultery. He immediately married Jane SEYMOUR, who bore him a son, EDWARD VI, but died in childbirth. Three years later, at Cromwell's instigation, he married ANNE OF CLEVES, but he hated her and demanded a quick divorce, and he had Cromwell beheaded in 1540. By now Henry was becoming paranoid, as well as enormously fat and unhealthy. In 1540 he married Catherine HOWARD, but had her beheaded for adultery in 1542. In 1542 he waged a financially ruinous war against Scotland. In 1543 he married Catherine PARR, who survived him.

Henry Beauclerc See HENRY I (ENGLAND)

Henry of Anjou See HENRY II (ENGLAND)

Henry Plantagenet See HENRY II (ENGLAND)

Henry the Navigator *Portuguese* Henrique o Navegador *orig.* Henrique, infante (Prince) de Portugal (1394–1460) Portuguese prince and patron of explorers. He helped his father JOHN I capture the Moroccan city of Ceuta in 1415 and served as governor of the Portuguese province of Algarve. From his own court at Sagres, he sponsored voyages of discovery to the Madeira Islands and the W coast of Africa. As grand master of the Order of Christ, he gained funds for voyages aimed at converting pagans. His patronage led to the development of the Portuguese caravel and improved navigational instruments and the advancement of cartography.

Henry the Navigator From a triptych attributed to Nuno Gonçalves, c.1465–70

Henry Tudor See HENRY VII (ENGLAND)

Henson, Jim (*orig.* James Maury) (1936–1990) U.S. puppeteer. Born in Greenville, Miss., he created a puppet show for a television station while in college and developed the first Muppets (melding "marionettes" and "puppets"). When PBS featured the Muppets on *Sesame Street* (from 1969), Henson achieved nationwide popularity. His *Muppet Show* (from 1976) gained audiences in over 100 countries. He also produced and directed *The Muppet Movie* (1979) and its sequels.

Henze \\'hent-sə\\, **Hans Werner** (b.1926) German-Italian composer. He studied with Wolfgang Fortner (1907–1987) and later René Leibowitz (1913–1972). After an early association with the avant-garde, his more traditional training reasserted itself. He moved permanently to Italy in 1953. He is best known for his operas, which include *Der König Hirsch* (1955), *Elegy for Young Lovers* (1961), *Der junge Lord* (1964), and *The Bassarids* (1965). He has also written numerous major symphonies and concertos. His longtime commitment to Marxism expressed itself in many of his works.

hepatitis INFLAMMATION of the LIVER. There are seven known types of viral hepatitis (A–G). Types A, spread mainly through food contaminated with feces, and B, transmitted sexually or by injection, cause JAUNDICE and flulike symptoms. The hepatitis C virus spreads mostly by shared needles in intravenous drug use and can cause liver CIRRHOSIS and cancer after a long latent period. Hepatitis D becomes active only in the presence of type B; it causes severe chronic liver disease. Type E, like Type A, is transmitted by contaminated food or water; its symptoms are more severe than Type A's and can result in death. The hepatitis F virus (HFV), first reported in 1994, is spread like Type A and E. The hepatitis G virus (HGV), isolated in 1996, is believed to be responsible for many sexually transmitted and bloodborne cases of hepatitis. HGV causes both acute and chronic forms of the disease and often infects persons already infected with Type C. VACCINES exist for types A and B (the second also prevents type D). Drug treatment for B and C is not always effective. The other types may not need drug treatment. Alcoholic hepatitis, from long-term overconsumption of alcohol, can be reversed and cirrhosis prevented by early treatment including quitting or sharply reducing drinking. An autoimmune hepatitis affects mainly young women and is treated with corticosteroids.

hepatolenticular degeneration See WILSON'S DISEASE

Hepburn, Audrey *orig.* Edda van Heemstra Hepburn-Ruston (1929–1993) British-U.S. (Belgian-born) actress. Discovered by COLETTE, who insisted she play the lead in *Gigi* on Broadway (1951), she made her U.S. film debut in *Roman Holiday* (1953, Academy Award), then returned to Broadway in *Ondine* (1954, Tony Award). She projected a radiant elfin innocence combined with elegance in such films as *Sabrina* (1954), *War and Peace* (1956), *Funny Face* (1957), *Breakfast at Tiffany's* (1961), *My Fair Lady* (1964), and *Wait Until Dark* (1967). She later devoted herself to international charity work.

Hepburn, Katharine (Houghton) (b.1907) U.S. actress. Born in Hartford, Conn., she made her Broadway debut in 1928 and became a star with her first film, *A Bill of Divorcement* (1932). Her following grew with *Morning Glory* (1933, Academy Award), *Little Women* (1933), and *Bringing Up Baby* (1938), to which she brought a spirited individuality. She starred in the Broadway hit *The Philadelphia Story* (1939; film, 1940). Other notable films include *The African Queen* (1951), *Summertime* (1955), and *Suddenly Last Summer* (1959). She made eight films with her longtime lover Spencer TRACY, including *Woman of the Year* (1942) and *Guess*

Katharine Hepburn

Who's Coming to Dinner (1967, Academy Award), and won two more Oscars for *The Lion in Winter* (1968) and *On Golden Pond* (1981).

Hephaestus *or* **Hephaistos** \\hi-'fes-təs\\ Greek god of fire. He was originally a deity of Asia Minor. His Roman counterpart was Vulcan. A cripple, he was cast out of heaven by his parents, ZEUS and HERA. His wife was APHRODITE. Pa-

tron of smiths and craftsman, he was often depicted working at his forge. Volcanoes were believed to be the fires of his workshops.

Hepplewhite, George (d.1786) British cabinetmaker. Little is known of his life before he opened a cabinet shop in London. His reputation is based on his *Cabinet-Maker and Upholsterer's Guide* (1788), containing some 300 designs. Pieces based on his designs are rare and none can be definitely attributed to him. The designs have the simplicity, elegance, and utility associated with the graceful Neoclassical style (e.g., chairs with straight, tapered legs and oval backs). His designs were borrowed by Thomas SHERATON and Duncan PHYFE.

heptathlon Women's athletics competition in which contestants take part in seven different TRACK-AND-FIELD events: 100-m hurdles (see HURDLING), SHOT PUT, HIGH JUMP, LONG JUMP, JAVELIN THROW, and 200- and 800-m runs. The two-day event replaced the women's PENTATHLON in the Olympic Games after 1981.

Hepworth, (Jocelyn) Barbara (*later* **Dame Barbara**) (1903–1975) British sculptor. Her work, naturalistic at first, had become abstract by the 1930s, when she produced severe geometrical pieces. Her sculptures became increasingly perforated, emphasizing interior space. By the 1950s she was receiving many prestigious commissions, including *Single Form* (1963), a memorial to Dag HAMMARSKJÖLD at the United Nations. She became, with Henry MOORE, a leader of the modern movement in England and one of the most influential sculptors of the mid-20th cent.

Hera Greek queen of the gods and sister-wife of ZEUS. Her Roman counterpart was JUNO. She was worshiped as queen of heaven and patron of marriage, women, and birth. Her sacred animal was the cow. In literature she vindictively pursued the women Zeus seduced.

Heracleitus *or* **Heraclitus** \\ˌher-ə-'klī-təs\\ (c.540–480 B.C.) Greek philosopher. In his cosmology, fire forms the basic material principle of an orderly universe; he called the world order an "ever-living fire kindling in measures and being extinguished in measures," and extended fire's manifestations to include the ether in the upper atmosphere. The persistence of unity despite change is illustrated by his famous analogy of life to a river: "Upon those who step into the same rivers, different and ever different waters flow down."

Heracles \\'her-ə-ˌklēz\\ *Latin* **Hercules** Legendary hero of ancient Greece and Rome. Known for his great strength, he was the son of ZEUS and Alcmeme, the granddaughter of PERSEUS. Zeus's jealous wife HERA plagued Heracles from babyhood. He grew up to marry a princess, but killed her in a fit of rage sent by Hera and was forced to become the servant of Eurystheus, ruler of Greece. Eurystheus set him 12 labors, including cleansing the Augean stables, fetching the golden apples of the Hesperides, and descending into Hades to bring back CERBERUS. Heracles burned himself to death on a pyre after donning a shirt that his second wife, Deianeira, had smeared with poison that she thought was a love potion. He then became an immortal and married HEBE.

heraldry Art and science of devising, displaying, and granting armorial insignia and of tracing and recording genealogies. The use of heraldic symbols for identification spread throughout the European nobility in the 13th cent. The principal vehicle for displaying the heraldic devices is the shield; the crest, a subsidiary device that emerged in the 14th cent., was modeled onto the helm (helmet). Pictorial representations show the shield with the helm and crest above. Arms are hereditary; all male descendants of the first person to whom they were granted bear the arms. As insignia of honor, they are protected by law in the European monarchies. In the Roman Catholic church, abbeys, priories, dioceses, and high functionaries have always had their own arms. See also coat of ARMS.

herb See SPICE AND HERB

herbaceous plant Plant that has little or no woody tissue and usually dies after a single growing season. Herbaceous plants are distinguished from woody plants, such as TREES and SHRUBS. Herbaceous perennials, such as many SPICES AND HERBS, die back after each growing season, but their

HIJ

roots remain alive and produce new plants the following year.

Herbert, George (1593–1633) British Metaphysical poet. As orator of Cambridge Univ., he was involved with the royal court. He was later ordained and became a rector at a rural parish, to which he devoted himself unstintingly until his death. His poems, published in *The Temple* (1633) only after his death, are noted for their mastery of metrical form, use of allegory and analogy, and religious devotion.

Herbert, Victor (August) (1859–1924) Irish-U.S. composer and cellist. Raised in Stuttgart, he studied at its conservatory. He and his wife moved to the U.S. in 1886, and he was soon a major figure in American musical life as conductor, cellist, composer, and teacher. His solid training, orchestrating skill, and melodic gift found natural expression in more than 40 popular operettas, including *Babes in Toyland* (1903), *Mlle Modiste* (1905), *The Red Mill* (1906), and *Naughty Marietta* (1910).

herbicide Agent for killing or inhibiting the growth of unwanted plants (weeds). Modern weed killers may be selective (affecting specific plant species) or nonselective (affecting plants generally). Contact herbicides (e.g., SULFURIC ACID, diquat, paraquat) kill only the plant organs they contact. Translocated herbicides (e.g., amitrole, picloram, 2,4-D) are effective against roots or other organs, to which they are transported from treated soil. See also DEFOLIANT.

herbivore \ˈər-bə-ˌvȯr\ Animal adapted to subsist solely on plant tissues. Herbivores range from insects (e.g., aphids) to large mammals (e.g., elephants), but the term is most often applied to UNGULATES. Adaptations for a herbivorous diet include the four-chambered stomach of RUMINANTS, the ever-growing incisor teeth of RODENTS, and the specialized grinding molars of cattle, sheep, and goats.

Herblock *orig.* Herbert (Lawrence) Block (1909–2001) U.S. editorial cartoonist. Born in Chicago, he first published his cartoons in the *Chicago Daily News* (1929). Later he worked for the *Washington Post* (from 1946). He attacked injustices in politics, big business, and labor throughout his 70-year career. He is best known for his 1950s cartoons attacking Sen. Joseph MCCARTHY. The winner of three Pulitzer Prizes (1942, 1954, 1979), he received the Presidential Medal of Freedom in 1994.

Herculaneum \ˌhər-kyu̇-ˈlā-nē-əm\ Ancient city, Campania, Italy. Located at the NW foot of VESUVIUS, it was destroyed and buried, together with POMPEII and Stabiae, by the eruption of A.D. 79. Excavation began in the 18th cent. and uncovered numerous artifacts, including paintings and furniture. Later work uncovered the palaestra (sports ground) and a vast central swimming pool.

Hercules See HERACLES

Herder, Johann Gottfried von (1744–1803) German critic and philosopher. He became the leading figure of the STURM UND DRANG literary movement with works such as *Plastik* (1778) and *Essay on the Origin of Language* (1772). With J. W. von GOETHE he helped lay the groundwork for German ROMANTICISM. His *Zerstreute Blätter* (1785–97; "Sporadic Papers") and the unfinished *Outlines of a Philosophy of the History of Man* (1784–91), attempting to show that nature and history obey one system of laws, mark him as an innovator in the philosophy of history and an early proponent of the idea that a common culture, rather than political boundaries, defines a people. His later estrangement from Goethe resulted in a bitter enmity toward the whole classical movement in German poetry and philosophy.

heredity Transmission of physical and mental traits from parents to offspring through GENES. In the late 19th cent., Gregor MENDEL derived certain basic laws of heredity, which eventually became the foundation of modern GENETICS. Each parent transmits only half its genes to its offspring, and different offspring of the same parents receive different combinations of genes. Many characteristics are polygenic (i.e., influenced by more than one gene), and many genes exist in numerous variations (ALLELES) throughout a population. There is thus a vast potential for variability among hereditary characteristics. While GENOTYPE determines the broad limits of features an individual may develop, the PHENOTYPE depends on complex interactions between genes and their environment. See also VARIATION.

heresy \ˈher-ə-sē\ Doctrine rejected as false by religious authorities. In Christianity, heretics are viewed as perversely rejecting the guidance of the church. Numerous Christian heresies appeared from the 2nd cent. onwards. Early heresies included ARIANISM, MONOPHYSITISM, and DONATISM. Some heresies, such as Montanism, expressed faith in a new prophet who added to the body of Christian revelation. The major means of combating heretics in the early church was EXCOMMUNICATION; this was supplemented in the 12th–13th cent. by the INQUISITION. In the 16th cent. the Protestant REFORMATION brought an end to the doctrinal unity of Western Christendom, and the concept of heresy became less important, though it continues to exist. The concept of heresy also exists in Judaism, Buddhism, Hinduism, and Islam.

Herman, Woody (*orig.* Woodrow Charles) (1913–1987) U.S. clarinetist, singer, and bandleader. Born in Milwaukee, Herman formed his first band in 1936. Known as "The Band That Plays the Blues," the group had a hit in 1939 with the riff tune "Woodchopper's Ball." His 1940s bands, the "Thundering Herds," evolved into powerful and colorful ensembles that played explosive, forward-looking arrangements. He led his band almost continuously for over 50 years.

hermaphroditism \hər-ˈma-frə-ˌdī-ˌti-zəm\ Condition of having both male and female reproductive organs (see REPRODUCTIVE SYSTEM). It is normal in most flowering plants and in some invertebrate animals. True human hermaphrodites are extremely rare. Tissue of the OVARY and TESTES may occur separately or be combined, external genitals may show traits of both sexes, and XY and XX SEX CHROMOSOME pairs are present. The sex of a hermophrodite infant can be chosen, usually on the basis of which sex organs dominate; those of the other sex are removed. Individuals who develop characteristics of the other sex at puberty may be treated with surgery, and SEX HORMONES may help them maintain their sexual identity. See also TRANSSEXUALISM.

hermeneutics \ˌhər-mə-ˈnü-tiks\ Study of the general principles of biblical interpretation. Its primary purpose is to discover the truths and values of the Bible, which is seen as a receptacle of divine revelation. Four major types of hermeneutics have emerged: literal (asserting that the text is to be interpreted according to the "plain meaning"), moral (seeking to establish the Bible's ethical principles), al-

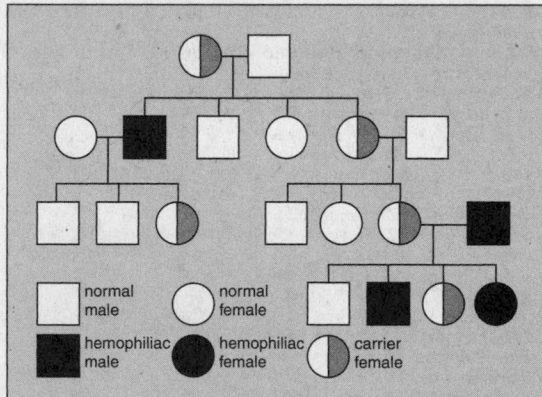

Heredity A pedigree chart tracing the inheritance of hemophilia, a sex-linked trait, through three familial generations. The recessive gene for hemophilia is carried on the X chromosome. Males inheriting one affected X chromosome from the mother and, less commonly, females inheriting an affected X chromosome from both mother and father experience the disease. Females who inherit an affected X chromosome from either mother or father are carriers for the disease. In the first generation here, a normal male and a female carrier produce a normal son and daughter, a son with hemophilia, and a carrier daughter.

legorical (interpreting narratives as having symbolical meaning), and mystical (seeking to link biblical events to the life to come). More recently the word has come to refer to all "deep" reading of literary and philosophical texts.

Hermes \'hər-ˌmēz\ Greek god, son of ZEUS and Maia. His cult emerged from Arcadia, where he was worshiped as a god of fertility. In HOMER's *Odyssey* he is the messenger of the gods and the conductor of the dead to HADES. As a messenger he also became the god of roads and doorways and the protector of travelers. He was also the god of dreams. His Roman counterpart was MERCURY.

Hermeticism \hər-'me-ti-ˌsi-zəm\ *or* **Hermetism** *Italian* **Ermetismo** Modernist poetic movement originating in Italy in the early 20th cent. Its works are characterized by unorthodox structure, illogical sequences, and highly subjective language. Its formalistic devices were partly derived from FUTURISM, but aspects of the Hermetics were forced on them by fascist censors. Giuseppe UNGARETTI, Salvatore QUASIMODO, and Eugenio MONTALE were its principal exponents.

Hermetic writings Occult texts on philosophical or theological subjects ascribed to Hermes Trismegistos ("Hermes the Thrice-Greatest"), identical to the Egyptian god THOTH. The collection, written in Greek and Latin, was probably put together in the 1st–3rd cent. A.D. Written in the form of dialogues, it synthesizes Near Eastern religion, PLATONISM, STOICISM, and other philosophies and reflects widely held beliefs on ASTROLOGY, ALCHEMY, and MAGIC. Its goal was the deification of humanity through knowledge of the transcendent God.

hermit *or* **eremite** Individual who shuns society to live in solitude, often for religious reasons. The first Christian hermits appeared in Egypt in the 3rd cent. A.D., escaping persecution by withdrawing to the desert and leading a life of prayer and penance. The first hermit was probably Paul of Thebes around A.D. 250. Other famous hermits included St. ANTHONY OF EGYPT and SIMEON STYLITES. The communal life of monasteries (see MONASTICISM) eventually tempered the austerities of the hermit's life. The eremitic life has persisted in Eastern Christianity.

Hermitage (museum) \er-mi-'tazh, *Engl* 'hər-mə-tij\ Largest museum in Russia. Located in St. Petersburg, it derives its name from the "Hermitage" pavilion adjoining the Winter Palace, built in 1767 for CATHERINE II the Great as a private gallery for her extensive collections. After the Winter Palace was destroyed by fire in 1837, the Hermitage was reconstructed and opened to the public by NICHOLAS I in 1852. After the Bolshevik Revolution, the collections were transferred to public ownership. The museum is now housed in five interconnected buildings. Along with thousands of art objects from Asia, the pre-Columbian Americas, Greece, and Rome, it houses outstanding collections of Western painting. Russian history is represented by archaeological material from prehistoric times on.

hermit crab Any CRAB (families Paguridae and Coenobitidae) that uses empty shells or other hollow objects as a shelter for partial containment and protection of the body. They have two pairs of antennae and four pairs of legs; the first pair of legs is modified to form pincers, shaped to cover the shell entrance when the animal is inside. As the crab grows, it periodically leaves its shell and finds a larger one to occupy. The reddish brown large hermit crab (*Pagurus pollicaris*; 4–5 in., or 10–12 cm, long) and the small hermit crab (*P. longicarpus*) are found in N. American Atlantic coastal waters.

Hermon, Mt. *Arabic* **Jabal al-Shaykh** \'jà-bàl-àsh-'shīk\ Snowcapped mountain on the Lebanon–Syria border. Located west of DAMASCUS, and rising to 9,232 ft (2,814 m), it is the highest point on the E coast of the Mediterranean Sea. A sacred landmark in Hittite, Palestinian, and Roman times, it represented the NW limit of Israelite conquest under MOSES and JOSHUA. Since the SIX-DAY WAR (1967), part of its S and W slopes have been within the Israeli-administered GOLAN HEIGHTS.

hernia Protrusion of any organ or tissue from its normal cavity. The term usually refers to an abdominal hernia, which may be a CONGENITAL DISORDER. Tissue may protrude through the abdominal muscle at the groin (inguinal),

upper thigh (femoral), or navel (umbilical); its circulation can become cut off, leading to INFLAMMATION, INFECTION, and GANGRENE. Surgery may be necessary. Other common hernias are hiatal hernia (protrusion of part or all of the stomach above the diaphragm) and herniated disk (protrusion of tissue from a disk in the vertebral column).

hero Mythological or legendary figure, often of divine descent, who is endowed with great strength or ability, like the heroes celebrated in early EPICS such as *Gilgamesh*, HOMER's *Iliad*, *Beowulf*, or the *Chanson de Roland*. Usually illustrious warriors or adventurers, heroes are often represented as fulfilling a quest (e.g., Beowulf ridding his people of their enemies). Inclined to boasting and foolhardiness, they defy pain and death to live fully, creating a moment's glory that survives in the memory of their descendants.

Hero and Leander \lē-'an-dər\ Lovers celebrated in Greek legend. Leander swam the Hellespont nightly to be with Hero, guided by a light from her tower. One stormy night the lamp was extinguished, and he drowned. When Hero discovered his body, she threw herself from the tower. The story was told by OVID and was subject material for Christopher MARLOWE and Lord BYRON.

Herod *or* **Herod the Great** (73–4 B.C.) Roman-appointed King of JUDAEA (37–4 B.C.). A practicing Jew, he was of Arab origin. Herod was critical to imperial control of Judaea, and he was a lifelong friend of Mark ANTONY. Judaea prospered under his early reign, during which he increased trade and built fortresses, aqueducts, and theaters. His grip on his kingdom weakened as he became increasingly mentally unstable and physically debilitated. He killed his wife, his eldest son, and other relatives, and he slew the infants of Bethlehem (see JESUS) shortly before his own death after a bungled suicide attempt.

Herod Antipas \'an-ti-pəs\ (21 B.C.–A.D. 39) Son of HEROD the Great and TETRARCH of GALILEE (4 B.C.–A.D. 39) throughout JESUS' ministry. He was responsible for the death of JOHN THE BAPTIST (demanded by his wife, Herodias, and stepdaughter, SALOME) but later refused to cooperate when Pontius PILATE pressed him to conduct the trial of Jesus. After denouncing Herod Agrippa I, (c.10 B.C.–A.D. 44), he was banished by CALIGULA to Gaul. A notable accomplishment was the building of the city of TIBERIAS.

Herodotus \hə-'rä-də-təs\ (484?–430/420 B.C.) Greek historian. He is the author of the first great narrative history produced in the ancient world, the *History* of the PERSIAN WARS. It is a unified artistic masterpiece, with many illuminating digressions and anecdotes skillfully worked into the narrative. Despite many inaccuracies, it remains the leading source of original information about the history of Greece between 550 and 479 B.C., as well as that of much of W Asia and Egypt.

heroin ORGANIC COMPOUND, a highly addictive ALKALOID derivative of MORPHINE that makes up a large portion of illicit NARCOTICS traffic. Easily made from morphine, it was developed and first used as an ANALGESIC, but its undesirable effects outweighed its value, and it is illegal in most countries. Injection brings an ecstatic, warm, glowing sensation, followed by relaxation and contentment. Within half a day withdrawal symptoms set in, with a craving for more. Development of tolerance, requiring ever greater amounts for the same effects, leads to DRUG ADDICTION. Illegal street heroin is usually only 2–5% pure; unwitting injection of relatively pure heroin is a major cause of overdose, resulting in depressed respiration, coma, and death.

heron Any of about 60 species of long-legged wading birds in the same family (Ardeidae) as EGRETS and BITTERNS. They are found worldwide but are most common in the tropics. They wade in the shallow waters of pools, marshes, and swamps, catching frogs, fishes, and other aquatic animals. They nest on rough stick platforms in bushes or trees near water. Herons commonly stand with their neck bent in an S shape and fly with their legs trailing and their head held back. They have broad wings and a long, straight, sharp-pointed bill.

Hero of Alexandria *or* **Heron of Alexandria** (fl.c.A.D. 60) Greek mathematician and inventor. He is remembered for his formula for the area of a triangle and for inventing the

first STEAM ENGINE. Of his many treatises, one contains a method for approximating the square root of a number. His writings include discussions of the simple MACHINES and the construction of many kinds of engines.

Herophilus \hə-'räf-ə-ləs\ (335?–c.280 B.C.) Alexandrian physician, often called the father of ANATOMY. He performed public dissections on human corpses; studied the cavities of the brain, which he regarded as the center of the nervous system; and classified nerve trunks as motor and sensory, distinguishing them from tendons and blood vessels. He described the eye, liver, salivary glands, pancreas, genitals, duodenum, and prostate gland (naming the last two) and was the first to measure the pulse. A student of HIPPOCRATES' doctrine, he emphasized the curative powers of drugs, diet, and gymnastics.

herpes simplex \'hər-ˌpēz\ Infection caused by herpes simplex VIRUS. Type I typically produces a cluster of small blisters (cold sores, or fever blisters), usually on the lips or face. Type II, transmitted mostly through sexual contact, causes painful genital blisters. Oral sex can give either type the chance to infect the usual site of the other. In both types, the virus remains after symptoms end and can reactivate. Babies born to mothers with active herpes can become infected during birth; this can be prevented by cesarean section. There is no cure, but drugs can reduce severity and risk of transmission.

herpes zoster See SHINGLES

Herrera \(h)ə-'rer-ə\, **Francisco** Name of two Spanish painters. Francisco Herrera the Elder (c.1590–1654) was a painter and engraver. Under the influence of Francisco ZURBARÁN, he developed the naturalistic style seen in his four scenes from the life of St. Bonaventure (1627). Around 1650 he moved to Madrid. His last documented work, a painting of St. Joseph (1648), features elongated forms and elaborate draperies. Diego VELÁZQUEZ was briefly his pupil. His son Francisco Herrera the Younger (1627–1685) worked as a painter and architect. His religious works are in the theatrical style of Roman baroque art, which he introduced in Seville. After 1660 he was active in Madrid as a painter of frescoes and altarpieces, becoming painter to CHARLES II (1672), and master of the Royal Works (1677). His greatest architectural achievement was the church of El Pilar at Saragossa (begun 1681).

Herrick, Robert (1591–1674) English poet. A country vicar in Devonshire and disciple of Ben JONSON, he wrote classically influenced lyrics whose appeal is in their freshness and their perfection of form and style. The only book he published was *Hesperides* (1648), containing 1,400 poems, mostly short, many of them EPIGRAMS. He is best remembered for the line "Gather ye rosebuds while ye may."

Herriman, George (Joseph) (1881–1944) U.S. cartoonist. Born in New Orleans, he started cartooning after a fall from a scaffold prevented him from working as a house painter. The first of his several comic strips, *Lariat Pete*, appeared in 1903. His best-known strip, *Krazy Kat*, appeared in 1910 and ran for more than 30 years in the W. R. HEARST newspapers. *Krazy Kat*'s fantasy, drawing, and dialogue were of such high quality that some people consider it the finest comic strip ever published.

herring Either the Atlantic or the Pacific subspecies of *Clupea harengus*, slab-sided, N fishes that are small-headed and streamlined, with silvery iridescent sides. The name also refers to other members of the family Clupeidae. Adults range in length from 8 to 15 in. (20–38 cm). One of the most abundant species of fish, herring travel in enormous schools. In Europe they are processed and sold as kippered herring; in E Canada and the NE U.S., most of the herring used are young fishes canned as sardines. Herring taken in the Pacific are used mainly to make fish oil and meal.

herring gull Most common of the Atlantic GULLS in the Northern Hemisphere. The herring gull (*Larus argentatus*) has a gray mantle and black-and-white-spotted wing tips. Its populations are increasing because of expanding food supplies, chiefly garbage and sewage in or near coastal waters.

Herriot \ˌer-ē-'ō\, **Édouard** (1872–1957) French politician and writer. He became mayor of Lyon in 1905 and kept the post for most of his life. Elected to the Chamber of Deputies (1919), he led the Radical Party opposition. As prime minis-

ter (1924–25) he led France to recognize the Soviet Union. In 1926 he was prime minister for three days, and he held the position in 1932 for six months. He abstained from voting when the National Assembly gave full powers to Philippe PÉTAIN at Vichy in 1940, then was arrested and deported to Germany (1942–45). He served as president of the National Assembly 1947–54.

Herriot \'her-ē-ət\, **James** *orig.* James Alfred Wight (1916–1995) British veterinarian and writer. Wight joined a veterinarian practice in the Yorkshire Dales and at age 50 began writing his humorous, fictionalized reminiscences, published in the U.S. under the name James Herriot as *All Creatures Great and Small* (1972). The instant best-seller inaugurated a series of highly popular books, which was adapted for two films and a long-running television series.

Herrmann, Bernard (1911–1975) U.S. composer. Born in New York City, he was one of a group of young composers around Charles IVES in the 1930s. His radio work with Orson WELLES led to a career in movies. His film scores included *Citizen Kane* (1941), *The Magnificent Ambersons* (1942), *All That Money Can Buy* (1941, Academy Award), and eight of Alfred HITCHCOCK's films, including *Vertigo* (1958), *North by Northwest* (1959), and *Psycho* (1960).

Herschel family \'hər-shəl\ British family of astronomers. The German-born William Herschel (1738–1822) emigrated to England in 1757. He ground his own mirrors to study distant celestial objects, producing the best telescopes of the day. His discovery of Uranus made him famous at 43. He hypothesized that nebulae are composed of stars, developed a theory of stellar evolution, and discovered infrared radiation. He was knighted in 1816. His sister, Caroline Lucretia Herschel (1750–1848), carried out calculations necessary to her brother's researches and detected by telescope three nebulae and eight comets. In 1787 the king recognized her work with an annual pension. She continued to work long after William died. William's son John (1792–1871) studied mathematics at Cambridge Univ. He journeyed to the Southern Hemisphere to survey its skies, and returned in 1838 having recorded the locations of 68,948 stars. Also an accomplished chemist, he invented (independently of Fox TALBOT) the process of photography on sensitized paper. He was knighted in 1831. His sons Alexander Stewart (1836–1907) and John (1837–1921) were also astronomers.

Hersey, John (Richard) (1914–1993) U.S. (Chinese-born) writer. Born to missionaries, he worked as a correspondent in the Far East, Italy, and Russia. His novel *A Bell for Adano* (1944, Pulitzer Prize) depicts the Allied occupation of a Sicilian town. *Hiroshima* (1946), about the experiences of atomic-blast survivors, and *The Wall* (1950), which deals with the Warsaw Ghetto uprisings, combine fact and fiction. His later novels include *A Single Pebble* (1956) and *The Child Buyer* (1960).

Hertz \'herts, *Engl* 'hərts\, **Heinrich (Rudolf)** (1857–1894) German physicist. While a professor at Karlsruhe Polytechnic (1885–89), he produced electromagnetic waves in the laboratory and measured their length and velocity. He showed that the nature of their vibration and their response to reflection and refraction were the same as those of light and heat waves, and proved that light and heat are electromagnetic radiations. He was the first to broadcast and receive radio waves. The hertz (Hz), a unit of frequency in cycles per second, is named for him.

Hertzog \'hert-ˌsȯk\, **J(ames) B(arry) M(unnik)** (1866–1942) Prime minister of the Union of S. Africa (1924–39). His political principles were "South Africa First" (i.e., ahead of the British Empire) and the "Two Streams Policy," under which British and AFRIKANER would be free from domination by each other. He broke with Louis Botha over his accommodationist policies and formed the NATIONAL PARTY in 1914. As prime minister, Hertzog gave the Union its flag, made AFRIKAANS an official language, and furthered APARTHEID. In 1933 he accepted a coalition with Jan SMUTS, but he resigned in 1939 over the issue of neutrality in World War II.

Hertzsprung-Russell diagram \'hert-sprüŋ-'rə-səl\ *or* **H-R diagram** Graph plotting the absolute MAGNITUDES of STARS against their color. Very important to stellar evolution theories, it evolved from charts begun independently in 1911 by Ejnar Hertzsprung (1873–1967) and Henry Norris Russell (1877–1957). It shows stars from bottom to top as brightness increases and from right to left as temperature increases. Stars tend to cluster in certain parts, mostly along a diagonal line, the "main sequence," the locus of hydrogen-burning stars of different masses.

Herzegovina See BOSNIA AND HERZEGOVINA

Herzen \\'hert-sən\\, **Aleksandr (Ivanovich)** (1812–1870) Russian writer and political activist. As a student, he joined a socialist group, for which he was exiled to work in the provincial bureaucracy (1834–42). Returning to Moscow, he turned to anarchist socialism. After inheriting a considerable fortune, he left Russia (1847). In Paris he proclaimed Western institutions "dead" and developed the theory of a unique Russian path to socialism known as peasant populism. He moved to London in 1852 and founded the influential newspaper *Kolokol* ("The Bell") in 1857; smuggled into Russia, the paper was read by both reformers and revolutionaries. He then turned his energies to writing *My Past and Thoughts* (1861–67), considered one of the greatest works of Russian prose.

Herzl \\'hert-səl\\, **Theodor** (1860–1904) Hungarian Zionist leader. Growing up as a Hungarian Jew, he believed that assimilation was the best strategy to deal with anti-Semitism. He became a Zionist while covering the Alfred DREYFUS affair as a journalist in Paris. In 1897 he organized a world congress of ZIONISM, attended by about 200 delegates, and became the first president of the World Zionist Organization. Herzl's indefatigable organizing, propagandizing, and diplomacy had much to do with making Zionism a political movement of worldwide significance.

Herzog \\'hert-sók\\, **Werner** *orig.* Werner H. Stipetic (b.1942) German filmmaker. He won two awards for his first feature film, *Signs of Life* (1967), which introduced the theme of descent into madness that would reappear in *Aguirre, the Wrath of God* (1972) and *Nosferatu* (1979). His own grand obsession with the filming of *Fitzcarraldo* (1982), which called for a ship to be dragged over the mountains in the Amazon rainforest, became legendary. His films were among the best of the postwar W. German cinema.

Hesiod \\'hē-sē-əd, 'he-sē-əd\\ (fl.c.700 B.C.) Greek poet. One of the earliest Greek poets, he is often called the father of Greek didactic poetry. He may have been a professional reciter of poetry. Two complete epics have survived: the *Theogony*, relating stories of the gods, and the *Works and Days*, describing peasant life and expressing his views on the proper conduct of men. His works, which portray a less glamorous world than HOMER's, won him renown during his lifetime.

Hess, (Walter Richard) Rudolf (1894–1987) German Nazi leader. He joined the fledgling NAZI PARTY in 1920. After participating in the BEER HALL PUTSCH (1923), he escaped but returned voluntarily to prison, where he took down dictation for Adolf HITLER's *Mein Kampf*. He became Hitler's private secretary and, in 1933, deputy party leader. In 1941 he created an international sensation when he secretly parachuted into Scotland on an abortive mission to negotiate peace between Britain and Germany. Held as a prisoner of war, he was given a life sentence at the NUREMBERG TRIALS; from 1966 he was the sole inmate at Spandau prison.

Hesse \\'hes\\ *German* **Hessen** State (pop., 1997 est.: 6,031,000), W central Germany. Occupying 8,152 sq mi (21,114 sq km), it was formed in 1945 through the amalgamation of former Prussian provincial units. Its capital is WIESBADEN. The Hessians are thought to be descended from a Frankish tribe Christianized by St. BONIFACE in the 8th cent. A.D. Hesse was twice partitioned in the 15th cent., but PHILIP OF HESSE reunited the territory. On the banks of the WESER RIVER are many ruined castles and old churches and palaces.

Hesse \\'hes-ə\\, **Eva** (1936–1970) U.S. (German-born) sculptor. She arrived in New York with her family in 1939, and attended Pratt Institute, Cooper Union, and Yale Univ. In 1961 she married and began making sculpture, developing a style featuring sensuous shapes and unconventional materials (including rubber tubing, synthetic resins, cord, cloth, and wire). In 1969 she underwent the first of three unsuccessful operations for a brain tumor. Her influence since her death has been widespread.

Hesse \\'hes-ə\\, **Hermann** (1877–1962) German novelist and poet. He left a seminary because of his inability to adapt to the life there. His early novels dealt with the inward and outward search of the artist. An opponent of militarism, he settled permanently in Switzerland at the outbreak of World War I. *Demian* (1919), influenced by his experience with psychoanalysis, made him famous. *Siddhartha* (1922), about the early life of the Buddha, reflects a visit to India. His later works, including *Steppenwolf* (1927), *Narcissus and Goldmund* (1930), and *The Glass Bead Game* (1943), concern the conflict between the contemplative and the active life. He won the Nobel Prize in 1946. His mysticism and his appeal for self-realization made him posthumously a cult figure among young people.

Hermann Hesse, 1957

Hestia Greek goddess of the hearth and one of the 12 chief deities of Mt. OLYMPUS. The daughter of RHEA and CRONUS, she rejected APOLLO and POSEIDON to remain a maiden forever, whereupon ZEUS gave her the honor of presiding over all sacrifices.

Heston, Charlton *orig.* John Charlton Carter (b.1924) U.S. actor. Born in Evanston, Ill., he made his Broadway debut in *Antony and Cleopatra* (1947) and his film debut in *Dark City* (1950). He became a star in *The Greatest Show on Earth* (1952) and was a muscular and dignified stalwart in *The Ten Commandments* (1956), *Ben-Hur* (1959, Academy Award), and *The Greatest Story Ever Told* (1965). He was president of the Screen Actors Guild (1966–71) and, as an outspoken conservative, was elected president of the National Rifle Assn. in 1998.

Hesychius of Alexandria \\hə-'si-kē-əs\\ (fl. 5th cent. A.D.) Greek scholar and linguist. His *Alphabetical Collection of All Words* is the most complete Greek lexicon known from antiquity. Though preserved only in a 15th-cent. abridgment by a Venetian editor, it is valued as a basic authority for ancient inscriptions and poetry as well as the writings of the Greek Church Fathers (see PATRISTIC LITERATURE).

heterozygote See HOMOZYGOTE AND HETEROZYGOTE

Hewlett-Packard Co. U.S. manufacturer of computers, computer printers, and measuring instruments. Founded in 1938 in Palo Alto, Cal., by William Hewlett (1913–2001) and David Packard (1912–1996), the company grew along with the electronics sector of the U.S. defense industry after World War II. In 1966 it developed its first computer, and in 1968 one of the earliest desktop electronic calculators. It entered the personal-computer market in 1980, and its HP Laser-Jet dominated the market for computer printers in the 1980s.

Heydrich \\'hī-drik\\, **Reinhard (Tristan Eugen)** (1904–1942) German Nazi official. He resigned from the navy in 1931 to join the SS, eventually becoming Heinrich HIMMLER's chief deputy. Noted for his ruthlessness, he organized mass executions in the German-occupied territories and became known as "the Hangman." In 1942 he chaired the notorious WANNSEE CONFERENCE. Appointed deputy adminstrator of Bohemia and Moravia, he was assassinated by Czech patriots; in retaliation the Gestapo demolished the village of Lidice and executed its male population of about 200.

Heyerdahl \\'hā-ər-ˌdäl\\, **Thor** (1914–2002) Norwegian ethnologist and adventurer. Convinced that Polynesian culture bore traces of S. American cultures, he built a raft, the *Kon-Tiki*, and sailed it from S. America to Polynesia in 1947 to demonstrate the possibility of such contact, a trip recounted in his best-selling *Kon-Tiki* (1950). In 1969 he sailed a reconstruction of an ancient Egyptian reed boat (the *Ra*) from Morocco to the Caribbean Sea to show that Mediterranean peoples could have preceded Christopher COLUMBUS to the New World. In 1977 he took the reed craft *Tigris* from the Tigris River in Iraq across the Arabian Sea to Pak-

istan and back to the Red Sea to demonstrate that trade could have spread ancient Sumerian culture eastward. His theories have not been generally accepted by anthropologists.

Hezbollah See HIZBULLAH

Hialeah \ˌhī-ə-ˈlē-ə\ City (pop., 2000: 226,000), SE Florida. It was settled in 1910 by the aviation pioneers James Bright and Glenn CURTISS. A suburb of MIAMI, it is the site of the horse-racing track Hialeah Park (1925).

Hiawatha \ˌhī-ə-ˈwȯ-thə\ Legendary chief (c.1450) of the Onondaga tribe of N. American Indians, regarded by native tradition as the founder of the IROQUOIS CONFEDERACY. His story is told in H. W. LONGFELLOW's popular poem *Song of Hiawatha* (1855), though Longfellow mistakenly placed Hiawatha in a Midwestern tribe.

hibernation State of greatly slowed METABOLISM and low body temperature in winter in certain animals. True hibernators include many cold-blooded animals and a few mammals (e.g., bats, hedgehogs) that go into a near-dead state with a near-freezing body temperature and very slow breathing and heart rate. Mammals such as bears that sleep in dens with only slightly lowered body temperature wake easily and are not considered true hibernators. Most hibernators build up a reserve of body fat or store food ahead of time. They may wake and eat several times during the winter. Cold-blooded animals must hibernate where the weather drops below freezing. Hibernation's warm-weather equivalent is estivation.

hibiscus \hī-ˈbis-kəs\ Any of about 250 species of shrubs, trees, and herbaceous plants that make up the genus *Hibiscus,* in the MALLOW FAMILY, native to warm temperate and tropical regions. Several are cultivated as ornamentals for their showy flowers. The tropical Chinese hibiscus, or China rose *(H. rosa-sinensis),* has large, somewhat bell-shaped reddish blossoms. Other members of the genus include OKRA, rose of Sharon, and many flowering plants known by the common name mallow.

hiccup Spasmodic contraction of the DIAPHRAGM that causes a sudden breath in, cut off when the vocal cords snap together, creating the characteristic sound. Causes include overdistended stomach, gastric irritation, and nerve spasms. Hiccups usually stop within minutes, though they may last days, weeks, or longer. The most common treatment is to hold one's breath. Prolonged severe hiccups are treated with nerve blocks or by surgically cutting the nerve that supplies the diaphragm.

Hickok, Wild Bill (*orig.* James Butler) (1837–1876) U.S. frontiersman. Born in Troy Grove, Ill., he moved to Kansas to farm. While working as a stage driver in 1861, he shot and killed the outlaw Dave McCanles, which launched legends of his marksmanship. He was a Union scout and spy in the Civil War. His ironhanded rule as sheriff of Hays City (1869–71) and marshal of Abilene (1871) helped tame these Kansas towns. Visiting the Dakota Territory, he was at a poker table in a Deadwood saloon when he was shot dead by a drunken stranger, Jack McCall.

hickory Any of about 18 species of deciduous timber and nut-producing trees that make up the genus *Carya,* in the WALNUT family. About 15 species are native to E N. America. The nuts of some species—principally shagbark hickory *(C. ovata),* shellbark hickory *(C. laciniosa),* mockernut hickory *(C. tomentosa),* and PECAN—contain large, sweet-tasting, edible seeds. The pecan is the most valuable species economically. The wood of other hickories is used as fuel and for tool handles, sports equipment, furniture, and flooring.

Hicks, Edward (1780–1849) U.S. folk painter. Born in Attleboro, Pa., he was a coach and sign painter who in middle age began to produce paintings of farm scenes and landscapes. Fearing that art was contrary to his Quaker religion, he often framed his pictures with edifying verse. He painted his best-known subject, *The Peaceable Kingdom,* about 100 times; some 25 versions survive. In this charming Quaker pageant, William PENN makes his treaty with the Indians, while little children play among a gathering of beasts.

Hidalgo \hi-ˈdal-gō\ State (pop., 2000: 2,231,000), E central Mexico. With an area of 8,036 sq mi (20,813 sq km), it was established as a separate state in 1869 in honor of Miguel

HIDALGO. Highly mountainous, it has extensive mineral deposits, including silver and gold. In pre-Columbian times it was the center of TOLTEC civilization; TULA, west of PACHUCA, the state capital, was once capital of the Toltecs. The state has major metalworking factories.

Hidalgo (y Costilla) \ē-ˈthäl-gō\, **Miguel** (1753–1811) Mexican priest, called the father of Mexican independence. In the town of Dolores (now Dolores Hidalgo), he joined a group plotting independence from Spain. On September 16, 1810, when his group was betrayed, he rang the church bell and addressed his parishioners with his *Grito de Dolores* (Cry of Dolores), calling them to revolution. Thousands of Indians and mestizos joined him, and he captured Guanajuato and other cities before reaching Mexico City, where his hesitation led to their defeat and his execution. The martyred Hidalgo became a potent symbol of the independence movement that eventually succeeded, and each September 16—now celebrated as Mexico's Independence Day—the president shouts a version of the *Grito de Dolores* from the National Palace balcony.

Hidatsa \hi-ˈdät-sə\ *or* **Gros Ventres (of the Missouri)** \ˈgrō-ˌvänt\ PLAINS INDIAN people who lived on the upper Missouri River in semipermanent villages. They raised corn, beans, and squash, and hunted bison. The SUN DANCE was the major religious ceremony. In the mid-1800s disease and war with the Dakota (SIOUX) sharply reduced their number. Today 1,200 Hidatsa live on a reservation in N. Dakota.

Hidatsa dancer, aquatint by Karl Bodmer, 1834

Hideyoshi See TOYOTOMI HIDEYOSHI

Hierakonpolis \ˌhī-ə-rə-ˈkän-pə-ləs\ Ancient city, Upper Egypt. Located south of THEBES, it was the prehistoric residence of the kings of Upper Egypt. It reveals the beginning of Egypt's historical period. It was at its height from 3400 B.C. to the Old Kingdom (c.2575 B.C.). THUTMOSE III later rebuilt the archaic temple. During the New Kingdom, Hierakonpolis retained its place as a religious and historic center.

Hierapolis \ˌhī-ə-ˈra-pə-ləs\ Ancient city, now in Syria. Its remains lie northeast of ALEPPO. As a center of the worship of the Syrian goddess Atargatis, it was one of the great cities of Syria in the 3rd cent. A.D., but thereafter declined. HARUN AL-RASHID restored it in the 8th cent. It later became the headquarters of the MONGOLS, who completed its ruin.

hieroglyph \ˈhī-rə-ˌglif\ Character in any of several systems of WRITING that is pictorial in nature. The term was originally used for the oldest system of writing Ancient Egyptian (see EGYPTIAN LANGUAGE). Egyptian hieroglyphs could be read iconically (the representation of a house enclosure stood for the word *pr,* "house"), phonetically (the "house" sign could have the phonetic value *pr*), or associatively (a sign representing one thing could stand for a homophone meaning something else). Unlike contemporary CUNEIFORM WRITING, phonetic hieroglyphs denoted consonants, not syllables, so there was no regular way to write vowels. The standardized writing of the Middle Kingdom (2050–1750 B.C.) employed about 750 hieroglyphs. The last dated hieroglyphic text is from A.D. 394, and the meaning of the signs was lost until the early 19th cent., when J.-F. CHAMPOLLION deciphered the ROSETTA STONE. The term "hieroglyph" has been applied to similar systems of writing, notably MAYAN HIEROGLYPHIC WRITING.

hierophant \ˈhī-ə-rə-ˌfant, hī-ˈer-ə-fənt\ Chief priest of the ELEUSINIAN MYSTERIES in ancient Greece. His main task was to display the sacred objects during the celebration of the mysteries and explain their secret meaning to initiates. The priest was usually an old, celibate man with a forceful voice.

high blood pressure See HYPERTENSION

high-definition television (HDTV) Any system producing significantly greater picture resolution than that of the ordinary 525-line (625-line in Europe) TELEVISION screen. Conventional television transmits signals in analog form. Digital HDTV systems, by contrast, transmit in the form of digital data. These numerical data are broadcast using the same high radio frequencies that carry analog waves, and computer processors in the television set then decode the data. Digital HDTV can provide sharper, clearer pictures and sound with very little interference or other imperfections. Digital television sets will potentially be able to send, store, and manipulate images, thereby merging the functions of the television set and the computer.

high-energy physics See PARTICLE PHYSICS

higher education Education beyond the secondary level. Institutions of higher education include COLLEGES and UNIVERSITIES, professional schools, teacher-training schools, COMMUNITY COLLEGES, and institutes of technology. At the end of a prescribed course of study, a DEGREE, diploma, or certificate is awarded. See also CONTINUING EDUCATION.

high jump Jump for height over a horizontal bar in a TRACK-AND-FIELD contest. The sport's equipment includes a semicircular runway allowing an approach run of at least 15 m (49 ft), the raised bar and its vertical supports, and a cushioned landing area. Jumpers must leave the ground from one foot. Early jumping styles were largely superseded from 1968 by the "Fosbury flop," a backward-twisting dive named for the U.S. jumper Dick Fosbury (b.1947).

high-rise building Multistory building taller than the maximum height people are willing to walk up, thus requiring vertical mechanical transportation. The introduction of safe passenger ELEVATORS made practical the erection of buildings more than four or five stories tall. The first high-rise buildings were constructed in the U.S. in the 1880s. Further developments were made possible by the use of steel structural frames and glass CURTAIN-WALL systems. See also SKYSCRAPER.

high school In the U.S., any three- to six-year SECONDARY SCHOOL serving students about 14–18 years of age. Four-year schools are by far the most common; their grade levels are designated freshman (9th grade), sophomore (10th), junior (11th), and senior (12th). Comprehensive high schools offer both general academic courses and specialized commercial, trade, and technical subjects. Most are tuition-free, supported by state funds. See also PAROCHIAL EDUCATION, PREPARATORY SCHOOL.

hijacking Crime of seizing possession or control of a vehicle from another by force or threat of force. Before the 1960s hijacking was limited to land vehicles and ships. In 1961 four U.S. airliners were hijacked and forced to fly to Cuba; later highly publicized cases involved Palestinian and other Arab hijackers who demanded the release of their comrades from jails in Israel and elsewhere. The world's most infamous hijacking took place on Sept. 11, 2001, when AL-QAEDA hijackers seized four airliners and crashed two into the WORLD TRADE CENTER and a third into the PENTAGON, killing some 3,000 people. See also PIRACY.

Hijaz, Al- See HEJAZ

Hijra See HEGIRA

Hilbert, David (1862–1943) German mathematician whose work aimed at establishing the formalistic foundations of mathematics. In 1900 at the International Mathematical Congress in Paris, he laid out 23 research problems as a challenge to the 20th cent. Many have since been solved, in each case to great fanfare. Hilbert's name is prominently attached to an infinite-dimensional space called a Hilbert space, a concept useful in mathematical analysis and QUANTUM MECHANICS.

Hildegard von Bingen \ˈhil-də-ˌgärt-fȯn-ˈbiŋ-ən\ (1098–1179) German abbess, visionary mystic, and composer. She became prioress at a Benedictine cloister in 1136. Having experienced visions since childhood, she was eventually permitted to write *Scivias* (1141–52), in which she recorded 26 prophetic, symbolic, and apocalyptic visions; it was followed by two more such collections. She founded a convent at Rupertsberg around 1147, where she continued to prophesy; her advice came to be sought by the most powerful and eminent figures of Europe. Her *Symphonia armonie celestium revelationum* consists of 77 lyrical poems, all with melodies; she is apparently the first woman composer in the Western tradition whose music is known. Though long regarded as a saint, she has never been formally canonized.

Hill, Joe *orig.* Joel Emmanuel Hägglund (1879–1915) Swedish-U.S. songwriter and organizer for the INDUSTRIAL WORKERS OF THE WORLD (IWW). Hill emigrated to the U.S. about 1902 and joined the IWW in 1910. His songs of protest and solidarity—including "The Preacher and the Slave," in which he coined the phrase "pie in the sky" as a mocking description of the reward awaiting the meek in the next world—became widely popular. Convicted of two murders on circumstantial evidence, Hill was executed by a firing squad despite mass demonstrations on his behalf. In death he became a martyr for the radical U.S. labor movement.

Hillary, Edmund (Percival) (*later* **Sir Edmund**) (b.1919) New Zealand mountain climber and explorer. A professional beekeeper, he enjoyed climbing in the New Zealand Alps. With TENZING NORGAY, he became the first person to reach the summit of Mt. EVEREST (1953), achieving worldwide fame. In 1958 he participated in the first crossing of Antarctica by vehicle. From the 1960s he has helped build schools and hospitals for the Sherpa people.

Hillel (fl.1st cent. B.C.–1st cent. A.D.) Jewish sage and architect of RABBINIC JUDAISM. Born in Babylonia, he went to Palestine to complete his studies under the PHARISEES. He became the revered head of the school known by his name, the House of Hillel. He liberated texts from a slavish literal interpretation and sought to make obedience to Law feasible for all Jews. His legal writings were very influential in the compilation of the TALMUD. He is remembered as a model scholar and communal leader, whose brilliance, patience, and goodness are to be emulated by all RABBIS.

Hilliard \ˈhil-yərd\, **Nicholas** (1547–1619) British painter. Trained as a jeweler, he began painting miniatures and in 1570 was appointed miniature painter to ELIZABETH I. He produced many portraits of her and of such members of her court as Francis DRAKE and Walter RALEIGH. The first great native-born English painter of the Renaissance, he raised the art of MINIATURE PAINTING to its highest point of development and influenced English portraiture through the early 17th cent.

Hilton, Conrad (Nicholson) (1887–1979) U.S. businessman, founder of one of the world's largest hotel organizations. Born in San Antonio, N.M., as a boy he helped his father turn the family's adobe house into an inn for traveling salesmen. In 1918 he bought several hotels in Texas, and by 1939 he was building, leasing, and buying hotels in California, New York, and Illinois. In 1946 the Hilton Hotels Corp. was organized; in 1948 it became Hilton International Co.

Hilton, James (Glen Trevor) (1900–1954) British novelist. He wrote numerous novels, but is principally remembered for three best-selling works that led to popular films: *Lost Horizon* (1933), *Good-Bye Mr. Chips* (1934), and *Random Harvest* (1941).

Himalayas \ˌhi-mə-ˈlā-əz, hi-ˈmä-lə-yəz\ *or* **the Himalaya** Mountain system, S Asia. It forms a barrier between the Tibetan Plateau to the north and the plains of the Indian subcontinent to the south. It constitutes the greatest mountain system on earth and includes 30 mountains rising to heights above 24,000 ft (7,300 m), including Mt. EVEREST. The system extends some 1,500 mi (2,400 km) from east to west and covers about 230,000 sq mi (595,000 sq km). It is traditionally divided into four parallel ranges: from north to south, the Trans-Himalayas, the Great Himalayas, the Lesser Himalayas, and the Outer Himalayas. It acts as a great climatic divide, causing heavy rain and snow on the Indian side but aridity in Tibet, and represents at many points a virtually impassable barrier, even by air. Its glaciers and snows are the source of 19 major rivers, including the INDUS, GANGES, and BRAHMAPUTRA.

Himmler, Heinrich (1900–1945) German Nazi police administrator. He joined the NAZI PARTY in 1925 and rose to become head of Adolf HITLER'S SS. He took charge of the GESTAPO in 1934, established the Third Reich's first con-

centration camp, at Dachau, and soon built the SS into a powerful network of state terror. By 1936 he commanded all the Reich's police forces and was second only to Hitler in power. In World War II he organized the death camps in Eastern Europe. In April 1945 he intrigued to surrender Germany to the Allies; Hitler ordered his arrest. Attempting to escape, he was captured by the British and committed suicide by taking poison.

Hinayana \ˌhē-nə-'yä-nə\ Name given to the more conservative schools of BUDDHISM. A Sanskrit word meaning "Lesser Vehicle" (because it is concerned with only the individual's salvation), it was applied pejoratively by followers of the more liberal MAHAYANA ("Greater Vehicle," because it is concerned with universal salvation) tradition. Of the ancient Hinayana schools, only THERAVADA Buddhism maintained a strong position after the collapse of Indian Buddhism in the 13th cent.

Hincmar of Reims \'hiŋk-ˌmär...'rēmz\ (806?–882) French archbishop and theologian. The most influential churchman of the Carolingian era, he advised the French kings LOUIS I and Charles II and was chosen archbishop of Reims in 845. He later secured the succession of Charles as Holy Roman Emperor. His theological writings included treatises on predestination, in which he argued that God does not damn a sinner in advance, and a defense of the Christian opposition to divorce.

Hindemith \'hin-də-ˌmit\, **Paul** (1895–1963) German composer. As a youth he mastered the viola, violin, clarinet, and piano, and he became concertmaster of the Frankfurt Opera at 20. His own music was considered "degenerate" by the Nazis, and he left Germany, reaching the U.S. in 1940. A professor at Yale, he advocated *Gebrauchsmusik* ("useful music"), and wrote solo sonatas and concertos for many neglected instruments. *Mathis der Maler* (1935) is the best known of his six operas; the symphony based on it is widely performed. His comprehensive tonal theories resulted in his rewriting (but not necessarily improving) many of his earlier compositions.

Hindenburg, Paul (Ludwig Hans Anton von Beneckendorff und) von (1847–1934) German field marshal and second president (1925–34) of the WEIMAR REPUBLIC. He retired from the Prussian army as a general in 1911. Recalled to duty in World War I, he became a national hero after the Battle of Tannenberg (1914). With Erich LUDENDORFF as his chief aide, he thenceforth nominally commanded all German forces, then retired again in 1919. Supported by conservative groups, he was elected president of Germany in 1925. When the GREAT DEPRESSION led to a political crisis, he was pressured to make the government more independent of parliamentary controls. In 1930 he allowed Chancellor Heinrich BRÜNING to dissolve the Reichstag. In 1932 he was reelected by opponents of the Nazis; however, in 1933 he was persuaded to appoint Adolf HITLER chancellor.

Hindenburg **disaster** Explosion of the dirigible *Hindenburg*, the largest rigid AIRSHIP ever constructed. Launched in 1936 in Germany, it started the first commercial air service across the N. Atlantic and made 10 successful round trips. On May 6, 1937, as it was landing in Lakehurst, N.J., its hydrogen gas burst into flames, destroying the airship and killing 36 of the 97 persons aboard. The disaster effectively ended the use of airships in commercial transportation.

Hindenburg in flames at Lakehurst, N.J., May 6, 1937

Hindi language INDO-ARYAN LANGUAGE of India, spoken or understood by more than 30% of the country's population. Modern Standard Hindi is a LINGUA FRANCA (as well as native language) of millions of people in N. India and the official language of the Indian Union. It developed from Hindustani, which in turn developed from Khari Boli, the speech of the Mughal court in the 16th–18th cent. A heavily Persianized variant of Khari Boli used by Muslim au-

thors formed the basis for URDU. A Sanskritized form of Hindustani (see SANSKRIT LANGUAGE) written in the Devanagari script (see INDIC WRITING SYSTEMS) became the progenitor of modern literary Hindi. During the Indian independence movement, Hindustani was regarded as a national unifying factor, but after the partition in 1947 this attitude changed, and the name has been replaced by either Hindi or Urdu. Linguists have also used the term Hindi to refer collectively to all the dialects and regional literary languages of the N Indian plain (see INDO-ARYAN LANGUAGES).

Hindu-Arabic numerals Set of 10 symbols—1, 2, 3, 4, 5, 6, 7, 8, 9, 0—that represent numbers in the decimal NUMBER SYSTEM. They originated in India in the 6th or 7th cent. and were introduced to Europe through Arab mathematicians around the 12th cent. (see AL-KHWARIZMI). They represented a profound break with previous methods of counting, such as the ABACUS, and paved the way for the development of ALGEBRA.

Hinduism Oldest of the world's major religions, with some 750 million adherents worldwide. It evolved from the VEDIC RELIGION of ancient India. Though each of the various Hindu sects relies on its own set of scriptures, all revere the ancient VEDAS. The philosophical Vedic UPANISHADS explored the search for a means to escape the cycle of REINCARNATION. Fundamental to Hinduism is the belief in a cosmic principle of ultimate reality called BRAHMAN, and its identity with the individual soul, or ATMAN. All creatures go through a cycle of rebirth (SAMSARA) that can only be broken by spiritual self-realization. The principle of KARMA determines a being's status within the cycle of rebirth. The greatest Hindu deities are BRAHMA, VISHNU, and SHIVA; the numerous other gods are mostly viewed as incarnations of the main deities. The major sources of classical mythology are the *MAHABHARATA* (which includes the BHAGAVAD-GITA, the most important religious text of Hinduism), the *RAMAYANA*, and the PURANAS. The important CASTE system is supported by the principle of DHARMA. The major branches of Hinduism are VAISHNAVISM and SHAIVISM. In the 20th cent. Hindu nationalism in India became a potent political force.

Major Hindu Holidays

Date	Name	Significance
Caitra (Mar.–Apr.) Shukla ("waxing fortnight") 9	Ramanavami ("ninth of Rama")	celebrates the birth of Rama
Asadha (June–July) Sh. 2	Rathayatra ("pilgrimage of the chariot")	famous Jagannatha festival of the temple complex at Puri, Orissa
Shravana (July–Aug.) Krsna ("waning fortnight") 8	Janmastami ("eighth day of the birth")	birthday of the god Krishna
Bhadrapada (Aug.–Sept.) Sh. 4	Ganeshacaturthi ("fourth of Ganesha")	honors Ganesha, a particular favorite in Maharashtra
Ashvina (Sept.–Oct.) Sh. 7-10	Durga-puja ("homage to Durga")	special to Bengal, in honor of the goddess Durga
Ashvina Sh. 7-10	Dashahra ("ten days"), or Dussera	celebrating Rama's victory over Ravana; traditional beginning of the warring season
Ashvina Sh. 15	Lakshmipuja ("homage to Lakshmi")	date on which commercial books are closed, and new annual records begun
Karttika (Oct.–Nov.) K. 15 and Sh. 1	Dipavali, Divali ("strings of lights")	festival of lights, when light is carried from the waning to the waxing fortnight
Margashirsa (Nov.–Dec.) K. 13	Maha-shivaratri ("great night of Shiva")	honors Shiva on the blackest night of the month
Pausa (Dec.–Jan.) Sh. 15	Guru Nanak Jayanti	birthday of Nanak, founder of Sikhism
Phalguna (Feb.–Mar.) Sh. 14	Holi (name of a demoness)	fertility and role-changing festival, scene of great teasing of superiors
Phalguna Sh. 15	Dolayatra ("swing festival")	scene of the famous hook-swinging rites of Orissa

Hindu Kush \'hin-dü-'kùsh\ *Latin* Caucasus Indicus. Mountain system, Central Asia. Some 600 mi (950 km) long, it runs from the PAMIRS in the east near the Pakistan–China border through Pakistan to W Afghanistan. Its passes have historically been of great military significance, providing access to the N plains of India. It includes about two dozen summits of more than 23,000 ft (7,000 m), including Tirich Mir, at 25,260 ft (7,699 m).

Hine, Lewis (Wickes) (1874–1940) U.S. photographer. Born in Oshkosh, Wis., he was trained as a sociologist. In 1904 he began to photograph immigrants at ELLIS ISLAND and the tenements and sweatshops where they lived and worked. In 1911 he was hired by the National Child Labor Committee to record child labor conditions, and produced appalling pictures of exploited children. In World War I he worked as a photographer with the Red Cross. On returning to New York, he photographed the construction of the EMPIRE STATE BUILDING.

Hines, Earl (Kenneth) (1903–1983) U.S. pianist and bandleader. Born in Duquesne, Pa., "Fatha" Hines became a pianist of amazing technical command and tireless energy. Breaking with the stride tradition, he emulated the single-note instruments (e.g., trumpet) in creating melodic variations of the melody with the right hand. Hines led a successful Chicago-based big band from 1928 to 1948. He and Louis ARMSTRONG performed together frequently; their recordings from the late 1920s, particularly "Weather Bird," are jazz classics.

hip-hop Cultural movement that became popular in the 1980s and '90s. Although widely considered a synonym for RAP music, the term also embraces such elements as "deejaying" or "turntabling," graffiti painting, and "B-boying," which includes hip-hop dance, style, and attitude. Emerging from New York's inner city in the late 1970s, graffiti and break dancing were the aspects that first caught public attention. By the late 1990s hip-hop was the best-selling genre of popular music in the U.S. and worldwide; fashions associated with hip-hop also generated huge sales.

Hipparchus *or* **Hipparchos** \hi-'pär-kəs\ (d. after 127 B.C.) Greek astronomer and mathematician. He discovered the precession of the EQUINOXES, calculated the year to within 6.5 minutes, and framed an early form of trigonometry. His observations were painstaking and extremely accurate. He rejected astrology but also a sun-centered universe; his views greatly influenced PTOLEMY. His star catalog, the first known, used celestial coordinates to give the positions and a system of magnitudes to specify the brightnesses of about 850 stars. He showed that the moon has an irregular elliptical orbit. He applied rigorous mathematical principles to determine geographical locations and was the first to use latitude and longitude to do so.

Hippocrates \hi-'pä-krə-ˌtēz\ (460?–377? B.C.) Greek physician regarded as the father of MEDICINE. His philosophy was to see the body as a whole. He apparently traveled widely in Greece and Asia Minor, practicing and teaching. The "Hippocratic Collection" supposedly belonged to the library of a medical school (probably at Cos, his birthplace) and then to the library at Alexandria. An unknown proportion of the 60 or so surviving manuscripts—the earliest dating from the 10th cent. A.D.—are actually by Hippocrates. The collection deals with anatomy, clinical subjects, diseases of women and children, prognosis, treatment, surgery, and medical ethics. The Hippocratic Oath (not actually written by Hippocrates), also part of the collection, sets out the physician's obligations to his students and their duties to him, and pledges him to prescribe only beneficial treatments, refrain from causing harm, and live an exemplary life.

hippopotamus Amphibious African mammal (*Hippopotamus amphibius*), the largest nonruminating, even-toed UNGULATE. Once found throughout sub-Saharan Africa, it is now restricted to parts of E and SE Africa. It has a barrel-shaped body, an enormous mouth, short legs, and four toes on each foot. It may reach a length of 15 ft (4.6 m), a height of 5 ft (1.5 m) at the shoulder, and a weight of 6,500–10,000 (3,000–4,500 kg). The ears and nostrils protrude above water when the rest of the body is submerged. Hippopotamuses live near bodies of water, usually in groups of seven to 15. During the day, they sleep in or near the water. At night they go on land to feed on grasses. In water they can swim fast, walk along the bottom, and remain submerged for as long as 10 minutes.

Hirohito \ˌhir-ō-'hē-tō\ *or* **Showa emperor** \'shō-ə\ (1901–1989) Longest-reigning of Japan's monarchs (1926–89). His rule, the SHOWA PERIOD, coincided with Japan's 20th-cent. militarism and its aggression against China and S.E. Asia and in the Pacific Ocean during World War II. Though the MEIJI CONSTITUTION invested the emperor with supreme authority, in practice he merely ratified the policies formulated by his ministers. Historians debate whether Hirohito could have diverted Japan from its militaristic path and what responsibility he should bear for its actions during the war. In 1946 he repudiated the traditional quasidivine status of Japan's emperors (see OCCUPATION).

Hiroshige Ando \ˌhir-ə-'shē-gä-'än-dō\ *orig.* Ando Tokutaro (1797–1858) Japanese artist and master of the color woodblock print. He became a pupil of the UKIYO-E master Utagawa Toyohiro about 1811. In 1833–34 a series of 55 landscape prints, *Fifty-three Stages on the Tokaido,* established him as one of the most popular *ukiyo-e* artists of all time. He produced more than 5,000 prints, and 10,000 copies were made from some of his woodcuts. His genius was first recognized in the West by the Impressionists and Postimpressionists, on whom he exerted much influence.

Hiroshima \hə-'rō-shə-mə, ˌhir-ə-'shē-mə\ City (pop., 1996 est.: 1,109,000), SW HONSHU, Japan. Founded as a castle town in the 16th cent., it was from 1868 a military center. In 1945 it became the first city ever to be struck by an ATOMIC BOMB, dropped by the U.S. in an effort to end World War II. Some 90% of the city was destroyed, and some 70–80,000 people are thought to have died. Hiroshima is now the largest industrial city in the region. It has become a spiritual center of the peace movement to ban atomic weapons; Peace Memorial Park is dedicated to those killed by the bomb.

Hirschfeld, Al(bert) (1903–2003) U.S. caricaturist. Born in St. Louis, he studied art in Europe. He is especially known for his stylish drawings, influenced by Japanese and Javanese art, in the *New York Times* over many decades (since 1929) portraying show-business personalities, in which readers have long enjoyed hunting for the name of his daughter, Nina. He also illustrated many books and produced watercolors, lithographs, etchings, and sculptures.

His \'his\, **Wilhelm** (1863–1934) Swiss cardiologist. His father, Wilhelm His (1831–1904), first realized that each nerve fiber stems from a single neuron, and invented the microtome. The younger His discovered (1893) the specialized muscle fibers (bundle of His) along the septum between the HEART's left and right chambers. He found that they help communicate a single rhythm of contraction throughout the heart, and recognized that the heartbeat originates in individual cells of heart muscle.

Hispaniola \ˌhis-pən-'yō-lə\ *Spanish* **Española** \ˌes-pä-'nyō-lä\ Island, central W. Indies, east of Cuba. It is divided into Haiti and the Dominican Republic. The island is some 400 mi (650 km) long and 150 mi (241 km) wide at its widest point. Christopher COLUMBUS landed there in 1492. The Spanish wiped out the natives and settled the island with African slaves. The slaves rebelled in the late 18th cent.; they won independence in 1804, forming the Republic of Haiti. In 1843 the E part rebelled and the Dominican Republic was formed.

Hiss, Alger (1904–1996) U.S. government official. Born in Baltimore, he worked at the U.S. State Department in the 1930s, attended the Yalta Conference as an adviser to Franklin Roosevelt, was briefly temporary secretary general of the fledgling U.N., and served as head of the Carnegie Endowment for International Peace 1946–49. In 1948 Whittaker CHAMBERS testified before the House Committee on Un-American Activities that Hiss had been a fellow member of a Communist spy ring in the 1930s. Hiss sued Chambers for slander. When Chambers produced State Department documents that Hiss had allegedly given him to pass to the Soviets, Hiss was indicted for perjury. His first trial ended with a hung jury in 1949; at his second trial (1950) he was found guilty. He was released from jail in 1954, still protesting his innocence. The Hiss case ushered in the Joseph MCCARTHY era and brought Richard NIXON fame as a congressional investigator.

HIJ

histamine \'his-tə-ˌmēn\ ORGANIC COMPOUND found in nearly all animal tissues, in microorganisms, and in some plants. Its release makes blood vessels dilate and become more permeable, causing the runny nose, watery eyes, and tissue swelling of HAY FEVER and some other ALLERGIES; histamine also affects gastric juice secretion and smooth muscle contraction and is implicated in anaphylactic shock (see ANAPHYLAXIS). Stinging nettles and certain insect VENOMS contain histamine. Its effects are counteracted by ANTIHISTAMINES.

histogram or **bar graph** GRAPH using vertical or horizontal bars whose lengths indicate quantities, frequently used to represent statistical data. It clearly shows the largest and smallest categories and gives an immediate impression of the distribution of the data. See also FREQUENCY DISTRIBUTION.

histology \his-'tä-lə-jē\ Branch of biology concerned with the composition and structure of plant and animal tissues in relation to their specialized functions. Its aim is to determine how tissues are organized at all structural levels, from CELLS and intercellular substances to organs. Histologists examine extremely thin slices of tissue under microscopes, using dye to increase the contrast between cellular components.

historiography \hi-ˌstōr-ē-'ä-grə-fē\ Writing of history, especially that based on the critical examination of sources and the synthesis of chosen particulars into an authoritative narrative. Two major tendencies are evident from the beginnings of the Western tradition: the concept of historiography as the accumulation of records and the concept of history as storytelling, filled with explanations of cause and effect. In the 5th cent. B.C. the Greek historians HERODOTUS and, later, THUCYDIDES emphasized firsthand inquiry in their efforts to impose a narrative on contemporary events. Christian historiography, which dominated the Western world by the 4th cent., introduced the idea of world history as a result of divine intervention in human affairs, an idea that prevailed throughout the Middle Ages. HUMANISM and the gradual secularization of critical thought influenced early modern European historiography. The 19th and 20th cent. saw the development of modern methods of historical investigation of scientific history based on the use of primary source materials. Modern historians often attempt to reconstruct a record of ordinary human activities and practices.

Hitchcock, Alfred (later **Sir Alfred**) (1899–1980) British-U.S. film director. He worked in the London office of a U.S. film company from 1920. His film The Lodger (1926) concerned an ordinary person caught in extraordinary events, a theme that was to recur in many of his films. He proved himself the master of the thriller with The Man Who Knew Too Much (1934), The 39 Steps (1935), and The Lady Vanishes (1938). For his first U.S. film, Rebecca (1940), he created a suspenseful psychological drama out of a romantic novel, and his virtuosity was evident in such celebrated later films as Spellbound (1945), Notorious (1946), Rear Window (1954), Vertigo (1958), North by Northwest (1959), Psycho (1960), and The Birds (1963).

Hitchings, George H(erbert) (1905–1998) U.S. pharmacologist. Born in Hoquiam, Wash. Over nearly 40 years, he and Gertrude ELION designed a variety of new drugs that work by interfering with replication or other vital functions of specific disease-causing agents, including drugs to treat leukemia, severe rheumatoid arthritis and other autoimmune diseases, gout, malaria, urinary and respiratory-tract infections, and herpes simplex. In 1988 he shared a Nobel Prize with Elion and Sir James Black (b.1924).

Hitler, Adolf (1889–1945) Dictator of Nazi Germany (1933–45). Born in Austria, he worked as an artist before moving to Munich in 1913 and fought with the German army in World War I. Resentful about defeat and the peace terms, he joined the German Workers' Party. In 1920 he became head of propaganda for the renamed NAZI PARTY, and in 1921 party leader. After leading the failed BEER HALL PUTSCH (1923), he served nine months in prison; there he started his virulent autobiography, Mein Kampf, exalting the "Aryan race" while propounding anti-Semitism, anti-communism, and extreme German nationalism. The economic slump of 1929 renewed his power. In the Reichstag elections of 1932 the Nazis became the country's largest party; Hitler failed to win the presidency, but in 1933 Paul von HINDENBURG invited him to be chancellor. Adopting the title of Führer ("Leader"), he gained dictatorial powers and suppressed opposition with assistance from Heinrich HIMMLER and Joseph GOEBBELS. His anti-Jewish measures foreshadowed the HOLOCAUST. His aggressive foreign policy led to the signing of the MUNICH AGREEMENT. He became allied with Benito MUSSOLINI in the Rome–Berlin Axis. The GERMAN–SOVIET NON-AGGRESSION PACT (1939) enabled him to invade Poland, precipitating WORLD WAR II. After early successes in the war, he often ignored his generals and met dissent with ruthlessness. As defeat grew imminent in 1945, he married Eva BRAUN in an underground bunker in Berlin, and the next day they committed suicide.

Adolf Hitler reviewing troops, 1939

Hitler–Stalin Pact See GERMAN–SOVIET NONAGGRESSION PACT

Hitler Youth German **Hitler-Jugend** \ˌyü-gent\ Organization set up by Adolf HITLER in 1933 for educating and training male youths aged 13–18 in Nazi principles. Under Baldur von Schirach (1907–1974), by 1936 it became a state agency that all young "Aryan" Germans were expected to join. They lived a spartan life of dedication, fellowship, and Nazi conformity, with little parental guidance. The parallel League of German Girls trained girls for domestic duties and motherhood.

Hittite \'hi-ˌtīt\ Indo-European people whose empire (Old Kingdom c.1700–1500 B.C., New Empire c.1500–1380 B.C.) was centered in Anatolia and N Syria. Hittite kings had absolute power and were deputies of the gods, at death becoming gods themselves. Hittite society was feudal and agrarian; iron-working technology was developed. The empire fell abruptly, possibly because of large-scale migrations of SEA PEOPLES and Phrygians to the area.

HIV in full **human immunodeficiency virus** RETROVIRUS associated with AIDS. HIV attacks and gradually destroys the IMMUNE SYSTEM. It is contracted mainly through exposure to blood and blood products (e.g., by sharing hypodermic needles or by accidental needle sticks), semen and female genital secretions, or breast milk. Fetuses can receive the virus across the placenta. The virus first multiplies in lymph nodes near the site of infection. Once it spreads through the body, usually about 10 years later, symptoms appear, marking the onset of AIDS. Multi-drug "cocktails" can delay onset, but missing doses can lead to DRUG RESISTANCE. A rapid MUTATION rate helps HIV foil both the immune system and treatment attempts. No vaccine or cure exists. Abstinence from sex, use of condoms or other means to prevent sexual transmittal of the disease, and avoidance of needle sharing have reduced infection rates in some areas.

hives or **urticaria** \ˌərt-ə-'kar-ē-ə\ Allergic skin reaction in which slightly raised, flat-topped, very itchy swellings appear suddenly. The acute form, most often caused by food ALLERGIES, lasts 6–24 hours, but the chronic form, possibly caused by autoimmune reactions and exacerbated by stress, lasts much longer. Acute hives may also be triggered by drugs, especially PENICILLIN. EPINEPHRINE and ANTIHISTAMINES may help the acute skin symptoms.

Hizbullah or **Hezbollah** \ˌhiz-bùl-'lä\ (Arabic: "Party of God") Militant Islamist organization founded in 1982 in S

Lebanon in response to the Israeli invasion and the Iranian Revolution (1979). Its goal is to form an Iranian-style Shiite Islamic republic in Lebanon. Its political stance is anti-West, and it is suspected of involvement in many of the terrorist activities of the 1980s in Lebanon, including kidnappings, bombings, and hijackings. In the 1990s Hizbullah candidates won seats in Lebanon's parliamentary elections. Increasingly anti-Semitic and international in reach, it has carried out bombings in S. America and elsewhere.

HMO See HEALTH MAINTENANCE ORGANIZATION

Hmong \'hmȯŋ\ or **Miao** \mē-'au̇\ Mountain-dwelling peoples of China, Vietnam, Laos, and Thailand who speak Sino-Tibetan dialects. Agriculture is the chief means of subsistence; they grow corn and rice and raise opium as a cash crop. Most venerate spirits, demons, and ancestral ghosts, and animal sacrifice is widespread. Households are multigenerational. The total Hmong population is about 5 million.

Hmong-Mien languages \'mȯŋ-'myen\ or **Miao-Yao languages** \mē-'au̇-'yau̇\ Language family of S China, N Vietnam, Laos, and N Thailand, with more than 9 million speakers. Hmong (Miao, Meo) has been divided into three dialect groups, Western, Central, and Northern. Beginning in the 18th cent., groups of Western dialect speakers emigrated into N Indochina. Though structurally similar to other languages of the area, most notably CHINESE, no genetic relationship between Hmong-Mien and any other language family has been demonstrated.

Hobart City (pop., 1998: 195,000), chief port, and capital, TASMANIA, Australia. Located at the base of Mt. Wellington, it is Tasmania's largest and Australia's most southerly city. Established in 1803, it became a major port for ships whaling in the S oceans. The city is the site of the first Jewish synagogue in Australia (built 1843–45).

Hobbema \'hä-bə-mə\, **Meindert** orig. Meyndert Lubbertsz(oon) (1638–1709) Dutch landscape painter. He worked principally in Amsterdam, painting quiet rural scenes studded with trees, rustic buildings, peaceful streams, and water mills. In 1689 he produced his masterpiece, *The Avenue, Middelharnis*. His work became popular and influential in England in the 19th cent.

Hobbes \'häbz\, **Thomas** (1588–1679) British philosopher and political theorist. He graduated from Oxford Univ., then became a tutor and traveled with his pupil in Europe, where he engaged GALILEO in philosophical discussions on the nature of motion. He later turned to political theory and wrote out his support for ABSOLUTISM, which put him at odds with the rising antiroyalist sentiment of the time. He fled to Paris in 1640, where he tutored the future CHARLES II of England and wrote his best-known work, *Leviathan* (1651), in which he reasserted his absolutist position, argued against separation of church and state, and conceived his theory of the SOCIAL CONTRACT. He returned to Britain in 1651 after the death of CHARLES I. He is regarded as a pioneer of UTILITARIANISM, modern POLITICAL SCIENCE, and RATIONALISM.

Hobby, Oveta Culp orig. Oveta Culp (1905–1995) U.S. publisher and government official. Born in Killeen, Texas, she married William P. Hobby, publisher of the *Houston Post-Dispatch*, and became its executive vice president (1938). She headed the Women's Auxiliary Army Corps (later WOMEN'S ARMY CORPS) 1942–45. She served as secretary (1953–55) of the new Department of Health, Education, and Welfare, the second woman to hold a U.S. cabinet position. She became chairman of the *Post*'s board in 1965.

Ho Chi Minh orig. Nguyen Sinh Cung (1890–1969) President (1945–69) of the Democratic Republic of Vietnam (N. Vietnam). Son of a poor scholar, in 1911 he found work on a French steamer

Ho Chi Minh, 1968

and traveled the world, then spent six years in France, where he became a communist (1920). He went to the Soviet Union (1923), and to China, where he organized exiled Vietnamese nationalists in Canton (1924–27). He founded the Indochina Communist Party in 1930 and its successor, the VIET MINH, in 1941. When the occupying Japanese surrendered to the Allies in 1945, Ho and his Viet Minh forces took Hanoi and proclaimed Vietnamese independence. France refused to relinquish its former colony, and the First INDOCHINA WAR broke out in 1946. Ho's forces defeated the French in 1954 at the Battle of DIEN BIEN PHU, after which the country was partitioned into N. and S. Vietnam. Ho, who ruled in the north, was soon embroiled in the VIETNAM WAR.

Ho Chi Minh City formerly **Saigon** \'sī-,gän\ City (pop., 1992 est.: 3,016,000), S Vietnam. It lies along the Saigon River north of the MEKONG RIVER delta. The Vietnamese first entered the region in the 17th cent. In 1862 the area was ceded to France. After the First INDOCHINA WAR, the Geneva conference in 1954 divided the country, and Saigon became the capital of S. Vietnam. In the VIETNAM WAR, it was the headquarters for U.S. military operations; captured by N. Vietnamese troops in 1975, it was renamed for HO CHI MINH. It remains the largest, richest, and most dynamic city in Vietnam.

Ho Chi Minh Trail Former trail system, extending from N Vietnam to S Vietnam. It was opened in 1959 and used by N. Vietnamese troops in the VIETNAM WAR as the major military supply route. Starting south of HANOI, the main trail traversed Laos and Cambodia and required more than a month's march to travel. With underground support facilities, including hospitals and weapons caches, it was the main route for the invasion of S. Vietnam in 1975.

Hockney, David (b.1937) British painter, printmaker, photographer, and stage designer. He studied art in London, and in the mid-1960s taught at several U.S. universities. In 1978 he settled in Los Angeles. His portraits, still lifes, and quiet scenes of friends are characterized by a frank, mundane realism and brilliant colors derived from Pop art. The California swimming pool became a favorite theme, as in *A Bigger Splash* (1967). A brilliant printmaker, he published series of etchings, including illustrations for *Six Fairy Tales of the Brothers Grimm* (1969). In the 1970s he achieved prominence as a set designer for the opera and ballet. He later experimented with photography and photocollage.

Hodgkin, Dorothy M(ary) orig. Dorothy Mary Crowfoot (1910–1994) English chemist. From 1942 to 1949 she worked on a structural analysis of penicillin. In 1948 she and her colleagues made the first X-ray photograph of vitamin B_{12}, one of the most complex nonprotein compounds, and they eventually completely determined its atomic arrangement. In 1969 she completed a similar three-dimensional analysis of insulin. Her work won her a 1964 Nobel Prize. She was known for her work for peace and international scientific cooperation. In 1965 she became the second woman ever awarded the Order of Merit.

Hodgkin's disease or **lymphoreticuloma** \,lim-fō-ri-,tik-yə-'lō-mə\ Most common LYMPHOMA. It starts with local, painless swelling of LYMPH NODES and sometimes of the spleen, liver, or other organs, followed by weight loss, weakness, and lassitude. Diagnosis is confirmed by biopsy. The cause remains unknown. Treatment with chemotherapy, radiation, or both depends on the stage of the disease; more than 90% of patients diagnosed early can be cured.

Hoe, Robert and Richard (March) (1784–1833, 1812–1886) British-U.S. inventors. Father and son, they were born respectively in Hoes, Leicestershire (England), and New York City. In New York Robert cofounded a printing-equipment company, and in 1827 he introduced the cast-iron frame, which would soon replace the standard wooden frames used for printing presses. His improved version of the Napier cylinder PRINTING press supplanted all English-made presses in the U.S. Richard replaced the flatbed press with the first successful ROTARY PRESS (patented 1847). He followed this with the web press (1865) and the web perfecting press (1871), revolutionary improvements that made possible the large-circulation daily newspaper.

HIJ

Hoff, Jacobus van't See Jacobus VAN'T HOFF

Hoffa, Jimmy (*orig.* James Riddle) (1913–1975?) U.S. labor leader. Born in Brazil, Ind., he moved with his family to Detroit in 1924 and left school at 14. He became a labor organizer in the 1930s, and rose in the TEAMSTERS UNION to hold the office of president 1957–71. A tough bargainer, he played a key role in forging the first national freight-hauling agreement and helped make the Teamsters the largest labor union in the U.S. Long associated with underworld figures, he was sent to prison in 1967 for jury tampering, fraud, and conspiracy; his sentence was commuted by Pres. Richard NIXON in 1971. In 1975 he disappeared from a restaurant near Detroit; he is believed to have been murdered to prevent his retaking control of the union. His son, James Riddle Hoffa, Jr. (b.1941), was elected president of the Teamsters in 1999.

Hoffman, Abbie (*orig.* Abbott) (1936–1989) U.S. political radical. Born in Worcester, Mass., he became active in the civil rights movement, and in 1968 organized the anarchic Youth International Party (Yippies), which protested the Vietnam War. Arrested for disrupting the Democratic Party convention in Chicago in 1968, he gained widespread media attention for his antics at the trial of the so-called Chicago Seven. Arrested for selling drugs (1973), he went underground, underwent plastic surgery, and worked as an environmentalist in New York under an alias. He resurfaced in 1980 and served a year in jail. Subject to depression, he committed suicide.

Hoffman, Dustin (b.1937) U.S. actor. Born in Los Angeles, he made his screen debut in *The Graduate* (1967), a phenomenal hit. He played a remarkable range of characters in such films as *Midnight Cowboy* (1969), *Little Big Man* (1970), *All the President's Men* (1976), *Kramer vs. Kramer* (1979, Academy Award), *Tootsie* (1982), *Rain Man* (1988, Academy Award), and *Wag the Dog* (1997). He returned to Broadway in *Death of a Salesman* (1984), repeating the role for television (1985, Emmy award).

Hoffmann \\'hȯf-män\\, **E(rnst) T(heodor) A(madeus)** (*orig.* Ernst Theodor Wilhelm) (1776–1822) German writer and composer, a major figure of German ROMANTICISM. His story collection *Fantasy Pieces in the Style of Callot* (1814–15) established his reputation as a writer. His later popular collections *Hoffmann's Strange Stories* (1817) and *The Serapion Brethren* (1819–21) combine wild flights of imagination with vivid examinations of human character. He also worked as a conductor, music critic, and theatrical musical director. His original musical works include the ballet *Arlequin* (1811) and the opera *Undine* (performed 1816). His often outlandish stories inspired notable operas and ballets by Jacques OFFENBACH *(Tales of Hoffmann)*, Leo DELIBES *(Coppélia)*, and P. I. TCHAIKOVSKY *(The Nutcracker)*.

Hoffmann \\'hȯf-män\\, **Josef** (1870–1956) Austrian architect and designer. He studied under Otto WAGNER, but in 1899 he helped found the Vienna SEZESSION, which broke free of Wagner's classicism. He cofounded, and for 30 years (1903–33) directed, the Wiener Werkstätte (Vienna Workshop), an important center for arts and crafts. His opulent Stoclet House (1905) in Brussels is considered his masterpiece; the exterior achieved an elegance not often associated with design based on straight lines and white squares and rectangles. He designed the Austrian pavilions for the 1914 Deutscher Werkbund Exhibition and the 1934 Venice Biennale. In 1920 he was appointed city architect of Vienna.

Hofmann, Hans (1880–1966) German-U.S. painter and art teacher. He studied art in Munich, and in 1904 he moved to Paris, where he was inspired by the work of Henri MATISSE and Robert DELAUNAY. In 1915 he opened his first school of painting in Munich. He moved to New York in 1930 and soon opened the Hans Hofmann School of Fine Art (1933–58), where he would exert strong influence on young abstract painters, including Willem DE KOONING and Jackson POLLOCK. His style evolved into total abstraction, and he pioneered the paint-dripping technique later associated with Pollock. He was one of the most influential art teachers of the 20th cent. and a significant figure in the development of ABSTRACT EXPRESSIONISM.

Hofmannsthal \\'hȯf-mäns-,täl\\, **Hugo von** (1874–1929) Austrian poet, dramatist, and essayist. He made his reputation with lyric poems and verse plays, including *The Death of Titian* (1892) and *Death and the Fool* (1893). He renounced lyrical poetry in a 1902 essay and thereafter turned to theater; his later plays include *Christina's Journey Home* (1910), *Everyman* (1911), and *The Tower* (1925). In 1906 he began a celebrated collaboration with the composer Richard STRAUSS; their remarkable first opera, *Elektra* (1908), was followed by *Der Rosenkavalier* (1910), *Ariadne auf Naxos* (1912), *Die Frau ohne Schatten* (1919), and four others. In 1920 he cofounded the Salzburg Festival with Max REINHARDT.

Hogan, Ben (*orig.* William Benjamin) (1912–1997) U.S. golfer. Born in Dublin, Texas, he won the U.S. PGA championship (1946, 1948), the U.S. Open (1948, 1950, 1951, 1953), the Masters Tournament (1951, 1953), and the British Open (1953), despite severe injuries suffered in a 1949 car accident. Known for his demanding practice regimen, singleminded determination, and extraordinary accuracy, he won 63 championships in his career.

Hogarth, William (1697–1764) British painter and engraver. He opened his own engraving and printing shop at 22. His first major work, *Masquerades and Operas*, attacking contemporary taste and questioning the art establishment, won him many enemies. In 1728 he embarked on a painting career with *A Scene from "The Beggar's Opera,"* revealing his interest in theater and comic subject matter. He also painted informal group portraits for wealthy clients. His engravings of modern morality subjects, often in sequential sets, were aimed at a wide public, and their outstanding success established his financial independence. He fought for leg-

William Hogarth, self-portrait, "The Painter and His Pug," 1745

islation protecting artists' copyright, and Britain's first copyright act was passed in 1735. His satirical series include *A Harlot's Progress* (1730–31), *The Rake's Progress* (1735), and *Marriage à la Mode* (1743–45). The teaching academy he established led to the founding of the Royal Academy (1768).

hog cholera *or* **swine fever** Often fatal viral disease of swine in Europe, N. America, and Africa, transmitted by vehicles used to carry pigs, people dealing with them, and uncooked garbage in feed. Fever progresses to symptoms that include appetite loss, respiratory difficulty, rash, and inflamed mouth and throat. The pig moves reluctantly and staggers; later it cannot rise; coma follows. Survivors become chronically ill and can spread the virus. Illness must be reported, infected animals slaughtered, and quarantine instituted. A vaccine can control it.

Hogg, James (1770–1835) Scottish poet. A shepherd, he was almost entirely self-educated. Hogg's talent as a balladeer was discovered by Walter SCOTT. His popularity accompanied the ballad revival of the early Romantic movement. His most significant work was *The Private Memoirs and Confessions of a Justified Sinner* (1824), a novel about religious mania with a psychopathic hero that anticipates the modern psychological thriller.

hognose snake Any of three or four species (genus *Heterodon*, family Colubridae) of harmless N. American snakes named for their upturned snout, which is used for digging. When threatened, they flatten the head and neck, then strike with a loud hiss, but rarely bite. If their bluff fails, they roll over, writhing, and then act dead, with mouth open and tongue lolling. Heavy-bodied and blotchy, they are usually about 24 in. (60 cm) long.

Hohenstaufen dynasty \\,hō-ən-'shtaü-fən\\ German dynasty that ruled the Holy Roman Empire (1138–1208, 1212–54). It was founded by Count Frederick (d.1105), who built Staufen Castle and was appointed duke of Swabia as Frederick I (1079). Hohenstaufen emperors included FREDER-

ICK I Barbarossa (r.1155–90), Henry VI (r.1191–97), and FREDERICK II (r.1220–50). The dynasty continued the struggle with the papacy begun under their predecessors (see GUELPHS AND GHIBELLINES).

Hohenzollern dynasty \ˌhō-ənt-ˈsó-lərn\ Dynasty prominent as the ruling house of Brandenburg-Prussia (1415–1918) and of imperial Germany (1871–1918). The first recorded ancestor, Burchard I, was count of Zollern in the 11th cent. The Franconian branch included electors of Brandenburg (see FREDERICK WILLIAM), kings of Prussia (see FREDERICK WILLIAM I, FREDERICK II the Great, FREDERICK WILLIAM II, and FREDERICK WILLIAM III), and German emperors (see WILLIAM I, WILLIAM II); the Swabian branch included princes and then kings of Romania.

Hohhot \ˈhə-ˈhót\ or **Hu-ho-hao-t'e** \ˈhü-ˈhə-ˈhaù-ˈtä\ or **Huhehot** \ˈhü-ˌhə-ˈhót\ Mongol **Kukukhoto** \ˌkü-kü-ˈḵō-tō\ City (pop., 1999 est.: 754,000), capital of Nei Monggol, N China. The original Mongol city was a religious center for Tibetan Buddhism (Lamaism) and later a Muslim trading community. After World War II it developed into an industrial and cultural center. Its university (1957) was the first in Nei Monggol.

Hohokam culture \ˈhō-hō-ˌkäm\ Culture of a group of N. American Indian peoples who lived around 300 B.C.–A.D. 1400 in the Sonoran Desert (Arizona), especially along the Gila and Salt rivers. The Hohokam Indians developed complex networks of canals for irrigation, an agricultural-engineering feat unsurpassed in pre-Columbian N. America. For unknown reasons, Hohokam culture disintegrated in the early 15th cent.

Hojo family Family of hereditary regents to the KAMAKURA SHOGUNATE of Japan who exercised actual power 1199–1333. Hojo Tokimasa (1138–1215) joined the cause of MINAMOTO YORITOMO, who defeated Taira Kiyomori to become Japan's new ruler in 1192, taking the title of SHOGUN. Tokimasa's daughter married Yoritomo, who died in 1199, and Tokimasa became regent to Yoritomo's heir, his own grandson. The position of shogunal regent became hereditary; it oversaw the constables and tax collectors that the shogunate placed in each province. The system worked well until the late 13th cent.; its decline was caused by the high cost of defending Japan against two Mongol invasions and the personal failings of the last Hojo regent. Hojo rule ended when Ashikaga Takauji (see ASHIKAGA FAMILY) captured Kyoto and assumed the title of shogun.

Hokan languages \ˈhō-kən\ Hypothetical superfamily of N. American Indian languages uniting a number of languages and language families of the W U.S. and Mexico. The Hokan hypothesis was first proposed in 1913; like PENUTIAN, it was an attempt to group a number of seemingly unrelated language families. Its core consisted of languages of aboriginal California and the Southwest, with others from Sonora and Oaxaca in Mexico. Most Hokan languages are now either extinct or spoken almost exclusively by older adults.

Hokkaido \hō-ˈkī-dō\ formerly **Yezo** \ˈye-zō\ Island (pop., 1999 est.: 5,694,000), N Japan. It has an area of 30,107 sq mi (77,978 sq km). Its administrative headquarters is SAPPORO. Its several high mountains include Asahi (7,513 ft, or 2,290 m). Long the domain of the aboriginal AINU, it attracted serious Japanese settlement beginning in 1869. It has a varied economy, supported by iron and steel, and the largest coal deposits in Japan. The Seikan Tunnel (1988) links it with HONSHU.

Hokusai \ˈhō-kù-ˌsī\ orig. Katsushika Hokusai (1760–1849) Japanese painter, printmaker, and book illustrator. He became a student of the leading UKIYO-E master, Katsukawa Shunsho, in 1778. His first published works, prints of kabuki actors (1779), were followed by historical and landscape subjects and prints of children. He achieved success with book illustrations and surimono prints ("printed things" for special occasions, such as cards and announcements), paintings, and ink sketches. He experimented with Western-style perspective and coloring and later concentrated on samurai themes and Chinese subjects. His Thirty-six Views of Mount Fuji (1826–33) were unsurpassed in concept and execution.

Holbein \ˈhōl-ˌbīn\, **Hans** German painters, father and son. Hans Holbein the Elder (c.1465–1524) was established as a painter in Augsburg by about 1493. He is best known for his large, multipaneled altarpieces, but some of his finest works are his insightful portraits, notably his silverpoint portrait drawings. Hans Holbein the Younger (1497/98–1543) trained with his father in Augsburg, moved to Basel (c.1515), and was executing important murals by 1521. He also designed book illustrations and woodcuts for publishers, notably a series of 49 scenes illustrating the medieval allegory of the Dance of Death (1523–26). His portraits, including that of Desiderius ERASMUS (1523), featured rich color, psychological depth, detailed accessories, and dramatic silhouette. In 1526 he went to England, and by 1533 he had entered the service of HENRY VIII. In his last 10 years he produced some 150 life-size and miniature portraits of the royalty and nobility. He was one of the greatest portraitists of all time.

Holberg \ˈhōl-berg\, **Ludvig** later Friherre (Baron) Holberg (1684–1754) Norwegian-Danish man of letters. Creator of a new class of humorous literature, his seriocomic epic Peder Paars (1719), a parody of VIRGIL's Aeneid, is the earliest classic of the Danish language. He produced a steady flow of stage comedies, including The Political Tinker (1723), The Weathercock (1723), Jeppe of the Hill (1723), and Erasmus Montanus (1731), many of which are still produced. His other works include the satirical novel The Journey of Niels Klim to the World Underground (1741). The outstanding Scandinavian literary figure of the ENLIGHTENMENT, he is claimed by both Norway and Denmark as a founder of their literatures.

Hölderlin \ˈhœl-dər-ˌlēn\, **(Johann Christian) Friedrich** (1770–1843) German poet. He produced works of passionate, expressive intensity, including his only novel, Hyperion (1797–99), and a number of odes, elegies, and verse translations. In these works he naturalized the forms of classical Greek verse in German and lamented the loss of an idealized classical Greek world. His behavior became erratic and in 1805 he succumbed irretrievably to schizophrenia. Little recognized in his lifetime, he later came to be ranked among the finest of German lyric poets.

holding company Corporation that owns enough voting STOCK in one or more other companies to exercise control over them. Compared with other means of gaining control, such as MERGERS or consolidations, holding companies are less complicated legally and less expensive. A holding company can reap the benefits of a subsidiary's goodwill and reputation while limiting its liability to the proportion of the subsidiary's stock that it owns. The parent company in a conglomerate corporation is usually a holding company.

Holiday, Billie orig. Eleanora Fagan (1915–1959) U.S. singer, one of the greatest interpreters of song in jazz. Born in Baltimore, Holiday was discovered singing in a Harlem nightclub in 1933. Recordings with Benny GOODMAN and Duke ELLINGTON led to a series of outstanding small-group records (1935–42) featuring such musicians as Lester YOUNG. Exposure with the big bands of Count BASIE (1937) and Artie Shaw (1938) brought greater public attention; for the rest of her short life, "Lady Day" would remain one of the best known of jazz singers. Personal crises and drug and alcohol addiction plagued her career. Her voice, in its prime, could reveal a sweet, often sensual expressiveness or disturbing bitterness, and project emotion to extraordinary effect.

Holiness movement Fundamentalist religious movement that arose in the 19th cent. in the U.S. Its doctrine of sanctification held that believers were enabled to live a perfect life after a conversion experience. It originated in the teachings of John WESLEY, founder of METHODISM. In 1843 a group of Holiness ministers founded the Wesleyan Methodist Church of America; another Holiness church of this era was the Free Methodist Church of N. America (1860). Between 1880 and World War I, new Holiness groups included the Church of the Nazarene, established to minister to the urban poor, and the Church of God.

Holinshed \ˈhä-lən-ˌshed\, **Raphael** (d.c.1580) English chronicler. He is remembered for his Chronicles of England, Scotlande, and Irelande (1577), compiled largely uncritically from many sources of varying degrees of trustworthiness. It enjoyed great popularity and was quarried by Elizabethan dramatists, especially William SHAKESPEARE, who

drew on it for *Macbeth, King Lear, Cymbeline,* and many of his historical plays.

holism \\'hō-,li-zəm\\ In the philosophy of the social sciences, the view that denies that all large-scale social events and conditions are ultimately explicable in terms of the individuals who participated in, enjoyed, or suffered them. Methodological holism maintains that at least some social phenomena must be studied at their own macroscopic level of analysis. Semantic holism denies that all meaningful statements about large-scale social phenomena (e.g., "The industrial revolution resulted in urbanization") can be translated into statements about the actions, attitudes, relations, and circumstances of individuals.

holistic medicine \\hō-'lis-tik\\ Doctrine of prevention and treatment that emphasizes looking at the whole person—body, mind, emotions, and environment—rather than a single function or organ. It promotes use of a wide range of health practices and therapies, including ACUPUNCTURE, HOMEOPATHY, and nutrition, stressing "self-care" with traditional commonsense essentials. It does not ignore mainstream Western medical practices, but does not see them as the only effective therapies. See also ALTERNATIVE MEDICINE.

Holland Historic region in the NW Netherlands. It originated in the early 12th cent. as a fief of the HOLY ROMAN EMPIRE. Members of the house of WITTELSBACH served as counts of Holland, Zeeland, and Hainaut until 1433, when they ceded the titles to PHILIP III the Good, duke of Burgundy. It passed to the HABSBURGS in 1482. With six other provinces, it declared independence from Spain in 1579, proclaiming the United Provinces of the Netherlands. Its capital, AMSTERDAM, became Europe's foremost commercial center in the 18th cent. The Napoleonic kingdom of Holland occupied the territory 1806–10.

Holley, Robert William (1922–1993) U.S. biochemist. Born in Urbana, Ill., Holley and others showed that transfer RNA was involved in the assembly of amino acids into proteins. He was the first to determine the sequence of NUCLEOTIDES in a NUCLEIC ACID. He shared a 1968 Nobel Prize with Marshall NIRENBERG and H. G. KHORANA.

Holliday, Doc (*orig.* John Henry) (1852–1887) U.S. gambler and gunman. Born in Griffin, Ga., he graduated from dental school, then moved west and soon abandoned dentistry for gambling. Settling in Tombstone, Ariz., in 1880, he joined Wyatt EARP in the famous gunfight at the O.K. Corral (1882). Having earned a reputation as a gunman, he continued to drift through the West until his death from tuberculosis at 35.

Hollweg, Theobald von Bethmann See Theobald von BETHMANN HOLLWEG

holly Any of approximately 400 species of red- or black-berried ornamental shrubs and trees that make up the genus *Ilex* (family Aquifoliaceae), including the popular Christmas hollies. English holly (*I. aquifolium*) bears shiny, spiny, dark, evergreen leaves; American holly (*I. opaca*) has oblong, prickly leaves; both have usually red fruits.

Holly, Buddy *orig.* Charles Hardin Holley (1936–1959) U.S. singer and songwriter. Born in Lubbock, Texas, he played in country-music bands before switching to rock and roll. In 1957 Holly and his band, the Crickets, had hits with such songs as "That'll Be the Day," "Peggy Sue," and "Oh, Boy!" Holly died at 22 in a plane crash, along with the singers Richie Valens (b.1941) and The Big Bopper (Jape Richardson, b.1930). He left behind many recordings which were released posthumously, and he soon attained legendary stature.

hollyhock Herbaceous plant (*Althaea rosea*) of the MALLOW FAMILY, native to China but widely cultivated for its handsome flowers. The stalk, growing about 5–9 ft (1.5–2.7 m) tall, bears leaves with five to seven lobes and, along the upper portion, commonly white, pink, red, or yellow flowers.

Hollywood District of the city of LOS ANGELES. Its name is synonymous with the U.S. movie industry. In 1887 it was laid out by Horace Wilcox (1832–1891), a prohibitionist who envisioned a community based on his religious principles. Consolidated with Los Angeles in 1910, it became the center of the movie industry by 1915. By the 1960s it was also the source of much television programming.

Hollywood City (pop., 2000: 139,000), SE Florida. The site was a coastal palmetto jungle when Joseph W. Young (1882–1934) laid out the town in 1921. It is now primarily a resort-residential city. Nearby are Port Everglades and a SEMINOLE reservation.

Hollywood Ten Group of U.S. movie producers, directors, and screenwriters who refused to answer questions about communist affiliations before the HOUSE UN-AMERICAN ACTIVITIES COMMITTEE in 1947. The Ten, including Edward Dmytryk, Ring Lardner, Jr., John Howard Lawson, and Dalton Trumbo, were charged with contempt and given prison sentences of six months to a year. Blacklisted, they were unable to find work in Hollywood until the early 1960s, though some wrote scripts under pseudonyms.

Holm, Hanya *orig.* Johanna Eckert (1898?–1992) German-U.S. choreographer. After teaching in Germany at Mary Wigman's Central Institute, she opened a Wigman school in New York, which became the Hanya Holm Studio in 1936. In addition to works for her own company, she choreographed such musicals as *My Fair Lady* (1956) and *Camelot* (1960). Her choreography for *Kiss Me, Kate* (1948) was the first to be copyrighted.

Holmes, Larry (b.1949) U.S. heavyweight boxing champion. Born in Cuthbert, Ga., from 1973 to 1978 Holmes won 28 consecutive bouts, culminating in a victory over the reigning champion, Ken Norton. He defended the title 17 times between 1978 and 1983. He lost the title to Michael Spinks in 1985. Only Joe LOUIS held the heavyweight crown longer than Holmes.

Holmes, Oliver Wendell (1809–1894) U.S. physician, poet, and humorist. A professor and later dean at Harvard Medical School, he was best known as a humorist and poet. He first won national acclaim with his poem "Old Ironsides" (1830). From 1857 he published his genial "Breakfast-Table" essays in the *Atlantic Monthly,* later republished in such collections as *The Professor of the Breakfast-Table* (1860). Other works include the poem "The Chambered Nautilus" and the novel *Elsie Venner* (1861). O. W. HOLMES, JR., was his son.

Holmes, Oliver Wendell, Jr. (1841–1935) U.S. jurist, legal historian, and philosopher. Born in Boston to O. W. HOLMES, he served heroically in the American Civil War, then practiced law in Boston, eventually serving as chief justice (1899–1902) of the state supreme court. In *The Common Law* (1881), he advanced the notion of law as accumulated experience rather than science. Appointed to the U.S. Supreme Court in 1902, Holmes advocated judicial restraint, maintaining that lawmaking was the business of legislative bodies rather than courts. In *Schenk vs. U.S.* (1919), he stated the "clear and present danger" test for FREEDOM OF SPEECH. Many of his vigorous and lucid opinions, including dissenting opinions (he was known as The Great Dissenter), became classic interpretations of the law, and he is regarded as one of the foremost jurists of the modern age. He served until 1932.

Oliver Wendell Holmes, Jr.

Holocaust *Hebrew* Sho'ah. Era of Nazi persecution of Jews and other minorities (1933–45). Marked by increasing barbarization of methods in the expanding territories under German rule, it climaxed in Adolf HITLER's "final solution," the attempted extermination of European Jewry. Hitler's persecution of Jews in Germany began soon after he became chancellor. Under the NUREMBERG LAWS (1935), Jews lost their citizenship. After the KRISTALLNACHT pogrom in 1938, Jews were increasingly imprisoned in CONCENTRATION CAMPS. In WORLD WAR II, as German armies moved eastward into Poland, the Balkans, and the Soviet Union, SS death squads rounded up and killed Jews, Gypsies, and many Slavs. After the notorious WANNSEE CONFERENCE (1942), Jews were systematically evacuated to concentration and extermination camps. RESISTANCE movements were active in several nations, and Jewish risings took place against overwhelming odds in the ghettos of Poland (see WARSAW GHETTO UPRISING). Individuals such as Raoul WALLENBERG saved thousands, but the Allied governments failed to provide effective aid to the Jews. By the end of the war, some 5.7 million Jews had been murdered.

Holocene epoch \\'hō-lə-ˌsēn\\ *formerly* **Recent epoch** Latest interval of geologic time, from 10,000 years ago to the present. Part of the QUATERNARY PERIOD, the Holocene follows the last glacial stage of the PLEISTOCENE EPOCH and is characterized by relatively warm climatic conditions. During this epoch humans refined the skills that led to the present level of civilization. See table at GEOLOGIC TIME.

holography \\hō-'lä-grə-fē\\ Method of recording or reproducing a three-dimensional image, or hologram, by means of a pattern of INTERFERENCE produced using a LASER beam. To create a hologram, a beam of coherent light (from a laser) is split; half falls on a recording medium (such as a photographic plate) unaltered, and the other half is first reflected off the object to be imaged. The two beams together produce an interference pattern of stripes and whorls on the plate. The developed plate is the hologram. When light shines on the hologram, a three-dimensional image is produced by the recorded interference pattern. Dennis Gabor (1900–1979) won a 1971 Nobel Prize for his 1947 invention.

Holst, Gustav(us Theodore von) (1874–1934) British composer. He played organ and conducted as a child. At the Royal College of Music he met Ralph VAUGHAN WILLIAMS, who became a friend for life. Always frail, he gave up teaching after a collapse in 1923 to devote the rest of his life to composition. His most popular piece is the vividly orchestrated suite *The Planets* (1916); other works include the *St. Paul's Suite* for strings (1913), the *Hymn of Jesus* (1917), and the *Choral Fantasia* (1930).

Holstein See SCHLESWIG-HOLSTEIN

Holstein \\'hōl-ˌshtīn\\, **Friedrich (August) von** (1837–1909) German diplomat. He never became foreign minister but exercised power behind the scenes, earning the nickname "the gray eminence." He broke with Otto von BISMARCK over his alignment with Russia, as Holstein advocated a firm alliance with Austria and Britain. After Bismarck's dismissal in 1890, Holstein held important posts under subsequent chancellors, but he proved powerless to oppose the policies of Emperor WILLIAM II and was dismissed in 1906.

Holy Communion See EUCHARIST

Holy Grail See GRAIL

Holy Island See LINDISFARNE

Holy Roman Empire *German* **Heiliges Römisches Reich.** Realm of varying extent in medieval and modern western and central Europe. Ruled initially by Frankish kings and later by Germans, it existed from CHARLEMAGNE's coronation by Pope Leo III in A.D. 800 until the renunciation of the imperial title by FRANCIS II in 1806. The reign of OTTO I the Great, who greatly enlarged the empire and succeeded in dominating his allies, is sometimes regarded as the beginning of the empire, whose name (not adopted until the reign of FREDERICK I Barbarossa) reflected Charlemagne's claim that his empire was the successor of the Roman empire, and that this temporal power was augmented by his status as God's principal vicar in the temporal realm. The empire's core consisted of Germany, Austria, Bohemia, and Moravia. Switzerland, the Netherlands, and N Italy sometimes formed part of it; France, Poland, Hungary, and Denmark were initially included. From the mid-11th cent. the emperors engaged in a great struggle with the papacy for dominance, and particularly under the powerful HOHENSTAUFEN DYNASTY (1138–1254) they fought with the popes over control of Italy. RUDOLF I became the first Habsburg emperor in 1273, and from 1438 the HABSBURG DYNASTY held the throne permanently. Until 1356 the emperor was chosen by the German princes; thereafter he was formally elected by the ELECTORS. During the REFORMATION, the German princes largely defected to the Protestant camp, opposing the Catholic emperor, and after 1562 emperors were no longer crowned by the pope. At the end of the THIRTY YEARS' WAR, the Peace of WESTPHALIA recognized the individual sovereignty of the empire's states; the empire

thereafter became a loose federation of states and the title of emperor principally honorific. In the 18th cent., issues of imperial succession resulted in the War of the AUSTRIAN SUCCESSION and the SEVEN YEARS' WAR. The greatly weakened empire was brought to an end by NAPOLEON.

Holy Roman Emperors

Carolingian dynasty			Henry Raspe	1246–47
Charlemagne			William of Holland	1247–56
(Charles I)	800–14		Conrad IV	1250–54
Louis I	814–40		*Great Interregnum*	
Civil War	840–43		Richard	1257–72
Lothair I	843–55		Alfonso (Alfonso X	
Louis II	855–75		of Castile)	1257–75
Charles II	875–77		*House of Habsburg*	
Interregnum	877–81		Rudolf I	1273–91
Charles III	881–87		*House of Nassau*	
Interregnum	887–91		Adolf	1292–98
House of Spoleto			*House of Habsburg*	
Guy	891–94		Albert I	1298–1308
Lambert	894–98		*House of Luxembourg*	
Carolingian dynasty			Henry VII	1308–13
Arnulf	896–99		*House of Habsburg*	
Louis III	901–5		Frederick (III)	1314–26
House of Franconia			*House of Wittelsbach*	
Conrad I	911–18		Louis IV	1314–46
Carolingian dynasty			*House of Luxembourg*	
Berengar	915–24		Charles IV	1346–78
House of Saxony			Wenceslas	1378–1400
(*Liudolfings*)			*House of Wittelsbach*	
Henry I	919–36		Rupert	1400–10
Otto I	936–73		*House of Luxembourg*	
Otto II	973–83		Jobst	1410–11
Otto III	983–1002		Sigismund	1410–37
Henry II	1002–24		*House of Habsburg*	
Salian dynasty			Albert II	1438–39
Conrad II	1024–39		Frederick III	1440–93
Henry III	1039–56		Maximilian I	1493–1519
Henry IV	1056–1106		Charles V	1519–56
Rival claimants			Ferdinand I	1556–64
Rudolf	1077–80		Maximilian II	1564–76
Hermann	1081–93		Rudolf II	1576–1612
Conrad	1093–1101		Matthias	1612–19
Henry V	1105/6–25		Ferdinand II	1619–37
House of Supplinburg			Ferdinand III	1637–57
Lothair II	1125–37		Leopold I	1658–1705
House of Hohenstaufen			Joseph I	1705–11
Conrad III	1138–52		Charles VI	1711–40
Frederick I			*House of Wittelsbach*	
(Barbarossa)	1152–90		Charles VII	1742–45
Henry VI	1190–97		*House of Habsburg*	
Philip	1198–1208		Francis I	1745–65
Welf dynasty			Joseph II	1765–90
Otto IV	1198–1214		Leopold II	1790–92
House of Hohenstaufen			Francis II	1792–1806
Frederick II	1215–50			
Rival claimants				
Henry (VII)	1220–35			

Holy Spirit *or* **Holy Ghost** *or* **Paraclete** In Christianity, the third person of the Holy TRINITY. Christian teaching about the Holy Spirit is derived mainly from the GOSPELS. The Holy Spirit descended on JESUS at his baptism, and outpourings of the Spirit, including healing, prophecy, exorcism, and speaking in tongues, are mentioned in the Acts of the Apostles. It also came to the disciples during PENTECOST. The definition of the Holy Spirit as being equal in substance to the Father and the Son was made at the Council of CONSTANTINOPLE (A.D. 381).

Home, Alec Douglas- See Alec DOUGLAS-HOME

Homeland Security, U.S. Department of Federal executive division responsible for coordinating security in the U.S. Proposed by a federal commission in early 2001, the idea gained impetus after the SEPTEMBER 11 ATTACKS, and the cabinet-level department was established by Congress in 2003. Its purpose is to effect a national strategy to fight TERRORISM in the U.S., in part by coordinating federal and state efforts in such areas as border and transportation security, emergency preparedness and response, and chemical, biological, radiological, and nuclear countermeasures. Agencies absorbed into the department include the Federal Emergency Management Agency, Immigration and Naturalization Services, U.S. Customs, the Coast Guard, and the Secret Service.

homeopathy \ˌhō-mē-ˈä-pə-thē\ System of therapeutics founded in 1796 by Samuel HAHNEMANN on the principle that "like cures like." That is, substances that in healthy persons would produce the symptoms from which the patient suffers are used to treat the patient; also, the potency of a curative agent increases as the substance is diluted. It has been criticized for focusing on symptoms rather than causes. With the rise of ALTERNATIVE MEDICINE, it has seen a resurgence.

homeostasis \ˌhō-mē-ō-ˈstā-səs\ Any self-regulating process by which a biological or mechanical system maintains stability. Systems in dynamic EQUILIBRIUM reach a balance in which internal change continuously compensates for external change in a feedback control process to keep conditions relatively uniform. For example, body temperature is regulated by a complex system controlled by the HYPOTHALAMUS, which adjusts breathing and metabolic rates, blood-vessel dilation, and blood-sugar level in response to changes in ambient temperature, hormones, and disease.

home page See WEB SITE

Homer (fl.9th or 8th cent. B.C.) Greek poet, one of the greatest and most influential writers of all time. He was probably an Ionian, and tradition holds that he was blind. The ancient Greeks attributed to him the great epic poems the *Iliad* (about the TROJAN WAR) and the *Odyssey* (about ODYSSEUS's return from the war). Modern scholars generally agree that he composed (but probably did not literally write) the *Iliad*, most likely relying on oral traditions, and at least inspired the composition of the *Odyssey*. The two epics provided the basis of Greek education and culture in the classical age and formed the backbone of humanistic education down to the Roman empire and the spread of Christianity.

Homer, Winslow (1836–1910) U.S. painter. Born in Boston, he became a freelance illustrator in New York and exhibited at the National Academy of Design in 1860. In France in 1866, he was attracted to French naturalism, but it had little effect on his generally bright and happy work, including *Snap the Whip* (1872). He became a master of watercolor and his oil paintings matured, focusing increasingly on solitary, withdrawn figures. He spent 1881–82 in England, on the North Sea, where the coastal atmosphere and stoic people became the subjects of some of his most powerful images. In 1883 he moved to Prout's Neck, Me., and his dominant theme became the sea. In his later years he continued to paint vigorously and in near-total isolation. Though he was recognized in his lifetime, appreciation of his enormous achievement came only after his death.

Home Rule, Irish Movement to secure internal autonomy for Ireland within the British empire. The slogan "Home Rule" was popularized in 1870 when the Home Government Assn. (later the Home Rule League) called for an Irish parliament. It was led from 1878 by C. S. PARNELL. After Home Rule bills introduced by Prime Minister William GLADSTONE in 1885 and 1893 were defeated, a third bill became law in 1914 but was militantly opposed by Ulster Unionists and republicans in Ireland. A system akin to home rule was established in the six counties of Ulster (Northern Ireland) in 1920. In 1921 the remaining 26 counties in the south achieved dominion status.

Homestead Movement Mid-19th-cent. drive for free land in the U.S. Midwest, Great Plains, and West. It began in the 1830s as laborers and reformers joined farmers in calling for public land to be given free to settlers. In 1848 the FREE SOIL PARTY advocated the homestead proposal. In 1862 the Homestead Act was passed, providing 160 acres of public land free to any adult citizen or head of family who had lived on the land for five years. By 1900, 600,000 homesteaders had claimed 80 million acres.

Homestead Strike Labor strike at Andrew CARNEGIE's steelworks in Homestead, Pa., in July 1892. When the steelworkers union went on strike following a wage cut, the company's manager, H. C. FRICK, hired strikebreakers, with Pinkerton detectives to protect them. A gun battle re-

sulted, in which several people were killed and many injured; the governor sent state militiamen to support the company. The broken strike represented a major setback to the union movement that was felt for decades.

homicide Killing of one human being by another. Homicide includes murder, manslaughter, and other criminal homicides as well as noncriminal killings. Murder is the crime of intentionally and unjustifiably killing another. First-degree murder is a homicide committed with premeditation or in the course of a serious FELONY (e.g., KIDNAPPING). Second- and third-degree murder involve lesser degrees of intent. Voluntary (or first-degree) manslaughter encompasses any homicide resulting from an intentional act done without malice or premeditation and while in the heat of passion or on sudden provocation; involuntary (second- or third-degree) manslaughter often includes an element of unlawful recklessness or negligence. Noncriminal homicides include killings committed in defense of oneself or another and most deaths resulting from accidents. See also SELF-DEFENSE.

hominid \ˈhä-mə-ˌnəd\ Any creature of the family Hominidae (order Primates), of which only one species exists today—HOMO SAPIENS, or human beings. Extinct species include *Ardipithecus ramidus*, various species of AUSTRALOPITHECUS, HOMO HABILIS, and HOMO ERECTUS. The family most closely related to the Hominidae today is the Pongidae, or anthropoid apes, including the GORILLA, chimpanzee, and ORANGUTAN. These are believed to have diverged from a common ancestral line 5–8 million years ago.

Homo Genus of the family Hominidae (see HOMINID) of PRIMATES characterized by a relatively large cranium (braincase), limb structure adapted to an erect posture and a two-footed gait, fully opposable thumb, hand capable of power and precision grips, and the ability to make precision tools. The genus includes modern humans (HOMO SAPIENS), the extinct species HOMO HABILIS and HOMO ERECTUS, and the extinct forms of *H. sapiens* called NEANDERTHAL and CRO-MAGNON.

Homo erectus ("erect man") Extinct species of early HOMINID, generally thought to be a direct ancestor of modern HOMO SAPIENS. *H. erectus* flourished about 1.6 million–250,000 years ago, ranging widely from Africa (where the species originated) to Asia to parts of Europe. It had a low, thick braincase (800–1,100 cc) with jutting brow ridges and a wide nose, palate, and jaw together with large teeth. The species was of medium stature and walked upright, and was the first hominid to master fire and inhabit caves. See also HUMAN EVOLUTION, JAVA MAN, ZHOUKOUDIAN.

Homo habilis \ˌhō-mō-ˈha-bə-ləs\ ("dexterous man") Extinct species of early HOMINID that inhabited parts of sub-Saharan Africa 2.5–1.5 million years ago and is generally regarded as the earliest member of the genus *Homo*. Remains of *H. habilis* were first discovered in 1959 at OLDUVAI GORGE in N Tanzania; additional fossils were later found in the LAKE TURKANA region of N Kenya. The cranial capacity of *H. habilis* was about 600–800 cc. Limb bones suggest that the species could walk upright. The fossil of a hand suggests that *H. habilis* was capable of precise manipulation of objects and could shape stone. See also HUMAN EVOLUTION, OLDOWAN INDUSTRY.

homology Similarity of the structure, physiology, or development of different species of organisms based on their descent from a common evolutionary ancestor. Analogy, by contrast, is a functional similarity of structure based on mere similarity of use. For example, the forelimbs of humans, bats, and deer are homologous; the form of construction and the number of bones in each are almost identical and represent adaptive modifications of the forelimb structure of their shared ancestor. The wings of birds and insects are merely analogous; both types are used for flight but they do not share a common origin.

Homo sapiens ("man the wise") Genus and species to which all modern human beings (*Homo sapiens sapiens*) belong and whose oldest known fossil remains date to at least 120,000 years ago. *H. sapiens* is distinguished from earlier HOMINID species by characteristics and habits such as bipedal stance and gait, brain capacity averaging about 1,350 cc, high forehead, small teeth and jaw, defined chin, construction and use of tools, and ability to use SYMBOLS. Many scholars believe that modern humans developed in Africa about 150,000 years ago and spread to the Middle East about 100,000 years ago and to other parts of Eurasia about 40,000–50,000 years ago (this is known as the "single-origin" model). Others contend that modern humans developed from various regional populations of archaic *H. sapiens* in Eurasia beginning about 250,000 years ago (the "regional-continuity" model). By about 11,000 B.C. *H. sapiens sapiens* had peopled virtually the entire globe. See also CRO-MAGNON, HUMAN EVOLUTION, NEANDERTHAL.

homosexuality Quality or state in some human beings characterized by a tendency to direct sexual desire toward another of the same sex. Female homosexuality is often called lesbianism (from Lesbos, the Aegean island where SAPPHO taught). At different times and in different cultures, homosexual behavior has variously been approved of, tolerated, and banned. The ancient Greeks accepted homosexuality between adult and adolescent males, whereas Judeo-Christian culture traditionally has viewed it as sinful. The American psychiatric establishment originally classified homosexuality as a mental illness, but dropped that designation in the mid-1970s amid increased political activity by homosexuals and advancing research. Traditional beliefs about homosexuals (such as that there is a homosexual "type" and that gay men are effeminate and gay women aggressive and masculine) have faded as a result of increased expression, experience, and acceptance of homosexuality as a normal variant of human sexuality. Homosexual orientation apparently results from a combination of hereditary or constitutional factors and environmental or social influences, and tends to coexist with heterosexual feelings in varying degrees in different individuals.

homozygote and heterozygote Two genetic possibilities for a fertilized egg. If the two sex cells (gametes) that fuse during FERTILIZATION carry the same form of a GENE for a specific trait, the organism is said to be a homozygote for that trait. If the gametes carry differing forms of the gene, the result is a heterozygote.

Honda Motor Co. Japanese manufacturer of motorcycles and automobiles. Founded as a maker of small, efficient engines by the engineer Honda Soichiro in 1946, the company was incorporated as Honda Motor Co. in 1948. The Honda C-100, a small-engine motorcycle, was introduced in 1953; by 1959 it was the largest-selling motorcycle in the world. Honda began making cars in 1963 and became especially known for the lightweight, reliable, fuel-efficient Civic and Accord. It is today one of the largest automobile companies in the world.

Honduras *officially* **Republic of Honduras** Republic. Area: 43,277 sq mi (112,088 sq km). Population (2000): 6,490,000. Capital: TEGUCIGALPA. The population is predominantly mestizo (mixed European and Indian). Language: Spanish (official). Religion: Roman Catholicism. Currency: Honduran lempira. The second-largest country of CENTRAL AMERICA, Honduras has a 400-mi (645-km) coastline on the Caribbean to the north and a 45-mi (72 km) coast on the Pacific to the south. More than three-fourths of Honduras is mountainous and wooded. The E lowlands include part of the MOSQUITO COAST. Most of the people live a generally isolated existence in the mountainous interior, where the climate is hot and rainy. The economy is primarily agricultural, with bananas, coffee, and sugar for export and corn as the chief domestic staple. It is a multiparty republic with one legislative house, and the head of state and government is the president. It was part of the MAYA civilization that flourished in the 1st millennium A.D. There are architectural and sculptural remains of a ceremonial center at COPÁN, in use from about 465 to 800. Christopher COLUMBUS reached Honduras in 1502, and permanent settlement followed. A major war between the Spaniards and the Indians broke out in 1537, culminating in the decimation of the Indian population through disease and enslavement. After 1570 it was part of the captaincy general of Guatemala until Central American independence in 1821. Part of the

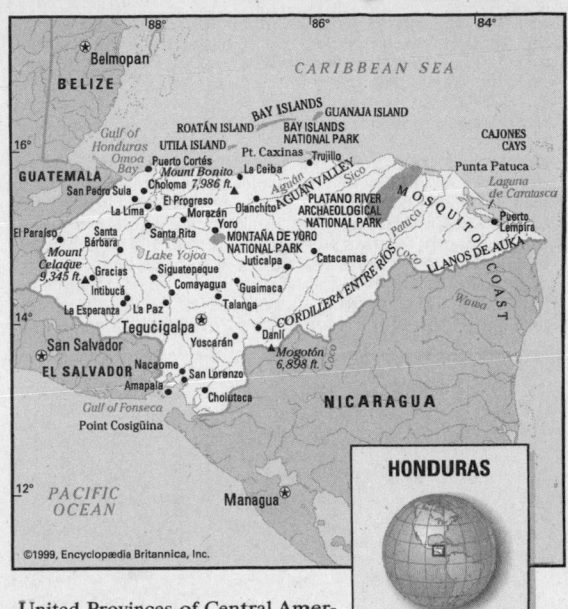

HONDURAS

Scale 1: 9,730,000

United Provinces of Central America, it withdrew in 1838 and declared its independence. In the 20th cent., under military rule, there was constant civil war and some intervention by the U.S. A civilian government was elected to offce in 1982. The military remained in the background, however, as the activity of leftist guerrillas increased. Flooding caused by a hurricane in 1998 devastated the country, killing over 7,000 people and leaving 500,000 homeless.

Honecker \'hō-nə-kər\, **Erich** (1912–1994) German communist head of E. Germany's Socialist Unity Party (1971–89) and chairman of the Council of State (1976–89). A member of the German Communist Party, he was imprisoned by the Nazis 1935–45. In 1946 he cofounded and led the Free German Youth movement in E. Germany. In 1961 he oversaw the building of the BERLIN WALL. He succeeded Walter ULBRICHT as head of E. Germany, which under his rule was one of the most repressive but also one of the most prosperous of the Soviet-bloc countries until the collapse of communism in 1989.

Honegger \ˌō-nā-'ger, *Engl* 'hä-ni-gər\, **Arthur** (1892–1955) French composer. Born to Swiss-French parents, he became part of the group known as Les SIX, and first gained renown for his oratorio *Le roi David* (1921). His *Pacific 231* (1923), portraying a locomotive, caused a sensation. Prolific throughout his life, he composed five symphonies, the oratorio *Jeanne d'Arc au bûcher* (1938), and numerous scores for ballet, theater, and films (including Abel GANCE's *Napoleon*).

honey Sweet, thick liquid food, golden in color, produced in the honey sacs of various bees from the nectar of flowers. Honey has played an enormous role in human nutrition since ancient times; until about 250 years ago, it was almost the sole sweetening agent. Commercial honeys are often produced from CLOVER by the domestic HONEYBEE. The nectar becomes honey by inversion of most of its SUCROSE into the sugars FRUCTOSE and GLUCOSE and the removal of excess moisture. Honey is stored in a honeycomb, a double layer of uniform hexagonal cells constructed of beeswax and propolis (a plant resin). The honey and comb are used in winter as food for the bee colony and their larvae. Honey extracted for human consumption is usually heated to destroy yeasts and then strained. See also BEEKEEPING.

honey bear See SUN BEAR

honeybee Broadly, any BEE that makes honey (any insect of the tribe Apini, family Apidae); more strictly, one of the four species constituting the genus *Apis*. The term is usually applied to one species, the domestic honeybee (*A. mellifera*). The other *Apis* species are confined to Asia. *A. mellifera* is usually about 0.5 in. (1.2 cm) long. All honeybees are social insects that live in nests or hives. They have three castes: queens, workers, and drones. See also BEE-KEEPING.

honeysuckle family Family Caprifoliaceae, containing approximately 500 species. It is well known for its many ornamental woody shrubs and vines, composed mostly of N temperate species. Japanese honeysuckle (*Lonicera japonica*) is a highly fragrant flowering vine that kills other plants by climbing over them and shutting out the light. Also included in this family is the ELDER.

Hong Kong *or* **Xianggang** \'shyäŋ-'gäŋ\ Special administrative region of China (pop., 2000: 6,782,000). Located off

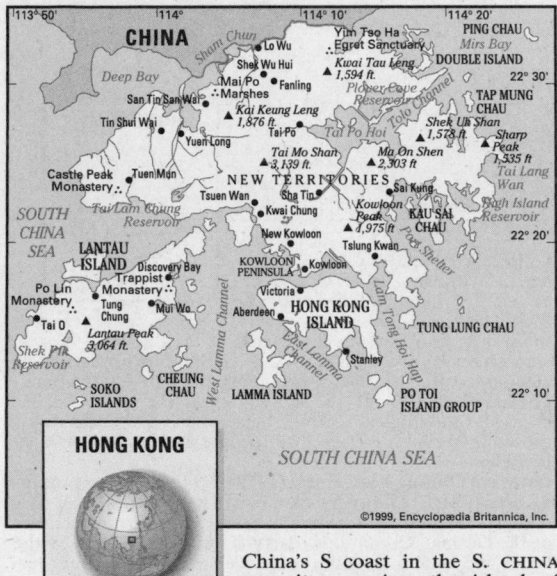

China's S coast in the S. CHINA SEA, it comprises the island of Hong Kong and adjacent islets, the KOWLOON Peninsula, and the New Territories, all of which were leased by the British from China for 99 years (1898–1997). The entire territory was returned to China in 1997. It covers 398 sq mi (1,031 sq km). The administrative center of VICTORIA on Hong Kong island's NW coast is also the center of economic activities. Hong Kong has an excellent natural harbor and is one of the world's major trade and financial centers. It has many educational institutions, including the Univ. of Hong Kong (1911).

Hongli See QIANLONG EMPEROR

Hong Xiuquan *or* **Hung Hsiu-ch'üan** \'huŋ-shē-'ü-chu̇e-'än\ (1814–1864) Chinese religious prophet, leader of the TAIPING REBELLION. After repeatedly failing the civil-service exams, he suffered an emotional collapse and had a vision in which he was instructed to rid the world of evil demons. He became the leader of his own brand of Christianity and promised an ultimate reward to his peasant followers. In 1850 he began plotting a rebellion; the next year he declared himself Heavenly King of the Heavenly Kingdom of Great Peace (Taiping Tianguo). His army of more than a million men and women soldiers captured Nanjing, which became Hong's new capital. He eventually withdrew from affairs of state in favor of his incompetent older brothers; he committed suicide in 1864.

Honiara \ˌhō-nē-'är-ə\ Town (pop., 1996 est.: 44,000), capital of the SOLOMON ISLANDS, SW Pacific Ocean. Situated at the mouth of the Mataniko River on the north coast of GUADALCANAL, it is a port and communications center trading chiefly in coconuts, timber, fish, and some gold. It became the capital in 1952.

Honolulu City (pop., 1996 est.: 423,000), capital, and principal port of Hawaii, on OAHU island. It is the crossroads of trans-Pacific shipping and air routes, the focus of inter-island services, and the commercial and industrial center of the state. Its area of 597 sq mi (1,545 sq km) includes some outlying islets. Honolulu's metropolitan area has almost 75% of the state's population. The area was settled from about 1100, according to Hawaiian legends. During the 19th cent., Honolulu flourished as a trade center especially for whalers. In Dec. 1941 the city and adjacent PEARL HARBOR were bombed by the Japanese. It became a prime staging area for the rest of WORLD WAR II, and later for the KOREAN and VIETNAM wars. Nearby Waikiki Beach is a prime tourist site.

Honor, Legion of See LEGION OF HONOR

Honorius III \hŏ-'nōr-ē-əs\ *orig.* Cencio Savelli (d.1227) Pope (1216–27). He extended INNOCENT III's policies on church reform and the recovery of the Holy Land, proclaiming a crusade to regain Jerusalem in 1215. He crowned FREDERICK II as Holy Roman Emperor (1220) but threatened to excommunicate him if he failed to join the crusade. Honorius also undertook a crusade against the Moors in Spain (1218) and continued the ALBIGENSIAN CRUSADE. He approved the Dominican, Franciscan, and Carmelite orders and authorized the first official book of canon law.

Honshu \'hŏn-ˌshü\ Island (pop., 1990: 100,254,000), Japan. The largest of the four main islands of Japan, it has an area of 87,992 sq mi (227,898 sq km). It is regarded as the Japanese mainland. The Pacific coast is the country's main economic center, lined with the metropolitan areas of TOKYO-YOKOHAMA and OSAKA-KOBE. Honshu contains Japan's largest mountain, Mt. FUJI, and its largest lake, Lake BIWA.

Honthorst \'hŏnt-ˌhȯrst\, **Gerrit van** (1592–1656) Dutch painter. In Italy (c.1610–20), he enjoyed the patronage of the nobility and assimilated the style of CARAVAGGIO. The dramatic effects of artificial light in his early paintings, as in such nocturnal scenes as *Supper Party* (1620), earned him the nickname Gherardo delle Notti ("Gerard of the Night Scenes"). He was court painter at The Hague 1637–52. With Hendrik TERBRUGGHEN, he was a leader of the UTRECHT SCHOOL.

Hooch \'hōk\, **Pieter de** (1629–1684) Dutch genre painter. He trained in Haarlem and was a member of the painters' guild of Delft 1655–57. He was noted for his small interiors and sunny outdoor scenes, with figures engaged in humble, domestic activities in settings of serene simplicity. In his best works, such as *A Woman and Her Maid in a Court* (1658) and *The Pantry* (c.1658), he was concerned with the effect of enclosures on light intensity, tonal variations, and linear perspective. After he moved to Amsterdam (c.1661), his paintings declined in quality.

Hood, Mt. Peak, NW Oregon. Located in the CASCADE RANGE, at 11,235 ft (3,424 m) high, it is an extinct volcano that last erupted around 1865. The highest mountain in the state, it is the focal point of Mt. Hood National Forest, a popular recreation area.

Hood, Raymond M(athewson) (1881–1934) U.S. architect. Born in Pawtucket, R.I., he studied at MIT. With John Mead Howells (1868–1959) he won first prize in the 1922 Chicago Tribune Building competition; their design would be one of their many Neo-Gothic skyscrapers. Later Hood turned away from the revival of past styles; his clean-lined Daily News (1930; with Howells) and McGraw-Hill (1930–31; with J. A. Fouilhoux) buildings, both in New York, foreshadow the ROCKEFELLER CENTER complex.

hoof-and-mouth disease See FOOT-AND-MOUTH DISEASE

Hooghly River See HUGLI RIVER

Hooke, Robert (1635–1703) English physicist. His achievements and theories were extraordinarily diverse. His important law of ELASTICITY, known as Hooke's law (1660), states that the stretching of a solid is proportional to the force applied to it. He was one of the first to build and use a reflecting telescope. He suggested that Jupiter rotates on its axis, and his detailed sketches of Mars were later used to determine its rate of rotation. He discovered DIFFRACTION, and proposed the wave theory of light to explain it. He was one of the first proponents of the theory of evolution. He was the first to state in general that all matter expands when heated and that air is made up of particles separated from each other by relatively large distances. He invented a marine barometer and anticipated the steam engine.

Hooker, Joseph (1814–1879) U.S. Army officer. Born in Hadley, Mass., he attended West Point. As brigadier general of volunteers at the outbreak of the Civil War, he participated in major campaigns. He succeeded Ambrose BURNSIDE as commander of the Army of the Potomac after the disastrous Battle of FREDERICKSBURG. He reorganized the army but failed to defeat Robert E. LEE at CHANCELLORSVILLE. He resigned just before the Battle of GETTYSBURG, but later helped secure the Union victory at CHATTANOOGA.

Hooker, Richard (1554?–1600) English clergyman and theologian. He attended Oxford Univ. and was ordained in 1581. He created a distinctive Anglican theology during a time when the Church of ENGLAND was threatened by both ROMAN CATHOLICISM and PURITANISM. His great work was *Of the Laws of Ecclesiastical Polity* (1594–97), in which he defended the threefold authority of the Bible, church tradition, and human reason.

Hoover, Herbert (Clark) (1874–1964) 31st president of the U.S. (1929–33). Born in W. Branch, Iowa, he became a mining engineer, and administered projects on four continents (1895–1913). He headed Allied relief operations in wartime England and Belgium; as U.S. national food administrator (1917–19), he furnished food to famine-stricken areas of Europe. As U.S. secretary of commerce (1921–27), he created divisions to regulate broadcasting and aviation. He oversaw commissions to build Boulder (later Hoover) Dam and the St. Lawrence Seaway. In 1928, as the Republican presidential candidate, he soundly defeated Alfred SMITH. His hopes for a "New Day" program were quickly overwhelmed by the GREAT DEPRESSION. As a believer in individual freedom, he vetoed bills to create a federal unemployment agency and to fund public-works projects. In 1932 he finally allowed relief to farmers through the RECONSTRUCTION FINANCE CORP. He was overwhelmingly defeated in 1932 by Franklin ROOSEVELT. After World War II he participated in famine-relief work in Europe and headed the HOOVER COMMISSION.

Herbert Hoover

Hoover, J(ohn) Edgar (1895–1972) U.S. director of the FEDERAL BUREAU OF INVESTIGATION. Born in Washington, D.C., he became a lawyer in the U.S. justice department. In 1924 he was named director of the Bureau of Investigation, which he remade into a professional, merit-based organization, successfully publicizing its achievements and expanding its size. Authorized to investigate the activities of communists and fascists, he added surveillance of all radicals and activists, including the KU KLUX KLAN and M. L. KING, but gave little attention to organized crime. He kept secret files on many politicians, which he used to discourage criticism of his work and conduct. He retained his post for 48 years until his death.

Hoover Commission (1947–49, 1953–55) Advisory body headed by former Pres. Herbert HOOVER to examine the organization of the U.S. executive branch. The first commission was appointed by Pres. Harry TRUMAN to reduce the number of federal departments. A second commission was appointed by Pres. Dwight EISENHOWER. Some agencies were consolidated and new bodies were created, including the Department of Health, Education, and Welfare and the General Services Administration.

Hoover Dam *formerly* **Boulder Dam** Highest concrete arch DAM in the U.S., built on the Colorado River at the Arizona–Nevada border. It impounds Lake MEAD. The dam, completed in 1936, is used for flood and silt control, electric power, irrigation, and domestic and industrial water supplies. It is 726 ft (221 m) high and 1,244 ft (379 m) long (along the crest).

hop In botany, either of two species of the genus *Humulus,* nonwoody annual or perennial vines in the HEMP family, native to temperate N. America, Eurasia, and S. America. The hops used to impart a mellow bitterness and delicate aroma to BEER are the dried female flower clusters (CONES) of the common hop (*H. lupulus*), a long-lived perennial. The Japanese hop (*H. japonicus*) is a quick-growing annual species used as a screening vine.

Hope, Bob (*orig.* Leslie Townes) (b.1903) U.S. (British-born) actor. Having moved to Ohio at 4, he created a song-and-comedy vaudeville act and in 1933 appeared in the musical *Roberta.* Success in radio led to his first film, *The Big Broadcast of 1938.* He hosted the highly rated *Bob Hope Show* (1938–50) on radio, and later appeared in numerous popular television specials. He costarred with Bing CROSBY and Dorothy Lamour in seven popular "Road" pictures, beginning with *The Road to Singapore* (1940), and won fans in *The Paleface* (1948) and *The Seven Little Foys* (1955). For over 40 years he performed with his variety show for U.S. troops overseas.

Hope diamond Blue diamond from India, one of the largest blue diamonds known. Named for the London banker Thomas Hope, who purchased it in 1830, the 45.5-carat diamond is on display in the Smithsonian Institution.

Hopewell culture *formerly* **Mound Builders** Most notable ancient Indian culture of E central N. America. It flourished around 200 B.C.–A.D. 500, chiefly in the Illinois and Ohio river valleys. The Hopewell Indians (named for an excavation site) built earthen mounds for enclosure, burial, religious rites, and defense. The inhabitants raised corn but still relied upon hunting and gathering. They produced pottery and metalwork. Trade routes were evidently well developed. After A.D. 400 Hopewell culture gradually disappeared. See also WOODLAND CULTURES.

Hopi \'hō-pē\ Westernmost group of PUEBLO INDIANS, living on reservation lands in NE Arizona surrounded by the NAVAJO Reservation. Most of their traditional settlements were on high mesas and consisted of terraced PUEBLO structures of stone and adobe. They supported themselves by growing corn, beans, squash, and melons and by sheepherding. Hopi life was steeped in religious ceremony and involved secret rites held in semi-underground KIVAS (pit-houses) and the use of masks and costumes to impersonate KACHINAS (ancestral spirits). The Hopi number about 6,000 today.

Hopkins, Anthony (*later* **Sir Anthony**) (b.1937) British actor. He joined London's National Theatre in 1965, where he starred in Shakespearean roles. A subtle actor able to convey volcanic emotion with a small gesture, he made an acclaimed Broadway debut in *Equus* (1974) and stayed on in the U.S. for such films as *The Elephant Man* (1980). His later films include *The Silence of the Lambs* (1991, Academy Award), *Howards End* (1992), *The Remains of the Day* (1993), and *Amistad* (1997).

Hopkins, Frederick Gowland (*later* **Sir Frederick**) (1861–1947) British biochemist. He discovered the AMINO ACID TRYPTOPHAN (1901) and showed that it and certain others are essential in the diet. For his discovery of VITAMINS, he shared a 1929 Nobel Prize with Christiaan EIJKMAN. He demonstrated that working muscles accumulate LACTIC ACID.

Hopkins, Gerard Manley (1844–1889) British poet. After studies at Oxford, he converted to Catholicism and eventually became a Jesuit priest. He burned his youthful verses as inappropriate to his profession, but remained troubled by his delight in the sensuous world. One of the most individual of Victorian writers, he is noted for intense language, compressed syntax, and innovations in prosody, including sprung rhythm. His best-known poems include "The Wreck of the Deutschland," "Pied Beauty," "God's Grandeur," and "The Windhover." He died of typhoid at 44. His work influenced many 20th-cent. poets.

Hopkins, Harry L(loyd) (1890–1946) U.S. NEW DEAL official. Born in Sioux City, Iowa, he directed New York's emergency relief agency from 1931. After Franklin ROOSEVELT became president, Hopkins became head of the Federal Emergency Relief Administration. In 1934 he created the

HIJ

WORKS PROGRESS ADMINISTRATION. He served as U.S. commerce secretary (1938–40), and later directed the LEND-LEASE program. He was regarded as Roosevelt's closest personal adviser during World War II.

Hopkins, Sarah Winnemucca *or* **Sarah Hopkins Winnemucca** *or* **Thocmectony** (1844?–1891) U.S. lecturer and writer. Born to a Northern Paiute family in Humboldt Sink, Mexico (now Nevada), she lived as a child with a white family and later served as an army interpreter and scout. Her lecture tours in the East in the 1880s publicized the plight of her tribe and protested government policies. Her writings, including *Life Among the Piutes* (1883), are valuable for their description of Indian life and their insights into the impact of white settlement.

hoplite \'hŏp-ˌlīt\ Heavily armed foot soldier of ancient Greece whose function was to fight in close formation. Hoplites probably appeared in the late 8th cent. B.C., equipped with new and heavier armor, including a metal helmet, breastplate, and shield, a sword, and a 6-ft (2-m) thrusting spear. From then on, battles were won not by individual champions but through massed hoplite phalanxes breaking through enemy ranks. Greek hoplites were the best fighters in the Mediterranean world.

Hopper, Edward (1882–1967) U.S. painter. Born in Nyack, N.Y., he was initially trained as an illustrator and later studied painting with Robert HENRI. He worked at advertising art and illustrative etchings before turning to watercolors and oil paintings of urban life in the mid-1920s. His *Room in Brooklyn* (1932) and *Office at Night* (1940) depict still, anonymous figures within geometric building forms, producing the haunting sense of isolation that was to be his hallmark. He used light to isolate figures and objects, as in *Early Sunday Morning* (1930) and *Nighthawks* (1942). He strongly influenced the Pop art and New Realist painters of the 1960s and '70s.

Hopper, Grace Murray *orig.* Grace Brewster Murray (1906–1992) U.S. mathematician and rear admiral. Born in New York City, she received her PhD from Yale Univ. in 1934 and taught at Vassar College 1931–44. As a U.S. Navy officer (1943–86), she worked on Harvard's Mark I (1944) and Mark II (1945) computers, and in 1949 helped design an improved COMPILER. She helped devise UNIVAC I, the first commercial electronic computer (1951). She received the National Medal of Technology in 1991.

Horace *Latin* Quintus Horatius Flaccus (65–8 B.C.) Latin lyric poet and satirist. The son of a former slave, he fought in BRUTUS' army in the upheaval after Julius CAESAR's murder, but later gained the favor of Brutus' conqueror, Octavian (later AUGUSTUS), and achieved virtually the status of poet laureate. His fame rests chiefly on his books of poetry, *Odes* and verse *Epistles*, including the treatise *Ars poetica*, which sets down rules for the composition of poetry. The *Odes* and *Epistles* significantly influenced Western poetry from the Renaissance through the 19th cent.

Horbat Qesari See CAESAREA

Horeb, Mt. See Mt. SINAI

horizontal integration See VERTICAL INTEGRATION

hormone Organic compound (often a STEROID or PEPTIDE) that is produced in one part of a multicellular organism and travels to another to exert its action. Hormones regulate physiological activities including growth, REPRODUCTION, and HOMEOSTASIS in vertebrates; molting and maintenance of the larval state (see LARVA) in insects; and growth, bud dormancy, and leaf shedding in plants. Most vertebrate hormones originate in specialized tissues (see ENDOCRINE SYSTEM, GLAND) and are carried through the CIRCULATION. Mammalian hormones include SEX HORMONES, INSULIN, and EPINEPHRINE. Insect hormones include ecdysone and juvenile hormone. Plant hormones include abscisin, auxins, and cytokinins.

Hormuz, Strait of *formerly* **Strait of Ormuz** Channel linking the PERSIAN GULF with the Gulf of OMAN and the Arabian Sea. It is 35–60 mi (55–95 km) wide and separates Iran from the Arabian Peninsula. It is strategically and economically important as a route for oil tankers.

Horn, Cape Cape, at the S extremity of S. America. Located on Horn Island, in S TIERRA DEL FUEGO archipelago, it projects into DRAKE PASSAGE. It was named Hoorn for the birthplace

of W. C. Schouten (c.1580–1625), who rounded it in 1616. Navigation around the cape is hazardous.

hornbill Any of about 45 species of Old World tropical birds (family Bucerotidae) noted for the bony helmet on the bill of some species. From 16 to 63 in. (40–160 cm) long, they typically have a large head, prominent bill, broad wings, long tail, and brown or black plumage with bold white markings. They nest in cavities, usually in large trees. The male of most species walls up the female in the nest with mud, leaving a small opening to convey food. The female breaks out after the eggs hatch, but the young may be walled up again.

Red-billed hornbill (*Tockus erythrorhynchus*)

hornblende Any of a subgroup of amphibole minerals that contain calcium, iron, and magnesium. It occurs widely in metamorphic and igneous rocks. Common hornblende is dark green to black in color and usually found in middle-grade metamorphic rocks (formed under medium conditions of temperature and pressure).

Horne, Marilyn (b.1934) U.S. mezzo-soprano. Born in Bradford, Pa., she studied with Lotte Lehmann (1888–1976) and dubbed the leading role in the film *Carmen Jones* (1954). Her long and influential association with the bel canto repertoire began in 1962, and she played an important role in the revival of operas by G. F. HANDEL and Gioacchino ROSSINI. Her distinctive, virtuosically flexible voice was even throughout its remarkably wide range. She retired in 2000 after a long career.

horned toad *or* **horned lizard** Any of about 14 species of LIZARDS (genus *Phrynosoma,* family Iguanidae) that usually have daggerlike head spines (horns) and a flattened oval body with pointed fringe scales. Species range from about 3 to 5 in. (8–13 cm) long. They are found from British Columbia to Guatemala, usually in desert or semidesert sandy country. They hide by changing their color pattern and wriggling into the sand. They may defend themselves by inflating the body quickly and (rarely) spurting blood from the eyes.

Horney \'hȯr-ˌnī\, **Karen** *orig.* Karen Danielsen (1885–1952) German-U.S. psychoanalyst. She conducted a private practice in Berlin 1920–32 and taught at the Berlin Psychoanalytic Institute. Settling in New York in 1934, she began teaching at the New School for Social Research. She departed from Sigmund FREUD in rejecting his concept of penis envy and emphasizing the need to help patients identify and cope with the specific causes of current anxieties rather than focus on childhood traumas and fantasies. Expelled from the New York Psychoanalytic Institute in 1941, she organized the Assn. for the Advancement of Psychoanalysis. Her works include *The Neurotic Personality of Our Time* (1937) and *New Ways in Psychoanalysis* (1939).

Hornsby, Rogers (1896–1963) U.S. baseball player. Born in Winters, Texas, he played second base most of his career, principally for the St. Louis Cardinals (1915–26). His career batting average of .358 is second only to Ty COBB's .367. For five years (1921–25) he averaged .401; his 1924 average of .424 was the highest attained in the 20th cent. He twice led his league in home runs, runs batted in, and batting average.

horoscope Astrological chart showing the positions of the sun, moon, and planets in relation to the signs of the ZODIAC at a specific time. It is used to analyze the character of individuals born at that time, provide information about the current state of their life, and predict their future. Basic to a horoscope is the belief that each heavenly body has its own character, which is modified according to its relation to other celestial bodies at a given moment. See also ASTROLOGY.

Horowitz, Vladimir (1903–1989) Russian pianist. He made his debut in 1921. His stunning technique gained him a large international reputation, and he became an inveterate touring performer. Always susceptible to nervous strain, in 1953 he decided to quit public performance; his return to the concert stage in 1965 was attended by great publicity. He favored the works of the Romantics, and was sometimes criticized for employing his dazzling capacities in insufficiently profound interpretations.

horror story Story that focuses on creating a feeling of fear. Such tales are of ancient origin and form a substantial part of folk literature. They may feature supernatural elements or address more realistic psychological fears. In Western literature, the literary cultivation of fear and curiosity for its own sake emerged in the 18th cent. with the GOTHIC NOVEL. Classic practitioners of the horror and gothic genres include Mary SHELLEY, Edgar Allan POE, Bram STOKER, Ambrose BIERCE, and Stephen KING.

horse EQUINE species (*Equus caballus*) long used by humans for transport and as a draft animal. Its earliest ancestor was the dawn horse (eohippus). The horse was apparently first domesticated in central Asia in the 3rd millennium B.C. The SADDLE was introduced in China in the first centuries A.D. Horses were reintroduced to the New World, after wild horses had become extinct there some 10,000 years earlier, by the Spanish in the 16th cent. A mature male is called a stallion; mature females are called mares. A castrated stallion is called a gelding. Young horses (foals) are also known as colts (males) and fillies (females). A horse's height is measured in 4-in. (10.2-cm) units, or hands, from the highest point of the back (withers) to the ground. Breeds are classified by size and build: draft (heavy) horses (e.g., Belgian, Percheron) are up to 20 hands high; PONIES (e.g., Shetland, Iceland) are less than 14.2 hands high; and light horses (e.g., ARABIAN, THOROUGHBRED) are intermediate, rarely taller than 17 hands. See also PRZEWALSKI'S HORSE.

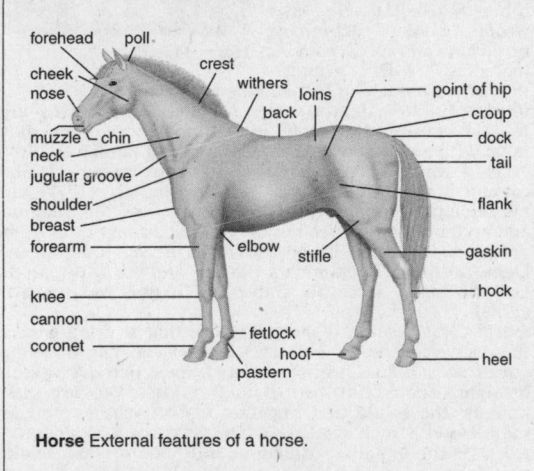

Labels: forehead, poll, crest, withers, loins, point of hip, cheek, nose, back, croup, muzzle, chin, dock, neck, tail, jugular groove, shoulder, flank, breast, forearm, elbow, stifle, gaskin, knee, hock, cannon, coronet, fetlock, hoof, heel, pastern

Horse External features of a horse.

horse-chestnut family Family Hippocastanaceae, composed of the buckeyes and the horse chestnuts (genus *Aesculus*), native to the N temperate zone. The best-known species of horse chestnut is the common, or European, horse chestnut (*A. hippocastanum),* native to SE Europe but widely cultivated as a large shade and street tree.

horsefly Any member of the DIPTERAN genus *Tabanus* or, more generally, of the family Tabanidae. These stout flies range from as small as a HOUSEFLY to as large as a BUMBLEBEE. They have metallic or iridescent eyes. Adults are fast, strong fliers usually found around streams, marshes, and wooded areas. They may carry animal diseases, including ANTHRAX. The bites of the bloodsucking females can be painful, and a swarm may suck more than 3 oz (about 90 ml) of blood a day from an animal. Horseflies of the genus *Chrysops,* usually called deerflies, are smaller.

horsepower Common unit of POWER, the rate at which WORK is done. In the English system, one horsepower

equals 33,000 foot-pounds of work per minute—that is, the power necessary to lift a total of 33,000 lbs mass one foot in one minute (actually about 50% more than the rate an average horse can sustain for a working day). The electrical equivalent is 746 watts in the INTERNATIONAL SYSTEM OF UNITS; the heat equivalent is 2,545 BTU per hour. The metric horsepower (see METRIC SYSTEM) equals 4,500 kg-m per minute (32,549 foot-pounds per minute), or 0.9863 horsepower.

horse racing Sport of running horses at speed, mainly THOROUGHBREDS with a rider astride or STANDARDBREDS with the horse pulling a conveyance with a driver. The first regularly organized national races were established in England, and the first in N. America were held on Long Island in 1665. Match events between two or three horses were run in heats. By the mid-18th cent., larger fields of runners and single-race "dash" events were the norm. HANDICAP racing emerged in the mid-18th cent. as well, as GAMBLING came to be a standard part of horse racing. PARI-MUTUEL betting was instituted in the 20th cent. Thoroughbred racing, conducted on a flat, elliptical, mile-long track, attracts the largest purses, followed by HARNESS RACING and quarter-horse racing. The most important U.S. Thoroughbred races are the KENTUCKY DERBY, PREAKNESS STAKES, and BELMONT STAKES. See also STEEPLECHASE.

horseradish Hardy perennial plant (*Armoracia lapathifolia*) of the MUSTARD FAMILY, native to Mediterranean lands and grown throughout the temperate zones. Its hotly pungent, fleshy root is used as a condiment and is traditionally considered medicinal. In many cool, moist areas it has become a troublesome weed. Its large, coarse, glossy-green basal leaves arise on long stems from the crown atop the large white root.

horseshoe crab Any of four extant species of marine ARTHROPODS (order Xiphosura, subphylum Chelicerata), found on the E coasts of Asia (three species) and N. America (one species). Despite the name, horseshoe crabs are not CRABS; they are more closely related to SCORPIONS. Fossil relatives date back 505 million years. The N. American species, *Limulus polyphemus,* can grow to more than 2 ft (60 cm) long. The body consists of three parts hinged together: a broad, horseshoe-shaped cephalothorax; a much smaller, segmented abdomen; and a long, sharp tail-spine, or telson.

horsetail Any of the 30 species of rushlike (see RUSH), conspicuously jointed, perennial herbaceous plants, also called scouring rushes, that make up the genus *Equisetum*. The stems contain abundant SILICATE and other minerals. The leaves are merely sheaths that encircle the shoots. An ancient plant, the horsetail's relatives date to the Carboniferous period. The common horsetail (*E. arvense*) is widespread along stream banks and in meadows in N. America and Eurasia. Though poisonous to livestock, horsetails are used by humans in folk medicines.

Horta, Victor, Baron (1861–1947) Belgian architect. His Hôtel Tassel (1892–93) was a pioneering example of the new ART NOUVEAU style. His Maison du Peuple (1896–99) was the first structure in Belgium with an iron-and-glass facade. From 1912 he directed the Académie des Beaux-Arts, and he designed the Palais des Beaux-Arts (1922–28).

horticulture Branch of agriculture concerned with the cultivation of garden plants—generally fruits, vegetables, flowers, and ornamentals such as plants used for landscaping. Propagation is the most basic horticultural practice. Its objectives are to increase the numbers of a plant and to preserve its essential characteristics. Propagation may be achieved sexually by use of SEEDS or asexually by use of techniques such as cutting, grafting (see GRAFT), and TISSUE CULTURE. Successful horticulture depends on extensive control of the environment, including light, water, temperature, soil structure and fertility, and pests. See also FLORICULTURE.

Horus Ancient Egyptian god with the head of a falcon, whose eyes were the sun and moon. The kings of Egypt were called living incarnations of Horus. After 2350 B.C. Horus became associated with the OSIRIS cult and was identified as the son of Osiris. He destroyed SETH, the killer of Osiris, and became ruler of all Egypt. In the Ptolemaic period, his victory over Seth became a symbol of Egypt triumphing over its occupiers.

Hosea \hō-ˈzā-ə, hō-ˈzē-ə\ (fl.8th cent. B.C.) First of the 12 Minor Prophets in the OLD TESTAMENT, traditional author of the Book of Hosea. (His prophecy is part of a larger book, The Twelve, in the Jewish canon.) The book, in which the prophet is presented as a man married to a harlot or an adulterous wife, allegorically describes the betrayal of God by Israel, which has "played the harlot" by dallying with Canaanite religion.

hosiery Knit or woven coverings for the feet and legs, worn inside shoes. In the 8th cent. B.C., HESIOD referred to linings for shoes; the Romans wrapped their feet, ankles, and legs in long strips of leather or woven cloth. After the invention of the KNITTING MACHINE, stockings were knitted flat, then shaped and seamed up the back by hand. In the 19th cent., seamless stockings, mostly of cotton, were knitted on circular machines, but seamless hose did not become popular until the 1940s, when nylon replaced silk. Panty hose were introduced in the 1960s.

hospice Home or HOSPITAL for relieving physical and emotional suffering of dying persons. In patients expected to live only months or weeks, hospice care offers an alternative to aggressive life-prolonging measures, which often only increase discomfort and isolation. Hospices provide a sympathetic environment in which prevention (not just control) of physical pain has top priority, along with patients' emotional and spiritual needs. Home hospice care is provided at the patient's home.

hospital Institution for diagnosing and treating the sick or injured, housing them during treatment, examining patients, and managing childbirth. Outpatients, who can leave after treatment, come in for emergency care or are referred for services not available in a private doctor's office. Hospitals may be public (government-owned) or private (profit-making or not-for-profit); in most nations except the U.S., most are public. They may also be general, accepting all types of medical or surgical cases, or special (e.g., children's hospitals, mental hospitals). See also HOSPICE.

Hospitallers See KNIGHTS OF MALTA, TEUTONIC ORDER

hosta \ˈhä-stə, ˈhō-stə\ Any of about 40 species of hardy herbaceous perennials of the genus *Hosta,* in the LILY FAMILY, native to E Asia. They prefer light shade but will grow under a variety of conditions. Their foliage may be light to dark green, yellow, blue, or variegated. The ribbed leaves grow in a cluster at the base, and stalks bearing clusters of tubular white or bluish-purple flowers emerge from the leaves.

hotel Building that provides lodging, meals, and other services to the traveling public on a commercial basis. Inns have existed since ancient times to serve merchants and other travelers. Medieval European monasteries operated inns to guarantee haven for travelers in dangerous regions. The spread of travel by stagecoach in the 18th cent. stimulated the development of inns, as did the Industrial Revolution. The modern hotel was largely the creation of the railroads; when traveling for pleasure became widely popular, large hotels were often built near railroad stations. In 1889 the Savoy Hotel in London set a new standard, with its own electricity and a host of special services; the Statler Hotel in Buffalo, N.Y. (1908), another landmark, catered to the growing class of business travelers. After World War II, new hotels tended to be larger and were often built near airports. Hotel chains became common, making purchasing, sales, and reservations more efficient. See also MOTEL.

hot rod Automobile rebuilt or modified for high speed, fast acceleration, or sporty appearance. A wide range of automobiles may be called hot rods, including some of those used in DRAG RACING as well as those used in recreational cruising. They may be composed of used or new parts. Some are intended primarily for exhibition.

hot spot Region of earth's upper mantle that upwells to melt through the crust to form a volcanic feature. The 5% of known world VOLCANOES not located on plate margins (see PLATE TECTONICS) are regarded as hot-spot volcanoes; Hawaiian volcanoes are the best examples. A chain of extinct volcanoes or volcanic islands (and seamounts), such as the Hawaiian chain, can form over millions of years where

a lithospheric plate moves over a hot spot. The active volcanoes all lie at one end of the chain or ridge.

hot spring *or* **thermal spring** Spring that issues water at temperatures substantially higher than the air temperature of the surrounding region. Most hot springs result from the interaction of groundwater with MAGMA or with still-hot igneous rocks. In some cases, deep circulation of water is thought to carry the water to the lower parts of the earth's CRUST, where the temperature of the rocks is high.

Hot Springs National Park National park, central Arkansas. Covering 5,839 acres (2,365 hectares), it is centered on 47 thermal springs with an average temperature of 143°F (62°C). The springs, long used by the Indians and probably visited by Hernando DE SOTO in 1541, drew Spanish and French visitors in search of health benefits in the 1700s. The town of Hot Springs (pop., 2000: 36,000) is a health and tourist resort.

Hottentots See KHOIKHOI

Houdini \hü-ˈdē-nē\, **Harry** *orig.* Erik Weisz (1874–1926) U.S. magician. Born in Hungary, from age 1 he lived with his family in Wisconsin. A trapeze and vaudeville performer, from about 1900 he earned an international reputation for his daring feats of escape from locked boxes, often submerged, while shackled in chains and handcuffed. His success depended on his great strength and agility and his unusual skill in manipulating locks. He exhibited his skills in several films (1916–23). He later wrote books debunking magicians and mind readers, including J.-E. ROBERT-HOUDIN, from whom he had taken his name.

Harry Houdini

Houdon \ü-ˈdōⁿ\, **Jean-Antoine** (1741–1828) French sculptor. Having won the Prix de Rome, he achieved immediate fame with an anatomical study of a standing man (c.1767), casts of which were widely used in art academies. He became a member of the Royal Academy in Paris (1777) with his reclining *Morpheus.* He produced numerous religious and mythological works, but his greatest strength was in the vivid individuality of his portrait busts of such luminaries as Denis DIDEROT, Benjamin FRANKLIN, and VOLTAIRE. In the U.S. he made a marble statue of George WASHINGTON (1788).

hound Classification of hunting dogs that is more general than setter, retriever, pointer, or other sporting dog categories. Most hounds were bred and trained to track by scent or sight. The BLOODHOUND and DACHSHUND are scent hounds; the saluki and AFGHAN HOUND chase game by sight. Hounds such as BEAGLES, BASSET HOUNDS, and FOXHOUNDS run in packs; Afghan hounds, borzois, and salukis run alone.

Houphouët-Boigny \üf-ˈwe-bwän-ˈyē\, **Félix** (c.1905–1993) President of Ivory Coast from independence until his death (1960–93). A rural doctor and planter, by the late 1950s he was president of the territorial assembly and mayor of Abidjan. As president, cooperating with the French, he pursued liberal free-enterprise politics and developed a strong cash-crop economy. Under his rule Ivory Coast became one of the most prosperous nations in Africa. His later years were marred by an economic downturn, civil unrest, and criticism of the enormous basilica he had built at YAMOUSSOUKRO, his birthplace.

house cat See DOMESTIC CAT

housefly Common DIPTERAN (*Musca domestica*), accounting for about 90% of all flies in human dwellings. Body size ranges from 0.2 to 0.3 in. (5–7 mm), and the conspicuous compound eyes have some 4,000 facets. Because it has sponging or lapping mouthparts, it cannot bite. Its feet may carry millions of microorganisms, some of which cause diseases, including CHOLERA, DYSENTERY, and TYPHOID.

Some insecticides are effective, but houseflies have developed resistance to others.

Houseman, John *orig.* Jacques Haussmann (1902–1988) U.S. producer and actor. Born in Romania and educated in England, he emigrated to the U.S. in 1924. In 1934 he directed the opera *Four Saints in Three Acts.* In 1937 he and Orson WELLES founded the Mercury Theatre. He later produced 19 films, including *Letter from an Unknown Woman* (1948), *They Live by Night* (1949), and *Lust for Life* (1956); he also produced and directed Broadway plays and TV specials (winning three Emmy awards), and directed the American Shakespeare Festival. His most notable acting role was in the film *The Paper Chase* (1973, Academy Award) and the later television series.

houseplant Plant adapted for growing indoors, commonly a member of a species that flourishes naturally only in warm climates. Successful houseplants must be easy to care for, and able to tolerate fairly low levels of light and humidity. Houseplants are selected for their foliage or flowers or both.

house sparrow *or* **English sparrow** One of the world's best-known and most abundant small birds (*Passer domesticus,* family Passeridae or Ploceidae). It lives in towns and on farms worldwide. It was introduced into N. America in 1852. It is about 6 in. (15 cm) long and buffy-brown; the male has a black bib. House sparrows breed nearly year-round in warm regions. See also SPARROW.

House Un-American Activities Committee (HUAC) Committee of the U.S. House of Representatives, established in 1938 under Martin DIES, that conducted investigations into alleged communist activities. Those investigated included many artists and entertainers, including the HOLLYWOOD TEN, Bertolt BRECHT, and Arthur MILLER. Richard NIXON was an active member in the late 1940s, and the committee's most celebrated case was that of Alger HISS. Its actions resulted in several contempt-of-Congress convictions and the blacklisting of many who refused to answer its questions. Highly controversial for its tactics, it was criticized for violating First Amendment rights. Its influence waning, in 1969 it was renamed the Internal Security Committee, and in 1975 it was dissolved.

Housing and Urban Development, U.S. Department of (HUD) Federal executive division responsible for carrying out government housing and community development programs. Established in 1965 under Pres. Lyndon JOHNSON, it ensures equal access to housing and community-based employment opportunities; finances new housing, public housing, and housing rehabilitation projects; insures mortgages; and carries out programs that serve the housing needs of low-income and minority families, the elderly, disabled, and mentally ill.

Housman, A(lfred) E(dward) (1859–1936) English scholar and poet. While working as a patent-office clerk, he studied Latin texts and wrote journal articles that led to his appointment as a professor at Univ. College, London, and later at Cambridge. His first poetry volume, *A Shropshire Lad* (1896), was based on classical and traditional models, and the lyrics express a Romantic pessimism in a spare, simple style. It gradually grew popular, and his second volume, *Last Poems* (1922), was extremely successful. His final collection was the posthumous *More Poems* (1936).

Houston City (pop., 2000: 1,953,000), S Texas. An inland port, it is linked by the Houston Ship Channel to the Gulf of MEXICO and the GULF INTRACOASTAL WATERWAY at GALVESTON. Founded in 1836, it was named for Sam HOUSTON; it was the capital of the Republic of Texas 1837–39. The nation's fourth-largest city and third-busiest port, it is a center for oil, petrochemical, and aerospace development (see NASA). It has several institutions for higher learning, including RICE UNIV. The Texas Medical Center is the largest in the world.

Houston, Charles H(amilton) (1895–1950) U.S. lawyer and educator. Born in Washington, D.C., he studied law at Harvard, where he became the first black editor of the *Harvard Law Review.* He served as special counsel to the NAACP 1935–40. Before the U.S. Supreme Court in *State ex rel. Gaines vs. Canada* (1939), he successfully questioned racial segregation in public schools in areas where no "separate but equal" fa-

cilities existed; the decision was a forerunner of *BROWN VS. BOARD OF EDUCATION* (1954). He served as teacher and mentor to Thurgood MARSHALL.

Houston, Sam(uel) (1793–1863) U.S. politician. Born in Rockbridge Co., Va., he lived as a youth with the Cherokee in Tennessee. He served in the U.S. House of Representatives (1823–27) and later as governor (1827–29). After his marriage failed, he resigned and again lived among the Cherokee. He exposed fraud perpetrated by government agents against the Indians, and in 1832 was sent by Pres. Andrew JACKSON to negotiate Indian treaties in Texas, then a Mexican province. When armed rebellion began in 1835, the Texan provisional government chose him to command its army, and he defeated the Mexicans at San Jacinto, securing Texas independence. He served as president of the Republic of Texas (1836–38, 1841–44) and helped win it statehood (1845), then served in the U.S. Senate (1846–59). He was elected governor in 1859 but when the state voted to secede in 1861, he refused to swear allegiance to the Confederacy and was deposed.

Sam Houston Photo by Mathew Brady

hovercraft See AIR-CUSHION VEHICLE

Hovhaness \hō-ʹvä-nəs\, **Alan** *orig.* Alan Hovhaness Chakmakjian (1911–2000) U.S. composer. Born in Somerville, Mass., he started to compose as a child. His interest in non-Western music began to influence his own work after he destroyed his early compositions in 1943. Affected by the music of his Armenian heritage and his own lifelong mysticism, he composed over 400 works, including more than 60 symphonies and many other orchestral works, often on sacred themes, sometimes incorporating aleatory or natural sounds, as in *And God Created Great Whales* (1970).

Howard, Catherine (c.1520–1542) Fifth wife of HENRY VIII of England. She was a maid of honor to ANNE OF CLEVES; after Henry had his marriage to Anne annulled, he married Catherine (1540). In 1541 he learned that Catherine had had several affairs before their marriage and had probably committed adultery as well. Incensed, he had Parliament pass a bill in 1542 declaring it treason for an unchaste woman to marry the king. Catherine was beheaded two days later.

Howard, Henry See Earl of SURREY

Howard, Oliver O(tis) (1830–1909) U.S. Army officer. Born in Leeds, Me., he served in the Civil War as a major general of Maine volunteers, fighting at Bull Run, Antietam, Chancellorsville, and Gettysburg. He commanded the Army of the Tennessee (1864) and marched with William T. SHERMAN through Georgia. During Reconstruction he was named commissioner of the FREEDMEN'S BUREAU. He helped found HOWARD UNIV. (1867) and served as its president 1869–74. He served as superintendent at West Point 1880–82.

Howard University Predominantly black university in Washington, D.C., the most prominent black educational institution in the U.S. It is financially supported by the U.S. government but is privately controlled. Founded in 1867, it has a college of liberal arts, a graduate school of arts and sciences, and schools or colleges of business and public administration, engineering, medicine, dentistry, and law, among others. Its library is the leading research library on black American history. Total enrollment is about 10,000.

Howe, Elias (1819–1867) U.S. inventor. Born in Spencer, Mass., in 1846 he was granted a patent for the first practical SEWING MACHINE. It attracted little attention, and he moved to England and worked to perfect his machine. When he returned the next year, he found that sewing machines were being widely made and sold; he finally established his patent rights in 1854. His invention soon revolutionized the garment industry. See also I. M. SINGER.

HIJ

Howe, Frederick W(ebster) (1822–1891) U.S. inventor and manufacturer. Born in Danvers, Mass., the son of a blacksmith, while still in his twenties he produced classic designs of a profiling machine, a barrel-drilling and -rifling machine, and the first commercially viable universal milling machine. His rifles built with interchangeable parts led to his establishing his own armory in Newark, N.J., in 1856. He perfected the manufacture of the SPRINGFIELD RIFLE during the Civil War, and as president of the Brown & Sharpe Co. created new sewing machines, milling machines, lathes, and other tools.

Howe, Gordie (*orig.* Gordon) (b.1928) Canadian-U.S. hockey player, regarded as one of the greatest of all time. Born in Floral, Saskatchewan, he began playing hockey at 5. In 26 seasons (1945–71) in the NHL, 25 of them playing right wing with the Detroit Red Wings, he set all-time career records for goals (801), assists (1,049), and points (1,850). Howe went on to play for or manage non-NHL teams before retiring in 1980.

Gordie Howe, 1969

Howe \ˈhaü\, **Irving** (1920–1993) U.S. critic. Raised in New York tenements, Howe helped found the left-wing magazine *Dissent,* which he edited from 1953. He wrote critical works on Sherwood ANDERSON (1951), William FAULKNER (1952), and Thomas HARDY (1967) and synthesized his political and literary interests in such works as *Politics and the Novel* (1957). *World of Our Fathers* (1976) is a major study of Jewish immigrants in New York.

Howe, James Wong *orig.* Wong Tung Jim (1899–1976) U.S. cinematographer. At age 5 he emigrated with his family from China to the U.S. He worked in Hollywood from 1917 and became a cameraman for C. B. DEMILLE. He pioneered the use of the wide-angle lens, deep focus, and the handheld camera. His low-key cinematography is seen in such films as *Kings Row* (1942), *Body and Soul* (1947), *The Rose Tattoo* (1955, Academy Award), and *Hud* (1963, Academy Award).

Howe, Julia Ward *orig.* Julia Ward (1819–1910) U.S. social reformer. Born in New York City, she worked in the abolitionist movement from her early years. She is best known for her stirring "Battle Hymn of the Republic" (1862). She became involved in the fight for equal opportunities for women, partly as a founder and first president (1868–77, 1893–1910) of the New England Woman Suffrage Assn. She also wrote travel books, biography, drama, verse, and children's songs, and edited *Woman's Journal* (1870–90). In 1908 she became the first woman elected to the American Academy of Arts and Letters. In 1843 she married Samuel Gridley Howe (1801–1876), the first director of the Perkins School for the Blind (1832–76).

Howe, Richard *later* Earl Howe (1726–1799) British admiral. As vice admiral (from 1775), he commanded in N. America 1776–78. After returning to England, he commanded the Channel fleet against the French and Spaniards and served as first lord of the admiralty 1783–88. In 1793 he again commanded the Channel fleet. His victory against the French on June 1, 1794, in the FRENCH REVOLUTIONARY WARS provided an example of tactical excellence for his successors, including Horatio NELSON.

Howe, William *later* Viscount Howe (1729–1814) British military commander. The brother of Adm. Richard HOWE, he served brilliantly as a general in the French and Indian War. In the AMERICAN REVOLUTION, he became supreme commander of British forces in N. America in 1776. He soon captured New York City and the surrounding area, and in 1777 he led British troops to victories at the BRANDYWINE and Germantown. By moving his forces to Philadelphia, he contributed to the British defeat at the Battle of SARATOGA. He resigned in 1778 and was succeeded by Henry CLINTON.

Howe Caverns Cavern system, E central New York. Located west of ALBANY, the limestone caves, discovered in 1842, have grotesque rock formations and underground channels. A second group, Secret Caverns, with underground waterfalls and fossilized marine life, is nearby.

Howel Dda See HYWEL DDA

Howells, William Dean (1837–1920) U.S. novelist and critic. Born in Martins Ferry, Ohio, he spent ten years as editor of the *Atlantic Monthly* (1871–81), becoming a preeminent figure in American letters. A champion of literary realism, he was one of the first to recognize the genius of Mark TWAIN and Henry JAMES. His own novels (from 1872) depict America as it changed from a simple, egalitarian society where luck and pluck were rewarded to one in which social and economic gulfs were becoming unbridgeable. His best-known work was *The Rise of Silas Lapham* (1885). He risked his livelihood with his plea for clemency for the anarchists involved in the HAYMARKET RIOT. His late novels, including *A Hazard of New Fortunes* (1890), reflected his deepening disillusionment with American society.

howler monkey Any of several species of slow-moving tropical American MONKEYS (genus *Alouatta*) noted for their roaring cries, which carry over a distance of 2–3 mi (3–5 km). Five species are the largest New World monkeys, generally reaching lengths of 16–28 in. (40–70 cm), excluding the 20–30-in. (50–75-cm) tail. Howlers are stoutly built and bearded, with a hunched appearance and a thickly furred, prehensile tail. They live in groups in territories mapped out by howling matches with neighboring clans.

Hoxha \ˈhȯ-jä\, **Enver** (1908–1985) Albanian communist chief of state (1944–85). He opposed the Albanian fascists in World War II and in 1941 helped found the Albanian Communist Party, which he controlled until his death. As prime minister (1944–54) he forced King ZOG to abdicate (1946). Hoxha transformed the semifeudal country into an industrialized economy; to enforce his radical programs he resorted to brutal Stalinist tactics. He broke with the Soviet Union in 1961 and with China in 1978, declaring that Albania would become a model socialist republic on its own.

Hoyle, Edmond (1671/72–1769) British writer on card games. He wrote *A Short Treatise on the Game of Whist* in 1742, and in 1760 established an important set of rules for whist. His codification of the laws of BACKGAMMON (1743) is still largely in force. Various game-rule books contain his name in the title as an indication of authority.

Hoyle, Fred (*later* **Sir Fred**) (1915–2001) British mathematician and astronomer. Within the framework of Albert EINSTEIN's theory of relativity, Hoyle formulated a mathematical basis for the STEADY-STATE THEORY of the universe. In the late 1950s and early 1960s, new observations of distant galaxies and other phenomena supported the BIG-BANG model; the steady-state theory has generally fallen out of favor. Though forced to alter some of his conclusions, Hoyle persistently tried to adapt his theory to new evidence. He is known also for his popular science works and fiction.

Hrabanus Maurus See RABANUS MAURUS

H-R diagram See HERTZSPRUNG-RUSSELL DIAGRAM

Hsia dynasty See XIA DYNASTY

Hsi-an See XI'AN

Hsi River See XI RIVER

Hsi-tsang See TIBET

Hsuan Tsung See XUANZONG

HTML *in full* HyperText Markup Language. MARKUP LANGUAGE derived from SGML that is used to prepare HYPERTEXT documents. Relatively easy for nonprogrammers to master, HTML is the language used for documents on the WORLD WIDE WEB. The text coding consists of commands contained in angle brackets <> that affect the display of elements such as text, color, and references to other documents, which can be interpreted by an Internet BROWSER according to style rules.

HTTP *in full* HyperText Transfer Protocol. Standard PROTOCOL used for exchanging files on the WORLD WIDE WEB. HTTP runs on top of the TCP/IP protocol. Web BROWSERS are HTTP clients that send file requests to Web SERVERS, which in turn handle the requests via an HTTP service. HTTP was originally proposed in 1989 by Tim BERNERS-LEE. HTTP in its first version was "stateless": each new request from a client established a new connection instead of handling all similar requests through the same connection between a specific client and server. Later versions allowed persistent connections, decompression of HTML files by client browsers, and multiple DOMAIN NAMES sharing the same IP address.

Huang Hai See YELLOW SEA

Huang River or **Hwang River** \\'hwän\\ *English* **Yellow River** River, N central and E China. The second-longest river in China, it flows 3,395 mi (5,464 km) from the Plateau of Tibet east to the YELLOW SEA (Huang Hai). In its lower reaches it has often overflowed its banks, flooding millions of acres of rich farmland, China's rice granary. Its outlet has shifted over the years to enter the Yellow Sea at points as far apart as 500 mi (800 km).

Hubbard, Elbert (Green) (1856–1915) U.S. editor, publisher, and author. Born in Bloomington, Ill., he worked as a freelance newspaperman and businessman before founding the Roycroft Press, modeled on William MORRIS's communal Kelmscott Press. In 1895 he began issuing his monthly "Little Journey" booklets, biographical essays on famous people. He started the magazine *The Philistine*, in which his well-known moralistic essay "A Message to Garcia" (1899) appeared. He died in the sinking of the *LUSITANIA*.

Hubbard, L(afayette) Ron(ald) (1911–1986) U.S. novelist and founder of the Church of SCIENTOLOGY. Born in Tilden, Neb., he grew up in Helena, Mont., and studied engineering at George Washington Univ. In the 1930s and '40s he became a successful science-fiction novelist. In 1950 he published the best-selling *Dianetics*, which detailed his theories of the human mind. In 1954 he founded the Church of SCIENTOLOGY to explore the spiritual dimension of Dianetics more fully. Often at odds with tax authorities as the church's wealth accumulated, he lived many years on a yacht.

Hubble, Edwin P(owell) (1889–1953) U.S. astronomer. Born in Marshfield, Mo., he earned his PhD at the Univ. of Chicago before beginning work at Mt. Wilson Observatory. In 1922–24 he discovered that certain nebulae contained CEPHEID VARIABLES, which he found were several hundred thousand light-years away, implying that the nebulae were actually other galaxies. His second remarkable discovery (1927) was that those galaxies were receding from the Milky Way at rates that increased with distance. This meant that the universe, long considered unchanging, was expanding. The ratio of the galaxies' speed to their distance, amazingly, was a constant (see HUBBLE'S CONSTANT), but Hubble's calculation of it was incorrect, making the Milky Way larger than all other galaxies and the universe younger than the earth. Later astronomers determined that galaxies were systematically more distant, resolving the discrepancy.

Hubble's constant Constant relating the velocities of remote galaxies to their distances from earth, estimated at about 9–19 mi/second (15–30 km/second) per million light-years. Denoted H and named for Edwin HUBBLE, it expresses the rate of expansion of the universe. Hubble used distant galaxies' RED SHIFTS and his estimates of their distance to establish the cosmological velocity-distance law (Hubble law): velocity = H × distance, so that the farther a galaxy, the faster it is receding. Derived theoretically and confirmed by observations, this law has made secure the concept of an EXPANDING UNIVERSE.

Hubble Space Telescope (HST) Most sophisticated optical observatory ever launched to orbit earth. Orbiting above the obscuring ATMOSPHERE, its images are much brighter, clearer, and more detailed than those from ground-based telescopes. It was built for NASA and deployed on a 1990 SPACE-SHUTTLE mission. Its mirror optics gather light from celestial objects and direct it into two cameras and two spectrographs (see SPECTROSCOPY).

Hubble Space Telescope, cutaway view

A defect made its first images fuzzy; correction of this and other problems on a 1993 mission has let it return spectacular photographs of cosmic phenomena.

huckleberry Small, fruit-bearing, branching shrub of the genus *Gaylussacia,* in the HEATH FAMILY. It bears fleshy fruit with 10 nutlike seeds, differing in this respect from the BLUEBERRY. The common huckleberry of the N U.S. is *G. baccata,* also called black, or highbush, huckleberry. The red huckleberry of the S U.S. is commonly called the southern cranberry.

HUD See U.S. Department of HOUSING AND URBAN DEVELOPMENT

Hudson, Henry (1565?–1611) English navigator and explorer. Sailing in search of the NORTHEAST PASSAGE to the Far East, in 1609 he set out in the *Half Moon* for the Dutch E. INDIA CO., but when stopped by storms he instead sought the NORTHWEST PASSAGE and cruised along the Atlantic coast and up the HUDSON RIVER. In 1610 he set out again for America, this time on behalf of the English E. INDIA CO., and discovered HUDSON BAY. Finding no outlet to the Pacific and in the close confinement of an Arctic winter, Hudson's crew mutinied and set Hudson adrift in a small boat, never to be found. His discoveries formed the basis for Dutch colonization of the Hudson River and for English claims to much of Canada.

Hudson, Rock *orig.* Roy Harold Scherer (1925–1985) U.S. film actor. Born in Winnetka, Ill., he made his film debut in *Fighter Squadron* (1948). His manly, wholesome good looks made him a popular star in such dramas as *Magnificent Obsession* (1954) and *Giant* (1956), and he displayed a flair for comedy in a series of films with Doris DAY, including *Pillow Talk* (1959). His death from AIDS greatly increased awareness of the disease.

Hudson Bay Inland sea, indenting E central Canada. With an area of 480,000 sq mi (1,243,000 sq km), it is bounded by Nunavut, Manitoba, Ontario, and Quebec. It is connected with the Atlantic Ocean via the Hudson Strait and with the Arctic Ocean via the Foxe Channel. Named for Henry HUDSON, who navigated its E coast in 1610, the bay and surrounding area, known as Rupert's Land, were controlled by the HUDSON'S BAY CO. 1821–69. Its islands are administratively part of Nunavut Territory. Its wildlife includes walrus, killer whales, and polar bears.

Hudson River River, New York. Originating in the ADIRONDACK MTNS. and flowing for about 315 mi (507 km) to NEW YORK CITY, it was named for Henry HUDSON, who explored it in 1609. Dutch settlement of the Hudson Valley began in 1629. The river became a strategic waterway during the AMERICAN REVOLUTION. Linked by canals with the GREAT LAKES, Delaware River, and lower ST. LAWRENCE RIVER, the Hudson is a major commercial route. The effect of the ocean's tides is felt as far north as Albany.

Hudson River school U.S. landscape painters, active around 1825–70. The first of them were inspired by the natural beauty of New York's Hudson River valley and Catskill Mtns. The leading figures were Thomas COLE, Asher DURAND, and Thomas Doughty (1793–1856). Others, such as Frederic CHURCH and George INNESS, had studied in Europe and found inspiration in the grandiose landscapes of J. M. W. TURNER. By mid-century they were widely admired for their depictions of the untamed U.S. landscape. The name is now often extended to artists who painted imposing scenes of the Rocky Mtns., Grand Canyon, and Yosemite Valley. The first native school of painting in the U.S., it remained the dominant school of landscape painting throughout the 19th cent.

Hudson's Bay Co. Corporation prominent in Canadian history. It was incorporated in England (1670) to seek the NORTHWEST PASSAGE to the Pacific, occupy lands adjacent to HUDSON BAY, and carry on commerce. The lands granted, known as Rupert's Land, extended from Labrador west to the Rocky Mtns. and from the S Canadian border north to include Hudson Bay. The company initially established fur-trading posts around Hudson Bay. By 1783 competitors had formed the NORTH WEST CO., and armed clashes continued until the two merged in 1821. The company was given exclusive fur-trade rights until 1858. In 1870 it sold its territories to the government in exchange for £300,000 and min-

eral rights to lands around the posts and a fertile portion of W Canada. It remained a large fur-collecting and marketing agency until 1991, with extensive real-estate interests and many department stores.

Hue \hü-'ā, 'wā\ City (pop., 1992 est.: 219,000), central Vietnam. The seat of the Chinese military authority in the kingdom of Nam Viet around 200 B.C., it passed to the Chams about A.D. 200. In 1306 it was ceded to Dai Viet (Vietnam). It is the site of the imperial citadel, from which the NGUYEN family reigned from the mid-16th to the mid-20th cent. It was occupied by the Japanese 1940–45. Hue was largely destroyed during the 1968 Tet offensive of the VIETNAM WAR; it has since been rebuilt.

Hueffer, Ford Madox See F. M. FORD

Huerta \'wer-tä\, **Victoriano** (1854–1916) Mexican president (1913–14). Born of Indian parents, he rose to become a general during the rule of Porfirio DÍAZ. He overthrew Díaz's successor, the liberal Francisco MADERO, and established a repressive military dictatorship. Constitutionalist forces united against him with support from U.S. Pres. Woodrow WILSON. Huerta was defeated in 1914 and fled to Spain; he moved to the U.S., where he was arrested for fomenting rebellion in Mexico and died in custody.

Hugh Capet \'kā-pət\ (938?–996) King of France (987–96) and founder of the CAPETIAN dynasty. The son of a Frankish duke, he inherited vast estates in the regions of Paris and Orléans, which made him a serious threat to the Carolingian king, Lothair. By 985 Hugh was the ruler of France in all but name, and two years later he was elected king. He immediately crowned his own son to ensure the line of succession, a practice continued until 1137. He mediated disputes among French nobles and survived a conspiracy to betray him to OTTO III.

Hughes, Charles Evans (1862–1948) U.S. jurist and statesman. Born in Glens Falls, N.Y., he won two terms as governor (1906–10), which were marked by extensive reform. He was appointed to the U.S. Supreme Court in 1910, but resigned in 1916 to run as the Republican presidential candidate, losing to Woodrow WILSON in a close race. As secretary of state (1921–25), he planned and chaired the Washington Conference (1921–22). Appointed chief justice of the U.S. Supreme Court in 1930, he led the Court through the great controversies arising out of Pres. Franklin ROOSEVELT's NEW DEAL legislation. He generally favored the exercise of government power, though he spoke for the Court in invalidating (in *Schechter Poultry Corp. vs. U.S.*) a principal New Deal statute. He attacked Roosevelt's court-packing plan (1937), and he wrote the opinion sustaining COLLECTIVE BARGAINING under the WAGNER ACT. He served until 1941.

Hughes, Howard (Robard) (1905–1976) U.S. manufacturer, aviator, and movie producer. Born in Houston, he left college at 17 to take control of his late father's Hughes Tool Co., which owned the patent to a profitable oil-drilling tool. In the early 1930s he founded Hughes Aircraft Co. In 1935 he set a speed record of 352 mph (567 kph) in a plane he designed. In 1938 he flew around the world in a record 91 hours. In 1947 he built and piloted the only flight of a wooden eight-engine flying boat dubbed "the Spruce Goose." He produced several movies in Hollywood in the 1930s, and later owned RKO Pictures. He held controlling stock in TRANS WORLD AIRLINES until 1966. After about 1950 he became a famously eccentric recluse, and after his death his forged memoirs and his several wills became a source of scandal.

Langston Hughes Photo by Jack Delano, 1942

Hughes, (James Mercer) Langston (1902–1967) U.S. poet and writer. Born in Joplin, Mo., he published the poem "The Negro Speaks of Rivers" when he was 19. His career was dramatically launched when Hughes, working as a busboy, presented his poems to Vachel LINDSAY as he dined. His poetry collections include *The Weary Blues* (1926) and *Montage of a Dream Deferred* (1951). His later *The Panther and the Lash* (1967) reflects black anger and militancy. Among his other works are short stories, autobiographies, many works for the stage, anthologies, and translations. His well-known comic character Jesse B. Semple appeared in his newspaper columns.

Hughes, Ted (*orig.* Edward James) (1930–1998) British poet. He married the American poet Sylvia PLATH in 1956. His first volumes of verse were *The Hawk in the Rain* (1957) and *Lupercal* (1960). His collections include *Wodwo* (1967), *Crow* (1970), *Cave Birds* (1975), and *Gaudete* (1977). His most characteristic work emphasizes the cunning and savagery of animal life in harsh, sometimes disjunctive lines. He wrote many volumes for children and edited the journal *Modern Poetry in Translation*. In 1984 he became Britain's poet laureate. *Birthday Letters* (1998), published shortly before his death, consists of revealing poems about his relationship with Plath.

Hugli River *or* **Hooghly River** \'hü-glē\ River, NE India. Commercially the most important arm of the GANGES RIVER, it provides access to CALCUTTA from the Bay of BENGAL. It flows south about 160 mi (260 km) through a heavily industrialized area with more than half of W. Bengal's population. The river is navigable to Calcutta by ocean liners.

Hugo, Victor (-Marie) (1802–1885) French poet, dramatist, and novelist. With his verse drama *Cromwell* (1827) he emerged as an important figure in ROMANTICISM. The production of his poetic tragedy *Hernani* (1830) was a famous victory for Romantics over traditional classicists. His best-known novels are *The Hunchback of Notre Dame* (1831), an evocation of medieval life, and *Les misérables* (1862), the story of the convict Jean Valjean; their huge popularity made him the most successful writer in the world. In later life he was a politician and

Victor Hugo Photo by Nadar

political writer. He spent the years 1851–70 in exile for his republican views, producing his most extensive and original poetry, including *Les châtiments* (1853) and *The Legend of the Centuries* (1859, 1877, 1883). He was made a senator in 1876, and he was buried in the Pantheon as a national hero.

Huguenots \'hyü-gə-ˌnäts\ French Protestants of the 16th–17th cent. The first French Huguenot community was founded in 1546, and the confession of faith drawn up by the first synod in 1559 was influenced by the ideas of John CALVIN. They rapidly became a political force, led by Gaspard de COLIGNY. Conflicts with the Roman Catholic government and others, including the House of GUISE, led to the Wars of RELIGION (1562–98). A Huguenot political party was formed in 1573 to fight for religious and civil liberties. In 1598 HENRY IV promulgated the Edict of NANTES, granting rights to Protestants. Civil wars occurred again in the 1620s, the Huguenots lost their political power, and they continued to be harassed and forcibly converted. In 1685 LOUIS XIV revoked the Edict of Nantes; over the next several years, more than 400,000 French Protestants left France.

Huhehot See HOHHOT

Hu-ho-hao-t'e See HOHHOT

Huitzilopochtli \ˌwēt-sē-lō-'pōcht-lē\ AZTEC sun and war god. He was usually portrayed as a hummingbird or as a warrior with a helmet of feathers and a turquoise snake staff. Some myths presented him as the divine leader of the tribe during the long migration that brought the Aztecs to the Valley of Mexico. The fifteenth month of the ceremonial year was dedicated to him, and human sacrifices were made in his honor, in keeping with the belief that he needed human blood and hearts as daily nourishment.

Huizinga \\'hœi-ziŋ-ȧ\\, **Johan** (1872–1945) Dutch historian. He was professor of history at Leiden from 1915 until 1942, when he was taken hostage by the Nazis. He became internationally recognized for *The Waning of the Middle Ages* (1919), a lively examination of life in France and Holland in the 14th–15th cent. His other works include *Erasmus* (1924), *In the Shadow of Tomorrow* (1935), and *Homo Ludens* (1938).

Hukbalahap Rebellion \\'hủk-bȧ-lȧ-'hȧp\\ (1946–54) Peasant uprising in Luzon, Philippines. The rich Luzon plain was farmed by a large tenant-farmer population working on vast estates, and the area became a focal point for communist organizers in the 1930s. The communist Hukbalahap (Huk) was a successful anti-Japanese guerrilla group during World War II, and by the war's end it had seized most of the Luzon large estates and established a government. When the Philippines became independent in 1946, the Huks, denied their elective legislative seats, began a rebellion. In 1950 they nearly seized Manila. Defeated by U.S. weaponry supplied to the government and by the rise of the popular Ramon MAGSAYSAY, the Huk leader, Luis Taruc (b.1913), surrendered in 1954, though the Huk movement continued into the 1970s.

hula Polynesian dance that combines undulating movement of the hips and mimetic hand gestures, often performed to chants and instruments such as the ukulele. Originally a religious dance performed to praise the chiefs, contemporary hulas tell a story or describe a place and are danced exclusively by women. The costume is typically a raffia skirt with a lei around the neck.

Hull *in full* **Kingston upon Hull** City (pop., 1999 est.: 266,000), seat of Humberside, England. It lies on the Humber Estuary 22 mi (35 km) from the North Sea. For more than 400 years it was the chief shipping port for nearby inland waterways. It is now a major national seaport, accommodating large oceangoing vessels. The medieval part of the city retains a number of historic buildings.

Hull, Bobby (*orig.* Robert Martin) (b.1939) Canadian hockey player. Born in Pointe Anne, Ontario, he played for the Chicago Black Hawks (1957–72), where his swinging slap shot and fast skating made him a dominant figure. By the time he retired from the NHL, he had scored 609 goals, 555 assists, and 1,164 points. He went on to play in the now-defunct World Hockey Assn. (1972–81).

Hull, Clark L(eonard) (1884–1952) U.S. psychologist. Born in Akron, N.Y., he taught at the Univ. of Wisconsin 1918–29, and was a member of Yale Univ.'s Institute of Human Relations 1929–52. His study of psychometrics culminated in *Aptitude Testing* (1929). His study of hypnosis resulted in *Hypnosis and Suggestibility* (1933). His intensive study of learning produced the dominant learning theory of the 1940s and '50s. His important *Mathematico-Deductive Theory of Rote Learning* (1940) was followed by his highly influential *Principles of Behavior* (1943). Attempting to develop a rigorous theory of learning that would account for all behaviors, human and animal, he and his followers dominated the experimental literature for more than two decades, but their theories eventually were replaced by a more cognitive psychology that provided a role for mental events.

Hull, Cordell (1871–1955) U.S. politician and diplomat. Born in Overton Co., Tenn., he served in the U.S. House of Representatives (1907–21, 1923–31), where he wrote the first income-tax bill (1913) and the inheritance-tax law (1916). As secretary of state under Franklin ROOSEVELT (1933–44), he initiated a reciprocal trade program that lowered tariffs and expanded world trade. He improved Latin American relations by fostering the GOOD NEIGHBOR POLICY. He began early in World War II to plan an international postwar peacekeeping body, causing Roosevelt to describe him as the "father of the UNITED NATIONS"; his work earned him the 1945 Nobel Peace Prize.

Hull, Isaac (1773–1843) U.S. naval officer. Born in Huntington, Conn., he was master of a ship by 19. In 1810 he became commander of the USS *CONSTITUTION*. Early in the War of 1812 he engaged the British frigate *Guerrière* and af-

ter a fierce battle rendered it a wreck. His victory united the U.S. behind the war effort. He commanded the U.S. squadrons in the Pacific (1824–27) and in the Mediterranean (1839–41).

human being See HOMO SAPIENS

human evolution Evolution of modern human beings from nonhuman and extinct HOMINID forms. Genetic evidence points to an evolutionary divergence between the lineages of humans and the great apes (Pongidae) on the African continent 5–8 million years ago. The oldest known hominid remains, dating to at least 4 million years ago, belong to the genus *AUSTRALOPITHECUS*. One of the species of australopithecines probably gave rise to *HOMO HABILIS*, which inhabited sub-Saharan Africa until about 1.5 million years ago. *H. habilis* was apparently supplanted by a taller and more human species, *HOMO ERECTUS*, which gradually migrated into Asia and parts of Europe. Archaic forms of *HOMO SAPIENS* with features resembling those of both *H. erectus* and modern humans appeared about 400,000 years ago in Africa and perhaps parts of Asia, but fully modern humans emerged only 250,000–150,000 years ago, probably descended from *H. erectus*.

Human Genome Project U.S. research effort initiated in 1990 by the U.S. Department of Energy and the National Institutes of Health to analyze the DNA of human beings. The project proposed to identify the chromosomal location of every human GENE, to determine each gene's precise chemical structure, and to determine the sequence of nucleotides of the entire set of genes (the genome). Another project was to address the ethical, legal, and social implications of the information obtained. The findings will be the basic reference for research in human biology and will provide fundamental insights into the genetic basis of disease. The new technologies developed will be widely applicable. In 2000 the government and the private corporation Celera Genomics jointly announced that the project had been virtually completed, five years ahead of schedule.

human growth hormone See GROWTH HORMONE

human immunodeficiency virus See HIV

humanism In Renaissance Europe, a cultural impulse characterized by a revival of classical letters, an individualistic and critical spirit, and a shift of emphasis from religious to secular concerns. It dates to the 14th cent. and the poet PETRARCH, though earlier figures are sometimes described as humanists. Today the term is often used loosely to mean an emphasis on a human-centered rather than a God-centered universe.

humanistic psychology 20th-cent. movement in psychology, developed in reaction against BEHAVIORISM and PSYCHOANALYSIS, that emphasizes the importance of values, intentions, and meaning to the individual. The concept of the "self" is a central focus. Its leading theorists included Abraham MASLOW, Carl ROGERS, and Rollo May (1909–1994). Humanistic therapies have included sensory awareness, encounter groups, Gestalt therapy, and various human-potential, holistic-health, and addiction-recovery schools.

humanities Branches of knowledge that investigate human beings, their culture, and their self-expression. Distinguished from the physical and biological sciences and, less decisively, from the social sciences, the humanities include the study of languages and literatures, the arts, history, and philosophy. The modern conception of the humanities has roots in classical Greek and Roman courses of education. The Renaissance humanists contrasted *studia humanitatis* ("studies of humanity") with studies of the divine; by the 19th cent. the distinction was instead drawn between the humanities and the sciences.

human nature Fundamental dispositions and traits of humans. Theories about the nature of humankind form a part of every culture. In the West, debate has traditionally centered on whether humans are selfish and competitive (see, e.g., Thomas HOBBES and John LOCKE) or social and altruistic (Karl MARX, Émile DURKHEIM). Recent research suggests that humans may be both, and that there is a complex interaction between genetically inherited factors ("nature") and developmental and social factors ("nurture"). Basic drives shared with other PRIMATES include food, sex, security, play, and social status. Traits unique to humans in-

HIJ

clude speech, tool manufacture, and CULTURE. GENDER differences include greater investment in reproduction and child-rearing among females, hence less risk-taking. See also *HOMO SAPIENS*, PERSONALITY.

human rights Rights that belong to an individual as a consequence of being human. The term came into wide use after World War II, replacing the earlier phrase "natural rights" (see NATURAL LAW). Today human rights are seen as universal, general, and fundamental. Some theorists limit human rights to the right to life, or to life and freedom of opportunity. In the 17th–18th cent., thinkers such as John LOCKE stressed civil and political rights (including freedom of speech and religion, and freedom from slavery, torture, and arbitrary arrest). In the 19th cent., the focus moved to economic and social rights (including the right to work and the right to a minimum standard of living). The adoption of the UNIVERSAL DECLARATION OF HUMAN RIGHTS in 1948 was a landmark. In the late 20th cent., the concept was sometimes extended to include such rights as self-determination, peace, and a healthy environment.

human sacrifice Offering of the life of a human being to a god. In some ancient cultures, it was an attempt to commune with the god and to participate in the divine life. It also sometimes served as an attempt to placate the god and expiate the sins of the people. It was especially common among agricultural peoples who sought to guarantee the fertility of the soil. The AZTECS sacrificed thousands annually, and the INCAS made human sacrifices on the accession of a ruler. In ancient Egypt, elsewhere in Africa, and in China, human sacrifice was connected with ANCESTOR WORSHIP, and slaves and servants were killed or buried alive along with dead kings in order to provide service in the afterlife. The Celts and Germanic peoples are among the European peoples who practiced human sacrifice.

Humbert See UMBERTO

Humboldt, (Friedrich Wilhelm Heinrich) Alexander, (Baron) von (1769–1859) German naturalist and explorer. In 1792 he joined the mining department of the Prussian government, where he invented a safety lamp and established a technical school for miners. From 1799 he explored Central and S. America, and discovered the connection between the Amazon and Orinoco river systems. He studied the oceanic current off the W coast of S. America, which became known as the Humboldt current (now the Peru current). He returned to Europe in 1804. His research helped lay the foundation for comparative climatology and added to an understanding of the devel-

Alexander von Humboldt
Painting by F. G. Weitsch, 1806

opment of the earth's crust. In Paris he used his financial resources to help Louis AGASSIZ and others launch careers. In 1829 he traveled to Russia and Siberia and made geographical, geological, and meteorological observations of Central Asia. During the 1830s he investigated magnetic storms. His last 25 years were spent writing *Kosmos,* an account of the structure of the universe.

Humboldt, (Karl) Wilhelm *later* **Freiherr (Baron) von Humboldt** (1767–1835) German linguist and educational reformer. The elder brother of Alexander von HUMBOLDT, he held various Prussian government posts. He raised elementary education standards and was instrumental in founding Friedrich Wilhelm Univ. (now Humboldt Univ., or Univ. of BERLIN). Humboldt also contributed greatly to the philosophy of language, contending that its character and structure express the speaker's culture and individuality and that humans perceive the world through the medium of language.

Humboldt River River, N Nevada. Rising in Elko county, it flows west and southwest for 290 mi (467 km) to Humboldt Lake. Named by J. C. FRÉMONT for Alexander von HUM-

BOLDT, it was an important route for emigrants going from Salt Lake City to the gold fields in central California.

Humboldt University of Berlin See Univ. of BERLIN

Hume, David (1711–1776) Scottish philosopher, historian, and economist. His first book was the important and comprehensive *Treatise of Human Nature* (1739–40). His well-received *Essays Moral and Political* (1741–42) strongly influenced the economic thinking of his friend Adam SMITH. His *Political Discourses* (1752) was followed by his huge *History of England* (5 vols., 1754–62). He conceived of philosophy as the inductive, experimental science of human nature. Employing Isaac NEWTON's scientific method and building on John LOCKE'S EMPIRICISM, he tried to describe how the mind works in acquiring knowledge. He concluded that no METAPHYSICS is possible, that there can be no knowledge of anything beyond experience, and that humans rely on sentiment more than reason. He was led to question the objective validity of the concepts of substance and causal necessity and of the method of INDUCTION. Immanuel KANT conceived his critical philosophy in direct reaction to Hume, and Hume was important in leading Auguste COMTE to POSITIVISM. In Britain, Hume's influence is seen in Jeremy BENTHAM, who was moved to UTILITARIANISM by Hume's *Treatise*, and in John Stuart MILL.

humidity Amount of water vapor in the air. An important factor in climate and weather; it regulates air temperature by absorbing thermal radiation both from the sun and the earth, and it is the ultimate source of condensation and precipitation. Humidity varies because the water-holding capacity of air is determined by temperature. When a volume of air at a given temperature holds the maximum amount of water vapor possible, the air is said to be saturated. Relative humidity is the water-vapor content of the air relative to its content at saturation; near the earth the relative humidity rarely falls below 30%.

Hummel \'hùm-əl\, **Johann Nepomuk** (1778–1837) Austrian composer, pianist, and conductor. Born in Pressburg (Bratislava), he was a piano prodigy. Moving at 8 to Vienna, he studied two years with W. A. MOZART. After five years of touring, he gave up public performance. He replaced F. J. HAYDN as music director at the Esterházy palace in 1804, while teaching and composing for the theater, and in 1814 he recommended performing with huge success. He composed a number of concertos and much chamber music.

Hummert, Anne and Frank (1905–1996, 1890?–1966) U.S. radio producers. Anne Schumacher was working for the Chicago advertising agency co-owned by Frank Hummert when the two began to write radio soap operas. Their *Just Plain Bill* (1932–55), *The Romance of Helen Trent* (1933–60), *Ma Perkins* (1933–60), and *Backstage Wife* (1935–59) became such hits that they formed Hummert Radio Productions. Creating the basic plots and overseeing an assembly line of writers, they produced more than 40 radio shows, including the soap opera *Stella Dallas* (1938–55), the mystery show *Mr. Keen, Tracer of Lost Persons* (1937–54), and the musical program *The American Album of Familiar Music* (1931–51).

hummingbird Any of about 320 species of New World birds (family Trochilidae), many of which have glittering colors. They are most abundant in S. America; about 12 species are found in the U.S. and Canada. They range in length from 2 in. (5 cm) to 8 in. (20 cm), weigh 0.07–0.7 oz (2–20 g), and have a long, slender bill. The bee hummingbird of Cuba is the smallest living bird. Hummingbirds can fly forward, straight up and down, sideways, and backward and can hover in front of flowers to obtain nectar and insects. Smaller species can beat their wings as fast as 80 times per second.

humor *or* **humour** (Latin: "fluid") One of the four body fluids thought to determine a person's temperament, according to a theory widely accepted in ancient and medieval times. According to GALEN, the four cardinal humors were blood, phlegm, choler (yellow bile), and melancholy (black bile). The mixture of these humors in each person determined his "complexion" or temperament and his mental and physical qualities. A disproportionate amount of one humor created a personality dominated by one set of related emotions (e.g., a choleric man was easily angered, proud, ambitious, and vengeful).

humpback whale Thickset BALEEN WHALE (*Megaptera novaeangliae,* or *M. nodosa*) that lives along all major ocean coasts, often close inshore. Humpbacks grow to 40–52 ft (12–16 m) long. They have very long, narrow pectoral fins and large knobs on the head and jaws. The humpback migrates between polar waters in summer and tropical or subtropical breeding grounds in winter. It is probably the most vocal of all whales (with "songs" of 5–35 minutes) and one of the most acrobatic (capable of turning a somersault). It has been protected since the 1960s as an endangered species.

Humpback whale (*Megaptera novaeangliae*)

Humperdinck, Engelbert (1854–1921) German composer. Having studied piano, organ, cello, and composition, in 1879 he met Richard WAGNER in Naples and became a member of his circle. Invited to help prepare *Parsifal* for its premiere, he came to be considered Wagner's chosen successor by some. He is known today for the highly popular opera *Hänsel und Gretel* (1892); his later works include the opera *Königskinder* (1897).

Humphrey, Doris (1895–1958) U.S. dancer and modern-dance choreographer. Born in Oak Park, Ill., she joined the Denishawn troupe in 1917. She left in 1928 to cofound, with Charles Weidman (1901–1975), a school and performing dance group, which was active until 1944. Her choreography expressed an innovative use of conflict between balance and imbalance, fall and recovery; her works included *Water Study* (1928) and *New Dance* (1935). She retired as a performer in 1945 but continued as artistic director for José LIMÓN's company.

Humphrey, Hubert H(oratio) (1911–1978) U.S. vice president (1965–69). Born in Wallace, S.D., he worked as a pharmacist before becoming Minnesota campaign manager for Pres. Franklin ROOSEVELT in 1944. He helped merge the state's Democratic and Farmer-Labor parties, and was elected mayor of Minneapolis (1945–48). In the U.S. Senate (1949–64), he proved to be a skilled parliamentary leader who helped forge bipartisan support for the Nuclear Test-Ban Treaty and the 1964 Civil Rights Act. As vice president under Lyndon JOHNSON, he defended the VIETNAM WAR, compromising his liberal reputation. He won the presidential nomination in 1968, but narrowly lost to Richard NIXON. He served again in the Senate 1971–78.

humus \\'hyü-məs\\ Nonliving, finely divided organic matter in soil, derived from microbial decomposition of plant and animal substances. It consists primarily of carbon but also contains nitrogen and smaller amounts of phosphorus and sulfur. As it decomposes, its components are changed into forms usable by plants. It is valued by farmers and gardeners because it provides nutrients essential for plant growth, increases the soil's water absorption, and improves soil workability.

Hundred Days *French* Cent Jours (1815) Period between NAPOLEON's arrival in Paris after escaping from exile on Elba and the return of LOUIS XVIII to Paris. Napoleon landed on French soil on March 1 and reached Paris on March 20. Austria, Britain, Prussia, and Russia swiftly concluded an alliance against him, and a series of battles led up to the Battle of WATERLOO. On June 22 Napoleon abdicated a second time and was removed to St. Helena; Louis returned to Paris on July 8.

Hundred Years' War (1337–1453) Intermittent armed conflict between England and France over territorial rights and the issue of succession to the French throne. It began when EDWARD III invaded Flanders in 1337 to assert his claim to the French crown; he won a major victory at the Battle of CRÉCY (1346). After the English victory at the Battle of POITIERS (1356), the French were obliged to surrender ex-

tensive lands under the treaties of BRÉTIGNY and Calais (1360). The French king CHARLES V refused to respect the treaties and reopened the conflict in 1369, putting the English on the defensive. After his death in 1380 both countries were preoccupied with internal power struggles, and the war lapsed into uncertain peace. In 1415, however, HENRY V took advantage of civil war in France to press English claims to the French throne (see Battle of AGINCOURT). By 1422 the English and their Burgundian allies controlled Aquitaine and all France north of the Loire, including Paris. A turning point came in 1429, when JOAN OF ARC raised the English siege of Orléans. The French king CHARLES VII conquered Normandy and then retook Aquitaine in 1453, leaving the English in possession only of Calais. The war laid waste to much of France and virtually destroyed the feudal nobility. By ending England's status as a power on the continent, it led the English to expand their reach and power at sea.

Hungarian language FINNO-UGRIC LANGUAGE of Hungary, with substantial minority populations in Slovakia, Transylvania, and N Serbia. Hungarian has about 14.5 million speakers worldwide, including 400,000–500,000 in N. America. The earliest known text in Hungarian dates from the late 12th cent.; a continuous literary tradition begins in the 15th cent. Though more heavily influenced by European languages than any other URALIC LANGUAGE, Hungarian retains some typical Uralic features, such as a complex nominal case system, expression of possession by suffixes, and a distinction in conjugation of verbs having definite and indefinite objects. Contact with other languages has given Hungarian many loanwords.

Hungarian Revolution (1956) Popular uprising in Hungary. Following a speech by Nikita KHRUSHCHEV in which he attacked the period of Joseph STALIN's rule, a rising tide of discontent in Hungary broke out into active fighting in October 1956. Rebels won the first phase of the revolution, and Imre NAGY became premier. On November 1 he declared Hungarian neutrality and appealed to the U.N. Western powers failed to respond, and on November 4 the Soviet Union invaded to stop the revolution. Nevertheless, Stalinist-type domination was replaced by a slow evolution toward some internal autonomy.

Hungary *officially* **Republic of Hungary** *Hungarian* **Magyar Koztarsasag** \\'mȯ-jȯr-kœs-'tär-shȯ-ˌshäg\\ Republic, central Europe. Area: 35,919 sq mi (93,030 sq km). Population (2000): 10,022,000. Capital: BUDAPEST. The people are an amalgam of Magyars and various Slavic, Turkish, and Germanic peoples. Language: Hungarian (Magyar) (official). Religions: Roman Catholicism, Protestantism. Currency: forint. The Great Alfold (Great Hungarian Plain), with fertile agriculture land, occupies nearly half the country. Hungary's two most important rivers are the DANUBE and TISZA. Lake Balaton, in the Transdanubian highlands, is the largest lake in central Europe. Forests cover nearly one-fifth of its land. It is one of the more prosperous nations of E Europe, and a major world producer of bauxite. A conversion from a socialist to a free-market economy was begun in the late 1980s. It is a multiparty republic with one legislative house; the chief of state is the president, and the head of government is the prime minister. The W part of Hungary was incorporated into the Roman empire in 14 B.C. The MAGYARS, a nomadic people, settled in the Great Alfold in the late 9th cent. STEPHEN I, crowned in 1000, Christianized the country and organized it into a strong and independent state. Invasions by the MONGOLS in the 13th cent. and by the Ottoman Turks in the 14th cent. devastated the country, and by 1568 the territory of modern Hungary had been divided into three parts: Royal Hungary fell to the HABSBURGS; TRANSYLVANIA gained autonomy in 1566 under the Trks; and the central plain remained under Turkish control until the late 17th cent., when the Austrian HABSBURGS took over. Hungary declared its independence from Austria in 1849, and in 1867 the dual monarchy of AUSTRIA-HUNGARY was established. Its defeat in World War I resulted in the dismemberment of Hungary, leaving it only those areas in which Magyars predominated. In an attempt to regain some of this lost territory, Hungary cooperated with the Germans against the Soviet Union during World

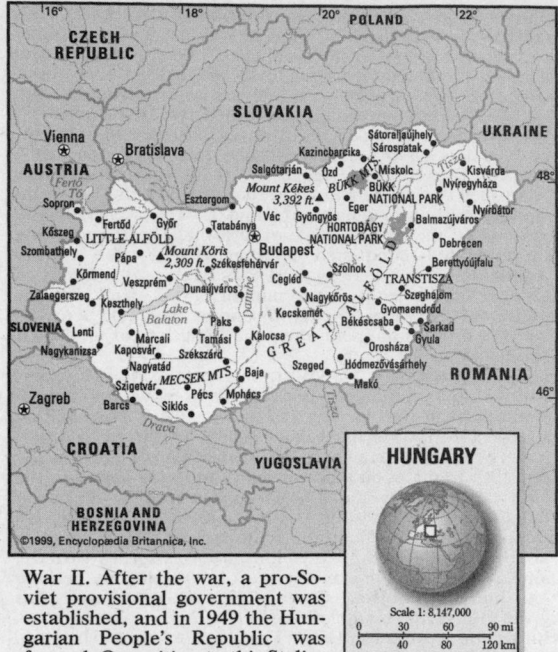

Scale 1: 8,147,000

0   30   60   90 mi
0   40   80   120 km

War II. After the war, a pro-Soviet provisional government was established, and in 1949 the Hungarian People's Republic was formed. Opposition to this Stalinist regime broke out in 1956 but was suppressed (see HUNGARIAN REVOLUTION). Nevertheless, in 1956–88 communist Hungary grew to become the most tolerant of the Soviet-bloc nations of E Europe. It gained its independence in 1989, and soon attracted the largest amount of direct foreign investment in E central Europe. In 1999 it joined NATO.

Hung Hsiu-ch'uan See HONG XIUQUAN

Huns Nomadic pastoralist people who invaded SE Europe about A.D. 370. Appearing from central Asia after the mid-4th cent., they first overran the Alani and then overthrew the OSTROGOTHS. About 376 they defeated the VISIGOTHS and reached the Danubian frontier of the Roman empire. As warriors they inspired almost unparalleled fear throughout Europe; they were accurate mounted archers, and their rapid, ferocious charges brought them overwhelming victories. They extended their power over many of the Germanic peoples of central Europe and allied themselves with the Romans. By 432 leadership had been centralized under a single king, Rua (Rugila), who was succeeded by his two nephews, Bleda and ATTILA. When the Romans apparently failed to pay the Huns stipulated subsidies, Attila launched a heavy assault on the Roman Danubian frontier (441). Other attacks spread the Huns' control into Greece and Italy. After Attila's death (453), his many sons divided up his empire and began a series of costly struggles with their subjects. The Huns were finally routed in 455 by an alliance in a great battle in PANNONIA. The E Roman government then closed the frontier to the Huns, who gradually disintegrated as a social and political unit.

Hunt, H(aroldson) L(afayette) (1889–1974) U.S. oilman. Born in Ramsey, Ill., Hunt purchased a tract of land in E Texas in 1930 that proved one of the richest oilfields in the U.S. He continued his shrewd investments through his Hunt Oil Co. (founded 1936), which became the largest independent oil and gas producer in the country. In the 1960s he exploited vast oil deposits in Libya. He promoted his ultraconservative views on his own radio programs and newspaper column in the 1950s. Two of his sons tried unsuccessfully to corner the world silver market in 1980, causing its near collapse.

Hunt, (James Henry) Leigh (1784–1859) British essayist, critic, journalist, and poet. He was an editor of influential journals, particularly the reformist weekly *The Examiner*

(1808–21), in an age when the periodical was at the height of its power. He was the first publisher of his friends P. B. SHELLEY and John KEATS. He was imprisoned (1813–15) for attacks in *The Examiner* on the prince regent. "Abou Ben Adhem" and "Jenny Kissed Me" are his best-known poems.

Hunt, Richard Morris (1827–1895) U.S. architect. Born in Brattleboro, Vt., he studied in Europe 1843–54, becoming the first U.S. architecture student at the École des Beaux-Arts in Paris. He returned to the U.S. to establish the BEAUX-ARTS STYLE. His work ranged from ornate early French Renaissance to monumental classicism to a picturesque villa style. He worked on the extension of the U.S. CAPITOL and designed the Tribune building in New York (1873), the facade of the METROPOLITAN MUSEUM OF ART (1900–2), and The Breakers mansion in Newport, R.I. (1892–95).

Hunt, William Holman (1827–1910) British painter, prominent in the PRE-RAPHAELITES. He attended the Royal Academy schools and achieved his first public success with *The Light of the World* (1854). His paintings are characterized by hard color, minute detail, and an emphasis on moral or social symbolism. He spent two years in Syria and Palestine painting biblical scenes, such as *The Scapegoat* (1855). His autobiographical *Pre-Raphaelitism and the Pre-Raphaelite Brotherhood* (1905) is the basic sourcebook of the movement.

Hunter, William (1718–1783) British obstetrician, educator, and medical writer. He introduced the French practice of providing individual medical students with cadavers for dissection to Britain. After 1756 his medical practice was devoted principally to obstetrics; he became the most successful specialist of his day. His work did much to remove obstetrics from the purview of midwives and establish it as an accepted branch of medicine.

hunting Pursuit of game, principally as sport. To early humans, hunting was a necessity, and it remained so in many societies until recently. In the modern era, hunters have learned to limit their means, and codes have been established that give the quarry a fair chance to escape and avoid unnecessary suffering of wounded game. Game laws now protect game and limit hunting. Weapons include the rifle and the bow and arrow, and methods include stalking, still-hunting (lying in wait), tracking, driving, and calling. Dogs are sometimes employed to track, flush, or capture prey.

hunting and gathering society Any human society that depends on hunting, fishing, or the gathering of wild plants for subsistence. Until about 8,000 years ago, all peoples were foragers of wild food. In the traditional hunting and gathering society, social groups were small, usually made up of either individual family units or a number of related families collected together in a band. The diet was well balanced and ample, and food was shared. The men usually did the hunting while the women gathered plants and did most domestic chores. The remainder of the time was spent on social and religious activities.

Huntington, Collis P(otter) (1821–1900) U.S. railroad magnate. Born in Harwinton, Conn., he became a prosperous merchant in Oneonta, N.Y. In 1849 he moved to Sacramento and joined Mark Hopkins (1814–1878) in selling miners' supplies during the gold rush. In 1861 he joined Hopkins, Leland STANFORD, and Charles Crocker (1822–1888)—called "the Big Four"—to form the Central Pacific Railroad. During its construction (1863–69), his lobbying secured funding and favorable federal legislation. In 1865 the Big Four formed the Southern Pacific Railroad. In 1869 Huntington bought the Chesapeake and Ohio Railway to link with the Southern Pacific, forming the first transcontinental railroad.

Huntsman, Benjamin (1704–1776) British inventor of the crucible process for steelmaking. A clockmaker, Huntsman opened a plant in SHEFFIELD around 1740, where he produced STEEL for clock springs. His new process yielded cast steel more uniform in composition and free from impurities than any previously produced. Sheffield steelmakers used the crucible process to achieve worldwide dominance in the production of high-quality steels.

Huntsville City (pop., 2000: 158,000), N Alabama. The first community in Alabama to be granted a city charter (1811), it was the site of Alabama's first constitutional convention (1819), and served briefly as the state capital. The George C. Marshall Space Flight Center is located there.

Hunyadi \'hủ-nyŏd-ē\, **Janos** (1407?–1456) Hungarian general. A knight under King SIGISMUND, he learned new military techniques while in Italy. Returning to S Hungary, he repelled Turkish attacks (1437–38) and was made governor of Transylvania. With aid from Venice and the pope, he mounted a campaign against the Turks (1441–43) that broke the Ottoman empire's hold on the S Balkan states, though he was defeated in a Turkish counterattack (1444). Elected regent for the young king, Laszlo V, he served as governor of the kingdom of Hungary 1446–52. In 1456 he raised the Turkish siege of Belgrade before dying of disease. For stopping the supposedly invincible Turkish armies, he is considered a Hungarian national hero.

hurdling TRACK-AND-FIELD sport of running races over a series of obstacles called hurdles. Runners must remain in assigned lanes, and, though they may knock hurdles down while running over them, they may do so only with a leg or foot, not a hand. Modern hurdlers use a double-arm forward thrust and exaggerated forward lean while clearing the hurdle, then bring a trailing leg through at nearly a right angle to the body, enabling them to continue forward without breaking stride.

hurdy-gurdy Pear-shaped fiddle whose strings are sounded by the rim of a rosined wooden wheel turned by a handle. A row of keys is used to produce the melody by stopping one or two strings; the remaining strings sound a constant drone. Known since the 12th cent., it has long been associated with street musicians and beggars. The name is also often used for the barrel organ, in which a hand crank rotates a barrel inside the case, on which several tunes are encoded, causing a small pipe organ to play.

hurling Irish game resembling both FIELD HOCKEY and LACROSSE, played between 15-player teams. The game dates back to at least the 13th cent. B.C. The stick used—a slightly curved device with a cupped blade—is called a hurley. A point is scored by hitting the ball over the crossbar of the opposing team's goalposts, three points by driving it under the crossbar.

Huron \'hyủr-,än\ N. American Indian people who lived in Huronia, between Georgian Bay and Lake Ontario. The Huron lived in villages, sometimes palisaded, consisting of large, bark-covered dwellings. Crops included corn, beans, squash, sunflowers, and tobacco. Hunting and fishing were of lesser importance. Clan matrons had the responsibility of selecting political leaders. The Huron were bitter enemies of tribes of the IROQUOIS CONFEDERACY, with whom they competed in the fur trade. Iroquois invasions in 1648–50 devastated the tribe, forcing a remnant westward. Today the Huron (or Wyandot) number about 2,000.

Huron, Lake Lake, U.S. and Canada. The second-largest of the GREAT LAKES, it is bounded by Michigan and Ontario, and is about 206 mi (330 km) long, with an area of 23,000 sq mi (59,570 sq km). Inflow comes from Lakes SUPERIOR and MICHIGAN; the lake discharges into Lake ERIE. It contains many islands, including MACKINAC. As part of the ST. LAWRENCE SEAWAY, it supports heavy commercial traffic from April to December. It was explored by the French (1615–79), who named it after the HURON Indians.

hurricane See TROPICAL CYCLONE

Hurston, Zora Neale (1903–1960) U.S. folklorist and writer. Born in Eatonville, Fla., she studied anthropology and became associated with the HARLEM RENAISSANCE, celebrating black culture in the voice of the rural South in the play *Mule Bone* (1931; with Langston HUGHES), the novels *Jonah's Gourd Vine* (1934) and the controversial but acclaimed *Their Eyes Were Watching God* (1937), and an autobiography, *Dust Tracks on a Road* (1942).

Hus \'həs, 'hủs\, **Jan** or **Jan Huss** (c.1370–1415) Bohemian religious reformer. Influenced by John WYCLIFFE, as rector of the Univ. of Prague from 1402 he became leader of a reform movement that criticized the corruption of the Roman Catholic clergy. The movement was threatened when Wycliffe's teachings were condemned by the church, and Hus's position was further undermined by his stand in the power struggles among rival popes. He was excommunicated in 1411, but continued to preach. He was invited to the Council of CONSTANCE to explain his views; though promised safe conduct, he was arrested, tried for heresy, and burned at the stake. His writings were important in the development of the Czech language as well as in the theology of church reform, and his followers were called HUSSITES.

Husayn ibn Ali \hủ-'sän-,ib-ən-à-'lē\, **al-** (626–680) Grandson of Muhammad and son of the fourth caliph, ALI. He accepted the rule of the first caliph of the UMAYYAD DYNASTY, MUAWIYAH I, but refused to accept Muawiyah's son, YAZID I. He was invited to join a revolt against the Umayyads, but was intercepted and killed. His martyrdom in the battle of KARBALA inspired Shiite Muslims and is commemorated during the month of Muharram. See also FITNAH, SHIITE.

Husaynid dynasty \hủ-'sā-nəd\ Ruling dynasty of Tunisia 1705–1957, established by the Ottoman al-Husayn ibn Ali. European pressure led later Husaynid rulers to suppress piracy (1819), abolish slavery, and ease restrictions on Jews (1837–55). When Tunisia became a French protectorate in 1883, Husaynid rulers became mere figureheads. The monarchy was abolished when Tunisia gained independence in 1957.

Hu Shi or **Hu Shih** \'hü-'shir\ (1891–1962) Chinese scholar and diplomat. Hu studied under John DEWEY at Columbia Univ. and was profoundly influenced by Dewey's pragmatic methodology. Back in China (1917), he began writing in vernacular Chinese, the use of which spread rapidly, and it soon became the official written language. Because he eschewed dogmas such as Marxism as solutions for China's problems, he was opposed by the Communists but also distrusted by the Nationalists. In 1937 he and the Nationalists were reconciled, and Hu served as ambassador to the U.S., and later as president of Taiwan's Academia Sinica.

Hussein, Saddam (b.1937) President of Iraq (from 1979). After joining the BAATH PARTY in 1957, he attended law school in Cairo and Baghdad. Jailed when the Baathists were overthrown, he escaped and helped reinstall them in 1968. He led the nationalization of the oil industry in 1972 and took over the presidency with the aims of replacing Egypt as leader of the Arab world and gaining hegemony over the Persian Gulf. He launched and ultimately lost the bloody IRAN–IRAQ WAR (1980–88). His extremely brutal dictatorship directed intensive campaigns against minorities within Iraq in the 1980s, particularly the KURDS. He invaded Kuwait in 1990, but suffered a humiliating defeat in the PERSIAN GULF WAR. U.S. fears regarding his development of weapons of mass destruction have led to continued Western sanctions against Iraq, and U.S. and British planes have patrolled most of Iraq's airspace since the Gulf War. See also PAN-ARABISM.

Hussein I \hủ-'sän\ *in full* Hussein ibn Talal (1935–1999) King of Jordan (1952–99). Educated in Britain, he succeeded his father, King Talal, in his teens. Jordan's geographic location and the politics of resident Palestinians forced him to chart a cautious course in international relations. Though he carried on secret talks with most Israeli leaders, he sided with other Arab nations in the SIX-DAY WAR. When the Jordan-based PALESTINE LIBERATION ORGANIZATION (PLO) threatened his reign, Hussein expelled it (1971). Thereafter he sought to repair relations with the PLO without unduly antagonizing Israel or the U.S. He surrendered Jordan's claim to the WEST BANK in 1988 to the PLO. He considered his 1994 peace treaty with Israel his crowning achievement. His son succeeded him as Hussein II.

Husserl \'hủ-sə-rəl\, **Edmund** (1859–1938) German philosopher, founder of PHENOMENOLOGY. He lectured at the Univ. of Halle 1886–1901. In *Logical Investigations* (1900–1), using a "phenomenological" method of analysis, he sought to resolve the opposition between EMPIRICISM and RATIONALISM by tracing all philosophical and scientific systems and developments of theory to their sources in pure experience. At the Univ. of Göttingen (1901–16), he spear-

HIJ

headed the PHENOMENOL-
OGY movement. In his *Ideas*
(1913) Husserl presented phenomenology as a universal
philosophical science. In *First
Philosophy* (1923–24) he proposed that phenomenology,
with its method of reduction,
is the way to the realization of
mankind's ethical autonomy.
His work was strongly influential, especially on Martin
HEIDEGGER.

Edmund Husserl, c.1930

Hussite \\'hə-ˌsīt, 'hü-ˌsīt\\
Member of a group of 15th-
cent. Bohemian religious reformers, followers of Jan
HUS. After Hus's death in
1415, the Hussites broke with Rome. They supported freedom of preaching, poverty of the clergy, civil punishment
of notorious sinners, and expropriation of church property.
Many were nobles and knights, and a papal crusade against
them failed in 1431. During peace negotiations in 1433 the
Hussites split into two factions, the moderate Utraquists
and the radical Taborites. The Utraquists joined the
Catholics and defeated the Taborites at Lipany in 1434; in
1620 they were absorbed by the Catholics. Another segment
of Hussites, Unitas Fratrum, set up an independent organization in 1467 and lasted until the COUNTER-REFORMA-
TION. The MORAVIAN CHURCH was founded in 1722 by a
group of Hussites in Saxony.

Huston \\'hyü-stən\\, **John** (1906–1987) U.S. film director and
screenwriter. Born in Nevada, Mo., the son of the actor
Walter Huston, he worked initially as a scriptwriter. His
first film as a director, *The Maltese Falcon* (1941), began an
illustrious career studded with film classics: *The Treasure of
the Sierra Madre* (1948, Academy Awards for best director
and screenplay), *Key Largo* (1948), *The Asphalt Jungle*
(1950), *The African Queen* (1951), *Moulin Rouge* (1952), *The
Night of the Iguana* (1964), *The Man Who Would Be King*
(1975), *Prizzi's Honor* (1985), and *The Dead* (1987). He
wrote screenplays for many of his own films and others, and
continued to act throughout his career. His daughter Anjel-
ica (b.1951) proved herself an accomplished actress in
Prizzi's Honor (1985, Academy Award), *The Dead* (1987),
and *The Grifters* (1990).

Hutchins, Robert Maynard (1899–1977) U.S. educator and
foundation president. Born in Brooklyn, N.Y., he became
dean of Yale Law School. At the Univ. of CHICAGO as president (1929–45) and chancellor (1945–51), he encouraged
liberal education based on study of the great books of the
Western tradition and dismantled the intercollegiate athletic program. Hutchins later headed the Ford Foundation.
He served as chairman of the board of editors of *ENCY-
CLOPÆDIA BRITANNICA* (1943–74) and edited the 54-vol-
ume *Great Books of the Western World* (1952).

Hutchinson, Anne *orig.* Anne Marbury (1591–1643) British-
American religious leader. In 1612 she married William
Hutchinson, and they followed John COTTON to the MASSA-
CHUSETTS BAY COLONY in 1634. She organized weekly religious meetings of Boston women, criticizing the narrow Puritan orthodoxy. Her opponents accused her of believing
that God's grace had freed Christians from the need to observe established moral precepts. Tried for "traducing the
ministers," she was sentenced to banishment. In 1638 she
and her husband established a colony at Aquidneck Island,
which became part of Rhode Island.

Hutchinson, Thomas (1711–1780) American colonial administrator. Son of a wealthy Boston merchant, he served
in local and provincial legislatures (1737–49), as lieutenant
governor (1758–71), and as chief justice of the state superior court (1760–69). After he was accused of initiating
the STAMP ACT, a mob sacked his home. As governor
(1771–74), he strictly enforced British rule. His insistence
that a shipment of tea be landed in Boston led to the
BOSTON TEA PARTY. He was replaced (1774) by Gen.
Thomas Gage.

Hutterite \\'hə-tə-ˌrīt\\ Member of the Hutterite Brethren, an
ANABAPTIST sect whose Austrian founder, Jakob Hutter,
was burned as a heretic in 1536. His followers held their
goods in common. Persecuted in Moravia and the Tirol,
they moved eastward to Hungary and the Ukraine. In the
1870s many emigrated to the U.S. and settled in S. Dakota.
The society still exists in the W U.S. and Canada, where its
members operate collective farms. Hutterites are pacifists
who remain separate from outside society.

Hutu Bantu-speaking people of Rwanda and Burundi, with a
large refugee population in the Congo (Zaire). Numbering
about 9.5 million, the Hutu comprise the vast majority in
both countries but were traditionally subject to the TUTSI
under German and Belgian colonial regimes. The two cultures both speak Rwanda and Rundi and adhere to similar
religious beliefs. The Tutsi remained dominant in Rwanda
until 1961, when the Hutu expelled most of them and took
over the government. A Hutu coup attempt in Burundi in
1965 was unsuccessful. Violent clashes occurred in Burundi
in 1972, 1988, and 1993, and in Rwanda in 1990. In 1994–96
a Hutu-initiated genocidal campaign led to the deaths of
over a million Rwandans, and 1–2 million Hutus were
forced into refugee camps in Zaire (now Congo) and Tanzania.

Huxley, Aldous (Leonard) (1894–1963) British novelist and
critic. Brother of Julian HUX-
LEY, he is known for works
of elegant, witty, pessimistic
satire, including *Crome Yellow* (1921), *Antic Hay* (1923),
and *Point Counter Point*
(1928). The celebrated *Brave
New World* (1932) is a nightmarish vision of a future society that expresses his distrust of trends in politics and
technology. Beginning with
Eyeless in Gaza (1936), his
works reveal a growing interest in Hindu philosophy and
mysticism. Later works include *The Doors of Perception*
(1954), about his experiences
with hallucinogens.

Aldous Huxley, 1959

Huxley, Julian (Sorell) (*later* **Sir Julian**) (1887–1975) British
biologist, philosopher, and author. He was a grandson of T.
H. HUXLEY and brother of Aldous HUXLEY. His research on
hormones, developmental processes, ornithology, and ecology influenced the modern development of embryology,
classification, and studies of behavior and evolution. He applied his scientific knowledge to social and political problems, formulating an ethical theory of "evolutionary humanism." Many of his books were written for the general
public.

Huxley, T(homas) H(enry) (1825–1895) British biologist. As
a surgeon on a surveying expedition in the S. Pacific (1846–
50), he carried out extensive studies of marine organisms. In
the 1850s he established his reputation with his important
papers on animal individuality, certain mollusks, the methods of paleontology, the methods and principles of science
and science education, the structure and functions of
nerves, and the vertebrate skull. He was one of the earliest
and strongest supporters of DARWINISM; his 1860 debate
with Bishop Samuel Wilberforce gained widespread attention. In the 1860s Huxley did valuable work in paleontology
and classification, especially classification of birds. Few scientists have been as influential over such a wide field of scientific development and as effective in the total movement
of thought and action within their own generation.

Huygens \\'hī-gənz, 'hȯi-gənz\\, **Christiaan** *or* **Christian
Huyghens** (1629–1695) Dutch mathematician, astronomer,
and physicist. He was the first to use a pendulum to regulate
a clock (1656). He invented a method of grinding and polishing telescope lenses, and used his telescopes to discover
the true shape of Saturn's rings (1659). He developed explanations of REFLECTION and REFRACTION based on the principle of secondary wave fronts, now called Huygens' princi-

ple. He developed the wave theory of light (1678) and contributed to the science of dynamics. He was also the first to determine acceleration due to gravity.

Hwange National Park \\'hwän-gä\\ National preserve, NW Zimbabwe. Located on the Botswana frontier, it was established in 1928 as a game reserve. Covering 5,657 sq mi (14,651 sq km), it is largely flat, with hardwood forests of mukwa and teak. It is one of Africa's largest elephant sanctuaries; its abundant wildlife can be observed from platforms overlooking the water holes.

Hwang River See HUANG RIVER

hyacinth Any of the approximately 30 species of bulbous ornamental herbaceous plants that make up the genus *Hyacinthus* (LILY FAMILY), native primarily to the Mediterranean region and tropical Africa. The common garden hyacinths are derived from *H. orientalis*. Most species have narrow, untoothed leaves at the base of the plant and fragrant flowers (usually blue) borne in a cluster at the top of the leafless stems.

Hyacinthus \\,hī-ə-'sin-thəs\\ In GREEK MYTHOLOGY, a young man of great beauty who attracted the love of APOLLO. The god killed him accidentally in discus throwing, and from his blood grew the flower *hyacinthos* (not the modern hyacinth), whose petals were marked with the words AI, AI ("Alas"). His death was commemorated with an early summer festival known as the Hyacinthia.

hyaline membrane disease See RESPIRATORY DISTRESS SYNDROME

hybrid Offspring of parents that differ genetically. The parents may be of two different species, genera, or (rarely) families. Because of basic biological incompatibilities, sterile hybrids (those that cannot produce living young) commonly result from crosses between species. Some species hybrids, however, are fertile and can be sources for the formation of new species. Many important cultivated plants (e.g., bananas, coffee, peanuts, dahlias, roses) originated through natural or artificially induced hybridization. Hybridization is important biologically because it increases necessary genetic VARIATION within a species.

Hyde, Edward See Earl of CLARENDON

Hyderabad \\'hī-də-rə-,bäd\\ City (pop., 1991: 3,146,000), capital of Andhra Pradesh state, S India. Founded by the sultans of GOLCONDA in the 16th cent., the town was destroyed following the Mughal occupation in 1685. In 1724 it became the capital of the independent kingdom of HYDERABAD. A walled city, it has many buildings in a blend of Hindu and Muslim styles. It is the site of Osmania Univ. (1918) and the Univ. of Hyderabad (1974).

Hyderabad *or* **Haydarabad** City (pop., 1981: 795,000), Pakistan. Located east of the INDUS RIVER, it was founded in 1768 and remained the capital of Sind until 1843 when it surrendered to the British and the capital was transferred to KARACHI. It is now Pakistan's third-largest city. Notable antiquities include the tombs and palaces of former rulers.

Hyderabad *formerly* **Haidarabad** *or* **Nizam's Dominions** \\ni-'zämz\\ Former princely state, S central India. Originally part of the ancient kingdom of GOLCONDA, it became part of the Mughal empire in 1687. The independent kingdom of Hyderabad was founded by NIZAM-AL-MULK in 1724. In 1798 it was placed under British protection. At Indian partition in 1947, the Nizams sought independence, but India invaded the state (1948) and took control. The area is now divided among three states.

hydrangea \\hī-'drān-jə\\ Any of approximately 23 species of erect or climbing woody shrubs that make up the genus *Hydrangea* (family Hydrangeaceae), native to the Western Hemisphere and E Asia. Several species are cultivated for their showy, usually ball-like flower clusters. The French hydrangea *(H. macrophylla),* bearing large globular flower clusters in various colors, is the florist's hydrangea.

hydraulics Branch of science concerned with the practical applications of FLUIDS, primarily LIQUIDS, in MOTION. It is related to FLUID MECHANICS, which in large part provides its theoretical foundation. Hydraulics deals with such matters as the flow of liquids in pipes, rivers, and channels and their confinement by dams and tanks. Some of its principles

apply also to GASES, usually when variations in density are relatively small.

hydride \\'hī-,drīd\\ Inorganic compound of HYDROGEN with another ELEMENT. Three common types are differentiated by their BONDING. In saline (ionic) hydrides (see IONIC BOND), the hydrogen is an ANION, H⁻, and behaves like a HALOGEN. Saline hydrides such as sodium hydride (NaH) and calcium hydride (CaH$_2$) react vigorously with water, giving off hydrogen gas (H$_2$), and are used as portable sources of it. Metallic hydrides, such as titanium hydride (TiH$_2$), are alloylike materials (see ALLOY) with some properties of METALS. Covalent hydrides (see COVALENT BOND) are mostly compounds of hydrogen and nonmetallic elements; they include WATER, AMMONIA, and METHANE. In polymeric hydrides, the hydrogen forms bridges between other atoms (e.g., hydrides of boron and aluminum). Those hydrides give off large amounts of energy when burned and may be useful as rocket fuels.

hydrocarbon Any of a class of organic compounds composed only of CARBON and HYDROGEN. The carbon atoms form the framework, and the hydrogen atoms attach to them. Hydrocarbons, the principal constituents of PETROLEUM and NATURAL GAS, serve as fuels, lubricants, and raw materials for production of plastics, fibers, rubbers, solvents, explosives, and industrial chemicals. All burn to CARBON DIOXIDE and WATER with enough OXYGEN or to CARBON MONOXIDE without it. The two major categories are aliphatic, with the carbon atoms in straight or branched chains or in nonaromatic rings, and aromatic (see AROMATIC COMPOUND). All but the simplest hydrocarbons have ISOMERS (see ISOMERISM). ETHYLENE, METHANE, ACETYLENE, BENZENE, toluene, and naphthalene are hydrocarbons.

hydrocephalus \\,hī-drō-'se-fə-ləs\\ Accumulation of cerebrospinal fluid (CSF) in the cavities of the brain, caused by overproduction, congenital blockage that prevents drainage (see NEURAL TUBE DEFECT), or complications of head injuries or infections. Normally, CSF circulates through the brain and spinal cord and drains into the circulation. Without surgery to divert the excess fluid into the blood or abdomen, accumulating fluid eventually compresses the brain, causing convulsions, mental retardation, and death.

hydrochloric acid *or* **muriatic acid** Solution in water of hydrogen chloride (HCl), a gaseous inorganic compound. It is a strong ACID, corrosive and irritating. The acid reacts with most METALS to produce HYDROGEN and the metal's chloride, and also reacts with OXIDES, HYDROXIDES, and many SALTS. It is used extensively in industrial processing of metals and concentrating of some ores; in boiler scale removal, food processing, metal cleaning and pickling; and as a chemical intermediate, laboratory reagent, and alcohol denaturant (see ETHANOL). Hydrochloric acid is present in the stomach's gastric juice and can cause PEPTIC ULCERS.

hydroelectric power ELECTRICITY produced from GENERATORS driven by water TURBINES that convert the energy in falling or fast-flowing water to mechanical ENERGY. Water at a higher elevation flows downward through large pipes or tunnels (penstocks). The falling water rotates turbines, which drive the generators, which convert the turbines' mechanical energy into electricity. The advantages of hydroelectric POWER over fossil fuels and nuclear fission are that it is continually renewable and produces no pollution. Such countries as Norway, Sweden, Canada, and Switzerland rely heavily on hydroelectricity because they have industrialized areas close to mountainous regions with heavy rainfall. See also TIDAL POWER. See diagram on next page.

hydrogen Lightest chemical ELEMENT, chemical symbol H, atomic number 1. A colorless, odorless, tasteless, flammable GAS, it occurs as the diatomic molecule H$_2$. Its ATOM consists of one PROTON (the nucleus) and one ELECTRON. Though only the ninth most abundant element on earth, it represents about 75% of all MATTER in the universe. It is used to synthesize AMMONIA, ETHANOL, ANILINE, and METHANOL; to treat PETROLEUM fuels; as a reducing agent (see REDUCTION) and to supply a reducing atmosphere, to make hydrogen chloride (see HYDROCHLORIC ACID) and hydrogen bromide; and in HYDROGENATION. Liquid hydro-

HIJ

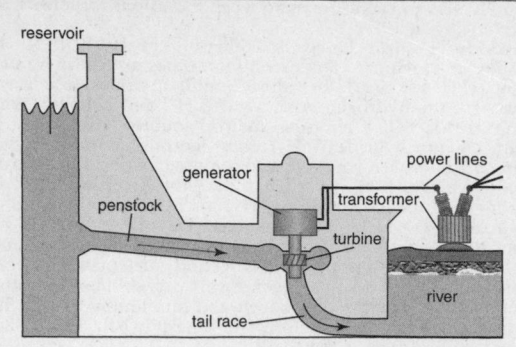

Hydroelectric power A hydro station generates power by the controlled release of water from the reservoir of a dammed river. The flowing water turns a turbine, which powers a generator, creating electricity. The voltage is stepped up by a transformer, to allow long-distance power transmission.

gen is used in the laboratory to produce extremely low temperatures, in BUBBLE CHAMBERS, and as a rocket fuel. Combustion of hydrogen with oxygen produces WATER. The properties of most ACIDS, especially in water solutions, arise from the hydrogen ION. See also DEUTERIUM, HYDRIDE, HYDROCARBON, TRITIUM.

hydrogenation \hī-ˌdrä-jə-'nā-shən\ CHEMICAL REACTION between molecular HYDROGEN (H_2) and another element or a compound, usually with a CATALYST. Hydrogen may be added at the sites of double or triple bonds (see BONDING) to make them single bonds (see SATURATION), or to AROMATIC COMPOUNDS to make them cyclic HYDROCARBONS. Edible OILS with unsaturated FATTY ACIDS are liquid at room temperature; food manufacturers use hydrogenation to make the product more solid. A second type of hydrogenation involves breaking up a compound and is of great importance in the PETROLEUM industry. Numerous processes in GASOLINE and PETROCHEMICAL manufacturing are based on it.

hydrogen bomb *or* **H-bomb** *or* **thermonuclear bomb** Weapon whose enormous explosive power is generated by the fusion of HYDROGEN ISOTOPES at high temperatures to form HELIUM. The high temperatures are produced by detonating an ATOMIC BOMB. The bomb's explosion produces a blast that can destroy any building within several miles, an intense white light that can cause blindness, and heat fierce enough to set off firestorms. It also creates radioactive FALLOUT that contaminates air, water, and soil. Hydrogen bombs, which may be thousands of times more powerful than atomic bombs, can be made small enough to fit in the warheads of ICBMs. Edward TELLER and other U.S. scientists tested the first H-bomb in 1952, followed by the Soviet Union (1953), Britain (1957), China (1967), and France (1968). By the late 1980s about 40,000 H-bombs existed; this number declined with the fall of the Soviet Union.

hydrogen bonding Interactions between pairs of ATOMS in adjoining MOLECULES, weaker than IONIC or COVALENT bonds but stronger than VAN DER WAALS FORCES, aligning them and keeping them together. One member of the pair (the donor) has HYDROGEN atoms covalently bonded to NITROGEN or OXYGEN atoms (–NH or –OH); the other member of the pair (acceptor) has N or O atoms or negatively charged particles. The donor molecule effectively shares its hydrogen with the acceptor by sharing its electrons with the acceptor nitrogen or oxygen atom. Water is a good SOLVENT because it forms hydrogen bonds readily. Hydrogen bonds between nitrogenous bases in NUCLEOTIDES on the two chains of DNA hold the key to the transmission of genetic information.

hydrologic cycle \ˌhī-drə-'lä-jik\ Cycle that involves the continuous circulation of WATER in the earth-atmosphere system. Water is transferred from the oceans through the

atmosphere to the continents and back to the oceans by means of EVAPORATION, TRANSPIRATION, PRECIPITATION, subterranean percolation, runoff, and other complex processes. Although the total amount of water within the cycle remains essentially constant, its distribution is continually changing.

hydrolysis \hī-'drä-lə-səs\ CHEMICAL REACTION in which WATER (H_2O or HOH) and another reactant exchange FUNCTIONAL GROUPS to form two products, one containing the H and the other the OH. For example, an ESTER can be hydrolyzed to form a CARBOXYLIC ACID and an ALCOHOL. Such reactions are often accelerated by ENZYMES (as in much of DIGESTION and METABOLISM in general) or other CATALYSTS. In hydrolyses of compounds with IONIC BONDS, the nonwater reactants are SALTS, ACIDS, or BASES.

hydroponics Cultivation of plants in nutrient-enriched water, with or without the mechanical support of an inert medium such as sand or gravel. Fertilizer solution is pumped through the system periodically. As the plants grow, concentration of the solution and frequency of pumping are increased. A wide variety of vegetables and florist crops can be grown satisfactorily in gravel. Automatic watering and fertilizing saves on labor, but installation costs are high and fertilizer solution must be tested frequently.

hydrosphere Discontinuous layer of water at or near the earth's surface. It includes all liquid and frozen surface waters, groundwater held in soil and rock, and atmospheric water vapor. Virtually all of these waters are in constant circulation through the HYDROLOGIC CYCLE. The components of the hydrosphere have been seriously affected by the water-polluting activities of modern society.

hydrostatics Branch of PHYSICS that deals with the characteristics of FLUIDS at rest, particularly with the pressure in a fluid or exerted by a fluid (gas or liquid) on an immersed body. In applications, the principles of hydrostatics are used for problems relating to pressure in deep water (pressure increases with depth) and high in the atmosphere (pressure lessens with altitude).

hydrotherapy External use of water for medical treatment. Wet heat helps relieve pain, improves circulation, and promotes relaxation. Wet cold causes blood vessels to constrict, reducing swelling and pain. Underwater exercise helps strengthen weak muscles, restore joint motion after injury, clean and heal burned flesh, and treat arthritic deformity and pain. Hydrotherapy is usually employed by specialists in PHYSICAL MEDICINE AND REHABILITATION.

hydroxide Any compound with one or more FUNCTIONAL GROUPS made up of one ATOM each of HYDROGEN and OXYGEN, bonded together and acting as the hydroxyl group or hydroxide ANION (OH^-). Hydroxides include the familiar ALKALIES of laboratory and industrial processes. Those of the ALKALI METALS, the strongest BASES, are the most stable and soluble; those of the ALKALINE EARTH METALS, also soluble strong bases, are less stable. The hydroxides of most other metals are only slightly soluble but neutralize ACIDS.

hyena Any of three species of coarse-furred, doglike CARNIVORES (family Hyaenidae) found in Asia and Africa. Actually more closely related to cats than to dogs, they have long forelegs, nonretractile claws, and enormously strong jaws and teeth. They live alone or in packs and may be active by night or day. Hyenas are noted for scavenging but will attack live prey. Calls of the spotted, or laughing, hyena, alternately resemble wailing and maniacal laughter. Yellowish or grayish with dark spots, it is about 6.5 ft (1.8 m) long, including the 12-in. (30-cm) tail, and weighs up to 175 lbs (80 kg). It has been known to attack people.

Hymen Greek god of marriage. In Attic legend he was a beautiful youth who res-

Spotted hyena (*Crocuta crocuta*)

cued a group of young women, including his beloved, from a gang of pirates. He obtained the girl in marriage, and their happy life was invoked in many wedding songs.

hymn Song used in Christian worship, usually sung by the congregation and written in stanzas with rhyme and meter. The term comes from the Greek *hymnos* ("song of praise"), but songs in honor of God or the gods exist in all civilizations. The earliest known Christian hymn dates from about A.D. 200. Hymns were prominent in the Byzantine liturgy, and in the Western church they were sung by congregations until the Middle Ages, when choirs took over hymn singing. Congregational singing was reestablished during the REFORMATION. Martin LUTHER and his followers were great hymn writers; the Calvinists preferred setting psalms to music. The compositions of Isaac WATTS and John and Charles WESLEY were notable in English hymnody. The Roman Catholic church restored congregational singing of hymns after the Second VATICAN COUNCIL in the 1960s.

Hypatia \hī-'pā-shə\ (c.A.D. 370–415) Egyptian-Greek philosopher. Daughter of a philosopher, she became head of the school of NEOPLATONISM at Alexandria about 400. Renowned for her intellect, eloquence, and beauty, she came to represent learning and science, which were then identified with PAGAN practices. When official policy promoted the destruction of non-Christian shrines, she became the symbol of paganism and was murdered by a mob incited by CYRIL OF ALEXANDRIA. Her writings, on such works as PTOLEMY's *Almagest* and especially on mathematics, have been lost.

hyperactivity See ATTENTION DEFICIT DISORDER

hyperbaric chamber \,hī-pər-'bar-ik\ *or* **decompression chamber** *or* **recompression chamber** Sealed chamber supplying a high-pressure atmosphere, to increase the oxygen level in tissues. This is used to inhibit growth of anaerobic bacteria (as in TETANUS or gas GANGRENE); to increase the chance that babies with certain heart malformations will survive heart surgery; or to get rid of air bubbles (as in air EMBOLISM or DECOMPRESSION SICKNESS).

hyperbola \hī-'pər-bə-lə\ Curve with two separate branches, one of the CONIC SECTIONS. It can be defined in terms of EUCLIDEAN GEOMETRY as the intersection of a plane and a right circular cone when the plane is parallel to the axis of the cone. If the cone's lines continue beyond its vertex to form a second, inverted cone, the cross section is the two arcs of a hyperbola. Hyperbolas have many important physical attributes that make them useful in the design of lenses and antennas.

hypertension *or* **high blood pressure** Condition in which BLOOD PRESSURE is abnormally high. Over time, it damages the kidneys, brain, eyes, and heart. Hypertension accelerates ARTERIOSCLEROSIS, increasing the risk of MYOCARDIAL INFARCTION, STROKE, and KIDNEY FAILURE. More common in the elderly and blacks, it usually has no symptoms but can be detected by a routine blood-pressure test. Secondary hypertension, usually caused by kidney disease or hormone imbalance, accounts for 10% of cases. The other 90% have no specific cause (essential hypertension). A low-salt diet, weight loss, quitting smoking, limiting alcohol intake, and exercise can prevent or treat it. Drug therapy may be necessary.

hypertext *or* **hyperlink** Linking of related information by electronic connections in order to allow a user easy access between them. Conceptualized by Vannevar BUSH (1945) and invented by Douglas Engelbart (b.1925) in the 1960s, hypertext is a feature of some computer programs that allows the user to select a word and receive additional information, such as a definition or related material. In Internet BROWSERS, hypertext links (hyperlinks) are usually denoted by highlighting a word or phrase with a different font or color. Hypertext links create a branching or network structure that permits jumps to related information. Hypertext has been used most successfully as an essential feature of the WORLD WIDE WEB (see HTML, HTTP).

HyperText Markup Language See HTML
HyperText Transfer Protocol See HTTP

hypnosis State that resembles SLEEP but is induced by a person (the hypnotist) whose suggestions are readily accepted by the subject. The hypnotized individual seems to respond in an uncritical, automatic fashion, ignoring aspects of the environment not pointed out to him or her by the hypnotist. Even the subject's memory and awareness of self may be altered by suggestion, and the effects of the suggestions may be extended into the subject's subsequent waking activity. Hypnotism is as old as the arts of sorcery and magic. It was popularized in the 18th cent. by F. A. MESMER (as "mesmerism"), and was studied in the 19th cent. by the Scottish surgeon James Braid (1795–1860). Sigmund FREUD relied on it in exploring the UNCONSCIOUS, and it came to be recognized as useful in helping to calm or anesthetize patients, modify unwanted behaviors, and uncover repressed memories.

hypochondriasis \,hī-pə-kən-'drī-ə-səs\ Mental disorder involving excessive preoccupation with one's health and a tendency to treat insignificant physical symptoms as evidence of a serious disease. The hypochondriac may have no symptoms at all, or may exaggerate the importance of minor aches and pains, becoming obsessed with the fear of a life-threatening illness. A doctor's reassurances often have only a slight or temporary effect. In some cases the disorder may represent a psychological coping mechanism that the individual adopts to deal with stressful life situations.

hypoglycemia \,hī-pō-glī-'sē-mē-ə\ Below-normal levels of blood GLUCOSE, quickly reversed by administration of oral or intravenous glucose. Fasting hypoglycemia can be life-threatening; it occurs most often in patients with DIABETES MELLITUS who mistime INSULIN therapy or miss meals. Reactive hypoglycemia occurs when the body produces too much insulin in response to sugar intake. Symptoms range from irritability to confusion and seizures, leading to coma and death in severe cases.

hypotension *or* **low blood pressure** Condition in which BLOOD PRESSURE is abnormally low. It may result from reduced blood volume (e.g., from heavy bleeding) or increased blood-vessel capacity (e.g., in SYNCOPE). Orthostatic hypotension—drop in blood pressure on standing—results from failure of the reflexes that contract muscles and constrict blood vessels in the legs to offset gravity as one rises. See also SHOCK.

hypothalamus \,hī-pō-'tha-lə-məs\ Region of the brain containing a control center for many AUTONOMIC-NERVOUS-SYSTEM functions, whose complex interaction with the PITUITARY GLAND makes it an important part of the ENDOCRINE SYSTEM. The hypothalamus regulates HOMEOSTASIS and stimulates the pituitary to release various HORMONES. The hypothalamus influences food intake, weight regulation, fluid intake and balance, thirst, body heat, and the SLEEP cycle. Disorders can produce pituitary dysfunction, INSOMNIA, and temperature fluctuations.

hypothermia Abnormally low body temperature. It is artificially induced (usually with ice baths) for certain surgical procedures and cancer treatments. Accidental hypothermia can result from falling into cold water or overexposure in cold weather. Hypothermia is serious when body temperature is below 95°F (35°C) and an emergency below 90°F (32.2°C), at which point shivering stops. Pulse, respiration, and blood pressure are depressed. Even when the victim appears dead, revival may be possible with very gradual passive rewarming (e.g., with blankets). See also FROSTBITE.

hypoxia \,hip-'äk-sē-ə, hī-'päk-sē-ə\ Condition in which tissues are starved of OXYGEN. There are four types: hypoxemic, from low blood oxygen content (e.g., in ALTITUDE SICKNESS); anemic, from low blood oxygen-carrying capacity (e.g., in carbon monoxide poisoning); stagnant, from low blood flow (e.g., generally in SHOCK or locally in ARTERIOSCLEROSIS); and histotoxic, from poisoning (e.g., with CYANIDE) that keeps cells from using oxygen. Hypoxia can lead to tissue death, as in MYOCARDIAL INFARCTION.

hysterectomy \,his-tə-'rek-tə-mē\ Surgical removal of the UTERUS, either completely (total hysterectomy) or leaving the cervix (subtotal hysterectomy). It is performed in the presence of cancer or in some cases of benign fibroid tumor. Hysterectomy may also be performed after CESAREAN SECTION in cases of complications. Once misused in the belief that removing the uterus (and often the OVARIES) would control what were considered inappropriate sexual urges, it is still the most common unnecessary surgery.

HIJ

hysteria Term formerly used in psychology to designate a NEUROSIS marked by emotional excitability and disturbances of psychic, sensory, vasomotor, and visceral functions. The concept was used frequently in the first half of the 20th cent. to explain a wide variety of symptoms and behaviors observed particularly in women. It was eventually dropped from the *Diagnostic and Statistical Manual of Mental Disorders* as overly broad. Disorders with similar symptoms include conversion disorder, factitious disorder, dissociative disorder, and PERSONALITY DISORDER (histrionic type).

Hywel Dda *or* **Howel Dda** \'hə-wel-'thä\ *or* **Hywel the Good** (d.950) Welsh chieftain called "king of all Wales." He inherited Seisyllwg and secured Dyfed by marriage; eventually Gwynedd and Powys also came under his rule. By 942 his realm was larger than that of any earlier Welsh ruler. He codified Welsh law during his peaceful reign and accepted the status of subking to the Anglo-Saxon king of Wessex.

I

Iacocca \ˌī-ə-ˈkō-kə\, **Lee** (*orig.* Lido Anthony) (b.1924) U.S. automobile executive. Born in Allentown, Pa., he rose rapidly in engineering and later sales at FORD MOTOR CO., becoming president in 1970, but was dismissed by Henry Ford II in 1978. Hired by the nearly bankrupt CHRYSLER CORP., he persuaded Congress to lend Chrysler $1.5 billion in 1980. After severe cost-cutting, a shift toward more fuel-efficient cars, and an aggressive advertising campaign, Chrysler began showing record profits, and Iacocca was a celebrity with a best-selling autobiography, *Iacocca* (1984). He led the national effort to restore the Statue of Liberty. He left Chrysler in 1992 to head EV Global Motors, a light electric vehicle company.

Iasi \ˈyäsh\ *German* **Jassy** \ˈyä-sē\ City (pop., 1997: 348,000), NE Romania. Located west of the border with MOLDOVA, it was settled as early as the 7th cent. From 1565 to 1862 it was the capital of Moldavia. It was burned by Tatars in 1513, by Turks in 1538, and by Russians in 1686. It is the site of a university, the 16th-cent. Church of St. Nicholas, and a national theater.

Ibadan \l-ˈba-dᵊn, ˌē-bä-ˈdän\ City (pop., 1996 est.: 1,432,000), SW Nigeria. Northeast of LAGOS, it is the nation's second largest city. The modern city grew from an 1829 camp taken by the British in 1893. A commercial center, it contains six parks, including Agodi Garden. It is the seat of the Univ. of Ibadan.

Ibárruri (Gómez) \ē-ˈbä-rü-rē\, **(Isidora) Dolores** *known as* **La Pasionaria** (1895–1989) Spanish Communist leader. Radicalized in her youth, in 1918 she published an article using her pseudonym ("The Passionflower"), and in 1920 she joined Spain's new Communist Party. By the outbreak of the Spanish Civil War in 1936 she had won fame as a fiery and even violent street orator, and she coined the Republican battle cry, "No pasarán!" ("They shall not pass!"). With Francisco FRANCO's victory in 1939 she fled to the Soviet Union; she returned in 1977 after his death and the party's relegalization, becoming honorary president of the party.

Iberian Peninsula *or* **Iberia** Peninsula, SW Europe, occupied by Spain and Portugal. Its name derives from its ancient inhabitants, whom the Greeks called IBERIANS, probably after the EBRO (IBERUS) RIVER. The PYRENEES form a land barrier in the northeast from the rest of Europe, and in the south at GIBRALTAR the peninsula is separated from N. Africa by a narrow strait. Cape da Roca, in Portugal, is the most westerly point of continental Europe.

Iberians Prehistoric people of S and E Spain. Culturally they were influenced by Greek and Phoenician trading colonies. On the E coast, tribes seem to have formed independent city-states; in the south, they formed monarchies. Their economy was based on agriculture, mining, and metallurgy.

Iberville \ē-ber-ˈvēl\, **Pierre Le Moyne d'** (1661–1706) French-Canadian colonist and explorer. He led raids on English fur-trading posts on Hudson Bay and by 1697 had expanded the area controlled by NEW FRANCE. He was sent south to fortify the Mississippi River delta and secure claims by R.-R. LA SALLE. The settlement he founded on Biloxi Bay (1699) and forts he built below present-day New Orleans (1700) and on the Mobile River (1702) led to the later colonization of Louisiana.

ibex \ˈī-ˌbeks\ Any of several species of surefooted, sturdy wild GOATS found in the mountains of Europe, Asia, and NE Africa. Ibex are typically about 3 ft (90 cm) tall at the shoulder and have brownish gray fur. The male has a beard and large, semicircular horns.

ibis \ˈī-bəs\ Any of about 20 species of medium-sized wading birds (subfamily Threskiornithinae) of the same family as the SPOONBILLS. Ibises are found in all warm regions except on S. Pacific islands. They wade in shallow lagoons, lakes, bays, and marshes, using their slender, down-curved bill to feed on small fishes and soft mollusks. Species range from 22 to 30 in. (55–75 cm) long. They usually breed in vast colonies.

Sacred ibis (*Threskiornis aethiopica*)

Ibiza \ē-ˈbē-zä\ Third-largest island (pop., 1995 est.: 70,000) of the BALEARIC ISLANDS, Spain. Lying southwest of MAJORCA, it has an area of 221 sq mi (572 sq km). A flourishing settlement in ancient times, it has notable archaeological sites. Its rugged N coast has cliffs exceeding 800 ft (245 m) in height. Its beaches and mild winter climate make it a popular tourist center.

IBM Corp. *in full* **International Business Machines Corp.** Leading U.S. computer manufacturer. It was incorporated in 1911 as the Computing-Tabulating-Recording Co. It adopted its present name in 1924 under the leadership of Thomas J. WATSON, who built it into the major U.S. manufacturer of punch-card tabulators. IBM bought an electric-typewriter company in 1933 and soon secured a large share of that market. In the early 1950s it entered the computer industry, and in the 1960s it produced 70% of the world's computers. In 1981 it produced its first PERSONAL COMPUTER, the IBM PC. IBM quickly became a leader in this field, but fierce competition forced the company to retrench in the 1990s. In 1995 IBM bought the software manufacturer Lotus Development Corp.

Ibn al-Arabi \ˌib-nùl-àr-à-ˈbē\ (1165–1240) Islamic mystic and theologian. Born in Spain, he traveled widely in search of masters of Sufism. In 1198 he began a pilgrimage to the Near East, eventually settling in Damascus in 1223. Honored as a spiritual master, he spent the rest of his life in contemplation, teaching, and writing. His great work *The Meccan Revelations* discussed the esoteric sciences in Islam and his own inner life. His *Bezels of Wisdom* (1229) was one of the most important works in Islamic mystical philosophy.

Ibn Ishaq \ˌi-bən-ēs-ˈhåk\ *in full* Muhammad ibn Ishaq ibn Yasar ibn Khiyar (704?–767) Arab biographer of Muhammad. His father and two uncles collected information about Muhammad in Medina, and Ibn Ishaq soon became an authority on the Prophet's campaigns. In Alexandria and Iraq, he met many people who provided him with information for what was to become the most popular biography of Muhammad in the Muslim world.

Ibn Khaldun \ˌib-ən-k̲ål-ˈdün\ *in full* Abu Zayd Abd al-Rahman ibn Khaldun (1332–1406) Arab historian. Born in Tunis, he was employed in court posts by various rulers in Tunis, Fez, and Granada. In his masterpiece, the *Muqaddimah* ("Introduction to History"), he developed one of the earliest nonreligious philosophies of history. He also wrote a definitive history of Muslim N. Africa, *Kitab al-ibar*. Caught in TIMUR's siege of Damascus in 1400, he negotiated the freedom of civilians before the sack of the city. He is regarded as the greatest of medieval Arab historians.

Ibn Rushd See AVERROËS

Ibn Saud \ˌib-ən-sä-'üd\, **Abdulaziz** (c.1880–1953) Founder of modern-day Saudi Arabia. Though the SAUD DYNASTY had ruled much of Arabia from 1780 to 1880, in Ibn Saud's infancy the family was forced out by its rivals, the Rashids. At 21 Ibn Saud led a daring raid against the Rashids and recaptured Riyadh. He was driven out two years later, but fought on, using religion to rally nomadic tribesmen to his cause. He defeated the Rashids and doubled his own territory (1920–22), then conquered the HEJAZ (1924). In 1932 he formally created the king-

Ibn Saud

dom of Saudi Arabia. He signed his first oil deal in 1933 but remained virtually penniless until the 1950s, when oil revenues began pouring in.

Ibn Sina See AVICENNA

Ibo See IGBO

Ibrahim Pasha \ib-rä-'hēm-'pash-ä\ (1789–1848) Egyptian general. He won military fame in Syria, defeating an Ottoman force, and Syria and Adana were ceded to Egypt, with Ibrahim as governor-general (1833). He created a consultative council and suppressed the feudal regime. When an Ottoman army invaded Syria, Ibrahim won his greatest victory (1839), forcing the Ottoman fleet to desert. However, the European powers, fearing the disintegration of the OTTOMAN EMPIRE, forced the Egyptians to evacuate the occupied territories. Ibrahim became viceroy of Egypt in 1848 shortly before his death.

Ibsen \'ip-sən, *Engl* 'ib-sən\, **Henrik (Johan)** (1828–1906) Norwegian playwright. At 23 he became theater director and resident playwright of the new National Theater at Bergen, and directed the Norwegian Theater 1857–63. He traveled in Europe, beginning a self-imposed exile that would last until 1891. In Italy he wrote the troubling moral tragedy *Brand* (1866) and the buoyant *Peer Gynt* (1867). He found an international audience with powerful studies of middle-class morality in *A Doll's House* (1879), *Ghosts* (1881), *An Enemy of the People* (1882), *The Wild Duck* (1884), and *Rosmersholm* (1886). His more symbolic

Henrik Ibsen, 1870

plays, most of them written after his return in 1891, include *Hedda Gabler* (1890), *The Master Builder* (1892), and *Little Eyolf* (1894). Emphasizing character over plot, Ibsen addressed social problems such as political corruption and the changing role of women as well as psychological conflicts stemming from frustrated love and destructive family relationships. He is regarded as the founder of modern prose drama.

ibuprofen \ˌī-byù-'prō-fən\ ANALGESIC, one of the NSAIDS, especially effective against DYSMENORRHEA, dental pain, and RHEUMATOID-ARTHRITIS pain. It may irritate the gastrointestinal tract and should not be taken by anyone who has an ALLERGY to ASPIRIN or takes ANTICOAGULANTS. Brand names include Advil, Motrin, and Nuprin. See also ACETAMINOPHEN.

IC See INTEGRATED CIRCUIT

Icarus See DAEDALUS

ICBM *in full* **intercontinental ballistic missile** Guided missile with a range of more than 3,300 mi (5,300 km). The MX

Peacekeeper has a range exceeding 6,000 mi (9,600 km). ICBMs include the silo-launched MINUTEMAN and the submarine-launched TRIDENT. The first ICBMs were developed by the Soviet Union in 1958.

ice SOLID form of WATER and water vapor. Below 32°F (0°C), liquid water forms a solid and water vapor forms frost on surfaces and snowflakes in clouds. Unlike most liquids, water expands on freezing, so ice is less dense than liquid water and therefore floats. It consists of compact aggregates of many CRYSTALS. Molecules in the crystal are held together by hydrogen bonds (see HYDROGEN BONDING). Ice conducts electricity much better than most nonmetallic crystals. At very high pressures, at least five other crystal forms of ice occur.

ice age *or* **glacial age** Any geologic period during which thick ice sheets cover vast areas of land. Such periods may last several million years and drastically reshape surface features of entire continents. A number of major ice ages have occurred throughout the earth's history; the most recent ended with the PLEISTOCENE EPOCH (1.8 million–10,000 years ago).

iceberg Floating mass of ice that has broken from a glacier or a polar ice sheet. Found especially around Greenland and Antarctica, icebergs form mostly during the spring and summer, when warmer weather increases the rate of calving (separation) of icebergs. About 10,000 icebergs are produced each year from the Greenland glaciers, and about 375 flow into the N. Atlantic shipping lanes, where they are a hazard to navigation, especially because only about 10% of an iceberg is exposed above the surface of the sea.

ice cream Frozen dairy food made from CREAM or butterfat, MILK, sugar, and flavorings. Nondairy fruit ices were introduced into Europe from the East in medieval times. Creation of the first true creamed ice is credited to a Parisian café owner named Tortoni in the late 18th cent. The ice-cream cone originated at the 1904 World's Fair in St. Louis, Mo. Commercial ice cream is made by heating, blending, and pasteurizing its ingredients, which are then agitated while being frozen to incorporate air; the highest-quality ice creams incorporate the least air.

ice hockey Game played on an ice rink by two teams of six players on skates whose object is to drive a puck (a small, hard rubber disk) into the opponents' goal with a hockey stick, thus scoring one point. The first true hockey game was played in 1875 at Montreal's McGill Univ. The NATIONAL HOCKEY LEAGUE was organized in 1917. Hockey was introduced at the Olympics in 1920. It is a very aggressive game; the puck is often stripped from a player by means of a hit (check) to the body, though some hits are illegal and draw penalties. A game consists of three 20-minute periods. See diagram on next page.

Iceland *officially* **Republic of Iceland** *Icelandic* **Ísland** \'ē-ˌslänt\ Island country, located in the N Atlantic Ocean, lying between Norway and Greenland. Area: 40,000 sq mi (100,000 sq km). Population (2000): 280,000. Capital: REYKJAVIK. The people are overwhelmingly Nordic. Language: Icelandic (official). Religion: Evangelical Lutheranism (official). Currency: krona. One of the most active volcanic regions in the world, Iceland contains about 200 volcanoes and accounts for one-third of the earth's total lava flow. One-tenth of its area is covered by cooled lava beds and glaciers, including Vatnajökull. Its rugged coastline is 3,700 mi (6,000 km) long. The economy is based heavily on fishing and fish products but also includes hydropower production, livestock, and aluminum processing. It is a republic with one legislative house; its chief of state is the president, and the head of government is the prime minister. Iceland was settled by Norwegian seafarers in the 9th cent. and was Christianized by 1000. Its legislature, the Althing, was founded in 930, making it one of the oldest legislative assemblies in the world. Iceland united with Norway in 1262 and with Denmark in 1380. It became an independent state of Denmark in 1918, but severed those ties to become an independent republic in 1944. Vigdís Finnbogadóttir became the world's first female elected president in 1980. Much of Iceland's recent economic growth has been in the expansion of its aluminum production.

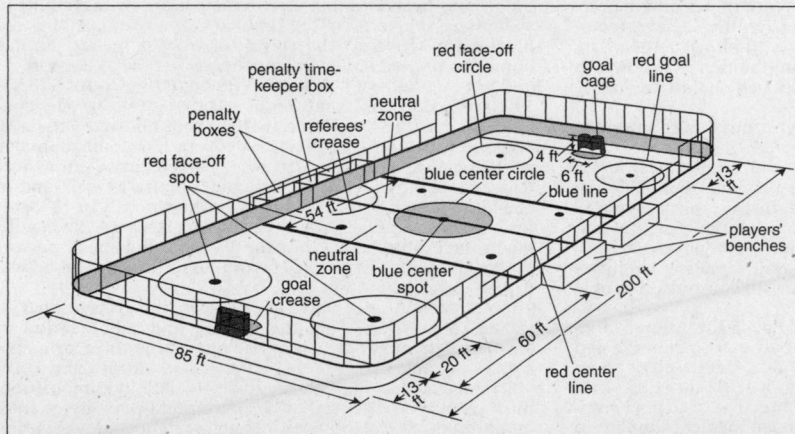

ICELAND

Scale 1: 7,540,000

0   20   40 mi

0   30   60 km

©1999, Encyclopædia Britannica, Inc.

tional acclaim for his antiwar films *The Burmese Harp* (1956) and *Fires on the Plain* (1959) and the documentary *Tokyo Olympiad* (1965).

I ching See YI JING

Ickes \\'i-kəs\\, **Harold L(eClair)** (1874–1952) U.S. public official. Born in Frankstown Township, Pa., he practiced law in Chicago, fighting for municipal reform. As a liberal Republican, he helped swing progressive votes to the Democrats in 1932. As secretary of the interior under Franklin ROOSEVELT (1933–46), he fought to preserve natural resources from private exploitation. He also headed the PUBLIC WORKS ADMINISTRATION (1933–39), spending over $5 billion on highways, public buildings, and dams. His scrutiny of each project ensured that it was graft-free but delayed the intended economic stimulus.

icon In EASTERN ORTHODOXY, the representation of sacred persons or events in murals, mosaics, or paintings on wood. After the Iconoclastic Controversy of the 8th–9th cent., which disputed the religious function and meaning of icons (see ICONOCLASM), the Eastern churches formulated an official doctrine that approved their use. Usually depicting Jesus or Mary but also sometimes saints, icons are relied on as objects of veneration and as tools for instruction.

iconoclasm Destruction of religious images. In Christianity and Islam, it was based on the Old Testament prohibition of graven images, which were associated with idolatry. The making of portraits of Christ and the saints was opposed in the early Christian church, but ICONS had become popular by the end of the 6th cent.; their defenders emphasized the symbolic nature of the images. Opposition by LEO III in 726 led to the Iconoclastic Controversy, which continued in the Eastern church for more than a century before icons were again accepted. Representations of saints and religious figures were also common in the Western church, though some Protestant sects eventually rejected them. Islam bans all icons.

ICU See INTENSIVE CARE UNIT

id In Freudian psychoanalytic theory, one of the three aspects of the personality, along with the EGO and SUPEREGO. The id is the source of instinctual impulses such as sex and aggression. It is entirely nonrational and functions according to the pleasure-pain principle, seeking immediate fulfillment of its impulses. Its processes are unconscious, but it supplies the energy for conscious mental life, and propels modes of expression that have a nonrational element, such as the making of art. The primary methods for unmasking its content, according to Sigmund FREUD, are dream analysis and free association.

Ida, Mt. Name of both a mountain in Turkey and the highest mountain in CRETE, Greece. The Turkish mountain, near the site of ancient TROY, was a classical shrine, where PARIS passed judgment on the rival goddesses. From its highest point, about 5,800 ft (1,800 m), the gods are said to have witnessed the TROJAN WAR. The Greek mountain, in W cen-

Icelanders' sagas *or* **family sagas** Class of heroic prose narratives written in the 13th cent. about the great families who lived in Iceland 930–1030. The family sagas represent the zenith of classical Icelandic saga writing and are far in advance of any contemporary medieval literature in their realism, controlled style, character delineation, and overwhelming tragic dignity. Justice, not courage, is often the primary virtue, as in the greatest of the sagas, *NJÁLS SAGA*.

Iceman, The Body of a man found sealed in a glacier in the Tirolean Alps in 1991 and dated to 3300–3200 B.C. It revealed significant details of everyday life during the NEOLITHIC PERIOD. The Iceman had tattoos and trimmed hair; it was previously thought that tattooing and hair cutting began much later in Europe. He wore neatly stitched deerskin clothing, a woven grass cape, and leather shoes stuffed with grass for insulation. He carried two (probably medicinal) fungi on leather thongs, a birchbark box for food, a copper ax, a flint dagger, a yew bow, and a deerskin quiver holding expertly finished arrows.

Ichikawa \\,ē-chē-'kä-wä\\, **Kon** (b.1915) Japanese film director. He directed his first film, *The Girl at Dojo Temple*, in 1946. He introduced sophisticated Western-style comedy to Japan in such films as *Mr. Pu* (1953). He gained interna-

Ice hockey A typical professional Amer. ice-hockey rink. U.S. college rinks are usually wider (100 ft), and international rinks vary in both length and width. Blue lines mark the respective off-sides areas; the space between them is called the neutral zone. The puck is put into play by being dropped between two players at the face-off spots; all players except those facing off must stand outside the face-off circle. A major penalty requires that a player go to the penalty box for five minutes while his team plays shorthanded.

tral Crete, reaches 8,058 ft (2,456 m). It too was a classical shrine, containing the legendary cave where ZEUS was reared.

Idaho State (pop., 2000: 1,294,000), NW U.S. It covers 83,557 sq mi (216,413 sq km); its capital is BOISE. It is dominated by the ROCKY MTNS., which extend from the Canadian border to S central Idaho and along the Wyoming border. Its most extensive valley surrounds the SNAKE RIVER, which flows through HELLS CANYON, the deepest gorge in N. America. First occupied by American Indians, the region was explored by the LEWIS AND CLARK EXPEDITION in 1805. It was part of the disputed Oregon Country that passed to the U.S. when Britain relinquished its claims by treaty in 1846. Discovery of gold in 1860 brought an influx of settlers. It became Idaho Territory in 1863 and was admitted to the Union as the 43rd state in 1890. Labor protests during 1890–1910 involving the INDUSTRIAL WORKERS OF THE WORLD erupted frequently. During the late 20th cent, Idaho developed its agriculture and industry, and promoted its natural wilderness.

ideal gas *or* **perfect gas** GAS whose physical behavior conforms to the general GAS LAW, which states that for a given quantity of gas, the product of the volume V and PRESSURE P is proportional to the absolute TEMPERATURE, or $PV = kT$, where k is a constant. A perfect gas is assumed to consist of a large number of MOLECULES in random motion, which obey NEWTON'S LAWS OF MOTION. Though no gas has these properties, real gases at sufficiently high temperatures and low pressures can be described this way (see KINETIC THEORY OF GASES).

idealism In METAPHYSICS, the view that stresses the central role of the ideal or the spiritual in the constitution of the world and in the interpretation of experience. Idealism may hold that the world or reality exists essentially as spirit or consciousness, and that abstractions are more fundamental than sensory things, or, at least, that whatever exists is known chiefly through and as ideas. Metaphysical idealism asserts the ideality of reality; epistemological idealism holds that the mind can grasp only its own contents. Metaphysical idealism is thus directly opposed to MATERIALISM, and epistemological idealism is opposed to REALISM. Absolute idealism (see G. W. F. HEGEL) holds that the everyday world of things and persons is not the world as it really is but merely as it appears, the best reflection of the world is in terms of a self-conscious mind, and truth consists in relationships between thoughts, rather than in a correspondence between thoughts and external realities. See also George BERKELEY.

ideology System of ideas that seeks both to explain the world and to change it. The word was coined in 1796 by the French writer A. L. C. Destutt de Tracy (1754–1836) as a label for his "science of ideas," which included a comprehensive theory of society, a political program, anticipation of a struggle to implement that program (thus requiring committed followers), and intellectual leadership. These ideas were adopted by the French DIRECTORY in building its version of a democratic, rational, and scientific society. Ideology is often contrasted unfavorably with PRAGMATISM. The significance of ideology follows from the fact that power is rarely exercised without some ideas or beliefs that justify support.

idiopathic respiratory distress syndrome See RESPIRATORY DISTRESS SYNDROME

idiot savant People of subnormal intelligence or severely limited emotional range who have prodigious intellectual gifts in a specific area, such as mathematics, music, art, and mechanics. Examples include performing rapid mental calculations of huge sums, playing lengthy compositions from memory after a single hearing, and repairing complex mechanisms without training. About 10% of autistic people are idiot savants. See also AUTISM.

Iditarod (Trail Sled-Dog Race) \ˌī-ˈdit-ə-ˌräd\ Annual dogsled race held in March on a route between Anchorage and Nome, Alaska. It originated in 1967 as a short race of 56 mi (90 km). By 1973 it had evolved into a 1,152-mi (1,855-km) trek roughly tracing an old mail route. The race also commemorates an emergency mission to get medical supplies to

Nome during a 1925 diphtheria epidemic. It typically takes 9–14 days to complete.

idol Image or statue of a deity used as an object of worship. In Judaism and Islam, the making of any representation of God is strictly forbidden. In Christianity, there has been a general acceptance of images of Jesus and the saints and, on occasion, God, though Christianity opposes their veneration as idols. In Jainism, Hinduism, and Buddhism, images of gods and saints are commonly venerated. In Hinduism, a statue may be treated as a god as an act of devotion but loses its special status when the act is finished.

Idris I \id-ˈrēs\ *in full* Sidi Muhammad Idris al-Mahdi al-Sanusi (1890–1983) King of Libya (1951–69). He succeeded his father in 1902 as leader of CYRENAICA but did not rule in his own name until 1916. Italy, which held the Libyan coast, confirmed Idris's authority in 1917 and established a parliament in 1919. His refusal to disarm his tribal supporters led to Italy's invasion of Tripolitania in 1922, and Idris went into exile. Cyrenaica and the other two Libyan provinces united under a constitutional monarchy headed by Idris and became independent in 1951. Idris was overthrown by Col. Muammar QADDAFI in a military coup in 1969. He died in exile in Egypt.

Idrisid dynasty \ˈid-ri-sid\ Dynasty that ruled BERBER areas of Morocco 788–921. The founder, Idris I, was a descendant of ALI and established the sharifian tradition in Morocco, by which the claim to descent from MUHAMMAD became the principle for monarchic rule. His son Idris II (r.803–28) founded FÈS in 808. The dynasty broke up into rival principalities, paving the way for the ALMORAVID DYNASTY.

Igbo \ˈig-bō\ *or* **Ibo** \ˈē-bō\ People of SE Nigeria who speak dialects of Igbo. During conflicts in 1966, many Igbo in N Nigeria were killed or forced into their traditional homelands in the east. In 1967 the E region tried to secede from Nigeria as the independent nation of BIAFRA; hundreds of thousands of Igbo were killed or starved. Today they number about 18.6 million, and include many farmers as well as traders, craftsmen, laborers, civil servants, and business entrepreneurs.

IG Farben World's largest chemical CARTEL from its founding in Germany until its dissolution by the Allies after World War II. It grew out of a complex merger of German manufacturers of chemicals, pharmaceuticals, and dyestuffs *(Farben)*. Its major members were the companies known today as BASF AG, BAYER AG, Hoechst AG, Agfa-Gevaert Group, and Cassella AG. They formed a loose association in 1916 and were formally united in 1925. During World War II, IG Farben established a synthetic oil and rubber plant at AUSCHWITZ to take advantage of available slave labor. After the war, several company officials were convicted of WAR CRIMES, and IG Farben was broken up into three independent companies.

igloo Temporary dome-shaped winter home or hunting-ground dwelling of Canadian and Greenland Inuit (ESKIMOS), made from blocks of compact snow. After a row of blocks has been laid in a circle, their tops are shaved off in a sloping angle to form the first rung of a spiral. Additional blocks are added to the spiral to draw it inward until a dome is completed, leaving a ventilation hole at the top.

Ignatyev \ig-ˈnät-yif\, **Nikolay (Pavlovich), Count** (1832–1908) Russian diplomat under ALEXANDER II. He concluded a treaty with China in 1860 that allowed Russia to construct the city of Vladivostok and become a major power in the N Pacific. He soon gained jurisdiction over Russia's relations with the Ottoman empire as well, and in 1864 he became ambassador to Constantinople. In 1878, after Russia's victory in the RUSSO–TURKISH WAR, he negotiated a favorable treaty; but the Western European powers replaced it with one far less favorable to Russia, and he was forced to resign.

igneous rock Any of various crystalline or glassy noncrystalline rocks formed by the cooling and solidification of MAGMA. Igneous rocks comprise one of the three principal classes of rocks, the others being METAMORPHIC and SEDIMENTARY rocks. Though they vary widely in composition, most igneous rocks consist of quartz, feldspars, pyroxenes, amphiboles, micas, olivines, nepheline, leucite, and apatite.

ignition system In a GASOLINE ENGINE, the means used for producing an electric spark to ignite the fuel-air mixture. It consists of a storage BATTERY recharged by a generator, an induction coil, a device to produce timed high-voltage discharges from the coil, a distributor, and a set of SPARK PLUGS. The battery provides an electric current of low voltage, usually 12 volts, that is converted by the system to some 40,000 volts. The distributor routes the successive bursts of current to each spark plug in the proper firing order.

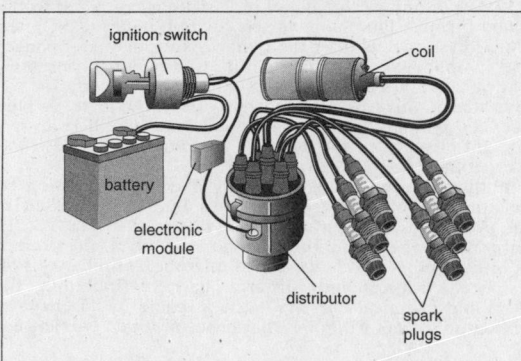

Ignition switch

coil

battery

electronic module

distributor

spark plugs

Ignition system An automobile ignition system. Electricity is provided to the spark plugs, which fire, igniting the fuel-air mixture in the combustion chamber. The induction coil consists of a transformer that steps up the voltage from the 12 volts supplied by the battery to the thousands of volts needed to fire the spark plugs. The distributor sends the current to the spark plugs in the proper firing order.

iguana \i-'gwä-nə\ Any of about 13 of the larger members of the LIZARD family Iguanidae. Best known is the common iguana *(Iguana iguana),* which ranges from Mexico to Brazil. It reaches a maximum length of 6 ft (1.8 m). It lives in trees, especially trees overhanging water, into which it will plunge if disturbed. It primarily eats tender leaves and fruits but will also eat small birds and crustaceans. Species of the SW U.S. and Mexico include the chuckwalla *(Sauromalus obesus)* and desert iguana *(Dipsosaurus dorsalis).*

Iguazú Falls *or* **Iguaçu Falls** \ₑē-gwə-'sü\ *formerly* **Victoria Falls** Cataract on the Iguazú River near the Argentina–Brazil border. The horseshoe-shaped falls were discovered by Á. N. CABEZA DE VACA in 1541. They are 269 ft (82 m) high and 2.5 mi (4 km) wide (four times the width of NIAGARA FALLS), and are divided into 275 waterfalls or cataracts. Their scenic beauty and wildlife are protected by national parks in both Brazil and Argentina.

Iguazú Falls

IJsselmeer \'ā-səl-ₘmer\ *English* **Lake IJssel** Shallow freshwater lake, N Netherlands. Fed by the IJSSEL RIVER, it was formed from the S part of the former ZUIDER ZEE by a dam, which separates it from both the Wadden Zee and the North Sea. Its total area (1,328 sq mi, or 3,440 sq km) has been reduced by the reclamation of 626 sq mi (1,620 sq km) of land. Regulated by sluices, the formerly brackish water has been replaced by fresh water from the IJssel River.

IJssel River \'ā-səl, *Engl* 'i-səl\ River, Netherlands. An important distributary of the RHINE RIVER, it leaves the Lower Rhine (Neder Rijn) just southeast of Arnhem and flows northeastward for 70 mi (113 km) to enter the IJSSELMEER.

ileitis \ₑi-lē-'ī-təs\ Chronic INFLAMMATION of part of the SMALL or LARGE INTESTINE (strictly, of the ILEUM). A more serious type, regional ileitis (Crohn's disease), involves both small and large intestines. Ileitis symptoms include chronic or intermittent, sometimes bloody, diarrhea and abdominal cramps. Fever, weight loss, and anemia may occur and in Crohn's disease can cause progressive deterioration. Simple ileitis has short-term causes, and many patients recover completely. In Crohn's disease, which may result from an autoimmune defect, remissions and relapses continue for years, causing the intestine's wall to thicken, its channel to narrow, and its lining to ulcerate. Drug treatment may help, but there is no known cure, and the disease often requires removal of part of the intestine.

ileum \'i-lē-əm\ Final and longest (about 13 ft or 4 m) segment of the SMALL INTESTINE, site of absorption of vitamin B_{12} and reabsorption of about 90% of conjugated BILE salts. Disorders produce B_{12} deficiency and extensive diarrhea (since bile salts in the large intestine interfere with water absorption).

Iliamna Lake \ₑi-lē-'am-nə\ Lake, Alaska. The second-largest freshwater lake entirely within the U.S., it is 80 mi (129 km) long and 25 mi (40 km) wide, and covers an area of 1,000 sq mi (2,600 sq km). Located at the base of the Alaska Peninsula, it drains into Bristol Bay. The active Iliamna Volcano, 10,016 ft (3,053 m) high, lies northeast of the lake.

Ilium See TROY

Illinois State (pop. 2000: 12,419,000), midwestern U.S. It covers 56,400 sq mi (146,076 sq km); its capital is SPRINGFIELD. The MISSISSIPPI RIVER forms the state's W boundary, the OHIO and WABASH rivers form its SE border, and the Illinois River traverses it. Located on its NE border is CHICAGO, the nation's third-largest city. Indian settlement dates from 8000 B.C. The MISSISSIPPIAN CULTURE was centered at Cahokia around A.D. 1300; all the tribes inhabiting the area at the time of European settlement were of Algonquian stock. The French explorers Jacques MARQUETTE and Louis JOLLIET entered the territory in 1673. France controlled it until 1763, when it passed to Britain after the FRENCH AND INDIAN WAR. It became part of the Northwest Territory in 1783, and part of Indiana Territory in 1800; Illinois Territory was formed in 1809 and it became the 21st state in 1818. Although politically divided during the AMERICAN CIVIL WAR, Illinois, the adopted home of Abraham LINCOLN, remained part of the Union. In the 20th cent. it was a major battleground in presidential elections. It is one of the largest U.S. industrial centers, and a top manufacturer of nonelectrical machinery. It is also a major insurance center.

Illinois, University of State system of higher education consisting of a main campus at Urbana-Champaign (founded 1867) and a second campus in Chicago (1946). Both campuses offer undergraduate, graduate, and professional degree programs. The main campus includes the National Center for Supercomputing Applications; the Chicago campus houses the Jane Addams School for Social Work. The main library is the third-largest academic collection in the U.S. Total enrollment is about 62,000.

illuminated manuscript Handwritten book decorated with gold or silver, brilliant colors, elaborate designs, or miniature paintings. "Illumination" originally denoted embellishment of text with gold or silver, which gave the impression that the page had been literally illuminated. In the Middle Ages, those who "historiated" (illustrated texts with paintings) were differentiated from those who "illuminated" (embellished the initial

Illuminated manuscript From the Winchester Bible, 12th cent.

capital letters with gold leaf or powder). Today the term denotes both historiation and illumination. Illumination was superseded by printed illustrations in the 15th cent.

Illustrated London News Picture magazine of news and the arts, published in London. Founded in 1842 as a weekly, it became a monthly in 1971. It was London's first illustrated periodical, the first periodical to make extensive use of woodcuts and engravings, and the first to use photographs. Initially focused mainly on English social life, it later broadened its scope to embrace general news and cultural activities.

illuviation Accumulation of dissolved or suspended soil materials in one area or layer as a result of leaching (percolation) from another. Usually CLAY, iron, or HUMUS wash out and form a line with a different consistency and color. These lines are important for studying the composition and ages of rock strata.

Illyria \ə-'lir-ē-ə\ Ancient country, NW BALKAN PENINSULA. It was inhabited from the 10th cent. B.C. by the Illyrians, an Indo-European people who later practiced piracy on Roman shipping. After a series of wars with Rome, it was defeated in 168 B.C. and established as the Roman province of Illyricum. From A.D. 395, Illyria east of the Drina River was part of the Eastern Empire. It was occupied by the Slavs from the 6th cent., and its name was eventually changed to Albania.

imaginary number Any number of the form $a + bi$ where a and b are real numbers, i is $\sqrt{-1}$ and b is not zero. If a is zero, the number is called a pure imaginary number. See also COMPLEX NUMBER.

Imagism \'im-i-,jiz-əm\ Movement in U.S. and English poetry characterized by the use of concrete language and figures of speech, modern subject matter, metrical freedom, and avoidance of romantic or mystical themes. It grew out of the SYMBOLIST MOVEMENT and was initially led by Ezra POUND, who formulated its credo around 1912. Later, Amy LOWELL took over leadership of the group. Imagism influenced the works of T. S. ELIOT, Marianne MOORE, D. H. LAWRENCE, and Wallace STEVENS.

imam \i-'mäm\ Head of the Muslim community. In SUNNI Islam the imam was identical with the CALIPH. The Sunnis held the imam to be a man capable of error but deserving obedience provided he maintained the ordinances of Islam. In SHIITE Islam the imam became a figure of absolute religious authority, possessed of unique insights into the Quran, divinely appointed, and preserved from sin. After the disappearance of the last imam (873), Shiites came to believe in a hidden imam, who is identified with the MAHDI. The term imam is also given to Muslims who lead prayers in mosques and is an honorary title.

IMF See INTERNATIONAL MONETARY FUND

Imhotep \im-'hō-,tep\ *Greek* Imouthes (fl.27th cent. B.C.) Egyptian sage and astrologer, later worshiped as the god of medicine. In Greece he was identified with ASCLEPIUS. Imhotep is remembered as a skilled physician and as the architect of the step-pyramid at SAQQARA in Memphis. He was deified around the time of the Persian conquest in 525 B.C., and his cult reached its zenith in Greco-Roman times, when sick people slept in his temples with the hope that the god would reveal remedies to them in dreams.

Immaculate Conception In ROMAN CATHOLICISM, the dogma that MARY was not tainted by ORIGINAL SIN. The belief was originally controversial, but in 1439 the Council of BASEL stated that it was in accordance with Catholic faith, and in 1709 Pope Clement XI made the feast of the Immaculate Conception a holy day of obligation. In 1854 PIUS IX issued a papal bull making it official church dogma. See also VIRGIN BIRTH.

immune system Cells, cell products, organs, and structures of the body involved in the detection and destruction of foreign invaders, such as bacteria, viruses, and cancer cells. IMMUNITY is based on the system's ability to launch a defense against such invaders. The system must be able to distinguish between the material of its own body (self) and other material (nonself). Failure to make this distinction can result in AUTOIMMUNE DISEASES. An exaggerated or inappropriate response by the immune system to nonharmful substances (e.g., pollen, animal dander) can result in ALLERGIES. The system's principal cells include LYMPHOCYTES that recognize ANTIGENS, and related accessory cells (such as phagocytic macrophages, which engulf and destroy foreign material). Lymphocytes (see B CELL, T CELL) arise from stem cells in the BONE MARROW. Mature lymphocytes enter the bloodstream, and many become lodged in various body tissues, including the SPLEEN, LYMPH NODES, TONSILS, and intestinal lining (termed LYMPHOID TISSUE). Fluid (LYMPH) draining from lymphoid tissues is conveyed to the blood through lymphatic vessels. Lymph nodes distributed along these vessels filter the lymph, exposing macrophages and lymphocytes contained within to any antigen present. The spleen plays a similar role, sampling the blood for the presence of antigens. The capability of lymphocytes to pass between lymphoid tissue, the blood, and lymph is an important element in the system's functioning. See also IMMUNODEFICIENCY, IMMUNOLOGY.

immunity Ability to resist attack or overcome infection by invading microbes or larger parasites. Immunity is based on the proper functioning of the body's IMMUNE SYSTEM. In natural or innate immunity, immune mechanisms present at birth combat a wide variety of microbes, familiar or not. Its mechanisms include physical barriers (including the skin) and chemical barriers (such as bactericidal enzymes present in saliva). Microbes that penetrate such barriers en-

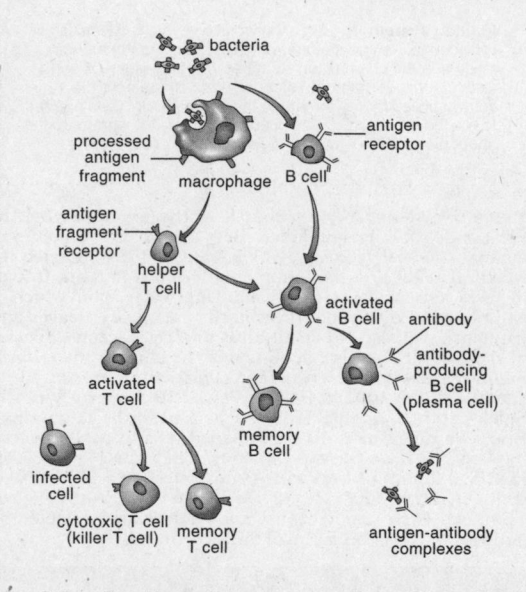

Cell-mediated Immunity   **Humoral Immunity**

Immune system Acquired immunity depends on the activities of T and B lymphocytes (T and B cells). One part of acquired immunity, humoral immunity, involves the production of antibodies by B cells. The other part, cell-mediated immunity, involves the actions of T cells. When an antigen (such as a bacterium) enters the body, it is attacked and engulfed by macrophages, which process and display parts of it on their cell surface. A helper T cell, recognizing the antigen displayed, initiates maturation and proliferation of other T cells. Cytotoxic (killer) T cells develop and attack foreign and infected cells. B cells stimulated by the presence of antigen are activated by helper T cells to divide and form antibody-producing cells (plasma cells). Released antibody binds to antigen, marking the cell for destruction. Helper T cells also induce the development of memory T and B cells needed to mount future immune responses on reinfection with the same pathogen.

counter substances (such as INTERFERON) that inhibit their growth or reproduction. Phagocytes (particle-engulfing cells) surround and destroy invading microbes, and natural killer cells pierce the microbe's outer membrane. Acquired immune responses are tailored to act against a specific microbe or its products. Previous infection, as well as VACCINES, produce this type of immunity, which is based on the recognition of ANTIGEN by B and T CELLS and is activated when innate mechanisms are insufficient to stem further invasion by pathogens. Killer or cytotoxic T cells destroy infected and foreign cells. Helper T cells induce B cells stimulated by the presence of antigen to proliferate into antibody-secreting cells, or plasma cells. ANTIBODIES produced by plasma cells bind to antigen-bearing cells, marking them for destruction. Acquired immunity relies on the long-term survival of sensitized T and B memory cells, which can proliferate quickly upon reinfection. See also IMMUNODEFICIENCY, IMMUNOLOGY, LEUKOCYTE, RETICULOENDOTHELIAL SYSTEM.

immunity In law, exemption or freedom from liability. Under international treaty, a diplomatic representative is exempt from local laws, both civil and criminal. A public prosecutor may grant immunity from prosecution to a witness who is suspected of criminal activity in return for testimony against other suspected criminals.

immunodeficiency Defect in IMMUNITY that impairs the body's ability to resist infection. The IMMUNE SYSTEM may fail to function for many reasons. Immune disorders caused by a genetic defect are usually evident early in life. Others can be acquired at any age through infections (e.g., AIDS) or IMMUNOSUPPRESSION. Aspects of the immune response that may be affected include LYMPHOCYTES, other LEUKOCYTES, and ANTIBODIES. Treatment for immunodeficiency may be administration of immunoglobulins, bone-marrow transplant, or therapy for the underlying disease.

immunology Science dealing with the body's defenses against disease-causing microorganisms and disorders of those defenses. Starting with Edward JENNER's use of a VACCINE against SMALLPOX in 1796, immunology has arrived at a comprehensive and sophisticated understanding of the role of microorganisms in disease and of the formation, mobilization, action, and interaction of ANTIBODIES and ANTIGEN-reactive cells. See also ALLERGIES, AIDS, AUTOIMMUNE DISEASE, IMMUNITY, IMMUNE SYSTEM, IMMUNODEFICIENCY, IMMUNOSUPPRESSION.

immunosuppression Suppression of IMMUNITY with drugs, usually to prevent rejection of an organ TRANSPLANT and allow the recipient to accept the organ permanently with no unpleasant side effects. Other uses are in the treatment of certain AUTOIMMUNE DISEASES. Its main drawback is the increased risk of infection for the duration of treatment and of LYMPHOMA in the case of long-term immunosuppression.

impact test Test of the ability of a material to withstand impact, used to predict its behavior under actual conditions. Many materials fail suddenly under impact, at flaws, cracks, or notches. The most common impact tests use a swinging pendulum to strike a notched bar; heights before and after impact are used to compute the energy required to produce a fracture. In the Charpy test, the test piece is held horizontally between two vertical bars; in the Izod test, it stands erect.

impala \im-ˈpa-lə\ Swift-running, graceful ANTELOPE *(Aepyceros melampus)* found in large herds, usually near water, on open country of central and S Africa. Impalas are noted for their jumping ability; when alarmed, they bound off in leaps up to 30 ft (9 m) long and 10 ft (3 m) high. Lightly built, the impala stands 30–40 in. (75–100 cm) high at the shoulder. It is

Male impala *(Aepyceros melampus)*

golden to reddish brown, with a vertical black stripe on each thigh. The male has long, lyre-shaped horns.

impatiens \im-ˈpā-shəns\ Any of about 900 species of herbaceous plants in the genus *Impatiens* (BALSAM family), so named because the seedpod bursts when slightly touched. Garden balsam *(I. balsamina),* native to the tropics of Asia, is a favorite showy annual in U.S. gardens; its flowers are irregular, single or clustered, and of almost every color but blue. Most impatiens have weak, hollow stems and require high moisture.

impeachment Criminal proceeding instituted against a public official by a legislative body. In the U.S., the president, vice president, and other federal officers, including judges, may be impeached by the U.S. House of Representatives. The House draws up articles of impeachment that itemize the charges and their factual bases. Once approved by a majority of House members, the articles are submitted to the Senate, which holds a trial. At its conclusion, each member votes for or against conviction on each article; conviction requires a two-thirds majority. A convicted official can be removed from office. The U.S. CONSTITUTION specifies that an officer is to be impeached for "high crimes and misdemeanors"; experts agree that impeachment is permitted for noncriminal misconduct (e.g., violation of the Constitution). Two U.S. presidents, Andrew JOHNSON and William CLINTON, have been impeached but acquitted. Articles of impeachment were drawn up against Pres. Richard NIXON in 1974, who resigned before formal proceedings could begin.

imperialism State policy, practice, or advocacy of extending power and dominion, especially by direct territorial acquisition or by gaining political and economic control of other areas. Because it always involves the use of power, whether military force or some subtler form, the term was often used in the 20th cent. to denounce and discredit an opponent's foreign policy. Theories such as those of Niccolò MACHIAVELLI and Adolf HITLER asserted that nations endowed with superior qualities are destined to rule over others. Arguments relating to strategy describe imperialism as a consequence of the quest for security. After World War II, imperialism through direct conquest gave way to so-called political, economic, and cultural imperialism. See also COLONIALISM.

Imperial Valley Valley extending from SE California to Mexico. It forms part of the Colorado Desert. Intensive irrigation began in 1901 with diversion of water from the COLORADO RIVER. Floodwaters in 1905–7 destroyed the irrigation channels and created the SALTON SEA. The valley is now watered by the HOOVER DAM and the All-American Canal. With 3,000 mi (4,800 km) of irrigation canals, it contains 500,000 acres (200,000 hectares) of cultivated land.

impetigo \im-pə-ˈtī-ˌgō, im-pə-ˈtē-ˌgō\ Bacterial inflammatory SKIN disease. Initial blisters rupture, drying to a crust. Caused by STAPHYLOCOCCUS or STREPTOCOCCUS, it is very contagious in newborns, becoming less so with age. Poor hygiene, crowding, and humid, hot weather may promote its spread. Treatment is with antibiotics.

impotence \ˈim-pə-təns\ Inability to achieve or maintain erection of the PENIS; hence, inability to participate fully in SEXUAL INTERCOURSE. Failure to achieve erection may have either physical causes (e.g., alcoholism, endocrine disease) or psychological ones (e.g., anxiety, hostility toward the partner). Inability to reach orgasm nearly always has an emotional cause. Incidence of impotence tends to increase with age. See also VIAGRA.

Impressionism Movement in art that developed in France in the late 19th cent. In painting it included works produced about 1867–86 by a group of artists who shared approaches, techniques, and discontent with academic teaching, originally including Claude MONET, Auguste RENOIR, Camille PISSARRO, Alfred SISLEY, and Berthe MORISOT. Later Edouard MANET, whose earlier style had strongly influenced several of them, Mary CASSATT, and others adopted the Impressionist style. The identifying feature of their work was an attempt to record the visual reality of a landscape or a scene from modern urban life accurately and objectively, capturing the transient effects of light on color and texture. They avoided muted browns, grays, and greens in favor of a

lighter, more brilliant palette; stopped using grays and blacks for shadows; and built up forms out of discrete flecks and dabs of color. They adopted Eugène BOUDIN's practice of direct observation, painting entirely out of doors. As the French Academy's SALON consistently rejected most of their works, they held their own exhibition in 1874; seven others followed. A critic described them derisively as "impressionists," and they adopted the name as an accurate description of their intent. Before dissolving in the late 1880s, the group had revolutionized Western painting.

Impressionism Term used for music written in a style initiated by Claude DEBUSSY at the end of the 19th cent. Introduced by analogy with contemporaneous French painting, the term (disliked by Debussy himself) usually implies such elements as static harmony, emphasis on instrumental timbres that creates a shimmering interplay of "colors," melodies that lack directed motion, surface ornamentation that obscures or substitutes for melody, and an avoidance of traditional musical form. Impressionism can be seen as a reaction against the rhetoric of Romanticism. The other composer most often associated with Impressionism is Maurice RAVEL.

impressment Enforcement of military or naval service on unwilling men. Until the early 19th cent., it flourished in port towns everywhere, as "recruiters" searched through waterfront boardinghouses, brothels, and taverns. Impressed men were forced into service through violence or coercion and were held to their duty by brutal discipline. In the early 19th cent., ROYAL NAVY ships halting U.S. vessels to search for British deserters frequently impressed naturalized U.S. citizens, one cause of the WAR OF 1812. See also CONSCRIPTION.

imprinting Rapid learning process wherein a very young animal fixes its attention on the first object with which it has visual, auditory, or tactile experience and thereafter follows that object. In nature, the object is almost always a parent; in experiments, other animals and inanimate objects have been used. It apparently takes place not only among birds but also among many mammals and some fishes and insects.

improvisation Creation of music in real time. Improvisation usually involves some preparation beforehand, particularly when there is more than one performer. Despite the central place of notated music in the Western tradition, improvisation has often played a role, from the earliest ORGANUM through the realization of FIGURED BASS. It has taken such forms as elaborate ornamentation added to a repeated section in an aria, keyboard variations on popular songs, concerto cadenzas, and free solo fantasias. Today improvisation is heard in "experimental" works and in "authentic" performances of older music. Its most important contemporary form is JAZZ.

incandescent lamp Any of various devices that produce light by heating a suitable material to a high temperature. In an electric incandescent lamp, or lightbulb, a filament is enclosed in a glass shell that is either evacuated or filled with an inert gas. The filament gives off light when heated by an electric current. The first practical electric incandescent lamps were independently produced in the late 1870s by Joseph Swan (1828–1914) and Thomas EDISON. Inefficient in comparison with FLUORESCENT LAMPS and ELECTRIC DISCHARGE LAMPS, incandescent lighting is today reserved mainly for domestic use. See also HALOGEN LAMP.

Incarnation Central Christian doctrine that God became man in the form of JESUS. In Jesus the divine and human nature are joined but neither is changed or diminished. This difficult doctrine gave rise to a variety of HERESIES, some denying Jesus's divine nature, others his human nature. The Councils of Nicaea (A.D. 325) and CHALCEDON (A.D. 451) defined the orthodox position.

Incas Group of S. American Indians who ruled a territory that extended along the Pacific coast and Andean highlands from what is now N Ecuador to central Chile. According to tradition, the founder of the Inca dynasty led the tribe to Cuzco, which became their capital. Under Topa Inca Yupanqui and his successor, the empire reached its southernmost and northernmost extent. By the early 16th cent. the Incas ruled an empire of 12 million subjects. They con-

structed a vast network of roads, which in the end facilitated the Spanish conquest in 1532. Their architecture was highly developed, and the remains of their irrigation systems, palaces, temples, and fortifications may still be seen. Inca society featured an aristocratic bureaucracy. Their pantheon, worshiped in a highly organized state religion, included a sun god, a creator god, and a rain god. Their descendants are the Quechua-speaking peasants of the Andes (see QUECHUA). In Peru about 45% of the population are of Inca descent; they are primarily farmers and herders, and their Roman Catholicism is infused with belief in pagan spirits and divinities. See also ANDEAN CIVILIZATION, ATAHUALLPA, AYMARÁ, Francisco PIZARRO.

incense Grains of RESINS (sometimes mixed with spices) that burn with a fragrant odor, widely used as religious offerings. Historically, the chief substances used as incense have been resins such as FRANKINCENSE and myrrh, along with fragrant wood and bark, seeds, roots, and flowers.

Inchon \'in-ˌchän\ *formerly* **Jinsen** \'jin-ˌsen\ *or* **Chemulpo** \jə-'mùl-pō\ Seaport city (pop., 1995: 2,308,000), S. Korea, near SEOUL. A fishing port since the 14th cent., it had developed as an international commercial port before the Japanese occupation (1910–45). During the KOREAN WAR, it was the site of a successful U.N. troop landing (1950).

Inclán, Ramón María del Valle- See R. M. del VALLE-INCLÁN

income tax Levy imposed by public authority on the incomes of persons or corporations within its jurisdiction. In nations with an advanced system of private enterprise, income tax is the chief source of government revenue. In 1799 Britain enacted a general income tax to finance the Napoleonic Wars. In the U.S. an income tax was first tried during the Civil War; the Supreme Court held it constitutional in 1881 but declared another income tax unconstitutional in 1894. In 1913 the 16th Amendment to the Constitution made the personal income tax permanent. The fairness of personal income taxation is based on the premise that one's income is the best single index of one's ability to contribute to the support of the government. Thus U.S. income taxes are PROGRESSIVE TAXES, falling more heavily on those who earn more money; deductions are allowed for items such as interest paid on home mortgage debt, unusual medical expenses, philanthropic contributions, and state and local income and property taxes. Enforcement has been facilitated by withholding the tax from wages and salaries. See also CAPITAL-GAINS TAX, REGRESSIVE TAX, SALES TAX, VALUE-ADDED TAX.

incontinence Inability to control EXCRETION. Starting and stopping URINATION relies on normal function in pelvic and abdominal muscles, diaphragm, and control nerves. Incontinence may reflect disorders (e.g., NEURAL TUBE DEFECT), paralysis of URINARY SYSTEM muscles, or certain urogenital malformations. Weak pelvic muscles can allow small urine losses on coughing or sneezing ("stress incontinence"). Uncontrolled DEFECATION can result from spinal or bodily injuries, old age, extreme fear, or severe DIARRHEA. See also ENURESIS.

incubus and succubus Demons (male and female, respectively) who seek to have sexual intercourse with sleeping humans. In medieval Europe some believed that union with an incubus resulted in the birth of witches, demons, and deformed human offspring.

Independence City (pop., 2000: 113,000), W Missouri. Settled in 1827, it served as the starting point for the SANTA FE TRAIL and the OREGON TRAIL, and was a rendezvous for wagon trains during the California GOLD RUSH. Home of a MORMON colony 1831–33, it is now the world headquarters of the Reorganized Church of Jesus Christ of Latter-day Saints. The hometown of Pres. Harry TRUMAN, it is the site of the Harry S. Truman Library and Museum.

Independence, Declaration of See DECLARATION OF INDEPENDENCE

Independence Day *or* **Fourth of July** Anniversary of the adoption of the DECLARATION OF INDEPENDENCE by the Second CONTINENTAL CONGRESS (July 4, 1776). It is the greatest secular holiday in the U.S. Celebrating the day became common only after the War of 1812, when it came to symbolize the ideals of democracy and citizenship.

independent school See PUBLIC SCHOOL (BRITISH)

indeterminacy principle See UNCERTAINTY PRINCIPLE

indexation Comparison of PRICE levels over time. In fiscal policy, indexation is used as a means of offsetting the effect of INFLATION or DEFLATION on social-security payments and taxes by measuring the real value of money from a fixed reference point, usually a PRICE INDEX. Without indexing, recipients of social-security benefits, for example, would suffer during inflation if their benefits remained at a fixed rate. Indexation is used in some countries to offset "bracket creep," which occurs in any PROGRESSIVE TAX system when inflation pushes taxpayers into higher tax brackets. Indexation may also refer to the linking of wage rates and financial instruments to a price index.

Index librorum prohibitorum \'in-deks-li-'brō-rəm-prō-,hi-bə-'tō-rəm\ (Latin: "Index of Forbidden Books") List of books once forbidden by Roman Catholic church authority as dangerous to the faith or morals of Catholics. The first catalog of banned books to be called an index was published in 1559. Publication of the list ceased in 1966, and it was relegated to the status of a historic document.

India *officially* **Republic of India** *Hindi* **Bharat** \'bər-ət\

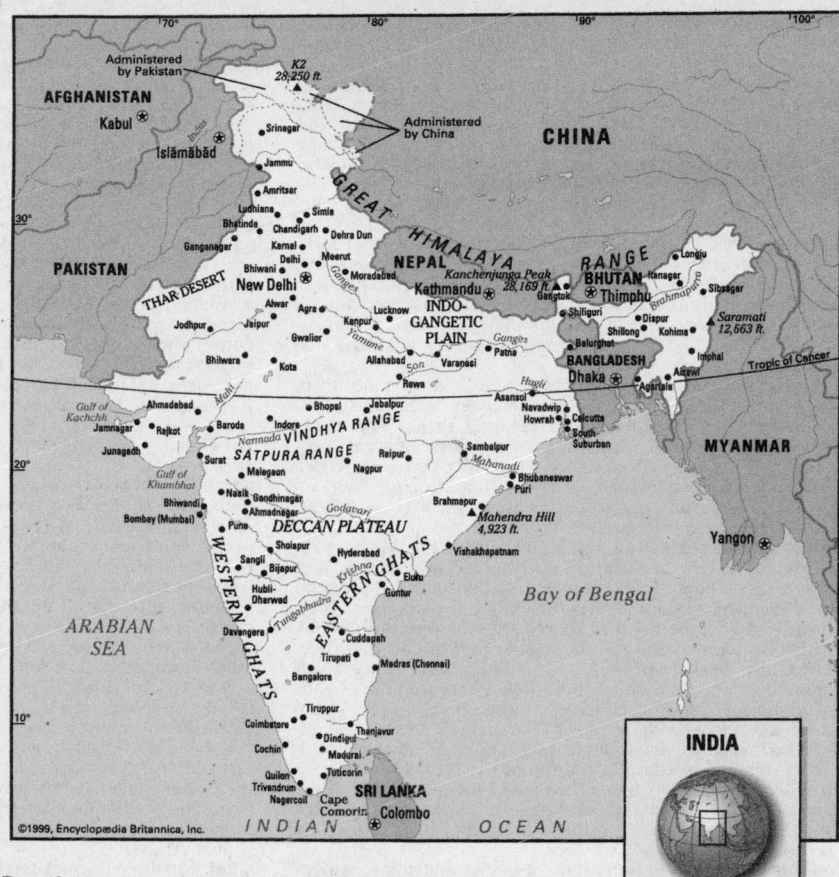

INDIA
Scale 1: 33,569,000
0   150   300 mi
0   250   500 km

Republic, S. Asia. It fronts the Bay of BENGAL on the southeast and the ARABIAN SEA on the southwest. Area: 1,222,559 sq mi (3,166,414 sq km). Population (2000): 1,014,004,000. Capital: NEW DELHI. The peoples of India comprise widely varying mixtures of ethnic strains drawn from peoples settled in the subcontinent before the dawn of history, or from invaders. Languages: Hindi, English (both official); many other languages, including Bengali, Marathi, and Urdu; DRAVIDIAN LANGUAGES; hundreds from several other language families. Religions: Hinduism, Islam, Christianity, Sikhism, Buddhism, Jainism. Currency: rupee. India has three major geographic regions: the HIMALAYAS, which form its N border; the Indo-GANGETIC PLAIN, formed by the alluvial deposits of three great river systems, including the GANGES; and the S region, noted for the DECCAN plateau. Agricultural products include rice, wheat, cotton, sugarcane, coconut, spices, jute, tobacco, tea, coffee, and rubber. Its manufacturing sector is highly diversified and includes both heavy and high-technology industries. It is a republic with two legislative houses; its chief of state is the president, and the head of government is the prime minister. India has been inhabited for thousands of years. Agriculture in India dates back to the 7th millennium B.C., and an urban civilization, that of the INDUS valley, was established by 2600 B.C. BUDDHISM and JAINISM arose in the 6th cet. B.C. in reaction to the caste-based society created by the VEDIC RELIGION and its successor, Hinduism. Muslim invasions began about A.D. 1000, establishing the long-lived DELHI SULTANATE in 1206 and the MUGHAL DYNASTY in 1526. Vasco da GAMA's voyage to India in 1498 initiated several centuries of commercial rivalry among the Portuguese, Dutch, English, and French. British conquests in the 18th and 19th cent. led to the rule of the British EAST INDIA CO. and direct administration by the BRITISH EMPIRE began in 1858. After Mohandas GANDHI helped end British rule in 1947, Jawaharlal NEHRU became its first prime minister and he, his daughter Indira GANDHI, and grandson Rajiv GANDHI guided the nation's destiny for all but a few years until 1991. In 1947 the subcontinent was partitioned into two countries—India, with a Hindu majority, and Pakistan, with a Muslim majority. A later clash with Pakistan resulted in the creation of Bangladesh in 1971. From the 1980s, Sikhs sought to establish an independent state in PUNJAB. Tensions with Pakistan over the disputed territory of KASHMIR have led to border clashes and development of nuclear weapons by both countries.

Indiana State (pop. 2000: 6,080,000) midwestern U.S. It covers 36,291 sq mi (93,994 sq km); its capital is INDIANAPOLIS. The OHIO RIVER and the WABASH RIVER define its southern E and W borders, respectively. Indiana was originally inhabited by Algonquian-speaking Indians, including the Miami, Potawatomi, and DELAWARE. R.-R. LA SALLE explored the region in 1679 and claimed it for France. It passed to Britain in 1763 and then to the U.S. in 1783, and became a territory in 1800. In 1811 U.S. forces won a final victory over the Indians at the Battle of TIPPECANOE. After it was admitted to the Union as the 19th state in 1816, its population began to grow. From 1850 its agriculture expanded, as did industrialization after the AMERICAN CIVIL WAR. For much of the 20th cent., steelmaking (see GARY) was important economically.

Indiana, Robert *orig.* Robert Clark (b.1928) U.S. painter, sculptor, and graphic artist. Born in New Castle, Ind., he studied in Chicago, then settled in New York and became a leading exponent of POP ART. He achieved wide recognition for paintings and graphics featuring geometric shapes, lettering, and vivid colors. In 1964 he collaborated with Andy WARHOL on the film *Eat* and produced an *EAT* sign for the

New York World's Fair. His most famous image, *LOVE*, first painted on canvas in 1965, became a universal symbol for the Pop generation.

Indiana Dunes State park and national lakeshore, S shore of Lake MICHIGAN, N Indiana. The state park includes 2,182 acres (883 hectares) of shoreline, marshland, dunes, and forests. At the Big Blowout in the E end of the park, lake winds drift sands over a wooded area, creating a "graveyard of trees"; the dunes may reach heights of 200 ft (60 m). The national lakeshore covers more than 12,857 acres (5,205 hectares).

Indianapolis City (pop., 2000: 791,000) and capital of Indiana. Located near the center of the state, it was founded in 1821 and made the state capital in 1825. It is a hub of road, rail, and air transportation, a leading grain market, and an industrial center. It hosts the annual INDIANAPOLIS 500 automobile race and is home to the Speedway Hall of Fame Museum.

Indianapolis 500 U.S. automobile race held annually from 1911 at the Indianapolis Motor Speedway, a 2.5-mi (4-km) asphalt oval with banked quarter-mile turns. The "Indy 500" is a 500-mi (805-km) race for top international competitors using specially designed Formula cars (open-wheel, open-cockpit, rear-engine vehicles). Traditionally held on or near Memorial Day, the race draws crowds of 300,000 and offers substantial prizes.

Indian architecture Building traditions of the Indian subcontinent, dating back to at least the 2nd millennium B.C. The earliest Indian buildings were Buddhist and Hindu temples made of wood and then brick. By the 4th cent. B.C., stone had become popular. Large STUPAS were built, along with cave temples and monasteries carved out of solid rock. The Gupta period (4th–6th cent. A.D.) saw the rapid development of temple architecture, often decorated with bands of elaborate carving. N India's most characteristic structure, a temple with a heavily decorated tower (see SIKHARA), reached its stylistic height in the 7th–11th cent. The extension of Islam into India in the 11th–12th cent. introduced typical Muslim architectural forms (e.g., the dome and pointed arch) and decoration. Such masterworks as the TAJ MAHAL resulted from the rule of the Muslim MUGHAL DYNASTY in the 16th–18th cent.

Indiana University State system of higher education consisting of a main campus in Bloomington (founded 1820) and several other campuses or schools, some operated in cooperation with PURDUE UNIV. The Bloomington and Indianapolis campuses award doctoral degrees. The medical school is in Indianapolis, the business and law schools in Bloomington. The Bloomington campus has a strong reputation in music and the fine arts and is one of the principal centers for folklore research in the U.S. Facilities include the Kinsey Institute for Research in Sex, Gender, and Reproduction. Total enrollment is approx. 86,000.

Indian buffalo See WATER BUFFALO

Indian Mutiny *or* **Sepoy Mutiny** (1857–58) Widespread rebellion against British rule in India begun by Indian troops (sepoys) in the service of the English E. INDIA CO. When sepoys refused to bite off the ends of new rifle cartridges lubricated with grease made of pigs' and cows' fat (taboo to Hindus and Muslims), they were shackled and imprisoned; their outraged comrades then shot their British officers and marched to Delhi. The ensuing fight was ferocious and ended in defeat for the Indians. Its immediate result was abolishment of the E. India Co. in favor of direct rule of India by the British government, as well as the beginning of a British policy of consultation with Indians and the easing of social measures that had antagonized Hindu society.

Indian National Congress *or* **Congress Party** Political party of India, founded in 1885. It was a moderate reform party until 1917, when it was taken over by its "nationalist" home-rule wing. In the 1920s and '30s, under Mohandas GANDHI, it promoted noncooperation to protest British policies. During World War II, the party announced that India would not support the war until granted complete independence, accomplished in 1947. Jawaharlal NEHRU dominated the party from 1951 to 1964. In 1969 Indira GANDHI broke with party leaders and formed the New Congress Party; in 1978 she and her followers seceded again and formed

the "real" Indian National Congress, popularly called the Congress (I) ("I" for Indira).

Indian Ocean Body of salt water stretching between Africa in the west, Australia in the east, Asia in the north, and Antarctica in the south. With an area of 28,360,000 sq mi (73,440,000 sq km), it covers approximately one-seventh of the earth's surface. Its greatest depth (24,442 ft or 7,450 m) is in the Java Trench. Its marginal seas include the RED SEA, ARABIAN SEA, PERSIAN GULF, Andaman Sea, Bay of BENGAL, and Great Australian Bight. Its major islands and island groups include Madagascar and Sri Lanka.

Indian philosophy Any of the numerous philosophical systems developed on the Indian subcontinent, including both orthodox *(astika)* systems, namely, the NYAYA, Vaisheshika, Samkhya, YOGA, Mimamsa, and VEDANTA schools of philosophy, and unorthodox *(nastika)* systems, such as BUDDHISM and JAINISM. In the history of Indian philosophy, the prelogical stage covers the pre-Mauryan and the Mauryan periods (c.321–185 B.C.), the logical period begins with the Kusanas (1st–2nd cent. A.D.) and finds its highest development in the Gupta era (3rd–5th cent.) and the age of imperial Kanauj (7th cent.), and the ultralogical age is the 11th–18th cent.

Indian Removal Act (May 28, 1830) First major legislation that reversed the U.S. policy of respecting the rights of American Indians. The act granted tribes unsettled W prairie land in exchange for their territories within state borders, mainly in the Southeast. Some tribes refused to trade their land, and U.S. troops forced such tribes as the CHEROKEE to march westward along the TRAIL OF TEARS (1838–39). In Florida the SEMINOLES fought resettlement in the SEMINOLE WARS (1835–42).

Indian Reorganization Act (June 18, 1934) Legislation to decrease federal control of American Indians and increase tribal self-government. The act sought to strengthen tribal structure by encouraging written constitutions and to undo the damage caused by the DAWES GENERAL ALLOTMENT ACT by returning surplus lands to the tribes. It gave Indians the power to manage their internal affairs and established a revolving credit fund for tribal land purchases and educational assistance. It remains the basic legislation concerning Indian affairs.

Indian Territory Former territory, U.S. West, including most of modern Oklahoma. The CHOCTAW, CREEK, SEMINOLE, CHEROKEE, and CHICKASAW tribes were forcibly moved to this area 1830–43. In 1866 its W portion was ceded to the U.S.; this became the Territory of Oklahoma in 1890. The areas were reunited and admitted to the Union as the state of Oklahoma in 1907.

India rubber plant See RUBBER PLANT

indicator, economic See ECONOMIC INDICATOR

indictment In criminal law, a formal written accusation of a crime affirmed by a GRAND JURY and handed up to the court for trial of the accused. In the U.S., the indictment is one of three principal methods of charging offenses, the others being the information (a written accusation resembling an indictment, prepared and presented to the court by a prosecuting official) and, for petty offenses, a complaint by the aggrieved party or by a police officer.

Indic writing systems Set of several dozen scripts used now or in the past to write many S. and S.E. Asian languages. Most extant writing of the region descends from the Brahmi script, first attested in the rock inscriptions of ASHOKA (3rd cent. B.C.). In the first six centuries after Ashoka, Brahmi appears to have diversified into N and S variants. The N types gave rise to the Gupta scripts (4th–5th cent.), which are the basis of the Devanagari script (now used to write SANSKRIT, HINDI, Marathi, and Nepali), the BENGALI and Oriya scripts, and Gurmukhi, used for modern Punjabi. The S types gave rise to the Sinhalese, TELUGU, and Kannada scripts on the one hand, and to the Pallava script on the other. The latter formed the basis of numerous other scripts, including those of the TAMIL and MALAYALAM languages, most S.E. Asian scripts, and a number used for AUSTRONESIAN LANGUAGES.

Indies, Laws of the Entire body of law promulgated by the Spanish crown in the 16th–18th cent. for the governance of its colonies. It consists of a compendium of decrees on church government and education, upper and lower courts, political and military administration, Indians, finance, navigation, and commerce. A summary promulgated in 1681 contained 6,377 laws; though criticized for inconsistencies, unenforceable details, and authoritarianism, it was the most comprehensive law code ever instituted for a colonial empire.

individualism Political and social philosophy that values individual freedom highly. Modern individualism emerged in Britain with the ideas of Adam SMITH and Jeremy BENTHAM, and Alexis de TOCQUEVILLE described it as fundamental to the American temper. It is expressed through a value system, a theory of human nature, and a belief in certain political, economic, social, and religious arrangements. All individualist values are people-centered; the individual is of supreme value, and all are morally equal. Individualism opposes authority without consent and views government as an institution whose power should be largely limited to maintaining law and order; society is seen as only a collection of morally equal individuals, with the right to live their lives as they choose. Individualistic ideas lost ground in the early 20th cent., when such directly opposing ideas as COMMUNISM and FASCISM arose, but they regained dominance with the near-universal appeal of representative democracy.

Indo-Aryan languages *or* **Indic languages** Major subgroup of the Indo-Iranian branch of the INDO-EUROPEAN LANGUAGE family. Indo-Aryan languages are spoken by over 800 million people, principally in India, Nepal, Pakistan, Bangladesh, and Sri Lanka. The Old Indo-Aryan period is represented by SANSKRIT. Middle Indo-Aryan (c.600 B.C.–A.D. 1000) consists principally of the Prakrit dialects, including PALI. Modern Indo-Aryan speech is spread over an undivided geographical space, so demarcations between languages and dialects are somewhat artificial. Complicating the situation are local language identification by native speakers (as in censuses) and supraregional languages such as Modern Standard HINDI and URDU. In the center of the Indo-Aryan speech area, the most common language of administration and education is Modern Standard Hindi. Important regional languages in the N Indian plain are Haryanvi, Kauravi, Braj, Awadhi, Chhattisgarhi, Bhojpuri, Magahi, and Maithili. Regional languages in Rajasthan include Marwari, Dhundhari, Harauti, and Malvi. Surrounding the Hindi zone, the most significant languages are, moving clockwise, Nepali, Assamese, BENGALI, Oriya, Marathi, Gujarati, Sindhi, PUNJABI, and Dogri. In JAMMU AND KASHMIR and the far north of Pakistan are the Dardic languages, including Kashmiri, Kohistani, Shina, and Khowar. Sinhalese (spoken on Sri Lanka), Divehi (spoken in the Maldive Islands), and ROMANY are also Indo-Aryan languages.

Indochina SE peninsula of Asia, occupied by Myanmar, Thailand, Laos, Cambodia, Vietnam, and W. Malaysia. The name refers to the region's intermingling of Indian and Chinese influences. The French gained control of the E part after 1858 and established a colonial empire (see FRENCH INDOCHINA). The W and S parts were controlled by the British.

Indochina wars 20th-cent. conflicts in Vietnam, Laos, and Cambodia. The French Indochina War, or First Indochina War (1946–54), involved France, which had ruled Vietnam as its colony, and the newly independent N. Vietnam under HO CHI MINH. After the Vietnamese victory in 1954 (see Battle of DIEN BIEN PHU), Vietnam was divided into the communist-dominated north and the U.S.-supported south; war soon broke out between the two. N. Vietnam won the Second Indochina War, or VIETNAM WAR (1955–75), after heavy U.S. involvement. Cambodia experienced its own civil war between communists and noncommunists during this period, which was won by the communist KHMER ROUGE in 1975. After years of horrifying atrocities under POL POT, the Vietnamese invaded in 1979 and installed a puppet government. Fighting between the Khmer Rouge and the Vietnamese continued throughout the 1980s. In 1993 U.N.-mediated elections established an interim government, and Cambodia's monarchy was reestablished. In Laos, N. Vietnam's victory over S. Vietnam brought the communist Pathet Lao complete control of Laos (1975).

Indo-European languages Family of languages with the greatest number of speakers, spoken in most of Europe and N. and S. America, and in much of SW and S Asia. They are descended from a single unrecorded language believed to have been spoken more than 5,000 years ago north of the Black Sea and to have split into a number of dialects by 3000 B.C. Carried by migrating tribes to Europe and Asia, these developed over time into separate languages. The main branches are Anatolian, Indo-Iranian (including INDO-ARYAN and IRANIAN), GREEK, ITALIC, GERMANIC, CELTIC, Albanian, the extinct Tocharian languages, BALTIC, and SLAVIC. The study of Indo-European began in 1786 with Sir William Jones's proposal that Greek, Latin, Sanskrit, Germanic, and Celtic were all derived from a "common source." In the 19th cent., linguists added other languages to the Indo-European family. Proto-Indo-European has since been partially reconstructed.

Indo-Gangetic Plain See GANGETIC PLAIN

Indonesia *officially* **Republic of Indonesia** *formerly* **Netherlands Indies** Archipelago nation, located off the coast of mainland SE Asia. It comprises about 13,670 islands, of which more than 7,000 are uninhabited. Area: 742,300 sq mi (1,922,600 sq km). Population (2000): 209,342,000. Capital: JAKARTA (on JAVA). It has more than 300 different ethnic groups which fall into three broad categories: the Muslim rice growers of Java and neighboring islands; the Islamic coastal peoples, including the MALAYS of Sumatra; and the Dayak and other isolated tribal peoples. Language: Bahasa Indonesia (official); some 250 languages from different ethnic groups. Religions: monotheism (official); Islam (more than 80%); Christianity; Hinduism; Buddhism. Currency: rupiah. Indonesia stretches 3,200 mi (5,100 km) from SUMATRA in the west to NEW GUINEA in the east. Other major islands include Java (with more than half of Indonesia's population), BALI, LOMBOK, SUMBAWA, W Timor, BORNEO (part), Celebes (SULAWESI), and the N MOLUCCAS. The islands are characterized by rugged volcanic mountains and tropical rain forests. Geologically unstable, Indonesia has frequent earthquakes and 220 active volcanoes, including KRAKATAU. Only one-tenth of its land is arable, and rice is the staple crop. Oil, natural gas, timber products, garments, and rubber are the country's major exports. It is a republic with two legislative houses; its head of state and government is the president. Proto-Malay peoples migrated to Indonesia from mainland Asia before 1000 B.C. About the 1st cent. A.D., commercial relations with China began, and Hindu and Buddhist cultural influences from India began to take hold. Indian traders brought Islam to the islands in the 13th cent.; it took hold over the islands, except for Bali which retained its Hindu religion and culture. European influence began in the 16th cent., and the Dutch ruled Indonesia from the late 17th cent. until 1942, when the Japanese invaded. SUKARNO declared Indonesia's independence in 1945. The Dutch granted Indonesia independence with nominal union to the Netherlands in 1949; Indonesia dissolved this union in 1954. An abortive coup in 1965 resulted in the deaths of over 300,000 alleged communists, and by 1968 Gen. SUHARTO had taken power. His government violently incorporated E. TIMOR into Indonesia in 1975–76. The country became increasingly beset by political, economic, and environmental problems; Suharto was deposed in 1998, E. Timor achieved independence in 1999, and democratic elections brought Sukarno's daughter Megawati (b.1947) to power in 2001, as separatist movements threatened to fragment the country. See map on following page.

Indonesian language See MALAY LANGUAGE

Indore \in-'dōr\ City (metro. area pop., 2001: 1,639,000), central India. Located northeast of BOMBAY, it was founded in 1715 as a trade market. It became the capital of the princely state of Indore. Under the British, it served as the headquarters of the British Central India Agency.

Indra In the ancient VEDIC RELIGION of India, chief of the gods and patron of warriors. Armed with lightning and thunderbolts and strengthened by drinking the elixir soma, he killed the dragon that kept the monsoon rains from breaking. Indra was later demoted to a rain god and regent of the heavens. He was father to ARJUNA, hero of the *MAHABHARATA*.

HIJ

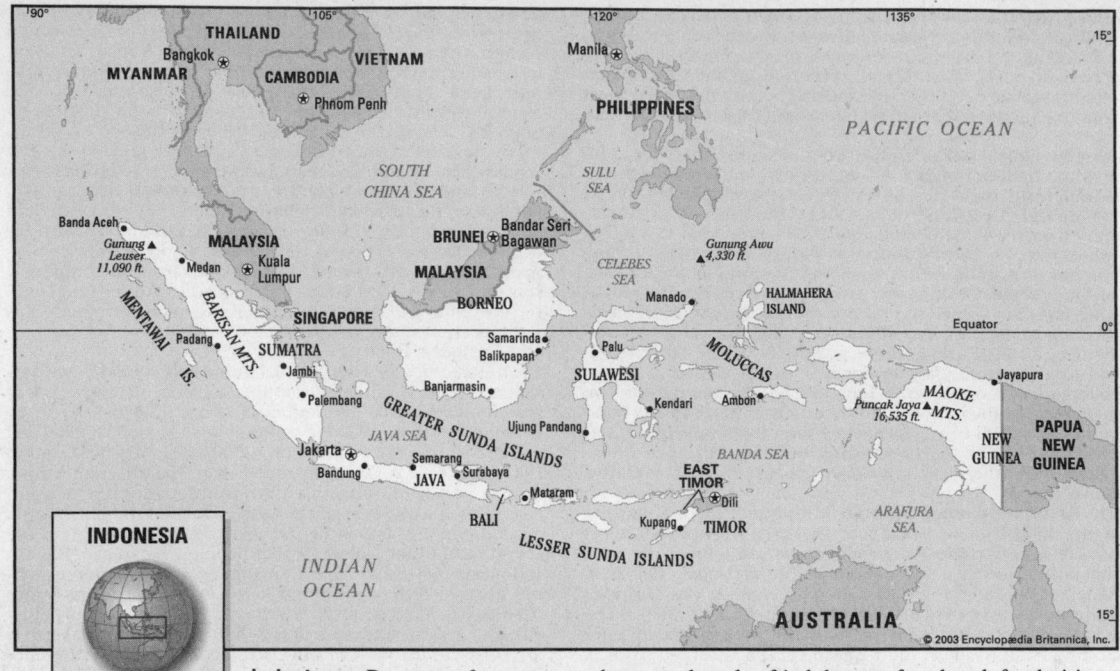

© 2003 Encyclopædia Britannica, Inc.

INDONESIA

Scale 1: 44,034,000

0   200   400 mi
0   300   600 km

inductance Property of a CON-DUCTOR, sometimes in the shape of a coil, that is measured by the size of the ELECTROMOTIVE FORCE (emf), or voltage, induced in it, compared with the rate of change of the ELECTRIC CURRENT that produces the voltage. A steadily changing electric current produces a varying MAGNETIC FIELD, which induces an emf in a conductor that is present in the field. The magnitude of this voltage is proportional to the rate of change of the current. The inductance is the proportionality factor.

induction In LOGIC, the method of reasoning from a part to a whole, from particulars to generals, from the individual to the universal, or from the characteristics of a sample to the characteristics of the larger population. Logicians traditionally distinguished between deductive logic (see DEDUCTION) and inductive logic, but induction is now considered the methodology of the natural sciences, and "logic" is generally taken to mean deductive logic.

induction See ELECTROMAGNETIC INDUCTION

induction heating Method of raising the temperature of an electrically conductive material by subjecting it to an alternating electromagnetic field. Energy in the ELECTRIC CURRENTS induced in the object is dissipated as HEAT. Induction heating is used in metalworking to heat METALS for soldering, tempering, and annealing, and in induction furnaces for melting and processing metals. Its principle resembles that of the TRANSFORMER. A water-cooled coil (inductor), acting as the primary winding of a transformer, surrounds the material to be heated (the workpiece), which acts as the secondary winding. Alternating current flowing in the primary coil induces eddy currents in the workpiece, causing it to become heated. The depth to which the eddy currents penetrate depends on the frequency of the primary alternating current and the magnetic permeability and resistivity of the material.

indulgence In ROMAN CATHOLICISM, the remission of temporal punishment for SINS that have been forgiven through the SACRAMENT of penance. The theology of indulgences is based on the concept that, even though sins are forgiven through penance, divine justice demands that the sinner pay for his crime either in this life or in PURGATORY. The first indulgences were intended to shorten times of penance by substituting periods of FASTING, private prayers, almsgiving, and payments of money. After the 12th cent. such abuses as the sale of indulgences for church fundraising or personal enrichment became common. Martin LUTHER'S NINETY-FIVE THESES (1517) were in part a protest against indulgences. The Council of TRENT put an end to the abuses in 1562 but not to the doctrine itself.

Indus civilization (c.2500–c.1700 B.C.) Earliest known urban culture of the Indian subcontinent and the most extensive of the world's three earliest civilizations, stretching from near the present-day Iran–Pakistan border on the Arabian Sea in the west to near Delhi in the east, and 500 mi (800 km) to the south and 1,000 mi (1,600 km) to the northeast. It is known to have included two large cities, Harappa and Mohenjo Daro. It was a literate civilization; the language may have been Dravidian. Wheat and barley were grown, many animals were domesticated, and cotton was cultivated. The best-known artifacts are seals depicting real and imaginary animals. How and when the civilization came to an end is unclear; Mohenjo Daro was attacked and destroyed in the mid-2nd millennium B.C., but in the south there was continuity between the Indus civilization and the Copper Age civilizations of central and W India.

Indus River Trans-Himalayan river of S Asia. It is one of the world's longest rivers, with a length of 1,800 mi (2,900 km). Its annual flow of 272 billion cu yards (207 billion cu m) is twice that of the NILE. It rises in SW Tibet and flows northwest along the slopes of the HIMALAYAS. After crossing the W Kashmir border it turns south to enter Pakistan; it empties into the Arabian Sea. It has supplied water for irrigation on the plains of Pakistan since early times. India and the Hindu religion derive their names from the Indus. See also INDUS CIVILIZATION.

industrialization Process of converting to a socioeconomic order in which INDUSTRY is dominant. Britain's INDUSTRIAL REVOLUTION led the way for the early industrializing nations of Western Europe and N. America. Industrialization entailed both technology and profound social developments. The freeing of laborers from feudal and customary obligations created a free market in labor, with a pivotal role for the entrepreneur. Cities attracted large numbers of people, massing workers in new industrial towns and FACTORIES. Later industrializers attempted to manipulate some of the elements: the Soviet Union eliminated the entrepreneur; Japan stimulated and sustained the entrepreneur's role; Denmark and New Zealand industrialized primarily by commercializing and mechanizing agriculture.

industrial melanism \'me-lə-ˌni-zəm\ Darkness of the skin, feathers, or fur developed by a population of animals living in an industrial region where the environment is soot-darkened. The melanization of a population offers protection in the form of camouflage; it takes place over many generations as the result of NATURAL SELECTION of the lighter, more conspicuous animals by predators.

industrial relations *or* **organizational relations** Study of human behavior in the workplace, focusing especially on its relation to PRODUCTIVITY. CLASSICAL ECONOMICS viewed workers as instruments of production, subject to the economic laws of SUPPLY AND DEMAND. Industrial relations first attracted scholarly attention in the late 1920s, when Elton Mayo (1880–1949) studied productivity at Western Electric Co.'s Hawthorne Works. Concluding that merely being chosen to participate in the study improved workers' productivity (the "Hawthorne effect"), Mayo became the first to show workers responding to psychosocial stimuli. Industrial relations also studies management styles and personnel administration (including developing job descriptions and structures of authority; recruiting, training, and general oversight of employees; negotiating terms of employment, and planning for the future).

Industrial Revolution Change from an agrarian, handicraft economy to one dominated by industry and machine manufacture. It began in England in the 18th cent. Technological changes included the use of iron and steel, new energy sources, invention of new machines (including the SPINNING JENNY), development of the factory system, and innovations in transportation and communication (including the STEAM ENGINE and TELEGRAPH). Other changes included agricultural improvements and a wider distribution of wealth. Largely confined to Britain from 1760 to 1830, it spread to Belgium and France. Once Germany, the U.S., and Japan achieved industrial power, they outstripped Britain's initial successes. Eastern European countries lagged into the 20th cent., and not until the mid-20th cent. did the Industrial Revolution spread to such countries as China and India.

Industrial Workers of the World (IWW) *known as* **the Wobblies** Radical labor organization founded in Chicago in 1905. The founders, who opposed moderate policies of the AFL, included William HAYWOOD, Daniel DE LEON, and Eugene DEBS. In 1908 the IWW split, and a militant group led by Haywood prevailed. To reach its goal of workers controlling the means of production, it advocated general strikes, boycotts, and sabotage. It opposed U.S. participation in World War I, and some of its leaders were prosecuted. By the 1920s membership had dwindled greatly.

industry Group of productive organizations that produce or supply goods, services, or sources of income. Industries are customarily classified as primary, secondary, and tertiary. Primary industry includes agriculture, forestry, fishing, mining, and quarrying. Secondary or manufacturing industry processes the raw materials supplied by primary industries into consumer goods (as well as energy and buildings), or further processes goods from other secondary industries, or builds capital goods used to manufacture consumer and nonconsumer goods. Tertiary or SERVICE INDUSTRY includes banking, finance, insurance, investment, and real estate services; wholesale, retail, and resale trade; transportation, information, and communications services; professional, consulting, legal, and personal services; tourism, hotels, restaurants, and entertainment; repair and maintenance services; education and teaching; and health, social welfare, administrative, police, security, and defense services.

inequality In mathematics, a statement of an order relationship—greater than, greater than or equal to, less than, or less than or equal to—between two numbers or algebraic expressions. Inequalities can be posed either as questions, much like EQUATIONS, and solved by similar techniques, or as statements of fact in the form of THEOREMS. Mathematical analysis relies on many inequalities in the proofs of its most important theorems.

inert gas See NOBLE GAS

inertia \i-'nər-shə\ Inherent property of a body (whether moving or at rest) that makes it oppose any FORCE that would cause a change (ACCELERATION) in its MOTION. The inertia of a body can be measured by its MASS, which governs its resistance to the action of a force, or by its moment of inertia about a specified axis, which measures its resistance to the action of a TORQUE about the same axis.

infancy Among humans, the period between birth and the acquisition of language usually one to two years later. At birth, infants display a set of reflexes involving such acts as sucking, blinking, and grasping. They are sensitive to light–dark contrasts and movements, and show a preference for gazing at the human face; they also early begin to recognize the human voice. By four months most babies are able to sit up, and most begin crawling in 7–10 months; most start walking by 12 months. Infants generally comprehend some words several months before they themselves speak their first meaningful words.

infanticide Killing of the newborn. Infanticide has often been interpreted as a primitive method of BIRTH CONTROL, but most societies actively welcome children and put them to death (or allow them to die) only when there is little or no likelihood of being able to provide support. As late as the 18th cent. in European countries, unwanted infants were disposed of by abandonment and exposure.

infantile paralysis See POLIOMYELITIS

infection Invasion of the body by various agents—including BACTERIA, fungi (see FUNGUS), PROTOZOANS, VIRUSES, and WORMS—and its reaction to them or their TOXINS. Infection can be local (e.g., an ABSCESS), confined to one body system (e.g., PNEUMONIA in the lungs), or generalized (e.g., SEPTICEMIA). Infectious agents can enter the body by inhalation, ingestion, sexual transmission, passage to a fetus during pregnancy or birth, wound contamination, or animal or insect bites. The body responds with an attack on the invader by LEUKOCYTES, production of ANTIBODIES or ANTITOXINS, and often FEVER. The antibodies may give short-term or lifelong IMMUNITY. Infectious diseases remain a major cause of illness and death, particularly in regions of poor sanitation, poor nutrition, and crowding.

inferiority complex Acute sense of personal inferiority, often resulting in timidity or (through overcompensation) exaggerated aggressiveness. Once a standard psychological concept, particularly among followers of Alfred ADLER, it has lost much of its usefulness through popular misuse.

infertility Inability of a couple to conceive and reproduce, defined as failure to conceive after one year of regular SEXUAL INTERCOURSE without CONTRACEPTION. Inability to conceive when desired can result from a defect at any of the stages required for FERTILITY. About one in every eight couples is infertile. Half the cases involve the female partner, 30–40% involve the male, and 10% are caused by unknown factors. In women, causes include ovulation or hormone problems, fallopian-tube disorders, and a chemical balance that is hostile to SPERM; in men, causes include IMPOTENCE, low sperm count, and sperm abnormalities. Either partner can have a blockage of the pathways the sperm must travel, often treatable by surgery. Emotional factors may contribute. Fertility drugs can stimulate the release of EGGS. If remedial methods are unsuccessful, couples may try ARTIFICIAL INSEMINATION, or IN VITRO FERTILIZATION, or choose ADOPTION.

infinite series In mathematics, the sum of infinitely many numbers, typically expressed as a formula or a FUNCTION. An infinite series that results in a finite sum is said to converge (see CONVERGENCE). One that does not, diverges. Mathematical analysis is largely taken up with studying the conditions under which a given function will result in a convergent infinite series (particularly useful in solving DIFFERENTIAL EQUATIONS).

infinity In mathematics, the useful concept of a process with no end. As represented by the symbol ∞, it is often mistakenly thought to be the largest number or a place on the real number line. Instead, it is the idea of a LIMIT. For example, the function $f(x) = 1/x$ (the reciprocal of x) tends toward 0 as x approaches infinity as a limit. This process of approaching is crucial to the definition of the DERIVATIVE and the INTEGRAL in CALCULUS, as well as to many other concepts of mathematical analysis.

inflammation Local reaction of living tissues to injury or illness. Its major signs are heat, redness, swelling, and pain.

HIJ

After brief contraction of nearby arterioles (see ARTERIES), dilation flushes the CAPILLARIES with blood, from which PLASMA, proteins, and LEUKOCYTES pass into the injured tissues, causing swelling as they attack the cause of injury. Initial acute inflammation can have any of four outcomes: resolution (return to normal), organization (new tissue buildup; see SCAR), suppuration (pus formation; see ABSCESS), or chronic inflammation. Treatment—including ANTIBIOTICS for bacteria, or surgical removal of an irritating foreign body—may eliminate the cause; anti-inflammatory drugs (e.g., CORTISONE or ASPIRIN) may be given.

inflation In astronomy, a hypothesized early period of exponential expansion of the universe, which may account for some of its properties, including energy and matter distribution. GRAND UNIFIED THEORIES suggest that inflation could have occurred in the first 10^{-32} of a second after the BIG BANG, when the STRONG FORCE was decoupling from the WEAK and ELECTROMAGNETIC forces, expanding the universe by over 100 orders of magnitude. Inflation is an effect of general RELATIVITY when the universe is trapped in a state of nonzero energy density (false vacuum).

inflation In economics, increase in the level of PRICES, especially an inordinate rise in the general level. Four theories are commonly used to explain inflation. The first and oldest, the quantity theory, promoted by David HUME, assumes that prices will rise as the supply of money increases. Milton FRIEDMAN refined this, arguing that the prescription for stable prices is to increase the money supply at a rate equal to that at which the economy is expanding. A second approach is J. M. KEYNES's theory of income determination, which assumes that inflation occurs when the demand for goods and services is greater than the supply. It calls for the government to control inflation by adjusting levels of spending and taxation and by raising or lowering interest rates. A third approach, the cost-push theory, traces inflation to the price-wage spiral, in which workers' demands for wage increases lead employers to increase prices to reflect their higher costs, thereby sowing the seeds of further wage demands. A fourth approach is the structural theory, which emphasizes structural maladjustments in the economy, as when in developing countries imports tend to increase faster than exports, causing prices to rise internally. See also DEFLATION, PRICE INDEX.

inflorescence \ˌin-flə-ˈre-sᵊns\ Cluster of flowers on one or a series of branches, which together make a large showy blossom. In determinate inflorescences, the youngest flowers are at the bottom or outside (e.g., ONION flowers). In indeterminate inflorescences, the youngest flowers are at the top or in the center (e.g., SNAPDRAGON, LILY OF THE VALLEY, and *Astilbe* flowers). Other indeterminate inflorescences are the dangling male and female catkins of OAK trees, the spike of BARLEY, and the flat head (capitulum) of the DANDELION.

influenza *or* **flu** *or* **grippe** Acute viral INFECTION of the upper or lower respiratory tract. Influenza VIRUSES A (the most common), B, and C produce similar symptoms, but infection with or vaccination against one does not give immunity against the others. Chills, fever, fatigue, and muscle aches begin abruptly, and may be accompanied by sore throat. Recovery starts in three to four days, and respiratory symptoms become more prominent. Bed rest, high fluid intake, and ASPIRIN or other anti-fever drugs are standard treatment. Influenza A and B occur in cycles and spread worldwide in wavelike epidemics. Mortality is usually low, but occasionally (see INFLUENZA EPIDEMIC OF 1918–19) it reaches immense proportions. Most deaths result from PNEUMONIA or BRONCHITIS.

Influenza Epidemic of 1918–19 *or* **Spanish Influenza Epidemic** Most severe INFLUENZA outbreak of the 20th cent. Flu pandemics occur every 30–40 years, but this one was unusually severe and spread very rapidly. U.S. troops sent to fight in World War I spread the virus to Western Europe, where a more lethal strain emerged. Outbreaks occurred in nearly every inhabited part of the world, spreading along transportation routes. PNEUMONIA often killed within two days. Perhaps the most deadly epidemic in history, it left an estimated 30 million dead; unusually, half the deaths were among 20- to 40-year-olds.

information retrieval Recovery of information, especially in a DATABASE stored in a computer. Two main approaches are matching words in the query against the database index (keyword searching), and traversing the database using HYPERTEXT or hypermedia links. Keyword searching has been the dominant approach to text retrieval since the early 1960s; hypertext is common in Internet databases. Evolving information-retrieval techniques using Internet SEARCH ENGINES combine natural language, hyperlinks, and keyword searching. Other techniques that seek higher levels of retrieval precision are studied by researchers involved with ARTIFICIAL INTELLIGENCE.

information science Discipline that deals with the processes of storing and transferring information. It attempts to bring together concepts and methods from such varied disciplines as library science, computer science and engineering, linguistics, and psychology to aid in the handling of information. In its early stages in the 1960s, information science was concerned primarily with applying computer technology to the processing and managing of documents. It has since entered many other disciplines. Computer science and engineering still dominate its theory- and technology-oriented subjects, and management science covers information-systems subjects.

infrared astronomy \ˌin-frə-ˈred\ Study of astronomical objects by observing their INFRARED RADIATION. It lets astronauts examine objects that emit energy at wavelengths in the infrared region of the ELECTROMAGNETIC SPECTRUM but not much optical light. Infrared astronomy derives from the work of William HERSCHEL, who discovered infrared radiation while studying sunlight. Systematic infrared observations of stellar objects were first made in the 1920s; the early 1960s saw advances like the use of filters in ground-based telescopes. Because atmospheric water vapor absorbs infrared rays, observations from spacecraft are more effective. Infrared astronomy has led to the discovery of evidence of planetary systems around certain stars, and of BROWN DWARFS.

infrared radiation Portion of the ELECTROMAGNETIC SPECTRUM that extends from the MICROWAVE range to the red end of the visible LIGHT range, with wavelengths from about 0.7 to 1,000 micrometers. Most of the radiation emitted by a moderately heated surface is infrared, with a continuous spectrum. Molecular excitation produces extensive infrared radiation but in a discrete spectrum of lines or bands. Infrared wavelengths are useful for night-vision equipment, heat-seeking missiles, molecular SPECTROSCOPY, and INFRARED ASTRONOMY. See also GREENHOUSE EFFECT.

Inge \ˈinj\, **William (Motter)** (1913–1973) U.S. playwright and screenwriter. Born in Independence, Kan., he initially worked as a schoolteacher (1937–49). His first play was revised for Broadway as *The Dark at the Top of the Stairs* (1957; film, 1960). He is best known for his plays *Come Back, Little Sheba* (1950; film, 1952), *Picnic* (1953, Pulitzer Prize; film, 1956), and *Bus Stop* (1955; film, 1956), and for his original screenplay for *Splendor in the Grass* (1961, Academy Award).

Ingres \ˈaⁿgrᵊ\, **Jean-Auguste-Dominique** (1780–1867) French painter. He studied with J.-L. DAVID in Paris before attending the École des Beaux-Arts (1799–1801), where he won a Prix de Rome scholarship. Critics condemned one of his first public works, the awe-inspiring portrait *Napoleon on His Imperial Throne* (1806), as stiff and archaic, but in Italy (1806–24) he prospered with portraits and history paintings. His small-scale portrait drawings are meticulously rendered. Back in Paris he received critical acclaim at last and won admission to the

J.-A.-D. Ingres, self-portrait, c.1800

Academy with *The Vow of Louis XIII* (1824). In 1825 he succeeded David as the leader of French Neoclassical painting and opened a teaching studio. It became one of the largest in Paris, and by the mid-1840s he was France's most sought-after society portraitist.

inheritance Devolution of property on an heir or heirs upon the death of its owner. In civil-law jurisdictions it is called succession. The concept depends on a common acceptance of the notion of private ownership of goods and property. Intestacy laws, which govern the INHERITANCE of estates whose distribution is not directed by a WILL, universally view kinship between the decedent and the beneficiary as a primary consideration. Inheritance usually entails payment of an inheritance tax. See also PROBATE.

inheritance tax Levy on the property accruing to each beneficiary of the estate of a deceased person. Inheritance tax may be more difficult to administer than ESTATE TAX because the value passing to each beneficiary must be fixed, and this often requires complex actuarial calculations. In the U.S. inheritance taxes have always been collected by the individual states, while the federal government has imposed an estate tax.

inhibition In enzymology, a phenomenon in which a compound (an inhibitor), usually similar in structure to the substance on which an ENZYME acts (the substrate), interacts with the enzyme so that the resulting complex cannot undergo the usual reaction or cannot form the usual product. The inhibitor may combine with the enzyme at the site at which the reaction usually occurs or at another site. See also ALLOSTERIC CONTROL, REPRESSION.

inhibition In psychology, the conscious or unconscious suppression of spontaneous thought or behavior through psychological impediments, including internalized social controls. Inhibition serves such useful social functions as protecting oneself and others from harm and enabling the delay of gratification from pleasurable activities. Both extreme lack of inhibition and excessive inhibition can be personally destructive. Inhibition also plays an important role in LEARNING, since an organism must learn to restrain certain instinctual behaviors or previously learned patterns in order to master new patterns.

initiation See SECRET SOCIETY

injunction In civil proceedings, a court order compelling a party to do or refrain from doing a specified act. It is an equitable remedy for harm for which no adequate remedy exists in law. Thus it is used to prevent a future harmful action (e.g., disclosing confidential information or violating a group's civil rights) rather than to compensate for an injury that has already occurred. It also provides relief from harm for which an award of money damages is not a satisfactory solution. A defendant who violates an injunction may be cited for contempt. See also EQUITY.

ink Fluid or paste of various colors used for writing and PRINTING, composed of a PIGMENT or DYE in a liquid "vehicle." Early inks used lampblack (a form of CARBON) or colored juices, extracts, or suspensions. Modern writing inks usually contain ferrous sulfate (see IRON) with a small amount of an acid; on paper, they darken and bond, becoming permanent. Colored and washable inks usually contain soluble synthetic dyes. Printing inks, with a base of quick-drying SOLVENT, are formulated for various requirements.

Inkatha Freedom Party \in-ˈkä-tə\ Political party in S. Africa consisting largely of the ZULU. Begun in 1924 as a cultural movement, it was revived as a political party by Mangosuthu BUTHELEZI to oppose the AFRICAN NATIONAL CONGRESS (ANC). Inkatha advocated a struggle against APARTHEID but accepted compromises that fell short of majority rule. From the late 1980s, Inkatha and ANC followers fought in bloody clashes with strong tribal overtones. In 1991 the white S. African government admitted that it had secretly subsidized Inkatha.

Inland Passage See INSIDE PASSAGE

inner ear *or* **labyrinth of the ear** Part of the EAR containing organs of HEARING and balance. The bony labyrinth has three sections (semicircular canals, vestibule, and cochlea); within each is a corresponding part of the membranous labyrinth (semicircular ducts, two saclike structures in the

vestibule, and cochlear duct). Sound vibrations are transmitted from the middle ear to fluid in the cochlea, whose motion stimulates hair cells, which trigger nerve impulses that travel to the brain, which interprets them as sound. Other hair cells, in the vestibule, indicate the head's position with respect to the rest of the body (see PROPRIOCEPTION). The three semicircular canals, at right angles to each other, signal motion of the head in three-dimensional space. If the motion sensed does not match with visual input, dizziness or MOTION SICKNESS result.

Inness, George (1825–1894) U.S. landscape painter. Born in Newburgh, N.Y., he was largely self-taught. His early paintings were influenced by the HUDSON RIVER SCHOOL. He spent much time in Europe studying the works of the BARBIZON SCHOOL, and from about 1855 developed the luminous, atmospheric quality for which his landscapes are known (see LUMINISM). His later works, such as *Autumn Oaks* (c.1875), are marked by the ascendancy of color over form, which steadily increased as his sense of mysticism intensified.

Innocent III *orig.* Lothair of Segni (c.1160–1216) Pope (1198–1216) who brought the medieval papacy to the height of its prestige and power. He crowned OTTO IV as Holy Roman Emperor, but Otto's determination to unite Germany and Sicily angered him, and in 1212 he gave his support to FREDERICK II. After he excommunicated King JOHN of England for refusing to recognize Stephen LANGTON as archbishop of Canterbury, John was obliged to declare England a fief of the Holy See (1213). Innocent launched the Fourth CRUSADE and the ALBIGENSIAN CRUSADE, approved the Dominican and Franciscan orders, and convoked the fourth LATERAN COUNCIL.

Innocent IV *orig.* Sinibaldo Fieschi (d.1254) Pope (1243–54) whose clash with Emperor FREDERICK II formed an important chapter in the conflict between papacy and empire. Frederick wanted the newly elected pope to lift his excommunication, but Innocent, feeling threatened, interrupted the negotiations and fled Rome for France (1244); from there he condemned Frederick and urged the election of a new emperor. He returned to Rome in 1253. He gave the Sicilian throne to Edmund, son of HENRY III of England. The papal army was defeated by Frederick's son Manfred in 1254.

Innsbruck City (pop., 1999 est.: 110,000) in W Austria, southwest of SALZBURG. A small market town in the 12th cent., it was located beside a bridge (*Brücke*) over the Inn River. In 1420 it became the capital of TIROL. Napoleon gave the city to BAVARIA in 1806, and in 1809 it was the site of an uprising of Tirolian patriots. Its narrow streets are lined with medieval houses. A winter sports center, it was the site of the Winter OLYMPIC GAMES in 1964 and 1976.

Inns of Court Four societies of British students and practitioners of law that have the exclusive right to admit people to practice. The four are Lincoln's Inn, Gray's Inn, Inner Temple, and Middle Temple. All are located in London and trace their origins to the Middle Ages. Until the 17th cent., when the Inn of Chancery developed (for training in the framing of documents used in EQUITY courts), they had a monopoly over legal education. By the 19th cent., modern law schools had emerged.

inorganic compound Any substance in which two or more chemical ELEMENTS other than CARBON are combined, nearly always in definite proportions (see BONDING), as well as some COMPOUNDS containing carbon but lacking carbon-carbon bonds (e.g., CARBONATES, CYANIDES). Inorganic compounds may be classified by the elements or groups they contain (e.g., OXIDES, SULFATES). SILICONES are one class of inorganic polymers. Coordination compounds, an important subclass of inorganic compounds, consist of a central METAL atom bonded to one or more LIGANDS (inorganic, organic, or both) and are often intensely colored. See also ORGANIC COMPOUND.

input-output analysis Economic analysis developed by Wassily LEONTIEF, in which the interdependence of an economy's various productive sectors is observed by viewing the product of each industry both as a commodity for CONSUMPTION and as a factor in the production of itself and other goods. For example, it will break down a nation's

HIJ

total production of trucks, showing that some trucks are used in the production of more trucks, some in farming, and so on. An analysis is usually summarized in a gridlike table showing what various industries buy from and sell to one another.

Inquisition Roman Catholic judicial institution established to combat HERESY and WITCHCRAFT. It was instituted by GREGORY IX in 1231 in response to the spread of heresies such as those of the CATHARI. Suspected heretics were arrested, interrogated, and tried; torture to obtain confessions was authorized by INNOCENT IV in 1252. Penalties ranged from prayer and fasting to imprisonment; convicted heretics who refused to recant could be executed by secular authorities. The papal Inquisition of the Middle Ages functioned most widely in N Italy and S France. The Spanish Inquisition was authorized by SIXTUS IV in 1478; the pope later tried to limit its powers, but it was successfully defended by the Spanish crown. The auto-da-fé, the public ceremony at which sentences were pronounced, became an elaborate celebration, and the grand inquisitor Tomás de TORQUEMADA was responsible for burning about 2,000 heretics at the stake. The Spanish Inquisition was also introduced in colonies such as Mexico and Peru as well as in Sicily (1517) and the Netherlands (1522), and it was not entirely suppressed in Spain until the early 19th cent.

insanity In criminal law, a disease, defect, or condition of the mind that renders one unable to understand the nature of a criminal act or the fact that it is wrong. Tests of insanity are not intended as medical diagnoses but rather serve only as determinations of whether a person may be held criminally responsible for his or her actions. Many U.S. states and several courts have now adopted the test proposed by the American Law Institute's Model Penal Code, under which the accused must lack "substantial capacity either to appreciate the criminality of his conduct or to conform his conduct to the requirements of the law." Some states have abolished the insanity plea, while others allow a finding of "guilty but mentally ill."

insect Any member of the class Insecta, the largest ARTHROPOD class, including nearly 1 million known species (about three-fourths of all animals) and an estimated 5–10 million undescribed species. Insect bodies have three segments:

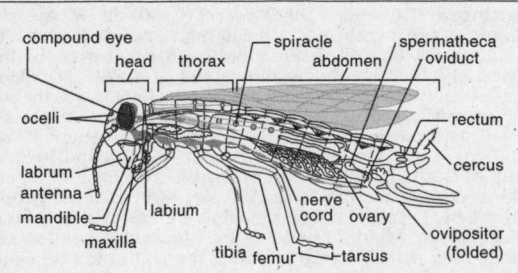

Insect Body plan of a generalized insect. The body is usually divided into a head, thorax, and abdomen. The head bears appendages modified into mouthparts and antennae bearing sense organs. Mouthparts include the toothed mandibles and bladelike maxillae found behind the "upper lip" or labrum. A second pair of maxillae, partly fused, form the "lower lip" or labium. An adult usually has both simple eyes (ocelli) and more complex faceted compound eyes, as well as a pair of wings on the thorax. The tarsal segment of the jointed leg often has claws with adhesive pads, enabling the insect to hold onto smooth surfaces. In some insects (incl. crickets and cockroaches), a pair of feelers (cerci) bearing sense organs are located at the rear of the abdomen. Tiny openings (spiracles) on the thorax and abdomen allow passage of oxygen to and release of carbon dioxide from internal air-filled tubules or tracheae. Sperm from the male is stored in the female's spermatheca until an egg released from the ovary passes through the oviduct. The female may have an ovipositor for depositing eggs.

head, thorax (which bears three pairs of legs and usually two pairs of wings), and many-segmented abdomen. Many species undergo complete METAMORPHOSIS. There are two subclasses: Apterygota (primitive, wingless forms, including SILVERFISH and bristletails) and Pterygota (more advanced, winged or secondarily wingless forms). The approximately 27 orders of Pterygota are generally classified by wing form: e.g., Coleoptera (BEETLES), Diptera (DIPTERANS), Heteroptera (bugs).

insecticide Any substance used to kill INSECTS, mainly to control pests that infest cultivated plants and crops or to eliminate disease-carrying insects in specific areas. Inorganic insecticides include ARSENIC, LEAD, and COPPER compounds. Organic insecticides may be natural, like rotenone, pyrethrins, and NICOTINE (see TOXIN), or synthetic, like chlorinated HYDROCARBONS, carbamates, and parathions. Insect HORMONES may be considered a separate class. Insecticides may affect the NERVOUS SYSTEM, inhibit essential ENZYMES, or prevent LARVAE from maturing. Some are stomach POISONS, some inhalation poisons, and others contact poisons. Agents like dormant oils act by blocking the breathing pores. Insecticides vary widely not only in effectiveness against target insects (which may develop resistance) but also in toxicity to nontarget species (including humans) and environmental effects; the worst (e.g., DDT) have been banned.

insectivore \in-'sek-tə-ˌvōr\ Any member of the mammalian order (Insectivora) that includes the HEDGEHOGS, MOLES, and sometimes SHREWS, or, more generally, any animal that eats mainly insects. The mammalian insectivores are generally small, active, and nocturnal. They are found in most parts of the world. Most species are solitary (except during the breeding season) and short-lived.

Inside Passage *or* **Inland Passage** Natural sheltered sea route from SEATTLE to Skagway, Alaska. Extending northwest for more than 1,000 mi (1,600 km), it is made up of channels and straits between the mainland and islands (including VANCOUVER ISLAND) that protect it from Pacific storms. It is the favored route for coastal shipping to and from Alaska.

insomnia Inability to sleep adequately. The causes may include poor sleeping conditions, circulatory or brain disorders, breathing disorders (e.g., sleep apnea), mental distress (e.g., tension or depression), or physical discomfort. Mild insomnia may be treated by improving sleeping conditions or through traditional remedies such as warm baths, milk, or systematic relaxation. Apnea may be treated surgically or mechanically with breathing apparatus. Severe or chronic insomnia may necessitate the temporary use of barbiturates or tranquilizers. Other methods of treatment include PSYCHOTHERAPY and HYPNOSIS.

instinct Involuntary ability of an animal to respond in a predictable and relatively fixed behavior pattern. Instinctive behavior is an inherited mechanism that serves to promote the survival of an animal or species. It is most apparent in fighting and sexual activity. The simplest form is the REFLEX. All animals have instinct, but, in general, the higher the animal form, the more flexible the behavior. Among mammals, learned behavior often prevails over instinctive behavior.

Institut Canadien \aⁿ-stē-'tǖ-kȧ-nȧd-'yaⁿ\ Literary and scientific society in 19th-cent. French Canada. It was founded in Montreal in 1844 as a discussion forum and free library, and established branches throughout French-speaking Canada, which criticized the institutionalism of the Catholic Church in Quebec. Church leaders, including Bishop Ignace Bourget, attacked the institute, which appealed to Rome. In 1869 the church condemned the movement, and most members withdrew.

Institutional Revolutionary Party (PRI) Political party that has dominated Mexican politics since its founding in 1929. It effectively institutionalized the power structure that emerged from the MEXICAN REVOLUTION of 1910–20. Until recently, nomination to public office by the PRI virtually guaranteed election. Since the 1970s, charges of deepening corruption eroded popular support and ended its monopoly of power. It is believed to have won the 1988 presidential election only by fraud, and in 2000 Vicente

FOX, candidate of the National Action Party (PAN), won the presidency.

instrumentalism *or* **experimentalism** Philosophy advanced by John DEWEY holding that what is most important in a thing or idea is its value as an instrument of action and that the truth of an idea lies in its usefulness. Dewey favored these terms over the term PRAGMATISM to label his educational philosophy. His school claimed that cognition evolved for the practical purpose of successful adjustment and that ideas are instruments for transforming the uneasiness arising from facing a problem into the satisfaction of solving it.

insulator Substance that blocks or retards the flow of ELECTRIC CURRENT or HEAT. An insulator is a poor CONDUCTOR because it has a high RESISTANCE to such flow. Electrical insulators hold conductors in place, separating them from one another and from surrounding structures to form a barrier between energized parts of an electric circuit and confine the flow of current. Electrical insulators include rubber, plastic, porcelain, and mica. Thermal insulators include fiberglass, cork, and rock wool.

insulin Polypeptide HORMONE (see PEPTIDE) that regulates blood GLUCOSE levels. Secreted by the islets of LANGERHANS in the PANCREAS when blood glucose rises, as after a meal, it helps transfer the glucose into the body's cells to be oxidized (see OXIDATION-REDUCTION) for energy or converted and stored as FATTY ACIDS or GLYCOGEN. When blood glucose falls, insulin secretion stops and the liver releases more glucose into the blood. Insulin-related disorders include DIABETES MELLITUS and HYPOGLYCEMIA. Frederick BANTING and J. R. MACLEOD won a Nobel Prize in 1923 for discovering insulin, and Frederick SANGER won one in 1958 for determining its amino acid sequence.

insurance Contract that, by redistributing RISK among a large number of people, reduces losses from accidents incurred by an individual. In return for a specified payment (premium), the insurer guarantees the insured against loss resulting from an event covered by the contract (policy). By pooling both the financial contributions and the risks of a large number of policyholders, the insurer is typically able to absorb losses much more easily than would the uninsured individual. Insurers may offer insurance to any individual able to pay, or may contract with members of a group (e.g., employees of a firm) to offer special rates for group insurance. Marine insurance, covering ships and voyages, is the oldest form of insurance; it originated in ancient times and was formalized in medieval Europe. Fire insurance arose in the 17th cent., and other forms of property insurance became common with the spread of industrialization in the 19th cent. It is now possible to insure almost any kind of property, including homes, businesses, motor vehicles, and goods in transit. See also CASUALTY INSURANCE, HEALTH INSURANCE, LIABILITY INSURANCE, LIFE INSURANCE.

intaglio \in-ˈtal-yō\ Engraved or incised work on gemstones, glass, ceramics, stone, or similar material in which the design is sunk beneath the surface, the opposite of CAMEO and RELIEF. The most ancient form of gem engraving, it appears in Mesopotamia by about 4000 B.C. The term is also used to describe printmaking processes in which the design is cut into a metal printing surface; ink is then rubbed into the incisions, the surface is wiped clean, and the paper is embossed into the incised lines with pressure from a roller press. Intaglio processes are the most versatile of printmaking methods, as they can produce a wide range of effects.

integer Whole-valued positive or negative number or 0. The integers are generated from the set of counting numbers 1, 2, 3, . . . and the operation of subtraction. When a counting number is subtracted from itself, the result is zero. When a larger number is subtracted from a smaller number, the result is a negative whole number. Thus, integers (derived from the counting numbers) are a set of numbers closed under the operation of subtraction (see GROUP THEORY).

integral Fundamental concept of CALCULUS related to areas and other quantities modeled by FUNCTIONS. A definite integral gives the area between the graph of a function and the horizontal axis between vertical lines at the endpoints of an interval. It also calculates the net change in a system

over an interval, and thus leads to formulas for the work done by a varying force or the distance traveled by an object moving at varying speeds. According to the fundamental theorem of calculus, a definite integral can be calculated using the indefinite integral, or antiderivative, of the function. The process of finding either a definite or an indefinite integral is called INTEGRATION.

integral calculus Branch of CALCULUS concerned with the theory and applications of INTEGRALS. While DIFFERENTIAL CALCULUS focuses on rates of change in a process, integral calculus deals with the total amount of change in the process over a prescribed interval. Integrating a velocity function yields the distance traveled by an object over an interval of time, for example. Much of integral calculus deals with the derivation of formulas for finding antiderivatives (indefinite integrals). Its applications include finding exact values for areas, lengths, and volumes defined by curves and probabilities associated with random variables.

integrated circuit (IC) *or* **microcircuit** *or* **chip** *or* **microchip** Assembly of microscopic electronic components (TRANSISTORS, DIODES, capacitors, and resistors) and their interconnections manufactured as a single unit on a wafer of semiconducting material such as a silicon COMPUTER CHIP, with no external connecting wires. Early ICs of the late 1950s consisted of about 10 components on a chip 0.12 in. (3 mm) square. Very large-scale integration (VLSI) vastly increased circuit density, giving rise to the MICROPROCESSOR. The first commercially successful IC chip (Intel, 1974) had 4,800 transistors; Intel's Pentium (1993) had 3.2 million. Over a billion are now achievable.

integrated pest management Technique for agricultural disease- and PEST-control in which as many pest-control methods as possible are used in an ecologically harmonious manner. Integrated pest management minimizes the use of chemical PESTICIDES and combines them with biological methods of pest control, including the breeding of pest-resistant crop varieties, the release of predators or parasites of the pest species, and the placement of traps baited with the pest's own sex attractants (PHEROMONES). Chemical insecticides generally are applied only as a last resort.

Integrated Services Digital Network See ISDN

integration In CALCULUS, the process of finding a FUNCTION whose DERIVATIVE is a given function. The term, sometimes used interchangeably with "antidifferentiation," is indicated symbolically with the integral sign ∫. (The DIFFERENTIAL dx usually follows to indicate x as the VARIABLE.) The basic rules of integration are: (1) $\int (f + g)\, dx = \int f\, dx + \int g\, dx$ (where f and g are functions of the variable x), (2) $\int kf\, dx = k \int f\, dx$ (k is a constant), and

$$(3)\ \int x^n\, dx = \left(\frac{1}{n+1}\right) x^{n+1} + C\ (C \text{ is a constant}).$$ Note that any constant value may be added onto an indefinite integral without changing its derivative. A definite integral is an indefinite integral evaluated over an interval. See also DIFFERENTIATION.

Intel Corp. U.S. manufacturer of semiconductor computer circuits. Intel was founded in 1968 as N M Electronics by Robert Noyce (1927–1990) and Gordon Moore (b.1929), inventors of the INTEGRATED CIRCUIT, to manufacture large-scale integrated (LSI) circuits. In the early 1970s it introduced the most powerful semiconductor chips then known, which soon replaced the magnetic cores previously used in computer memories. IBM chose to use Intel's 8088 MICROPROCESSOR (introduced 1978) in its first PERSONAL COMPUTER (the IBM PC), and Intel microprocessors became standard for all PC-type machines. Intel later developed faster, more powerful microprocessors, notably the Pentium family of chips (from 1993).

intellectual property Property that derives from the work of the mind or intellect. Early COPYRIGHT law aimed to protect the economic interests of book publishers rather than the intellectual rights of authors. Current copyright law protects the labor of elaborating an idea, not the idea itself. The concept of discovery also plays a role in intellectual property rights: PATENTS are awarded to those who can demonstrate that they have invented something not previously known. The WORLD TRADE ORGANIZATION goes fur-

HIJ

ther in its principles and rules for intellectual property than had the World Intellectual Property Organization. See also TRADEMARK.

intelligence Ability to learn or understand or to deal with new or trying situations. In psychology, the term may more specifically denote the ability to apply knowledge to manipulate one's environment or to think abstractly as measured by objective criteria (such as the IQ test). Intelligence is usually thought of as deriving from a combination of inherited characteristics and environmental (developmental and social) factors. The subject remains hotly debated. Particularly contested have been studies purporting to show links between RACE and intelligence, most of which have not been accepted in the scientific community. General intelligence is often said to comprise various specific abilities (verbal ability, ability to apply logic in solving problems, etc.), but critics contend that better models, perhaps based on information processing, are needed. High intelligence (as measured by tests) is sometimes shown to correlate with social achievement, but intelligence is no guarantor of success (and its lack is no guarantor of failure). See also ARTIFICIAL INTELLIGENCE, CREATIVITY.

intelligence quotient See IQ

intensive care unit *or* **critical care unit** HOSPITAL facility for care of critically ill patients at a more intensive level than is needed by other patients. Staffed by specialized personnel, the intensive care unit contains a complex assortment of monitors and life-support equipment that can sustain life in once-fatal situations.

interactionism In sociology, a theory that social processes (such as conflict, cooperation, and identity formation) are derived from human interaction. Georg SIMMEL first stated that "society is merely the name for a number of individuals connected by interaction." In the U.S., John DEWEY and especially George Herbert Mead (1863–1915) developed symbolic interactionism, the theory that mind and self arise only through social interaction, or the communication with others using SYMBOLS. For symbolic interactionists, the individual is always engaged in socialization or the modification of his or her mind, role, and behavior through contact with others.

intercontinental ballistic missile See ICBM

interest Price paid for the use of CREDIT or MONEY. It is usually figured as a percentage of the money borrowed and is computed annually. Interest is charged by the lender as payment for the use of this money for a period of time. The interest rate reflects the risk of lending and is higher for loans that are considered higher-risk. Like the prices of goods and services, interest rates are responsive to SUPPLY AND DEMAND. Interest rates may also be used as a tool for implementing MONETARY POLICY (see DISCOUNT RATE). High interest rates may dampen the economy by making it difficult for consumers, businesses, and home buyers to secure loans, while lower rates tend to stimulate the economy and encourage both INVESTMENT and CONSUMPTION.

interference In physics, the net effect of combining two or more WAVE trains moving on intersecting or coincident paths. Constructive interference occurs if two components have the same FREQUENCY and PHASE; the wave amplitudes are reinforced. Destructive interference occurs when the two waves are out of phase by one-half period; if the waves are of equal amplitude, they cancel each other. Two waves moving in the same direction but having slightly different frequencies interfere constructively at regular intervals (see BEAT). Two waves traveling in opposite directions but having equal frequencies interfere constructively in some places and destructively in others, resulting in a standing wave.

interferon \ˌin-tər-ˈfir-ˌän\ Any of several related PROTEINS produced by all vertebrates and possibly some invertebrates. They play an important role in resistance to infection. The body's most rapidly produced and important defense against VIRUSES, they can also combat BACTERIA and parasites (see PARASITISM), inhibit cell division, and promote or impede cell differentiation. Various types of interferons are distinguished by their characteristics as proteins and by which cells produce them. Initial hopes that interferon would be a wonder drug for a wide variety of diseases were deflated by its serious side effects, but a few rare conditions respond to it.

Interior, U.S. Department of the Federal executive division responsible for most of the nation's federally owned lands and natural resources, as well as Indian reservations. Created in 1849, it includes the Bureau of Land Management, the Bureau of Indian Affairs, the U.S. Fish and Wildlife Service, the National Park Service, and the U.S. Geological Survey.

interior design Design of interior spaces, closely related to architecture and sometimes including interior decoration. The designer's goal is to produce a coordinated and harmonious whole in which the architecture, site, function, and visual aspects of the interior are unified, pleasing, and appropriate. Design criteria include harmony of color, texture, lighting, scale, and proportion. The design of such nonresidential spaces as offices, hospitals, stores, and schools places clear organization of functions ahead of purely aesthetic concerns.

interleukin \ˌin-tər-ˈlü-kən\ Any of a class of naturally occurring PROTEINS important in regulation of LYMPHOCYTE function. ANTIGENS and microbes stimulate production of interleukins, which induce production of various types of lymphocytes in a complex series of reactions that ensure a plentiful supply of T CELLS that fight specific infectious agents. See also IMMUNITY.

intermediate-range nuclear weapons Class of NUCLEAR WEAPONS with a range of 620–3,400 mi (1,000–5,500 km). Some multiple warheads developed by the Soviet Union could strike several targets anywhere in Western Europe in less than 10 minutes. The U.S. could send a single nuclear warhead from central Europe to Moscow. U.S.–Soviet arms-control negotiations (1980–87) led to the intermediate nuclear forces (INF) treaty to completely remove and dismantle these and shorter-range weapons.

internal-combustion engine Any ENGINE in which a fuel-air mixture is burned in the engine proper so that the hot gaseous products of combustion act directly on the surfaces

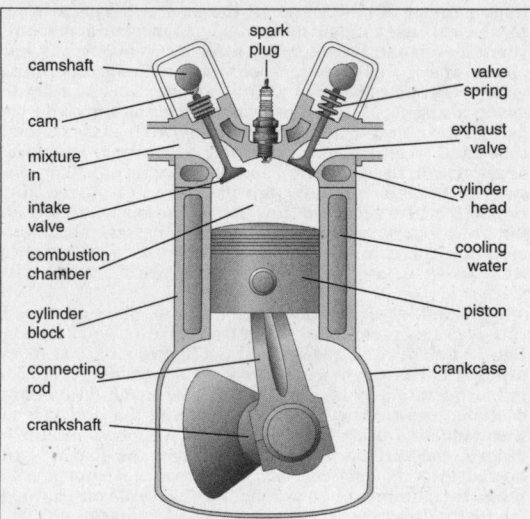

Internal-combustion engine Cross section showing one cylinder of a four-stroke internal-combustion engine. In the first stroke (shown), a cam (left) compresses a valve spring, opening the intake valve to admit the fuel-air mixture to the cylinder. Both valves then close, the mixture is compressed by the piston, and current is sent to the spark plug. Ignited by the spark plug, the burning mixture forces the piston down, producing power to turn the crankshaft and run the car. Another cam (right) opens the exhaust valve and the burned exhaust gases exit.

of its moving parts, such as those of pistons (see PISTON AND CYLINDER) or TURBINE rotor blades. Internal-combustion engines include GASOLINE ENGINES, DIESEL ENGINES, gas turbine engines, pure JET ENGINES, and ROCKET engines and motors. They are commonly divided into continuous-combustion engines and intermittent-combustion engines. In the first type (e.g., jet engines) fuel and air flow steadily into the engine, where a stable flame is maintained for continuous combustion. In the second (e.g., gasoline-reciprocating-piston engines), discrete quantities of fuel and air are periodically ignited.

Internal Revenue Service (IRS) Agency of the U.S. Department of the TREASURY charged with administering and enforcing federal tax laws, except those relating to alcohol, tobacco, firearms, and explosives. It issues rulings and regulations to supplement the provisions of the Internal Revenue Code; determines, assesses, and collects internal revenue taxes; and determines exempt organization status.

International, Communist See FIRST INTERNATIONAL, SECOND INTERNATIONAL, COMINTERN

International Bank for Economic Cooperation (IBEC) International bank instituted by Bulgaria, Hungary, E. Germany, Mongolia, Poland, Romania, Czechoslovakia, and the Soviet Union in 1963 to facilitate economic cooperation and promote development. Cuba and Vietnam joined later. Its functions included making multilateral settlements in transferable rubles, advancing credit, accepting deposits, and conducting ARBITRAGE and other financial operations. After the fall of the Soviet Union it became a Russian bank with a new charter.

International Brigades Foreign volunteers who fought on the Republican side against the Nationalist forces in the SPANISH CIVIL WAR (1936–39). Groups initially came from some 50 countries, organized by the COMINTERN. The U.S. contingent called itself the Abraham Lincoln Batallion. Many of the mostly young recruits were communists. The total number of volunteers reached about 60,000. The brigades were formally withdrawn from Spain late in 1938.

International Court of Justice *or* **World Court** Principal judicial body of the UNITED NATIONS, located at The Hague. Successor to the Permanent Court of International Justice, the LEAGUE OF NATIONS' judicial body, it held its first session in 1946. Its jurisdiction is limited to disputes between states willing to accept its authority on matters of INTERNATIONAL LAW. Its decisions are binding, but it has no enforcement power; appeals must be made to the U.N. Security Council. Its 15 judges, each of whom serves a nine-year term, are elected by the U.N. General Assembly.

international date line Imaginary line from the N. Pole through the Pacific Ocean to the S. Pole that arbitrarily separates each calendar day from the next. It corresponds along most of its length to the 180th meridian of longitude, with deviations to avoid dividing Siberia, to include the Aleutian Islands with Alaska, and to give certain S island groups the same day as New Zealand. The date line is arranged so that local noon corresponds approximately to the time at which the sun crosses the local meridian of longitude. See also STANDARD TIME.

International Herald Tribune Daily newspaper published in Paris. It has long been the staple source of English-language news for Americans in Europe. Its roots are in the *Paris Herald* (established 1887); a merger in 1924 between its parent, the *New York Herald,* and the *New York Tribune* created the *New York Herald-Tribune* and the *Paris Herald Tribune.* The Paris edition survived its parent's demise in 1966, rescued by a joint venture of the *New York Times,* the *Washington Post,* and Whitney Communications. It is now printed simultaneously in 16 sites around the world.

international law Body of laws, rules, or legal principles that are based on custom, treaties, or legislation and that control or affect the rights and duties of nations in relation to each other. Important elements include SOVEREIGNTY, recognition (which allows a country to honor the claims of another), consent (which allows for modifications in international agreements to fit the customs of a country), freedom of the high seas, self-defense (which ensures that measures may be taken against illegal acts committed against a sovereign nation), freedom of commerce, and protection of nationals abroad. International courts, such as the INTERNATIONAL COURT OF JUSTICE, resolve disputes on these and other matters, including WAR CRIMES. See also ASYLUM, IMMUNITY.

International Monetary Fund (IMF) Specialized agency of the U.N. system. Conceived at the Bretton Woods Conference (1944) as a voluntary cooperative institution to help ensure the smooth international buying and selling of currency, it provides temporary financial assistance to countries with balance-of-payments problems. Its over 180 member countries contribute operating funds and receive voting rights according to their volume of international trade, national income, and international reserve holdings; the U.S. has over 18% of the voting rights, more than twice that of any other member. The IMF has no coercive power over member nations, but it can refuse to lend money to non-compliant members. See also WORLD BANK.

International Organization for Standardization (ISO) Organization concerned with determining standards in most technical and nontechnical fields. Founded in Geneva in 1947, it has over 100 member countries. An appropriate national body represents each country, the U.S. member being the American National Standards Institute (ANSI). Standardization affects units of measurement, alphabetization and transliteration, and specifications for parts, materials, surfaces, processes, tools, methods of testing, and machines.

International Phonetic Alphabet (IPA) Set of symbols intended as a universal system for transcribing speech sounds. The promulgation and updating of the IPA has been a principal aim of the International Phonetic Assn., founded in Paris in 1886. The first IPA chart was published in 1888. IPA symbols are based on an extended version of the LATIN ALPHABET, with modifications of some letters and the use of additional symbols, some from earlier phonetic ALPHABETS.

International Space Station (ISS) Space station to be built largely by the U.S., with international assistance and components. After funding and technical delays, in-orbit construction began in 1998 when a Russian control module (*Zarya*) and the U.S. *Unity* connecting node were launched and joined in orbit. The station will ultimately involve at least 16 nations. It will be over 350 ft (over 100 m) long, accommodating seven crew members in orbit about 220 mi (350 km) above earth. Smaller crews began staying on board in late 2000 to complete construction and conduct experiments. The station's purpose is to conduct long-term materials and life-science research in very low gravity, conduct medical research in space, and enable long-term space exploration.

International Style Architectural style that developed in the 1920s and '30s and dominated Western architecture in the mid-20th cent. The term was first used in 1932 in Henry-Russell Hitchcock and Philip JOHNSON's *The International Style: Architecture Since 1922.* Its characteristics include rectilinear forms, open interior spaces, large expanses of glass, and steel and REINFORCED-CONCRETE construction. Walter GROPIUS, Ludwig MIES VAN DER ROHE, and LE CORBUSIER are among those associated with the style. See also BAUHAUS.

International Style Schroeder House by G. T. Rietveld, 1924

International System of Units *or* **Système International d'Unités** \sēs-ˈtem-aⁿ-ter-nä-syȯ-ˈnál-dū̄e̅-nē̄-ˈtä\ *or* **SI** International decimal system of weights and measures derived from and extending the METRIC SYSTEM of units. Adopted in 1960, its fundamental units include the meter (m) for length, the kilogram (kg) for mass, and the second (s) for time. Derived units include those for force (newton, N), energy (joule, J), and power (watt, W).

International Telephone and Telegraph Corp. (ITT) Former U.S. telecommunications company. Founded in 1920 by Sosthenes and Hernand Behn as a HOLDING COMPANY for their Caribbean-based telephone and telegraph companies, it expanded into Europe. In the 1960s and '70s ITT became a conglomerate, acquiring such firms as the Sheraton Corp.

and the Hartford Fire Insurance Co. It divested its telecommunications businesses in 1987, and in 1995 it split into three companies: ITT Hartford Group Inc. (insurance); ITT Industries Inc. (defense electronics and auto parts); and a "new" ITT Corp. (hotels, gaming, and entertainment) which merged with Starwood Lodgings in 1997.

international unit Any of several precision standards used in measuring physical quantities, such as mass, length, and time (see INTERNATIONAL SYSTEM OF UNITS), and also lighting systems, radiation processes, and pharmacology. The luminous intensity of a light is expressed in candelas. The second is based on the frequency of radiation emitted by cesium-133 atoms. In radioactive decay, the international unit is the number of disintegrations per second in a sample. In pharmacology, the unit is the quantity of a substance that produces a specified effect when tested according to an accepted procedure.

Internet Publicly accessible computer NETWORK connecting many smaller networks from around the world. It grew out of a U.S. Defense Department program called ARPANET (Advanced Research Projects Agency Network), established in 1969 with connections between computers at four universities. ARPANET's purpose was to conduct research into computer networking in order to provide a secure and survivable communications system in case of war. As the network quickly expanded, academics and researchers in other fields began to use it. In 1971 the first program for sending E-MAIL over a distributed network was developed. In 1973 the first international connections to ARPANET were made (from Britain and Norway). The 1970s also saw the development of mailing lists, NEWSGROUPS and BULLETIN-BOARD SYSTEMS, and the TCP/IP communications PROTOCOLS, which were adopted as standard protocols for ARPANET in 1982–83. In 1984 the DOMAIN NAME addressing system was introduced. In 1986 the National Science Foundation established a distributed network of networks capable of handling far greater traffic, and within a year more than 10,000 hosts were connected to the Internet. In 1988 real-time conversation over the network became possible (see CHAT). In 1990 the first commercial dial-up access to the Internet became available. In 1991 the WORLD WIDE WEB was released to the public. The Mosaic BROWSER was released in 1993, and its popularity led to the proliferation of World Wide Web sites and users. In 1995 Internet traffic began to be routed through network providers rather than NSF supercomputers. That year the Web became the most popular part of the Internet. By 2000 there were over 30 million hosts on the Internet and over 20 million registered domain names. Internet access can now be gained via radio signals, cable-television lines, satellites, and fiber-optic connections, though most traffic still uses a part of the public telephone network. The Internet is widely regarded as a development of vast significance that will affect nearly every aspect of human culture and commerce in ways not yet known.

Internet Protocol address See IP ADDRESS

Internet service provider (ISP) Company that provides INTERNET connections and services to individuals and organizations. For a monthly fee, ISPs provide computer users with a connection to their site, as well as a log-in name and password. They may also provide software packages (such as BROWSERS), E-MAIL accounts, and a WEB SITE or home page. ISPs are all connected to each other through network access points (NAPs), public network facilities on the Internet backbone.

Interpol *officially* International Criminal Police Organization. Organization whose purpose is to fight international crime by promoting cooperation of its members' police forces. Founded in Austria in 1923 with 20 member nations, it moved to France in 1946 and today has over 175 members. It hunts criminals who operate in more than one country (e.g., smugglers), those who stay home but whose crimes affect other countries (e.g., counterfeiters of foreign currency), and those who commit a crime in one country and flee to another.

interpolation In mathematics, ESTIMATION of a value between two known data points. A simple example is calculating the mean (see MEAN, MEDIAN, AND MODE) of two

population counts made 10 years apart to estimate the population in the fifth year. Estimating outside the data points (e.g., predicting the population five years after the second population count) is called extrapolation. If more than two data points are available, a curve may fit the data better than a straight line.

interstate commerce In the U.S., commerce, traffic, transportation, and exchange between states. Government regulation of interstate commerce began with legislation enacted during RECONSTRUCTION. From 1887 until 1995 the INTERSTATE COMMERCE COMMISSION oversaw all interstate surface transportation. In the 20th cent., court decisions have interpreted interstate commerce broadly, thus allowing Congress to regulate internal or local activities that affect it. For example, cattle crossing a state line while grazing and the movements of pollutants across state lines have been considered interstate commerce.

Interstate Commerce Commission (ICC) (1887–1995) First REGULATORY AGENCY established in the U.S. and a prototype for independent government regulatory bodies. Responsible for the economic regulation of interstate surface transportation, including railroads, trucking companies, and bus lines, it certified carriers, regulated rates, oversaw mergers, and approved railroad construction. The ICC was dissolved in 1995; its functions were assigned to the new Surface Transportation Board and the Federal Highway Administration.

interstellar medium Content of the region between the stars, including vast, diffuse clouds of gases and minute solid particles. Such tenuous matter accounts for about 5% of the MILKY WAY's total mass. By no means a complete vacuum, the interstellar medium contains mainly hydrogen gas, with a smaller amount of helium and dust particles of uncertain composition. Primary COSMIC RAYS also travel through interstellar space, and magnetic fields extend across much of it. Most interstellar matter occurs in clouds that can condense to form STARS, which lose mass back to the interstellar medium through stellar winds (see SOLAR WIND), SUPERNOVAS, and shedding of planetary nebulae (see PLANETARY NEBULA).

interval In music, two tones heard in relation to one other, and specifically their distance in musical space. In Western music, intervals are generally named according to the number of scale-steps within a given KEY that they embrace; thus, the ascent from C to G (C–D–E–F–G) is called a 5th since the interval embraces five scale degrees (inclusive of those at both ends). An interval with a simple numerical designation will also have a more precise name; thus, C–E is a major 3rd (since it consists of four semitones), C-sharp–E is a minor 3rd (three semitones), C–E-sharp is an augmented 3rd (five semitones), and C-sharp–E-flat is a diminished 3rd (two semitones). 2nds and 6ths are classified like 3rds; 4ths and 5ths are classified instead as perfect (a perfect 4th consisting of five semitones, a perfect 5th of seven semitones), augmented (when expanded by a semitone), or diminished (when contracted by a semitone).

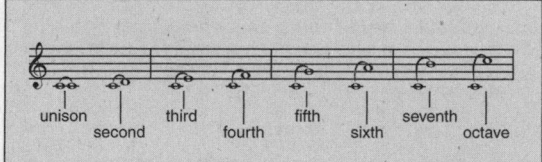

Interval Examples of simple musical intervals.

intestine See LARGE INTESTINE, SMALL INTESTINE

intifada \ˌin-ti-ˈfä-də\ (Arabic: "shaking off") (1987–93) Periodic revolts of Palestinians in the GAZA STRIP and WEST BANK against Israeli rule. Initially (1987) a spontaneous reaction to 20 years of occupation and recent unemployment, it was soon taken over by the PALESTINE LIBERATION ORGANIZATION (PLO). Its tactics included strikes, boycotts, and confrontation of Israeli troops. Some 800 Palestinians had been killed by Israeli security forces by 1990. Intifada pressure helped make possible the 1993 Israeli–PLO agreement on Palestinian self-determination. A "Second Intifada," a wave of suicide bombings that began in the autumn of 2000, led to the election of Ariel SHARON in 2001 and an Israeli invasion of the West Bank in 2002. See also Yasir ARAFAT, FATAH, HAMAS.

Intolerable Acts *or* **Coercive Acts** (1774) Four punitive measures enacted by Britain against the American colonies. Boston's harbor was closed until restitution was made for the BOSTON TEA PARTY; the Massachusetts colony's charter was annulled and a military governor installed; and arrangement for housing British troops in American houses was revived. The QUEBEC ACT added to these oppressive measures. The acts, called "intolerable" by the colonists, led to a convening of the CONTINENTAL CONGRESS.

intonation In PHONETICS, the melodic pattern of speech, measured by variation in the pitch level of the voice (see TONE). In languages such as English, stress and rhythm are also involved. Intonation conveys differences of expressive meaning (e.g., surprise, doubtfulness) and may serve a grammatical function, distinguishing one type of sentence from another. Thus, "it's gone" is an assertion when spoken with a drop in pitch at the end, but a question when spoken with a rise in pitch at the end.

introvert and extrovert Basic personality types, according to the theories of C. G. JUNG. The introvert is often shy, contemplative, and reserved. The extrovert is usually outgoing, responsive, and aggressive. This typology is now regarded as simplistic because almost no one can be described as wholly introvert or extrovert.

intrusive rock IGNEOUS ROCK formed from MAGMA forced into older rocks at depths within the earth's crust. It slowly solidifies below the earth's surface, though it may later be exposed by erosion. Igneous intrusions form a variety of rock types. See also EXTRUSIVE ROCK.

intuition In philosophy, the power of obtaining knowledge that is not or cannot be acquired either by inference or observation. As such, intuition is thought of as an original, independent source of knowledge. Knowledge of basic moral principles is sometimes explained in this way. A technical sense of intuition, deriving from Immanuel KANT, refers to immediate acquaintance with individual entities; intuition (*Anschauung*) in this sense may be empirical (e.g., consciousness of sense-data) or pure (e.g., consciousness of space and time as forms of all empirical intuitions). As conceived by Benedict de SPINOZA and Henri BERGSON, intuition is concrete knowledge of the world as an interconnected whole, as contrasted with the piecemeal, "abstract" knowledge obtained by science and observation.

Inuit See ESKIMO

inventory In business, any supply held by a firm, including finished goods for sale, goods in the process of production, raw materials, and items that will be consumed in the process of producing salable goods. Inventories appear on a company's BALANCE SHEET as assets. Inventory turnover is a key factor in appraising a firm's financial condition. For financial statements, inventories may be priced either at cost or at market value.

Inverness \ˌin-vər-ˈnes\ City (pop., 1991 est.: 63,000), N Scotland. Located on the River Ness and the Caledonian Canal, it is the headquarters for the Highlands administrative region. In the 6th cent. it was the capital of the Pictish kingdom of King Brude. By the 12th cent. it had become a burgh near the castle of MALCOLM III CANMORE. It has expanded as the offshore oil industry develops.

inverse function Mathematical FUNCTION that undoes the effect of another function. For example, the inverse function of the formula that converts Celsius temperature to Fahrenheit temperature is the formula that converts Fahrenheit to Celsius. Inverse procedures are essential to solving EQUATIONS because they allow mathematical operations to be reversed (e.g. LOGARITHMS, the inverses of EXPONENTIAL FUNCTIONS, are used to solve exponential equations).

invertebrate Any animal that lacks a vertebral column, or backbone. More than 90% of living animals are invertebrates. They include the PROTOZOANS, ANNELIDS, CNIDARIANS, ECHINODERMS, FLATWORMS, NEMATODES, MOLLUSKS, and ARTHROPODS. They range in size from minute

protozoans to giant squids. Apart from the absence of a vertebral column, invertebrates have little in common. They are generally soft-bodied and have an external skeleton for muscle attachment and protection. See also VERTEBRATE.

Investiture Controversy Struggle between the papacy and the Holy Roman Emperor over the ruler's presentation of the symbols of office to churchmen. Pope GREGORY VII condemned lay investiture in 1075 as an unjustified assertion of secular authority over the church, a key issue in his dispute with the emperor HENRY IV. HENRY I of England renounced lay investiture (1106) in return for the guarantee that homage would be paid to the king before consecration; the Concordat of WORMS (1122) forged a similar compromise.

investment Process of exchanging income for an asset that is expected to produce earnings at a later time. An investor refrains from CONSUMPTION in the present in hopes of a greater return in the future. Investment may be influenced by rates of INTEREST, with the rate of investment rising as interest rates fall, but other factors more difficult to measure may also be important—for example, businessmen's expectations about future demand and profit, technical changes in production methods, and expected relative costs of LABOR and CAPITAL. Investment cannot occur without SAVING, which provides funding. Because investment increases an economy's capacity to produce, it is the factor responsible for economic growth.

investment bank Firm that originates, underwrites, and distributes new SECURITY issues of corporations and government agencies. The Banking Act of 1933 required the separation of investment banking and COMMERCIAL BANKING, but the Gramm-Leach Bliley Act of 1999 repealed its last vestiges. Investment banks purchase a new security issue from a corporation, set the public offering price, and sell the issue in smaller units to the investing public. A syndicate of investment-banking firms underwrites and distributes most security issues in order to divide the RISK. See also BANK, CENTRAL BANK, SAVINGS BANK.

investment credit Tax incentive that permits businesses to deduct a specified percentage of certain investment costs from their tax liability, in addition to the normal allowances for DEPRECIATION. Investment credits are similar to investment allowances, which permit businesses to deduct a specified percentage of certain capital costs from their taxable income. In effect, both are SUBSIDIES for investment. Both were adopted by the U.S. in 1962 in order to protect domestic business from foreign competition, but they were eliminated in the Tax Reform Act of 1969 in an attempt to counteract rising INFLATION.

in vitro fertilization (IVF) \in-ˈvē-trō\ *or* **test-tube conception** Procedure, used to overcome INFERTILITY, in which EGGS are removed from a woman, fertilized with SPERM outside the body, and inserted into the UTERUS of the same or another woman. In a successful procedure, the embryo is implanted in the uterine wall, and pregnancy begins. The most common problem is failed implantation. IVF has been a source of moral, ethical, and religious controversy since its development in 1978.

Io \ˈī-ō\ In GREEK MYTHOLOGY, the daughter of the river god Argos, who drew HERA's jealousy when ZEUS fell in love with her. Zeus changed her into a white heifer to protect her. When Hera set the many-eyed Argus to watch her, Zeus sent HERMES to lull Argus to sleep and kill him. Hera then sent a gadfly, which pursued Io across Europe and the bodies of water later named the Ionian Sea and the BOSPORUS ("Ford of the Cow") in her honor. In Egypt she resumed her original form.

iodine Nonmetallic chemical ELEMENT, chemical symbol I, atomic number 53. The heaviest nonradioactive HALOGEN, it is a nearly black crystalline solid that sublimes to a deep violet, irritating vapor. It is never found in nature uncombined. Its sources (mostly in brines and seaweeds) and compounds are usually iodides; iodates and periodates also occur. Dietary iodine is essential for THYROID GLAND function, so table salt usually has potassium iodide added to prevent IODINE DEFICIENCY. Elemental iodine is used in medicine, in synthesizing some organic chemicals, in manufacturing dyes, in analytical chemistry (see ANALYSIS), and

HIJ

in photography. The radioactive ISOTOPE I-131 (see RA-DIOACTIVITY), with an eight-day half-life, is very useful in medicine (see NUCLEAR MEDICINE) and other applications.

iodine deficiency Inadequate intake or metabolism of IODINE. It directly affects THYROID secretions; simple GOITER is the most frequent result. Severe, prolonged deficiency can cause hypothyroidism. Lack of iodine during infancy may cause CRETINISM. Eating seafood regularly or using iodized table salt will prevent iodine deficiency. Some countries have made dietary iodine additives mandatory.

ion ATOM or group of atoms with one or more positive (CATION) or negative (ANION) ELECTRIC CHARGES. Ions are formed when ELECTRONS are added to or removed from neutral MOLECULES or other ions; when ions combine with other particles; and when a COVALENT BOND between two atoms is ruptured in such a way that the resulting particles are charged. Many crystalline substances (see CRYSTAL) are composed of ions held in regular geometric patterns by the attraction of the oppositely charged particles for each other. Ions migrate to the electrode of opposite charge in an ELECTRIC FIELD and are the conductors of current in electrolytic cells (see ELECTROLYSIS). Compounds that form ions are called ELECTROLYTES. Ions are also formed in gases when an electrical discharge passes through them.

Ionesco \yȯ-nes-'kō\, **Eugène** orig. Eugen Ionescu (1909–1994) Romanian-French playwright. His first one-act "antiplay," *The Bald Soprano* (1950), helped inaugurate the theater of the ABSURD. He followed it with other one-act plays in which illogical events create an atmosphere both comic and grotesque, including *The Lesson* (1951), *The Chairs* (1952), and *The New Tenant* (1955). His most popular full-length play, *Rhinoceros* (1959), concerns a provincial French town in which all the citizens are metamorphosing into rhinoceroses. Other plays include *Exit the King* (1962) and *A Stroll in the Air* (1963).

ion-exchange resin Any of a wide variety of synthetic POLYMERS containing positively or negatively charged sites that can interact with or bind to an ION of opposite charge from a surrounding solution. Light, porous solids, they absorb the solution and swell as they attract the target ions; when exhausted, they are removed from it and regenerated by an inexpensive brine or carbonate solution. Industrially, these resins are used to soften HARD WATER, purify SUGAR, and concentrate valuable elements (gold, silver, uranium) from their ores. In the laboratory, they are used to separate and concentrate substances and sometimes as catalysts.

Ionia \ī-'ō-nyə\ Ancient region, W coast of ASIA MINOR (modern Turkey) bordering on the AEGEAN SEA. It consisted of a coastal strip of 100 mi (160 km). In the 8th cent. B.C. there were 12 major Greek cities in the region, including PHOCAEA and MILETUS on the mainland, and the islands CHIOS and SAMOS. Until 500 B.C. Ionic philosophy and architecture and the Ionic dialect were highly influential in Greece. In the mid-6th cent. B.C., it fell to LYDIA; it later fell to the Persians, and subsequently became part of the SELEUCID kingdom. In 133 B.C. it passed to the Romans and became part of the Roman province of Asia. It was devastated during the Turkish conquest of Asia Minor.

Ionian Islands \ī-'ō-nē-ən\ *ancient* Heptanesos. Group of seven Greek islands (pop., 1991: 191,000) in the Ionian Sea: CORFU, Cephalonia, Zacynthus, Leucas, Ithaca, Cythera, and Paxos. They were controlled by Venice in the 15th–18th cent. In 1815 they came under the control of Britain, which ceded them to Greece in 1864. The islands have fertile land and good harbors, but are subject to earthquakes.

Ionians Ancient Greek inhabitants of IONIA, from the collapse of MYCENAEAN civilization. Their contributions to Greek culture included the epics of HOMER and the earliest elegiac and iambic poetry. They began the study of geography, philosophy, and historiography in the 6th cent. After ALEXANDER THE GREAT their literary language was the basis of koine, or "common speech," the language of practically all Greek writing to the present day.

Ionian Sea Part of the MEDITERRANEAN SEA lying between Greece, Sicily, and Italy. The Mediterranean reaches its greatest depth (16,000 ft or 4,900 m) in the Ionian south of Greece. Along its E shore are the IONIAN ISLANDS.

ionic bond Electrostatic attraction among oppositely charged IONS in which an ELECTRON is transferred from one neutral ATOM (usually a METAL, which becomes the CATION) to another (a nonmetallic element or a group, which becomes the ANION). The two types of ion are held together by electrostatic forces in a solid that does not contain MOLECULES as such; rather, each ion has neighbors of the opposite charge in an ordered overall structure. See also BONDING, COVALENT BOND.

ionization Process by which electrically neutral ATOMS or MOLECULES are converted to IONS by the removal or addition of ELECTRONS. It is one of the principal ways in which RADIATION transfers energy to matter, and hence of detecting radiation. In general, ionization occurs whenever sufficiently energetic charged particles or radiant energy travels through matter. A certain minimal level of ionization is present in the earth's atmosphere because of continuous absorption of COSMIC RAYS from space and ULTRAVIOLET RADIATION from the sun.

ionization potential *or* **ionization energy** Amount of ENERGY required to remove an ELECTRON from an isolated ATOM or MOLECULE. The ionization potential of an ELEMENT is a measure of its ability to enter into chemical reactions requiring ION formation or donation of electrons and is related to the nature of the chemical bonding in the compounds formed by elements. See also BINDING ENERGY, IONIZATION.

ionosphere \ī-'än-ə-ˌsfir\ Region of the earth's atmosphere in which the number of IONS is large enough to affect the propagation of RADIO WAVES. It begins at an altitude of about 30 mi (50 km) but is most distinct above about 50 mi (80 km). The IONIZATION is caused mainly by solar radiation at X-ray and ultraviolet wavelengths. The ionosphere is responsible for the long-distance propagation, by reflection, of radio signals in the shortwave and broadcast bands.

Iowa State (pop. 2000: 2,926,000), midwestern U.S. It covers 56,275 sq mi (145,752 sq km); its capital is DES MOINES. The DES MOINES RIVER flows across the state from northwest to southeast. The MISSISSIPPI RIVER forms its E boundary, while the MISSOURI and the Big Sioux rivers define portions of its W boundary. The SAUK, FOX, Iowa, and SIOUX Indians lived in the region when French explorers Louis JOLLIET and Jacques MARQUETTE arrived in 1673. The U.S. acquired Iowa as part of the LOUISIANA PURCHASE in 1803. Following the Black Hawk War and purchase of E Iowa from the Sauk and Fox Indians in the 1830s, white settlement advanced rapidly. It became a territory in 1838 and was made the 29th state in 1846. After the Civil War, railroad expansion drew large waves of immigrants from the east and from Europe. After World War I population growth slowed. Its economy is based on agriculture, and Iowa is a leader in the U.S. production of livestock.

Iowa, University of Public university in Iowa City. Founded in 1847, it was the first public university in the U.S. to admit men and women on an equal basis and the first to award advanced degrees in the creative arts. It comprises a college of liberal arts and many specialized colleges and schools. The campus is home to the renowned Writer's Workshop and International Writing Program. Total enrollment is about 28,000.

Iphigeneia \ˌi-fə-jə-'nī-ə\ In GREEK MYTHOLOGY, the eldest daughter of AGAMEMNON and sister of ELECTRA and ORESTES. When the Achaean fleet was becalmed at Aulis, her father sacrificed her to ARTEMIS in order to secure favorable winds to carry the ships to Troy. Iphigeneia's story is treated in plays by AESCHYLUS, SOPHOCLES, and EURIPIDES. According to Euripides, she did not die but was saved by Artemis; later, in Tauris, she saved Orestes from madness and death after he killed their mother.

IQ *in full* **intelligence quotient** Number intended as a measure of relative INTELLIGENCE as determined by the subject's responses to a series of test problems. Originally computed as the ratio of a person's mental age to his or her chronological (physical) age, multiplied by 100, IQ is now generally assessed on the basis of the statistical distribution of scores. Most widely used are the Stanford-Binet test (1916), for children, and the Wechsler test (1939). A score above 130 is considered to reflect "giftedness," while a score below 70 is considered to reflect mental impairment or MENTAL RETARDATION. Intelligence tests have provoked great controversy, particularly about what kinds of mental ability constitute intelligence and whether IQ adequately represents these abilities, and about cultural and class bias in test construction.

Iqaluit \ē-ˈkä-lü-it\ *formerly* **Frobisher Bay** Town (pop., 1998: 5,000), capital of Nunavut territory. Situated on SE BAFFIN ISLAND, it is the largest community in the E Canadian Arctic. It was established as a trading post in 1914 and became an air base during World War II. It is the site of a meteorological station and a hospital. It became Nunavut's capital in 1999.

Iqbal \ˈik-ˌbäl\, **Muhammad** (*later* **Sir Muhammad**) (1877–1938) Indian poet and philosopher. He first won fame for his poetry, which was widely recited and became known even among the illiterate. His perspective grew increasingly Pan-Islamic, as revealed in the long poem *The Secrets of the Self* (1915). He advocated the separate Muslim state that would eventually be realized with the founding of Pakistan in 1947, and he was acclaimed after his death as the father of Pakistan. His poetic masterpiece is *The Song of Eternity* (1932). He is considered the greatest 20th-cent. poet to write in Urdu.

IRA See IRISH REPUBLICAN ARMY

Iran *officially* **Islamic Republic of Iran** *formerly* **Persia** Country, SW Asia. Area: 634,562 sq mi (1,643,510 sq km). Population (2000 est.): 62,704,000. Capital: TEHRAN. Iranians

IRAN

Scale 1: 25,935,000
0   100   200 mi
0 100 200 300 km

©1999, Encyclopædia Britannica, Inc.

(Persians) constitute 51% of its population; other ethnic groups include the Azerbaijani and the KURDS. Language: Farsi (Persian) (official). Religion: Islam (official); most are Shiites. Currency: rial. Iran occupies a high plateau more than 1,500 ft (460 m) above sea level and is surrounded by mountains. More than half of its surface area consists of salt deserts and other wasteland. About one-tenth of its land is arable, and another one-fourth is suitable for grazing. Iran's rich petroleum reserves account for about 9% of world reserves and are the basis of its economy. It is an Islamic republic with one legislative house; its head of state and government is the president, but the supreme political and religious authority is the religious leader. Habitation in Iran dates to around 100,000 B.C., but recorded history began with the Elamites about 3000 B.C. The Medes flourished from around 728 B.C. but were overthrown (550 B.C.) by the Persians, who were in turn conquered by ALEXANDER THE GREAT in the 4th cent. B.C. The Parthians (see PARTHIA) created a Greek-speaking empire

that lasted from 247 B.C. to A.D. 226, when control passed to the SASANIANS. Arab Muslims conquered them in 640 and ruled Iran for 850 years. In 1502 the SAFAVIDS established a dynasty that lasted until 1736. The QAJARS ruled from 1779, but in the 19th cent. the country was economically controlled by the Russian and British empires. Reza Khan (see Reza Shah PAHLAVI) seized power in a coup (1921). His son M. R. Shah PAHLAVI alienated religious leaders with a program of modernization and westernization and was overthrown in 1979; Shiite cleric Ruhollah KHOMEINI then set up a fundamentalist Islamic republic, and Western influence was suppressed. The destructive IRAN–IRAQ WAR (1980–88) ended in a stalemate. After Khomeini's death (1989), the elected government sought to liberalize, while the powerful mullahs resisted change.

Iran-Contra Affair U.S. political scandal in the mid-1980s involving secret weapons transactions. In 1985 Robert McFarlane, head of the National Security Council, authorized sales of weapons to Iran in an attempt to secure release of U.S. hostages held in Lebanon by pro-Iranian terrorist groups, contravening stated policy regarding terrorists and aid to Iran. Part of the $48 million paid for the arms was diverted to the Nicaraguan CONTRAS with the assistance of Oliver NORTH, violating a 1984 law banning aid to the contras. A Senate investigation resulted in convictions for North and others (later overturned because of immunity agreements). The affair significantly damaged Ronald REAGAN's administration.

Iran hostage crisis (1979–81) Conflict between the U.S. and Iran. More than 20 years of friendly relations between the U.S. and M. R. Shah PAHLAVI fueled opposition to the shah's rule, and he went into exile in January 1979. On Nov. 4, after the shah had been permitted to enter the U.S. for cancer treatment, Iranian revolutionaries stormed the U.S. embassy in Tehran, seizing 69 hostages. They demanded the return of the shah and his money to Iran. Pres. Jimmy CARTER refused to accede, and froze all Iranian assets in the U.S. In April 1980 the U.S. launched an unsuccessful military strike on the embassy. Negotiations began after the shah's death in July. Carter lost his bid for reelection partly because of the crisis. After 444 days in captivity, the remaining hostages were released on the day of Ronald REAGAN's inauguration.

Iranian languages Major subgroup of the Indo-Iranian branch of the INDO-EUROPEAN LANGUAGE family. Iranian languages are spoken by over 80 million people in SW and S Asia. Modern Iranian languages have been divided into four groups. The SW group includes Modern PERSIAN (Farsi), Dari (in N Afghanistan), Tajiki (in Tajikistan and other Central Asian republics), Luri and Bakhtiari (in SW Iran), and Tat. The NW group includes Kurdish (spoken in KURDISTAN) and Baluchi (in SW Pakistan, SE Iran, and S Afghanistan). The SE group includes Pashto (in Afghanistan and NW Pakistan) and the 10 or so Pamir languages (in E Tajikistan and adjacent parts of Afghanistan and China). The NE group includes Ossetic, spoken by the Ossetes in the central Caucasus Mtns. Nearly all the Modern Iranian languages have been written—if at all—in adaptations of the ARABIC ALPHABET.

Iran–Iraq War (1980–90) War begun by Iraq with Iran, stemming from Iraq's desire for control of an oil-rich Iranian border territory and control of both sides of the SHATT AL-ARAB, and from fear of the effects of the SHIITE Iranian revolution (1979) on Iraq's Shiite minority. Iraq was backed by Saudi Arabia, the U.S., and the Soviet Union, Iran by Syria and Libya. After early gains (1980–82), Iraq lost ground and announced itself ready to negotiate peace, but Iran refused. Stalemated fighting continued until 1988, when Iran agreed to a cease-fire. After Iraq invaded Kuwait in 1990, it agreed to Iran's settlement terms. The war was devastating on both sides. See also Saddam HUSSEIN, Ruhollah KHOMEINI.

Iraq *officially* **Republic of Iraq** Middle Eastern country, northwest of the PERSIAN GULF. Area: 167,975 sq mi (435,052 sq km). Population (2000): 22,676,000. Capital: BAGHDAD. The population consists mainly of an Arab majority and a KURD minority. Language: Arabic (official). Religion: Islam (official); 60% Shiites, 30% Sunni, who dominate the government. Currency: dinar. The country can be

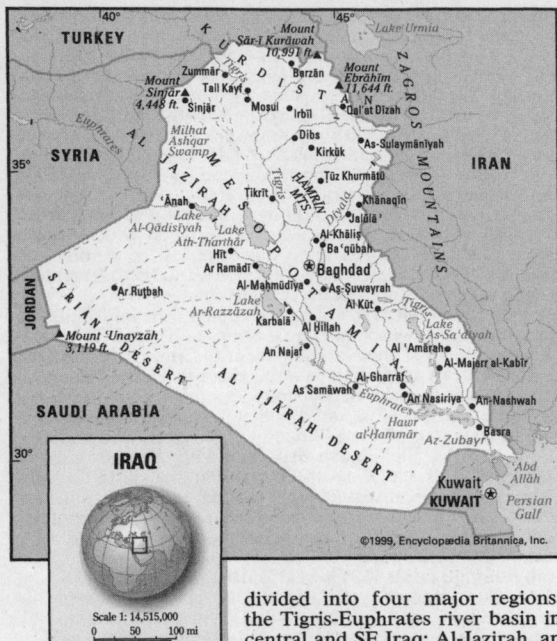

IRAQ

©1999, Encyclopædia Britannica, Inc.

Scale 1: 14,515,000
0   50   100 mi
0   80   160 km

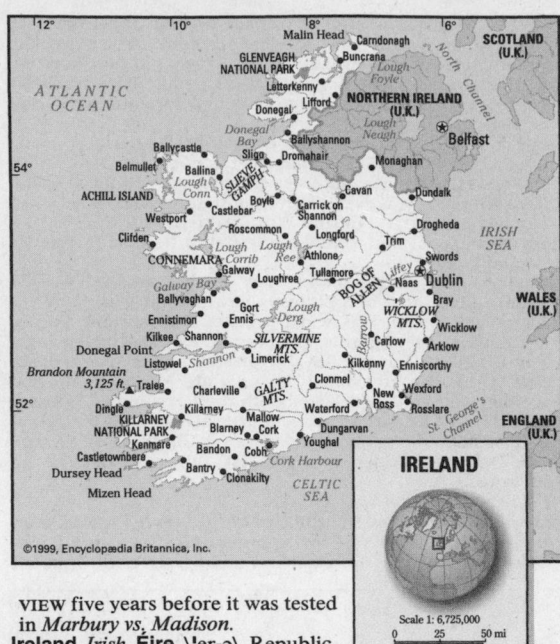

IRELAND

©1999, Encyclopædia Britannica, Inc.

Scale 1: 6,725,000
0   25   50 mi
0   40   80 km

divided into four major regions: the Tigris-Euphrates river basin in central and SE Iraq; Al-Jazirah, an upland region in the north between the TIGRIS and the EUPHRATES rivers; deserts in the west and south, covering about two-fifths of the country; and highlands in the northeast. Iraq has the world's second-largest proven reserves of petroleum; it also has substantial reserves of natural gas. Agriculture employs one-eighth of the labor force. It is a republic with one legislative house; its head of state and government is the president. Called MESOPOTAMIA in classical times, the region gave rise to the world's earliest civilizations, including those of SUMER, AKKAD, and BABYLON. Conquered by ALEXANDER THE GREAT in 330 B.C., the area later became a battleground between Romans and Parthians, then between Sasanians and the Byzantines. Arab Muslims conquered it in the 7th cent. A.D., and ruled until the Mongols took over in 1258. The Ottomans took control in the 16th cent. and ruled until 1917. The British occupied the country during World War I and created the kingdom of Iraq in 1921. The British occupied Iraq again during World War II. A king was restored following the war, but a revolution ended the onarchy in 1958. Following a series of military coups, the socialist BAATH PARTY, led by Saddam HUSSEIN, took control and established totalitarian rule in 1968. The IRAN–IRAQ WAR of the 1980s and the PERSIAN GULF WAR (precipitated by the Iraqi invasion of Kuwait in 1990) brought heavy casualties and disrupted the economy. U.N. trade sanctions led to severe economic hardship. U.N. inspectors of purported factories of biological and chemical weapons were expelled in 1997, leading to threats of invasion by the U.S.

Irbid City (pop., 1994: 208,000), N Jordan. Built on Early Bronze Age settlements, it may have been the biblical city of Beth Arbel and the Arbila of the ancient DECAPOLIS. Modern Irbid is an industrial and agricultural center. The many local springs provide water for irrigation. It is the seat of Yarmuk Univ.

Iredell \ˈīr-ˌdel\, **James** (1751–1799) U.S. (British-born) jurist. He helped draft and revise the laws of the new state of N. Carolina and led the state's Federalists in supporting ratification of the U.S. CONSTITUTION. He served on the U.S. Supreme Court 1790–99, and wrote several notable dissents, including those for *Chisholm vs. Georgia* (1793; affirming the subordination of the states to the federal government) and *Ware vs. Hylton* (1796; upholding the primacy of U.S. treaties over state statutes). His opinion in *Calder vs. Bull* (1798) helped establish the principle of JUDICIAL RE-

VIEW five years before it was tested in *Marbury vs. Madison*.

Ireland *Irish* **Éire** \ˈer-ə\ Republic, occupying the greater part of an island west of England. The republic's only neighbor is Northern IRELAND, which occupies the NE portion of the island. Area: 27,137 sq mi (70,285 sq km). Population (2000): 3,783,000. Capital: DUBLIN. Although it has been invaded and colonized by Celts, Norsemen, Normans, English, and Scots, racial and ethnic distinctions are nonexistent. Languages: Irish, English (both official). Religions: Roman Catholicism (95%), Church of Ireland Episcopalianism, Presbyterianism, Methodism, Judaism. Currency: euro. Ireland's topography consists largely of broad lowlands, drained by rivers that include the SHANNON; its coasts are fringed with mountains. Almost 60% of the population is urban, and agriculture employs one-eighth of the workforce. Mining, manufacturing, construction, public utilities, and tourism are important industries. It is a republic with two legislative houses; its chief of state is the president, and the head of government is the prime minister. Human settlement in Ireland began about 6000 B.C., and Celtic migration dates from around 300 B.C. St. PATRICK is credited with Christianizing the country in the 5th cent. Norse domination began in 795 and ended in 1014, when the Norse were defeated by BRIAN BORU. Gaelic Ireland's independence ended in 1171 when English king HENRY II proclaimed himself overlord of the island. Beginning in the 16th cent., Irish Catholic landowners fled religious persecution by the English and were replaced by English and Scottish Protestant migrants. The United Kingdom of Great Britain and Ireland was established in 1801. The Great Famine of the 1840s led over 2 illion people to emigrate and built momentum for Irish HOME RULE. The EASTER RISING (1916) was followed by civil war (1919–21) between the Catholic majority in S Ireland who favored complete independence and the Protestant majority in the north who preferred continued union with Britain. S Ireland was granted dominion status and became the Irish Free State in 1921, and in 1937 it adopted the name Éire and became a sovereign independent nation. It remained neutral during World War II. Britain recognized the status of Ireland in 1949 but declared that cession of the N six counties (see Northern IRELAND) could not occur without consent of the Parliament of Northern Ireland. The late 20th cent. was dominated by sectarian hostilities between the island's Catholics and Protestants.

Ireland, Northern Division of the United Kingdom of Great Britain and Northern Ireland occupying the NE portion of

the island of Ireland. It is bounded by the republic of Ireland, the Irish Sea, the N. Channel, and the Atlantic Ocean. Northern Ireland is often referred to as the province of Ulster. Area: 5,452 sq mi (14,120 sq km). Population (1998 est.): 1,663,000. Capital: BELFAST. The people are descended from indigenous Irish and those who emigrated from England and Scotland. Language: English (official). Religions: Protestantism (three-fifths) and Roman Catholicism (two-fifths). Currency: pound sterling. Northern Ireland's industries include engineering, shipbuilding, auto manufacturing, textiles, food and beverage processing, and clothing. Agriculture is important, with most farm income derived from livestock. Northern Ireland shares most of its history with the republic of IRELAND, though the 16th–17th cent. immigration of Protestant English and Scots tended to settle in Ulster. In 1801 the Act of Union created the United Kingdom, which united Great Britain and Ireland. In response to mounting Irish sentiment in favor of HOME RULE, the Government of Ireland Act was adopted in 1920, providing for two partially self-governing units in Ireland: the N six counties constituting Northern Ireland, and the S counties now making up the Republic of Ireland. In 1968 civil-rights protests by Roman Catholics sparked violent conflicts with Protestants and led to occupation by British troops in the early 1970s. The IRISH REPUBLICAN ARMY (IRA) mounted a prolonged terrorist campaign in an effort to force the withdrawal of British troops as a prelude to Northern Ireland's unification with Ireland. In 1972 Northern Ireland's constitution and parliament were suspended, bringing it under direct rule by the British. Violence continued for three decades. A 1998 peace agreement provided for extensive home rule in the province, but it was threatened by renewed sectarian strife.

Irgun Zvai Leumi \ir-ʹgün-tsvə-ʹē-lə-ù-ʹmē\ (Hebrew: "National Military Organization") Jewish right-wing underground militant movement that advocated force in the establishment of a Jewish state on both sides of the Jordan River. In 1943 Menachem BEGIN became its leader. It opposed the British and the Arabs; its activities included a 1946 attack on the King David Hotel, leaving 91 dead, and a 1947 raid on an Arab village in which all 254 inhabitants were killed. With Israeli independence it reorganized as the Herut Party. See also LIKUD.

Irian See NEW GUINEA

iridium \i-ʹri-dē-əm\ Chemical ELEMENT, one of the TRANSITION ELEMENTS, chemical symbol Ir, atomic number 77. A very rare, precious, silvery-white, hard, brittle METAL that even resists most ACIDS, it is one of the densest substances known on earth. It probably does not occur uncombined in nature but is found in natural ALLOYS. The pure metal has no significant uses; alloys with platinum are used in jewelry, pen points, surgical pins and pivots, electrical contacts and sparking points, and extrusion dies. The discovery of abnormally high amounts of iridium in rocks dating to between the CRETACEOUS and TERTIARY PERIODS has given rise to a controversial hypothesis that an iridium-containing METEORITE crashing into the earth led to a catastrophic chain of events including extinction of dinosaurs and many other forms of life.

iris family Family Iridaceae, composed of about 1,700 species of mostly perennial herbaceous plants in some 80 genera. It is known for ornamentals such as irises (genus *Iris*), gladioli (see GLADIOLUS), CROCUSES, and freesias. Irises have swordlike, smooth leaves and bear showy flowers in a great variety of colors and sizes on a smooth stem. Most abundant and diverse in Africa, they are found nearly worldwide. The underground stems may be RHIZOMES, BULBS, or corms.

Irish Free State See IRELAND
Irish Home Rule See Irish HOME RULE
Irish language *or* **Irish Gaelic language** CELTIC LANGUAGE of Ireland, written in the LATIN ALPHABET introduced with Christianity in the 5th cent. Irish is conventionally divided into three periods: Old Irish (7th cent.–c.950), Middle Irish (c.950–1200), and Modern Irish (from c.1200). Old and Middle Irish are the vehicles of a rich literature of prose tales and verse. Classical Modern Irish was a literary medium in Ireland and Scottish Gaeldom into modern

times (see SCOTTISH GAELIC LANGUAGE). Literacy in Irish declined under English rule; by 1800 it was all but an unwritten language. The deaths and emigration resulting from the IRISH POTATO FAMINE further reduced the number of Irish-speakers. Irish was revived as a literary language in the late 19th cent., and with Irish independence (1921) it was made official. Hundreds of thousands of Irish citizens and people of Irish descent have some competence in Irish, and its value as a token of cultural identity most likely ensures its survival well into the 21st cent.

Irish Literary Renaissance Flowering of Irish literary talent in the late 19th and early 20th cent., closely allied with a strong political nationalism and a revival of interest in Ireland's Gaelic heritage. Given impetus by the GAELIC REVIVAL, it developed into a vigorous literary force centered on W. B. YEATS; other important figures were Lady Augusta GREGORY, J. M. SYNGE, and Sean O'CASEY. See also ABBEY THEATRE.

Irish Potato Famine (1845–49) Famine that occurred in Ireland when the potato crop failed in successive years. Almost half the Irish population, particularly the rural poor, depended almost entirely on the potato for nourishment. A reliance on only one or two high-yielding varieties made the crop vulnerable to disease, including the late blight fungus, which ruined the crop. The British government provided minimal relief to the starving Irish, limited to loans and soup kitchens. More than a million people died from starvation or famine-related diseases, and perhaps as many as 1.5 million emigrated to N. America and Britain. By 1921 the Irish population was barely half of the 8.4 million it had been before the famine.

Irish Republican Army (IRA) Unofficial semimilitary organization based in the Republic of Ireland. Founded in 1919 to fight for independence from Britain, it used armed force to achieve the same objectives as SINN FÉIN. After the establishment of the Irish Free State (1922), it refused to accept a separate Northern IRELAND. Declared illegal in 1931, it gained popular support in the 1960s when Catholics in Northern Ireland began a civil-rights campaign against discrimination by the Protestant majority. In 1969 the IRA split into the Marxist Official wing, which eschewed violence, and the Provisionals (Provos), Ulster Catholics committed to terror tactics against Ulster Protestants and British military, tactics that included the 1979 assassination of Louis MOUNTBATTEN and the killing of over 3,000 before the 1994 cease-fire.

Irish Sea Arm of the N. Atlantic Ocean that separates Ireland from Great Britain. Connected with the Atlantic by North Channel and St. George's Channel, it is about 130 mi (210 km) long and 150 mi (240 km) wide. The Isle of MAN and ANGLESEY are its two principal islands.

Irish terrier Breed of TERRIER developed in Ireland, one of the oldest terrier breeds. It stands 16–18 in. (42–46 cm) high and weighs 22–26 lbs (10–12 kg), and has a wiry golden-red to reddish brown coat. It is reputedly adaptable, loyal, spirited, and recklessly courageous. It served as a messenger and sentinel in World War I.

Irish wolfhound Tallest of all dog breeds, a keen-sighted HOUND used in Ireland to hunt wolves and other game and noted for its speed and strength. An ancient breed, first mentioned about the 2nd cent. A.D., it is similar in build to the GREYHOUND but far more powerful. The male stands at least 32 in. (81 cm) high. The colors of its rough coat include gray, brindle, red-brown, black, and white. The dog is valued as a gentle, even-tempered companion.

Irkutsk \ir-ʹkütsk\ City (pop., 1997 est.: 591,000), E central Russia. Founded in 1652, it soon became a commercial center for the fur trade and a base on the Russian trade route to China and Mongolia. Its importance grew after the opening of the TRANS-SIBERIAN RAILROAD in 1898. Now an industrial and cultural center, it is the seat of Irkutsk State Univ.

iron Chemical ELEMENT, one of the TRANSITION ELEMENTS, chemical symbol Fe, atomic number 26. Iron is the most used and cheapest METAL, the second most abundant metal and fourth most abundant element in the earth's crust. It occurs rarely as the free metal, occasionally in ALLOYS (especially in meteorites), and in hundreds of minerals and

ores, including HEMATITE and MAGNETITE. The human body contains 4.5 g of iron, mostly in HEMOGLOBIN and its precursors; iron in the diet is essential to health. Iron is ferromagnetic at ordinary temperatures and the only metal that can be tempered (see TEMPERING). Its uses in STEELS of various types, as well as in CAST and WROUGHT IRON, are numerous. Iron in compounds usually has VALENCE 2 (ferrous) or 3 (ferric). Rust is ferric oxide containing water; ferrites, made from an intermediate oxide, are used in computer memories and magnetic tapes. Ferrous and ferric sulfates and chlorides are all of industrial importance.

Iron Age Period of human culture in which IRON largely replaced BRONZE in implements and weapons. The start of the Iron Age varied geographically, beginning in the Middle East and SE Europe about 1200 B.C. but in China not until about 600 B.C. The large-scale production of iron implements brought new patterns of more permanent settlement, but the widespread use of iron for weapons set off a series of large-scale movements and conquests that lasted 2,000 years and changed the face of Europe and Asia. See also BRONZE AGE.

ironclad Warship developed in Europe and the U.S. in the mid-19th cent., characterized by iron armor protecting the hull. In the Crimean War (1853–56) the French and British successfully deployed ironclad barges mounting heavy guns. In 1859 the French completed the first iron warship, the *Gloire*, with iron plates 4.5 in. (11 cm) thick. Britain and the U.S. soon followed. Union forces

Ironclad The *Gloire*, after a painting by A. W. Weedon

launched armored gunboats in the American Civil War, and a flotilla captured Ft. Henry (1862). The first battle between ironclads was the Battle of the *Monitor* and *Merrimack* (1862). See also MONITOR.

Iron Curtain Political, military, and ideological barrier erected by the Soviet Union after World War II to seal off itself and its Eastern European allies from open contact with the West. Winston CHURCHILL employed the term in a speech in Fulton, Mo., in 1946. The rigidity of the Iron Curtain eased slightly between Joseph STALIN's death in 1953 and the construction of the BERLIN WALL in 1961. It largely ceased to exist in 1989–90 with the communists' abandonment of one-party rule in Eastern Europe.

iron pyrite See PYRITE

Irons, Jeremy (b.1948) British actor. He made his London stage debut in *Godspell* (1973) and appeared on Broadway in *The Real Thing* (1984, Tony Award). After his screen debut in *Nijinsky* (1980), he became widely popular in the hit television series *Brideshead Revisited* (1980–81). His later films include *Dead Ringers* (1988), *Reversal of Fortune* (1990, Academy Award), *Waterland* (1992), and *Lolita* (1997).

ironweed Any of about 500 species of perennial plants constituting the genus *Vernonia* (family Asteraceae). Small herbaceous species are found throughout the world. Ironweed species have lance-shaped, toothed leaves that alternate along the stem; clusters of white, purple, or pink flower heads composed only of disk flowers; and a ring of overlapping BRACTS below the flower heads. Some autumn-blooming species are cultivated as border plants.

ironwood Any of numerous trees and shrubs that have exceptionally tough or hard wood useful for timber, fence posts, and tool handles. Most familiar is the eastern, or American, hop hornbeam *(Ostrya virginiana)*, which has bright yellow to orange and scarlet autumn foliage.

irony Language device in which the real intent is concealed or contradicted by the literal meaning of words or a situation. Verbal irony arises from an awareness of contrast between what is and what ought to be, as when expressions of praise are used when blame is meant. Dramatic irony, an incongruity in a theatrical work between what is expected and what occurs, is often created by the audience's awareness of a fate in store for the characters that they themselves do not suspect. See also FIGURE OF SPEECH.

Iroquois \ˈir-ə-ˌkwȯi\ Any member of the IROQUOIS CONFEDERACY or, more broadly, any speaker of Iroquoian languages. Iroquoian-speaking peoples were semisendentary, practiced agriculture, palisaded their villages, and dwelled in LONGHOUSES that lodged many families. Women worked the fields and helped determine the makeup of village councils. Men built houses, hunted, fished, and made war. Warfare was ingrained in Iroquois society, and war captives were often tortured or made permanent slaves. Today the various Iroquois tribes include about 20,000 members.

Iroquois Confederacy *or* **League of the Iroquois** Confederation of five (later six) Indian tribes across upper New York that in the 17th–18th cent. played a strategic role in the struggle between the French and British for supremacy in N. America. The five original nations were the MOHAWK, ONEIDA, Onondaga, Cayuga, and SENECA; the Tuscarora joined in 1722. According to tradition, the idea of the confederacy was originally conceived by HIAWATHA. United mainly by their desire to stand together against invasion, the tribes created a common council composed of 50 sachems (chiefs). A number of tribes were subdued, dispersed, or destroyed by the league. A schism developed as member tribes took opposing sides during the AMERICAN REVOLUTION. The Loyalist Iroquois were defeated in 1779, and the confederacy came to an end.

irrational number Among the REAL NUMBERS, any of those that cannot be represented as quotients of INTEGERS. In decimal form, irrational numbers are represented by nonterminating, nonrepeating decimals. Examples include square roots of prime numbers and such TRANSCENDENTAL NUMBERS as π and e.

Irrawaddy River \ˌir-ä-ˈwä-dē\ River, Myanmar. It flows 1,350 mi (2,170 km) across the center of the country and empties into the Bay of BENGAL. The country's most important commercial waterway, it is formed by the confluence of the Nmai and the Mali rivers, and is later joined by the Chindwin. Its chief port is MANDALAY.

irrigation Artificial supply of water to land, to maintain or increase yields of food crops. Irrigation can compensate for the naturally variable rate and volume of rain. Water is pumped from natural ponds, lakes, streams, and wells; or alternatively, through canals that flow from huge constructed reservoirs. Today portable irrigation systems of lightweight aluminum pipe are in wide use. Drip irrigation, a newer method, uses narrow tubing to supply water directly to the base of each plant. Agricultural irrigation, water towers, and machines invented to lift and distribute water are ancient innovations. Early Egyptians were irrigating with Nile River water by 5000 B.C., and such other ancient civilizations as Babylon and China seem to have developed largely as a result of irrigation-based agriculture.

IRS See INTERNAL REVENUE SERVICE

Irving City (pop., 2000: 191,000), NE Texas. Established in 1903, the city developed into an industrial hub during the 1950s. A suburb of DALLAS, it is the site of the Univ. of Dallas and of Texas Stadium, home of the Dallas Cowboys football team.

Irving, John (Winslow) (b.1942) U.S. novelist. Born in Exeter, N.H., he won fame with *The World According to Garp* (1978; film, 1982), a best-seller notable, like his other works, for its engaging story line, colorful characterizations, macabre humor, and examination of contemporary issues. Later novels include *The Hotel New Hampshire* (1981; film, 1984), *The Cider House Rules* (1985; film, 1999), and *A Widow for One Year* (1999).

Irving, Washington (1783–1859) U.S. author, called the "first American man of letters." Born in New York City, he became a leader of the group that published *Salmagundi* (1807–8), a periodical containing whimsical essays and poems. His best-known stories, "The Legend of Sleepy Hollow" and "Rip van Winkle," are contained in *The Sketch Book* (1819–20), which was followed by *Bracebridge Hall* (1822). He held diplomatic positions in Madrid, where his writings reflected his interest in Spain's past.

Isaac Second of the patriarchs of Israel, the only son of ABRAHAM and SARAH, husband of Rebecca, and father of Esau and JACOB. His story is told in the Book of GENESIS. As a test of Abraham's faith and obedience, God commanded him to sacrifice Isaac; at the last minute, Abraham was told to sacrifice a ram instead. God is called the God of Abraham, Isaac, and Jacob, because with them God's relationship of promise and purpose was fixed for all those who descended from them.

Isaac \ē-'zäk\, **Heinrich** (c.1450–1517) Flemish composer. He spent much of his career in Italy, especially Florence, but was known as a leading representative of the Netherlandish style. As court composer to Emperor MAXIMILIAN I (from 1497), he was allowed to travel. His historical importance in Germany is as the main disseminator of the progressive Northern style there. His works, notable for their beauty and craft, include over 100 masses, dozens of motets, and secular songs.

Isabela Island Island, GALÁPAGOS ISLANDS. The largest in the group, it has an area of 1,650 sq mi (4,274 sq km). Its N tip is crossed by the equator. It has unique species of flightless cormorants and penguins, and large numbers of iguanas and flamingos.

Isabella I *known as* **Isabella the Catholic** *Spanish* Isabel la Católica (1451–1504) Queen of Castile (1474–1504) and of Aragon (1479–1504). Daughter of John II of Castile and León, she married the future FERDINAND V in 1469. In 1479 the kingdoms of Castile and Aragon came together in the persons of their rulers. In a long campaign (1482–92), Isabella and Ferdinand succeeded in conquering Granada, the last Muslim stronghold in Spain. In 1492 Isabella approved support of Christopher COLUMBUS's journey to the New World. That same year she was involved in the expulsion of the Jews under the INQUISITION.

Isabella I Portrait by an unknown artist

Isabella II *Spanish* **Isabel** \ē-sä-'bel\ (1830–1904) Queen of Spain (1833–68). She was the daughter of FERDINAND VII, and the issue of her succession precipitated the First Carlist War (see CARLISM). Liberal opposition to the regime's authoritarianism, scandalous reports about her private life, and her arbitrary political interference led to the Revolution of 1868, which drove her into exile.

Isabella Farnese See ELIZABETH FARNESE

Isaiah \ī-'zā-ə\ (fl.8th cent. B.C.) PROPHET of ancient Israel after whom the biblical Book of Isaiah is named, although Isaiah is believed to have written only some of its chapters. Isaiah's call to prophesy came around 742 B.C. He denounced economic and social injustice among the Israelites and urged them to obey the Law or risk cancellation of God's COVENANT. He correctly predicted the destruction of Samaria, or N Israel, in 722 B.C., and he declared the Assyrians to be the instrument of God's wrath. The Christian Gospels lean more heavily on Isaiah than on any other prophet, and his "swords-into-plowshares" passage has universal appeal.

ischemic heart disease See CORONARY HEART DISEASE

ISDN *in full* Integrated Services Digital Network. Digital telecommunications network that operates over standard copper telephone wires or other media. ISDN connections can provide digital voice telephone, FAX, E-MAIL, digital video, and access to the INTERNET. Speeds up to about 128 kilobits per second (kbps) are possible, making ISDN faster than an ordinary dial-up connection (at about 56 kbps), but much slower than cable modem or DSL connections.

Isfahan See ESFAHAN

Isherwood, Christopher (William Bradshaw-) (1904–1986) British-U.S. writer. He became close friends with W. H. AUDEN, with whom he collaborated on three verse dramas. He lived in Berlin 1929–33; his two novels about this period, later published together as *The Berlin Stories* (1946), inspired the play *I Am a Camera* (1951; film, 1955) and the musical *Cabaret* (1966; film, 1972). A pacifist, he moved to S California at the beginning of World War II, where he

wrote screenplays. A follower of Swami Prabhavananda, he wrote and translated works on Indian VEDANTA.

Ishtar In Mesopotamian religion, the goddess of war and sexual love. She was called ASTARTE by W Semitic peoples. In early Sumeria she was the goddess of the storehouse as well as of rain and thunderstorms. She evolved into a deity of contradictory qualities, of joy and sorrow, fair play and enmity. In Akkadia she was the patroness of prostitutes and alehouses. Her popularity became universal in the ancient Middle East, and she was called Queen of the Universe.

Isidore of Seville, St. (c.560–636) Spanish prelate and scholar, last of the Western Fathers of the Church. He became archbishop of Seville around 600 and presided over several councils that shaped church policy, including the fourth Council of Toledo (633). His best-known work was an encyclopedia called *Etymologies;* he also wrote biographies and treatises on natural science, cosmology, and history. He was declared a Doctor of the Church in 1722.

isinglass See MUSCOVITE

Isis \'ī-səs\ One of the major goddesses of ancient Egypt, the wife of OSIRIS. When Osiris was killed by SETH, she gathered up the pieces of his body and brought him back to life. She hid their son HORUS from Seth until Horus could avenge his father. She was invoked to heal the sick or protect the dead. By Greco-Roman times she was dominant among Egyptian goddesses, and her cult reached much of the Roman world as a MYSTERY RELIGION.

ISKCON See HARE KRISHNA MOVEMENT

Isla de Pascua See EASTER ISLAND

Islam Major world religion founded by MUHAMMAD in Arabia in the early 7th cent. A.D. The word *islam* means "submission" — specifically, submission to the will of the one God, called ALLAH in Arabic. Islam is strictly monotheistic, and its adherents (Muslims) regard the Prophet Muhammad as the last and most perfect of God's messengers, who include ADAM, ABRAHAM, MOSES, JESUS, and others. Its sacred scripture is the QURAN, which contains God's revelations to

Isis with Horus, bronze figurine, Late Period

HIJ

Muhammad. Muhammad's sayings and deeds recounted in the SUNNA are also an important source of belief and practice. Basic religious obligations are summed up in the Five Pillars of ISLAM. Islamic law, or SHARIA, embraces the total way of life commanded by God. Observant Muslims pray five times a day and worship together on Fridays at the MOSQUE. Every believer must make a pilgrimage to MECCA at least once in a lifetime, barring poverty or physical incapacity. The month of RAMADAN is set aside for fasting. Alcohol and pork are always forbidden, as are gambling, usury, fraud, slander, and the making of images. In addition to celebrating the beginning and end of Ramadan, Muslims celebrate Muhammad's birthday and his ascension into heaven. Muslims are enjoined to defend Islam against unbelievers through JIHAD. Divisions occurred early in Islam, brought about by disputes over the succession to the caliphate (see CALIPH). About 90% of Muslims belong to the SUNNI branch. The SHIITES broke away in the 7th cent. and later gave rise to other sects, including the ISMAILIS. SUFISM is an important mystical movement. In the late 20th cent., fundamentalist movements (see Islamic FUNDAMENTALISM) threatened or toppled a number of secular Middle

Eastern governments; some have been associated with terrorism.

Islam, Nation of *or* **Black Muslims** African-American religious movement that mingles elements of ISLAM and black nationalism. It was founded in 1931 by Wallace D. Fard (1877?–1934?) in Detroit. After Fard's mysterious disappearance in 1934, it was taken over by his assistant Elijah MUHAMMAD, who founded a second temple in Chicago. He asserted the superiority of Africans over whites and urged American blacks to renounce Christianity as a tool of the oppressors. The sect grew quickly after World War II and achieved national prominence through the work of MALCOLM X, who later split off and formed a separate organization before being assassinated in 1965. In the 1970s Elijah was succeeded by his son, Wallace D. Muhammad (b.1933), who renamed and eventually dissolved the organization (1985), urging its members to become orthodox Muslims. A splinter group headed by Louis FARRAKHAN retains the movement's original name and principles.

Islam, Pillars of Five duties imposed on every Muslim. They are: profession of faith in one God and in MUHAMMAD as his Prophet, prayer five times a day, the giving of alms to the poor, fasting during the month of RAMADAN, and the HAJJ.

Islamabad \is-'lä-mə-ˌbäd\ Capital (pop., 1998: 525,000) of Pakistan, located northeast of RAWALPINDI. Established in 1959 to replace KARACHI as the capital, the city itself is small, but the planned capital area is a 350-sq-mi (910-sq-km) expanse of natural terraces and meadows. It is the seat of the Univ. of Islamabad (founded 1965).

Islamic architecture Building traditions of the Muslim Middle East and elsewhere. It finds its highest expression in religious buildings such as the MOSQUE and MADRASAH. Early Islamic religious architecture, exemplified by Jerusalem's DOME OF THE ROCK (A.D. 691) and the Great Mosque (705) in Damascus, drew on Christian architectural features such as domes, columnar arches, and mosaics, but also included large courts for congregational prayer. Religious architecture came into its own with the creation in Iraq and Egypt of the hypostyle mosque, whose roof rests on rows of columns. In Iran a mosque plan consisting of four *eyvans* (vaulted halls) opening onto a central court, incorporating domes and decorated squinches across the corners of the rooms, was used. Persian architectural features spread to India, as seen in the TAJ MAHAL and Mughal palaces. Ottoman architecture, derived from Islamic and Byzantine traditions, is exemplified by mosques with a great central dome and slender minarets. One of the greatest examples of secular Islamic architecture is the ALHAMBRA.

Islamic law See SHARIA

Islamic Salvation Front (FIS) Algerian religious-political group that won most of the seats in the National Assembly in the first round of balloting in 1991. The government canceled the second round and arrested many of the group's leaders. Since then, FIS and more extreme Islamist groups have waged civil war, in which both sides have committed atrocities.

island Any land area smaller than a continent that is entirely surrounded by water. A group of islands is called an archipelago. Continental islands are unsubmerged parts of a continental mass; Greenland, the world's largest island, is an example. Oceanic islands are produced by volcanic activity, by lava accumulating to enormous thickness until it protrudes above the ocean surface; the piles of lava that form Hawaii rise 32,000 ft (9,700 m) above the ocean floor.

island arc Long, curved chain of oceanic ISLANDS associated with intense volcanic and seismic activity and mountain-building processes. Examples include the Aleutian-Alaska Arc and the Kuril-Kamchatka Arc. Most consist of two parallel rows of islands; the inner row is a string of volcanoes, and the outer row is made up of nonvolcanic islands. An island arc typically has a landmass or a partially enclosed, unusually shallow sea on its concave side. Along the convex side there usually exists a long, narrow DEEP-SEA TRENCH.

Islas Baleares See BALEARIC ISLANDS

Isle of Wight See Isle of WIGHT

Isle Royale National Park Island national park located in NW Lake SUPERIOR, NW Michigan. Established in 1931, it has an area of 571,790 acres (231,575 hectares) and includes Isle Royale, measuring 45 mi (72 km) long and 9 mi (14 km) across. Its forested wilderness, with streams and inland lakes, contains more than 200 species of birds. Travel is possible only on foot or by canoe.

islets of Langerhans See islets of LANGERHANS

Ismail I \is-'mä-ˌel\ (1487–1524) Shah of Iran (1501–24) and founder of the SAFAVID DYNASTY. He became head of a Shiite military force at 14. He captured Tabriz in 1501 and proclaimed himself shah of Iran, bringing the whole country and portions of modern-day Iraq under his control. In 1510 his troops defeated the Uzbek Sunnis. He proclaimed Shia the established religion, which provoked the Ottoman Turks to invade in 1514. Ismail lost the battle, but mutiny among the Ottoman troops forced their withdrawal. The conflict between the Safavids and their Sunni neighbors continued for over a century.

Ismaili \ˌis-mä-'ē-lē\ Member of a sect of the SHIITE branch of Islam. It came into existence after the death of the sixth IMAM in 765. His son Ismail was accepted as successor only by a minority, who became known as Ismailis. Their doctrine made a distinction between ordinary Muslim believers and the elect, who shared a secret wisdom. Subsects arose over the issue of the descent of the caliph. The Fatimid subsect conquered Egypt in 969 and established the FATIMID DYNASTY. A subgroup of the Fatimids was the Nizaris, who were known as ASSASSINS. The major Nizari line survives under the leadership of the AGA KHAN. The DRUZE broke away early in the 11th cent. and formed a closed society of their own.

Ismail Pasha \is-'mä-ˌel-pä-'shä\ (1830–1895) Viceroy of Egypt (1863–79). After an education and diplomatic missions in Europe, he was appointed viceroy and became involved with work on the SUEZ CANAL (1859–69). His plan to unify the Nile valley through creation of a new S Egyptian province failed but helped promote nationalist feeling. The sultan dismissed him after the national debt increased by a factor of more than 10.

Ismay \'iz-mä\, **Hastings Lionel** *later* Baron Ismay (of Wormington) (1887–1965) British soldier. As Winston CHURCHILL's chief of staff (1940–46) and closest military adviser, he participated in most major policy decisions of the Allied powers, particularly in the decision to make Germany the Allies' first-priority target and in planning for the Normandy invasion. After the war he served as secretary-general of NATO 1952–57.

ISO See INTERNATIONAL ORGANIZATION FOR STANDARDIZATION

Isocrates \ī-'sä-krə-ˌtēz\ (436–338 B.C.) Athenian author, rhetorician, and teacher. His school, unlike PLATO's more philosophical Academy, provided an education for the practical needs of society; it was given over almost entirely to RHETORIC. He promoted Greek political unity and cultural superiority and advocated a unified Greek attack on Persia. When Greece lost its independence after the Battle of Chaeronea, Isocrates, in despair, starved himself to death.

isolationism National policy of avoiding political or economic entanglements with other countries. Though isolationism is a recurrent force in American history, the term is most often applied to the sentiment that gripped the U.S. in the 1930s. The failure of Pres. Woodrow WILSON's internationalism, liberal opposition to warfare, and the rigors of the GREAT DEPRESSION were among the reasons for Americans' reluctance to concern themselves with the growth of FASCISM abroad. Congressional acts (1934, 1935) effectively prevented economic or military aid to any country involved in the European disputes that were to escalate into World War II. U.S. isolationism reinforced British APPEASEMENT and French paralysis in response to Nazi Germany's aggression, but did not ultimately prevent the U.S. from mobilizing the Western Hemisphere to fight the Depression and resist German encroachments. See also NEUTRALITY.

Isole Eolie See LIPARI ISLANDS

isomer \'ī-sə-mər\ One of two or more substances with identical molecular formulas but different CONFIGURATIONS, differing only in the arrangement of their component atoms. It usually refers to stereoisomers, of which there are two types. Optical isomers, or enantiomers (see OPTICAL ACTIVITY), occur in mirror-image pairs. Geometric isomers are often the result of rigidity in the molecular structure; in organic compounds, this is usually due to a double bond (see BONDING) or a ring structure. In the case of a double bond between two carbon atoms, if each has two other groups bonded to it and all are rigidly in the same plane, the corresponding groups can be on the same side *(cis)* of the C=C bond or across the C=C bond *(trans)* from each other. An analogous distinction can be made for ring structures that are all in a plane. See also ISOMERISM.

isomerism \ī-ˈsä-mə-ˌri-zəm\ Existence of sets of two or more substances with identical molecular formulas (see CHEMICAL FORMULA) but different CONFIGURATIONS and hence different properties. J. J. BERZELIUS first recognized and named it (1830). In constitutional (structural) isomerism, the atoms present are the same, but the BONDING differs. For example, C_2H_6O is the molecular formula for both ETHANOL (CH_3CH_2OH) and methyl ETHER (CH_3OCH_3). In the second type, stereoisomerism, substances with the same atoms are bonded in the same ways but different in their three-dimensional configurations. See also ISOMER.

isoprenoid \ˌī-sə-ˈprē-ˌnȯid\ *or* **terpene** Class of organic compounds made up of two or more isoprene units. Isoprene is a five-carbon HYDROCARBON with a branched-chain structure and two double bonds (see BONDING). Isoprenoids play a wide variety of roles in plant and animal physiological processes. ESSENTIAL OILS with flavors and fragrances such as menthol (from peppermint oil) and limonene (from lemon and orange oils), as well as pinene (from TURPENTINE) and CAMPHOR, have two isoprene units. Examples with more units include phytol, a precursor of CHLOROPHYLL; squalene, a precursor of STEROIDS; lycopene, the red pigment in tomatoes; and CAROTENE, the pigment in carrots and a precursor of VITAMIN A. Natural RUBBER is a polyisoprene with many thousands of isoprene units.

isostasy \ī-ˈsäs-tə-sē\ Theory describing the mass balance in the earth's CRUST, which treats all large portions of the crust as though they were floating on a denser underlying layer, about 70 mi (110 km) below the surface. In this theory, high mountains must be regions where the crust is very thick, with deep roots extending into the MANTLE. This is analogous to an iceberg, in which the greater part is under water.

isotope \ˈī-sə-ˌtōp\ One of two or more species of ATOMS of a chemical ELEMENT having nuclei with the same number of PROTONS but different numbers of NEUTRONS. They have the same ATOMIC NUMBER and hence nearly identical chemical behavior but different atomic MASSES. Most elements found in nature are mixtures of several isotopes. In most cases, only stable isotopes of elements are found in nature. The radioactive forms break down spontaneously (see RADIOACTIVITY). Isotopes of all elements heavier than bismuth are radioactive.

Isozaki \ˌē-sō-ˈzä-kē\, **Arata** (b.1931) Japanese avant-garde architect. His first notable building is the Oita Prefectural Library (1966). Later works, which often synthesize Eastern and Western elements, use bold geometric forms and frequently make historical allusions. Among his innovative structures are the Los Angeles Museum of Contemporary Art (1986) and Art Tower in Mito, Japan (1990).

ISP See INTERNET SERVICE PROVIDER

Israel *officially* **State of Israel** Republic, at the E end of the Mediterranean Sea. Area: 7,992 sq mi (20,700 sq km). Population (2000): 6,107,000 (includes pop. of GOLAN HEIGHTS and E. Jerusalem; excludes Israelis in WEST BANK Jewish localities and GAZA STRIP). Capital: JERUSALEM. Jews constitute more than four-fifths of the population, and Arabs about one-sixth. Languages: Hebrew, Arabic (both official). Religions: Judaism, Islam (mainly Shiite), Christianity. Currency: new shekel. Israel can be divided into four major regions: the Mediterranean coastal plain in the west; a hill region extending from the N border into central Israel; a RIFT VALLEY, containing the DEAD SEA, in the east; and the arid NEGEV, occupying nearly the entire S half of the country.

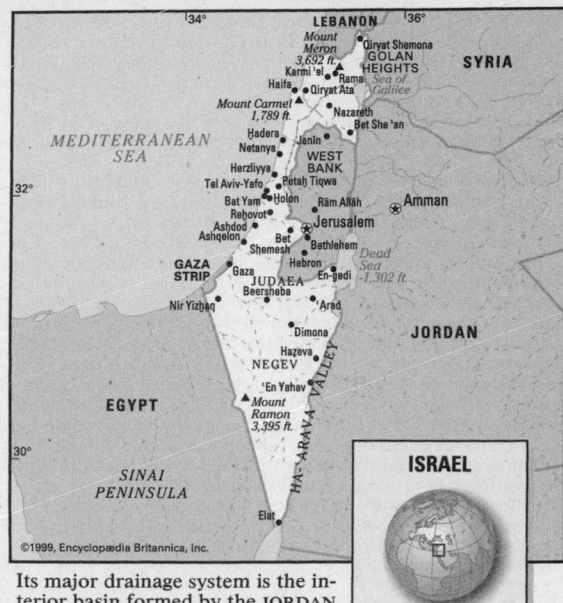

©1999, Encyclopædia Britannica, Inc.

ISRAEL

Scale 1: 6,301,000
0   25   50 mi
0   40   80 km

Its major drainage system is the interior basin formed by the JORDAN RIVER; the Sea of GALILEE provides water to almost half of the country's agricultural land. It has a mixed economy based largely on services and manufacturing; exports include machinery and electronics, diamonds, chemicals, citrus fruits and vegetables, and textiles. Its population is nine-tenths urban and is concentrated in the Mediterranean coastal plain. It is a republic with one legislative house; its chief of state is the president, and the head of government is the prime minister. The record of human habitation in Israel (Palestine) is at least 100,000 years old (see PALESTINE for history). Efforts by Jews to establish a national state there began in the late 19th cent. Britain supported ZIONISM, and in 1923 assumed political responsibility for what was Palestine. Migration of Jews there during NAZI persecution led to deteriorating relations with Arabs. In 1947 the U.N. voted to partition the region into separate Jewish and Arab states, a decision opposed by neighboring Arab countries. The State of Israel was proclaimed in 1948, and Egypt, Transjordan, Syria, Lebanon, and Iraq immediately declared war on it. Israel won this war (see ARAB–ISRAELI WARS) as well as the 1967 SIX-DAY WAR, in which it claimed the W. BANK from Jordan and the GAZA STRIP from Egypt. Another, indecisive war with its Arab neighbors followed in 1973, but the CAMP DAVID ACCORDS led to the signing of a peace treaty between Israel and Egypt in 1979. Israel invaded Lebanon to quell the PALESTINE LIBERATION ORGANIZATION (PLO) in 1982, and in the late 1980s a Palestinian resistance movement (see INTIFADA) arose in the occupied territories. Peace negotiations began in 1992. Israel and the PLO agreed in 1993 upon a five-year extension of self-government to the Palestinians of the W. Bank and the Gaza Strip. Israel signed a full peace treaty with Jordan in 1994. Israeli soldiers and Lebanon's HIZBULLAH forces clashed in 1997. A new uprising in 2000 led to a wave of HAMAS-sponsored suicide bombings in response to hardening government policies.

Israel, tribes of In the Bible, the 12 tribes of the ancient Hebrew people, 10 of which were named for sons of JACOB (Reuben, Simeon, Judah, Issachar, Zebulun, Gad, Asher, Dan, Naphtali, and Benjamin) and two of which were named for sons of Jacob's son JOSEPH (Ephraim and Manasseh). The tribes of Judah and Benjamin formed a S kingdom called JUDAH, while the 10 N tribes formed the kingdom of Israel. After being conquered by Assyria in 721 B.C., the N tribes vanished from history and became known as the 10 lost tribes of Israel. Only Judah and Benjamin remained; they became the source of modern JUDAISM.

Israelite In early Jewish history, a member of the 12 tribes of ISRAEL. After the establishment (930 B.C.) of two Jewish kingdoms (Israel and Judah) in Palestine, only the ten N tribes constituting the kingdom of Israel were known as Israelites. After Israel was conquered by the Assyrians (721 B.C.), the term Israelite came to refer to those who were still distinctively Jewish—the descendants of the kingdom of Judah.

Istanbul *formerly* **Constantinople** *ancient* **Byzantium** City and seaport (pop., 1996: 8,023,000), Turkey. Situated on a peninsula at the entrance to the BLACK SEA, Turkey's largest city lies on either side of the BOSPORUS, in both Europe and Asia. Byzantium was founded as a Greek colony in the 8th cent. B.C. It passed to the Persian empire in 512 B.C. and then to ALEXANDER THE GREAT. CONSTANTINE I made it the seat of the Roman empire in 330, later naming it Constantinople. It remained the capital of the BYZANTINE EMPIRE after the fall of Rome in the late 5th cent. Frequently besieged by Persians, Arabs, Bulgars, and Russians, it was captured by the Fourth CRUSADE (1203) but returned to Byzantine rule in 1261. In 1453 it was made the capital of the OTTOMAN EMPIRE and dubbed Istanbul. The Turkish capital was moved to ANKARA in 1923, and Constantinople was officially renamed Istanbul in 1930. Among its architectural treasures are the HAGIA SOPHIA, the Mosque of Suleyman (1550–57), and the Blue Mosque. The Univ. of Istanbul (founded 1453) is Turkey's oldest university.

Italian Communist Party See DEMOCRATIC PARTY OF THE LEFT

Italian language ROMANCE LANGUAGE spoken in Italy (including Sicily and Sardinia), Switzerland, and parts of France (including Corsica). Its 66 million speakers worldwide include many immigrants and their descendants in the Americas. Written Italian dates from the 10th cent. The standard literary form is based on the dialect of Florence, but many Italians do not speak it, instead using regional dialects. Italian has a sound system similar to that of Latin and Spanish and a grammar with noun-adjective agreement, masculine and feminine genders, and an elaborate system of perfect and progressive verb tenses. See also ITALIC LANGUAGES.

Italian Popular Party (PPI) *formerly (1943–93)* **Christian Democratic Party** Centrist political party. United by Roman Catholicism and anticommunism, its factions advocate programs ranging from social reform to the defense of free enterprise. The original party was founded in 1919 and quickly won popularity, but in 1926 the Fascists banned all political parties. In 1943 former party leaders, along with Catholic organizations, founded the Christian Democratic Party. It largely dominated Italian politics until the mid-1990s, when some of its leading members were implicated in financial scandals and political corruption. In 1993 the struggling party reverted to its original name, but in 1994 it fell from power and became a minor party. See also CHRISTIAN DEMOCRACY.

Italian Somaliland Former Italian colony, E Africa. It extended south from Cape Asir to the boundary of Kenya, occupying 178,218 sq mi (461,585 sq km). Italy obtained control of it in 1889 and it became a state in Italian E. Africa in 1936. Britain invaded in 1941 and retained control until it became a U.N. trust territory in 1950. In 1960 it was united with British Somaliland to form Somalia.

Italian Wars (1494–1559) Series of violent wars for control of Italy. Largely fought by France and Spain, but involving much of Europe, they resulted in Italy's domination by the Spanish Habsburgs and shifted power from Italy to NW Europe and its Atlantic world. The wars began with the invasion of Italy by the French king CHARLES VIII in 1494. He took Naples, but an alliance between MAXIMILIAN I, Spain, and the pope drove him out of Italy. In 1499 LOUIS XII invaded Italy and took Milan, Genoa, and Naples, but was driven out of Naples in 1503 by Spain under FERDINAND V. In 1516 a peace was concluded by which France held onto Milan and Spain kept Naples. Fighting began in 1521 between Emperor CHARLES V and FRANCIS I. Francis was captured and forced to sign the Treaty of Madrid (1526), renouncing all claims in Italy, but once freed he repudiated the treaty and formed a new alliance with HENRY VIII of

England, Pope CLEMENT VII, Venice, and Florence. Charles sacked Rome in 1527 and forced the pope to come to terms, and Francis gave up all claims to Italy in 1529. By the Treaty of Cateau-Cambrésis (1559), the wars finally ended.

Italic languages \i-'ta-lik\ INDO-EUROPEAN LANGUAGES spoken in the Apennine Peninsula (Italy) during the 1st millennium B.C., after which only LATIN survived. These languages may represent three independent members of the Indo-European family: Latin, Osco-Umbrian, and Venetic. Latin, the language of Latium and Rome, began to emerge as the predominant language as early as the 3rd cent. B.C. By A.D. 100 it had replaced all dialects (except Greek) between Sicily and the Alps. Until then, Oscan dialects were most widely spoken. Venetic was spoken in the region of Venice. These languages were written in various alphabets, including the GREEK and LATIN alphabets and modified versions of the Etruscan.

Italic War See SOCIAL WAR

Italo–Turkish War (1911–12) War undertaken by Italy to gain colonies in N. Africa by conquering the Turkish provinces of Tripolitana and Cyrenaica (modern Libya). The Italian victory unleashed the nationalist-expansionist sentiment that guided Italy's policy in the following decades.

Italy *officially* **Italian Republic** *Italian* **Italia** Country, S Europe. It comprises the boot-shaped peninsula extending into the Mediterranean Sea as well as SICILY, SARDINIA, and a

ITALY

Scale 1: 18,825,000

©1999, Encyclopædia Britannica, Inc.

number of smaller islands. Area: 116,324 sq mi (301,277 sq km). Population (2000): 57,723,000. Capital: ROME. Language: Italian (official). Religion: Roman Catholicism. Currency: euro. More than three-quarters of Italy is mountainous or highland country. The ALPS stretch from east to west along Italy's N boundary, and the APENNINES stretch southward the length of the peninsula. Most of the country's lowlands lie in the valley of its major river, the PO. Three tectonic plates converge in S Italy and Sicily, creating intense geologic activity; S Italy's four active volcanoes include Mt. VESUVIUS and Mt. ETNA. The economy is based largely on services and manufacturing; exports include machinery and transport equipment, chemicals, textiles, clothing and shoes, and food products (olive oil, wine, fruit, and tomatoes). It is a republic with two legislative houses; the chief of state is the president and the head of government, the prime minister. Italy has been inhabited since Paleolithic times. The ETRUSCAN civilization arose in the 9th cent. B.C. and was overthrown by the Romans in the 4th–3rd cent. B.C. (see ROMAN RE-

PUBLIC AND EMPIRE). Barbarian invasions of the 4th–5th cent. A.D. destroyed the W Roman empire. Italy's political fragmentation lasted for centuries but did not diminish its impact on European culture, notably during the RENAISSANCE. In 15th–18th cent., Italian lands were ruled by France, the HOLY ROMAN EMPIRE, Spain, and Austria. When Napoleonic rule ended in 1815, Italy was again a grouping of independent states. The RISORGIMENTO successfully united most of Italy, including Sicily and Sardinia, by 1861, and the unification of peninsular Italy was completed by 1870. Italy joined the Allies during WORLD WAR I, but in the 1920s social unrest brought Benito MUSSOLINI's Fascist movement to power, and Italy formed an alliance with Nazi Germany in WORLD WAR II. Defeated by the Allies in 1943, Italy proclaimed itself a republic in 1946. It completed the process of setting up regional legislatures with limited autonomy in 1970. Since World War II it has had a rapid change of governments but has remained socially stable. It has worked with other European countries to establish the EUROPEAN UNION.

Itasca \ī-'tas-kə\, **Lake** Lake, NW Minnesota. Occupying an area of 1.8 sq mi (4.7 sq km), it is located 1,475 ft (450 m) above sea level. The theory of Henry Rowe Schoolcraft (1793–1864) that Lake Itasca is the source of the MISSISSIPPI RIVER has been widely accepted. He is generally credited with originating the name Itasca.

Ito Hirobumi \'ē-tō-hē-'rō-bù-mē\ (1841–1909) Japanese statesman and writer of the MEIJI CONSTITUTION. He played a minor role in the MEIJI RESTORATION, then served as home minister (1878–82). He persuaded the government to adopt a constitution, which he drafted; in 1889 the emperor promulgated the resultant document. Later, as prime minister, Ito negotiated an end to extraterritoriality with Britain; other Western nations soon followed suit. Frustrated with political parties' ability to impede passage of government programs in the Diet, in 1900 Ito founded his own party, the Rikken Seiyukai. In 1906 Ito became resident general in Korea, where he was assassinated in 1909 by a Korean nationalist.

ITT See INTERNATIONAL TELEPHONE AND TELEGRAPH CORP.

Iturbide \ē-tür-'bē-thä\, **Agustín de** or **Agustín I** (1783–1824) Leader and hero of the conservative factions in the Mexican independence movement. An army officer when the independence movement emerged in 1810, he fought for the royalists, but in 1820, reacting to a liberal coup in Spain, the conservatives reversed themselves and advocated immediate independence. Iturbide joined the insurgents and won Mexico's independence in 1821. In 1822 he crowned himself emperor, but his arbitrary and extravagant ways cost him support. His abdication in 1823 did not save him from execution.

Ivan III \'ī-vən\ known as **Ivan the Great** (1440–1505) Grand prince of Moscow (1462–1505). Determined to enlarge the territory he inherited, Ivan led successful military campaigns against the TATARS, subdued Novgorod (1478), and had gained control of most of Great Russia by 1485. He also renounced Moscow's subjection to the khan of the GOLDEN HORDE (1480) and won a final victory over the khan's sons in 1502. Stripping the BOYARS of much of their authority, he laid the administrative foundations of a centralized Russian state.

Ivan IV Russian Ivan Vasilyevich known as **Ivan the Terrible** (1530–1584) Grand prince of Moscow (1533–84) and first CZAR of Russia (1547–84). Crowned czar in 1547 after a long regency (1533–46), he embarked on wide-ranging reforms, including a centralized administration, church councils that systematized the church's affairs, and the first national assembly (1549). He also instituted reforms to limit the powers of the BOYARS. After conquering KAZAN (1552) and ASTRAKHAN (1556), he engaged in an unsuccessful

Ivan IV Icon, late 16th cent.

war to control LIVONIA, fighting against Sweden and Poland (1558–83). After the suspected treason of several Russian boyars, Ivan withdrew into his own entourage and left Russia's management to others. At the same time, he instituted a reign of terror, executing thousands of boyars and ravaging the city of Novgorod. During the 1570s he married five wives in nine years, and in a fit of rage, he murdered his son and heir, Ivan, in 1581.

Ives, Charles E(dward) (1874–1954) U.S. composer. Born in Danbury, Conn., Ives got his early training from his father, George, a highly imaginative Army bandmaster. At Yale Univ. he studied with Horatio Parker (1863–1919) and composed his first symphony. Under the influence of Transcendentalism, he decided to forgo a music career, and in 1907 he founded a successful insurance firm. With music as a "sideline," he felt free to pursue his unusual interests. A heart attack in 1918 curtailed all activities, and he stopped composing around 1926. His dissonant, atmospheric, and nostalgic music runs the gamut from sentimental or quirkily humorous songs to exciting tone poems (The Fourth of July, 1913) and weighty meditations (Concord Sonata, 1915). He apparently made many remarkable tonal innovations, though he may have antedated some works to give a misleading impression. His music was rediscovered late in his life; the third of his four symphonies won a Pulitzer Prize in 1947.

IVF See IN VITRO FERTILIZATION

ivory Hard white substance, a variety of dentin, that makes up the tusks of such animals as ELEPHANTS, WALRUSES, and preserved MAMMOTHS. It is prized for its beauty, durability, and suitability for carving. Most ivory used commercially once came from Africa; sales of ivory declined in the 20th cent. as the populations of African elephants shrank, and its export and import are now generally banned. The once-thriving markets of Europe have shifted to SE Asia, where skilled artisans, often trading illegally, carve ivory into figurines and other objects.

Ivory, James (Francis) (b.1928) U.S. film director. Born in Berkeley, Cal., he joined with the Indian producer Ismail N. Merchant (b.1936) to make a series of films written by Ivory and R. P. JHABVALA. Their first international success, Shakespeare Wallah (1965), was followed by a series of high-quality, well-acted films noted for their lush cinematography, including The Europeans (1979), The Bostonians (1984), A Room with a View (1986, Academy Award), Maurice (1987), Howards End (1992), and The Remains of the Day (1993).

ivory-billed woodpecker Black-and-white WOODPECKER (Campephilus principalis) with a flaring crest (red on the male) and a long whitish bill. The largest N. American woodpecker, it was declared extinct in 1995, its decline coinciding with the logging of virgin forest, where it subsisted on deadwood insects. A subspecies, the Cuban ivory-billed woodpecker, may likewise be extinct. A related species, the imperial woodpecker of Mexico, is critically endangered.

Ivory Coast or **Côte d'Ivoire** \kōt-dē-'vwär\ officially **Republic of Côte d'Ivoire** Republic, W Africa. Area: 123,847 sq mi (320,763 sq km). Population (2001): 16,400,000. Capital: YAMOUSSOUKRO, seat of government, ABIDJAN. There are about 60 independent tribes, including the Beti, Senufo, Baule, Anyi, Malinke, Dan, and Lobu. Languages: French (official), various native languages. Religions: Islam, Roman Catholicism, traditional animistic beliefs. Currency: CFA franc. Ivory Coast can be divided into four major regions: a narrow coastal region, an equatorial rain forest in the west, a cultivated forest zone in the east, and a savanna region in the north. Agriculture employs more than 60% of the workforce. The country is the world's largest producer of cocoa and a major producer of coffee; other exports include bananas, cotton, rubber, timber, and diamonds. It is a republic with one legislative house; its chief of state is the president, and its head of government is the prime minister. European powers came to the area to trade in ivory and slaves beginning in the 15th cent., and local kingdoms gave way to French influence in the 19th cent. The French colony of Côte d'Ivoire was founded in 1893, and full French occupation took place 1908–18. In 1946 it became a territory in the French Union; in 1947 the N part of the country separated and became the nation of Upper Volta

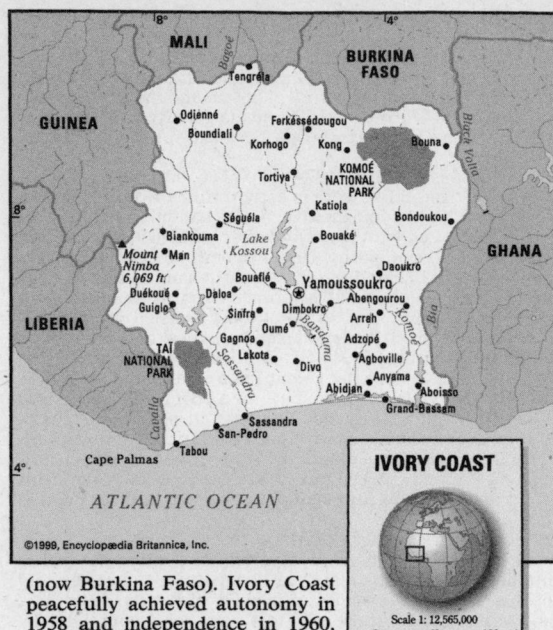

©1999, Encyclopædia Britannica, Inc.

IVORY COAST

Scale 1: 12,565,000

0   60   120 mi
0   80   160 km

(now Burkina Faso). Ivory Coast peacefully achieved autonomy in 1958 and independence in 1960, when Félix HOUPHOUËT-BOIGNY was elected president. The country's first multiparty presidential elections were held in 1990. A military coup in 1999, the country's first, was followed in 2000 by new democratic elections.

ivy Any of about five species of evergreen woody vines that make up the genus *Hedera* in the GINSENG family, commonly grown as ground covers and on stone walls, especially English ivy *(H. helix)*, which climbs by aerial roots with adhering disks that develop on the stems. The tough, dark-green leaves of English ivy have three to five lobes and tend to droop horizontally from the stem. See also POISON IVY.

Ivy League Group of eight universities in the NE U.S., high in academic and social prestige, that formed a football conference in the 1870s. It consists of HARVARD, YALE, PRINCETON, COLUMBIA, BROWN, and CORNELL universities, the Univ. of PENNSYLVANIA, and DARTMOUTH COLLEGE.

Iwo Jima Island, Japan. Lying 759 mi (1,221 km) south of Tokyo, it has an area of 8 sq mi (20 sq km). It was the scene of one of the severest campaigns of WORLD WAR II. After extensive bombing by U.S. planes (Dec. 1944–Feb. 1945), it was invaded by U.S. marines and its airfield was captured. In 1968 it was returned to Japan.

IWW See INDUSTRIAL WORKERS OF THE WORLD

Izmir \iz-'mir\ *formerly* **Smyrna** City (pop., 1996: 2,073,000), W Turkey. On the Aegean seacoast, it is one of Turkey's largest ports. Founded as early as 3000 B.C., it was settled by the Greeks before 1000 B.C., and captured by the Lydians around 600 B.C. Refounded by ALEXANDER THE GREAT in the 4th cent. B.C., it became one of the principal cities of ASIA MINOR. After being conquered in turn by the Crusaders and by TIMUR (Tamerlane), it was annexed to the Ottoman empire about 1425. It has grown rapidly since 1945.

Izvestiya \iz-'ves-tē-ə\ Russian daily newspaper published in Moscow, the official national publication of the Soviet government until 1991. Founded in 1917, it grew rapidly in circulation, and eventually became a lively, readable daily under Alexei Adzhubei, Nikita KHRUSHCHEV's son-in-law, while remaining an instrument of the state. Following the Soviet Union's breakup, it became an independent, employee-owned publication with a liberal editorial policy.

J

Jabrail See JIBRIL

jack Portable hand-operated device for raising heavy weights through short distances, exerting great pressures, or holding assembled work firmly in position. The ratio of the load to the amount of force applied to the handle can be made quite high by using a GEAR or SCREW. A RATCHET allows a heavy weight to be raised in short successive stages. Though limited by the requirements of portability and ease of operation, jacks may exert a force of several tons. A familiar example is the automobile jack, used to raise one end of a car to change a tire.

jackal Any of three CANINE species of the genus *Canis*. They inhabit open country and live alone, in pairs, or in packs. They hunt at night, feeding on small animals, plant material, or carrion. A pack can bring down larger prey. The golden, or Asiatic, jackal is found from E Europe and NE Africa to SE Asia. The black-backed jackal and side-striped jackal are found in S and E Africa. Jackals are 34–37 in. (85–95 cm) long, including the 12–14-in. (30–35-cm) tail, and weigh 15–24 lbs (7–11 kg).

jackdaw *or* **daw** Crowlike black bird (*Corvus monedula*) with pearly eyes. About 13 in. (33 cm) long, jackdaws breed in colonies in treeholes and on cliffs and tall buildings; their flocks fly in formation around the site. Their cry sounds like their name: "chak." They range from the British Isles to central Asia.

jack-in-the-pulpit N. American plant (*Arisaema triphyllum*) of the ARUM FAMILY, noted for the unusual shape of its flower. It grows in wet woodlands and thickets from Nova Scotia to Minnesota and south to Florida and Texas. Three-part leaves on each of two long stalks overshadow the flower, which consists of a conspicuous green- and purple-striped structure called a spathe ("pulpit"). The spathe curves in a hood over a club-shaped spadix ("jack") that, at its base, bears minute flowers. In late summer the plant produces a cluster of brilliant red, poisonous berries.

Jackson City (pop., 2000: 184,000) and capital, Mississippi. It lies along the PEARL RIVER in the W central part of the state. Settled in 1792 as a trading post, it was made the state capital in 1822 and named for Andrew JACKSON. During the AMERICAN CIVIL WAR it was burned by Union forces (1863). The state's largest city, it is the seat of Jackson State Univ. (1877).

Jackson, A(lexander) Y(oung) (1882–1974) Canadian landscape painter. Born in Montreal, he traveled to every region of Canada, often returning to a favorite spot on the St. Lawrence River, where he produced sketches that he later executed in paint (e.g., *Early Spring, Quebec*, 1926; *Laurentian Hills, Early Spring*, 1931). His easy style, featuring rolling rhythms and rich, full color, exerted a strong influence on Canadian landscape painting.

Jackson, Andrew (1767–1845) Seventh president of the U.S. (1829–37). Born in Waxhaw, S.C., he became a lawyer in Tennessee and was elected to the U.S. House of

Andrew Jackson

Representatives (1796–97) and Senate (1797–98). In 1802 he was elected major general of the Tennessee militia; when the WAR OF 1812 began, he offered the U.S. the services of his 50,000-volunteer militia. Sent to fight the Creek Indians allied with the British in Mississippi Territory, he defeated them at the Battle of Horseshoe Bend. After capturing Pensacola, Fla., from the British-allied Spanish, he marched overland to engage the British in Louisiana. A decisive victory at the Battle of NEW ORLEANS made him a national hero, dubbed "Old Hickory" by the press. After U.S. acquisition of Florida, he was named governor of the territory (1821). One of four candidates in the 1824 presidential election, he won an electoral-vote plurality, but the House gave the election to J. Q. ADAMS. In 1828 Jackson defeated Adams after a fierce campaign and became the first president elected from west of the Appalachian Mtns. His election was considered a triumph of grassroots democracy. He replaced many federal officeholders with his supporters, introducing the SPOILS SYSTEM. He pursued a policy of moving Indians westward with the INDIAN REMOVAL ACT. He split with his vice president, John C. CALHOUN, over the NULLIFICATION movement. His reelection in 1832 was due in part to support for his anticapitalistic fiscal policies (see BANK WAR). His popularity continued to build throughout his presidency. During his tenure a strong DEMOCRATIC PARTY developed that led to a vigorous two-party system.

Jackson, Glenda (b.1936) British actress. Discovered by Peter BROOK, she appeared as the mad Charlotte Corday in his celebrated production of Peter WEISS's *Marat/Sade* (1964; film, 1967). She became known for her tense portrayals of complex women, gaining international acclaim in the film *Women in Love* (1969, Academy Award) and such later successes as *Sunday Bloody Sunday* (1971), *A Touch of Class* (1973, Academy Award), and the television series *Elizabeth R*. In 1992 she won a seat in the House of Commons.

Jackson, Jesse (Louis) *orig.* Jesse Louis Burns (b.1941) U.S. civil rights leader. Born in Greenville, S.C., he took his adoptive father's name. Involved with the CIVIL RIGHTS MOVEMENT as a college student, he marched with M. L. KING and worked for the SOUTHERN CHRISTIAN LEADERSHIP CONFERENCE (SCLC). In 1967–71 he was national director of Operation Breadbasket, the SCLC's economic arm. He was ordained a Baptist minister in 1968. In 1971 he founded Operation PUSH. He led a 1983 voter-registration drive in Chicago that helped elect the city's first black mayor. Jackson be-

Jesse Jackson, 1988

came the first black man to run for president by entering the Democratic primaries in 1984 and 1988; he won 6.7 million votes in 1988. In 1989 he moved to Washington, D.C., and was elected the city's unpaid "statehood senator" to lobby Congress for statehood.

Jackson, Mahalia (1911–1972) U.S. gospel singer. As a child, Jackson sang in the New Orleans church where her father preached, but was also exposed to blues recordings. In Chicago she joined a touring gospel quintet and opened several small businesses. Her warm, powerful voice first came to wide public attention in the 1930s, when she toured widely singing such songs as "He's Got the Whole World in His Hands." Closely associated with Thomas A. DORSEY, she sang many of his songs. "Move on up a Little Higher" (1948) sold over a million copies, and she became one of the best-selling singers of the 1950s and '60s. She was active in the civil-rights movement from 1955.

Jackson, Michael (Joseph) (b.1958) U.S. singer. Born in Gary, Ind., the 9-year-old Jackson became the lead singer of The Jackson Five, a family group formed by his father. Their hits on the MOTOWN label included "I Want You Back" and "ABC." They had their own TV series in the 1970s and were the subject of a cartoon series. He began making solo recordings in 1971. His successful album *Off the Wall* (1979) was followed by *Thriller* (1982), which sold more than 40 million copies, more than any other album in history. He bought the publishing rights to more than 250 Beatles songs in 1985. He later released such albums as *Bad* (1987), *Dangerous* (1991), *HIStory* (1995), and *Invincible* (2001). A child-molestation lawsuit was dropped in 1994 when he settled with the parents of a 14-year-old boy. His sister Janet (b.1966) has also enjoyed great solo success.

Jackson, Reggie (*orig.* Reginald Martinez) (b.1946) U.S. baseball player. Born in Wyncote, Pa., he excelled in track, football, and baseball in high school. In the major leagues, playing outfield, he helped three teams (Oakland Athletics, 1968–75; New York Yankees, 1976–81; California Angels, 1982–87) win five World Series. Nicknamed "Mr. October" for his reliable prowess in play-off and World Series games, he hit a career total of 563 home runs, placing him eighth-highest of all time.

Jackson, Robert H(oughwout) (1892–1954) U.S. jurist. Born in Spring Creek, Pa., he became general counsel for the U.S. Bureau of Internal Revenue (1934), and successfully prosecuted Andrew W. MELLON for income-tax evasion. After serving as U.S. attorney general (1940–41), he was appointed to the U.S. Supreme Court, where he served until 1954. He infused his well-worded opinions with a blend of liberalism and nationalism. In 1945–46 he served as chief U.S. prosecutor in the NUREMBERG TRIALS.

Jackson, Shirley (Hardie) (1916–1965) U.S. writer. Born in San Francisco, she is best known for her story "The Lottery" (1948), a chilling tale that provoked outrage when first published, and *The Haunting of Hill House* (1959; films, 1963, 1999). These and her other five novels confirmed her reputation as a master of gothic horror and psychological suspense.

Jackson, Stonewall (*orig.* Thomas Jonathan) (1824–1863) U.S. and Confederate army officer. Born in Clarksburg, Va., he attended West Point and served with distinction in the Mexican War. At the start of the Civil War, he organized Virginia volunteers into an effective brigade. At the first Battle of BULL RUN he withstood a Union assault, earning the nickname "Stonewall" and promotion to major general. Robert E. LEE used Jackson's troops to encircle the Union forces to win the second Battle of Bull Run, and Jackson assisted Lee at Antietam and Fredericksburg. Moving his troops around the flank of the Union army at CHANCELLORSVILLE, he was accidentally shot and mortally wounded by his own men.

Jacksonville City (pop., 2000: 735,000), NE Florida. It is the site of Florida's first European (French Huguenot) settlement (1564). Named for Andrew JACKSON, it was laid out in 1822 and incorporated in 1832. It covers 841 sq mi (2,178 sq km), making it one of the largest U.S. cities in land area. A deepwater port with major shipyards, it is Florida's chief transportation and commercial center. It is the site of Jacksonville Univ. and the Univ. of N. Florida.

Jack the Ripper Pseudonymous murderer of at least seven prostitutes in or near London's Whitechapel district, Aug. 7–Nov. 10, 1888. Each victim had her throat cut, and usually the body was mutilated in a manner indicating the murderer's knowledge of human anatomy. Authorities received a series of taunting notes from a person calling himself Jack the Ripper. Though strenuous efforts were made to identify and trap the killer, he remained unknown. In 2002 the mystery writer Patricia Cornwell presented evidence that pointed to the prominent painter Walter Sickert (1860–1942) as the likely murderer.

Jacob Hebrew PATRIARCH, son of Isaac and grandson of ABRAHAM, and the traditional ancestor of the people of Israel. The younger twin brother of Esau, he used trickery to gain Isaac's blessing and Esau's birthright. On a journey to CANAAN he wrestled all night with an angel, who blessed him and gave him the name Israel. Jacob had 13 children, 10 of whom founded tribes of ISRAEL. His favorite son was JOSEPH.

Jacob \zhä-'kòb\, **François** (b.1920) French biologist. He worked with Jacques MONOD studying the regulation of bacterial enzyme synthesis. They discovered regulator genes, so called because they control the activities of other genes. Jacob and Monod also proposed the existence of an RNA messenger, a partial copy of DNA that carries genetic information to other parts of the cell. The two shared a 1965 Nobel Prize with André Lwoff (1902–1995).

Jacobean age \ja-kə-'bē-ən\ Period in the visual and literary arts during the reign of JAMES I (Latin, *Jacobus*) of England (r.1603–25). Jacobean architecture included classical details, Tudor pointed arches, and interior paneling. Inigo JONES introduced the classical style of Renaissance architecture into England. Jacobean furniture, made of oak, featured heavy forms and bulbous legs. Most Jacobean portraitists and sculptors were foreign-born or foreign-influenced, and their efforts faded when such Flemish painters as Peter Paul RUBENS and Anthony VAN DYCK worked in England for James's successor, CHARLES I. See also JACOBEAN LITERATURE.

Jacobean literature \ja-kə-'bē-ən\ Body of works written during the reign of JAMES I of England (1603–25). The successor to ELIZABETHAN LITERATURE, Jacobean literature was often dark in its questioning of the stability of the social order and its occupation with the problem of evil; some of William SHAKESPEARE's greatest tragedies may date from the beginning of the period. Jacobean poetry included the graceful verse of Ben JONSON and the CAVALIER POETS, but also the intellectual complexity of the METAPHYSICAL POETRY of John DONNE and others. Its dramatists included Jonson, John WEBSTER, and Francis BEAUMONT. In prose, writers such as Francis BACON and Robert BURTON showed a new toughness and flexibility of style. The era's monumental prose achievement was the King James Version of the Bible (1611).

Jacobin Club \'ja-kə-bən\ *or* **Jacobins** Political group of the FRENCH REVOLUTION identified with extreme radicalism and violence. Formed in 1789 as the Society of the Friends of the Constitution, it was known as the Jacobin Club because it met in a former convent of the Dominicans (known in Paris as Jacobins); it later changed its name to Society of the Jacobins, Friends of Liberty and Equality. It admitted leftist MONTAGNARD deputies of the NATIONAL CONVENTION and agitated for the king's execution and the overthrow of the GIRONDINS. In 1793, with about 8,000 clubs and 500,000 members, the Jacobins became instruments of the REIGN OF TERROR. The Parisian club supported Maximilien ROBESPIERRE, but it closed after his fall in 1794.

Jacobite In British history, a supporter of the exiled Stuart king JAMES II (Latin, *Jacobus*) and his descendants after the GLORIOUS REVOLUTION of 1688. The Jacobites, especially under WILLIAM III and Queen ANNE, could offer a feasible alternative title to the crown, and several attempts were made to restore the Stuarts. In 1689 James's army was defeated at the Battle of the Boyne. In the Fifteen Rebellion (1715), Jacobites tried to seize the crown for J. E. STUART, the Old Pretender. In the Forty-five Rebellion (1745) his son C. E. STUART took Scotland, but the Jacobite army was crushed at the Battle of Culloden (1746).

Jacobs, Jane *orig.* Jane Butzner (b.1916) U.S.-Canadian writer on urban life. Born in Scranton, Pa., she became active in urban community work while living in New York City with her architect husband. For 10 years she was an editor at *Architectural Forum*. Her highly influential *Death and*

Life of Great American Cities (1961) presented a highly original reinterpretation of the multiple needs of modern urban places. *The Economy of Cities* (1969) discussed the importance of diversity to a city's prospects. Later works included *Cities and the Wealth of Nations* (1984) and *Edge of Empire* (1996).

Jacopo da Pontormo See Jacopo da PONTORMO

Jacopo della Quercia \\'yä-kō-pō-däl-lä-'kwer-chä\ *orig.* Jacopo di Piero di Angelo (c.1374–1438) Italian sculptor. His earliest major work is the tomb of Ilaria del Carretto in Lucca Cathedral (c.1406–8). His most important commission for Siena was the fountain known as Fonte Gaia (1408–19) in the Piazza del Campo. His last and greatest work was the sculptural reliefs around the portal of San Petronio in Bologna (1425–30). In 1435 he was appointed supervising architect of Siena Cathedral. The greatest non-Florentine sculptor of the 15th cent., he was a major influence on the young MICHELANGELO.

Jacquard \zha-'kär, *Engl* 'ja-ˌkärd\, **Joseph-Marie** (1752–1834) French inventor. In 1801 he demonstrated an automatic loom that utilized interchangeable punched cards to control the weaving of the cloth so that any desired pattern could be obtained automatically. This became the basis of the modern automatic loom and a precursor of the modern computer. Jacquard's punched cards were adapted by Charles BABBAGE as in input-output medium for his proposed analytical engine, and punched cards were used for inputting data into early digital computers.

Jacquard loom \\'ja-ˌkärd\ LOOM incorporating a special device to control individual warp YARNS. It enabled production of fabrics with intricate woven patterns such as TAPESTRY, BROCADE, and damask, and has also been adapted to the production of patterned knitted fabrics. Developed by J.-M. JACQUARD in 1804–5, it used interchangeable punched cards that controlled the weaving of the cloth so that any desired pattern could be obtained automatically. It aroused violent hostility among weavers, who feared that its labor-saving capabilities would deprive them of jobs. Eventually the loom's advantages led to its general acceptance; by 1812 there were 11,000 in use in France, and from there use of the loom spread virtually worldwide.

jade Either of two tough, compact, typically green gemstones that take a high polish. Both have been carved into jewelry, ornaments, small sculptures, and utilitarian objects from earliest recorded times. The more highly prized is JADEITE; the other is NEPHRITE.

jadeite \\'jād-ˌīt\ Gem-quality SILICATE MINERAL, one of the two forms of JADE. Jadeite (imperial jade), sodium aluminum silicate, may contain impurities that give it a variety of colors: white, green, red, brown, and blue; the most highly prized is emerald green. Jadeite occurs only in metamorphic rocks, most often those deep below the earth's surface. An area in N Myanmar has long been the main source of gem-quality jadeite.

jaeger \\'yä-gər\ *or* **skua** Any of three species (genus *Stercorarius,* family Stercorariidae) of seabirds resembling dark GULLS with a forward-set black cap and projecting central tail feathers. They nest in the Arctic tundra and then go to sea, many as far as Australia. While nesting along coasts they force TERNS and kittiwakes to disgorge their food, destroy the eggs and young of other seabirds, and capture land birds and rodents. The species range from 14 to 20 in. (35–50 cm) long.

Jaffa See TEL AVIV-JAFFA

Jagannatha \\'jə-gə-ˌnät-ə\ *or* **Jagannath** Form under which KRISHNA is worshiped at Puri, Orissa, a famous religious center of India. The Rathayatra, or Chariot Festival, is held in his honor in June or July. An image of the god is placed on a cart so heavy that it takes thousands of devotees several days to move it to a temple outside the city. According to legend, pilgrims sometimes throw themselves under the wagon in hopes of attaining instant salvation, a practice that gave rise to the word juggernaut.

Jagiello I See WLADISLAW II JAGIELLO

Jagiellon dynasty \yäg-'ye-lȯn\ Family of monarchs of Poland-Lithuania, Bohemia, and Hungary powerful in the 15th–16th cent. It was founded by Jogaila, grand duke of Lithuania, who became WLADYSLAW II JAGIELLO of Poland. Wladyslaw III (1424–1444) extended the dynasty by also assuming the throne of Hungary (1440). He was succeeded by CASIMIR IV, who placed his son on the thrones of Bohemia (1471) and Hungary. Sigismund I (1467-1548) strengthened the Polish government and saw the TEUTONIC ORDER convert its lands into the secular Duchy of Prussia (1525), a Polish fief. In 1526 Jagiellon rule ended in Bohemia and Hungary. In 1561 Sigismund II Augustus incorporated Livonia into Poland, but when he died, leaving no heirs, the dynasty ended (1572).

jaguar Largest New World CAT. The jaguar (*Panthera onca*) survives, in reduced numbers, only in remote areas of Central and S. America, principally in the Amazon rain forest. The male is 5.5–9 ft (1.7–2.7 m) long, including the 23–35-in. (60–90-cm) tail, and weighs 220–350 lbs (100–160 kg). The coat is typically orange-tan with black spots arranged in rosettes. A solitary predator, the jaguar usually hunts rodents, deer, birds, and fish; it will also take cattle, horses, and dogs.

jai alai \\'hī-ˌlī, ˌhī-ə-'lī\ (Basque: "merry festival") Court game resembling HANDBALL, played between two or four players with a ball, and a hurling device, a long, curved wicker basket, strapped to the wrist. Of BASQUE origin, it developed from PELOTA. The ball may reach speeds up to 150 mph (240 kph). The court, 53.3 m (58.3 yards) long, is three-walled; the object is to bounce the ball off the front wall with such speed and English (spin) as to defeat an opponent's attempt to return it. PARI-MUTUEL betting is permitted in the U.S.

Jainism \\'jī-ˌni-zəm\ Religion of India established in the 6th cent. B.C. by Vardhamana, who was called Mahavira (599?–527 B.C.). Jainism's core belief is AHIMSA, or noninjury to all living things. It was founded as a reaction against the VEDIC RELIGION, which required animal sacrifices. Jainism has no belief in a creator god, though there are a number of lesser deities. Jains believe that their religion was revealed in stages by a number of Conquerors, of whom Mahavira was the 24th. Mahavira preached the need for rigorous penance and self-denial as the means of perfecting human nature, escaping the cycle of rebirth, and attaining MOKSHA, or liberation. Jains view KARMA as an invisible material substance that interferes with liberation and can only be dissolved through asceticism. In keeping with their principle of reverence for life, Jains are known for their charitable works, including building shelters for animals. Jainism preaches universal tolerance and does not seek to make converts. It has about 4 million adherents.

Jaipur \\'jī-ˌpur\ Capital (pop., 1991: 1,458,000) of Rajasthan state, NW India. It was founded in 1727 by Maharaja Sawai Jai Singh to replace Amber as the capital of the princely state of Jaipur. The city, known for its beauty, is unique in its straight-line planning; its buildings are mostly rose-colored, and it is sometimes called the "pink city." Its historic structures include the city palace, the Hall of Winds, Ram Bagh palace, and Nahargarh, or Tiger Fort.

Jakarta *formerly (1949–72)* **Djakarta** \jə-'kär-tə\ Capital (pop., 1996: 9,341,000) and largest city of Indonesia. Located on the NW coast of JAVA, it was founded in 1527 by the sultan of Bantam. The Dutch took control in 1619, renaming it Batavia and establishing it as the headquarters of the Dutch E. INDIA CO. In 1949 the city, one of the world's largest, was renamed and made Indonesia's capital. The country's principal port, it is also a major industrial and financial center, and the seat of many universities.

Jakobson \\'yä-kəb-sən\, **Roman (Osipovich)** (1896–1982) Russian-U.S. linguist. Born and educated in Moscow, Jakobson moved to the U.S. in 1941. He taught at Harvard Univ. 1949–67. His interests ranged from folk epics and the cultural history of the Slavs to general PHONOLOGY, the MORPHOLOGY of the Slavic languages, and speech acquisition. Other important contributions include his analysis of the Russian case system (1938) and a brilliant analysis of the Russian verbal system (1948).

Jalal al-Din al-Rumi See Jalal al-Din al-RUMI

Jalapa (Enríquez) \hä-'lä-pä\ City (pop., 1990 est.: 279,000), capital of VERACRUZ state, E central Mexico. It is located in the SIERRA MADRE Oriental, at 4,681 ft (1,427 m) above sea

HIJ

level. A market city, it was famous in colonial days for its annual fair, held to dispose of the goods brought from CÁDIZ by the returning Spanish silver fleet. It is notable for its massive Spanish-Moorish architecture.

Jalisco \hä-ˈlēs-kō\ State (pop., 2000: 6,321,000), W central Mexico. It has an area of 31,211 sq mi (80,836 sq km); its capital is GUADALAJARA. The SIERRA MADRE Occidental mountain range traverses the state. The Sierra region is largely volcanic. The state's many lakes include Chapala, Mexico's largest. It was first invaded by Spaniards in 1526. In 1889 its territory of Tepic was separated, and in 1917 it became NAYARIT state. Its economy is based on agriculture, livestock-raising, forest products, and mining.

jam See JELLY AND JAM

Jamaica Island nation, W. Indies. Located south of Cuba, it is 146 mi (235 km) long and 35 mi (56 km) wide, the third-

[map of Jamaica]

largest island in the Caribbean. Area: 4,471 sq mi (11,580 sq km). Population (2000): 2,619,000. Capital: KINGSTON. The population consists mostly of descendents of African slaves. Languages: English (official), CREOLE. Religions: Christianity, spiritual sects, RASTAFARIAN movement. Currency: Jamaica dollar. Jamaica has three major regions: the coastal lowlands, which encircle the island and are heavily cultivated; a limestone plateau, which covers half the island; and the interior highlands, with forested mountain ranges, including the Blue Mtns. Agriculture employs one-fourth of the workforce, and the major agricultural export is raw sugar, with molasses and rum as by-products. Industry focuses on the production of bauxite and alumina, and on the garment industry. Tourism is very important, and half of the population is employed in services. It is a constitutional monarchy with two legislative houses. Its chief of state is the British monarch, represented by the governor-general, and its head of government is the prime minister. The island was settled by Arawak Indians around A.D. 600. It was sighted by Christopher COLUMBUS in 1494; Spain colonized it in the early 16th cent. but neglected it because it lacked gold reserves. Britain gained control in 1655, and by the end of the 18th cent. it had become a prized colonial possession due to the volume of sugar produced by slave laborers. Slavery was abolished in the late 1830s, and the plantation system collapsed. Jamaica gained full internal self-government in 1959 and became an independent country within the British COMMONWEALTH in 1962. In the late 20th cent., the government, led by Michael MANLEY, nationalized many businesses.

James, Harry (Haag) (1916–1983) U.S. trumpeter and bandleader. Born in Albany, Ga., he joined Benny GOODMAN's band in 1937 before forming his own group in 1938. It achieved commercial success through recordings featuring Frank SINATRA, virtuoso set pieces, and ballads performed with James's trademark wide vibrato. He married actress Betty Grable in 1943 and appeared in several films. A technically brilliant improviser, he continued to perform with his band for over 40 years.

James, Henry (1843–1916) U.S.-British novelist. Born in New York City, the brother of William JAMES, he traveled frequently to Europe from childhood on; after 1876 he lived primarily in England. His fundamental theme was the innocence and exuberance of the New World in conflict with the corruption and wisdom of the Old. *Daisy Miller* (1879) won him international renown; it was followed by *The Europeans* (1879), *Washington Square* (1880), and *The Portrait of a Lady* (1881). In *The Bostonians* (1886) and *The Princess Casamassima* (1886), his sub-

Henry James, 1905

jects were social reformers and revolutionaries. In *The Spoils of Poynton* (1897), *What Maisie Knew* (1897), and *The Turn of the Screw* (1898), he made use of complex moral and psychological ambiguity. *The Wings of the Dove* (1902), *The Ambassadors* (1903), and *The Golden Bowl* (1904) were his great final novels. Perhaps his chief technical innovation was his strong focus on the individual consciousness, which reflected his sense of the decline of public and collective values in his time.

James, Jesse (Woodson) (1847–1882) U.S. outlaw. Born near Centerville (now Kearny), Mo., Jesse and his brother Frank (1843–1915) were Confederate guerrillas during the Civil War. In 1866 they assembled a gang to rob banks, and later trains and stagecoaches. In 1876 Jesse led a failed attempt on a bank in Northfield, Minn.; only the brothers escaped. In 1881 Missouri's governor offered a $10,000 reward for their capture, and in 1882 Jesse was shot in the back of the head by a member of his gang. Frank was subsequently tried and acquitted three times. Their exploits were romanticized by pulp-fiction writers and in movies.

James, St. *or* **James the Great** (d.c.A.D. 44) One of the 12 APOSTLES of JESUS. He and his brother John (see St. JOHN THE APOSTLE) were fishermen on the Sea of Galilee and were among the first disciples to be called. James witnessed the major events in the ministry of Jesus. He was beheaded by order of Herod Agrippa. By tradition, his body was taken to SANTIAGO DE COMPOSTELA, Spain, where his shrine has long been a place of pilgrimage.

James, William (1842–1910) U.S. philosopher and psychologist. Brother of Henry JAMES, he was born in New York City and studied medicine at Harvard, where he taught from 1872. His *Principles of Psychology* (1890) treated thinking and knowledge as instruments in the struggle to live. His famous *Varieties of Religious Experience* (1902) discussed the religious impulse as psychologically innate in humans. In *Pragmatism* (1907), he generalized the PRAGMATISM of C. S. PEIRCE by asserting that the meaning of any idea must be analyzed in terms of its consequences; that truth and error depend solely on these consequences. He applied pragmatism to change and chance, freedom, variety, pluralism, and novelty. Pragmatism was also the basis for his polemic against monism, and all views that presented reality as a static whole. He was also a leader of the psychological movement of functionalism.

James I *Spanish* Jaime *known as* **James the Conqueror** (1208–1276) King of ARAGON and CATALONIA (1214–76), the most renowned of the medieval kings of Aragon. Educated by the Knights TEMPLAR, James helped to subdue rebellious nobles and took over the government of his kingdoms in 1227. He reconquered the Balearic Islands (1229–

35) and Valencia (1233–38) but renounced his claims to lands in S France. He also helped ALFONSO X to suppress a Moorish rebellion in Murcia (1266).

James I (1566–1625) King of Scotland, as James VI (1567–1625), and first Stuart king of England (1603–25). Son of MARY, QUEEN OF SCOTS, at age 1 James succeeded his mother to the Scottish throne and was controlled by a succession of regents. In 1583 he began to pursue his own policies as king, allying himself with England. He succeeded to the English throne on the death of ELIZABETH I, as great-great-grandson of HENRY VII. He quickly achieved peace and prosperity by ending England's war with Spain (1604). He rejected most of the Puritans' demands for reform of the Church of England but permitted a new translation of

James I Painting attributed to John de Critz, c.1620

the Bible, the King James Version. His policies toward Catholics led to the GUNPOWDER PLOT. His conflicts with an increasingly self-assertive Parliament led to his dissolution of Parliament (1611–21). With the death of Robert CECIL (1612), he came under the influence of incompetent favorites.

James I (1394–1437) King of the Scots (1406–37). The son of Robert III, he was captured by the English in 1406 and held prisoner until 1424. During the 13 years in which he truly ruled Scotland (1424–37), he established the first strong monarchy the Scots had known in nearly a century. He weakened the nobility but did not entirely subdue the Highland lords, and he greatly improved the administration of justice. His murder in a friary by a group of nobles led to an uprising in favor of his widow and 6-year-old son, who succeeded him as James II.

James II (1633–1701) King of Great Britain (1685–88). The brother of CHARLES II, he became lord high admiral in the ANGLO–DUTCH WARS. He converted to Catholicism (c.1668), and resigned in 1673 rather than take the TEST ACT oath. By 1678 his Catholicism had created a climate of hysteria about a POPISH PLOT, and successive Parliaments sought to exclude him from succession, but when Charles died (1685), James came to the throne with little opposition. Rebellions caused him to fill the army and high offices with Roman Catholics. The birth of his son, a possible Catholic heir, brought about the GLORIOUS REVOLUTION in 1688, and he fled to France. In 1689 he landed in Ireland to regain his throne, but his army was defeated at the Battle of the Boyne, and he returned to exile in France.

James II (1430–1460) King of Scotland (1437–60). He succeeded his father, JAMES I of Scotland, but because he was so young, the strong central authority his father had established quickly collapsed. His first adult task was the restoration of monarchical authority; he established a strong central government and improved the administration of justice. Turning his attention to the English, who had renewed their claims to rule Scotland, he attacked English outposts in Scotland and was killed during a siege of Roxburgh Castle.

James III (1452–1488) King of Scotland (1460–88). He succeeded his father, JAMES II. A weak monarch, he was confronted with two major rebellions. He evidently offended his nobles by his interest in the arts and by taking artists for his favorites. In 1488 two powerful border families raised a rebellion and won to their cause his son, the future JAMES IV; James III was captured and killed at 36.

James IV (1473–1513) King of Scotland (1488–1513). He unified his country, gaining control over all N and W Scotland by 1493. His marriage (1503) to MARGARET TUDOR, helped stabilize relations with England, but in 1512 he allied with France against England. He invaded England in support of the French in 1513; his army was defeated at the Battle of Flodden, and James was killed.

James Bay Extension of HUDSON BAY, between N Ontario and Quebec. It is 275 mi (443 km) long and 135 mi (217 km) wide, with numerous islands. The many rivers that empty into the bay are the cause of its low salinity. Visited by Henry HUDSON in 1610, it is named for Capt. Thomas James (1593?–1635?), who explored it in 1631.

Jameson, Leander Starr (*later* **Sir Leander**) (1853–1917) British administrator in S Africa. As Cecil RHODES's representative, Jameson negotiated mineral concessions in present-day Zimbabwe before becoming the first administrator of the new colony of RHODESIA in 1893. In 1895 Rhodes and Jameson plotted with British leaders in the Transvaal to overthrow the Boer government of Paul KRUGER; the plan was postponed, but Jameson launched his own unsuccessful invasion and was captured. After imprisonment in England, he returned to participate in S. African politics.

James the Conqueror See JAMES I (ARAGON)

Jamestown Site on Virginia's James River, the first permanent British settlement in N. America. Founded in May 1607 and named after King JAMES I, it initiated the cultivation of tobacco and established the continent's first representative government (1619). It was the capital of Virginia until 1698. In 1936 it was incorporated into the Colonial National Historical Park.

Jamison \ˈjā-mə-sən\, **Judith** (b.1943) U.S. dancer and choreographer. Born in Philadelphia, she danced with Alvin AILEY's American Dance Theater from 1965 to 1980, becoming celebrated for her energetic grace and inspiring many of Ailey's new dances. She starred in the Broadway musical *Sophisticated Ladies* (1980). She toured worldwide in the 1980s and choreographed for various companies. In 1989 she succeeded Ailey as the troupe's artistic director.

Janacek \ˈyä-nə-ˌchek\, **Leos** (*orig.* Leo Eugen) (1854–1928) Czech (Moravian) composer. Until age 40 he worked as a teacher and choral conductor. In 1894 he began his first mature opera, *Jenufa*; a decade later it had a successful premiere (1904), and he retired to compose full-time, becoming music's most extraordinary late bloomer. In his last two decades he composed the *Glagolitic Mass* (1927) and the operas *Katya Kabanova* (1921), *The Cunning Little Vixen* (1924), *The Makropulos Affair* (1925), and *From the House of the Dead* (1928).

Leos Janacek

Janissary *or* **Janizary** \ˈja-nə-ˌser-ē, ˈja-nə-ˌzer-ē\ Elite corps of the OTTOMAN EMPIRE's army from the late 14th cent. to 1826. Its original soldiers were Balkan Christians forcibly converted to Islam. Strict early rules, later abandoned, included celibacy. In 1826 they rebelled rather than accept Westernization of the army, and all of them were killed when the sultan, Mahmud II, bombed their barracks and executed the survivors.

Jansen \ˈyän-sən, *Engl* ˈjan-sən\, **Cornelius Otto** (1585–1638) Dutch leader of the Roman Catholic reform movement known as JANSENISM. At the Univ. of Louvain he absorbed the teachings of St. AUGUSTINE, especially those concerning original sin and the need for grace. He spent 1611–14 in Bayonne, France, where he directed the episcopal college. He became rector at Louvain in 1635 and a year later was appointed bishop of Ypres. His major work, the *Augustinus*, was published in 1640; in 1642 Pope Urban VIII forbade the reading of the book.

Jansenism Roman Catholic reform movement inspired by the writings of Cornelius JANSEN. Jansen adopted St. AUGUSTINE's doctrines of PREDESTINATION and the necessity of God's GRACE, a stance considered uncomfortably close to CALVINISM by Roman Catholic authorities, who banned his book the *Augustinus* in 1642. Blaise PASCAL, the most famous Jansenist, defended Jansenism's teachings in his *Provincial Letters* (1656–57). In 1709 LOUIS XIV ordered its home abbey at Port Royal, France, demolished. Followers of Jansen started a Jansenist Church in 1723 that has endured to the present day.

Jansky, Karl (Guthe) (1905–1950) U.S. engineer. Born in Red Bank, N.J., he was assigned by Bell Telephone Laboratories to track down static that interfered with telephone calls and discovered (1932) the first extraterrestrial source of radio waves, coming from the constellation Sagittarius. This proof that celestial bodies could emit radio waves marked the beginning of radio astronomy.

Janus \'jā-nəs\ Roman god of doorways and archways, after whom the month of January is named. Often depicted as a double-faced head, he was a deity of beginnings. Rome had many freestanding ceremonial gateways called *jani*, used for symbolically auspicious entrances or exits. The Janus Geminus had double doors that were left open in time of war and closed when Rome was at peace.

Janus Roman coin

Japan *Japanese* **Nippon** \ni-'pón\ *or* **Nihon** \nē-'hòn\ Island country, lying off the E coast of Asia in the W Pacific Ocean. It consists of four main islands—HOKKAIDO, HONSHU, Shikoku, and KYUSHU. It is separated from China by the E. CHINA SEA and from S. Korea, N. Korea, and Russia by the Sea of JAPAN. Area: 145,883 sq mi (377,835 sq km). Population (2000): 126,920,000. Capital: TOKYO. The Japanese overwhelmingly are a single Asian ethnic group. Language: Japanese (official). Religions: SHINTO, BUDDHISM. Currency: yen. Situated in one of the earth's most geologically active zones, Japan experiences volcanic eruptions and earthquakes. Mountain ranges cover more than four-fifths of Japan's land surface; the country's highest mountain is Mt. FUJI. The nation's economy, one of the world's biggest, is based largely on manufacturing and services; exports include electronic and electrical equipment, motor vehicles, chemicals, and iron and steel products. The government's involvement in banking results in unique cooperation between the public and private sectors. It is also one of the world's principal seagoing nations, with an important marine fishing industry. It is a constitutional monarchy with two legislative houses; its chief of state is the emperor, and the head of government is the prime minister. Japan's history began with the accession of the legendary first emperor, JIMMU, in 660 B.C. The Yamato court established the first unified Japanese state in the 4th–5th cent. A.D.; during this period, Buddhism arrived in Japan by way of Korea. For centuries Japan borrowed heavily from Chinese culture, but it began to sever its links with the mainland by the 9th cent. The FUJIWARA FAMILY held sway through the 11th cent. In 1192 MINAMOTO YORITOMO established Japan's first BAKUFU, or shogunate (see KAMAKURA SHOGUNATE). The ASHIKAGA SHOGUNATE (1338–1573) was marked by warfare among powerful families. Unification was achieved in the late 1500s under the leadership of Oda Nobunaga, TOYOTOMI HIDEYOSHI, and TOKUGAWA IEYASU. During the TOKUGAWA SHOGUNATE, beginning in 1603, the government imposed a policy of isolation. Under the leadership of Emperor MEIJI (1868–1912), it adopted a constitution (1889) and began a program of modernization and Westernization. Japanese imperialism led to war with China (1894–95) and Russia (1904–5) as well as to the annexation of Korea (1910) and Manchuria (1931). During WORLD WAR II Japan attacked U.S. forces in Hawaii and the Philippines (Dec. 1941) and occupied European colonial possessions in SE Asia. In 1945 the U.S. dropped ATOMIC BOMBS on HIROSHIMA and NAGASAKI, and Japan surrendered to Allied powers. U.S. postwar occupation of Japan led to a new democratic constitution in 1947. In rebuilding Japan's ruined industrial plant, new technology was used in every major industry. A tremendous economic recovery followed. Japan was able to maintain a favorable balance of trade until a deep recession set in in the 1990s. It remains the world's second-largest economy. See map on following page.

Japan, Sea of Branch of the W Pacific Ocean, bounded by Japan, the island of SAKHALIN, and by Russia and Korea on the Asian mainland. It covers about 377,600 sq mi (978,000 sq km) and has a maximum depth of 12,276 ft (3,742 m). Its relatively warm waters contribute greatly to the mild climate of Japan. Growing trade has increased its use as a commercial waterway.

Japanese architecture Building traditions of Japan. Early building types were the grass-roofed pit house, raised thatched-roof granary (c.400 B.C.), and mound tomb *(kofun)*. Buddhist temples imitated Chinese and Korean form, a symmetrical complex bordered by a continuous roofed cloister usually containing a PAGODA, Golden Hall *(kondo)*, belfry, and living quarters. Roof tiles, stone, and wood were the essential materials. Around A.D. 700 appeared the distinctive Japanese approach: asymmetrical layouts following the contours of the land. Domestic architecture became marked by unpretentiously rustic buildings, meticulously designed viewing gardens, verandas, and sliding panels offering vistas on nature. The need for a place of contemplation led to the evolution of both the tea room and study room *(tsuke shoin)*. The late 19th cent. saw a rapid assimilation of Western technology, with brick, stone, and reinforced concrete displacing wood. Postwar Japan's finest architectural achievements are in contemporary interpretations of traditional forms.

Japanese beetle SCARAB BEETLE (Popillia japonica) that is a major PEST of plants. Introduced accidentally from Japan into the U.S. in 1916, it is known to feed on more than 200 species of plant. It ranges from Maine to S. Carolina, and infestations have occurred in other parts of N. America. The adult, about 0.4 in. (10 mm) long, is bright metallic green with coppery-brown wing covers. Control efforts include use of poisonous sprays and a disease-inducing bacterium and introduction of the beetle's natural enemies.

Japanese language Language spoken by about 125 million people on the islands of Japan, including the Ryukyus. Japanese is not closely related to any other language but may have a distant kinship to KOREAN and an even more remote relationship to the ALTAIC LANGUAGES. Japanese is first attested in the 8th cent. A.D., when Middle CHINESE characters were utilized solely for their phonetic value to write native Japanese words. Japanese retains a huge stock of loanwords from Middle Chinese, long adapted to native phonetics. Typologically, Japanese is an agglutinative language with basic subject-object-verb word order; modifiers regularly precede what they modify.

Japanese music Traditional music of Japan. Absorbing the influences of China, India (by way of Buddhism), and the West, Japan has refined them into something distinct during its periods of withdrawal from outside contact. Its earliest music was apparently religious; by the 6th cent. this had been codified into a body of music associated with SHINTO called *mikagura*. After the imperial state was established, GAGAKU was imported from China by way of Korea (612). *Heikebiwa*, a narrative form of singing by minstrel-like figures (often blind) accompanying themselves on the *biwa* (lute), grew in importance as court music declined. In the EDO PERIOD (1615–1868), a new merchant class supported popular entertainments such as KABUKI and bunraku, while NO DRAMA was supported by the nobility. Genres associated with certain solo instruments also arose, particularly for the shakuhachi (bamboo flute), KOTO, and samisen (a three-stringed lute). With Japan's reopening in the 19th cent., Western influences became predominant and almost displaced traditional forms.

Jarmusch \'jär-mùsh\, **Jim** (b.1953) U.S. film director and screenwriter. Born in Akron, Ohio, he established his reputation as a new voice in independent film with his first film, *Stranger Than Paradise* (1984). His later films include the offbeat comedies *Down by Law* (1986), *Mystery Train* (1989), and *Night on Earth* (1992), as well as *Dead Man* (1995) and *Ghost Dog* (1999).

Jarrell \ja-'rel\, **Randall** (1914–1965) U.S. poet and critic. Born in Nashville, Tenn., he published his early poems in *Little Friend, Little Friend* (1945) and *Losses* (1948), both drawing on his wartime experiences. As a critic, he revitalized the reputations of Robert FROST, Walt WHITMAN, and

W. C. WILLIAMS in the 1950s; his criticism is collected in *Poetry and the Age* (1953), *A Sad Heart at the Supermarket* (1962), and the posthumous *Third Book of Criticism* (1969). Later poetry collections include *The Seven-League Crutches* (1951) and *The Woman at the Washington Zoo* (1960).

Jarry \zhȧ-'rē\, **Alfred** (1873–1907) French writer. He went to Paris to live on his inheritance at 18; after exhausting it, he led a life of calculated buffoonery. His farce *Ubu Roi* (1896) and two sequels, which featured the grotesque Père Ubu, are considered a forerunner of theater of the AB-SURD and of SURREALISM. The brilliant imagery and wit of his stories, novels, and poems usually lapse into incoherence and unintelligible symbolism. A heavy drinker, he died at 34.

Jaruzelski \ˌyär-ü-'zel-skē\, **Wojciech (Witold)** (b.1923) Polish chief of state (1981–89) and president (1989–90). As Poland came under increasing pressure from the SOLIDAR-ITY movement, he declared martial law (1981–83), carrying out mass arrests of dissidents. Unable to restore Poland's stagnant economy, in 1988 he began negotiations with Solidarity and agreed to reforms. In 1990 Lech WALE-SA was elected president and Jaruzelski relinquished the last of communist power in Poland.

jasmine \'jaz-mən\ Any of about 300 tropical and subtropical species of fragrant, flowering, woody, climbing shrubs that make up the genus *Jasminum* of the OLIVE family, native to all continents except N. America. The jasmine used in perfumery and aromatherapy comes from the fragrant white flowers of common jasmine (*J. officinale*), native to Iran. The dried flowers of Arabian jasmine (*J. sambac*) make jasmine tea.

Jason In Greek legend, the leader of the ARGONAUTS. He was the son of the king of Iolcos. Raised by CHIRON after his father's half-brother Pelias seized Iolcos, he returned as a young man and was promised his inheritance if he could bring back the fleece of a miraculous winged golden ram, owned by King Aeetes of Colchis. He won the Golden Fleece with the help of MEDEA, whom he married, and the two returned to Iolcos, where Medea murdered Pelias. Driven out by Pelias's son, they sought refuge in Corinth, where Jason deserted Medea, leading her to kill her children by Jason.

jasper Opaque, fine-grained or dense variety of CHERT that is chiefly brick red to brownish red. Long used for jewelry and ornamentation, it has a dull luster but takes a fine polish; its physical properties are those of QUARTZ. Jasper is widely distributed, occurring in the Ural Mtns., N. Africa, Sicily, and Germany. For thousands of years, black jasper was used to test gold-silver alloys for their gold content. Rubbing the alloys on the stone, called a touchstone, produces a streak the color of which determines the gold content within 1 part in 100.

Jasper National Park National park, W Alberta. Located on the E slopes of the ROCKY MTNS., it occupies 4,200 sq mi (10,878 sq km), including the ATHABASCA RIVER valley and the surrounding mountains. It encompasses part of the great Columbia Icefield. The park's wildlife includes bear, elk, moose, caribou, and cougar.

Jaspers \'yäs-pərs\, **Karl (Theodor)** (1883–1969) German-Swiss philosopher and psychiatrist. As a research psychiatrist, he promoted rigorous, scientifically descriptive methods in his *General Psychopathology* (1913). He taught philosophy at the Univ. of Heidelberg from 1921 until 1937, when the Nazi regime forbade him to work, and at the Univ. of Basel from 1948. In his magnum opus, *Philosophy* (3 vols., 1969), he argues that the aim of philosophy is practical; its purpose is the fulfillment of human existence. For Jaspers, philosophical illumination is achieved in the experience of limit situations that define the human condition—conflict, guilt, suffering, and death. One of the most important existentialists (see EXIS-TENTIALISM), he approached the subject from mankind's direct concern with its own existence.

Jassy See IASI

jaundice Excess BILE pigments (bilirubin) in the bloodstream and tissues, causing a yellow to orange color in the skin and the whites of the eyes. Bilirubin may be overproduced or inadequately removed by the LIVER (retention jaundice), or may leak back into the bloodstream (regurgitation jaundice); jaundice may also be due to impaired bile flow (obstructive jaundice). Causes include ANEMIA, PNEU-MONIA, and CIRRHOSIS). Bilirubin excess usually does no harm, but retention jaundice signals severe liver malfunction.

Jaurès \zhȯ-'res\, **(Auguste-Marie-Joseph-) Jean** (1859–1914) French socialist leader. He served in the Chamber of Deputies (1885–89, 1893–98, 1902–14). After 1899 the socialists split into two groups, and Jaurès headed the FRENCH SOCIALIST PARTY. In the newspaper *L'Humanité*, which he cofounded in 1904, he espoused democratic so-

Map

128° 134° 140° 146°

CHINA RUSSIA SEA OF OKHOTSK

La Perouse Strait

KITAMI MTS

KURIL ISLANDS (Occupied by Russia since 1945; claimed by Japan)

Ishikari Bay

Sapporo HOKKAIDO

HIDAKA RANGE

44°

OSHIMA PENINSULA Cape Erimo

NORTH KOREA

Seikan Tunnel Tsugaru Strait

⊛ P'yongyang Aomori

OGA PENINSULA OU MTS.

Akita Morioka

SEA OF JAPAN (EAST SEA)

SADO Yamagata Sendai

⊛ Seoul Niigata Fukushima

38° NOTO PENINSULA HONSHU

SOUTH KOREA Toyama Nagano Utsunomiya

Kanazawa Maebashi Mito

Fukui Urawa Tokyo

Matsue Tottori Mt. Fuji Gifu Otsu Nagoya Chiba

12,388 ft. Kyoto Kobe Tsu Shizuoka Yokohama

Strait Hiroshima Okayama Osaka Nara

Korea Yamaguchi Takamatsu SHIKOKU Wakayama IZU ISLANDS

Kitakyushu Matsuyama Kochi KII PENINSULA

EAST CHINA SEA TSUSHIMA Fukuoka Saga Oita PACIFIC OCEAN

Nagasaki Kumamoto

32° GOTO ISLANDS KYUSHU Bungo Channel

Kagoshima Miyazaki

Osumi Strait

OSUMI ARCHIPELAGO TANEGA-SHIMA

YAKU-SHIMA

RYUKYU IS.

AMAMI GREAT ISLAND

TOKUNO-SHIMA

KERAMA ISLANDS OKINO-ERABU ISLAND

Naha ● OKINAWA

©1999, Encyclopædia Britannica, Inc.

JAPAN

Scale 1: 21,741,000

0   100   200 mi

0   150   300 km

cialism. In 1905 the two French socialist parties united, and his authority continued to grow. On the eve of World War I, he espoused peace through arbitration and championed Franco-German rapprochement, which earned him the hatred of French nationalists, and he was assassinated in 1914 by a young nationalist fanatic. He wrote several books, including the influential *Socialist History of the French Revolution* (1901–7).

Java Indonesian **Djawa** \ˈjä-vä\ Island (pop., 1988 est.: 105,560,000), Indonesia. Lying southeast of Malaysia and Sumatra, it is Indonesia's fourth-largest island and contains more than half of its population. Its area, including offshore Madura Island, is 51,038 sq mi (132,187 sq km). The capital of Java and of the republic is JAKARTA. The island's highest point is Mt. Semeru, an active volcano 12,060 ft (3,676 m) high. The remains of *Homo erectus*, or "Java man," indicate that the island was occupied 800,000 years ago. The Majapahit dynasty was founded in E Java in 1293; it fell early in the 16th cent. when Muslim kingdoms arose. In 1619 the Dutch E. INDIA CO. took control of Batavia (Jakarta), and extended its influence. Ruled by the Dutch until the 1940s when it was occupied by Japan, it became part of the newly independent Republic of Indonesia in 1950.

Java Modular OBJECT-ORIENTED PROGRAMMING language developed by Sun Microsystems in 1995 specifically for the INTERNET. Java is based on the idea that the same SOFTWARE should run on many different kinds of computers, consumer gadgets, and other devices; its code is translated according to the needs of the machine on which it is running. The most visible examples of Java software are the interactive programs called "applets" that animate sites on the WORLD WIDE WEB, where Java is a standard creative tool. Java provides an interface to HTML.

Java man Common name of fossilized *HOMO ERECTUS* remains found in 1891 at Trinil, Java. The remains of Java man represent the first known fossils of *H. erectus* (though originally assigned to *Pithecanthropus erectus*). Together with numerous other finds along Java's Solo River, they suggest that *H. erectus* was present in E Asia about 1 million years ago and persisted there for 500,000–800,000 years. Java man predates the finds at ZHOUKOUDIAN (Peking Man) in China.

Javanese Largest ethnic group on the island of JAVA, Indonesia. The Javanese are Muslim, though few are strictly observant. Traditional Javanese social organization varied in structure from relatively egalitarian villages to the highly stratified society of the cities; these differences find expression in the many Javanese styles of speech still in use. Javanese villages are compact groups of single-family houses, generally built of bamboo, surrounding a central square. In large cities, Javanese workers live in makeshift huts in enclosed neighborhoods called kampongs.

JavaScript Computer PROGRAMMING LANGUAGE developed by Netscape in 1995 for use in HTML pages. JavaScript is a scripting language, which is not as fast as compiled languages (such as JAVA or C++) but easier to learn and use. It is only loosely related to Java. JavaScript can be quickly added to an HTML page to provide dynamic features. The JavaScript code must be interpreted and executed by a BROWSER as it reads the Web page or by a Web server before it delivers the page to the browser.

Java Sea Part of the W Pacific Ocean between JAVA and BORNEO islands. It occupies 167,000 sq mi (433,000 sq km). A shallow sea, it has a mean depth of 151 ft (46 m). It was the scene of a World War II naval battle (1942) that resulted in Japan's invasion of Java.

javelin See PECCARY

javelin throw TRACK-AND-FIELD sport of throwing a wooden or metal spear for distance. It is hurled after a short run and must land point first. Included in the ancient Greek Olympic Games as part of the PENTATHLON, it has been part of the modern Olympic program since its inception in 1896. A women's event was added in 1932. See also DECATHLON, HEPTATHLON.

jaw Either of two bones that frame the MOUTH: a movable lower jaw (mandible) and a fixed upper jaw (maxilla). These hold the teeth (see TOOTH) and are used for biting and chewing and in speech. Vertical portions at the back of the lower jaw form hinge joints at the temples. The upper jaw is attached to bones at the bridge of the nose, in the eye sockets and roof of the mouth, and the cheekbones. It contains the large maxillary SINUS.

Jawlensky \yəv-ˈlän-skē\, **Alexey** (1864–1941) Russian-German painter. He gave up a military career to study painting, and in 1896 moved to Munich. In France in 1905 he worked with Henri MATISSE. Back in Munich he produced such works as *Mme. Turandot* (1912), featuring flat areas of vibrant Fauve color outlined with simple, thick contours. Such semiabstract faces as *Looking Within Night* (1923) had a mystical intensity reminiscent of Russian icon painting. In 1924 he joined Vassily KANDINSKY, Paul KLEE, and Lyonel FEININGER to form Der Blaue Vier ("The Blue Four"); they exhibited together until arthritis forced Jawlensky to abandon painting.

jay Any of 35–40 bird species (family Corvidae) that inhabit woodlands in the New World and Eurasia and are known for their bold, raucous manner. Jays are nearly omnivores; some steal eggs, and many store seeds and nuts for winter use. The 12-in. (30-cm) blue jay, bright blue and white, is found in N. America east of the Rockies; westward it is replaced by the dark-blue, black-crested Steller's jay. The scrub jay is found throughout W N. America and in Florida.

Jay, John (1745–1829) First chief justice of the U.S. SUPREME COURT. Born in New York City, he practiced law there and became a staunch supporter of independence. Elected New York's first chief justice in 1777, he was chosen president of the CONTINENTAL CONGRESS. He helped Benjamin FRANKLIN negotiate terms for a peace treaty with Britain and then served as secretary for foreign affairs (1784–90). Convinced of the need for a stronger centralized government, he urged ratification of the U.S. Constitution and joined with James MADISON and Alexander HAMILTON to write *The FEDERALIST* essays. In 1789 he was appointed the first chief justice of the U.S. Supreme Court, where he set legal precedent in affirming subordination of the states to the federal government. In 1794 he was sent to Britain to negotiate a treaty dealing with commercial disputes; the Jay Treaty helped avert war, but Jeffersonian Republicans criticized it as pro-British. Jay resigned from the court in 1795 and was elected governor of New York (1795–1801).

Jayavarman VII \ˌjä-yä-ˈvär-män\ (c.1120–c.1215) King of the Khmer (Cambodian) empire of Angkor (r.1181–1215?). Born into the royal family of Angkor, he settled in the Champa kingdom (central Vietnam) and engaged in military campaigns. Returning to Angkor (c.1177), he led the struggle for independence against the Cham, and was crowned king of a reconstituted Khmer empire (1181). He brought the empire to its zenith in terms both of territorial extent and of royal architecture and construction. Champa, S Laos, and portions of the Malay Peninsula and Burma came under his control. He built temples, hospitals, and rest houses, and rebuilt the city of ANGKOR. His dedication to both the spiritual and physical needs of the people has made him a national hero to modern Cambodians.

Jazairi, Abdelqadir al- See ABDELQADIR AL-JAZAIRI

jazz Music developed in the U.S. usually incorporating improvisation and syncopated rhythmic momentum. It developed principally as an amalgam in late-19th- and early-20th-cent. New Orleans. Elements of the BLUES and RAGTIME provided harmonic and rhythmic structures upon which to improvise. Whether for dancing or marching, celebration or ceremony, the music was tailored to suit the occasion. Instrumental technique combined Western tonal values with emulation of the human voice. Emerging from the collective routines of DIXIELAND, Louis ARMSTRONG became the first great soloist in jazz, which thereafter became primarily a vehicle for profoundly personal expression. Elaboration of the role of the soloist in both small and large ensembles occurred during the SWING era (c.1930–45), when the music of Duke ELLINGTON demonstrated the combination of composed and improvised elements. In the mid-1940s Charlie PARKER pioneered the technical complexities of BEBOP, his extremes of tempo and harmonic sophistication challenging both performer and listener. Miles DAVIS led groups that established the relaxed aesthetic and lyrical phrasing of cool jazz in the 1950s, later incorporating modal and electronic elements. John COLTRANE's music explored many of the directions jazz would take in the 1960s, including experimental free improvisation.

Jeddah See JIDDA

Jeffers, (John) Robinson (1887–1962) U.S. poet. Born in Pittsburgh, he settled on the California coast. His poetry expresses contempt for humanity and love of the harsh, eternal beauties of nature. *Tamar and Other Poems* (1924) brought him fame and revealed the unique style and eccentric ideas later developed in *Cawdor* (1928), *Thurso's Landing* (1932), and *Be Angry at the Sun* (1941). He made a theatrically successful adaptation of Euripides' *Medea* (1946).

Jefferson, Thomas (1743–1826) Third president of the U.S. (1801–9). Born in Shadwell, Va., he was a planter and lawyer from 1767, as well as a slaveholder who opposed slavery. While a member of the House of BURGESSES (1769–75), he helped initiate the COMMITTEES OF CORRESPONDENCE (1773). A delegate to the second Continental Congress, he was appointed to the committee to draft the DECLARATION OF INDEPENDENCE and became its primary author. He was elected governor of Virginia (1779–81). Again a member of the Continental Congress (1783–85), he proposed territorial provisions incorporated in the NORTHWEST ORDINANCES. He traveled in Europe on diplomatic missions and became U.S.

Thomas Jefferson Painting by Rembrandt Peale, 1800

minister to France (1785–89). Pres. George WASHINGTON made him secretary of state (1790–93). His conflict with Alexander HAMILTON about interpretation of the Constitution led to the rise of factions and political parties, with Jefferson representing the Democratic-Republicans. He was elected vice president (1797–1801), but opposed Pres. John ADAMS's ALIEN AND SEDITION ACTS and codrafted the VIRGINIA AND KENTUCKY RESOLUTIONS. In 1801 he became president after an electoral-vote tie with Aaron BURR was settled by the U.S. House of Representatives. As president, he initiated frugal fiscal policies and sought to pay off the national debt. He oversaw the LOUISIANA PURCHASE and authorized the LEWIS AND CLARK EXPEDITION. He sought to avoid involvement in the NAPOLEONIC WARS by signing the EMBARGO ACT. He retired to his plantation, MONTICELLO, where he pursued his many interests in science, philosophy, and architecture. In 1819 he founded and designed the Univ. of VIRGINIA. After a long estrangement, he and Adams became reconciled in 1813 and exchanged views on national issues that illuminated much of the founders' philosophies. They both died on July 4, 1826, the 50th anniversary of the Declaration of Independence.

Jefferson City Capital (pop., 2000: 39,000), Missouri. Lying near the center of the state, it was selected as the site of the state capital in 1821. Loyalties were divided during the AMERICAN CIVIL WAR, but it remained in the Union. The Capitol, completed in 1918, contains murals by T. H. BENTON. Lincoln Univ. was founded there by black Union Army veterans in 1866.

Jeffreys, Harold (*later* **Sir Harold**) (1891–1989) British astronomer and geophysicist. He established that the four large outer planets (Jupiter, Saturn, Uranus, and Neptune) are very cold and devised models of their planetary structure. He also investigated the thermal history of the earth, was coauthor (1940) of the standard tables of travel times for earthquake waves, and was the first to hypothesize that the earth's core is liquid. He explained the origin of monsoons and sea breezes and showed how cyclones are vital to the general circulation of the atmosphere.

Jehovah's Witness Member of an international religious movement founded in Pittsburgh, Pa., by Charles T. RUSSELL in 1872. The Witnesses are a millennialist sect with a belief system based primarily on the apocalyptic sections of the Bible, notably Daniel and the Book of REVELATION. They regard all political parties and governments as unwitting allies of Satan, and refuse to perform military service or salute the flag. They are famous for their door-to-door evangelizing and for refusing blood transfusions on a scriptural basis. Their goal is the establishment of God's kingdom on earth. Their headquarters is in Brooklyn, N.Y.; their major publications, *The Watchtower* and *Awake!*, are published in about 80 languages. See also MILLENNIALISM.

Jekyll, Gertrude (1842–1932) British landscape architect. Initially a painter, she helped William Robinson (1838–1935) in his writings about the natural garden, and wrote several successful books herself, including *Wood and Garden* (1899) and *Home and Garden* (1900). She later worked closely with Edwin LUTYENS, developing a modern, informal style of garden marked by rhythmic use of color and form.

jelly and jam Foods consisting of the strained juice of various fruits or vegetables that are sweetened, boiled, slowly simmered, and congealed, often with the aid of PECTIN or GELATIN. Jam differs from jelly in its inclusion of fruit pulp or whole fruit; whole-fruit jam is sometimes called preserve. Fruit and berry jellies and jams are eaten in sandwiches or with other breads. Vegetable and herb jellies traditionally complement lamb and other meat dishes.

jellyfish Any of about 200 described species of marine CNIDARIANS (in the classes Scyphozoa and Cubozoa), many of which have a bell-shaped body. The term is also frequently applied to other similar cnidarians (e.g., PORTUGUESE MAN-OF-WAR) and some unrelated forms (e.g., CTENOPHORES). In scyphozoan jellyfish, the free-swimming MEDUSA form is the dominant stage, with the sessile POLYP form found only during larval development. Free-swimming jellyfish live in all oceans and include the familiar disk-shaped animals that are often found drifting along the

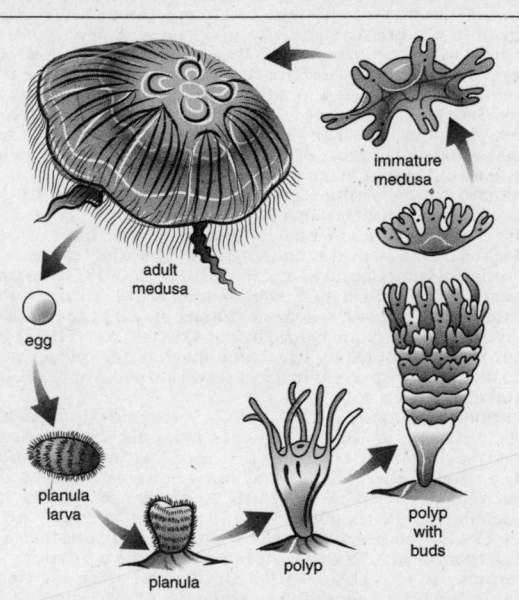

Jellyfish Life cycle of the common jellyfish *Aurelia*. Eggs released by females pass out through the mouth and become lodged in pits on the tentacles. Sperm released from male jellyfish fertilize the eggs, which remain on the tentacles during early development. A fertilized egg develops into a ciliated larva, or planula, which settles on and attaches to a substrate (such as a rock) and develops into a polyp with a mouth and tentacles. The polyp reproduces asexually by budding off saucer-shaped immature medusae, which develop into mature sexually reproducing forms.

shoreline. Most species are 1–16 in. (2–40 cm) in diameter; some are 6 ft (1.8 m) in diameter. Most feed on small animals that they catch in their tentacles, whose stinging cells immobilize the animals; contact can be irritating and sometimes dangerous to humans. The cubozoan jellyfish include 50 species of box jellies (with squared-off bodies), usually 1–2 in. (2–4 cm) in diameter.

Jenner, Edward (1749–1823) English surgeon, discoverer of the SMALLPOX VACCINE. Jenner had noticed as a youth that people who had been sick with the relatively harmless disease cowpox did not contract smallpox. In 1796 he inoculated a young boy with matter taken from a dairymaid's fresh cowpox lesions. The boy caught cowpox and, when subsequently inoculated with smallpox, did not contract it. Despite early difficulties, the procedure became accepted and the death rate from smallpox fell. Jenner received worldwide recognition.

Jensen \\'yen-sən\\, **Georg** (1866–1935) Danish silversmith and designer. Apprenticed to a goldsmith, he later opened his own workshop in Copenhagen. Exhibiting his silverware and jewelry at major foreign exhibitions, he quickly built a reputation as an outstanding and original silversmith and was among the first to fashion steel into handsome, serviceable cutlery. By 1935 his firm had stores all over the world and carried more than 3,000 patterns.

Jephtha \\'jef-thə\\ One of the judges in ancient Israel. According to the Book of Judges, he was the illegitimate son of a Gileadite. Cast out by his father's legitimate sons, he joined a band of brigands. When the Gileadites were oppressed by an Ammonite army, they asked Jephtha to aid them. He was victorious after promising God a sacrifice of the first thing he saw on leaving his house, which turned out to be his daughter. Jephtha represents an exemplar of Israel's fidelity to God.

Jeremiah (c.650 B.C.–c.570 B.C.) Hebrew PROPHET and reformer, author of the Old Testament Book of Jeremiah. Born into a priestly family in a village near Jerusalem, he began to preach around 627 B.C., charging his fellow citizens with injustice and false worship and calling on them to reform. He accurately predicted the destruction of JUDAH by Babylonia. He stayed in Jerusalem even after it fell in 586 B.C., but left when the new governor of the region was assassinated. His most significant prophecy looked to a time when God would make a new covenant with Israel.

Jericho *Arabic* **Ariha** Town (pop., 1995 est.: 25,000), W. Bank of the JORDAN RIVER. Inhabited since about 9000 B.C., it is famous in biblical history as the first town attacked by the Israelites under JOSHUA after they crossed the Jordan River. Captured by the British in 1918, it became part of the British mandate of PALESTINE. Incorporated into Jordan in 1949, it became the site of two huge camps of Arab refugees from Israel. In the SIX-DAY WAR (1967) the town was occupied by Israel, and much of the refugee population was dispersed. In 1994 it was turned over to Palestinian rule.

Jerome, Chauncey (1793–1868) U.S. inventor. Born in Canaan, Conn., in 1824 he designed a popular bronze clock, and he formed a company that soon became the leading U.S. clockmaker. His one-day brass movement was an improvement over the wood clock. Applying mass-production techniques, he flooded the U.S. with low-priced brass clocks, which quickly spread to Europe and so astonished the English that "Yankee ingenuity" became a byword.

Jerome, St. (c.A.D. 347–419/420) Church Father and translator. Born into a wealthy Christian family in Dalmatia, he was baptized around 366 and spent most of the next 20 years in travel. He lived two years as a hermit in the desert of Chalcis. From 377 to 379, while in Antioch, he studied biblical texts and translated the works of ORIGEN and others. He lived in Rome 382–85, but theological controversy and opposition to his ascetic views led him to depart for the Holy Land, and he settled in Bethlehem, where he lived until his death. Traditionally regarded as the most learned of the Latin Fathers, in 406 he completed his translation of the Bible into Latin. Jerome's Latin Bible is known as the Vulgate.

Jersey Largest and southernmost island (pop., 1993 est.: 86,000) of the English CHANNEL ISLANDS. It occupies 44 sq mi (115 sq km); its capital is St. Helier (pop., 1991: 28,000). Separated from NORMANDY in 1204, it kept its Norman law and local customs but was administered for the British king by a warden. It was given legislative authority in 1771. Jersey fabric and Jersey cattle take their names from the island.

Jersey City City (pop., 2000: 240,000), NE New Jersey, opposite NEW YORK CITY. Occupied by Dutch trappers (1618) as Paulus Hook, it was a permanent settlement by 1660. In 1779, during the AMERICAN REVOLUTION, Gen. Henry LEE won a victory there over the British. Renamed Jersey City in 1836, it is a manufacturing center.

Jerusalem *Hebrew* **Yerushalayim** \\ye-ˌrü-shä-'lī-im\\ *Arabic* **Al-Quds** \\äl-'küts\\ City (pop., 1999: 633,000) and capital of Israel. Lying west of the DEAD SEA and east of the Mediterranean Sea, it is a holy city of JUDAISM, CHRISTIANITY, and ISLAM. For Jews it is the ancient capital of the Hebrews and the site of the Temple of JERUSALEM; for Christians it was the scene of the ministry and crucifixion of JESUS; for Muslims it was the site of MUHAMMAD's ascension to heaven. In 1000 B.C. King DAVID captured it and made it the capital of Israel; his son SOLOMON built the Temple. The Romans captured it in 63 B.C. Muslim Arabs took it in 637, and Crusaders in 1099 (see CRUSADES). Occupied by the British in 1917, it became the capital of the British mandate of PALESTINE. During the ARAB–ISRAELI WARS, it was divided between Transjordan (later JORDAN) and Israel. Israel took E. Jerusalem from Jordan in the SIX-DAY WAR of 1967. Its capital status has remained a point of international contention. Sacred Jewish shrines include the site of the First and Second Temples and the WESTERN WALL; Islamic holy places include the DOME OF THE ROCK and Al-Aqsa Mosque.

Jerusalem, Temple of Either of two temples that were at the center of worship and national identity in ancient Israel. When DAVID captured Jerusalem, he selected as a temple site Mt. Moriah, or Temple Mount, where it was believed that ABRAHAM had built his altar to sacrifice Isaac. The First Temple was completed there under David's son SOLOMON in 957 B.C. It contained three rooms: a vestibule, the main room for religious services, and the inner sanctum known as the Holy of Holies. It was destroyed during the Babylonian conquest in 586 B.C. When the Jews returned from exile in 538, they built the Second Temple (finished 515). Desecrated by the Syrians (167 B.C.) and plundered by CRASSUS (54 B.C.), it was rebuilt and enlarged by HEROD the Great; construction lasted 46 years. The Jewish rebellion in A.D. 66 led to its destruction by Roman legions in A.D. 70. All that remains is the WESTERN WALL. The Temple Mount is now occupied by a Muslim mosque, al-Aqsa, and the DOME OF THE ROCK.

Jerusalem artichoke SUNFLOWER (Helianthus tuberosus) native to N. America and grown for its edible TUBERS. The aboveground part of the plant is 7–10 ft (2–3 m) tall with numerous showy flower heads of yellow ray flowers and yellow, brownish, or purplish disk flowers. Jerusalem artichoke is popular as a cooked vegetable in Europe and has long been cultivated in France as a stock feed.

Jervis Bay Inlet of the S. Pacific, NEW S. WALES, Australia. It occupies 28 sq mi (73 sq km). It was discovered in 1770 and named Long Nose, but renamed in 1791 for Adm. John Jervis (1735–1823). It provides the Australian Capital Territory with access to the sea. The bay is a resort area and the site of the Royal Australian Naval College (founded 1915).

Jespersen \\'yes-pər-sən\\, **(Jens) Otto (Harry)** (1860–1943) Danish linguist. He led a movement for basing foreign-language teaching on conversation rather than textbook study, helping to revolutionize language teaching in Europe. An authority on English grammar, Jespersen contributed greatly to the advancement of phonetics and linguistic theory. His many published works include *Modern English Grammar* (7 vols., 1909–49), *Language: Its Nature, Development, and Origin* (1922), and *The Philosophy of Grammar* (1924).

jester See FOOL

Jesuit \\'je-zü-ət\\ Member of the Roman Catholic order called the Society of Jesus. First organized by St. Ignatius of LOYOLA in 1534, the order was approved by Pope PAUL III in 1540. It discontinued such medieval practices as obligatory penances, fasts, and a common uniform to focus on military-style mobility and adaptability. Its organization was characterized by centralized authority, probation lasting many years before final vows, and special obedience to the pope. A preaching, teaching, and missionary society, the Jesuits actively promoted the COUNTER-REFORMATION, and by the time of Ignatius's death in 1556 their efforts were already worldwide. Their success earned them much hostility from religious and political foes. Under pressure, Pope Clement XIV abolished the order in 1773, but it was restored by Pius VII in 1814. The Jesuits have since become the largest male religious order.

Jesus In CHRISTIANITY, the son of God and the second person of the Holy TRINITY, who by his CRUCIFIXION and resurrection paid for the sins of all mankind. His life and ministry are recounted in the four GOSPELS of the NEW TESTAMENT. He was born a Jew in Bethlehem before the death of HEROD the Great in 4 B.C., and he died while Pontius PILATE was Roman governor of Judaea (A.D. 28–30). His mother, MARY, was married to Joseph, a carpenter of Nazareth (see St. JOSEPH). Jesus was a carpenter until he began his ministry about age 30, becoming a preacher, teacher, and healer. He gathered disciples in the region of GALILEE, including the 12 APOSTLES, and preached the coming of the Kingdom of God. His moral teachings, outlined in the SERMON ON THE MOUNT, and his reported miracles won him a growing number of followers, who believed that he was the promised MESSIAH. On Passover he entered Jerusalem, where he shared the Last Supper with his disciples and was betrayed to the Roman authorities by JUDAS ISCARIOT. Condemned to death as a political agitator, he was crucified and buried. Three days later, visitors to his tomb found it empty. According to the Gospels, he appeared several times to his disciples before ascending into heaven.

jet engine Any of a class of INTERNAL-COMBUSTION ENGINES that propel aircraft by means of the rearward discharge of a jet of fluid, usually hot exhaust gases generated by burning fuel with air drawn in from the atmosphere. Jets rely on the third of NEWTON'S LAWS OF MOTION (action and reaction are equal and opposite). The first jet-powered airplane was introduced in 1939 in Germany. The jet engine significantly simplified propulsion and enabled substantial increases in aircraft speed, size, and operating altitudes. Modern types of jet engines include TURBOJETS, turbofans, TURBOPROPS, turboshafts, and RAMJETS. See diagram at AIRPLANE.

jet lag Period of adjustment of BIOLOGICAL RHYTHM after moving from one time zone to another, experienced as fatigue and lowered efficiency. It reflects a delay in the synchronization of changes in the level of blood cortisol, the major STEROID produced by the adrenal cortex (see ADRENAL GLAND), with the local day-night cycle. Duration and severity depend on how much distance is covered in how little time.

jet stream Any of several long, narrow, high-speed air currents that flow eastward in the STRATOSPHERE or upper TROPOSPHERE. Jet streams are characterized by wind motions that generate strong vertical shearing action (see WIND SHEAR), considered largely responsible for the clear-air turbulence experienced by aircraft. They circle the earth in meandering paths, shifting position as well as speed with the seasons; in the winter they are nearer the equator and their speeds are higher than in the summer.

Jew Any person whose religion is JUDAISM. In a wider sense the term refers to any member of a worldwide ethnic and cultural group descended from the ancient Hebrews who traditionally practiced the Jewish religion. In Jewish tradition, any child born of a Jewish mother is considered a Jew; in REFORM JUDAISM a child is considered a Jew if either parent is Jewish.

jewelry Objects designed for the adornment of the body, usually made of gold, silver, or platinum, often with precious or semiprecious stones. Jewelry evolved from shells, animal teeth, and other objects used as adornment in prehistoric times. Over the centuries it came to be a sign of social or religious rank. In Renaissance Italy, jewelry making reached the status of a fine art. By the 19th cent., industrialization brought jewelry within the reach of the middle class. Firms opened by such jewelers as Carl FABERGÉ and L. C. TIFFANY achieved great success by making fine jewelry for the wealthy. It has played an important role in world history: in the 16th cent. the Spaniards established an empire to acquire the gold and jeweled objects of pre-Columbian Mexico and Peru.

Jewett, (Theodora) Sarah Orne (1849–1909) U.S. writer. Born in S. Berwick, Me., she virtually never left the state. Concerned to capture the folkways of a vanishing culture, she wrote realistic sketches of aging Maine natives, notable for their pungency and humor. Outstanding among her 20 volumes are *Deephaven* (1877), *A White Heron* (1886), and *The Country of the Pointed Firs* (1896).

Jewish calendar See Jewish CALENDAR

Jezebel \ˈje-zə-ˌbel\ (d.c.843 B.C.) In the Old Testament, the wife of King AHAB of Israel. She persuaded Ahab to introduce the worship of the Tyrian god BAAL-Melkart into Israel, thus interfering with the exclusive worship of Yahweh. She was opposed by ELIJAH. After Ahab's death Jezebel's son Jehoram became king of Israel, but ELISHA encouraged a general, Jehu, to revolt. Jehoram was killed, and Jezebel was thrown from a window to her death. In history and literature, she became the archetype of the wicked woman.

Jhabvala \ˈjäb-vä-lə\, **Ruth Prawer** *orig.* Ruth Prawer (b.1927) German-British-U.S. novelist and screenwriter. Born in Germany, she emigrated to England with her family in 1939. She later moved to India, where she lived until 1975. Many of her novels, including *Heat and Dust* (1975, Booker Prize), are set in India. She has written many short stories, original screenplays for such films as *Shakespeare Wallah* (1965), and film adaptations of such novels as *The Bostonians* (1984) and *Howards End* (1992). Later novels include *Shards of Memory* (1995).

Jhelum River \ˈjā-ləm\ River, India and Pakistan. The westernmost of the "Five Rivers" of the PUNJAB, it rises in the HIMALAYAS and crosses from the Indian to the Pakistani portion of KASHMIR, then joins the Chenab River after a course of 450 mi (725 km). It is believed to be the Hydaspes mentioned by Arrian, ALEXANDER THE GREAT's historian, and the Bidaspes mentioned by PTOLEMY.

Jiang Jieshi See CHIANG KAI-SHEK

Jiang Jinguo See CHIANG CHING-KUO

Jiang Qing *or* **Chiang Ch'ing** \jē-ˈäŋ-ˈchiŋ\ (1914?–1991) Third wife of MAO ZEDONG and member of the radical GANG OF FOUR. Jiang married Mao in 1939 but entered politics only in 1963. As first deputy head of the CULTURAL REVOLUTION, she acquired far-reaching powers over China's cultural life and oversaw the total suppression of many traditional cultural activities. Arrested after Mao's death and accused of fomenting the widespread civil unrest of the Cultural Revolution, she refused to confess guilt and was sentenced to life imprisonment. Her death was a suicide.

Jiang Zemin \jē-ˈäŋ-zə-ˈmin\ (b.1926) General secretary of the CHINESE COMMUNIST PARTY (CCP) (1989–2002) and president of China (1993–2003). He started his career as an engineer and gradually rose through the ranks of the CCP. He was named mayor of Shanghai in 1985 and chairman of China's Central Military Commission in 1989. His support of the forcible suppression of pro-democracy student demonstrations of 1989 won him the support of DENG XIAOPING. He has combined a commitment to continued free-market reform with a determination to preserve the CCP's monopoly on political power.

Jibril *or* **Jabrail** \ji-ˈbrēl\ In Islam, the archangel who acts as intermediary between God and mankind. His biblical counterpart is GABRIEL. Jibril aided MUHAMMAD in times of crisis and guided him during his ascent into heaven. Muslim legend holds that Jibril also aided ADAM after his expulsion from Paradise and MOSES in delivering the Israelites from Egypt.

jícama \ˈhē-kə-mə\ Leguminous vine (*Pachyrhizus erosus*), also called yam bean. A native of Mexico and Central and S. America, it is grown for its edible root. The brown-skinned tubers are white-fleshed, crisp, and juicy, and can be eaten raw or cooked. Sometimes very young seedpods of the plant are eaten, but the mature seeds are highly toxic.

HIJ

Jidda *or* **Jeddah** City (pop., 1991 est.: 1,500,000), W Saudi Arabia. Located on the Red Sea, it is a major port and the nation's diplomatic capital. Jidda has long been a point of entry for Muslim pilgrims journeying to the holy cities of MECCA and MEDINA. It belonged to Turkey until 1916, when it yielded to British forces. Captured by Abdulaziz IBN SAUD in 1925, it was incorporated into Saudi Arabia in 1927.

jihad \ji-ʹhäd\ In ISLAM, the central doctrine that calls on believers to combat the enemies of their religion. According to the QURAN and the HADITH, jihad is a duty that may be fulfilled in four ways: by the heart, the tongue, the hand, and the sword. The first way involves struggling against evil desires. The ways of the tongue and hand call for verbal defense and right actions. The jihad of the sword involves waging war against enemies of Islam. In the 20th cent. the concept of jihad has sometimes been used as an ideological weapon in the effort to combat Western influences and secular governments.

Jim Crow laws Laws that enforced racial segregation in the U.S. South. "Jim Crow," taken from a minstrel-show routine, became a derogatory epithet for blacks. After RECONSTRUCTION, Southern legislatures passed laws requiring segregation of whites and "persons of color" on public transportation and in schools, restaurants, and other public places. In 1954 the U.S. Supreme Court declared segregation in public schools unconstitutional in *BROWN VS. BOARD OF EDUCATION*; later rulings struck down other Jim Crow laws.

Jiménez \k̲ē-ʹmä-näs, *Engl* hē-ʹmä-nəs\, **Juan Ramón** (1881–1958) Spanish poet. His early poetry reflects the influence of Rubén DARÍO; this highly emotional style gave way to a more austere tone around 1917. His popular *Platero ànd I* (1917) is a prose story of a man and his donkey. After the Spanish Civil War (1936–39) he moved to Puerto Rico. His poetic output was immense. He was awarded the Nobel Prize in 1956.

Jimmu \ʹjēm-ˌmü\ Legendary first emperor of Japan and founder of the imperial dynasty. He is credited with establishing his state in 660 B.C. on the plains of Yamato. (An actual state on the Yamato plains dates from the 3rd cent. A.D.) Jimmu was believed to be a descendant of the sun goddess AMATERASU.

Jinan *or* **Tsinan** \ʹjē-ʹnän\ City (pop., 1999: 1,713,000), capital of Shandong province, NE China. It has been an administrative center since the 8th cent. B.C. Nearby Mt. Tai was one of China's greatest holy mountains; many Buddhist cave temples were built in the hills south of the city in the 4th–7th cent. A.D. It was made the capital of Shandong under the MING DYNASTY (1368–1644). Opened to foreign commerce in 1904, it developed further after becoming a railroad junction in 1912. It is now a major administrative, industrial, educational and cultural center.

Jin dynasty *or* **Chin dynasty** \ʹjin\ First of two major Chinese dynasties to bear the name Jin. The dynasty had two distinct phases: the Western Jin (A.D. 265–317) and the Eastern Jin (A.D. 317–420). China was reunited under Sima Yan (Ssu-ma Yen), first of the Jin emperors, but after his death the empire rapidly crumbled. Nomads of the north overran the Jin capital of Luoyang. For the next two centuries China was divided into two societies, northern (plagued by barbarian invasions) and southern. The Eastern Jin, one of the SIX DYNASTIES, was founded by another Sima prince at Nanjing; it suffered revolts, court intrigues, and frontier wars, but also saw the flourishing of Buddhism in China and the birth of China's first great painter, Gu Kaizhi (344–406?).

Jinnah, Mohammed Ali (1876–1948) Indian Muslim politician, founder and first governor-general of Pakistan (1947–48). After studies in Bombay and London, he returned to India (1896), practiced law, and was elected to India's Imperial Legislative Council in 1910. Committed to home rule for India and to maintaining Hindu-Muslim unity, he joined the MUSLIM LEAGUE in 1913 and worked to ensure its collaboration with the INDIAN NATIONAL CONGRESS. Opposed to Mohandas GANDHI's noncooperation movement, he withdrew from both groups in 1920. He led a reformed League from 1935. When the Congress Party refused to form coalition governments with the Muslim League in the provinces (1937), Jinnah began to work for the partitioning of India and the creation of a Muslim nation. Pakistan emerged as an independent country in 1947, and Jinnah became its first head of state. He is revered as the father of the nation.

Mohammed Ali Jinnah

jinni *or* **genie** In Arabic mythology, any of the supernatural spirits less powerful than angels or devils. Evil spirits of air or fire, they could take animal or human form and could dwell in inanimate objects or under the earth. They had the bodily needs of human beings and could be killed, but were otherwise free of physical restraints. The jinn were popular subjects for folklore, notably in the tale of AL-ADDIN in *THE THOUSAND AND ONE NIGHTS*.

jitterbug Dance variation of the two-step in which couples swing, balance, and twirl in standardized patterns. It originated in the U.S. in the mid-1930s and became internationally popular in the 1940s. Danced to syncopated music in 4/4 time, it originally included acrobatic lifts and swings, but became modified in ballroom versions.

Jiulong See KOWLOON

Joan, Pope Legendary female pontiff who supposedly reigned, as Pope John VIII, for about 25 months from 855 to 858. The tale held that she was an Englishwoman who fell in love with a Benedictine monk, disguised herself as a man, and joined his order. After acquiring great learning she moved to Rome, where she became cardinal and then pope. The legend was regarded as fact until the 17th cent.

Joan I *or* **Joanna I** *Italian* Giovanna (1326–1382) Countess of Provence and queen of Naples (1343–82). She belonged to the house of Anjou, and her marriage to the brother of the king of Hungary was intended to reconcile Hungarian and Angevin claims on Naples. Suspected of her husband's murder, she fled to Provence (1348), sold Avignon to the papacy in return for being cleared of the crime, then went back to Naples in 1352. When she recognized the antipope (1378), Pope URBAN VI crowned Charles of Durazzo king of Naples (1381); Charles captured Naples and had Joan killed.

Joan of Arc, St. *French* **Jeanne d'Arc** \zhän-ʹdȧrk\ (1412?–1431) French military heroine. She was a peasant girl who from an early age believed she heard the voices of Sts. Michael, Catherine, and Margaret. When she was about 16, her voices began urging her to aid France's Dauphin (crown prince) and save France from the English in the HUNDRED YEARS' WAR. Dressed in men's clothes, she visited the Dauphin and convinced him and the church authorities to support her. With her inspiring conviction, she rallied the French troops and raised the English siege of Orléans in 1429. The Dauphin was crowned king

St. Joan of Arc From *La vie des femmes célèbres*, c.1505

at Reims as CHARLES VII, with Joan beside him. Her siege of Paris was unsuccessful, and in 1430 she was captured by the Burgundians and sold to the English. Abandoned by Charles, she was turned over to the ecclesiastical court at Rouen, controlled by French clerics who supported the English, and tried for witchcraft and heresy (1431). She fiercely defended herself, but finally recanted and was sentenced to life imprisonment; when she again asserted that she had been divinely inspired, she was burned at the stake.

Job \'jōb\ Central character of the Book of Job in the OLD TESTAMENT. Initially Job is a wealthy man with a large family. Satan challenges God to allow him to take away Job's blessings as a test of his faith. Soon Job is desolate, his wealth gone and his family dead. Three comforters arrive; he disputes with them, denying he has done anything to deserve this misery but maintaining his faith in God. In a confrontation with God, the power and mystery of the deity are memorably reasserted, but the problem of why the innocent suffer is left unresolved.

Jobim \zhō-'biⁿ\, **Antônio Carlos** (1927–1994) Brazilian songwriter and composer. He played guitar and piano in clubs before becoming music director of Odeon Records. In 1959 he cowrote "Manha de Carnaval" for the film *Black Orpheus*, and his worldwide success soon followed. He transformed samba music into bossa nova, whose fusion of understated samba pulse, gentle singing, and the sophisticated harmonies of cool jazz found a long-lasting niche in U.S. popular music. He also composed classical works and film scores. His more than 400 songs include "One-Note Samba," "Meditation," and "The Girl from Ipanema."

Jobs, Steven P(aul) (b.1955) U.S. computer innovator. Adopted in infancy, he grew up in Los Altos, Cal. He dropped out of Reed College and went to work for Atari Corp. designing video games. In 1976 he cofounded (with Stephen WOZNIAK) APPLE COMPUTER, INC. The first Apple computer, created when Jobs was only 21, changed the public's idea of a computer from a machine for scientific use to a home appliance. Apple's Macintosh computer (1984) introduced a GRAPHICAL USER INTERFACE and MOUSE technology that became the standard for all applications interfaces. In 1980 Apple made an initial public offering, and Jobs became the company's chairman. He left Apple in 1985 to form NeXT Computer Inc., but he returned in 1996 and became CEO in 1997.

Joel Second of the 12 Minor Prophets in the OLD TESTAMENT, author of the Book of Joel. (His prophecy is part of a larger book, The Twelve, in the Jewish canon.) He lived sometime during the period of the Second Temple of JERUSALEM (516 B.C.–A.D. 70). He opens his prophecy by describing a plague of locusts, an allegory of the disasters to come upon a faithless people. The end of the book looks forward to the final days, when all Israel will share in the knowledge of God.

Joffre \'zhòfrᵃ\, **Joseph (-Jacques-Césaire)** (1852–1931) French general in WORLD WAR I. He was responsible for the calamitous initial French campaign, but he shifted his forces and created a new French army under his direct command that won a great victory in the First Battle of the MARNE (1914). As commander in chief (1915–16), he ordered the French armies to burst through the German positions, at ruinous cost. His prestige waned, and because of the lack of French preparation for the Battle of VERDUN (1916) he was stripped of his direct command and resigned.

Joffrey, Robert *orig.* Abdullah Jaffa Bey Khan (1930–1988) U.S. dancer and choreographer. Born in Seattle to an Afghan father, he studied dance there and later in New York. In 1956 he founded the Robert Joffrey (later simply Joffrey) Ballet with Gerald Arpino (b.1928), and the company soon gained international fame. Joffrey's ballets include *Persephone* (1952), *Astarte* (1967), and *Postcards* (1980). After his death, Arpino became director; in 1995 he moved the company to Chicago.

Johannesburg City (pop. 1991: 712,000; metro. area pop., 1991: 1,920,000), NE Republic of S. Africa. One of the country's largest cities, it lies on the S slopes of the Witwatersrand highland region. It was founded in 1886 after the discovery of gold nearby and was occupied by the British during the S. AFRICAN WAR in 1900. It was a legally segregated city until 1991, with nonwhites restricted to living in outlying areas called townships, including SOWETO. It is a leading industrial and financial center with notable cultural and educational institutions including the Univ. of Witwatersrand.

Johannsen, Wilhelm Ludvig (1857–1927) Danish botanist and geneticist. He supported Hugo DE VRIES's discovery that variation in genotype can occur by mutation; the new character, while independent of natural selection in its initial occurrence, is then subject to natural selection. Johannsen's *Elements of Heredity* (1909) became an influential text.

John *known as* **John Lackland** (1167–1216) King of England (1199–1216). The youngest son of HENRY II, he joined his brother Richard (later RICHARD I) in a rebellion against Henry (1189). John became lord of Ireland, and during Richard's absence, he tried to seize control of England (1193). On Richard's return John was banished (1194), but the two were later reconciled. Crowned king in 1199, John lost Normandy (1204) and most of his other French lands in a war with PHILIP II Augustus. After INNOCENT III excommunicated him for refusing to recognize Stephen LANGTON as archbishop of Canterbury, John was obliged to declare England a fief of the Holy See (1213). His heavy taxes and aggressive assertion of feudal privileges led to civil war (1215), and the barons forced him to sign the MAGNA CARTA.

John, Augustus (Edwin) (1878–1961) Welsh painter. By the age of 20 he had won a reputation for his brilliant drawing technique. A colorful personality, he roamed Britain, living with Gypsies and learning their language; the painting *Encampment on Dartmoor* (1906) is based on these experiences. His most significant portraits include those of James JOYCE and G. B. SHAW.

John, Elton (Hercules) *orig.* Reginald Kenneth Dwight (*later* **Sir Elton**) (b.1947) British rock singer, pianist, and songwriter. He won a scholarship to the Royal Academy of Music at 11. In the late 1960s he began the partnership with lyricist Bernie Taupin (b.1950) that would produce such hit albums as *Goodbye Yellow Brick Road* (1973) and such songs as "Rocket Man," "Bennie and the Jets," and "Philadelphia Freedom." His new version of 1973's "Candle In the Wind" at the 1997 funeral of his friend DIANA, PRINCESS OF WALES became the best-selling single of all time.

John I *Portuguese* João *known as* **John of Aviz** \ə-'vēzh\ (1357–1433) King of Portugal (1385–1433). The illegitimate son of Pedro I, he was elected king in 1385. He fought off a Castilian invasion (1385) and preserved Portugal's independence. He signed a 10-year truce with Castile in 1389, but frontier warfare was intermittent until 1411. He and his sons (including HENRY THE NAVIGATOR) captured Ceuta in Morocco in 1415, thus beginning the era of Portuguese expansion.

John II Comnenus \käm-'nē-nəs\ (1088–1143) Byzantine emperor (1118–43). The son of ALEXIUS I COMNENUS, he made it his mission to reconquer Byzantine territory lost to the Arabs, Turks, and crusaders. He sought to strengthen Byzantine finances by ending Venetian trading privileges in the empire but was forced to restore them after an unsuccessful war (1122). He reconquered Cilicia (1137) and won homage from Antioch.

John III Ducas Vatatzes \'dyü-kəs-və-'tat-sēz\ (1193–1254) Emperor of NICAEA (1222–54). He succeeded THEODORE I LASCARIS and defeated rivals for the imperial throne and their allied Latin forces (1225) to gain control of Asia Minor. He briefly besieged Constantinople (1235). He acquired territory in Bulgaria (1241) and Epirus (1242) and supported a cultural revival from his capital at Nicaea, paving the way for the eventual reestablishment of the Byzantine empire. Venerated by his people, he was canonized in the Eastern Church.

John III Sobieski \sòb-'yä-skē\ *Polish* Jan Sobieski (1629–1696) Elective king of Poland (1674–96). Named commander in chief of the Polish army (1668), he distinguished himself by victories over the Cossacks and Turks. His reputation was so great that he was elected king in preference to the Habsburgs' candidate. In 1683 he concluded a treaty with Emperor LEOPOLD I against the Ottoman Turks. When a Turkish army approached Vienna later that year, he rushed there with troops and achieved a brilliant victory. He was later unsuccessful in a Hungarian campaign (1683–91) to liberate Moldavia and Walachia from Ottoman rule.

John V Palaeologus \ˌpā-lē-'ä-lə-gəs\ (1332–1391) Byzantine emperor (1341–91). He inherited the throne at age 9 and was co-emperor until 1354. He offered to end the schism between the Byzantine and Latin churches in return for Western help against the Ottoman Turks, but no mili-

tary aid was given. Impoverished by war, he was arrested as a debtor when he visited Venice (1369). In 1371 he was forced to recognize Turkish overlords, who later helped him to regain the throne (1379) after he was deposed by his son.

John XXII *orig.* Jacques Duèse (d.1334) Second Avignon pope (1316–34). The successor to CLEMENT V, he established the papal court at Avignon on a permanent basis (see AVIGNON PAPACY). He upheld papal authority over imperial elections against the opposition of the emperor, LOUIS IV. When John excommunicated Louis, the emperor retaliated by declaring him deposed (1328) and sponsoring the election of an ANTIPOPE. John is remembered for centralizing church administration and adding to the body of canon law.

John XXIII *orig.* Angelo Giuseppe Roncalli (1881–1963) Pope (1958–63). In 1944 he was named papal nuncio to newly liberated France, where he successfully revived sympathy for the Vatican. He was elected pope after the death of PIUS XII in 1958. Because of his advanced age, he was expected to be little more than a caretaker in the office, but instead he became the major reforming pope of the century. Eager to lead the church into the modern era, he called the Second VATICAN COUNCIL in 1962 and invited Eastern Orthodox and Protestant observers to join Catholic delegates. He also

John XXIII, 1963

sought to repair relations with the Jews. An energetic advocate of world peace, John was one of the most popular popes in history.

John Damascene, St. See St. JOHN OF DAMASCUS

John Lackland See JOHN (ENGLAND)

John of Aviz See JOHN I (PORTUGAL)

John of Damascus, St. *or* **St. John Damascene** (c.675–749) Monk and theological doctor of the Greek and Latin churches. He spent his entire life under Muslim rule. As a writer of hymns and theology, he had great influence in the Eastern and Western churches, especially through *De fide orthodoxa* ("The Orthodox Faith"), a summary of the teachings of the Greek fathers. He also wrote against the iconoclasts (see ICONOCLASM).

John of Gaunt *later* Duke of Lancaster (1340–1399) English prince. The fourth son of EDWARD III, whose additional name "Gaunt" (a corruption of his birthplace, Ghent) became the popularly accepted form of his name through its use in William SHAKESPEARE's *Richard II*, John served as a commander in the Hundred Years' War, then returned to become an important influence in his father's last years as king and in the reign of his nephew RICHARD II. Through his first wife, John acquired the duchy of Lancaster in 1362, becoming the immediate ancestor of the 15th-cent. monarchs of the House of LANCASTER.

John of the Cross, St. *Spanish* San Juan de la Cruz *orig.* Juan de Yepes y Álvarez (1542–1591) Spanish mystic, poet, Doctor of the Church, and reformer of monasticism. A CARMELITE monk, he was ordained a priest in 1567. Joining St. TERESA OF ÁVILA in her effort to restore the Carmelites to their original austerity, he cofounded the Discalced Carmelite order in 1568. Reform caused friction within the order and led to his imprisonment; he escaped in 1578. In his great mystical poetry, including "The Dark Night of the Soul," he traced the steps of the soul's ascent to union with God.

John Paul II *orig.* Karol Wojtyla (b.1920) Pope (from 1978), the first non-Italian pope in 456 years and the first Polish pope ever. He studied for the priesthood at an underground seminary in Kraków during World War II, and later earned a doctorate in ethics. He became archbishop of Kraków in 1964 and cardinal in 1967. Elected pope after the brief term of John Paul I (1912–1978), he became known for his energy, charisma, and intellect as well as for his conservative

theological views and fervent anticommunism. He recovered from an attempted assassination by a Turkish terrorist (1981), and became the most traveled pope in history, visiting all parts of the world and championing economic justice in developing nations.

Johns, Jasper (b.1930) U.S. painter and printmaker. Born in Augusta, Ga., he began his career as a commercial artist. In 1958 he had his first one-man exhibition, a rousing success. With his friend Robert RAUSCHENBERG, he is considered largely responsible for the vogue for POP ART. His images depict commonplace two-dimensional objects (e.g., flags, maps, targets, numbers) in simple colors. His banal subject matter and rejection of emotional expression departed radically from the dominant ABSTRACT EXPRESSIONISM. Among his best-known works is *Painted Bronze* (1960), a cast sculpture of two Ballantine Ale cans. From 1961 he began to attach real objects to his canvases. In the 1970s he produced paintings composed of clusters of parallel lines that he called "crosshatchings."

Johns Hopkins University Private university in Baltimore, Md. It was founded as a graduate school in 1876, endowed by the Baltimore merchant Johns Hopkins (1795–1873). It became coeducational after a group of women, in 1893, provided funds for a medical school. Today its school of medicine and the affiliated Johns Hopkins Hospital constitute one of the nation's leading medical research centers. Total enrollment is about 6,000.

Johnson, Andrew (1808–1875) 17th president of the U.S. (1865–69). Born in Raleigh, N.C., and reared in Tennessee, he was self-educated and worked as a tailor before entering the state legislature (1835–43), where he became a spokesman for small farmers. He served in the U.S. House of Representatives (1843–53) and as governor of Tennessee (1853–57). In the U.S. Senate (1857–62), he opposed Southern secession, even after Tennessee seceded in 1861. In 1862 he was appointed military governor of Tennessee, then under Union control. In 1864 he was se-

Andrew Johnson

lected to run for vice president with Pres. Abraham LINCOLN; he assumed the presidency after Lincoln's assassination. During RECONSTRUCTION he favored a moderate policy that readmitted former Confederate states to the Union with few provisions for reform or civil rights for freedmen. In 1867 the RADICAL REPUBLICANS passed civil rights legislation and established the FREEDMEN'S BUREAU. His veto angered Congress, which passed the TENURE OF OFFICE ACT. In 1868 in defiance of the act, Johnson dismissed secretary of war Edwin STANTON. The House responded by impeaching the president for the first time in U.S. history. In his Senate trial, the two-thirds vote needed for conviction failed by one vote. Though Johnson remained in office, his effectiveness had ended.

Johnson, Jack (*orig.* John Arthur) (1878–1946) U.S. heavyweight boxing champion, the first black to hold the title. Born in Galveston, Texas, he won the national heavyweight crown in 1908 by knocking out Tommy Burns. A cry for a "Great White Hope" to defeat him produced numerous opponents. In 1915 he was knocked out in Havana by Jess Willard in 26 rounds. Excoriated by the press for twice marrying white women, in 1912 he was convicted of violating the Mann Act for transporting his fiancée across state lines. He fled abroad, continuing to fight as a fugitive before surrendering in 1920 to serve a one-year sentence. He died in a car crash.

Johnson, James P(rice) (1894–1955) U.S. pianist and composer, a chief figure in the transition of RAGTIME to JAZZ. Born in New Brunswick, N.J., Johnson was performing in New York saloons while still in his teens. He created the stride piano technique, a development of ragtime, in such pieces as "Carolina Shout." He composed music for stage revues, including *Keep Shufflin'* (1928) with his student Fats WALLER. His songs include "The Charleston" (largely responsible for the 1920s dance craze); his large-scale works include the *Harlem Symphony* (1932).

Johnson, James Weldon (1871–1938) U.S. writer. Born in Jacksonville, Fla., he collaborated with his brother, the composer J. Rosamond Johnson (1873–1954), on some 200 songs for the Broadway stage. After holding diplomatic posts, he served as executive secretary of the NAACP 1920–30. His writings include the novel *Autobiography of an Ex-Colored Man* (1912) and his best-known work, *God's Trombones* (1927), black-dialect sermons in verse. The brothers collaborated on pioneering anthologies of black poetry and spirituals. Their most famous original song, "Lift Every Voice and Sing," became an anthem of the civil rights movement.

Johnson \ˈjän-sən\, **John H(arold)** (b.1918) U.S. publisher. Born in Arkansas City, Ark., he introduced *Negro Digest*, a periodical for blacks, in 1942. Three years later he launched *Ebony*, which he modeled on *Life;* by the 1990s it had a circulation of about 2 million. Through Johnson Publishing Co., he has also published books and other magazines, and he later moved into radio broadcasting, insurance, and cosmetics.

Johnson, Lyndon B(aines) (1908–1973) 36th president of the U.S. (1963–69). Born in Gillespie Co., Texas, he taught school before going to Washington, D.C., as a congressional aide. There he was befriended by Sam RAYBURN and his political career blossomed. He won a seat in the U.S. House of Representatives (1937–49), and Pres. Franklin ROOSEVELT made him a protégé. He won election to the U.S. Senate in 1949. As majority leader (1955–61), he developed a talent for consensus building among dissident factions with methods both tactful and ruthless.

Lyndon B. Johnson

In 1960 he was elected vice president; he became president after the assassination of John KENNEDY. He quickly won from Congress passage of a huge quantity of important civil rights, tax-reduction, antipoverty, and conservation legislation. He defeated Barry GOLDWATER in 1964 by the largest popular majority to that time and announced his GREAT SOCIETY program. He was diverted from overseeing its enactment by the escalation of U.S. involvement in the VIETNAM WAR, beginning with the GULF OF TONKIN RESOLUTION. He pursued strategies criticized on both the left and the right. His falling approval ratings led to his decision not to seek reelection in 1968.

Johnson, Magic (*orig.* **Earvin**) (b.1959) U.S. basketball player. Born in Lansing, Mich., he led the Los Angeles Lakers to five championships in the 1980s. Standing 6 ft 9 in., he was an all-around player who brought a new vitality to the game and became one of the sport's first international stars. His no-look passes helped him become the NBA's all-time leader in assists (10,141). His announcement of his infection with HIV in 1991 and consequent retirement were greeted with shock. Johnson has since devoted much time to youth and AIDS work and to reviving impoverished neighborhoods.

Johnson, Michael (Duane) (b.1967) U.S. sprinter. Born in Dallas, he broke the 200-m indoor record in 1989 while attending Baylor Univ. He shared an Olympic gold medal in 1992 on the world-record-setting 4 × 400-m relay team, and in 1996 he became the first man to win gold medals in both the 200-m and 400-m, setting a world record of 19.32 seconds in the 200-m. In 1999 he set a new world record of 43.18 seconds in the 400-m. In the 2000 Olympics he again won two gold medals.

Johnson, Philip (Cortelyou) (b.1906) U.S. architect and critic. Born in Cleveland, he studied philosophy and architecture at Harvard Univ. As director of the architecture department at the Museum of Modern Art (1932–34, 1946–57), he did much to familiarize Americans with modern Eu-

ropean architecture. He gained fame with his own "Glass House" (1949), which combined Classical allusion and the influence of Ludwig MIES VAN DER ROHE (later his collaborator on the SEAGRAM BUILDING). His style took a striking turn with the AT&T headquarters, New York (1982), a controversial postmodernist landmark. Johnson was the first recipient of the Pritzker Architecture Prize, in 1979.

Johnson, Rafer (Lewis) (b.1935) U.S. decathlete. Born in Hillsboro, Texas, he won the decathlon gold medal in the Pan-American Games in 1955 while at UCLA. He won the gold medal at the 1960 Olympic Games, and was the first black athlete to carry the U.S. flag in the Olympic procession.

Johnson, Robert (1911?–1938) U.S. BLUES guitarist. Born in Hazlehurst, Miss., to a sharecropping family, he learned harmonica and guitar, probably influenced by personal contact with such bluesmen as Son House and Charley Patton. He traveled widely, playing at house parties, juke joints, and lumber camps. In 1936–37 he recorded songs by House and others, as well as such originals as "Hellhound on My Trail" and "Love in Vain." He is said to have died, at 27, after drinking strychnine-laced whiskey in a juke joint. His eerie falsetto and masterly slide guitar influenced many later musicians.

Johnson, Samuel *known as* **Dr. Johnson** (1709–1784) British man of letters, one of the outstanding figures of 18th-cent. England. The son of a poor bookseller, he worked eight years to produce the first great English dictionary, which brought him fame. He contributed to such periodicals as *The Gentleman's Magazine* and *The Universal Chronicle*, and almost single-handedly wrote and edited the biweekly *The Rambler* (1750–52). In 1765 he produced a critical edition of William SHAKESPEARE; its preface did much to establish Shakespeare as the center of the literary canon. His *Lives*

Samuel Johnson Painting by Joshua Reynolds, 1775

of the Most Eminent English Poets (10 vols., 1779–81) was a significant critical work. Other important works include the philosophical tale *Rasselas* (1759). A brilliant conversationalist, he helped found the Literary Club (c.1763), which became famous for its members of distinction. His aphorisms helped make him one of the most frequently quoted of English writers. His companion James BOSWELL wrote Johnson's biography, the most admired biography of all time.

Johnson, Walter (Perry) (1887–1946) U.S. baseball pitcher. Born in Humboldt, Kan., he developed perhaps the most effective fastball ever; "Big Train" holds the all-time record for most shutouts (110), ranks second to Cy YOUNG in wins (416), and established the record for his time for most strikeouts (3,508). He played for the Washington Senators 1907–27.

Johnstown Flood Disastrous flood (1889) in the town of Johnstown, Pa. At the time of the flood Johnstown was a leading steelmaking center. At 3:10 p.m. on May 31, the S. Fork Dam, a poorly maintained earthfill dam, collapsed after heavy rains, sending a wall of water rushing down the Conemaugh River Valley at speeds of 20–40 mph (30–60 kph). A 30-ft (9-m) wall of water smashed into Johnstown at 4:07 p.m., killing 2,209 people.

John the Apostle, St. *or* **St. John the Evangelist** *or* **St. John the Divine** (fl.1st cent. A.D.) One of the original 12 APOSTLES of JESUS, traditionally credited with writing the fourth GOSPEL and three New Testament epistles. The Book of REVELATION was also traditionally assigned to him. John and his brother James (see St. JAMES) were among the first disciples called by Jesus, and John appears to have held a position of authority in the early church after the resurrection. He is said to have died in EPHESUS, and his tomb became a site of pilgrimage. John's Gospel, unlike the other three, presents a well-developed theological point of view.

HIJ

His explications of issues such as the significance of the Son of God greatly influenced the development of Christian doctrine.

John the Baptist, St. (fl. early 1st cent. A.D.) Jewish PROPHET revered in Christianity as the forerunner of JESUS. Sources for his life are the four GOSPELS, the Acts of the Apostles, and the historian JOSEPHUS. As a young man John lived in the Judaean desert, either as a hermit or in a Jewish monastic community. He attracted much public notice around A.D. 28 as a prophet in the Jordan Valley. He preached the imminent wrathful judgment of God and called on his hearers to repent and be baptized. Jesus was baptized by John shortly before beginning his own mission. John was imprisoned for criticizing the illegal marriage of HEROD ANTIPAS, and was executed after Herod's stepdaughter, SALOME, demanded his head as a reward for dancing for the king's guests.

joint In geology, a brittle fracture surface in rocks along which little or no displacement has occurred. Present in nearly all surface rocks, joints may have smooth, clean surfaces, or they may be scarred by slickensides, or striations. Jointing does not extend far into the earth's crust, because at about 7.5 mi (12 km) even rigid rocks tend to flow plastically in response to stress.

joint Structure connecting two or more BONES. Most joints, including synovial (fluid-containing) joints and those between vertebrae, which incorporate a disk, can move. Immovable joints include the sutures of the SKULL. LIGAMENTS connect the bones of a joint, but MUSCLES keep them in place. See also ARTHRITIS, DISLOCATIONS, FRACTURES.

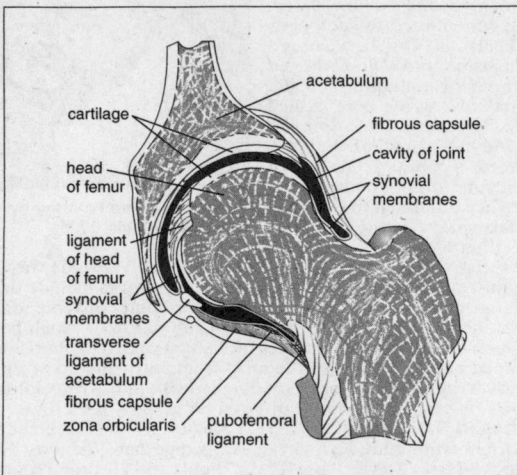

Joint Section through a hip joint. The hip joint, a synovial joint, is of the ball-and-socket type, the head of the femur articulating with the cup-shaped acetabulum. The joint cavity is enclosed by a fibrous capsule lined with a type of connective tissue (synovial membrane) that produces a fluid (synovial fluid) which lubricates the cartilage-covered opposing surfaces of bone. The fibrous capsule is made up of internal circular fibers (zona orbicularis) and external longitudinal fibers, strengthened by ligaments, and covered by muscles.

joints and joinery In architecture, the connection of construction materials. All joints are carefully detailed by the architect with concern for strength, movement, and protection from the elements. The term joinery refers especially to carpentry. Common joints include the dovetail, used for interlocking two flat members at right angles, as in the sides of a drawer; the doweled joint, in which doweling is employed for strength; and the mortise and tenon, used to join a horizontal member with the vertical member of a frame.

Joinville \zhwaⁿ-'vēl\, **Jean, Sire de** (1224?–1317) French chronicler. A nobleman, Joinville became friends with LOUIS IX while taking part in the Seventh Crusade (1248–54). His famous *Histoire de Saint Louis*, completed around 1309, is a prose chronicle that provides a supreme account of the Crusade, including vivid descriptions of the financial hardships, the dangers of sea voyages, the ravages of disease, the confusion and lack of discipline in the crusading army, and Muslim customs.

Joliba River See NIGER RIVER

Joliot-Curie \zhól-yó-kūē-'rē\, **(Jean-) Frédéric** *orig.* Jean-Frédéric Joliot (1897–1956) French physical chemist. In 1926 he married Irene Curie (1900–1958), daughter of Pierre and Marie CURIE. In 1932 he first observed production of an electron-positron pair. The two are remembered for their discovery of new radioactive isotopes prepared artificially, for which they were jointly awarded a 1935 Nobel Prize. Both died of conditions caused by their long exposure to radioactivity.

Jolliet \zhòl-'yā\, **Louis** (1645–1700) French-Canadian explorer. Born near Quebec, he was appointed to explore the Mississippi River with Jacques MARQUETTE and five others. In 1673 they set out in birchbark canoes across Lake Michigan, following the Fox and Wisconsin rivers to the Mississippi, then down the Mississippi to its confluence with the Arkansas, concluding that the river flowed south to the Gulf of Mexico and not, as hoped, into the Pacific Ocean.

Jolson, Al *orig.* Asa Yoelson (1886–1950) U.S. (Russian-born) singer, songwriter, and blackface comedian. Jolson's family arrived in the U.S. in 1893 and settled in Washington, D.C.

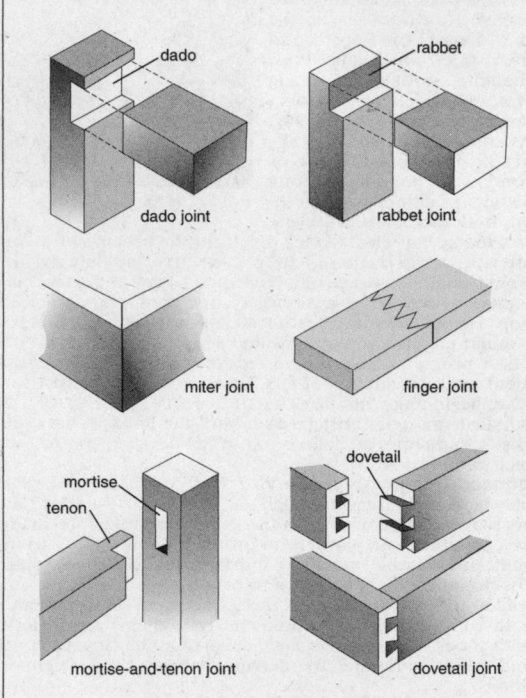

Joints and joinery Some common woodworking joints. The dado joint is made by inserting the end of one piece into a rectangular groove (dado) in another. The rabbet joint involves joining pieces along a channel or notch (rabbet) along an edge of one or both members. The miter joint is formed by butting two ends cut at an angle. The finger joint is used to lengthen a board by interlacing fingerlike projections. The mortise-and-tenon joint is made by inserting a projection (tenon) on one piece into a notch or hole (mortise) in the other. The dovetail joint consists of one or more fan-shaped tenons fitting tightly into corresponding mortises.

He performed in vaudeville before joining a minstrel troupe in 1909. In New York he was featured in such musicals as *La Belle Paree* (1911) and *Big Boy* (1925). In *Sinbad* (1918) he made "Swanee" into his trademark number; in *Bombo* (1921) he introduced "Toot, Toot, Tootsie" and "California, Here I Come." In 1927 he starred in *The Jazz Singer*, the first feature film with synchronized speech. Perhaps the greatest singing star of the teens and '20s, his life story was filmed in *The Jolson Story* (1946) and *Jolson Sings Again* (1949).

Jomini \ˌzhō-mə-ˈnē\, **(Antoine-) Henri, baron de** (1779–1869) Swiss-French general and military theorist. After a stint with the French army (1798–1800), he wrote his *Treatise on Grand Military Operations* (5 vols., 1805). He was appointed staff colonel in 1805 by NAPOLEON I, who had read his book. He was created a baron after the Treaties of Tilsit (1807). He rose to the post of chief of staff, but unjust treatment prompted him to resign (1813), and thereafter he fought for France's enemy, Russia. His works include *Principles of Strategy* (1818) and *Summary of the Art of War* (1838). A founder of modern military thought, he was the first to fix divisions between strategy, tactics, and LOGISTICS.

Jonah (fl.c.785 B.C.) One of the 12 Minor Prophets in the OLD TESTAMENT, whose story is told in the Book of Jonah. (His narrative is part of a larger book, The Twelve, in the Jewish canon.) God ordered Jonah to prophesy against the wickedness of NINEVEH, but Jonah refused to believe that this hated foreign city deserved salvation, and sailed away in the opposite direction. When a great storm threatened the ship, he confessed his fault and asked the crew to throw him overboard. A great fish swallowed him, but he prayed for deliverance and was spat out on dry ground, whereupon he went to Nineveh and persuaded its sinful people to repent.

Jonathan (c.10th cent. B.C.) In the Old Testament, the eldest son of King SAUL and closest friend of DAVID from the time David joined Saul's household. Saul became jealous of David's popularity and sought to kill him, but Jonathan prevented him. He died in battle at Mt. Gilboa before he could become David's prime minister.

Jones, Bill T. (*orig.* William Tass) (b.1952) U.S. dancer and choreographer. Born in Bunnell, Fla., he cofounded the Bill T. Jones/Arnie Zane Dance Co. with his companion Arnie Zane (1948–1988) in 1982. His works often make explicit reference to social issues; his controversial *Still/Here* (1995) dealt with the sufferings caused by AIDS, with which Jones is infected and which was the cause of Zane's death.

Jones, Bobby (*orig.* Robert Tyre) (1902–1971) U.S. golfer. Born in Atlanta, he won 13 major championships between 1923 and 1930, a feat unequaled until 1973. In 1930 he became the first golfer to achieve the Grand Slam of his time, winning the British and U.S. Open and Amateur championships. He retired at 28. Jones helped establish the MASTERS TOURNAMENT.

Jones, Chuck (*orig.* Charles M.) (1912–2002) U.S. animator. Born in Spokane, Wash., as a cartoonist for Warner Brothers (1933–62) he helped develop such characters as Bugs Bunny, Road Runner, and Wile E. Coyote. Three of his cartoon films, noted for their speed and action, won Academy Awards. He later formed his own company and directed such animated features as *The Phantom Tollbooth* (1971) and specials for television. He received an Academy Award for lifetime achievement in 1996.

Jones, Inigo (1573–1652) British painter, architect, and designer. Beginning in 1605, he designed the scenes and costumes for masques by Ben JONSON and others. From 1615 to 1642, he was the King's Surveyor of Works. His first important undertaking was the Queen's House at Greenwich (begun 1616), England's first Palladian-style building. His greatest achievement, the Banqueting House at Whitehall (1619–22), consists of one great raised chamber with colonnades set against the walls, which support a flat, beamed ceiling. For his design for COVENT GARDEN (1630), London's first square, Jones is credited with the introduction of town planning in England.

Jones, James Earl (b.1931) U.S. actor. Born in Arkabutla, Miss., he made his Broadway debut in 1957. Praised for his performance in *Othello* (1964) and in roles with the New York Shakespeare Festival (1961–73), he starred in *The Great White Hope* (1969, Tony Award; film, 1970), and later in *Paul Robeson* (1978) and *Fences* (1985, Tony Award). He also starred in the television series *Gabriel's Fire* (1990–91, Emmy award). He has appeared in numerous films; his sonorous voice lent gravity to the *Star Wars* series (1977–83) and *The Lion King* (1994).

Jones, Jim *orig.* James Warren Jones (1931–1978) U.S. cult leader. Born near Lynn, Ind., he became a preacher in Indianapolis. He established the evangelical group the People's Temple. Accused of defrauding church members, he led his group from San Francisco to Guyana in 1977 and set up the agricultural commune of Jonestown, using threats and manipulation to control his followers. When an investigating committee led by Congressman Leo Ryan arrived in Jonestown, cult members killed Ryan and four others. The next day Jones commanded his followers to drink a cyanide-laced drink; the Jonestown Massacre's death toll was 913, including many children.

Jones, John Paul *orig.* John Paul (1747–1792) Scottish-American naval hero. He went to sea at 12, and joined his brother in Virginia in 1775. When the American Revolution began, he joined the new Continental Navy; in 1776, sailing the *Providence*, he captured eight ships and sank eight more. In 1779 he commanded the *Bonhomme Richard* and intercepted a merchant fleet off the E coast of England. He engaged the escort ship *Serapis* and, though outgunned, forced its surrender after a fierce battle, answering its challenge to surrender with "I have not yet begun to fight!" His ship sank soon after, and he sailed two British prizes to the Netherlands.

John Paul Jones Portrait by Charles Wilson Peale, 1781

Jones, LeRoi See BARAKA, AMIRI

Jones, Mary Harris *orig.* Mary Harris *known as* **Mother Jones** (1830–1930) U.S. labor organizer. Born in Ireland, she was brought to the U.S. in 1835. In 1867 she lost her children and husband to yellow fever in Memphis; four years later she lost all her possessions in the great Chicago fire. She turned for assistance to the KNIGHTS OF LABOR, and became a highly visible organizer for the UNITED MINE WORKERS, supporting strikes all across the country. At 93 she was still working among striking coal miners in W. Virginia. She was a founder of the Social Democratic Party (1898) and the INDUSTRIAL WORKERS OF THE WORLD (1905). Her autobiography was published in 1925. She lived to the age of 100.

jongleur \zhōⁿ-ˈglœr, *Engl* ˈjäŋ-glər\ Professional storyteller or public entertainer in medieval France. His roles included those of musician, juggler, acrobat, and reciter of literary works. Jongleurs were most important in the 13th cent.; in the 14th cent., the various facets of their role were taken over by other performers. See also GOLIARD, TROUVÈRE.

Jonson, Ben(jamin) (1572–1637) English playwright and poet. In 1598 his comedy *Every Man in His Humour* established his reputation. He wrote several MASQUES for the court of James I and created the "antimasque" to precede the masque proper. His classic plays *Volpone* (1605–6), *The Alchemist* (1610), and *Bartholomew Fair* (1614) use satire to expose the follies and vices of his age, attacking greed, charlatanism, and religious hypocrisy. The era's leading dramatist after William SHAKESPEARE, Jonson influenced the later Restoration playwrights (see RESTORATION LITERATURE). He was also a lyric poet whose works include two famous elegies for his son and daughter.

Joplin, Janis (Lyn) (1943–1970) U.S. rock and blues singer. Born in Port Arthur, Texas, she left home at 17 and began singing in Austin and later Los Angeles. She joined the band Big Brother and the Holding Company in San Francisco in 1966, and soon became famous for her raw, powerful, emotional blues style, as heard on the album *Cheap Thrills*

HIJ

(1968). Leaving the band, she continued to record hit songs, including "Me and Bobby McGee." Joplin died from an overdose of heroin at 27.

Joplin, Scott (1868–1917) U.S. composer, the outstanding exponent of RAGTIME music. Born near Linden, Texas, Joplin was a classically trained pianist and composer. His compositions, including "Maple Leaf Rag" (1899), ragtime's first hit, and "The Entertainer" (1902), transcend the sometimes mechanical dimension of the genre. He also wrote a ballet and two operas, including *Treemonisha* (1911). He suffered a nervous collapse in 1911 and was institutionalized in 1916.

Jordaens \'yòr-ˌdàns\, **Jacob** (1593–1678) Flemish painter active in Antwerp. By the 1620s he had a flourishing studio with many students. After the death of Peter Paul RUBENS, to whose style he was indebted, he became the leading painter in Flanders. His paintings, crowded with robust figures, are noted for strong contrasts of light and shade and an air of sensual vitality bordering on coarseness. He also produced religious paintings and portraits. His most important commissions were two enormous murals for the royal country house near The Hague.

Jordan *officially* **Hashemite Kingdom of Jordan** *Arabic* **Al-Urdun** \àl-'ùr-dùn\ Arab state, SW Asia, lying east of the JORDAN RIVER. It is bordered by Syria, Iraq, Saudi Arabia, and Israel. Jordan has 12 miles (19 km) of coastline on the Gulf of AQABA. Area: 34,342 sq mi (88,946 sq km). Population (2000): 4,982,000. Capital: AMMAN. The vast majority

JORDAN

Scale 1: 7,562,000

©1999, Encyclopædia Britannica, Inc.

of the population are Arabs, about 60% of whom are Palestinian Arabs who emigrated to Jordan from Israel and the W. Bank as a result of the ARAB–ISRAELI WARS. Language: Arabic (official). Religion: Islam (official), with more than 95% of the population Sunnite. Currency: Jordan dinar. Four-fifths of Jordan is occupied by desert, and less than one-tenth of the country's land is arable. The country's highest point, Mt. Ramm (5,755 ft, or 1,754 m), lies in the uplands region on the E. Bank of the Jordan River. The Jordan Valley region contains the DEAD SEA. Jordan's economy is based largely on manufacturing and services (including tourism); exports include phosphate, potash, pharmaceuticals, fruits and vegetables, and fertilizers. It is a constitutional monarchy with two legislative houses; the head of state and government is the king, assisted by the prime minister. Jordan shares much of its history with IS-RAEL, since both occupied the area known historically as PALESTINE. Much of present-day E Jordan was incorporated into Israel under DAVID and SOLOMON around 1000

B.C. It fell to the Seleucids in 330 B.C. and to Muslim Arabs in the 7th cent. A.D. The Crusaders extended the kingdom of Jerusalem east of the Jordan River in 1099. Jordan submitted to Ottoman Turkish rule during the 16th cent. In 1920 the area comprising Jordan (then known as the Transjordan) was established within the British mandate of Palestine. Transjordan became an independent state in 1927, although the British mandate did not end until 1948. After hostilities with the new state of Israel ceased in 1949, Jordan annexed the W. Bank of the Jordan River, administering the territory until Israel gained control of it in the SIX-DAY WAR of 1967. In 1970–71 Jordan was wracked by fighting between the government and guerrillas of the PALESTINE LIBERATION ORGANIZATION (PLO), a struggle that ended in the expulsion of the PLO from Jordan. In 1988 King HUSSEIN I renounced all Jordanian claims to the W. Bank in favor of the PLO. In 1994 Jordan and Israel signed a full peace agreement.

Jordan, Jim (*orig.* James Edward) **and Marian** *orig.* Marian I. Driscoll (1896–1988, 1898–1961) U.S. radio comedians. Both were born near Peoria, Ill.; they married in 1918 and adapted their vaudeville comedy act for radio in 1924. In collaboration with the writer Don Quinn they produced a comedy series that evolved into *Fibber McGee and Molly* (1935–57), a weekly show that delighted a huge national audience with its running gags in skits involving the McGees and their neighbors.

Jordan, Michael (Jeffrey) (b.1963) U.S. basketball player, considered the greatest all-around player in basketball history. Born in Brooklyn, N.Y., he was an outstanding star at the Univ. of N. Carolina before joining the Chicago Bulls in 1984. He holds the all-time NBA record for scoring average (32 points), and in 1987 became the second player to score 3,000 points in a single season. Nicknamed "Air Jordan" for his extraordinary leaping ability and his acrobatic evasive maneuvers, he led the Bulls to six championships (1991–93, 1996–98) and led the 1984 and 1992 U.S. Olympic teams to gold medals. He retired briefly in 1993, hoping to play professional baseball, but returned to the Bulls from 1995 until 1999, by which time he was the most famous athlete in America and an international icon. In 2001 he returned to play for the Washington Wizards, of which he was part-owner.

Jordan River River, SW Asia. It rises in Syria and flows through the Sea of GALILEE before receiving the Yarmuk River. It drains into the DEAD SEA at a depth of 1,312 ft (400 m) below sea level, after a total course of 223 mi (360 km). Revered in many religions, in Christianity it is known as the place where JESUS baptized JOHN the Baptist.

José Bonifácio See J. B. de ANDRADA E SILVA

Joseph In the OLD TESTAMENT, the son of JACOB and his wife, RACHEL. He was favored by his father, and his brothers became bitterly jealous when he was given a resplendent "coat of many colors." They sold him into slavery in Egypt, telling Jacob he had been killed by a wild beast. In Egypt Joseph rose to high office, owing to his ability to interpret the pharaoh's dreams, and his acquisition of grain supplies enabled Egypt to withstand a famine. When famine forced Jacob to send his sons to Egypt to buy grain, the family was reconciled with Joseph and settled there. The story begins the history of the Israelites in Egypt.

Joseph, Chief (1840–1904) NEZ PERCÉ chief. In 1877 the U.S. attempted to force the Nez Percé to move to a reservation in Idaho. Chief Joseph at first agreed, but finally decided instead to lead his followers on a trek to Canada. During the three-month, 1,000-mile journey, he outmaneuvered and outfought federal troops and won the admiration of many whites by his humane conduct. His group was finally surrounded near the Canadian border and subsequently removed to Indian Territory (Oklahoma), and later to Washington.

Joseph, St. (fl.1st cent. B.C.–1st cent. A.D.) In the NEW TESTAMENT, the husband of MARY and the earthly father of JESUS. Descended from the house of DAVID, he was a carpenter in Nazareth. He was betrothed to Mary, and when he found her already pregnant an angel appeared to him in a vision and told him the expected child was the son of God. The last mention of Joseph occurs in the

Gospel of Luke when he and Mary take the 12-year-old Jesus to Jerusalem.

Joseph II (1741–1790) Holy Roman emperor (1765–90). He succeeded his father, FRANCIS I, and initially coruled with his mother, MARIA THERESA (1765–80). An advocate of ENLIGHTENED DESPOTISM, he abolished serfdom, established religious equality before the law, granted freedom of the press, and emancipated the Jews. He came into conflict with the Roman Catholic Church by attempting to impose state controls over it, and traditional countries such as the Austrian Netherlands and Hungary resisted his far-reaching reforms.

Joséphine *orig.* Marie-Josèphe-Rose Tascher de la Pagerie (1763–1814) Consort of NAPOLEON and empress of the French. Born in Martinique, she married Alexandre, vicomte de BEAUHARNAIS, in 1779. She was guillotined during the French Revolution, and Joséphine was imprisoned briefly. A leader of Paris society, she married Napoleon in a civil ceremony in 1796. She was an indifferent and extravagant wife, but used her social position to advance her husband's political fortunes. After he became emperor (1804), she persuaded him to marry her again, with religious rites. In 1810 he had their marriage nullified to make a politically convenient marriage with MARIE-LOUISE.

Josephson effect Flow of electric current between two pieces of superconducting material (see SUPERCONDUCTIVITY) separated by a thin layer of insulating material. This flow was predicted by Brian Josephson (b.1940) in 1962. According to Josephson, pairs of ELECTRONS can move from one superconductor to the other across what is called a Josephson junction. The Josephson current flows only if no battery is connected across the two conductors. A major application of this discovery is in superfast switching devices used in computers.

Josephus \jō-'sē-fəs\, **Flavius** *orig.* Joseph Ben Matthias (A.D. 37/38–c.100) Jewish priest, scholar, and historian. Born of a priestly family in Jerusalem, he was favored in the courts of emperors VESPASIAN, TITUS, and DOMITIAN. His *History of the Jewish War* (79) is the principal source on the Jewish revolt of A.D. 66–70 and includes much on Roman tactics and strategy. *The Antiquities of the Jews* (93), his greatest work, traces Judaism from creation up to the revolt. *Against Apion* defends Judaism against Hellenism.

Joshua Leader of the Israelite tribes after the death of MOSES. According to the Old Testament Book of Joshua, Joshua led the people of Israel westward across the Jordan River to invade CANAAN and gain control of the Promised Land. The book begins by recounting the battles, including the famous demolition of the walls of JERICHO. Joshua then divides Canaan among the 12 tribes of ISRAEL, makes his farewell speech, and dies. The book was probably compiled in the 6th cent. B.C.

Joshua Tree National Park National park, SE California. Situated on the border between the MOJAVE and Colorado deserts, it has an area of 1,241 sq mi (3,214 sq km). It is noted for its variety of desert plant life, including the Joshua tree, creosote bush, and Mojave yucca. Its fauna include coyotes, bobcats, and tarantulas.

Josiah \jō-'sī-ə\ (c.640–609 B.C.) King of JUDAH and religious reformer. He became king at 8 after the assassination of his father, Amon. As the Assyrian empire crumbled, Judah gained a measure of independence, and in 621 B.C. Josiah began a program of national renewal. He drove out foreign cults, abolished local sanctuaries, and centered the worship of Yahweh (God) in the Temple of JERUSALEM. Josiah hoped to reunify Judah and Israel, but he was killed in a battle against the Egyptians.

Josquin des Prez \zhȯs-'kaⁿ-de-'prā\ (c.1440–1521) Northern French composer. He spent his life working as a singer, moving from post to post in Italy, including the Papal Chapel (1486–94), before returning to Condé in 1504, where he would spend the rest of his life. Josquin was able to balance complexity of imitative counterpoint with an inexhaustible melodic gift. He left over 60 motets, some 18 complete masses (including *Missa Pange lingua*), and many superb secular songs in the chordal "Italian" style (including "El grillo"). His posthumous reputation was the greatest of any composer up to his time.

Jotunheim Mountains \'yō-tᵊn-ˌhām\ Mountain range, S central Norway. Extending for 80 mi (130 km), it is the highest range in Scandinavia; its tallest peaks are Glitter Mtn. (8,045 ft, or 2,452 m) and Galdhø Mtn. (8,100 ft, or 2,470 m). The mountains are mentioned in early Norse sagas.

Joule \'jül\, **James (Prescott)** (1818–1889) English physicist. After studying under John DALTON, in 1840 he described "Joule's law," which stated that the heat produced in a wire by an electric current is proportional to the product of the resistance of the wire and the square of the current. In 1843 he published his value for the amount of work required to produce a unit of heat, and established that heat is a form of energy. He established that the various forms of energy are basically the same and can be changed from one into another, a discovery that formed the basis of the CONSERVATION LAW. In his honor, a standard unit of work is called the joule.

jousting Medieval mock battle between two horsemen who charged at each other with leveled lances in an attempt to unseat the other. It probably originated in France in the 11th cent., and it flourished in much of Europe in the 12th–15th cent. Though the lances were blunted, knights were often seriously wounded or killed. Tournaments were mounted only by royalty and nobility; ladies of the court would sponsor individual knights, in a ritual of COURTLY LOVE. Characterized by striking pageantry, jousting tournaments represented the preeminent display of CHIVALRY.

Jove See JUPITER

Joyce, James (Augustine Aloysius) (1882–1941) Irish novelist. In 1902 he moved to Paris, which would become his principal home after years spent in Trieste and Zurich. His life was a difficult one, marked by financial troubles, chronic eye diseases that occasionally left him totally blind, censorship problems, and his daughter Lucia's mental illness. The remarkable story collection *The Dubliners* (1914) and the autobiographical novel *Portrait of the Artist as a Young Man* (1916) brought new techniques to the English novel and short story which he would later develop much further. He spent seven years writing *Ulysses* (1922), the controversial masterpiece (initially banned in the U.S. and Britain) now widely regarded as

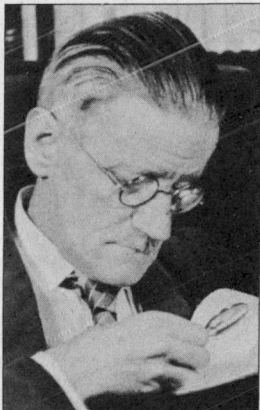

James Joyce Photo by Gisèle Freund, 1939

the greatest 20th-cent. English-language novel. It embodies a highly experimental use of language and exploration of such new literary methods as stream-of-consciousness narrative. He spent 17 years on his final work, *Finnegans Wake* (1939), famous for its extremely demanding linguistic virtuosity. He also published three poetry collections and the play *Exiles* (1918).

Joyner, Florence Griffith See Florence GRIFFITH JOYNER

Joyner-Kersee, Jackie *orig.* Jacqueline Joyner (b.1962) U.S. athlete, considered by some the greatest female athlete ever. Born in E. St. Louis, Ill., she won four consecutive National Junior Heptathlon championships and starred in basketball at UCLA. In 1986 she became the first HEPTATHLON competitor ever to score 7,000 points. She broke that barrier six times, four times establishing a new world record, and won heptathlon gold medals at the 1988 and 1992 Olympics. Her best single event was the long jump (world record, 1987; Olympic gold medal, 1988).

JPEG \'jā-ˌpeg\ *in full* Joint Photographic Experts Group. Standard computer file format for storing graphic images in a compressed form. JPEG images are compressed using a mathematical ALGORITHM. A variety of encoding processes can be used, depending on whether the user's goal is the highest quality of image or smallest file size. The JPEG and

GIF formats are the most commonly used graphics formats on the Internet.

Juan Carlos I (b.1938) King of Spain from 1975. The grandson of ALFONSO XIII, he lived in exile until 1947. After Francisco FRANCO declared Spain a representative monarchy, he prepared Juan Carlos for his future role. In 1969 Juan Carlos was designated prince; he acceded to the Spanish throne two days after Franco's death. Though he had sworn loyalty to Franco's National Movement, he proved to be relatively liberal and helped restore parliamentary democracy. In 1981 he deflated a potential military coup and preserved the democracy.

Juan de Fuca Strait \ˌhwän-də-ˈfyü-kə\ Strait, N. Pacific Ocean. Located between the Olympic Peninsula of Washington and Canada's VANCOUVER ISLAND, it is 11–17 mi (18–27 km) wide and 80–100 mi (130–160 km) long. It is named for a Greek who sailed in the service of Spain and who may have visited the passage in 1592. It is used by ships to and from VANCOUVER and SEATTLE.

Juan Fernández Islands Island group, S. Pacific Ocean. Located 400 mi (650 km) west of Chile, it consists of two islands and an islet. They were discovered in 1563 by Juan Fernández (c.1536–1604). Alexander Selkirk, a Scottish seaman, lived there alone from 1704 until 1709; his adventures are believed to have inspired Daniel DEFOE's *Robinson Crusoe*. Possessions of Chile since the early 19th cent., they have since often been used as penal settlements.

Juárez *or* **Ciudad Juárez** \ˌsyü-ˈthäth-ˈhwär-ˌes\ City (pop., 1995: 995,000), N CHIHUAHUA, Mexico. Located on the RIO GRANDE opposite EL PASO, Texas, it was known until 1888 as El Paso del Norte. It is an important border city and functions as the marketing center for a cotton-growing area.

Juárez \ˈhwär-əs\, **Benito (Pablo)** (1806–1872) National hero and president (1861–72) of Mexico. A ZAPOTEC Indian, Juárez initially studied for the priesthood but later became a legislator, judge, and cabinet minister. From 1854 he led the social revolution known as La Reforma, and in 1855, when liberal forces took control of the government, he was able to put his ideas into practice. An 1856 LAND-REFORM law broke up large landed estates and forced the Roman Catholic Church to sell its land. In 1857 a liberal constitution was promulgated. Conservatives ousted the president in 1858, but Juárez restored the liberal government.

Benito Juárez

He was elected president in 1861 and twice reelected. The French under NAPOLEON III invaded and occupied Mexico, putting MAXIMILIAN of Austria in power in 1864, but when French troops withdrew in 1867 Juárez had Maximilian executed. His final years were marred by waning support and personal tragedy.

Jubayl See BYBLOS

Juchen dynasty \ˈzhü-ˈjen\ *or* **Jin dynasty** (1115–1234) Dynasty that ruled an empire formed by the Tungus Juchen tribes of Manchuria. It covered much of Central Asia and all of N China. Like the Liao, an earlier Central Asian dynasty, the Juchen maintained a Chinese-style bureaucracy to rule over the S part of their conquests; to preserve their ethnic identity, they maintained their language, developed their own script, and banned Chinese clothes and customs from their army.

Judaea *or* **Judea** \jü-ˈdē-ə\ S division of ancient PALESTINE successively under Persian, Greek, and Roman rule. It was bounded on the north by Samaria and on the west by the Mediterranan Sea. It succeeded the kingdom of JUDAH, which was destroyed by the Babylonians in 586 B.C. The revived kingdom of Judaea was established by the MACCABEES. Family disputes led to Roman intervention in 63 B.C. Under Roman control, HEROD was made king of Judaea in 37 B.C. As a result of the Jewish revolt in A.D. 66, the city of Jerusalem was destroyed (A.D. 70).

Judah One of the 12 tribes of ISRAEL, descended from Judah, the fourth son of JACOB. The tribe of Judah entered CANAAN with the other Israelites and settled in the region south of Jerusalem. It eventually became the most powerful tribe, producing the kings DAVID and SOLOMON, and it was prophesied that the MESSIAH would come from among its members. After the 10 northern tribes were dispersed by the Assyrian conquest of 721 B.C., the tribes of Judah and Benjamin were left as the sole inheritors of the Mosaic covenant. The kingdom of Judah flourished until 586 B.C., when it was overrun by the Babylonians and many of its people were carried into exile. CYRUS THE GREAT allowed them to return in 538 B.C.; the history of Judah from that time forward is the history of the JEWS and JUDAISM. The kingdom of Judah was succeeded by JUDAEA.

Judaism \ˈjü-də-ˌi-zəm, ˈjü-dē-ˌi-zəm\ Religious beliefs and practices of the JEWS. One of the three great monotheistic world religions, Judaism began as the faith of the ancient Hebrews, and its sacred text is the Hebrew BIBLE, particularly the TORAH. Fundamental to Judaism is the belief that the people of Israel are God's chosen people, who must serve as a light for other nations. God made a COVENANT first with ABRAHAM, then renewed it with Isaac, JACOB, and MOSES. The worship of Yahweh (God) was centered in Jerusalem from the time of DAVID. The Babylonians destroyed the First Temple of JERUSALEM in 586 B.C.; during the BABYLONIAN EXILE the Jews hoped for national restoration under a MESSIAH. The Jews were allowed to return by the Persians, but an unsuccessful rebellion against Roman rule led to the destruction of the Second Temple in A.D. 70 and the Jews' dispersal throughout the world in the Jewish DIASPORA. RABBINIC JUDAISM emerged to replace the temple cult at Jerusalem. The great body of oral law and commentaries were committed to writing in the TALMUD and MISHNA. Two branches of Judaism emerged in the Middle Ages: the SEPHARDI, centered in Spain, and the ASHKENAZI, centered in France and Germany. Elements of mysticism appeared in the esoteric writings of the KABBALA and the movement known as HASIDIS. CONSERVATIVE and REFORM JUDAISM emerged in 19th-cent. Germany as an effort to modify the strictness of ORTHODOX JUDAISM, and ZIONISM arose as an outgrowth of reform. European Judaism suffered terribly during the HOLOCAUST, when millions were put to death by the Nazis, and the rising flow of Jewish emigrants to Palestine led to declaration of the State of Israel in 1948.

Jewish Festivals

Tishri (Sept.–Oct.)	1–2	Rosh Hashanah (New Year)
	3	Fast of Gedaliah
	10	Yom Kippur (Day of Atonement)
	15–21	Sukkot (Tabernacles)
	22	Shemini Atzereth (Eighth Day of Solemn Assembly)
	23	Simhath Torah (Rejoicing of the Law)
Kislev (Nov.–Dec.)	25	Hanukkah (Festival of Lights) begins
Tebet (Dec.–Jan.)	2 or 3	Hanukkah ends
	10	Fast
Shebat (Jan.–Feb.)	15	New Year for Trees
Adar (Feb.–Mar.)	13	Fast of Esther
	14–15	Purim (Feast of Lots)
Second Adar (Adar Sheni) or Veadar (intercalated month); Adar holidays fall in Veadar during leap years.		
Nisan (Mar.–Apr.)	15–22	Pesach (Passover)
Iyar (Apr.–May)	5	Israel Independence Day
	18	Lag b'Omer (33rd Day of the Omer Counting)
Sivan (May–June)	6–7	Shabuoth (Feast of Weeks, or Pentecost)
Tammuz (June–July)	17	Fast
Ab (July–Aug.)	9	Fast

Judas Iscariot (d.c.A.D. 30) Disciple who betrayed JESUS. He was one of the original 12 disciples. Judas betrayed Jesus to the Jewish authorities for 30 pieces of silver, bringing the armed guard to the Garden of GETHSEMANE and identifying Jesus with a kiss. He later regretted his deed and committed suicide; according to Matthew, he returned the money to the priests before hanging himself.

Judas Maccabaeus \ˌma-kə-ˈbē-əs\ (d.161/160 B.C.) Leader of a Jewish rebellion against the Syrians. On his father's death, Judas became leader of the rebels fighting ANTI-OCHUS IV EPIPHANES and won a series of victories in 166–164 B.C. In 166 he purified the Temple of JERUSALEM, an event celebrated at HANUKKAH. On Antiochus' death in 164, the Seleucids offered the Jews freedom of worship, but Judas continued the war, hoping to gain political freedom. The history of the dynasty is told in the two books of MAC-CABEES in the APOCRYPHA.

Judd, Donald (1928–1994) U.S. sculptor. Born in Excelsior Springs, Mo., he studied in New York and had his first one-man exhibition of paintings in 1957. In 1960–62 he made the transition from painting to sculpture, and became a leading exponent of MINIMALISM. Much of his work consists of simple cubes or other geometric units, in stainless steel or metal and plexiglass, sometimes painted, which stand on the floor or are cantilevered from the wall, often in stacks or horizontal progressions.

Judea See JUDAEA

judgment In law, a formal decision or determination on a matter or case by a court. Judgments are classified as *in personam, in rem,* and *quasi in rem.* A judgment in personam determines the rights and liabilities of a particular person. A judgment in rem affects the status of a particular thing (e.g., an item of property). Quasi in rem describes a judgment in which property is subject to court control to satisfy a claim against its owner. The court may punish for CONTEMPT any party that does not adhere to its orders. See also APPEAL.

Judgment, Day of In Christianity, the final judgment of God on all people at the end of history. It will occur at the second coming of Christ, when the dead are resurrected. It is especially important in millennialist denominations (see MILLENNIALISM). In Islam, the Day of Judgment is described in the QURAN and the HADITH.

judicial review Examination by a country's courts of the actions of the legislative, executive, and administrative branches of government to ensure that those actions conform to the provisions of the constitution. Actions that do not conform are unconstitutional and therefore null and void. The practice is usually considered to have begun with the U.S. Supreme Court's ruling in *Marbury vs. Madison* (1803). Especially subject to scrutiny in the U.S. have been actions bearing on civil rights (or CIVIL LIBERTY), DUE PROCESS of law, EQUAL PROTECTION under the law, freedom of religion, FREEDOM OF SPEECH, and rights of PRIVACY.

judiciary Branch of government in which judicial power is vested. The principal work of any judiciary is the adjudication of disputes or controversies. Typically present in court are the presiding judge, the parties to the matter (sometimes called litigants), the lawyers representing the parties, and other individuals including witnesses, clerks, bailiffs, and jurors when the proceeding involves a jury. Though the courts' stated function is to administer justice according to rules enacted by the legislative branch, courts in effect make law by laying down rules for future cases; this is known as the doctrine of precedent.

Judith Legendary Jewish heroine, the central character in the Book of Judith in the APOCRYPHA. (The book is excluded from the Hebrew Bible.) When her city is besieged by the Assyrians under their general, Holofernes, Judith leaves in pretended flight and foretells victory to Holofernes. Invited into his tent, she cuts off his head as he lies in a drunken sleep, and the Jews defeat the Assyrians. The story may have been written in the 2nd cent. B.C.

judo MARTIAL ART that emphasizes the use of quick movement and leverage to throw an opponent. Its techniques are generally intended to turn an opponent's force to one's own advantage rather than to oppose it directly. The opponent must be thrown cleanly, pinned, or mastered through pressure on arm joints or the neck.

Judo National championship match, Japan

Judo evolved out of JUJITSU in late-19th-cent. Japan; it is now practiced primarily as sport.

Jugendstil \\'yü-gǝnt-₁shtēl\\ Artistic style in Germany and Austria. Its name was derived from the Munich magazine *Die Jugend* ("Youth"), founded in 1896, which featured ART NOUVEAU designs. Its early phase, primarily floral in character, was rooted in English Art Nouveau and Japanese prints; a more abstract phase emerged after 1900. Primarily a style in architecture and the decorative arts, it also included the painter Gustav KLIMT.

Jugurtha \\jŭ-'gǝr-thǝ\\ (c.160–104 B.C.) Ruler of the N. African kingdom of NUMIDIA threatened by the Romans (118–105 B.C.). Jugurtha shared rule with his cousins. He had one killed and captured the capital city of the other. Rome intervened with troops, which Jugurtha successfully outwitted until he was captured in 105 B.C. See also Gaius MARIUS, Lucius Cornelius SULLA.

Juilliard School \\'jü-lē-₁ärd\\ Internationally renowned school of the performing arts in New York City. It has its roots in the Institute of Musical Art (founded 1905) and a graduate school (1924) endowed by the financier Augustus D. Juilliard (1840–1919). Housed at the LINCOLN CENTER FOR THE PERFORMING ARTS, it offers bachelor's degrees in music, dance, and drama and postgraduate degrees in music. Total enrollment is about 900.

jujitsu \\jü-'jit-sü\\ MARTIAL ART that employs holds, throws, and paralyzing blows to subdue or disable an opponent. It evolved among the SAMURAI in Japan from about the 17th cent. Its ruthless techniques included the use of hard or tough parts of the body (e.g., knuckles, fists, elbows, and knees) against an enemy's vulnerable points. Jujitsu declined in the mid-19th cent., but many of its methods were incorporated into JUDO, KARATE, and AIKIDO.

Julia (39 B.C.–A.D. 14) Only daughter of AUGUSTUS. She briefly wed MARCELLUS (25–23 B.C.), then AGRIPPA (21), Augustus' chief lieutenant. When Agrippa died (12), Augustus forced his stepson and heir TIBERIUS to divorce his wife and marry Julia (11). The unhappy Julia became promiscuous, and Tiberius went into self-imposed exile. When Augustus discovered Julia's behavior, he banished her to an island off Campania (2 B.C.), then to Rhegium. On becoming emperor, Tiberius withheld her allowance, and she starved to death.

Julian *or* **Julian the Apostate** *Latin* Julianus Apostata *orig.* Flavius Claudius Julianus (A.D. 331/332–363) Last pagan Roman emperor (361–63). The nephew of CONSTANTINE I, he was raised a Christian but converted to mystical paganism. As caesar (subemperor) in the west, he restored the Rhine frontier and was proclaimed augustus (senior emperor) by his armies. At Constantinople, Julian proclaimed freedom of worship for pagans and Christians in 361; he nevertheless committed acts of violence and persecution against Christians. To reassert Roman power in the east he attacked Persia; the effort failed, and he was killed in a retreat near Baghdad.

Juliana (Louise Emma Marie Wilhelmina) (b.1909) Queen of the Netherlands (1948–80). During World War II she took refuge in Ottawa, while her husband, Prince BERNHARD, remained with Queen WILHELMINA's London government. Returning to the Netherlands in 1945, Juliana became queen when Wilhelmina abdicated. In 1980 she abdicated in favor of her daughter BEATRIX.

Julian of Norwich *or* **Juliana of Norwich** (1342–after 1416) English mystic. After being healed of a serious illness (1373), she wrote two accounts of her visions; her *Revelations of Divine Love* is remarkable for its clarity, beauty, and profundity. She spent her later life as a recluse in Norwich.

Julio-Claudian dynasty (A.D. 14–68) Successors of AUGUSTUS, the first Roman emperor: TIBERIUS, CALIGULA, CLAUDIUS, and NERO. It was a loosely defined set of kin relations rather than a direct bloodline. Tiberius' rule was competent but ended in cruel tyranny. The insane Caligula was wild and capricious. Under Claudius Rome experienced marked development. Under Nero the empire prospered, but he was given to excesses, and his reign ended amid rebellion and civil war.

Julius II *orig.* Giuliano della Rovere (1443–1513) Pope (1503–13). The nephew of SIXTUS IV, he was elected pope in 1503. Julius set out to restore the Papal States, subjugating

HIJ

Perugia and Bologna (1508) and defeating Venice (1509). A popular revolt drove the French from N Italy in 1512, and Parma and Piacenza were added to the Papal States. The greatest art patron of all the popes, Julius was a close friend of MICHELANGELO, from whom he commissioned the sculpture of Moses and the paintings in the Sistine Chapel. He also commissioned RAPHAEL's Vatican frescoes.

Julius Caesar See Julius CAESAR

July monarchy In French history, the reign of LOUIS-PHILIPPE (1830–48), brought about by the July Revolution that toppled CHARLES X. Also known as the "bourgeois monarchy," the new regime rested on a broad social base centered on the wealthy bourgeoisie. The 1830s were marked by challenges to the regime by the legitimists and republicans, as well as attempts to assassinate the king. There were several labor uprisings, and Louis-Napoléon (later NAPOLEON III) made two attempts to take the crown. A period of remarkable stability began about 1840. François Guizot (1787-1874) became the key figure in the ministry; he imposed high protective tariffs that resulted in an economic boom, beginning France's transformation to an industrial society. In foreign affairs, the regime maintained friendly relations with Britain and supported Belgian independence. However, in 1848 general unrest led to the FEBRUARY REVOLUTION and the end of the July monarchy.

July Plot *or* **Rastenburg Assassination Plot** Abortive attempt on July 20, 1944, to assassinate Adolf HITLER and seek favorable peace terms from the Allies. Col. Claus von Stauffenberg (1907-1944) left a bomb in a briefcase in a conference room at Rastenburg, E. Prussia, where Hitler was meeting with top military aides. But the briefcase was pushed behind a table support, and Hitler survived the blast with minor injuries. Meanwhile, the other conspirators in Berlin failed to act. The chief conspirators, including Stauffenberg and Gen. Erwin ROMMEL, were promptly shot or forced to commit suicide. In subsequent days, about 200 conspirators were shot, hanged, or viciously strangled.

junco Any of several species of finchlike birds (genus *Junco,* family Fringillidae), about 6 in. (15 cm) long, of Canada and the U.S. Usually gray, they have white outer tail feathers that are flashed in flight to the accompaniment of snapping or twittering calls. Common winter birds, they are found in forests, fields, thickets, and city parks.

Juneau \ˈjü-nō\ City (pop., 2000: 31,000), capital of Alaska. Located in SE Alaska, it was settled in 1880. Mining was important until the Alaska-Juneau gold mine closed in 1944. Juneau was made the state capital in 1959. In 1970 Juneau merged with Douglas, on an island across the channel, to form the largest U.S. city in area (3,108 sq mi, or 8,050 sq km).

June beetle *or* **May beetle** *or* **June bug** Any insect of the genus *Phyllophaga* belonging to a widely distributed, plant-feeding SCARAB BEETLE subfamily (Melolonthinae). They appear in the Northern Hemisphere on warm spring evenings and are attracted to lights. Heavy-bodied, they are 0.5–1 in. (1.2–2.5 cm) long and have shiny wing covers. They feed on foliage and flowers at night, sometimes causing considerable damage. The larvae live in the soil, and can destroy crops, lawns, and pastures.

Jung \ˈyu̇ŋ\, **Carl Gustav** (1875–1961) Swiss psychiatrist. After taking his medical degree (1902), Jung pursued research on mental illness that led to his notion of the complex, or cluster of emotionally charged (and largely unconscious) associations. Between 1907 and 1912 he was Sigmund FREUD's close collaborator and most likely successor, but he broke with Freud over the latter's insistence on the sexual basis of neuroses. He founded the field of ANALYTIC PSYCHOLOGY in response to Freud's

Carl Gustav Jung

PSYCHOANALYSIS, advancing the concepts of the introvert and extrovert personality, archetypes, and the collective unconscious. His new psychotherapeutic techniques were designed to reacquaint the person with his or her unique "myth" or place in the collective unconscious, as expressed in dream and imagination. Sometimes criticized for its lack of verifiability, his work has been influential in religion and literature as well as psychiatry. His books include *The Psychology of the Unconscious* (1912; revised as *Symbols of Transformation*), *Psychological Types* (1921), *Psychology and Religion* (1938), and *Memories, Dreams, Reflections* (1962).

junior college See COMMUNITY COLLEGE

juniper Any of 60–70 species of aromatic evergreen trees or shrubs that make up the genus *Juniperus* of the CYPRESS family, found throughout the Northern Hemisphere. Juvenile leaves are needlelike; mature leaves are awl-shaped, spreading, and arranged in pairs or in whorls of three. Common juniper (*J. communis*) is a sprawling shrub whose fragrant, spicy-smelling berries are used to flavor foods and alcoholic beverages, particularly GIN. The fragrant wood of eastern red cedar (*J. virginiana*) is made into cabinets, fence posts, and pencils.

junk bond BOND with a rating below BBB. Often issued by smaller, newer companies, junk bonds offer higher rates of interest than more secure bonds, but are considered too risky by the large institutional investors (savings and loan associations, pension funds, insurance companies, and MUTUAL FUNDS) that provide U.S. corporations with much of their investment capital.

Juno In ROMAN RELIGION, the chief goddess and female counterpart of JUPITER. She was identified with the Greek goddess HERA. Probably introduced into Rome by the ETRUSCANS, she was connected with all aspects of the lives of women, particularly marriage. Individualized, she became a female guardian spirit; as every man had his genius, so every woman had her juno. Her temple in Rome eventually housed the Roman mint.

Jupiter Fifth PLANET from the sun. With 318 times the mass and over 1,400 times the volume of earth, it has over 2.5 times the gravity of earth at the top of its atmosphere and exerts strong effects on other members of the SOLAR SYSTEM, causing the KIRKWOOD GAPS in the asteroid belt and changing the motions of COMETS; it may pull in bodies that might otherwise collide with other planets. Jupiter has at least 16 moons (see GALILEAN SATELLITE) and a narrow, diffuse ring system. A gas giant, it has hydrogen and helium in proportions near those of the sun, which it orbits every 12 years at an average distance of 484 million mi (778 million km). Its rapid rotation (9 hours, 55.5 minutes) acts on electric currents to give it the largest magnetic field of any of the planets and causes intense storms, including one that has lasted hundreds of years (the GREAT RED SPOT). The planet is presumed to have a solid core. Its central temperature is estimated to be 45,000°F (25,000°C).

Jupiter Photo by Voyager I from 20.3 million miles, 1979

Jupiter *or* **Jove** Chief god of ancient Rome and Italy. Like his Greek counterpart, ZEUS, he was worshiped as a sky god. Probably introduced into Rome by the ETRUSCANS, Jupiter was associated with treaties, alliances, and oaths; he was the protecting deity of the republic and later of the reigning emperor. He was worshiped on the summits of hills throughout Italy, and all places struck by lightning became his property.

Jura Mountain range, central Europe. It extends 143 mi (230 km) along the boundary of France and Switzerland. Its highest peak is Mt. Neige, 5,652 ft (1,723 m) high. Its W slopes are the source of the Doubs and Ain rivers in France.

Jurassic period Interval of geologic time, 208–144 million years ago, in the MESOZOIC ERA. During the Jurassic, PAN-

GAEA began to break up into the continents we know today. Marine invertebrates flourished, and large reptiles dominated many marine habitats. On land, FERNS, MOSSES, and CONIFERS thrived. The DINOSAURS rose to supremacy, and by the end of the Jurassic the largest species had evolved. ARCHAEOPTERYX, the first primitive bird, appeared before the end of the period. Early mammals, tiny shrewlike creatures that appeared late in the preceding TRIASSIC PERIOD, managed to survive and evolve. See table at GEOLOGIC TIME.

Jurchen dynasty See JUCHEN DYNASTY

jurisdiction Authority of a court to hear and determine cases. This authority is constitutionally based. Examples of judicial jurisdiction are: appellate jurisdiction, in which a superior court has power to correct legal errors made in a lower court; concurrent jurisdiction, in which a suit might be brought to any of two or more courts; and federal jurisdiction. A court may also have authority to operate within a certain territory. Summary jurisdiction, in which a magistrate or judge has power to conduct proceedings resulting in a conviction without jury trial, is limited in the U.S. to petty offenses.

jury In law, a body of individuals selected and sworn to inquire into a question of fact and to render a verdict according to the evidence. Modern juries may deal with questions of law in addition to questions of fact, though federal juries in the U.S. are usually limited to dealing with questions of fact. The modern jury can vary in size depending on the proceeding, but usually has either six or 12 members. By U.S. law, federal grand and petit juries must be "selected at random from a fair cross-section of the community in the district or division wherein the court convenes." State jury selection varies somewhat. See also GRAND JURY, PETIT JURY.

justice In philosophy, the concept of a proper proportion between a person's deserts (what is merited) and the good and bad things that befall or are allotted to him or her. ARISTOTLE's view of justice has been central—that the key element of justice is treating like cases alike. Later thinkers have worked out which similarities (need, desert, talent) are relevant. Aristotle distinguishes between justice in the distribution of wealth or other goods (distributive justice) and justice in reparation, as, for example, in punishing someone for doing a wrong (retributive justice). The concept of justice is essential to that of the just state, a central formulation in POLITICAL PHILOSOPHY.

Justice, U.S. Department of Federal executive division responsible for law enforcement. Headed by the U.S. attorney general, it investigates and prosecutes cases under federal antitrust, civil rights, criminal, tax, and environmental laws. It controls the FEDERAL BUREAU OF INVESTIGATION, the Bureau of Prisons, and the DRUG ENFORCEMENT ADMINISTRATION.

justice of the peace In Anglo-American legal systems, a local magistrate empowered chiefly to administer justice in minor cases. In the U.S., justices of the peace are elected or appointed and hear minor civil matters and petty criminal cases. They may also officiate at weddings, issue arrest warrants, deal with traffic offenses, and hold inquests.

Justinian, Code of Collections of laws and legal interpretations developed under the sponsorship of the Byzantine emperor JUSTINIAN I from 529 to 565. Strictly speaking, they did not constitute a new legal code, but rather two collections of past laws and extracts of the opinions of the great Roman jurists. Also included were an elementary outline of the law and a collection of Justinian's new laws.

Justinian I orig. Petrus Sabbatius (483–565) Byzantine emperor (527–65). Determined to regain former Roman provinces, Justinian, with BELISARIUS, conquered the VANDALS in N Africa (534) and defeated the OSTROGOTHS in Italy (540). He did not gain control of the whole of Italy un-

til 562, and he was unable to prevent barbarian raids along the empire's N frontier. He also carried on an intermittent war with Persia until 561. He reorganized the imperial government and sponsored the Code of JUSTINIAN. His efforts to root out corruption triggered an abortive revolt in Constantinople in 532; his wife, THEODORA, helped him put down the revolt. Among his many public works was the church of HAGIA SOPHIA.

Justinian I Mosaic, 6th cent.

Justin Martyr, St. (c.100– c.165) Early Christian theologian. A pagan born in Palestine, he studied philosophy before becoming a Christian in 132. One of the first Apologists for Christianity, he was the first to blend Greek philosophy and Christian doctrine. He addressed two *Apologies* to Roman emperors, asserting that Christian faith can be in harmony with human reason and that Christianity is a purer form of the truth glimpsed in pagan philosophy. While living in Rome he was denounced as subversive and condemned to death.

just-in-time manufacturing (JIT) Production-control system, developed by TOYOTA MOTOR CORP., that has revolutionized manufacturing methods in some industries. By relying on daily deliveries of most supplies, it eliminates waste due to overproduction and lowers warehousing costs. Supplies are closely monitored and quickly altered to meet changing demands, and small and accurate resupply deliveries must be made just as they are needed. Because there are no spares, the components must be free of defects. Plants wholly dedicated to the JIT concept require a logistics staff to schedule production, balancing product demand with plant capacity and availability of inputs. JIT has worked most effectively for large automobile manufacturers.

jute Either of two herbaceous annuals (*Corchorus capsularis* and *C. olitorius*) in the LINDEN family, or their fiber. The plants grow 10–12 ft (3–4 m) high and have long, serrated, tapered, light-green leaves and small yellow flowers. Jute has been grown and processed in India and Bangladesh since ancient times. Its biggest use is in burlap sacks and bags. High-quality jute cloths are used as backing for tufted carpets and hooked rugs.

Jutland *Danish* **Jylland** \'yē-,lȧn\ Peninsula, N Europe. Forming the Danish mainland and the German state of SCHLESWIG-HOLSTEIN, it is bounded to the west and north by the North Sea. Politically, its name applies only to the mainland of Denmark. In World War I, the Battle of Jutland was fought off its coast.

Juvenal \'jü-və-nəl\ *Latin* Decimus Junius Juvenalis (c.A.D. 55–130) Roman poet. He is chiefly known for his 16 *Satires*, indignant attacks on human brutality and folly, particularly the corruption of Roman society under DOMITIAN and his more humane successors NERVA, TRAJAN, and HADRIAN. His verses are technically fine, vivid, and often ruthless, and many of his phrases and epigrams ("bread and circuses," "who will guard the guards themselves?" etc.) have entered common parlance.

juvenile court Special court handling problems of delinquent, neglected, or abused children. Two types of cases are processed: civil matters, often concerning care of an abandoned or impoverished child; and criminal matters arising from antisocial behavior by the child. Most statutes provide that all persons under a given age (often 18 years) must first be processed by the juvenile court, which can then, at its discretion, assign the case to an ordinary court.

HIJ

K

K2 *or* **Dapsang** \ˌdäp-ˈsäng\ Mountain in the KARAKORAM RANGE. The world's second-highest peak, it reaches 28,251 ft (8,611 m). It was measured in 1856 by Col. T. G. Montgomerie (1830–1878) and called K2 because it was the second peak measured in the Karakoram Range. In 1954 the Italians Achille Compagnoni (b.1914) and Lino Lacedelli (b.1925) became the first to reach its summit.

Kaaba Most sacred Muslim shrine, located near the center of the Great Mosque in MECCA. All Muslims face toward it in their daily prayers. The cube-shaped structure is made of gray stone and marble; the interior contains only pillars and silver and gold lamps. Pilgrims to Mecca walk around the Kaaba seven times and touch the Black Stone of Mecca on its E side, which may date from the pre-Islamic religion of the Arabs. In 630 MUHAMMAD purged the place of its pagan idols and rededicated it to ISLAM.

Kabalega National Park \ˌkä-bä-ˈlā-gä\ National park, NW Uganda. Established in 1952, it occupies 1,483 sq mi (3,840 sq km) of rolling grassland. Kabalega Falls, on the Victoria Nile River, drop 400 ft (120 m) in three cascades.

Kabbala *or* **Cabbala** \kä-ˈbä-lə\ Jewish MYSTICISM as it developed in the 12th cent. and after. Essentially an oral tradition, it laid claim to secret wisdom of the unwritten TORAH communicated by God to ADAM and MOSES. It provided Jews with a direct approach to God, a notion regarded as heretical and pantheistic by ORTHODOX JUDAISM. A major text was the 12th-cent. *Book of Brightness,* which introduced the doctrine of transmigration of souls to Judaism and provided Kabbala with extensive mythical symbolism. In the 16th cent. the center of Kabbala was Safed, Galilee, where it was based on the esoteric teachings of Isaac LURIA. The doctrines of Lurianic Kabbala, which called for Jews to achieve a cosmic restoration *(tiqqun)* through an intense mystical life and an unceasing struggle against evil, were influential in the development of modern HASIDISM.

Kabila \kə-ˈbē-lə\, **Laurent (Désiré)** (1939–2001) Rebel leader and president (1997–2001) of Congo (Zaire). He attended schools abroad, including military school in China, before participating in several Marxist-inspired uprisings in Zaire in the 1960s and '70s. He later became a trader in precious minerals and ivory. In the Rwandan civil war, Kabila collaborated with Paul KAGAME in attacking HUTU guerrilla groups in Zaire as well as Zairean government forces. His troops ousted MOBUTU SESE SEKO in 1997, and Kabila proclaimed himself president. His repressive policies led to a major war involving many African states. Kabila was assassinated, and his son Joseph (b.1971) succeeded him.

kabuki \kä-ˈbü-kē\ Popular Japanese entertainment that combines music, dance, and mime in highly stylized performance. The word is formed

Kabuki Warrior hero in *Shibaraku,* written in 1697

of three Japanese characters—*ka* (song), *bu* (dance), and *ki* (skill). It developed in the early 1600s from the nobility's NO DRAMA and became the theater of townspeople. In its early years it had a licentious reputation, its actors often being prostitutes; women and young boys were consequently forbidden to perform, and kabuki is today performed by an adult all-male cast. The lyrical but fast-moving and even acrobatic plays, noted for their spectacular staging and elaborate costumes and with striking makeup in place of masks, are vehicles in which the actors demonstrate a wide range of skills. Kabuki employs two musical ensembles, one onstage and the other offstage.

Kabul \ˈkä-bəl\ City (pop. 1994 est.: 700,000), capital of Afghanistan. Located on the Kabul River in a valley strategically located between mountain passes, including the KHYBER PASS, it has existed for 3,500 years. It was briefly the capital of the MUGHAL DYNASTY's empire in the 16th cent. In 1738 Iran gained control. Kabul has been the capital of Afghanistan since 1776. After the country's occupation by the Soviet Union (1979–89), factional fighting among Afghan guerrillas caused widespread destruction in the city. Under the TALIBAN (1996–2001) the country was effectively ruled from Kandahar. More damage was inflicted by U.S. bombing in 2001.

Kachchh, Rann of *or* **Rann of Kutch** \ˈkəch\ Large salt marsh, W central India, with a small portion in S Pakistan. The N portion, Great Rann, occupies 7,000 sq mi (18,000 sq km); the E section, Little Rann, occupies 2,000 sq mi (5,100 sq km). Originally an extension of the Arabian Sea, it has been closed off by centuries of silting.

kachina \kə-ˈchē-nə\ Ancestral spirit of the PUEBLO INDIANS. There are more than 500 of these spirits, who act as intermediaries between humans and the gods. Each tribe has its own kachinas. Kachina masks, when worn, allow the performer to be temporarily transformed by the kachina's spirit. Kachinas are also represented by small wooden dolls, carved and decorated by the men of the tribe.

Kaczynski \kə-ˈzin-skē\, **Theodore** *known as* **the Unabomber** (b.1942) U.S. criminal. Born in Evergreen Park, Ill., he earned a PhD in mathematics and taught at UC–Berkeley 1967–69, then abruptly left to become a hermit in a tiny, isolated shack in Montana. Over 17 years, he sent mail bombs to people he perceived as enemies of humanity, most of them researchers in science and technology, killing three people and injuring 23. His manifesto excoriating industrial society was published in 1995. Arrested in 1996 on a tip from his brother, he was sentenced to life in prison.

Kadar \ˈkä-ˌdår\, **Janos** *orig.* Janos Czermanik (1912–1989) Premier of Hungary (1956–58, 1961–65) and first secretary (1956–88) of Hungary's Communist Party. He entered the Hungarian Politburo in 1945. In 1950 he came into conflict with the Stalinists and was jailed (1951–53). Rehabilitated in 1954, he joined Imre NAGY's short-lived government. After Soviet troops took over the country in 1956, Kadar formed a new government. He later convinced the Soviet Union to withdraw its troops and allow Hungary a modicum of internal independence.

Kaddish \ˈkä-dish\ Jewish prayer of mourners, recited for a period of 11 months and one day after the death of a parent or close relative. Spoken in the ARAMAIC LANGUAGE, it is a hymn of praise to God and a prayer for the speedy coming of the MESSIAH. The association of the arrival of the mes-

642

siah and the resurrection of the dead led to its becoming the prayer of mourners.

Kadet See CONSTITUTIONAL DEMOCRATIC PARTY

Kafka \\'käf-kä\\, **Franz** (1883–1924) Czech writer who wrote in German. Born into a middle-class Jewish family in Prague (then part of Austria-Hungary), he earned a doctorate and then worked unhappily for many years at a government insurance office. Hypersensitive and neurotic, he reluctantly published only a few works in his lifetime, including the symbolic story *The Metamorphosis* (1915), the allegorical fantasy *In the Penal Colony* (1919), and the story collection *A Country Doctor* (1919). He died of tuberculosis at age 40. His unfinished novels *The Trial* (1925), *The Castle* (1926), and *Amerika* (1927), published posthumously against his wishes, express the anxieties

Franz Kafka

and alienation of 20th-cent. humanity. Kafka's posthumous reputation and influence have been enormous.

Kagame \\kä-'gä-mä\\, **Paul** (b.1957?) Leader of the TUTSI-dominated military campaign that won control of Rwanda from the HUTU majority in 1994. Kagame grew up in exile in Uganda, where he helped overthrow Milton OBOTE in 1986. In 1990 he assisted a coup attempt in Rwanda. When civil war broke out in 1994 he led the joint Tutsi-Hutu opposition forces. In the midst of genocidal campaigns, Kagame refused to condone ethnic violence. As vice president and defense minister of the new government, he was instrumental in the overthrow of MOBUTU'SESE SEKO in neighboring Zaire (Congo) in 1997, but soon turned against Laurent KABILA, whom he had helped install. In 2000 he was elected president of Rwanda.

Kaganovich \\kə-gə-'nȯ-vich\\, **Lazar (Moiseyevich)** (1893–1991) Soviet political leader. As head of the Moscow party organization (1930–35), he brought it firmly under Joseph STALIN's control. Until 1953 he was largely responsible for heavy industry in the Soviet Union. Under Nikita KHRUSHCHEV, he held administrative posts, but he opposed de-Stalinization and joined the unsuccessful attempt to depose Khrushchev in 1957, after which he lost all his offices.

Kahlo (y Calderón de Rivera) \\'kä-lō\\, **(Magdalena Carmen) Frida** (1907–1954) Mexican painter. The daughter of a German-Jewish photographer, at 18 she suffered a serious bus accident. She subsequently underwent some 35 operations; during her recovery, she taught herself to paint. Her marriage to Diego RIVERA (from 1929) was tumultuous but artistically rewarding. Often identified as a Surrealist, she is noted for her intense, bizarre, brilliantly colored self-portraits, many reflecting her physical ordeal, which incorporate primitivistic elements. André BRETON and Marcel DUCHAMP helped arrange exhibits of her work in the U.S. and Europe.

Kahn, Albert (1869–1942) U.S. (German-born) industrial architect. In 1904 he received a commission for the Packard Motor Car factory and originated the prototypical modern factory building, a rapidly and inexpensively built reinforced-concrete steel-frame structure with an unobstructed floor plan and large windows and skylights where all production takes place on one floor. For 30 years he was the principal architect for the major U.S. auto companies, and by 1937 his firm was producing a fifth of all architect-designed industrial buildings in the U.S.

Kahn, Louis I(sadore) (1901–1974) U.S. (Estonian-born) architect. One of the century's most original architects, Kahn turned from the INTERNATIONAL STYLE to a timeless, elegant Brutalism. His Richards Medical Research Building at the Univ. of Pennsylvania (1960–65) isolated "servant" spaces (stairwells, elevators, vents, and pipes) in four towers distinct from "served" spaces (laboratories and offices). His

fortresslike National Assembly Building in Dhaka, Bangladesh (1962–74), utilized geometric shapes to admit light to its inner domed mosque. Concerned about wasteful use of natural resources, he proposed geodesic skyscrapers and huge car "silos." He taught at Yale Univ. (1947–57) and the Univ. of Pennsylvania (1957–74), where his intellect elevated him to cult status.

Kaieteur Falls \\'kī-ə-ˌtu̇r\\ Cataract on the Potaro River, W central Guyana. After a sheer drop of 741 ft (226 m), the falls pass into a gorge 5 mi (8 km) long. The falls are 300 to 350 ft (90 to 105 m) wide at the top.

Kaifeng *or* **K'ai-feng** \\'kī-'fəŋ\\ City (pop., 1999: 569,000), N Henan province, China. In the 4th cent. B.C. it became the capital of the state of Wei, and the first of its many canals was built. It was destroyed by the QIN DYNASTY in the late 3rd cent. B.C., but became an important commercial center in the 7th cent. A.D., enriched by traffic along the GRAND CANAL, and it was the capital of the FIVE DYNASTIES and the SONG DYNASTY. Kaifeng was the site of China's only large Jewish community (12th–15th cent.).

Kairouan \\ker-'wän\\ Town (pop., 1994: 103,000), NE Tunisia. A holy city of ISLAM, it was founded in 670 and became the first Arab center in the MAGHREB. It was chosen as the Maghreb capital by the Aghlabid dynasty around 800. It served as an administrative, commercial, religious, and intellectual center under the FATIMID and Zirid dynasties. The rise of TUNIS, the new capital, led to Kairouan's decline and its devastation by Bedouins in the 11th cent. Its 9th-cent. Great Mosque is one of the city's 150 mosques.

Kaiser \\'kī-zər\\, **Henry J(ohn)** (1882–1967) U.S. industrialist. Born in Sprout Brook, N.Y., he undertook his first public-works projects in 1914, eventually building dams in California, levees on the Mississippi River, and highways in Cuba. Between 1931 and 1945, he organized the construction of the HOOVER, Bonneville, and Grand Coulee dams. During World War II he ran seven shipyards, using his own integrated steel mill and assembly-line production to build ships in less than five days. He established the first HEALTH MAINTENANCE ORGANIZATION, the Kaiser plan, for his shipyard employees; it served more than a million people and became a model for later programs. In the postwar era he dealt profitably in aluminum, steel, and automobiles.

Kalahari Desert \\ˌkä-lä-'hä-rē\\ Arid region, S Africa. It covers 360,000 sq mi (930,000 sq km) and lies mostly in Botswana but also in Namibia and S. Africa. Not truly desert, it supports trees, low scrub, and grasses as well as abundant wildlife, including gnu, gemsbok, giraffe, and elephant. It includes Kalahari Gemsbok National Park, GEMSBOK NATIONAL PARK, and Central Kalahari Game Reserve.

Kalaupapa Peninsula \\kä-ˌlä-ü-'pä-pä\\ Promontory, Molokai island, Hawaii. It is isolated from the rest of the island by 2,000-ft (600-m) cliffs. It was the site of the original leper colony (see LEPROSY) established by King Kamehameha V in 1866; Father DAMIEN ministered to the lepers there 1873–89. The entire peninsula is now the state leprosarium.

kale Loose-leafed, edible plant (*Brassica oleracea* 'acephala') derived from the CABBAGE, in the MUSTARD FAMILY. It has stems up to 2 ft (60 cm) long, carrying a rosette of elongated, dark-bluish-green, wavy or frilled leaves. Kale is usually served cooked and is highly nutritious. See also BRASSICA, COLLARD.

Kalevala \\'kä-lä-ˌvä-lä\\ Finnish national epic. It was compiled by Elias LÖNNROT from the songs and ballads of Finland's oral tradition and published in complete form in 1849. Kalevala, the dwelling place for the poem's chief characters, is also a poetic name for Finland, meaning "land of heroes." The epic contains a creation story and adventures of legendary heroes. Though the *Kalevala* depicts conditions during the pre-Christian era, it also seems to foretell the decline of the old religions.

Kalf \\'kälf\\, **Willem** (1619–1693) Dutch painter. He is among the best-known Dutch painters of still lifes, a choice of subject matter influenced by a stay in Paris. His early works depict kitchen interiors. His later paintings feature luxurious, expensive objects such as Venetian glass, painted with restraint and richness of texture. Works such as *Still Life with a Nautilus Cup* (c.1660) were popular among Amsterdam's wealthy.

Kali Destructive and devouring Hindu goddess. She is a terrifying aspect of DEVI, who in other forms appears as peaceful and benevolent. Kali is commonly associated with death, violence, sexuality, and, paradoxically, with motherly love. She is usually depicted nearly naked, wearing a garland of skulls and a girdle of severed hands. Kali developed her taste for blood from killing the demon Raktavija. Until the 19th cent. the thugs of India worshiped Kali and offered their victims to her.

Kalidasa \ˌkä-lē-ˈdä-sä\ (fl.c.5th cent.) Indian poet and dramatist. Many works are traditionally ascribed to him, but scholars have identified only six or seven as genuine. The Sanskrit drama *The Recognition of Sakuntala*, his most famous creation, is traditionally judged the major Indian literary effort of any period, and Kalidasa is regarded as perhaps the greatest of all Indian writers.

Kalinga Ancient and medieval kingdom, E central India. It was conquered by Mahapadma, the founder of the Nanda Dynasty, in the 4th cent. B.C. Beginning in the mid-11th cent. A.D., the Eastern GANGA DYNASTY assumed control. The temple of the sun-god at Konarak was built in the 13th cent. by Narasimha I. The dynasty collapsed when the sultan of Delhi invaded Kalinga from the south in 1324.

Kaliningrad \kə-ˈlē-nin-ˌgrát\ *formerly* **Königsberg** \ˈkœ̄-niks-ˌberk\ City (pop., 1997 est.: 424,000), W Russia, situated on the Pregolya River. Founded in 1255 as Königsberg, it was the capital of the dukes of Prussia and later the capital of E. Prussia. Virtually destroyed in World War II, it was rebuilt by the U.S.S.R. in 1946 as Kaliningrad. It is the seat of the Univ. of Kaliningrad and the birthplace of Immanuel KANT.

Kalmar Union \ˈkäl-ˌmär\ (1397–1523) Scandinavian union that joined the kingdoms of Norway, Sweden, and Denmark under a single monarch. Margaret I became ruler of the three kingdoms in 1387; she chose her grandson Erik of Pomerania to become their king, and he was crowned at Kalmar, Sweden, in 1397. Each country kept its own laws, customs, and administration. Sweden rebelled and claimed independence in 1523, and Norway became a Danish province in 1536.

Kamakura shogunate \ˌkä-mä-ˈkùr-ä\ (1192–1333) Military government of Japan from the city of Kamakura. It was established by MINAMOTO YORITOMO after his 1185 defeat of the rival Taira family. To assert his authority, Yoritomo had stewards assigned to all the estates (SHOEN) in the land to collect taxes, and protectors assigned to one or more provinces to lead them in times of war. This system was improved by the HOJO FAMILY, which later took control of the shogunate. The shogunate marks the start of Japan's medieval or feudal period, characterized by a warrior ethic of duty, loyalty, and stoicism. ZEN Buddhism, SAMURAI, SEPPUKU, and the TEA CEREMONY date from this period. The True Pure Land and NICHIREN sects of Buddhism, which emphasized salvation through faith alone, provided solace to the masses, while tales of warrior exploits provided them with entertainment.

Kama River River, W central Russia. The largest tributary of the VOLGA, it flows for 1,122 mi (1,805 km) before entering the Volga below Kazan. Navigation is possible for about 955 mi (1,535 km). It is important historically as the route to the Urals and Siberia and economically as part of the vast Volga system of waterways.

Kamchatka \kəm-ˈchät-kə\ Peninsula, E Russia. It lies between the Sea of Okhotsk on the west and the Pacific Ocean and BERING SEA on the east. It has an area of 140,000 sq mi (370,000 sq km). Its mountain ranges, with 22 active volcanoes, include Klyuchevskaya Volcano (15,584 ft, or 4,750 m), the highest peak in SIBERIA.

Kamehameha I \kä-ˈmā-hä-ˈmā-hä\ *orig.* Paiea *known as* **Kamehameha the Great** (1758?–1819) Hawaiian conqueror and king who united all the Hawaiian islands. As a young man he fought his cousin over control of the island of Hawaii; by 1795 he had conquered all but two of the Hawaiian islands, and in 1810 those were ceded to him. He retained the harsh traditional legal system but protected the common people from the brutality of powerful chiefs and outlawed human sacrifice. He enriched his kingdom through a government monopoly on the sandalwood trade and through port duties imposed on visiting ships, and maintained its independence throughout the difficult period of European discovery and exploration.

Kamehameha IV *orig.* Alexander Liholiho (1834–1863) Hawaiian ruler (1855–63). The adopted child of Kamehameha III (1813–1854), as king he sought to curb the power of the U.S. missionaries, inviting the Church of England to establish itself in the islands, and expanded trade with other countries. Popular and benevolent, he improved harbors to accommodate a growing whaling industry and provided free medical care for Hawaiians.

Kamenev \ˈkä-myə-ˌnyef\, **Lev (Borisovich)** *orig.* Lev Borisovich Rosenfeld (1883–1936) Russian political leader. A member of the Bolsheviks from 1903, he worked with Vladimir LENIN in Europe 1909–14. He served as head of the Moscow soviet 1919–25. When Lenin became seriously ill in 1922, Kamenev joined Joseph STALIN and Grigory ZINOVYEV to form the ruling triumvirate, attacking Leon TROTSKY. In 1925 Stalin shifted his attack to Kamenev and Zinovyev; in 1926 Kamenev was expelled from the party after conspiring with Zinovyev and Trotsky against Stalin. In 1936 he was tried in the first of the PURGE TRIALS and confessed to fabricated charges, hoping to save his family. He was executed, and his wife, Trotsky's sister, perished in the GULAG.

kamikaze \ˌkä-mi-ˈkä-zē\ Any of the Japanese pilots in World War II who made deliberate suicidal crashes into enemy targets, usually ships. The word means "divine wind," a reference to a typhoon that dispersed a Mongol invasion fleet threatening Japan in 1281. Most kamikaze planes were loaded with bombs or extra gasoline tanks. Such attacks sank 34 ships and damaged hundreds; at Okinawa they inflicted the greatest losses ever suffered by the U.S. Navy in a single battle, killing almost 5,000 men.

Kampala \käm-ˈpä-lä\ City (pop., 1998: 1,154,000), capital of Uganda. The country's largest city, it is in S Uganda, north of Lake VICTORIA. It was selected in 1890 by F. D. LUGARD as the headquarters of the British E. Africa Co. In 1962 Kampala became the capital of independent Uganda. It is the headquarters for most of Uganda's large firms and the site of Makerere Univ. and the Uganda Museum.

Kampuchea See CAMBODIA

Kampuchean See KHMER

Kanawa, Kiri Te See Kiri TE KANAWA

Kanchenjunga \ˌkən-chən-ˈjəŋ-gə\ Peak in the HIMALAYAS. The world's third-highest mountain, it reaches 28,169 ft (8,586 m). It is located on the Nepalese border with Sikkim, India. In 1955 a British expedition led by Charles Evans (1918–1995) made the first successful climb.

Kander, John (b.1927) U.S. songwriter. Born in Kansas City, he studied music at Columbia Univ. With lyricist Fred Ebb (b.1932), a native New Yorker who also studied at Columbia, he scored some of Broadway's most successful musicals, including *Cabaret* (1966; film, 1972), *Zorba* (1968), *Chicago* (1975), and *Kiss of the Spider Woman* (1992), and films such as *Funny Lady* (1975) and *New York, New York* (1977).

Kandinsky \kan-ˈdin-skē\, **Vasily (Vasilievich)** (1866–1944) Russian painter, a pioneer of pure abstraction in modern painting. Though offered a law professorship, he chose painting instead. After art studies in Munich, he achieved moderate success with his series of *Compositions, Improvisations,* and *Impressions* (1909–14). In 1911 he and Franz MARC founded the influential BLAUE REITER group. In 1914 he returned to Russia. After being briefly lionized by the Soviet government, he returned to Germany in 1921, taught at the BAUHAUS 1921–33, then emigrated to Paris. Through the years, Kandinsky's work evolved from fluid organic forms to geometric and finally pictographic forms. His

Vasily Kandinsky

book *Concerning the Spiritual in Art* (1912) explains his theories on the expressiveness of forms and color, which he likened to qualities of sound (e.g., comparing yellow to a blaring trumpet). His influence on 20th-cent. art was profound.

Kane, Paul (1810–1871) Canadian (Irish-born) painter. His family emigrated to Canada in 1819. He worked mainly in Toronto, but traveled widely, depicting landscapes, American Indian subjects, fur traders, and missionaries; *Wanderings of an Artist* (1859) is his memoir. His portraits, works of great historical value, record the dress and ornaments of his subjects in accurate detail. He excelled at composing large figurative groups in a genre-painting style.

kangaroo Any of about 47 species of Australasian MARSUPIALS (family Macropodidae). Most are terrestrial and all are herbivores. They generally have long, powerful hind legs and feet and a long tail, thickened at the base. The hind legs enable their spectacular leaps and are also useful for self-defense; the tail is used for balance. Females have one young annually; it is suckled in its mother's pouch for six months, and later often returns to the pouch. The gray kangaroo, the best-known and second-largest species, can leap more than 30 ft (9 m). The red kangaroo, the largest species, may stand 6 ft (1.8 m) tall and weigh 200 lbs (90 kg). Tree kangaroos climb trees and leap from branch to branch. Kangaroo populations have declined severely. See also WALLABY, WALLAROO.

Kangaroo Island Island (pop., 1986: 2,000), S. Australia. Located southwest of ADELAIDE, it is 90 mi (145 km) long and occupies an area of 1,970 sq mi (5,102 sq km). Visited in 1802 by Matthew FLINDERS, it was named for its many kangaroos.

kangaroo rat Any of about 25 species (genus *Dipodomys*, family Heteromyidae) of RODENTS that leap about on their hind legs. Found in dry regions of N. America, they have large heads, large eyes, short forelimbs, long hind limbs, and fur-lined external cheek pouches. They are 4–6.5 in. (10–16 cm) long without the long tail, which usually ends in a furry tuft. They forage by night for seeds and leaves, carrying food in their cheek pouches to store in their burrows, but seldom drink water.

Kangxi emperor *or* **K'ang-hsi emperor** \'käŋ-'shē\ (1654–1722) Second emperor of China's QING DYNASTY. One of China's most capable rulers, Kangxi reigned from 1661 and laid the foundation for a long period of political stability and prosperity. A peace treaty was signed with Russia, parts of Outer Mongolia were added to China's territory, and control was extended over Tibet. His public works included the repairing of the GRAND CANAL to permit transportation of rice to feed the N population, and the banking of the Huang (Yellow) River to prevent destructive flooding. He reduced taxes many times and opened four ports to foreign ships for trade. Though an ardent proponent of NEO-CONFUCIANISM, he also welcomed Jesuit missionaries, permitting the propagation of Roman Catholicism in China. He commissioned many books, including the Kangxi dictionary.

Kang Youwei *or* **K'ang Yu-wei** \'käŋ-'yō-'wä\ (1858–1927) Chinese scholar and reformer. In 1895 Kang led a protest against the humiliating terms of China's treaty with Japan after the SINO-JAPANESE WAR and to petition for reforms. In 1898 the Qing emperor launched a reform program that included streamlining the government, strengthening the armed services, and promoting local self-government, but the empress CIXI annulled the reforms; six reform leaders were executed, and Kang fled the country. He returned in 1914 and participated in an abortive restoration of the emperor; his fears of a divided country led him to oppose the government of SUN YAT-SEN in S China. Kang is also known for his reappraisal of Confucius, whom he saw as a reformer.

Kannon See AVALOKITESVARA

Kano \'kä-nō\ City (pop., 1996 est.: 674,000), N Nigeria. Its traditional founder was Kano, a blacksmith of the Gaya tribe in ancient times. It became the capital of the Hausa state of Kano in the early 12th cent. It was the capital of an emirate in the 19th cent. before being captured by the British in 1903. The old city is enclosed by a massive city wall dating from the 15th cent.; the central mosque is Nigeria's largest.

Kanpur \'kän-ˌpúr\ *or* **Cawnpore** City (pop., 1991: 1,874,000), Uttar Pradesh, N India. The British acquired it in 1801; in 1857, during the INDIAN MUTINY, it was the site of the massacre of British troops and civilians by native forces. One of the largest cities in India, it is a major commercial, industrial, and educational center, with a university and a campus of the Indian Institute of Technology.

Kansas State (pop., 2000: 2,688,000), central U.S. It covers 82,277 sq mi (213,097 sq km); its capital is TOPEKA. It is part of the GREAT PLAINS, rising more than 3,000 ft (900 m) from its E prairies to the high plains of the west. The region was occupied by the Kansa, OSAGE, PAWNEE, and Wichita Indians before European settlement. The first European explorer was Francisco CORONADO, who came from Mexico in 1541 in search of gold. R.-R. LA SALLE claimed the region for France in 1682. Kansas was acquired by the U.S. as part of the LOUISIANA PURCHASE in 1803. In the early 19th cent. the federal government relocated displaced E Indians to Kansas. The KANSAS-NEBRASKA ACT of 1854 created Kansas Territory and opened it to white settlement. It was the site of conflicts over slavery, including one spurred by John BROWN (see BLEEDING KANSAS). It entered the Union as the 34th state in 1861. After the Civil War, the coming of the railroads promoted the growth of cow towns; Texas cattlemen drove herds to WICHITA and ABILENE to reach the railheads. Agriculture became important as farmers worked on the Great Plains. During and following World War II, airplane production expanded, and the market for farm products remained strong.

Kansas, Bleeding See BLEEDING KANSAS

Kansas City City (pop., 2000: 441,000), W Missouri, on the MISSOURI RIVER. The city is contiguous with Kansas City, Kan. (pop., 2000: 147,000). First settled by French fur traders in 1821, it was a river port and the terminus for the SANTA FE TRAIL and the OREGON TRAIL. It was named Kansas City in 1889. The state's second-largest city, it is a railroad center with stockyards, packinghouses, and grain-storage facilities.

Kansas-Nebraska Act (1854) Legislation that organized the territories of Kansas and Nebraska according to the doctrine of POPULAR SOVEREIGNTY. Introduced by Sen. Stephen DOUGLAS to stop the sectional division over slavery, it was criticized as a capitulation to proslavery advocates. Groups on both sides rushed to settle Kansas Territory with their adherents, leading to the chaotic BLEEDING KANSAS period and the formation of the REPUBLICAN PARTY to oppose the expansion of slavery to any U.S. territory.

Kant \'känt\, **Immanuel** (1724–1804) German philosopher, the foremost thinker of the ENLIGHTENMENT. Son of a saddler, he studied at the Univ. of Königsberg and taught there from 1755 to 1797. Much of Kant's work was devoted to arguing that METAPHYSICS, understood as knowledge of things supersensible, is an impossibility. Yet he held that metaphysics could be put on "the sure path of science", and that it is also possible, even necessary, to hold certain beliefs about God, freedom, and immortality, though to know about the intelligible world is entirely beyond human capacity. Though the Ideas of God,

Immanuel Kant Portrait by H. V. Schnorr von Carolsfeld

freedom, and immortality are dismissed in his great *Critique of Pure Reason* (1781) as objects that humans can never know, he argued in *The Critique of Practical Reason* (1788) that they are essential postulates for the moral life. His *Groundwork of the Metaphysics of Morals* (1785) is among the most influential ethical treatises ever written. His last great work was *The Critique of Judgment* (1790). One of the

K L

greatest philosophers of all time, he synthesized new trends that had begun with the RATIONALISM of René DESCARTES and the EMPIRICISM of Francis BACON. His comprehensive and systematic work in epistemology, ethics, and aesthetics greatly influenced all subsequent philosophy, especially the various German schools of KANTIANISM and IDEALISM.

Kantianism \\'kan-tē-ə-ˌni-zəm, kän-tē-ə-ˌni-zəm\\ System of critical philosophy created by Immanuel KANT and those philosophies strongly influenced by it. All Kantian philosophies share Kant's concern to explore the nature and limits of human knowledge in the hope of raising philosophy to the level of a science. In the 1790s, there emerged in Germany the so-called semi-Kantians, who altered features of Kant's system that they viewed as inadequate, unclear, or even wrong; its members included Friedrich SCHILLER, Friedrich Bouterwek (1766–1828), and Jakob Friedrich Fries (1773–1843). The period 1790–1835 was the age of the post-Kantian idealists (see IDEALISM). A major revival of interest in Kantian philosophy began about 1860. See also Johann Gottlieb FICHTE, G. W. F. HEGEL.

Kantorovich \\ˌkän-tə-'rȯ-vich\\, **Leonid (Vitalyevich)** (1912–1986) Soviet mathematician and economist. A professor at Leningrad State Univ. (1934–60), he developed the linear programming model as a tool of economic planning. He used mathematical techniques to show how decentralizing decision making in a planned economy requires basing prices on the relative scarcity of resources. His most notable work is *The Best Use of Economic Resources* (1959). In 1975 he and Tjalling Koopmans (1910–1985) shared the Nobel Prize for their work on optimal allocation of scarce resources. He published over 300 papers and books on mathematics, economics, and computers.

kaolinite \\'kā-ə-lə-ˌnīt\\ Group of common CLAY MINERALS that are hydrous aluminum silicates and constitute the principal ingredients of kaolin (china clay). They are natural alteration products of feldspars, feldspathoids, and other silicates.

kapok \\'kā-ˌpäk\\ Fiber obtained from the large Asian tropical silk cotton, or kapok, tree (*Ceiba pentandra,* family Bombacaceae), which bears hundreds of seedpods filled with fibrous seeds. Sometimes called silk cotton or Java cotton, this moisture-resistant, quick-drying, resilient, buoyant fiber is used in life preservers and other water-safety equipment. Kapok is also used to stuff pillows, mattresses, and upholstery, and as insulation. However, it is highly flammable, and the fibers are too brittle for spinning.

Kaposi's sarcoma \\'ka-pə-sēz\\ Usually lethal CANCER appearing as red-purple or blue-brown spots on the skin and other organs. It has been linked to one of the herpes viruses. When described in 1872 by Moritz Kaposi, it was extremely rare, confined to specific Mediterranean and African populations. Since about 1980, it has become common in AIDS patients. More homosexual male HIV patients (about 25%) have developed it than heterosexual intravenous-drug-using HIV patients (3%). Remissions have occurred, but there is no known cure.

Karachi \\kä-'rä-chē\\ City (pop., 1998: 9,269,000), Pakistan. Located in S Pakistan on the Arabian Sea, it grew from a small fishing village in the early 18th cent. to a major port of the British empire by 1914. The provincial capital of Sind from 1936, it was also the capital of Pakistan 1947–59. Today it is one of the world's largest cities. A major industrial and commercial center, the seat of the Univ. of Karachi, and the terminus of Pakistan's railway system, it is the port for virtually all shipping from and to Pakistan and Afghanistan.

Karadzic \\kä-'rä-jētʸ, *Engl* kä-'rad-zich\\, **Radovan** (b.1945) Bosnian Serb politician. He trained as a psychiatrist and also wrote poetry and children's books. In 1992, when the Bosnian Serbs declared an independent state, he became its president. With the support of Yugoslav president Slobodan MILOSEVIC and with Bosnian Serb military leader Gen. Ratko Mladic, Karadzic undertook a campaign of "ethnic cleansing" in Bosnia to purge it of non-Serb peoples. In 1995 he was indicted by a U.N. war-crimes tribunal and forced to resign. However, he continued to influence the Serb-controlled part of Bosnia and Herzegovina from a mountain hideaway outside Sarajevo. See also BOSNIAN CONFLICT.

Karajan \\'kär-ə-ˌyän\\, **Herbert von** (1908–1989) Austrian conductor. Born in Salzburg, he was a piano prodigy, and he took his first conducting post in Ulm in 1929. In 1933 he joined the Nazi Party, and under the Third Reich his reputation grew swiftly. After World War II he initially was not allowed to conduct, but in 1947 he began recording with the Vienna Philharmonic, the start of a legacy of some 800 recordings. In 1955 he assumed leadership of the Berlin Philharmonic, and he headed the Salzburg Festival from 1964 until his death.

Karakoram Range Mountain system, Central Asia. Extending 300 mi (480 km) from E Afghanistan to KASHMIR, it is one of the highest mountain systems in the world; its loftiest peak is K2. Surrounded by other steep mountain ranges, the Karakorams are virtually inaccessible, although the completion of the Karakoram Highway in 1978 improved transportation in the region.

Karakorum \\ˌkä-rä-'kȯr-əm\\ Ancient capital, MONGOL empire. Its ruins lie on the upper Orhon River in N central Mongolia. It was first settled about 750; GENGHIS KHAN established his headquarters there in 1220. In 1235 OGODEI enclosed the city with walls and built a palace. Chinese forces invaded Mongolia and destroyed Karakorum in 1388. It was abandoned by the 16th cent.

Karakum Desert or **Kara-Kum Desert** \\ˌkär-ə-'küm\\ Desert area, central Asia. Located in TURKMENISTAN, it is bordered on the east by the AMU DARYA valley. It can be divided into three major regions: the elevated and wind-eroded Trans-Unguz in the north; the low-lying central plain; and salt marshes of the southeast.

Karamanlis \\ˌkär-ə-män-'lēs\\, **Konstantinos** or **Constantine Caramanlis** (1907–1998) Greek prime minister (1955–63, 1974–80) and president (1980–85, 1990–95). In various cabinet posts after World War II, he helped rebuild Greece's war-torn economy. Chosen prime minister in 1955, he formed a new conservative party, the National Radical Union. In 1960 he established an independent republic on Cyprus to ease tensions with Britain and Turkey over the island. He resigned in 1963 and lived in exile in Paris until 1974. Recalled as prime minister (1974), he subordinated the military to civilian authority, averted war with Turkey over Cyprus, and oversaw the adoption of a new constitution that strengthened the presidency and a referendum that abolished the monarchy. In 1980 he resigned as prime minister and was elected president; he resigned in 1985, then was reelected in 1990.

karate MARTIAL ART in which an attacker is disabled by crippling kicks and punches. Emphasis is on concentration of as much of the body's power as possible at the point and instant of impact. Striking surfaces include hands (particularly the knuckles and the outer edge), ball of the foot, heel, forearm, knee, and elbow. In sporting matches and in sparring, blows and kicks are stopped short. Developed from older forms, karate was first systematized in Okinawa in the 17th cent. See also TAE KWON DO.

Karbala \\ˌkär-bä-'lä\\, **Battle of** (680) Battle between forces of the second Umayyad caliph, YAZID I, and HUSAYN IBN ALI. Husayn was on his way to Kufah to become caliph when he was attacked and killed in the town of Karbala, Iraq, by a Umayyad army. Shiites regard the battle's date as a holy day of mourning, and Husayn's tomb as the holiest place in the world. See also ALI, FITNAH, al-MUAWIYAH I.

Kardelj \\'kär-ˌdelʸ\\, **Edvard** (1910–1979) Yugoslav administrator. He helped organize the resistance to the German occupation in World War II and joined TITO in much of the Partisans' fighting. In 1946 he drew up the Soviet-inspired constitution after Tito became premier. He was the main architect of socialist self-management, which distinguished Yugoslavia's system from the Soviet system. In foreign affairs, he pioneered the concept of Yugoslav nonalignment.

Karisimbi \\ˌkä-rē-'sim-bē\\, **Mt.** Peak, E central Africa. The highest peak in the Virunga Mtns. at 14,787 ft (4,507 m), it lies on the boundary between Rwanda and the Congo (Zaire). It is the habitat of gorillas and is known for its exotic plants.

Karl Franz Josef See CHARLES I (AUSTRIA)

Karl-Marx-Stadt See CHEMNITZ

Karloff, Boris *orig.* William Henry Pratt (1887–1969) British-U.S. actor. He emigrated to Canada from England in 1909 and later moved to Hollywood, where he acted in films from 1919 and won fame in Hollywood's first important monster film, James Whale's *Frankenstein* (1931). He acted in over 100 films, specializing in such horror pictures as *The Mummy* (1932), *The Mask of Fu Manchu* (1932), and *Bride of Frankenstein* (1935), and his name became synonymous with the horror genre. He gave highly acclaimed performances on Broadway in *Arsenic and Old Lace* (1941) and as Captain Hook in *Peter Pan* (1950).

Boris Karloff

Karlovy Vary \'kär-lȯ-vē-'vär-ē\ *German* **Karlsbad** *or* **Carlsbad** \'kärls-ˌbät\ City (pop., 1991: 56,000), W Czech Republic. A health resort with sulfur springs, it was developed in 1358 by the Holy Roman emperor CHARLES IV.

karma In Indian philosophy, the influence of an individual's past actions on his future lives or REINCARNATIONS. It is based on the conviction that the present life is only one in a chain of lives (see SAMSARA). The accumulated moral energy of a person's life determines his or her character, class status, and disposition in the next life. The process is automatic, and no interference is possible. The concept of karma, basic to Hinduism, was also incorporated into Buddhism and Jainism.

Karman \'kär-mȧn\, **Theodore von** (1881–1963) Hungarian-U.S. engineer. After directing the Aeronautical Institute at Aachen, Germany (1912–30), he emigrated to the U.S., where he taught at Caltech (1930–44) and later headed NATO's aeronautical advisory group (1951–63). His pioneering work included important contributions to fluid mechanics, turbulence theory, supersonic flight, and aircraft structures. His jet-assisted takeoff (JATO) ROCKET provided the prototype for engines used in present-day long-range missiles. He contributed to the first assisted takeoff of U.S. aircraft with solid- and liquid-propellant rockets, the flight of aircraft with rocket propulsion alone, and the development of spontaneously igniting liquid propellants. In 1963 he was awarded the first National Medal of Science.

Karma-pa See DGE-LUGS-PA

Karnak Village in Upper Egypt, which has given its name to the N half of the ruins of THEBES (c.3200 B.C.) on the Nile's E bank. Here stood the largest of all Egyptian temples, the Temple of AMON. Itself a complex of temples, its alterations reflect the fluctuating fortunes of the Egyptian empire. There are no fewer than 10 pylons, separated by courts and halls. The vast hypostyle hall built by Ramses I (14th cent. B.C.), has an area of 52,000 sq ft (4,850 sq m); fourteen enormous columns raised the roofing slabs of the central aisle to produce a CLERESTORY.

Karpov \'kär-ˌpȯf\, **Anatoly (Yevgenyevich)** (b.1951) Russian chess master. A child prodigy, he became world champion in 1975 when Bobby FISCHER declined to meet him in tournament play. He lost his title to Garry KASPAROV in 1985, but regained it in 1993 after Kasparov was stripped of the title for organizing a new chess federation. In 1999 Karpov refused to defend his title in a world tournament.

Karsavina \kär-'sä-və-nə\, **Tamara (Platonovna)** (1885–1978) Russian-British dancer best known as the leading ballerina in the BALLETS RUSSES (1909–22). She trained at the Imperial Ballet school in St. Petersburg and later joined the Ballets Russes. Dancing with Vaslav NIJINSKY until 1913, she created most of the leading roles in Michel FOKINE's neo-Romantic repertoire, including *Les sylphides*, *The Firebird*, and *Daphnis and Chloe*. She settled in London, where she helped found the Royal Academy of Dancing in 1920 and later coached Margot FONTEYN.

Karsh, Yousuf (1908–2002) Turkish-Canadian photographer. He emigrated at 16 to join his photographer uncle in Canada, worked for a Boston portrait photographer (1928–31), then opened his own studio in Ottawa. In 1935 he was appointed official portrait photographer of the Canadian government. His portrait of Winston CHURCHILL (1941) brought him international fame. "Karsh of Ottawa" went on to photograph hundreds of the world's most prominent figures, employing his subtle lighting to produce idealized likenesses.

Kasai River \kȧ-'sī\ River, central Africa. It is the chief S tributary of the CONGO RIVER, measuring 1,338 mi (2,153 km) from its source in Angola to its confluence with the Congo. It forms part of the border between Angola and Congo (Zaire). It is unnavigable in the north, but water traffic is heavy from KINSHASA to Ilebo. After joining the Kwango River, it is known as the Kwa.

Kasanje \kä-'sän-jä\ Historical African kingdom, on the upper Kwango River in what is now Angola. Founded in 1620 by a group from Lunda, by the mid-17th cent. it had developed a monopoly of inland Portuguese-African trade that lasted until 1850, when Ovimbundu people opened alternative routes and markets. Occupied by the Portuguese, it was incorporated into Portuguese Angola in 1910–11.

Kasavubu \kȧ-sȧ-'vü-bü\, **Joseph** (c.1910–1969) First president of the Congo republic (later Zaire), 1960–65. He held various administrative posts before serving as president in Patrïce LUMUMBA's government. When Katanga province under Moise TSHOMBE seceded, Kasavubu supported Tshombe and, with Col. Joseph Mobutu (see MOBUTU SESE SEKO), ousted Lumumba. Four years later a split between Kasavubu and Tshombe enabled Mobutu to seize control.

Kashmir Former princely state, NW Indian subcontinent, now divided among India, Pakistan, and China. The land is predominantly mountainous, and includes K2 and other mountains of the Karakoram Range. Pakistan occupies the N and W portions, China holds the NE section, and India controls the largest portion, in the south and southeast, organized as the state of Jammu and Kashmir (pop., 2001: 10,070,000), including the Jammu plain and the fertile and heavily populated Vale of Kashmir. In recent years the Indian state has seen guerrilla actions by Muslim Kashmiri separatists and foreign terrorists.

kashruth \kä-'shrüt, 'kä-shrúth\ In JUDAISM, the rules forbidding the eating of certain foods and requiring that other foods be prepared in a specific way. These rules, derived from the Hebrew Bible, determine which foods can be called kosher. Jews observing kashruth may eat only fish with scales and fins and animals that chew the cud and have cloven feet; shellfish and pork are thus forbidden. Animals and birds must be slaughtered according to ritual and with prayer. Meat and dairy products must be strictly separated; they may not be eaten at the same meal or from the same set of dishes.

Kasparov \kas-'pär-ȯf\, **Garry** (*orig.* Garri Kimovich) (b.1963) Russian chess master. Born in Baku, Azerbaijan, he was an international grandmaster by 17. After failing to beat the reigning champion, Anatoly KARPOV, in a 48-game draw in 1984–85, he returned later in 1985 to take the title, becoming at 22 the youngest champion in history. The International Chess Federation stripped him of his title in 1993 when he left it to form a new federation. In 1996 he defeated the computer DEEP BLUE in a match that attracted worldwide attention; in 1997 an upgraded Deep Blue prevailed.

Kathmandu *or* **Katmandu** \ˌkat-man-'dü\ City (pop., 1993 est.: 535,000), capital of Nepal. Situated at an elevation of 4,344 ft (1,324 m), it was founded in 723. Its name (*kath*, "wood"; *mandir*, "temple") refers to a temple said to have been built from the wood of a single tree in 1596. The seat of the ruling Shah family of the Gurkha people since 1768, it is Nepal's business and commercial center, a thriving tourist destination, and the site of Tribhuvan Univ.

Katmai National Park and Preserve \'kat-ˌmī\ National park, SW Alaska, at the head of the Alaska Peninsula. It occupies an area of 4,090,000 acres (1,655,000 hectares). The eruption of Mt. Katmai in 1912, the largest eruption in N. America in the 20th cent., produced the wasteland known

K L

as the Valley of TEN THOUSAND SMOKES. The park, with some 14 active volcanoes, abounds in wildlife, including large numbers of brown and grizzly bears.

Katowice \\kä-tȯ-ˈvēt-sə\ City (pop., 1999 est.: 345,000), S central Poland. Located in the midst of the coalfields of Upper Silesia, it was settled by 1598. It became a city in 1865 and part of Poland in 1922. It is a center of mining and heavy industry and an important rail junction.

Katsina \\ˈkät-sē-nä\ City (pop., 1996 est.: 207,000), N Nigeria. Probably founded around 1100, it was the capital of the kingdom of Katsina, one of the earliest HAUSA states, and an ancient center of learning. The city's Fulani emirs retain traditional and advisory roles. It is a market and crafts center.

Kattegat Arm of the NORTH SEA, between Sweden and JUTLAND, Denmark. Its maximum width is 88 mi (142 km). It is connected by straits with the BALTIC sea. Its chief ports are GÖTEBORG and Halmstad in Sweden, and ÅRHUS in Denmark. It is important for commercial navigation and is a popular vacation area.

katydid Any of numerous species in several subfamilies of the long-horned GRASSHOPPER family (Tettigoniidae). Generally green with long wings, many species resemble leaves. They are powerful jumpers, but many species do not fly. They feed chiefly on plant matter. The true katydids of E N. America are considered great singers; each species has its own repetitive song, produced only at night.

Fork-tailed bush katydid (*Scudderia furcata*)

Katyn Massacre \\ka-ˈtin\ Mass execution of Polish military officers by the Soviet Union in WORLD WAR II. After the GERMAN–SOVIET NONAGGRESSION PACT (1939) and Germany's defeat of Poland, Soviet forces occupied E Poland and interned thousands of Polish military personnel. The Germans invaded the Soviet Union in 1941, and in 1943 they discovered mass graves in the Katyn forest in W Russia. Over 4,000 corpses were recovered, later identified as Polish officers. Russia claimed the invading German army had killed them, but refused Polish requests to have the Red Cross investigate. In 1992 the government released documents proving the Soviet secret police was responsible for the executions.

Kauffmann \\ˈkau̇f-ˌmän\, **(Maria Anna) Angelica (Catharina)** (1741–1807). Swiss-Italian painter. Highly precocious, she studied art in Italy before moving to London in 1766. There she became known for her decorative work with such architects as Robert ADAM. Her pastoral compositions incorporate delicate and graceful depictions of gods and goddesses. Her portraits of female sitters are among her finest works. After marrying the painter Antonio Zucchi (1726–1795), she returned to Italy in 1781.

Kaufman, George S(imon) (1889–1961) U.S. playwright and director. Born in Pittsburgh, he was drama critic for the *New York Times* 1917–30. Known for his wit and satirical eye, he collaborated with other writers on numerous plays and directed most of them. With Marc CONNELLY he wrote *Dulcy* (1921), *Merton of the Movies* (1922), and *Beggar on Horseback* (1924), and he cowrote the book for George GERSHWIN's musical *Of Thee I Sing* (1931, Pulitzer Prize). He cowrote *The Royal Family* (1927) and *Dinner at Eight* (1932) with Edna FERBER, and *Once in a Lifetime* (1930), *You Can't Take It with You* (1936, Pulitzer Prize), and *The Man Who Came to Dinner* (1939) with Moss HART. The MARX BROTHERS films *The Cocoanuts* (1929) and *Animal Crackers* (1930) were based on his collaborative plays.

Kaunas \\ˈkau̇-nəs\ *Russian* **Kovno** \\ˈkȯv-nō\ City (pop., 2000 est.: 412,000), S Lithuania. Founded as a fortress in 1030, it passed to Russia in 1795 after the third Partition of POLAND. It was the capital of independent Lithuania 1920–40, then it was annexed by the U.S.S.R. Many historic buildings survive in the Old Town. It is an industrial, educational, and cultural center.

Kaunda \\kä-ˈün-də\, **Kenneth (David)** (b.1924) Politician who led Zambia to independence and was its president for 27 years (1964–91). Prominent in the movement to stop Britain from consolidating the Rhodesias and Nyasaland (1959–60), Kaunda was elected the first president of independent Zambia. He helped avert civil war in the late 1960s, but ended up imposing single-party rule. From the 1970s he led other nations in confronting the white-minority governments of Rhodesia and S. Africa. His regime allowed agriculture, education, and social services to languish and poverty to increase. Several attempted coups were crushed,

Kenneth Kaunda

but in 1990 Kaunda was forced to allow opposition parties, and in 1991 he was voted out of office.

Kautsky \\ˈkau̇t-skē\, **Karl** (1854–1938) German Marxist theorist and leader. He was the author of the Erfurt Program adopted by Germany's Social Democrat Party in 1891, which committed the party to an evolutionary form of Marxism. He founded the Marxist review *Neue Zeit* in 1883, which he edited in various European cities until 1917, and wrote several books about Marx's doctrines.

kava *or* **kava kava** \\ˈkä-və\ Nonalcoholic, yellow-green, somewhat bitter beverage made from the root of the PEPPER plant (mainly *Piper methysticum*) in most S. Pacific islands. It is traditionally consumed in the kava ceremony, which includes a ceremonial feast. In the West, it is taken to relieve stress and anxiety and as a mood elevator.

Kavaratti Island \\kə-və-ˈrə-tē\ Island of the Laccadive group, off the coast of SW India. It is 3.5 miles (5.6 km) long. The town Kavaratti (pop., 1991: 9,000), administrative center of the territory of Lakshadweep, is noted for the ornate pillars and roofs of its mosques.

Kaveri River \\ˈkä-və-rē\ *or* **Cauvery River** \\ˈkȯ-və-rē\ River, S India. Rising in N Kerala, it flows southeast 475 mi (764 km) to enter the Bay of BENGAL. On the border of Karnataka are the Kaveri (Cauvery) Falls, which descend about 320 ft (515 m). The river is the source for an extensive irrigation system. It is considered one of India's sacred rivers.

Kawabata \\ˈkä-wä-ˌbä-tä\, **Yasunari** (1899–1972) Japanese novelist. His writing echoes ancient Japanese forms in prose influenced by post–World War I French literary currents such as DADA and EXPRESSIONISM. His best-known novel is *Snow Country* (1948), the story of a forlorn geisha. His other major works (published together in 1952) are *A Thousand Cranes* and *The Sound of the Mountain*. He was awarded the Nobel Prize in 1968. He died a suicide.

Kawasaki \\kä-wä-ˈsä-kē\ City (pop., 1995: 1,203,000) and port, Honshu, Japan. It lies on Tokyo Bay, between TOKYO and YOKOHAMA. Almost completely destroyed in World War II, it has since been rebuilt. It is a major industrial center for machinery, chemicals, and shipbuilding. It is the site of a 12th-cent. Buddhist temple.

Kawatake Mokuami \\kä-wä-ˈtä-kä-ˌmō-kü-ˈä-mē\ *orig.* Yoshimura Yoshisaburo (1816–1893) Japanese playwright. He became chief playwright of the Kawarasaki Theatre in 1843. His domestic plays featured ordinary townspeople, and his picaresque plays portrayed the lives of thieves. After 1868 he wrote historical plays that emphasized factual accuracy and pioneered the production of domestic plays that described the modernization of early MEIJI-PERIOD society. He wrote over 360 plays, and his works account for half the current KABUKI repertory.

Kay, John (1704–1764?) British machinist and engineer. In 1733 he patented a "New Engine or Machine for Opening and Dressing Wool" that incorporated his flying shuttle, an important step toward automatic WEAVING. Kay's invention so increased yarn consumption that it spurred the invention of the SPINNING JENNY and spinning mule, but its true importance lay in its adaptation in power LOOMS.

Kay, Ulysses (Simpson) (1917–1995) U.S. composer. Born in Tucson, a nephew of King OLIVER, he was an all-around musician from childhood. He studied under William Grant Still (1895–1978) and with Paul HINDEMITH, and he taught principally at the City Univ. of New York. His music—neoclassical in style but characterized by verve and warmth—received many awards; mostly orchestral or choral, it includes five operas and several film and television scores.

kayak \ˈkī-ˌak\ Type of CANOE covered by a deck except for a cockpit in which the paddler sits. It has a pointed bow and stern and no keel; the paddler faces forward, grasping a double-bladed paddle and dipping the blades alternately on either side. Kayaks were used for fishing and hunting by ESKIMOS, who crafted them of stretched seal skins over a driftwood or whalebone frame. A snug "skirt" allows a paddler to right an overturned kayak without taking on water. Now often made of molded plastic or fiberglass, kayaks are widely used for recreation.

Kaye, Danny *orig.* David Daniel Kaminski (1913–1987) U.S. actor and comedian. Born in New York City, he worked in vaudeville and nightclubs, developing his trademark pantomimes, rapid-fire nonsense songs, and physical antics. After success on Broadway in *The Straw Hat Revue* (1939) and *Lady in the Dark* (1940), he starred in the films *Up in Arms* (1944), *The Secret Life of Walter Mitty* (1947), *The Inspector General* (1949), *Hans Christian Andersen* (1952), and *White Christmas* (1954). He starred on television in *The Danny Kaye Show* (1963–67). Much of his comedy material was written by his wife, Sylvia Fine.

Kaysone Phomvihan \kä-ˈsō-ne-ˈpòm-vē-hàn\ (1920–1992) Laotian revolutionary, prime minister (1975–91) and president (1991–92). He met HO CHI MINH while studying law in Hanoi and returned to Laos to become the leader of the Pathet Lao, an anti-French revolutionary movement. In 1975 it overthrew Laos's 600-year-old monarchy, and Kaysone became prime minister of the Lao People's Democratic Republic. He kept the country isolated from Western influence until 1989, when he first looked to France and Japan for financial aid. As president, he relaxed some government controls and released most political prisoners.

Kazakstan *or* **Kazakhstan** \kə-ˌzäk-ˈstän\ *officially* **Republic of Kazakstan** Country, W central Asia. Area: 1,052,100 sq

RUSSIA
KAZAKSTAN
Scale 1: 43,241,000
0 200 400 mi
0 200 400 600 km

mi (2,724,900 sq km). Population (2000): 14,913,000. Capital: ASTANA. Kazaks, a Turkic-speaking people, the original inhabitants, are less than one-half the population; an equal number of Russians live there with small minorities of Germans and Ukrainians. Language: Kazak (of-

ficial), Russian. Religion: Islam (Sunnite). Currency: tenge. From the steppe and desert lands of W and central Kazakstan, the country rises to high mountains in the southeast along the border with Kyrgyzstan and China. Its highest point is Mt. Khan-Tengri, at 22,949 ft (6,995 m) high. It is intensively agriculturally developed, but much of the country's land area is used for pasture, with sheep and goats as the main livestock. Manufacturing includes cast iron and rolled steel; mining and oil drilling are also important. It is a republic with a parliament consisting of two chambers; its head of state and government is the president, assisted by the prime minister. Named for its earliest inhabitants, the Kazaks, the area came under Mongol rule in the 13th cent. The Kazaks consolidated a nomadic empire in the 15th–16th cent. Under Russian rule by the mid-19th cent., it became part of the Kirgiz Autonomous Republic formed by the Soviets in 1920, and in 1925 its name was changed to the Kazakh Autonomous Soviet Socialist Republic. Kazakstan obtained its independence from the Soviet Union in 1991. By 2000 it had managed to stabilize its economy.

Kazan \kə-ˈzän\ City (pop., 1997 est.: 1,085,000), capital of the Tatarstan republic, W Russia. Founded in the 13th cent. by Mongols of the GOLDEN HORDE, Kazan became the capital of an independent khanate in the 15th cent. In 1552 it was captured by IVAN IV. The city was burned in a revolt (1773–74), but after its reconstruction it grew as a trading center, and by 1900 it was one of the chief manufacturing cities of Russia. It is home to Kazan State Univ. (1804).

Kazan \kə-ˈzan\, **Elia** *orig.* Elia Kazanjoglous (b.1909) U.S. (Greek-born) stage and film director. He emigrated to the U.S. as a child. Initially an actor, he became a noted Broadway director with such plays as *The Skin of Our Teeth* (1942), *A Streetcar Named Desire* (1947; film, 1951), *Death of a Salesman* (1949), *J.B.* (1958, Tony Award), and *Sweet Bird of Youth* (1959). In 1947 he cofounded the ACTORS STUDIO. He was praised for his naturalistic style in such movies as *A Tree Grows in Brooklyn* (1945), *Gentleman's Agreement* (1947, Academy Award), *On the Waterfront* (1954, Academy Award), and *East of Eden* (1955). Though bitterly attacked for his cooperation with the House Un-American Activities Committee in the early 1950s, he received an Academy Award for lifetime achievement in 1999.

Kazantzákis \kä-zänt-ˈzä-kēs\, **Níkos** (1885–1957) Greek writer. He is best known for his widely translated novels, including *Zorba the Greek* (1946; film, 1964), *The Greek Passion* (1954), and *The Last Temptation of Christ* (1955; film, 1988). His works also include essays, travel books, tragedies, and translations of such classics as DANTE's *Divine Comedy* and J. W. von GOETHE's *Faust*. He also wrote lyric poetry and the poetic epic *Odyssey* (1938), a sequel to the Homeric epic.

Kazin \ˈkā-zən\, **Alfred** (1915–1998) U.S. literary critic. Born in Brooklyn, N.Y., he wrote an early sweeping historical study of modern American literature, *On Native Grounds* (1942), which won him instant recognition. Much of his criticism appeared in *Partisan Review, The New Republic,* and *The New Yorker*. His books include *Starting Out in the Thirties* (1965), *New York Jew* (1978), and *A Writer's America* (1988).

Kazvin See QAZVIN

Kean, Edmund (1789–1833) British actor. In 1814 he won acclaim in London with his innovative portrayal of Shylock in *The Merchant of Venice*. He went on to specialize in other Shakespearean villains, and also excelled at playing Othello and Hamlet, as well as Barabas in *The Jew of Malta*. Though praised for his passionate and sensational stage portrayals, he became unpopular for his ungovernable behavior offstage. His son Charles (1811–1868) was an actor-manager noted for his Shakespeare revivals.

Keaton, Buster (*orig.* Joseph Francis) (1895–1966) U.S. film actor and director. Born in Picqua, Kan., he acted with his parents in vaudeville (1899–1917), where he developed his mastery of comic falls and subtle timing and his trademark never-smiling face. His film debut in *The Butcher Boy* (1917) was followed by several short films (1917–19) with Fatty Arbuckle. As head of his own production company (1920–28) he directed and starred in such classic silent movies as *The Navigator* (1924), *Sherlock, Jr.* (1924), *The General* (1927),

K L

Steamboat Bill, Jr. (1928), and *The Cameraman* (1928). He later appeared in *Sunset Boulevard* (1950) and *Limelight* (1952). He is now regarded as one of the greatest silent comedy stars.

Keaton, Diane *orig.* Diane Hall (b.1946) U.S. film actress. Born in Santa Ana, Cal., she acted on Broadway with Woody ALLEN in *Play It Again, Sam* (1969; film, 1972). After supporting roles in *The Godfather* (1972) and its sequels, she starred in such Allen movies as *Annie Hall* (1977, Academy Award), *Interiors* (1978), and *Manhattan* (1979). Her other films include *Reds* (1981), *Mrs. Soffel* (1984), and *The First Wives Club* (1996).

Keats, John (1795–1821) English Romantic poet. The son of a livery-stable manager, his formal education was limited. His first mature work was the sonnet "On First Looking into Chapman's Homer" (1816). During a few intense months of 1819 he produced many of his greatest works: several great odes (including "Ode on a Grecian Urn," "Ode to a Nightingale," and "To Autumn"), two unfinished versions of the story of the titan Hyperion, and "La Belle Dame Sans Merci." Most were published in the landmark collection *Lamia, Isabella, The Eve of St. Agnes, and Other Poems* (1820). Marked by vivid imagery, great sensuous appeal, and a yearning for the lost glories of the classical world, his finest works are among the greatest of the English tradition. His letters are among the best by any English poet. He died of tuberculosis at 25.

keep See DONJON

Keillor \'kē-lər\, **Garrison (Edward)** (b.1942) U.S. radio entertainer and writer. Born in Anoka, Minn., he wrote for *The New Yorker* before creating the long-running public-radio humor and variety show *A Prairie Home Companion,* about the fictional Minnesota town Lake Wobegon, in 1974. His books include the best-selling *Lake Wobegon Days* (1985), *Leaving Home* (1987), and *WLT: A Radio Romance* (1991).

Keitel \'kī-t*əl\, **Wilhelm** (1882–1946) German field marshal. He became minister of war in 1935 and head of the German armed forces high command in 1938. Though one of Adolf HITLER's most trusted lieutenants, he was a weak officer and served chiefly as Hitler's lackey. He signed the act of Germany's military surrender in 1945. He was convicted at the NUREMBERG TRIALS and executed as a war criminal.

Keller, Helen (Adams) (1880–1968) U.S. author and educator. Deprived by illness of sight and hearing at the age of 19 months, Keller soon became mute as well. At 6 she began to be instructed by Anne Sullivan (1866–1936), who taught her the names of objects by pressing the manual alphabet into her palm. Eventually Keller graduated from Radcliffe College, wrote several books, including *The Story of My Life* (1902), and lectured widely on behalf of progressive causes.

Helen Keller at 66

Kellogg, John Harvey and W(ill) K(eith) (1852–1943, 1860–1951) U.S. cereal manufacturers. John, born in Tyrone, Mich., was a physician and vegetarian who in 1876 helped found a Seventh-Day Adventist sanitarium in Battle Creek, Mich. There he developed various products, including a flaked-wheat CEREAL, to serve to patients, one of whom was C. W. POST. John's younger brother, W. K., born in Battle Creek, founded the W. K. Kellogg Co. in 1906 to manufacture cornflakes. It soon became a leading U.S. producer of breakfast cereals and other convenience foods. The W. K. Kellogg Foundation is one of the country's largest philanthropic institutions.

Kells, Book of ILLUMINATED MANUSCRIPT version of the four Gospels, late 8th–early 9th cent. A masterpiece of the ornate Hiberno-Saxon style, it features geometric design rather than naturalistic representation, flat areas of color, and complex interlaced patterns. Probably begun at the Irish monastery on the Scottish island of Iona, the book was apparently taken to the monastery of Kells in Co. Meath, Ireland, after a Viking raid, and completed there. See also LINDISFARNE GOSPELS.

Kelly, Ellsworth (b.1923) U.S. painter and sculptor. Born in Newburgh, N.Y., in the 1960s he became a leading exponent of the hard-edge style of painting, in which abstract contours are sharply and precisely defined. He rejected illusionism in his paintings, which typically consist of adjacent rectangular panels of flat, uninflected primary colors. He used the clean geometric lines of his paintings in his painted, cut-out sheet-metal sculptures.

Kelly, Gene (*orig.* Eugene Curran) (1912–1996) U.S. dancer, choreographer, actor, and movie director. Born in Pittsburgh, he moved to New York in 1938 and danced in Broadway musicals, creating the title role in *Pal Joey* in 1940. His athletic style and carefree acting—exemplified in the popular *On the Town* (1949), *An American in Paris* (1951), and *Singin' in the Rain* (1952), which he also helped choreograph and direct—soon became hallmarks of the movie musical. His achievements earned him a special Academy Award in 1951.

Kelly, Grace *later* **Princess Grace of Monaco** (1929–1982) U.S. film actress. Born in Philadelphia, she made her Broadway debut in 1949. Her movie debut in *Fourteen Hours* (1951) was followed by roles in *High Noon* (1952), *Mogambo* (1953), and *The Country Girl* (1954, Academy Award). Noted for her stately beauty and alluring reserve, she starred in Alfred HITCHCOCK's *Dial M for Murder* (1954), *Rear Window* (1954), and *To Catch a Thief* (1955). She made her last movie, *High Society* (1956), before marrying Prince Rainier of Monaco. She died in a car accident after suffering a stroke.

Kelly, Walt(er Crawford) (1913–1973) U.S. cartoonist. Born in Philadelphia, from 1935 he produced animation drawings for Walt Disney Productions, and in the 1940s he worked as a commercial artist in New York. His best-known character, the opossum Pogo, first appeared in a comic book (c.1943), and in 1948 *Pogo* began to be published as a daily comic strip. Skillfully drawn, with witty and literate text, it featured Pogo and his winning animal friends in Okefenokee Swamp, characters Kelly often used to satirize prominent political figures.

kelp Any of about 30 genera of large seaweeds that make up the order Laminariales (brown ALGAE), found in colder seas. *Laminaria,* abundant along the Pacific coasts and the British Isles, is a source of commercial IODINE. Its stipe (stemlike structure) is 3–10 ft (1–3 m) long. The largest known kelp, *Macrocystis,* grows up to 215 ft (65 m) long. Kelp is rich in minerals and algin, a complex carbohydrate used as an emulsifier to prevent crystal formation in ice cream. Species of kelp are widely eaten in E. Asia.

Kelvin (of Largs), Baron *orig.* William Thomson *known as* **Lord Kelvin** (1824–1907) British physicist. Teaching at the Univ. of Glasgow, he helped develop the second law of THERMODYNAMICS, and in 1848 he invented the absolute temperature scale named after him (see ABSOLUTE ZERO). He served as chief consultant for the laying of the first Atlantic cable (1857–58). His patent for a mirror galvanometer for receiving telegraph signals (1858) made him wealthy. His work in electricity and magnetism led ultimately to J. C. MAXWELL's theory of ELECTROMAGNETISM. He also contributed to the determination of the age of earth and the study of hydrodynamics.

Kempe \'kemp\, **Margery** (1373?–1440?) English mystic. She had 14 children before beginning a series of pilgrimages to Jerusalem, Rome, Germany, and Spain in 1414. Apparently illiterate, she dictated her autobiography, *Book of Margery Kempe,* describing her travels and her religious ecstasies in an unaffected style (c.1432–36). It is one of the earliest autobiographies in English literature.

Kempis, Thomas à See THOMAS À KEMPIS

Kenai Fjords National Park \'kē-,nī\ National park, S Alaska. Located on the S coast of the Kenai Peninsula, it extends over 670,000 acres (271,100 hectares), including the Harding Icefield and its outflowing glaciers as well as coastal fjords. The park's wildlife includes sea otters, seals, and seabirds.

Kennan, George F(rost) (b.1904) U.S. diplomat and historian. Born in Milwaukee, he entered the U.S. foreign service in 1925. Assigned to the U.S. embassy in Moscow (1933–35), he returned there during and after World War II. His concept of CONTAINMENT, published in an anonymous article in 1947, became the basis of U.S. policy toward the Soviet Union. He taught at the Institute of Advanced Study at Princeton, 1956–74. He won simultaneous Pulitzer Prizes and National Book Awards for *Russia Leaves the War* (1956) and *Memoirs, 1925–50* (1967).

Kennedy, Anthony M(cLeod) (b.1936) U.S. jurist. Born in Sacramento, Cal., he was appointed to the U.S. Circuit Court of Appeals in 1975. Nominated to the U.S. Supreme Court in 1988, he established a record that has reflected his conservative outlook, and he has consistently voted against such policies as AFFIRMATIVE ACTION and abortion rights.

Kennedy, Edward M(oore) *known as* **Ted Kennedy** (b.1932) U.S. senator. Born in Brookline, Mass., the son of Joseph P. KENNEDY and the brother of John F. KENNEDY and Robert KENNEDY, he was elected to the U.S. Senate in 1962, where he served for decades as an unswerving advocate for liberal causes and social-welfare legislation. In 1969 his car plunged off a Chappaquiddick (Martha's Vineyard), Mass., bridge at night and a young woman in it drowned, an incident that probably cost him his party's presidential nomination.

Kennedy, John F(itzgerald) (1917–1963) 35th president of the U.S. (1961–63). Born in Brookline, Mass., the son of Joseph P. KENNEDY, he attended Harvard and joined the navy in World War II, where he earned medals for heroism. In the U.S. House of Representatives (1947–53) and Senate (1953–60), he supported social legislation and became increasingly committed to civil rights legislation. In 1960 he won the Democratic nomination for president; after a vigorous campaign, aided financially by his father, he narrowly defeated Richard NIXON. He was the youngest person and the first Roman Catholic

John F. Kennedy

elected president. In his inaugural address he called on Americans to "ask not what your country can do for you, ask what you can do for your country." He established the PEACE CORPS and the ALLIANCE FOR PROGRESS. His foreign policy began with the abortive BAY OF PIGS INVASION (1961), which emboldened the Soviet Union to move missiles to Cuba, sparking the CUBAN MISSILE CRISIS, and to build the BERLIN WALL. In 1963 he successfully concluded the NUCLEAR TEST-BAN TREATY. He was assassinated while riding in a motorcade in Dallas by a sniper, allegedly L. H. OSWALD. Kennedy's youth, energy, humor, and idealism made him a charismatic figure worldwide.

Kennedy, Joseph P(atrick) (1888–1969) U.S. financier. Born in Boston, he graduated from Harvard and was a bank president by 25. He acquired a large fortune by speculating in the stock market and was a heavy contributor to the Democratic Party. As chairman of the Securities and Exchange Commission (1934–35), he outlawed the speculative practices that had made him rich. He was ambassador to Britain 1937–40. With his wife, Rose, he encouraged his children—including John F. KENNEDY, Robert KENNEDY, and Edward KENNEDY—to strive competitively for public leadership.

Kennedy, Robert F(rancis) (1925–1968) U.S. politician. Born in Brookline, Mass., he earned a law degree (1951) and managed his brother John F. KENNEDY's successful 1952 Senate campaign. He was chief counsel (1957–60) to the Senate committee investigating labor racketeering before managing his brother's 1960 presidential campaign. As U.S. attorney general (1961–64), he led a drive against organized crime that convicted Jimmy HOFFA. After his brother's as-

sassination, he was elected to the Senate from New York (1964) and became a spokesman for liberals and a critic of Lyndon JOHNSON's Vietnam War policy. Campaigning for the presidential nomination in Los Angeles, he was assassinated by Sirhan Sirhan, a Palestinian immigrant.

Kennedy Center for the Performing Arts Huge cultural complex (opened 1971) in Washington, D.C., with a total of six stages, designed by Edward Durell STONE. The complex, surfaced in marble, makes use of the ornamental facade screens for which the architect was known. The great Concert Hall has been designated a national monument; its acoustics are considered exceptional, and its embossed ceiling and crystal chandeliers have been much admired.

Kenneth I *or* **Kenneth MacAlpin** (d.858?) First king of the united Scots of Dalriada and the PICTS. He inherited (834?) the Scottish kingdom of Dalriada from his father, Alpin, and gained control over Pictavia. From 843 the two kingdoms were gradually joined, an important step in the making of a unified SCOTLAND. The union was probably accomplished both by intermarriage and by conquest.

Kent County (pop. 1998 est.: 1,332,000), SE England. It lies along the ENGLISH CHANNEL; the county seat is MAIDSTONE. The Romans ruled the area from A.D. 43, using CANTERBURY as a base. It was invaded by Jutes and Saxons in the 5th cent.; it became one of the seven kingdoms of Anglo-Saxon Britain. The king of Kent welcomed St. AUGUSTINE OF CANTERBURY's Christian mission in 587. Highly fertile, it has long been known as the "Garden of England."

Kent, Earl of See ODO OF BAYEUX

Kent, Rockwell (1882–1971) U.S. painter and illustrator. Born in Tarrytown Heights, N.Y., he studied architecture and painting. He worked variously as an architectural draftsman, lobsterman, and ship's carpenter in Maine, and traveled in Tierra del Fuego, Newfoundland, Alaska, and Greenland, gathering material for his paintings and travel books. His dramatic woodcut-like pen-and-ink drawings appeared in many books by contemporary and classic writers and made him one of the most popular artists in the U.S., despite harassment for his radical leftist politics.

Kenton, Stan(ley Newcombe) (1912–1979) U.S. pianist, composer, arranger, and bandleader. Born in Wichita, Kan., Kenton formed his first band in 1941. The group gained a reputation for a bombastic orchestral approach, often playing arrangements by Pete Rugolo. His players included saxophonist Art Pepper, trumpeter Maynard Ferguson, drummer Shelly Manne, and singers Anita O'Day and June Christy. Kenton was also a pioneer in formal jazz education.

Kentucky *officially* **Commonwealth of Kentucky** State (pop. 2000: 4,041,000), SE central U.S. It covers 40,395 sq mi (104,623 sq km); its capital is FRANKFORT. Among its geographical features are the APPALACHIAN MTNS. of the east, the interior lowlands, including the BLUEGRASS REGION, and the rich lowlands along the MISSISSIPPI RIVER. Before the arrival of white settlers, the region was a hunting ground for Indian tribes, including the SHAWNEE, IROQUOIS, and CHEROKEE. Daniel BOONE, among the first white settlers, arrived in 1769; a wave of immigration followed the AMERICAN REVOLUTION. Settlements began as part of a district of Virginia, but in 1792 Kentucky entered the Union as the 15th state. It was a border state during the AMERICAN CIVIL WAR, remaining in the Union but providing troops to both sides. The opening of rail lines into the E coal country and the introduction of a tobacco economy spurred growth in the late 19th cent. In the 1970s a nationwide energy shortage created a demand for coal, from which Kentucky prospered, but demand dropped in the 1980s and many jobs were lost. Manufacturing is the leading source of income, while tobacco is the chief crop. Kentucky is known for its bourbon whiskey and Thoroughbred horses; the KENTUCKY DERBY is run annually at Churchill Downs.

Kentucky Derby Classic U.S. THOROUGHBRED horse race, run annually since 1875 on the first Saturday in May at Churchill Downs track in Louisville. With the PREAKNESS and the BELMONT STAKES, it makes up U.S. racing's coveted TRIPLE CROWN. The field is limited to 3-year-olds. The track distance is 1.25 mi (2,000 m).

Kenya *officially* **Republic of Kenya** Republic, E Africa. It is bounded by Ethiopia, Sudan, Somalia, the Indian Ocean, Tanzania, and Uganda. Area: 224,961 sq mi (582,646 sq km). Population (2000): 30,340,000. Capital: NAIROBI. With a small group of European settlers' descendents, there are

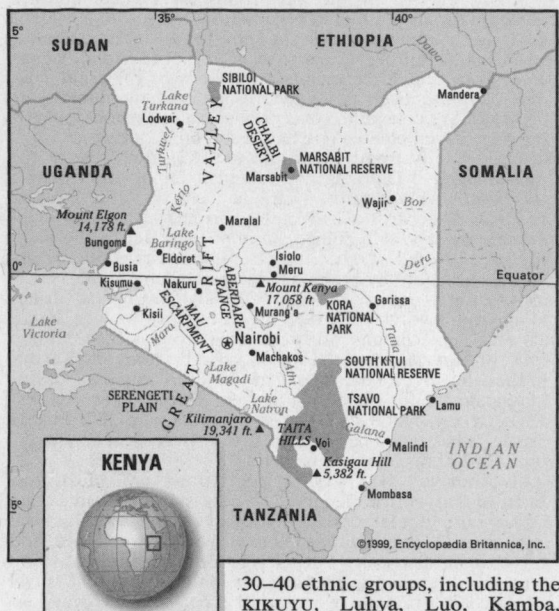

KENYA

Scale 1: 17,833,000

| 0 | 50 | 100 | 150 mi |
| 0 | 100 | 200 km |

©1999, Encyclopædia Britannica, Inc.

30–40 ethnic groups, including the KIKUYU, Luhya, Luo, Kamba, Kalenjin, and MASAI. Languages: Swahili, English (both official); others belonging to the Bantu, Nilotic, and Cushitic language groups. Religions: Christianity, animism, Islam, Hinduism. Currency: shilling. Kenya can be divided into five regions: the Lake VICTORIA basin in the SW corner; the vast plateau of E Kenya; the 250-mi (400-km) coastal belt along the Indian Ocean; the highlands of the Mau Escarpment on the W side of the GREAT RIFT VALLEY in W Kenya; and the highlands and mountains of the Aberdare Range on the E side of the Rift Valley, including Mt. KENYA. It is noted for such wildlife as lion, leopard, elephant, buffalo, rhinoceros, zebra, hippopotamus, and crocodile. Only about 4% of the land is arable, and about 7% of the land is used for grazing cattle, goats, and sheep. Agriculture employs four-fifths of the workforce, and tea and coffee are the leading exports. It is a republic with one legislative house; its head of state and government is the president. The coastal region was dominated by Arabs until it was seized by the Portuguese in the 16th cent. The Masai people held sway in the north and moved into central Kenya in the 18th cent., while the Kikuyu expanded from their home region in S central Kenya. The interior was explored by European missionaries in the 19th cent. After the British took control, Kenya was established as a British protectorate (1890) and a crown colony (1920). The MAU MAU rebellion of the 1950s was directed against European colonialism. In 1963 the country became fully independent, and a year later a republican government under Jomo KENYATTA was elected. In 1992 president Daniel arap MOI allowed the country's first multiparty elections in three decades, though the elections were marred by violence and fraud. Political turmoil and widespread corruption occurred over the next decade. In the 2002 election Moi was replaced by Mwai Kibaki (b.1931).

Kenya, Mt. *Swahili* **Kirinyaga** Extinct volcano, central Kenya. Lying just south of the equator, it is the highest mountain in Kenya, rising to 17,058 ft (5,199 m). Mt. Kenya National Park, occupying an area of 277 sq mi (718 sq km), contains a variety of big game. Nanyuki lies at the mountain's NW foot and is the chief base for ascents.

Kenyatta \ken-ˈyä-tə\, **Jomo** (1894?–1978) First prime minister (1963–64) and then president (1964–78) of indepen-

dent Kenya. Of KIKUYU descent, Kenyatta left the E African highlands to become a civil servant and political activist in Nairobi around 1920. He opposed a union of the British colonies of Kenya, Uganda, and Tanganyika. In 1945 he helped organize the sixth Pan-African Congress. In 1953 he was sentenced to a seven-year prison term for directing the MAU MAU rebellion, though he denied the charges. In 1962 he negotiated terms leading to Kenya's independence. As its leader he rejected calls to nationalize property, and made Kenya one of the most stable and economically dynamic African states, though critics complained of the dominance of his Kenya African National Union (KANU) party and the creation of a political and economic elite.

Jomo Kenyatta

Kenyon College Private liberal-arts college in Gambier, Ohio. Founded in 1824, it is affiliated with the Episcopal church. It offers arts and sciences programs, and cooperative engineering programs with three universities. The literary journal *The Kenyon Review* was founded by John Crowe RANSOM in 1939. Enrollment is about 1,600.

Keokuk \ˈkē-ə-ˌkək\ (1790?–1848?) SAUK Indian leader. Born near present-day Rock Island, Ill., he engaged in a lifelong struggle for power with BLACK HAWK, who advocated resistance to white settlement on tribal lands. For his refusal to fight U.S. forces, the government named Keokuk leader of the Sauk nation in 1837. He continued to give away land until the Sauk and Fox had to settle on a Kansas reservation. Though wealthy and powerful, he died in disgrace among his people.

Kepler, Johannes (1571–1630) German astronomer. Born into a poor family, he received a scholarship to the Univ. of Tübingen. He developed a mystical theory that the cosmos was constructed of the five regular polyhedrons, enclosed in a sphere, with a planet between each pair. He sent his paper on the subject to Tycho BRAHE, who invited Kepler to join his research staff. He was the first to explain accurately how the eye sees, how eyeglasses improve vision, and what happens to light in a telescope. In 1609 he published his finding that the orbit of Mars was an ellipse, not the perfect circle presumed for all celestial bodies. This fact became the basis of the first of Kepler's laws of planetary motion. He also showed that planets move faster nearer the sun and developed a simple mathematical formula relating the planets' orbital periods to their distance from the sun. In 1620 he defended his mother from charges of witchcraft, thereby preserving his own reputation as well.

keratin \ˈker-ə-tən\ Fibrous structural PROTEIN of hair, nails, hooves, wool, feathers, and skin. A quarter of the AMINO ACIDS in keratin are cystine, whose ability to form strong bridging (disulfide) bonds with other cystine units accounts for keratin's great stability. Its fibers are 10–12% longer at maximum water content (about 16%) than when dry. The sulfurous smell of burning keratin is distinctive.

Kerensky \ˈke-ryən-skē, *Engl* ker-ˈen-skē\, **Aleksandr (Fyodorovich)** (1881–1970) Russian political leader. A prominent lawyer, he joined the SOCIALIST REVOLUTIONARY PARTY and was elected to the fourth Duma (1912), where he became a noted orator. After the start of the RUSSIAN REVOLUTION OF 1917, he held posts in the provisional government; a popular figure, in July he became prime minister. He sought to unify the factions but lost the support of the moderates and officers by dismissing the army commander in chief, Lavr Kornilov (1870–1918), and of the left by refusing to implement their radical programs. When the BOLSHEVIKS seized power in October, he went into hiding, then emigrated in 1918. In 1940 he moved to the U.S., where he lectured and wrote books on the revolution.

Kern, Jerome (David) (1885–1945) U.S. composer, one of the major creators of the MUSICAL. Kern studied music in his native New York and in Heidelberg, and gained theatrical experience in London. In New York, he worked as a pianist for music publishers and wrote new numbers for European operettas. His own very successful show *Very Good Eddie* (1915) was followed by *Oh, Boy!* (1917), *Sally* (1920), and *Sunny* (1925). In 1927 his *Show Boat* became the first American musical with a serious plot drawn from a literary source; it represents a landmark in

Jerome Kern

the history of musical theater. It was followed by *The Cat and the Fiddle* (1931), *Music in the Air* (1932), and *Roberta* (1933). After 1933 he composed for Hollywood. Kern's classic songs include "All the Things You Are," "Smoke Gets in Your Eyes," and "Ol' Man River."

kerosene Organic compound, a clear, oily, highly flammable liquid with a strong odor, distilled from PETROLEUM (10–25% of total volume). It is less volatile than GASOLINE, boiling at 285–610°F (140–320°C). It is burned in lamps, heaters, and furnaces and used as a fuel or fuel component for diesel and tractor engines, jet engines, and rockets and as a SOLVENT for greases and insecticides.

Kerouac \'ker-ə-ˌwak\, **Jack** (*orig.* Jean-Louis) (1922–1969) U.S. poet and novelist. Born in Lowell, Mass., he attended Columbia Univ., served as a merchant seaman, and roamed the U.S. and Mexico before his first book appeared. A spokesman of the BEAT MOVEMENT (a term he coined), he celebrated its code of poverty and freedom in *On the Road* (1957); his best-known novel, and the first written in the nonstop, unedited style that he advocated, it enjoyed a huge success among young people, for whom Kerouac became a romantic hero. All his novels, including *The Dharma Bums* (1958) and *Desolation Angels* (1965), are autobiographical. His death at 47 resulted from alcoholism.

Kertesz \ker-ˈtesh\, **André** (1894–1985) Hungarian-U.S. photographer and photojournalist. He moved from Budapest to Paris in 1925 and became a major contributor to European illustrated periodicals. He arrived in New York in 1936 and did fashion photography for major U.S. magazines. He returned to his creative style about 1962, and in 1964 the Museum of Modern Art gave an exhibition of his works. His spontaneous, unposed pictures exerted a strong influence on magazine photography.

Kesey \'kē-zē\, **Ken (Elton)** (1935–2001) U.S. writer. Born in La Junta, Col., in 1962 he published *One Flew over the Cuckoo's Nest* (film, 1975), which became one of the most widely read countercultural novels of the 1960s. It was followed by *Sometimes a Great Notion* (1964). His entourage, the Merry Pranksters, toured the U.S. in a brightly painted bus from the 1960s, and were the subject of Tom WOLFE's *Electric Kool-Aid Acid Test* (1968).

Kesselring, Albert (1885–1960) German field marshal. Chief of the German air staff, he commanded early attacks on Poland, France, Britain, and the Soviet Union. He codirected the Axis campaign in N. Africa with Erwin ROMMEL. After the Allied invasion of Italy in 1943, he fought an effective defensive action that prevented an Allied victory there until 1944. Unable to stop the Allies' drive into Germany, he surrendered the S half of the German forces in May 1945. He was imprisoned for war crimes 1947–52.

kestrel \'kes-trəl\ Any of several BIRDS OF PREY (genus *Falco*) known for hovering while hunting. Kestrels prey on large insects, birds, and small mammals. They are Old World birds except for one species, the American kestrel (*F. sparverius*), often called SPARROW HAWK. It is about 12 in. (30 cm) long, reddish brown and slate-gray above with colorful markings on the head. The common kestrel (*F. tinnunculus*) of the Old World is larger and less colorful. See also FALCON.

Ket See SIBERIAN PEOPLES

ketone \'kē-ˌtōn\ Any of a class of organic compounds containing a carbonyl group (–C=O; see FUNCTIONAL GROUP) bonded to two CARBON atoms. Ketones can participate in many CHEMICAL REACTIONS, though to a lesser extent than the related ALDEHYDES. Many more complex organic compounds have ketones as building blocks. Their chief industrial use is as solvents and in the manufacture of explosives, lacquers, paints, and textiles. ACETONE is the most important ketone; several SUGARS and some natural and synthetic STEROIDS are ketones.

Kettering, Charles F(ranklin) (1876–1958) U.S. engineer. Born near Loudonville, Ohio, in 1904 he developed the first electric cash register. With Edward Deeds he founded Delco around 1910; in 1916 Delco became a subsidiary of General Motors, and Kettering served as director of research for GM 1920–47. Many of his inventions were instrumental in the evolution of the modern automobile, including the first electric starter (1912), antiknock fuels, leaded gasoline, the high-speed, two-cycle diesel engine, and a revolutionary high-compression engine (1951). He later cofounded the Sloan-Kettering Institute for Cancer Research.

kettledrums See TIMPANI

Kevlar Trademarked name of a nylonlike POLYMER first produced by Du Pont in 1971. Kevlar can be made into strong, tough, stiff, high-melting fibers, five times stronger per weight than steel; they are used in radial tires, heat- or flame-resistant fabrics, bulletproof clothing, and fiber-reinforced composite materials for aircraft panels and boat hulls.

Kevorkian, Jack (b.1928) U.S. pathologist, advocate and practitioner of physician-assisted suicide. Born in Pontiac, Mich., in the 1980s he devised his "suicide machine," with which a person could commit suicide by merely pushing a button, and in the 1990s he assisted in the deaths of over 100 terminally ill persons. His actions provoked furious controversy and led to legislation and referenda; he was tried, convicted twice, and jailed, and his medical license was revoked. In 1998 he was convicted of murder for administering a lethal injection himself and was sentenced to 10–25 years in jail.

Kew Gardens *officially* **Royal Botanic Gardens, Kew** Botanic garden located at Kew, site of a former royal estate in SW London. In 1759 Augusta, mother of George III, laid out a portion of her estate as a botanic garden. It became an eminent scientific institution under the unofficial directorship of Joseph BANKS. In 1840 the gardens were donated to the nation. Under Sir William Jackson Hooker (1785–1865), they became the world's leading botanical institution. Today they are home to 50,000 different types of plants, a herbarium of more than 5 million dried specimens, a massive library, and three museums.

key System of PITCHES and HARMONIES generated from a scale of seven tones, one of which is paramount. Keys are a basic element of TONALITY. When a given piece is "in C," C is its central tone. In Western music after about 1600, most music has been written either in a major or a minor key. The major scale consists of the interval pattern *tone-tone-semitone-tone-tone-tone-semitone*. The minor scale consistently differs from it by beginning with the pattern *tone-semitone-tone*, producing a minor 3rd rather than a major 3rd above the tonic.

key, cryptographic Secret value used by a computer together with a complex ALGORITHM to encrypt and decrypt messages. Since confidential messages might be intercepted during transmission, they require encryption so that they will be meaningless to third parties. If someone encrypts a message with a key, only someone else with a matching key should be able to decrypt the message. See also DATA ENCRYPTION.

Key, Francis Scott (1779–1843) U.S. author of "The Star-Spangled Banner." Born in Frederick Co., Md., he practiced law from 1802. After the burning of Washington, D.C., in the WAR OF 1812, he was sent to secure the release of a friend from a British ship, and watched the British shelling of Ft. McHenry during the night of Sept. 13–14, 1814; when he saw the U.S. flag still flying the next morning, he wrote the poem "Defense of Fort M'Henry." Later set to the tune

K L

of an English drinking song, "To Anacreon in Heaven," it was adopted as the U.S. national anthem in 1931.

Keynes \\'kānz\\, **John Maynard** *later* Baron Keynes (of Tilton) (1883–1946) British economist. Son of a distinguished economist, he served in the British treasury during World War I and attended the Versailles Peace Conference, but resigned in protest over the Treaty of VERSAILLES, denouncing its provisions in *The Economic Consequences of the Peace* (1919). The Great Depression prompted him to write *The General Theory of Employment, Interest and Money* (1935–36), the most influential economic treatise of the 20th cent. It refuted laissez-faire economic theories, arguing that the treatment for depression was either to enlarge private investment or to create public substitutes for private investment. In mild economic downturns, MONETARY POLICY in the shape of easier CREDIT and lower interest rates might stimulate investment. More severe crises called for deliberate public deficits (see DEFICIT FINANCING) either in the shape of public works or subsidies to the poor and unemployed. Keynes's theories were put into practice by many Western democracies, notably by the U.S. in the NEW DEAL. Keynes helped design the WORLD BANK and INTERNATIONAL MONETARY FUND at the Bretton Woods Conference in 1944.

Key West City (pop., 2000: 25,000), SW Florida. The southernmost city of the continental U.S., it lies on an island about 4 mi (6.5 km) long and 1.5 mi (2.4 km) wide in the W Florida Keys. In 1822 a U.S. naval depot was set up on Key West as a base of operations against pirates. It is now a winter resort and tourist destination. Many writers and artists have lived there, and the homes of Ernest HEMINGWAY and J. J. AUDUBON have been preserved.

KGB *Russian* Komitet Gosudarstvennoy Bezopasnosti ("Committee for State Security") Soviet agency responsible for intelligence, counterintelligence, and internal security. Its predecessors were the Cheka, established in 1917 to investigate counterrevolution and sabotage; the GPU (later OGPU), the Soviet Union's first secret-police agency (1923), which also administered corrective labor camps and by 1931 had its own army; the NKVD (1934), which carried out extensive purges; and the MGB (1941), with responsibility for both state security and espionage. In 1954 the KGB was created. At its peak, it was the world's largest secret-police and espionage organization. It lost power under Mikhail GORBACHEV. It was renamed after the dissolution of the Soviet Union, and its internal-security functions were segregated from its espionage and counterespionage operations.

Khachaturian \\ˌkä-chə-'tur̄-ē-ən\\, **Aram (Ilyich)** (1903–1978) Soviet (Armenian) composer. Born in Tbilisi (Tiflis), Georgia, he gained international notice when Sergey PROKOFIEV recommended a piece for a Paris concert. He was criticized by the government in 1948 for "formalist tendencies," though his music was in fact always conservative and accessible. After Joseph STALIN's death (1953), he published a call for greater artistic freedom. His ballet scores include *Masquerade* (1944) and *Spartacus* (1954); *Gayane* (1943) contains the well-known "Sabre Dance."

Khadafy, Muammar al- See Muammar al-QADDAFI

khan Historically, the ruler or monarch of a Mongol tribe. Later, the term was adopted by the SELJUQ and Khwarezm-Shah dynasties as a title for the highest nobility. Gradually it became an affix to the name of any Muslim property owner; today it is often used as a surname.

Khanty See SIBERIAN PEOPLES

Kharkiv \\'kär-kəf\\ City (pop., 1998: 1,521,000), NE Ukraine. Founded in 1655 as a military stronghold, it became a seat of provincial government in 1732. It served as the capital of the Ukrainian S.S.R. (1921–34). The second-largest city in Ukraine, it is a heavy industry center.

Khartoum \\kär-'tüm\\ City (pop., 1993: 925,000), capital of the Sudan. Located just south of the confluence of the Blue and White NILE rivers, it was originally an Egyptian army camp (1821). The Mahdi besieged the town for 10 months in 1884–85, eventually overrunning it and killing C. G. GORDON, the British governor-general. Reoccupied by the British in 1898, it served as the seat of the Anglo-Egyptian government until 1956, when it became the capital of an in-

dependent Sudan. A major trade and communications center, it is the seat of several universities.

Khatami \\kä-tä-'mē\\, **Muhammad al-** (b.1943) President of Iran (from 1997). He graduated from Qom Theology School (1961) and began political activities while studying philosophy at Esfahan Univ. He headed an Islamic center in Germany during the Iranian Revolution (1979) and returned home to seek election to the Majlis (parliament) in 1980. He served in government posts during the IRAN–IRAQ WAR and as cultural adviser to Pres. Rafsanjani and head of the National Library (1992–97) before winning the presidency as a moderate.

Khayr al-Din See BARBAROSSA

Khayyam, Omar See OMAR KHAYYAM

Khios See CHIOS

Khmelnytsky \\ˌkmyel-'nit-skē\\, **Bohdan (Zinoviy Mykhaylovych)** (c.1595–1657) Ukrainian Cossack leader (1648–57). From the fortress of the Zaporozhian Cossacks in 1648, he organized a rebellion with support from Ukrainian peasants and townspeople, and marched against Poland. After years of war, he sought aid from the Russians in 1654, and they subsequently invaded Poland, winning control of Ukrainian lands. His attempts to secure autonomy for his Cossack followers resulted only in their later subjection to Russian rule.

Khmer \\kə-'mer\\ *or* **Cambodian** *or* **Kampuchean** Ethnolinguistic group that constitutes most of the population of Cambodia. Smaller numbers of Khmer also live in SE Thailand and S Vietnam. Traditional Khmer are a predominantly agricultural people; their crafts include weaving, pottery making, and metalworking. They follow THERAVADA Buddhism, which coexists with pre-Buddhist animistic beliefs. Indian culture has historically been a strong influence on Khmer culture.

Khmer Rouge \\kə-'mer-'rüzh\\ (French: "Red Khmer") Radical communist movement that ruled Cambodia 1975–79. The Khmer Rouge, under the leadership of POL POT, opposed the government of NORODOM SIHANOUK and gained support after Sihanouk was toppled by LON NOL (1970). In 1975 the Khmer Rouge ousted Lon Nol. Their extraordinarily brutal regime led to over 1.5 million deaths from starvation, hardship, and executions. Overthrown in 1979 by the Vietnamese, they retreated to remote areas and continued guerrilla warfare until 1997.

Khoikhoi \\'kòi-ˌkòi\\ *or* **Khoikhoin** *formerly* **Hottentots** Group of peoples speaking closely related KHOISAN LANGUAGES who were among the first indigenous S Africans encountered by Europeans. The pre-contact Khoikhoi tended large herds of cattle and sheep. By 1800 the Khoikhoi south of the Orange River in Cape Colony had been largely destroyed by disease and warfare; the remnants either served as bonded laborers for white farmers or blended into mixed-race frontier communities.

Khoisan languages \\'kòi-ˌsän\\ Group of more than 20 languages spoken by several hundred thousand KHOIKHOI and SAN peoples of S Africa. A remarkable feature of all Khoisan languages is their use of suction sounds known as CLICKS completely integrated into their consonant systems. The genetic unity of the Khoisan languages remains disputed.

Khomeini \\kō-'mā-nē\\, **Ruhollah** *orig.* Ruhollah Musawi (1900–1989) Iranian cleric and revolutionary. After receiving a religious education, he settled in Qom in the early 1920s, where he became known as a Shiite scholar and opponent of M. R. Shah PAHLAVI. Acclaimed a grand AYATOLLAH in the early 1960s, he was imprisoned and then exiled (1964) for his antigovernment stance. He settled in Iraq, and later near Paris. From exile he sent tape-recorded messages to his followers to foment revolution. Iranian unrest increased until the shah fled in 1979; Khomeini returned two weeks later to be named Iran's political and religious leader for life. His extremely conservative domestic policies were based on Islamic fundamentalism, and his foreign policies were both anti-Western and anticommunist. The first years of his rule saw the taking of 66 U.S. hostages (1979–81), a move that greatly angered the U.S., and the commencement of the devastating IRAN–IRAQ WAR (1980–90).

Khorana \\kō-'rä-nə\\, **Har Gobind** (b.1922) Indian-U.S. biochemist. He shared a 1968 Nobel Prize with Marshall

NIRENBERG and Robert HOLLEY for research that helped show how the genetic components of the cell nucleus control the synthesis of proteins. His contribution was to synthesize small nucleic-acid molecules whose exact structure was known. Combined with the proper materials, his synthetic nucleic acids caused protein synthesis, just as in the cell; comparing these proteins with the nucleic acid showed which portions of the nucleic acid were the codes for each part of the protein.

Khosrow I \kòs-ʼraù\ *or* Khosrow Anushirvan (d.579) Persian king (r.531–79) of the SASANIAN DYNASTY. He reformed taxation, reorganized the army, and launched military campaigns in Armenia, the Caucasus, and Yemen. Astronomy and astrology flourished during his reign. Anything pre-Islamic in Iran whose origin is unknown is credited to him.

Khosrow II *or* **Khosrow Parviz** (d.628) Sasanian king (r.590–628) of Persia who extended the empire to its maximum. He came to the throne in troubled times, assisted by Byzantium. Khosrow then launched a war against the BYZANTINE EMPIRE, taking Armenia and central Asia Minor. In 613 he took Damascus; Jerusalem fell in 614. Later Byzantine forces recaptured lost ground and his ablest generals were killed. Revolution within the royal family followed, and Khosrow was executed. After his death the empire rapidly declined, falling to the Arabs in 640. See also SASANIAN DYNASTY.

Khrushchev \krùsh-ʼchóf, *Engl* ʼkrüsh-chef\, **Nikita (Sergeyevich)** (1894–1971) Soviet leader. Son of a miner, in 1935 he became first secretary of the Moscow party organization. He participated in Joseph STALIN's purges of party leaders. In 1938 he became head of the Ukrainian party and in 1939 a member of the Politburo. After Stalin's death in 1953, he emerged from a bitter power struggle as the party's first secretary. In 1955, on his first trip outside the Soviet Union, Khrushchev showed his flexibility and the brash, extroverted style of diplomacy that would become his trademark. At the party's TWENTIETH CONGRESS in 1956, he

Nikita Khrushchev, 1960

delivered a secret speech denouncing Stalin for his "intolerance, his brutality, his abuse of power." Supporting de-Stalinization, Khrushchev allowed the Poles relative freedom, but he crushed the HUNGARIAN REVOLUTION by force (1956). Opposition within the party crystallized in 1957, but Khrushchev secured the dismissal of his enemies and in 1958 assumed the premiership himself. Asserting a doctrine of peaceful coexistence, he toured the U.S. in 1959, but a planned Paris summit was canceled after the U-2 AFFAIR. In 1962 he attempted to place Soviet missiles in Cuba, causing the CUBAN MISSILE CRISIS. Ideological differences and the signing of the NUCLEAR TEST-BAN TREATY (1963) led to a split with the Chinese. Agricultural failures, the China quarrel, and his often arbitrary administrative methods led to his forced retirement in 1964.

Khulna \ʼkùl-nə\ City (pop., 1991: 731,000), SW Bangladesh. Located northeast of CALCUTTA, India, it is an important river port and trade center, connected by road and rail to the major cities of the S Ganges Delta.

Khwarizmi, al- See AL-KHWARIZMI

Khyber Pass \ʼkī-bər\ Pass in the Safed Koh Range on the border between Afghanistan and Pakistan. About 33 mi (53 km) long, it has historically been the gateway for invasions of the Indian subcontinent from the northwest; it was traversed by Persians, Greeks, Mughals, Afghans, and the British. In 1879 the Khyber tribes finally came under British rule. The pass is now controlled by Pakistan.

kibbutz \ki-ʼbùts\ Israeli communal settlement in which wealth is held in common and profits are reinvested. The

first kibbutz was founded in 1909; currently there are some 200, with a total population exceeding 100,000. Adults live in private quarters; children are generally housed and cared for as a group. Meals are communal. Members have regular meetings to discuss business and make decisions. Jobs may be assigned by rotation, by choice, or by skill. The kibbutz movement has declined in recent decades.

Kiche See QUICHE

Kidd, Michael *orig.* Milton Gruenwald (b.1919) U.S. dancer, choreographer, and director. Born in Brooklyn, N.Y., he danced with American Ballet Theatre, for which he choreographed *On Stage I* (1945). He choreographed many Broadway musicals, winning Tony awards for *Guys and Dolls* (1951), *Can-Can* (1953), *Li'l Abner* (1956), and *Destry Rides Again* (1959). His film credits include *The Bandwagon* (1953), *Seven Brides for Seven Brothers* (1954), and *Hello, Dolly!* (1969).

Kidd, William *known as* **Captain Kidd** (1645?–1701) British privateer and pirate. A legitimate privateer for Britain, he was commissioned in 1695 to apprehend pirates in the E. Indies. He himself turned pirate on the voyage, took several ships, and mortally wounded his gunner. He surrendered in New York in 1699, having been promised a pardon. Sent to England for trial, he was found guilty of murder and five piracy counts, and was hanged. Much of his treasure has apparently never been found. He was later romanticized as a dashing swashbuckler.

Kidder, Alfred V(incent) (1885–1963) U.S. archaeologist. Born in Marquette, Mich., Kidder received his PhD from Harvard Univ. (1914) for developing the first effective pottery typology relating to the prehistory of the SW U.S. He later extended these interests to a classic study (1924) of the PUEBLO INDIANS and to the creation (1927) of a widely used archaeological classification system (the Pecos system) for the Southwest. He also organized (1929) a far-reaching survey of cultural history of the Maya empires.

kidnapping Crime of seizing, confining, abducting, or carrying away a person by force or fraud, often to subject him or her to involuntary servitude, in an attempt to demand a ransom, or in furtherance of another crime. In most countries it is punishable by a long prison sentence or death.

kidney One of a pair of organs that maintain water balance and expel metabolic wastes. Human kidneys are bean-shaped organs about 4 in. (10 cm) long, in the small of the back. They filter the entire 5-quart (4.5-liter) water content of the blood every 45 minutes. Glucose, minerals, and needed water are returned to the blood by reabsorption. The remaining fluid and wastes pass into collecting ducts, flowing to the ureter and bladder as URINE. Each kidney has over 1 million functional units (NEPHRONS). The kidneys also secrete renin, an enzyme involved in blood pressure regulation. See also KIDNEY FAILURE, KIDNEY STONE, NEPHRITIS, URINARY SYSTEM. See diagram next page.

kidney failure *or* **renal failure** Partial or complete loss of KIDNEY function. Acute failure causes reduced URINE output and blood chemical imbalance, including UREMIA. Most patients recover within six weeks. Damage to various kidney structures can result from chemical exposure, major blood loss, injury, HYPERTENSION, severe BURNS, severe kidney infections, DIABETES MELLITUS, renal artery or urinary tract blockage, and liver diseases. Chronic failure usually results from long-term kidney diseases. The kidneys can sustain life until they lose about 90% of their function. If one is removed, the other enlarges to compensate. Failure of both usually requires DIALYSIS or KIDNEY TRANSPLANT.

kidney stone *or* **renal calculus** Mass of minerals and organic matter that may form in a KIDNEY. Low URINE volume or high mineral concentration can cause dissolved SALTS to precipitate and grow, forming stones. Large stones can block urine flow at various points, be a focus for infection, or cause painful spasms. Treatment deals with any underlying problem (e.g., infection or obstruction), tries to dissolve stones with drugs or ULTRASOUND, or removes large ones surgically.

kidney transplant *or* **renal transplant** Replacement of a diseased or damaged KIDNEY with one from a living relative or a legally dead donor. The former's tissue type is more likely to match, and gives the patient more time for DIALYSIS be-

K L

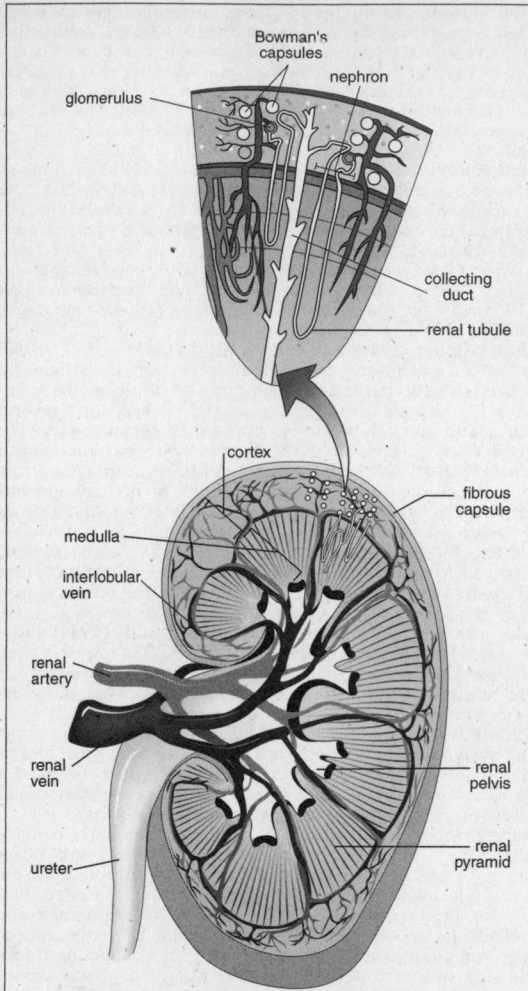

Kidney Cross section of a kidney. The kidney is made up of an outermost cortex, a middle medulla, and an inner pelvis. Blood enters via the renal artery, which branches into smaller vessels, each of which terminates in a tuft of capillaries (glomerulus). Fluids from the blood are forced out of the glomerulus into the surrounding Bowman's capsule during filtration. The glomerulus, Bowman's capsule, and associated renal tubule make up the nephron. Any important substances filtered from the blood (incl. glucose, minerals, and much of the water) are returned to it by reabsorption in the renal tubule. The medulla is divided into triangular masses of tissue (renal pyramids) that contain the collecting ducts for the fluid (urine) not reabsorbed into the blood. Water is further removed from the urine as it passes through the collecting ducts into the funnel-shaped renal pelvis, which leads to the ureter.

fore surgery to control existing disease; but removal puts the donor at risk, and a kidney from a dead donor is more likely to be available. The new kidney is implanted and its blood vessels and ureter sewn in place. A near-normal life may be resumed within two months. See also TRANSPLANT.

Kiefer \ˈkē-fər\, **Anselm** (b.1945) German painter. In 1970 he studied under the conceptual artist Joseph BEUYS. In such huge paintings as *Germany's Spiritual Heroes* (1973) he used visual symbols, somber colors, and naïve drawing to comment with irony and sarcasm on Germany's tragic past. In the 1980s his colossal paintings acquired an intense physical presence. He is one of the most prominent figures of NEO-EXPRESSIONISM.

Kiel \ˈkēl\ City (pop., 1998 est.; 240,000), capital of SCHLESWIG-HOLSTEIN state, N Germany. A port and naval base, it was founded in 1242. It entered the HANSEATIC LEAGUE in 1284; in 1773 it became part of Denmark. Schleswig-Holstein passed to Prussia in 1866, and Kiel became its capital in 1917. It is the site of St. Nicholas Church (c.1240), a ducal palace (c.1280), and the Christian-Albrechts Univ. of Kiel (founded 1665).

Kienholz \ˈkēn-ˌhôlts\, **Edward** (1927–1994) U.S. sculptor. Born in Fairfield, Wash., he moved to Los Angeles in 1954 and began producing large wooden reliefs for walls. His later controversial environmental sculptures were elaborately detailed three-dimensional assemblages that harshly indicted U.S. society. His most famous walk-in scenes included *Roxy's* (1961), a replica of a 1943 Los Angeles bordello. His brutal images of sex, death, and decay were criticized as repulsive.

Kieran the Younger See St. CIARAN OF CLONMACNOISE

Kierkegaard \ˈkir-kə-ˌgärd\, **Søren (Aabye)** (1813–1855) Danish religious philosopher, regarded as the founder of EXISTENTIALISM. He studied theology at the Univ. of Copenhagen. He is famous for his critique of systematic rational philosophy. He attacked G. W. F. HEGEL's attempt to systematize the whole of existence, declaring that existence is constantly developing. In *Concluding Unscientific Postscript* (1846), he proposed that subjectivity is truth, thereby intending to clear the ground for an adequate consideration of faith and religion, specifically Christianity. His most famous works include *Either/Or* (1843), *Fear and Trembling* (1843), and *The Sickness unto Death* (1849). He insistently attacked the organized church in his later years; exhausted by the strain, he died at 42. His greatest influence was felt in the 20th cent., on such thinkers as Karl BARTH, Karl JASPERS, Martin HEIDEGGER, and Martin BUBER.

Søren Kierkegaard Drawing by Christian Kierkegaard, c.1840

kieselguhr See DIATOMACEOUS EARTH

Kiev \ˈkē-ef\ *Ukrainian* **Kyyiv** \ˈkyiv\ City (pop., 1998 est.: 2,620,000), capital of UKRAINE. Located along the DNIEPER RIVER, it was founded in the 8th cent., and by the late 9th cent. was the capital of KIEVAN RUS. In 1240 it was destroyed by the GOLDEN HORDE; rebuilt, it came successively under Lithuanian, Polish, and Cossack rule. Incorporated into Russia in 1793, in 1934 it became the capital of the Ukrainian S.S.R. It remained the capital on Ukraine independence in 1991. An industrial, educational, and cultural center, it is the seat of a state university and the Academy of Sciences of Ukraine.

Kievan Rus \ˈkē-vən-ˈrüs\ First E Slavic state. It was founded by the Viking Oleg, ruler of NOVGOROD from about 879, who seized SMOLENSK and KIEV (882); Kiev became the capital of Kievan Rus. Kievan Rus peaked in the 10th–11th cent. under VLADIMIR I and YAROSLAV, when Kiev became E Europe's chief political and cultural center. At Yaroslav's death in 1054, his sons divided the empire into warring factions. The 13th-cent. MONGOL conquest ended its power.

Kigali \kē-ˈgä-lē\ City (pop., 1991: 233,000), capital of RWANDA. It was a trading center during the German colonial administration (after 1895), and a regional center during the Belgian colonial period (1919–62). It became the capital of independent Rwanda in 1962. It was the site of bloody Hutu–Tutsi clashes in the 1990s.

Kikuyu \ki-'kü-yü\ Bantu-speaking people of the highland area of S central Kenya. Numbering over 6 million, they are the largest ethnic group in Kenya. They traditionally lived in separate domestic family homesteads, but during the MAU MAU rebellion they were moved into villages for security purposes, by the British colonial government. Many Kikuyu serve in government posts.

Kilauea \ˌkē-laů-'ä-ə\ Crater, E side of MAUNA LOA, HAWAII VOLCANOES NATIONAL PARK. The world's largest active volcanic crater, it is about 3 mi (5 km) long, 2 mi (3.2 km) wide, and 500 ft (150 m) deep. In its floor is the vent known as Halemaumau Pit, legendary home of the fire goddess Pele. Its frequent eruptions are usually contained, but since 1983 eruptions have produced lava that reached the sea 30 mi (48 km) away.

Kilby, Jack (St. Clair) (b.1923) U.S. inventor. Born in Jefferson City, Mo., he studied at the Univ. of Wisconsin. In 1958 he joined Texas Instruments; there he envisioned all of a circuit's components integrated on a single surface, which led to the invention of the COMPUTER CHIP. He also coinvented a handheld calculator with a thermal printer. The owner of more than 60 patents, in 2000 he shared a Nobel Prize with Herbert Kroemer (b.1928) and Zhores Alferov (b.1930).

kilim \kē-'lēm\ Pileless floor covering handwoven by TAPESTRY techniques in Anatolia, the Balkans, and parts of Iran. The name is also given to a variety of brocaded, embroidered, warp-faced, and other flat-woven rugs and bags. A common characteristic is a slit that occurs wherever two colors meet along a vertical line in the pattern. The finest examples are silk 16th–17th-cent. pieces from Kashan, Iran. The largest kilims are produced in Turkey, as are smaller examples and prayer kilims (prayer rugs). The kilims of the S Balkans, originally copies of Turkish types, gradually developed individual styles.

Kilimanjaro \ˌki-lə-mən-'jä-rō\ Volcanic mountain, NE Tanzania. It includes the peaks of three extinct volcanoes: Kibo, Mawensi, and Shira. Its highest peak is Kibo, which rises to 19,340 ft (5,895 m) and is the highest point in Africa. Kibo was first scaled in 1889.

killdeer Bird (*Charadrius*, sometimes *Oxyechus, vociferus*) that frequents grassy mudflats, pastures, and fields. Its name is suggestive of its loud, insistent whistle. It is about 10 in. (25 cm) long and has a brown back, a white belly, and two black breast bands. Killdeers breed throughout N. America and in NW S. America. To protect their young, killdeers will feign injury and flutter awkwardly away from the nest, luring predators with the promise of an easy kill.

killer whale *or* **orca** Toothed whale (*Orcinus orca*) found in all seas, the largest of the oceanic DOLPHINS. The male may be 30 ft (9 m) long and weigh over 10,000 lbs (4,500 kg). The killer whale is black, with white on the underparts, above each eye, and on each flank. Its strong jaws have 40–50 large, sharp, conical teeth. Killer whales live in groups of up to 50 individuals. They feed on fishes, cephalopods, penguins, seals, and even other whales, but there is no recorded instance of a killer whale killing a human. They are often trained as performers in marine shows.

Killy \kē-'lē\, **Jean-Claude** (b.1943) French skier. Reared in an Alpine ski resort, he became the European champion in 1965, and in 1966 he won the world-combined championship (downhill, slalom, and giant slalom). In 1967 he won the first World Cup for men, repeating this triumph in 1968. In the 1968 Winter Olympics he became the second skier in history to sweep the Alpine events.

kilt Knee-length, skirtlike garment worn by men as part of the traditional national garb, or Highland dress, of Scotland. Made of permanently pleated wool in a TARTAN pattern, it is wrapped around the wearer's waist; it is usually worn with the plaid, a rectangular length of cloth draped over the left shoulder. The ensemble, which developed in the 17th cent., is worn for ordinary purposes as well as for special occasions. Highland dress is the uniform of Scottish regiments in the British army, worn into battle as recently as World War II.

Kimberley City (pop., 1996: 170,000), S. Africa. Founded in 1871 shortly after the discovery of diamonds in the area, it became part of Cape Colony. It was besieged by the Boers (1899–1900) during the S. AFRICAN WAR. It housed the country's first stock exchange. It is still a diamond-mining center; the DE BEERS and Kimberley mines are nearby.

kimberlite *or* **blue ground** Dark, heavy, often fragmented igneous rock that may contain DIAMONDS in the rock matrix. Kimberlite is a MICA peridotite. It occurs in the Kimberley district of S. Africa and the Kimberley and Lake Argyle regions of Australia, as well as near Ithaca, N.Y.

Kim Dae Jung \'kim-'dī-'jəŋ\ (b.1925) S. Korean politician. He first entered politics in 1954, opposing the policies of Syngman RHEE, but did not win a seat in government until 1961. After several arrests in the 1970s, Kim was imprisoned. In 1985, after a brief exile in the U.S., he resumed his role as a leader of the political opposition. He served as president of S. Korea 1997–2003. In 2000 he received the Nobel Peace Prize for improving relations with N. Korea.

Kim Il-sung \'kim-'il-'sůŋ\ (1912–1994) Communist leader of N. Korea (1948–94). After World War II, Kim helped establish a communist provisional government in N. Korea and became its first premier. His invasion of S. Korea in an attempt to reunify the country initiated the KOREAN WAR. After the war, Kim introduced a philosophy of self-reliance under which N. Korea tried to develop its economy with little help from foreign countries. His omnipresent personality cult enabled him to rule unchallenged for 46 years in one of the world's most isolated and repressive societies.

Kim Jong Il \'kim-'chəŋ-'il\ (b.1941) N. Korean leader. Son of KIM IL-SUNG, he was designated his father's successor in 1980 and became N. Korea's leader on his father's death in 1994. Some 2 million N. Koreans may have died of starvation under his highly secretive administration. He has begun to relax his country's extreme isolationism, and in 2000 he met with KIM DAE JUNG to pursue reunification with S. Korea. In 2002 tensions mounted with revelations of N. Korea's ongoing nuclear weapons program, in breach of an agreement with the U.S.

kimono Garment worn by Japanese men and women from the Early Nara period (645–724) to the present. The essential kimono is an ankle-length gown with long, full sleeves and a V-neck. It is lapped left over right across the chest and secured at the waist by a broad sash, or obi. Though the kimono is originally of Chinese origin, its great beauty is attributable to 17th- and 18th-cent. Japanese designers.

Kim Young Sam \'kim-'yəŋ-'sam\ (b.1927) S. Korean president (1993–98). He served in S. Korea's National Assembly from 1954 until his expulsion in 1979 by Pres. Park Chung Hee, which touched off riots that preceded Park's assassination. After a military takeover in 1980, Kim was put under house arrest until 1983. In 1990 he merged his party with the ruling Democratic Justice Party, which helped him win the presidency in 1992. He enacted reforms to end political corruption, and his term was initially one of rising prosperity for Korea.

kindergarten School or class for children aged 4–6, a prominent part of PRESCHOOL EDUCATION. It began in the early 19th cent. as an outgrowth of the ideas and practices of Robert OWEN in Britain, J. H. PESTALOZZI in Switzerland and his pupil Friedrich FROEBEL in Germany, and Maria MONTESSORI in Italy. Kindergartens generally encourage self-understanding through play activities and greater freedom rather than the imposition of adult ideas.

Kindi, al- *in full* Yakub ibn Ishaq al-Sabah al-Kindi (d.c.870) First prominent Islamic philosopher. He worked in Iraq under the caliphs al-MAMUN and al-Mutasim. One of the first Arab students and translators of the Greek philosophers, he tried to combine the views of PLATO and ARISTOTLE into a new system. His short treatises concerned NEOPLATONISM. He also wrote over 270 scientific treatises on such subjects as astrology, Indian arithmetic, sword manufacturing, and cooking.

kinesiology \ki-ˌnē-zē-'ä-lə-jē\ Study of the mechanics and anatomy of human movement and their roles in promoting health and reducing disease. Kinesiology has direct applications to fitness and health, including developing exercise programs for people with and without disabilities, preserving the independence of older people, preventing disease due to trauma and neglect, and rehabilitating people after disease or injury. Research encompasses the biochemistry

K L

of muscle contraction and tissue fluids, bone mineralization, responses to exercise, how physical skills are developed, and work efficiency.

kinetic energy \kə-ˈnet-ik\ Form of ENERGY that an object has by reason of its MOTION. The kind of motion may be translation (motion along a path from one place to another), rotation about an axis, vibration, or any combination of motions. The kinetic energy of an object depends on its MASS and VELOCITY. For instance, the amount of kinetic energy KE of an object in translational motion is equal to one-half the product of its mass m and the square of its velocity v, or $KE = \frac{1}{2}mv^2$, provided the speed is low relative to the speed of light. At higher speeds, RELATIVITY changes the relationship.

kinetic sculpture Sculpture in which movement (as of a motor-driven part or a changing electronic image) is a basic element. Actual movement became an important aspect of sculpture in the 20th cent. Pioneers such as Naum GABO and Alexander CALDER produced movement by such means as water, mechanical devices, and air currents (as in Calder's MOBILES). Jean TINGUELY's self-destructing sculpture *Homage to New York* (1960) functioned as both an object and an event—a "happening."

kinetic theory of gases Theory based on a simple description of a GAS, from which many properties of gases can be derived. The theory is one of the most important concepts in modern science. The simplest kinetic model is based on the assumptions that (1) a gas is composed of a large number of identical MOLECULES moving in random directions, separated by distances that are large compared to their size; (2) the molecules undergo perfectly elastic (no energy loss) collisions with each other and with the walls of the container; and (3) the transfer of KINETIC ENERGY between molecules is HEAT. This model describes an IDEAL GAS but is a reasonable approximation to a real gas.

King, B. B. (*orig.* Riley B.) (b.1925) U.S. BLUES guitarist. Born in Itta Bena, Miss., and reared in the Mississippi Delta, he was influenced early by gospel music. His first hit, "Three O'Clock Blues" (1951), was followed by a long succession of others, including "Every Day I Have the Blues" and "The Thrill Is Gone." To his own impassioned vocal calls, King plays single-string guitar responses with a distinctive vibrato. By the late 1960s rock guitarists were acknowledging his influence and introducing King and his guitar, Lucille, to the white public. He remains the most successful bluesman of all time.

King, Billie Jean *orig.* Billie Jean Moffitt (b.1943) U.S. tennis player. Born in Long Beach, Cal., she won her first Wimbledon doubles championship in 1961. She went on to capture a record 20 Wimbledon titles from the mid-1960s to the mid-1970s. She also won several U.S. singles titles (1967, 1971–72, 1974) and the Australian (1968) and French (1972) titles. She was ranked no. 1 in the U.S. seven times and no. 1 in the world five times. In 1973 she defeated the 55-year-old former men's champion Bobby Riggs in a hugely publicized "battle of the sexes." Her later public announcement of her lesbianism gained her further attention. In 1974 she founded the Women's Sports Foundation, cofounded the Women's Tennis Assn., and, with her husband, founded World TeamTennis.

King, Martin Luther, Jr. *orig.* Michael Luther King, Jr. (1929–1968) U.S. civil rights leader. Born in Atlanta, he became an adherent of nonviolence philosophies while in college. Ordained in 1954, he became pastor of a church in Montgomery, Ala. He received his doctorate from Boston Univ. in 1955. Through his efforts, Montgomery ended its public-transport segregation policies. In 1957 he formed the SOUTHERN CHRISTIAN LEADERSHIP CONFERENCE and began lecturing nationwide, urging active nonviolence to achieve civil rights for blacks. In 1960 he returned to Atlanta and was arrested for protesting segregation at a lunch counter and jailed; the case drew national attention, and presidential candidate John F. KENNEDY interceded to obtain his release. In 1963 King helped organize the March on Washington, an assembly of more than 200,000 protestors at which he made his famous "I have a dream" speech. The march influenced the passage of the 1964 CIVIL RIGHTS ACT, and King was awarded the 1964 Nobel Peace Prize. From 1965 he was criticized by radicals within the CIVIL

RIGHTS MOVEMENT. He broadened his advocacy to address the plight of the poor of all races and oppose the Vietnam War. Having gone to Memphis, Tenn., to support a strike by sanitation workers, he was assassinated by J. E. RAY.

Martin Luther King, Jr.

King, Stephen (Edwin) (b.1947) U.S. writer. Born in Portland, Me., he won fame early with his enormously popular books, blending horror, the macabre, fantasy, and science fiction, which have made him one of the world's best-selling writers. *Carrie* (1974) was his first published novel and an immediate success; later works include *The Shining* (1977), *The Dead Zone* (1979), *Cujo* (1981), *It* (1986), *Misery* (1987), the series *The Dark Tower* (1992–97), *Rose Madder* (1996), and the series *The Green Mile* (1996). Many have become highly successful films.

King, W(illiam) L(yon) Mackenzie (1874–1950) Prime minister of Canada (1921–26, 1926–30, 1935–48). Born in Berlin, Ontario, the grandson of W. L. MACKENZIE, he was appointed Canada's first minister of labor (1909–11). A member of the Canadian Parliament from 1919, he served as leader of the Liberal Party 1919–48. As prime minister, he effected a more independent relationship between the Commonwealth nations and Britain. During and after World War II he unified a country often divided between English and French constituents.

King Cotton Phrase used before the AMERICAN CIVIL WAR to denote the economic supremacy of Southern cotton production. The concept was touted by Southern politicians, who believed that cotton's economic and political power would bring victory if secession led to war. The South expected support from Britain, a major cotton importer, but Britain instead developed alternative sources of cotton within its empire. Its one-crop economy contributed to the South's weak position after the Civil War.

kingfish Any of various fishes, among them certain species of MACKEREL and a drum. The king mackerel, or kingfish (*Scomberomorus cavalla*), is a W Atlantic fish about 65 in. (170 cm) long and weighing 80 lbs (36 kg) or more. The kingfish, or whiting (*Menticirrhus saxatilis*), is notable among drums in that it lacks an air bladder.

kingfisher Any of about 90 species of birds (family Alcedinidae), many of which fish for their food. Solitary birds, kingfishers are chiefly tropical. They have a large head and compact body. Species range from 4 to 18 in. (10–45 cm) long; most have bright, boldly patterned plumage, and many are crested. They utter rattling or piping calls. The only widespread N. American species, the belted kingfisher (*Megaceryle alcyon*), is bluish gray above and white below. The forest kingfishers (e.g., KOOKABURRA) have a broader bill.

King George's War (1744–48) Inconclusive struggle between France and Britain (under King GEORGE II) for mastery of N. America. The war involved disputes over boundaries of Nova Scotia and N New England and control of the Ohio Valley. After bloody border raids by both sides, aided by their Indian allies, they signed a treaty that restored conquered territory but failed to resolve colonial issues.

Belted kingfisher (*Megaceryle alcyon*)

King Philip's War (1675–76) Bloodiest conflict between American colonists and Indians. By 1660 colonial settlers had pushed into Indian territory in Massachusetts, Connecticut, and Rhode Island. To protect their lands, the Wampanoag chief King Philip (METACOM) organized a federation of tribes, which in 1675 destroyed several frontier settlements. In retaliation the colonial militia burned Indian villages and crops. After Philip's death in 1676, Indian resistance collapsed. Some 600 settlers and 3,000 Indians were killed in the conflict.

Kings, Valley of the Defile, W THEBES, Egypt. It is the burial site of nearly all the pharaohs of the 18th–20th dynasties (1539–1075 B.C.), from Thutmose I to Ramses XI. The valley contains 60 tombs. Only the tomb of TUTANKHAMEN escaped pillage, and its treasures now reside in the Egyptian Museum in CAIRO. The longest tomb, nearly 700 ft (215 m) long, belongs to Queen HATSHEPSUT. The largest tomb, built for the sons of RAMSES II, contains 67 burial chambers.

Kings Canyon National Park National park, SIERRA NEVADA, S central California. It occupies 722 sq mi (1,870 sq km) adjacent to SEQUOIA NATIONAL PARK. Established in 1940, it contains giant sequoia trees. The spectacular Kings Canyon, on the Kings River, was carved by glacial action.

kingship, divine See DIVINE KINGSHIP

Kingsley, Charles (1819–1875) English clergyman and novelist. He served as chaplain to Queen Victoria, professor of modern history at Cambridge, and canon of Westminster. He published several novels about social problems before writing the very successful historical novels *Hypatia* (1853) and *Westward Ho!* (1855). Fearing the Anglican church's trend in the direction of Catholicism, he engaged in a famous controversy with J. H. NEWMAN. His wholehearted acceptance of Charles DARWIN's theory of evolution inspired his popular children's book *The Water-Babies* (1863).

king snake Any of seven species of SNAKE (genus *Lampropeltis,* family Colubridae) found from SE Canada to Ecuador. They kill by constriction, and eat other snakes, small mammals, amphibians, birds, and birds' eggs. Strikingly marked and smooth-scaled, they are usually less than 4 ft (1.2 m) long, but can approach 7 ft (2 m). The common king snake, found throughout the U.S. and in N Mexico, is usually black or dark brown, variously blotched, ringed, or speckled with yellow or white.

Kingston City (pop., 1991: 104,000; metro. area pop.: 588,000), capital, and chief port of JAMAICA. Founded in 1692, it soon became the commercial center of Jamaica, and was made the political capital in 1872. Historic buildings include a 17th-cent. church, a moated fortress, and the 18th-cent. Headquarters House. It is the seat of the Univ. of the W. Indies.

Kingston, Maxine Hong orig. Maxine Hong (b.1940) U.S. writer. Born to an immigrant family in Stockton, Cal., she has written novels and nonfiction works that explore the myths, realities, and cultural identities of Chinese and American families. Her widely admired *The Woman Warrior* (1976) and *China Men* (1980) blend fact and fantasy to tell aspects of her family's history; *Tripmaster Monkey* (1988) concerns a young Chinese-American man.

Kingstown Capital (pop., 1995: 16,000), chief port of ST. VINCENT AND THE GRENADINES, W. Indies. It is located on St. Vincent island. Its Botanic Gardens (1763) are the oldest in the W Hemisphere; Capt. William BLIGH made his 1787 voyage on the *Bounty* to obtain breadfruit trees from TAHITI for this garden.

King William's War (1689–97) Inconclusive battle for N. American territory between Britain, under King WILLIAM III, and France. The N. American extension of the War of the GRAND ALLIANCE, it involved French Canadians and New England colonists and their Indian allies. The British captured Port Royal, Acadia (later Nova Scotia), but failed to take Quebec. The French won skirmishes at Schenectady, N.Y., and in New England but failed to take Boston.

Kinsey \'kin-zē\, **Alfred (Charles)** (1894–1956) U.S. expert on human sexual behavior. After earning a Ph.D. from Harvard Univ. in 1920, he taught zoology at Indiana Univ., where he became the founder-director of its Institute for Sex Research in 1942. His *Sexual Behavior in the Human Male* (1948) and *Sexual Behavior in the Human Female* (1953), based on 18,500 personal interviews, received extraordinary publicity for their revelations about contemporary sexual behavior.

Kinshasa \kin-'shä-sə\ *formerly* **Léopoldville** Capital and largest city (pop., 1994 est.: 4,655,000), Democratic Republic of the Congo (Zaire). Situated on the CONGO RIVER, it was founded as Léopoldville in 1881 by H. M. STANLEY. It became the capital of the Belgian Congo in the 1920s. After World War II it emerged as the largest city in sub-Saharan Africa. It was given its present name in 1966. The chief port on the Congo, it is the seat of the Univ. of Kinshasa.

Kiowa \'kī-ə-ˌwȯ\ N. American Indian people who lived on the S Great Plains, one of the last PLAINS INDIAN tribes to capitulate to the U.S. They hunted buffalo on horseback and lived in large three-poled TEPEES. They believed that dreams and visions gave them supernatural power, and they participated in the SUN DANCE ceremony. They were also noted for their pictographic portrayals, or "calendar histories," of important tribal events. About 5,000 Kiowa live today on an Oklahoma reservation shared with the CO-MANCHE.

Kipling, (Joseph) Rudyard (1865–1936) British novelist, short-story writer, and poet. Born in India, he was reared in England but returned to India as a journalist. He soon became famous for volumes of stories, beginning with *Plain Tales from the Hills* (1888; including "The Man Who Would Be King"), and later for the poetry collection *Barrack-Room Ballads* (1892; including "Gunga Din" and "Mandalay"). During a residence in the U.S., he published *The Light That Failed* (1890), the two *Jungle Book*s (1894, 1895), *Captains Courageous* (1897), and *Kim* (1901), one of the great novels of India. He wrote six other volumes of short stories and several other verse collections.

Rudyard Kipling

His children's books include the famous *Just So Stories* (1902). His poems, often strongly rhythmic, are frequently narrative ballads. He was awarded the Nobel Prize in 1907. After World War I his image as a jingoistic imperialist impaired his extraordinary popularity and reputation.

Kirchhoff \'kiṙk-hȯf\, **Gustav Robert** (1824–1887) German physicist. KIRCHHOFF'S CIRCUIT RULES (1845) allow calculation of the currents, voltages, and resistances of electrical networks. With Robert BUNSEN, he demonstrated that every element emits colored light when heated at wavelengths specific to it, a fact that is the basis of spectrum analysis. They used this new research tool to discover CESIUM (1860) and rubidium (1861), and began a new era in astronomy when they applied it to the spectrum of the sun.

Kirchhoff's circuit rules \'kiṙ-ˌkȯfs\ *or* **Kirchhoff's laws** Two statements, developed by Gustav KIRCHHOFF, about complex CIRCUITS that embody the laws of conservation (see CONSERVATION LAW) of ELECTRIC CHARGE and energy. They are used to determine the value of the ELECTRIC CURRENT in each branch of the circuit. The first states that the sum of the currents into a junction in the circuit equals the sum of the currents out of the junction. The second states that around each loop in an electric circuit, the total ELECTROMOTIVE FORCE is equal to the sum of all the potential drops (changes in voltage) across components in the loop.

Kirchner \'kiṙk-nər\, **Ernst Ludwig** (1880–1938) German painter and printmaker. A founder of the Expressionist group Die BRÜCKE, he was influenced by Albrecht DÜRER and Edvard MUNCH; his style was noted for its psychological tension and eroticism. He used simple, powerfully drawn forms and often garish colors to create intense, sometimes threatening works, such as his two versions of *Street, Berlin* (1907, 1913). Highly strung and often depressed, he took his own life when the Nazis declared his work "decadent."

Kiribati \ˌkir-ə-'bä-tē, ˌkir-i-'bas, 'kir-i-ˌbas\ *officially* **Republic of Kiribati** Independent nation, consisting of 33 islands, central Pacific Ocean. The three major island groups are the

GILBERT, Phoenix, and Line Islands (excluding the three Line islands that are U.S. territories); Kiribati also includes Banaba Island, the former capital of the Gilbert and Ellice Islands colony. Area (land): 313 sq mi (811 sq km). Population (2000): 92,000. Capital: Bairiki, on TARAWA atoll. The native people are mostly Micronesians. Languages: English (official), Gilbertese. Religions: Roman Catholicism, Protestantism, Baha'i. Currency: Australian dollar. With the exception of Banaba (which is a coral island and higher in elevation), all the islands of Kiribati are low-lying coral atolls built on a submerged volcanic chain and encircled by reefs. Only about 20 of the islands are inhabited; more than 95% of the population of Kiribati live in the Gilbert Islands. The economy is based on subsistence farming and fishing. It is a republic with one legislative house; its head of state and government is the president. The islands were settled by Austronesian-speaking peoples before the 1st cent A.D. Fijians and Tongans arrived around the 14th cent. In 1765 the British commodore John Bryon (1723–1786) discovered the island of Nikunau; the first permanent European settler arrived in 1837. In 1916 the Gilbert and Ellice islands and Banaba became a crown colony of Britain; the Phoenix Islands joined the colony in 1937. Most of the Line Islands joined the colony in 1972, but in 1976 the Ellice Islands were separated to form the country of Tuvalu. The colony became self-governing in 1977, and in 1979 it became the nation of Kiribati. See also map at OCEANIA.

Kiriwina Islands See TROBRIAND ISLANDS

Kirkland, (Joseph) Lane (1922–1999) U.S. labor-union leader. Born in Camden, S.C., he joined the AFL in 1948, was elected secretary-treasurer of the AFL-CIO in 1969, and succeeded George MEANY as president in 1979. During Kirkland's tenure (1979–95), the AFL-CIO's membership and political influence waned, owing to shrinking employment in the U.S. manufacturing sector.

Kirkuk \kir-'kük\ City (pop., 1987: 419,000), NE Iraq. Situated north of BAGHDAD, it was in one of the first Arab areas where oil was discovered in the 20th cent. Kirkuk is a trade and export center as well as a center of Iraq's petroleum industry, with oil pipeline connections to Tripoli and to Yumurtalik on the Turkish coast.

Kirkwood gaps Interruptions in the distribution of ASTEROIDS where their orbital periods would be a simple fraction of Jupiter's. Daniel Kirkwood (1814–1895) noticed several zones of low density in the asteroid belt around 1860 and explained them as resulting from perturbations by Jupiter. Any object that revolved in one of these locations would be influenced by the planet's gravitational pull to move to another orbit.

Kirov \'kē-róf\, **Sergey (Mironovich)** orig. Sergey Mironovich Kostrikov (1886–1934) Soviet political leader. He extended the Communist Party's control in Transcaucasia, and Joseph STALIN appointed him head of the Leningrad party organization (1926). He modernized the city's industries, was elected to the Politburo (1930), and acquired power that nearly rivaled Stalin's. In 1934 he was assassinated by a young party member. Stalin, claiming a widespread conspiracy to assassinate the entire Soviet leadership, used the assassination as a pretext to institute the PURGE TRIALS. In 1956 Nikita KHRUSHCHEV suggested that Stalin had engineered Kirov's assassination.

Kirov Theater See MARIINSKY THEATER

Kirstein \'kir-,stēn\, **Lincoln (Edward)** (1907–1996) U.S. dance impresario and writer. Born in Rochester, N.Y., to a wealthy family, in 1933 he persuaded George BALANCHINE to come to the U.S. to found the School of American Ballet, which Kirstein directed 1940–89. He and Balanchine jointly established a series of ballet companies, culminating in the NEW YORK CITY BALLET (1948), which he served as general director until 1989. He wrote seven books on ballet, including the classic history *Dance* (1935). His influence on the growth of ballet in the U.S. remains unmatched.

Kisangani \,kē-sän-'gä-nē\ formerly (until 1966) **Stanleyville** City (pop., 1994 est.: 418,000), NE Democratic Republic of the Congo (Zaire). The nation's chief inland port after KINSHASA, it is located on the CONGO RIVER, below Boyoma Falls. Founded in 1883 and long known as Stanleyville (for H. M. STANLEY), it has been the major center of the N

Congo since the late 1800s. It is the seat of the Univ. of Kisangani (1963).

Kish Ancient Mesopotamian city-state located east of BABYLON in what is now S central Iraq. City ruins date back to the 4th millennium B.C. and the Sumerian culture; archaeological evidence of the palace of SARGON and the temple of NEBUCHADNEZZAR II has also been found.

Kishinev See CHISINAU

Kishon River See QISHON RIVER

Kissinger \'ki-s°n-jər\, **Henry A(lfred)** (b.1923) U.S. (German-born) foreign-policy adviser. He emigrated with his family to the U.S. in 1938. He taught at Harvard Univ. 1954–69. In 1968 he was appointed assistant for national security affairs by Pres. Richard NIXON and later served as secretary of state (1973–77). His policy of DÉTENTE toward the Soviet Union led to the SALT agreements, and he developed the first official U.S. contact with Communist China. He negotiated the cease-fire agreement that ended the VIETNAM WAR, for which he shared the Nobel Peace Prize in 1973. Such initiatives as the secret bombing of Cambodia (from 1969) and connivance in the overthrow of Salvador ALLENDE earned him a reputation for deviousness.

Kitaj \ki-'tī\, **R(onald) B(rooks)** (b.1932) U.S.-British painter. Born in Cleveland, he studied in New York and Europe. In the 1960s he was a prominent member of the POP ART movement in Britain. He developed an evocative pictorial language of figurative imagery filled with references to historical, artistic, and literary topics executed in a brightly colored, semiabstract style. He has taught at various British art schools.

Kitakami Mountains \kē-'tä-kä-mē\ Mountain range, NE HONSHU, Japan. It parallels the Pacific coast and extends for about 155 mi (250 km) to the Ojika Peninsula. Its highest peak rises to 6,280 ft (1,914 m). It is the most culturally isolated region of Honshu. Until the mid-20th cent. such practices as the serf system known as Nago survived there.

Kitakyushu \kē-'tä-,kyü-shü\ City (pop., 1995: 1,020,000), KYUSHU, Japan. It was created in 1963 by the amalgamation of several cities. It is one of Japan's leading manufacturing centers. Undersea tunnels link the city with Shimonoseki, Honshu.

Kit-Cat Club Association of early-18th-cent WHIG leaders that met in London. Members included the writers Richard STEELE, Joseph ADDISON, and William CONGREVE and such political figures as Robert WALPOLE and the duke of MARLBOROUGH. They first met in the tavern of Christopher Cat, whose mutton pies were called kit-cats. Portraits of the 42 members were painted by Godfrey Kneller (1646–1723), and the specific size of the canvas used (36″ x 28″) became known as a kit-cat.

Kitchener City (pop., 1996: 178,000), SE Ontario. It is situated in the Grand River valley, southwest of TORONTO. Settled by German immigrants beginning about 1807, it was renamed in honor of H. H. KITCHENER in 1916. The boyhood home of W. L. M. KING is now preserved in Woodside National Historic Park.

Kitchener, H(oratio) H(erbert) later **Earl Kitchener (of Khartoum and of Broome)** (1850–1916) British field marshal and imperial administrator. Kitchener served in the Middle East and Sudan before taking charge of the Egyptian army in 1892. In 1898 he crushed the MAHDIST MOVEMENT in the Battle of OMDURMAN and forced concessions from France in the FASHODA INCIDENT. In 1899 he entered the S. AFRICAN WAR as chief of staff, becoming commander in chief a year later. Late in the war, he resorted to brutal methods, burning Boer farms and establishing concentration camps. He was later sent to India to reorganize the army there. In 1911 he returned to Khartoum as proconsul of Egypt and the Sudan. As secretary of state for war during World War I, he organized armies on an unprecedented scale and became a symbol of the national will to victory. He died when his ship was sunk by a German mine.

kite Light frame covered with paper or cloth, often provided with a balancing tail, and designed to be flown in the air at the end of a long string; it is held aloft by wind. Kites have been in use in Asia from time immemorial, and religious significance is still connected to some ceremonial kite-flying there. Kites were used to carry weather-recording devices aloft before the advent of balloons and airplanes. Types of kite commonly in use today include the hexagonal (or three-sticker), the malay (modified diamond), and the box kite, invented in the 1890s. Newer wing-like kites use pairs of controlling strings for superior maneuverability.

kite Any of numerous lightly built BIRDS OF PREY that have a small head, short beak, and long, narrow wings. They are found worldwide in warm regions. In flight, kites slowly flap and then glide with wings angled back. Kites belong to three subfamilies of the family Accipitridae: Milvinae (true kites and snail kites), Elaninae (including the white-tailed kite), and Perninae (including the swallow-tailed kite of the New World). See also HAWK.

Swallow-tailed kite
(Elanoides forficatus)

kithara \'ki-thə-rə\ Large LYRE, the principal STRINGED INSTRUMENT of the Greeks and later of the Romans. It had a box-shaped resonating body from which extended two parallel arms connected by a crossbar to which 3–12 strings were attached. It was held vertically and plucked with a plectrum. It was played by singers of the Greek epics, as well as by later professional accompanists and soloists.

kiva \'kē-və\ Underground chamber of the PUEBLO INDIAN villages of the SW U.S., notable for the murals that decorate its walls. Though the kiva's primary purpose is for ritual ceremonies, men also use it for meetings; women are almost always excluded. The traditional round slope of the earliest kiva, in contrast to the otherwise square or rectangular Pueblo architecture, recalls the circular pit houses of the prehistoric basket-weaving culture from which these tribes, primarily HOPI and ZUNI, descend.

kiwi Any of three species (genus *Apteryx*) of chicken-sized, grayish brown RATITE birds, found in New Zealand. Their Maori name refers to the male's shrill call. Kiwis have vestigial wings, soft hairlike feathers, and stout, muscular legs. Each of the four toes has a large claw. Kiwis live in forests, where they sleep by day and forage for worms, insects and their larvae, and berries at night. They run swiftly and use their claws in defense when cornered.

kiwi fruit Edible fruit of the vine *Actinidia chinensis* (family Actinidiaceae), native to China and Taiwan and widely grown commercially. It has a slightly acid taste and is high in vitamin C. Kiwi can be eaten raw or cooked, and the juice is sometimes used as a meat tenderizer.

KKK See KU KLUX KLAN

klebsiella \ˌkleb-zē-'e-lə\ Any of the rod-shaped BACTERIA of the genus *Klebsiella*. Gram-negative (see GRAM STAIN) COLIFORM BACTERIA, they thrive better without oxygen than with it, and do not move. *K. pneumoniae* can infect the human respiratory tract and cause pneumonia and urinary-tract and wound infections.

Klee \'klā\, **Paul** (1879–1940) Swiss painter. After studies in Germany and Italy, he settled in Munich, where he became associated with Der BLAUE REITER (1911). He taught at the BAUHAUS (1920–31), but returned to Switzerland in 1933. One of the foremost artists of the 20th cent., he belonged to no movement, yet he assimilated and even anticipated some of the major artistic tendencies of his time. Using both representational and abstract approaches, he produced some 9,000 paintings, drawings, and watercolors in a great variety of styles. His works, usually small in scale, are remarkable for their delicate nuances of line, color, and tonality. In Klee's highly sophisticated art, irony and a sense of the absurd are joined to an intense evocation of the mystery and beauty of nature.

Klein, Calvin (Richard) (b.1942) U.S. fashion designer. Born in New York City, he attended the Fashion Institute of Technology. He opened his own company in 1968, when casual, hippie-style clothing was in fashion, but took a different direction by designing simple, understated, elegant clothing. The first designer to win three consecutive Coty Awards for womenswear (1973–75), he is known for his clothing, cosmetics, linens, and other designer collections.

Klein, Melanie *orig.* Melanie Reizes (1882–1960) Austrian-British psychoanalyst. She underwent psychoanalysis with Sandor FERENCZI in Budapest before World War I. She joined the Berlin Psychoanalytic Institute (1921–26) and later moved to London. In *The Psychoanalysis of Children* (1932) and *Narrative of a Child Analysis* (1961), she asserted that children's play was a symbolic way of controlling anxiety and that observation of free play with toys could reveal early psychological impulses.

Klein, Yves (1928–1962) French painter, sculptor, and performance artist. With no formal artistic training, he began in the mid-1950s to exhibit nonobjective paintings in which a canvas was uniformly covered in a single color, usually blue; he also used the technique for sculptural figures and reliefs. In 1958 he produced a near-riot with an "exhibition of emptiness," an empty gallery painted white, titled *Le vide* ("The Void"). His work was deliberately extreme and experimental. A member of FLUXUS, he greatly influenced the development of MINIMALISM.

Kleist \'klīst\, **(Bernd) Heinrich (Wilhelm von)** (1777–1811) German writer. His grim and intense drama *Penthesilea* (1808) contains some of his most powerful poetry, and *The Broken Pitcher* (1808) is a masterpiece of dramatic comedy; they were followed by *Katherine of Heilbronn* (1810), *Die Hermannsschlacht* (1821), and *The Prince of Homburg* (1821). In 1811 he published a collection of eight masterly novellas, including *Michael Kohlhaas, The Earthquake in Chile*, and *The Marquise of O*. Embittered by a lack of recognition, he died in a joint suicide with a young woman at 34. He is now considered the first of the great 19th-cent. German dramatists, and his densely written fictions are widely admired by writers.

Klemperer, Otto (1885–1973) German conductor. After studying composition with Hans Pfitzner (1869–1949), in 1905 he met Gustav MAHLER, who had him appointed chief conductor at the Hamburg Opera (1910). At the short-lived Kroll Opera (1927–31) he conducted the Berlin premieres of many important works. In 1933 he fled Germany for the U.S. A brain tumor in 1939 left him partly paralyzed. From the 1950s, though seated on the podium, he created a much-admired recorded legacy with London's Philharmonia Orchestra.

klezmer music Traditional music played in the Jewish and German ghettos of Eastern Europe, especially for weddings and other ceremonies. The Yiddish term means basically "professional musican," and klezmer music has included liturgical music as well as boisterous dance music. Klezmer ensembles have varied considerably; today in the U.S., a typical band specializes in dance music and consists of four to six musicians playing clarinet, trumpet, trombone, tuba, and percussion.

Klimt, Gustav (1862–1918) Austrian painter. In 1897, after a period as an academic muralist, he revolted against academic art in favor of a decorative style similar to ART NOUVEAU and founded the Vienna SEZESSION. His later murals are characterized by precisely linear drawing and flat, decorative patterns of color. His most successful works include *The Kiss* (1908) and a series of portraits, in which he treats the human figure without shadow, conveying the sensuality of skin by surrounding it with areas of flat, highly ornamental areas of decoration. See also JUGENDSTIL.

Kline, Franz (1910–1962) U.S. painter. Born in Wilkes-Barre, Pa., he studied art in London before settling in New York City. A leading artist of ABSTRACT EXPRESSIONISM, he used inexpensive commercial paints and large house-painter's brushes to build graphic networks of rough bars of black paint on white backgrounds, achieving a sense of majesty and power in such large-scale works as *Mahoning* (1956). In the late 1950s he introduced color into his paintings.

Klinefelter's syndrome Chromosomal disorder that occurs in one out of 500 males. With an extra X CHROMOSOME in each cell (XXY), patients look male, with firm, small TESTES, but produce no sperm and may have enlarged breasts and buttocks and very long legs. TESTOSTERONE levels are low. Social adjustment can be difficult. Rarer variants cause additional abnormalities. All variants are treated with ANDROGENS.

K L

Klinger, Max (1857–1920) German painter, sculptor, and printmaker. He is known for his use of symbol, fantasy, and dreamlike situations, reflecting a late-19th-cent. awareness of psychological depths. His vivid, frequently morbid imaginings and his interest in the gruesome and grotesque can be seen in his Goyaesque etchings.

Klondike gold rush Canadian gold rush of the late 1890s. Gold was discovered on August 17, 1896, near the confluence of the Klondike and YUKON rivers in W Yukon Territory. The news spread quickly, and by late 1898 more than 30,000 prospectors had arrived. Annual production peaked in 1900, and soon prospectors began moving on to Alaska. Mining ended in 1966.

Kluane National Park \klü-ˈȯ-nē\ National park, SW Yukon. Located on the Alaskan border, it encompasses some 5,440,000 acres (2,203,000 hectares). Its focal point is Mt. LOGAN, the highest peak in Canada. Kluane also has a large glacier system and abundant wildlife.

knight *French* **chevalier** \shə-ˈval-ˌyā\ *German* **Ritter** In the European Middle Ages, a formally professed cavalryman, generally a vassal holding land as a FIEF from the lord he served (see FEUDALISM). At about 7 a boy bound for knighthood became a page, then at 12 a varlet or valet, and subsequently a shieldbearer or esquire. When judged ready, he was dubbed knight by his lord in a solemn ceremony. The Christian ideal of knightly behavior (see CHIVALRY) required devotion to the church, loyalty to military and feudal superiors, and preservation of personal honor. By the 16th cent. knighthood had become honorific.

Knight, Frank H(yneman) (1885–1972) U.S. economist. Born in McLean Co., Ill., he taught at the Univ. of Chicago 1927–52; Milton FRIEDMAN was one of the many students he influenced. His book *Risk, Uncertainty and Profit* (1921) distinguished between insurable and uninsurable RISKS and asserted that profit was the reward entrepreneurs earned for bearing uninsurable risk. His monograph *The Economic Organization* is a classic exposition of MICROECONOMICS. He is considered the founder of the Chicago school of economics.

Knights of Labor U.S. labor organization. Founded in 1869 as the Noble Order of the Knights of Labor, it proposed a system of workers' cooperatives to replace capitalism. To protect its members from employers' reprisals, it originally maintained secrecy. Under Terence Powderly (1879–93) it favored open arbitration with management and discouraged strikes. National membership reached 700,000 in 1886. Strikes by militant groups and the HAYMARKET RIOT rapidly reduced its influence. A splinter group left to form the AFL (later AFL-CIO).

Knights of Malta *or* **Hospitallers** \ˈhäs-ˌpi-təl-ərz\ *in full (since 1961)* Sovereign Military Hospitaller Order of St. John of Jerusalem, of Rhodes and of Malta. Religious order founded at Jerusalem in the 11th cent. to care for sick pilgrims. Recognized by the pope in 1113, the order built hostels along the routes to the Holy Land. The Hospitallers acquired wealth and lands and began to combine the task of tending the sick with waging war on Islam, eventually becoming a major military force in the CRUSADES. They ruled Rhodes from 1309 until it fell to the Turks in 1523; thereupon they moved to Malta, where they ruled until their defeat by NAPOLEON in 1798. In 1834 they moved to their present headquarters in Rome.

Knight Templar See TEMPLAR

knitting machine Machine for TEXTILE and garment production. Flatbed machines may be hand-operated or power-driven, and, by selection of color, type of stitch, cam design, and Jacquard device (see JACQUARD LOOM), almost unlimited variety is possible. Modern circular machines may have 100 feeders, allowing each needle to pick up 100 threads per revolution. Small bladelike units (sinkers) are inserted between every two needles to engage and hold the completed fabric. Machines may have pattern wheels controlling needle action to produce special stitches, and also a Jacquard mechanism.

Knopf \kə-ˈnəpf, kə-ˈnȯpf\, **Alfred A.** (1892–1984) U.S. publisher. Born in New York City, he and his wife, Blanche, founded the publishing firm Alfred A. Knopf, Inc., in 1915. His appreciation of contemporary literature and his literary contacts helped make the firm renowned for publishing works of high literary quality. By the time of his death, its authors had won 16 Nobel and 27 Pulitzer prizes. Knopf also published the influential periodical *American Mercury* (1924–34).

Knossos \ˈnä-səs\ Ancient royal city, CRETE. It was King MINOS' capital and the center of the MINOAN civilization. Settled by migrants from ASIA MINOR in the 7th millennium B.C., it gave rise to a sophisticated BRONZE AGE culture. Two great palaces were built in the Middle Minoan period, the second around 1720 B.C. after an earthquake leveled the city. After its palace was destroyed by fire around 1400 B.C., Aegean political focus shifted to MYCENAE. Knossos was the site of the legendary labyrinth of DAEDALUS.

Knossos Faience statuette of a "snake goddess," c.1600 B.C.

knot Interlacement of parts of one or more ropes, cords, or other pliable materials, commonly used to bind objects together. Humans first used knots in vines and cordlike fibers to bind stone heads to wood in primitive axes, and in the making of nets and traps. Knot making became sophisticated when it began to be used in the rigging that controlled the sails of early sailing vessels. Knots are still depended on by campers and hikers, mountaineers, fishermen, and weavers.

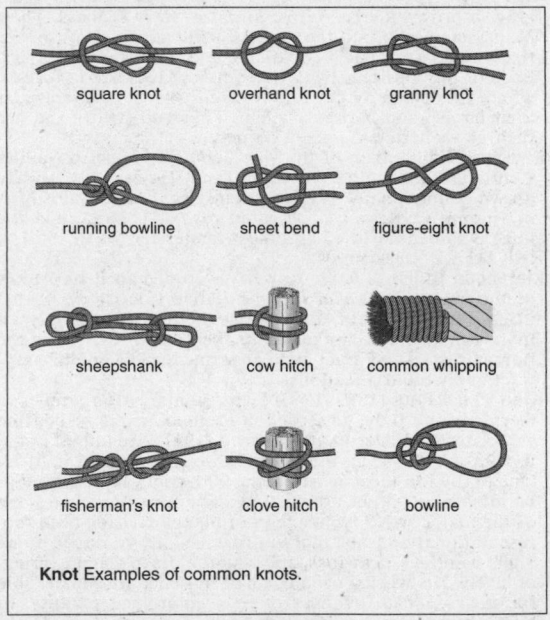

Knot Examples of common knots.

Knowles \ˈnōlz\, **John** (1926–2001) U.S. author. Born in Fairmont, W.V., he gained prominence for his first novel, *A Separate Peace* (1959), about the competitive friendship of two private-school students. Most of his novels are psychological examinations of characters caught in conflict between the wild and the pragmatic sides of their personalities.

Know-Nothing Party *or* **American Party** U.S. political party of the 1850s. Developed from the anti-immigrant and anti-Roman Catholic movement of the 1840s, the secret Order of the Star-Spangled Banner was formed in New York in 1849. Members were instructed to reply to queries about their group with "I know nothing." The group, which officially became the American Party, called for restrictions on immigration and naturalized citizenship. By 1855 there were 43 Know-Nothing congressmen. At its 1856 convention the party split over the slavery issue, and by 1859 its influence was limited to the border states.

Knox, Henry (1750–1806) American Revolutionary officer. Born in Boston, he joined the Continental Army. Sent by George WASHINGTON to transport British artillery captured in the Battle of Ticonderoga, he oversaw the transport of 120,000 lbs (55,000 kg) of artillery by oxen and horses over snow and ice 300 mi (480 km) to Boston. Promoted to general, he commanded the artillery in the battles of Monmouth and Yorktown, and in 1783 he succeeded Washington as commander of the army. He served as the first U.S. secretary of war (1789–95).

Knox, John (c.1514–1572) Scottish clergyman, leader of the Scottish Reformation and founder of Scottish PRESBYTERIANISM. Probably trained for the priesthood at the Univ. of St. Andrews, he was ordained in 1540. He joined a group of Protestants who fortified St. Andrews Castle, but they were captured by French Catholics in 1547. After his release in 1549, he spent four years preaching in England, where he influenced developments in the Church of England. With the accession of the Catholic MARY I, he fled to the Continent, returning to Scotland in 1559. Knox survived conflicts with MARY, QUEEN OF SCOTS and spent the rest of his life setting up the Presbyterian church.

Knoxville City (pop., 2000: 173,000), E Tennessee. In 1785 a treaty with the CHEROKEE Indians opened the region to settlers, and in 1791 a frontier outpost was renamed Knoxville after Henry KNOX. It served as the state capital 1796–1812 and 1817–19. It is the seat of the Univ. of Tennessee and headquarters of the TENNESSEE VALLEY AUTHORITY.

Knut See CANUTE THE GREAT

Knuth \kə-ˈnüth\, **Donald E(rvin)** (b.1938) U.S. computer scientist. Born in Milwaukee, he studied mathematics at Case Institute of Technology, where he first encountered computers. He earned a PhD in 1963 from Caltech. He applied his knowledge of mathematics and programming to typeface design and typesetting to develop a document-preparation system that gave computers their first ability to control text layouts and to print with typeset quality, leading to the revolution in DESKTOP PUBLISHING. He has received such awards as the Kyoto Prize (1996), the Turing Award (1974), and the National Medal of Science (1979). His ongoing multivolume series *The Art of Computer Programming* has been widely acclaimed.

koala Tree-dwelling MARSUPIAL *(Phascolarctos cinereus)* of coastal E Australia. About 21–33 in. (60–85 cm) long and tail-less, the koala has a stout, pale gray or yellowish body; broad face; big, round, leathery nose; small, yellow eyes; and fluffy ears. Its feet have strong claws and some opposable digits. The koala feeds only on EUCALYPTUS leaves. The offspring (one born at a time) remains in the rearward-opening pouch for up to seven months. Koala populations have dwindled seriously.

koan \ˈkō-ˌän\ In ZEN Buddhism, a brief paradoxical statement or question used as a discipline in MEDITATION.

Koala *(Phascolarctos cinereus)*

The effort to solve a koan is designed to exhaust the analytic intellect and the will, leaving the mind open for response on an intuitive level. Of some 1,700 traditional koans, probably the best-known example is "When both hands are clapped a sound is produced; listen to the sound of one hand clapping."

Kobe \ˈkō-bā\ City (pop., 1995: 1,424,000), S central HONSHU, Japan. It is situated on Osaka Bay and occupies a narrow shelf of land between mountains and the sea. With neighboring OSAKA and KYOTO, it is the center of an industrial zone. After the MEIJI RESTORATION it grew rapidly. It was severely bombed during World War II and suffered a major earthquake in 1995. Kobe is an important Japanese port and a center of shipbuilding and steel production; it is the seat of Kobe Univ.

Koblenz *or* **Coblenz** \ˈkō-ˌblents\ *ancient* Confluentes. City (pop., 1998 est.: 109,000), W Germany. Situated at the junction of the RHINE and MOSELLE rivers, it was founded by the Romans in 9 B.C. It was a Frankish royal seat in the 6th cent. A.D. The French occupied it in 1794; it passed to Prussia in 1815. Devastated in World War II, it has since been restored. It is a center for the German wine trade.

Kobo Daishi See KUKAI

Kobuk Valley National Park \kō-ˈbük\ National park, NW Alaska. Located north of the Arctic Circle, it occupies 1,750,421 acres (708,920 hectares), and preserves the Kobuk and Salmon rivers, forest lands, and the Great Kobuk Sand Dunes. Archaeological sites reveal more than 10,000 years of human occupation. It protects caribou migration routes; other wildlife include grizzly and black bears, fox, moose, and wolves.

Koch \ˈkȯk, *Engl* ˈkȯk\, **(Heinrich Hermann) Robert** (1843–1910) German physician, considered a founder of BACTERIOLOGY. As the first to isolate the ANTHRAX bacillus, observe its life cycle, and develop a preventive inoculation for it, he first proved a causal relation between a germ and a disease. He perfected pure-culture techniques, based on Louis PASTEUR's concept. He isolated the TUBERCULOSIS and CHOLERA organisms and developed a vaccination for RINDERPEST. Koch's postulates remain fundamental to PATHOLOGY: the organism should always be found in

Robert Koch

sick animals and never in healthy ones; it must be grown in pure culture; the cultured organism must make a healthy animal sick; and it must be reisolated from the newly sick animal and recultured and still be the same. He received a Nobel Prize in 1905.

Kocher \ˈkȯ-kər\, **Emil Theodor** (1841–1917) Swiss surgeon. He was the first surgeon to remove the thyroid gland to treat GOITER (1876). He introduced a surgical method for reducing shoulder dislocations, as well as many new surgical techniques, instruments, and appliances. A type of forceps and a gallbladder surgery incision named for him are still used. He adopted Joseph LISTER's principles of complete asepsis in surgery. In 1909 he won a Nobel Prize.

Kodak Co., Eastman See EASTMAN KODAK CO.

Kodaly \ˈkō-ˌdī\, **Zoltan** (1882–1967) Hungarian composer, ethnomusicologist, and music educator. He played various instruments as a child, and earned a doctorate in Hungarian folk song. With Bela BARTOK, a lifelong friend, he compiled the important *Hungarian Folk Songs* (1906). He came to international attention with his *Psalmus hungaricus* (1923) and the opera *Háry János* (1926), which, like his other works, are based on folk music. The "Kodaly method," his school music curriculum for developing children's musicality, remains in wide use today.

Kodiak Island Island (pop., 2000: 14,000), in the Gulf of ALASKA. It has an area of 3,588 sq mi (9,293 sq km). The Kodiak National Wildlife Refuge covers 75% of the island and is the habitat of the Kodiak bear. Discovered in 1763 by a Russian fur trader, the island became the site in 1784 of the first Russian colony in America. Russian control ended in 1867. In 1964 a destructive earthquake lowered the island by 5–6 ft (1.5–1.8 m).

Koestler \ˈkest-lər\, **Arthur** (1905–1983) Hungarian-British writer. He is best known for *Darkness at Noon* (1940); a political novel examining the moral danger in a totalitarian system that sacrifices means to an end, it reflects his experiences in the Communist Party and his imprisonment by Spanish fascists. He also wrote of his disillusionment with communism in the essay collection *The God That Failed* (1949). His later works include *The Act of Creation* (1964) and *The Ghost in the Machine* (1967). He died with his wife in a suicide pact.

Koguryo \ˌkō-gùr-ˈyō\ Largest of the three kingdoms of ancient Korea. Tradition sets its founding at 37 B.C., but modern historians believe it was founded in the 2nd cent. B.C. Eventually the N half of the Korean peninsula and much of Manchuria were under Koguryo's rule. Buddhism, Confucianism, and Taoism all influenced the kingdom, which fell to the allied forces of China's TANG DYNASTY and the S Korean kingdom of SILLA in 668. Numerous surviving tomb paintings depict Koguryo's forceful, horse-riding N people.

kohen See COHEN

Koh-i-noor \ˈkō-ə-ˌnùr\ Famous Indian DIAMOND with a history dating perhaps as far back as the 14th cent. Originally a 191-carat stone, it was recut to 109 carats in 1852 to enhance its fire (flashes of color) and brilliance. The Koh-i-noor (Hindi for "mountain of light") was acquired by the British in 1849 and became part of the crown jewels.

Kohl \ˈkōl\, **Helmut** (b.1930) Chancellor of W. Germany (1982–90) and of the reunified Germany (1990–98). After earning a doctorate at the Univ. of Heidelberg, he rose to become chair of the Christian Democratic Union in 1973, and in 1982 became German chancellor of a centrist coalition government. After the fall of the Berlin Wall in 1989, Kohl concluded a treaty with E. Germany that unified the two countries' economic systems. Absorption of the moribund E. German economy led to increased taxes and cuts in government spending. In 1998 his coalition government was defeated by the Social Democrats under Gerhard SCHRÖDER. Revelations of serious financial irregularities during Kohl's chancellorship soon emerged, tainting his reputation and weakening his party.

Köhler \ˈkœ-lər\, **Wolfgang** (1887–1967) German psychologist. His studies of problem solving by chimpanzees (*The Mentality of Apes,* 1917) led to a radical revision of learning and perception theory, and Köhler became a key figure in the development of Gestalt psychology (*Gestalt Psychology,* 1929). He emigrated to the U.S. after the Nazi takeover and taught at Swarthmore College 1935–55. His other writings include *Dynamics in Psychology* (1940), *The Place of Values in a World of Facts* (1938), and *The Task of Gestalt Psychology* (1969).

kohlrabi \kōl-ˈrä-bē\ Form of CABBAGE (*Brassica oleracea*), native to Europe. Its most distinctive feature is the greatly enlarged stem that grows just above the soil. Its flesh resembles that of a turnip but is sweeter and milder. Kohlrabi is an excellent source of vitamin C, minerals, and dietary bulk. The young tender leaves may be eaten as greens; the thickened stem is served raw or cooked. See also BRASSICA.

Kokand See QUQON

Kokoschka \kə-ˈkòsh-kə\, **Oskar** (1886–1980) Austrian painter and writer. He studied and taught at the Vienna School of Arts and Crafts but was dissatisfied because the school omitted study of the human figure, his primary artistic interest. After about 1912 he became a leading exponent of EXPRESSIONISM; his portraits were painted with increasingly broader strokes of more varied color and heavier outlines. While recovering from a wound received in World War I, he wrote, produced, and staged three plays, including *Orpheus and Eurydice* (1918). The landscapes he produced during 10 years of teaching and travel mark the second peak of his career. In 1938 he fled to London, where his paintings became increasingly political and antifascist. He continued his political art after moving to Switzerland in 1953.

kola nut *or* **cola nut** CAFFEINE-containing NUT of two evergreen trees (*Cola acuminata* and *C. nitida*) of the cocoa family (Sterculiaceae), native to tropical Africa and cultivated extensively in the New World tropics. The trees grow to 60 ft (18 m) in height and have oblong leathery leaves and star-shaped fruit. The nut has been used in medicines and in soft drinks, though American "colas" today instead use synthetic flavorings that mimic its taste. Kola nuts are also chewed to diminish sensations of hunger and fatigue, aid digestion, and combat intoxication, hangover, and diarrhea.

Kolbe \ˈkòl-bə\, **St. Maksymilian Maria** *orig.* Rajmund Kolbe (1894–1941) Polish Franciscan priest martyred by the Nazis. Ordained in 1918, he founded the City of Mary Immaculate religious center (1927) and became director of Poland's chief Roman Catholic publishing complex. Arrested by the Gestapo on charges of aiding Jews and the Polish underground, he was shipped to Auschwitz, where he volunteered his life in place of that of a condemned inmate. Kolbe was canonized in 1982.

Kolchak \kòl-ˈchäk\, **Aleksandr (Vasilyevich)** (1874–1920) Russian naval officer and political leader. In 1917 he was forced to resign as commander of the Black Sea fleet after the RUSSIAN REVOLUTION began. After a coup d'état in Omsk in 1918, he was recognized by the counterrevolutionary White Russians as supreme ruler of Russia. After initial successes against the Red Army (see RUSSIAN CIVIL WAR), his armies were routed in 1919, and he was captured and executed.

Kollwitz \ˈkòl-ˌvits, *Engl* ˈkòl-ˌwits\, **Käthe** *orig.* Käthe Schmidt (1867–1945) German graphic artist and sculptor. She studied painting in Berlin and Munich but devoted herself primarily to etchings, drawings, lithographs, and woodcuts. She became the last great practitioner of German EXPRESSIONISM and an outstanding artist of social protest. Two early series of prints, *Weavers' Revolt* (1895–98) and *Peasants' War* (1902–8), portray the plight of the oppressed with the powerfully simplified, boldly accentuated forms that became her trademark. After her son died in World War I, she created a cycle of prints dedicated to the theme of a mother's love. The first woman elected to the Prussian Academy of Arts, she headed its Master Studio for Graphic Arts 1928–33. The Nazis banned her works from exhibition. The bombing of her home and studio in World War II destroyed much of her work.

Köln See COLOGNE

Kol Nidre \ˈkòl-ˌni-drä\ Prayer sung in Jewish synagogues at the start of services on the eve of YOM KIPPUR. It begins with an expression of repentance for all unfulfilled vows, oaths, and promises to God during the previous year. It was in use as early as the 8th cent.

Kolyma River \ˌkä-li-ˈmä\ River, NE SIBERIA, E Russia. Rising in the Kolyma Mtns. and emptying in the E. Siberian Sea, it is 1,323 mi (2,129 km) long. It is ice-free only from June to September. Under Joseph STALIN, area goldfields held labor camps where more than one million prisoners died (1932–54).

Komodo dragon \kə-ˈmō-dō\ Largest living LIZARD (*Varanus komodoensis*) of the monitor lizard family Varanidae. It lives on Komodo Island and a few neighboring islands in Indonesia. Driven almost to extinction, it is now protected. Komodos grow to 10 ft (3 m) long, weigh up to 300 lbs (135 kg), and may live 100 years. Carrion is their main diet, but adults may attack large game and occasionally kill humans.

Komodo dragon (*Varanus komodoensis*)

Komsomol \ˈkäm-sə-ˌmäl\ Organization in the former Soviet Union for young people aged 14–28 that was primarily a political organ for spreading Communist teachings and preparing future members of the COMMUNIST PARTY. It was organized in 1918. Members participated in health, sports, education, and publishing activities and various industrial projects. They were frequently favored over nonmembers for employment, scholarships, and the like. It disbanded with the collapse of Soviet communism in the early 1990s.

Konbaung dynasty See ALAUNGPAYA DYNASTY

Kongo *or* **Bakongo** Bantu-speaking peoples living along the Atlantic coast in Congo (Zaire), Congo (Brazzaville), and Angola. They engage in subsistence agriculture and cash cropping; many work in towns. A Kongo kingdom existed from the 14th cent., trading in ivory, hides, slaves, and a shell currency; it broke into warring chiefdoms in 1665.

Königsberg See KALININGRAD

Konya \ˈkon-yä\ *ancient* Iconium. City (pop., 1997: 623,000), central Turkey. First settled in the 3rd millennium B.C., it is one of the oldest urban centers in the world. Iconium came under Roman rule by 25 B.C. It was taken by the Seljuq Turks about 1072. Renamed Konya, it was a major cultural center in the 13th cent. and home to the mystics known as "whirling DERVISHES." It was annexed to the Ottoman empire around 1467. Revived after the Istanbul–Baghdad railway opened in 1896, it is an important industrial and agricultural center.

kookaburra *or* **laughing jackass** E Australian species (*Dacelo gigas*) of forest KINGFISHER (subfamily Daceloninae). Its call, which sounds like fiendish laughter, can be heard early in the morning and just after sunset. It reaches a length of 17 in. (43 cm), with a 3.2–4-in. (8–10-cm) beak. In its native habitat it eats invertebrates and small vertebrates, including venomous snakes. It has been introduced into W Australia and New Zealand.

Koolhaas \ˈkōl-ˌhäs\, **Rem** (b.1944) Dutch architect. He first achieved recognition with his book *Delirious New York* (1978), which profiled Manhattan's architectural development. His best-known projects are large-scale structures, including the Kunsthal in Rotterdam, the Grand Palais exhibition hall in Lille (France), and a plan for the MCA/Universal Studios site in Los Angeles. His book *S, M, L, XL* (1996) addressed the theme of size. In 1998 he won the competition for a campus center at the Illinois Institute of Technology. In 2000 he won the Pritzker Architecture Prize.

Kooning, Willem de See Willem DE KOONING

Kootenay National Park National park, SE British Columbia. Centered around the Kootenay River, the park occupies the W slopes of the ROCKY MTNS., adjacent to BANFF and Yoho national parks. It covers 543 sq mi (1,406 sq km). From prehistoric times, the area was a major north–south travel route. Pictographs indicate settlements near the hot springs 11,000–12,000 years ago. The park's scenery is characterized by snowcapped peaks, glaciers, cascades, canyons, and verdant valleys. Wildlife includes wapiti (elk) and mountain goats.

Koraïs \kȯ-ˈrä-ēs\, **Adamántios** (1748–1833) Greek scholar. His advocacy of a revived classicism, with the goal of awakening national aspirations and an awareness of their heritage in modern Greeks, had a great influence on Greek language and culture. His anthologies include the *Library of Greek Literature* (17 vols., 1805–26) and the *Parerga* (9 vols., 1809–37). Largely through his *Atakta* (composed 1828–35), the first Modern Greek dictionary, he created a new Greek literary language out of Demotic and Classical Greek.

Koran See QURAN

Korbut, Olga (Valentinovna) (b.1956) Soviet gymnast. Born in Grodno, Belarus, she first competed in the 1969 championships at 13. Appealingly diminutive, with a captivating smile, she was the first person ever to do a backward somersault on the balance beam. In the 1972 Olympic Games she won three gold medals and a silver. In the 1976 Olympics she won a team gold medal and a silver for the balance beam.

Korda, Alexander *orig.* Sandor Laszlo Kellner (*later* **Sir Alexander**) (1893–1956) Hungarian-British film director and producer. After becoming manager of the Corvin movie studio in Budapest, he eventually arrived in Hollywood, where he directed such movies as *The Private Life of Helen of Troy* (1927). Moving to England in 1931, he founded London Film Productions and helped broaden Britain's film industry, directing and producing such successful films as *The Private Life of Henry VIII* (1933), *The*

Scarlet Pimpernel (1934), and *Rembrandt* (1936), and producing *The Third Man* (1949) and *Richard III* (1955).

Kordofan \ˌkȯr-də-ˈfan\ *or* **Kurdufan** \ˌkȯr-dů-ˈfän\ Region, central Sudan, west of the White NILE RIVER. Controlled by the Christian Tungur dynasty 900–1200 A.D., it was later taken by Arabs. Egyptian rule began in the 1820s. The slave trade was important to the region's economy until its eradication in 1878 by C. G. GORDON. Egyptian rule was ended by a revolt in 1882 led by Al-Mahdi.

Korea *Korean* **Choson** \ˈchō-sŏn\ Former kingdom, a peninsula (Korean Peninsula) on the E coast of Asia. According to tradition, the ancient kingdom of Choson was established in the N part of the peninsula in the 3rd millennium B.C. It later developed into the Three Kingdoms of SILLA, KOGURYO, and PAEKCHE. Invaded by the Mongols in 1231, the Kingdom of Choson, with its capital at SEOUL, was ruled by the Yi dynasty (see YI SONG-GYE) from 1392 to 1910. From about 1637 it shut out foreign contacts; it was forced in 1876 to open ports to Japan. Rivalry over Korea brought on the RUSSO–JAPANESE WAR, after which Korea became a Japanese protectorate. Formally annexed to Japan in 1910, it was freed from Japanese control in 1945. In 1948 it was partitioned into two republics, N. Korea and S. Korea.

Korea, North *officially* **Democratic People's Republic of Korea** Country, occupying the N half of the Korean Peninsula, E. Asia. Area: 47,399 sq mi (122,762 sq km). Population (2000): 21,688,000. Capital: PYONGYANG. Ethnically, the population is almost completely Korean. Language: Ko-

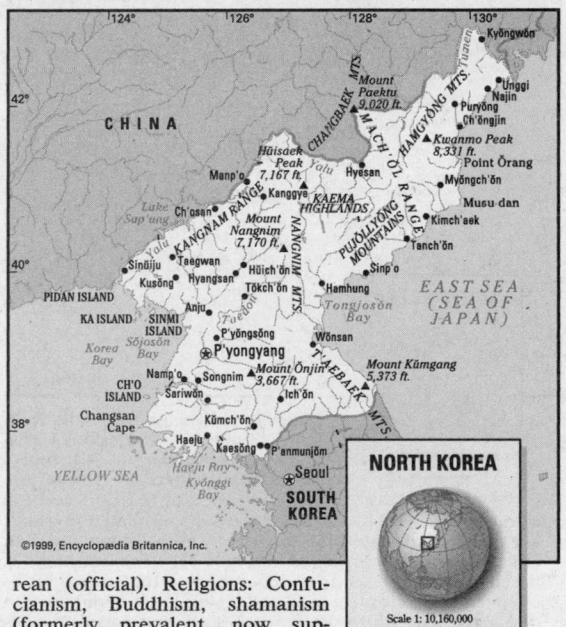

rean (official). Religions: Confucianism, Buddhism, shamanism (formerly prevalent, now suppressed), CH'ONDOGYO. Foreign missionaries were expelled during World War II. Currency: won.

Four-fifths of N. Korea's land area consists of mountain ranges and uplands; its highest peak is the volcanic Mt. Paektu (9,022 ft, or 2,750 m). N. Korea has a centrally planned economy based on heavy industry (iron and steel, machinery, chemicals, and textiles) and agriculture. Cooperative farms raise crops such as rice, corn, barley, and vegetables. The country is also rich in mineral resources, including coal, iron ore, and magnesite. It is a republic with one legislature; the chief of state is the Chairman of the National Defense Commission, and the head of state and government is the premier; its early history is that of KOREA. After the Japanese defeat in World War II, the Soviet Union occupied Korea north of latitude 38° N while the U.S. occupied the area south of it. The Democratic People's Republic of Korea was established as a communist state in 1948. Seeking to unify the peninsula by force, N. Korea launched an invasion of S. Korea in 1950, initiating the KO-REAN WAR. U.N. troops intervened on the side of S. Korea, and Chinese soldiers reinforced the N. Korean army in the war, which ended with an armistice in 1953. Under KIM IL-SUNG, N. Korea became one of the most harshly regimented societies in the world, with a state-owned economy that failed to produce adeqate supplies of food and consumer goods for its citizens. In the late 1990s, under Kim Il-sung's son KIM JONG IL, the country endured a serious famine; over a million Koreans may have died. In 2000, 50 years after the start of the Korean War, a summit between the leaders of N. and S. Korea raised hopes for an end to N. Korea's long isolation.

Korea, South *officially* **Republic of Korea** Country, occupying the S half of the Korean peninsula, E. Asia. It is located northwest of Japan and includes Cheju Island, located about 60 mi (97 km) south of the peninsula. Area: 38,330 sq mi (99,274 sq km). Population (2000): 47,275,000. Capital: SEOUL. The population is almost entirely ethnically Korean.

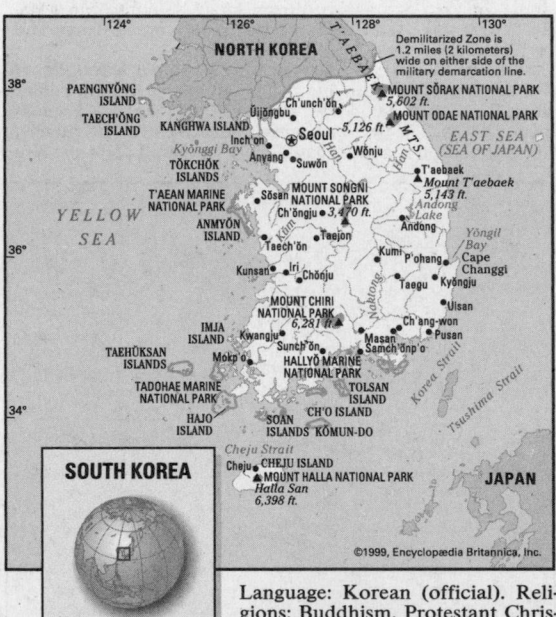

Language: Korean (official). Religions: Buddhism, Protestant Christianity, Confucianism. Currency: won. Nearly three-fourths of the total land area of S. Korea consists of mountains and uplands; the densely populated lowlands are heavily cultivated for wet rice. The Naktong and Han are the country's principal rivers. S. Korea's economy is based largely on services and industry (including petrochemicals, electronic goods, and steel). It is a republic with one legislative house; its head of state and government is the president, assisted by the prime minister; its early history is that of KOREA. The Republic of Korea was established in 1948 in the S portion of the Korean peninsula, which had been occupied by the U.S. after World War II. In 1950 N. Korean troops invaded S. Korea, precipitating the KOREAN WAR. U.N. forces intervened on the side of S. Korea, while Chinese troops backed N. Korea in the war, which ended with an armistice in 1953. The devastated country was rebuilt with U.S. aid, and S. Korea prospered in the postwar era, developing a strong export-oriented economy. It experienced an economic downturn in the mid-1990s that affected many economies in the area. In 2000 the leaders of N. and S. Korea held a summit that revived hopes for reunification.

Korean language Official language of N. and S. Korea, spoken by over 75 million people. Korean is not closely related to any other language, but may have a distant kinship to JAPANESE and an even more remote relationship to the AL-TAIC LANGUAGES. Korean was written with CHINESE characters as early as the 12th cent. A unique phonetic script for it was invented in 1443; now called hangul, it represents syllables by arranging simple symbols for each PHONEME into a square form like that of a Chinese character. Grammatically, Korean has a basic subject-object-verb word order and places modifiers before the element they modify.

Korean War (1950–53) Conflict arising after the post-World War II division of Korea into N. Korea and S. Korea. In 1950 N. Korea, a Soviet client state, invaded S. Korea, which was backed by the U.S. The U.N. Security Council, minus the absent Soviet delegate, passed a resolution calling for the assistance of all U.N. members in halting the invasion, and Pres. Harry TRUMAN ordered U.S. troops to the assistance of S. Korea. At first the N. Korean forces drove the S. Korean and U.N. forces down to the S tip of the Korean peninsula, but the brilliant tactics of Gen. Douglas MACARTHUR turned the tide in favor of the U.N. troops, who advanced to near the border of N. Korea and China. The Chinese then entered the war and drove the U.N. forces back south; the front line stabilized at the 38th parallel. MacArthur favored bombing China at this point, and was relieved of his command when he refused to accept Truman's decision to the contrary. Pres. Dwight EISENHOWER helped conclude an armistice that accepted the front line as the de facto boundary between the two Koreas. The war resulted in the deaths of 1.3 million S. Koreans, 1 million Chinese, 500,000 N. Koreans, and 37,000 Americans.

Kornberg, Arthur (b.1918) U.S. biochemist and physician. Born in Brooklyn, N.Y., he joined the faculty at Stanford Univ. in 1959. The problem of how NUCLEOTIDES are strung together to form DNA molecules led him to add radioactive nucleotides to an enzyme mixture prepared from cultures of *E. coli*. He found evidence of a reaction catalyzed by the enzyme that adds nucleotides to a preexisting DNA chain. He was the first to accomplish the cell-free synthesis of DNA. He shared a 1959 Nobel Prize with Severo OCHOA.

Korolyov \kə-rəl-'yóf\, **Sergey (Pavlovich)** (1907–1966) Soviet designer of guided missiles, rockets, and spacecraft. In 1933 he and F. A. Tsander launched the Soviet Union's first liquid-propellant rocket. During World War II Korolyov designed and tested liquid-fuel rocket boosters for military aircraft. After the war he modified the German V-2 MISSILE. His work led to the Soviet Union's first ICBM. He directed systems engineering for Soviet launch vehicles and spacecraft, and was the guiding genius behind the Soviet spaceflight program.

Koror \'kór-,ór\ Island (pop., 1995: 12,000) and town of the same name, capital of PALAU, W Pacific Ocean. It has a land area of 3 sq mi (8 sq km). The administrative capital of all Japanese mandated islands in the Pacific 1921–45, it was devastated during World War II.

Korsakov, Nicolai Rimsky- See Nicolai RIMSKY-KORSAKOV

Koryo \'kór-yō\ Korean kingdom ruled by a dynasty of the same name from 935 to 1392, when Korea began to form a distinctively Korean cultural tradition. Gen. Wang Kon of Later Koguryo defeated the kingdoms of SILLA and Later Paekche to create a unified Korean peninsula in 936. A centralized bureaucratic system replaced the old aristocratic tribal system. The kingdom saw a flowering of the arts, particularly ceramics (Koryo celadon). In the 13th cent. Koryo suffered a series of Mongol invasions, and in 1392 YI SONG-GYE overthrew the shaky dynasty.

Kosala \'kō-sə-lə\ Ancient kingdom, N India. Roughly corresponding to the historical region of Oudh, in what is now S central Uttar Pradesh state, it extended into present-day Nepal. In the 6th cent. B.C. it rose to become one of the dominant states in N India. MAGADHA conquered Kosala around 490 B.C., and it became known as Northern Kosala to distinguish it from a larger kingdom to the south. The BUDDHA was born there.

Kosciusko \,kä-zē-'əs-kō\, **Mt.** Peak, in the Snowy Mtns., AUSTRALIAN ALPS, SE NEW S. WALES, Australia. The highest mountain in mainland Australia, it reaches 7,310 ft (2,228 m). It is near Mounts Townsend, Twynam, N. Ramshead, and Carruthers, whose melting snows feed the rivers and reservoirs that make up the Snowy Mtns. Hydroelectric Scheme.

Kosciuszko \kȯsh-'chu̇sh-kō, *Engl* ˌkä-sē-'əs-kō\, **Tadeusz** (1746–1817) Polish patriot who fought in the AMERICAN REVOLUTION. He studied military engineering in Paris and went to America in 1776 to join the colonial army. He helped build fortifications in Philadelphia and at West Point, N.Y. As chief of engineers, he twice rescued Gen. Nathanael GREENE's army by directing river crossings. At the war's end he was made a brigadier general. He returned to Poland in 1784, became a major general in the Polish army, and in 1794 led a rebellion against occupying Russian and Prussian forces. From France in his later years, he continued efforts to secure Polish independence.

Tadeusz Kosciuszko
Lithograph by C. Motte, 1826

kosher See KASHRUTH

Kosovo \'kȯ-sō-ˌvȯ\ Autonomous province (pop., 1997 est.: 2,227,000), within the republic of SERBIA, Yugoslavia. It occupies an area of 4,203 sq mi (10,887 sq km); its capital is PRISTINA. Before 1999, ethnic Albanians, most of whom are Muslims, made up nine-tenths of its population and Serbs (mostly Christian) one-tenth. In the late 1980s the Albanians protested Serbia's control of Kosovo, and in 1992 they voted to secede from Yugoslavia. Serbia responded by tightening its control, which led to the KOSOVO CONFLICT. Since the conflict's end, strong sentiment for full independence has been discouraged by the U.N.

Kosovo \'kȯ-sə-ˌvō\, **Battle of** Name of two battles fought in the Serbian province of KOSOVO. The first (June 13, 1389), between the Serbs and the Ottoman Turks, ended in the collapse of Serbia. The battle, which led to three centuries of Serbian vassaldom, has remained a central event to Serbian nationalists. The second battle (Oct. 17–20, 1448), between the Ottomans and a Hungarian-Walachian coalition, halted the last major Christian effort to free the Balkans from Ottoman rule. See also OTTOMAN EMPIRE.

Kosovo conflict (1998–99) Ethnic war in KOSOVO, Yugoslavia. In 1989 the Serbian president Slobodan MILOSEVIC abrogated Kosovo's constitutional autonomy and began systematic oppression of its ethnic Albanian majority. Growing tensions led in 1998 to armed clashes, involving the Kosovo Liberation Army (KLA). The U.S., Britain, Germany, France, Italy, and Russia demanded cessation of fighting, withdrawal of Serbian forces, return of refugees, and unlimited access for international monitors. Milosevic agreed to meet most of the demands, but did not. The U.N. condemned Serbia's so-called ethnic cleansing (killing and expulsion) and imposed a comprehensive arms embargo, but the violence increased. When negotiations at Rambouillet, France, broke down, Serbia launched military forces in a renewed assault, and NATO forces began bombing to prevent a humanitarian catastrophe. Refugees fled amid reports of extensive Serbian atrocities. An 11-week NATO bombing campaign extended to Belgrade and significantly damaged Serbia's infrastructure. It halted after NATO and Yugoslavia signed an accord outlining Serbian troop withdrawal and the return of over a million ethnic Albanian refugees.

Kossuth \'kȯ-ˌshu̇t, *Engl* 'kä-ˌsüth\, **Lajos** (1802–1894) Hungarian patriot. A lawyer from a noble family, he developed a radical political philosophy. Imprisoned 1837–40, he later wrote for a reform journal and gained a devoted following. Elected to the Diet (1847–49), he led the "national opposition," and after the FEBRUARY REVOLUTION (1848) he persuaded the delegates to vote for independence from Austria. Appointed provisional governor, he became virtual dictator of Hungary. In 1849 Russian armies intervened on behalf of Austria, forcing Kossuth to resign. He fled to Turkey, where he was interned for two years. After his re-

lease, he lectured in the U.S. and England, and later settled in Italy.

Kosygin \kə-'sē-gən\, **Aleksey (Nikolayevich)** (1904–1980) Soviet premier (1964–80). He joined the Communist Party in 1927, and by 1939 was a member of the Central Committee. After 1957 he worked closely with Nikita KHRUSHCHEV on economic matters, and in 1964, after Khrushchev's forced resignation, became head of the Soviet government. A competent and pragmatic economic administrator, he introduced reforms designed to modernize the Soviet economy. He shared power with Leonid BREZHNEV and Nikolay Podgorny, but his role decreased as Brezhnev's authority increased.

koto Japanese musical instrument, a long zither with movable bridges and usually 13 strings. It lies on the ground or a low table, and the strings are plucked by plectra while the left hand alters the pitch or ornaments the sound of individual strings by pressing or manipulating them. It is played solo, in chamber ensembles (especially with the shakuhachi and samisen), and in GAGAKU music. The koto is Japan's national instrument.

Koufax \'kō-ˌfaks\, **Sandy** (*orig.* Sanford) (b.1935) U.S. baseball player. Born to Jewish parents in New York City, he joined the Brooklyn (later Los Angeles) Dodgers in 1955 as a left-handed thrower with a blazing fastball and a sharp breaking curveball. He set several season records for strikeouts (including 382 in 1965). In 1965 he pitched his fourth no-hit game, until 1981 a major-league record. Despite his early retirement in 1966 because of arthritis, he is regarded as one of baseball's greatest pitchers.

kouros \'kü-ˌrȯs\ Archaic Greek statue representing a standing nude male youth. These large stone figures began to appear in Greece about 700 B.C. and closely followed the Egyptian style of geometrical, rigid figures. Later naturalistic forms reflect the Greeks' increased understanding of human anatomy. Kouroi sometimes represented the god Apollo, but more commonly served as votive offerings or grave markers. The kore was the kouros's clothed female counterpart.

Koussevitzky \ˌkü-sə-'vit-skē\, **Sergey (Alexandrovich)** (1874–1951) Russian-U.S. conductor. A virtuoso double-bass player, he was self-taught as a conductor. He founded his own orchestra, which toured the Volga by riverboat. Leaving the Soviet Union in 1920, he established the Concerts Koussevitzky series in Paris before becoming conductor of the Boston Symphony Orchestra (1924–49). He gave about 100 premieres there, and inspired his musicians to legendary performances by the force of his personality. The Tanglewood Music Center in Lenox, Mass., was established during his tenure in Boston.

Kovno See KAUNAS

Kowloon \'kau̇-'lün\ *or* **Jiulong** \'jyō-'lu̇ŋ\ Small peninsula on the Chinese mainland, administratively part of HONG KONG. The city of Kowloon (pop., 1996: 1,987,000) extends north into the New Territories and includes New Kowloon and Kowloon City. It is an important modern commercial center.

Koxinga See ZHENG CHENGGONG

Kpelle \kə-'pel-ə\ People occupying central Liberia and part of Guinea. Numbering about 400,000, they are primarily rice farmers; cash crops include peanuts, sugarcane, and kola nuts. They are known for elaborate SECRET SOCIETIES that serve a variety of social and political functions.

kraal \'krȯl, 'kräl\ In S Africa, an enclosure or group of houses surrounding an enclosure for livestock, the social unit that inhabits these structures, or the associated way of life. Among some ZULUS, the traditional kraal consists of a number of huts arranged in a circle around a cattle corral. The word kraal has also been applied to the temporary encampments of the MASAI of E Africa.

Krafft-Ebing \'kräft-'ā-biŋ\, **Richard, Freiherr (Baron) von** (1840–1902) German neuropsychiatrist. He taught psychiatry at Strasbourg, Graz, and Vienna, and studied subjects ranging from epilepsy and syphilis to genetic functions in insanity and sexual deviation. He is best remembered for his *Psychopathia sexualis* (1886), a groundbreaking examination of sexual aberrations.

kraft process Method for producing wood pulp using CAUSTIC SODA and sodium sulfide as the liquor in which the pulpwood is cooked to loosen the fibers. The process produces particularly strong and durable PAPER. Another advantage is its capability of digesting pine chips; RESINS dissolve in the alkaline liquor and are recovered as tall oil, a valuable by-product. Recovery of sodium compounds is important in the economy of the process. In modern kraft mills, operations are completely contained; waste streams are recycled and reused, eliminating water pollution.

Krakatau \ˌkra-kə-ˈtaů\ *or* **Krakatoa** \ˌkra-kə-ˈtō-ə\ Island volcano in the Sunda Strait, between JAVA and SUMATRA, Indonesia. Its eruption in 1883 was one of the most catastrophic in history. Its explosions were heard in Australia, Japan, and the Philippines, and large quantities of ash fell over 300,000 sq mi (800,000 sq km). It caused a tidal wave 120 ft (36 m) high that took 36,000 lives in Java and Sumatra. It erupted again in 1927 and is still active.

Krakow *or* **Cracow** \ˈkrä-ˌküf, *Engl* ˈkra-ˌkaů\ City (pop., 1999: 740,000), S Poland. Located on both sides of the upper VISTULA RIVER, it survived a Mongol invasion in 1241, and was made the capital of a reunited Poland in 1320. Its importance diminished after the capital was moved to WARSAW in 1609. In 1846 it came under Austrian rule; it was returned to Poland in 1918. Rebuilt since World War II, it is an industrial center with a giant steelworks on the city's outskirts. Its university was founded in 1364.

Krasnoyarsk City (pop., 1997 est.: 874,000), N central Russia. Located on the upper YENISEY RIVER, it was founded by COSSACKS in 1628. The TRANS-SIBERIAN RAILROAD brought rapid growth in the 1890s. The site of one of the world's largest hydroelectric stations, it is now a commercial and industrial center.

Krebs, Hans Adolf (*later* **Sir Hans**) (1900–1981) German-British biochemist. He was the first to describe the urea cycle (1932). He and Fritz Lipmann (1899–1986) received a 1953 Nobel Prize for their discovery of the series of chemical reactions in living organisms known as the TRICARBOXYLIC ACID CYCLE, or Krebs cycle, a discovery of vital importance to a basic understanding of cell metabolism and molecular biology.

Krebs cycle See TRICARBOXYLIC ACID CYCLE

kremlin Central fortress in medieval Russian cities, usually located at a strategic point along a river and separated from the surrounding parts of the city by a wall with ramparts, moat, towers, and battlements. Several capitals of principalities were built around old kremlins. The Moscow Kremlin (established 1156) served as the center of Russian government until 1712 and again after 1918. Its crenellated brick walls and 20 towers were built in the 15th cent. by Italian architects. The palaces, cathedrals, and government buildings within the walls encompass Byzantine, Russian baroque, and Classical styles.

Krieghoff \ˈkrēg-hóf\, **Cornelius** (1815–1872) Dutch-Canadian painter. He emigrated to New York around 1837 and later moved to Canada. Working in Montreal and Quebec, he produced over 2,000 images of American Indian and French-Canadian life and colorful landscapes in a detailed, romanticized, anecdotal style that became very popular, and his work was much imitated and forged.

krill Any member of the CRUSTACEAN suborder Euphausiacea, composed of shrimplike animals that live in the open sea. The name also refers to the genus *Euphausia* within the suborder and sometimes to a single species, *E. superba.* The described species, numbering more than 80, range in size from about 0.25 to 2 in. (8–60 mm). Most have bioluminescent organs on the lower side, making them visible at night. They are important as food for various fishes, birds, and whales, particularly BLUE and FIN WHALES. Krill may occur in vast swarms at the ocean surface, where they feed at night, and at depths greater than about 6,000 ft (2,000 m).

Krishna One of the most widely venerated Hindu gods, worshiped as the eighth incarnation of VISHNU and as the supreme deity. Many Krishna legends are drawn from the *MAHABHARATA* and the PURANAS. Raised by a cowherd, as a child Krishna was beloved for his pranks; he also performed miracles and slew demons. As a youth he was famous as a lover. He killed the wicked king of Mathura (as had been prophesied), then set up his court at Dvaraka, marrying the princess Rukmini and taking other wives as

well. He was killed when a huntsman shot him in the heel, his one vulnerable spot. In art Krishna is often depicted with blue-black skin, wearing a loincloth and a crown of peacock feathers. As a divine lover he is shown playing the flute surrounded by adoring females.

Krishnamurti \ˌkrish-nə-ˈmůr-tē\, **Jiddu** (1895–1986) Indian spiritual leader and theosophist. He was educated in theosophy by Annie BESANT, who proclaimed him the coming "World Teacher" who would bring about world enlightenment. He broke with formal theosophy in 1929 and renounced any claims to being a World Teacher. His desire, he said, was to set people free, a goal that could only be achieved through unflinching self-awareness. He established a number of Krishnamurti foundations in the U.S., Britain, and India to further his aims. His books include *The Songs of Life* (1931) and *Commentaries on Living* (1956–60).

Kristallnacht \krēs-ˈtäl-ˌnäkt\ *or* **Crystal Night** *or* **Night of Broken Glass** Night of violence against Jews carried out by the German NAZI PARTY on Nov. 9–10, 1938. The violence, instigated by Joseph GOEBBELS, left 91 Jews dead, 7,500 Jewish businesses gutted, and 177 synagogues demolished. The GESTAPO arrested 30,000 wealthy Jews, offering to release them only if they emigrated and surrendered their wealth. The incident marked a major escalation in Nazi persecution, foreshadowing the HOLOCAUST.

Krivoy Rog See KRYVYY RIH

Kroc, Ray(mond Albert) (1902–1984) U.S. restaurateur, a pioneer of the fast-food industry. Born in Chicago, he was working as a blender salesman when he discovered a restaurant in San Bernardino, Cal., owned by Maurice and Richard McDonald, that used an assembly-line format to prepare and sell a large volume of hamburgers, french fries, and milk shakes. Kroc opened his first MCDONALD'S restaurant in Des Plaines, Ill., in 1955, paying the brothers a percentage of the receipts. He soon began selling franchises and instituted a training program in standardization for owner-managers. He lived to see 7,500 McDonald's restaurants worldwide.

Kroeber \ˈkrō-bər\, **A(lfred) L(ouis)** (1876–1960) U.S. anthropologist. Trained under Franz BOAS, he later taught at UC–Berkeley, where he made valuable contributions to American Indian ethnology, New World archaeology, and the study of linguistics. Kroeber's career coincided with the emergence of academic, professionalized anthropology in the U.S. and contributed significantly to its development. His most influential books were *Anthropology* (1923) and *The Nature of Culture* (1952).

Kronos See CRONUS

Kronshtadt Rebellion \ˈkrón-ˌshtät\ (1921) Uprising against Soviet rule after the RUSSIAN CIVIL WAR, conducted by sailors from the Kronshtadt naval base. Disillusionment with the government and inadequate food supplies led them to demand economic and labor reform and political freedoms. The rebels were crushed by a force led by Leon TROTSKY; the survivors were shot or imprisoned. The rebellion, along with several other internal uprisings, led to the adoption of the NEW ECONOMIC POLICY.

Kronstadt See BRASOV

Kropotkin \krə-ˈpót-kən\, **Peter (Alekseyevich)** (1842–1921) Russian theorist of ANARCHISM. The son of a prince, in 1871 he renounced his aristocratic heritage. Though he achieved renown in such fields as geography, zoology, sociology, and history, he shunned material success for the life of a revolutionist. Imprisoned on political charges (1874–76), he escaped and fled to Western Europe. In 1886 he settled in England, where he remained until the RUSSIAN REVOLUTION OF 1917. He wrote several influential books, including *Memoirs of a Revolutionist* (1899) and *Mutual Aid* (1902), in

Peter Kropotkin

which he attempted to put anarchism on a scientific basis and argued that cooperation rather than conflict is the chief factor in the evolution of species. On his return to Russia he was bitterly disappointed that the Bolsheviks had made their revolution by authoritarian methods.

Kru Group of peoples of Liberia and the Ivory Coast, including the Bassa, Krahn, Grebo, Klao (Kru), Bakwe, and Bete. Several groups are known as stevedores and fishermen all along the W coast of Africa and have established colonies in most ports from Dakar to Douala.

Kruger, Paul (*orig.* Stephanus Johannes Paulus) (1825–1904) S. African soldier and statesman, builder of the AFRIKANER nation. Kruger took part in the GREAT TREK and was impressed by the Boers' ability to defend themselves against hostile tribes and establish an orderly government. When the British annexed the TRANSVAAL in 1877, Kruger championed his people's efforts to regain independence. After leading a series of armed attacks, he obtained limited independence and was elected president of the restored republic (1883–1902). In 1895 he fended off an attempt by Cecil RHODES to end Boer control of the republic. During the S. AFRICAN WAR he fled to the Netherlands.

Kruger National Park National park, S. Africa. Located on the Mozambique border, it became a national park in 1926. It covers an area of 7,523 sq mi (19,485 sq km), contains six rivers, and has a wide variety of wildlife, including elephant, lion, and cheetah.

Krupp family \\'krúp\\ German steel-manufacturing dynasty. Friedrich Krupp (1787–1826) founded a steel factory in Essen in 1811. On his death his son Alfred (1812–1887) took charge at 14 and made a fortune supplying steel to railways and manufacturing cannons; Krupp guns performed well in the Franco–German War of 1870–71. At Alfred's death he had armed 46 nations. The rise of the German navy and the need for armor plates further enriched the company under his son Friedrich Alfred (1854–1902). When Friedrich Alfred's daughter Bertha (1886–1957) inherited control of the firm, it employed 40,000 people. Her husband, Gustav von Bohlen (1870–1950), ran the Krupp empire until 1943, when he was succeeded by their son Alfried Krupp (1907–1967). The Krupp works used slave labor during World War II and were a major part of the Nazi war machine; Alfried was later convicted of war crimes. An Allied order to break up the company in 1953 found no buyer, and Alfried eventually restored the Krupp fortune. See also THYSSEN KRUPP STAHL.

Krupp GmbH See THYSSEN-KRUPP STAHL

Krupskaya \\'krúp-skə-yə\\, **Nadezhda (Konstantinovna)** (1869–1939) Russian revolutionary, wife of Vladimir LENIN. A Marxist activist, she met Lenin about 1894. Sentenced to three years in exile in 1898, she obtained permission to spend her term with Lenin in Siberia, where they were married. She helped found the BOLSHEVIK party faction, spread Bolshevik propaganda after the 1917 revolution, and later served in the educational bureaucracy.

krypton \\'krip-ˌtän\\ Chemical ELEMENT, chemical symbol Kr, atomic number 36. One of the NOBLE GASES, it is colorless, odorless, tasteless, and almost completely inert. Krypton occurs in slight traces in the atmosphere and in rocks and is obtained by fractional distillation of liquefied air. It is used in luminescent tubes, flash lamps, lasers, and tracer studies.

Kryvyy Rih \\kri-'vi-'rik\\ *Russian* **Krivoy Rog** \\kri-'vòi-'ròk\\ City (pop., 1998 est.: 715,000), SE central Ukraine. Founded as a village by Cossacks in the 17th cent., it grew after a railway was constructed to the DONETS BASIN in 1884. It soon became a significant iron-mining city; it is now also the site of a major uranium mine and numerous metallurgical plants, foundries, mills, and chemical works.

Ktesibios of Alexandria \\te-'sib-ē-ˌōs\\ *or* **Ctesibius of Alexandria** \\te-'sib-ē-əs\\ (fl.c.270 B.C.) Greek physicist and inventor. He was the first great figure of the ancient engineering tradition of Alexandria, Egypt. He discovered the ELASTICITY of air, and invented several devices using compressed air, including force PUMPS and an air-powered CATAPULT; an improvement of the water clock, in which water dripping at a constant rate raised a float with a pointer; and a hydraulus (water organ), in which the weight of water forced air through the organ pipes.

Kuala Lumpur \\'kwä-lə-'lùm-ˌpùr\\ City (pop., 1991: 1,145,000), capital of MALAYSIA. Founded as a tin-mining camp in 1857, it was made capital of the Federated Malay States in 1895, of the independent Federation of Malaya in 1957, and of Malaysia in 1963. It is the site of the world's tallest buildings, the PETRONAS TOWERS. Its educational institutions include the Univ. of Malaya and Universiti Kebangsaan.

Kuang-chou See GUANGZHOU

Kuan Han-ch'ing See GUAN HANQING

Kuan-yin See AVALOKITESVARA

Kuan Yu See GUAN YU

Kubitschek (de Oliveira) \\'kü-bə-ˌchek\\, **Juscelino** (1902–1976) President of Brazil (1956–61). A doctor, he became mayor of Belo Horizonte and governor of Minas Gerais. As president he promoted rapid development of the hydroelectric, steel, and other heavy industries and built 11,000 mi (18,000 km) of roads. He moved the government from Rio de Janeiro to BRASÍLIA, 600 mi (1,000 km) inland, to accelerate development of Brazil's vast interior. One result was rapid and persistent inflation, exacerbated by the cost of aiding the drought-stricken NE region.

Kublai Khan \\'kü-blə-'kän\\ (1215–1294) Grandson of GENGHIS KHAN who conquered China and established the YUAN (Mongol) DYNASTY. His brother, the emperor MONGKE, gave Kublai the task of conquering and administering SONG-DYNASTY China. Recognizing the superiority of Chinese thought, he gathered around himself Confucian advisers who convinced him of the importance of clemency toward the conquered. In subduing China and establishing himself there, he alienated other Mongol princes; but he succeeded in reunifying China, subduing first the North and then the South by 1279. To

Kublai Khan

restore China's prestige, Kublai engaged in wars on its periphery with Burma, Java, Japan, and the nations of Indochina, suffering some disastrous defeats. At home, he set up a four-tiered society, with the Mongols and other Central Asian peoples forming the top two tiers, the inhabitants of N China ranking next, and those of S China on the bottom. Posts of importance were allotted to foreigners, including Marco POLO. Kublai repaired the GRAND CANAL and public granaries and made BUDDHISM the state religion; his reign was one of brilliant prosperity.

Kubrick \\'kyü-brik\\, **Stanley** (1928–1999) U.S. film director. Born in New York City, he directed his first feature film, *Fear and Desire*, in 1953. He won fame with *Paths of Glory* (1957); it was followed by *Spartacus* (1960), *Lolita* (1962), *Dr. Strangelove* (1964), *2001: A Space Odyssey* (1968), *A Clockwork Orange* (1971), *Barry Lyndon* (1975), *The Shining* (1980), *Full Metal Jacket* (1987), and *Eyes Wide Shut* (1999). His films are characterized by a cool visual style, meticulous attention to detail, and a detached, often ironic pessimism. He lived in England from 1961.

kudu Slender African ANTELOPES of the genus *Tragelaphus*. The greater kudu lives in small groups in hilly bush country or open woods. It stands about 50 in. (1.3 m) high at the shoulder and is reddish brown to blue-gray, with narrow vertical white stripes on the body. The male has long, corkscrewlike horns. The lesser kudu lives in pairs or small groups in open bush country; it stands about 40 in. (1 m) high and has more tightly spiraled horns. Both species browse on shrubs and leaves.

kudzu vine \\'kùd-ˌzü\\ Fast-growing, twining, perennial, woody vine (*Pueraria lobata*, or *P. thunbergiana*) belonging to the pea family (see LEGUME). Transplanted from China and Japan to N. America in the 1870s as an attractive ornamental that could be planted on steep soil banks to prevent erosion, kudzu has become a rampant weed in the SE U.S, where it readily spreads to form great canopies over trees

K L

and exposed soil. Roots survive even N winters, and the hairy vine grows to a length of 60 ft (18 m) in one season. In its native range kudzu is grown for its edible, starchy roots and for a fiber made from its stems, and used as a fodder crop.

Kuei-yang See GUIYANG

Kuhn \'kün\, **Thomas (Samuel)** (1922–1996) U.S. historian and philosopher of science. Born in Cincinnati, he taught at Berkeley (1956–64), Princeton (1964–79), and MIT (1979–91). In his highly influential *The Structure of Scientific Revolutions* (1962), he questioned the accepted view of scientific progress as a gradual accumulation of knowledge based on methodical experimentation, claiming that progress was often achieved by far-reaching "paradigm shifts." His other works include *The Copernican Revolution* (1957) and *The Essential Tension* (1977).

Kuiper belt \'kī-pər\ *or* **Edgeworth-Kuiper belt** Disk-shaped belt of billions of small, icy bodies orbiting the sun beyond the orbit of NEPTUNE, mostly at 30–100 astronomical units, believed to extend thinly out to the OORT CLOUD. Gerard Peter Kuiper (1905–1973) proposed its existence in 1949 as part of a theory of the origin of the solar system (see SOLAR NEBULA); Kenneth Edgeworth (1880–1972) reached the same conclusions independently. Disturbances by Neptune's gravity of objects in the belt probably give rise to many of the short-period COMETS. The first Kuiper-belt object was discovered in 1992, though some astronomers regard PLUTO as the largest known Kuiper-belt object rather than a planet.

Kukai \'kü-ˌkī\ *or* **Kobo Daishi** (774–835) Japanese Buddhist saint and founder of the Shingon school of esoteric Buddhism. After studying in China (804–6) with Huiguo (746–805), he returned home to spread his doctrines, which emphasized magic formulas, ceremonials, and services for the dead. In 816 he built a temple on Mt. Koya. His *Ten Stages of Consciousness* traces the development of Confucianism, Taoism, and Buddhism, representing Shingon as the highest stage. He was also a gifted poet, artist, and calligrapher.

Ku Klux Klan (KKK) Either of two U.S. terrorist groups. The first was organized by veterans of the Confederate Army, first as a social club and then as a secret means of resistance to RECONSTRUCTION, with the goal of restoring white supremacy. Dressed in robes and sheets, Klansmen whipped and killed freedmen and their white supporters in nighttime raids. Having largely accomplished its goals by the 1870s, it gradually faded away. The second KKK arose in 1915, partly out of fear of the Russian Revolution and the changing ethnic character of U.S. society; it counted Catholics, Jews, foreigners, and labor unions among its enemies. Its membership peaked in the 1920s, with over 4 million members, but declined during the GREAT DEPRESSION. It became active again during the CIVIL-RIGHTS MOVEMENT, with bombings, whippings, and shootings attributed to it, but growing racial tolerance and a government crackdown reduced its numbers to a few thousand.

kulak (Russian: "fist") Wealthy or prosperous landed peasant in Russia. Before the RUSSIAN REVOLUTION OF 1917, kulaks were major figures in peasant villages. The early Soviet government undermined the kulaks' position by organizing poor peasants to administer the villages. The kulaks regained their position under the NEW ECONOMIC POLICY, but in 1929 the government began a drive for rapid collectivization and "liquidation of the kulaks as a class." By 1934 most kulaks had been deported to remote regions and their land confiscated.

Kulturkampf \kúl-'túr-ˌkämpf\ (German: "culture struggle") Bitter struggle by Otto von BISMARCK to subject the Roman Catholic church to state controls. Bismarck, a staunch Protestant, doubted the loyalty of Catholics in his new German empire; in 1872 the state dissolved the JESUIT order in Germany, and in 1875 it mandated civil marriage services. Bismarck retreated in the face of strong Catholic resistance, especially by the Center Party. By 1887 many anti-Catholic laws had been repealed.

Kumasi \kü-'mä-sē\ *formerly* **Coomassie** \kü-'ma-sē\ City (pop., 1988 est.: 385,000), S central Ghana. A 17th-cent. ASHANTI king chose the site for his capital and conducted land negotiations under a kum tree, which gave the town its name. The British gained control of the city in 1874. Called

the "Garden City of W. Africa," it has one of the largest central markets in W Africa.

Kumin \'kyü-min\, **Maxine** *orig.* Maxine Winokur (b.1925) U.S. poet. Born in Philadelphia, she has written poetry in traditional forms that deals with loss, fragility, family, and the cycles of life and nature. Her New Hampshire farm inspired *Up Country* (1972, Pulitzer Prize); later collections include *The Retrieval System* (1978) and *Our Ground Time Here Will Be Brief* (1982). She has written numerous children's books, some with Anne SEXTON, as well as novels and short stories.

kumquat \'kəm-ˌkwät\ Any of several evergreen shrubs or small trees of the genus *Fortunella* (RUE, or citrus, FAMILY), or their fruit. Native to E Asia, kumquats are cultivated throughout the subtropics. They bear white, orange-like flowers followed by small, orange-yellow, oval fruit that has mildly acid, juicy pulp and an edible skin. Kumquats may be eaten fresh, preserved, or candied, or made into jams and jellies.

Kun \'kün\, **Bela** (1886–1939?) Hungarian communist leader. In World War I he was captured by the Russians, and became a Bolshevik. Returning to Hungary, in March 1919 Kun headed the new Hungarian Soviet Republic. He created a Red Army that reconquered much of the territory lost to Czechoslovaks and Romanians and eliminated moderates in the government. In August the regime collapsed, and Kun fled to Russia and became a leader of the COMINTERN. He later fell victim to Joseph STALIN's PURGE TRIALS.

kundalini \ˌkún-də-'lē-nē\ In some tantric forms of YOGA, the cosmic energy believed to be within everyone. Through a series of exercises involving posture, meditation, and breathing, a practitioner can force this energy up through the body to the top of the head. This brings about a sensation of bliss, as the ordinary self is dissolved into its eternal essence, ATMAN.

Kundera \'kün-de-rä\, **Milan** (b.1929) Czech-French writer. He worked as a jazz musician and taught film, but gradually turned to writing. His works were banned after he participated in Czechoslovakia's short-lived liberalization movement (1967–68), and he emigrated to France in 1975. His novels combine erotic comedy with political criticism. *The Joke* (1967) describes life under Stalin. *The Book of Laughter and Forgetting* (1979) and *The Unbearable Lightness of Being* (1984; film, 1988) were banned in his homeland until 1989. His later books include *Immortality* (1990), *Slowness* (1994), and *Identity* (1996).

kung fu *pinyin* gongfu. Ancient Chinese MARTIAL ART that is simultaneously a spiritual and a physical discipline. Its prescribed stances and actions are based on keen observations of human skeletal and muscular anatomy and physiology, and many of its movements are imitations of the fighting styles of animals. Its combative techniques resemble those used in KARATE and TAE KWON DO; kung fu performed as exercise resembles T'AI CHI CH'UAN.

Kunitz \'kyü-nits\, **Stanley (Jasspon)** (b.1905) U.S. poet. Born in Worcester, Mass., his verse was collected in such volumes as *Selected Poems 1928–1958* (1958, Pulitzer Prize). With *The Testing-Tree* (1971), he began to write shorter, looser, more emotional poetry. Among his later collections, noted for their subtle craftsmanship, are *The Coat Without a Seam* (1974), *Next-to-Last Things* (1985), and *Passing Through* (1995). In 2000 he was named U.S. poet laureate.

Kunlun Mountains *or* **K'un-lun Mountains** \'kün-'lün\ Mountain system, W Asia. It extends for 1,250 mi (2,000 km) through the W regions of China. From the PAMIRS of Tajikistan, it runs east to the Sino-Tibetan ranges in the province of Qinghai. It divides the Plateau of Tibet from the interior plains of central Asia. Its highest peak measures 25,348 ft (7,726 m).

Kunming *or* **K'un-ming** \'kün-'miŋ\ *formerly* **Yunnan** \'yü-'nän\ City (pop., 1999 est.: 1,350,000), capital of Yunnan province, S China. It has long been a commercial center at the junction of major trading routes. Known as Tuodong in the 8th–9th cent. A.D., it came under Chinese control in 1253; it became the provincial capital of Yunnan in 1276 and was visited by Marco POLO. It was transformed into a modern city in 1937 during the SINO–JAPANESE WAR, when Chinese evacuees from the north brought industrial plants and universities to Kunming.

Kunstler, William (Moses) (1919–1995) U.S. radical lawyer. Born in New York City, he earned a Bronze Star in World War II. In the 1950s and '60s he became involved with the AMERICAN CIVIL LIBERTIES UNION and with such clients as M. L. KING. He represented the black activists Stokely Carmichael and Bobby Seale, and later such notorious clients as Sheikh Omar Abdel Rahman, accused of conspiring to blow up the World Trade Center in 1993.

Kuomintang See GUOMINDANG

Kuo Mo-jo See GUO MORUO

Kurdistan Mountainous region with indefinite boundaries forming a nonpolitical region in SE Turkey, and in adjoining areas of NW Iran, NE Iraq, and NE Syria. It covers about 74,000 sq mi (191,660 sq km). Its chief towns include Van in Turkey and MOSUL and KIRKUK in Iraq. Since early times the region has been the home of the KURDS. The Treaty of Sèvres, signed in 1920, provided for the recognition of the Kurdistan state, but this treaty was never ratified. Kurdistan independence movements have been harshly repressed in all four countries.

Kurds Stateless ethnic and linguistic group numbering over 15 million people and living primarily in Iran, Iraq, and Turkey (see KURDISTAN). Traditionally nomadic, they were forced into farming by the redrawing of national borders after World War I. Most Kurds are Sunni Muslims; some are Sufis or adhere to other sects. Plans for a Kurdish state, promised by the Treaty of Sèvres (1920), which dissolved the Ottoman empire, were never realized. Kurds in Turkey, Iran, and Iraq have been persecuted and pressured to assimilate; Iraqi attacks were particularly severe during the IRAN–IRAQ WAR and the PERSIAN GULF WAR.

Kurdufan See KORDOFAN

Kuril Islands \'kyu̇r-ˌēl\ Archipelago, E Russia. It extends for 750 mi (1,200 km) from the S tip of Russia's KAMCHATKA peninsula to the NE coast of Japan's HOKKAIDO island. The 56 islands cover 6,000 sq mi (15,600 sq km). The Kurils were originally settled by the Russians in the 17th–18th cent. Japan seized the S islands and in 1875 traded SAKHALIN for the entire chain. After World War II, they were ceded to the Soviet Union, and the Japanese population was repatriated. Japan has tried repeatedly to regain the S islands.

Kurosawa \ˌku̇r-ə-'sau̇-ə\, **Akira** (1910–1998) Japanese film director. He studied painting before making his first film in 1943. He won notice with *Drunken Angel* (1948), starring Toshiro MIFUNE, and was internationally acclaimed for *Rashomon* (1950). His later classic films, including *Seven Samurai* (1954), *Throne of Blood* (1957), *The Hidden Fortress* (1958), *Kagemusha* (1980), and *Ran* (1985), combine Japanese aesthetic and cultural elements with a Western sense of action and drama. He received an honorary Academy Award for lifetime achievement in 1990.

Kush See CUSH

Kushner, Tony (b.1956) U.S. dramatist. Born in New York City, he grew up in Lake Charles, La. His major work, *Angels in America*, consists of two lengthy and ambitious plays that deal with political issues and the catastrophe of AIDS in the 1980s. The first part, *Millennium Approaches* (1991), won a Pulitzer Prize. Later works include *Slavs!* (1995), *Henry Box Brown* (1997), and *Homebody/Kabul* (2001).

Kutch, Rann of See Rann of KACHCHH

Kutuzov \kə-'tü-zȯf\, **Mikhail (Illarionovich Golenishchev-)** *later* **Prince Kutuzov** (1745–1813) Russian army commander. In 1805 he was given command of the joint Russian-Austrian army that opposed the French advance on Vienna. Following the French victory at AUSTERLITZ (1805) Kutuzov was partly blamed, but after NAPOLEON's army entered Russia in 1812 he was appointed commander in chief. When Napoleon led his troops in retreat from Moscow, Kutuzov forced the French army to leave Russia along the path it had devastated when it entered the country. He pursued the French into Prussia, destroying his opponent without fighting another major battle. Considered the finest Russian commander of his day, he appears as a major character in Leo TOLSTOY's *War and Peace*.

Kuwait *officially* **State of Kuwait** Country, NW coast of the PERSIAN GULF. Area: 6,880 sq mi (17,818 sq km). Population (2000): 1,984,000. Capital: KUWAIT city. Its population is about 80% Arab. Languages: Arabic (official), Persian,

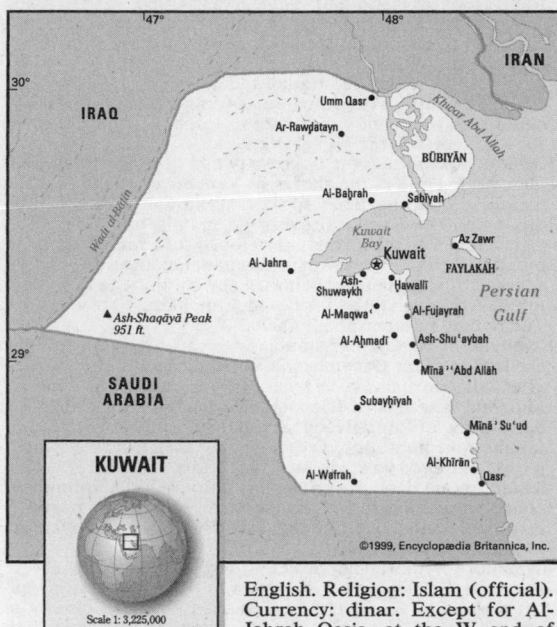

KUWAIT
Scale 1: 3,225,000
0   10   20   30 mi
0   15   30   45 km
©1999, Encyclopædia Britannica, Inc.

English. Religion: Islam (official). Currency: dinar. Except for Al-Jahrah Oasis, at the W end of Kuwait Bay, and a few fertile patches in the SE and coastal areas, it is largely desert; annual precipitation totals 1–7 in (25–180 mm). One-twelfth of the country serves as pastureland for livestock, including sheep and goats. Kuwait has almost no agricultural soil; its extensive petroleum and natural-gas deposits are the basis of its economy. Its estimated reserves of petroleum represent 10% of global reserves, ranking Kuwait third after Iraq and Saudi Arabia. It is a constitutional monarchy with one legislative body; the head of state and government is the emir, assisted by the prime minister. Faylakah island, in Kuwait Bay, had a civilization dating back to the 3rd millennium B.C. It flourished until 1200 B.C., when it disappeared from the historical record. Greek colonists again settled the island in the 4th cent. B.C. The nomadic Anizah tribe of central Arabia founded Kuwait city in 1710, and Abd Rahim of the SABAH DYNASTY became sheikh in 1756, the first of a family that continues to rule Kuwait. In 1899, to thwart German and Ottoman influences, Kuwait agreed to give Britain control of its foreign affairs. Following the outbreak of war with the Ottomans in 1914, Britain established a protectorate there. In 1961, after Kuwait gained full independence from Britain, Iraq laid claim to Kuwait. British troops were sent to defend Kuwait; the ARAB LEAGUE recognized its independence, and Iraq dropped its claim. During the IRAN–IRAQ WAR of the 1980s, Kuwait made large loans to Iraq. After talks on the repayment of war debts broke down, Iraqi forces invaded and occupied Kuwait in 1990. A U.S.-led military coalition drove the Iraqi army out of Kuwait in 1991 (see PERSIAN GULF WAR). The destruction of nearly half of Kuwait's 1,300 oil wells complicated reconstruction efforts.

Kuwait *or* **Kuwait City** City (pop., 1995: 29,000), capital of Kuwait. Located at the head of the PERSIAN GULF, it was founded in the 18th cent., and became a trading city relying on sea and caravan traffic. Development of the oil industry after World War II transformed the city. Almost all of the country's population is concentrated near the capital. The city was heavily damaged in 1990–91 during the Iraqi occupation and the PERSIAN GULF WAR.

KL

Kuybyshev See SAMARA

Kuznets \\'kəz-nets\\, **Simon (Smith)** (1901–1985) Russian-U.S. economist and statistician. He emigrated to the U.S. in 1922 and taught at the Univ. of Pennsylvania (1930–54), Johns Hopkins (1954–60), and Harvard (1960–71). His work emphasized the complexity of underlying data in the construction of economic models, stressing the need for information on population structure, technology, labor quality, government structure, trade, and markets. He described cyclical variations in growth rates (now called "Kuznets cycles") and their links with factors such as population. In 1971 he received the Nobel Prize.

Kwakiutl \\kwä-kē-'yü-t°l\\ NORTHWEST COAST INDIAN people who live along the shores of Vancouver Island and the mainland opposite. They speak a Wakashan language. Traditionally, the Kwakiutl subsisted mainly by fishing. The POTLATCH was elaborately developed and was often combined with dances and songs dramatizing ancestral experiences with supernatural beings. They continue to be known for their highly stylized art, which includes TOTEM POLES. Today they number about 4,000.

Kwanzaa or **Kwanza** \\'kwän-zə\\ African-American holiday celebrated from December 26 to January 1 and patterned after African harvest festivals. It was created in 1966 by Maulana Karenga, a black-studies professor at California State Univ. at Long Beach, as a nonreligious celebration of family and community. The name was taken from the Swahili phrase *matunda ya kwanzaa* ("first fruits"). Each day is dedicated to one of seven principles: unity, self-determination, collective responsibility, cooperative economics, purpose, creativity, and faith. Kwanzaa is now observed by more than 15 million people.

kwashiorkor \\,kwä-shē-'òr-kər\\ Condition caused by severe PROTEIN deficiency. It is common in tropical and subtropical regions in young children weaned on a diet chiefly of starchy foods. It causes potbelly, EDEMA, weakness, irritability, dry skin with rash, reddish-orange hair discoloration, DIARRHEA, ANEMIA, and fat deposits in the liver. Mental development may be stunted. Adults who had the disease in childhood may be at risk of diseases such as CIRRHOSIS. Treatment is protein supplementation, often in the form of dried skim milk. Nondietary causes include inadequate absorption of nutrients by the intestines, chronic alcoholism, kidney disease, and trauma (e.g., infection, burns) causing abnormal protein loss.

Kworra River See NIGER RIVER

Kyd \\'kid\\, **Thomas** (1558–1594) English dramatist. With *The Spanish Tragedie* (1592), one of the most popular plays of its time, he initiated the revenge tragedy, a favorite dramatic form in the Elizabethan and Jacobean eras. The only other play certainly by Kyd is *Cornelia* (1594). He was arrested and tortured in 1593 after "atheistical" documents were found in his room. His reputation ruined, he died the next year at 36.

Kynewulf See CYNEWULF

Kyoto City (pop., 1995: 1,464,000), W central HONSHU, Japan. The center of Japanese culture and Japanese Buddhism, Kyoto was the capital of Japan and the site of the imperial family residence for more than 1,000 years (794–1868). The modern city has theaters that present NO DRAMA and KABUKI. Many small workshops produce textiles and porcelain. Buddhist temples and Shinto shrines are found throughout the city. It is also a manufacturing center. Its educational institutions include Kyoto Univ. (founded 1897) and Doshisha Univ. (1875).

Kyrgyzstan \\,kir-giz-'stan\\ *officially* **Kyrgyz Republic** Country, central Asia. On the southeast, the Kok Shaal-Tau Range, part of the Tian Shan, forms the border with China. Area: 76,600 sq mi (198,500 sq km). Population (2000): 4,895,000. Capital: BISHKEK. The Kyrgyz make up about

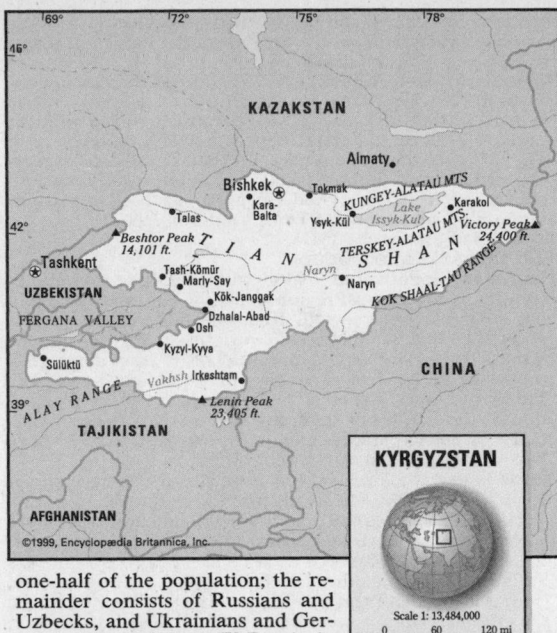

©1999, Encyclopædia Britannica, Inc.

KYRGYZSTAN

Scale 1: 13,484,000

one-half of the population; the remainder consists of Russians and Uzbeks, and Ukrainians and Germans deported from W Russia in 1941. Languages: Kyrgyz, Russian (both official). Religion: Islam (Sunnite). Currency: som. Kyrgyzstan is a largely mountainous country. At its E edge rises Pobeda Peak, which at 24,406 ft (7,439 m) is the country's highest peak. The country's valleys and plains, occupying only one-seventh of the total area, are home to most of its people. The economy is based largely on agriculture, including livestock raising and the cultivation of cereals, potatoes, cotton, and sugar beets. Coal mining and industries such as food processing and the production of machinery are also important. It is a republic with two legislative houses; its head of state and government is the president, assisted by the prime minister. The Kyrgyz, a nomadic people of central Asia, settled in the Tian Shan region in ancient times. They were conquered by GENGHIS KHAN's son Jochi in 1207. The area became part of the Qing empire of China in the mid-18th cent. The region came under Russian control in the 19th cent., and its rebellion against the Soviet Union in 1916 resulted in a long period of brutal repression. Kirgiziya became an autonomous province of the Soviet Union in 1924 and was made the Kirgiz Soviet Socialist Republic in 1936. Kyrgyzstan gained independence in 1991. It has since struggled with its democratization process and with establishing a thriving economy.

Kyushu Island (pop., 1995: 13,420,000), southernmost of Japan's four main islands. Located off the E coast of Asia, it is separated from HONSHU to the north by the Shimonoseki Strait and from Shikoku to the east by the Bungo Strait. The island, with an area of 14,177 sq mi (36,719 sq km), is mountainous with several famous peaks of 5,000–6,000 ft (1,525–1,980 m). Its chief cities include FUKUOKA and KITAKYUSHU.

Kyzil Kum \\ki-'zil-'küm\\ Desert in Kazakstan and Uzbekistan. Occupying 115,000 sq mi (300,000 sq km), it lies southeast of the ARAL SEA. Desert plants support sheep, horses, and camels; there are several small oasis settlements. Its resources include natural gas deposits and gold.

L

labor In economics, the general body of wage earners. In CLASSICAL ECONOMICS, labor is one of the three factors of production, along with CAPITAL and LAND. Labor can also be used to describe work performed, including any valuable service rendered by a human agent in the production of wealth, other than accumulating and providing capital. Labor is performed for the sake of its product or, in modern economic life, for the sake of a share of the total product of the community's industry. The price per unit of time, or wage rate, commanded by a particular kind of labor in the MARKET depends not only on the technical efficiency of the laborer but also on the demand for his services and on the supply of other workers. Other variables include the training, skill, and intelligence of workers and the social status, prospects for advancement, and relative difficulty of the work.

labor See PARTURITION

Labor, Knights of See KNIGHTS OF LABOR

Labor, U.S. Department of Federal executive division responsible for enforcing labor statutes and promoting the general welfare of U.S. wage earners. Established in 1913, it controls the Occupational Safety and Health Administration (OSHA) and numerous other agencies involved in administration of programs concerning employment and training, trade adjustment assistance, unemployment insurance, veterans and senior citizens, and mine safety.

Labor Day Annual holiday devoted to the recognition of working people's contribution to society. It is observed on the first Monday in September in the U.S. and Canada. It was first celebrated in New York in 1882, under the sponsorship of the KNIGHTS OF LABOR; in 1894 Congress made it a national holiday. In most other countries, workers are honored on MAY DAY.

labor economics Study of how workers are allocated among jobs, how their rates of pay are determined, and how their efficiency is affected by various factors. Critical considerations include qualities of the labor force itself (such as health, level of education, distribution of special training and skills, and degree of mobility), structural characteristics of the economy (e.g., proportions of heavy manufacturing, high-technology, and service industries), and institutional factors (including the extent and effect of LABOR UNIONS, employers' associations, and minimum-wage laws). Custom and variations in the BUSINESS CYCLE are also considered. Certain general trends are widely accepted by labor economists; for instance, wage levels tend to be higher in industries that require higher levels of education or training, in economies that have high proportions of such industries, and in industries that are heavily unionized.

labor law Body of law applied to employment, wages, conditions of work, LABOR UNIONS, labor-management relations, and so on. Employment laws cover such matters as hiring, training, advancement, and UNEMPLOYMENT compensation. Wage laws cover the forms and methods of payment, pay rates, SOCIAL SECURITY, PENSIONS, and other matters. Legislation on working conditions regulates hours, rest periods, vacations, child labor, equality in the workplace, and health and safety. Laws on trade unions and labor-management relations deal with the status of unions, the rights and obligations of workers' and employers' organizations, COLLECTIVE-BARGAINING agreements, and rules for settling STRIKES and other disputes. See also ARBITRATION, MEDIATION.

Labor Relations Act, National See WAGNER ACT

labor union Association of workers in a particular trade, industry, or plant, formed to obtain improvements in pay, benefits, and working conditions. The first fraternal and self-help associations of laborers appeared in Britain in the 18th cent., and the era of modern labor unions began in Britain, Europe, and the U.S. in the 19th cent. The movement met with hostility from employers and governments, and union organizers were regularly prosecuted. British unionism received its legal foundation in the Trade-Union Act of 1871. In the U.S. the same effect was achieved more slowly through a series of court decisions. The founding of the American Federation of Labor (AFL) in 1886 marked the beginning of a large-scale labor movement in the U.S. The unions brought together in the AFL were craft unions, representing workers skilled in a particular craft or trade. Early organizers showed little interest in unions representing all workers, skilled or unskilled, in a single industry, but in 1935 the Congress of Industrial Organizations (CIO) was founded by unions expelled from the AFL for attempting to organize unskilled workers, and by 1941 it had organized the entire steel and automobile industries (see AFL-CIO). The use of COLLECTIVE BARGAINING to settle wages, working conditions, and disputes became standard in all non-communist industrial countries. In Britain, labor unions demonstrated political activity that culminated in the formation of the LABOUR PARTY in 1906. In France, too, the major unions are highly politicized; the Confédération Générale du Travail (formed in 1895) was allied with the Communist Party for many years. Japan developed a form of union organization known as enterprise unionism, which represents workers in a single plant or multiplant setting rather than within a craft or industry.

Labour Party British political party. In opposition to the CONSERVATIVE PARTY, it is Britain's major democratic socialist party. Formed from two trade-union groups, it took the name Labour Party in 1906. In 1918 it became a socialist party with a democratic constitution, and by 1922 it had supplanted the LIBERAL PARTY as the official opposition party. In 1924 Ramsay MACDONALD formed the first Labour government, with Liberal support. The party was out of power 1935–45; then a spectacular recovery brought in Clement ATTLEE's government (until 1951), which introduced a system of social welfare, including a national health service, and extensive nationalization of industry. Labour regained power under Harold WILSON (1964–70) and later James CALLAGHAN (1974–79), but foundered because of economic problems and worsening relations with its trade-union allies. Only in 1997 did Tony BLAIR and his "New Labour" agenda succeed in returning Labour to power.

Labrador Large peninsula, NE Canada. It is divided between Quebec and Newfoundland provinces and occupies an area of about 625,000 sq mi (1,620,000 sq km). Its highest mountains are over 5,000 ft (1,520 m), and its coast is lined with islands. The N portion is tundra; the S portion is coniferous forest. A few tiny settlements dot the coast. The peninsula is rich in mineral and timber resources. Politically, Labrador refers to the Newfoundland portion of the peninsula; the Quebec portion is Ungava Peninsula.

Labrador Current Surface oceanic current flowing southward along the W side of the Labrador Sea. It maintains temperatures of less than 32°F (0°C) and has a low salinity. The current is limited to the CONTINENTAL SHELF and reaches depths of about 2,000 ft (600 m). It carries several thousand ICEBERGS southward each year.

La Brea Tar Pits \lə-'brā-ə\ Fossil field in Hancock Park (formerly Rancho La Brea), LOS ANGELES. It is the site of "pitch springs" oozing crude oil. The tar pits contain the fossilized bones of PLEISTOCENE mammals that became entrapped there; they include MAMMOTHS, MASTODONS, and SABER-TOOTHED CATS. The George C. Page Museum contains more than one million specimens exhumed from the pits.

La Bruyère \lä-brüē-'yer\, **Jean de** (1645–1696) French satiric moralist. Employed in a royal household, he observed aristocratic idleness, fads, and fashions. His *The Characters, or Manners of the Age, with the Characters of Theophrastus* (1688) was appended to his translation of Theophrastus and written in the latter's style. A masterpiece of French literature, it was an indictment of the vanity and pretensions around him.

labyrinth *or* **maze** System of intricate passageways and blind alleys. Ancient Greek and Roman labyrinths were buildings, entirely or partly underground, with many chambers and passages, making exit difficult. From the European Renaissance on, formal gardens featured labyrinths or mazes consisting of intricate paths separated by high hedges.

Lacan \lä-'kän\, **Jacques (Marie Émile)** (1901–1981) French psychoanalyst. Lacan introduced the study of language into psychoanalytic theory. His major achievement was his reinterpretation of Sigmund FREUD's work in terms of structural LINGUISTICS. He became a celebrity in France with *Écrits* (1966; *The Language of the Self*) and in the 1970s was a dominant figure in French cultural life as well as a strong influence on American psychoanalytic and literary theory.

lace Ornamental openwork fabric formed by the looping, interlacing, braiding, or twisting of threads, originally primarily of linen. Almost all high-quality artistic lace is made by one of two techniques: needle lace involves a difficult technique that originated in Italy; bobbin lace is a more widespread craft that originated in Flanders. By 1600 lace had become a fabric of luxury and an important article of commerce. After the Industrial Revolution, machines produced less-expensive lace made of cotton, and lace gradually disappeared from fashion. By 1920 the industry was dying. Fine handmade lace is still made in Belgium, Italy, and elsewhere, but chiefly as souvenirs.

Lacedaemon See SPARTA

lacemaking Methods of producing LACE. The popularity of handmade laces led to the invention of lacemaking MACHINES in the 19th cent. Later improvements included Nottingham-lace machines, primarily for coarse lace, and Barmens machines. Schiffli lace, a type of embroidery, is made by modern machines, using needles with points at each end. Machine-made laces frequently have geometrically shaped nets forming their backgrounds. The high strength and low cost of man-made fiber yarns has made sheer laces widely available.

lacewing Any of many species of insects in the order Neuroptera, especially those in the green lacewing and brown lacewing families. The lacewing has long, delicate antennae, a slender body, and two pairs of veined wings. It is found worldwide, flying near grasses and shrubs. It is also known as a stinkfly because it emits a disagreeable odor. The larva, with prominent sucking mouthparts, drains body fluids from aphids and other soft-bodied insects.

Lachaise \lä-'shez\, **Gaston** (1882–1935) French-U.S. sculptor. Trained in the decorative arts, he studied sculpture in Paris and was a designer of Art Nouveau decorative objects for René LALIQUE before emigrating to the U.S. in 1906. His most famous work, *Standing Woman* (1912–27), a female nude with enormous breasts and thighs and sinuous, tapered limbs, typifies the image he worked and reworked throughout his career. He is also known for his portrait busts of John MARIN, Marianne MOORE, E. E. CUMMINGS, and others.

lachrymal duct and gland See TEAR DUCT AND GLAND

Lackland, John See JOHN (ENGLAND)

Laclos \lä-'klō\, **Pierre (-Ambroise-François) Choderlos de** (1741–1803) French writer. He chose an army career, but soon left it to become a writer. His *Les liaisons dangereuses* (1782; *Dangerous Liaisons*), one of the earliest psychological novels, is the EPISTOLARY NOVEL of a noble seducer and his female accomplice who take unscrupulous delight in their victims' misery. It caused an immediate sensation and was banned for years. Returning to the army, Laclos ultimately rose to the rank of general under Napoleon.

La Coruña \lä-kō-'rü-nyä\ Seaport city (pop., 1998 est.: 243,000), NW Spain. It was part of the caliphate of CORDOBA. The point of departure for the SPANISH ARMADA in 1588, it was sacked by Francis DRAKE in 1589. In the PENINSULAR WAR, it was the site of a notable victory by the English over the French.

lacquerwork Decorative objects or surfaces, usually of wood, to which a colored, highly polished, and opaque type of varnish called lacquer has been applied. Chinese or Japanese in origin, the lacquerwork technique was copied in Europe, where it was known as "japanning," but European lacquerwork lacks the hardness and brilliance of Asian lacquer. True lacquer is the purified and dehydrated sap of the *Rhus verniciflua* tree, native to China and cultivated in Japan. Many thin layers of lacquer are applied, allowed to dry, and smoothed before the surface is ready for decoration by carving, engraving, or inlay.

lacrosse Outdoor team sport in which players use a long-handled stick that has a triangular head with a mesh pouch for catching, carrying, and throwing a hard rubber ball with the object of slinging it into an opponent's goal. Adapted by French settlers in Canada from an ancient American Indian event that was at once sport, combat training, and mystical ceremony, it became an organized sport in the late 19th cent. Modern teams have 10 players. The game is divided into four periods of 15 minutes each. Especially popular as a collegiate sport, it is played by both men and women.

lactation Production of milk by female mammals after giving birth. The milk is discharged by the MAMMARY GLANDS in the breasts. Hormones triggered by delivery of the placenta and by nursing stimulate milk production. Colostrum (milk that the mother produces in the first few days after

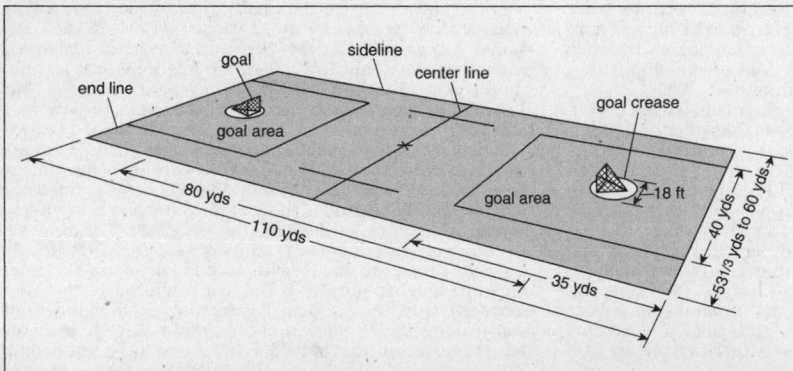

Lacrosse A typical men's lacrosse field. The women's game is often played on a larger field (120 x 82 yards), with the goals 100 yards apart, and usually without the outside boundary lines marked. The ball is put into play by a face-off at the middle of the field, and play is continuous except for goals, fouls, and timeouts. Players may kick the ball, but only the goalie may use his hands.

end line · goal · sideline · center line · goal area · goal crease · goal area · 80 yds · 110 yds · 35 yds · 18 ft · 40 yds · 53⅓ yds to 60 yds

giving birth) has more proteins, minerals, and antibodies and fewer calories and fats than the mature milk that develops later. Mature milk supplies nutrients, hormones, and substances that provide the infant with IMMUNITY against infectious agents. The American Academy of Pediatrics recommends that babies be fed mother's milk exclusively for the first six months and that nursing continue through the first year. Mothers taking certain drugs or with some diseases (e.g., AIDS) should not nurse, because of risks to the baby.

lactic acid CARBOXYLIC ACID found in certain plant juices, in blood and muscle, and in soil. Stiffness and soreness after prolonged heavy exercise are due to accumulated lactic acid in muscles. The end product of bacterial FERMENTATION, lactic acid is the commonest acidic constituent of fermented milk products (e.g., sour milk and cream, cheese, buttermilk, yogurt). It is used in other foods as a flavoring or preservative and industrially in tanning leather and dyeing wool and as a raw material or catalyst in many chemical processes.

lactobacillus \,lak-tō-bə-'si-ləs\ Any of the rod-shaped, gram-positive (see GRAM STAIN) bacteria of the genus *Lactobacillus*, widely distributed in animal feeds, manure, and milk and milk products. Various species are used to produce sour milks, cheeses, yogurt, fermented vegetables (pickles and sauerkraut), beverages (beer, wine, and juices), sourdough breads, and some sausages. They inhabit but do not damage animal and human intestinal tracts. Lactobacilli may be used to restore normal intestinal flora after antibiotic therapy.

lactose Slightly sweet SUGAR (disaccharide) composed of two MONOSACCHARIDES, GLUCOSE and galactose, linked together. Lactose-intolerant people cannot digest lactose because they lack the ENZYME (lactase) that splits it into simpler sugars and suffer DIARRHEA and bloating when they eat foods containing it. Lactose, which makes up 2–8% of the milk of mammals, is the only common sugar of animal origin. It is used in foods, in pharmaceuticals, and in nutrient broths used to produce penicillin, yeast, and riboflavin, and other products.

Ladakh \lə-'däk\ Region, E Kashmir, part of KASHMIR state, N India. It covers about 45,000 sq mi (117,000 sq km) and includes the W Himalayan Ladakh Range (see HIMALAYAS), the KARAKORAM RANGE, and the upper INDUS RIVER valley. India and Pakistan fought over it; a treaty in 1949 gave its S portion to India and the rest to Pakistan. In the Sino–Indian War of 1962 China gained a portion of NE Ladakh. The region's boundaries are still in dispute.

Ladd-Franklin, Christine *orig.* Christine Ladd (1847–1930) U.S. scientist and logician. Born in Windsor, Conn., she fulfilled PhD requirements at Johns Hopkins Univ. in the 1880s, but because women candidates were not recognized, was not awarded her degree until 1926. In symbolic logic, she reduced syllogistic reasoning to an inconsistent triad with the introduction of the antilogism, a form that made the testing of deductions easier. The Ladd-Franklin theory of color vision stressed increasing color differentiation with evolution and assumed a photochemical model for the visual system.

Ladies' Home Journal U.S. monthly magazine. Founded in 1883 as a supplement to the *Tribune and Farmer* (1879–85), it became an independent publication in 1884. Under Edward BOK (1889–1919), it became an outstanding success, with a circulation surpassing that of any other U.S. publication. Bok revolutionized the women's-magazine field by offering high-quality fiction and nonfiction, establishing service departments that answered letters from readers, and conveying a sense of intimacy.

Ladislas I *or* **St. Ladislas** \'lä-dē-,släs\ (1040–1095) King of Hungary (1077–95). He greatly expanded the boundaries of the kingdom, gaining land in Transylvania and occupying Croatia (1091). Ladislas introduced Roman Catholicism to Croatia and persecuted pagans in his dominions. He also promulgated a legal code that brought order and prosperity to Hungary. He died while preparing for the First CRUSADE.

Ladoga \'lä-də-gə\, **Lake** Lake, W Russia. The largest lake in Europe, it covers an area of 6,700 sq mi (17,600 sq km). It contains 660 islands of more than 2.5 acres (1 hectare) in area. Its outlet is the NEVA RIVER, in the SW corner. Formerly divided between the U.S.S.R. and Finland, it now lies entirely within Russia. During the Siege of LENINGRAD (1941–44), the lake was the lifeline that connected the city with the rest of the Soviet Union.

Ladrone Islands See MARIANA ISLANDS

ladybug *or* **ladybird beetle** Any of about 5,000 widely distributed BEETLES of the family Coccinellidae. In the Middle Ages the beetle was dedicated to the Virgin Mary and called "beetle of Our Lady." Ladybugs are hemispheric, and are usually 0.3–0.4 in. (8–10 mm) long. They have short legs and are usually brightly colored with black, yellow, or reddish markings. Several generations are produced each summer. Ladybugs are often used to control such pests as APHIDS, SCALE INSECTS, and MITES, which they eat.

lady's slipper Any member of several genera of ORCHIDS in which the lip of the flower is slipper-shaped. The genus *Cypripedium* has about 50 temperate and subtropical species. Two well-known species, the yellow lady's slipper (*C. calceolus*) and the pink lady's slipper, or moccasin flower (*C. acaule*), are found in temperate coniferous woods in early spring. Many hybrids have been developed.

Laemmle \'lem-lē\, **Carl** (1867–1939) German-U.S. film producer. Emigrating to the U.S. in 1884, he opened a nickelodeon in Chicago in 1906 and became a leading film distributor. He founded the Independent Motion Picture Co. in 1909 and induced such stars as Mary PICKFORD to join his studio. He produced 100 short films by 1910, then merged with smaller companies to form UNIVERSAL PICTURES, and in 1915 he opened its 230-acre studio. His employees included Irving THALBERG and Harry COHN.

Lafayette, marquis de *orig.* Marie-Joseph-Paul-Yves-Roch-Gilbert du Motier (1757–1834) French military leader. A courtier at the court of LOUIS XVI, he sought glory as a soldier. In 1777 he went to Philadelphia, became a close friend of George WASHINGTON, and fought with distinction at the Battle of BRANDYWINE. He returned to France in 1779, persuaded Louis to send a 6,000-man force, and returned to America in 1780 to command an army in Virginia and help win the Siege of YORKTOWN. Hailed as "the Hero of Two Worlds," he returned to France in 1782. Elected to the Estates General in 1789, he presented the DECLARATION OF THE RIGHTS OF MAN AND OF THE CITIZEN to the National Assembly. As commander of the national guard of Paris, he sought to protect the king, but when his guards fired on a crowd of petitioners in the Champ de Mars (1791), he lost popularity and resigned his position. He commanded the army against Austria (1792), then defected to the Austrians, who held him captive until 1797. Returning to France, Lafayette became a gentleman farmer. In the BOURBON RESTORATION, he served in the Chamber of Deputies (1814–24) and commanded the national guard in the July Revolution (1830).

Laffite \lə-'fēt\, **Jean** (1780?–1825?) French pirate. He led a band of privateers that preyed on Spanish ships and smuggled goods and slaves through New Orleans. In the War of 1812 the British offered Laffite $30,000 for his allegiance in their planned attack on the city. He warned Louisiana officials but was not believed. He then offered his aid to Gen. Andrew JACKSON, who accepted Laffite's help in the Battle of NEW ORLEANS. After the war Laffite returned to privateering against the Spanish.

Laffitte \lä-'fēt\, **Jacques** (1767–1844) French banker and politician. As governor of the Bank of France (1814–19), he raised large sums of money for the provisional government in 1814 and for LOUIS XVIII during the HUNDRED DAYS. He saved Paris from a financial crisis in 1818. An influential early partisan of a constitutional monarchy under LOUISPHILIPPE, he served as premier (1830–31) in the JULY MONARCHY.

La Follette \lə-'fäl-ət\, **Robert M(arion)** (1855–1925) U.S. politician. Born in Primrose, Wis., he served as a U.S. Representative (1885–91) and as governor of Wisconsin (1901–6). In the U.S. Senate (1906–24), he sponsored bills to restrict the railroads' power. He founded *La Follette's Weekly* (1909) to broaden his reform movement, and led Republican opposition to the policies of Pres. W. H. TAFT. He opposed U.S. entrance into World War I and policies of Pres.

K L

Woodrow WILSON that favored big business, and he vigorously exposed postwar corruption, including the TEAPOT DOME SCANDAL. As the PROGRESSIVE PARTY's presidential candidate in 1924, he won 5 million votes. He died the next year; his son Robert (1895–1953) held his Senate seat until 1947.

La Fontaine \là-fōⁿ-'ten\, **Jean de** (1621–1695) French poet. He is best known for his *Fables* (1668–94), which rank among the masterpieces of French literature. Comprising some 240 poems, they include timeless tales about simple countryfolk, heroes of Greek mythology, and the familiar animals of FABLES. Their chief theme is the everyday moral experience of humankind. His many lesser works include *The Loves of Cupid and Psyche* (1669) and the often licentious *Tales and Novels in Verse* (1664–74).

Jean de La Fontaine Painting by François De Troy

LaFontaine \là-fòⁿ-'tan\, **Louis Hippolyte** (*later* **Sir Louis**) (1807–1864) Canadian statesman. Born in Boucherville, Lower Canada (now Quebec), he was elected to the provincial assembly in 1830. He supported French-Canadian grievances against the British but opposed the rebellions of 1837–38. Appointed joint prime minister with Robert Baldwin (1842–43, 1848–51), he established responsible (i.e., representative) government for Canada. His Rebellion Losses Bill, to compensate property owners for damages in 1837–38, provoked riots in Montreal but affirmed the strength of the government.

Lagash \'lä-ˌgash\ *modern* **Telloh** \'tel-ō\ Ancient capital in SUMER. It was located midway between the TIGRIS and EUPHRATES rivers in BABYLONIA, now modern SE Iraq. Excavations have uncovered palace and temple ruins as well as CUNEIFORM texts that provide knowledge of Sumer in the 3rd millennium B.C. Founded in the Ubaid Period (c.5200–c.3500 B.C.), it was occupied as late as the Parthian era (247 B.C.–A.D. 224).

Lagerkvist \'lä-gər-ˌkvēst\, **Pär (Fabian)** (1891–1974) Swedish writer. Though his early works are characterized by extreme pessimism, he declared his faith in humanity with his great prose monologue *The Triumph over Life* (1927). In the 1930s and '40s his writings protested fascism and brutality. The novel *The Dwarf* (1944) was his first best-seller and his first undisputed critical success. He won world recognition with the novel *Barabbas* (1950). He was awarded the Nobel Prize in 1951.

Lagerlöf \'lä-gər-ˌlœf\, **Selma (Ottiliana Lovisa)** (1858–1940) Swedish novelist. Her first novel, *Gösta Berlings saga* (1891), chronicles life in her native Värmland. Later works include *Jerusalem* (1901–2), which established her as Sweden's foremost novelist. A gifted storyteller, she rooted her work in legend and saga. In 1909 she became the first woman to win the Nobel Prize for Literature.

Selma Lagerlöf, 1909

lagoon Area of relatively shallow, quiet water with access to the sea but separated from it by sandbars, barrier islands, or CORAL REEFS. Coastal lagoons have low to moderate tides and constitute about 13% of the world's coastline. Their water is colder than the sea in winter and warmer in summer. In warm regions, evaporation may result in hypersaline water and even the buildup of thick salt deposits. Coral-reef lagoons occur on marginal reefs such as the Great Barrier Reef, but the most spectacular examples, some more than 30 mi (50 km) across, are associated with Pacific atolls.

Lagos \'lä-ˌgäs, 'lä-gəs\ City (pop., 1996 est.: 1,518,000) and chief port, Nigeria. It is Nigeria's largest city, built on four main islands on the Bight of Benin connected by bridges. Settled in the 15th cent., it was dominated by Benin in the 16th–19th cent. The Portuguese established a slave trade there in 1472. It was ceded to Britain in 1861, became a crown colony, and was governed from Sierra Leone (1866–74) and as part of the Gold Coast colony (1874–86). It was made the capital of the colony of Nigeria in 1914. It was the capital (1960–91) of independent Nigeria, until ABUJA became the new capital. It is a major trade and industrial center.

Lagrange \là-'gräⁿzh\, **Joseph-Louis** *later* comte (Count) de L'Empire (1736–1813) Italian-French mathematician who made important contributions to NUMBER THEORY and to classical and celestial mechanics. By age 25 he was recognized as one of the greatest living mathematicians because of his papers on wave propagation and maxima and minima (see MAXIMUM, MINIMUM) of curves. His prodigious output included his textbook *Mécanique analytique* (1788; "Analytical Mechanics"), the basis for all later work in this field.

La Guardia \lə-'gwär-dē-ə\, **Fiorello H(enry)** (1882–1947) U.S. politician, mayor of New York (1933–45). Born in New York City, he practiced law there before serving in the U.S. House of Representatives (1917, 1918–21, 1923–33) as a progressive Republican. As New York's mayor, he fought Tammany Hall corruption and introduced reform programs for civic improvement through low-cost housing, social-welfare services, and new roads and bridges. A colorful figure with a flair for the dramatic, he enjoyed enormous popularity for his fearless forthrightness and lack of pretension. He is regarded as the greatest of New York's mayors.

Laguna Madre See Laguna MADRE

Lahore \lə-'hōr\ City (pop., 1998: 5,063,000), capital of PUNJAB province, NE Pakistan. The second-largest city of Pakistan, it lies in the upper Indus plain on the RAVI RIVER. An ancient city, it became prominent under the Mughals in the 11th–12th cent. It was captured by BABUR's troops in 1524, and was later ruled by AKBAR and Jahangir. Ruled by Sikhs in the early 19th cent., it passed to the British in 1849, and to newly independent Pakistan in 1947. It is the site of the mosque of Wazir Khan (1634); a mosque built by AURANGZEB; and the Shalimar gardens, laid out in 1641.

Laing \'lan\, **R(onald) D(avid)** (1927–1989) Scottish psychiatrist. In his highly controversial *The Divided Self* (1960), his analysis of SCHIZOPHRENIA led him to theorize that insecurity about one's existence prompts a defensive reaction in which the self splits into separate components, generating psychotic symptoms. He opposed standard schizophrenia treatments such as hospitalization and electroshock, and even opposed the concept of mental illness. He later modified some of his controversial positions.

laissez-faire \ˌle-sā-'fer\ (French: "allow to do") Policy dictating a minimum of governmental interference in the economic affairs of individuals and society. It was promoted by the PHYSIOCRATS and strongly supported by Adam SMITH and J. S. MILL. It held that society as a whole is best served by permitting individuals to pursue their interests and limiting the state to maintaining order and property rights. The wide popularity of the laissez-faire doctrine waned in the late 19th cent. in the face of social and economic problems caused by INDUSTRIALIZATION. See also CLASSICAL ECONOMICS.

lake Relatively large body of slow-moving or standing water that occupies an inland basin. Lakes are most abundant in high N latitudes and in mountain regions, particularly those that were covered by GLACIERS. The primary sources of lake water are melting ice and snow, springs, and rivers. In the upper part of lakes there is a good supply of light, heat, oxygen, and nutrients, which support a large number of diverse aquatic organisms; the most abundant forms are PLANKTON (chiefly DIATOMS), ALGAE, and flagellates. In the lower levels and in the sediments, the main forms of life are bacteria.

Lake Clark National Park National park, S Alaska. Located on the W shore of Cook Inlet, it occupies 3,653,000 acres

(1,478,900 hectares). Lake Clark, more than 40 mi (65 km) long, is the largest of its glacial lakes; it feeds rivers that provide the most important spawning ground for red salmon in N. America. The park includes waterfalls and active volcanoes.

Lake District Mountainous region, Cumbria, NW England. It occupies 866 sq mi (2,243 sq km). It contains numerous lakes, including Grasmere, WINDERMERE, and Coniston Water, as well as the region's highest mountains. It was home to several English poets, including William WORDSWORTH, Robert SOUTHEY, and S. T. COLERIDGE, who celebrated its beautiful landscape. The district became a national park in 1951.

Lake Dwellings Remains of various pre- and post-BRONZE AGE settlements within the margins of lakes in S Germany, Switzerland, France, and Italy. The dwellings appear to have been built on platforms supported by piles above the water surface or above swampy areas along the water's edge. The platforms supported one- or two-room rectangular huts with beaten clay floors. Through study of the Lake Dwellings, archaeologists were able to work out a cultural sequence confirming that the Bronze Age immediately followed the STONE AGE. See also CRANNOG.

Lake of the Ozarks See Lake of the OZARKS

Lake of the Woods See Lake of the WOODS

Lake Placid Village (pop., 2000: 2,500), NE New York, on Mirror Lake and Lake Placid, in the ADIRONDACK MTNS. The site was first settled in 1800. It was promoted in 1850 as a summer resort, and Melvil DEWEY founded the Lake Placid Club there in 1895. A year-round recreational area with golf courses, ski resorts, and mountain scenery, it hosted the OLYMPIC GAMES in 1932 and 1980.

Lake Turkana remains Collection of HOMINID fossils found along the shores of Lake Turkana in NW Kenya. The Koobi Fora site, excavated by Richard Leakey (see LEAKEY FAMILY) and others, has proved to be the richest fund of hominid remains found anywhere in the world, yielding fossils that represent perhaps 230 individuals, including members of *HOMO HABILIS, HOMO ERECTUS,* and *AUSTRALOPITHECUS.* On the W shore was found a well-preserved skeleton of an 11-year-old boy (the "Turkana Boy") later dated to about 1.8 million years ago. See also HUMAN EVOLUTION.

Lakshmi *or* **Laksmi** \'lәk-shmē\ Hindu and Jain goddess of wealth and good fortune. She is the consort of VISHNU. She is a principal object of worship during DIVALI, when her presence is sought in homes, temples, and businesses for the whole of the year to come.

Lalique \lä-'lēk\, **René (Jules)** (1860–1945) French jeweler and glassmaker. Trained in Paris and London, he opened his own firm in Paris in 1885. Reacting against machine-produced jewelry featuring precious gems, he designed elegant and fantastic jewelry with less conventional gemstones and materials. His designs contributed significantly to the ART NOUVEAU and ART DECO movements. His interest in architectural glass led him to develop the style of molded glass for which he is famous, characterized by iced surfaces, elaborate patterns in relief, and occasionally applied or inlaid color.

lama In TIBETAN BUDDHISM, a spiritual leader. Some lamas are considered to be reincarnations of their predecessors; others have won respect for their high level of spiritual development. The most honored of the reincarnate lamas is the DALAI LAMA. The process of discovering the new incarnation of a reincarnated lama involves considering oracular messages, unusual signs during the lama's death or during a birth thereafter, and examinations of candidates. The child thus identified is given extensive monastic training from an early age.

Lamarck \lә-'märk\, **Jean-Baptiste de Monet, chevalier (knight) de** (1744–1829) French biologist. He is credited with the first use of the word biology (1802). He was an originator of the modern concept of the museum collection. He seems to have been the first to relate fossils to the living organisms to which they corresponded most closely. His notion that acquired traits could be inherited (called Lamarckism) was discredited after the 1930s by most geneticists except in the Soviet Union, where it dominated Russian genetics until the 1960s (see Trofim LYSENKO). See also Charles DARWIN, DARWINISM.

Lamartine \lä-mär-'tēn\, **Alphonse de** (1790–1869) French poet and statesman. He is chiefly remembered for his very successful first collection of poetry, the musical, evocative *Méditations poétiques* (1820), which established him as a key figure in French ROMANTICISM. From 1830 he was active in politics; after France's SECOND REPUBLIC was proclaimed in 1848, he briefly headed the provisional government until the revolution was crushed. In later years he published novels, poetry, and historical works in a vain struggle against bankruptcy.

Lamashtu \lä-'mäsh-tü\ In Mesopotamian religion, the most terrible of all female demons. Lamashtu killed children, consumed human flesh and blood, blighted plants, spoiled rivers and streams, sent nightmares, caused miscarriages, and brought disease. She had seven names and was often described in incantations as "seven witches." She was portrayed as a lion- or bird-headed female figure.

Lamb, Charles (1775–1834) English essayist and critic. From 1796 he was guardian of his sister, the writer Mary Lamb (1764–1847), who in a fit of madness had killed their mother. He is best known for the often autobiographical essays he wrote under the pseudonym Elia for *London Magazine,* first collected in *Essays of Elia* (1823). Among the greatest of English letter writers, he included some of his most perceptive literary criticism in letters. He collaborated with Mary on *Tales from Shakespear* (1807), a highly popular retelling of the plays for children.

Lamb, William See Viscount MELBOURNE

Lamennais \läm-'ne\, **(Hugues-) Félicité (-Robert de)** (1782–1854) French priest and philosopher. With his brother Jean, he sketched a program of church reform in *Reflections on the State of the Church* (1808). Ordained in 1816, he wrote the acclaimed *Essay on Indifference Toward Religion* (1817–23), which argued for the necessity of religion. In 1830, he cofounded the journal *L'Avenir* to advocate democratic principles and church-state separation. Its principles were condemned by the pope in 1832. Lamennais's *The Words of a Believer* (1834), written in response to papal condemnation, led to his severance from the church. Thereafter he wrote in the cause of republicanism and socialism.

L'Amour \lä-'mör-, lä-'mùr\, **Louis** *orig.* Louis Dearborn LaMoore (1908–1988) U.S. author of westerns. Born in Jamestown, N.D., he left school at 15 and traveled the world before beginning his writing career in the 1940s. His more than 100 works, mostly formula westerns that convincingly portray frontier life, have sold nearly 300 million copies in 20 languages, and more than 30—including *Hondo* (1953), *The Burning Hills* (1956), and *How the West Was Won* (1963)—were the basis of films.

lamprey \'lam-prē, 'lam-ˌprā\ Any of about 22 species of primitive, jawless fishes (with HAGFISHES in class Agnatha). Lampreys live in coastal waters and freshwater in temperate regions. Eel-like and scaleless, they are 6–40 in. (15–100 cm) long. Lampreys have well-developed eyes, a single nostril on top of the head, a cartilaginous skeleton, and a sucking mouth with horny teeth surrounding the round opening. They attach to fish with their mouth and feed on their host's blood and tissues. Some species remain in freshwater, notably the sea lamprey, which entered the Great Lakes and nearly eliminated several commercially important fishes there.

Lampsacus \'lamp-sә-kәs\ Ancient Greek colony on the Asian shore of the Hellespont (DARDANELLES). It was famous for its wines and was the chief seat of the worship of PRIAPUS. Colonized in 654 B.C. by Ionian Phocaea, it later joined the DELIAN LEAGUE. When Athens fell in 405, it came under Persian control until ALEXANDER THE GREAT freed it in 334.

LAN See LOCAL AREA NETWORK

Lancang Jiang See MEKONG RIVER

Lancashire \'laŋ-kә-ˌshir\ County (pop. 1998 est.: 1,136,000), NW England. Its county seat is Preston. In the early Middle Ages it was part of the kingdom of NORTHUMBRIA. It included the ancestral lands of the House of LANCASTER. In the Industrial Revolution it became a center of the textile industry. Lancaster and Preston are its major cities; it also has resort towns, including Blackpool, on the Irish Sea.

Lancaster, Burt(on Stephen) (1913–1994) U.S. film actor. Born in New York City, he toured with circuses as an acrobat. His movie debut in *The Killers* (1946) made him a star, and he became noted for his portrayals of physically tough, emotionally sensitive characters. His many films include *Come Back, Little Sheba* (1952), *From Here to Eternity* (1953), *The Rose Tattoo* (1955), *Elmer Gantry* (1960, Academy Award), *The Birdman of Alcatraz* (1962), *The Swimmer* (1968), *Atlantic City* (1981), and *Local Hero* (1983).

Lancaster, House of Cadet branch of the House of PLANTAGENET that provided three kings of England (HENRY IV, HENRY V, HENRY VI). The title earl of Lancaster was granted to HENRY III's son Edmund (1245–1296); Edmund's grandson Henry (d.1361) became the 1st duke of Lancaster, and the inheritance fell to his daughter Blanche and her husband, JOHN OF GAUNT. John's son became King Henry IV, and the duchy of Lancaster was merged in the crown. The Lancaster dynasty ended after the defeat of Henry VI in the Wars of the ROSES, and the Lancaster claims were passed on to the House of TUDOR.

Lancelot *or* **Launcelot** \'lan-sə-ˌlät, 'lan-sə-ˌlət\ One of the greatest knights in ARTHURIAN LEGEND, the lover of Guinevere and the father of GALAHAD. He first appeared in a 12th-cent. romance by CHRÉTIEN DE TROYES, and he is a major character in Thomas MALORY's *Morte Darthur.* His full name, Sir Lancelot du Lac, refers to his upbringing by the Lady of the Lake, the enchantress who trained him to be a model of chivalry. His adultery with Guinevere caused him to fail in the quest for the GRAIL and set in motion the events that led to the destruction of CAMELOT. He was displaced as the model knight by Galahad.

Lan-chou See LANZHOU

land In economics, the resource that encompasses the natural resources used in production. In CLASSICAL ECONOMICS, the three factors of production are land, LABOR, and CAPITAL. Land was considered to be the "original and inexhaustible gift of nature." In modern economics, it is broadly defined to include all that nature provides, including minerals, forest products, and water and land resources. While many of these are renewable resources, no one considers them "inexhaustible."

Land, Edwin (Herbert) (1909–1991) U.S. inventor and physicist. Born in Bridgeport, Conn., he cofounded the Land-Wheelwright Laboratories in Boston in 1932. Interested in light POLARIZATION, he developed the polarizer, for which he envisioned numerous uses. By 1936 Land was using types of Polaroid material in sunglasses and other optical devices. In 1937 he founded the POLAROID CORP. in Cambridge, Mass. In 1947 he demonstrated the revolutionary Polaroid Land Camera, which produced a finished print in 60 seconds; he introduced color Polaroid film in 1963. His interest in light and color resulted in a new theory of color perception. He received more than 500 patents.

Landau \län-'daù\, **Lev (Davidovich)** (1908–1968) Soviet physicist. He is known for his work in low-temperature physics, atomic and nuclear physics, and solid-state, stellar-energy, and plasma physics. For explaining the phenomenon of liquid helium, he was awarded a 1962 Nobel Prize. For his work in many areas of physics, his name is applied to Landau diamagnetism, Landau levels, Landau damping, the Landau energy spectrum, Landau cuts, and the Landau Institute for Theoretical Physics in Moscow.

Landers, Ann *orig.* Esther Friedman (1918–2002) U.S. newspaper columnist. Born in Sioux City, Iowa, she took over an advice column in the *Chicago Sun-Times* in 1955, adopting her now-familiar pseudonym, and made it into the most widely syndicated advice column in the U.S. Her twin sister Pauline wrote the competitive and equally well-known "Dear Abby" advice column from 1956.

land grant college See MORRILL ACT OF 1862

Landis, Kenesaw Mountain (1866–1944) U.S. federal judge and first commissioner of professional baseball. Born in Millville, Ohio, he was named for a Georgia mountain where his father had been wounded as a Civil War soldier. He practiced law in Chicago (1891–1905) before being appointed a U.S. district judge (1905–22). He was named baseball commissioner in 1920 in the aftermath of the BLACK SOX SCANDAL, and became noted for his uncompro-

mising measures to preserve the game's integrity. Though widely disliked for his stern, autocratic rule, he kept the post until his death.

landlord and tenant Parties to the leasing of real estate, whose relationship is bound by contract. The landlord, or lessor, is the owner; the tenant, or lessee, supplies payment in order to enjoy possession and use of the property for a specified period. Important forms of tenancy include tenancy for a fixed period, periodic (seasonal) tenancy, tenancy at will, and holdover tenancy (whereby a tenant remains after the contract has ended). See also REAL AND PERSONAL PROPERTY, RENT.

land mine Explosive charge buried just below the surface of the earth. It may be fired by the weight of vehicles or troops on it, the passage of time, or remote control. Though used in World War I, landmines became important only beginning in World War II. Early mines had metal cases; later models were sometimes made of other materials to prevent magnetic detection. They are typically used to disrupt or prevent attack of tanks or infantry but have also been used to render land useless to civilian populations. A treaty banning land mines—not signed by the U.S., Russia, and China—went into effect in 1997. See also SUBMARINE MINE.

Landon, Alf(red Mossman) (1887–1987) U.S. politician. Born in W. Middlesex, Pa., he entered the oil business in Kansas (1912) and became active in Progressive Party politics. He was elected governor of Kansas in 1932 and again in 1934, the only incumbent Republican governor to succeed that year. As the Republican presidential nominee in 1936, he lost to Franklin ROOSEVELT in a landslide.

Landowska \lan-'dȯf-skə\, **Wanda** (*orig.* Alexandra) (1879–1959) Polish-U.S. harpsichordist. After establishing herself as a pianist, she had a harpsichord made for her by Pleyel in Paris, and first performed on it at the Breslau Bach Festival in 1912, thus beginning the 20th-cent. revival of the instrument and sparking interest in authentic performance practice. Her many recordings included the first recording of J. S. BACH's *Goldberg Variations*, and she commissioned works for harpsichord from important composers. As a Jew she was forced to flee the Nazis, and after 1940 she lived and taught in the U.S.

land reform Deliberate change in the way agricultural land is held or owned, the methods of its cultivation, or the relation of agriculture to the rest of the economy. The most common political objective of land reform is to abolish feudal or colonial forms of landownership, often by taking land away from large landowners and redistributing it to landless peasants. Other goals include coordinating agricultural production with industrialization programs. The earliest record of land reform is from 6th-cent.-B.C. Athens, where SOLON abolished the debt system that forced peasants to mortgage their land and labor. Large landowners were the norm in the ancient world, however, and through the Middle Ages and the Renaissance as well. The FRENCH REVOLUTION brought land reform to France. Serfdom was abolished throughout most of Europe in the 19th cent. The RUSSIAN REVOLUTION OF 1917 introduced collectivization of agriculture, attended by loss of capital and devastating famines. Land reform was instituted at various times throughout Latin America and in countries where communists came to power, notably China. It remains a potent political issue in many parts of the world.

Landsat *officially* **Earth Resources Technology Satellites** Series of unmanned U.S. scientific satellites. The first three were launched in 1972, 1975, and 1978. Designed mainly to collect data about earth's natural resources, they were also equipped to monitor atmospheric and oceanic conditions and detect ecological changes. Four more Landsat satellites were launched (in 1982, 1984, 1993, and 1999), but radio communication with Landsat 6 was lost just after launch.

Landseer, Edwin (Henry) (*later* **Sir Edwin**) (1802–1873) British painter and sculptor. After studies at the Royal Academy, he specialized in animals and developed great skill in depicting animal anatomy, but humanized his subjects to the point of sentimentality or moralizing (e.g., *Dignity and Impudence*, 1839). He achieved great success, and was a favorite painter of Queen VICTORIA. As a sculptor he is best known for his bronze lions at the base of Nelson's Column in Trafalgar Square (unveiled 1867).

Land's End Westernmost peninsula, CORNWALL, England. Its tip is the southwesternmost point of England. Off its coast lie dangerous reefs, one group of which is marked by the Longships lighthouse.

Lanfranc \\'lan-ˌfraŋk\\ (c.1005–1089) Archbishop of Canterbury (1070–89). An Italian scholar who settled in Normandy, he became prior of the Benedictine monastery of Bec. A trusted adviser of WILLIAM I the Conqueror, he was nominated as archbishop of Canterbury after the Norman Conquest. Lanfranc reorganized the English church, ensuring its independence from the crown. He uncovered a conspiracy against the king (1075), and he secured the succession for WILLIAM II (1087).

Lanfranco \\län-'frän-kō\\, **Giovanni** (1582–1647) Italian painter. He studied with the CARRACCI family and in 1602 went to Rome to work with Annibale Carracci in the Farnese Palace, soon becoming the leading fresco painter in Rome. His work shows the influence of CORREGGIO's dynamic illusionism. His masterpiece is the *Assumption of the Virgin* in the dome of Sant'Andrea della Valle (1625–27); with its vigorously painted figures floating in the clouds over the viewer, it is a pivotal work of the baroque era. He worked in Naples 1633–46; his best-known work there is the dome of the chapel of San Gennaro in the cathedral (1641–46).

Lang, Fritz (1890–1976) Austrian-U.S. film director. He studied architecture and wrote screenplays before finding work at a movie studio in Berlin, where he later directed such successful films as *Between Two Worlds* (1921), *Dr. Mabuse* (1922), the two-part *The Nibelungen* (1924), the expressionistic *Metropolis* (1926), and *M* (1931). After making the anti-Nazi film *The Last Will of Dr. Mabuse* (1933), he left Germany for Paris and later Hollywood. His U.S. films, which equal his German films in their intensity, pessimism, and visual mastery, include *Fury* (1936), *You Only Live Once* (1937), *Ministry of Fear* (1944), *Rancho Notorious* (1952), and *The Big Heat* (1953).

Fritz Lang checking model for *Hangmen Also Die*, 1943

Lange \\'laŋ\\, **Dorothea** (1895–1965) U.S. documentary photographer. Born in Hoboken, N.J., she studied photography and opened a portrait studio in San Francisco in 1919. During the Great Depression, her photos of homeless men led to her employment by a federal agency to bring the plight of the poor to public attention. Her photographs were so effective that California established camps for migrants; her *Migrant Mother* (1936) was especially widely reproduced. Another of her photo essays documents the World War II internment of Japanese-Americans.

Lange, Jessica (b.1949) U.S. film actress. Born in Cloquet, Minn., she made her movie debut in *King Kong* (1976) and won praise in *The Postman Always Rings Twice* (1981), *Frances* (1982), *Tootsie* (1982, Academy Award), *Country* (1984), *Sweet Dreams* (1985), *Music Box* (1989), and televised versions of *Cat on a Hot Tin Roof* (1984) and *O Pioneers!* (1992). Later films include *Blue Sky* (1994, Academy Award), *A Thousand Acres* (1997), and *Titus* (1999).

Langer, Susanne K(nauth) orig. Susanne Katherina Knauth (1895–1985) U.S. philosopher. Born in New York City, she taught at Harvard Univ. (1927–42) and other institutions. In *Philosophy in a New Key* (1942), she presented a novel interpretation of the meaning of art. Her *Feeling and Form* (1953) proposed that art, especially music, symbolizes intuitive knowledge of life patterns. Her *Mind: An Essay on Human Feeling* (3 vols., 1967–82) traced the development of the mind.

Langerhans, islets of *or* **islands of Langerhans** Irregularly shaped patches of endocrine tissue in the PANCREAS, which contains about 1 million of them. Beta cells, the most common type, produce INSULIN; inadequate production causes DIABETES MELLITUS. Alpha cells produce an opposing hormone, glucagon, which releases glucose from the liver and fatty acids from fat tissue. Delta cells produce somatostatin; its metabolic role is not clear. Small numbers of F cells secrete pancreatic polypeptide, which slows down nutrient absorption. See also ENDOCRINE SYSTEM.

Langland, William (c.1330–c.1400) Presumed author of the poem known as *Piers Plowman*. Little is known of his life. One of the greatest Middle English alliterative poems, *Piers Plowman* is an allegorical work in the form of a series of dream visions with a complex variety of religious themes; written in simple, colloquial language, it contains powerful imagery.

Langton, Stephen (d.1228) English cardinal and archbishop of Canterbury (1207–28). Langton was living at Rome when INNOCENT III nominated him as archbishop of Canterbury (1207) to settle a disputed election. When King JOHN refused to allow him into England, the pope excommunicated John (1209). John finally submitted and received Langton in 1213. The new archbishop encouraged baronial opposition to the king but opposed violence. He was present at the signing of the MAGNA CARTA (1215) and influenced its provisions on ecclesiastical liberties.

Langtry, Lillie orig. Emilie Charlotte Le Breton (1853–1929) British actress. Born on the Isle of Jersey (and later known as the "Jersey Lily"), she married Edward Langtry in 1874. A famous beauty, she caused a sensation when she became the first society woman to go on the stage, starring in *She Stoops to Conquer* (1881). She played to enthusiastic audiences in England and the U.S., notably in *As You Like It*. Her lovers included the Prince of Wales (later EDWARD VII). She later managed the Imperial Theatre (1901–17).

language System of conventional spoken or written symbols used by people in a shared culture to communicate with each other. A language both reflects and affects a culture's way of thinking. Related languages become more differentiated when their speakers are isolated from each other. When speech communities come into contact, their languages influence each other. Most existing languages are grouped with other languages descended "genetically" from a common ancestral language. For example, all the ROMANCE LANGUAGES are derived from Latin, which in turn belongs to the Italic branch of the INDO-EUROPEAN LANGUAGE family, descended from the ancient parent language, Proto-Indo-European. Other major families include, in Asia, SINO-TIBETAN, AUSTRONESIAN, DRAVIDIAN, ALTAIC, and AUSTROASIATIC; in Africa, NIGER-CONGO, AFRO-ASIATIC, and NILO-SAHARAN; and in the Americas, UTO-AZTECAN, MAYAN, Otomanguean, and Tupian. Relationships between languages are traced by comparing GRAMMAR and SYNTAX and especially by looking for cognates (related words) in different languages. Language has a complex structure that can be analyzed and systematically presented (see LINGUISTICS). All languages begin as SPEECH, and many go on to develop WRITING systems. The principal resources of language are word order, word form, syntactic structure, and, in speech, INTONATION. Different languages keep indicators of number, person, GENDER, TENSE, MOOD, and other categories separate from the root word or attach them to it. Languages learned after about age 10 are usually not spoken as well as those learned earlier. See also DIALECT.

Languedoc \\lä⁻g-'dȯk\\ Historical region, S central France. Languedoc's name is derived from the traditional OCCITAN LANGUAGE of S France, in which the word *oc* means "yes." Part of the Roman province of Gallia Narbonensis, it was controlled by the Visigoths in the 5th cent. During the Middle Ages it came under the counts of Toulouse. Religious wars (see ALBIGENSIAN CRUSADE) in the 13th cent. brought it under the French crown. In the 16th–18th cent. it was the scene of Protestant persecution which culminated in the war of the CAMISARDS.

La Niña Cyclic counterpart to EL NIÑO, consisting of a cooling of surface waters of the Pacific Ocean along the W coast of S. America. Its local effects on weather and climate are generally the opposite of those associated with El Niño; its global effects can be more complex. La Niña events often follow El Niños, which occur at irregular intervals of about 5–10 years.

Lan Na One of the first major TAI kingdoms in Thai history. It was founded by Mangrai (r.c.1259–1317) in the N region of present-day Thailand; its capital was Chiang Mai. A powerful state and a center for the spread of THERAVADA Buddhism, under Tilokaracha (r.1441–87) it was famous for its Buddhist scholarship and literature. It was conquered by the Myanmar in the 16th cent. The Siamese did not reassert control over the area until the 19th cent.

Lansdowne, Marquess of *orig.* Henry Charles Keith Petty-Fitzmaurice (1845–1927) Irish nobleman and British diplomat. He served in William GLADSTONE's Liberal administration and as governor-general of Canada (1883–88). As viceroy of India (1888–94), he reorganized the police, reconstituted legislative councils, and extended railway and irrigation works. As secretary of war (1895–1900), he was blamed for British unpreparedness in the S. AFRICAN WAR. As foreign secretary (1900–6), he concluded the ENTENTE CORDIALE.

L'Anse aux Meadows \ˌlans-ō-ˈme-ˌdōz\ Site on the N tip of Newfoundland where Norse settlers established as many as three settlements near the end of the 10th cent., the first known European settlements in the New World. After initially fighting each other, the Norse settlers and the Inuit established a regular trade relationship. The settlements were soon abandoned, probably as the Norse withdrew from Greenland.

Lansing City (pop., 2000: 119,000), capital of Michigan. Located on the Grand River at its junction with the Red Cedar River, it was a recently settled site when the state capital was moved there from DETROIT in 1847. Since the late 19th cent. it has been a major automobile production center. It is the site of the first U.S. agricultural college, MICHIGAN STATE UNIV. (now in E. Lansing).

Lansky, Meyer *orig.* Maier Suchowljansky (1902–1983) U.S. (Russian-born) gangster. As a young man he joined Bugsy SIEGEL in auto theft, burglary, and liquor smuggling. In 1931 he allegedly organized the murder of crime boss Joe Masseria and joined Lucky LUCIANO in forming a national crime syndicate. By 1936 he had developed gambling operations in Cuba and the U.S., putting Siegel in charge of Las Vegas. In the 1960s he extended his gambling empire in the Caribbean, while continuing to run narcotics, prostitution, labor-racketeering, and extortion rackets. Though convicted of income-tax evasion in 1973, he remained free on appeals.

lanthanide \ˈlan-thə-ˌnīd\ Any of the series of 15 consecutive chemical ELEMENTS in the PERIODIC TABLE from lanthanum to lutetium (atomic numbers 57–71). With scandium and yttrium, they make up the RARE EARTH METALS. Their atoms have similar configurations and similar physical and chemical behavior; the most usual VALENCES are 3 and 4.

Lan-Ts'ang Chiang See MEKONG RIVER

Lanzhou *or* **Lan-chou** \ˈlän-ˈjō\ City (pop., 1999 est.: 1,429,000), capital of Gansu province, N central China. Situated on the upper HUANG RIVER, it developed as a major trade center on the SILK ROAD. It became the seat of Lanzhou prefecture under the Sui dynasty (581–618 A.D.) and the capital of Gansu province in 1666. It was the terminus of the 2,000-mi (3,200-km) Chinese–Soviet highway that was used during the SINO–JAPANESE WAR for the transport of Soviet supplies. It developed as an industrial and cultural center after World War II.

Laocoön \lā-ˈä-kō-ˌän\ In Greek legend, a seer and priest of APOLLO. Laocoön offended Apollo by breaking his priestly vow of celibacy and begetting children, and by warning the Trojans not to accept the wooden horse presented by the Greeks. While preparing a sacrifice to POSEIDON, he and his two sons were crushed to death by sea serpents sent by Apollo.

Laos \ˈlä-ōs, ˈlaùs\ *officially* **Lao People's Democratic Republic** Country, S.E. Asia. Area: 91,429 sq mi (236,800 sq km). Population (2000): 5,497,000. Capital: VIENTIANE. Laos's major ethnic groups include the Lao-Lum (valley Lao), who make up two-thirds of the population; the Lao-Tai, a highland tribal people; the Lao-Theung (Mon-

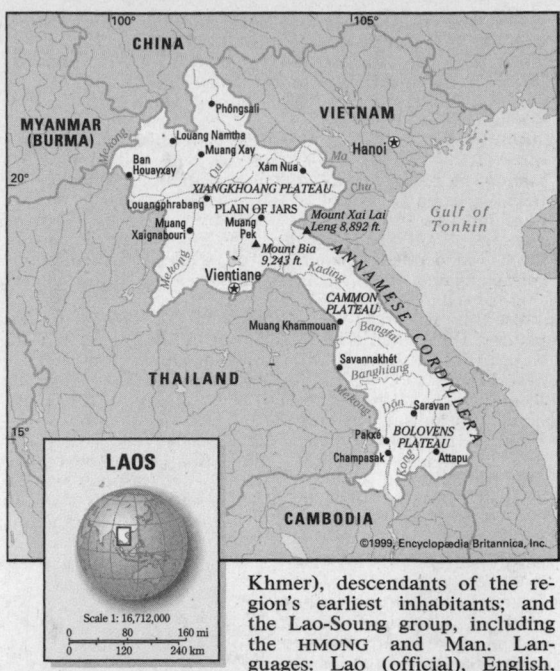

LAOS

Scale 1: 16,712,000

0   80   160 mi
0   120   240 km

©1999, Encyclopædia Britannica, Inc.

Khmer), descendants of the region's earliest inhabitants; and the Lao-Soung group, including the HMONG and Man. Languages: Lao (official), English, Vietnamese, French. Religions: Theravada Buddhism (much of the population), animism. Currency: kip. Laos is largely mountainous, especially in the north; its highest point is Mt. Bia (9,245 ft, or 2,818 m). Tropical forests cover more than half of the country's total land area; only 4% of its total area is suitable for agriculture. The floodplains of the MEKONG RIVER provide the country's only lowlands and its major wet-rice fields. Laos has a centrally planned economy based primarily on agriculture (including rice, sweet potatoes, sugarcane, cassava, and opium) and international aid. It is a people's republic with one legislative house; its chief of state is the president and its head of government is the prime minister. The Lao people migrated into Laos from S China after the 8th cent. A.D., displacing indigenous tribes now known as the Kha. In the 14th cent. Fa Ngum founded the first Laotian state, Lan Xang. Except for a period of rule by Burma (1574–1637), the Lan Xang kingdom ruled Laos until 1713, when it split into three kingdoms—Vientiane, Champassak, and Luang Prabang. During the 18th cent. the rulers of the three Laotian kingdoms became vassals of Siam. France gained control of the region in 1893, and Laos became a French protectorate. In 1945 Japan seized control and declared Laos independent. The area reverted to French rule after World War II. By the end of the First INDOCHINA WAR, the leftist Pathet Lao movement controlled two provinces of the country. The Geneva Conference of 1954 unified and granted independence to Laos. Pathet Lao forces fought the Laotian government and took control in 1975, establishing the Lao People's Democratic Republic; about one-tenth of the population fled into neighboring Thailand. Laos held its first election in 1989 and promulgated a new constitution in 1991. Although its economy was adversely affected by the mid-1990s Asian monetary crises, it realized a longtime goal in 1997 when it joined the ASSOCIATION OF SOUTHEAST ASIAN NATIONS.

Laozi *or* **Lao-tzu** \ˈlaù-ˈdzə\ (fl.c.6th cent. B.C.) First philosopher of Chinese TAOISM. He is traditionally named as the author of the TAO-TE CHING, though the work probably had more than one author. The historical Laozi, if he existed, may have been a scholar and caretaker of sacred books at the royal court of the ZHOU DYNASTY. According to legend, he met CONFUCIUS as a young man. He is venerated as a philosopher by the Confucianists; as a saint or god by the common people of China; and as a divinity and the representative of the tao by Taoists.

laparoscopy \,la-pə-'räs-kə-pē\ *or* **peritoneoscopy** \,per-ət-ᵊn-,ē-'äs-kə-pē\ Procedure for inspecting the ABDOMINAL CAVITY using a laparoscope; also surgery using a laparoscope. Laparoscopes use fiber-optic lights and small video cameras, inserted through small incisions, to show tissues and organs on a monitor. Laparoscopic surgical procedures include gallbladder, appendix, and tumor removal; tubal ligation; and hysterectomy. Less invasive than traditional (open) surgery, laparoscopy reduces postoperative pain, recovery time, and length of hospital stay.

La Paz (de Ayacucho) \lä-'päs\ City (pop., 2000: 1,000,000), administrative capital of Bolivia. Located in W central Bolivia, it is the world's highest capital, built at over 12,000 ft (3,650 m) above sea level. Founded in 1548 by the Spanish on the site of an Inca village, since 1898 it has been the administrative capital of Bolivia, though SUCRE remains the legal capital. It is Bolivia's principal industrial center, and also the site of the Univ. of San Andrés and national museums.

La Paz City (pop., 1995: 154,000), capital of BAJA CALIFORNIA SUR state, NW Mexico. Situated on La Paz Bay of the Gulf of CALIFORNIA, it is a popular resort and the largest urban center in the state. The bay was first visited by the Spanish in 1596.

Lapidus \'la-pi-dəs\, **Morris** (1902–2001) U.S. (Russian-born) architect. Reared in New York City, he worked in New York architectural firms 1928–42, then moved to Miami Beach, where he ran his own firm until 1986. He designed numerous buildings there in the Art Deco style, including the Fontainebleau and Eden Roc hotels, as well as office buildings, shopping centers, hospitals, and over 200 hotels worldwide.

lapis lazuli \,la-pəs-'la-zə-lē\ Semiprecious stone valued for its deep blue color. It is not a single mineral but an intergrowth lazurite with calcite, pyroxene, and commonly small grains of PYRITE. The most important mines are in Afghanistan and Chile. Much of what is sold as lapis is an artificially dyed JASPER from Germany that shows colorless specks of quartz, not the goldlike flecks of pyrite that are characteristic of lapis lazuli and have been compared to stars in the sky.

Laplace \lə-'pläs\, **Pierre-Simon, marquis de** (1749–1827) French mathematician, astronomer, and physicist. He is best known for his investigations into the stability of the solar system and the theory of magnetic, electrical, and heat wave propagation. In his major lifework he applied Newtonian gravitational theory to the solar system to explain deviations of the planets from the orbits predicted by the theory (1773). He continued to work on elucidating planetary perturbations through the 1780s. A work published in 1796 included his nebular hypothesis, which attributed the origin of the solar system to the cooling and contracting of a gaseous nebula, a theory that strongly influenced future thought on planetary origins.

Lapland Region (pop., 1992 est.: 113,000), N Europe. Located within the Arctic Circle, it stretches across N Norway, Sweden, and Finland, and into Russia's Kola Peninsula. Occupying 150,000 sq mi (390,000 sq km), it is bounded by the Norwegian Sea, the BARENTS SEA, and the White Sea. It is named for the Sami (Lapp) people, who have inhabited the region for several thousand years. Those who still herd reindeer can move freely across national boundaries. Industries include mining and fishing.

La Plata City (pop., 1999: 556,000), Argentina. After BUENOS AIRES became the national capital, La Plata was chosen (1882) as the new provincial seat and modeled after Washington, D.C. Located near the Río de la PLATA estuary, it is a seaport with a large artificial harbor. Its industries include meatpacking and oil refining.

L'Aquila \'lä-kwē-lä\ City (pop., 1991: 67,000), capital of the ABRUZZI region, central Italy. The area was settled by the Sabini, an ancient Italic tribe, and the city was founded about 1240. It became part of the kingdom of Italy in 1861. It is a skiing center and summer resort. Historic sites include a 14th-cent. cathedral and a 16th-cent. castle.

Laramide orogeny \'lar-ə-,mīd-ò-'rä-jə-nē\ Series of mountain-building events that affected much of W N. America in the late CRETACEOUS and early TERTIARY PERIODS (c.65 million years ago). The Laramide orogeny consisted of many separate pulses of deformation that varied in intensity and age from place to place. Laramide rocks, however, were generally created around the Cretaceous–Tertiary time boundary.

larch Any of about 10–12 species of coniferous trees that make up the genus *Larix* of the PINE family, native to cool temperate and sub-Arctic regions of the Northern Hemisphere. Larches shed their short, light-green, needlelike leaves in autumn. The most widespread N. American larch, the tamarack, or eastern larch (*L. laricina*), matures in 100–200 years and may grow 40–100 ft (12–30 m) tall. Larch wood is useful in ship construction and for telephone poles, mine timbers, and railroad ties.

Lardner, Ring(gold Wilmer) (1885–1933) U.S. writer. Born in Niles, Mich., he won popular success with comic stories about a baseball player, some collected in *You Know Me, Al* (1916). Later collections, noted for their satire, narrative skill, and convincing vernacular language, include *How to Write Short Stories* (1924) and *The Love Nest* (1926). He collaborated on such Broadway plays as *June Moon* (1929; with George S. KAUFMAN). His son, the screenwriter Ring Lardner, Jr. (1915–2000), was one of the HOLLYWOOD TEN, and later wrote such hit movies as *M*A*S*H* (1970).

Laredo \lə-'rā-dō\ City (pop., 2000: 176,000), S Texas. Located on the RIO GRANDE opposite Nuevo Laredo, Mexico, it was established in 1755. After the Texas revolt against Mexican rule in 1836, it became the seat of the Republic of the Rio Grande (1839–41). It was occupied by the Texas Rangers in 1846. Today its manufacturing includes electronic components and oil refining.

Lares \'lar-,ēz\ In ROMAN RELIGION, guardian deities. Originally gods of cultivated fields, Lares were later worshiped in association with the PENATES, the gods of the household. The household Lar, considered the center of the family cult, was often represented as a youthful figure holding a drinking horn and cup. A prayer was said to the Lar or Lares every morning, and offerings were made at family festivals. Public Lares presided over local districts marked by a crossroad; state Lares (*praestites*) were worshiped in a temple on the Via Sacra.

large intestine End section of the intestine, about 5 ft (1.5 m) long, wider than the SMALL INTESTINE, with a smooth inner wall. In the first half, ENZYMES complete digestion, and bacteria produce many B vitamins and vitamin K. Over 24–30 hours, churning movements break down tough cellulose fibers and expose the contents to the COLON's walls, which absorb water and electrolytes. The more vigorous "mass movement" (gastrocolic reflex) occurs only two or three times a day to propel waste material toward the anal canal. See also COLITIS, DIVERTICULUM, POLYP, TUMOR.

lark Any of about 75 species of songbirds (family Alaudidae) found throughout the Old World. Only the horned, or shore, lark (*Eremophila alpestris*) is native to the New World. The bill may be small and narrowly conical or long and downward-curving. The plumage is plain brownish or streaked. Its body is 5–9 in. (13–23 cm) long. Flocks of larks forage for insects and seeds on the ground. All species have a high, thin, melodious voice.

Larkin, Philip (Arthur) (1922–1985) English poet. Educated at Oxford, he worked his whole life as a librarian. He wrote two novels before becoming well known with his third volume of verse, *The Less Deceived* (1955), which expressed the antiromantic sensibility prevalent in English verse of his time. Later poetry volumes, including *The Whitsun Weddings* (1964), *High Windows* (1974), and *Aubade* (1980), brought him a popularity rare among serious poets.

larkspur *or* **delphinium** Any of about 300 species of herbaceous plants that make up the genus *Delphinium* in the BUTTERCUP family, many of which are grown for their showy flower stalks. Annual larkspurs include the common rocket larkspur (*D. ajacis*) and its varieties, up to 2 ft (60 cm) tall, with bright blue, pink, or white flowers on branching stalks. Perennial larkspurs, often with blue flowers, include species that grow to 4.5 ft (1.4 m).

K L

La Rochefoucauld \la-ròsh-fü-'kō\, **François, duc (duke) de** (1613–1680) French writer. Of a noble family, he joined the army and later played a leading part in the FRONDE, but gradually won his way back into royal favor. He turned his energies to intellectual pursuits and became the leading exponent of the *maxime*, a French form of EPIGRAM that concisely expresses a harsh or paradoxical truth. *Maximes* (five eds., 1665–78), his principal achievement, consists of 500 reflections on human behavior.

Larousse \lə-'rüs\, **Pierre (Athanase)** (1817–1875) French publisher, lexicographer, and encyclopedist. Son of a blacksmith, he received a scholarship to study in Versailles. He founded a publishing house, Librairie Larousse, in 1852. His major work was the combined dictionary and encyclopedia *Grand dictionnaire universel du XIXe siècle* (17 vols., 1866–76). Librairie Larousse continues to publish a multivolume encyclopedia as well as dictionaries and smaller encyclopedias.

Lartigue \lär-'tēg\, **Jacques-Henri (-Charles-Auguste)** (1894–1986) French painter and photographer. He was given a Brownie camera at 7; from the beginning, his photographs were invariably informal shots of everyday subjects. When his work was discovered in the 1960s, he was acclaimed for his departure from formal, posed portraits and for the ingenuous charm and beguiling spontaneity and humor of his boyhood photos of family and friends, and even his documentation of World War I.

larva Active, feeding stage in the development of many animals, occurring after birth or hatching and before the adult form is reached. Larvae are structurally different from adults and often are adapted to a different environment. Some species have free-living larvae but sessile (affixed) adults, the moving larvae thus helping to spread the species; others have aquatic larvae but terrestrial adults. Many INVERTEBRATES (e.g., CNIDARIANS) have simple larvae. FLUKES have several larval stages, and ANNELIDS, MOLLUSKS, and CRUSTACEANS have various larval forms. Insect larvae are called CATERPILLARS, grubs, maggots, or worms; the larval stage of many insects may last much longer than the adult stage. ECHINODERMS also have larval forms. The larvae of FROGS and TOADS are called tadpoles. See also METAMORPHOSIS, PUPA.

laryngitis \ˌlar-ən-'jī-təs\ INFLAMMATION of the LARYNX, causing hoarseness. Simple laryngitis usually occurs with infections (see COLD) or inhalation of irritants. The larynx's lining becomes swollen and secretes mucus. In chronic laryngitis, caused by excessive smoking, drinking, or vocal-cord use, the larynx is dry and has POLYPS.

larynx \'lar-inks\ *or* **voice box** Hollow, tubular structure connecting the PHARYNX with the TRACHEA, through which air passes on the way to the lungs. The larynx consists of a framework of cartilage plates, with a ridge in front (Adam's apple); the epiglottis, a flaplike projection up into the throat that covers the airway during swallowing; and the VOCAL CORDS (see SPEECH).

La Salle \lə-'säl\, **René-Robert Cavelier, Sieur (Lord) de** (1643–1687) French explorer. In 1666 he left France for N. America and was granted land near Montreal. He explored the Ohio River region (1669), then helped establish Ft. Frontenac on Lake Ontario, where he controlled the fur trade. With Henri de Tonty (1650?–1704), he canoed down the Mississippi River to the Gulf of Mexico and in 1682 claimed the entire Mississippi Basin for France, naming it Louisiana after Louis XIV. Back in France, he received authority to build a fort at the mouth of the Mississippi. Beset by losses of men and ships, he mistakenly landed at Matagorda Bay, Texas. After fruitless attempts to locate the Mississippi, he was killed by mutineers.

Las Casas, Bartolomé de (1474–1566) Spanish historian and missionary, called the Apostle of the Indies. He sailed on Christopher COLUMBUS's third voyage (1498) and later became a planter on Hispaniola (1502). In 1510 he became the first priest ordained in the Americas. He devoted his life to protesting the mistreatment of the Indians, with whom he worked in Guatemala, Peru, Cuba, Nicaragua, and Mexico. His call for an end to the ENCOMIENDA system aroused implacable opposition. His *Brief Report on the Destruction of the Indians* (1552) and his unfinished *History of the Indians* inspired Simón BOLÍVAR and other revolutionary heroes.

Lascaux Grotto \lä-'skō\ Cave near Montignac, France, that contains perhaps the most outstanding known display of prehistoric art. Discovered in 1940, it consists of a main cavern and several steep galleries, all magnificently decorated with engraved, drawn, and painted animals, including four great aurochs, a curious unicorn-type animal that may represent a mythical creature, and a rare narrative composition involving a bird-man figure and a speared bison. The site has been dated to the late AURIGNACIAN period (c.15,000 B.C.). Because of heavy tourist traffic, the cave was closed to the public in 1963, but a full-scale facsimile, Lascaux II, was opened in 1983. See also ROCK ART.

laser Device that produces an intense beam of coherent LIGHT (light composed of waves having a constant difference in PHASE). Its name (from "light amplification by stimulated emission of radiation") describes how its beam is produced. The first laser was constructed in 1960 by Theodore Maiman (b.1927) based on earlier work by Charles Townes (b.1915). Light of a suitable WAVELENGTH excited ruby ATOMS to higher energy levels. The excited atoms decayed swiftly to slightly lower energies and then fell more slowly to the ground state, emitting light at a specific wavelength. The light bounced back and forth between the polished ends of the ruby rod, stimulating further emission. The laser has found valuable applications in microsurgery, compact-disc players, communications, holography, drilling, alignment in tunnel drilling, long-distance measurement, and mapping fine details.

Lasker, Emanuel (1868–1941) German chess master. He first won the world championship in 1894 and retained the title until his defeat by José Capablanca in 1921; his term remains the longest reign as world champion in chess history. He wrote the classic *Common Sense in Chess* (1896) as well as books on mathematics and philosophy. He was forced to leave Nazi Germany in 1933 as a Jew. He returned to chess at age 66 with impressive success.

Las Palmas (de Gran Canaria) Seaport city (pop., 1998 est.: 352,000), NE Grand Canary Island, Spain. It is the largest city of the CANARY ISLANDS. Founded in 1478, it served as a base for the Spanish conquest of Tenerife and La Palma islands. It is a year-round resort; historic sites include a 15th-cent. cathedral and the house of Christopher COLUMBUS.

Lassen Peak *or* **Mt. Lassen** Volcano, S end of the CASCADE RANGE, NE California. It erupted in 1914 and intermittently thereafter until 1921. The peak, 10,457 ft (3,187 m) high, is part of Lassen Volcanic National Park, which occupies

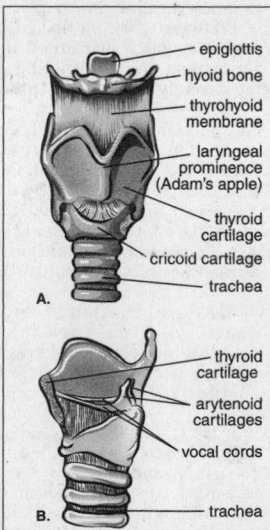

epiglottis
hyoid bone
thyrohyoid membrane
laryngeal prominence (Adam's apple)
thyroid cartilage
cricoid cartilage
trachea
A.

thyroid cartilage
arytenoid cartilages
vocal cords
trachea
B.

Larynx A. Frontal view. The larynx is composed of cartilage plates that are joined together by muscles and ligaments. The thyroid cartilage, the largest, forms a prominence in front called the Adam's apple. The leaf-shaped epiglottis, attached to the upper part of the thyroid cartilage, closes during swallowing. B. Cutaway side view. The vocal cords in the cavity of the larynx are large folds in the mucous membrane lining the larynx. They stretch between the thyroid cartilage in front and the arytenoid cartilages in the back. As air passes between them, they vibrate to emit sound.

106,372 acres (43,081 hectares). It is named for Peter Lassen, an explorer who guided settlers through the area.

Lassus \'lä-sūes\, **Orlande de** *or* **Orlando di Lasso** \'lä-sō\ (1532–1594) Flemish composer. As a choirboy, he had such a beautiful voice that he is said to have been kidnapped to sing elsewhere. After 1556 he was chapel master to the duke of Bavaria, but pursued an international career, traveling in Italy, Germany, Flanders, and France. He wrote more than 1,200 works, in every contemporary style and genre, including some 60 masses, 500 motets, and hundreds of madrigals and chansons. Because of his range of styles and because his works were printed so widely, he influenced many composers, and he is regarded as one of the greatest masters of his century.

Last Mountain Lake Lake, S central Saskatchewan. With an average width of 2 mi (3.2 km) and a length of 60 mi (96 km), it occupies 89 sq mi (231 sq km). It is a popular fishing and resort area.

Las Vegas City (pop., 2000: 478,000), SE Nevada. Nevada's largest city, it is famous for its luxury hotels, casinos, and nightclubs, located in the downtown area known as "The Strip." It became a railroad town in 1905. Gambling was legalized in 1931, and Las Vegas expanded rapidly after 1940. Its connections to crime syndicates began in 1946, when Bugsy SIEGEL opened the Flamingo Hotel. The city's flamboyant architecture has become increasingly extraordinary. By the late 20th cent. it was one of the country's fastest-growing metropolitan areas, attracting a year-round population as well as tourists.

Late Baroque See ROCOCO STYLE

La Tène \lä-'ten\ (French: "The Shallows") Archaeological site at the E end of Lake Neuchâtel, Switzerland. The name now applies to a Late IRON AGE culture of European CELTS. La Tène culture originated in the mid-5th cent. B.C., when the Celts came into contact with Greeks and ETRUSCANS. It passed through several phases and regional variations during the next 400 years, as the Celts populated N Europe and the British Isles, and ended in the mid-1st cent. B.C. when most of the Celts came under Roman control.

La Tène Gold disk, 5th cent. B.C.

latent heat Characteristic amount of ENERGY absorbed or released by a substance during a change in physical state that occurs without a change in TEMPERATURE. Heat of fusion is the latent heat associated with melting a solid or freezing a liquid. Heat of VAPORIZATION is the latent heat associated with vaporizing a liquid or condensing (see CONDENSATION) a vapor. For example, when water reaches its BOILING POINT and is kept boiling, it remains at that temperature, and all the heat added to it is absorbed as latent heat of vaporization and carried away by the vapor molecules.

laterality *or* **hemispheric asymmetry** Characteristic of the human BRAIN in which certain functions are localized on one side. One example is handedness (the tendency to use one hand or the other to perform activities): Since the left and right cerebral hemispheres control the right and left sides of the body, respectively, right-handed people are left-dominant in terms of hemispheric control of various motor functions and ordinarily also with respect to seeing (right-eyed) and language comprehension. Paul BROCA first identified the brain center for articulate SPEECH in what is now called Broca's area. Later researchers discovered that functions involving logical analysis generally reside in the left hemisphere, while the right hemisphere seems to control processing of spatio-visual information and musical relations. There is no agreement about whether laterality is genetically transmitted, developed during gestation, or learned.

Lateran Council Any of five ecumenical councils of the Roman Catholic church held in the Lateran Palace in Rome. The First Lateran Council (1123) reiterated decrees of earlier ecumenical councils (condemning SIMONY, forbidding clergymen to marry, etc.). The second (1139) was called by Innocent II to end the schism created by the election of a rival pope. The third (1179), held during the papacy of ALEXANDER III, established a two-thirds majority of the College of Cardinals as a requirement for papal election and condemned the heresies of the CATHARI. INNOCENT III called the fourth (1215); its decrees obliged Catholics to make a yearly CONFESSION, sanctioned the doctrine of TRANSUBSTANTIATION, and made preparations for a new CRUSADE. The fifth (1512–17), convoked by JULIUS II, affirmed the immortality of the soul and restored peace among warring Christian rulers.

Lateran Treaty *or* **Lateran Pact of 1929** Pact of mutual recognition between Italy and the Vatican, signed in the Lateran Palace, Rome. The Vatican agreed to recognize the state of Italy in return for, among other provisions, formalizing ROMAN CATHOLICISM as the state religion, instituting religious instruction in the public schools, banning divorce, and recognizing papal sovereignty over Vatican City. A concordat signed in 1985 ended Catholicism's status as the state religion.

Later Le dynasty \'lē\ (1428–1788) Greatest and longest-lasting dynasty of traditional Vietnam. Its founder, LE LOI, drove the Chinese out of Vietnam and began recovering the S portion of the Indochinese peninsula from the kingdom of Champa. In 1471 the dynasty's greatest ruler, Le Thanh Tong (d.1497), completed that work. He divided the country into provinces patterned on the Chinese model. After 1533 the Le rulers were only theoretically supreme, real power being held by the Trinh and NGUYEN families. In 1771–78 a peasant uprising toppled the dynasty.

latex Any of several natural or synthetic colloidal suspensions (see COLLOID). Some latexes occur naturally in the cells of plants such as chicle and RUBBER TREES. They are complex mixtures of organic compounds, including various RESINS, FATS, or WAXES, suspended in a watery medium with dissolved salts, sugars, tannins, alkaloids, enzymes, and other substances from which the latex (or natural RUBBER, the only available rubber until 1926) can be concentrated, coagulated, and vulcanized. Synthetic latexes are used as paints and coatings; the PLASTIC, dispersed in the water, forms films by fusion as the water evaporates.

lathe \'lāth\ MACHINE TOOL that performs turning operations in which unwanted material is removed from a workpiece rotated against a cutting tool. Lathes are among the oldest and most important machine tools, used in France from 1569 and important in the INDUSTRIAL REVOLUTION, when they were adapted for metal cutting. Lathes today have a power-driven, variable-speed horizontal spindle to which the workholding device is attached. Operations include turning straight or tapered cylindrical shapes, grooves, shoulders, and screw threads and facing flat surfaces on the ends of cylindrical parts. Internal cylindrical operations include drilling, boring, reaming, counterboring, countersinking, and threading with a single-point tool or tap.

Latin alphabet *or* **Roman alphabet** Most widely used ALPHABET, the standard script of most languages that originated in Europe. It developed before 600 B.C. from the Etruscan alphabet (in turn derived from the N. Semitic alphabet by way of the Phoenician and GREEK alphabets). The earliest known Latin inscriptions date from the 7th–6th cent. B.C. The classical Latin alphabet had 23 letters. In medieval times the letter J became differentiated from I, and U and W became differentiated from V, producing the 26-letter alphabet of modern English. In ancient Roman times there were two types of Latin script, capital letters and cursive. Uncial script, mixing both types, developed in the 3rd cent. A.D.

Latin America Countries of S. AMERICA and N. AMERICA (including CENTRAL AMERICA and the islands of the CARIBBEAN SEA) south of the U.S. The colonial era in Latin America began in the 15th–16th cent. with voyages of discovery by explorers, including Christopher COLUMBUS and Amerigo VESPUCCI. The CONQUISTADORES who followed, including Hernán CORTÉS and Francisco PIZARRO, brought Spanish rule to much of the region. In 1532 the first Portuguese settlement was made in Brazil. The Roman

K L

Catholic Church soon established many missions in Latin America; ROMAN CATHOLICISM is still the region's chief religion. Spanish and Portuguese colonists enslaved the native Indian population, which was soon greatly reduced by ill treatment and disease, and then imported African slaves to replace them. Movements for independence, led by José de SAN MARTÍN, Simón BOLÍVAR, and others, swept Latin America in the early 19th cent. Many of the new federal republics collapsed into political chaos and were taken over by dictators, a situation that persisted into the 20th cent. In the 1990s a trend toward democratic rule reemerged; many state-owned industries were privatized, and efforts toward regional economic integration were accelerated.

Latin American Free Trade Association (LAFTA) International association of Latin American nations founded in 1960 to improve its members' economic well-being through free trade. It originally comprised Argentina, Brazil, Chile, Mexico, Paraguay, Peru, and Uruguay; by 1970 Ecuador, Colombia, Venezuela, and Bolivia had joined. Unable to remove all trade barriers because of its members' economic diversity, LAFTA was superseded in 1980 by the Latin American Integration Assn., which established bilateral trading agreements between the members, divided into three groups according to their level of economic development.

Latin language INDO-EUROPEAN LANGUAGE of the ITALIC group, ancestor of the modern ROMANCE LANGUAGES. Originally spoken by small groups of people living along the lower TIBER RIVER, Latin spread with the growth of Roman political power through most of W and S Europe and the W Mediterranean region. The earliest known Latin inscriptions date from the 7th cent. B.C.; Latin literature dates from the 3rd cent. B.C. The Romance languages developed from DIALECTS of Vulgar Latin, the popular spoken language. During the Middle Ages and much of the Renaissance, Latin was the language most widely employed in the West for scholarly and literary purposes. Until the latter part of the 20th cent., its use was required in the liturgy of the Roman Catholic church. Latin has a complex system of noun declensions and verb conjugations, with three genders.

latitude and longitude Coordinate system by which the location of any place on the earth's surface can be determined. Latitude is a measurement of location north or south of the equator. Longitude is a measurement of location east or west of the prime meridian, which passes through Greenwich, England. Together they establish a grid by which exact positions can be determined: for example, a point described as 40°N, 30°W is located 40° of arc north of the equator and 30° of arc west of the Greenwich meridian.

Latium \'lā-shē-əm\ Ancient area, W central Italy, on the Tyrrhenian Sea. The Latins (or Latini) came from Indo-European tribes that settled in the Italian peninsula before 1000 B.C. By 500 B.C. the cities of Latium had formed the Latin League. War between Rome and the Latins ended in 338 B.C. with the defeat of the Latins and dissolution of the league.

La Tour \lə-'tür\, **Georges de** (1593–1653) French painter. He was well known in his lifetime, especially for his depictions of candlelit subjects, then was forgotten until the 20th cent., when the identification of works previously misattributed established his reputation as a giant of French painting. His early works were painted in a realistic manner and influenced by CARAVAGGIO; his later work is more geometric and simplified, as in *St. Joseph the Carpenter* (1645). Little is known of his life, and only four or five of his paintings are dated.

Latreille \lä-'trāy\, **Pierre-André** (1762–1833) French zoologist, regarded as the father of entomology. An ordained priest, in 1796 he published his *Summary of the Generic Characteristics of Insects,* which led to his becoming head of entomology at the National Museum of Natural History. He later published the *Comprehensive Natural History of Crustaceans and Insects* (14 vols., 1802–5). These two works of classification mark the beginnings of modern entomology.

Latrobe \lə-'trōb\, **Benjamin (Henry)** (1764–1820) British-U.S. architect. His first important building was the State Penitentiary in Richmond, Va. In 1798 he designed the Bank of Pennsylvania, considered the first U.S. monument of the Greek Revival. Appointed surveyor of public buildings, Latrobe completed the U.S. CAPITOL, and later rebuilt it after its destruction by the British. In Baltimore he designed the country's first cathedral (1818). He was active as an engineer, especially in the design of waterworks. He is regarded as having established architecture as a profession in the U.S.

Latter-day Saints, Church of Jesus Christ of See MORMON

Latvia *officially* **Republic of Latvia** Country, NE Europe, along the shores of the BALTIC SEA and the Gulf of Riga. Area: 24,946 sq mi (64,610 sq km). Population (2000): 2,375,000. Capital: RIGA. Just over half of the population

©1999, Encyclopædia Britannica, Inc.

are Latvians, or Letts, who speak Latvian, one of two surviving Baltic languages. Ethnic Russians make up about one-third of the population. Languages: Latvian (official), Russian. Religions: Lutheranism, Roman Catholicism, Orthodoxy. Currency: lats. Latvia is an undulating plain, with fairly flat lowlands alternating with hills. It is a fully industrialized nation; its leading manufacturing activities are machine building and metal fabrication. Other manufactured goods include ships, transportation equipment, motors, agricultural implements, and textiles. It is a republic with one legislative body; its chief of state is the president, and the head of government is the prime minister. Latvia was settled by the Balts in ancient times. They came under the overlordship of the Varangians, or Vikings, in the 9th cent. and were later dominated by their German-speaking neighbors to the west, who Christianized Latvia in the 12th–13th cent. The Knights of the Sword conquered Latvia by 1230 and established German rule. From the mid-16th to the early 18th cent., the region was split between Poland and Sweden, but by the end of the 18th cent. all of Latvia had been annexed by Russia. Latvia declared its independence after the RUSSIAN REVOLUTION OF 1917. In 1939 it was forced to grant military bases to the Soviet Union, and in 1940 the Soviet Red Army invaded. Held by Nazi Germany 1941–44, the country was recaptured by the Soviets and incorporated into the Soviet Union (the U.S. did not recognize this takeover). With the Soviet Union breakup, Latvia gained its independence in 1991, then set about privatizing the economy and building ties with Western Europe.

Laud, William (1573–1645) Archbishop of Canterbury (1633–45) and religious adviser to CHARLES I. He became bishop of London in 1628, devoting himself to combating PURITANISM and enforcing strict Anglican ritual. By the time he became archbishop of Canterbury he had extended his authority over the whole country. He had Puritan writers such as William PRYNNE imprisoned. Aided by his close ally Thomas WENTWORTH, he influenced the king to change government social policy. By 1637, opposition to Laudian suppression had grown. In 1640 the LONG PARLIAMENT met, and Laud was accused of high treason. His trial, managed by Prynne, resulted in Laud's conviction and beheading.

Laue \ˈlaủ-ə\, **Max (Theodor Felix) von** (1879–1960) German physicist. He was the first to use a CRYSTAL to diffract X RAYS, demonstrating that X rays are ELECTROMAGNETIC RADIATION similar to light and that the molecular structure of crystals is a regularly repeating arrangement. For his work in crystallography he received a 1914 Nobel Prize. He championed Albert EINSTEIN's theory of relativity and studied the quantum theory, the COMPTON EFFECT, and the disintegration of atoms.

laughing gas See NITROUS OXIDE

laughing jackass See KOOKABURRA

Laughton \ˈlȯ-tᵊn\, **Charles** (1899–1962) British-U.S. actor. He made his London stage debut in 1926 and in New York in 1931. He acted in movies from 1929 and earned international acclaim in *The Private Life of Henry VIII* (1933, Academy Award). He was noted for his wide diversity of character roles in such films as *Mutiny on the Bounty* (1935), *The Hunchback of Notre Dame* (1939), and *Witness for the Prosecution* (1957). He directed the memorable *Night of the Hunter* (1955).

Launcelot See LANCELOT

Laurana \laủ-ˈrä-nä\, **Francesco** (c.1430–1502) Italian sculptor and medalist. His early life is obscure. In 1453 he was commissioned to work on the Castel Nuovo in Naples. At the court of the duke of Anjou (1461–66) he executed a series of medals. His other works include Madonnas and bas-reliefs in Italy and tombs and architectural sculptures in France. He is best known for his portrait busts of women, characterized by serene, detached dignity and aristocratic elegance.

Laurasia N subcontinent of the hypothetical protocontinent PANGAEA. Formed in the late PALEOZOIC ERA by the merger of Laurussia with several Asian landmasses, it separated from GONDWANA in the early MESOZOIC ERA. It then slowly fragmented into the present landmasses of N. America, Europe, and Asia (except peninsular India).

Laurel and Hardy U.S. film comedians. Stan (born Arthur Stanley Jefferson) Laurel (1890–1965) performed in vaudeville before moving to the U.S. from Britain in 1910, where he began appearing in silent movies. Oliver Norvell Hardy, Jr. (1892–1957), born in Harlem, Ga., acted in silent comedy films from 1913. They joined Hal ROACH's studio in 1926 and were soon performing together, the skinny Laurel playing the bumbling and innocent foil to the fat, pompous Hardy as they converted simple, everyday situations into disastrous tangles of stupidity. They made over 100 comedies, including *Leave 'em Laughing* (1928), *The Music Box* (1932), *Sons of the Desert* (1933), and *Way Out West* (1937), and are considered Hollywood's first great comedy team.

laurel family Family Lauraceae, composed of about 2,200 species of often aromatic and evergreen flowering plants in 45 genera. The genus *Laurus* includes bay laurel (*L. nobilis*), native to the Mediterranean, which provides bay leaves for cooking, essential oils for perfumery, and the wreaths that crowned heroes in antiquity. Another genus, *Cinnamomum*, includes the CAMPHOR tree and CINNAMON. Also included in this family are the AVOCADO, MOUNTAIN LAUREL, and SASSAFRAS.

Laurence, Margaret *orig.* Jean Margaret Wemyss (1926–1987) Canadian writer. Born in Neepawa, Manitoba, she is best known for depicting the lives of women struggling for self-realization in the male-dominated world of W Canada. Her works include the novels *The Stone Angel* (1964), *A Jest of God* (1966), and *The Fire-Dwellers* (1969) and the stories collected in *A Bird in the House* (1970) and *The Diviners* (1974). In the 1970s she turned to writing children's books.

Laurence, St. See St. LAWRENCE

Laurentian Mountains \lȯ-ˈren-chən\ Range forming the Quebec portion of the CANADIAN SHIELD, bounded by the Ottawa, ST. LAWRENCE, and Saguenay rivers. One of the oldest mountain ranges in the world, it consists of PRECAMBRIAN rocks over 544 million years old. Erosion has left its highest peak measuring only 3,905 ft (1,190 m). Nearby parks are popular vacation areas.

Laurentide Ice Sheet Principal glacial cover of N. America during the PLEISTOCENE EPOCH (1.8 million–10,000 years ago). It spread as far south as latitude 37°N and covered an area of more than 5 million sq mi (13 million sq km). In some areas its thickness reached 8,000–10,000 ft (2,400–3,000 m) or more.

Laurier \ˈlȯr-ē-ˌā\, **Wilfrid** (*later* **Sir Wilfrid**) (1841–1919) Prime minister of Canada (1896–1911). Born in St.-Lin, Canada East (now Quebec), he studied law at McGill Univ., then served in the Canadian House of Commons 1874–1919. He led the Liberal Party to victory in the 1896 election and became prime minister, the first French Canadian and Roman Catholic to hold that office. He advocated unity between English and French Canadians, development of the W territories, protection of Canadian industry, and an expanded transportation system. He championed Canadian autonomy and helped shape the British Commonwealth of independent states. He is remembered as one of Canada's most outstanding statesmen.

Wilfrid Laurier

Lautrec, Henri de Toulouse- See Henri de TOULOUSE-LAUTREC

lava Molten rock originating as MAGMA in the earth's MANTLE that pours out onto the earth's surface from a VOLCANO at temperatures of about 1,300–2,200°F (700–1,200°C). Lavas such as BASALT form flows known by the Hawaiian names *pahoehoe* and *aa*. Pahoehoe is smooth and gently undulating; the lava moves through natural pipes (lava tubes). Aa is very rough, covered with a layer of loose, irregular fragments (clinker), and flows in open channels. Lavas of intermediate composition form a block lava flow, which also has a top consisting largely of loose rubble.

Laval \lə-ˈväl\ City (pop., 1996: 330,000), S Quebec. It occupies the whole of Jesus Island, 20 mi (32 km) long and 8 mi (12 km) wide, just north of MONTREAL. First settled in 1681, it was granted to the Society of Jesus (JESUITS) in 1699 and named for François de Laval, the first Roman Catholic Canadian bishop. The island's Montreal suburbs were merged to form Laval in 1965. Development has accelerated with the opening of industrial parks.

Laval \lä-ˈväl\, **Carl Gustaf Patrik de** (1845–1913) Swedish scientist, engineer, and inventor. Laval built his first impulse steam TURBINE in 1882. A Laval reaction turbine attained a speed of 42,000 revolutions per minute. By 1896 he was operating a complete power plant using an initial steam pressure of 3,400 lbs per sq in. He invented the divergent nozzle to deliver steam to the turbine blades. His flexible shaft and double-helical gear formed the foundation for most subsequent steam turbine development.

Laval \lä-ˈväl\, **Pierre** (1883–1945) French politician. He was premier of France 1931–32 and 1935–36. The Hoare-Laval Pact (1935), an initially secret attempt to appease Fascist Italy by granting it most of Ethiopia, was widely denounced. In 1940, as minister of state in Philippe PÉTAIN's government (see VICHY FRANCE), he began his own negotiations with the Germans; Pétain dismissed him, but in 1942 he returned as head of the government. He agreed to provide French laborers for German industries, and announced that he desired a German victory. In 1945 he was executed as a traitor.

Laval University French-language university in Quebec City. Its predecessor institution, the Seminary of Quebec (founded 1633), is considered Canada's first institution of higher learning. Today the university has undergraduate and graduate degree programs in numerous fields. Total enrollment is about 35,000.

lavender Any of about 20 species of evergreen shrubs that make up the genus *Lavandula* in the MINT family, the needles, leaves, and flowers of which contain scented oil glands. Native to the Mediterranean, lavender is cultivated widely. Several species yield essential oil for fine perfumes and cosmetics. The narrow fragrant leaves are dried for use in sachets, and spikes of purple flowers distilled in alcohol constitute lavender water.

Laver, Rod(ney George) (b.1938) Australian tennis player. He joined Australia's Davis Cup team at 18 and remained on the squad until 1962. He became the second male player (after Don BUDGE) to win the Grand Slam (1962) and the first to repeat the feat (1969). He had become tennis's all-time leading money winner by the time of his retirement.

La Vérendrye \lä-ˌver-ən-ˈdrē\, **Pierre Gaultier de Varennes et de** (1685–1749) French-Canadian explorer. Born in Trois-Rivières, New France, he became a fur trader. From the Indians he heard of a river that might lead to the Pacific Ocean, and with his sons he built a string of fur-trading posts from Ontario to Manitoba (1731–38). Two sons sent farther west became the first Europeans to explore areas of present-day Nebraska, Montana, and Wyoming. The 30,000 beaver pelts La Vérendrye annually sent to Quebec broke the monopoly of the HUDSON'S BAY CO. He is now considered one of the greatest explorers of the Canadian West.

Lavoisier \lə-ˈvwä-zē-ˌā\, **Antoine (-Laurent)** (1743–1794) French chemist, regarded as the father of modern chemistry. His work on combustion, oxidation (see OXIDATION-REDUCTION), and GASES (especially those in AIR) overthrew the century-old phlogiston doctrine, which held that a component of matter (phlogiston) was given off when a substance burned. He formulated the principle of the conservation of MASS (i.e., the weights of reactants must equal the weights of products) in CHEMICAL REACTIONS, clarified the distinction between ELEMENTS and COMPOUNDS, and was instrumental in devising the modern system of chemical nomenclature (naming oxygen, hydrogen, and carbon). He was among the first to use quantitative procedures in chemical investigations, and his experimental ingenuity, exact methods, and cogent reasoning, along with the resultant discoveries, revolutionized chemistry. He also worked on physical problems, especially heat, and on fermentation and respiration. He had a remarkable simultaneous career as a public servant. A reformer and political liberal, he was active in the FRENCH REVOLUTION, but came under increasing attack from extremists and was guillotined.

law Discipline and profession concerned with the customs, practices, and rules of conduct that are recognized as binding by the community. Enforcement of the body of rules is through a controlling authority, such as a group of elders, a regent, a court, or a judiciary. Important areas in the study and practice of law include ADMINISTRATIVE LAW, ANTITRUST LAW, BUSINESS LAW, constitutional law, CRIMINAL LAW, environmental law, family law, health law, immigration law, intellectual property law, INTERNATIONAL LAW, LABOR LAW, MARITIME LAW, PROCEDURAL LAW, property law, public-interest law, tax law, TRUSTS and estates, and TORTS. See also CANON LAW, CIVIL LAW, COMMON LAW, EQUITY, Islamic law (SHARIA), MILITARY LAW.

Law, John (1671?–1729) Scottish monetary reformer. His *Money and Trade Considered* (1705), proposed a central bank as an agency for manufacturing money, as banknotes rather than as gold and silver. France agreed to try his plan in 1716, and he founded the Banque Générale. He soon combined it with a company empowered to develop France's N. American territories, particularly the lower Mississippi valley. His plan foundered; held responsible for the "Mississippi Bubble" speculative disaster, he fled and died in poverty in Venice.

Lawamon See LAYAMON

law code Systematic compilation of law or legal principles. The oldest extant fragments of a code, from the ancient city of Ebla, date to around 2400 B.C. The best-known ancient code is that of HAMMURABI. Though Roman legal records began in the 5th cent. B.C., the first formal codification was ordered by JUSTINIAN I in the 6th cent. A.D. In the Middle Ages and into the modern era, only local or provincial compilations were attempted. The first major national code was the NAPOLEONIC CODE. In COMMON-LAW countries such as England and the U.S., law codes have traditionally been less important than the record of judicial decisions, or precedents, but in the 20th cent. major codifications have been completed (e.g., the *U.S. Code*, the *Uniform Commercial Code*). See also CIVIL LAW.

lawn Fine-textured expanse of grass that is kept mowed. A common element of Western-style gardens and parks, lawns aid in giving a sense of scale and proportion. Made popular in the 18th cent. by Capability BROWN, the lawn is the antithesis of the French PARTERRE. In the 20th cent. it became a ubiquitous adjunct to U.S. single-family detached houses, serving to denote ownership and provide a buffer zone between street and private space.

law of the sea See law of the SEA

Lawrence, D(avid) H(erbert) (1885–1930) English novelist, short-story writer, poet, and essayist. The son of a Midlands coal miner and an educated mother, he began to write in 1905. He often drew his themes from his early life history or from his relationship with his German wife, Frieda, whom he married in 1914. The object of hostility and suspicion during World War I because of his pacifism and her origins, the couple lived in various countries after 1919, never returning to England. *Sons and Lovers* (1913) is an autobiographical novel about working-class family life. *The Rainbow* (1915) and its sequel, *Women in Love* (1920), trace the sickness of modern civilization to the effects of industrialization upon the human psyche. Lawrence's writing is notable for its intensity and its erotic sensuality; several of his works, including *Lady Chatterley's Lover* (1928), were banned as obscene. He died of the tuberculosis that had plagued him from an early age.

Lawrence, Ernest O(rlando) (1901–1958) U.S. physicist. Born in Canton, S.D., he taught at UC–Berkeley from 1929. In 1929 he developed the CYCLOTRON, with which he accelerated protons to speeds high enough to cause nuclear disintegration. He later produced radioactive isotopes for medical use, instituted the use of neutron beams to treat cancer, invented a color-television picture tube, and worked with the MANHATTAN PROJECT. He received a 1939 Nobel Prize. Lawrence Berkeley Laboratory and Lawrence Livermore National Laboratory were named in his honor, as was element 103, lawrencium.

Lawrence, Jacob (1917–2000) U.S. painter. Born in Atlantic City, N.J., he moved with his family at 13 to New York's Harlem. Art classes sponsored by the WORKS PROGRESS ADMINISTRATION developed his talent. His works portray scenes of African-American life and history with vivid, stylized realism. His series on historical and social themes include *Life in Harlem* (1942) and *War* (1947). Gouache and tempera are his characteristic mediums.

Lawrence, James (1781–1813) U.S. naval officer. Born in Burlington, N.J., he served in the WAR OF 1812 and commanded the USS *Hornet* in the capture of the British *Peacock*. As captain of the USS *Chesapeake*, in 1813 he accepted a challenge by the British *Shannon* off the coast of Boston. The *Chesapeake* was defeated in less than an hour, and Lawrence was mortally wounded; his last words were "Don't give up the ship."

Lawrence, John (Laird Mair) *later* Baron Lawrence (of the Punjab and of Grately) (1811–1879) British viceroy and governor-general of India (1864–69). An administrator in Delhi, after the First SIKH WAR (1845–46) he was made commissioner of the newly annexed district of Jullundur, where he subdued the hill chiefs, established courts and police posts, and curbed female infanticide and suttee. Appointed to the Punjab board of administration (1849), he introduced a uniform currency and encouraged road and canal construction. As viceroy and governor-general from 1864, he promoted education for Indians but resisted their appointment to high civil-service posts.

Lawrence, St. *or* **St. Laurence** (d.258) Roman martyr. He was one of seven deacons in Rome during the papacy of Sixtus II. When the pope was executed during VALERIAN's persecution of Christians, the authorities asked Lawrence to turn the churches' treasures over to the state. When he distributed the money to the poor instead, he was condemned to death. According to legend, he was roasted to death on a gridiron, remarking to his torturers, "I am cooked on that side; turn me over, and eat."

Lawrence, T(homas) E(dward) *known as* **Lawrence of Arabia** (1888–1935) British scholar, military strategist, and author. He studied at Oxford and learned Arabic on an archaeological expedition. During World War I he conceived the plan of supporting Arab rebellion against the Turks as a way of undermining Turkey, Germany's ally, and led Arab forces in a guerrilla campaign behind Turkish lines. In 1917 his forces had their first major victory, capturing Aqaba. He was captured later that year, but escaped. His troops reached Damascus in 1918, but European politics prevented the

T. E. Lawrence

Arabs from forming a unified nation despite their victory. Lawrence retired, declining royal decorations. Under the names Ross and Shaw, he enlisted in the Royal Air Force. He finished his autobiography, *The Seven Pillars of Wisdom,* in 1926. He was eventually posted to India; his experiences provided grist for his semifictional *The Mint.* He died at 46 in a motorcycle accident three months after his discharge.

laxative Substance that promotes DEFECATION. These include irritants (stimulants) such as cascara sagrada and castor oil, bulk formers such as bran and psyllium, saline laxatives such as Epsom salts or milk of magnesia, glycerin, lubricants such as mineral oil and some vegetable oils, and stool softeners. See also dietary FIBER.

Laxness \'läks-nɛs\, **Halldór** *orig.* Halldór Kiljan Guthdjónsson (1902–1998) Icelandic novelist. He converted to Roman Catholicism while traveling in Europe as a young man, but later dissociated himself from Christianity and turned to socialism. Works exploring the social issues of Iceland include *Salka Valka* (1936) and *Independent People* (1935). The nationalist trilogy *Íslandsklukkan* (1943–46; "Iceland's Bell") established him as the foremost writer of Iceland. His later works were more lyrical and introspective. He received the Nobel Prize in 1955.

Layamon \'lā-ə-mən\ *or* **Lawamon** \'lȯ-mən\ (fl.12th cent.) Middle English poet. A priest, he was the author of the romance-chronicle the *Brut* (c.1200), the outstanding product of the 12th-cent. English literary revival and the first work in English to treat the ARTHURIAN LEGEND. In some 16,000 long alliterative lines, the *Brut* tells of Britain from the landing of Brutus, great-grandson of AENEAS, to the final Saxon victory over the Britons in 689.

Lazarus In the Gospel of JOHN THE APOSTLE, the man whom JESUS raised from the dead. Lazarus' sister Mary lamented that if only Jesus had visited them four days earlier, surely he could have prevented her brother from dying. Jesus went to where Lazarus was entombed and commanded him to "come forth," and he did. The miracle inspired many Jews to accept Jesus as the MESSIAH.

Lazio \'lät-sē-ō\ Autonomous region (pop., 1996 est.: 5,202,000), W central Italy. Established in 1948, its capital is ROME. In the east are the central APENNINES, and in the west lies a coastal plain. In the early 20th cent. its malarial lowlands were drained and repopulated. Situated in the region previously known as LATIUM, it supports light industry, but the area is dominated by Rome.

LCD See LIQUID CRYSTAL DISPLAY

L-dopa See DOPA

leaching Loss of soluble substances and colloids from the top layer of soil by percolating precipitation. The materials are generally redeposited in a lower layer resulting in a porous and open top layer and a dense, compact lower layer. In areas of extensive leaching, the remaining quartz and hydroxides of iron, manganese, and aluminum form laterite. In such areas rapid bacterial action results in the absence of HUMUS in the soil.

Leacock, Stephen (Butler) (1869–1944) Canadian (British-born) writer and lecturer. A professor at McGill Univ. (1903–36), he wrote extensively on history and political economy, but his true calling was humor. His fame rests on his many books of lighthearted sketches and essays, beginning with *Literary Lapses* (1910) and *Nonsense Novels* (1911), which reflect the incongruity between appearance and reality in human conduct.

lead Chemical ELEMENT, chemical symbol Pb, atomic number 82. Lead is a soft, silvery-white or grayish, malleable, ductile, dense METAL that conducts electricity poorly. Its stable ISOTOPES are all end products of radioactive decay of URANIUM and other heavy elements. Known since ancient times, lead is so durable and resistant to corrosion that Roman lead pipes are still usable. Lead is used in roofing, as cable coverings, and in pipes, conduits, and structures; in storage BATTERIES, ammunition, and low-melting-point ALLOYS (e.g., solder, pewter); and as shielding against sound, vibrations, and radiation. Lead is rarely found free in nature; its major ore is GALENA. Because it and its compounds are poisons (see LEAD POISONING), lead-based paints and gasoline additives have been banned. Lead in compounds has VALENCE 2 and 4; an OXIDE (litharge) is the most widely used. Lead compounds have many varied uses. Almost half of all lead is recovered from recycled scrap. The "lead" in pencils is GRAPHITE.

lead-210 dating Method of DATING that makes use of the ratio of the amount of the radioactive lead isotope lead-210 to that of the stable isotope lead-206. Particularly useful for determining the ages of relatively recent marine sediments, it has been applied to studies concerned with the impact of human activity on the aquatic environment.

Leadbelly *orig.* Huddie (William) Ledbetter (1885–1949) U.S. folk-blues singer and songwriter. Born in Mooringsport, La., he worked as an itinerant musician with Blind Lemon Jefferson. In 1918 he was imprisoned for murder; he was pardoned in 1925 by the governor of Texas, who had heard him sing. Resuming a life of drifting, he was imprisoned for attempted murder in 1930; he was discovered in 1933 by John and Alan LOMAX, who secured his release. Under their guidance he embarked on a concert tour and recorded extensively, with Woody GUTHRIE among others. Leadbelly died penniless, but several of his songs, including "Goodnight, Irene" and "The Midnight Special" soon became standards.

lead glance See GALENA

lead poisoning *or* **plumbism** Poisoning by accumulation of LEAD in the body. Large doses cause gastroenteritis in adults and brain disorders in children. Anemia, constipation and abdominal spasm, confusion, a progressive paralysis, and sometimes brain cancer result from chronic exposure. Children are particularly susceptible to nerve and brain damage; sensitive tests show that even low levels of lead can harm children and are linked to behavioral problems. Sources in the home include lead-based paint, lead drinking-water pipes, and lead-glazed tableware. The U.S. phaseout of lead in gasoline was completed in 1996. Treatment involves giving ANTIDOTES that bind the lead in the tissues.

leaf Any flattened, green outgrowth from the stem of a VASCULAR PLANT. Leaves manufacture oxygen and GLUCOSE, which nourishes and sustains both plants and animals. Leaves and stem tissue grow from the same apical BUD. A typical leaf has a broad, expanded blade (lamina), attached to the stem by a stalklike petiole. The leaf may be simple (a single blade), compound (separate leaflets), or reduced to a spine or scale. Veins transport materials to and from the leaf tissues, radiating from the petiole through the blade. They are arranged in a netlike pattern in dicot leaves and are parallel in monocot leaves (see COTYLEDON). The leaf's outer layer (epidermis) protects the interior (mesophyll), whose soft-walled, unspecialized green cells (parenchyma) produce carbohydrate food by PHOTOSYNTHESIS. In autumn the green CHLOROPHYLL pigments of deciduous leaves break down, revealing other pigment colors, and the leaves drop off. In CONIFERS, evergreen needles, a type of leaf, persist for two or three years. See diagram next page.

leaf-footed bug See SQUASH BUG

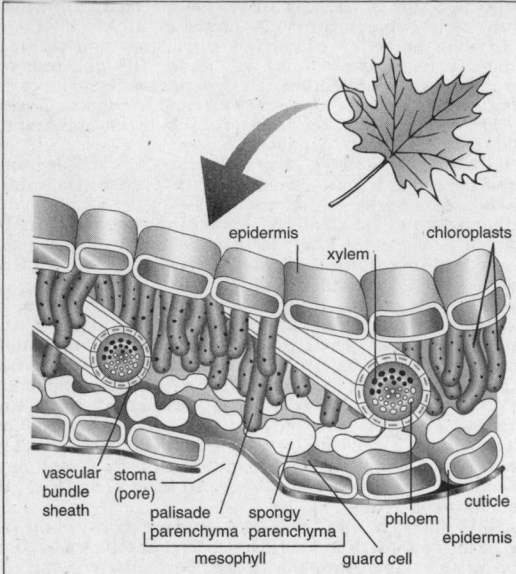

epidermis

xylem

chloroplasts

vascular bundle sheath

stoma (pore)

palisade parenchyma

spongy parenchyma

mesophyll

phloem

cuticle

epidermis

guard cell

Leaf Structures of a leaf. The epidermis is often covered with a waxy protective cuticle that helps prevent water loss from inside the leaf. Oxygen, carbon dioxide, and water enter and exit the leaf through pores (stomata) scattered mostly along the lower epidermis. The vascular or conducting tissues are known as xylem and phloem; water and minerals travel up to the leaves from the roots through the xylem, and sugars made by photosynthesis are transported to other parts of the plant through the phloem. Photosynthesis occurs within the chloroplast-containing mesophyll layer.

League of Arab States See ARAB LEAGUE

League of Nations Organization for international cooperation established by the ALLIED POWERS at the end of WORLD WAR I. A league covenant, embodying the principles of collective security and providing for an assembly, a council, and a secretariat, was formulated at the PARIS PEACE CONFERENCE (1919) and contained in the Treaty of VERSAILLES. Headquartered at Geneva, the League was weakened by the nonadherence of the U.S., which had not ratified the treaty. Discredited by its failure to prevent Japanese expansion in Manchuria and China, Italy's conquest of Ethiopia, and Germany's seizure of Austria, it was replaced in 1946 by the UNITED NATIONS.

Leakey family Family of paleontologists and anthropologists known for their discoveries of HOMINID and other fossil remains in E Africa. Louis S. B. Leakey (1903–1972), born of British missionary parents, grew up in Kenya, was educated at Cambridge Univ., and eventually (1931) came to do field research at OLDUVAI GORGE in Tanzania. He was joined there by his wife, Mary D. Leakey (1913–1996), who in 1959 uncovered remains of a form of AUSTRALOPITHECUS. The couple later uncovered the first known remains of HOMO HABILIS, as well as those of Proconsul, a common ancestor of both humans and apes (lived about 25 million years ago). Louis persuaded both Jane GOODALL and Dian FOSSEY to undertake their pioneering studies of chimpanzees and gorillas. Mary continued to make important discoveries after her husband's death. Their son Richard (b.1944) is known for his work on the LAKE TURKANA REMAINS in Kenya, where he uncovered evidence of H. habilis in Africa as early as 2 million years ago.

Lean, David (later *Sir David*) (1908–1991) British film director. He worked at Gaumont Studios from 1928, becoming head film editor. He codirected *In Which We Serve* (1942) with Noël COWARD and directed Coward's *Blithe Spirit*

(1945) and *Brief Encounter* (1945), as well as *Great Expectations* (1946) and *Oliver Twist* (1948). He won wide acclaim for *The Bridge on the River Kwai* (1957, Academy Award), *Lawrence of Arabia* (1962, Academy Award), *Dr. Zhivago* (1965), and *A Passage to India* (1984).

Leaning Tower of Pisa White marble CAMPANILE in Pisa, Italy, famous for the uneven SETTLING of its foundation, which causes it to lean 15 ft (4.5 m) from the perpendicular. Begun in 1173, it was designed to stand 185 ft (56 m) high. Work was suspended several times; the tower, still leaning, was completed in the 14th cent. In 2001 it was reopened after an 11-year stabilizing operation.

Lear, Edward (1812–1888) English painter and comic poet. From age 15 he earned his living by drawing. Employed to illustrate the earl of Derby's private menagerie in the 1830s, he later produced *Book of Nonsense* (1846) for the earl's grandchildren. Later volumes include *Nonsense Songs, Stories, Botany and Alphabets* (1871), containing "The Owl and the Pussy-Cat," and *Laughable Lyrics* (1877). He is best known for popularizing the LIMERICK.

Lear, Norman (Milton) (b.1922) U.S. television producer, writer, and director. Born in New Haven, Conn., he worked in television as a comedy writer and director (1950–59) and wrote and produced such movies as *Come Blow Your Horn* (1963) and *Divorce American Style* (1967) before returning to television to create the hit series *All in the Family* (1971–83), for which he received four Emmy awards; *Maude* (1972–78); *Sanford and Son* (1972–77); *Good Times* (1974–79); and *The Jeffersons* (1975–85).

Lear, William Powell (1902–1978) U.S. engineer and industrialist. Born in Hannibal, Mo., he founded the Lear Avia Corp. to make radio and navigational devices for aircraft. In World War II, the company manufactured precision devices for Allied aircraft, and later a miniaturized autopilot that could be used on small fighter aircraft. In 1963 Lear formed Lear Jet, Inc., whose jets became the world's most popular private jet aircraft.

learned helplessness In psychology, a mental state in which a laboratory subject forced to bear noxious stimuli becomes unable or unwilling to avoid subsequent applications, even if "escapable," presumably through having "learned" that control is out of his or her hands. Experiments have led some researchers, including Martin Seligman (b.1942) in *Helplessness* (1975), to believe that chronic failure, depression, and similar conditions are forms of learned helplessness. Critics have argued that broad generalizations are unwarranted.

learning Process of modifying existing knowledge, skills, or habits through experience, practice, or exercise. Learning includes associative processes (see ASSOCIATION, CONDITIONING), discrimination of sense-data, psychomotor and perceptual learning (see PERCEPTION), imitation, concept formation, problem solving, and insight learning. The first experiments with associative learning were conducted by Ivan PAVLOV in Russia and Edward L. Thorndike (1874–1949) in the U.S. Critics of the early stimulus-response (S-R) theories claimed they ignored a subject's inner activities. GESTALT-PSYCHOLOGY researchers drew attention to the importance of pattern in learning, while structural linguists argued that language learning was grounded in a genetically inherited "grammar." Developmental psychologists, such as Jean PIAGET, highlighted stages of growth in learning. More recently, cognitive scientists have explored learning as a form of information processing, while some brain researchers, such as Gerald Edelman (b.1929), have proposed that thinking and learning involve an ongoing process of cerebral pathway building. Related topics include attention, comprehension, and MOTIVATION. See also BEHAVIORISM, EDUCATIONAL PSYCHOLOGY, IMPRINTING, INSTINCT, INTELLIGENCE.

learning disabilities Chronic difficulties in learning to read, write, spell, or calculate. Though their causes are still not fully understood, it is widely agreed that they do not indicate subnormal intelligence, but rather that the learning-disabled have a neurologically based difficulty in processing language or figures, which must be compensated for with special learning strategies. Examples of learning disabilities include difficulty in reading (DYSLEXIA), writing (dysgraphia), and mathematics (dyscalculia). They may be diagnosed through testing, and children may be enrolled in programs offering special help; left unrecognized, disabilities may result not only in poor classroom performance but also in low self-esteem and disruptive behavior.

leather Animal skins and hides treated to preserve them and make them suitable for use. TANNING converts the perishable skin to a stable and nondecaying material. The most common leathers come from cattle, sheep and lamb, goat and kid, horse, mule, zebra, buffalo, pig, seal, walrus, whale, and alligator. Leather making has been practiced for more than 7,000 years.

Leavis \'lē-vəs\, **F(rank) R(aymond)** (1895–1978) British literary critic. Teaching at Cambridge Univ., he brought a new seriousness to criticism, believing that the critic's duty is to assess works according to the author's moral position. He cofounded *Scrutiny*, a journal (1932–53) often regarded as his greatest contribution to English letters. His influential books include *New Bearings in English Poetry* (1932) and *The Great Tradition* (1948).

Lebanese civil war (1975–91) Conflict resulting from the presence in Lebanon in the 1970s of the PALESTINE LIBERATION ORGANIZATION (PLO) and exacerbated by tensions among Lebanon's Christian and Muslim populations. In 1975 Lebanon's Muslims supported the PLO and sought more political power; its Christians opposed the PLO. The factions fought fiercely and Lebanon became effectively partitioned, with the Christians in power in the north and Muslims in the south. Israel invaded S Lebanon in 1982 to destroy Palestinian bases; PLO leaders and troops were driven out of Beirut, and by 1985 Israel had withdrawn from most of Lebanon, which by then was split internally over whether to accept Syria's leadership. In 1989 the Christian leader Gen. Michel Aoun failed to drive Syria from Lebanon, and the ARAB LEAGUE mediated a peace deal (1990). In S Lebanon, fighting between Israeli and HIZBULLAH forces continued through the 1990s.

Lebanon *officially* **Republic of Lebanon** Country, E shore of the Mediterranean Sea. It is bounded by Syria and Israel. Area: 3,950 sq mi (10,230 sq km). Population (2000): 3,578,000. Capital: BEIRUT. The Lebanese are ethnically a mixture of Phoenician, Greek, Armenian, and Arab ele-

[Map of Lebanon]

ments. Languages: Arabic (official), French, English. Religions: Islam (Sunnite and Shiite), Christianity (Maronite, Greek Orthodox). Currency: Lebanese pound. Its mountains include the LEBANON MTNS. in the central region and the Anti-Lebanon and Mt. Hermon ranges along

the E border; a low coastal plain stretches along the Mediterranean. The Litani River flows southward through the fertile BEKAA VALLEY. Originally much of the country was forested (the cedars of Lebanon were famous), but forests now cover only about 8% of the terrain. Lebanon is not agriculturally self-sufficient and must rely on food imports. Its traditional role as the financial center of the Middle East has been undermined by civil strife and foreign intervention in recent decades. It is a republic with one legislative house; its chief of state is the president, and the head of government is the prime minister. Much of present-day Lebanon corresponds to ancient PHOENICIA, which was settled around 3000 B.C. In the 6th cent. A.D., Christians fleeing Syrian persecution settled in N Lebanon and founded the MARONITE CHURCH. Arab tribesmen settled in S Lebanon and by the 11th cent. had founded the DRUZE faith. Part of the medieval crusader states, Lebanon was later ruled by the Mamluks. In 1516 the Ottoman Turks seized control; the Turks ended the local rule of the Druze Shihab princes in 1842. Poor relations between religious groups resulted in the massacre of Maronites by Druze in 1860. France intervened, forcing the Ottomans to form an autonomous province for the Christian area known as Mt. Lebanon. Following World War I, it was administered by the French military, but by 1946 it was fully independent. After the ARAB–ISRAELI WAR of 1948–49, over 200,000 Palestinian refugees settled in S Lebanon. In 1970 the PALESTINE LIBERATION ORGANIZATION (PLO) moved its headquarters to Lebanon and began raids into N Israel. The Christian-dominated Lebanese government tried to curb them, and in response the PLO sided with Lebanon's Muslims in their conflict with Christians, sparking a civil war by 1975. In 1976–82 Syrian and U.N. troops tried to maintain a cease-fire. In 1982 Israeli forces invaded in an effort to drive Palestinian forces out of S Lebanon; Israeli troops withdrew in 1985, leaving the conflict unresolved. Israeli troops returned, but a cease-fire was agreed to in 1996. It was broken when Israeli soldiers and Lebanon's HIZBULLAH forces clashed in 1997. Following numerous contentious talks between Lebanon and Israel, Israeli troops abruptly withdrew from Lebanon in 2000.

Lebanon Mountains *Arabic* **Jabal Lubnan** \'ja-bəl-ˌlüb-'nän\ *ancient* Libanus. Mountain range, Lebanon. Running parallel to the Mediterranean coast, it is about 100 mi (160 km) long. The N section is the highest part of the range and includes the tallest peak, Qurnet al-Sauda, at 10,131 ft (8,088 m) high. On the W flanks are the remaining groves of the Cedars of Lebanon.

Lebrun \lə-'brœn\, **Albert** (1871–1950) Last president (1932–40) of France's THIRD REPUBLIC. He was elected president as a compromise candidate and served as a mediator and symbol of unity, rarely influencing policy. In 1940 he complied with the cabinet's decision to seek an armistice with Germany and his replacement by the VICHY FRANCE government. In 1944 he acknowledged Charles DE GAULLE as head of the provisional government.

Le Brun \lə-'brœn\, **Charles** (1619–1690) French painter and designer. After study in Paris and Rome, he received large decorative and religious commissions that made his reputation. Possessing extraordinary organizational as well as technical skills, as the first painter to LOUIS XIV he created or supervised the production of most of the paintings, sculptures, and decorative objects commissioned by the French government for three decades (see LOUIS XIV STYLE). As director of the Academy of Painting and Sculpture from 1648, he was instrumental in establishing the characteristic homogeneity of French art in the 17th cent.

Lebrun, Elisabeth Vigée- See Elisabeth VIGÉE-LEBRUN

Le Carré \lə-kä-'rā\, **John** *orig.* David John Moore Cornwell (b.1931) British novelist. As a member of the foreign service in W. Germany from 1959, he acquired firsthand knowledge of international espionage. His novels include the realistic, suspenseful *The Spy Who Came in from the Cold* (1963; film, 1965); the trilogy of *Tinker, Tailor, Soldier, Spy* (1974), *The Honourable Schoolboy* (1977), and *Smiley's People* (1980); *The Little Drummer Girl* (1983; film, 1984); *The Russia House* (1989; film, 1990); and *The Tailor of Panama* (1996; film 2001).

K L

lecithin \'le-sə-thən\ Any of a class of PHOSPHOLIPIDS important in cell structure and METABOLISM. They are composed of PHOSPHATE, CHOLINE, GLYCEROL (as the ESTER), and two FATTY ACIDS. Various fatty acids pairs distinguish the various lecithins. Commercial lecithin is used in animal feeds, baking products and mixes, chocolate, cosmetics and soap, insecticides, paint, and plastics.

Leclerc \lə-'kler\, **Jacques-Philippe** orig. Philippe-Marie, vicomte (Viscount) de Hauteclocque (1902–1947) French general in World War II. He was captured by the Germans in 1939, but escaped to England, where he took the pseudonym Leclerc to protect his family and joined the FREE FRENCH forces. He achieved a number of military victories in Africa, and in 1944 commanded a French division in the Normandy invasion. On August 25 he received the surrender of the German commander in Paris. He died in an airplane accident.

Le Corbusier \lə-kȯr-bū̄es-'yä\ orig. Charles-Édouard Jeanneret (1887–1965) Swiss-French architect and city planner.

Le Corbusier Photo by Yousuf Karsh, 1954

After settling in Paris, he and the painter Amédée Ozenfant (1886–1966) formulated the ideas of Purism, with an aesthetic based on modern technology. His early work included theoretical plans for skyscraper cities and mass-produced housing; he declared that "a house is a machine for living in." The Villa Savoye at Poissy (1929–30), with its structure raised on slender pillars, open floor plan, long strip windows, and roof terrace, embodied his principles of modern housing. Later works include the Unité d'Habitation and the lyrical chapel of Notre-Dame-du-Haut at Ronchamp (1950–55). His government buildings at Chandigarh, India (begun 1950), with their enormous concrete sunshades, sculptural facades, and swooping rooflines, represent the first large-scale application of his city-planning principles. Le Corbusier's many writings gave a firm foundation to the worldwide avant-garde architectural movement he created.

LED See LIGHT-EMITTING DIODE

Leda \'lē-də\ In Greek legend, a queen who was visited by ZEUS in the form of a swan and conceived HELEN of Troy. Zeus was also sometimes said to be the father of her son Pollux, while Leda's husband Tyndareus was held to be the father of his twin, Castor (see DIOSCURI). Leda's daughter by Tyndareus, Clytemnestra, married AGAMEMNON.

Lederberg \'lā-dər-ˌberg\, **Joshua** (b.1925) U.S. geneticist. Born in Montclair, N.J., he earned his PhD at Yale Univ. With Norton Zinder (b. 1928), Lederberg found that certain viruses could carry a bacterial gene from one bacterium to another, a discovery that made bacteria an important tool of genetic research. He also developed ingenious breeding techniques for bacterial genetics. In 1958 he shared the Nobel Prize with George BEADLE and Edward TATUM for discovery of the mechanisms of genetic recombination in bacteria.

Ledo Road See STILWELL ROAD

Ledoux \lə-'dü\, **Claude-Nicolas** (1736–1806) French architect. In the 1760s and early 1770s he designed private houses in an innovative Neoclassical style, among them Madame du Barry's famous château at Louveciennes (1771–73). In the mid-1770s he planned a new saltworks and surrounding town at the Salines de Chaux, Arc-et-Senans; the design, in which rings of workers' dwellings enclosed a central factory, was designed both to facilitate production and ensure healthy living conditions. His theater at Besançon (1771–73) was revolutionary in providing seats for the ordinary public as well as the upper classes.

Lee, Ang (b.1954) Taiwanese-U.S. film director. He moved to the U.S. in 1978, where he initially worked writing screenplays. He wrote and directed *Pushing Hands* (1992) and the acclaimed offbeat comedies *The Wedding Banquet* (1993) and *Eat Drink Man Woman* (1994), and directed the well-received *Sense and Sensibility* (1995) and the award-winning *Crouching Tiger, Hidden Dragon* (2000).

Lee, Ann (1736–1784) British-American religious leader. A factory worker in Manchester, England, she joined the SHAKERS in 1758 and was acknowledged as their leader in 1770. Persecuted by the authorities and commanded by a vision, she emigrated to America in 1774. With a band of followers, she founded a settlement at Niskeyuna (present-day Watervliet), N.Y., in 1776. "Mother Ann" is said to have performed miracles, including healing the sick by touch. She was imprisoned briefly for treason because of her pacifism and refusal to sign an oath of allegiance.

Lee, Bruce orig. Lee Yuen Kam (1940–1973) U.S. film actor. Born to a touring Chinese opera star in San Francisco, he grew up in Hong Kong. He became the very popular star of martial-arts action films, including *The Chinese Connection* (*Fist of Fury,* 1972) and *Enter the Dragon* (1973), which gained an international cult following. His career was cut short by his sudden death at 33 from a brain edema. His son Brandon Lee (1965–1993) was emerging as an action-movie star when he died in a shooting accident on a movie set.

Lee, Gypsy Rose orig. Rose Louise Hovick (1914–1970) U.S. striptease artist. Born in Seattle, she made her debut in BURLESQUE in 1929, becoming the headliner at Billy Minsky's Republic Theatre on Broadway (1931). Noted for her grace and style, she became the most famous stripper of all time. After retiring from burlesque (1937), she appeared in nightclubs and on television. Her autobiography *Gypsy* (1957) was the basis for a successful musical.

Lee, Henry (1756–1818) American army officer and politician. Born in Prince William Co., Va., in the AMERICAN REVOLUTION he rose to cavalry commander (earning the nickname "Light-Horse Harry") and led victories at Paulus Hook, N.J., and in the South. He served as governor of Virginia 1791–94, and commanded the army to suppress the WHISKEY REBELLION (1794). As a U.S. Representative (1799–1801), he wrote the resolution eulogizing George WASHINGTON as "first in war, first in peace, and first in the hearts of his countrymen." He was the father of Robert E. LEE.

Lee, Richard Henry (1732–1794) American statesman. Born in Stratford, Va., he served in the Virginia House of Burgesses (1758–75) and helped initiate the COMMITTEES OF CORRESPONDENCE. In the Continental Congress, on June 7, 1776, he introduced a resolution calling for independence. It led to the Declaration of Independence, which he signed, as he did the Articles of Confederation. He served in the Congress 1784–89 and as its president 1784–85. He opposed ratification of the U.S. Constitution because it lacked a bill of rights but later served in the first U.S. Senate (1789–92).

Lee, Robert E(dward) (1807–1870) U.S. and Confederate military leader. Born in Stratford, Va., the son of Henry LEE, he graduated from West Point, then served in the engineering corps and in the Mexican War under Winfield SCOTT. In 1859 he led U.S. troops to suppress John BROWN's insurgents at Harpers Ferry. In 1861 he was offered command of U.S. troops to force the seceded Southern states back into the Union. Though opposed to secession, he refused. After Virginia seceded, he became commander of Virginia's forces in the AMERICAN CIVIL WAR. He repulsed the Union forces in the SEVEN DAYS' BATTLES, then won victories at BULL RUN, FREDERICKSBURG, and CHANCELLORSVILLE. His attempts to draw Union forces out of Virginia by invading the North resulted in failures at ANTIETAM and GETTYSBURG. In 1864–65 he conducted defensive campaigns against Union forces under U. S. GRANT that caused heavy casualties. Lee ended his retreat behind the fortifications built at Petersburg and Richmond (see PETERS-

Robert E. Lee, 1865

BURG CAMPAIGN). By April 1865 dwindling forces and supplies forced Lee, now general of all Confederate armies, to surrender at APPOMATTOX. Still a hero to the South, he became president of Washington College (later WASHINGTON AND LEE UNIV.).

Lee, Spike (*orig.* Shelton Jackson) (b.1957) U.S. film director. Born in Atlanta, he grew up in Brooklyn, N.Y. At NYU he began writing, directing, producing, and acting in his movies about African-American life. *She's Gotta Have It* (1986) was followed by *School Daze* (1988), the highly successful *Do the Right Thing* (1989), *Mo' Better Blues* (1990), the epic *Malcolm X* (1992), *Crooklyn* (1994), *He Got Game* (1998), and *Summer of Sam* (1999), confirming his reputation as the foremost black American film director.

leech Any ANNELID of the class Hirudinea (about 300 known species), with a small sucker containing the mouth at the front end and a large sucker at the back end. Species range from tiny to about 8 in. (20 cm) long. Leeches live primarily in freshwater or on land. Aquatic leeches may feed on the blood of fishes, amphibians, birds, and mammals, or they may eat snails, insect larvae, and worms. True land leeches feed only on the blood of mammals. Substances in the leech's saliva anesthetize the wound area, dilate the blood vessels, and prevent the blood from clotting. Some species have been used by doctors to drain off blood for centuries.

Leeds City (pop., 1999 est.: 680,000), W. Yorkshire, England. It lies northeast of MANCHESTER. Incorporated as a city in 1626, it was an early center of the woolen industry. The Leeds and Liverpool Canal (1816) stimulated its growth, and the end of the century saw rapid expansion in the factory production of ready-made clothing. It is the seat of the Univ. of Leeds.

leek Hardy, vigorous, biennial plant (*Allium porrum*) of the LILY FAMILY, native to the E Mediterranean and the Middle East. It has a mild, sweet, onionlike flavor prized in cooking. It became the national emblem of Wales following an ancient victory by an army of Welshmen who wore leeks as a distinguishing sign. The long, narrow leaves and nearly cylindrical bulb of the first season are replaced in the second season by a tall, solid, flower-bearing stalk.

Lee Kuan Yew (b.1923) Prime minister of Singapore (1959–90). A lawyer and a socialist, he worked as a legal adviser to labor unions and won election to Singapore's legislative council in 1955, while the country was still a British crown colony. He helped Singapore achieve self-government and, running as an anticolonialist and anticommunist, was elected prime minister in 1959. His numerous reforms included the emancipation of women. Lee industrialized the country and made Singapore the most prosperous nation in S.E. Asia. He achieved both labor peace and a rising standard of living for workers, though his mildly authoritarian government at times infringed on civil liberties.

Lee Teng-hui \'lē-'dən-'hwē\ (b.1923) First Taiwan-born president (1988–2000) of the Republic of China (Taiwan). He became president after the death of CHIANG CHING-KUO, was reelected in 1990, and won a landslide victory in 1996 in the first direct presidential election. Lee favored "flexible diplomacy" in dealing with the People's Republic of China.

Leeuwenhoek \'lā-vən-ˌhùk\, **Antonie van** (1632–1723) Dutch microscopist. With his simple microscopes he observed protozoa in rainwater and pond and well water, and bacteria in the human mouth and intestine. He also discovered blood corpuscles, capillaries, and the structure of muscles and nerves, and in 1677 he first described the spermatozoa of insects, dogs, and humans. How he enhanced the power of his lenses sufficiently to achieve such results remains unknown. His research on lower animals argued against the doctrine of spontaneous generation, and his observations helped lay the foundations for the sciences of bacteriology and protozoology.

Leeward Islands \'lü-ərd, 'lē-wərd\ Arc of W. Indian islands in the Lesser ANTILLES, NE Caribbean Sea. The major islands are, from north to south, the VIRGIN ISLANDS OF THE U.S. and the British VIRGIN ISLANDS, ANGUILLA, ST. MARTIN, ST. KITTS-NEVIS, ANTIGUA AND BARBUDA, MONTSER-

RAT, and GUADELOUPE. Just south is DOMINICA, usually designated as part of the WINDWARD ISLANDS.

Lefkosía See NICOSIA

left The portion of the political spectrum associated with SOCIALISM. The term derives from the seating arrangement of the French revolutionary parliament in the 1790s, where the socialistic representatives sat to the presiding officer's left. The left favors greater popular sovereignty and more effective democracy and regards social welfare as the most important goal of government. Modern liberalism may shade off into socialism, the standard ideology of the left in most countries of the world; COMMUNISM is a more radical and sharply defined leftist ideology.

legend Traditional story or group of stories told about a particular person or place. Formerly the term referred to a tale about a saint. Legends resemble folktales in content; they may include supernatural beings, elements of mythology, or explanations of natural phenomena, but they are associated with a particular locality or person. They are popularly regarded as historical, though they are not entirely verifiable.

Léger \lā-'zhā\, **Fernand** (1881–1955) French painter. He worked as an architectural draftsman in Paris before studying art. Influenced by Paul CÉZANNE and the early Cubists, he developed a painting style that combined bold colors with geometric and cylindrical forms arranged in highly disciplined compositions. His best-known works celebrated modern industrial technology by emphasizing shapes derived from machine parts. Though he was seriously injured in World War I, his art continued to affirm his faith in modern life and popular culture.

Leghorn See LIVORNO

legion Military organization, originally the largest permanent unit in the Roman army. It was the basis of the military system by which imperial Rome conquered and ruled its empire. The early Roman Republic found the Greek phalanx too unwieldy for fragmented fighting in the hills and valleys of central Italy, and evolved small and flexible infantry units called maniples. These were grouped in larger units called cohorts, which ranged from 360 to 600 men, depending on the era. Ten cohorts made up a legion. See also FOREIGN LEGION.

Legionnaires' disease Type of PNEUMONIA first identified in American Legion conventioneers in 1976, 29 of whom died. The cause was identified as a previously unknown bacterium, *Legionella pneumophila*. Usually, malaise and headache are followed by high fever and often chills, dry cough, shortness of breath, and pain. Contaminated water (e.g., in water-distribution systems, humidifiers, and whirlpool spas) is usually suspected as the source. The disease is treated with antibiotics.

Legion of Honor *officially* **Order of the Legion of Honor** Highest-ranking order and decoration of the French republic, created by NAPOLEON in 1802. Membership is open to men and women, French citizens and foreigners; admission requires 20 years of civil achievement in peacetime or extraordinary military bravery and service in times of war.

legislature Lawmaking branch of a government. Early European legislatures include the English PARLIAMENT and the Icelandic Althing (founded c.930). Legislatures may have one or two houses (see BICAMERAL SYSTEM). Their powers may include passing laws, establishing the government's budget, confirming executive appointments, ratifying treaties, impeaching and removing from office members of the executive branch and judiciary, and redressing constituents' grievances. Members may be appointed or elected; they may represent the people as a whole, particular groups, or territorial subdistricts. In presidential systems, the executive and legislative branches are clearly separated; in parliamentary systems, members of the executive branch are chosen from the legislative membership.

Le Guin \lə-'gwin\, **Ursula K(roeber)** *orig.* Ursula Kroeber (b.1929) U.S. writer of science fiction and fantasy. Born in Berkeley, Cal., the daughter of anthropologist A. L. KROEBER, she was influenced by the methods of anthropology and has often included highly detailed descriptions of alien societies in her works. Among her novels are *The Left Hand of Darkness* (1969), *The Dispossessed* (1974), and the Earthsea series.

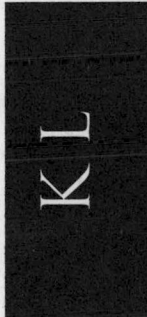

K L

legume \'le-ˌgyüm\ Any of about 18,000 species in about 650 genera of flowering plants that make up the order Fabales, consisting of the single family Leguminosae, or Fabaceae (the pea family). The term also refers to their characteristic fruit, also called a pod. Legumes are widespread on all habitable continents. Leaves of many members appear feathery, and flowers are almost universally showy. In the production of food, the legume family is the most important of any family. The pods are part of the diet of nearly all humans and supply most dietary protein in regions of high population density. In addition, legumes perform the invaluable act of NITROGEN FIXATION. Legumes also provide edible oils, GUMS, fibers, and raw material for plastics, and some are ornamentals. Included in this family are ACACIA, ALFALFA, BEANS, CAROB, CLOVER, LUPINE, MIMOSA, PEAS, PEANUTS, SOYBEANS, TAMARIND, and VETCH.

Lehar \'lā-ˌhär\, **Franz (Christian)** orig. Ferencz Christian Lehar (1870–1948) Austro-Hungarian composer. Born in Hungary, he became a military bandmaster like his father, but soon moved to Vienna, where he became a popular composer of marches and waltzes. After 1901 he concentrated on orchestra conducting and on composing, especially of 40 witty and melodic operettas that embody the prewar Viennese spirit, including *The Merry Widow* (1905), *The Countess of Luxembourg* (1909), and *The Land of Smiles* (1929).

Le Havre \lə-'hävrᵊ\ Seaport city (pop., 1999: 190,000), N France. It lies along the ENGLISH CHANNEL and the SEINE RIVER estuary, northwest of PARIS. The second port of France (after MARSEILLE), it is also an important industrial center. The harbor was built in 1517 by FRANCIS I; enlarged and fortified in the 17th cent., it was adapted to accommodate bigger vessels in the late 18th cent. Most of the city was destroyed during World War II; its 17th-cent. Church of Notre-Dame is one of the few old buildings to survive.

Lehmbruck \'lām-brük\, **Wilhelm** (1881–1919) German sculptor, painter and printmaker. His youthful work was academically realistic, but he grew to admire the works of Auguste RODIN, and in 1910 he moved to Paris. One of the most important German Expressionist sculptors, he is best known for his elongated nudes, such as *Kneeling Woman* (1911), which suggests a resigned pessimism. He returned to Germany at the outbreak of World War I and tended wounded soldiers in a hospital. *Seated Youth* (1917) reveals his profound depression; he committed suicide two years later.

Leiber \'lē-bər\, **Jerry** (b.1933) U.S. songwriter and producer. Born in Baltimore, he grew up in Los Angeles, where he met Mike Stoller (b.1933), who had moved there from New York. In 1950, while still in their teens, Leiber and Stoller became a songwriting and production team, among the first to combine pop music with rhythm and blues. Their "Hound Dog" was recorded by Elvis PRESLEY, who would record more than 20 of their songs. They wrote numerous songs for the Coasters, including "Yakety-Yak." Other hits included "Stand By Me" and "Is That All There Is?"

Leibniz \'līb-nəts, *Ger* 'līp-nits\, **Gottfried Wilhelm** *later* Freiherr (baron) von Leibniz (1646–1716) German philosopher and mathematician. He earned a doctorate in law at 20. In *De arte combinatoria* (1666) he set forth the fundamental concepts of the computer. While working for the elector of Mainz (1667–76), he codified the laws of Mainz. He served the dukes of Braunschweig-Lüneburg as librarian and privy councillor (1676–1716). He invented the differential and integral calculus simultaneously with Isaac NEWTON; Leibniz's work was published three years earlier (1684) and his notation was universally adopted. He also contributed to optics and mechanics. In 1700 he helped found the German Academy of Sciences in Berlin and became its first president. His *Theodicy* (1710) expressed an optimistic faith in reason and became an important text of the Enlightenment. He worked energetically to reconcile the Protestant churches in several countries. His chief philosophical contributions were in logic and metaphysics, in which he provided an alternative to the rationalism of Benedict de SPINOZA and René DESCARTES. In metaphysics he espoused pluralism (as opposed to Descartes's dualism and Spinoza's

monism). His universal mind and astonishing achievements make him one of the most extraordinary figures of Western civilization.

Leicester \'les-tər\ City (pop., 1999 est.: 270,000), seat of Leicestershire, central England. Settled by Romans, it was the site of a Norman castle and abbey built in 1143. It was where King RICHARD III spent the night before the Battle of BOSWORTH FIELD. It was incorporated in 1589, and became an industrial center after the arrival of the railway in 1832. The Univ. of Leicester (founded 1957) is nearby.

Leicester \'les-tər\, **Earl of** orig. Robert **Dudley** (1532?–1588) English courtier and favorite of ELIZABETH I. Sentenced to death in 1553 for aiding the attempt to put Lady Jane GREY on the throne, he was released in 1554. Handsome and ambitious, he soon won the queen's affection and was made a privy councillor in 1559. When his wife died in 1560, it was rumored that he had murdered her in order to marry Elizabeth. Dudley failed to win the queen's hand but they remained close friends. In 1585 he commanded an English force to assist the Netherlands against Spain, but proved incompetent and was recalled (1587).

Leicester, Earl of See Simon de MONTFORT

Leiden or **Leyden** \'līd-ᵊn, *Dutch* 'lā-də\ Commune (pop., 1999 est.: 117,000), W Netherlands. It was governed by the court of Holland until 1420. It became a printing center after the ELZEVIR FAMILY set up their press around 1581. The Univ. of Leiden was founded in 1575, and the town became a center of theology, science, and art. The birthplace of REMBRANDT VAN RIJN and J. J. van GOYEN, it was the residence of the PILGRIMS for 11 years before they sailed to America in 1620.

Leif Eriksson the Lucky *Norwegian* Leiv Eriksson den Hepne (10th–11th cent.) Icelandic explorer, possibly the first European to reach N. America. Son of ERIK THE RED, he was on his way back from Norway to Greenland (c.1000) when he sailed off course and landed probably at Nova Scotia, which he called VINLAND. This standard account comes from the Icelandic *Eiriks saga*. Another account, the *Groenlendinga saga* ("Tale of the Greenlanders"), says he learned of Vinland from a man who had been there 14 years earlier and that Leif reached N. America after 1000.

Leigh \'lē\, **Mike** (*orig.* Michael) (b.1943) British film director and playwright. His *The Box Play* (1965) began the process of improvisation with his actors that marks his works for stage, television, and film, which usually depict working-class life with sharp intelligence, humor, and pathos. His offbeat movies *High Hopes* (1988), *Life Is Sweet* (1991), and *Naked* (1993), were followed by the internationally acclaimed *Secrets and Lies* (1996), *Career Girls* (1997), *Topsy-Turvy* (1999), and *All or Nothing* (2002).

Leigh, Vivien *orig.* Vivian Mary Hartley (1913–1967) British actress. She made her film debut in 1934 and her London stage debut in 1935. She was chosen after a well-publicized search for the role of Scarlett in *Gone with the Wind* (1939, Academy Award), which brought her great fame. Noted for her delicate beauty, she later starred in *That Hamilton Woman* (1941), *Anna Karenina* (1948), and *A Streetcar Named Desire* (1951, Academy Award). She was married (1940–60) to Laurence OLIVIER, with whom she appeared in many successful London stage productions.

Leinster \'len-stər\ Province (pop., 1996: 1,922,000), E Ireland. Some of its disparate parts maintained their independence until the 16th cent. Its counties include Carlow, Dublin, Kildare, Kilkenny, Laoighis, Longforth, Louth, Meath, Offaly, Westmeath, Wexford and Wicklow.

Leipzig \'līp-sik, 'līp-sig\ City (pop., 1996 est.: 471,000), E central Germany. Situated in W SAXONY state, it was, in the 11th cent., a fortified town. Its location on the principal trade routes of central Europe made it an important commercial center. Several battles of the THIRTY YEARS' WAR were fought near the city, which was also the site of the Battle of Leipzig (1813). Massive demonstrations in Leipzig in 1989 helped end the communist regime in E. Germany. For centuries it has been one of the leading musical centers of Europe. It is the site of the Univ. of Leipzig (1409), the 13th-cent. Church of St. Thomas, and the annual Leipzig Fair.

Leipzig, University of State-supported university in Leipzig, Germany, founded in 1409. In the 1500s it was a center of

Reformation thought, and in the 18th and 19th cent. it became one of Europe's leading literary and cultural centers, attracting such students as G. W. LEIBNIZ, J. W. von GOETHE, J. G. FICHTE, and Richard WAGNER. It was named Karl Marx Univ. of Leipzig 1953–90. Enrollment is about 21,000.

leishmaniasis \ˌlēsh-mə-ˈnī-ə-səs\ Human protozoal infection spread by the bite of a bloodsucking sandfly. It occurs worldwide but is especially prevalent in tropical areas. It is caused by various species of the flagellate PROTOZOAN genus *Leishmania*, which infect rodents and canines. Visceral leishmaniasis, or kala-azar, affects the liver, spleen, and bone marrow and is usually fatal if not treated. Cutaneous leishmaniasis, or Oriental sore, is characterized by lesions on the skin of the legs, feet, hands, and face, most of which heal spontaneously after many months.

Leland \ˈlē-lənd\, **Henry M(artyn)** (1843–1932) U.S. engineer and manufacturer. Born in Danville, Vt., he founded Leland & Faulconer Manufacturing Co. in Detroit in 1890 to build automobile engines. In 1904 he merged it into his new Cadillac Motor Car Co. In 1917 he founded the Lincoln Motor Co., which was purchased by Henry FORD in 1922. He was known for his rigorous standards; his innovations included the V-8 engine and adoption of the electric starter.

Lelang See NANGNANG

Le Loi \ˈlā-ˈlȯi\ (d.1443) Vietnamese general and emperor who won back independence for Vietnam from China and founded the LATER LE DYNASTY. A wealthy landowner, he was affected by the social conditions of the common people, who suffered under the Chinese overlords and the Vietnamese aristocracy. He led a series of revolts, begun in 1418, that drove the Chinese out. He maintained diplomatic relations with the Chinese Ming dynasty, which acknowledged his kingdom in 1428. Among his achievements were land reforms to help the peasants. He is the most honored Vietnamese hero of the medieval period.

Le Mans \lə-ˈmän\ **(Grand Prix d'Endurance)** Automobile race, perhaps the best known in the world, run annually since 1923 at the 8.3-mi (13.4-km) Sarthe road-racing circuit, near Le Mans, France. The winner is the sports car that travels the greatest distance in a 24-hour period.

LeMay, Curtis E(merson) (1906–1990) U.S. Air Force officer. Born in Columbus, Ohio, in World War II he developed advanced strategic bombardment techniques and led bomber commands in Europe and the Pacific, where he launched fire-bombing raids on Japanese cities. As commander of U.S. air forces in Europe (1945–48), he directed the Berlin airlift (see BERLIN BLOCKADE AND AIRLIFT). As head of the Strategic Air Command (1948–57) he built it into a global strike force. He was chief of staff of the U.S. Air Force (1961–65). In 1968 he ran on the third-party ticket headed by George WALLACE.

Lemieux \lə-ˈmyü\, **Mario** (b.1965) Canadian hockey player. Born in Montreal, in 12 seasons with the Pittsburgh Penguins (1984–94, 1995–97) he scored 613 goals and set the all-time record for goals per game (.823). Despite serious back injuries, he led his team to STANLEY CUP victories (1991–92). In 1992 he was found to have Hodgkin's disease, but after surgery and radiation he led his team on a 17-game winning streak, an NHL record. After retiring in 1996, he acquired the Penguins in 1999 and returned to play on the team in 2000.

lemming Any of several species of small RODENTS belonging to the family Cricetidae and found primarily in N temperate and polar regions. Lemmings have short legs and long, soft fur. They are 4–7 in. (10–18 cm) long, including the stumpy tail. They feed on roots, shoots, and grasses and live in burrows or rock crevices. They are noted for regular population fluctuations, and for their spring and fall migrations. During those of the Norway lemming (*Lemmus lemmus*) many of the migrants drown in the sea. However, lemmings are hesitant to enter water and, contrary to legend, do not plunge into the sea in a deliberate death march.

Lemmon, Jack (*orig.* John Uhler) (1925–2001) U.S. actor. Born in Boston, he made his Broadway debut in 1953. He established his movie career in *Mister Roberts* (1955, Academy Award), and became noted for his character portrayals, often playing excitable, baffled individuals in such

movies as *Some Like It Hot* (1959), *The Apartment* (1960), and *The Odd Couple* (1968). His many other films included *Save the Tiger* (1973, Academy Award), *The China Syndrome* (1979), *Missing* (1982), and *Glengarry Glen Ross* (1992).

lemon Small thorny tree or spreading bush (*Citrus limon*) of the RUE FAMILY (citrus family), and its edible fruit. Under the yellow outer rind is the white, spongy inner peel, the source of commercial PECTIN. The juicy pulp is acidic and rich in vitamin C. The climates of coastal Italy and California are especially favorable for lemon trees, which in these regions produce fruit 6–10 times a year. Lemon juice enhances many drinks and dishes, and lemon by-products are used in beverages (citric acid), fruit jellies (pectin), and furniture polish (lemon oil).

lemon balm See BALM

Le Moyne de Bienville, Jean-Baptiste See J.-B. Le Moyne de BIENVILLE

Le Moyne d'Iberville, Pierre See Pierre Le Moyne d'IBERVILLE

lemur \ˈlē-mər\ In general, any of the prosimian PRIMATES (including galagos), all of which have a moist tip to their muzzle, forward-directed lower front teeth, and clawlike nails on the second toes of the feet. More strictly, the name refers to the nine species in the family Lemuridae, found only on Madagascar and the Comoro Islands, which have large eyes, a foxlike face, a slender monkeylike body, and long hind limbs. All lemurs are docile and gregarious. Species range from 5 in. (13 cm) to about 2 ft (60 cm) long. The bushy tail may be longer than the body. Most are active at night and spend most of their time in trees, eating fruits, leaves, buds, insects, and small birds and birds' eggs. A number of species are endangered.

Le Nain brothers \lə-ˈnaⁿ\ French painters. By 1630 the three brothers—Antoine (c.1600–1648), Louis (c.1603–1648), and Mathieu (c.1607–1677)—had established a workshop together in Paris. Most notable of their works are the dignified and sympathetic genre paintings of peasant life. Their realism is unique in 17th-cent. French art. None of the brothers' works bears more than a surname, and today they are treated as a single painter.

Lena River \ˈlē-nə, ˈlā-nə\ River, E central Russia, one of the longest rivers in the world. From its source west of Lake BAIKAL, it flows 2,734 mi (4,400 km) north across Russia to enter the Arctic Ocean. Its basin covers 961,000 sq mi (2,490,000 sq km). The land along its upper course and tributaries is rich in minerals, including gold and coal.

lend-lease System promulgated by Pres. Franklin ROOSEVELT to give aid to U.S. allies in WORLD WAR II. Faced with Britain's inability to pay cash for war materials and food, as required by U.S. law, Roosevelt asked Congress to allow repayment "in kind or property" from countries vital to U.S. defense. The Lend-Lease Act was passed in March 1941. Much of the aid went to British Commonwealth countries; the Soviet Union, China, and 40 other countries also received assistance.

L'Enfant \läⁿ-ˈfäⁿ, *Engl* ˈlän-ˌfänt\, **Pierre Charles** (1754–1825) French-U.S. engineer and architect. After studies in Paris, he volunteered in the American Revolutionary Army. Congress made him major of engineers in 1783. In 1791 George WASHINGTON had him prepare a plan for the federal capital. He designed a gridiron of blocks with broad diagonal avenues superimposed; focusing on the Capitol and presidential mansion, the plan incorporated green spaces and provided vistas of intersections where monuments and fountains could be placed. Though he was dismissed in 1792, his plan was generally followed.

L'Engle \ˈleŋ-gəl\, **Madeleine** *orig.* Madeleine Camp (b.1918) U.S. author of children's books. Born in New York City, she became known for works that explore such themes as the conflict of good and evil, the nature of God, and individual responsibility. In *A Wrinkle in Time* (1962), she introduced a group of children who engage in a cosmic battle against a great evil; their adventures continue in *A Swiftly Tilting Planet* (1978) and other books. She also has written adult fiction, poetry, and autobiography.

Lenin, Vladimir (Ilich) *orig.* Vladimir Ilich Ulyanov (1870–1924) Founder of the Russian Communist Party and leader of the RUSSIAN REVOLUTION OF 1917. Influenced by his

K L

brother Aleksandr, who was hanged in 1887 for conspiring to assassinate the czar, he became a Marxist in 1889 while practicing law. He was arrested as a subversive in 1895 and exiled to Siberia, where he married Nadezhda KRUPSKAYA. They lived in Western Europe after 1900. At the 1903 meeting in London of the RUSSIAN SOCIAL-DEMOCRATIC WORKERS' PARTY, he emerged as the leader of the BOLSHEVIK faction. In several revolutionary newspapers that he founded and edited, he put forth his ideas, known as LENINISM. With the outbreak of the RUSSIAN REVOLUTION OF 1905, he returned to Russia, but he resumed his exile in 1907 and continued his agitation for the next 10 years. In the RUSSIAN REVOLUTION OF 1917, he led the Bolshevik coup that overthrew the provisional government of Aleksandr KERENSKY. As revolutionary dictator of the Soviet state, he ended its war with Germany (1918) and repulsed counterrevolutionary threats in the RUSSIAN CIVIL WAR. He founded the COMINTERN in 1919. In 1921, to forestall economic disaster, he launched the NEW ECONOMIC POLICY. In ill health from 1922, he died of a stroke in 1924.

Leningrad See SAINT PETERSBURG

Leningrad, Siege of (Sept. 8, 1941–Jan. 27, 1944) Prolonged siege of the city of Leningrad (now St. Petersburg) by German forces in World War II. German forces invaded the Soviet Union in June 1941, and by November the city was almost completely encircled and its supply lines cut off. In 1942 alone, over 650,000 Leningrad citizens died from starvation, disease, and shelling from distant German artillery. Sparse supplies reached the city by barge in the summer and by sled in winter across Lake Ladoga; they kept the city's arms factories operating and its 2 million inhabitants barely alive, while another 1 million children, sick, and elderly were evacuated. In January 1944 a successful Soviet attack drove the Germans westward from the city's outskirts, ending the siege.

Leninism Principles expounded by Vladimir LENIN to guide the transition of society from CAPITALISM to COMMUNISM. The tenets of MARXISM, which Lenin embraced, provided no concrete guidelines for the transition. Lenin believed that a small, disciplined, professional group of revolutionaries was needed to violently overthrow the capitalist system, and that a "dictatorship of the proletariat" must guide society until the day when the state would wither away. Leninism in practice meant state control of all aspects of life by the COMMUNIST PARTY and the creation of the first modern totalitarian state.

Lenni Lenape See DELAWARE

Lennon, John (Winston) (1940–1980) British singer and songwriter. Born in Liverpool, he initially wanted to be a sailor like his father. In 1957 he formed the band that became the BEATLES, and in the 1960s he enjoyed enormous success performing with the group and writing songs with Paul MCCARTNEY. In the mid-1960s he began working on side projects in film and music, notably with the avant-garde artist Yoko Ono (b.1933), whom he married in 1969. Their political activism was reflected in his early solo work, including the hit "Imagine," and the government sought to have him deported. After 1975 he withdrew from public life; he and Ono returned with the album *Double Fantasy* shortly before his murder by a deranged fan.

Le Nôtre \lə-'nō-tr³\, **André** (1613–1700) French landscape architect. In 1637 he became master gardener to LOUIS XIII at the Tuileries Palace; he redesigned its gardens and extended the main avenue that later became the CHAMPS-ÉLYSÉES. LOUIS XIV placed Le Nôtre in charge of planning the gardens at the Palace of VERSAILLES, which he transformed from a muddy swamp to a park of splendid vistas. His many other parks and gardens included St.-Germain-en-Laye, St. Cloud, and FONTAINEBLEAU.

lens Piece of glass or other transparent substance that is used to form an image of an object by converging or diverging rays of LIGHT from the object. Because of the curvature of its surface, different rays of light are refracted (see REFRACTION) through different angles. A convex lens causes rays to converge on a single point, the focal point. A concave lens causes rays to diverge as though they are coming from a focal point. Both types cause the rays to form a visual image of the object, either real or virtual.

Lent In the Christian church, a period of penitential preparation for EASTER, observed since apostolic times. Western churches once provided for a 40-day fast (excluding Sundays), in imitation of JESUS' fasting in the wilderness; one meal a day was allowed. These rules have gradually been relaxed, and only Ash Wednesday—the first day of Lent in Western Christianity—and GOOD FRIDAY are now kept as fast days. Rules of fasting are stricter in the Eastern churches.

lentil Small annual LEGUME *(Lens esculenta)* and its lens-shaped, protein-rich, edible seed. One of the most ancient of cultivated foods, it is a good source of vitamin B, iron, and phosphorus. The lentil is widely cultivated throughout Europe, Asia, and N. Africa. Growing 6–18 in. (15–45 cm) high, the plant has compound leaves and pale blue flowers. Animals are fed the stalks and leaves as fodder.

Lenya, Lotte *orig.* Karoline Blamauer (1898–1981) Austrian-U.S. actress-singer. Born into poverty, Lenya worked as a dancer and actress in Zurich and later Berlin. She married Kurt WEILL in 1926 and began appearing in such Bertolt BRECHT-Weill works as *Mahagonny* (1927) and *The Three-penny Opera* (1928; film, 1930). They fled Nazi Germany in 1933, reaching New York in 1935. After Weill's death, she lent her inimitably husky voice to revivals throughout the 1950s, including a long-running production of *The Three-penny Opera*, and later *Brecht on Brecht* (1962) and *Cabaret* (1966), as well as films.

Leo I, St. *known as* **Leo the Great** (c.400–461) Pope (440–61). He was a champion of orthodoxy and a doctor of the church. To counter Eutyches of Constantinople, Leo wrote the *Tome* (449), which established the coexistence of Christ's human and divine natures. Leo's teachings were embraced by the Council of CHALCEDON (451), which also accepted his teaching as the "voice of Peter." Leo dealt capably with the invasions of barbaric tribes, persuading the HUNS not to attack Rome (452) and the VANDALS not to sack the city (455).

Leo III *known as* **Leo the Isaurian** \ī-'sör-ē-ən\ (c.675–741) Byzantine emperor (717–41). A military commander, he seized the throne with the help of Arab armies who hoped to subjugate the Byzantine empire. He then successfully defended Constantinople against the Arabs (717–18). Having crowned his son CONSTANTINE V co-emperor (720), Leo used his son's marriage to cement an alliance with the Khazars. Victory over the Arabs at Akroïnos (740) was crucial in preventing their conquest of Asia Minor. His policy of ICONOCLASM (730), which banned the use of sacred images in churches, engendered a century of conflict within the empire.

Leo IX, St. *orig.* Bruno, Graf (Count) von Egisheim und Dagsburg (1002–1054). Pope (1049–54). He was named pope by Emperor Henry III but insisted on election by the clergy and people of Rome. He strengthened the papacy and instituted reforms, seeking to eradicate clerical marriage and SIMONY. His assertion of papal primacy and his military campaign against the Normans in Sicily (1053) alienated the Eastern Church. His representatives excommunicated the patriarch of Constantinople, an act that triggered the SCHISM OF 1054.

Leo X *orig.* Giovanni de' Medici (1475–1521) Pope (1513–21), one of the most extravagant of the Renaissance pontiffs. Son of Lorenzo de' MEDICI, he was named a cardinal in 1492, and in 1494 he was exiled from Florence by the revolt of Girolamo SAVONAROLA. He returned in 1500 and soon consolidated Medici control of the city. As pope, he became a patron of the arts, accelerating construction of ST. PETER'S BASILICA. His lavish spending depleted his treasury. He discouraged reforms at the fifth LATERAN COUNCIL, and he responded inadequately to the REFORMATION, excommunicating Martin LUTHER in 1521 and failing to address the need for change, a lapse that signaled the end of the unified Western church.

León City (pop., 1995 : 124,000), W Nicaragua. The second-largest city in Nicaragua, it is the country's political and intellectual center. It was founded by the Spanish on the edge of Lake Managua in 1524; it was later destroyed by an earthquake and rebuilt in 1610 northwest of MANAGUA. It was the capital of Nicaragua until 1855. The seat of the Univ. of León, it is the burial place of Rubén DARÍO.

León Medieval kingdom, NW Spain. It began as a Christian kingdom in the early 10th cent. when García I established his court on a former Roman legion campsite. It was united with the kingdom of CASTILE in 1037–1157, then regained its independence and was ruled by its own kings. It was permanently reunited with Castile in 1230. The modern autonomous community of CASTILLA Y LEÓN covers roughly the same area.

Leonard, Sugar Ray (*orig.* Ray Charles) (b.1956) U.S. boxer. Born in Rocky Mount, N.C., he was an outstanding amateur, winning 145 of 150 bouts, including a 1976 Olympic championship. He gained the world welterweight title in 1979 by defeating Wilfred Benítez, lost it to Roberto Duran in 1980, but recaptured it from him later that year. After retiring because of a detached retina, he made a comeback in 1984. In 1987, as a middleweight, he defeated Marvin Hagler in one of boxing's great matches. He retired again in 1991. Known for his agility and finesse, he won 36 of his 40 professional matches.

Leonardo da Vinci \ˈvin-chē\ (1452–1519) Renaissance painter, sculptor, draftsman, architect, engineer, and scientist. Born in the town of Vinci, near Florence, he received training in painting, sculpture, and mechanical arts as an apprentice to Andrea del VERROCCHIO. In 1482, having made a name for himself in Florence, he entered the service of the duke of Milan as "painter and engineer." In Milan his artistic and creative genius unfolded. Around 1490 he began his project of writing treatises on the "science of painting," architecture, mechanics, and anatomy, believing that the painter, able to pictorialize his observations, was uniquely qualified to probe nature's secrets. His numerous surviving manuscripts—

Leonardo da Vinci, self-portrait

full of remarkable inventions, including the submarine and the telescope, that were never built—are noted for being written in a backward script that requires a mirror to be read. In 1502–3, as military architect and engineer for Cesare BORGIA, he helped lay the groundwork for modern cartography. After five years back in Florence (1503–8), he returned to Milan, where his scientific work flourished. In 1516 he entered the service of FRANCIS I of France; he never returned to Italy. Though only some 15 completed paintings survive, they are universally seen as masterpieces. The power of *The Last Supper* (1495–97) comes in part from its masterly composition. In the *Mona Lisa* (c.1503–6) the features and symbolic overtones of the subject achieve a complete synthesis, as did art and science in the unparalleled achievement of Leonardo's career.

Leoncavallo \lā-ˌōn-kä-ˈväl-lō\, **Ruggero** (1857–1919) Italian composer. After earning a doctorate in literature, he toured as a pianist while writing operas. His first, *Chatterton* (1878), attracted the interest of the publisher Ricordi. His one-act opera *I pagliacci* (1892) was his only enduring success.

Leone \lā-ˈō-nā\, **Sergio** (1921?–1989) Italian film director. After a directing debut in 1961, he won a wide audience with *A Fistful of Dollars* (1964), the first of the violent Italian-made "spaghetti westerns"; the equally popular *For a Few Dollars More* (1965) and *The Good, the Bad, and the Ugly* (1966) similarly starred Clint EASTWOOD. Among his other films are the epics *Once upon a Time in the West* (1968) and *Once upon a Time in America* (1984).

Leonidas \lē-ˈä-nə-dəs\ (d.480) King of SPARTA (c.490–480 B.C.). He is noted for his heroic stand against the Persians at the Battle of THERMOPYLAE in 480. Finding his army in a hopeless situation, he sent most of his troops in retreat, and with his 300-man royal guard withstood the Persian army for two days, battling valiantly to the last man. He became the object of a hero cult at Sparta. The legend that Spartans never surrender derived from this episode.

Leontief \lē-ˈän-tē-ˌef\, **Wassily** (1906–1999) Russian-U.S. economist. He emigrated to the U.S. in 1931. At Harvard Univ. (1931–75) he articulated his INPUT-OUTPUT ANALYSIS. He also described what is known as the Leontief paradox: that capital rather than labor is the scarce factor of production in the U.S. He was awarded the 1973 Nobel Prize. From 1975 until his death he taught at New York Univ.

leopard *or* **panther** Big CAT (*Panthera pardus*) of the bush and forest, found throughout sub-Saharan Africa, in NE Africa, and in Asia. The average leopard weighs 110–200 lbs (50–90 kg) and is about 6 ft (210 cm) long, excluding the 35-in. (90-cm) tail. The background color is typically yellowish above and white below, with dark spots arranged in rosettes over much of the body. The leopard is solitary and mainly nocturnal. An agile climber, it frequently stores the remains of its kills in tree branches. It preys on antelope and deer, but also hunts dogs and baboons. Several leopard races are endangered. See also CHEETAH, COUGAR, JAGUAR, SNOW LEOPARD.

Leopardi \ˌlä-ō-ˈpär-dē\, **Giacomo** (1798–1837) Italian poet, scholar, and philosopher. Congenitally deformed, he suffered throughout his life from chronic ailments and frustrated hopes. His usually pessimistic poetry is admired for its brilliance, intensity, and effortless musicality. His finest poems are probably the lyrics called "Idillii." *Operette morali* (1827; "Minor Moral Works") is an influential philosophical exposition of his doctrine of despair. He is considered among the great Italian writers of the 19th cent.

Leopold, (Rand) Aldo (1886–1948) U.S. environmentalist. Born in Burlington, Iowa, he worked for the U.S. Forest Service 1909–28, mainly in the Southwest, helping create the first national wilderness area (Gila Wilderness Area in New Mexico) in 1924. He taught at the Univ. of Wisconsin 1933–48. A fervent campaigner for wildlife and wilderness preservation, he cofounded the Wilderness Society in 1935. His posthumous *Sand County Almanac* (1949) eloquently called for the preservation of ecosystems; read by millions, it had an important influence on the budding environmental movement.

Leopold I *orig.* Léopold-Georges-Chrétien-Frédéric (1790–1865) First king of the Belgians (1831–65). The son of Francis, duke of Saxe-Coburg-Saalfeld, he married Charlotte, daughter of the future English king GEORGE IV, in 1816. After her death in 1817 Leopold continued to live in England until elected king of the newly formed Belgium. He helped strengthen the nation's new parliamentary system and scrupulously maintained Belgian neutrality. Influential in European diplomacy, in 1832 he married the daughter of LOUIS-PHILIPPE, and in 1840 he helped arrange the marriage of his niece, VICTORIA, to his nephew, Prince ALBERT of Saxe-Coburg-Gotha.

Leopold I (1640–1705) Holy Roman emperor (1658–1705). Son of FERDINAND III, Leopold was a devout Catholic destined for the church, but when his elder brother died unexpectedly (1654) he was crowned king of Hungary (1655) and of Bohemia (1656); with his father's death, Leopold became emperor in 1658. During his lengthy reign Austria emerged from a series of struggles to become a great European power. In 1683 the Turks besieged Vienna and were repulsed; they ceded control of Hungary in 1699. His third marriage, to Eleonore of Palatinate-Neuburg, was a happy union that produced 10 children, including the future emperors Joseph I and CHARLES VI.

Leopold II *orig.* Léopold-Louis-Philippe-Marie-Victor (1835–1909) King of the Belgians (1865–1909). Succeeding his father, LEOPOLD I, in 1876 he founded an association to explore the Congo River area, with H. M. STANLEY as his main agent. Leopold formed the Congo Free State in 1885 and ruled as its sovereign, allowing barbarous cruelty by the colonial masters; when news of the conditions there broke (c.1905), it provoked an international scandal. Under British and U.S. pressure, the region was removed from Leopold's personal rule and annexed to Belgium in 1908.

Leopold II (1747–1792) Holy Roman emperor (1790–92). Son of MARIA THERESA and Emperor FRANCIS I, he became

K L

a practitioner of ENLIGHTENED DESPOTISM, and built an efficient state government and encouraged representative institutions. In 1790 he succeeded his brother JOSEPH II as emperor and retained many of Joseph's reforms. In 1792 he allied with Prussia against revolutionary France, precipitating the FRENCH REVOLUTIONARY WARS.

Leopold III *orig.* Léopold-Philippe-Charles-Albert-Meinrad-Hubertus-Marie-Miguel (1901–1983) King of the Belgians (1934–51). In World War II he assumed command of the Belgian army, but surrendered his encircled forces 18 days after the German invasion in May 1940. The Belgian government repudiated his decision to remain with his forces, rather than join the government-in-exile in London. Under house arrest through the war, he later went to Switzerland (1945–50) to await resolution of the controversy. Though 58% of voters voted for his return to the throne, he abdicated in favor of his son BAUDOUIN.

Leopoldville See KINSHASA

lepidopteran \ˌle-pə-ˈdäp-tə-rən\ Any of the more than 100,000 species constituting the order Lepidoptera (Greek: "scaly wing"): BUTTERFLIES, MOTHS, and SKIPPERS. A slender proboscis is used for sucking. Nearly all lepidopterans are plant eaters, and species are found on every continent except Antarctica. Females may lay up to a thousand or more eggs at a time. All lepidopterans undergo complete METAMORPHOSIS. Many types move from one region to another, sometimes crossing thousands of miles of ocean, but the only species that truly migrates is the MONARCH BUTTERFLY.

Lepidus \ˈle-pə-dəs\, **Marcus Aemilius** (d.13/12 B.C.) Roman CONSUL (46, 42 B.C.) and triumvir (43–36). After the death of Julius CAESAR, Lepidus controlled parts of Gaul, Spain, and Africa and wielded great influence. He and Mark ANTONY opposed republican conspirators and in 43 formed the Second TRIUMVIRATE with Octavian (later AUGUSTUS). Lepidus lost Spain and Gaul to Antony and Octavian; he later challenged Octavian (36), but his soldiers defected, and he was forced to retire.

leprechaun \ˈlep-rə-ˌkän\ In Irish folklore, a FAIRY in the form of a tiny old man wearing a cocked hat and leather apron. Leprechauns lived in remote places and worked as shoemakers. Each was believed to possess a hidden crock of gold, whose location he would reveal if captured, provided his captor never took his eyes off him. Usually the captor was tricked into glancing away, and the leprechaun vanished.

leprosy *or* **Hansen's disease** Chronic disease of the SKIN and superficial nerves, caused by the bacterium *Mycobacterium leprae*. In the lepromatous (cutaneous) type, grainy masses infiltrate inflamed tissue under the skin, in the lining of the upper respiratory tract, and in the testes; untreated, the outlook is poor. The tuberculoid type, marked by spots having raised, reddish borders and patches that spread and lose feeling, may not progress or may improve. Long-term SULFA-DRUG therapy usually helps; rehabilitation is usually also needed. How it spreads is still unclear; prolonged close contact with an infected person usually precedes infection. Prevention depends on recognizing cases for isolation and treatment.

lepton \ˈlep-tän\ Any member of a class of FERMIONS that respond only to gravitational (see GRAVITATION), ELECTROMAGNETIC, and WEAK FORCES and do not take part in strong interactions. Leptons have a half-integral SPIN and obey the PAULI EXCLUSION PRINCIPLE. They can either carry one unit of ELECTRIC CHARGE or be neutral. The charged leptons are the ELECTRONS, muons, and taus. Each has a negative charge and a distinct MASS. Each charged lepton has an associated neutral partner, or NEUTRINO.

Lerma River River, W central Mexico. It rises southeast of Toluca and flows for 350 mi (560 km) to empty into Lake Chapala. The Río Grande de Santiago is sometimes considered an extension of the Lerma. With its major tributaries, it constitutes Mexico's largest river system.

Lermontov \ˈlʸer-mən-təf\, **Mikhail (Yuryevich)** (1814–1841) Russian poet and novelist. His first volume of verse, *Vesna* ("Spring"), was published in 1830. As a guards officer, he was twice exiled to regiments in the Caucasus because of his passionately libertarian verse. He became popular for having suffered for his poetry, which combined civic and philosophical themes with deeply personal motifs. His mature poems include *Mtsyri* (1840) and *Demon* (1841). His novel *A Hero of Our Time* (1840) is written in superb prose, and the portrait of its alienated hero profoundly influenced later Russian writers. He died in a duel at 26. He is remembered as his country's leading Romantic poet.

Lerner, Alan Jay (1918–1986) U.S. librettist and lyricist. Born in New York City, he studied at Juilliard and Harvard. He wrote more than 500 radio scripts before meeting the composer Frederick Loewe (1904–1988) in 1942. Their first Broadway successes were *Brigadoon* (1947; film, 1954) and *Paint Your Wagon* (1951; film, 1969). *My Fair Lady* (1956) set a record for the longest original run of any musical; the film version (1964) won seven Academy Awards. Their film musical *Gigi* (1958) received nine Academy Awards. *Camelot* followed in 1960 (film, 1967). Lerner also collaborated with Kurt WEILL (*Love Life*, 1948) and Burton Lane (*On a Clear Day You Can See Forever*, 1965; film, 1970), among others. His film scripts included *An American in Paris* (1951, Academy Award).

Lesage, Alain-René *or* **Alain René Le Sage** \lə-ˈsäzh\ (1668–1747) French novelist and playwright. His classic *The Adventures of Gil Blas of Santillane* (1715–1735), one of the earliest realistic novels, was influential in making the PICARESQUE NOVEL a European literary fashion. A prolific satirical dramatist, he adapted Spanish models for his early plays, including the comedy *Crispin, Rival of His Master* (1707). He also composed more than 100 *comédies-vaudevilles* in the tradition of MOLIÈRE.

Lesbos \ˈlez-ˌbäs\ *or* **Mytilene** \ˌmit-ᵊl-ˈē-nē\ *or* **Mitilíni** \ˌmē-tē-ˈlē-nē\ Third-largest island (pop., 1991 est.: 104,000) in the Aegean Sea. It occupies 630 sq mi (1,640 sq km). Its main town is Mytilene. It is the birthplace of the poet SAPPHO and thus is the source of the term "lesbian." Inhabited since about 3000 B.C., it was settled around 1050 B.C. by the Aetolians. After being under Persian rule (527–479 B.C.), it joined the DELIAN LEAGUE. In the PELOPONNESIAN WAR, it fell to SPARTA (405 B.C.), then was recovered for ATHENS (389 B.C.). It was ruled by the Turks 1462–1911, then was annexed by Greece.

Lesotho \lə-ˈsü-ˌtü, lə-ˈsō-ˌtō\ *officially* **Kingdom of Lesotho** *formerly* **Basutoland** Independent kingdom, S Africa, an

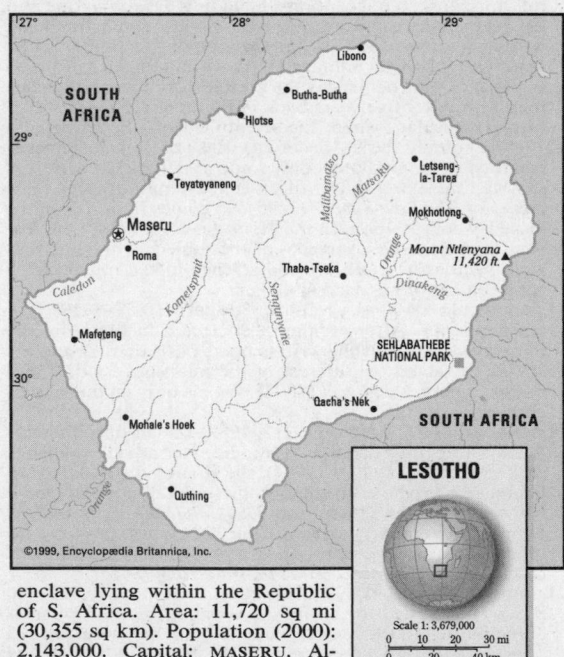

©1999, Encyclopædia Britannica, Inc.

LESOTHO
Scale 1: 3,679,000
0   10   20   30 mi
0   20   40 km

enclave lying within the Republic of S. Africa. Area: 11,720 sq mi (30,355 sq km). Population (2000): 2,143,000. Capital: MASERU. Almost all of its population belong to the SOTHO, a Bantu-speaking people. Languages: Sotho, English (both official), Africaans, Zulu, Xhosa, French. Religions: Christianity (official), including Roman Catholicism, Lesotho Evangelical Church, Anglicanism. Currency: loti. About two-thirds of Lesotho's total area is mountainous; its highest point is Mt. Ntlenyana (11,424 ft, or 3,482 m). The Maloti Mtns. in the central northwest are the source of two of S. Africa's largest rivers, the Tugela and the ORANGE. It has scant mineral resources. Agriculture employs two-thirds of the workforce; its chief farm products are corn, sorghum, and wheat. Livestock provide exports (cattle, wool, and mohair). Industries include food processing, textiles and apparel, and furniture. It is a republic with two legislative houses; its chief of state is the king, and the head of government is the prime minister. Bantu-speaking farmers began to settle the area in the 16th cent., and a number of chiefdoms arose. The most powerful organized the Basotho in 1824, and obtained British protection in 1843, as tension between the Basotho and the S. African Boers increased. It became a British territory in 1868 and was annexed to the Cape Colony in 1871. The colony's effort to disarm the Basotho resulted in revolt in 1880, and four years later it separated from the colony and became a British High Commission Territory. In 1964 it declared its independence as a constitutional monarchy. A new constitution, effective 1993, ended seven years of military rule, but Lesotho continues to suffer from internal political stagnation and stalemate and a deteriorating economy.

Lesseps \\'le-səps\\, **Ferdinand (-Marie), vicomte (Viscount) de** (1805–1894) French diplomat, builder of the SUEZ CANAL. Authorized by the viceroy of Egypt to build a canal across the isthmus of the Suez, he organized a company in 1858, with half its capital from the French people; the Suez Canal was inaugurated in 1869. In 1879 Lesseps organized another company to build a Panama canal, but gave up the project because of political and economic difficulties.

Lessing, Doris orig. Doris May Tayler (b.1919) British novelist and short-story writer. Born in Iran, she lived on a farm in Southern Rhodesia (now Zimbabwe) 1924–49 before settling in England. Her works, which have often reflected her leftist political activism, are largely concerned with people caught in social and political upheavals. *Children of Violence* (1952–69), an admired semiautobiographical five-novel series, reflects her African experience. *The Golden Notebook* (1962), her most widely read novel, is regarded as a feminist classic. A master of the short story, she has published several collections.

Lessing, Gotthold Ephraim (1729–1781) German playwright and critic. He was a theater critic in Berlin when he wrote *Miss Sara Sampson* (1755), the first German domestic tragedy. After studying philosophy and aesthetics in Breslau, he wrote the influential treatise on painting and poetry *Laocoön* (1766). His finest play, *Minna von Barnhelm* (1767), marks the beginning of classical German comedy. He was adviser to the first Hamburg national theater and published his reviews as essays on the principles of drama in *Hamburg Dramaturgy* (1767–69). His attacks on orthodox Christianity aroused great controversy. He also wrote the famous dramatic poem *Nathan the Wise* (1779).

Lethe \\'lē-thē\\ Ancient Greek personification of oblivion. Her name was also applied to a river or plain in the realm of the dead. In the Orphic mysteries it was believed that the newly dead who drank from the River Lethe would lose all memory of their past existence.

Leto \\'lē-tō\\ In classical mythology, the mother of APOLLO and ARTEMIS by ZEUS. She gave birth on the floating island of DELOS, which was fixed to the bottom of the sea for the birth.

Letterman, David (b.1947) U.S. talk-show host. Born in Indianapolis, he began his career as a stand-up comedian and was a guest host of Johnny CARSON's *Tonight Show* from 1979. He hosted NBC's *Late Night with David Letterman* 1982–93, winning six Emmy awards and great popularity with his ironic, abrasive, flippant style of interviewing. Since 1993 he has hosted *The Late Show* on CBS.

letterpress printing *or* **relief printing** In commercial PRINTING, process by which many copies are produced by repeated direct impression of an inked, raised surface against PAPER. Letterpress is the oldest traditional printing tech-

nique, the only important one from the time of Johannes GUTENBERG (c.1450) until LITHOGRAPHY (late 18th cent.) and especially OFFSET PRINTING (early 20th cent.). The ink-bearing surface for a page of text was originally assembled letter by letter and line by line. The Monotype and Linotype were the first keyboard-activated TYPESETTING machines. Letterpress can produce high-quality work at high speed, but requires much time to prepare and adjust the press, so newspapers are now printed by the offset process.

lettuce Cultivated annual salad plant (*Lactuca sativa*) of the COMPOSITE FAMILY that produces clusters of crisp, water-filled leaves. The best-known varieties are head lettuce (variety *capitata*), which includes the popular iceberg lettuce; leaf, or curled, lettuce (variety *crispa*); cos, or romaine, lettuce (variety *longifolia*); and asparagus lettuce (variety *asparagina*). Lettuce is an early annual crop that grows best in cool weather and with ample water. Though usually consumed in salads, it may also be cooked.

leukemia CANCER of blood-forming tissues with high levels of LEUKOCYTES. Radiation exposure and hereditary susceptibility are factors in some cases. In acute leukemias, ANEMIA, fever, bleeding, and LYMPH-NODE swelling develop rapidly. Acute lymphocytic leukemia, found mostly in children, was once over 90% fatal in six months; drug therapy can now cure more than half these children. Acute myelogenous (granulocytic) leukemia, found mostly in adults, has frequent remissions and recurrences, and few patients survive long. Chronic myelogenous leukemia most often begins in the 40s; weight loss, low fever, weakness, and other symptoms may not develop immediately; CHEMOTHERAPY helps the symptoms but may not prolong life. Chronic lymphocytic leukemia, mostly in the elderly, may be inactive for years; most deaths are caused by infection or hemorrhage.

leukocyte \\'lü-kə-ˌsīt\\ *or* **white blood cell** *or* **white corpuscle** Any of several types of blood cells that help defend the body from INFECTION. The different mature forms—granulocytes (of several types), monocytes (of several types), and LYMPHOCYTES—have different functions, including ingesting BACTERIA, PROTOZOANS, or infected or dead body cells; producing ANTIBODIES; and regulating the action of other leukocytes. They act mostly in the tissues and are in the bloodstream only for transport. Blood normally contains 5,000–10,000 leukocytes per cu mm.

leukoderma See VITILIGO

Levant \\lə-'vänt\\ Historical name for the countries along the shores of the E MEDITERRANEAN SEA. Applied to the coastlands of ASIA MINOR and Syria, the term was often associated with Venetian trading ventures. It was also used as a synonym for the Middle or Near East. The name Levant States was given to the French mandate of Syria and Lebanon after World War I.

level Device for establishing a horizontal plane. It consists of a small, sealed glass tube containing liquid and a small air bubble; the tube is fixed horizontally in a block or frame. When the bubble is in the middle of the glass tube, the device is on a level surface. The glass tube is slightly bowed, and the level's sensitivity is proportional to the radius of curvature.

lever Simple MACHINE used to amplify physical FORCE. All early peoples used the lever in some form, for moving heavy stones or as digging sticks. Balance beams for weighing were probably used in Egypt around 5000 B.C.; they consist of a bar pivoted at its center with weights on one end balancing the object on the other. By 1500 B.C. people were raising water and lifting soldiers over battlements using a long lever pivoted near one end with a platform or container hanging from the short arm and counterweights attached to the long arm.

Levi \\'lē-ˌvī\\ In ancient Israel, the third son of the patriarch JACOB. Levi became head of the clans of religious functionaries known as Levites. Unlike the 12 tribes of ISRAEL, the Levites were given no allotment of land when CANAAN was conquered. They are thought to have served as musicians, guardians, Temple officials, judges, and craftsmen.

Levi \\'lā-vē\\, **Primo** (1919–1987) Italian writer and chemist. Two years after obtaining a degree in chemistry, Levi, a Jew, was captured by the Nazis and sent to Auschwitz. His autobiographical works including *Survival in Auschwitz*

K L

(1947) and *The Drowned and the Saved* (1986) are restrained and moving accounts of and reflections on survival in the Nazi camps. His best-known work, *The Periodic Table* (1975), is a collection of 21 meditations, each named for a chemical element. He died a suicide.

Levine \lə-'vīn\, **James (Lawrence)** (b.1943) U.S. conductor. Born in Cincinnati, he debuted as a pianist at 10 with the Cincinnati Symphony Orchestra. He was assistant conductor of the Cleveland Orchestra 1964–70. A 1971 guest appearance led to his appointment as principal conductor (1973) of the Metropolitan Opera. He built the flagging Met orchestra into a virtuoso ensemble and became recognized as one of the world's greatest conductors. In 2001 he was chosen as the next director of the Boston Symphony Orchestra.

Lévi-Strauss \'lā-vē-'straüs\, **Claude** (b.1908) Belgian-French social anthropologist and leading exponent of STRUCTURALISM. Lévi-Strauss originally studied philosophy at the Univ. of Paris (1927–32) but went on to teach sociology at the Univ. of São Paulo (1934–37) and to conduct field research on the Indians of Brazil. He came to view CULTURE as a system of communication, analogous to a language. His work is an effort to identify universal structures of the mind as reflected in MYTHS, cultural SYMBOLS, and social organization. He was director of studies at the École Pratique des Hautes Études (1950–75) and taught at the Collège de France. Among his major works are *The Elementary Structures of Kinship* (1949), *Tristes Tropiques* (1955), *Structural Anthropology* (1961), and the four-volume *Mythologiques* (1964–71).

Claude Lévi-Strauss

Levi Strauss & Co. World's largest maker of pants, noted especially for its blue-denim jeans. Its founder, Levi Strauss (1829–1902), a Bavarian immigrant, sold dry goods to miners during the California GOLD RUSH. Hearing of their need for durable pants, he provided garments made of tent canvas, later substituting DENIM. In 1873 he patented the copper riveting used to strengthen the pants. The company achieved spectacular growth after 1946. In 1959 it began exporting, and during the 1960s jeans became enormously popular worldwide. The company went public in 1971 but was returned to private control (by Strauss's descendants) in 1985.

Levittown Extensive suburban housing development in Hempstead, Long Island, N.Y. Developed 1946–51 by the firm of Levitt and Sons, Inc., it was an example of a preplanned, mass-produced housing complex. It contained thousands of low-cost homes (with nearby shopping centers, playgrounds, swimming pools, community halls, and schools). Levitt repeated the formula in Bucks County, Pa. (1951–55). The name Levittown became equated with the monotonous developments of the postwar building boom, but its towns differ from others in their meandering roads and lush plantings.

levodopa See DOPA

levulose See FRUCTOSE

Lewinsky affair \lə-'win-skē\ Scandal involving U.S. Pres. William CLINTON and Monica Lewinsky (b.1973). She began an internship at the White House in 1995, which led to a sexual relationship with Clinton. Transferred to the Pentagon, she was befriended by a coworker, Linda Tripp, who secretly recorded conversations about the affair. In 1998 Tripp turned the tapes over to special prosecutor Kenneth Starr as evidence that Clinton had committed perjury in denying the relationship in a sexual-harassment suit brought by Paula Jones. The investigation led to Clinton's impeachment.

Lewis, (Frederick) Carl(ton) (b.1961) U.S. track-and-field athlete. Born in Birmingham, Ala., he qualified for the 1980 Olympics but did not participate because of the U.S. boycott of the Moscow games. At the 1984 Olympics he won the 100-m and 200-m races, the long jump, and the 4×100 relay. In 1988 he won the long jump and the 100-m race and received a silver medal in the 200-m. In 1992 he again won the long jump and anchored the winning U.S. 4×100-relay team, and in 1996 he astounded observers by winning a fourth consecutive long-jump title.

Lewis, C(live) S(taples) (1898–1963) British scholar and writer. Lewis taught at both Oxford and Cambridge. Many of his books defend Christian faith and theology; *The Screwtape Letters* (1942) is a satirical EPISTOLARY NOVEL in which an experienced devil instructs his young charge in the art of temptation. Also well known are *The Chronicles of Narnia* (1950–56), a series of seven children's stories (including *The Lion, the Witch, and the Wardrobe*) that have become classics of fantasy. The critical *Allegory of Love* (1936), on medieval and Renaissance literature, is often considered his greatest work.

Lewis, Jerry *orig.* Joseph Levitch (b.1926) U.S. actor, director, and producer. Born in Newark, N.J., in 1946 he developed a nightclub comedy routine with Dean Martin (1917–1995), who played the suave, romantic singer to Lewis's zany clown; they appeared together in 16 movies, including *My Friend Irma* (1949), *Jumping Jacks* (1952), and *Pardners* (1956), before ending their partnership. Lewis then directed, produced, and acted in such movies as *The Bellboy* (1960), *The Nutty Professor* (1963), and *The Big Mouth* (1967). Since 1966 he has hosted the U.S. annual Muscular Dystrophy Telethon.

Lewis, Jerry Lee (b.1935) U.S. rock-and-roll musician. Born in Ferriday, La., he began playing piano early, influenced by blues and gospel musicians. Expelled from school, he played in several bands, perfecting his signature "pumping" piano technique. His first hits came in 1957 with "Whole Lotta Shakin' Goin' On" and "Great Balls of Fire." In 1958 it was discovered that he had married a 13-year-old relative, and his record sales dropped. Though he had a few more hits, he concentrated on his famously energetic and uninhibited live performances. Later controversies included the deaths of two wives.

Lewis, John L(lewellyn) (1880–1969) U.S. labor leader. Born near Lucas, Iowa, to Welsh immigrants, he became a coal miner at 15. He rose through the ranks of the UNITED MINE WORKERS OF AMERICA (UMWA) and from 1911 was also an organizer of the American Federation of Labor (AFL). As president of the UMWA (1920–60), Lewis joined several other AFL union leaders in organizing workers in mass-production industries. On breaking with the AFL (see AFL-CIO) in 1935, they founded the Committee for Industrial Organization, later renamed the Congress of Industrial Organizations. As president of the CIO (1936–40), Lewis presided over the often-violent struggle to introduce unionism into previously unorganized industries such as steel and automobiles.

Lewis, Meriwether (1774–1809) U.S. explorer. Born near Charlottesville, Va., he served in the army and in 1801 became private secretary to Pres. Thomas JEFFERSON, who selected him to lead the first overland expedition to the Pacific Northwest. William CLARK was appointed to share the command. The success of the LEWIS AND CLARK EXPEDITION (1804–6) was greatly due to Lewis's preparation and skill. At its conclusion, he and Clark each received 1,600 acres of land. Lewis was named governor of Louisiana Territory in 1808. His death in an inn while en route to Washington was either a murder or a suicide.

Lewis, (Harry) Sinclair (1885–1951) U.S. novelist and social critic. Born in Sauk Center, Minn., he made his literary reputation with *Main Street* (1920), a portrayal of Midwestern provincialism. Among his other popular satirical novels puncturing middle-class complacency are *Babbitt* (1922), a scathing study of a conformist businessman; *Arrowsmith* (1925), a look at the medical profession; *Elmer Gantry* (1927), an indictment of fundamentalist religion; and *Dodsworth* (1929), the story of a rich American couple in Europe. He won the 1930 Nobel Prize for Literature, the first given to an American. His later novels include *Cass Timberlaine* (1945).

Lewis, (Percy) Wyndham (1882–1957) English artist and writer. He was the founder of VORTICISM. His first novel, *Tarr,* appeared in 1918. *The Childermass* (1928) was followed by the huge satirical novel *The Apes of God* (1930) and *The Revenge for Love* (1937). In the 1930s he produced some of his most noted paintings, including "The Surrender of Barcelona" (1936). Notorious in the 1930s for championing fascism, he later recanted those beliefs.

Lewis and Clark Expedition (1804–6) First overland expedition to the U.S. Pacific coast, led by Meriwether LEWIS and William CLARK. Initiated by Pres. Thomas JEFFERSON, the expedition set out to find an overland route to the Pacific, documenting its exploration through the new LOUISIANA PURCHASE. About 40 men, skilled in various trades, left St. Louis in 1804. They traveled up the Missouri River into present-day N. Dakota, where they built Ft. Mandan (later Bismarck) and wintered over. They left the next spring, hiring Toussaint Charbonneau and his Indian wife, SACAGAWEA, who served as guide and interpreter. They traveled through Montana and by horse over the Continental Divide to the Clearwater River. They canoed to the Snake River and thence to the mouth of the Columbia River, where they spent the winter. On the return the group divided, then reunited to canoe down the Missouri to St. Louis, arriving to great acclaim. Only one member had died. Their journals documented the Indian tribes, wildlife, and geography and did much to dispel the myth of an easy water route to the Pacific.

Lexington City (pop., 2000: 260,000), N central Kentucky. Named in 1775 for Lexington, Mass., it was chartered in 1782 and was the site of the first session of the Kentucky legislature (1792). It is the seat of the Univ. of Kentucky, and also the headquarters of the American Thoroughbred Breeders Association.

Lexington and Concord, Battles of (April 19, 1775) Initial skirmishes that marked the beginning of the AMERICAN REVOLUTION. En route from Boston to seize the colonists' military stores at Concord, Mass., a British force of 700 was met at Lexington by 77 local MINUTEMEN alerted by Paul REVERE and others. Who fired the first shot is unclear, and resistance soon ended. The British moved on to Concord, where they were met by over 300 American patriots and forced to withdraw. Marching back to Boston, they were continually harried by colonists firing from behind barns, trees, and walls. Losses totaled 273 British and 95 Americans.

Leyden See LEIDEN

Leyden, Lucas van See LUCAS VAN LEYDEN

Leyster \'lā-stər\, **Judith** (1609–1660) Dutch painter. A brewer's daughter, she had gained membership in the Haarlem painters' guild by age 24. Many of her known works, primarily portraits, genre paintings, and still lifes, were formerly attributed to her male contemporaries. She embraced a greater range of subjects than other Dutch painters of the era, and was one of the first to depict domestic scenes.

Leyte \'lā-tē\ Island (pop., 1990: 1,810,000) of the VISAYAN group, E Philippines. Occupying 2,785 sq mi (7,214 sq km), it is linked to SAMAR Island by a 7,093-ft (2,162-m) bridge. Known to 16th-cent. Spanish explorers as Tandaya, it was under Spanish rule until the late 19th cent. In the early 20th cent., its population grew rapidly. During World War II the occupying Japanese were ousted by U.S. forces in the Battle of Leyte Gulf.

Lhasa \'lä-sə\ Capital (pop., 1999 est.: 121,000), Tibet autonomous region, China. It is located at an elevation of 11,975 ft (3,650 m) in the Tibetan HIMALAYAS near the Lhasa River. It has served as the religious center of Tibet since at least the 9th cent. A.D. It became independent Tibet's capital in 1642 and remained so until the Chinese occupied the city (1951) and took over the government (1959). The 7th-cent. temple of Gtsug-lag-khang is considered the holiest in Tibet. Other landmarks include the temple of Klu-khang, the POTALA PALACE, and monasteries. It is traditionally known as the "Forbidden City."

Lhasa apso \'lä-sə-'äp-sō\ Breed of dog from Tibet. Hardy, intelligent, and watchful, it stands 10–11 in. (25–28 cm) high and weighs 13–15 lbs (6–7 kg). It has a heavily haired tail that curls over its back, and its very long coat covers its eyes.

Lhotse \'lōt-'sā\ Peak in the Himalayas. Located on the Nepal–Tibet boundary and reaching 27,890 ft (8,501 m), it is the world's fourth-highest mountain. It is sometimes considered part of Mt. EVEREST's massif because it is joined to that peak by a 25,000-ft (7,600-m) ridge. Swiss climbers made the first ascent in 1956.

liability, limited See LIMITED LIABILITY

liability insurance Provision against claims of loss or damage for which a policyholder might have to compensate another party. The policy covers losses resulting from acts or omissions that are legally deemed to be negligent and that result in damage to the person, property, or legitimate interests of others. Besides automobile-related issues, it extends to MALPRACTICE insurance for doctors and other professionals, marine liability for boat owners and operators, and product liability for manufacturers of consumer goods. See also CASUALTY INSURANCE, CONSUMER PROTECTION.

liana \lē-'ä-nə\ *or* **liane** \lē-'än\ Any of various longstemmed, woody VINES, especially of tropical rain forests, that are rooted in the soil and climb or twine around other plants as they grow upward. Lianas often form a tangled network, up to 330 ft (100 m) high, around and among the trees that support them.

Liard River \'lē-ərd\ River, NW Canada. Rising in the Yukon Territory, it dips into British Columbia before flowing northeast into the MACKENZIE RIVER in the Northwest Territories, after a course of 693 mi (1,115 km). Its upper course has rapids and canyons; its lower course is navigable for small boats. It is named for the liards (poplar trees) along its course.

Libby, Willard (Frank) (1908–1980) U.S. chemist. Born in Grand Valley, Col., for the MANHATTAN PROJECT he helped develop a method for separating URANIUM ISOTOPES and showed that TRITIUM is a product of cosmic radiation. In 1947 he and his students developed CARBON-14 DATING, which proved an extremely valuable tool for archaeology, anthropology, and earth science, and earned him a 1960 Nobel Prize.

libel See DEFAMATION

liberal arts College or university curriculum aimed at imparting general knowledge and developing general intellectual capacities rather than professional, vocational, or technical skills. In classical antiquity the term designated the education proper to a freeman (Latin, *liber:* "free") as opposed to a slave. In the medieval university, the seven liberal arts were grammar, rhetoric, and logic (the *trivium*) and geometry, arithmetic, music, and astronomy (the *quadrivium*). Today the liberal arts include literature, languages, philosophy, history, mathematics, and science as the basis of a general, or liberal, education.

liberalism Political philosophy that favors maximizing individual liberties. Liberals believe the state's primary function is to protect the rights of its citizens. The ideology of liberalism is a product of the ENLIGHTENMENT; John LOCKE laid the philosophical foundations of British liberalism, and Adam SMITH expounded economic liberalism (see LAISSEZFAIRE). The U.S. Constitution is a product of classical liberalism. Economic liberalism in the U.S. today, which endorses unregulated markets, is generally embraced by those who call themselves conservatives; those who call themselves liberals usually believe in restrictions on corporate freedom, as well as in civil liberties, social-welfare supports, consumer protection, and environmental conservation. See also CONSERVATISM.

Liberal Party British political party that emerged in the mid-19th cent. as the successor to the WHIGS. It was the major party in opposition to the CONSERVATIVE PARTY until 1918, after which it was supplanted by the LABOUR PARTY. It was initially supported by the middle class enfranchised by the REFORM BILL OF 1832. The first unequivocally Liberal government was formed in 1868 by William GLADSTONE. Until 1894, the party's hallmark was reform; after 1884, it espoused Irish HOME RULE. It championed individualism, private enterprise, human rights, and promotion of social justice. During World War I it split into two camps, centered on H. H. ASQUITH and David LLOYD GEORGE. It continued as a minor party until 1988, when it merged with the Social Democratic Party to form the Liberal Democratic Party.

K L

Liberal Party of Canada One of the two major Canadian political parties. Advocating "responsible government" and pressing for parliamentary representation, the first Liberal government was headed by Alexander MACKENZIE (1873–78). The party regained power under Wilfrid LAURIER (1896–1911) and was the ruling party for much of the 20th cent. under such prime ministers as W. L. M. KING, Louis ST. LAURENT, Lester PEARSON, Pierre TRUDEAU, and Jean CHRÉTIEN.

liberation theology Roman Catholic movement that originated in the late 20th cent. in Latin America and seeks to express religious faith by helping the poor and working for political and social change. It began in 1968, when bishops attending a conference in Medellín, Colombia, affirmed the rights of the poor and asserted that industrialized nations were enriching themselves at the expense of the Third World. Its central text, *A Theology of Liberation* (1971), was written by Gustavo Gutiérrez (b.1928). The Vatican has sought to curb its influence by appointing more conservative prelates.

Liberia *officially* **Republic of Liberia** Republic, W Africa. Area: 38,250 sq mi (99,067 sq km). Population (2000): 3,164,000. Capital: MONROVIA. Liberia's ethnic groups in-

SIERRA LEONE

GUINEA

Voinjama

Zorzor

Yekepa — Mount Nimba 6,069 ft.

Lofa

Bopolu

Tubmanburg   Kle   Bong RANGE   Gbarnga   Sanniquellie

IVORY COAST

Robertsport   Bensol

Monrovia   Careysburg

Harbel

Buchanan

Zwedru

SAPO NATIONAL PARK   PUTU RANGE

ATLANTIC OCEAN

GRAIN COAST

Greenville

Grand Cess

LIBERIA

Harper   Cape Palmas

©1999, Encyclopædia Britannica, Inc.

Scale 1: 10,783,000
0   50   100 mi
0   80   160 km

clude the Americo-Liberians, descendants of the black freedmen who emigrated from the U.S. in the 19th cent.; and indigenous peoples, including the Kpelle, Bassa, and Grebo. Languages: English (official), native languages. Religions: Christianity, Islam, traditional beliefs. Currency: Liberian dollar. Liberia has coastal lowlands extending 350 mi (560 km) along the Atlantic; farther inland are hills and low mountains. Roughly one-fifth of Liberia consists of tropical rain forest. Less than 4 percent of Liberia is considered arable, but the country has rich iron-ore reserves, which are a major source of exports. The principal cash crops are rubber, coffee, and cacao; the staple crops are rice and cassava. It is a republic with two legislative houses; its head of state and government is the president. Africa's oldest republic, Liberia was established on land bought from local tribes as a home for freed U.S. slaves under the American Colonization Society, which founded a colony at Cape Mesurado in 1821. In 1822 Jehudi Ashmun, a Methodist minister, became the director of the settlement and Liberia's real founder. In 1824 it was named Liberia, and its main settlement was named Monrovia. Joseph Jenkins Roberts (1809–1876), Liberia's first nonwhite governor, proclaimed Liberian independence in 1847 and expanded its boundaries. Border disputes with the French and British

lasted until 1892, when its boundaries were officially established. In 1980 a coup led by Gen. Samuel K. DOE marked the end of the Americo-Liberians' long political dominance over the indigenous Africans. A rebellion in 1989 escalated into a destructive civil war. A peace agreement led to elections in 1997 but battles with rebels and exiles in Guinea continued.

libertarianism Political philosophy that stresses the principles of personal liberty. Libertarians believe that individuals should have complete freedom of action, provided their actions do not infringe on the freedom of others. Libertarianism's distrust of government reveals its roots in 19th-cent. ANARCHISM. Libertarians not only oppose such government impositions as income tax but also such programs as social security and the postal service. Their views often cross traditional party boundaries (e.g., they oppose gun control and support legalization of prohibited drugs). The U.S. Libertarian Party was formed in 1971; in 1980 its presidential candidate was on the ballot in all 50 states.

libido \lə-'bē-dō\ Physiological and emotional energy associated with the sex drive. The concept was originated by Sigmund FREUD, who saw the libido as linked with all constructive human activity and believed that psychiatric illnesses were the result of misdirecting or suppressing it. C. G. JUNG used the term more broadly to encompass all life processes in all species.

Li Bo *or* **Li Po** \'lē-'bō\ *or* **Li Taibo** \'lē-'tī-'bō\ (701–762) Chinese poet. A student of Taoism, he spent long periods wandering and served as an unofficial court poet. His lyrics are celebrated for their exquisite imagery, rich language, allusions, and cadence. A romantic, he was a famous wine drinker and wrote of the joys of drinking, as well as about friendship, solitude, nature, and the passage of time. He rivals DU FU for the title of China's greatest poet.

library Collection of information resources in print or in other forms that is organized and made accessible for reading or study. The keeping of written records dates at least to the 3rd millennium B.C. in Babylonia. The first repositories of books were those of the Greek temples and those established in conjunction with the Greek schools of philosophy in the 4th cent. B.C. Today's libraries frequently contain periodicals, microfilms, tapes, videos, and compact discs, and library users may often search electronically linked databases worldwide. See also LIBRARY SCIENCE.

library classification System of arrangement adopted by a library to enable patrons to locate its materials quickly and easily. Classifications may be natural (e.g., by subject), artificial (e.g., by alphabet, form, or numerical order), or accidental (e.g., chronological or geographic). Widely used systems include the DEWEY DECIMAL CLASSIFICATION, the Library of Congress Classification, the Bliss Classification, and the Colon Classification.

Library of Alexandria See Library of ALEXANDRIA

library science Principles and practices of library operation and administration, and their study. The first training program for librarians in the U.S. was established by Melvil DEWEY in 1887. In the 20th cent., library science was gradually subsumed under the more general field of INFORMATION SCIENCE. Today's graduate programs in library and information science prepare students for professional positions in other areas of the information industry as well.

Libreville \'lē-brə-ˌvil\ City (pop., 1993: 362,000), capital of GABON. Pongoue people first settled the region after the 16th cent., followed by the Fang in the 19th cent. The French built a fort there in 1843, and in 1849 a settlement of freed slaves and a group of Pongoue villages were given the name Libreville. In 1850 France abandoned its fort and resettled on the plateau. Libreville was the capital of French Equatorial Africa 1888–1904. The city is well industrialized and is Gabon's educational center.

Libya *officially* **Socialist People's Libyan Arab Jamahiriya** \ja-mə-hi-'rē-yə\ Country, N. Africa. Area: 678,400 sq mi (1,757,000 sq km). Population (2000): 5,115,000. Capital: TRIPOLI. Berbers, once the major ethnic group, have been assimilated into the Arab culture. Italians, Greeks, Jews, and black Africans are among the other ethnic groups. Languages: Arabic (official), Hamitic (Berbers). Religion: Islam (official). Currency: dinar. All but two tiny fractions

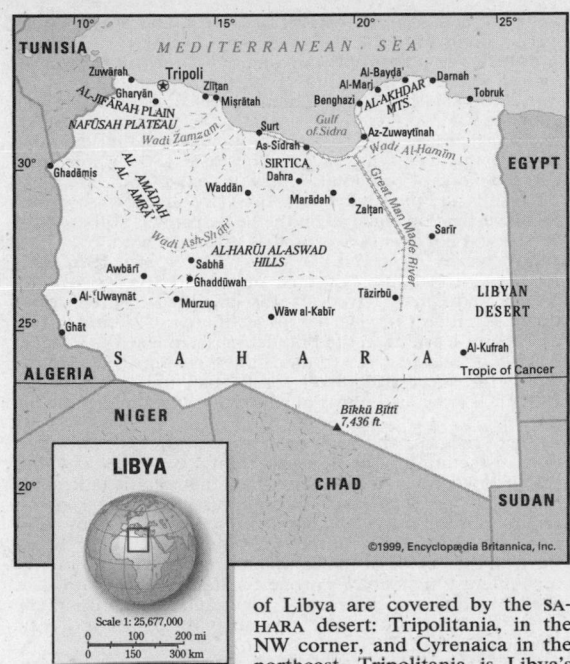

©1999, Encyclopædia Britannica, Inc.

LIBYA

Scale 1: 25,677,000
0   100   200 mi
0   150   300 km

of Libya are covered by the SA-HARA desert: Tripolitania, in the NW corner, and Cyrenaica in the northeast. Tripolitania is Libya's most important agricultural region and its most populated area. The production and export of petroleum are the basis of Libya's economy; other resources include natural gas, manganese, and gypsum. The rearing of livestock, including sheep and goats, is important in the north. It is a socialist state with one policy-making body; the chief of state is Muammar al-QADDAFI (de facto), and the head of government is the prime minister (for early history, see CYRENAICA, TRIPOLITANIA). In the 16th cent. the Ottoman Turks combined Fezzan, Cyrenaica, and Tripolitania under one regency in Tripoli. In 1911 Italy claimed control of Libya, and by the outbreak of World War II 150,000 Italians had immigrated there. The scene of much fighting in the war, it became an independent state in 1951 and a member of the ARAB LEAGUE in 1953. The discovery of oil in 1959 brought wealth to Libya. A decade later a group of army officers led by Qaddafi deposed the king and made the country an Islamic republic. Under Qaddafi's rule it supported the PALESTNIAN LIBERATION ORGANIZATION (PLO) and terrorist groups, bringing protests from many countries, particularly the U.S. Intermittent warfare with Chad (1970s–1980s) ended with Chad's defeat of Libya in 1987. International relations in the 1990s were dominated by the consequences of the 1988 bombing of a U.S. airliner over Lockerbie, Scotland; the U.S. accused Libyan nationalists of the deed and imposed a trade embargo on Libya, upheld by the U.N. 1992–1999.

Libyan Desert NE portion of the SAHARA desert, extending from E Libya through SW Egypt into NW Sudan. The highest point is Mt. Al-Uwaynat (6,345 ft, or 1,934 m). Harsh and arid, it is characterized by bare rocky plateaus and sandy plains.

lichee See LITCHI.

lichen \'lī-kən\ Any of about 15,000 species of small, colorful, scaly, extremely hardy plants that consist of a symbiotic association of ALGAE (usually green) and fungi (see FUNGUS). Fungal cells, anchored to the substrate with hairlike growths (rhizines), form the base. Numerous algal cells are distributed among fewer fungal cells in the fungal body. Through PHOTOSYNTHESIS the algal cells provide simple sugars and vitamins for both partners. The fungal cells protect the algal cells from environmental extremes. Lichens may form a tightly bound crust over their substrate (e.g., rocks), or they may be small and leafy, with loose attachments to the substrate. Their colors range from brown to bright orange or yellow. In far N Europe and Asia, lichens provide two-thirds of caribou and reindeer food. They have been the source of medicines and dyes.

Lichtenstein \'lik-tən-,stīn, 'lik-tən-,stēn\, **Roy** (1923–1997) U.S. painter, sculptor, and graphic artist. Born in New York, he briefly embraced Abstract Expressionism, but in the 1960s he turned to the POP ART for which he is best known. Especially popular are his brilliantly colored paintings in the style of large-scale comic strips, such as *Whaam* (1963). In the 1970s he also made sculptures, in which he reproduced ART DECO forms. In the 1980s he painted a five-story-high mural in a New York office building.

Licinius \lə-'si-nē-əs\ *in full* Valerius Licinianus Licinius (d. A.D. 325) Roman emperor (308–24). Licinius was appointed augustus (senior emperor) by his friend the emperor GALERIUS. Because the empire was split up among several emperors at that time (see TETRARCH), his domain was confined to Pannonia. After GALERIUS' death (311) he allied with CONSTANTINE I, defeated his competitor Maximinus in Asia Minor, and partitioned the empire (313). Though reputedly a Christian, he launched a mild campaign of persecution against the Christians around 320. Constantine soon drove him from power and had him executed.

licorice \'li-krish\ Perennial herb (*Glycyrrhiza glabra*) of the pea family (see LEGUME), and the flavoring, confection, and medicine made from its roots. Native to S Europe, the plant is widely cultivated elsewhere. It grows to 3 ft (1 m) and bears graceful compound leaves, blue-violet flower clusters, and flat, flexible seedpods 3–4 in. (7–10 cm) long. It is 42 times sweeter than table sugar, and its flavor can mask unpleasant medicinal tastes.

Li Dazhao *or* **Li Ta-chao** \'lē-'dä-'jaú\ (1888 1927) Cofounder with CHEN DUXIU of the CHINESE COMMUNIST PARTY. Chief librarian and professor of history at Beijing Univ., Li became inspired by the success of the Russian Revolution and began to lecture on Marxism. In 1921 the study groups Li had created became the Chinese Communist Party. Li helped the new party carry out the policy of the COMINTERN and cooperated with SUN YAT-SEN and the GUOMINDANG. His career was cut short when he was seized and hanged by the warlord ZHANG ZUOLIN, but his ideas of a revolution of the peasantry were brought to fruition by MAO ZEDONG.

Liddell Hart \,lid-əl-'härt\, **Basil (Henry)** (*later* **Sir Basil**) (1895–1970) British military historian and strategist. He joined the British army in World War I, retiring in 1927. An early advocate of air power and mechanized tank warfare, he wrote for London newspapers 1925–45. His focus on mobility and surprise was most influential in Germany; his "expanding torrent" theory of attack became the basis for German BLITZKRIEG warfare in 1939–41. The author of more than 30 books, he was knighted in 1966.

Lie \'lē\, **Trygve** (1896–1968) First secretary-general of the UNITED NATIONS (1946–52). Born in Norway, Lie was active in the Labor Party before being appointed foreign minister of Norway's government-in-exile during World War II. In 1945 he helped draft the provisions for the UNITED NATIONS SECURITY COUNCIL. As secretary-general, he helped coax Soviet troops out of Iran and dealt with the first ARAB–ISRAELI WAR. The Soviet Union stopped cooperating with him when he supported U.N. intervention in the KOREAN WAR, and his effectiveness was further hampered by the strident anticommunism of the postwar U.S. He resigned in 1952.

Liebig \'lē-bik\, **Justus** *later* Freiherr (Baron) von Liebig (1803–1873) German chemist. He made many important contributions to the early systematization of organic chemistry and to biochemistry, chemical education, and agricultural chemistry. He was the first to demonstrate the existence of FREE RADICALS and did much to clarify the properties of ACIDS. He developed simple analytical methods (see ANALYSIS) that greatly aided his work, analyzed many tissues and body fluids, and showed that plants use carbon dioxide, water, and ammonia.

Liebknecht \'lēp-,knekt\, **Karl** (1871–1919) German socialist leader. A Marxist, in 1912 he entered the Reichstag and led the opposition to Germany's pre–World War I policy. In 1916 he was expelled from the SOCIAL DEMOCRATIC PARTY

K L

for opposing its leadership and came into close alliance with Rosa LUXEMBURG. He was imprisoned 1916–18 for advocating the overthrow of the government. In 1918 he helped form the German Communist Party. A series of bloody clashes culminated in the January 1919 putsch, in which Liebknecht resorted to force and was shot while in custody.

Liechtenstein \'lik-tən-ˌshtīn\ *officially* **Principality of Liechtenstein** Principality, W Europe. It is located between Switzerland and Austria. Area: 62 sq mi (160 sq km). Population (2000): 32,000. Capital: VADUZ. The Liechtensteiners

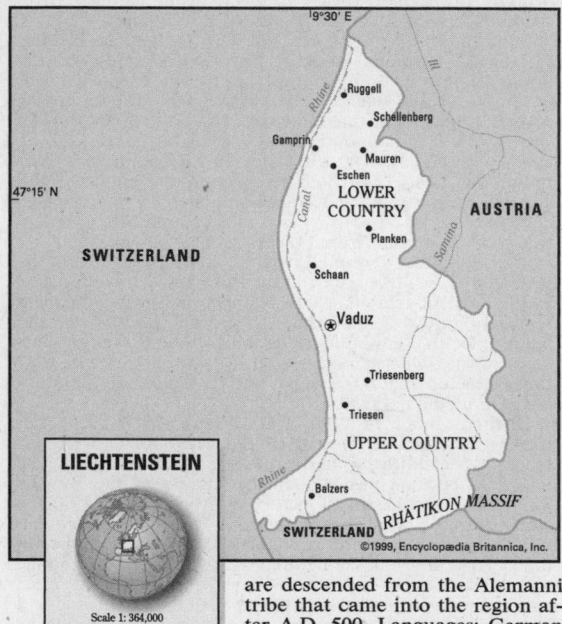

©1999, Encyclopædia Britannica, Inc.

are descended from the Alemanni tribe that came into the region after A.D. 500. Languages: German (official), Alemanni dialect, Walser dialect. Religion: Roman Catholicism. Currency: Swiss franc. The E two-thirds of Liechtenstein's small territory is composed of the foothills of the Rhätikon Massif, part of the central ALPS. The W section of the country is occupied by the RHINE RIVER floodplain. It has no natural resources of commercial value, and virtually all raw materials, including wood, have to be imported. Manufacturing includes metalworking, pharmaceuticals, optical lenses, electronics, and food processing. Liechtenstein, a tourist center, is also a center of banking because of its stable political situation and its absolute bank secrecy. It is a constitutional monarchy with one legislative house; its chief of state is the prince, and the head of government is the prime minister. The Rhine plain was occupied for centuries by two independent lordships of the HOLY ROMAN EMPIRE, Vaduz and Schellenberg. The principality of Liechtenstein, consisting of these two lordships, was founded in 1719 and remained part of the Holy Roman Empire. It was included in the GERMAN CONFEDERATION (1815–66). In 1866 it became independent. In 1921 it adopted Swiss currency, and in 1923 it joined the Swiss customs union. An almost 60-year ruling coalition dissolved in 1997, and the prince urged adoption of constitutional reforms. In recent years the government has confronted charges of money laundering.

lied \'lēt\ German song, particularly an art song for voice and piano of the late 18th or 19th cent. The Romantic movement fostered serious popular poetry by such poets as J. W. von GOETHE and Heinrich HEINE. Composers often set such poetry to folklike music, but lieder music could also be highly sophisticated. At first generally performed at private gatherings, they eventually moved into the concert-hall repertoire. The most influential lieder composer was Franz SCHUBERT, who wrote over 600; Robert SCHUMANN,

Felix MENDELSSOHN, Johannes BRAHMS, and Hugo WOLF were prominent in the lied's subsequent history.

lie detector *or* **polygraph** Instrument for recording physiological phenomena (including BLOOD PRESSURE, PULSE rate, and RESPIRATION) of a human subject as he or she answers questions asked by an operator. These data (recorded as graphs) are used as the basis for judging whether the subject is lying. The types of questions asked, their wording, and the mode of presentation have a tremendous effect on the results and their reliability. Used in police interrogation and investigation since 1924, the lie detector is still controversial and not always accepted as evidence in courts.

Liège \'lyezh\ *Flemish* **Luik** \'lȯik\ City (pop., 1996 est.: 191,000), E Belgium. Located at the confluence of the MEUSE and Ourthe rivers, it was inhabited in prehistoric times. St. Hubert transferred his see there in 721, and it was a center of learning in the Middle Ages. Annexed to France in 1795, it was assigned to the Netherlands in 1815. A center of the successful revolt for Belgian independence in 1830, it is now an industrial research center and a major port.

lien \lēn\ In law, a charge or encumbrance on PROPERTY for the satisfaction of a debt or other duty. COMMON LAW developed two kinds of possessory lien: the specific (a lien on the specific property involved in a transaction) and the general (a lien for the satisfaction of a balance due, not confined to any specific property). Courts of EQUITY may, through the device of the equitable lien, recognize a creditor's interest in a debtor's property. Statutory liens are also available; building contractors, for example, may use their interest in an improved site as security for payment (a mechanic's lien).

Lifar \'lē-ˌfär\, **Serge** (1905–1986) Russian-French dancer and choreographer. From 1923 he danced with the BALLETS RUSSES, creating title roles in several of George BALANCHINE's ballets. As lead dancer and ballet master at the Paris Opera Ballet (1929–45, 1947–58), he choreographed over 50 works, including, *Icare* (1935), *Les mirages* (1947), and *Les noces fantastiques* (1955), and rebuilt the company as a separate performing group, emphasizing the importance of male dancers.

Life Weekly picture magazine (1936–72) published in New York City. Founded by Henry LUCE, it became one of the most popular and widely imitated of U.S. magazines. From the start it emphasized photography, with gripping, superbly chosen news photographs, photo features, and photo essays by the best photographers. Its war coverage was notably vivid, authentic, and moving. It ceased publication largely because its costs outstripped revenues, and reappeared in 1978 as a monthly.

life State characterized by the ability to metabolize nutrients (process materials for energy and tissue building), grow, reproduce, and respond and adapt to environmental stimuli. Fossil evidence suggests that earth's first living organisms, BACTERIA and CYANOBACTERIA, arose about 3.5 billion years ago. All known life-forms possess either DNA or RNA. VIRUSES, which possess both, cannot reproduce without a host cell and do not metabolize nutrients, and it is uncertain whether they should be classified as living. See also DRAKE EQUATION.

life insurance Method by which large groups of individuals lessen the burden of financial loss from death by distributing funds to the beneficiaries of those who die. There are three basic types of life-insurance contract. Term insurance is issued for a specified number of years; protection expires at the end of the period and no cash value remains. Whole-life contracts run for the whole of the insured's life and also accumulate a cash value, which is paid when the contract matures or is surrendered; the cash value is less than the policy's face value. Endowment contracts run for a specified time period and pay their full face value at the end of the period.

Liffey River River, Ireland. Rising southwest of DUBLIN, it flows west and then northeast into Dublin, where it is channeled into canals, and empties into Dublin Bay after a course of 50 mi (81 km). The river is personified as Anna Livia Plurabelle in James JOYCE's *Finnegans Wake*.

lift Upward-acting FORCE on an aircraft wing or airfoil. An aircraft in flight experiences an upward lift force, as well as the thrust of the engine, the force of its own weight, and a DRAG force. The lift force arises because the speed at which the displaced air moves over the top of the airfoil (and the attached BOUNDARY LAYER) is greater than the speed at which it moves over the bottom and because the pressure acting on the airfoil from below is therefore greater than the pressure from above.

ligament Tough fibrous band of CONNECTIVE TISSUE that supports internal organs and holds bones together properly in JOINTS. It is composed of dense bundles of fibers and spindle-shaped cells (fibroblasts). White ligament is rich in sturdy, inelastic COLLAGEN fibers; yellow ligament is rich in tough elastic fibers. See also TENDON.

ligand \'li-gənd, 'lī-gənd\ ATOM or MOLECULE attached to a central atom, usually of a TRANSITION ELEMENT, in a coordination COMPOUND, or complex ion (see BONDING). It is almost always the electron-pair donor (NUCLEOPHILE) in a COVALENT BOND. Common ligands include the neutral molecules WATER (H_2O), ammonia (NH_3), and carbon monoxide (CO) and the ANIONS cyanide (CN^-), chloride (Cl^-), and hydroxide (OH^-). Organic ligands include EDTA and nitrilotriacetic acid. Biological systems rely on ligands such as the porphyrin in HEMOGLOBIN and CHLOROPHYLL. The ligands in a complex may be the same or different.

Ligeti \lē-'gä-tē\, **Gyorgy (Sandor)** (b.1923) Hungarian (Transylvanian) composer. By 1950 he was teaching at the Budapest Academy, but not until he met Karlheinz STOCKHAUSEN and others in Vienna in 1956 did he find his compositional path and gain international recognition for pieces composed in his characteristic "planes" of sound, avoiding traditional pitch and rhythm but using traditional instruments. IIis *Atmosphères* (1961) was used in the film *2001*. The opera *Le grand macabre* (1978) has been widely performed in Europe.

light Any ELECTROMAGNETIC RADIATION, but especially that portion of the SPECTRUM visible to the human eye. It is a form of ENERGY that travels through empty space at a speed of about 186,000 miles per second (300,000 km/s). In the early 19th cent., light was described in terms of waves, but experiments later showed that it exhibits properties of particles as well. Light is the basis for the sensation of sight, and for the perception of COLOR. See also OPTICS, WAVE-PARTICLE DUALITY.

light-emitting diode (LED) SEMICONDUCTOR DIODE that produces visible or infrared light when subjected to an electric current. Visible-light LEDs are used in many electronic devices as indicator lamps (e.g., an on/off indicator) and, when arranged in a matrix, to spell out letters or numbers on alphanumeric displays. Infrared LEDs are used in optoelectronics (e.g., in auto-focus cameras and television remote controls) and as light sources in some long-range fiber-optic communications systems. LEDs consume little power and are long-lasting and inexpensive.

light-frame construction System of construction using many small and closely spaced members that can be assembled by nailing. It is the standard for U.S. suburban housing. The balloon-frame house with wood cladding, invented in Chicago in the 1840s, aided the rapid settlement of the W U.S. In contrast to balloon framing, in which the studs (vertical members) extend the full height of the building, in platform framing, each floor is framed separately. Freed from the heavy timbers of the POST-AND-BEAM SYSTEM, this system offers ease of construction. Carpenters first fabricate a floor, which consists of wood joists and subflooring, then the stud wall frames are fabricated in sections and then lifted into place. On top of this is placed a second floor or the roof. The roof is formed of rafters (sloping joists) or wood TRUSSES. The standard interior wall sheathing is gypsum board (drywall), which provides fire-resistance, stability, and a surface ready for finishing.

lighthouse Structure, usually with a tower, built onshore or on the seabed to signal danger or provide aid to seafarers. The first known lighthouse was the Pharos of Alexandria. The modern lighthouse dates only from the early 18th cent. Wooden towers were often washed away in severe storms. The first lighthouse made of interlocking masonry blocks was built on the treacherous Eddystone Rocks reef, off Plymouth, England (1759). Masonry blocks were replaced by concrete and steel in the 20th cent. The most common illuminant is the electric-filament lamp. Refinements in lenses and reflectors made it possible to substantially increase the light's intensity. Radio and satellite-based navigation systems have greatly reduced the need for large lighthouses in sighting land.

lighting Use of an artificial source of light for illumination. It is a key element of architecture and interior design. Residential lighting uses mainly either INCANDESCENT LAMPS or FLUORESCENT LAMPS and often depends heavily on movable fixtures plugged into outlets; built-in lighting is typically found in kitchens, bathrooms, and corridors and as hanging pendants in dining rooms. Lighting in nonresidential buildings is predominantly fluorescent. High-pressure sodium-vapor lamps (see ELECTRIC DISCHARGE LAMP) have higher efficiency and are used in streetlight fixtures and commercial and industrial applications. HALOGEN LAMPS have residential, industrial, and photographic applications. Depending on their fixtures, lamps (bulbs) produce a variety of lighting conditions. Incandescent lamps placed in translucent glass globes create diffuse effects; in recessed ceiling-mounted fixtures with reflectors, they can light walls or floors evenly. Fluorescent fixtures are typically recessed and rectangular, with prismatic lenses, but other types include luminous ceilings, in which lamps are placed above suspended translucent panels.

lightning Visible discharge of electricity when part of the atmosphere acquires enough electrical charge to overcome the resistance of the air. During a THUNDERSTORM, lightning flashes can occur within clouds, between clouds, between clouds and air, or from clouds to the ground. Lightning is usually associated with cumulonimbus CLOUDS (thunderclouds) but also occurs in nimbostratus clouds, in snowstorms and dust storms, and sometimes in the dust and gases emitted by a volcano. A typical lightning flash involves a potential difference between cloud and ground of several hundred million volts; temperatures in the lightning channel may reach 50,000°F (30,000K). A cloud-to-ground flash comprises at least two strokes: a pale leader stroke that strikes the ground and a highly luminous return stroke. Thunder is caused by rapid heating of air along the length of the lightning channel. As the heated air expands at supersonic speeds, the shock wave decays into a sound wave which, modified by the intervening air and topography, produces a series of rumbles and claps.

lightning bug See FIREFLY

light quantum See PHOTON

light-year Distance traveled by LIGHT moving in a vacuum in one year. At its speed of 186,282 mi/second (298,051 km/second), it equals about 5.88×10^{12} mi (9.46×10^{12} km), 63,240 ASTRONOMICAL UNITS, or 0.307 PARSECS.

lignin \'lig-nən\ Complex oxygen-containing organic compound, a mixture of POLYMERS of poorly known structure. After CELLULOSE, it is the most abundant organic material on earth, making up a quarter to a third of the dry weight of wood. Removed from wood pulp in the manufacture of PAPER, it is used as a binder in particleboard and similar products and as a soil conditioner, filler in certain plastics, and adhesive for linoleum.

lignite Brown to black COAL that has been formed from PEAT under moderate pressure. Dry lignite contains about 60–75% carbon. About 45% of the world's total coal reserves are lignitic, but these reserves have not been exploited to any great extent because lignite is inferior to higher-rank coals (e.g., BITUMINOUS COAL) in heating value and storage stability. In some areas, however, the scarcity of fuel has led to extensive developments.

Liguria Autonomous region (pop., 1996 est.: 1,659,000), NW Italy. Located between France and Tuscany, its capital is GENOA. It was under Roman rule from the 1st cent. B.C. Genoa emerged as a leading power as early as the 11th cent., and by 1400 the entire region was benefiting from its maritime and commercial importance. In 1815 the Congress of VIENNA gave Liguria to the kingdom of Piedmont-Sar-

K L

dinia. Its economy is based on agriculture, tourism, and industry. La Spezia is home to a major naval base.

Li Hongzhang *or* **Li Hung-chang** \lē-ˈhùŋ-ˈjäŋ\ (1823–1901) Chinese statesman who represented China in the series of humiliating negotiations at the end of the SINO–FRENCH WAR (1883–85), SINO–JAPANESE WAR (1894–95), and BOXER REBELLION (1900). Much earlier in his career, Li helped with the suppression of the TAIPING REBELLION (1850–64) and put down the Nian Rebellion (c.1852–68). Coming into contact with Westerners (notably England's C. G. GORDON), he became convinced that China needed Western-style firepower if it wanted to protect its sovereignty. As governor-general of the capital province, Zhili, from 1870, he built arsenals, established two modern naval bases, and purchased warships, hoping to preserve traditional China through modernization, but he was fatally hampered by the system he was trying to protect.

Likud \li-ˈküd\ Coalition of Israeli right-wing political parties. It was created by the 1973 merger of the Herut Party (1948) and other Zionist groups. It alternated electoral victories with Israel's Labour Party from the 1980s until 1992. Under Benjamin Netanyahu (b.1949) it opposed formation of a Palestinian state and supported continued Jewish settlement of occupied territories. Other leaders have included Menachem BEGIN, Yitzhak SHAMIR, and Ariel SHARON. See also ARAB–ISRAELI WARS, IRGUN ZVAI LEUMI.

lilac Any of about 30 species of fragrant N spring-flowering garden shrubs and small trees that make up the genus *Syringa* in the OLIVE family, native to E Europe and temperate Asia. Lilacs have large, oval clusters of compound blooms colored deep purple, lavender, blue, red, pink, white, or creamy yellow; they are often highly fragrant. The common lilac (*S. vulgaris*) reaches 20 ft (6 m) in height.

Lilith In Jewish folklore, a female DEMON. In rabbinic literature she is depicted either as Adam's first wife or as the mother of his demonic offspring after he separated from Eve outside Paradise (see ADAM AND EVE). A cult associated with Lilith survived into the 7th cent. A.D.

Liliuokalani \li-ˌlē-ə-wō-kə-ˈlä-nē\ *orig.* Lydia Kamakaeha (1838–1917) Hawaiian queen, the last Hawaiian monarch to govern the islands (1891–93). Born in Honolulu, she succeeded her brother on the throne and tried to restore the traditional monarchy. Opposing commercial concessions to the U.S., in 1893 she was declared deposed by Sanford DOLE and the Missionary Party, which favored annexation by the U.S. An uprising in her name was suppressed; to win pardons for her supporters, she formally abdicated in 1895. She composed the song "Aloha Oe."

Liliuokalani

Lille \ˈlēl\ City (pop., 1999: 182,000), N France. Fortified in the 11th cent., it changed hands several times during the Middle Ages. LOUIS XIV besieged and captured the city in 1667. It was taken by the duke of MARLBOROUGH in 1708 and ceded to France in 1713. It was occupied by the Germans during both World Wars. It is traditionally France's textile center; other industries include machinery and chemical manufacturing. Its museum has a rich art collection.

Lilongwe \li-ˈlöŋ-gwā\ Capital and second-largest city (metro. area pop., 1994 est.: 396,000), Malawi. An agricultural market for the fertile Central Region Plateau, it replaced Zomba as the national capital in 1975. The old part of the city functions as a service and commercial center, while the newer district houses government buildings and embassies.

Lily, William (1468?–1522?) English Renaissance scholar and classical grammarian. He became a pioneer of Greek learning in England and was appointed master of the school of St. Paul's in 1510. His grammars, one in English and the other in Latin, first appeared about 18 years after his death. Their widespread use by royal order led to the name "the

King's Grammar." With corrections and revisions, they continued to be used as late as the 19th cent., and influenced generations of English people's views of all languages.

lily family Family Liliaceae (order Liliales), which contains about 4,000 species of flowering herbs and shrubs in 280 genera. The genus *Lilium* includes the true lilies. Native primarily to temperate and subtropical regions, these monocots (see COTYLEDON) usually have six-segmented flowers and three-chambered capsular fruits. True lilies are erect perennials with leafy stems, scaly bulbs, usually narrow leaves, and solitary or clustered, often fragrant flowers in a variety of colors. Most species store nutrients underground in a bulb, corm, or tuber. The family includes the ALOE, BLUEBELL, CROCUS, DAY LILY, HOSTA, and TULIP. Food-producing members include ONION, GARLIC, and ASPARAGUS.

lily of the valley Fragrant perennial herb and sole species (*Convallaria majalis*) of the genus *Convallaria* (LILY FAMILY), native to Eurasia and E N. America. White, bell-shaped flowers droop in a row from one side of a leafless stalk, which bears usually two glossy leaves at its base. The fruit is a single red berry.

Lily of the valley (*Convallaria majalis*)

Lima \ˈlē-mə\ City (metro. area pop., 1993: 5,706,000), capital of Peru, located inland from the Pacific port of CALLAO, near the ANDES. Its nickname, El Pulpo ("The Octopus"), refers to its sprawling metropolitan area of 1,506 sq mi (3,900 sq km). It was founded by Francisco PIZARRO in 1535 and later became the capital of the new viceroyalty of Peru. It was destroyed by an earthquake in 1746 but was rebuilt. It now accounts for about one-third of Peru's population, and is its economic and cultural center. Historic sites include the cathedral (begun in the 16th cent.), and the National Univ. of San Marcos (founded 1551).

Limbaugh \ˈlim-ˌbò\, **Rush** *orig.* Rush Hudson Limbaugh III (b.1951) U.S. talk-show host. Born in Cape Girardeau, Mo., he began his career as a disc jockey in 1971 and became a top radio host in Sacramento (1985–88), known for his sarcastic right-wing political commentary and his combative replies to listeners' call-in comments. He began national broadcast of *The Rush Limbaugh Show* in 1988; by 1993 it was radio's most popular and influential talk show, and had spawned numerous conservative shows nationwide. He hosted a television spin-off show from 1992 and wrote best-selling books such as *The Way Things Ought to Be* (1992).

limbo In ROMAN CATHOLICISM, a region between HEAVEN and HELL, the dwelling place of SOULS not condemned to punishment but deprived of the joy of existence with God in heaven. The concept probably developed in the Middle Ages. Two distinct kinds of limbo were proposed: one where Old Testament saints were confined until liberated by JESUS in his "descent into hell," and another for children too young to have sinned but whose original sin had never been washed away by BAPTISM or whose free will was restricted by mental deficiency. Limbo is not an official part of modern church doctrine.

Limbourg brothers *or* **Limburg brothers** \ˈlim-ˌbùrk\ (fl.c.1400–1416) Flemish illuminators. The three brothers—Pol, Herman, and Jehanequin de Limbourg—learned the goldsmith's art in Paris and entered the service of the duc (duke) de Berry, for whom they produced one of the most famous of all ILLUMINATED MANUSCRIPTS, a book of hours (private prayer book) known as the "Très riches heures du duc de Berry" (c.1410–16). Characterized by tall, aristocratic figures with lavish, curvilinear draperies, and by highly naturalistic seasonal landscapes and scenes of peasant life, their style influenced the course of early Netherlandish art. Their deaths in the same year suggest that they died of plague.

lime Small shrublike tree *(Citrus aurantifolia)* widely grown in tropical and subtropical areas, and its edible acid fruits. Clusters of small white flowers produce small oval fruits with a greenish-yellow rind. The juicy pulp is sweeter and more acidic than that of the LEMON. Limes are used to flavor many foods. High in vitamin C, they were formerly used in the British Navy to prevent SCURVY; hence the nickname "Limey" for British sailors.

lime *or* **quicklime** Inorganic compound, white or grayish lumps, chemical formula CaO, made by roasting LIMESTONE (calcium carbonate, $CaCO_3$) until all the carbon dioxide (CO_2) is driven off. One of the four most important basic chemical commodities, it has numerous uses, including to remove sulfur dioxide from stack gases and to neutralize various acids. Adding water to lime yields calcium hydroxide (slaked lime, calcium hydrate, hydrated lime, or caustic lime), which has uses in mortar, plasters, and cements, among many other applications.

limerick Popular form of short, humorous verse, often nonsensical and frequently ribald. It consists of five lines, rhyming *aabba,* and the dominant meter is anapestic, with two feet in the third and fourth lines and three feet in the others. A group of poets in Co. Limerick, Ireland, wrote limericks in Irish in the 18th cent. The first collections in English date from around 1820. Among the most famous are those in Edward LEAR's *Book of Nonsense* (1846).

limestone Sedimentary rock composed mainly of calcium carbonate, usually in the form of CALCITE. It may contain much magnesium carbonate (DOLOMITE) as well. Most limestones have a granular texture; in many cases, the grains are tiny fragments of fossil animal shells. Much knowledge of the earth's history has been derived from FOSSILS embedded in limestone and other carbonate rocks. Limestone is used as a soil conditioner, in the manufacture of glass, and in agriculture. Ornamental varieties are used for flooring, facings of buildings, and monuments.

limit Mathematical concept based on the idea of closeness, used mainly in studying the behavior of FUNCTIONS close to values at which they are undefined. For example, the function $1/x$ is not defined at $x = 0$. For positive values of x, as x is chosen closer and closer to 0, the value of $1/x$ begins to grow rapidly, approaching INFINITY as a limit. Limits provide the means of defining the DERIVATIVE and INTEGRAL of a function.

limitations, statute of Legislative act restricting the time within which legal proceedings may be brought after the occurrence of the events that gave rise to proceedings. Such statutes are enacted to protect persons against claims made after evidence has been lost, memories have faded, or witnesses have disappeared. The periods prescribed for different actions in different jurisdictions vary considerably.

limited liability Condition under which the loss that an owner (shareholder) of a business may incur is limited to the capital invested in the business and does not extend to personal assets. The forerunners of limited-liability companies were limited partnerships, in which one partner was entirely liable for losses and the other partners were liable only for the amounts they invested. After the Joint-Stock Companies Act (1844) in England made incorporation easier, joint-stock companies with limited liability for all members became widespread. The development of the limited-liability company (LLC) was crucial to the rise of large-scale industry in the late 19th cent., since it enabled businesses to mobilize capital from a variety of investors who were unwilling to risk their entire personal fortunes.

limited obligation bond See REVENUE BOND

limnology \lim-'nä-lə-jē\ Study of freshwaters, specifically lakes and ponds, including their biological, physical, and chemical aspects. François-Alphonse Forel (1841–1912) established the field with his studies of Lake Geneva. Limnology traditionally is closely related to hydrobiology, which applies the principles and methods of physics, chemistry, geology, and geography to ecological problems.

Limoges ware PORCELAIN, largely serviceware, produced in Limoges, France. FAIENCE of undistinguished quality was produced there from 1736, but the manufacture of

hard-paste, or true, porcelain dates only from 1771. In 1784 the factory was acquired by the royal factory at Sèvres (see SÈVRES PORCELAIN), and the decorations of the two wares became similar. After 1858 Limoges became a mass exporter of porcelain to the U.S. under the name Haviland.

Limón \li-'mōn\, **José (Arcadio)** (1908–1972) U.S. dancer and choreographer. Born in Mexico, he moved to the U.S. at age 7. He studied with Doris HUMPHREY and Charles Weidman and danced with their company 1930–40. He established the José Limón Dance Co. in 1947, with Humphrey as artistic director. His choreography conveyed modern-dance expression within a well-defined structure, in such works as *The Moor's Pavane* (1949) and *Missa Brevis* (1958). The company has remained active since Limón's death.

Limousin \ˌli-mə-'zēn, *French* ˌlē-mə-'zeⁿ\ Historical region, central France. Conquered by Rome around 50 B.C., under the CAROLINGIANS it was part of AQUITAINE. On ELEANOR OF AQUITAINE's marriage to the English king HENRY II in 1152, it passed to English control. Subsequently fought over, it was finally annexed to the French crown under HENRY IV.

limpet \'lim-pət\ Any of various species of SNAILS that have a flattened shell. Most marine species (subclass Prosobranchia) cling to rocks near shore. A common U.S. species is the Atlantic plate limpet *(Acmaea testudinalis)* of cold waters. Keyhole limpets have a slit or hole at the apex of the shell. See also MOLLUSK.

Limpopo River River, SE Africa. Rising as the Crocodile (Krokodil) River in the Witwatersrand, S. Africa, it flows northeast, forming S. Africa's border with Botswana and Zimbabwe, and then southeast across Mozambique to empty into the Indian Ocean. It is 1,100 mi (1,800 km) long but is navigable only 130 mi (208 km) from the coast.

Lin, Maya (b.1959) U.S. architect and sculptor. Born in Athens, Ohio, she achieved fame when her class assignment at Yale Univ. won the VIETNAM VETERANS MEMORIAL competition in 1981. Her subsequent designs include the Civil Rights Memorial, Montgomery, Ala. (1989), The Women's Table at Yale (1993), and an extraordinary translucent clock, *Eclipsed Time,* for New York's Pennsylvania Station (1994).

linac See LINEAR ACCELERATOR

Linacre \'li-ni-kər\, **Thomas** (c.1460–1524) English physician and classical scholar. He was one of the first propagators of the humanist "New Learning" in England; his students included Desiderius ERASMUS and Thomas MORE. His patients included HENRY VIII, whose approval he obtained in 1518 to found the Royal College of Physicians, which licensed physicians throughout the kingdom, ending the indiscriminate practice of medicine by barbers, clergymen, and others.

Lin Biao *or* **Lin Piao** \'lin-bē-'aù\ (1907–1971?) Chinese military leader. He joined CHIANG KAI-SHEK's NORTHERN EXPEDITION in 1926, but when Chiang turned on the Communists in 1927, Lin fled to join MAO ZEDONG. During the LONG MARCH Lin became legendary for never losing a battle, and he prevailed against the Japanese in the 1930s and the Nationalists in the 1940s. In the early 1960s his indoctrination of the army in accordance with Mao's teachings became a model for the rest of society, and during the CULTURAL REVOLUTION he was designated Mao's successor. It is speculated that Mao feared the power Lin had amassed and that Lin plotted a coup to avoid being purged. The government claimed he died in a 1971 plane crash in Mongolia, but Mongolian officals found no proof of his presence on the plane.

Lincoln City (pop., 2000: 225,000), capital of Nebraska. Laid out in 1859, it was renamed for Abraham LINCOLN when it was chosen as the capital in 1867. It was the home of W. J. BRYAN 1887–1921. It is a railroad junction and commercial center. Its institutions of higher education include the Univ. of Nebraska.

Lincoln *ancient* Lindum. City (pop., 1991: 82,000), seat of Lincolnshire, E England. Lindum served as a Roman fortress, later came under Danish rule, and in the Middle Ages was one of England's major towns. HENRY II gave the

KL

city its first charter in 1154. It has many medieval buildings, including the cathedral (begun c.1075).

Lincoln, Abraham (1809–1865) 16th president of the U.S. (1861–65). Born in a log cabin in Hodgenville, Ky., he moved to Indiana in 1816 and to Illinois in 1830, working as a storekeeper, rail-splitter, postmaster, and surveyor. Though largely self-taught, he practiced law in Springfield, Ill., and served in the state legislature (1834–40) and the U.S. House of Representatives (1847–49). As a circuit-riding lawyer from 1849, he became one of the state's most successful lawyers, noted for his shrewdness, common sense, and honesty (earning the nickname "Honest Abe"). In 1856 he joined the Republican Party, which nominated him as its Senate candidate in 1858. He debated Stephen

Abraham Lincoln, 1863

DOUGLAS on such issues as slavery; though he was not elected, the LINCOLN-DOUGLAS DEBATES brought him national notice. As the Republican presidential nominee in 1860, he opposed slavery's extension into new territories; his election was soon followed by secession of the Confederate states and the start of the AMERICAN CIVIL WAR. The war dominated Lincoln's administration, from choosing competent generals to conciliating radical congressional factions. He pioneered in the creation of a high command for amassing all the energies and resources of a people for war, and he brilliantly combined statecraft and overall direction of armies. To unite the North and influence foreign opinion, he issued the EMANCIPATION PROCLAMATION (1863); his GETTYSBURG ADDRESS (1863) further ennobled the war's purpose. The continuing war affected some Northerners' resolve and his reelection was not assured, but strategic victories turned the tide and he easily defeated George MCCELLAN in 1864. His platform included passage of the 13th Amendment outlawing slavery (ratified 1865). At his second inaugural, he spoke of moderation in reconstructing the South and building a harmonious Union. Five days after the war ended, he was shot by J. W. BOOTH. His reputation among U.S. presidents remains unsurpassed.

Lincoln Center for the Performing Arts Cultural complex on the W side of Manhattan (1962–68), built by a board of architects headed by Wallace K. Harrison (1895–1981). The buildings house the METROPOLITAN OPERA, the New York City Opera, the New York Philharmonic, the NEW YORK CITY BALLET, and the JUILLIARD SCHOOL. Harrison designed the Metropolitan Opera building, Eero SAARINEN designed the Vivian Beaumont Theater, and Philip JOHNSON designed the New York State Theater. Johnson also rebuilt Avery Fisher Hall (home of the New York Philharmonic), originally designed by Max Abramovitz, to correct acoustic deficiencies.

Lincoln-Douglas Debates Seven debates between Abraham LINCOLN and Sen. Stephen DOUGLAS in the 1858 Illinois senatorial campaign. They focused on slavery and its extension into the W territories. Lincoln criticized Douglas for his support of POPULAR SOVEREIGNTY and the KANSAS-NEBRASKA ACT, while Douglas accused Lincoln of advocating racial equality and disruption of the Union. Douglas won reelection, but Lincoln's oratorical brilliance made him a national figure in the young REPUBLICAN PARTY.

Lind, James (1716–1794) Scottish naval surgeon and physician. Having observed thousands of SCURVY, TYPHUS, and DYSENTERY cases and the shipboard conditions that caused them, he published *A Treatise on Scurvy* in 1754, a time when scurvy killed more British sailors than combat. He recommended giving citrus fruits and juices to sailors on long voyages, a practice long known to the Dutch, and quickly eradicated the disease. Lind also suggested shipboard delousing and use of hospital ships.

Lind, Jenny (*orig.* Johanna Maria) (1820–1887) Swedish soprano. She became prima donna at the Royal Opera in Stockholm at 18. Her career expanded to Germany, then to Vienna and London, where she created a sensation. P. T. BARNUM arranged a U.S. tour (dubbing her "the Swedish Nightingale") that launched many modern publicity techniques.

Lindbergh, Charles A(ugustus) (1902–1974) U.S. aviator who made the first nonstop solo flight across the Atlantic Ocean. Born in Detroit, he became an airmail pilot in 1926. He obtained backing from St. Louis businessmen to compete for a prize for flying from New York to Paris, and in 1927 in the monoplane *Spirit of St. Louis* he made the flight in 33 1/2 hours, becoming an instant hero in the U.S. and Europe. In 1929 he married the writer Anne Morrow (1906–2001), who would later serve as his copilot and navigator. In 1932

Charles A. Lindbergh, 1927

their child was kidnapped and murdered, a crime that received worldwide attention. They moved to England to escape the publicity, returning to the U.S. in 1940 to criticism over his speeches calling for U.S. neutrality in World War II. Lindbergh later was a consultant to Pan American Airways and the U.S. Department of Defense and served on many aeronautical boards and committees. In 1953 he wrote the Pulitzer Prize–winning *The Spirit of St. Louis*.

linden Any of about 30 species of deciduous trees that make up the genus *Tilia* (family Tiliaceae), native to the Northern Hemisphere. A few are outstanding deciduous ornamental and shade trees, with heart-shaped, coarsely toothed leaves, fragrant cream-colored flowers, and small globular fruit. Species native to England are called lime trees. See also BASSWOOD.

Lindisfarne *or* **Holy Island** Historic small island 2 mi (3 km) from the English Northumbrian coast. It became a religious center in 635, when St. Aidan established a monastery and church there. It was abandoned in 875, but the monastery was refounded in 1082 and survived until the dissolution of the monasteries (1536–40) under HENRY VIII. The manuscript of the Lindisfarne Gospels (c.696–98) is one of the finest surviving illuminated manuscripts of the period.

Lindisfarne Gospels ILLUMINATED MANUSCRIPT version of the four Gospels, produced in the late 7th cent. for the monastery of LINDISFARNE. Designed and executed by Eadfrith, who became bishop of Lindisfarne in 698, the Lindisfarne Gospels (now in the British Library) show the fusion of Irish, classical, and Byzantine elements. See also Book of KELLS.

Lindsay, Howard (1889–1968) U.S. playwright, known for his collaboration with Russel Crouse (1893–1966). Born in Waterford, N.Y., Lindsay was an actor, director, and playwright, and Crouse, born in Findlay, Ohio, was a journalist before they teamed up to write librettos for the successful Cole PORTER musicals *Anything Goes* (1934) and *Red, Hot and Blue* (1936). Their *Life with Father* (1939) ran for over seven years; it was followed by *Arsenic and Old Lace* (1940) and later by librettos for such musicals as *State of the Union* (1945, Pulitzer Prize), *Call Me Madam* (1950), and *The Sound of Music* (1959).

Lindsay, (Nicholas) Vachel (1879–1931) U.S. poet. Born in Springfield, Ill., Lindsay in his youth began traveling the country reciting his poems in return for food and shelter, in an attempt to revive poetry as an oral art form of the common people. He first received widespread recognition for "General William Booth Enters into Heaven" (1913). His works are full of powerful rhythms, vivid imagery, and bold rhymes and express a passion for progressive democracy and a romantic view of nature. His collections include *The Congo* (1914) and *The Chinese Nightingale* (1917). Depressed and unstable in later years, he committed suicide by drinking poison.

line Basic element of EUCLIDEAN GEOMETRY. EUCLID defined a line as an interval between two points and claimed it could be extended indefinitely in either direction. Such an extension in both directions is now thought of as a line, and Euclid's original definition is considered a line segment. A ray is part of a line extending indefinitely from a point on the line in only one direction. In a COORDINATE SYSTEM on a plane, a line can be represented by the linear EQUATION $ax + by + c = 0$. This is often written in the slope-intercept form as $y = mx + b$, in which m is the SLOPE and b is the value where the line crosses the y-axis.

Linear A and Linear B Linear forms of WRITING used by AEGEAN CIVILIZATIONS during the 2nd millennium B.C. The unknown language represented by Linear A, a syllabary written from left to right, date from 1850 B.C.–1400 B.C. Linear B, adapted from Linear A, was borrowed from the MINOAN civilization by the MYCENAEAN Greeks, probably around 1600 B.C., and used to write the Mycenaean Greek dialect. Examples of Linear B script 1400–1200 B.C. represent the oldest known form of Greek.

linear accelerator or **linac** Type of PARTICLE ACCELERATOR that imparts a series of relatively small increases in energy to SUBATOMIC PARTICLES as they pass through a sequence of alternating electric fields set up in a linear structure. The small accelerations add together to give the particles a greater energy than could be achieved by the voltage used in one section alone. One of the world's longest linacs is the 2-mi (3.2-km) machine at the Stanford Linear Accelerator Center, which can accelerate electrons to energies of 50 billion electron volts.

linear algebra Branch of ALGEBRA concerned with methods of solving systems of linear EQUATIONS; more generally, the mathematics of LINEAR TRANSFORMATIONS and vector spaces. "Linear" refers to the form of the equations involved—in two dimensions, $ax + by = c$. Geometrically, this represents a line. If the variables are replaced by VECTORS, FUNCTIONS, or DERIVATIVES, the equation becomes a linear transformation. A SYSTEM OF EQUATIONS of this type is a system of linear transformations. Because it shows when such a system has a solution and how to find it, linear algebra is essential to the theory of mathematical analysis and DIFFERENTIAL EQUATIONS. Its applications extend into such fields as biology and economics.

linear transformation In mathematics, a rule for changing one geometric figure (or MATRIX or VECTOR) into another using a formula with a specified format. The format must be a linear combination, in which the original components (e.g., the x and y coordinates of each point of the original figure) are changed via the formula $ax + by$ to produce the coordinates of the transformed figure. Examples include flipping the figure over the x or y axis, stretching or compressing it, and rotating it. Every such transformation has an inverse, which undoes its effect.

linen Fiber, YARN, and fabric made from the FLAX plant. Flax is one of the oldest TEXTILE fibers used by humans; evidence of its use has been found in Switzerland's prehistoric lake dwellings. The fiber is obtained by subjecting plant stalks to a series of operations, including retting (a fermentation process), drying, crushing, and beating. Linen is stronger than COTTON, dries more quickly, and is more slowly affected by exposure to sunlight. Low elasticity, imparting a hard, smooth texture, makes linen subject to wrinkling. Because linen absorbs and releases moisture quickly and is a good conductor of heat, linen garments feel cool to wearers. Fine grades of linen are made into woven fabrics and laces for apparel and household furnishings.

linga or **lingam** In HINDUISM, the phallus, symbol of the god SHIVA and of generative power. Lingas are the main objects of worship in temples to Shiva and family shrines throughout India. Linga worship dates from at least the 1st–2nd cent. A.D. The female YONI often forms the base of the erect linga, a reminder that the male and female principles together represent the totality of existence. In linga worship, the purity of the offerings and the cleanliness of the worshipers are particularly stressed.

lingonberry Fruit of a small creeping plant (*Vaccinium vitisidaea*) of the HEATH FAMILY, related to the BLUEBERRY and CRANBERRY. Also known as cowberry, foxberry, and mountain, or rock, cranberry, the lingonberry is a wild plant used for jelly and juice by N Europeans. The plants grow densely in the forest understory.

lingua franca \'liŋ-gwə-'fraŋ-kə\ Language used for communication between two or more groups that have different native languages. It may be a standard language—for example, English and French are often used for international diplomacy, and SWAHILI is used by speakers of many local languages in E Africa. A lingua franca may also be a PIDGIN. The term lingua franca (Latin: "Frankish language") was first applied to a pidgin based on French and Italian developed in the Mediterranean. See also CREOLE.

linguistics Study of the nature and structure of language. Linguists use a synchronic (describing a language as it exists at a given time) or a diachronic (tracing a language's history) approach to language study. Greek philosophers in the 5th cent. B.C. were the first in the West to be concerned with linguistic theory. The first complete Greek GRAMMAR, written by Dionysius Thrax in the 1st cent. B.C., inspired Roman grammarians, whose work led to the medieval and Renaissance vernacular grammars. With the rise of historical linguistics in the 19th cent., linguistics became a science. In the late 19th and early 20th cent., Ferdinand de SAUSSURE established the structuralist school of linguistics, which analyzed actual speech to learn about the underlying structure of language. In the 1950s, Noam CHOMSKY argued that linguistics should study native speakers' unconscious knowledge of their own language (competence), not their actual production of language (performance).

linkage System of solid links (bars) connected to two or more other links by pin joints (hinges), sliding joints, or ball-and-socket joints to form a closed chain or a series of closed chains. When one link is fixed, the possible movements of the other links relative to it and to one another depend on the number of links and the number and types of joints. With four pin-connected links, the links all move in parallel planes, and regardless of which link is fixed, the others move in a fixed way relative to the fixed link. With various relative lengths of the links, this four-bar linkage becomes a useful mechanism for converting uniform rotary to non-uniform rotary motion or continuous rotary to oscillatory motion.

Linnaeus \lə-'nē-əs\, **Carolus** *Swedish* Carl von Linné (1707–1778) Swedish botanist and explorer. He became the first to develop principles for defining genera and species of organisms and to create a uniform system for naming them, BINOMIAL NOMENCLATURE. His system was based mainly on flower parts, which tend to remain unchanged during evolution. Linnaeus not only systematized the plant and animal kingdoms, but also classified the mineral kingdom and wrote a study of the diseases known in his day. His works include *Systema Naturae* (1735), *Fundamenta Botanica* (1736), and *Species Plantarum* (1753).

linoleum Smooth-surfaced floor covering made principally from a mixture of oxidized linseed oil and resins, applied to a felt or canvas backing. Linoleum is flexible, warm, and unaffected by ordinary floor temperatures. It is specially hardened to resist indentation and is not susceptible to damage from fats, oils, greases, or organic solvents.

Linux \'li-nəks\ OPERATING SYSTEM for digital computers. Developed by Linus Torvalds (b.1969) and modified by hundreds of developers around the world, the Linux core program was first released in 1994. A true multiuser, multitasking system, Linux contains features consistent with UNIX-type systems. It has a reputation as a reliable, fast-performing system with good security features. It can be installed on personal computers as well as more powerful machines. Its source code is freely available to anyone; however, several companies sell prepackaged Linux products. Linux has gained popularity particularly as an operating system for business applications and Web servers.

Lin Yutang or **Lin Yü-t'ang** (1895–1976) Chinese writer. He studied in the U.S. and Europe and in 1932 established a highly successful Western-style satirical magazine of a type totally new to China. A prolific writer of works in Chinese and English, he produced his first English-language book, *My Country and My People,* in 1935. From 1936 he lived chiefly in the U.S. His other works include *The Wisdom of*

K L

China and India (1942) and highly acclaimed English translations of Chinese literary masterpieces.

Linz \'lints\ *ancient* Lentia. City (pop., 1999 est.: 190,000), N central Austria. Located on the DANUBE RIVER west of VIENNA, and on the direct rail route between the Baltic and Adriatic seas, it originated as a Roman fortress. It was noted for its fairs in the 15th cent. It is now a cultural center and the seat of Johannes Kepler Univ.

Lin Zexu *or* **Lin Tse-hsü** \'lin-'dzə-'shü\ (1785–1850) Chinese official of the QING DYNASTY. Having suggested to the emperor ways to suppress the British opium trade, Lin was appointed imperial commissioner (1838) and dispatched to Canton to deal with the problem directly. He was so successful that, in retaliation for his destruction of their opium stocks, the British ravaged large parts of S China (see OPIUM WARS) and Lin was quickly dismissed, but was soon called back to important service. He is regarded as a national hero.

lion Large, powerfully built CAT (*Panthera leo*), the proverbial "king of beasts." It is now found mainly in parts of sub-Saharan Africa, though a few hundred constitute an Asiatic race in India. Lions inhabit grassy plains and open savanna. The male is 6–7 ft (1.8–2.1 m) long, excluding the 3-ft (1-m) tail, stands about 4 ft (1.2 m) high at the shoulder, and weighs 370–500 lbs (170–230 kg). The female, or lioness, is considerably smaller. The male's outstanding characteristic is his mane. Lions are unique among cats in that they live in a group, or pride, often consisting of about 15 individuals. Lionesses are the chief hunters; they prey particularly on wildebeests, antelopes, and zebras.

lionfish Any of several species of showy Indo-Pacific fish of the SCORPION-FISH family (Scorpaenidae), noted for their venomous fin spines, which can inflict painful puncture wounds. Lionfish have enlarged pectoral fins and elongated dorsal fin spines, and each species bears a particular pattern of bold stripes. When disturbed, they display their fins and may attack with the dorsal spines. *Pterois volitans,* sometimes kept by fish fanciers, is striped with red, brown, and white and grows to about 12 in. (30 cm) long.

Lions Clubs, International Association of Civilian service club. The nation's largest service-club organization, it was founded in 1917 to foster a spirit of "generous consideration" among peoples of the world and promote good government, good citizenship, and an active interest in civic welfare. Its activities include aid to the blind and support of the U.N. Lions Clubs operate in over 150 countries.

Lipari Islands \'li-pə-rē\ *Italian* **Isole Eolie** \'ē-zō-,lā-ā-'ô-lē-,ä\ Volcanic island group, Tyrrhenian Sea. Located off the N coast of SICILY, it includes seven major islands and several islets, with a total land area of 34 sq mi (88 sq km). Vulcano and Stromboli are active volcanoes. The Greeks believed the islands to be the home of the god Aeolus, who kept the winds confined in one of their caves. They have been inhabited since NEOLITHIC times and were held successively by the Greeks, Carthaginians, Romans, Saracens, Normans, and Aragonese.

Lipchitz \'lip-shits\, **Jacques** *orig.* Chaim Jacob Lipchitz (1891–1973) Lithuanian-French-U.S. sculptor. Trained as an engineer, he turned to sculpture after moving to Paris in 1909. His early style was Cubist. Around 1925 he began producing his "transparents," open-spaced, curvilinear bronzes, such as *Harpist* (1928), which would greatly influence the course of sculpture in the following quarter-century. After settling near New York City in 1941, he produced such massive works as *The Prayer* (1943) and *Bellerophon Taming Pegasus* (1966).

lipid \'lip-əd\ Any of a diverse class of organic compounds, found in all living things, that are greasy and insoluble in water. Of the three large classes of substances in foods and living cells, lipids contain more than twice as much energy (CALORIES) per unit of weight as the other two, PROTEINS and CARBOHYDRATES. They include the FATS and edible OILS (e.g., butter, olive oil, corn oil), which are primarily TRIGLYCERIDES; phospholipids (e.g., LECITHIN, CHOLINE); WAXES of animal or plant origin; and sphingolipids, complex substances that are components of cell membranes.

Lipizzaner *or* **Lippizaner** \,li-pət-'sä-nər\ Breed of light HORSE named for the Austrian imperial stud farm at Lip-

izza, near Trieste, formerly part of Austria-Hungary. The founding of the breed, which has six strains, dates to 1580. Lipizzaners have a long back and a short, thick neck, average 15–16 hands (about 60–64 in., or 152–164 cm) in height and 1,000–1,300 lbs (450–585 kg) in weight, and are usually gray. Best known are those trained at Vienna's Spanish Riding School.

Li Po See LI BO

lipoprotein \,lī-pə-'prō-,tēn\ Any of a class of organic compounds that contain both LIPID (FAT) and PROTEIN. They may dissolve in water and water solutions (those in egg yolk and blood plasma) or not (those in cell membranes). Lipoproteins in blood plasma are the mode of transport for CHOLESTEROL, insoluble by itself. Low-density lipoproteins (LDLs) carry cholesterol from the liver, where it is made, to the cells, where it is used; high-density lipoproteins (HDLs) may carry excess cholesterol back to the liver for breakdown and excretion.

Lippi, Filippino (c.1457–1504) Italian painter. After the death of his father, Fra Filippo LIPPI, Filippino entered the workshop of Sandro BOTTICELLI and absorbed many aspects of his style. He completed the frescoes in the Brancacci Chapel in Florence's Santa Maria del Carmine (c.1485–87), left unfinished when MASACCIO died. His most popular painting is the *Vision of St. Bernard* altarpiece (c.1480). His highly decorative frescoes in the Carafa Chapel in Rome (1488–93) and the Strozzi Chapel in Florence (completed 1502) anticipated Tuscan Mannerism of the 16th cent.

Lippi, Fra Filippo (c.1406–1469) Italian painter. In 1421 he became a Carmelite monk at Santa Maria del Carmine in Florence, where MASACCIO was soon decorating the Brancacci Chapel with frescoes. Lippi himself painted frescoes in the church, then disappeared from the monastery in 1432. In 1437 he returned to Florence under the protection of the MEDICI FAMILY and was commissioned to execute several works. His *Madonna and Child* (1437) and *Annunciation* (c.1442) show a maturing style characterized by warm coloring and attention to decorative effects. In 1456, while painting in a convent in Prato, he fled with one of the nuns. They were later released from their vows and permitted to marry; their son was Filippino LIPPI. The former friar's frescoes in the Prato cathedral stand among his finest achievements.

Lippmann, Walter (1889–1974) U.S. newspaper commentator and author. Born in New York City, he became an editor at the fledgling *New Republic* (1914–17). His thinking influenced Woodrow WILSON, and he took part in the negotiations that culminated in the Treaty of Versailles. In 1931 he began his "Today and Tomorrow" column at the *New York Herald-Tribune;* eventually widely syndicated, it would win two Pulitzer Prizes (1958, 1962), and Lippmann would become one of the most respected political columnists in the world. His books include *Public Opinion* (1922), perhaps his most influential work, and *The Good Society* (1937).

Lipton, Thomas J(ohnstone) (*later* **Sir Thomas**) (1850–1931) British merchant who built the Lipton tea empire. He opened a small grocery in Glasgow, which grew into a chain of retail shops throughout Britain. To supply his shops cheaply, Lipton bought tea, coffee, and cocoa plantations in Ceylon as well as English fruit farms, jam factories, and bakeries. A keen yachtsman, he raced his "Shamrock" yachts five times unsuccessfully for the AMERICA'S CUP.

liqueur \li-'kər\ Alcoholic beverage produced by combining a DISTILLED LIQUOR, usually BRANDY, with fruit- or herb-flavored sugar syrup. Alcohol content is 24–60% by volume. Liqueurs were probably first produced commercially by medieval monks and alchemists. They are popular as after-dinner drinks and are also used in mixed drinks and dessert dishes. Varieties include crème de menthe (mint-flavored), curaçao (flavored with green orange peel), and proprietary brands such as Benedictine (a plant liquor), Grand Marnier (a curaçao from France's Cognac region), and Kahlúa (coffee-flavored).

liquid One of the three principal states of matter, intermediate between a GAS and a SOLID (see PHASE). A liquid has neither the orderliness of a solid nor the randomness of a gas. Liquids flow under the action of very small shear stresses. Liquids in contact with their own vapor or air have a SURFACE TENSION that causes the interface to assume the configuration of minimum area (i.e., spherical). Surfaces between liquids and solids have interfacial tensions that determine whether the liquid will wet the other material. See also BOILING POINT, CAPILLARITY, FREEZING POINT.

liquid crystal Substance that flows like a liquid but maintains some of the ordered structure characteristic of a CRYSTAL. Some organic substances do not melt directly when heated but instead turn from a crystalline solid to a liquid crystalline state. When heated further, a true liquid is formed. Liquid crystals have unique properties. See also LIQUID CRYSTAL DISPLAY.

liquid crystal display (LCD) Device used in displays for watches, calculators, notebook computers, and other electronic devices. Current passed through specific portions of a liquid-crystal solution causes the crystals to align, blocking the passage of light, thereby producing visual images on the display screen. Since LCDs are much lighter and consume less power than other display technologies (e.g., CATHODE-RAY TUBES), they are ideal for flat-panel displays, as in portable computers.

liquor See DISTILLED LIQUOR

Lisbon *Portuguese* **Lisboa** City (pop., 1991: 678,000), capital of Portugal. The country's chief seaport and largest city, it lies on the TAGUS RIVER near the Atlantic Ocean. It was under Rome from 205 B.C., ruled by barbarian tribes from the 5th cent., and taken by Moors in the 8th cent. The Crusaders under AFONSO I gained control of it in 1147, and it became the national capital in 1256. It flourished as a leading European trading city in the 14th–16th cent. One of the greatest earthquakes ever recorded struck Lisbon in 1755, killing 30,000.

Lissitzky, El *orig.* Lazar Markovich Lisitsky (1890–1941) Russian painter, typographer, and designer. As a teacher at Marc CHAGALL's revolutionary art school in Vitebsk, he met Kazimir MALEVICH, whose influence is seen in a series of abstract paintings that were Lissitzky's major contribution to CONSTRUCTIVISM. In 1922 he went to Germany, where Theo van DOESBURG and László MOHOLY-NAGY transmitted his ideas to the West through classes at the BAUHAUS. In 1925 he returned to Russia and devoted himself to devising new techniques of printing, photomontage, and architecture.

List, (Georg) Friedrich (1789–1846) German-U.S. economist. He first gained prominence as the founder of an association of German industrialists that favored abolishing tariff barriers between the German states. Exiled in 1825 for his liberal views, he went to the U.S., where he wrote *Outlines of American Political Economy* (1827), maintaining that emerging industrial economics require tariff protection. His best-known work was *The National System of Political Economy* (1841). Financial and other difficulties eventually drove him to suicide.

Lister, Joseph *later* Baron Lister (of Lyme Regis) (1827–1912) British surgeon and medical scientist. In 1861 he was appointed surgeon to the Glasgow Royal Infirmary, where he observed that 45–50% of amputation patients died from sepsis (infection). Initially he theorized that airborne dust might cause sepsis, but in 1865 he learned of Louis PASTEUR's theory that microorganisms caused infection. Using PHENOL as an antiseptic, Lister reduced mortality in his ward to 15% within four years. By the time of his retirement in 1893, he had seen his principle accepted almost universally.

Lister, Samuel Cunliffe *later* **Baron Masham (of Swinton)** (1815–1906) British inventor. His wool-combing machine (1845) helped lower the price of clothing and contributed greatly to the development of Australian sheep farming. Another invention (c.1865) permitted the use of silk waste to make goods that could compete with those manufactured from the perfect cocoon. His velvet loom for making pile fabrics (c.1878) was another important innovation.

Liszt \'list\, **Franz** (*orig.* Franciscus) (1811–1886) Hungarian-French composer and pianist. Karl CZERNY recognized Liszt's talent at age 8, and Liszt studied with Czerny and Antonio SALIERI in Vienna. After an 1823 Paris success, he toured Europe. Hearing Niccolò PAGANINI in 1832, he was inspired to develop his technique to the utmost and compose his first mature pieces, including the *Transcendental Études* (1837) and *Paganini Études* (1839). An affair with Countess Marie d'Agoult resulted in the birth of his daughter, Cosima (1837–1930), who would marry his friend Richard WAGNER. The 1840s were the height of "Lisztmania," the unprecedented frenzy of his audiences sparked by his

Franz Liszt Lithograph by Joseph Kriehuber, 1846

blazing technique and dashing style. Seeing himself as a messenger of the future, he ceased concertizing in the late 1840s to devote himself to composition and furthering the work of progressive composers. In the 1850s he wrote many of his most ambitious works, including *A Faust Symphony* (1854) and the piano sonata in B minor (1853). In 1865 he took minor church orders. His later output anticipated many 20th-cent. developments.

Li Ta-chao See LI DAZHAO

Li Taibo See LI BO

litchi *or* **lichee** *or* **lychee** \'lē-chē, 'lī-chē\ Fruit of the tree *Litchi chinensis* (family Sapindaceae), believed to be native to S China, but now also cultivated elsewhere. It has been a favorite fruit of the Cantonese Chinese since ancient times. The fresh pulp tastes musky; when dried, it is acidic and very sweet. The handsome tree bears leaves that are bright green year-round. Clusters of small, inconspicuous flowers form small, oval red fruits.

literacy Ability to read and write. The term may also refer to a basic level of education obtained through the written word. In ancient civilizations such as those of the Sumerians and Babylonians, only an elite group of scholars and priests were literate. In classical Greece and Rome, literacy was often limited to members of the upper classes. The spread of literacy in Europe in the Middle Ages led to the use of writing for functions once conducted orally, such as the indenture of servants and the notation of evidence. The spread of literacy during the Reformation and the Renaissance was greatly facilitated by the development of PRINTING from movable type and by the adoption of vernacular languages in place of Latin. Compulsory schooling, widely established in the 19th cent., has led to high rates of literacy in the modern industrialized world.

literary criticism Discipline concerned with philosophical, descriptive, and evaluative inquiries about literature. The Western critical tradition began with PLATO's *Republic* (4th cent. B.C.). A generation later, ARISTOTLE, in his *Poetics*, developed a set of principles of composition that had a lasting influence. European criticism since the Renaissance has primarily focused on the moral worth of literature and the nature of its relationship to reality. Sir Philip SIDNEY argued that literature offers an imagined world that is in some respects superior to the real one. A century later, John DRYDEN proposed that literature must primarily offer an accurate representation of the world for "the delight and instruction of mankind." The criticism of the Romantic period is epitomized by William WORDSWORTH's assertion that the object of poetry is "truth . . . carried alive into the heart by passion." The later 19th cent. saw two divergent developments: an aesthetic theory of "art for art's sake," and Matthew ARNOLD's view that literature must assume the moral and philosophical functions previously filled by religion. The later years of the 20th cent. saw the development of a multiplicity of critical factions (see STRUCTURALISM, POSTSTRUCTURALISM, DECONSTRUCTION).

lithification Complex process whereby loose grains of sediment are converted into ROCK. Cementation is one of the main processes involved, particularly for sandstones and conglomerates. In addition, reactions take place within a sediment between various minerals and between minerals and the fluids trapped in the pores to form new minerals.

K L

lithium Chemical ELEMENT, lightest ALKALI METAL, chemical symbol Li, atomic number 3. It is soft, white, lustrous, and very reactive (VALENCE 1). The metal is used in certain ALLOYS, as a coolant in nuclear reactors, and as a reagent, scavenger, and rocket fuel. Lithium HYDRIDE is used as a source of hydrogen; lithium hydroxide is used as an additive in storage BATTERIES and to absorb carbon dioxide. Lithium carbonate is an important drug for treating DEPRESSION and BIPOLAR DISORDER.

lithography \li-'thä-grə-fē\ PRINTING process that makes use of the immiscibility of grease and water. Aloys Senefelder of Prague (1771–1834) exploited the properties of a stone with a calcium carbonate base and a fine, porous surface. In Senefelder's process, perfected in 1798, the stone, with a design drawn on it with crayon or greasy ink, was wetted with water; after various etching and protecting steps, it was brushed with oily ink; it retained the ink only on the design. This inked surface was then printed—either directly on paper, by a special press (as in most fine-art PRINTMAKING), or onto a rubber cylinder and thence onto paper (as in commercial printing). The method of preparing stones for hand printing is still the lithographic method preferred by artists. Commercial lithographic printing on a modern rotary OFFSET PRINTING press can produce high-quality impressions at high speed. It now accounts for more than 40% of all printing, packaging, and publishing.

litho-offset See OFFSET PRINTING

lithosphere Rigid, rocky outer layer of the earth, consisting of the CRUST and the solid outermost layer of the upper MANTLE. It extends to a depth of about 60 mi (100 km). It is broken into about a dozen separate rigid blocks, or plates (see PLATE TECTONICS). Slow convection currents deep within the mantle, generated by radioactive heating of the interior, are believed to cause the lateral movements of the plates.

Lithuania *officially* **Republic of Lithuania** Nation, NE Europe. Area: 25,213 sq mi (65,301 sq km). Population (2000): 3,697,000. Capital: VILNIUS. Ethnic Lithuanians make up

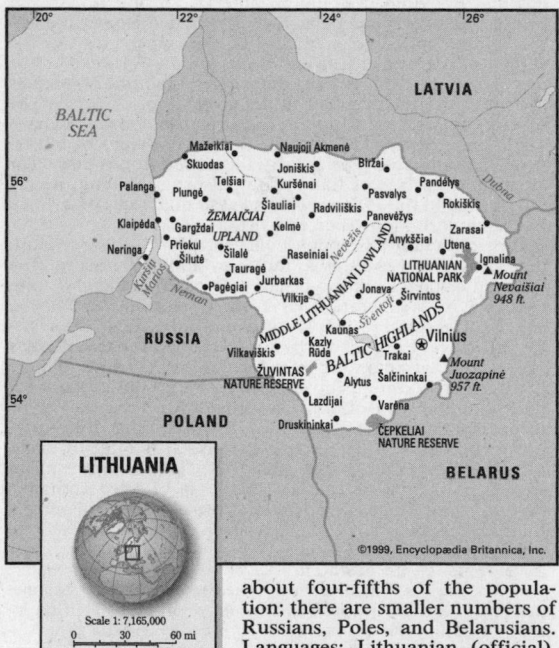

LITHUANIA

Scale 1: 7,165,000

©1999, Encyclopædia Britannica, Inc.

about four-fifths of the population; there are smaller numbers of Russians, Poles, and Belarusians. Languages: Lithuanian (official), Russian, Polish, Belarusian. Religion: Roman Catholicism (a majority of the population). Currency: litas. The country consists of low-lying plains alternating with hilly uplands, watered by rivers that meander westward to the Baltic Sea. Manufacturing, including metalworking, woodworking, and textile production, is the most important sector of the economy, especially in the east and south. Agriculture focuses on livestock breeding, especially dairy farming and pigs, and the cultivation of cereals, flax, sugar beets, potatoes, and fodder crops. It is a republic with one legislative house; its head of state is the president, and the head of government is the prime minister. Lithuanian tribes united in the mid-13th cent. to oppose the TEUTONIC knights. Gediminas, one of the grand dukes, expanded Lithuania into an empire that dominated much of E Europe in the 14th–16th cent. In 1386 the Lithuanian grand duke became the king of Poland, and the two countries remained closely associated for the next 400 years. It was acquired by Russia in the Third Partition of POLAND in 1795 and joined in the Polish revolt in 1863. Occupied by Germany during World War I, it declared its independence in 1918. In 1940 the Soviet Red Army gained control of Lithuania, which was soon incorporated into the Soviet Union as the Lithuanian S.S.R. Germany occupied Lithuania again in 1941–44, but the Red Army regained control in 1944. With the breakup of the U.S.S.R., Lithuania declared its independence in 1990 and gained full independence in 1991. During the 1990s it sought economic stability. It signed a border treaty with Russia in 1997.

litmus \'lit-məs\ Mixture of colored organic compounds obtained from several species of LICHEN. In water solution or as litmus paper, it is the oldest and most used indicator of whether a substance is an ACID or a BASE. It turns red or pink in acid solutions and blue or purple-blue in alkaline solutions.

Little Bighorn, Battle of the *or* **Custer's Last Stand** (June 25, 1876) Battle at the Little Bighorn River, Montana Territory, between federal troops led by Col. G. A. CUSTER and a band of Eastern SIOUX and Northern CHEYENNE Indians. The U.S. government had ordered the N Plains tribes to return to designated reservations, sending troops under Gen. Alfred H. Terry to enforce the order. A party of some 200 soldiers led by Custer launched an early attack and was slaughtered. Government troops subsequently flooded the area, forcing the Indians to surrender.

Little League International baseball organization for children and youth, started in 1939 in Williamsport, Pa., by Carl E. Stotz. The league originally included boys aged 8–12; girls were admitted in 1974. It now includes two upper divisions for youths aged 13–15 and 16–18. In the junior division the game is played on a field two-thirds the size of a professional diamond. A season comprises about 15 games. The organization expanded rapidly after World War II; today there are Little League clubs in some 100 countries.

Little Missouri River River, NW U.S. It rises in NE Wyoming and flows across the corners of Montana and S. Dakota into N. Dakota, emptying into the MISSOURI RIVER after a course of 560 mi (900 km). The Theodore Roosevelt National Park lies along its shores in N. Dakota.

Little Richard *orig.* Richard Wayne Penniman (b.1932) U.S. RHYTHM-AND-BLUES singer and pianist. Born into a strict religious family in Macon, Ga., he sang and played piano in church. Ejected from home by his father, he performed in nightclubs and recorded as a blues artist from the early 1950s. His hit "Tutti Frutti" (1956) was followed by "Long Tall Sally," "Lucille," and "Good Golly, Miss Molly," and his energy and penchant for the outrageous set a standard for the emerging rock idiom. After a religious conversion, he was ordained a minister, but soon returned to music and has continued to tour with much success. He was an original inductee into the Rock and Roll Hall of Fame.

Little Rock City (pop., 2000: 183,000), capital of Arkansas, located on the ARKANSAS RIVER. In 1722 a French explorer named the site for a rock formation on the riverbank. It became the capital of Arkansas in 1821. It was strongly anti-Union in the AMERICAN CIVIL WAR; Federal troops occupied the city in 1863. It grew as a commercial center and hub of railway and river transportation. In 1957 federal troops were used to prevent state authorities from interfering with desegregation at Central High School. The state's largest city, it has many institutions of higher learning.

Little Turtle (1752–1812) American Indian leader. Born near Ft. Wayne, Ind., he became chief of the Miami tribe and led raids on settlements in the Northwest Territory in the early

1790s. Defeated at the Battle of FALLEN TIMBERS (1794), he was obliged to sign a treaty that ceded to the U.S. much of Ohio and parts of Illinois, Indiana, and Michigan. He then advocated peace and kept the Miami from joining the Shawnee confederacy of TECUMSEH.

Litvinov \lyit-'vē-nȯf\, **Maksim (Maksimovich)** *orig.* Meir Walach (1876–1951) Soviet diplomat. He joined the RUSSIAN SOCIAL DEMOCRATIC WORKERS' PARTY (1898), was arrested for revolutionary activity (1901), and fled to Britain. After World War I he led Soviet delegations to disarmament conferences. As commissar for foreign affairs (1930-39), he established diplomatic relations with the U.S. (1934), negotiated anti-German treaties with France and Czechoslovakia (1935), and urged the League of Nations to resist Germany (1934–38). Dismissed before the signing of the German–Soviet Nonaggression Pact, he served as ambassador to the U.S. 1941–43.

Liu Bang *or* **Liu Pang** \lē-'ü-'bäŋ\ *or* **Han Gaozu** \'hän-'gaù-'dzü\ (256–195 B.C.) Founder of China's HAN DYNASTY (206 B.C.–A.D. 220). When the first emperor of the QIN DYNASTY died, Liu joined rebels led by Xiang Yu to overthrow the Qin. Xiang Yu won and rewarded Liu with the kingdom of Han in W China, but the two allies subsequently turned against each other. Liu's pragmatic shrewdness triumphed, and he became the Han dynasty's first ruler in 206 B.C.

Liu Shaoqi *or* **Liu Shao-ch'i** \lē-'ü-'shaù-'chē\ (1898–1969) Chairman of the People's Republic of China (1959–68). An activist Communist from the 1920s, Liu rose within the CHINESE COMMUNIST PARTY, and his studies in the Soviet Union made him an effective spokesman for the new government in China. When MAO ZEDONG resigned as chairman after the failure of his GREAT LEAP FORWARD, Liu assumed the title (1959). His policies for revitalizing agriculture by permitting peasants to cultivate private plots and giving them monetary incentives were later rejected by Mao. In 1968 Liu was purged from power for being a "capitalist roader." Not until 1974 was Liu's death in 1969 made public.

live oak Any of several N. American ornamental and timber trees in the red-oak group of the genus *Quercus* in the BEECH family. The southern live oak *(Q. virginiana)* is a massive (50 ft, or 15 m, tall) evergreen tree. The trunk divides near the ground into several limbs that extend horizontally as much as two to three times the height of the tree, whose elliptical leaves are dark green above, whitish and hairy below. It is planted as a timber, shade, and avenue tree in the S U.S. The oldest trees are 200–300 years old.

liver Largest GLAND in the body. It secretes BILE; metabolizes PROTEINS, CARBOHYDRATES, and FATS; stores GLYCOGEN and VITAMINS; synthesizes COAGULATION factors; removes wastes and toxic matter from the BLOOD; regulates blood volume; and destroys old red blood cells. The portal vein carries blood from the gastrointestinal tract, gallbladder, pancreas, and spleen to the liver to be processed. A duct system carries bile from the liver to the duodenum and the GALLBLADDER. Liver tissue consists of a mass of cells tunneled with bile ducts and blood vessels. About 60% are hepatic cells, which have more metabolic functions than any other cells. A second type, Kupffer cells, play a role in blood-cell formation, ANTIBODY production, and ingestion of foreign particles and cell debris. The liver manufactures plasma proteins, including ALBUMIN and clotting factors, and synthesizes enzymes that modify substances such as nutrients and toxins, filtered from the blood. Liver disorders include JAUNDICE, HEPATITIS, and CIRRHOSIS.

Liverpool City (pop., 1999 est.: 452,000), NW England, on the estuary of the MERSEY RIVER. King JOHN granted its charter in 1207. In the 18th cent. it became Britain's most important port after LONDON. The Liverpool and Manchester Railway (opened 1830) was the first in England to link two major cities. Heavily damaged in World War II, it declined as a port and an industrial center in the postwar era. The birthplace of the BEATLES, it is also the seat of the Univ. of Liverpool (1903).

Livingston, Robert R. (1746–1813) American lawyer and diplomat. Born in New York City, he served in the Continental Congress and helped draft the DECLARATION OF INDEPENDENCE. As New York's first chancellor (1777–1801),

he administered the oath of office to George WASHINGTON (1789). As minister to France (1801–4), he helped effect the LOUISIANA PURCHASE. In partnership with Robert FULTON, he received a steamboat monopoly for New York waters; the first vessel to operate on the Hudson River (1807) was named the *Clermont,* after his ancestral home.

Livingstone, David (1813–1873) Scottish missionary and explorer in Africa. Livingstone studied theology and medicine before being ordained (1840) and deciding to help open up the African interior for colonization, extend the Gospel, and abolish the slave trade. By 1842 he had penetrated farther north of the Cape Colony than any other white man. He was the first European to reach Lake Ngami (1849) and to reach LUANDA from the interior (1854). He discovered VICTORIA FALLS (1855), crossed the continent to E Mozambique (1856, 1862), explored the Lake MALAWI region (1861–

David Livingstone

63), discovered Lakes Mweru and Bangweulu (1867), and reached points farther east of Lake Tanganyika than any previous expedition (1871). When found by Henry Morton STANLEY in 1871, his health was failing but he refused to leave. Livingstone produced a complex body of knowledge—geographic, technical, medical, and social—that took decades to mine. In his lifetime he was celebrated as one of the great figures of British civilization.

living will Document specifying medical measures to be taken or withheld in the event the writer is disabled. Advances in technology now allow the body to be kept alive in circumstances that would normally result in death, but many people do not want to be kept alive if there is no chance of recovery. Because it is impossible to express one's wishes when in a vegetative state, a living will allows them to be stated in advance. It usually specifies conditions under which a do-not-resuscitate (DNR) order is to take effect and authorizes another person to make decisions on the patient's behalf.

Livonia Region, E coast of Baltic Sea, north of Lithuania. Originally inhabited by the Livs, a Finno-Ugric people, it eventually expanded to include nearly all of modern Latvia and Estonia. In the 13th cent. it was organized into the Livonian confederation. A Russian invasion set off the Livonian War (1558–82), in which Russia, Poland, and Sweden seized portions of it. Sweden eventually gained control of most of it but ceded the region to Russia in 1721. In 1918 the N portion became part of independent Estonia and the S portion joined independent Latvia.

Livorno *English* **Leghorn** City (pop., 1998 est.: 163,000), TUSCANY region, central Italy, on the Ligurian Sea. It came under Florentine rule in 1421. Cosimo I de' MEDICI began construction of the Medici Harbor in the 16th cent., and in the 18th cent. Leopold II enlarged the harbor and gave privileges to foreign merchants. Livorno became part of Italy in 1860. One of Italy's largest ports, it has a large shipbuilding yard.

Livy \'li-vē\ *Latin* Titus Livius (59/64 B.C.–A.D. 17) Roman historian. His lifework was a history of the city, written in 142 books, most of which have been lost. Having played no part in politics, Livy presented history not as partisan politics but in terms of character and morality. His history, a classic in his lifetime, profoundly influenced the style and philosophy of historical writing down to the 18th cent.

lizard Any of about 3,000 species of four-legged REPTILES (suborder Sauria), most abundant in the tropics but found worldwide. Like SNAKES, lizards have scales, paired male copulatory organs, and a flexible skull. Typical lizards have well-developed legs, a tail slightly longer than the body, and movable lower eyelids. They range in size from 1-in. (3-cm) GECKOS to the 10-ft (3-m) KOMODO DRAGON, but most are about 12 in. (30 cm) long. Ornamentation includes crests,

K L

spines, brightly colored throat fans, and throat frills. Most species feed on insects and rodents, but some, such as the IGUANA, eat plants. See also GILA MONSTER, HORNED TOAD.

Ljubljana \lē-ˌü-blē-'ä-nə\ City (pop., 1999 est.: 258,000), capital of SLOVENIA. The site of a Roman city in the 1st cent. B.C., it was destroyed in the 5th cent. A.D. and rebuilt by the Slavs, passed to Carniola in the 12th cent., and came under HABSBURG rule in 1277. It was the capital of the kingdom of Illyria 1816–49. The center of Slovene nationalism under Austrian rule, in 1918 it became part of what would become Yugoslavia. It remained the Slovenian capital after Slovenia's independence in 1992. A railroad and commercial center, it is the site of the Univ. of Ljubljana (founded 1595).

llama \'lä-mə\ Domesticated S. American lamoid (see AL-PACA), maintained in herds in Bolivia, Peru, Ecuador, Chile, and Argentina. The llama (*Lama glama*) is used primarily as a pack animal but also as a source of food, wool, hides, tallow for candles, and dried dung for fuel. A 250-lb (113-kg) llama can carry a load of 100–130 lbs (45–60 kg) and travel 15–20 mi (25–30 km) a day. It has a high thirst tolerance and can subsist on a wide variety of plant materials. It is usually gentle, but when overloaded or mistreated it will lie down, hiss, spit and kick, and refuse to move. It appears to have been bred from the guanaco (*Lama guanacoe*).

Llano Estacado \'la-nō-ˌes-tə-'kä-dō\ *or* **Staked Plain** Plateau, SE New Mexico, W Texas, and NW Oklahoma. Occupying about 30,000 sq mi (78,000 sq km), it is a semiarid plain with occasional pools filled by rainwater. Its soil supports grazing, dryland farming of grains, and irrigated cotton production. Production of petroleum and natural gas is also important. The area includes LUBBOCK and AMARILLO, Tex. The meaning of its name, conferred by F.V. de CORONADO, is uncertain.

Llosa, Mario Vargas See Mario VARGAS LLOSA

Lloyd, Chris Evert See Chris EVERT

Lloyd, Harold (Clayton) (1893–1971) U.S. film comedian. Born in Burchard, Neb., he began his film career in 1913, mastering the comic chase scene as a member of Mack SEN-NETT's troupe. He created his Lonesome Luke character in popular movies such as *Just Nuts* (1915), and developed his trademark white-faced character in round glasses in 1918. Using physical danger as a source of laughter, he performed his own daring stunts, hanging from the hands of a clock far above the street in *Safety Last* (1923) and standing in for a football tackling-dummy in *The Freshman* (1925). He received a special Academy Award in 1952.

Lloyd George, David *later* Earl Lloyd-George of Dwyfor (1863–1945) British prime minister (1916–22). Raised in Wales, he entered Parliament in 1890 as a Liberal and retained his seat for 55 years. He served as president of the Board of Trade 1905–8, then as chancellor of the exchequer 1908–15. He devised the National Insurance Act of 1911, which laid the foundation of the British WELFARE STATE. As minister of munitions (1915–16), he used unorthodox methods to ensure that war supplies were forthcoming. He replaced H. H. ASQUITH as prime minister in 1916, with Conservative support in his coalition government. His small war cabinet ensured speedy decisions. Distrustful of the British high command, he was constantly at odds with Gen. Douglas HAIG. He was one of the three great statesmen responsible for the Treaty of VERSAILLES at the PARIS PEACE CONFERENCE. He began the negotiations for the Anglo–Irish treaty of 1921. He resigned in 1922 and headed an ailing Liberal Party 1926–31.

Lloyd's of London Insurance marketing association in London, specializing in high-risk insurance services. Its history dates to 1688, when Edward Lloyd kept a London coffeehouse where merchants, seafarers, and marine-insurance underwriters met to transact business. The underwriters at Lloyd's eventually formed a marine-insurance association (incorporated 1871); it expanded to include other forms of insurance in 1911. After a series of financial scandals, the corporation was reorganized 1982. Today individual members of several hundred syndicates, rather than the corporation, are liable for losses. Until record losses in the 1980s and '90s bankrupted some members, they had unlimited li-

ability for business transacted for them; in 1993 that liability was limited.

Lloyd Webber, Andrew *later* Baron Lloyd-Webber (b.1948) British composer of musicals. Born in London, he studied at the Royal College of Music, which his father directed. His first collaboration with lyricist Tim Rice (b.1944), *Joseph and the Amazing Technicolor Dreamcoat* (1968), was followed by the "rock opera" *Jesus Christ Superstar* (1971), which blended classical forms with rock music. Their last major collaboration was *Evita* (1978). *Cats* (1981) became the longest-running musical ever in London and New York. Later collaborations include *Starlight Express* (1984), *Phantom of the Opera* (1986), and *Sunset Boulevard* (1993).

Llull \'lyül\, **Ramon** *English* **Raymond Lully** (1232/33–1315/16) Spanish (Catalan) mystic, poet, and missionary. In his youth he wrote lyrical troubadour poetry. He later traveled widely, attempting to convert Muslims to Christianity; he is said to have been stoned to death at Bejaïa. As a philosopher, he is best known as the inventor of an "art of finding truth," designed to unify all branches of knowledge. In his principal work, *Ars magna* (1305–8), he tried to relate all forms of knowledge as mutually analogous and manifestations of the godhead. His writings influenced Neoplatonic mysticism throughout medieval and 17th-cent. Europe. In Catalan culture, his allegorical novels *Blanquerna* (c.1284) and *Felix* (c.1288) enjoy wide popularity; he is also known for his treatise on chivalry, his animal fables, and an encyclopedia of medieval thought.

Llywelyn ap Gruffudd \hlə-'we-lin-ap-'gri-fith\ (d.1282) Prince of Wales (1258–77). As prince of Gwynedd in N Wales from 1255, he sought to extend his rule, and he proclaimed himself prince of Wales in 1258. He fought the English lords of S Wales (1262), but after the death of his ally Simon de MONTFORT he signed a treaty recognizing HENRY III as overlord (1267). Llywelyn rebelled against EDWARD I but was defeated by him in 1277. He was killed in a final rebellion in 1282, and Wales soon fell entirely under English rule.

Llywelyn ap Iorwerth \hlə-'we-lin-ap-'yòr-werth\ *known as* **Llywelyn the Great** (d.1240) Welsh prince. Exiled as a child from Gwynedd in N Wales, he returned in 1194 and deposed his uncle, gaining control of most of N Wales by 1202. Though he married King JOHN's daughter, the English king later invaded Wales (1211). Llywelyn soon recovered his lands and allied with John's baronial opponents. HENRY III acknowledged his rule in most of Wales (1218), but by 1223 Llywelyn was forced to withdraw to the north.

loam Rich, crumbly soil with nearly equal parts of sand and silt, and somewhat less clay. The term is sometimes used imprecisely to mean earth or soil in general. Loam in subsoil receives varied minerals and amounts of clay by leaching (percolation) from the topsoil above.

Loanda See LUANDA

Lobachevsky \ˌlō-bə-'chev-skē\, **Nikolay (Ivanovich)** (1792–1856) Russian mathematician. In 1829 he published his groundbreaking theory, a geometry that rejected EUCLID's parallel postulate (see NON-EUCLIDEAN GEOMETRY). It was the final solution to a problem that had baffled mathematicians for 2,000 years. Lobachevsky also did distinguished work in the theory of infinite series, especially trigonometric series, as well as in INTEGRAL CALCULUS, ALGEBRA, and PROBABILITY THEORY. He was largely ignored during his lifetime; acceptance of his new geometry came a decade after his death, though much of the credit went to others.

Lobamba Town (pop., 1995 est.: 10,000), legislative capital of Swaziland. Located near MBABANE, it is, according to traditional SWAZI customs, the residence of the Queen Mother, and thereby, the spiritual home of the Swazi nation. It is also an official residence of the king.

lobbying Any attempt by a group or individual to influence the decisions of government. The term originated in 19th-cent. efforts to influence the votes of legislators, generally in the lobby outside a legislative chamber. The effort may be a direct appeal to a decision maker in either the executive or legislative branches, or it may be indirect (e.g., through attempts to influence public opinion). It may include oral or written efforts of persuasion, campaign contributions, public-relations campaigns, research supplied to legislative committees, and formal testimony before such committees. In the U.S., the Federal Regulation of Lobbying Act (1946) requires that lobbyists and the groups they represent register and report contributions and expenditures.

lobotomy \lə-'bä-tə-mē\ Operation to cut nerve pathways linking one or more lobes to the rest of the BRAIN. Introduced in 1935 and favored for grossly disturbed patients who did not respond to SHOCK THERAPY, it reduced agitation but often caused increased apathy and passivity, inability to concentrate, and decreased emotional response. It was widely performed until about 1956, when drugs that were more effective in calming patients became available.

lobster Any of numerous species of marine shrimplike DECAPODS that are bottom-dwellers and mostly nocturnal. Lobsters scavenge for dead animals but also eat live fish, small mollusks, and seaweed. One or more pairs of legs are often modified into pincers, usually larger on one side than the other. True lobsters have a distinct snout on the upper body shell. The American lobster (*Homarus americanus*) and SCAMPI are highly prized as food. The American lobster is found from Labrador to N. Carolina. Most deepwater specimens weigh about 6 lbs (2.5 kg); some may weigh 40 lbs (20 kg). See also SHELLFISH.

local area network (LAN) Communications network consisting of many computers within a local area, such as a single building or company complex. Individual users can share data or files on a LAN as if the data or files resided on their respective computers; a central computer used for this purpose is called a SERVER. Laser printers and other peripheral equipment can be connected to a LAN for common use. See also computer NETWORK.

Loch Lomond See Loch LOMOND

Lochner \'lök-nər\, **Stefan** (c.1400–1451) German painter. He settled in Cologne about 1430. Flemish influence, especially that of Jan van EYCK, is seen in *The Adoration of the Magi*, his altarpiece for Cologne's great cathedral, but Lochner adds his own naturalistic observation and masterly sense of color and design. Known for his highly mystical religious paintings, he is considered the greatest representative of the school of Cologne.

Lochner vs. New York U.S. Supreme Court decision (1905) that struck down a New York law setting 10 hours of labor a day as the legal maximum in the baking trade. It declared that the 14th Amendment prohibited states from curtailing employers' freedom to make their own economic arrangements with employees. The opinion drew a stinging rebuke from O. W. HOLMES, JR., whose dissent became the prevailing interpretation of the 14th Amendment by the 1930s, when maximum-hours laws were held constitutional.

Loch Ness See Loch NESS

lock Mechanical or electronic device for securing a door or receptacle so that it cannot be opened except by a key or a code. The oldest known lock was found near Nineveh; possibly 4,000 years old, it is of the pin tumbler (or Egyptian) type. The Romans were the first to use metal locks and to make small keys for them. They also invented wards, projections in the keyhole that prevent a key from turning unless it has slots that avoid the projections. The familiar cylinder lock is a pin tumbler lock opened by a flat key with a serrated edge; the serrations raise pins in the cylinder to the proper heights, allowing the cylinder to turn. On a combination lock, the user dials a sequence of numbers or letters. Electronic locks that open with magnetic card keys are popular for banks and hotel rooms.

Locke, John (1632–1704) English philosopher. Educated at Oxford, he became physician and adviser to the future 3rd Earl of Shaftesbury (1667–72). Forced to flee to the Netherlands in 1684, he returned after the Glorious Revolution to become commissioner of appeals under WILLIAM III. In his famous *Essay Concerning Human Understanding* (1690) he rejected the rationalist view that a thinker could work out by reason alone the truth about the universe, arguing the need for experience. In EPISTEMOLOGY, Locke laid the foundations of British EMPIRICISM and of PRAGMATISM. His important *Two Treatises of Government* (1690) refutes ABSOLUTISM and the divine right of monarchs; this classic expression of LIBERALISM inspired the leaders of the American and French Revolutions and the authors of the U.S. Constitution. An initiator of the ENLIGHTENMENT in England and France, Locke was also a strong influence on David HUME, George BERKELEY, and many other 18th-cent. figures.

lockjaw See TETANUS

locomotion Animal movements that result in progression from one place to another. Aquatic protozoans move by ciliary or flagellar appendages or by pseudopods, footlike appendages. Other forms of aquatic locomotion include walking on legs, crawling, and swimming by either hydraulic propulsion (as with JELLYFISH) or undulation (FISHES). Terrestrial ARTHROPODS and VERTEBRATES move on jointed appendages, the legs. Snakes and other limbless vertebrates crawl by means of muscular thrusts against the substrate. Flight is achieved by the forward thrust of WINGS.

locomotive Self-propelled vehicle used for hauling railroad cars on tracks. Early experimental steam locomotives were built by Richard TREVITHICK from 1803. The first practical steam locomotive, the *Rocket*, was developed in 1829 by George STEPHENSON, in whose "steam blast" system the steam from a multitube boiler drove pistons connected to a pair of flanged driving wheels. The first U.S. steam locomotive was built by John STEVENS in 1825, and the first commercially usable locomotive, the *Tom Thumb*, by Peter COOPER in Baltimore in 1830. Steam from wood or coal fuel was the main source of power until the mid-20th cent., though electric power had been used from the early 20th cent., especially in Europe. After World War II DIESEL-ENGINE power replaced steam, though diesel-electric and gas turbine–electric combinations were also used.

locoweed Any of several species of poisonous plants of the genera *Astragalus* and *Oxytropis*, in the pea family (see LEGUME), native to the prairies of N central and W N. America. These low-growing plants have variably hairy, fernlike leaves and spikes of pealike flowers. They pose a danger to grazing animals because they contain a toxin that affects muscle control, producing frenzied behavior, impaired vision, and sometimes death.

locust In botany, any of about 20 species of trees in the genus *Robinia* of the pea family (see LEGUME), all occurring in E N. America and Mexico. Best known is the black locust (*R. pseudoacacia*), often called false acacia, or yellow

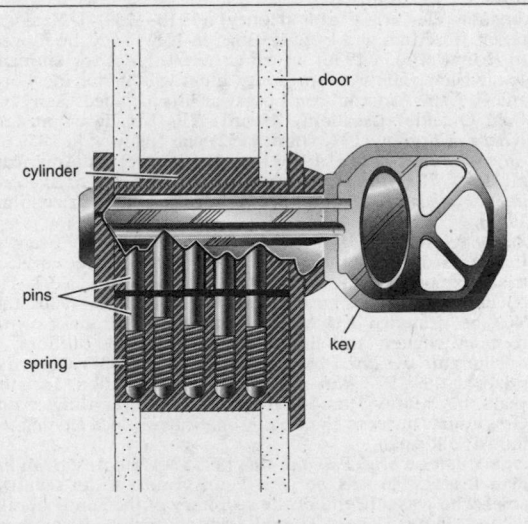

Lock A cylinder lock's tumbler consists of a series of pins arranged in pairs. The pins are spring-loaded to press against the contours of the inserted key. A wrong key will cause one or more of the pins to block the cylinder from turning; only when the tops of all the lower pins line up with the edge of the cylinder can the cylinder turn.

locust. It grows to 80 ft (24 m) high and bears long, compound leaves. The fragrant white flowers hang in loose clusters. The black locust has long been used for erosion control and as a timber tree. The so-called honey locust *(Gleditsia triacanthos),* also of the pea family, is a N. American ornamental tree.

locust Species (family Acrididae) of short-horned GRASSHOPPER that often increases greatly in number and migrates long distances in destructive swarms. In N. America the names locust and grasshopper are used for any acridid; a CICADA may also be called a locust. In Europe, locust refers to large species and grasshopper to small ones. Locusts are found on all continents. Migratory swarms form when overcrowding results in a scarcity of resources. Swarms may be almost unimaginably large; in 1889 a Red Sea swarm was estimated to cover 2,000 sq mi (5,000 sq km), and swarms may form huge towers 5,000 ft (1,500 m) high. Locust plagues can be extremely destructive of crops.

lodestone See MAGNETITE

Lodge, Henry Cabot (1850–1924) U.S. politician. Born in Boston, he received the first PhD in political science from Harvard Univ. He served in the U.S. House of Representatives (1887–93) and Senate (1893–1924). As chairman of the Senate's foreign relations committee, he delayed action on adopting the Treaty of Versailles with its covenant establishing the LEAGUE OF NATIONS and proposed amendments (the "Lodge reservations") requiring Senate approval before the U.S. would accept certain League decisions. Pres. Woodrow WILSON refused to accept the amendments, and the Senate rejected the treaty.

Lódz \\'wüch, *Engl* 'lōdz\\ City (pop., 1999 est.: 806,000), central Poland. The Russian-ruled Congress Kingdom of Poland established it as a center of the textile industry in 1820, and it soon led Poland in the production of cotton textiles. It was occupied by the Germans during World Wars I and II. It is now a cultural center and Poland's second-largest city.

loess \\'les, 'lō-əs\\ Unstratified, geologically recent deposit of silty or loamy material that is usually buff or yellowish brown and is deposited chiefly by the wind. Composed largely of silt-sized grains that are loosely cemented by calcium carbonate, it is highly porous and is traversed by vertical capillaries that permit the sediment to fracture and form vertical bluffs.

Loesser \\'le-sər\\, **Frank (Henry)** (1910–1969) U.S. composer, librettist, and lyricist. Born in New York, he moved to Hollywood in 1936, where he wrote lyrics for eminent songwriters. His wartime songs included "Praise the Lord and Pass the Ammunition"; postwar hits included "Baby It's Cold Outside" (Academy Award). His Broadway musical *Where's Charley?* (1948; film, 1952) was followed in 1950 by *Guys and Dolls* (film, 1955), one of the greatest American musicals, *The Most Happy Fella* (1956), and *How to Succeed in Business Without Really Trying* (1962, Pulitzer Prize; film, 1967).

Loewy \\'lō-ē\\, **Raymond (Fernand)** (1893–1986) French-U.S. industrial designer. With an advanced degree in electrical engineering, he emigrated in 1919 in New York. He opened his own design firm in 1929, and in the 1930s and '40s he designed a variety of household products with rounded corners and simplified, "streamlined" outlines. A refrigerator designed for Sears, Roebuck (1934) won first prize at the 1937 Paris International Exposition. In later years his highly functional designs for everything from Greyhound buses to the Coca-Cola bottle helped shape U.S. industrial design.

Logan, James *orig.* Tah-gah-jute (1725?–1780) American Indian leader. He was born in Pennsylvania to an ONEIDA chief who was a friend of the secretary of the Pennsylvania colony, James Logan. Though friendly with white settlers, after his family was massacred by a frontier trader in 1774 he led Indian raids on white settlements in LORD DUNMORE'S WAR. He refused to participate in peace negotiations, sending his grievances in a message known as "Logan's Lament." He was allied with the British in the American Revolution.

Logan, Mt. Peak, ST. ELIAS MTNS., SW Yukon Territory, near the Alaskan boundary. Reaching 19,524 ft (5,951 m), it is the highest mountain in Canada and is second in N. America only to Mt. MCKINLEY. It is located in KLUANE NATIONAL PARK. The summit was first reached in 1925. The peak was named for William Logan (1798–1875), founder of the Geological Survey of Canada.

logarithm In mathematics, the power to which a base must be raised to yield a given number (e.g., the logarithm to the base 3 of 9, or $\log_3 9$, is 2, because $3^2 = 9$). A common logarithm is a logarithm to the base 10. Thus, the common logarithm of 100 (log 100) is 2, because $10^2 = 100$. Logarithms to the base *e,* in which $e = 2.71828 \ldots$, called natural logarithms (ln), are especially useful in CALCULUS. Logarithms were invented to simplify cumbersome calculations, since exponents can be added or subtracted to multiply or divide their bases.

log cabin Small, one-room house built of logs notched at the ends and laid one upon another with the spaces filled with plaster, moss, mortar, mud, or dried manure. In N. America they were built by early settlers, hunters, loggers, and other wilderness dwellers. They have also been built in Europe, particularly Scandinavia. A common style features a sloping, single-gabled timbered roof and small windows.

loggia \\'lō-jē-ə\\ Hall, gallery, or porch open to the air on one or more sides. It evolved in the Mediterranean region as an open sitting room with protection from the sun. It is often a roofed, arcaded open gallery on an upper story overlooking a court, though it can also be a separate arcaded or colonnaded structure. In medieval and Renaissance Italy, loggias often form the borders of public squares.

logic Study of inference and argument. In logic, an argument consists of a set of statements (the premises) whose truth is claimed to be sufficient for the truth of a further statement (the conclusion of the argument). Logic may be divided into deductive logic, inductive logic, and the study of what are often called informal fallacies (see DEDUCTION, INDUCTION, FALLACY). Modern formal logic takes as its main subject matter propositions and deductive arguments, and it abstracts from their content the logical forms they embody. The logician uses a symbolic notation to express these logical forms and to facilitate inference and tests of validity. Subfields include propositional calculus and predicate calculus. Logic is fundamental to the fields of philosophy and mathematics.

logical positivism Early form of ANALYTIC PHILOSOPHY, inspired by David HUME, the logic of Bertrand RUSSELL and Alfred North WHITEHEAD, and Ludwig WITTGENSTEIN's *Tractatus* (1921). The school, instituted at the Univ. of Vienna in 1922, continued there as the VIENNA CIRCLE until 1938. It proposed several revolutionary theses: (1) All meaningful discourse consists either of (a) the formal sentences of logic and mathematics or (b) the factual propositions of the special sciences; (2) Any assertion that claims to be factual has meaning only if it is possible to say how it might be verified; (3) Metaphysical assertions, coming under neither of the two classes of (1), are meaningless; and (4) All statements about moral, aesthetic, or religious values are scientifically unverifiable and meaningless.

logic design Basic organization of the circuitry of a DIGITAL COMPUTER. All digital computers are based on a two-valued logic system—1/0, on/off, yes/no (see BINARY CODE). Computers perform calculations using components called logic gates, which are made up of INTEGRATED CIRCUITS that receive an input signal, process it, and change it into an output signal. The components of the gates pass or block a clock pulse as it travels through them, and the output bits of the gates control other gates or output the result. There are three basic kinds of logic gates, called "and," "or," and "not." By connecting logic gates together, a device can be constructed that can perform arithmetic.

logicism \\'lä-ji-,si-zəm\\ Thesis that mathematics is derivable from LOGIC. As early as 1666, G. W. LEIBNIZ had conceived of logic as a universal science. Richard Dedekind in 1888, and Gottlob FREGE in 1884 and 1893, derived arithmetic from logic. Bertrand RUSSELL claimed that all mathematics is reducible to logic alone.

logistics \\lō-'jis-tiks, lə-'jis-tiks\\ In military science, all the activities of armed-force units in support of combat units, including transport, supply, communications, and medical aid. Its importance grew in the 20th cent. with the increasing complexity of modern warfare. The ability to mobilize large populations has escalated military demands for supplies and provisions, and sophisticated technology has added to the cost and intricacy of weapons, communications systems, and medical care, creating the need for a vast support system. In World War II only about three in 10 U.S. soldiers served in a combat role.

logistic system See FORMAL SYSTEM

logos (Greek: "word," "reason," "plan") In Greek philosophy and theology, the divine reason that orders the cosmos and gives it form and meaning. The concept is also found in Persian, Indian, and Egyptian philosophical and theological systems. In Christian theology it is used to describe the role of JESUS as the principle of God active in the creation and ordering of the cosmos and in the revelation of the divine plan of salvation. The Gospel of JOHN THE APOSTLE identifies Christ as the Word (Logos) made flesh.

Lohengrin \'lō-ən-ˌgrēn, *Engl* 'lō-ən-ˌgrin\ Hero-knight of medieval Germanic legends. He was called the knight of the swan because he arrived in a boat drawn by a swan to help a noble lady in distress. He married her but forbade her to ask his origin; when she forgot this promise, he left her forever. The legend first appeared around 1210 in WOLFRAM VON ESCHENBACH's *Parzival,*. The 15th-cent. epic *Lorengel* provided the basis for Richard WAGNER's opera *Lohengrin* (1850).

Loire River \'lwär\ River, SE France. The longest river in France, it flows north and west for 634 mi (1,020 km) to the Bay of BISCAY. Though it was long used extensively for the transport of goods, a canal system built in the 17th–18th cent. is inadequate for modern vessels. Its valley contains rich farmland and is famous for its splendid châteaus.

Loki \'lō-kē\ In Norse mythology, a trickster who was able to change his shape and sex. His father was a giant, but he was included among the AESIR, a tribe of the gods. Loki helped ODIN and THOR with his clever plans but sometimes embarrassed them. He also appeared as the enemy of the gods. After causing the death of the god BALDER, he was punished by being bound to a rock. Loki's three evil progeny were HEL, the goddess of death; Jörmungand, the evil serpent surrounding the world; and Fenrir, the wolf.

Lo-lang See NANGNANG

Lollards Followers of John WYCLIFFE in late-medieval England. The disrespectful name (from Middle Dutch, *lollaert:* "mumbler") had been applied earlier to European groups suspected of heresy. The first Lollard group centered on some of Wycliffe's colleagues at Oxford; in 1382 the archbishop of Canterbury forced them to renounce their views, but the sect continued to multiply. In 1414 a Lollard rising was quickly defeated by HENRY V; it brought severe reprisals and marked the end of the Lollards' overt political influence. A Lollard revival began about 1500, and by 1530 it was merging with the new Protestant forces. The Lollard tradition predisposed opinion in favor of HENRY VIII's anticlerical legislation.

Lomax \'lō-ˌmaks\, **John** (1867–1948) U.S. ethnomusicologist. Born in Goodman, Miss., he attended Harvard Univ. and soon began publishing collections of cowboy songs. In the 1930s he and his teenage son Alan (1915–2002) collected folk songs of the Southwest and Midwest. Jelly Roll MORTON, LEADBELLY, and Muddy WATERS were perhaps the most important of their discoveries. Their many books and anthologies spurred the folk-music revival of the 1950s and '60s.

Lombard, Carole *orig.* Jane Alice Peters (1908–1942) U.S. film actress. Born in Ft. Wayne, Ind., she made her screen debut in 1921 and appeared in comedy shorts from 1925. After starring in *Twentieth Century* (1934), she appeared in such popular screwball comedies as *My Man Godfrey* (1936), *Nothing Sacred* (1937), *Mr. and Mrs. Smith* (1941), and *To Be or Not to Be* (1942). Married to Clark GABLE, she died in a plane crash while on tour to sell war bonds.

Lombard, Peter See PETER LOMBARD

Lombardi, Vince(nt Thomas) (1913–1970) U.S. football coach. Born in Brooklyn, N.Y., he played at Fordham Univ. on the famous "Seven Blocks of Granite" line. As head coach of the Green Bay Packers (1959–67), he imposed a strenuous regimen on the disheartened players and led them to five NFL championships (1961, 1962, 1965, 1966, 1967) and to victories in Super Bowls I and II (1967, 1968). In 1969 he coached the Washington Redskins to its first winning season in 14 years. His career was cut short by cancer.

Lombard League Italian league that resisted attempts by the Holy Roman Emperors to curtail the liberties of the communes of Lombardy in N Italy. Founded in 1167, it was backed by Pope ALEXANDER III, who saw it as an ally against FREDERICK I Barbarossa. After several military setbacks at the hands of the league, Frederick was forced to grant the Lombard cities communal liberties and jurisdiction (1183). It was renewed in 1226 and resisted FREDERICK II's attempt to reassert imperial power in N Italy.

Lombards Germanic people who from 568 to 774 ruled a kingdom in the Halian region of LOMBARDY. In the 6th cent. they moved from Germany into N Italy, conquering the cities that had been left defenseless after the overthrow of the OSTROGOTHS by the BYZANTINE EMPIRE. In the 8th cent, Liudprand, probably the greatest of the Lombard kings, steadily reduced the area of Italy still under Byzantine rule. In 773 they were defeated by the Franks, and CHARLEMAGNE became their king.

Lombardy \'läm-bər-dē\ Autonomous region (pop., 1996 est.: 8,925,000), N Italy. Bounded on the north by Switzerland, it contains many alpine peaks as well as the fertile valley of the PO RIVER. Its capital is MILAN. Inhabited by Celtic peoples from the 5th cent. B.C., it was conquered by Rome and became part of Cisalpine Gaul. In A.D. 568–774 it was the center of the kingdom of the LOMBARDS. Several of its towns formed the LOMBARD LEAGUE in the 12th cent. and won autonomy by defeating FREDERICK I Barbarossa in 1176. The area was later ruled by Spain (1535–1713), Austria (1713–96), and France (1796–1814). In 1859 Lombardy joined the newly unified Italy. It is Italy's most populous region.

Lombok \'lòm-ˌbòk\ Island (pop., 1980: 1,960,000), Indonesia. It is one of the Lesser SUNDA ISLES, separated from BALI by the Lombok Strait and from SUMBAWA by the Alas Strait. It is 70 mi (115 km) long and 50 mi (80 km) wide. It includes Mt. Rindjani (12,224 ft, or 3,726 m), Indonesia's highest mountain. It was ruled by the sultan of Makasar in 1640. Later the Balinese seized control. The Dutch ruled the kingdom of Mataram from 1843 and gained control of the entire island by the late 19th cent. Following World War II, it became part of Indonesia.

Lomé \lō-'mā\ City (metro. area pop., 1990 est.: 513,000), capital of Togo. Located on the Gulf of GUINEA, it was chosen as the capital of German Togoland in 1897. Its port was modernized in the 1960s, and its deepwater harbor is a major shipping center. An oil refinery was opened in 1978. It is the site of the Univ. of Bénin (1965).

Lomond \'lō-mən\, **Loch** Lake, Scotland. The country's largest lake, located at the S edge of the Highlands, it is 24 mi (39 km) long and 0.75 to 5 mi (1.2 to 8 km) wide. It drains by the River Leven into the Firth of Clyde at Dumbarton. Its E shore near Ben Lomond is the region made famous by the outlaw ROB ROY.

Lomonosov \lə-ˌmə-'nò-səf\, **Mikhail (Vasilyevich)** (1711–1765) Russian scientist, poet, and grammarian, considered the first great Russian linguistic reformer. He established what became the standards for Russian verse in his *Letter Concerning the Rules of Russian Versification.* In 1745 he joined the faculty at the St. Petersburg Imperial Academy of Sciences, where he made substantial contributions to the physical sciences. He later wrote a Russian grammar and worked to systematize the Russian literary language. He founded Moscow State Univ. (which now bears his name).

London Capital and largest city (metro. area pop., 1998 est.: 7,187,000), United Kingdom, situated in SE England on the River THAMES. Inner London includes the original City of London and 13 of London's 33 boroughs; Greater London includes all 33 boroughs. Founded by the Romans as Londinium in the 1st cent. A.D., it passed to the Saxons in the 6th cent. WILLIAM I the Conqueror established the central stronghold of the TOWER OF LONDON. Norman kings selected Westminster as their seat of government, and ED-

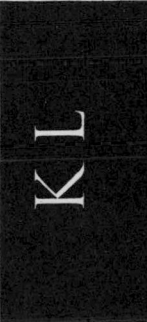

K L

WARD THE CONFESSOR built WESTMINSTER ABBEY. London was struck by the BLACK DEATH in 1348–49. Trade grew in the mid-16th cent., fueled by Britain's new overseas empire. In 1664–65 the plague killed about 70,000 Londoners, and in 1666 the GREAT FIRE OF LONDON consumed five-sixths of the City; it was afterwards rebuilt (see Christopher WREN). It was the center of world trade from the late 18th cent. to 1914. It opened the world's first electric underground railway in 1890. It was severely damaged by German bombs in the Battle of BRITAIN (1940–41). Among its sites of interest are BUCKINGHAM PALACE, the TATE GALLERY, the National Gallery, the BRITISH MUSEUM, and the VICTORIA AND ALBERT MUSEUM.

London City (pop., 1996: 325,000), SE Ontario. It lies on the Thames River, near several of the GREAT LAKES. First settled in 1826, it was incorporated as a city in 1855. It became an important transportation and industrial center as a result of its interlake location. It is the seat of the Univ. of Western Ontario.

London, Great Fire of See GREAT FIRE OF LONDON

London, Great Plague of See GREAT PLAGUE OF LONDON

London, Jack *orig.* John Griffith Chaney (1876–1916) U.S. writer. Born to poverty and illegitimacy in San Francisco, he became a sailor, hobo, Alaskan gold miner, and militant socialist. He gained a wide audience with his first book, *The Son of the Wolf* (1900), and the story "To Build a Fire" (1908). Thereafter he wrote steadily; his 50 books of fiction and nonfiction, including many romantic depictions of elemental struggles for survival as well as socialist tracts, include *The Call of the Wild* (1903), *The Sea-Wolf* (1904), *White Fang* (1906), *The Iron Heel* (1907), and *Martin Eden* (1909). Though his work brought him wealth and fame, his death at 40 was a suicide.

London, University of Federation of more than 50 British institutions of higher learning, located primarily in London. Established by liberals and religious dissenters in 1828, it accepted for enrollment Roman Catholics, Jews, and other non-Anglicans. The first two colleges were Univ. College and King's College. From 1849 a student enrolled in any university in the British Empire could be awarded a Univ. of London degree after examination. Many important institutions became affiliated with the university, including Bedford College, the renowned London School of Economics and Political Science, and the Imperial College of Science and Technology. Total enrollment is about 95,000.

London Bridge Any of several successive structures spanning the River Thames. The Old London Bridge of nursery-rhyme fame was built by Peter of Colechurch between 1176 and 1209, replacing an earlier timber bridge. Despite frequent need for repair, the bridge survived more than 600 years, its roadway loaded with houses and shops, many projecting out over the river. It was replaced in the 1820s by New London Bridge, designed and built by John Rennie, Sr. (1761–1821), and his son John Rennie, Jr. (1794–1874). In the 1960s it was again replaced; the old masonry facing was dismantled and reerected at Lake Havasu City, Ariz., as a tourist attraction.

London Co. British trading company chartered by JAMES I in 1606 to colonize the E American coast. Three ships with 120 colonists, led by John SMITH, reached Virginia in 1607 and founded JAMESTOWN. The company expanded its territory with new charters (1609, 1612) and authorized a two-part legislature (1619), including a House of BURGESSES. Divided by internal disputes, it was dissolved in 1624, whereupon Virginia became a royal colony. See also PLYMOUTH CO.

Londonderry See DERRY

London Stock Exchange London marketplace for SECURITIES. It was formed in 1773 by a group of stockbrokers who had been meeting informally in local coffeehouses. In 1801 its members raised money for construction of a building in Bartholomew Lane. In 1973 the London Stock Exchange merged with several regional British stock exchanges. It is governed by a council of members and not subject to government regulation.

Long, Huey (Pierce) (1893–1935) U.S. politician. Born near Winnfield, La., he became railroad commissioner at 25. His call for state regulation of utilities and attacks on Standard Oil Co. won him widespread popularity. Elected governor (1928–31), he became known for his fiery oratory and unconventional behavior. He implemented public-works projects and education reform, but used autocratic methods and pervasive patronage to control state government. In the U.S. Senate (1932–35), he sought national power with a Share-the-Wealth program at the height of the GREAT DEPRESSION. In 1935 he was assassinated by Carl A. Weiss, whose father Long had vilified. His brother Earl K. Long (1895–1960) later served as governor (1939–40, 1948–52, 1956–60).

Long Beach City (pop., 2000: 461,000), SW California. The site was part of Spanish ranches in the 18th cent. Incorporated as a city in 1888, it was renamed for its 8.5-mi (13.5-km) beach. The discovery of oil nearby in 1921 led to rapid growth. An earthquake in 1933 caused extensive damage. Connected to the LOS ANGELES harbor, it is the site of a U.S. naval station and shipyard. The ocean liner *Queen Mary* has been moored in the harbor since 1969.

longbow Leading missile weapon of the English in the 14th–16th cent. It was usually 6 ft (2 m) tall and shot arrows more than a yard long. The best were made of YEW, might require a force of 100 lbs (45 kg) to draw, and had an effective range of 200 yards (180 m). English archers used longbows in the HUNDRED YEARS' WAR, notably at CRÉCY, Poitiers, and AGINCOURT. See also BOW AND ARROW, CROSSBOW.

Longfellow, Henry Wadsworth (1807–1882) U.S. poet. Born in Portland, Mass. (now in Maine), he taught modern languages at Harvard 1836–54. His *Voices of the Night* (1839) first won him popularity. *Ballads and Other Poems* (1841), including "The Wreck of the Hesperus" and "The Village Blacksmith," swept the nation, as did his long poem *Evangeline* (1847). With *Hiawatha* (1855), *The Courtship of Miles Standish* (1858), and *Tales of a Wayside Inn* (1863), including "Paul Revere's Ride," he became the best-loved American poet of the 19th cent. He later translated DANTE's *Divine Comedy* (1867). The hallmarks of his verse are gentleness, simplicity, and an idealized vision of the world.

Henry Wadsworth Longfellow

Longhi \'lȯn-gē\, **Pietro** *orig.* Pietro Falca (1700/02–1785) Italian painter. He became known for his scenes of everyday life among Venice's upper class and bourgeoisie. Popular for their charm, these genre paintings manifest the interest in social observation characteristic of the Enlightenment. He also painted landscapes and portraits.

longhouse Traditional communal dwelling of the IROQUOIS Indians until the 19th cent. The longhouse was a rectangular box up to 200 ft (60m) long, built out of poles, with doors at each end and saplings stretched over the top to form the roof, the whole structure being covered with bark. Down the middle of the house were fires, which were shared by families on either side. The term is also applied today to an Iroquois building designated as church and meeting hall, though its form is entirely different. See also POLE CONSTRUCTION.

Long Island Island (pop., 2000: 7,448,000), SE New York, lying between LONG ISLAND SOUND and the Atlantic Ocean. Of its four counties, Kings Co. (the borough of BROOKLYN) and Queens Co. (the borough of QUEENS) form part of NEW YORK CITY. It is separated from the BRONX and MANHATTAN by the EAST RIVER and from STATEN ISLAND by the Narrows. It is 118 mi (190 km) long and 12–23 mi (19–37 km) wide, and has an area of 1,401 sq mi (3,629 sq km). Its E portion has many beaches; it serves as a recreation area for New York City. Its S shore, lined by sand spits (see FIRE ISLAND), shelters several bays, including Jamaica Bay. Originally inhabited by Indians, it was included in a grant to the PLYMOUTH CO. The island became part of the British colony of New York in 1664. The Battle of Long Island (Aug. 27, 1776) was an American defeat in the AMERICAN REVOLUTION.

Long Island Sound Body of water between Connecticut and LONG ISLAND, New York. It is 90 mi (145 km) long and 3–20 mi (5–32 km) wide. Its shores have many residential communities and summer resorts.

longitude See LATITUDE AND LONGITUDE

long jump *or* **broad jump** TRACK-AND-FIELD sport consisting of a horizontal jump for distance. It was formerly performed from both standing and running starts, as separate events, but the standing long jump is no longer included in major competitions. The running long jump was an event in the OLYMPIC GAMES of 708 B.C. and in the modern Games from 1896. In 1948 the women's long jump became an Olympic event.

Long March (1934–35) Trek of 6,000 mi (10,000 km) by Chinese Communists from SE China to NW central China. Having withstood four of CHIANG KAI-SHEK's campaigns against their base area in SE China, the Communists were nearly defeated by his fifth attack. The remaining 85,000 troops broke through Nationalist lines and fled first westward under ZHU DE and then north under MAO ZEDONG. By the time Mao arrived at Shaanxi, he was followed by only about 8,000 survivors, most of the rest having been killed by fighting, disease, and starvation. At their new base the Communists, with Mao as their undisputed leader, were able to build up their strength in preparation for their eventual victory in 1949.

Long Parliament Session of the English Parliament summoned in November 1640 by CHARLES I, so-named to distinguish it from the Short Parliament of April–May 1640. Charles called the session to raise the money needed for his war against the Scots. Resistant to Charles's demands, the Parliament passed an act forbidding its own dissolution without its members' consent. Tension increased until the ENGLISH CIVIL WAR broke out in 1642. After the king's defeat (1646), the army, led by Thomas PRIDE, exercised political power and in 1648 expelled all but 60 members of the Long Parliament. The remaining group, called the Rump, brought Charles to trial and execution (1649); it was forcibly ejected in 1653.

Longshan culture *or* **Lung-shan culture** (2500–1900 B.C.) Neolithic culture of China's Huang (Yellow) River valley. Large sites with rammed-earth walls have been found. Characteristic Longshan pottery has thin walls and is well crafted; there are tall-stemmed black cups with eggshell-thin walls as well as polished black beakers. Jade artifacts and traces of metallurgy have also been found.

longship *or* **Viking ship** Vessel widely used in N Europe for more than 1,500 years. It was a 45–75-ft (14–23-m) GALLEY with up to 10 oars on a side, a square sail, and a 50–60-man capacity. Double-ended and built with overlapped planks, it was exceptionally sturdy in high seas. Examples date back to 300 B.C. It carried the Vikings on their piratical raids of the 9th cent., and Dutch, French, English, and German merchants and warriors also used it.

Longstreet, James (1821–1904) U.S. army officer. Born in Edgefield District, S.C., he resigned from the U.S. Army when S. Carolina seceded. Appointed brigadier general in the Confederate army, he fought in the battles of Bull Run, Antietam, and Fredericksburg. He was second in command to Robert E. LEE at GETTYSBURG, where his delay in attacking contributed to the Confederate defeat. He directed the attack at Chickamauga and was badly wounded in the Battle of the Wilderness but later resumed command.

Lon Nol (1913–1985) Cambodian military and political leader. A magistrate in the French colonial service, he became head of the national police (1951), army chief of staff (1955), and commander in chief (1960). Twice premier (1966–67, 1969–70) under NORODOM SIHANOUK, he was the chief architect of the U.S.-supported coup that deposed Sihanouk. He abandoned Sihanouk's policy of neutrality in the Vietnam War and supported the U.S. and S. Vietnam. In 1972 he assumed total power in Cambodia; he fled to the U.S. in 1975 when the KHMER ROUGE takeover was imminent.

Lönnrot \ˈlœn-rût\, **Elias** (1802–1884) Finnish folklorist and philologist. While living in a remote part of E Finland, Lönnrot collected linguistic information and folk poetry from the region's inhabitants. Believing that the short poems were fragments of a continuous epic, he added connective material of his own and assembled them into the *Kalevala* (1835, enlarged 1849), which became the Finnish national epic.

Lonsdale, Kathleen *orig.* Kathleen Yardley (*later* **Dame Kathleen**) (1903–1971) British crystallographer. In 1929 her X-ray CRYSTALLOGRAPHY techniques established the regular hexagonal arrangement of carbon atoms in molecules of benzene compounds. She developed a technique with which she measured (to seven figures) the distance between carbon atoms in diamond. She also applied crystallographic techniques to medical problems, in particular the study of bladder stones and certain drugs.

loom Machine for WEAVING cloth. The earliest looms (5th millennium B.C.) consist of bars or beams forming a frame to hold a number of parallel threads in two alternating sets. By raising one set of these threads (which together formed the warp), it was possible to run a cross thread (a weft, or filling) between them. A shuttle carried the filling strand through the warp. The drawloom, probably invented in Asia for SILK weaving, provided a means for raising warp threads in groups as required by a pattern. In the 18th cent., Jacques de VAUCANSON and J.-M. JACQUARD mechanized this function by the ingenious use of punched cards; the cards programmed the mechanical drawboy, saving labor and eliminating errors (see JACQUARD LOOM). In England the inventions of John KAY (flying shuttle), Edmund CARTWRIGHT (power drive), and others contributed greatly to the INDUSTRIAL REVOLUTION.

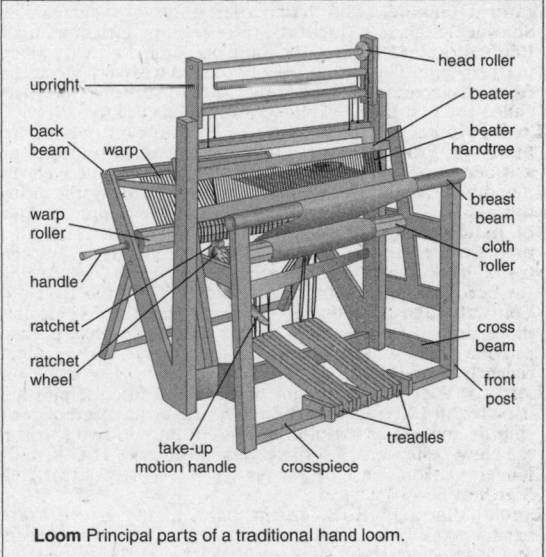

Loom Principal parts of a traditional hand loom.

loon *or* **diver** Any of four species (genus *Gavia*) of diving birds of N. America and Eurasia. Loons range in length from 2 to 3 ft (60–90 cm). They have small pointed wings and legs placed far back on the body, making walking awkward. They are black or gray above and white below. They feed mainly on fishes, crustaceans, and insects. They can swim long distances underwater and can dive to a depth of 200 ft (60 m). They are known for their eerie, "laughing" cries.

Loos \ˈlōs\, **Adolf** (1870–1933) Austrian architect. He practiced in Vienna, with extended periods in the U.S. and Paris. Opposed to both Art Nouveau and Beaux-Arts historicism, he announced as early as 1898 his intention to avoid use of unnecessary ornament. His Steiner House, Vienna (1910), is a skillful composition of austere Cubistic forms. His well-known Goldman and Salatsch Building (1910) features large areas of blank, polished marble.

KL

loosestrife Any ornamental plant of the family Lythraceae, especially in the genera *Lythrum* and *Decodon*. Purple loosestrife (*Lythrum salicaria*), native to Eurasia, grows 2–6 ft (0.6–1.8 m) high on riverbanks and in ditches. Its branched stem bears whorls of narrow, pointed, stalkless leaves and ends in tall, tapering spikes of red-purple flowers. It is a noxious weed in wetlands in many parts of the U.S. and Canada.

Lopez (Knight), Nancy (b.1957) U.S. golfer. Born in Torrance, Cal., in her first full season in 1978 she won a record total of nine tournaments. She became a three-time winner of the Ladies' Professional Golf Assn. championship (1978, 1985, 1989) and a four-time LPGA Player of the Year. Her success and personality helped rejuvenate women's golf.

López Portillo (y Pacheco) \lō-ˌpez-pór-'tē-yō\, **José** (b.1920) President of Mexico (1976–82). A professor, he joined the governments of Gustavo Díaz Ordaz (1911–1979) and Luis Echeverría (b.1922). As president, he emphasized foreign investment, tax concessions for industrial development, creation of nonagricultural jobs, and exploitation of oil and natural gas. He increased participation of minority parties, facilitating later challenges to the INSTITUTIONAL REVOLUTIONARY PARTY. Most of the wealth from expanded oil exports was lost to corruption, and his administration was discredited by the huge foreign debt it amassed. See also PEMEX.

Lorca, Federico García See Federico GARCÍA LORCA

lord See FEUDALISM

Lord Chamberlain's Men See CHAMBERLAIN'S MEN

Lord Dunmore's War (1774) Attack by Virginia militia on the SHAWNEE in Kentucky. The militiamen seized Ft. Pitt on the W border, renaming it after their royal governor, Lord Dunmore, who had ordered attacks against the Shawnee, seen as a threat to white settlers. Defeated at the Battle of Point Pleasant, the Shawnee signed a treaty giving up their land. The war, probably started to divert Virginians from disagreements with royal administrators, has been called the first battle of the AMERICAN REVOLUTION.

Lords, House of Upper house of Britain's bicameral PARLIAMENT. From the 13th–14th cent. it was the house of the aristocracy. Until 1999, its membership included clergy, hereditary peers, life peers (peers appointed by the prime minister since 1958), and the judges of the Supreme Court of Judicature (Britain's final court of appeal). Though it predates the House of COMMONS and dominated it for centuries, its power diminished greatly in the 20th cent. In 1999 the hereditary peers lost their right to sit in the House of Lords, though an interim reform retains their voice in a more limited fashion. The body's chief value has been to provide additional consideration to bills that may be insufficiently formulated.

Lord's Prayer Prayer taught by JESUS to his disciples and used by all Christians as the basic prayer in common worship. It appears as a model of how to pray in two forms in the New Testament: a shorter version in Luke 11:2–4, and a longer version, part of the SERMON ON THE MOUNT, in Matthew 6:9–13.

Lorelei \'lōr-ə-ˌlī\ Rock on the bank of the RHINE RIVER near Sankt Goarshausen in Germany. It produces an echo and is associated with the legend of a beautiful maiden who drowned herself over a faithless lover. She was transformed into a SIREN who lured fishermen to their death. Clemens BRENTANO claimed to have invented the essentials of the legend.

Loren \lō-'ren\, **Sophia** *orig.* Sofia Scicolone (b.1934) Italian film actress. She became a model and movie extra in Rome; coached by the producer Carlo Ponti (later her husband), she acted in Italian movies from 1950. Noted for her statuesque beauty and earthy femininity, she starred in *The Black Orchid* (1959), *El Cid* (1961), *Two Women* (1961, Academy Award), *Yesterday, Today, and Tomorrow* (1964), *Marriage Italian Style* (1964), and *A Special Day* (1977). She received a lifetime-achievement Oscar in 1991.

Lorentz \'lōr-ˌents\, **Hendrik Antoon** (1853–1928) Dutch physicist. In 1875 he refined J. C. MAXWELL's theory of ELECTROMAGNETIC RADIATION so that it explained the reflection and refraction of light. Aiming to devise a single theory to explain the relationship of electricity, magnetism, and light, he suggested that atoms might consist of charged particles that oscillate and produce light. In 1896 Pieter Zeeman (1865–1943) demonstrated this phenomenon, and in 1902 the two were awarded the second Nobel Prize for Physics. In 1904 Lorentz developed the Lorentz transformations, formulas that relate space and time measurements of one observer to those of a second observer moving relative to the first. These formed the basis of Albert EINSTEIN's special theory of RELATIVITY.

Lorenz, Edward (Norton) (b.1917) U.S. meteorologist. Born in W. Hartford, Conn., he taught at MIT from 1946. In the 1960s he discovered that long-range weather forecasting is impossible. He showed that a simple model of heat convection possesses intrinsic unpredictability, a circumstance he called the butterfly effect, suggesting that the mere flapping of a butterfly's wing can change the weather. His ideas became basic to the emerging field of CHAOS THEORY.

Lorenz \'lōr-ents\, **Konrad (Zacharias)** (1903–1989) Austrian zoologist and founder (with Nikolaas TINBERGEN) of modern ETHOLOGY. In 1935 he demonstrated the phenomenon of IMPRINTING in ducklings and goslings. He later examined the roots of human aggression (in the best-selling *On Aggression*, 1963). His other popular works include *King Solomon's Ring* (1949) and *Man Meets Dog* (1950). He shared a 1973 Nobel Prize with Tinbergen and Karl von FRISCH.

Lorenzetti \ˌlō-ränt-'set-tē\, **Pietro and Ambrogio** (fl.c.1306–1345, c.1317–1348) Italian painters. Both brothers were possibly pupils of DUCCIO, whose influence is seen in Pietro's altarpiece at Arezzo and in Ambrogio's early works. Ambrogio's works reveal an individualistic realism and preoccupation with three-dimensional space and form, most evident in his fresco series in Siena's Palazzo Pubblico (1338–39), the most important of Sienese frescoes. Pietro's *Birth of the Virgin* and Ambrogio's *Presentation in the Temple*, for Siena Cathedral (1342), are notable for their handling of perspective. The brothers were among the principal exponents of Sienese art in the years before the BLACK DEATH, in which both presumably died.

Lorenzo the Magnificent See Lorenzo de' MEDICI

loris Any of three species of nocturnal, arboreal PRIMATES in the family Lorisidae. Lorises have soft gray or brown fur, huge eyes encircled by dark patches, and no tail. They move slowly and often hang by their feet, leaving their hands free to grasp branches or food. The slender loris (*Loris tardigradus*) of India and Sri Lanka is 8–10 in. (20–25 cm) long; it eats insects and small animals. It is an endangered species. The slow lorises (*Nycticebus pygmaeus* and *N. coucang*) of SE Asia and the Malay Peninsula also eat fruit and vegetation.

Lorrain, Claude See CLAUDE LORRAIN

Lorraine Duchy, W Europe. It was formed by the division of Lorraine (Lotharingia) into two duchies in 959. Upper Lorraine, in the region of the MEUSE and MOSELLE rivers, was ruled by one ducal family from the 11th cent. METZ, Toul, and Verdun, outside the dukes' control, were seized by France in 1552. It came permanently under the French crown in 1766. After the FRANCO–PRUSSIAN WAR, part of it was ceded to Germany as part of ALSACE-LORRAINE.

Lorre \'lōr-ē\, **Peter** *orig.* Laszlo Loewenstein (1904–1964) Hungarian-U.S. film actor. After earning international fame as the psychotic murderer in the German film *M* (1931), he left Germany in 1933 and made his English-language debut in *The Man Who Knew Too Much* (1934). In Hollywood he played malevolent characters in such movies as *Mad Love* (1935), *The Maltese Falcon* (1941), *Casablanca* (1942), and *The Beast with Five Fingers* (1946). He also starred in the eight Mr. Moto detective movies (1937–39).

Los Alamos Town (pop., 2000: 12,000), N central New Mexico, northwest of SANTA FE. The site was chosen by the U.S. government in 1942 as the location for the MANHATTAN PROJECT, which developed the first ATOMIC BOMB. After World War II, the Los Alamos Scientific Laboratory developed the first NUCLEAR FUSION bomb. The town is still the site of a major nuclear research facility.

Los Angeles City (pop., 2000: 3,694,000); metro. area pop. 16,374,000), S California. The second-largest city in the U.S., it is situated between the San Gabriel Mtns. and the

Pacific Ocean. Bisected by the Santa Monica Mtns., which separate the neighborhoods of HOLLYWOOD, BEVERLY HILLS, and Pacific Palisades from the SAN FERNANDO VALLEY, it is near the SAN ANDREAS FAULT and earthquakes are frequent. It began in 1771 as a Spanish mission. Taken by U.S. forces in the MEXICAN WAR, it prospered with the 1849 GOLD RUSH and the arrival of the railroads in 1876 and 1885. In 1913 an aqueduct was built to supply it with water from the slopes of the SIERRA NEVADA. It was struck by a major earthquake in 1994. A city of immense ethnic diversity, it is perhaps best-known as the center of the American film and television industry. Sites of interest include the GETTY MUSEUM, the Los Angeles Co. Museum of Art, and the Museum of Contemporary Art. Educational institutions include the Univ. of SOUTHERN CALIFORNIA and the Univ. of CALIFORNIA at Los Angeles.

Lost Generation Group of U.S. writers who established their reputations in the 1920s; more broadly, the entire post–World War I American generation. Believing that their inherited values could not operate in the postwar world, they felt spiritually alienated from a country they considered hopelessly provincial and emotionally barren. The term embraces Ernest HEMINGWAY, F. Scott FITZGERALD, John DOS PASSOS, E. E. CUMMINGS, and Hart CRANE, among others.

lost-wax casting Traditional method of producing MOLDS for METAL SCULPTURE and other CASTINGS. It requires a positive, a core made of refractory material and an outer layer of wax. The positive can be produced either by direct modeling in wax over a prepared core or by casting in a mold taken from a master cast. The wax positive is invested with a mold made of refractory materials and heated to melt the wax, leaving a narrow cavity between the core and the investment. Molten metal is poured into this cavity; when it has solidified, the investment and core are broken away.

Lot Nephew of ABRAHAM. He emigrated with Abraham from Ur and settled in Sodom, a city so evil that God decided to destroy it. Warned by angels, Lot fled with his family. His wife disobeyed God's orders by looking back at the burning city and was turned into a pillar of salt. Lot's children by his own daughters became the founders of the Moabite and Ammonite nations, enemies of Israel. See also SODOM AND GOMORRAH.

Lotharingia See LORRAINE

Loti \lȯ-ˈtē\, **Pierre** orig. Louis-Marie-Julien Viaud (1850–1923) French novelist. As a naval officer, Loti visited the Middle East and E. Asia, which later provided the exotic settings of his novels and reminiscences. His first novel, *Aziyadé* (1879), won him critical and popular success. Other novels include *An Iceland Fisherman* (1886) and *Japan: Madam Chrysanthemum* (1887). Among his recurring motifs are love, death, and despair at the passing of sensuous life. His themes anticipated some of the preoccupations of French literature between the world wars.

lottery Drawing of lots in which prizes are distributed to the winners among persons buying a chance. A form of GAMBLING, lottery in its modern form may be traced to 15th-cent. Europe. A lottery was established to raise funds for the American Revolution. By the mid-19th cent., in the wake of abuses by private organizers, U.S. states began passing antilottery laws. A revival began in the mid-1960s, as state governments seeking revenues instituted lotteries. In most such operations, the bettor buys a numbered receipt or writes down his or her number choices, a drawing is held, and the winners identify themselves. The value of the prizes is the amount remaining after expenses and the state's share are deducted; winnings are usually subject to taxes. While prizes can grow into the tens of millions, causing a buying frenzy, the odds against winning remain astronomical.

Lotto, Lorenzo (c.1480–1556) Italian painter. Born in Venice, he worked in several other cities as well and developed an idiosyncratic style. His nervous temperament is evident in such works as the *Crucifixion* in Monte San Giusto (c.1530), with its highly charged mysticism and crowded composition. In 1554 he became a lay brother at the Santa Casa in Loreto to escape his critics and his debts. Though

primarily a religious painter, he is best known today for his psychologically acute portraits.

lotus Any of several different plants. The lotus of the Greeks was the shrub *Ziziphus lotus* (family Rhamnaceae); wine made from its fruit was thought to produce contentment and forgetfulness. The Egyptian lotus is a white WATER LILY (*Nymphaea lotus*). The sacred lotus of the Hindus is an aquatic plant (*Nelumbo nucifera*) with white or delicate pink flowers; the lotus of E N. America is related. *Lotus* is also a genus of the pea family (see LEGUME), containing about 100 species found in temperate regions. The lotus is a common ornament in architecture, and since ancient times it has symbolized fertility, purity, sexuality, birth, and rebirth of the dead.

Lotus Sutra Text central to the Japanese Tendai (Chinese Tiantai) and NICHIREN sects of MAHAYANA Buddhism. It represents the BUDDHA as divine and eternal, having attained perfect enlightenment eons ago. All beings are invited to become fully enlightened Buddhas through the grace of innumerable BODHISATTVAS. It became extremely popular in China and Japan, where the simple act of chanting it was thought to bring salvation.

loudspeaker *or* **speaker** In SOUND reproduction, device for converting electrical energy into acoustical (sound) signal energy that is radiated into a room or open air (see ACOUSTICS). The motor, or voice coil, converts electrical into mechanical energy, vibrating a diaphragm that vibrates the air in immediate contact with it and producing a sound wave corresponding to the pattern of the original speech, music, or other acoustic signal.

Louganis \lü-ˈgä-nəs\, **Greg(ory Efthimios)** (b.1960) U.S. diver, considered the greatest diver in history. Born in San Diego, he was trained early in dancing, tumbling, and acrobatics. During his diving career, he won an unprecedented 47 national and 13 world championships, including two Olympic gold medals (1984). In 1982 he became the first diver ever to earn a perfect score of 10, and the following

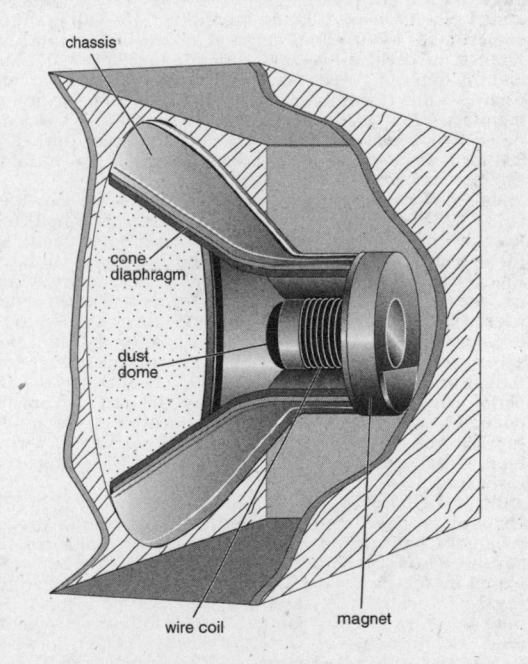

chassis

cone diaphragm

dust dome

wire coil   magnet

Loudspeaker Electrical signals sent through the coil cause it to act as an electromagnet, which is alternately repelled by or attracted to the permanent magnet. This movement causes the cone diaphragm to vibrate, creating sound waves.

K L

year he received 99 points in springboard competition. In 1995 he revealed that he had AIDS.

Lou Gehrig's disease See AMYOTROPHIC LATERAL SCLEROSIS

Lough Neagh See Lough NEAGH

Louis, Joe *orig.* Joseph Louis Barrow (1914–1981) U.S. boxer. Born into a sharecropper's family in Lexington, Ala., he began boxing after his family moved to Detroit. He won the U.S. Amateur Athletic Union heavyweight title in 1934. On the road to his first title bout he defeated six previous or subsequent champions, including Max Baer, Jack Sharkey, and Jersey Joe Walcott. Nicknamed "the Brown Bomber," he gained the title by defeating James J. Braddock in 1937, and held it until 1949. He lost to Max Schmeling in 1936 but defeated him in one round in 1938. He successfully defended his title 25 times (21 by knockout) before retiring in 1949.

Joe Louis, 1946

Louis, Morris *orig.* Morris Louis Bernstein (1912–1962) U.S. painter. Born in Baltimore, he worked as an easel painter for the WPA FEDERAL ART PROJECT. Inspired by Helen FRANKENTHALER's color stain technique, in 1954 he began a series of paintings titled *Veils*, featuring stained vertical waves of color. His later work featured diagonal parallel streams of color that flowed across the bottom corners of the picture plane. In his last series, *Stripes*, bunched, straight vertical bands of color are surrounded by empty canvas.

Louis, St. See LOUIS IX

Louis I \'lü-ē\ *known as* **Louis the Pious** (778–840) Frankish emperor (814–40). The son and successor of CHARLEMAGNE, he divided his empire among his nephew Bernard and his four sons—Lothair, Pepin, Louis the German, and Charles—but this only increased their appetite for power, manifested in a series of revolts beginning in 817. Twice deposed by his sons, he recovered the throne each time (830, 834), but at his death the Carolingian empire was in disarray. See also Treaty of VERDUN.

Louis IV *German* Ludwig *known as* **Louis the Bavarian** (1283?–1347) German king (1314–47) and uncrowned Holy Roman Emperor (1328–47). As the Luxembourg candidate for emperor, he was opposed by the Habsburg candidate Frederick III of Austria; both men were elected and crowned king in 1314, and Louis's forces defeated Frederick's army in 1322. A conflict with Pope JOHN XXII led to his excommunication (1324). To placate his opponents Louis agreed to corule with Frederick, an arrangement that continued until Frederick's death (1330). He accepted the imperial crown from the Roman people instead of from the pope (1328) and backed the appointment of an ANTIPOPE. In 1346 Pope CLEMENT VI secured the election of a rival king, Charles of Moravia, and Louis died while preparing for war.

Louis IX *or* **St. Louis** (1214–1270) King of France (1226–70). His mother served as regent until 1234, helping to subdue rebellious barons and Albigensian heretics. Louis led the Seventh CRUSADE (1248–50), but his troops were badly defeated by the Egyptians. On his return he reorganized the royal administrative system and standardized coinage. He built the extraordinary Sainte-Chapelle to house a religious relic. He made peace with the English (1259), allowing HENRY III to keep Aquitaine. He died of plague in Tunisia during a crusade. His reputation for justness and piety led the French to venerate him as a saint even before his canonization in 1297.

Louis XI (1423–1483) King of France (1461–83). He plotted against his father, CHARLES VII, and was exiled to Dauphiné (1445), which he ruled as a sovereign state until Charles approached its borders with an army (1456). Louis then fled to the Netherlands, returning to France to become king on his father's death in 1461. He fought rebellious French princes (1465) and destroyed the power of the Burgundians in 1477. He also took control of Anjou (1471), Maine and Provence (1481), and Franche-Comté and Artois (1482).

Louis XII (1462–1515) King of France (1498–1515). Succeeding his cousin CHARLES VIII, he married Charles's widow, Anne of Brittany, to reinforce the union of her duchy with France. He continued France's part in the ITALIAN WARS, often with disastrous results. He concluded a treaty with FERDINAND V that partitioned Naples (1500), but the two kings went to war and Louis lost all of Naples (1504). In 1510 England joined a Holy League against France, invading it several times. Despite his failures, Louis was highly popular with the French, who called him the "Father of the People."

Louis XIII (1601–1643) King of France (1610–43). He was the son of HENRY IV and MARIE DE MÉDICIS. His mother was regent until 1614 but continued to govern until 1617; she arranged Louis's marriage to the Spanish ANNE OF AUSTRIA in 1615. Resentful of his mother's power, Louis exiled her, but Cardinal de RICHELIEU, her principal adviser, reconciled them in 1620. In 1624 Louis made Richelieu his principal minister; the two cooperated closely to make France a leading European power, consolidating royal authority in France and fighting to break the dominant rule of the Spanish and Austrian Habsburgs in the THIRTY YEARS' WAR, despite his mother's pleas on behalf of Spain. France declared war on Spain in 1635, and had won substantial victories by the time Richelieu died in 1642.

Louis XIV *known as* **the Sun King** (1638–1715) King of France (1643–1715). He succeeded his father, LOUIS XIII, at age 4, under the regency of his mother, ANNE OF AUSTRIA. In 1648 the nobles and the Paris Parlement, who hated the prime minister, Cardinal MAZARIN, rose against the crown and started the FRONDE. In 1653, victorious over the rebels, Mazarin gained absolute power, though the king was of age. In 1660 Louis married Marie-Thérèse of Austria (1638–1683), daughter of PHILIP IV of Spain. When Mazarin died in 1661, Louis astonished his ministers by assuming full responsibility for ruling the

Louis XIV Portrait by Hyacinthe Rigaud, 1701

kingdom. He was assisted by his able ministers, J.-B. COLBERT and the marquis de LOUVOIS. A patron of the arts, he protected writers and built splendid palaces, including VERSAILLES, where he kept most of the nobility under his watchful eye. In 1667 and again in 1672 he invaded the Spanish Netherlands. The Sun King was at his zenith; he had extended France's N and E borders and was adored at his court. In 1680, a scandal involving his mistress, the marquise de Montespan (1641–1707), made him fearful for his reputation and he openly renounced pleasure. The queen died in 1683, and he secretly married the pious marquise de MAINTENON. After trying to convert French Protestants by force, he revoked the Edict of NANTES in 1685. Fear of his expansionism led to alliances against France during the War of the GRAN ALLIANCE (1688–97) and the War of the SPANISH SUCCESSION (1701–14). Louis died at 77 at the end of the longest reign in European history.

Louis XIV style Style of the visual arts produced in France during the reign of LOUIS XIV. In 1648 Charles LE BRUN founded the Royal Academy of Painting and Sculpture, which rigidly dictated styles for the rest of the reign. The most influential painter was Nicolas POUSSIN. Sculpture reached a new zenith with the works of François GIRARDON and Pierre PUGET. A national style in the decorative arts evolved through the Gobelin factory (see GOBELIN FAMILY). Furniture was veneered, inlaid, and heavily gilded, commonly decorated with shells, satyrs, garlands, and dolphins. In architecture, the renovation of the Palace of VERSAILLES was most notable.

Louis XV (1710–1774) King of France (1715–74). Louis succeeded to the throne on the death of his great-grandfather LOUIS XIV. His marriage to Princess Marie Leszczynska of Poland (1703–1768) in 1725 led to involvement in the War of the POLISH SUCCESSION. He chose A.-H. de Fleury as his chief minister in 1726, and his own influence became perceptible only after Fleury's death in 1744. Louis's mistresses, particularly Madame de POMPADOUR, held considerable political influence. Louis brought France into the War of the AUSTRIAN SUCCESSION (1740–48) and the SEVEN YEARS' WAR (1756–63), by which it lost to Britain almost all its colonial possessions. As the crown's moral and political authority declined, the Parlement's gained in power. The king died hated by his subjects.

Louis XV style ROCOCO STYLE of French decorative arts during the reign of LOUIS XV. Emphasis was laid on the ensemble, so that paintings and sculptures became part of the decorative arts. Decorative techniques included superb carving, ornamentation of all types of metal, inlay work in exotic woods, metal, mother-of-pearl, and ivory, and exquisite lacquered chinoiserie that rivaled products from the Far East. Notable artists included J.-H. FRAGONARD and François BOUCHER.

Louis XVI (1754–1793) Last king of France (1774–92) preceding the FRENCH REVOLUTION. In 1770 he married MARIE-ANTOINETTE, and in 1774 he succeeded his grandfather, LOUIS XV. Immature and lacking in strength of character, he was unable to give the necessary support to his ministers, including A.-R.-J. TURGOT and Jacques NECKER, in their efforts to stabilize France's tottering finances. Aristocratic opposition to the economic reforms of C.-A. de Calonne forced the king to summon the Estates General in 1788, setting the Revolution in motion. Dominated by the reactionary court faction, he refused to sanction the achievements of the NATIONAL ASSEMBLY.

Louis XVI Portrait by J.-S. Duplessis

His resistance to popular demands led to the royal family's forcible transfer from Versailles to the Tuileries palace in Paris. He lost credibility further when he attempted to escape the capital in 1791 and was caught at Varennes. Thereafter he was dominated by the queen, who encouraged him to a policy of subterfuge instead of implementing the Constitution of 1791. When proof of his counterrevolutionary intrigues with foreigners was found, he was tried for treason. Condemned to death, he went to the guillotine in 1793. His dignity during his trial and execution only somewhat redeemed his reputation.

Louis XVI style Style of the visual arts produced in France from about 1760 to the French Revolution. The predominant style in painting, architecture, sculpture, and the decorative arts was Neoclassicism—a reaction against the excesses of the Rococo style and a response to J.-J. ROUSSEAU's call for "natural" virtue, as well as a response to the excavations at POMPEII and HERCULANEUM. The most prominent painter was J.-L. DAVID; the foremost sculptor was J.-A. HOUDON. The style in furniture was classical, yet workmanship was more complex than in any earlier period. See also CLASSICISM AND NEOCLASSICISM.

Louis XVII orig. Louis-Charles (1785–1795) Titular king of France (1793–95). The second son of LOUIS XVI and MARIE-ANTOINETTE, he was imprisoned with the rest of the royal family in the FRENCH REVOLUTION. When his father was beheaded in 1793, the French ÉMIGRÉ NOBILITY proclaimed Louis-Charles king. He died in prison at age 10, but rumors arose that he was not dead, and over the

next few decades more than 30 persons claimed to be Louis XVII.

Louis XVIII orig. Louis-Stanislas-Xavier, comte (Count) de Provence (1755–1824) King of France by title from 1795 and in fact 1814–24. He fled the country in 1791, during the French Revolution, and organized ÉMIGRÉ-NOBILITY associations. He became regent for his nephew LOUIS XVII in 1793 and at the dauphin's death in 1795 he proclaimed himself king. When the allied armies entered Paris in 1814, C.-M. de TALLEYRAND negotiated the BOURBON RESTORATION and Louis was received with jubilation. The CHARTER OF 1814 was adopted; after the interruption of the HUNDRED DAYS, he resumed his constitutional monarchy. The legislature included a strong right-wing majority, which exercised increasing control and thwarted Louis's attempts to heal the wounds left by the Revolution.

Louisiana State (pop., 2000: 4,469,000), S U.S. It covers 48,523 sq mi (125,674 sq km); its capital is BATON ROUGE. It can be divided physically into the MISSISSIPPI RIVER flood plain and delta, and the low hills of the Gulf of Mexico coastal plain. It is the only U.S. state to be governed under the NAPOLEONIC CODE. Indian occupancy in the area probably spanned 16,000 years; at the time of European settlement the region was inhabited by Caddo and CHOCTAW Indians. French explorer R.-R. LA SALLE descended the Mississippi River in 1682 and claimed the entire river basin for France. The city of NEW ORLEANS was founded in 1718, and Louisiana became a French crown colony in 1731. Colonization increased in the 1760s with the arrival of French-speaking Acadians (CAJUNS) from Nova Scotia. Spain controlled the territory 1762–1800; then it passed back to the French. The lands that constitute modern Louisiana were acquired by the U.S. as part of the LOUISIANA PURCHASE in 1803 and became the Territory of Orleans in 1804. Louisiana became the 18th U.S. state in 1812. It seceded from the Union in 1861 at the start of the AMERICAN CIVIL WAR and was readmitted in 1868. The plantation economy continued with the farmer class denied ownership, which contributed to the rise of the populist Huey LONG in the 1920s. After World War II Louisiana experienced more rapid development with the rise of offshore oil and gas drilling. Major agricultural products are soybeans and cotton; tree farming and shrimp fishing are also important. Petroleum and natural gas are the chief mineral resources.

Louisiana Purchase Territory purchased by the U.S. from France in 1803, for $15 million. It extended from the MISSISSIPPI RIVER to the ROCKY MTNS. and from the Gulf of Mexico to British America (Canada). In 1762 France had ceded Louisiana west of the Mississippi River to Spain, but Spain returned it to French control in 1800. Alarmed by this potential increase in French power, Pres. Thomas JEFFERSON threatened to form an alliance with Britain. NAPOLEON then sold the U.S. the entire Louisiana Territory. The purchase doubled the area of the U.S.

Louisiana State University State university system with 10 campuses in five cities, the main institution being Louisiana State Univ. and Agricultural and Mechanical College in Baton Rouge. The university opened in 1860. It now has about 28,000 students at the main university and 57,000 in the entire system. It operates some 800 sponsored research projects and includes a Center for Coastal, Energy, and Environmental Resources.

Louis-Napoléon See NAPOLEON III

Louis-Philippe known as the Citizen King (1773–1850) King of the French (1830–48). Eldest son of the duc d'ORLÉANS, he joined the Revolutionary army in 1792, but deserted during the war with Austria (1793) and lived in exile in Switzerland, the U.S., and England. He returned to France on the restoration of LOUIS XVIII and joined the liberal opposition. Following CHARLES X's abdication, he was proclaimed the "citizen king" by Adolphe THIERS and elected by the legislature. During the JULY MONARCHY, he consolidated his power by steering a middle course, but resorted to repressive measures because of numerous rebellions and attempts on his life. Though he strengthened France's position in Europe, mounting middle-class opposition to his arbitrary rule and his inability to win allegiance from the new indus-

K L

trial classes caused his abdication during the FEBRUARY REVOLUTION of 1848.

Louis the Bavarian See LOUIS IV

Louis the Pious See LOUIS I

Louisville \'lü-i-ˌvil\ City (pop., 2000: 256,000), N central Kentucky, located on the OHIO RIVER. Settled in 1778 and named for LOUIS XVI of France, it became an important river trading center. During the AMERICAN CIVIL WAR it served as a Union military headquarters and supply depot. The largest city in Kentucky, it is a leading producer of bonded bourbon whiskey and cigarettes. It is home to the Univ. of Louisville (founded 1798) and Churchill Downs, site of the KENTUCKY DERBY.

Lourdes PILGRIMAGE site in SW France, situated southwest of Toulouse at the foot of the Pyrenees. Its modern significance dates from 1858, when the 14-year-old BERNADETTE OF LOURDES had repeated visions of the Virgin MARY. The underground spring in the grotto where Bernadette had her visions was declared to have miraculous qualities, and Lourdes has since become one of the foremost destinations for Roman Catholic pilgrims. Nearly 3 million visit annually, many hoping to be healed. A basilica was built above the grotto in 1876, and a vast underground church was added in 1958.

Lourenço Marques See MAPUTO

louse Any member of some 3,300 species of small, wingless, parasitic insects of the order Phthiraptera, which consists mainly of biting, or chewing, lice (parasites of birds and mammals) and the sucking lice. Most species spend their entire lives on the body of host animals. Infestations cause much irritation and may lead to secondary infections. In moving from host to host, lice may spread many diseases, including tapeworm infestation in dogs and murine typhus in rats. See also human LOUSE.

louse, human Any of three types of sucking louse that infest humans. The body louse (mainly *Pediculus humanus humanus,* also called human louse or cootie) and head louse (*P. h. capitis*) are spread by person-to-person contact and through shared clothing, bedding, combs, and other personal items. Body lice carry the organisms that cause relapsing fever, trench fever, and TYPHUS. Head lice may cause IMPETIGO. Both are readily spread under conditions of overcrowding, especially among children. The crab louse, or pubic louse (*Phthirus pubis*) infests primarily the pubic region and is transmitted chiefly through sexual intercourse. Lice infestations can be cured with shampoos, soaps, and lotions containing benzene hexachloride, along with the thorough washing of bedding and clothing.

Louvois \lüv-'wä\ **marquis de** *orig.* **François-Michel Le Tellier** \lə-tāl-'yā\ (1639–1691) French secretary of state for war under LOUIS XIV and his most influential minister 1677–91. The son of one of the most powerful officials in France, he was groomed by his father to replace him as war secretary. A brilliant administrator, Louvois realized reforms that made the French army one of the most formidable in Europe. Complicit in the military policy that led up to the revocation of the Edict of NANTES (1685), he was also responsible for a policy that led to the War of the GRAND ALLIANCE.

Louvre Museum \'lüvrˀ\ National museum and art gallery of France, in Paris. It was built as a royal residence, begun under FRANCIS I in 1546 on the site of a 12th-cent. fortress. The court moved to Versailles in 1682, and plans were made in the 18th cent. to turn it into a public museum. In 1793 the revolutionary government opened the Grand Gallery; Napoleon built the N wing; and two major W wings were completed and opened by Napoleon III. The completed Louvre included a vast complex of buildings, enclosing two large courtyards. A controversial steel-and-glass pyramid entrance designed by I. M. PEI opened in 1989. The painting collection is one of the richest in the world.

lovebird Any of nine species of small PARROTS (genus *Agapornis,* subfamily Psittacinae) of Africa and Madagascar. Popular as pets for their pretty colors and the seemingly affectionate closeness of pairs, most have a red bill and prominent eye ring. The two sexes look alike. Large flocks forage for seeds and may damage crops. Hardy and long-lived, they have a loud, squawky voice. Though not easy to tame, they can be taught to perform tricks and mimic human speech to a limited extent.

Lovebird (*Agapornis personata*)

Love Canal Neighborhood in NIAGARA FALLS, N.Y., site of the worst disaster involving chemical wastes in U.S. history. An abandoned canal, it became a dumping ground for nearly 22,000 tons of chemical waste in the 1940s and 1950s. Later it was filled in, and housing was built on it. The leakage of toxic chemicals into these homes was detected in 1978, and residents were discovered to have a high incidence of chromosomal damage. After their evacuation, 1,300 former residents obtained a $20 million settlement. In the early 1990s New York state ended its cleanup and declared parts of the area safe for residence.

Lovejoy, Elijah P(arish) (1802–1837) U.S. abolitionist. Born in Albion, Me., he moved to St. Louis and in 1833 became editor of the *St. Louis Observer,* in which he wrote articles strongly condemning slavery. Under threat of mob violence (1836), he moved his paper across the river to Alton, in the free state of Illinois. There mobs repeatedly destroyed his presses; he was killed while defending his building against a mob attack. News of his death strengthened abolitionist sentiment.

Lovelace, Ada King, Countess of *orig.* Lady Augusta Ada Byron (1815–1852) English mathematician. Her absentee father was the poet Lord BYRON. She became a countess when her husband, William King, was created an earl. Interested in Charles BABBAGE's analytical machines, in 1843 she translated and annotated an important Italian article about them. For creating a program for Babbage's prototype of a digital computer, she has been called the first female computer programmer. The programming language ADA is named for her.

Lovell \'lə-vəl\, **(Alfred Charles) Bernard** (*later* **Sir Bernard**) (b.1913) British radio astronomer. He worked for the Air Ministry during World War II, and lectured at the Univ. of Manchester after the war. He built the first giant RADIO TELESCOPE (1957) at Jodrell Bank; its bowl diameter is 250 ft (76 m).

low blood pressure See HYPOTENSION

Low Countries Coastal region, NW Europe, consisting of Belgium, the Netherlands, and Luxembourg. Much of the land along the North Sea is below or at sea level. They are often called the Benelux countries, from the initial letters of their names.

Lowell City (pop., 2000: 105,000), NE Massachusetts. Settled in 1653 as E. Chelmsford, it became a major center of cotton-textile manufacturing in the 19th cent. It was renamed for industrialist Francis LOWELL. In the 20th cent. it diversified into other industries. The Lowell National Historical Park (established 1978) commemorates the Industrial Revolution in the U.S. It is the birthplace of the artist J. A. M. WHISTLER and the seat of the Univ. of Massachusetts–Lowell.

Lowell, Amy (1874–1925) U.S. critic and poet. Born into the prominent Lowell family of Boston, she published her first volume of poetry, *A Dome of Many-Coloured Glass,* in 1912. *Sword Blades and Poppy Seed* (1914) included her first poems in free verse and what she called "polyphonic prose." She became a leader of IMAGISM and was noted for her vivid and powerful personality and her scorn for conventional behavior. Her critical works include *Six French Poets* (1915) and *John Keats* (2 vols., 1925).

Lowell, Francis Cabot (1775–1817) U.S. businessman. Born in Newburyport, Mass., Lowell closely studied the British textile industry while visiting Britain. With Paul Moody (1779–1831) he devised an efficient power LOOM and spinning apparatus. His Boston Manufacturing Co. was apparently the world's first mill in which were performed all operations converting raw COTTON into finished cloth. His example greatly stimulated the growth of New England industry.

Lowell, James Russell (1819–1891) U.S. poet, critic, editor, and diplomat. Born in Cambridge, Mass., he wrote extensively against slavery, including the *Biglow Papers* (1848), satirical verses in Yankee dialect. His other most important works are *The Vision of Sir Launfal* (1848), a long poem on the brotherhood of mankind; and *A Fable for Critics* (1848), a witty evaluation of contemporary authors. A highly influential man of letters, he taught at Harvard, cofounded *The Atlantic Monthly*, edited *The North American Review,* and served as minister to Spain and ambassador to Britain.

Lowell, Percival (1855–1916) U.S. astronomer. Born in Boston, in the 1890s he built a private observatory in Flagstaff, Ariz., to study Mars. He championed the theory that inhabitants of a dying Mars had built a planetwide irrigation system and that the "canals" of Mars were bands of vegetation it nourished. Lowell's theory, long disputed, was finally put to rest by data from the U.S. Mariner spacecraft. His prediction of a planet beyond Neptune was vindicated when Pluto was discovered in 1930.

Lowell, Robert *orig.* Robert Traill Spence Lowell, Jr. (1917–1977) U.S. poet. Born in Boston, Lowell was a descendant of a distinguished family that included J. R. LOWELL and Amy LOWELL. Though he turned away from his Puritan heritage, it forms the subject of much of his poetry. *Lord Weary's Castle* (1946, Pulitzer Prize) was his first major work. *Life Studies* (1959) contains an autobiographical essay and 15 complex, confessional poems. His activities in liberal causes in the 1960s influenced his next three volumes, including *For the Union Dead* (1964). His later collections include *The Dolphin* (1973, Pulitzer Prize).

Lower Canada See CANADA EAST

low relief See BAS-RELIEF

Lowry \'laù-rē\, **(Clarence) Malcolm** (1909–1957) British writer. In his youth the rebellious Lowry shipped to China as a cabin boy; he later lived in various countries. His reputation rests on the novel *Under the Volcano* (1947); its images of social decay and alcoholic self-destructiveness were seen as a symbolic vision of Europe on the verge of World War II. It received popular recognition only after Lowry's death at 47.

Loyalists American colonists loyal to Britain in the AMERICAN REVOLUTION. About one-third of colonists were Loyalists, including officeholders who served the British crown, large landholders, wealthy merchants, Anglican clergy and their parishioners, and Quakers. Loyalists were most numerous in the South, New York, and Pennsylvania. At first they urged moderation; when denounced by radical patriots, they became active partisans. Some joined the British army, including 23,000 from New York; when captured, they were treated as traitors. All states passed laws against them, confiscating or heavily taxing their property. About 100,000 Loyalists fled into exile, many to Canada. Punitive state laws were repealed by 1814.

Loyola, St. Ignatius of *orig.* Iñigo de Oñaz y Loyola (1491–1556) Spanish founder of the Society of Jesus (JESUITS). Born into the nobility, he began his career as a soldier. While convalescing from wounds in 1521, he experienced a religious conversion. After a pilgrimage to Jerusalem, he pursued religious studies in Spain and France. In Paris he gathered about him the companions (including Francis XAVIER) who were to join him in founding the Jesuits in 1539. The new order received papal approval in 1540, and Loyola served as its general until his death, by which time it had branches in Italy, Spain, Germany, France, Portugal, India, and Brazil.

LSD *in full* lysergic acid diethylamide. Highly potent HALLUCINOGEN. An organic compound, LSD can be derived from the ALKALOIDS ergotamine and ergonovine, found in the ERGOT fungus, but most LSD is produced synthetically. It can block the action of the NEUROTRANSMITTER SEROTONIN and produces marked deviations from normal perceptions and behavior lasting 8–10 hours or longer. Mood shifts, time and space distortions, and impulsive behavior may progress to suspicions of the intentions and motives of other people and aggression against them. LSD is not an approved drug, and no clinically valuable uses have been found for it.

Lualaba River \ˌlü-ä-'lä-bä\ River, central Africa. The headstream of the CONGO RIVER, its 1,100-mi (1,800-km) course lies entirely within the Democratic Republic of the Congo (Zaire).

Luanda \lù-'än-də\ *or* **Loanda** \lō-'än-də\ Seaport and capital (pop., 1995 est.: 2,081,000), Angola. It is Angola's largest city. Founded in 1576 by Paulo Dias de Novais, it became the administrative center for the colony of Angola in 1627. It was a major outlet for slave traffic to Brazil until the 19th cent. Many Mbundu live in the city, and there is a sizable Cuban community. It is the seat of the Univ. of Luanda; the old fortress of São Miguel lies beyond the port. Luanda's economy has been devastated by Angola's long civil war.

Luba-Lunda states \'lü-bə-'lün-də\ Complex of kingdoms that flourished in Central Africa in the 16th–19th cent. In the late 15th cent. a group of ivory hunters founded a kingdom around which a number of satellites proliferated, spreading by the 17th cent. into the S Congo Basin, W Angola, and Zambia. The NE portion was inhabited by the Luba, the SW portion by the Lunda. The kingdom traded slaves and ivory to the Portuguese. In the 18th cent., migrants founded the Kazembe kingdom farther southeast.

Lubbock \'lə-bək\ City (pop., 2000: 199,000), NW Texas. Located south of AMARILLO, it was named for Tom S. Lubbock (1817–1862), a signer of the Texas declaration of independence. Formed in 1890, it developed as a ranching center and is today one of the nation's leading cotton markets. It is the seat of Texas Tech Univ. (1923).

Lübeck \'lū-ˌbek\ City (pop. 1996: 216,000), N Germany. Founded in 1143, it developed as a trading post. It became a free city in 1226 and the seat of the HANSEATIC LEAGUE in 1358. It declined after the 16th cent., and its trade was ruined during the NAPOLEONIC WARS. It revived after the Elbe–Lubeck canal was built in 1900. In 1937 the Nazis revoked its self-governing status and made it part of SCHLESWIG-HOLSTEIN. It is one of Germany's largest Baltic ports.

Lubitsch \'lü-bich\, **Ernst** (1892–1947) German-U.S. film director. He acted with Max REINHARDT's German stage company (1911–14), then turned to directing costume dramas which were the first German films shown abroad, including *Passion* (1919), *Deception* (1920), and *The Loves of Pharaoh* (1921). He moved to Hollywood in 1923 and developed a style of sophisticated wit and unerring narrative timing—the famous "Lubitsch touch"—in such successful comedies as *Trouble in Paradise* (1932), *Ninotchka* (1939), *The Shop Around the Corner* (1940), *To Be or Not to Be* (1942), and *Heaven Can Wait* (1943).

Lublin \'lü-blin\ City (pop., 1999 est.: 356,000), E Poland. Founded in the late 9th cent., the settlement received town rights in 1317. In 1795 it passed to Austria and in 1815 to Russia. The first independent temporary Polish government was proclaimed there in 1918. In World War II the Nazi CONCENTRATION CAMP Majdanek was established in one of its suburbs. It is now an industrial and cultural center for SE Poland.

lubrication Introduction of a substance between sliding surfaces to reduce wear and FRICTION. Lubricants may secondarily control corrosion, regulate temperature, electrically insulate, remove contaminants, or damp shock. Prehistoric peoples used mud and reeds to lubricate sledges, timbers, or rocks. Animal fat lubricated the first axles and continued in wide use until crude OIL became the chief source of lubricants. Crude oil has been the basis of lubricants for automobiles, aircraft, and all other power machinery. There are three basic varieties of lubrication: fluid-film (in which a fluid film completely separates sliding surfaces), boundary (in which the friction between surfaces is determined by the properties of the surfaces and properties of the lubricant other than VISCOSITY), and solid (used when liquid lubricants lack adequate resistance to load or temperature extremes). The principal lubricants are liquid, oily materials (petroleum-based or synthetic, and including greases); solids (such as graphite, soft metals, waxes, and plastics); and gases.

Lubumbashi \ˌlü-büm-'bä-shē\ *formerly (until 1966)* **Elisabethville** City (pop., 1994 est.: 851,000), Democratic Republic of the Congo (Zaire). Established by Belgian

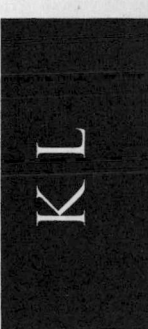

K L

colonists in 1910, it became the site of one of the world's largest copper mining and smelting operations. It was the center of Katanga province's secession movement in the early 1960s.

Luca da Cortona See Luca SIGNORELLI

Lucas, George (b.1944) U.S. film director and producer. Born in Modesto, Cal., he studied filmmaking at USC. His *THX 1138* (1971) was followed by the surprise success *American Graffiti* (1973). He wrote and directed the immensely popular *Star Wars* (1977), which made innovative use of computerized special effects. Having formed the production company Lucasfilms (1978) and its special-effects division Industrial Light and Magic, he produced the *Star Wars* sequels, *The Empire Strikes Back* (1980) and *Return of the Jedi* (1993), as well as Steven SPIELBERG's *Raiders of the Lost Ark* (1981) and its sequels. He returned to directing with the *Star Wars* "prequels" *The Phantom Menace* (1999) and *Attack of the Clones* (2002).

Lucas (Huyghszoon) van Leyden \\'lū̄e-käs-vän-'lī-dən\\ (c.1494–1533) Netherlandish painter and engraver. Born in Leiden, he was trained as a painter, but his great talent was as an engraver. Even such youthful prints as *Muhammad and the Monk Sergius* (1508) show great technical skill. In 1510, under the influence of Albrecht DÜRER, he produced two masterpieces, *The Milkmaid* and *Ecce Homo*. He is thought to have developed the technique of etching on copper (instead of iron) plates, whose softness let him combine etching and line engraving in the same print. *The Last Judgment* (1526–27) is his most celebrated painting.

Luce, Clare Boothe *orig.* Ann Clare Boothe (1903–1987) U.S. politician and dramatist. She worked as a magazine editor before marrying Henry LUCE in 1935. Three of her witty plays were adapted into films: *The Women* (1936), *Kiss the Boys Goodbye* (1938), and *Margin for Error* (1939). A U.S. Representative (1943–47) and ambassador to Italy (1953–56), she was influential in Republican Party politics. In 1983 she was awarded the Presidential Medal of Freedom.

Luce, Henry R(obinson) (1898–1967) U.S. (Chinese-born) magazine publisher. Born to missionary parents, Luce attended Yale Univ., where he met Briton Hadden (1898–1929); together they launched *TIME* in 1923. He expanded his publishing empire with the business magazine *Fortune* (1929) and *LIFE*, (1936). Among other Luce magazines was *Sports Illustrated* (1954). His publications had many imitators, and Luce became one of the most powerful figures in the history of U.S. journalism. Both he and his wife, C. B. LUCE, had a major influence on the Republican Party and on national affairs.

Lucerne \\lü-'sərn\\ *German* **Luzern** \\lüt-'sern\\ City (pop., 1995 est.: 61,000), central Switzerland. Located southwest of ZURICH, on a river outlet of Lake LUCERNE, it developed around an 8th-cent. monastery. It joined the Swiss Confederation in 1332. It was a stronghold of Catholicism during the REFORMATION. It is a tourist center, with medieval walls, towers, and covered bridges; the famous "Lion of Lucerne," carved in rock, commemorates Swiss Guards slain in the French Revolution.

Lucerne, Lake *German* **Vierwaldstätter See** \\'fēr-vält-ˌshtet-ər-ˌzā\\ Lake, central Switzerland. It is 24 mi (39 km) long and 0.5–2 mi (0.8–3 km) wide, with an area of 44 sq mi (114 sq km). The "Cross of Lucerne" is formed by its four main basins in four cantons. LUCERNE lies at its W end. It is in a region of resorts and tourist attractions.

Lucian \\'lü-shən\\ *Latin* Lucianus (c.A.D. 120–after 180) Ancient Greek rhetorician, pamphleteer, and satirist. His essays, outstanding for their mordant wit, are a sophisticated critique of the shams and follies of the literature, philosophy, and intellectual life of his day. In such works as *Charon*, *Dialogues of the Dead*, *True History*, and *Nigrinus*, he satirized nearly every aspect of human behavior. His best work of literary criticism is *How to Write History*.

Luciano \\lü-'chä-nō\\, **Lucky** *orig.* Salvatore Lucania *later* Charles Luciano (1896–1962) U.S. (Italian-born) gangster. He emigrated to New York in 1906, and was soon involved in crime. In 1916 he joined Frank Costello and Meyer LANSKY, earning the nickname "Lucky" by evading arrest and winning at craps. By 1920 he was directing Joe Masseria's bootlegging, narcotics, and prostitution rackets. In 1931 he planned the assassinations of Masseria and rival boss Salvatore Maranzano, and began developing a national crime syndicate. Jailed in 1936, he directed crime operations from his cell. Deported to Italy in 1946, he continued to direct drug traffic and the smuggling of aliens into the U.S.

Lucifer In classical mythology, the morning star (the planet VENUS at dawn), personified as a male figure. Lucifer (Latin: "Light-Bearer") carried a torch and served as herald of the dawn. In Christian times, Lucifer came to be regarded as the name of Satan before his fall.

Lucknow \\'lək-ˌnaú\\ City (metro. area pop., 1995: 2,029,000) and capital, Uttar Pradesh state, N India, southeast of Delhi. It was captured by the Mughal ruler BABUR in 1528. In 1775 it became the capital of Oudh province. It is now a rail center with paper factories and other industries. Notable sites include the Great Imambara (tomb) of one of the nabobs of Oudh and the Univ. of Lucknow.

Lucretius \\lu-'krē-shəs\\ *in full* Titus Lucretius Carus (96?–c.55 B.C.) Latin poet and philosopher. His long poem *On the Nature of Things* is the fullest statement of the physical theory of EPICURUS. In it he established the principles of atomism and refuted the rival theories of HERACLEITUS, EMPEDOCLES, and ANAXAGORAS; demonstrated the mortality of the soul; described the mechanics of sense perception and thought and condemned sexual passion; and described the creation and working of the celestial bodies and the evolution of life and human society.

Lucullus \\lü-'kə-ləs\\, **Lucius Licinius** (117?–58/56 B.C.) Roman general who served as CONSUL in 74 B.C. He fought alongside SULLA and was the only officer to take part in Sulla's march on Rome. After Sulla's death, Lucullus drove MITHRADATES from Roman provinces and later invaded Armenia. Mutinies prevented complete victory, and Lucullus was replaced by POMPEY. His legendary hedonism and extravagance made "Lucullan" a synonym of "lavish."

Lucy Nickname for a 40%-complete HOMINID skeleton found at Hadar, Ethiopia, in 1974 and dated to 3.2 million years ago. The specimen is usually classed as *AUSTRALOPITHECUS afarensis*, and suggests—by virtue of its long arms, short legs, apelike chest and jaw, small brain, but relatively human pelvis—that bipedal locomotion preceded the development of a larger (humanlike) brain in hominid evolution. Lucy stood about 3 ft 7 in. (109 cm) and weighed about 60 lbs (27 kg).

Luda See DALIAN

Luddite Member of organized groups of English craftsmen who destroyed the textile machinery that was replacing them. The movement began in Nottingham in 1811. The Luddites, named after a probably mythical leader, Ned Ludd, often enjoyed local support. Harsh repressive measures by the government included a mass trial at York in 1813 that resulted in many hangings and banishments.

Ludendorff \\'lü-dᵊn-ˌdòrf\\, **Erich** (1865–1937) German general. In World War I he was appointed chief of staff to Paul von HINDENBURG, and in 1916 the two generals were given supreme military control. In 1917 Ludendorff approved unrestricted submarine warfare against the British, which led to the U.S.'s entry into the war. In 1918 his offensive on the Western Front failed and he demanded an armistice, but then insisted the war continue when he realized the severity of the ARMISTICE conditions. Political leaders opposed him, and he resigned his post. Insisting he

Erich Ludendorff, c.1930

had been betrayed, for the next 20 years he led a bizarre life, becoming a leader of reactionary political movements and taking part in the BEER HALL PUTSCH (1923). He served in Parliament as a Nazi (1924–28) and developed a belief that "supernatural powers"—Jewry, Christianity, Freemasonry—had deprived him and Germany of victory in World War I.

Ludlum, Robert (1927–2001) U.S. author of spy thrillers. Born in New York City, he worked as an actor and producer before turning to writing. Among his best-sellers were *The Osterman Weekend* (1972; film, 1983) and *The Bourne Identity* (1980; films, 1988, 2002). Though critics often found his plots unlikely and his prose uninspired, his fast-paced combination of international espionage, conspiracy, and mayhem led to sales exceeding 200 million copies.

Ludwig, Carl F(riedrich) W(ilhelm) (1816–1895) German physician. He invented devices to record arterial blood-pressure changes, measure blood flow, and separate gases from blood. He was the first to keep animal organs alive outside the body, and he hypothesized a filtering role for the kidney. Nearly 200 of Ludwig's students became prominent scientists, and he is regarded as the founder of the physicochemical school of PHYSIOLOGY.

Ludwig I \\'lüt-vik\\ *or* **Louis I** (1786–1868) King of Bavaria (1825–48). The son of MAXIMILIAN I, Ludwig won early acclaim as a liberal, but after his accession he came to distrust all democratic institutions. An outstanding patron of the arts, he collected the art works that fill Munich's museums and transformed Munich into the artistic center of Germany; his planning created the city's present layout and classic style. He caused scandal by his affair with Lola MONTEZ, and at the outbreak of the REVOLUTIONS OF 1848 he abdicated in favor of his son Maximilian II.

Ludwig II *or* **Louis II** *known as* **Mad King Ludwig** (1845–1886) King of Bavaria (1864–86). The son of Maximilian II, he supported Prussia in the FRANCO–PRUSSIAN WAR (1870–71). He brought his territories into the new German empire in 1871 but concerned himself only intermittently with affairs of state, preferring a life of increasingly morbid seclusion. He was a lifelong patron of the composer Richard WAGNER. He developed a mania for extravagant building projects, including NEUSCHWANSTEIN CASTLE. Formally declared insane, he drowned himself three days later.

Ludwig IV See LOUIS IV

Lugano \\lü-'gä-nō\\, **Lake** *or* **Lago Ceresio** \\che-'res-yō\\ Lake in Switzerland and Italy, located between MAGGIORE and COMO lakes. Straddling the border of the two countries, it has an area of 19 sq mi (49 sq km) and a maximum depth of 945 ft (288 m). The resort town of Lugano (pop., 1990: 26,000), Switzerland, is Italian in appearance.

Lugard \\lü-'gärd\\, **F(rederick) (John) D(ealtry)** *later* **Baron Lugard (of Abinger)** (1858–1945) British colonial administrator. He fought in Asia and N. Africa and later worked for the British E. Africa Co. and Royal Niger Co. He preceded the French in establishing trade routes centered at Buganda, the Middle Niger, and Bechuanaland. In Nigeria he served as high commissioner (1900–6) and governor and governor-general (1912–19). He succeeded in uniting the disparate N and S districts and greatly influenced British colonial policy by exercising control through native rulers and respecting native customs.

Lugdunensis \\ˌləg-də-'nen-sis\\ Roman province in GAUL. It extended northwest from its capital at Lugdunum (modern LYON) and included the land between the SEINE and LOIRE rivers up to BRITTANY and the Atlantic coast. It was conquered by Julius CAESAR and became a Roman province in 27 B.C. under Caesar AUGUSTUS.

luge \\'lüzh\\ Sled-racing using a small sled (luge) that is ridden in a supine position and steered with the feet and a hand rope. Dating to the 16th cent., luge is a traditional winter sport especially in Austria. The course used is similar to a BOBSLEDDING course, and speeds above 60 mph (100 kph) are common. Luge became an Olympic sport in 1964.

Lugosi \\lə-'gō-sē\\, **Bela** *orig.* Bela Ferenc Dezso Blasko (1882–1956) Hungarian-U.S. film actor. He acted with the National Theater in Budapest (1913–19) before coming to the U.S. in 1921. He directed and starred in the play *Dracula* in New York in 1927; he reprised the role, ideally suited for his aristocratic manner and heavy accent, in the movie *Dracula* (1931). His other horror movies included *The Black Cat* (1934), *Mark of the Vampire* (1935), *Son of Frankenstein* (1939), and *The Ape Man* (1943).

Lukacs \\'lü-ˌkäch\\, **Gyorgy** (1885–1971) Hungarian philosopher and critic. In *History and Class Consciousness* (1923), he developed a Marxist philosophy of history and laid the basis for his literary criticism by linking the development of form in art with the history of the class struggle. A major figure during the 1956 Hungarian uprising, he was exiled until 1957. His works include the essay collection *Soul and Form* (1911) and *The Historical Novel* (1955). His earlier work, including *Theory of the Novel* (1920), is now considered superior to his later Stalinist-influenced criticism.

Luke, St. (fl.1st cent. A.D.) In Christian tradition, the author of the third GOSPEL and the Acts of the Apostles. He wrote in Greek and is considered the most literary of the NEW TESTAMENT writers. He was not an eyewitness to the ministry of JESUS, but was a companion to St. PAUL, who called him the "beloved physician." Tradition holds that he was a gentile and a native of Antioch in Syria, and that he died a martyr.

Lully \\lü-'lē\\, **Jean-Baptiste** *orig.* Giovanni Battista Lulli (1632–1687) French (Italian-born) composer. Born in Florence, he was sent to a noble French household at age 13 as valet. Having learned guitar, organ, violin, and dancing, Lully became a dancer and musician for the king and at 30 was put in charge of all royal music. In the 1660s he composed the incidental music for MOLIÈRE's plays as well as those of France's great tragedians. In the 1670s he obtained the sole patent to present opera and began the series of "lyric tragedies," most with librettos by Philippe Quinault

Jean-Baptiste Lully Portrait by an unknown artist, 17th cent.

(1635–1688), for which he is known, including *Alceste* (1674), *Atys* (1676), and *Armide* (1686). The orchestra he developed was an important forerunner of the modern orchestra. His style prevailed in France for many decades after his death.

Lully, Raymond See Raymond LLULL

lumber Collective term for harvested WOOD, whether cut into logs, heavy timbers, or members used in light-frame construction. Lumber is classified as hardwood or softwood. The term often refers specifically to the products derived from logs in a sawmill. Conversion of logs to sawed lumber involves debarking, sawing into boards or slabs, edging, crosscutting to square the ends and remove defects, grading according to strength and appearance, and drying. Drying below the fiber-saturation point results in shrinkage and greater strength, stiffness, and density and better prepares the wood for finishing.

Lumet \\'lü-mət\\, **Sidney** (b.1924) U.S. television and film director. Born in Philadelphia, he directed over 200 television dramas for CBS (1951–57), including *Playhouse 90* and *Studio One* productions, before making his debut as a movie director with the acclaimed *Twelve Angry Men* (1957). He showed himself a master of psychological drama with such films as *The Fugitive Kind* (1960), *Fail Safe* (1964), *The Pawnbroker* (1965), *Serpico* (1973), *Dog Day Afternoon* (1975), *Network* (1976), *Prince of the City* (1981), and *The Verdict* (1982).

Lumière \\lᵫ-'myer\\, **Auguste and Louis** (1862–1954, 1864–1948) French inventors. In 1882 Louis developed a method of making photographic plates, and by 1894 the brothers' factory was producing 15 million plates a year. They patented their combination movie camera and projector, the Cinématographe, in 1895; their film "Workers Leaving the Lumière Factory" is considered the first movie. In 1896 the brothers, led by Louis, made over 40 films recording everyday French life. They also made the first newsreels, sending crews all over the world. In addition to the films he directed, Louis served as producer for some 2,000 films.

luminescence Process by which an excited material emits light in a process not caused solely by a rise in temperature.

K L

The excitation is usually achieved with ULTRAVIOLET RADIATION, X RAYS, ELECTRONS, alpha particles, ELECTRIC FIELDS, or chemical energy. The color of the light emitted is determined by the material; the intensity depends on both the material and the input energy. Light emissions from neon lamps, television and computer screens, fluorescent lamps, and fireflies are examples. See also BIOLUMINESCENCE, FLUORESCENCE, PHOSPHORESCENCE.

Luminism Painting style that emphasizes a particular clarity of light, characteristic of a group of U.S. painters of the later 19th cent., influenced by the HUDSON RIVER SCHOOL. Typically landscapes or seascapes, with sky occupying nearly half of the composition, Luminist works are distinguished by cool, clear colors and meticulously detailed objects modeled by light. The most prominent Luminists were M. J. HEADE and FitzHugh Lane (1804–1865).

Lumumba \lə-'mùm-bə\, **Patrice (Hemery)** (1925–1961) African nationalist leader, first prime minister of the Democratic Republic of the Congo (June–Sept. 1960). A labor organizer, Lumumba founded the Mouvement National Congolais, Congo's first nationwide political party, in 1958. His militant nationalism at a PAN-AFRICAN MOVEMENT conference attracted attention, and in 1960 he was asked to form the first independent Congolese government. His rival Moise TSHOMBE immediately announced the secession of Katanga province. When Belgian troops arrived to sustain the secession, Lumumba appealed to the U.N. and then to the Soviet Union. He was dismissed by Pres. Joseph KASAVUBU and soon thereafter assassinated by Tshombe loyalists. His death caused a scandal throughout Africa, where he was looked on as a leader of Pan-Africanism.

Luna Any of a series of 24 unmanned Soviet lunar probes, launched between 1959 and 1976. Luna 2 (1959) was the first spacecraft to strike the MOON; Luna 3 (1959) was the first to circle it and took the first pictures of its far side. Luna 9 (1966) made the first lunar soft landing. Luna 16 (1970) was the first unmanned spacecraft to carry lunar soil samples back to earth. Luna 17 (1970) soft-landed a robot vehicle for exploration; its television equipment sent live pictures of the moon's surface.

Luna See SELENE

Lunacharsky, Anatoly (Vasilyevich) (1875–1933) Russian politician and writer. Deported in 1898 for his revolutionary activities, he joined the Bolsheviks in 1904 and disseminated propaganda to Russian students and political refugees abroad. Appointed commissar for education in 1917, he did much to preserve works of art during the Russian Civil War, encouraged innovation in the theater and in education, and published plays of his own.

Lunda empire See LUBA-LUNDA STATES

lung Either of two light, spongy, elastic organs in the chest, used for breathing. Contraction of the DIAPHRAGM and the muscles between the ribs draws air into the lungs through the TRACHEA, which splits into two primary bronchi, one per lung. Each bronchus branches repeatedly, eventuating in the PULMONARY ALVEOLI. There, oxygen in the inspired gas is exchanged for carbon dioxide from the blood in the surrounding CAPILLARIES (see PULMONARY CIRCULATION). Adequate tissue oxygen supply depends on sufficient distribution of air (ventilation) and blood (perfusion) in the lungs. Lung injuries or diseases (e.g., EMPHYSEMA, EMBOLISM, PNEUMONIA) can affect either or both.

lung cancer Malignant tumor of the LUNG, the leading cause of CANCER-related death in the U.S. Four major types (squamous-cell carcinoma, adenocarcinoma, large-cell carcinoma, and small-cell carcinoma) have roughly equal prevalence. Most cases are due to long-term cigarette SMOKING. Other risk factors include passive inhalation ("secondhand smoke") and exposure to RADON or ASBESTOS. Symptoms, including coughing, chest pain, and shortness of breath, seldom appear until lung cancer is advanced, when treatment with surgery, chemotherapy, and radiation or some combination of the three is less effective.

Lung-shan culture See LONGSHAN CULTURE

Lunt, Alfred and Lynn Fontanne (*orig.* Lillie Louise) (1892–1977, 1887–1983) U.S. acting team. Born in Milwaukee, Lunt starred in *Clarence* on Broadway in 1919. Fontanne, born in England, made her New York debut in 1910. She

and Lunt married in 1922 and performed with the THEATRE GUILD in 1924–29. They acted together in more than 25 plays, including *Arms and the Man* (1925), *Elizabeth the Queen* (1930), *Design for Living* (1933), *Idiots Delight* (1936), and *The Visit* (1958). Considered the foremost acting couple of the U.S. theater, they were acclaimed for the subtlety and effortless cooperation of their performances, especially in comedies by G. B. SHAW and Noël COWARD.

Lunyu \'lùn-'yǖ\ *English* **Analects** One of four Confucian texts that made up the FOUR BOOKS. Scholars consider *Lunyu* the most reliable source of the doctrine of CONFUCIUS. It covers almost all the basic ethical concepts of CONFUCIANISM, including benevolence, the superior man, heaven, the doctrine of the mean, and rectification of names. It also contains many direct quotations from Confucius. See also NEO-CONFUCIANISM.

Luo \lə-'wō\ People of the flat country near Lake Victoria in W Kenya and N Uganda. Numbering 3.2 million, the Luo are the third-largest ethnic group in Kenya. Many work as agricultural laborers and in urban occupations. Most are Christians. See also NILOTES.

Lupercalia \ˌlü-pər-'kā-lē-ə\ Ancient Roman festival held each February 15. Its origins are uncertain, but it may have been connected with a primitive deity who protected herds from wolves or with the legendary she-wolf who nursed ROMULUS AND REMUS. The festival began with the sacrifice of goats and a dog. After all had feasted, the priests cut thongs from the skins of the sacrificed animals and ran around the Palatine hill, striking at any woman who came near them; a blow from the thong was supposed to bestow fertility.

lupine *or* **lupin** \'lü-pən\ Any of about 200 species of herbaceous and partly woody plants that make up the genus *Lupinus* in the pea family (see LEGUME), found throughout the Mediterranean and especially on the prairies of W N. America. Many are grown in the U.S. as ornamentals, and a few species are useful as cover or forage crops. Herbaceous lupines, which grow up to 4 ft (1.25 m) tall, have low, divided leaves and an upright flower spike.

lupus erythematosus \'lü-pəs-ˌer-ə-ˌthē-mə-'tō-səs\ Either of two inflammatory AUTOIMMUNE DISEASES, both more common in women. In the discoid type, a skin disease, red patches with grayish brown scales appear on the upper cheeks and nose, scalp, lips, and/or inner cheeks. Sunlight worsens it. Antimalarial drugs may help. The second type, systemic lupus erythematosus (SLE), may affect any organ or structure, especially the skin (with marks like those of the discoid type), kidneys, heart, nervous system, and lymph nodes, with acute episodes and remissions. Symptoms vary widely. Treatment includes pain relief, control of inflammation, and trying to limit damage to vital organs.

Luria \'lür-yä\, **Isaac (ben Solomon)** (1534–1572) Jewish mystic and founder of a school of KABBALA. He pursued rabbinic studies in Egypt, dedicating himself to the study of the Kabbala with messianic fervor, and in 1570 he journeyed to a center of the movement in Galilee. He died two years later in an epidemic, having written little. The Lurianic Kabbala, a collection of Luria's doctrines recorded after his death by a pupil, had great influence on later Jewish mysticism and on HASIDISM. It calls for restoration of the world's original harmony through ritual meditation and secret combinations of words.

Luria \'lùr-ē-ə\, **Salvador (Edward)** (1912–1991) Italian-U.S. biologist. In 1942 he obtained an electron micrograph of bacteriophage particles that confirmed earlier descriptions of their structure. In 1943 he and Max DELBRÜCK showed that viruses can undergo permanent changes in their hereditary material. He also proved that the simultaneous existence of phage-resistant bacteria with phage-sensitive bacteria in the same culture was a result of the selection of spontaneous bacterial mutants. In 1945 he and A. D. Hershey (1908–1997) demonstrated the existence not only of such bacterial mutants but also of spontaneous phage mutants. The three shared a 1969 Nobel Prize.

Lusaka \lü-'sä-kä\ City (pop., 1990: 982,000), capital of Zambia. In the 1890s the area was taken by the British S. Africa Co. during the formation of Northern RHODESIA; it became the capital in 1935. After the federation of Northern and Southern Rhodesia in 1953, it was a center of the civil-disobedience movement that led to the creation of independent Zambia in 1960. The Univ. of Zambia (founded 1965) is located nearby.

Lüshun *or* **Lü-shun** \ˈlüˈ-ˈshùn\ *formerly* **Port Arthur** Former city, Liaoning province, NE China. Situated at the S tip of the Liaodong Peninsula, near DALIAN, it was a staging post as early as the 2nd cent. B.C. Fortified under the MING DYNASTY, it was captured by the MANCHUS in 1633. In 1878 it became the chief base for China's first modern naval force. Leased to Russia in 1898, it was captured by Japan (1905) in the RUSSO–JAPANESE WAR. It was a Sino-Soviet military base 1945–55. The city was incorporated into Dalian in 1960.

Lusitania British ocean liner sunk by a German submarine off Ireland on May 7, 1915. Despite warnings to avoid the area and to use the evasive tactic of zigzagging, the crew ignored these recommendations. Though unarmed, the ship was carrying munitions for the Allies. The loss of life—1,198 people drowned, including 128 U.S. citizens—outraged public opinion. The U.S. protested, and Germany limited its submarine campaign. When it renewed unrestricted submarine warfare, the U.S. entered World War I in April 1917.

Lussac, Joseph Gay- See Joseph GAY-LUSSAC

luster Appearance of a mineral surface in terms of its light-reflecting qualities. Luster depends on a mineral's refractivity (see REFRACTION), transparency, and structure. Variations in these properties produce different kinds of luster, from metallic (e.g., gold) to dull (e.g., chalk).

lustered glass *or* **lustred glass** Art glass of the ART NOUVEAU style, delicately iridescent with rich colors, mimicking the iridescent sheen produced by the corrosion of ancient buried glassware. In 1893 L. C. TIFFANY founded the Stourbridge Glass Co. to produce lustered drinking glasses, bowls, vases, lamps, and jewelry. His lustered glass was produced by metallic pigments applied to opaque glass. Tiffany's wares were so popular that he made thousands of pieces annually until 1933.

Lu-ta See DALIAN

lute Plucked STRINGED INSTRUMENT popular in 16th–17th-cent. Europe. It originated from the Arab ud, which reached Europe in the 13th cent. It has a deep pear-shaped body with an ornamental soundhole and a fretted neck with a bent-back pegbox. In later years it acquired several unstopped bass strings. It became the preferred instrument for cultivated amateurs, who often used it to accompany songs.

Luther, Martin (1483–1546) German priest who sparked the REFORMATION. The son of a miner, he entered an Augustinian monastery in 1505, and later became a professor of biblical theology at the Univ. of Wittenberg. He was shocked by the clerical corruption he witnessed in Rome in 1510, and became troubled by fear of divine retributive justice. His spiritual crisis was resolved when he hit on the idea of justification by faith, the doctrine that salvation is granted as a gift through God's grace. He urged church reform, protesting the sale of INDULGENCES and other abuses, and in 1517 he posted his NINETY-FIVE THESES on the door of the castle church in Wittenberg. In 1521 he was excommunicated by Pope LEO X, and under a storm of criticism he took refuge in a castle in Eisenach, the Wartburg. There he translated the Bible into German so that the common people would be able to read it; his superb translation is regarded as the greatest landmark in the history of the GERMAN LANGUAGE. In 1525 he married a former nun, Katherina von Bora. Though his preaching sparked the PEASANTS' WAR (1524–26), his denunciation of the peasants contributed to their defeat. His break with the papacy led to the founding of the Lutheran Church (see LUTHERANISM), whose confession of faith, or AUGSBURG CONFESSION, was produced in 1530. Luther's writings included hymns and a liturgy as well as many theological works.

Lutheranism Protestant movement founded on the principles of Martin LUTHER. Lutheranism arose at the start of the REFORMATION, after Luther posted his NINETY-FIVE THESES in Wittenberg. It spread through much of Germany and into Scandinavia, where it was established by law. It was brought to the New World by Dutch and Scandinavian colonists. Its doctrines are contained in the catechisms of Luther and in the AUGSBURG CONFESSION. Lutheran doctrine emphasizes salvation by faith alone and the primacy of the BIBLE as the church's authority. The Lutheran World Federation is based in Geneva. See also PIETISM.

Lutoslawski \ˌlü-tə-ˈsläv-skē\, **Witold** (1913–1994) Polish composer. He initially became known as a pianist. His international reputation was secured by his colorful *Concerto for Orchestra* (1954), and later his *Funeral Music* (1958). From the late 1950s his works incorporate limited aleatory, often using it as a contrast to traditional genres, such as fugue. His four brilliantly orchestrated symphonies, *Livre pour orchestra* (1968), and string quartet (1964) are widely admired.

Lutuli \lə-ˈtü-lē\, **Albert (John Mvumbi)** (1898–1967) ZULU chief and president of the AFRICAN NATIONAL CONGRESS (1952–60). Lutuli taught and served a small community as chief before being elected ANC president. Frequently imprisoned for anti-apartheid activities, in 1960 he became the first African to win a Nobel Peace Prize. He wrote *Let My People Go* (1962).

Lutyens \ˈlə-chənz\, **Edwin L(andseer)** (*later* **Sir Edwin**) (1869–1944) British architect. The house at Munstead Wood (1896), designed for Gertrude JEKYLL, established his reputation. For his later country houses, many designed in collaboration with Jekyll, Lutyens adapted past styles to contemporary domestic life in delightful ways. For the new Indian capital at Delhi, he devised a plan based on hexagons separated by broad avenues; his Viceroy's House (1912–30) combined Classical and Indian motifs. After World War I he became architect to the Imperial War Graves Commission, designing the Cenotaph in London (1919–20) and other memorials.

Luxembourg \ˈlʌk-səm-ˌbürk, *Engl* ˈlək-səm-ˌbərg\ *officially* **Grand Duchy of Luxembourg** Country, W Europe. Area: 998 sq mi (2,586 sq km). Population (2000): 439,000. Capital: LUXEMBOURG. Most of the population are ethnically

French or German. Languages: Luxembourgian, French, German. Religions: Roman Catholicism, Protestantism (Lutheranism), Judaism (a small minority). Currency: euro. At 51 mi (82 km) long and 35 mi (56 km) wide, it is divided into two regions: the Oesling, an extension of the Ardennes Mtns. in the N third of the country, consisting of a high plateau dissected by river valleys; and the Bon Pays, or Gutland, a rolling plateau that occupies the rest of the country. Luxembourg's economy is largely based on heavy industry and international trade and banking, and its per capita income is the second highest in the world (after Switzerland). It is a constitutional monarchy with two legislative houses; its chief of state is the Grand Duke, and the head of government is the prime minister. At the time of Roman conquest (57–50 B.C.), the Luxembourg area was inhabited by a Belgic tribe, the Treveri. After A.D. 400, Germanic tribes invaded the region. It later came under CHARLEMAGNE's empire. Made a duchy in 1354, it was ceded to the house of BURGUNDY in 1441 and to the HABSBURGS in 1477. In the mid-16th cent. it became part of the Spanish Netherlands. The Congress of VIENNA in 1815 made it a grand duchy and awarded it to the Netherlands. After an uprising in 1830, its W portion became part of Belgium, while the remainder was held by the Netherlands. In 1867 the European powers guaranteed the neutrality and independence of Luxembourg. In the late 19th cent. it built a great steel industry by exploiting its extensive iron-ore deposits. It was invaded and occupied by Germany in both World Wars. Following World War II, it abandoned its neutrality by joining NATO in 1949. It joined the Benelux Economic Union in 1944 and the EUROPEAN ECONOMIC COMMUNITY in 1957. A member of the EUROPEAN UNION, its economy has continued to expand.

Luxembourg City (pop., 1997 est.: 78,000), capital of LUXEMBOURG. A rocky promontory along the Alzette River was the site of a Roman fortress and later of a Frankish castle, around which the medieval town developed. Under Siegfried, count of Ardennes, the duchy of Luxembourg became independent in 963. The strongest in Europe after GIBRALTAR, the castle was garrisoned by the Prussians as a bulwark of the GERMAN CONFEDERATION 1815–66. The city is an industrial and financial center. It is the seat of the European Court of Justice and several administrative offices of the EUROPEAN COMMUNITY.

Luxemburg \'lük-səm-ˌbürk, *Engl* 'lək-səm-ˌbərg\, **Rosa** (1871–1919) Polish-German political radical. As a Jew in Russian-controlled Poland, she was drawn early into underground political activism. Having obtained her doctorate, in 1892 she cofounded what would become the Polish Communist Party. The RUSSIAN REVOLUTION OF 1905 convinced her that the world revolution would originate in Russia. An advocate of the mass strike as the proletariat's most important tool, she was imprisoned in Warsaw for agitation, then moved to Berlin to teach and write (1907–14). Early in World War I, she cofounded the Spartacus League, and in 1918 she oversaw its transformation into the German Communist Party; she was assassinated less than a month later. She believed in a democratic path to socialism and opposed what she recognized as Vladimir LENIN's emerging dictatorship.

Luxor \'lək-ˌsȯr, 'lük-ˌsȯr\ City (pop., 1991 est.: 142,000), Upper Egypt. Its name has been given to the S half of the ruins of THEBES. It is centered on the Great Temple of AMON, built on the E bank of the NILE RIVER by King AMENHOTEP III in the 14th cent. B.C. TUTANKHAMEN and Horemheb completed the temple, and RAMSES II added to it. The town is a tourist and market center. See also KARNAK.

luxury tax Excise levy on goods or services considered to be luxuries rather than necessities (e.g., jewelry and perfume). Luxury taxes may be levied with the intent of taxing the rich or in a deliberate effort to alter consumption patterns, either for moral reasons or in times of national emergency.

Luzon \lü-'zȯn\ Island (pop., 2000: 42,839,000), PHILIPPINES. The country's largest island, with an area of 40,420 sq mi (104,688 sq km), it is the site of QUEZON CITY and MANILA, the nation's capital. Located in the N Philippine archipelago, it is separated from TAIWAN by the Luzon Strait. It represents 35% of the nation's land area and over 50% of its population. It is largely mountainous; in 1991 the eruption of Mt. PINATUBO altered the island's geography.

Lviv \lə-'vē-ü, *Engl* lə-'vēf\ *or* **Lvov** \lə-'vȯf\ City (pop., 1998 est.: 793,000), W Ukraine. Founded about 1256 by Prince Daniel of Galicia, it came under Polish rule in 1349. It became one of the great medieval trading towns and changed hands many times. It was taken by the COSSACKS in 1648 and by the Swedes in 1704. Given to Austria in 1772, it passed to Poland in 1919. It was seized by the Soviet Union in 1939 and, after German occupation, annexed by the So-

viets in 1945. It is now a center for Ukrainian culture and the seat of a university (founded 1661).

Lvov \lə-'vȯf\, **Georgy (Yevgenyevich), Prince** (1861–1925) Russian politician, first head of the provisional government established during the RUSSIAN REVOLUTION OF 1917. Chairman of the All-Russian Union of Zemstvos (1914) he won the respect of political liberals and army commanders. In March 1917 he became premier but was unable to satisfy the increasingly radical demands of the populace. He resigned in July, in favor of Aleksandr KERENSKY. Arrested when the Bolsheviks seized power, he escaped and settled in Paris.

Lyallpur See FAISALABAD

Lyautey \lyō-'tā\, **Louis-Herbert-Gonzalve** (1854–1934) French soldier and first colonial administrator in Morocco under the Protectorate (1912–56). Early in his career he served in Indochina, Madagascar, and Algeria. As resident general in Morocco (1912–24), he pacified the colony and advocated the principle of indirect rule.

lyceum movement \lī-'sē-əm\ Form of adult education popular in the U.S. during the mid-19th cent. The lyceums were local associations that sponsored lectures and debates on current issues. The first was founded in 1826, and by 1834 there were around 3,000 in the Northeast and Midwest. They attracted such speakers as Ralph Waldo EMERSON, Frederick DOUGLASS, Henry David THOREAU, Daniel WEBSTER, Nathaniel HAWTHORNE, and Susan B. ANTHONY. After the Civil War, the movement blended into the CHAUTAUQUA MOVEMENT.

lychee See LITCHI

Lycurgus \lī-'kər-gəs\ (fl.7th cent. B.C.?) Legendary founder of the legal institutions of ancient SPARTA. Because sources give differing accounts of his career, some scholars conclude that he never existed, but many believe that a man named Lycurgus instituted drastic reforms in Sparta after the revolt of the HELOTS in the 7th cent. B.C. He is thought to have devised the militarized communal system that made Sparta unique among Greek city-states and to have determined the powers of the council and the assembly.

Lydia Ancient land, W ASIA MINOR, in present-day Turkey. It profoundly influenced the Ionian Greeks in the 7th–6th cent. B.C., through such developments as metallic COINAGE and permanent retail shops. Conquered by the Persians under CYRUS THE GREAT in 546 B.C., it later passed to Syria, Pergamum, and the Romans.

lye Alkaline (see ALKALI) liquid extracted by soaking wood ashes in water, commonly used for washing and in making SOAP. More generally, lye is any strong alkaline solution or solid, such as sodium hydroxide (CAUSTIC SODA) or potassium hydroxide (caustic potash).

Lyell \'lī-əl\, **Charles** (*later* **Sir Charles**) (1797–1875) Scottish geologist. While studying law at Oxford Univ., he became interested in geology. He came to believe that there were natural (as opposed to supernatural) explanations for all geologic phenomena, a position he supported with many examples in his three-volume *Principles of Geology* (1830–33). A recognized leader in his field, he gained the friendship of other well-known men of science, including Charles DARWIN, whose *Origin of Species* (1859) persuaded Lyell to accept evolution. Lyell was largely responsible for the general acceptance of UNIFORMITARIANISM in geology.

Lyly \'li-lē\, **John** (1554?–1606) English writer. Lyly gained fame with two prose romances, *Euphues* (1578) and *Euphues and His England* (1580). The novels inspired "euphuism," an elegant, extravagant Elizabethan literary style, and made Lyly the first English prose stylist to leave an enduring impression on the language. As a dramatist he contributed to the development of prose dialogue in English comedy. *Endimion* (performed 1588) is considered his finest play.

Lyme disease Tick-borne bacterial disease identified in 1975, named for Old Lyme, Conn. It is caused by a SPIROCHETE, *Borrelia burgdorferi,* transmitted by tiny deer TICKS, which pick it up in the blood of infected animals. Humans can be bitten by deer ticks in tall grass or fallen leaves. Lyme disease has three stages: a target-shaped rash, often with flulike symptoms; migrating arthritic pain and neurological symptoms, and crippling ARTHRITIS, with symptoms like those of multiple sclerosis. Most cases do not progress beyond the first stage, but those that do reach the third within two years. Prevention involves avoiding tick bites. Diagnosis can be difficult, especially if the initial rash is not noticed. Early antibiotic treatment can prevent progression. Advanced cases need more powerful antibiotics, and symptoms may recur.

lymph Pale fluid that bathes tissues, maintaining fluid balance and removing bacteria. It enters the BLOOD system at a vein under the collarbone that it reaches via channels and ducts, being driven through them mainly by surrounding muscle activity. Lymph contains LYMPHOCYTES and macrophages, the primary cells of the IMMUNE SYSTEM. See also LYMPHATIC SYSTEM.

lymphatic system System of LYMPH NODES, vessels, and nodules, and LYMPHOID TISSUE, including the THYMUS, SPLEEN, TONSILS, and BONE MARROW, through which LYMPH circulates and is filtered. Its primary function is to return proteins, waste products, and fluids to the blood; molecules too big to enter the CAPILLARIES pass through the more permeable walls of lymphatic vessels. Valves keep lymph flowing in one direction, more slowly than blood and at a lower pressure. The lymphatic system also has a role in the IMMUNE SYSTEM. Nodes filter bacteria and foreign matter from lymph. Blockage of a lymph vessel may cause fluid to collect in the tissues, producing tissue swelling. Other lymphatic-system disorders include lymphocytic LEUKEMIAS and LYMPHOMA. See also RETICULOENDOTHELIAL SYSTEM.

lymph node Small, rounded mass of LYMPHOID TISSUE contained in CONNECTIVE TISSUE. Lymph nodes occur all along lymphatic vessels, with clusters in certain areas (e.g., neck, groin, armpits). They filter bacteria and other foreign materials out of LYMPH and expose them to LYMPHOCYTES and macrophages that can engulf them; these cells multiply in response to accumulation of such materials, which is why lymph nodes swell during INFECTIONS. The nodes also produce lymphocytes and ANTIBODIES, to be carried by lymph throughout the LYMPHATIC SYSTEM. Many cancers may invade lymphatic vessels, which carry cells to lymph nodes, where they grow into secondary tumors. Lymph nodes are therefore removed in cancer surgery to detect or prevent tumor spread. See also HODGKIN'S DISEASE, LYMPHOMA.

lymphocyte Type of LEUKOCYTE fundamental to the IMMUNE SYSTEM, regulating and participating in acquired IMMUNITY. Each has receptor molecules on its surface that bind to a specific ANTIGEN. The two primary types are B and T CELLS. When a B cell binds to an antigen, it multiplies to form a clone of identical cells. Some of these, acted on by helper T cells, differentiate into plasma cells that produce ANTIBODIES against the antigen. Others (memory cells) multiply, providing long-term IMMUNITY to the antigen.

lymphoid tissue Cells, tissues, and organs composing the IMMUNE SYSTEM, including the BONE MARROW, THYMUS, SPLEEN, and LYMPH NODES. The most highly organized components are the thymus and lymph nodes, and the least organized are the cells that wander in the loose CONNECTIVE-TISSUE spaces under membranes lining most body systems, where they can establish lymph nodules (local LYMPHOCYTE production centers) in response to ANTIGENS. The most common lymphoid tissue cell is the lymphocyte. See also IMMUNITY, LYMPHATIC SYSTEM.

lymphoma \lim-'fō-mə\ Any of a group of malignant diseases (see CANCER) that usually start in the LYMPH NODES or LYMPHOID TISSUES. The two major types, HODGKIN'S DISEASE and non-Hodgkin's lymphoma, each have several subtypes. Diagnosis of either type requires BIOPSY, usually from the lymph nodes.

lymphoreticuloma See HODGKIN'S DISEASE

lynching Execution of a presumed offender by a mob without trial, under the pretense of administering justice. Lynching has often occurred under unsettled conditions. The term derives from the name of Charles Lynch, a Virginian who headed an irregular court to persecute Loyalists during the American Revolution. In the U.S., lynching was widely used in the post-Reconstruction South against blacks, often to intimidate other blacks from exercising their civil rights.

Lynn, Loretta *orig.* Loretta Webb (b.1935) U.S. COUNTRY-MUSIC singer. Born in a coalminer's shack in Butcher Hollow, Ky., Lynn married at 13 and bore the first of six children the next year. In 1960 she released her first single, "Honky Tonk Girl." In 1962 she joined the GRAND OLE OPRY, and by the mid-1960s such hits as "Don't Come Home A-Drinkin'" had made her one of country's biggest stars. Her signature song, "Coal Miner's Daughter," provided the title of a bestselling autobiography and a popular film (1980).

Lynn Canal Deep fjord, SE Alaska. A gateway to the Klondike region, it is 80 mi (129 km) long and 6 mi (10 km) wide. The northernmost fjord to penetrate the Coast Mtns., it was named in 1794 by Capt. George Vancouver (1757–1798) for his birthplace, King's Lynn, England.

lynx Short-tailed forest CAT (*Felis lynx*) of Europe, Asia, and N N. America. The Canada lynx is sometimes regarded as a distinct species (*Felis canadensis*). The lynx has long legs, large paws, tufted ears, hairy soles, and a broad, short head and a bushy ruff on the neck. Its fur has been used for trimming garments. Lynx are approximately 30–40 in. (80–100 cm) long, without the 4–8-in. (10–20-cm) tail, and stand about 24 in. (60 cm) high at the shoulder. They weigh 20–45 lbs (10–20 kg). Nocturnal and silent except during mating season, lynx live alone or in small groups. They climb and swim well, and feed on birds, small mammals, and occasionally deer.

Lyon \'lyōⁿ\ *English* **Lyons** \'lyōⁿ, 'lī-ənz\ City (pop., 1999: 445,000), E central France. Located at the confluence of the RHÔNE and SAÔNE rivers, it was founded as the Roman military colony Lugdunum in 43 B.C. and became a principal city of Gaul. It was incorporated into the Holy Roman Empire in 1032 and into the kingdom of France in 1312. By the 17th cent. it was the silk-manufacturing center of Europe. It was a center of the French RESISTANCE during World War II. A major river port, it has a diversified economy. Its buildings include a Roman theater, a 12th-cent. Gothic cathedral, and a 15th-cent. palace.

Lyon, Mary (Mason) (1797–1849) U.S. pioneer in higher education for women. Born in Buckland, Mass., she supported herself from age 17 by teaching. The demand for the young women she had trained led to her plan for a permanent instructional institution for women. The school she founded in S. Hadley, Mass., opened in 1837 as the Mount Holyoke Female Seminary (see MOUNT HOLYOKE COLLEGE), and she served as its principal until her death.

lyre Stringed musical instrument consisting of a resonating body with two arms and a crossbar to which the strings extending from the resonator are attached. Lyrelike instruments existed in Sumer before 2000 B.C. Greek lyres were of two types, the KITHARA (for the professional) and the lyra (for the amateur). The latter had a rounded body and a curved back—often a tortoiseshell—and a skin belly.

lyrebird Either of two species of insectivorous suboscine PASSERINES (family Menuridae) named for the shape of their extremely long tail when spread in courtship display. Found in forests in SE Australia, lyrebirds are ground dwellers with chickenlike bodies. The male superb lyrebird displays in a small clearing, bringing his tail forward so that the beautiful white plumes form a lyre-shaped canopy over his head. While prancing in rhythm, he sings far-carrying melodious notes interspersed with perfect mimicry of other creatures and even of mechanical sounds.

Lysander \lī-'san-dər\ (d.395 B.C.) Spartan leader in the PELOPONNESIAN WAR. In his first year as admiral he won the support of the Persian king Cyrus the Younger and defeated the Athenian fleet at Notium (406). He destroyed the Athenian fleet at the Battle of AEGOSPOTAMI in 405, closing Athens's grain route and starving the city into surrender. He installed the THIRTY TYRANTS, and made his friends governors of Athens's former empire. He suffered a defeat when Sparta allowed the restoration of democracy in Athens (403). Having led his forces into Boeotia, he was killed while attacking Haliartus.

Lysenko \lə-'seŋ-kō\, **Trofim (Denisovich)** (1898–1976) Russian agronomist. During the Soviet famines of the 1930s he proposed imaginative techniques for enhancing crop yields, rejecting Mendelian GENETICS on the basis of unconfirmed

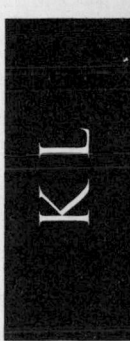

KL

experiments, and gained a large popular following. As director of the Soviet Academy of Sciences' Institute of Genetics (1940–65), he became the controversial "dictator" of Stalinist biology. He promised greater, more rapid, and less costly increases in crop yields than other biologists believed possible, claiming, among other things, that wheat plants under the right conditions would produce seeds of rye. Eventually his "grassland" system of crop rotation was abandoned in favor of cultivation with mineral fertilizers, and a hybrid-corn program based on the U.S. example was pursued. In 1964 his doctrines were officially discredited.

Trofim Lysenko, 1938

Lysias \'li-sē-əs\ (c.445–after 380 B.C.) Greek rhetorician. A metic, or resident foreigner, in Athens, he was forbidden to speak for himself; all his speeches were delivered by others. He was seized by the ruling oligarchy in 404 as a disaffected alien, but he escaped. He ranks with ANTIPHON as a writer of clear, simple prose of great effectiveness; many of his writings survive.

lysine \'lī-ˌsēn\ One of the essential AMINO ACIDS, present in many common PROTEINS. The lysine content of some important food plants (including wheat and corn) is so small that populations dependent on these grains for dietary protein suffer from lysine deficiency, affecting growth in children and general well-being in adults. It is used in biochemical and nutritional research, in pharmaceuticals, in fortified foods, and as a nutritional supplement and feed additive.

Lysippus *or* **Lysippos** \lī-'si-pəs\ (fl.c.370–300 B.C.) Greek sculptor. Famous for his figures' new and slender proportions and lifelike naturalism, he reportedly made more than 1,500 works, most in bronze. None survive, but some copies may be reliably ascribed to him, including *Apoxyomenos,* a young athlete scraping oil from his skin, and the colossal Heracles at Sikyon. He made many portrait busts of ALEXANDER THE GREAT from boyhood on; it was said that Alexander would have no other sculptor portray him.

lysogeny \lī-'sä-jə-nē\ Type of life cycle that takes place in a BACTERIOPHAGE after it infects certain types of BACTERIA. The bacteriophage's entire collection of genes enters the CHROMOSOME of the host bacterium and replicates with it. No offspring viruses are produced; the infecting virus lies dormant until the host is exposed to certain stimuli, such as ultraviolet light. At that point, the virus genome is unmasked and begins to multiply, forming new viruses. Finally, the bacterial host is destroyed (lysed), releasing virus particles to infect new bacterial cells.

lysosome \'lī-sə-ˌsōm\ Membrane-enclosed organelle found in all eukaryotic cells (see EUKARYOTE) that is responsible for the cell's digestion of macromolecules, old cell parts, and microorganisms. Lysosomes therefore contain a wide variety of enzymes. Many of the products of lysosomal digestion, including amino acids and nucleotides, are recycled back to the cell for reuse.

M

M16 rifle *or* **AR-15** ASSAULT RIFLE adopted as a standard weapon by the U.S. Army in 1967. It has semiautomatic and fully automatic capabilities. It weighs less than 8 lbs (3.6 kg), is 39 in. (99 cm) long, and fires .22-caliber ammunition at the rate of 700-950 rounds per minute. The M4/M4A1 is gradually replacing it. See also SPRINGFIELD RIFLE.

M31 See ANDROMEDA GALAXY

Ma, Yo-Yo (b.1955) U.S. (French-born) cellist. Born to Chinese parents in Paris, he made his cello debut when he was 5. His huge repertoire includes many works written especially for him. He is known for his collaborations with an unusual range of other musicians and artists and his energetic work on behalf of music programs for young people.

Maasai See MASAI

Maastricht Treaty \mä-'strikt, *Engl* 'mä-strikt\ *officially* Treaty on European Union. Agreement that established the EUROPEAN UNION (EU) as successor to the EUROPEAN COMMUNITY. It bestowed EU citizenship on every national of its member states, provided for the introduction of a central banking system and a common currency (see EURO), and committed the member states to work toward a common foreign and security policy. Signed in 1991, it took effect in 1993.

Mabuse See Jan GOSSART

macadam \mə-'ka-dəm\ Form of PAVEMENT invented by John MCADAM. McAdam's road cross-section consisted of a compacted subgrade of crushed granite or greenstone designed to support the load, covered by a surface of light stone to absorb wear and tear and shed water to the drainage ditches. Today crushed stone or gravel is placed on the compacted base course and bound together with ASPHALT cement or hot tar. A third layer to fill the spaces is then added and rolled.

macadamia \,ma-kə-'dā-mē-ə\ Any of about 10 species of ornamental evergreen trees in the family Proteaceae, and their edible, richly flavored NUTS. Macadamias originated in the coastal rain forests and scrubs of NE Australia. Those grown commercially are principally the smooth-shelled *Macadamia integrifolia* and the rough-shelled *M. tetraphylla.* Hard to propagate and slow to bear, the trees grow only in rich, well-drained soil with 50 in. (130 cm) of rain annually. Fragrant pink or white flower clusters on trees with large, shiny, leathery leaves produce bunches of 1–20 fruits. The nuts contain much fat but are a good source of minerals and vitamin B.

MacAlpin, Kenneth See KENNETH I

Macao \mə-'kaù\ *Portuguese* **Macau** \mə-'kaù\ *Chinese* **Aomen** \'aù-'men\ Former Portuguese territory (pop., 1996 est.: 433,000), S coast of China. It consists of a small peninsula and two small islands, about 40 mi (64 km) west of HONG KONG. It occupies a total land area of 6.5 sq mi (17 sq km). Portuguese traders first arrived in 1513, and it soon became a market center. It was declared a Portuguese colony in 1849 and an overseas territory in 1951. In Dec. 1999 Portugal returned it to Chinese rule. Tourism and gambling are the mainstays of its economy.

macaque \mə-'kak\ Any of about 12 primarily Asian species of omnivorous, diurnal MONKEYS (genus *Macaca*) with cheek pouches. Some species have long tails, some have short tails, and some have none. Males are 15–30 in. (40–70 cm) long (excluding the tail) and weigh 8–40 lbs (3.5–18 kg). Some species, including the RHESUS MONKEY, are important to humans. Malays train pigtailed macaques (*M. nemestrina*) to pick coconuts. See also BARBARY APE.

MacArthur, Charles (Gordon) (1895–1956) U.S. playwright and screenwriter. Born in Scranton, Pa., he worked as a reporter in Chicago and New York (1914–26) before collaborating with Ben HECHT on such Broadway hits as *The Front Page* (1928; film, 1931) and *Twentieth Century* (1932; film, 1934), noted for their graphic, crisp dialogue. Their many screenplays included *Wuthering Heights* (1939), and they wrote and directed such movies as *The Scoundrel* (1935).

MacArthur, Douglas (1880–1964) U.S. general. Born in Little Rock, Ark., son of a general, he graduated from West Point, of which he became superintendent (1919–22). He rose to become army chief of staff (1930–35). In 1932 he commanded the troops that evicted the BONUS ARMY. In 1937 he took command of the Philippine military. When World War II broke out, he led the combined Philippine-U.S. forces in the Philippines until it was overrun by the Japanese (1942). From Australia, he commanded U.S. forces in the SW Pacific, returning as promised ("I shall return") to liberate the Philippines in 1944. As general of the army, he received Japan's surrender in 1945. As Allied commander of the OCCUPATION of Japan (1945–51), he directed the restoration of its economy. Commander of U.N. forces in the KOREAN WAR, he stemmed the advance of N. Korean troops. His desire to bomb China was rejected by Pres. Harry TRUMAN; when MacArthur made the dispute public, Truman relieved him of his command for insubordination (1951). He was twice (1948, 1952) seriously considered for the Republican nomination for president.

Macassar See UJUNG PANDANG

Macaulay \mə-'kô-lē\, **Thomas Babington** *later* Baron Macaulay of Rothley (1800–1859) English politician, historian, and poet. He published the first of his essays, on John MILTON (1825), and gained immediate fame. In Parliament from 1830, he became known as a leading orator. He served on the Supreme Council in India 1834–38, supporting the equality of Europeans and Indians before the law and inaugurating a national educational system. He published *Lays of Ancient Rome* (1842) before retiring to begin his brilliant *History of England* (5 vols., 1849–61); covering the period 1688–1702, it established a WHIG interpretation of English history that influenced generations.

Thomas Babington Macaulay
Painting by J. Partridge, 1840

macaw \mə-'kô\ Any of about 18 species of large tropical New World PARROTS (subfamily Psittacinae) with very long tails and big sickle-shaped beaks. Macaws eat fruits and nuts. They are easily tamed and often kept as pets; some learn to mimic human speech, but most only screech. A few have lived 65 years. Best known is the scarlet macaw (*Ara macao*), found from Mexico to Brazil, a 36-in. (90-cm) bright-red bird with blue and yellow wings, blue and red tail, and white face.

MacBride, Seán (1904–1988) Irish statesman. Born to Irish patriots—his mother was W. B. YEATS's beloved Maud Gonne (1866–1953), and his father was Maj. John MacBride, executed for his part in the 1916 Easter Rising—he became chief of staff of the IRISH REPUBLICAN ARMY at 24. In 1936 he founded the Irish Republican Party; he served in the Irish legislature 1947–58, and as minister of external affairs 1948–51. The first chairman of AMNESTY INTERNATIONAL (1961–75), he was awarded the 1974 Nobel Peace Prize for his efforts on behalf of human rights.

Maccabees \'ma-kə-ˌbēz\ (fl.2nd cent. B.C.) Priestly family of Jews who organized a rebellion against ANTIOCHUS IV EPIPHANES in Palestine and reconsecrated the defiled Temple of JERUSALEM. The rebellion began under the Jewish priest Mattathias after Antiochus forbade all Jewish practices and desecrated the temple (167 B.C.). Mattathias's son JUDAS MACCABAEUS recaptured Jerusalem and reconsecrated the temple, and the war continued intermittently under his brothers Jonathan and Simon.

MacDiarmid \mək-'dər-məd\, **Hugh** *orig.* Christopher Murray Grieve (1892–1978) Scottish poet. In 1922 he founded the monthly *Scottish Chapbook,* in which he published his lyrics and sparked the Scottish literary renaissance. A radical leftist, for a time he rejected English as a medium and scrutinized modern society in verse written in "synthetic Scots," an amalgam of various dialects. A noted work is the extended rhapsody *A Drunk Man Looks at the Thistle* (1926). He later returned to standard English in such volumes as *A Kist of Whistles* (1947).

MacDonald, (James) Ramsay (1866–1937) British politician, first LABOUR PARTY prime minister of Britain (1924, 1929–31, 1931–35). He joined the precursor of the Labour Party in 1894 and was its secretary 1900–11. He served in the House of Commons 1906–18, and as leader of the Labour Party 1911–14, but was forced to resign after opposing Britain's participation in World War I. Reelected to Parliament in 1922, he led the Labour opposition. He served as prime minister in 1924 with Liberal Party support and returned in 1929. In 1931 he offered his resignation during the Great Depression but decided instead to remain in office as head of a national coalition until 1935.

Macdonald, John (Alexander) (*later* **Sir John**) (1815–1891) Canadian (Scottish-born) politician, first prime minister of the Dominion of Canada (1867–73, 1878–91). He emigrated to Canada as a child and practiced law in Kingston, Upper Canada (now Ontario). He served in the province's assembly 1844–54, advocating the unification of Canada. He co-founded the Liberal-Conservative Party and became premier of the province in 1857. He helped secure passage of the BRITISH N. AMERICA ACT, which created the Dominion of Canada (1867). As prime minister, he supported trade protectionism and advocated Canadian unity, loyalty to the British Commonwealth, and independence from the U.S.

Macdonnell Ranges Mountain system, S central Northern Territory, Australia. Extending east and west of the town of ALICE SPRINGS for 230 mi (380 km), its highest peak is Mt. Ziel (4,954 ft, or 1,510 m).

MacDowell, Edward (Alexander) *orig.* Edward Alexander McDowell (1860–1908) U.S. composer. Born in New York City, he studied in Germany, where Franz LISZT assisted him with performances and publication of his early works. In 1896 he became Columbia Univ.'s first professor of music. Paresis made him unable to perform or compose after 1904, and he lapsed into insanity and died at 47. His farm in Peterborough, N.H., became the MacDowell Colony for artists after his death. His most popular works are the Second Piano Concerto (1886), the Second Orchestral ("Indian") Suite (1895), and such piano sets as *Woodland Sketches* (1896) and *Sea Pieces* (1898).

Macedonia *officially* **Republic of Macedonia** Country, SE Europe, S Balkans region. Area: 9,928 sq mi (25,713 sq km). Population (2000): 2,041,000. Capital: SKOPJE. Two-thirds of the population are Slavic Macedonians and about one-fifth are Albanians. Languages: Macedonian (official). Religions: Serbian Orthodoxy, Islam. Currency: denar. Located on a high plateau studded with mountains, Macedonia has few mineral resources and is one of the poorest countries in Europe. Agriculture is central to its economy, and includes

©1999, Encyclopædia Britannica, Inc.

the production of tobacco, rice, fruit, vegetables, and wine; sheep herding and dairy farming are also important. It is a republic with one legislative house; its head of state is the president, and the head of government, the prime minister. Macedonia has been inhabited since before 7000 B.C. Under Roman rule, part of the region was incorporated into the province of MOESIA in A.D. 29. It was settled by Slavic tribes by the mid-6th cent. A.D. and was Christianized during the 9th cent. Seized by the Bulgarians in 1185, it was ruled by the Ottoman empire 1371–1912. The north and center of the region were annexed by Serbia in 1913 and became part of the Kingdom of Serbs, Croats, and Slovenes (later YUGOSLAVIA) in 1918. When Yugoslavia was partitioned by the AXIS POWERS in 1941, Yugoslav Macedonia was occupied principally by Bulgaria. Macedonia once again became a republic of Yugoslavia in 1946. After Croatia and Slovenia seceded from Yugoslavia, fear of Serbian dominance drove Macedonia to declare its independence in 1991. In order to appease Greece, which has an area traditionally known as Macedonia, it adopted as its formal title Former Yugoslav Republic of Macedonia, and normalized relations with Greece in 1995. During the 1999 KOSOVO CONFLICT tens of thousands of ethnic Albanians fled to Macedonia, threatening to destabilize the government.

Macedonian language See BULGARIAN LANGUAGE

Macedonian Wars Three wars fought by PHILIP V of Macedonia and his successor, PERSEUS, against Rome (215–205, 200–197, 171–167 B.C.). The first war, fought by Rome in the context of the Second PUNIC WAR, ended favorably for the Macedonians; Rome was victorious in the next two wars. After Rome's victory at the Battle of Pydna (168), Macedonian territory was divided into four republics. Another conflict, fought in 149–148, may be considered a fourth Macedonian War; it resulted in a decisive Roman victory, and in its aftermath Macedonia became the empire's first province.

Macfadden, Bernarr (*orig.* Bernard Adolphus) (1868–1955) U.S. publisher and champion of physical health. Born in Mill Spring, Mo., in 1898 he began publishing *Physical Culture* magazine, in which he promoted his ideas of exercise, diet, and fasting. He built up a publishing empire, bringing out the first confession magazine, *True Story* (1919), followed by *True Romances* (1923), *True Detective* (1925), and other periodicals. Physically fit into old age, he parachuted into Paris on his 84th birthday.

Mach \'mäk, *Engl* 'mäk\, **Ernst** (1838–1916) Austrian physicist and philosopher. In the 1860s he discovered the physiological phenomenon known as Mach's bands, the tendency of the human eye to see bright or dark bands near the boundaries between areas of sharply differing illumination. He later developed techniques for measuring sound waves and wave propagation. In 1887 he established the principles of supersonics and the Mach number, the ratio of the velocity of an object to the velocity of sound. He also proposed the theory of inertia known as Mach's principle. In *Contributions to the Analysis of the Sensations* (1886), he asserted that all knowledge is derived from sensory experience or observation.

Machado de Assis \mȧ-'shä-dō-dē-ȧ-'sēs\, **Joaquim Maria** (1839–1908) Brazilian poet and novelist. His witty, pessimistic works, rooted in European cultural traditions, include the eccentric first-person narrative *Epitaph of a Small Winner* (1881) and the novels *Philosopher or Dog?* (1891) and *Dom Casmurro* (1899), his masterpiece. Considered the classic master of Brazilian literature, he became the first president of the Brazilian Academy of Letters in 1896.

Machaut \mȧ-'shō\, **Guillaume de** (c.1300–1377) French poet and composer. After taking holy orders, he traveled throughout Europe as secretary to the king of Bohemia. From 1340 he settled in Reims, supported by royal patrons, including CHARLES V. Beside 14 narrative poems incorporating short lyrics, he wrote more than 400 separate lyric poems. His musical output numbers many chansons in the FORMES FIXES, as well as the first complete setting of the mass for four voices, and he was the outstanding figure of the ARS NOVA.

Machiavelli \ˌmä-kē-ə-'vel-ē\, **Niccolò** (1469–1527) Italian statesman, historian, and political theorist. Born in Florence, he rose to power after the overthrow of Girolamo SAVONAROLA in 1498. A diplomat for 14 years, he came in contact with the most powerful figures in Europe. He was dismissed when the MEDICI FAMILY returned to power in 1512. His famous treatise *The Prince* (1513, published 1532) is a handbook for rulers. He viewed *The Prince* as reflecting political reality; because he viewed human nature as venal, grasping, and thoroughly self-serving, he suggested that ruthless cunning is appropriate to the conduct of government. Though admired for its brilliance, the book has long been condemned as cynical and amoral. His other works include discourses on LIVY (c.1518), the comedy *Mandragola* (c.1518), and *The Art of War* (published 1521).

Niccolò Machiavelli Painting by Santi di Tito

machine Device that amplifies or replaces human or animal effort to accomplish a physical task. A machine may be further defined as a device consisting of two or more parts that transmit or modify force and motion in order to do work. The six simple machines are the LEVER, the WEDGE, the WHEEL and AXLE, the PULLEY, the inclined plane, and the SCREW; all complex machines are combinations of these basic devices. The operation of a machine may involve the transformation of chemical, thermal, electrical, or nuclear ENERGY into mechanical energy, or vice versa. All machines have an input, an output, and a transforming or modifying and transmitting device. Machines that receive their input energy from a natural source (such as air currents, moving water, coal, petroleum, or uranium) and transform it into mechanical energy are known as prime movers; examples include WINDMILLS, WATERWHEELS, TURBINES, STEAM ENGINES, and INTERNAL-COMBUSTION ENGINES.

machine gun Automatic weapon of small caliber capable of rapid, sustained fire, usually 500–1,000 rounds per minute. Developed in the late 19th cent., it profoundly altered modern warfare. Hand-cranked machine guns, notably the GATLING GUN, were used in the American Civil War. The invention in the 1880s of smokeless GUNPOWDER, with its even combustion, allowed Hiram MAXIM to harness the recoil. The World War I battlefield was dominated by the belt-fed machine gun, which remained little changed into World War II. See also SUBMACHINE GUN.

machine language *or* **machine code** Elemental language of computers, consisting of a string of 0's and 1's. Because machine language is the lowest-level computer language and the only language that computers directly understand, a program written in a more sophisticated language (e.g., C, PASCAL) must be converted to machine language prior to execution. This is done via a compiler or assembler. The resulting binary (or executable) file can then be executed by the CPU. See also ASSEMBLY LANGUAGE.

machine tool Stationary, power-driven machine used to cut, shape, or form materials such as metal and wood. Machine tools date from the invention of the STEAM ENGINE in the 18th cent. Today dozens of different machine tools are used in the workshops of home and industry. They are frequently classified into seven types: turning machines such as LATHES; shapers and planers; power DRILLS or drill presses; milling machines; GRINDING MACHINES; power SAWS; and presses (e.g., punch presses).

machismo \mä-'chēz-mō\ Exaggerated pride in masculinity, perceived as power, often coupled with a minimal sense of responsibility and disregard of consequences and denigration of the feminine. It has for centuries been a strong current in Latin American politics and society. CAUDILLOS, prominent in the history of Latin America, have typified machismo with their bold and authoritarian approach to government and their willingness to employ violence to achieve their ends.

Machu Picchu \'mä-chü-'pēk-chü\ Ancient fortress city of the INCAS in the ANDES, S central Peru, northwest of CUZCO. Perched spectacularly in a narrow saddle between two sharp peaks, at an altitude of 7,710 ft (2,350 m), it was discovered only in 1911 by Hiram Bingham (1875–1956). One of the few pre-Columbian urban centers found nearly intact, it is about 5 sq mi (13 sq km) in area, and includes a temple and a citadel. Its construction relies on an ingenious system of terraces, sheer walls, and some 3,000 steps.

Mac ind Og See MAPONOS

Mack, Connie *orig.* Cornelius (Alexander) McGillicuddy (1862–1956) U.S. baseball manager. Born in E. Brookfield, Mass., he played professional baseball 1886–96 before becoming manager of the Milwaukee Brewers (1897–1900) and the Philadelphia Athletics (1901–50; president, 1937–53). His teams won 3,776 games and lost 4,025, both all-time records. He helped establish the AMERICAN LEAGUE as a major league.

Mackenzie, Alexander (*later* **Sir Alexander**) (1755?–1820) Scottish-Canadian explorer. He entered a Canadian fur-trading firm in 1779, and in 1788 set up a trading post, Ft. Chipewyan, on Lake Athabasca. There began his 1789 expedition, which followed the Mackenzie River from Great Slave Lake to the Arctic Ocean. In 1793 he journeyed from Ft. Chipewyan to the Pacific coast, becoming the first European to reach the Pacific after crossing the Rocky Mtns.

Mackenzie, Alexander (1822–1892) Scottish-Canadian politician, first Liberal prime minister of Canada (1873–78). He emigrated to Canada West (now Ontario) in 1842. In 1852 he became editor of a local Liberal newspaper and befriended George BROWN, leader of the Reform Party. In 1867 he was elected to the House of Commons, where he led the Liberal opposition. As prime minister, his efforts at renewed reciprocity with the U.S. failed to address economic concerns. He served in Parliament until his death.

Mackenzie, (Edward Montague) Compton (*later* **Sir Compton**) (1883–1972) British novelist and playwright. He gave up legal studies to finish his first play, *The Gentleman in Grey* (1906). During World War I he directed the Aegean Intelligence Service in Syria; he was prosecuted when he wrote about those experiences in *Greek Memories* (1932). He founded *Gramophone* magazine in 1923 and edited it until 1962. His more than 100 novels, plays, and biographies include ten volumes of memoirs.

Mackenzie, William Lyon (1795–1861) Scottish-Canadian insurgent leader. He emigrated to Canada in 1820 and became a merchant in Upper Canada (later Ontario). He founded the *Colonial Advocate,* in which he assailed the administration (1824–34); elected to the province's assembly (1828–36), he was expelled six times by the conservative majority for his editorial invective. In 1837 he led 800 followers in an unsuccessful attempt to overthrow the provincial government. He tried to rally his forces on Navy Island in the Niagara River, N.Y., and was jailed for breaking U.S. neutrality laws. He served in the Canadian Parliament 1851–58.

Mackenzie River River system, Northwest Territories. It flows northward 1,025 mi (1,650 km) from GREAT SLAVE LAKE into the BEAUFORT SEA. Its basin, with an area of 697,000 sq mi (1,805,200 sq km), is the largest in Canada. With the Finlay River, its farthest headstream, the entire system is 2,635 mi (4,241 km) long, the second-longest in N. America. It was visited by Alexander MACKENZIE in 1789.

mackerel Swift-moving, carnivorous, torpedo-shaped food and sport fishes of temperate and tropical seas worldwide. Mackerels (family Scombridae, order Perciformes) are 1–5.5 ft (30–170 cm) long. Such species as the common mackerel *(Scomber scombrus)* of the N. Atlantic and the chub mackerel *(S. colias)* of California and the Atlantic are economically important. Others are favorite game fish. The name mackerel also refers to certain shark species, TUNA, and BONITO.

Mackinac \'ma-kə-,nò\, **Straits of** Channel connecting Lake MICHIGAN with Lake HURON. Forming an important waterway between the Upper and Lower peninsulas of Michigan, the straits are spanned by the Mackinac Bridge, a 3,800-ft (1,158-m) suspension bridge built in 1957.

Mackinac Island Island in the Straits of MACKINAC, SE Upper Peninsula of Michigan. It is 3 mi (5 km) long. It was an ancient Indian burial ground when the British built a fort there in 1780. After the U.S. took possession in 1783, it became the headquarters of the American Fur Co. It has been a state park since 1895; automobiles are banned from the island.

Mackintosh, Charles Rennie (1868–1928) Scottish architect, furniture designer, and artist. A giant of the ARTS AND CRAFTS MOVEMENT, he is especially revered for his glass-and-stone studio building at the Glasgow School of Art (1896–1909). In the 1890s he achieved an international reputation creating unorthodox posters, craftwork, and furniture. Considered Britain's first designer of true ART NOUVEAU architecture, he produced work of an unrivaled lightness, elegance, and originality, as exemplified by four remarkable Glasgow tearooms (1896–1904). By 1914 he was dedicating all his energies to watercolor painting.

MacLaine, Shirley *orig.* Shirley MacLean Beaty (b.1934) U.S. film actress. Born in Richmond, Va., the sister of Warren BEATTY, she worked as a dancer on Broadway, replacing the injured star in *The Pajama Game* (1954). She made her movie debut in *The Trouble with Harry* (1955) and played comic and dramatic roles in *Some Came Running* (1959), *The Apartment* (1960), *Irma La Douce* (1963), *Sweet Charity* (1969), and *Terms of Endearment* (1983, Academy Award). Her best-selling books, often about her mystical experiences, include *Out on a Limb* (1983) and *Going Within* (1989).

Maclean, Donald See Guy BURGESS

Maclean's \mə-'klānz\ Weekly newsmagazine published in Toronto, the leading Canadian magazine. It provides coverage of Canadian and world news. Founded in 1905 in a large-page format, it presented feature articles and fiction reflecting a conservative view of Canadian life and values and developed a reputation for outstanding photography. In the 1970s its format was reduced and revised.

MacLeish \mə-'klēsh\, **Archibald** (1892–1982) U.S. poet, playwright, teacher, and public official. Born in Glencoe, Ill., he moved to France in 1923, where he wrote such poems as "Ars Poetica" (1926) and "You, Andrew Marvell" (1930). He expressed his concern for democratic ideals in such "public" verse as *Conquistador* (1932, Pulitzer Prize) and *Public Speech* (1936). Other works include the radio verse play *Air Raid* (1938), *Collected Poems* (1952, Pulitzer Prize), and the verse drama *J.B.* (1958, Pulitzer Prize). He served as librarian of Congress (1939–44) and assistant secretary of state (1944–45).

MacLennan \mə-'klen-ən\, **(John) Hugh** (1907–1990) Canadian novelist and essayist. Born in Glace Bay, Nova Scotia, he taught at McGill Univ. 1951–81. His novels include *Barometer Rising* (1941), *Two Solitudes* (1945), *The Watch That Ends the Night* (1959), and *Voices in Time* (1980). He won five Governor-General's awards, and is regarded as the first major English-speaking novelist to use Canadian themes.

Macleod \mə-'klaùd\, **J(ohn) J(ames) R(ickard)** (1876–1935) Scottish physiologist. He taught in several universities, becoming noted for his work on carbohydrate metabolism. With Frederick BANTING and Charles Best (1899–1978) he discovered INSULIN, an achievement for which he and Banting shared a Nobel Prize in 1923.

Mac-Mahon \màk-mä-'ōⁿ\, **(Marie-Edme-Patrice-) Maurice, comte (Count) de** *later* duc (Duke) de Magenta (1808–1893) French soldier and second president (1873–79) of the THIRD REPUBLIC. Descended from an Irish Jacobite family, he distinguished himself in the Crimean War and in the Italian campaign at the Battle of Magenta (1859). He was governor-general of Algeria 1864–70. As head of the Versailles Army, he defeated the PARIS COMMUNE in 1871. He was elected president after the resignation of Adolphe THIERS. During his term the Constitutional Laws of 1875 were promulgated. Mac-Mahon resigned following a constitutional crisis that was resolved in favor of parliamentary control of the government.

Macmillan, Daniel and Alexander (1813–1857, 1818–1896) Scots-British publishers. In 1843 the two brothers founded Macmillan & Co., a successful bookshop in Cambridge that began publishing textbooks in 1844 and novels in 1855. After Daniel's death, Alexander founded *Macmillan's Magazine* (1859–1907), a literary periodical, and *Nature* (1869–), a leading scientific journal. He published many important Victorian writers. Long led by Daniel's descendants, the company grew into one of the largest publishing firms in the world.

Macmillan, (Maurice) Harold *later* Earl of Stockton (1894–1986) British prime minister (1957–63). He served in the House of Commons 1924–29 and 1931–64, and held posts in Winston CHURCHILL's wartime coalition government. After serving as minister of housing (1951–54) and chancellor of the exchequer (1955–57), he became prime minister and leader of the CONSERVATIVE PARTY. He worked to improve relations with the U.S. and supported Britain's postwar social programs. His government began to lose popularity in 1961 because of a wage freeze and a Soviet espionage scandal involving John Profumo, secretary of state for war. In 1963 Charles DE GAULLE vetoed British entry into the EUROPEAN ECONOMIC COMMUNITY. Demands for a new party leader led to his resignation in 1963. He later served as chair (1963–74) of his family's publishing house, Macmillan & Co.

MacMillan, Kenneth (*later* **Sir Kenneth**) (1929–1992) British dancer and choreographer. After studies at the Sadler's Wells ballet school, he danced with its ballet companies from 1946. He choreographed his first work, *Somnambulism,* in 1953, and *Danses concertantes* in 1955. His *Romeo and Juliet* (1965) made an international impact. In 1970 he was appointed director of the ROYAL BALLET; in 1977 he resigned to become its principal choreographer.

MacNeice, (Frederick) Louis (1907–1963) British poet and playwright. In the 1930s he became known as one of a group of socially committed young poets that included W. H. AUDEN, Cecil DAY-LEWIS, and Stephen SPENDER. His volumes include *Blind Fireworks* (1929), *Autumn Journal* (1939), and *The Burning Perch* (1963). He wrote and produced radio verse plays for the BBC, notably *The Dark Tower* (1947). Among his prose works are the *Letters from Iceland* (1937; with Auden) and *The Poetry of W.B. Yeats* (1941).

Macon \'mā-kən\ City (pop., 2000: 97,000), central Georgia. In 1806 a settlement grew up around an existing fort. During the AMERICAN CIVIL WAR, it was a Confederate supply depot. It is the site of several colleges and Robins Air Force Base, as well as the birthplace of the poet Sidney Lanier (1842–1881).

Macphail, Agnes Campbell (1890–1954) Canadian politician. Born in Grey Co., Ontario, she became a schoolteacher and entered politics to represent the region's farmers. She was elected to the Canadian House of Commons as its first female member in 1921, and served until 1940, advocating prison reform and women's rights as well as a protective tariff. In the Ontario legislature (1943–45, 1948–51), she sponsored Ontario's first equal-pay legislation.

Macquarie \mə-'kwar-ē\, **Lachlan** (1761–1824) British colonial governor. Appointed governor of New S. Wales, Australia, in 1809, he replaced the corrupt military corps that had overthrown the previous governor, William BLIGH. He began public-works programs that gave opportunities to Emancipists (freed convicts), established the colony's currency, and encouraged exploration and settlement. His policy favoring Emancipist agriculture angered the large landowners and sheep farmers (Exclusionists), and he was recalled in 1821.

Macready \mə-'krē-dē\, **William (Charles)** (1793–1873) English ACTOR-MANAGER. He made his debut in 1810, and by 1820 he was famous for his performances as Hamlet, Lear, and Macbeth. As theater manager of London's COVENT GARDEN (1837–39) and DRURY LANE (1841–43), he introduced such reforms as full rehearsals, historically accurate costumes and sets, and a reversion to the original Shakespeare texts. His diary provides a view of 19th-cent. theatrical life.

macrobiotics Diet based on the Chinese philosophy of balancing yin and yang (see YIN–YANG). It stresses avoiding foods that are classified as strongly yin (e.g., ALCOHOLIC BEVERAGES) or yang (e.g. MEAT) and relying mainly on near-neutral foods such as grains and foods that grow naturally in one's own climate. Macrobiotics was first developed in Asia in the 1930s and swept Europe and the U.S. in the late 1960s. Adherents maintain that macrobiotics can enhance the quality of life and even cure serious disease; critics counter that uninformed attempts to practice such a diet can lead to MALNUTRITION.

macroeconomics Study of the entire economy in terms of the total value of goods and services produced, total income earned, level of employment of productive resources, and movement of prices. Until the 1930s, most economic analysis focused on specific firms and industries. With the GREAT DEPRESSION and the development of national income and product statistics, the field of macroeconomics began to expand. Macroeconomic policy promotes economic growth, price stability, and full employment. See also MICROECONOMICS.

macrophage system See RETICULOENDOTHELIAL SYSTEM.

macular degeneration Degeneration of the macula (central part of the RETINA). It is the leading cause of BLINDNESS in old age. It is now known to have a genetic component. It is twice as common in smokers as in nonsmokers, and is also correlated with lifelong sun exposure. Peripheral vision usually remains, but loss of central visual acuity makes reading or fine work difficult or impossible. Some forms of macular degeneration can be halted (but not reversed) by laser surgery.

Macumba \mə-'küm-bə\ Afro-Brazilian religion, combining traditional AFRICAN RELIGIONS, Brazilian SPIRITUALISM, and ROMAN CATHOLICISM. CANDOMBLÉ is the best-known sect. African elements include an outdoor ceremonial site, the sacrifice of animals, spirit offerings (e.g., candles and flowers), and dances. Macumba rites are led by mediums, who enter trances and communicate with holy spirits. Roman Catholic elements include the worship of saints, who are given African names.

Macy and Co. *in full* **R. H. Macy and Co., Inc.** Major U.S. DEPARTMENT-STORE chain. Its 11-story store in New York's Herald Square was for many years the largest single store in the country. Rowland H. Macy (1822?–1877) established the business in 1858; its red star trademark was derived from a tattoo he bore. Isidor and Nathan STRAUS acquired part ownership in 1887 and full control in 1896, and expanded nationwide. Bankrupt in 1992, Macy's merged with Federated Department Stores Inc. in 1994.

Madagascar *officially* **Republic of Madagascar** Nation, occupying the island of Madagascar, off the SE coast of

©1999, Encyclopædia Britannica, Inc.

MADAGASCAR

Scale 1: 25,920,000
0   100   200 mi
0   150   300 km

Africa. The island of Madagascar, the world's fourth-largest island, is about 976 mi (1,570 km) long and 355 mi (571 km) wide. It is separated from the African coast by the Mozambique Channel. Area: 226,658 sq mi (587,041 sq km). Population (2000): 15,506,000. Capital: ANTANANARIVO. Almost all the population belongs to about 20 Malayo-Indonesian groups. Languages: Malagasy, French. Religions: Traditional animism; Christianity (Roman Catholicism, Protestantism); Islam. Currency: Malagasy franc. Madagascar's high central plateau rises to 9,436 ft (2,876 m) at the volcanic Tsaratanana massif; the island was once heavily forested, and forests still cover one-fourth of the land area. Agriculture dominates the economy, with staple crops, including rice and cassava, and cash crops, including coffee, cloves, and vanilla. It is a republic with one legislative house; its chief of state is the president, and the head of government is the prime minister. Indonesians migrated to Madagascar around A.D. 700. The first European to visit the island was Portuguese navigator Diogo Dias in 1500. Trade in arms and slaves allowed the development of Malagasy kingdoms at the beginning of the 17th cent. In the 18th cent. the Merina kingdom became dominant; with British assistance, it gained control of a large part of Madagascar in the early 19th cent. In 1868 Merina signed a treaty granting France control over the NW coast, and in 1895 French troops took the island. Madagascar became a French overseas territory in 1946. In 1958 France agreed to let the territory decide its own fate; as the Malagasy Republic, it gained independence in 1960. It severed ties with France in the 1970s, taking its present name in 1975. A new constitution was adopted in 1992. The country has since been politically and economically unstable and victimized by drought, disease, and tropical storms.

mad cow disease *or* **bovine spongiform encephalopathy (BSE)** \'spən-ji-,fórm-in-,sef-ə-'läp-ə-thē\ Fatal neurodegenerative disease of cattle. Symptoms include behavioral changes (e.g., agitation), gradual loss of coordination and locomotive function, and, in advanced stages, weight loss, small-scale muscle contractions, abnormal gait, and isolation from the herd. Brain tissue becomes pitted and spongy. Death usually follows within a year. No treatment is known. A BSE epidemic in Britain that began in the mid-1980s is believed to have been caused by the use of cattle feed containing animal remains, including those of sheep with a similar disease, scrapie. Both diseases are caused by PRIONS. See also CREUTZFELDT-JAKOB DISEASE.

M

madder family Family Rubiaceae, composed of about 6,500 species of herbs, shrubs, and trees in 500 genera. The leaves usually are large and evergreen in tropical species, deciduous in temperate species, and needlelike or scalelike in desert species. The plants may bear a single flower or many small flowers clustered together. Economically important products of the family include COFFEE, QUININE, ipecac, the red dye alizarin, and ornamentals including GARDENIAS.

Maddux, Greg(ory Alan) (b.1966) U.S. baseball player. Born in San Angelo, Texas, he pitched for the Chicago Cubs (1986–92) before joining the Atlanta Braves in 1993 as a free agent. He is the only pitcher ever to win the Cy Young pitching award four years in a row (1992–95). Since coming to the Braves he has won over 150 games and lost less than half that number.

Madeira \mä-'där-ə\ Island (pop., 1993 est.: 253,000), largest of the Madeira Island group, an autonomous region of Portugal. Lying off the coast of Morocco, it is the site of the region's capital, FUNCHAL. It is 34 mi (55 km) long and 14 mi (22 km) wide and has deep ravines and rugged mountains. It allegedly had the world's first sugarcane plantation. Its Madeira wine has been an important export since the 17th cent. Tourism is also important. Porto Santo is the only other island of the group that is inhabited.

Madeira River River, W Brazil. It is formed by the junction of the Mamoré and Beni rivers in Bolivia, flows north along the border with Brazil, and meanders northeast in Brazil to join the AMAZON east of MANAUS. Measured from the upper reaches of the Mamoré River, it is 2,082 mi (3,352 km) long.

Madero \mə-'der-ō\, **Francisco (Indalecio)** (1873–1913) Mexican revolutionary and president (1911–13). Son of a wealthy landowner, in 1908 he called for honest elections and an end to the long dictatorship of Porfirio DÍAZ. He incited an armed insurrection that led to Díaz's resignation and was elected president in 1911, but was quickly overwhelmed by conflicting pressures from conservatives and revolutionaries. His administration ended in national disaster with his assassination in 1913. See also MEXICAN REVOLUTION, Pancho VILLA, Emiliano ZAPATA.

Madison City (pop., 2000: 208,000), capital of Wisconsin. It lies in the S central part of the state, on an isthmus between lakes Mendota and Monona. Founded in 1836, it became the capital of Wisconsin Territory the same year. Steady development followed the 1854 arrival of the railroad. Noted for its parks and wooded lakeshore, it is the seat of the Univ. of WISCONSIN's main campus.

Madison, James (1751–1836) Fourth president of the U.S. (1809–17). Born in Port Conway, Va., he served in the state legislature (1776–80, 1784–86). At the Constitutional Convention (1787), his active participation and careful notes earned him the title "father of the Constitution." To promote ratification, he collaborated with Alexander HAMILTON and John JAY on *The FEDERALIST*. In the U.S. House of Representatives (1789–97), he sponsored the Bill of Rights. In reaction to the ALIEN AND SEDITION ACTS, he drafted one of the VIRGINIA AND KENTUCKY RESOLUTIONS (1798). As secretary of state (1801–9) under Thomas JEFFERSON, he developed U.S. foreign policy.

James Madison

Elected president in 1808, he was occupied by the trade and shipping embargo problems that led to the WAR OF 1812. He was reelected in 1812; his second term was marked principally by the war, during which he reinvigorated the U.S. Army. He retired to his Virginia estate, Montpelier, with his wife, Dolley (1768–1849), whose political acumen he had long prized, and served as rector of the Univ. of Virginia (1826–36).

Madonna In Christian art, a depiction of the Virgin MARY. Though often shown with the infant JESUS, the Madonna (Italian: "My lady") may also be represented alone. Byzantine art developed a set of Madonna types—the Madonna and child enthroned, the Madonna as intercessor, the Madonna nursing the child, and so on. Western art adapted and added to the Byzantine types, producing images that sought to inspire piety through beauty and tenderness.

Madonna orig. Madonna Louise Ciccone (b.1958) U.S. pop singer, songwriter, and actress. Born in Bay City, Mich., she studied dance with Martha GRAHAM and Alvin AILEY in New York. Her first two albums, *Madonna* (1983) and *Like a Virgin* (1984), were among the most popular of the 1980s. Her provocatively sexual showmanship made her one of the most controversial figures in pop. Her films have included *Desperately Seeking Susan* (1985), *Dick Tracy* (1990), and *Evita* (1996).

Madras \mə-'dräs\ or **Chennai** \ˌchen-'nī\ City (metro. area pop., 2001: 6,424,000), capital of Tamil Nadu state, S India, on the Coromandel Coast of the Bay of BENGAL. Founded in 1639 by the British E. INDIA CO., it was known as Ft. St. George and was used as a base for the company's expansion in S India. The English made Madras their administrative and commercial capital about 1800. It is an industrial center, especially known for its cotton fabrics, and the site of numerous educational and cultural institutions.

madrasah \'mád-rə-sə\ (Arabic: "school") Islamic theological seminary and law school attached to a MOSQUE. The residential madrasah was a newer building form than the mosque, flourishing in most Muslim cities by the end of the 12th cent. The Syrian madrasahs in Damascus tended to follow a standardized plan: An elaborate facade led into a domed hallway and then into a courtyard where instruction took place. Madrasah instruction centers on the Quran. Room, board, and tuition are provided free of charge.

Madre, Laguna Long narrow inlet of the Gulf of Mexico along the Texas-Mexico coast. Sheltered by barrier islands, including PADRE ISLAND, it is divided by the delta of the RIO GRANDE; the U.S. portion extends south for 120 mi (190 km) from Corpus Christi Bay, and the Mexican portion extends north for 100 mi (160 km) from the Soto la Marina River. The GULF INTRACOASTAL WATERWAY runs through it.

Madre de Dios River River, SE Peru and NW Bolivia. Rising in the easternmost range of the ANDES, in Peru, it flows east to cross the tropical rain forest of NW Bolivia, joining the Beni River after a course of 700 mi (1,100 km).

Madrid \mä-'threth, *Engl* mə-'drid\ City (pop., 1998: 2,881,000), capital of Spain, and of Madrid autonomous community. At 2,100 ft (635 m) above sea level, it is one of Europe's highest capitals. The original town grew up around the Moorish alcazar (castle). King ALFONSO VI captured it from the Muslims in 1083. PHILIP II moved the Spanish court to Madrid in 1561, and in 1607 Philip III made it the official capital. During the SPANISH CIVIL WAR, it was held by the Loyalists 1936–39. It is an important transportation, commercial, industrial, and cultural center. Major institutions include the PRADO MUSEUM and the Univ. of Madrid.

madrigal Form of vocal chamber music, usually polyphonic and unaccompanied, of the 16th–17th cent. It originated and developed in Italy. Usually for three to six voices, madrigals came to be sung widely by cultivated amateurs, male and female. The texts, almost always about love, were by such poets as PETRARCH and Torquato TASSO. Orlande de LASSUS, Luca MARENZIO, and Claudio MONTEVERDI were among the greatest Italian madrigalists; Thomas MORLEY and others created a distinguished body of English madrigals.

Madura *Dutch* **Madoera** \mä-'dùr-ə\ Island (pop., 1980: 2,690,000), Jawa Timur province, Indonesia, off NE JAVA. Its capital is Pamekasan. It has an area of 2,042 sq mi (5,290 sq km). Dutch influence dates from the late 17th cent. Madura became part of Indonesia in 1949. Bull races, usually held in September, attract huge crowds.

Maecenas \mi-'sē-nəs\, **Gaius (Cilnius)** (c.70–8 B.C.) Roman diplomat and literary patron. Though highly influential in the state, he held no title, nor did he wish to be a senator. From 43 on, he helped Octavian (later AUGUSTUS) diplomatically and domestically, administering Rome and Italy while Octavian was fighting Pompeius in 36 and Mark ANTONY in 31. He is best remembered as the generous patron of such writers as VIRGIL, HORACE, and PROPERTIUS.

Maekawa \ˌmä-ä-ˈkä-wä\, **Kunio** (1905–1986) Japanese architect. Maekawa worked for LE CORBUSIER in Paris and for Antonin RAYMOND in Tokyo. His works, large Brutalist masses teeming with activity, strive to use concrete in a manner appropriate to the material. The Harumi Flats, Tokyo (1959), and Saitama Cultural Center (1966) provide fine examples. His community centers influenced his assistant Kenzo TANGE.

maenads and bacchantes \ˈmē-ˌnadz...bə-ˈkänts, bə-käntēz\ Female followers of the Greek wine-god DIONYSUS. During the orgiastic rites of Dionysus, maenads roamed the mountains and forests performing frenzied, ecstatic dances, supposedly possessed by the god. While in this state, it was said they could tear animals or people to pieces (the fate met by ORPHEUS). As bacchantes they were named for Bacchus, the Roman counterpart of Dionysus.

Maes \ˈmäs\, **Nicolaes** (1634–1693) Dutch painter. After study with REMBRANDT (c.1650–53), he returned to his native Dordrecht and painted a few life-size Rembrandtesque genre scenes. In 1655–60 he painted smaller domestic scenes, usually of women spinning, eavesdropping, reading the Bible, or cooking. In 1673 he moved to Amsterdam and devoted himself to portraiture, abandoning intimacy and the deep glowing colors characteristic of Rembrandt for elegance and cooler tones reminiscent of Anthony VAN DYCK.

Maeterlinck \ˈmä-tər-ˌliŋk\, **Maurice** *later* **comte (Count) Maeterlinck** (1862–1949) Belgian playwright and poet. His *Pelléas et Mélisande* (1892), considered the masterpiece of Symbolist drama, became the basis of Claude DEBUSSY's opera (1902) and works by other composers. He wrote a collection of Symbolist poems, *Hothouse Blooms* (1899), and plays such as *Monna Vanna* (1902), *The Blue Bird* (1908), and *The Burgomaster of Stilmonde* (1918). He was also noted for his popular treatments of scientific subjects, including *The Life of the Bee* (1901) and *The Intelligence of Flowers* (1907). He was awarded the Nobel Prize in 1911.

Ma-fa-mu-ts'o See MAPAM YUMCO

Mafia Society of criminals of primarily Italian or Sicilian origin, and criminal organizations in Sicily and the U.S. The Mafia arose in Sicily in the late Middle Ages; it drew its members from the small private armies, or *mafie*, hired by landlords to protect their estates. By 1900 the Mafia "families" of W Sicily controlled the economies of their localities. In the 1920s Benito MUSSOLINI jailed most of the members, but after World War II they resumed their activities. In the 1970s their control of the heroin trade led to fierce rivalry among the clans. In the 1990's, a series of murders led to a sweeping government crackdown that greatly weakened the Sicilian organization. In the U.S., Sicilian immigrants included former Mafia members who set up similar criminal operations. Their operations expanded from bootlegging in the 1920s to gambling, narcotics, and prostitution, and the Mafia, or Cosa Nostra, became the largest U.S. syndicated crime organization (see ORGANIZED CRIME). About 24 Mafia "families" controlled operations in the U.S. In the late 20th cent. the Mafia's power was greatly diminished through convictions of top officials, defections, and murderous internal disputes.

mafic rock \ˈma-fik\ Any IGNEOUS ROCK dominated by the silicates pyroxene, amphibole, olivine, and mica. These minerals are high in magnesium and ferrous iron, which give mafic rock its characteristic dark color; examples include BASALT and GABBRO. It is usually contrasted with light-gray felsic rock.

Magadha \ˈmə-gə-də\ Ancient kingdom, India, situated in present-day Bihar state, NE India. An important kingdom in the 7th cent. B.C., it absorbed the kingdom of Anga in the 6th cent. B.C. Pataliputra (PATNA) was its capital. Under the MAURYAN dynasty (4th–2nd cent. B.C.), it made up nearly the entire Indian subcontinent. It was conquered by the Muslims in the late 12th cent. It was the scene of many events in the life of BUDDHA.

Magadi \mä-ˈgä-dē\, **Lake** Lake, GREAT RIFT VALLEY, S Kenya, east of Lake VICTORIA. It is 20 mi (32 km) long and 2 mi (3 km) wide. Its bed is mainly soda deposits, which dye the waters a vivid pink.

magazine *or* **periodical** Printed collection of texts (essays, articles, stories, poems), often illustrated, that is produced at regular intervals. One of the first magazines was the German *Erbauliche Monaths-Unterredungen* ("Edifying Monthly Discussions"), issued 1663–68. In the early 18th cent., Joseph ADDISON and Richard STEELE brought out the influential periodicals *The Tatler* and *The Spectator;* other critical reviews began in the mid-1700s. By the 19th cent., magazines catering to less learned audiences had developed, including the women's weekly, the religious and missionary review, and the illustrated magazine. In the late 19th and 20th cent., advertisements became a means of financial support. Subsequent developments included lavish illustrations and vastly greater specialization.

Magdalena River \ˌmag-də-ˈlā-nə\ River, Colombia. It rises in the ANDES in S Colombia and flows northward 956 mi (1,534 km) into the Caribbean Sea near Barranquilla. Navigable for 930 mi (1,496 km), it has been a major commercial artery since the Spanish conquest.

Magdalenian culture \ˌmag-də-ˈlē-nē-ən\ STONE-TOOL INDUSTRY and artistic tradition of the Upper PALEOLITHIC PERIOD in Europe, named after the type-site La Madeleine in SW France. The Magdalenians lived about 11,000–17,000 years ago, at a time when reindeer, wild horses, and bison formed large herds. They killed animals with spears, snares, and traps and lived in caves, rock shelters, and tents. Magdalenian stone tools include blades, burins, scrapers, borers, and projectile points. Their bone tools—often engraved with animal images—include adzes, hammers, spearheads, harpoons, and eyed needles. Cave art in the early period is characterized by coarse black drawings, while that of the later period includes beautifully rendered realistic figures in polychrome, such as those at ALTAMIRA.

Magdalen Islands \ˈmag-də-lən\ *French* **Îles de la Madeleine** \ˌēl-də-lä-mȧd-ˈlen\ Island group (pop., 1991: 14,000) of E Quebec. Located in the Gulf of ST. LAWRENCE between Prince Edward Island and Newfoundland, the group includes several islands and islets, with a total area of 88 sq mi (228 sq km). Discovered by Jacques CARTIER in 1534, they are inhabited mainly by French Canadians.

Magdeburg \ˈmäg-də-ˌburk\ City (pop., 1996: 255,000), capital of Saxony-Anhalt state, E central Germany. Located on the ELBE RIVER, it was a trading settlement as early as the 9th cent., and a leading member of the HANSEATIC LEAGUE by the 13th cent. It embraced the REFORMATION in 1524. In 1631, during the THIRTY YEARS' WAR, it was burned and sacked. In 1815 it became the capital of the province of SAXONY. It was heavily bombed during World War II. An important inland port, it is also a railroad junction.

Magellan \mə-ˈjel-ən\, **Ferdinand** *Portuguese* Fernão de Magalhães *Spanish* Fernando de Magallanes (c.1480–1521) Portuguese navigator and explorer. From 1505 he served in expeditions to the E. Indies and Africa. When his requests for a higher rank were refused, he offered his services to King Charles I of Spain (later Emperor CHARLES V), proposing to sail west to the Moluccas (Spice Islands) to prove that they lay in Spanish rather than Portuguese territory. In 1519 he left Seville with five ships and 270 men and sailed around S. America. With three ships left, he crossed the sea he later called the Pacific Ocean because of their calm crossing. He was killed by natives in the Philippines, but two ships reached the Moluccas, and one, the *Victoria*, commanded by Juan de Elcano (1476?–1526), continued west to Spain, accomplishing the first circumnavigation of the world in 1522.

Magellan, Strait of *Spanish* **Estrecho de Magallanes** \ä-ˈstrā-chō-thä-ˌmä-gä-ˈlyä-näs\ Strait linking the Atlantic and Pacific oceans, between the S tip of S. America and TIERRA DEL FUEGO. Lying mostly within Chilean territorial waters, it is 350 mi (560 km) long and 2–20 mi (3–32 km) wide. Discovered in 1520 by Ferdinand MAGELLAN, it was an important route before the building of the PANAMA CANAL.

Magellanic Cloud \ˌma-jə-ˈla-nik\ Either of two irregular companion GALAXIES of the Milky Way, named for Ferdi-

nand MAGELLAN, whose crew discovered them during the first voyage around the world. Visible only in the Southern Hemisphere, they share a gaseous envelope and lie about 22° apart near the S celestial pole (see CELESTIAL SPHERE). The Large Magellanic Cloud is over 150,000 and the Small Magellanic Cloud some 200,000 light-years from earth. They are excellent laboratories for the study of the evolution of STARS.

Maggiore \mä-'jō-rä\, **Lake** ancient Lacus Verbanus. Lake, N Italy and S Switzerland, bordered on the north by the Swiss ALPS. Occupying 82 sq mi (212 sq km), and 34 mi (54 km) long, it is Italy's second-largest lake. Traversed from north to south by the Ticino River, it is also fed by the Tresa River from Lake LUGANO on the east. It is a popular resort area.

Maghreb \'mə-grəb\ Region of N. Africa bordering the Mediterranean Sea. Encompassing the coastal plain of Morocco, Algeria, Tunisia, and Libya, it was known to the ancients as Africa Minor. It later included Moorish Spain. It was absorbed into Muslim civilization in the 7th–8th cent.

Magi \'mā-ˌjī\ In Christian tradition, wise men from the East who came to pay homage to the infant JESUS. According to Matthew 2:1–12, they followed a miraculous guiding star to BETHLEHEM and brought gifts of "gold and frankincense and myrrh." HEROD asked them to report the location of Jesus' birth on their return journey, but an angel warned them of his evil intentions. In later Christian tradition they were said to be kings. Their visit was seen as evidence that the Gentiles as well as the Jews would worship Jesus; it is celebrated in the feast of Ephiphany. See also MAGUS.

magic Use of means (such as charms or spells) believed to have supernatural power over natural forces. Magic forms the core of many religious systems and plays a central social role in many nonliterate cultures. It emphasizes techniques that are means to specific ends (an enemy's defeat, rainfall, etc.), although some believe that its character is primarily symbolic and expressive. Thus, a rainmaking ritual may both elicit rainfall and stress the symbolic importance of rain and the agricultural activities associated with it. Both the magician and the magical rite are typically surrounded by TABOOS, purification procedures, and other activities that draw the participants into the magical sphere. Strains of magic in Western tradition, formerly associated with heretics, alchemists, witches, and sorcerers, persist in modern times in the activities of satanists and others. The art of entertaining by performing apparently magical feats (see CONJURING) relies on sleight of hand and other means. See also SHAMAN, WITCHCRAFT AND SORCERY.

magic realism or **magical realism** Latin-American literary phenomenon characterized by the matter-of-fact incorporation of fantastic or mythical elements into otherwise realistic fiction. The term was first applied to literature in the 1940s by Alejo Carpentier (1904–1980), who recognized his contemporaries' tendency to illuminate the mundane by means of the fabulous. Prominent practitioners include Gabriel GARCÍA MÁRQUEZ, Jorge AMADO, J. L. BORGES, M. A. ASTURIAS, and Julio CORTÁZAR.

magic show See CONJURING

Maginot Line \'ma-zhə-ˌnō\ Elaborate defensive, concrete barrier along the German frontier in NE France built in 1929–34. Named after its principal creator, André Maginot (1877–1932), it was supplied with heavy guns and had living quarters, supply storehouses, and underground rail lines. However, it ended at the French–Belgian frontier, which German forces crossed in May 1940.

magma Molten rock from which IGNEOUS ROCKS form, usually consisting of silicate liquid. Magma migrates either at depth or to the earth's surface, where it is ejected as LAVA. The interactions of such physical properties as chemical composition, viscosity, content of dissolved gases, and temperature determine its characteristics.

Magna Carta (Latin: "Great Charter") Document guaranteeing English political liberties, drafted at Runnymede, a meadow by the Thames, and signed by King JOHN in 1215 under pressure from his rebellious barons. Resentful of the king's high taxes and aware of his waning power, the barons were encouraged by the archbishop of Canterbury, Stephen LANGTON, to demand a solemn grant of their rights. Among the charter's provisions were clauses providing for a free church, reforming law and justice, and controlling the behavior of royal officials. Though it reflects the feudal order rather than democracy, the Magna Carta is traditionally regarded as the foundation of British constitutionalism.

Magna Graecia \'mag-nə-'grē-shə\ Group of ancient Greek cities along the coast of S Italy. Euboeans founded the first colonies, including CUMAE, around 750 B.C., and subsequently Spartans settled at Tarentum (TARANTO); Achaeans at Metapontum, SYBARIS, and Croton; Locrians at Locri Epizephyrii; and Chalcidians at Rhegium (REGGIO DI CALABRIA). After the 5th cent. B.C., most of the cities declined in importance.

Magnani \män-'yä-nē\, **Anna** (1908–1973) Italian film actress. A nightclub singer noted for her bawdy street songs, she made her film debut in The Blind Woman of Sorrento (1934). She earned international fame for her role in Roberto ROSSELLINI's Open City (1945), and became known for her forceful portrayals of earthy lower-class women in such films as The Miracle (1948), Bellissima (1951), The Rose Tattoo (1955, Academy Award), and The Fugitive Kind (1960).

magnesium Chemical ELEMENT, one of the ALKALINE EARTH METALS, chemical symbol Mg, atomic number 12. The silvery-white METAL does not occur free in nature, but compounds such as the SULFATE (Epsom salts), OXIDE (magnesia), and CARBONATE (magnesite) have long been known. The metal is used in photographic flash devices, bombs, flares, and pyrotechnics and in lightweight alloys for aircraft, spacecraft, cars, machinery, and tools. The compounds (VALENCE 2) are used as insulators and refractories, in fertilizers, cement, rubber, and plastics and in foods and pharmaceuticals (antacids, purgatives, LAXATIVES). Magnesium is an essential element in human nutrition.

magnet Any material capable of attracting IRON and producing a MAGNETIC FIELD outside itself. By the end of the 19th cent., all known elements had been tested for MAG-

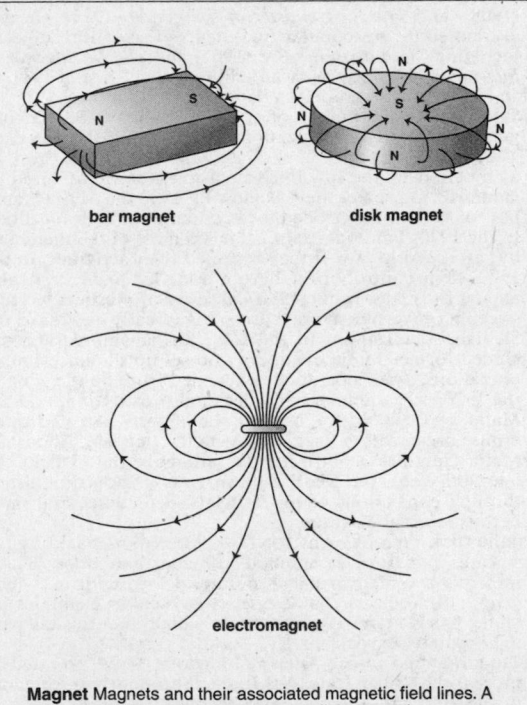

bar magnet   disk magnet

electromagnet

Magnet Magnets and their associated magnetic field lines. A permanent magnet (such as a bar or disk magnet) possesses a magnetic field by virtue of the alignment of all the magnetic particles it is composed of. An electromagnet is generated by a current flowing through a wire loop at the center of the field.

NETISM, and all were found to have some magnetic property. However, only three elements—iron, NICKEL, and COBALT—exhibit FERROMAGNETISM. See also ELECTROMAGNET.

magnetic field Region around a magnet, ELECTRIC CURRENT, or changing ELECTRIC FIELD, in which MAGNETIC FORCES are observable. The field around a permanent magnet or wire carrying a steady DIRECT CURRENT is stationary; that around an ALTERNATING CURRENT or changing direct current is continuously changing. Magnetic fields are commonly represented by continuous lines of force, or magnetic flux, between north-seeking and south-seeking magnetic poles. The density of the lines indicates the magnitude of the field.

magnetic force Attraction or repulsion that arises between electrically charged particles that are in motion. Only electric forces exist among stationary ELECTRIC CHARGES, but both electric and magnetic forces exist among moving electric charges. The magnetic force between two moving charges is the force exerted on one charge by a MAGNETIC FIELD created by the other. Magnetic force is responsible for the action of electric motors and the attraction between magnets and iron.

magnetic resonance Absorption or emission of ELECTROMAGNETIC RADIATION by electrons or atomic nuclei in response to certain MAGNETIC FIELDS. Its principles are used to study the atomic and nuclear properties of matter; two common laboratory techniques are NUCLEAR MAGNETIC RESONANCE and electron spin resonance. See also MAGNETIC RESONANCE IMAGING.

magnetic resonance imaging (MRI) Production of images from MAGNETIC RESONANCE. Lacking the possibly harmful effects of X RAYS or GAMMA RAYS, it is invaluable in detecting and delineating tumors and in providing images of the brain, the heart, and other soft-tissue organs. MRI may produce anxiety because the patient must often lie perfectly still inside a narrow tube. It requires a longer scanning time than other computer-assisted forms of scanning, which makes it more sensitive to motion and of less value in scanning the chest or abdomen, but MRI images provide better contrast between normal and diseased tissue.

magnetism Phenomenon associated with MAGNETIC FIELDS, the effects of such fields, and the motion of ELECTRIC CHARGES (see DIAMAGNETISM, PARAMAGNETISM, FERROMAGNETISM, and FERRIMAGNETISM). Magnetic fields exert forces on moving ELECTRIC CHARGES; the effects are evident in the deflection of an electron beam in a CATHODE-RAY TUBE and the motor force on a current-carrying CONDUCTOR. Other applications of magnetism range from the simple magnetic door catch to medical imaging devices and electromagnets used in high-energy PARTICLE ACCELERATORS.

magnetite or **lodestone** or **magnetic iron ore** Iron oxide mineral, the chief member of a series of the spinel group. Minerals in this series form black to brownish, metallic, moderately hard octahedrons and masses in igneous and metamorphic rocks. Magnetite, as the name implies, is strongly attracted to a MAGNET, and is a common constituent of iron ores. Magnetite with an intrinsic magnetic field (a natural magnet) is known as lodestone.

magneto \mag-ˈnē-tō\ Permanent-magnet alternating generator used mainly to produce electrical current for the IGNITION SYSTEM in various types of INTERNAL-COMBUSTION ENGINES, such as aircraft, marine, tractor, and motorcycle engines. Its main parts are a permanent-magnet rotor, a primary winding of a small number of turns of coarse wire, a secondary winding with a large number of turns of fine wire, a cam-type circuit breaker, and a capacitor. As the rotor turns, it produces a current in the primary winding, charging the capacitor. The cam breaks the circuit, and the magnetic field around the primary winding collapses. The capacitor releases its stored current into the primary winding, causing a reversed magnetic field. The collapse and reversal of the magnetic field produce a current in the secondary winding that is sent to the SPARK PLUGS.

magnetosphere Region around a PLANET where magnetic phenomena and the high atmospheric conductivity caused by IONIZATION strongly influence how charged particles act

(see ELECTRIC CHARGE). A planet's MAGNETIC FIELD becomes weaker farther from the planet. The SOLAR WIND sweeps the magnetosphere away from the sun in a "tail" well beyond the planet.

magnitude Measure of the brightness of a star or other celestial body. The brighter the object, the lower the number of its magnitude. In ancient times, six magnitude classes were used. Today a difference of one magnitude is defined as a ratio of brightness of 2.512 times. Apparent magnitude is brightness as seen from earth (e.g., −26.7 for the sun, about −11 for the moon). Absolute magnitude is brightness as seen at a distance of 10 PARSECS (e.g., 4.8 for the sun). See also ALBEDO, PHOTOMETRY.

magnolia Any of about 80 species of trees and shrubs in the widely distributed genus *Magnolia*. They are valued for their fragrant flowers and handsome leaves. *Magnolia* is one of 12 genera in the family Magnoliaceae, which contains 210 species. Magnolias are among the most primitive of flowering plants; their primitive features include spiral arrangement of flower parts and simple water-conducting cells.

Magnus Eriksson (1316–1374) King of Sweden (1319–63, as Magnus II) and Norway (1319–55, as Magnus VII). Grandson of Norway's Haakon V, and nephew of the Swedish king, Magnus became ruler of both countries. Since he spent almost all his time in Sweden, Norwegian nobles arranged for his son Haakon's succession, and Magnus abdicated in 1355. After curbing the economic power of the church and nobility, in 1356 he was forced to cede half his Swedish kingdom to his son Erik. When he renewed his efforts to control the Swedish nobles, they deposed him.

magpie Any of several genera of long-tailed songbirds of the CROW family (Corvidae). The black-billed magpie (*Pica pica*) is 18 in. (45 cm) long and strikingly pied (black-and-white), with an iridescent blue-green tail. It is found in NW Africa, across Eurasia, and in W N. America. A bird of farmlands and tree-studded open country, it may eat the eggs and young of other birds and fresh carrion. It is known for hoarding small, bright objects. Other species (in the genera *Cyanopica*, *Cissa*, and *Urocissa*) include the brilliant blue or green magpies of Asia.

Magritte \mȧ-ˈgret\, **René (-François-Ghislain)** (1898–1967) Belgian painter. After art study in Brussels, he designed wallpaper and did advertising sketches until the support of an art gallery enabled him to become a full-time painter. His early works were in the Cubist and Futurist styles, but in 1922 he discovered the work of Giorgio de CHIRICO and embraced SURREALISM with *The Menaced Assassin* (1927). Certain images reappear in Magritte's works—the sea, wide skies, the female torso, the bourgeois "little man" in a bowler hat—and dislocations of space, time, and scale were common elements in his enigmatic paintings.

Magsaysay \mäg-ˈsī-ˌsī\, **Ramon** (1907–1957) President of the Philippines (1953–57). A guerrilla leader during World War II, he served as a liberal congressman 1946–50. In 1950, as secretary of defense, he launched one of the most successful antiguerrilla campaigns in modern history against insurgents of the HUKBALAHAP REBELLION. He deprived them of popular support by offering peasants land and tools and insisting that the army treat them with respect. In 1953 Magsaysay was elected president. His efforts at land reform were frustrated by a conservative congress. He died in an airplane crash.

magus \ˈmā-gəs\ Member of an ancient Persian clan specializing in cultic activities. The magi were a priestly caste during the SELEUCID, Parthian, and SASANIAN dynasties. Their PRIESTHOOD is believed to have served several religions, including ZOROASTRIANISM. From the 1st cent. A.D. onward, the word was applied to magicians and soothsayers, chiefly from BABYLONIA. The Persian magi were credited with profound religious knowledge, but the Babylonian magi were often considered outright imposters. See also MAGI.

Magyars \ˈmag-ˌyärz, ˈmä-ˌjärz\ People who form the dominant ethnic group in Hungary. Speakers of a FINNO-UGRIC LANGUAGE, they migrated from their early home in E European Russia across the steppes into the N Balkans in the 9th cent. After collisions with neighboring peoples, the

Magyars settled in the middle basin of the Danube River in the late 9th cent., subjugating Slavs and other peoples there. They adopted Christianity in the 11th cent.

Mahabharata \mə-ˌhä-ˈbä-rə-tə\ One of the two major SANSKRIT epics of India, valued for its literary merit and its religious inspiration. It tells of the struggle for supremacy between two groups of cousins, incorporating many myths and legends along with didactic material on topics such as the proper conduct of a warrior. Together with the RAMAYANA, it is an important source of information about the evolution of HINDUISM. It contains the BHAGAVADGITA, Hinduism's single most important religious text. The sage Vyasa (fl.c.5th cent. B.C.) is traditionally named as the *Mahabharata*'s author. The poem reached its present form around A.D. 400.

Mahan \mə-ˈhan\, **Alfred Thayer** (1840–1914) U.S. naval officer and historian. Born in West Point, N.Y., he studied at the U.S. Naval Academy. His nearly 40 years of active naval duty included fighting in the American Civil War. He was president of the Naval War College in Newport, R.I. (1886–89). His books *The Influence of Sea Power upon History, 1660–1783* (1890) and *The Influence of Sea Power upon the French Revolution and Empire, 1793–1812* (1892) were avidly read in Britain and Germany, and greatly influenced the buildup of naval forces before World War I.

Maharishi Mahesh Yogi *orig.* Mahad Prasad Varma (b.1911?) Indian religious leader, founder of TRANSCENDENTAL MEDITATION (TM). He took a degree in physics before going to the Himalayas to study with the yogi Guru Dev for 13 years. He arrived in the U.S. in 1959, preaching the virtues of TM; in the 1960s the BEATLES were his most celebrated followers. He returned to India in the late 1970s and moved to the Netherlands in 1990. His organization was worth more than $3 billion in the late 1990s.

Mahathir bin Mohamad \mä-ˈhä-tēr-bin-mō-ˈhä-məd\ *in full* Datuk (Headman) Seri Mahathir bin Mohamad (b.1925) Malaysian politician, prime minister from 1981. A physician, he entered Parliament in 1964, where he became a forceful advocate of policies to ensure ethnic Malay economic success. Under his leadership as prime minister, Malaysia acquired one of the most prosperous economies in S.E. Asia, rising literacy rates, and increased life expectancies. The economy plunged in the late 1990s, but Mahathir kept a tenacious grip on his power.

Mahayana \mə-ˌhä-ˈyä-nə\ One of the three major Buddhist traditions. It arose in the 1st cent. A.D. and is widely followed today in China, Korea, Japan, and Tibet. Mahayanists distinguish themselves from the more conservative THERAVADA Buddhists of Sri Lanka, Burma, Thailand, Laos, and Cambodia. Whereas the Theravadins view the historical Buddha as a (merely) human teacher of the truth, Mahayanists see him as an earthly manifestation of a celestial Buddha. Mahayanists revere BODHISATTVAS, key figures in universal salvation. Compassion, the chief virtue of the bodhisattva, is valued as highly as wisdom, the virtue emphasized by the ancient Buddhists. See also NICHIREN BUDDHISM, TIBETAN BUDDHISM, ZEN.

mahdi (Arabic: "divinely guided one") In Islamic eschatology, a messianic deliverer who will bring justice to the earth, restore true religion, and usher in a short golden age before the end of the world. The mahdi is not mentioned in the QURAN and is questioned by SUNNI theologians, but is important in SHIITE doctrine. The doctrine of the mahdi gained currency during the upheavals of early ISLAM (7th–8th cent.) and received new emphasis in periods of crisis. The title has been claimed by Islamic revolutionaries, notably in N. Africa (see MAHDIST MOVEMENT).

Mahdist movement \ˈmä-dəst\ Religious and political movement founded by the Sudanese prophet al-Mahdi (1844–1885). He adopted the name (meaning "Divinely Inspired One") believing that he had been divinely chosen to lead a holy war against Sudan's Egyptian ruling class for deserting the Islamic faith. His uprising began in 1881; within four years he had conquered almost all the territory formerly occupied by Egypt, his crowning victory being the capture of KHARTOUM from Gen. Charles GORDON in 1885. He became head of an armed theocracy based at OMDURMAN. When he died from illness, his disciple Abd Allah succeeded

him. Following initial victories, Abd Allah's forces were hunted down by Anglo-Egyptian armies under H. H. KITCHENER and destroyed in the Battle of Omdurman.

Mahfouz \mä-ˈfüz\, **Naguib** (b.1911) Egyptian writer. His major work, the *Cairo Trilogy* (1956–57), represents a penetrating overview of 20th-cent. Egyptian society. Subsequent works, including *Children of Gebelawi* (1959) and *Miramar* (1967), offer critical views of the Egyptian monarchy, colonialism, and contemporary Egypt. He has also written short-story collections, more than 30 screenplays, and stage plays. In 1988 he became the first Arabic writer to win the Nobel Prize.

Mahican \mə-ˈhē-kən\ *or* **Mohican** \mō-ˈhē-kən\ N American Indian people of the upper Hudson River Valley. They lived in strongholds of 20–30 houses situated on hills or in woodlands. In 1664 they were forced by the MOHAWK to move to what is now Stockbridge, Mass.; later they moved to Wisconsin, where they now number about 1,000. James Fenimore COOPER drew a romanticized portrait of the declining Mahican in *The Last of the Mohicans* (1826).

Mahilyow *or* **Mogilev** \mə-gi-ˈlyóf\ City (pop., 1998: 369,000), E central Belarus, on the DNIEPER RIVER. It was founded in 1267 as a fortress and became a town in 1526 under Lithuanian rule. Later passing to Poland, it became Russian in 1772. In 1812 a major battle between NAPOLEON's troops and Russian forces was fought nearby. It is now a major industrial city.

Mahler, Gustav (1860–1911) Austro-Hungarian composer and conductor. Born in Bohemia, he attended the Vienna Conservatory. In 1880 he decided to become a conductor, and though critics found his interpretations extreme, by 1886 he had achieved success in Prague. He also began the first of his ten symphonies (1888–1910), his main compositional legacy. In 1897 he was named director of the Vienna Opera; his stormy reign there was acknowledged as an artistic success. He moved to the Metropolitan Opera in 1908 and the New York Philharmonic in 1909–10. Ill with heart disease and mourning

Gustav Mahler

his daughter's death, he wrote the masterly orchestral song cycle *Das Lied von der Erde* (1908–9) and his ninth symphony. His orchestral songs *Des Knaben Wunderhorn* (1892–98) and *Kindertotenlieder* (1904) are frequently performed. His emotionally charged and subtly orchestrated music waited decades to be widely accepted.

Mahmud of Ghazna \mä-ˈmüd\ (971–1030) Son of the founder of the GHAZNAVID dynasty, Sebuktigin. He ascended the throne in 998 and was granted autonomy by the ABBASID caliph. He expanded his kingdom into the Punjab and NE India, carrying with him the banner of Islam. With the treasures he amassed, he transformed the city of Ghazna (modern Ghazni, Afghanistan) into a brilliant cultural center. At his court were the scholar al-BIRUNI and the poet FERDOWSI.

mahogany family Family Meliaceae (order Sapindales), composed of 575 species of trees in 51 genera, native to tropical and subtropical regions. Trees of the genus *Swietenia* and *Entandrophragma*, commonly called mahogany, and of the genus *Cedrela* (especially the cigar-box cedar, *C. odorata*) are economically important timber trees. The China tree (*Melia azedarach*) is an ornamental Asian tree with lilac-colored flowers and poisonous yellow fruits. Most members of the family have large compound leaves and branched flower clusters. A few have edible fruits.

Maidstone Town (pop., 1994 est.: 139,000), seat of KENT, SE England. Lying southeast of LONDON, it was a residence of the Norman archbishops of CANTERBURY until the REFORMATION, and grew as a market town. It is located in England's largest hops-growing area, and brewing is important to its economy. Among many sites of architectural interest is the medieval archbishop's palace.

mail, chain See CHAIN MAIL
Mailer, Norman (b.1923) U.S. novelist. Born in Long Branch, N.J., he drew on his wartime service in the Pacific for his celebrated novel *The Naked and the Dead* (1948), which established him as one of the major postwar Jewish-American writers. A flamboyant and controversial figure who has enjoyed antagonizing critics and readers, he has since commanded less respect for his fiction than for journalistic works that convey actual events with the richness of novels, including *The Armies of the Night* (1968, Pulitzer Prize); *Miami and the Siege of Chicago* (1968); and *The Executioner's Song* (1979, Pulitzer Prize), about the execution of a murderer.

Maillol \mä-ˈyȯl\, **Aristide** (1861–1944) French sculptor, painter, and printmaker. He was a painter and tapestry designer until he was almost 40, when eyestrain persuaded him to turn to sculpture. He rejected the highly emotional style of Auguste RODIN and attempted to preserve and purify the classical sculpture of Greece and Rome. Most of his works depict the mature female form, and are characterized by emotional restraint and serene surfaces. After 1910 he was internationally famous. Later in life, he produced excellent woodcut illustrations for fine editions of Latin poets.

Maimonides \mī-ˈmä-nə-ˌdēz\, **Moses** orig. Moses ben Maimon (1135–1204) Jewish philosopher, jurist, and physician. Born in Spain, he settled in Egypt (1165), where he was free to practice his faith. There his medical skill led to his becoming SALADIN's court physician. Maimonides' first major work was an Arabic commentary on the MISHNA. His other writings included a monumental code of Jewish law called the *Mishne Torah* (in Hebrew) and the classic *Guide of the Perplexed* (in Arabic), which called for a more rational approach to Judaism and sought to reconcile science, philosophy, and religion. He is considered the greatest intellectual figure of medieval Judaism.

Maine State (pop., 2000: 1,274,000), NE U.S. One of the NEW ENGLAND states, it covers 33,265 sq mi (86,156 sq km); its capital is AUGUSTA. The APPALACHIAN MTNS. cross the state, rising to 5,268 ft (1,606 m) at Mt. Katahdin; Maine's upland region has many lakes and valleys, and its Atlantic coast is rocky and scenic. Algonquian Indians were the earliest-known inhabitants of the area. European settlers found the Penobscot and Passamaquoddy tribes living along the river valleys and coasts. The French included Maine as part of the province of ACADIA in 1603, and Britain included it in territory granted to the PLYMOUTH CO. in 1606. During the 17th cent. Britain established scattered settlements, but the area was a constant battleground until the British conquered the French in E Canada in 1763. Maine was governed as a district of MASSACHUSETTS from 1652 until it was admitted as the 23rd state of the Union under the MISSOURI COMPROMISE in 1820. Its Canadian boundary was established in 1842. The AMERICAN CIVIL WAR and the INDUSTRIAL REVOLUTION diverted workers and capital from Maine in the 19th cent. In the 20th cent. it has seen slow but steady economic gains, especially in the SW coastal region. Its economy is based on agriculture and natural resources. Chief products include timber and wood products, potatoes, and lobsters. Tourism is also an important source of income.

Maine \ˈmen\ Historical region, NW France. A hereditary countship in the 10th cent., it was united with ANJOU in 1126 and came under England in 1154. It fell to France early in the 13th cent. After alternating between English and French rule, it reverted to France in 1481 and was made a duchy under LOUIS XIV.

Maine, **destruction of the** (Feb. 15, 1898) Incident preceding the SPANISH–AMERICAN WAR in which a mysterious explosion sank the U.S. battleship *Maine* in the harbor of Havana, Cuba, killing 260 sailors. The U.S. had sent the *Maine* in January 1898 to protect U.S. citizens and property after riots in Cuba's struggle for independence from Spain. U.S. anti-Spanish sentiment was inflamed by newspapers proclaiming "Remember the *Maine*, to hell with Spain!" and armed intervention followed in April. Investigation has since shown that the explosion was caused internally.

Maine coon cat N. America's only native breed of long-haired DOMESTIC CAT. It was first shown in Boston in 1878.

Maines are large, muscular, and heavy-boned; they may have been named for their raccoon-like tail. Excellent mousers, they are known for their gentleness and intelligence, and are especially good with children and dogs.

mainframe DIGITAL COMPUTER designed for high-speed, high-volume data processing. They have been used for such applications as payroll computations, accounting, business transactions, information retrieval, airline reservations, and scientific and engineering computations. Mainframe systems, with remote "dumb" terminals, have been displaced in many applications by CLIENT-SERVER ARCHITECTURE.

Main River \ˈmīn\ River, central Germany. Rising in N Bavaria, and flowing west, it passes through FRANKFURT before emptying into the RHINE RIVER; it is 326 mi (524 km) long. It forms part of the Main-Danube Canal, which links the Rhine and DANUBE rivers to create a 2,200-mi (3,500-km) waterway from the North Sea to the Black Sea.

Maintenon \maⁿ-tə-ˈnōⁿ\, **marquise de** orig. Françoise d'Aubigné known as **Madame de Maintenon** (1635–1719) Second wife of LOUIS XIV of France. In 1652 she married the poet Paul Scarron, 25 years her senior, and presided over his literary salon. Widowed in 1660, she was left penniless, but managed to become governess in 1668 to the king's children born to his mistress. In 1675 Louis bestowed the Château de Maintenon and lands on her, and after the queen's death in 1683 he secretly married her, either in 1683 or 1697. Though blamed for being a bad influence on Louis politically, she maintained a climate of dignity and piety around him.

Mainz \ˈmīnts\ French **Mayence** \mä-ˈyäⁿs\ City (pop., 1998 est.: 186,000), W central Germany. Situated on the RHINE RIVER opposite the mouth of the MAIN RIVER, it was established as a Roman military camp around 14 B.C. It became an archbishopric in A.D. 775, a free city in 1244, and the head of the Rhenish League in 1254. It served as a fortress of the GERMAN CONFEDERATION and later of the German empire until 1918. Severely damaged during World War II, it was rebuilt. It is the birthplace of Johannes GUTENBERG.

maiolica See MAJOLICA
Maipuran languages See ARAWAKAN LANGUAGES
maize See CORN
majolica \mə-ˈjä-li-kə\ Italian **maiolica** \mə-ˈyä-li-kə\ Tin-glazed EARTHENWARE introduced from Moorish Spain by way of the island of Majorca and produced in Italy from the 14th cent. It is usually restricted to five colors: cobalt blue, antimony yellow, iron red, copper green, and manganese purple. White tin enamel was used also for highlights. Its most common shape was a display dish, decorated in the *istoriato* style, a 16th-cent. Italian narrative style that uses the pottery body solely as support for a purely pictorial effect. Majolica from the cities of Faenza and Urbino has long been particularly prized. The name faience is given to Faenza-style majolica from elsewhere in Europe and to the glazed earthenware tiles, ornaments, and figurines of ancient Egypt.

Major, John (b.1943) British prime minister (1990–97). He was elected to the House of Commons as a Conservative in 1979, and in 1989 Margaret THATCHER appointed him foreign secretary and then chancellor of the exchequer. He won the party leadership after Thatcher's resignation in 1990 and in 1992 won in the general election. Major's first years in office coincided with a long recession (1990–93), and Major himself was perceived as colorless and indecisive. In 1997 the Conservatives lost by a landslide to the Labour Party, led by Tony BLAIR.

Majorca \mä-ˈjȯr-kə, mä-ˈyȯr-kə\ Spanish **Mallorca** \mä-ˈlyȯr-kə\ ancient Balearis Major. Island (pop., 1994 est.: 737,000) and autonomous community, Spain. Its capital is PALMA. The largest of the BALEARIC ISLANDS, it occupies 1,405 sq mi (3,640 sq km). The kingdom of Majorca was established by JAMES I of Aragon in the 13th cent. It is now a popular tourist center.

Majuro \mä-ˈjü-rō\ Atoll (pop., 1999: 23,000), SE MARSHALL ISLANDS, W Pacific Ocean. It comprises 64 islets on a 25-mi (40-km) reef and has a total land area of 4 sq mi (10 sq km). It has the largest population of any of the Marshall Islands; the city Majuro is the capital of the republic.

Makalu \\'mə-kə-ˌlü\\ Peak in the HIMALAYAS, on the Nepalese–Tibetan border. Located east-southeast of Mt. EVEREST, it reaches 27,766 ft (8,463 m), making it the world's fifth-highest mountain. Two French climbers—Jean Couzy (1923–1958) and Lionel Terray (1921?–1965)—reached the summit in 1955.

Makarios III \\mä-'kär-ē-ˌōs\\ *orig.* Mikhai Khristodolou Mouskos (1913–1977) Archbishop and primate of the Orthodox Church of Cyprus. Son of a poor shepherd, he was ordained in 1946; he became bishop in 1948 and archbishop in 1950. A supporter of Cyprus's union with Greece, opposing both independence and partition, he negotiated with the British governor of Cyprus (1955–56), but was arrested for sedition and exiled. In 1959 he accepted independence and was elected president, with a Turkish vice president, serving a total of three terms.

Makarova \\mä-'kär-ə-və\\, **Natalia (Romanovna)** (b.1940) Russian ballerina, considered one of the greatest of classical dancers. She trained in Leningrad (St. Petersburg), joining the Kirov Ballet in 1959 to become a leading ballerina. She defected in London in 1970, and soon joined the AMERICAN BALLET THEATRE. She is best known for her leading role in *Giselle*.

Makassar Strait \\mə-'ka-sər\\ Narrow ocean passage, Indonesia. Located between BORNEO and SULAWESI, it is 500 mi (800 km) long and 80–230 mi (130–370 km) wide. It contains numerous islands. In 1942, during World War II, it was the scene of naval and air battles as the Allies tried to prevent the Japanese from occupying BORNEO.

mako shark \\'mä-kō\\ Any of certain potentially dangerous SHARKS (genus *Isurus*) in the mackerel shark family (Isuridae). Two species are generally recognized: the Atlantic *I. oxyrinchus* and the Indo-Pacific *I. glaucus*. They are about 13 ft (4 m) long and weigh about 1,000 lbs (450 kg). They prey on herring, mackerel, and swordfish. Outstanding game fish, they are prized for their fighting qualities and their spectacular leaps out of the water.

Malabar Coast \\'ma-lə-ˌbär\\ Region, SW coast of India, stretching from the Western GHATS to the Arabian Sea. It now includes most of Kerala state and the coastal region of Karnataka state. The term has sometimes been used to mean the entire W coast of peninsular India. The Portuguese established trading posts there; they were followed by the Dutch in the 17th cent., the French in the 18th cent., and the British in the late 18th cent.

Malabo \\mä-'lä-bō\\ *formerly (until 1973)* **Santa Isabel** City (pop., 1995 est.: 48,000), capital of EQUATORIAL GUINEA. Located on the island of BIOKO, it is the republic's commercial and financial center. The main activity of its harbor is the export of cocoa, timber, and coffee. Its European population declined after 1969 riots there.

Malacca \\mə-'lä-kə\\, **Strait of** Channel connecting the Indian Ocean and the S. CHINA SEA. It separates SUMATRA from the MALAY PENINSULA. It is 500 mi (800 km) long; numerous islets hinder passage at its S entrance. The shortest sea route between India and China, it is one of the most heavily traveled shipping channels in the world.

Malacca, sultanate of (1403?–1511) Malay dynasty that ruled the great trading port of Malacca (Melaka) and its dependencies. Commanding the main sea route between India and China, Malacca was founded by Paramcsvara (d.1424), who converted to Islam and took the title Sultan Iskandar Shah in 1414. It benefited from China's trade with the West, and became a major commercial emporium; by the 1450s it was an important territorial power as well. The wealthy state encouraged literature, learning, and a lively political and religious life; the period of its ascendancy is considered the golden age of Malay history. The city fell to the Portuguese in 1511.

Malachi \\'ma-lə-ˌkī\\ (5th cent. B.C.) One of the 12 Minor Prophets in the OLD TESTAMENT. (His prophecy is part of a larger book, The Twelve, in the Jewish canon.) The book consists of dialogues in question-and-answer form, in which the prophet defends the justice of God to a community doubtful because its expectations of salvation for Israel are unfulfilled. Malachi calls for faithfulness to God's covenant and promises that the day of judgment will soon arrive. The book was probably written in the 5th cent. B.C.

malachite \\'ma-lə-ˌkīt\\ Widespread CARBONATE MINERAL of copper, a hydrous copper carbonate. Its distinctive bright green color and its presence in nearly all copper deposits make it useful as a prospecting guide. It is found in Siberia, France, Namibia, and Arizona in the U.S. Malachite has been used as an ornamental stone and as a gemstone.

Málaga \\'mä-lä-gä\\ Port city (pop., 1998 est.: 528,000), S Spain. It lies on the Costa del Sol of the Mediterranean Sea. Founded by the PHOENICIANS in the 12th cent. B.C., it was later conquered by the Romans and the Visigoths. Under Moorish rule from 711 A.D., it became a chief city of ANDALUSIA. It fell to FERDINAND II and ISABELLA I in 1487. It is the foremost Spanish Mediterranean port after BARCELONA; among its exports are fruit and Malaga wine. It was the birthplace of Pablo PICASSO.

Malagasy peoples \\ˌma-lə-'ga-sē\\ Complex of about 20 ethnic groups in Madagascar. The largest group is the Merina ("Elevated People"), who primarily inhabit the central plateau. The second-largest are the Betsimisaraka, who live generally in the east. The third is the Betsileo, who inhabit the plateau around Fianarantsoa. Others include the Tsimihety, the Sakalava, the Antandroy, the Tanala, the Antaimoro, and the Bara. Most Malagasy peoples live in rural areas and grow rice, cassava, and other crops. About half are Christian, while the rest practice traditional religion based on ancestor worship.

Malamud \\'ma-lə-ˌməd\\, **Bernard** (1914–1986) U.S. novelist and short-story writer. Born to Russian-Jewish immigrants in Brooklyn, N.Y., he wrote novels that often make parables out of Jewish immigrant life. These include *The Natural* (1952), about a baseball hero; *The Assistant* (1957), about a Jewish grocer and a Gentile hoodlum; and *The Fixer* (1966, Pulitzer Prize), often considered his finest novel. His genius is most apparent in his stories, collected in *The Magic Barrel* (1958), *Pictures of Fidelman* (1969), and other volumes.

malamute, Alaskan See ALASKAN MALAMUTE

Malan \\mə-'lan\\, **Daniel F(rançois)** (1874–1959) S. African politician. A Dutch Reformed minister before entering parliament (1918), Malan joined J. B. M. HERTZOG's cabinet (1924–33), broke with Hertzog to form the Purified Nationalist Party (1934), then reconciled with him in 1939 and assumed leadership of the NATIONAL PARTY. His party won the 1948 elections; Malan formed S. Africa's first exclusively Afrikaner government (1948–54) and instituted APARTHEID.

malaria Protozoal disease, a serious, relapsing infection caused by protozoa of the genus *Plasmodium* (see PLASMODIUM), transmitted by the bite of *Anopheles* MOSQUITOES. It occurs in tropical and subtropical regions near swamps. The roles of the mosquito and the parasite were not proven until the early 20th cent. Annual cases worldwide are estimated at 250 million and deaths at 2 million. The parasites have an extremely complex life cycle; in one stage they develop synchronously inside red blood cells. Their mass fissions at 48- or 72-hour intervals cause attacks lasting 4–10 hours. Shaking and chills are followed by fever of up to 105°F (40.6°C), with severe headache, then profuse sweating. Patients often have anemia, spleen enlargement, and general weakness. Complications can be fatal. Malaria is diagnosed by detecting the parasites in blood. QUININE was long used to alleviate the fevers. Synthetic drugs, such as chloroquine, have replaced it, but many strains are now resistant. Malaria prevention requires eliminating mosquito breeding places and using insecticides or natural predators, window screens, netting, and insect repellent.

Malawi \\mä-'lä-wē\\ *officially* **Republic of Malawi** *formerly* **Nyasaland** \\nī-'a-sə-ˌland\\ Country, SE Africa. Area: 45,747 sq mi (118,484 sq km). Population (2000): 10,386,000. Capital: LILONGWE. Almost the entire population consists of BANTU-speaking black Africans. Languages: English, Chichewa. Religions: Protestantism, Roman Catholicism, Islam, animism. Currency: kwacha. Malawi's terrain is characterized by dramatic highlands and extensive lakes, with forests occupying about two-fifths of the total land area. The GREAT RIFT VALLEY runs north–south and contains Lake MALAWI. Agriculture employs four-fifths of the workforce; staple crops include corn, peanuts, beans, and peas, and cash crops include tobacco, tea, sugarcane, and

MALAWI

Scale 1: 13,300,000

0   50   100 mi
0 50 100 150 km

©1999, Encyclopædia Britannica, Inc.

cotton. Coal mining and the quarrying of limestone also contribute to the economy. Major industrial products are sugar, beer, cigarettes, soap, chemicals, and textiles. It is a republic with one legislative house; its head of state and government is the president. Inhabited since 8000 B.C., the region was settled by Bantu-speaking peoples between the 1st and 4th cent. A.D. They established separate states, and about 1480 they founded the Maravi Confederacy, which encompassed most of central and S Malawi. In N Malawi the Ngonde people established a kingdom around 1600, and in the 18th cent. the Chikulamayembe state was founded. The slave trade flourished during the 18th–19th cent., the same era in which Islam and Christianity arrived in the region. Britain established colonial authority in 1891, creating the Nyasaland Districts Protectorate. It became the British Central Africa Protectorate in 1893 and Nyasaland in 1907. The colonies of Northern and Southern Rhodesia and Nyasaland formed a federation (1951–53), which was dissolved in 1963. The next year Malawi achieved independence as a member of the British COMMONWEALTH. In 1966 it became a republic, with Hastings BANDA as president. In 1971 he was designated president for life, and he ruled for three decades before being defeated in multiparty presidential elections in 1994. A new constitution was adopted in 1995.

Malawi, Lake *or* **Lake Nyasa** \nī-'a-sə\ Lake, SE Africa, bounded by Malawi, Mozambique, and Tanzania. The southernmost and third-largest of the GREAT RIFT VALLEY lakes, it is about 360 mi (580 km) long and covers 11,430 sq mi (29,604 sq km). It contains Likoma Island, site of an Anglican cathedral completed in 1911. Fed by 14 rivers, its sole outlet is the Shire River. There are about 200 recorded species of fish in the lake.

Malayalam language \ˌmä-lə-'yä-ləm\ DRAVIDIAN LANGUAGE spoken by more than 34 million people mainly in the Indian state of Kerala. Malayalam is closely related to TAMIL. The earliest literary composition in the language is from the 13th cent. Like other major Dravidian languages, Malayalam has a number of dialects that reflect differences in caste and religion. Literacy among Malayalam-speakers is believed to be higher than literacy among speakers of any other Indian language.

Malayan Emergency (1948–60) Period of unrest following the creation of the Federation of Malaya (precursor of Malaysia) in 1948. The Communist Party of Malaya, which was mostly Chinese, was alarmed at the special guarantees of Malay rights and began a guerrilla insurgency. British efforts to suppress the insurgency militarily were unpopular,

especially their relocation of rural Chinese into tightly controlled "New Villages"; when the British addressed political and economic grievances, the rebels became isolated and the emergency ended.

Malay Archipelago Largest group of islands in the world, located off the SE coast of Asia. It consists of the more than 13,000 islands of INDONESIA and some 7,000 islands of the PHILIPPINES. Sometimes called the E. Indies, the archipelago extends along the equator for more than 3,800 mi (6,100 km). Principal islands include SUMATRA, JAVA, BORNEO, SULAWESI, the MOLUCCAS, NEW GUINEA, LUZON, MINDANAO, and the VISAYAN ISLANDS.

Malay language \mə-'lā, 'mā-ˌlā\ AUSTRONESIAN LANGUAGE with over 30 million first-language speakers in the Malay Peninsula, Sumatra, Borneo, and other parts of Indonesia and Malaysia. Malay became a LINGUA FRANCA in Indonesian ports, giving rise to a range of PIDGINS and CREOLES known as Bazaar Malay (Melayu Pasar). In 20th-cent. Indonesia, a standardized form of Malay was adopted as the national language, Indonesian, written in Latin letters. Similar standardizations of Malay are the national languages of Malaysia and Brunei. The oldest known Malay texts are 7th-cent. inscriptions from S Sumatra; a continuous Malay literary tradition did not begin until the Islamicization of the Malay Peninsula in the 14th cent.

Malayo-Polynesian languages See AUSTRONESIAN LANGUAGES

Malay Peninsula Peninsula, S.E. Asia. Containing W. Malaysia, SW Thailand, and Singapore, it occupies an area of 70,000 sq mi (180,000 sq km) and extends south for 700 mi (1,100 km) to Cape Balai, the southernmost point of the Asian continent. Its central mountain range is the source of many rivers. Both its W and E coast are exposed to monsoons. It has large tracts of tropical rain forest and is a major producer of rubber and tin.

Malays \mə-'lā, 'mā-ˌlā\ Members of an ethnic group that probably originated in Borneo and expanded into Sumatra and the Malay Peninsula. They constitute more than half the population of Peninsular Malaysia. They are mainly a rural people, growing rice for food and rubber as a cash crop. Influenced by India, they were Hinduized before converting to Islam in the 15th cent. Their culture has also been influenced by the Siamese, Javanese, and Sumatrans. Malay class distinctions are still marked, and marriages have traditionally been arranged by parents.

Malaysia Country, S.E. Asia. It is composed of two regions—Peninsular or W. Malaysia and E. Malaysia—separated by 400 mi (650 km) of the S. CHINA SEA. W. Malaysia has 11 states on the S half of the MALAY PENINSULA, and is bordered on the north by Thailand. E. Malaysia occupies the NW part of the island of BORNEO and consists of the states of Sarawak and Sabah. Area: 127,584 sq mi (330,442 sq km). Population (2000): 23,260,000. Capital: KUALA LUMPUR. Because it lies on the heavily traveled Strait of MALACCA, the country's population is a very diverse mix, in which ethnic Malays and Chinese form the largest groups. Smaller ethnic groups include Indians, Pakistanis, and Tamils. Languages: Malay (official), Chinese, Indo-European languages. Religions: Islam (official), Buddhism, Taoism, Confucianism, Hinduism. Currency: ringgit. W. Malaysia is largely mountainous; E. Malaysia has coastal plains rising to hills and then to a mountainous core. Much of Malaysia is covered by rain forest. Tree crops, notably rubber and palm oil, are the country's most important cash crops; rice is the chief staple crop. Petroleum drilling and production and tin mining are important, as is the manufacture of rubber goods, cement, and iron and steel products. It is a constitutional monarchy with two legislative houses; the chief of state is the Paramount Ruler, and the head of government is the prime minister. Malaya has been inhabited for 6,000–8,000 years, and small kingdoms existed in the 2nd–3rd cent. A.D., when adventurers from India first arrived. Sumatran exiles founded the city-state of Malacca about 1400, and it flourished as a trading and Islamic religious center until its capture by the Portuguese in 1511. Malacca passed to the Dutch in 1641. The British founded a settlement on Singapore island in 1819, and by 1867 they had established the Straits Settlements, including

M

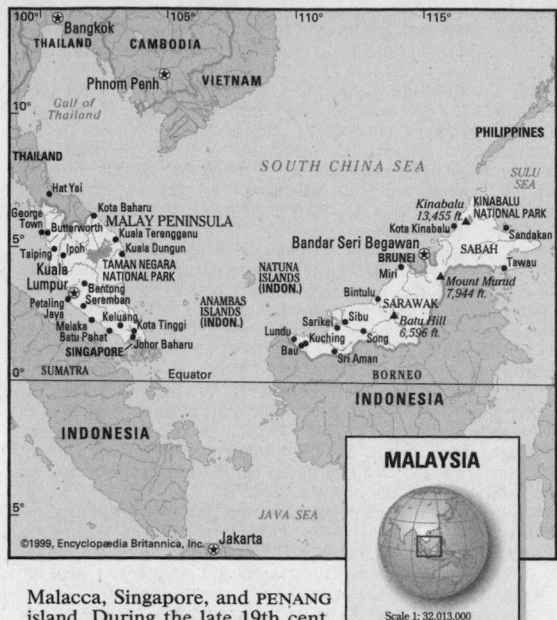

MALAYSIA

Scale 1: 32,013,000

0   150   300 mi
0   200   400 km

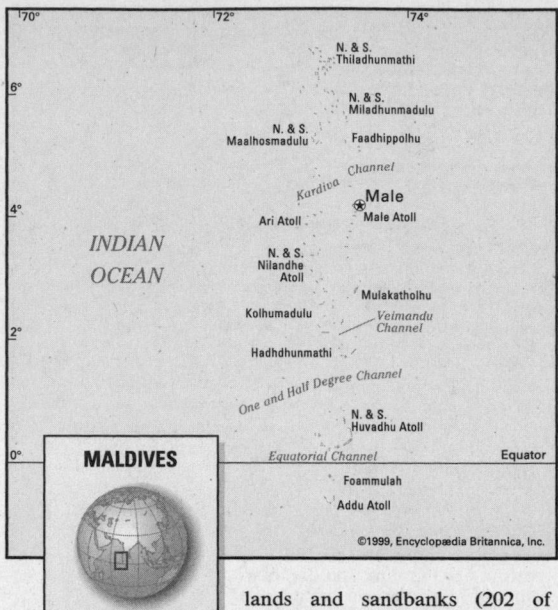

MALDIVES

Scale 1: 14,001,000

0   60   120 mi
0   80   180 km

©1999, Encyclopædia Britannica, Inc.

©1999, Encyclopædia Britannica, Inc.

Malacca, Singapore, and PENANG island. During the late 19th cent. Chinese began to migrate to Malaya. Japan invaded Malaya in 1941 and captured Singapore in 1942. Opposition to British rule led to the creation of the United Malaya National Organization (UMNO) in 1946, and in 1948 the peninsula was federated with Penang. Malaya gained independence from Britain in 1957, and the federation of Malaysia was established in 1963. Its economy expanded greatly from the late 1970s, and it is now a major exporter of semiconductors.

Malcolm II (954?–1034) King of Scotland (1005–34). He acquired the throne after killing Kenneth III and defeating a Northumbrian army at Carham (c.1016). He became the first king to reign over territory roughly equivalent to modern SCOTLAND. He tried to eliminate rivals to his grandson DUNCAN I, but Macbeth (d.1057) survived to challenge the succession.

Malcolm III Canmore (1031?–1093) King of Scotland (1058–93). The son of King DUNCAN I, he lived in exile in England after Macbeth killed his father (1040). He defeated and killed Macbeth in 1057 and was crowned king, founding a dynasty. He gave refuge to EDGAR THE AETHELING in 1066. Though he recognized WILLIAM I as overlord in 1072, Malcolm made five raids into England, during the last of which he was killed.

Malcolm X *orig.* Malcolm Little *later* El-Hajj Malik El-Shabazz (1925–1965) U.S. black militant leader. Born in Omaha, Neb., he was raised in Michigan, where his father was murdered and his mother was institutionalized. He moved to Boston, and was sent to prison for burglary in 1946. There he became a member of the black nationalist Nation of ISLAM the same year. On his release in 1952, he changed his last name to X, rejecting his "slave name." He became the Nation of Islam's most effective speaker and organizer, denouncing white exploitation of blacks, deriding the civil rights movement and integration, and calling for black separatism, black pride, and the use of violence for self-protection. Differences with the sect's leader, Elijah MUHAMMAD, prompted Malcolm to leave the Nation of Islam in 1964. A pilgrimage to Mecca led him to acknowledge the possibility of world brotherhood and to convert to orthodox Islam. Rival Black Muslims made death threats, and he was shot to death at a rally. His celebrated autobiography (1965) was written by Alex HALEY.

Maldives \\'mȯl-ˌdēvz\\ *officially* **Republic of Maldives** Independent island nation in the Indian Ocean, situated southwest of Sri Lanka. It is a chain of about 1,300 small coral is-

lands and sandbanks (202 of which are inhabited), grouped in clusters, or atolls. Area (land): 115 sq mi (298 sq km); the islands extend more than 510 mi (820 km) north–south and 80 mi (130 km) east–west. Population (2000): 285,000. Capital: MALE. The population is ethnically mixed; ancestors include Dravidian and Sinhalese peoples as well as Arabs, Chinese, and others from surrounding Asian areas. Languages: Divehi (official), Arabic, Hindi, English. Religion: Islam (official). Currency: rufiyaa. All of the islands are low-lying, none rising to more than 6 ft (1.8 m) above sea level. The atolls have sandy beaches, lagoons, and a luxuriant growth of coconut palms, together with breadfruit trees and tropical bushes. One of the world's poorest countries, the Maldives has a developing economy based on fishing, tourism, boatbuilding, and boat repairing. It is a republic with one legislative house; its head of state and government is the president. The archipelago was settled in the 5th cent. B.C. by Buddhists from Sri Lanka and S India, and Islam was adopted in 1153. The Portuguese held sway in Male in 1558–73. The islands were a sultanate under the Dutch rulers of Ceylon (now Sri Lanka) during the 17th cent. After the British gained control of Ceylon in 1796, the area became a British protectorate, a status formalized in 1887. The islands won full independence from Britain in 1965, and in 1968 a republic was founded and the sultanate was abolished. The Maldives joined the British COMMONWEALTH in 1982. From the 1990s its economy has gradually improved.

Male \\'mä-lē\\ Chief atoll (pop., 1995: 63,000) and capital of Maldives. It consists of two groups of islets: N. Male, 32 mi (51 km) by 23 mi (37 km); and S. Male, 20 mi (32 km) by 12 mi (19 km). It is a trade and tourist center.

Malenkov \\mə-'len-ˌkȯf\\, **Georgy (Maksimilianovich)** (1902–1988) Soviet prime minister (1953–55). He joined the Communist Party in 1920 and rose swiftly through the ranks as a close associate of Joseph STALIN. After Stalin's death (1953), he was forced to yield his post as senior party secretary to Nikita KHRUSHCHEV, but as prime minister Malenkov worked to reduce arms appropriations, increase the production of consumer goods, and provide more incentives for collective farm workers. Opposed by other party leaders, he was forced to resign (1955). Involved in the unsuccessful effort to depose Khrushchev, he was expelled from the party (1961) and exiled to central Asia to manage a hydroelectric plant.

Malevich \\mə-'lyä-vich\\, **Kazimir (Severinovich)** (1878–1935) Russian painter and designer. He returned from a trip to Paris in 1912 to lead the Russian Cubist movement. In 1915 he exhibited paintings more abstractly geometrical than any seen before, in a style he called SUPREMATISM. In 1917–18 he created his well-known *White on White* series, austere, unearthly images of a white square floating on a white background. In 1919 he joined Marc CHAGALL's art school in Vitebsk, where he influenced El LISSITZKY. In the 1920s he returned to representational painting but rejected the government's demand for SOCIALIST REALISM. Though his career was doomed, he greatly influenced Western art and design.

Mali *officially* **Republic of Mali** Country, W. Africa. Area: 482,077 sq mi (1,248,574 sq km). Population (2000): 10,686,000. Capital: BAMAKO. The BAMBARA constitute about one-third of the country's total population. Other ethnic groups include the FULANI, the BERBERS, and the MOORS. Languages: French (official), indigenous languages

and dialects, Arabic. Religions: Islam (90%), traditional beliefs. Currency: CFA franc. Mali's terrain is largely flat, and in the N part of the country its plains stretch into the SAHARA. The Upper Niger River basin is situated in the south, and nearly one-third of the total length of the NIGER RIVER flows through Mali. Only about 2% of Mali's total land area is considered arable. Its mineral reserves, which are largely unexploited, include iron ore, bauxite, petroleum, gold, nickel, and copper. Agriculture is the largest industry; staple crops include millet, sorghum, corn (maize), and rice; cash crops include cotton and peanuts. It is a republic with one legislative house; its head of state is the president, and the head of government is the prime minister. Inhabited since prehistoric times, the region was situated on a caravan route across the Sahara. In the 12th cent. the MALINKE empire of Mali was founded on the Upper and Middle Niger. In the 15th cent. the SONGHAI EMPIRE in the Timbuktu-Gao region gained control. In 1591 Morocco invaded the area, and Timbuktu (now TOMBOUCTOU) remained under the Moors for two centuries. In the mid-19th cent. the French conquered the area, which became part of French W. Africa. In 1946 the area, known as the French Sudan, became an overseas territory of the French Union. In 1958 it was proclaimed the Sudanese Republic and joined with Senegal (1959–60) to form the Mali Federation. Senegal seceded, and in 1960 the independent Republic of Mali was formed. The government was overthrown by military coups in 1968 and 1991. During the 1990s elections were held, the second time in 1997, but political instability continued.

Mali empire Trading empire that flourished in W. Africa in the 13th–16th cent. It developed from the state of Kangaba, on the Upper NIGER RIVER, and was probably founded before A.D. 1000. Its MALINKE inhabitants acted as middlemen in the GHANA EMPIRE's gold trade of the 13th–14th cent., when it absorbed Gao and Timbuktu (now TOMBOUCTOU). Its boundaries extended to the HAUSA people in the east and to the FULANI and Tukulor peoples in the west. By around 1550 it had ceased to be an important political entity.

Malinke \mə-ˈliŋ-kē\ *or* **Mandinka** *or* **Mandingo** Cluster of peoples occupying parts of Mali, Guinea, Ivory Coast, Senegal, Gambia, and Guinea-Bissau. They number 4.7 million. One group, the Kangaba, has one of the world's oldest dynasties, virtually continuous since the 7th-cent. founding of the MALI EMPIRE. Most Malinke grow millet and sorghum and tend cattle. Many practice Islam.

Malinowski \ˌma-lə-ˈnȯf-skē\, **Bronislaw (Kasper)** (1884–1942) Polish-British anthropologist principally associated with studies of the peoples of Oceania and with the school of thought known as FUNCTIONALISM. After taking degrees in philosophy, physics, and mathematics in Poland, Malinowski studied anthropology at the London School of Economics and Political Science (1910–16). Doing research in the Trobriand Islands, he lived in a tent among the TROBRIANDERS, spoke the vernacular fluently, recorded "texts" freely on the scene as well as in set interviews, and observed reactions with an acute clinical

Bronislaw Malinowski

eye. His work, presenting a dynamic picture of social institutions that clearly separated ideal norms from actual behavior, laid much of the basis for modern anthropological field research. He taught at the London School of Economics (1922–38) and Yale Univ. (1938–42). Among his books are *Argonauts of the Western Pacific* (1922), *Sex and Repression in Savage Society* (1927), and *Magic, Science and Religion* (1948).

Malla era Period of Nepal's history when the Malla dynasty ruled (10th–18th cent.). The Malla ruler Jaya Sthiti (r.1382?–95) introduced a legal and social code strongly influenced by contemporary Hindu principles. In the early 18th cent. one of Nepal's independent principalities, the Gurkha, began to challenge the Mallas, who were weakened by familial, social, and economic discontent; they were overthrown by the Gurkha in 1769.

mallard \ˈmal-ərd\ Abundant "wild duck" (*Anas platyrhynchos,* family Anatidae) of the Northern Hemisphere, ancestor of most domestic DUCKS. The mallard is a typical DABBLING DUCK in its general habits and courtship display. The drake of the common mallard (subspecies *A. p. platyrhynchos*) has a metallic green or purplish head, reddish breast, and light-gray body; the hen is mottled yellowish brown. Males and females of the Greenland mallard (*A. p. conboschas*) also differ markedly in plumage. In the other subspecies, both sexes resemble the female common mallard.

Mallarmé \ma̤-la̤r-ˈma̤\, **Stéphane** (1842–1898) French poet, an originator and leader of the SYMBOLIST MOVEMENT. Most of his verse expresses an intellectual longing to transcend reality and find refuge in an ideal world, as in the dramatic poems *Hérodiade* (1869) and *L'après-midi d'un faune* (1876; "The Afternoon of a Faun"), which inspired Claude DEBUSSY's famous prelude, and the typographically innovative *Un coup de dés* (1897). After 1868 he devoted himself to writing complex, exquisitely wrought, and extraordinarily difficult poems about the nature of imagination itself.

Malle \ˈma̤l\, **Louis** (1932–1995) French film director. He gained commercial success with *The Lovers* (1958), starring Jeanne MOREAU, becoming a leading figure in the French NEW WAVE. In such films as *The Fire Within* (1963), *Murmur* *of the Heart* (1971), and *Lacombe, Lucien* (1973), he achieved emotional realism and stylistic simplicity. In the U.S. he directed such admired films as *Pretty Baby* (1978), *Atlantic City* (1980), *My Dinner with André* (1981), *Au revoir les enfants* (1987), and *Vanya on 42nd Street* (1994).

Mallorca See MAJORCA

mallow family Family Malvaceae (order Malvales), which contains about 95 widely distributed genera of herbs, shrubs, and small trees. Hairs that branch into starlike patterns commonly cover some nonflower parts of these plants. The flowers are regular and often showy. COTTON is the most important member of the family economically. The green fruits of OKRA are edible. Many species are valued as ornamentals, including HIBISCUS, HOLLYHOCK, and rose of Sharon.

Malmö \'mäl-ˌmœ\ Port city (pop., 1999: 254,000), S Sweden, located across from COPENHAGEN. Chartered in the late 13th cent., it suffered an economic decline following its union with Sweden in 1658, owing in part to the loss of trade. The building of the harbor in 1775 and the arrival of the railroad after 1800 stimulated development. Sweden's third-largest city, it has an economy based on export products, shipbuilding, and textile manufactures. Its historic buildings include a 16th-cent. fortress, the town hall, and the 14th-cent. St. Peter's Church.

malnutrition Condition resulting from inadequate diet or from inability to absorb or metabolize nutrients because of disease. Food intake may be insufficient to supply CALORIES or PROTEIN (see KWASHIORKOR), or deficient in one or more essential VITAMINS or minerals. The latter case can lead to specific nutritional-deficiency diseases (including BERIBERI, PELLAGRA, RICKETS, and SCURVY). See also NEURAL TUBE DEFECT, NUTRITION, PERNICIOUS ANEMIA.

Malory, Sir Thomas (fl.c.1470) English author of *Le morte darthur* ("The Death of Arthur"). Even in the 16th cent. Malory's identity was unknown, but he was probably a Welshman and knight. *Le morte darthur* (completed c.1470) was the first account of ARTHURIAN LEGEND in English prose. Though based on French romances, it differs from its models in its emphasis on the brotherhood of the knights rather than on courtly love, and on the conflicts of loyalty that destroy the fellowship.

Malpighi \mal-ˈpē-gē\, **Marcello** (1628–1694) Italian physician and biologist. In 1661 he identified the pulmonary capillary network, proving William HARVEY's theory on blood CIRCULATION. He discovered the taste buds and was the first to see red blood cells and realize that they gave blood its color. He studied subdivisions of the liver, brain, spleen, kidneys, bone, and deeper skin layers (Malpighian layers), concluding that even the largest organs are composed of minute glands. Malpighi also studied insect larvae, chick embryology, and plant anatomy. He is regarded as the founder of microscopic ANATOMY and the first histologist.

malpractice NEGLIGENCE, misconduct, lack of ordinary skill, or breach of duty in performing a professional service that results in injury or loss. The plaintiff must usually demonstrate a failure to perform according to the field's accepted standards. Physicians, lawyers, accountants, and other professionals became increasingly subject to malpractice suits in the U.S. in the late 20th cent.

Malraux \mäl-ˈrō\, **André (-Georges)** (1901–1976) French writer and statesman. Imprisoned at 21 by French colonial authorities in Cambodia, Malraux became a fervent anticolonialist. He became involved with revolutionary movements in Indochina and later fought in the Spanish Civil War and with the French Resistance during World War II. He was Charles DE GAULLE's minister of cultural affairs 1958–68. His novels, which often draw on his experiences, include *The Conquerors* (1928) and *Man's Fate* (1933), his masterpiece. After

André Malraux, 1967

1945 he abandoned fiction for art history and criticism; *The Voices of Silence* (1951) is his major work of the period.

Malta Independent state, located on a small archipelago, south of Sicily in the Mediterranean Sea. It consists of three inhabited islands, Malta (the largest), Gozo, and Comino, and two uninhabited islets, Comminotto and Filfla. Area: 122 sq mi (316 sq km). Population (2000): 382,000. Capital:

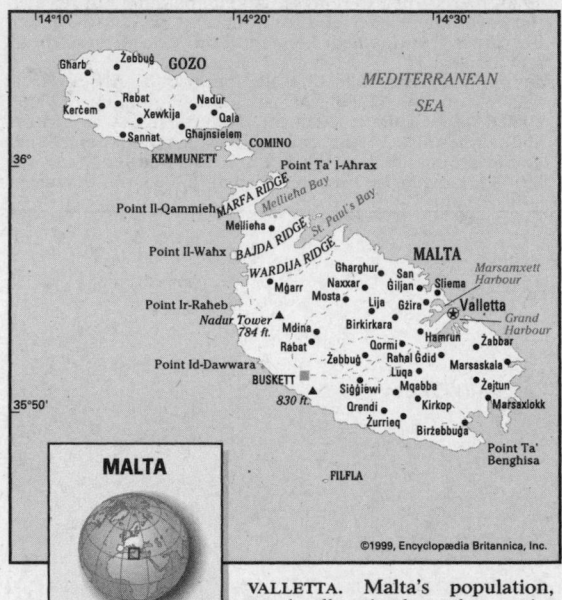

MALTA

Scale 1: 572,700

©1999, Encyclopædia Britannica, Inc.

VALLETTA. Malta's population, nearly all native-born, has a mixture of Italian, Arab, British, and Phoenician heritages. Languages: Maltese, English (both official). Religion: Roman Catholicism (official). Currency: Maltese lira. Although two-fifths of the total land area is arable, it imports most of its food; tourism is its major industry. It is a republic with one legislative house; its chief of state is the president, and its head of government is the prime minister. Inhabited as early as 3800 B.C., it was ruled by the Carthaginians around the 8th–7th cent. B.C. It came under Roman control in 218 B.C. In A.D. 60 the apostle PAUL was shipwrecked on the island and converted the inhabitants to Christianity. It was under Byzantine rule until the Arabs seized control in 870. In 1091 the Normans defeated the Arabs, and it was ruled by a succession of feudal lords until the early 16th cent. In 1530 it came under the KNIGHTS OF MALTA; NAPOLEON seized control in 1798, and the British took it in 1800. The 1802 Treaty of Amiens returned the islands to the Knights. The Maltese protested and acknowledged the British as sovereign; this arrangement was ratified in the 1814 Treaty of Paris. It became self-governing in 1921 but reverted to a colonial regime in 1936. Malta was severely bombed by Germany and Italy during World War II, and in 1942 it received Britain's George Cross; the medal had previously only been conferred upon individuals. In 1964 it gained independence within the Commonwealth, and in 1974 became a republic. When its alliance with Britain ended in 1979, Malta proclaimed its neutral status.

Malta, Knights of See KNIGHTS OF MALTA

Maltese Breed of TOY DOG named for the island of Malta, where it may have originated about 2,800 years ago. Delicate-looking but vigorous, affectionate, and lively, it was once the valued pet of the wealthy and aristocratic. It has a long, silky, pure-white coat, hanging ears, a compact body, and a plumed tail that curves over its back. It stands about 5 in. (13 cm) and weighs up to 7 lbs (3 kg).

Malthus \'mal-thəs\, **Thomas Robert** (1766–1834) British economist and demographer. In 1798 he published *An Essay on the Principle of Population*, in which he argued that population will always tend to outrun the food supply—that the increase of population will take place, if unchecked, in a geometrical progression, while the means of subsistence will increase only in an arithmetical progression. He believed population would expand to the limit of subsistence and would be held there by famine, war, and ill health. He argued that relief measures for the poor tended to encourage the growth of excess population. His theories, though erroneous, had great influence on contemporary social policy and on such economists as David RICARDO.

Malvinas, Islas See FALKLAND ISLANDS

mamba \\'mäm-bə\\ Any of four or five species of slender, agile elapid snakes (genus *Dendroaspis,* or *Dendraspis)* having large scales and long front teeth. They inhabit sub-Saharan Africa, where they hunt small animals. The aggressive black mamba *(D. polylepis)* grows up to 14 ft (4.2 m) long. It rears up to strike, biting a person's head or trunk. Its bite is nearly always fatal without antivenin treatment. The green mamba (e.g., *D. angusticeps*) is smaller (to 9 ft, or 2.7 m) and more arboreal.

Mamet \\'mam-it\\, **David (Alan)** (b.1947) U.S. playwright and screenwriter. Born in Chicago, he won notice with *Sexual Perversity in Chicago* (1976) and followed it with such plays as *American Buffalo* (1977; film, 1996), and *Glengarry Glen Ross* (1983, Pulitzer Prize; film, 1992). He became known for rapid-fire dialogue studded with obscenities and for his preoccupation with power relationships and corporate corruption. His later plays include *Speed-the-Plow* (1987), *Oleanna* (1992; film, 1994), and *The Cryptogram* (1994). He wrote screenplays for such movies as *The Verdict* (1980), *Tin Men* (1987), *The Untouchables* (1986), and *Wag the Dog* (1997) and directed *House of Games* (1987), *Homicide* (1991), and *The Spanish Prisoner* (1997), among other films.

Mamluk regime \\'mam-ˌlük\\ *or* **Mameluke regime** \\'mam-ə-ˌlük\\ (1250–1517) Rule of Syria and Egypt that originated from the ranks of Turkish slave soldiers who exploited the military power vested in them to seize control. Mamluk generals seized the throne on the death of the Ayyubid sultan Al-Malik al-Salih Ayyub (r.1240–49). The Mamluks revived the caliphate in 1258 and patronized the rulers of Mecca and Medina. Under Mamluk rule the remaining crusaders were expelled from the E Mediterranean coast and the Mongols were driven back from Palestine and Syria. They oversaw achievement in historical writing (see IBN KHALDUN) and architecture. A shift in their ethnic makeup from Turkish to Circassian corresponded with their slow decline; their failure to adopt field artillery as weapons permitted their defeat by the Ottomans in 1517 (see OTTOMAN EMPIRE). Thereafter they were only one of several forces influencing Egyptian political life. See also BAYBARS I.

mammal Any member of a class (Mammalia) of warm-blooded VERTEBRATES having four limbs (except for some aquatic species) and distinguished from other CHORDATE classes by the female's milk-secreting glands and the presence of hair at some stage of development. Other unique characteristics include a jaw hinged directly to the skull, a muscular diaphragm separating the pectoral and abdominal cavities, and nonnucleated mature red blood cells. Mammals range in size from the tiny SHREW to the enormous BLUE WHALE. MONOTREMES (PLATYPUS and ECHIDNA) lay eggs; all other mammals bear live young. MARSUPIAL newborns complete their development outside the womb. The earliest mammals date from the late TRIASSIC PERIOD (ended 208 million years ago); their immediate ancestors were the reptilian therapsids. For 70 million years mammals have dominated terrestrial ecosystems, thanks to the behavioral adaptability provided by the ability of mammalian young to learn from their elders, and the physical adaptability to a wide range of conditions provided by their warm-bloodedness. See also CARNIVORE, CETACEAN, HERBIVORE, INSECTIVORE, OMNIVORE, PRIMATE, RODENT.

mammary gland \\'mam-ə-rē\\ MILK-producing GLAND of female mammals, undeveloped and nonfunctional in males. Regulated by the ENDOCRINE SYSTEM, it is derived from a modification of SWEAT GLANDS. The gland is made up of lobes drained by separate ducts that meet at the nipple. Pregnancy causes the cells lining the lobes to multiply, and LACTATION begins in response to hormones released starting at the time of birth. At the end of lactation, the glands return almost to their state before pregnancy. After MENOPAUSE, they atrophy and are largely replaced by connective tissue and fat.

mammoth Any of several species of extinct ELEPHANT (genus *Mammuthus*) whose fossils have been found in Pleistocene deposits (beginning 1.8 million years ago) on every continent except Australia and S. America. The woolly, Northern, or Siberian mammoth *(M. primigenius)* is the best-known species because the Siberian permafrost preserved numerous carcasses intact. Most species were about the size of modern elephants. The N. American imperial mammoth *(M. imperator)* grew to a shoulder height of 14 ft (4 m). Mammoths had a high, domelike skull, small ears, and long, downward-pointing tusks. Cave paintings show them traveling in herds. Mammoths survived until about 4,000 years ago; hunting by humans may have been a cause of their extinction. See also MASTODON.

Mammoth Cave National Park National park, SW central Kentucky. It occupies a surface area of 82 sq mi (212 sq km) covering a system of limestone caverns. In 1972 a passage was discovered linking the Mammoth Cave and the Flint Ridge Cave System; the explored underground passages have a combined length of some 329 mi (530 km). Various animals living there have undergone adaptation to the dark, including cave crickets, blindfish, and blind crayfish. Mummified Indian bodies, possibly pre-Columbian, have been found in the caves.

Mamoulian \\mə-'mü-lē-ən\\, **Rouben** (1897–1987) Russian-U.S. director. He moved to London in 1918, where he directed operettas and musicals. After emigrating to the U.S. in 1923, he directed the play *Porgy* (1927) and its later musical adaptation, *Porgy and Bess* (1935), and such musicals as *Oklahoma!* (1943) and *Carousel* (1945). Invited to direct the film musical *Applause* (1929), he won acclaim for his innovative camera work; his later films include *City Streets* (1931), *Queen Christina* (1933) with Greta GARBO, *Blood and Sand* (1941), and *Silk Stockings* (1957).

Mamun \\mä-'mün\\, **al-** (786–833) Son of HARUN AL-RASHID. After his father's death (809) he became the seventh ABBASID caliph (813). Attempting to reconcile Sunni and Shiite Muslims, he designated as his heir a Shiite, to whom he married his daughter; the move, which failed to satisfy Shiite extremists and angered Sunnis, was nullified by the heir's death. His sponsorship of translations of Greek philosophical and scientific works and his building of observatories proved a lasting legacy.

Man, Isle of Island (pop., 2000: 73,000), in the IRISH SEA, off the NW coast of England. It is a self-governing crown possession of Britain. Its capital is Douglas (pop., 1996: 23,000). It is about 30 mi (48 km) long and 10 mi (16 km) wide. The Manx breed of tailless cats is believed to have originated there. The isle was home to Irish missionaries beginning in the 5th cent. A.D. It was later held by the Norse (9th–13th cent.), Scots (13th–14th cent.), and English settlers (from the 14th cent.).

Man, Paul de See Paul de MAN

Managua \\mä-'nä-gwä\\ City (pop., 1995: 864,000), capital of Nicaragua, on the S shore of Lake Managua. It was selected as the nation's capital in 1857. It was devastated by earthquake and fire in 1931 and by another major earthquake in 1972. It was the scene of fighting in 1978–79 during the civil war. The largest city and commercial center of Nicaragua, it has several institutions of higher education, including the Univ. of Managua. Sites of interest include Darío Park and the National Palace.

Manama \\mä-'nä-mə\\ *or* **Al-Manamah** City (pop., 1995 est.: 148,000), capital of Bahrain. Bahrain's largest city and one of the PERSIAN GULF's most important ports, it is a commercial and financial center enriched by Bahrain's oil wealth. First mentioned in Islamic chronicles around 1345, it was taken by the Portuguese in 1521 and by the Persians in 1602. It has been held, with brief interruptions, by the Al Khalifah dynasty since 1783. The seat of the British political resident for the Persian Gulf 1946–71, it became the capital of independent Bahrain.

Manasarowar See MAPAM YUMCO

manatee Any of three species (family Trichechidae) of slow-moving, shallow-water herbivorous mammals. Manatees

have a tapered body ending in a rounded flipper, no hind flippers, and foreflippers near the head. The Caribbean manatee *(Trichechus manatus)* lives along coasts of the SE U.S. and N S. America; the Amazonian manatee *(T. inunguis)* and the W. African manatee *(T. senegalensis)* inhabit rivers and estuaries. Adults are 8–15 ft (2.5–4.5 m) long and weigh up to 1,500 lbs (700 kg). Manatees are protected by law in most areas.

Manaus \mȧ-ˈnaús\ City (pop., 1996: 1,150,000), NW Brazil. Located in the heart of the Amazon rain forest, it lies on the NEGRO RIVER above its junction with the AMAZON RIVER. European settlement dates from 1669. It became the capital of the Rio Negro captaincy general in 1809. It prospered from 1890 to 1920 as the world's only supplier of rubber, after which it declined. Though 1,000 mi (1,600 km) from the sea, it has revived as a major inland port and commercial center. Notable features include botanical gardens (c.1669), an opera house, and Univ. of the Amazon.

Mancha, La See CASTILLA-LA MANCHA

Manche, La See ENGLISH CHANNEL

Manchester City (pop., 1999 est.: 404,000), NW England. Lying east of LIVERPOOL, it was the site of a Roman fort A.D. 78–86. By 919 the town of Manchester had sprung up nearby. In the 16th cent. it was important in the wool trade, and with the INDUSTRIAL REVOLUTION in the 18th cent. it became perhaps the world's leading center for textile manufacture. The world's first modern railroad, the Liverpool and Manchester, opened in 1830. Beset by urban problems, it now is undergoing redevelopment. Its Manchester United football (soccer) team is known worldwide.

Manchester City (pop., 2000: 107,000), S New Hampshire. The state's largest city, it was settled in 1722–23. One of America's first textile mills was built there in 1805, beginning a period of rapid industrial growth. Canals built in the early 19th cent. opened navigation to BOSTON. The textile industry's decline in the 1930s spurred economic diversification.

Manchu People, many of JUCHEN ancestry, who acquired a Manchu identity in the 17th cent. before conquering China and forming the QING DYNASTY (1644–1911/12). Though official policy aimed to maintain the Manchus as a distinct people, this did not prevent intermarriage and adoption of Chinese customs. China today recognizes the Manchu as a distinct ethnic group with over 10 million members living mainly in NE China (see MANCHURIA). See also BANNER SYSTEM.

Manchu dynasty See QING DYNASTY

Manchuguo *or* **Manchukuo** \ˈman-ˈchü-ˈgwō\ Puppet state created in 1932 by Japan out of the three historical Manchurian provinces. After the RUSSO–JAPANESE WAR, Japan gained control of the Russian-built S. Manchurian Railway and established its army in the area. In 1931 the Japanese army created an excuse to attack Chinese troops, and in 1932 Manchuguo was proclaimed an independent state. The last Qing emperor was brought out of retirement and made Manchuguo's ruler, but the state was rigidly controlled by the Japanese, who used it as their base for expansion into Asia. An underground guerrilla movement opposed the occupying Japanese. After Japan's defeat in 1945 the area returned to China.

Manchuria \man-ˈchur̄-ē-ə\ *Chinese* **Dongbei** *or* **Tung-Pei** \ˈdùṇ-ˈbā\ Historical region, NE China. It consists of the modern provinces of Liaoning, Jilin, and Heilongjiang; the NE portion of Nei Monggol is sometimes also included. In 1211 GENGHIS KHAN invaded and occupied Manchuria. Chinese rebellions overthrew the YUAN DYNASTY of the Mongols in 1368, and established the MING DYNASTY. The QING (MANCHU) DYNASTY originated there in the early 17th cent. Russia and Japan fought each other there in the RUSSO–JAPANESE WAR of 1904–5; after its defeat, Russia ceded S Manchuria to Japan. The Japanese occupied all of Manchuria in 1931 and created the puppet state of MANCHUGUO in 1932. The Soviets captured Manchuria in 1945, and Chinese Communist guerrillas soon came to power. It is now one of China's most important industrial areas.

Mancini, Henry (1924–1994) U.S. composer. Born in Cleveland, he worked as pianist and arranger with the postwar Glenn Miller Band. He gained wide attention with his jazz-

inflected music for the television series *Peter Gunn* (1958), but is perhaps best known for his scores for the *Pink Panther* movies. Other scores include *Touch of Evil* (1958), *Breakfast at Tiffany's* (1961; with "Moon River"), and *Days of Wine and Roses* (1962). He contributed music to some 200 films and won four Academy Awards.

mandala \ˈmən-də-lə\ In tantric Hinduism and Buddhism, a diagram representing the universe, used in sacred rites and as an instrument of MEDITATION. By mentally "entering" the mandala and moving toward its center, one is guided through the cosmic processes of disintegration and reintegration. Mandalas may be painted on paper or cloth, drawn on the ground, or fashioned of bronze or stone. In one type of mandala, the movement is from one to the many; in another, the movement is from the many into one.

Mandalay City (pop., 1983: 533,000), central Myanmar, on the IRRAWADDY RIVER. The nation's second-largest city, it was built in 1857 by King Mindon to replace Amarapura as his capital. It fell to Britain in 1885. It was nearly destroyed during the Japanese occupation in World War II. An important Buddhist religious center, it is the site of the famous Mahamuni pagoda and of 730 pagodas housing marble tablets with Buddhist scriptures.

Mandan \ˈman-ˌdan\ PLAINS INDIAN people who lived along the Missouri River in what is now SW N. Dakota. They lived in dome-shaped, earth-covered lodges clustered in stockaded villages; planted corn, beans, pumpkins, and sunflowers; hunted buffalo; and made pottery and baskets. They held elaborate ceremonies, including the SUN DANCE and the bear ceremony, a healing and war-preparation rite. George CATLIN portrayed Mandan life and people in a series of paintings. By the mid-19th cent. the Mandan, reduced by smallpox, were removed to a N. Dakota reservation, where today they number about 1,000.

Mandarin In imperial China, a public official drawn from the ranks of the lesser officeholders who had achieved success in the CHINESE EXAMINATION SYSTEM. The word has come to mean a pedantic official, a bureaucrat, or a person of position and influence (and usually a traditionalist or reactionary mindset) in intellectual or literary circles. The Mandarin dialect is the most widely spoken of the CHINESE LANGUAGES.

Mandel \mäⁿ-ˈdel\, **Georges** *orig.* Louis-Georges Rothschild (1885–1944) French political leader. A member of a prosperous Jewish family, he served as a personal aide to Georges CLEMENCEAU (1906–9, 1917–20), in the National Assembly (1919–24, 1928–40), and in cabinet posts (1934–40). As minister of the interior (1940), he supported Paul Reynaud's refusal to accept an armistice with Germany. Imprisoned in 1940, he was shot on orders of the Vichy police chief.

Mandela \man-ˈdel-ə\, **Nelson** (b.1918) S. African black nationalist leader and statesman. The son of a XHOSA chief, Mandela studied law and joined the AFRICAN NATIONAL CONGRESS (ANC) in 1944. After the Sharpeville massacre (1960), he abandoned his nonviolent stance and helped found the ANC's military wing. In 1962 he was sentenced to life imprisonment. From prison he retained broad support among S. Africa's black population and gained worldwide fame. Released by Pres. F. W. DE KLERK in 1990, he became president of the ANC in 1991. In 1993 Mandela and de Klerk were awarded the Nobel Peace Prize for their

Nelson Mandela, 1990

efforts to end APARTHEID and promote nonracial democracy. In 1994 Mandela was elected president in the country's first all-race elections; by the time he stepped down in 1999, he was the most universally respected figure of postcolonial Africa.

Mandelbrot \'man-dəl-ˌbròt\, **Benoit B.** (b.1924) Polish-U.S. mathematician. He is best known for his work with fractals (see FRACTAL GEOMETRY), which, he showed, can occur in many different places in mathematics and in nature. He was influenced by Gaston Maurice Julia (1893–1978), author of a 1918 paper on dynamical systems theory. Julia's work was forgotten until the 1970s, when Mandelbrot's fundamental computer experiments and use of computer graphics revived it. The Mandelbrot set is a mathematical set of imaginary numbers generated from a simple equation; it appears infinitely complex when graphed on a computer.

Mandelstam \mən-dyil-'shtàm\, **Osip (Emilyevich)** (1891–1938) Russian poet and critic. A leader of the Acmeist poets, who rejected the mysticism and abstraction of Russian Symbolism, he wrote intellectually demanding, apolitical verse in such volumes as *Tristia* (1922). In 1934 he was arrested for an epigram about Joseph STALIN. While suffering from mental illness brought on by his interrogation, he composed the *Voronezh Notebooks*, which contain some of his finest lyrics. Arrested again in 1938, he died in custody at 47.

Mandingo See MALINKE

Mandinka See MALINKE

mandolin \ˌman-də-'lin\ Small STRINGED INSTRUMENT related to the LUTE. It has a pear-shaped body with a deeply vaulted back, a short fretted fingerboard, and four pairs of steel strings. (The American folk mandolin is a shallow, flat-backed version.) It is played with a plectrum; each pair of strings is strummed rapidly back and forth to produce a characteristic tremolo.

mandrake Any of six poisonous plant species of the genus *Mandragora* (NIGHTSHADE FAMILY), native to the Mediterranean and the Himalayas. The best-known species, *M. officinarum*, has a thick, fleshy, often forked root. The mandrake has long been known for its poisonous properties. In ancient times it was used as a narcotic and an aphrodisiac, and it was believed to have magical powers. When pulled from the ground, its forked root, supposed to resemble the human form, was said to utter a shriek that killed or drove mad anyone who heard it. Once pulled, however, the plant was said to provide soothing sleep, heal wounds, induce love, and facilitate pregnancy.

mandrill Diurnal MONKEY (family Cercopithecidae, usually genus *Mandrillus*) of equatorial African rain forests, known for its striking coloring. The ribbed bare skin on the adult male's cheeks is bright blue, with scarlet on the nose; the buttock pads are pink to crimson, shading to bluish; the beard and neck are yellow. The adult male is about 3 ft (90 cm) long and weighs about 45 lbs (20 kg); the female is duller and smaller. Mandrills eat fruit, roots, insects, and small reptiles and amphibians.

Manes See MANI

Manet \mà-'nā\, **Édouard** (1832–1883) French painter and printmaker. Son of a prosperous civil servant, Manet was a poor student interested only in drawing. In 1856, after six years of study, he opened a studio. The SALON rejected his first submission, *The Absinthe Drinker* (1859), but in 1861 he exhibited his *Spanish Singer* (1860). When it rejected his *Luncheon on the Grass* in 1863, he exhibited it at the Salon des Refusés. It aroused critical hostility and the enthusiasm of a group of young painters who later formed the nucleus of IMPRESSIONISM. Manet uncomfortably found himself a

Édouard Manet, "A Bar at the Folies Bergères," 1882

leader of the avant-garde, though he continued to seek the Salon's approval. His *Olympia* (1863) caused a scandal at the Salon of 1865. His friendship with Claude MONET led to his luminous open-air painting *Boating* (1874). His last great work, *A Bar at the Folies Bergère* (1882), appeared at the Salon. Manet broke new ground in choosing subjects from his

own time and in stressing the arrangement of paint areas on a canvas over and above its function as representation.

manganese \'maŋ-gə-ˌnēz\ Chemical ELEMENT, one of the TRANSITION ELEMENTS, chemical symbol Mn, atomic number 25. It is a silvery white, hard, brittle METAL, widely distributed in the earth's crust in combination with other elements. NODULES rich in manganese occur in huge quantities on the sea floor, but no economical way to exploit them has been devised. More than 95% of the manganese produced is used in iron and steel alloys and much of the rest in nonferrous alloys. Manganese compounds (of various VALENCES) are used in fertilizers and textile printing and as reagents and raw materials. Potassium permanganate is used for disinfecting, deodorizing, and bleaching and as a reagent in ANALYSIS. Manganese is essential to plants for growth and to higher animals to promote the action of many ENZYMES.

mango Evergreen tree and fruit (*Mangifera indica*) of the SUMAC, or cashew, family, one of the most important and widely cultivated fruits of the tropics. The sweet, juicy fruit is a rich source of vitamins A, C, and D, varying in shape, color, and size from ovoid to long, from vividly red and yellow to dull green, and from plum- to melon-sized. The long-lived tree reaches 50–60 ft (15–18 m) and has long, lance-shaped leaves and clusters of small, pinkish, fragrant flowers.

mangrove Any of certain shrubs and trees of the families Rhizophoraceae, Verbenaceae, Sonneratiaceae, and Arecaceae (PALM) that grow densely along tidal estuaries, in salt marshes, and on muddy coasts. The term also applies to the thickets and forests of such plants. Mangroves characteristically have prop roots (exposed, supporting roots). In many species, respiratory, or knee, roots project above the mud and have small openings for air that passes to the roots beneath the mud. Mangrove fruits put out an embryonic root before they fall from the tree; the root may fix itself in the mud before the fruit separates from the parent. Likewise, branches and trunks put out random roots which, once they are secure in the mud, send up new shoots. The fruit of the common mangrove (*Rhizophora mangle*) is sweet and wholesome.

Mangu See MONGKE

Manhattan Borough (pop., 2000: 1,537,000) of NEW YORK CITY, including Manhattan island and three smaller islands in the EAST RIVER. It is said to have been purchased by Peter MINUIT in 1626 from the Manhattan Indians with trinkets valued at 60 guilders. Incorporated as New Amsterdam in 1653, it was obtained by Britain in 1664 and renamed New York City. In 1898 Manhattan was chartered as one of five boroughs comprising Greater New York. It is one of the world's great commercial, financial, and cultural centers. Among its many points of interest are CENTRAL PARK, the EMPIRE STATE BUILDING, the UNITED NATIONS headquarters, WALL ST., the METROPOLITAN MUSEUM, LINCOLN CENTER for the Performing Arts, CARNEGIE HALL, COLUMBIA UNIV., and the JUILLIARD SCHOOL.

Manhattan Project (1942–45) U.S. government research project that produced the first ATOMIC BOMB. In 1939 U.S. scientists urged Pres. Franklin ROOSEVELT to establish a program to study the potential military use of fission, and $6,000 was appropriated. By 1942 the project was code-named for the site of Columbia Univ., where much early research was done. Research was also carried out at the Univs. of California and Chicago. In 1943 a laboratory to construct the bomb was established at LOS ALAMOS, N.M., and staffed by scientists headed by J. Robert OPPENHEIMER. Production was also carried out at Oak Ridge, Tenn., and Hanford, Wash. By its end the project had cost some $2 billion and involved 125,000 people.

Mani \mà-'nē\ *or* **Manes** \mà-'nē, 'mā-nēz\ *or* **Manichaeus** \ˌma-nə-'kē-əs\ (A.D. 216–274?) Persian founder of MANICHAEISM. Born in S Babylonia, he had his first vision of an angel in his boyhood. When he was 24 the angel called him to preach a new religion. He traveled to India and made converts there. The Persian king Shapur I permitted him to preach in the Persian empire, but during the reign of Bahram I he was attacked by Zoroastrian priests. He died in prison.

manic-depressive psychosis See BIPOLAR DISORDER

Manichaeism \'ma-nə-ˌkē-ˌi-zəm, ˌma-nə-'kē-ˌi-zəm\ Dualistic religion founded by MANI in Persia in the 3rd cent. A.D. Mani viewed himself as the last in a line of prophets that included ADAM, BUDDHA, ZOROASTER, and JESUS. Manichaeism held that the world was a fusion of spirit and matter, the original principles of good and evil, and that the fallen soul, trapped in the evil, material world, could only reach the transcendent world by way of the spirit. Its zealous missionaries were vigorously opposed by both the Christian church and the Roman state, and Manichaeism disappeared almost entirely from Western Europe by the end of the 5th cent., though it survived in Asia until the 14th cent.

Manifest Destiny Concept of U.S. territorial expansion westward to the Pacific Ocean. The phrase was coined in 1845 by the editor John L. O'Sullivan, who described the U.S. annexation of Texas and, by extension, the occupation of the rest of the continent as a divine right of the American people. The term was used to justify the U.S. annexation of Oregon, New Mexico, and California and later U.S. involvement in Alaska, Hawaii, and the Philippines.

Manila City (pop., 2000: 1,673,000), capital of the PHILIPPINES. Located on LUZON island, it is the chief port and the economic, political, and cultural center of the Philippines. The original walled Muslim settlement was destroyed by 16th-cent. Spanish CONQUISTADORES. During the SPANISH–AMERICAN WAR, U.S. forces gained control of Manila in 1898. Occupied by the Japanese in 1942, it was widely damaged during its recapture in 1945. In 1946 it became the capital of the newly independent Philippines. QUEZON CITY became the capital in 1948, but Manila regained that position in 1976. Its industries include shipbuilding and food processing; it is the seat of several universities.

Manila Bay Inlet extending into SW LUZON island, Philippines. One of the world's great harbors, it covers 770 sq mi (2,000 sq km). The decisive Battle of MANILA BAY, in the SPANISH-AMERICAN WAR, took place there in 1898. Corregidor Island, the scene of intense fighting in World War II, marks the bay's entrance.

Manila Bay, Battle of (May 1, 1898) Naval engagement in the SPANISH–AMERICAN WAR. The U.S. Asiatic squadron under George DEWEY was ordered to sail from its Hong Kong base to destroy the Spanish fleet then in the Philippines, and in one morning the U.S. destroyed the Spanish ships anchored in Manila Bay. Manila was occupied by U.S. troops in August. The battle established the U.S. as a major naval power.

manioc See CASSAVA

Manitoba \ˌma-ni-'tō-bə\ Province (pop., 1999 est.: 1,143,000), central Canada. Its capital is WINNIPEG. Three-fifths of its territory is covered by the CANADIAN SHIELD, an area of rocks, forests, and rivers. The region was first inhabited by the Inuit (ESKIMO) and by the CREE, ASSINIBOIN, and OJIBWA Indians. The HUDSON'S BAY CO. opened Manitoba to European influence, and the region became a focus of French and British competition for Canadian fur trade dominance; it was ceded by France to Britain in 1763. The Métis rebellion led to the passage of the Manitoba Act in 1870, making it the fifth province of the Dominion of Canada. Steamboat and rail transportation opened the province to settlers from Europe in the late 19th cent. Though much of the economy is based on farming, lumbering and mining, heavy industry has become important to an expanding Winnipeg.

Manitoba, Lake Lake, S central MANITOBA. Located northwest of WINNIPEG, it drains into Lake WINNIPEG. It is more than 125 mi (200 km) long, with an area of 1,785 sq mi (4,624 sq km). It was visited in 1738 by Pierre LA VÉRENDRYE.

Manizales \ˌmä-nē-'sä-läs\ City (pop., 1999 est.: 361,000), central Colombia. It sits on a ridge of the ANDES, 6,975 ft (2,126 m) above sea level. Founded in 1848, it is the center of Colombia's most important coffee-growing district.

Mankiewicz \'man-ki-ˌwits\, **Joseph L(eo)** (1909–1993) U.S. film director, producer, and screenwriter. Born in Wilkes-Barre, Pa., he wrote scripts for Paramount from 1929 and later produced such movies as *Fury* (1936), *The Philadelphia Story* (1940), and *Woman of the Year* (1942). He wrote and directed such films as *A Letter to Three Wives* (1949,

Academy Awards for best director and screenplay), *All About Eve* (1950, Academy Awards for best picture, director, and screenplay), *The Barefoot Contessa* (1954), and *Guys and Dolls* (1955), and directed the disastrously expensive *Cleopatra* (1963). His brother Herman (1897–1953) was a screenwriter and a famous wit, best remembered as the principal author of *Citizen Kane* (1941, Academy Award).

Manley, Michael (Norman) (1924–1997) Jamaican political leader. Son of a prime minister, Manley become a leader of the People's National Party and the National Worker's Union before becoming prime minister in 1972. His leftist government made advances in housing, education, and health care, but a dramatic rise in oil prices created an economic crisis. Much of the middle class fled the country, unemployment rose to 30%, and in 1980 he was defeated. He was reelected in 1989, this time as a moderate; he stepped down in 1992 for health reasons.

Mann, Horace (1796–1859) U.S. educator, the first great American advocate of public education. Raised in poverty, Mann educated himself at the Franklin, Mass., town library, attended Brown Univ., and later studied law. As state secretary of education he vigorously argued that education should be free and universal, nonsectarian, and reliant on well-trained, professional teachers; his work revolutionized public-school organization and teaching, and he helped establish the nation's first normal school (1839). He served in the U.S. Congress (1849–53) and as first president of ANTIOCH UNIV. (1853–59).

Mann \'män\, **Thomas** (1875–1955) German novelist and essayist, considered the greatest German novelist of the 20th cent. *Buddenbrooks* (1901), his first novel, was an elegy for old bourgeois virtues. In the remarkable novella *Death in Venice* (1912), he took up the tragic dilemma of the artist in a collapsing society. Though ardently patriotic at the start of World War I, after 1919 he slowly revised his views of the authoritarian German state. His great novel *The Magic Mountain* (1924) clarified his growing espousal of Enlightenment principles as one strand of a complex and multifaceted whole. An outspoken opponent of Nazism, he fled to Switzerland on Adolf HITLER's accession. His tetralogy *Joseph and His Brothers* (1933–43) concerns the biblical Joseph. *Doctor Faustus* (1947), his most directly political novel, analyzes the darker aspects of the German soul. The often hilarious *Felix Krull, Confidence Man* (1954) remained unfinished. He is noted for his finely wrought style enriched by humor, irony, and parody and for his subtle, many-layered narratives of vast intellectual scope. He received the Nobel Prize in 1929.

Mannerheim \'mä-nər-ˌhām\, **Carl Gustaf (Emil), Baron** (1867–1951) Finnish soldier and president of Finland (1944–46). He commanded the anti-Bolshevik forces (1918) in the Finnish Civil War and expelled the Soviet forces. He served as regent of Finland (1918–19) until the new republic was declared. He later oversaw construction of the Mannerheim line of fortifications across the Karelian Isthmus. As commander in chief of Finnish forces (1939–40, 1941–44), he won initial successes against greatly superior Soviet forces in the Russo–Finnish War (1939–40). As president of the Finnish republic, he negotiated a peace agreement with the Soviets.

Mannerism Artistic style predominant in Italy from the 1520s to about 1590. It originated in Florence and Rome but ultimately spread as far as central and N Europe. A reaction to the harmonious classicism and idealized naturalism of High Renaissance art, Mannerism is characterized by artificiality, a self-conscious cultivation of technical facility, and a sophisticated indulgence in the bizarre. After being superseded by the baroque style, it was seen as decadent. By the 20th cent., it was appreciated anew for its technical bravura and elegance.

Mannheim City (pop., 1998 est.: 310,000), SW Germany. One of Europe's largest inland ports, it is situated on the RHINE RIVER at the mouth of the NECKAR RIVER. Chartered in 1607, the town was twice destroyed in wars during the 17th cent. The Palatine electors (see PALATINATE) moved their residence there in 1720. Destroyed again in 1795, the city was rebuilt and became a center of the revolutionary movement in 1848. Today it is an industrial center.

manorialism *or* **seignorialism** \sän-'yȯr-ē-əl-i-zəm\ Political, economic, and social system by which the peasants of medieval Europe were tied to their land and their lord through SERFDOM. The basic unit was the manor, a self-sufficient landed estate, or FIEF, under the control of a lord. Free tenants paid rent or provided military service in exchange for the use of the land. Peasants farmed small plots of land and owed rent and labor to their lord, and most were not free to leave the estate. The manorial system flourished in Western Europe in the 8th–13th cent., while in Eastern Europe it achieved its greatest strength after the 15th cent. See also FEUDALISM.

Man o' War U.S. Thoroughbred racehorse. In 1919–20 he won 20 of 21 races, including the Preakness and Belmont Stakes. He sired 64 stakes horses, including War Admiral, a TRIPLE CROWN winner (1937). In a 1950 Associated Press poll, Man o' War was voted the greatest horse of the first half of the 20th cent.

man-o'-war bird See FRIGATE BIRD

Man Ray See Man RAY

Mansa Musa See MUSA

Mansfield, Katherine *orig.* Kathleen Mansfield Beauchamp (1888–1923) New Zealand–British writer. After moving to England at 19, she secured her reputation with the story collection *Bliss* (1920). She reached the height of her powers in the collection *The Garden Party* (1922). Her delicate stories, which focus on psychological conflicts, show the influence of Anton CHEKHOV. She died of tuberculosis at 34.

Mansfield, Mike (*orig.* Michael Joseph) (1903–2001) U.S. politician. Born in New York City, he worked in Montana copper mines and later taught history at Montana State Univ. He served in the U.S. House of Representatives 1943–53 and in the Senate 1953–77, where he was majority leader 1961–77. He became an outspoken critic of the Vietnam War, and a persistent critic of Pres. Richard NIXON, especially during the Watergate investigation. After retiring, he served as U.S. ambassador to Japan (1977–88).

Mansi See SIBERIAN PEOPLES

manslaughter See HOMICIDE

Manson, Charles (b.1934) U.S. cult leader. Born in Cincinnati, in 1967 he formed a communal cult, the Manson Family. He tried to become a pop musician in Los Angeles, but when the producer Terry Melcher failed to help him, Manson decided to launch a racial war by murdering prominent white people, for which he believed blacks would be blamed. In 1969 he sent cult members to Melcher's house, which was rented to the actress Sharon Tate and Roman POLANSKI; they murdered Tate and five friends and elsewhere killed three others. Manson's death sentence (1971) was later commuted to life imprisonment.

manta ray *or* **devil ray** *or* **devilfish** Any of several genera of warm-water marine RAYS, constituting the family Mobulidae, that are wider than they are long. Extensions of the pectoral fins project from the front of the head, looking like devils' horns; these sweep plankton and small fishes into their mouths. The long, whiplike tail may have one or more stinging spines. Mantas swim near the surface. The largest species, the powerful but inoffensive Atlantic manta, or giant devil, ray (*Manta birostris*), may grow to over 23 ft (7 m) wide.

Mantegna \män-'tān-yə\, **Andrea** (1431?–1506) Italian painter. Adopted by Francesco Squarcione, a tailor-turned-painter, Mantegna was one of several pupils who later sued him for exploitation. At about 17 he established his own workshop. His frescoes in Padua's Eremitani Church (1448–57), with their monumental figures and detailed treatment of classical architecture, show that he had fully mastered perspective and foreshortening and was successfully experimenting with illusionistic effects, best seen in his frescoes of the GONZAGA family (completed 1474) in the Palazzo Ducale in Mantua, which transform a small interior room into an open-air pavilion. He later became court painter to Ludovico Gonzaga. His humanistic approach to antiquity and his spatial illusionism were to have far-reaching influence.

Mantinea \man-tə-'nē-ə\ Ancient Greek city of ARCADIA, situated north of modern Tripolis. At the first Battle of Mantinea in 418 B.C., SPARTA defeated the coalition of Mantinea, Elis, Argos, and Athens. In 362 B.C. the Theban army defeated Spartan troops in an encounter nearby. In 207 B.C. the ACHAEAN LEAGUE defeated the Spartans there. Mantinea later dwindled under the Romans and disappeared under Ottoman rule.

mantis *or* **praying mantis** Any of over 1,500 species of the INSECT suborder Mantodea (order Orthoptera). The long-bodied, slow-moving mantis (or mantid) eats only living insects, using its large forelimbs to capture and hold its struggling prey. The female is likely to eat the male after mating. The Chinese mantis (*Tenodera aridifolia sinensis*), introduced to N. America, grows to 3–8 in. (7–10 cm) long. The name mantis ("diviner") reflects an ancient Greek belief in its supernatural powers.

mantle That part of the earth that lies beneath the CRUST and above the central CORE. On average, the mantle begins about 22 mi (35 km) below the surface and ends at a depth of about 1,800 mi (2,900 km). Predominant in the rock material are OLIVINES and PYROXENES. See also LITHOSPHERE.

Mantle, Mickey (Charles) (1931–1995) U.S. baseball player. Born in Spavinaw, Okla., he had to play with his legs heavily taped for much of his career because of ankle and knee injuries. He joined the New York Yankees in 1951 and became a powerful switch-hitting outfielder and first baseman. Between 1954 and 1961 "the Mick" led the American League four times in home runs and six times in runs; in 1956 he won the triple crown for home runs, RBI, and batting average (.353). In 1961 he hit 54 home runs, trailing his teammate Roger MARIS, who broke Babe RUTH's season record that year. He retired in 1968 with a lifetime total of 536 home runs.

mantra In HINDUISM and BUDDHISM, a sacred utterance (syllable, word, or verse) believed to possess mystical or spiritual power. Mantras may be spoken aloud or uttered in thought, and they may be either repeated or sounded only once. Most have no apparent verbal meaning. Repetition of a mantra can induce a trancelike state and can lead to a higher level of spiritual awareness. OM is a well-known and widely used mantra.

Manu \'mə-nü\ In the mythology of India, the first man and the legendary author of the *MANU-SMRTI*. In the VEDAS Manu performs the first sacrifice. He is also known as the first king. In the story of the great flood, Manu built a boat after being warned of the flood by a fish. His boat came to rest on a mountaintop, and Manu poured out an oblation of milk and butter. A year later a woman calling herself the "daughter of Manu" was born from the waters, and these two became the parents of a new human race.

Manuel I \mən-'wel\ *known as* **Manuel the Fortunate** (1469–1521) King of Portugal (1495–1521). He opened trade with India and Brazil, sending P. A. CABRAL on a voyage to the Orient (1500), and gained riches from Vasco da GAMA's voyage around Africa. In order to marry the daughter of FERDINAND V and Isabella, he agreed to expel Jews and Muslims from Portugal (1496). His reign saw the founding of Portuguese outposts in India and the Malay Peninsula, and his explorers reached China in 1513. Manuel also centralized Portuguese administration, reformed the courts, and revised the legal code.

Manuel I Comnenus \'man-yü-əl...käm-'nē-nəs\ (1122?–1180) Byzantine emperor (1143–80). The son of JOHN II COMNENUS, he renewed alliances in the West against the Normans in Sicily and Antioch. He took Apulia briefly (1155) but was defeated at Brindisi (1156), ending Byzantine influence in Italy. He reasserted his authority over the crusader states (1158–59) and added Dalmatia, Croatia, and Bosnia to the empire in 1167. He launched a campaign against the Seljuq Turks (1176); his defeat showed the waning of Byzantine power and ended his plan of restoring the Roman empire.

manure Organic material used to fertilize land, consisting of the feces and urine of domestic livestock, with or without litter such as straw, hay, or bedding. Some countries also use human excrement ("night soil"). Livestock manure is rich in organic matter, or HUMUS, and thus improves the capacity of the soil to absorb and store water, thereby preventing erosion. Because manure must be carefully stored and spread in order to derive the most benefit, some farmers do not bother with it. Manufactured chemical fertilizers, though more concentrated and efficient, are also more costly and more likely to cause excess runoff and pollution.

Manu-smrti \'mə-nü-'smri-tē\ *officially Manava-dharmashastra.* Most authoritative of the books of the Hindu law code. It is attributed to MANU. In its present form it dates from the 1st cent. B.C. It prescribes the DHARMA of each Hindu, stating the obligations attached to his or her social class and stage of life. It also deals with cosmogony, SACRAMENTS, and other religious topics as well as with marriage, hospitality, dietary restrictions, the conduct of women, and the law of kings.

Manutius \mə-'nü-shəs\, **Aldus, the Elder** *Italian* Aldo Manuzio il Vecchio (1449–1515) Italian printer, the leading figure of his time in printing, publishing, and typography. In 1490 he settled in Venice and gathered around him a group of compositors and Greek scholars. He produced the first printed editions of many Greek and Latin classics and is particularly associated with the production of small, excellently edited pocket-size books printed in inexpensive editions. The Aldine Press remained in his family's hands for generations.

Manzanar Relocation Center \'man-zə-ˌnär\ Internment facility for Japanese-Americans during WORLD WAR II. Fear that Japan would invade the W U.S. with the aid of domestic spies led the government to force Japanese-Americans in W states to relocate to ten camps, of which Manzanar, in California, was the first and the best known. During its operation, over 11,000 people were confined there.

Manzoni, Alessandro (1785–1873) Italian novelist and poet. Though he wrote tragedies and religious poems, he is best known for the novel *The Betrothed* (3 vols., 1827), a masterpiece of world literature and the most famous Italian novel of its century, in which, prompted by a patriotic urge to forge a language accessible to a wide readership, he employed a clear, expressive prose that became a model for many subsequent Italian writers. Manzoni's advocacy of a united Italy made him a hero of the RISORGIMENTO; his death prompted Giuseppe VERDI's great *Requiem.*

Alessandro Manzoni Painting by Francesco Hayez

Manzù \'mänd-zü\, **Giacomo** *orig.* Giacomo Manzoni (1908–1991) Italian sculptor. In 1950, after making a name for himself with sculptures of more than 50 Roman Catholic cardinals and a series of female nudes, he was commissioned to create sculptural bronze doors for ST. PETER'S BASILICA. His sober realism and delicate modeling achieved both severity and sensuousness of form.

Mao Dun or **Mao Tun** \'maů-'důn\ *orig.* Shen Dehong or Shen Yanbing (1896–1981) Chinese author. He served as MAO ZEDONG's first minister of culture (1949–64). Many Western critics consider his trilogy of novellas *Shi* (1930; "The Canker") to be his masterpiece, though it was attacked by Marxists. His other works include *Spring Silkworms and Other Stories* (1956) and the novel *Rainbow* (1992). He is generally considered China's greatest novelist of REALISM.

Maoism \'maů-ˌi-zəm\ Variation of MARXISM and LENINISM developed by MAO ZEDONG. Mao substituted the dormant power of the peasantry (discounted by traditional Marxists) for the urban proletariat that China largely lacked. The Maoist faith in revolutionary enthusiasm and the positive value of the peasants' lack of sophistication fueled the GREAT LEAP FORWARD and the CULTURAL REVOLUTION, whose disastrous consequences led Mao's successors to abandon Maoism as counterproductive to economic growth and social order. Maoism was embraced by insurgent guerrilla groups worldwide (see KHMER ROUGE).

Maori \'maů-rē\ Polynesian people of New Zealand. Maori traditional history describes their arrival from a mythical land in the 12th–14th cent., but archaeologists have dated habitations in New Zealand back to at least A.D. 800. Their first European contact was with A. J. TASMAN (1642). Later Europeans were initially welcomed, but the arrival of muskets, disease, Western agricultural methods, and missionaries corroded Maori culture and social structure, and conflicts arose. After the British assumed formal control of New Zealand (1840), war over land broke out repeatedly; by 1872 all fighting had ended and great tracts of Maori land had been confiscated. Today, about 9% of New Zealanders are classified as Maori; nearly all have some European ancestry.

Mao Zedong or **Mao Tse-tung** \'maů-dzə-'důn\ (1893–1976) Chinese soldier and statesman, chairman of the People's Republic of China (1949–59) and the CHINESE COMMUNIST PARTY (1931–76). The son of a peasant, Mao joined the revolutionary army that overthrew the QING DYNASTY but soon left to acquire more education. At Beijing Univ. he met LI DAZHAO and CHEN DUXIU, founders of the Chinese Communist Party, and in 1921 he committed himself to MARXISM. In 1925 Mao concluded that in China it was the peasantry, not the urban proletariat, that had to be mobilized (see MAOISM). He became chairman of a Chinese Soviet Republic formed in rural Jiangxi; its Red Army withstood repeated attacks from CHIANG KAI-SHEK's Nationalist army but at last undertook the LONG MARCH to a more secure position in NW China. Here Mao became the undisputed head of the Communist Party. Guerrilla-warfare tactics and Mao's agrarian policies gained the party military advantages against their Nationalist and Japanese enemies and broad support among the peasantry. When Mao and the Communists succeeded in taking power in 1949, the Soviet Union agreed to provide technical assistance. Later Mao's GREAT LEAP FORWARD and his criticism of "new bourgeois elements" in the Soviet Union and China alienated the Soviet Union, which withdrew aid in 1960. Mao clung to his vision, inaugurating the equally disastrous CULTURAL REVOLUTION. After Mao's death, DENG XIAOPING introduced socil and economic reforms and the cult of Mao was greatly diminished.

map Graphic representation, usually on a flat surface, of geographic, geologic, or geopolitical features of an area of the earth or of any celestial body. Globes are maps represented on the surface of a sphere. Major types of maps include topographic maps (showing features of the earth's land surface), nautical charts (coastal and marine areas), hydrographic charts (ocean depths and currents), and aeronautical charts (surface features and air routes). See also CARTOGRAPHY.

Mapam Yumco \'mä-ˌpäm-'yùm-kō\ or **Manasarowar** \ˌmä-nä-sä-'rō-ˌwär\ or **Ma-fa-mu-ts'o** \'ma-ˌfä-'mü-tsō\ Lake in the HIMALAYAS, SW Tibet, China. Lying nearly 15,000 ft (4,570 m) above sea level, it is considered the world's highest body of fresh water. It is one of the most sacred places of pilgrimage for Hindus.

maple family Family Aceraceae, composed of about 200 species (in the genera *Dipteronia* in China and *Acer* across the Northern Hemisphere) of ornamental, shade, and timber trees. Maples offer a great variety of form, size, and foliage; many display striking autumn color. The red maple (*A. rubrum*) is one of the most common trees in its native E N. America, where it tolerates compact, wet soils and city pollution. Box elder (*A. negundo*) grows quickly and resists drought, so early prairie settlers planted many for shade and for wood. The watery, sweet sap of the sugar maple (*A. saccharum*) is boiled down for syrup; the wood of certain sugar maples is used for furniture.

mapmaking See CARTOGRAPHY

Mapplethorpe \'mä-pəl-ˌthôrp\, **Robert** (1946–1989) U.S. photographer. Born in New York City, he attended Pratt Institute (1963–70) and soon became noted for his austere black-and-white photographs of flowers, celebrities, and male nudes; the explicit homoeroticism of some of his nudes aroused controversy. His death resulted from AIDS. A retrospective exhibition of his work in 1990, funded partly by the National Endowment for the Arts (NEA), stirred a debate about government subsidies of "obscene" art and provoked Congress to enact restrictions on future NEA grants.

mappo \'mäp-ˌpō\ In Japanese Buddhism, the age in which the BUDDHA's law will degenerate. The period following the death of the Buddha is divided into three ages: the age of the true law, the age of the copied law, and the age of degeneration of the law. A new period, in which true faith will again flower, will then be ushered in. Japanese Buddhists calculate that the 10,000-year age of mappo began in A.D. 1052.

Maputo \mä-'pü-tō\ *formerly (until 1976)* **Lourenço Marques** \lō-'rāⁿ-sü-'mär-kish\ Port city (pop., 1997: 966,000), capital of Mozambique. Its former name is that of the Portuguese trader who explored the region in 1544. The town developed around a fortress completed in 1787. Created a city in 1887, it became the capital of Portuguese E. Africa in 1907. Since Mozambique achieved independence in 1975, decreased tourism and trade have damaged the city's economy.

Mara Buddhist Lord of the Senses, who repeatedly tempted the BUDDHA Gautama. When Gautama seated himself under the BODHI TREE to await enlightenment, the evil Mara attempted to deceive him into abandoning his quest, raised a terrifying storm, and sent his three daughters to seduce Gautama, but to no avail. After the Buddha had achieved enlightenment, Mara pressed him to abandon any attempt to preach, but the gods successfully persuaded him to preach the law.

marabou \'mär-ə-ˌbü\ African STORK (*Leptoptilos crumeniferus*). At 5 ft (1.5 m) tall, with a wingspread of 8.5 ft (2.6 m), the marabou is the largest of all storks. Mainly gray and white, it has a naked pinkish head and neck; a reddish, inflatable throat pouch; and a straight, heavy bill.

Maracaibo \ˌmä-ra-'kī-bō\ City (pop., 2000 est.: 1,764,000), NW Venezuela, situated on the channel connecting Lake Maracaibo with the Gulf of Venezuela. It is Venezuela's second-largest city. Founded in 1571, it soon became a center for inland trade. It changed hands several times during Venezuela's struggle for independence from Spain. Within a decade of the discovery of oil in 1917, it became the oil metropolis of S. America.

Marat \mä-'rä\, **Jean-Paul** (1743–1793) French leader of the radical MONTAGNARD faction in the FRENCH REVO-

Marabou (*Leptoptilos crumeniferus*)

LUTION. A well-known doctor in London in the 1770s, he returned to France as physician at the court of the comte d'Artois (later CHARLES X). Marat wrote scientific publications as well as political pamphlets. From 1789, as editor of the newspaper *L'Ami du Peuple*, he became an influential voice for radical measures against the aristocrats and advocated the execution of counterrevolutionaries. Highly influential, he was actively supported by Parisians in street demonstrations. In April 1793 the GIRONDINS brought him before a Revolutionary tribunal, but he was acquitted. In July a young Girondin supporter, Charlotte CORDAY, stabbed him to death in his bath, making him a martyr to the people's cause.

Maratha Wars (1775–82, 1803–5, 1817–18) Three conflicts between the British and the Maratha confederacy. At the time, the confederacy of ruling families controlled large portions of the DECCAN and the W coast of the Indian peninsula. The British lost the first conflict, in which they supported one contender's bid for the office of peshwa (chief minister). They won the second, restoring an ousted peshwa. The third war was caused by the British invasion of Maratha territory in pursuit of robber bands. Maratha forces were defeated, Maratha territory was annexed, and British supremacy in India became complete.

marathon Long-distance footrace run on an open course of 26 miles 385 yards (42.2 km). First held at the revived Olympic Games in 1896, it commemorates the legendary feat of a Greek soldier who is said to have run from Marathon to Athens to report the Greek victory at MARATHON, after which he dropped dead. Marathons today are usually open events, often run by thousands, including the venerable Boston Marathon (established 1897). Women's marathons became an Olympic event in 1984.

Marathon, Battle of (490 B.C.) Decisive battle on the plain of Marathon outside Athens in the PERSIAN WARS. DARIUS I led his enormous army against a much smaller Athenian force led by Miltiades. The Athenians attacked with great speed, devastating the Persian line and resulting in Darius' departure from Greece. It is said that a messenger ran about 25 miles (40 km) back to Athens, where he announced the overwhelming victory before dying of exhaustion (see MARATHON). In another version, an Athenian runner was sent to Sparta before the battle to ask for help, running 150 mi (240 km) in two days; Sparta refused, so Athens fought with help only from PLATAEA.

marble Granular LIMESTONE or DOLOMITE that has recrystallized under the influence of heat, pressure, and aqueous solutions. Its main mineral is CALCITE. Commercially, "marble" includes all decorative calcium-rich rocks that can be polished, as well as some SERPENTINES. Marbles are used principally for buildings and monuments, interior decoration, and statuary. Statuary marble, the most valuable variety, must be pure white and of uniform grain size.

Marbury vs. Madison First U.S. Supreme Court decision to declare an act of Congress unconstitutional (1803), thus establishing the doctrine of JUDICIAL REVIEW. The case, involving a man appointed justice of the peace by an outgoing administration whose appointment was not honored by the incoming administration, hinged on authority granted by the Judiciary Act of 1789. Chief Justice John MARSHALL, writing for the Court, held that a section of the act contravened the Constitution and was thus invalid, declaring that the Constitution must always take precedence in any conflict between it and a law passed by Congress.

Marc, Franz (1880–1916) German painter. His early works were academic, but exposure to IMPRESSIONISM and JUGENDSTIL lightened his style. In 1911 he helped found the BLAUE REITER group. He believed that spiritual essence is best revealed through abstraction. His work consisted primarily of animal studies, since he believed nonhuman forms of life to be the most expressive manifestation of the vital force of nature. He was killed in action in World War I.

Marceau \mär-'sō\, **Marcel** (b.1923) French MIME. After studying with the pantomimist Étienne Decroux, he formed a mime troupe (1948–64) and earned worldwide acclaim in the 1950s with his production of the "mimodrama" of Nikolay GOGOL's *Overcoat*. In 1978 he founded a school of mimodrama in Paris. He is noted for his eloquent, deceptively simple portrayals, including his celebrated white-faced character Bip.

Marcel, Gabriel (-Honoré) (1889–1973) French philosopher, dramatist, and critic. His philosophical works explore aspects of human existence (e.g., trust, fidelity, hope, and despair) which had traditionally been dismissed as not amenable to philosophical consideration. His use of PHENOMENOLOGY was independent of the work of Edmund HUSSERL. Marcel is considered the first French proponent of EXISTENTIALISM.

Marcellus, Marcus Claudius (268?–208 B.C.) Roman general. He served as CONSUL in 222, 215, 214, 210, and 208. In 222 he fought in Gaul and won the *spolia opima* ("spoils of honor"), awarded for killing an enemy chief in single combat, for the third and last time in Roman history. In Sicily (214–211) in the Second PUNIC WAR, his troops sacked Syracuse and carried its art treasures to Rome. While fighting HANNIBAL near Venusia, he was caught in an ambush and killed.

march Musical form with an even meter with strongly accented beats to facilitate military marching. Marches were not notated until the late 16th cent., time being generally kept by percussion alone, often with improvised fife embellishment. With the extensive development of BRASS INSTRUMENTS especially in the 19th cent., marches became widely popular and were often elaborately orchestrated. Important composers incorporated them into their operas, sonatas, and symphonies. The later popularity of J. P. SOUSA's band marches was unmatched.

Marche \'märsh\ Historical region, central France. It was made a frontier countship (march) in the 10th cent. It was held by the Bourbons 1342–1435 and by the Armagnacs 1435–77. Confiscated by FRANCIS I in 1527, it was granted to the widows of French kings 1574–1643. It was a province of France until the FRENCH REVOLUTION.

Marche \'mar-kā\ Autonomous region (pop., 1996 est.: 1,443,000), central Italy. Situated between the Adriatic Sea and UMBRIA, it is crossed by the APENNINES; its only level land is along river valleys and on the Adriatic shore near Ancona, its capital. It came under Roman rule by A.D. 292. Conflicts arose in 12th–13th cent. among powerful feudal families and the popes; in 1631 the duchy of Urbino was incorporated into the PAPAL STATES. Marche joined the kingdom of Italy in 1860. An agricultural area, it has some industrial development.

March on Rome See March on ROME

Marciano \ˌmär-shē-'ä-nō\, **Rocky** orig. Rocco Francis Marchegiano (1923–1969) U.S. boxer. Born in Brockton, Mass., he developed into an unscientific but hard-punching and exceptionally durable fighter. He won the heavyweight championship title in 1952 by defeating Jersey Joe Walcott and relinquished it on retiring in 1956. He was undefeated in 49 professional fights, scoring 43 knockouts.

Marconi, Guglielmo (1874–1937) Italian physicist and inventor. He began experimenting with radio waves in 1894. In 1896 he went to England, where he developed a successful system of radio telegraphy. His improved aerials greatly extended the range of radio signaling. In 1899 he established communication across the English Channel. In 1901 he sent signals across the Atlantic for the first time. He acquired numerous patents, though his famous patent for an apparatus that enabled several stations to operate on different wavelengths without interference was later overturned. In his later years he worked on developing shortwave wireless communication, which is the basis of nearly all modern radio broadcasting. Marconi shared a 1909 Nobel Prize. He was made a marquis, nominated to the Italian senate (1929), and elected president of the Royal Italian Academy (1930).

Marco Polo See Marco POLO

Marcos, Ferdinand (Edralin) (1917–1989) Philippine head of state (1966–86). A trial lawyer before serving under Manuel ROXAS, first president of the independent Philippines, he was himself elected president in 1966. At first he made progress in agriculture, industry, and education, but in 1972 he imposed martial law, and his later years in power were noted for rampant government corruption and political repression. The outcry over the assassination of the opposition leader Benigno Aquino (1983) and Marcos's apparently fraudulent electoral victory over Corazon AQUINO forced him into exile in Hawaii, where he and his wife, Imelda, were indicted for embezzling billions of dollars from the Philippine economy. After his death, she returned to the Philippines, where she was tried and sentenced to 18 years in prison (1993); the sentence was later overturned.

Marcus Aurelius \ˌmär-kəs-ò-'rēl-yəs\ in full Caesar Marcus Aurelius Antoninus Augustus orig. Marcus Annius Verus (A.D. 121–180) Roman emperor (161–80). HADRIAN arranged that he and Lucius Verus be adopted by the designated future emperor ANTONINUS PIUS. On his accession, Marcus shared power with his adoptive brother as coemperor. His reign was marked by numerous military crises, all the major frontiers being threatened by invasion, and by a plague that devastated Rome. Verus died in 169; Marcus made his son COMMODUS coemperor in 177. Though a man of gentle character and wide learning, Marcus opposed Christianity and supported persecution of its adherents. His *Meditations* on STOICISM, considered one of the great books

of all time, gives a full picture of his religious and moral values. His reign is often thought to mark the Golden Age of Rome.

Marcuse \mär-'kü-zə\, **Herbert** (1898–1979) German-U.S. political philosopher. A member of the FRANKFURT SCHOOL, he fled Germany in 1933. His writings include *Eros and Civilization* (1955), *One-Dimensional Man* (1964), and *Counterrevolution and Revolt* (1972). He believed that Western society was unfree and repressive, and that its technology had bought the complacency of the masses with material goods. He was also hostile to the Soviet system. His Marxist philosophy and Freudian analyses of 20th-cent. Western society were popular among 1960s student leftists.

Mar del Plata Coastal city (pop., 1999 est.: 579,000), E central Argentina. The site of a Spanish mission (1746–51), it was established in 1874, became a city in 1907, and was promoted as a seaside resort. It is famous for its luxurious casino, one of the largest in the world.

Mardi Gras \'mär-dē-ˌgrä\ (French: "Fat Tuesday") CARNIVAL celebrated on or culminating on Shrove Tuesday, the day before the start of LENT. Traditionally, households consumed all the remaining foods that would be forbidden during Lent (e.g., eggs) on that day. In New Orleans it lasts several days and is marked by parades, street celebrations, and extravagant costumes.

Marduk \'mär-ˌdük\ or **Bel** In Mesopotamian religion, the chief god of the city of BABYLON and the national god of BABYLONIA. He began as a god of thunderstorms, and became lord of all the gods after conquering the monster of primeval chaos, Tiamat. Marduk's sacred animals (horses, dogs, and a dragon with a forked tongue) adorned Babylon's walls.

mare \'mär-ā\ Any flat, low, dark plain on the MOON. Its largest surface features, maria are huge lava flows marked by ridges, depressions (graben), and faults. The best known is probably Mare Tranquillitatis ("Sea of Tranquility"), where APOLLO 11 landed. All 14 are on the side of the moon that always faces earth and can be seen from earth with the unaided eye. The features of the "man in the moon" are maria.

Marenzio \mä-'rents-yō\, **Luca** (1553?–1599) Italian composer. He moved to Rome in the mid-1570s to work for Cardinal Luigi d'Este. He is best known for his 25 books of MADRIGALS, whose style became influential in Italy and England. His later madrigals, more serious in tone, use dissonance and chromaticism to reflect their texts, and are sometimes linked into cycles.

Marfan's syndrome Rare hereditary CONNECTIVE-TISSUE disorder. Patients are tall, with long, thin limbs and spiderlike fingers. The lens of the eye is dislocated, and many patients have GLAUCOMA or DETACHED RETINA. Heart-muscle abnormalities and various malfunctions and malformations occur; some can be corrected surgically. Severity varies; affected individuals may die young or live essentially normal lives. Rupture of the AORTA is the commonest cause of death.

Margaret of Angoulême \äⁿ-gü-'lem\ or **Margaret of Navarre** French Marguerite d'Angoulême (1492–1549) Queen consort of Henry II of Navarre and an outstanding figure of the French Renaissance. When her brother FRANCIS I acceded to the crown in 1515, she became highly influential in his court. After her first husband died, she married Henry in 1525. She was noted as a patron of humanists and reformers and of such writers as François RABELAIS. She was a writer herself; her most important work was the *Heptaméron* (published 1558–59), 72 tales modeled on BOCCACCIO's *Decameron*.

Margaret of Scotland, St. (1045?–1093) Patron saint of Scotland. Sister of EDGAR THE AETHELING, she married MALCOLM III CANMORE, and three of their sons succeeded to Scotland's throne. She founded abbeys, improved conditions for the poor, and persuaded Malcolm to initiate ecclesiastical reforms that transformed Scotland's religious and cultural life.

Margaret of Valois \väl-'wä\ or **Margaret of France** French Marguerite known as **Queen Margot** \mär-'gō\ (1553–1615) Queen consort of Navarre who played a secondary part in the Wars of RELIGION. The daughter of HENRY II of France, she was married in 1572 to the Protestant king of Navarre, the future HENRY IV of France, to seal the peace between Catholics and Protestants, but days later the SAINT BARTHOLOMEW'S DAY Massacre began. Aware of her involvement in conspiracies, HENRY III banished her to the castle at Usson in 1586. She granted her husband an annulment in 1600 and lived out her life in Paris. She was known for her beauty, learning, and licentious life; her *Mémoires* provide a vivid picture of contemporary France.

Margaret Tudor (1489–1541) Queen consort of King JAMES IV of Scotland (1503–13). The daughter of HENRY VII of England, she was married to James to improve relations with Scotland. After his death (1513), she briefly served as regent for her son, James V (1512–1542). She married the pro-English earl of Angus (1514), and played a key role in the conflict between the pro-French and pro-English factions in Scotland, shifting her allegiances to suit her financial interests. Obtaining an annulment (1527), she married Henry Stewart, Baron Methven, who became James's chief adviser.

margarine Food made from vegetable or animal fat mixed with milk and other ingredients, used as a substitute for BUTTER. It was developed by the French chemist H. Mège-Mouriès in the late 1860s. Polyunsaturated oils such as corn and sunflower oil, considered more healthful than saturated fats, are common today for making margarine.

margin In finance, the amount by which the value of collateral pledged as security for a loan exceeds the amount of the loan. This excess provides the lender a "margin" of safety over and above the collateral offered. The term is used especially with reference to transactions in SECURITIES and commodity FUTURES. When securities are purchased "on margin," the buyer supplies a percentage of the purchase price in cash and borrows the remainder from his broker, pledging the security as collateral. The U.S. Federal Reserve Board (see FEDERAL RESERVE SYSTEM) sets minimum margin requirements on loans made for buying securities, to prevent excessive use of credit for speculation in STOCKS, as happened before the stock-market crash of 1929. Dealings on margin are not allowed on British stock exchanges.

mariachi \ˌmär-ē-ˈä-chē\ Traditional Mexican street ensemble. In the 19th cent., mariachis consisted solely of stringed instruments, including violin, guitar, guitarrón, vihuela, mandolin, and double bass; since the 1920s they have generally included trumpets and often other wind instruments as well. The mariachi repertoire includes songs and lively dance music.

Mariam, Mengistu Haile See MENGISTU HAILE MARIAM

Mariana Islands \ˌmar-ē-ˈa-nə\ *formerly* **Ladrone Islands** \lə-ˈdrōn\ Island group, W Pacific Ocean. East of the Philippines, it includes 15 islands, divided politically into GUAM and the NORTHERN MARIANA ISLANDS. The population is descended from the pre-Spanish Chamorro people and Spanish, Mexican, German, Philippine, and Japanese settlers. Spanish cultural traditions are strong. Ferdinand MAGELLAN discovered the group in 1521. In 1668 colonizing Jesuit missionaries changed its name to honor Mariana of Austria, regent of Spain.

Mariana Trench Depression in the floor of the W Pacific Ocean. It is the deepest known depression on the surface of the earth, with a maximum depth of 36,198 ft (11,033 m). The trench extends over 1,580 mi (2,550 km) from southeast of GUAM to northwest of the MARIANA ISLANDS, and has a mean width of 43 mi (69 km). See also DEEP-SEA TRENCH.

Maria Theresa \tə-ˈrā-sə\ *German* Maria Theresia (1717–1780) Archduchess of Austria and queen of Hungary and Bohemia (1740–80). She was the daughter of Emperor CHARLES VI, whose PRAGMATIC SANCTION allowed her to succeed to the Habsburg domains; opposition to her succession led in 1740 to the War of the AUSTRIAN SUCCESSION. In 1745 she obtained the imperial crown for her husband, who became FRANCIS I. She helped initiate financial and educational reforms, promoted commerce and agriculture, and reorganized the army, all of which strengthened Austria's resources. Continued conflict with Prussia led to the SEVEN YEARS' WAR. After her husband's death (1765),

her son became emperor as JOSEPH II. A key figure in the power politics of 18th-cent. Europe, Maria Theresa brought unity to the Habsburg monarchy and was considered one of its most capable rulers. Her 16 children included MARIE-ANTOINETTE and LEOPOLD II.

Marib \ˈmar-ib\ Ancient city ruins, N central Yemen. The ancient fortified city was the center of the pre-Islamic state of Saba, or Sheba (950–115 B.C.). It was located on one of the caravan routes between the Mediterranean world and the Arabian Peninsula, and it prospered through its monopoly on frankincense and myrrh. The Marib Dam, built about the 7th cent B.C. to regulate the waters of the Wadi Sadd, irrigated more than 4,000 acres (1,600 hectares).

Marie-Antoinette (-Josèphe-Jeanne d'Autriche-Lorraine) (1755–1793) Queen consort of LOUIS XVI of France. The daughter of Emperor FRANCIS I and MARIA THERESA, she was married in 1770 to the French dauphin. After he became king (1774), she was criticized for her extravagance, but was unjustly implicated in the Affair of the DIAMOND NECKLACE (1786). After the FRENCH REVOLUTION began, she influenced Louis to resist attempts to restrict the royal prerogative. She became the target of agitators, who attributed to her the celebrated remark, after being told the people had no bread, "Let them eat cake!" She tried to save the crown by negotiating secretly with monarchist factions and with

Marie-Antoinette Portrait by Elisabeth Vigée-Lebrun

her brother, Emperor LEOPOLD II; news of her intrigues led to the overthrow of the monarchy (1792). After a year in prison, she was tried and guillotined.

Marie de France (fl. late 12th cent.) French poet, the earliest known woman poet of France. She wrote verse narratives on romantic and magical themes and may have inspired lyrics of the later TROUBADOURS. She probably wrote in England; her verses were dedicated to a "noble" king, either HENRY II of England or his son. She also wrote fables called *Ysopets*.

Marie de Médicis \də-mā-dē-ˈsēs\ *Italian* Maria de' Medici (1573–1642) Queen consort of HENRY IV of France. A member of the noted MEDICI FAMILY, she was married in 1600 to Henry as his second wife. As regent for their son, LOUIS XIII, after Henry's assassination in 1610, she squandered state revenues and bought the loyalty of rebellious nobles. After Louis assumed the throne (1617), she was exiled to Blois. She tried to raise a revolt and won favorable peace terms through her adviser, the future Cardinal de RICHELIEU. Restored to the king's council (1622), she persuaded Louis to make Richelieu chief minister. Richelieu gradually withdrew from Marie's influence and by 1628 was opposing her policies. When she attempted to have him dismissed, Louis banished Marie from court. In 1631 she fled to Brussels, where she later died in poverty.

Marie-Louise *German* Maria-Luise (1791–1847) Austrian archduchess and second wife of NAPOLEON. The eldest daughter of Emperor FRANCIS II, she was married to Napoleon (1810) and gave birth to his long-desired heir, the future NAPOLEON II, in 1811. When Napoleon abdicated (1814), Marie-Louise returned to Vienna with her son, ignoring Napoleon's entreaties to join him in exile. Made duchess of Parma, Piacenza, and Guastalla (1816), she ruled in accordance with Austrian prescriptions.

marigold Any of about 30 species of annual herbaceous plants that make up the genus *Tagetes* in the COMPOSITE FAMILY, native to SW N. America. Marigolds include popular garden ornamentals such as African marigold *(T. erecta)* and French marigold *(T. patula),* which have solitary or clustered red, orange, and yellow flowers and usually finely cut leaves. Because the strongly scented leaves discourage

M

insect pests, marigolds are often planted among vegetable crops.

Mariinsky Theater \mär-'yin-skē\ *formerly* **Kirov Theater** Russian imperial theater in St. Petersburg. The theater, named for the wife of the reigning czar, opened in 1860. Ballet was presented there after 1880. It housed the ballet company whose dancers had been trained at the affiliated Imperial Ballet school. From 1935 to 1991 it was known as the Kirov Theater. Its resident ballet company, the celebrated Kirov (or Mariinsky) Ballet, tours worldwide.

marijuana \ˌmar-ə-'wä-nə\ HEMP plant *(Cannabis sativa),* or the crude drug made of its dried and crushed leaves or flowers. The active ingredient is tetrahydrocannabinol (THC). Also called pot, grass, and weed, the drug has long been used as a sedative or analgesic; it was in use in China by the 3rd millennium B.C., and today it is used worldwide, though it is generally illegal. Its psychological and physical effects, including mild euphoria and alterations in vision and judgment, vary with strength and amount consumed, the setting, and the user's experience. Chronic use can be psychologically habit-forming. Marijuana has been shown to be medically therapeutic for patients suffering from glaucoma, AIDS, and the side effects of CHEMOTHERAPY. A resin from the plant is the source of HASHISH.

marimba XYLOPHONE with resonators under each bar. The original African instrument uses tuned calabash resonators. In Mexico and Central America, where it was brought by African slaves, the wooden bars may be affixed to a frame supported by legs or hung at the player's waist. The orchestral marimba uses long metal tubes as resonators.

Marin \'mar-ən\, **John** (1870–1953) U.S. painter and printmaker. Born in Rutherford, N.J., he studied painting in New York. After exposure to Cubism and German Expressionism, he developed a personal form of expressionism, consisting of semiabstract images based on objective reality. While watercolor usually produces delicate, transparent effects, Marin used the medium to render the monumental power of New York City (e.g., *Lower Manhattan,* 1922) and the relentless surge of the sea (e.g., *Maine Islands,* 1922).

Marín, Luis Muñoz See Luis MUÑOZ MARÍN

marine Member of a military force trained for service at sea and in land operations related to naval campaigns. In the 5th cent. B.C. Greek fleets were manned by *epibatai,* or heavily armed sea soldiers, but not until the naval wars of the 17th cent. was the distinct role of marines rediscovered by the British and the Dutch, who raised the first two modern marine corps, the Royal Marine (1664) and the Koninklijke Nederlandse Corps Mariniers (1665). See also UNITED STATES MARINE CORPS.

marine biology Science that deals with the animals and plants of the sea and estuaries and with airborne and terrestrial organisms that depend directly on bodies of saltwater for food and other necessities. Of particular interest are adaptations of organisms to the chemical and physical properties of seawater, the movements and currents of the ocean, and the availability of light at various depths. Other important areas of study are marine food chains, the distribution of economically important fish and crustaceans, and the effects of pollution. In the later 19th cent., the emphasis was on collecting and cataloging marine organisms. In the 20th cent., improved diving equipment, submersible craft, and underwater cameras and television made direct observation possible.

marine geology *or* **geologic oceanography** Scientific discipline concerned with the geology of the CONTINENTAL SHELF, CONTINENTAL SLOPE, and ocean basins. It originally focused on marine sedimentation and the interpretation of bottom samples, but the advent of the concept of SEAFLOOR SPREADING broadened its scope. Many investigations of the OCEANIC RIDGE system, the magnetism of rocks on the seafloor, geochemical analyses of deep brine pools, and CONTINENTAL DRIFT are considered part of marine geology.

Mariner \'mar-ə-nər\ Any of a series of 10 unmanned U.S. space probes sent near VENUS, MARS, and MERCURY. Mariners 2 (1962) and 5 (1967) passed close to Venus and made measurements of temperature and atmospheric density. Mariners 4 (1965), 6 and 7 (1969), 9 (1971–72), and 10 (1973–75) sent striking pictures of the surface of Mars and analyzed its atmosphere and magnetic field. Mariner 10 (1974–75) is the only spacecraft ever to visit Mercury.

Marinetti \ˌmä-rē-'nät-tē\, **Filippo Tommaso (Emilio)** (1876–1944) Italian-French writer, the ideological founder of FUTURISM. In early poetry such as *Destruction* (1904), he showed the vigor and anarchic experimentation with form that would characterize his later work. Futurism officially began with the 1909 publication of his manifesto in a Paris newspaper; he later elaborated on his theory in a novel and several dramatic works. Arguing that FASCISM was Futurism's natural extension, he lost most of his following in the 1920s.

Marini, Marino (1901–1980) Italian sculptor and painter. Working primarily in bronze, he concentrated on two major images: the earthbound woman and the horse and rider. His sensitivity to form and surface owes much to Etruscan and Roman works, but his bold, straining figures reflect an expressionist sensibility. His portrait busts capture the spiritual side of his subjects. In the 1940s he turned to painting nearly abstract works.

Marino, Dan *orig.* Daniel Constantine Marino, Jr. (b.1961) U.S. football quarterback. Born in Pittsburgh, he played at the Univ. of Pittsburgh. Drafted by the Miami Dolphins in 1983, he set all-time career records for passes completed (4,967 in 8,358 attempts), yards passing (61,261), and touchdown passes (420), and in 21 other categories. In 1984 he became the first quarterback to pass for more than 5,000 yards (5,084) and to complete over 40 touchdown passes (48) in a season.

Marino, Giambattista (1569–1625) Italian poet, founder of the school of Marinism (later *secentismo*), which dominated 17th-cent. Italian poetry. His most important work, a labor of 20 years, is *Adonis* (1623), an enormous poem (45,000 lines) that relates, with many digressions, the love story of Venus and Adonis. His work, praised throughout Europe, far surpassed that of his imitators, who carried his complicated wordplay and elaborate conceits and metaphors to such extremes that Marinism became a pejorative term.

Mariology \ˌmar-ē-'ä-lə-jē\ Study of doctrines concerning MARY, the mother of JESUS, or the content of those doctrines. The New Testament says little about Mary, though the tradition that she remained a virgin despite giving birth to Jesus was accepted early on. She became an especially important figure in ROMAN CATHOLICISM. PIUS IX proclaimed the doctrine of the IMMACULATE CONCEPTION in 1854. For Catholics, Mary is seen as the spiritual mother and heavenly intercessor and a partner with Jesus in the redemption of human beings. In 1950 PIUS XII proclaimed the doctrine that at her death Mary was bodily assumed into heaven.

Marion, Francis *known as* **the Swamp Fox** (1732?–1795) American Revolutionary commander. Born in Winyah, S.C., in the AMERICAN REVOLUTION he commanded troops in S. Carolina and escaped after the British victory at Charleston. Gathering a band of guerrillas, he harassed British troops with surprise raids, escaping into the region's swamps when pursued. In 1781 he led a daring rescue of American troops surrounded by the British at Parkers Ferry, S.C., and was appointed a brigadier general.

marionette Puppet figure manipulated from above by strings attached to a wooden cross or control. Also called a string puppet, it is usually manipulated by nine strings, attached to each leg, hand, shoulder, and ear and at the base of the spine. Early marionettes were controlled by an iron rod instead of strings, a form that survived in Sicily. In the 18th cent., marionette operas were extremely popular, and they are still performed today in Salzburg to Mozart's music. See also PUPPETRY.

Marionette Scheherazade, snake charmer, and snake by Bil Baird

Maris \'mar-əs\, **Roger (Eugene)** (1934–1985) U.S. baseball player. Born in Hibbing, Minn., he played outfield for the

Cleveland Indians (1957–59), the New York Yankees (1960–66), and the St. Louis Cardinals (1967–68). In 1961 his one-season total of 61 home runs broke Babe RUTH's long-standing record of 60, edging out his teammate Mickey MANTLE. Maris's record stood until 1998.

Maritain \mà-rē-'taⁿ\, **Jacques** (1882–1973) French philosopher. A devout Roman Catholic, his thought was based on Aristotelianism and THOMISM and drew on anthropology, sociology, and psychology. He emphasized the importance of the individual as well as the Christian community. Among his works are *Art and Scholasticism* (1920), *The Degrees of Knowledge* (1932), *Art and Poetry* (1935), *Man and the State* (1951), and *Moral Philosophy* (1960).

maritime law *or* **admiralty law** *or* **admiralty** Body of legal rules that governs ships and shipping. Maritime law deals mainly with the eventualities of loss of a ship (e.g., through collision) or cargo, with insurance and liability relating to those eventualities, and with collision compensation and salvage rights. There is an increasing tendency to make maritime laws uniform; the chief organization overseeing maritime law is the International Maritime Committee, composed of the maritime-law associations of several nations.

Maritime Provinces Canadian provinces of New Brunswick, Nova Scotia, and Prince Edward Island. They are located on the Atlantic Coast and the Gulf of ST. LAWRENCE. With Newfoundland and Labrador they form the Atlantic Provinces. Under France, much of the area was called ACADIA.

Marius \'mar-ē-əs\, **Gaius** (157?–86 B.C.) General and consul who redesigned the Roman army. He secured command of the army in Africa (107) and solved the chronic manpower shortage by enlisting landless citizens for the first time. He defeated JUGURTHA in 106. At Rome he held unconstitutional successive consulships (104–100) while it was threatened by the Cimbri and the Teutones, whom he defeated. In 88 he replaced SULLA as Asian commander and confronted MITHRADATES. When an outraged Sulla marched on Rome, Marius fled for his life. He returned forcibly in 87, was elected consul for the seventh time, and ruthlessly murdered his opponents.

Marivaux \mà-rē-'vō\, **Pierre (Carlet de Chamblain de)** (1688–1763) French playwright. Born into an aristocratic family, he lost his fortune in 1720 and embarked on a serious literary career. He wrote his first plays, including the tragedy *Annibal* (1720), for the COMÉDIE-FRANÇAISE, but preferred to write for the Italian COMMEDIA DELL'ARTE theater in Paris, for which he produced *Harlequin Brightened by Love* (1723) and *The Game of Love and Chance* (1730). His nuanced feeling and clever wordplay became known as *marivaudage*. He also wrote the satires *Isle of Slaves* (1725), *Isle of Reason* (1727), and *The New Colony* (1729).

marjoram *or* **sweet marjoram** \'mär-jə-rəm\ Perennial herb (*Majorana hortensis*) of the MINT family, or its fresh or dried leaves and flowering tops. It is used to flavor many foods. Various other aromatic herbs or undershrubs of the genera *Origanum* (see OREGANO) and *Majorana* of the mint family are also called marjoram.

Mark, St. (fl.1st cent. A.D.) Christian evangelist to whom the second GOSPEL is traditionally ascribed. He joined Sts. PAUL and BARNABAS on their first missionary journey but left them at Perga and returned to Jerusalem. He may also have aided St. PETER in Rome, and some scholars believe that his Gospel is based on Peter's account of his experiences as one of the 12 disciples. If this is true, it was probably written shortly after Peter's death around A.D. 65. The Egyptian church claims Mark as its founder.

Mark Antony See Mark ANTONY

market Means by which buyers and sellers are brought into contact with each other and goods and services are exchanged. No longer a specific place, today a market may be any arena for transactions. Dealers at commodity exchanges in London and New York, for example, communicate by telephone and computer links as well as in person. Markets trade not only in tangible commodities such as grain and livestock but also in financial instruments such as SECURITIES and CURRENCIES. CLASSICAL ECO-

NOMICS developed the theory of perfect competition, in which free markets were seen as places where large numbers of buyers and sellers communicated easily with each other and traded in readily transferable commodities, with prices determined only by SUPPLY AND DEMAND. Since the 1930s, economists have focused more on the theory of imperfect competition, in which supply and demand are not the only factors that influence the operations of the market, the number of sellers or buyers is limited, rival products are differentiated (by design, quality, brand name, etc.), and various obstacles hinder new producers' entry into the market.

marketing Activities that direct the flow of goods and services from producers to consumers. Marketing issues can play a major role in determining organizational policy and success. Once primarily concerned with ADVERTISING and promotion, marketing efforts now focus on CREDIT policies, product development, customer support, distribution, and corporate communications. Marketers may look for sales and promotional outlets including retail stores, direct-mail marketing, WHOLESALING, and partnering. They may conduct demographic studies, experiment with marketing strategies, and interview target audiences. Marketing is used both to increase awareness and sales of existing concepts and products and to introduce new ones. See also MERCHANDISING.

marketing board Organization set up by a government to regulate the buying and selling of a certain commodity. The simplest type of board conducts MARKET RESEARCH, promotes sales, and furnishes information. It is usually supported by fees from sales of the product concerned. Examples include the Tea Propaganda Board of Sri Lanka and the Tobacco Export Promotion Council of Zimbabwe. Other boards may establish packing standards and quality analysis. The primary goal is usually to stabilize PRICES, especially of products intended for the export market, where price fluctuations are often violent. The boards may raise average prices by manipulating commodity flows to maintain high levels of demand. Marketing boards are also helpful in setting up outlets for time-sensitive perishables. See also CARTEL.

market research Study of the requirements of specific markets, the acceptability of products, and methods of developing and exploiting new markets. Past sales may be projected forward; surveys may be made of consumer attitudes and product preferences; and new or altered products may be introduced into test-market areas. Formal market research dates back to the 1920s in Germany. After World War II, U.S. firms led in the refinement of market-research techniques, which then spread throughout much of Western Europe and Japan.

Markham, Beryl *orig.* Beryl Clutterbuck (1902–1986) British pilot, adventurer, and writer. Raised in British E. Africa, she became a horse trainer and breeder. Turning to aviation, she carried goods, people, and mail to far corners of Africa, and in 1936 she made a historic east-to-west solo flight across the N. Atlantic from England to Cape Breton Island. In 1942 she published her celebrated memoir *West with the Night*.

Markova \mär-'kō-və\, **Alicia** (*later* **Dame Alicia**) *orig.* Lilian Alicia Marks (b.1910) British ballerina. She made her debut with the BALLETS RUSSES in 1924 and became a leading ballerina, noted for her ethereal lightness. At the Vic-Wells Ballet (1931–35) she became the first English dancer to dance the lead in *Giselle*. With her frequent partner Anton DOLIN, she formed and directed several companies (1935–38) and London's Festival Ballet (1949–52). As a guest artist with companies worldwide, she won admiration in such works as *Les sylphides* and *Pas de quatre*. She directed the Metropolitan Opera Ballet 1963–69.

markup language Standard text-encoding system consisting of a set of symbols inserted in a text document to control its structure, formatting, or the relationship among its parts. The most widely used markup languages are SGML, HTML, and XML. The markup symbols can be interpreted by a device (computer, printer, browser, etc.) to control how a document looks when printed or displayed on a monitor. A marked-up document thus contains two types of text: text to be displayed and markup language specifying how to display it.

Marlborough, Duke of *orig.* John Churchill (1650–1722) British military commander. He served with distinction at Maastricht (1673), was promoted rapidly, and advanced at court, in part because his wife was a confidant of Princess (later Queen) ANNE. In 1688 his allegiance to WILLIAM III, was rewarded with the earldom of Marlborough and a succession of commands in Flanders and Ireland. Queen Anne appointed him commander of English and Dutch forces in the War of the SPANISH SUCCESSION, and for his successes he was created duke of Marlborough (1702). His victory at the Battle of Blenheim (1704) helped change the balance of power in Eu-

Duke of Marlborough
Painting attributed to J. Closterman

rope. In gratitude, he was granted a royal manor, where BLENHEIM PALACE was built. His outstanding military tactics continued to produce victories. His influence with Queen Anne was undermined by intrigue between Tories and Whigs; after his Whig allies lost the election of 1710, he was dismissed. He retired from public life, though he was restored to favor by GEORGE I in 1714. Considered one of England's greatest generals, he secured a reputation in Europe that was unrivaled until the rise of Napoleon.

Marley, Bob (*orig.* Robert Nesta) (1945–1981) Jamaican singer and songwriter. Raised in the Kingston slums, Marley worked as a welder before forming the Wailers with Peter Tosh and others. In the 1970s they became the first international REGGAE stars with such releases as *Catch a Fire* (1973), *Exodus* (1977), and *Uprising* (1980). He died of cancer at 36. Marley's music, an amalgamation of American, African, and Jamaican styles, reflected his RASTAFARIAN beliefs in universal peace and empowerment for the black race. Since his death he has attained near-legendary stature.

marlin Any of four species (genus *Makaira,* family Istiophoridae) of deep-blue to blue-green marine fish with a long body, a long dorsal fin, and a rounded spear extending from the snout, which it uses to club the fish it feeds on. It is highly prized for sport and food. Species range in weight from about 100 lbs (45 kg) to more than 1,500 lbs (700 kg).

Marlowe, Christopher (1564–1593) English playwright. From 1587 he wrote plays for the London theaters, starting with *Tamburlaine the Great* (published 1590), in which he established dramatic blank verse. *Tamburlaine* was followed by *Dido, Queen of Carthage* (published 1594), cowritten with Thomas NASHE; *The Massacre at Paris* (c.1594); and *Edward II* (1594). His *Tragical History of Doctor Faustus* (published 1604) is one of the most admired English dramas of all time. *The Jew of Malta* (published 1633) may have been his final work. His poetry includes the unfinished long poem *Hero and Leander.* He died a violent death at 29 in a tavern brawl, which may have been an assassination for his service as a government spy. He was William SHAKESPEARE's most important contemporary in English drama.

Marmara \ˈmär-mə-rə\, **Sea of** Inland sea lying between the Asian and European parts of Turkey. It is connected with the BLACK SEA through the BOSPORUS, and with the AEGEAN SEA through the DARDANELLES. It is 175 mi (280 km) long and nearly 50 mi (80 km) wide. Its Kizil Islands are primarily resort areas. The Marmara Islands are rich in granite, slate, and marble, all quarried since antiquity.

marmoset Any species of arboreal, diurnal, long-tailed S. American MONKEY (family Callitrichidae) classified in two groups: eight species with short tusks (lower canine teeth), called marmosets, and 25 with long tusks, called TAMARINS. Members of the common marmoset genus *Callithrix* are 6–10 in. (15–25 cm) long, excluding the 10–16-in. (25–40-cm) tail. The dense, silky fur is white, reddish, or blackish; the

ears are generally tufted. Marmosets have been kept as pets since the early 17th cent. Some are endangered.

marmot \ˈmär-mət\ Any of about 14 species (genus *Marmota*) of stout-bodied, terrestrial SQUIRRELS found in N. America, Europe, and Asia. Marmots are 12–24 in. (30–60 cm) long, excluding the short tail, and weigh 7–17 lbs (3–7.5 kg). Most species live in burrows or among boulders. They frequently sit upright and emit a whistling alarm call. The black-and-white hoary marmot *(M. caligata),* of Siberia and NW N. America, hibernates for up to nine months. The yellow-bellied marmot *(M. flaviventris)* inhabits the W U.S. and British Columbia. See also WOODCHUCK.

Marne, First Battle of the (Sept. 6–12, 1914) Military offensive by French and British troops in WORLD WAR I. After German forces had moved to within 30 mi (50 km) of Paris at the MARNE RIVER, Joseph JOFFRE counterattacked. French reinforcements were driven to the front by 600 Paris taxis, the first automotive transport of troops. The Germans were forced to retreat north of the Aisne River, where they dug in to conduct the TRENCH WARFARE of the next three years. The Allied success thwarted Germany's plan for a quick victory on the Western Front.

Marne River \ˈmärn\ River, NE France. It flows northwest into the SEINE RIVER near PARIS. It is navigable for 220 mi (350 km) of its total length of 326 mi (525 km) and has extensive canals. Its valley was the scene of crucial battles in WORLD WAR I.

Maroni River \mä-ˈrō-nē\ River forming the boundary between French Guiana and Suriname. It rises near the Brazilian border and descends northward to enter the Atlantic Ocean after a course of 450 mi (725 km). Its upper course is known as the Litani in Suriname, or Itany in French Guiana; its middle course is called the Lawa, or Aoua.

Maronite Church \ˈmar-ə-ˌnīt\ Eastern-rite community centered in Lebanon (see EASTERN RITE CHURCH). It traces its origin to St. Maron, a Syrian hermit of the 4th–5th cent. A.D., and St. John Maron, under whom the invading Byzantine forces were defeated in 684. For several centuries the Maronites were considered heretics because they believed that Jesus had only a divine will and not a human will. No permanent affiliation with Rome took place until the 16th cent. In 1860 the Ottoman government incited a massacre of the Maronites by the DRUZE, which led to the establishment of Maronite autonomy within the Ottoman empire. The Maronites obtained self-rule under French protection in the early 20th cent. They are a major religious group in present-day Lebanon. Their spiritual leader (after the pope) is the patriarch of Antioch, and the church retains the ancient W. Syrian liturgy.

Marot \mà-ˈrō\, **Clément** (1496?–1544) French poet. While imprisoned in 1526 for defying Lenten abstinence regulations, he wrote some of his best-known works, including "L'Enfer" ("The Inferno"), an allegorical satire on justice. He held several court posts; his long service to FRANCIS I was only briefly interrupted. One of the greatest poets of the French Renaissance, he markedly influenced the style of his successors with his use of the forms and imagery of Latin poetry.

Marquesas Islands \mär-ˈkā-səz\ Group (pop., 1996: 8,000) of 10 islands in FRENCH POLYNESIA, northeast of Tahiti. The SE group includes Hiva Oa, the largest and most populated and the burial place of artist Paul GAUGUIN. Álvaro de Mendaña de Neira (1541–1595) named the islands for the Marquesa de Mendoza in 1595. They were annexed by France in 1842.

marquess \ˈmär-kwəs\ *or* **marquis** \mär-ˈkē\ European title of nobility, ranking below a DUKE and above a COUNT or earl. The wife of a marquess is a marchioness or marquise. The term originally denoted a count holding a march, or mark (frontier district).

Marquette \mär-ˈket\, **Jacques** *known as* **Père Marquette** (1637–1675) French missionary and explorer. A Jesuit, he arrived in Quebec in 1666 to preach among the Ottawa. He helped found missions at Sault Ste. Marie (1668) and St. Ignace (1671) (both now in Michigan). In 1673 he accompanied Louis JOLLIET down the Mississippi River to the mouth of the Arkansas River. They returned via the Illinois River to Green Bay on Lake Michigan, where Marquette remained. In 1674 he set out to found a mission among the Illinois Indians, reaching the site of present-day Chicago.

Márquez, Gabriel García See Gabriel GARCÍA MÁRQUEZ

Marrakech *or* **Marrakesh** \mə-ˈrä-kish, ˌmar-ə-ˈkesh\ City (metro. area pop., 1994: 672,000), S Morocco. It was founded in 1062 by Yusuf ibn Tashufin as the African capital of the ALMORAVID DYNASTY. It fell to the ALMOHADS in 1147, passed to the Marinids in 1269, and was the capital under the Saadians in the 16th cent. In the medieval era, it was one of Islam's great cities. It was held by the French 1912–1956. Now a popular resort, it has many historical buildings and a well-known souk (marketplace).

marriage Legally and socially sanctioned union between, usually, a man and one or more women that accords status to their offspring and is regulated by laws and customs that prescribe the rights and duties of the partners. The universality of marriage is attributed to the many basic social and personal functions it performs, such as procreation and provision for sexual gratification and regulation, care of children and their education and socialization, regulation of lines of DESCENT, division of labor between the sexes, and satisfaction of personal needs for social status, affection, and companionship. Until modern times, marriage was rarely a matter of free choice. In Western society, love has come to be associated with marriage; however, romantic love has not been a primary motive for matrimony in most eras. In societies in which the extended FAMILY remains the basic unit, marriages are usually arranged by the family, and much thought is given to the socioeconomic advantages accruing to the larger family from the match. Some form of DOWRY or BRIDEWEALTH almost always accompanies arranged marriages. The ceremonies surrounding marriage are associated primarily with fertility and validate the importance of marriage for the continuation of a family, clan, TRIBE, or society. See also DIVORCE, POLYGAMY.

marriage law Body of legal specifications and requirements that regulate the initiation, continuation, and validity of marriages. Modern Western European and U.S. marriage law allows only monogamous unions; partners must be above a certain age and not within prohibited degrees of blood relationship, and must be free to marry and give consent to the marriage. DIVORCE is now almost universally allowed. Islamic law regards marriage as a purely civil contract for the "legalization of intercourse and the procreation of children." The practice of POLYGAMY, though historically permitted, has waned, though polygamous marriages are still permitted in many African nations. Marriage law in present-day China and Japan resembles that in the West.

Mars Ancient Roman god of war and protector of Rome, second only to JUPITER in importance. Until the time of AUGUSTUS, Mars had only two temples in Rome. His sacred spears were kept in a sanctuary; on the outbreak of war, the consul had to shake the spears, saying "Mars vigila!" ("Mars, awake!") Under Augustus, Mars became the emperor's personal guardian. He was identified with the Greek god ARES.

Mars Fourth PLANET from the sun, named after the Roman god of war. Its mean distance from the sun is 141 million mi (228 million km); its day is 24.6 earth hours and its year about 687 earth days. It has two small moons, Phobos and Deimos. Mars's mean diameter (4,244 mi, or 6,790 km), is about half that of earth, and its mass is about one-tenth of earth's; it is less dense than earth and its surface gravity about one-third as strong. Its lack of a magnetic field and its low density suggest it has no substantial metallic core. Mars has seasons and a thin atmosphere, mainly carbon dioxide with some nitrogen and argon and traces of water vapor; its mean surface temperature is −9°F (−23°C). No life has been detected on it. Images from MARINER, Viking, and other spacecraft show a cratered surface like the moon's, with volcanoes, including Olympus Mons, the largest known volcano in the solar system; lava plains; channels and canyons; and remnants of landslides. Wind is an important element on Mars; it can cause global dust storms and form dunes and crater streaks.

Mars, canals of Apparent systems of markings on MARS, now known to be an illusion caused by the chance align-

ment of surface features. Giovanni Virginio Schiaparelli (1835–1910) observed about 100 "channels." Percival LOWELL called them canals and believed them to be evidence of intelligent life. Most astronomers could not see them, and many doubted their reality. Their existence was disproved by pictures from MARINER spacecraft.

Marsalis \mär-ˈsa-ləs\, **Wynton** (b.1961) U.S. trumpeter and composer, a major figure in the renewal of interest in jazz. Born in New Orleans, Marsalis was recognized as an important classical and jazz soloist at an early age. He joined Art BLAKEY's Jazz Messengers (1980–82) before leading his own groups. As a composer he has written ballet and concert works and won the 1997 Pulitzer Prize for his oratorio *Blood on the Fields*.

Marseille *or* **Marseilles** \mär-ˈsā\ City (pop., 1999: 807,000), SE France. One of the Mediterranean's major seaports and the second-largest city in France, it lies just west of the French RIVIERA. Settled by Greeks during the 7th cent. B.C. and annexed by the Romans in 49 B.C., it thrived as a commercial port during the CRUSADES era and passed to the French crown in 1481. The plague of 1720 killed half of its population. In the 19th cent. the development of France's colonial empire added to the city's importance. Following World War II its rapid growth was fueled by the construction of a huge steelworks and an oil pipeline.

marsh Freshwater or marine wetland ecosystem characterized by poorly drained mineral soils and by plant life dominated by grasses. Fewer plant species grow in marshes than on well-watered but not water-logged land; grasses, sedges, and reeds or rushes are most common. Commercially, rice is by far the most important freshwater marsh plant. Salt marshes are formed on intertidal land by seawater flooding and draining. See also SWAMP.

Marsh, O(thniel) C(harles) (1831–1899) U.S. paleontologist. Born in Lockport, N.Y., he spent his entire career at Yale Univ. (1866–99) as the first professor of vertebrate paleontology in the U.S. In 1871 one of his field expeditions discovered the first pterodactyl found in the U.S. He maintained a fierce rivalry with E. D. COPE. Credited with discovering more than 1,000 fossil vertebrates, Marsh published major works on toothed birds, gigantic horned mammals, and N. American dinosaurs. His books include *Fossil Horses in America* (1874) and *Introduction and Succession of Vertebrate Life in America* (1877).

Marsh, Reginald (1898–1954) U.S. painter and printmaker. Born to American parents in Paris, from 1922 to 1925 he produced a daily column of drawings of vaudeville acts for the *New York Daily News*. As an original staff member of *The New Yorker* magazine (1925), he drew humorous illustrations and metropolitan scenes. In 1929 he began painting scenes of city life, including Coney Island crowds and Bowery derelicts. He taught at the Art Students League from 1934.

Marshall, George C(atlett) (1880–1959) U.S. Army officer and statesman. Born in Uniontown, Pa., he graduated from Virginia Military Institute, and served in World War I. He was an aide to Gen. John PERSHING (1919–24) and assistant commandant of the army's infantry school (1927–33), where he taught many future World War II commanders. As chief of staff of the U.S. Army (1939–45), he directed army operations throughout World War II. After he retired (1945), Pres. Harry TRUMAN sent him to mediate the civil war in China (1945–47). As secretary of state (1947–49), he proposed the European aid program known as the MARSHALL PLAN and initiated discussions that led to NATO.

George C. Marshall

He resigned because of ill health but was called back to become secretary of defense (1950–51) and to prepare for the

KOREAN WAR. In 1953 he was awarded the Nobel Peace Prize.

Marshall, John (1755–1835) U.S. patriot, politician, and jurist. Born near Germantown, Va., he served as a lieutenant under Gen. George WASHINGTON in the American Revolution. He later served in the Virginia legislature and on Virginia's executive council (1782–95), gaining a reputation as a leading Federalist. He was one of three commissioners sent to France 1797–98 (see XYZ AFFAIR). After serving Pres. John ADAMS as secretary of state (1800–1), Marshall was appointed chief justice of the U.S. Supreme Court in 1801. He participated in more than 1,000 decisions, writing 519 himself. During his tenure the Court set forth the main structural lines of the government; its groundbreaking decisions included *MARBURY VS. MADISON, MCCULLOCH VS. MARYLAND*, and the DARTMOUTH COLLEGE CASE. Marshall is remembered as the principal founder of the U.S. system of constitutional law, including the doctrine of JUDICIAL REVIEW.

Marshall, Thurgood (1908–1993) U.S. jurist and civil-rights advocate. Born in Baltimore, he went to work for the NAACP in 1936 and became its chief counsel in 1940. He won 29 of the 32 cases he argued before the U.S. Supreme Court, including the landmark *BROWN VS. BOARD OF EDUCATION* (1954) and others that established EQUAL PROTECTION for blacks in housing, voting, employment, and graduate study. He became the first black Supreme Court justice in 1967. A steadfast liberal, he championed the rights of the individual, 1st-Amendment freedoms, and AFFIRMATIVE ACTION. He retired in 1991.

Marshall Islands *officially* **Republic of the Marshall Islands,** *Marshallese* **Majol** \'mä-jȯl\ Independent republic, central Pacific Ocean. It is composed of two parallel chains of low-lying coral atolls: the Ratak, or Sunrise, to the east and the Ralik, or Sunset, to the west. The chains lie 125 mi (200 km) apart and extend some 800 mi (1,290 km) northwest to southeast. The islands and islets number more than 1,200. Area: 70 sq mi (181 sq km). Population (2000): 51,000. Capital: MAJURO. The indigenous people are Micronesian. Languages: Marshallese, English (both official). Religion: Christianity (a majority). Currency: U.S. dollar. The largest atoll is Kwajalein, consisting of about 90 islets, with a total land area of 6 sq mi (16 sq km). Much of Kwajalein is used as a missile-testing range by the U.S. military, which provides a major source of revenue. Subsistence farming, fishing, and the raising of pigs and poultry are the principal economic activities. It is a republic with two legislative houses; its head of state and government is the president. The islands were sighted in 1529 by the Spanish navigator Álvaro Saavedra. Germany declared the islands a protectorate in 1885 and purchased them from Spain in 1899. Japan seized them in 1914 and after 1919 administered them as a League of Nations mandate. During World War II the U.S. seized Kwajalein and Enewetak, and the Marshall Islands were made part of the U.N. Trust Territory of the Pacific Islands under U.S. jurisdiction in 1947. BIKINI and Enewetak atolls served as testing grounds for U.S. nuclear weapons 1946–58. The country became an internally self-governing republic in 1979. It signed a compact of free association with the U.S. in 1982 and became fully self-governing in 1986. See also map at OCEANIA.

Marshall Plan (1948–51) U.S.-sponsored program to provide economic aid to European countries after World War II. The idea of a European self-help plan financed by the U.S. was proposed by George MARSHALL in 1947 and was authorized by Congress as the European Recovery Program. It provided almost $13 billion in grants and loans to 17 countries and was a key factor in reviving their economies and stabilizing their political structures. The plan's concept was extended to less-developed countries under the POINT FOUR PROGRAM.

marsh gas See METHANE

Marsic War See SOCIAL WAR

Mars Pathfinder and Rover First spacecraft to attempt landing on MARS since Viking in 1976. Launched in 1996 by NASA, Pathfinder landed in July 1997 using parachutes, rockets, and airbags and deployed instruments, including Sojourner, a small, six-wheeled Rover, which explored as far as 1,600 ft (500 m) from the lander and sent pictures back for over a month. Its success showed that low-cost Mars landings and exploration are feasible.

Marston, John (1576–1634) English dramatist. One of the most vigorous satirists of his era, his best-known work is the tragicomedy *The Malcontent* (1604), which rails at the iniquities of a lascivious court. *The Dutch Courtezan* (produced 1603–4), was one of the cleverest comedies of its time. Though he feuded with Ben JONSON, the two collaborated on *Eastward Hoe* (1605; with George Chapman) and *Love's Martyr* (1607). He took holy orders in 1609.

Marston Moor, Battle of (July 2, 1644) First major Royalist defeat in the ENGLISH CIVIL WAR. Royalist forces under Prince RUPERT relieved the siege of York and pursued the Parliamentary forces to nearby Long Marston. A surprise counterattack by Parliamentary forces under Oliver CROMWELL caused heavy losses to Royalist troops. With the fall of York, CHARLES I lost control of the north, and Cromwell emerged as the leading Parliamentary general.

marsupial \mär-'sü-pē-əl\ Any MAMMAL of the infraclass Marsupialia, characterized by premature birth, with the young remaining attached to the mother's teats for a period corresponding to the late stages of fetal development of a placental mammal. More than 170 species (e.g., BANDICOOTS, KANGAROOS, KOALAS, WOMBATS) are found in Australia, New Guinea, and nearby islands; about 65 species of OPOSSUM occur in the Americas. Many species have a pouch (marsupium), a fold of skin covering the nipples on the mother's lower belly, where the young continue their development.

marten Any of several forest-dwelling CARNIVORE species (genus *Martes,* family Mustelidae). Larger than WEASELS, their total length is 20–40 in. (50–100 cm); they may weigh 2–5 lbs (1–2.5 kg) or more. Martens hunt alone, feeding on animals, fruit, and carrion. The fur of the American marten *(M. americana)* of N N. America is sometimes sold as sable. Other species include the pine, baum, or sweet marten *(M. martes)* of Europe and central Asia and the yellow-throated marten, or honey dog *(M. flavigula),* of S Asia. See also FISHER.

Martha's Vineyard Island off the SE coast of Massachusetts. Situated across Vineyard Sound from CAPE COD, it is nearly 20 mi (32 km) long and 2–10 mi (3–16 km) wide. It was first described in 1602; it was named for its wild grapevines. It was considered part of New York before being ceded to Massachusetts in 1692. Once a whaling and fishing center, it is now a popular summer resort.

Martí (y Pérez) \mär-'tē\, **José (Julián)** (1853–1895) Cuban poet, essayist, and patriot. Involved in an 1868 revolutionary uprising, Martí was deported to Spain; he later lived in New York City (1881–95). He organized and unified the movement for Cuban independence and died in battle. As a writer, he is noted for his personal prose and deceptively simple verse on themes of a free and united America. His essays are often considered his greatest contribution to Latin-American letters. He is the national hero of Cuba.

Martial \'mär-shəl\ *Latin* Marcus Valerius Martialis (c.A.D. 38/41–c.103) Roman poet. Born in a Roman colony in Spain, Martial went to Rome as a young man, where he enjoyed the patronage of the emperors TITUS and DOMITIAN. He is renowned for his 12 books of EPIGRAMS (86–102?), a form he virtually created. Pointed and often obscene, they provide a picture of Roman society during the early empire that is remarkable both for its completeness and for its accurate portrayal of human foibles.

martial art Any of several arts of combat and self-defense that are widely practiced as sport. There are armed and unarmed varieties, most based on traditional fighting methods used in E. Asia. Derivatives of armed martial arts include kendo (fencing) and kyudo (archery). Unarmed varieties include AIKIDO, JUDO, KARATE, KUNG FU, and TAE KWON DO. Because of the influence of Taoism and Zen Buddhism, there is a strong emphasis on the practitioner's mental and spiritual state. A hierarchy of expertise, ranging from the novice ("white belt") to the master ("black belt"), is usually recognized. See also T'AI CHI CH'UAN, JUJITSU.

martial law Temporary rule of a designated area by military authorities in time of emergency when the civil authorities are deemed unable to function. Under martial law, civil rights are usually suspended and the activities of civil courts restricted or supplanted entirely by military tribunals. See also HUMAN RIGHTS, WAR CRIMES.

martin Any of several species of songbirds in the family Hirundinidae. The purple martin (*Progne subis*), at 8 in. (20 cm) long, is the largest U.S. SWALLOW. The sand martin (*Riparia riparia*), a 5-in. (12-cm) brown-and-white bird, breeds throughout the Northern Hemisphere, nesting in sandbank burrows. The European house martin (*Delichon urbica*) is blue-black above and white-rumped. The African river martin (*Pseudochelidon eurystomina*) of the Congo is black.

Martin, Agnes (b.1912) Canadian-U.S. painter. Born in Saskatchewan, she came to the U.S. in 1932. She lived in New Mexico and New York City, where she had her first solo exhibition in 1958. She is a prominent exponent of MINIMALISM and geometric abstraction; for her, a gray grid of intersecting penciled lines became the ultimate geometric composition. In the 1970s she produced printed equivalents of her paintings, as well as a notable series of silkscreens, *On a Clear Day* (1973).

Martin, Steve (b.1945) U.S. comedian and writer. Born in Waco, Texas, in the 1970s he wrote for and performed on such shows as *Saturday Night Live*. His slapstick and absurdist humor were showcased in *The Jerk* (1979), which he both wrote and starred in. His other film comedies include *All of Me* (1984), *Roxanne* (1987), *Little Shop of Horrors* (1986), *Dirty Rotten Scoundrels* (1988), and *Parenthood* (1989). He wrote the stage play *Picasso at the Lapin Agile* (1995).

Martin V *orig.* Oddo Colonna (1368–1431) Pope (1417–31). His election at the Council of Constance marked the end of the Western SCHISM, and he chose to reside in Rome rather than Avignon. He condemned conciliar theory (see CONCILIAR MOVEMENT) and any appeals of papal judgment on matters of faith. He helped to rebuild Rome and tried to recover control of the PAPAL STATES. He organized crusades against the HUSSITES, and asserted the rights of the church against the crown.

Martin du Gard \mȧr-taⁿ-dǖ-ˈgȧr\, **Roger** (1881–1958) French novelist and dramatist. Originally trained as a paleographer and archivist, he first attracted attention with the novel *Jean Barois* (1913), the story of an intellectual torn between the Catholic faith of his childhood and the scientific materialism of his maturity. He is best known for the eight-novel family saga *Les Thibault* (1922–40), which chronicles the social and moral issues facing the French bourgeoisie in the pre–World War I era. He received the 1937 Nobel Prize.

Martineau \ˈmär-ti-ˌnō\, **Harriet** (1802–1876) English essayist, novelist, and economic and historical writer. She became prominent among English intellectuals of her time despite her deafness and heart disease. She first gained a large reading public with a series popularizing classical economics. Her chief historical work was *The History of the Thirty Years' Peace, A.D. 1816–1846* (1849), a widely read popular treatment. Her best-regarded novel is *Deerbrook* (1839).

Martínez Montañés, Juan See J. M. MONTAÑÉS

Martinique \ˌmär-tə-ˈnēk\ Island (pop., 2000: 385,000) of the WINDWARD ISLANDS, W. INDIES, and overseas department of France. It is 50 mi (80 km) long and 22 mi (35 km) wide and occupies an area of 436 sq mi (1,128 sq km). Largely mountainous, its highest point, Mt. PELÉE, is an active volcano. Its capital is FORT-DE-FRANCE. Tourism is the basis of its economy. Carib Indians resided on the island when Christopher COLUMBUS visited it in 1502. In 1635 a Frenchman established a colony there, and in 1674 it passed to the French crown. Made a department of France in 1946, it remained under French rule despite a communist-led independence movement in the 1970s.

Martin of Tours \ˈtu̇r\, **St.** (A.D. 316–397) Patron saint of France. Born a pagan, he converted to Christianity at 10. After being imprisoned by the Romans, he became a missionary. He founded the first monastery in Gaul, at Poitiers. In 371 he was made bishop of Tours. A second monastery he founded, at Mormoutier, became a great monastic complex. St. Martin was known as a miracle worker in his own

lifetime and was one of the first saints to be revered who was not a martyr.

Martins, Peter (b.1946) Danish-U.S. dancer, choreographer, and director. After dancing with the Royal Danish Ballet, he joined the NEW YORK CITY BALLET in 1969 as a principal dancer and soon became a major star. He began choreographing for the company in 1977 with *Calcium Light Night;* other works include *L'histoire du soldat* and *Symphony No. 1.* Chosen by George BALANCHINE as his successor, Martins became codirector (1983–1990) and then sole director of the company.

Martinu \mär-ˈtē-nü\, **Bohuslav (Jan)** (1890–1959) Czech (Bohemian) composer. His early pieces combined the influences of folk music and Claude DEBUSSY. In Paris from 1923, he gained a reputation for his colorful ballet scores, and experimented with neoclassicism, jazz, and ragtime. After World War II he lived in France, Italy, and Switzerland, and his Czech heritage reasserted itself. He wrote much music, including six symphonies, operas, and large choral works, but did little to promote it.

Martov \ˈmär-ˌtȯf\, **L.** *orig.* Yuly Osipovich Tsederbaum (1873–1923) Russian revolutionary. After his arrest and exile to Siberia (1896–99), he joined Vladimir LENIN in Switzerland as an editor of *Iskra*. From 1903 Martov supported the MENSHEVIK faction of the RUSSIAN SOCIAL-DEMOCRATIC WORKERS' PARTY and was its leader 1905–7. After the RUSSIAN REVOLUTION OF 1917, he supported the BOLSHEVIK government but later opposed many of its dictatorial measures. He left Russia in 1920 and edited the *Socialist Courier* in Berlin.

martyr Person who voluntarily suffers death rather than deny his or her religion. Readiness for martyrdom was a collective ideal in ancient Judaism, and its importance has continued into modern times. ROMAN CATHOLICISM sees the suffering of martyrs as a test of their faith. Many SAINTS of the early church underwent martyrdom during the persecutions of the Roman emperors. In Islam, martyrs are thought to comprise two groups of the faithful: those killed in JIHAD and those killed unjustly.

Marvell \ˈmär-vəl\, **Andrew** (1621–1678) English poet and politician. After tutoring Oliver CROMWELL's ward and serving as assistant to John MILTON in the foreign office, he gained a seat in Parliament. His reputation as one of the finest secular Metaphysical poets (see METAPHYSICAL POETRY) is based on a small body of brilliant lyric verse, including "To His Coy Mistress" (1681) and "The Garden." Among his other works are classical odes, political verse satires opposing the government after the Restoration, and prose satires.

Marx, Karl (Heinrich) (1818–1883) German political theorist and revolutionary. He studied law and philosophy at the Univ. of Berlin (1836–41), where he was exposed to the works of G. W. F. HEGEL. Working as a writer in Cologne and Paris (1842–45), he became active in leftist politics. In Paris he met Friedrich ENGELS, who would become his lifelong collaborator. Expelled from France in 1845, he moved to Brussels, where he and Engels made names for themselves through their writings.

Karl Marx

Marx was invited to join a secret left-wing group in London, for which he and Engels wrote the *Communist Manifesto* (1848). That same year he organized the first Rhineland Democratic Congress in Germany and opposed the king of Prussia. Exiled, he and his family moved to London in 1849, where he would live the rest of his life, much of it in poverty. Marx worked part-time as a correspondent for the *New York Tribune* (1851–62) while writing his major critique of CAPITALISM, *Das Kapital* (3 vols., 1867–94). He was a leading figure in the FIRST INTERNA-

TIONAL 1864–72. See also COMMUNISM, DIALECTICAL MATERIALISM, MARXISM.

Marx Brothers U.S. comedy team. The original five brothers—Chico (*orig.* Leonard) (1886–1961), Harpo (*orig.* Adolph Arthur) (1888–1964), Groucho (*orig.* Julius Henry) (1890–1977), Gummo (*orig.* Milton) (1893–1977), and Zeppo (*orig.* Herbert) (1901–1979)—initially performed as a vaudeville act 1904–18. After Gummo left the act, "The Four Marx Brothers" won fame with their first Broadway play, *I'll Say She Is* (1924), followed by *The Cocoanuts* (1925; film, 1929) and *Animal Crackers* (1926; film, 1930). They later starred in *Monkey Business* (1931), *Horse Feathers* (1932), *Duck Soup* (1933), *A Night at the Opera* (1935), and *Room Service* (1938), among other films, developing a skillful blend of visual and verbal humor, with Groucho supplying wisecracks and a running commentary as counterpoint to the frantic, anarchic activities of the silent Harpo and the Italian-accented Chico. Zeppo left the act in 1934, and the brothers disbanded in 1949. Groucho later hosted the successful television quiz program *You Bet Your Life* (1950–61).

Marxism Ideology and socioeconomic theory developed by Karl MARX and Friedrich ENGELS. The fundamental ideology of COMMUNISM, it holds that all people are entitled to enjoy the fruits of their labor but are prevented from doing so in a capitalist economic system, which divides society into two classes: nonowning workers and nonworker owners. When the workers repossessed the fruits of their labor, such "alienation" would be overcome and class divisions would cease. The Marxist theory of history posits class struggle as history's driving force, and sees CAPITALISM as the most recent and most critical historical stage, when the proletariat will at last arise united. The failure of the 1848 European revolutions and an increasing need to elaborate on Marxist theory (generally more analytical than practical) led to such adaptations as LENINISM and MAOISM. The collapse of the Soviet Union and China's adoption of many elements of a free-market economy marked the end of Marxism as an applicable economic or governmental theory, though it retains interest as a critique of market capitalism and a theory of historical change. See also DIALECTICAL MATERIALISM.

Mary *or* **St. Mary** *or* **Virgin Mary** Mother of JESUS. According to the GOSPELS, she was betrothed to St. JOSEPH when the archangel GABRIEL appeared to her to announce the coming birth of Jesus. Other Gospel accounts of Mary include the visit to Elizabeth, mother of JOHN THE BAPTIST; the birth of Jesus and his presentation in the Temple; the coming of the MAGI and the flight to Egypt; the marriage at Cana in Galilee; the attempt to see Jesus while he was teaching; and watching at the cross. Most Christian denominations hold Jesus to have been divinely conceived and Mary to have remained a virgin. The Roman Catholic church also holds to the doctrine of her IMMACULATE CONCEPTION and her bodily assumption into heaven. See also MARIOLOGY.

Mary See MERV

Mary I *or* **Mary Tudor** (1516–1558) Queen of England (1553–58). The daughter of King HENRY VIII and CATHERINE OF ARAGON, she was declared illegitimate after Henry's divorce and new marriage to Anne BOLEYN (1533). In 1544 she was restored to court and granted succession to the throne. After becoming queen (1553), she married PHILIP II of Spain, restored Roman Catholicism, and revived the laws against heresy. The resulting persecution of Protestant rebels and the execution of some 300 heretics earned her the hatred of her subjects and the nickname "Bloody Mary.".

Mary II (1662–1694) Queen of England (1689–94). The daughter of King JAMES II, a Catholic convert, she was reared as a Protestant and in 1677 married to her cousin, William of Orange. They lived in Holland until English nobles opposed to James's pro-Catholic policies invited William and Mary to assume the English throne; Mary and William (as King WILLIAM III) became corulers in 1689. Mary enjoyed great popularity, and her Dutch tastes had an influence on English pottery, landscape gardening, and interior design. She died of smallpox at 32.

Maryinsky Theater See MARIINSKY THEATER

Maryland State (pop., 2000: 5,296,000), E U.S. A middle-Atlantic state, it covers 10,460 sq mi (27,091 sq km); its capital is Annapolis. The state's main geographic regions are the coastal plain along CHESAPEAKE BAY, the rich farming country of the Piedmont plateau, and the APPALACHIAN MTNS. First occupied by late Ice Age hunters around 10,000 B.C., the area was later inhabited by the Nanticoke and Piscataway tribes. Capt. John SMITH charted the Chesapeake Bay region in 1608. Maryland was included in a charter given by the British king to Cecil Calvert, Lord Baltimore. Leonard Calvert, his brother, founded the first settlement in 1634 at St. Marys City. Maryland became the first American colony to establish religious freedom. Its boundary dispute with Pennsylvania was settled in the 1760s with the drawing of the MASON-DIXON LINE. In 1788 Maryland became the 7th state to ratify the U.S. Constitution. The state ceded the DISTRICT OF COLUMBIA as the site for a new federal capital in 1791. It was involved in the WAR OF 1812 (see FT. MCHENRY). The U.S. NAVAL ACADEMY was founded at Annapolis in 1845. Maryland remained in the Union during the AMERICAN CIVIL WAR, but strong Southern sentiments resulted in the imposition of martial law. After the war, it prospered as a transshipment center for consumer goods to the South and Midwest. During the 20th cent. its proximity to the national federal government spurred population growth. Its economy is based primarily on government services and manufacturing.

Mary Magdalene, St. (fl.1st cent. A.D.) Follower of JESUS and the first person to see the resurrected Christ. After Jesus cleansed her of seven demons, she accompanied him in Galilee, and she witnessed his crucifixion and burial. On EASTER morning she was among the women who found the tomb empty. Christ later appeared to her and instructed her to tell the APOSTLES that he was ascending to God. Popular tradition has long associated her with the repentant prostitute who anointed Christ's feet.

Mary, Queen of Scots *orig.* **Mary Stuart** (1542–1587) Queen of Scotland (1542–67). She became queen when her father, James V (1512–42), died six days after her birth. Sent by her mother to be raised at the court of the French king HENRY II, she was married in 1558 to his son Francis II. After Francis's brief rule as king (1559–60) ended with his premature death, Mary returned to Scotland (1561), where she was distrusted because of her Catholic upbringing. In 1565 the beautiful, redhaired queen married her ambitious cousin Henry Stewart, Lord Darnley. After the birth of her son James (later JAMES I of England) in 1566, Mary was estranged from Darnley, who was murdered in 1567. Ignoring objections by the jealous Scottish nobility, she married James Hepburn, earl of Bothwell (1535?–1578), a suspect in Darnley's murder. The rebellious nobles forced her to abdicate (1567). After failed attempts to win back the throne, she sought refuge in England with her cousin ELIZABETH I, who arranged to keep her in captivity. After several uprisings by English Catholics in Mary's favor, she was tried and condemned; she was beheaded at Fotheringhay Castle in 1587.

Masaccio \mə-ˈzä-chē-ˌō\ *orig.* Tommaso di Giovanni di Mone Cassai (1401–1428) Italian painter. Little is known about him until 1422, when he entered the artists' guild in Florence. In his most famous work, the frescoes in the Brancacci Chapel of Florence's Santa Maria del Carmine (c.1425–28), his massive figures are constructed with strongly differentiated areas of light and dark that give them a three-dimensional effect. His *Trinity* fresco (c.1427–28) in Florence's Santa Maria Novella is the first known example of the systematic use of one-point PERSPECTIVE in a painting. He went to Rome in 1428 and died there at age 26 so suddenly that some people suspected he had been poisoned. The rationality, realism, and humanity of the art he created in his brief six years of work inspired the major Florentine painters of the mid-15th cent., and ultimately influenced the course of Western painting.

Masada \mə-ˈsä-də\ Ancient mountaintop fortress, SE Israel. It occupies the entire top of a mesa 1,424 ft (434 m) tall, with an area of 18 acres (7 hectares). Its fortifications were built by HEROD the Great; it was captured by the Zealots, a Jewish sect, in their revolt against Rome in A.D. 66. After the fall of JERUSALEM, Masada, the last remnant of Jewish rule in Palestine, refused to surrender. In A.D. 73, after a lengthy siege, it was finally taken by the Romans, who are said to have found that nearly all of the 1,000 Zealots had committed suicide rather than be captured. It has become a symbol of Jewish heroism.

Masai *or* **Maasai** \ma-'sī\ Nomadic herders of S Kenya and N Tanzania. Numbering about 450,000, the Masai subsist almost entirely on the meat, blood, and milk of their cattle herds. A Masai KRAAL holds four to eight families and their herds. POLYGAMY is common among older men. Young men traditionally spend time in isolation in the bush to develop strength, courage, and endurance. See also NILOTES.

Masaryk \'mä-sə-rik\, **Jan (Garrigue)** (1886–1948) Czech statesman. The son of Tomas MASARYK, he served as ambassador to Britain 1925–38, and foreign minister of the Czechoslovak provisional government in London (1940–45) and Prague (1945–48). At the request of Pres. Edvard BENEŠ, he remained at his post after the communist takeover in 1948. Two weeks later he either jumped or was pushed to his death from a window in the foreign office.

Masaryk, Tomas (Garrigue) (1850–1937) First president of Czechoslovakia (1918–35). He taught philosophy at the Czech Univ. of Prague (1882) and wrote on the Czech Reformation; his most important works were a study of Marxism (1898) and *Russia and Europe* (1913). After serving in the Austrian Reichsrat (1891–93, 1907–14), in 1915 he went to Western Europe, where he organized the Czech national council, which in 1918 gained recognition as the de facto government of the future Czechoslovakia. He negotiated its liberation as one of the FOURTEEN POINTS. Elected president of the new country (1918–35), he was occupied with settling conflicts between the Czech and Slovak parties.

Mascagni \mäs-'kän-yē\, **Pietro** (1863–1945) Italian composer. At the Milan Conservatory he studied with Amilcare Ponchielli (1834–1886) but was expelled. He won a contest with his one-act opera *Cavalleria rusticana* (1890), his most lasting work. His later operas *L'amico Fritz* (1891) and *Iris* (1899) also enjoyed some success.

Masefield, John (1878–1967) English poet. He went to sea in his youth, and is best known for his poems of the sea, *Salt-Water Ballads* (1902; including "Sea Fever"), as well as his long narrative poems, such as *The Everlasting Mercy* (1911), containing phrases of colloquial coarseness unknown in earlier 20th-cent. English verse. After he became poet laureate in 1930, his poetry became more austere. He also wrote adventure novels and works for children.

maser \'mā-zər\ Device that produces and amplifies ELECTROMAGNETIC RADIATION in the MICROWAVE range of the spectrum. The first maser was built in 1951 by Charles Townes (b.1915). Its name is an acronym for "microwave amplification by stimulated emission of radiation." The wavelength produced by a maser is exceptionally constant and reproducible. Masers have been used to amplify faint signals returned from radar and communications satellites, and have enabled measurement of the temperature of the planet Venus. The maser was the principal precursor of the LASER.

Maseru \'ma-zə-rü\ City (metro. area pop., 1999 est.: 373,000), capital of Lesotho. It lies near the border of S. Africa. It was founded in 1869 by MOSHOESHOE. Diamond-mining is important economically. Maseru is the nation's only urban center. Roma, to the southeast, is the seat of the National Univ. of Lesotho.

Mashhad \'mäsh-hàd, mə-'shad\ *or* **Meshed** \mə-'shed\ City (pop., 1996: 1,887,000), NE Iran. For centuries it has been an important trade center along regional caravan routes and highways. It was sacked by Turkmen and Uzbeks in the 16th–17th cent. Nadir Shah, who reigned 1736–47, made it his capital. The city is the burial place of HARUN AL-RASHID and is a site of pilgrimage.

mask Object worn either to disguise or protect the face or to project the image of another personality or being. Masks have been used in art and religion since the Stone Age. In most primitive societies, they are thought to have supernatural power. Death masks, associated with the return of the spirit to the body, were used in ancient Egypt, Asia, and the Inca civilization, and were sometimes kept as portraits of the dead. Masks worn on holidays such as Halloween and Mardi Gras signal festivity and license. They have also been

widely used in the Western theater, beginning with the Greek drama, as well as in other theater traditions (e.g., Japanese NO DRAMA).

Maslow \'maz-lō\, **Abraham H(arold)** (1908–1970) U.S. psychologist. Born in New York City, he became a practitioner of HUMANISTIC PSYCHOLOGY, known for his theory of "self-actualization." In *Motivation and Personality* (1954) and *Toward a Psychology of Being* (1962), Maslow argued that each person has a hierarchy of needs, ranging from basic physiological requirements to love, esteem, and, finally, self-actualization. As each need is satisfied, the next higher level dominates conscious functioning.

masochism \'ma-sə-ki-zəm, 'ma-zə-ki-zəm\ Psychosexual disorder in which an individual achieves erotic release by being subjected to pain or humiliation. The term is derived from the name of Leopold von Sacher-Masoch (1836–1895), whose novels center on the practice. The pain involved can vary from ritual humiliation with little violence to severe beating; it is usually sought out and to some degree controlled by the masochist. The traits of masochism and SADISM often occur in the same individual.

Mason, George (1725–1792) American Revolutionary statesman. Born in Fairfax Co., Va., he owned a large plantation and became active in promoting W expansion. He helped George WASHINGTON draft the Fairfax Resolves (1774) for a boycott of English goods. In 1776 he drafted the state constitution and the Virginia Declaration of Rights, which influenced Thomas JEFFERSON and provided a model for other states. In the Virginia House of Delegates (1776–88), he opposed Virginia's ratification of the U.S. Constitution.

Mason-Dixon Line Originally, the boundary between Maryland and Pennsylvania. The 233-mi (375-km) line was surveyed by Charles Mason and Jeremiah Dixon in 1765–68 to define the disputed boundaries between the lands of the Penns, proprietors of Pennsylvania, and the Baltimores, proprietors of Maryland. The term was first used in debates leading to the MISSOURI COMPROMISE (1820) to describe the line between the slave states to its south and the free-soil states to its north.

masonry Craft of building in stone, BRICK, or block. By 4000 B.C., Egypt had developed an elaborate cut-stone technique. In Crete, Italy, and Greece, cyclopean work, the use of enormous irregularly shaped stones without mortar, reduced the number of joints. African stonemasons also were skilled at mortarless work, and Japanese mortarless castle walls resisted collapse during earthquakes. The Roman inventions of concrete and mortar permitted the development of the ARCH, and led to many variations in the facing used for walls. The Assyrian and Persian empires used sun-dried clay bricks. Stone and clay were the primary masonry materials in the Middle Ages and later. Precast-concrete blocks, often used as infill in modern steel framing, did not effectively compete with brick until the 20th cent. Glass-block walls, which utilize steel rods to reinforce the mortar joints, admit light. See also ADOBE.

Masqat *or* **Muscat** \'məs-kät\ City (metro. area pop., 1999: 887,000), capital of Oman, located on the Gulf of Oman. It came under Persian control in the 6th cent. B.C. and was converted to Islam in the 7th cent. A.D. The Portuguese gained control in 1508 and made Masqat their Arabian headquarters 1622–48. Held by the Persians 1650–1741, it later became part of the sultanate of Oman. The sultan's Indian-style palace is built at the edge of the sea.

masque Short dramatic entertainment performed by masked actors. It originated in the MUMMING PLAY and evolved into elaborate court spectacles in the 16th–17th cent. It presented an allegorical theme using speeches, dances, and songs, in a performance often embellished with rich costumes and spectacular scenery. In 17th-cent. England the court poet Ben JONSON, collaborating with Inigo JONES on many notable masques (1605–34), gave it literary force. The masque later merged with OPERA, also influencing ballet and pantomime.

mass Quantitative measure of INERTIA, or the resistance of a body to a change in motion. The greater the mass, the smaller is the change produced by an applied force. Unlike WEIGHT, the mass of an object remains constant regardless of its location. Thus, as a satellite moves away from the gravitational pull of earth, its weight decreases but its mass remains the same. In ordinary, classical chemical reactions, mass can be neither created nor destroyed (see CONSERVATION LAW). Albert EINSTEIN's special theory of RELATIVITY shows that mass and energy are equivalent, so mass can be converted into energy and vice versa. Mass is converted into energy in NUCLEAR FUSION and NUCLEAR FISSION. In these instances, conservation of mass is seen as a special case of a more general conservation of mass-energy.

mass Celebration of the EUCHARIST in the Roman Catholic church. A sacramental reenactment of the death and resurrection of JESUS, it is also seen as a true sacrifice in which the body and blood of Jesus (the bread and wine) are offered to God and as a sacred meal that unifies and nourishes the community of believers. The rite was greatly changed after the Second VATICAN COUNCIL, notably in the adoption of vernacular languages in place of Latin. See also SACRAMENT, TRANSUBSTANTIATION.

Massachusetts *officially* **Commonwealth of Massachusetts** State (pop., 2000: 6,349,000), NE U.S. One of the NEW ENGLAND states, it covers 8,284 sq mi (21,456 sq km); its capital is BOSTON. Bounded on the east by the Atlantic Ocean, the state's soils are poor and rocky, and agriculture plays a limited role in the economy, although cranberry farming is important. The region was inhabited by Algonquian Indian tribes when the first English settler, Bartholomew Gosnold (1572–1607), arrived in 1602. PLYMOUTH was settled by the PILGRIMS, who came on the *Mayflower* in 1620. The MASSACHUSETTS BAY COLONY was founded and governed by the Massachusetts Bay Co. spurring Puritan settlement. It joined the NEW ENGLAND CONFEDERATION in 1643 and acquired Maine in 1652. The SE and central state's settlements experienced KING PHILIP'S WAR in 1675. After losing its first charter in 1684, it became part of the Dominion of New England in 1686. Its second charter in 1691 granted the colony jurisdiction over Maine and Plymouth. In the 18th cent. Massachusetts became a center of resistance to British colonial policy; it was the scene of the BOSTON TEA PARTY, and of uprisings at the Battles of LEXINGTON AND CONCORD that marked the beginning of the AMERICAN REVOLUTION. In 1788, it became the sixth state to ratify the U.S. Constitution. It was in the forefront of the 19th-cent. INDUSTRIAL REVOLUTION and was known for its textile mills. Today its major industries are electronics, high tehnology, and communications. It is the location of many well-known institutions of higher learning. Tourism is important especially in the CAPE COD region and the BERKSHIRE HILLS.

Massachusetts Bay Colony Early English colony in MASSACHUSETTS. It was settled in 1630 by a group of 1,000 Puritan refugees from England (see PURITANISM). In 1629 the Massachusetts Bay Co. had obtained an English charter allowing it to trade and colonize in New England, envisioning the colony as a refuge from religious persecution. Led by John WINTHROP, the colonists founded their colony on the Charles River at what would become BOSTON. In 1684 England annulled the company's charter and in 1691 established royal government under a new charter, which merged PLYMOUTH colony and Maine into the Massachusetts Bay Colony.

Massachusetts Institute of Technology (MIT) Private university in Cambridge, Mass., famous for its scientific and technological training and research. Founded in 1861, MIT has schools of architecture and planning, engineering, humanities and social sciences, management (the Sloan School), and science, and a college of health sciences and technology. Best known for its programs in engineering and the physical sciences, it also excels in such other areas as economics, political science, and linguistics. Among its facilities are a nuclear reactor, geophysical and astrophysical observatories, a linear accelerator, supersonic wind tunnels, and an artificial-intelligence laboratory. Total enrollment is about 10,000.

massage \mə-ˈsäzh\ Systematic, scientific manipulation of body tissues with the hands to relieve pain and reduce swelling, relax muscles, and speed healing after strains and sprains. It was used in ancient China. The Swedish physician Per Henrik Ling (1776–1839) devised a massage system for joint and muscle ailments, which was later extended to relieve deformities of arthritis and re-educate muscles following paralysis. Manipulations include light or hard stroking, compression (kneading, squeezing, and friction), and percussion (striking with the edges of the hands in rapid alternation). See also ACUPRESSURE, PHYSICAL MEDICINE AND REHABILITATION.

Massasoit \ˌmas-ə-ˈsóit\ (c.1590–1661) American Indian chief. Born near present Bristol, R.I., he became the grand sachem (intertribal chief) of the Wampanoag Indians. Several months after the *Mayflower* landed, he journeyed to Plymouth and established peaceful relations with the settlers. Having shared techniques of planting, fishing, and cooking, in 1623 he was nursed back to health from a serious illness by grateful Pilgrims. Peace dissolved after his death; KING PHILIP'S WAR (1675) was led by his son METACOM.

Masséna \má-sā-ˈná\, **André** *later* prince d'Essling (1758–1817) French general. He became a general in the Revolutionary army, and in campaigns against the Austrians in Italy he became NAPOLEON's most trusted officer. Commanding the French army in Switzerland, he defeated the Russians at Zurich (1799). Sent by Napoleon to restore the demoralized army of Italy, he enabled the crucial French victory at Marengo. He displayed heroism against the Austrians, notably at Aspern-Essling and Wagram (1809), and Napoleon made him prince d'Essling (1810). In command of the French forces in Portugal and Spain (1810–11), he was defeated by the British. Relieved of his command, he returned to Paris, where he supported the restoration of the monarchy.

mass-energy equation See EINSTEIN'S MASS-ENERGY RELATION

Massenet \ˌma-sᵊn-ˈä\, **Jules** (Émile Frédéric) (1842–1912). French composer. When his family left Paris in 1854, he ran away to continue his studies. He won the Prix de Rome in 1863, and he began writing operas in 1867. His reputation was established with his oratorio *Marie-Magdeleine* (1873), and his *Le roi de Lahore* was performed at the Paris Opéra in 1877. There followed the series of successes for which he is chiefly known, including *Hérodiade* (1881), *Manon* (1884), *Le Cid* (1885), *Esclarmonde* (1889), *Werther* (1892), and *Thaïs* (1894).

Massey, (Charles) Vincent (1887–1967) Canadian administrator, first Canadian governor-general of Canada (1952–59). Born in Toronto, he taught history at the Univ. of Toronto and operated a farm-machinery business. An active Liberal, he served in W. L. M. KING's cabinet (1925), as Canada's first minister to the U.S. (1926–30), and as high commissioner for Canada in Britain (1935–46). After serving as chancellor of the Univ. of Toronto (1947–52), he was named governor-general. His brother was the actor Raymond Massey (1896–1983).

Massif Central \ma-ˈsēf-säⁿ-ˈträl\ Plateau region, S central France. It is bordered by the lowlands of AQUITAINE, the Loire Basin, the Rhône-Saône Valley, and the Mediterranean coastlands of LANGUEDOC. It occupies 35,006 sq mi (90,665 sq km), about one-sixth of France. Its highest peak is Puy de Sancy, which reaches 6,184 ft (1,885 m). It is the source of many rivers, including the LOIRE.

Massine \ma-ˈsēn\, **Léonide** *orig.* Leonid Fyodorovich Miassin (1896–1979) Russian-French dancer and choreographer. He joined the BALLETS RUSSES in 1914 and produced his first ballet, *Le soleil de nuit*, in 1915; this was followed by *Parade* (1917), *The Three-Cornered Hat* (1919), and *Pulcinella* (1920). During 1932–38 he was principal dancer and choreographer for the Ballet Russe de Monte Carlo. His innovative ballets *Les présages* (1933), *Choreartium* (1933), and *Rouge et noir* (1939) were among the first dances based on symphonies. From 1938 to 1963 he directed his reformed Ballet Russe de Monte Carlo, and he became artistic director of a new Ballets de Monte Carlo in 1966.

Masson \má-ˈsōⁿ\, **André (-Aimé-René)** (1896–1987) French painter and graphic artist. He was severely wounded in World War I, and an overriding pessimism penetrated his art. He joined the Surrealist movement in the 1920s and produced turbulent images of violence, psychic pain, and eroticism, using sinuous lines to delineate abstract forms. He lived in Spain (1934–36) and later the U.S. (1941–45), where he became an important link between SURREALISM and Abstract Expressionism, then returned to France and concentrated on landscape painting.

mass production Application of the principles of specialization, DIVISION OF LABOR, and standardization of parts to the manufacturing of goods on a large scale. Modern mass-production methods have led to such improvements in the cost, quality, quantity, and variety of goods available that the largest global population in history is now sustained at the highest general standard of living ever. The requirements for mass production of a particular product include the existence of a large market; a product design that can use standardized parts and processes; a physical layout that minimizes materials handling; division of labor into simple, short, repetitive steps; and continuous flow of work. See also ASSEMBLY LINE.

mass spectrometry *or* **mass spectroscopy** Analytic technique by which chemical substances are identified by sorting gaseous IONS by mass using ELECTRIC and MAGNETIC FIELDS. A mass spectrometer uses electrical means to detect the sorted ions; a mass spectrograph uses photographic or other nonelectrical means; either device is a mass spectroscope. The process is widely used to measure masses and relative abundances of different ISOTOPES and to analyze products of a separation by liquid or gas CHROMATOGRAPHY.

mass transit Transportation systems, usually publicly owned and operated, designed to move large numbers of people in various types of vehicles in cities and suburbs. In the 1830s early mass transit in New York City included horse-drawn buses, which were soon replaced by fixed-rail horse-drawn trolleys. By 1900 motorized BUSES had appeared in Europe and America. With the advent of electricity, STREETCARS and SUBWAYS were introduced in many large cities. In the 20th cent. the AUTOMOBILE's increasing popularity undermined mass-transit development; fixed-rail streetcar systems were widely removed to provide space for cars. In the late 20th cent., concern over air pollution revived interest in light-rail transit and led to regional mass transit systems.

mastectomy \ma-'stek-tə-mē\ Surgical removal of a breast, usually because of BREAST CANCER. Radical mastectomy removes surrounding tissue and/or nearby structures, including chest muscles and LYMPH NODES. Modified radical mastectomy leaves at least the main chest muscle. Simple mastectomy is removal of the breast only; lumpectomy is removal of the tumor only. Breast reconstruction employs the patient's own tissue and often implants.

Masters, Edgar Lee (1869–1950) U.S. poet and novelist. Born in Garnett, Kan., he became a lawyer in Chicago. In 1915 he published *Spoon River Anthology* (1915), his major work. Its 245 free-verse epitaphs in the form of monologues are spoken from the grave by the former inhabitants of a fictitious small town, who tell of their bitter, unfulfilled lives. Among his novels are *Mitch Miller* (1920) and *The Nuptial Flight* (1923).

Masters, William H(owell) and Virginia E(shelman) Johnson *orig.* Virginia Eshelman (1915–2001, b.1925) U.S. human-sexuality research team. Born in Cleveland, Ohio, and Springfield, Mo., respectively, together (as physician and psychologist), they founded and codirected the Masters & Johnson Institute in St. Louis. They observed couples having sex under laboratory conditions, using biochemical equipment to record sexual stimulations and reactions. Their book *Human Sexual Response* (1966) was considered the first comprehensive study of the physiology and anatomy of human sexual activity.

Masterson, Bat (*orig.* Bartholomew) (1853–1921) U.S. (Canadian-born) lawman and gambler. Born in Henryville, Canada East (now Quebec), he grew up in the U.S. In Dodge City, Kan., he worked as a buffalo hunter (1873–75) and sheriff (1877–79). In Tombstone, Ariz. (1880), he was associated with Wyatt EARP and became known as a defender of order. He lived a gambler's life in Denver (1887–1902), then moved to New York, where he was a prominent sports editor for the *Morning Telegraph*.

Masters Tournament Invitational golf competition held since 1934 at the Augusta National Golf Club, Augusta, Ga. One of the world's most prestigious golf contests, it com-

prises 72 holes of stroke play. The course, famous for its beauty and for the speed and difficulty of its greens, was designed by Bobby JONES and Alister MacKenzie.

mastodon \'mas-tə-ˌdän\ Any of several extinct ELEPHANT species (genus *Mastodon*) that lived worldwide 23.7 million–10,000 years ago or later in N. America, where they were contemporaneous with historic American Indian groups. Well-preserved remains are quite common. Mastodons ate leaves and had small grinding teeth and long, parallel, upward-curving upper tusks; males also had short lower tusks. Shorter than modern elephants, they had long, heavily built bodies and short, pillarlike legs. The ears were small. Human hunting may have played a role in the mastodon's extinction. See also MAMMOTH.

Mastroianni \mäs-trȯy-'ä-nē\, **Marcello** (1924–1996) Italian film actor. He made his film debut in 1947 and soon became popular in Italy. Darkly handsome, with a screen persona alternately winning and morose, he won international fame in such films as Luchino VISCONTI's *White Nights* (1957) and Federico FELLINI's *La Dolce Vita* (1960). He acted in over 100 movies, including *La Notte* (1960), *Divorce—Italian Style* (1961), *8 1/2* (1963), *Yesterday, Today, and Tomorrow* (1963), *A Special Day* (1977), *Ginger and Fred* (1985), and *Dark Eyes* (1987).

masturbation Erotic stimulation of one's own genital organs, usually to achieve orgasm. Masturbation is common in infants, adolescents, and adults; studies indicate that over 90% of U.S. males and 60–80% of U.S. females have masturbated. Christian teaching traditionally condemned masturbation as the sin of Onan, who in the Old Testament was censured for spilling his seed.

matador In BULLFIGHTING, the principal performer, who works the capes and attempts to dispatch the bull with a sword thrust between the shoulder blades. Most of the techniques used today were established in the 1910s by Juan Belmonte of Spain (1894–1962). The traditional costume, which offers no protection, is known as the "suit of lights." The audience judges the matador according to his skill, grace, and daring. Almost every matador is gored at least once a season.

Mata Hari *orig.* Margaretha Geertruida Zelle (1876–1917) Dutch courtesan and alleged spy in World War I. In 1895 she married and lived in Java and Sumatra (1897–1902). In 1905 she began to dance in Paris, calling herself Mata Hari (a Malay expression for the sun). Beautiful and exotic and willing to dance virtually nude, she soon had numerous lovers, including military officers. She apparently spied for Germany from 1916. She was arrested by the French in 1917, tried, and shot.

Matamoros City (pop., 1995: 323,000), Mexico. Sited on the RIO GRANDE, across from Brownsville, Texas, it was the scene of bitter fighting in the MEXICAN WAR and was occupied by U.S. troops in 1846. It is now one of Mexico's chief ports of entry for tourists, and a trade center.

Matapédia Valley \ˌma-tə-'pē-dē-ə\ Valley of the Notre Dame Mtns., GASPÉ PENINSULA, E Quebec province. Extending for some 60 mi (100 km), it forms a direct lowland passage from the ST. LAWRENCE RIVER to the Atlantic coast. It serves as an important transportation route between the MARITIME PROVINCES and the Canadian mainland.

maté *or* **yerba maté** \'mä-tā\ Stimulating tealike beverage, popular in many S. American countries, brewed from the dried leaves of an evergreen shrub or tree *(Ilex paraguariensis)* related to HOLLY. It contains caffeine and tannin but is less astringent than tea. Though usually served plain, maté is sometimes flavored with milk, sugar, or lemon juice.

materialism In METAPHYSICS, the doctrine that reality is essentially of the nature of matter. In the philosophy of mind, materialism typically asserts that states of mind are identical to states of the brain. Supporters of this theory (called central-state materialism) agree that mind and body are conceptually distinct but argue, usually on grounds of economy (see OCKHAM'S RAZOR), that they are identical. What seems to be a state of mind is really a state of the brain, and the mental is thus reduced to the physical. See also MIND–BODY PROBLEM.

materials science Study of the properties of solid materials and how those properties are determined by the material's

composition and structure. Materials science grew out of solid-state physics, metallurgy, ceramics, and chemistry, since the numerous properties of materials cannot be understood within the context of any single discipline. With a basic understanding of the origins of properties, materials can be selected or designed for an enormous variety of applications, from structural steels to computer microchips. Materials science is therefore important to many ENGINEERING fields, including electronics, aerospace, telecommunications, information processing, and nuclear power.

mathematics Science of structure, order, and relation that has evolved from counting, measuring, and describing the shapes of objects. It deals with logical reasoning and quantitative calculation. Since the 17th cent. it has been an indispensable adjunct to the physical sciences and technology, to the extent that it is considered the underlying language of science. Among the principal branches of mathematics are ALGEBRA, ARITHMETIC, EUCLIDEAN and NON-EUCLIDEAN GEOMETRIES, GAME THEORY, NUMBER THEORY, NUMERICAL ANALYSIS, OPTIMIZATION, PROBABILITY, SET THEORY, STATISTICS, TOPOLOGY, and TRIGONOMETRY.

Mather \\'ma-thər\\, **Cotton** (1663–1728) American Puritan leader. The son of Increase MATHER, he was ordained a Congregational minister in 1685 and assisted his father at Boston's North Church (1685–1723). Though his writings on witchcraft fed the hysteria that resulted in the SALEM WITCH TRIALS, he disapproved of the trials and argued against the use of "spectral evidence." His best-known writings include *Magnalia Christi Americana* (1702), a church history of New England, and his *Diary* (1711–12). His *Curiosa Americana* (1712–24) won him membership in the Royal Society of London. He was an early supporter of smallpox inoculation. See also CONGREGATIONALISM, PURITANISM.

Cotton Mather Portrait by Peter Pelham

Mather, Henry See C. S. GREENE

Mather, Increase (1639–1723) American Puritan leader. The son of a Puritan cleric, he was born in the MASSACHUSETTS BAY COLONY and was educated at Harvard College and at Trinity College, Dublin. He returned to New England and served as minister of Boston's North Church (1661–1723). He served as president of Harvard College 1685–1701. His *Case of Conscience Concerning Evil Spirits Personating Men* (1693) helped end the SALEM WITCH TRIALS. Cotton MATHER was his son. See also PURITANISM.

Mathewson, Christy (*orig.* Christopher) (1880–1925) U.S. baseball pitcher. Born in Factoryville, Pa., he attended Bucknell Univ. and was one of the first college men to enter the major leagues. With the New York Giants (1900–16), he won more than 20 games in each of 13 seasons, and 30 or more in four of those years. He ranks third in all-time wins (373) and shutouts (80) and fourth in earned run average (2.13). He played for and managed the Cincinnati Reds 1916–18. He died of tuberculosis at 45.

Mathias \\mə-'thī-əs\\, **Bob** (*orig.* Robert Bruce) (b.1930) U.S. athlete. Born in Tulare, Cal., he suffered from anemia as a child and turned to athletics to gain strength. In 1948, at 17, he won a gold medal in the Olympic DECATHLON, becoming the youngest Olympic track-and-field gold medalist ever. In 1952 he won a second decathlon gold medal and played fullback on Stanford Univ.'s football team at the Rose Bowl. He later served in the U.S. House of Representatives.

Matilda *or* **Maud** (1102–1167) Daughter of HENRY I of England and claimant to the English throne. She married Emperor Henry V (1114–25) and later Geoffrey Plantagenet (1128). Her brother's death in 1120 left her as Henry I's sole legitimate heir, and Henry named her as his successor in 1127. STEPHEN of Blois seized the throne on Henry's death

in 1135, and his army defeated her supporters in 1141. Matilda retired to Normandy in 1148; by agreement, her son became HENRY II of England.

Matilda of Canossa \\kə-'nä-sə\\ *known as* **Matilda the Great Countess** (1046–1115) Countess of Tuscany. A close friend of Pope GREGORY VII, she backed him in his struggle against the emperor HENRY IV (see INVESTITURE CONTROVERSY), and it was at her castle at Canossa that the emperor performed his barefoot penance before Gregory (1077). She was intermittently at war with Henry 1080–1106, sometimes donning armor to lead her own troops, and she helped to finance the pope's military operations. Her unwavering support for the popes of Rome was honored by her reburial in St. Peter's Basilica in 1634.

Matisse \\mà-'tēs\\, **Henri (-Émile-Benoît)** (1869–1954) French painter, sculptor, and graphic artist. After study with Gustave MOREAU at the École des Beaux-Arts, he exhibited four paintings at the SALON and scored a triumph when the government bought his *Woman Reading* (1895). He experimented with pointillism but eventually abandoned it in favor of the swirls of spontaneous brushwork and riots of color that became known as FAUVISM. He also took up sculpture, and would produce some 60 pieces during his lifetime. In 1917 he moved to the French Riviera, where his paintings became less daring but his output remained prodigious. After 1939 he became increasingly active as a graphic artist, and in 1947 published *Jazz*, a book of reflections on art and life with brilliantly colored illustrations made by "drawing with scissors": the motifs were pasted together after being cut out of sheets of colored paper. He was ill during most of his last 13 years; as thanks to the Dominican nuns who cared for him, he designed the magnificent Chapelle du Rosaire at Vence (1948–51). His well-known paintings include *Joy of Life* (1906), *The Red Studio* (1915), *Piano Lesson* (1916), and *The Dance I* and *II* (1931–33).

Mato Grosso \\'mä-tü-'grō-sü\\ State (pop., 1996: 2,235,000), SW Brazil. It occupies 352,400 sq mi (912,716 sq km), and is bounded by Bolivia on the southwest and west. Its capital is Cuiabá (pop., 1996: 426,000). In 1748 Mato Grosso became an independent captaincy. One of the few great frontier regions still in existence, it consists of grassland, dense forest, and highland plains, with some areas that remain largely unexplored.

matriarchy \\'mā-trē-,är-kē\\ Hypothetical social system in which familial and political authority is wielded by women. Under the influence of Charles DARWIN's theories of evolution, and particularly the work of the Swiss anthropologist J. J. Bachofen (1815–1887), some 19th-cent. scholars believed that matriarchy followed a stage of general promiscuity and preceded male ascendancy (patriarchy) in human society's evolutionary sequence. This notion of matriarchy as a universal stage of development is now generally discredited, and the modern consensus is that a strictly matriarchal society has never existed. Nevertheless, societies organized by matrilineal DESCENT trace socially powerful positions through the maternal line.

matrix Set of numbers arranged in rows and columns to form a rectangular array. Matrix elements may also be differential operators, vectors, or functions. Matrices have wide applications in engineering, physics, economics, and statistics, as well as in various branches of mathematics. They are usually first encountered in the study of SYSTEMS OF EQUATIONS represented by matrix equations of the form $Ax = B$.

Matsushita Electric Industrial Co., Ltd. \\mät-'sü-shi-tə\\ Major Japanese manufacturer of electric appliances and consumer electronics. Founded in 1918 by Matsushita Konosuke (1894–1989) and incorporated in 1935, its early products included radios and phonographs. In the 1950s it added television sets, tape recorders, and household appliances; a decade later it brought out microwave ovens, air conditioners, and videotape recorders. Matsushita is noted for its heavy investment in research and development. Through worldwide subsidiaries, it markets products under the brand names Panasonic and Quasar.

matter Material substance that constitutes the observable universe and, together with ENERGY, forms the basis of all objective phenomena. ATOMS are the basic building blocks of matter. Matter in bulk occurs in several states; the most familiar are the gaseous (see GAS), LIQUID, and SOLID states (PLASMAS, GLASSES, and various others are less clearly defined), each with characteristic properties. According to Albert EINSTEIN's special theory of RELATIVITY, matter and energy are equivalent and interconvertible (see CONSERVATION LAW).

Matterhorn *French* **Mont Cervin** \ˌmôⁿ-ser-ˈveⁿ\ *Italian* **Monte Cervino** \ˈmȯn-tä-cher-ˈvē-nō\ Mountain in the ALPS, on the border between Italy and Switzerland. It rises to 14,692 ft (4,478 m). It was first scaled in 1865 by Edward Whymper (1840–1911), from the Swiss side, and three days later by Giovanni A. Carrel (1829–1890), from the Italian side. Its dramatically chiseled form makes it, with Mt. FUJI, perhaps the world's most photographed mountain.

Matterhorn reflected in one of the Riffel lakes, Switzerland

Matthau \ˈma-thaù\, **Walter** *orig.* Walter Matuschanskavasky (1920–2000) U.S. actor. Born in New York City, he appeared on Broadway in plays such as *Once More, with Feeling* (1958) before winning stardom in *The Odd Couple* (1965), which he reprised on film (1968) with his frequent costar, Jack LEMMON. His other films include *The Fortune Cookie* (1966, Academy Award), *Kotch* (1971), *The Sunshine Boys* (1975), *Grumpy Old Men* (1993), and *I'm Not Rappaport* (1996).

Matthew, St. (fl.1st cent. A.D.) One of the Twelve APOSTLES, traditional author of the first GOSPEL. According to the Gospels, he was a tax collector known as Levi when Jesus called him to be a disciple. Other information about him is scarce. The Gospel of Matthew is directed at a Jewish-Christian audience in a Jewish environment and may have been written originally in Hebrew, but it is now doubted that the Apostle Matthew was its author.

Matthias I *or* **Matthias Corvinus** \mə-ˈthī-əs...kȯr-ˈvī-nəs\ *Hungarian* Mátyás Corvin *orig.* Mátyás Hunyadi (1443–1490) King of Hungary (1458–90). He spent much of his reign combating the claims of the HABSBURG DYNASTY and attempting to reconstruct the Hungarian state after decades of feudal anarchy. He modernized the army and codified Hungarian law. He fought off Turks on Hungary's S border, and gained control of Bosnia (1463) and most of Bohemia (1469). Long a rival of Emperor FREDERICK III, he occupied Vienna and other Habsburg lands, but after his death his conquests were lost.

Matthiessen \ˈmath-ə-sən\, **Peter** (b.1927) U.S. writer. Born in New York City, he became a dedicated world traveler early on. His concerns about the environment and primitive societies led to such nonfiction books as *Wildlife in America* (1959), *The Tree Where Man Was Born* (1972), *The Snow Leopard* (1978), and *African Silences* (1991), and such novels as *At Play in the Fields of the Lord* (1965; film, 1991), *Far Tortuga* (1975), and *Killing Mister Watson* (1990).

Maud See MATILDA

Maudslay \ˈmȯdz-lē\, **Henry** (1771–1831) British engineer and inventor. The son of a workman, he became the inventor of machines fundamentally important to the INDUSTRIAL REVOLUTION, most outstandingly the metal LATHE. He also invented methods for printing calico cloth and for desalting seawater for ships' boilers, as well as a measuring machine that was accurate to 0.0001 in. (0.00025 cm), and he designed and built many stationary and marine engines.

Maugham \ˈmȯm\, **W(illiam) Somerset** (1874–1965) English novelist, playwright, and short-story writer. His reputation rests primarily on the novels *Of Human Bondage* (1915), *The Moon and Sixpence* (1919), *Cakes and Ale* (1930), and *The Razor's Edge* (1944). His many short stories (including "Rain") often portray the confusion of Europeans in alien surroundings. His plays, mainly Edwardian social comedies, brought him financial security. His works are characterized by a clear, unadorned style, cosmopolitan settings, and a shrewd understanding of human nature.

Mauldin \ˈmȯl-din\, **Bill** (*orig.* William Henry) (1921–2003) U.S. cartoonist. Born in Mountain Park, N.M., he worked as a cartoonist before World War II, when he enlisted in the army. His sardonic cartoons for *Stars and Stripes,* featuring Willie and Joe, disheveled enlisted men who managed to retain their humanity between the onslaughts of war and an often fatuous army hierarchy, were widely republished. After the war he became a widely syndicated political cartoonist. He won Pulitzer Prizes in 1945 and 1959.

Mau Mau \ˈmaù-ˌmaù\ Militant KIKUYU-led nationalist movement of the 1950s in Kenya. The Mau Mau advocated violent resistance to British domination in Kenya, and the British Kenya government responded militarily. During 1952–56, some 11,000 Kikuyu, 100 Europeans, and 2,000 African loyalists were killed; another 20,000 Kikuyu were put into detention camps. Kikuyu resistance nonetheless spearheaded the independence movement, and Jomo KENYATTA, jailed as a Mau Mau leader in 1953, became prime minister of independent Kenya in 1963.

Mauna Kea \ˌmaù-nä-ˈkē-ə\ Dormant volcano, N central HAWAII island, Hawaii. Rising to 13,796 ft (4,205 m), it is the highest point in the state and is the chief feature of a state park occupying 500 acres (202 hectares). Its dome is 30 mi (48 km) across, and is the site of a major astronomical observatory. Its W and S slopes are covered with lava from its neighbor, MAUNA LOA.

Mauna Loa Volcano, S central HAWAII island, Hawaii. Located in HAWAII VOLCANOES NATIONAL PARK, it is the world's largest mountain in cubic content. It rises to 13,678 ft (4,169 m) and has a dome 75 mi (120 km) long and 64 mi (103 km) wide. Its pit crater has an area of nearly 4 sq mi (10 sq km) and a depth of 500–600 ft (150–180 m). It has averaged one eruption every 3 1/2 years since 1832. Its lava flows occupy more than 2,000 sq mi (5,120 sq km). See also KILAUEA.

Maupassant \mō-pà-ˈsäⁿ\, **(Henry-René-Albert-) Guy de** (1850–1893) French writer of short stories. His law studies were interrupted by the FRANCO–PRUSSIAN WAR; his experience as a volunteer provided him with material for some of his best works. Later he became a protégé of Gustave FLAUBERT. He first gained attention with "Boule de Suif" (1880), probably his finest story. In the next 10 years he published some 300 short stories, six novels, and three travel books. Taken together, his stories present a broad, naturalistic picture of French life from 1870 to 1890. Maupassant was phenomenally promiscuous, and before he was 25 his health was being eroded by syphilis. He attempted suicide in 1892 and was committed to an asylum, where he died at 42. He is generally considered France's greatest master of the short story.

Guy de Maupassant Photo by Nadar, c.1885

Mauretania Ancient region of N. Africa corresponding to present-day N Morocco and W and central Algeria. It was settled by the Phoenicians and Carthaginians from the 6th cent. B.C. It was annexed to Rome around A.D. 42. It had become virtually independent in the 5th cent., but it was overrun by the VANDALS and Arabs in the 7th cent.

Mauriac \mȯr-ˈyàk\, **François** (1885–1970) French writer. Mauriac grew up in a pious and strict Catholic family, and he subsequently placed at the heart of all his works the soul grappling with the problems of sin, grace, and salvation. He is best known for his austere, psychological novels, including *The Kiss to the Leper* (1922) and *Vipers' Tangle* (1932), often considered his masterpiece. He wrote polemical works against totalitarianism and fascism in the 1930s and worked with the Resistance during World War II. He was awarded the 1952 Nobel Prize.

Maurice of Nassau *Dutch* Maurits, Prins (Prince) van Oranje, Graaf (Count) van Nassau (1567–1625) Dutch general and statesman. The son of WILLIAM I THE SILENT, he was invested in 1585 as stadtholder (chief executive) of the N provinces of the Netherlands. With political direction from Johan van OLDENBARNEVELT, Maurice consolidated the power of the provinces against Spain and made them trade and shipping centers. His development of military strategy and tactics made the Dutch army the most modern in Europe. In 1618 he consolidated his political power after removing Oldenbarnevelt from office, and as prince of Orange, count of Nassau, he became effectively king of the Netherlands.

Maurier, Daphne Du See Daphne DU MAURIER

Maurier, George Du See George DU MAURIER

Mauritania *officially* **Islamic Republic of Mauritania** Republic, NW Africa. It is bordered by the Atlantic Ocean. Area: 398,000 sq mi (1,030,700 sq km). Population (2000): 2,668,000. Capital: NOUAKCHOTT. The Moors (of mixed Arab-Berber and Sudanic black descent) constitute the great majority of the population. Languages: Arabic (official); Fulani, Soninke, Wolof (all national). Religion: Islam (official). Currency: ouguiya. Most of Mauritania is made up of low-lying desert that forms the westernmost part of the Sahara. Only a tiny fraction of its land is arable, but almost 40% is rangeland or pasture, and the nomadic herding of goats, sheep, and camels occupies a large portion of the population. Ocean fishing and iron-ore production are major sources of revenue. It is a republic with two legislative houses; its head of state and government is the president, assisted by the prime minister. Inhabited in ancient times by Sanhadja BERBERS, in the 11th–12th cent. it was the center of the Berber ALMORAVID movement, which imposed Islam on many of the neighboring peoples. Arab tribes arrived in the 15th cent. and formed several powerful confederations: Trarza and Brakna, which dominated the Sénégal River region; Kunta in the east; and Rigaibat in the north. The Por-

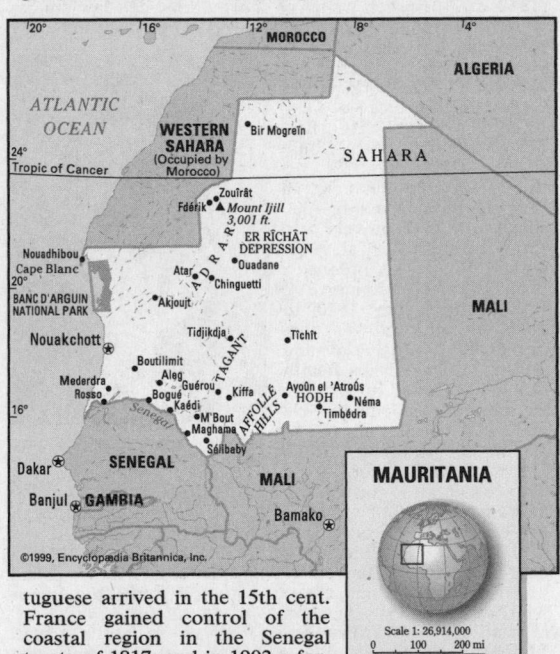

©1999, Encyclopædia Britannica, Inc.

MAURITANIA

Scale 1: 26,914,000

tuguese arrived in the 15th cent. France gained control of the coastal region in the Senegal treaty of 1817, and in 1903 a formal protectorate was extended over the territory. In 1904 it was added to French W. Africa, and in 1920 it became a colony. In 1960 Mauritania achieved independence and left the French Community. The country's first president, Moktar Ould Daddah, was ousted in a coup in 1978, and a military government was established. In 1980 a civilian government was set up and in 1991 a new constitution was adopted. Relations between the government and opposition groups deteriorated, and the country's huge foreign debt and periodic severe droughts continued to cause deep concern.

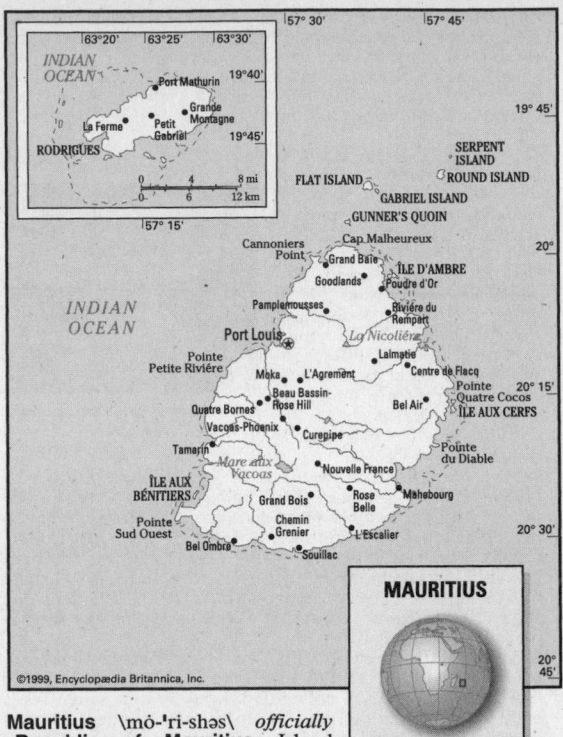

©1999, Encyclopædia Britannica, Inc.

MAURITIUS

Scale 1: 1,353,000

Mauritius \mȯ-'ri-shəs\ *officially* **Republic of Mauritius** Island country, lying east of Madagascar in the Indian Ocean. The central independent island state of the Mascarene group, it extends 38 mi (61 km) north–south and 29 mi (47 km) east–west. Its outlying territories are Rodrigues Island to the east, the Cargados Carajos Shoals to the northeast, and the Agalega Islands to the north. Area: 788 sq mi (2,040 sq km). Population (2000): 1,184,000. Capital: PORT LOUIS. About three-fifths of the population are either Creole or of French descent, and two-fifths are Indian. Languages: English (official), Creole (lingua franca), various ethnic languages. Religions: Hinduism (one-half the population), Christianity (one-third), Islam. Currency: rupee. Volcanic in origin and almost surrounded by coastal reefs, Mauritius rises to 2,711 ft (826 m) at the Petite Rivière-Noire Peak; its chief water source is Lake Vacoas. About half of its land is arable, and sugarcane is the major crop, though the government has sponsored agricultural diversification. The country is heavily dependent on food imports, mainly rice. The nation's population density is one of the highest in the world. The island was visited, but not settled, by the Portuguese in the early 16th cent. The Dutch took possession 1598–1710, called it Mauritius after the governor Maurice of Nassau, and attempted to settle it (1638–58, 1664–1710) before abandoning it to pirates. The French E. India Co. occupied it, renamed it Île de France in 1721, and governed it until the French ministry of marine took over its administration in 1767. Sugar planting was the main industry, and the colony prospered. The British captured the island in 1810 and were granted formal control of it under the Treaty of Paris in 1814; the name Mauritius was reinstated, and slavery was abolished. In the late 19th cent. competition from beet sugar caused an economic decline, compounded by the opening of the SUEZ CANAL in 1869. After World War II, Mauritius adopted political and economic reforms, and in 1968 it became an independent state within the COMMONWEALTH. In 1992 it became a republic. Political unrest marked the 1990s.

Maurois \mȯr-'wä\, **André** *orig.* Émile Herzog (1885–1967) French writer. He is best known for biographies with the narrative interest of novels, including those of P. B. SHELLEY, Lord BYRON, and Victor HUGO; *The Quest for Proust*

(1949) is considered by many his finest biography. His novels include *Bernard Quesnay* (1926) and *Whatever Gods May Be* (1928). He also wrote histories of England and the U.S., essays, and children's tales.

Maurras \mȯ-ˈräs\, **Charles (-Marie-Photius)** (1868–1952) French writer and political theorist. In 1891 he cofounded a group of poets opposed to the SYMBOLISTS and later known as the *école romane*. An ardent monarchist, he cofounded *L'Action Française* (1899), a review that promoted the supremacy of the state and became the party organ of Maurras's reactionary Action Française movement. During World War II he was a strong supporter of the government of Philippe PÉTAIN, for which he was imprisoned 1945–52.

Maurya See CANDRA GUPTA

Mauryan empire \ˈmau̇-rē-ən\ (321?–c.185 B.C.) In ancient India, a state centered at Pataliputra (later Patna), the first Indian empire. About 322 B.C. CANDRA GUPTA, the dynastic founder, carved out an empire that encompassed most of the Indian subcontinent. ASHOKA (r.c.265–238? B.C.), the famous Buddhist emperor, left stone edicts that describe his reign and include some of the oldest deciphered original texts of India. The empire declined after Ashoka's death, but for almost 100 years it was an efficient and highly organized autocracy.

mausoleum Large, impressive tomb, especially a stone building with places for entombment of the dead aboveground. The word is derived from Mausolus, whose widow raised a splendid tomb at HALICARNASSUS (c.353–350 B.C.). Probably the most ambitious mausoleum is the TAJ MAHAL.

Mauss \ˈmōs\, **Marcel** (1872–1950) French sociologist and anthropologist. Mauss was the nephew of Émile DURKHEIM, who contributed much to his intellectual formation and with whom he collaborated in such important works as *Suicide* (1897) and *Primitive Classification* (1901–2). His most influential independent work was *The Gift* (1925), a comparative study of the relation between forms of GIFT EXCHANGE and social structure. He taught at the École Pratique des Hautes Études and the Collège de France, and cofounded the Univ. of Paris's Institut d'Ethnologie.

Mawlana See Jalal al-Din al-RUMI

Maxim, Hiram (Stevens) (*later* **Sir Hiram**) (1840–1916) U.S.-British inventor. Son of a Maine farmer, he became chief engineer of the U.S. Electric Lighting Co. (1878–81), for which he introduced carbon filaments for electric lightbulbs. Working on a fully automatic MACHINE GUN, in 1884 he achieved a design that used the recoil of the barrel to eject the spent cartridges and reload the chamber. He also developed his own smokeless GUNPOWDER, cordite. Soon every army was equipped with Maxim guns or adaptations. His other inventions included an early airplane (1894). His son Hiram Percy (1869–1936) invented the Maxim silencer for rifles and designed the Columbia electric automobile.

Maximilian *orig.* Ferdinand Maximilian Joseph (1832–1867) Archduke of Austria and emperor of Mexico (1864–67). Brother of FRANCIS JOSEPH I of Austria-Hungary, he accepted the offer of the Mexican throne, naively thinking the Mexicans had chosen him king. In fact, the offer was a scheme between Mexican conservatives, who wanted to overthrow Pres. Benito JUÁREZ, and NAPOLEON III, who wanted to collect a debt from Mexico and had imperialist ambitions there. Maximilian upheld Juárez's reforms, to the fury of the conservatives. The U.S. intervened on Juárez's behalf; French forces supporting Maximilian left at the request of the U.S., and Juárez's army retook Mexico City. Refusing to abdicate, Maximilian was defeated and executed.

Maximilian I (1459–1519) German king and Holy Roman Emperor (1493–1519). The eldest son of FREDERICK III, he gained BURGUNDY's lands in the Netherlands by marriage in 1477, but was later forced to give Burgundy to LOUIS XI (1482). He retook most of the Habsburg lands

Maximilian I Drawing by Albrecht Dürer, 1518

in Austria from the Hungarians and drove the Turks from the empire's SE borders. He fought a series of wars against the French, helping to force them out of Italy in 1496 but losing Milan to them in 1515. He lost Switzerland as well, but acquired the TIROL peacefully. He acquired Spain for the Habsburgs through his children's marriages, gained influence in Hungary and Bohemia, and built an intricate network of European alliances. A popular monarch, he encouraged culture and the arts.

Maximilian I *orig.* Maximilian Joseph (1756–1825) First king of Bavaria (1806–25). A member of the House of WITTELSBACH, in 1799 he inherited its territories as Maximilian IV Joseph, elector of Bavaria. He supported the French war effort (1805–9), and received territories by which he crowned himself king of Bavaria (1806). After 1813 he allied with Austria to guarantee the integrity of his kingdom. Aided by his chief minister, Count von Montgelas (1759–1838), Maximilian made Bavaria into an efficient, liberal state under a new constitution (1808) and charter (1818) that established a bicameral parliament.

maximum In mathematics, a point at which a FUNCTION's value is greatest. If the value is greater than or equal to all other function values, it is an absolute maximum. If it is merely greater than any nearby point, it is a relative, or local, maximum. In CALCULUS, the DERIVATIVE equals zero or does not exist at a function's maximum point. Techniques for finding maximum and minimum points motivated the early development of calculus and have made it easier to solve many problems. See also MINIMUM, OPTIMIZATION.

Maxwell, James Clerk (1831–1879) Scottish physicist. At Cambridge Univ. he supervised the building of Cavendish Laboratory. His most revolutionary achievement was his demonstration that light is an electromagnetic wave, and he originated the concept of ELECTROMAGNETIC RADIATION. His field equations (see MAXWELL'S EQUATIONS) paved the way for Albert EINSTEIN's special theory of relativity. He established the nature of Saturn's rings, did important work on color perception, and produced the KINETIC THEORY OF GASES. His ideas formed the basis for QUANTUM MECHANICS and ultimately for the modern theory of the structure of atoms and molecules.

Maxwell's equations Four equations, formulated by J. C. MAXWELL, that together form a complete description of the production and interrelation of ELECTRIC and MAGNETIC FIELDS. The statements of these four equations are (1) electric field diverges from ELECTRIC CHARGE, (2) there are no isolated magnetic poles, (3) electric fields are produced by changing magnetic fields, and (4) circulating magnetic fields are produced by changing electric fields and by electric currents. See also ELECTROMAGNETISM.

Maya \ˈmī-ə\ Group of Mesoamerican Indians who between A.D. 250 and 900 developed one of the Western Hemisphere's greatest civilizations. By A.D. 200 they had developed cities with palaces, temples, plazas, and ball courts. Their sculpture and relief carving were highly developed. MAYAN HIEROGLYPHIC WRITING survives in books and inscriptions. Mayan mathematics used positional notation and the zero; Mayan astronomy featured an accurately determined solar year and precise tables of the positions of Venus and the moon. Calendrical accuracy was important for the elaborate rituals of the Mayan religion, which was based on a pantheon of gods. Mayan bloodletting, torture, and human sacrifice were employed to propitiate the gods, ensure fertility, and stave off cosmic chaos. At the height of its Classic period, Mayan civilization included more than 40 cities of 5,000–50,000 people. After 900 the civilization declined rapidly for unknown reasons. Descendants of the Maya are now subsistence farmers in S Mexico and Guatemala. See also CHICHÉN ITZÁ, COPÁN, MAYA CODICES, MAYAN LANGUAGES, QUICHE, TIKAL, UXMAL.

Maya Codices Books in MAYAN HIEROGLYPHIC WRITING that survived the Spanish conquest. They are made of figbark paper folded like an accordion, with covers of jaguar skin. Though most Mayan books were destroyed as pagan by Spanish priests, four are known to have survived, dating from approximately the 11th to the 15th cent. They deal with astronomical calculations, divination, and ritual.

Mayakovsky \mə-ˌyə-ˈkȯf-skē\, **Vladimir (Vladimirovich)** (1893–1930) Russian poet. Repeatedly jailed for subversive activity, he began writing poetry during solitary confinement in 1909. On his release he became the spokesman for FUTURISM in Russia. He was the leading poet of the Russian Revolution of 1917 and the early Soviet period, producing political works aimed at mass audiences, including "Ode to Revolution" (1918) and "Left March" (1919) and the drama *Mystery Bouffe* (performed 1921). Increasingly alienated from Soviet reality, he committed suicide at 36.

Mayan hieroglyphic writing \\'mī-ən\\ System of writing used by people of the MAYA civilization from about the 3rd cent. A.D. to the 17th cent. It has about 800 signs that have been inventoried in more than 5,000 instances (see MAYA CODICES). Signs are either logographic, representing words, or syllabic, representing consonant-vowel sequences. Typically, up to five signs are fit into tight square or rectangular clusters, which are further arranged into rows or grids. The language of Classic Period writing (c.A.D. 250–900) is an ancestral MAYAN LANGUAGE; later inscriptions were in Yucatec. By the 1990s, scholars had an accurate grasp of 60–70% of Mayan inscriptions. Most inscriptions record significant events and dates in the lives of Mayan rulers.

Mayan languages Family of about 30 American Indian language complexes, spoken by more than 3 million people, mainly in S Mexico and Guatemala. While some have few remaining speakers, Yucatec in Mexico, and K'iche (Quiché), Kaqchikel (Cakchiquel), Mam, and Q'eqchi' (Kekchí) in Guatemala count speakers in the hundreds of thousands. Mayan languages were recorded in an indigenous script (see MAYA CODICES, MAYAN HIEROGLYPHIC WRITING), as well as in colonial documents in a Spanish-based spelling, including the *Popol Vuh* and the Yucatec prophetic texts known as the *Books of Chilam Balam.*

May beetle See JUNE BEETLE

May Day In Europe, the day (May 1) for traditional springtime celebrations. It probably originated in pre-Christian agricultural rituals. Celebrations included a May king and queen and a Maypole. Designated an international labor day by the International Socialist Congress of 1899, it remains the standard Labor Day worldwide, with a few exceptions, including Canada and the U.S. A major holiday in the Soviet Union and other communist countries, it was the occasion for important political demonstrations.

Mayer, Louis B(urt) (*orig.* Eliezer *or* Lazar) (1885–1957) U.S. (Russian-born) film executive. He emigrated to Canada and then the U.S. with his parents. He bought a small nickelodeon near Boston in 1907, and by 1918 owned the largest chain of movie theaters in New England. He founded a film production company in Hollywood in 1917 and merged it with other companies in 1925 to form MGM, which became Hollywood's largest and most prestigious studio. The creator of the star system, Mayer had under contract many of the outstanding screen stars of the day, including Greta GARBO, Clark GABLE, and Judy GARLAND. He was considered the most powerful Hollywood executive until his forced retirement in 1951. He was the chief founder of the Academy of Motion Picture Arts and Sciences.

Mayerling affair See RUDOLF

Mayflower Compact (1620) Document signed by 41 male passengers on the *Mayflower* before landing at PLYMOUTH, Mass. Concerned that some members might leave to form their own colonies, William BRADFORD and others drafted the compact to bind the group into a political body and pledge members to abide by any laws that would be established. It became the basis of the colony's government.

mayfly Any INSECT of the order Ephemeroptera, found around streams and ponds. The approximately 2,000 species are up to 1.6 in. (4 cm) long, have triangular membranous forewings, smaller round hind wings, and two or three long, threadlike tails. The adult lives just long enough to mate and reproduce. Males "dance" in large swarms to attract females. The adult's entire life span is usually only a few hours, and poets have used the mayfly as a symbol of life's ephemeral nature.

May Fourth Movement Chinese intellectual revolution and sociopolitical reform movement. In 1915 young intellectuals inspired by CHEN DUXIU began agitating for reform through acceptance of Western science, democracy, and schools of thought, to make China strong enough to resist Western imperialism. On May 4, 1919, reformist zeal found focus in a protest by Beijing's students against the Versailles Peace Conference's decision to transfer former German concessions in China to Japan. After more than a month of demonstrations, the government gave way and refused to sign the peace treaty with Germany. The movement gave birth to the CHINESE COMMUNIST PARTY.

Mayo family Family of U.S. physicians. William Worrall Mayo (1819–1911) opened a surgical practice in Rochester, Minn., in 1863, and in 1889 he opened St. Mary's Hospital with his two sons. The elder son, William James (1861–1939), specialized in surgery of the abdomen, pelvis, and kidney, and served as administrator. Charles Horace (1865–1939), a gifted surgeon in all areas, originated modern procedures in goiter surgery, neurosurgery, and orthopedic surgery. Around 1900 the partnership was changed to what became the Mayo Clinic, which currently includes about 500 physicians, treating more than 200,000 patients a year.

Mayon Volcano \\mä-'yōn\\ *or* **Mt. Mayon** Active volcano, SE LUZON, Philippines. One of the world's most perfect volcanic cones, it has a base 80 mi (130 km) in circumference and rises to 7,943 ft (2,421 m). It is popular with climbers and campers. It has erupted more than 30 times since 1616; an eruption in 1993 caused 75 deaths. Its most destructive eruption was in 1814, burying the town of Cagsawa.

mayor Political leader of a municipal corporation. Mayors are either appointed or elected for a limited term. In Europe until the mid-19th cent., most mayors were appointed by the central government. In the U.S., they are either directly elected by the populace or chosen by an elected council. Some mayors fulfill only ceremonial functions, executive power being held by a professional manager hired by the legislature; others may make appointments, veto legislation, administer budgets, and manage administrative functions.

Mayotte \\mä-'yöt\\ Southeasternmost island (pop., 1991 est.: 86,000) of the COMOROS archipelago, a French overseas territorial collectivity. Located northwest of Madagascar, it occupies 144 sq mi (373 sq km); Mamoutzo is its chief town. Originally inhabited by descendants of BANTU and Malayo-Indonesian peoples, it was converted to Islam by Arab invaders in the 15th cent. Taken by a Malagasy tribe from Madagascar in the 18th cent., it came under French control in 1843. With the other Comoros islands and Madagascar, it became part of a French overseas territory in the early 20th cent. It has been administered separately since 1975, when the three northernmost islands of the Comoros declared independence.

maypole Tall wooden pole garlanded with flowers and greenery and often hung with ribbons that are woven into complex patterns by dancers in a ceremonial folk dance. The custom probably originated in ancient fertility rites. In many European countries, the pole is set up on May 1 as part of MAY DAY festivities. Similar ribbon dances were performed in India and in pre-Columbian Latin America.

Mayr \\'mīr\\, **Ernst (Walter)** (b.1904) German-U.S. biologist. He emigrated to the U.S. in 1932 and held positions at the American Museum of Natural History (1932–53) and Harvard Univ. (1953–75). He wrote more than 100 papers on avian taxonomy. His early studies of speciation and of founder populations made him a leader in the development of the modern synthetic theory of EVOLUTION. In 1940 Mayr proposed a definition of species that won wide acceptance. His influential works include *Systematics and the Origin of Species* (1942) and *The Growth of Biology Thought* (1982).

Mays, Willie (Howard) (b.1931) U.S. baseball player. Born in Westfield, Ala., he played in the Negro Leagues when he was only 16. The "Say Hey Kid" later played center field principally for

Willie Mays

the New York (later San Francisco) Giants in the major leagues (1951–72). One of the greatest all-around players in history, he ranks among the all-time top five in home runs (660), runs (2,062), and extra-base hits (1,323) and among the top ten for runs batted in (1,903) and hits (3,283).

Maysles \\'mā-zəlz\\, **Albert and David** (b.1926, 1932–1987) U.S. documentary filmmakers. The brothers were born in Boston, and Albert made his first documentary, *Psychiatry in Russia*, in 1955. The two thereafter collaborated on documentaries in the CINÉMA VÉRITÉ (or "direct cinema") style, notably *Salesman* (1969) and *Gimme Shelter* (1970), both made with Charlotte Zwerin. Their later films include *Christo's Valley Curtain* (1972), and *Grey Gardens* (1975).

Mazarin \\ˌma-zə-'raⁿ\\, **Jules, Cardinal** *orig.* Giulio Raimondo Mazarini (1602–1661) Italian-French cardinal and statesman. A member of the papal diplomatic service (1627–34), he served as papal nuncio to the French court (1634–36), where he admired Cardinal de RICHELIEU. He entered the service of France and became a naturalized French citizen (1639) and a cardinal (1641). After the deaths of Richelieu (1642) and LOUIS XIII (1643), Mazarin was appointed first minister of France by ANNE OF AUSTRIA, regent for LOUIS XIV. A highly influential adviser to the young king, he helped train a staff of able administrators. His foreign policy established France's supremacy among the European powers, effecting the Peace of WESTPHALIA (1648). A patron of the arts, Mazarin founded an academy of painting and sculpture and compiled a large library.

Mazatlán \\ˌmä-sä-'tlän\\ Seaport city (pop., 1995: 302,000), SW SINALOA state, Mexico. Sited on the Gulf of CALIFORNIA, it is Mexico's largest Pacific port, and its island-studded harbor is known for its fine sandy beaches. Called the Pearl of the Pacific, it is a fishing center and a popular tourist resort.

maze See LABYRINTH

Mazrui \\màz-'rü-ē\\, **Ali (Al Amin)** (b.1933) Kenyan-U.S. political scientist. After receiving a doctorate from Oxford Univ., he taught at Uganda's Makerere Univ. (1963–73) and the Univ. of Michigan (1974–91). At SUNY–Binghamton he founded the Institute of Global Cultural Studies. He has taught and consulted worldwide, and is the author of many books on African politics and society and postcolonial development. For television he wrote the nine-hour BBC-PBS coproduction *The Africans* (1986).

Mazzini \\mät-'sē-nē\\, **Giuseppe** (1805–1872) Italian patriot. A lawyer, he joined the secret independence group CARBONARI, was imprisoned for its activities, then moved to Marseille (1831), where he founded the YOUNG ITALY movement. He later expanded his plan for a world republican federation and in Switzerland founded Young Europe. In London (from 1837), he continued his revolutionary activities by correspondence with agents worldwide. In 1848 he returned briefly to Italy to help govern the short-lived Republic of Rome. He founded the Friends of Italy (1851) and backed unsuccessful uprisings in Milan, Mantua, and Genoa. An uncompromising republican, he disapproved of the new united Kingdom of Italy (1861). See also RISORGIMENTO.

Mbabane \\əm-bä-'bä-nä\\ Capital and largest town (pop., 1998 est.: 60,000) of Swaziland. It developed near the cattle kraal of the Swazi king Mbandzeni in the late 19th cent. The actual town was founded in 1902, when the British assumed control of Swaziland and set up an administrative headquarters there. A Mozambican railway link near Mbabane was established in 1964.

Mbeki \\em-'bek-ē\\, **Thabo** (b.1942) President of S. Africa (from 1999). The son of an anti-APARTHEID activist, he studied economics at Sussex Univ. in Britain, then received military training in the Soviet Union. Mbeki was appointed deputy president by Nelson MANDELA following S. Africa's first all-race elections in 1994. Less charismatic than Mandela, he alarmed many by his insistence that HIV was probably not the cause of AIDS, which has ravaged the country.

McAdam, John (Loudon) (1756–1836) Scottish inventor of the MACADAM road surface. He made an early fortune in his uncle's New York countinghouse (1770–83). Back in Scotland, he noted the poor condition of its highways and undertook experiments in road making. He recommended that roads be raised above the adjacent ground for good drainage and covered, first with larger stones and then with smaller stones, the whole mass to be bound with fine gravel or slag. In 1823 his views were officially adopted, and in 1827 he was appointed Britain's Surveyor General of Metropolitan Roads.

McCarthy, Cormac *orig.* Charles McCarthy, Jr. (b.1933) U.S. novelist. Born in Providence, R.I., he grew up in Tennessee. His novels, known for their morbid realism and violence, are in the Southern gothic tradition. They include *Outer Dark* (1968), *Blood Meridian* (1985), and the widely read Border Trilogy (*All the Pretty Little Horses*, 1992; *The Crossing*, 1994; *Cities of the Plain*, 1999).

McCarthy, Eugene J(oseph) (b.1916) U.S. politician. Born in Watkins, Minn., he taught college before serving in the U.S. House of Representatives (1949–59) and later the Senate (1959–71). A liberal Democrat, he became an outspoken critic of the Vietnam War. In 1967 he entered the Democratic primaries for the presidential nomination. His initial successes convinced Pres. Lyndon JOHNSON not to seek reelection. Failing to win the nomination, he left the Senate in 1971.

McCarthy, Joseph R(aymond) (1908–1957) U.S. politician. Born near Appleton, Wis., he practiced law before becoming a state circuit judge and serving with the Marines in World War II. Elected to the U.S. Senate in 1946, in 1950 he began charging that communists had infiltrated the U.S. State Department. His anticommunist crusade gained wide popular support, and his subcommittee on investigations held hearings to question government officials and others about suspected communist activities, in a campaign of persecution and slander that became known as McCarthyism. The 1954 televised hearings on charges of subversion by U.S.

Joseph McCarthy

Army officers revealed McCarthy's irresponsible tactics, and he was censured by the Senate that year. A heavy drinker, he died at 48.

McCarthy, Mary (Therese) (1912–1989) U.S. novelist and critic. Born in Seattle, she served on the editorial staff of the *Partisan Review* 1937–48. Her work is noted for bitingly satiric commentaries on marriage, the impotence of intellectuals, and the role of women in contemporary urban America. Her novels include *The Company She Keeps* (1942); *The Group* (1963), her most popular work; and *Cannibals and Missionaries* (1979). She also wrote two autobiographies, *Memories of a Catholic Girlhood* (1957) and *How I Grew* (1987).

McCartney, (James) Paul (*later* **Sir Paul**) (b.1942) British singer and songwriter. Born to a working-class Liverpool family, he learned piano but switched to guitar after hearing American rock-and-roll recordings. In the mid-1950s he met John LENNON, with whom he formed the Quarrymen, which evolved into the BEATLES. He and Lennon cowrote scores of songs, including some of the most popular songs of the 20th cent. He released his first solo album in 1970. With his wife, Linda Eastman (1941–1998), he formed the group Wings; their hit albums included *Band on the Run* (1973). After the band dissolved, McCartney achieved extraordinary worldwide popularity in the 1980s.

McCarty, Maclyn (b.1911) U.S. biologist. Born in South Bend, Ind., he received his MD at Johns Hopkins. With Oswald AVERY and Colin MacLeod he provided the first experimental evidence that the genetic material of living cells is composed of DNA. In their classic experiments (1944), the introduction of certain material from one type of pneumococcus bacteria into another type transformed the receiving bacteria into the type from which the material had been taken.

McClellan, George B(rinton) (1826–1885) U.S. Army officer. Born in Philadelphia, he served in the Mexican War and conducted military engineering surveys. In the AMERICAN CIVIL WAR he was named commander of the department of the Ohio. He defeated Confederate forces in W Virginia and helped keep Kentucky in the Union. Appointed general in chief by Abraham LINCOLN (1861), he reorganized the army into an efficient force, but his lack of offensive action led Lincoln to issue his General War Order (1862) calling for forward movement of all armies. McClellan's cautious Peninsular Campaign failed to take Richmond, and he fought indecisively in the SEVEN DAYS' BATTLES. At the Battle of ANTIETAM he failed to destroy Robert E. LEE's army, and Lincoln removed him from command. In 1864 he was the Democratic candidate for president against Lincoln.

McClintock, Barbara (1902–1992) U.S. geneticist. Born in Hartford, Conn., she pursued experiments with variations in the coloration of kernels of corn in the 1940s and '50s that revealed that genetic information is not stationary. She isolated two control elements in genetic material and found not only that they moved but that the change in position affected the behavior of neighboring genes, and suggested that these elements were responsible for the diversity in cells during an organism's development. Her pioneering research eventually resulted in her being awarded a 1983 Nobel Prize.

McClung, Nellie *orig.* Nellie Mooney (1873–1953) Canadian writer. Born in Chatsworth, Ontario, she married in 1896 and became prominent in the temperance movement. Her *Sowing Seeds in Danny*, a 1908 novel about life in a small W town, became a national best-seller; she would write 15 more books. She lectured widely on women's suffrage and other reforms in Canada and the U.S. and served in the Alberta legislature (1921–26).

McCormick, Cyrus H(all) (1809–1884) U.S. industrialist and inventor. Born in Rockbridge Co., Va., he is generally credited with the development (from 1831) of the mechanical reaper, which revolutionized the harvesting of grain. The McCormick reaper was soon famous around the world. In 1902 the McCormick Harvesting Co. joined with other companies to form International Harvester Co., with McCormick's son Cyrus, Jr., as its first president.

Cyrus McCormick

McCormick, Robert R(utherford) *known as* **Colonel McCormick** (1880–1955) U.S. newspaper editor and publisher. Born in Chicago, the grandson of Joseph Medill, editor and publisher of the *Chicago Tribune,* he was president of the Chicago Tribune Co. from 1911 and sole editor and publisher of the *Tribune* from 1925. Under his direction the paper achieved the largest circulation among U.S. standard-sized newspapers. His idiosyncratic editorials made him the personification of reactionary journalism in the U.S.

McCullers, Carson *orig.* Lula Carson Smith (1917–1967) U.S. novelist and short-story writer. Born in Columbus, Ga., she eventually settled in New York's Greenwich Village. A series of strokes suffered as a child left her partly paralyzed. She typically set her stories in small Southern communities and depicted the inner lives of lonely people. Her novels include *The Heart Is a Lonely Hunter* (1940; film, 1968), perhaps her finest work; *Reflections in a Golden Eye* (1941; film, 1967); *The Member of the Wedding* (1946; film, 1952); and *The Ballad of the Sad Café* (1951; film, 1991).

McCulloch vs. Maryland U.S. Supreme Court decision (1819) that affirmed the constitutional doctrine of Congress's implied powers. The case concerned the legitimacy of the authority of a newly created national bank to control the issuance of currency by the states, including Maryland. The decision established that Congress possesses not only the powers expressly conferred on it by the Constitution but also the authority appropriate to the utilization of such powers, in this case the creation of such a bank. This doctrine, drawn from the "elastic clause" of Article 1, became a powerful force in the steady growth of federal powers.

McDonald's Corp. Fast-food restaurant chain. Established in 1955 by Ray KROC, who soon began selling franchises to owner-managers, the chain expanded throughout the U.S. and abroad. Today it is the world's largest food-service retailer; by 2001 the company was serving nearly 45 million customers a day at more than 25,000 restaurants in 120 countries.

McEnroe, John (Patrick), Jr. (b.1959) U.S. tennis player. Born in Wiesbaden, Germany, in three consecutive years (1979–81) he won the U.S. Open, winning it a fourth time in 1984. He also won the Wimbledon singles in 1981, 1983, and 1984. Known for his temper tantrums and invective, he became the first player ejected from a Grand Slam match in nearly 30 years. He has become well known as a television tennis commentator.

McGill University Privately endowed but state-supported university in Montreal. Founded in 1821 through the gift of James McGill (1744–1813), it is known for its work in chemistry, medicine, and biology. It has additional faculties in a wide range of arts, humanities, and professional fields. Instruction is in English, though students may write examinations in French. Total enrollment is about 31,000.

McGovern, George S(tanley) (b.1922) U.S. politician. Born in Avon, S.D., he earned a doctorate in history and taught at Dakota Wesleyan Univ. Active in Democratic politics from 1948, he served in the U.S. House of Representatives (1957–61) and Senate (1963–81), where he held important hearings on hunger in the U.S. A leading opponent of the Vietnam War, he won the 1972 Democratic presidential nomination but lost to Pres. Richard NIXON by a large margin.

McGraw, John (Joseph) (1873–1934) U.S. baseball player and manager. Born in Truxton, N.Y., he was a star infielder for the Baltimore National League team; his .391 average in 1899 remains the highest ever for a third baseman. As manager of the New York Giants (1902–32), he led the team to 10 National League championships and three World Series titles (1905, 1921, 1922).

McGuffey, William Holmes (1800–1873) U.S. educator remembered chiefly for his series of elementary readers. Born near Claysville, Pa., McGuffey taught in the Ohio frontier schools and then at Miami Univ. (1826–36). The six "McGuffey's Readers," published 1836–57, were collections of didactic tales and excerpts from great books, intended to introduce young people to a wide variety of topics and practical matters. They became standard texts in nearly all states for the next 50 years and sold over 125 million copies.

McGwire, Mark (David) (b.1963) U.S. baseball player. Born in Pomona, Cal., he joined the Oakland Athletics in 1987 and quickly displayed the strength that would become his trademark. His 49 home runs that year set a rookie record, and he was named the American League's Rookie of the Year. In 1989 his batting guided Oakland to the World Series championship. Traded to the St. Louis Cardinals in 1997, he hit 58 homers. In 1998, racing Sammy SOSA to top Roger MARIS's season record of 61 home runs, McGwire achieved the new record with 70. He retired in 2001.

McKay, Claude (1890–1948) Jamaican-U.S. poet and novelist. He moved to the U.S. in 1912, and with the publication of the poetry volumes *Spring in New Hampshire* (1920) and *Harlem Shadows* (1922), he emerged as the first and most militant voice of the HARLEM RENAISSANCE. An advocate of full civil rights, in his writings he searched among the common folk for a distinctive black identity. His *Home to Harlem* (1928) was the most popular novel by an American black to that time.

McKim, Charles Follen (1847–1909) U.S. architect. Born in Chester Co., Pa., in 1879 he joined William Rutherford Mead (1846–1928) and Stanford WHITE to found McKim, Mead & White, the most successful U.S. architectural firm of its time. Until 1887 the firm excelled at SHINGLE-STYLE residences. It later championed the formal Renaissance tradition and its Classical antecedents. Among its widely admired successes are the Boston Public Library (1887), the

Columbia Univ. Library (1893), the Morgan Library (1903), and New York's magnificent Pennsylvania Railway Station (1904–10; demolished 1963).

McKinley, Mt. *Athabascan* **Denali** \də-ˈnä-lē\ Highest mountain in N. America. Located in the ALASKA RANGE, in S central Alaska, and in DENALI NATIONAL PARK, it rises to 20,320 ft (6,194 m). The N peak was first scaled in 1910, and in 1913 Hudson Stuck (1863–1920) and Harry Karstens (1878–1955) ascended the S peak, the true summit. It was named in honor of Pres. William MCKINLEY.

McKinley, William (1843–1901) 25th president of the U.S. (1897–1901). Born in Niles, Ohio, he served in the Civil War as an aide to Col. Rutherford B. HAYES, who later encouraged his political career. In the U.S. House of Representatives (1877–91), he favored protective tariffs and sponsored the McKinley Tariff of 1890. With the support of Mark HANNA, he was elected governor of Ohio (1892–96). In 1896 he won the Republican presidential nomination and the general election, defeating W. J. BRYAN. He was soon involved in events in Cuba that led to the SPANISH–AMERICAN WAR. At the war's end, he advocated U.S. dependency status for the Philippines and Puerto Rico. He again defeated Bryan by a large majority in 1900. In Buffalo, N.Y., on a tour to urge control of trusts and commercial reciprocity to boost foreign trade, issues neglected during the war, he was fatally shot by an anarchist, Leon Czolgosz. He was succeeded by Theodore ROOSEVELT.

William McKinley

McLuhan \mək-ˈlü-ən\, **(Herbert) Marshall** (1911–1980) Canadian communications theorist and educator. Born in Edmonton, Alberta, he taught from 1946 at the Univ. of Toronto. His aphorism "the medium is the message" summarized his view of the potent influence of television, computers, and other electronic media in shaping styles of thinking and thought. He regarded the printed book as fated to disappear. His highly influential works include *The Gutenberg Galaxy* (1962), *Understanding Media* (1964), and *The Medium Is the Massage* (*sic*; with Quentin Fiore, 1967).

McMahon Line Frontier between TIBET and ASSAM in British India, negotiated between Tibet and Britain in 1913–14, and named after the chief British negotiator, Sir Henry McMahon. China refused to recognize the boundary on the grounds that Tibet, being subordinate to China, could not make treaties. The 1962 Indo–Chinese conflict failed to resolve the border dispute; China still considers the boundary illegal.

McMurdo Sound Inlet of the SW Ross Sea, Antarctica. Lying at the edge of ROSS ICE SHELF, the 92-mi (148-km) channel has been a major center for Antarctic explorations. Discovered in 1841 by James C. Ross, it served as one of the main access routes to the Antarctic continent. Ross Island was the site of headquarters for R. F. SCOTT and Ernest SHACKLETON.

McMurtry, Larry (Jeff) (b.1936) U.S. novelist. Born on a ranch in Wichita Falls, Tex., he is noted for novels set in the American West. *The Last Picture Show* (1966; film, 1971) examines the isolation of small-town life. *Lonesome Dove* (1985, Pulitzer Prize) is part of an epic frontier series that also includes *Streets of Laredo* (1993). His other novels include *Horseman, Pass By* (1961; filmed as *Hud,* 1963) and *Terms of Endearment* (1975; film, 1983).

McPhee, John (Angus) (b.1931) U.S. journalist and nonfiction writer. Born in Princeton, N.J., he became a staff writer at *The New Yorker* in 1965 and has written for it since. His admired nonfiction covers a wide variety of topics, particularly science, the environment, and profiles of figures in sports. He has taught journalism at Princeton since 1975.

McPherson, Aimee Semple *orig.* Aimee Elizabeth Kennedy (1890–1944) U.S. (Canadian-born) Pentecostal evangelist. Born near Ingersoll, Ontario, she began preaching at 17. After serving as a missionary to China with her first husband, she came to the U.S., where she became an itinerant evangelist and healer. She settled in Los Angeles and founded the International Church of the Foursquare Gospel. For nearly 20 years she preached to large audiences at her Angelus Temple; she also built a radio station and established about 200 missions. In 1926 she disappeared mysteriously for five weeks; her tale of kidnapping on her reappearance was greeted with skepticism. She faced numerous trials for financial irregularities.

McQueen, (Terrence) Steve(n) (1930–1980) U.S. film actor. Born in Beech Grove, Ind., he won notice on Broadway in *A Hatful of Rain* (1955) and made his screen debut in *Somebody up There Likes Me* (1956), then starred in the television series *Wanted: Dead or Alive* (1958–61). He played the heroic loner in such films as *The Great Escape* (1963), *The Sand Pebbles* (1966), *Bullitt* (1968), *The Thomas Crown Affair* (1968), and *Papillon* (1973).

McVeigh \mək-ˈvā\, **Timothy (James)** (1968–2001) U.S. terrorist. Born in Pendleton, N.Y., he served in the army 1988–91, then worked at odd jobs. In 1995 he was arrested as a suspect in the OKLAHOMA CITY bombing, in which a massive homemade bomb in a rental truck destroyed the Alfred P. Murrah Federal Building, killing 168 people. He and Terry Nichols (b.1955) were found guilty in separate trials in 1997. McVeigh claimed that the building was targeted to avenge the deaths of more than 70 BRANCH DAVIDIANS at WACO, Texas, in 1993. He was executed in 2001.

mead Alcoholic beverage fermented from HONEY and water. It can be light or rich, sweet or dry, or even sparkling. Alcoholic drinks made from honey were common in ancient Europe, particularly in N Europe, where grapevines do not flourish. By the 14th cent., ale and sweetened wine were surpassing mead in popularity. Today mead is made as a sweet or dry wine of low alcoholic strength.

Mead, Lake Reservoir of the HOOVER DAM, on the Arizona–Nevada border. One of the largest man-made lakes in the world, it was formed by the damming of the COLORADO RIVER. Lake Mead is 115 mi (185 km) long and 1–10 mi (1.6–16 km) wide; it has a capacity of over 31 million acre ft (38 billion cubic m). Lake Mead National Recreation Area (established 1936) has an area of 2,338 sq mi (6,055 sq km) and extends 240 mi (386 km) along the river.

Mead, Margaret (1901–1978) U.S. anthropologist. Born in Philadelphia, she studied under Franz BOAS and Ruth BENEDICT at Columbia Univ., and did fieldwork in Samoa before completing her PhD (1929). The first and most famous of her 23 books, *Coming of Age in Samoa* (1928), presents evidence in support of cultural determinism with respect to the formation of personality. Her other books include *Sex and Temperament in Three Primitive Societies* (1935), *Male and Female* (1949), and *Culture and Commitment* (1970). Her observational methods and conclusions were posthumously questioned by other anthropologists. She became a prominent voice on such issues as women's rights and nuclear proliferation, and her great fame owed as much to her outspokenness as to the quality of her scientific work. She served in curatorial positions at the American Museum of Natural History for over 50 years.

Meade, George G(ordon) (1815–1872) U.S. general in the AMERICAN CIVIL WAR. Born in Cádiz, Spain, to U.S. parents, he graduated from West Point. As brigadier general of Pennsylvania volunteers, he fought at Bull Run, Antietam, and Chancellorsville. Three days before the Battle of GETTYSBURG, he replaced Joseph HOOKER as commander of the Army of the Potomac. At Gettysburg he repulsed the Confederate attack, turning the tide of the war, but was criticized for failing to pursue Robert E. LEE's forces. After 1864 he was subordinate to Gen. U. S. GRANT, whom he served loyally.

mealybug Any insect of the family Pseudococcidae (order Homoptera). Not a true bug, the mealybug is covered by a white sticky powder resembling cornmeal. The females, about 0.4 in. (1 cm) long, and "crawlers" (the active young) cluster along the veins and undersides of leaves, especially

M

of citrus trees and potted plants; the males are active two-winged fliers.

mean, median, and mode In mathematics, the three principal ways of designating the average value of a list of numbers. The arithmetic mean is found by adding the numbers and dividing the sum by the number of numbers in the list. The median is the middle value in a list ordered from smallest to largest. The mode is the most frequently occurring value on the list. There are other types of means. A geometric mean is found by multiplying all values in a list and then taking the root of that product equal to the number of values (e.g., the square root if there are two numbers). In STATISTICS, the mean of a random variable is its expected value—i. e., the theoretical long-run arithmetic mean of the outcomes of repeated trials, such as a large number of tosses of a die.

meander \mē-'an-dər\ Extreme U-bend in a stream, usually occurring in a series. Meanders form in stream-deposited sediments and may occur upstream of an obstruction, resulting in a gooseneck. A cutoff may form through the gooseneck and allow the former meander bend to be sealed off as an OXBOW LAKE. Silt deposits may eventually fill the lake to form a MARSH or a meander scar.

Meany, George (1894–1980) U.S. labor leader. Born in New York City, he joined the United Assn. of Plumbers and Steam Fitters in 1915. He was elected secretary-treasurer of the American Federation of Labor (AFL) in 1939 and president in 1952. He led the challenging merger of the AFL and CIO in 1955. Conservative and anticommunist, as president of the AFL-CIO (1955–79) he steered the U.S. labor movement away from radicalism. Feisty and often dictatorial, he expelled the TEAMSTERS UNION in 1957, and he lost the UNITED AUTOMOBILE WORKERS in 1967 after disputes with Walter REUTHER. Meany wielded considerable influence in the Democratic Party through the 1970s.

measles *or* **rubeola** \,rü-bē-'ō-lə, rü-'bē-ə-lə\ Highly contagious childhood VIRAL DISEASE. It initially resembles a severe cold with red eyes and fever; a blotchy rash and higher fever later develop. After recovery, patients have lifelong immunity. ANTIBIOTICS now prevent death from secondary infections but there is no drug for measles itself. A vaccine developed in the 1960s proved not to give permanent immunity and is too heat-sensitive for use in tropical areas. The worldwide incidence of measles continues to rise, causing at least a million deaths annually. See also RUBELLA.

meat Flesh and other edible parts of animals, particularly MAMMALS, used for food. Not only the MUSCLES and FAT but also such organs as the liver, kidney, and heart are eaten. Meat is valued as a complete-PROTEIN food. It digests slowly, largely because of the presence of fats. BEEF is the most widely consumed meat; PORK is second; mutton and lamb, goat, and venison are other common meats. The U.S. produces and consumes about a third of the world's meat, while much of the world's population eats little if any.

Mecca *Arabic* **al-Makkah** \,al-'mä-kə\ City (pop., 1991 est.: 630,000), W Saudi Arabia. The holiest city of ISLAM, it was the birthplace of the Prophet MUHAMMAD. In A.D. 622 he was forced to flee to MEDINA (see HEGIRA); he returned and captured the city in 630. It came under the control of the Egyptian Mamluks in 1269 and of the Ottoman Turks in 1517. King Abdulazīz IBN SAUD occupied it in 1925, and it became part of the Kingdom of Saudi Arabia. It is a religious center to which Muslims must attempt a pilgrimage (see HAJJ) once during a lifetime. It is the site of the Al-Haram Mosque, which contains the KAABA.

mechanical efficiency See EFFICIENCY

mechanical energy Sum of a system's KINETIC ENERGY (KE) and POTENTIAL ENERGY (PE). Mechanical energy is constant in a system that experiences no dissipative forces such as FRICTION or air resistance. For example, a swinging pendulum that experiences only GRAVITATION has greatest KE and least PE at its lowest point, where its speed is greatest and its height least. It has least KE and greatest PE at the extremities of its swing, where its speed is zero and its height is greatest. As it moves, energy passes continuously between the two forms.

mechanical engineering Branch of ENGINEERING concerned with the design, manufacture, installation, and oper-

ation of ENGINES, MACHINES, and manufacturing processes. It involves application of the principles of DYNAMICS, THERMODYNAMICS and heat transfer, FLUID MECHANICS, MATERIALS SCIENCE, ELECTRONICS, and MATHEMATICS. It is concerned with MACHINE TOOLS, motor vehicles, textile machinery, metalworking machines, welding, refrigerators, agricultural machinery, and many other machines and processes essential to an industrial economy.

mechanics Science of the action of FORCES on material bodies. Beginning with NEWTON'S LAWS OF MOTION in the 17th cent., the theory has been modified and expanded by the theories of QUANTUM MECHANICS and RELATIVITY. Newton's theory ("classical mechanics") accurately represented the effects of forces under all conditions known in his time. It consists of statics, the study of EQUILIBRIUM, and DYNAMICS, the study of MOTION caused by forces. Though classical mechanics fails on the scale of ATOMS and molecules, it remains the framework for much of modern science and technology.

mechanism Means of transmitting and modifying motion in a MACHINE or an assembly of mechanical parts. The chief characteristic of the mechanism of a machine is that the parts can move only in certain ways in relation to each other. The mechanism of a machine can always be analyzed as a group of simple basic mechanisms, each of which contains members that transmit motion from one moving link to another, generally in one of three ways: by a wrapping connector such as a CHAIN DRIVE or belt drive, by direct contact as in a CAM or GEAR, or by a pin-connected LINKAGE.

Mecherino See Domenico BECCAFUMI

medal Piece of metal struck with a design to commemorate a person, place, or event. Medals can range in size and shape from large medallions to small plaques. Most medals are made of gold, silver, bronze, or lead, the precious metals being used for the finer productions. The art of the medalist began in the mid-15th cent. with bronze medals of Italian Renaissance rulers and humanists.

Medan \mä-'dän\ City (pop., 1995: 1,909,000), NE Sumatra, Indonesia. After the introduction of tobacco plantations in 1873, Medan became the commercial center of an agricultural region where cash crops, including tobacco and rubber, were raised for export. It was occupied by the Japanese during World War II. It is the seat of the Univ. of N. Sumatra and the Islamic Univ. of N. Sumatra.

Medawar \'me-də-wər\, **Peter B(rian)** (*later* **Sir Peter**) (1915–1987) British (Brazilian-born) zoologist. His finding (1953) that adult animals injected with foreign cells early in life accept skin grafts from the original donor or its twin lent support to Macfarlane BURNET's hypothesis that, during and just after birth, cells learn to distinguish "own" from "foreign." He proved that ANTIGENS "leak" between twin embryos' yolk sacs, and showed with mice that each cell contains genetic antigens important to immunity. His work deflected IMMUNOLOGY from dealing with the fully developed immunity mechanism to attempting to alter the mechanism itself (e.g., suppression of transplant rejection). He and Burnet shared a 1960 Nobel Prize.

Medea \mə-'dē-ə\ In GREEK MYTHOLOGY, the daughter of King Aeetes of Colchis. After helping JASON to obtain the Golden Fleece from her father, the two were married. In Iolcos, she killed the king who had deprived Jason of his inheritance. In EURIPIDES' tragedy *Medea*, Jason later deserts her for the daughter of King Creon, and Medea takes revenge by killing Creon, his daughter, and her own two children by Jason.

Médecins Sans Frontières See DOCTORS WITHOUT BORDERS

Medellín \,mā-thā-'yēn, *Engl* ,mā-də-'lēn\ City (pop., 1999: 1,957,000), NW Colombia. It is the nation's second-largest city. Founded in 1675 as a mining town, it grew rapidly after the completion of the PANAMA CANAL and the arrival of the railroad in 1914. It is now noted for its textile mills, clothing factories, and steel mills. It was a major center for the illegal cocaine trade from the 1970s until 1993.

Med fly See MEDITERRANEAN FRUIT FLY

Media \'mē-dē-ə\ Ancient country, S Asia. It was situated in modern NW Iran and occupied by the Medes, an Iranian people. In 625 B.C. Cyaxares united the area's tribes into a kingdom. In 614 B.C. he captured ASHUR; he later defeated ASSYRIA and seized territory in Iran, N Assyria, and Armenia. In 550 B.C. Media became part of the new ACHAEMENIAN empire under Persia's CYRUS THE GREAT. ALEXANDER THE GREAT occupied it in 330 B.C. Later S Media passed to the SELEUCIDS; N Media passed to Parthia, Armenia, and Rome. In 226 B.C. the whole of Media passed to the SASANIANS.

median See MEAN, MEDIAN, AND MODE

mediation In law, a nonbinding intervention between parties to promote resolution of a grievance, reconciliation, settlement, or compromise. In many industrialized nations, the government provides mediation services in order to protect the public interest. In the U.S., the National Mediation Board functions in this capacity. Mediation is commonly used to resolve labor disputes and international conflicts. See also ARBITRATION.

medical examiner See CORONER

medical imaging See DIAGNOSTIC IMAGING

Medicare and Medicaid U.S. government programs in effect since 1966. Medicare covers most people 65 or older and those with long-term disabilities. Part A, a hospital insurance plan, also pays for home health visits and hospice care. Part B, a supplementary plan, pays for doctors' services, tests, and other services. Requirements and benefits are complex. Patients pay deductibles and copayments. Medicaid, a joint federal-state program, covers low-income people under age 65 and those who have exhausted Medicare benefits. It pays for hospital care, doctors' services, nursing-home care, home health services, family planning, and screening. Participating states must offer Medicaid to all persons on public assistance but decide their own eligibility guidelines. Many physicians refuse to treat Medicaid patients because of low reimbursement levels.

Medici \'me-də-,chē\, **Cosimo de'** *known as* **Cosimo the Elder** (1389–1464) Founder of one of the main lines of the MEDICI FAMILY. Cosimo represented his father's bank and handled papal finances, becoming the wealthiest man of his time. Another leading family, the Albizzi, had him imprisoned (1433) and tried to assassinate him, but a year later the Medici regained power in Florence and Cosimo triumphantly returned. An alliance with the SFORZA FAMILY of Milan provided him with troops to crush a coup d'état in 1458, after which he created a Senate composed of 100 loyal supporters (the Cento). He was a patron of scholarship and the arts, including such figures as DONATELLO and Filippo BRUNELLESCHI.

Medici, Cosimo I de' (1519–1574) Second duke of Florence (1537–74) and first grand duke of Tuscany (1569–74). Of the powerful MEDICI FAMILY, he became head of the Florentine republic in 1537. Seeking to expand his power, he attacked Siena in 1554 and brought nearly all of Tuscany under his control. He used his despotic power to improve the government's efficiency and to sponsor artistic projects. Far advanced for the time as an administrator, he united all public services into one building, the UFFIZI ("Offices"). He promoted the talents of such artists as Il BRONZINO, sponsored excavations of Etruscan sites, and established the Florentine Academy for linguistic studies. In 1569 he was given the title grand duke of Tuscany.

Medici, Lorenzo de' *known as* **Lorenzo the Magnificent** (1449–1492) Florentine statesman and patron of arts and letters. The grandson of Cosimo de' MEDICI, he was the most brilliant of the MEDICI FAMILY. He ruled FLORENCE with his brother Giuliano from 1469. Giuliano was assassinated in 1478 by the Pazzi, a leading Florentine banking family in league with SIXTUS IV and the king of Naples. Lorenzo's direct appeal to the king allowed him to regain power in

Lorenzo de' Medici Bust by Andrea del Verrocchio, c.1485

Florence as sole ruler. His 13-year-old son Giovanni was created a cardinal and later became pope as LEO X. Lorenzo used the Medici riches to patronize many artists, including Sandro BOTTICELLI, LEONARDO DA VINCI, and MICHELANGELO, and he remains perhaps the most famous patron of all time. His policies bankrupted the Medici bank, but Medici political power remained strong in Florence and Tuscany.

Medici family Italian bourgeois family that ruled Florence and later Tuscany from about 1430 to 1737. Noted for its often tyrannical rulers and its beneficent patrons of the arts, it also provided the church with four popes (LEO X, CLEMENT VII, Pius IV, and Leo XI) and married into the royal families of Europe, notably in France. The effective founder of the family was Giovanni di Bicci de' Medici (1360–1429), a merchant who amassed great wealth in trade and was the virtual ruler of Florence 1421–29. From his two sons derived the major branches of the family. The so-called elder branch began with Cosimo de' MEDICI. His grandson, Lorenzo de' MEDICI greatly expanded the family's power; his great-granddaughter became CATHERINE DE MÉDICIS. Another of Cosimo's grandsons, Giulio, became pope as Clement VII. The so-called younger branch of the family began with Giovanni's younger son Lorenzo whose son married into the powerful SFORZA FAMILY; their son Giovanni de' Medici (1498–1526) became a noted general. His son Cosimo I de' MEDICI became duke of Florence, and the grandfather of MARIE DE MÉDICIS. Cosimo I's grandson Cosimo II (1590–1621) gave up the family practice of banking and commerce, and Tuscany's power gradually declined. The childless Gian Gastone de' Medici (1671–1737) was the last grand duke of Tuscany.

medicine Set of scientific fields related to prevention, diagnosis, and treatment of disease and maintenance of health, practiced in doctors' offices, HEALTH-MAINTENANCE-ORGANIZATION facilities, HOSPITALS, and clinics. In addition to FAMILY PRACTICE, internal medicine, and specialties for specific body systems, it includes research, PUBLIC HEALTH, EPIDEMIOLOGY, and PHARMACOLOGY. Each country sets its own requirements for medical degrees and licenses. Medical boards and councils set standards and oversee medical education. Boards of certification have stringent requirements for physicians seeking to practice a specialty and stress continuing education.

Medicine Bow Mountains NW section of the Front Range, in the central ROCKY MTNS. Averaging a height of 10,000 ft (3,000 m), the mountains run southeast for about 100 mi (160 km) from Medicine Bow, Wyo., to Cameron Pass, Col., just northwest of Rocky Mtn. National Park. The highest summit, Medicine Bow Peak, reaches 12,014 ft (3,662 m).

medicine man Priestly healer or SHAMAN, especially among the American Indians. The medicine man (often a woman in some societies) commonly carries a kit of objects such as feathers, stones, or hallucinogenic plants that have magical associations. The work of healing often involves the extraction—by sucking, pulling, or other means—of offending substances from the patient's body. Singing, recitation of myths, and other ceremonies often accompany the healing rite.

Médicis, Catherine de See CATHERINE DE MÉDICIS

Médicis, Marie de See MARIE DE MÉDICIS

Medina *Arabic* **Al-Madinah** \,al-mȧ-'dē-nə\ *ancient* Yathrib. City (pop., 1991: 400,000), W Saudi Arabia, north of MECCA. It developed from an oasis settled by Jews around A.D. 135. In 622 MUHAMMAD fled from Mecca to Medina (see HEGIRA). It served as capital of the Islamic state until 661. It was held chiefly by the Ottoman Turks from 1517 until World War I, and in 1925 it fell to Abdulaziz IBN SAUD. A sacred city of ISLAM, it is second only to Mecca as a place of Muslim pilgrimage; the Prophet's Mosque contains the tomb of MUHAMMAD.

meditation Private religious devotion or mental exercise, in which techniques of concentration and contemplation are used to reach a heightened level of spiritual awareness. The practice has existed in all religions since ancient times. In Hinduism it has been systematized in the school of YOGA. One aspect of Yoga gave rise to a school of its own among the Buddhists, becoming the basis of ZEN. In many reli-

gions, meditation involves verbal or mental repetition of a single syllable, word, or text (e.g., a MANTRA). MANDALAS, PRAYER WHEELS, or ROSARIES can be useful in focusing concentration. Movements such as TRANSCENDENTAL MEDITATION teach meditation techniques outside a religious context.

Mediterranean fruit fly *or* **Med fly** FRUIT FLY (*Ceratitis capitata*) proven to be particularly destructive to citrus crops, at great economic cost. The Med fly lays up to 500 eggs in citrus fruits (except lemons and sour limes), and the larvae tunnel into the fruit, making it unfit for human consumption.

Mediterranean Sea Inland sea enclosed by Europe, Africa, and Asia. It measures as much as 2,300 mi (3,700 km) east–west, and occupies an area of about 970,000 sq mi (2,512,000 sq km). It has a maximum depth of 16,896 ft (5150 m). In the west the Strait of GIBRALTAR connects the Mediterranean with the Atlantic Ocean. In the northeast the Sea of MARMARA, the DARDANELLES, and the BOSPORUS link it with the BLACK SEA. The SUEZ CANAL connects it with the RED SEA in the southeast. Its largest islands are MAJORCA, CORSICA, SARDINIA, SICILY, CRETE, CYPRUS, and RHODES. The RHÔNE, PO, and NILE rivers form its only large deltas.

Medusa In GREEK MYTHOLOGY, one of the monsters known as GORGONS. Anyone who looked directly at Medusa turned to stone. PERSEUS, looking only at her reflection in a shield given to him by ATHENA, killed her by cutting off her head. Athena later placed the head in her shield; according to another account, Perseus buried it in the marketplace of ARGOS.

medusa \mi-'dü-sə\ In zoology, one of the two principal CNIDARIAN body forms; the typical form of the JELLYFISH. Its name derives from its tentacles, resembling the snakes borne by MEDUSA in place of hair. The medusoid body is bell- or umbrella-shaped. Hanging downward from the center is a stalklike structure, the manubrium, bearing the mouth at its tip. The medusa moves by rhythmic muscular contractions of the bell, providing a slow propulsive action against the water. The other principal cnidarian body type is the POLYP.

meerkat Certain carnivore species of the CIVET family (Viverridae), specifically the suricate and various MONGOOSE species (in the genera *Mungos, Cynictis,* and others). The colonial, burrowing suricate *(Suricata suricatta),* or slender-tailed meerkat, found in S. Africa, differs from mongooses in having four (rather than five) toes on each foot. The suricate grows to a total length of 17–24 in. (43–60 cm). It is diurnal and is easily tamed as a pet.

megalith Huge, often undressed stone used in various types of NEOLITHIC PERIOD and Early BRONZE AGE monuments. The most ancient form of megalithic construction may be the dolmen, a type of burial chamber consisting of several upright supports and a flat roofing slab. Another form is the menhir, a simple upright stone usually placed with others to form a circle, as at STONEHENGE and Avebury in England, or a straight alignment, as at Carnac in France. The meaning of megalithic monuments remains largely unknown, but all share features suggesting that their creators sought to impose a human design on the landscape and imbue it with cultural symbols. See also ROCK ART.

Megalópolis \ˌme-gä-'lö-pȯ-lēs\ Ancient city, central Peloponnese, Greece. It was founded in 371–368 B.C. by EPAMINONDAS of THEBES as the seat of the ARCADIAN LEAGUE. Attacked several times by SPARTA, it joined the ACHAEAN LEAGUE in 234 B.C. It was plundered by Sparta in 223 B.C., and by the 2nd cent A.D. it lay in ruins.

Mégara \'me-gə-rə\ Port city (pop., 1991: 26,000), Greece. Situated west of Athens, it served as the capital of ancient Megaris. A maritime power, by the 7th cent. B.C. it had established colonies in Sicily, Chalcedon, Byzantium, Bithynia, and Crimea. During the PELOPONNESIAN WAR (431–404 B.C.), it was subjugated by Athens and forced into financial ruin. In the 4th cent. A.D. it recovered, but in 1500 it was depopulated by the Venetians.

Megiddo \mi-'gi-dō\ City, ancient Palestine, in present-day N Israel. It occupied a strategic location at the crossing of military and trade routes; it was also famous as a battlefield

and is thought to be the biblical ARMAGEDDON. The first town was built early in the 4th millennium B.C. It was captured by THUTMOSE III about 1468 B.C. King SOLOMON later rebuilt it as a military center. British general E. H. H. ALLENBY defeated the Turks near the site in 1918.

Mehmed II \me-'met\ (1432–1481) Ottoman sultan. His father, Murad II, abdicated in his favor when Mehmed was 12, but reclaimed the throne two years later after a Christian Crusade. Mehmed regained the throne when his father died (1451). In 1453 he captured Constantinople; he restored its grandeur, and in fifty years it was Europe's largest city. In the next 25 years he conquered the Balkans. Under his reign, criminal and civil laws were codified; he collected a library of Greek and Latin works and had eight colleges built.

Meier \'mī-ər\, **Richard (Alan)** (b.1934) U.S. architect. Born in Newark, N.J., Meier worked with the firm of Skidmore, Owings & Merrill and with Marcel BREUER. The crisp whiteness of his houses contrasts sharply with the natural setting; the Douglas House, Harbor Springs, Mich. (1973), is a dramatically sited example. The Getty Center in Los Angeles (1992–97), with its terraced gardens, is a resplendent acropolis in travertine stone. Meier received the 1984 Pritzker Architecture Prize.

Meiji Constitution \'mā-jē\ Constitution of Japan 1890–1947. After the MEIJI RESTORATION, Japan's leaders wanted a constitution that would define Japan as a modern nation deserving of Western respect while preserving their own power. The resultant document, drafted by ITO HIROBUMI, called for a bicameral parliament (the Diet) with an elected lower house and a prime minister and cabinet appointed by the emperor. A privy council composed of the Meiji leaders advised the emperor and wielded actual power. Voting restrictions, which limited the electorate to about 5% of the adult male population, were loosened over the next 25 years, resulting in universal male suffrage. Political parties enjoyed limited power in the 1920s, but in the 1930s the military exerted control without violating the constitution. After World War II, a U.S.-approved constitution (see OCCUPATION) giving power to the people replaced the Meiji Constitution.

Meiji emperor *orig.* Mutsuhito (1852–1912) Emperor of Japan (1867–1912). With the end of the TOKUGAWA SHOGUNATE, the imperial throne came to the forefront of the political scene after centuries of being overshadowed by shogunal rule. The Meiji emperor believed in the need to modernize Japan along Western lines; a new school system was introduced, and the MEIJI CONSTITUTION was promulgated. His reign also saw the annexation of Taiwan after the SINO–JAPANESE WAR (1894–95), the annexation of Korea (1910), and Japan's defeat of Russia in the RUSSO–JAPANESE WAR (1904–5).

Meiji period (1868–1912) Period in Japanese history corresponding to the reign of the MEIJI EMPEROR. It was a time of rapid modernization and westernization. Feudal domains were replaced with prefectures; DAIMYO and SAMURAI were relieved of their special privileges. A national army was formed, universal conscription was enacted, and a new agricultural tax was instituted to finance the new government. Eager to encourage economic growth, the government aided the textile industry, established railways and shipping lines, and founded an ironworks. Education was also reformed, and compulsory coeducational elementary schools were introduced. By 1912 the goals of the MEIJI RESTORATION had been largely accomplished: the unequal treaties with Western powers had been revised, the country was developing well economically, and its military power had won the respect of the West.

Meiji Restoration Overthrow of Japan's TOKUGAWA SHOGUNATE and restoration to power of the MEIJI EMPEROR in 1868. In the 19th cent., the shogunate's policy of isolation made Japanese feudal leaders aware of Japan's vulnerability to superior Western firepower. After the visit of Matthew PERRY, the country was forced to sign a series of unequal treaties giving Western nations special privileges in Japan. In response, young SAMURAI hostile to the Tokugawa regime took up arms against the government. In January 1868 they announced the restoration of the emperor to power. The revolutionaries had the emperor issue the CHARTER OATH, which promised an end to feudal class restrictions and a search for knowledge that could transform Japan into a "rich country with a strong military." The Restoration ushered in the MEIJI PERIOD of rapid modernization.

meiosis \mī-'ō-səs\ *or* **reduction division** Division of a gamete-producing cell in which the NUCLEUS splits twice, resulting in four sex cells (gametes, or EGGS and SPERM), each possessing half the number of CHROMOSOMES of the original cell. Meiosis is characteristic of organisms that reproduce sexually and have a diploid (paired) set of nuclear chromosomes. The chromosomes in each pair consist of joined sister strands (chromatids). Meiosis begins as the paired chromosomes line up along the midline of the cell. The chromosome pairs exchange genetic material by the process of crossing-over. The pairs then separate and are pulled to opposite ends of the cell, which pinches in to form two daughter cells, each containing half the usual number of double-stranded chromosomes. In the second round of meiotic division, the double-stranded chromosomes of each daughter cell are pulled apart into their separate chromatids, resulting in four haploid gametes from the initial cell. When two gametes unite during FERTILIZATION, each contributes its haploid set of chromosomes to the new individual, restoring the diploid number. See also MITOSIS.

Meïr \mā-'ir\ (fl.2nd cent. A.D.) Rabbi and scholar of Palestine. He fled Palestine during the persecutions that followed the BAR KOKHBA revolt in A.D. 132–35, but returned to help reestablish the SANHEDRIN. Its patriarch eventually threatened him with excommunication over a question of protocol, and he left for Asia Minor, where he had been born. He is cited repeatedly in the Talmud and is remembered as the greatest of the *tannaim*, a group of masters of the Jewish oral law. Legends of his miraculous powers sprang up during the Middle Ages.

Meir \me-'ir\, **Golda** *orig.* Goldie Mabovitch *later* Goldie Myerson (1898–1978) U.S.-Israeli (Ukrainian-born) stateswoman, fourth prime minister of Israel (1969–74). Her family emigrated to Milwaukee in 1906, where she became a leader of the local Zionist party. In 1921 she and her husband emigrated to Palestine. She was a forceful negotiator with British authorities during World War II. A signer of Israel's independence declaration in 1948, she served in the Knesset 1949–74 and was foreign minister 1956–66. As prime minister, she sought diplomatic solutions to ease the region's tensions; unable to prevent the Yom Kippur War of 1973 (see ARAB–ISRAELI WARS), she resigned six months later.

Meissen porcelain \'mī-s°n\ German hard-paste, or true, PORCELAIN produced at the Meissen factory, near Dresden, from 1710 until the present day. The first successfully produced true porcelain in Europe, it dominated the style of European porcelain until about 1756. The high point of the Meissen factory was reached after 1731 with the modeling of J. J. Kändler (1706–1775); its onion pattern (c.1739) was widely copied.

meistersinger \'mī-stər-,siŋ-ər, 'mī-stər-,ziŋ-ər\ (German: "master singer") Member of a German guild whose function was to continue the tradition of the minnesingers, poet-musicians of the 12th–14th cent. In the 14th–16th cent., these amateur guilds spread throughout Germany until most towns had one. The guilds held monthly singing contests. Concerned with fostering morality and religious belief, they were instrumental in promulgating the Protestant message during the REFORMATION, though their music lacks distinction.

Meitner \'mīt-nər\, **Lise** (1878–1968) German physicist. Working at Berlin's Kaiser Wilhelm Institute (1912–38), she and Otto HAHN isolated the radioactive isotope protactinium-231; later, with Fritz Strassmann (1902–1980), they investigated the products of neutron bombardment of URANIUM. In 1938 she left Germany for Sweden. After Hahn and Strassmann showed that barium appears in neutron-bombarded uranium, she and her nephew Otto Frisch (1904–1979) explained the physical characteristics of this division, which they named FISSION. Element 109, meitnerium, is named in her honor.

Mekong River \'mā-'kóŋ\ *Chinese* **Lancang Jiang** *or* **Lan-Ts'ang Chiang** \'län-'tsäŋ-'jē-'äŋ\ Longest river, S.E. Asia. Rising in E Tibet, it flows south and forms part of the border between Myanmar and Laos, as well as between Laos and Thailand, then runs through Laos and Cambodia before entering the S. CHINA SEA south of HO CHI MINH CITY in Vietnam after a course of 2,700 mi (4,350 km). VIENTIANE and PHNOM PENH stand on its banks. In 1957 the U.N. initiated the Mekong River Development Project to harness the river for hydroelectricity and irrigation.

Melanchthon \mə-'laŋk-thən, *German* mä-'läŋk-tón\, **Philipp** *orig.* Philipp Schwartzerd (1497–1560) German Protestant reformer. He was named professor of Greek at Wittenberg in 1518. A friend and defender of Martin LUTHER, he wrote *Loci communes* (1521), the first systematic treatment of the principles of the REFORMATION, as well as the AUGSBURG CONFESSION (1530). He reorganized Germany's educational system, founding and reforming several of its universities. His willingness to compromise with Catholics on theological issues in his later years became controversial.

Melanesia \,me-lə-'nē-zhə\ Collective name for the islands in the SW Pacific Ocean, northeast of Australia and south of the equator. A subdivision of OCEANIA, it includes NEW GUINEA, ADMIRALTY ISLANDS, BISMARCK and Louisiade archipelagoes, SOLOMON ISLANDS, Santa Cruz Islands, NEW CALEDONIA and the Loyalty Islands, VANUATU, FIJI, NORFOLK ISLAND, and numerous others. The PAPUANS have inhabited the area for 40,000 years. Other, seafaring peoples with an AUSTRONESIAN LANGUAGE and a S. E. Asian cultural tradition settled in the area about 3,500 years ago.

melanin \'me-lə-nən\ Any of several organic compounds, dark biological PIGMENTS that give coloration (shades of yellow to brown) to skin, hair, feathers, scales, eyes, and some internal tissues. In humans, melanins help protect the skin against the damaging effects of ULTRAVIOLET RADIATION, but MELANOMA may arise from cells that produce it. The amount in the skin depends on both genetic and environmental factors. Melanin is produced from the AMINO ACID tyrosine; albinos lack the ENZYME that catalyzes that reaction (see ALBINISM).

melanism, industrial See INDUSTRIAL MELANISM

melanoma \,me-lə-'nō-mə\ Dark-colored tumor most often derived from MELANIN-pigmented SKIN cells. A melanoma may or may not be malignant. It may develop from irritation of a MOLE or WART. Melanomas are prone to metastasize (see CANCER) and are associated with the highest death rate of any skin cancer. Removal, together with a collar of surrounding healthy skin, cures melanoma if done early. Melanomas are very rare in persons with dark skin.

melatonin \,me-lə-'tō-nən\ Only HORMONE secreted by the PINEAL GLAND of most vertebrates. It appears to be important in regulating sleeping cycles; more is produced at night, and test subjects injected with it become sleepy. Melatonin may be involved in SEASONAL AFFECTIVE DISORDER. It also appears to regulate sexual maturation. In mammals other than humans, melatonin may act as a cue to breeding and mating in season.

Melbourne \'mel-bərn\ City (pop., 1996: 2,865,000), SE Australia. The area was discovered by Europeans in 1802. The first settlement was founded in 1835 by settlers from Tasmania, and in 1837 it was named for the British prime minister, Lord MELBOURNE. Made the capital of Victoria in 1851, it grew rapidly with the gold rush of the early 1850s. It served as the first capital of the Australian commonwealth 1901–27, until CANBERRA became the new capital. Second in size to SYDNEY, it is an industrial, commercial, and financial center, and is the seat of several universities, including the Univ. of Melbourne.

Melbourne (of Kilmore), Viscount *orig.* **William Lamb** (1779–1848) British prime minister (1834, 1835–41). Though a Whig, he served in Tory governments as chief secretary for Ireland (1827–28) and advocated political rights for Roman Catholics. As prime minister (1834), he gained the support of Whigs and moderate Tories. In his second administration (1835–41), he became the young Queen VICTORIA's valued chief political adviser. His firm stand in foreign policy averted war with France over Syria (1840). His wife, Lady Caroline Lamb (1785–1828), was a minor novelist, famous for her affair with Lord BYRON in 1812–13.

Melchizedek \mel-'ki-zə-ˌdek\ Canaanite king and priest. In the Book of Genesis, Abraham receives bread and wine from Melchizedek, king of Salem (probably another name for Jerusalem), who blesses him in the name of "God Most High." St. PAUL's Epistle to the Hebrews treats Melchizedek as a foreshadowing of Christ.

Méliès \māl-'yes\, **Georges** (1861–1938) French filmmaker. He was a professional magician and manager-director of the Théâtre Robert-Houdin in Paris when he saw the first movies made by the LUMIÈRE brothers in 1895. In his film experiments he exploited the basic camera tricks of slow motion, dissolve, and fade-out. From 1899 to 1912 he made over 400 films, which combined illusion, comic burlesque, and pantomime in fantasy productions, including *A Trip to the Moon* (1902). He also filmed reconstructed news events as an early form of newsreel.

Melilla \mə-'lē-yä\ Spanish enclave (pop. 1998 est.: 60,000), N. Africa. A military station and seaport, it constitutes with CEUTA an autonomous community of Spain. Located on Morocco's N coast, it was successively colonized by the Phoenicians, Greeks, and Romans. It fell to Spain in 1497, and remained Spanish despite a long history of siege. It was the first Spanish town to rise against the Popular Front government in 1936, helping to precipitate the SPANISH CIVIL WAR.

Mellon, Andrew W(illiam) (1855–1937) U.S. financier. Born in Pittsburgh, he entered his father's banking house and built up a financial empire by supplying capital for corporations to expand in fields such as aluminum, steel, and oil. He helped found ALCOA and the GULF OIL CORP., and he joined H. C. FRICK to found Union Steel Co. and Union Trust Co. As secretary of the Treasury (1921–32), he persuaded Congress to lower taxes in order to encourage business expansion. He was praised for the economic boom of the 1920s but criticized during the GREAT DEPRESSION. A noted art collector and philanthropist, Mellon donated an extensive art collection and $15 million to establish the NATIONAL GALLERY OF ART.

melodrama Sentimental drama marked by extravagant theatricality. The term originally (in the 18th cent.) referred to a drama with a musical background, but the use of background music soon ended. Later melodramas usually have improbable plots that feature such stock characters as the noble hero, the long-suffering heroine, and the hardhearted villain. Written by such playwrights as Dion BOUCICAULT, melodramas were popular in Europe and the U.S. during the 19th cent. They often featured spectacular events such as shipwrecks, battles, fires, earthquakes, and horse races. Melodrama became popular in silent film, in which live musical accompaniment again became standard.

melody Rhythmic succession of single tones organized as an aesthetic whole. The melody is often the highest line in a musical composition. Melodies may suggest their own HARMONY or COUNTERPOINT. As fundamental as RHYTHM AND METER (and more so than harmony), melody is common to all musical cultures.

melon Any of the seven groups of *Cucumis melo,* a trailing vine grown for its edible, sweet, musky-scented fruit. Members of the horticulturally diverse GOURD family, melons are frost-tender annuals native to central Asia but widely cultivated worldwide. They have soft, hairy, trailing stems, lobed leaves, yellow flowers, and large flat seeds. The fruits of the numerous cultivated varieties differ greatly in size, shape, surface texture, flesh color, flavor, and weight. Examples include cantaloupe, honeydew, and casaba. See also WATERMELON.

melting point Temperature at which the solid and liquid states of a pure substance can exist in EQUILIBRIUM. As HEAT is applied to a solid, its temperature increases until it reaches the melting point. At this temperature, additional heat converts the solid into a liquid without a change in temperature. The melting point of solid water (ice) is 32°F (0°C). Though the melting point is usually the same as the FREEZING POINT of the corresponding liquid, they may differ because a liquid may freeze into different crystal systems, or impurities may lower the freezing point.

Melville, Herman *orig.* Herman Melvill (1819–1891) U.S. writer. Born to a wealthy New York family that suffered great financial losses, Melville began a period of wanderings at sea in 1839. In 1841 he sailed on a whaler bound for the South Seas; the next year he jumped ship in the Marquesas Islands. His adventures in Polynesia were the basis of his successful first novels, *Typee* (1846) and *Omoo* (1847). *Moby-Dick* (1851), his masterpiece, is both an intense whaling narrative and a symbolic examination of the problems and possibilities of American democracy; it brought him neither acclaim nor reward when published. Increasingly reclusive and despairing, he wrote the unpopular *Pierre* (1852), followed by *Israel Potter* (1855), *The Confidence-Man* (1857), and magazine stories, including "Bartleby the Scrivener" (1853) and "Benito Cereno" (1855). After 1857 he wrote verse. He returned to prose for his last work, the novel *Billy Budd, Foretopman,* which remained unpublished until 1924. Neglected for much of his career, Melville came to be regarded by modern critics as one of the greatest U.S. writers.

Melville Island Island in the Timor Sea, off the coast of Australia. It is 80 miles (130 km) long and 55 mi (88 km) wide. It was sighted by the Dutch in 1644; the British built Ft. Dundas there in 1824. It is one of the few areas of Australia still occupied by AUSTRALIAN ABORIGINES. In 1978 the island's ownership passed from the Australian government to the Tiwi Land Council.

membrane In biology, the thin layer that forms the outer boundary of a living CELL or of an internal cell compartment. The outer boundary is the plasma membrane, and the compartments enclosed by internal membranes are called organelles. Biological membranes have a dual function: separation of vital but incompatible metabolic processes conducted in the organelles; and passage of nutrients, wastes, and metabolic products between organelles and between the cell and the outside environment. See also CYTOPLASM, EUKARYOTE.

Memling \'mem-liŋ\, **Hans** *or* **Hans Memlinc** \'mem-liŋk\ (c.1430/40–1494) Flemish painter. He settled in Bruges in 1465 and established a large workshop that made him one of the city's wealthiest citizens. Though somewhat derivative of the works of contemporary Flemish painters, his art has great charm and a distinctive character. Memling's religious paintings and portraits of wealthy patrons (e.g., *Tommaso Portinari and His Wife,* c.1468) remain enormously popular.

Memnon In GREEK MYTHOLOGY, a king of the Ethiopians. The son of Eos (Dawn), he fought bravely for his uncle PRIAM against the Greeks, and was slain by ACHILLES; ZEUS granted him immortality. His companions, changed into birds, came every year to fight and lament over his grave. In Egypt his name was connected with the colossal stone statues of AMENHOTEP III near THEBES; the harplike sounds these statues emitted when touched by the rays of the rising sun were believed to be the voice of Memnon responding to the greeting of Eos.

Memorial Day *or* **Decoration Day** U.S. holiday. Originally held in commemoration of soldiers killed in the AMERICAN CIVIL WAR (1868), its observance later extended to all U.S. war dead. Most states conform to the federal practice of observing it on the last Monday in May, but some retain the traditional day of celebration, May 30. National observance is marked by the placing of a wreath on the Tomb of the Unknowns in Arlington National Cemetery.

memory In DIGITAL COMPUTERS, a physical device used to store such information as data or programs on a temporary or permanent basis. Most digital computer systems have two types of memory, the main memory and one or more auxiliary storage units. The main memory is usually a high-speed RAM. Auxiliary storage units include HARD DISKS, FLOPPY DISKS, and magnetic tape drives. Other forms of memory include ROM and optical storage media such as VIDEODISCS and COMPACT DISCS (see CD-ROM).

memory Power or process of recalling or reproducing what has been learned or experienced. Research indicates that the ability to retain information is fairly uniform among normal individuals; what differs is the degree to which persons learn or take account of something to begin with and the kind and amount of detail that is retained. Attention, MOTIVATION, and especially ASSOCIATION facilitate this process. Visual images are generally better remembered than are other forms of sense-data. Memory prodigies, or people with "photographic" or "eidetic" memories, often draw heavily on visual associations, including mnemonics. Various models of memory have been proposed, from the Enlightenment notion of impressions made on brain tissues (restyled as "memory molecules" or coded "engrams" in the 20th cent.) to B. F. SKINNER's "black box," to more recent ideas concerning information processing or the formation of neuronal groups. Disorders of or involving memory include ALZHEIMER'S DISEASE, AMNESIA, POST-TRAUMATIC STRESS DISORDER, and SENILE DEMENTIA.

Memphis Capital of ancient Egypt during the Old Kingdom (c.2575–c.2130 B.C.), located on the W bank of the NILE RIVER, south of CAIRO. The town of Mit Rahina now occupies the site. Founded about 2925 B.C. by Menes, it was by the 3rd dynasty a flourishing community. Despite rivalry with Heracleopolis and THEBES, it remained important, particularly in the worship of PTAH. Beginning in the 8th cent. B.C., it fell successively to Nubia, Assyria, Persia, and ALEXANDER THE GREAT. It was abandoned after the Muslim conquest of Egypt in A.D. 640. Its ruins are extensive. Nearby are the pyramids of SAQQARA and GIZA.

Memphis City (pop., 2000: 650,000), SW Tennessee. Situated above the Mississippi River where Arkansas, Mississippi, and Tennessee meet, it was founded in 1819. A Confederate military center at the start of the AMERICAN CIVIL WAR, it was captured by Union forces in 1862. In the 1870s yellow fever killed 8,000 residents, and the city was forced into bankruptcy. Rechartered in 1893, it was the state's largest city by 1900. Sites of interest include Beale St., made famous by W. C. HANDY as the birthplace of the blues; and Graceland, the mansion of Elvis PRESLEY.

Menander \mə-'nan-dər\ (342?–292? B.C.) Athenian dramatist, considered by ancient critics the supreme poet of Greek NEW COMEDY. He produced his first play in 321 B.C., and in 316 won a prize with *Dyscolus* ("The Misanthrope"), the only one of his 100 plays for which a complete text still exists. He excelled at presenting such characters as stern fathers, young lovers, and intriguing slaves. As adapted by the Romans PLAUTUS and TERENCE, his plays influenced the later Renaissance comedy.

Mencius \'men-shē-əs\ *Chinese* **Mengzi** *or* **Meng-tzu** \'mən-'tsə\ *orig.* Meng K'o (372?–289? B.C.) Chinese philosopher. The book *Mencius* records his activities and statements on innate human goodness, with focus on the four principles *(si duan)*—the inborn feelings of commiseration, shame, courtesy, and right and wrong. Mencius taught that the four principles, when properly cultivated, will develop into the four cardinal virtues of *ren* (benevolence), righteousness, decorum, and wisdom. His development of orthodox CONFUCIANISM earned him the title "second sage," and he has long been revered as the cofounder of Confucianism.

Mencius Ink and color on silk

Mencius or Mengzi or Meng-tzu Chinese Confucian text concerning government, written by MENCIUS. The book maintains that the welfare of the common people comes before every other consideration. When a ruler no longer practices benevolence and righteousness, he should be removed. *Mencius* did not become a classic until the 12th cent., when it was published as one of the FOUR BOOKS. See also CONFUCIANISM.

Mencken, H(enry) L(ouis) (1880–1956) U.S. controversialist and critic. A native of Baltimore, Mencken worked on the staff of the *Baltimore Sun* for much of his life. He coedited *The Smart Set* (1914–23) and cofounded and edited (1924–

33) the *American Mercury*, both important literary magazines. He often used criticism to jeer at the nation's social and cultural weaknesses. *Prejudices* (1919–27) collects many of his reviews and essays. In *The American Language* (1919; supplements 1945, 1948), he brought together American expressions and idioms; by the time of his death, he was perhaps the leading authority on the language of his country.

Mendel \'men-dəl\, **Gregor (Johann)** (1822–1884) Austrian botanist and plant experimenter. He became an Augustinian monk in 1843 and later studied at the Univ. of Vienna. Working in his monastery's garden, he did the experiments that led to his formulation of the basic principle of HEREDITY. He crossed varieties of the garden pea that had maintained constant differences in such single alternative traits as height, flower color, and pod form. He theorized that the occurrence of the alternative traits was due to the occurrence of paired elementary units of heredity, now known as GENES. What was new in Mendel's interpretation of his data was his recognition that genes obey simple statistical laws. His system proved to be of general application and is one of the basic principles of biology. He achieved fame only after his death, through the work of Carl Erich CORRENS, Erich TSCHERMAK VON SEYSENEGG, and Hugo DE VRIES.

Mendele Moykher Sforim \'men-də-lə-mō-'ker-sfä-'rēm\ *or* **Mendele Mokher Sefarim** \ˌsef-ə-'rēm\ ("Mendele the Itinerant Bookseller") *orig.* Shalom Jacob Abramovitsh (1835–1917) Russian author. He lived much of his life as a rabbi in Ukraine. His stories, written with lively humor and gentle satire, are invaluable in the study of Jewish life in Eastern Europe. His greatest work is *The Travels and Adventures of Benjamin the Third* (1875), a panorama of Jewish life in Russia. He is considered the founder of both modern Yiddish and modern Hebrew narrative literature and the creator of modern literary Yiddish.

Mendeleyev \ˌmen-də-'lā-əf\, **Dmitry (Ivanovich)** (1834–1907) Russian chemist. He made a fundamental contribution to chemistry by establishing in 1869 the principle of periodicity of the ELEMENTS. His first PERIODIC TABLE was based on arranging the elements in ascending order of ATOMIC WEIGHT and grouping them by similarity of properties. Mendeleyev's theory allowed him to predict the existence and atomic weights of several elements not discovered until years later.

Mendelsohn \'men-dəls-ˌzōn\, **Erich** (1887–1953) German architect. He was influenced by the BLAUE REITER group of Expressionist artists. Mendelsohn's Einstein Tower, Potsdam (1919–21), a highly sculptured structure, reflects his early interest in science fiction. In the 1920s he designed the Schocken stores in Stuttgart (1927) and Chemnitz (1928), notable for their prominent use of glass in strongly horizontal compositions. His American works include the Maimonides Hospital, San Francisco (1946).

Mendelssohn (-Bartholdy), (Jakob Ludwig) Felix (1809–1847) German composer. Grandson of Moses MENDELSSOHN, he grew up in a wealthy Jewish family that had converted to Protestantism. He began to compose at 11, and at 16 he wrote his first masterpieces, the Octet and the overture to *A Midsummer Night's Dream*. In 1829 he conducted the first performance of J. S. BACH's *St. Matthew Passion* in 100 years, greatly contributing to the Bach revival. His "Reformation" (1832) and "Italian" (1833) symphonies date from this period. As music director of the city of Leipzig (1835–41), he built up the Gewandhaus Orchestra, with which he established the historical concert programming that has remained standard to the present day. His last decade produced such great works as the "Scottish" Symphony (1842), the violin concerto (1844), and the oratorio *Elijah* (1846). His other works include several concert overtures, the large piano set *Songs Without Words*, and two piano concertos. His beloved and musically talented sister, Fanny (1805–1847), discouraged from composing until her marriage to the painter Wilhelm Hensel (1794–1861), eventually wrote more than 500 works. Her death was a severe shock to Mendelssohn, and he died at 38.

Mendelssohn, Moses *orig.* Moses ben Menachem (1729–1786) German Jewish philosopher and scholar. The son of an impoverished scribe, he began his career as a tutor but eventually won fame for his philosophical writings, which would become influential among the 19th-cent. U.S. Transcendentalists. He combined Judaism with the rationalism of the Enlightenment; his works helped bring Jews into the mainstream of European culture. His works include *Phädon* (1767), a defense of the immortality of the soul, and *Jerusalem* (1783), on the relationship of religion and the state. Felix MENDELSSOHN was his grandson.

Mendenhall Glacier Blue ice sheet, 12 mi (19 km) long, 1.5 mi (2.4 km) wide, and more than 100 ft (30 m) high. It flows from the S half of the huge Juneau Icefield, which lies in the Boundary Ranges in SE Alaska. A relic of the Little Ice Age (1500–1750), it recedes up to 90 ft (27 m) a year.

Menelaus \ˌme-nə-ˈlā-əs\ In GREEK MYTHOLOGY, the king of SPARTA and the younger son of ATREUS. When his wife, HELEN, was abducted by PARIS, he asked the other Greek kings to join him in an expedition against Troy, thus beginning the TROJAN WAR. He served under his brother AGAMEMNON. At the war's end he recovered Helen and brought her back to Sparta instead of killing her as he had intended.

Menem \ˈme-nem\, **Carlos (Saúl)** (b.1930) President of Argentina (1989–99). The son of Syrian immigrants, he joined the PERONIST movement in 1956, favoring nationalism, expansion of the government, large raises for wage earners, and tax breaks for businesses. By the time he took office, however, inflation had risen to 28,000% and Argentina was in crisis; he abandoned party orthodoxy for fiscal conservatism to stabilize the economy. A flamboyant figure, he enjoyed great popularity despite his controversial pardoning of human-rights violators from the period of military rule. In 2001 he was indicted for illegal arms dealing.

Mengele \ˈmeŋ-gə-lə\, **Josef** (1911–1979) German Nazi doctor. In 1934 Mengele joined the research staff of the newly founded Institute for Hereditary Biology and Racial Hygiene. An ardent Nazi, he served as medical officer with the SS. In 1943 he was appointed chief doctor at AUSCHWITZ-Birkenau, where he selected incoming Jews for labor or extermination, becoming known as the "Angel of Death," and conducted medical experiments on inmates in pseudoscientific racial studies. After the war he escaped to S. America.

Mengistu Haile Mariam \men-ˈgis-ˌtü-ˈhī-lē-ˈmär-yàm\ (b.1937) Ethiopian head of state (1974–91). After overthrowing HAILE SELASSIE (1974) and assassinating his rivals, Mengistu became the new regime's acknowledged strongman. By 1978 he had crushed a major rebellion in Eritrea and, with Soviet and Cuban help, a Somali invasion of the OGADEN region. In the 1980s he faced new rebellions, and devastating famines drew attention to his failed agricultural policies. After the withdrawal of Soviet support in 1991, he fled to Zimbabwe.

Mengs \ˈmeŋs\, **Anton Raphael** (1728–1779) German painter. He became painter to the Saxon court in Dresden in 1745. In Rome in the 1750s, he developed an enthusiasm for classical antiquity. His fresco *Parnassus* (1760–61) at the Villa Albani helped establish the ascendancy of Neoclassical painting. He also worked for the Spanish court in Madrid. He was regarded as Europe's greatest living painter in his day, but his reputation has since declined.

Mengzi See MENCIUS

menhaden \men-ˈhā-dᵊn\ *or* **pogy** Any of several species of Atlantic coastal fishes (genus *Brevoortia* of the HERRING family), used for oil, fish meal and fertilizer. Menhaden have a deep body, sharp-edged belly, large head, and toothedged scales. Adults are about 15 in. (38 cm) long and weigh 1 lb (0.5 kg) or less. Dense schools of menhaden range from Canada to S. America.

menhir \ˈmen-ˌhir\ Ancient megalithic stone monument (see MEGALITH). Menhirs were simple upright stones, sometimes of great size, erected chiefly in Western Europe, often in vast circles, semicircles, or ellipses. In Britain, the best-known sites are STONEHENGE and Avebury in Wiltshire. Menhirs were also placed in parallel rows, called alignments, the most famous being the Carnac alignments in NW France, with 2,935 menhirs.

Menilek II \ˈmen-ə-ˌlek\ *orig.* Sahle Miriam (1844–1913) King of the semi-independent state of Shewa, or Shoa (1865–89),

and emperor of Ethiopia (1889–1913). The son of deposed King Malakot of Shewa, he escaped prison in 1865 and returned to Shewa as *negus* (king). In 1889 he succeeded Yohannes IV as emperor of Ethiopia, taking his crown name from the legendary son of Solomon and the Queen of Sheba. When Italy sought to annex Ethiopia, Menilek defeated its forces at the Battle of Adowa (1896). He later expanded the empire, funding education and building up its infrastructure.

meningitis \ˌme-nən-ˈjī-təs\ INFLAMMATION of the brain's covering membrane. BACTERIA, often from infection elsewhere, produce the most dangerous forms. Symptoms develop rapidly: vomiting, then severe headache, then stiff neck. The patient may die within hours. Pus in cerebrospinal fluid can block brain passages and spinal spaces. Speedy diagnosis (by lumbar puncture) and treatment (with ANTIBIOTICS) can prevent brain damage and death. Viral meningitis usually has a short course and requires no therapy.

Menninger family \ˈmen-iŋ-ər\ U.S. physicians and pioneers in psychiatric treatment. Charles Frederick Menninger (1862–1953), born in Tell City, Ind., began practicing medicine in Topeka, Kan., in 1889. He saw the benefit of group medical practice after visiting the MAYO FAMILY's clinic in 1908. With his son Karl (1893–1990), he founded the Menninger Diagnostic Clinic for the group practice of general medicine (1920). With Karl's brother William (1899–1966), they established the Menninger Sanitarium and Psychopathic Hospital, to link the understanding of behavior as applied to the treatment of patients and the use of the hospital's social environment as a part of therapy. Their treatment of the mentally ill attracted other scientists, and they made significant strides in establishing psychiatry as a legitimate science. In 1941 they formed the Menninger Foundation, followed by the Menninger School of Psychiatry, which Karl directed (1946–69).

Mennonite \ˈme-nə-ˌnīt\ Member of a Protestant church named for MENNO SIMONSZ. They trace their origins to the Swiss Brethren (established 1525), nonconformists who rejected infant baptism and stressed the separation of church and state. Persecution scattered them across Europe; they found political freedom first in the Netherlands and N Poland, then in Ukraine and Russia. They first emigrated to N. America in 1663. Today Mennonites are found in many parts of the world, especially in N. and S. America. Their creed stresses the authority of the Scriptures, the example of the early church, and baptism as a confession of faith. They value simplicity of life, and many refuse to swear oaths or serve in the military. Mennonite groups include the strictly observant AMISH and HUTTERITES.

Menno Simonsz. \ˈsī-mənz, ˈsē-mȯns\ *or* **Menno Simons** *or* **Menno Simonszoon** (1496–1561) Dutch ANABAPTIST leader. He was ordained a Roman Catholic priest, but came under the influence of Lutheranism and withdrew from the church in 1536. Convinced that only people of mature faith were eligible for membership in the church, he became a leader in the peaceful wing of the Anabaptist movement in 1537. Pronounced a heretic, he was in constant danger of arrest for the rest of his life. He wrote and printed many theological works, and his followers founded the MENNONITE Church.

menopause Final cessation of MENSTRUATION, ending female FERTILITY, usually between ages 45 and 55. A gradual decline in function of the OVARIES reduces ESTROGEN production. Ovulation becomes irregular and gradually ceases. The length of the menstrual cycle and periods may vary; flow may lessen or increase. Adjustment of the ENDOCRINE SYSTEM to estrogen reduction causes hot flashes, often at night, with a warm sensation, flushing, and sweating. Removal or destruction of the ovaries to treat disease causes artificial menopause, with similar but more sudden effects. The protective effect of ESTROGEN against OSTEOPOROSIS and atherosclerosis (see ARTERIOSCLEROSIS) is lost, and risk of fracture and CORONARY HEART DISEASE increases. Hormone replacement therapy, once widely prescribed to reduce these risks, raises the risk of endometrial (see UTERUS) and BREAST CANCER.

menorah \mə-'nōr-ə\ Candelabra used during HANUKKAH. It holds nine candles (or has nine receptacles for oil). Eight of the candles stand for the eight days of Hanukkah. The ninth, usually set in the center and raised above the others, is used to light the others. The menorah is an imitation of the seven-branched golden candelabra of the TABERNACLE, which signified the seven days of creation.

Menotti \mə-'nä-tē\, **Gian Carlo** (b.1911) Italian-U.S. composer, librettist, and stage director. He wrote his first opera by age 10. At the Curtis Institute he met Samuel BARBER, who would become his lifelong companion. In 1939 he produced the radio opera *The Old Maid and the Thief*. *The Medium* (1946) had a Broadway run, and *The Consul* was also successful (1950, Pulitzer Prize). The highly popular *Amahl and the Night Visitors* (1951), for television, was followed by *The Saint of Bleecker Street* (1955, Pulitzer Prize). In 1958 he founded the Festival of Two Worlds in Spoleto, Italy; it enjoyed great success, and in 1977 he founded a New World counterpart in Charleston, S.C.

Menshevik \'men-shə-vik\ Member of the non-Leninist wing of the RUSSIAN SOCIAL-DEMOCRATIC WORKERS' PARTY. The group evolved in 1903 when L. MARTOV called for a mass party modeled after Western European groups, as opposed to Vladimir LENIN's plan to restrict the party to professional revolutionaries. When Lenin's followers obtained a majority on the party central committee, they called themselves BOLSHEVIKS ("those of the majority"), and Martov and his group became the Mensheviks ("those of the minority"). Active in the RUSSIAN REVOLUTION OF 1905, they divided over World War I and the RUSSIAN REVOLUTION OF 1917. In 1922 they were permanently suppressed.

Menshikov \'myen-shi-kȯf\, **Aleksandr (Danilovich)** (1673-1729) Russian soldier and administrator. Fighting for PETER I the Great, Menshikov commanded troops to victories in the Second NORTHERN WAR, after which he received the title of field marshal (1709). As an administrator from 1714, he was criticized for corrupt practices as he amassed power and wealth. After Peter's death in 1725, he succeeded in having his ally Catherine I proclaimed empress, making him the virtual ruler of Russia. After her death in 1727, Menshikov's enemies forced him into exile in Siberia.

menstruation Periodic discharge from the VAGINA of blood, secretions, and shed mucous lining of the UTERUS (endometrium). The endometrium prepares to receive a fertilized EGG by thickening and producing secretions. If the egg released by the OVARY is not fertilized, the endometrium breaks down and is expelled. The first menstruation occurs after other changes of PUBERTY, usually at 11–13 years of age, apparently triggered by the passing of a weight threshold. In adult women, menstrual periods begin at an average interval of 28 days and last about five days; some variation among women and in the same woman is normal. Uterine contractions are felt as cramps. The amount of blood lost is usually less than 1.7 oz (50 ml). Menstruation ends with MENOPAUSE. See also PREMENSTRUAL SYNDROME.

mental disorder Any illness with a psychological origin, manifested either in symptoms of emotional distress or in abnormal behavior. Most mental disorders can be classified as either psychoses or neuroses (see NEUROSIS, PSYCHOSIS). Psychoses (e.g., SCHIZOPHRENIA and BIPOLAR DISORDER) produce such severe symptoms as delusions, HALLUCINATIONS, and inability to objectively evaluate reality. Neuroses, less severe and more treatable, include DEPRESSION, ANXIETY, and PARANOIA as well as OBSESSIVE-COMPULSIVE DISORDERS and POST-TRAUMATIC STRESS DISORDERS. Some mental disorders, such as ALZHEIMER'S DISEASE, are caused by organic disease, but the causes of most others are still unclear. Schizophrenia appears to be partly caused by genetic factors. Some mood disorders, such as mania and depression, may be caused by imbalances of NEUROTRANSMITTERS; they are treatable by drugs (see PSYCHOPHARMACOLOGY). Neuroses often appear to be caused by emotional deprivation, frustration, or abuse during childhood, and they may be treated through PSYCHOTHERAPY. PHOBIAS may represent maladaptive responses built up into the equivalent of conditioned reflexes.

mental retardation Subaverage intellectual ability that is present from birth or infancy and is manifested by abnormal development, learning difficulties, and problems in social adjustment. Mildly retarded individuals, with IQ scores of 53–70, are able to learn academic and pre-vocational skills with some SPECIAL EDUCATION. The moderately retarded, with scores of 36–52, are able to learn functional academic skills and undertake semiskilled work under supervised conditions. Those in the severe (21–35) and profound (below 21) ranges require progressively more supervision or full-time care. Retardation can be caused by genetic disorders (such as DOWN'S SYNDROME), infectious diseases (such as MENINGITIS), metabolic disorders, poisoning from lead or radiation, injuries to the head, and MALNUTRITION.

Menuhin \'men-yə-wən\, **Yehudi** *later* Baron Menuhin (1916–1999) U.S.-British violinist and conductor. Born in New York and raised in San Francisco, he made his debut at 7. After study with George Enescu (1881–1955), he went on to astound audiences worldwide with his precocious depth and mastery. From 1959 he lived in London. He directed the Bath Festival 1958–68 and the Gstaad Festival from 1956. In 1958 he founded his own chamber orchestra. Often accompanied by his pianist sister, Hephzibah (1920–1981), he also recorded with the sitarist Ravi SHANKAR. In later years he devoted much energy to the cause of international cooperation and world peace.

Menzies \'men-ˌzēz\, **Robert (Gordon)** (*later* **Sir Robert**) (1894–1978) Australian prime minister (1939–41, 1949–66). He served as Australia's attorney general 1934–39, then as prime minister 1939–41. He organized the Liberal Party in 1944 and again became premier in 1949. He fostered industrial growth in Australia and immigration from Europe, strengthened military ties with the U.S., and encouraged the ANZUS PACT and Australia's membership in the SOUTHEAST ASIA TREATY ORGANIZATION. He retired in 1966 after the longest ministry in Australian history.

mercantile agency Organization that supplies information on the creditworthiness and financial strength of business firms. The first, the Mercantile Agency, was founded in New York City in 1841. It provided information to businesses expanding nationally that needed to assess the credit histories of prospective customers in distant locations. Under the name Dun & Bradstreet, Inc., it is today the best-known mercantile agency. Mercantile agencies may limit their investigations to firms in a particular line of trade or a particular region. Most agencies provide both general and special reports. General reports, issued periodically on all firms investigated by the agency, assign a rating to the firm's financial statement and creditworthiness. Special reports containing more detailed information are issued to clients of the agency on request. See also CREDIT BUREAU.

mercantile law See BUSINESS LAW

mercantilism Economic theory and policy influential in Europe from the 16th to the 18th cent., calling for government regulation of a nation's economy to increase its power at the expense of rivals. The term was given currency by Adam SMITH in his *Wealth of Nations* (1776). Mercantilism's emphasis on the importance of gold and silver holdings as a sign of a nation's power led to policies designed to obtain precious metals through trade by ensuring "favorable" trade balances (see BALANCE OF TRADE), meaning an excess of exports over imports, with payments for the goods or services made with gold or silver. Colonial possessions were to serve as markets for exports and as suppliers of raw materials to the mother country, a policy that created conflict between the European colonial powers and their colonies, in particular fanning resentment of Britain in its colonies and helping bring about the American Revolution. Thrift and SAVING were virtues in mercantilism because they made possible the creation of CAPITAL. Mercantilism provided a favorable climate for the early development of CAPITALISM, but was later severely criticized, especially by advocates of LAISSEZ-FAIRE, who argued that all trade was beneficial and that strict government controls were counterproductive.

Mercator \mər-'kā-tər\, **Gerardus** *orig.* Gerhard Kremer (1512–1594) Flemish cartographer. A skilled engraver and

scientific-instrument maker, he and his colleagues made Louvain a center for construction of maps, globes (terrestrial and celestial), and astronomical instruments. He was appointed court cosmographer to Duke Wilhelm of Cleve in 1564, and in 1569 he perfected the Mercator projection (see CARGOGRAPHY), in which parallels and meridians are rendered as straight lines spaced to produce at any point an accurate ratio of latitude to longitude. It permitted mariners to steer a course over long distances by plotting straight lines. While the meridians are equally spaced parallel vertical lines, the lines of latitude are spaced farther apart as their distance from the equator increases; on world maps the projection greatly enlarges areas distant from the equator.

mercenary \'mər-sᵊn-,er-ē\ Hired professional soldier who fights in foreign service without regard to political principles. From the earliest days of warfare, governments supplemented their military forces with mercenaries. After the Hundred Years' War (1337–1453), Swiss soldiers were hired out all over Europe. The German state of Hesse also hired out its soldiers; Hessian troops fought for the British in the AMERICAN REVOLUTION. Later mercenaries have been individual soldiers of fortune.

Mercer, Johnny (*orig.* John Herndon) (1909–1976) U.S. songwriter. Born in Georgia, Mercer began to write lyrics in New York in the late 1920s, and later joined Paul Whiteman's orchestra as singer and master of ceremonies. In 1942 Mercer cofounded Capitol Records. On Broadway, he collaborated with Harold ARLEN on *St. Louis Woman* (1946) and *Saratoga* (1959), and also provided lyrics for *Li'l Abner* (1956). His songs for films won four Academy Awards. He collaborated with such composers as Hoagy CARMICHAEL and Jerome KERN, and is credited with over 1,000 lyrics, including "One for My Baby," "Autumn Leaves," and "Moon River."

mercerization \,mər-sə-rə-'zā-shən\ Treatment applied to COTTON fibers or fabrics to make them permanently able to accept dyes and various chemical finishes more easily. The method, patented in 1850 by John Mercer (1791–1866), also imparts increased TENSILE STRENGTH and greater absorptive properties. Higher-quality cotton goods are usually mercerized. The treatment consists of dipping the yarn or fiber in a solution of sodium hydroxide and then treating the material with water or acid to neutralize it.

merchandising Element of MARKETING concerned especially with the sale of goods and services to customers. One aspect of merchandising is ADVERTISING aimed at capturing the interest of those most likely to buy the product. Merchandising also involves product visibility; companies provide display and promotional materials to retailers and negotiate shelf space. Overall strategies include the determination of pricing, discounts, and special offers; the invention of sales pitches; and the identification of avenues for sales, including store-based RETAILING and alternative means such as direct-mail marketing, telemarketing, commercial Web sites, vending machines, and door-to-door sales.

Merchant, Ismail See James IVORY

merchant marine Commercial ships of a nation, whether privately or publicly owned, and the personnel who operate them, as distinct from naval vessels. Merchant ships are used to transport people, raw materials, and manufactured goods. By carrying the commerce of other nations on the seas, a merchant fleet contributes to its home nation's foreign-exchange earnings, promotes trade, and provides employment. The U.S. Merchant Marine Academy (founded 1943) is in Kings Point, N.Y.

Mercia \'mər-shə\ Ancient Anglican kingdom, central England. One of a group of seven Anglo-Saxon kingdoms, it originally comprised the border areas of modern STAFFORDSHIRE, Derbyshire, NOTTINGHAMSHIRE, and N West Midlands and WARWICKSHIRE. OFFA, who ruled 757–796, created a single state from the Humber to the English Channel. After Offa's death, Mercia declined. In the early 10th cent., it came under the rule of WESSEX.

Mercury In ROMAN RELIGION, the god of merchants, commonly identified with the Greek messenger of the gods, HERMES. His temple on Rome's Aventine Hill was dedicated

in 495 B.C. Mercury is sometimes depicted holding a purse, symbolic of his business functions. More often, he is given the attributes of Hermes and portrayed wearing winged sandals or a winged cap and carrying a CADUCEUS.

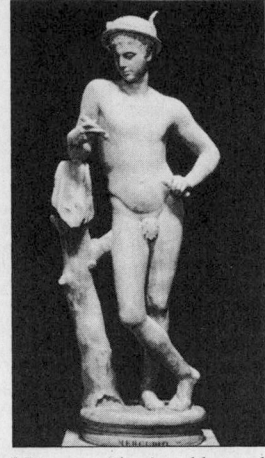
Mercury with winged hat and staff

mercury *or* **quicksilver** Chemical ELEMENT, chemical symbol Hg, atomic number 80. Mercury is the only elemental METAL that is liquid at ordinary temperatures. Silvery white, dense, toxic (see MERCURY POISONING), and a good conductor of electricity, mercury is occasionally found free in nature but usually occurs as the sulfide ore. It has many uses, in dental and industrial AMALGAMS, as a CATALYST, in electrical and measuring apparatus and instruments, as the CATHODE in electrolytic cells, in mercury-vapor lamps, and as a coolant and neutron absorber in nuclear power plants. Many of mercury's compounds (VALENCE 1 or 2) are pigments, pesticides, and medicinals. It is a dangerous pollutant because it concentrates in animal tissues in increasing amounts up the food chain.

Mercury Innermost PLANET of the SOLAR SYSTEM. With a highly elliptical orbit, it is 28.5 million mi (46 million km) from the sun at its nearest and about 43.5 million mi (70 million km) away at its farthest. The second-smallest major planet (after Pluto), it has a diameter of about 3,050 mi (4,870 km) and a mass about one-eighteenth of earth's. With a year 88 earth days long and the highest average orbital speed (30 mi/second, or 48 km/second) of any planet, it is aptly named for the swift Roman messenger god. It makes a complete rotation relative to the stars every 59 earth days, but its day relative to the sun is 176 earth days, owing to its revolution around the sun. It has numerous craters, including the 800-mi (1,300-km) Caloris Basin. Mercury also has steep cliffs that extend for hundreds of miles. The magnetic field found in its vicinity suggests a large iron core, which would account for a mean density almost as high as earth's. Its surface gravity, about one-third of earth's, holds only a thin atmosphere. Surface temperatures range from about 756°F (402°C) on the side facing the sun to about −279°F (−173°C) at the end of its night.

Mercury First series of U.S. manned spaceflights (1961–63). In May 1961, about three weeks after Yury GAGARIN's pioneering flight, Alan SHEPARD rode the first Mercury space capsule, Freedom 7, on a 15-minute, 302-mi (486-km) flight, to an altitude of 116 mi (186 km). The first U.S. manned flight to orbit earth was Friendship 7's, in February 1962, in which John GLENN completed three orbits. The last Mercury flight, Faith 7, in May 1963, was the longest, making 22 orbits in about 34 hours.

mercury poisoning Harmful effects of MERCURY compounds. Manufacture of paints, various household items, and pesticides uses mercury compounds; the finished product and the waste products released into air and water may contain them. The aquatic FOOD CHAIN can concentrate organic mercury compounds in fish and seafood, which, if eaten by humans, can affect the central NERVOUS SYSTEM, leading to PARALYSIS and sometimes death (see MINAMATA DISEASE). Acute mercury poisoning causes severe digestive-tract inflammation. Mercury accumulates in the kidneys, causing UREMIA and death. Chronic poisoning, from occupational inhalation or skin absorption, causes metallic taste, oral inflammation, blue gum line, extremity pain and tremor, weight loss, and mental changes (depression and withdrawal).

Meredith, George (1828–1909) English novelist and poet. The novel *The Ordeal of Richard Feverel* (1859) is typical of his best work, rich in allusion, metaphor, lyrical prose, witty dialogue, and psychological insight. After writing the comedy *Evan Harrington* (1860) and a volume of poems, *Modern Love* (1862), he finally won fame and fortune with the novels *The Egoist* (1879) and *Diana of the Crossways* (1885). His works are noted for their use of interior monologue and their treatment of women as equals of men.

Meredith, James (Howard) (b.1933) U.S. civil rights activist. Born in Kosciusko, Miss., and raised in poverty, in 1961 he took aim at the system of racial segregation by applying to the all-white Univ. of Mississippi. He won a legal battle to be admitted, but federal troops and Justice Department officials had to be brought in to enforce the court order. At a voter-registration drive after his graduation, he was shot and wounded by a white supremacist.

merengue \mə-'reŋ-gā\ Couple dance from the Dominican Republic or Haiti, danced throughout Latin America. Originally a folk dance, it has become a ballroom dance, where it is danced with a limping step, the weight always on the same foot. Dominican merengue music became widely popular in the late 20th cent.

merganser *or* **fish duck** Any species of the DIVING DUCK genus *Mergus*. Essentially freshwater birds, they are classified as a sea duck (tribe Mergini). Mergansers have a narrow, serrated, hooked bill for catching fish. The males of all but the common merganser *(M. merganser)* are crested. The common merganser, the hooded merganser *(M. cucullatus)*, the red-breasted merganser *(M. serrator),* and the smew *(M. albellus)* live in N regions. Mergansers are called trash ducks because their flesh is rank.

merger Combination of two or more independent business corporations into a single enterprise. The dominant firm may purchase the other firm's assets with cash or SECURITIES, purchase the other firm's STOCK, or issue its own stock to the other firm's stockholders in exchange for their shares in the acquired firm. In horizontal mergers, both firms produce the same commodity or service for the same market. In vertical mergers, a firm acquires either a supplier or a customer. If the merged business is not related to that of the acquiring firm, the new corporation is called a conglomerate. The reasons for mergers are various: the acquiring firm may seek to eliminate a competitor, to increase its efficiency, to diversify its products, services, and markets, or to reduce its taxes.

Mergui Archipelago \mər-'gwē\ Group of more than 200 islands in the Andaman Sea off the coast of SE Myanmar. Trade in elephants, china, spices, and silk flourished in the 16th–17th cent. The region has been largely inaccessible since Burma (now Myanmar) became independent in 1948. Its largely unexploited ecosystems exhibit great biodiversity. Mountainous and jungle-covered, the islands are inhabited chiefly by the Selungs.

Mérida \'mā-rē-thä\ *ancient* Emerita Augusta. Town (pop., 1991: 48,000), capital of the autonomous community of Extremadura, W Spain. Founded by the Romans in 25 B.C., it served as the capital of the province of Lusitania and became one of the most important towns in Iberia. Occupied in A.D. 713 by the Moors, it was recaptured in 1228 by Alfonso IX of Leon, who granted it to the Knights of Santiago. It is known for its Roman ruins, including a bridge, an amphitheater, and an aqueduct.

Mérida City (pop., 1995: 612,000), capital of YUCATÁN state, SE Mexico. It lies in NW YUCATÁN PENINSULA near the Gulf of Mexico. It was founded in 1542 on the site of the ancient MAYA city of T'ho. It is the site of numerous colonial buildings, a 16th-cent. cathedral, and Yucatán Univ. It serves as a tourist base for trips to nearby Maya cities, including CHICHÉN ITZÁ and UXMAL.

Mérimée \mā-rē-'mā\, **Prosper** (1803–1870) French short-story writer and dramatist. His passions were mysticism, history, and the unusual. His stories, many of which are mysteries, include *Mateo Falcone* (1829), the collection *Mosaïque* (1833), and the novellas *Colomba* (1840) and *Carmen* (1845), the basis of Georges BIZET's opera. He also wrote works of history and archaeology, historical fiction, and literary criticism. He became a senator in 1853.

Merleau-Ponty \mer-lō-pōⁿ-'tē\, **Maurice** (1908–1961) French philosopher. With Jean-Paul SARTRE and Simone de BEAUVOIR he founded the journal *Les Temps Modernes* in 1945. From 1949 he taught at the Sorbonne. One of France's leading exponents of PHENOMENOLOGY, he claimed that perception is the source of knowledge and the ultimate foundation of the constructions of the natural sciences. His most influential work was *The Phenomenology of Perception* (1945), a major treatment of AESTHETICS.

Merlin Magician and wise man in ARTHURIAN LEGEND. In GEOFFREY OF MONMOUTH's *History of the Kings of England,* Merlin was an adviser to King Arthur and possessed magical powers. Later narratives made him a prophet of the GRAIL and gave him credit for the idea of the Round Table. In Thomas MALORY's *Morte Darthur* he brought Arthur to the throne and served as his mentor. He was imprisoned by an enchantress who had learned the magic arts from him.

Merman, Ethel *orig.* Ethel Agnes Zimmerman (1909–1984) U.S. singer and actress. Born in Queens, N.Y., Merman worked as a secretary before her first professional singing engagement in 1929. She made her stage debut in *Girl Crazy* (1930), and her brassy, ebullient style and powerful voice soon made her a favored performer for Irving BERLIN, Cole PORTER, and others. In addition to screen appearances, she starred on her own radio show. Her many Broadway successes include *Anything Goes* (1934), *Annie Get Your Gun* (1946), *Call Me Madam* (1950), and *Gypsy* (1959).

Merovingian dynasty (476–750) Frankish dynasty considered the first French royal house. It was named for Merovech (fl. c.450), whose son Childeric I (d.482?) ruled a tribe of Salian FRANKS from his capital at Tournai. His son, CLOVIS I, united nearly all of Gaul in the late 5th cent. On his death the realm was divided among his sons, but by 558 it was united under his youngest son, Chlotar I. The pattern of dividing and then reuniting the realm continued for generations. After the reign of DAGOBERT I (623–39), the Merovingian kings were little more than puppets, and the real power lay in the hands of the mayors of the palace. In 750 Childeric III was deposed by PEPIN III, the first of the CAROLINGIAN DYNASTY.

Merrick, David *orig.* David Margulois (1912–2000) U.S. theatrical producer. Born in St. Louis, Mo., he practiced law until 1949, when he became a producer in New York. His first independent production, *Clutterbuck* (1949), was followed by more than 85 other Broadway shows, including *Look Back in Anger* (1957), *Gypsy* (1959), *Becket* (1960), *Oliver!* (1963), *Hello, Dolly!* (1964), *Play It Again, Sam* (1969), and *42nd Street* (1980). Many were critical and commercial successes, and he was known for his skillful use of publicity.

Merrick, Joseph See ELEPHANT MAN

Merrill, Charles E(dward) (1885–1956) U.S. investment banker. Born in Green Cove Springs, Fla., in 1914 he cofounded the investment-banking firm Merrill, Lynch & Co., which soon became the broker for some of the largest chain-store SECURITIES. He helped create Safeway Stores in 1926 and founded *Family Circle* magazine six years later. Foreseeing the crash of 1929, he advised his clients accordingly. In the 1930s the firm focused on underwriting and investment banking, but in 1940 it returned to brokerage. As Merrill Lynch, Pierce, Fenner & Smith, the company is today the largest retail brokerage house in the U.S. Charles was the father of the poet James MERRILL.

Merrill, James (Ingram) (1926–1995) U.S. poet. Born in New York to a wealthy family, he devoted his life to poetry. His lyric and epic poems are known for their craftsmanship, erudition, and wit. Many of his later works were stimulated by sessions with a Ouija board. His collections include the trilogy of *Divine Comedies* (1976, Pulitzer Prize), *Mirabell: Books of Number* (1978), and *Scripts for the Pageant* (1980), published together in *The Changing Light at Sandover* (1982). *A Different Person*, a memoir, was published in 1994.

Mersey River River, NW England. It flows west through the S suburbs of MANCHESTER and is joined by the Irwell in its canalized form as the Manchester Ship Canal. Joined by the Weaver, it forms the Mersey Estuary, the harbor of LIVERPOOL. It enters the Irish Sea after a course of 70 mi (110 km).

Merton, Thomas *later* Father M. Louis (1915–1968) U.S. (French-born) monk and Roman Catholic writer. Merton taught English at Columbia Univ. before entering a

monastery in Kentucky. His early works, on spiritual themes, include poetry collections and the autobiographical *Seven Storey Mountain* (1948), which brought him international fame and led many readers to the monastic life. In the 1960s his writings tended toward social criticism, Oriental philosophy, and mysticism.

Merv *modern* **Mary** \mä-ᵊrē\ Ancient city, central Asia. Lying near the modern town of Mary (formerly Merv) in Turkmenistan, it was the seat of a satrapy of the Persian empire. Under the Arabs in the 7th cent. A.D., it was a base for Muslim expansion into central Asia. A great center of Islamic learning under the ABBASID caliphs, it reached its zenith under the SELJUQ sultan Sanjar (r.1118–59). It was destroyed by the MONGOLS in 1221, then rebuilt in the 17th cent. It was occupied by Russia from 1884.

Merwin, W(illiam) S(tanley) (b.1927) U.S. poet and translator. Born in New York City, he earned critical acclaim with his first poetry collection, *A Mask for Janus* (1952). He became known for the spare style of his poetry, which often expresses concerns about the natural environment. His volumes include *The Lice* (1967), *The Carrier of Ladders* (1970, Pulitzer Prize), and *Travels* (1993). His translations include ancient and modern works from Chinese, Sanskrit, and Japanese.

mesa \ᵊmä-sə\ (Spanish: "table") Flat-topped tableland with one or more steep sides, common in the Colorado Plateau regions of the U.S. A BUTTE is similar but smaller. Both are formed by erosion; during downcutting and stripping, areas of harder rock in a plateau act as flat protective caps for portions of underlying land situated between such places as stream valleys, where erosion is especially active.

Mesa Verde National Park \ᵊmä-sə-ᵊver-dē\ National park, SW Colorado. It was established in 1906 to preserve prehistoric Indian cliff dwellings. Occupying a high tableland area of 52,085 acres (21,078 hectares), it contains hundreds of PUEBLO ruins up to 13 centuries old. The most striking are multistoried apartments built under overhanging cliffs; Cliff Palace, the largest, contains hundreds of rooms.

mescaline \ᵊmes-kə-lin\ HALLUCINOGEN from the PEYOTE cactus. An ALKALOID related to EPINEPHRINE and NOREPINEPHRINE, mescaline is usually extracted from the peyote and purified, but can also be synthesized. Its hallucinogenic effects begin in two to three hours and may last over 12 hours; the hallucinations vary greatly among individuals and from one time to the next, but are usually visual rather than auditory. Side effects include nausea and vomiting.

Meselson \ᵊme-sel-sən\, **Matthew Stanley** (b.1930) U.S. molecular biologist. Born in Denver, he taught at Harvard Univ. from 1964. He conducted imaginative research with Franklin STAHL that showed that, during cell division (MITOSIS), DNA splits into its two component strands, each of which acquires a newly synthesized partner strand before passing into one of the daughter cells.

Meshed See MASHHAD

Mesmer \ᵊmez-mər\, **Franz Anton** (1734–1815) German physician. His theory of "animal magnetism" held that an invisible fluid in the body acted according to the laws of magnetism and that disease was caused by obstacles to the free circulation of this fluid. In Mesmer's view, harmony could be restored by inducing "crises" (trance states often ending in delirium or convulsions). In the 1770s he carried out dramatic demonstrations of his ability to "mesmerize" his patients using magnetized objects. Accused of fraud, he left Austria and settled in Paris (1778). His theories were eventually discredited, but his ability to induce trance states led to the modern use of HYPNOSIS.

Mesoamerican civilization Complex of aboriginal cultures that developed in parts of Mexico and Central America. With the ANDEAN CIVILIZATION it constitutes a New World counterpart to those of ancient Egypt, Mesopotamia, and China. Humans have been present in Mesoamerica from as early as 21,000 B.C.; a shift from hunting and gathering to agriculture, which began around 7000 B.C. with the end of the Ice Age, was completed by about 1500 B.C. The earliest great Mesoamerican civilization, the OLMEC, dates from around 1150 B.C. The Middle Formative period (900–300 B.C.) saw increased cultural regionalism and the rise of the ZAPOTEC people. Civilizations of the Late Formative and Classic periods (lasting until about A.D. 900) include the MAYA and the civilization centered at TEOTIHUACÁN; later societies include the TOLTECS and the AZTECS.

Mesolithic period \ᵊme-zə-ᵊli-thik\ ("Middle Stone Age") Ancient technological and cultural stage (c.8000–2700 B.C.) between the PALEOLITHIC and NEOLITHIC PERIODS in NW Europe. The Mesolithic hunter, using a tool kit of chipped and polished stone together with bone, antler, and wooden tools, achieved a greater efficiency than his predecessors and was able to exploit a wider range of animal and vegetable food sources. Immigrant Neolithic farmers probably absorbed many indigenous Mesolithic hunters and fishers. There is no direct counterpart to the Mesolithic outside Europe.

meson \ᵊme-ˌzän\ Any member of a family of SUBATOMIC PARTICLES composed of a QUARK and an antiquark (see ANTIMATTER). Mesons are sensitive to the STRONG FORCE, have integral SPIN, and differ widely in MASS. Though unstable, many mesons last a few billionths of a second, long enough to be observed with particle detectors.

Mesopotamia Region between the TIGRIS and EUPHRATES rivers, constituting most of modern Iraq. Known as the "cradle of civilization," it was the site of settlements by 5000 B.C., and from about 4000 B.C. to 625 B.C. its location and its fertility, much enhanced by a great system of irrigation canals, made it the seat of the important early civilizations of SUMER, AKKAD, BABYLONIA, and ASSYRIA. It was held by Persia from 538 B.C. until taken by Alexander the Great in 331 B.C. It fell to a succession of conquerors before being overrun by Arabs in the 7th cent. A.D. Under the ABBASID DYNASTY (from 762), BAGHDAD became the splendid capital of the Islamic world. The region declined under the MONGOLS (from 1258). It became part of the OTTOMAN EMPIRE in 1638. The object of a British campaign in World War I, it became a British mandate in 1920, and in 1921 Britain set up the kingdom of Iraq.

Mesozoic era \ˌme-zə-ᵊzō-ik\ Second of the earth's three major geologic eras, 248–65 million years ago. It is divided into three periods: the TRIASSIC (the earliest), JURASSIC, and CRETACEOUS. The Mesozoic saw the evolution of widely diversified and advanced flora and fauna. The continental landmasses as known today were probably separated from the supercontinents LAURASIA and GONDWANA by CONTINENTAL DRIFT. See table at GEOLOGIC TIME.

mesquite \mə-ᵊskēt\ Any of the spiny shrubs or small trees that make up the genus *Prosopis* of the pea family (see LEGUME). Mesquites form extensive thickets in areas from S. America to the SW U.S. Two races occur: one of tall trees (50 ft, or 15 m), the other low and far-reaching, called running mesquite. Water-seeking roots grow to depths of up to 70 ft (20 m). Stems bear hairy leaves, then cream-colored catkins of flowers, followed by clusters of long, narrow, pale-yellow beans. Cattle eat the beans, which contain a sweet pulp; the wood has value only for unusual furniture and trinkets and as aromatic firewood.

Mesrob \mes-ᵊrōp\, **St.** *or* **St. Mesrop Mashtots** \mash-ᵊtōts\ (c.360–440) Armenian theologian and linguist. A scholar of classical languages, he became a monk (c.395) and eventually founded several monasteries. He systematized or invented the Armenian alphabet and sponsored the first translation of the Bible into Armenian (c.410). He helped establish Armenia's golden age of Christian literature.

Messene \me-ᵊsä-nā, mə-ᵊsē-nē\ Ancient city, SW PELOPONNESE, Greece, located north of the modern city of the same name. Founded about 369 B.C. as the site of the new capital of Messenia, it formed a strategic barrier against SPARTA, along with MEGALOPOLIS, MANTINEA, and ARGOS. It fell to PHILIP II of Macedonia in 338 B.C.

Messenia \mə-ᵊsē-nē-ə\, **Gulf of** Gulf of the Ionian Sea, on the coast of the SW PELOPONNESE, Greece. On the west side of the gulf is the port of Koroni, originally settled by Argives after the First Messenian War (c.735–715 B.C.). The French landed at the Gulf of Messenia in 1828 during the War of GREEK INDEPENDENCE to drive the Turks from the Peloponnese.

Messerschmitt, Willy (1898–1978) German aircraft designer. From 1926 he was chief designer at an aircraft factory in Augsburg, which in 1938 became Messerschmitt AG. In 1939 his first military aircraft, the Messerschmitt 109, set a speed record of 481 mph (775 kph). In World War II his factory produced 35,000 Me 109s for the German air force, as well as the Me 110 bomber, the Me 163 rocket-propelled plane, and the Me 262, the first combat jet.

Messiaen \mes-'yäⁿ\, **Olivier (Eugéne Prosper Charles)** (1908–1992) French composer. In 1931 he became principal organist at the church of the Sainte Trinité, where he would remain for 40 years. He wrote his *Quartet for the End of Time* in a German POW camp. After the war, he taught at the Paris Conservatory (1947–78), where his students included Pierre BOULEZ and Karlheinz STOCKHAUSEN. His music's main sources of inspiration were his devout Catholic faith and his love of nature, many works being inspired by birdsong. He also was influenced rhythmically by study of Indian music. Major works include *Vingt regards sur l'enfant Jésus* (1944) and *Catalogue d'oiseaux* (1958) for piano, the *Turangalîla* Symphony (1948), and the opera *Saint François d'Assise* (1983).

messiah In JUDAISM, the expected king of the line of DAVID who will deliver the Jews from foreign bondage and restore Israel's golden age. The term used for the messiah in the Greek NEW TESTAMENT, *christos,* was applied to JESUS, who is accepted by Christians as the promised redeemer. Messiah figures in other religions include the MAHDI, for SHIITE Muslims, and Maitreya, the Buddha of the future, for Buddhists.

Messier catalog \mäs-'yā, *Engl* 'me-sē-,ā\ List of about 109 STAR clusters, nebulae (see NEBULA), and GALAXIES compiled by the French astronomer Charles Messier (1730–1817), who discovered many of them. Still valuable for amateurs, it has been superseded by the New General Catalogue (NGC); both NGC and M numbers are commonly used.

Messina *ancient* Zankle. City (pop., 1998 est.: 262,000), NE SICILY, Italy. Founded by Greeks in the 8th cent. B.C., it was destroyed by Carthaginians in 397 B.C. The Romans took the city in 264 B.C., precipitating the First PUNIC WAR. It was taken successively by the Goths, Byzantines, Arabs, Normans, Spaniards, and finally the Italians in 1860. Heavily bombed during World War II, it was rebuilt. It is now an important Italian port. Sites of interest include the cathedral and the university (founded 1548).

Messina, Antonello da See ANTONELLO DA MESSINA

Messina, Strait of *ancient* Siculum Fretum. Channel between S Italy and NE Sicily. MESSINA lies on its bank in SICILY, opposite REGGIO DI CALABRIA. See also SCYLLA AND CHARYBDIS.

mestizo \mes-'tē-zō\ Any person of mixed blood. In Spanish America, the term denotes a person of combined Indian and European extraction. In Mexico the term's meaning has varied so greatly that it has been abandoned in census reports. In the Philippines it denotes a person of mixed foreign (e.g., Chinese) and native ancestry.

metabolism \mə-'ta-bə-,li-zəm\ Sum of all the CHEMICAL REACTIONS that take place in every CELL of a living organism, providing energy for the processes of life and synthesizing new cellular material. "Intermediary metabolism" refers to the vast web of interconnected chemical reactions by which all the cell's constituents, many rarely found outside it, are created and destroyed. Anabolic reactions use energy (usually as ATP) to build complex MOLECULES from simpler organic compounds; catabolic reactions break complex molecules down into simpler ones, releasing chemical energy (ATP). For most organisms, the energy comes ultimately from the sun, whether they obtain it by PHOTOSYNTHESIS and store it in organic compounds or consume those that photosynthesize for the energy stored in their organic compounds. In some BACTERIA in special environments such as DEEP-SEA VENTS, the energy comes from chemical bonds instead. Every cellular chemical reaction is mediated by a specific ENZYME. See also DIGESTION, FERMENTATION, TRICARBOXYLIC ACID CYCLE.

Metacom \'me-tə-,käm\ *or* **Metacomet** *or* **King Philip** (1638?–1676) Wampanoag Indian chief who led the most severe Indian war in New England history, known as KING PHILIP'S WAR (1675–76). His father, MASSASOIT, had negotiated peace with the Pilgrims in 1621. Embittered by the humiliations to which he and his people were continually subjected by whites, Metacom in June 1675 led a group of warriors into battle. He was killed in the final confrontation. His body was quartered and his head displayed on a pole for 25 years at Plymouth.

metal Any of a class of substances with, to some degree, the following properties: good heat and electricity conduction, malleability, ductility, high light reflectivity, and capacity to form positive IONS in solution and HYDROXIDES rather than ACIDS when their OXIDES meet water. About three-quarters of the ELEMENTS are metals; these are usually fairly hard and strong crystalline (see CRYSTAL) solids with high chemical reactivity that readily form ALLOYS with each other. Metallic properties increase from lighter to heavier elements in each vertical group of the PERIODIC TABLE and from right to left in each row. The most abundant metals are aluminum, iron, calcium, sodium, potassium, and magnesium. The vast majority are found as ORES rather than free. Metals fall into the following classifications (not mutually exclusive and most not rigidly defined): ALKALI METALS, ALKALINE EARTH METALS, TRANSITION ELEMENTS, noble (precious) metals, platinum metals, lanthanides (RARE EARTHS), ACTINIDES, light metals, and heavy metals. Many have essential biochemical roles, often in trace amounts, and many are toxic as both elements and compounds (see MERCURY POISONING, LEAD POISONING).

metal fatigue Weakened condition of METAL parts of MACHINES, vehicles, or structures caused by repeated stresses or loadings, ultimately resulting in fracture under a stress much weaker than that necessary to cause fracture in a single application. Fatigue-resistant metals have been developed and their performance improved by surface treatments, and fatigue stresses have been significantly reduced in aircraft and other applications by designing to avoid stress concentrations.

metallography \,me-t°l-'ä-grə-fē\ Study of the structure of METALS and ALLOYS. Visual and optical microscopic observation of metal surfaces and fractures can reveal valuable information about the crystalline, chemical, and mechanical makeup of the material. In electron microscopes a beam of electrons instead of a beam of light is directed onto the specimen; transmission electron microscopes have made it possible to examine internal details of very thin metal foils. X-RAY DIFFRACTION techniques are used to study phenomena related to the grouping of the atoms themselves.

metallurgy \'me-t°l-,ər-jē\ Art and science of extracting METALS from their ORES and modifying the metals for use. It also concerns the chemical, physical, and atomic properties and structures of metals and the principles by which metals are combined to form ALLOYS. Metals are extracted from crude ore in two phases. In ore dressing, the ore is broken down to isolate the desired metallic elements from the crude ore. In process metallurgy, the resulting minerals are reduced to metal, alloyed, and made available for use. See also SMELTING.

metal point *or* **silverpoint** Method of drawing with a small sharpened metal rod—of lead, copper, gold, or most commonly silver—on specially prepared paper. Silverpoint produces a fine gray line that oxidizes to a light brown; the technique is best suited for small-scale work. It achieved great popularity in the 15th cent.; Albrecht DÜRER and LEONARDO DA VINCI were its greatest exponents. Out of fashion in the 17th cent., it was revived in the 18th cent. by the miniaturists.

metalwork Useful and decorative objects fashioned of various metals. The oldest technique is hammering; after about 2500 B.C., CASTING was also used. GOLD and SILVER objects have been produced since ancient times; they were in such demand in the 12th cent. that gold- and silversmiths organized guilds. COPPER was worked in ancient Egypt and was widely used for household utensils in 17th–18th-cent. Europe. Both BRONZE and BRASS were widely used in ancient Greece. PEWTER plates and tankards were made in the Middle Ages and remained popular until superseded by cheaper EARTHENWARE and PORCELAIN in the

18th cent. WROUGHT IRON has been used for decorative hinges, gates, and railings since the 16th cent. LEAD has traditionally been used for roof coverings.

metamorphic rock Any of a class of rocks that result from the alteration of preexisting rocks in response to variations in temperature, pressure, and mechanical stress. The preexisting rocks may be IGNEOUS, SEDIMENTARY, or other metamorphic rocks. The structure and mineralogy reflect the particular type of METAMORPHISM that produced the rock and the composition of the parent rock. Metamorphic rocks are commonly classified by type of facies, predictable mineral assemblages associated with certain temperature and pressure conditions.

Metalwork Statue of Krishna, gilded bronze, 18th cent.

metamorphism Mineralogic and structural changes in solid rocks caused by physical conditions different from those under which the rocks originally formed. The most important agents of metamorphism are temperature, pressure, and stress. Dynamic metamorphism results from mechanical deformation with little long-term temperature change. Contact metamorphism results from increases in temperature by contact with IGNEOUS ROCKS. Regional metamorphism results from the general increase of temperature and pressure over a large area and a long period of time, as in mountain-building processes. See also METAMORPHIC ROCK.

metamorphosis In biology, any striking developmental change of an animal's form or structure, accompanied by physiological, biochemical, and behavioral changes. The best-known examples occur among insects, which may exhibit complete or incomplete metamorphosis (see NYMPH). The complete metamorphosis of butterflies, moths, and some other insects involves four stages: EGG, LARVA (CATERPILLAR), PUPA (chrysalis or cocoon), and adult. The change from tadpole to frog is an example of metamorphosis among amphibians.

metaphor FIGURE OF SPEECH in which a word or phrase denoting one kind of object or action is used in place of another to suggest a likeness or analogy between them (as in "the ship plows the seas" or "a volley of oaths"). A metaphor is an implied comparison (as in "a marble brow"), in contrast to the explicit comparison of the SIMILE ("a brow white as marble"). Metaphor is common at all levels of language and is fundamental in poetry.

Metaphysical poetry Highly intellectualized poetry written chiefly in 17th-cent. England. Less concerned with expressing feeling than with analyzing it, Metaphysical poetry is marked by bold and ingenious, metaphors, complex and subtle thought, frequent use of paradox, and a dramatic directness of language whose rhythm derives from living speech. John DONNE was the leading Metaphysical poet; others include George HERBERT, Henry VAUGHAN, Andrew MARVELL, and Abraham COWLEY.

metaphysics Branch of philosophy whose object is to determine the real nature of things. In the history of Western philosophy, metaphysics has been understood as: (1) an inquiry into what basic kinds of things (e.g., the mental and the physical) exist; (2) the science of reality, as opposed to appearance; (3) the study of the world as a whole; and (4) a theory of first principles. ARISTOTLE distinguished two tasks for the philosopher: to investigate the nature and properties of what exists in the natural, or sensible, world, and to explore the characteristics of "being as such" and inquire into the character of the unmoved mover. The first was carried out primarily in his *Physics*; the second, which

he also called "theology" (because God was the unmoved mover), is discussed in his *Metaphysics*.

Metastasio \\mā-tä-'stäz-yō\\, **Pietro** *orig.* Antonio Domenico Bonaventura Trapassi (1698–1782) Italian opera librettist. His first libretto, *Didone abbandonata* (1724), was so successful that he was soon known throughout Italy. Such important librettos as *Enzio* (1728) and *Semiramide* (1729) soon followed. He was invited to Vienna as court poet by CHARLES VI. His 27 three-act librettos were set in more than 800 operas in the 18th and early 19th cent. by such composers as Antonio VIVALDI, G. F. HANDEL, and W. A. MOZART.

Metaxas \\met-äk-'säs\\, **Ioannis** (1871–1941) Greek general and premier (1936–41). Named army chief of staff in 1913 he left Greece when King CONSTANTINE I was deposed in 1917, but returned in 1920. After the monarchy's fall in 1923, he led an opposition ultraroyalist party until the monarchy was restored in 1935. Appointed premier in 1936, he established a repressive dictatorship, carried out some beneficial reforms, and brought a united country into the Western alliance in World War II.

Metchnikoff \\'mech-ni-ˌkóf\\, **Élie** *orig.* Ilya Ilich Mechnikov (1845–1916) Russian zoologist and microbiologist. He directed the Pasteur Institute from 1895. Working with starfish, he discovered amoebalike cells in their systems that engulf foreign bodies such as bacteria. He established that these "phagocytes" are the first line of defense against acute infection in most animals. This phenomenon, now known as phagocytosis, is fundamental to immunology. He shared a 1908 Nobel Prize with Paul EHRLICH.

metempsychosis See REINCARNATION

meteor or **shooting star** or **falling star** Streak of light in the sky seen when a particle or small chunk of matter (meteoroid) enters earth's ATMOSPHERE and is vaporized by FRICTION. Most meteoroids, traveling at five times the speed of sound or more, burn up in the upper atmosphere, but a large one may reach the surface (see METEORITE). See also METEOR SHOWER.

meteorite Any interplanetary particle or chunk of matter (meteoroid) that strikes the surface of a planet or moon. A meteoroid falling toward earth travels at least 7 mi/second (11 km/second) and is vaporized by air FRICTION, producing a streak of light (METEOR). Though vast numbers of meteoroids enter the atmosphere each year, only a few hundred reach the ground.

meteorite crater Depression that results from the impact of a METEORITE with any planetary body. Impact craters have been discovered on many planets and satellites; they probably occur throughout the universe. Impact craters are uncommon on the earth because friction burns up most of the smaller bodies that enter the earth's atmosphere. Thus, any craters formed on the earth's surface tend to be larger than the average size of all entering meteorites.

meteoritics \\ˌmē-tē-ə-'ri-tiks\\ Study of the chemistry and mineralogy of METEORITE samples that have been collected on the earth and of METEORS as they pass through the earth's atmosphere. It provides information about the age of meteorites, the conditions under which they formed, and the geological history of their original planets. It is especially important for understanding the early geological history of the solar system.

meteorology Scientific study of atmospheric phenomena, particularly of the TROPOSPHERE and lower STRATOSPHERE. Meteorology entails the systematic study of WEATHER and its causes, and provides the basis for weather forecasting. See also CLIMATOLOGY.

meteor shower Entry into earth's atmosphere of multiple meteoroids (see METEOR), traveling in parallel paths, usually over hours or days. Most meteor showers come from matter released from a COMET and recur annually as the earth crosses the comet's orbit. They are usually named for a constellation (e.g., Leonid for Leo) or star in their direction of origin. Usually a few dozen meteors are seen per hour, but in the great Leonid meteor shower of 1833 hundreds of thousands were seen in one night all over N. America.

meter In poetry, the rhythmic pattern of a poetic line. Various principles have been devised to organize poetic lines into rhythmic units. Quantitative verse, the meter of classical Greek and Latin poetry, measures the length of time required to pronounce syllables, regardless of their stress; combinations of long and short syllables form the basic rhythmic units. Syllabic verse is most common in languages that are not strongly accented, such as French or Japanese; it is based on a fixed number of syllables within a line. Accentual verse occurs in strongly stressed languages such as the Germanic; only stressed syllables within a line are counted. Accentual-syllabic verse is the usual form in English poetry; it combines syllable counting and stress counting. The most common English meter, iambic pentameter, is a line of 10 syllables, or five iambic feet; each foot contains an unstressed syllable followed by a stressed syllable. See also PROSODY.

meter Basic unit of length in the METRIC SYSTEM and the INTERNATIONAL SYSTEM OF UNITS. In 1983 the General Conference on Weights and Measures decided that the accepted value for the speed of light would be exactly 299,792,458 meters per second, so the meter is now defined as the distance traveled by light in a vacuum in 1/299,792,458 second. One meter is equal to about 39.37 in. in U.S. units.

meter See RHYTHM AND METER

methadone \'me-thə-ˌdōn\ Organic compound, a potent synthetic NARCOTIC drug, the most effective form of treatment for addiction to HEROIN and other narcotics (see DRUG ADDICTION). It has been widely used in heroin-addiction programs in the U.S. since the 1960s. Though addictive itself, it is easier to stop using than heroin and causes no euphoric effects. A person taking a daily maintenance dose does not experience either heroin withdrawal symptoms or a heroin rush from any attempt to resume heroin, so heroin's psychological hold can be broken.

methanal See FORMALDEHYDE

methane *or* **marsh gas** Organic compound, chemical formula CH_4, colorless, odorless GAS that occurs naturally in NATURAL GAS and from bacterial decomposition of vegetation in the absence of oxygen (including in the rumens of cattle and other RUMINANTS). Methane burns readily, forming CARBON DIOXIDE and WATER with enough OXYGEN, and CARBON MONOXIDE without it. Mixtures of 5–14% methane in air are explosive and have caused many mine disasters. Abundant, cheap, and clean, methane is used widely as a fuel in homes, commercial establishments, and factories; it is mixed with trace amounts of an odorant to allow its detection. It is also a raw material for many industrial materials, including fertilizers, explosives, methanol, chloroform, carbon tetrachloride, and carbon black, and is the principal source of METHANOL.

methanol *or* **methyl alcohol** *or* **wood alcohol** Simplest of the ALCOHOLS, chemical formula CH_3OH. Methanol is an important industrial material; its derivatives are used in great quantities for making a vast number of compounds, among them many important synthetic dyes, resins, drugs, and perfumes. It is also used in automotive antifreezes, in rocket fuels, and as a solvent. It is flammable and explosive. A clean-burning fuel, it may substitute (at least in part) for GASOLINE. It is also used for denaturation of ETHANOL. A violent poison, it causes blindness and eventually death when drunk.

Method acting See STANISLAVSKY METHOD

Methodism Protestant religious movement originated by John WESLEY. Wesley, an Anglican clergyman, underwent an epiphany in 1738 in which he felt an assurance of personal salvation, and he soon began open-air preaching. Methodism did not formally break with the Church of ENGLAND until 1795. The Methodists' well-organized system of church government combined a strong central authority with effective local organization and the employment of lay preachers. Especially successful among the industrial working class, the movement expanded rapidly in the 19th cent. The Methodist Episcopal Church was founded in the U.S. in 1784; British and U.S. missionaries have since spread Methodism throughout the world. Methodism emphasizes the power of the Holy Spirit, the need for a personal relationship with God, simplicity of worship, and concern for the underprivileged.

Methodius, St. See Sts. CYRIL AND METHODIUS

Methuselah \mə-'thü-zə-lə\ Old Testament patriarch who lived to the age of 969. He is mentioned in GENESIS as a descendant of Seth, the son of Adam and Eve begotten after CAIN. He is remembered as the world's oldest human being. He was the grandfather of NOAH and the ancestor of ABRAHAM, JACOB, and DAVID.

methyl alcohol See METHANOL

Métis \mā-'tēs\ Canadian of mixed Indian and French or Scottish ancestry. The first Métis were the offspring of local Indian women and European fur traders in what is now S Manitoba. For over half a century they cultivated a distinctive way of life and came to think of themselves as a nation. They set up a provisional government under the leadership of Louis RIEL, and in 1870 negotiated a union with Canada that resulted in the establishment of the province of Manitoba. Today there are about 100,000 Métis in W Canada.

metrical foot See metrical FOOT

metric space In mathematics, a set of objects equipped with a concept of distance. The objects can be thought of as points in space, with the distance between points given by a distance formula, such that: (1) the distance from point A to point B is zero if and only if A and B are identical, (2) the distance from A to B is the same as from B to A, and (3) the distance from A to B plus that from B to C is greater than or equal to the distance from A to C (the triangle inequality). Two- and three-dimensional EUCLIDEAN SPACES are metric spaces, as are certain topological spaces (see TOPOLOGY).

metric system International decimal system of weights and measures, based on the METER (m) for length and the kilogram (kg) for mass, originally adopted in France in 1795. All other metric units were derived from the meter, including the GRAM (g) for weight and the liter (l, or L) for capacity (0.0001 cu m). In the 20th cent., the metric system became the basis for the INTERNATIONAL SYSTEM OF UNITS.

Metric and U.S. Customary Systems: Conversion Factors for Length, Weight, Area, Volume, Capacity, Power

To convert	Multiply by	To convert	Multiply by
inches to millimeters	25.4	millimeters to inches	0.03937
inches to centimeters	2.54	centimeters to inches	0.3937
feet to meters	0.3048	meters to feet	3.28
yards to meters	0.9144	meters to yards	1.0936
miles to kilometers	1.61	kilometers to miles	0.621

To convert	Multiply by	To convert	Multiply by
ounces to grams	28.35	grams to ounces	0.03527
pounds to kilograms	0.4536	kilograms to pounds	2.2046

To convert	Multiply by	To convert	Multiply by
square inches to square centimeters	6.4516	square centimeters to square inches	0.155
square feet to square miles	0.0929	square meters to square feet	10.764
square yards to square meters	0.836	square meters to square yards	1.196
square miles to square kilometers	2.5887	square kilometers to square miles	0.3863
acres to hectares	0.4047	hectares to acres	2.471

To convert	Multiply by	To convert	Multiply by
cubic inches to cubic centimeters	16.387	cubic centimeters to cubic inches	0.061
cubic inches to liters	0.016387	liters to cubic inches	61.024
cubic feet to cubic meters	0.0283	cubic meters to cubic feet	35.3357
cubic yards to cubic meters	0.7646	cubic meters to cubic yards	1.3079

To convert	Multiply by	To convert	Multiply by
quarts to liters	0.946	liters to quarts	1.0565
gallons to liters	3.785	liters to gallons	0.26413
gallons to cubic meters	0.003785	cubic meters to gallons	264.13

To convert	Multiply by	To convert	Multiply by
horsepower to kilowatts	0.7457	kilowatts to horsepower	1.341

M

Metro-Goldwyn-Mayer, Inc. See MGM

Metropolitan Museum of Art Most comprehensive art museum in the U.S. and one of the foremost in the world. It was incorporated in New York City in 1870, and the present building in Central Park on Fifth Avenue was opened in 1880. Much of the medieval collection is housed at The Cloisters in Manhattan's Ft. Tryon Park; its building (1938) incorporates parts of medieval monasteries and churches. The Metropolitan was built with the private fortunes of businessmen; today it is owned by the city but supported mainly by private endowment. Its outstanding collections from all periods include—in addition to paintings, sculpture, and graphic arts—architecture, glass, ceramics, clothing, textiles, metalwork, furniture, arms and armor, and musical instruments. It also incorporates one of the world's greatest art and archaeology reference collections.

Metropolitan Opera Oldest opera company in New York. Founded in 1883 by a group of millionaires who had failed to get boxes at the Academy of Music, the Met was soon second to no opera house in the world in the quality of the singers it attracted. Originally sited at Broadway and 39th Street, it moved to LINCOLN CENTER FOR THE PERFORMING ARTS in 1966.

Metsys \'met-sīs\, **Quentin** (c.1465–1530) Flemish artist. According to tradition, Metsys (whose name was also spelled Massys and Matsys) was trained as a blacksmith but studied painting after falling in love with an artist's daughter. He was admitted to the Antwerp artists' guild in 1491. His most celebrated paintings, the triptychs *The Holy Kinship* (1507–9) and *The Entombment of Christ* (1508–11), exhibit strong religious feelings and precision of detail. He also painted many notable portraits. He was the first Flemish artist to effect a genuine synthesis of the N European and Italian Renaissance traditions.

Metternich (-Winneburg-Beilstein) \'me-tər-,nik\, **Klemens (Wenzel Nepomuk Lothar), Fürst (Prince) von** (1773–1859) Austrian statesman. He served as Austrian minister in Saxony (1801–3), Berlin (1803–5), and Paris (1806–9). In 1809 Francis I of Austria (see Francis II) appointed him minister of foreign affairs, a position he held until 1848. By skillful diplomacy and deceit, he kept Austria neutral in the war between France and Russia (1812) and secured its position of power before finally allying with Prussia and Russia (1813). As the organizer of the Congress of VIENNA (1814–15), he was largely responsible for the policy of balance of power in Europe to ensure the stability of European governments. After 1815 he remained firmly opposed to liberal ideas. He was forced to resign by the REVOLUTION OF 1848. He is remembered for his role in restoring Austria as a leading European power.

Metz \'metz, *French* 'mes\ City (pop., 1999: 124,000), NE France. Fortified by the Romans, it became a bishopric in the 4th cent. A.D. and the capital of Frankish Lorraine in 843. It prospered as a free town within the HOLY ROMAN EMPIRE. Taken by the French in 1552, it was formally ceded to France in 1648. It fell to German rule in 1871, but was returned to France after World War I. It was the birthplace of Paul VERLAINE.

Meuse River \'mœz, *Engl* 'myüz\ *Dutch* **Maas** \'mäs\ River, W Europe. Rising in NE France, it flows north into Belgium, then the Netherlands, one branch flowing into the Hollandsch Canal (an outlet of the North Sea), and another joining the Waal River, eventually emptying into the North Sea after 590 mi (950 km). It is an important waterway in W Europe. Its valley was the scene of heavy fighting in World War I; in World War II the crossing of the Meuse was critical to Germany's 1940 invasion of France.

Mexicali City (pop., 1995: 505,000), NW Mexico. It lies in the Mexicali Valley, an extension of the IMPERIAL VALLEY of the U.S., in NE Baja California. It extends across the Mexico–U.S. border to Calexico, Cal. Its economy is chiefly based on tourism and the processing and distribution of cotton, fruits, vegetables, and cereals. It is the seat of the Autonomous Univ. of Baja California.

Mexican Revolution (1910–20) Lengthy struggle that began with the overthrow of the conservative Porfirio DÍAZ. Francisco MADERO, Pancho VILLA, and Emiliano ZAPATA amassed supporters, and in 1911 Madero was declared pres-

ident, but his slow-paced reforms alienated many. He was deposed by Gen. Victoriano HUERTA, whose own despotic dictatorship quickly fell to Villa, Álvaro Obregón (1880–1928), and Venustiano CARRANZA. Carranza declared himself president in 1914 over Villa's objections; he enacted the liberal constitution of 1917 but did little to implement its key provisions, and in 1920 he was killed while fleeing a rebellion. With the election of the reform-minded Obregón, the revolutionary period ended.

Mexican War *or* **Mexican–American War** War between the U.S. and Mexico, 1846–48. After the U.S. annexed Texas in 1845, Mexico claimed the S border of Texas was the Nueces River, while the U.S. claimed it was the Rio Grande. A secret U.S. mission to negotiate the dispute and purchase New Mexico and California was aborted by Mexico. In response to the snub, Pres. J. K. POLK sent troops under Zachary TAYLOR to occupy the land between the two rivers. In April 1846 Mexican troops crossed the Rio Grande and attacked Taylor's troops; Congress approved a declaration of war in May. Ordered to invade Mexico, Taylor captured Monterrey and defeated a large force under Antonio SANTA ANNA at Buena Vista in Feb. 1847. Gen. Winfield SCOTT moved his army by sea to Veracruz, captured the city, and marched inland to Mexico City in September. Under the Treaty of GUADALUPE HIDALGO, Mexico ceded nearly all of present New Mexico, Utah, Nevada, Arizona, California, Texas, and Colorado. Casualties included about 13,000 American deaths; all but 1,700 were caused by disease. The war, which made a national hero of Taylor, reopened the slavery-extension issue.

Mexico *Spanish* **México** \'me-hē-,kō\ *officially* **United Mexican States** Republic, S N. America. The RIO GRANDE forms part of its NE border with the U.S. Area: 756,066 sq mi (1,958,201 sq km). Population (2000 est.): 98,881,000. Capital: MEXICO CITY. About three-fifths of Mexico's population is MESTIZO, one-third is American Indian, and the rest is of European ancestry. Languages: Spanish (official); more than 50 Indian languages are spoken. Religion: Roman Catholicism. Currency: Mexican peso. Mexico has two major peninsulas, the YUCATÁN in the southeast and BAJA CALIFORNIA in the northwest. The high Mexican Plateau forms the core of the country and is enclosed by mountain ranges: the SIERRA MADRE Occidental, the Sierra Madre Oriental, and the Cordillera Neo-Volcánica. The last has the nation's highest peak, the volcano CITLALTÉPETL. Mexico has a mixed economy based on agriculture, manufacturing, and petroleum extraction. About one-eighth of the land is arable; its major crops include corn, wheat, rice, beans, coffee, cotton, fruits, and vegetables. It is the world's largest producer of silver, bismuth, and celestite, and its crude-oil reserves rank seventh in the world. Manufactures include processed foods, chemicals, transport vehicles, and electrical machinery. It is a republic with two legislative houses; its chief of state and head of government is the president. Inhabited for more than 20,000 years, the area produced great civilizations in A.D. 100–900, including the OLMEC, TLTEC, MAYAN, and AZTEC. The Aztec were conquered in 1521 by Hernán CORTÉS, who established Mexico City on the site of the Aztec capital, TENOCHTITLÁN. Francisco de Montejo (1479–1553) conquered the remnants of Maya civilization in 1526, and Mexico became part of the viceroyalty of NEW SPAIN. In 1821 rebels negotiated a status quo independence from Spain, and in 1823 a new congress declared Mexico a republic. In 1845 the U.S. voted to annex Texas,

Mexican Presidents from 1917

President	Term	President	Term
Venustiano Carranza*	1917–20	Adolfo Ruiz Cortines	1952–58
Adolfo de la Huerta	1920	Adolfo López Mateos	1958–64
Álvaro Obregón	1920–24	Gustavo Díaz Ordaz	1964–70
Plutarco Elías Calles	1924–28	Luis Echeverría Álvarez	1970–76
Emilio Portes Gil	1928–30	José López Portillo	1976–82
Pascual Ortíz Rubio	1930–32	Miguel de la Madrid	1982–88
Abelardo L. Rodríguez	1932–34	Carlos Salinas de Gortari	1988–94
Lázaro Cárdenas	1934–40	Ernesto Zedillo	1994–2000
Manuel Ávila Camacho	1940–46	Vicente Fox	2000–
Miguel Alemán	1946–52		

*Claimed the presidency as early as 1914.

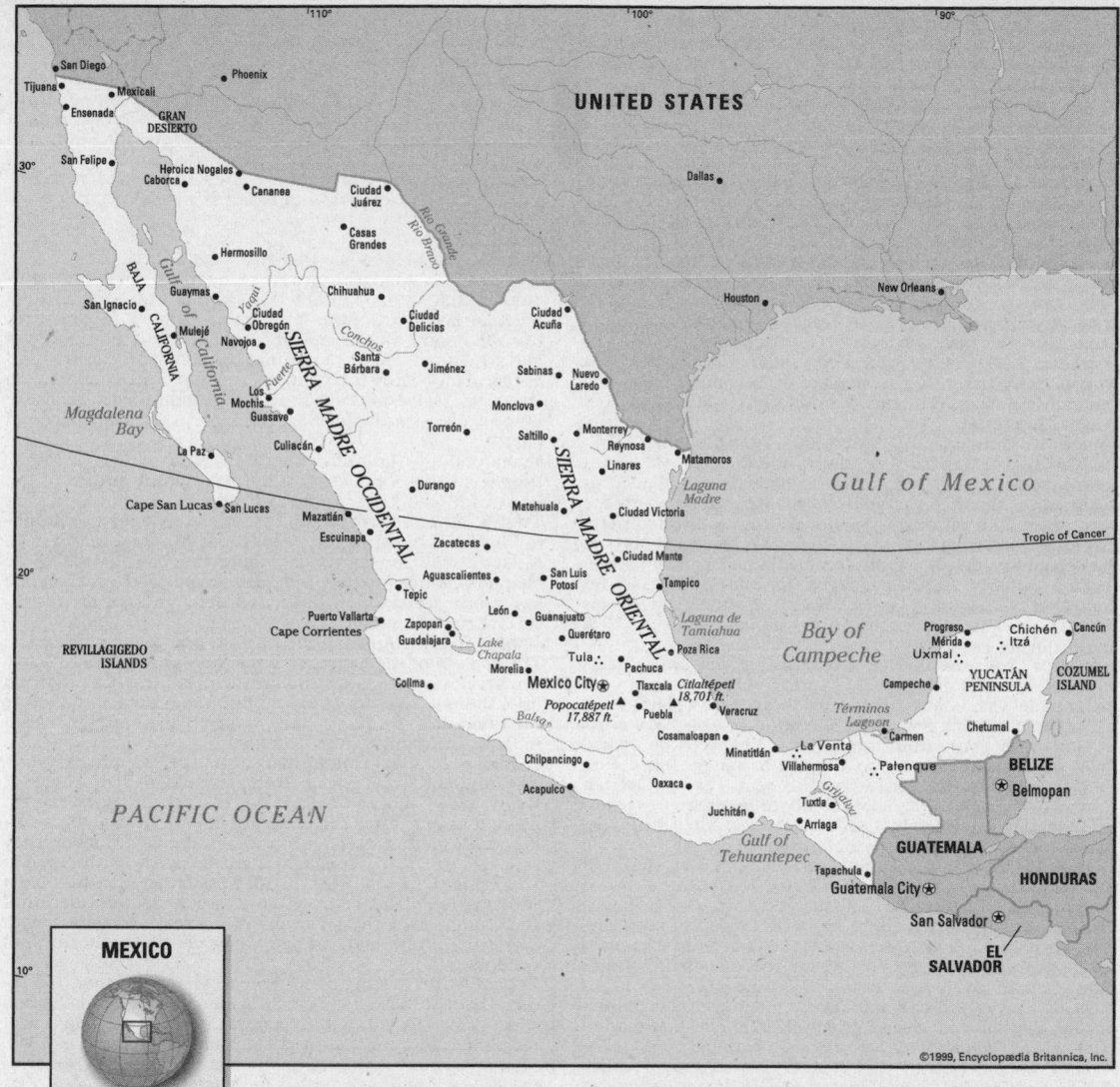

©1999, Encyclopædia Britannica, Inc.

MEXICO

Scale 1: 23,766,000
0   100   200 mi
0   150   300 km

initiating the MEXICAN WAR. Under the Treaty of GUADALUPE HIDALGO in 1848, it ceded a vast territory in what is now the W and SW U.S. The Mexican government endured several rebellions and civil wars in the late 19th and early 20th cent. (see MEXICAN REVOLUTION). During World War II it declared war on the AXIS POWERS (1942), and in the postwar era it was a founding member of the UNITED NATIONS (1945) and the ORGANIZATION OF AMERICAN STATES (1948). In 1993 it ratified the N. AMERICAN FREE TRADE AGREEMENT. The election of Vicente Fox (2000) ended 71 years of rule by the INSTITUTIONAL REVOLUTIONARY PARTY.

México \'me-hē-ˌkō\ State (pop., 2000: 13,083,000), central Mexico, surrounding the Federal District and MEXICO CITY. Its capital is TOLUCA. Occupying an area of 8,245 sq mi (21,355 sq km), it contains many preconquest ruins, including TEOTIHUACAN. The state's elevation at more than 10,000 ft (3,000 m) above sea level creates a cool climate; its population density is the highest of any Mexican state.

Mexico, Gulf of Gulf, SE coast of N. America. Covering an area of 600,000 sq mi (1,550,000 sq km), it is bounded by the U.S., Mexico, and Cuba. It has a maximum depth, in the

Mexico Basin, of 17,070 ft (5,203 m). The GULF STREAM enters it from the Caribbean Sea and flows out to the Atlantic. Its major ports are VERACRUZ in Mexico, and GALVESTON, NEW ORLEANS, Pensacola, and TAMPA in the U.S. It is an important source of fish, offshore oil, and natural gas.

Mexico, National Autonomous University of Government-financed university in Mexico City, founded in 1551. The university was controlled by the Roman Catholic Church (1553–1867). After 1867, the government established professional schools of law, medicine, engineering, and architecture. The university was given administrative autonomy in 1929; it moved to a new campus in 1954. Total enrollment is about 270,000.

Mexico City officially **Ciudad de México, D.F.** \ˌsyü-'thäth-thä-'me-hē-ˌkō\ Capital (pop., 1995: 8,489,000; metro. area pop., 16,560,000) of the Federal District and of Mexico. Located at an elevation of 7,350 ft (2,240 m), and occupying an area of 571 sq mi (1,479 sq km), it is the world's largest city proper and one of the world's fastest-growing metropolitan areas. It generates about one-third of Mexico's industrial production. It lies on an ancient lake bed, the site of the AZTEC capital, TENOCHTITLÁN, taken by the Spanish explorer Hernán CORTÉS in 1521. It was the seat of the viceroyalty of NEW SPAIN. Captured by revolutionaries un-

M

der Gen. Agustín de ITURBIDE in 1821, it was seized by the U.S. in 1847 during the MEXICAN WAR and by the French 1863–67 under MAXIMILIAN. It was greatly improved during the presidency of Porfirio DÍAZ. In 1985 it was struck by a severe earthquake that killed 9,500 people. The old city center, the Zócalo, has many historic buildings. The city is home to the huge National Autonomous Univ. of Mexico (founded 1551).

Meyerbeer \'mī-ər-ˌbār\, **Giacomo** *orig.* Jakob Liebmann Meyer Beer (1791–1864) German-French composer. Brother of the astronomer Wilhelm Beer (1797–1850) and the playwright Michael Beer (1800–1833), he achieved early success as a pianist. After studying vocal writing in Italy, he produced successful Italian operas. He moved to Paris around 1825, and his *Robert le diable* (1831) was one of opera's greatest triumphs. Three later French grand operas also became international successes: *Les Huguenots* (1836), *Le prophète* (1849), and *L'africaine* (1864). Though Richard WAGNER's criticism led to neglect of his music for many years, Meyerbeer influenced both Giuseppe VERDI and Wagner himself.

Meyerhold \'mī-ər-ˌhōlt\, **Vsevolod (Yemilyevich)** (1874–1940?) Russian theatrical producer and director. He joined the MOSCOW ART THEATRE in 1898 and formulated his avant-garde theories of symbolic theater. Opposed to the naturalism of Konstantin STANISLAVSKY, he directed plays in a nonrepresentational style. After 1908 he staged plays in St. Petersburg that drew on commedia dell'arte and Asian theater, notably *The Magnificent Cuckold* (1920) and his controversial *Queen of Spades* (1935). Condemned for his opposition to socialist realism, he was imprisoned in 1938 and probably executed.

mezzotint \'met-sō-ˌtint\ (from Italian, *mezza tinta:* "halftone") Engraving produced by pricking the surface of a metal plate with innumerable small holes that will hold ink; when the engraving is printed, the ink produces large areas of tone with soft, subtle gradations. Engraved or etched lines are often introduced to give the design greater definition. Invented in Holland in the 17th cent., it was practiced primarily in England. Its adaptability to making color prints made it ideal for reproduction of paintings. After the invention of photography it was rarely used.

MGM *in full* **Metro-Goldwyn-Mayer, Inc.** U.S. film studio. It was formed when the film distributor Marcus Loew, who bought Metro Pictures in 1920, merged it with the Goldwyn production company in 1924 and with Louis B. Mayer Pictures in 1925. L. B. MAYER was executive head of the studio for 25 years, assisted by production manager Irving THALBERG. It reached its peak in the 1930s and '40s, when it had most of Hollywood's famous stars under contract. It produced such hits as *Grand Hotel* (1932), *The Good Earth* (1937), *The Philadelphia Story* (1940), *Gaslight* (1944), *The Asphalt Jungle* (1950), *Ben-Hur* (1959), *Doctor Zhivago* (1965), and *2001: A Space Odyssey* (1968). It was celebrated for its lavish musicals, including *The Wizard of Oz* (1939), *Easter Parade* (1948), *On the Town* (1949), *An American in Paris* (1951), *Singin' in the Rain* (1952), and *Gigi* (1958). It sold off many of its assets in the 1970s, and later merged with UNITED ARTISTS CORP. Since 1986 it has had a succession of owners.

MI-5 *in full* **Military Intelligence (Unit 5)** British Security Service. Originally organized in 1909 to counter German espionage, in 1931 it assumed wider responsibility for assessing threats to national security. Today, as Britain's domestic-security intelligence agency, its purpose is to protect against such threats as terrorism, espionage, and subversion. The Security Service Act (1996) expanded its role to assist in fighting organized crime.

Miami City (pop., 2000: 362,000), SE Florida, on BISCAYNE BAY. The southernmost large city in the continental U.S., it has a beach 7 mi (11 km) long. A Spanish mission was founded near the site in 1567, but permanent settlement did not begin until 1835. The arrival of the railway in 1896 spurred development. The city has been damaged by hurricanes, notably in 1926, 1935, and 1992. Nearly 300,000 Cuban refugees have arrived since 1959, establishing "Little Havana" within the city. It is a major resort and retirement center, and its port handles the world's largest number of cruise-ship passengers. It is also a banking center. Educational institutions include the Univ. of Miami and Florida International Univ.

Miami Beach City (pop., 2000: 88,000), SE Florida. It is situated on an island across BISCAYNE BAY from MIAMI. Until 1912 the site was a mangrove swamp. The bay was dredged to form an island measuring 7.4 sq mi (19 sq km), with an 8-mi (13-km) beach. The city, incorporated in 1915, is now a luxury resort and convention center. Connected with Miami by several causeways, it is noted for its ART DECO architecture.

Miao See HMONG

Miao-Yao languages See HMONG-MIEN LANGUAGES

mica \'mī-kə\ Any of a group of hydrous potassium, aluminum SILICATE MINERALS that exhibit a two-dimensional sheet, or layer, structure. A common variety is MUSCOVITE; two others are biotite and phlogopite. Micas have various industrial uses. The varieties that contain little iron are used as thermal or electrical insulators in appliances and in such electrical devices as capacitors. In ground form, micas are used in the manufacture of wallpaper, roofing paper, and paint.

Micah \'mī-kə\ (late 8th cent. B.C.) One of the 12 Minor Prophets in the OLD TESTAMENT, traditional author of the Book of Micah. (His prophecy is part of a larger book, The Twelve, in the Jewish canon.) He probably began to prophesy before the fall of the N kingdom of Israel in 721 B.C. Modern scholars usually attribute the book's first three chapters, which predict judgment from God on idolaters and unjust leaders, to Micah, and date much of the rest to several centuries later.

Michael In the BIBLE and the QURAN, one of the archangels. The captain of the heavenly hosts, he was invoked by early Christian armies against the heathen. In Christian tradition he is thought to escort the soul into the presence of God at the time of death. In art he is depicted as a warrior, sword in hand, in triumph over a dragon.

Michael *or* **Michael Romanov** \rō-'mä-nəf, 'rō-mə-ˌnäf\ *Russian* Mikhail Fyodorovich Romanov (1596–1645) Czar of Russia (1613–45) and founder of the ROMANOV DYNASTY. Elected as czar after the chaotic Time of TROUBLES, he allowed his mother's relatives to direct the government; they restored order to Russia and made peace with Sweden (1617) and Poland (1618). In 1619 his father, released from captivity in Poland, returned to Russia and, as coruler until 1633, dominated the government, increasing contact with Western Europe and strengthening central authority and serfdom.

Michael (b.1921) King of Romania. After his father, the future Carol II (1893–1953), had been excluded from succession (1926), the young Michael was proclaimed king. Carol reclaimed the throne in 1930, but abdicated in 1940. Michael again became king but was in effect a prisoner of the military regime; in 1944 he helped lead the coup that overthrew it. He strongly opposed the communists' subsequent rise to power, but was forced to abdicate in 1947. He went into exile in Switzerland and joined a U.S. brokerage firm.

Michael VIII Palaeologus \ˌpā-lē-'äl-ə-gəs\ (1224?–1282) Byzantine emperor (1261–82). Appointed regent for the 6-year-old son of Theodore II (1258), he seized the throne and blinded the rightful heir. He recovered Constantinople from the Latins (1261) and allied with the pope against his rivals, briefly reuniting Greek and Roman churches in 1274. In 1281 the new pope, Martin IV, excommunicated him and declared Charles of Anjou's planned campaign against Byzantium to be a holy crusade. The SICILIAN VESPERS prevented Charles's expedition and thus saved Byzantium from a second occupation by the Latins.

Michelangelo (di Lodovico Buonarroti) (1475–1564) Italian sculptor, painter, architect, and poet. Born in Caprese, he served a brief apprenticeship with Domenico GHIRLANDAIO in Florence before beginning the first of several sculptures for Lorenzo de' MEDICI. Later, in Rome, his *Bacchus* (1496–97) established his fame and led to a commission for the *Pietà* now in ST. PETER'S BASILICA, the masterpiece of his early years. His *David* (1501–4), commissioned for the cathedral of Florence, is still considered the prime example of the Renaissance ideal of perfect humanity. He also produced several Madonnas for private patrons and his only universally accepted easel painting, *The Holy Family* (known as the *Doni Tondo*). He then agreed to paint the ceiling of the SISTINE CHAPEL (1508–12). The first scenes, depicting the story of Noah, are relatively stable and on a small scale, but the later scenes evince boldness and complexity. His figures for the tombs in Florence's Medici Chapel (1519–33), which he designed, are among his most accomplished creations. He devoted his last 30 years largely to the *Last Judgment*

Michelangelo, detail, "Pietà," c.1550–55, reputed self-portrait

fresco in the Sistine Chapel, to writing over 300 sonnets and madrigals, and to architecture. He was commissioned to complete St. Peter's Basilica, begun in 1506; though it was not quite finished at his death, its exterior owes more to him than to any other architect. He is regarded today as among the most exalted of artists.

Michelet \mēsh-'le\, **Jules** (1798–1874) French nationalist historian. His life's work was the 17-volume *Histoire de France* (1833–67). His method, an attempt to resurrect the past by immersing his own personality in his narrative, resulted in a historical synthesis of great dramatic power, though the 11 volumes that appeared in 1855–67 are distorted by his hatred of priests and kings, hasty or abusive treatment of documents, and mania for symbolic interpretation. His other works include the vivid and impassioned *Histoire de la révolution française* (7 vols., 1847–53). A later series of lyrical books on nature displays his superb prose style.

Michelin \ˌmē-shə-'laⁿ\ Leading French manufacturer of tires and other rubber products. Founded in 1888 by the Michelin brothers, André (1853–1931) and Édouard (1859–1940), it introduced pneumatic tires for automobiles in the 1890s. Today it operates plants in many countries. It was reorganized as a HOLDING COMPANY in 1951. It also publishes a famous series of travel guides and road maps.

Michelson \'mī-kəl-sən\, **A(lbert) A(braham)** (1852–1931) U.S. (Prussian-born) physicist. He taught principally at the Univ. of Chicago (1892–1931). He invented the interferometer, with which he used light to make extremely precise measurements. He is best remembered for the MICHELSON-MORLEY EXPERIMENT. Using a more refined interferometer, Michelson measured the diameter of the star Betelgeuse, the first substantially accurate determination of the size of a star. In 1907 he became the first American scientist to receive a Nobel Prize.

Michelson-Morley experiment Attempt to detect the VELOCITY of the earth with respect to ether, a hypothetical medium in space formerly proposed to carry light waves. It was first performed in 1881 by A. A. MICHELSON and refined in 1887 by Michelson and Edward W. Morley (1838–1923). The procedure assumed that if the speed of light were constant with respect to the ether, the motion of the earth could be detected by comparing the speed of light in the direction of earth's motion and the speed of light at right angles to earth's motion. No difference was found, discrediting the ether theory. As a result, Albert EINSTEIN proposed in 1905 that the speed of light is a universal constant.

Michener \'mich-nər\, **James A(lbert)** (1907?–1997) U.S. writer. Michener was a foundling discovered in Doylestown, Pa., and raised as a Quaker. During 1944–46 he was a naval historian in the S. Pacific; his *Tales of the South Pacific* (1947, Pulitzer Prize) was adapted as the musical *South Pacific* (1949; film, 1958). He is known for his best-selling epic and detailed novels drawing on extensive research, including *Hawaii* (1959; film, 1966), *Chesapeake* (1978), and *Mexico* (1992).

Michigan State (pop., 2000: 9,938,000), midwestern U.S. Surrounded almost entirely by the GREAT LAKES, it covers 58,527 sq mi (151,585 sq km); its capital is LANSING. Michigan is divided into two large land segments: the Upper and Lower peninsulas. The W region of the Upper Peninsula is a rugged upland rich in minerals, and the remainder of the state consists of lowlands and rolling hills. The area was originally inhabited by ALGONQUIAN-speaking Indians. The French arrived in the 17th cent., founding SAULT STE. MARIE in 1668 and DETROIT in 1701; fur trading was their primary activity. The English gained control of Michigan in 1763 following the FRENCH AND INDIAN WAR, and it passed to the U.S. in 1783. It was included in the NORTHWEST TERRITORIES in 1787 and in Indiana Territory in 1800. Michigan Territory was organized on the Lower Peninsula in 1805. Though surrendered to the British in the WAR OF 1812, U.S. rule was restored in 1813 by the victory of O. H. PERRY at the Battle of Lake Erie. A boundary dispute with Ohio, known as the Toledo War, was settled by Congress, with Michigan receiving the Upper Peninsula and statehood as compensation. In 1837 it became the 26th U.S. state. Throughout the AMERICAN CIVIL WAR, it made major contributions to the Union cause. In the 20th cent. its economy was dominated by the automotive industry and suffered with its decline.

Michigan, Lake Third-largest of the five GREAT LAKES, and the only one lying wholly within the U.S. Bordered by Michigan, Wisconsin, Illinois, and Indiana, it connects with Lake HURON through the Straits of MACKINAC in the north. It is 321 mi (517 km) long and up to 118 mi (190 km) wide, with a maximum depth of 923 ft (281 m). Its first European visitor was the French explorer Jean Nicolet in 1634; R.-R. LA SALLE brought the first sailing ship there in 1679. It now attracts international shipping as part of the Great Lakes-St. Lawrence Seaway.

Michigan, University of State university with its main campus in Ann Arbor and branch campuses in Flint and Dearborn. Established in Ann Arbor in 1837, today it is one of the nation's leading research universities. Facilities include a nuclear reactor, a hospital complex, an aerospace engineering laboratory, a Great Lakes research center, and the Gerald R. Ford Presidential Library. Enrollment at the main campus is about 37,000.

Michigan State University Public university in E. Lansing. Chartered in 1855, it became the prototype for land-grant colleges created under the MORRILL ACT OF 1862. Facilities include a plant research laboratory, the National Superconducting Cyclotron laboratory, and centers for international studies, economic development, and environmental toxicology. Total enrollment is about 42,000.

Michizane See SUGAWARA MICHIZANE

Michoacán \ˌmē-chō-ä-'kän\ State (pop., 2000: 3,979,000), SW Mexico. Bounded by the Pacific Ocean, and occupying an area of 23,138 sq mi (59,928 sq km), it rises from a narrow coastal plain to the SIERRA MADRE. Its capital is MORELIA. In the 1530s Vasco de Quiroga established the first successful missions among the Tarascan Indians. The state lies in an area of great volcanic activity: Mt. Jorullo was formed by an eruption in 1759, and PARICUTÍN was created by an eruption that lasted from 1943 to 1952.

Mickey Mouse Famous character of Walt DISNEY's animated cartoons. Introduced in *Steamboat Willie* (1928), the first animated cartoon with sound, Mickey was created by Disney, who also provided his high-pitched voice, and was usually drawn by the studio's head animator, Ub Iwerks. With his overlarge head and round black ears, he became the star of over 100 cartoon shorts. In 1932 Disney received an honorary Academy Award for his creation.

Mickiewicz \mʸēts-'kʸe-vʸēch\, **Adam (Bernard)** (1798–1855) Polish poet. A lifelong apostle of Polish national freedom and one of Poland's greatest poets, Mickiewicz was deported to Russia for his revolutionary activities in 1823 and later settled in Paris. His *Poezja* (2 vols., 1822–23; "Poetry") was the first major Polish Romantic work. Other works include his masterpiece, the poetic epic *Pan Tadeusz* (*Master Thaddeus*; 1834), which describes the life of the Polish gentry in the early 19th cent. He also was a professor, edited a radical newspaper, and undertook missions on behalf of Poland.

Micmac Largest of the Indian tribes of Canada's E Maritime Provinces. Early chronicles describe them as fierce and warlike, but they were among the first Indians to accept Jesuit teachings and intermarry with the settlers of New France. In winter they hunted caribou, moose, and small game; in summer they fished, gathered shellfish, and hunted seals. In the 17th–18th cent. they were allies of the French against the English. Today their descendants, mixed with whites, number about 15,000.

microbiology Scientific study of microorganisms, a diverse group of simple life-forms including PROTOZOANS, ALGAE, MOLDS, BACTERIA, and VIRUSES. Microbiology is concerned with their structure, function, and classification and with ways of controlling and using their activities. Its foundations were established with the work of Louis PASTEUR and Robert KOCH. Since then, many disease-causing microorganisms have been identified and means of controlling their harmful effects developed. Means of channeling the activities of various microorganisms to benefit medicine, industry, and agriculture have been discovered. See also BACTERIOLOGY, GENETIC ENGINEERING.

microchip See INTEGRATED CIRCUIT

microcircuit See INTEGRATED CIRCUIT

microclimate Climatic condition in a relatively small area, within a few feet above and below the earth's surface and within canopies of vegetation. Microclimates are affected by such factors as temperature, humidity, wind and turbulence, the nature of the soil and vegetation, elevation, and season. Weather and climate are sometimes influenced by microclimatic conditions, especially by variations in topography.

microcomputer Small DIGITAL COMPUTER whose CPU is contained on a single integrated COMPUTER CHIP. The processing capacity of microcomputers has grown immensely since their introduction. The PERSONAL COMPUTER is the most common example of a microcomputer, but high-performance microcomputer systems are widely used in business, in engineering, and in "smart" machines in manufacturing. See also INTEGRATED CIRCUIT, MICROPROCESSOR.

microeconomics Study of the economic behavior of individual consumers, firms, and industries and the distribution of total production and income among them. It considers individuals both as suppliers of LAND, LABOR, and CAPITAL and as consumers of the final product, and it examines firms both as suppliers of products and as consumers of labor and capital. Microeconomics seeks to analyze the MARKET or other mechanisms that establish relative prices among goods and services and allocate society's resources. See also MACROECONOMICS.

micromanipulation See MICROSURGERY

Micronesia Group of W Pacific islands. A subdivision of OCEANIA, it consists of KIRIBATI, GUAM, NAURU, the Northern MARIANAS, the Federated States of MICRONESIA, the MARSHALL ISLANDS, and PALAU. First colonized in the 17th cent. by Spain, it passed to Germany in 1885–99. Japan occupied the islands in 1914 and was granted a mandate to govern them in 1920. The U.S. occupied Micronesia in 1944 and received a trusteeship mandate in 1947. In 1973–74 the Congress of Micronesia adopted guidelines for independence, but regional differences led to a division of the islands into several constituencies after 1978.

Micronesia, Federated States of Republic, W Pacific Ocean. It includes the four island states of Yap, Chuuk (Truk), Pohnpei (Ponape), and Kosrae, all in the CAROLINE ISLANDS. Area: 271 sq mi (701 sq km). Population (2000): 118,000. Capital: PALIKIR on Pohnpei, the largest island. The people of the Federated States are Micronesian. Languages: Malayo-Polynesian languages, English. Religions: Christianity (predominant). Currency: U.S. dollar. The islands and atolls extend about 1,750 mi (2,800 km) east–west and about 600 mi (965 km) north–south. U.S. government grants constitute the main source of revenue; subsistence farming and fishing are the principal economic activities. It is a republic in free association with the U.S., and has one legislative house; its head of state and government is the president. The islands were probably settled by people from E Melanesia some 3,500 years ago. They were colonized by Spain in the 17th cent. and came under Japanese rule after World War I. They were captured by U.S. forces during World War II, and in 1947 they became part of the U.N. Trust Territory of the Pacific Islands, administered by the U.S. The islands became an internally self-governing federation in 1979. In 1982 the Federated States signed a compact of free association through which the U.S. is responsible for Micronesia's defense. See also map at OCEANIA.

microphone Device for converting sound waves into electric power that has wave characteristics similar to those of the sound. A microphone may be given directional characteristics so that it will pick up sound primarily from a single direction, from two directions, or uniformly from all directions. In addition to their use in telephones, microphones are widely applied in hearing aids, sound-recording systems, dictating machines, and public-address systems.

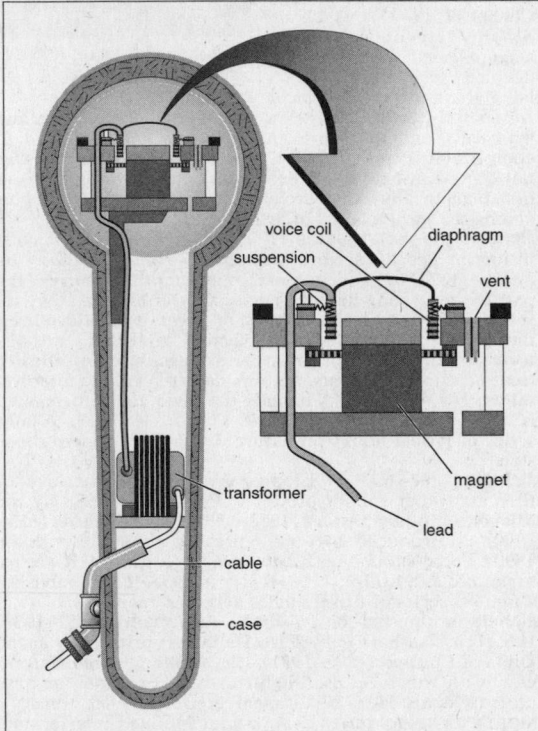

voice coil
diaphragm
suspension
vent
transformer
magnet
lead
cable
case

Microphone In a moving-coil microphone, sound causes the diaphragm to move, and the wire voice coil attached to the diaphragm thus moves through a magnetic field, generating a current. At the other end of the circuit, the process is reversed to generate sound with a loudspeaker.

microprocessor Miniature electronic device that functions as a DIGITAL COMPUTER's CPU. Microprocessors are INTEGRATED CIRCUITS that can interpret and execute program instructions as well as handle arithmetic operations. Their development in the late 1970s enabled computer engineers to develop MICROCOMPUTERS. Microprocessors led to "intelligent" terminals, such as bank ATMs, and to automatic control of much industrial instrumentation and hospital equipment, programmable appliances, and electronic games.

microscope Instrument that produces enlarged images of small objects, allowing them to be viewed at a scale convenient for examination and analysis. Formed by various means, the image is received by direct imaging, electronic processing, or a combination of these methods. The familiar optical, or light, microscope uses LENSES to form the image. Other types of microscopes use the wave nature of various physical processes, the most important being the electron microscope (see ELECTRON MICROSCOPY). Crude microscopes date to the mid-15th cent., but not until 1674 were the powerful microscopes of Antonie van LEEUWENHOEK able to detect phenomena as small as protozoa.

Microsoft Corp. U.S. computer firm, the leading developer of PERSONAL COMPUTER (PC) software systems and applications. It was founded in 1975 by Bill GATES and Paul G. Allen (b.1954), who adapted BASIC for PC use. In 1981 they released the operating system MS-DOS for the IBM PC. The subsequent adoption of MS-DOS by most other PC manufacturers generated vast revenues for Microsoft, which became a publicly owned corporation in 1986. It issued the first version of Microsoft Word, its popular word-processing program, in 1983, and Microsoft Windows, a GRAPHICAL USER INTERFACE which would eventually absorb the operating system, in 1985. In 2000 Microsoft was found culpable in an antitrust suit brought by the U.S. government, and uncertainty as to the possible consequences severely reduced its earnings.

microsurgery *or* **micromanipulation** Surgical technique for operating with specialized, tiny precision instruments under observation through a microscope, sometimes equipped with cameras to show the operation on a monitor. Microsurgery permits operations on the delicate bones of the inner and middle ear, reattachment of severed parts, repair of the retina, and removal of tumors intricately embedded in vital structures.

microtubule \ˌmī-krō-ˈtü-byül\ Thin tubular intracellular structure enclosed by a membrane, found within animal and plant cells. They help give shape to many cells and are major components of cilia and flagella (see CILIUM, FLAGELLUM), participate in cell division (MITOSIS), and assist the flow of materials from the cell bodies of nerve cells toward the ends of those cells' long extensions (axons).

microwave Portion of the spectrum of ELECTROMAGNETIC RADIATION with frequencies between about 1 gigahertz (10^9 Hz) and 1 terahertz (10^{12} Hz). Microwaves are the principal carriers of television, telephone, and data transmissions between stations on earth, and between earth and satellites. RADAR beams are short pulses of microwaves. Materials such as glass and ceramics do not absorb microwaves and are not heated by them; metals reflect microwaves, so metal containers block them out. See also MASER, MICROWAVE OVEN.

microwave oven Appliance that cooks food by means of high-frequency ELECTROMAGNETIC RADIATION. It is a relatively small, boxlike oven that raises the temperature of food by subjecting it to a high-frequency electromagnetic field. The microwaves are absorbed by water, fats, sugars, and certain other molecules, whose resulting vibrations produce heat. The heating thus occurs inside the food, without warming the surrounding air. This process greatly reduces cooking time.

Midas \ˈmī-dəs\ In Greek and Roman legend, a king of PHRYGIA. Granted a wish by DIONYSUS, he asked that everything he touched turn to gold. After turning his daughter to gold when she embraced him, he asked to be released from his wish. In another legend Midas was punished for judging APOLLO's music inferior to that of the satyr Marsyas by being given donkey's ears.

Midas See MISSILE DEFENSE ALARM SYSTEM

Mid-Atlantic Ridge Submarine ridge lying along the floor of the central Atlantic Ocean. It is a long mountain chain running for about 10,000 mi (16,000 km) in a north–south direction, curving from the Arctic Ocean to the S tip of Africa. The mountains sometimes reach above sea level, forming such islands as Ascension and ST. HELENA.

Middle Ages Period in European history from the 5th cent. A.D. to the RENAISSANCE. The sack of Rome by the VISIGOTHS in 410 destroyed the centralized structure provided by the Roman empire and marked the beginning of the Middle Ages. The early Middle Ages (c.410–1000) were formerly called the Dark Ages because of the eclipse of European civilization. The empire's systems of agriculture, roads, water supply, and shipping routes gradually decayed, and the unity of imperial society, government, and culture was replaced by the conflicting powers of the various Ger-

manic tribes that now dominated S and W Europe. Artistic and scholarly work also faded. The Roman Catholic Church gradually strengthened, providing the foundations of social unity. A 12th-cent. cultural and economic revival saw a growth of population, the flourishing of towns and farms, the emergence of merchant classes, and the beginnings of the erosion of FEUDALISM. Medieval civilization reached its apex in the 13th cent. with classic GOTHIC ARCHITECTURE and organizations such as GUILDS, civic councils, and monastic chapters. The church dominated intellectual life, producing the SCHOLASTICISM of St. THOMAS AQUINAS. The demise of feudalism and the rise of nationalism, secular education, and other cultural developments produced a new age, the Renaissance.

Middlebury College Private liberal-arts college in Middlebury, Vt., founded in 1800. One of the best-regarded colleges in the U.S., it is known for its curriculum emphasizing modern languages, and for its annual Bread Loaf Writers' Conference. Student enrollment is about 2,100.

Middle East *or* **Mideast** Region comprising the countries of SW Asia and NE Africa. It is an unofficial and imprecise term that now generally encompasses the lands around the S and E shores of the Mediterranean Sea, notably Libya, Egypt, Jordan, Israel, Lebanon, and Syria, as well as Iran, Iraq, and the countries of the Arabian Peninsula.

Middle English Vernacular spoken and written in England around 1100–1500, the descendant of OLD ENGLISH and the ancestor of Modern English. Its central period was marked by the borrowing of many Anglo-Norman words and the rise of the London dialect, used by such poets as John GOWER and Geoffrey CHAUCER in a 14th-cent. flowering of English literature.

Middlesex Former county, SE England, situated along the THAMES RIVER. Its earliest settlements date from 500 B.C.; Belgic tribes arrived in the 1st cent. B.C., followed by the Romans; SAXONS came in the early 5th cent. A.D. Situated between the E. and W. Saxons, it obtained its name (meaning "middle Saxons") by A.D. 704. Middlesex was an administrative county 1888–1965.

Middleton, Thomas (1570?–1627) English playwright. He wrote three books of poetry by 1600, then turned to writing plays in collaboration with John WEBSTER and others. His tragedies *Women Beware Women* (c.1621) and *The Changeling* (1622, with William Rowley) are considered his masterpieces. His comedies, which picture a society dazzled by money, included *Michaelmas Terme* (c.1605), *A Trick to Catch the Old-one* (1608), *A Mad World, My Masters* (1608), and *A Game at Chess* (1625).

Middle West See MIDWEST

Mideast See MIDDLE EAST

Midgard In Norse mythology, the dwelling place of humankind, between ASGARD and Niflheim. According to legend, it was made from the body of the first created being, the giant AURGELMIR (Ymir). The gods killed him and rolled his body into the central void of the universe, forming the land from his flesh, the oceans from his blood, the mountains from his bones, and so on. Aurgelmir's skull, held up by four dwarfs, became the dome of the heavens.

midge Any of a group of tiny DIPTERANS, sometimes called GNATS and classified as nonbiting (family Chironomidae), biting (family Ceratopogonidae), or gall (family Cecidomyiidae) midges. Nonbiting midges resemble mosquitoes; humming swarms can be found around water in late afternoon. The often blood-red, aquatic larvae (bloodworms) are important food for aquatic animals. Biting midges (no-see-ums) are the smallest bloodsucking insect (about 0.04 in., or 1 mm, long). Punkies or sand flies (genera *Culicoides* and *Leptoconops*) attack humans. Gall-midge larvae cause tissue swellings (galls) in plants.

Midgley, Thomas, Jr. (1889–1944) U.S. engineer and chemist. Born in Beaver Falls, Pa., in 1921 he discovered the effectiveness of tetraethyl lead as an antiknock additive for GASOLINE. He also discovered dichlorodifluoromethane—a refrigerant sold commercially as Freon-12 (see FREON), which with related compounds came into universal use as refrigerants and later as aerosol propellants—and one of the first CATALYSTS for "cracking" (breaking down) HYDROCARBONS.

MIDI \\'mi-dē\ *in full* Musical Instrument Digital Interface. PROTOCOL for transmission of musical data between digital components, such as SYNTHESIZERS and a computer's sound card. MIDI uses 8-bit asynchronous serial transmission with a data rate of 31.25 kilobytes per second. The transmitted data do not represent musical sound but specify aspects of it (a given pitch, its loudness, its duration). The data are then processed by a computer chip to create a specific sound.

Midler, Bette (b.1945) U.S. actress and singer. Born in Honolulu, she developed a popular though bawdy nightclub act in New York. Her Broadway show *The Divine Miss M* (1974) won a Tony Award as well as a Grammy award for the album. Her films include *The Rose* (1979), *Down and Out in Beverly Hills* (1986), *Stella* (1990), and *The First Wives Club* (1996). "The Rose" and "Wind Beneath My Wings" were among her hit singles.

mid-ocean ridge See OCEANIC RIDGE

Midrash \mē-'dräsh, 'mi-ˌdräsh\ In JUDAISM, a large collection of writings that examine the Hebrew BIBLE in the light of oral tradition. Midrashic activity reached its height in the 2nd cent. A.D. with the schools of Ishmael ben Elisha and AKIBA BEN JOSEPH. The Midrashim are divided into two groups: HALAKHAH, which clarify legal issues; and HAGGADAH, nonlegal writings intended simply to enlighten.

Midway *formerly* **Brooks Islands** Unincorporated U.S. territory (no permanent population), central Pacific Ocean. It consists of two coral islands with a total land area of 2 sq mi (5 sq km). Claimed for the U.S. in 1859, the islands were formally annexed in 1867. Their location gave them strategic importance for U.S. forces during World War II, and in 1941 the U.S. Navy established an air and submarine base there. The Battle of Midway (1942) took place in nearby waters. Its airfield was closed in 1993.

Midwest *or* **Middle West** Region, N and central U.S., lying midway between the APPALACHIAN and ROCKY mountains, and north of the OHIO RIVER. As defined by the federal government, it includes the states of Illinois, Indiana, Iowa, Kansas, Michigan, Minnesota, Missouri, Nebraska, N. Dakota, Ohio, S. Dakota, and Wisconsin. It includes much of the GREAT PLAINS, the region of the GREAT LAKES, and the upper MISSISSIPPI RIVER valley.

midwifery \mid-'wif-ər-ē\ Art of attending women in childbirth (see PARTURITION). With 20th-cent. advances in OBSTETRICS AND GYNECOLOGY, most women gave birth in hospitals. In the 1960s, the NATURAL CHILDBIRTH movement, feminism, and other factors renewed interest in the personal care given by midwives. In the U.S., certified nurse-midwives (CNMs)—registered nurses trained in midwifery—accept only low-risk patients. If problems develop, a physician is called. CNMs also provide pre- and postnatal care and reproductive health advice. Lay midwives usually have no formal training, are unlicensed, and deliver (at home) about three-fourths of infants born throughout the world, mostly in developing countries and rural areas of developed nations.

Mies van der Rohe \ˌmēs-ˌvan-də-'rō-ə\, **Ludwig** *orig.* Maria Ludwig Michael Mies (1886–1969) German-U.S. architect, undisputed leader of the INTERNATIONAL STYLE. Mies worked in the office of Peter BEHRENS. His first great work was the Barcelona Pavilion for the 1929 International Exposition. His steel-and-leather Barcelona chair became a 20th-cent. classic. He directed the BAUHAUS 1930–33. In 1937 Mies moved to the U.S. While teaching at Chicago's Armour Institute (now Illinois Institute of Technology), he designed the school's new campus (1939–41). Other projects include Chicago's Lake Shore Drive Apartments (1949–51), the SEAGRAM

Ludwig Mies van der Rohe, Lake Shore Drive Apartments, Chicago, 1949–51

BUILDING, and Berlin's New National Gallery (1963–68). Steel skeletons sheathed in glass curtain-wall facades, these buildings exemplify Mies's dictum that "less is more." Steel-and-glass office buildings influenced by his work were built all over the world.

Mifune \mi-'fü-nā\, **Toshiro** (1920–1997) Japanese film actor. He made his screen debut in 1947 and achieved international fame in *Rashomon* (1950). He acted in over 100 films and was best known for his portrayals of samurai in those of Akira KUROSAWA, including *Seven Samurai* (1954), *The Hidden Fortress* (1958), *Yojimbo* (1961), and *Sanjuro* (1962), which made him Japan's greatest international film star. His other films include *Throne of Blood* (1957), *Red Beard* (1965), and *Hell in the Pacific* (1969).

Mighty Five, The Group of Russian composers that joined together in 1875 to produce a Russian national music: César Cui (1835–1918), Aleksandr BORODIN, Mily BALAKIREV, Modest MUSSORGSKY, and Nikolai RIMSKY-KORSAKOV. A larger group around this core was labeled "the Mighty Handful," and the names have tended to merge.

migraine Recurrent vascular HEADACHE, usually on one side of the head. Severe throbbing pain is sometimes accompanied by nausea and vomiting. Some people have warning symptoms (an "aura") before the headache, including visual disturbance, weakness, numbness, or dizziness. Drugs may be taken as an attack begins (to abort it) or daily by patients with very frequent attacks (to prevent them or reduce their severity).

migrant labor Unskilled workers who move from one region to another offering their services on a temporary, usually seasonal, basis. In N. America, migrant labor is generally employed in agriculture, and moves seasonally from south to north following the harvest. In Europe and the Middle East, migrant labor usually involves urban employment and calls for longer periods of residence. The migrant labor market is often disorganized and exploitative. Laborers frequently endure long hours, low wages, poor working conditions, and substandard housing. In some countries child labor is widespread, and even in the U.S. those children who do not work may not go to school, since schools are usually open only to local residents. Workers who accept such employment are driven by even worse conditions in their home countries. Labor organizing is made difficult by mobility and by low rates of literacy and political participation, though some migrant laborers in the U.S. have been unionized.

migration, human Permanent change of residence by an individual or group. Migrations may be classed as internal or international, and as voluntary or forced. Voluntary migration is usually undertaken in search of a better life; forced migrations include expulsions during war and transportation of slaves or prisoners. The earliest humans migrated from Africa to all the continents except Antarctica within about 50,000 years. Modern mass migrations include the Great Atlantic Migration from Europe to N. America, a total of 37 million people between 1820 and 1980, and the forced migration of 20 million people from Africa to N. America as slaves. War-related forced migrations and refugee flows continue to be very large, as are voluntary migrations from developing nations to industrialized ones.

Mikan \'mī-kən\, **George (Lawrence)** (b.1924) U.S. basketball player. Born in Joliet, Ill., he earned a law degree at DePaul Univ. Standing about 6 ft 10 in. (2 m 8 cm) he played for the Minneapolis Lakers 1947–56, leading them to six championships. He was later named first commissioner of the American Basketball Assn. (1967–69). An Associated Press poll named him the greatest basketball player of the first half of the 20th cent.

Mikoyan \ˌmē-kō-'yän\, **Anastas (Ivanovich)** (1895–1978) Russian statesman. After joining the Bolsheviks in 1915, he became a supporter of Joseph STALIN. Commissar of trade from 1926 and a member of the Politburo from 1935, he was deputy premier 1946–64 and directed the country's trade. He supported Nikita KHRUSHCHEV's rise to power and became his close adviser and a first deputy premier of the Soviet Union.

Milan \mə-'lan, mə-'län\ *Italian* **Milano** \mē-'lä-nō\ Capital (metro. area pop., 1998 est.: 1,302,000), LOMBARDY region,

N Italy. The area was settled by the Gauls around 600 B.C. It was conquered by the Romans in 222 B.C. Attacked in A.D. 452 by ATTILA and in 539 by the Goths, it fell to CHARLEMAGNE in 774. It was destroyed by the HOLY ROMAN EMPIRE in 1162. Rebuilt as part of the LOMBARD LEAGUE in 1167, it achieved independence in 1183. In 1450 Francesco Sforza founded a new dynasty; after 1499 it was ruled alternately by the French and the SFORZA FAMILY until 1535, when the HABSBURGS obtained it. In 1805 it became the capital of NAPOLEON's kingdom of Italy. It was incorporated into Italy in 1860. It is Italy's most important manufacturing area. It is noted for its fashion industry and electronic goods production, and is Italy's financial center. Its historic sites include the medieval Duomo, Europe's third-largest cathedral; the 15th-cent. monastery that houses LEONARDO DA VINCI's *Last Supper*; and La Scala opera house.

mildew Conspicuous mass of filaments and fruiting structures produced by various fungi (see FUNGUS). Mildew grows on cloth, fibers, leather goods, and plants, using these substances as food for growth and reproduction. Downy mildew and powdery mildew are plant diseases that affect hundreds of species.

mile Any of various units of distance, including the statute mile of 5,280 ft (1.61 km). It originated from the Roman *mille passus*, or "thousand paces," which measured 5,000 Roman ft, or 4,840 English ft (1,475 km). A nautical mile is the length on earth's surface of one minute of arc, or, by international definition, 1,852 m (6,076.12 ft, or 1.1508 statute mi); it remains in universal use in both marine and air transportation.

Miletus \mī-ˈlē-təs\ Ancient Greek city of W ASIA MINOR. Before 500 B.C., it was the greatest Greek city in the east, distinguished as a commercial and colonial power and also for its intellectual figures, including THALES, ANAXIMANDER, and ANAXIMENES. It later passed successively to LYDIA and PERSIA. About 499 B.C. Miletus led the Ionian revolt that sparked the PERSIAN WARS, and it was destroyed by the Persians in 494 B.C. After the Greeks defeated the Persians, it joined the DELIAN LEAGUE. It fell to ALEXANDER in 334 B.C. but retained its commercial importance until the 6th cent. A.D.

Milhaud \mē-ˈyō\, **Darius** (1892–1974) French composer. He accompanied Paul CLAUDEL to Brazil (1916) and wrote *Saudades do Brazil* (1921) on his return, when he was becoming known as one of Les SIX. The influence of jazz is audible in his best-known work, *La création du monde* (1923). He wrote many ballets, operas, and film scores in the 1920s, culminating in the grand opera *Christophe Colomb* (1928). In 1940 he moved to the U.S. He helped found the Aspen Music Festival in 1949.

Military Academy, U.S. See UNITED STATES MILITARY ACADEMY

military law Law prescribed by statute for governing the armed forces and their civilian employees. It in no way relieves military personnel of their obligations to their country's civil code or to the codes of INTERNATIONAL LAW. MUTINY, insubordination, desertion, misconduct, and other offenses injurious to military discipline constitute violations of military law; offenders may be subject to COURT-MARTIAL.

military unit Group of a prescribed size with a specific combat role within a larger military organization. The chief units in the ancient world were the Greek phalanx and the Roman LEGION. The basic units—company battalion, brigade, and division—have remained in use since their emergence in the 16th–18th cent. The smallest unit today is the squad, which has 7–14 soldiers and is led by a sergeant. Three or four squads make up a platoon, and two or more platoons compose a company, which has 100–250 soldiers and is commanded by a captain or a major. Two or more companies constitute a battalion, and several battalions form a brigade. Two or more brigades, along with specialized battalions, make up a division, which has 7,000–22,000 troops and is commanded by a major general. Two to seven divisions make up an army corps, commanded by a lieutenant general, which with 50,000–300,000 troops is the largest regular army formation.

militia \mə-ˈli-shə\ Military organization of citizens with limited military training who are available for emergency service, usually for local defense. The Anglo-Saxons required every able-bodied free male to serve. In colonial America, it was the only defense against hostile Indians. In the AMERICAN REVOLUTION, the militia, called the MINUTEMEN, provided most of the American forces. Militias played a similar role in the WAR OF 1812 and the AMERICAN CIVIL WAR. State-controlled volunteer militias became the U.S. NATIONAL GUARD. The U.S. in recent decades has seen a rise in so-called civilian or unorganized militias, paramilitary organizations whose members profess to be patriots training to protect the U.S. from threats from within and without. Many have white-supremacist leanings, and some have been implicated in terrorist attacks.

milk Liquid secreted by the MAMMARY GLANDS of female mammals to nourish their young. The milk of domesticated animals is also an important food source for humans. Most milk consumed in Western countries is from the cow; sources important elsewhere include the sheep, goat, water buffalo, and camel. Milk is essentially an emulsion of FAT and PROTEIN in water, along with dissolved sugar, minerals (including CALCIUM and PHOSPHORUS), and VITAMINS (particularly VITAMIN B COMPLEX); commercial cow's milk is commonly enriched with vitamins A and D. Many countries require PASTEURIZATION to protect against microorganisms. Fat from whole milk (about 3.5% fat content) can be removed to leave low-fat milk (1–2% fat) or skim milk (0.5% fat). Commercially sold milk is usually homogenized, forced under high pressure through small openings to distribute the fat evenly. It may also be condensed or dehydrated for preservation and ease of transport.

Milk, Harvey (Bernard) (1930–1978) U.S. political leader. Born in Woodmere, N.Y., he settled in San Francisco and soon became a leader of its gay community. In 1977 he was elected to the city's Board of Supervisors, becoming one of the first openly gay elected officials in U.S. history. In 1978 Milk and the city's mayor, George Moscone (1929–1978), were shot and killed in City Hall by Dan White, a conservative former city supervisor. After White was convicted only of voluntary manslaughter, riots broke out in the city.

Milken, Michael R. (b.1946) U.S. financier. Born in Encino, Cal., he went to work in 1969 for what was to become Drexel Burnham Lambert Inc., an investment-banking company. As head of its bond-trading department from 1971, he persuaded many clients to invest in JUNK BONDS. The capital he raised financed a new class of "corporate raiders" who carried out numerous mergers, acquisitions, hostile takeovers, and leveraged buyouts. In 1986 the firm's client Ivan Boesky, convicted of insider trading, implicated Milken and the firm in his dealings. Heavily fined, the firm declared bankruptcy in 1990 when the junk-bond market collapsed. Milken pleaded guilty to securities fraud and was sentenced to 10 years in prison and a $600 million fine; released after 22 months, he made a second fortune.

milkweed family Family Asclepiadaceae, composed of about 2,000 species of flowering herbaceous plants or shrubby climbers in more than 280 genera. Most family members have milky juice, podlike fruits, and tufted silky-haired seeds that drift on wind currents. Common milkweed (*Asclepias syriaca*) and bloodflower (*A. curassavica*) often are cultivated as ornamentals. The family also includes some SUCCULENTS and PITCHER PLANTS.

Milky Way galaxy Large spiral GALAXY (roughly 150,000 light-years across) containing our SOLAR SYSTEM and the multitude of stars whose light is seen as the Milky Way, the luminous band encircling the sky in the plane of the galactic disk. The sun lies in one of its spiral arms, about 27,000 light-years from the center. The Milky Way system contains about 100 billion stars and much interstellar gas and dust. The dust obscures our view of large areas, which could not be studied without INFRARED ASTRONOMY and radio astronomy (see RADIO AND RADAR ASTRONOMY). Its constituents, shape, and true size and mass are not precisely known; it is believed to contain large amounts of DARK MATTER.

Mill, James (1773–1836) Scottish philosopher, historian, and economist. He went to London in 1802, where he met Je-

remy BENTHAM and became a major promulgator of UTILI-TARIANISM. He helped found London Univ. in 1825. After completing his *History of British India* (3 vols., 1817), he was appointed an official in India House (1819) and later became head of the examiner's office (1830). His criticism of British rule led to changes in the government of India. His *Elements of Political Economy* (1821) summarized the views of David RICARDO, and his *Analysis of the Phenomena of the Human Mind* (1829) associated psychology with utilitarianism, a doctrine continued by his son, J. S. MILL. Mill is considered the founder of philosophical radicalism.

Mill, John Stuart (1806–1873) British philosopher and economist. He was educated by his father, James MILL. In *A System of Logic* (2 vols., 1843), he seeks to formulate a logic of the human sciences based on causal explanation. Intended by his father as the philosophical successor to Jeremy BENTHAM, he cofounded the Utilitarian Society with Bentham (1823), though he later significantly modified the UTILITARIANISM he inherited from both men to meet the criticisms it encountered. In 1825 he and Bentham cofounded University College London. In *On Liberty* (1859) Mill eloquently defended individual freedom. His *Utilitarianism*

John Stuart Mill

(1863) sought to answer objections to his ethical theory; he was especially insistent that "utility" include the pleasures of the imagination and the gratification of the higher emotions, and that his system include a place for settled rules of conduct. His *The Subjection of Women* (1869) made a controversial call for women's rights. His other works include *Principles of Political Economy* (1848), *Three Essays on Religion* (1874), and an autobiography (1873).

Millais \'mi-₁lā, mi-'lā\, **John Everett** (*later* **Sir John**) (1829–1896) British painter and illustrator. In 1848 he became a founding member of the PRE-RAPHAELITES. His period of greatest achievement came in the 1850s, with *The Return of the Dove to the Ark* (1851) and *The Blind Girl* (1856), a tour de force of Victorian sentiment and technical facility. He was popular as a portraitist and also as a book illustrator.

Millay, Edna St. Vincent (1892–1950) U.S. poet and dramatist. She was born in Rockland, Maine, and her work is filled with the imagery of coast and countryside. In the 1920s, when she lived in Greenwich Village, she came to personify the romantic rebellion and bravado of youth. Among her volumes are *Renascence* (1917), *A Few Figs from Thistles* (1920), *The Harp Weaver* (1923, Pulitzer Prize), and the sonnet sequence *Fatal Interview* (1931). Other works include three verse plays and the libretto for Deems Taylor's opera *The King's Henchman* (1927).

Mille, Agnes See Agnes DE MILLE

millennialism *or* **millenarianism** Belief in the millennium of Christian prophecy (Rev. 20), the 1,000 years when Christ is to reign on earth. The millennium will see the rule of righteousness on earth; at its end, Satan will for a time deceive the nations, but he will be defeated and the dead will be gathered for the final judgment. Periods of social change or crisis have tended to lead to a resurgence in millennialism; it is now associated especially with such Protestant denominations as the ADVENTISTS, JEHOVAH'S WITNESSES, and MORMONS.

millennium bug See Y2K BUG

miller *or* **owlet moth** Any of the more than 20,000 MOTH species in the LEPIDOPTERAN family Noctuidae. Some species have a 1-ft (30-cm) wingspan, the largest wingspan of any moth, but most species have a wingspan of 1.5 in. (4 cm) or less. Adults feed on fruits, sap, or nectar. The larvae of many species are agricultural pests (e.g., CUTWORM, boll-worm) that feed on foliage and seeds, bore into stems and

fruits, and eat or sever roots. A few species prey on SCALE INSECTS.

Miller, Arthur (b.1915) U.S. playwright. Born in New York City, he wrote his first important play, *All My Sons*, in 1947. His most famous work, *Death of a Salesman* (1949, Pulitzer Prize), was the tragedy of the aging salesman Willy Loman. Noted for combining social awareness with a searching concern for his characters' inner lives, Miller wrote many other plays, including *The Crucible* (1953), *A View from the Bridge* (1955), *After the Fall* (1964), *Incident at Vichy* (1964), *The Price* (1968), and *The Ride Down Mount Morgan* (1991). He also wrote the screenplay for *The Misfits* (1961), which starred his former wife Marilyn MONROE.

Miller, (Alton) Glenn (1904–1944) U.S. trombonist and leader of one of the most popular SWING bands. Born in Clarinda, Iowa, Miller formed his band in 1937 and had soon recorded such hits as "In the Mood," "Moonlight Serenade," and "Chattanooga Choo-Choo." Miller disbanded in 1942 to join the war effort leading a military band. Traveling from London to Paris, his plane disappeared over the English Channel.

Miller, Henry (Valentine) (1891–1980) U.S. writer and perennial bohemian. Miller wrote about his Brooklyn childhood in *Black Spring* (1936). *Tropic of Cancer* (1934), a monologue about his life as an impoverished expatriate in Paris, and *Tropic of Capricorn* (1939), which draws on his earlier New York phase, were banned as obscene in the U.S. and Britain. *The Air-Conditioned Nightmare* (1945) is a critical account of a tour of the U.S. He settled in Big Sur, Cal., and his later works include his *Rosy Crucifixion* trilogy: *Sexus*, *Plexus*, and *Nexus* (U.S. ed., 1965).

millet Any of various GRASSES (family Gramineae or Poaceae), that produce small edible seeds used as forage crops and as food CEREALS. Except for pearl millet (*Pennisetum glaucum*, or *P. americanum*), seeds remain enclosed in hulls after threshing. Cultivated in China since at least the 3rd millennium B.C., millets are today an important food staple in much of Asia, Russia, and W Africa. High in carbohydrates, they are consumed mainly in flatbreads and porridges or prepared and eaten much like rice. In the U.S. and W Europe they are used chiefly for pasture or to produce HAY.

Millet \mē-'yā, *Engl* mi-'lā\, **Jean-François** (1814–1875) French painter. He studied with a painter in Paris, but when one of his two submissions to the SALON was rejected (1840), he returned to Cherbourg. His first success came with *The Milkmaid* (1844), and in 1848 another peasant scene, *The Winnower,* was shown at the Salon. In 1849 he settled in the village of Barbizon (see BARBIZON SCHOOL). Because he continued to exhibit peasant scenes that emphasized the labors of rustic life, he was accused of being a socialist, but his aims were not political. His *Angelus* (1859) became one of the most popular paintings of the 19th cent.

Millikan oil-drop experiment \'mil-ə-kən\ First method for direct measurement of the ELECTRIC CHARGE of a single ELECTRON, originally performed in 1909 by Robert Millikan (1868–1953). He used a microscope to measure the rate of descent of tiny oil droplets through a box. By halting the descent of droplets carrying their own electric charge by precisely adjusting the voltage between the box's metal top and bottom, he discovered that the electric charges on the drops were all whole-number multiples of a lowest value, the elementary electric charge.

millipede Any of about 10,000 species of the ARTHROPOD class Diplopoda. Most species live in and eat decaying plant matter; some injure living plants. Millipedes are 1–11 in. (2.5–28 cm) long and have from 11 to more than 100 diplosomites, double segments formed from the fusion of two segments. The head is legless; the next three segments have one pair of legs each; and the remaining segments have two pairs each. In defense, many species secrete a pungent, toxic liquid or gas.

Mills, C(harles) Wright (1916–1962) U.S. sociologist. Born in Waco, Texas, Mills joined the faculty of Columbia Univ.; there he became associated with the theories of Max WEBER and with issues regarding the role of intellectuals in modern life, and contributed to the development of a critical sociology. He believed social scientists should shun "abstracted empiricism" and become activists on behalf of social change. His radical analysis of U.S. business and society appeared in *White Collar* (1951) and *The Power Elite* (1956). A colorful public figure, he wore black leather and rode a motorcycle. His death at 45 resulted from heart disease.

Milne \\'miln\\, **A(lan) A(lexander)** (1882–1956) English writer. He produced successful light comedies and a memorable detective novel, *The Red House Mystery* (1922), before publishing the verse collections *When We Were Very Young* (1924) and *Now We Are Six* (1927), which became beloved children's classics. Tales of his son Christopher Robin and the toy animals Pooh, Piglet, Kanga, Roo, and Eeyore are told in the immensely popular *Winnie-the-Pooh* (1926) and *The House at Pooh Corner* (1928).

A. A. Milne Drawing by P. Evans, c.1930

Milon of Croton \\'mī-ˌlän\\ *or* **Milo of Croton** (fl. late 6th cent. B.C.) Ancient Greek athlete. The most renowned wrestler of antiquity, he won numerous Olympic and Pythian Games. His name has long been synonymous with extraordinary strength, and he is said to have carried an ox on his shoulders across the Olympic stadium.

Milosevic \\mi-'lō-sə-ˌvich\\, **Slobodan** (b.1941) Serbian politician. A Communist at 18, he later became head of the state-owned gas company and president of a major Belgrade bank. Advised by his wife, a party ideologue, he became head of the Communist Party in Belgrade (1984) and Serbia (1987). He replaced party leaders with his supporters, and in 1989 became the republic's president. His opposition to a confederation with Croatia and Slovenia led to the breakup of Yugoslavia (1991). He supported Serb militias fighting the Muslims in Bosnia and Croatia (see BOSNIAN CONFLICT), but after the Serbs were forced from Croatia in 1995, he signed a peace agreement for the Bosnia Serbs. As president of the new Federal Republic of Yugoslavia, he maintained his power by repression and control of the mass media. In his zeal to reclaim territory to Serbia, in 1998 he instituted the policy of "ethnic cleansing" in Kosovo (see KOSOVO CONFLICT). His hate-mongering and near-genocidal policies earned him worldwide loathing as a war criminal. In 2000 he was defeated in national elections. In 2001 he was arrested and moved to The Hague, where his trial before the International Tribunal began in 2002.

Milosz \\'mē-lòsh\\, **Czeslaw** (b.1911) Polish-U.S. author, translator, and critic. During the Nazi occupation of Poland, he was active in the resistance. After serving briefly as a diplomat for communist Poland, he emigrated to the U.S., where he taught for decades at UC–Berkeley. His poetry is noted for its classical style and preoccupation with philosophical and political issues. His essay collection *The Captive Mind* (1953) condemned the accommodation of many Polish intellectuals to communism. He was awarded the Nobel Prize in 1980.

Milstein \\'mil-ˌstīn, 'mil-ˌstēn\\, **César** (1927–2002) Argentine-British immunologist. In 1975 Milstein and Georges Köhler (1946–1995) fused highly specific LYMPHOCYTES with the cells of a myeloma. The hybrid cells, like lymphocytes, secreted ANTIBODIES to a single antigen and, like myeloma cells, perpetuated themselves. This enabled production of large quantities of pure antibodies against single antigenic characteristics (monoclonal antibodies). Milstein, Köhler, and Niels K. Jerne (1911–1994) shared a Nobel Prize in 1984.

Milton, John (1608–1674) English poet. As a young man he wrote poems in Latin, Italian, and English; these included *L'Allegro* and *Il Penseroso,* both published later in *Poems* (1645). During 1632–38 he engaged in private study—writing the masque *Comus* (1637) and the extraordinary elegy "Lycidas" (1638)—and toured Italy. Concerned with the Puritan cause in England, he spent much of 1641–60 pam-

phleteering for civil and religious liberty and serving in Oliver CROMWELL's government. His best-known prose is in the pamphlets *Areopagitica* (1644), on freedom of the press, and *Of Education* (1644). He lost his sight around 1651, and thereafter dictated his works. After the Restoration he was arrested as a noted defender of the Commonwealth, but was soon released. In *Paradise Lost* (1667), his epic masterpiece on the Fall of Man written in blank verse, he uses his sublime "grand style" with superb power; his characterization of Satan is a supreme achievement. He further expressed his purified faith in God and the regenerative strength of the individual soul in *Paradise Regained* (1671) and *Samson Agonistes* (1671). Considered second only to William SHAKESPEARE in the history of English-language poetry, Milton had an immense influence on later literature.

Milwaukee City (pop., 2000: 597,000) and lake port, SE Wisconsin. The state's largest city, it is situated on Lake MICHIGAN. The site was visited by French missionaries and fur traders in the 17th cent. and settled in 1800; it was incorporated in 1846. It was a center of German immigration until about 1900. It is a major GREAT LAKES port, shipping especially grain; it also produces electrical machinery. Its educational institutions include Marquette Univ. and the Univ. of Wisconsin–Milwaukee.

mime and pantomime Dramatic performance in which a story is told solely by expressive body movement. Mime appeared in Greece in the 5th cent. B.C. as a comic entertainment that also included song and spoken dialogue; a separate Roman form (from c.100 B.C.) centered on crude and licentious subjects. Roman pantomime differed from Roman mime by its loftier themes and its use of masks, which called for expression through posture and hand gestures. Mime also forms an element in Chinese and Japanese drama (e.g., NO DRAMA). Roman pantomime was modified in the 16th-cent. COMMEDIA DELL'ARTE. The 19th-cent. pantomime was a children's entertainment emphasizing spectacle. Modern Western mime developed into a purely silent art. Famous mimes include Étienne Decroux (who developed a systematic language of gesture) and Marcel MARCEAU, as well as Charlie CHAPLIN, Sid CAESAR, and the clown Emmett Kelly.

mimicry Similarity between organisms that confers a survival advantage on one. In Batesian mimicry, an organism lacking defenses mimics a species that does have defenses. In Müllerian mimicry, all species in a group are similar even though all individually have defenses. In aggressive mimicry, a predatory species mimics a benign species so that it can approach its prey without alarming it, or a parasitic species mimics its host. Some plant species mimic the color patterns and scents of animals for the purposes of pollination and dispersal.

mimosa \\mə-'mō-sə\\ Any member of the more than 450 species that make up the genus *Mimosa* in the family Mimosaceae, native to tropical and subtropical areas throughout both hemispheres. Most are herbaceous plants or undershrubs; some are woody climbers; a few are small trees. They are often prickly. Mimosas are widely cultivated for the beauty of their foliage and for their interesting response to light and mechanical stimuli: the leaves of some species droop in response to darkness and close up their leaflets when touched. Many ACACIAS are incorrectly called mimosas.

Minamata disease \\ˌmi-nə-'mä-tə\\ Disease first identified in 1956 in Minamata, Japan. A fishing port, Minamata was also the home of a chemical plant. Methyl mercury discharged from the factory contaminated fish and shellfish, which in turn caused illness in the local inhabitants who consumed them and birth defects in their children. The sometimes fatal disease (see MERCURY POISONING) was the first whose cause was recognized as industrial pollution of seawater. It stimulated the development of the worldwide environmental movement.

Minamoto Yoritomo \\ˌmē-nä-'mō-tō-ˌyò-rē-'tō-mō\\ (1147–1199) Founder of the KAMAKURA SHOGUNATE of Japan. A member of the Minamoto warrior clan, Yoritomo was banished in his youth when his father revolted against the reigning Taira family. In exile Yoritomo found support in Hojo Tokimasa (see HOJO FAMILY), and in 1185 he defeated

the Taira (see GEMPEI WAR). In 1192 the cloistered emperor granted him the title of SHOGUN, which made him the supreme authority over all military forces in the country. By creating a governmental infrastructure in competition with, and gradually superseding, that of the imperial court, he was able to rule without actually overthrowing the emperor, a pattern emulated by later shogunates.

Minamoto Yoshitsune \ˌmē-nä-ˈmō-tō-ˌyō-shēt-ˈsùn-ä\ (1159–1189) Japanese military leader. Brother of MINAMOTO YORITOMO, he was raised in a monastery but ran away at 15 to join Yoritomo in the GEMPEI WAR. Yoshitsune seized Kyoto and then defeated the remaining Taira forces along Japan's Inland Sea. Yoritomo became jealous of Yoshitsune and eventually had him killed. Yoshitsune is the epitome of the Japanese underdog hero; many legends, stories, and kabuki plays celebrate his adventures with his faithful follower, the monk Benkei.

Minangkabau \ˌmē-näŋ-kä-ˈbaù\ Largest ethnic group on the island of SUMATRA, Indonesia. Though Muslim, the Minangkabau are matrilineal. Traditionally, the wife remained with her maternal relatives after marriage; her husband lived with his mother but visited his wife. Today, more men have left their villages to establish their own households with wives and children. Traditional Minangkabau are farmers, and their crafts include wood carving, metalwork, and weaving. Some migrated to Malaya (Peninsular Malaysia) in the 1850s to work as tin miners. In the 20th cent. they came to control most of Malaya's retail trade. The Minangkabau number 2–5 million.

Minas Basin \ˈmī-nəs\ E inlet of the Bay of FUNDY, Nova Scotia. Up to 25 mi (40 km) wide and more than 50 mi (80 km) long, it has some of the highest tides in the world, with fluctuations exceeding 50 ft (15 m). Samuel de CHAMPLAIN named it in 1604 after nearby mineral deposits.

Mindanao \ˌmin-də-ˈnä-ˌō, ˌmin-də-ˈnaù\ Island (pop., 2000: 15,593,000), S Philippines. The second-largest island in the Philippines, it has an area of 36,537 sq mi (94,630 sq km). It is mountainous and contains active volcanoes, including Mt. Apo. Islam spread throughout Mindanao in the 16th cent. It was visited by Ferdinand MAGELLAN in 1521. It was later claimed by Spain, but the resistance of its Muslim inhabitants kept it largely independent of Spanish authority. The autonomous region of Muslim Mindanao was created in 1990.

mind–body problem Metaphysical problem of the relationship between mind and body. The modern problem stems from the thought of René DESCARTES, who gave dualism its classical formulation. Thomas HOBBES argued that there was no such thing as mental substance, only material substance (see MATERIALISM). Benedict de SPINOZA posited a single substance of which the mental and the material are attributes; his theory is known as psycho-physical parallelism.

Mindon \ˈmin-ˈdòn\ (1814–1878) King of Myanmar (1853–78). He came to power after the Second ANGLO–BURMESE WAR. He was unable to persuade the British to return Pegu (in S Myanmar) and was also forced to make large economic concessions. Domestically, his reign saw numerous reforms and great cultural and religious flowering. In 1857 he built the new capital, Mandalay, with superb palaces and monasteries. He held the fifth Buddhist Council there in 1871 in an effort to revise and purify the Pali scriptures.

Mindoro Island (pop., 1990: 833,000), W central Philippines, south of LUZON. It is 80 mi (130 km) long and 50 mi (80 km) wide. It came under U.S. rule in 1901. It was occupied by the Japanese during World War II. The tamaraw, a small water buffalo, is unique to the island.

Mindszenty \mēnd-ˈshen-tē\, **Jozsef** orig. Jozsef Pehm (1892–1975) Hungarian cardinal. Arrested as an enemy of totalitarian governments in 1919 and again in 1944, he was appointed primate of Hungary in 1945 and made a cardinal in 1946. Refusing to permit Hungary's Catholic schools to be secularized by the communists, he was arrested in 1948 and convicted of treason. Sentenced to life imprisonment, he was freed in the Hungarian Revolution (1956). When the communists regained control, he sought asylum in the U.S. embassy and lived there for 15 years, refusing Vatican requests to leave Hungary. He relented in 1971 and settled in Vienna.

mine See LAND MINE, SUBMARINE MINE

mineral Any naturally occurring homogeneous solid that has a definite (but not fixed) chemical composition and a distinctive internal crystal structure. Minerals are usually formed by inorganic processes. Although most minerals are chemical compounds, a small number (e.g., sulfur, copper, gold) are elements. Minerals combine with each other to form rocks. For example, granite consists of the minerals feldspar, quartz, mica, and amphibole in varying amounts. Rocks are generally, therefore, an intergrowth of various minerals.

mineralogy Scientific study of MINERALS, including their physical properties, chemical composition, internal crystal structure, occurrence and distribution in nature, and origins or conditions of formation. Mineralogic studies range from description and classification of new or rare minerals to analysis of crystal structure and laboratory or industrial synthesis of mineral species.

Minerva In ROMAN RELIGION, the goddess of handicrafts, the professions, the arts, and, later, war. She was commonly identified with the Greek ATHENA. Some scholars believe that worship of Minerva began when Athena's cult was introduced at Rome from Etruria. Minerva was one of the Capitoline triad, along with JUPITER and JUNO; her worship attained its greatest vogue under the emperor DOMITIAN, who claimed her special protection.

Ming dynasty (1368–1644) Chinese dynasty that provided an interval of native rule between eras of MONGOL and MANCHU dominance. The Ming extended Chinese influence farther than any other native rulers of China. The capital of China was moved from Nanjing to Beijing, and the FORBIDDEN CITY was constructed. Naval expeditions led by ZHENG HE paved the way for trade with S.E. Asia, India, and E Africa. The era saw the creation of novels in the vernacular, while philosophy benefited from the work of WANG YANGMING in NEO-CONFUCIANISM. Ming monochrome porcelain became famous the world over.

Mingus, Charles (1922–1979) U.S. jazz bassist, composer, and bandleader. Born in Nogales, Ariz., Mingus played in the groups of Lionel HAMPTON and Duke ELLINGTON, ultimately working with many of the innovators of BEBOP. In 1953 he organized the Jazz Workshop ensemble, which played a spirited combination of loosely arranged passages and improvisation. As a pioneering bandleader and virtuoso bassist, Mingus remained an uncompromising and innovative force in jazz for the rest of his career.

miniature painting Small, detailed painting, usually a portrait, executed in watercolor on vellum (parchment), prepared card, copper, or ivory. The name derives from the *minium,* or red lead, used to emphasize initial letters in medieval illuminated manuscripts. Combining the traditions of illumination and the Renaissance medal, it flourished from the early 16th to the mid-19th cent. The earliest datable examples were painted in France by Jean CLOUET at the court of FRANCIS I; in England, Hans HOLBEIN the Younger produced masterpieces in miniature under HENRY VIII. Nicholas HILLIARD served as miniature painter to ELIZABETH I for more than 30 years. In the 17th–18th cent., painting in enamel on metal became popular in France. In Italy Rosalba CARRIERA, painting on ivory, stimulated a great revival of the medium in the late 18th cent. In the mid-19th cent., miniature paintings were rendered obsolete by the new medium of photography.

Minimalism 20th-cent. movements in art and music characterized by extreme simplicity of form and rejection of emotional content. In the visual arts, it originated in New York in the 1950s as a form of abstract art. The Minimalists believed that a work of art should be entirely self-referential; personal elements were stripped away to reveal the objective, purely visual elements. Leading sculptors include Carl ANDRE and Donald JUDD; painters include Ellsworth KELLY, Agnes MARTIN, and Frank STELLA. In music, Minimalism was an entirely separate movement that arose in the 1960s. It employs a steady pulsing beat, incessant repetition of tones and chords with only gradual changes in their components, a slow rate of harmonic change, and little or no counterpoint. Its principal antecedents are the musics of India and S.E. Asia. Its most important practitioners include La Monte Young (b.1935), Terry Riley (b.1935), whose *In C* (1964) is perhaps its most seminal work, Steve REICH, Philip GLASS, and John ADAMS.

minimum In mathematics, a point at which the value of a function is lowest. If the value is less than or equal to all other function values, it is an absolute minimum. If it is merely less than at any nearby point, it is a relative, or local, minimum. In CALCULUS, the DERIVATIVE equals zero or does not exist at a function's minimum point. See also MAXIMUM, OPTIMIZATION.

minimum reserve system See FRACTIONAL RESERVE SYSTEM

minimum wage Wage rate established by COLLECTIVE BARGAINING or by government regulation, specifying the lowest rate at which workers may be employed. A legal minimum wage is one mandated by government for all workers, with few exceptions. The modern minimum wage, combined with compulsory arbitration of labor disputes, first appeared in Australia and New Zealand in the 1890s. In 1909 Britain established trade boards to set minimum wage rates in certain trades and industries. The first minimum wage in the U.S. (which applied only to women) was enacted by Massachusetts in 1912. Minimum-wage laws or agreements now exist in most nations.

mining Excavation of materials from the earth's crust, including those of organic origin, such as coal and petroleum. Modern mining is costly and complicated. First, a mineral vein that can likely produce enough of the desired substance to justify the cost of extraction must be located. Then mining engineers decide the best way to mine it. Excavating a mine and extracting mineral substances involve different combinations of drilling, blasting, hoisting, and hauling. A vital consideration in mining is how to ventilate the underground tunnels and caverns, to provide fresh air to miners and to disperse harmful gases. Separation techniques often involve the leaching of valuable trace minerals from crushed ore using solvents. See also STRIP MINING.

mink Either of two species of nocturnal, semiaquatic carnivores in the WEASEL family (Mustelidae) that are trapped and raised commercially for their pelts. *Mustela vison*, found throughout N. America except in arid parts of the SW U.S., is 17–29 in. (43–74 cm) long and weighs up to 3.5 lbs. (1.6 kg). The Eurasian species (*M. lutreola*) is slightly smaller. Generally wild mink fur is more valuable than "ranch mink."

Minneapolis City (pop., 2000: 382,000), E Minnesota. The state's largest city, it is situated on the MISSISSIPPI RIVER near the mouth of the MINNESOTA RIVER. With ST. PAUL across the river it forms the Twin Cities area. It was visited by Louis HENNEPIN in 1680. The city of Minneapolis (formed in 1872) developed as a center of the lumber and wheat industries. Today it is also a manufacturing and finance center. Its educational institutions include the Univ. of MINNESOTA. The city is noted for its 18 lakes and its extremely cold winters.

Minnelli, Vincente (1910–1986) U.S. film director. Born in Chicago, he achieved success as a Broadway director (c.1935) and moved to Hollywood in 1940. He combined a daring use of color with imaginative camera work in such films as *Cabin in the Sky* (1943), *Meet Me in St. Louis* (1944), *An American in Paris* (1951), *The Band Wagon* (1953), *Brigadoon* (1954), and *Gigi* (1958, Academy Award). He was married to Judy GARLAND 1945–51. Their daughter, the singer and actress Liza Minnelli (b.1946), won a Tony Award at 19 in *Flora, the Red Menace* (1965). Her movie roles have included *The Sterile Cuckoo* (1969) and *Cabaret* (1972, Academy Award), and she won a wide following through her energetic concert performances.

Minnesota State (pop., 2000: 4,919,000), midwestern U.S. It covers 84,068 sq mi (217,736 sq km); its capital is ST. PAUL. The most northerly of the 48 contiguous U.S. states, it has extensive woodlands, fertile prairies, and numerous lakes. Before European settlement, the region was inhabited by the Ojibwa (Chippewa) and the Dakota (SIOUX) tribes. French explorers arrived in search of the NORTHWEST PASSAGE in the mid-17th cent. The NE portion passed to the British in 1763 and then to the U.S. in 1783, becoming part of the Northwest Territories in 1787. The SW portion was

acquired by the U.S. in 1803 as part of the LOUISIANA PURCHASE, and the NW portion was ceded to the U.S. by the British by treaty in 1818. The first permanent U.S. settlement was made in 1819, when Ft. Snelling was founded. The Minnesota Territory, established in 1849, included present-day Minnesota and the E sections of N. and S. Dakota. Minnesota became the 32nd U.S. state in 1858. The Sioux Uprising in S Minnesota in 1862 resulted in the death of 500 civilians, soldiers, and Indians. Commercial iron-ore production began in 1884 and after the huge iron reserves of the Mesabi Range were discovered in 1890, the population at DULUTH and Superior grew rapidly. Today agriculture, especially grains, meat, and dairy products, is the basis of the economy. Mineral resources include iron ore, granite, and limestone.

Minnesota, University of State university system consisting of a main campus in the Twin Cities district and three branch campuses. The main campus received land-grant status in 1862. Its noted undergraduate programs include chemical engineering, medical technology, geography, economics, psychology, and architecture. There are over 100 research facilities, and its library houses about 5 million volumes. Enrollment at the main campus is about 37,000.

Minnesota Mining & Manufacturing Co. (3M) Diversified U.S. corporation. Incorporated under its present name in 1902, it first made sandpaper, then added the original cellophane tape—Scotch tape—and masking tape to its product line. Today its products include photographic film, videocassettes, computer-synthesized graphics, and health-care products. It is notable in that its diversification has been primarily by internal means rather than by large-scale acquisitions.

Minnesota River River, S Minnesota. Rising on the S. Dakota–Minnesota boundary, it joins the MISSISSIPPI RIVER just south of ST. PAUL, after a course of 332 mi (534 km). Once known as the St. Peter or St. Pierre, it was important to early explorers and fur traders.

Minoans \mi-ˈnō-ənz\ Non-Indo-European people who flourished (c.3000–c.1100 B.C.) on the island of Crete during the BRONZE AGE. The sea was the basis of their economy and power. Named for the legendary King MINOS, their sophisticated culture represented the first high civilization in the Aegean area. The Minoans exerted great influence on MYCENAEAN culture. Minoan culture reached its peak around 1600 B.C. and was noted for its cities and palaces, extended trade contacts, and use of writing (see LINEAR A AND LINEAR B). Familiar Minoan art motifs, seen especially in the vibrant palace frescoes, are the snake (symbol of the goddess) and the bull and leaping dancer, also of mystical significance.

Mino da Fiesole \ˈmē-nō-dä-fyä-ˈzō-lä\ (1429–1484) Italian sculptor. He was active both in Florence and Rome, where he created monuments (especially wall tombs) and busts of cardinals and other prominent individuals. Among the earliest Renaissance portrait sculptures, his works were greatly admired in the 19th cent. but are now considered less inspired than those of his eminent contemporaries.

Minos \ˈmī-nəs\ In Greek legend, a king of Crete, the son of ZEUS and EUROPA. His wife Pasiphaë fell in love with a bull and gave birth to the MINOTAUR, which was imprisoned in the Labyrinth. Minos waged war against Athens and exacted a tribute of youths and maidens to feed the Minotaur until THESEUS killed the monster with the aid of Minos's daughter ARIADNE. Many scholars now consider that Minos was a royal or dynastic title for the priestly rulers of Bronze Age or MINOAN CIVILIZATION in KNOSSOS (Minoan means "of Minos").

Minot \ˈmī-nət**, George (Richards)** (1885–1950) U.S. physician. Born in Boston, he and William Murphy (1894–1987) found that eating raw liver reversed PERNICIOUS ANEMIA in humans, and shared a Nobel Prize in 1934 with George H. Whipple (1878–1976) for their treatment of the previously invariably fatal disease. Liver extracts were the main treatment for pernicious anemia until 1948, when vitamin B_{12} was isolated.

Minotaur \ˈmi-nə-ˌtȯr\ In GREEK MYTHOLOGY, a monster of Crete with the body of a man and the head of a bull. It was the offspring of Pasiphaë, wife of King MINOS, and a snow-

white bull sent by POSEIDON and intended for sacrifice. The Minotaur (whose name means "Minos bull") was imprisoned in the Labyrinth built by DAEDALUS. After defeating Athens in a war, Minos forced the Athenians to send human tribute to be devoured by the Minotaur. The third year the tribute was sent, THESEUS volunteered to go, and with the help of ARIADNE he killed the monster.

Minsk Capital (pop., 1998: 1,717,000) and largest city of Belarus. Settled before 1067, it became the seat of a principality in 1101. It passed to Lithuania in the 14th cent. and later to Poland. Annexed by Russia in 1793, it grew in importance as an industrial center after the arrival of the railways in 1870. During World War I it was occupied first by the Germans and then by the Poles. It was almost entirely destroyed in World War II. Once the capital of the Belorussian S.S.R., it remained the capital when Belarus gained independence in 1991.

Minsky, Marvin (Lee) (b.1927) U.S. computer scientist. Born in New York City, he received his PhD from Princeton Univ. and joined the faculty at MIT, where he has remained for his entire career. His research has contributed to advances in ARTIFICIAL INTELLIGENCE, cognitive psychology, and NEURAL NETWORKS (he built the first neural-network simulator in 1951). A pioneer in robotics, he built some of the first mechanical hands with tactile sensors, visual scanners, and accompanying software and computer interfaces. He influenced many robotic projects and has worked to build into machines the human capacity for commonsense reasoning. In his *The Society of Mind* (1987), 270 interconnected one-page ideas reflect the structure of his theory. He received the Turing Award in 1969.

minstrel show Form of entertainment popular in the U.S. in the 19th and early 20th cent. It originated in the 1830s with the popular white performer Thomas D. Rice, known as "Jim Crow," who wore the stylized makeup called blackface and performed songs and dances in a stereotyped imitation of black Americans. Blackfaced white minstrel troupes were particularly popular in the U.S. and England in 1840–80; the Christy Minstrels played on Broadway for 10 years and had songs composed for them by Stephen FOSTER. Black minstrel troupes also performed after the Civil War. The minstrel show included frequent exchanges of jokes, interspersed with ballads, comic songs, and instrumental numbers (usually on the banjo and violin), as well as individual acts, soft-shoe dances, and specialty numbers.

mint In botany, any fragrant, strong-scented herb of the genus *Mentha*, composed of about 25 species of perennial herbs, and certain related genera of the mint family (Lamiaceae, or Labiatae), which contains about 3,500 species of flowering plants in about 160 genera. Mints are important to humans as herb plants useful for flavor, fragrance, and medicinal properties. True mints have square stems, opposite, aromatic leaves, and small flowers usually arranged in clusters. All *Mentha* species contain volatile oil in resinous dots in the leaves and stems. Included in this genus are PEPPERMINT, SPEARMINT, MARJORAM, ROSEMARY, and THYME; other members of the mint family include LAVENDER and CATNIP.

mint In economics, a place where coins are made according to exact compositions, weights, and dimensions, usually specified by law. The first state mint was probably established by the Lydians in the 7th cent. B.C. The Romans laid the foundations of modern minting standards. Coining spread across the Mediterranean, as well as to Persia and India. It originated independently in China in the 7th cent. B.C. and spread to Japan and Korea. In medieval Europe, mints proliferated as kings, counts, bishops, and free cities all exercised the mint privilege; the resulting variation in coinage often handicapped commerce. Most countries now operate only one mint; the U.S. has mints in Philadelphia and Denver, and proof sets of coins for collectors are minted in San Francisco. Some small countries contract to have their coins struck in foreign mints. See also CURRENCY, MONEY.

minuet \ˌmin-yə-'wet\ Dignified couple dance derived from a French folk dance, dominant in European court ballrooms in the 17th–18th cent. Using small, slow steps to music in 3/4 time, dancers often performed choreographed figures combined with stylized bows and curtsies. The most popular dance of the 18th-cent. aristocracy, it fell from favor after the French Revolution. Of great importance in art music, it was the only dance form retained in the SYMPHONY, SONATA, and STRING QUARTET up to about 1800.

Minuit \'min-yə-wət\, **Peter** (1580?–1638) Dutch colonial governor of New Netherland. In 1626 the Dutch W. India Co. named him director of the colony on MANHATTAN Island. To legitimize his occupation of the island, he persuaded the Indians to sell it for a few trinkets worth (according to legend) 60 guilders ($24). At the island's S tip he founded New Amsterdam. Later sent to establish the colony of New Sweden on Delaware Bay, he again purchased land from the Indians and built Ft. Christina (later Wilmington, Del.) in 1638.

Minuteman missile U.S. ICBM first deployed in 1962. Its three generations—I (1962), II (from 1966), and III (from 1970)—dominated the U.S. land-based nuclear arsenal through the 1980s. It was the first U.S. ICBM to be based in underground silos. From 1986 it began to be replaced by the Peacekeeper.

minutemen Colonial soldiers of the AMERICAN REVOLUTION, first organized in Massachusetts in Sept. 1774, when revolutionary leaders sought to eliminate British sympathizers from the militia by replacing all officers. One-third of the members of each new regiment was to be ready for military duty "at a minute's warning." After their first great test at the Battles of LEXINGTON AND CONCORD, the Continental Congress recommended that other colonies organize minuteman units.

Miocene epoch \'mī-ə-ˌsēn\ Major division of the TERTIARY PERIOD, 24–5 million years ago. The extensive fossil record of terrestrial life during the Miocene provides a fairly complete picture of the development of vertebrates, especially mammals; half of the known modern mammal families are present. The horse evolved, mainly in N. America, and advanced primates, including apes, were present in S Europe. Some interchange of faunas occurred in the Northern Hemisphere between the Old and New Worlds. Free communication was possible between Africa and Eurasia, but S. America and Australia remained isolated. See table at GEOLOGIC TIME.

Miquelon See SAINT-PIERRE AND MIQUELON

Mir Russian SPACE STATION whose core module, launched in 1986, and other attached modules formed a large, flexible laboratory in space. The third generation of Russian space stations, Mir had six docking ports, living quarters for up to six, more power, and modernized research equipment. Late in 1987, Yury Romanenko (b.1944) spent 326 days in space, aboard Mir. In the 1990s several U.S. space shuttles docked with Mir for Russian-U.S. collaborative studies. Equipment and systems problems made the station increasingly unsafe in the late 1990s, and it was guided to a final reentry in March 2001.

Mirabeau \mē-rà-'bō\, **comte (Count) de** *orig.* Honoré-Gabriel Riqueti (1749–1791) French politician and orator. Son of the economist Victor Riqueti (1715–1789), he was often imprisoned for intrigues and wild behavior (1774–80); he wrote several essays on prison life. In 1789 he was elected to the Estates General from the Third Estate. A skilled orator, he was influential in the early years of the French Revolution, and tried to mediate between the absolute monarchists and the revolutionaries. He was elected president of the National Assembly in 1791, but died soon after.

miracle Extraordinary event attributed to a supernatural power. Belief in miracles exists in all cultures and nearly all religions. Popular HINDUISM attributes miraculous powers to the ascetic yogis. CONFUCIANISM had little room for miracles; TAOISM, however, admits a rich crop of miracles. Miracles are taken for granted throughout the OLD TESTAMENT and were fairly common in the Greco-Roman world. Accounts of the BUDDHA Gautama's miraculous birth and life were later woven into his legend and into those of later Buddhist saints. The NEW TESTAMENT attributes many miracles to JESUS. Miracles also attest to the holiness of Christian SAINTS. MUHAMMAD renounced miracles as a matter of principle (the QURAN was the great miracle), but his life was later invested with miraculous details. Muslim popular religion, particularly under the influence of SUFISM, abounds in miracles and wonder-working saints.

miracle play Vernacular drama performed in the Middle Ages, presenting a real or fictitious account of the life, miracles, or martyrdom of a saint. It evolved from the liturgical dramas of the 10th–11th cent.; by the 13th cent. the plays were separated from church services and performed at public festivals by members of craft guilds and other amateur actors. Most concerned either the Virgin Mary or St. NICHOLAS, both of whom had active cults in the Middle Ages. See also MORALITY PLAY, MYSTERY PLAY.

mirage \mə-'räzh\ In optics, the deceptive appearance of a distant object caused by the bending of light rays (REFRACTION) in layers of air of varying density. Under certain conditions, such as over a stretch of hot pavement or in the desert, the air cools rapidly with elevation and therefore increases in density and refractive power. Sunlight reflected down from the upper portion of an object curves upward after it enters the rarefied hot air near the ground, thus being refracted to the observer's eye as though it had originated below the heated surface. When the sky is the object of the mirage, the land is mistaken for a lake or sheet of water.

miraj \'mi-räj\ Ascension of MUHAMMAD into heaven. One night Muhammad was visited by two archangels, who opened his body and purified his heart. He was carried to heaven, where he ascended the seven levels to reach the throne of God. Along the way he and the archangel Jibril met the earlier prophets and visited hell and paradise. He learned that he was more highly regarded by God than all the other prophets. The miraj is popularly celebrated with readings of the legend on the Laylat al-Miraj ("Night of the Ascension").

Miranda \mi-'ran-də\, **Carmen** *orig.* Maria do Carmo Miranda da Cunha (1909–1955) Brazilian singer and actress. The most popular recording artist in Brazil, she was recruited by a Broadway producer and starred in *The Streets of Paris* (1939), then made her U.S. film debut in *Down Argentine Way* (1940). She became typecast as the "Brazilian Bombshell" in such caricature roles as "The Lady in the Tutti-Frutti Hat" in *The Gang's All Here* (1943).

Miranda vs. Arizona U.S. Supreme Court decision (1966) that established that the police are required to inform arrested persons that they have the right to remain silent, that anything they say may be used against them, and that they have the right to an attorney. The plaintiff claimed that the state of Arizona, by obtaining a confession from him without having informed him of his right to have a lawyer present, had violated his rights under the 5th Amendment regarding SELF-INCRIMINATION. The 5–4 decision shocked the law-enforcement community; later decisions have limited its scope somewhat.

Miró \mē-'rō\, **Joan** (1893–1983) Spanish (Catalan) artist. Born in Barcelona, he worked as an office clerk until a mental breakdown persuaded his artisan father to permit him to study art. From the beginning he sought to express concepts of nature metaphorically. From 1919 on he lived alternately in Spain and Paris, where he came under the influence of Dada and Surrealism. The influence of Paul KLEE is apparent in his "dream pictures" and "imaginary landscapes" of the late 1920s. His mature style evolved from the tension between this fanciful, poetic impulse and his vision of the harshness of modern life. He worked extensively in lithography and produced numerous murals, tapestries, and sculptures for public spaces.

Joan Miró Photo by Yousuf Karsh, 1966

MIRV \'mərv\ *in full* **Multiple Independently Targetable Reentry Vehicle** Any of several nuclear warheads carried on the front end of a ballistic missile. The technique allows separately targeted nuclear warheads to be fired independently. MIRV technology was first developed in the U.S.; today all U.S. and Russian ICBMs and submarine-launched ballistic missiles can be equipped with MIRVs.

miscarriage *or* **spontaneous abortion** Spontaneous expulsion of an EMBRYO or FETUS from the UTERUS before it can live outside the mother. More than 60% are caused by an inherited defect in the fetus, which might result in a fatal abnormality. Other causes may include acute infectious disease, abnormalities of the uterus, and death of the fetus from umbilical-cord knotting. The main sign of impending miscarriage is vaginal bleeding.

misdemeanor See FELONY AND MISDEMEANOR

Mises \'mē-zes\, **Ludwig (Edler) von** (1881–1973) Austrian-U.S. libertarian economist. He taught at the Univ. of Vienna (1913–38) before emigrating to the U.S. and joining the NYU faculty (1945–69). In *The Anti-Capitalistic Mentality* (1956), he dealt with the opposition to the free market of intellectuals, who, in his view, bear an unwarranted resentment toward the necessity of obeying mass demand, which is the basis of prosperity in big business.

Mishima \'mē-shē-mä\, **Yukio** *orig.* Hiraoka Kimitake (1925–1970) Japanese writer. He won acclaim with his first novel, *Confessions of a Mask* (1949), about a homosexual youth. Many of his characters are obsessed with unattainable ideals and erotic desires, as in *The Temple of the Golden Pavilion* (1956). His epic *The Sea of Fertility* (4 vols., 1965–70) is perhaps his most lasting achievement. Strongly opposed to Japan's imitation of the West, he formed a small private army, hoping to preserve Japan's martial spirit and protect the emperor. After seizing a military headquarters, he died by committing SEPPUKU. He is often considered his nation's most important 20th-cent. novelist.

Mishna *or* **Mishnah** \mēsh-'nä, 'mish-nə\ Oldest authoritative collection of Jewish oral law, supplementing the written laws in the OLD TESTAMENT. It was given final form in the 3rd cent. A.D. Later annotations resulted in the Gemara; the Mishna and Gemara are usually said to make up the TALMUD. The Mishna has six major sections: on daily prayer and agriculture, SABBATH and other religious ritual, married life, civil and criminal law, the Temple of JERUSALEM, and ritual purification.

Miskito Coast See MOSQUITO COAST

missile ROCKET-propelled weapon designed to deliver an explosive warhead with great accuracy at high speed. Missiles vary from small tactical weapons effective out to only a few hundred feet to much larger strategic weapons with ranges of several thousand miles. They first became significant after World War II. Almost all contain some guidance and control mechanism and are therefore often called guided missiles. An unguided military missile or launch vehicle is usually called a rocket.

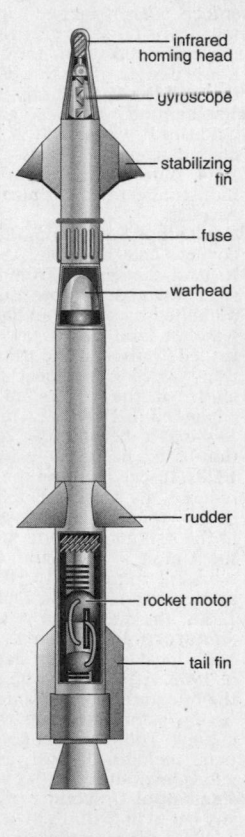

infrared homing head

gyroscope

stabilizing fin

fuse

warhead

rudder

rocket motor

tail fin

Missile A heat-seeking air-to-air missile, designed to home in on the hot exhaust from an enemy plane's jet engines.

With the development of ICBMs, missiles became central to COLD WAR strategy. See also ANTIBALLISTIC MISSILE, CRUISE MISSILE, MINUTEMAN MISSILE, TORPEDO, V-1 MISSILE, V-2 MISSILE.

Missile Defense Alarm System (Midas) Series of unmanned U.S. military satellites developed to warn of surprise attacks by Soviet intercontinental ballistic missiles, the world's first such warning system. Launched in the early 1960s, the reconnaissance satellites had infrared sensors to detect the heat of a missile's rocket exhaust shortly after firing.

mission Organized effort to spread the Christian faith. The new religion spread rapidly along the trade routes of the Roman empire, but its advance slowed with the disintegration of the Roman empire after 500 and the growth of Arab power in the 7th–8th cent. Celtic and British missionaries continued to spread the faith in W and N Europe, while missionaries of the Greek church in Constantinople worked in E Europe and Russia. Missions to Islamic areas and the Orient began in the medieval period, and Roman Catholic missionaries were active in the 16th-cent. colonies of Spain, Portugal, and France. Roman Catholic missionary work in the 19th cent. focused on Africa and Asia. Protestant missionary work experienced an upsurge in the 19th and early 20th cent. Missionary work continues today, though it is often discouraged by the governments of former European colonies that have won independence.

Mission style *or* **Spanish Mission style** Style of the missions established by Spanish Franciscans in Florida, Texas, Arizona, New Mexico, and especially California (1769–1823). It featured simple geometric volumes of white stucco, sharply incised windows, and simplified interior details. Mission style also refers to a style largely created in the early 20th cent. by Gustav STICKLEY, who marketed house designs and a line of plain oak furnishings inspired by those of the Spanish missions.

Mississauga \ˌmi-sə-ˈsȯ-gə\ City (pop., 1996: 544,000), SE Ontario. It was settled in the early 19th cent. on land purchased from the Mississauga Indians. It became a city in 1974. A residential suburb of TORONTO and an important industrial center, it is also the site of Toronto International Airport.

Mississippi State (pop., 2000: 2,844,000), S central U.S. It covers 47,689 sq mi (123,514 sq km); its capital is JACKSON. Its landscape ranges from hills and pine woods to plains and river lowlands. Before European settlement, the area was inhabited by several Indian tribes, including the CHOCTAW, Natchez, and Chickasaw. It became part of French-controlled Louisiana, and Biloxi was settled in 1699. The N portion was ceded to the U.S. in 1783; the S portion was included in the Mississippi Territory (created 1798), which expanded in 1804 to include most of the present-day state. Mississippi became the 20th U.S. state in 1817. A plantation-based economy using slave labor developed in the 1820s. It seceded from the Union in 1861 and gave the Confederacy its president, Jefferson DAVIS. The Union victory in the VICKSBURG CAMPAIGN (1863) proved a turning point in the AMERICAN CIVIL WAR. Mississippi was readmitted to the Union in 1870 and adopted a constitution aimed at blocking RECONSTRUCTION in 1890. The state became a battleground in the struggle against racial segregation in the 1960s: the state's effort to block the admission of James MEREDITH to the Univ. of MISSISSIPPI triggered riots in 1962; local civil rights leader Medgar EVERS was murdered in 1963. After 1969, when the federal government ordered the integration of the state's segregated school system, Mississippi's long-standing racial traditions began a gradual change. Today, its economy is based on agricultural products, including cotton and soybeans, and manufactured goods, including textiles and electrical equipment.

Mississippi, University of *known as* **Ole Miss** Public university based in Oxford, Miss. Chartered in 1844 and opened in 1848, it offers undergraduate, graduate, and professional degrees and manages more than 15 research units, including the Center for Study of Southern Culture. Its law school was established in 1854. Women were first admitted in 1882; racial segregation was forcibly ended in 1962. William FAULKNER attended classes at the university, which now operates his home as a museum.

Mississippian culture Last major prehistoric cultural development in N. America, around 800–1550. It spread over much of the Southeast and the mid-continent and was based on intensive cultivation of corn, beans, squash, and other crops. Each large town dominated a group of satellite villages and had a temple within a central ceremonial plaza, indicating a connection to Central America. The Cahokia Mounds, which lie along the Mississippi River near present-day Collinsville, Ill., was the culture's largest urban center. Craftwork was executed in copper, shell, stone, wood, and clay. The culture had already begun to decline by the time Europeans first penetrated the Southeast. See also WOODLAND CULTURES.

Mississippi River River, central U.S. It rises at Lake ITASCA in Minnesota and flows south, meeting its major tributaries, the MISSOURI and OHIO rivers, about halfway along its journey to the Gulf of MEXICO. It enters the Gulf southeast of NEW ORLEANS, after a course of 2,350 mi (3,780 km). It is the largest river in N. America. Spanish explorer Hernando DE SOTO was the first European to discover the river, in 1541. Jacques MARQUETTE and Louis JOLLIET traveled down it in 1673 as far as the ARKANSAS RIVER. R.-R. LA SALLE reached the delta in 1682 and claimed the entire Mississippi region for France, as Louisiana. France sold it to the U.S. in 1803 as part of the LOUISIANA PURCHASE. During the AMERICAN CIVIL WAR, Union forces captured VICKSBURG in 1863, breaking the Confederate hold on the river. A powerful river, it was immortalized by Mark TWAIN in *Huckleberry Finn*. As the central river artery of the U.S, it is one of the busiest commercial waterways in the world.

Missouri State (pop., 2000: 5,595,000), midwestern U.S. It covers 69,697 sq mi (180,515 sq km); its capital is JEFFERSON CITY. The MISSOURI RIVER runs from west to east across the state. The area north of it has rolling hills and fertile plains, the area south has deep valleys and swift streams. The region was originally inhabited by various Indian tribes, one of which, the Missouri, gave the state its name. The first permanent European settlement was made in 1735 at Ste. Genevieve by French hunters and lead miners. ST. LOUIS was founded in 1764. The U.S. gained control of the region in 1803 as part of the LOUISIANA PURCHASE. It was part of Louisiana Territory in 1805 and Missouri Territory in 1812. An influx of U.S. settlers occurred after the WAR OF 1812. Missouri became the 24th state in 1821, but only after the MISSOURI COMPROMISE allowed its admission as a slave state. It suffered much tension between slaveholders and abolitionists, evidenced in the DRED SCOTT DECISION in 1857. Missouri remained in the Union during the AMERICAN CIVIL WAR, though its citizens fought on both sides. After the war, its economic growth expanded and was celebrated in the St. Louis Exhibition of 1904. After World War II, its economy shifted from agriculture to manufacturing. It leads the nation in lead production, based mainly in the OZARKS region.

Missouri Compromise (1820) Act passed by the U.S. Congress admitting Missouri to the Union as the 24th state. After the territory requested statehood without slavery restrictions, Northern congressmen tried to attach amendments restricting further slaveholding. When Maine (originally part of Massachusetts) requested statehood, a compromise led by Henry CLAY allowed Missouri admission as a slave state and Maine as a free state, with slavery prohibited from then on in territories north of Missouri's S border. Clay's compromise appeared to settle the slavery-extension issue but highlighted the sectional division.

Missouri River River, central U.S. The longest tributary of the MISSISSIPPI RIVER, it is formed in the ROCKY MTNS. of SW Montana. It flows east to central N. Dakota and south across S. Dakota, forming sections of the boundaries of S. Dakota, Nebraska, Missouri, and Kansas. It then crosses Missouri to join the Mississippi River north of ST. LOUIS, after a total course of 2,315 mi (3,726 km). It has been nicknamed "Big Muddy" because of the amount of silt that it carries. The first Europeans to visit its mouth were Jacques MARQUETTE and Louis JOLLIET in 1673. The first exploration of the river from its mouth to its headwaters was made in 1804–5 by the LEWIS AND CLARK EXPEDITION. Efforts continue to check its turbulent flooding.

Missouri River, Little See LITTLE MISSOURI RIVER
Misti \'mēs-tē\, **El** *or* **Volcán Misti** Volcano, ANDES, S Peru. It rises to 19,098 ft (5,821 m) above sea level, towering over the city of AREQUIPA. Its pristine, snowcapped cone is thought to have had religious significance for the INCAS, and it has inspired legends and poetry. Now dormant, it last erupted in 1600.

mistletoe Any of many species of semiparasitic green plants of the families Loranthaceae and Viscaceae, especially those of the genera *Viscum, Phoradendron,* and *Arceuthobium. V. album,* the traditional mistletoe of literature and Christmas celebrations, is found throughout Eurasia. This bush droops on the branch of a host tree, bearing small, leathery, evergreen leaves and yellowish flowers, which produce poisonous, waxy-white berries. A modified root penetrates the bark of the host tree and forms tubes through which water and nutrients pass from the host to the parasite. The N. American counterpart is *P. serotinum.* Mistletoe was formerly believed to have magical and medicinal powers, and kissing under hanging mistletoe was said to lead inevitably to marriage.

Mistral \mēs-'träl\, **Gabriela** *orig.* Lucila Godoy Alcayaga (1889–1957) Chilean poet. A diplomat and professor, her reputation as a poet was established in 1914 when she won a prize for three "Sonetos de la muerte" ("Sonnets of Death"). Her passionate lyrics, with love of children and of the downtrodden as principal themes, are collected in such volumes as *Desolación* (1922), *Tala* (1938), and *Lagar* (1954). In 1945 she became the first Latin-American woman to win the Nobel Prize.

MIT See MASSACHUSETTS INSTITUTE OF TECHNOLOGY

Gabriela Mistral, 1941

Mitanni \mi-'ta-nē\ Ancient kingdom of upper MESOPOTAMIA, extending from the EUPHRATES RIVER nearly to the TIGRIS RIVER. Founded by Indo-Iranians, it competed with Egypt for control of Syria. In the 15th cent. B.C., its soldiers looted the Assyrian palace in ASHUR. In the mid-14th cent. B.C., its capital was sacked by the Hittites; the kingdom became part of the HITTITE empire and later an Assyrian province.

Mitchell, Arthur (b.1934) U.S. dancer, choreographer, and director. Born in New York City, he danced in Broadway musicals before joining the NEW YORK CITY BALLET in 1956 as its first black dancer. He created roles in several of George BALANCHINE's ballets, including *A Midsummer Night's Dream* (1962) and *Agon* (1967), before leaving the company in 1972. His own company, Dance Theatre of Harlem, made its debut in 1971.

Mitchell, Billy (*orig.* William) (1879–1936) U.S. aviator. Born in France to U.S. parents, he became the top U.S. air commander in World War I, initiating mass-bombing formations and leading an attack involving 1,500 planes. An outspoken advocate for a separate air force, he foresaw that the bomber would replace the battleship. When a navy dirigible was lost in a storm (1925), he accused the war and navy departments of incompetence. Charged with insubordination, he was court-martialed and suspended from duty. He resigned in 1926 but continued to champion air power and warned of advances by foreign air forces. In 1948 he was posthumously honored by the new U.S. Air Force with a special medal.

Mitchell, Joni *orig.* Roberta Joan Anderson (b.1943) Canadian singer and songwriter. Born in Fort Macleod, Alberta, Mitchell studied art in Calgary, where she began to sing in clubs. Several early songs, including "Both Sides Now" and "Woodstock," became hits for other artists. While her early recordings, such as *Clouds* (1969) and *Blue* (1971), were folk-oriented and reflected the idealism of the time, later releases, such as *Court and Spark* (1974), *Hejira* (1976), and *Turbulent Indigo* (1994), were marked by strong pop and jazz influences. Her notably original songs have made her perhaps the preeminent female songwriter of her time.

Mitchell, Margaret (1900–1949) U.S. writer. Born in Atlanta, Mitchell spent 10 years writing her one book, *Gone with the Wind* (1936, Pulitzer Prize; film, 1939). A story of the American Civil War and Reconstruction from the Southern point of view, it became the largest-selling novel in U.S. history to that time. She died when she was struck by a car.

Mitchell, Mt. Peak, W N. Carolina. The highest U.S. peak east of the Mississippi River, it rises to 6,684 ft (2,037 m). It is situated in the Black Mtns., part of the BLUE RIDGE system. Formerly called Black Dome, it was renamed for Elisha Mitchell (1793–1857), who surveyed it in 1835; he is buried at its summit.

Mitchum, Robert (1917–1997) U.S. film actor. Born in Bridgeport, Conn., he made his screen debut in 1943, acting in several Hopalong Cassidy westerns. He won praise for his role in *The Story of G.I. Joe* (1945). With his trademark sleepy-eyed, tough-guy appearance, he usually played loners and villains, in such movies as *Out of the Past* (1947), *Crossfire* (1947), *The Big Steal* (1949), *The Night of the Hunter* (1955), *Thunder Road* (1958), *Cape Fear* (1962), *The Friends of Eddie Coyle* (1973), and *Farewell, My Lovely* (1975).

mite Any of about 20,000 species of tiny ARACHNIDS (subclass Acari, sometimes Acarina or Acarida). Species range from microscopic to 0.25 in. (6 mm) long. Mites live in water and soil, on plants, and as plant and animal parasites. Itch mites (family Sarcoptidae), which burrow into the skin of humans and animals, cause the highly contagious disease scabies. A few species transmit tapeworms to cattle. Grain mites (family Glycyphagidae) damage stored products. House dust allergy is caused by species of the common genus *Dermatophagoides.* See also CHIGGER.

Mithra \mē-'trä, 'mith-rə\ In Indo-Iranian myth, the god of light. He was born bearing a torch and armed with a knife, beside a sacred stream and under a sacred tree. He soon rode, and later killed, the life-giving cosmic bull, whose blood fertilizes all vegetation. This deed became the prototype for a bull-slaying fertility ritual. As god of light, Mithra was associated with the Greek HELIOS and the Roman Sol Invictus. The first written reference to Mithra dates to 1400 B.C. See also MITHRAISM.

Mithradates VI Eupator \mith-rə-'dā-tēz...'yü-pə-ˌtȯr\ *known as* **Mithradates the Great** (d.63 B.C.) King of PONTUS (120–63 B.C.) and enemy of Rome. As a boy he was coruler with his mother from around 120 B.C., then overthrew her to become sole ruler in 115. He waged three wars against Rome, called the Mithradatic Wars (88–85, 83–82, 74–63). Though he originally seemed a champion to Greeks seeking relief from the Roman threat, his cruel treatment of them and his defeat by SULLA (86) destroyed that hope. Greece turned to Rome after 86 but suffered the harsh demands of both until Mithradates' final defeat by POMPEY. He was one of the few leaders successfully to challenge Roman expansion in Asia.

Mithraism \'mith-rə-ˌi-zəm\ Ancient Iranian religion based on the worship of MITHRA, the greatest of Iranian deities before the coming of ZOROASTER in the 6th cent. B.C. It spread from India through Persia and the Hellenic world; in the 3rd–4th cent. A.D., soldiers of the Roman empire carried it as far west as Spain, Britain, and Germany. The most important Mithraic ceremony was the sacrifice of the bull, an event associated with the creation of the world. Mithraic ceremonies were held by torchlight in subterranean caverns. After CONSTANTINE I accepted CHRISTIANITY in the early 4th cent., Mithraism rapidly declined.

Mitilíni See LESBOS

Mitla \'mēt-lä\ Village and archaeological site, OAXACA state, S Mexico. It is surrounded by the mountains of the SIERRA MADRE del Sur. It was established as a sacred burial site by the ZAPOTECS, who used it until about A.D. 900. The Mixtecs moved down from N Oaxaca 900–1500 and took possession of Mitla. The modern village serves as a base for study of the ruins.

mitochondrion Structure within a eukaryotic CELL (see EUKARYOTE) that is the location of energy production for the cell. Mitochondria appear in both plant and animal cells as

elongated cylindrical bodies, roughly one micrometer long and closely packed in regions actively using metabolic energy. Oxidizing the products of cytoplasmic metabolism (see OXIDATION-REDUCTION, TRICARBOXYLIC ACID CYCLE), they convert the energy so liberated into ATP. Mitochondria and CHLOROPLASTS have a structural resemblance, and both have a somewhat independent existence within the cell, synthesizing some proteins and dividing according to instructions in their own DNA, which appears to resemble that of BACTERIA. This has led to the hypothesis that these organelles are descendants of bacteria that entered primitive nucleated cells and developed stable, symbiotic associations between nucleated hosts and bacterial parasites.

mitosis \mī-'tō-səs\ Cell division in which a cell gives rise to two genetically identical daughter cells. Strictly, the term describes the duplication and distribution of CHROMOSOMES. Prior to mitosis, each chromosome is replicated, producing two strands (chromatids) attached at a CENTROMERE. During mitosis, the membrane around the cell's nucleus dissolves and the chromatids of each chromosome are separated and pulled to opposite ends of the cell. As the nuclear membrane re-forms around each set of chromosomes, the cytoplasm of the parent cell begins to divide and the cell membrane inches in to separate the daughter cells. Mitosis is essential to life because it provides new cells for growth and for replacement of worn-out cells. See also MEIOSIS.

Mitsubishi group Loose consortium of independent Japanese companies. The first Mitsubishi company was a trading and shipping concern established in 1873 by Iwasaki Yataro (1835–1885). Several subsidiaries were created after World War I, and by the 1930s Mitsubishi was Japan's second-largest ZAIBATSU. During World War II it was a major military contractor, producing the Zero fighter plane, and came to control some 200 companies. The zaibatsu was broken up by U.S. occupation forces, but after the postwar U.S. occupation some companies began to reassociate. The group today consists of more than two dozen independent companies, including Bank of Tokyo and Kirin Brewery. It suffered severe losses in the 1990s.

Mitterrand \mē-tə-'räⁿ\, **François (-Maurice-Marie)** (1916–1996) President of France (1981–95). Elected to the National Assembly (1946), he held cabinet posts in 11 Fourth Republic governments (1947–58). Moving to the political left, he opposed Charles DE GAULLE's government. In 1971 he became secretary of the FRENCH SOCIALIST PARTY and made it the majority party of the left, which led to his election as president in 1981. He introduced radical economic reforms, which were modified when a right-wing majority regained legislative power in 1986. Reelected in 1988, he strongly promoted the European Union. His domestic policy was less successful, and France experienced high unemployment. He appointed Edith Cresson (b.1934) prime minister, the first woman to hold that office (1991–92). An electoral defeat for the Socialists in 1993 further moderated his policies.

Mix, Tom (*orig.* Thomas Hezikiah) (1880–1940) U.S. film actor. Born in Mix Run, Pa., he worked as a cowhand and Texas Ranger before joining a Wild West show in 1906. He made his screen debut as a roughriding hero in 1910 and soon became a star of silent westerns, along with his famous horse, Tony. Mix appeared in more than 200 one- and two-reelers and feature films, many of which he also produced or directed.

Mizoguchi Kenji \ˌmē-zō-'gù-chē-'ken-jē\ (1898–1956) Japanese film director. Initially an actor, he made his debut as a director in 1922. His early films included *Tokyo March* (1929), *Osaka Elegy* (1936), and *The Story of the Last Chrysanthemums* (1939). His pictorially beautiful films, of which he made over 80, often dealt with the conflict between modern and traditional values. He won international acclaim for *Ugetsu monogatari* (1953), an allegorical commentary on postwar Japan. He was also noted for his films about women, including *Street of Shame* (1956).

moa Any of 13–25 species of extinct RATITE of New Zealand constituting the order Dinornithiformes. Species ranged from turkey-sized to 10 ft (3 m) high. Moas were swift run-

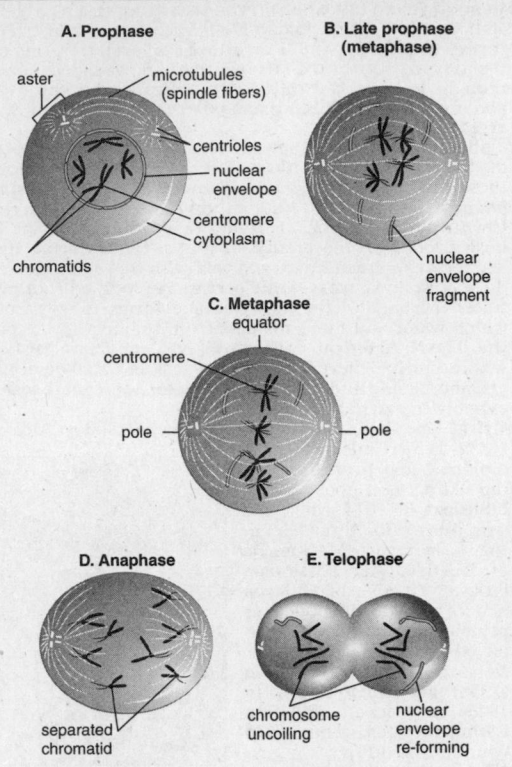

Mitosis Stages of mitosis. A. Prophase. Replicated chromosomes, consisting of two daughter strands (chromatids) attached by a centromere, coil and contract. Two pairs of specialized organelles (centrioles) begin to move apart, forming a bridge of hollow protein cylinders known as microtubules (spindle fibers) between them. Microtubules also extend in a radial array (aster) from the centrioles to the poles of the cell. B. Late prophase. As the centrioles move apart, the nuclear envelope breaks down and microtubules extend from each centromere to opposite sides or poles of the cell. C. Metaphase. The centromeres align in a plane midway between the poles known as the equator or metaphase plate. During late metaphase, each centromere divides into two, freeing sister chromatids from each other. D. Anaphase. Sister chromatids are drawn to opposite ends as centromeric microtubules shorten and polar microtubules lengthen, causing the poles to move farther apart. E. Telophase. Chromosomes uncoil, microtubules disappear, and the nuclear envelope reforms around each set of daughter chromosomes. The cytoplasm begins to pinch in to create two daughter cells. The process of cytoplasmic division is completed during cytokinesis.

ners that defended themselves by kicking. They were hunted for their flesh (eaten as food), bones (used as weapons and ornaments), and eggs (used for water vessels). Some species survived into the 19th cent. Moas browsed and grazed on seeds, fruits, leaves, and grasses. They laid a single large egg in a hollow in the ground.

Moab \'mō-ˌab\ Ancient kingdom, Syria. Located east of the DEAD SEA, in what is present-day SW Jordan, it was bounded by EDOM and the country of the Amorites. MOABITES were closely related to the Israelites; they were sometimes allies and sometimes adversaries. Moab was conquered by BABYLONIA in 582 B.C.

Moabites \'mō-ə-ˌbīts\ Semitic people who lived in the highlands east of the DEAD SEA (now in W-central Jordan). The Moabites' culture dates from the late 14th cent. B.C. to 582

B.C., when they were conquered by the Babylonians. Though their language, religion, and culture were closely related to those of the Israelites, the Moabites were not part of the Israelite community. The Moabite Stone, a stela discovered in 1868, is the only written document of any length that survives from Moab; it tells of King Omri of Israel's reconquest of Moabite lands, which the Moabites ascribed to the anger of their god, Chemosh.

Mobile \'mō-ˌbēl, mō-'bēl\ City and seaport (pop., 2000: 198,000), SW Alabama, situated on MOBILE BAY at the mouth of the Mobile River. The site was explored by Spaniards in 1519. It served as the capital of French Louisiana until 1720. It was ceded to the British in 1763 and was captured by the Spanish during the AMERICAN REVOLUTION. It passed to the U.S. with the purchase of Florida from Spain in 1819. During the AMERICAN CIVIL WAR it was an important Confederate port, but Federal forces won the Battle of Mobile Bay. It is the state's only seaport.

mobile \'mō-ˌbēl\ Abstract sculpture that has moving parts, driven either by motors or natural air currents. Its revolving parts create a constantly changing visual experience. The term was initially suggested by Marcel DUCHAMP for a 1932 Paris exhibition of such works by Alexander CALDER, who became the mobile's greatest exponent.

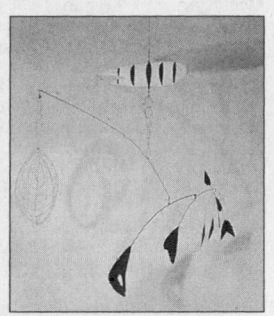

Mobile "Lobster Trap and Fish Tail" by Alexander Calder, 1939

Mobile Bay Inlet of the Gulf of MEXICO, extending 35 mi (56 km) north to the mouth of the Mobile River in SW Alabama. It is 8–18 mi (13–29 km) wide. During the AMERICAN CIVIL WAR it was the scene of the Battle of Mobile Bay.

Möbius \'mœ̄-bē-ûs, *Engl* 'mō-bē-əs\, **August Ferdinand** (1790–1868) German mathematician and theoretical astronomer. He introduced homogeneous coordinates into ANALYTIC GEOMETRY and dealt with geometric TRANSFORMATIONS, in particular projective transformations. He was a pioneer in TOPOLOGY; in a memoir discovered after his death he discussed the properties of one-sided surfaces, including the famous Möbius strip.

Mobutu Sese Seko \mə-'bü-tü-'sä-sä-'sä-kō\ *orig.* **Joseph Mobutu** (1930–1997) President of Zaire (now Congo), 1965–97. Mobutu served in the Belgian Congolese army before joining Patrice LUMUMBA in independence negotiations in 1960. When independence was achieved, the coalition government of Joseph KASAVUBU and Lumumba put Mobutu in charge of defense. In the rift between Kasavubu and Lumumba, Mobutu helped Kasavubu seize control. Four years later, he removed Kasavubu and assumed the presidency. He established single-party rule and suppressed attempted coups. He Africanized all European names, changing his own to Mobutu Sese Seko ("All-Powerful Warrior"). Repression, corruption, mismanagement, and neglect led to Zaire's decline, while Mobutu himself amassed one of the largest fortunes in the world. He was overthrown by Laurent KABILA in 1997 and died in exile.

mocambo See QUILOMBO

mockingbird Any of several versatile songbirds of a New World family (Mimidae). The common, or northern, mockingbird (*Mimus polyglottos*) can imitate the songs of 20 or more species within 10 minutes. It is gray, with darker, white-marked wings and tail. It ranges from the N U.S. to Brazil, and thrives in suburban areas. Other *Mimus* species range from Central America to Patagonia, and the blue mockingbird (genus *Melanotis*) inhabits much of Mexico.

Moctezuma II See MONTEZUMA II

mode In music, any of a variety of concepts used to classify SCALES and melodies. In Western music, the term is particularly used for the medieval CHURCH MODES. KEYS in tonal music are normally said to be in either major or minor mode. Indian RAGAS can be regarded as modes. The concept of mode may extend to embrace an entire vocabulary of melodic formulas and perhaps other aspects of music that traditionally occur in tandem with a given set of formulas. The term has also been used for purely rhythmic patterns such as those of the ARS ANTIQUA.

mode See MEAN, MEDIAN, AND MODE

Model T Automobile built by the FORD MOTOR CO. from 1908 until 1927, the first widely affordable mass-produced car. ASSEMBLY-LINE production methods introduced by Henry FORD in 1913 enabled the price of this five-seat touring car to drop from $850 in 1908 to $300 in 1925. Over 15 million Model Ts were built. The car was offered in several body styles, all mounted on a standard chassis. It was replaced by the popular Model A in 1928.

modem \'mō-ˌdəm\ Electronic device that converts digital data into analog (modulated-wave) signals suitable for transmission over traditional phone lines, and demodulates received analog signals to recover the digital data transmitted. The "*modulator/dem*odulator" thus makes it possible for existing communications channels to support digital communications, including E-MAIL, INTERNET access, and FAX transmissions. An ordinary modem has a data transmission speed limit of about 56 kilobits per second. ISDN lines allow communications at over twice that rate, and cable modems and DSL lines have transmission rates of over a million bits per second.

Modena \'mō-dä-nä\ City (pop., 1998 est.: 175,000), EMILIA-ROMAGNA region, N Italy. An ancient Etruscan city, it was made a Roman colony in 183 B.C. Attacked and pillaged by the Huns under ATTILA and later by the Lombards, it passed to the ESTE FAMILY in 1288. It was taken by France in 1796 and made part of Napoleon's kingdom of Italy in 1805. It joined Italy in 1860. The automobile industry is important to its economy. Its university, founded in 1175, is the third-oldest in Europe.

modern art Painting, sculpture, architecture, and graphic arts characteristic of the later 19th and 20th cent. It embraces a wide variety of movements, theories, and attitudes that tend to reject traditional or academic forms and conventions. Its origins can be traced to IMPRESSIONISM; a succession of movements and styles emerged, including POSTIMPRESSIONISM, NEO-IMPRESSIONISM, SYMBOLISM, FAUVISM, CUBISM, FUTURISM, EXPRESSIONISM, SUPREMATISM, CONSTRUCTIVISM, De STIJL, DADA, SURREALISM, SOCIAL REALISM, ABSTRACT EXPRESSIONISM, POP ART, OP ART, MINIMALISM, and NEO-EXPRESSIONISM.

modern dance Theatrical dance that developed in the U.S. and Europe in the 20th cent. as a reaction to traditional BALLET. Precursors included Loie FULLER and Isadora DUNCAN. Formal teaching of modern dance began with the establishment of the Denishawn schools by Ruth Saint DENIS and Ted SHAWN in 1915. Many of their students, principally Doris HUMPHREY and Martha GRAHAM, contributed importantly to its development. Their works often stressed contemporary themes and the expression of emotional intensity. Later developments included a revolt against Expressionism in the 1950s led by Merce CUNNINGHAM, and a profusion of pop and postmodern influences in the last quarter of the 20th cent.

modernism In the arts, experimentation that flouted traditional conventions, from the late 19th cent. to the mid-20th cent. Its rise owed greatly to the factors that made the era modern: industrialization, rapid social change, advances in science and the social sciences, and the accompanying sense of alienation. Modernist works tended no longer to speak for a society, nation, or people, but to be either individualistic and idiosyncratic or broadly universal. MODERN ART and MODERN DANCE are manifestations of modernism. In literature, the works of T. S. ELIOT, James JOYCE, and Virginia WOOLF are considered typically modernist; in music, the compositions of Arnold SCHOENBERG, and Igor STRAVINSKY; and in architecture, buildings in the BAUHAUS and INTERNATIONAL STYLE.

Modernismo Spanish-language literary movement of the late 19th and early 20th cent., founded by Rubén DARÍO. Reacting against the sentimental romantic writers then popular, *modernistas* often wrote about exotic worlds, such as the ancient past and the lands of childhood fancy. With "art

M

for art's sake" as their creed, they brought about the greatest revitalization of language and poetic technique in Spanish since the 17th cent. Its adherents included Peru's José Santos Chocano (1875–1934) and Cuba's José MARTÍ. Though the movement was over by 1920, its influence continued well into the 20th cent.

Modersohn-Becker \'mō-dər-ˌzōn-'be-kər\, **Paula** *orig.* Paula Becker (1876–1907) German painter. After studying art in London and Paris, she became one of the first artists to introduce French POSTIMPRESSIONISM into German art. Her later paintings, such as *Self-Portrait with a Camellia* (1907), combine a lyrical naturalism with the broad areas of simplified color characteristic of Paul GAUGUIN and Paul CÉZANNE. She died at 31 giving birth to her first child.

Modesto City (pop., 2000: 189,000), central California, east of SAN FRANCISCO. Founded in 1870 by the Central Pacific Railway, it was called Modesto (Spanish: "modest") when W. C. Ralston (1826–1875), a railway director, modestly declined to have it named in his honor. Incorporated as a city in 1884, it is an agricultural center.

Modigliani \ˌmō-dēl-'yä-nē\, **Amedeo** (1884–1920) Italian painter and sculptor. After studying art in Italy, he settled in Paris (1906). Following the advice of Constantin BRANCUSI, he studied African sculpture and in 1912 exhibited 12 stone heads whose simplified and elongated forms reflect African influence. When he returned to painting, his portraits and nudes reflected the style of his sculpture. In 1917 he began painting a series of female nudes that, with their warm, glowing colors and sensuous, rounded forms, are among his best works. His work reflects his lifelong admiration for Italian Renaissance masters, as well as the influence of Paul CÉZANNE and Brancusi. He died at 35 of tuberculosis.

modulation In electronics, a technique for impressing information (voice, music, picture, or data) on a radio-frequency carrier wave by varying one or more characteristics of the WAVE in accordance with the signal. There are various forms of modulation, each designed to alter a particular characteristic of the carrier wave, such as amplitude (see AM), frequency (see FM), PHASE, pulse sequence, and pulse duration.

modulation In music, a temporary change of MODE or KEY. Of the seven lettered pitches in a given key, six are shared with the most closely related keys; modulation to those keys thus requires changing the letter whose pitch is not shared. For example, if "The Star-Spangled Banner" is played in C major, whose fourth step is F, the F-sharp on "-ly" ("dawn's ear*ly* light") creates a fleeting modulation to the key of G major, which differs from C major only in that one note.

Moesia \'mē-shə\ Province of the Roman empire, SE Europe. Bordered by the DANUBE RIVER and the BLACK SEA, it was conquered by Rome 30–28 B.C. and became a Roman province in A.D. 15. Despite barbarian invasions, it remained part of the eastern Roman empire until the 7th cent., when it was occupied by Slavs and Bulgarians.

Mogadishu \ˌmō-gə-'dē-shü\ City (pop., 1999 est.: 1,162,000), seaport and capital of Somalia. Founded in the 10th cent., it carried on trade with the Arab states and later with the Portuguese. It fell to the sultan of Zanzibar in 1871. Subsequently the capital of Italian SOMALILAND and of the Somalia trust territory, it became the capital of independent Somalia in 1960. Since the 1980s civil war in Somalia has devastated the city, and fierce fighting among warlords continues to impede government.

Mogilev See MAHILYOW

Mogollon culture \ˌmō-gə-'yōn\ Culture of a group of N. American Indians who lived in what is now SE Arizona and SW New Mexico around 200 B.C.–A.D. 1200. The first pottery in the Southwest was made by the Mogollon. The early economy was based on gathering wild plant foods and hunting small game. Corn cultivation emerged around A.D. 500. In the final, or Mimbres, period (1050–1200) new patterns of house design (multilevel PUEBLOS centered around a plaza) and pottery (crisp black-on-white designs) emerged, suggesting contact with the ANASAZI peoples to the north. For unknown reasons, Mogollon culture came to an end in the 13th cent.

Mogul dynasty See MUGHAL DYNASTY

Mohammed See MUHAMMAD

Mohave See MOJAVE

Mohawk N. American Indian people, the easternmost group of the IROQUOIS CONFEDERACY. The Mohawk lived near what is now Schenectady, N.Y. Women practiced corn agriculture while men hunted during the fall and winter and fished during the summer. Related families lived together in LONGHOUSES. Most Mohawk sided with the British in both the FRENCH AND INDIAN WAR and the AMERICAN REVOLUTION. Today they number about 10,000 and work in various fields, notably the structural steel industry.

Mohawk River River, E central New York. The HUDSON RIVER's largest tributary, it flows 148 mi (238 km) to join the Hudson north of Troy. The Mohawk Valley (Mohawk Trail) was the historic route of westbound pioneers. The Five Nations of the IROQUOIS CONFEDERACY lived in the valley, which was a major battleground during the FRENCH AND INDIAN WAR and the AMERICAN REVOLUTION.

Mohegan \mō-'hē-gən\ N. American Indian people who once inhabited the area of SE Connecticut. They later seized land in Massachusetts and Rhode Island from other tribes. Their economy was based on corn cultivation, hunting, and fishing. In the 17th cent. the Mohegan and the PEQUOT tribes were ruled jointly by a Pequot chief, but a rebellion led to Mohegan independence and the destruction of the Pequot. Allied with the English, the Mohegan were the only important tribe remaining in S New England after KING PHILIP'S WAR (1675–76). About 1,000 Mohegans now live near Norwich, Conn.

Mohican See MAHICAN

Moho \'mō-ˌhō\ *or* **Mohorovicic discontinuity** \ˌmō-hə-'rō-və-ˌchich\ Boundary between the earth's CRUST and its MANTLE. It lies at a depth of about 22 mi (35 km) below continents and about 4.5 mi (7 km) beneath the oceanic crust. Modern instruments have determined that the velocity of SEISMIC WAVES increases rapidly at the Moho, named for Andrija MOHOROVICIC.

Moholy-Nagy \'mȯ-hȯi-'näd^y\, **Laszlo** (1895–1946) Hungarian painter, photographer, and art teacher. After studying law in Budapest, he went to Berlin in 1919. In 1923–28 he taught at the BAUHAUS and edited its publications. As a painter and photographer he worked predominantly with light. His "photograms" were composed directly on film, and his "light modulators" (oil paintings on transparent or polished surfaces) included mobile light effects. As an educator, he developed a widely accepted curriculum to develop students' natural visual gifts. Fleeing Nazi Germany in 1935, he went to London and then to Chicago, where he organized the New Bauhaus.

Mohorovicic, Andrija (1857–1936) Croatian meteorologist and geophysicist. A professor in Zagreb, he was also director of its meteorological observatory from 1892. From observations of SEISMIC WAVES, he deduced that the solid earth consisted of an outer and inner layer and that between them lay a distinct boundary, later named the Mohorovicic discontinuity, or MOHO. He also devised a technique for locating earthquake epicenters and calculated the travel time of seismic waves.

Mohs hardness \'mōz\ Rough measure of the resistance of a smooth surface to scratching or abrasion, expressed in

Mohs Hardness Table

Mineral	Mohs no.	Description
Talc	1	very easily scratched by the fingernail; has a greasy feel
Gypsum	2	can be scratched by the fingernail
Calcite	3	very easily scratched with a knife and just scratched with a copper coin
Fluorite	4	very easily scratched with a knife but not as easily as calcite
Apatite	5	scratched with a knife with difficulty
Orthoclase	6	cannot be scratched with a knife, but scratches glass with difficulty
Quartz	7	scratches glass easily
Topaz	8	scratches glass very easily
Corundum	9	cuts glass
Diamond	10	used as a glass cutter

terms of a scale devised by German mineralogist Friedrich Mohs (1773–1839) in 1812. Minerals are compared with the Mohs scale, which is made up of 10 minerals given arbitrary hardness values from 1 (least hard, or talc) to 10 (hardest, or diamond).

Moi \'moi\, **Daniel arap** (b.1924) President of Kenya (1978–2002). Moi served as vice president under Jomo KENYATTA before succeeding him as president. Head of the dominant Kenyan African National Union party, he governed autocratically, finally permitting multiparty elections only when forced to by international pressure in 1991. His subsequent electoral victories led to civil unrest and charges of fraud. Under Moi some sectors of the economy have grown, but critics attribute this to the strong political patronage system.

Moiseyev \moi-'sä-ef\, **Igor (Aleksandrovich)** (b.1906) Russian dancer, choreographer, and director. In 1936 he became head choreographer at Moscow's Theater of Folk Art, and he later founded the State Academic Folk Dance Ensemble, or Moiseyev Ensemble. In over 170 dances created for the ensemble, he combined authentic folk-dance steps with theatrical effects. The company served as a model for other national folk-dance ensembles.

Mojave *or* **Mohave** \mō-'hä-vē\ American Indian farmers of the Mojave Desert along the lower Colorado River. This valley was a patch of green surrounded by barren desert. The Mohave farmed, fished, hunted, and gathered wild plants. There were no settled villages; wherever there was suitable floodland for farming, the Mojave built scattered houses. They believed in a supreme creator; dreams were considered the source of all special powers. About 2,000 Mojave now live on or near the Colorado River reservation in Arizona.

Mojave Desert *or* **Mohave Desert** \mō-'hä-vē\ Arid region, SE California. Occupying more than 25,000 sq mi (65,000 sq km), it extends from the SIERRA NEVADA to the Colorado Plateau and merges with the Great Basin Desert to the north and the SONORAN DESERT to the south and southeast. It receives an average annual rainfall of 5 in. (13 cm). It is the location of JOSHUA TREE NATIONAL PARK.

moksha *or* **moksa** \'mōk-shə\ In HINDUISM and JAINISM, the ultimate spiritual goal, the soul's release from the bonds of transmigration. The soul, once entered upon a bodily existence, remains trapped in a chain of successive rebirths until it attains the perfection that allows it release. The methods by which release is sought and attained differ from one philosophical school to the next.

mol See MOLE

mold In biology, a conspicuous mass of mycelium and fruiting structures produced by various fungi (see FUNGUS). Molds of the genera *Aspergillus, Penicillium,* and *Rhizopus* are associated with food spoilage and plant diseases, but some have beneficial uses, as in the manufacture of ANTIBIOTICS (e.g., PENICILLIN) and certain cheeses. *Neurospora,* or orange bread mold, has been invaluable in the study of biochemical genetics. See also SLIME MOLD.

mold In manufacturing, a cavity or surface in which a fluid or plastic substance is shaped into a desired finished product. A molten substance is poured or forced into a mold and allowed to harden. Molds are made of various materials; sand is frequently used for metal CASTING, hardened steel for molds for plastic materials, and plaster for various purposes. See also TOOL AND DIE MAKING.

Moldavia \mäl-'dā-vē-ə\ Former principality, SE central Europe. Located on the lower DANUBE RIVER, it was founded in the 14th cent. Later taken by the OTTOMAN EMPIRE, in 1774 it came under Russian control; it soon lost its NW territory, Bukovina, to Austria, and its E portion, BESSARABIA to Russia. In 1859 Moldavia and WALACHIA formed the state of Romania. That part east of the Dniester River now lies within Ukraine; lands west of the Dniester form present-day Moldova.

molding In architecture and the decorative arts, a defining, transitional, or terminal element that serves to contour or outline edges and surfaces. The surface of a molding may be plain or modeled with recesses and reliefs, which either maintain a constant profile along its length or are set in rhythmically repeated patterns. The profiles of moldings

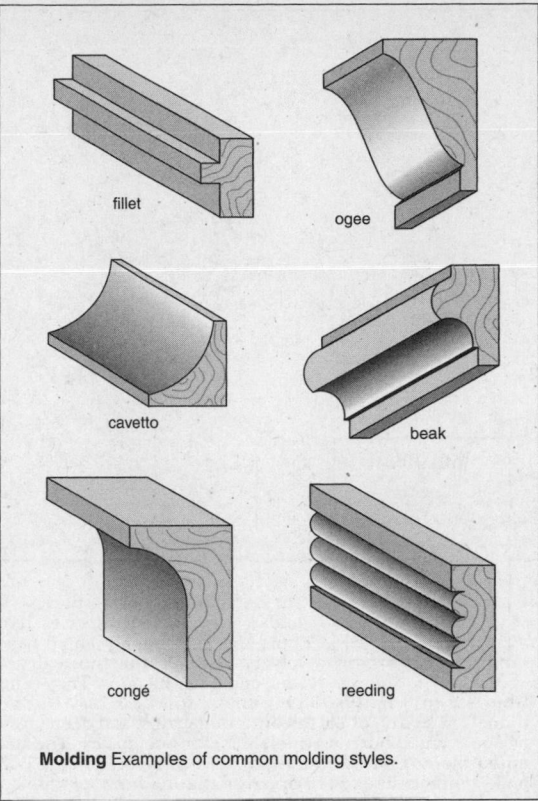

Molding Examples of common molding styles.

are traditionally enhanced by flower forms or geometric motifs.

Moldova \mol-'do-və\ *officially* **Republic of Moldova** Republic, central Europe. It is bordered by Ukraine and Romania. Area: 13,000 sq mi (33,700 sq km). Population (2000): 4,298,000. Capital: CHISINAU. The majority of the people are ethnic Moldovans; the Transdniester region, east of the DNIESTER RIVER, has large numbers of Russians and Ukrainians. Languages: Romanian (official), Russian, Ukrainian. Religion: Eastern Orthodoxy. Currency: leu. Most of Moldova is a fertile region lying between the Dniester and Prut rivers; the N and central regions of the country are forested. The economy is based on agriculture; the major farm products are grapes, winter wheat, corn, and dairy products. Industry is centered on food processing. It is a parliamentary republic with one legislative body; its head of state is the president, and the head of government is the prime minister. The area of present-day Moldova consists of that part of the principality of Moldavia lying east of the Prut River (part of Romania before 1940) and, adjoining it on the south, the region of BESSARABIA along the Black Sea coast (see MOLDAVIA for history prior to 1940). The two regions were incorporated as the Moldavian S.S.R. in 1940. In 1991 Moldavia declared independence from the Soviet Union. Having legitimized use of the Roman rather than the Cyrillic alphabet, it adopted the Romanian spelling of Moldova. The republic was admitted to the U.N. in 1992. See map on following page.

mole *or* **mol** \'mōl\ Standard unit for measuring everyday quantities of such minute entities as ATOMS or MOLECULES. For any substance, the number of atoms or molecules in a mole is AVOGADRO'S NUMBER (6.02×10^{23}) of particles. For each substance, a mole is its ATOMIC WEIGHT, MOLECULAR WEIGHT, or FORMULA WEIGHT in GRAMS. See also STOICHIOMETRY.

mole Any burrowing, often blind, INSECTIVORE in the families Talpidae (including 22 species of true moles) or

M

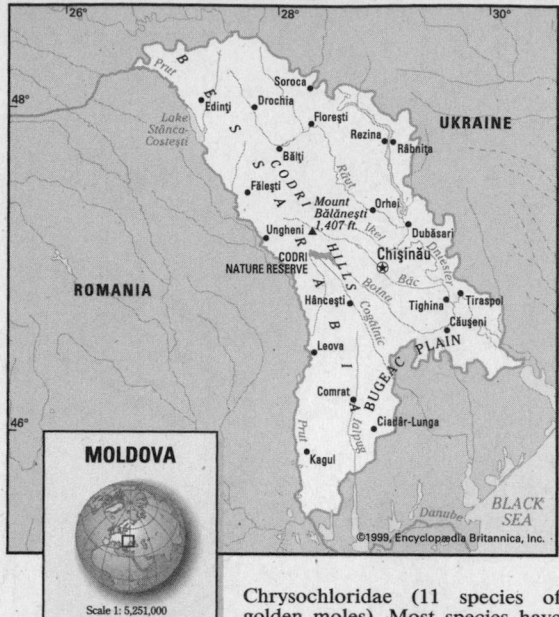

MOLDOVA

Scale 1: 5,251,000
0 — 20 — 40 mi
0 — 30 — 60 km

©1999, Encyclopædia Britannica, Inc.

Chrysochloridae (11 species of golden moles). Most species have short legs and tail, a pointed head, velvety grayish fur, no external ears, and a strong odor. They range from 3.5 to 8 in. (9–20 cm) long. Moles dig both surface tunnels in search of earthworms and grubs, and deep (10-ft, or 3-m) vented burrows (molehills) for occupancy. The star-nosed mole *(Condylura cristata)* of NE N. America has 22 pink, tentacle-like touch organs radiating from its nose.

mole Pigmented flat or fleshy SKIN mark, made up mostly of cells that produce MELANIN, which gives moles their light to dark brown or black color. Thicker moles also contain nerve elements and connective tissue. Moles often begin in childhood, usually as flat spots between the dermis and epidermis. Those that remain there are more likely to become malignant. Most move into the dermis and become slightly raised. In children, moles may undergo changes resembling cancer but are benign. Malignant MELANOMA can begin in moles, but almost never before puberty. During pregnancy, moles may enlarge and new ones may appear. Moles sometimes disappear with age.

molecular biology Field of science concerned with the chemical structures and processes of biological phenomena at the molecular level. Having developed out of BIOCHEMISTRY, GENETICS, and BIOPHYSICS, the discipline is particularly concerned with the study of PROTEINS, ENZYMES, NUCLEIC ACIDS, and GENES. In the early 1950s, growing knowledge of the structure of proteins enabled the structure of DNA to be described. See also BIOTECHNOLOGY, GENETIC ENGINEERING, RECOMBINATION.

molecular electronics *or* **moletronics** *or* **nanoelectronics** Use of individual molecules as electronic components and assembled especially into computer circuits to perform calculations and store data. The technology, still in its infancy, may eventually supersede even the smallest silicon-based microchips. A computer chip the size of a grain of sand may acquire hundreds of times the capacity of chips now operating desktop computers. The primary theoretical advantage of molecular electronics is the capacity to manufacture chips with a much higher density of transistors operating with lower power needs. Other potential advantages are low manufacturing costs, higher-speed circuitry, and lower operating temperatures. Potential uses of miniature molecular computers include insertion into the human bloodstream to monitor or control biochemical functions. While some individual circuit components (including molecular logic gates, transistors, and even wires) have been created, commercial applications may not be available for a decade or more.

molecular weight MASS of a molecule of a substance, based on 12 as the ATOMIC WEIGHT of carbon-12. It is calculated by summing the atomic weights of the atoms making up the substance's molecular formula. The molecular weight of hydrogen (chemical formula H_2) is 2; for many complex organic molecules (e.g., PROTEINS, POLYMERS) it may be in the millions.

molecule Smallest identifiable unit into which a pure substance can be divided and retain its composition and chemical properties. Division into still smaller parts, eventually ATOMS, involves destroying the BONDING that holds the molecule together. For NOBLE GASES, the molecule is a single atom; all other substances have two (diatomic) or more (polyatomic) atoms in a molecule. The atoms are the same in ELEMENTS, such as hydrogen (H_2), and different in COMPOUNDS, such as glucose ($C_6H_{12}O_6$). Atoms always combine into molecules in fixed proportions. Molecules of different substances can have the same constituent atoms, either in different proportions, as in carbon monoxide (CO) and carbon dioxide (CO_2), or bonded in different ways (see ISOMER). ANALYSIS with modern techniques and computers can determine and display the size, shape, and CONFIGURATION of molecules. ELECTRON MICROSCOPY can even produce images of individual molecules and atoms. See also MOLECULAR WEIGHT.

Molière \mȯl-ʹyer\ *orig.* Jean-Baptiste Poquelin (1622–1673) French playwright, actor, and director. He became an actor

CH₃   CH₃   CH₃
CH₂OH
CHO
CH₃
CH₃   CH₃

bond-line formula of vitamin A

Kekulé structure of benzene

H —— OH
HO —— H
H —— OH
H —— OH
CH₂OH

Fischer projection of glucose

ball-and-stick model of methane

Lewis structures of methane

H
..
H : C : H
..
H

or

H
|
H — C — H
|
H

Molecule Several methods of representing a molecule's structure. In Lewis structures, element symbols represent atoms, and dots represent electrons surrounding them. A pair of shared electrons (covalent bond) may also be shown as a single dash. The ball-and-stick model better illustrates the spatial arrangement of the atoms. For aromatic compounds, the Kekulé structure is common, in which each bond is represented by a dash, carbon atoms are implied where two or more lines meet, and hydrogen atoms are usually omitted. Bond-line formulas, similar to the Kekulé structure, are often used for complex nonaromatic organic compounds. Sugars are often drawn as Fischer projections, in which the carbon "backbone" is drawn as a straight vertical line, with carbon atoms implied where horizontal lines intersect the vertical one.

in 1643, cofounded the Illustre Théâtre troupe, and toured the French provinces (1645–58), writing plays and acting in them. After his troupe was established in a permanent theater in Paris under the patronage of LOUIS XIV, he won acclaim for his comedy *The Affected Young Ladies* (1659). His other major plays included *The School for Wives* (1662), *Tartuffe* (1664; initially banned by religious authorities), *The Misanthrope* (1666), *Amphitryon* (1668), *The Miser* (1669), *The Bourgeois Gentleman* (1670), and *The Imaginary Invalid* (1673). His plays composed a portrait of all levels of 17th-cent. French society, and were marked by their good-humored and intelligent mockery of human vices, vanities, and follies. He is considered the greatest French dramatist and the father of modern French comedy.

Molière Painting by Pierre Mignard

Molise \mō-'lē-zä\ Autonomous region (pop., 1996 est.: 331,000), S central Italy. Its W sector is part of the APENNINES, and the remainder consists mostly of low mountains and hills. Under LOMBARD rule during the early Middle Ages, it was controlled by the duchy of Benevento. In 1860 it was joined to ABRUZZI; in 1965 they were separated. It is one of Italy's most rural regions; its capital is Campobasso.

mollusk *or* **mollusc** Any of some 75,000 species of soft-bodied INVERTEBRATE animals (phylum Mollusca), many of which are enclosed in a calcium carbonate shell secreted by the mantle, a soft covering formed from the body wall. Between the mantle and the body is the mantle cavity. Mollusks occur in most habitats, from the deep sea to high mountains. Living mollusks are usually grouped into eight classes: Gastropoda (see GASTROPOD), Bivalvia or Pelecypoda (see BIVALVE), Cephalopoda (see CEPHALOPOD), Scaphopoda (tusk shells), Aplacophora (Solenogasters), Caudofoveata (sometimes included in the Aplacophora order), Polyplacophora (chitons), and Monoplacophora. Mollusks are economically important as food, and their shells are used in decorative items.

Molly Maguires (1862–76) Secret organization of U.S. coal miners in Pennsylvania and W. Virginia. To protest poor working conditions and discrimination, the Irish-American miners formed a group named for an Irish widow who had led antilandlord agitators in Ireland. Acts of sabotage and terrorist murders in the coalfields were blamed on the group, and mine owners hired a Pinkerton detective to infiltrate it. After widely publicized trials (1875–77), 10 "Mollies" were convicted of murder and hanged.

Moloch \'mō-ˌlōk, 'mä-lək\ Ancient Middle Eastern deity to whom children were sacrificed. The laws given to MOSES by God expressly forbade the Israelites to sacrifice children to Moloch, as the Egyptians and Canaanites did.

Molotov \'mȯ-lə-ˌtȯf\, **Vyacheslav (Mikhaylovich)** *orig.* Vyacheslav Mikhaylovich Skryabin (1890–1986) Soviet political leader. A member of the Bolsheviks from 1906 and staunch supporter of Joseph STALIN, he was promoted to the Politburo in 1926. In 1928–30 he purged the Moscow party organization of anti-Stalinists. He served as prime minister 1930–41, and as foreign minister 1939–49 and 1953–56. He negotiated the GERMAN–SOVIET NONAGGRESSION PACT in 1939, and in World War II he ordered the production of the crude bottle bombs later called "Molotov cocktails." He arranged Russia's wartime alliances with the U.S. and Britain. Dismissed in 1956 by Nikita KHRUSHCHEV, Molotov joined an unsuccessful attempt to depose Khrushchev (1957) and lost all his party offices.

Moltke \'mōlt-kə\, **Helmuth (Karl Bernhard) von** *later* **Graf (Count) von Moltke** (1800–1891) Prussian general. Appointed to the army general staff in 1832, he later traveled widely and wrote several books on history and travel. In 1855 he served as personal aide to the Prussian prince Frederick William, then was selected as chief of the Prussian general staff (1857–88). Highly intelligent and militarily cre-

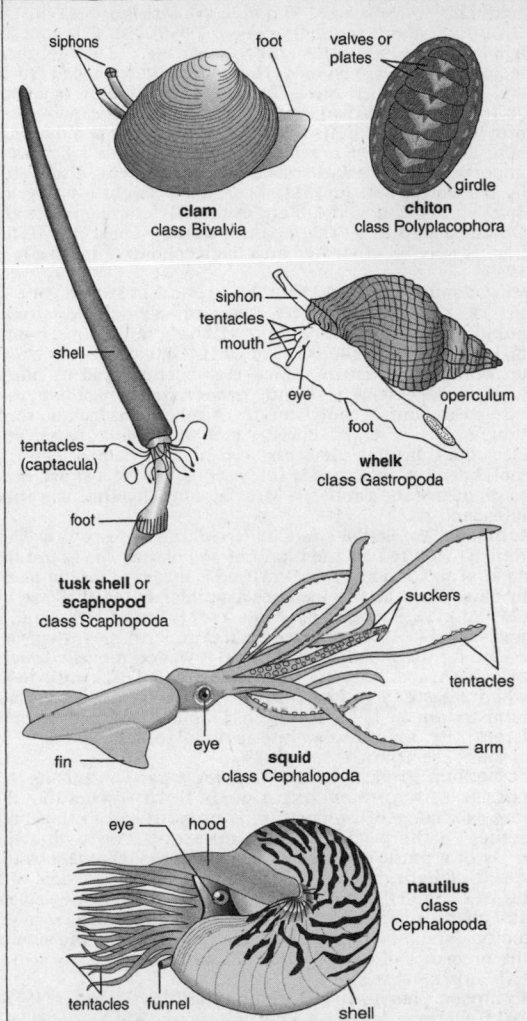

clam
class Bivalvia

chiton
class Polyplacophora

siphons · foot · valves or plates · girdle

whelk
class Gastropoda

siphon · tentacles · mouth · shell · eye · operculum · foot

tusk shell or **scaphopod**
class Scaphopoda

tentacles (captacula) · foot

squid
class Cephalopoda

suckers · tentacles · arm · eye · fin

nautilus
class Cephalopoda

eye · hood · tentacles · funnel · shell

Mollusk Representative mollusks. Bivalves have a shell with two halves. Filter feeders, they take in food and water through a tubular siphon. In the clam, a muscular foot is used for burrowing and creeping. The chitons, typically found adhering to rocks and shells, have shells divided into eight overlapping plates. Tusk or tooth shells are burrowing mollusks with a shell open at both ends; with the larger end buried in the sand, they feed on microorganisms captured by the tentacles. The whelks, like most gastropods (univalves), have a single shell, which is usually coiled; when threatened, the body can be pulled into the shell, which is closed by a plate (operculum). Cephalopods have a well-developed head and a foot divided into numerous tentacles. The two long tentacles of the squid are used to capture prey, and the short arms transfer food to the mouth. The nautilus is the only cephalopod that has retained an exterior shell; by regulating the amount of gas and fluid in the interior chambers, it can regulate its buoyancy.

ative, he reorganized the Prussian army and devised new strategic and tactical command methods for modern mass armies. His strategies produced victories against Austria in the SEVEN WEEKS' WAR (1866) and against France in the FRANCO–PRUSSIAN WAR (1870–71).

Moluccas \mō-'lə-kəz\ *Indonesian* **Maluku** \mä-'lü-kü\ Group of islands (pop., 1995 est.: 2,095,000), E Indonesia, lying between SULAWESI and NEW GUINEA. The Moluccas include three large islands (Halmahera, CERAM, and Buru) and many smaller ones. Their combined area is about 28,767 sq mi (74,505 sq km). They constitute the Indonesian province of Maluku; its capital is AMBON. The population is ethnically diverse. Known as the "Spice Islands," they were important to the Asian spice trade before being discovered by the Portuguese in 1511. They were fought over by the Spanish, English, and Dutch, eventually coming under the Dutch. Occupied by the Japanese during World War II, the islands were incorporated into the Republic of Indonesia in 1949.

molybdenum \mə-'lib-də-nəm\ Chemical ELEMENT, one of the TRANSITION ELEMENTS, chemical symbol Mo, atomic number 42. It is a silvery gray, relatively rare METAL with a high melting point (4,730°F, or 2,610°C) that does not occur uncombined in nature. Since molybdenum and its alloys have useful strength at high temperatures, high-temperature steels contain molybdenum. Applications include reaction vessels; aircraft, missile, and automobile parts; and electrodes, heating elements, and filament supports. Some molybdenum compounds (of various VALENCES) are used as pigments and catalysts. Molybdenum disulfide is a solid lubricant.

Mombasa \mŏm-'bä-sə\ City (pop., 1991 est.: 600,000), Kenya, centered on the island of Mombasa. The island has an area of 5.5 sq mi (14 sq km) and is linked to the mainland by causeway; the city includes a mainland area of 100 sq mi (259 sq km). Founded by Arab traders in the 11th cent., it was visited in 1498 by Vasco da GAMA. With its strategic location for the Indian Ocean trade, it was continually fought over by Arabs, Persians, Portuguese, and Turks until 1840, when ZANZIBAR gained control. It came under British administration in 1895. It is Kenya's chief port and second-largest city, known as an international tourist resort.

moment See TORQUE

momentum Product of the MASS of a particle and its VELOCITY. NEWTON'S SECOND LAW OF MOTION states that the rate of change of momentum is proportional to the force acting on the particle. Albert EINSTEIN showed that the mass of a particle increases as its velocity approaches the speed of light, but at the speeds treated in classical MECHANICS the effect of speed on the mass can be neglected, and changes in momentum are the results of changes in velocity alone. For a rigid body, the momentum is the sum of the momenta of each particle in the body. See also ANGULAR MOMENTUM.

Mommsen \'mŏm-zən\, **(Christian Matthias)Theodor** (1817–1903) German historian and writer. In 1848 he became a professor of law at Leipzig, but he was soon dismissed for his participation in liberal political activities. He is most famous for his *History of Rome* (4 vols., 1854–56, 1885), his masterpiece. His *Corpus Inscriptionum Latinarum* (from 1863), a comprehensive collection of Latin inscriptions, greatly advanced understanding of life in the ancient world. His *Roman Constitutional Law* (3 vols., 1871–88) represented the first codification of Roman law. His lifetime output was immense, his publications numbering close to 1,000. In 1902 he received the second Nobel Prize for Literature.

Mon \'mŏn\ People thought to have originated in W China and currently living in the E delta region of Myanmar and in W-central Thailand. They have lived in their present area for the last 1,200 years and brought Myanmar its writing (Pali) and its religion (Buddhism). Today they number more than 1.1 million. See also MON KINGDOM.

Monaco \'mä-nə-,kō\ *officially* **Principality of Monaco** Independent principality, on the Mediterranean Sea near the France–Italy border. Area: .73 sq mi (1.9 sq km). Population (2000): 32,000. The majority of Monaco's population is composed of French citizens, with a small minority of Italians. About 15% are of Monagesque descent. Language: French (official). Religion: Roman Catholicism (official). Currency: French franc. Inhabited since prehistoric times, the area was known to the Phoenicians, Greeks, Carthaginians, and Romans. In 1191 the Genoese took possession of it;

in 1297 the reign of the Grimaldi family began. The Grimaldis allied themselves with France except for the period 1524–1641, when they were under the protection of Spain. France annexed Monaco in 1793, and it remained under French control until the fall of NAPOLEON, when the Grimaldis returned. In 1815 it was put under the protection of Sardinia. A treaty in 1861 called for the sale of the towns of Menton and Roquebrune to France and the establishment of Monaco's independence. Monaco is one of Europe's most luxurious resorts, known for its MONTE CARLO gambling center, international sports-car races, and beaches. In 1997 the 700-year rule of the Grimaldis, now under Prince RAINIER III, was celebrated. Lax banking laws have led to charges of major money-laundering.

monarch butterfly Species (*Danaus plexippus,* family Danaidae) of milkweed BUTTERFLY, occurring worldwide but mainly in the Americas. Monarchs are the only LEPIDOPTERAN that individually make a true round-trip migration. In N. America, millions of monarchs gather in autumn, migrate more than 1,800 mi (2,900 km), mostly to central Mexico, and return north in spring. The distinctive pattern of the adult's reddish brown wings warns predators of its bad taste.

monarchy Undivided SOVEREIGNTY or rule by a single person, who is the permanent head of state. The term is now used to refer to countries with hereditary sovereigns. The monarch was the ideal head of the new nation-states of the 16th–17th cent.; his powers tended toward ABSOLUTISM, though in Britain PARLIAMENT limited that power from early on. The old idea that the monarch represented the rule of God culminated in the 17th-cent. doctrine of the divine right of kings, exemplified by LOUIS XIV. Monarchical absolutism adapted to the ENLIGHTENMENT by evolving into "benevolent despotism," as typified by the rule of CATHERINE II of Russia. The French Revolution dealt absolute monarchy a crushing blow, and World War I effectively destroyed what remained of it, the rulers of Russia, Germany, and Austria-Hungary being held responsible.

monarchy, constitutional See CONSTITUTIONAL MONARCHY

monastery Residence of a religious order, particularly an order of monks. Christian monasteries originally developed in the Middle East and Greece from the streets of hermits' huts. Walls were built for defense, and monks' cells were later constructed against the walls, leaving a central space for church, chapels, fountain, and dining hall. The *vihara* was an early type of Buddhist monastery, consisting of an open court surrounded by open cells. Small STUPAS and images of the Buddha were later installed in the central court. In W India, viharas were often excavated into rock cliffs. See also ABBEY.

monasticism Institutionalized religious movement whose members are bound by vows to an ascetic life of prayer, meditation, or good works. Members of monastic orders (monks) are usually celibate, and they live apart from society either in a community of monks or nuns or as religious recluses. The earliest Christian monastic communities were founded in the deserts of Egypt, most notably by the 4th-cent. hermit St. ANTHONY OF EGYPT. Monasticism spread throughout the BYZANTINE EMPIRE and Western Europe. The BENEDICTINE order, founded by St. BENEDICT OF NURSIA in the 6th cent., called for moderation of ascetic practices. Throughout the Middle Ages, monasticism played a vital role not only in spreading Christianity but also in preserving and adding to literature and learning. Monasticism has also been important in Eastern religions. In early Hindu times (c.600–200 B.C.) there were hermits who lived in groups (ashrams), though they did not lead a strictly organized communal life. Jainism may be the first religion to have had an organized monastic life; it was characterized by extreme asceticism. Buddhist monks avoid extremes of self-indulgence and self-mortification.

Monck \'mənk\, **George** *later* **Duke of Albemarle** (1608–1670) English general. After suppressing a rebellion in Ireland (1642–43), he fought in the ENGLISH CIVIL WARS, then served in Scotland as commander (1650) and governor (1654). Appointed a general at sea (1652) in the ANGLO–DUTCH WARS, he played a leading part in the English naval victories. In 1660 he was the chief architect of the RESTORATION of the Stuart monarchy.

Mondale, Walter F(rederick) (b.1928) U.S. politician. Born in Ceylon, Minn., he became active in Minnesota's Farmer-Labor Party and worked for Hubert HUMPHREY's U.S. Senate campaign in 1948. He served in the U.S. Senate from 1964 to 1976, when he won election as vice president with Jimmy CARTER. In 1984 he won the Democratic presidential nomination, but lost to Ronald REAGAN. He served as ambassador to Japan 1993–96.

Monde \'mōⁿd\, **Le** (French: "The World") Daily newspaper published in Paris, one of the most important and widely respected newspapers in the world. Established in 1944, it has covered national and world news in depth from the start and earned a reputation for accuracy and independence. Its writers present their own views, with the result that the paper reveals no unified policies or consistent ideological outlook, though it is usually associated with the left.

Mondrian \'mȯn-drē-ˌän\, **Piet** orig. Pieter Cornelis Mondriaan (1872–1944) Dutch painter. His first paintings, which followed the prevailing trend of Dutch landscape and still-life painting, were exhibited in 1893. Later he broke away from tradition and became a leading figure in De STIJL. In Paris (1919–38), his mature style emerged in "Neoplasticism," based on the simplest harmonies of straight line, right angle, and the primary colors plus black, white, and gray (e.g., *Composition in Yellow and Blue*, 1929). He fled war-torn Paris for London and then New York in 1940. Inspired by the city's pulsating life and the new rhythms of U.S. music, he replaced his austere patterns with a series of small squares and rectangles that coalesced into a flow of colorful vertical and horizontal lines (e.g., *Broadway Boogie-Woogie*, 1942–43). His work exerted a profound influence on 20th-cent. art, architecture, and graphic design.

moneran See BACTERIA, PROKARYOTE

Monet \mō 'nā\, **Claude** (1840–1926) French Impressionist landscape painter. He spent his early years in Le Havre, where his first teacher, Eugène BOUDIN, taught him to paint in the open air. Moving to Paris, he formed lifelong friendships with other young painters, including Auguste RENOIR, Alfred SISLEY, and Paul CÉZANNE. An early Monet canvas, *Impression: Sunrise,* shown at the first Impressionist Exhibition in 1874, gave its name to the movement of which he was the leader. Restless by nature, he painted outdoors around France (often at Argenteuil) and also in England, Venice, Holland, and elsewhere. In his mature works Monet de-

Claude Monet with one of his water-lily paintings, 1920

veloped his method of producing several studies of the same motif in series, changing canvases with the light or as his interest shifted. These series, including *Haystacks* (1891) and *Rouen Cathedral* (1894), were often exhibited together. In the garden at his home in Giverny, Monet created the water-lily pond that inspired his most famous works, the lyrical *Nymphéas* (water lilies) paintings. His work exerted huge influence internationally, and he is regarded as the emblematic representative of IMPRESSIONISM.

monetarism School of economic thought that maintains that the money supply is the chief determinant of economic activity. Milton FRIEDMAN and his followers promoted monetarism as an alternative to Keynesian economics (see J. M. KEYNES); their economic theories became influential in the 1970s and early 1980s. Monetarism holds that a change in the money supply directly affects and determines production, employment, and price levels, though its influence is slow to be felt. Fundamental to the monetarist approach is the rejection of FISCAL POLICY in favor of "monetary rule." Friedman and others asserted that fiscal measures such as tax-policy changes or increased government

spending have little significant effect on the fluctuations of the BUSINESS CYCLE, and thus that government intervention in the economy should be minimal. Steady, moderate growth of the money supply, in their view, offered the best hope of assuring steady economic growth with low inflation. U.S. economic performance in the 1980s cast doubts on monetarism, and the proliferation of new types of bank deposits made it difficult to calculate the money supply.

monetary policy Measures employed by governments to influence economic activity, specifically by manipulating the money supply and interest rates. Monetary and FISCAL POLICY are two ways in which governments attempt to achieve or maintain high levels of employment, price stability, and economic growth. Monetary policy is directed by a nation's CENTRAL BANK. In the U.S., monetary policy is the responsibility of the FEDERAL RESERVE SYSTEM, which uses three main instruments: open-market operations (the purchase and sale of government securities), the DISCOUNT RATE, and reserve requirements (see FRACTIONAL RESERVE SYSTEM). Inflation tends to result when the money supply grows at too rapid a rate. See also MONETARISM.

money Commodity accepted by general consent as a medium of economic exchange. It is the medium in which PRICES and values are expressed. Throughout history various commodities have been used as money, including seashells, beads, and cattle, but since the 17th cent. the most common forms have been metal coins, paper notes, and bookkeeping entries. Money is held to have four functions: to serve as a medium of exchange universally accepted in return for goods and services; to act as a measure of value, making possible the operation of the price system and the calculation of COST, PROFIT, and loss; to serve as a standard of deferred payments, the unit in which loans are made and future transactions are fixed; and to provide a means of storing wealth not immediately required for use. Metals, especially gold and silver, have been used for money for at least 4,000 years; standardized coins have been minted for perhaps 2,600 years. In the late 18th cent. banks began to issue notes redeemable in gold or silver, but from the 1930s most nations abandoned the GOLD STANDARD. To most individuals today, money consists of coins, notes, and bank deposits. In terms of the economy, however, since most of the deposits placed in banks are loaned out, the total money supply is several times larger.

money market Set of institutions, conventions, and practices whose aim is to facilitate the lending and borrowing of money on a short-term basis. It is different from the capital market, which is concerned with medium- and long-term CREDIT. Money-market transactions involve not only banknotes but assets that can be turned into cash at short notice, such as short-term government SECURITIES and BILLS OF EXCHANGE. The market enables those with surplus short-term funds to lend and those with the need for short-term credit to borrow, through middlemen who provide their services for a profit. In most countries the government plays a major role, acting both as a lender and borrower and often using its position to influence the money supply and INTEREST rates according to its MONETARY POLICY. The U.S. money market covers financial instruments ranging from bills of exchange and government securities to funds from clearinghouses and CERTIFICATES OF DEPOSIT; the FEDERAL RESERVE SYSTEM provides considerable short-term credit directly to the banking system. The international money market facilitates the borrowing, lending, and exchange of currencies between countries.

money order Certificate requiring the issuer to pay a certain sum of money on demand to a specific person or organization. Money orders provide a fast, safe, and convenient means of transferring small sums of money. They are issued by governments (usually through postal authorities), banks, and other qualified institutions to buyers who pay the issuer the face amount of the money order plus a service charge. The AMERICAN EXPRESS CO., which began issuing money orders in 1882, is the largest nonbank issuer. See also CURRENCY.

Mongke \'mȯṇ-kā\ (1208–1259) MONGOL leader. Grandson of GENGHIS KHAN, he was elected great khan in 1251. Un-

der Mongke, the Mongols conquered Iran, Iraq, and Syria as well as the Thai kingdom of Nanchao and the area of present-day Vietnam. He died before the Mongols could complete the conquest of China, and was succeeded by his brother KUBLAI KHAN.

Mongkut \ˌmȯn-ˈküt\ *or* **Phrachomklao** \ˌprä-ˌkȯm-ˈklaù\ *or* **Rama IV** (1804–1868) King of Siam (r.1851–68). The 43rd child of King Rama II, he was a Buddhist monk and scholar before he ascended the throne. His reformed Buddhism grew into the Thammayut order, which today occupies the intellectual center of Thai Buddhism. As king, he fully opened Siam to Western commerce and combined tolerance and shrewdness to help ensure its survival as an independent nation. The reminiscences of an English governess he employed became the basis for the musical *The King and I.*

Mongol Member of an Asian people from the Mongolian plateau who share a common language and a nomadic herding tradition. Mongol power was greatest in the 13th cent., when GENGHIS KHAN, his sons (including OGODEI), and his grandsons BATU and KUBLAI KHAN, created one of the world's largest empires. It declined greatly in the 14th cent., when China was lost to the MING DYNASTY and the GOLDEN HORDE was taken by Muscovites; by the 15th–16th cent. only a loose federation existed. Today the plateau is divided between independent Mongolia and China. Other Mongols live in Siberia. Tibetan Buddhism is the principal Mongol religion. See also TATARS.

Mongol dynasty See YUAN DYNASTY

Mongolia *or* **Outer Mongolia** Country (pop., 2000: 2,399,000), N central Asia, between Russia and China. Area: 604,800 sq mi (1,566,500 sq km). Capital: ULAANBAATAR. Almost four-fifths of the population are Mongols; minorities consist of

Kazaks, Russians, and Chinese. Languages: Khalkha Mongolian (official), Turkic languages, Russian, Chinese. Religions: Tantric Buddhism (Lamaism) 96%; Islam. Currency: tugrik. Mongolia averages an elevation of about 5,200 ft (1,580 m) above sea level. Three mountain ranges stretch across the north and west: the Altai, the Hangayn (Khangai), and the Hentiyn (Khentei). The south and east are occupied by the GOBI DESERT. Livestock raising, especially sheep raising, accounts for about 70% of the total value of agricultural production; wheat is the major crop. Mongolia's rich mineral resources include coal, iron ore, and tin. It is a republic with one legislative house; its chief of state is the president, and the head of government is the prime minister. In Neolithic times it was inhabited by small groups of hunters and no-

mads. During the 3rd cent. B.C. it became the center of the Xiongnu empire. Turks held sway in the 4th–10th cent. A.D. In the early 13th cent. GENGHIS KHAN united the Mongol tribes and conquered central Asia. His son, OGODEI, conquered the JIN (CHIN) DYNASTY of CHINA in 1234. KUBLAI KHAN established the YUAN (MONGOL) DYNASTY in China in 1279. After the 14th cent., the MING DYNASTY of China confined the Mongols to their original homeland in the steppes. Ligdan Khan (r.1604–34) united Mongol tribes in defense against the MANCHU, but after his death, the Mongols became part of the Chinese QING DYNASTY. Inner Mongolia was incorporated into China in 1644. After the fall of the Manchu dynasty in 1912, Mongol princes, supported by Russia, declared Mongolia's independence from China, and in 1921 Russian forces helped drive off the Chinese. The Mongolian People's Republic was established in 1924, and was recognized by China in 1946. Dominated by the Soviet Union until 1991, the nation adopted a new constitution in 1992 and shortened its name to Mongolia.

Mongolian languages Family of about eight ALTAIC LANGUAGES spoken by 5–7 million people in central Eurasia. All Mongolian languages are relatively closely related. The languages of several ethnic groups in NW China, E Qinghai, and adjacent parts of Gansu and Inner Mongolia are spoken by under a half-million people. The core language is Mongolian proper, the dominant dialect in the Republic of Mongolia and the basis of Modern Standard Mongolian. Classical Mongolian is written in a vertical alphabetic script borrowed from the Uighurs (see TURKIC LANGUAGES). In 1946 the People's Republic of Mongolia introduced a script using a modified CYRILLIC ALPHABET. With political democratization in the 1990s, the old script has been revived.

Mongoloid See RACE

mongoose Any of more than 40 species in 15 genera of the CIVET family (Viverridae), carnivores found in Africa, Asia, and S Europe. Rudyard KIPLING's famous "Rikki-tikki-tavi" was an Indian, or gray, mongoose (*Herpetes edwardsi*). Species range from 7 to 35 in. (17–90 cm) long, excluding the furry 6–12-in. (15–30-cm) tail. Mongooses have short legs, a pointed nose, and small ears. Mongooses eat small mammals, birds, reptiles, eggs, and fruit. A few species are semiaquatic. Though not immune to venom, some species attack and kill poisonous snakes by cracking the skull with a powerful bite. See also MEERKAT.

monitor IRONCLAD warship originally used in shallow harbors and rivers to blockade the Confederate states in the AMERICAN CIVIL WAR. The original ironclad, built by John ERICSSON, was named *Monitor.* Its design included minimal exposure above the waterline and a revolving gun turret. The Battle of the *Monitor* and *Merrimack* (1862) was the first between ironclad warships. The U.S. Navy built many improved monitors during the war; the British navy kept its monitors in service as late as World War II.

Monitor and Merrimack, Battle of (Mar. 9, 1862) Naval engagement in the AMERICAN CIVIL WAR at Hampton Roads, Va. The *Merrimack,* originally a federal frigate, had been salvaged by the Confederates, fitted with iron armor, and renamed the *Virginia.* It sank several wooden warships before meeting the Union's *Monitor.* After a four-hour battle both ships were damaged, but each side claimed victory. Both ships were destroyed later in 1862, the *Virginia* by its crew to avoid capture and the *Monitor* in a storm.

monk See MONASTICISM

Monk, Thelonious (Sphere) *orig.* Thelious Junior Monk (1917–1982) U.S. jazz pianist and composer. Born in Rocky Mount, N.C., Monk grew up in New York City. He worked as house pianist at Minton's Playhouse (1940–43), where the expanding harmonic vocabulary of BEBOP was developed. He performed with Coleman HAWKINS and Dizzy GILLESPIE before making recordings under his own name beginning in 1947. His highly idiosyncratic, percussive playing made frequent use of sharp dissonances and insistent rhythms unusual in jazz and became widely influential.

monkey Any member of two tropical anthropoid PRIMATE groups: OLD WORLD MONKEYS and NEW WORLD MONKEYS. Most species are arboreal, using all four limbs to leap from tree to tree. They can sit upright and stand erect. Most species run along branches rather than swinging arm over arm like the APES. Monkeys are highly social omnivores, organized in clans as large as several hundred individuals headed by an old male. Most species bear a single young, which is reared by the mother for years.

monkey puzzle tree Evergreen ornamental and timber CO-NIFER (*Araucaria araucana*) of the family Araucariaceae, native to the Andes Mtns. of S. America. The tree may grow to 150 ft (45 m) in height. The rigid, overlapping, needle-pointed leaves are spirally arranged on stiff branches, which form a tangled, prickly network that discourages animals from climbing the tree.

monkfish Any of 10–12 species of SHARKS (genus *Squatina*, family Squatinidae) having a flattened head and body, with winglike pectoral and pelvic fins that make them resemble RAYS. Behind each eye is a prominent spiracle. Monkfish grow up to 6 ft (2.5 m) long. They inhabit tropical and warm temperate waters of the continental shelf worldwide. The angelfish, or angel shark (*S. squatina*), is often caught for food in Mediterranean waters. Two species of goosefishes (*Lophius americanus* and *L. piscatorius*), popular as food fishes, are also called monkfish.

Mon-Khmer languages \'mōn-kə-'mer\ Family of about 130 AUSTROASIATIC LANGUAGES, spoken by more than 80 million people in S. and S.E. Asia, of whom three-quarters speak VIETNAMESE. Other languages with many speakers are Muong in N Vietnam; Khmer in Cambodia; Kuay (Kuy); and Mon in S Myanmar and parts of Thailand. Only Mon, Khmer, and Vietnamese have written traditions dating earlier than the 19th cent. Old Mon, attested from the 7th cent., was written in a script of S. Asian origin that was later adapted by the Burmese (see MON KINGDOM, INDIC WRITING SYSTEMS). Typical phonetic features of Mon-Khmer languages are a large vowel inventory and lack of TONE distinctions.

Mon kingdom Kingdom of the MON people, who were powerful in Myanmar in the 9th–11th cent. and the 13th–16th cent. By 825 they had founded their capital city, Thaton, and the city of Pegu. The Mon kingdom was defeated by the Burman kingdom of PAGAN (1057), but when Pagan fell to the Mongols (1287) the Mon regained their independence and their former territory. Defeated again in 1539, they reestablished Pegu briefly (c.1747), but it was destroyed by the ALAUNGPAYA in 1757.

Monmouth \'män-məth\, **Duke of** *orig.* James Fitzroy *or* James Crofts *later* James Scott (1649–1685) British military leader. The illegitimate son of CHARLES II of England, he lived in Paris with his mother. In 1662 he was brought to England as a favorite of the king, who created him duke of Monmouth. A member of the king's guard from 1668, he was championed for the royal succession by the anti-Catholic Whigs, but after the unsuccessful Rye House Plot against Charles, he took refuge in the Netherlands (1684). Returning to challenge JAMES II, he and his army of peasants were defeated and he was captured and beheaded.

Monnet \mó-'nā\, **Jean** (1888–1979) French economist and diplomat. Born in Cognac, he managed his family's brandy business before becoming a partner of an investment bank (1925). In 1947 he created and directed the successful Monnet Plan to rebuild and modernize France's economy. In 1950, with Robert SCHUMAN, he proposed the plan for the European Coal and Steel Community, predecessor of the EUROPEAN ECONOMIC COMMUNITY, and served as its first president (1952–55). Founder and president of the action committee for the United States of Europe (1955–75), he is remembered as the "father of Europe."

monocot See COTYLEDON, FLOWERING PLANT

Monod \mó-'nō\, **Jacques (Lucien)** (1910–1976) French biochemist. In 1961 he and François JACOB proposed the existence of messenger RNA (mRNA), which carries the information encoded in the base sequence to the RIBOSOMES, where the sequence of bases is translated into the sequence of amino acids of a protein. They suggested the existence of a class of genes (OPERONS) that regulate the function of other genes by regulating the synthesis of mRNA. The two shared a 1965 Nobel Prize with André Lwoff (1902–1994).

monogram Originally a cipher consisting of a single letter, later a design or mark consisting of two or more letters in-

tertwined. The letters thus interlaced may be used on notepaper, seals, or elsewhere. Many early Greek and Roman coins bear the monograms of rulers or towns. The famous sacred monogram is formed by the conjunction of chi and rho, the first two Greek letters of ΧΡΙΣΤΟΣ (Christ), usually with the α (alpha) and ω (omega) of the Apocalypse on each side of it. The Middle Ages were extremely prolific in inventing ciphers for ecclesiastical, artistic, and commercial use. Related devices are the hallmarks of metalsmiths and the logos of corporations.

monomer \'mä-nə-mər\ MOLECULE of any of a class of mostly organic compounds that can react with other molecules of the same or other compounds to form very large molecules (POLYMERS). The essential feature of monomer molecules is the ability to form chemical bonds (see BONDING) with at least two other monomer molecules (polyfunctionality). Those able to react with two others can form only chainlike polymers; those able to react with three or more can form cross-linked, network polymers.

Monongahela River \mə-ˌnän-gə-'hē-lə\ River, N W. Virginia. It flows north into Pennsylvania and joins the ALLEGHENY RIVER at PITTSBURGH to form the OHIO RIVER, after a total course of 128 mi (206 km). Navigable for 106 mi (170 km), it serves as a hydroelectric source and major barge route.

mononuclear phagocyte system See RETICULOENDOTHELIAL SYSTEM

mononucleosis \ˌmä-nō-ˌnü-klē-'ō-səs\, **infectious** *or* **glandular fever** Common infection, caused by EPSTEIN-BARR VIRUS. It occurs most often at ages 10–35. Infected young children usually have little or no illness but become immune. It is spread mostly by oral contact with exchange of saliva. It usually lasts 7–14 days. The most common symptoms are malaise, sore throat, fever, and lymph-node enlargement. Liver involvement is usual but rarely severe. The spleen often enlarges and in rare cases ruptures fatally. Diagnosis may require blood analysis. There is no specific therapy.

Monophysitism \mə-'nä-fə-ˌsīt-i-zəm\ Doctrine that emphasized the single nature (the term means literally "of one nature") of Christ, as a wholly divine being rather than part-divine and part-human. It began to appear in the 5th cent.; though condemned as a heresy at the Council of CHALCEDON (451), it was tolerated by such Byzantine leaders as THEODORA, resulting in a schism between East and West. Several Monophysite churches, including the COPTIC ORTHODOX CHURCH, were founded in the 6th cent.

monopoly Exclusive possession of a market by a supplier of a product or service for which there is no substitute. In the absence of competition, the supplier usually restricts output and increases PRICE in order to maximize PROFITS. In situations where having more than one supplier is inefficient (e.g., for electricity, gas, or water), economists refer to "natural monopoly" (see PUBLIC UTILITY). For monopoly to exist there must be a barrier to the entry of competing firms. In the case of natural monopolies, the government creates that barrier. Either local government provides the service itself, or it awards a franchise to a private company and regulates it. In some cases, the barrier is attributable to an effective PATENT. In other cases, the barrier that eliminates competing firms is technological. Large-scale, integrated operations that increase efficiency and reduce production costs confer a benefit on firms that adopt them and may confer a benefit on consumers if the lower costs lead to lower product prices. In many cases, the barrier is a result of anticompetitive behavior on the part of the firm. Most free-enterprise economies have adopted laws such as the U.S. ANTITRUST LAWS to prevent abuse of monopoly power. Antitrust law prohibits MERGERS and acquisitions that lessen competition. See also OLIGOPOLY.

monorail Electric railway that runs on a single rail either above or under the railway cars. The earliest system probably opened in 1901 in Wuppertal, Germany. Short-run monorails have since been built in such cities as Tokyo and Seattle. Because of higher costs and slower speeds than conventional rail systems, the monorail has not gained wide support. High-speed monorail vehicles that use magnetic levitation have been undergoing research for many years.

M

monosaccharide \ˌmä-nə-ˈsa-kə-ˌrīd\ Any of the simple SUGARS that serve as building blocks for CARBOHYDRATES. They are classified based on their backbone of carbon (C) atoms: Trioses have three carbon atoms, tetroses four, pentoses five, hexoses six, and heptoses seven. The carbon atoms are bonded to hydrogen atoms (–H), hydroxyl groups (–OH; see FUNCTIONAL GROUP), and carbonyl groups (–C=O), whose combinations, order, and CONFIGURATIONS allow a large number of stereoisomers (see ISOMER) to exist. Pentoses include ribose, a component of RNA and several VITAMINS; and deoxyribose, a component of DNA. Important hexoses include GLUCOSE and FRUCTOSE. Monosaccharides combine with each other and other groups to form a variety of disaccharides, POLYSACCHARIDES, and other carbohydrates.

monotheism \ˈmä-nə-ˌthē-ˌi-zəm\ Belief in the existence of one god. It is distinguished from POLYTHEISM. The earliest known instance of monotheism dates to the reign of AKHENATON of Egypt in the 14th cent. B.C. Monotheism is characteristic of JUDAISM, CHRISTIANITY, and ISLAM, all of which view God as the creator of the world and the source of the highest good. In Judaism, Yahweh was first adopted as the single object of worship; other gods were not to be worshiped, but their existence was not initially denied. Islam is clear in confessing one, eternal, unbegotten, unequaled God, while Christianity holds that a single God is reflected in the three persons of the Holy TRINITY.

monotreme \ˈmä-nə-ˌtrēm\ Any of three living species of egg-laying MAMMALS (order Monotremata): the PLATYPUS and two species of ECHIDNA. Monotremes are found only in Australia, Tasmania, and New Guinea. Except for their egg laying, they have mammalian characteristics, such as mammary glands, hair, and a complete diaphragm. They lack teats; the young suck milk through pores on the mother's skin. Monotremes probably originated from a line of mammal-like reptiles different from those that gave rise to placental mammals and MARSUPIALS.

Monroe, Bill (*orig.* William Smith) (1911–1996) U.S. singer, songwriter, and mandolin player, inventor of the BLUEGRASS style. Born in Rosine, Ky., Monroe began to play professionally in 1927, and later toured with his brother Charlie. He formed the Blue Grass Boys in 1939. His bluegrass sound emerged fully in 1945, when Earl Scruggs and Lester FLATT joined his band. The Blue Grass Boys established the classic makeup of a bluegrass group—mandolin, fiddle, guitar, banjo, and upright bass—and bequeathed its name to the genre itself.

Monroe, James (1758–1831) Fifth president of the U.S. (1817–25). Born in Westmoreland Co., Va., he fought in the American Revolution and studied law under Thomas JEFFERSON. He served in the Congress (1783–86) and U.S. Senate (1790–94), where he opposed George WASHINGTON's administration. He was governor of Virginia 1799–1802. Pres. Jefferson sent him to France, where he helped negotiate the LOUISIANA PURCHASE (1803), then named him minister to Britain (1803–7). He later served as U.S. secretary of state (1811–17) and secretary of war (1814–15). He served two terms as president, presiding in a period that became known as

James Monroe

the Era of GOOD FEELINGS. He oversaw the SEMINOLE WAR (1817–18) and the acquisition of the Floridas (1819–21), and signed the MISSOURI COMPROMISE (1820). With secretary of state J. Q. ADAMS, he developed the principles of U.S. foreign policy later called the MONROE DOCTRINE.

Monroe, Marilyn *orig.* Norma Jean Mortenson (1926–1962) U.S. film actress. Born in Los Angeles, she made her screen debut in 1948. She achieved stardom as a blonde sex symbol in the comedies *Gentlemen Prefer Blondes* (1953), *How to Marry a Millionaire* (1953), and *The Seven Year Itch* (1955).

After studying at the ACTORS STUDIO, she starred in more ambitious films, including *Bus Stop* (1956), *Some Like It Hot* (1959), and *The Misfits* (1961). Her private life, which included marriages to Joe DIMAGGIO and Arthur MILLER, was widely publicized. She died at 36 of a barbiturate overdose.

Monroe Doctrine U.S. foreign-policy statement enunciated by Pres. James MONROE on Dec. 2, 1823. He declared that any attempt by a European power to control any nation in the Western Hemisphere would be viewed as a hostile act against the U.S. It was reiterated in 1845 and 1848 by Pres. James K. POLK to discourage Spain and Britain from establishing footholds in Oregon, California, or Mexico's Yucatán peninsula. In 1865 the U.S. massed troops on the Rio Grande to persuade France to withdraw from Mexico. In 1904 Pres. Theodore ROOSEVELT added the Roosevelt Corollary, stating that in case of flagrant wrongdoing by a LATIN AMERICAN state, the U.S. had the right to intervene in its internal affairs. As the U.S. became a world power, the Monroe Doctrine came to define the Western Hemisphere as a U.S. sphere of influence. See also GOOD NEIGHBOR POLICY.

Monrovia Port city (pop., 1999: 479,000), capital of Liberia. It was founded in 1822 as a settlement for freed U.S. slaves and named for Pres. James MONROE. Bushrod Island contains the artificial harbor and free port of Monrovia, the only such port in W. Africa. It is Liberia's largest city and its administrative and commercial center. Many of the city's buildings were damaged during the civil war that began in 1990; political strife continues to disrupt city life. It is the seat of the Univ. of Liberia.

monsoon Major wind system that seasonally reverses its direction (e.g., one that blows for six months from the northeast and six months from the southwest). The most prominent examples occur in Africa and S Asia. The primary cause is the difference between annual temperature trends over land and sea. Seasonal changes in temperature are large over land but small over oceans. A monsoon blows from sea toward land in summer, producing heavy rains, and from land toward sea in winter, causing drought.

montage \män-ˈtäzh\ (French: "mounting") Technique in which cut-out pictures, or fragments of them, are arranged together to produce a composite picture. It differs from COLLAGE in using only ready-made images chosen for their subject or message; it is widely used in advertising. Photomontage uses photographs only. In motion pictures, montage is the sequential assembling of separate pieces of thematically related film to produce visual juxtapositions and complex audio patterns.

Montagnais and Naskapi \ˌmän-tən-ˈyä...ˈnas-kə-pē\ Two related Indian peoples of E Canada. The Montagnais, traditionally occupying a large forested area above the N shores of the Gulf of St. Lawrence, lived in birch-bark wigwams and subsisted on moose, salmon, eel, and seal. The Naskapi, living farther north on the Labrador plateau, hunted caribou and fished. Religious belief centered on *manitou,* or supernatural power; much importance was attached to nature and animal spirits. Today there are some 11,000 Montagnais and 1,000 Naskapi.

Montagnard \ˌmōⁿ-ˌtän-ˈyär\ (French: "Mountain Man") Radical deputy in the NATIONAL CONVENTION during the FRENCH REVOLUTION. So-called because as deputies they sat on the higher benches (the Mountain) above the uncommitted deputies of the PLAIN, the Montagnards emerged in 1792 as opponents of the moderate GIRONDINS and later associated with the radical JACOBINS. After the THERMIDORIAN REACTION, many Montagnards were executed or purged, and they became a minority called the *crête* ("crest").

Montagu \ˈmän-tə-ˌgyü\, **Lady Mary Wortley** *orig.* Lady Mary Pierrepont (1689–1762) English writer, the most colorful Englishwoman of her time. A prolific letter writer, Montagu is remembered chiefly for 52 superb letters chronicling two years she spent in Constantinople with her husband. On their return, they introduced the Near Eastern practice of smallpox vaccination into Europe. Among her writings are six "town eclogues," witty adaptations of VIRGIL; a lively attack on Jonathan SWIFT (1734); and essays dealing with feminism and the moral cynicism of her time.

Montaigne \mōⁿ-'tenʸ, *Engl* män-'tän\, **Michel (Eyquem) de** (1533–1592) French courtier and author. While serving as counselor at the Bordeaux Parliament he met the lawyer Étienne de La Boétie, with whom he formed an extraordinary friendship; the void left by La Boétie's death in 1563 likely led Montaigne to begin his writing career. He retired to his château in 1571 to work on his *Essais* (1580, 1588), a series of short prose reflections on many subjects that form one of the most captivating and intimate self-portraits ever written. At once deeply critical of his time and deeply involved in its struggles, he sought un-

Michel de Montaigne Portrait by an unknown artist, 16th cent.

derstanding through self-examination, which he developed into a description of the human condition and an ethic of authenticity, self-acceptance, and tolerance. He served as mayor of Bordeaux during the troubled period 1581–85. See also ESSAY.

Montale \mōn-'tä-lā\, **Eugenio** (1896–1981) Italian poet and prose writer. His first book of poems, *Cuttlefish Bones* (1925), expressed the bitter pessimism of the postwar period. He was identified with HERMETICISM in the 1930s and '40s, before his works became progressively introverted and obscure. *The Storm and Other Poems* (1956) and subsequent works showed increasing skill, warmth, and directness. His stories and sketches were collected in *The Butterfly of Dinard* (1956). He received the Nobel Prize in 1975.

Montana State (pop., 2000: 902,000), NW U.S. It covers 147,046 sq mi (380,849 sq km); its capital is HELENA. Montana straddles the GREAT PLAINS to the east and the ROCKY MTNS. to the west. Unique among the states, its rivers flow into three of the continent's primary watersheds: the Pacific, the Gulf of Mexico, and Hudson Bay. At the time of European settlement the region was inhabited by various Indian tribes, including the CHEYENNE, BLACKFOOT, NEZ PERCÉ, and CROW. Most of Montana was obtained by the U.S. through the LOUISIANA PURCHASE of 1803. The W part was disputed until 1846, when Britain relinquished its claim to the area. The LEWIS AND CLARK EXPEDITION explored Montana in 1804–6. St. Mary's Mission, established in 1841 by Roman Catholic missionaries, became the first permanent town as Stevensville. Gold was discovered in the early 1860s; cattle and sheep grazing were introduced later that decade, leading to bitter battles with the Indians, whose hunting grounds were destroyed. Montana Territory was established in 1864. Though the U.S. troops of G. A. CUSTER were defeated and slain at the Battle of the LITTLE BIGHORN in 1876, the Indians ceased fighting in 1877 and were placed on reservations. Montana became the 41st state in 1889. Vast deposits of copper were found in the 1890s, and mining was the economic mainstay for almost a century. The state's economy now emphasizes tourism.

Montana, Joe *orig.* Joseph Clifford Montana, Jr. (b.1956) U.S. football quarterback. Born in New Eagle, Pa., he played for the Univ. of Notre Dame. Playing with the San Francisco 49ers 1979–93, he led the team to Super Bowl championships in 1982, 1985, 1989, and 1990. He maintained one of the highest passing-completion rates in the NFL, with a career average of 63.2. His career totals for passes completed (3,409), yards passing (40,551), and touchdown passes (273) are among the highest on record. He finished his career with the Kansas City Chiefs (1993–95).

Montañés \mōn-tän-'yäs\, **Juan Martínez** (1568–1649) Spanish sculptor. After studying in Granada, he established his studio in Seville. Known as *el dios de la madera* ("the god of wood") because of his great skill at wood carving, he is remembered for his wood altars and altar figures covered with polished gold and colored paint, which are realistic yet idealized. His output and influence over 50 years were enormous, and his work influenced not only the sculptors and

altar makers of Spain and Latin America but also the Spanish painters of his century.

Mont Blanc See Mont BLANC

Montcalm (de Saint-Véran) \mänt-'kälm\, **Marquis de** *orig.* Louis-Joseph de Montcalm-Grozon (1712–1759) French military leader. He joined the French army at 12 and fought in several European conflicts. In 1756 he was placed in command of French troops in N. America. He forced the British to surrender their post at Oswego and captured Ft. William Henry (1757). At the Battle of Ticonderoga, N.Y. (1758), he repulsed an attack by 15,000 British troops with 3,800 French forces. In 1759, while opposing Gen. James WOLFE in the Battle of QUEBEC, Montcalm was mortally wounded after fighting with conspicuous gallantry.

Monte Albán \'mȯn-tä-äl-'bän\ Ridgetop site of the ruins of the ancient center of ZAPOTEC culture, located near Oaxaca, Mexico. Construction began around the 8th cent. B.C.; Monte Albán reached its height A.D. 250–700. The site contains great plazas, temples, truncated pyramids, a *tlachtli* court for an ancient ballgame, underground passageways, and about 170 tombs, the most elaborate yet uncovered in the New World. In its final phase, Monte Albán was inhabited by the Mixtec.

Monte Carlo Resort (pop., 1990: 15,000), one of the four sections of Monaco. In 1856 Charles III of Monaco granted a charter allowing a joint stock company to build a casino, which opened in 1861. The district around it, called Monte Carlo, became a luxurious playground for the world's rich.

Monte Cassino Principal monastery of the BENEDICTINE order, located in Latium, central Italy. It was founded around 529 by St. BENEDICT OF NURSIA and reached its peak under Desiderius (later Pope Victor III), who was abbot 1058–87. Its buildings were destroyed many times, most recently in World War II, but were rebuilt each time. It was reconsecrated in 1964.

Montego Bay \män-'tē-gō\ Seaport (pop., 1991: 83,000), NW Jamaica. It lies on the site of a large ARAWAK village visited by Christopher COLUMBUS in 1494. The Spanish, ousted by the British after 150 years, destroyed most of the original buildings. One of Jamaica's largest cities, it is a commercial center and popular beach resort.

Montenegro \ˌmȯn-tä-'nä-grō\ *Serbo-Croatian* **Crna Gora** \ˌtsȯr-nə-'gȯr-ə\ Constituent republic (pop., 1997 est.: 879,000) of the Federal Republic of Yugoslavia. Area: 5,333 sq mi (13,812 sq km). Capital: PODGORICA. The republic's name ("Black Mtn.") refers to Mt. Lovcen (5,738 ft, or 1,749 m), its ancient stronghold near the Adriatic Sea. Its economy is based on agriculture, especially sheep and goat raising and cereal grains. The majority of its population are Montenegrins who follow the Eastern Orthodox church; there are sizable Muslim and Albanian minorities. The region was part of the Roman province of ILLYRIA. Settled by Slavs in the 7th cent., it was incorporated into the Serbian empire in the late 12th cent. It retained its independence following the Turkish defeat of the Serbians in 1389 (see Battle of KOSOVO). It began an alliance with Russia in 1711. In the BALKAN WARS of 1912–13, it cooperated against Turkey. It supported SERBIA during and after World War I. It was then absorbed into Serbia as part of the Kingdom of Serbs, Croats, and Slovenes (from 1929, Yugoslavia). During World War II it was occupied by the Italians and was the scene of heavy fighting. In 1946 Montenegro became one of Yugoslavia's six federated units. After the breakup of Yugoslavia, Montenegro and Serbia formed the new Federal Republic of Yugoslavia in 1992.

Monterrey City (pop., 1995: 1,088,000), capital of NUEVO LEÓN state, N Mexico. Mexico's fifth-largest city, it was founded in 1579. In 1846 it was taken by U.S. Gen. Zachary TAYLOR in the MEXICAN WAR. In 1882 rail connections were established with Laredo, Tex., and in 1930 construction began on the Inter-American Highway, leading to the development of large-scale smelting and heavy industry.

Montesquieu \ˌmän-təs-'kyü\, **baron de (La Brède et de)** *orig.* C(harles)-L(ouis) de Secondat (1689–1755) French PHILOSOPHE and satirist. Born into a noble family, from 1726 he traveled widely to study social and political institutions. His huge *L'esprit des lois* (1750; *The Spirit of the Laws*) profoundly influenced European and American political thought; it advocated the separation of the legislative, judicial, and executive powers and was relied on by the framers of the U.S. Constitution. His other works include the satirical *Persian Letters* (1721) and *Causes of the Greatness and Decadence of the Romans* (1734).

Montessori \ˌmän-tə-ˈsȯr-ē\, **Maria** (1870–1952) Italian educator. Montessori took a degree in medicine (1894) and worked with retarded children before teaching at the Univ. of Rome. In 1907 she opened her first children's school, and for the next 40 years she traveled throughout Europe, India, and the U.S. lecturing, writing, and setting up Montessori schools. Today there are hundreds of such schools in the U.S. and Canada alone; their principal focus is on PRESCHOOL EDUCATION, but some provide ELEMENTARY EDUCATION to grade 6. The Montessori system is based on belief in children's creative potential, their drive to learn, and their right to be treated as individuals.

Maria Montessori

Monteverdi \ˌmän-tə-ˈver-dē\, **Claudio (Giovanni Antonio)** (1567–1643) Italian composer. The first of his nine books of madrigals appeared in 1587; his third book (1592) shows freer use of dissonance and close coordination of music and words. In 1599 he settled at the Gonzaga court in Mantua. Attacked in 1600 for the even freer dissonance in his newest works, he replied that music now had two "practices," a strict practice for sacred works and a more expressive practice for secular music. The year 1607 saw the premiere of *Orfeo*, his landmark first opera. In 1610 he completed his great *Vespers*. Released from Mantua in 1612, the next year he was put in charge of music at ST. MARK'S BASILICA, Venice. After the first opera house opened in Venice (1637), he wrote his last three operas, including *Il ritorno d'Ulisse in patria* (1640) and *L'incoronazione di Poppea* (1643). Monteverdi is the first great figure of baroque music, a remarkable innovator and synthesizer who created the first baroque masterpieces of both sacred and secular music.

Montevideo \ˌmän-tə-vi-ˈdā-ō\ Seaport (pop., 1996: 1,379,000), capital of Uruguay, situated on the N shore of the Río de la PLATA Estuary. Founded by the Spanish in 1726, from 1807 to 1830 it was alternately occupied by British, Spanish, Argentine, Portuguese, and Brazilian forces. It became the capital of the newly independent Uruguay in 1830. A major seaport of S. America, it is the commercial, political, and cultural center of Uruguay, and the site of Uruguay's only institutions of higher education.

Montez \ˈmän-ˌtez\, **Lola** *orig.* Marie Eliza Gilbert (1818–1861) Irish adventuress and dancer. After a few dance lessons in Spain, she toured Europe, billing herself as a Spanish dancer. While in Munich in 1846 she became the mistress of LUDWIG I of Bavaria. Her influence over the king provoked angry reactions in the government in 1848, forcing her to flee and causing his abdication. After further tours, she settled in New York.

Montezuma II *or* **Moctezuma II** (1466–1520) Ninth emperor of the AZTECS. In 1502 he inherited an empire of 5–6 million people that stretched from present-day Mexico to Nicaragua. Aztec belief in the return of the god QUETZALCÓATL, whose description the conquistador Hernán CORTÉS resembled, contributed to his downfall. Cortés, who had made alliances with disaffected tribes, took Montezuma prisoner, and he died in custody.

Montfort, Simon de *later* **Earl of Leicester** (c.1208–1265) His father, Simon de Montfort (1165?–1218), was a leader of the ALBIGENSIAN CRUSADE. The younger Simon gave up Montfort lands in France but revived the family claim to the English earldom of Leicester. He distinguished himself on a crusade to the Holy Land (1240–42) and joined HENRY III's failed invasion of France (1242). Sent to pacify Gascony

(1248), he was censured for his harsh methods there and recalled. He later joined other leading barons in forcing Henry to accept the Provisions of OXFORD; when they were annulled, Simon defeated and captured Henry (1264) and summoned what became the beginning of the modern Parliament (1265). He governed England for less than a year before being defeated and killed by Henry's son Edward.

Montgolfier \mōⁿ-gȯl-ˈfyā\, **Joseph-Michel and Jacques-Étienne** (1740–1810, 1745–1799) French designers of the hot-air balloon. Having discovered that heated air collected in a lightweight bag would cause the bag to rise, the brothers demonstrated their discovery in 1783 with a balloon that rose 3,000 ft (1,000 m) and remained aloft 10 minutes. After sending a sheep, a duck, and a rooster up as passengers, they conducted the first manned untethered balloon flight.

Montgomery City (pop., 2000: 201,000), capital of Alabama. The site was inhabited by Indian mound builders in prehistoric times. In 1715 the French built Ft. Toulouse near the present site of Montgomery. The city was founded in 1819 and named for Gen. Richard Montgomery (1736–1775); it became the state capital in 1847. In 1861, during the AMERICAN CIVIL WAR, it served briefly as the capital of the Confederacy. It was a center of the CIVIL RIGHTS MOVEMENT, notably the protests organized by M. L. KING, Jr.

Montgomery, Bernard Law *later* **Viscount Montgomery (of Alamein, of Hindhead)** (1887–1976) British general in WORLD WAR II. Having distinguished himself in World War I, he became known as a tough and efficient leader. In World War II he commanded the British army in the N. AFRICA CAMPAIGN, notably at EL ALAMEIN (1942); in the Allied invasion of Sicily and Italy (1943); and in the NORMANDY CAMPAIGN, leading the British-Canadian army group across N France to Germany. He later became deputy commander of NATO (1951–58). A cautious, thorough strategist, "Monty" often exasperated fellow Allied commanders, including Dwight EISENHOWER, but his insistence on complete readiness ensured his popularity with his troops.

Montgomery Ward & Co. U.S. retail merchandising company. It was founded in Chicago in 1872 by A. M. WARD (1844–1913), who bought merchandise wholesale and sold it directly to farmers. He distributed the world's first mail-order catalog and offered a money-back guarantee. The company opened its first retail stores in 1926, and by 1930 retail sales exceeded catalog sales. It ended its mail-order business in 1985, and closed in 2000.

month See DAY

Monticello \ˌmän-tə-ˈse-lō, ˌmän-tə-ˈche-lō\ Home of Thomas JEFFERSON, located southeast of Charlottesville, Va. Designed by Jefferson and constructed 1768–1809, it is one of the finest examples of the early Classical Revival style in the U.S. The facade was influenced by the work of Andrea PALLADIO. The final structure is a three-story brick-and-frame building with 35 differently shaped rooms. An octagonal dome dominates the structure.

Montmorency \mōⁿ-mȯ-rāⁿ-ˈsē *Engl* ˌmänt-mə-ˈren-sē\, **Anne, duc de** (1493–1567) French soldier and Constable of France. Named for his godmother, Queen Anne of Brittany, he served three kings—FRANCIS I, HENRY II, and CHARLES IX. He fought in numerous wars in N Italy and S France against Emperor CHARLES V, and in campaigns against the HUGUENOTS. In 1529 he helped negotiate the Peace of Cambrai between France and Charles V. He was created Constable of France in 1538. Wounded at the Battle of Saint-Denis, in the Wars of RELIGION, he died two days later.

Montpelier \mänt-ˈpēl-yər\ City (pop., 2000: 8,000), capital of Vermont. Named for MONTPELLIER, France, it commanded the main pass through the GREEN MTNS. It became the state capital in 1805 and defeated attempts by other cities, including Burlington, to succeed it as capital. It was the birthplace of Adm. George DEWEY.

Montpellier \mōⁿ-pel-ˈyā\ City (pop., 1999: 225,000), S France, near the Mediterranean coast. Founded in the 8th cent., it later came under control of ARAGON and the king of MAJORCA. A trading station for spice imports in the 10th cent., it reverted to France in the 14th cent. and served as a HUGUENOT stronghold until its capture by LOUIS XIII in 1622. It then became the administrative capital of

LANGUEDOC. The city's schools of medicine and law date from the 12th cent., and the Univ. of Montpellier was founded in 1220. It is a tourist center, with France's oldest botanical gardens (founded 1593) and a 14th-cent. Gothic cathedral.

Montreal \ˌmän-trē-ˈȯl\ City (pop., 1996: 1,016,000), SE Canada. It occupies about one-third of Île de Montréal (Montreal Island), near the confluence of the Ottawa and ST. LAWRENCE rivers. It is built on the slopes of a mountain, Mont-Royal. English and French are spoken throughout the city, which is the chief center of French-Canadian industry and culture. The site was occupied by the HURON Indian settlement of Hochelaga when visited by French explorer Jacques CARTIER in 1535. The first European settlement was founded by the French in 1642. Rapid colonization based on the fur trade began in the first half of the 18th cent. The city surrendered to British forces in 1760 and, with all of NEW FRANCE, became part of the British N. American empire in 1763. Montreal served as the capital of Canada 1844–49. It is Canada's second-largest city, one of its chief ports, and a major cultural center. It is the seat of the English-language universities MCGILL UNIV. and Concordia Univ., and of the French-language Univ. de Montréal and the Univ. du Québec à Montréal.

Montreux \ˈmȯⁿ-ˈtrœ̄\ Resort town (pop., 1990: 20,000), W Switzerland, E shore of Lake GENEVA. The nearby 13th-cent. Château de Chillon was made famous by Lord BYRON's poem "Prisoner of Chillon." The town is perhaps best known for its summer jazz festival.

Mont-Saint-Michel \mōⁿ-saⁿ-mē-ˈshel\ Rocky islet rising out of Mont-Saint-Michel Bay between Brittany and Normandy, NW France. It becomes an island only at high tide. Above medieval walls and towers rise the village's clustered buildings, with an ancient ABBEY crowning the mount. Over the centuries it has been a pilgrimage center, fortress, and prison. The abbey church has an imposing 11th-cent. Romanesque nave and an elegant Gothic choir. The Gothic monastery combines the power of a military fortress and the simplicity of a religious building.

Montserrat Island (pop., 2000 est.: 6,400), British crown colony, W. Indies. Situated in the E Caribbean Sea, it is 11 mi (18 km) long and 7 mi (11 km) wide. It was visited and named by Christopher COLUMBUS in 1493 and was colonized by the British and Irish in 1632. Its cotton and sugar plantations used African slave labor. It was part of the Leeward Islands 1871–1956, and then of the Federation of the W. Indies 1958–62. It was rebuilt after a devastating hurricane in 1989. A major eruption of the Soufriere Hills volcano in 1996 led more than two-thirds of the population to leave the island by 1998.

Monty Python('s Flying Circus) British comedy troupe. Its members, most of whom met while attending Cambridge Univ., included Graham Chapman (1941–1989) and John Cleese (b.1939), coauthors of most of their skits and films, Terry Jones (b.1942), Terry Gilliam (b.1940), Eric Idle (b.1943), and Michael Palin (b.1943). The troupe's parodies of celebrity interviews and their array of absurd characters surprised and delighted international television audiences. Their films included *Monty Python and the Holy Grail* (1975) and *Monty Python's Life of Brian* (1979).

mood *or* **mode** In GRAMMAR, a category that reflects the speaker's view of an event's reality, likelihood, or urgency. Often marked by special verb forms (inflections), moods include the indicative, for factual or neutral situations (e.g., "You did your work"); the imperative, to convey commands or requests ("Do your work"); and the subjunctive, which may express doubt, possibility, necessity, desire, or future time.

Moody, Dwight L(yman) (1837–1899) U.S. Protestant evangelist. Born in E. Northfield, Mass., he converted to evangelical Christianity in 1856, and he engaged in missionary work with the YMCA 1861–73. He founded Chicago's Moody Church (1864) and preached in the slums. In 1870 he and the hymn writer Ira D. Sankey (1840–1908) began a series of highly popular revival tours in Britain and the U.S. Moody also founded the Northfield and Mt. Hermon schools (1879, 1881) as well as the Chicago Bible Institute (1889, now the Moody Bible Institute).

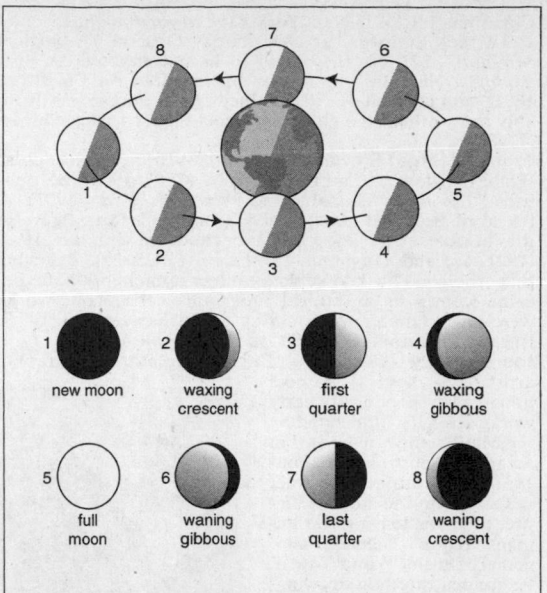

Moon As the moon revolves around the earth, the amount of its illuminated half seen from the earth slowly increases and decreases (waxes and wanes). The cycle takes about 29½ days.

moon Sole natural SATELLITE of earth, which it orbits from west to east at a mean distance of about 239,900 mi (384,400 km). It is less than one-third the size of earth (diameter about 2,160 mi, or 3,476 km), about one-eightieth as massive, and about two-thirds as dense. Its gravity, about one-sixth of earth's at its surface, causes earth's TIDES. The moon shines by reflected sunlight, with an ALBEDO of 7.3%. It rotates relative to the sun in about 29.5 days, the same time it takes to orbit earth, so the same side always faces earth. That side is lit by the sun at different angles as the moon revolves, displaying different phases over the month, from new to full. The moon is thought to have formed from fragments ejected from the proto-earth when a Mars-sized body struck it early in its history. Its surface has been studied by telescope since GALILEO first observed it in 1609, and APOLLO missions brought lunar rocks back to earth. Micrometeorite impacts grind rock fragments into fine dust, and METEORITE strikes produced the many craters on its surface. The maria (see MARE) are huge, ancient lava flows. In 1998, possible signs of water ice near the moon's poles were found.

Moon, Sun Myung (b.1920) S. Korean religious leader. Convinced that he was a successor to JESUS, Moon began to preach a new religion loosely based on Christianity in N. Korea in 1946. After being imprisoned, he fled to S. Korea, where he founded the UNIFICATION CHURCH in 1954. In 1973 he moved his headquarters to Tarrytown, N.Y., where he became the focus of controversies over fund-raising techniques, tax evasion, and the indoctrination of followers. In 1982 Moon was convicted of tax evasion; he has since been accused of extensive sexual misconduct. In the 1990s he moved to Brazil, where his church has purchased large tracts of rain forest.

Moore, Archie *orig.* Archibald Lee Wright (1913–1998) U.S. boxer. Born in Benoit, Miss., he began boxing in the 1930s. In 1952 he defeated Joey Maxim to win the world light-heavyweight championship. He held the crown until 1962, when he was disqualified for failing to meet the leading contender, Harold Johnson. From 1936 to 1963 he fought 229 bouts and won 194, 141 by knockouts. He later became a film actor.

Moore, Clement Clarke (1779–1863) U.S. scholar remembered for the ballad that begins "'Twas the night before

Christmas." Born in New York City, Moore taught Oriental and Greek literature at New York's General Theological Seminary 1821–50. He is said to have composed "A Visit from St. Nicholas" to amuse his children on Christmas 1822, but in 2000 it was determined that the poem was probably the work of the gentleman poet Henry Livingston, Jr. (1748–1828).

Moore, G(eorge) E(dward) (1873–1958) British philosopher. While a fellow at Cambridge Univ. (1898–1904), he published his major ethical work, *Principia Ethica* (1903). A friend of Bertrand RUSSELL, he became a leading figure in the BLOOMSBURY GROUP. He edited the journal *Mind* (1921–47) and taught at Cambridge (1925–39). Believing that "the good" is knowable by direct apprehension, he became known as an ethical intuitionist. His major works were important in undermining the influence of G. W. F. HEGEL and Immanuel KANT on British philosophy.

Moore, Henry (1898–1986) English sculptor and graphic artist. The son of a coal miner, he produced early works strongly influenced by the Maya sculpture he saw in a Paris museum. From about 1931 he combined abstract shapes with the human figure, at times leaving the human figure behind altogether. During World War II, he concentrated on drawings of Londoners sheltering from bombs in Underground stations. Commissions for a *Madonna and Child* and a

Henry Moore, mid-1960s

family group turned his style from abstraction to the more humanistic approach that became the basis of his international reputation. He returned to experimentation in the 1950s with angular, pierced standing figures in bronze. Much of his work is monumental, and he is particularly well known for a series of reclining nudes. Among his major commissions were sculptures for UNESCO's Paris headquarters (1957–58), Lincoln Center (1963–65), and the National Gallery of Art (1978).

Moore, Marianne (Craig) (1887–1972) U.S. poet. Born in St. Louis, she attended Bryn Mawr College. She edited the influential journal *The Dial* 1925–29. Her poetry volumes include *Observations* (1924) and *Collected Poems* (1951; Pulitzer and Bollingen Prizes). In her highly disciplined poems, she distilled moral and intellectual insights from close observation of objective detail, often in innovative stanzaic forms. In "Poetry" (1921) she calls for poems presenting "imaginary gardens with real toads in them." In her late years, the winningly eccentric Moore, in her cape and tricornered hat, became an icon of sprightly gentility.

Moore, Mary Tyler (b.1936) U.S. television and film actress. Born in Brooklyn, N.Y., she costarred in the television hit *Dick Van Dyke Show* (1961–66; two Emmy awards), then achieved even greater success in *The Mary Tyler Moore Show* (1970–77; four Emmy awards), the most popular situation comedy of the 1970s. Her films include *Ordinary People* (1980).

Moore, Thomas (1779–1852) Irish poet, satirist, composer, and singer. While studying law in London, he became a close friend of Lord BYRON and P. B. SHELLEY. His collections *Irish Melodies* and *National Airs* (1807–34) consist of 130 original poems set to folk melodies, including "The Minstrel Boy," "Believe Me, if All Those Endearing Young Charms," and "The Last Rose of Summer." Performed by Moore for London's aristocracy, they aroused support for Irish nationalists. His reputation among his contemporaries was immense; his poem *Lalla Rookh* (1817) became the most translated poem of its time. He later brought out biographies of Byron and others, as well as a *History of Ireland* (1827).

Moors Muslim population of Spain, of mixed Arab, Spanish, and Berber origins. N. African Muslims (called in Latin *Mauri*, i.e., natives of Roman Mauretania) invaded Spain in the 8th cent. and, under the UMAYYAD and ALMORAVID DYNASTIES, created the great Arab Andalusian civilization in such cities as Córdoba, Toledo, Granada, and Seville. The Christian reconquest of Spain under ALFONSO VI began in the 11th cent.; from then until the Moors' final defeat in 1492, and for another century thereafter, many Moors settled as refugees in N. Africa.

moose Largest species *(Alces alces)* in the DEER family (Cervidae) found in N N. America and Eurasia; called ELK in Europe. Moose have long legs, a pendulous muzzle, and a brown, shaggy coat. They stand 5–7 ft (1.5–2 m) and weigh up to 1,800 lbs (800 kg). Males have enormous flattened, tined antlers that are shed and regrown annually. Moose wade in forest-edged lakes and streams, eating submerged aquatic plants, and browse on leaves, twigs, and bark. They are usually solitary, but N. American moose often assemble in bands in winter. See also WAPITI.

moraine \mə-'rān\ Accumulation of rock debris (till) carried or deposited by a GLACIER. The material may range in size from boulders to sand, and it shows no sorting or bedding. Depending on how they are deposited by the glacier, moraines may be lateral (along the margins of the glacier) or terminal (at its leading edge).

Morales \mō-'rä-läs\, **Luis de** (c.1520–1586) Spanish painter. He lived all his life in Badajoz, leaving only for occasional commissions. He is considered Spain's greatest Mannerist painter and is known especially for his emotional religious paintings of such subjects as the Ecce Homo, the Pietà, and the Virgin and Child. His paintings are marked by detailed execution and the anguished asceticism of 16th-cent. Spain.

morality play Vernacular allegorical drama of 15th–16th-cent. Europe. The plays' characters personified moral qualities (such as charity or vice) or abstractions (such as death or youth). Representing a transition from liturgical drama to professional secular drama, the plays were short works, usually performed by semiprofessional acting troupes. *Everyman* (c.1495), featuring Everyman's summons by Death and his journey to the grave, is considered the greatest morality play. See also MIRACLE PLAY, MYSTERY PLAY.

Morava River \'mò-rä-vä\ *German* **March** \'märk\ River, E Czech Republic. It flows south to enter the DANUBE RIVER just above BRATISLAVA, Slovakia, after a course of 227 mi (365 km). In its lower course it first divides the Czech Republic from Slovakia and then divides Slovakia from Austria.

Morava River River, Serbia, Yugoslavia. Formed by the confluence of the S. (Juzna) Morava and W. (Zapadna) Morava rivers, it flows north to enter the DANUBE RIVER, after a course of 137 mi (221 km). Its basin is almost the size of SERBIA.

Moravia \mə-'rä-vē-ə\ Region, central Europe. Bounded by Bohemia, Silesia, Slovakia, and NE Austria, it was inhabited from the 4th cent. B.C. Dominated by the Avars in the 6th–7th cent. A.D., it was later settled by Slavic tribes. It was destroyed by the MAGYARS in 906. In 1526 it came under HABSBURG rule. After the Revolution of 1848 it became an Austrian crown land with its capital at BRNO. In 1918 it was incorporated into the new state of Czechoslovakia. It was included in the Czech Socialist Republic created in 1968, and in the Czech Republic in 1993.

Moravia \mō-'räv-yä\, **Alberto** *orig.* Alberto Pincherle (1907–1990) Italian writer. He worked as a journalist in Turin and London. *Time of Indifference* (1929), his first novel, is a scathing study of middle-class moral corruption. His works were censored by Benito MUSSOLINI's fascists and centured by the Catholic church. Later important novels, many of them portrayals of social alienation and loveless sexuality, include *The Conformist* (1951; film, 1971) and *Two Women* (1957; film, 1961). His books of short stories include *Roman Tales* (1954).

Moravian Church Protestant denomination founded in the 18th cent. It traces its origins to the Unity of Brethren, a 15th-cent. HUSSITE movement in Bohemia and Moravia. In America the Moravians founded Bethlehem, Pa. (1740), and several other settlements, and carried out missionary work among the Indians. The Moravians ordain bishops but are governed by synods of elected representatives; they are guided by the Bible as their only rule of faith and worship.

moray \mə-'rā, 'mòr-ā\ Any of about 80 species (family Muraenidae) of shallow-water EELS inhabiting all tropical and subtropical seas, where they live among reefs and rocks, hiding in crevices. Their skin is usually vividly marked or colored. Most species lack pectoral fins. Morays have a wide mouth and strong, sharp teeth for seizing and holding prey (chiefly fishes). They attack humans only when disturbed. Most species are less than 5 ft (1.5 m) long, but one may grow to more than 11 ft (3.5 m). Moray flesh can be toxic.

Moray Firth \\'mər-ē\\ Inlet of the NORTH SEA, NE Scotland. It extends inland for 39 mi (63 km). Its inner reaches are divided by a peninsula into Cromarty Firth and the Firth of Inverness; the city of INVERNESS lies there.

Mordecai \\'mȯr-də-ˌkī\\ In the Old Testament Book of Esther, the cousin or guardian of ESTHER. Mordecai was a Jew who offended Haman, minister of King Ahasuerus. Haman persuaded the king to order Mordecai's execution and the destruction of all the Jews in the Persian Empire, but thanks to the pleading of Esther, Ahasuerus's beloved Jewish queen, it was Haman who was hanged. See also PURIM.

More, St. Thomas (1477–1535) English statesman and humanist. He studied at Oxford and was successful as a lawyer from 1501. He served as an undersheriff of London (1510–18) and endeared himself to Londoners as a fair judge. He wrote the notable *History of King Richard III* (1513–18) and the renowned *Utopia* (1516). In 1517 More was named to the king's council, and he became HENRY VIII's secretary and confidant. After the fall of Cardinal WOLSEY (1529), More succeeded him as lord chancellor, but he resigned in 1532 when he could not affirm Henry's divorce from Catherine. He also refused to accept the Act of Supremacy, recognizing Henry as head of the Church of England. In 1534 More was charged with high treason and imprisoned in the Tower, where he wrote his *Dialogue of Comfort Against Tribulation.* In 1535 he was tried and sentenced to death by hanging, which the king commuted to beheading.

Moreau \\mȯ-'rō\\, **Gustave** (1826–1898) French painter. He developed a distinctive style in the Symbolist mode, becoming known for his erotic paintings of mythological and religious subjects. Such works as *Oedipus and the Sphinx* (1864) and *Dance of Salome* (1876) have often been described as decadent. His nonfigurative paintings, done in a loose manner with thick impasto, led some to call him a herald of Abstract Expressionism.

Moreau, Jeanne (b.1928) French film actress. At age 20 she became the youngest member of the COMÉDIE-FRANÇAISE. She made her screen debut in 1949 and won acclaim in Louis MALLE's *Frantic* (1957) and *The Lovers* (1958). Noted for her sensuality and sophistication, she starred in *Moderato cantabile* (1960), *La notte* (1961), and *Jules et Jim* (1961), playing a woman loved by two men in the movie that established her as an international star, and later in *The Trial* (1962), *Diary of a Chambermaid* (1964), and *The Bride Wore Black* (1968). She has also directed films, including *Lumière* (1976).

Morelia \\mō-'rāl-yä\\ City (pop., 1995: 512,000), capital of MICHOACÁN state, W central Mexico. It was founded in 1541 as Valladolid and became the provincial capital in 1582. During the Mexican wars for independence it served briefly as the base of operations for the revolution; in 1828 its name was changed in honor of revolutionary leader José María Morelos (1765–1815). It is home to the Univ. of Michoacán and the Colegio San Nicolás (founded 1540), Mexico's oldest institution of higher learning.

Morelos \\mō-'rā-lōs\\ State (pop., 2000: 1,553,000), central Mexico. It occupies 1,911 sq mi (4,950 sq km). Its capital is CUERNAVACA. It is one of the country's most productive agricultural states. It was named after José María Morelos (1765–1815) and was the birthplace of Emiliano ZAPATA, both heroes of Mexico's war for independence.

Morgan, Henry (*later Sir Henry*) (1635–1688) British buccaneer. In the second ANGLO–DUTCH WAR, he commanded buccaneers against the Dutch colonies in the Caribbean. In 1670, with 36 ships and 2,000 buccaneers, he defeated a large Spanish force, and sacked and burned the major Spanish colonial city of Panamá. On the return journey, he deserted his followers and took most of the booty. An exaggerated account of Morgan's exploits created his popular reputation as a bloodthirsty pirate.

Morgan, John (1735–1789) U.S. medical educator. Born in Philadelphia, he studied medicine in Europe before returning to found the American colonies' first medical school in 1765 at the Univ. of Pennsylvania, where he separated medicine, surgery, and pharmacology into distinct disciplines. He was made head of the army's medical system in 1775; however, the Continental Congress did not let him organize the system and dismissed him in 1777, holding him responsible for the war's high death rate. Though absolved in 1779, he never recovered and died an impoverished recluse. Morgan was one of the first U.S. physicians to advocate Edward JENNER's smallpox vaccination method.

Morgan, J(ohn) P(ierpont) (1837–1913) U.S. financier. Born in Hartford, Conn., he became an agent for his father's banking company in 1861. In 1871 he was named a partner in the firm of Drexel, Morgan, which became the chief source of U.S. government financing. In 1895 it became J. P. Morgan and Co. In the 1880s and '90s Morgan reorganized several major railroads and became one of the world's most powerful railroad magnates, controlling about 5,000 mi (8,000 km) of railway by 1902. After the panic of 1893, Morgan formed a syndicate to supply the U.S. Treasury's depleted gold reserves. He led the financial community in averting a general financial collapse following the stock-market panic of 1907. He financed a series of giant industrial consolidations, organizing the mergers that formed GENERAL ELECTRIC, U.S. STEEL CORP., and International Harvester Co. A noted art collector, he donated many artworks to the METROPOLITAN MUSEUM OF ART; his book collection and the building that housed it became the Pierpont Morgan Library.

Morgan, Julia (1872–1957) U.S. architect. Born in San Francisco, she became California's first licensed woman architect. Following the San Francisco earthquake of 1906, she designed hundreds of buildings in the Bay area. She also designed and supervised the building of William Randolph HEARST's 150-room private castle at SAN SIMEON (1919–38).

Morgan, Lewis Henry (1818–1881) U.S. ethnologist and a principal founder of scientific anthropology. Born near Aurora, N.Y., and trained as an attorney, Morgan developed a deep interest in the American Indians and in 1846 was adopted by the SENECA. His *Systems of Consanguinity and Affinity of the Human Family* (1871) sought to establish connections between cultures and particularly to establish the Asiatic origin of the American Indians. This work led to a comprehensive theory of SOCIOCULTURAL EVOLUTION, set forth in *Ancient Society* (1877). He claimed that advances in social organization arose primarily from changes in food production, and that society had progressed from a hunting-and-gathering stage ("savagery") to one of settled agriculture ("barbarism") to modern "civilization." This theory is now obsolete, but for many years Morgan was the dean of American anthropology.

Morgan, Thomas Hunt (1866–1945) U.S. zoologist and geneticist. Born in Lexington, Ky., Morgan found Charles DARWIN's theory of natural selection implausible because it could not be tested experimentally, and objected to Mendelian and CHROMOSOME theories, arguing that no single chromosome could carry specific hereditary traits. His opinion changed as a result of his studies of drosophila. He developed the hypothesis of sex-linked traits. He adopted the term gene, and concluded that genes were possibly arranged in a linear fashion on chromosomes. He was awarded the Nobel Prize in 1933. See also Calvin BRIDGES.

Morgan le Fay ("Morgan the Fairy") Enchantress in ARTHURIAN LEGEND. Skilled in the arts of healing and changing shape, she ruled AVALON, the island where King Arthur retreated to be healed of his wounds after his last battle. In some stories she is Arthur's sister and enemy, and seduces him to produce a son who later kills Arthur.

Morison, Samuel Eliot (1887–1976) U.S. biographer and historian. Born in Boston, he taught at Harvard Univ. for 40 years. To give authenticity to his maritime writings, he undertook numerous voyages and served in the wartime navy. His works include *Admiral of the Ocean Sea* (1942, Pulitzer Prize), on Christopher COLUMBUS; *John Paul Jones* (1959, Pulitzer Prize); *History of U.S. Naval Operations in World*

War II (15 vols., 1947–62); and *The Oxford History of the American People* (1965).

Morisot \mȯ-rē-ˈzō\, **Berthe** (1841–1895) French painter. Granddaughter of J.-H. FRAGONARD, she studied with Camille COROT, but the major influence over her work was Édouard MANET, whose brother she later married. She exhibited regularly with the Impressionists. Her coloring was delicate and subtle, often with a subdued emerald glow, and her subjects were often members of her family (e.g., *The Artist's Sister Edma and Their Mother*, 1870). She is best known for her extremely loose brushwork, and for the sensitivity she brought to her female subjects.

Berthe Morisot, "The Artist's Sister, Mme Pontillon, Seated on the Grass," 1873

Morley, John *later* **Viscount Morley (of Blackburn)** (1838–1923) English politician and historian. He was editor of the liberal *Fortnightly Review* 1867–82. As chief secretary for Ireland (1886, 1892–95), he helped prepare the Irish HOME RULE bills. As secretary for India (1905–10), he brought elected Indian representation into the government. His acclaimed historical works include biographies of William GLADSTONE, VOLTAIRE, J.-J. ROUSSEAU, and Oliver CROMWELL.

Morley, Thomas (1557?–1602) English composer and music theorist. A student of William BYRD, he is best known for his secular songs, including the *First Booke of Ayres* (1600), and for the treatise *A Plaine and Easie Introduction to Practicall Musick* (1597). By compiling several anthologies of Italian music, he was instrumental in bringing the Italian madrigal to England. *The Triumphes of Oriana* (1601) was his collection of works by 23 English composers.

Mormon Member of the Church of Jesus Christ of Latter-day Saints or of a sect closely related to it. The Mormon religion was founded by Joseph SMITH, who received an angelic vision telling him the location of golden plates containing God's revelation; this he published in 1830 as the Book of MORMON. Smith and his followers diverged significantly from orthodox Christianity; their many unique doctrines include the belief in salvation of the dead through retroactive baptism. The sect became notorious for its practice of POLYGAMY, though polygamy was only officially sanctioned 1852–90. Smith and his followers migrated westward from Palmyra, N.Y.; he was killed by a mob in 1844. In 1846–47, under Brigham YOUNG, the Mormons made a 1,100-mi (1,800-km) trek to Utah, where they founded SALT LAKE CITY. Today the church has a worldwide membership of nearly 10 million, swelled yearly by the missionary work usually required (for two years) of all male members. Mormons look forward to the establishment of God's kingdom in America, to be ruled in person by Jesus.

Mormon, Book of Holy scripture of the MORMONS, supplemental to the BIBLE. First published in 1830, it is held by all branches of Mormonism to be a divinely inspired work translated by the founder of their religion, Joseph SMITH. It relates the history of a tribe of Hebrews who migrated from Jerusalem to America around 600 B.C. They eventually split into two groups: the Lamanites, who were ancestors of the American Indians; and the Nephites, who were instructed by JESUS before being destroyed by the Lamanites. The prophet Mormon recorded their history on gold tablets; his son Moroni appeared to Smith in angelic form and revealed their location.

morning-glory family Family Convolvulaceae, composed of about 1,400 species of flowering plants in 50 genera, widely distributed and cultivated for their colorful, funnel-shaped flowers. Most are twining and erect herbaceous plants; a few are woody vines, trees, or shrubs. Most popular morning glories are of the genus *Ipomoea*, as is the SWEET POTATO. Several species of BINDWEEDS are agricultural pests. The seeds of two species, *Rivea corymbosa* and *I. violacea*, contain hallucinogenic compounds.

Moro, Aldo (1916–1978) Italian politician and premier of Italy (1963–64, 1964–66, 1966–68, 1974–76, 1976). Elected to the legislature in 1946, he became secretary of the Christian Democrat Party (1959–63). As premier of Italy, he included socialists in his coalition governments. In 1976 he became president of the Christian Democrats. In 1978 he was kidnapped in Rome by RED BRIGADES terrorists; after the government refused to release Brigades members on trial in Turin, he was murdered by his captors.

Moroccan Crises (1905–6, 1911) Two incidents centering on Germany's attempt to block France's control of Morocco. While visiting Tangiers in 1905, the German emperor WILLIAM II issued a statement of support for Moroccan independence, which caused international panic; the Algeciras Conference (1906) recognized France's special political interests in Morocco. In 1911 a German gunboat arrived in Agadir, ostensibly to protect German economic interests during a local uprising. The French objected and made preparations for war, as did Britain. A settlement gave France a protectorship over Morocco; in return, Germany acquired part of the French Congo.

Morocco *officially* **Kingdom of Morocco** *Arabic* **Al-Mamlakah al-Maghribiyah** \al-ˈmäm-lä-kə-äl-ˌmä-grē-ˈbē-yə\ Country, NW Africa. Area: 177,117 sq mi (458,730 sq km). Population (2000): 29,067,000. Capital: RABAT. Arabized

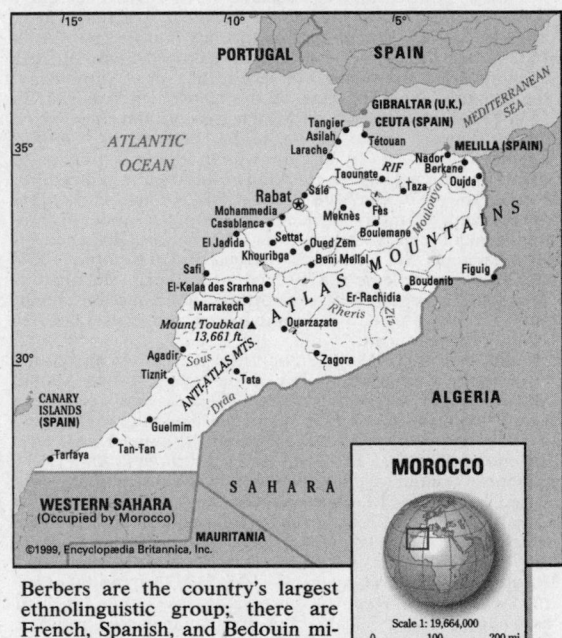

MOROCCO

Scale 1: 19,664,000

Berbers are the country's largest ethnolinguistic group; there are French, Spanish, and Bedouin minorities. Languages: Arabic (official), Berber. Religion: Islam (official), mostly Sunni. Currency: dirham. Morocco is a mountainous country with an average elevation of 2,600 ft (800 m) above sea level. The Er Rif runs along the N coast; the ATLAS MTNS. rise in the nation's center and include Mt. Toubkal (13,665 ft, or 4,165 m), the country's highest peak. The area is a zone of severe seismic activity, and earthquakes are frequent. Its fertile lowlands support agriculture; major crops include barley, wheat, and sugar beets. Morocco is the world's largest supplier of phosphate. The nation's industrial center is CASABLANCA, its largest city. It is a constitutional monarchy with two legislative houses; its chief of state and head of government is the king, assisted by the prime minister. The Berbers entered Morocco near the end of the 2nd millennium B.C. PHOENICIANS established trading posts along the Mediterranean during the 12th cent. B.C., and CARTHAGE had settlements along the Atlantic in the 5th cent. B.C. After the fall of Carthage, Morocco became a loyal ally of Rome, and in A.D. 46 it was annexed by Rome as part of the province of MAURETANIA. It was invaded by Muslims in the 7th cent. The ALMORAVIDS conquered it and the Muslim areas of Spain in the mid-11th cent.; in the 12th cent. the ALMOHADS overthrew the Almoravids. They in turn were conquered by the Marinids in the 13th cent. After the fall of the Marinids in the mid-15th cent., the Sa'dis ruled for a century after 1550. Association with the BARBARY COAST states compelled Europeans to enter the area: the French fought Morocco over the Algerian boundary, Britain obtained trading rights in 1856, and the Spanish seized part of Moroccan territory in 1859. It was a French protectorate from 1912 until its independence in 1956. In the late 1970s it reasserted claim to the Spanish Sahara (see WESTERN SAHARA), and in 1976 Spanish troops withdrew from the region, leaving behind the Algerian-supported Saharan guerrillas of the Polisario Front. Relations with Mauritania and Algeria deteriorated, and fighting over the region has continued.

Moroni Town (pop., 1995: 34,000), capital of the COMOROS Islands, in the Indian Ocean. Founded by Arabic-speaking settlers, it is the largest settlement of the Comoros and has served as the capital since 1958. The town retains an Arabic character, and it has several mosques, including Chiounda, a pilgrimage center.

Moros Several Muslim peoples living in the S Philippines. Constituting about 5% of the Philippine population, they are not racially different from other Filipinos but, with a separate Islamic faith and local cultures, they have been the object of prejudice. They have often opposed the ruling powers: first Roman Catholic Spanish colonialists (16th–19th cent.), then U.S. occupation troops, and finally the independent Philippine government. The Moro National (later Islamic) Liberation Front espoused Moro separatism and led a violent insurgency from 1968 to 1977, then split into factions but continued the insurgency. The Autonomous Region of Muslim MINDANAO was established in 1990 to appease the Moros, but some extremists continue to fight for complete independence.

morpheme In linguistics, the smallest grammatical unit of speech. It may be an entire word (*cat*) or an element of a word (*re-* and *-ed* in *reappeared*). In so-called isolating languages, like Vietnamese, each word contains a single morpheme; in agglutinating languages, words often contain multiple morphemes. The study of morphemes is included in MORPHOLOGY.

Morpheus In Greek and Roman mythology, the god of dreams. He was a son of the god of sleep. Morpheus sent human shapes of all kinds to the dreamer, while his brothers Phobetor and Phantasus sent the forms of animals and inanimate objects.

morphine Organic compound, NARCOTIC ANALGESIC ALKALOID originally isolated from OPIUM. It is among the most powerful naturally occurring compounds in its ability to reduce pain and distress; its calming effect protects the system against exhaustion in traumatic shock, internal hemorrhage, congestive heart failure, and other debilitating conditions. Its most serious drawback is its addictiveness; many doctors are reluctant to use amounts adequate to relieve severe pain, even though short-term use in such cases rarely leads to DRUG ADDICTION. See also HEROIN.

morphology In linguistics, the study of the internal construction system of words. Languages vary widely in the number of MORPHEMES a word can have. English has many words with multiple morphemes (e.g., *replacement* is composed of *re-*, *place*, and *-ment*). Many American Indian languages have a highly complex morphology; other languages, such as Chinese, have a very simple one. Morphology includes the grammatical processes of inflection, marking categories like person, tense, and case, and derivation, the formation of new words from existing words.

Morrill (Land-Grant College) Act of 1862 U.S. congressional enactment that provided grants of land to state colleges specializing in the teaching of "agriculture and the mechanic arts." It was named for its sponsor, Vermont congressman Justin Smith Morrill (1810–1898). Since 1862 some 12 million acres have been distributed, on which some 70 landgrant colleges currently flourish.

Morris, Gouverneur (1752–1816) American statesman. Born in New York City, he served in the Continental Congress

(1778–79). As assistant superintendent of finance (1781–85), he proposed the decimal coinage system that became the basis for U.S. currency. At the Constitutional Convention, he helped write the final draft of the U.S. Constitution. He served as minister to France (1792–94) and was the first chairman of the Erie Canal commission (1810–16).

Morris, Mark (b.1956) U.S. dancer and choreographer. Born in Seattle, he danced with various companies before forming the Mark Morris Dance Group in 1980. In 1990 Morris cofounded the White Oak Dance Project with Mikhail BARYSHNIKOV. Known for his daring and highly imaginative style, he has choreographed over 90 works for his own company, now located in New York.

Morris, Robert (1734–1806) American (British-born) financier and politician. He emigrated to Maryland as a boy and entered a Philadelphia mercantile firm in 1748. As a member of the Continental Congress in the AMERICAN REVOLUTION, he raised money to buy supplies for the Continental Army. As U.S. superintendent of finance (1781–84) he established the Bank of N. America. A delegate to the Constitutional Convention, he later served in the U.S. Senate (1789–95). He went bankrupt speculating in real estate and was confined to debtors' prison 1798–1801.

Morris, Robert (b.1931) U.S. artist. His studies took him from his native Kansas City to San Francisco and later New York, where he began in 1960 to produce large monochromatic geometric sculptures. From the late 1960s, he experimented with a wide variety of forms, including the "happening," "dispersal pieces" (in which materials were strewn on the gallery floor), and environmental sculpture. He is also a prominent exponent of Minimalism, conceptual art, and performance art.

Morris, William (1834–1896) British painter, designer, craftsman, poet, and social reformer, founder of the ARTS AND CRAFTS MOVEMENT. Born into a wealthy family, he studied medieval architecture at Oxford, but visits to Europe turned him toward painting. In 1861, with D. G. ROSSETTI, Edward BURNE-JONES, F. M. BROWN, and others, he founded an association of "fine art workmen" based on the medieval guild, which produced furniture, tapestry, stained glass, fabrics, carpets, and most notably wallpaper designs. In 1891 Morris founded the Kelmscott Press; the press's 53 titles included *The Works of Geoffrey Chaucer*, one of the greatest examples of the art of the printed book. Though he sought to produce fine art objects for the masses, only the rich could afford his expensive handmade products. A utopian socialist, he did much to develop British socialism; in 1884 he formed the Socialist League. In 1877 he founded the Society for the Protection of Ancient Buildings, one of the world's first preservationist groups. He wrote several volumes of poetry and many prose romances, as well as the four-volume epic *Sigurd the Volsung* (1876). Morris revolutionized Victorian taste, and he ranks as one of the largest cultural figures of 19th-cent. Britain.

morris dance Ritual folk dance mainly danced in rural England from about the 15th cent. The name, a variant of "Moorish," refers to the dancers' blacking their faces as part of the ritual disguise. It is principally a spring fertility dance. Traditionally danced by groups of men often dressed in white and wearing bells on their legs, the steps are varied and intricate and are maintained in a jog-trot while handkerchiefs are waved in both hands.

Morris Jesup, Cape Cape, N GREENLAND. Situated 440 mi (710 km) from the NORTH POLE, it is the world's most northerly point of land. Robert PEARY was the first explorer to reach it (1900); it was named for Morris K. Jesup (1830–1908), a merchant-banker who financed polar expeditions.

Morrison, Jim (*orig.* James Douglas) (1943–1971) U.S. rock singer and songwriter. Born in Melbourne, Fla., the son of a rear admiral, he studied film at UCLA, where he met Ray Manzarek (b.1935), and they formed the psychedelic rock group the Doors. Morrison's haunted voice made the band one of the most popular of the 1960s, with such hits as "Light My Fire." His drug use and outrageous stage behavior led to arrests. In 1971 he left the Doors and moved to Paris, where he died of a heart attack at 27.

Morrison, Toni *orig.* Chloe Anthony Wofford (b.1931) U.S. writer. Born in Lorain, Ohio, she taught at various universi-

ties before publishing *The Bluest Eye* (1970), a novel dealing with some of the shocking realities of the lives of poor blacks, and *Sula* (1973). The brilliant *Song of Solomon* (1977) brought her fame. Her novels, which also include *Tar Baby* (1981), *Beloved* (1987, Pulitzer Prize), *Jazz* (1992), and *Paradise* (1998), explore the African-American experience, particularly that of women, enriched by fantasy and myth. She was awarded the Nobel Prize in 1993.

Morristown National Historical Park Historical park, Morristown, N.J. In the AMERICAN REVOLUTION, the Continental army under George WASHINGTON had its main winter campsite here in 1776–77 and 1779–80. The park includes the house that served as Washington's headquarters.

Morse, Samuel F(inley) B(reese) (1791–1872) U.S. painter and inventor. Born in Charlestown, Mass., he attended Yale Univ. and studied painting in England 1811–15. His portraits still rank among the finest produced in the U.S. He cofounded the National Academy of Design and served as its first president (1826–45). Independent of similar efforts in Europe, he developed an electric TELEGRAPH (1832–35), believing his to be the first, and also devised the MORSE CODE (1838). He received congressional support for the first U.S. telegraph line, from Baltimore to Washington; on its completion in 1844 he sent the message "What hath God wrought!"

Morse code System for representing text by a sequence of dots, dashes, and spaces. It is transmitted as electrical pulses of varied lengths or analogous mechanical or visual signals, such as flashing lights. The original system was invented by Samuel MORSE in 1838; the International Morse Code, a simpler and more precise variant with codes for letters with diacritic marks, was devised in 1851. This code remains in use for certain types of radiotelegraphy, including amateur radio.

mortar Short-range ARTILLERY piece with a short barrel that fires an explosive projectile in a high-arched trajectory. Large mortars were used from medieval times through World War I. Since 1915, portable models have been standard infantry weapons. Medium mortars, with a caliber of about 3–4 in. (70–90 mm), a range of up to about 2.5 mi (4 km), and a bomb weight of up to 11 lbs (5 kg), are now widely used.

mortar Material used in building construction to bond brick, stone, tile, or concrete blocks into a structure. The ancient Romans are credited with its invention. Consisting of sand mixed with cement and water, mortar must be sufficiently flexible to flow slightly but not collapse under the weight of the masonry units. Before the 19th-cent. invention of PORTLAND CEMENT, masons used thin joints of lime mortar, which required greater precision than the thicker joints of portland-cement mortar and were not as strong.

mortgage In Anglo-American law, the method by which a debtor (mortgagor) conveys an interest in property to a creditor (mortgagee) as security for the payment of a money debt. In medieval Europe, the mortgagor gave the mortgagee ownership of the land on the condition that the mortgagee would return it once the mortgagor's debt was paid off. Over time, it became the practice, and later the mortgagor's right, to remain in possession of the land so long as there was no default on the debt.

Morton, Earl of *orig.* James Douglas (1516?–1581) Scottish nobleman. Appointed chancellor by MARY, QUEEN OF SCOTS, in 1563, he conspired with other Protestant nobles against her and probably was involved in the murder of her husband Lord Darnley. He led the nobles that forced her to abdicate in favor of her infant son, James (later JAMES I of England); he became regent for James in 1572. Resented by the other nobles, he was forced to resign in 1578; he was later charged with complicity in Darnley's murder and executed.

Morton, Jelly Roll *orig.* Ferdinand Joseph Lemothe (1890–1941) U.S. pianist and the first important composer in jazz. Born in New Orleans, he was apparently active as a gambler, pool shark, and procurer in his youth. He toured the country as a pianist from 1904, making his first recordings in Chicago in 1923 with his ensemble the Red Hot Peppers, achieving success by integrating elements of ragtime with improvised and arranged ensemble passages. By the early 1930s, Morton's fame had been overshadowed by that of Louis ARMSTRONG and other emerging innovators.

Mosaddeq \'mȯs-ad-ˌdek\, **Muhammad** (1880–1967) Iranian opposition leader. He served in the government until Reza Shah PAHLAVI became shah (1925). After Pahlavi was deposed in 1941, he was reelected to the parliament (1944). His popularity forced M. R. Shah PAHLAVI to appoint him premier (1951) following Mosaddeq's nationalization of the British-owned Anglo-Iranian Oil Co. Tension between the two led to his dismissal, but the resulting unrest sent the shah into exile until Mosaddeq's U.S.-backed opponents could overthrow him and restore the shah (1953). He spent three years in prison and the rest of his life under house arrest.

mosaic Surface decoration of small colored pieces of stone, glass, tile, or shell, closely set into an adhesive ground. Mosaic pieces, or tesserae, are usually small squares, triangles, or other regular shapes. Glass tesserae can achieve a great brilliance, especially those to which gold and silver foil have been applied, as in the great shimmering mosaics of the Byzantine period. The earliest known mosaics date from the 8th cent. B.C. and were made of pebbles, a technique refined by the Greeks in the 5th cent. The Romans used mosaics widely, particularly for floors. Pre-Columbian Americans favored mosaics of garnet, turquoise, and mother-of-pearl, which usually encrusted shields, masks, and cult statues.

Mosconi, Willie (*orig.* William Joseph) (1913–1993) U.S. pocket billiards player. Born in Philadelphia, he began playing professionally in the early 1930s. Known for his accurate rapid-fire shooting, he was world champion 15 times between 1941 and 1957, and once had a run of 526 consecutive balls.

Moscow \'mäs-kō, 'mäs-kau̇\ *Russian* **Moskva** \mȧs-'kvȧ\ Capital and largest city (pop., 1997: 8,405,000) of Russia and the Russian Republic. It is located on the MOSKVA RIVER, in W Russia, about 400 mi (640 km) southeast of ST. PETERSBURG. The site was first mentioned as a village in 1147 and became the capital of the principality of Moscow (Muscovy) in the late 13th cent. It expanded in the 15th–16th cent. under its grand dukes IVAN III and IVAN IV and became the capital of a united Russia (1547–1712). In 1812 it was occupied by the French under NAPOLEON and almost entirely destroyed by fire. In 1918 it became the capital of the UNION OF SOVIET SOCIALIST REPUBLICS (U.S.S.R.) and expanded greatly. It suffered much damage from German bombing in World War II. The spiritual home of the Russian Orthodox Church for more than 600 years, it is a political, industrial, transportation, and cultural center. Its most notable structure is the KREMLIN, a medieval fortress, with Red Square along its E wall. The Lenin Mausoleum is nearby, and St. Basil's Cathedral is at the S end of the square. It is also home to the BOLSHOI Theater and MOSCOW STATE UNIV.

Moscow Art Theatre Russian theater specializing in naturalism, founded in 1898 by Konstantin STANISLAVSKY and Vladimir Nemirovich-Danchenko (1858–1943). Replacing old-fashioned histrionic acting and heavy-handed staging with a simpler and truer style, it won its first major success with Anton CHEKHOV's *The Seagull*. Along with other plays by Chekhov, the theater mounted new works by writers such as Maxim GORKY and Maurice MAETERLINCK. Its company received acclaim on European and U.S. tours in 1922 and influenced later theatrical development worldwide.

Moscow River See MOSKVA RIVER

Moscow school School of late-medieval Russian ICON and mural painting. It flowered first under the influence of the painter Theophanes the Greek (c.1330/40–1405), who moved to Moscow from Novgorod about 1400 and introduced complexity of composition, subtle color, and almost impressionistic rendering of figures. His most distinguished successor was Andrei RUBLEV. From 1430 to 1500 Moscow grew in prestige and sophistication as the Mongols were driven out of Russia. When Constantinople fell to the Turks in 1453, Moscow became the center of EASTERN ORTHODOXY, which led to a new didactic iconography that expounded mysteries, rites, and dogma. By the 17th cent., the Stroganov school of Moscow artists had assumed the leadership of Russian art, producing small, exquisitely detailed icon paintings.

Moscow State University State-operated university in Moscow. Founded in 1755 by the linguist M. V. LOMONOSOV, it is the oldest, largest, and most prestigious university in Russia. It maintained its 19th-cent. preeminence, especially in the sciences, following the Russian Revolution, and continued to expand during the Soviet period. It now has more than 350 laboratories. Its library is one of the largest in the world (8.5 million vols.). Enrollment is about 28,000.

Moselle River *or* **Mosel River** \mō-'zel, *German* 'mō-zǝl\ River, W Europe, about 340 mi (545 km) long. Rising in NE France, it flows north, forming part of the border between Germany and Luxembourg, then northeast into the RHINE RIVER at KOBLENZ. In this part of the valley are the vineyards that produce the famous Moselle wines. Among its chief tributaries are the ORNE and the SAAR.

Moses (fl.13th cent. B.C.) Prophet of JUDAISM. According to the Book of EXODUS, he was born in Egypt to Hebrew parents, who set him afloat on the Nile in a reed basket to save him from an edict calling for the death of all newborn Hebrew males. Found by the pharaoh's daughter, he was reared in the Egyptian court. After killing a brutal Egyptian taskmaster, he fled to Midian, where Yahweh (God) revealed himself in a burning bush and called Moses to deliver the Israelites from slavery in Egypt. With the help of his brother AARON, Moses pleaded with the pharaoh for the Israelites' release. The pharaoh let them go after a series of plagues sent by God, but then sent his army after them. God parted the Red Sea to let the Israelites pass, then drowned the pursuing Egyptians. God made a COVENANT with the Israelites at Mt. SINAI and delivered the TEN COMMANDMENTS to Moses. After 40 years of wandering, Moses led his people to the edge of CANAAN.

Moses, Grandma *orig.* Anna Mary Robertson (1860–1961) U.S. folk painter. Born in Greenwich, N.Y., she began to produce embroidery pictures after her husband died in 1927. When arthritis impaired her embroidering, she turned to painting. After her first exhibition in a drugstore at age 78, she went on to produce more than 1,000 nostalgic scenes of turn-of-the-century rural life (e.g., *Catching the Thanksgiving Turkey, Over the River to Grandma's House*), which were exhibited internationally and regularly reproduced on holiday greeting cards. She died at 101.

Moses, Robert (1888–1981) U.S. public official. Born in New Haven, Conn., he began his long career in public service in New York City's bureau of municipal research. In 1924 Gov. Alfred SMITH appointed him head of both the New York and Long Island state park commissions. For 40 years in these and related positions, Moses supervised the vast expansion of the park system and the construction of numerous roads, bridges, tunnels, and housing projects in and around the city, reshaping it on a grand scale in often controversial ways.

Moshoeshoe \mō-'shwā-,shwā\ *or* **Mshweshwe** \em-'shwā-,shwā\ (1786?–1870) Founder and first paramount chief of Sotho (later Basutoland; now Lesotho). In the 1830s and '40s he played off British and Boer interests to advantage, but in 1868 the British annexed Sotho, and his power waned. His descendant Moshoeshoe II (1938–1996) was the first king of independent Lesotho.

Moskva River \mäs-'kvà\ *or* **Moscow River** River, W Russia. It is 315 mi (507 km) long and flows through MOSCOW to join the OKA RIVER just below Kolomna. It is navigable from Moscow.

Mosley, Sir Oswald (Ernald) (1896–1980) British politician and fascist. He served in the House of Commons 1918–31. After a visit to Italy, he founded the British Union of Fascists in 1932. With his followers, he distributed anti-Semitic propaganda, conducted hostile demonstrations in the Jewish sections of E London, and wore Nazi-style uniforms. During World War II, he was interned (1940–43) with his wife, Diana Guinness, a friend of Adolph HITLER. In 1948 Mosley founded the Union Movement, an amalgam of right-wing book clubs.

mosque Islamic public place of prayer. The *masjid jami,* or "collective mosque," is the center of community worship and the site of Friday prayer services. Originally simply a sacred plot of ground, the mosque building has remained essentially an open space, usually roofed, with a minaret sometimes attached. The *minbar,* a seat at the top of steps placed near the mihrab, a prayer niche, is used by the preacher *(khatib)* as a pulpit. Occasionally there is also a *maqsurah,* a box or wooden screen originally used to shield a worshiping ruler from assassins. The

Mosque Inside the Blue Mosque, Cairo

minaret is used by the muezzin (crier) to proclaim the call to worship five times each day. During prayer, Muslims orient themselves toward the KAABA. See also ISLAMIC ARCHITECTURE.

Mosque of Omar See DOME OF THE ROCK

mosquito Any of 2,500 DIPTERAN species in the family Culicidae. The females of most species require a blood meal to mature their eggs. Through bloodsucking, females of various species (genera *Aedes, Anopheles,* and *Culex*) transmit human diseases, including DENGUE FEVER, ENCEPHALITIS, filariasis, MALARIA, YELLOW FEVER, and elephantiasis. The adult has a long proboscis, a slender, elongated body, and long, fragile legs. The males (and sometimes the females) feed on plant juices. The female's characteristic sound is made by the vibration of thin membranes on the thorax. The females lay their eggs on the surface of usually stagnant water, and the eggs hatch into aquatic larvae (wrigglers). Control measures have included elimination of breeding sites and application of surface films of oil to clog the larvae's breathing tubes.

Mosquito Coast *or* **Miskito Coast** Region along the coast of E Nicaragua and Honduras. It consists of a lowland about 40 mi (65 km) wide that skirts the Caribbean Sea for about 225 mi (360 km). In 1655 England established a protectorate there. It is named for the Miskito Indians. Spain, Nicaragua, and the U.S. disputed England's protectorate until 1850. In 1894 it was incorporated into Nicaragua, but the N part was granted to Honduras in 1960 by the International Court of Justice.

moss Any of at least 10,000 species of small, spore-bearing land plants in the BRYOPHYTE division, found worldwide except in salt water since the PERMIAN PERIOD. Commonly found in moist, shady locations, mosses may range in size from microscopic forms to plants more than 40 in. (1 m) long. They prevent erosion and release nutrients. The life cycle shows clear ALTERNATION OF GENERATIONS between the sexual GAMETOPHYTE, with stemlike and leaflike structures, and the SPOROPHYTE, a raised stalk that ends in a spore case (sporangium). Mosses also reproduce asexually by branching. The economically important genus *Sphagnum* forms PEAT. Many so-called mosses are not bryophytes, including Irish moss (a red form of ALGAE) and various LICHENS. Spanish moss is an EPIPHYTE, and club moss is an evergreen herb of the family Lycopodiaceae.

Moss, Stirling (b.1929) British Formula One racing driver. He won his first event in 1950 in England and went on to win scores of races, including the British Grand Prix and the Monaco Grand Prix (three times). In 1962 an accident ended his career.

Mossi \'mô-sē\ People of Burkina Faso and other parts of W Africa. Mossi society is organized as in the former Mossi States (c.1500–1895), being divided into royalty, nobles, commoners, and formerly slaves. The *morho naba* ("big lord") occupies a court in OUAGADOUGOU. In the colonial era the Mossi acted as trading intermediaries between forest states and cities of the Niger. Today most of the 5.4 million Mossi are farmers.

M

Mossi states Complex of independent W African kingdoms (c.1500–1895) around the headwaters of the VOLTA RIVER, within present-day Burkina Faso and Ghana. The MOSSI people harassed the empires of MALI and SONGHAI and vied for control of the NIGER RIVER. From about 1400 the states acted as trading intermediaries between the forest states and the cities of the Niger. They remained independent until the French invasions of the late 19th cent.

Mosul \mō-ˈsül, ˈmō-səl\ *Arabic* **Al-Mawsil** \ˌȧl-maů-ˈsēl\ City (pop., 1987: 664,000), N Iraq. Located across the TIGRIS RIVER from the ruins of ancient NINEVEH, Mosul prospered until 1258, when it was ravaged by the MONGOLS. It was a center of the OTTOMAN EMPIRE from about 1534 to 1918. After World War I it was occupied by the British, and in 1926 ceded to Iraq. Iraq's third-largest city, it has an oil refinery and nearby oil fields. Its many ancient buildings include the Great Mosque and the Red Mosque.

motel Hotel designed for persons traveling by automobile, with convenient parking space (the name blends the words "motor hotel"). Originally usually consisting of modest roadside cabins, motels serve commercial and business travelers as well as vacationers and tourists. By 1950 the automobile was the principal mode of travel in the U.S., and motels were being built near large highways, just as hotels had been built near railroad stations.

motet Latin choral composition, generally in one movement. Its origins are in the 13th cent., when words (French, *mots*) began to be added to polyphonic lines in settings of plainchant. It grew directly out of a polyphonic decoration of a portion of ORGANUM, but soon split off to become a separate composition, while retaining a meaningless fragment of chant text and melody in the tenor part. The upper texts often became a confusing mixture of sacred and secular poems, indicating its intended performance in courtly as well as ecclesiastical settings. The most important musical genre of the 13th cent., it was an essential vehicle for the development of polyphony. Renaissance sacred motets, employing a single text, were written by such composers as JOSQUIN DES PREZ and Orlande de LASSUS. In the 17th–18th cent., motets were written by J.-B. LULLY, Heinrich SCHÜTZ, and J. S. BACH.

moth Any of several thousand LEPIDOPTERAN species found in all but polar habitats. Moths are chiefly nocturnal and have a stouter body, duller coloring, and proportionately smaller wings than BUTTERFLIES. They have distinctive feathery antennae and, when at rest, fold their wings, wrap them around the body, or hold them extended at their sides. Wingspans range from less than an inch to about 1 ft (30 cm). The life cycle has four stages: egg, LARVA (caterpillar, or worm), PUPA (chrysalis), and adult (imago). Many larvae and adults seriously damage forests, agricultural crops, and fabrics. See also GYPSY MOTH, HAWK MOTH, MILLER.

Mother Goose Fictitious old woman, reputedly the source of the body of traditional children's songs and verses known as NURSERY RHYMES. Often pictured as a beak-nosed, sharp-chinned old woman riding on the back of a flying gander, she was first associated with nursery rhymes in *Mother Goose's Melody* (1781), published by the successors of John NEWBERY. The name derived from the title of Charles PERRAULT's collection of fairy tales *Ma mère l'oye, or "My Mother Goose"* (1697).

Mother Jones See M. H. JONES

Mother Lode Country Former gold-rush belt, SIERRA NEVADA foothills, central California. It was about 150 mi (240 km) long, but only a few miles wide. The GOLD RUSH was sparked by the 1848 discovery of placer gold on John SUTTER's property. The term "mother lode" evolved from the miners' concept of one main quartz vein with subsidiary offshoot veins. Mining operations ceased there in the 1930s. The area is dotted with ghost camps and old mining towns.

Mother's Day and Father's Day U.S. holidays. A nationwide observance of Mother's Day was suggested by Anna Jarvis of Grafton, W.V., and in 1908 formal observances were held in churches in Grafton and Philadelphia. By 1911 every state celebrated the occasion on the second Sunday in May. It was formalized by Congress in 1914. Father's Day was first celebrated in 1910 in Spokane, Wash., through efforts of Sonora Dodd and the YMCA. Celebrated on the third Sunday in June, it was signed into law in 1972.

Motherwell, Robert (1915–1991) U.S. painter and writer. Born in Aberdeen, Wash., he earned degrees from Stanford and Harvard before deciding to become a serious painter. He espoused ABSTRACT EXPRESSIONISM from the beginning, and his erudite writings were largely responsible for the intellectual tone of the movement. In his *Elegy to the Spanish Republic* series of over 100 paintings, begun in 1949, he developed a limited repertory of simple, serene black forms that were applied to the picture plane in a way that created a sense of slow, solemn movement.

motion Change in position of a body relative to another body or with respect to a REFERENCE FRAME or COORDINATE SYSTEM. Motion occurs along a definite path, the nature of which determines the character of the motion: translational motion occurs if all points in a body have similar paths relative to another body; rotational motion occurs when any line on a body changes its orientation relative to a line on another body. Motion relative to a moving body is called relative motion. Indeed, all motions are relative, but motions relative to the earth or to any body fixed to it are often assumed to be absolute. See also BROWNIAN MOTION.

motion, equation of Mathematical formula that describes the MOTION of a body relative to a given REFERENCE FRAME, in terms of the position, VELOCITY, or ACCELERATION of the body. In classical MECHANICS, the basic equation of motion is Newton's second law (see NEWTON'S LAWS OF MOTION). Other equations of motion include the position-time equation, the velocity-time equation, and the acceleration-time equation of a moving body.

motion picture *or* **movie** Series of still photographs on film, projected in rapid succession onto a screen. Filmed with a movie camera, which makes rapid exposures of people or objects in motion, it is shown with a movie projector, which reproduces sound synchronized with the images. The principal inventors of motion-picture machines were Thomas EDISON in the U.S. and the LUMIÈRE brothers in France. Film production was centered in France in the early 20th cent., but by 1920 the U.S. had become dominant. The HOLLYWOOD movie studios reached their zenith in the 1930s and '40s, when they also typically owned extensive theater chains. The U.S. film industry, with its immense technical resources, has continued to dominate the world market to the present day. See also COLUMBIA PICTURES, MGM, PARAMOUNT COMMUNICATIONS, RKO, UNITED ARTISTS, WARNER BROTHERS.

motion sickness Sickness caused by contradiction between external data from the eyes and internal cues from the balance center in the INNER EAR. For example, in seasickness the inner ear senses the ship's motion, but the eyes see the still cabin. This stimulates stress hormones and accelerates stomach-muscle contraction, leading to dizziness, pallor, cold sweat, and nausea and vomiting. Minimizing changes of speed and direction, reclining, not turning the head, closing the eyes, or focusing on distant objects may help. Drugs can prevent or relieve it. Pressing an ACUPUNCTURE point on the wrist helps some people.

motion study See TIME-AND-MOTION STUDY

motivation Factors within a human being or animal that arouse and direct goal-oriented behavior. Early researchers, influenced by Charles DARWIN, ascribed much of animal and human behavior to INSTINCT. Sigmund FREUD believed that much of human behavior was also based on irrational instinctive urges and unconscious motives. Walter CANNON proposed that basic human drives direct energies toward the reduction of physiological tensions. Behavioral psychologists stress the importance of external goals in prompting action, while humanistic psychologists examine the role of felt needs. Cognitive psychologists have found that a motive sensitizes a person to information relating to that motive. See also HUMAN NATURE, LEARNING.

motorcycle Bicycle propelled by an INTERNAL COMBUSTION ENGINE. The first gasoline-engine motorcycle was built by Gottlieb DAIMLER in 1885. Motorcycles were widely used after 1910, especially by the armed forces in World War I. After 1950 a larger, heavier motorcycle was used mainly for touring and sport competitions. The moped, a light, low-speed motor bicycle that can also be pedaled, was developed mainly in Europe, as was the sturdier Italian-made motor scooter.

Motown First large black-owned music company in the U.S., the originator of a regional variant of black popular music that achieved enormous popularity in the 1960s. It was founded in Detroit (for which Motown is a nickname) in 1959 by the songwriter Berry Gordy, Jr. (b.1929). It scored its first nationwide hit with "Shop Around" (1960) by the Miracles. Its roster soon included the Temptations, the Four Tops, the SUPREMES, Marvin Gaye, and Stevie WONDER, who, with the songwriting teams Holland-Dozier-Holland and Nick Ashford and Valerie Simpson, helped create the infectious "Motown sound." Later Motown names included Gladys Knight and the Pips, the Jackson Five, and Lionel Ritchie. Gordy moved its headquarters to Los Angeles in 1971, and sold the label to MCA in 1988.

Mott, Lucretia *orig.* Lucretia Coffin (1793–1880) U.S. social reformer. Born in Nantucket, Mass., she taught at a Quaker boarding school, and in 1811 married a fellow teacher, James Mott. She became a Quaker minister in 1821. The Motts were active in the antislavery campaign, and Lucretia lectured widely on social reform. In 1848 she and E. C. STANTON organized the SENECA FALLS CONVENTION, and she thereafter devoted her attention primarily to women's rights, writing articles and lecturing widely.

Mound Builders See HOPEWELL CULTURE

Mount, William Sidney (1807–1868) U.S. painter. Born in Setauket, Long Island, N.Y., he studied drawing at the newly opened National Academy of Design. He turned to genre painting and achieved immediate success with such works as *Rustic Dance After a Sleigh Ride* (1830). His portrayals of country life, affectionate and humorous without being sentimental, are a valuable record of his time. He was one of the first and most notable U.S. genre painters.

mountain Landform that rises well above its surroundings, generally exhibiting steep slopes, a relatively small summit area, and considerable local relief (inequalities of elevation). Mountains are considered larger than hills, but the term has no standardized geologic meaning. Mountains are formed by the folding, faulting, or upwarping of the earth's surface due to the movement of plates (see PLATE TECTONICS). The HIMALAYAS were formed by a collision between plates that caused extreme compressional folding and the uplifting of large areas. The mountain ranges around the Pacific basin are attributed to the sinking of one plate beneath another.

mountaineering *or* **mountain climbing** Sport of scaling mountains. It is a group activity, with each member both supporting and supported by the group's efforts. Its pleasures include the physical and spiritual satisfactions brought about through intense personal effort, ever-increasing proficiency, and contact with natural grandeur. The greater rewards entail considerable risk. The first great peak ascended in modern times was Mont BLANC, in 1786. Other Alpine peaks followed, capped by the ascent of the MATTERHORN in 1865. By the 1910s, most peaks of the Andes, the Rockies, and other Western Hemisphere ranges had been climbed. Ascents in the Himalayas began in the 1930s, culminating in the 1953 ascent of Mt. EVEREST. From the 1960s mountaineering became an increasingly technical sport, emphasizing the use of specialized gear in the ascent of vertical rock or ice faces.

mountain goat *or* **Rocky Mountain goat** RUMINANT (BOVID species *Oreamnos americanus*) of the Yukon to the N Rockies that is more closely related to ANTELOPES than to GOATS. Mountain goats stand about 40 in. (1 m) at the shoulder. Both sexes bear short, hollow, slightly backward-curving, black horns. The shaggy, coarse white hair covers a thick,

Mountain goat (*Oreamnos americanus*)

woolly underfur. Mountain goats are agile climbers and can leap more than 12 ft (3.5 m). They live above the timberline, eating moss, lichen, and scrub foliage.

mountain laurel Flowering evergreen shrub (*Kalmia latifolia*) of the HEATH FAMILY, occurring in most mountainous regions of E N. America. It grows to about 3–18 ft (1–6 m) in height and has oval leaves. The rosy, pink, or white flowers appear in large clusters above the foliage. The shrub is popular in landscape plantings.

mountain lion See COUGAR

mountain sickness See ALTITUDE SICKNESS

Mountbatten, Louis *later* **Earl Mountbatten (of Burma)** *orig.* Louis Francis Albert Victor Nicholas, Prince of Battenberg (1900–1979) British statesman. A great-grandson of Queen VICTORIA, he entered the Royal Navy in 1913. In World War II he was allied commander for S.E. Asia (1943–46) and directed the recapture of Burma. As viceroy of India (1947), he administered the transfer of power from Britain to the independent nations of India and Pakistan and served as the first governor-general of India 1947–48. He became first sea lord (1955–59) and chief of the United Kingdom Defense Staff (1959–65). In 1979, while on a sailing visit to Ireland, he was assassinated by Irish terrorists.

Mount Cook National Park Park, W central SOUTH ISLAND, New Zealand. It has an area of 270 sq mi (700 sq km). There are some 27 peaks higher than 10,000 ft (3,000 m), including Mt. Cook, the highest point in New Zealand, at 12,349 ft (3,764 m). More than one-third of the park is covered by permanent snow and glacial ice.

Mount Holyoke College Private liberal-arts college for women in S. Hadley, Mass. Founded by Mary LYON as a female seminary in 1837, it was one of the first institutions of higher education for women in the U.S. Mount Holyoke is part of an educational consortium with nearby AMHERST, Hampshire, and SMITH colleges and the Univ. of Massachusetts. Enrollment is about 2,000.

Mounties See ROYAL CANADIAN MOUNTED POLICE

Mount of Olives See Mount of OLIVES

Mount Vernon Home and burial place of George WASHINGTON. It is located in N Virginia, on the POTOMAC RIVER near WASHINGTON, D.C. The estate was inherited by Washington in 1751. After the U.S. government declined to buy it, in 1858 the Mt. Vernon Ladies' Association of the Union purchased the house and 200 acres (80 hectares) of the estate; the association still maintains the site.

mouse Any of many species (family Muridae) of small, scampering RODENTS. They are distinguished from RATS principally by their smaller size. Mice are basically Asian in origin. Species in other rodent families (e.g., DEER MOUSE, POCKET MOUSE) are called mice without scientific basis. They are mostly beneficial; they are the main prey of predators that might otherwise take more valuable prey. The white laboratory mouse is a form of the house mouse (*Mus musculus*), which inhabits buildings worldwide. See also FIELD MOUSE.

mouse Hand-controlled electromechanical device for interacting with a DIGITAL COMPUTER that has a GRAPHICAL USER INTERFACE. The mouse can be moved around on a flat surface to control the movement of a cursor on the computer display screen. Its buttons can be used to select text, activate programs, or move items around the screen by quickly pressing and releasing one of them ("clicking") or by keeping a button depressed while moving the mouse ("clicking and dragging").

mouse deer See CHEVROTAIN

Mousterian industry \mü-ˈstir-ē-ən\ Tool culture traditionally associated with NEANDERTHALS in Europe, W Asia, and N Africa about 40,000 B.C. Mousterian tools included small hand axes made from disk-shaped cores; flake tools such as scrapers and points; toothed, sawlike instruments produced by making notches in a flake; and round limestone balls, believed to have served as bolas. Wooden spears were used to hunt large game such as the MAMMOTH and woolly rhinoceros. Mousterian implements disappeared abruptly from Europe with the passing of the Neanderthals.

mouth *or* **oral cavity** *or* **buccal cavity** \ˈbək-əl\ Orifice through which food and air enter the body. Its chief structures are the teeth (see TOOTH), TONGUE, and palate. It is

the site of chewing and SPEECH formation. The mouth is lined by mucous membranes containing small GLANDS that, along with the SALIVARY GLANDS, keep it moist and clear of food and other debris.

mouth organ See HARMONICA

movie See MOTION PICTURE

Moyers, Bill (Don) (b.1934) U.S. journalist. Born in Hugo, Okla., he originally trained for the ministry. He served as special assistant and press secretary to Pres. Lyndon JOHNSON 1963–67. He created the public-affairs program *Bill Moyers' Journal* on public television (1971–76, 1978–81), and later served as a news analyst for CBS News (1981–86). He formed Public Affairs TV, Inc., in 1987, producing such television specials and series as *A World of Ideas* (1989), *Healing and the Mind* (1990), and *Genesis* (1996), and numerous best-selling books derived from them. He has won more than 30 Emmy awards.

Mozambique \ˌmō-zäm-ˈbēk\ *officially* **Republic of Mozambique** *formerly* **Portuguese East Africa** Nation, SE coast of Africa. Area: 297,846 sq mi (771,421 sq km). Population

MOZAMBIQUE

Scale 1: 26,326,000
0   75   150   225 mi
0   100   200   300 km

©1999, Encyclopædia Britannica, Inc.

(2000 est.): 19,105,000. Capital: MAPUTO. About half the people are Bantu-speaking Africans. Ethnolinguistic groups include the Makua, Tsonga, Malawi, Shona, and Yao peoples. Languages: Portuguese (official), BANTU, SWAHILI. Religions: traditional beliefs, Islam, Christianity. Currency: metical. Mozambique may be divided into two broad regions: the lowlands in the south and the highlands in the north, separated by the ZAMBEZI RIVER. It has a centrally planned, developing economy based on agriculture, international trade, and light industries. Several industries were nationalized after 1975. It is a republic with one legislature; its head of state and government is the president, assisted by the prime minister. Inhabited in prehistoric times, it was settled by Bantu peoples around the 3rd cent. A.D. Arab traders occupied the coastal region from the 14th cent., and the Portuguese controlled the area from the early 16th cent. The slave trade later became an important part of the economy. Outlawed in the mid-18th cent., it continued illegally. In the late 19th cent. private trading companies began to administer parts of the inland areas. It became an overseas province of Portugal in 1951. An independence movement became active in the 1960s, and after years of war, the country was granted independence in 1975. A single-party state under the Frelimo, or Mozambique Liberation Front party, it was wracked by civil war in the 1970s and 1980s. In 1990 a new constitution ended its Marxist collectivism and introduced privatization, a market economy,

and multiparty government. A peace treaty was signed with the rebels in 1992.

Mozambique Channel Strait, W Indian Ocean. Located between Madagascar and Mozambique, it is about 950 mi (1,530 km) long and 250–625 mi (400–1,000 km) wide. An important shipping route for E Africa, it serves the ports of Mahajanga and Toliara in Madagascar, and MAPUTO and Beira in Mozambique.

Mozart \ˈmōt-ˌsärt\, **Wolfgang Amadeus** *orig.* Joannes Chrysostomus Wolfgangus Theophilus Mozart (1756–1791) Austrian composer. Son of the violinist and composer Leopold Mozart (1719–1787), he and his older sister, Maria Anna (1751–1829), were prodigies, and at 5 he began to compose and gave his first public performance. From 1762 Leopold toured throughout Europe with them, showing off the "miracle that God allowed to be born in Salzburg." The first round of touring (1762–69) took them as far as France and England, where Wolfgang met J. C. BACH and wrote his first symphonies (1764). Tours of Italy followed (1769–74); there he wrote his first Italian opera. He returned to Salzburg as cathedral organist and in 1781 wrote his opera *Idomeneo*. Chafing under the archbishop's rule, he was released from his position in 1781 and moved to Vienna to begin his independent career. While giving piano lessons, he wrote *The Abduction from the Seraglio* (1782) and many of his great piano concertos. The later 1780s saw the height of his success, with the "Haydn quartets," the three great operas on Lorenzo DA PONTE's librettos—*The Marriage of Figaro* (1786), *Don Giovanni* (1787), and *Così fan tutte* (1790) —and his superb late symphonies. In his last year he composed the opera *The Magic Flute* and his great *Requiem* (left unfinished). Despite his success, he always lacked money and had to borrow heavily from friends. His death at 35 may have resulted from a kidney infection. No other composer left such an extraordinary legacy in so short a lifetime.

MP3 Standard technology and format for the compression of audio signals into very small computer files. Sound data from a COMPACT DISK (CD) can be compressed to one-twelfth the original size without sacrificing sound quality. MP3 files have become the most popular type of sound files on the Internet. Recording companies now provide sample songs in MP3 format to promote CD sales, and some musicians bypass recording companies and issue their songs in MP3 format only.

MRI See MAGNETIC RESONANCE IMAGING

MS See MULTIPLE SCLEROSIS

Mshweshwe See MOSHOESHOE

MTV *in full* **Music Television** U.S. cable television network. Established in 1980 to present videos of musicians and singers performing new rock music, MTV won a huge young audience worldwide. Soon virtually every major pop or rock performer was making videos to be shown on MTV, and the reception of their videos directly affected record sales. An additional channel now offers more conventional programming. MTV is controlled by the media conglomerate Viacom Inc.

Muawiyah I \mù-ˈä-wē-yə\, **al-** (602?–680) First CALIPH (661–80) of the UMAYYAD DYNASTY. He converted to Islam only after Muhammad had conquered Mecca. As governor of Damascus he built up the Syrian army to resist Byzantine attacks. Opposed to ALI's caliphate, he eventually overthrew Ali and became CALIPH. He channeled tribal aggressiveness into anti-Byzantine campaigns and captured parts of N. Africa. To administer his large empire, he adopted Roman and Byzantine procedures. By securing his son as his successor, he established hereditary rule. Though disliked by pious Muslim historians for deviating from Muhammad's leadership style and by Shiites for his role in Ali's death, he is praised in Arabic literature as the ideal ruler. See also AMR IBN AL-AS, FITNAH, HUSAYN IBN ALI, Battle of KARBALA.

Mubarak \mù-ˈbä-räk\, **Hosni** (b.1928) President of Egypt (from 1981). As air-force commander (from 1972) he planned Egypt's opening moves in the 1973 ARAB–ISRAELI WAR. Named vice president in 1975, he became president on Anwar al-SADAT's assassination in 1981. He has maintained relations with Israel while working to restore Egypt to its traditional position as the most influential of the Arab states. Islamic fundamentalism in the 1990s weakened his power base.

Mucha \'mü-ka̱\, **Alphonse** (*orig.* Alfons Maria) (1860–1939) Czech painter and designer. After study in Prague, Munich, and Paris, he became the principal designer of posters advertising the stage appearances of Sarah BERNHARDT; he designed sets and costumes for her as well. His many opulent posters and magazine illustrations made him one of the foremost designers in the ART NOUVEAU style. After Czechoslovakia became independent, he designed its stamps and banknotes.

muckraker Any of a group of U.S. writers identified with pre–World War I reform and exposé literature. The term originated in an allusion Theodore ROOSEVELT made in 1906 to a passage in John BUNYAN's *Pilgrim's Progress* about a man with a muckrake who "could look no way but downward." Later it took on favorable connotations of social concern and exposure of injustice. The movement emerged from the YELLOW JOURNALISM of the 1890s and from popular magazines such as *McClure's* and articles by writers such as Lincoln STEFFENS and Ida TARBELL on municipal government, labor, and trusts. The best-known muckraking novel is Upton SINCLAIR's *The Jungle* (1906).

mucoviscidosis See CYSTIC FIBROSIS

mudra \mü-'drä\ In BUDDHISM and HINDUISM, a symbolic gesture of the hands and fingers. Hundreds of mudras are used in ceremony and dance, often in combination with movements of the wrists, elbows, and shoulders. In ceremonies, especially in Buddhism, a mudra acts as a kind of seal, affirming a mystical or magical vow or utterance, such as a prayer to ward off evil.

mufti \'muf-te\ Islamic legal authority charged with issuing an opinion (*fatwa*) in answer to an inquiry. A mufti must have extensive knowledge of the QURAN, the HADITH, and legal precedents. During the Ottoman empire the mufti of Istanbul was Islam's chief legal authority. The development of modern legal codes in Islamic countries has significantly reduced the authority of mufti, and they now deal only with questions of personal status such as inheritance, marriage, and divorce.

Mugabe \mü-'gä-bā\, **Robert (Gabriel)** (b.1924) First prime minister (1980–87) and executive president (from 1987) of Zimbabwe. With Joshua NKOMO, Mugabe led a guerrilla war that forced the white-dominated government of Ian SMITH to accept universal elections, which Mugabe's party easily won. He formed a coalition government with Nkomo's party, but ousted Nkomo in 1982. Mugabe soon moved to convert Zimbabwe from a parliamentary democracy to a one-party socialist state. His rule has been marked by increasing authoritarianism. In 2000 he began a campaign to seize all remaining white-owned farms, drawing international condemnation.

Muggeridge, Malcolm (Thomas) (1903–1990) British writer and social critic. A journalist, he served as editor of *Punch* 1953–57. An outspoken and controversial iconoclast, he targeted liberalism and other aspects of contemporary life with his stinging wit and elegant prose. He was early an avowed atheist but moved gradually to embrace Roman Catholicism. He wrote some 30 books, including satiric novels and religious accounts, and from the 1950s was a popular figure on British television.

Mughal dynasty \'mü-gəl\ *or* **Mogul dynasty** \'mō-gəl\ Muslim dynasty that ruled most of N India from 1526 to around 1760. Descended from TIMUR and GENGHIS KHAN, the dynasty was distinguished by its administrative efficiency and by its emperors' efforts to integrate Hindus and Muslims into a united Indian state. Prominent among the Mughal rulers were the founder, BABUR (r.1526–30), his grandson AKBAR (r.1556–1605), and SHAH JAHAN (r.1628–58). Under AURANGZEB (r.1658–1707) the empire reached its greatest extent, but his intolerance sowed the seeds for its decline. It broke up under pressure from factional rivalries, dynastic warfare, and the invasion of N India in 1739 by Nadir Shah.

Mugwumps Reform faction of the REPUBLICAN PARTY. In 1884 the Mugwumps refused to support the Republican presidential candidate, James BLAINE, whom they considered corrupt, and campaigned for Democratic nominee

Grover CLEVELAND, whom they saw as a reformer. The term, derived from an Indian word for "war leader," had been used as slang for "kingpin" and was applied to the breakaway group by a New York newspaper.

Muhammad *or* **Mohammed** (c.570–632) Arab prophet and founder of ISLAM. He was born in MECCA, son of a merchant of the ruling tribe. He was married with children when he heard a voice telling him he was the messenger of ALLAH, whereupon he became the prophet of a new religion. His revelations and teachings, recorded in the QURAN, are the basis of Islam. He began to preach publicly around 613, urging the rich to give to the poor and calling for the destruction of idols. His enemies' plan to murder him forced him to flee to MEDINA in 622. This flight, the HEGIRA, marks the beginning of the Islamic era. Muhammad's followers won control of Mecca by 629 and of all Arabia by 630. Muhammad died in 632 and was buried at Medina. His life, teachings, and miracles have been the subjects of Muslim devotion and reflection ever since.

Muhammad, Elijah *orig.* Elijah Poole (1897–1975) U.S. black separatist and leader of the Nation of ISLAM. Born in Sandersville, Ga., son of sharecroppers, he moved to Detroit in 1923. He joined the Nation of Islam and established its second temple in Chicago; on the disappearance of its founder, Wallace D. Fard, in 1934, he became head of the movement. His relentless call for a separate nation for African-Americans, whom he declared to be Allah's chosen people, prompted his most famous disciple, MALCOLM X, to break with the group in 1964. He moderated his views in his later years.

Muhammad Ali (1769–1849) OTTOMAN viceroy of Egypt (1805–48) and founder of the dynasty that ruled Egypt until 1953. He reorganized Egyptian society in the aftermath of the Napoleonic occupation, eliminated the MAMLUKS, and stamped out peasant rebellions. He nationalized most land, introduced cash crops, and attempted industrialization. He succeeded in securing the hereditary right to rule Egypt and Sudan (1841), which opened the way to eventual independence from Ottoman and British domination.

Muir \'myu̇r\, **John** (1838–1914) U.S. naturalist and conservationist. Born in Scotland, Muir emigrated with his family to Wisconsin in 1849. An 1867 accident caused him to abandon an industrial career and devote himself to nature. He began his efforts to establish a federal forest conservation policy in 1876. His writings swung public opinion in favor of Pres. Grover CLEVELAND's proposal for national forest reservations and influenced Pres. Theodore ROOSEVELT's conservation program, and he was largely responsible for establishing SEQUOIA and YOSEMITE NATIONAL PARK (1890). He was the chief founder and first president of the SIERRA CLUB (1892–1914).

mujahidin \mü-ja-hi-'dēn\ Warrior in a JIHAD; in Afghanistan, the guerrilla rebel fighters who opposed invading Soviet forces and the Afghan communist government (1979–92). Politically fragmented, their military efforts remained uncoordinated throughout the Afghan War. In 1992 various rebel groups drove the communist president, Mohammad Najibullah, from power. Rival factions fought from 1992 to 1994, when the TALIBAN emerged.

Mukden See SHENYANG

Mukden Incident \'mu̇k-dən\ (1931) Seizure of the Manchurian city of Mukden (now Shenyang, China). Responding to the increasingly successful unification of China by CHIANG KAI-SHEK, the Japanese garrison in Manchuria used the pretext of a railway explosion to occupy Mukden. With reinforcements from the Japanese colony of Korea, its army occupied all of Manchuria within three months, and soon established the state of MANCHUGUO.

mulberry family Family Moraceae, composed of about 1,000 species of deciduous trees or evergreens in about 40 genera, found mostly in tropical and subtropical regions. Plants of the family contain a milky latex and produce multiple fused fruits. Edible fruits grow on the common mulberries (genus *Morus*), FIG (in the largest genus, *Ficus*), and BREADFRUIT. Other species include the India RUBBER TREE and the wide-spreading BANYAN tree.

mule Hardy offspring of a male ASS and a female HORSE. The less common cross of a female ass and a male horse is

M

called a hinny. The mule resembles the horse in height and in shape of neck and croup (rump); it resembles the ass in its long ears, small hooves, and short mane. Mules are 12–17.5 hands (50–70 in., 120–180 cm) high and weigh 600–1,500 lbs (275–700 kg). They have been used as pack animals for at least 3,000 years.

mule deer Large-eared DEER *(Odocoileus hemionus)* of W N. America that lives alone or in small groups at high altitudes in summer and lower altitudes in winter. Mule deer stand 3–3.5 ft (90–105 cm). The male's antlers fork twice above a short tine near the base; a mature male normally has five tines on each antler. It is related to the WHITE-TAILED DEER.

mullah \\'mə-lə\ Muslim title applied to a scholar or religious leader, especially in the Middle East and the Indian subcontinent. It means "lord" and has also been used in N. Africa as an honorific attached to the name of a king, sultan, or member of the nobility. The title is now given to a variety of religious leaders. The word can also refer to the entire class that upholds the traditional interpretation of Islam.

Muller \\'mə-lər\, **Hermann Joseph** (1890–1967) U.S. geneticist. Born in New York City, he was initially motivated by the possibility of consciously guiding human evolution, and for a time worked in the Soviet Union's Institute of Genetics. In 1926 he first induced genetic mutations through the use of X rays, and he demonstrated that mutations are the result of breakages in chromosomes and of changes in individual genes. His receipt of the Nobel Prize in 1946 increased his opportunities to publicize the dangers posed by accumulating spontaneous mutations in the human gene pool as a result of industrial processes and radiation.

Mulligan, Gerry *(orig.* Gerald Joseph) (1927–1996) U.S. saxophonist, pianist, composer, arranger, and bandleader. Born in Queens, N.Y., he worked as staff arranger for Gene Krupa's band in 1946, later writing arrangements and playing for Miles DAVIS's "Birth of the Cool" recordings (1949). He formed a pianoless quartet in Los Angeles featuring trumpeter Chet Baker in 1952.

Mullis, Kary B(anks) (b.1944) U.S. biochemist. Born in Lenoir, N.C., in 1983 he invented the POLYMERASE CHAIN REACTION (PCR), with which scientists can determine the order of nucleotides in a gene, use genetic fingerprinting to identify individuals by their DNA patterns, study evolution, and make medical diagnoses. He shared a 1993 Nobel Prize with Michael Smith (b.1932).

Mulroney \mǝl-'rü-nē\, **(Martin) Brian** (b.1939) Prime minister of Canada (1984–93). Born in Baie-Comeau, Quebec, he became a lawyer in Montreal, and was president of the Iron Ore Co. 1977–83. Elected leader of the Progressive Conservative Party in 1983, he became prime minister when the party won a majority in 1984. He created a coalition of Quebec nationalists and W conservatives and advocated unification while recognizing Quebec as a "distinct society." He sought U.S. cooperation on acid rain and trade policies and helped negotiate the N. AMERICAN FREE TRADE AGREEMENT.

Multan \mùl-'tän\ City (pop., 1998: 1,182,000), central Pakistan. An ancient city, it was taken by ALEXANDER THE GREAT in 326 B.C. It fell to the Muslims about A.D. 712. For three centuries it remained the outpost of ISLAM in what was then India. It has textile mills, glass factories, and cottage industries, including pottery and camelskin work. It is the site of many Muslim shrines and an ancient Hindu temple.

multimedia Computer-delivered electronic system that allows the user to control, combine, and manipulate different types of media, such as text, sound, video, computer graphics, and animation. The most common multimedia machine consists of a PERSONAL COMPUTER with a sound card, MODEM, digital speaker unit, and CD-ROM. More advanced systems include television services with computer interfaces that enable viewers to interact with TV programs and VIRTUAL-REALITY systems that create small-scale artificial sensory environments.

multiple personality disorder *or* **dissociative identity disorder** Rare condition in which two or more independent and distinct PERSONALITY systems develop in the same individual. The various personalities typically differ from one another in outlook, temperament, and body language, and give themselves different first names. The condition is viewed as resulting from the splitting off from conscious awareness and control of thoughts, feelings, memories, and other mental components in response to situations that are painful or disturbing. Treatment is aimed at integrating the disparate personalities.

multiple sclerosis (MS) \sklə-'rō-səs\ Disease of the BRAIN and SPINAL CORD in which gradual, patchy destruction of the myelin sheath of nerve fibers causes interruption or disordered transmission of nerve impulses. Its early symptoms may include limb weakness or trembling, visual problems, sensory disturbances, unsteady walking, and defective bladder control, which come and go irregularly. Attacks grow more severe, and some symptoms become permanent, with eventual complete PARALYSIS. Average survival from onset is about 25 years, but a rare acute form progresses over months. The cause remains uncertain and treatment unsatisfactory. Corticosteroids may ease symptoms.

multiplexing Process of transmitting multiple (but separate) signals simultaneously over a single channel or line, to be separated at the receiving end. The two main types of multiplexing methods are time-division multiplexing (TDM) and frequency-division multiplexing (FDM). In TDM (typically used for digital signals), a device is given a specific time slot to use the channel. In FDM (typically used for analog signals), the channel is subdivided into subchannels, each assigned to a specific signal. Optical-fiber networks can use DWDM (dense wavelength-division multiplexing), in which different data signals are sent in different wavelengths of light.

multiplier In economics, a numerical coefficient showing the effect of a change in one economic variable on another. The autonomous expenditures multiplier is the ratio of the change in the nation's total income to the change in its total investment. If, for example, the total investment in an economy is increased by $1 million, producers of raw materials used in the investment projects and workers employed in them gain $1 million in income. If they spend three-fifths of that income, $600,000 will be added to the incomes of others. The makers of the goods they buy will in turn spend three-fifths of their new income. The amount by which total income increases may be computed by an algebraic formula. In this case, the multiplier is 1/(1–3/5), or 2.5. Thus a $1 million increase in investment creates a $2.5 million increase in total income. Other multipliers include the money multiplier, which measures money creation resulting from a change in MONETARY POLICY, and the government spending multiplier, which measures the change in national income resulting from changes in FISCAL POLICY. The concept of the multiplier process was popularized in the 1930s by J. M. KEYNES.

Mumbai See BOMBAY

Mumford, Lewis (1895–1990) U.S. architectural critic and cultural historian. Born in Flushing, N.Y., he taught at various universities and wrote for *The New Yorker* and other magazines. In works such as *Technics and Civilization* (1934), *The City in History* (1961), and *The Myth of the Machine* (3 vols., 1967–70), Mumford analyzed the effects of technology and urbanization on human societies, criticizing the dehumanizing tendencies of modern technological society.

mumming play *or* **mummers' play** Traditional dramatic entertainment, still performed in a few villages of England and Northern Ireland, in which a champion is killed in a fight and then restored to life by a doctor. It probably has links with primitive ceremonies marking important stages in the agricultural year. Mummers were originally bands of masked persons who during winter festivals in Europe paraded through the streets and entered houses to dance or play dice in silence.

mummy Body embalmed or preserved for burial in the manner of the ancient Egyptians. The process involved removing the internal organs, treating the body with resin, and wrapping it in linen bandages. Among the many other peoples who practiced mummification were the INCAS.

mumps *or* **epidemic parotitis** \ˌpar-ə-'tīt-əs\ Acute contagious viral disease with inflammatory swelling of the SALIVARY GLANDS. Epidemics often occur, mostly among 5- to

15-year-olds. Cold symptoms with low fever are followed by swelling and stiffening in front of the ear, often on both sides. This rapidly spreads toward the neck and under the jaw. Pain is seldom severe, with little redness, but chewing and swallowing are difficult. During recovery in patients past puberty, other glands including the testes, may be affected, but usually not seriously. Mumps needs no special treatment, and patients usually develop immunity. Vaccination can prevent it.

Munch \\'muŋk\\, **Edvard** (1863–1944) Norwegian painter and printmaker. His life and art were marked by the early deaths of both parents, his brother, and his sister, and the mental illness of another sister. He received little formal training, but exposure to Impressionism and Postimpressionism helped him develop a highly original style. It was principally through his work of the 1890s, a series of paintings on love and death in which he gave form to mysterious and dangerous psychic forces, that he made crucial contributions to modern art. *The Scream* (1893) is his most famous work. His etchings, lithographs, and

Edvard Munch, self-portrait, lithograph, 1895

woodcuts closely resemble his paintings in style and subject matter. After a nervous breakdown in 1908–9, therapy lent his work a more positive tone, but his art never recovered its former intensity.

Munda languages \\'mun-də\\ Family of about 17 languages spoken in India, Bangladesh, and Nepal that together with MŌN-KHMER comprises the AUSTROASIATIC superfamily. Munda languages are spoken by more than 7 million people, all members of tribal groups living mainly in hilly and forested regions of NE India, NW Bengal, and the Nepal–Assam border. Munda languages differ from all other Austroasiatic languages in complexity of MORPHOLOGY and in having basic subject-object-verb rather than subject-verb-object word order.

Munich \\'myü-nik\\ *German* **München** \\'men-kən\\ City (pop., 1998 est.: 1,206,000), capital of Bavaria, Germany. Founded about 1158, it became the capital of Bavaria under the ruling WITTELSBACH family. The city developed as a center of music and theater through the 19th cent. After World War I, it became a center of right-wing political ferment; it was the site of Adolf HITLER's abortive BEER HALL PUTSCH (1923) and subsequent NAZI PARTY activities. In World War II it suffered heavily from Allied bombing. It is a trade, cultural, educational, and industrial center known for its many museums as well as for its beer and ale brewing and its famous Oktoberfest.

Munich, University of *German* Ludwig-Maximilians Universität München. Autonomous university supported by the state of Bavaria, Germany. It was founded in Ingolstadt in 1472 and modeled on the Univ. of VIENNA. During the Protestant Reformation it was a center of Roman Catholic opposition to Martin LUTHER. In 1826 it moved to Munich. Enrollment is about 60,000.

Munich agreement (1938) Settlement reached in Munich by Germany, France, Britain, and Italy permitting German annexation of Czechoslovakia's SUDETENLAND. Adolf HITLER's threats to occupy the German-populated part of Czechoslovakia stemmed from his broader goal of reuniting Europe's German-populated areas. Though Czechoslovakia had a defense treaty with France, Britain and France agreed that majority-German areas in the Sudetenland should be returned. When Czechoslovakia refused to evict all Czechoslovaks from the areas, Britain's Neville CHAMBERLAIN negotiated an agreement permitting Germany to occupy the areas but promising that all future differences would be resolved through consultation. Ignoring the agreement, Hitler annexed the rest of Czechoslovakia the next year. See also APPEASEMENT.

Munich Putsch See BEER HALL PUTSCH
Muñoz Marín \\mün-'yōs-mə-'rēn\\, **Luis** (1898–1980) Statesman and four-term governor of Puerto Rico (1948–64). Son of Luis MUÑOZ RIVERA, he was educated in the U.S. Editor of the newspaper *La Democracia,* he was elected to the Puerto Rican senate in 1932. He initially advocated independence but later worked closely with the U.S.-appointed governor. He achieved success with Operation Bootstrap, a program for rapid economic growth. When Puerto Rico won the right to elect its own governor, he was overwhelmingly elected and repeatedly reelected. In 1952 he achieved his goal of making Puerto Rico a commonwealth.

Muñoz Rivera \\mün-yōs-rē-'ver-ä\\, **Luis** (1859–1916) Puerto Rican statesman, publisher, and patriot. In 1889 he founded the newspaper *La Democracia,* which crusaded for Puerto Rican freedom from Spanish domination. He was instrumental in obtaining Puerto Rico's charter of home rule in 1897, and was president of the first autonomist cabinet, but died just before the U.S. Congress passed the Jones Bill, for which he had fought, giving Puerto Rico a large measure of self-government. His son was Luis MUÑOZ MARIN.

Munro \\mən-'rō\\, **Alice** *orig.* Alice Anne Laidlaw (b.1931) Canadian writer. Born in Wingham, Ont., she is known for exquisitely drawn short stories, usually set in rural Ontario and peopled by characters of Scotch-Irish stock. Her collections *Dance of the Happy Shades* (1968), *Who Do You Think You Are?* (1978), and *The Progress of Love* (1986) won the Governor General's Award. Her other collections include *The Moons of Jupiter* (1982) and *Open Secrets* (1994).

Münster \\'men-stər\\ City (pop., 1998 est.: 265,000), W Germany. Founded in 804 as a bishopric, it was named Münster in 1068. A member of the HANSEATIC LEAGUE from the 13th cent., it was seized by the ANABAPTISTS in 1535. The Peace of WESTPHALIA was signed there in 1648, and in 1815 Münster became the capital of Prussian WESTPHALIA. Although it suffered heavy damage in World War II, most of its historic buildings were restored or rebuilt.

Munster Province (pop., 1996: 1,033,000), S Ireland. In the 10th cent. Vikings invaded and eventually settled in Waterford and Limerick. After the 12th cent. Anglo-Norman invasion, it was ruled by the feudal families of Fitzgerald and Butler. Munster now includes the counties of Clare, Cork, Kerry, Limerick, Tipperary (North Riding and South Riding), and Waterford.

muntjac \\'mənt-ˌjak\\ *or* **barking deer** Any of about seven species of solitary, nocturnal DEER, native to Asia and introduced into England and France, that constitute the genus *Muntiacus* (family Cervidae). Named for their cry, most species stand 15–25 in. (40–65 cm) high and weigh 33–77 lbs (15–35 kg). Males have tusklike upper canine teeth and short one-branched antlers. The giant muntjac (88–110 lbs, or 40–50 kg) was discovered in N Vietnam in 1993–94. Fea's muntjac (*M. feae*), of Myanmar and Thailand, is endangered.

mural Painting applied to and made integral with the surface of a wall or ceiling. The Romans produced large numbers of murals in Pompeii and Ostia, but mural painting (not synonymous with FRESCO) reached its high point in Europe with the work of MASACCIO, Fra ANGELICO, LEONARDO DA VINCI, MICHELANGELO, and RAPHAEL. In the 20th cent., the mural was embraced by artists of the Cubist and Fauve movements in Paris, revolutionary painters in Mexico (e.g., Diego RIVERA, J. C. OROZCO, D. A. SIQUEIROS), and Depression-era artists under the sponsorship of the U.S. government (e.g., Ben SHAHN, T. H. BENTON).

Murasaki Shikibu \\mu-'rä-sä-kē-'shē-kē-bu\\ (978?–1014?) Japanese writer. Her real name is unknown. Her *Tale of Genji* (completed c.1010) is a long and complex tale concerned mostly with the many loves of Prince Genji. Supremely sensitive to human emotions and the beauties of nature, it provides delightful glimpses of life at the court of the empress Joto mon'in. It is considered one of the world's oldest and greatest novels.

Murat \\mē-'rä\\, **Joachim** (1767–1815) French soldier and king of Naples (1808–15). He served in Italy and Egypt as a daring cavalry commander, and later aided NAPOLEON in his coup d'état (1799) and married Napoleon's sister Caroline BONAPARTE. After victories at Austerlitz (1805) and

Jena (1806), he was made king of Naples (1808), where he carried out administrative and economic reforms and encouraged Italian nationalism. He led troops in Napoleon's Russian campaign, and supported Napoleon again during the HUNDRED DAYS in 1815, but was defeated with his Neapolitan forces at the Battle of Tolentino, and was later taken prisoner and shot.

Murcia City (pop., 1998 est.: 349,000), capital of MURCIA, SE Spain. The site was settled before the 3rd cent. B.C. In 825 A.D. it was made a provincial Muslim capital by the emir of CÓRDOBA. It was the birthplace of IBN AL-ARABI (1165). The Segura River divides the city into older and newer parts. The 14th-cent. cathedral was restored in the 18th cent. Its silk industry, dating from Moorish times, continues today.

Murcia \'mər-shə\ Autonomous community (pop., 1998 est.: 1,115,000), province, and historical region, SE Spain. It covers 4,369 sq mi (11,316 sq km), and its capital is the city of MURCIA. It was an independent Moorish kingdom until its annexation by CASTILE in 1243. The Segura River flows through its center, irrigating rich farmland and orchards. Its ports of CARTAGENA, Mazarrón, and Aguilas have grown with the development of shipping and mining.

murder See HOMICIDE

Murder, Inc. Popular name for an arm of the U.S. national crime syndicate founded about 1930 in Brooklyn, N.Y., to threaten, maim, or murder designated victims for a price. Its services were available to any syndicate member anywhere in the country; many of its victims were syndicate members. Its principal figures were Louis Buchalter, known as Louis Lepke, and Albert Anastasia. Investigated by Thomas DEWEY, it was exposed in 1940–41 by a former member, Abe "Kid Twist" Reles, who described some 70 murders; he himself died mysteriously in the middle of the investigation.

Murdoch \'mər-ˌdäk\, **(Jean) Iris** (later **Dame Iris**) (1919–1999) British novelist and philosopher. Her novels, which typically have convoluted plots featuring philosophical and comic elements, include *Under the Net* (1954), *A Severed Head* (1961), *A Fairly Honourable Defeat* 1970, *The Black Prince* (1973), and *The Sea, The Sea* (1978). Her other philosophical works include *The Sovereignty of Good* (1970) and *Metaphysics as a Guide to Morals* (1992). Her decline under Alzheimer's disease was chronicled by her husband, the critic John Bayley, in *Elegy for Iris* (1999).

Murdoch, (Keith) Rupert (b.1931) Australian-U.S. newspaper publisher and media entrepreneur. He inherited two Adelaide newspapers in 1954 and boosted their circulation by emphasizing crime, sex, scandal, and sports, while taking an outspokenly conservative editorial stance. He used this approach with soaring success with papers bought in Australia, Britain, and the U.S. by his global media holding company, The News Corporation. He also acquired conventional and respected publications, including *The Times* of London. In the 1980s and '90s he expanded into book and electronic publishing, television, and film production. His holdings include the *New York Post*, Fox, Inc. (see FOX BROADCASTING CO.), and HarperCollins Publishers.

Mures River \'mü-resh\ River, rising in the E CARPATHIAN MTNS., E central Romania. It flows west about 450 mi (725 km) to join the TISZA RIVER at Szeged, Hungary. The Tisza's most important tributary, it is navigable for small boats for more than 200 mi (320 km).

muriatic acid See HYDROCHLORIC ACID

Murillo \mü-'rē-ō, *Engl* myù-'ri-lō\, **Bartolomé Esteban** (c.1618–1682) Spanish painter. The most popular baroque religious painter of 17th-cent. Spain, he is noted for his idealized figures, most of them painted for religious orders and societies. His early works were executed in the naturalistic style of Francisco de ZURBARÁN, but from the 1650s he surpassed the older master in fame and popularity. The softly modeled forms, rich colors, and broad brushwork of the later paintings, such as the *Immaculate Conception* of 1652 (his favorite subject), reveal the influence of 16th-cent. Venetian and Flemish baroque painters. Murillo's works were copied throughout Spain and its empire, and he was the first Spanish painter to achieve fame outside the Spanish world.

Murmansk Seaport (pop., 1997 est.: 394,000), NW Russia. Situated on the BARENTS SEA, about 125 mi (200 km) from Finland and Norway, it is the world's largest city north of the ARCTIC CIRCLE. Its ice-free harbor makes it Russia's only port with unrestricted access to the Atlantic. It served as a major supply base during World War II. In addition to a Russian naval base, it has a large fishing fleet and fish-processing industry.

Muromachi period See ASHIKAGA SHOGUNATE

Murphy, Audie (Leon) (1924–1971) U.S. war hero and actor. Born near Kingston, Texas, he enlisted in the army in 1942 and became the most decorated U.S. soldier of World War II, killing hundreds of Germans and once jumping onto a burning tank destroyer to turn its machine gun on the enemy troops. In 1945 he received the Medal of Honor. After the war he starred in such films as *The Red Badge of Courage* (1951), *To Hell and Back* (1955), and *The Quiet American* (1958). He died when his private plane crashed.

Murray, James (Augustus Henry) (later **Sir James**) (1837–1915) Scottish lexicographer. He taught in a grammar school 1855–85. His *Dialect of the Southern Counties of Scotland* (1873) established him as a leading philologist. He was hired to edit the vast *New English Dictionary on Historical Principles*, later called the *Oxford English Dictionary*, in 1879, and applied himself to the work with legendary energy and resourcefulness. The first volume appeared in 1884, and by his death he had completed about half the dictionary.

Murray River Principal river of Australia. Rising near Mt. KOSCIUSKO, it flows east across SE Australia from the Snowy Mtns. to the Indian Ocean; it is 1,610 mi (2,590 km) long. It forms the boundary between Victoria and NEW S. WALES and then turns south and flows into Encounter Bay through Lake Alexandrina. River shipping was important in the 19th cent. The river valley is of great economic importance, fostering the production of grains, fruit, and wine, and the raising of cattle and sheep.

Murrow, Edward (Egbert) R(oscoe) (1908–1965) U.S. broadcaster. Born in Greensboro, N.C., he became head of CBS's European Bureau in 1937. He became famous for his eyewitness reportage of events leading to and during World War II. After the war, with Fred FRIENDLY, he produced *Hear It Now,* an authoritative radio news digest, and on television the comparable *See It Now*. In the 1950s he was an influential force for the free dissemination of information, producing a notable exposé of the tactics of Sen. Joseph MCCARTHY.

Murrumbidgee River \ˌmə-rəm-'bi-jē\ River, SE NEW S. WALES, Australia. It flows west from the GREAT DIVIDING RANGE near CANBERRA to join the MURRAY RIVER; it is 980 mi (1,578 km) long. The Murrumbidgee Irrigation Area involves more than 1,000 sq mi (2,600 sq km), supporting livestock pastures, grapes, citrus fruits, wheat, cotton, and rice.

Musa \'mü-sä\ *or* **Mansa Musa** (d.1332/37?) Emperor (*mansa*) of the MALI EMPIRE from 1307 (or 1312). Musa left a realm notable for its extent and riches. The splendor of his pilgrimage to Mecca (1324) awakened the world to Mali's stupendous wealth and stimulated a desire among N. Africans and Europeans to locate its source. Under Musa, Mali became one of the largest empires in the world and TOMBOUCTOU a major commercial city.

Muscat See MASQAT

Muscat and Oman See OMAN

muscle Contractile tissue that produces motion for functions including body movements, digestion, focusing, circulation, and body warmth. It can be classified as striated, cardiac, and smooth; or as phasic and tonic (responding quickly or gradually to stimulation, respectively). Striated muscle, whose fibers appear striped under a microscope, is responsible for voluntary movement. Most of these muscles are phasic. They are attached to the skeleton and move the body by contracting in response to signals from the central NERVOUS SYSTEM; contraction is achieved by the sliding of thin filaments (of actin) between thick ones (of myosin); stretch receptors in the tissue provide feedback, allowing smooth motion and fine motor control. The branched fibers of cardiac muscle give it a netlike structure; contraction originates in the heart's muscle tissue itself with a signal

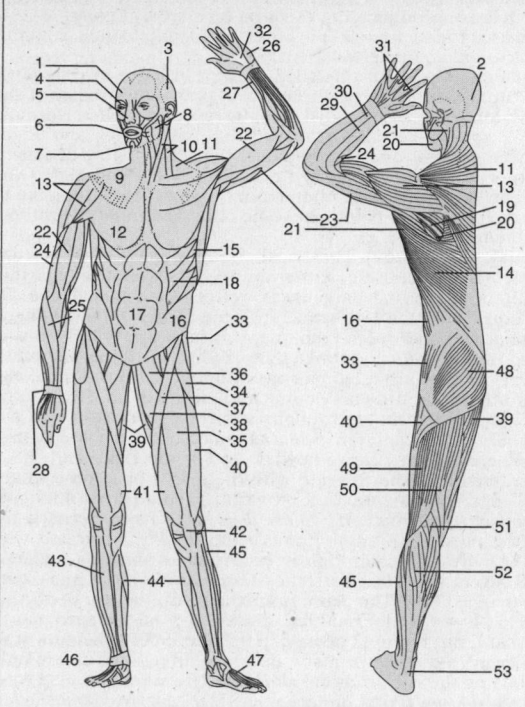

Muscle Major muscles of the human body.
(1) frontalis, (2) occipitalis, (3) temporalis, (4) orbicularis of eye,
(5) nasalis, (6) orbicularis of mouth, (7) mentalis, (8) masseter,
(9) platysma, (10) sternocleidomastoid, (11) trapezius, (12) pectoralis
major, (13) deltoid, (14) latissimus dorsi, (15) anterior serratus,
(16) external oblique, (17) rectus abdominis, (18) internal oblique,
(19) infraspinatus, (20) teres minor, (21) teres major, (22) biceps,
(23) triceps, (24) brachialis, (25) long radial extensor of wrist,
(26) short palmaris, (27) pronator quadratus, (28) annular ligament of
the carpus, (29) common extensor of digits, (30) ulnar extensor of wrist,
(31) tendons of extensors of digits and wrists, (32) palmar aponeurosis,
(33) gluteus medius, (34) tensor of the fascia lata, (35) rectus femoris,
(36) pectineus, (37) sartorius, (38) long adductor of thigh, (39) gracilis,
(40) vastus lateralis, (41) vastus medialis, (42) patella, (43) anterior tibialis,
(44) medial head of gastrocnemius, (45) soleus,
(46) annular ligament of ankle, (47) short extensor, (48) gluteus
maximus, (49) biceps of thigh, (50) semitendinosus, (51) plantaris,
(52) lateral head of gastrocnemius, (53) Achilles' tendon

from the natural pacemaker. Smooth muscle, the muscle of internal organs and blood vessels, is generally involuntary and tonic; its cells can operate either collectively or individually. Disorders of voluntary muscle cause weakening, atrophy, pain, and twitching.

Muscle Shoals Former rapids, TENNESSEE RIVER, NW Alabama. About 37 mi (60 km) long, it was a navigation hazard but is now submerged under at least 9 ft (3 m) of water by dams that eliminated the rapids. Hydroelectric power facilities are administered by the TENNESSEE VALLEY AUTHORITY (TVA). Since the 1960s the city of Muscle Shoals (2000 pop.: 12,000) has been a major center for music recording.

muscovite \\'məs-kə-₁vīt\\ or **common mica** or **potash mica** or **isinglass** Abundant SILICATE MINERAL that contains potassium and aluminum, the most common member of the MICA group. Because it occurs in thin, transparent sheets, it was used in Russia for window panes and became known as Muscovy glass (isinglass). Muscovite is usually colorless. Its low iron content makes it a good electrical and thermal insulator.

muscular dystrophy \\'dis-trə-fē\\ Inherited disease that causes progressive weakness in the skeletal (and occasionally heart) muscle. Muscle tissue degenerates and regenerates randomly and is replaced by scar tissue and fat. There is no specific treatment. Physical therapy, braces, and corrective surgery may help. Duchenne's muscular dystrophy, the most common of the many types, strikes only males. Symptoms start in boys 3–7 years old; muscle wasting progresses from the legs to the arms and then the diaphragm. Pulmonary infection or respiratory failure usually causes death before age 20. Becker's dystrophy, also sex-linked, is less severe and begins later. Patients usually survive into their 30s and 40s. Myotonic muscular dystrophy, which causes difficulty in contracting voluntary muscles, affects adults of both sexes. Limb-girdle dystrophy affects the pelvic or shoulder muscles in both sexes. Facioscapulohumeral (face, shoulder-blade, and upper-arm) dystrophy starts in childhood or adolescence and affects both sexes.

Muse In Greco-Roman religion and myth, any of a group of sister goddesses, daughters of ZEUS and Mnemosyne (Memory). They probably began as the patron goddesses of poets, though later their range was extended to include all the liberal arts and sciences. Nine Muses are usually named: Calliope (heroic or epic poetry), Clio (history), Erato (lyric or love poetry), Euterpe (music or flutes), Melpomene (tragedy), Polyhymnia (sacred poetry or mime), Terpsichore (dancing and choral song), Thalia (comedy), and Urania (astronomy).

museum Public institution dedicated to preserving and interpreting the primary tangible evidence of humans and their environment. Types of museums include general (multidisciplinary) museums, natural-history museums, science and technology museums, history museums, and art museums. In Roman times the word referred to a place devoted to scholarly occupation (see MUSEUM OF ALEXANDRIA). The public museum as it is known today did not develop until the 17th–18th cent. The first organized body to receive a private collection, erect a building to house it, and make it publicly available was Oxford Univ.; the resulting Ashmolean Museum opened in 1683. The 18th cent. saw the opening of such great museums as the BRITISH MUSEUM, LOUVRE, and UFFIZI GALLERY. By the early 19th cent. the granting of public access to formerly private collections had become common. The next 100 years saw the worldwide founding of museums intended for the public. In the 20th cent., museums broadened their roles as educational facilities, sources of leisure activity, and information centers.

Museum of Alexandria Ancient center of classical learning at ALEXANDRIA in Egypt. Organized into faculties and headed by a president-priest, the Museum, with its renowned library, was built near the royal palace either by PTOLEMY II PHILADELPHUS about 280 B.C. or by his father, PTOLEMY I SOTER. The best surviving description is by STRABO. In A.D. 270 its buildings were probably destroyed by ZENOBIA.

Musgrave, Thea (b.1928) Scottish-U.S. composer. She studied with Nadia BOULANGER and Aaron COPLAND, and later taught at colleges in the U.S. Her dramatic concertos often reflect her interest in music's spatial dimension. She is best known for her operas, including *The Voice of Ariadne* (1973), *Mary, Queen of Scots* (1977), and *Simón Bolívar* (1995).

mushroom Fleshy spore-bearing structure of certain fungi (see FUNGUS), typically of the class Basidiomycetes. It arises from the mycelium, which may live hundreds of years or a few months, depending on its food supply. Some species grow cellular strands (hyphae) in all directions, forming a circular mat with a "fairy ring" of fruiting bodies around the outside. Popularly, "mushroom" refers to edible fungi while "toadstool" refers to inedible or poisonous ones, but there is no scientific distinction between the two names. Mushrooms are classified by cap shape. Umbrella-shaped sporophores with spore-shedding gills on the undersurface are found chiefly in the AGARIC family (Agaricaceae). Mushrooms that bear spores in an easily detachable layer on the underside of the cap belong to the family Boletaceae. Together the agarics and boletes include most of the forms known as mushrooms. Mushroom poisoning can cause nau-

M

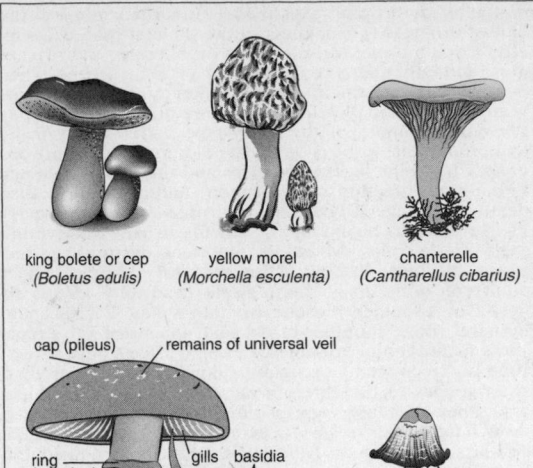

king bolete or cep
(*Boletus edulis*)

yellow morel
(*Morchella esculenta*)

chanterelle
(*Cantharellus cibarius*)

cap (pileus) — remains of universal veil

ring
(annulus)

gills   basidia

stalk
(stipe)

mycelium

basidiospores

gill

meadow mushroom
(*Agaricus campestris*)

shaggy mane
(*Coprinus comatus*)

Mushroom A mushroom typically consists of a stalk (stipe) and a cap (pileus). As the mushroom develops from an underground mycelium and pushes upward, it is protected by a thin membrane (universal veil), which eventually ruptures, leaving fragments on the cap. Another membrane, attaching the cap to the stalk, also ruptures, allowing the cap to expand and leaving a remnant ring (annulus) on the stalk. Radiating rows of gills are found on the cap's undersurface; these bear the club-shaped reproductive structures (basidia) which form minute spores known as basidiospores, of which a single mushroom may produce millions.

sea, diarrhea, vomiting, cramps, hallucinations, coma, and sometimes death.

mushroom poisoning *or* **toadstool poisoning** Sometimes fatal effect of eating any of the 70–80 species of poisonous MUSHROOMS, or toadstools. Many contain toxic ALKALOIDS. The most deadly, *Amanita phalloides* (death cap), causes violent abdominal pain, vomiting, and bloody diarrhea. Severe liver, kidney, and central-nervous-system damage lead to coma. Over half the victims die. Treatments may be effective. *A. muscaria* causes vomiting, diarrhea, excessive perspiration, and confusion, with recovery within 24 hours. *Gyromitra esculenta* toxin is usually destroyed by cooking. Some poisonous mushrooms resemble harmless ones, so extreme caution is needed in wild-mushroom gathering.

Musial \'myü-zē-əl\, **Stan(ley Frank)** (b.1920) U.S. baseball player. Born in Donora, Pa., he played his entire career for the St. Louis Cardinals (1941–63), starting as a pitcher but switching to the outfield and ultimately first base. Popular among fans for his unfailing graciousness, "Stan the Man" became one of the game's great hitters; at his retirement his lifetime totals of hits (3,630) and runs (1,949) were second only to those of Ty COBB, his total of runs batted in (1,951) was the fourth-highest of all time, and his total of extra-base hits (1,477) was unsurpassed.

music Organization of sound. Music most often implies sounds with distinct PITCHES that are arranged into MELODIES and organized into patterns of RHYTHM AND METER. The melody will usually be in a certain KEY or MODE,

and will usually suggest HARMONY that may be made explicit as accompanying CHORDS or COUNTERPOINT. Music is used for such social purposes as worship, dance, communication, and entertainment.

musica ficta (Latin: "feigned music") Practice of unnotated CHROMATICISM in performance of polyphonic music of the Middle Ages and Renaissance. It was left to the performers to "correct" certain INTERVALS, but which ones, and under what circumstances, varied over time. The highly dissonant interval of the diminished 5th (e.g., B–F), considered the "devil in music," was often made "perfect" by flatting the B, and the interval below the tonic often had to be altered to a semitone.

musical (comedy) Theatrical production, normally sentimental and amusing, with a simple but distinctive plot, that offers music and dancing as well as spoken dialogue. Its roots lie in such 18th- and 19th-cent. genres as ballad opera, singspiel, and opéra comique, in which dialogue is mostly spoken. *The Black Crook* (1866), often called the first musical comedy, attracted patrons of opera, serious drama, and BURLESQUE SHOWS. Victor HERBERT, Rudolf FRIML, and Sigmund ROMBERG brought a form of OPERETTA to the U.S. that became an essential source. George M. COHAN ushered in the genre's heyday, and in the 1920s and '30s it entered its richest period with the works of Jerome KERN, George GERSHWIN, Cole PORTER, Richard RODGERS, and Oscar HAMMERSTEIN. *Show Boat* (1927) was perhaps the first musical to employ music thoroughly integrated with the narrative; later tightly constructed musicals included Rodgers and Hammerstein's *Oklahoma!* (1943) and *South Pacific* (1949). The genre flourished with the works of Alan J. LERNER and of Frederick Loewe and of Leonard BERNSTEIN, but began to decline in the late 1960s, when musicals began to diverge in many different directions, as exemplified by the rock musical *Hair* (1967), Andrew LLOYD WEBBER's *Jesus Christ Superstar* (1971), Marvin Hamlisch's *A Chorus Line* (1975), Stephen SONDHEIM's *Sweeney Todd* (1979), and Jonahan Larson's *Rent* (1995).

musical notation System of symbols with which music is written down. There are two basic approaches to notating music. Tablature (seen in guitar chord diagrams) depicts the actions a performer is to take (in particular, showing where to put the fingers to produce a given sound). Symbolic notation describes the sounds themselves. The Western notation system combines rhythmic notation (the appearance of a note indicates its duration) with pitch notation (the line or space on a staff where a note is placed indicates its pitch). Thus, a single symbol shows both pitch and duration, and a string of these symbols notates both melody and rhythm. See diagram on next page.

music hall and variety theater Popular entertainment that featured successive acts by singers, comedians, dancers, and actors. The form derived from the taproom concerts given in city taverns in 18th–19th-cent. England, when tavern owners began to annex nearby buildings as music halls, where drinking and smoking were permitted. The originator of the English music hall was Charles Morton, who built Morton's Canterbury Hall (1852) and Oxford Hall (1861) in London. Leading performers included Lillie LANGTRY, Harry Lauder (1870–1950), and Gracie Fields. Music halls evolved into larger, more respectable variety theaters, such as London's Hippodrome and the Coliseum. Variety acts combined music, comedy acts, and one-act plays and featured such celebrities as Sarah BERNHARDT. See also VAUDEVILLE.

musicology Scholarly study of music. In the late 18th and early 19th cent., such study was done by amateurs. As interest about earlier music grew, greater professionalism was required, including the ability to decipher and assess manuscript sources of both music itself and writing about it. Today musicology combines elements of older disciplines, such as music theory, music history, and sociology, and utilizes the latest scientific methods. The best modern performers continue to use the tools musicology puts at their disposal.

musket Muzzle-loading shoulder firearm developed in 16th-cent. Spain. Muskets were initially fired with matchlocks (which ignited with a slow-burning match), then flintlocks

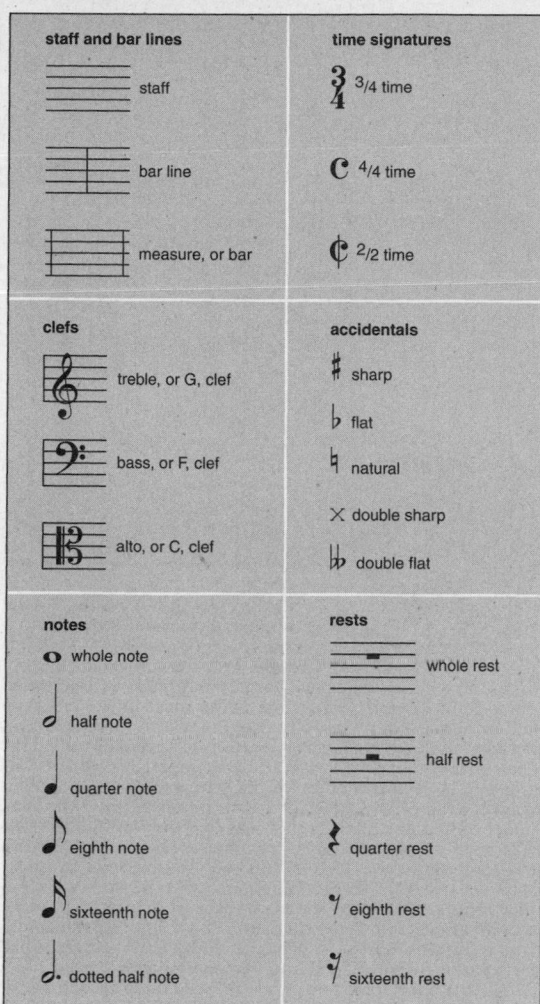

staff and bar lines		time signatures	
	staff	**3/4**	3/4 time
	bar line	**C**	4/4 time
	measure, or bar	**¢**	2/2 time

clefs		accidentals	
	treble, or G, clef	♯	sharp
	bass, or F, clef	♭	flat
		♮	natural
	alto, or C, clef	✕	double sharp
		𝄫	double flat

notes		rests	
𝅝	whole note	▬	whole rest
𝅗𝅥	half note	▬	half rest
𝅘𝅥	quarter note	𝄽	quarter rest
𝅘𝅥𝅮	eighth note	𝄾	eighth rest
𝅘𝅥𝅯	sixteenth note	𝄿	sixteenth rest
𝅗𝅥.	dotted half note		

Musical notation Common symbols used in modern musical notation.

(which struck a spark from flint) in the 17th cent., and finally percussion locks in the early 19th cent. Early muskets often required two people and a portable rest. Typically 5.5 ft (1.7 m) long and weighing about 20 lbs (9 kg), they fired a ball about 175 yards (160 m) with little accuracy. Later types were lighter and able to hit a person at 80–100 yards (75–90 m). The musket was replaced in the mid-19th cent. by the breech-loading RIFLE.

musk ox Arctic RUMINANT (BOVID species *Ovibos moschatus*) with a musky odor, large head, and small ears. The neck, legs, and tail are short. Males stand 5 ft (1.5 m) and may weigh almost 900 lbs (400 kg). Both sexes have horns. The broad-based horns of males, up to 2 ft (60 cm) long, start at the middle of the head, dip downward along the sides, and then curve upward. The shaggy coat reaches nearly to the feet. Musk oxen travel in herds of 20–30, eating lichen and low-growing plants.

muskrat Either of two semiaquatic, brown RODENT species (family Cricetidae) native to marshes, shallow lakes, and streams of N. America. The compact, heavy-bodied muskrat, or musquash *(Ondatra zibethica),* is about 12 in. (30 cm) long, not including the long, scaly, flat tail. The hind feet are partially webbed. Anal sacs produce a musky secretion. The fur is commercially valuable. Muskrats live in either a burrow dug into the bank or a reed-and-rush mound built in the water, and eat mostly sedges, reeds and roots. The round-tailed muskrat, or Florida water rat *(Neofiber alleni),* is smaller.

Muslim Brotherhood *Arabic* al-Ikhwan al-Muslimun. Organization founded in Egypt in 1928 by Hasan al-Banna (1906–1949) that promoted the QURAN and HADITH as the proper basis for society. It quickly gained many followers throughout N. Africa and the Middle East. It became politicized after 1938, rejecting Westernization, modernization, and secularization. Suppressed in Egypt after a 1954 assassination attempt on G. A. NASSER, it operated clandestinely in the 1960s and '70s. In the 1980s it experienced an upsurge, competing in elections in Egypt and Jordan.

Muslim calendar See Muslim CALENDAR

Muslim League *orig.* All India Muslim League. Political group in British India. Founded in 1906 to protect Indian Muslims' rights, it soon adopted self-government for India as its goal, and such leaders as M. A. JINNAH supported Hindu-Muslim unity in an independent India. In 1940, fearing Hindu domination, the league called for a separate nation for India's Muslims. After the creation of Pakistan in 1947, the Muslim League (as the All Pakistan Muslim League) became Pakistan's dominant political party, but it gradually declined in popularity and by the 1970s had disappeared altogether.

mussel Any of numerous BIVALVE species of either the marine family Mytilidae, found worldwide, or the freshwater superfamily Unionacea, called naiads, found mostly in the U.S. and S.E. Asia. Marine mussels are usually wedge-shaped or pear-shaped and 2–6 in. (5–15 cm) long. They often have a hairy covering. The shells of many species are dark blue or greenish brown. Mussels attach themselves to solid objects or to one another, often forming dense clusters. Some burrow into soft mud or wood. Some species are raised commercially for food.

Mussolini, Benito (Amilcare Andrea) (1883–1945) Italian dictator (1922–43). An unruly but intelligent youth, he became an ardent socialist and served as editor of the party newspaper, *Avanti!* (1912–14). When he reversed his opposition to World War I, he was ousted by the party. He founded the pro-war *Il Popolo d'Italia* and served with the Italian army 1915–17. Advocating dictatorship, he formed a political group in 1919 that marked the beginning of FASCISM. A dynamic orator at rallies, he organized the March on ROME (1922) to prevent a Socialist-led general strike. After the government fell, he was appointed prime minister. He obtained a law to establish the Fascists as the majority party and became known as *Il Duce* ("The Leader"). He restored order to the country and introduced social reforms and public-works improvements that won widespread popular support. His dreams of empire led to the invasion of Abyssinia (later Ethiopia) in 1935. Supported in his fascist schemes by Adolf HITLER but wary of German power, Mussolini agreed to the Rome–Berlin Axis and declared war on the Allies in 1940. Italian defeats led to growing disillusionment with Mussolini, and after the Allied invasion of Sicily (1943) the Fascist Grand Council dismissed him from office. Imprisoned, he was rescued by German commandos, then became head of the Hitler-installed puppet government at Salò in N Italy. Trying to escape to Austria, he was captured and executed by Italian partisans.

Mussorgsky \mu̇-'sȯrg-skē\, **Modest (Petrovich)** (1839–1881) Russian composer. Inspired by folktales, he composed without training in his teens before meeting several of the composers with whom he later made up the MIGHTY FIVE. He resigned from his military regiment after a breakdown in 1858 and held a series of government jobs, but his worsening alcoholism eventually made him unemployable. Personal decline was accompanied by maturity as a composer, and he wrote his major works, including *Night on Bald Mountain* (1867), the great opera *Boris Godunov* (1868), and the famous piano cycle *Pictures at an Exhibition* (1874). His opera *Khovanshchina* was left unfinished when he died at 42.

mustard family Family Brassicaceae (or Cruciferae), composed of 350 genera of mostly herbaceous plants with peppery-flavored leaves. The pungent seeds of some species are spices. Mustard flowers take the form of a Greek cross,

with four petals, usually white, yellow, or lavender, and an equal number of sepals. The seeds are produced in podlike fruits. Many members of the mustard family have been extensively altered and domesticated by humans. The most important genus is BRASSICA; TURNIPS, RADISHES, and RUTABAGAS are also members of the family. As a spice, mustard is sold in seed, powder, or paste form.

mutagen \\'myü-tə-jen\\ Any agent capable of causing MUTATION, that is, altering a cell's genetic makeup by changing the structure of the hereditary material, DNA. Many forms of electromagnetic RADIATION are mutagenic, as are various chemical compounds. The effects of some mutagens are increased or suppressed in some organisms by the presence of certain other, nonmutagenic substances.

Mutanabbi \\ˌmü-tä-ˈnáb-bē\\, **(Abu al-Tayyib Ahmad ibn Husayn) al-** (915–965) Poet regarded by many as the greatest in the Arabic language. Born in Iraq, he received an education because of his poetic talent. He lived among the Bedouin and, claiming to be a prophet, led an unsuccessful Muslim revolt in Syria. He later became a wandering poet. He primarily wrote PANEGYRICS in a flowery style marked by improbable metaphors. Proud and arrogant in tone, his verse is crafted with consummate skill and artistry.

mutation Alteration in the genetic material of a cell that is transmitted to the cell's offspring. Mutations may be spontaneous, or induced by outside factors (MUTAGENS). They take place in the GENES, occurring when one base is added, deleted, or substituted for another in the sequence of bases that determines the GENETIC CODE. Many mutations are harmless; some have serious consequences. Only mutations that occur in the sex cells (EGGS or SPERM) can be transmitted to the individual's offspring. Alterations caused by these mutations are usually harmful. In the rare instances in which a mutation produces a beneficial change, the percentage of organisms with this gene will tend to increase through NATURAL SELECTION until the mutated gene becomes the norm in the population. In this way, beneficial mutations serve as the raw material of EVOLUTION.

mutiny Any concerted resistance to lawful military authority. Mutiny was formerly regarded as a most serious offense, especially aboard ships at sea. Wide disciplinary powers were given the commanding officer, including the power to inflict CAPITAL PUNISHMENT without a COURT-MARTIAL. With the development of radio communications, the threat diminished and harsh punishment was prohibited in the absence of a court-martial.

Mutsuhito See MEIJI EMPEROR

mutual fund *or* **unit trust** *or* **open-end trust** Company that invests the funds of its subscribers in diversified SECURITIES and issues units representing shares in those holdings. It differs from an investment trust, which issues shares in the company itself. While investment trusts have a fixed capitalization and a limited number of shares for sale, mutual funds make a continuous offering of new shares and redeem their shares on demand, both at net asset value.

Muybridge \\'mī-ˌbrij\\, **Eadweard** *orig.* Edward James Muggeridge (1830–1904) British-U.S. photographer. He emigrated to the U.S. as a young man, and in 1868 his photos of Yosemite Valley made him famous. Hired by Leland STANFORD to prove that a trotting horse lifted all four legs simultaneously, he developed a special fast shutter for his battery of 12–24 cameras, and in 1877 was able to prove Stanford right. He lectured widely on animal locomotion, using his zoopraxiscope, a predecessor of the movie projector. His photographic studies of human movement (1884–87) have been useful to artists and scientists.

Myanmar \\'myän-ˌmär\\ *or* **Burma** *officially* **Union of Myanmar** Nation, S.E. Asia, on the Bay of BENGAL and the Andaman Sea. Area: 261,789 sq mi (678,034 sq km). Population (2000): 41,735,000. Capital: YANGON (Rangoon). Inhabitants are chiefly Burman; others include Shan, Karen, and Chin. Languages: Burmese (official), many indigenous languages. Religions: Buddhism (the majority), Christianity, animism, Islam, and Hinduism. Currency: kyat. Myanmar may be divided into four main regions: the N mountains, the W mountains, the central lowlands, and the Shan Plateau in the east. Its major rivers are the IRRAWADDY and the SALWEEN. Myanmar's tropical climate is greatly influ-

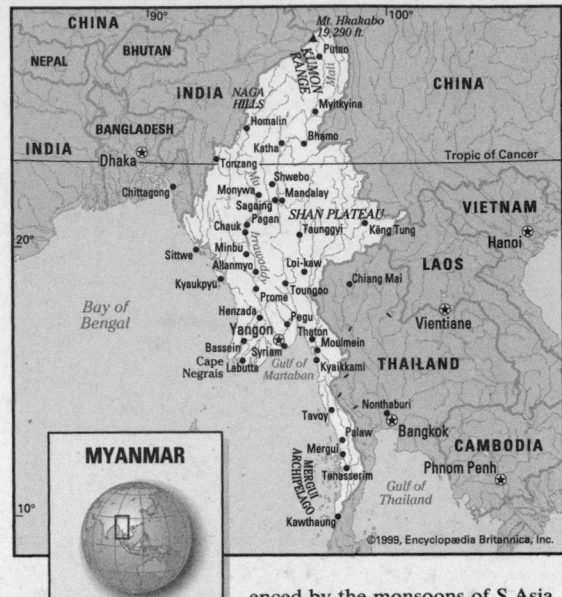

enced by the monsoons of S Asia, and only about one-sixth of its extremely mountainous land is arable. It has a centrally planned, developing economy that is largely nationalized and based on agriculture and trade. Rice is the most important crop and principal export; teak is also important. It is ruled by a military regime; its head of state and government is the chairman of the State Peace and Development Council. The area was long inhabited, with the Mon and Pyu states dominant after the 1st cent. A.D. It was united in the 11th cent. under a Burmese dynasty that was overthrown by the Mongols in the 13th cent. The Portuguese, Dutch, and English traded there in the 16th–17th cent. The modern Burmese state was founded in the 18th cent. by ALAUNGPAYA. Conflict with the British over ASSAM resulted in a series of wars, and Myanmar fell to the British in 1885. Under British control, it became Burma, a province of India. It was occupied by Japan in World War II and became independent in 1948. A military coup took power in 1962 and nationalized major economic sectors. Civilian unrest in the 1980s led to antigovernment rioting that was suppressed by force. In 1990 opposition parties won in national elections, but the army continued in control. Trying to negotiate for an end to the brutally repressive regime, AUNG SAN SUU KYI was awarded the Nobel Peace Prize in 1991.

myasthenia gravis \\ˌmī-əs-ˈthē-nē-ə-ˈgra-vəs\\ Chronic AUTOIMMUNE DISEASE causing MUSCLE weakness. Muscles weaken with repeated use but regain their strength after rest. The pattern varies, but usually muscles used in eye movements, facial expressions, chewing, swallowing, and respiration are affected first, then neck, trunk, and limb muscles. Severe cases impede breathing. Anticholinesterase drugs stimulate nerve-impulse transmission, and corticosteroids may help. Remission lasting several years may occur.

Mycenae \\mī-ˈsē-nē\\ Prehistoric city, NE PELOPONNESE, Greece. A natural rock citadel, it was the legendary capital of AGAMEMNON. It flourished during the BRONZE AGE, building the distinctive MYCENAEAN civilization. It was at its height in the Aegean around 1400 B.C. and declined about 1100 B.C. with the invasion of the DORIANS from the north. Ruins include the Lion Gate, acropolis, granary, and several royal tombs.

Mycenaeans \\ˌmī-sə-ˈnē-ənz\\ Warlike Indo-European peoples who entered Greece from the north starting around 1900 B.C. and established a BRONZE AGE culture on the mainland and nearby islands. Their culture was dependent on that of the MINOANS of Crete, who for a time politically

MYANMAR

Scale 1: 32,508,000
0   150   300 mi
0   150 300 450 km

©1999, Encyclopædia Britannica, Inc.

dominated them. They threw off Minoan control around 1400 and were dominant in the Aegean until around 1150. By the 2nd cent. A.D., MYCENAE was in ruins. Mycenaean myths and legends lived on through oral transmission into later stages of Greek civilization and form the basis of Homeric epic and Greek tragedy. Their language is believed to be the most ancient form of Greek.

mycobacteria \ˌmī-kō-bak-ˈtir-ē-ə\ Rod-shaped gram-positive (see GRAM STAIN) BACTERIA of the genus *Mycobacterium.* The two most important species cause TUBERCULOSIS and LEPROSY in humans; another causes tuberculosis in both cattle and humans. Most are found in soil and water in a free-living form, or in diseased tissue of animals. Various antibiotics have had some success against mycobacterial infections.

mycology \mī-ˈkä-lə-jē\ Study of fungi (see FUNGUS), including MUSHROOMS and YEASTS. Many fungi are useful in medicine and industry. Fungi were the initial source of such antibiotic drugs as PENICILLIN, cephalosporin, and griseofulvin. Mycology also has important applications in the dairy, wine, and baking industries and in the production of dyes and inks.

mycoplasma \ˌmī-kō-ˈplaz-mə\ Any of the BACTERIA of the genus *Mycoplasma,* among the smallest of bacterial organisms. Mycoplasma species are gram-negative (see GRAM STAIN) and do not require oxygen. They are colonial microorganisms that lack cell walls. They are parasites of joints and the mucous membranes lining the respiratory, genital, or digestive tracts of cud-chewing animals, carnivores, rodents, and humans. They excrete toxic by-products that accumulate in the host's tissues and cause damage. One species causes a widespread but rarely fatal pneumonia in humans.

myeloid tissue See BONE MARROW

My Lai incident \ˈmē-ˈlī\ (Mar. 16, 1968) Massacre of 502 unarmed villagers by U.S. soldiers in the village of Song My during the VIETNAM WAR. William Calley was the platoon leader who directed the killing in the hamlet of My Lai, where soldiers shot men, women, and children. The incident was initially covered up by high-ranking Army officers. Calley was tried and sentenced to life in prison, but Pres. Richard NIXON intervened and he was paroled after three years. The massacre shocked the U.S. public and contributed to opposition to the war.

mynah *or* **myna** \ˈmī-nə\ Any of several Asian songbird species of the STARLING family (Sturnidae). The hill mynah (*Gracula religiosa*) of S Asia, called the grackle in India, is glossy black with white wing patches and yellow wattles. In the wild, it chuckles and shrieks; caged, it learns to imitate human speech far better than its chief rival, the gray PARROT. The common, or Indian, mynah (*Acridotheres tristis*) was introduced into Australia, New Zealand, and Hawaii. The crested mynah (*A. cristatellus*) is native to China and Indonesia.

myocardial infarction \ˌmī-ə-ˈkär-dē-əl-in-ˈfärk-shən\ *or* **heart attack** Death of a section of HEART muscle when its blood supply is cut off, usually by a blood clot in a coronary artery narrowed by ARTERIOSCLEROSIS. HYPERTENSION, DIABETES MELLITUS, high CHOLESTEROL, cigarette SMOKING, and CORONARY HEART DISEASE increase the risk. Symptoms include severe chest pain, often radiating to the left arm, and shortness of breath. Up to 20% of victims die before reaching the hospital. Treatment aims to limit the area of tissue death (infarct) and prevent and treat complications. Thrombolytic (clot-dissolving) drugs may be administered. BETA-BLOCKERS alleviate pain and slow the heart rate. Follow-up may include drugs, exercise programs, and counseling on diet and lifestyle changes. See also ANGIOPLASTY, CORONARY BYPASS.

Myra \ˈmī-rə\ Ancient city, Lycia, S coast of ASIA MINOR, now SW Turkey. Ancient ruins dating from the 5th–3rd cent. B.C. include an acropolis, a magnificent theater, and rock-cut tombs resembling wooden houses and shrines. St. NICHOLAS was bishop of the city in the 4th cent. A.D.

Myrdal \ˈmūͤr-ˌdäl, *Engl* ˈmir-ˌdäl\, **(Karl) Gunnar** (1898–1987) Swedish economist and sociologist. He taught at Stockholm Univ. 1933–67. He explored the social and economic problems of blacks in the U.S. (1938–40) and in 1944

published the classic study *An American Dilemma,* which theorizes that poverty breeds poverty. He argued elsewhere that rich and poor countries, rather than converging economically, might well diverge, the poor countries becoming poorer as the rich countries enjoyed economies of scale and the poor ones were forced to rely on primary products. In 1974 he shared the Nobel Prize with Friedrich von HAYEK. His wife, Alva Myrdal (1902–1986), was a sociologist, diplomat, U.N. administrator, and antiwar activist; she shared the 1982 Nobel Peace Prize with Alfonso García Robles (1911–1991).

Myron \ˈmī-rən\ (c.480–440 B.C.) Greek sculptor. Considered by the ancients one of the most versatile and innovative of all Attic sculptors, he was the first Greek sculptor to combine a mastery of movement with a gift for harmonious composition. Working almost exclusively in bronze, he is best known for his studies of athletes in action, particularly the *Discobolos* (*Discus Thrower,* c.450 B.C.).

myrtle Any of the evergreen shrubs in the genus *Myrtus* (family Myrtaceae). Most occur in S. America, some in Australia and New Zealand. Common myrtle (*M. communis*) is native to the Mediterranean and the Middle East and is cultivated elsewhere.

Myron, "Discobolos," c.450 B.C., Roman copy

Other plants known as myrtle include the MOUNTAIN LAUREL and PERIWINKLE. The family Myrtaceae, commonly called the myrtle family, includes the plants that produce the spices ALLSPICE and CLOVES, and the genus *Eucalyptus.*

Mysore \mī-ˈsōr\ City (pop., 1991: 607,000), S Karnataka state, S India. Situated midway between the KAVERI and Kabbani rivers, the city was the capital of the princely state of Mysore 1799–1831, then was occupied by the British. It is an important industrial center. Sites of interest include the 17th-cent. British residency, the maharaja's palace, the Univ. of Mysore (founded 1916), and a monolith representing Nandi, the sacred bull of SHIVA.

mystery play Vernacular drama of the Middle Ages. It developed from the liturgical drama, and usually represented a biblical subject. In the 13th cent., craft guilds began producing mystery plays at sites removed from the church, adding apocryphal and satirical elements to the dramas. In England groups of 25–50 plays were later organized into lengthy cycles, such as the Chester plays and the Wakefield plays. In France and Italy they were acted on stages with scenery representing heaven, earth, and hell. Technical flourishes such as flying angels and fire-spouting devils kept the spectators' attention. See also MIRACLE PLAY, MORALITY PLAY.

mystery religions Secret cults of the Greco-Roman world. They reached their peak in Greece in the first three centuries A.D. Their members met secretly to share meals and take part in dances and ceremonies, especially initiation rites. The cult of DEMETER produced the most famous of the mystery religions, the ELEUSINIAN MYSTERIES. Festivals of DIONYSUS included wine, choral singing, sexual activity, and mime. The Orphic cult, by contrast, based on writings attributed to ORPHEUS, required chastity and abstinence. Mystery cults also attached to ATTIS, ISIS, and others.

mystery story Work of fiction in which the evidence related to a crime or to a mysterious event is so presented that the reader has an opportunity to consider solutions to the problem, the author's solution being the final phase of the piece. The mystery story is an age-old popular genre; elements of mystery may be present in narratives of horror, pseudoscientific fantasies, crime stories, or any situation involving an enigma. See also DETECTIVE STORY, GOTHIC NOVEL.

mysticism Spiritual quest for union with the divine, found in all major religions. HINDUISM, with its goal of absorption

of the soul in the All, is inherently predisposed to mystical experience. BUDDHISM emphasizes MEDITATION as a means of moving toward NIRVANA. In ISLAM, SUFISM employs metaphors of intoxication and love to express the desire for union with the divine. In JUDAISM, mysticism found special expression in the KABBALA and in HASIDISM. Mysticism has appeared intermittently in CHRISTIANITY, notably in the writings of St. AUGUSTINE, St. TERESA OF ÀVILA, and Meister ECKHART.

myth Traditional story of ostensibly historical events that serves to unfold part of the worldview of a people or explain a practice, belief, or natural phenomenon. Myths relate the events and deeds of gods or superhuman beings that are outside ordinary human life and yet basic to it. These events are usually set at the beginning of creation or at an early stage of prehistory. A people's myths are usually closely related to their religious beliefs and rituals. The modern study of myth arose with early-19th-cent. ROMANTICISM. J. G. FRAZER and others later employed a more comparative approach. Sigmund FREUD viewed myth as an expression of repressed ideas, a view later expanded by C. G. JUNG in his theory of the "collective unconscious" and the mythic ARCHETYPES that arise out of it. Bronislaw MALINOWSKI emphasized how myth fulfills common social functions, providing a model or "charter" for human behavior. Claude LÉVI-STRAUSS discerned underlying structures in myths throughout the world. Features of myth are shared by other kinds of literature. Origin tales explain the source or causes of various aspects of nature or human society and life. FAIRY TALES deal with extraordinary beings and events but lack the authority of myth. SAGAS and EPICS claim authority and truth but reflect specific historical settings.

Mytilene See LESBOS

Myxomycetes See SLIME MOLD

myxovirus \ˌmik-sō-ˈvī-rəs\ Any of a group of VIRUSES that are agents of INFLUENZA and can cause the common COLD, MUMPS, and MEASLES in humans, canine DISTEMPER, rinderpest in cattle, and Newcastle disease in fowl. The virus particle is variable in shape from spheroidal to threadlike, studded with spikelike protein projections; it contains RNA. These viruses react with a protein on the surface of red blood cells.

NAACP *in full* **National Association for the Advancement of Colored People** Oldest and largest U.S. civil-rights organization. It was founded in 1909 to secure political, educational, social, and economic equality for blacks; W. E. B. DU BOIS was among its 60 founders. Its most successful efforts have been lawsuits, political activity, and public-education programs. Its independent Legal Defense and Education Fund sued for school desegregation in *Brown vs. Board of Education* (1954), argued by its general counsel Thurgood MARSHALL. Its goal of desegregating the armed forces was achieved in 1948.

Nabis \'nä-bēz\ (from Hebrew, *navi*, "prophet, seer") Group of French artists who paved the way for the development of abstract art in the early 20th cent. The Nabis preached that a work of art is the visual expression of an artist's synthesis of nature and his or her personal aesthetic. They were influenced by Paul GAUGUIN, Japanese woodcuts, Symbolist painting, and the Pre-Raphaelites. Paul Sérusier (1865–1927), the group's founder, painted the first Nabi work, *Landscape at the Bois d'Amour at Pont-Aven* (also called *Talisman;* 1888). Members included Pierre BONNARD, Édouard VUILLARD, and Aristide MAILLOL.

Nabisco See RJR NABISCO, INC.

Nabokov \nə-'bȯ-kəf, 'na-bə-ˌkȯf\, **Vladimir (Vladimirovich)** (1899–1977) Russian-U.S.-Swiss novelist and critic. Born to an aristocratic family, he had an English-speaking governess. He left Russia permanently in 1919. Initially a poet, by 1925 he had turned to prose. His life before coming to the U.S. in 1940 is recalled in his superb autobiography, *Speak, Memory* (1951). Beginning with *King, Queen, Knave* (1928), his writing began to feature intricate stylistic devices. His novels are principally concerned with the problem of art itself, presented in various disguises, as in *Invitation to a Beheading* (1938). His novels written in English include the notorious and greatly admired best-seller *Lolita* (1955), which

Vladimir Nabokov, 1968

brought him wealth and international fame; *Pale Fire* (1962); and *Ada* (1969). His critical works include a translation of Aleksandr PUSHKIN's *Eugene Onegin* (4 vols., 1964).

Nadar \nȧ-'dȧr\ *orig.* Gaspard-Félix Tournachon (1820–1910) French photographer, caricaturist, and writer. In 1842 he settled in Paris and began selling caricatures to humor magazines. By 1853 he had become an expert photographer and had opened a portrait studio. His studies of prominent Parisians such as Charles BAUDELAIRE (1855) and Eugène DELACROIX (1855) were exceptional in their naturalness. His studio became a favorite meeting place of the Paris intelligentsia, and was the site of the first Impressionist exhibit. A tireless innovator, in 1858 he made the first successful aerial photograph, from a balloon. He also wrote novels, essays, satires, and autobiographical notes.

Nader, Ralph (b.1934) U.S. consumer advocate. Born in Winsted, Conn., he began working in public-interest law in Washington, D.C., in 1963. His best-selling book *Unsafe at Any Speed* (1965) led directly to the passage of national auto-safety standards. He and his associates, known as "Nader's Raiders," then turned their attention to other consumer, safety, and environmental issues. He was instrumental in the passage of the Freedom of Information Act (1966) and in establishing OSHA, the Consumer Product Safety Commission, and the ENVIRONMENTAL PROTECTION AGENCY. He also founded the consumer organization Public Citizen and the U.S. Public Interest Research Group, an umbrella organization for other public-interest research groups. His presidential campaign in 2000 won 2.6% of the vote and influenced the outcome of the race.

NAFTA See NORTH AMERICAN FREE TRADE AGREEMENT

naga \'nä-gə\ In Hindu and Buddhist mythology, a semidivine being, half human and half serpent. Nagas can assume either wholly human or wholly serpentine form. They live in an underground kingdom filled with beautiful palaces adorned with gems. BRAHMA is said to have commanded them to bite only the truly evil or those destined to die prematurely. They are also associated with sources of water and are regarded as guardians of treasure.

Naga Hills Hill region, India and Myanmar. A N extension of the Arakan Yoma system, the densely forested hills reach a height of 12,552 ft (3,826 m) at Mt. Saramati on the frontier. The area is inhabited by villages of Naga tribes.

Nagasaki City and seaport (pop., 1995: 439,000), W KYUSHU, Japan. It was the only Japanese port open to foreign trade 1639–1859. After 1639, only the Dutch, Chinese, and Koreans were allowed into the harbor. In the 19th cent. it was the winter port of the Russian Asian fleet. It became a major shipbuilding center in the early 20th cent. In 1945 the second atomic bomb was dropped there by the U.S. in WORLD WAR II, killing about 39,000 people and injuring about 25,000 others. The bomb also destroyed about 40% of its buildings. The city has been rebuilt and is a spiritual center for movements to ban NUCLEAR WEAPONS.

Nag Hammadi \'näg-häm-'ma-dē\ Town in Upper Egypt on the Nile. In 1945 a collection of 13 codices containing 53 Gnostic texts was found nearby. Written in Coptic, the texts were copied in the 4th cent. They include accounts of the life of JESUS and his sayings after his resurrection, predictions of the APOCALYPSE, and theological treatises. The only surviving documents written by Gnostics themselves, they constitute a major source of knowledge about GNOSTICISM.

Nagorno-Karabakh Region (pop., 1991 est.: 193,000), SW Azerbaijan. It occupies 1,700 sq mi (4,400 square km) on the Karabakh Range. Russia annexed it from Persia in 1813, and in 1923 it became an autonomous province of the Azerbaijan S.S.R. In 1988 its Armenian majority demonstrated against Azerbaijani rule, and in 1991, after the breakup of the U.S.S.R. brought independence to Armenia and Azerbaijan, war broke out between the two ethnic groups. Since 1994 it has been held by ethnic Armenians, though officially it remains part of Azerbaijan.

Nagoya City (pop., 1995: 2,152,000), S HONSHU, Japan. It is one of Japan's leading industrial cities. Nagoya dates from 1610, when a great castle was erected by the Owari branch of the TOKUGAWA SHOGUNATE; the castle was destroyed during World War II and rebuilt in 1959. The city's institutions include Nagoya Univ. and the Tokugawa Art Museum. The Atsuta Shrine and the Ise Shrine are the oldest and most highly esteemed SHINTO shrines in Japan.

Nagpur \'näg-,pûr\ City (pop., 1991: 1,625,000), NE Maharashtra state, India. It is situated almost at the geographic center of India. Founded in the 18th cent., it became the capital of members of the Maratha Confederacy. It is dominated by the former British fort built at its center.

nagual \nä-'gwäl\ *or* **nahual** \nä-'wäl\ In some Mesoamerican religions, a personal guardian spirit that resides in an animal. The person who wishes to find his nagual goes to sleep in an isolated spot, and the animal that appears in a dream or that confronts him when he awakens will thereafter be his guardian spirit. In some areas, nagual refers to the animal into which men with magical powers can transform themselves to do evil.

Nagy \'näd^y\, **Imre** (1896–1958) Hungarian politician. He fought in World War I, was captured by the Russians, and joined the Red Army. He lived in Moscow 1929–44, then returned to Hungary under the Soviet occupation and held several ministerial posts. An advocate for peasants' rights, he became premier (1953–55) but was ousted for his independent ideas. Premier again during the HUNGARIAN REVOLUTION (1956), he made an unsuccessful appeal to the West for help against the invading Soviet troops, but was arrested, tried, and executed.

Nagy, Laszlo Moholy- See Laszlo MOHOLY-NAGY

Nahua \'nä-wə\ Indian population of Mexico and Central America, of whom the AZTECS are the best known. Modern-day Nahua are agriculturalists and skilled weavers, using fibers of the maguey plant, wool, and cotton. Though they profess Roman Catholicism, the Nahua believe in witchcraft and recognize a variety of supernatural beings. See also NAHUATL LANGUAGE.

nahual See NAGUAL

Nahuatl language \'nä-,wä-t^əl\ UTO-AZTECAN LANGUAGE of Mexico with more than a million speakers in various dialects. Nahuatl was a main language of pre-Conquest central Mexico, including Tenochtitlán (now MEXICO CITY), the capital of the AZTEC empire. Soon after the Conquest in the 1520s, Nahuatl began to be written in a Spanish-based spelling, and an abundance of documents survive from the colonial period.

Nahum \'nä-(h)əm\ (late 7th cent. B.C.) One of the 12 Minor Prophets in the OLD TESTAMENT, traditional author of the Book of Nahum. (His prophecy is part of a larger book, The Twelve, in the Jewish canon.) His subject is the collapse of the Assyrian empire and the fall of its capital, NINEVEH (612 B.C.), which he views as a demonstration of God's desire to punish Israel's longtime enemies.

nail Structure made of KERATIN that grows on the end of each finger and toe. Nails consist of a root, under the skin; a translucent plate, attached to a nail bed beneath; and a free edge. Nail plate cells are produced at the root and pushed forward as new cells form behind them. They die as they reach the free edge and lose contact with the richly vascularized nail bed, which supplies them with nutrients. Fingernails grow continuously at about 0.5 mm per week; toenails grow more slowly. Nails help the fingers pry, pick up small objects, and scratch.

Nain brothers, Le See LE NAIN BROTHERS

Naipaul \'nī-,pól\, **V(idiadhar) S(urajprasad)** (*later* **Sir Vidiadhar**) (b.1932) Trinidadian-British novelist. Of Indian descent, Naipaul left Trinidad in 1950 to settle in England. He won critical recognition with *A House for Mr. Biswas* (1961), about an immigrant's attempt to assert his identity and independence. Other novels that explore, in an often harshly critical tone, the disintegration and alienation typical of postcolonial nations include *In a Free State* (1971; Booker Prize), *A Bend in the River* (1979), and *The Enigma of Arrival* (1987). His nonfiction works include several studies of India and the Mideast. Naipaul received the Nobel Prize in 2001.

Nairobi \nī-'rō-bē\ City (pop., 1999: 1,505,000), capital of Kenya. It is located in S central Kenya at an elevation of about 5,500 ft (1,680 m). Founded around 1899, it became the capital of BRITISH E. AFRICA in 1905. When Kenya gained independence in 1963, it remained the capital, with its area greatly expanded by the new constitution. It is Kenya's principal commercial and industrial city, producing beverages, processed food, cigarettes, and furniture. The city exports many products via the port of MOMBASA.

Noted institutions include the Univ. of Nairobi and the National Museum of Kenya. Tourism is important, and nearby Nairobi National Park attracts many visitors.

Naismith \'nā-,smith, 'nāz-məth\, **James A.** (1861–1939) Canadian-U.S. inventor of BASKETBALL. Born in Almonte, Ontario, he studied theology. At the YMCA Training School (later Springfield College) in Springfield, Mass. (1890–95), he was asked to devise a new indoor winter sport. His new game called for nine players per team and the use of peach baskets as goals. He later coached basketball at the Univ. of Kansas (1898–1937). He later invented the protective helmet for football players. The Naismith Memorial Basketball Hall of Fame was incorporated in Springfield in 1959.

Najd See NEJD

Namath \'nā-məth\, **Joe** (*orig.* Joseph William) (b.1943) U.S. football quarterback. Born in Beaver Falls, Pa., he developed his quarterback skills at the Univ. of Alabama. An exceptional passer, in his third season with the New York Jets (1965–77) he threw for a record 4,007 yards. Though long hampered by knee injuries, he set seasonal and career records for most games with 300 yards or more gained in passing.

Namib Desert \'nä-mib\ Desert region, along the entire coast of Namibia. It is about 800 mi (1,300 km) long and 30–100 mi (50–160 km) wide. It is a smooth platform of bedrock of various types and ages. In the S half the platform is covered with sand. The E part, the Inner Namib, supports large numbers of antelope. The shore area has a dense population of marine birds, including flamingos, pelicans, and penguins.

Namibia \nə-'mi-bē-ə\ *officially* **Republic of Namibia** *formerly* (1915–68) **South-West Africa** Nation, SW coast of Africa. Area: 318,580 sq mi (825,118 sq km). Population (2000): 1,771,000. Capital: WINDHOEK. More than half the people are Ovambo. Others include Nama, Kavango, Herero, and San. Languages: English (official), Afrikaans, Bantu,

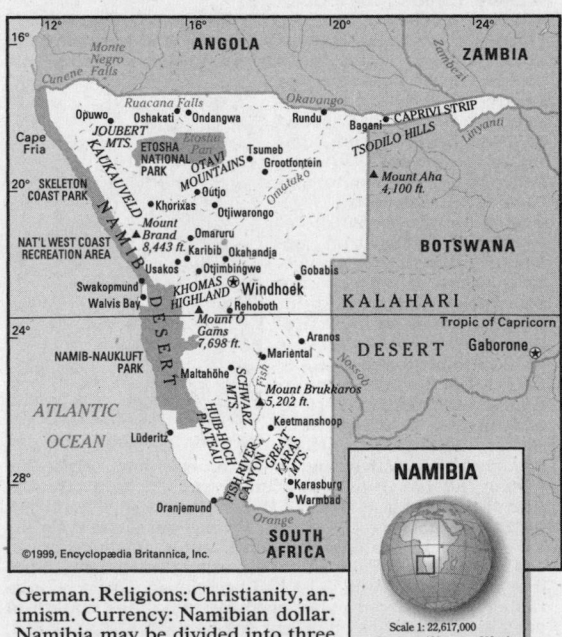

©1999, Encyclopædia Britannica, Inc.

NAMIBIA

Scale 1: 22,617,000

German. Religions: Christianity, animism. Currency: Namibian dollar. Namibia may be divided into three broad regions: the NAMIB DESERT, the Central Plateau, and the KALAHARI DESERT. The economy is based largely on agriculture and on the production and export of diamonds. It is a republic with two legislative houses; its head of state and government is the president. Long inhabited by indigenous peoples, it was explored by the Portuguese in the late 15th cent. In 1885 it was annexed by Germany as German Southwest Africa. It was captured in World War I by S. Africa, which received it as a mandate from the LEAGUE OF NATIONS in 1918 and refused to give it up after World War II. A U.N. resolution in 1966 ending the mandate was challenged by S. Africa in the 1970s and '80s. Through long negotiations involving many factions and interests, it achieved independence in 1990.

Nanak \'nä-nək\ (1469–1539) Indian founder of SIKHISM. Born into a Hindu merchant caste, he underwent a spiritual experience that caused him to leave his job and family and begin a 20-year phase of travel. He eventually settled in Kartarpur, a village in Punjab, to which he attracted many disciples, and became the first GURU of the Sikhs. His doctrine stressed the unity and uniqueness of God and offered salvation through disciplined meditation on the divine name. It rejected all external aids such as idols, temples, mosques, scriptures, and set prayers.

Nanchang or **Nan-ch'ang** City (pop., 1999 est.: 1,265,000), capital of Jiangxi province, SE China. An old walled city, it was founded in 201 B.C. In A.D. 959 under the TANG regime, it became the S capital. At the end of the MONGOL period it was a battleground between the founder of the MING DYNASTY and local warlords. Nanchang suffered from the TAIPING REBELLION. In 1927 it was the site of revolutionary activities of the Chinese Communist Party. Since 1949 it has become industrialized.

Nan-ching See NANJING

Nanga Parbat \'nəŋ-gə-'pər-bət\ Peak, W HIMALAYAS. The world's 10th-highest mountain, it is located in the region of KASHMIR under Pakistani control. Severe weather and frequent avalanches caused the deaths of at least 31 climbers before Hermann Buhl (1924–1957) reached the 26,660-ft (8,126-m) summit in 1953.

Nangnang or **Lo-lang** Colony of HAN-DYNASTY China in N Korea, near modern-day Pyongyang, from which the Chinese incorporated S Korea and parts of Japan into their sphere of influence. From 108 B.C. the Chinese maintained a presence there for 400 years, introducing the local people to wet-rice cultivation, iron technology, and high-fired ceramic technology.

Nanjing or **Nan-ching** \'nän-'jiŋ\ or **Nanking** \'nan-'kiŋ\ formerly **Chian-ning** \'jyän-'niŋ\ City (pop., 1999 est.: 2,389,000), capital of Jiangsu province, E central China. Located on the CHANG (Yangtze) River, northwest of SHANGHAI, the site has been inhabited for thousands of years. The present city was the capital of the MING DYNASTY 1368–1421. Taken by the British in the OPIUM WARS of 1842, it was largely destroyed during the TAIPING REBELLION, 1853–64. It was the GUOMINDANG capital 1928–37, then was taken by the Japanese. It was the site of the NANJING MASSACRE in the SINO–JAPANESE WAR. It is a port city and a major industrial center with a university and several colleges.

Nanjing, Treaty of (Aug. 29, 1842) Treaty that ended the first OPIUM WAR, the first of the unequal treaties between China and foreign imperialist powers. China paid the British an indemnity, ceded the territory of Hong Kong, and agreed to establish a "fair and reasonable" tariff. British merchants, who had previously been allowed to trade only at Guangzhou (Canton), were now permitted to trade at five "treaty ports" and with whomever they pleased. The treaty was supplemented in 1843 to grant Britain any rights in China that China might grant to other nations.

Nanjing Massacre or **Rape of Nanjing** (Dec. 1937–Jan. 1938) Mass killing and rape of Chinese people in Nanjing by Japanese soldiers during their destruction of the city. An estimated 100,000–300,000 were killed, and tens of thousands of rapes were committed. Japanese brutality in China continued to contribute to cool relations between the two countries into the 21st cent.

Nanning or **Nan-ning** \'nän-'niŋ\ formerly (1913–45) **Yung-ning** \'yùŋ-'niŋ\ City (pop., 1999 est.: 984,000), capital of Guangxi province, SE China. Located on the Yung River, about 100 mi (160 km) north of Vietnam, it was the site of a county seat first established in A.D. 318. It was opened to foreign trade in 1907. Occupied by the Japanese during the SINO–JAPANESE WAR, it was a supply base for Communist forces during the anti-French war in INDOCHINA and the VIETNAM WAR.

Nansen \'nän-sən\, **Fridtjof** (1861–1930) Norwegian explorer and statesman. In 1888 he led the first expedition to cross the ice fields of Greenland. In 1895 he reached the farthest N latitude then attained. He engaged in scientific research 1896–1917, and led oceanographic expeditions in the N. Atlantic. He served as Norway's first minister to Britain (1906–8) and as head of Norway's delegation to the new League of Nations (1920). He directed the repatriation from Russia of over 400,000 prisoners of war for the League and organized famine relief in Russia for the Red Cross. In 1922 he was awarded the Nobel Peace Prize. In 1931 the Nansen International Office for Refugees was established in Geneva.

Nantes \'näⁿt\ Breton **Naoned** \'nȧ-ned\ ancient Condivincum. City (pop., 1999: 269,000), NW France. Located on the LOIRE RIVER, it was settled by the Namnetes, a Gallic tribe, before the Romans conquered GAUL. It passed to France in 1499 and rallied to King HENRY IV of France after he signed the Edict of NANTES in 1598. During the FRENCH REVOLUTION its populace suffered many executions. Occupied by German troops in World War II, it was heavily damaged by Allied bombing. It has important industrial plants and shipbuilding yards, a castle, a cathedral, a university, and a museum of fine arts.

Nantes, Edict of (April 13, 1598) Law promulgated by HENRY IV of France to grant religious liberty and full civil rights to the Protestant HUGUENOTS, ending the Wars of RELIGION. It stipulated that Protestant pastors were to be paid by the state, and public worship was permitted in most of the kingdom, though not in Paris. The edict was resented by the Catholic clergy; Cardinal de RICHELIEU annulled its political clauses in 1629, and the full edict was revoked by LOUIS XIV in 1685.

Nantucket Island (pop., 2000: 9,500), Atlantic Ocean, south of CAPE COD, Mass. Of glacial origin, it has sandy beaches and a good harbor. Purchased from the PLYMOUTH colony in 1641, it became part of New York and was settled in 1659 by Quakers, then ceded to Massachusetts in 1692. It was a whaling center in the 18th and 19th cent. The summer tourist trade is now its economic mainstay.

napalm \'nä-ˌpäm\ Organic compound, the aluminum SOAP or SALT of a mixture of FATTY ACIDS, used to thicken GASOLINE for use as an incendiary in flamethrowers and firebombs. The thickened mixture, itself also called napalm, burns more slowly and can be propelled more accurately and over greater distances than gasoline. It was developed and first used by the U.S. in World War II. Its use in the Vietnam War became highly controversial.

Napier \'nä-pər\, **John** (1550–1617) Scottish mathematician and champion of PROTESTANTISM. He divided his life between attacks on the Church of Rome and the pursuit of numerical calculations. From 1594 he worked on developing secret weapons, including a metal chariot with small holes through which shot could be fired. He developed the concept of the LOGARITHM to facilitate calculations involving multiplication, division, roots, and powers. He also introduced the decimal point as a notation for decimal FRACTIONS.

Naples Italian **Napoli** \'nä-pō-lē\ ancient Neapolis. City (pop., 2000: 1,002,000) and capital, CAMPANIA, S Italy. It lies on the beautiful Bay of NAPLES, southeast of Rome; its skyline is dominated by Mt. VESUVIUS. Founded around 600 B.C. by refugees from an ancient Greek colony, it was conquered by the Romans in the 4th cent. B.C. Part of the realms of the Byzantines and then the Saracens, in the 11th cent. it was conquered by the Norman ruler of Sicily and through the 19th cent. it was the capital of the kingdom of The Two SICILIES and the kingdom of NAPLES. It was heavily damaged in World War II by Allied and German bombing, and suffered severe earthquake damage in 1980. It is a commercial center and a major port; its industries include shipbuilding and textiles. It has had a notable musical history; its conservatory (1537) is the oldest in the West. The Univ. of Naples (1224) is one of the oldest in Europe.

Naples, Bay of Semicircular inlet of the Tyrrhenian Sea, S Italy. It extends about 20 mi (32 km). Its noted scenic beauty is enhanced by the volcanic hills surrounding it, including Mt. VESUVIUS. Its major port is NAPLES, and along its shore are ruins of POMPEII and HERCULANEUM.

Naples, Kingdom of Former kingdom composed of the S portion of the Italian peninsula. The region was held successively by Romans, Byzantines, Lombards, and Saracens, then incorporated into the Norman kingdom of SICILY in the 11th cent. Separated in 1282, it was reunited with Sicily in 1442 as one of The Two SICILIES. Again separating from Sicily in 1458, it was ruled by Spain for two centuries. Ceded to the Austrian HABSBURGS in 1713, it was conquered in 1734 by the Spanish BOURBONS, who reestablished the kingdom of The Two Sicilies. Napoleon made it an independent kingdom 1806–15, after which the Bourbons were restored. In 1860 it was united with N Italy.

Napoleon *orig. Italian* Napoleone Buonaparte *French* **Napoléon Bonaparte** (1769–1821) French general and emperor (1804–15). Born in Corsica to parents of Italian ancestry, he was educated in France and became an army officer in 1785. He fought in the FRENCH REVOLUTIONARY WARS and was promoted to brigadier general in 1793. In 1796 he married JOSÉPHINE. After victories against the Austrians in N Italy (1797), he attempted to conquer Egypt (1798–99) but was defeated by the British under Horatio NELSON in the Battle of the NILE. In 1799 he installed a military dictatorship, with himself as First Consul (see CONSULATE). He introduced numerous reforms in government, including the NAPOLEONIC CODE, and reconstructed the French education system. After victory against the Austrians at Marengo (1800), he embarked on the NAPOLEONIC WARS. The formation of coalitions of European countries against him led Napoleon to declare France a hereditary empire and to crown himself emperor in 1804. He won great victories at AUSTERLITZ (1805), Jena and Auerstedt (1806), and Friedland (1807). He installed as rulers in his conquered territories his brothers Joseph BONAPARTE and Louis BONAPARTE and his stepchildren Eugene de BEAUHARNAIS and Hortense de BEAUHARNAIS. Despite his loss to Britain at TRAFALGAR, he sought to weaken British commerce and established the CONTINENTAL SYSTEM of port blockades. He consolidated his European empire until 1810, but became embroiled in the PENINSULAR WAR (1808–14). In 1809 he had his marriage to Joséphine annulled, and married MARIE-LOUISE (1810). He led an army of over 450,000 into Russia in 1812, winning the Battle of Borodino, but was forced to retreat from Moscow with disastrous losses, and a strong coalition of allied powers defeated him at the Battle of Leipzig (1813). After Paris was taken by the allied coalition, Napoleon was forced to abdicate in 1814 and was exiled to the island of Elba. In 1815 he mustered a force and returned to France to reestablish himself as emperor for the HUNDRED DAYS, but was decisively defeated at the Battle of WATERLOO and exiled to the remote island of St. Helena, where he died six years later. One of the most celebrated figures in history, Napoleon revolutionized military organization and brought about reforms that permanently influenced civil institutions throughout Europe.

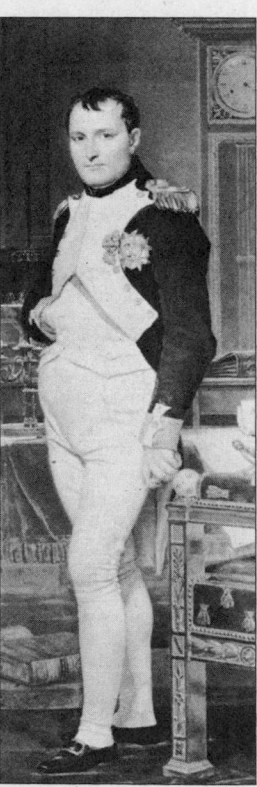

Napoleon "Napoleon in His Study" by J.-L. David, 1812

Napoleon II *or* **Duke of Reichstadt** *orig.* Napoléon-François-Charles-Joseph Bonaparte (1811–1832) The only son of NAPOLEON and MARIE-LOUISE, he received the title King of Rome. On his father's abdication (1814), he was named his successor, but the Allies refused to accept him. His mother took him to live at the court of her father, Emperor FRANCIS II. Given the Austrian title of duke of Reichstadt, he was controlled by Klemens von METTERNICH. In 1830 Bonapartist insurgents attempted to restore him as Napoleon II, but he was already ill with the tuberculosis that would kill him.

Napoleon III *or* **Louis-Napoléon** *orig.* Charles-Louis-Napoléon Bonaparte (1808–1873) Emperor of France (1852–70). Son of Louis BONAPARTE and nephew of NAPOLEON, he lived in exile in Switzerland and Germany 1815–30. With the death in 1832 of NAPOLEON II, he became the claimant to the French throne. After an abortive coup (1836), he was exiled by King LOUIS-PHILIPPE. After another attempted coup (1840), he was imprisoned. He escaped in 1846 and returned to Paris in 1848. He evoked the legend of Napoleon to win the popular vote as president of the SECOND REPUBLIC. Attempting to expand his power, he staged a coup in 1851 and made himself dictator; in 1852, as Napoleon III, he became emperor of the SECOND EMPIRE. Seeking to reestablish French power, he led France into the CRIMEAN WAR. He aided Italy in achieving unity and annexed Savoy and Nice (1860). He promoted liberalized policies within France, which enjoyed prosperity during much of his reign. He expected material rewards from his "Latin empire" by installing MAXIMILIAN as emperor of Mexico, but was disappointed. He kept France neutral in the Austro–Prussian War (1866), but in 1870 was drawn into the disastrous FRANCO–PRUSSIAN WAR. After leading his troops to defeat in the Battle of Sedan, he surrendered and was deposed.

Napoleonic Code *French* **Code Civil** French civil code enacted by NAPOLEON in 1804. It clarified and made uniform the private law of France and followed Roman law in being divided into three books: the law of persons, things, and modes of acquiring ownership of things. In Louisiana, the only civil-law state in the U.S., the civil code of 1825 (revised in 1870 and still in force) is closely connected to the Napoleonic Code.

Napoleonic Wars (1799–1815) Series of wars that ranged France against shifting alliances of European powers. Originally an attempt to maintain French strength established by the FRENCH REVOLUTIONARY WARS, they became efforts by NAPOLEON to affirm his supremacy in Europe. A victory over Austria at the Battle of Marengo (1800) left France the dominant power on the continent. Britain's victory at the Battle of TRAFALGAR (1805) ended Napoleon's threat to invade England. Napoleon won major victories in the Battles of Austerlitz (1805), Jena and Auerstedt (1806), and Friedland (1807) against an alliance of Russia, Austria, and Prussia. The resulting Treaties of TILSIT (1807) and Schönbrunn (1809) left most of Europe either part of the French Empire, controlled by France, or allied to it by treaty. Napoleon's successes resulted from a strategy of moving his army rapidly, attacking quickly, and defeating each of the disconnected enemy units. His enemies' responding strategy was to avoid engagement while withdrawing, forcing Napoleon's supply lines to be overextended; the strategy was successfully used by the Duke of WELLINGTON in the PENINSULAR WAR and, most devastatingly, by Mikhail BARCLAY DE TOLLY and Mikhail KUTUZOV in Russia. In 1813 the QUADRUPLE ALLIANCE amassed armies that outnumbered Napoleon's. He was forced to withdraw west of the Rhine River, and after the invasion of France (1814) he abdicated. He rallied a new army to return in the HUNDRED DAYS (1815), but a revived Quadruple Alliance defeated him at the Battle of WATERLOO.

Nara period (710–784) Period of Japanese history during which the emperor resided in Nara. The capital city was modeled on the capital of TANG-DYNASTY China, Changan, and the Japanese borrowed extensively from China in this period. Buddhism rose in popularity, and many temples and statues were commissioned. The CHINESE WRITING SYSTEM was introduced and modified, allowing the production of two official histories and the earliest Japanese poetry collections. The Taiho Code, (701) was based on Chinese law. The imperial state extended its frontiers to include S Kyushu and N Honshu.

Narayan(swami) \nə-'rī-ən\, **R(asipuram) K(rishnaswami)** (1906–2001) Indian writer. His novels, which typically portray the ironies of Indian daily life, in which modern urban existence clashes with ancient tradition, include *The English Teacher* (1945), *The Guide* (1958), *The Man-Eater of Malgudi* (1961), *The Vendor of Sweets* (1967), and *A Tiger for Malgudi* (1983). He also wrote short stories, memoirs, and modern prose versions of Indian epics.

Nara period Painted clay Shukongojin, 733

Narbonensis \ˌnär-bə-'nensəs\ *or* **Gallia Narbonensis** Ancient Roman province between the Alps, the Mediterranean Sea, and the Cévennes Mtns., constituting what is now SE France. Part of Roman Gallia (see GAUL), it was originally called Provincia (see PROVENCE) and was renamed Gallia Narbonensis under Caesar AUGUSTUS. Vineyards prospered, olive groves were cultivated, and splendid buildings were erected. The province was also famous for its culture, especially the schools at Massilia (see MARSEILLE).

narcissism \'när-sə-ˌsi-zəm\ Mental disorder characterized by extreme self-absorption, an exaggerated sense of self-importance, and a need for attention and admiration. First identified by Havelock ELLIS in 1898, it is named for the mythological NARCISSUS, who fell in love with his own reflection. In addition to an inflated self-image and addiction to fantasy, narcissism is characterized by the tendency to take others for granted or to exploit them, and by an unusual coolness and composure. According to Sigmund FREUD, narcissism is a normal stage in children's development, but constitutes a disorder after puberty.

narcissus \när-'si-səs\ Any of about 40 species of bulbous, fragrant, ornamental plants that make up the genus *Narcissus* in the AMARYLLIS FAMILY, native mainly to Europe. Popular species include the DAFFODIL, or narcissus (*N. pseudonarcissus*), the jonquil (*N. jonquilla*), and poet's narcissus (*N. poeticus*). The stem bears one large blossom, which ranges in shape from the form of a trumpet to a ringlike cup. Rushlike or flattened leaves arise from the base of the plant. The bulbs were once used in medicines.

Narcissus \när-'si-səs\ In GREEK MYTHOLOGY, a beautiful youth who fell in love with his own reflection. His callous rejection of the nymph ECHO or of his lover Ameinias drew upon him the gods' vengeance: he fell in love with his own image in the waters of a spring and wasted away. The NARCISSUS flower sprang up where he died.

narcolepsy SLEEP disorder with sudden, uncontrollable spells of daytime sleep and disturbances of nighttime sleep. It usually begins in youth or early adulthood and is presumably due to dysfunction of certain brain structures. Narcoleptics can fall asleep anywhere and anytime (e.g., while talking, eating, or driving), usually for only a moment. Sleep paralysis, normal when falling asleep or waking, occurs during full consciousness, with brief but complete inability to move.

narcotic DRUG that produces analgesia (see ANALGESIC), narcosis (stupor or sleep), and DRUG ADDICTION. In most people narcotics also produce euphoria. Those that occur naturally in the OPIUM POPPY, notably MORPHINE, have been used since ancient Greek times. The main therapeutic use of narcotics is for pain relief. Most countries limit the production, sale, and use of narcotics because of their ad-

dictive properties and detrimental effects and the incidence of drug abuse. A narcotic overdose can cause central nervous system depression, respiratory failure, and death. See also HEROIN.

Narmada River \nər-'mə-də\ *or* **Nerbudda River** River, central India. Rising in Madhya Pradesh state, it flows west 801 mi (1,289 km) into the Gulf of Khambhat, and forms the traditional boundary between Hindustan and the DECCAN. Long an important route between the Arabian Sea and the GANGES RIVER valley, it is also a pilgrimage route for Hindus, who regard it as their most sacred river after the Ganges.

Narodnik See POPULIST

Narragansett Bay \ˌnar-ə-'gan-sət\ Inlet of the Atlantic Ocean, Rhode Island. It extends 28 mi (45 km) into the state and includes Mt. Hope Bay, which is crossed by one of New England's longest bridges. Since colonial times it has been an active shipping center; its chief ports are PROVIDENCE and NEWPORT. Much of the bay's area is devoted to fishing and recreation.

Narses \'när-ˌsēz\ (c.480–574) Byzantine general under JUSTINIAN I. A eunuch, he commanded the imperial bodyguard and rose to become grand chamberlain. He helped to quell a riot in 532 and save Justinian's throne. Narses led military expeditions against barbarians in the Balkans, and he returned to Italy in 551 to conquer the OSTROGOTHS completely. He held power in Italy until removed by Justinian's successor (567).

narwhal *or* **narwal** \'när-ˌwäl\ *or* **narwhale** \'när-ˌwāl\ Toothed WHALE (*Monodon monoceros*, family Monodontidae) of the Arctic, found in groups of 15–20 along coasts and sometimes in rivers. Narwhals are 11.5–16 ft (3.5–5 m) long, and have no dorsal fin. They have only two teeth. The male's left tooth is a straight, protruding tusk, 8.9 ft (2.7 m) long, that is grooved on the surface in a left-handed spiral. Prized in medieval times as the unicorn horn, it is thought to have evolved as a sexual display. Narwhals are hunted by humans for their tusks and meat.

NASA *in full* **National Aeronautics and Space Administration** Independent U.S. government agency established in 1958 for aeronautics and space exploration. Its goals include improving our understanding of the universe, the solar system, and earth, and establishing a manned SPACE STATION. NASA, previously the National Advisory Committee for Aeronautics (NACA), was created largely in response to Russia's launch of SPUTNIK in 1957. In 1961, Pres. John F. KENNEDY proposed that the U.S. put a man on the moon by the end of the 1960s (see APOLLO). Later unmanned programs (e.g., Viking, MARINER, VOYAGER, GALILEO) explored other planets, and orbiting observatories (e.g., the HUBBLE SPACE TELESCOPE) study the cosmos. Various other NASA SATELLITES have earth applications, such as LANDSAT and communications and weather satellites. See also SPACE SHUTTLE.

NASDAQ \'naz-dak\ *in full* **National Association of Securities Dealers Automated Quotations** U.S. OVER-THE-COUNTER MARKET for securities. Established in 1971, NASDAQ is an automated quotation system that reports on the trading of domestic securities not listed on the regular stock exchanges. It publishes two composite PRICE INDEXES daily as well as bank, insurance, transportation, utilities, and industrial indexes. The market for major computer and electronics firms, by the 1990s it had surpassed the AMERICAN STOCK EXCHANGE (AMEX) to become the second-largest U.S. securities market. In 1999 it merged with AMEX to form the Nasdaq-Amex Market Group.

Nash, John (1752–1835) British architect and city planner. From 1798, Nash was employed by the Prince of Wales. Acquiring considerable wealth, he built for himself E. Cowes Castle, Isle of Wight (1798), which influenced the GOTHIC REVIVAL, and he dotted England and Ireland with castles, houses, and cottages in Gothic or Italianate style. Regent's Park (1811) comprises a canal, lake, wooded area, botanical garden, and, on the periphery, shopping arcades and residences. In 1821 he began to reconstruct Buckingham House as a royal palace but was dismissed before completing the project.

Nash, John F(orbes) (b.1928) U.S. mathematician. Born in Bluefield, W.V., he began teaching at MIT in 1951, but left in the late 1950s because of mental illness; thereafter he was informally associated with Princeton. Beginning in the 1950s with his influential thesis "Non-cooperative Games," Nash established the mathematical principles of GAME THEORY. His "Nash solution" attempted to explain the dynamics of threat and action among competitors; it was widely applied by business strategists. He shared the 1994 Nobel Prize in Economics with John C. Harsanyi (1920–2000) and Reinhard Selten (b.1930).

Nash, (Frederic) Ogden (1902–1971) U.S. writer of humorous poetry. Born in Rye, N.Y., he worked at the *New Yorker* for many years. In his 20 collections, including *The Bad Parents' Garden of Verse* (1936) and *I'm a Stranger Here Myself* (1938), his audacious, quotable verse employs delightfully impossible rhymes, puns, and ragged stanzas, often interrupted by digressions. He wrote several children's books and the lyrics for the musicals *One Touch of Venus* (1943) and *Two's Company* (1952).

Nashe \'nash\, **Thomas** (1567–1601?) English pamphleteer, poet, dramatist, and novelist. The first of the English prose eccentrics, Nashe wrote in a vigorous combination of colloquial diction and idiosyncratic coined compounds that was ideal for controversy. Among his works are the satire *Pierce Penilesse His Supplication to the Divell* (1592) and *The Unfortunate Traveller* (1594), the first picaresque novel in English. The play *Dido, Queen of Carthage* (1594) was a collaboration with Christopher MARLOWE.

Nashville City (pop., 2000: 545,000), capital of Tennessee. It is located on the CUMBERLAND RIVER. Founded in 1779, it became the state capital in 1843. During the AMERICAN CIVIL WAR, it was occupied by Federal troops (1862); the war's last major battle (1864) took place outside the city. Important industries include printing, publishing, and recording. Well known for COUNTRY MUSIC, it is the site of Opryland U.S.A. and the Country Music Hall of Fame and Museum. It is the home of VANDERBILT and FISK universities.

Nasir Hamid Abu Zayd \'na-sir-hȧ-'mēd-ˌab-ü-'zīd\ (b.1943) Egyptian scholar. His research and writings, including his well-known *Critique of Islamic Discourse* (1995), have offended some Islamic conservatives. In 1993 a colleague denounced him in a major Cairo mosque. Islamic radicals successfully sought a nullification of his marriage on the grounds that his writings demonstrated his apostasy. Eventually the divorce was confirmed by the Egyptian Supreme Court. The case attracted widespread concern among intellectuals and human-rights groups. Since 1995 Abu Zayd and his wife have lived in exile.

Naskapi See MONTAGNAIS AND NASKAPI

Nassau Historical region of Germany, former duchy, W part of modern HESSE. It is a thickly forested and hilly area north and east of the Rhine. The title "Count of Nassau" was first assumed in the 12th cent. Nassau became a duchy in 1806. It was annexed by Prussia in 1866. The descendants of the house of Nassau are royal heads of the Netherlands and Luxembourg to this day.

Nassau City (pop., 1990: 172,000), capital of the Bahamas. Located on New Providence island, it was settled by the English in the 17th cent. and became a rendezvous for pirates in the 18th cent. During the AMERICAN CIVIL WAR, it became a base for Confederate blockade-runners. It is now a popular resort; its economy is based on tourism.

Nasser, Gamal Abdel *Arabic* Jamal Abd al-Naser (1918–1970) Egyptian leader. As an army officer, he led a coup that deposed the royal family (1952) and installed Gen. Mohammad Naguib as a puppet head of state. In 1954 he deposed Naguib and made himself prime minister. The MUSLIM BROTHERHOOD tried to assassinate him but failed. In 1956 he established a constitution that made Egypt a one-party socialist state with himself as president. He nationalized the Suez Canal (see SUEZ CRISIS) and secured Soviet assistance to build the ASWAN HIGH DAM. A charismatic figure, he dreamed of becoming leader of the Muslim world, and succeeded briefly in forming the United Arab Republic with Syria (1958–61). He had tentatively accepted a U.S. peace plan for Egypt and Israel when he died of a heart attack. See also ARAB–ISRAELI WARS, Anwar al-SADAT.

Nasser, Lake *or in Sudan* **Lake Nubia** Lake, S Egypt and N Sudan. About 300 mi (480 km) long, it was formed in the 1960s as a result of the construction of the ASWAN HIGH DAM. Its waters have brought 800,000 acres (324,000 hectares) of land under irrigation. It has flooded a number of archaeological sites, including ABU SIMBEL.

Nast, Thomas (1840–1902) U.S. (German-born) political cartoonist. He arrived in the U.S. at 6, and from 1862 to 1886 he worked as a cartoonist for *Harper's Weekly*. His cartoons in support of the Union cause in the Civil War led Abraham LINCOLN to call him "our best recruiting sergeant." Many of his most effective cartoons were attacks on the New York political machine of W. M. TWEED in the 1870s; one led to Tweed's identification and arrest in Spain. Nast originated the Republican Party's elephant and one of the most popular images of Santa Claus, and popularized the Democratic Party's donkey, and his cartoons have been credited with several victories in presidential elections.

nasturtium \nas-'tǝr-shǝm\ Any of various annual plants of the genus *Tropaeolum* (family Tropaeolaceae), native to Mexico, Central America, and N S. America, and cultivated elsewhere. Brilliant yellow, orange, or red flowers are funnel-shaped and have a long spur that contains sweet nectar. The peppery-tasting leaves and flowers are sometimes used in salads.

Natal \nǝ-'täl\ Seaport city (pop., 1996: 656,000), NE Brazil. Founded by the Portuguese in 1597, it is the capital and commercial center of the state of Rio Grande do Norte; it is also a busy port and naval base. The Marine Research Institute and the Barreira do Inferno rocket base are located in the vicinity.

Natal \nǝ-'täl\ Former province, SE Republic of S. Africa. Long occupied by BANTU-speaking peoples, it was named Natal by Vasco da GAMA on Christmas Day (Portuguese, *Natal*) in 1497. In 1837 AFRIKANERS established the Republic of Natal. It was annexed by the British in 1843. During the S. AFRICAN WAR, Natal was invaded by Afrikaner forces, which were stopped by the British. In 1910 it became a province of the Union of S. Africa, and in 1961 of the Republic of S. Africa. The fragmented black "homeland" of KwaZulu was later created within Natal, which was the scene of clashes by rival black factions. In 1994 the region was united to form the province of KwaZulu-Natal.

Natchez Trace Old road, SE U.S. It follows an Indian trail (or trace) to the northeast from Natchez, Miss., across NW Alabama to Nashville, Tenn., and is more than 500 mi (800 km) long. A wagon road constructed in the early 19th cent. was used by traders and settlers. Among its historical landmarks is Chickasaw Village, in Mississippi.

Nation, Carry (Amelia) *orig.* Carry Amelia Moore (1846–1911) U.S. temperance advocate. Born in Garrard Co., Ky., she married in 1867 but soon left her alcoholic husband. In 1877 she married David Nation, a lawyer. She joined the TEMPERANCE MOVEMENT in the prohibition state of Kansas and came to believe that the illegality of saloons meant they could be destroyed with impunity. A tall and heavy woman, she would march alone or with hymn-singing supporters into saloons and proceed to pray, shout, and smash their fixtures and stock with a hatchet. She was jailed many times, paying her fines with proceeds from her lectures and sales of souvenir hatchets.

Nation, The U.S. journal of opinion, the oldest continuously published U.S. weekly. Founded in 1865 by F. L. OLMSTED and Edwin L. Godkin (1831–1902) as a reformist publication, it was sold to the *New York Evening Post* in 1881 and was a weekly edition of the paper until 1914. While Oswald Garrison Villard (1872–1949) was owner and editor (1918–34), it moved decisively to the political left, where it remained. In circulation it is now one of the largest intellectual journals in America.

National Aeronautics and Space Administration See NASA

National Assembly *French* Assemblée nationale. French parliamentary body. The name was first used during the FRENCH REVOLUTION to designate the revolutionary assembly formed by the THIRD ESTATE (1789), and then as a short form for the National Constituent Assembly (1789–91). In the THIRD REPUBLIC (1875–1940), it designated the two houses of parliament, the Senate and the

Chamber of Deputies. In the FOURTH REPUBLIC (1946–58) and FIFTH REPUBLIC (from 1958), it was applied only to the lower house (the former Chamber of Deputies).

National Association for the Advancement of Colored People See NAACP

national bank In the U.S., any COMMERCIAL BANK chartered and supervised by the federal government and operated by private individuals. Created under the National Bank Act of 1863 to combat financial instability and help finance the Civil War, these banks purchased federal BONDS and deposited them with the comptroller of the currency. They then issued national bank notes, creating a stable, uniform national CURRENCY. After the Civil War, the government began to retire the bonds, reducing the number of national bank notes that could be issued. Concern over the inflexibility of national bank notes led to the formation of the FEDERAL RESERVE SYSTEM in 1913, which all national banks were required to join. The U.S. Treasury assumed the obligation of issuing national bank notes in 1935.

National Basketball Association (NBA) U.S. professional basketball league formed in 1949 by the merger of the National Basketball League (founded 1937) and the Basketball Assn. of America (1946). Membership is divided into two conferences. The Eastern Conference consists of the Atlantic Division (Boston Celtics, Miami Heat, New Jersey Nets, New York Knicks, Orlando Magic, Philadelphia 76ers, and Washington Wizards) and the Central Division (Atlanta Hawks, Chicago Bulls, Cleveland Cavaliers, Detroit Pistons, Indiana Pacers, Milwaukee Bucks, New Orleans Hornets, and Toronto Raptors). The Western Conference consists of the Midwest Division (Dallas Mavericks, Denver Nuggets, Houston Rockets, Memphis Grizzlies, Minnesota Timberwolves, San Antonio Spurs, and Utah Jazz), and the Pacific Division (Golden State Warriors, Los Angeles Clippers, Los Angeles Lakers, Phoenix Suns, Portland Trail Blazers, Sacramento Kings, and Seattle SuperSonics).

National Broadcasting Co. See NBC

National Collegiate Athletic Association (NCAA) Organization that administers U.S. intercollegiate athletics. It was formed in 1906, but did not acquire significant powers to enforce its rules until 1942. Headquartered at Overland Park, Kan., it functions as a general administrative authority, formulating and enforcing rules of play for various sports and eligibility criteria for athletes. It has more than 800 member schools and conducts about 80 national championships in about 20 sports.

National Convention *French* Convention nationale. Governing assembly (1792–95) of the FRENCH REVOLUTION. It consisted of 749 deputies elected after the overthrow of the monarchy (1792) to provide a new constitution for France. The struggle between the radical MONTAGNARDS and the moderate GIRONDINS initially dominated the Convention. After the THERMIDORIAN REACTION (1794), the balance of power was held by members of the PLAIN. In 1795 a new Constitution was approved for the DIRECTORY regime that replaced the Convention.

national debt *or* **public debt** Total indebtedness of a government, especially as evidenced by SECURITIES issued to investors. The national debt grows whenever government spending exceeds revenues in a year. To finance its debt, the government can issue securities such as BONDS or TREASURY BILLS. The level of national debt varies from country to country, from less than 10% to more than 200% of the GROSS DOMESTIC PRODUCT (GDP). Public borrowing is often used during RECESSIONS to stimulate CONSUMPTION, INVESTMENT, and employment. See also DEFICIT FINANCING.

National Education Association (NEA) Voluntary association of U.S. teachers, administrators, and other educators associated with elementary, secondary, and higher education. Founded in 1857 as the National Teachers Assn., it is the world's largest professional organization (around 2.4 million members). Operating much like a LABOR UNION, it represents its members through state and local affiliates. It seeks to improve schools and working conditions and advance the cause of public education. See also AMERICAN FEDERATION OF TEACHERS.

National Film Board of Canada Canadian department of film production. Established in 1939 and directed by John

Grierson (1898–1972), it developed into a leading producer of documentaries, including the World War II propaganda films *Canada Carries On* and *The World in Action*. It also made high-quality animated movies by Norman McLaren (1914–1987) and others, and later such feature films as *The Luck of Ginger Coffey* (1964) and *The Apprenticeship of Duddy Kravitz* (1974).

National Football League (NFL) Major professional football organization in the U.S. It was founded in 1920 at Canton, Ohio; in 1970 it merged with the rival American Football League (founded 1959). Today it is divided into two conferences. The National Conference consists of a North Division (Chicago Bears, Detroit Lions, Green Bay Packers, and Minnesota Vikings), a South Division (Atlanta Falcons, Carolina Panthers, New Orleans Saints, and Tampa Bay Buccaneers), an East Division (Dallas Cowboys, New York Giants, Philadelphia Eagles, and Washington Redskins), and a West Division (Arizona Cardinals, St. Louis Rams, San Francisco 49ers, and Seattle Seahawks). The American Conference likewise consists of a North Division (Baltimore Ravens, Cincinnati Bengals, Cleveland Browns, and Pittsburgh Steelers), a South Division (Houston Texans, Indianapolis Colts, Jacksonville Jaguars, and Tennessee Titans), an East Division (Buffalo Bills, Miami Dolphins, New England Patriots, and New York Jets), and a West Division (Denver Broncos, Kansas City Chiefs, Oakland Raiders, and San Diego Chargers).

national forest, U.S. Any of numerous forest areas under federal supervision for the purposes of conserving water, timber, wildlife, fish, and other renewable resources, and providing public recreation areas. Administered by the U.S. Department of AGRICULTURE's Forest Service, the forests numbered 156 in 2000 and occupied 352,000 sq mi (911,700 sq km) in 44 states and Puerto Rico. The country's first forest reserves were established in 1891. See also Gifford PINCHOT.

National Gallery of Art Museum in Washington, D.C., part of the SMITHSONIAN INSTITUTION. It was founded in 1937 when Andrew W. MELLON donated his collection of European paintings and funds to construct the gallery's neoclassical building, opened in 1941. Now known as the West Building, it is connected by plaza and underground concourse to the East Building, designed by I. M. PEI (completed 1978). The museum houses an extensive collection of U.S. and European paintings, sculpture, decorative arts, and graphic arts from the 12th to the 20th cent.

National Geographic Society U.S. scientific society founded in 1888 in Washington, D.C., by a small group of eminent explorers and scientists "for the increase and diffusion of geographic knowledge." Today it has more than 9 million members. It has supported more than 5,000 major scientific projects and expeditions, including those of Robert PEARY, Richard BYRD, the LEAKEY family, J.-Y. COUSTEAU, Jane GOODALL, and Dian FOSSEY. It has published numerous books, atlases, and bulletins and has created hundreds of television documentaries. *National Geographic Magazine* is a monthly magazine of geography, archaeology, anthropology, and exploration. It became a leader in reproducing color photographs and printing photographs of undersea life, views from the stratosphere, and animals in their natural habitats.

National Guard, U.S. Volunteer reserve group organized by the U.S. Army and Air Force. Every U.S. state and territory has a National Guard, which can be called on by state governors during emergencies such as riots and natural disasters. Guard units may also be ordered into active duty for up to two years by the U.S. president in the event of a national emergency.

National Hockey League (NHL) Organization of professional N. American ice-hockey teams, formed in Canada in 1917. It today consists of 30 teams. Its Eastern Conference includes the Atlantic Division (New Jersey Devils, New York Islanders, New York Rangers, Philadelphia Flyers, and Pittsburgh Penguins), the Northeast Division (Boston Bruins, Buffalo Sabres, Montreal Canadiens, Ottawa Senators, and Toronto Maple Leafs), and the Southeast Division (Atlanta Thrashers, Carolina Hurricanes, Florida Panthers, Tampa Bay Lightning, and Washington Capitals). Its Western Conference includes the Central Division (Chicago Blackhawks, Columbus Blue Jackets, Detroit Red Wings, Nashville Predators, and St. Louis Blues), the Northwest Division (Calgary Flames, Colorado Avalanche, Edmonton Oilers, Minnesota Wild, and Vancouver Canucks), and the Pacific Division (Mighty Ducks of Anaheim, Dallas Stars, Los Angeles Kings, Phoenix Coyotes, and San Jose Sharks). At the end of the season, the top teams in each division engage in a play-off for the STANLEY CUP.

national income accounting Set of principles and methods used to measure a country's income and production. The expenditure approach measures the money value of the total output of goods and services in a given period (usually a year). The income approach measures the total income derived from economic activity after allowing for capital CONSUMPTION. The standard indicator of national output is the GROSS DOMESTIC PRODUCT (GDP). National income may be derived from gross national product (GNP) by subtracting from the GNP such non-income costs as indirect taxes, SUBSIDIES, and DEPRECIATION. National income thus calculated represents the total income of the owners of the factors of production; it is the sum of wages, salaries, PROFITS, INTEREST, DIVIDENDS, RENT, and so on. Common uses of such data include breakdowns of GDP according to type of product, breakdowns of national income by type of income, and analyses of the sources of financing (e.g., personal savings, company funds, or national deficits).

National Institutes of Health (NIH) U.S. government agency made up of numerous specialized institutes (e.g., National Cancer Institute, National Institute of Mental Health) that conduct or support biomedical research in their fields. Part of the Department of HEALTH AND HUMAN SERVICES, it also trains health researchers, disseminates information, and maintains other offices and divisions and the National Library of Medicine (foremost source of medical information in the U.S.).

nationalism Loyalty and devotion to one's nation or country, especially as above loyalty to other groups or individual interests. Before the era of the nation-state, the primary allegiance of most people was to their immediate locality or religious group. The rise of large, centralized states weakened local authority and religious loyalty. Early nationalist movements in 18th- and early 19th-cent. Europe were liberal and internationalist, but they gradually became more conservative and chauvinistic. Nationalism was a major contributing cause of both world wars. In Africa and Asia in the 20th cent., it often arose in opposition to COLONIALISM. After the fall of the Soviet Union, it made a powerful resurgence in Eastern Europe, contributing (with ethnicity) to increased conflict in such territories as Yugoslavia.

Nationalist China See TAIWAN

Nationalist Party (Chinese) See GUOMINDANG

National Labor Relations Act See WAGNER ACT

National League Oldest existing U.S. major-league baseball organization, founded in 1876. Of several rival organizations, only the AMERICAN LEAGUE has survived; since 1903 their two champions have engaged in an annual WORLD SERIES competition. Today the league consists of 16 teams. In its Eastern Division are the Atlanta Braves, Florida Marlins (Miami), Montreal Expos, New York Mets, and Philadelphia Phillies. In its Central Division are the Chicago Cubs, Cincinnati Reds, Houston Astros, Milwaukee Brewers, Pittsburgh Pirates, and St. Louis Cardinals. In its Western Division are the Arizona Diamondbacks (Phoenix), Colorado Rockies (Denver), Los Angeles Dodgers, San Diego Padres, and San Francisco Giants.

National Liberation Front (NLF) Title used by nationalist, usually socialist, movements in various countries since World War II. A communist-sponsored NLF operated in occupied Greece during the war. In Vietnam, the National Front for the Liberation of the South was formed (1960) to overthrow the S. Vietnamese government. In Algeria, the NLF succeeded the independence force in the ALGERIAN WAR to become the only constitutionally legal party 1962–89. In Uruguay, the leftist guerrilla TUPAMARO NLF (1963) battled police and the army 1967–72; it later became a legal political party. In the Philippines, the MORO NLF (1968) espoused separatism; its terrorist insurgency (1973–76) left

50,000 dead. The Corsican NLF (1976), the largest and most violent Corsican nationalist movement, remained active through the 1990s. See also SANDINISTAS.

National Organization for Women (NOW) U.S. women's-rights organization. It was founded in 1966 by Betty FRIEDAN to challenge sex discrimination in all areas of society, particularly in employment. With about half a million members, it addresses, through lobbying and litigation, child care, pregnancy leave, and abortion and pension rights. In the 1970s it focused on the EQUAL RIGHTS AMENDMENT. It has had greater success on the state level, with such issues as equal-pay legislation.

national park Area set aside by a national government for the preservation of its natural environment. Most are kept in their natural state. Those in the U.S. and Canada focus on land and wildlife preservation; those in Britain focus mainly on the land, those in African nations primarily on animals. The world's first national park, YELLOWSTONE, was established in the U.S. in 1872. Canada's first, BANFF, was established in 1885. Japan and Mexico established their first national parks in the 1930s; Britain, in 1949. The U.S. National Park Service (1916) also manages U.S. national monuments, recreation areas, seashores, historic sites, and battlefields. See also NATIONAL FOREST.

National Party of South Africa S. African political party that ruled the country 1948–94. Its following includes most AFRIKANERS and many other whites. It was founded in 1914 by J. B. M. HERTZOG to rally Afrikaners against the Anglicizing policies of Louis Botha and Jan SMUTS. During 1933–39 Hertzog and Smuts joined a coalition government, creating the United Party. Daniel MALAN and others, however, kept the National Party alive, and in 1939 accepted Hertzog back as their leader. After winning the 1948 elections and enacting a mass of racial legislation, the party named its policy APARTHEID. In 1961 it broke S. Africa away from the Commonwealth, making it a republic. In 1982 much of its right wing left to form the Conservative Party. Under F. W. DE KLERK, it began to seek repeal of racial laws. Defeated in the multiracial elections of 1994, it joined a coalition government with the AFRICAN NATIONAL CONGRESS, but enactment of a new constitution in 1996 caused the Nationalists to resign from the government.

National Recovery Administration (NRA) (1933–35) U.S. government agency established to stimulate business recovery during the GREAT DEPRESSION. As part of the National Industrial Recovery Act (1933), the NRA established codes to eliminate unfair trade practices, reduce unemployment, and set minimum wages and maximum hours. The U.S. Supreme Court invalidated the act in 1935 because it gave quasi-legislative powers to the executive branch. Many of its provisions appeared in subsequent legislation.

National Security Agency U.S. intelligence agency responsible for cryptographic and communications intelligence and security. Established in 1952 by presidential directive rather than by law, it has remained relatively free from congressional oversight. Its mission includes the protection and formulation of codes and ciphers and the interception of coded transmissions. It conducts research into all forms of electronic transmission, operating listening posts around the world. A target for penetration by foreign intelligence services, until recently it maintained no contact with the public or the press. Though its budget is secret, it is acknowledged to be far larger than that of the CENTRAL INTELLIGENCE AGENCY.

National Socialism or **Nazism** Totalitarian movement led by Adolf HITLER as head of Germany's NAZI PARTY (1920–45). It had its roots in Prussian militarism and German Romanticism, which celebrated a mythic past and proclaimed the rights of the exceptional individual over all rules and laws. Its ideology was shaped by Hitler's beliefs in German superiority and the dangers of communism. It rejected democracy, the rule of law, and human rights, stressing instead the subordination of the individual to the state. It emphasized the inequality of individuals and races and the right of the strong to rule the weak. Politically, it favored rearmament, reunification of the German areas of Europe, expansion into non-German areas, and the purging of "undesirables," especially Jews. See also FASCISM.

Nation of Islam See Nation of ISLAM
Native American See AMERICAN INDIAN
NATO *in full* **North Atlantic Treaty Organization** International military alliance created to defend Western Europe from Soviet expansion. A 1948 collective-defense alliance between Britain, France, the Netherlands, Belgium, and Luxembourg was recognized as inadequate to deter potential Soviet aggression, and in 1949 the U.S. and Canada agreed to join them in an enlarged alliance. The treaty stated that an attack on one signatory should be regarded as an attack on the rest. The admission of W. Germany in 1955 led to the Soviet Union's creation of the opposing WARSAW PACT. France withdrew from military participation in 1966. Since NATO ground forces were smaller than those of the Warsaw Pact, the balance of power was maintained by superior weaponry. After the Warsaw Pact's dissolution in 1991, NATO withdrew its nuclear weapons from Europe and refined its mission. It involved itself in the Balkan conflicts of the 1990s. The admission of three former Warsaw Pact members in 1999 and seven more countries in 2002 brought the number of full members to 26.

natural childbirth Any of the systems (e.g., the Lamaze method) of managing PARTURITION without drugs or surgery. All begin with classes to teach pregnant women about the birth process. The goal is to reduce fear and muscle tension, which can increase the pain of labor, and to make the mother an active participant in the process. The father usually attends the classes with the mother and coaches her during the birth.

natural gas Colorless, highly flammable gaseous HYDROCARBON consisting primarily of methane and ethane. It commonly occurs in association with crude oil (see PETROLEUM). Natural gas is extracted from wells drilled into the earth. Some natural gas can be used as it comes from the well, without any refining, but most requires processing. It is transported either in its natural gaseous state by pipeline or, after liquefaction by cooling, by tankers. It occupies only 1/600 of the volume of the gas. It has grown steadily as a source of energy since the 1930s.

naturalism Aesthetic movement of the late 19th to early 20th cent. inspired by the adaptation of the principles and methods of natural science, especially DARWINISM, to literature and art. In literature it extended the tradition of REALISM, aiming at an even more faithful representation of reality, presented without moral judgment. Characters in naturalistic literature typically illustrate the deterministic role of heredity and environment on human life. Naturalism originated in France, where its leading exponent was Émile ZOLA. In America it is associated with the work of Stephen CRANE and Theodore DREISER. Visual artists associated with naturalism chose themes from life, capturing subjects unposed and not idealized, thus giving their works freshness and immediacy. Following the lead of Gustave COURBET, painters chose themes from contemporary life, and many deserted the studio for the open air, finding subjects among peasants and tradespeople. While naturalism was short-lived as a historical movement, it contributed to art an enrichment of realism and new areas of subject matter.

naturalism In philosophy, the theory that affirms that all beings and events are natural and therefore can be fully known by the methods of scientific investigation. Naturalism has been equated with MATERIALISM, but is much broader in scope. Naturalism has no bias toward any particular set of categories of reality: dualism and monism, ATHEISM and THEISM, IDEALISM and materialism are all compatible with it. Naturalism's greatest vogue occurred in the 1930s and '40s, chiefly in the U.S. among philosophers such as John DEWEY, Sidney Hook (1902–1989), and W. V. O. QUINE.

naturalization Process of granting nationality or CITIZENSHIP to an ALIEN. It may be granted after voluntary application or through legislation, marriage to a citizen, or parental action. Qualifications for naturalization may include a minimum residency period, a minimum age, lawabiding character, good health, self-sufficiency, satisfactory knowledge of the new country, and willingness to give up one's former nationality.

natural law In philosophy of science, a universal statement that describes and/or explains the course of natural events (e.g., NEWTON'S LAWS OF MOTION); in jurisprudence and POLITICAL PHILOSOPHY, a system of right or justice common to all humankind and derived from nature rather than from the rules of society. This concept can be traced back to ARISTOTLE, who held that what was "just by nature" was not always the same as what was "just by law." Natural law was asserted by the Stoics (see STOICISM), CICERO, St. PAUL, St. AUGUSTINE, GRATIAN, THOMAS AQUINAS, John DUNS SCOTUS, and William of OCKHAM. Hugo GROTIUS and Thomas HOBBES constructed a system of natural law by deduction from a "state of nature" followed by a SOCIAL CONTRACT. John LOCKE described the state of nature as a state of society based on natural law. Jean-Jacques ROUSSEAU postulated a savage who was virtuous in isolation and actuated by self-preservation and compassion. The DECLARATION OF INDEPENDENCE refers to "the Laws of Nature" before citing equality and other "unalienable" rights as "self-evident."

natural selection Process that results in adaptation of an organism to its environment. VARIATIONS that increase an organism's chances of survival and procreation are preserved and multiplied down the generations. As proposed by Charles DARWIN, natural selection is the mechanism by which EVOLUTION occurs. It may arise from differences in survival, fertility, rate of development, mating success, or any other aspect of the life cycle. Random processes such as MUTATION, gene flow, and GENETIC DRIFT also alter GENE abundance; natural selection moderates their effects because it multiplies the incidence of beneficial mutations and eliminates harmful ones, since the organisms that carry the latter leave few or no descendants. See also SELECTION.

Nature Conservancy Nonprofit organization dedicated to environmental conservation and the preservation of biodiversity, founded in 1951, that operates the largest private system of nature sanctuaries in the world. It owns and manages 1,400 preserves throughout the U.S., and has expanded into Latin America and the Pacific, overseeing some 90 million acres (37 million hectares) of ecologically significant land. Government-administered programs identify the relative abundance of plant and animal species and the habitats they need to survive, and the Conservancy then acquires—through gifts, exchanges, easements, and other nonconfrontational arrangements—areas that are home to threatened species.

Naucratis \ˈnȯ-krə-təs\ Ancient Greek settlement, Egypt, in the NILE delta. It was founded in the 7th cent. B.C. and flourished as a center of trade between Greece and Egypt. It declined after ALEXANDER THE GREAT's founding of ALEXANDRIA in 332 B.C. In 1884 Flinders PETRIE discovered the site and helped excavate it.

Nauru \nä-ˈü-rü\ *Nauruan* **Naoero** \nä-ˈür-ō\ *officially* **Republic of Nauru** Island republic, SE MICRONESIA, SW Pacific Ocean. Area: 8 sq mi (21 sq km). Population (2000): 12,000. Capital: Yaren. About three-fifths of the population are indigenous Nauruans of Polynesian, Micronesian, and Melanesian ancestry. Language: Nauruan, English. Religion: Christianity (predominantly). Currency: Australian dollar. Nauru is a coral island with a central plateau 100–200 ft (30–60 m) high. A thin strip of fertile land encircling the island is the major zone of human settlement. It lacks harbors, and ships must anchor to buoys beyond a reef. Nauru had the world's largest concentration of phosphate, and its economy was formerly based on its mining and processing; deposits are now depleted, and the economy is being converted to fishing and other ventures. It is a republic with one legislative house; its head of state and government is the president. Nauru was inhabited by Pacific islanders when the first British explorers arrived in 1798 and named it Pleasant Island after their friendly welcome. Annexed by Germany in 1888, it was occupied by Australia at the start of World War I, and in 1919 it was placed under a joint mandate of Britain, Australia, and New Zealand. During World War II it was occupied by the Japanese. Made a U.N. trust territory under Australian administration in 1947, it gained complete independence in 1968 and joined the British Commonwealth in 1969. In recent years it has

N
O
Z

gained notoriety as a money-laundering center. See also map at OCEANIA.

nausea Discomfort in the pit of the stomach associated with disgust for food and a feeling that VOMITING will follow, as it often does. Nausea results from irritation of nerve endings in the stomach or duodenum, which stimulate brain centers that control nausea and vomiting. Nausea can be a symptom of minor or serious disorders. Common causes include indigestion, FOOD POISONING, MOTION SICKNESS, and PREGNANCY (morning sickness). Nausea may also arise from any cause of abnormal lack of appetite (e.g., shock, pain, influenza).

Nautilus Any of at least three historic SUBMARINES. Robert FULTON built one of the earliest submersible craft in 1800 in France; his *Nautilus* used a hand-turned propeller for power. Andrew Campbell and James Ash of Britain built a *Nautilus* submarine driven by battery-powered electric motors in 1886. A *Nautilus* was also the world's first nuclear-powered submarine, launched by the U.S. Navy in 1954. It made a historic trip under the polar ice cap from Alaska to the Greenland Sea in 1958.

nautilus \'nȯ-tᵊl-əs\ Either of two genera of CEPHALOPODS. The pearly, or chambered, nautilus (genus *Nautilus*) lives in the outermost chamber of its smooth, coiled, usually 36-chambered shell, about 10 in. (25 cm) in diameter, which it can employ as a float. Nautiluses search the ocean bottom for shrimp or other prey, which they capture with up to 94 small, suckerless, contractile tentacles. The paper nautilus (genus *Argonauta*) feeds on plankton near the surface of tropical and subtropical seas. The female resembles an OCTOPUS but has a thin, unchambered, coiled shell, 12–16 in. (30–40 cm) in diameter.

Navajo *or* **Navaho** \'na-və-ˌhō\ Most populous Indian group in the U.S., with about 200,000 individuals in NW New Mexico, Arizona, and SE Utah. The Navajo and Apache migrated to the Southwest from Canada around A.D. 900–1200, after which the Navajo came under the influence of the PUEBLO INDIANS. Painted pottery and the famous Navajo rugs, as well as SANDPAINTING, are products of this influence. Their traditional economy was based on farming, and later herding of sheep, goats, and cattle. Religion focused on the emergence of the first people from worlds beneath the earth's surface. In 1863, the U.S. government ordered Col. Kit CARSON to put an end to Navajo and Apache raiding; his offensives resulted in the incarceration of about 8,000 Navajo and the destruction of crops and herds. Today many Navajo live on or near the Navajo Reservation (24,000 sq mi; 64,000 sq km); thousands earn their living as transient workers. Their language has been tenaciously preserved.

Naval Academy, U.S. See UNITED STATES NAVAL ACADEMY

Navarra \nä-'vä-rä\ Autonomous community (pop., 1998 est.: 531,000) and province, N Spain. It is approximately co-extensive with the Spanish part of the historical kingdom of NAVARRE. It has an area of 4,024 sq mi (10,422 sq km). The PYRENEES dominate its N half, and a Mediterranean climate prevails in the south. Its capital is PAMPLONA.

Navarre \nə-'vär\ *Spanish* **Navarra** Ancient kingdom, N Spain, bordered by France, ARAGON, CASTILE, and the BASQUE COUNTRY. It encompassed modern NAVARRA and part of the French department of Pyrénées-Atlantiques. It was conquered by the Romans, the Visigoths, and CHARLEMAGNE. French dynasties ruled Navarre after 1234. Incorporated into Castile in 1515, it was united to France when Henry of Navarre became King HENRY IV of France in 1589.

nave Main part of a Christian church, extending from the entrance to the chancel (area around the altar). In a BASILICA, which has side aisles, nave refers only to the central section. Medieval naves were generally divided into many bays, producing the effect of great length. During the Renaissance, the nave was divided into fewer compartments, giving a feeling of spaciousness and balanced proportion, as in ST. PAUL'S CATHEDRAL.

navigation Science of directing a craft by determining its position, course, and distance traveled. Early mariners followed landmarks visible on shore; the Phoenicians and Polynesians used the stars. The COMPASS (first used by the Chinese around 1100) gave a constant reference point; modern compasses are stabilized by GYROSCOPES. Ship speed was first calculated by dropping overboard a log attached to a line knotted at regular intervals; the number of knots exposed while a sandglass emptied gave the vessel's speed in knots (nautical mph). Fixing a position requires charts detailing known locations and instruments that calculate a vessel's bearing relative to them. The earliest instrument for determining latitude was the quadrant, which measured the altitude of the polestar or the noonday sun. Other early instruments included the SEXTANT and the ASTROLABE. Longitude (used for navigation with increasing success in the 17th–18th cent.) was fixed using CHRONOMETERS and tables showing positions of celestial bodies. In the 20th cent., radio beacons and satellite networks allowed aircraft and ships to determine their position. Dead reckoning uses a history of a vessel's headings and speeds drawn from gyroscopes and from computerized measurements of the craft's acceleration. See also GLOBAL POSITIONING SYSTEM.

Navratilova \ˌnav-rə-ti-'lō-və\, **Martina** (b.1956) Czech-U.S. tennis player. She became the undisputed top-seeded player in the world in 1979 after winning the Wimbledon women's singles and doubles. In 1982 she won 90 of 93 matches, and in 1983 she won 86 of 87 matches. In 1984 she was honored for winning the Grand Slam, but later was denied the title on a technicality. Her lifetime total of 56 Grand Slam championships placed her second only to Margaret Smith COURT. She retired from active singles competition in 1994 with 167 titles, more than any other player, male or female, in tennis history.

navy Warships and craft of every kind maintained by a nation for fighting on, under, or over the sea. A large modern navy includes AIRCRAFT CARRIERS, cruisers, DESTROYERS, frigates, SUBMARINES, minesweepers and minelayers, gunboats, and various support, supply, and repair ships, as well as naval bases and ports essential to sea control and sea denial. Sea control enables a nation to carry on maritime commerce, amphibious assaults, and other wartime seaborne operations. Sea denial deprives enemy merchant vessels and warships of safe navigation. See also UNITED STATES NAVY.

Naxos \'nak-säs\ Largest island (pop., 1981: 14,000) of the CYCLADES, Greece. It is about 22 mi (35 km) long and 16 mi (26 km) wide. The capital is Náxos. In ancient times, it was famous for its wines and the worship of DIONYSUS. In mythology, it is where THESEUS abandoned ARIADNE. In the 7th–6th cent. B.C., it exported white marble for statuary. It was captured by the Persians in 490 B.C. and by Athens in 471 B.C. A Venetian duchy ruled 1207–1566; it was later ruled by the Turks. In 1830 it joined the Greek kingdom. Mycenaean ruins (see MYCENAE) have been found there.

Nayarit \ˌnī-ə-'rēt\ State (pop., 2000: 920,000), W central Mexico. Located on the Pacific Ocean, it has an area of 10,664 sq mi (27,620 sq km). The capital is Tepic. The SIERRA MADRE cuts the state's terrain into gorges and valleys. Its volcanoes Ceboruco and Sangangüey are notable, and the coastal lagoons are well-known bird refuges. Nayarit is primarily agricultural.

Nazarenes \'na-zə-ˌrēnz\ Members of the Brotherhood of St. Luke, an association formed in 1809 by young German, Swiss, and Austrian painters in reaction against Neoclassicism. Moving to Rome (1810), they acquired the nickname Nazarenes because of their biblical style of hair and dress. They admired medieval and early Renaissance painters and rejected most subsequent painting, believing it abandoned religious ideals and morality in favor of artistic virtuosity. Members lived and worked together in a semimonastic existence, in imitation of the medieval workshop. Its leading members were Friedrich Overbeck (1789–1869), Franz Pforr (1788–1812), and Peter von Cornelius (1783–1867).

Nazareth *Hebrew* **Nazerat** \ˌnä-zə-'rät\ *Arabic* **En Nasira** \en-'nä-sē-ˌrä\ Town (pop., 1992 est.: 50,000), N Israel, southeast of HAIFA. It is Israel's largest Arab city. In the NEW TESTAMENT, it is the childhood home of JESUS. It contains many Christian churches and is a pilgrimage center. Christian Arabs form the majority of the population.

Nazi Party German political party of NATIONAL SOCIALISM. Founded in 1919 as the German Workers' Party, it changed its name to the National Socialist German Workers' Party (Nationalsozialistische Deutsche Arbeiter-Partei, source of the nickname Nazi) when Adolf HITLER became leader (1920–21). It grew from its home base in Bavaria and attracted members from disaffected elements throughout Germany. It organized strong-arm groups (later the SA) to protect its rallies. Though the failed BEER HALL PUTSCH diminished the party's influence, the GREAT DEPRESSION brought millions of new members, and in 1932 the party became the largest bloc in the Reichstag. After Hitler was named chancellor in 1933, it became the only political party allowed in Germany. It controlled virtually all activities in Germany until the end of World War II (1945), after which the party was banned.

NBA See NATIONAL BASKETBALL ASSN.

NBC *in full* **National Broadcasting Co.** Major U.S. BROADCASTING network. Formed in 1926 by RCA CORP., GENERAL ELECTRIC CO., and WESTINGHOUSE ELECTRIC CORP., it was the first U.S. company to operate a broadcast network. Directed by RCA's president David SARNOFF, it became wholly owned by RCA in 1930. NBC was initially divided into the semi-independent Blue Network and Red Network. By 1938 the Red Network carried 75% of NBC's programs; the Blue Network was sold in 1941 and became ABC. NBC continued to lead the networks with its popular comedy, variety, and drama programs, but in the late 1940s it lost several leading performers to CBS. NBC entered television broadcasting in a weakened position, but gradually regained its leading position. In 1986 RCA was sold to GE.

NCAA See NATIONAL COLLEGIATE ATHLETIC ASSN.

NCR Corp. U.S. manufacturer of cash registers, computers, and information-processing systems. It was founded in 1884 as National Cash Register Co. by John H. Patterson (1844–1922). The company expanded in the 20th cent., introducing accounting machines in the 1920s, electronic products during World War II, computer hardware and software in the 1960s, and microelectronics in the 1970s. In 1991 it was purchased by AT&T CORP. and renamed AT&T Global Information Solutions. In 1996, NCR Corp. was spun off with its original name.

N'Djamena \ˈn-jä-ˈmä-nä\ *formerly* **Fort-Lamy** \ˌför-lə-ˈmē\ City (metro. area pop., 1993 est.: 531,000), capital of Chad. It lies adjacent to Cameroon. Founded in 1900 as Fort-Lamy, it remained a small settlement until after Chad's independence in 1960. It was occupied by Libyan forces in 1980–81 during the civil war that began in the 1960s. It is an important marketplace for cotton, cattle, and fish. It is the site of the nation's only university, the Univ. of Chad (founded 1971).

Ndongo \ˈn-ˈdȯŋ-gō\ Historical African kingdom of Mbundu people. Established around 1500 in what is now Angola, it traded with the Portuguese of SÃO TOMÉ. When Portugal tried to take it over, a century of fighting ensued. It was absorbed into Angola about 1670.

NEA See NATIONAL EDUCATION ASSN.

Neagh \ˈnä\, **Lough** Lake, E central Northern Ireland. It is the largest lake in the British Isles, with an area of 153 sq mi (396 sq km). Ancient deposits on its NW shore have yielded the oldest recorded human artifacts in Ireland. In 1959 flood-control works lowered the lake level.

Neanderthal \nē-ˈan-dər-ˌthȯl, nä-ˈän-dər-ˌtäl\ Species of the genus *Homo* that inhabited much of Europe and the Mediterranean lands in the late PLEISTOCENE, about 100,000–35,000 years ago. The name derives from the discovery in 1856 of remains in a cave above Germany's Neander Valley. Some scholars designate the species as *Homo neanderthalensis* and do not consider them direct human ancestors, while others regard them as an early form of *HOMO SAPIENS*. Neanderthals were short, stout, and powerful. Cranial capacity equaled or surpassed that of modern humans, though their braincases were long, low, and wide. They seem to have walked fully erect. They were cave dwellers who used fire, hunted animals using stone tools and wooden spears (see MOUSTERIAN INDUSTRY), buried their dead, and cared for their sick or injured. They probably used language and may have practiced religion.

near-death experience Mystical or transcendent experience reported by people who have been on the threshold of death. Characteristics frequently include hearing oneself declared dead, feelings of peacefulness, the sense of leaving one's body, the sense of moving through a dark tunnel toward a bright light, a life review, the crossing of a border, and meetings with deceased friends and relatives. Near-death experiences are reported by about one-third of those who come close to death. The causes remain uncertain. Typical aftereffects include greater spirituality and decreased fear of death.

Nebraska State (pop., 2000: 1,711,000), W central U.S. It covers 77,355 sq mi (200,349 sq km); its capital is LINCOLN. The MISSOURI RIVER is on its E boundary. The N. Platte and S. Platte unite in SW central Nebraska to form the Platte River. Various prehistoric peoples inhabited the area as early as 8000 B.C. Indian tribes living in the area include PAWNEE, UTE, and Omaha in the east and SIOUX, ARAPAHO, and COMANCHE in the west. The U.S. bought the territory from France as part of the LOUISIANA PURCHASE in 1803. In 1804 the LEWIS AND CLARK EXPEDITION visited the Nebraska side of the Missouri River. It became part of Nebraska Territory with the KANSAS-NEBRASKA ACT of 1854. Nebraska was admitted to the Union as the 37th state in 1867. Soon after, population increased, and as Indian resistance on the frontier was broken, settlement extended to Nebraska's panhandle. At the turn of the 20th cent., it experienced a short but influential POPULIST MOVEMENT. In 1937 it established a unicameral legislature, the only one in the nation. Most of the state is agricultural; its industries include food processing and machinery. Petroleum is the principal mineral resource. In addition to Lincoln, OMAHA is the state's other cultural and industrial center.

Nebuchadnezzar II \ˌneb-yə-kəd-ˈne-zər\ *or* **Nebuchadrezzar** \ˌneb-yə-kəd-ˈre-zər\ (c.630–561? B.C.) Second and greatest king of the Chaldean dynasty of BABYLONIA. He began his military career as an administrator (c.610 B.C.) and ascended the throne on his father's death, just after winning Syria from the Egyptians (605 B.C.). He attacked Judah, finally capturing Jerusalem in 587/6, and deporting prominent citizens to BABYLON. He devoted time and energy to rebuilding Babylon's infrastructure, and may have built the Hanging Gardens of Babylon.

nebula \ˈneb-yə-lə\ Tenuous cloud of gas and dust in interstellar space. Nebulae constitute a small part of a GALAXY's mass. Dark nebulae are very dense, cold molecular clouds that appear as large, obscure, irregular areas in the sky. Bright nebulae appear as faintly glowing surfaces; they emit light or reflect that of nearby stars. See also PLANETARY NEBULA.

nebular hypothesis See SOLAR NEBULA

Neckar River \ˈne-kär\ River, SW Germany. It rises in the BLACK FOREST and flows north and northeast 228 mi (367 km), passing STUTTGART and HEIDELBERG to enter the RHINE RIVER at MANNHEIM. Many of the hills above its picturesque valley are crowned with castles.

Necker \nä-ˈker, ˈne-kər\, **Jacques** (1732–1804) Swiss-French finance minister under LOUIS XVI. Born in Geneva, he became a banker in Paris, amassed wealth from speculating during the Seven Years' War, and retired from banking in 1772. He became France's director-general of finance in 1777. He was forced to resign in 1781 over opposition to his scheme to help finance the AMERICAN REVOLUTION. Recalled in 1788 to rescue the almost-bankrupt France, he proposed financial and political reforms that included a limited constitutional monarchy. Court opposition led to Necker's dismissal on July 11, 1789, an event that provoked the storming of the BASTILLE. Germaine de STAËL was his daughter.

necropolis \ni-ˈkrä-pə-ləs\ (Greek: "city of the dead") Extensive and elaborate burial place serving an ancient city. Many in Egypt were situated across the Nile River opposite the cities. In Greece and Rome a necropolis often lined the roads leading out of town. A necropolis was discovered in the 1940s under ST. PETER'S BASILICA in Rome.

necropsy See AUTOPSY

nectarine Smooth-skinned PEACH (*Prunus persica* 'nectarina'), grown throughout warmer temperate regions. They result when some peaches self-pollinate or are crossed so that they express a genetic factor for smooth skin. Com-

N

monly eaten fresh or cooked in desserts and jams; they are a good source of vitamins A and C.

needlefish Any of about 60 species (family Belonidae) of primarily marine, edible, carnivorous fishes found throughout temperate and tropical waters. Needlefish are adept jumpers and have a long, slender jaw with sharp teeth. They are long, slim, and silvery, with a blue or green back. The largest species grows to 4 ft (1.2 m) long.

needlepoint Embroidery in which the stitches are counted and worked with a needle over the threads, or mesh, of a canvas foundation. If the canvas has 16 or more mesh holes per linear inch, the embroidery is called petit point, a style dominant in the 16th–18th cent. Needlepoint as it is known today originated in the 17th cent., with the fashion for furniture upholstered with embroidered fabrics. Wool is generally used for needlepoint, silk yarn less often. Needlepoint kits, containing canvas stamped with a design and all the materials needed for the project, were sold as early as the mid-18th cent.

Nefertiti \ˌne-fər-ˈtē-tē\ (14th cent. B.C.) Queen of Egypt and wife of AKHENATON (r.1353–1336 B.C.). She is known from her portrait bust found at TELL EL-AMARNA, the king's new capital. She may have been an Asian princess from Mitanni. Of her six daughters, two became queens of Egypt. In the 12th year of Akhenaton's reign, she either retired after losing favor or died.

Negev \ˈne-ˌgev\ or **Ha-Negev** Desert region, S Israel. Bounded by the SINAI Peninsula and the Jordan Rift Valley, it has an area of about 4,700 sq mi (12,200 sq km). It was a pastoral region in biblical times and a source of grain for the Roman empire. After the Arab conquest of Palestine (7th cent. A.D.), for more than 1,200 years it had only a small population of BEDOUIN. Modern agricultural development began with three KIBBUTZES in 1943; irrigation projects were initiated after World War II. It was the scene of clashes between Israeli and Egyptian forces in 1948–49. It is the site of many planned Israeli settlements, including Elat, Israel's outlet to the Red Sea. Beersheba is an important administrative center.

negligence In law, failure to exercise the degree of care expected of a person of ordinary prudence in protecting others from a risk of harm. It may render one civilly and sometimes criminally liable for resulting injuries. The doctrine of negligence does not require the elimination of all risk, but rather only foreseeable and unreasonable risk.

Negritude \nā-grē-ˈtüed\ Literary movement of the 1930s, '40s, and '50s that began among French-speaking African and Caribbean writers living in Paris as a protest against French colonial rule and the policy of assimilation. Its leading figures were Léopold SENGHOR of Senegal, Aimé Césaire (b.1913) of Martinique, and Léon Damas (1912–1978) of French Guiana. The group believed that Africans must look to their own heritage for values and traditions, and that writers should use African subject matter and poetic traditions. The movement faded in the early 1960s after its objectives had been achieved in most African countries.

Negro \ˈnā-grō\, **Río** or **Río Guainía** \ˈrē-ù-gwī-ˈnē-ə\ River, NW S. America. It rises in the rain forest of E Colombia, forms a section of the Colombia–Venezuela boundary, crosses Brazil, and enters the AMAZON RIVER at MANAUS. It is about 1,400 mi (2,250 km) long and is a major transport artery. Its name comes from its jet-black color, caused by the decomposition of organic matter and its low silt content.

Negroid See RACE

Negro Leagues Associations of teams of African-American baseball players active largely between 1920 and the late 1940s. The principal leagues were the Negro National League, organized in 1920, and the Negro American League, organized in 1937. The Homestead (Pa.) Grays won nine pennants in the years 1937–45 and included the great hitters Cool Papa Bell, Buck Leonard, and Josh GIBSON. In the mid-1930s the Pittsburgh Crawfords included Satchel PAIGE. The Kansas City Monarchs, after winning four national championships, lost Jackie ROBINSON to the Brooklyn Dodgers; the breaking of the color barrier led to the Negro Leagues' quick decline.

Negros \ˈnā-grōs\ Island (pop., 1990: 3,170,000) in the VISAYAN group, central Philippines. It has an area of 4,907

sq mi (12,710 sq km). It produces about 50% of Philippine sugar and is one of the wealthiest and most politically influential regions in the nation.

Nehemiah \ˌnē-ə-ˈmī-ə\ (fl.5th cent. B.C.) Jewish leader who supervised the rebuilding of JERUSALEM. His story is told in the Old Testament Book of Nehemiah. He was cupbearer to the Persian ruler Artaxerxes I soon after the end of the BABYLONIAN EXILE. Around 444 B.C. he was put in charge of Jerusalem's reconstruction, and he organized the rebuilding of the city walls. He also revived adherence to Mosaic law and forbade intermarriage with non-Jews.

Nehru \ˈnā-rü\, **Jawaharlal** (1889–1964) First prime minister of independent India (1947–64). Son of the independence advocate Motilal Nehru (1861–1931), Nehru became a lawyer in 1912. More interested in politics than law, he was impressed by Mohandas GANDHI's approach to Indian independence. He joined the INDIAN NATIONAL CONGRESS in 1919, and in 1929 he became its president. Proclaiming complete independence (rather than dominion status) as India's political goal, he was imprisoned nine times between 1921 and 1945 for his political activity. When India was granted limited self-government in 1935, the Congress Party under Nehru unwisely refused to form coalition governments with the MUSLIM LEAGUE in some provinces; the hardening of relations between Hindus and Muslims that followed ultimately led to the partition of India and the creation of Pakistan. As the first prime minister of independent India, he attempted a foreign policy of nonalignment during the COLD WAR. During his tenure India clashed with Pakistan over Kashmir and with China over the Brahmaputra River valley. Domestically he promoted democracy, socialism, secularism, and unity, adapting modern values to Indian conditions. His daughter, Indira GANDHI, became prime minister two years after his death.

Neiman Marcus \ˌnē-mən-ˈmär-kəs\ Prestigious U.S. department-store chain. It was founded in Dallas in 1907 by Herbert Marcus, his sister Carrie Marcus Neiman, and her husband A. L. Neiman. From the beginning it featured extravagant and outlandish gifts (including camels and Chinese junks) to appeal to the rich, in addition to more standard merchandise for moderate-income customers.

Nei Monggol \ˈnā-ˈmùŋ-ˈgól\ or **Nei-meng-ku** \ˈnā-ˈməŋ-ˈgü\ English **Inner Mongolia** Autonomous region (pop., 1999 est.: 23,620,000), N China. Its capital is HOHHOT. A vast inland plateau about 3,000 ft (900 m) above sea level, it lies partly in the GOBI DESERT to the north and is partly bordered along the south by the GREAT WALL. In 1664 Inner Mongolia was separated from MONGOLIA (or Outer Mongolia); it became an autonomous region in 1947. Its population of mainly Mongols and Chinese lives mostly in the agricultural belt near the HUANG RIVER. Industrial development has centered around its largest city, Baotou (pop., 1999 est.: 1,093,000).

Nejd \ˈnezhd\ or **Najd** \ˈnäzhd\ Region of central Saudi Arabia. Composed of a rocky plateau sloping eastward from the mountains of the HEJAZ, it is sparsely settled. It became the center of the fundamentalist WAHHABI movement in the mid-18th cent. Nejd was captured by Abdulaziz IBN SAUD around 1905 and united with the Hejaz to become the kingdom of Saudi Arabia in 1932.

Nelson, (John) Byron (b.1912) U.S. golfer. Born in Fort Worth, Texas, "Lord Byron" won the U.S. Open (1939), the Masters (1937, 1942), and the PGA championship (1940, 1945), setting records in 1945 when he won 18 out of 30 tournaments, 11 in succession.

Nelson, Horatio later Viscount Nelson known as **Lord Nelson** (1758–1805) British naval commander. In 1793 he was sent to support the British allies against the French in the Mediterranean and helped win the Battle of Cape St. Vincent (1797). In 1798 he pursued Napoleon's fleet to Egypt, where he won the decisive Battle of the NILE. During a prolonged stay in Naples for his ships' repairs, he pursued a love affair with Emma, Lady HAMILTON. He helped restore the Neapolitan king FERDINAND I to power (1799), and later defeated the Danes at the Battle of Copenhagen (1801). Appointed commander in chief of the navy, in 1805 he was sent to the Mediterranean to meet the threat posed by Napoleon's scheme to invade England. In the Battle of

TRAFALGAR, Nelson, aboard his flagship *Victory,* was shot by a French sniper and died just as the British fleet secured its victory. Widely mourned, he became England's most popular hero. His brilliant tactical command assured British naval supremacy for over 100 years.

Nelson, Willie (b.1933) U.S. COUNTRY-MUSIC singer and songwriter. Born in Abbott, Texas, he learned guitar from his grandfather and by 10 was performing at local dances. In 1961 he moved to Nashville, where he wrote hit songs for dozens of singers, including "Hello Walls," "Night Life," and "Crazy." Returning to Texas, he released the hit album *Red Headed Stranger* (1975); it was followed by *Wanted: The Outlaws* (1976), which outsold every previous country album, and *Stardust* (1978). He has recorded with at least 75 other singers, including Waylon Jennings (b.1937).

Nelson River River, N central Manitoba. Flowing out of N Lake WINNIPEG into HUDSON BAY, it is 400 mi (644 km) long. A trading post of the HUDSON'S BAY CO. was established there about 1670. Fur traders used the river as an inland route. The Hudson Bay Railway now follows most of its course.

Neman River \'ne-mən\ *Lithuanian* **Nemunas** \'ne-mü-ˌnäs\ River, central Europe. Rising in Belarus, south of MINSK, it flows west into Lithuania, and between Lithuania and Kaliningrad province, Russia, to empty into the BALTIC SEA. It is 582 mi (936 km) long and navigable for most of its length. It was the scene of many battles between Russian and German forces in World War I.

nematode \'ne-mə-ˌtōd\ *or* **roundworm** Any of more than 15,000 named and many more unnamed species of WORMS in the class Nematoda (phylum Aschelminthes). Nematodes include plant and animal parasites and free-living forms found in soil, freshwater, and saltwater. Some species have separate sexes; others are hermaphroditic. They range from microscopic to about 23 ft (7 m) long. Nematode parasites are most common in the digestive, circulatory, or respiratory system. Hookworms, PINWORMS, filarial worms, guinea worms, trichina, and eelworms are nematodes.

Nemerov \'nem-ər-ˌóf\, **Howard** (1920–1991) U.S. poet. Born in New York City, the brother of Diane ARBUS, he taught principally at Bennington. His poetry appears in volumes beginning with *The Image and the Law* (1947) and including *Collected Poems* (1977, Pulitzer Prize, National Book Award). His verse, marked by irony and self-deprecatory wit, is often about nature. His fiction includes *The Homecoming Game* (1957). He was poet laureate of the U.S. 1988–90.

Nemesis \'ne-mə-səs\ Greek goddess of retribution. In the earliest Greek religion she was worshiped as a fertility goddess. According to one legend, she was the mother of HELEN of Troy. Nemesis dealt out punishments that expressed the gods' disapproval of human presumption. Her cult was also popular in Rome, particularly among soldiers.

Nen River *formerly* **Nonni River** River, NE China, main tributary of the Songhua River. It rises in N Heilongjiang province and flows south, watering the fertile N section of the Manchurian plain. It is about 740 mi (1,190 km) long, and much of it is navigable.

Neoclassical architecture Modern classicism (as it was known at the time) of the 18th and early 19th cent. The movement concerned itself with the logic of entire Classical volumes, unlike Classical Revivalism (see GREEK REVIVAL), which tended to reuse Classical parts. Neoclassical architecture is characterized by grandeur of scale; simplicity of geometric forms; Greek, especially Doric (see ORDER), or Roman detail; dramatic use of columns; and a preference for blank walls. The new taste represented a general reaction to the excesses of ROCOCO STYLE. Russia's CATHERINE II transformed St. Petersburg into an unparalleled collection of Neoclassical buildings. By 1800 nearly all new British architecture reflected the Neoclassical spirit (see Robert ADAM, John SOANE). France's boldest innovator was Claude-Nicolas LEDOUX. In the U.S., Neoclassicism continued to flourish throughout the 19th cent.

Neoclassicism See CLASSICISM AND NEOCLASSICISM

Neo-Confucianism In China, a rationalistic revival of CONFUCIANISM in the 11th cent. A.D. that influenced Chinese thought for 800 years. The movement sought to reestablish the supremacy of the Confucian heritage over the increasingly popular BUDDHISM and TAOISM. Its two principal schools of thought were the Li Xue (School of Principle), as taught by ZHU XI, and the Xin Xue (School of Mind), represented by WANG YANGMING. Introduced into Japan by ZEN Buddhists, Neo-Confucianism became the guiding philosophy of the TOKUGAWA SHOGUNATE (1603–1867). Its emphasis on classical literature led to renewed interest in the Japanese classics and a revival of SHINTO studies.

Neo-Expressionism Art movement, chiefly of painters, dominant in the early to mid-1980s. It was controversial both in its quality and its commercialization. Its practitioners, including Julian SCHNABEL and Anselm KIEFER, returned to portraying the human body and other recognizable objects, in reaction to the abstract art of the 1970s. Their art was characterized by a tense yet playful presentation of objects in a primitivist manner, painted in vivid color harmonies, conveying inner tension and alienation. See also EXPRESSIONISM.

Neo-Impressionism Movement in French painting of the late 19th cent., in reaction against the realism of IMPRESSIONISM. The Neo-Impressionists, led by Georges SEURAT and Paul SIGNAC, applied paint to canvas in dots of contrasting pigments, scientifically chosen so that adjacent dots would blend from a distance into a single color, a technique called pointillism. Whereas the Impressionists captured the fugitive effects of color and light, the Neo-Impressionists crystallized them into immobile monumentality.

Neolithic period \ˌnē-ə-'li-thik\ ("New Stone Age") Final stage of technological development among prehistoric humans, characterized by stone tools shaped by polishing or grinding, domestication of plants or animals, permanent villages, and such crafts as pottery and weaving. It followed the PALEOLITHIC PERIOD (and in NW Europe the MESOLITHIC) and preceded the BRONZE AGE. Neolithic villages emerged in SW Asia about 9000 B.C. and flourished in the TIGRIS and EUPHRATES river valleys from about 7000 B.C. Farming spread northward throughout Eurasia, not reaching Britain and Scandinavia until after 3000 B.C. Neolithic technologies also spread to the Indus River valley of India by 5000 B.C. and to the Huang (Yellow) River valley of China by about 3500 B.C.

neon Chemical ELEMENT, chemical symbol Ne, atomic number 10. One of the NOBLE GASES, neon is colorless, odorless, tasteless, and completely unreactive. It occurs in minute amounts in the atmosphere and is obtained by fractional DISTILLATION of liquefied air. When under low pressure, it glows a bright orange-red if an electric current is passed through it. Its chief use is in luminous tubes and bulbs.

Neo-Paganism Any of several movements that attempt to revive the polytheistic religions of Europe and the Middle East. Largely a product of the 1960s, contemporary Neo-Paganism has flourished particularly in the U.S., Britain, and Scandinavia. Its adherents often have deep ecological concerns and an attachment to nature. Neo-Paganism has also attracted feminists open to goddess worship. Neo-Pagan groups include the Church of All Worlds, Feraferia, Pagan Way, the Reformed Druids of N. America, the Church of the Eternal Source, and the Viking Brotherhood. See also WICCA.

neoplasm See TUMOR

Neoplatonism Form of PLATONISM developed by PLOTINUS in the 3rd cent. A.D. and modified by his successors. It came to dominate the Greek philosophical schools and remained predominant until the late 6th cent. It postulated an all-sufficient unity, the One, from which emanated the Divine Mind, or LOGOS, and below that, the World Soul. Individual souls could rise to mystical union with the One through contemplation. Though Plotinus's thought resembles GNOSTICISM in some respects, he was a passionate opponent of Gnosticism.

Neorealism *or* **neorealismo** Italian literary movement that flourished especially after World War II. Rooted in the 1920s, it was similar to the *verismo* ("realism") movement but differed in that its upsurge resulted from the intense feelings inspired by fascist repression, the Resistance, and the war. Neorealist writers include Italo CALVINO, Alberto

MORAVIA, Cesare PAVESE, Salvatore QUASIMODO, and Ignazio SILONE. The movement reemerged after the war in full strength.

Neosho River \nē-'ō-shō\ *or* **Grand River** River, SE Kansas and NE Oklahoma. It rises in E central Kansas and flows about 460 mi (740 km) to join the ARKANSAS RIVER near Ft. Gibson, Okla. Neosho is an OSAGE word meaning "clear and abundant water." The river crossing at Council Grove was a starting point for the SANTA FE TRAIL.

Nepal \nə-'pȯl\ *officially* **Kingdom of Nepal** Nation, S Asia. Area: 54,362 sq mi (140,798 sq km). Population (2000): 24,702,000. Capital: KATHMANDU. Most of the people are Nepalese of Indo-Aryan ancestry; there is a significant mi-

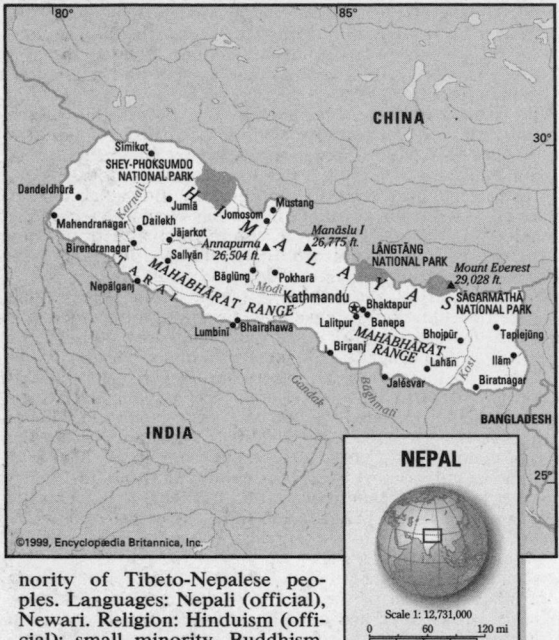

nority of Tibeto-Nepalese peoples. Languages: Nepali (official), Newari. Religion: Hinduism (official); small minority, Buddhism. Currency: Nepalese rupee. Nepal contains some of the most rugged mountainous terrain in the world. The great HIMALAYAS, including Mt. EVEREST, are in its central and N parts. As a result of its years of geographic and self-imposed isolation, it is one of the least-developed nations of the world. Its market economy is mostly based on agriculture, and it is a major producer of medicinal herbs, which grow on the slopes of the Himalayas. It is a constitutional monarchy with a bicameral parliament; its chief of state is the king, and the head of government is the prime minister. The region developed under early Buddhist influence, and dynastic rule dates from about the 4th cent. A.D. It was formed into a single kingdom in 1769 and fought border wars with China, Tibet, and British India in the 18th–19th cent. Its independence was recognized by Britain in 1923. A new constitution in 1990 restricted royal authority, stated basic human and civil rights, and accepted a democratically elected parliamentary government. In its national outreach, it signed trade agreements with India in 1997. In 2001 the king and queen were murdered by their son, the heir apparent.

nephrite \'ne-ˌfrīt\ Gem-quality, usually green SILICATE MINERAL. The less prized but more common of the two types of JADE, it may be distinguished from JADEITE by its splintery fracture and oily luster. Nephrite occurs in low-grade (formed under low-temperature, low-pressure conditions), regionally metamorphosed rocks. Important deposits occur in China, Siberia, New Zealand, Switzerland, Alaska, and Wyoming.

nephritis \ni-'frī-təs\ INFLAMMATION of the KIDNEYS. The most common type is BRIGHT'S DISEASE. Symptoms vary with the type of nephritis; severe cases can result in KIDNEY

FAILURE. Causes include infection, ALLERGY or AUTOIMMUNE DISEASE, blockage in the URINARY SYSTEM, and hereditary diseases. Treatment addresses the cause where possible.

nephrology \ni-'frä-lə-jē\ Branch of medicine dealing with KIDNEY function and diseases. An understanding of kidney physiology is important not only in treating kidney disease but in knowing the effect of drugs, diet, and HYPERTENSION on kidney disease, and vice versa. A key development in nephrology was the permanent arteriovenous shunt (1960), which made repeated hemodialysis feasible, instantly changing the outlook for chronic-renal-disease patients from certain death to 90% survival. See also DIALYSIS, KIDNEY FAILURE, KIDNEY STONE, KIDNEY TRANSPLANT, NEPHRON.

nephron Functional unit of the KIDNEY that removes waste and excess substances from the blood to produce URINE. Each of the million or so nephrons in each kidney is a tubule 1.2–2.2 in. (30–55 mm) long. At one end it forms a double-walled cuplike structure (Bowman's capsule) enclosing a cluster of CAPILLARIES (glomerulus). Fluid forced out of the blood through the capillary walls into Bowman's capsule flows into the adjacent renal tubule, where water and nutrients are selectively reabsorbed back into the blood, and ELECTROLYTES such as sodium and potassium are balanced in several distinct sections along its length. The final concentrated product is urine. See also URINARY SYSTEM.

Neptune Eighth PLANET from the sun, discovered in 1846 and named after the Roman sea god. It takes 165 years to orbit the sun, at an average distance of 2.8 billion mi (4.5 billion km), and rotates every 16.11 hours. Neptune has over 17 times earth's mass, 58 times its volume, and 12% stronger gravity at the top of its atmosphere, with a diameter of 30,775 mi (49,528 km). Largely hydrogen and helium, it has no apparent solid surface but may have a frozen, rocky core. Methane gas in its atmosphere absorbs red light, causing Neptune's deep blue color. Voyager 2 found winds of over 700 meters per second, the fastest on any of the sun's planets, and dark spots that may be storms like Jupiter's GREAT RED SPOT. Neptune receives little solar radiation, but temperatures around −353°F (−214°C) suggest an internal heat source. A weak magnetic field traps a belt of SOLAR WIND and COSMIC RAYS. Neptune has eight known satellites; the largest is TRITON.

Neptune In ROMAN RELIGION, the god of water. Neptune was originally the god of fresh water, but by 399 B.C. he was identified with the Greek god POSEIDON and thus became a deity of the sea. Neptune's festival (Neptunalia) took place in the heat of summer (July 23), when fresh water was scarcest. In art Neptune is often given Poseidon's attributes, the trident and dolphin.

Nerbudda River See NARMADA RIVER

Nereid \'nir-ē-əd\ In GREEK MYTHOLOGY, any of the daughters of the sea god NEREUS and of Doris, daughter of Oceanus. The Nereids, who numbered 50 or 100, were depicted as young girls, inhabiting any water, salt or fresh, and benign toward humanity. The best known were Amphitrite, consort of POSEIDON; THETIS; and Galatea, loved by POLYPHEMUS.

Nereus \'nir-ē-əs\ Greek sea god. He was noted for his gift of prophecy and his ability to change his shape. He lived at the bottom of the sea with his daughters, the NEREIDS. HERACLES wrestled with him in a variety of shapes in order to gain his advice about recovering the golden apples of the Hesperides.

Neri \'nā-rē\, **St. Philip** (1515–1595) Roman Catholic mystic. In 1548 he cofounded a society of laymen dedicated to the care of pilgrims, the poor, and the sick. He was ordained in 1551; from 1564 to 1575 he was rector of the church of San Giovanni. In 1575 GREGORY XIII granted him Santa Maria in Vallicella, where he established his Congregation of the Oratory (see ORATORIO), a group of priests and clerics engaged in devotion and charitable activities. He was noted for his eloquence as a preacher.

Nernst \'nernst\, **Walther Hermann** (1864–1941) German scientist, one of the founders of modern PHYSICAL CHEMISTRY. Nernst's researches on the theory of electric cells (see BATTERY), the thermodynamics of chemical EQUILIB-RIUM, the properties of vapors at high temperatures and of solids at low temperatures, and the mechanism of photochemistry have had important applications. His formulation of the third law of thermodynamics earned a Nobel Prize (1920).

Nero *in full* Nero Claudius Caesar Augustus(*or* Drusus) Germanicus *orig.* Lucius Domitius Ahenobarbus (A.D. 37–68) Roman emperor (54–68). He became CLAUDIUS' adoptive son when the emperor married Nero's mother, AGRIPPINA THE YOUNGER, and took the throne after she had Claudius poisoned. He was guided by his tutor, SENECA, and by Agrippina until he murdered her. By respecting the Senate and leaving imperial administration alone, he became popular in the east, but BOUDICCA's revolt in Britain (61), unemployment, and contempt for his excesses caused dissatisfaction. In 64 a fire, possibly lit at his orders, destroyed much of Rome; he blamed and persecuted the Christians and proceeded to build a garish palace, the Domus Aurea. With his reign in decline, he murdered his wife, Octavia, as well as her successor, Poppaea, ordered Seneca to kill himself, and executed senators. Revolts in Gaul and Spain were led by GALBA, who was declared emperor by his army. Now regarded as mad, Nero gave public lyre and theatrical performances to the disgust of his subjects. Condemned by the Senate, he chose suicide over execution.

Nerses I the Great \'ner-sēz\, **St.** (c.310–373?) Patriarch of the Armenian church from about 353. A descendant of St. Gregory the Illuminator (240–332), Nerses established monastic and charitable institutions and schools. He was a supporter of King Pap of Armenia but broke with him over his fostering of religious ties with the court of Constantinople, which led to Pap's instigating the murder of Nerses.

Neruda \nä-'rü-thä\, **Pablo** *orig.* Neftalí Ricardo Reyes Basoalto (1904–1973) Chilean poet and diplomat. At 20 he published his most widely read work, *Twenty Love Poems and a Song of Despair* (1924). In 1927 he took his first diplomatic post; late in life he was ambassador to France. In Asia he began *Residence on Earth* (1933, 1935, 1947), which examined social decay and personal isolation. In 1945 he was elected senator and joined the Communist Party; he later spent years in exile when the government turned toward the right. *Canto General* (1950), his great epic poem about the American continents, is the culminating expression of his political beliefs. He was awarded the Nobel Prize in 1971.

Pablo Neruda

Nerva \'nər-və\ *in full* Nerva Caesar Augustus *orig.* Marcus Cocceius Nerva (c.A.D. 30–98) Roman emperor (96–98), first of the Five Good Emperors. Nerva served twice as consul (71, 90). After an undistinguished career, he was chosen to succeed DOMITIAN because of his age, dignity, and lack of children who would succeed him. He rejected Domitian's autocratic tyranny but completed Domitian's building projects and instituted administrative and financial reforms. He adopted TRAJAN as his heir.

nerve See NEURON

nerve gas Organophosphate that interferes with normal nerve transmission and induces intense and fatal bronchial spasm. A derivative of fluorophosphoric acid developed by Germany during World War II, nerve gas was banned from warfare by the Geneva Protocol. Gases include VX, soman, tabun, and sarin, used for a lethal attack in the Tokyo subways (1995) by the AUM SHINRIKYO.

Nervi \'ner-vē\, **Pier Luigi** (1891–1979) Italian engineer and building contractor. He became internationally renowned for inventing ferrocement, a type of concrete reinforced with steel mesh, for use in thin shell design. His projects in-

cluded a series of airplane hangars in Italy (1935–41), conceived as concrete vaults with huge spans; a sailboat with a ferroconcrete hull only .5 in (1.25 cm) thick; and his complex for the Turin Exhibition (1949–50). Nervi worked on the UNESCO headquarters in Paris (1950) with Marcel BREUER and helped design Italy's first skyscraper, the Pirelli Building in Milan (1955–59).

nervous system System of specialized cells (NEURON, or nerve cells) that conduct stimuli from a sensory receptor through a network to the site (e.g., a gland or muscle) where the response occurs. In humans, it consists of the central nervous system (BRAIN and SPINAL CORD) and the peripheral nervous system (nerves, which carry impulses to and from the central nervous system). Most cranial nerves handle head and neck sensory and motor activities; the vagus nerve conducts signals to visceral organs. Each spinal nerve is attached to the spinal cord by a sensory and a motor root. These exit between the vertebrae and merge to form a large mixed nerve, which branches to supply a defined area of the body. Disorders include AMYOTROPHIC LATERAL SCLEROSIS, CHOREA, EPILEPSY, MYASTHENIA GRAVIS, NEURAL TUBE DEFECT, PARKINSONISM, and POLIOMYELITIS.

Ness, Eliot (1903–1957) U.S. crime fighter. Born in Chicago, he was hired at 26 as a special agent of the U.S. Department of Justice to head its Chicago prohibition bureau, with the express purpose of breaking up Al CAPONE's bootlegging network. He formed a nine-man team of extremely dedicated and unbribable officers, "the Untouchables." Evidence they collected helped send Capone to prison. After the end of Prohibition in 1933, Ness held other federal posts and was director of public safety in Cleveland (1935–41).

Ness, Loch Lake, INVERNESS district in the Highland region, Scotland. At 788 ft (240 m) deep and about 23 mi (36 km) long, it has the largest volume of fresh water in Britain. It forms part of the Caledonian Canal system. Surface oscillations, or seiches, caused by differential heating, are common. Reports of an aquatic monster inhabiting Loch Ness date back to the 6th cent. but remain unproved.

Nesselrode \nyis-syilʸ-'rôd-yi, *Engl* 'ne-səl-ˌrōd\, **Karl (Robert Vasilyevich), Count** (1780–1862) Russian statesman. He served as minister of foreign affairs 1822–56, and as chancellor 1845–62. He sought to influence the Ottoman empire with treaties favoring Russia, and supported aid to Austria in suppressing the Hungarian uprising (1848). His policy of promoting Russia's influence in the Balkans helped precipitate the CRIMEAN WAR.

nest Structure built by an animal as a permanent home or for bearing and rearing offspring. The social insects build systems of chambers and tunnels, above or below ground. Fishes' nests vary from shallow depressions in sand to enclosed structures constructed of vegetation. Certain frog species build mud-basin nests. Bird nests are commonly cup-shaped or domed structures of twigs, leaves, mud, and feathers. Many mammals, especially small ones, build nests in trees, on the ground, or in burrows.

Nestlé SA Multinational manufacturer of food products. Headquartered in Vevey, Switzerland, it operates in more than 70 countries. Its products include condensed and powdered milk, baby foods, chocolate, cheese, instant coffee and tea, condiments, and frozen foods. Henri Nestlé founded the company in 1866 to manufacture the first infant formula; in 1905 it merged with the Anglo-Swiss Condensed Milk Co. Nestlé created the first milk chocolate, and in 1937 the first instant coffee, Nescafé. The company acquired Crosse & Blackwell in 1960, Stouffer Corp. in 1973, and Carnation Co. in 1984. Today it claims to be the world's largest food company.

Nestor In Greek legend, the king of Pylos in Elis. All his brothers were killed by HERACLES, but Nestor survived. In HOMER's *Iliad* he appeared as an elder statesman who entertained the warriors with tales of his youthful exploits. In the *Odyssey* Telemachus, son of ODYSSEUS, came to Elis looking for his father, and Nestor entertained him.

Nestorian Member of a Christian sect that originated in Asia Minor and Syria in the 5th cent. A.D., inspired by the views of NESTORIUS. Nestorians stressed the independence of Christ's divine and human natures. Nestorianism spread as far east as India and China; in Central Asia, certain tribes were almost entirely converted. Today the Nestorians are represented by the Church of the East, or Persian Church, usually referred to in the West as the Assyrian or Nestorian Church. Most of its 170,000 members live in Iraq, Ṣyria, and Iran.

Nestorius (late 4th cent. A.D.–c.451) Founder of NESTO-RIAN Christianity. Born of Persian parents, as bishop of Constantinople (from 428) he aroused controversy when he objected to MARY's receiving the title of Theotokos (God-Bearer), which he believed compromised Christ's full humanity. In 431 the Council of Ephesus condemned his teaching as heresy on the ground that he denied the reality of Christ's incarnation, and Nestorius went into exile. The Persian Church still adheres to his teachings.

Netherlands *officially* **Kingdom of the Netherlands** *Dutch* **Nederland** \'nā-dər-ˌlänt\ Kingdom, NW Europe. Area: 16,033 sq mi (41,525 sq km). Population (2000): 15,896,000. Capital: AMSTERDAM; Seat of Government: The HAGUE.

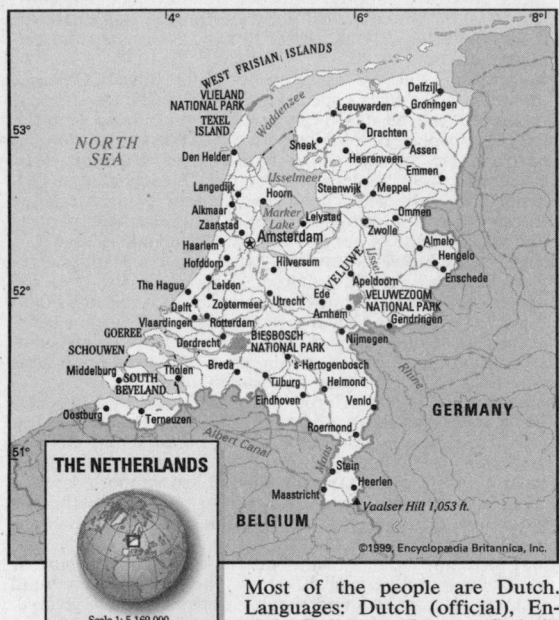

THE NETHERLANDS

Scale 1: 5,169,000

©1999, Encyclopædia Britannica, Inc.

Most of the people are Dutch. Languages: Dutch (official), English. Religions: Roman Catholicism, Protestantism. Currency: euro. The Netherlands' S and E region consists mostly of plains and a few high ridges; its W and N region is lower and includes the ZUIDER ZEE and the common delta of the RHINE, MEUSE, and SCHELDE rivers. Coastal areas are almost completely below sea level and are protected by dunes and artificial dikes. The country has a developed market economy based largely on financial services, light and heavy industries, and trade. It is a constitutional monarchy with a parliament composed of two legislative houses; its chief of state is the monarch, and the head of government is the prime minister. Celtic and Germanic tribes inhabited the region at the time of the Roman conquest. Under the Romans trade and industry flourished, but by the mid-3rd cent. A.D. Roman power had waned, eroded by resurgent German tribes and the encroachment of the sea. A Germanic invasion (406–7) ended Roman control. The MEROVINGIAN DYNASTY followed the Romans, but was supplanted in the 7th cent. by the CAROLINGIAN DYNASTY, which converted the area to Christianity. After CHARLEMAGNE's death (814), the area was increasingly the target of VIKING attacks. It became part of the medieval kingdom of Lotharingia, which avoided incorporation into the HOLY ROMAN EMPIRE by investing its bishops and abbots with secular powers, leading to the establishment of an Imperial Church. In the 12th–14th cent. large areas of land in the Holland-Utrecht peat-bog plain were made available for agriculture, and dike-building occurred on a large scale; FLANDERS developed as a textiles center. The dukes of BURGUNDY gained control in the late 14th cent. By the early 16th cent. the Low Countries were ruled by the Spanish HABSBURGS. By this time the Dutch had taken the lead in fishing, shipbuilding, and beer brewing, laying the basis for Holland's remarkable 17th-cent. prosperity. Culturally, it was the period of Jan van EYCK, THOMAS À KEMPIS, and Desiderius ERASMUS. CALVINISM and the ANABAPTISTS' doctrines attracted many followers. In 1581 the seven N provinces, led by Calvinists, declared their independence from Spain, and Spain recognized Dutch independence in 1648, following the THIRTY YEARS' WAR. The 17th cent. was the golden age of Dutch civilization. Benedict de SPINOZA and René DESCARTES enjoyed the country's intellectual freedom, and REMBRANDT and Johannes VERMEER painted their masterpieces. The Dutch E. INDIA CO. secured Asian colonies, and the country's standard of living soared. In the 18th cent., Dutch maritime power declined; the region was conquered by the French during the FRENCH REVOLUTIONARY WARS and became the kingdom of Holland under NAPOLEON (1806). The Netherlands remained neutral in World War I and declared neutrality in World War II but was occupied by Germany. After the war it lost the Netherlands Indies, which became Indonesia (1949), and Netherlands New Guinea (1962). It joined NATO in 1949 and the EUROPEAN ECONOMIC COMMUNITY in 1958. It is a member of the EUROPEAN UNION.

Netherlands, Republic of the United See DUTCH REPUBLIC

Netherlands, Spanish See SPANISH NETHERLANDS

Netherlands Antilles \an-'ti-lēz\ *formerly* **Curaçao** \ˌkûr-ə-'sō, ˌkyûr-ə-'saů\ Five islands (pop., 2000: 221,000), in the CARIBBEAN SEA. Part of the Netherlands, they have a combined area of 309 sq mi (800 sq km). St. Eustatius, the S section of ST. MARTIN, and SABA are at the N end of the LEEWARD ISLANDS; about 500 mi (800 km) southwest, off the coast of Venezuela, are CURAÇAO and Bonaire. The capital, on Curaçao, is WILLEMSTAD. The islands were claimed for Spain by Christopher COLUMBUS in 1493. In the 17th cent. the Dutch gained control, and in 1845 the islands became the Netherlands Antilles. In 1954 they became an integral part of the Netherlands, with full autonomy in domestic affairs. Aruba seceded from the group in 1986.

Neto \'nā-tü\, **(Antônio) Agostinho** (1922–1979) Poet, physician, and first president of Angola. In 1948 Neto joined a movement aimed at rediscovering indigenous Angolan culture. In 1960 he was arrested by colonial authorities, who opened fire when his patients protested. He was imprisoned in Portugal for two years before escaping to join Angola's Marxist party, whose president he became in 1962. When Angola became independent in 1975, he was proclaimed president. His poems were widely recognized in the Portuguese-speaking world.

nettle family Family Urticaceae, composed of about 45 genera of herbaceous plants, shrubs, small trees, and a few vines, found mostly in tropical regions. Many species have on their stems and leaves stinging hairs that break the skin and release a fluid that irritates it for hours. Ornamental species include artillery plant (*Pilea microphylla*) and baby tears (*Helxine soleiroli*), both creeping plants. Ramie, or China grass (*Boehmeria nivea*), produces a valuable fiber. Some nettles can be cooked and eaten.

network, computer Two or more computers and peripheral equipment (e.g., printers) connected with one another for the purpose of exchanging data. Two basic network types are LOCAL AREA NETWORKS (LANs) and wide-area networks. Wide-area networks connect computers and smaller networks to larger networks over greater geographical areas, including different continents. Communications may occur over cables, fiber optics, or satellites, but most computer users access the network via a modem. The largest wide-area network is the INTERNET.

network, neural See NEURAL NETWORK

Neubrandenburg \'noi-ˌbrän-dən-ˌbûrk\ City (pop., 1998 est.: 77,000), NE Germany, near Tollense Lake. Founded in 1248, it became part of Mecklenburg in 1292, and prospered from its weaving industry. It was plundered during the THIRTY YEARS' WAR, devastated by fire, and battered by the NAPOLEONIC WARS. Its medieval fortifications are well preserved; most of its buildings were destroyed by bombing in World War II, but much was rebuilt after 1952.

Neuchâtel, Lake \ˌnœ-shä-ˈtel\ Lake, W Switzerland. With an area of 84 sq mi (218 sq km), it is the largest lake entirely within Switzerland. It is a survivor of a former glacial lake at the base of the JURA Mtns. On the N shore is La Tène, a major Iron Age site.

Neue Sachlichkeit \ˌnȯi-ə-ˈzäk-lik-ˌkīt\ (German: "New Objectivity") Movement in German painting of the 1920s reflecting the cynicism and resignation of the post–World War I period. The term was coined by the museum director Gustav Hartlaub for a 1925 exhibition including works by George GROSZ, Otto DIX, and Max BECKMANN. They worked in a realistic style, as opposed to the prevailing styles of abstraction and EXPRESSIONISM, using meticulous detail to portray evil in smooth, cold, and static images for the purpose of violent social satire. The movement ended in the 1930s with the rise of Nazism.

Neumann \ˈnȯi-ˌmän\, **(Johann) Balthasar** (1687–1753) German architect. In 1719 he began work on the prince-bishop's new palace in Würzburg, noted for its grand staircase. He was eventually put in charge of all major building projects in Würzburg and Bamberg, including palaces, public buildings, bridges, a water system, and many churches. A master of the ROCOCO STYLE, his best work was the pilgrimage church at Vierzehnheiligen (1743–53), featuring ingenious use of domes and barrel vaults to create sequences of round and oval spaces whose airy elegance is lit by huge windows and accented by lavish decoration.

Neumann, John von See John VON NEUMANN

neuralgia \nyu̇-ˈral-jə\ Pain, often of unknown cause, in the area covered by a peripheral sensory nerve. In trigeminal neuralgia (tic douloureux), brief attacks of severe shooting pain along a nerve in front of the ear usually begin after middle age, more often in women. Attacks become more frequent and easily triggered by touching the affected area, talking, eating, or cold. ANALGESICS help, but cure requires surgery. Glossopharyngeal neuralgia most often affects men over 40. Excruciating pains begin in the throat and radiate to the ears or down the neck, with or without a trigger (e.g., sneezing, yawning, chewing). Attacks subside before analgesics take effect. Surgery may help in extreme cases. See also NEURITIS.

neural network Type of parallel computation in which computing elements are modeled on the network of NEURONS that constitute animal NERVOUS SYSTEMS. This model, intended to simulate the way the brain processes information, enables the computer to "learn." A neural network typically consists of a number of interconnected processors, or nodes. Each handles a particular sphere of knowledge, with several inputs and one output to the network. Based on the inputs it gets, a node can "learn" about the relationships between sets of data, sometimes using the principles of FUZZY LOGIC. For example, a backgammon program can store and grade results from moves in a game and then play a move based on its stored result. Neural networks have been used in pattern recognition, speech analysis, weather prediction, and the modeling of thinking and consciousness.

neural tube defect Congenital defect of the BRAIN or SPINAL CORD from abnormal growth of their precursor, the neural tube (see EMBRYOLOGY), usually with spine or skull defects. The tube may fail to close properly, have parts missing, or have a blockage (see HYDROCEPHALUS). In spina bifida, vertebrae are open over the back of the spinal cord, usually at the base. This may not affect function if no further defects exist. The more serious forms can cause paralysis and impair bladder and bowel function. Adequate FOLIC-ACID intake by women of childbearing age reduces the risk of neural tube defects. Early surgery can prevent or minimize disability.

neuritis \nyu̇-ˈrī-təs\ INFLAMMATION of one or several nerves. The cause may be mechanical, vascular, allergic, toxic, metabolic, or viral. Symptoms—tingling, burning, or stabbing pains with sensory nerves, and anything from muscle weakness to paralysis with motor nerves—are usually confined to the part of the body served by the inflamed nerve. In Bell's palsy, facial nerve inflammation causes a characteristic facial muscle distortion. ANALGESICS can relieve the pain. Recovery is usually rapid. See also NEURALGIA.

neurology Medical specialty concerned with NERVOUS-SYSTEM function and disorders. Clinical neurology did not begin to develop until the mid-19th cent., when mapping of the functional areas of the brain first began and understanding of the causes of conditions such as EPILEPSY improved. The development of the ELECTROENCEPHALOGRAPH in the 1920s aided in the diagnosis of neurological disease, as did the development of COMPUTED AXIAL TOMOGRAPHY and nuclear MAGNETIC RESONANCE IMAGING. Greater understanding of the brain chemistry of disorders such as SCHIZOPHRENIA and DEPRESSION has led to effective drugs that nevertheless work best in conjunction with PSYCHOTHERAPY. Side effects of drugs or surgery can be serious, and many nervous-system disorders have no effective treatment.

neuron *or* **nerve cell** Any of the cells of the NERVOUS SYSTEM. Sensory neurons relay information from sense organs, motor neurons carry impulses to muscles and glands, and interneurons transmit impulses between sensory and motor neurons. A typical neuron consists of dendrites (fibers that receive stimuli and conduct them inward to the cell body), a cell body, and an axon (a fiber that relays the nerve impulse from the cell body outward to its terminals, the synaptic knobs). Impulses are conducted by NEUROTRANSMITTER chemicals released by the axon's synaptic knobs across the SYNAPSES. Most neurons are insulated by a myelin sheath surrounding the axons. Bundles of fibers from neurons held together by CONNECTIVE TISSUE form nerves.

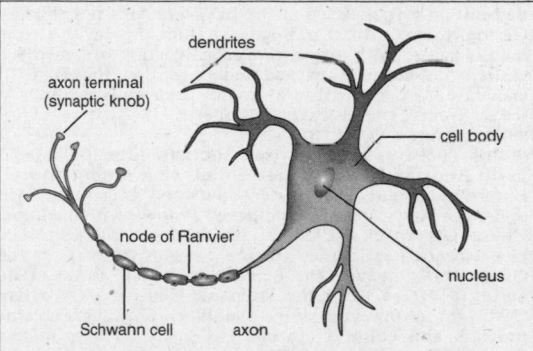

Neuron Structure of a neuron. Dendrites, usually branching fibers, receive and conduct impulses to the cell body, which integrates inputs arriving from various dendrites and sends nerve impulses out to the axon. When an impulse reaches the end of the axon, terminals release neurotransmitters into a gap (synapse) between the neuron and a neighboring cell. The neurotransmitter diffuses across the gap to start an impulse in an adjacent neuron or effector cell (as of a muscle or gland). Schwann cells surround the axon, forming an insulating myelin sheath. A space (node of Ranvier) between two Schwann cells serves to conduct the nerve impulse quickly along the axon.

neuropathy \nu̇-ˈrä-pə-thē\ Disorder of the peripheral NERVOUS SYSTEM. It may be genetic or acquired, progress quickly or slowly, involve motor, sensory, and/or autonomic (see AUTONOMIC NERVOUS SYSTEM) nerves, and affect only certain nerves or all of them. It can cause pain or loss of sensation, weakness, PARALYSIS, loss of REFLEXES, or, in autonomic neuropathies, disturbances of varied functions. Some types damage the NEURON itself, others the myelin sheath that insulates it. Examples include CARPAL TUNNEL SYNDROME, AMYOTROPHIC LATERAL SCLEROSIS, POLIOMYELITIS, SHINGLES, and nerve DEAFNESS. Causes include diseases (e.g., DIABETES MELLITUS, LEPROSY,

SYPHILIS), injury, TOXINS, and VITAMIN deficiency. See also NEURALGIA, NEURITIS.

neuropsychology Science concerned with the integration of psychological observations on behavior with neurological observations on the central NERVOUS SYSTEM (CNS), including the BRAIN. The field emerged through the work of Paul BROCA and Carl Wernicke (1848–1905), who identified sites on the CEREBRAL CORTEX involved in the production or comprehension of language. The related field of neuropsychiatry addresses such disorders as APHASIA, Korsakoff's syndrome, and TOURETTE'S SYNDROME. See also LATERALITY.

neurosis Mental and emotional disorder that affects only part of the PERSONALITY, is less severe than a PSYCHOSIS, and is characterized by various physiological and mental disturbances. Neuroses include ANXIETY attacks, certain forms of DEPRESSION, HYPOCHONDRIASIS, hysterical reactions, OBSESSIVE-COMPULSIVE DISORDERS, PHOBIAS, sexual dysfunctions, and some TICS. They have traditionally been viewed as based on emotional conflict in which a blocked impulse seeks expression in a disguised response or symptom. Behavioral psychologists regard them as learned responses to stress that can be unlearned.

neurotransmitter Chemical released by NEURONS to stimulate neighboring neurons, allowing impulses to be passed from one cell to the next. A nerve impulse arriving at the axon terminal of one neuron stimulates release of a neurotransmitter, which crosses the microscopic gap (see SYNAPSE) in milliseconds to the adjoining neuron's dendrite. Many chemicals, including acetylcholine, DOPAMINE, and SEROTONIN, act as neurotransmitters. Some mind-altering drugs act by changing synaptic activity.

Neuschwanstein Castle \ˈnȯi-ˈshvän-ˌshtīn\ Elaborate castle built on a rock ledge in the Bavarian Alps near Füssen, Germany, by LUDWIG II. Begun in 1869, this lavish stronghold is an eccentric romantic reconstruction of a medieval castle, with walled courtyard, indoor garden, towers, artificial cave, two-story throne room, and. wall paintings of scenes from Richard WAGNER's operas.

neutering See CASTRATION

Neutra \ˈnȯi-trä, *Engl* ˈnü-trə\, **Richard (Joseph)** (1892–1970) Austrian-U.S. architect. From white Cubistic forms, he moved to light cages of steel and wood, in harmony with their lush landscaping. He achieved renown with the Lovell House, Los Angeles (1927–29), using glass expanses and cable-suspended balconies in the INTERNATIONAL STYLE. Other works include the Kaufmann Desert House, Palm Springs (1946–47), and the Tremaine House, Santa Barbara (1947–48), along with office buildings, churches, housing projects, and cultural centers. His many writings include *Survival Through Design* (1954).

neutralism See NONALIGNMENT

neutrality Legal status arising from a country's abstention from all participation in a war between other countries and an attitude of impartiality toward the belligerents. In the past, rights of a neutral country included freedom of its territory from use or occupation by any warring party, maintenance of diplomatic relations with other neutrals and belligerents, and respect for its intent to be neutral. In the two world wars, many of the basic concepts of neutrality ceased to be respected; the freedom of the neutral was sharply reduced in the later 20th cent.

neutrino \nü-ˈtrē-nō\ Fundamental particle with no ELECTRIC CHARGE, little or no MASS, and a SPIN value of $^1/_2$. Neutrinos belong to the LEPTON family of SUBATOMIC PARTICLES. There are three types, each associated with a charged lepton: the electron, the muon, and the tau. Neutrinos are the most penetrating of subatomic particles because they react with matter only by the WEAK force. They do not cause IONIZATION, because they are not charged.

neutron One of the constituent particles of every atomic NUCLEUS except ordinary hydrogen. Discovered in 1932 by James Chadwick (1891–1974), it has no ELECTRIC CHARGE and has nearly 1,840 times the mass of the ELECTRON. Free neutrons undergo BETA DECAY with a half-life of about 10 minutes. Thus, they are not readily found in nature, except in COSMIC RAYS. They are a penetrating form of radiation.

When bombarded with neutrons, various elements undergo NUCLEAR FISSION and release more free neutrons (see CHAIN REACTION, NUCLEAR POWER, ATOMIC BOMB). Neutron beams produced in CYCLOTRONS and nuclear reactors are important probes of matter.

neutron bomb *or* **enhanced radiation warhead** Small thermonuclear weapon that produces minimal blast and heat but large amounts of lethal RADIATION. The blast and heat are confined to a few hundred yards; within a somewhat larger area, the bomb throws off a massive wave of neutron and gamma radiation extremely destructive to living tissue. It could be used with deadly efficiency on the battlefield without endangering cities only a few miles away. It can be delivered by missile, howitzer, or aircraft.

neutron star Any of a class of extremely dense STARS thought to be composed mainly of NEUTRONS with a thin atmosphere of mostly iron atoms, electrons, and protons. They are usually about 12 mi (20 km) across, with a mass roughly twice the sun's, and a density about a hundred trillion times that of water. Neutron stars have very strong MAGNETIC FIELDS and, unlike BLACK HOLES, a solid surface. Below it, gravity causes pressure so high it compacts atoms' protons and electrons into neutrons. The discovery of PULSARS in 1967 provided the first evidence of the existence of neutron stars, predicted in the early 1930s and generally thought to be formed in SUPERNOVA explosions. See also WHITE DWARF STAR.

Nevada State (pop., 2000: 1,998,000), W U.S. It covers 110,561 sq mi (286,353 sq km); its capital is CARSON CITY. The Black Rock Desert is in the northwest; the COLORADO RIVER forms its extreme SE boundary. Human settlement in the area has spanned more than 20,000 years, and evidence of prehistoric inhabitants include dwelling remains and ROCK ART. Early inhabitants included the SHOSHONE and PAIUTE Indians. Spanish missionaries in the 18th cent. and fur traders in the 1820s arrived before major exploration and mapping were done by J.C. FREMONT and Kit CARSON 1843–45. Nevada was part of the land ceded to the U.S. by Mexico in 1848 and was included in the Utah Territory (1850–61). Settlements increased after the discovery of the Comstock Lode, a rich silver deposit, at Virginia City in 1859. It became the Territory of Nevada in 1861 and the 36th U.S. state in 1864. It began its transition to a modern economy during the GREAT DEPRESSION when gambling was legalized. Construction of the HOOVER DAM aided the economy of S Nevada. In the 1950s the state became the main testing site for atomic-energy experiments. The traditional bases of its economy, mining and agriculture, are overshadowed by governmental activity and tourism, the latter centered on LAS VEGAS, RENO, and Lake TAHOE.

Neva River \nye-ˈvä\ River, NW Russia. It flows 46 mi (74 km) from Lake LADOGA west to the Gulf of Finland in the BALTIC SEA. It is usually frozen from November to April. The city of ST. PETERSBURG is at its mouth. Its banks were the scene of a battle in 1240 in which ALEXANDER NEVSKY, prince of NOVGOROD, defeated the Swedes.

Nevelson, Louise *orig.* Leah Berliawsky (1899–1988) U.S. (Ukrainian-born) sculptor. She moved with her family to Maine in 1905 and studied art with Hans HOFMANN (1931). Her early figurative sculptures feature blockish, interlocking masses and found objects (e.g., *Ancient Figure,* 1932; *The Circus Clown,* 1942). She is best known for large, monochromatic abstract sculptures consisting of open-faced wooden boxes stacked to make freestanding walls. Within the boxes are collections of abstract-shaped objects mingled with pieces of architectural debris and other found objects skillfully arranged to produce a sense of mystery (e.g., *Sky Cathedral,* 1958; *Silent Music II,* 1964) and then painted a single color, usually black. She is recognized as one of the foremost sculptors of the 20th cent.

Neville, Richard See Earl of WARWICK

Nevins, Allan (1890–1971) U.S. historian. Born in Camp Point, Ill., he worked nearly 20 years as a journalist before joining the faculty at Columbia Univ. (1928–58). His best-known works include biographies of U.S. political and industrial figures, including *Grover Cleveland* (1932, Pulitzer Prize) and *Hamilton Fish* (1936, Pulitzer Prize), and his eight-volume history of the American Civil War (1947–71).

In 1948 he inaugurated at Columbia the first oral history program in the U.S.

Nevsky, Alexander See St. ALEXANDER NEVSKY

nevus See MOLE

New Age Eclectic group of cultural attitudes that arose in late-20th-cent. Western society. It is usually seen as having emerged from the youth culture of the 1960s, though its antecedents date from much earlier. It has drawn on such belief systems as holism, PANTHEISM, OCCULTISM, and THEOSOPHY as well as Eastern mysticism and American Indian beliefs, and practitioners have pursued alternative approaches to spirituality, right living, and health (see HOLISTIC MEDICINE). New Age music is a typically soft, soothing form of instrumental music used to promote relaxation.

Newark \\'nü-ərk\\ City (pop., 2000: 274,000) and port of entry, NE New Jersey, west of NEW YORK CITY. It was founded in 1666 by Puritans. In 1776 the city served as a supply base for Gen. George WASHINGTON. The largest city in the state, it was the scene of major civil disturbances in 1967. It was the birthplace of Aaron BURR and Stephen CRANE.

Newbery, John (1713–1767) English publisher. In 1744 he set up a book shop and publishing house in London, where he published some of the first children's books, including *Little Goody Two-Shoes*. In 1781 his firm published the first collection of nursery rhymes associated with MOTHER GOOSE. The Newbery Medal has been awarded annually since 1922 for outstanding children's literature in the U.S.

New Britain *formerly* **Neu-Pommern** \\nòi-'pò-mərn\\ Largest island (pop. 1989 est.: 264,000) in the BISMARCK ARCHIPELAGO, Papua New Guinea. It was visited and named by William DAMPIER in 1700. After periods under German, Australian, and Japanese rule, it became part of Papua New Guinea in 1975 when that nation attained independence. Its highest peak, Mt. Sinewit, at 7,999 ft (2,438 m), erupted violently in 1937. Commercial products include coconuts and cocoa.

New Brunswick Province (pop., 1996: 762,000), one of the four MARITIME PROVINCES, E Canada. It is connected with Nova Scotia by the Isthmus of Chignecto. Its capital is FREDERICTON. New Brunswick was part of the original ACADIA; it was colonized by the French in the 18th cent., then captured by the British, who expelled the French-speaking Acadians in 1755 and incorporated the area into Nova Scotia. After the AMERICAN REVOLUTION, some 14,000 loyalists from the U.S. settled there. As a result of this large influx, it was separated from Nova Scotia, and the province of New Brunswick was established in 1784. In 1867 it became an original member of the Dominion of Canada. Forests cover 90% of the province, whose chief cities include ST. JOHN and Moncton. Forestry and lumbering are the largest industries, followed by commercial fishing.

New Caledonia *French* **Nouvelle Calédonie** \\nü-'vel-kà-lā-dô-'nē\\ French overseas territory (pop., 2000: 211,000), SW Pacific Ocean. It consists of the islands of New Caledonia and Walpole, the Isle of Pines, and several other island groups; its capital is NOUMÉA. The main island, New Caledonia, has huge deposits of nickel. Excavations indicate an Austronesian presence in the area about 2000–1000 B.C. The islands were visited by Capt. James COOK in 1774. Occupied by France in 1853, they were a penal colony 1864–94. New Caledonians joined the FREE FRENCH cause of Charles DE GAULLE in 1940; the islands were the site of Allied bases (1942–44). They became part of the French overseas territory in 1946.

Newcastle *or* **Newcastle upon Tyne** City (pop., 1999 est.: 259,000) and port, N England. It dates from the Roman period and derives its name from the NORMAN castle built in 1080 by ROBERT II of Normandy. At first an important wool trade center, it became a major mining area and coal-shipping port in the 16th cent. It was among the world's largest ship-repairing facilities; its economy now rests on associated marine and heavy engineering industries.

New Comedy Greek drama from around 320 B.C. to 250 B.C. that offers a mildly satiric view of contemporary Athenian society. Unlike Old Comedy, which parodies public figures and events (see ARISTOPHANES), New Comedy features fictional average citizens in domestic life. Plays usually involve the conventionalized situation of thwarted lovers and contain stock characters. MENANDER introduced the New Comedy and became its most famous exponent. PLAUTUS and TERENCE translated its plays for the Roman stage.

Newcomen \\'nü-kə-mən\\, **Thomas** (1663–1729) British engineer. In 1712 he built his atmospheric STEAM ENGINE, a precursor of James WATT's engine. In the Newcomen engine, atmospheric pressure pushed the piston down after the condensation of steam had created a vacuum in the cylinder. Newcomen engines were used for some years to drain mines and raise water to power waterwheels.

New Criticism *or* **formalism** Post–World War I school of Anglo-American literary theory that insisted on the intrinsic value of a work of art. New Critics were opposed to the practice of bringing historical or biographical data to bear on the interpretation of a work. The primary critical technique was analytic (or "close") reading of the text, concentrating on its language, imagery, and emotional or intellectual tensions. The New Critics included I. A. RICHARDS, William EMPSON, J. C. RANSOM, and R. P. Blackmur (1904–1965).

New Deal U.S. domestic program of Pres. Franklin ROOSEVELT to bring economic relief (1933–39). The term was taken from a 1932 speech in which he promised "a new deal for the American people." New Deal legislation was enacted mainly in the first three months of 1933 (Roosevelt's "hundred days") and established such agencies as the PUBLIC WORKS ADMINISTRATION and CIVILIAN CONSERVATION CORPS to alleviate unemployment, the NATIONAL RECOVERY ADMINISTRATION to revive industrial production, the FEDERAL DEPOSIT INSURANCE CORP. and SECURITIES AND EXCHANGE COMMISSION to regulate financial institutions, the Agricultural Adjustment Administration to support farm production, and the TENNESSEE VALLEY AUTHORITY to provide public power and flood control. A second period of legislation (1935–36) established the National Labor Relations Board, the WORKS PROGRESS ADMINISTRATION, and the SOCIAL SECURITY system. Though some legislation was declared unconstitutional, many reforms endured and permanently changed the role of government.

New Delhi \\'de-lē\\ City (pop., 1991 est.: 301,000), capital of India, S of Delhi in Delhi union territory. Built from 1912 to 1929, it was formally opened in 1931, when it became the capital. It has an orderly, diagonal street pattern and gives a feeling of openness and quiet. The main east–west axis is Central Vista Park, a thoroughfare with government buildings, museums, and research centers.

New Economic Policy Economic policy of the Soviet Union, 1921–28. A temporary retreat from the failed War Communism policy of extreme centralization and doctrinaire socialism, it returned most agriculture, retail trade, and light industry to private ownership (though the state retained control of heavy industry, banking, transport, and foreign trade) and reintroduced money into the economy. In 1928 chronic grain shortages prompted Joseph STALIN to begin to collectivize agriculture under state control. By 1931 state control was reimposed over all industry and commerce.

New England Region, NE U.S. It consists of Maine, New Hampshire, Vermont, Massachusetts, Rhode Island, and Connecticut, and has an area of 66,667 sq mi (172,668 sq km). Named by John SMITH, who explored its shores in 1614, it was later settled by English Puritans (see PURITANISM). Its colonies, peopled by self-sufficient farmers, evolved representative governments. Its harbors promoted the growth of overseas commerce and a vigorous shipbuilding industry. In the 18th cent. it became a hotbed of agitation for independence from Britain, and its patriots played leading roles in the AMERICAN REVOLUTION.

New England Confederation *or* **United Colonies of New England** Organization of four American colonies. In 1643 delegates from Massachusetts, Connecticut, New Haven, and Plymouth met to solve trade, boundary, and religious disputes and form a common defense against the French, Dutch, and Indians. They drew up articles of agreement and established a directorate. The confederation was weakened by its advisory status and by the 1665 merger of Connecticut and New Haven. It was dissolved in 1684.

N
O

New England Renaissance See AMERICAN RENAISSANCE

Newfoundland and Labrador \ˈnü-fənd-lənd\ Province (pop., 1996: 564,000), one of the four Atlantic provinces, Canada. Consisting of the island of Newfoundland and LABRADOR on the mainland, and bounded by Quebec, it extends into the N. Atlantic Ocean and is the easternmost part of N. AMERICA. Its capital is ST. JOHN'S. It was originally settled by Indians and ESKIMOS. VIKING ruins from around A.D. 1000 have been found in the N part of the island. John CABOT claimed the island for England in 1497; the first colony was established at St. John's in 1583. France and England disputed possession of the area, and though England retained control with the 1713 Peace of UTRECHT, controversies over fishing rights continued through the 19th cent. A province since 1949, it includes the GRAND BANKS fishing grounds. Fishing, mainly for cod, was virtually the only industry until the early 20th cent., when W Labrador's vast iron reserves began to be exploited.

New France Possessions of France in N. America from 1534 to the Treaty of PARIS in 1763. After the first land claim for France by Jacques CARTIER (1534), the company of New France was established in 1627. With the explorations by Samuel de CHAMPLAIN, Jacques MARQUETTE, R.-R. LA SALLE, Louis JOLLIET, and others, the boundaries of New France expanded beyond the lower ST. LAWRENCE RIVER to include the GREAT LAKES and the Mississippi Valley. The FRENCH AND INDIAN WAR (1754–63) resulted in the loss, to England and Spain, of all French territory except the islands of St.-Pierre and Miquelon.

New Goa See PANAJI

New Granada Spanish viceroyalty in NW S. America during colonial times. Conquered by the Spaniards in 1537–38, it was subject to the viceroyalty of PERU until 1740. It then became a separate viceroyalty that included modern Colombia, Panama, Venezuela, and Ecuador. Its capital was Santa Fé (modern BOGOTÁ). It was liberated from Spain in 1823.

New Guinea *Indonesian* **Irian** \ˌir-ē-ˈän\ Island, E MALAY ARCHIPELAGO, W Pacific, north of Australia, divided between Irian Jaya in its W half, and Papua New Guinea in its E half. The second-largest island in the world, it is about 1,500 mi (2,400 km) long, with an area of about 342,000 sq mi (885,000 sq km). The terrain ranges from lowland rainforest to fertile highlands and its climate is tropical. Copper and gold are its chief mineral resources.

New Hampshire State (pop., 2000: 1,236,000), NE U.S. One of the NEW ENGLAND states, it covers 9,279 sq mi (24,033 sq km); its capital is CONCORD. The CONNECTICUT RIVER forms its W boundary with Vermont. The White Mtns., in its central part, contain Mt. WASHINGTON. The region was inhabited by Algonquian Indian tribes (see ALGONQUIAN LANGUAGES) when the first English people settled near Portsmouth in 1623. The area came under the jurisdiction of Massachusetts in 1641 and became a separate crown colony in 1679. It was the first colony to declare its independence from Britain in 1776. Following the nation's establishment, the state grew rapidly. Agriculture flourished and manufacturing developed along the rivers. Portsmouth became a major shipbuilding center. The economy is now based primarily on manufacturing and tourism, although dairy farming and granite quarrying are also important. Because it holds the nation's earliest presidential primary, it has furnished the first testing ground for many candidacies. DARTMOUTH and the Univ. of New Hampshire are two of the state's prominent educational institutions.

New Haven City (pop., 2000: 124,000), S central Connecticut. Settled in 1638, it became part of the colony of Connecticut in 1664. It was the co-capital with HARTFORD until 1875. It was sacked by LOYALIST forces during the AMERICAN REVOLUTION (1779). During the AMERICAN CIVIL WAR it was a center of Abolitionist activity. A number of famous inventors made it a center of industrial technology, including Charles GOODYEAR, Eli WHITNEY, and Samuel MORSE. It is the home of YALE UNIV.

New Hebrides See VANUATU

Newhouse family U.S. family of publishers. Samuel Irving Newhouse (1895–1979), born in New York City, took over a failing New Jersey newspaper while in his teens and made it profitable, and was soon buying and turning around other papers. In 1959 he purchased the Condé Nast magazines, including *Vogue* and *House & Garden*. At his death Advance Publications owned 31 newspapers, seven magazines, five radio stations, and six television stations. His sons Samuel I., Jr. (b.1928), and Donald E. (b.1930) greatly expanded the company, buying several book publishers, including RANDOM HOUSE, and buying or starting such magazines as *The NEW YORKER* and *Gentleman's Quarterly*.

Ne Win \ˈnä-ˈwin\, **U** *or* **Shu Maung** \ˈshü-ˈmauṅ\ (1911–2002) Leader of Burma (Myanmar) 1962–88. Involved in the Burmese independence movement in the mid-1930s, during World War II he initially served in the Japanese-sponsored army, but he later helped organize underground resistance to the Japanese. General of the army, he served as temporary prime minister 1958–60. In 1962 he ousted the elected prime minister U NU; his subsequent regime combined military dictatorship with a socialist economic program, which isolated and impoverished the country. He resigned in 1988, but continued to exercise power behind the scenes.

New Jersey State (pop., 2000: 8,414,000), E U.S. It covers 7,787 sq mi (20,168 sq km); its capital is TRENTON. The HUDSON RIVER forms its NE boundary; the Delaware River, its W boundary. Before European colonization, the region was inhabited by DELAWARE Indian tribes. Although it was sighted by Giovanni da VERRAZZANO and Henry HUDSON, it was first settled by Dutch and Swedish traders. It was the site of numerous battles during the AMERICAN REVOLUTION, including one led by Gen. George WASHINGTON in 1776, after crossing the Delaware (see Battles of TRENTON and PRINCETON). It was the third state to ratify the U.S. Constitution in 1787. Between the Revolutionary and Civil wars, it underwent tremendous industrialization, abetted by the construction of canals and, later, railways. Although known as the "Garden State," a name influenced by its 18th-cent. agricultural fertility, its economy is based primarily on manufacturing, and it has many research facilities and laboratories. Tourism, led by ATLANTIC CITY, is also important. Chief cities include NEWARK, JERSEY CITY, PATERSON, and Elizabeth.

Newman, Arnold (Abner) (b.1918) U.S. photographer. Born in New York, he studied art at the Univ. of Miami. In 1946 he opened his own studio in New York, where he specialized in portraits of well-known people posed in settings associated with their work; these included Georgia O'KEEFFE, Igor STRAVINSKY, Pablo PICASSO, and Jean COCTEAU. His "environmental portraiture" greatly influenced 20th-cent. portrait photography.

Newman, Barnett (*orig.* Baruch) (1905–1970) U.S. painter. Born in New York City, he studied at the Art Students League and City College. With Robert MOTHERWELL and Mark ROTHKO, he cofounded the school called "Subject of the Artist" (1948), which held open sessions and lectures for other artists. He developed a style of mystical abstraction and achieved his breakthrough with *Onement I* (1948), in which a single stripe (or "zip") of orange vertically bisects a field of dark red. This austerely geometric style became his trademark.

Newman, John Henry *known as* **Cardinal Newman** (1801–1890) English churchman and man of letters. In 1833 he became the leader of the OXFORD MOVEMENT, which stressed the Catholic elements in the English religious tradition and sought to reform the Church of England. He was received into the Roman Catholic church in 1845, but he came under suspicion among the more rigorous clergy because of his quasi-liberal spirit. A challenge from Charles KINGSLEY prompted him to write an eloquent exposition of his spiritual history, the widely admired *Apologia pro Vita Sua* (1864). The work assured his place in the church, and in 1879 he became a cardinal-deacon.

Newman, Paul (b.1925) U.S. film actor. Born in Cleveland, he first appeared on Broadway in *Picnic* (1953) and began acting in films in 1955. His performances in such successful films as *Cat on a Hot Tin Roof* (1958), *The Hustler* (1961), *Hud* (1963), *Cool Hand Luke* (1967), *Butch Cassidy and the Sundance Kid* (1969), *The Sting* (1973), *The Verdict* (1982), and *The Color of Money* (1986; Academy Award) made him one of the most popular and enduring stars of his time. He directed and produced such films as *Rachel, Rachel* (1968) and *The Glass Menagerie* (1987), both of which starred his wife, Joanne Woodward (b.1930).

New Mexico State (pop., 2000: 1,819,000), SW U.S. It covers 121,593 sq mi (314,926 sq km); its capital is SANTA FE. In the west, it is crossed north–south by the CONTINENTAL DIVIDE. The RIO GRANDE bisects the state and for a short distance forms the boundary with Texas. Human settlement in the area has probably spanned 10,000 years. Before the NAVAJO and APACHE arrived in the 15th cent., an agricultural Indian civilization had developed irrigation systems, PUEBLOS, and CLIFF DWELLINGS whose ruins still dot the state. Spaniards from Mexico claimed the area for Spain in the 16th cent., and in 1540 F. V. de CORONADO explored it. The first settlement was at Santa Fe in 1610. Missionaries were active in the 1600s. It became part of Mexico in 1821 and was ceded to the U.S. in 1848 at the end of the MEXICAN WAR. The Territory of New Mexico was established by Congress in 1850. It became the 47th U.S. state in 1912, and retained its frontier image. World War II spurred economic and social change, bringing research facilities, including that at LOS ALAMOS. The economy today is largely dependent on the export of raw materials and on federal government expenditures; oil and natural gas are also important. The Univ. of New Mexico and a fine-arts community are in ALBUQUERQUE.

New Model Army (1645) Parliamentary army in the ENGLISH CIVIL WARS. Formed to provide a well-trained force drawn from all parts of England instead of the limited local militias, it also replaced the private armies raised by individual generals that lacked a unified command. Under Thomas FAIRFAX and Oliver CROMWELL, it won the Battle of Naseby, ending the first phase of the civil wars.

New Orleans City (pop., 2000: 485,000), SE Louisiana. Situated between the MISSISSIPPI RIVER and Lake PONTCHARTRAIN, it is the state's largest city and a major deepwater port. Founded in 1718 by French colonist J.-B. BIENVILLE, it was the state capital 1812–49. During the AMERICAN CIVIL WAR it was captured by Union forces in 1862. It is famed as the birthplace of JAZZ. A notable tourist center, its attractions include the MARDI GRAS and the French Quarter, a popular tourist area noted for its nightclubs and Creole architecture. Its French and Caribbean heritage make it uniquely exotic among U.S. cities. It is also a major industrial center.

New Orleans, Battle of (1815) U.S. victory over Britain in the WAR OF 1812. Late in 1814 a British fleet of more than 50 ships sailed into the Gulf of Mexico and prepared to attack New Orleans. Gen. Andrew JACKSON, commanding chiefly militiamen and volunteers, fought the British regulars who stormed their position on Jan. 8, 1815. His troops were so effectively entrenched behind earthworks and the British troops so exposed that the fighting was brief, ending in a decisive U.S. victory. The battle was without military value, since the Treaty of Ghent ending the war had been signed in December, but the news had been slow to arrive. The victory nevertheless contributed to national morale, enhancing Jackson's reputation as a hero.

New Orleans jazz See DIXIELAND

Newport City (pop., 2000: 26,000), SE Rhode Island, at the mouth of NARRAGANSETT BAY. Founded in 1639, it became a haven for religious refugees. With PROVIDENCE, it was the joint capital of the state until 1900. Newport has held many of the AMERICA'S CUP yacht races, and has been the site of long-running folk-music and jazz festivals. It is famous for its many opulent mansions. The Touro synagogue is the oldest in the U.S.

Newport News City (pop., 2000: 180,000) and port of entry, SE Virginia, at the mouth of the James River. The site was settled in 1621. It was an important embarkation point in both World Wars. With NORFOLK and PORTSMOUTH, it constitutes the Port of HAMPTON ROADS. It is the site of one of the largest shipyards in the world.

New Republic, The Weekly journal of opinion, founded in 1914 by Willard Straight, with Herbert Croly as editor. Long one of the most influential liberal magazines in the U.S., it early reflected the progressive movement, declining in the 1920s when liberalism was out of favor but reviving in the 1930s. After initially opposing Franklin D. ROOSEVELT's administration, it supported his NEW DEAL. In the 1980s, the magazine began to display an array of commentary reflecting the resurgence of conservatism in U.S. politics.

New River River, SW Virginia and S W. Virginia. It is formed in N. Carolina and flows north about 320 mi (515 km) into W. Virginia, where it joins the Gauley River to form the Kanawha River. The longest steel-arch bridge in the world, the River Gorge bridge near Fayetteville, W. Va., has a main span of 1,700 ft (518 m).

news agency *or* **news service** *or* **wire service** Organization that gathers, writes, and distributes news to newspapers, periodicals, radio and television broadcasters, government agencies, and other users. By sharing costs, its subscribers obtain services they could not otherwise afford. All the mass media depend on agencies for the bulk of the news they carry. Many are cooperatives, with members providing news from their area to a pool for general use. The largest news agencies are United Press International, ASSOCIATED PRESS, REUTERS, and Agence France-Presse.

New School University *formerly* **New School for Social Research** Private university in New York City. It was established in 1919 as an informal center for adult education and soon became the first American university to specialize in CONTINUING EDUCATION. In 1934 it established a graduate faculty of political and social sciences. It now includes a liberal-arts college, a graduate school of management, the Mannes College of Music, and the Parsons School of Design. Total enrollment is about 7,000.

newsgroup INTERNET forum for discussion of specific subjects. Newsgroups are organized into subjects (e.g., automobiles); each typically has several subgroups (e.g., classic cars, Formula One racing cars). A person starts a discussion by "posting" (uploading) an article; the follow-up replies (including replies to replies) constitute the discussion. A newsgroup name usually consists of an abbreviation (e.g., "rec" for the recreation newsgroup) followed by subgroup names separated by dots (e.g., "rec.music.jazz"). Most newsgroups are connected via Usenet, a worldwide network. See also BULLETIN-BOARD SYSTEM.

New Siberian Islands Island group, Arctic Ocean, NE Russia. They are separated from the Siberian mainland by Dmitry Laptev Strait. With an area of about 14,500 sq mi (38,000 sq km), they are snow-covered for most of the year. Arctic fox, northern deer, LEMMING, and many species of birds inhabit the islands.

New South Wales State (pop., 1998 est.: 6,342,000), SE Australia. It has an area of 309,433 sq mi (801,428 sq km); the capital is SYDNEY. The dominant geographic feature is the GREAT DIVIDING RANGE. Inhabited from prehistoric times, it was claimed for Britain by Capt. James COOK in 1770. In 1901 it became part of Commonwealth of Australia. The state ceded the area of the Australian Capital Territory (Canberra) beginning in 1911. It is the center of Australia's commercial farming, industry, and culture.

New Spain Former Spanish viceroyalty (1535–1821), principally in N. America, including the SW U.S., Mexico, Central America north of Panama, much of the W. Indies, and the Philippines. MEXICO CITY was the seat of the government. The first viceroy sent F. V. de CORONADO on his northern expeditions. The viceroyalty fell to Agustín de ITURBIDE in 1821.

newspaper Publication usually issued daily or weekly that provides news, views, and features. Forerunners of the modern newspaper appeared in ancient Rome. Regular papers printed from movable type appeared in Germany, Italy, and the Netherlands in the early 17th cent. The first English daily was *The Daily Courant* (1702–35); the *New-England Courant* (1721) was the first independent newspaper in the English colonies. By 1800 the principles of a free press and a basic formula for both serious and popular papers were taking root in Europe and the U.S. In the 19th cent. the number of U.S. papers and their circulations rose dramatically, owing to wider literacy, broadening appeal, lower prices, and technological advances, and newspapers achieved great power. Competition for readers often led to sensationalism and, in the 20th cent., gave rise to the so-

NO

called tabloids (see YELLOW JOURNALISM). Since 1900 newspaper publishing worldwide has expanded greatly.

New Sweden Only Swedish colony in N. America, extending from the site of TRENTON, N.J., to the mouth of the Delaware River. It was established by Peter MINUIT in 1638, when Ft. Christina was built at what is now WILMINGTON, Del. It was captured by the Dutch in 1655 under Peter STUYVESANT, but the Swedish colonists were allowed to keep their lands and customs.

Newsweek U.S. newsweekly, published in New York City. Founded in 1933 by Thomas J. C. Martyn, it initially offered a rather drab survey of the news with columns of analysis. After World War II it grew livelier, especially after its purchase by Philip Graham, publisher of the *WASHINGTON POST*, in 1961. Like *TIME*, it presents news in terse summary form and has a reputation for accurate, brisk, and vivid reporting.

newt *or* **eft** Any of more than 40 SALAMANDER species (family Salamandridae) prevalent in the SE U.S. and Mexico and also found in Asia and Great Britain. Aquatic species are called newts; terrestrial species are called efts. Newts have a long, slender body, and the tail is higher than it is wide. They eat earthworms, insects, and snails. Both aquatic and terrestrial species breed in ponds. The red eft *(Notophthalmus viridescens)* of E N. America is bright red during its terrestrial youth, after which it becomes permanently aquatic and dull green.

New Testament Second of the two major divisions of the Christian BIBLE. Christians see the New Testament as the fulfillment of the promise of the OLD TESTAMENT. It recounts the life and ministry of JESUS and interprets their meaning, focusing especially on the new COVENANT created between God and the followers of Jesus. The New Testament comprises four GOSPELS; the Acts of the Apostles, a narrative of the church's first years; 21 epistles, or letters of advice and instruction to early Christians; and the Book of REVELATION. Most were written in the later 1st cent. A.D. Only two authors are known for certain: St. PAUL, credited with 13 epistles; and St. LUKE, writer of the third gospel and the Book of Acts. These documents circulated among the early churches and were used as preaching and teaching sources. The earliest known list of the current New Testament canon dates from A.D. 367; a church council of 382 gave final approval to the list.

Newton, Huey P(ercy) (1942–1989) U.S. black activist. Born in New Orleans, he attended the San Francisco School of Law, and in 1966 cofounded the BLACK PANTHER PARTY. In 1974 Newton was accused of murder and fled to Cuba; on his return in 1977, he was freed after two trials ended in hung juries. In 1989 he was convicted of misusing funds intended for a Black Panther–founded school; later that year he was found shot dead on a street in Oakland, Cal.

Newton, Isaac (*later* **Sir Isaac**) (1642–1727) English physicist and mathematician. His experiments passing sunlight through a prism led to the discovery of the heterogeneous, corpuscular nature of white light and laid the foundation of physical OPTICS. He built the first reflecting telescope in 1668. He worked out the fundamentals of CALCULUS, though this work went unpublished for more than 30 years. His most famous publication, *Principia Mathematica* (1687), grew out of correspondence with Edmond HALLEY. It describes his works on the laws of motion (see NEWTON'S LAWS OF MOTION), orbital dynamics, tidal theory, and the theory of universal GRAVITATION, and is regarded as the seminal work of modern science. He became the first scientist ever to be knighted in 1705. During his career he engaged in heated arguments with several of his colleagues. The battle with

Isaac Newton Painting by Godfrey Kneller, 1702

G. W. LEIBNIZ (over the authorship of calculus) dominated the last 25 years of his life; it is now well established that Newton developed calculus first, but that Leibniz was the first to publish on the subject. Newton is regarded as one of the greatest scientists of all time.

Newton's law of gravitation Statement that any particle of MATTER in the universe attracts any other with a FORCE (F) that is proportional to the product of their masses (m_1 and m_2) and inversely proportional to the square of the distance (R) between them. In symbols: $F = G(m_1m_2)/R^2$, where G is the gravitational constant. Isaac NEWTON put forth the law to explain the observed motions of the planets and their moons. See also GRAVITATION.

Newton's laws of motion Relations between the FORCES acting on a body and the MOTION of the body, formulated by Isaac NEWTON. The laws describe only the motion of a body as a whole and are valid only for motions relative to a REFERENCE FRAME (usually the earth). The first law (called the law of INERTIA) states that a body at rest or moving at constant speed in a straight line will continue to do so unless it is acted upon by a force. The second law states that the force F acting on a body is equal to the MASS m of the body times its ACCELERATION a, or $F = ma$. The third law (the action-reaction law) states that the actions of two bodies on each other are always equal in magnitude and opposite in direction. See also MECHANICS.

New Wave *French* nouvelle vague. Group of individualistic French film directors of the late 1950s, including Claude CHABROL, François TRUFFAUT, J.-L. GODARD, Louis MALLE, and Alain RESNAIS. Most were associated with the important film magazine *Cahiers du Cinéma,* in which they developed the highly influential AUTEUR THEORY. Their films were characterized by a brilliance of technique that sometimes overshadowed the subject matter. Among the most important were Godard's *Breathless* (1959), Truffaut's *The 400 Blows* (1959), and Resnais's *Hiroshima mon amour* (1959).

New World monkey Any S. American MONKEY (platyrrhine) species in either of two families: MARMOSETS (Callitrichidae) or cebids (Cebidae), including CAPUCHINS and SPIDER MONKEYS. Platyrrhines have a broad nose, with a wide septum separating the outwardly directed nostrils, and relatively unopposable thumbs. Most species have a long tail. See also OLD WORLD MONKEY.

New Year's Day First day of the new year, celebrated with religious, cultural, and social observances around the world. It is usually marked by rites and ceremonies that symbolize casting off the old year and rejoicing in the new. Judaism, Christianity, and Islam all use different calendars and celebrate the new year on different dates. In the West January 1 is now the accepted date. The Jewish New Year, ROSH HASHANAH, can fall anytime from September 6 to October 5 in the Western calendar. The Muslim new year falls on the first day of the month of Muharram, which gradually regresses through the Western calendar year. The Chinese New Year falls from late January to early February.

New York State (pop., 2000: 18,976,000), E U.S. It covers 49,576 sq mi (128,402 sq km); its capital is ALBANY. The HUDSON, ST. LAWRENCE, Delaware, and NIAGARA rivers all form parts of its boundaries. The ADIRONDACK MTNS. are in the northeast; the CATSKILLS are in the east. Before European colonization, Algonquians (see ALGONQUIAN languages) and IROQUOIS inhabited the area. In 1524 Giovanni da VERRAZZANO visited New York Bay. The 1609 explorations of Henry HUDSON and Samuel de CHAMPLAIN led to settlement. In 1664 the Dutch colony, New Netherland, led by Peter STUYVESANT, surrendered to the British and was renamed New York. The FRENCH AND INDIAN WAR resulted in skirmishes in N and central New York; its conclusion confirmed English dominance in the region. In the AMERICAN REVOLUTION, it was the scene of many battles, including those of Ticonderoga and SARATOGA, and of Benedict ARNOLD's treason at West Point. New York adopted the first state constitution (1777). The capital moved from NEW YORK CITY to Albany in 1797. The opening of the ERIE CANAL in 1825 spurred development of the W part of the state. In the 19th cent. the growing influence in New York City of TAMMANY HALL caused tension between the city and the state. The economy was once based largely on manufacturing in cities, including BUFFALO, ROCHESTER, and SYRACUSE. It is now dominated by service industries concentrated in New York City.

New York, State University of (SUNY) Largest university system in the U.S. (total enrollment about 400,000). Founded in 1948, it consists of university centers in Albany, Binghamton, Buffalo, and Stony Brook; 12 colleges of arts and sciences; three medical centers (two in New York City and one in Syracuse); several two-year agricultural and technical colleges; over 30 community colleges; and various specialized units.

New York City City (pop., 2000: 8,008,000), SE New York, at the mouth of the HUDSON RIVER. The largest city in the U.S. and an important seaport, it consists of five boroughs: the BRONX, BROOKLYN, MANHATTAN, QUEENS, and STATEN ISLAND. The site of a Dutch trading post on Manhattan Island, it was colonized as New Amsterdam by Dutch director general Peter MINUIT, who bought it from the Indians in 1626. The colony surrendered to the British in 1664 and was renamed New York. It was the capital of the state 1784–1797 and of the U.S. 1789–90. The economy grew after the opening of the ERIE CANAL in 1825, and the city expanded rapidly after the AMERICAN CIVIL WAR. In 1898 the five boroughs were merged into a single city. Long a magnet for immigrants to the U.S., it is a center of world trade and finance, media, art, entertainment, and fashion. In 2001 the city's tallest landmark, the WORLD TRADE CENTER, was destroyed by AL-QAEDA terrorists.

New York City Ballet Preeminent U.S. ballet company. Descended from companies founded by George BALANCHINE and Lincoln KIRSTEIN, it assumed its current name in 1948 and moved to its permanent home, Lincoln Center's New York State Theater, in 1964. Under Balanchine's direction, the company became the leading U.S. ballet troupe, combining European classical ballet with American characterization and innovation. Later artistic directors Jerome ROBBINS and Peter MARTINS contributed numerous works to its repertoire. Its dancers have included Maria TALLCHIEF, Edward VILLELLA, Jacques D'AMBOISE, and Suzanne FARRELL.

New Yorker, The U.S. weekly magazine, famous for its varied literary fare and humor. It was founded in 1925 by Harold ROSS, who was its editor until 1951; he was succeeded by William Shawn (1952–87). Initially focused on New York City's amusements and social and cultural life, it gradually acquired a broader scope, encompassing literature, current affairs, and other topics. Aimed at a sophisticated, liberal audience, it became renowned for its short fiction, cartoons, major nonfiction pieces, and detailed reviews in the arts. It was sold in 1985 to Samuel I. Newhouse, Jr. (see NEWHOUSE FAMILY). It is perhaps the most admired of all American magazines today.

New York Public Library Largest city public library in the U.S. and one of the great libraries of the world. It was established in 1895, and its central building opened in 1911. Its holdings include more than 10 million books and more than 10 million manuscripts.

New York Stock Exchange (NYSE) World's largest marketplace for SECURITIES. The exchange began as an informal meeting of 24 men in 1792 on what is now WALL STREET in New York City. It was formally constituted as the New York Stock and Exchange Board in 1817. Since 1868 membership has been obtained by purchasing a seat from an existing number; membership has been limited to 1,366 since 1953. After the Panic of 1837, the exchange began to demand that companies disclose financial data as a condition of offering stock. The stock-market crash of 1929 led to regulation by the SECURITIES AND EXCHANGE COMMISSION. To be listed on the NYSE, a company must earn $2.5 million before taxes, have at least one million shares of stock outstanding, give common stockholders voting rights, and publish periodic financial statements. See also AMERICAN STOCK EXCHANGE, NASDAQ.

New York Times, The Morning daily newspaper, long the U.S. newspaper of record. From its establishment in 1851 it has aimed to avoid sensationalism and to appeal to cultured, intellectual readers. In 1896 it was bought by Adolph

S. OCHS, who built it into an internationally respected daily. Its prestige was notably enhanced by its coverage of the sinking of the TITANIC and of the two world wars. In the 1970s it became involved in controversy with its publication of the PENTAGON PAPERS. Under A. O. SULZBERGER, its organization and staff underwent sweeping changes, including the introduction of a national edition printed at regional sites. Today it is the most respected and influential newspaper in the world.

New York University (NYU) Private university in New York City, founded in 1831. It consists of 13 schools, colleges, and divisions at six major centers in Manhattan. Its graduate and professional programs include business, public administration, medicine, dentistry, law, social work, and the fine arts. The Gallatin Division, organized in 1972, offers degrees through innovative study programs. Total enrollment is about 30,000.

New Zealand Island nation, S. Pacific Ocean. Area: 104,454 sq mi (270,534 sq km). Population (2000): 3,835,000. Capi-

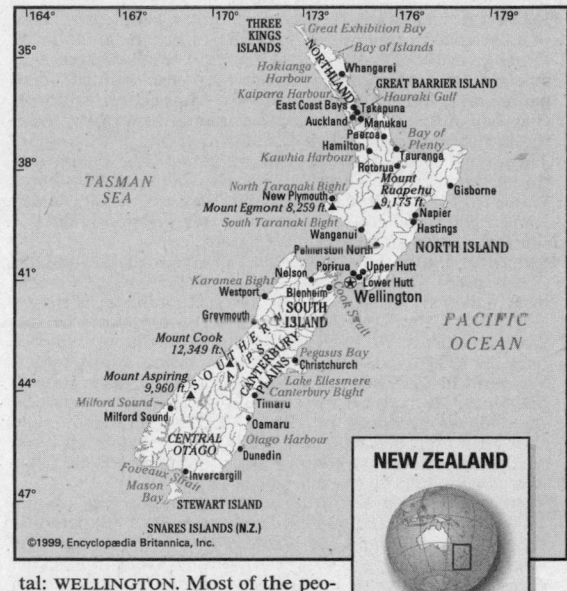

NEW ZEALAND

©1999, Encyclopædia Britannica, Inc.

Scale 1: 23,005,000
0   100   200 mi
0   150   300 km

tal: WELLINGTON. Most of the people are of European origin; about 10% are MAORI, and some are Pacific Islanders and Chinese. Languages: English and Maori (both official). Religion: Christianity. Currency: New Zealand dollar. New Zealand consists of the NORTH ISLAND and the SOUTH ISLAND, which are separated by Cook Strait, and several smaller islands. Both main islands are bisected by mountains in the south and hills in the north. New Zealand has a developed market economy largely based on agriculture, dominated by sheep raising, small-scale industries, and services. It is a constitutional monarchy with one legislative house; its chief of state is the British monarch represented by the governor-general, and the head of government is the prime minister. Polynesian occupation dates to around A.D. 1000. First sighted by Dutch explorer A. J. TASMAN in 1642, the main islands were charted by Capt. James COOK in 1769. Named a British crown colony in 1840 at Wellington, the area was the scene of warfare between colonists and native Maori through the 1860s. The capital was moved from AUCKLAND to Wellington in 1865, and in 1907 the colony became the Dominion of New Zealand. It administered Western SAMOA 1919–62 and participated in both world wars. The literacy rate is nearly 100%, and the cultural milieu is predominantly European, although a revival of traditional Maori culture and art is underway. CHRISTCHURCH is the major city on South Island. When Britain joined the EUROPEAN ECONOMIC COMMUNITY in the early 1970s, its influence led New Zealand to expand its export markets and diversify its economy. It has also become more independent in its foreign relations.

Ney, Michel *later* prince de la Moskowa (1769–1815) French army officer. He distinguished himself in the FRENCH REVOLUTIONARY WARS. A supporter of NAPOLEON, he was created marshal of France after victories in the NAPOLEONIC WARS. He led French forces at the Battle of Borodino (1812); in the French retreat from Moscow, he commanded the exposed rear guard and earned Napoleon's praise as "the bravest of the brave." After Napoleon's abdication, Ney favored LOUIS XVIII but rallied to Napoleon's support in the HUNDRED DAYS and at the Battle of WATERLOO. After the BOURBON RESTORATION, he was court-martialed and shot.

Nezahualcóyotl \nä-ˌsä-wäl-ˈkō-ˌyō-tᵊl\ City (pop., 1995: 1,233,000), central Mexico, suburb of MEXICO CITY. It is Mexico's third-largest municipality. Settlement began just after 1900, when Lake Texcoco was reduced in size and large areas of land became available. Xochiaca Dam to the north protects the city from floods.

Nez Percé \ˈnez-ˈpərs\ N. American Indian people who lived in an area centering on the Snake River in central Idaho, W Oregon, and W Washington. They built small villages near streams with abundant salmon; they also hunted small game and collected wild plant foods. After acquiring horses they began to hunt bison and became more warlike, eventually becoming one of the dominant tribes in the region. Through a series of treaties in the mid-1800s, their traditional territory was severely reduced; the tragic Nez Percé War (1877), led by Chief JOSEPH, was the result. Today some 2,500 Nez Percé remain on a reservation in Idaho.

NFL See NATIONAL FOOTBALL LEAGUE

Ngo Dinh Diem \ˈŋō-ˈdin-dē-ˈem, *Engl* en-ˈgō-ˈdin-dē-ˈem\ (1901–1963) President of S. Vietnam (1955–63). Of noble birth, Diem served as Emperor BAO DAI's minister of the interior (1933), but resigned when the French opposed his legislative reforms. He lived in self-imposed exile until invited back in 1954 by Bao Dai to serve as prime minister of S. Vietnam. In 1955 he ousted the emperor and made himself president. He refused to carry out elections mandated by the Geneva Accords of 1954, ruled autocratically, and showed preference to fellow Roman Catholics in an overwhelmingly Buddhist country. An unpopular leader, Diem was assassinated by his generals in 1963.

Ngugi wa Thiong'o \ˈŋ-ˈgü-gē-wä-ˈthyòŋ-gō\ *orig.* James Thiong'o Ngugi (b.1938) Kenyan novelist. Educated in Uganda and England, he wrote the first major novel in English by an E. African; the popular *Weep Not, Child* (1964) is the story of a family drawn into the struggle for Kenyan independence. His other novels include *A Grain of Wheat* (1967) and *Petals of Blood* (1977). As he became more sensitive to the effects of colonialism, he adopted his traditional name and wrote in the language of the Kikuyu people.

Nguyen dynasty \ˈŋūē-ən, *Engl* ˈnü-ən, en-gī-ˈen\ (1802–1945) Last Vietnamese dynasty. During the 16th cent., while the emperors of the LATER LE DYNASTY were nominally in control, the Nguyen family came to rule S Vietnam in an essentially independent fashion. Emperor Gia Long (1762–1820), founder of the dynasty, conquered all of Vietnam in 1802; his successors modeled their administration on the Chinese QING DYNASTY. The French invaded in 1858 and eventually took control of the entire country. They retained the Nguyen emperors as rulers of central and N Vietnam, but not S Vietnam. BAO DAI, the last emperor, abdicated in 1945.

NHL See NATIONAL HOCKEY LEAGUE

niacin \ˈnī-ə-sən\ *or* **nicotinic acid** \ˌni-kə-ˈtē-nik, ˌni-kə-ˈtinik\ *or* **vitamin B₃** ORGANIC COMPOUND essential to growth and health in animals, including humans. It is found in the body only in combined form as a coenzyme, nicotinamide adenine dinucleotide (NAD), which is involved in the METABOLISM of CARBOHYDRATES and SUGARS. One of the most stable vitamins (see VITAMIN B COMPLEX), it survives cooking and most preserving processes. It is widely found in dietary sources, especially lean meat. Deficiency causes PELLAGRA. It is used as a drug to raise high-density-LIPOPROTEIN CHOLESTEROL levels.

Niagara Falls Great falls of the NIAGARA RIVER, on the U.S.–Canadian border. They are divided by Goat Island into the Horseshoe (or Canadian) Falls and the American Falls. At the foot of the American Falls is the Cave of the Winds, a large rocky chamber formed by erosion. The river below the falls flows between high cliffs, forming Whirlpool Rapids. Tourism is a major industry, and it is a hydroelectric center.

Niagara River River forming the U.S.–Canada boundary between W New York and S Ontario. Its high flow and steep descent make it one of the best sources of hydroelectric power in N. America. It connects Lake ERIE with Lake ONTARIO, and NIAGARA FALLS lies about halfway along its course.

Niamey \ˈnyä-mä\ City (metro. area pop., 1999: 731,000), capital of Niger, along the NIGER RIVER. It became the capital of Niger colony in 1926 and grew rapidly after World War II. At the intersection of trade routes, it is home to YORUBA and HAUSA traders, merchants, officials, and craftsmen from Nigeria, Benin, and Togo. It is a commercial center with a university.

Nibelungenlied \ˈnē-bə-ˌlùŋ-ən-ˌlēt\ ("Song of the Nibelungs") Middle High German epic poem written around 1200 by an unknown poet. It contains elements traceable to Old Norse literature, stories in the *Poetic Edda,* and Scandinavian SAGAS. The principal characters are Prince SIEGFRIED, Queen BRUNHILD, Princess Kriemhild, her brother King Gunther, and his henchman Hagen; the story focuses on deceit, revenge, and slaughter. Many versions of the poem appeared in later centuries, including Richard WAGNER's opera cycle *Der Ring des Nibelungen* (1853–74).

Nicaea \nī-ˈsē-ə\ Independent principality (1204–61) of the fragmented BYZANTINE EMPIRE. It was founded in 1204 by THEODORE I LASCARIS. It was the political and cultural center from which a restored Byzantium arose in the mid-13th cent. under MICHAEL VIII PALAEOLOGUS. It extended from the BLACK SEA coast east of the Sangarius River southwest across W Asia Minor to MILETUS and the Maeander. It declined after 1261, when Michael VIII regained Constantinople.

Nicaragua *officially* **Republic of Nicaragua** Republic, Central America. Area: 50,464 sq mi (130,700 sq km). Popula-

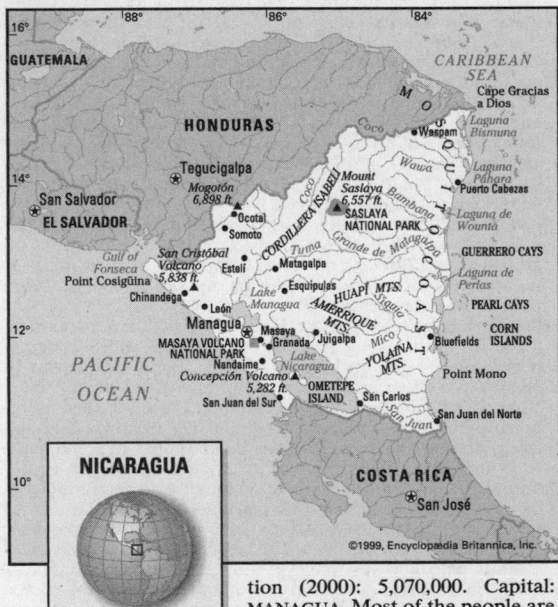

©1999, Encyclopædia Britannica, Inc.

NICARAGUA

Scale 1: 11,073,000

0　50　100 mi
0　80　160 km

tion (2000): 5,070,000. Capital: MANAGUA. Most of the people are MESTIZOS. Languages: Spanish (official), indigenous Indian languages, English. Religion: Roman Catholicism. Currency: córdoba oro. Nicaragua's W half consists of thickly forested mountain ranges and fertile valleys. Parallel to the Pacific coast is a belt of about 40 dormant and active volcanoes. The E coastline along the Caribbean is known as the MOSQUITO COAST. Earthquakes are common. Nicaragua has a developing market economy based largely on agriculture, light industries, and trade. It is a republic with one legislative house; its head of state and government is the president. The area has been inhabited for thousands of years, most notably by the MAYA. Christopher COLUMBUS arrived in 1502, and Spanish explorers discovered Lake NICARAGUA soon thereafter. Nicaragua was governed by Spain until 1821, when it declared its independence. It was part of Mexico and then the United Provinces of Central America until 1938 when full independence was achieved. The U.S. intervened in political affairs by maintaining troops there 1912–33. Ruled by the dictatorial SOMOZA dynasty 1936–79, it was taken over by the SANDINISTAS after a popular revolt. They were opposed by armed insurgents, the U.S.-backed CONTRAS, from 1981. The Sandinista government nationalized several sectors of the economy but lost the national elections in 1990. The new coalition government returned many economic activities to private control, but unrest between the ruling government and the Sandinistas continued, along with high unemployment and corruption.

Nicaragua, Lake Lake, SW Nicaragua. It is 102 mi (164 km) long, with a surface area of about 3,100 sq mi (8,000 sq km). The largest freshwater lake between the U.S. and Peru, it is the only freshwater lake containing oceanic animal life, including sharks, swordfish, and tarpon. Its largest island, Ometepe, is the preeminent pre-Columbian archaeological site in Nicaragua.

Nice \ˈnēs\ *ancient* Niceaea. City (pop., 1999: 343,000) SE France. It is located on the CÔTE D'AZUR of the Mediterranean Sea, near the Italian border. Founded by Greeks around 350 B.C., it was conquered by Romans in the 1st cent. A.D. It was later held by the counts of PROVENCE, then the counts of SAVOY, before being ceded to France in 1860. It is the leading resort of the French RIVIERA.

Nicene Creed \ˈnī-ˌsēn, nī-ˈsēn\ Ecumenical Christian statement of faith accepted by the Roman Catholic, Eastern Orthodox, Anglican, and major Protestant churches. It was long thought to have been drafted at the Council of Nicaea (325), but is now believed to have been issued by the Council of CONSTANTINOPLE (381).

Nichiren Buddhism \ˈnē-chē-ˌren\ One of the largest schools of Japanese BUDDHISM, founded by the monk Nichiren (1222–1282). It believes that the essence of the BUDDHA's teachings are contained in the LOTUS SUTRA and that the beliefs of other Buddhist schools are erroneous. In Nichiren Buddhism, the chanting of the title of the Lotus Sutra can lead to salvation. After Nichiren's death the school split into various subsects; one, Nichiren-sho-shu, has adherents in the U.S. In Japan its lay organization is the SOKA-GAKKAI.

Nicholas *Russian* Nikolay Nikolayevich (1856–1929) Russian grand duke. The nephew of ALEXANDER II, he became inspector general of calvary (1895–1905), and introduced reforms in training and equipment. In 1914 he was appointed head of all Russian forces. A popular commander, he led the army to early successes in World War I but was hampered by shortages. Dismissed in 1915 by NICHOLAS II, he commanded in the Caucasus 1915–17. After the Russian Revolution he moved to France, where he led an organization to unite anticommunist Russian émigrés.

Nicholas, St. *or* **Santa Claus** (fl.4th cent.) Minor saint associated with CHRISTMAS. He was probably bishop of Myra in Asia Minor. He is reputed to have provided dowries for three poor girls to save them from prostitution and to have restored to life three children who had been chopped up by a butcher. He became the patron saint of Russia and Greece. After the Reformation, his cult disappeared in all the Protestant countries except Holland, where he was known as Sinterklaas. Dutch colonists brought the tradition to New York, and English-speaking Americans adopted him as Santa Claus, who lives at the North Pole and brings gifts to children at Christmas.

Nicholas I *Russian* Nikolay Pavlovich (1796–1855) Czar of Russia (1825–55). In 1825 he succeeded his brother ALEXANDER I and suppressed the DECEMBRIST REVOLT. His reign came to represent autocracy, militarism, and bureaucracy. To enforce his policies, he created such agencies as the THIRD SECTION (political police). He quelled an uprising in Poland (1830–31) and aided Austria against a Hungarian uprising (1849). His designs on Constantinople led to war with Turkey (1853) and drew other European powers into the CRIMEAN WAR.

Nicholas II *Russian* Nikolay Aleksandrovich (1868–1918) Czar of Russia (1894–1917). Son of ALEXANDER III, he succeeded his father in 1894. He was an autocratic but indecisive ruler, strongly influenced by his wife, ALEXANDRA. His interest in Asia led to construction of the TRANS-SIBERIAN RAILROAD and helped cause the disastrous RUSSO–JAPANESE WAR. After the RUSSIAN REVOLUTION OF 1905, he agreed reluctantly to a representative DUMA but restricted its powers. His prime minister, Piotr STOLYPIN, attempted reforms, but Nicholas, increasingly influenced by Alexandra and Grigory RASPUTIN,

Nicholas II

opposed him. After setbacks in WORLD WAR I, Nicholas ousted the popular grand duke NICHOLAS as commander in chief of Russian forces and assumed command himself. His absence from Moscow and Alexandra's mismanagement of the government caused increasing civil unrest and culminated in the RUSSIAN REVOLUTION OF 1917. Nicholas abdicated in March 1917 and was detained by Georgy LVOV's provisional government. Plans for the royal family to be sent to England were overruled. Sent to Yekaterinburg, the family was executed in a cellar there in July 1918.

Nicholas V *orig.* Tommaso Parentucelli (1397–1455) Pope (1447–55). Soon after his election, he ended the schism caused by the rivalry between popes and church councils. He restored peace to the Papal States, won Poland's allegiance, and gained the support of Austria. He initiated the Peace of Lodi (1455) to end strife in Italy, and tried to stamp out SIMONY and other corrupt practices in the church. A patron of art and scholarship, he rebuilt many of Rome's architectural treasures and founded the Vatican Library.

Nicholas of Cusa (1401–1464) German cardinal, mathematician, scientist, and philosopher. Ordained a priest in 1440, he was made a cardinal in Italy and became bishop in 1450. In *On Catholic Concordance* (1433), he supported the supremacy of the general councils of the church over the papacy's authority. Skilled in nearly every branch of learning, he anticipated the work of COPERNICUS by discerning a movement in the universe that did not center on the earth.

Nichols, Mike *orig.* Michael Igor Peschkowsky (b.1931) U.S. (German-born) director. He came to the U.S. with his family in 1938. He formed a comic improvisational group in Chicago, and with Elaine May (b.1932) toured and recorded a set of brilliant social-satire routines. He later directed several Broadway hits, including *Barefoot in the Park* (1963), *The Odd Couple* (1965), and *Plaza Suite* (1968). His film debut, *Who's Afraid of Virginia Woolf?* (1966), was followed by *The Graduate* (1967, Academy Award); his later films included *Catch-22* (1970), *Silkwood* (1983), *Working Girl* (1988), and *Primary Colors* (1998).

Nicholson, Jack (b.1937) U.S. film actor. Born in Neptune, N.J., he first won acclaim for his role in *Easy Rider* (1969). He followed it with such successful films as *Five Easy Pieces* (1970), *Chinatown* (1974), *One Flew over the Cuckoo's Nest* (1975, Academy Award), *The Shining* (1980), *Terms of Endearment* (1983, Academy Award), *Prizzi's Honor* (1985), *Batman* (1989), *Hoffa* (1992), and *As Good As It Gets* (1997, Academy Award). Noted for his devilish grin and his portrayals of unconventional outsiders, he has become one of the most admired stars of his time.

nickel Chemical ELEMENT, one of the TRANSITION ELEMENTS, chemical symbol Ni, atomic number 28. Nickel is silvery white, tough, harder than iron, ferromagnetic (see FERROMAGNETISM), and highly resistant to corrosion. As pure METAL, it is used to coat other metals and as a catalyst. In alloys, it is used in coins, stainless steels, and cutlery. Its compounds (usually VALENCE 2) have a variety of industrial uses, as catalysts and mordants (see DYE) and in ELECTRO-PLATING.

nickelodeon Early motion-picture theater, so named because admission typically cost a nickel. Nickelodeons offered continuous showings of one- and two-reel films, lasting from 15 minutes to one hour and accompanied by a piano. The first opened in Pittsburgh in 1905; by 1910 they numbered 10,000, fueling a huge demand for silent films and providing the impetus for the development of the film industry.

Nicklaus \\'nik-ləs\\, **Jack (William)** (b.1940) U.S. golfer. Born in Columbus, Ohio, he won the U.S. Amateur Championship twice (1959, 1961) while attending Ohio State Univ. As a professional, he won the U.S. Open four times (1962, 1967, 1972, 1980), the Masters Tournament six times (1963, 1965, 1966, 1972, 1975, 1986), the PGA championship five times (1963, 1971, 1973, 1975, 1980), and the British Open three times (1966, 1970, 1978). He was a record three-time individual World Cup winner (1963, 1964, 1971). By 1986 "the Golden Bear" had played in 100 major championships, finishing in the top three 45 times. Combining skill and power with remarkable concentration and composure under pressure, he is widely regarded as the greatest golfer in history.

Nicobar Islands See ANDAMAN AND NICOBAR ISLANDS

Nicopolis (Actia) \\nə-'kä-pə-lis\\ Ancient city, NW Greece. Its ruins lie about 4 mi (6 km) north of Préveza. It was founded in 31 B.C. by Octavian (later Caesar AUGUSTUS) to commemorate his victory over Mark ANTONY and CLEOPATRA at the Battle of ACTIUM. It became the capital of the coastal region and was famous for its buildings and for the Actian games. Its ruins include a basilica, a Roman theater, and an aqueduct.

Nicosia \\ˌni-kə-'sē-ə\\ *or* **Lefkosía** \\'lef-kō-'sē-ə\\ City (metro. area pop., 1998 est.: 194,000), capital of Cyprus. It was a kingdom in the 7th cent. B.C. and has been the capital of the island since the 10th cent. A.D. During the 20th cent. the city has grown beyond the existing circular Venetian walls. A U.N. buffer zone has separated the city's Greek and Turkish sectors since 1974.

nicotine Principal ALKALOID of TOBACCO, occurring throughout the plant but mostly in the leaves. Nicotine is the chief addictive ingredient (see DRUG ADDICTION) in cigarettes, cigars, and snuff. It has a unique biphasic effect: Inhaled in short puffs it is a stimulant, but when inhaled slowly and deeply it can be a tranquilizer. In larger doses, nicotine is a highly toxic poison, used as an insecticide, fumigant, and vermifuge.

nicotinic acid See NIACIN

Niebuhr \\'nē-ˌbür\\, **Reinhold** (1892–1971) U.S. theologian. Born in Wright City, Mo., the son of an evangelical minister, he was ordained in 1915 and led Bethel Evangelical Church in Detroit until 1928. His years in that industrial city made him a critic of capitalism and an advocate of socialism. His influential writings, which forcefully criticized liberal Protestant thought and emphasized the persistence of evil in human nature and social institutions, include *Moral Man and Immoral Society* (1932), *The Nature and Destiny of Man* (1941–43), and *The Self and the Dramas of History* (1955).

niello \\nē-'e-lō\\ Black enamel-like alloy of sulfur with silver, copper, or lead, used to fill designs that have been engraved on the surface of a metal object, usually of silver. The contrast of the black niello against the bright surface produces an attractive decorative effect. During the height of its popularity in the Renaissance, the technique was widely used for embellishing religious as well as utilitarian objects. Nielli (objects decorated with niello) were produced in ancient Rome and 9th-cent. England. In Russia niello work is known as Tula work.

Nielsen, Carl (August) (1865–1931) Danish composer. He studied violin and trumpet as a child. In 1890 he went to Germany and met Johannes BRAHMS, whose music came to influence his own. His individual style—following classical forms but using intense chromaticism combined with a lyric, melodic strain—emerged after 1900. His six symphonies are the core of his work, but he also composed many short orchestra pieces and concertos for violin, flute, and clarinet.

Nielsen ratings National rating of the popularity of television shows. Developed by A. C. Nielsen in 1950, the system now samples television viewing in about 5,000 homes. A meter attached to each television set records the channel being watched and sends the data to a computer center. The ratings project each program's total audience; for example, a rating of 20 denotes that 20% of U.S. households tuned in to a particular program. Commercial television networks use the ratings to set advertising rates for each program as well as to determine which programs to continue and to cancel.

Niemeyer (Soares Filho) \\'nē-ˌmī-ər\\, **Oscar** (b.1907) Brazilian architect. Niemeyer's first major independent project was the plan for Pampulha (1941), a suburb of Belo Horizonte. He is famous for his work on BRASÍLIA (1956–61), a series of rather plain, isolated monuments surrounded by vast space. The mushroomlike Museum of Contemporary Art in Niterói, Brazil (1991) is a late work. With its lyrical and sculptural forms, his work is free-flowing and optimistic. Niemeyer received the Pritzker Architecture Prize in 1988.

Niemöller \\'nē-ˌmœl-ər\\, **(Friedrich Gustav Emil) Martin** (1892–1984) German theologian. A war hero in World War I, he became a minister in 1924. When the Nazis came to power, he protested their interference in church affairs, helped combat discrimination against Christians of Jewish background, and founded the anti-Nazi Confessing Church. He was interned 1937–45. After the war he helped rebuild the Evangelical Church and became a controversial pacifist; for his efforts to extend friendship ties to Eastern-bloc countries, he received the Lenin Peace Prize (1967) and W. Germany's Grand Cross of Merit (1971).

Niepce \\'nyeps\\, **(Joseph-) Nicéphore** (1765–1833) French inventor. In 1807 Niepce and his brother invented an internal-combustion engine (fueled with lycopodium powder). In 1826–27, using a camera, he made a view from his workroom window on a pewter plate—the first permanently fixed image from nature. In 1829 he began a partnership with Louis DAGUERRE, but he died before they had achieved any further advance.

Nietzsche \\'nē-chə, 'nē-chē\\, **Friedrich (Wilhelm)** (1844–1900) German-Swiss philosopher and writer. The brilliant son of a Lutheran pastor, at 24 he became professor of classical philology at the Univ. of Basel. He became close to Richard WAGNER, in whose operas he saw the potential for the revival of Western civilization, but broke with Wagner angrily in 1876. His *Birth of Tragedy* (1872) contained major insights into ancient Greek drama; like *Untimely Meditations* (1873), it is dominated by a Romantic perspective also influenced by Arthur SCHOPENHAUER. Mental and physical problems forced him to leave his position in 1878, and he spent 10 years attempting to recover his health in various resorts. His works from *Human, All Too Human* (1878) to *The Gay Science* (1882) extol reason and science and experiment with literary genres. His mature writings, particularly *Beyond Good and Evil* (1886), *A Genealogy of Morals* (1887), and *Thus Spake Zarathustra* (1883–92), were preoccupied with the origin and function of values in human life. He fulminated against Christianity and announced the death of God. His mental breakdown in 1889 marked the virtual end of his productive life. He was revered by Adolf HITLER for his dislike of democracy and his heroic ideal of the *Übermensch* (Superman), though the Nazis ignored much in Nietzsche's thought that was hostile to their aims. His analyses of the values that underlie traditional Western religion, morality, and philosophy affected generations of theologians, philosophers, psychologists, poets, novelists, and playwrights.

Niger \\'nī-jər, nē-'zher\\ *officially* **Republic of Niger** Nation, W Africa, on the S edge of the SAHARA. Area: 459,073 sq mi (1,188,999 sq km). Population (2000): 10,076,000. Capital: NIAMEY. More than half the people are HAUSA; there are

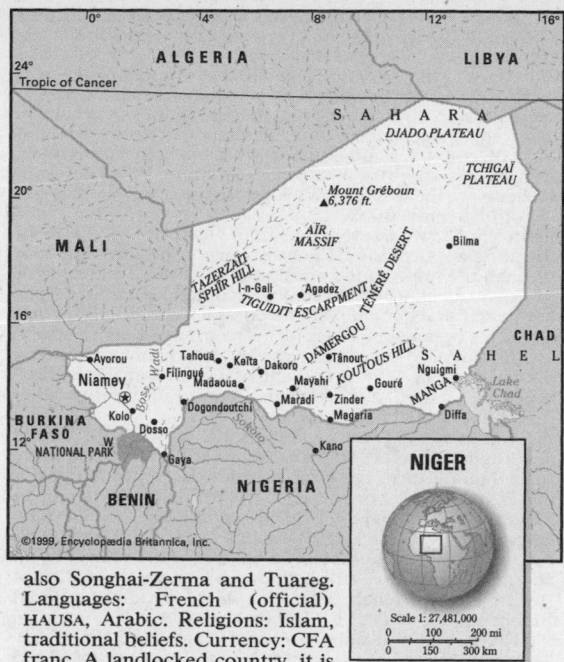

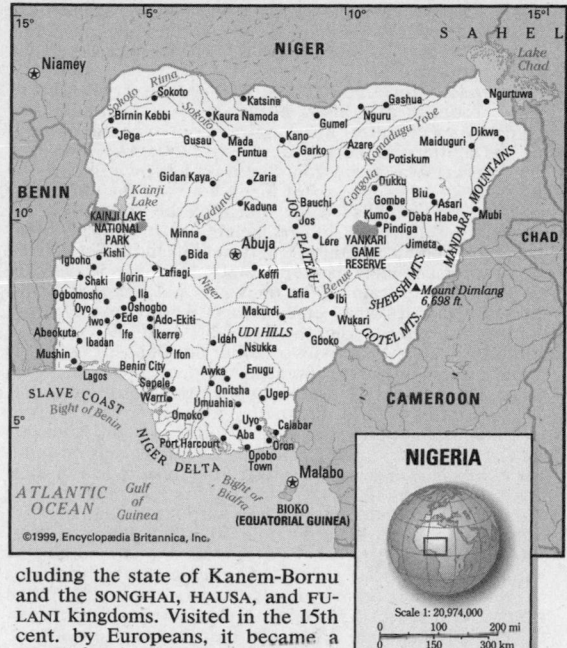

NIGER

Scale 1: 27,481,000

0   100   200 mi
0   150   300 km

NIGERIA

Scale 1: 20,974,000

0   100   200 mi
0   150   300 km

also Songhai-Zerma and Tuareg. Languages: French (official), HAUSA, Arabic. Religions: Islam, traditional beliefs. Currency: CFA franc. A landlocked country, it is characterized by savanna in the south and desert in the center and north; most of the population lives in the south. The NIGER RIVER dominates in the southwest, and the Aïr Massif, a mountainous region, in the N central part of the country. Niger has a developing economy based largely on agriculture and mining. It is a republic with one legislative body; its head of state and government is the president, assisted by the prime minister. There is evidence of NEOLITHIC culture in the region, and there were several precolonial kingdoms. First explored by Europeans in the late 18th cent., it became part of FRENCH W. AFRICA in 1904. It became an overseas territory of France in 1946 and gained independence in 1960. The first multiparty elections were held in 1993, but military coups followed in 1996 and 1999. By 2000 Niger was seen as the second-poorest country in Africa.

Niger-Congo languages Superfamily of 900–1,300 languages spoken by most of the population of sub-Saharan Africa, from N Senegal and Kenya in the north to Namibia and Eastern Cape province (S. Africa) in the south. The name Niger-Congo was introduced by J. H. GREENBERG. Niger-Congo has nine branches: ADAMAWA-UBANGI, Atlantic (20 million speakers in W coastal Africa), BENUE-CONGO, Gur (5 million speakers around the upper Volta), Ijoid (2 million speakers on the Niger delta), Kordofanian (200,000 speakers in S Sudan), Kru (1–2 million speakers mainly in Ivory Coast and Liberia), Kwa (30 million speakers in Nigeria and adjacent countries), and Mande (10 million speakers in W central Africa).

Nigeria *officially* **Federal Republic of Nigeria** Nation, W Africa. Area: 356,669 sq mi (923,773 sq km). Population (2000): 123,338,000. Capital: ABUJA. There are more than 250 ethnic groups, including HAUSA, YORUBA, IGBO (Ibo), and FULANI. Languages: English (official), HAUSA. Religions: Islam, Christianity, animism. Currency: naira. Nigeria consists of plateaus and the lowlands between them, which are major river basins fed especially by the NIGER RIVER. It has a developing, mixed economy based largely on petroleum production and agriculture. Manufacturing remains undeveloped. Services, trade, and transportation employ more than two-fifths of the workforce. Nigeria is a republic with two legislative bodies; its head of state and government is the president. Inhabited for thousands of years, the region was the center of the Nok culture from 500 B.C. to A.D. 200 and several precolonial empires, in-

cluding the state of Kanem-Bornu and the SONGHAI, HAUSA, and FULANI kingdoms. Visited in the 15th cent. by Europeans, it became a center for the slave trade. The area began to come under British control in 1861, and was entirely British-controlled by 1906. Nigeria gained independence in 1960 and became a republic in 1963, with Nnamdi Azikiwe (1904–1996) as president. Ethnic strife soon led to military coups, and military groups ruled the country 1966–79 and 1983–99. Civil war between the central government and the former E region, BIAFRA, in 1967–70 ended in Biafra's surrender after the death by starvation of a million Biafrans. In 1991 the capital was moved from LAGOS to Abuja. The execution of writer and activist Ken Saro-Wiwa in 1995 led to international sanctions, and civilian government was reestablished in 1999 after nearly 16 years of military rule. By far the most populous nation in Africa, Nigeria suffers from rapid population increase, political instability, foreign debt, slow economic growth, a high rate of violent crime, and rampant government corruption.

Niger River *or* **Joliba** \ˈjäl-ə-bə\ *or* **Kworra** \ˈkwȯr-ə\ Principal river of W Africa. The third-longest on the continent, it rises in Guinea near the Sierra Leone border and flows into Nigeria and the Gulf of GUINEA. It is 2,600 mi (4,180 sq km) long. Peoples living along the Niger include the BAMBARA, the MALINKE, and the SONGHAI.

nighthawk Any of several species of N. and S. American birds in the WHIPPOORWILL family (Caprimulgidae) that are buff, reddish, or grayish brown, usually with light spots or patches, and 6–14 in. (15–35 cm) long. They fly about at night, especially at evening and dawn, catching flying insects. The common nighthawk (*Chordeiles minor*) inhabits most of N. America. It has a white throat and wing patches, and a sharp nasal call. During courtship it dives swiftly, creating audible whirring sounds.

nightingale Any of several small Old World THRUSHES (family Turdidae) renowned for their song. The name refers in particular to the Eurasian nightingale (*Erithacus*, or *Luscinia*, *megarhynchos*), a brown bird 6.5 in. (16 cm) long. It sings day and night from perches in shubbery. Its strong and varied song, with prominent cre-

Eurasian nightingale
(*Erithacus megarhynchos*)

©1999, Encyclopædia Britannica, Inc.

©1999, Encyclopædia Britannica, Inc.

scendo effects, has been regarded for centuries throughout Europe and Asia as the most beautiful of all birdsongs. The term is also applied to other birds with rich songs (e.g., the WOOD THRUSH).

Nightingale, Florence (1820–1910) British (Italian-born) nurse, founder of trained NURSING as a profession for women. As a volunteer nurse, she was put in charge of nursing the military in Turkey during the CRIMEAN WAR. Her first concern was sanitation. She used her own finances to purchase supplies. She spent many hours in the wards; her night rounds established her image as the "Lady with the Lamp." Her efforts on soldiers' behalf led to the Army Medical School and a Sanitary Department in India. She started the first scientifically based nursing school, was instrumental in setting up training for midwives and nurses in workhouse infirmaries, and helped reform workhouses. She was the first woman awarded the Order of Merit (1907).

nightjar *or* **goatsucker** Any of about 60–70 species of birds (family Caprimulgidae) found in temperate to tropical regions. The name is sometimes applied to all birds in the order Caprimulgiformes. The name goatsucker derives from an old belief that they sucked goat's milk at night. Nightjars eat flying insects at night. The common nightjar (*Caprimulgus europaeus*) has soft plumage that results in noiseless flight. It is about 12 in. (30 cm) long. Its N. American relatives include the NIGHTHAWK and WHIPPOORWILL.

Night of the Long Knives (June 30, 1934) Purge of Nazi leaders by Adolf HITLER. Fearing that the paramilitary SA had become too powerful, Hitler ordered his elite SS guards to murder the organization's leaders, including Ernst RÖHM. Also killed that night were hundreds of other perceived opponents of Hitler, including Kurt von SCHLEICHER and Gregor STRASSER.

nightshade family Family Solanaceae, composed of at least 2,400 species of flowering plants in about 95 genera, found worldwide, especially in tropical Latin America. The medicinally significant nightshades are potent sources of such ALKALOIDS as NICOTINE, atropine, and scopolamine; they include deadly nightshade (BELLADONNA), jimsonweed, henbane, and MANDRAKE. The most important nightshades are the POTATO, EGGPLANT, TOMATO, garden PEPPER, TOBACCO, and many garden ornamentals, including PETUNIAS. The genus *Solanum* contains almost half the species in the family. The species usually called nightshade in N. America and England is *S. dulcamara*.

nihilism \'nī-ə-ˌli-zəm, 'nē-ə-ˌli-zəm\ Any of various philosophical positions that deny that there are objective foundations for human value systems. In 19th-cent. Russia, the term was applied to a philosophy of skepticism that negated all forms of aestheticism and advocated utilitarianism and scientific rationalism. Rejecting the social sciences, classical philosophical systems, and the established social order, nihilism negated all authority exercised by the state, the church, or the family and based its belief on nothing but scientific truth. It gradually became associated with political terror and degenerated into a philosophy of violence.

Nijinska \nə-'zhin-skə\, **Bronislava (Fominitshna)** (1891–1972) Russian-U.S. dancer, choreographer, and teacher. After training at the Imperial Ballet school in St. Petersburg, she joined the BALLETS RUSSES with her brother, Vaslav NIJINSKY, in 1911. She choreographed several ballets for the company, including *Les noces* (1923) and *Les biches* (1924), and also created works for other companies, including her own (1932–37). She moved to Los Angeles in 1938, where she opened a school.

Nijinsky \nə-'zhin-skē\, **Vaslav (Fomich)** (1889–1950) Russian ballet dancer. He and his sister, Bronislava NIJINSKA, trained in St. Petersburg, and he joined the MARIINSKY THEATER company in 1907. With his spectacular leaps and unrivaled grace, he was an immediate sensation, dancing leading roles in *Giselle, Swan Lake,* and *Sleeping Beauty,* often with Anna PAVLOVA and Tamara KARSAVINA. He joined the BALLETS RUSSES in 1909 and created many roles in Michel FOKINE's ballets, including *Le spectre de la rose* and *Petrushka.* In 1912–13 he choreographed *The Afternoon of a Faun, Jeux,* and *The Rite of Spring,* all of which caused scandals. His marriage in 1913 led to his dismissal by his mentor, Sergey DIAGHILEV. His intensifying mental illness led to his

retirement in 1919, and he lived mostly in mental institutions until his death. Nijinsky's legendary reputation is unequaled in the history of dance.

Nike \'nī-kē, 'nē-kā\ Greek goddess of victory. Nike was originally an attribute of both ATHENA and ZEUS, represented as a small figure carried in their hand. She gradually came to be recognized as a mediator between gods and mortals, and was frequently shown carrying a palm branch, wreath, or staff as the messenger of victory. When depicted on her own, she was often a winged figure hovering over the victor in a competition.

Nikon \'nyē-kən\ *orig.* Nikita Minin (1605–1681) Leader of the Russian Orthodox Church. Born a peasant, he rose through the ranks of the priesthood to become patriarch of Moscow and all Russia in 1652. He purged Russian religious books and practices of what he considered corruptions and exiled his opponents. His reforms so troubled many believers that they led to a schism in the church and widespread disaffection. In 1666 a council of Greek patriarchs convened by Czar ALEXIS stripped Nikon of all priestly functions but retained his reforms.

Nile, Battle of the (Aug. 1, 1798) Battle between the British fleet under Horatio NELSON and French Revolutionary forces. In a plan to constrict British trade routes by invading Egypt, NAPOLEON ordered the French fleet to sail to Alexandria; it eluded the British fleet to reach Abu Qir Bay, where it anchored in a defensive line. Nelson discovered the French at twilight and ordered an immediate attack. In an all-night battle, the British destroyed or captured all but two of the 13 French ships. The decisive victory secured British control of the Mediterranean.

Nile River *Arabic* **Al-Bahr** \al-'bär\ River, E and NE Africa. The longest river in the world, it is about 4,160 mi (6,693 km) long from its remotest headstream and 3,473 mi (5,588 km) from Lake VICTORIA to the Mediterranean Sea. It flows generally north from E Africa through Uganda, Sudan, and Egypt. It receives major tributaries, including the Blue Nile and the Atbara River before entering Lake NASSER near the Egypt–Sudan border. After the ASWAN HIGH DAM impounds the lake, it continues northward to its delta near CAIRO, where it empties into the Mediterranean. It has supported continuous human settlement for at least 5,000 years; canals and waterworks were built in the 19th cent. The Nile is also a vital waterway for the transport of people and goods.

Nilo-Saharan languages \ˌnī-lō-sə-'hä-rən\ Hypothesized superfamily of perhaps 115 African languages spoken by more than 27 million people from Mali west to Ethiopia and from southernmost Egypt south to Tanzania. The concept of Nilo-Saharan was introduced in 1963 by J. H. GREENBERG; most Africanists accept it as a working hypothesis. Nilo-Saharan is divided into two large families, Central Sudanic and Eastern Sudanic, and a number of small families and single languages, including Songhai and Kanuri. Central Sudanic comprises languages of S Chad, S Sudan, and NE Congo (Zaire). Eastern Sudanic includes the Nubian family, spoken along the Nile in N Sudan and S Egypt, and the Nilotic languages, spoken by about 14 million people (see NILOTES), including the DINKA, LUO, and MASAI.

Nilotes \'nī-lə-ˌtēz\ Cluster of E central African peoples living in S Sudan, N Uganda, and W Kenya. The name refers to the region of the Upper Nile and its tributaries, where most of them live. Nilotic men commonly reach a height of 7 ft (210 cm). The Acholi, DINKA, LUO, MASAI, Nandi, Nuer, and Shilluk are classed as Nilotes. Altogether they number about 7 million.

Nilsson, Birgit *orig.* Märta Birgit Svennsson (b.1918) Swedish soprano. She made her debut in Stockholm in 1946, and she sang her first Brünnhilde in a complete *Ring of the Nibelungen* in Munich (1954–55). She went on to sing most of the major Wagnerian soprano roles at Bayreuth between 1959 and 1970, acclaimed as the greatest Wagnerian soprano of her time for the astonishing power and capacities of her steely voice. Her other great roles included Elektra, Salome, Turandot, and Leonora.

Nîmes \'nēm\ *ancient* Nemausus. City (pop., 1999: 133,000), S France. It was the capital of a Gaulish tribe that submitted to Rome in 121 B.C. Caesar AUGUSTUS founded a new city there, and for five centuries it was one of the principal cities of Roman GAUL. Plundered by the VANDALS and VISIGOTHS and occupied by SARACENS in the 8th cent., it passed to the French crown in 1229. It prospered with the coming of the railways in the late 19th cent. It is noted for its Roman remains, including the Maison Carée (an ancient temple).

Nimitz \'ni-mits\, **Chester W(illiam)** (1885–1966) U.S. naval officer. Born in Fredericksburg, Texas, he graduated from Annapolis in 1905 and rose to become chief of the navy's bureau of navigation in 1939. After the Japanese attack on Pearl Harbor, he was made commander in chief of the Pacific fleet, which won the battles of MIDWAY and the CORAL SEA. He led later naval operations in the Pacific that ended with the Japanese surrender, signed aboard his flagship, the USS *Missouri*.

Nin \'nēn, 'nin\, **Anaïs** (1903–1977) French-U.S. author. Daughter of the Cuban composer Joaquín Nin (1878–1949), she became closely associated with Henry MILLER in bohemian Paris. Her writing, including the huge novel *Cities of the Interior* (5 vols., 1959), shows the influence of Surrealism and psychoanalysis. She won late recognition with the publication of eight volumes of her personal diaries. Her account of her long incestuous relationship with her father was published posthumously. Though admired by some, her work has been criticized as narcissistic and pretentious.

Niña, La See LA NIÑA

Ninety-five Theses Propositions for debate on the question of INDULGENCES, written by Martin LUTHER and posted on the door of the Castle Church in Wittenberg, Germany, on October 31, 1517. This event is now seen as the beginning of the Protestant REFORMATION. The theses, written in response to the selling of indulgences to pay for the rebuilding of ST. PETER'S BASILICA, represented an implicit criticism of papal policy and stressed the spiritual, inward character of the Christian faith. Widely circulated, they aroused much controversy.

Nineveh \'ni-nə-və\ *ancient* Ninus. Oldest and most populous city of ancient ASSYRIA, on the TIGRIS RIVER opposite modern MOSUL, Iraq. Its greatest development was under SENNACHERIB and ASHURBANIPAL in the 7th cent. B.C. It was destroyed by Nabopolassar of BABYLONIA and his allies, the Scythians and Medes, in 612 B.C. Excavations have revealed palaces, a library, and city walls.

Niño, El See EL NIÑO

Niobe \nī-'ō-bē\ In GREEK MYTHOLOGY, the prototype of the bereaved mother. The mother of six sons and six daughters, she boasted of her fertility to the Titaness LETO, who had only two children, APOLLO and ARTEMIS. As punishment for her pride, Apollo killed all of Niobe's sons and Artemis all her daughters. Niobe was so overwhelmed with grief that the gods turned her into a rock on Mt. Sipylus that weeps endlessly as the snow above it melts.

Niobrara River \,nī-ə-'brar-ə\ River, Wyoming and Nebraska. Flowing east across Wyoming's high plains and Nebraska's sandhills and low plains, it joins the MISSOURI RIVER at the S. Dakota line. It is 431 mi (694 km) long. The Agate Fossil Beds National Monument is located on its banks.

Nippur \ni-'pùr\ Ancient city of MESOPOTAMIA, now in SE Iraq, southeast of the site of BABYLON. It was originally on the EUPHRATES RIVER, whose course later changed. By 2500 B.C. it was the center of worship of the important Sumerian storm god Enlil (see SUMER). The city was abandoned in the 12th or 13th cent. A.D. Excavations have revealed temples, a ZIGGURAT, and thousands of clay tablets that are a primary source of knowledge of ancient Sumerian civilization. Also uncovered were an Akkadian tomb (see AKKAD) and a large temple to the Mesopotamian goddess of healing.

Nirenberg \'nir-ən-,bərg\, **Marshall W(arren)** (b.1927) U.S. biochemist. Born in New York City, he received his PhD from the Univ. of Michigan. He demonstrated that each possible triplet (codon) of the four different kinds of nitrogen-containing bases found in DNA and (in some viruses) in RNA (with three exceptions) ultimately causes the incorporation of a specific amino acid into a cell protein. His research earned him a Nobel Prize in 1968, shared with Robert HOLLEY and Har Gobind KHORANA.

nirvana \nir-'vä-nə\ (Sanskrit: "extinction") In Indian religious thought, the transcendent state of freedom achieved by the extinction of desire and of individual consciousness. Nirvana is the supreme goal in BUDDHISM. Release from desire (and consequent suffering) and the continuous round of rebirths constitutes enlightenment, or the experience of nirvana.

Nis *or* **Nish** \'nēsh\ *ancient* Naissus *or* Nissa. City (pop., 2000 est.: 182,000), southeast of BELGRADE, Yugoslavia. An ancient Roman city, it was the birthplace of CONSTANTINE I the Great (c.280), who adorned it with many buildings. Under the Turks it became an important station on the route from Istanbul to Hungary. It was ceded to Serbia by the Treaty of Berlin in 1878 and was its capital until 1901. Bomb damage in World War II and postwar construction erased much of its Turko-Byzantine style.

NIST See BUREAU OF STANDARDS

niter See SALTPETER

nitrate Any SALT or ESTER of NITRIC ACID (HNO₃). The salts are inorganic compounds with IONIC BONDS, containing the nitrate ION (NO₃⁻) and any CATION. Many, particularly ammonium nitrate, are used as agricultural fertilizers (see SALTPETER). The esters are organic compounds with COVALENT BONDS, having the structure R–O–NO₂, in which R represents an organic combining group such as methyl, ethyl, or phenyl.

nitric acid \'nī-trik\ Inorganic compound, colorless, fuming, highly corrosive liquid, chemical formula HNO₃. It is used to manufacture fertilizers and explosives (including NITROGLYCERIN), as well as in organic syntheses, metallurgy, ore flotation, and reprocessing of spent nuclear fuel. A strong ACID, it is toxic and can cause severe burns. It attacks most metals and is used for etching steel and photoengraving.

nitrifying bacteria \'nī-trə-,fī-iŋ\ Small group of oxygen-requiring BACTERIA that use nitrogen compounds as an energy source. These microorganisms are important in the NITROGEN CYCLE as converters of soil AMMONIA to NITRATES. The nitrification process requires two distinct groups: bacteria that convert ammonia to NITRITES, and bacteria that convert nitrites to nitrates. Nitrifiers increase the nitrate content of soils irrigated with ammonia and thus increase crop yields. See also DENITRIFYING BACTERIA.

nitrite \'nī-,trīt\ Any SALT or ESTER of nitrous acid (HNO₂). The salts are inorganic compounds with IONIC BONDS, containing the nitrite ION (NO₂⁻) and any CATION. The esters are organic compounds with COVALENT BONDS, having the structure R–O–N–O, in which R represents a carbon-containing combining group and the BONDING is from carbon to oxygen. Nitrites are used as food preservatives and color enhancers, though they are so toxic they have caused deaths and combine with AMINES to produce CARCINOGENS. They are used in medicine to dilate blood vessels.

nitrogen Gaseous chemical ELEMENT, chemical symbol N, atomic number 7. A colorless, odorless, tasteless GAS, it makes up 78% of the earth's atmosphere and is a constituent of all living matter. As the almost inert diatomic molecule N₂, it is useful as an inert atmosphere or to dilute other gases. Nitrogen is commercially produced by DISTILLATION of liquefied air. NITROGEN FIXATION is achieved naturally by soil microbes and industrially by the HABER-BOSCH PROCESS. AMMONIA is the starting material for most other nitrogen compounds (especially NITRATES and NITRITES), whose main uses are in agricultural fertilizers and explosives. Nitrogen forms several OXIDES: NITROUS OXIDE; nitric oxide (NO), recently found to play key roles in physiology; and nitrogen dioxide (NO₂) and other forms (including N₂O₃ and N₂O₅) notorious for causing air pollution, especially when acted on by sunlight. Other compounds include the nitrides, exceptionally hard materials made from nitrogen and a metal; CYANIDES; azides, used in detonators and percussion caps; and thousands of organic compounds containing nitrogen in FUNCTIONAL GROUPS or in a linear or ring structure. See also NITROGEN CYCLE.

nitrogen cycle Circulation of NITROGEN in various forms throughout nature. Nitrogen is essential to life, but most is inert and unavailable in AIR. NITROGEN FIXATION by microbes turns this nitrogen into NITRATES and other compounds, which plants or algae assimilate into their tissues.

Animals that eat plants incorporate the compounds into their tissues. Microbes decompose the remains and waste of all living things into AMMONIA (ammonification); the ammonia may leave the soil through vaporization into the air or leaching into water or be converted through nitrogen fixation so that the cycle can start again. Once fixed from the air, nitrogen can go through the cycle repeatedly without reverting to the gaseous state. In waterlogged, oxygen-deficient soils, there are bacteria that convert nitrates into free nitrogen (denitrification).

nitrogen fixation Any natural or industrial process that causes free NITROGEN in the air to combine chemically with other elements to form compounds such as AMMONIA, NITRATES, or NITRITES. Soil microorganisms (e.g., *Rhizobium* bacteria living in root nodules of LEGUMES) are responsible for more than 90% of all nitrogen fixation. Though nitrogen is part of all PROTEINS and essential in both plant and animal METABOLISM, plants and animals cannot use the nitrogen that forms 80% of the atmosphere. Symbiotic nitrogen-fixing bacteria invade the root hairs of host plants, and the resulting nodules convert free nitrogen to nitrates, which the host plant uses for its development. Nitrogen fixation in legumes is of prime importance in agriculture. Before the use of synthetic FERTILIZERS in the industrial countries, usable nitrogen was supplied as MANURE and by CROP ROTATION that included a legume crop.

nitrogen narcosis *or* **nitrogen euphoria** *or* **raptures of the deep** Effects of breathing NITROGEN under increased pressure. In divers breathing compressed air, nitrogen saturates the nervous system, causing a light-headed, numb feeling, then slowed reasoning and dexterity, and then emotional instability and irrationality. Severe cases progress to convulsions and blackout. Severity increases with depth, but there are no aftereffects. Physical function remains normal, and unaware divers may rise too fast (see DECOMPRESSION SICKNESS) or let their air supply run out. HELIUM, which dissolves less easily in body tissues, is used for deep dives.

nitroglycerin \ˌnī-trə-ˈgli-sə-rən\ *or* **glyceryl trinitrate** Organic compound, powerful explosive and ingredient of most forms of DYNAMITE. It is a colorless, oily, somewhat toxic liquid with a sweet, burning taste. Its safe use as a blasting explosive became possible after Alfred NOBEL developed dynamite. Nitroglycerin is also used in rocket propellants. In medicine, it is used to dilate blood vessels, especially to ease ANGINA PECTORIS.

nitrous oxide \ˈnī-trəs\ *or* **laughing gas** Inorganic compound, one of the OXIDES of NITROGEN. A colorless gas with a pleasantly sweetish odor and taste, it has an ANALGESIC effect when inhaled, and is used as an ANESTHETIC in dentistry and surgery. This effect is preceded by mild hysteria, hence the name "laughing gas." It is also used as a propellant in food aerosols and as a leak detector.

Nivernais \ˌnē-vər-ˈnā\ Historical region, central France. Originally part of BURGUNDY, it became a county about the 10th cent. FRANCIS I of France made it a duchy in 1539. In 1659 it was sold to Cardinal MAZARIN. His descendants possessed it until the FRENCH REVOLUTION, when it was the last great FIEF to be reunited to the French crown.

Nixon, Richard M(ilhous) (1913–1994) 37th president of the U.S. (1969–74). Born in Yorba Linda, Cal., he practiced law in California 1937–42. He was elected to the U.S. House of Representatives in 1947, employing harsh campaign tactics. He came to national attention with the Alger HISS case, and was elected to the Senate in 1950, again following a bitter campaign. He won the vice presidency in 1952 on a ticket with Dwight EISENHOWER, and again in 1956. As presidential candidate in 1960, he lost narrowly to John F. KENNEDY. After losing the 1962 California gubernatorial race, he retired from politics, but returned to run for president in 1968, and

Richard Nixon, 1970

defeated Hubert HUMPHREY with his "southern strategy" of seeking votes from S and W conservatives in both parties. As president, he began to gradually withdraw U.S. military forces in an effort to end the VIETNAM WAR while ordering the secret bombing of N. Vietnamese military centers in Laos and Cambodia. Economic problems caused by inflation made the U.S. budget deficit the largest to date, and in 1971 Nixon established unprecedented peacetime controls on wages and prices. He won reelection in 1972 with a landslide victory over George MCGOVERN. Assisted by secretary of state Henry KISSINGER, he concluded the war. He reopened communications with Communist China and made a state visit there, the first by a U.S. president. On his visit to the Soviet Union, he signed the bilateral SALT agreements. The WATERGATE SCANDAL overshadowed his second term; to avoid impeachment, he became the first president to resign from office. Though never convicted, he was pardoned by his successor, Gerald FORD. He retired to write his memoirs and books on foreign policy.

Nizam al-Mulk \nē-ˈzåm-ủl-ˈmülk\ *orig.* Abu Ali Hasan ibn Ali (c.1018–1092) Persian VIZIER of the Turkish SELJUQ DYNASTY sultans. He served ALP-ARSLAN as governor of Khorasan before becoming VIZIER (1063), a position he occupied for 30 years. He recorded his views on authoritarian rule in the *Seyasat-hameh* ("Book of Government"). He is seen as the quintessential vizier. He was assassinated after falling out of favor with Malik-Shah, Alp-Arslan's son and successor.

Nizam's Dominions See HYDERABAD.

Nizhniy Novgorod \ˈnizh-nē-ˈnòv-gə-rət\ *formerly (1932–90)* **Gorki** City (pop., 1997 est.: 1,371,000), central Russia. It is located on the VOLGA RIVER at its confluence with the OKA RIVER. Founded in 1221, it was annexed to MOSCOW in 1392. It was important in the Russian conquest of the Volga through the mid-16th cent. In 1932 it was renamed for Maxim GORKY, who was born there. It was a place of internal exile for Andrey SAKHAROV. It is a major industrial center.

Njáls saga \ˈnyaůls\ *or* **Njála** \ˈnyaů-lä\ *or* **Burnt Njáll** \ˈbərnt-ˈnyaůl\ ICELANDERS' SAGA, one of the longest and perhaps the finest. Set in a society where blood ties impose inescapable obligations and honor demands vengeance for past injuries, it presents the most comprehensive picture of Icelandic life in the heroic age. Its vividly drawn characters range from comic to sinister; its overriding mood is tragic pessimism.

Nkomo \en-ˈkō-mō\, **Joshua (Mqabuko Nyongolo)** (1917–1999) Zimbabwean (formerly Rhodesian) black nationalist. Nkomo helped lead the guerrilla war against white rule in Rhodesia. As leader of the Zimbabwe African People's Union (ZAPU), he became Robert MUGABE's longtime rival. They participated in a coalition government from 1980 to 1982, when Nkomo was ousted. ZAPU and Mugabe's Zimbabwe African National Union (ZANU) merged in 1987; Nkomo became a vice president in Mugabe's government in 1990.

Nkrumah \en-ˈkrü-mə\, **Kwame** (1909–1972) Nationalist leader and first president of Ghana. A student of literature and socialism, in 1949 he formed the Convention People's Party, to advocate nonviolent protests, strikes, and noncooperation with the British. Elected prime minister of the Gold Coast (1952–60), then president of independent Ghana (1960–66), Nkrumah built new roads, schools, and health facilities, but after 1960 he promoted the PAN-AFRICAN MOVEMENT at the expense of Ghana's economy. Following an attempted coup in 1962, he increased authoritarian controls, increased contacts with communist countries, and wrote works on political phi-

Kwame Nkrumah, 1962

losophy. With the country facing economic ruin, he was deposed in 1966.

Noah Biblical character from GENESIS. He was a man of blameless piety, who was chosen by God to perpetuate the human race after his wicked contemporaries had perished in the flood. On God's instructions, Noah built an ark and took into it one male and one female of each of the world's animals. After the waters receded, God set a rainbow in the sky as a guarantee of his promise never again to curse the earth. The entire human race is supposed to have descended from Noah's sons, Shem, Ham, and Japheth.

Nobel \ˌnō-ˈbel\, **Alfred (Bernhard)** (1833–1896) Swedish chemist, engineer, and industrialist. His attempts to find a safe way to handle NITROGLYCERIN resulted in the invention of DYNAMITE and the blasting cap. He built a network of factories to manufacture dynamite and corporations to produce and market his explosives. He went on to develop more powerful explosives and to construct and perfect detonators for explosives that did not explode on simple firing. Nobel registered over 350 patents, many unrelated to explosives. He left most of his immense fortune, from worldwide explosives and oil interests, to establish the NOBEL PRIZES, which would become the most highly regarded of all international awards.

Nobel Prize Any of the prizes awarded annually by four institutions (three Swedish and one Norwegian) from a fund established under the will of Alfred P. NOBEL intended for those who "have conferred the greatest benefit on mankind." Since 1901, prizes have been awarded for physics, chemistry, physiology or medicine, literature, and peace; since 1969, a sixth prize, established by the Bank of Sweden, has been awarded in economic sciences. They are regarded as the most prestigious prizes in the world.

noble gas *or* **inert gas** Any of the six chemical ELEMENTS that make up the rightmost group of the PERIODIC TABLE as usually arranged: HELIUM, NEON, ARGON, KRYPTON, XENON, and RADON. All are colorless, odorless, and nonflammable and occur in tiny amounts in the atmosphere (though helium is the most plentiful element in the universe). Their stable electronic CONFIGURATIONS make them extremely unreactive, though the three heaviest can form compounds (mainly with FLUORINE). They are used in fluorescent lighting devices and discharge lamps, because they glow with a characteristic color when confined in a glass tube at low pressure with an electric current passing through it. Their very low boiling and melting points make them useful as refrigerants for low-temperature research.

No drama *or* **Noh drama** Classic Japanese theatrical form. One of the world's oldest extant theatrical forms, No drama has a heroic theme, a chorus, and highly stylized action, costuming, and scenery. Its all-male performers are storytellers who use their visual appearances and movements to suggest their tale rather than enact it. No (meaning "talent" or "skill") developed from ancient forms of dance-drama and became a distinctive form in the 14th cent. Kanami (1333–1384) and his son Zeami (1363–1443) wrote many of the most beautiful No texts; over 200 remain in the modern No repertoire.

nodule \ˈnä-jül\ A rounded mineral concretion that is distinct from, and may be separated from, the formation in which it occurs. Nodules usually are elongated and have a knobby irregular surface. CHERT AND FLINT, clay ironstone, and phosphorites commonly occur as nodules. Manganese-rich nodules are found on the ocean floor.

Noguchi \nō-ˈgü-chē\, **Isamu** (1904–1988) U.S. sculptor and designer. Though born in Los Angeles, he spent his early years in Japan. He served as Constantin BRANCUSI's assistant in Paris 1927–28. His earlier premedical training suggested to him the interrelatedness of bone and stone, as seen in *Kouros* (1945). Much of his work, such as *Bird C(MU)* (1953–58), consists of elegantly abstracted, rounded forms in highly polished stone. His long collaboration with Martha GRAHAM resulted in stage sets for many ballets, and he also designed public sculptures, sculptural gardens, and playgrounds, as well as furniture.

noise Undesired SOUND that is intrinsically objectionable or that interferes with other sounds. In electronics and information theory, noise refers to random, unpredictable, and undesirable signals, or changes in signals, that mask the desired information content. In radio, this is called static; in television, snow. White noise is a complex signal or sound covering the entire range of component frequencies, all of equal intensity.

Noland, Kenneth (b.1924) U.S. painter of the ABSTRACT EXPRESSIONIST school. Born in Asheville, N.C., he studied at Black Mountain College and in Paris. He was one of the first to use the technique of staining the canvas with thinned paints. He is best known for works in which he deploys his colors in concentric rings and parallel bands in a minimalist style.

Nolde \ˈnōl-də\, **Emil** *orig.* Emil Hansen (1867–1956) German Expressionist painter, printmaker, and watercolorist. Born to a peasant family in Nolde, he carved wood for a living and came late to painting. Fervently religious, he created such works as *Dance Around the Golden Calf* (1910), in which the figures' erotic frenzy and demonic faces are rendered with deliberately crude draftsmanship and dissonant colors. On an expedition to the E. Indies (1913–14), he was impressed by the power of unsophisticated belief. Back in Europe, he produced brooding landscapes (e.g., *Marsh Landscape,* 1916) and colorful paintings of flowers. As a graphic artist he was noted for the stark effect of his crudely incised woodcuts. Though he was a Nazi, the party declared his art "degenerate" and forbade him to paint.

nomadism Way of life of peoples who move cyclically or periodically. It is based on temporary centers whose stability depends on the availability of food supply. HUNTING AND GATHERING SOCIETIES form one class of nomadic group. Pastoral nomads, who depend on domestic livestock, move in an established territory to find pasturage for their animals. Tinker or trader nomads, such as the GYPSIES and the Irish Tinkers, are associated with a larger society but maintain their mobile way of life. Nomadism has declined in the 20th cent. as urban centers have expanded and governments have sought to regulate or eliminate it.

Nome Seaport (pop., 2000: 3,500), W Alaska, on the S side of the Seward Peninsula. Founded as a goldmining camp, it became a center of the Alaskan gold rush of 1899–1903. Its population, estimated at 20,000 in 1900, had dwindled to 852 by 1920. Gold mining remained the chief occupation until 1962. The finish line for the IDITAROD trail race; it also serves as a supply center for NW Alaska.

nonalignment *or* **neutralism** Peacetime policy of avoiding political or ideological affiliations with major power blocs. In the 20th cent., nonalignment was adopted primarily by Asian and African states that had once been colonies of the Western powers and were wary of being drawn into a new form of dependence by the West or the communist bloc. The nonaligned movement, founded by Jawarharlal NEHRU, Gamal Abdel NASSER, and others, held its first official meeting in 1961; it was attended by 25 nations. Meetings have since been held on a three-year schedule. While the Soviet Union existed, the nations tended to seek development assistance from both sides. The movement today counts over 110 members, whose current concerns include debt forgiveness and fairer trade relationships. See also THIRD WORLD.

Nonconformist Any English Protestant who does not conform to the doctrines or practices of the established Church of ENGLAND. The term was first used after the RESTORATION of the monarchy in 1660 to describe congregations that had separated from the national church. Such congregations, also called Separatists or Dissenters, often rejected Anglican rites and doctrines as being too close to Catholicism. In England and Wales the term is generally applied to all Protestant denominations outside Anglicanism.

non-Euclidean geometry Any theory of the nature of geometric space differing from the traditional view held since EUCLID's time. These geometries arose in the 19th cent. when several mathematicians working independently explored the possibility of rejecting Euclid's parallel postulate by making different assumptions about how many lines through a point not on a given line could be parallel to that line. Mathematicians were forced to abandon the idea of a single correct geometry; they created mathematical systems by selecting consistent axioms and studying the theorems that could be derived from them. The development of these alternative geometries had a profound impact on the notion of space and paved the way for the theory of RELATIVITY. See also Nikolay LOBACHEVSKY, Bernhard RIEMANN.

Nonni River See NEN RIVER

nonobjective art See ABSTRACT ART

nonrepresentational art See ABSTRACT ART

nonsense verse Humorous or whimsical verse that features absurd characters and actions and often contains evocative but meaningless words coined for the verse. It differs from other comic verse in its resistance to any rational or allegorical interpretation. Most nonsense verse has been written for children and is modern, dating from the beginning of the 19th cent. Examples include Edward LEAR's *Book of Nonsense* (1846), Lewis CARROLL's "Jabberwocky" (1871), and Hillaire BELLOC's *Bad Child's Book of Beasts* (1896). See also LIMERICK.

nonsteroidal anti-inflammatory drugs See NSAIDS

noradrenaline See NOREPINEPHRINE

Nordenskiöld \'nür-dən-ˌshœld\, **(Nils) Adolf Erik** *later* Baron Nordenskiöld (1832–1901) Finnish-Swedish geologist and explorer. In 1858 he became professor and curator of mineralogy at the Swedish State Museum. He led several geologic expeditions to the Arctic island of Spitsbergen between 1864 and 1873. In 1878–79, on the steam vessel *Vega,* he sailed from Norway to Alaska on the first expedition to successfully navigate the NORTHEAST PASSAGE. In 1883 he became the first to break through the great sea ice barrier of the SE Greenland coast.

norepinephrine \ˌnòr-ˌep-ə-'nef-rən\ *or* **noradrenaline** One of two HORMONES (EPINEPHRINE is the other) secreted by the ADRENAL GLANDS, as well as at nerve endings, as a NEUROTRANSMITTER. It resembles epinephrine chemically and in its actions on the body. It constricts most blood vessels, and is given for certain types of SHOCK.

Norfolk City and port (pop., 2000: 234,000), SE Virginia. It lies just south of HAMPTON ROADS. Founded in 1682, it was destroyed by fires in 1776 and 1799. YELLOW FEVER killed 10% of the population in 1855. During the AMERICAN CIVIL WAR it was occupied by Union troops. Prosperity resumed after 1870 with railroad service. With NEWPORT NEWS and PORTSMOUTH it makes up the Port of Hampton Roads. Shipping and shipbuilding are the major economic activities. Norfolk is the headquarters of the U.S. Atlantic Fleet and NATO's Supreme Allied Command, Atlantic.

Norfolk, 2nd Duke of *orig.* Thomas Howard (1443–1524) English noble prominent in the reigns of HENRY VII and HENRY VIII. While fighting for RICHARD III, he was taken prisoner (and his father killed) in the Battle of BOSWORTH FIELD (1485). After his release in 1489, he commanded the defense of the Scottish borders and later defeated the Scots at the Battle of Flodden (1513). He later served as lord treasurer and a privy councillor. In 1520 he was guardian of England during Henry VIII's absence in France.

Norfolk, 3rd Duke of *orig.* Thomas Howard (1473–1554) English noble prominent in the reign of HENRY VIII. Son of the 2nd duke of NORFOLK, he was made lord high admiral in 1513 and helped rout the Scots at the Battle of Flodden. He led the faction opposed to Thomas WOLSEY, whom he replaced as president of the royal council in 1529. He supported the marriage of his niece Anne BOLEYN to Henry (1533), but later presided over her trial (1536). By 1540 he was the most powerful of Henry's councillors. His position weakened after his niece Catherine HOWARD was put to death (1542); when his son Henry Howard (1517–1547) was executed for treason, he was imprisoned as an accessory.

Norfolk Island S Pacific island, a territory of Australia. Located midway between New Caledonia and New Zealand, it has an area of 13 sq mi (35 sq km). Discovered by Capt. James COOK in 1774, it became a British penal colony (1788–1814, 1825–55). The population of PITCAIRN ISLAND was moved here in 1856, and many residents are descended from crew members of HMS *Bounty*. It has abundant Norfolk Island Pine.

Noricum Ancient kingdom and Roman province, W central Europe. It was located roughly south of the DANUBE RIVER and north of modern Italy. Annexed by Caesar AUGUSTUS around 15 B.C., it had rich iron and gold mines worked by the Romans. Latin inscriptions on coins indicate a Romanized culture. Emperor CLAUDIUS recruited soldiers from the area for the PRAETORIAN GUARD. The FRANKS settled there by the end of the 5th cent. A.D.

Noriega (Morena) \ˌnòr-ē-'ä-gə\, **Manuel (Antonio)** (b.1938) Panamanian general and strongman. As chief of military intelligence in the 1970s, he cooperated with the CENTRAL INTELLIGENCE AGENCY and negotiated the release of U.S. freighter crews held by Cuba, but was tainted by reports of drug trafficking and brutality. In 1989, as head of the armed forces, he canceled election results that displeased him. The U.S. government then invaded Panama, primarily to capture Noriega. He was brought to trial in the U.S., convicted of racketeering, drug trafficking, and money laundering, and sentenced to 40 years in prison.

normal distribution In STATISTICS, a FREQUENCY DISTRIBUTION in the shape of the classic bell curve. It accurately represents most variations in such attributes as height and weight. Any random variable with a normal distribution has a mean (see MEAN, MEDIAN, AND MODE) and a standard deviation that indicates how much the data as a whole deviate from the mean.

Norman, Jessye (b.1945) U.S. soprano. Born in Augusta, Ga., she debuted in Berlin in *Tannhäuser* (1969). Having garnered extraordinary praise for years, she made her Metropolitan Opera debut in *Les Troyens* in 1983, confirming her reputation as perhaps the greatest soprano of her generation. An imposing stage presence, she ranges with equal conviction and musicality across an exceptionally wide operatic and concert repertoire.

Norman Conquest (1066) Military conquest of England by William, duke of Normandy (later WILLIAM I), mainly through his victory over HAROLD II at the Battle of HASTINGS. After defeating Harold's army and advancing to London, Willliam was crowned king in Westminster Abbey on Christmas Day, 1066. Native revolts continued until 1071, notably in Northumbria. The Norman Conquest brought great social and political changes to England, linking the country more closely with Western Europe, strengthening feudalism, and replacing the old English aristocracy with a Norman aristocracy. The English language was subjected to a long period of influence by Anglo-French, which remained in literary and courtly use until the reign of EDWARD III.

Normandy *French* **Normandie** \nòr-mäⁿ-'dē\ Historic region, NW France. The capital was ROUEN. Its Celtic population was conquered by the Romans around 56 B.C., when it became part of the Roman province of LUGDUNENSIS. It was ceded to the VIKINGS in 911 by Charles III the Simple of France; they became known as NORMANS, hence the region's name. After the NORMAN CONQUEST (1066), it was united to England by WILLIAM I of Normandy. It became a province of France in 1450. It was the site of the World War II NORMANDY CAMPAIGN.

Normandy Campaign (June 6, 1944) Allied invasion of N Europe in WORLD WAR II that began in Normandy, France. Also called Operation Overlord, the largest amphibious landing in history transported 156,000 U.S., British, and Canadian troops across the English Channel in over 5,000 ships and 10,000 planes; it was directed by Gen. Dwight EISENHOWER. The D-Day invasion was preceded by airborne commando units that crippled German communications. Assault forces landed at five beaches on the Normandy coast and soon established beachheads, despite stiff German resistance and heavy losses at the code-named Omaha Beach. Allied air supremacy prevented rapid German reinforcements, and discord between Adolf HITLER and his generals stalled crucial counterattacks. Though delayed by heavy fighting around Caen and near Cherbourg, the Allied ground troops had begun their rapid advance across France by mid-July.

Normans VIKINGS, or Norsemen, who settled in N France (or the Frankish kingdom) and their descendants. As pagan pirates from Denmark, Norway, and Iceland, they raided the European coast in the 8th cent. They settled in the lower Seine valley by about 900 and then extended their territory westward. They founded the duchy of NORMANDY. Though the Normans converted to Christianity and adopted the French language, they continued to display the appetite for conquest of their Viking ancestors. In the 11th cent. they seized England in the NORMAN CONQUEST and colonized S Italy and Sicily.

Norodom \ˈnȯr-ə-dəm\ *orig.* Vody (1834–1904) King of Cambodia (r.1860–1904). Cambodia had been under the joint vassalage of Vietnam and Siam (Thailand) since 1802. After the death of Norodom's father, King Duong, in 1860, the Siamese asserted sole dominion over Cambodia, but France opposed Siamese claims and forced Norodom to accept French protection. He was crowned in 1864, and during his reign France dominated Cambodian affairs.

Norodom Sihanouk \ˌsē-ə-ˈnük\ (b.1922) Cambodia's king (1941–55, from 1993) and head of state (1955–70). He abdicated in favor of his father in 1955, becoming prime minister, then head of state. During the Vietnam War he steered a neutral course in both his foreign and internal policies. Overthrown by LON NOL in 1970, he campaigned for the KHMER ROUGE but was imprisoned after they came to power, and most of his family was killed. Released in the face of a Vietnamese invasion (1979), he denounced both the Vietnamese and the Khmer Rouge. In 1982 he became president of a fragile coalition of resistance groups. Following U.N.-sponsored elections in 1993, Cambodia's National Assembly voted to restore the monarchy, and Sihanouk again became king.

Norris, (Benjamin) Frank(lin) (1870–1902) U.S. writer. Born in Chicago, he became the first important American author to embrace NATURALISM. *McTeague* (1899; film, *Greed*, 1924) is a portrait of an acquisitive society. He adopted a more humanitarian ideal beginning with *The Octopus* (1901), the first novel of a projected trilogy dealing with the economic and social forces involved in the wheat industry. The second part, *The Pit*, appeared in 1903. His works present a vivid picture of life in California in his day. He died in surgery at 32.

Norsemen See VIKINGS

North (of Kirtling), Frederick *later* Earl of Guilford *known as* **Lord North** (1732–1792) English prime minister (1770–82). He served as lord of the treasury 1759–65 and chancellor of the exchequer 1767–70. As prime minister, he gave vacillating support to both harsh and conciliatory measures toward the American colonies before the American Revolution. Though only a halfhearted supporter of the war, he was a pliant agent of GEORGE III. He resigned on hearing of the British defeat at Yorktown.

North, Oliver (Laurence) (b.1943) U.S. marine involved in the IRAN-CONTRA AFFAIR. Born in San Antonio, he graduated from the U.S. Naval Academy and served in the Vietnam War. In 1981 he was assigned to the National Security Council. Embracing the cause of the Nicaraguan contras, he raised private donations for them. In 1986, after Congressional investigation of the Iran-Contra Affair, he was reluctantly dismissed by Ronald REAGAN. In 1988 he was indicted for conspiracy to defraud the government; found guilty, he was sentenced to two years' probation. In 1991, after a prosecution witness claimed that his testimony had been tainted, all charges against North were dropped. From 1995 he hosted a radio talk show.

North, Simeon (1765–1852) U.S. firearms manufacturer. Born in Berlin, Conn., he supplied pistols and rifles to the U.S. government from 1799. He developed the use of interchangeable parts in manufacturing and the first known milling machine. In 1825 he built a breech-loading rifle with fully interchangeable parts.

North Africa Campaigns (1940–43) Battles in WORLD WAR II for control of N. Africa. After the 1940 victory by Italian troops in Egypt, the Italians were driven back into Libya by British troops. German reinforcements led by Erwin ROMMEL forced the British to retreat into Egypt after the defense of Tobruk. In 1942 the British under Bernard MONTGOMERY successfully counterattacked at the Battles of EL ALAMEIN. In November 1942 U.S. and British forces landed in Algeria and Morocco. In May 1943 the Allies, advancing from east and west, defeated the Axis forces and forced the surrender of 250,000 Axis troops.

North America Continent, Western Hemisphere. The third-largest continent on earth, it lies mostly between the ARCTIC CIRCLE and the TROPIC OF CANCER. It is almost completely surrounded by bodies of water, including the Pacific Ocean, the Bering Strait, the Arctic Ocean, the Atlantic Ocean, the Gulf of Mexico, and the Caribbean Sea. Area: 9,361,791 sq mi (24,247,039 sq km). Population (2000): 440,554,000. Its geologic structure is built around a stable platform of Precambrian rock called the CANADIAN SHIELD. To the southeast are the APPALACHIAN MTNS., and to the west are the younger and much taller Cordilleras. These mountains extend the length of the continent and occupy about one-third of the total land area. The ROCKY MTNS. constitute the E Cordillera. The highest point is Mt. MCKINLEY. The MISSISSIPPI RIVER basin, with its major tributaries, the MISSOURI and OHIO, occupies more than one-eighth of the continent's total area. Generally temperate climatic conditions prevail. Arable land accounts for about one-eighth of the land area and forests for about one-third. English, the primary language of the U.S., predominates, followed by Spanish; French is spoken in parts of Canada. N. America has a mixture of developed and developing economies, adequate reserves of most metallic resources, and the world's largest reserves of cadmium, copper, lead, molybdenum, silver, and zinc. It is the world's leading food producer. Among the continent's democratically governed states are Canada, Mexico, Costa Rica, and the U.S. The nations of N. America have sought hemispheric unity as members of the ORGANIZATION OF AMERICAN STATES, which also includes S. AMERICAN countries. The first inhabitants were AMERICAN INDIANS, who migrated from Asia about 20,000 years ago. The greatest pre-Columbian civilizations were in Mesoamerica (see MESOAMERICAN CIVILIZATION) and included the OLMEC, MAYA, TOLTEC, and AZTEC, who were conquered by the Spanish. Beginning in the 17th cent. the continent underwent a profound transformation with the coming of Europeans and the Africans they introduced as slaves. The style of life became Latin American south of the RIO GRANDE and Anglo-American to the north, with enclaves of French culture in Canada and Louisiana. Slavery, practiced in the 16th–19th cent., added a significant minority culture of African origin, especially in the U.S. and the Caribbean (see W. INDIES). The huge industrial economy of the U.S., its abundant resources, and its military strength give the continent considerable global influence. See map on following page.

North American Free Trade Agreement (NAFTA) Trade pact signed by Canada, the U.S., and Mexico in 1992, which took effect in 1994. Inspired by the European Community's success in reducing trade barriers among its members, NAFTA created the world's largest free-trade area. It basically extended to Mexico the provisions of a 1988 Canada–U.S. free-trade agreement; it calls for elimination of all trade barriers over a 15-year period, grants U.S. and Canadian companies access to certain Mexican markets, and incorporates agreements on labor and the environment.

Northampton, Earl of *orig.* **Henry Howard** (1540–1614) English noble noted for his intrigues in the reigns of ELIZABETH I and JAMES I. Implicated in efforts to free MARY, QUEEN OF SCOTS, he successfully sought favor with the Scottish king James VI, who on his accession as James I of England made Howard a privy councillor (1603) and earl of Northampton (1604). As a judge at the trials of Walter RALEIGH (1603) and Guy FAWKES (1605), he pressed for conviction.

North Atlantic Treaty Organization See NATO

North Carolina State (pop., 2000: 8,049,000), U.S., S Atlantic region. It covers 52,669 sq mi (136,413 sq km); its capital is RALEIGH. Ranges of the APPALACHIAN MTNS., including the GREAT SMOKY MTNS., are in the west; the BLUE RIDGE MTNS. are in the east. Several Indian tribes, including the Algonquians, SIOUX, and IROQUOIS, inhabited the area before Europeans arrived. The coast was explored by Giovanni da VERRAZZANO in 1524, and the first English settlement in the New World was established at ROANOKE ISLAND in 1585. It formed part of the Carolina grant of 1663. A provincial congress in April 1776 gave the first explicit sanction of independence by an American colony, and it was invaded by British troops in 1780. An original state of the Union, it was the 12th to ratify the Constitution. Its 18th

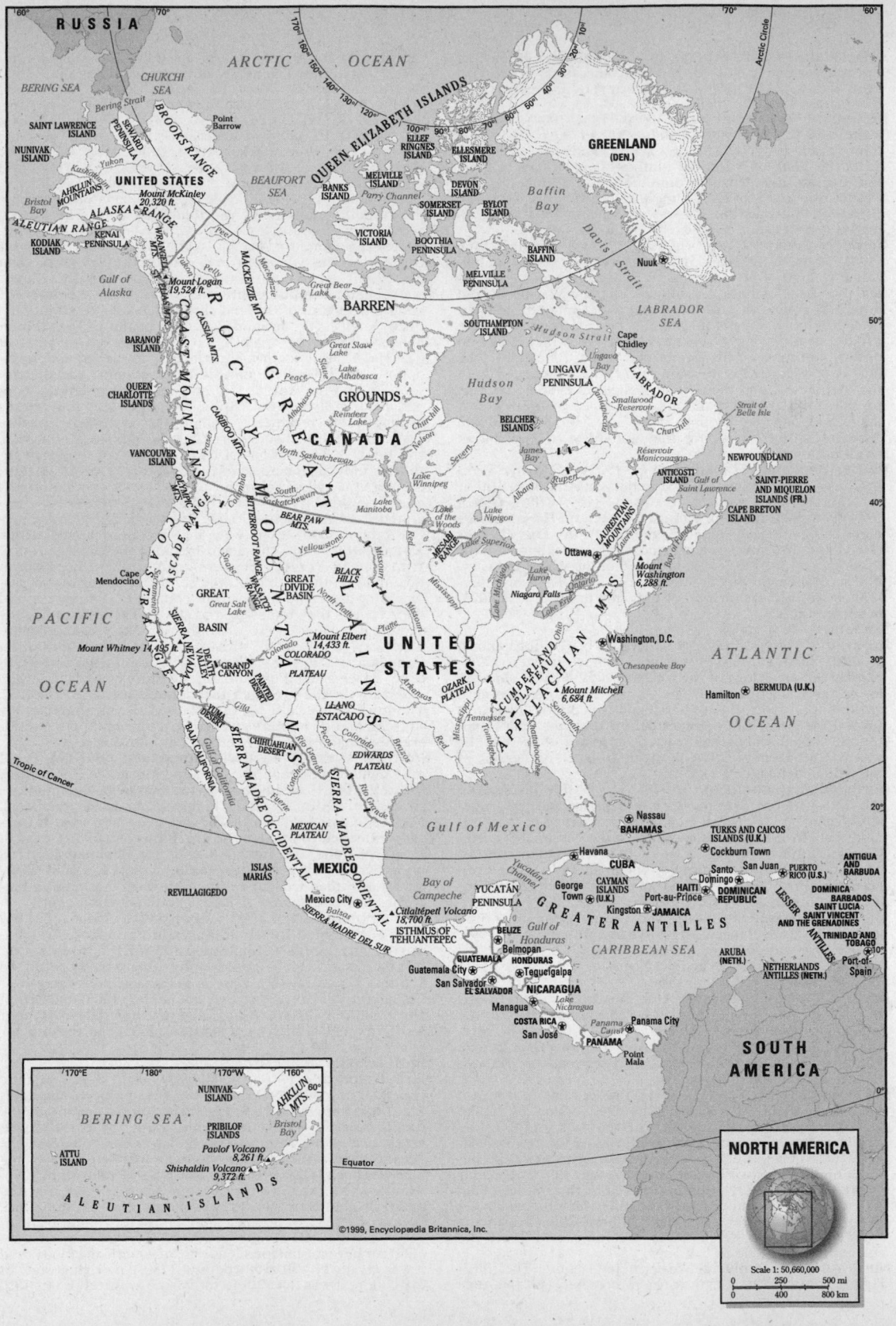

RUSSIA

ARCTIC OCEAN

BERING SEA

CHUKCHI SEA

SAINT LAWRENCE ISLAND

Bering Strait

Point Barrow

BEAUFORT SEA

QUEEN ELIZABETH ISLANDS

GREENLAND (DEN.)

NUNIVAK ISLAND

SEWARD PENINSULA

BROOKS RANGE

Kobuk

Yukon

Kuskokwim

AHKLUN MOUNTAINS

UNITED STATES

Mount McKinley 20,320 ft.

ALASKA RANGE

ELLEF RINGNES ISLAND

BANKS ISLAND

MELVILLE ISLAND

Parry Channel

SOMERSET ISLAND

DEVON ISLAND

ELLESMERE ISLAND

Baffin Bay

Bristol Bay

Kenai Peninsula

Gulf of Alaska

ALEUTIAN RANGE

KODIAK ISLAND

KENAI PENINSULA

WRANGELL MTS.

Mount Logan 19,524 ft.

ST. ELIAS MTS.

VICTORIA ISLAND

BOOTHIA PENINSULA

BYLOT ISLAND

BAFFIN ISLAND

MELVILLE PENINSULA

Davis Strait

Nuuk

BARANOF ISLAND

CASSIAR MTS.

MACKENZIE MTS.

Peel

Liard

Peace

BARREN

Great Bear Lake

Great Slave Lake

SOUTHAMPTON ISLAND

Hudson Strait

Cape Chidley

LABRADOR SEA

QUEEN CHARLOTTE ISLANDS

COAST MOUNTAINS

CARIBOO MTS.

Lake Athabasca

Reindeer Lake

GROUNDS

Hudson Bay

UNGAVA PENINSULA

Ungava Bay

LABRADOR

VANCOUVER ISLAND

Fraser

Peace

North Saskatchewan

CANADA

Churchill

Nelson

BELCHER ISLANDS

Smallwood Reservoir

Réservoir Manicouagan

NEWFOUNDLAND

Cape Mendocino

OLYMPIC RANGE

CASCADE RANGE

South Saskatchewan

BEAR PAW MTS.

Lake Winnipeg

Lake Manitoba

Lake of the Woods

James Bay

Albany

Rupert

Churchill

LAURENTIAN MOUNTAINS

Strait of Belle Isle

Gulf of St. Lawrence

ANTICOSTI ISLAND

SAINT-PIERRE AND MIQUELON ISLANDS (FR.)

CAPE BRETON ISLAND

PACIFIC OCEAN

SIERRA NEVADA

COAST RANGES

Snake

BITTERROOT RANGE

WASATCH RANGE

Yellowstone

GREAT DIVIDE BASIN

BLACK HILLS

Missouri

Red

Lake Superior

Lake Nipigon

Lake Michigan

Lake Huron

Lake Ontario

Lake Erie

Niagara Falls

Ottawa

St. Lawrence

Mount Washington 6,288 ft.

Bay of Fundy

GREAT BASIN

Great Salt Lake

ROCKY MOUNTAINS

GREAT PLAINS

North Platte

Platte

UNITED STATES

APPALACHIAN MTS.

CUMBERLAND PLATEAU

Washington, D.C.

Chesapeake Bay

ATLANTIC OCEAN

Mount Whitney 14,495 ft.

DEATH VALLEY

GRAND CANYON

PAINTED DESERT

COLORADO PLATEAU

Colorado

Mount Elbert 14,433 ft.

COLORADO

Arkansas

OZARK PLATEAU

Ohio

Tennessee

Mount Mitchell 6,684 ft.

Hamilton

BERMUDA (U.K.)

OCEAN

Gila

LLANO ESTACADO

EDWARDS PLATEAU

Pecos

Brazos

Red

Mississippi

HUMPHREYS DESERT

SIERRA MADRE OCCIDENTAL

BAJA CALIFORNIA

CHIHUAHUAN DESERT

Rio Grande

Conchos

Colorado

Tropic of Cancer

ISLAS MARÍAS

MEXICAN PLATEAU

Fuerte

SIERRA MADRE ORIENTAL

Gulf of California

Gulf of Mexico

Bay of Campeche

Yucatán Channel

Nassau

BAHAMAS

TURKS AND CAICOS ISLANDS (U.K.)

Cockburn Town

ANTIGUA AND BARBUDA

REVILLAGIGEDO

MEXICO

Mexico City

Balsas

Citlaltépetl Volcano 18,700 ft.

SIERRA MADRE DEL SUR

Havana

CUBA

George Town

CAYMAN ISLANDS (U.K.)

Santo Domingo

San Juan

PUERTO RICO (U.S.)

DOMINICA

YUCATÁN PENINSULA

GREATER ANTILLES

HAITI

Port-au-Prince

Kingston

JAMAICA

DOMINICAN REPUBLIC

BARBADOS

SAINT LUCIA

SAINT VINCENT AND THE GRENADINES

LESSER ANTILLES

TRINIDAD AND TOBAGO

Port-of-Spain

ISTHMUS OF TEHUANTEPEC

BELIZE

Belmopan

Gulf of Honduras

GUATEMALA

Guatemala City

San Salvador

EL SALVADOR

HONDURAS

Tegucigalpa

NICARAGUA

Managua

Lake Nicaragua

CARIBBEAN SEA

ARUBA (NETH.)

NETHERLANDS ANTILLES (NETH.)

COSTA RICA

San José

PANAMA

Panama Canal

Panama City

Point Mala

SOUTH AMERICA

170°E   180°   170°W   160°

NUNIVAK ISLAND

AHKLUN MTS.

BERING SEA

PRIBILOF ISLANDS

Bristol Bay

ATTU ISLAND

Pavlof Volcano 8,261 ft.

Shishaldin Volcano 9,372 ft.

ALEUTIAN ISLANDS

Equator

©1999, Encyclopædia Britannica, Inc.

NORTH AMERICA

Scale 1: 50,660,000

0   250   500 mi

0   400   800 km

cent. agricultural economy based on slave labor continued into the 19th cent. It seceded from the Union in 1861; in 1865, following the AMERICAN CIVIL WAR, it annulled the secession order and abolished slavery, and it was readmitted to the Union in 1868. In the 1940s its economy improved as some of the nation's largest military installations, including Ft. Bragg, were located there. After World War II the long struggle to eliminate racial segregation began. It has a large rural population but is also the leading industrial state of its region, and has an expanding high-technology industry in the Raleigh-Durham area. Products include tobacco, corn, and furniture.

North Carolina, University of State system of higher education, consisting of a main campus in Chapel Hill and branches in five other locations. The Chapel Hill campus, chartered in 1789, is a major research university, with schools of law, medicine, dentistry, and business. Total enrollment is about 24,000. The system also includes N. Carolina State Univ. in Raleigh, founded in 1887, and its various sister institutions. Enrollment at the Raleigh campus is about 27,000.

Northcliffe (of Saint Peter), Viscount *orig.* **Alfred Charles William Harmsworth** (1865–1922) British newspaper publisher, the most successful in British history. He joined his brother, Harold Sidney Harmsworth (1868–1940), in publishing popular periodicals that formed the basis of Amalgamated Press, at the time the world's largest periodical publishing empire. In 1896 he started the *Daily Mail,* one of the first British newspapers to appeal to a mass readership. He also founded the *Daily Mirror* (1903) and bought *The TIMES* (1908), transforming it into a modern newspaper. His influence was greatest in shifting the press away from its traditional informative role to that of the commercial exploiter and entertainer of mass publics.

North Dakota State (pop., 2000: 642,000), U.S. Situated in the N central region, it covers 70,665 sq mi (183,022 sq km); its capital is BISMARCK. The MISSOURI RIVER crosses it; the RED RIVER OF THE NORTH forms its E boundary. There is evidence of prehistoric inhabitation throughout the state. At the time of European contact, it was inhabited by various tribes of PLAINS INDIANS. It became part of the U.S. with the LOUISIANA PURCHASE of 1803. The NE corner was added by a treaty with Great Britain in 1818. In 1804–5 the LEWIS AND CLARK EXPEDITION wintered there among the Indians. In 1861 it became part of the Dakota Territory. Separated from S. Dakota, it was admitted to the Union in 1889 as the 39th state. In the 20th cent. N. Dakota's history has been marked by the increasing mechanization of agriculture, the enlargement of farms, and the loss of a rural population. In the 1950s it became an oil-producing state, and in the 1960s air bases and missile sites were built there. Its larger cities include FARGO, Grand Forks, and Minot.

Northeast Passage Maritime route along the N coast of Europe and Asia. It lies mainly off N Russian SIBERIA. Early explorers included Willem Barents (c.1550–1597), Olivier Brunel (c.1540–1585), and Henry HUDSON. In 1778 Capt. James COOK saw both sides of the Bering strait and demonstrated that Asia and N. America are separate continents. The passage was first traversed by A. E. NORDENSKIÖLD 1878–79. It is kept open in summer by icebreakers.

Northern Expedition (1926–27) Campaign of the Chinese Nationalist army, led by CHIANG KAI-SHEK, that advanced north from Guangzhou (Canton) to the Chang (Yangtze) River battling WARLORD forces. It was aided by Soviet arms and advisers. After defeating the warlords, the Nationalist army turned on Britain as the chief imperialist power and primary enemy. In response, the British returned their concessions in Hankou and Jiujiang but prepared to defend Shanghai. Communist-led labor unions captured Shanghai for Chiang, but he attacked and suppressed them; when he set up his new government in Nanjing he expelled the Communists, ending their alliance.

Northern Ireland See Northern IRELAND

Northern Mariana Islands Self-governing commonwealth (pop., 2000: 72,000) in political union with the U.S., in the W Pacific Ocean. Composed of 22 islands north of GUAM, only five of which are inhabited, the islands extend 450 mi (720 km) and have an area of 184 sq mi (477 sq km). The capital is on SAIPAN. The indigenous people are Micronesian. The islands were discovered by Ferdinand MAGELLAN in 1521. They were colonized by Spain in 1668. Sold by Spain to Germany in 1899, they were occupied by Japan in 1914 and became a Japanese mandate from the LEAGUE OF NATIONS after 1919. They were the scene of fierce fighting in World War II; Tinian was the base for U.S. planes that dropped atomic bombs on HIROSHIMA and NAGASAKI. They were granted to the U.S. in 1947 by the U.N. as a trust territory, and became a commonwealth under U.S. sovereignty in 1986, when its residents became U.S. citizens.

Northern Rhodesia See ZAMBIA

Northern Territory Territory (pop. 1998 est.: 190,000), N Australia. It covers 519,800 sq mi (1,346,200 sq km). Its capital is DARWIN; the only other sizeable town is ALICE SPRINGS. Most residents are of European descent; about one-fifth are AUSTRALIAN ABORIGINES. It includes Simpson Desert in the southeast and ARNHEM LAND in the north. It was inhabited by Aborigines for thousands of years; they held AYERS ROCK as central to their culture. The coast was explored by the Dutch in the 17th cent. and surveyed in the early 19th cent. by Matthew FLINDERS. The N parts were bombed by the Japanese in World War II and occupied by Allied troops. It was granted self-government within the Commonwealth in 1978. It remains sparsely inhabited; its economy rests on cattle farming and mining.

Northern War, Second *or* **Great Northern War** (1700–1721) Military conflict to challenge Sweden's supremacy in the Baltic area. Sweden's expansion on the Baltic coast antagonized Russia, Denmark-Norway, and Saxony-Poland, which formed an anti-Swedish coalition in 1698. They attacked Swedish-held regions in 1700, but Sweden's CHARLES XII successfully countered the attacks. The Russians eventually succeeded in establishing their power on the E Baltic coast. Sweden renewed its attack on Russia in 1707, but was defeated at Poltava (1709). Despite an alliance with Turkey (1710–11), Swedish forces suffered further defeats by the revived anti-Swedish coalition, which by then included England and Prussia. Charles opened peace negotiations in 1717, but in 1718 he invaded Norway, where he was killed. His successor, Frederick I (1676–1751), negotiated peace settlements in 1719–21 and ceded Estonia, Livonia, and other territory to Russia. The war marked the decline of Swedish influence and the emergence of Russia as a major power.

Northern Wei dynasty *or* **Toba dynasty** (A.D. 386–534/35) Longest-lived and most powerful of the N Chinese dynasties that ruled after the HAN DYNASTY fell. Founded by Toba tribesmen, the Northern Wei defended its territory against other N nomads and by 439 had unified all of N China. The Wei lifestyle became more sedentary, and the Toba people, impressed by Chinese culture, began to emulate the Chinese. To bring into cultivation land abandoned during war, hundreds of thousands of peasants were relocated and given their own land. The rulers of the Northern Wei were great patrons of Buddhism, and the period is noted for its Buddhist art, particularly at the YUNGANG CAVES).

North Island Island (pop., 1998 est.: 2,866,000), New Zealand. The smaller of the nation's two principal islands, it has an area of 44,297 sq mi (114,729 sq km) and an increasing majority of the national population, concentrated in the cities of WELLINGTON and AUCKLAND.

North Korea See North KOREA

North Platte River River, Colorado, Wyoming, and Nebraska. It rises in N Colorado, flows north into Wyoming, and joins the S. Platte in SW central Nebraska to form the Platte River. It is 680 mi (1,094 km) long and is part of an irrigation, power, and flood-control project of the MISSOURI RIVER basin.

North Pole N end of the earth's geographic axis, located at 90°N latitude, the N point from which all meridians of longitude start. Covered with drifting pack ice, it has six months of constant sunlight and six months of total darkness each year. Robert PEARY claimed to have reached the pole by dogsled in 1909, but that is now in dispute; Roald AMUNDSEN and possibly Richard BYRD claimed to have reached it by air in 1926. The geographic pole does not coincide with the magnetic North Pole, which in 1993 lay about 78°27′N, 104°24′W, or with the geomagnetic North Pole, which is about 79°13′N, 71°16′W.

North Sea *ancient* Mare Germanicum. Arm of the Atlantic Ocean. Extending south from the NORWEGIAN SEA between Norway and the British Isles, it connects the Skagerrak Channel with the ENGLISH CHANNEL. It is about 600 mi (970 km) long and 350 mi (560 km) wide. The sea contains renowned fisheries and extensive oil and natural gas deposits.

North Star See POLARIS

Northumberland County (pop., 1998 est.: 310,000), N England. It includes much of the ancient Anglo-Saxon kingdom of NORTHUMBRIA. Its islands include LINDISFARNE. The landscape is varied, with coastal plains in the east, the rugged CHEVIOT HILLS and moors in the west, and industrial areas in the S Tyne River valley. It was the site of prehistoric settlement before Roman rule began in A.D. 122, when HADRIAN'S WALL was built. It was the scene of border warfare with Scotland until 1603. Good farmland is limited, but sheep pasture is plentiful.

Northumberland, Duke of *orig.* John Dudley (1502–1553) English politician. After serving as lord high admiral (1542), he fought in the invasion of Scotland (1544) and captured the French city of Boulogne (1544). As a member of the regency council that governed for the young EDWARD VI, he engineered the fall of the duke of SOMERSET and took control of the regency (1550); he ordered Somerset's arrest and execution in 1552. He imposed strict conformity to Protestant doctrine in support of the Reformation. In 1553 he persuaded the dying Edward VI to will the crown to Northumberland's daughter-in-law, Lady Jane GREY. Thwarted by supporters of Mary Tudor (MARY I), he was executed for treason.

Northumbria Anglo-Saxon kingdom of Britain. Located between the Humber River and the Firth of Forth, it extended from the Irish Sea to the North Sea. Its religious, artistic, and intellectual achievements in the 7th–8th cent. were epitomized by LINDISFARNE and the monasteries of Wearmouth and Jarrow. Jarrow, with its fine library, was the home of the Venerable BEDE. It became the most powerful of the Anglo-Saxon kingdoms before being destroyed by the Danes, who captured YORK in 866. In 944 Northumbria became an earldom within the kingdom of England.

Northwest Coast Indians Any of the AMERICAN INDIAN peoples who inhabited a narrow but rich belt of coastland and offshore islands from SE Alaska to NW California. From north to south: TLINGIT, HAIDA, TSIMSHIAN, N KWAKIUTL (Heiltsuq), Bella Coola, S Kwakiutl, Nootka, Coast Salish, a series of lesser divisions, and CHINOOK.

North West Co. (1783–1821) British-Canadian fur-trading company. Centered around Lake Superior and the valleys of the Red, Assiniboine, and Saskatchewan rivers, it later spread north and west to the Arctic and Pacific oceans. When its competitor, the HUDSON'S BAY CO., established a colony on the Red River (1811–12), North West workers destroyed it in the SEVEN OAKS MASSACRE. Hudson's Bay workers retaliated by destroying the North West post at Ft. Gibraltar. Britain pressured the two companies to merge in 1821 as the Hudson's Bay Co.

Northwestern University Private university in Evanston, Ill., founded in 1851. A comprehensive research institution, it includes schools of music, education, social policy, graduate studies, law, medicine, and dentistry, as well as the Medill School of Journalism, the McCormick School of Engineering and Applied Science, and the Kellogg Graduate School of Management. Total enrollment is about 12,000.

Northwest Ordinances (1784, 1785, 1787) Measures enacted for the division and settlement of the Northwest Territory, extending north of the Ohio River to the Great Lakes and west of Pennsylvania to the Mississippi River. The original ordinance, written by Thomas JEFFERSON, divided the territory into self-governing districts and set population requirements for statehood. The final ordinance provided public land for schools, outlawed slavery, and guaranteed civil liberties. It established the principle of admitting new states on equal terms with the original 13 states.

Northwest Passage Sea passage between the Atlantic and Pacific oceans along the N coast of America. The search for a commercial sea route around the American land barrier attracted explorers such as Jacques CARTIER, Francis DRAKE, Martin FROBISHER, and Capt. James COOK. The passage was finally navigated successfully in 1906 by Roald AMUNDSEN. As a modern trade route it has been marginally useful because of the polar ice cap and giant icebergs, though it would significantly shorten many international shipping distances.

Northwest Territories Territory (pop., 1999 est.: 42,000), N Canada. Bounded by the YUKON TERRITORY, HUDSON BAY, and NUNAVUT, it stretches across the roof of the N. American continent. The capital is YELLOWKNIFE. It includes many islands, including VICTORIA ISLAND; the MACKENZIE RIVER; and GREAT BEAR and GREAT SLAVE lakes. More than half the people are Inuits (ESKIMOS) and American Indians. European settlers were mainly whalers, fur traders, and missionaries until the 1920s, when oil was discovered. Mining is the principal industry and centers on the petroleum and natural gas fields in the W Arctic coastal regions.

North York City (pop., 1996: 590,000), part of metropolitan TORONTO. Planned development protects more than 4,000 acres (1,600 hectares) of parks and open space. York Univ. and the Black Creek Pioneer Village are among its attractions.

Norton, Edwin (1845–1914) U.S. inventor and manufacturer. Born in Illinois, he and his brother opened a number of successively larger canmaking plants. By 1890 he had perfected the first automatic can-making line. He invented the solder-trimmed cap and the machinery for making it, revolutionizing can manufacturing. He received more than 300 patents. Socially, he was an influential supporter of shorter working hours for laborers.

Norway *officially* **Kingdom of Norway** *Norwegian* **Norge** \'nȯr-gə\ Nation, NW Europe. Area: 125,050 sq mi (323,878 sq km). Population (2000): 4,487,000. Capital: OSLO. Most of

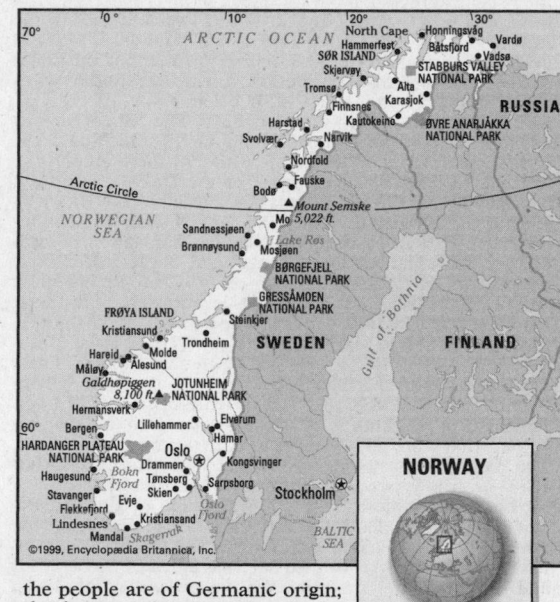

the people are of Germanic origin; the largest minority group is the Sami (Lapps). Language: Norwegian (official). Religion: Evangelical Lutheranism (official). Currency: Norwegian krone. In the W part of the Scandinavian Peninsula, Norway is Europe's fifth-largest country. It is a mountainous land with extensive plateau regions in its SW and central parts. Traditionally a fishing and lumbering country, it has greatly increased its mining and manufacturing activities since World War II. It has a developed economy largely based on services, petroleum and natural gas production, and light and heavy industries. Literacy is virtually 100%. It is a constitutional monarchy with one legislative house; its chief of state is the king, and the head of government is the prime minister. Several principalities were united into the kingdom of Norway in the 11th cent. From 1380 it had the same king as Denmark until it was ceded to Sweden in 1814. The union with Sweden was dissolved in 1905, and Norway's economy grew rapidly. It remained neutral during World War I, although its shipping industry played a vital role in the conflict. It declared its neutrality in World War II but was invaded and occupied by German troops. Norway maintains a comprehensive welfare system and is a member of NATO. It turned down membership in the EUROPEAN UNION in 1994. Its economy has grown consistently since then.

Norway lobster See SCAMPI

Norwegian language N. GERMANIC LANGUAGE of the W. Scandinavian branch, spoken in Norway. Modern Norwegian has two rival forms. Dano-Norwegian (Bokmål, or Riksmål), the more popular, stems from written Danish used during the union of Denmark and Norway (1380–1814; see KALMAR UNION). It is used in national newspapers and most literary works. New Norwegian (Nynorsk), based on W rural dialects, was created by Ivar Aasen in the mid-19th cent. to carry on the tradition of Old Norse. Both languages are used in government and education. Plans to unite them gradually in a common language, Samnorsk, are controversial.

Norwegian Sea Open sea, bordered by Greenland, Iceland, Spitsbergen, and Norway. A submarine ridge linking Greenland, Iceland, the Faeroe Islands, and N Scotland separates it from the Atlantic Ocean. The warm Norway Current off the Norway coast produces generally ice-free conditions. Colder currents mixing with this warm water create excellent fishing grounds.

Norwich \'nȯr-ich\ City (pop., 1994 est.: 128,000), England. Located northeast of LONDON, it was among the most prosperous English provincial towns for centuries; its economy was fostered by EDWARD III, who induced Flemish weavers to settle there, and by the influx of immigrants during the reign of ELIZABETH I. A center of footwear manufacturing, it features a Norman castle and cathedral. It is the traditional regional capital of E. ANGLIA.

nose Prominent structure between and below the eyes. With the nasal cavity behind it, it functions for breathing and smelling. Behind the front section it is divided vertically by three convoluted ridges into air passages. In the highest one, the olfactory region, a small segment of mucous membrane lining contains NEURONS covered by a moisture layer, in which particles in inhaled air dissolve and stimulate the neurons. The rest of the cavity warms and moistens inhaled air and filters particles and bacteria out of it. See also PALATE, SINUS.

Nostradamus \ˌnäs-trə-'dā-məs\ orig. Michel de Notredame (1503–1566) French astrologer and physician. As a doctor in S France, he gained a reputation for his innovative treatment of plague victims in 1546–47. He began making prophecies in 1547, and in 1555 they were published in a book titled *Centuries*. He wrote them in rhymed quatrains, using a cryptic style that mingled French, Latin, Spanish, and Hebrew. CATHERINE DE MÉDICIS invited him to her court, and in 1560 he was appointed physician to CHARLES IX. His prophecies are still widely read; readers have discovered apparent predictions of such events as the French Revolution and World War I.

notary public Public officer who certifies and attests to the authenticity of writings (e.g., deeds) and takes affidavits, depositions, and protests of negotiable instruments, such as bank notes or checks. The notary is commissioned by the state and may act only within the territory authorized by state statutes.

notation, musical See MUSICAL NOTATION

no-till farming or **till-less agriculture** Cultivation technique in which the soil is disturbed only along the slit or hole into which seeds are planted, one of several primitive farming methods revived as conservation measures in the 20th cent. Reserved detritus from previous crops covers and protects the seedbed. Primary benefits are a decreased rate of soil erosion; reduced need for equipment, fuel, and fertilizer; significantly less time required for tending crops; and im-

proved soil-aggregate formation, microbial activity in the soil, and water infiltration and storage. HERBICIDES are used selectively to kill weeds and the remains of the previous crop.

Nôtre, André Le See André LE NÔTRE

Notre Dame, University of Private university in Notre Dame, near South Bend, Ind. It was founded in 1842; it became coeducational in 1972. It is affiliated with the Roman Catholic church. It has a range of colleges, a graduate school, and a law school. Total enrollment is about 10,000.

Notre-Dame de Paris \nȯ-trᵊ-'däm-də-pá-'rē\ (1163–c.1350) Gothic cathedral in Paris. Probably the most famous Gothic cathedral, Notre-Dame is a superb example of the RAYONNANT STYLE. Two massive Early Gothic towers (1210–50) crown the three-story W facade, which has doors adorned with Early Gothic carvings and surmounted by figures of Old Testament kings. Its flying buttresses are notable for their boldness and grace, and its three great 13th-cent. ROSE WINDOWS are of awe-inspiring beauty.

Notre-Dame de Paris

Notre-Dame school Composers of medieval ORGANUM at the Cathedral of NÔTRE-DAME DE PARIS. Léonin (c.1135–1201?) composed two-voice organum characterized by a rhythmically patterned melisma added to each sustained note of the plainchant. He may have devised the rhythmic notation that made this possible, or at least codified the important system of rhythmic modes. Pérotin (fl.c.1200) edited, extended, and added parts to Léonin's *Magnus liber organi* ("Great Book of Organum") and created the first three- and four-voice textures known in world music. See also ARS ANTIQUA.

Notte, Gherardo delle See Gerrit van HONTHORST

Nottingham \'nä-tiŋ-em\ City (pop., 1999 est.: 284,000), England. Lying northeast of BIRMINGHAM, the original Saxon town was held by the Danes in the 9th cent. It was the scene of three parliaments in the 14th cent. In 1642 King CHARLES I raised his standard here at the outbreak of the ENGLISH CIVIL WARS; Nottingham Castle stands on that site. The link between Nottingham and ROBIN HOOD is commemorated by a statue on Castle Green. The city has a distinctive lace quarter. It is home to the Univ. of Nottingham.

Nottinghamshire \'nä-tiŋ-em-ˌshir\ County (pop., 2000: 1,033,000), N central England. It has coalfields and railway lines in the west; in medieval times, the forest of Sherwood, haunt of ROBIN HOOD, stretched north from the city of NOTTINGHAM. Agriculture in the Vales of Trent and Belvoir includes dairy farming. The Trent river powers thermal electric stations. The SW area is densely populated and heavily industrialized.

Nouakchott \nú-'äk-ˌshät\ City (pop., 1999 est.: 881,000), capital of Mauritania. It lies near the Atlantic coast, northeast of DAKAR, Senegal. It was a small village until Mauritania gained independence from France (1960). It was a major refugee center during the Saharan droughts of the 1970s and grew rapidly. A port facility was built nearby.

Nouméa \nü-'mā-ə\ formerly **Port-de-France** \ˌpȯr-də-'fräⁿs\ Town (pop., 1996: 76,000), port, and capital of NEW

CALEDONIA territory. Located on New Caledonia Island, it was founded in 1854 as Port-de-France on an excellent deepwater harbor. It has modern buildings, a large public market, and an old stone cathedral.

nova STAR whose luminosity temporarily increases by several thousand to a million times. Most such stars appear to be BINARY STARS, one of which is a WHITE DWARF STAR drawing in matter from the other until it becomes unstable. It then sheds its outer layer in an outburst, reaching maximum luminosity in hours, shining intensely for days to weeks, and then slowly returning to its former level, usually too faint to see with the unaided eye. The sudden brightening may make it visible from earth for the first time, so it appears to be a new star; "nova" is Latin for "new." See also SUPERNOVA.

Novalis \nō-'vä-lis\ orig. Friedrich Leopold, Freiherr (baron) von Hardenberg (1772–1801) German Romantic poet and theorist. He took his pseudonym from a former family name. His beautiful *Hymns to the Night* (1800) express his grief on the death of his young fiancée. In the years before his own death from tuberculosis at 28, he drafted a philosophical system based on idealism and produced his most significant poetic work. His mythical romance *Heinrich von Ofterdingen* (1802) describes a young poet's mystical and romantic searchings.

Nova Scotia \ˌnō-və-'skō-shə\ Province, (pop., 1999 est.: 941,000), Canada, one of the MARITIME PROVINCES. It includes the peninsula of Nova Scotia, Cape Breton Island, and a few small adjacent islands, and it is bounded by the Northumberland Strait, the Gulf of St. Lawrence, the Atlantic Ocean, the Bay of Fundy, and New Brunswick. Its capital is HALIFAX. The region was first visited by VIKINGS about A.D. 1000 and was inhabited by MICMAC Indians when John CABOT claimed it for England in 1497. French settlers in 1605 adopted the Micmac name ACADIA for the region. English and Scottish colonists arrived by 1621. The conflict between France and England over control of the area was ended by the 1713 Peace of UTRECHT, which awarded it to England. In the 1750s, the British expelled most of the French settlers. Following the AMERICAN REVOLUTION, many Loyalists emigrated there. It joined the Dominion of Canada in 1867 as one of the original members. The province's economic mainstays are fishing, shipbuilding, and transatlantic shipping.

novel Fictional prose narrative of considerable length and some complexity that deals imaginatively with human experience through a connected sequence of events involving a group of persons in a specific setting. The genre encompasses a wide range of types and styles, including PICARESQUE, EPISTOLARY, GOTHIC, romantic, realist, and historical novels. Though forerunners of the novel appeared in a number of places, including classical Rome, the European novel is usually said to have begun with Miguel de CERVANTES's *Don Quixote*. The novel was established as a literary form in England in the 18th cent. through the work of Daniel DEFOE, Samuel RICHARDSON, and Henry FIELDING. The novel has remained popular because of its capacity for providing a faithful image of everyday reality.

Noverre \nò-'ver\, **Jean-Georges** (1727–1810) French choreographer. In the 1750s he choreographed ballets in Paris, London, and Stuttgart; in Vienna (1767–74) he collaborated with the composer Christoph Willibald GLUCK. His *Letters on Dancing and Ballets* (1760) stressed the need for unified dramatic structure by integrating story, music, choreography, and set design, as opposed to the loosely connected episodes of the usual dance suite that then prevailed. Called *ballet d'action,* or "ballet with a story," this innovation brought major reforms in ballet production. In 1776 he became ballet master of the Paris Opera. In all he choreographed over 150 ballets.

Novgorod \'nòv-gə-rət\ City (pop., 1997 est.: 232,000), NW Russia. One of the oldest Russian cities, it came under RURIK around 862. It was of great importance in the 11th–15th cent., when it was the capital of the principality of Novgorod. It prospered by trade with the Orient, Constantinople, and the HANSEATIC LEAGUE. The center of the Novgorod School of medieval icon painting, it was ruled by ALEXANDER NEVSKY in the 13th cent. It became a rival of MOSCOW, and was destroyed by IVAN IV in 1570. In World War II it suffered heavy damage. Many historic buildings were later restored, and it is a center of tourism.

Novi Sad \'nò-vē-'säd\ *Hungarian* **Uvidek** \'ü-ē-ˌvē-ˌdāk\ City (pop., 2000 est.: 183,000), Serbia, N Yugoslavia. The administrative capital of VOJVODINA, it is a transit port on the DANUBE RIVER, northwest of BELGRADE. Founded in the 17th cent., it was part of Hungary until the formation of Yugoslavia in 1918. Its economy suffered badly during the 1990s Balkan upheavals.

Novosibirsk \ˌnō-vò-si-'birsk\ *formerly (1895–1925)* **Novonikolayevsky** City (pop., 1997 est.: 1,367,000), S central Russia in Asia. The chief city of W SIBERIA, it lies where the TRANS-SIBERIAN RAILROAD crosses the OB RIVER. The city began in 1893. During World War II many Russian factories from the west were moved there. It is renowned for industry and scientific research. As Siberia's cultural and educational center, it developed the satellite town Akademgorodok with research institutes and a university.

NOW See NATIONAL ORGANIZATION FOR WOMEN

NRA See NATIONAL RECOVERY ADMINISTRATION

NSAIDs \'en-ˌsedz, 'en-ˌsädz\ *or* **nonsteroidal anti-inflammatory drugs** Drugs that reduce INFLAMMATION and are neither STEROIDS nor opioids (natural and synthetic opiates). They are also effective against pain (see ANALGESIC) and FEVER. Most are usually used for short periods for mild pain. ASPIRIN is technically an NSAID, but the term is generally applied to a newer class of drugs, including IBUPROFEN and similar drugs. They act with fewer side effects, but aspirin-sensitive people should not use them.

Nu See NUN

Nu, U *orig.* Thakin Nu (1907–1995) Burmese independence leader and prime minister (1948–58, 1960–62). A prominent nationalist activist since his student days, U Nu became the first prime minister of independent Burma (now Myanmar) in 1948. Though an able statesman, he was plagued by ethnic-minority insurrections and economic difficulties. He resigned in 1958, was reinstated in 1960, and was overthrown and imprisoned by NE WIN in 1962. After his release he organized resistance to Ne Win and made an unsuccessful bid for power in 1988.

Nubia Ancient region, Nile Valley, NE Africa. It extended north to include Aswan and the first cataract of the Nile in Upper Egypt. Now part of Sudan and Egypt, it contains the NUBIAN DESERT. For about 1,800 years in ancient times it was subject to Egypt as a part of Ethiopia. CUSH was in the S part. Nubia was the center of a powerful state from the 6th to the 14th cent., when it was captured by the Arabs. The region was conquered by Egypt in 1820–22.

Nubia, Lake See Lake NASSER

Nubian Desert Desert, NE Sudan. It is separated from the LIBYAN DESERT by the NILE RIVER valley to the west. Rocky and rugged, it is essentially a sandstone plateau interspersed with many wadis (seasonal rivers) that die out before reaching the Nile.

nuclear energy *or* **atomic energy** Energy released from atomic nuclei in significant amounts. In 1919 Ernest RUTHERFORD discovered that alpha rays could split the NUCLEUS of an ATOM. This led to the discovery of the NEUTRON and the release of huge amounts of energy by NUCLEAR FISSION. Nuclear energy is also released in NUCLEAR FUSION. The energy release can be controlled or uncontrolled. Nuclear reactors carefully control the release of energy, but the energy release of a NUCLEAR WEAPON or a core meltdown in a nuclear reactor is uncontrolled. See also CHAIN REACTION, NUCLEAR POWER, RADIOACTIVITY.

nuclear fission Division of a heavy atomic NUCLEUS into two fragments of roughly equal MASS, accompanied by the release of a large amount of energy, the BINDING ENERGY of the SUBATOMIC PARTICLES. The energy released in the fission of one uranium nucleus is about 50 million times greater than that released when a carbon atom combines with oxygen atoms in the burning of coal. The energy appears as KINETIC ENERGY of the fragments, which converts to thermal energy as the fragments collide in matter and slow down. Fission also releases two or three free NEUTRONS (see CHAIN REACTION). Nuclear fission is used to generate electricity and to propel ships and submarines, and

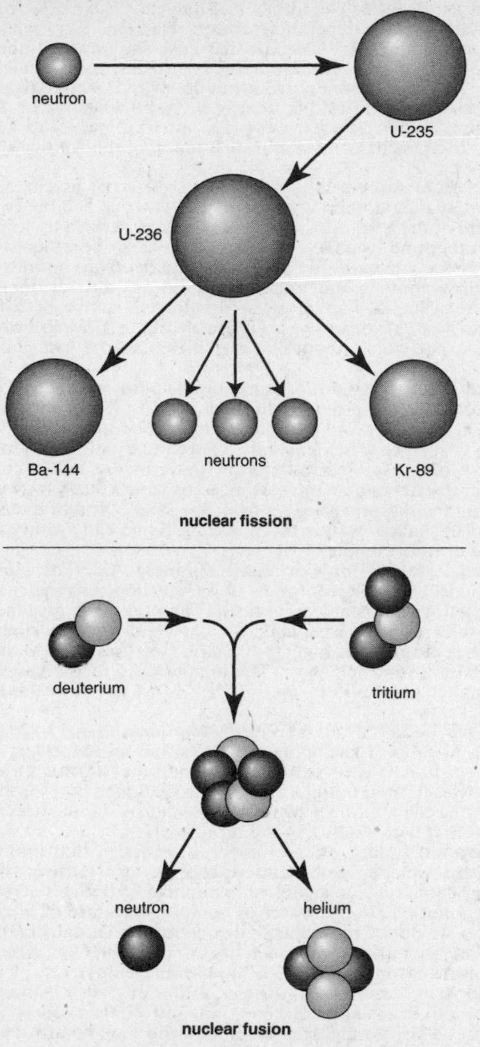

nuclear fission

nuclear fusion

Nuclear fission and fusion Top: Uranium-235 combines with a neutron to form an unstable intermediate, which quickly splits into barium-144 and krypton-89 plus three neutrons in the process of nuclear fission. Bottom: Deuterium and tritium combine by nuclear fusion to form helium plus a neutron.

is a source of the vast destructive power of NUCLEAR WEAPONS.

nuclear fusion Process by which nuclear reactions between light elements form heavier ones, releasing huge amounts of energy. In 1939 Hans BETHE suggested that the energy output of the sun and other stars is a result of fusion reactions among HYDROGEN nuclei. In the early 1950s American scientists produced the HYDROGEN BOMB by inducing fusion reactions in a mixture of the hydrogen isotopes DEUTERIUM and TRITIUM, forming a heavier helium nucleus. Though fusion is common in the sun and other stars, it is difficult to produce artificially and is very difficult to control. If controlled nuclear fusion is achieved, it might provide an inexpensive energy source.

nuclear magnetic resonance (NMR) Selective ABSORPTION of very high-frequency RADIO WAVES by certain atomic nuclei subjected to a strong stationary MAGNETIC FIELD. NMR is used to study the molecular structure of various solids and liquids. MAGNETIC RESONANCE IMAGING is a version of NMR used to view soft tissues of the body in a hazard-free, noninvasive way.

nuclear medicine Medical specialty using radioactive ELEMENTS or ISOTOPES for diagnosis and treatment of disease. A radioisotope is introduced into the body (usually by injection). The radiation it emits, detected by a scanner and recorded, reflects its distribution in different tissues and can reveal much about abnormalities in various organs. The isotopes used have short half-lives and decay before RADIOACTIVITY causes any damage. Radioactive substances are also implanted to treat small, early-stage cancers. This yields a slow, continuous dose that limits damage to normal cells while destroying tumor cells. See also COMPUTED AXIAL TOMOGRAPHY, DIAGNOSTIC IMAGING, POSITRON EMISSION TOMOGRAPHY, RADIATION THERAPY, RADIOLOGY.

Nuclear Nonproliferation Treaty *officially* Treaty on the Nonproliferation of Nuclear Weapons. Agreement intended to prevent the spread of nuclear technology, signed by the U.S., Britain, the Soviet Union, and 59 other countries in 1968. The three major signatories agreed not to assist states lacking nuclear weapons to obtain them; the nonnuclear signatories agreed not to develop them, in exchange for assistance in developing nuclear power for peaceful purposes. France and China ratified the treaty in 1992, but some nuclear powers, including Israel, India, and Pakistan, have never signed. In 1995 it was extended indefinitely by a consensus vote of 174 countries at the U.N. See also NUCLEAR TEST-BAN TREATY.

nuclear power Energy produced by NUCLEAR FISSION of heavy atomic nuclei. About one-third of all electric power worldwide now comes from nuclear power plants. The navies of many countries include nuclear-powered warships. Most commercial nuclear reactors are thermal reactors, including light-water reactors of two types, the boiling-water reactor and the pressurized-water reactor. In the liquid-metal fast-breeder reactor, fuel is utilized 60 times more effectively than in light-water reactors. See also NUCLEAR ENERGY.

nuclear reactor Device that can initiate and control a self-sustaining series of NUCLEAR-FISSION reactions. Neutrons released in one fission reaction may strike other heavy nuclei, causing them to fission. The rate of this CHAIN REACTION is controlled by introducing materials, usually control rods, to absorb neutrons if the series of fissions begins to proceed at too great a rate, which could lead to meltdown of the core. The heat released by fission is removed from the reactor core by a circulating coolant, and some of it is used to heat water and convert it to high-pressure steam. This steam drives a turbine, and a GENERATOR converts the mechanical energy into electricity. Besides providing electric power for commercial use, nuclear reactors also serve to propel certain types of ships, submarines, and unmanned spacecraft. Reactors also produce radioactive ISOTOPES for scientific research, medical therapy, and industry.

nuclear species See NUCLIDE

Nuclear Test-Ban Treaty *officially* Treaty Banning Nuclear Weapons Tests in the Atmosphere, in Outer Space and Under Water. Treaty that bans NUCLEAR WEAPONS tests except those conducted underground. Britain, the U.S., and the Soviet Union signed the treaty in 1963, as did more than 100 other governments soon after. France and China were notable nonsignatories. In 1996 the treaty was replaced by the Comprehensive Test-Ban Treaty, which will not take effect until ratified by all 44 countries with nuclear-power plants. By 2003 13 of the 44 countries, including the U.S., China, and India, had yet to ratify the document. See also NUCLEAR NONPROLIFERATION TREATY.

nuclear weapon *or* **atomic weapon** *or* **thermonuclear weapon** Bomb or other warhead that derives its force from NUCLEAR FISSION or NUCLEAR FUSION and is delivered by aircraft, missile, or other strategic delivery system. Nuclear weapons are the most potent explosive devices ever invented. Fission-dependent devices break heavy-element nuclei down into fragments; fusion devices fuse hydrogen nuclei to form helium nuclei. Destructive effects include not only the blast but also blinding light, searing heat, and lethal FALLOUT. See also ATOMIC BOMB, HYDROGEN BOMB.

nuclear winter Environmental devastation that many scientists contend would probably result from a nuclear war. As hypothesized, huge fireballs created by exploding nuclear warheads would ignite great fires (firestorms); smoke and dust would be lifted to high altitudes and driven by winds to form a uniform belt encircling the Northern Hemisphere. The clouds could block most of the sun's light, and surface temperatures would plunge for several weeks. The semidarkness and subfreezing temperatures, combined with high doses of RADIATION, would interrupt plant photosynthesis and could thus destroy much of the earth's vegetation and animal life. Other scientists dispute the results of the original calculations.

nucleic acid \nü-'klē-ik, nü-'klā-ik\ Any of the organic compounds making up the genetic material of living cells. Nucleic acids direct the course of PROTEIN synthesis, thereby regulating all cell activities. Their transmission from one generation to the next is the basis of HEREDITY. The two main types, DNA and RNA, are composed of similar materials but differ in structure and function. Both are long chains of repeating NUCLEOTIDES. The sequence of PURINES and PYRIMIDINES (bases)—ADENINE (A), GUANINE (G), and CYTOSINE (C) and THYMINE (T) or URACIL (U)—in the nucleotides, in groups of three (triplets, or codons), constitutes the GENETIC CODE.

nucleolus See NUCLEUS

nucleophile \'nü-klē-ə-,fīl\ ATOM or MOLECULE that contains an ELECTRON pair available for BONDING and in CHEMICAL REACTIONS therefore seeks a positive center, such as the NUCLEUS of an atom, or the positive end of a polar molecule (see ELECTRIC DIPOLE). In the Lewis electron theory (see ACID-BASE THEORY), nucleophiles are by definition Lewis bases. Examples include the hydroxide ion (OH$^-$), the halogen ions (Cl$^-$, Br$^-$, and I$^-$), ammonia (NH$_3$), and water (H$_2$O). See also BASE, ELECTROPHILE.

nucleoside \'nü-klē-ə-,sīd\ Any of a class of organic compounds, including structural subunits of NUCLEIC ACIDS. Each consists of a molecule of a five-carbon SUGAR (RIBOSE in RNA, deoxyribose in DNA) and a nitrogen-containing base, either a PURINE or a PYRIMIDINE. Nucleosides usually have a PHOSPHATE group attached, forming NUCLEOTIDES. Usually obtained by decomposition of nucleic acids, nucleosides are important in physiological and medical research. Those that are not part of nucleic acids include puromycin and certain other ANTIBIOTICS produced by fungi.

nucleosynthesis \,nü-klē-ō-'sin-thə-səs\ Production on a cosmic scale of all the chemical ELEMENTS from one or perhaps two simple types of atomic nuclei (see NUCLEUS). Elements differ in the number of PROTONS and ISOTOPES of each element by the number of NEUTRONS in their nuclei. One type of nucleus can be transformed into another by adding or removing protons, neutrons, or both, processes that go on in stars. Many of the lighter elements and their present cosmic abundances can be accounted for by successive NUCLEAR-FUSION reactions, beginning with HYDROGEN. Heavier elements are created by capture of successive neutrons and decay of some of these into protons.

nucleotide \'nü-klē-ə-,tīd\ Any of a class of organic compounds, including the structural units of NUCLEIC ACIDS. Each consists of a NUCLEOSIDE and one or more PHOSPHATE groups. In nucleic acids, the phosphate of one nucleotide joins to the sugar of the next to form the backbone. Other important nucleotides include ATP, cyclic AMP (needed in GLYCOGEN breakdown), and certain coenzymes.

nucleus Specialized structure occurring in most CELLS (except BACTERIA) and separated from the rest of the cell by the nuclear MEMBRANE. This membrane seems to be continuous with the cell's ENDOPLASMIC RETICULUM and has pores that permits the passage of large molecules. The nucleus controls and regulates the cell's activities (e.g., growth and metabolism) and carries the GENES. A cell normally contains only one nucleus.

nucleus Central, positively charged core of an ATOM. It consists of positively charged PROTONS and neutral NEUTRONS, known collectively as nucleons, held together by the STRONG FORCE. The number of nucleons can range from 1 to about 270, depending on the element. ISOTOPES are atoms of the same element that have the same number of protons but different numbers of neutrons. Some nuclei, especially heavier ones, are unstable, or radioactive (see RADIOACTIVITY), emitting energy by ALPHA DECAY or BETA DECAY, or as GAMMA RAYS. The nucleus makes up nearly all the MASS but only a minute fraction of the volume of the atom.

nuclide or **nuclear species** Species of ATOM as characterized by the number of PROTONS, NEUTRONS, and the energy state of the NUCLEUS. A nuclide is characterized by its mass number and its ATOMIC NUMBER. Nuclear ISOMERS, which have the same number of protons and neutrons but differ in energy content and RADIOACTIVITY, are also distinct nuclides. Nuclides are associated with radioactive decay and may be stable or unstable. There are about 1,700 known nuclides, of which about 300 are stable and the rest radioactive.

nudibranch \'n(y)ü-də-,braŋk\ or **sea slug** Any marine GASTROPOD in the order Nudibranchia. Most lack a shell, mantle cavity (see MOLLUSK), and gills, and breathe through the body surface. The delicately colored body, up to 16 in. (43 cm) long, has bizarre defensive outgrowths, called cerata, that discharge nematocysts ingested from CNIDARIAN prey. Antennalike organs arise from the head. Nudibranchs occur in shallow waters of all oceans. Some can swim; others are bottom creepers.

nuée ardente \nü-'ā-är-'dänt\ (French: "fiery or glowing clouds") Incandescent mass of gas-enveloped particles associated with volcanic eruptions. These glowing avalanches, as they are sometimes called, can move down even slight inclines at speeds as high as 100 mph (160 kph), killing all living things in their path. The temperature of the gases can reach 1,100–1,300°F (600–700°C). Most occur in the RING OF FIRE.

Nuevo León \'nwä-vō-lā-'ōn\ State (pop., 2000: 3,826,000), NE Mexico. It has an area of 25,067 sq mi (64,924 sq km); its capital is MONTERREY. The SIERRA MADRE Oriental crosses it. A state since 1824, it was occupied by U.S. troops during the MEXICAN WAR. Its iron and steel industries were the first heavy industry in Latin America.

nuisance In law, an act, object, or practice that interferes with another's rights or interests by being offensive, annoying, dangerous, obstructive, or unhealthful. Such activities as polluting air and water or operating a house of prostitution are public nuisances and constitute criminal violations. A private nuisance is an activity or condition (e.g., excessive noise) that interferes with the use and enjoyment of one's property; it may be a cause of action in civil litigation. An attractive nuisance is something on one's property that poses a risk to children or others who may be attracted to it.

Nuku'alofa \,nü-kü-ä-'lō-fə\ Town (metro. area pop., 1999: 37,000), capital and chief port of Tonga. Located on Tongatapu Island, it has a deep-draft harbor protected by reefs. The town exports copra and bananas. Landmarks include the 19th-cent. royal palace.

nullification Doctrine upholding the right of a U.S. state to declare null and void an act of the federal government. First enunciated in the VIRGINIA AND KENTUCKY RESOLUTIONS (1798), it was expanded by John C. CALHOUN in response to the Tariff of 1828. The S. Carolina legislature agreed by passing the Ordinance of Nullification (1832), threatening to secede if the federal government forced collection of the 1828 tariff duties. The U.S. Congress passed a compromise tariff bill reducing the duties but also passed the Force Bill, which authorized federal enforcement of the law. The S. Carolina legislature rescinded its ordinance, but the conflict highlighted the danger of nullification.

number Basic element of mathematics used for counting, measuring, solving EQUATIONS, and comparing quantities. The counting numbers are the familiar 1, 2, 3 . . . ; whole numbers are the counting numbers and ZERO; INTEGERS are the whole numbers and the negative counting numbers; and the RATIONAL NUMBERS are all possible quotients formed by integers, including FRACTIONS. These numbers can be symbolically represented by terminating or repeating decimals. IRRATIONAL NUMBERS must be represented by special symbols such as $\sqrt{2}$, e, and π. Together, the rational and irrational numbers constitute the REAL NUMBERS, which form an algebraic field (see FIELD THEORY), as do the COMPLEX NUMBERS. See also TRANSCENDENTAL NUMBER.

number system Method of writing numerals to represent numbers. The use of ZERO as a placeholder was the greatest advance in number systems. The most common system is the decimal system, in which 10 symbols (the HINDU-ARABIC NUMERALS) denote multiples of powers of 10 by their position relative to the decimal point. Computers have brought greater awareness of the binary number system, in which two symbols, 0 and 1, represent multiples of powers of 2.

number theory Branch of mathematics concerned with properties of and relations among INTEGERS. It is popular among amateur mathematicians and students because of its wealth of seemingly simple problems. It has been said that any unsolved mathematical problem of any interest more than a century old belongs to number theory. One of the best examples is FERMAT'S LAST THEOREM.

numerical analysis Branch of applied mathematics that studies methods for solving complicated equations using arithmetic operations, often requiring a computer, to approximate the processes of analysis (i.e., CALCULUS). The arithmetic model for the approximation is called an ALGORITHM. An example is an algorithm for deriving π by calculating the perimeter of a regular polygon as its number of sides becomes very large. Numerical analysis is also concerned with determining whether the ERROR at any stage is within acceptable bounds.

numerology Use of numbers to interpret a person's character or divine the future. It is based on the assertion by PYTHAGORAS that all things can be expressed in numerical terms because they are ultimately reducible to numbers. Modern numerology attaches a series of digits to an inquirer's name and uses these, along with the date of birth, to reveal the person's true nature and prospects.

Numidia \nǔ-'mi-dē-ə\ Ancient country, N Africa, approximately coextensive with modern Algeria. During the Second PUNIC WAR, its two great tribes divided, one supporting the Romans and the other the Carthaginians. After the destruction of CARTHAGE, thousands fled to Numidia, which became a Roman province in 46 B.C. Its chief city was Hippo, the see of St. AUGUSTINE. After its conquest by the VANDALS in A.D. 429, its Roman civilization declined rapidly.

numismatics \ˌnü-məz-'ma-tiks\ Systematic accumulation and study of coins, tokens, paper money, and objects of similar form and purpose. During the 15th–16th cent., nobles collected coins from Greece and Rome, whose cultures they admired. In the 17th cent., catalogs and systematic analysis became more common, and false coins were more easily distinguished. In the 20th cent. museums have formed large collections of great detail and range. London is the world's largest numismatic market. Because the number of a particular coin issue decreases as coins are worn, damaged, lost, or destroyed, the issue's value generally increases over time. Coins are also usually worth at least face value for their metal alone.

Nun \'nün\ or **Nu** Oldest of the Egyptian gods and father of RE, the sun god. Nun represented the dark, turbulent waters out of which the cosmos was churned. Since it was believed that the primeval ocean continued to surround the ordered cosmos, the creation myth was reenacted each day as the sun rose from the waters. Nun was also thought to be the source of the annual flooding of the NILE.

Nunavut \'nü-nə-ˌvüt\ Territory (pop., 1999 est.: 27,000), N central Canada. Nunavut (Inuit for "our land") is the result of Canada's largest land-claim settlement, created to give the Inuit (see ESKIMO), representing 85% of its population, a greater voice in Canadian government. Occupying an area of 733,600 sq mi (1.9 million sq km), or one-fifth of Canada's landmass, it consists of the central and E parts of the former NORTHWEST TERRITORIES, including BAFFIN and ELLESMERE islands. Its capital is IQALUIT. The area was settled by Inuits from 4500 B.C. to A.D. 1000. Vikings prob-

ably visited during the Middle Ages, but the first records of exploration are from Martin FROBISHER's 1576 search for the NORTHWEST PASSAGE. The mainland was explored by Englishman Samuel Hearne (1745–1792) in 1770–72. After passing through British possession, it was transferred to Canada in 1870. The territory was inaugurated on April 1, 1999.

Nuremberg *German* **Nürnberg** \'nǖrn-ˌberk\ City (pop., 1998 est.: 490,000), BAVARIA, S Germany. It grew up around a castle in the 11th cent., and in 1219 it received its first charter. It became one of the greatest of the German free imperial cities, reaching the height of its power and cultural eminence in the 16th cent. In 1806 it became part of the kingdom of Bavaria. In the 1930s it was a center of the NAZI PARTY; it was the site of the annual NUREMBERG RALLIES, and in 1935 it gave its name to the anti-Semitic NUREMBERG LAWS. It was severely damaged in World War II, but its medieval walls still stand. After the war, it was the scene of the NUREMBERG TRIALS. Its Academy of Arts (founded 1662) is the oldest in Germany.

Nuremberg Laws (1935) Two measures designed by Adolf HITLER and approved by a NAZI PARTY convention at Nuremberg. The laws deprived Jews of German citizenship and forbade marriage or sexual relations between Jews and "citizens of German or cognate blood." Supplementary decrees defined a Jew as a person with at least one Jewish grandparent and declared that Jews could not vote or hold public office.

Nuremberg Rallies Massive NAZI PARTY rallies held in Nuremberg, Germany, to showcase its power. The first large-scale rally was held in 1929 and featured the nationalistic pageantry that marked subsequent annual rallies (1933–38). Attended by hundreds of thousands of party members, the rallies were carefully staged to reinforce party enthusiasm, with martial songs, massed banners and flags, goose-step marches, torchlight processions, and lengthy orations.

Nuremberg Trials (1945–46) Trials of former NAZI PARTY leaders held in Nuremberg, Germany. At the end of World War II, the International Military Tribunal was established by the U.S., Britain, France, and the Soviet Union to try former Nazis as war criminals. It defined the offenses as crimes against peace (planning and waging of war in violation of treaties); crimes against humanity (extermination, deportation, and GENOCIDE); and WAR CRIMES. After 216 court sessions, three of the original 22 defendants were acquitted, four (including Karl DÖNITZ and Albert SPEER) were sentenced to prison for 10–20 years, three (including Rudolf HESS) were sentenced to life imprisonment, and 12 (including Wilhelm KEITEL, Joachim von RIBBENTROP, Arthur SEYSS-INQUART, and Julius STREICHER) were sentenced to death. Hermann GÖRING committed suicide before he could be executed, and Martin BORMANN was convicted in absentia.

Nureyev \nǔ-'rä-yef\, **Rudolf (Hametovich)** (1938–1993) Russian ballet dancer of charismatic virtuosity. He trained in Leningrad and joined the Kirov Ballet as a soloist in 1958. He defected during a tour in Paris in 1961. Thereafter he danced as a guest artist with many companies, especially the ROYAL BALLET from 1962 to the mid-1970s, where he regularly partnered Margot FONTEYN. His electrifying performances, combining an intensely romantic sensibility with stunning technique, made him a huge international star. He also performed on television and in movies. He was artistic director of the Paris Opera Ballet 1983–89. He was widely acclaimed as the greatest ballet virtuoso since Vaslav NIJINSKY.

Rudolf Nureyev with Margot Fonteyn

Nu River See SALWEEN RIVER

Nurmi, Paavo (Johannes) (1897–1973) Finnish track athlete. "The Flying Finn" captured nine gold medals and three silvers in three Olympic Games (1920, 1924, 1928), and held the world record for the mile run for eight years (1923–31).

Nürnberg See NUREMBERG

nursery Place where plants are grown for transplanting, for use as stocks for budding and grafting, or for sale. While most nursery-grown plants are ornamental, the nursery business also includes fruit plants and certain PERENNIAL vegetables used in home gardens (e.g., asparagus, rhubarb). See also FLORICULTURE.

nursery rhyme Verse customarily told or sung to small children. Though the oral tradition of nursery rhymes is ancient, the largest number date from the 16th, 17th, and (most frequently) 18th cent. Apparently most rhymes were originally composed for adults, many as popular ballads and songs. The earliest known published collection is *Tommy Thumb's (Pretty) Song Book* (London, 1744). The most influential collection was *Mother Goose's Melody* (1781).

nursing Health-care profession providing physical and emotional care to the sick and disabled and promoting health in all individuals through activities including research, health education, and patient consultation. Nurse-practitioners, clinical nurse specialists, nurse-anesthetists, and nurse-midwives now perform tasks traditionally performed by physicians. The American Nurses Assn. sets standards, gives examinations, provides continuing education, and promotes legislation. Registered nurses (RNs) earn a degree and pass an exam. Licensed practical nurses (LPNs) complete a year of training and assist RNs. In addition to health-care settings, nurses practice in schools, the military, industry, and private homes. Community (PUBLIC HEALTH) nurses educate the public on topics such as nutrition and disease prevention.

nursing home Facility for care (usually long-term) of patients who are not sick enough to need hospital care but are not able to remain at home. Historically, most residents were elderly or ill or had chronic irreversible and disabling disorders, and medical and nursing care was minimal. Today nursing homes often help patients prepare to live at home or with a family member when possible. They help conserve hospital facilities for the acutely ill and improve the prospects of the chronically disabled.

nut Dry, hard, one-seeded FRUIT consisting of a kernel, usually oily, surrounded by a hard or brittle shell that does not split open at maturity. Nuts include CHESTNUTS, FILBERTS, PECANS, and WALNUTS; but other so-called nuts are botanically seeds (BRAZIL NUT, PISTACHIO), LEGUMES (PEANUT), or drupes (ALMOND and COCONUT). Not all nuts are edible; some are used for ornament.

nuthatch Any of about 22 species (genus *Sitta*, family Sittidae) of songbirds that are 4–7.5 in. (9.5–19 cm) long and have a short, square tail, short neck, and thin, pointed bill. Most are forest dwellers. Nuthatches search tree trunks and rocks for insects, often descending headfirst. They also eat seeds. Four species occur in N. America. Most are bluish above and white or reddish below; there may be a black eye stripe or a cap.

nutmeg Spice consisting of the seed of a tropical evergreen tree *(Myristica fragruns),* native to the Moluccas in Indonesia. It has a distinctive, pungent fragrance and is used in cooking and sachets and as incense. The tree yields fruit eight years after sowing, reaches its prime in 25 years, and bears fruit for 60 years or longer.

nutria *or* **coypu** Semiaquatic S. American RODENT *(Myocastor coypus)* in the hutia family (Capromyidae). The nutria has reddish brown fur, small ears, a long, rounded, scaly tail, partially webbed hind feet, and broad orange incisors. It is about 40 in. (1 m) long, including the tail, and may weigh 18 lbs (8 kg). The nutria lives in a shallow burrow along a pond or river. Because their fur is valuable, nutrias were introduced into N. America and Europe, and in some places have become pests that damage crops and compete with other wildlife.

nutrition Processes of taking in and utilizing food substances. CALORIES are supplied by CARBOHYDRATES (SUG-

ARS and STARCHES), FATS, and PROTEINS. Other nutrients include minerals, VITAMINS, and dietary FIBER. Minerals are used in many ways—IRON for HEMOGLOBIN; CALCIUM for bones, teeth, and cellular processes; SODIUM and POTASSIUM to regulate HOMEOSTASIS; IODINE to produce thyroid HORMONES. Trace minerals have less well understood functions. Fiber aids DIGESTION, lowers blood CHOLESTEROL, and may help prevent some CANCERS and HYPERTENSION. Different amounts of these nutrients exist in different foods; a varied diet ensures an adequate supply. Nutritional supplements, required by some people, do not compensate for an unhealthy diet. Sufficient WATER is always essential. The U.S. FOOD AND DRUG ADMINISTRATION and other agencies assess nutritional requirements. See also MALNUTRITION.

Nuuk \'nük\ *or* **Godthåb** \'gȯt-ˌhȯp\ City (pop., 1999 est.: 13,000), capital of GREENLAND. Located on the SW coast, it is Greenland's main port. The modern town dates from 1721. It is the seat of the parliament and supreme court and has foreign consulates, a teachers' college, and research stations. Most transportation is by boat or helicopter.

Nyasa, Lake See Lake MALAWI

Nyasaland See MALAWI

Nyaya \'nyä-yə\ One of the six DARSHANS (orthodox systems) of Indian philosophy, important for its analysis of logic and epistemology and for its detailed model of the reasoning method of inference. It recognizes four valid means of knowledge: perception, inference, comparison, and testimony.

Nyerere \ni-'rar-ē\, **Julius (Kambarage)** (1922–1999) First prime minister of independent Tanganyika (1961), first president of Tanzania (1964–85), and the major force behind the ORGANIZATION OF AFRICAN UNITY (OAU). As leader of the Tanganyika African National Union (TANU), he advocated peaceful change, social equality, and ethnic harmony. In elections in 1958–60 TANU won many seats in the legislature. As president he collectivized village farmlands and instituted universal education, but his efforts to make Tanzania economically self-sufficient ultimately failed. In 1979 he authorized the invasion of Uganda to overthrow Idi AMIN. Within the OAU he advocated the overthrow of white-supremacist governments in S. Africa, Rhodesia, and S.W. Africa.

Julius Nyerere, 1981

Nykvist \'nūē-kvist, *Engl* 'nī-kvist\, **Sven** (b.1922) Swedish cinematographer. He shot his first film in 1945, and his first for Ingmar BERGMAN in 1953, becoming Bergman's regular cinematographer in 1960. Best known for his subtle, luminous camera work in a long series of Bergman films, he won Academy Awards for *Cries and Whispers* (1972) and *Fanny and Alexander* (1983). With U.S. directors, he has filmed such movies as *The Unbearable Lightness of Being* (1988) and *Crimes and Misdemeanors* (1989).

nylon Any synthetic PLASTIC material composed of polyamides of high MOLECULAR WEIGHT. Nylons were developed by Du Pont in the 1930s. The successful production of a useful fiber from compounds readily available from air, water, and coal or petroleum stimulated expansion of research on POLYMERS, leading to a rapidly growing family of synthetics. Nylon can be made to form fibers, filaments, bristles, or sheets to be manufactured into YARN, TEXTILES, and cordage, and can also be formed into molded products. It has high resistance to wear, heat, and chemicals. Most applications are in the form of filaments in such articles as hosiery, parachutes, and outerwear.

nymph In GREEK MYTHOLOGY, any of a large class of minor female divinities. Nymphs were usually associated with features of the natural world, such as trees and water. Though not immortal, they were extremely long-lived, and they tended to be well disposed toward humans.

nymph In entomology, the sexually immature form of insects that undergo incomplete METAMORPHOSIS (e.g., GRASSHOPPERS). The nymph is similar to the adult but differs in body proportions and (in winged species) has only wing buds, which develop into wings after the first few molts. With each successive growing stage (instar), the nymph resembles the adult more closely. The nymphs of aquatic species (also called naiads), such as DRAGONFLIES, have gills and other modifications for an aquatic existence.

nymphaeum \nim-ˈfē-əm\ Ancient Greek and Roman sanctuary consecrated to water nymphs. Nymphaea also served as reservoirs and assembly chambers for weddings. The name, originally denoting a natural grotto with springs, later referred to an artificial grotto or building filled with plants, sculpture, fountains, and paintings.

Nystad, Treaty of See Second NORTHERN WAR

NYU See NEW YORK UNIV.

O

Oahu \ō-'wä-hü\ Island (pop., 2000: 876,000), Hawaii. Situated between the islands of Kauai and Molokai, it occupies 607 sq mi (1,574 sq km) and is the most densely populated of the Hawaiian Islands. Its two mountain groups are connected by a central plateau. It is the site of HONOLULU, PEARL HARBOR, and WAIKIKI. Military installations, tourism, pineapples, and sugar are important to its economy.

oak Any of about 450 species of ornamental and timber trees and shrubs that make up the genus *Quercus* in the BEECH family, found throughout temperate climates. Oaks are mostly DECIDUOUS TREES that bear spring catkins (male flowers) and spikes (female flowers) on the same tree. The leaves have lobed, toothed, or smooth margins. The fruit is the acorn. They are hardy and long-lived shade trees. Red- and white-oak lumber is used in construction, flooring, furniture, and millwork. The genus includes many ornamentals and natural hybrids.

Oakland City (pop., 2000: 399,000), W California, on the E side of SAN FRANCISCO BAY. Settled by the Spanish in 1820 and incorporated in 1854, in 1869 it was chosen as the terminus of the first transcontinental railroad, which led to the development of its deepwater port. It suffered damage and loss of life in the earthquake of 1989. The Bay Bridge connects it with San Francisco. Lake Merritt is a wildfowl refuge surrounded by parkland.

Oakley, Annie *orig.* Phoebe Anne Oakley Moses (1860–1926) U.S. sharpshooter. Born in Darke Co., Ohio, she won acclaim for her marksmanship as a girl and toured vaudeville circuits with her marksman husband, Frank Butler. In 1885 they joined Buffalo Bill's WILD WEST SHOW, where they remained for 17 years. Oakley's famous act included hitting the thin edge of a playing card from 30 paces, and shooting distant targets while looking into a mirror.

OAS See ORGANIZATION OF AMERICAN STATES

oasis Fertile tract of land that occurs in a desert wherever a permanent supply of freshwater is available. Oases vary in size from about 2 acres (1 hectare) around small springs to vast areas of naturally watered or irrigated

Annie Oakley

land. Underground springs and wells are supplied from sandstone AQUIFERS whose intake areas may be more than 500 mi (800 km) away. Two-thirds of the population of the Sahara lives in oases, where the DATE PALM is the main source of food and provides shade for growing other fruits, vegetables, and grains.

Oates, Joyce Carol (b.1938) U.S. writer. Born in Lockport, N.Y., she has written more than 60 novels and story collections, often portraying people whose intensely experienced lives end in bloodshed and self-destruction owing to forces beyond their control. Her major novels include *A Garden of Earthly Delights* (1967), *them* (1969), and *Do with Me What*

You Will (1973). Also significant is a parodic gothic series including *Bellefleur* (1980).

oats Hardy CEREAL plant *(Avena sativa),* cultivated in temperate regions, that is able to live in poor soil. The edible starchy grain is used primarily as livestock feed, but is also processed into rolled oats, oat bran, and oat flour for human consumption. High in carbohydrates, oats also provide protein, fat, calcium, iron, and B vitamins. Oat STRAW is used for animal feed and bedding.

OAU See ORGANIZATION OF AFRICAN UNITY

Oaxaca \wä-'hä-kä\ State (pop., 2000: 3,432,000), S Mexico. It occupies 36,820 sq mi (95,364 sq km) and includes most of the Isthmus of Tehuantepec. The capital is OAXACA. Remains of pre-Columbian ZAPOTEC and Mixtec structures are found at MITLA and MONTE ALBÁN. It has the largest population of Indian descent in Mexico.

Oaxaca (de Juárez) City (pop., 1995: 242,000), capital of OAXACA state, S Mexico. It lies in the fertile Oaxaca Valley, 5,085 ft (1,550 m) above sea level. Conquered by the Spanish in 1521, it was the home of Benito JUÁREZ and Porfirio DÍAZ. It is noted for its 16th-cent. architecture and its handicraft market.

Obadiah \ˌō-bə-'dī-ə\ (between 9th and 6th cent. B.C.) One of the 12 Minor Prophets in the OLD TESTAMENT, traditional author of the Book of Obadiah. The Old Testament's shortest book, it consists of one chapter of 21 verses. (It is part of a larger book, The Twelve, in the Jewish canon.) It castigates Edom for failing to help Israel repel foreign invaders, announces that the Day of Judgment is near, and predicts the restoration of the Jews to their native land.

O'Bail, John See CORNPLANTER

obelisk Tapered four-sided pillar, originally erected in pairs at the entrance to ancient Egyptian temples. The Egyptian obelisk was carved from a single piece of stone and embellished with hieroglyphics. It was wider at its square or rectangular base than at its pyramidal top, and could be over 100 ft (30 m) high. A well-known modern obelisk is the WASHINGTON MONUMENT.

Oberammergau See PASSION PLAY

Oberlin College Private liberal-arts college in Oberlin, Ohio. Founded in 1833, it was the first U.S. college to admit women and the first to admit black students on an equal footing with whites. It was a station on the UNDERGROUND RAILROAD. Oberlin's music conservatory is renowned. Enrollment is about 3,000.

obesity Excessive body FAT, defined as weight at least 20% more than optimum. It is usually caused by sedentary habits and a diet high in fat, alcohol (see ETHANOL), or total CALORIES. Rare causes include glandular defects and excess STEROIDS (see CUSHING'S SYNDROME). Obesity raises the risk of HEART DISEASE and DIABETES MELLITUS.

object-oriented programming (OOP) Computer programming that emphasizes the structure of data. It is a departure from traditional or procedural programming. OOP languages incorporate objects that are self-contained collections of commands and data. Programs can be written by assembling sets of these predefined objects in far less time than is possible using conventional languages. See also C++, JAVA.

oblation In Christianity, the offering up by the faithful of any gift for use usually by the clergy, the church, or the sick or poor. The bread and wine offered for consecration in the EUCHARIST are oblations. In the Middle Ages children dedicated to a monastery and left there to be brought up were called oblates. Later, oblates were laity who lived at or in close connection with a monastery but who did not take religious vows.

oboe Double-reed WOODWIND INSTRUMENT. The oboe developed out of the more powerful shawm in the early 17th cent. Intended for indoor use with stringed instruments, its tone was softer and less brilliant. In its early form it had as few as two keys; today it has about 13. With its sweet but piercing sound, it was by the end of the 17th cent. the principal wind instrument of the orchestra and military band, and a leading solo instrument. Today the orchestra generally includes two oboes. The modern alto oboe is the ENGLISH HORN.

Obote \ō-'bō-tā\, **(Apollo) Milton** (1924–1996) First prime minister (1962–70) and president (1966–71, 1980–85) of Uganda. Elected to the legislative council in 1958, he led Uganda to independence in 1962. He accepted a constitution granting federal status to five traditional kingdoms, including Buganda, but in 1966 he sent troops under Gen. Idi AMIN to subdue Buganda's ruler, Mutesa II, and abolished all the kingdoms. He was overthrown by Amin in 1971, but returned in 1979 to establish a repressive government. Having failed to quell ethnic strife despite his own often brutal policies, which resulted in 300,000-400,000 deaths, he was again ousted in 1985.

Obrecht \'ō-ˌbreḵt\, **Jacob** (c.1450–1505) Flemish composer. Little is known of his origins or education. Most outstanding among his works are his 29 masses; he also wrote about 30 motets. Despite his contemporary renown, he had little influence on later composers, and his intellectual but exuberant music came to seem old-fashioned with the advent of JOSQUIN DES PREZ.

O'Brian, Patrick orig. Richard Patrick Russ (1914–2000) British-French writer. He received little critical notice until age 54, when he began publishing his 18th-cent. seafaring series featuring Capt. Jack Aubrey and ship's surgeon Stephen Maturin; it eventually numbered 20 books (1969–99) and was compared with the works of Herman MELVILLE and Anthony TROLLOPE.

Ob River \'ȯb\ River, W Russia. Flowing across W SIBERIA northwestward from the ALTAY SHAN of central Asia, it courses into the Kara Sea of the Arctic Ocean. It is about 2,287 mi (3,680 km) long. Its middle course is through swampy TAIGA; in the north are vast stretches of icy, treeless TUNDRA. The Ob is an important source of hydroelectric power and a major transportation route when not frozen.

obscenity Act, utterance, or matter that is deeply offending according to contemporary community standards of morality and decency. The U.S. Supreme Court has ruled that materials are obscene if they appeal predominantly to a prurient interest in sexual conduct, depict or describe sexual conduct in a patently offensive way, and lack serious literary, artistic, political, or scientific value. Material deemed obscene by the Court is not protected by the free-speech guarantee of the 1st Amendment. See also FREEDOM OF SPEECH, PORNOGRAPHY.

observatory Structure with TELESCOPES and other instruments for observing the skies. Optical observatories receive the visible part of the ELECTROMAGNETIC SPECTRUM. Some are equipped to detect RADIO WAVES. Orbiting astronomical observatories are earth SATELLITES whose special telescopes and detectors study celestial sources of high-energy radiation from above the ATMOSPHERE. STONEHENGE may have been an early optical observatory. HIPPARCHUS built (c.150 B.C.) perhaps the first observatory that used instruments. Tycho BRAHE built (1576) the first notable premodern European observatory. The HERSCHELS' Observatory House, in Slough, England, was one of the technical wonders of the 18th cent. Today's largest groupings of optical telescopes are on Mauna Kea, Hawaii, and Cerro Tuldo, Chile. Other major observatories include ARECIBO, Mt. Wilson, Palomar, and ROYAL GREENWICH OBSERVATORIES.

obsessive-compulsive disorder Mental disorder characterized by recurring obsessions and compulsions. An obsession is a persistent preoccupation with an unreasonable idea or feeling (e.g., being contaminated through shaking hands

with someone). A compulsion is an irresistible impulse to perform an irrational act (e.g., repeatedly washing the hands). The two phenomena are usually linked. The illness has been linked to malregulation of the neurotransmitter SEROTONIN as well as to high STRESS.

obsidian Natural glass of volcanic origin that is formed by the rapid cooling of viscous LAVA. It is typically jet black, but the presence of hematite (iron oxide) produces red and brown varieties; it is sometimes used as a semiprecious stone. Obsidian was used by American Indians and others for weapons, implements, tools, and ornaments, and by the ancient Aztecs and Greeks for mirrors.

obstetrics and gynecology \ˌgī-nə-'kä-lə-jē\ Medical and surgical specialty concerned with the management of PREGNANCY and childbirth (see PARTURITION) and with the health of the female REPRODUCTIVE SYSTEM. Obstetricians confirm pregnancy, diagnose ECTOPIC PREGNANCY, conduct prenatal care, perform AMNIOCENTESIS, deliver babies, and perform ABORTIONS. Gynecologists do routine pelvic exams, take samples for PAP SMEARS, advise on and prescribe birth control, and treat reproductive system disorders (e.g., ENDOMETRIOSIS, hormonal imbalances, problems with MENSTRUATION and MENOPAUSE). They perform surgery to prevent conception (tubal ligation), repair pelvic injuries, and remove cysts and tumors from the UTERUS, cervix, and OVARIES. Both specialties are involved in diagnosis and treatment of INFERTILITY. See also CESAREAN SECTION, CONTRACEPTION, HYSTERECTOMY, MIDWIFERY, NATURAL CHILDBIRTH.

O'Casey, Sean orig. John Casey (1880–1964) Irish playwright. Born to a poor Protestant family, he worked from age 14 at manual labor. He embraced the Irish nationalist cause, changing his name to its Irish form. By 1915 he had turned to writing realistic tragicomedies about Dublin slum dwellers in war and revolution. The ABBEY THEATRE produced three of his earliest and best plays—*The Shadow of a Gunman* (1923), *Juno and the Paycock* (1924), and *The Plough and the Stars* (1926)—which caused riots by Irish patriots. When his antiwar play *The Silver Tassie* was rejected, O'Casey moved to England. His later plays include *Within the Gates* (1934), *The Star Turns Red* (1940), and *Red Roses for Me* (1946).

Occam, William of See William of OCKHAM

Occam's razor See OCKHAM'S RAZOR

Occitan language \'äk-sə-ˌtan\ or **Provençal language** \ˌprō-vän-'säl, ˌprä-vən-'säl\ ROMANCE LANGUAGE spoken in Occitania, a region of S France, whose 1.5 million speakers use it as a vernacular. The name Provençal originally referred to the dialects of the Provence region, used by medieval TROUBADOURS and as a standard and literary language in France and N Spain in the 12th–14th cent. Gascon, spoken in SW France, is sometimes considered a distinct language. Occitan is closely related to Catalan and has more in common with Spanish than with French.

occultism Theories, practices, and rituals based on esoteric knowledge of the world of spirits and unknown forces. The wide range of occult beliefs and practices includes ASTROLOGY, ALCHEMY, DIVINATION, MAGIC, and WITCHCRAFT AND SORCERY. The Western tradition of occultism has its roots in Hellenistic magic and alchemy (especially the HERMETIC WRITINGS) and in the Jewish mysticism associated with the KABBALA.

Occupation (of Japan) (1945–52) Occupation of Japan after its defeat in World War II. Theoretically an international occupation, in fact it was carried out almost entirely by the U.S. general Douglas MACARTHUR. The Occupation oversaw the dismantling of arms industries and the release of political prisoners; wartime leaders stood trial for WAR CRIMES and seven were executed. A new constitution, vesting power in the people, replaced the MEIJI CONSTITUTION; in it Japan renounced its right to wage war, the emperor was reduced to ceremonial status, and women were given the right to vote. The Occupation also carried out land reform, reducing the number of farmers who were tenants from 46% to 10%, and began the breakup of the ZAIBATSU. Labor unions were initially encouraged. The education system was revised to resemble the U.S. system. Though the U.S. wanted to end the Occupation in 1947, the Soviet

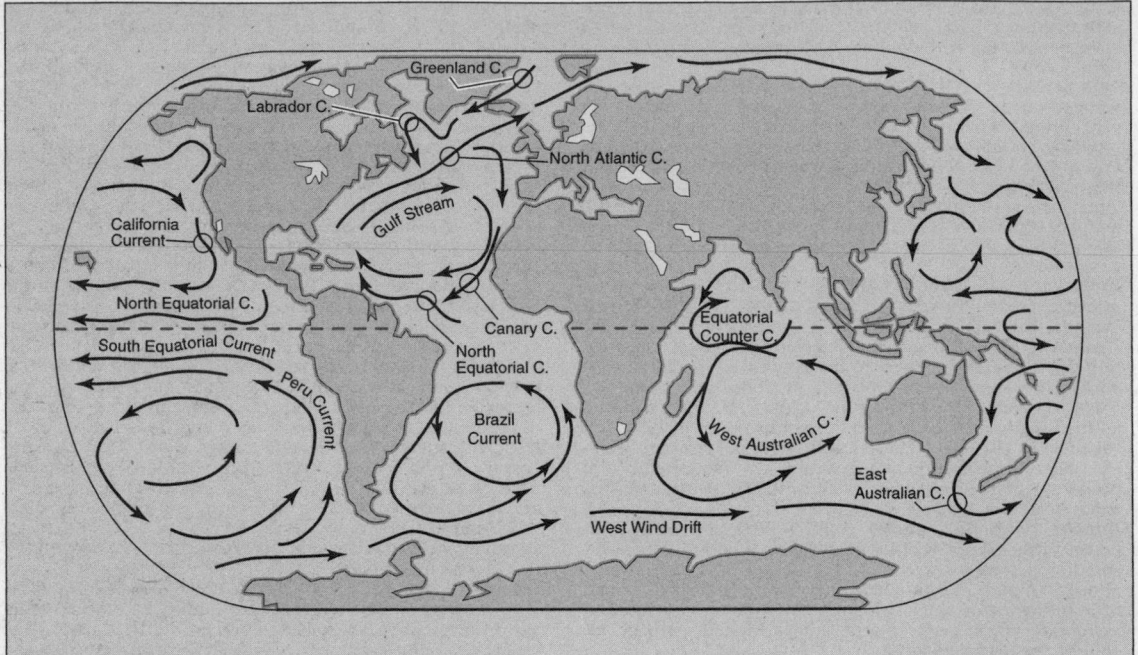

Ocean current Major surface currents of the world's oceans. Subsurface currents also move vast amounts of water, but are not known in such detail.

Union vetoed a peace treaty; in 1951 a treaty was signed, and the Occupation ended the following year.

occupational disease Illness associated with a particular occupation. The Industrial Revolution's long working hours, dim light, lack of fresh air, and dangerous machinery fostered illness and injury in general, but certain occupations (e.g., mining) carry particular risks (e.g., black lung, SILICOSIS). 20th-cent. innovations (including use of new chemicals and radioactive materials) have caused an increase in certain cancers and injuries. So-called "sick buildings" (in which pathogens grow in air circulation systems) contribute to health problems among office workers. See also ASBESTOSIS.

occupational therapy Use of activities to promote health and independence, particularly after the acute phase of illness, to reorient patients unable to work for long periods. Occupational therapists tailor programs to restore physical function and devise ways to help those with permanent limitations carry out everyday functions. See also PHYSICAL MEDICINE AND REHABILITATION.

ocean Large, continuous body of salt water. Ocean covers nearly 71% of the earth's surface and is divided into major oceans and smaller seas. The three principal oceans, the Pacific, Atlantic, and Indian, are largely delimited by land and submarine topographic boundaries. All are connected to the so-called Southern Ocean, the waters encircling Antarctica. Important marginal seas, primarily in the Northern Hemisphere, are partially enclosed by landmasses or ISLAND ARCS. The largest are the Arctic Ocean and adjacent seas, the Caribbean Sea, and the Mediterranean Sea.

ocean current Horizontal and vertical circulation system of ocean waters, produced by gravity, wind friction, and water density variation. CORIOLIS FORCES cause ocean currents to move clockwise in the Northern Hemisphere and counterclockwise in the Southern Hemisphere. Major ocean currents include the GULF STREAM–N. Atlantic–Norway Current in the Atlantic Ocean, the Peru (Humboldt) Current off S. America, and the W Australian Current.

Oceania \ˌō-shē-ˈa-nē-ə\ Collective name for the islands scattered throughout most of the Pacific Ocean. These include MICRONESIA, MELANESIA, and POLYNESIA, and some-

times Australia, New Zealand, and the MALAY ARCHIPELAGO. In its most restricted sense, excluding Australia, but including Papua New Guinea, it encompasses more than 10,000 islands, with an area of about 317,000 sq mi (821,000 sq km) and a population (1990 est.) of 9,400,000.

oceanic plateau \ˌō-shē-ˈa-nik\ *or* **submarine plateau** Large submarine elevation rising sharply at least 650 ft (200 m) above the surrounding seafloor and having an extensive, relatively flat or gently tilted summit. Most plateaus are steplike interruptions of the CONTINENTAL SLOPES. Some, however, stand alone, and are believed to be fragments of continent that were isolated during CONTINENTAL DRIFT and SEAFLOOR SPREADING.

oceanic ridge *or* **mid-ocean ridge** Continuous submarine mountain chain extending approximately 50,000 mi (80,000 km) through all the world's oceans, separating them into distinct basins. The main ridge extends down the middle of the Atlantic Ocean, passes between Africa and Antarctica, turns north to the Indian Ocean, then continues between Australia, New Zealand, and Antarctica and across the Pacific basin to the mouth of the Gulf of California. Lateral ridges extend to adjacent continents. The oceanic ridge system is explained by the theory of PLATE TECTONICS as a boundary between diverging plates where molten rock is brought up from deep beneath the earth's crust.

oceanic trench See DEEP-SEA TRENCH

ocean liner Large merchant ship that visits designated ports on a regular schedule, carrying whatever cargo and passengers are available on the date of sailing. The first liners were operated in the N. Atlantic, notably by Samuel CUNARD of Britain, beginning in 1840. Their heyday lasted from the late 19th to the mid-20th cent. Many were extraordinarily luxurious. Among the most famous were Cunarders such as the *Mauretania* and the *Queen Mary;* the German *Vaterland* (later *Leviathan*); the ill-fated *TITANIC;* and the *United States*. Their reign ended in the 1960s with the rise of jet travel.

oceanography Scientific discipline concerned with the world's OCEANS and seas, including their physical and chemical properties, origin and geology, and life forms. Research entails sampling seawater and marine life, studying oceanic processes, and exploring the seafloor. Oceanography aids in predicting weather and climate, exploiting the

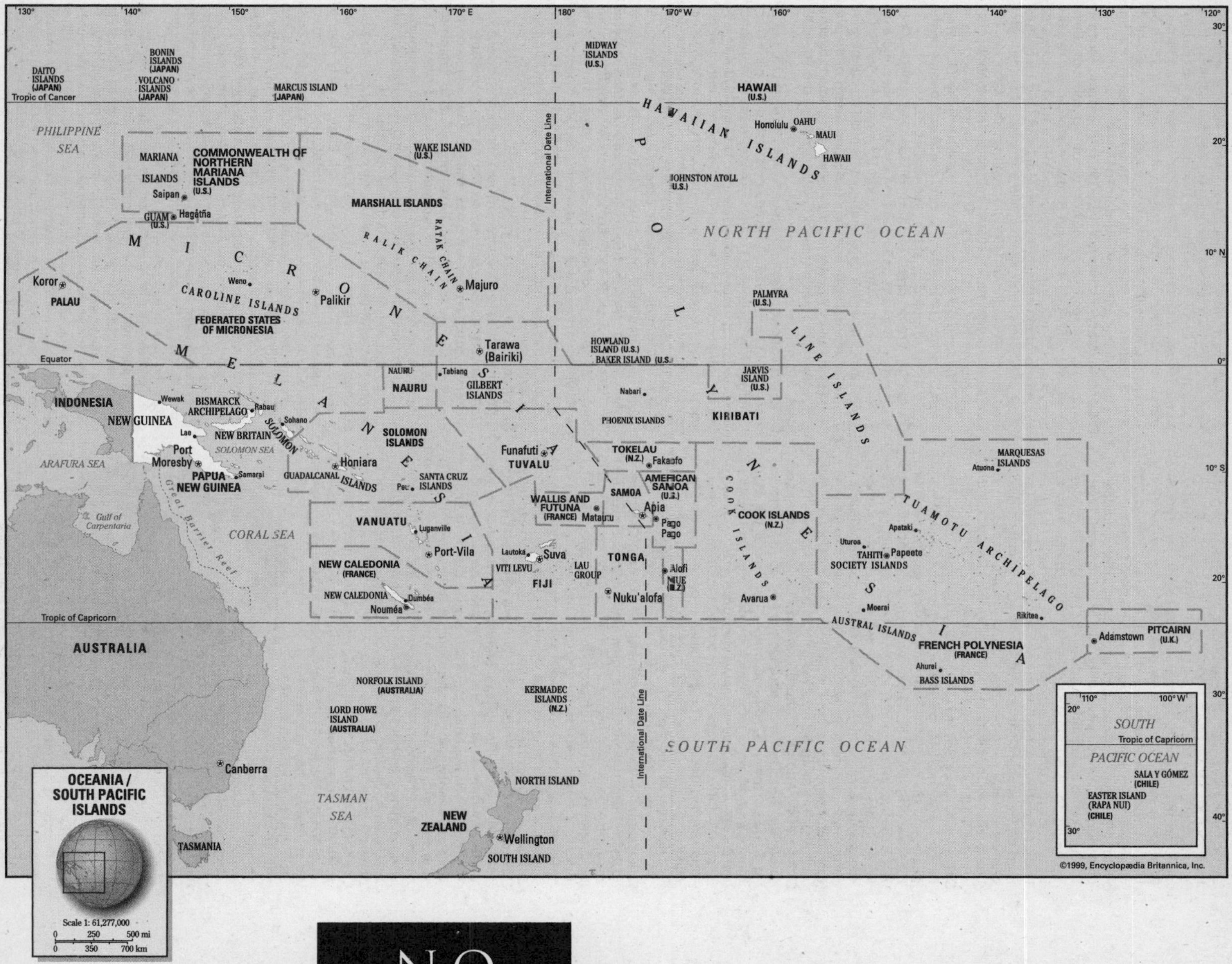

30° 20° N 10° N 0° 10° S 20°

120° 130° 140° 150° 160° 170° W 180° 170° E 160°

©1999, Encyclopædia Britannica, Inc.

PITCAIRN (U.K.)
Adamstown

SOUTH
Tropic of Capricorn
PACIFIC OCEAN
SALA Y GÓMEZ (CHILE)
EASTER ISLAND (RAPA NUI) (CHILE)

NORTH PACIFIC OCEAN

SOUTH PACIFIC OCEAN

HAWAII (U.S.)
HAWAIIAN ISLANDS
Honolulu OAHU MAUI HAWAII

MIDWAY ISLANDS (U.S.)

JOHNSTON ATOLL (U.S.)

International Date Line

PALMYRA (U.S.)
JARVIS ISLAND (U.S.)
LINE ISLANDS
KIRIBATI

MARQUESAS ISLANDS
Atuona

TUAMOTU ARCHIPELAGO
Rikitea
Apataki Papeete
TAHITI
Uturoa SOCIETY ISLANDS
Moorea
AUSTRAL ISLANDS
FRENCH POLYNESIA (FRANCE)
Aiurui
BASS ISLANDS

P O L Y N E S I A

COOK ISLANDS (N.Z.)
Avarua
COOK ISLANDS

HOWLAND ISLAND (U.S.)
BAKER ISLAND (U.S.)
Nahari
PHOENIX ISLANDS
TOKELAU (N.Z.) Fakaofo
AMERICAN SAMOA (U.S.)
Pago Pago
SAMOA Apia
Alofi
NIUE (N.Z.)
TONGA
Nuku'alofa

Tabiang Tarawa (Bairiki)
GILBERT ISLANDS

WALLIS AND FUTUNA (FRANCE) Mata'utu
LAU GROUP
Lautoka
VITI LEVU Suva
FIJI

Funafuti TUVALU

M I C R O N E S I A

MARSHALL ISLANDS
WAKE ISLAND (U.S.)
Majuro
RATAK CHAIN
RALIK CHAIN

NAURU Yaren
SANTA CRUZ ISLANDS
Luganville
Port-Vila
VANUATU
Dumbéa
Nouméa
NEW CALEDONIA (FRANCE)
NEW CALEDONIA

M E L A N E S I A

SOLOMON ISLANDS
Honiara
GUADALCANAL ISLAND

KERMADEC ISLANDS (N.Z.)

NORFOLK ISLAND (AUSTRALIA)
LORD HOWE ISLAND (AUSTRALIA)

NORTH ISLAND
Wellington
SOUTH ISLAND
NEW ZEALAND

TASMAN SEA

DAITO ISLANDS (JAPAN)
VOLCANO ISLANDS (JAPAN)
BONIN ISLANDS (JAPAN)
MARCUS ISLAND (JAPAN)
Tropic of Cancer

PHILIPPINE SEA

MARIANA ISLANDS (U.S.)
Saipan
GUAM (U.S.) Hagåtña

COMMONWEALTH OF NORTHERN MARIANA ISLANDS (U.S.)

Weno
Palikir
CAROLINE ISLANDS
FEDERATED STATES OF MICRONESIA

Koror
PALAU

Equator

INDONESIA

NEW GUINEA
Wewak
Lae
Port Moresby
PAPUA NEW GUINEA
BISMARCK ARCHIPELAGO
NEW BRITAIN
Sohano
SOLOMON ISLANDS
Samarai
SOLOMON SEA
Bougainville
Pac.

ARAFURA SEA
Gulf of Carpentaria
CORAL SEA
Great Barrier Reef

AUSTRALIA
Canberra
Tropic of Capricorn
TASMANIA

OCEANIA / SOUTH PACIFIC ISLANDS

Scale 1: 61,277,000
0 250 500 mi
0 350 700 km

120° W 110° 100°
20° 30°

earth's resources, and understanding the effects of pollutants. See also MARINE GEOLOGY.

Oceanside City (pop., 2000: 161,000), SW California. Located north of SAN DIEGO, it is a beach resort. Incorporated in 1888, it grew notably after 1942 with the opening of a U.S. Marine Corps base, Camp Pendleton, to the north. Nearby is the restored Mission San Luis Rey (1798).

ocelot \'ä-sə-‚lät\ Species *(Felis, or Leopardis, pardalis)* of CAT found in forests, grasslands, and brush-covered regions from Texas to N Argentina. It is 36–52 in. (90–130 cm) long, excluding the 12–16-in. (30–40-cm) tail. It stands about 18 in. (45 cm) and weighs 24–35 lbs (11–16 kg). The upper body varies from whitish to tawny yellow to gray. The fur is marked by specific patterns of black stripes and spots, including oblong spots arranged in chainlike bands on the body. The ocelot hunts at night for small mammals, birds, reptiles, and fish. It is an endangered species in the U.S.

Ochoa \ō-'chō-ə\, **Severo** (1905–1993) Spanish-U.S. molecular biologist. In 1955, while researching high-energy phosphates, he discovered an enzyme in bacteria that enabled him to synthesize RNA. The enzyme normally breaks down RNA, but in a test tube it runs its natural reaction in reverse. It has been valuable in enabling scientists to understand and recreate the process whereby the hereditary information contained in genes is translated into enzymes that determine each cell's functions and character. With Arthur KORNBERG he received a 1959 Nobel Prize.

Ochs \'äks\, **Adolph S(imon)** (1858–1935) U.S. newspaper publisher. Born in Cincinnati, Ochs grew up in Tennessee. At 20 he borrowed $250 to become proprietor of the moribund *Chattanooga Times,* which he developed into one of the South's leading newspapers. He gained control of the financially faltering *NEW YORK TIMES* in 1896. Despising YELLOW JOURNALISM, he emphasized comprehensive and trustworthy news gathering. Under his ownership the *Times* became one of the world's outstanding newspapers. From 1900 he was a director of the ASSOCIATED PRESS.

Ockeghem \'ō-kə-gem\, **Johannes** or **Jean d'Ockeghem** (c.1415–1497) Flemish composer and singer. He is first mentioned as a member of an Antwerp choir in 1443, and he later held a series of posts in the Low Countries and France. Though universally admired, his output, over a career of more than 50 years, was small, comprising 14 masses, about 10 motets, and about 20 chansons. His richly sonorous works often reflect intricate structural principles.

Ockham \'ä-kəm\, **William of** or **William of Occam** (c.1285–1347/49) English Franciscan philosopher, theologian, and political writer. A late Scholastic thinker, he is regarded as the founder of nominalism, which denies that UNIVERSALS have any reality apart from individual things. With his passion for logic, he placed great trust in mankind's natural reason. As a theologian, he believed that God's GRACE consists in giving without any obligation and is already profusely demonstrated in the creation of nature. See also OCKHAM'S RAZOR.

Ockham's razor Methodological principle of parsimony in scientific explanation. Traditionally attributed to William of OCKHAM, the principle prescribes that entities are not to be multiplied beyond necessity. That is, if a phenomenon can be explained without assuming the existence of an entity, then philosophers and scientists should not assume the entity's existence. The history of science provides many examples of the principle's application. See also MATERIALISM.

O'Connell, Daniel *known as* **the Liberator** (1775–1847) Irish nationalist leader. Involved in the struggle for CATHOLIC EMANCIPATION, he organized nationwide "aggregate meetings" of Irish Catholics to petition for their legal rights, and in 1823 co-

Daniel O'Connell Portrait by B. Mulrenin, 1836

founded the Catholic Association. After helping win passage of the 1829 Emancipation Act, which allowed Irish Catholics to serve in the British Parliament, he was elected to the House of Commons. Disenchanted with the administration's inaction on Irish reform measures, in 1839 he formed the Repeal Association to dissolve the Anglo-Irish Act of UNION. A series of illegal mass meetings in Ireland led to his being jailed for sedition 1843–44.

O'Connor, (Mary) Flannery (1925–1964) U.S. writer. Born in Savannah, she spent most of her life on her mother's farm in Milledgeville, Ga. A devout Roman Catholic, she usually set her works in the rural South and often tried to examine the relationship between the individual and God by putting their characters in grotesque and extreme situations. Her first novel, *Wise Blood* (1952), combines the keen ear for common speech and caustic religious imagination that characterize her later work. With the story collections *A Good Man Is Hard to Find* (1955) and *Everything That Rises Must Converge* (1965), she was acclaimed as a master of the form. Long crippled by lupus, she died at 39.

O'Connor, Frank *orig.* Michael O'Donovan (1903–1966) Irish writer. Brought up in poverty, O'Connor became a director of Dublin's ABBEY THEATRE. He won popularity for short stories in which apparently trivial incidents illuminate Irish life, appearing in volumes including *Guests of the Nation* (1931) and *Crab Apple Jelly* (1944). He also wrote critical studies and translations of Gaelic works of the 9th–20th cent.

O'Connor, Sandra Day *orig.* Sandra Day (b.1930) U.S. jurist. Born in El Paso, Texas, she graduated first in her class from Stanford Law School. The first woman in the U.S. to hold the position of state senate majority leader (1972–74), she was nominated in 1981 to the U.S. Supreme Court and became the first female justice in the Court's history. She has proved to be a moderate conservative. She is known for dispassionate and meticulously researched opinions.

OCR *in full* **optical character recognition** Scanning technique that identifies and stores printed text or numerical data. It avoids the need to retype already printed material for data entry. OCR software attempts to identify characters and words by comparing them to those stored in its software library and will try to reconstruct the original page layout. High accuracy can be obtained with high-quality originals, but accuracy decreases as the quality of the original declines.

Octavian See Caesar AUGUSTUS

October Manifesto Document issued by Czar NICHOLAS II in October 1905. In response to the unrest caused by the RUSSIAN REVOLUTION OF 1905 and on the advice of his minister Sergey WITTE, Nicholas promised to guarantee civil liberties and establish a popularly elected DUMA. The Duma was in fact given only a limited voice in the government, and the civil rights actually granted were far less substantial than those promised by the manifesto.

October Revolution See RUSSIAN REVOLUTION OF 1917

octopus Any eight-armed CEPHALOPOD of the order Octopoda; specifically, members of the large, widely distributed genus *Octopus.* Species range from about 2 in. (5 cm) to 18 ft (5.5 m) long with an armspan up to 30 ft (9 m). The head is usually only slightly demarcated from the body. Each arm bears fleshy suckers. Two sharp beaks and a filelike organ in the mouth drill crustacean shells and rasp away flesh. Most octopuses crawl along the bottom; when alarmed, they may jet-propel themselves backward, and they sometimes eject an inky substance to cloud the water and escape predators. They can change color rapidly, a reflection of their environment or mood. The common octopus (*O. vulgaris*) is thought to be the most intelligent of all INVERTEBRATES.

ode Ceremonious lyric poem on an occasion of dignity in which personal emotion and universal themes are united. The form is usually marked by exalted feeling and style, varying line length, and complex stanza forms. Forms of odes include the PINDARIC ODE, written to celebrate public events such as the Olympic games, and the form associated with HORACE, whose intimate, reflective odes have two- or four-line stanzas and polished meters. Both were revived during the Renaissance and influenced Western lyric poetry into the 20th cent.

Odense \'u̇-ən-zə, *Engl* 'ō-den-sə\ City (metro. area pop., 1999 est. : 184,000), Fyn Island, Denmark. Sacred in pagan times as the sanctuary of ODIN, it first appears in records about A.D. 1000. A bishop's seat, it became a center of pilgrimage to the shrine of CANUTE THE GREAT. It was burned in 1247. It grew after its port and harbor were built and the Odense Canal was opened in 1804. Denmark's third-largest city, it is a shipbuilding center. The home of H. C. ANDERSEN is now a museum.

Oder River \'ō-dər\ *or* **Odra River** \'ȯ-drä\ *ancient* Viadua. River, N Europe. It flows from its source in the Oder Mtns. in the Czech Republic north through W Poland, where it forms the boundary between Poland and Germany. As the second-largest river emptying into the BALTIC SEA, it is economically important as a transport route. Navigable for 475 mi (765 km), it is connected by canal with the VISTULA RIVER and with the W European waterway system. It was partially internationalized under the Treaty of VERSAILLES in 1919.

Odessa City (pop., 1998 est.: 1,027,000), SW Ukraine. A Tatar fortress was established there in the 14th cent. The city was ceded to Russia in 1791 and became its second most important port after ST. PETERSBURG. It was a center of revolutionary activity in 1905 (see RUSSIAN REVOLUTION OF 1905). It suffered heavy damage in World War II but remains a major seaport, with shipbuilding and oil refineries. It is also a cultural center.

Odets \ō-'dets\, **Clifford** (1906–1963) U.S. playwright. Born in Philadelphia, he joined New York's Group Theatre in 1931. His first play, the social-protest drama *Waiting for Lefty* (1935), helped establish his and the theater's reputation. He followed it with *Awake and Sing!* (1935) and *Golden Boy* (1937). He moved to Hollywood, where he wrote screenplays and directed movies, including *None but the Lonely Heart* (1944). His later plays included *The Big Knife* (1949; film, 1955), *The Country Girl* (1950; film, 1954), and *The Flowering Peach* (1954).

Odin \'ō-din\ *or* **Wotan** \'vō-ˌtän\ One of the principal Norse gods. A war god from earliest times, Odin appeared in Scandinavian heroic literature as the protector of heroes. Fallen warriors were believed to join him in VALHALLA. Odin was the great magician among the gods and was associated with RUNIC WRITING. Odin was usually depicted as a tall old man with a flowing beard and only one eye (the other he gave in exchange for wisdom); he wore a cloak and a wide-brimmed hat and carried a spear.

Odoacer \ˌō-dō-'ā-sər\ *or* **Odovacar** \ˌō-dō-'vä-kər\ (433?–493) First barbarian king of Italy (476–93). A German warrior in the Roman army, he led a revolt against the usurper Orestes (475) and was proclaimed king by his troops in 476, the date that traditionally marks the end of the Western Roman empire. He conquered Dalmatia (482) and retook Sicily from the Vandals. By attacking the Eastern empire he alienated the emperor Zeno, who encouraged the Ostrogothic king THEODORIC to invade Italy (489). Theodoric captured almost the entire peninsula and killed Odoacer after inviting him to a banquet.

Odo of Bayeux \'ō-dō...bà-'yœ̄\ *or* **Earl of Kent** (1036?–1097) Bishop of Bayeux, Normandy, and half brother of WILLIAM I the Conqueror. He fought in the Battle of HASTINGS and probably commissioned the BAYEUX TAPESTRY. Made earl of Kent in 1067, he ruled England (with others) in William's absence. William imprisoned him (1082–87) for raising troops without royal permission. He helped organize the First CRUSADE and died on his way to the Holy Land.

Odra River See ODER RIVER

Odysseus \ō-'di-sē-əs\ *Roman* **Ulysses** \yü-'li-sēz\ Hero of HOMER's *Odyssey*. According to Homer, Odysseus was the king of Ithaca. His shrewdness, resourcefulness, and endurance enabled him to capture TROY (using the Trojan horse) and endure nine years of wandering and adventures before reaching his home. He evades disaster at the hands of, among others, POLYPHEMUS the Cyclops, CIRCE, the SIRENS, and SCYLLA AND CHARYBDIS. He arrives home disguised as a beggar and, with the help of his son, Telemachus, kills the many suitors of his faithful wife, Penelope. Odysseus was treated by numerous Greek and Roman poets and many later writers.

Oe \'ō-e\, **Kenzaburo** (b.1935) Japanese novelist. His works, written in a rough prose style that at times nearly violates the natural rhythms of Japanese, reflect his life and epitomize the rebellion of the post–World War II generation. They include *A Personal Matter* (1964), which investigates the problem of culturally disinherited youth; *Hiroshima Notes* (1965); and *The Silent Cry* (1967). He received the Nobel Prize in 1994.

Oedipus \'e-də-pəs, 'ē-də-pəs\ In GREEK MYTHOLOGY, a king of THEBES who unwittingly killed his father and married his mother. In the most familiar version of the story, an oracle warned Laius, king of Thebes, that his son would slay him. When his wife, Jocasta, bore a son, he exposed the baby on a mountainside, but the infant Oedipus was saved and later adopted by the king of Corinth. In early manhood, Oedipus met Laius while traveling; Laius provoked a quarrel, and Oedipus killed him. Later he received the hand of the widowed queen of Thebes—his mother—as a reward for besting

Oedipus and the Sphinx, Attic cup, c.470–430 B.C.

the SPHINX. When at last they learned the truth, Jocasta committed suicide and Oedipus blinded himself and went into exile. ANTIGONE was his daughter.

Oedipus complex In psychoanalytic theory, a desire for sexual involvement with the parent of the opposite sex and a sense of rivalry with the other parent. The term was introduced by Sigmund FREUD in his *Interpretation of Dreams* (1899) and is derived from the mythological OEDIPUS, who killed his father and married his mother; its female analogue is the Electra complex. Freud considered it a normal stage in the development of children ages 3–5, and believed that the process of overcoming the complex gave rise to the SUPEREGO.

O'Faolain \ō-'fā-lən, ō-'fa-lən\, **Sean** *orig.* John Francis Whelan (1900–1991) Irish writer. He is known for carefully crafted, lyrical short stories about Ireland's lower and middle classes, often examining the decline of the nationalist struggle or the oppressive provincialism of Irish Catholicism. He achieved success with his first story collection, *Midsummer Night Madness* (1932), and the novel *A Nest of Simple Folk* (1933). His other works include *A Life of Daniel O'Connell* (1938) and *Vive moi!* (1964), his autobiography.

Offa \'ȯ-fə\ (d.796) King of Mercia (757–96) in Anglo-Saxon England. He extended his rule over most of S England and married his daughters to the rulers of Wessex and Northumbria. Eager to form European diplomatic ties, Offa signed a commercial treaty with CHARLEMAGNE (796) and allowed the pope to increase his control over the English church. He built OFFA'S DYKE to divide Mercia from Welsh lands.

Offa's Dyke Earthwork in W England. It stretches 169 mi (270 km) from the SEVERN RIVER near Chepstow to the Dee River estuary. It was built by OFFA of Mercia to fortify the boundary between his kingdom and the lands of the Welsh; for centuries it marked the England–Wales boundary. It consisted of a plain bank (in places some 60 ft, or 18 m, high) and a ditch (12 ft, or 3.7 m, deep). Many sections remain, and a walking path now runs its length.

Off-Broadway Small-scale theatrical productions in New York. The term was first used to refer to experimental plays produced on low budgets in small theaters, as an alternative to the commercially oriented BROADWAY theaters. Off-Broadway theaters grew after 1952 with the success of José QUINTERO's productions. Plays by Edward ALBEE and Sam SHEPARD were first produced off-Broadway, as were avant-garde works by Eugène IONESCO, Samuel BECKETT, and Harold PINTER. Many new plays are now staged in well-equipped off-Broadway houses. Smaller and more experimental theaters are now labeled off-off-Broadway.

Offenbach \'ȯ-fən-ˌbäk\, **Jacques** (*orig.* Jacob) (1819–1880) German-French composer. Son of a cantor, he first wrote theater music as conductor of the Théâtre-Français (from 1850); he later opened his own Bouffes Parisiens, for which he wrote 22 one-act works (1855–58). He began writing longer operettas and had a string of hits, including *Orpheus in the Underworld* (1858), *La belle Hélène* (1864), *La vie Parisienne* (1866), and *The Grand Duchess of Gérolstein* (1868). He spent his last three years on his masterpiece, *The Tales of Hoffmann* (1881).

offset printing *or* **offset lithography** *or* **litho-offset** PRINTING technique in which the inked image on a printing plate is imprinted on a rubber cylinder and then transferred (offset) to PAPER or other material. The rubber cylinder gives great flexibility, permitting printing on wood, cloth, metal, or leather. The matter to be printed is neither raised above the surface of the printing plate (as in LETTERPRESS PRINTING) nor sunk below it (as in GRAVURE PRINTING). Offset printing, a development of LITHOGRAPHY, is based on the principle that water and grease do not mix, so that a greasy ink can be deposited on grease-treated printing areas of the plate, while nonprinting areas, which hold water, reject the ink. The surface of the metal offset plate is treated to render it porous and then coated with a photosensitive material. Exposure to an image hardens the coating on printing areas; the coating on nonprinting areas is washed away, leaving wetted metal that will reject ink.

offshore bar See SANDBAR

O'Flaherty, Liam (1896–1984) Irish novelist and short-story writer. He abandoned his training for the priesthood and became a soldier in World War I, a migrant laborer, and a revolutionary in Ireland. A leading writer of the IRISH LITERARY RENAISSANCE, he combined brutal naturalism, psychological analysis, poetry, and biting satire with an abiding respect for the Irish people. His novels include *Thy Neighbour's Wife* (1923), *The Informer* (1925; film, 1935), and *Skerrett* (1932).

Ogaden \ō-gə-ˈden\ Region, E Ethiopia. In the triangular wedge that juts into Somalia, it is a dry, barren plain. Conquered in the late 19th cent. by MENILEK II, it was invaded by Italy in 1935 and made part of Italian E. Africa. Liberated in 1941, it remained under British administration until 1948. It was invaded by Somalia in 1977 and retaken by Ethiopia in 1978.

Ogbomosho \ōg-bō-ˈmō-shō\ City (pop., 1996 est.: 730,000), SW Nigeria. Founded in the mid-17th cent., it was an outpost of the OYO EMPIRE until the Muslim FULANI conquests in the early 19th cent. Located northeast of IBADAN, the walled town is one of Nigeria's largest urban centers, a trading center, and a rail junction.

Ogilvy \ˈō-gəl-vē\, **David M(ackenzie)** (1911–1999) British advertising executive. After an Oxford education, he and Anderson Hewitt (1908–1984) formed Hewitt, Ogilvy, Benson & Mather (1948), which became one of the world's largest advertising firms. He is noted for reminding his colleagues that "the consumer is not a moron." His ads for brands such as Schweppes and Rolls-Royce were admired for their creativity.

Oglethorpe, James (Edward) (1696–1785) English colonist. As a member of Parliament, he became interested in prison reform. In 1732 he secured a charter for a colony in what became Georgia, where debtors could start a new life and persecuted Protestants could practice freely. He accompanied the first settlers to found Savannah (1733) and led the defense of his territory against attacks by Spain (1739, 1742).

Ogodei \ˈō-gə-ˌdā\ (1185–1241) Son of GENGHIS KHAN who succeeded his father in 1229 and greatly expanded the MONGOL empire. He built the capital city of KARAKORUM. Like his father, he carried out simultaneous campaigns by relying on generals who acted independently but were subject to his orders. Allying himself with S China's SONG DYNASTY, Ogodei attacked the JUCHEN DYNASTY in N China, taking its capital in 1234. His nephew BATU defeated Russia while other generals were attacking Iran and Iraq. Only Ogodei's death prevented the invasion of Western Europe. See also KUBLAI KHAN, MONGKE.

Ogooué River *or* **Ogowe River** \ō-gō-ˈwä\ River, W central Africa, mainly in Gabon. It rises in Gabon and flows northwest, then west, emptying into the Atlantic Ocean south of Port-Gentil after a course of 750 mi (1,200 km). It is heavily used for shipping lumber to the coast.

O'Hara, John (Henry) (1905–1970) U.S. novelist and short-story writer. A native of Pottsville, Pa., he worked as a critic and reporter in New York City. His works stand as a social history of upwardly mobile Americans of the 1920s through the 1940s. Among them are the popular novels *Appointment in Samarra* (1934); *Butterfield 8* (1935; film, 1960); *Pal Joey* (1940), adapted as a successful musical; *Ten North Frederick* (1955; film, 1958); and *From the Terrace* (1958; film, 1960).

O'Higgins, Bernardo (1776?–1842) S. American revolutionary leader and first Chilean head of state (1817–23). The illegitimate, European-educated son of a Spanish officer of Irish origin, he joined Chile's new congress when NAPOLEON invaded Spain (1808) and Spanish control of Chile relaxed. He led the defensive forces when Chile was invaded by royalists from Peru in 1814; defeated, he fled to Argentina. He returned in 1817 with José de SAN MARTÍN and defeated the Spanish. Elected supreme director of Chile, he established a working governmental organization, but his reforms antagonized conservatives and he resigned.

Ohio State (pop., 2000: 11,353,000), U.S., N central region. It covers 41,222 sq mi (106,765 sq km); its capital is COLUMBUS. Lake ERIE is on its N boundary; the OHIO RIVER forms part of its SE and S boundary. Ohio was originally inhabited by prehistoric HOPEWELL mound builders, who disappeared around A.D. 400. The earliest European explorers found the area occupied by Miami, SHAWNEE, and other Indian tribes. The region was ceded to Britain by France after the FRENCH AND INDIAN WAR. In 1803 it became the 17th state, and the first state carved out of the Northwest Territory (see NORTHWEST ORDINANCES). During the 19th cent., it became one of the first great industrial states because of its location, transport facilities, and natural resources, including coal, petroleum, and natural gas. Although manufacturing is its most important economic activity, nearly two-thirds of the state is still farmland. It was the birthplace or residence of eight U.S. presidents—W. H. HARRISON, U. S. GRANT, R. B. HAYES, James GARFIELD, Benjamin HARRISON, William MCKINLEY, W. H. TAFT, and W. G. HARDING. Its major cities include COLUMBUS, CLEVELAND, CINCINNATI, TOLEDO, AKRON, and DAYTON.

Ohio River Major river, E central U.S. Formed by the ALLEGHENY and MONONGAHELA rivers, it flows northwest out of Pennsylvania, and west and southwest to shape the state boundaries of Ohio–West Virginia, Ohio–Kentucky, Indiana–Kentucky, and Illinois–Kentucky. After 975 mi (1,569 km), it empties into the MISSISSIPPI RIVER at Cairo, Ill. It has supported commerce since the earliest settlements, and its strategic importance was recognized by the 1750s.

Ohio State University, The State university system consisting of a main campus in Columbus and five branch locations. It was established in 1870 as a land-grant institution. The main campus is a comprehensive research institution, with a transportation research center, freshwater laboratory, supercomputer center, and polar research center. The Columbus campus has the highest enrollment in the U.S., around 48,000.

Ohm's law Relationship between the potential difference (voltage), ELECTRIC CURRENT, and RESISTANCE in an electric CIRCUIT. In 1827 Georg Ohm (1789–1854) discovered that at constant temperature, the current I in a circuit is directly proportional to the potential difference V, and inversely proportional to the resistance R, or $I = V/R$. Resistance is generally measured in ohms (Ω). In an ALTERNATING-CURRENT circuit, when the combination of resistance and reactance, called impedance Z, is constant, Ohm's law is applicable and $V/I = Z$.

oil Any greasy substance liquid at room temperature and insoluble in water. It may be a fixed (nonvolatile) oil, an ESSENTIAL OIL, or a mineral oil (see PETROLEUM). Fixed oils and (animal) FATS are both ESTERS of GLYCEROL and FATTY ACIDS. These oils have a variety of industrial and food uses. Linseed, tung, and other drying oils are used in paints and varnishes. When exposed to air they absorb oxygen and polymerize (see POLYMERIZATION), forming a tough coating. Some specialty oils and oil derivatives are also used in leather dressing and textile manufacture.

oil-drop experiment See MILLIKAN OIL-DROP EXPERIMENT

oil painting Painting in oil colors, a medium consisting of pigments suspended in drying oils. Oil paint enables both fusion of tones and crisp effects, and is unsurpassed for textural variation. It is applied with brushes or a thin palette knife, usually onto a stretched linen canvas. Finished oil paintings are often coated with varnish. Oil as a painting medium is recorded as early as the 11th cent., though the practice of easel painting with oil colors stems directly from 15th-cent. TEMPERA PAINTING. In the 16th cent., oil color emerged as the basic painting material in Venice; it has since been the most widespread medium for easel paintings.

oil shale Any fine-grained SEDIMENTARY ROCK that contains solid organic matter (kerogen) and yields significant quantities of SHALE OIL. Because the present methods of mining and refining it are expensive, damage the land, pollute the water, and produce carcinogenic wastes, oil shale will probably not be exploited on a wide scale until other petroleum resources have been nearly depleted. Estonia, China, and Brazil produce limited quantities, and the U.S. government operates an experimental plant in Colorado.

Oise River \\'wäz\\ River, N France. Formed by two streams, one rising in Belgium and the other in France, it flows southwest into the SEINE, and is 188 mi (302 km) long. It is a link in the canal system between the Seine and the canals of N France. Several battles of World War I were fought nearby.

Ojibwa \\ō-'jib-wä\\ or **Chippewa** \\'chi-pə-,wò\\ N American Indian people who formerly inhabited a region north of the Great Lakes but who during the 17th–18th cent. moved west to what is now N Minnesota. They hunted and fished in migratory bands, grew corn, and collected wild rice. The Midewiwin, or Grand Medicine Society, was the major Ojibwa religious organization. The Ojibwa are one of the largest Native American groups in N. America today, numbering about 50,000 in the U.S. and over 100,000 in Canada.

Ojukwu \\ō-'jùk-wü\\, **Odumegwu** (b.1933) Governor of the Eastern Region of Nigeria (1966–67) and head of the secessionist state of BIAFRA (1967–70). An IGBO, the Oxford-educated Ojukwu was appointed head of the traditional Igbo homelands in the east following the Igbo overthrow of Nigeria's civilian government. After opposition HAUSA and YORUBA leaders staged a successful countercoup, secessionist pressures led him to declare the Eastern Region independent in 1967. Following the Biafra conflict he fled, but returned to Nigeria in 1982.

okapi \\ō-'kä-pē\\ RUMINANT species (*Okapia johnstoni*) of the GIRAFFE family that lives in Congo rain forests. Its neck and legs are proportionately shorter than the giraffe's, and females, which are larger than males, stand about 5 ft (1.5 m) at the shoulder. The upper legs are black-and-white-striped, and the lower legs are white. The male's short horns are largely covered with skin.

Oka River \\ō-'kä\\ River, central Russia. The largest right-bank tributary of the VOLGA RIVER, it flows 932 mi (1,500 km) north to Kaluga, then east to join the Volga at NIZHNIY NOVGOROD. It is an

Okapi (*Okapia johnstoni*)

important trade artery for lumber and grain.

Okavango River \\,ō-kä-'väŋ-gō\\ *in Angola* **Cubango River** River, SW central Africa. Rising in central Angola, it forms a section of the boundary between Angola and Namibia, and empties into the Okavango Swamp in N Botswana, after a course of about 1,000 mi (1,600 km). A major problem for area residents is control of the TSETSE FLY. The Moremi Wildlife Reserve in the NE corner of the swamp teems with wildlife.

Okeechobee \\,ō-kə-'chō-bē\\, **Lake** Lake, S central Florida. The largest lake in the S U.S., at 730 sq mi (1,890 sq km), it

drains to the sea through the EVERGLADES. The source of drinking water for six million people, it has fallen significantly and pollution has greatly increased.

O'Keeffe, Georgia (1887–1986) U.S. painter. Born in Sun Prairie, Wis., she studied art in Chicago and New York, where she met and married the photographer Alfred STIEGLITZ. By the early 1920s, her highly individualistic painting style had emerged, as typified by such works as *Black Iris* (1926). Her mysteriously suggestive images of bones and flowers set against a perspectiveless space have inspired a variety of erotic, psychological, and symbolic interpretations. Her later works celebrate the clear skies and desert landscapes of New Mexico, where she moved after her husband's death in 1946. She is regarded by critics as one of the most original and important American artists, and her works are highly popular among the general public.

Okefenokee Swamp \\,ō-kə-fə-'nō-kē\\ Swamp and wildlife refuge, SE Georgia and NE Florida. Located about 50 mi (80 km) inland from the Atlantic coast, it has an area of more than 600 sq mi (1,550 sq km). It has diverse and abundant wildlife. Exotic flowers, such as rare orchids, abound. In 1937 a large area of the swamp, almost all in Georgia, was made the Okefenokee National Wildlife Refuge.

Okhotsk \\ə-'ḳótsk\\, **Sea of** Arm of the NW Pacific Ocean. Bounded by the Siberian coast, the KAMCHATKA Peninsula, and the KURIL ISLANDS, it covers 611,000 sq mi (1.58 million sq km). It connects the ports of the Russian Far East. In winter ice floes impede navigation, and dense fog is a hindrance in summer.

Okinawa \\,ō-kē-'nä-wä\\ Island of Japan, the largest island in the RYUKYU archipelago. It is about 70 mi (112 km) long and 7 mi (11 km) wide. It was the site of severe fighting in WORLD WAR II. In April 1945 U.S. troops made an amphibious landing on the heavily defended island. In a three-month long campaign, the Japanese lost 94,000 soldiers and the U.S. 12,500 before U.S. forces gained control. In 1972 the U. S. returned Okinawa to Japan, though U.S. military installations remained.

Oklahoma State (pop., 2000: 3,450,000), U.S., SW central region. It covers 69,956 sq mi (181,186 sq km); its capital is OKLAHOMA CITY. The RED RIVER forms its S boundary; the ARKANSAS RIVER flows across NE Oklahoma. Its highest point is Black Mesa (4,973 ft, or 1,516 m), located in the Panhandle. Evidence of inhabitation by the CLOVIS and FOLSOM COMPLEX cultures, 15,000–10,000 years ago, has been found. In more modern times, until the expedition of F. V. de CORONADO in 1541, the area was home to representatives of at least three major Indian language groups. Spanish control of the area lasted until 1800, when it passed to the French. In 1803 the area became part of the U.S. with the LOUISIANA PURCHASE. In 1828 the U.S. Congress reserved Oklahoma for settlement by Indians, and it became known as INDIAN TERRITORY. In 1890 the W part was organized as Oklahoma Territory. The two were merged and admitted to the union as the 46th state in 1907. Cattle raising and farming are the mainstays of the economy. Mineral products include natural gas, petroleum, coal, and stone. The state's heritage is reflected in Indian and cowboy museums. A barge system links the state's second major city, TULSA, to the Gulf of Mexico.

Oklahoma City City (pop., 2000: 506,000), capital of Oklahoma. Settled during the Oklahoma land rush in 1889, it became the state capital in 1910. It expanded rapidly after the discovery of petroleum (1928). The largest city in the state, it is the chief marketing and processing point for the livestock industry. It is home to the National Cowboy Hall of Fame, Myriad Gardens, and an annual rodeo competition. In 1995 the Murrah Federal Building was bombed by Timothy MCVEIGH, killing 168 people and injuring 500.

okra Herbaceous, hairy, annual plant (*Hibiscus,* or *Abelmoschus, esculentus*) of the MALLOW FAMILY, grown for its edible, gummy, unripe fruit. Okra leaves are heart-shaped; flowers are yellow with a crimson center. The fruit or pod is a tapering, 10-angled capsule, 4–10 in. (10–25 cm) long. Because of its large amount of mucilage, okra is used as a broth and soup thickener. In some countries the seeds are used as a substitute for coffee.

Olaf I Tryggvason \ˈō-läf...ˈtrēg-və-sȯn\ (964?-c.1000) Viking king of Norway (995-c.1000). The son of a Norwegian chieftain, he joined Viking attacks on England in 991 and 994. He was accepted as king on the death of Haakon the Great in 995. Olaf imposed Christianity on the Norwegian coast but had little influence in the interior. His missionaries included LEIF ERIKSSON THE LUCKY. He was killed in the Battle of Svolder, celebrated in medieval Scandinavian poetry.

Olaf II Haraldsson \ˈhä-räl-sȯn\ or **St. Olaf** (c.995-1030) King of Norway (1016-28). A Viking warrior, he fought in England, then returned to Norway after his conversion to Christianity and gained control over the country by 1016. Olaf sent out missionaries throughout his realm, and his religious code (1024) established the Church of Norway. Driven out of Norway by CANUTE THE GREAT (1028), he was killed trying to reconquer the country two years later. He became a national hero and the patron saint of Norway.

Old Church Slavic language Oldest attested SLAVIC LANGUAGE, known from 10th- or 11th-cent. manuscripts mostly written in an ancestor of the CYRILLIC ALPHABET). The Old Church Slavic (or Old Church Slavonic) documents, all translations from Christian ecclesiastical texts, resulted from the mission to the Moravian Slavs of Sts. CYRIL AND METHODIUS. The influence of the vernacular languages in Serbia, Bulgaria-Macedonia, Ukraine, and Russia soon led to regional variations in Church Slavic. Church Slavic remained a literary language of EASTERN ORTHODOXY into modern times and is still the liturgical language of the Slavic EASTERN RITE CHURCH.

Oldenbarnevelt \ˌōl-dən-ˈbär-nə-vəlt\, **Johan van** (1547-1619) Dutch statesman and a founding father of Dutch independence. In 1579 he helped WILLIAM I negotiate the Union of Utrecht, which founded the Dutch Republic. Appointed "great pensionary" of Holland, he mobilized Dutch resources for the military goals of MAURICE OF NASSAU. As foreign secretary of the Union's seven provinces, he negotiated a triple alliance with France and England against Spain (1596). He later concluded a truce with Spain (1609) reaffirming Holland's dominant role in the republic. In 1617 he sided

Johan van Oldenbarnevelt
Painting by M. J. van Mierevelt

with the moderate Arminians in religious strife against the stricter Calvinists and Prince Maurice; convicted of religious subversion, he was beheaded.

Oldenburg Former German state, since 1946 part of Lower SAXONY, Germany. It was held by the counts of Oldenburg from around 1100 until 1667, when it passed to Denmark. In the late 18th cent. it was ruled by the bishop of Lübeck. It became a grand duchy in the early 19th cent. It joined the German empire in 1871. Its last grand duke abdicated in 1918. The 17th-cent. grand-ducal palace in the city of Oldenburg (pop., 1998 est.: 153,000) is now a state museum of art and culture.

Oldenburg, Claes (Thure) (b.1929) Swedish-U.S. POP ART sculptor. The son of a consular official, he spent part of his early life in the U.S. and graduated from Yale Univ. After art studies, he moved to New York in 1956. Like other practitioners of Pop art, he chose banal subjects from consumer culture, but for "soft sculptures" such as *Giant Clothespin* (1976) and *Giant Soft Shuttlecock* (1995) he chose subjects with close human associations, and his frequent use of soft, yielding vinyl gave the objects human, often sexual overtones.

Old English or **Anglo-Saxon** Language spoken and written in England before A.D. 1100. It belongs to the Anglo-Frisian group of W. GERMANIC LANGUAGES. Most extant Old English writings are in the W. Saxon dialect. The great epic poem of Old English is *Beowulf*; the first period of extensive literary activity occurred in the 9th cent. Old English had three genders (masculine, feminine, neuter) for nouns and adjectives; nouns, pronouns, and adjectives were also inflected for case. Old English had a greater proportion of irregular verbs than does Modern English, and its vocabulary was more heavily Germanic. See also ENGLISH LANGUAGE.

Old English sheepdog Shaggy WORKING DOG developed in early-18th-cent. England and used primarily to drive sheep and cattle to market. It has a shuffling, bearlike gait. It stands 21-26 in. (53-66 cm) and weighs over 55 lbs (25 kg). Its long, dense, weather-resistant coat covers the eyes but does not obscure vision. The tail is usually removed soon after birth.

Old Ironsides See USS CONSTITUTION

Oldowan industry \ˈäl-də-wən\ STONE-TOOL INDUSTRY of the early PALEOLITHIC PERIOD (beginning c.2.5 million years ago) characterized by crudely worked pebble tools made of quartz, quartzite, or basalt and chipped in two directions to form simple, rough implements for chopping, scraping, or cutting. The industry is associated with early HOMINIDS and has been found at OLDUVAI GORGE (from which its name derives), Lake Turkana (see LAKE TURKANA REMAINS), and the Afar region of Ethiopia. Oldowan tools were made for nearly 1.5 million years before the emergence of the Acheulian industry about 1 million years ago.

Old Testament Sacred scriptures of JUDAISM and, with the NEW TESTAMENT, of CHRISTIANITY. Written almost entirely in Hebrew between 1200 and 100 B.C., the Old Testament (or Hebrew Bible) is an account of God's dealings with the Hebrews as his chosen people. In the Hebrew Bible, the first six books tell how the Israelites became a people and settled in the Promised Land, the following seven describe the development of Israel's monarchy and the messages of the prophets, and the last 11 contain poetry, theology, and some additional historical works. Christians divided some of the original Hebrew books into two or more parts. The content of the Old Testament varies according to religious tradition, the Jewish, Roman Catholic, and Protestant canons all differing as to which books they include. See also APOCRYPHA, BIBLE.

Olduvai Gorge \ˈōl-də-ˌwä, ˈōl-də-ˌvī\ Archaeological site in the E Serengeti Plains, N Tanzania. It is a steep-sided ravine about 30 mi (50 km) long and 300 ft (90 m) deep. Deposits exposed in the sides of the gorge cover a time span from about 2.1 million to 15,000 years ago and have yielded the remains of more than 50 HOMINIDS as well as the most complete sequence of STONE-TOOL INDUSTRIES. The site first came to public notice when Louis and Mary Leakey (see LEAKEY FAMILY), after nearly 30 years of work, uncovered the remains of the first australopithecine (see *AUSTRALOPITHECUS*) found outside S Africa. See also OLDOWAN INDUSTRY.

Old Vic London theater company. The company's theater opened in 1818 as the Royal Coburg; renamed the Royal Victoria in 1833, it became popularly known as the Old Vic. Under Lilian BAYLIS it began a regular Shakespeare season in 1914. It was later noted for its memorable productions of classics with such actors as John GIELGUD, Laurence OLIVIER, and Ralph RICHARDSON. Dissolved in 1963, it formed the nucleus of the new National Theatre, which performed at the Old Vic theater until moving to a new building in 1976.

Old World monkey Any of certain anthropoid PRIMATES of Africa and Asia, also called catarrhines. Catarrhines are generally distinguished from NEW WORLD MONKEYS (platyrrhines) in having a narrow nose, narrow septum, close-set nostrils directed forward or down, two premolars in each half of each jaw, a nonprehensile tail (if any), and hard patches of naked skin (ischial callosities) on the buttocks. They include the families Cercopithecidae (monkeys with cheek pouches: guenons, BABOONS, and others) and Colobidae (leaf monkeys), but may also include the Hylobatidae (GIBBONS), Pongidae (APES), and Hominidae (human beings). See also COLOBUS MONKEY, PROBOSCIS MONKEY.

oleander \ˈō-lē-ˌan-dər\ Any of the ornamental evergreen shrubs of the genus *Nerium* (DOGBANE FAMILY), which have poisonous milky juice. Numerous varieties of flower color in the common oleander, or rosebay (*N. oleander*), have been introduced from greenhouse culture and are grown outdoors in warmer climates. All parts of the plant are very toxic if eaten, and contact with them may cause skin irritation.

Olga, St. (c.890–969) Princess of Kiev. She served as regent of Kiev (945–64) after the assassination of her husband Igor I (877?–945); she avenged his death by having his murderers scalded to death. Probably baptized (c.957) at Constantinople, she became the first member of the ruling family of Kiev to adopt Christianity. She was canonized as the first Russian saint of the Orthodox Church.

oligarchy \'ä-li-ˌgär-kē, 'ō-li-ˌgär-kē\ Rule by the few, often seen as having self-serving ends. Aristotle used the term pejoratively for unjust rule by bad men. Most classic oligarchies have resulted when governing elites were recruited exclusively from a ruling class, which tends to exercise power in its own interest. The term is often avoided today because "few" fails to describe the ruling group.

Oligocene epoch \'ä-li-gō-ˌsēn\ Major division of the TERTIARY PERIOD, 34–24 million years ago. The term (from the Greek for "few recent forms") refers to the small number of modern animals that originated during this epoch. Oligocene climates appear to have been temperate, and many regions were nearly tropical. Grasslands expanded, and forested regions dwindled. See table at GEOLOGIC TIME.

oligopoly \ˌäl-ə-'gä-pə-lē\ Market situation in which producers are so few that the actions of any of them affect pricing and competition. A cut in price by one may lead to an equal reduction by the others, with the result that each firm will retain about the same market share but with a lower profit margin. Competition thus occurs mainly in advertising and product differentiation. Oligopolies in the U.S. include the steel, aluminum, and automobile industries. See also CARTEL, MONOPOLY.

olive Subtropical, broad-leaved, evergreen tree *(Olea europaea)* and its edible fruit. The edible olive may have been domesticated 10,000 years ago, and it was used by the ancient Greeks and Romans, after which olive growing spread to all the Mediterranean countries. Today olives are grown primarily for olive oil, which is valued for its distinctive taste and fragrance and its healthful properties. Fresh olives must be treated to neutralize their extreme bitterness before they can be eaten. The olive family (Oleaceae) comprises about 900 species in 24 genera of woody plants. They grow worldwide except in the Arctic, as evergreens in tropical and warm temperate climes and as deciduous trees in colder zones. ASH trees yield HARDWOOD timber; horticultural favorites include LILACS, JASMINES, privets, and FORSYTHIA. Many members of the family are cultivated for their beautiful and fragrant flowers.

Oliver, King (*orig.* Joseph) (1885–1938) U.S. jazz cornetist and bandleader. Oliver grew up in New Orleans and established himself as the city's preeminent cornetist, coleading a band with trombonist Kid Ory before moving to Chicago in 1918. In 1922, Oliver hired his New Orleans protégé Louis ARMSTRONG to join him in Chicago in his Creole Jazz Band. Their recordings together are jazz classics.

Olives, Mount of Limestone ridge, east of JERUSALEM. Frequently mentioned in the BIBLE, it is holy both in Judaism and in Christianity. Its slopes have been the most sacred burial ground in Judaism for centuries. The peak generally regarded as the Mount of Olives is 2,652 ft (808 m) high. Nearby is the traditional site of the Garden of GETHSEMANE.

Olivier \ə-'li-vē-ˌā\, **Laurence (Kerr)** *later* **Baron Olivier (of Brighton)** (1907–1989) British actor and director. He began his professional career in 1926 and joined the OLD VIC company in 1937, playing many major Shakespearean roles. He codirected the Old Vic 1944–50, and he acted in some of its greatest productions, including *Richard III, Henry IV,* and *Oedipus Rex.* From 1950 he directed and

Laurence Olivier as Edgar in *The Dance of Death,* 1967

acted under his own management; his notable productions included *Antony and Cleopatra* (1957). He was the founding director of the National Theatre (1962–73). In 1970 he was created a life peer, the first actor ever to be so honored. His many films included *Wuthering Heights* (1939), *Rebecca* (1940), *Henry V* (1944), *Hamlet* (1948, Academy Award), *Richard III* (1955), *The Entertainer* (1960), *Othello* (1965), and *Sleuth* (1972).

olivine \'ä-lə-ˌvēn\ Any member of a group of common magnesium and iron silicate minerals. Olivines occur in many IGNEOUS ROCKS and are a major constituent of the earth's upper MANTLE. Olivine forms yellow to greenish yellow crystals and is sometimes used in making bricks. Transparent green olivine is called PERIDOT.

Olmec \'äl-ˌmek\ First elaborate pre-Columbian culture of Mesoamerica. The Olmec lived in the lowlands of S Mexico's Gulf Coast. Through trade their cultural influence spread north to the Valley of Mexico and south to Central America; later native religions and art throughout Mesoamerica have Olmec roots. The site of San Lorenzo, which dates to about 1150 B.C., is remarkable for colossal stone sculptures of human heads. The dominant motif in Olmec art is the figure of a god that is a hybrid of a jaguar and a human infant.

Olmsted, Frederick Law (1822–1903) U.S. landscape architect. Born in Hartford, Conn., he traveled in the South and won fame for several books describing its slaveholding culture. Profoundly impressed with English landscaping, he wrote *Walks and Talks of an American Farmer in England* (1852). In 1857 he was hired as superintendent of New York's planned CENTRAL PARK. With the architect Calvert Vaux (1824–1895), he won a competition to design the park; the result was a nature-lover's paradise incorporating lawns, woods, ponds, and meandering paths. Other Olmsted parks include Prospect Park in Brooklyn, Niagara Falls, an extensive park system in Boston, and the World's Columbian Exposition (later Jackson Park) in Chicago. In 1865 he founded the magazine *The Nation.* As chairman of the first Yosemite commission, he helped secure the area as a permanent public park.

Olympia Ancient sanctuary and site of the OLYMPIC GAMES, NW Peloponnese, S Greece. Located 10 mi (16 km) inland from the Ionian Sea, on the ALPHEUS RIVER, it held the primarily athletic contests in honor of ZEUS every four years, beginning in 776 B.C. In the temple of Zeus, built around 460 B.C., was the statue of Zeus by PHIDIAS, one of the SEVEN WONDERS OF THE WORLD.

Olympia City (pop., 2000: 42,000), capital of Washington state. It lies at the S end of PUGET SOUND. A city from 1859, it developed port facilities and a lumber-based economy, supplemented by oyster farming and other industries. Its harbor is the site of a large merchant reserve fleet. Located at the base of the Olympic Peninsula, it is the gateway to OLYMPIC NATIONAL PARK.

Olympic Games In ancient Greece, a Panhellenic festival held in OLYMPIA every fourth year and made up of contests

Sites of the Modern Olympic Games

Year	Summer	Winter	Year	Summer	Winter
1896	Athens	*	1960	Rome	Squaw Valley
1900	Paris	*	1964	Tokyo	Innsbruck
1904	St. Louis	*	1968	Mexico City	Grenoble
1908	London	*	1972	Munich	Sapporo
1912	Stockholm	*	1976	Montreal	Innsbruck
1916	†	*	1980	Moscow	Lake Placid
1920	Antwerp	*	1984	Los Angeles	Sarajevo
1924	Paris	Chamonix	1988	Seoul	Calgary
1928	Amsterdam	St. Moritz	1992	Barcelona	Albertville
1932	Los Angeles	Lake Placid	1994	‡	Lillehammer
1936	Berlin	Garmisch-Partenkirchen	1996	Atlanta	‡
			1998	‡	Nagano
1940	†	†	2000	Sydney	‡
1944	†	†	2002	‡	Salt Lake City
1948	London	St. Moritz	2004	Athens	‡
1952	Helsinki	Oslo	2006	‡	Turin
1956	Melbourne	Cortina	2008	Beijing	‡

†Games were not held during World Wars I and II.
‡After 1992 the Summer and Winter Games were held on a staggered two-year schedule.

of sports, music, and literature. Since 1896, the name has been used for a modified revival of the ancient games consisting of international athletic contests held at four-year intervals. The original Greek games included footraces, the discus and javelin throws, the long jump, boxing, wrestling, the pentathlon, and chariot races. After the subjugation of Greece by Rome, the games declined; they were finally abolished in A.D. 393. They were revived in the late 19th cent. through the efforts of the baron de COUBERTIN. The first Winter Games were held in 1924. The direction of the modern Olympic movement and the regulation of the games is vested in the International Olympic Committee. Until the 1970s the games adhered to a strict code of amateurism, but since that time professional players have also been allowed to participate.

Olympic Mountains Segment of the COAST RANGES, NW Washington. The mountains cross the Olympic Peninsula south of the Strait of JUAN DE FUCA within OLYMPIC NATIONAL PARK. The chief peaks are Mt. Olympus, at 7,965 ft (2,428 m), and Mt. Constance, at 7,743 ft (2,360 m). Some Douglas fir and Sitka spruce in its rain forests are nearly 300 ft (90 m) high and 8 ft (2.5 m) in diameter.

Olympic National Park Park, NW Washington. Established in 1938 to preserve the OLYMPIC MTNS. and their forests and wildlife, it covers 1,442 sq mi (3,735 sq km). There are more than 60 glaciers in the park. The W part includes rain forests; the E slopes feature lakes; and the ocean shore section contains scenic beaches and three Indian reservations.

Olympus, Mt. Mountain peak, NE Greece. At 9,570 ft (2,917 m), it is the highest mountain in Greece. It is near the Gulf of Salonika. The summit is snowcapped and often has cloud cover. In ancient Greece, it was regarded as the abode of the gods and the site of the throne of ZEUS.

Olynthus \ō-ˈlin-thəs\ Ancient Greek city, MACEDONIA, on the Chalcidice Peninsula, NE Greece. From the late 5th cent. B.C. until 348 B.C. it was the head of a strong confederacy known as the Chalcidian League. Excavations have unearthed the town plan and provided material for studying the relationship between Classical and Hellenistic Greek art.

om \ˈōm\ In HINDUISM and other Indian religions, a sacred syllable considered the greatest of all MANTRAS. The syllable om is composed of the three sounds *a-u-m* (in Sanskrit, the vowels *a* and *u* join to become *o*), which represent three important triads: earth, atmosphere, and heaven; the major Hindu gods, BRAHMA, VISHNU, and SHIVA; and the sacred Vedic scriptures, Rig, Yajur, and Sama (see VEDIC RELIGION). Thus om mystically embodies the essence of the universe.

Omaha \ˈō-mə-ˌhȯ, ˈō-mə-ˌhä\ City (pop., 2000: 390,000), E Nebraska, on the Missouri River, bordering Iowa. The city's name, meaning "upstream people," referred to the Omaha Indians. Omaha was founded in 1854. In 1863 it became the starting point for the UNION PACIFIC RAILROAD Co.'s first transcontinental railroad. The largest city in the state, it is a major livestock and grain market. It is home to the Univ. of Nebraska.

Oman \ō-ˈmän\ *officially* **Sultanate of Oman** *formerly* **Muscat and Oman** Nation, SE coast of the ARABIAN PENINSULA. Area: 119,500 sq mi (309,500 sq km). Population (2000): 2,416,000. Capital: MASQAT, or Muscat. The Omanis are predominantly Arab and tribal in organization. There are also many people from S.E. Asia and E. Africa working there. Language: Arabic (official), Baluchi. Religions: Islam (official), Hinduism. Currency: rial Omani. Oman is a hot, arid country with high humidity along the coasts. The Al-Hajar Mtns. parallel the Gulf of Oman coast, reaching a height of more than 10,000 ft (3,000 m). A broad expanse of gravel desert extends southwestward to cover three-fourths of the country. It has a developing mixed economy, with the production and export of petroleum as its largest sector. It is a monarchy, with two advisory councils; its head of state and government is the sultan. The land has been inhabited for at least 10,000 years. The Arab migration to Oman began in the 9th cent. B.C. Tribal warfare continued until the conversion to Islam in the 7th cent. A.D. It was ruled by Ibadi IMAMS until 1154, when a royal dynasty was established. The Portuguese controlled the coastal areas from

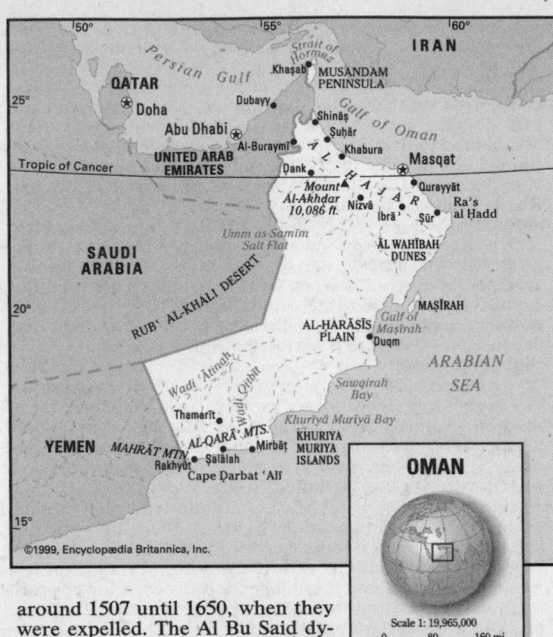

©1999, Encyclopædia Britannica, Inc.

OMAN

Scale 1: 19,965,000
0   80   160 mi
0   120   240 km

around 1507 until 1650, when they were expelled. The Al Bu Said dynasty, founded in the mid-18th cent., still rules Oman. The kingdom expanded into E Africa in the 18th–19th cent., and the capital was in ZANZIBAR. Oil was discovered in 1964. In 1970 the sultan was deposed by his son, who began a policy of modernization and joined the ARAB LEAGUE and the UNITED NATIONS. In the PERSIAN GULF WAR, Oman cooperated with the allied forces against Iraq. Continuing to expand its foreign relations, in 2000 it achieved membership in the World Trade Organization.

Oman, Gulf of NW arm of the ARABIAN SEA, between Oman and Iran. About 230 mi (370 km) wide and 340 mi (545 km) long, it connects with the PERSIAN GULF through the Strait of HORMUZ. It is crucial as a shipping route for the oil-producing area around the Persian Gulf.

Omar, Mosque of See DOME OF THE ROCK

Omar Khayyam \ˌō-ˌmär-ˌkī-ˈyäm\ *Persian* Abu ol-Fath Omar ebn Ebrahim ol-Khayyami (1048–1131) Persian poet, mathematician, and astronomer. He was renowned in his country and time for his scientific achievements. His verses attracted little attention until his *robaiyat* ("quatrains") were loosely translated into English by Edward FITZGERALD (1859). Many of the quatrains (each of which was intended as an independent poem) are of doubtful attribution; most scholars agree on the authenticity of about 50.

ombudsman \ˈäm-ˌbu̇dz-mən\ (Swedish: "representative") Representative assigned by a large organization or a government to investigate citizen complaints and suggest solutions. An ombudsman's office was established by the Swedish constitution of 1809. The idea soon spread to other Scandinavian countries, and later to other countries and some U.S. states. An ombudsman's responsibility is to serve as an independent and impartial arbiter in recommending how to satisfy the complainant or to explain why no action is necessary. Its use has spread to universities, corporations, municipalities, and institutions such as hospitals.

Omdurman \ˌäm-dər-ˈman\ City (pop., 1993: 1,267,000), E central Sudan. It is situated on the NILE RIVER opposite KHARTOUM. An insignificant village until the victory of al-Mahdi over the British in 1885, it grew rapidly after al-Mahdi and his successor, Abd Allah, made it their capital. It was captured by Anglo-Egyptian forces in 1898 but continued to develop into the cultural, religious, and commercial center of Sudan. Sites of interest include Abd Allah's house and the tomb of al-Mahdi.

omen Observed phenomenon that is interpreted as signifying good or bad fortune. The many omens that the ancients noted included lightning, cloud movements, the flights of birds, and the paths of sacred animals. Each type of omen was gauged according to specific meaningful characteristics (such as the kinds of bird or direction of flight).

omnivore \\'äm-nə-ˌvȯr\\ Animal that eats both plant and animal matter. Many animals generally considered CARNIVORES are actually omnivorous; for example, the red fox eats fruits and berries as well as mammals and birds. See also HERBIVORE.

Omsk \\'ȯmsk\\ City (pop., 1997 est.: 1,158,000), SW Russia, at the confluence of the Irtysh and Om rivers. Founded in 1716, it remained the headquarters of the Siberian COSSACKS until the late 19th cent. It grew with the building of the TRANS-SIBERIAN RAILROAD in the 1890s and the onset of World War II. In 1918–19 it was the seat of the anti-Bolshevik government of Adm. A. V. KOLCHAK. Pipelines from the Volga-Urals and W Siberian oil fields supply its petrochemical industry.

On See HELIOPOLIS

Onassis, Aristotle (Socrates) (1906–1975) Greek shipping magnate and international businessman. Born in Smyrna, Greece (now Turkey), he started a tobacco-importing business in Buenos Aires, and was made consul general after negotiating a trade agreement for Greece. A millionaire by age 25, he bought his first freight ships in 1932. By the 1950s his fleet was larger than the navies of many countries. During 1957–74 he owned Olympic Airways, the Greek national airline. He conducted a long affair with Maria CALLAS, and in 1968 married Jacqueline Kennedy (see J. K. ONASSIS).

Onassis, Jacqueline Kennedy *orig.* Jacqueline Bouvier (1929–1994) U.S. public figure. Born in Southampton, N.Y., in 1953 she married Sen. John F. KENNEDY, who became president in 1961. As first lady, she restored the WHITE HOUSE to its original Federal style. Her graciousness, culture, and beauty endeared her to the American public and foreign leaders. After her husband's assassination, she moved to New York with their children, Caroline (b.1957) and John, Jr. (1960–1999). In 1968 she married Aristotle ONASSIS. After his death in 1975, she returned to New York, where she became noted as a book editor.

onchocerciasis See RIVER BLINDNESS

oncogene \\'äŋ-kə-ˌjēn\\ GENE that can cause CANCER. It is a sequence of DNA that has been altered or mutated from its original form, the proto-oncogene (see MUTATION). Proto-oncogenes promote the specialization and division of normal cells. In humans, proto-oncogenes can become oncogenes in three ways: point mutation (alteration of one nucleotide base pair), translocation (in which a segment of the chromosome breaks off and attaches to another chromosome), or amplification (increase in the number of copies of the proto-oncogene). Oncogenes were first discovered in RETROVIRUSES and were later identified as cancer-causing agents in many animals. About 60 human oncogenes have been identified, including some that cause breast and lung cancer. See also Harold VARMUS.

Onega \\ə-'nye-gə\\, **Lake** Lake, NW Russia. Located between Lake LADOGA and the WHITE SEA, it is the second-largest lake in Europe. It has an area of 3,753 sq mi (9,720 sq km) and is 154 mi (248 km) long. It is connected with the BALTIC and White seas and with the VOLGA RIVER basin, enabling it to play an important part in international trade and transport.

Oneida \\ō-'nī-də\\ N. American Indian people of what is now central New York, one of the original five nations of the IROQUOIS CONFEDERACY. The Oneida are semisedentary and practiced corn agriculture. LONGHOUSES sheltered families related through maternal descent. They supported the colonist cause in the American Revolution. By the mid-19th cent., most Oneida had dispersed. They number about 5,000 today, with concentrations in Canada, Wisconsin, and central New York.

Oneida Community Utopian religious community founded by John Humphrey Noyes (1811–1886) in Oneida, N.Y., in 1847. Noyes and his disciples formed their first religious society in Putney, Vt., in 1841, but their practice of communal marriage aroused local hostility, and they were obliged to move to Oneida. The Oneida group flourished for 30 years; after it broke up in 1879, remaining members reorga-

nized it as a commercial enterprise, which is noted for the manufacture of silver plate.

O'Neill, Eugene (Gladstone) (1888–1953) U.S. playwright. Born in New York City, the son of a touring actor, he spent an itinerant youth as a seaman, heavy drinker, and derelict, then began writing plays while recovering from tuberculosis (1912). His early plays were produced by the PROVINCETOWN PLAYERS. *Beyond the Horizon* (1920) earned him his first Pulitzer Prize. Enormously prolific, he often wrote about tortured family relationships and the conflict between idealism and materialism. His many plays include *The Emperor Jones* (1921), *The Hairy Ape* (1922), *Anna Christie* (1922, Pulitzer Prize), *Desire Under the Elms* (1925), *The Great God Brown* (1926), *Strange Interlude* (1928, Pulitzer Prize), *Mourning Becomes Electra* (1931), *Ah, Wilderness!* (1933; his only comedy), *The Iceman Cometh* (1946), and the autobiographical *Long Day's Journey into Night* (produced 1956; Pulitzer Prize), considered his masterpiece. O'Neill was awarded the Nobel Prize in 1936, the first U.S. playwright so honored.

Onin War \\'ō-nin\\ (1467–77) Civil war in central Japan that destroyed the remnants of central governmental authority and led to 100 years of warfare. The war sprang from a shogunal succession dispute, with one powerful clan supporting the brother of the ruling SHOGUN and another supporting the shogun's infant son. It ended in stalemate, but clans across Japan became involved in hopes of increasing their territory. The nation was later reunified under Oda Nobunaga, TOYOTOMI HIDEYOSHI, and TOKUGAWA IEYASU.

onion Herbaceous biennial plant (*Allium cepa*) of the LILY FAMILY, probably native to SW Asia but now grown worldwide, and its edible bulb. Onions bear a cluster of small, greenish-white flowers on one or more leafless stalks. The leaf base swells to form the underground mature, edible onion. Onions are pungent and cause eye tearing when peeled or sliced because they contain a sulfur-rich volatile oil. Though low in standard nutrients, they are valued for their flavor. Closely related to GARLIC, onions have been claimed to cure colds, earaches, and laryngitis and have been used to treat animal bites, powder burns, and warts.

Onsager \\'ȯn-ˌsä-gər\\, **Lars** (1903–1976) Norwegian-U.S. chemist. His development of a general theory of irreversible chemical processes, described as the "fourth law of THERMODYNAMICS," gained him a 1968 Nobel Prize. He also applied the laws of thermodynamics to systems not in EQUILIBRIUM. His explanation of the movement of IONS in SOLUTION as related to TURBULENCE and fluid DENSITY had a major effect on the development of PHYSICAL CHEMISTRY.

Ontario Province (pop., 1999 est.: 11,561,000), the second-largest in Canada. It is situated between HUDSON and JAMES bays and the ST. LAWRENCE RIVER–Great Lakes chain; its capital is TORONTO. Before European settlement, the area was inhabited by IROQUOIS and Algonquian Indian tribes. In the 17th cent. it was visited by French explorers and missionaries. It passed to the British in 1763 after the FRENCH AND INDIAN WAR. It was the scene of many battles in the WAR OF 1812. Known as CANADA WEST 1841–67, in 1867 it became one of four provinces of the new Dominion of Canada. N Ontario has a rocky and rugged terrain with thick forests, bogs, lakes, and extensive mineral reserves. S Ontario is an important farming and industrial region and is the center of Canada's population and urban development. OTTAWA, the national capital, is also in Ontario.

Ontario, Lake Smallest and easternmost of the GREAT LAKES of N. America. Bounded by New York and Ontario, the lake is 193 mi (311 km) long; its greatest width is 53 mi (85 km). The NIAGARA RIVER is the lake's main feeder; it discharges into the ST. LAWRENCE RIVER. The Welland Canal and the Niagara River connect it to Lake ERIE to the southwest. It was visited by Samuel de CHAMPLAIN in 1615. Ports on the lake include TORONTO and HAMILTON, Ont., and ROCHESTER and Oswego, N.Y.

ontology Theory of being as such. Ontology is synonymous with METAPHYSICS as defined by ARISTOTLE, but metaphysics came to include such other studies as philosophical COSMOLOGY and rational psychology. In the 18th cent. Christian Wolff saw ontology as leading to necessary truths about the essences of beings. Immanuel KANT presented influential refutations of ontology, but it became important again in the 20th cent. among students of PHENOMENOLOGY and EXISTENTIALISM, particularly Martin HEIDEGGER.

onyx \'ä-niks\ Striped, semiprecious variety of the silica mineral AGATE with white and black alternating bands. Other varieties include carnelian onyx, with white and red bands, and sardonyx, with white and brown bands. Onyx is used in carved cameos and intaglios because its layers can be cut to show a color contrast. It is found worldwide, but chiefly in India and S. America.

Oort cloud Vast spherical cloud of small, icy bodies orbiting the sun at about 0.1 to one light-year away, probably the source of most long-period COMETS. In 1950 Dutch astronomer Jan Hendrik Oort (1900–1992), noting that no comet's orbit indicated an interstellar origin, proposed that the sun is surrounded by billions of objects, detectable only when they enter the inner solar system. The bodies composing the Oort cloud are believed to date from the formation of the solar system (see SOLAR NEBULA). Its inner region merges into the more disk-shaped KUIPER BELT.

opal Hydrated, noncrystalline silica mineral used extensively as a gemstone. Pure opal is colorless, but impurities generally give it various dull colors ranging from yellow and red, the most common, to black, the rarest and most valuable. Various forms are widely used as abrasives, insulation material, and ceramic ingredients. Opal is most abundant in volcanic rocks, especially in areas of hot-spring activity. The finest gem opals have been found in Australia.

Op art Mid-20th-cent. geometric abstract art that deals with optical illusion. Op (i.e., optical) art painters used repetitive forms such as parallel lines, checkerboard patterns, and concentric circles, and the juxtaposition of complementary colors to create the illusion of movement. Principal artists in the late 1950s and 1960s included Victor VASARELY, Bridget Riley (b.1931), and Larry Poons (b.1937).

OPEC See ORGANIZATION OF PETROLEUM EXPORTING COUNTRIES

open cluster *or* **galactic cluster** Any group of Population I (see POPULATIONS I AND II) stars with a common origin, held together by their gravity. Stars in open clusters are more scattered than those in GLOBULAR CLUSTERS. Known open clusters have about 10 to 1,000 or more stars (about half contain fewer than 100) and diameters of 5–75 light-years. The Milky Way galaxy has over 1,000, including the PLEIADES and the Hyades.

Open Door policy Statement of U.S. foreign policy toward China. Initiated by U.S. secretary of state John HAY (1899), the policy reaffirmed the principle that all nations should have equal access to Chinese ports open to trade. The U.S. sent notes to Britain, Germany, France, Italy, Japan, and Russia explaining the policy to prevent them from establishing separate spheres of influence in China. Their replies were evasive, but the U.S. considered them acceptances of the policy.

open-heart surgery Surgical procedure opening the HEART and exposing one or more of its chambers, most often to repair valve disease or correct congenital malformations. Invention of the heart-lung machine (see ARTIFICIAL HEART) made it possible. The first successful open-heart surgery was performed in the U.S. in 1953.

opera Musical drama made up of vocal pieces with orchestral accompaniment and interludes. Opera was invented around 1600 in an attempt by the Camerata, an academy of Florentine poets, musicians, and scholars, to imitate ancient Greek drama, which was known to have been largely sung or chanted, though no actual Greek music was known. Imitations of Greek pastoral poetry became the basis for early opera libretti. The first operas, by Jacopo Peri (*Dafne,* 1598; lost) and Giulio CACCINI (*Euridice,* 1600), consisted throughout of lightly accompanied melody imitating inflected speech. Claudio MONTEVERDI, the greatest early operatic figure, composed the first masterpiece, *Orfeo,* in 1607; RECITATIVE here begins to be clearly distinguished from ARIA, an achievement that would prove decisive for opera's future success. In France, the style of J.-B. LULLY would dominate French opera through the mid-18th cent. J.-P. RAMEAU, G. F. HANDEL, and C. W. von GLUCK were the most significant opera composers of the early 18th cent.; their works were surpassed by the brilliant operas of W. A. MOZART. In the early 19th cent., Gioacchino ROSSINI and Gaetano DONIZETTI dominated Italian opera. The later 19th cent. saw the great works of Giuseppe VERDI and Richard WAGNER; Richard STRAUSS and Giacomo PUCCINI wrote the most popular 20th-cent. operas.

operating system (OS) SOFTWARE that controls the operation of a COMPUTER, directs the input and output of data, keeps track of files, and controls the processing of computer PROGRAMS. It also serves as an interface between the computer and the user, and allocates computer resources to various functions. When several jobs reside in the computer simultaneously and share resources (multitasking), the OS allocates fixed amounts of CPU time and MEMORY in turn, or allows one job to read while another prints and still another performs computations. Through a process called time-sharing, a large computer can handle hundreds of users simultaneously. Modern computer operating systems are becoming increasingly machine-independent; such systems as UNIX are capable of running on different kinds of computers. Most personal computers run on Microsoft's Windows operating system. See also LINUX.

operations management See PRODUCTION MANAGEMENT

operetta Musical drama similar to OPERA, usually with a romantically sentimental plot and spoken dialogue. The modern tradition begins with Jacques OFFENBACH, whose 90 operettas inspired a Viennese tradition that began with the works of Franz von Suppé (1819–1895) and Johann STRAUSS. In Britain, many of the 14 comic operettas (1871–96) of W. S. GILBERT and Arthur SULLIVAN have been enduringly popular. In the U.S., the works of such immigrant composers as Victor HERBERT and Rudolf FRIML were widely popular in the early 20th cent. See also MUSICAL.

operon \'ä-pər-ˌän\ Genetic regulatory system of single-celled organisms (PROKARYOTES) and their viruses, in which GENES coding for functionally related proteins are clustered along the DNA, enabling their expression to be coordinated. By providing a means to produce proteins only when and where they are required, the operon allows the cell to conserve energy. A typical operon consists of a group of structural genes that code for enzymes involved in a metabolic pathway. A single unit of messenger RNA is transcribed from the operon and is then translated into separate proteins. Operons are controlled by various regulatory elements that respond to environmental cues.

ophthalmology \ˌäf-thəl-'mä-lə-jē\ Medical specialty dealing with the EYES. Ophthalmologists test visual function and examine the eye for faulty development, disease, injury, degeneration, aging, or refractive errors. They prescribe treatment for eye disease (including congenital defects) and lenses for refraction and perform surgery when needed. See also OPTOMETRY.

Ophüls \'ō-fᵫels\, **Max** *orig.* Max Oppenheimer (1902–1957) German film director. He gained renown with *Liebelei* (1932), then left Germany for France, where he made *The Tender Enemy* (1936). In Hollywood he directed *The Exile* (1947), *Letter from an Unknown Woman* (1948), and *The Reckless Moment* (1949). He returned to France to make *La ronde* (1950), *Le plaisir* (1952), and *Lola Montez* (1955), considered his masterpiece. His son, Marcel (b.1927), has worked in France making documentaries; *The Sorrow and the Pity* (1971), examining French conduct under German occupation, earned him international acclaim, as did *Hotel Terminus* (1988, Academy Award).

opium Organic compound, a NARCOTIC drug known since ancient Greek times, obtained from OPIUM POPPIES. Opium has legitimate medical uses, as the source of CODEINE and MORPHINE and their derivatives. It is also used illicitly, either raw or purified as alkaloids and their derivatives (including HEROIN). Opium ALKALOIDS of one type (e.g., morphine, codeine) act on the NERVOUS SYSTEM, mimicking the effects of ENDORPHINS; they are ANALGESIC, narcotic, and potentially addicting (see DRUG ADDICTION). Those of a second type, including papaverine and noscapine, relieve smooth muscle spasms and are not analgesic, narcotic, or addicting. Opium overdoses can cause death by depressing RESPIRATION.

opium poppy Flowering plant *(Papaver somniferum)* of the POPPY FAMILY, native to Turkey. OPIUM, MORPHINE, CODEINE, and HEROIN are all derived from the milky fluid in the unripe seed capsule. A common garden annual, the opium poppy bears wide (5 in., or 13 cm) blue-purple or white flowers on plants about 3–16 ft (1–5 m) tall, with lobed or toothed silver-green foliage. It is also grown for its tiny nonnarcotic ripe seeds, used in cooking and for bird-seed.

Opium Wars Two trading wars (1839–42, 1856–60), the first between China and Britain and the second between China and a British-French alliance. Historically, China believed that the West had nothing of interest to offer in trade, and required Western nations to pay for Chinese goods in hard currency. The British took to the illegal importation of opium, which the Chinese population was eager to buy. When China tried to stop the practice, hostilities broke out. Britain triumphed, and the resultant Treaty of NANJING was a blow to China. The second opium war resulted in further Chinese concessions. When China refused to sign the treaties, Beijing was captured and the emperor's summer palace burned. A deeper reason for the Opium Wars was mutual arrogance: China saw itself as the center of the world to which peripheral nations came humbly to trade; Britain and the West saw China as backward and therefore coercible.

Oporto See PORTO

opossum Any of about 66 species (family Didelphidae) of New World, mostly arboreal, nocturnal MARSUPIALS. Opossums have changed little in millions of years. The N. American species, the stout-bodied common, or Virginia, opossum *(Didelphis marsupialis),* grows to 40 in. (100 cm) long. It is largely white; with its long, naked, prehensile tail, it resembles a large rat. Up to 25 grublike newborns compete for the 13 nipples in the pouch, where the survivors spend four or five weeks; they spend the following eight to nine weeks clinging to the mother's back. The common opossum may feign death ("play possum") if surprised. It eats small animals, insects, and fruit.

Oppenheimer, J(ulius) Robert (1904–1967) U.S. theoretical physicist. Born in New York City, he taught at Caltech 1929–47. His research focused on energy processes of subatomic particles, and he trained a generation of American physicists. In World War II he was named director of the Army's atomic-bomb project, later known as the MANHATTAN PROJECT, and set up its laboratory in LOS ALAMOS, N.M. He directed the Institute for Advanced Study in Princeton 1947–66. He strongly opposed the development of the hydrogen bomb, and in 1953 he was suspended from secret nuclear research as an alleged communist; the case, which pitted him against Edward TELLER, became a worldwide cause célèbre. In 1963 he was reinstated and honored with the Enrico Fermi Award.

optical activity Ability of a substance to rotate the plane of POLARIZATION of a beam of LIGHT passed through it, either as CRYSTALS or in SOLUTION. Louis PASTEUR was the first to recognize that molecules with optical activity are stereoisomers (see ISOMERISM). Optical ISOMERS occur in mirror-image pairs whose physical and chemical properties are the same except that they rotate the plane of polarized light in opposite directions and interact differently with other stereoisomers.

optical character recognition See OCR

optical scanner See optical SCANNER

optics Science concerned with the production and propagation of LIGHT, the changes it undergoes and produces, and closely related phenomena. Physical optics deals with the nature and properties of light; geometric optics deals with the formation of images by mirrors, LENSES, and other devices. Optical data processing involves manipulation of the information content of an image formed by coherent (one-wavelength) optical systems. See also BINOCULARS, CAMERA, CONTACT LENS, FIBER OPTICS, LASER, MICROSCOPE, TELESCOPE.

Optimates and Populares \ˌäp-ti-ˈmä-tēz...ˌpäp-yə-ˈlar-ēz\ Ideological positions in ancient Rome that became defined in the early 1st cent. B.C. The Optimates (Latin: "Best Ones," "Aristocrats") promoted the dominance of the Sen-ate and the proper balance of the constitution; the Populares ("Demagogues," "Populists") defended the powers of the popular assemblies and the office of tribune and advocated such measures as land distribution and debt cancellation. Their polarization led to civil wars—notably between Julius CAESAR and POMPEY and between Octavian (AUGUSTUS) and Mark ANTONY—and to the fall of the republic with Augustus' accession.

optimization Field of applied mathematics whose principles and methods are used to solve quantitative problems in disciplines including physics, biology, engineering, and economics. Questions of maximizing or minimizing FUNCTIONS arising in the various disciplines can be solved using the same mathematical tools (see MAXIMUM, MINIMUM). Typically, the goal is to find the values of controllable factors determining the behavior of a system (e.g., a physical production process, an investment scheme) that maximize productivity or minimize waste. The simplest problems may be solved with DIFFERENTIAL CALCULUS.

optometry \äp-ˈtä-mə-trē\ Profession concerned with examining the EYES for defects or faults of refraction. Optometrists prescribe optical aids (e.g., eyeglasses, CONTACT LENSES), and examine the eyes for disorders such as GLAUCOMA and CATARACTS. They generally do not prescribe drugs or perform surgery. See also OPHTHALMOLOGY.

oracle Source of a divine communication delivered in response to a petitioner's request. Ancient Greece and Rome had many oracles. The most famous was that of APOLLO at DELPHI, where the medium was a woman over 50 called the Pythia. After bathing in the Castalian spring, she apparently would descend into a basement cell, mount a sacred tripod, and chew the leaves of the laurel, sacred to Apollo. Her often ambiguous utterances were interpreted by priests. Other oracles, including those of OLYMPIA (Zeus) and EPIDAURUS (ASCLEPIUS), were consulted through other methods; the oracle of ZEUS at Dodona spoke through the whispering of the leaves of a sacred oak. At some shrines, the inquirer would sleep in the holy precinct and receive an answer in a dream.

oral tradition Cultural information passed on from one generation to the next by word of mouth. The forms of oral tradition include POETRY (often chanted or sung), folktales, and PROVERBS as well as magical spells, religious instruction, and recollections of the past. Music and rhyme commonly serve as both entertainment and aids to memory. A culture's epic poems often began as oral tradition and were later written down. In oral cultures, oral tradition is the only means of communicating knowledge. The rise of print and electronic media has led to the decline of oral tradition, but it survives among old people and some minority groups as well as among children, whose games and songs are transmitted orally from generation to generation.

Oran \ȯ-ˈrän\ City (pop., 1998: 692,000), NW Algeria. Situated on the Mediterranean Sea, it is about midway between TANGIER, Morocco, and ALGIERS. With the adjacent Mers el-Kebir, it is the country's second-largest port. Founded in the 10th cent. by Andalusians, it was held by the Spanish until 1708, when it fell to the Turks. It was devastated by a 1790 earthquake. In 1831 it was occupied by the French and became a modern port and naval base. Most of its European inhabitants left after Algerian independence in 1962. Old and new city sections are built on terraces above a waterfront.

orange Any of several species of small trees or shrubs in the genus *Citrus* of the RUE FAMILY (or citrus), grown in tropical and subtropical regions, and their round fruits, with leathery, oily rinds and edible, juicy inner flesh rich in vitamin C. Key commercial species include the China (or sweet, or common) orange; the mandarin orange (including TANGERINES); and seedless navel oranges. The tree has broad, glossy, medium-sized evergreen leaves and very fragrant flowers. It bears fruit abundantly for 50–80 years. By-products include essential oils, pectin, candied peel, orange marmalade, and stock feed.

Orange Free State Former province, central Republic of S. Africa. Before the arrival of the Europeans, the area was the home of BANTU-speaking peoples. AFRIKANERS came in large part during the GREAT TREK of the 1830s. The independent Orange Free State was established in 1854. In 1910 it became the Orange Free State province of the Union of S. Africa. After the elections of 1994, it became the province of Free State. Blacks make up about 80% of the population. The province's capital is BLOEMFONTEIN.

Orange-Nassau, House of Princely dynasty and royal family of the Netherlands. The title began with WILLIAM I the Silent, prince of Orange-Nassau, who was stadtholder (viceroy) of the Netherlands, as were his descendants until 1795. In 1815 William VI became WILLIAM I, king of the Netherlands. The male line of the dynasty continued until 1890, when WILHELMINA, daughter of William III, became queen. In 1908 she decreed that her descendants should be styled princes and princesses of Orange-Nassau.

Orange River River, S Africa. It rises in the Lesotho Highlands as the Sinqu River and flows west as the Orange across S. Africa. It passes the S edge of the KALAHARI DESERT, and winds through the NAMIB DESERT before draining into the Atlantic Ocean. It forms the border between S. Africa and Namibia. It is about 1,300 mi (2,100 km) long.

orangutan \ə-ˈraŋ-ə-ˌtaŋ\ *or* **orang** Species (*Pongo pygmaeus,* family Pongidae) of diurnal, mostly arboreal great APE, now found only in the lowland swamp forests of Borneo. The orangutan (Malaysian for "man of the forest") has a short thick body, long arms, short legs, and shaggy reddish hair. Males are about 4.5 ft (137 cm) tall and weigh about 185 lbs (85 kg); females are smaller. Orangutans are placid, deliberate, ingenious, and persistent. Orangutans use all four limbs to walk and climb. They eat mostly figs and other fruits. They sleep in trees on a platform built of interwoven branches. Adults

Orangutan *(Pongo pygmaeus)*

are solitary and live far apart. The mother carries and nurses the single young for almost three years. The orangutan is an endangered species.

Oranjestad \ō-ˈrän-yə-ˌstät\ Seaport and chief administrative town (pop., 1996 est.: 21,000), ARUBA, Netherlands Antilles. It is a free port and a petroleum processing and shipping center.

oratorio Large-scale sacred musical composition for solo voices, chorus, and orchestra. The term derives from the oratories, community prayer halls set up by St. Philip NERI in a COUNTER-REFORMATION attempt to provide locales for religious edification outside the church itself, and the oratorio remained a nonliturgical (and non-Latin) form for moral musical entertainment. The first oratorio was written in 1600 by Emilio de' Cavalieri (c.1550–1602), and the oratorio's development closely followed that of OPERA. Giacomo CARISSIMI produced an important body of Italian oratorios, and M.-A. CHARPENTIER transferred the oratorio to France. In Germany Heinrich SCHÜTZ anticipated the oratorio-like Passions of J. S. BACH. The most celebrated oratorio composer was G. F. HANDEL; his great English works include the incomparable *Messiah* (1742). Handel inspired F. J. HAYDN's great *Creation* (1798) and influenced the 19th-cent. oratorio, whose composers include Hector BERLIOZ, Felix MENDELSSOHN, and Franz LISZT.

orbital Mathematical expression, called a WAVE FUNCTION, that describes properties characteristic of no more than two ELECTRONS near an atomic NUCLEUS or molecule. An orbital can be considered a three-dimensional region in which there is a 95% probability of finding an electron. Atomic orbitals are designated by a combination of numerals and letters (e.g., 1*s*, 2*p*, 3*d*, 4*f*). The numerals are the principal QUANTUM number and are related to the atomic energy level and distance from the nucleus; the letters indicate the orbital's angular momentum and hence its shape. Molecular orbitals have geometries determined by the overlap of two or more atomic orbitals, and are designated by Greek symbols, e.g., σ and π.

orca See KILLER WHALE

Orcagna \ȯr-ˈkän-yä\, **Andrea** *orig.* Andrea di Cione (c.1315/20–1368) Florentine painter, sculptor, and architect. The leading member of a family of painters, he was the most prominent Florentine artist of the mid-14th cent. His altarpiece for the Strozzi Chapel in Florence's Santa Maria Novella (1354–57) shows his ability to unify the multiple panels of a polyptych. As a sculptor he is known for the tabernacle in the guild oratory of Or San Michele (1352–60), a decorative structure of great complexity. He was employed as architect on Florence's Duomo (cathedral) in 1357 and 1364–67.

orchestra Instrumental ensemble of varying size and composition. Today the term usually refers to the traditional large Western ensemble of bowed STRINGED INSTRUMENTS with BRASS, WOODWIND, and PERCUSSION INSTRUMENTS, with several players to each string part. The development of the early orchestra coincides with that of OPERA. The modern orchestra owes most to that of the mid-17th-cent. French court, which was dominated by 24 bowed strings but also often included woodwind instruments. Trumpets, horns, and timpani were often added in the early 18th cent. The 19th cent. saw a considerable expansion, particularly in the number and variety of wind and percussion instruments; some works called for well over 100 musicians. The symphony orchestra changed little in the 20th cent.

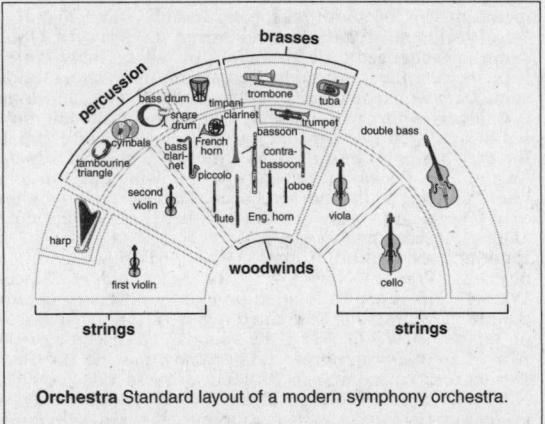

Orchestra Standard layout of a modern symphony orchestra.

orchestration Art and science of choosing which instruments to use for a given piece of music. Once entirely dependent on what was available or customary, composers began to explore the musical potential of instrumental combinations with the advent of the modern orchestra in the mid- to late 18th cent. The sections of the orchestra historically were separate ensembles: the stringed instruments for indoors, the woodwind instruments for outdoors, the horns for hunting, and trumpets and drums for battle or royal ceremony. The first great orchestration text was written by Hector BERLIOZ (1843).

orchid Any of the 15,000–35,000 species in 400–800 genera of nonwoody perennial plants that make up the family Orchidaceae. Orchids grow in most of the nonpolar world, especially in tropical regions. Hybrids with showy flowers for the commercial trade come from the genera *Cattleya, Cymbidium, Vanda,* and *Laelia.* Flowers vary widely in size, color, and shape, but all are bilaterally symmetrical and have three sepals. Most orchids photosynthesize, but some live on dead organic material or absorb food from a fungus living in their roots. VANILLA is extracted from the seedpod of the genus *Vanilla.*

ordeal In customary law, a test of guilt or innocence in which the accused undergoes dangerous or painful tests believed to be under supernatural control. Ordeals by fire or water are the most common. Burns suffered while passing through fire (as in Hindu custom) or rejection (i.e., being buoyed up) by a body of water (as in witch trials) would be regarded as proof of guilt. In ordeal by combat, as in the medieval DUEL, the victor is said to win not by his own strength but because supernatural powers have intervened on the side of the right.

order In CLASSICAL ARCHITECTURE, a style defined by its base, COLUMN, capital, and ENTABLATURE. There are five major orders: Doric, Ionic, and Corinthian (all developed in Greece), and Tuscan and Composite (developed in Rome). The capital is an order's most distinguishing characteristic. The Doric order is squat and simple. The Ionic, distinguished by its scrolls, resembles a capital I. The Corinthian capital is ornate, with carved acanthus leaves and scrolls. The Tuscan order is a simplified form of Doric; the Composite combines Ionic and Corinthian.

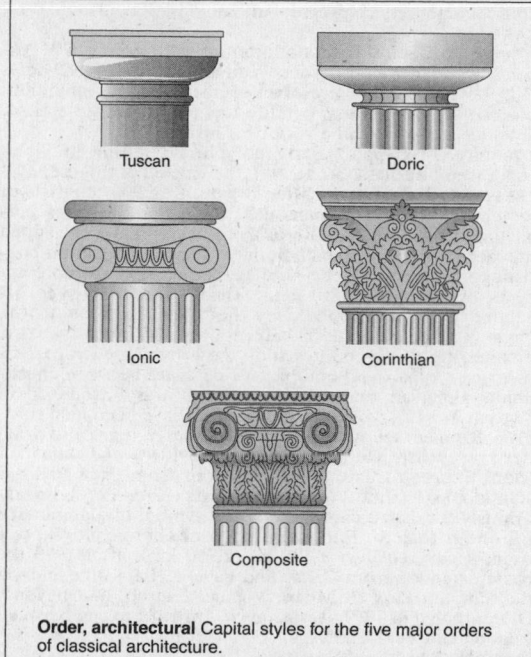

Order, architectural Capital styles for the five major orders of classical architecture.

Order of the Garter See Order of the GARTER
Ordovician period \ˌȯr-də-ˈvi-shən\ Interval of geologic time, 505–438 million years ago, in the PALEOZOIC ERA. Many of the landmasses were aligned in the tropics. Life was dominated by marine invertebrates, but some forms of land plants may have appeared during the middle of the period. Spores suggesting a tropical terrestrial environment have been found in rocks of that age. See table at GEOLOGIC TIME.

ore Aggregate of economically important MINERALS that is sufficiently rich to separate for a profit. Although more than 3,500 mineral species are known, only about 100 are considered ore minerals. The term originally applied only to metallic minerals but now includes such nonmetallic substances as SULFUR, FLUORITE, and BARITE. Ore is always mixed with unwanted rocks and minerals, known collectively as gangue. The ore and the gangue are mined together and then separated (see MINING), and the desired element is extracted.

oregano Flavorful dried leaves and flowering tops of any of various perennial herbs of the MINT family, particularly *Origanum vulgare*. Oregano is an essential ingredient of Mediterranean and Mexican cuisines. Native to the Mediterranean and W Asia, the herbs are now naturalized in parts of Mexico and the U.S.

Oregon State (pop., 2000: 3,421,000), U.S., NW region. It covers 97,073 sq mi (251,419 sq km); its capital is SALEM. The COLUMBIA RIVER forms its N boundary; the SNAKE RIVER is its upper E boundary. The CASCADES RANGE, with Mt. HOOD, is in W central Oregon. First sighted by Spanish explorers, it was visited by Francis DRAKE in 1579

and by James COOK in 1778. The area was inhabited by many American Indian peoples when in 1792 Capt. Robert Gray (1755–1806) explored the COLUMBIA RIVER, giving the U.S. a claim to the region. The river's mouth was reached by the LEWIS AND CLARK EXPEDITION in 1805. The first white settlement was founded at Astoria in 1811 by the fur trader J. J. ASTOR. Settlement of the area accelerated from around 1843 with mass migration over the OREGON TRAIL. It was part of the Oregon Territory and was admitted to the Union as the 33rd state in 1859. The state's economy is dependent on its forests, farms, and livestock. Salmon and shellfish are the bases of the fishing industry. Centers of population, arts, and education are PORTLAND, EUGENE, and Medford.

Oregon Question Dispute over ownership of the Pacific Northwest region of N. America. Spain, Russia, the U.S., and Britain all had claims to the region based on exploration or settlement. Spain vacated its claims in an 1819 treaty with the U.S. Russia abandoned its claims in 1824–25. The U.S. and Britain established a joint claim over the Oregon Country in 1818; a compromise Oregon Treaty (1846) drew the U.S.–Canada land boundary at 49°N.

Oregon Trail Major U.S. route to the Northwest in the 19th cent. It stretched about 2,000 mi (3,200 km), from Independence, Mo., to Oregon. First used by fur traders and missionaries, it was heavily used in the 1840s by travelers to Oregon, including settlers of the "great migration," led by Marcus WHITMAN. Of all W trails, it was in use for the longest period, particularly as a trail for eastward cattle and sheep drives.

Orestes \ȯ-ˈres-tēz\ In GREEK MYTHOLOGY, the son of AGAMEMNON and Clytemnestra. According to HOMER, Orestes was away when his father returned from TROY and was killed by Aegisthus, Clytemnestra's lover. On reaching manhood, Orestes avenged his father by killing Aegisthus and Clytemnestra. AESCHYLUS' *Oresteia* recounts the murder and the pursuit of Orestes by the FURIES for the crime of matricide. In EURIPIDES' *Iphigeneia in Tauris,* Orestes regains his father's kingdom.

Øresund \ˈœ-rə-ˌsən\ *English* **The Sound** Almost tideless strait between SJÆLLAND island, Denmark, and Sweden, connecting the KATTEGAT with the BALTIC SEA. It is one of the busiest sea lanes in the world, though ice sometimes impedes navigation. COPENHAGEN and Helsingør are ports on the Danish side, MALMÖ and Hälsingborg on the Swedish side.

Orff, Carl (1895–1982) German composer and educator. In the 1920s he grew interested in early Baroque music and the association of music with movement; from 1930 he rewrote his earlier pieces to conform to these interests. His comprehensive music-education program (Orff Schulwerk) involving improvisation on special percussion instruments has come into wide international use. After writing his best-known work, *Carmina Burana* (1937), he withdrew all his earlier compositions. His later propulsively rhythmic theater works include the operas *Der Mond* (1939) and *Die Kluge* (1943).

organ Keyboard instrument in which pressurized air produces notes by means of a series of tuned pipes. Organs include the largest and most complex of all instruments. The simplest organs consist of a single rank of pipes, each corresponding to a single key. They are arranged over a wind chest connected to the keys by a set of valves and fed with a supply of air by electrically or mechanically activated bellows. By pulling out knobs, called stops, the player engages new ranks of pipes. Flue pipes produce sound by directing air against the edge of an opening in the pipe, whereas reed pipes sound by means of a thin metal tongue inside the pipe that vibrates against a fixed projection next to it. Different shapes and materials produce a variety of tone colors. A large organ may have five or more banked keyboards, or manuals, each of which controls a distinctive group of pipes. Most organs also have pedalboards played with the feet. A large organ's pipes may vary in length from about 1 in to 32 ft (2.5 cm–10 m), resulting in a huge nine-octave range. In the earliest organs (c.250 B.C.) the wind was regulated by water pressure. The bellows-fed organ appeared around the 7th cent. A.D. The organ became firmly associated with the church by the 10th cent.

organic compound Substance whose MOLECULES contain one or more (often many more) CARBON ATOMS (excluding carbonates, cyanides, carbides, and a few others; see INORGANIC COMPOUND). Until 1828 (see UREA), scientists believed that organic compounds could be formed only by life processes (hence the name). Since carbon has a far greater tendency to form chains and rings than other elements, its COMPOUNDS are vastly more numerous (many millions have been described) than all others known. Living organisms consist mostly of water and organic compounds: PROTEINS, CARBOHYDRATES, FATS, NUCLEIC ACIDS, HORMONES, VITAMINS, and a host of others. Natural and synthetic fibers and most fuels, drugs, and plastics are organic. See also ALCOHOL, ALDEHYDE, AMINO ACID, CARBOXYLIC ACID, ETHER, HYDROCARBON, ISOPRENOID, KETONE, PHENOL.

organic farming *or* **organic gardening** System of crop cultivation that uses biological methods of fertilization and pest control as substitutes for chemical FERTILIZERS and PESTICIDES. It was initiated as a rejection of modern agri-chemical techniques in the 1930s by the British agronomist Sir Albert Howard. Organic materials, including animal MANURE, COMPOST, grass turf, STRAW, and other crop residues, are applied to fields to improve both soil structure and moisture-holding capacity and to nourish soil life, which in turn nourishes plants. (Chemical fertilizers, by contrast, feed plants directly.) Biological pest control is achieved through preventive methods, including diversified farming, CROP ROTATION, the planting of pest-deterrent species, and the use of INTEGRATED PEST MANAGEMENT techniques. Bioengineered strains are avoided. Organic produce formerly accounted for a minuscule portion of total American farm output, but has seen a huge proportional increase in sales in recent years.

organizational relations See INDUSTRIAL RELATIONS

Organization for Economic Cooperation and Development (OECD) International organization founded in 1961 to stimulate economic progress and world trade. Based in Paris, the OECD serves as a consultative assembly and a clearinghouse for economic data, and also coordinates economic aid to developing countries. It promotes international stability by assisting governments in tackling the economic, social, and governance challenges of a globalized economy. Its current members are Australia, Canada, Japan, Mexico, New Zealand, S. Korea, Turkey, the U.S., and 21 European countries.

Organization of African Unity (OAU) Intergovernmental organization established in 1963 to promote unity among African states and eliminate vestiges of colonialism. Its headquarters are in Addis Ababa, Ethiopia. It hosts an annual assembly of heads of state and government and maintains caucuses at the U.N. The OAU successfully mediated the Algeria–Morocco dispute of 1964–65 and the Somalia–Ethiopia and Kenya–Somalia border disputes of 1965–67, but failed in its efforts to deal with BIAFRA (1968–70). From the 1970s it has concentrated on economic cooperation and human rights. See also PAN-AFRICAN MOVEMENT.

Organization of American States (OAS) International organization formed in 1948 to replace the Pan-American Union. It aims to strengthen hemispheric peace and security through a pro-U.S., anticommunist policy, settle disputes among its members, provide for collective security, and encourage socioeconomic cooperation. It has promoted democracy among its members (e.g., by monitoring elections and safeguarding human rights), which include all the countries in the Western Hemisphere, though Cuba's membership is only nominal.

Organization of Petroleum Exporting Countries (OPEC) Multinational organization established in 1960 to coordinate the petroleum policies of its members. Iran, Iraq, Kuwait, Saudi Arabia, and Venezuela were later joined by Qatar (1961), Indonesia and Libya (1962), Abu Dhabi (1967; membership transferred to the United Arab Emirates, 1974), Algeria (1967), and Nigeria (1971). The dominant Middle Eastern members used oil price increases as a political weapon in retaliation against Western support of Israel in the 1973 ARAB–ISRAELI WAR, and OPEC members' income greatly increased as a result. Internal dissent, the development of alternative energy sources, and the exploitation of non-OPEC oil sources subsequently reduced OPEC's influence.

organized crime Crime committed on a national or international scale by a criminal association; also, the associations themselves. Characteristics include a hierarchy of ranks with assigned responsibilities, a conspiracy among groups to coordinate activities, a commitment to secrecy, and corruption of law-enforcement authorities. One source of income is the provision of illegal goods and services, including narcotics, gambling, and prostitution; other sources include extortion, fraud, theft, and robbery. Organized crime arose in the U.S. during PROHIBITION to provide bootlegged liquor. In recent years organized crime has become immensely powerful in Russia. See also MAFIA, YAKUZA.

Organ Pipe Cactus National Monument Preserve, SW Arizona, at the Mexican border. With an area of 330,689 acres (133,929 hectares), it preserves segments of the mountainous SONORAN DESERT. Wildlife includes GILA MONSTERS, antelope, coyotes, and a variety of birds.

organum \ˈȯr-gə-nəm\ Early polyphonic setting of plainchant (see GREGORIAN CHANT), the earliest form of COUNTERPOINT. The oldest written organum (c.900) consists of two lines moving simultaneously, the added line often paralleling the chant line a 4th or a 5th below. Later the added line acquired greater melodic individuality. Organum consisting of more than one note against each chant note appears by the early 12th cent. Three- and four-voice organum was first composed by the NOTRE-DAME SCHOOL. Organum died out with the advent of the 13th-cent. MOTET.

orienteering Cross-country footrace in which each participant uses a map and compass to navigate between checkpoints along an unfamiliar course. It was introduced in Sweden in 1918; world championships have been held since 1966. Runners set out at intervals. Orienteering is also practiced by cyclists, canoeists, horseback riders, and skiers.

Orient Express Luxury train that ran from Paris to Constantinople (Istanbul) for over 80 years (1883–1977). Its luxuriously furnished cars became the symbol of glamour for European society. Europe's first transcontinental express train, it covered over 1,700 mi (2,750 km); after 1919 the route extended from Calais and Paris to Lausanne and via the Simplon Pass to Milan, Venice, Zagreb, and beyond. Discontinued in 1977, it was revived in 1982 to run between London and Venice.

origami See PAPER FOLDING

Origen \ˈȯr-i-jən\ *orig.* Oregenes Adamantius (c.A.D. 185–254?) Greek theologian, one of the Fathers of the Church. Probably the son of a Christian martyr, Origen studied philosophy in Alexandria and served as head of its catechetical school for 20 years. He later founded a school of philosophy and theology in Palestine. His greatest work, the *Hexapla,* is a synopsis of six versions of the Old Testament. His writings, influenced by Neoplatonism and Stoicism, stress that providence seeks to restore all souls to their original blessedness; he was condemned for holding that even Satan was not beyond repentance and salvation.

original sin In Christian doctrine, the condition or state of SIN into which each human being is born, or its origin in ADAM's disobedience to God when he ate the fruit of the tree of knowledge of good and evil. His guilt was transmitted to his descendants. The main scriptural basis of the doctrine is found in the writings of St. PAUL; St. AUGUSTINE helped make humanity's sinful nature a central element in orthodox Christian theology.

Orinoco River \ˌȯr-ē-ˈnō-kō\ Major river, S. America. It rises in the Sierra Parima Mtns. along the Venezuela–Brazil border, flows in a giant arc through Venezuela for 1,700 mi (2,740 km), and enters the Atlantic Ocean near the island of Trinidad. It forms part of the Colombia–Venezuela border. With its tributaries, it is the northernmost of S. America's four major river systems. The water fauna include the PIRANHA and the Orinoco CROCODILE.

oriole Any songbird of 24 species in the Old World genus *Oriolus* (family Oriolidae) or 30 species in the New World genus *Icterus* (family Icteridae). Males typically are black and yellow or black and orange, with some white. Orioles are not easily seen but may be detected by their loud whistling and jarring notes. The only European species is the 9.5-in. (24-cm) golden oriole (*O. oriolus*). Other *Oriolus* species are found in Africa, Asia, and Australia. The Baltimore oriole (*I. galbula*) breeds in N. America east of the Rockies.

Orion \ə-'rī-ən\ In GREEK MYTHOLOGY, a powerful hunter. He drove the wild beasts out of the island of Chios and fell in love with Merope, the king's daughter. The king had him blinded, but his vision was restored by the rays of the rising sun. He later went to Crete to live and hunt with ARTEMIS. Some legends hold that he was killed by Artemis or APOLLO out of jealousy; another tells that he was fatally bitten by a scorpion. After his death the gods placed him in the sky as a constellation.

Orion Nebula \ə-'rī-ən\ Bright NEBULA, faintly visible to the unaided eye in the "sword" of the constellation Orion. About 1,500 light-years from earth, it contains hundreds of very hot young stars clustered about a group of four massive stars, whose radiation excites it to glow. Discovered in the early 17th cent., it was the first nebula to be photographed (1880).

Orizaba See CITLALTÉPETL

Orkney Islands Group of more than 70 islands and islets (pop., 1995 est.: 20,000), Scotland, lying north of the Scottish mainland. Only 17 are inhabited. They were the Orcades of ancient classical literature. Their abundant Neolithic remains include those at SKARA BRAE. Norse raiders arrived in the late 8th cent. A.D. Thereafter they were ruled by Norway and Denmark until Scotland annexed them in 1472. They played a major role in both world wars (see SCAPA FLOW). The islands are known for their beef, ales, and whiskies.

Orlando City (pop., 2000: 186,000), central Florida. Settlement began around 1844. Its name honors Orlando Reeves, an army sentry killed during the SEMINOLE WARS. The development of the aerospace complex at Cape CANAVERAL after 1950, and of nearby DISNEY WORLD and other theme parks after 1971, boosted the city's population and economy.

Orléans \ȯr-lā-'äⁿ\ *ancient* Aurelianum. City (pop., 1999: 113,000), N central France. Located on the LOIRE RIVER in a fertile valley, it became an intellectual center under CHARLEMAGNE and a major cultural center in the Middle Ages. During the HUNDRED YEARS' WAR, the English siege in 1429 was relieved by JOAN OF ARC, known as the Maid of Orléans.

Orléans, Louis-Philippe-Joseph, duc (Duke) d' *known as* **Philippe Égalité** (1747–1793) French Bourbon prince who supported popular democracy in the FRENCH REVOLUTION. A cousin of LOUIS XVI, he disapproved of MARIE-ANTOINETTE and lived away from the royal court at Versailles. In 1789 he was elected to the Estates General. After joining the Jacobins (1791), he renounced his title of nobility (1792) and accepted the name Philippe Égalité from the Paris Commune. In the National Convention, he supported the radicals, but after his son LOUIS-PHILIPPE defected to the Austrians, he was accused of conspiracy, arrested, and guillotined.

Orlov, Grigory (Grigoryevich), Count (1734–1783) Russian military officer and lover of CATHERINE II. While stationed in St. Petersburg, he met the future PETER III and his wife, Catherine, whose lover Orlov became about 1760. After Peter ascended the throne (1762), Orlov planned the coup d'état that overthrew Peter and made Catherine empress of Russia. As Catherine's close adviser, he proposed agrarian reforms to help the serfs, but little was accomplished. He lost favor at court about 1772.

Ormandy, Eugene *orig.* Jenö Blau (1899–1985) Hungarian-U.S. conductor. A violin prodigy, he became professor of violin at the Budapest Royal Academy at 17. He came to New York in 1921 and eventually served as conductor of the Minneapolis Symphony (1931–36). He succeeded Leopold STOKOWSKI at the Philadelphia Orchestra in 1938, and led the orchestra until 1980. His violin background had much to do with maintaining the rich "Philadelphia sound" created by his predecessor.

ormolu \'ȯr-mə-ˌlü\ (from French, *dorure d'or moulu:* "gilding with gold paste") Gold-colored alloy made up of copper, zinc, and sometimes tin in various proportions, but usually at least 50% copper. It is used in mounts (ornaments on borders, edges, and as angle guards) for furniture and for other decorative purposes. After the molten alloy has been poured into a mold and allowed to cool, it is gilded with powdered gold, then fired. Ormolu was first produced in France in the mid-17th cent., and France remained its main center of production.

Orne River \'ȯrn\ River, NW France. It is 94 mi (152 km) long, and flows past Caen into the English Channel. Its bridges were seized by the Allied forces during the NORMANDY CAMPAIGN in June 1944.

ornithischian \ˌȯr-nə-'this-kē-ən\ Any "bird-hipped" DINOSAUR species (order Ornithischia), herbivores with hip bones arranged like those of modern birds, with the pubis bone pointed backward. They flourished from the Late Triassic to the Late Cretaceous periods (227–65 million years ago). Many species had a toothless, horny beak and powerful cheek teeth. Many species (in the suborder Cerapoda) were bipedal, and defensive armor, if present, was only on the massive head and culminated in a great bony frill. Other species (in the suborder Thyreophora) were heavily plated and armored along the back, and some species also had armor on the flanks and head. See also PROTOCERATOPS, SAURISCHIAN, STEGOSAUR, TRICERATOPS.

ornithology Branch of ZOOLOGY dealing with the study of birds. Early writings were largely anecdotal (including folklore) or practical (e.g., treatises on falconry and game-bird management). From the mid-18th cent. on, ornithology progressed from the description and classification of newly discovered species to examination of internal anatomy to the study of the bird ecology and ethology. The field observations of amateur birders provide valuable information on behavior, ecology, distribution, and migration. Other information is gained by radar, radio transmitters, portable audio equipment, and bird banding, which provides information on longevity and movements.

orogeny \ȯ-'rä-jə-nē\ Mountain-building event, generally one that occurs in a GEOSYNCLINE. Orogeny is usually accompanied by folding and faulting of strata and by the deposition of sediments in areas adjacent to the orogenic belt. Orogenies may result from continental collisions, the underthrusting of continents by oceanic plates, or the overriding of oceanic ridges by continents (see PLATE TECTONICS).

Oromo \ō-'rō-mō\ *or* **Galla** Major ethnic group of Ethiopia, numbering 20 million, or nearly half the population. They have assimilated and intermarried with various other peoples since the 16th cent. Traditionally nomadic herders, today most are farmers. Politically they are largely subjugated to the dominant AMHARA.

Orozco \ō-'rōs-kō\, **José Clemente** (1883–1949) Mexican mural painter. As a caricaturist for a revolutionary paper, he explored Mexico City's slums and painted a series of watercolors, *House of Tears,* on the lives of prostitutes. In 1919 he joined Diego RIVERA and D. A. SIQUEIROS in creating large-scale murals for public buildings, in which he continued his radical social commentary. Forced to abandon Mexico in 1927, he worked until 1934 in the U.S., where his style evolved and matured in murals from coast to coast. His international reputation firmly established, he returned to Mexico and embarked on his most technically impressive and emotionally expressive murals, including *Catharsis* (1934), in the Palacio de Bellas Artes. He was a leader among those who raised Mexican art to a position of international eminence.

Orpheus Greek legendary hero who sang and played the lyre so beautifully that animals, trees, and rocks danced around him. When his wife, Eurydice, was killed by a snake, he sought her in the underworld, and his music and grief so moved HADES that he agreed to let Orpheus take Eurydice to the land of the living on condition that neither of them was to look back as they left. When Orpheus did, Eurydice disappeared. Orpheus was later torn to pieces by MAENADS, and his head, still singing, floated to LESBOS, where an oracle of Orpheus was established. By the 5th cent. B.C., a Hellenistic MYSTERY RELIGION (the Orphic mysteries) had arisen based on his songs and teachings.

Orphic mysteries See MYSTERY RELIGIONS

ON

Orr, Bobby (*orig.* Robert Gordon) (b.1948) Canadian-U.S. ice-hockey player. Born in Parry Sound, Ontario, he was signed to a junior amateur contract by Boston Bruins scouts when he was 12. He joined the Bruins in 1966 and played with them for 10 seasons, helping them to the play-offs in eight consecutive seasons and to two Stanley Cup victories. He is the only player ever recognized as the most valuable defenseman eight years in a row.

Ortega (Saavedra) \òr-'tä-gə\, **Daniel** (b.1945) President of Nicaragua (1984–90). In 1963 he became a member of the SANDINISTAS and organized resistance to the corrupt dictatorship of the SOMOZA FAMILY. Exiled, he returned secretly and helped unite opposition to Pres. Anastasio Somoza. After the Sandinistas prevailed in 1979, Ortega coordinated the ruling junta; in 1984 he was elected president. U.S. efforts destabilized his government, and he lost the election of 1990 to Violeta CHAMORRO. See also CONTRAS.

Ortega y Gasset \òr-'tä-gä-ē-gä-'set\, **José** (1883–1955) Spanish philosopher. He taught at the Univ. of Madrid from 1911, and lived abroad 1931–46. Though influenced by Neo-Kantianism, he diverged from it in such works as *Adam in Paradise* (1910), *Quixote's Meditations* (1914), and *The Modern Theme* (1923). Sharing his generation's preoccupation with Spain's problems, he founded the periodicals *España* (1915), *El sol* (1917), and *Revista de Occidente* (1923). His best-known work, *The Revolt of the Masses* (1929), foreshadowed the Spanish Civil War. He greatly influenced Spain's 20th-cent. cultural and literary renaissance.

orthoclase \'òr-thə-ˌklās\ Common alkali FELDSPAR mineral, potassium aluminosilicate, that usually occurs as variously colored grains in granite. Orthoclase is used in the manufacture of glass and ceramics; occasionally, transparent crystals are cut as gems. It is primarily important as a rock-forming mineral, however, and is abundant in IGNEOUS ROCKS, PEGMATITES, and GNEISSES. Microcline is a lower temperature structural form of the same chemical composition as orthoclase and yields the green gemstone variety amazonite.

Orthodox Catholic Church See EASTERN ORTHODOXY

Orthodox Judaism Religion of Jews who adhere strictly to traditional beliefs and practices; the official form of JUDAISM in Israel. Orthodox Jews hold that both the written law (TORAH) and the oral law (codified in the MISHNA and interpreted in the TALMUD) are immutably fixed and remain the sole norm of religious observance. Orthodox Judaism has held fast to such practices as daily worship, dietary laws, intensive study of the Torah, and separation of men and women in the synagogue. It also enjoins strict observance of the SABBATH.

orthopedics \ˌòr-thə-'pē-diks\ *or* **orthopedic surgery** Medical specialty concerned with the SKELETON and its associated structures. It treats FRACTURES, strained MUSCLES, torn LIGAMENTS and TENDONS, and other injuries, and deals with acquired and congenital skeletal deformities and the effects of degenerative diseases such as OSTEOARTHRITIS. It uses bone grafts, hip and other joint replacements, prostheses (see PROSTHESIS), special footwear, and braces to enhance mobility. Orthopedics also uses the techniques of PHYSICAL MEDICINE AND REHABILITATION and OCCUPATIONAL THERAPY.

Orton, Joe (*orig.* John Kingsley) (1933–1967) British dramatist. His three full-length black comedies, *Entertaining Mr. Sloane* (1964), *Loot* (1965), and *What the Butler Saw* (produced 1969), scandalized audiences with their examination of moral corruption, violence, and sexual rapacity. Orton's career was cut short when he was murdered by K. L. Halliwell, his companion.

Orwell, George *orig.* Eric Arthur Blair (1903–1950) British novelist and essayist. Orwell served in the Indian Imperial Police in Burma 1922–27, an experience that changed him into a literary and political rebel. On returning to Europe, he lived in self-imposed poverty, gaining material for *Down and Out in Paris and London* (1933), and became a socialist. He went to Spain to report on the Spanish Civil War and stayed to join the Republican militia. His war experiences, which gave him a dread of totalitarian communism, are recounted in *Homage to Catalonia* (1938). His novels typically portray a sensitive, emotionally isolated individual at odds with an oppressive or dishonest social environment. His most famous works are the anti-Soviet satirical fable *Animal Farm* (1945) and *Nineteen Eighty-four* (1949), a dystopic vision of totalitarianism. His literary essays are also admired. He died of tuberculosis at 46.

George Orwell

oryx Any of four species (genus *Oryx*) of large stocky ANTELOPES living in herds on African and Arabian deserts and plains. Oryxes are 40–47 in. (102–120 cm) high. They have a mane and a tufted tail, dark patches on the face and forehead, and a dark streak on either side of the eye. Both sexes have long, sharp-tipped, straight or curved horns.

Osage \ō-'sāj\ N. American Indian people who lived variously in the Piedmont and Ozark plateaus and the W Missouri and SE Kansas prairies. Osage culture was of the prairie type, marked by the combination of village agriculture and buffalo hunting. Their villages consisted of LONGHOUSES; TEPEES were used during the hunting season. In the late 19th cent. the Osage were removed to a reservation in Oklahoma. The discovery of oil there made them a uniquely prosperous tribe. Today they number about 8,000.

Osage River \ō-'sāj, 'ō-ˌsāj\ River, W Missouri. About 500 mi (800 km) long, it is the largest tributary of the MISSOURI RIVER. It flows east and northeast through Lake of the OZARKS and enters the Missouri just east of Jefferson City, Mo.

Osaka \ō-'sä-kä, *Jap* 'ō-sä-kä\ *ancient* Naniwa. City (pop., 1995 est.: 2,602,000) and seaport, S central HONSHU, Japan. Naniwa was made a castle town by TOYOTOMI HIDEYOSHI in the 16th cent. It was the leading commercial city of Japan during the feudal era and the leading industrial city from the late 19th cent. It was badly damaged by U.S. bombing during World War II. It is now a leading financial center with heavy industries. With KOBE and KYOTO, it is part of Japan's second-largest urban and industrial complex. It is also a cultural and educational hub, with several universities and theaters.

Osborne, John (James) (1929–1994) British playwright. He cowrote his first play, *The Devil Inside Him* (1950), with Stella Linden. His *Look Back in Anger* (1956; film, 1959) ushered in a spate of vigorously realistic plays about British working-class life that typified the ANGRY YOUNG MEN. *The Entertainer* (1957; film, 1960) starred Laurence OLIVIER as a failing music-hall comedian. He wrote the screenplay for *Tom Jones* (1963, Academy Award). His later plays include *Luther* (1961) and *Inadmissible Evidence* (1964).

Oscars See ACADEMY AWARDS

Osceola \ˌä-sē-'ō-lə\ (1804?–1838) SEMINOLE Indian leader during the Second SEMINOLE WAR (1835–37). When the U.S. government attempted to force the Seminole to leave Florida, Osceola and his followers employed brilliant guerrilla tactics against government forces for two years and forced a truce. Emerging for negotiations under a flag of truce, he was arrested and removed to a military fort at Charleston, S.C., where he died, possibly murdered.

oscillator Mechanical or electronic device that produces a back-and-forth periodic motion. A PENDULUM is a simple mechanical oscillator that swings with a constant amplitude, requiring the addition of energy at each swing only to compensate for the energy lost because of air resistance or FRICTION. In electronic oscillators, ELECTRONS oscillate with a constant period and also require the addition of energy to replace energy loss. Electronic oscillators are used to generate ALTERNATING CURRENT and high-frequency currents for carrier waves in radio broadcasting.

oscilloscope \ə-'si-lə-ˌskōp\ *or* **cathode-ray oscilloscope** Electronic display device used to produce patterns on a screen that are the graphical representations of electrical signals. Time is normally on the horizontal axis, and a function of the voltage generated by the input signal to the oscilloscope on the vertical axis. Because almost any physical phenomenon can be converted into a corresponding electric voltage, oscilloscopes find commercial, engineering, and scientific applications in a variety of fields.

Oshogbo \ō-ˈshȯg-bō\ City (pop., 1996 est.: 477,000), Nigeria. Located northeast of IBADAN, it lies along the Oshun River. It grew in the early 19th cent. with an influx of YORUBAS fleeing from FULANI conquerors. In 1840 it was the scene of a critical battle in the Fulani–Yoruba wars. It was made the capital of the new state of Osun in 1991. It is a trade center for cocoa, palm oil, tobacco, and textiles.

Osiris \ō-ˈsī-rəs\ Ancient Egyptian god of the underworld. According to myth, Osiris was slain by the god SETH, who tore apart the corpse and flung the pieces all over Egypt. ISIS, consort of Osiris, and her sister found the pieces and gave new life to Osiris, who became the ruler of the underworld. Isis and Osiris then conceived HORUS. In the Egyptian concept of divine kingship, the king at death became Osiris and the new king was identified with Horus. Osiris also represented the power that brought life out of the earth.

Osler \ˈōs-lər\, **William** (*later* **Sir William**) (1849–1919) Canadian physician and professor. Born in Bond Head, Ontario, he became the first to identify blood PLATELETS (1873). At Johns Hopkins Univ.'s new medical school (1889–1905), he helped transform clinical teaching; students studied patients in the wards and took their problems to the lab, and experts pooled their knowledge to benefit both patient and student in public teaching sessions. Osler's *Principles and Practice of Medicine* (1892) became the most popular medical textbook of its day. He later taught at Oxford Univ. (1905–19). He was a cofounder of two physicians' associations and the *Quarterly Journal of Medicine*.

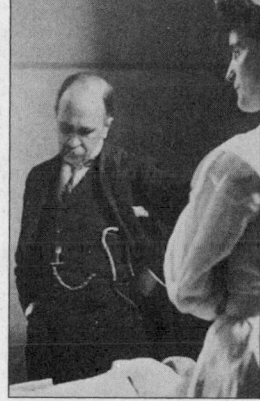

William Osler at a patient's bedside

Oslo \ˈäz-lō, *Norwegian* ˈüs-lü\ *formerly (1624–1925)* **Christiania** *or* **Kristiania** City (metro. area pop., 1999 est.: 503,000), capital of Norway. It lies at the N end of Oslo Fjord. It was founded by King HARALD III SIGURDSSON around 1050. After a destructive fire in 1624, King CHRISTIAN II of Denmark-Norway built a new town farther west and called it Christiania. In the 19th cent. it surpassed BERGEN as Norway's largest and most influential city. It was renamed Oslo in 1925. It is the country's principal commercial, industrial, and transportation center, and its harbor is the largest and busiest in Norway.

osmosis \äz-ˈmō-səs\ Spontaneous passage or DIFFUSION of water or other SOLVENT through a semipermeable membrane. If a solution is separated from a pure solvent by a membrane that passes the solvent but not the solute, the solvent will go through the membrane, diluting the solution. The pressure caused by the migration of solvent through the membrane is called osmotic pressure.

osprey \ˈäs-prē, ˈäs-prā\ *or* **fish hawk** Species (*Pandion haliaetus*) of long-winged HAWK found along seacoasts and large interior waterways. Ospreys are about 26 in. (65 cm) long and brown above and white below. An osprey flies over the water, hovers above its prey, and then plunges feet first, seizing the fish in its long, curved talons. Ospreys breed on all continents except S. America, where they live only in winter. They usually nest, singly or in colonies, high in trees or on cliffs.

Osroene *or* **Osrhoene** \äz-rə-ˈwē-nē\ Ancient kingdom, NW MESOPOTAMIA. Located between the TIGRIS and EUPHRATES rivers, it was situated across the modern frontier of Turkey and Syria, with its capital at EDESSA. Founded about 136 B.C., it commanded strategic trade and military routes from the 1st cent. B.C. to the 2nd cent. A.D. At dif-

ferent times it was allied with either PARTHIA or ROME. The kingdom was abolished by Roman emperor CARACALLA in A.D. 216. In the 4th–7th cent. A.D. it was dominated by the wars between Byzantium and Persia. It fell to the Muslims in 638.

Ossianic ballads \ˌä-sē-ˈa-nik, ˌä-shē-ˈa-nik\ Irish Gaelic and Scottish lyric and narrative poems dealing with the legendary Finn MacCumhaill and his war band. They are named for Oisín (Ossian), the chief bard of the FENIAN CYCLE. The ballads consist of more than 80,000 lines dating from the 11th to the 18th cent. They are pagan and anticlerical, full of lament for past glories and contempt for the Christian present. Most of the poetry claimed for Oisín was in fact written by the Scottish poet James Macpherson (1736–1796).

Ossianic cycle See FENIAN CYCLE

Ostade \ȯs-ˈtä-də\, **Adriaen van** (1610–1685) Dutch painter and printmaker. Known for his genre paintings of peasant life, he also did religious subjects, portraits, and landscapes. Influenced by Adriaen BROUWER, he delighted in scenes such as tavern brawls in dimly lit interiors, as in *Carousing Peasants in an Interior* (c.1638). He employed a broad, vigorous technique in a subdued range of colors. Later he adopted a brighter palette, his subjects became less ribald, and from the 1650s he painted many of them in outdoor settings (e.g., *The Itinerant Fiddler*, 1672).

osteitis deformans See PAGET'S DISEASE OF BONE

osteoarthritis \ˌäs-tē-ō-är-ˈthrī-təs\ *or* **osteoarthrosis** *or* **degenerative joint disease** Most common JOINT disorder, afflicting over 80% of those who reach age 70. Overweight, sports injuries, and genetic predisposition are risk factors. CARTILAGE softens and wears away, and BONE grows in its place, distorting the joint's surface and causing pain, stiffness, and limited movement, usually in weight-bearing joints (vertebrae, knees, hips). Treatment may include ANALGESICS, rest, weight loss, corticosteroids, PHYSICAL MEDICINE AND REHABILITATION or an exercise program, and sometimes surgery.

osteopathy \ˌäs-tē-ˈä-pə-thē\ Health-care profession founded by the U.S. physician Andrew Taylor Still (1828–1917) as a reform movement against the rather primitive 19th-cent. drugs and surgical techniques. It emphasizes the relationship between musculoskeletal structure and organ function. Osteopathic physicians learn to recognize and correct structural problems through manipulative and other therapies and earn a doctor of osteopathy (DO) degree. They are licensed to practice in all U.S. states, with the same professional rights and responsibilities as MDs in most.

osteoporosis \ˌäs-tē-ō-pə-ˈrō-səs\ Generalized loss of BONE density, causing skeletal weakness. Around age 40, the rate of bone resorption starts to exceed the rate of bone formation. Women experience accelerated bone loss after menopause. When the amount of bone falls below a certain threshold, FRACTURES occur with little or no trauma. Prevention involves adequate CALCIUM intake in youth and throughout life, as well as weight-bearing exercise and VITAMIN D. In women, hormone-replacement therapy helps arrest it, as ESTROGEN deficiency is a major cause of accelerated bone loss. Bisphosphonates inhibit bone resorption or prevent bone loss in patients not yet suffering from osteoporosis.

Ostia \ˈä-stē-ə\ Ancient Roman town. It lay near the modern seaside resort of Ostia, on the TIBER RIVER. Probably founded in the 4th cent. B.C., it developed as a naval station, major port, and center of the grain trade. It reached the height of its prosperity in the 2nd cent. A.D. with a population of about 50,000. It suffered from barbarian raids in the 5th cent. Its Roman ruins were quarried for building materials in the Middle Ages and for sculptors' marble during the Renaissance. About two-thirds of the Roman town has been excavated.

ostomy \ˈäs-tə-mē\ Operation creating a surgical opening in the body, usually to allow discharge of wastes through the abdominal wall. It may be temporary, to relieve strain on damaged organs, or permanent, to replace normal channels surgically removed (usually to treat cancer). A loop of bowel (the COLON in COLOSTOMY and the ILEUM in ileostomy) is cut and the end brought through to the abdominal surface. Waste usually exits into a self-adhering bag worn over the opening, or an internal pouch may be made from body tissue.

Ostpolitik \'òst-pò-li-,tēk\ (German: "Eastern Policy") W. German foreign policy begun in the late 1960s. Initiated by Willy BRANDT as foreign minister and then chancellor, the policy was one of détente with Soviet-bloc countries, recognizing the E. German government and expanding commercial relations with other Soviet-bloc countries. The policy was continued by Chancellor Helmut SCHMIDT.

Ostrasia See AUSTRASIA

Ostrava \'ò-strə-və\ City (pop., 1999 est.: 322,000), NE Czech Republic, on the ODER RIVER near the border with Poland. It was founded about 1267 as a fortified town by Bruno, bishop of Olomouc, to protect the entry to MORAVIA from the north. Historic buildings include a 13th-cent. church. The major industry is coal mining.

ostrich Two-toed, long-necked RATITE (*Struthio camelus,* family Struthionidae) found in Africa, the largest living bird. An adult male ostrich may be 8 ft (2.5 m) tall and weigh up to 350 lbs (155 kg). Males are black, with white wing and tail plumes; females are brown. Ostriches live in flocks of 5–50. Roaring, hissing males fight for three to five hens, which lay 15–60 eggs in a communal nest. One-month-old chicks can run with adults, at 40 mph (65 kph). To escape detection, ostriches may lie on the ground with neck outstretched, a habit that may have given rise to the notion that they bury their head in the sand.

Ostrogoths \'äs-trə-,gäths\ E division of the GOTHS (Ostrogoth means "Eastern Goth"). They built an empire north of the Black Sea in the 3rd cent.; at its zenith in the 4th cent., it included most of present-day Ukraine. After their subjugation by the HUNS (c.370), some Ostrogoths settled along the Danube River (c.450). When the Hun empire collapsed (455), THEODORIC led the Ostrogothic invasion of Italy and declared himself king (493). JUSTINIAN I fought the Ostrogoths in Italy for almost 20 years (c.535–54) and ended their national existence. See also VISIGOTHS.

Ostrovsky \,ə-'strof-skē\, **Aleksandr (Nikolayevich)** (1823–1886) Russian playwright. His second play, *The Bankrupt* (1850), exposed bogus bankruptcy cases. His later plays, most of which treat characters from the Russian merchant class, include the comedies *Poverty Is No Disgrace* (1853), *The Thunderstorm* (1859), and *The Snow Maiden* (1873). With his 47 plays Ostrovsky created a Russian national repertoire, and he is considered the greatest representative of the Russian realistic period.

Ostwald \'òst-,vält\, **(Friedrich) Wilhelm** (1853–1932) Russian-German physical chemist. He wrote the influential *Textbook of General Chemistry* (1885–87). With Jacobus VAN'T HOFF he founded the *Zeitschrift für physikalische Chemie,* which became for many years the most important journal in the field. His work at the Univ. of Leipzig (1887–1906) established it as a great school of PHYSICAL CHEMISTRY. In 1888 he discovered Ostwald's law of dilution of an electrolyte. He gave the first modern definition of a catalyst in 1894, and was awarded the Nobel Prize (1909) for his work on CATALYSIS. His process for the conversion of ammonia to nitric acid proved of great industrial importance.

Oswald, Lee Harvey (1939–1963) U.S. assassin of Pres. John F. KENNEDY. Born in New Orleans, he served in the U.S. Marines, then moved to the Soviet Union and unsuccessfully tried to become a Soviet citizen. He returned to the U.S. in 1962 with his Russian wife but retained his radical political beliefs. In October 1963 he took a job at the Texas School Book Depository in Dallas. On November 22, from a window on its sixth floor, he allegedly fired three shots that killed Kennedy and wounded Gov. John B. Connally. Soon afterward he killed a patrolman, and he was soon captured and arraigned. While being transferred to an interrogation office, he was fatally shot by Jack Ruby, a nightclub owner.

Otis, James (1725–1783) American Revolutionary statesman. Born in W. Barnstable, Mass., he argued before the colonial court against the British-imposed Writs of ASSISTANCE (1761), reportedly stating "Taxation without representation is tyranny." A leader with Samuel ADAMS in opposing the STAMP ACT, he wrote political pamphlets

upholding the colonists' cause. Struck on the head in a scuffle in 1769, he later became mentally unbalanced.

otitis \ō-'tī-təs\ INFLAMMATION of the EAR. Otitis externa is DERMATITIS, usually bacterial. It can cause a foul discharge, pain, fever, and sporadic DEAFNESS. Otitis media is due to allergy or viral or bacterial infection of the middle ear. The bacterial form may be acute (causing earache, fever, and pus and requiring antibiotics) or chronic. It can invade the bone, requiring surgery. Otitis in the INNER EAR (labyrinthitis) has symptoms including vertigo, vomiting, and hearing loss. Recovery is usually quick unless there is pus formation, which can cause permanent deafness in an ear.

otolaryngology \,ō-tō-,lar-ən-'gä-lə-jē\ *or* **otorhinolaryngology** \,ō-tō-,rī-nō-,lar-ən-'gä-lə-jē\ Medical specialty dealing with the EAR, NOSE, and throat (see LARYNX, PHARYNX). Otolaryngologists use an otoscope to examine the eardrum and a laryngoscope to inspect the larynx. They also test hearing and prescribe HEARING AIDS. The operating microscope and flexible ENDOSCOPY permit them to operate on delicate internal structures.

O'Toole, Peter (Seamus) (b.1932) British actor. The son of a bookie, he made his London debut in 1956, and played Hamlet in the National Theatre's inaugural production in 1963. He won international acclaim for *Lawrence of Arabia* (1962). Noted for his wit and intensity, he often played eccentrics and heavy drinkers, starring in such films as *Becket* (1964), *The Lion in Winter* (1968), *The Ruling Class* (1972), *The Stunt Man* (1980), and *My Favorite Year* (1982).

otorhinolaryngology See OTOLARYNGOLOGY

ottava rima \ō-'tä-və-'rē-mə\ Italian stanza form composed of eight 11-syllable lines, rhyming *ababab cc*. It originated in the late 13th cent. and was established by Giovanni BOCCACCIO as the standard form for Italian epic and narrative verse. When the form appeared in English, the lines were shortened to 10 syllables. In the 17th–18th cent., English ottava rima was written in iambic pentameter and used for heroic poetry. Notably effective is Lord BYRON's *Beppo* (1818) and *Don Juan* (1819–24).

Ottawa \'ä-tə-wə\ City (pop., 1996: 323,000), capital of Canada. It is located in SE Ontario, on the OTTAWA, Gatineau, and Rideau rivers. It was visited by Samuel de CHAMPLAIN in 1613, and the nearby rivers served traders and explorers over the next two centuries. Its settlement developed after the construction of the Rideau Canal in 1826. To resolve political disputes between TORONTO and QUEBEC CITY, and MONTREAL and Kingston, it was selected as Canada's capital by Queen VICTORIA in 1857. The federal government is the major employer. Its educational and cultural institutions include the National Arts Centre and the National Gallery of Canada.

Ottawa River River, E central Canada, the chief tributary of the ST. LAWRENCE RIVER. It rises in the Laurentian plateau of W QUEBEC and flows west to form the Quebec–Ontario border before joining the St. Lawrence west of MONTREAL. It is 790 mi (1,271 km) long and forms innumerable lakes. Explored by Samuel de CHAMPLAIN in 1613, it became a major route for explorers, fur traders, and missionaries to the GREAT LAKES. It is now a source of hydroelectric power.

otter Any of several carnivore species in four genera of semi-aquatic, web-footed members of the WEASEL family (Mustelidae), found throughout Africa, N. and S. America, Europe, and Asia. Total length is typically 3–7 ft (1–2 m) and weight is 7–60 lbs (3–27 kg); the large SEA OTTER is an exception. Otter fur, especially that of N animals, is highly valued. Most species live near rivers; some live near lakes or streams; the sea otter is completely marine. Otters eat small aquatic animals. They are inquisitive and playful; a favorite sport is sliding down a mudbank and plunging into water.

Otto, Nikolaus (August) (1832–1891) German engineer. He built his first gasoline-powered engine in 1861, and in 1876 he built an INTERNAL-COMBUSTION ENGINE using the four-stroke cycle (four strokes of the piston for each explosion), which offered the first practical alternative to the STEAM ENGINE. Though the four-stroke cycle was patented in 1862 by Alphonse Beau de Rochas (1815–1893), it is commonly known as the Otto cycle since Otto was the first to build such an engine.

Otto, Rudolf (1869–1937) German theologian, philosopher, and historian of religion. His theories on religion were influenced by his journeys to Africa and Asia to study non-Christian faiths and by the writings of Immanuel KANT and Friedrich SCHLEIERMACHER. In *The Idea of the Holy* (1917), Otto coined the term "numinous" to designate the nonrational element of religious experience—the blissful exaltation inspired by the perception of the divine. He believed that religion provided an understanding of the world beyond that of science. His other books include *Mysticism East and West* (1926) and *The Kingdom of God and Son of Man* (1938).

Otto I *known as* **Otto the Great** (912–973) German king (936–73) and Holy Roman Emperor (962–73). He extended the frontiers of the German kingdom, winning territory from the Slavs in the east and forcing the Bohemians to pay tribute (950). In 951 Otto became king of the Lombards and married the queen of Italy. He defeated the MAGYARS in the Battle of Lechfeld (955). Crowned emperor by Pope John XII in 962, he deposed John in 963 and replaced him with Leo VIII. He returned to Italy (966–72) to subdue Rome.

Otto III (980–1002) German king (983–1002) and Holy Roman Emperor (996–1002). Elected German king at age 3, he went to Rome to put down a rebellion in 996 and installed his cousin as Gregory V, the first German pope. He made Rome the center of his empire. He saw himself as leader of world Christianity and hoped to revive the glory of ancient Rome in a universal Christian state. When Rome rebelled against him (1001), he requested help from Bavaria but died before it arrived.

Otto IV *or* **Otto of Brunswick** (c.1175–1218) German king and Holy Roman Emperor. He was elected German king in 1198 but was opposed by the HOHENSTAUFENS, who elected Philip of Swabia; after Philip's murder in 1208 a new election gave the throne to Otto. He was crowned emperor (1209) by INNOCENT III after agreeing not to claim Sicily. When he violated this pact and conquered S Italy (1210), the German princes invited FREDERICK II to replace him. With his uncle, JOHN of England, Otto invaded France, Frederick's ally; defeated at the Battle of Bouvines, he was deposed in 1215.

Ottoman empire Former Turkish empire centered in ASIA MINOR. It was named for Osman I (1259–1326), a Muslim prince who conquered regions once held by the SELJUQ DYNASTY. Ottoman troops first invaded Europe in 1345, sweeping through the Balkans. By 1453, they had destroyed the BYZANTINE EMPIRE and captured Constantinople (ISTANBUL), which became the Ottoman capital. Under Selim I (1467–1520) and SULEYMAN I the Magnificent, the Ottoman empire became the largest in the world, Suleyman taking control of Persia, Arabia, Hungary, and the Balkans. By the early 16th cent. the Ottomans had also defeated the MAMLUKS in Syria and Egypt; and their navy under BARBAROSSA soon seized control of much of the BARBARY COAST. Beginning with Selim, the Ottoman sultans also held the title of CALIPH. Ottoman power began to decline with the destruction of the imperial fleet by allied European forces in 1571 at Lepanto. The Ottoman siege of Vienna in 1683 ended in defeat, and they relinquished Hungary in 1699. Corruption and decadence gradually undermined the government, and the RUSSO–TURKISH WARS and wars with Austria and Poland further weakened the empire. Most of its remaining European territory was lost in the BALKAN WARS (1912–13). Treaties following World War I dissolved the empire, and in 1922 the sultanate was abolished by M. K. ATATURK, who proclaimed the Republic of Turkey.

Otway, Thomas (1652–1685) English dramatist and poet. A failed actor, he turned to writing and had immense success with *Don Carlos* (produced 1676), considered the best of his rhymed heroic plays. His other plays include *The Orphan* (1680) and his masterpiece, *Venice Preserv'd* (1682), one of the greatest theatrical successes of the period. A forerunner of sentimental drama, he is outstanding for his convincing presentations of human emotions in an age of heroic but artificial tragedies.

Ouachita River \ˈwä-shə-ˌtȯ\ *formerly* **Washita River** River, SW Arkansas and E Louisiana. Rising in the Ouachita Mtns., it flows southeast to join the RED RIVER after 605 mi (973 km). It has been a navigation route since the late 18th cent.; six locks and dams were built on it by 1924.

Ouagadougou \ˌwä-gä-ˈdü-gü\ City (pop., 1993 est.: 690,000), capital of Burkina Faso, W Africa. It was the capital of the historic MOSSI kingdom of Wagadugu, which was founded in the 15th cent. The Mossi king still lives in the city. A manufacturing center, it is the nation's largest city.

Ouija board \ˈwē-jə\ Device for obtaining messages from the spirit world. The name derives from the French and German words for "yes" (oui/ja). The oblong Ouija board has letters of the alphabet inscribed in a half-moon along the edge. A small board is placed on top of it. Participants each lightly place a finger on the small board, which spirits supposedly move around on the larger board. As it touches the letters it may spell out words or sentences.

ounce See SNOW LEOPARD

Ouranus See URANUS

Outer Banks Chain of barrier islands, N. Carolina coast. It stretches 175 mi (282 km) from the Virginia border to Cape Lookout. Generally covered with sand dunes, most of the islands are linked by causeways; numerous beaches make the Outer Banks a popular resort area. Once a hideout for pirates and a place of shipwrecks, the islands have such historical sites as ROANOKE ISLAND and Kitty Hawk, scene of Wilbur and Orville WRIGHT's first powered flight. Most of the chain is protected as national seashore.

Outer Mongolia See MONGOLIA

Ouyang Xiu *or* **Ou-yang Hsiu** \ˈō-ˈyäŋ-ˈshyü\ (1007–1072) Chinese poet, historian, and statesman. Repeatedly demoted from various official positions for outspokenness and personal scandals, he took to drink and built a pavilion that he named Cuiweng ting ("Old Drunkard Pavilion") and made the subject of an essay that became one of the most celebrated works in Chinese literature. Later put in charge of the CHINESE EXAMINATION SYSTEM, he favored those who wrote in the simple, ancient style known as *guwen* and failed those who used literary embellishments, thus setting a new course in Chinese literature. His own writings in the *guwen* style became a stylistic model.

ovary \ˈō-və-rē\ In zoology, the female reproductive organ (see REPRODUCTIVE SYSTEM) that produces EGGS and SEX HORMONES (ESTROGEN and PROGESTERONE). Humans have two ovaries, almond-shaped organs about 1.5 in. (4 cm) long. They contain hollow balls of cells (follicles) that hold immature eggs. At ovulation, a follicle matures and releases an egg, which develops into an EMBRYO if fertilized or, if not, passes from the body with MENSTRUATION. At MENOPAUSE the few remaining follicles decay and the ovaries shrink and produce far less estrogen. In botany, an ovary is the enlarged base of a flower's female organ (PISTIL). It contains ovules, which develop into SEEDS when fertilized, and matures into a fruit.

over-the-counter market Trading in STOCKS and BONDS that does not take place on STOCK EXCHANGES. Such trading occurs most often in the U.S., where requirements for listing stocks on the exchanges are strict. Schedules of fees for buying and selling SECURITIES are not fixed in the over-the-counter market, and dealers derive their profits from the markup of their selling price. Many bond issues and preferred-stock issues, including U.S. government bonds, are listed on the NEW YORK STOCK EXCHANGE but are chiefly sold over-the-counter. Other U.S. government securities, as well as state and municipal bonds, are traded over-the-counter exclusively. Institutional investors such as MUTUAL FUNDS often trade over-the-counter to gain volume discounts. Regulation is carried out largely by the National Assn. of Securities Dealers. See also NASDAQ.

overtone *or* **harmonic** In acoustics, a series of higher tones contained within almost any musical tone. A body producing a musical pitch—such as a taut string, or a column of air within the tubular body of a wind instrument—vibrates not only as a unit but simultaneously also as integral fractions (half, third, etc.), producing a series of overtones within the fundamental tone. These contribute greatly to the TIMBRE of a given sound source, though few listeners notice any pitch except the fundamental. The second harmonic sounds an octave higher than the fundamental; the third sounds a 5th above the second; the fourth sounds a

4th above the third; the 5th sounds a major 3rd above the fourth; and so on. The special consonance of the octave and the 5th, and even the major 3rd, probably result from their strength in the overtone series (see CONSONANCE AND DISSONANCE).

overture Musical introduction to a larger, often dramatic, work. Originating with Claudio MONTEVERDI's *Orfeo* (1607), overtures served as openings for operas. The large-scale two- or three-part "French overture" invented by J.-B. LULLY (1658) was widely imitated for a century. The sinfonia, which became the standard Italian overture form, was a principal precursor of SONATA FORM, which itself became the standard form for later overtures. In the 19th cent., overtures independent of any larger work usually illustrated a literary or historical theme (see SYMPHONIC POEM).

Ovid \'ä-vid\ *Latin* Publius Ovidius Naso (43 B.C.–A.D. 17) Roman poet. His first work, *The Loves,* was an immediate success. It was followed by *Epistles of the Heroines; The Art of Beauty; The Art of Love,* one of his best-known works; and *Remedies for Love*, all reflecting the sophisticated, pleasure-seeking society in which he lived. He was a well-established poet when he undertook perhaps his greatest work, *Metamorphoses*, on legends of transformations of human beings into nonhuman forms by gods. His verse had immense influence because of its imaginative interpretations of classical myth and its supreme technical accomplishment. For unclear reasons, in A.D. 8 AUGUSTUS banished him to Tomis on the Black Sea. He described his life in an autobiographical poem in *Sorrows.* Extensively read and imitated in the Renaissance, he is the classical poet who most influenced William SHAKESPEARE.

ovum See EGG

Owen, Robert Dale (1801–1877) Scottish-American social reformer. In 1825 he emigrated with his father, Robert OWEN, to establish a community at New Harmony, Ind. He moved to New York with Fanny Wright (1795–1852) and edited the *Free Enquirer,* an advocate for radical free thought; they were active in the Workingmen's Party. In the U.S. House of Representatives (1843–47) he introduced a bill establishing the SMITHSONIAN INSTITUTION. A strong advocate of emancipation, he wrote *The Wrong of Slavery* (1864).

Owen, Robert (1771–1858) Welsh manufacturer and philanthropist. At his New Lanark cotton mills (Lanarkshire, Scotland), in partnership with Jeremy BENTHAM, he set up innovative social and industrial welfare programs, including improved housing and schools for young children. In *A New View of Society* (1813) he contended that character is wholly formed by one's environment. By 1817 his work had evolved into ideas presaging socialism and the cooperative movement. He sponsored several experimental utopian communities of "Owenites" in Britain and the U.S., including one at New Harmony, Ind. (1825–28), all of which proved short-lived. He was the father of R. D. OWEN.

Owen, Wilfred (1893–1918) British poet. He enlisted in the army in 1915, and the experience of trench warfare brought him to rapid maturity; the poignant poems he wrote after January 1917 are full of anger at the cruelty and waste of war and pity for its victims. A week before the armistice, he died in action at 25. His single volume of poems, published posthumously, is noted for its experiments in assonance.

Owens, Jesse (*orig.* James Cleveland) (1913–1980) U.S. track-and-field athlete. Born in Oakville, Ala., he broke or equaled four world track records in one day at Ohio State Univ. in 1935, setting a long-jump record that would stand for 25 years. In the 1936 Olympics in Berlin he won four gold medals, tying the Olympic record in the 100-m run, breaking the Olympic record in the 200-m run, running the final segment for the world-record-breaking U.S. 400-m relay team, and break-

Jesse Owens, 1936

ing the listed world record for the long jump. As a black man, he thereby dramatically foiled Adolf HITLER's intention to use the games to show Aryan racial superiority.

owl Any of the mostly nocturnal BIRDS OF PREY in the order Strigiformes: typical owls (family Strigidae), BARN and grass owls (Tytonidae), and bay owls (Phodilidae). Their virtually noiseless flight aids in capturing insects, birds, and small mammals. Owls have round, forward-looking eyes, a sharply hooked beak, and acute hearing and vision. They are 5–28 in. (13–70 cm) long. Some species have a disk framing the face or ear tufts that help locate prey by reflecting sound to the ears. Some species can turn the head as much as 270°. They nest in buildings, trees, or on the ground.

owlet moth See MILLER

ox Domesticated form of large BOVID (species *Bos taurus*) that once moved in herds across N. America and Europe (where they have disappeared) and Asia and Africa (where some still exist in the wild). The docile castrated male is used as a draft animal. The term is also applied to a castrated male of any CATTLE breed. See also AUROCHS, YAK.

oxalis \äk-'sa-ləs\ Any of about 850 species of small herbaceous plants that make up the genus *Oxalis,* native mostly to S Africa and tropical and S. America. Most members are familiar garden ornamentals. The common wood sorrel (*O. acetosella*) of E N. America and Britain is a small, stemless plant with cloverlike three-part leaves, whose edible leaflets fold back and droop at night. The flowers have five white, purple-veined petals.

oxbow lake Small crescent-shaped lake located in a former MEANDER loop of a river or stream channel. It is generally formed as a river cuts through a meander neck to shorten its course, blocks off the old channel, and then migrates away from the lake. Eventually, oxbow lakes silt up to form MARSHES.

Oxenstierna (af Södermöre) \'ük-sen-,sher-nä\, **Axel (Gustafsson), Count** (1583–1654) Swedish statesman. In 1612 he was appointed chancellor by GUSTAV II ADOLF, and helped stabilize administrative reforms. As a diplomat, he negotiated peace treaties with Denmark (1613) and Poland (1622). In the THIRTY YEARS' WAR, he was appointed governor-general of Prussia (1626) and military commander in Germany (1631). He directed Swedish policy in Germany until 1636. As a regent during Queen CHRISTINA's minority (1636–44), he effectively ruled the country.

Oxford *ancient* Oxonia. City (pop., 1994 est.: 133,000), county seat of OXFORDSHIRE, England. Situated on the THAMES RIVER, it is best known for the Univ. of OXFORD. From a fording point it became a burg, built to defend the N frontier of WESSEX from Danish attack; it was first mentioned in the Anglo-Saxon Chronicle of A.D. 912. It is known as the "City of Spires" because of its skyline of 15th–17th-cent. Gothic towers and steeples, most of which belong to the university. The city was the Royalist headquarters in the ENGLISH CIVIL WARS. Its modern economy includes printing and publishing.

Oxford, Earl of *orig.* Edward de Vere (1550–1604) English lyric poet. A brilliantly gifted linguist and one of the most dashing figures of his time, he was a patron of actors as well as of such writers as John LYLY and Edmund SPENSER. He wrote highly praised poems and plays in his earlier years, though none of the plays are known to have survived. A 1920 book by J. Thomas Looney made Oxford the leading candidate, next to William SHAKESPEARE himself, for the authorship of Shakespeare's plays, a theory supported by the coincidence that Oxford's literary output apparently ceased just before Shakespeare's work began to appear.

Oxford, Earl of See Robert HARLEY

Oxford, Provisions of (1258) Plan of reform accepted by HENRY III of England. On the verge of bankruptcy, Henry asked Parliament for a grant of revenue and agreed in return to a program of reform drafted by a royal commission. Regarded as England's first written constitution, the Provisions placed the government under the direction of the king and a 15-member baronial council, provided for Parliament to meet three times a year, and reformed local administration. They were annulled in 1266.

Oxford, University of Autonomous university at Oxford, England. It was founded in the 12th cent. and modeled on the Univ. of PARIS, with initial faculties of theology, law, medicine, and the liberal arts. Of the earliest colleges, Univ. College was founded in 1249, Balliol about 1263, and Merton in 1264. Early scholars of note include Roger BACON, John DUNS SCOTUS, William of OCKHAM, and John WYCLIFFE. In the Renaissance, Desiderius ERASMUS and Thomas MORE helped enhance its already considerable reputation. The first women's college, Lady Margaret Hall, was established in 1878. There are now 32 other colleges and collegial institutions. Oxford houses the BODLEIAN LIBRARY and the Ashmolean Museum of Art and Archaeology. Oxford Univ. Press (1478) is the world's oldest and largest university publisher. Oxford has been associated with many of the greatest names in British history. Enrollment is about 16,000.

Oxford English Dictionary, The (OED) Definitive historical DICTIONARY of the English language. It was conceived by London's Philological Society in 1857, and sustained editorial work began in 1879 under James A. H. MURRAY. It was published in 10 volumes between 1884 and 1928; its second edition was published in 20 volumes in 1989. Its definitions are illustrated with dated quotations from English-language literature and records.

Oxford movement *or* **Tractarian movement** (1833–45) Movement within the Church of ENGLAND that aimed to emphasize the church's Catholic inheritance as a source of legitimacy and deeper spirituality. Its main intent was to defend the Church of England as a divine institution against the threats of liberal theology, rationalism, and government interference. Though some in the movement (notably J. H. NEWMAN) ended up converting to Catholicism, most did not. Their concern for a higher standard of worship also influenced other British Protestant sects. The movement was instrumental in the establishment of Anglican monasteries and convents.

Oxfordshire \'äks-fərd-ˌshir\ County (pop., 1998 est.: 616,000), S central England. It consists of two upland areas divided by a broad vale. Evidence of inhabitation dates from the Paleolithic era. Dorchester was an important Roman settlement; Saxons later lived along the THAMES RIVER valley. The county saw action during the ENGLISH CIVIL WARS. The economy is basically agricultural, with sheep farming and wool production. The county seat is OXFORD.

oxidation-reduction *or* **redox** Any CHEMICAL REACTION in which ELECTRONS are transferred. Addition of hydrogen or electrons is reduction, and removal of hydrogen or electrons is oxidation. The processes always occur simultaneously: one substance is oxidized by the other, which it reduces. The conditions of the substances before and after are called oxidation states, to which numbers are given and with which calculations can be made. (VALENCE is a similar but not identical concept.) Strong oxidizing agents include FLUORINE, OZONE, and OXYGEN; strong reducing agents include ALKALI METALS such as SODIUM and LITHIUM.

oxide Any chemical compound in which OXYGEN is combined with another ELEMENT. METAL oxides contain the metal CATION and the oxide ANION (O_2^-); they typically react with water to form BASES or with acids to form SALTS. Oxides of nonmetallic elements are volatile compounds in which a COVALENT BOND joins the oxygen and the nonmetal; they react with water to form acids or with bases to form salts. A few substances (e.g., ALUMINUM, ZINC) form amphoteric oxides, which form salts with both acids and bases.

Oxus River See AMU DARYA

oxygen Gaseous chemical ELEMENT, chemical symbol O, atomic number 8. It constitutes 21% (by volume) of air and over 46% (by weight) of the earth's crust, where it is the most plentiful element. It is a colorless, odorless, tasteless GAS, occurring as the diatomic molecule O_2. In RESPIRATION, it is taken up by animals and some bacteria (and by plants in the dark), which give off CARBON DIOXIDE (CO_2). In PHOTOSYNTHESIS, green plants assimilate carbon dioxide in the presence of sunlight and give off oxygen. The small amount of oxygen that dissolves in water is essential for the respiration of fish and other aquatic life. Oxygen takes part in combustion and corrosion but does not itself burn. It has VALENCE 2 in compounds; the most important is WATER. It forms OXIDES and is part of many other molecules and FUNCTIONAL GROUPS, including NITRATE, SULFATE, PHOSPHATE, and CARBONATE; ALCOHOLS, ALDEHYDES, CARBOXYLIC ACIDS, and KETONES; and PEROXIDES. Obtained from liquefied air, oxygen is used in steelmaking and other metallurgical processes and in the chemical industry. Medical uses include respiratory therapy, incubators, and inhaled ANESTHETICS.

Oxyrhynchus \ˌäk-si-'riŋ-kəs\ Archaeological site, Egypt, on the W bank of the NILE RIVER. Many ancient papyri dating from 250 B.C. to A.D. 700 have been discovered here. Mainly in Greek and Latin, they contain both religious texts and masterpieces of Greek classical literature, some by PINDAR and CALLIMACHUS. The modern village of Al-Bahnasa is located on the site.

Oyo empire YORUBA state in present-day SW Nigeria. Two waves of immigrants probably entered the area around A.D. 700–1000, the second wave forming a state at Oyo. Oyo became preeminent among Yoruba states because of its good trading position, natural resources, and industrious inhabitants. By 1700 its ruler, Orompoto, had used trade-derived wealth to maintain a trained army. In the 18th cent. Oyo subjugated the DAHOMEY KINGDOM and began trading with European merchants at Dahomey's ports. Neglect of the army and of possibilities for territorial expansion by Abiodun (reigned c.1770–90) weakened central authority, and soon after 1800 Oyo was captured by FULANI Muslims from Hausaland.

oyster Any BIVALVE of two families, Ostreidae (true oysters) or Aviculidae (pearl oysters), found in temperate and warm coastal waters worldwide. Both valves (halves) have a rough, often dirty-gray outer surface and a smooth white lining (nacre). The oyster filters its food, minute organic particles, from the water. Cultivated as a food, oysters are regarded as a delicacy. PEARLS are the accumulation of nacre around a piece of foreign matter.

oystercatcher Any of about seven species (genus *Haematopus,* family Haematopodidae) of stout-bodied shorebirds inhabiting temperate and tropical seacoasts and inland waters worldwide. Oystercatchers are 16–20 in. (40–50 cm) long, with long pointed wings and a long orange-red bill. Their plumage varies from black-and-white to entirely black. They attack mollusks as the tide ebbs, when the shells are exposed and still partially open.

Ozark Mountains *or* **Ozark Plateau** Heavily forested highlands, S central U.S. Extending southwest from ST. LOUIS to the ARKANSAS RIVER, they occupy an area of about 50,000 sq mi (130,000 sq km) in Missouri, Arkansas, Illinois, and Kansas. The mountains were formed by the erosion of the original plateau; many of the highest peaks exceed 2,000 ft (600 m). Its scenic beauty makes it popular among tourists. Lake of the OZARKS provides power and recreational facilities.

Ozarks, Lake of the Lake, S central Missouri. One of the largest man-made lakes in the U.S., it is located in the scenic OZARK MTNS. Formed by the Bagnell Dam in the OSAGE RIVER, it is about 125 mi (200 km) long. The area has recreational fishing and water sport facilities and is a popular resort destination. Nearby are several limestone caverns.

Ozawa \ō-'zä-wə\, **Seiji** (b.1935) Japanese-U.S. (Manchurian-born) conductor. After study with Herbert von KARAJAN, he became assistant to Leonard BERNSTEIN (1961–65), then held posts in Toronto (1965–69) and San Francisco (1970–76) before taking over the Boston Symphony Orchestra in 1973. In 2002 he retired from the BSO to direct the Vienna State Opera.

Ozick \'ō-zik\, **Cynthia** (b.1928) U.S. novelist and short-story writer. Born in New York City, she has stressed Jewish themes in such works as *Trust* (1966), *Leviathan* (1982), *The Messiah of Stockholm* (1987), *The Shawl* (1990), and *The Puttermesser Papers* (1997). Collections of her essays include *Metaphor and Memory* (1989) and *Fame and Folly* (1996).

ozone Pale blue GAS (O_3) that is irritating, explosive, and toxic. Like ordinary OXYGEN gas (O_2), it contains oxygen atoms, but the BONDING differs. It is formed in electrical discharges, and accounts for the odor of the air after thunderstorms or near electrical equipment. It is used in water purification, deodorization, bleaching, and various CHEMICAL REACTIONS that require a strong oxidizing agent (see OXIDATION-REDUCTION). Small amounts that occur naturally in the OZONE LAYER absorb ULTRAVIOLET (UV) RADIATION, which otherwise could severely damage living organisms. Ozone contributes to AIR POLLUTION as a component of SMOG.

ozone layer or **ozonosphere** Region in the upper ATMOSPHERE, about 6–30 mi (10–50 km) high, with significant concentrations of OZONE, formed from OXYGEN by solar ULTRAVIOLET (UV) RADIATION. Ozone strongly absorbs such radiation, preventing much of it from reaching earth's surface and injuring living things. CHLOROFLUOROCARBONS, or CFCs, and some other air pollutants destroy ozone. In the mid-1980s, scientists discovered that a "hole"—where the ozone layer is up to 50% thinner than normal—develops periodically above Antarctica. A natural seasonal depletion, apparently exacerbated by the effects of CFCs, it may have led to an increase in SKIN CANCER.

Ozu \'ō-zü\, **Yasujiro** (1903–1963) Japanese film director. He directed his first film in 1926. He originated the genre known as *shomin-geki* ("common-people's drama"), which treated lower-middle-class Japanese family life, with such films as the silent comedies *I Graduated, But* . . . (1929) and *I Was Born, But* . . . (1932). His later films, noted for their detailed character portrayals, pictorial beauty, and quiet, contemplative mood, include *Late Spring* (1949), *Tokyo Story* (1953), *Early Spring* (1956), and *An Autumn Afternoon* (1962).

P

Paasikivi \\'pä-si-ki-vē\\, **Juho Kusti** (1870–1956) Finnish statesman. He served as independent Finland's first prime minister in 1918. Later he was prominent as a banker and businessman. As minister to Sweden (1936–39), he negotiated a treaty to end the Russo–Finnish War (1940). He later served as Finland's prime minister (1944–46) and later president (1946–56). While maintaining friendly relations with the Soviet Union, he was uncompromising in his defense of Finnish independence and resisted the growth of communist influence in Finland.

Pabst \\'päpst\\, **G(eorg) W(ilhelm)** (1885–1967) Austrian film director. Initially an actor and stage director, he later directed films in Berlin, beginning with *The Treasure* (1923) and continuing with *The Joyless Street* (1925), *Secrets of a Soul* (1926), and *The Love of Jeanne Ney* (1927). His masterpieces, *Pandora's Box* (1929) and *Diary of a Lost Girl* (1929), both starred Louise BROOKS. Later films include *The Threepenny Opera* (1931). He moved to France in 1933, and to Austria after the war.

pacemaker Source of rhythmic electrical impulses that trigger HEART contractions. In the heart's electrical system, impulses generated at a natural pacemaker are conducted to the atria and ventricles. Heart surgery or certain diseases can interrupt conduction, requiring an artificial pacemaker. A small electrode attached to an electric generator is threaded through a vein into the heart. The generator, inserted beneath the skin, produces regular pulses of electric charge to maintain the heartbeat. Permanent pacemakers can also be implanted on the heart's surface.

Pachelbel \\päk-'el-,bel, *Engl* 'pä-kəl-,bel\\, **Johann** (1653–1706) German composer and organist. Conservative musically, he taught J. S. BACH's relative and teacher J. C. Bach (1671–1721). Though he wrote a huge amount of music, including superb organ chorale variations and Magnificat settings, he is principally known today for a single piece, the Canon in D.

Pacher \\'päk-ər\\, **Michael** (1435–1498) Austrian painter and sculptor. His colossal altarpiece for the Pilgrimage Church of St. Wolfgang (1479–81) is a masterpiece of late Gothic painting, sculpture, and architecture. The painted panels, with their deep architectural perspective and dramatic foreshortening, indicate knowledge of Andrea MANTEGNA, and the sculptural portions, with their intricate detail, bright polychrome, and sweeping draperies, show his attachment to N traditions. Pacher was one of the earliest artists to introduce the principles of Renaissance painting into German-speaking regions.

Pachuca (de Soto) City (pop., 1995: 210,000), capital of HIDALGO state, central Mexico. Founded in 1534, it was one of the first settlements in NEW SPAIN. It lies in the Sierra Madre Oriental, 8,150 ft (2,484 m) above sea level. Its silver mines date from the 16th cent., when the Mexican process of separating silver from the ore by amalgamation with mercury was perfected there.

Pacific, War of the (1879–83) Conflict involving Chile, Bolivia, and Peru over disputed territory on the Pacific coast. In the 1870s Chile controlled nitrate fields located in Peru and Bolivia. As demand for nitrates rose, war broke out over the territory. Chile defeated both countries, and Bolivia lost its entire Pacific coast. A 1904 treaty gave Bolivian commerce freedom of transit through Chilean territory, but it continued to try to escape its landlocked status (see CHACO WAR). Peru foundered economically for decades af-

ter the war. A final accord between Peru and Chile was reached only in 1929 through U.S. mediation.

Pacification of Ghent See Pacification of GHENT

Pacific Coast Ranges See COAST RANGES

Pacific Islands, Trust Territory of the Former UNITED NATIONS trusteeship, administered by the U.S. 1947–86. It consisted of more than 2,000 islands scattered over the W Pacific Ocean, north of the equator. It covered the region known as MICRONESIA and consisted of three major island groups: the MARIANAS, the CAROLINES, and the MARSHALLS. The seat of government was SAIPAN. In 1986 the Federated States of Micronesia and the Republic of the Marshall Islands became sovereign states and the Northern Mariana Islands became a commonwealth of the U.S. The Republic of PALAU became a sovereign state in 1994.

Pacific Ocean Body of salt water extending from the Antarctic region in the south to the Arctic circle in the north and lying between Asia and Australia on the west and N. and S. America on the east. It occupies about one-third of the earth's surface and is by far the largest of the world's OCEANS. Its area, excluding adjacent seas, is approximately 63,800,000 sq mi (165,250,000 sq km), twice that of the ATLANTIC OCEAN and more than the whole land area of the globe.

Pacific Railway Acts (1862, 1864) Measures providing federal aid for construction of a U.S. transcontinental railroad. The first act granted rights-of-way to the UNION PACIFIC RAILROAD to build westward from Omaha, Neb., and to the Central Pacific Railroad to build eastward from Sacramento, Cal. The second act doubled the size of the land grants and allowed the railroads to sell bonds. Investigations later showed that some railroad owners had illegally profited from the acts.

Pacific Security Treaty See ANZUS PACT

pacifism \\'pa-sə-,fi-zəm\\ Opposition to war and violence as a means of settling disputes. BUDDHISM was the first genuinely pacifist movement; the Buddhist king ASHOKA renounced war, though Buddhist doctrines did not prevent later rulers from waging war. The Greek conception of peace was an individual one, while the Pax Romana of the Roman empire did not apply to so-called barbarians. Aspects of Christianity supported pacifism, but only for those within the fold. In the 17th–18th cent., pacifist thought focused on the idea that transferring power from sovereigns to the people would result in peace, because, it was claimed, wars were a product of sovereigns' ambitions and pride. In the 19th–20th cent., the pacifist theme led to interest in general disarmament and the founding of the LEAGUE OF NATIONS and the UNITED NATIONS. Personal pacifism may lead one to become a CONSCIENTIOUS OBJECTOR. Leo TOLSTOY, Mohandas GANDHI, and Martin Luther KING became well known for their pacifism.

Pacino \\pə-'chē-nō\\, **Al(fredo James)** (b.1940) U.S. actor. Born in New York City, he began as a stage actor, winning Tony awards for *Does a Tiger Wear a Necktie?* (1969) and later for *The Basic Training of Pavlo Hummel* (1977). He won the important film role of Michael Corleone in *The Godfather* (1972) and its sequels (1974, 1990), and also starred in such films as *Serpico* (1973), *Dog Day Afternoon* (1975), *Scarface* (1983), *Glengarry Glen Ross* (1992), *Scent of a Woman* (1992, Academy Award), and *The Insider* (1999), earning a reputation as one of the finest of U.S. actors.

pack ice Floating mass of ice formed from seawater in polar regions. Pack ice expands during winter to cover about 5%

of the N oceans and 8% of the S oceans. In the Northern Hemisphere it covers an average area of about 4 million sq mi (10 million sq km), filling the Arctic Ocean basin and adjacent N. Atlantic Ocean. The maximum area of Antarctic pack ice is about 7.5 million sq mi (20 million sq km).

Paderewski \ˌpa-də-ˈref-skē\ **Ignacy Jan** (1860–1941) Polish pianist, composer, and statesman. While teaching at the Warsaw Conservatory (1878–83), he wrote most of the pieces he is remembered for (including the famous Minuet in G). On a 117-concert N. American tour, his pianism and dashingly extended Romantic image brought him a wild popularity. In 1919 he served briefly as the first premier of the new Polish state, representing it at the Paris Peace Conference.

Padre Island \ˈpä-drē, ˈpä-drā\ Barrier island, S Texas. It is 113 mi (182 km) long, and extends south from CORPUS CHRISTI to Port Isabel. It contains a recreational preserve with a large variety of birdlife, excellent fishing, and a broad beach.

Padua \ˈpa-dyü-wə\ *Italian* **Padova** \ˈpä-dō-vä\ *ancient* Patavium. City (pop., 1998: 212,000), N Italy. Legend holds that it was founded by the Trojan hero Antenor. First mentioned in 302 B.C., it prospered as a Roman city. A leading Italian commune in the 11th–13th cent., it passed to VENICE, which held it from 1405 to 1797. Under Austrian rule 1815–66, it was active in the RISORGIMENTO. Its historic buildings contain works by GIOTTO, TITIAN, DONATELLO, and MANTEGNA. The Univ. of Padua (1222), the second-oldest in Italy, had GALILEO among its teachers and DANTE, PETRARCH, and TASSO among its students. Padua's botanical garden (1545) is the oldest in Europe.

Paekche \ˈpak-ˌchə\ One of three kingdoms into which Korea was divided before 660. It is traditionally said to have been founded in 18 B.C. by the legendary leader Onjo. In the 3rd cent. A.D. Paekche emerged as a fully developed kingdom, and by the 4th cent. it extended from the SW tip to central Korea and was a centralized aristocratic state. Confucianism and Buddhism flourished, and Paekche's visual arts revealed technical maturity and warm human qualities. In the 5th cent. it was pushed south by the N Korean kingdom of KOGURYO, and in 660 it fell to an alliance of the S Korean state of SILLA and TANG-DYNASTY China.

Paestum \ˈpes-təm, ˈpēs-təm\ Ancient city, S Italy, on the Gulf of Salerno. It was founded in the 6th cent. B.C. by Greek colonists from SYBARIS, who called it Poseidonia, and later taken by the Lucanians, an indigenous Italic people. In 273 B.C. the city was captured by the Romans. It was sacked by Muslim raiders in A.D. 871. It is known for its three Doric temples and its city walls of travertine blocks.

Pagan \pə-ˈgän\ Village, central Myanmar. Extending along the IRRAWADDY RIVER, southwest of MANDALAY, it was founded about A.D. 849 and was the capital of a powerful dynasty from the 11th cent. until it was conquered by the MONGOLS in 1287. As a center of Buddhist learning, it is a pilgrimage destination. Ruined and restored shrines and pagodas cover a wide area. An earthquake in 1975 destroyed or damaged more than half of the important structures.

pagan Follower of a religion other than CHRISTIANITY, JUDAISM, and ISLAM. The early Christians often used the term to refer to non-Christians who worshiped multiple deities. Christian missionaries frequently sought to stamp out pagan practices by building churches on the sites of pagan shrines or by associating Christian holidays with pagan rituals. The term pagan was also used to refer to non-Christian philosophers.

Paganini \ˌpa-gə-ˈnē-nē\ **Niccolò** (1782–1840) Italian violinist and composer. A prodigy, he joined an orchestra by age 9. He toured Italy 1810–28, renowned as its greatest

Niccolò Paganini After a drawing by J.-A.-D. Ingres, 1818

violin virtuoso in the world though dismissed by serious musicians as a showman. His long-deferred international tour (1830–34) created frenzy, and some believed he had made a pact with the devil for his amazing talent. Paganini greatly extended violin technique; his numerous compositions include 24 solo *Caprices* and six violin concertos.

Paget's disease of bone *or* **osteitis deformans** \ˌäs-tē-ˈīt-əs\ Chronic disease of middle age, with locally disorganized BONE destruction alternating with disordered bone construction. The long bones, vertebrae, pelvis, and skull are most often affected, more often in men. The risk of cancer, usually osteosarcoma, is high. Calcitonin (which regulates bone growth) and bisphosphonates (which block excessive bone breakdown) are drugs of treatment.

pagoda Towerlike, multistoried structure, usually associated with a Buddhist temple complex and enshrining sacred relics. It evolved from the Indian STUPA. The pagoda's crowning ornament is bottle-shaped in Tibet and pyramidal or conical in S.E. Asia. In China, Korea, and Japan, a pagoda is a tall tower repeating a basic story unit in diminishing proportions. The pagoda form is intended mainly as a monument and has very little usable interior space.

Pago Pago \ˌpäŋ-ō-ˈpäŋ-ō, ˈpä-gō-ˈpä-gō\ Town (pop., 1990: 4,000), capital of AMERICAN SAMOA. Located on Tutuila Island, it was a U.S. Navy coaling station from 1872 and an active naval base until 1951. Its airport, opened in 1964, has stimulated tourism and modernization.

Pahlavi \ˈpa-lə-ˌvē\ **Mohammad Reza Shah** (1919–1980) Shah of Iran (1941–79). After an education in Switzerland, he replaced his father, Reza Shah PAHLAVI, as ruler when the latter was forced into exile. His rule was marked by a power struggle with his premier, Muhammad MOSADDEQ, who briefly deposed him in 1953. His program of rapid modernization and oil-field development initially brought him popular support, but his autocratic style, along with corruption and the unequal distribution of oil wealth, led to increasing opposition, led by the exiled Ruhollah KHOMEINI. In 1979 he was forced into exile, where he died of cancer.

Pahlavi, Reza Shah (1878–1944) Shah of Iran (1926–41). Born to a family of tribal chiefs, he rose through the army ranks and in 1921 led a coup that overthrew the QAJAR dynasty. He constructed roads, schools, and hospitals, opened a university, and built the Trans-Iranian Railway. He emancipated women and banned the veil, nationalized several economic sectors, and reduced the clergy's power by repressive methods. During World War II the U.S. and Britain occupied Iran to prevent an alliance with Germany, forcing him to abdicate in favor of his son, M. R. Shah PAHLAVI.

Paige, Satchel (*orig.* Leroy Robert) (1906?–1982) U.S. baseball pitcher. Born in Mobile, Ala., he earned legendary fame during his many years in the NEGRO LEAGUES. He was 42 when he was finally allowed to enter the major leagues in 1948. Joining the Cleveland Indians, he helped that team win the World Series that year. He retired after six seasons. A right-handed, loose-jointed "beanpole" standing 6 ft 4 in. (1 m 93 cm), Paige had considerable pitching speed and a comprehensive mastery of slow-breaking deliveries. He is reputed to have won 2,000 of a total of 2,500 games pitched during his nearly 30-year career.

Paik \ˈpāk, ˈpīk\ **Nam June** (b.1932) Korean-U.S. sculptor and video and performance artist. He studied music at the Univs. of Tokyo and Munich, and came to the U.S. in 1964. Inspired by Joseph BEUYS and John CAGE, he joined the FLUXUS group. He is considered the father of video art. His sophisticated video displays, such as *TV Buddha* (1974), an installation with a Buddha contemplating himself on television, were seen as uniquely appropriate to the despiritualized Information Age.

pain Physical suffering associated with disease or injury and accompanied by mental or emotional distress. Pain, in its simplest form, is a warning mechanism that helps protect an organism by influencing it to withdraw from harmful stimuli. In its more complex form, as in a chronic condition accompanied by depression or anxiety, it can be difficult to isolate and treat. Pain receptors, found in the skin and other tissues, are nerve fibers that react to mechanical, thermal, and chemical stimuli. Pain impulses enter the spinal cord and are transmitted to the brain stem and thalamus. The perception of pain is highly variable among individuals; it is influenced by previous experiences, cultural attitudes, and genetic makeup. Medication, rest, and emotional support are the standard treatments. Pain-relieving drugs range from OPIUM and MORPHINE to ANALGESICS such as ASPIRIN and IBUPROFEN.

Paine, Thomas (1737–1809) British-American political philosopher. After an early life of failed prospects in England, he arrived in Philadelphia in 1774, where he helped edit the *Pennsylvania Magazine.* In 1776 he wrote *Common Sense,* a 50-page pamphlet eloquently advocating independence; more than 500,000 copies were quickly sold, and it greatly strengthened the colonists' resolve. In the AMERICAN REVOLUTION he served as an aide to Gen. Nathanael GREENE and wrote the 16 *Crisis* papers (1776–83), each signed "Common Sense." Paine traveled to England in 1787. His *The Rights of Man* (1791–92) defended the French Revolution and

Thomas Paine Portrait by J. W. Jarvis

espoused republicanism; seen as an attack on the monarchy, it was banned and Paine was declared an outlaw in England. He went to France, where he was elected to the National Convention (1792–93). He criticized the REIGN OF TERROR and was soon imprisoned (1793–94). After his release, he wrote *The Age of Reason* (1794, 1796), a work on DEISM and an attack on organized religion. He returned to the U.S. in 1802; criticized for his Deist writings and little remembered for his service to the Revolution, he died in poverty.

paint Decorative and protective coating commonly applied to rigid surfaces as a liquid consisting of a PIGMENT suspended in a vehicle, or binder. The vehicle, usually a RESIN dissolved in a SOLVENT, dries to a tough film, binding the pigment to the surface. Paint was used for pictorial and decorative purposes in the caves of France and Spain as early as 15,000 B.C.

Painted Desert Region, N central Arizona. It stretches about 150 mi (240 km) from the GRAND CANYON to PETRIFIED FOREST NATIONAL PARK and has an area of about 7,500 sq mi (19,425 sq km). Its name describes the area's brilliantly colored rock surfaces, exposed by erosion. Much of the desert lies within NAVAJO and HOPI reservations. Navajo tribes use the variegated sands in ceremonial sand paintings.

painting Art consisting of representational, imaginative, or abstract designs produced by application of colored paints to a flat surface. The elements of design (i.e., line, color, tone, texture) are used in various ways to produce sensations of volume, space, movement, and light. The range of media (e.g., TEMPERA, FRESCO, OIL, WATERCOLOR) and the choice of a particular form (e.g., MURAL, easel, panel, MINIATURE) combine to realize a unique visual image. The early cultural traditions of tribes, religions, guilds, royal courts, and states controlled the craft and subject matter of painting and determined its function (e.g., ritualistic, devotional, decorative). Painters were considered merely skilled artisans until eventually, in the Far East and Renaissance Europe, the creative artist emerged with the social status of a scholar and courtier.

Paisiello \ˌpä-ēz-ˈye-lō\, **Giovanni** (1740–1816) Italian composer. He served CATHERINE II as chapel master in St. Petersburg (1776–84), writing many short operas. He enjoyed his first operatic success in Vienna in 1784, but returned to Naples to work for Ferdinand IV, and remained there despite changes in regime until 1815. His 80 operas include a very popular *Barber of Seville* (1782).

Paisley, Ian (Richard Kyle) (b.1926) Protestant leader in Northern Ireland. A minister, he cofounded a new sect, the

Free Presbyterian Church of Ulster (1951), which soon grew to over 30 churches. In the 1960s he became the voice of extreme Protestant opinion in Northern Ireland, opposed to any concessions to the Catholics. He led demonstrations throughout Northern Ireland and was repeatedly imprisoned for unlawful assembly. Elected to the House of Commons, he cofounded the Democratic Unionist Party in 1971, which continues to oppose peace agreements in Northern Ireland.

Paiute \ˈpī-ˌyüt\ Either of two distinct American Indian groups. The Southern Paiute occupied what is now S Utah, NW Arizona, S Nevada, and SW California; the Northern Paiute occupied E central California, W Nevada, and E Oregon. Both groups subsisted on wild plant foods, supplemented by small game. They occupied temporary brush shelters, used rabbit-skin clothing, and made baskets for food gathering. Most Paiute were directed onto reservations in the 19th cent.; today they number about 7,500. See also UTE.

Pakistan *officially* **Islamic Republic of Pakistan** Nation, S Asia. Area: 307,374 sq mi (796,095 sq km). Population (2000): 141,554,000. Capital: ISLAMABAD. The population is a complex mix of indigenous peoples that have been affected by

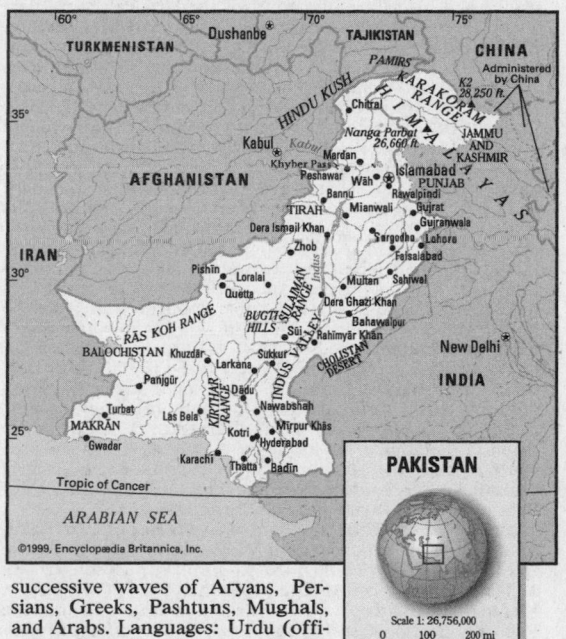

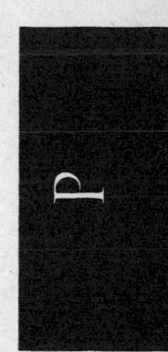

successive waves of Aryans, Persians, Greeks, Pashtuns, Mughals, and Arabs. Languages: Urdu (official), Punjabi, Pashto, Sindhi, Balochi. Religions: Islam (official), Hinduism, Christianity. Currency: Pakistan rupee. Pakistan may be divided into four regions: the great highlands, the Baluchistan Plateau, the Indus Plain, and the desert areas. The Himalayan and Trans-Himalayan ranges form the great highlands, in the northernmost part of the country; the highest peaks include K2 and NANGA PARBAT. It has a developing mixed economy based largely on agriculture, light industries, and services. Unemployment is widespread and emigration has depleted the workforce; remittances from Pakistanis working abroad are a major source of foreign exchange. It is an Islamic republic with two legislative houses; its chief of state and government is the chief executive, assisted by the national security council. The area has been inhabited since about 3500 B.C. From the 3rd cent. B.C. to the 2nd cent. A.D., it was part of the Mauryan and Kushan kingdoms. The first Muslim conquests were in the 8th cent. A.D. The British EAST INDIA CO. subdued the reigning MUGHAL DYNASTY in 1757. During the period of British colonial rule, what is now (Muslim) Pakistan was part of (Hindu) India. The new state of Pakistan came into existence in 1947 by act of the British Parliament. Kashmir remained a disputed territory between Pakistan and India, resulting in military clashes and full-scale war in 1965. Civil war between E. and W. Pakistan in 1971 resulted in independence for Bangladesh (formerly E. Pakistan) in 1972. Many Afghan refugees migrated to Pakistan during the Soviet–Afghan War in the 1980s. Pakistan elected Benazir BHUTTO, the first woman to head a modern Islamic state, in 1988. She was ousted in 1990 by a conservative coalition. From the 1990s political conditions were volatile and the economy precarious. Border flare-ups with India continued and Pakistan conducted nuclear tests. The army carried out a coup in 1999. Having sponsored the TALIBAN in neighboring Afghanistan, Pakistan joined the U.S. in overthrowing it in 2001.

palace Royal residence, and sometimes a seat of government or religious center. The earliest known palaces are those of the Egyptian kings at Thebes. Other ancient cultures also built vast palaces—the Assyrian palaces at Nimrud, Khorsabad, and Nineveh; the Minoan palace at Knossos; and the Persian palaces at Persepolis and Susa. In Rome and Constantinople, palaces reached their peak as centers of power. In Western Europe after the Middle Ages, palaces tended to be single buildings. In Renaissance Italy every prince had his palace; the court of the Pitti Palace in Florence (1560) is a fine example of Mannerist architecture. French palaces include the LOUVRE and VERSAILLES; Spanish palaces include EL ESCORIAL and the ALHAMBRA. In contrast to the typical Western format, E. Asia's palaces, such as the imperial palaces of Japan and those in Beijing's FORBIDDEN CITY, consist of many buildings (often highly decorated wooden pavilions) within vast, walled gardens.

palate \'pa-lət\ Roof of the MOUTH, separating the oral and nasal cavities (see NOSE). The front two-thirds, the hard palate, is a plate of bone covered by mucous membrane. It gives the TONGUE a surface to act against and keeps pressures in the mouth from closing off the nasal passage. The flexible soft palate behind it is made of muscle and connective tissue and ends in the uvula, a fleshy projection. It rises to block the nasal cavity and upper PHARYNX off from the mouth and lower pharynx for swallowing or to create a vacuum for drinking. See also CLEFT PALATE.

Palatinate \pə-'la-tᵊn-ət\ *German* **Pfalz** \'pfälts\ Historical region, now part of Germany. It was once under the jurisdiction of the counts palatine, who in the 14th cent. became ELECTORS of the HOLY ROMAN EMPIRE. The Lower, or Rhenish, Palatinate, lay along the RHINE RIVER in the area south of the MAIN RIVER, the Upper Palatinate in N Bavaria around Amberg and Regensburg. The capital of the Lower Palatinate was HEIDELBERG until the 18th cent.

Palau \pə-'laù\ *or* **Belau** \bə-'laù\ *officially* **Republic of Palau** *formerly* **Pelew** Independent island republic, W Pacific Ocean. Area: 188 sq mi (487 sq km). Population (2000): 19,000. Capital: KOROR. The population is of mixed Malay, Melanesian, Filipino, and Polynesian ancestry. Languages: Palauan, Sonsorolese-Tobian, English (all official). Religions: Roman Catholicism, Protestantism, Modekne. Currency: U.S. dollar. Of its more than 200 islands, fewer than 10 are permanently populated. The islands are fertile, with mangrove swamps along the coasts, backed by savanna and palms rising to rain forests in the hills. The major source of employment is government service. Subsistence farming and fishing are the main occupations in rural areas. It is a republic with two legislative houses; its head of state and government is the president. The islands were under nominal Spanish ownership for more than three centuries when they were sold to Germany in 1899. They were seized by Japan in 1914 and taken by Allied forces in 1944 during World War II. Palau became part of the U.S. Trust Territory of the PACIFIC ISLANDS in 1947 and became a sovereign state in 1994; the U.S. provides economic assistance and maintains a military presence in the islands. See also map at OCEANIA.

Palembang \ˌpä-lem-'bäŋ\ City (pop., 1995 est.: 1,352,000) and river port, S Sumatra, Indonesia. It was the capital of a Buddhist kingdom in the 7th–14th cent. A.D. before being overthrown by the Hindu Majapahit empire. The Dutch EAST INDIA CO. built a fort there in 1659. It was included in the Republic of Indonesia in 1950. The port is accessible to

ocean traffic and has considerable trade with the MALAY PENINSULA, Thailand, and China.

Palenque \pä-'leŋ-kä\ Ruined ancient Mayan city of the Late Classic period (c.A.D. 600–900) in Chiapas state, Mexico, considered the most beautiful of Mayan sites. The principal structure is the Palace, a labyrinth of galleries with interior courts, a four-story square tower, and walls embellished with delicate stucco reliefs of rulers, gods, and ceremonies. The great Temple of the Inscriptions is noted for its hieroglyphics and a vast funerary crypt filled with jade.

Paleocene epoch \'pā-lē-ə-ˌsēn\ Earliest division of the TERTIARY PERIOD, 65–55 million years ago. It was characterized by a generally warming climate, with little or no frost; seasonal variation probably consisted of alternating dry and wet seasons. The epoch saw the rapid proliferation and evolution of mammals. See table at GEOLOGIC TIME.

paleoclimatology Scientific study of the extended climatic conditions of past geologic ages. It seeks to explain climate variations for all parts of the earth during any given geologic period. The basic research data are drawn mainly from geology and paleobotany; speculative attempts at explanation have come largely from astronomy, atmospheric physics, meteorology, and geophysics.

paleogeography Geography of selected portions of the earth's surface at specific times in the geologic past. The simplest paleogeographic map shows the locations of ancient lands and seas, but it may also show the distribution of fossil, plant, and animal communities; environments of sedimentation (e.g., deltas, reefs, deserts, or deep-sea basins); areas undergoing uplift and erosion or subsidence and deposition; and major climatic zones.

Paleolithic period \ˌpā-lē-ə-'li-thik\ ("Old Stone Age") Ancient technological or cultural stage characterized by the use of rudimentary chipped stone tools. During the Lower Paleolithic (c.2.5 million–200,000 years ago), simple pebble tools and crude stone choppers were made by the earliest human ancestors. About 700,000 years ago, the first rough hand ax appeared. A flake-tool tradition emerged in the Middle Paleolithic (see MOUSTERIAN INDUSTRY). The Upper Paleolithic (40,000–10,000 B.C.) saw the emergence of more complex, specialized, and diverse regional stone-tool industries, such as the AURIGNACIAN and MAGDALENIAN. The two principal forms of Paleolithic art are small sculptures, including the so-called Venus figurines and various carved or shaped animals, and monumental paintings and reliefs in caves such as ALTAMIRA and LASCAUX. The end of the Paleolithic is marked by the emergence of the settled agricultural villages of the NEOLITHIC PERIOD.

paleontology Scientific study of life of the geologic past, involving analysis of plant and animal FOSSILS preserved in rocks. It is concerned with the biology of ancient life forms, including their shape and structure, evolutionary patterns, taxonomic relationships, and geographic distribution. Paleontology has played a key role in reconstructing the earth's history and has provided evidence to support the theory of evolution. It has also aided petroleum geologists in locating deposits of oil and natural gas, which are frequently associated with the remains of certain ancient life forms.

Paleozoic era \ˌpā-lē-ə-'zō-ik\ Major interval of geologic time, 544–248 million years ago. From the Greek for "ancient life," it is the earliest era of the PHANEROZOIC EON and is divided into six periods: the CAMBRIAN (the earliest), ORDOVICIAN, SILURIAN, DEVONIAN, CARBONIFEROUS, and PERMIAN. During the early Paleozoic, much of N. America was covered by a warm, shallow sea with many coral reefs. Fossils include marine invertebrates and primitive fish; the plants were predominantly algae, with some mosses and ferns. During the late Paleozoic, huge, swampy forest regions covered much of the N continents. Amphibians left the oceans to live on land, reptiles became fully terrestrial, insect life began, and precursors of the conifers appeared. See table at GEOLOGIC TIME.

Palermo *ancient* Panormus. City (metro. area pop., 1998 est.: 688,000), seaport, and capital of SICILY, Italy. Founded by Phoenician traders in the 8th cent. B.C., it was taken by the Romans in 254 B.C. Conquered by the Arabs in A.D. 831, it flourished as a center of trade with N. Africa. It enjoyed its golden age as capital of the Norman kingdom of Sicily founded by King ROGER II in 1130. In 1194 Germany's Hohenstaufen ruler FREDERICK II took over. In 1282 the SICILIAN VESPERS uprising ended the subsequent French rule. It was taken by Giuseppe GARIBALDI in 1860 and made part of the kingdom of Italy. Heavily bombed during World War II, it was captured by Allied forces in 1943. Ship repair is a leading industry.

Palestine *biblical* **Canaan** Region, at the E end of the MEDITERRANEAN SEA. It extends east to the JORDAN RIVER, north to Lebanon, west to the Mediterranean, and south to the NEGEV desert, reaching the Gulf of AQABA. The political status and geographical area designated by the term have changed considerably over three millennia. The E boundary has been particularly fluid, often understood as lying east of the Jordan and extending at times to the edge of the ARABIAN DESERT. A land of sharp contrasts, it includes the DEAD SEA and, 2,000-ft (600-m) mountain peaks. In the 20th cent. it has been the object of conflicting claims by Jewish and Arab national movements. The region is sacred to Judaism, Christianity, and Islam. Settled since early prehistoric times, it was occupied in biblical times by the kingdoms of Israel, JUDAH, and JUDAEA. It was subsequently held by the Assyrians, Persians, Romans, Byzantines, Crusaders, and Ottoman Turks, among others. It was governed by Britain under a League of Nations (later U.N.) mandate from the end of World War I until 1948, when the state of Israel was proclaimed.

Palestine Liberation Organization (PLO) *Arabic* Munazzamat al-Tahrir Filastiniyah. Umbrella political organization representing the aspiration for a Palestinian state. It was formed in 1964 to centralize the leadership of various groups. In 1969 Yasir ARAFAT, leader of FATAH, the PLO's largest component group, became its chairman. From the late 1960s the PLO engaged in terrorist attacks on Israel from bases in Jordan; in 1971 King HUSSEIN I expelled it, and PLO headquarters moved to Lebanon. In 1974 Arafat advocated limiting terrorism, and the Arab community recognized the PLO as representing all Palestinians. It was admitted to the ARAB LEAGUE in 1976. In 1982 Israel invaded Lebanon to neutralize the PLO presence there. The PLO leadership, having moved to Tunis, declared a State of Palestine in 1988, and in 1989 elected Arafat president. It also recognized Israel's right to exist, though militant factions dissented. In 1993 Arafat and Yitzhak RABIN signed an accord calling for transition to Palestinian self-rule of the WEST BANK and GAZA STRIP. See also LEBANESE CIVIL WAR.

Palestinian Talmud See TALMUD

Palestrina See PRAENESTE

Palestrina \ˌpa-lə-ˈstrē-nə\, **Giovanni Pierluigi da** (1526?–1594) Italian composer. Having worked as an organist in his hometown of Palestrina, he was appointed director of the Vatican's Cappella Giulia by Pope Julius II in 1551, and later worked at the other great Roman churches. When the Council of TRENT dictated a musical style that permitted the words to be readily understood, a legend grew up that Palestrina's *Pope Marcellus Mass*, written in the simpler style, had actually saved church polyphony from being banned altogether. He wrote 104 masses, almost 400 motets, and at least 140 madrigals. After his death, his superbly balanced and serene music was proclaimed as a model for Catholic church music. The modern study of counterpoint dates from the codification of his practice in the 18th cent.

Paley, William S(amuel) (1901–1990) U.S. broadcaster. Born in Chicago, he worked in his family's cigar business from 1922. His success at increasing sales through radio advertisements led him to invest in a small radio network, Columbia Broadcasting System, and he built CBS into one of the world's leading radio and television networks, serving as president 1928–46 and chairman of the board 1946–90. He launched CBS News in 1933 and built its outstanding staff, and he hired top entertainment stars for CBS's other radio and television shows.

Pali canon See TRIPITAKA

Palikir \ˌpä-lē-ˈkir\ Capital of the Federated States of MICRONESIA. It is located on the island of Pohnpei (formerly Ponape, pop., 1998: 34,000). Scuba diving is popular at Palikir Pass.

Pali language \ˈpä-lē\ Middle INDO-ARYAN LANGUAGE of the 5th cent. B.C. in which the most essential documents of THERAVADA Buddhism are written. Linguistically, Pali is a homogenization of the N Middle Indo-Aryan dialects in which the BUDDHA's teachings were orally recorded and transmitted. No single script was ever developed for Pali; scribes used scripts of their own languages to copy canonical texts and commentaries, and most extant palm-leaf manuscripts of Pali are of relatively recent date. See also TRIPITAKA.

Palladio \pä-ˈläd-yō\, **Andrea** *orig.* Andrea di Pietro della Gondola (1508–1580) Italian architect. His first palace design, the Palazzo Civena (1540–46), was innovative for its use of an arcaded area behind the main elevation, in imitation of a Roman forum. In his villas, Palladio tried to recreate the Roman villa based on ancient descriptions. His first, Villa Godi at Lonedo (c.1540–42), contained elements for which he is famous, including symmetrical wings and a walled court. His most widely copied villa was the Villa Rotonda (1550–51), near Vicenza. His reconstruction of the Basilica (town hall) in Vicenza (begun 1549) employs a two-story arcade with a motif that came to be known as Palladian: rounded arches flanked by rectangular openings. His facades for three Venetian churches became prototypes for attaching classical temple fronts to basilicas. Palladio was the first to systematize the plan of a house and to use the ancient Greco-Roman temple front as a portico. His *Four Books of Architecture* was possibly the most influential architectural pattern book ever printed. His influence climaxed during the 18th-cent. Classical Revival; the resulting Palladianism spread through Europe and the U.S.

palm Any of about 2,800 species of flowering, subtropical trees, shrubs, and vines that make up the family Arecaceae (or Palmae). Many are economically important. Palms furnish food, shelter, clothing, timber, fuel, building materials, fibers, starch, oils, waxes, and wines. Many species have very limited ranges; some grow only on single islands. The usually tall, unbranched, columnar trunk is crowned by a tuft of large, pleated, fan- or feather-shaped leaves, the bases of which remain after leaves drop, often clothing the trunk. Trunk height and diameter, leaf length, and seed size vary greatly. Small flowers are produced in large clusters. Among the most important palms are the sugar palm (*Arenga pinnata*, or *saccharifera*), COCONUT PALM, DATE PALM, and PALMETTO.

Palma (de Mallorca) City (pop., 1998 est.: 319,000), capital of the BALEARIC ISLANDS and of MAJORCA island, Spain, in the W Mediterranean Sea. It lies on the SW coast of Majorca. The city has notable homes built in the 16th and 18th cent. as well as a historic Gothic cathedral and Bellver Castle.

Palmas, Las See LAS PALMAS

Palme \ˈpäl-mə\, **(Sven) Olof (Joachim)** (1927–1986) Swedish prime minister (1969–76, 1982–86). Elected to the Swedish parliament (1958) he became a leader of the Swedish Social Democratic Workers' Party. He became prime minister in 1969. A strong pacifist, he attacked U.S. policy in the Vietnam War and later acted as a U.N. special envoy to mediate in the Iran–Iraq War. After his reelection in 1982, he tried to reinstate socialist policies. He was shot to death by an assassin; his murder remains unsolved.

Palmer, A(lexander) Mitchell (1872–1936) U.S. politician. Born in Moosehead, Pa., he served in the U.S. House of Representatives (1909–15) and helped secure the Democratic nomination for Woodrow WILSON in 1912. As attorney general (1919–21), Palmer used the espionage and sedition acts (1917, 1918) to attack political radicals, dissidents, and aliens in the "Red Scare" period after World War I, when roundups of suspected communists became known as the "Palmer raids."

Palmer, Arnold (Daniel) (b.1929) U.S. golfer. Born in Youngstown, Ohio, he turned professional in 1954 after winning the U.S. Amateur championship. He was the first player to win the MASTER'S TOURNAMENT four times (1958, 1960, 1962, 1964); his other titles include the U.S. Open (1960) and the British Open (1961–62). From 1954 through 1975, he won 61 tournaments. His exciting play and amiable personality won him wide popularity among fans who became known as "Arnie's Army."

P

Palmerston (of Palmerston), Viscount *orig.* Henry John Temple *known as* **Lord Palmerston** (1784–1865) English politician and prime minister (1855–58, 1859–65). Initially a Tory but associated with the Whig Party from 1830, he served many years as foreign secretary (1830–34, 1835–41, 1846–51) and supported British interests and liberal causes abroad. He played a key role in establishing the independence of Belgium (1830–31) and Greece (1832). As prime minister, he brought an end to the Crimean War, approved the creation of the independent kingdom of Italy, and supported a policy of neutrality in the American Civil War. Nicknamed "Pam," he was one of Britain's most popular leaders.

palmetto \pal-'me-tō\ *or* **cabbage palmetto** Tree *(Sabal palmetto)* of the PALM family, occurring in the SE U.S. and the W. Indies. Commonly grown for shade and as ornamentals, palmettos grow to about 80 ft (24 m) tall and have fan-shaped leaves. The water-resistant trunk is used as wharf piling. Mats and baskets are sometimes made from the leaves, and stiff brushes are made from the stems. The buds are edible.

palmistry Reading of an individual's character and DIVINATION of the future by interpreting lines on the palm of the hand. Palmistry may have originated in ancient India, and the GYPSIES (of Indian origin) have long been known as palm readers. It was also practiced in China, Tibet, Persia, Mesopotamia, Egypt, and ancient Greece. In medieval Europe, pigmentation spots on the hand were believed to reveal a witch. Though palmistry is still practiced, there is no known scientific basis for it.

palm PC Computer small enough to fit in a person's palm. Palm PCs (also called palmtops, handheld computers, or personal data assistants) typically use pens instead of keyboards for input. They have limited memory and lack built-in peripheral devices (e.g., disk drives and modems), though such devices can be plugged in. They run a limited set of application programs, such as calendars, address books, and memo pads. Many now provide wireless Internet access.

Palm Springs Resort city (pop., 2000: 43,000), S California. Known for its hot springs, it was a stagecoach stop by 1872. In 1884 John G. McCallum (1826–1897) established the Palm Valley Colony there. It developed into a glamorous desert resort and residential area, frequented by Hollywood stars. Nearby is JOSHUA TREE NATIONAL PARK.

Palm Sunday *or* **Passion Sunday** In Christianity, the Sunday before EASTER, commemorating JESUS' triumphal entry into Jerusalem. It usually includes a procession of members of the congregation carrying palms, representing the palm branches the crowd scattered in front of Jesus as he rode into the city. Palm Sunday was celebrated in Jerusalem as early as the 4th cent. and in the West by the 8th cent.

Palmyra \pal-'mī-rə\ *biblical* Tadmor. Ancient city, Syria, northeast of DAMASCUS, at the modern city of Tadmur. Said to have been built by King SOLOMON, it became prominent in the 3rd cent. B.C., when the road through Palmyra became a route of east–west trade. Under Roman control by the reign of TIBERIUS, it briefly regained autonomy in the 3rd cent. A.D. under the Arab queen ZENOBIA. The main military station on the road that linked Damascus to the EUPHRATES RIVER, it was conquered by the Muslims in 634. Inscriptions supply knowledge of the city's extensive trade.

palsy See CEREBRAL PALSY, PARALYSIS

Pamirs \pə-'mirz\ High-altitude region, central Asia, mostly in Tajikistan. Lying partly on the borders of China, India, and Afghanistan, it contains many peaks over 20,000 ft (6,000 m) high and many glaciers. COMMUNISM PEAK rises in the northwest. It is sparsely populated, and almost all the inhabitants are Tajiks. From it extend several great ranges, including the KARAKORAMS and HINDU KUSH.

Pamlico Sound \'pam-li-,kō\ Shallow body of water, E shore of N. Carolina. It is separated from the Atlantic Ocean by the OUTER BANKS. It extends 80 mi (130 km) south from ROANOKE ISLAND and is 8–30 mi (13–48 km) wide. Numerous waterfowl nest along the coastal waters.

Pampas Vast, grass-covered plain extending west from the Atlantic coast to the Andean foothills, primarily in Argentina. The Argentine pampas covers 295,000 sq mi (760,00 sq km). The W portion is dry and largely barren; the humid E portion is the nation's economic heart. Herds of wild cattle and horses, rounded up by Argentina's famed GAUCHOS, roamed the pampas until the later 19th cent., when the land was fenced into huge *estancias* (ranches). The region is prominent in Argentina's literature and musical folklore.

Pamplona *ancient* Pompaelo. City (pop., 1998 est.: 171,000), capital of NAVARRA, N Spain. According to tradition, it was founded in 75 B.C. by POMPEY THE GREAT. It was captured from the Moors by CHARLEMAGNE in A.D. 778 and later became the capital of the kingdom of NAVARRE. The citadel built by King PHILIP II of Spain in 1571 made it the most strongly fortified town of the north. Its world-famous attraction is the Fiesta de San Fermín, honoring its first bishop, which is celebrated with bullfights and the "running of the bulls" through the city streets.

Pan Greek fertility deity with a half-human, half-animal form. The Romans associated him with FAUNUS. Pan was often represented as a vigorous and lustful figure with the horns, legs, and ears of a goat. Some Christian depictions of the devil bear a striking resemblance to Pan. Pan haunted the high hills, where he was chiefly concerned with flocks and herds. Like a shepherd, Pan was a piper, and he rested at noon. He could inspire irrational terror *(panic)* in humans.

pan See PLAYA

Pan-African movement Movement dedicated to establishing independence for African nations and unity among black people worldwide. It originated in conferences held in London (1900, 1919, 1921, 1923) and other cities; W. E. B. DU BOIS was an early leader. The sixth conference (Manchester, 1945) included Jomo KENYATTA and Kwame NKRUMAH. The 1958 conference in Accra, Ghana, featured Patrice LUMUMBA. The Pan-Africanist Congress (PAC) was founded in S. Africa in 1959 as an alternative to the AFRICAN NATIONAL CONGRESS, seen as tainted by non-African influences. The ORGANIZATION OF AFRICAN UNITY (OAU) was founded in 1963 and became the most important Pan-Africanist organization.

Panaji \pä-'nä-jē\ *or* **New Goa** Town (pop., 1991: 43,000), seaport, and capital of GOA, W India. It replaced Old Goa as the residence of the Portuguese viceroy in 1759 and as the capital of Portuguese India in 1843.

Panama *officially* **Republic of Panama** Nation, CENTRAL AMERICA. It is bounded by the Caribbean Sea, Colombia, the Pacific Ocean, and Costa Rica. Area: 29,157 sq mi (75,517 sq km). Population (2000): 2,823,000. Capital: PANAMA CITY. The people are mostly mestizo (mixed Spanish-Indian) and Indian groups, including the Guaymí, Cuna, and Chocó. The introduction of black Africans produced mixed races, while the building of the PANAMA CANAL brought N. Americans, French, and Chinese. Languages: Spanish (official), English, and indigenous Indian languages. Religion: Roman Catholicism (the majority). Currency: balboa (U.S. dollar). Panama consists of three distinct areas: the lowlands, or hot lands (more than 85% of the country); the temperate lands; and the highlands, or cold lands. It has a market economy based on agriculture and services. Most of the latter are transportation, communications, and storage connected with the Panama Canal, as well as international banking and tourism. It is a republic with one legislative house; its head of state and government is the president, assisted by vice presidents. The land was inhabited by American Indians when the Spanish arrived in 1501. The first successful Spanish settlement was founded by V. N. de BALBOA in 1510. Panama was part of the viceroyalty of NEW GRANADA until it declared its independence from Spain in 1821 to join Colombia. In 1903 it revolted against Colombia and was recognized by the U.S., to whom it ceded the CANAL ZONE. The completed canal was opened in 1914; its jurisdiction reverted from the U.S. to Panama in 1999. An invasion by U.S. troops in 1989 overthrew the de facto ruler, Gen. Manuel NORIEGA. Panama joined the WORLD TRADE ORGANIZATION in 1997. See map on next page.

Panama Canal Ship canal, Panama. Extending across the Isthmus of Panama, it connects the Atlantic and Pacific oceans. It is about 51 mi (82 km) long, with a minimum width of 300 ft (91 m) and a minimum depth of 41 ft (12 m).

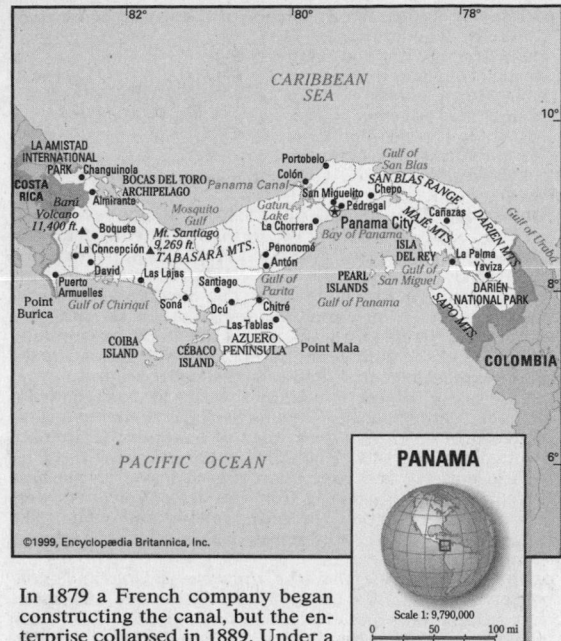

PANAMA

Scale 1: 9,790,000

In 1879 a French company began constructing the canal, but the enterprise collapsed in 1889. Under a 1903 treaty Panama granted the U.S. the Panama CANAL ZONE and the rights to build and operate a canal. Work began in 1904; facing enormous obstacles, George GOETHALS directed the construction from 1907 and the canal opened on Aug. 15, 1914. Panama gained control of the canal in 1999. Ships are towed through the canal by electric locomotives; it takes 15–20 hours to complete the passage. Duplicate locks permit two-way traffic. The canal allows ships sailing between the E and W coasts of the U.S. to save about 8,000 nautical miles.

Panama Canal Zone See CANAL ZONE

Panama City City (pop., 2000: 463,000), capital of Panama. Near the Pacific entrance of the PANAMA CANAL, the site was originally an Indian fishing village. The old city was founded in 1519 and completely destroyed by British buccaneer Henry MORGAN in 1671. Rebuilt in 1674, in 1751 it became part of NEW GRANADA and later part of Colombia. It was the center of the Panamanian revolt against Colombia in 1903, when it became the capital of Panama. After the opening of the canal in 1914, it developed rapidly as the commercial and transportation center of the country.

Pan American (Sports) Games Quadrennial sports event for the nations of the Western Hemisphere, patterned after the Olympic Games and sanctioned by the International Olympic Committee. The games, conceived in 1940 but first held in 1951, are conducted by the Pan American Sports Organization (PASO), headquartered in Mexico City. They are held the year preceding the Olympics, in various host cities.

Pan-American Highway International highway system connecting N. and S. America. Though conceived in 1923 as a single route, it includes other highways such as the Inter-American Highway from Nuevo Laredo, Mexico, to Panama City. The whole system, extending from Alaska to Argentina, totals nearly 30,000 mi (48,000 km). Only some 240 mi (400 km) in the Panama–Colombia border area remains uncompleted.

Pan American World Airways, Inc. *known as* **Pan Am** Former U.S. airline. It was founded in 1927 by the colorful former World War I pilot Juan Trippe (1899–1981). In 1929 he established passenger service to the Caribbean and Central America. He inaugurated the first transpacific flights (San Francisco–Manila) in 1936, the first transatlantic flights (New York City–Lisbon) in 1939, and the first round-the-world flights in 1947, and pioneered commercial jet travel in the 1950s. Business later declined, and despite selling its Asian and S. Pacific routes to UNITED AIRLINES and its transatlantic, European, and Middle Eastern routes to Delta Air Lines, Pan Am was forced to declare bankruptcy in 1991.

Pan-Arabism Concept of cultural and religious unity among Arab countries that developed after their liberation from Ottoman and European dominance. An important event was the founding in 1943 of the BAATH PARTY, which now has branches in several countries and rules in Syria and Iraq. Another was the founding of the ARAB LEAGUE in 1945. Pan-Arabism's most charismatic and effective proponent was Egypt's G. A. NASSER. Since Nasser's death, Syria's Hafiz al-ASSAD, Iraq's Saddam HUSSEIN, and Libya's Muammar al-QADDAFI have all tried to assume his mantle.

Panchen Lama \'pän-chən-'lä-mə\ Any of the line of reincarnated LAMAS who are second only to the DALAI LAMA in spiritual authority in the dominant sect of TIBETAN BUDDHISM. A Panchen Lama installed by the Chinese government remained in Tibet after the 13th Dalai Lama fled into exile in 1959. He refused to brand the Dalai Lama a traitor and was imprisoned in 1964. Released in the late 1970s, he died in 1989. The six-year-old boy chosen as the new Panchen Lama in 1995 was seized by the government and a different boy was substituted.

pancreas \'paŋ-krē-əs\ Compound GLAND functioning as both an exocrine (secreting through a duct) and an endocrine (ductless) gland. It continuously secretes pancreatic juice (containing digestive enzymes) through the pancreatic duct to the DUODENUM. Scattered among the enzyme-producing cells are the islets of LANGERHANS, which secrete INSULIN and glucagon directly into the bloodstream.

panda *or* **giant panda** Species (*Ailuropoda melanoleuca*, family Ursidae) of white-and-black forest-dwelling mammal, found in W central China, that subsists mainly on bamboo. Because they cannot digest cellulose, wild pandas (of which there are fewer than 1,000) spend 10–12 hours a day eating up to 65 lbs (30 kg) of bamboo leaves, stems, and shoots to obtain needed nutrients. Pandas in captivity (currently about 100) eat cereals, milk, and garden vegetables. They grow to 5 ft (1.5 m) long and

Giant panda (*Ailuropoda melanoleuca*)

weigh over 200 lbs (100 kg). Having a slow reproductive cycle, they are difficult to breed in captivity. The name panda is also used for a long-tailed Asian mammal (*Ailurus fulgens*) resembling the related raccoon.

Pandora In GREEK MYTHOLOGY, the first woman. After PROMETHEUS stole fire from heaven and bestowed it on mortals, ZEUS had HEPHAESTUS fashion a woman out of earth, upon whom the gods bestowed their choicest gifts. After marrying Prometheus' brother, Pandora opened a jar containing all kinds of misery and evil, which escaped and flew out over the earth.

panegyric \,pa-nə-'jir-ik\ Eulogistic oration or laudatory discourse, originally a speech delivered at an ancient Greek general assembly *(panegyris),* such as the Olympic festivals. Speakers frequently expounded on the former glories of Greek cities, often in elaborate and flowery language. Later Roman speakers praised and flattered eminent persons in panegyrics. The form was also used in the European Middle Ages, Renaissance, and Baroque era.

Pangaea \pan-'jē-ə\ Hypothetical protocontinent proposed by Alfred WEGENER in 1912 as part of his theory of CONTINENTAL DRIFT. Pangaea (from Greek: *pangaia,* "all earth") supposedly covered about half the earth and was completely surrounded by a world ocean called Panthalassa. Late in the TRIASSIC PERIOD (248–208 million years ago), Pangaea began to break apart into LAURASIA (the present-day N continents) and GONDWANA (the S continents).

Pan-Germanism Movement to politically unify all German-speaking people. The Pan-German League was organized in

1894 by Ernst Hasse (1846–1908) to heighten German nationalist awareness, especially among German-speaking people outside Germany. The movement, which pressed for German expansion in Europe, gained support after World War I and was actively promoted by Adolf HITLER and the NAZI PARTY. After Germany's defeat in 1945 and the expulsion of Germans from formerly German areas of Eastern Europe, the movement declined.

pangolin \'paŋ-gə-lən\ *or* **scaly anteater** Any of about eight species of armored placental MAMMALS (genus *Manis*, order Pholidota) of tropical Asia and Africa. Scales formed of cemented hairs cover the upper body, legs, and tail. Pangolins are 2–6 ft (60–180 cm) long and weigh 10–60 lbs (5–27 kg). They have a conical head, no teeth, a long tongue, short legs, and a long prehensile tail. Nocturnal animals, pangolins locate prey, mainly termites, by smell, ripping open nests with their front claws. When threatened, they curl up or emit an odoriferous secretion. See also ANTEATER, ECHIDNA.

panic In economics, a severe financial disturbance, such as widespread bank failures, feverish stock speculation followed by a market crash, or a climate of fear caused by economic crisis or anticipation of such a crisis. The term is applied only to an initial, violent upheaval rather than an entire decline in a BUSINESS CYCLE (see DEPRESSION and RECESSION). Until the 19th cent., economic fluctuations were largely connected with shortages of goods, market expansion, and speculation. Panics in the advanced economies of the 19th–20th cent. have been more complex. The Panic of 1857 in the U.S. had its seeds in the decline in the value of railroad SECURITIES; its effects included the closing of many banks, severe unemployment in the U.S., and a money-market panic in Europe. The Panic of 1873 began with financial crises in Vienna and New York and led to a long-term contraction in the world economy. The greatest panic began with the U.S. stock-market crash of 1929 (see GREAT DEPRESSION).

Panjabi language See PUNJABI LANGUAGE

Pankhurst, Emmeline *orig.* Emmeline Goulden (1858–1928) British WOMEN'S SUFFRAGE MOVEMENT leader. In 1879 she married Richard Pankhurst (1834–1898), a women's suffrage advocate. In 1889 she founded the Women's Franchise League, which in 1894 secured for married women the right to vote in local elections. In 1903 she founded the Women's Social and Political Union. From 1912 she advocated extreme militancy, mainly in the form of arson, and was arrested 12 times in one year. Her daughter Christabel H. Pankhurst (1880–1958)—later Dame Christabel—organized the militant tactics of the WSPU and directed actions that included hunger strikes and huge outdoor rallies. She later became a religious evangelist and moved to the U.S.

Pannonia Province, Roman empire, corresponding to modern W Hungary and parts of E Austria, Slovenia, and N Yugoslavia. Conquered by Rome beginning in 35 B.C., it revolted in A.D. 6, posing the greatest threat to Italy since HANNIBAL's invasion. It was split in A.D. 106, and Pannonia Superior figured in the Roman wars of MARCUS AURELIUS. The Romans withdrew after 395.

Panofsky \pə-'nôf-skē\, **Erwin** (1892–1968) German-U.S. art historian. A professor at the Univ. of Hamburg (1926–33), he fled Nazi Germany and in 1935 began teaching at Princeton's Institute for Advanced Study. He gained prominence for his studies in iconography, the study of symbols and themes in works of art. His writings are distinguished by their variety of subjects, critical penetration, and erudition. Among his major works are the groundbreaking *Studies in Iconology* (1939), *Albrecht Dürer* (1943), and *Early Netherlandish Painting* (1953).

panorama Painted narrative scene or landscape which surrounds or is unrolled before the viewer. The true panorama is exhibited on the walls of a large cylinder, and the viewer stands on a platform in the cylinder's center and turns around to see all points of the horizon. The first panorama, a view of Edinburgh, was executed in 1788 by the Scottish painter Robert Barker (1739–1806). In the mid-19th cent. the rolled panorama became popular: a painting on canvas was wound between two poles and slowly unrolled behind a frame.

panpipe *or* **syrinx** Wind instrument consisting of pipes of different lengths made of cane (less often wood, clay, or metal) arranged in a row. It is blown across the top, each pipe producing a different note. The panpipe dates from about 2000 B.C. and is found worldwide.

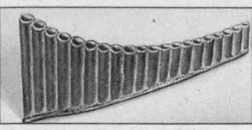
Romanian panpipe

Pan-p'o See BANPO

Pan-Slavism Movement to unite Slav peoples of Eastern and central Europe. Political goals for Slavic unity increased in 1848, when a Slav congress met in Prague to press for equal rights under Austrian rule. In the 1860s the movement became popular in Russia, to which Pan-Slavs looked for protection from Turkish and Austro-Hungarian rule; this led Russia and Serbia into wars against the Ottoman empire in 1876–77. In the 20th cent., nationalist rivalries among the Slav peoples prevented their effective collaboration.

pansy Any of several popular cultivated VIOLETS (genus *Viola*). The garden pansy (*V. wittrockiana*) is probably a cultivated form of *V. tricolor*, a weed of European grainfields. Annuals or short-lived perennials, pansies grow 6–12 in. (15–30 cm) tall and have heart-shaped leaves at the base and oblong leaves growing from the stems. Velvety flowers occur in combinations of blue, yellow, and white. The smaller, mildly toxic wild pansy is also known as Johnny-jump-up, or heartsease.

pantheism Doctrine that the universe is God and, conversely, that there is no god apart from the substance, forces, and laws manifested in the universe. Pantheism characterizes many Buddhist and Hindu doctrines. Numerous Greek philosophers contributed to the foundations of Western pantheism, a tradition that continued in NEOPLATONISM and Judeo-Christian MYSTICISM. In the 17th cent. Benedict de SPINOZA formulated the most thoroughly pantheistic philosophical system, arguing that God and Nature are merely two names for one reality.

Pantheon Temple in Rome begun 27 B.C. and completely rebuilt by HADRIAN (A.D. 118–28). It is remarkable for its size and design. A circular building of concrete faced with brick, it has a great concrete dome, 142 ft (43 m) in diameter, and a porch of Corinthian columns with a triangular pediment. The vast space is lit solely by the 27-ft (8-m) oculus at the dome's center. The interior is lined with colored marble; the walls are marked by seven deep recesses screened by pairs of columns.

panther See COUGAR, LEOPARD

pantomime See MIME AND PANTOMIME

Paoli \'pau̇-lē\, **Pasquale** (1725–1807) Corsican patriot. Son of Giacinto Paoli, who led the Corsicans against Genoa in 1735, he lived with his father in exile in Naples 1739–55. On his return, he overcame the Genoese faction and was elected to rule Corsica. He suppressed the vendetta system, substituted order and justice, and instituted national schools. After France invaded in 1769 he fled to England, where he lived until 1790. Recalled as military commandant, he expelled the French with British naval support (1794) and offered the island's sovereignty to England.

Paolo, Giovanni di See GIOVANNI DI PAOLO

papacy \'pā-pə-sē\ System of central government of the Roman Catholic church. BISHOPS led the early Church, with the bishop of Rome being accorded special respect by the end of the 1st cent. In the 4th–5th cent. the power of the see of Constantinople rose to challenge that of Rome; the rivalry would culminate in the SCHISM OF 1054 between the Eastern and Western Churches. After the collapse of the Roman empire, the papacy found protection under the wing of CHARLEMAGNE and his successors; in the 9th–10th cent. the German emperors controlled it. In 1059 Pope LEO IX responded by vesting the right to name a new pope exclusively with the College of CARDINALS. GREGORY VII decreed in 1075 that civil rulers could not invest churchmen with temporal power and excommunicated HENRY IV of Germany. In the next centuries, the worldliness and corruption of the papal court led to the Western SCHISM and eventually to the REFORMATION. In the 19th cent. the papacy lost its remaining temporal powers when the PAPAL

STATES were incorporated into the new Kingdom of Italy. It maintained a conservative and authoritarian religious position until the Second VATICAN COUNCIL gave the bishops, clergy, and laity more voice. See also ROMAN CATHOLICISM.

Papal Curia See ROMAN CURIA

papal infallibility In ROMAN CATHOLICISM, the doctrine that the pope, under certain specific conditions, cannot err when he teaches in matters of faith or morals. It is based on the belief that the church, entrusted with the teaching mission of Jesus, will be guided by the Holy Spirit in remaining faithful to that teaching. The doctrine was established by the First Vatican Council (1869–70). A pope only speaks infallibly when he intends to demand irrevocable assent from the entire church in some aspect of faith or morals. The doctrine remains a major obstacle to ecumenical endeavors and is controversial even among Roman Catholic theologians.

Papal Inquisition See INQUISITION

Papal States *Italian* **Stati Pontifici** \'stä-tē-pōn-'tē-fē-chē\ Territories of central Italy over which the POPE had sovereignty 756–1870. The extent of the territory and the degree of papal control varied over the centuries. The temporal power of the medieval papacy was based on the DONATION OF PEPIN in A.D. 754. The papacy acquired the duchy of Benevento in 1077, and Popes INNOCENT III and JULIUS II expanded the papal domain. The rise of communes and rule by local families weakened papal authority, and by the 16th cent. the papal territory was one of a number of petty Italian states. They were an obstacle to Italian unity until 1870, when ROME was taken by Italian forces and became the capital of Italy. In 1929 the LATERAN TREATY settled the pope's relation to the Italian state and set up an independent city-state (see VATICAN CITY).

Papandreou, Georgios (1888–1968) Greek prime minister (1944, 1963, 1964–65). In 1935 he founded the Democratic Socialist Party, then went into exile. He briefly headed a coalition government in 1944, then held ministerial posts 1946–52. He merged his party with the Liberal Party and formed the Center Union in 1961. As prime minister in 1964 he introduced far-reaching social reforms, but he was dismissed by the king in 1965. His son, Andreas Papandreou (1919–1996), was prime minister in 1981–89 and 1993–96.

papaw *or* **pawpaw** \'pä-,pô\ Deciduous tree or shrub (*Asimina triloba*) of the custard apple family, native to the E and midwestern U.S. It can grow to 40 ft (12 m) tall and has drooping leaves up to 12 in. (30 cm) long. The purple flowers bloom with a foul odor before the leaves emerge in spring. The edible fruit looks like a stubby banana; its skin turns black as it ripens.

papaya \pə-'pī-ə\ Large palmlike plant (*Carica papaya;* family Caricaceae), cultivated throughout the tropics and warm subtropics, and its succulent juicy fruit. The juice of the unripe fruit contains an enzyme that is useful in various remedies for indigestion and in meat tenderizers.

Papeete \,pä-pā-'ā-tā\ Seaport (pop., 1988: 24,000), capital of FRENCH POLYNESIA, on TAHITI. A tropical city with tall palms and exotic flowers, it is one of the largest commercial centers in the S. Pacific. By 1829 its excellent harbor made it a port of call for whalers. It is a major tourist base and a center for Pacific Rim trade.

Papen \'pä-pən\, **Franz von** (1879–1969) German politician. A monarchist member of the German Reichstag (1921–32), he was chosen chancellor in 1932, but was soon ousted by Kurt von SCHLEICHER. In revenge, Papen persuaded Paul von HINDENBURG to appoint Adolf HITLER as chancellor and himself as vice chancellor. Papen resigned in 1934 when he was unable to restrain the Nazis' push for power. As ambassador to Austria 1934–38, he worked for Austria's annexation to Germany. Arrested in 1945, he was acquitted at the NUREMBERG TRIALS, but spent four years in prison.

paper Matted or felted sheet, usually made of CELLULOSE fibers, formed on a wire screen from water suspension. Source materials include wood pulp, rags, and recycled paper. The fibers are separated (by mechanical or chemical means) and wetted to produce paper pulp, or stock. The pulp is filtered on a woven screen to form a sheet of fiber, which is pressed and compacted to squeeze out most of the water. The remaining water is removed by evaporation, and the dry sheet is further compressed and often coated or infused with other substances. Types of paper in common use include bond paper, book paper, newsprint, kraft paper, and sanitary paper (for towels, napkins, etc.). See also CALENDERING, FOURDRINIER MACHINE, KRAFT PROCESS.

paper folding *Japanese* **origami** Art of folding objects out of paper without cutting, pasting, or decorating. Probably developed from the older art of folding cloth, origami has reached its greatest development in Japan, with hundreds of traditional folds and an extensive literature dealing with the art. There are two types of Japanese folds: figures used in ceremonial etiquette, and objects such as animals, flowers, furniture, and human figures. Paper folding has also flourished in Spain, S. America, and Germany.

Paper folding "Peafowl" by Akira Yoshizawa, 1942

Paphlagonia Ancient district, N ASIA MINOR, on the BLACK SEA. A mountainous country, one of the oldest in Asia Minor, it submitted to ALEXANDER THE GREAT in 333 B.C. In 65 B.C. the coastal districts, including the capital, Sinope, were attached to Roman Bithynia. The area was incorporated into the Roman province of GALATIA around 6 B.C.; the interior regions were left under native rulers. It later became part of the Byzantine empire.

papillomavirus \,pa-pə-'lō-mə-,vī-rəs\ Any of a group of VIRUSES that cause WARTS and other harmless tumors in humans. More than 50 distinct types are known, responsible for warts of the hands, plantar warts (of the feet), flat warts, and throat warts. Genital warts are caused by other types, which are spread by sexual intercourse. Some papillomaviruses have been linked with various cancerous tumors, especially cervical cancers; their presence can be detected by a PAP SMEAR.

papillon \,pä-pē-'yō⁸\ Breed of TOY DOG known from the 16th cent., when it was called a dwarf SPANIEL. A favorite of MARIE-ANTOINETTE, it appeared in paintings by Old Masters. It acquired its name (French for "butterfly") when a variety with large, flaring ears became fashionable. A slender, graceful dog with a plumed tail and a soft, full coat, it stands 11 in. (28 cm) or less and weighs up to 11 lbs (5 kg).

Papineau \,pá-pē-'nō\, **Louis Joseph** (1786–1871) Canadian politician. Born in Montreal, he served as speaker of the legislative assembly of Lower Canada (now Quebec) from 1815 to 1837. A leader of the French-Canadian Party, he opposed the British-dominated government and in 1834 helped draft the 92 Resolutions, demanding control of revenues and an elective provincial council. When the British governor rejected the demands, hostilities broke out. Papineau escaped to the U.S., then to France, but later returned and served in the Canadian House of Commons (1848–54).

Papp, Joseph *orig.* Joseph Papirofsky (1921–1991) U.S. theatrical producer and director. Born in Brooklyn, N.Y., in 1954 he founded the New York Shakespeare Festival, which gave free performances of Shakespeare's plays in city parks, and produced and directed most of the plays. In 1967 he founded the Public Theater to produce new and classic dramas, creating a seven-theater complex; several productions traveled to Broadway, including *Hair* (1967) and *A Chorus Line* (1975). Papp remained one of OFF-BROADWAY's most active producers into the 1980s, championing many young playwrights and actors. He served as artistic director of the Shakespeare Festival and the Public Theater until his death.

Pap smear *or* **Papanicolaou's stain** \,päp-ə-'nē-kə-,laủz\ Sample of cells from the VAGINA and cervix of the UTERUS for laboratory staining and examination to detect genital herpes and early-stage CANCER, especially of the cervix but also of the endometrium and OVARIES. The technique also can be applied to cells obtained from other surfaces.

Papua New Guinea \'pa-pyủ-wə...'gi-nē\ *officially* **Independent State of Papua New Guinea** Island nation, SW Pacific Ocean. Area: 178,704 sq mi (462,840 sq km). Population

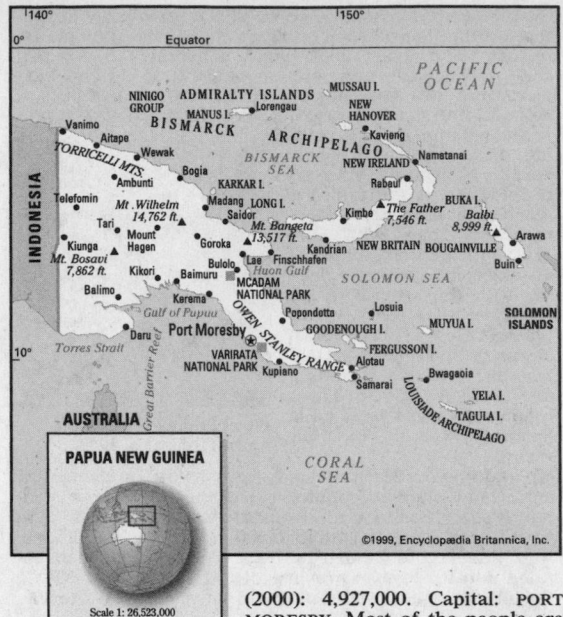

140° 150°

Equator

PACIFIC OCEAN

NINIGO GROUP
ADMIRALTY ISLANDS
MUSSAU I.
Lorengau
NEW HANOVER
MANUS I.
Vanimo
BISMARCK
Kavieng
Aitape
Wewak
ARCHIPELAGO
Namatanai
TORRICELLI MTS.
BISMARCK SEA
NEW IRELAND
Bogia
Ambunti
KARKAR I.
Rabaul
Telefomin
Madang LONG I.
Kimbe
BUKA I.
Balbi
Tari
Mt. Wilhelm
14,762 ft.
The Father
7,546 ft.
8,999 ft.
Mount
Hagen
Mt. Bangeta
13,517 ft.
Arawa
Kiunga
Goroka
Kandrian
NEW BRITAIN
BOUGAINVILLE
Mt. Bosavi
7,862 ft.
Kikori
Bulolo Lae
Finschhafen
Buin
Kerema
Baimuru
Huon Gulf
Balimo
MCADAM NATIONAL PARK
SOLOMON SEA
Daru
Kerema
Popondetta
Losuia
MUYUA I.
SOLOMON ISLANDS
Port Moresby
GOODENOUGH I.
Torres Strait
VARIRATA NATIONAL PARK
FERGUSSON I.
Kupiano Alotau
Bwagaoia
Samarai
YELA I.
AUSTRALIA
LOUISIADE ARCHIPELAGO
TAGULA I.
CORAL SEA

INDONESIA

Gulf of Papua

OWEN STANLEY RANGE

Great Barrier Reef

0°

10°

PAPUA NEW GUINEA

©1999, Encyclopædia Britannica, Inc.

Scale 1: 26,523,000
0   100   200 mi
0   150   300 km

(2000): 4,927,000. Capital: PORT MORESBY. Most of the people are Papuan (four-fifths) and Melanesian; minorities are Polynesian, Chinese, and European. Languages: English (official), Tok Pisin, Motu, indigenous languages. Religions: Protestantism, Roman Catholicism. Currency: kina. About 85% of the total land area is on the island of NEW GUINEA; the nation also includes BOUGAINVILLE island and the BISMARCK ARCHIPELAGO. The New Guinea terrain ranges from swampy lowland plains in the south and north to high central mountains, the Highlands, in the northwest and southeast. Much of the land is covered with tropical rain forest. Some of the outlying islands are volcanic. It has a developing mixed economy based largely on the export of mineral and agricultural products. It is a constitutional monarchy with one legislative house; its chief of state is the British monarch represented by the governor-general, and the head of government is the prime minister. The area has been inhabited since prehistoric times, with hunters as the earliest settlers. The Portuguese sighted the coast in 1512, and in 1545 the Spanish claimed the island. In 1828 the Dutch claimed the W half as part of the Dutch E. Indies. In 1884 Britain annexed the SE part and Germany took over the NE sector. The British part became the Territory of Papua in 1906 and passed to Australia, which also governed the German sector after World War I. After World War II, Australia governed both sectors as the Territory of Papua and New Guinea. Dutch New Guinea was annexed to Indonesia in 1969 as the province of Irian Jaya. Papua New Guinea achieved independence in 1975 and joined the British COMMONWEALTH. Bougainville's long war for independence won a treaty granting increased autonomy in 2001.

papyrus \pə-'pī-rəs\ Writing material of ancient times and the plant from which it comes, *Cyperus papyrus* (SEDGE FAMILY). This grasslike aquatic plant has woody, bluntly triangular stems and grows to about 15 ft (4.5 m) high in quietly flowing water up to 3 ft (90 cm) deep. Paper made from papyrus was the chief writing material in ancient Egypt, Greece, and Rome. In the 8th–9th cent. A.D., other plant fibers replaced papyrus in the manufacture of paper. The plant is now often used as a pool ornamental.

parabola \pə-'ra-bə-lə\ Open curve, one of the CONIC SECTIONS. It results when a right circular cone intersects a plane that is parallel to an edge of the cone. In ANALYTIC GEOMETRY its equation is $y = ax^2 + bx + c$. Such a curve has the useful property that any line parallel to its axis of SYMMETRY reflects through its focus, and vice versa. Rotating a parabola about its axis produces a surface (parabo-

loid) with the same reflection property, making it an ideal shape for satellite dishes and reflectors in headlights. Parabolas occur naturally as the paths of projectiles. The shape is also seen in the design of bridges and arches.

Paracel Islands \ˌpar-ə-'sel\ *Chinese* **Xisha Qundao** \'shē-ˌshä-'chün-'daú\ *Vietnamese* **Quan Dao Hoang Sa** \'kwän-'daú-'hwäŋ-'sä\ Group of about 130 small coral islands and reefs, S. CHINA SEA, east of central Vietnam. They lack fresh water and have no permanent human residents. In 1932 they were claimed by FRENCH INDOCHINA, and Japan occupied some during World War II. China, Taiwan, and Vietnam all claim them. In 1974 China assumed control, and they remain a matter of contention.

Paracelsus \ˌpar-ə-'sel-səs\ *orig.* Philippus Aureolus Theophrastus Bombastus von Hohenheim (1493–1541) German-Swiss physician and alchemist. Adopting the name "para-Celsus"—meaning "beyond Celsus" (the Roman authority on medicine)—he wandered throughout Europe and the Middle East, studying with alchemists. He valued the common sense of common people more than the dry teachings of ARISTOTLE, GALEN, and AVICENNA, and stressed nature's healing power. All were welcome at his lectures (which he gave in German, not Latin) at the Univ. of Basel, but such broadmindedness scandalized the authorities, and eventually he was forced to flee the city. He anticipated by centuries the treatment of syphilis by mercury compounds, the identification of the causes of goiter and of miners' silicosis, and homeopathy.

parachute Umbrella-like device for slowing the descent of a body falling through the atmosphere. Separate panels sewn together form a canopy attached by suspension lines to a harness worn by the user. Originally designed to provide a safe escape from a disabled aircraft, parachutes are also used for dropping supplies and for slowing returning space capsules. In 1797 a 3,200-ft (1,000-m) exhibition jump from a balloon was made by André-Jacques Garnerin (1769–1823). Early parachute material was canvas, which was later replaced by silk and then nylon. See also SKYDIVING.

Paraclete See HOLY SPIRIT

paradox Apparently self-contradictory statement whose underlying meaning is revealed only by careful scrutiny. Its purpose is to arrest attention and provoke fresh thought, as in the statement "Less is more." In poetry, paradox functions as a device encompassing the tensions of error and truth simultaneously. A paradox compressed into two words, as in "living death," is called an oxymoron.

Paraguay \ˌpä-rä-'gwī, *Engl* 'par-ə-ˌgwā\ *officially* **Republic of Paraguay** Nation, S central S. America. Area: 157,043 sq mi (406,741 sq km). Population (2000): 5,496,000. Capital: ASUNCIÓN. Most of the people are mestizo (mixed Spanish and GUARANÍ Indian); there are much smaller groups of Indians, blacks, Caucasians, and Asians. Languages: Spanish and Guaraní (both official). Religion: Roman Catholicism (88% of the population). Currency: Guaraní. Paraguay is a landlocked country of plains and swampland. The PARAGUAY RIVER, flowing from north to south, divides the country into two geographic regions: the Eastern Region, which is an extension of the Brazilian Plateau; and the Western Region, which forms the N part of the GRAN CHACO plains. It has a developing market economy that is based largely on agriculture, trade, and light industries. It is a republic with two legislative houses; its chief of state and government is the president. Seminomadic tribes speaking Guaraní were in the area long before it was settled by Spain in the 16th–17th cent. Paraguay was part of the viceroyalty of RIO DE LA PLATA until it became independent in 1811. It suffered from dictatorial governments in the 19th cent. and from the 1865 war with Brazil, Argentina, and Uruguay. The CHACO WAR with Bolivia over disputed territory was settled primarily in Paraguay's favor by the peace treaty of 1938. Military governments, including that of Alfredo STROESSNER, predominated in the mid-20th cent. until the election of a civilian president, Juan Carlos Wasmosy, in 1993. A series of coups has confirmed that the country is only nominally a democracy. See map on following page.

Paraguayan War *or* **War of the Triple Alliance** (1864/65–70) Bloodiest conflict in Latin American history, fought between Paraguay and the allied countries of Argentina,

PARAGUAY

Scale 1: 13,300,000
0   50   100 mi
0   80   160 km

©1999, Encyclopædia Britannica, Inc.

paramagnetism Kind of MAGNETISM that occurs in materials weakly attracted by a strong magnet. Compounds containing iron, palladium, platinum, and the rare-earth elements exhibit strong paramagnetism because they have atoms with some incomplete inner ELECTRON shells. Their unpaired electrons make the atoms behave like tiny permanent magnets that align with and strengthen an applied MAGNETIC FIELD. As temperature rises, strong paramagnetism decreases. Weak paramagnetism is independent of temperature.

Paramaribo \ˌpä-rä-ˈmä-rē-bō\ City (pop., 1999 est.: 233,000), seaport, and capital of Suriname. Settled by the French around 1640, in 1651 it became a British colony; it was ceded to the Dutch in 1667. It is built on a shingle reef that stands 16 ft (5 m) above the river at low tide. Distinctive Dutch colonial architecture and a canal system remain. Since 1945 the city has grown considerably because of tourism and industry.

paramecium \ˌpar-ə-ˈmē-sē-əm\ Any of the free-living single-celled PROTOZOANS of the genus *Paramecium*, all easily cultivated in the laboratory. Most are about the size of the period at the end of this sentence. They vary in shape and are surrounded by a rigid protein layer (pellicle) covered with hundreds of cilia (see CILIUM) that beat rhythmically to propel them and to direct bacteria and other food particles into their oral groove. Food particles are collected into food VACUOLES, where digestion takes place. Two (occasionally three) contractile vacuoles near the ends of the cell expand and contract as they discharge metabolic wastes and excess fluid.

Brazil, and Uruguay. The Paraguayan dictator Francisco Solano López (1827–1870), objecting to Brazil's interference in Uruguay, declared war on Brazil in 1864. Argentina organized the Triple Alliance, which after three years, annihilated the Paraguayan forces, but Solano López fought on until he was killed. Paraguay was devastated by the war; its population was halved and 55,000 sq mi (140,000 sq km) was annexed by Brazil and Argentina.

Paraguay River River, S. America. It is 1,584 mi (2,550 km) long and the principal tributary of the PARANÁ RIVER. Rising in the Mato Grosso region of Brazil, it crosses Paraguay to meet the Paraná near the Argentine border. The GRAN CHACO plain extends west from the river.

parakeet Any of 115 species in 30 genera (subfamily Psittacinae) of small, slender seed-eating PARROTS with a long, tapering tail. Parakeets typically form large flocks. Most species lay four to eight eggs in a tree hole. The most popular caged parakeet is the budgerigar (*Melopsittacus undulatus*), mistakenly called LOVEBIRD; about 8 in. (19 cm) long, it may be any color.

parallax \ˈpar-ə-laks\ Difference in the direction of a celestial object as seen from two widely separated points, used to find its distance. The two positions of the observer and the object form a triangle; its apex angle (at the object) is twice the parallax, which becomes smaller at greater distances. Observations for calculating solar parallax can be made simultaneously from two places on the earth's surface, to a maximum of 8,794 seconds of arc for points diametrically opposed. A star's distance can be calculated from the difference in its position as seen from earth at points six months apart in its orbit (stellar, or annual, parallax). The parallax of stars over 30 PARSECS from earth has been determined from the EUROPEAN SPACE AGENCY's Hipparcos satellite.

paralysis *or* **palsy** Loss or impairment of voluntary use of one or more MUSCLES. It may be flaccid (with loss of muscle tone) or spastic (stiff). Hemiplegia (one-sided paralysis) is usually caused by STROKE or brain TUMOR on the opposite side. Diplegia (two-sided paralysis, as in CEREBRAL PALSY) results from generalized brain disease. SPINAL-CORD damage paralyzes the body at and below the level of the damage (paraplegia if the legs and lower body only; quadriplegia if arms and legs). POLIOMYELITIS and polyneuritis (NEURITIS of multiple nerves) result in paralysis with muscle wasting. Bell's palsy paralyzes the muscles of one side of the face. Paralysis may also have psychiatric causes (see HYSTERIA). See also MUSCULAR DYSTROPHY, MYASTHENIA GRAVIS.

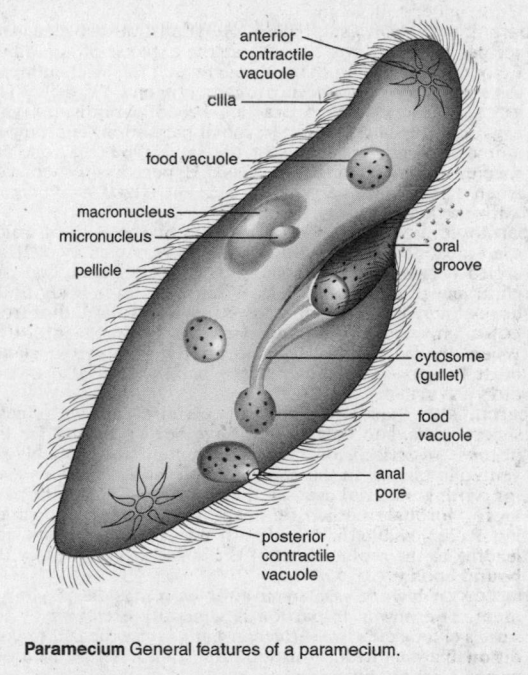

Paramecium General features of a paramecium.

Paramount Pictures Motion picture studio. It was founded by W. W. Hodkinson (1881–1971) in 1914 as a film distributor. It became a motion-picture company two years later and won attention with stars such as Mary PICKFORD, Gloria SWANSON, and Rudolph VALENTINO. In the late 1920s and 1930s the studio added Claudette Colbert, Gary COOPER, and Marlene DIETRICH to its roster. Among its successes of the 1940s and '50s were the films of Preston STURGES and Billy WILDER. In 1966 Gulf & Western Industries took control of Paramount, and the new company later changed its name to Paramount Communications. In 1994 it was acquired by Viacom Inc., which in 2000 merged with CBS.

Paraná River \,pä-rä-'nä\ River, S. America, the second-longest after the AMAZON RIVER. It rises on the plateau of SE central Brazil, at the confluence of the Rio Grande and Paranaíba River, and flows generally south 3,032 mi (4,880 km), forming part of Paraguay's border with Brazil and Argentina, to join the URUGUAY RIVER and form the Río de la PLATA estuary. Its huge drainage basin includes most of SE Brazil, Paraguay, E Bolivia, and N Argentina. The PARAGUAY RIVER is its largest tributary. The Itaipú Dam (completed 1982), one of the world's largest hydroelectric projects, submerged the massive Guaíra Falls and created a vast reservoir.

paranoia Mental disorder characterized by delusions of persecution or grandeur, usually without HALLUCINATIONS. Once classified as a distinct PSYCHOSIS, it is now generally treated as one of several varieties of SCHIZOPHRENIA or, in milder cases, of PERSONALITY DISORDER. The paranoid generally suffers from an exaggerated tendency to construe events and acts as pertaining to him- or herself.

parapsychology \,par-ə-,sī-'kä-lə-jē\ Discipline concerned with investigating events that cannot be accounted for by natural law, and knowledge that cannot have been obtained through the usual sensory abilities. Parapsychology studies the cognitive phenomena often called EXTRASENSORY PERCEPTION, as well as physical phenomena such as the levitation of objects and the bending of metal through psychokinesis. It became a subject of serious research when the Society of Psychical Research was established in London in 1882, partly in reaction to the growth of the spiritualist movement. In the 20th cent. research into parapsychology was also conducted at some universities, notably at Duke Univ. under J. B. Rhine.

parasitism \'par-ə-sə-,ti-zəm\ Relationship between two species in which one benefits at the expense of the other. Ectoparasites live on the body surface of the host; endoparasites live in their hosts' organs, tissues, or cells. The CUCKOO and COWBIRD practice brood parasitism, laying eggs in other birds' nests. In social parasitism, one type of animal parasitizes animals of the same type (e.g., one ant species on different ant species). Hyperparasitism occurs when parasites are parasitized (e.g., PROTOZOANS hyperparasitize a flea on a dog).

parathyroid gland Endocrine GLAND, two to eight of which are embedded in each side of the THYROID GLAND. It secretes parathyroid HORMONE, which regulates blood calcium and phosphorus levels. When calcium in body fluids drops, increased hormone secretion releases calcium from BONE into the bloodstream (see CALCIUM DEFICIENCY). When thyroid removal is required, the parathyroid glands must be separated out and left in place. See also ENDOCRINE SYSTEM.

parchment Processed skins of certain animals (chiefly sheep, goats, and calves) that have been prepared for the purpose of writing on them. Parchment was probably invented in Greece in the 2nd cent. B.C. Skins had been used for writing material even earlier (c.2400 B.C.), but the new, more thorough method of cleaning, stretching, and scraping made possible the use of both sides of a manuscript leaf, leading to the replacement of the rolled manuscript by the bound book (CODEX).

pardon In law, release from guilt or remission of punishment. The power to pardon is generally exercised by the state's chief executive officer. A pardon may be full or conditional; a conditional pardon imposes a lesser punishment or some other obligation.

Paré \pä-'rā\, **Ambroise** (1510–1590) French physician and surgeon. Employed as an army surgeon, Paré preferred less drastic measures than those then in use (including searing of large arteries with hot irons during amputation) and operated only when necessary. He introduced artificial limbs and eyes and the implantation of gold and silver teeth, and invented many instruments, popularized the truss for hernias, and first suggested that syphilis caused aneurysms. He published books on a wide variety of medical and surgical matters.

Parícutin \pä-'rē-kü-,tēn\ Volcano, W Michoacán state, W central Mexico, on the site of the former village of Parícutin. It is about 9,100 ft (2,775 m) high and is one of the youngest volcanoes on earth. It began to erupt in an open field in 1943 and buried the village. Eruptions ceased in 1952.

pari-mutuel \,par-i-'myü-chə-wəl\ Betting pool in which those who bet on competitors finishing in the first three places share the total amount bet minus a percentage for the management. First introduced in France around 1870, it soon became one of the most popular methods of betting on horse races internationally. Today computers calculate betting pools and current odds on each horse and flash the figures to the public at regular intervals. The system is used largely for off-track betting.

Paris City (pop., 1999: 2,123,000; metro. area pop., 1990: 9,060,000), river port, and capital of France, on the SEINE RIVER. Lutetia, the original settlement, existed by the late 3rd cent. B.C. By the early 4th cent. A.D. it was known as Paris. It withstood several Viking sieges 885–87 and became the capital of France in 987, when HUGH CAPET, the count of Paris, became king. The city was improved during the reign of PHILIP II, who formally recognized the Univ. of PARIS about 1200. In the 14th–15th cent. its development was hindered by the BLACK DEATH and the HUNDRED YEARS' WAR. In the 17th–18th cent. it was improved and beautified. Leading events of the FRENCH REVOLUTION took place there 1789–99. NAPOLEON III commissioned Georges HAUSSMANN to modernize the city's infrastructure and lay out its grand boulevards. During World War II it was occupied by German troops. It has long been the undisputed financial, commercial, artistic, and intellectual center of France. Paris is widely admired as the most beautiful large city in the world. Its many attractions include the EIFFEL TOWER, NOTRE-DAME DE PARIS, the LOUVRE, POMPIDOU CENTER, and PARIS OPERA, as well as boulevards, public parks, and gardens.

Paris In GREEK MYTHOLOGY, a son of King PRIAM of TROY. ZEUS chose him to determine which of three goddesses was most beautiful—HERA, ATHENA, or APHRODITE. In the famous "judgment of Paris," he chose Aphrodite because she offered to help him win the most beautiful woman alive. His seduction of HELEN was the cause of the TROJAN WAR. Near the end of the war, Paris shot the arrow that killed ACHILLES and soon afterward was himself killed.

Paris, Treaty of (1763) Treaty concluding the SEVEN YEARS' WAR (including the FRENCH AND INDIAN WAR). France renounced to Britain the mainland of N. America east of the Mississippi, its conquests in India since 1749, and four W. Indian islands. Britain restored to France four other W. Indian islands and the W. African colony of Gorée (Senegal). In return for recovering Havana and Manila, Spain ceded Florida to Britain and received Louisiana from the French.

Paris, University of Second-oldest European university (after the Univ. of BOLOGNA), founded about 1170. It grew out of the cathedral schools of Notre-Dame, and soon became a great center of Christian orthodox teaching; its professors included St. BONAVENTURE, ALBERTUS MAGNUS, and THOMAS AQUINAS. Its most celebrated early college was the Sorbonne, founded around 1257. The university declined during the Reformation and Counter-Reformation. With the French Revolution and Napoleon's reforms, teaching became more independent of religion and politics. By the mid-20th cent. the university had again become a preeminent scientific and intellectual center. In May 1968 a Sorbonne student protest led to replacement of the old university in 1970 by a system in Paris and its suburbs called the Universities of Paris I–XIII. Enrollment systemwide is about 310,000.

Paris Commune *or* **Commune of Paris** (Mar. 18–May 28, 1871) Insurrection of Paris against the French government. After the collapse of the SECOND EMPIRE, the republican Parisians feared that the conservative National Assembly would restore the monarchy. On March 18 the National Guard in Paris resisted orders to disarm, and after municipal elections were won by the revolutionaries, they formed the Commune government. Factions included the so-called Jacobins, who wanted the Paris Commune to control the revolution; the Proudhonists, socialist followers of P.-J. PROUDHON who supported a federation of communes; and the Blanquistes, socialist followers of Auguste BLANQUI who demanded violent action. Government forces quickly suppressed communes elsewhere in France, then entered Paris on May 21. In a week of fierce fighting, they crushed the Communards, who had set up barricades in the streets and burned public buildings, including the Tuileries Palace. About 20,000 insurrectionists and 750 government troops were killed. In the aftermath, the government took harsh repressive action; 38,000 suspects were arrested and over 7,000 were deported.

Paris Opera *or* **Opéra Garnier** \ō-per-'ä-gàrn-'yä\ Opera house in Paris, designed by Charles Garnier (1825–1898). The extraordinarily lavish building, considered one of the masterpieces of the Second Empire (BEAUX-ARTS STYLE), was begun in 1861 and opened in 1875. The interior, with its grand staircase and numerous richly decorated galleries, foyers, and corridors, provided a place to be seen as well as a splendid performance space.

Paris Peace Conference (1919–20) Meeting that inaugurated the international settlement after WORLD WAR I. It opened on Jan. 12, 1919, with representatives from over 30 countries; the principal delegates were France's Georges CLEMENCEAU, Britain's David LLOYD GEORGE, and the U.S.'s Woodrow WILSON. Commissions were appointed to study specific financial and territorial questions, including REPARATIONS. The major products of the conference were the LEAGUE OF NATIONS; the Treaty of VERSAILLES, presented to Germany; and treaties presented to Austria and Bulgaria. The inauguration of the League of Nations on Jan. 16, 1920, brought the conference to a close.

parity In economics, equality in price, rate of exchange, purchasing power, or wages. In international exchange, parity exists when the EXCHANGE RATE between two CURRENCIES makes the purchasing power of both currencies equal. Adjustments to maintain parity can occur in the marketplace as prices change in response to SUPPLY AND DEMAND, or through the intervention of governments or agencies such as the INTERNATIONAL MONETARY FUND. In U.S. agricultural economics, the term parity is used for a system of maintaining the prices of farm commodities, usually by government price supports and production quotas. Parity is also used in personnel administration to establish equitable wage rates for various classes of employees.

parity In physics, a property related to the symmetry of the WAVE FUNCTION representing a system of fundamental particles. It plays an important role in QUANTUM MECHANICS in the description of a physical system. Parity transformation replaces a system with a type of mirror image in which the spatial coordinates describing the system are inverted, so that the coordinates x, y, and z are replaced with $-x$, $-y$, and $-z$, but the physical observables of the system remain unchanged. In 1957 Chien-Shiung Wu (1912–1997) made the surprising discovery that BETA DECAY reactions do not conserve parity; in other words, the inverted image of the process does not exist in nature. This is a general property of the WEAK FORCE.

park Large outdoor area set aside for recreation. The earliest parks were hunting grounds of the Persian kings. In Greece, the functions of an area for exercise, social concourse, and athletes' training ground were combined with elements of a sculpture gallery and religious center. Parks of post-Renaissance times featured extensive woods, raised galleries, and often elaborate aviaries and cages for wild animals. Present-day parks accommodate active recreation; facilities may include outdoor theaters, zoos, concert shells, concessions for dining and dancing, amusement areas, boating areas, and areas for sports. See also NATIONAL PARK.

Park, Mungo (1771–1806) Scottish explorer of the Niger. A surgeon, Park was chosen by the African Assn. to head an expedition to find the source of the NIGER RIVER (1795–97). He lost most of his crew and supplies, was imprisoned and tortured by Arabs, and suffered severe illness, reaching Ségou (now in Mali) but not the river's source. His *Travels in the Interior Districts of Africa* (1797) became a great popular success. On a second expedition (1805–6) he reached BAMAKO, but was killed on the return trip.

Parker, Charlie (*orig.* Charles Christopher) (1920–1955) U.S. jazz saxophonist and composer. Born in Kansas City, Parker played with several big bands before leading his own

small groups in New York. With Dizzy GILLESPIE in the mid-1940s, he made a series of small-group recordings that heralded the arrival of BEBOP as a mature outgrowth of the improvisation of the late swing era. His direct, cutting tone and unprecedented dexterity made rapid tempos and fast flurries of notes trademarks of bebop, and his complex, subtle harmonic understanding brought an altogether new sound to the music. Easily the most influential jazz musician of his generation, his chronic drug addiction and early death contributed to making him a tragic legend.

Charlie Parker, 1949

Parker, Dorothy *orig.* Dorothy Rothschild (1893–1967) U.S. writer. Born in West End, N.J., she was a drama critic for *Vanity Fair* and wrote book reviews for the *New Yorker* (1927–33). Her poetry volumes include *Enough Rope* (1926) and *Death and Taxes* (1931). Her short stories were collected in *Laments for the Living* (1930) and *After Such Pleasures* (1933). She also collaborated on several plays. She is chiefly remembered for her wit.

parkinsonism Neurological disorder causing progressive loss of control of movement. The cause of primary parkinsonism, or Parkinson's disease, is unknown. The mean age of onset is about 57, but juvenile parkinsonism is also known. NEURONS in the brain that normally produce DOPAMINE deteriorate. When 60–80% are destroyed, signals suppressing unintended movement are disrupted and symptoms appear, including tremor at rest, muscle rigidity, trouble in starting movements, and loss of balance. Known causes include SLEEPING SICKNESS; certain poisons; repeated blows to the head, as in boxing; and the "designer drug" MPTP. Environmental toxins or genetic susceptibility may contribute. Drug therapy requires careful scheduling and combinations to delay development of tolerance and side effects. Surgical treatments remain experimental.

Parkman, Francis (1823–1893) U.S. historian. A native of Boston, Parkman embarked on a journey to the West in 1846 that resulted in *The California and Oregon Trail* (1849). He is noted for his seven-part history *France and England in North America*, covering the colonial period up to 1763; its volumes include *Montcalm and Wolfe* (1884), which demonstrates how biography can penetrate the spirit of an age.

Parks, Gordon (b.1912) U.S. writer, photographer, and film director. Born in Fort Scott, Kan., Parks worked as a photographer for *Life* (1948–72), becoming known for his portrayals of ghetto life and the civil rights movement. His first work of fiction was the novel *The Learning Tree* (1963). He has combined poetry and photography in collections such as *A Poet and His Camera* (1968). He has also directed several motion pictures, including *Shaft* (1971).

Parks, Rosa *orig.* Rosa McCauley (b.1913) U.S. civil rights activist. Born in Tuskegee, Ala., she worked as a seamstress in Montgomery, where she was active in the NAACP (1943–56). In 1955 she was arrested after refusing to give her seat on a public bus to a white man. The resultant boycott of the bus system organized by M. L. KING brought the CIVIL RIGHTS MOVEMENT to new prominence. She was later a staff assistant (1965–88) to U.S. Rep. John Conyers. She was awarded the Congressional Gold Medal in 1999.

Parliament Legislative assembly of Britain and of other governments modeled after it. The British Parliament consists of the monarch, the House of LORDS, and the House of COMMONS, and traces its roots to the union (c.1300) of the Great Council and the King's Court. Parliament soon was split into two houses, with the lords spiritual and temporal (i.e., not only the nobility but also high officials of the church) debating in one and the knights and burgesses in the other. In the 14th cent. Parliament also began to present petitions ("bills") to the king, which with his assent would become law. Robert WALPOLE was the first party leader to head the government as PRIME MINISTER (1721–42). See also PARLIAMENTARY DEMOCRACY.

Parliament, Canadian Legislature of Canada, created by the BRITISH N. AMERICA ACT. The 301 members of its House of Commons are elected for maximum terms of five years from the provinces on the principle of representation by population. The 105 members of its Senate are appointed by Canada's governor-general from the regions of Canada and serve until age 75. The parliament has authority over the armed forces, regulates trade and commerce, levies taxes, and is in charge of banking, criminal law, postal services, and other spheres. It also retains powers not specifically assigned to provincial legislatures. The leader of the party winning the most seats in a general election becomes prime minister. The party winning the second-largest number of seats in the House becomes the official opposition party.

parliamentary democracy Democratic form of government in which the party with the greatest representation in the parliament forms the government, its leader becoming PRIME MINISTER or chancellor. Executive functions are exercised by members of the parliament appointed by the prime minister to the CABINET. The parties in the minority serve in opposition to the majority and have the duty to regularly challenge it. Parliamentary democracy originated in Britain (see PARLIAMENT) and was adopted in almost all its former colonies, as well as in many other countries.

parliamentary procedure *or* **rules of order** Generally accepted rules and practices used in the governance of deliberative assemblies. They are intended to maintain decorum, ascertain the will of the majority, preserve the rights of the minority, and facilitate the orderly transaction of business. Such rules originated in Britain in the 16th–17th cent., and were subsequently adopted by legislatures around the world. *Robert's Rules of Order*, codified in 1876 by U.S. Gen. Henry M. Robert (1837–1923) and regularly refined, remains the standard in the U.S.

Parma City (pop, 1998 est.: 167,000), EMILIA-ROMAGNA region, N Italy, on the Parma River. Founded by the Romans in 183 B.C., it was destroyed by the Ostrogoths under THEODORIC but rebuilt. Made part of the duchy of Parma and Piacenza in 1545, it was held by the FARNESE FAMILY and later passed to the Austrians. In 1861 it became part of united Italy. It was badly damaged during World War II. Sites of interest include the 12th-cent. Romanesque cathedral, the 13th-cent. baptistery, and the university (founded in the 11th cent.).

Parmenides \pär-'men-ə-,dēz\ (b.c.515 B.C.) Greek philosopher, leader of the ELEATICS. His teaching was reconstructed from surviving fragments of his long poem *On Nature*. He held that the multiplicity of existing things, their changing forms and motion, are but an appearance of a single eternal reality ("Being"), thus giving rise to the Parmenidean principle that "all is one." He is considered a founder of METAPHYSICS. PLATO's dialogue *Parmenides* deals with his thought.

Parmigianino \,pär-mi-jä-'nē-nō\ *orig.* Girolamo Francesco Maria Mazzola (1503–1540) Italian painter and etcher. Born in Parma (the source of his nickname), he painted some of his early frescoes for San Giovanni Evangelista; they were influenced by CORREGGIO, who had recently worked in the same church. His originality is seen in his *Self-Portrait in a Convex Mirror* (1524). His *Madonna of the Long Neck* (1534) is typical of his later work, which is characterized by ambiguity of spatial composition, elongation of the human figure, and a sensuous beauty beyond nature. Among the most remarkable portrait painters of his age, he developed an elegant version of MANNERISM that influenced later painters. He was also one of the first Italian artists to practice etching.

Parnaíba River \,pär-nà-'ē-bə\ River, NE Brazil. It rises in the Serra da Tabatinga and flows northeast for 600 mi (965 km) to empty into the Atlantic Ocean, forming a delta at its mouth. The river has great economic importance. The port of Parnaíba (pop., 1996: 112,000), near its mouth, is a commercial center.

Parnassian poets \pär-'na-sē-ən\ Members of a French school of poetry of the later 19th cent. Led by C.-M.-R. Leconte de Lisle (1818–1894) and Théophile GAUTIER, they stressed restraint, objectivity, technical perfection, and precise description as a reaction against the emotionalism and verbal excess of ROMANTICISM. Their name came from the anthology *Le Parnasse contemporain* (1866, 1871, 1876). Their influence led to experimentation in meters and verse forms and the revival of the SONNET.

Parnassus \pär-'na-səs\, **Mt.** Mountain in central Greece. Located in the Pindus range, it rises to a height of 8,061 ft (2,457 m). In the ancient world it was sacred to APOLLO, probably because of its proximity to DELPHI and its oracle. For Roman poets the Castalian spring on Parnassus was a source of inspiration, and the mountain was regarded as the home of the MUSES.

Parnell \pär-'nel\, **Charles Stewart** (1846–1891) Irish nationalist leader. He served in the British Parliament (1875–91), introducing obstructionist legislative tactics to call attention to Ireland's needs. In 1877 he became president of the Home Rule Confederation. He was jailed for making violent speeches against the new land act (1881–82), then released to curb an increase in terrorist acts. He united factions in Ireland to win support for parliamentary measures, such as William GLADSTONE's HOME RULE proposals. He remained popular in Ireland until he was named in the divorce suit of his mistress, Katherine O'Shea (1890).

parochial education Education offered institutionally by a religious group. In the U.S. and Canada, parochial education refers to elementary and secondary schools maintained by Roman Catholic parishes, Protestant churches, or Jewish organizations and are separate from the public school system.

parody In literature, a work in which the style of an author is closely imitated for comic effect or in ridicule. Differing both from BURLESQUE (by the depth of its technical penetration) and from travesty (which treats dignified subjects in a trivial manner), parody mercilessly exposes the tricks of manner and thought of its victim, and therefore cannot be written without a thorough appreciation of the work it ridicules.

parole Supervised conditional liberty from prison granted prior to the expiration of a prisoner's sentence. Modern use of parole stems from a change in penal philosophy to emphasize rehabilitation rather than retribution. In some jurisdictions, those convicted of certain crimes (e.g., rape or murder) are not eligible for parole. Conditions of parole vary, but in all cases their violation may constitute grounds for reincarceration. See also PROBATION.

Parr, Catherine (1512–1548) Sixth and last wife of HENRY VIII of England. The daughter of an official in the royal household, she had been widowed twice by the time she married Henry in 1543. She exerted a beneficial influence on the increasingly paranoid king. After Henry's death in 1547, she married Baron Thomas Seymour but died shortly after giving birth to a daughter.

Parrish \'par-ish\, **(Frederick) Maxfield** (1870–1966) U.S. illustrator and painter. Born in Philadelphia and trained in art there, he was the highest-paid commercial artist in the U.S. by the 1920s. He is best known for his depictions of fantasy landscapes populated by attractive young women. He used meticulously defined outlines and intricately detailed natural backgrounds; his unusual colors, especially the luminous "Parrish blue," give his pictures a dreamlike quality. Though his popularity declined in the late 1930s, appreciation of his work revived in the 1960s and '70s.

parrot Any of some 300 species of birds in the family Psittacidae. About 220 species of true parrots (subfamily Psittacinae) are found worldwide in warm regions (see PARAKEET). Many are brilliantly colored. They have a blunt tongue; their vocal apparatus permits many species to mimic human speech with great accuracy. The African gray parrot (*Psittacus erithacus*), almost unsurpassed as a talker, has a red tail and white face; it lives up to 80 years. The 26 species of Amazon parrots (genus *Amazona*), also good mimics, are predominantly green. See also COCKATIEL, COCKATOO, LOVEBIRD, MACAW.

parrot fish Any of about 80 species (family Scaridae) of slender, blunt-headed, deep-bodied fishes found on tropical reefs. They are often brightly colored and have large scales. The fused teeth form a "beak" used to scrape algae and the soft part of coral from reefs. The Indo-Pacific surf, or rivulated, parrot fish (Callyodon fasciatus) grows to 18 in. (46 cm) or more. Some species grow to 4 ft (1.2 m) long and weigh 45 lbs (20 kg).

parsec Unit of measure used to express distances to stars and galaxies, the distance at which the radius of earth's orbit would subtend an angle of 1 second of arc. An object 1 parsec away has a PARALLAX of 1 second. Distance in parsecs is the reciprocal of parallax in seconds of arc. For example, ALPHA CENTAURI, with a parallax of 0.76 second, is 1.33 parsecs away. One parsec equals 3.26 light-years, or $1.92 \times 1,013$ mi $(3.09 \times 1,013$ km).

Parsi or **Parsee** Zoroastrian of India. The Parsis, whose name means "Persians," are descended from Persian Zoroastrians who emigrated to India to escape persecution by Muslims. The migration occurred sometime between the 8th and 10th cent. The Parsis initially settled in Gujarat, but when the British E. INDIA CO. took control of the region around Bombay in the late 17th cent., establishing religious freedom, many Parsis moved there. The Parsis still live chiefly in the Bombay area. See also ZOROASTRIANISM AND PARSIISM.

Parsiism See ZOROASTRIANISM AND PARSIISM

parsley Hardy biennial herb (Petroselinum crispum) of the family Apiaceae, or Umbelliferae, native to Mediterranean lands. The compound leaves are used in cooking. The family Apiaceae, sometimes called the parsley family, contains 300–400 genera of plants found mostly in N temperate regions. The flowers are often arranged in a conspicuous umbel (a flat-topped cluster). Many species are poisonous, including POISON HEMLOCK. Popular members of the family include CARROT, CELERY, PARSNIP, and FENNEL. Species used as herbs and spices include ANISE, DILL, coriander, CARAWAY, and cumin.

parsnip Plant (Pastinaca sativa) of the PARSLEY family, cultivated for its carrot-shaped edible white root. At the end of summer the solids of the root consist largely of starch, but a period of low temperature changes much of the starch to sugar. The root is hardy and not damaged by hard freezing of the soil.

Parsons, Charles Algernon (later **Sir Charles**) (1854–1931) British engineer. He developed the multiple-stage turbine in 1884, and had introduced it in power plants to generate electricity by 1891. Modern steam and nuclear power plants still use turbines of this type to turn their generators. He demonstrated his marine turbine in "Turbinia," a vessel that attained a speed of over 34 knots in 1897; Parsons turbines made high-speed ocean liners possible.

Partch, Harry (1901–1974) U.S. composer and instrument maker. Born in Oakland, Cal., he was largely self-taught musically. He traveled as a hobo, conceiving many of his musical ideas while doing so. Around 1930 he began building a remarkable instrumentarium of original percussion and string instruments, tunable to 43 divisions of the octave. His works often involve theatrical elements, reflecting his interest in African, Japanese, and Native American ritual. They include Lyrics by Li Po (1931), and On the 7th Day Petals Fell on Petaluma (1966).

parterre \pär-'ter\ Division of garden beds in an ornamental pattern. It grew out of the medieval knot garden, in which various plant types were separated by hedges. In the 16th cent., the hedges were replaced by wooden or leaden shapes or by lines of shells or coal, and the areas between were filled with colored sand or stone chips. The naturalistic English garden of the 18th cent. displaced the elaborate parterre.

Parthenon \'pär-thə-ˌnän\ Chief temple of ATHENA on the ACROPOLIS at Athens. Built 447–432 B.C. by Ictinus and Callicrates under Pericles, it is considered the culmination of the Doric ORDER. Though the white marble temple has suffered damage over the centuries, including the loss of most of its sculpture, its basic structure remains intact. The

Parthenon

colonnade consists of eight columns on the ends and 17 on the sides; the interior originally held a great gold-and-ivory statue by PHIDIAS. Its sculpture rivaled its architecture. The pediment sculptures represent the birth of Athena and her battle with Poseidon; a continuous frieze shows the annual procession of citizens honoring Athena. The entire work is a marvel of harmony and clarity. See also ELGIN MARBLES.

Parthia Ancient land, W Asia. Corresponding roughly to modern NE Iran, it formed a province of PERSIA and later of the empire of ALEXANDER THE GREAT. After the dissolution of the SELEUCID empire around 250 B.C., a new Parthian kingdom was founded. At its height in the early 1st cent. B.C., it was known as the Parthian empire and included the area between the EUPHRATES and INDUS rivers and between the AMU DARYA and the Arabian Sea. It was overthrown by Persia about A.D. 226. The ruins of CTESIPHON, a major Parthian city, are in modern Iraq. The Parthians were famous as horsemen and archers.

particle accelerator Device that accelerates a beam of fast-moving, electrically charged atoms (IONS) or SUBATOMIC PARTICLES. Accelerators are used to study the structure of atomic nuclei (see ATOM) and the nature of subatomic particles and their fundamental interactions. At speeds close to that of light, particles collide with and disrupt atomic nuclei and subatomic particles, allowing physicists to study nuclear components and to make new kinds of subatomic particles. Accelerators are also used for radioisotope production, cancer therapy, biological sterilization, and one form of radiocarbon dating. See also CYCLOTRON, LINEAR ACCELERATOR.

particle physics or **high-energy physics** Study of the fundamental SUBATOMIC PARTICLES, including both MATTER (and ANTIMATTER) and the carrier particles of the fundamental interactions as described by QUANTUM FIELD THEORY. Fundamental particles possess properties such as ELECTRIC CHARGE, SPIN, MASS, MAGNETISM, and other complex characteristics, but are regarded as pointlike. All theories in particle physics involve QUANTUM MECHANICS, in which symmetry is of primary importance. See also ELECTROWEAK THEORY, LEPTON, MESON, QUANTUM CHROMODYNAMICS, QUARK, STANDARD MODEL.

Parti Québécois \pàr-tē-kā-be-'kwä\ Minor Canadian political party founded in 1968 by René Lévesque (1922–1987) and other French-Canadian separatists in the province of Quebec. In the 1976 provincial election it won a majority in the assembly, which then decreed French as the province's only official language. After a separatist referendum on independence failed (1980), the party lost membership. It revived to win the 1994 provincial election. A 1995 referendum on secession was narrowly defeated.

partnership Association of two or more persons or entities that conduct a business for profit as co-owners. Except in the case of the LIMITED LIABILITY partnership, a partnership is traditionally viewed as an association of individuals rather than an entity with a separate and independent existence. The partners are taxed as individuals and are personally liable for TORTS and contractual obligations. Each is viewed as the agent of the others. See also AGENCY.

partridge Any of certain species of Old World game bird in the family Phasianidae. The European gray partridge (Perdix perdix), introduced into N. America, has a reddish face and tail, and barred sides; males may be 12 in. (30 cm) long. Family groups (coveys) forage for seeds and insects. The five Asian and 35 African species of francolins (genus Francolinus) are 10–16 in. (25–40 cm) long. The snow partridge (Lerwa lerwa) inhabits high Asian mountains. Partridges are larger than QUAIL and have a stronger bill and feet. GROUSE and BOBWHITES are often erroneously called partridge.

Parton, Dolly (orig. Dollie Rebecca) (b.1946) U.S. singer and actress. Born on a farm in Locust Ridge, Tenn., she began singing with Porter Wagoner (b.1927) in 1967 and pursued a

solo singing career from 1974. By the mid-1970s she was the top female country music singer and had crossed over to the pop-music market. She appeared in such films as *Nine to Five* (1980) and *Steel Magnolias* (1989) and produced several television specials. She has written hit songs, and is also noted for her bluegrass recordings.

parturition *or* **birth** *or* **childbirth** *or* **labor** *or* **delivery** Process of bringing forth a child from the UTERUS, ending PREGNANCY. It has three stages. In dilation, uterine contractions lasting about 40 seconds begin 20–30 minutes apart, and progress to severe labor pains about every three minutes. The opening of the cervix widens as contractions push the FETUS. Dilation averages 13–14 hours in first-time mothers, less for later births. When the cervix dilates fully, expulsion begins. The "water" (amniotic sac) breaks (if it has not already), and the woman may actively push. Expulsion lasts 1–2 hours or less. Normally, the baby's head emerges first. In the third stage, the PLACENTA is expelled, usually within 15 minutes. Within six to eight weeks, the mother's REPRODUCTIVE SYSTEM returns to nearly the pre-pregnancy state. See also CESAREAN SECTION, LACTATION, MIDWIFERY, MISCARRIAGE, NATURAL CHILDBIRTH, OBSTETRICS AND GYNECOLOGY.

party system Political system in which individuals who share a common set of political beliefs organize themselves into parties to compete in elections for the right to govern. Single-party systems are found in countries that do not allow genuine political conflict. Multiparty and two-party systems, representing means of organizing political conflict, are indicative of democracy. Multiparty systems allow for greater representation of minority viewpoints, but the coalitions they must form to achieve a governing majority are often fragile.

Pasadena City (pop., 2000: 134,000), SW California, at the base of the SAN GABRIEL MTNS. Founded in 1874, it grew as a winter resort and citrus center after the construction of the Santa Fe Railway and the freeway that links it to LOS ANGELES. It is home to the CALIFORNIA INSTITUTE OF TECHNOLOGY and its Jet Propulsion Laboratory. It is the site of the annual college football ROSE BOWL and the Tournament of Roses, a flower festival begun in 1890.

Pasargadae \pə-'sär-gə-ˌdē\ Ruined city, ancient Persia, northeast of PERSEPOLIS and of modern SHIRAZ, Iran. It was the capital of CYRUS THE GREAT, supposedly founded on the site of his victory over the last king of the Medes (c.550 B.C.). It was known for the majestic simplicity of its architecture; its ruins include the bases of several large buildings and the nearly intact tomb of Cyrus.

Pascal \pas-'kal\ Computer PROGRAMMING LANGUAGE named for Blaise PASCAL and based partly on ALGOL. It was developed by Niklaus Wirth of Switzerland (b.1934) in the late 1960s as an educational tool for the teaching of programming. It was published in 1974 and used by many universities for the next 15 years. Pascal strongly influenced languages developed later, such as ADA. Complex data and ALGORITHMS can be described concisely by Pascal, and its programs are easy to read and debug.

Pascal \pas-'kal\, **Blaise** (1623–1662) French mathematician, physicist, and religious philosopher. A child prodigy, he earned the envy of René DESCARTES at age 17 with an essay on conic sections. In the 1640s and '50s he made contributions to physics (formulating Pascal's Law of fluid mechanics) and mathematics (working on the arithmetic triangle, inventing a calculating machine, and contributing to differential calculus), for which he is regarded as the founder of the modern theory of probability. *Les provinciales* (1656–57) is a series of letters defending JANSENISM and attacking the JESUITS. His great defense of Christianity, *Apologie de la religion chrétienne,* was never finished, but notes and fragments assembled in 1657–58 were later published as *Pensées* (1670). He contributed to the *Éléments de géométrie* and published his findings on cycloid curves, but he soon returned to devotional life and spent his last years helping the poor. A unit of pressure and a computer programming language were named for him.

Pascin \pás-'kaⁿ\, **Jules** *orig.* Julius Pincas (1885–1930) Bulgarian painter. He lived in Austria and Germany, producing drawings for satirical journals, before moving to Paris in 1905, where he became associated with other Jewish artists, including Marc CHAGALL and Amedeo MODIGLIANI. He painted portraits and a series of large-scale biblical and mythological scenes, but his most notable works are thinly painted ironic studies of women. Though financially successful, he was emotionally unstable; he hanged himself at 45.

Pashtuns \ˌpàsh-'tûnz\ Pashto-speaking people of SE Afghanistan and NW Pakistan. They number about 7.5 million in Afghanistan, constituting the majority of its population, and 14 million in Pakistan. Most scholars believe that they arose from an intermingling of ancient ARYANS from the north or west with subsequent invaders. Each Pashtun tribe is divided into clans, subclans, and patriarchal families. Disputes over property, women, and personal injury often result in blood feuds between families and whole clans. Most tribesmen are sedentary farmers; some are migratory herdsmen and caravaners. Many have always been attracted to military service.

Pasic \'pà-shĕtʸ, *Engl* 'pä-shich\, **Nikola** (1845–1926) Serbian and Yugoslav statesman. The editor of a socialist newspaper in Serbia, he was elected to the legislature, where he advocated a parliamentary democracy. In 1881 he helped found the Radical Party, but he was forced to flee to Bulgaria in 1883. Returning in 1889 under a new king, he served as premier (1891–92). Forced into exile again because of his radicalism (1899–1903), he returned to support King PETER I. As leader of the Radical Party, he served as premier of Serbia during most of the period 1904–18, then helped create the new Kingdom of Serbs, Croats, and Slovenes (later Yugoslavia). As premier again (1921–26), he pushed for a unitary constitution that confirmed Serbia's dominance.

Pasionaria, La See Dolores IBÁRRURI

Pasolini \ˌpä-sō-'lē-nē\, **Pier Paolo** (1922–1975) Italian writer and film director. He wrote novels about Rome's slum life as well as poetry; as a screenwriter, he collaborated on Federico FELLINI's *Nights of Cabiria* (1956). His directorial debut, *Accattone* (1961), was based on his novel *A Violent Life* (1959). His best-known film is the stylistically unorthodox *The Gospel According to Saint Matthew* (1964). Later films include *Oedipus Rex* (1967), *Teorema* (1968), *Medea* (1969), and *The Arabian Nights* (1974). His use of eroticism, violence, and depravity were criticized by Italian religious authorities.

pasqueflower See ANEMONE

passage, rite of Any of numerous ceremonial events, existing in all societies, that mark the passage of an individual from one social or religious status to another. The term was coined by Arnold van Gennep (1873–1957) in 1909. Many of the most important rites are connected with the biological stages of life—birth, maturity, reproduction, and death. Other rites celebrate changes that are wholly cultural, such as initiation into SECRET SOCIETIES. Rites of passage may allow societies to confront and incorporate change without disrupting the equilibrium necessary to social order.

passenger pigeon Extinct species (*Ectopistes migratorius*) of PIGEON (subfamily Columbinae, family Columbidae). Billions inhabited E N. America in the early 19th cent.; migrating flocks darkened the skies for days. Gunners began to slaughter them in huge numbers for shipping by railway carloads for sale in city meat markets. Martha, the last known passenger pigeon, died in 1914 in the Cincinnati Zoo. The bird's extinction was largely responsible for ending the marketing of game birds and gave major impetus to the conservation movement.

Passenger pigeon (*Ectopistes migratorius*), mounted

passerine Any perching bird. All passerines belong to the largest order of birds, Passeriformes, and have feet specialized for holding onto a horizontal branch (perching). The passerine foot has three forward-directed toes and one backward-directed toe. Most passerines have moderately curved, sharp claws. Some ground-dwelling species (e.g., LARKS) have flatter, longer feet. Species that spend much time airborne (e.g., SWALLOWS) have small, weak feet. Species that cling and climb (e.g., NUTHATCHES) have strong, sharp, curved claws. Passerines include about 4,000 species of oscines (songbirds; suborder Passere, or Oscines) and 1,100 species of suboscines. Suboscines lack the syrinx of the songbirds or have only a poorly developed one, but some can utter complex vocalizations. All passerines are land birds; most are insectivorous.

passionflower family Family Passifloraceae, composed of about 600 species of herbaceous or woody vines, shrubs, and trees in 20 genera. Members of this family grow mostly in warm regions. Many species produce edible fruits. Members of the largest genus, *Passiflora*, are highly prized for their showy, unusual flowers, often used to symbolize events in the last hours (Passion) of JESUS.

Passion play Religious drama of medieval origin. Early Passion plays were written in Latin and consisted of Gospel readings alternating with poetic descriptions of the events of JESUS's Passion (i.e., his sufferings between the Last Supper and his death). Latin was eventually replaced by the local language, and by the 16th cent. many of the plays had become mere popular entertainments. Some survived into the 20th cent., most notably one performed by local villagers every 10 years at Oberammergau, Germany.

passive resistance See CIVIL DISOBEDIENCE, SATYAGRAHA

Passover In JUDAISM, the holiday commemorating the liberation of the Hebrews from slavery in Egypt. God sent a plague to destroy the firstborn of the Egyptians, but his angel of death passed over (i.e., spared) the Israelites, who had specially marked their doors. The festival of Passover begins on the 15th and ends on the 22nd (in Israel, the 21st) day of the month of Nisan (March or April). The unleavened bread eaten during Passover symbolizes the Hebrews' suffering in bondage and the haste with which they left Egypt. On the first night of Passover, a SEDER is held, and the HAGGADAH is read aloud.

passport Document issued by a national government identifying a traveler as a citizen with a right to protection while abroad and a right to return to the country of citizenship. It is normally a small booklet containing a description and photograph of the bearer. Most nations require entering travelers to obtain a visa, an endorsement on the passport permitting the bearer to enter the country and remain for a specified period.

pasta Any of several starchy food pastes made from semolina, the purified middlings (endosperm) of a hard WHEAT called durum. Pasta is traditionally associated with Italian cuisine, though it entered Europe from Asia in the 13th cent. In making pasta, semolina dough is compacted and forced through dics that form it into ribbons, cords, tubes, and other shapes, each with its own name (e.g., spaghetti, macaroni). The formed dough is then dried under controlled conditions, or cooked immediately by boiling.

pastel Drawing medium consisting of fragile, finger-size crayons called pastels, made of powdered pigments combined with a minimum of nongreasy binder. Because pigment applied with pastel does not change in color value, the final effect can be seen immediately. Pastel remains on the surface of the paper and thus can be easily obliterated unless protected by glass or a fixative. When applied in short strokes or linearly, it is usually classed as drawing; when rubbed, smeared, and blended to achieve painterly effects, it is often regarded as a painting medium.

Pasternak, Boris (Leonidovich) (1890–1960) Russian poet and prose writer. His early poetry, though avant-garde, was admired and successful, but in the 1930s a gap widened between his work and officially approved literary modes, and he supported himself by doing translations. The banned novel *Doctor Zhivago* (1957; film, 1965), an epic of wandering, spiritual isolation, and love amid the harshness of the revolution and its aftermath, became a best-seller in the West. He was awarded the Nobel Prize in 1958, but was forced to decline it by his government.

Pasteur \pas-'tər\, **Louis** (1822–1895) French chemist and microbiologist. Early in his career, he researched the effects of polarized light on chemical compounds. His studies of FERMENTATION of alcohol and milk (souring) showed that yeast could reproduce without free oxygen; he deduced that fermentation and food spoilage were due to the activity of microorganisms and could be prevented by excluding or destroying them. His work overturned the concept of spontaneous generation (life arising from nonliving matter) and led to heat PASTEURIZATION, allowing vinegar, wine, and beer to be produced and transported without spoiling. He saved the French silk industry by his work on silkworm diseases. In 1881 he perfected a way to isolate and weaken germs, and went on to develop VACCINES against anthrax in sheep and cholera in chickens following Edward JENNER's example. Turning his attention to rabies, he saved the life of a boy bitten by a rabid dog by inoculating the boy with weakened virus. In 1888 he founded the Pasteur Institute for rabies research, prevention, and treatment.

Pasteurella \ˌpas-chə-'rel-ə\ Genus (named after Louis PASTEUR) of rod-shaped BACTERIA that cause several serious diseases in domestic animals and milder infections in humans. Members are gram-negative (see GRAM STAIN), do not move, and do not require oxygen. The widespread infections they cause are transmitted by direct contact and, in some cases, by ticks and fleas. Control by vaccine is variable, as is treatment with antibiotics.

pasteurization Partial STERILIZATION of a substance by using heat to destroy microorganisms without altering its chemical makeup. The process is named for Louis PASTEUR, its originator. Pasteurization of milk requires temperatures of about 145°F (63°C) for about 30 minutes, or higher temperatures for shorter periods. The treatment destroys any disease-causing organisms as well as organisms that cause spoilage.

pastoral \ˌpas-tə-'räl\ Literary work dealing in a usually artificial manner with shepherds or rural life, typically contrasting the innocence and serenity of the simple life with the misery and corruption of city or court life. The characters are often the vehicles for the author's moral, social, or literary views. The poet and his friends are often presented as shepherds and shepherdesses; two or more shepherds sometimes contend in "singing matches." The conventions of pastoral poetry were largely established by THEOCRITUS, whose bucolics are its earliest examples; VIRGIL's *Eclogues* were influential as well, as was Edmund SPENSER's *Shepheardes Calender* in the Renaissance. See also ECLOGUE.

Patagonia Semi-arid scrub plateau, S Argentina. It is the largest desert region in the Americas, with an area of over 300,000 sq mi (775,000 sq km). Its approximate boundaries are the Río Colorado in the north, the Atlantic Ocean in the east, the Río Coig in the south, and the ANDES in the west. It has a variety of wildlife, including llamas, pumas, and eagles. Natural resources include petroleum, iron ore, copper, uranium, and manganese.

Patel \pə-'täl\, **Vallabhbhai (Jhaverbhai)** *known as* **Sardar** ("Leader") **Patel** (1875–1950) Indian statesman. A lawyer, he did not become involved in politics until 1917. Like Mohandas GANDHI and unlike Jawaharlal NEHRU, he advocated dominion status within the British Commonwealth rather than independence for India. He opposed armed struggle on practical grounds, and was not interested in Hindu-Muslim unity. The leader of a landowners' revolt against increased taxes (1928), he was active in the Indian National Congress and was imprisoned with other leaders (1932–34, 1940–41, 1942–45). After Indian independence (1947), he held several cabinet positions. He is remembered for achieving the peaceful integration of the princely Indian states into the Indian Union and the political unification of India.

Patenier, Joachim de See Joachim de PATINIR

patent Government grant to an inventor of the exclusive right to make, use, or sell an invention, usually for a specified term. It may be granted for a process or method that is new, useful, and not obvious, or for a new use of a known process, machine, or composition of matter or material, including genetically engineered organisms. It may also be granted for any new, original, and ornamental design for an article of manufacture. In the U.S., design patents are issued for 14 years, other patents for 20 years. Patents are

P

considered personal property and may be sold, assigned, or otherwise transferred. See also COPYRIGHT.

Pater \'pā-tər\, **Walter (Horatio)** (1839–1894) English art critic. Pater made his reputation with essays collected in *Studies in the History of the Renaissance* (1873). Written in a delicate, fastidious style, it introduced his influential advocacy of "art for art's sake," which contrasted with the prevailing emphasis on art's moral or educational values and became a cardinal doctrine of AESTHETICISM. *Marius the Epicurean* (1885), a philosophical romance, is his most substantial work.

Paterson City (pop., 2000: 149,000), NE New Jersey. Located on the Passaic River, it was founded in 1791 as an industrial settlement by advocates of U.S. industrial independence from Europe. The successful enterprise, begun by Alexander HAMILTON, was known as the Society for Establishing Useful Manufactures. In the 19th cent. it was a center of the textile industry and locomotive manufacturing. It was the scene of many labor disputes. Its industries are now widely diversified.

Pathan See PASHTUN

Pathé \pà-'tā, *Engl* pa-'thā\, **Charles** (1863–1957) French film executive. In 1896 he and his brother Émile founded Pathé Frères, which soon entered film production using the camera developed by the LUMIÈRE brothers. In 1909 Pathé produced his first "long film," *Les misérables,* and launched the *Pathé Gazette,* an internationally popular newsreel that ran until 1956. With facilities throughout the world, Pathé Frères dominated the film market in the early 20th cent., and it remained a leading film distributor after Charles's retirement in 1929.

pathology Medical specialty dealing with causes of disease and structural and functional changes in abnormal conditions. In the mid-19th cent., the humoral theories of infection were replaced first by cell-based theories (see Rudolf VIRCHOW) and then by the bacteriologic theories of Robert KOCH and Louis PASTEUR. Today, pathologists work mostly in the laboratory and consult with a patient's physician after examining specimens including surgically removed body parts, blood and other fluids, urine, feces, and discharges. Culturing of infectious organisms, staining, fiber optic endoscopy, and electron microscopy have greatly expanded the information available to the pathologist. See also AUTOPSY.

Patinir \ˌpà-tə-'nir\, **Joachim** (c.1480–1524) Netherlandish painter. Nothing is known of his early life. He is the first Western artist known to have specialized in landscape painting, though his work has a nominal religious subject. His novelty lay in the fact that the religious motif in such works as *Flight into Egypt* (1515–20) was overshadowed by the phenomena of the natural world. He apparently supplied landscape settings for figure compositions painted by other Flemish masters. His landscapes combine realistic detail with a sense of fantasy that suggests his familiarity with the works of Hieronymus BOSCH.

patio In Spanish and Latin-American architecture, a courtyard open to the sky within a building. A development of the Roman ATRIUM, it is comparable to the Italian *cortile* but provides more seclusion. The patio of the contemporary U.S. house is a paved outdoor area adjoining the building and often used for outdoor dining.

Patna \'pət-nə\ City (pop., 1991: 1,100,000) and capital of Bihar state, NE India. Lying on the GANGES RIVER, it was founded in the 5th cent. B.C. as Pataliputra; it was the capital of MAGADHA until the 1st cent. B.C. A center of learning, it became the GUPTA DYNASTY's capital in the 4th cent. A.D. Deserted by the 7th cent., it was revived as Patna in 1541 by an Afghan ruler, became prosperous under the MUGHAL DYNASTY, and passed to the British in 1765.

Paton, Alan (Stewart) (1903–1988) S. African writer and political activist. While principal of a reformatory housing black youths, Paton introduced controversial progressive reforms and wrote his best-selling novel *Cry, the Beloved Country* (1948), focusing international attention on the issue of APARTHEID. He helped found the Liberal Party of S. Africa in 1953 and led the organization until it was banned in 1968. His other works include the novel *Too Late the Phalarope* (1953).

patriarch Title applied to OLD TESTAMENT leaders such as METHUSELAH, ABRAHAM, and JACOB. It was once given also to the most powerful Roman Catholic BISHOPS, and is still used in EASTERN ORTHODOXY, which now has nine patriarchates: Constantinople, Alexandria, Antioch, Jerusalem, Moscow, Georgia, Serbia, Romania, and Bulgaria.

patrician In ancient Rome, any member of a group of citizen families who, in contrast to the PLEBEIANS, formed a privileged nobility. They attempted to hold on to magistracies, priesthoods, and legal and religious knowledge, and the great civil struggle of the ROMAN REPUBLIC was the plebeians' effort to achieve equality. The patricians gradually lost their monopoly except in a few areas. After 27 B.C., patrician rank was necessary for ascent to the imperial throne.

Patrick, St. (fl.5th cent.) Patron saint of Ireland. Born in Britain, he was captured at 16 and carried into slavery in Ireland. He spent six years as a herdsman before escaping to Britain. Called in a dream to bring Christianity to the Irish, he returned to Ireland, where he baptized chiefs and kings and converted whole clans. He is said to have explained the notion of the Holy Trinity using the shamrock, now the national flower of Ireland, and to have rid Ireland of snakes.

patristic literature Body of literature comprising those works (excluding the New Testament) written by Christians before the 8th cent. A.D. The term refers to the works of the Church Fathers. Significant patristic authors include JUSTIN MARTYR, ORIGEN, ATHANASIUS, BASIL THE GREAT, John CHRYSOSTOM, AMBROSE, AUGUSTINE, JEROME, CYRIL OF ALEXANDRIA, and GREGORY I.

patronage system See SPOILS SYSTEM

pattern recognition In computer science, the identification of input data, such as speech, images, or a stream of text on the basis of patterns they contain and their relationships. Stages in pattern recognition involve picking out distinguishing attributes and comparing them with known patterns to determine a match or mismatch. Pattern recognition has extensive application in astronomy, medicine, and robotics. See also SPEECH RECOGNITION.

Patterson, Floyd (b.1935) U.S. boxer. Born in Waco, N.C., he was reared in Brooklyn, N.Y. He won an Olympic gold medal as a middleweight in 1952. In 1956 he succeeded Rocky MARCIANO as world heavyweight champion by knocking out Archie MOORE. He lost the title to Ingemar Johansson in 1959, regained it in 1960, and lost it again in 1962 to Sonny Liston.

Patton, George S(mith) (1885–1945) U.S. Army officer. Born in San Gabriel, Cal., he graduated from West Point and fought in World War I with the newly formed tank corps. He later became a major general in command of the 2nd Armored Division (1940). In World War II, he led military operations in Morocco (1942) and Sicily (1943), then commanded the 3rd Army in its sweep across N France into Germany. His bold use of mobile tank warfare strategies, coupled with his highly disciplined leadership, earned him his troops' respect. Criticized for striking a hospitalized soldier he suspected of malingering, he publicly apologized. He died in a car crash in Germany.

George Patton, 1945

Paul, Les *orig.* Lester Polfus (b.1916) U.S. guitarist and inventor. Born in Waukesha, Wis., he played many styles of popular music, initially country but later jazz. He invented the first solid-body electric guitar, and was instrumental in developing modern-day multitrack recording. His overdubbed, sped-up records—including "Brazil" (1948), "Nola" (1950), and "How High the Moon" (1951), often with his wife, Mary Ford (1924–1977), singing harmony with herself—demonstrated the potential of tape.

Paul, St. *orig.* Saul (c.A.D. 10–67?) Early Christian missionary and theologian, "Apostle to the gentiles." Born a Jew in TARSUS, Asia Minor, he was trained as a rabbi but earned his living as a tentmaker. A zealous PHARISEE, he persecuted the first Christians until a vision of Jesus, experienced while on the road to Damascus, converted him to Christianity. Three years later he met St. PETER and Jesus' brother James, and was henceforth recognized as the 13th Apostle. By asserting that non-Jewish disciples of Christ did not have to observe Jewish law, he helped to establish Christianity as a separate religion rather than a Jewish sect. On a journey to Jerusalem, he aroused such hostility among the Jews that he was arrested and imprisoned for two years. Paul's letters, or epistles, collected in the NEW TESTAMENT, are the first Christian theological writing and the source of much Christian doctrine. It was due to Paul more than anyone else that Christianity became a world religion.

Paul I *Russian* Pavel Petrovich (1754–1801) Czar of Russia (1796–1801). He was the son of PETER III and CATHERINE II the Great, whom he succeeded in 1796. He reversed many of Catherine's policies, strengthened the autocracy, and established the law of succession within the ROMANOV DYNASTY. He provoked the hostility of the nobles and the army with his tyrannical rule and capricious foreign policy. In a plot to depose him and place his son Alexander (later ALEXANDER I) on the throne, Paul was assassinated.

Paul III *orig.* Alessandro Farnese (1468–1549) Pope (1534–49). The son of a noble Tuscan family, he was made a cardinal-deacon in 1493 and served as bishop in Parma and Ostia before being named dean of the College of Cardinals by LEO X. He was unanimously elected pope in 1534. Though loose in morals in earlier years, he became an efficient promoter of reform, convening the Council of TRENT in 1545 and initiating the COUNTER-REFORMATION. He also supported the newly founded JESUITS and was a patron of the arts.

Paul VI *orig.* Giovanni Battista Montini (1897–1978) Pope (1963–78). He was a church diplomat for much of his career, until he was named archbishop of Milan in 1954. He became a cardinal in 1958, and in 1963 he was elected pope. Paul VI presided over the final sessions of the Second VATICAN COUNCIL and appointed commissions to carry out its reforms. He also relaxed rules on fasting and removed a number of questionable saints from the church's calendar. He promoted ECUMENISM and was the first pope to travel widely.

Pauli, Wolfgang (1900–1958) Austrian-U.S. physicist. In 1924 he proposed that a SPIN QUANTUM number, $+1/2$ or $-1/2$, is necessary to specify electron energy states; and in 1930 he proposed that the energy and momentum apparently lost when an electron is emitted from an atomic nucleus in BETA DECAY is carried away by an almost massless, uncharged, and difficult-to-detect particle (the NEUTRINO). He was awarded a 1945 Nobel Prize for his 1925 discovery of the PAULI EXCLUSION PRINCIPLE.

Pauli exclusion principle Assertion proposed by Wolfgang PAULI that no two ELECTRONS in an ATOM can be in the same state or configuration at the same time. The principle has since been generalized to all FERMIONS. The SPIN of such particles is always an odd whole-number multiple of $1/2$. For example, electrons have spin $1/2$, and can occupy two distinct states with opposite spin directions. The principle indicates that only two electrons are allowed in each atomic energy state, leading to the successive buildup of ORBITALS around the NUCLEUS. This prevents matter from collapsing to an extremely dense state.

Pauling, Linus (Carl) (1901–1994) U.S. chemist. Born in Portland, Ore., he was one of the first to apply quantum mechanics to the study of molecular structures, and calculated interatomic distances and the angles between chemical bonds (see BONDING), effectively using X-RAY DIFFRACTION and other techniques. His book *The Nature of the Chemical Bond* (1939) became one of the century's most influential chemistry texts. He was the first recipient of the American Chemical Society's Langmuir Prize (1931), and later the first recipient of its Lewis medal (1951), and in 1954 he received the Nobel Prize for Chemistry. In 1962 his efforts on behalf of control of NUCLEAR WEAPONS and against nuclear testing brought him the Nobel Peace Prize, making him the first recipient of two unshared Nobel Prizes. He later studied the prevention of illness by taking high doses of vitamins and minerals.

Pausanias \pȯ-'sā-nē-əs\ (fl.A.D. 143–176) Greek traveler and geographer. His *Description of Greece* is an invaluable guide to ancient ruins. He describes the religious art and architecture of OLYMPIA and DELPHI, the pictures and inscriptions at ATHENS, the statue of Athena on the ACROPOLIS, and monuments outside the city. According to James Frazer (1854-1941), without Pausanias the ruins of Greece would be "a labyrinth without a clue, a riddle without an answer."

Pavarotti, Luciano (b.1935) Italian tenor. He started out as a schoolteacher, beginning his vocal training only in his twenties. He made his professional debut in 1961, debuted at La Scala in 1965, and at the Metropolitan Opera in 1968. He retained the beautiful tone and thrilling high notes that his audiences loved into his sixties. The most famous male classical singer of the late 20th cent., he came to personify the Italian tenor worldwide.

pavement Durable surfacing of a road, path, court, patio, plaza, airstrip, or other such area. The Romans built their roads of stone and concrete. By A.D. 75 India was using brick and stone slab pavements. Smaller cobblestones began to be used for European paving in the late Middle Ages. The 18th–19th cent. saw the development of pavement systems (e.g., MACADAM) that used light surfaces of broken or crushed stone. Modern pavements, containing sand and gravel or crushed stone with a bituminous binder (e.g., asphalt or tar), have enough plasticity to absorb shock. Rigid pavements are made of concrete, usually reinforced with steel rod or mesh.

Pavese \pä-'vā-sā\, **Cesare** (1908–1950) Italian poet, critic, novelist, and translator. Pavese founded the publishing house of Einaudi and edited the antifascist review *La Cultura*. He was imprisoned in 1935. His translations in the 1930s and '40s introduced many modern U.S. and English writers to Italy. Much of his own work appeared between the end of World War II and his death by suicide at 41. His best works include *Dialogues with Leucò* (1947), poetic conversations on the human condition, and the novel *The Moon and the Bonfire* (1950). The Pavese Prize for literature was established in 1957.

Pavia \pä-'vē-ə\ *ancient* Ticinum. City (pop., 1991: 76,000), LOMBARDY, N Italy. Pillaged by ATTILA and ODOACER in the 5th cent. A.D., it became a center of Gothic resistance against the Byzantine empire. Ruled by the Visconti family from around 1359, it became a leading Italian city-state. In 1525 it was the scene of a decisive victory by CHARLES V over the French under FRANCIS I. It was active in the RISORGIMENTO and joined the kingdom of Italy in 1859. It retains the plan of the Roman fortified town, and medieval structures remain. The Univ. of Pavia (founded 1361) is linked with the ancient law school, which dates to 825.

Pavlov \'päv-ˌlȯf\, **Ivan (Petrovich)** (1849–1936) Russian physiologist. He is known chiefly for the concept of the conditioned REFLEX: he showed that a hungry dog trained to associate the sound of a bell with food salivated at the sound even in the absence of food. He expanded on Charles SHERRINGTON's explanation of the spinal reflex. He also tried to apply his laws to human psychoses and language function. His ability to devise simple experiments and his pioneering studies relating human behavior to the nervous system laid the basis for the scientific analysis of behavior. He won a 1904 Nobel Prize for his work on digestive secretions.

Pavlova \'pav-lə-və\, **Anna (Pavlovna)** (1881–1931) Russian ballerina, considered the greatest ballerina of the early 20th cent. She studied at the Imperial Ballet school and joined the MARIINSKY THEATER company in 1899, be-

Anna Pavlova

P

coming prima ballerina in 1906. From 1908 she toured in Europe as a guest artist with many companies. In 1913 she left Russia to tour with her own company, which showcased her outstanding classical performances in such ballets as M. FOKINE's *Dying Swan*. She brought ballet to audiences in many countries for the first time and did much to popularize ballet worldwide.

pawnbroking Business of advancing loans to customers who have pledged household goods or personal belongings as security. One of the oldest trades known, it existed 2,000–3,000 years ago in China, as well as in ancient Greece and Rome. Pawnbroking was common in medieval Europe despite laws against USURY. Private pawnbrokers were usually those exempt from the laws, notably the Jews. Public pawnshops existed briefly in the Middle Ages but were reestablished in the 18th cent. to free debtors from the high interest rates of private pawnshops. Most European countries now maintain public pawnshops; in the U.S. only private pawnshops exist. Social-welfare programs and increased access to easy CREDIT has led to a decline in pawnbroking's importance.

Pawnee \pô-'nē\ PLAINS INDIAN people who traditionally lived along the Platte River in what is now Nebraska. They lived in large, dome-shaped, earth-covered lodges but used TEPEES on buffalo hunts. Women raised corn, squash, and beans. Pawnee religion focused on a variety of deities, including the supreme being Tirawa, the sun god, and morning and evening stars. Many Pawnee served as scouts for the U.S. armies of the frontier. Pawnee lands were ceded to the U.S. in the mid-19th cent., and most Pawnee were relocated to a reservation in Oklahoma. Today they number about 2,300.

pawpaw See PAPAW

Pax Romana \'paks-rō-'ma-nə, 'päks-rō-'mä-nə\ (Latin: "Roman Peace") State of comparative tranquility throughout the Mediterranean world, N Africa, and Persia from the reign of AUGUSTUS (27 B.C.–A.D. 14) to that of MARCUS AURELIUS (A.D. 161–80). The empire protected and governed provinces, each of which legislated and administered its own laws while accepting Roman taxation and military control. It was the Pax Romana that ensured the survival and eventual transmission of the classical Greek and Roman heritage.

payments, balance of See BALANCE OF PAYMENTS

Payton, Walter (Jerry) (1954–1999) U.S. football player. Born in Columbia, Miss., from 1975 to 1987 he played for the Chicago Bears. He ranks second in all-time career totals for yardage (16,726), combined yardage (rushing and pass receiving; 21,803 yds), seasons with 1,000 or more yards rushing (10), and yards gained in a single game (275). He died at 45 of a rare liver disease. He is considered by some the greatest running back in history.

Paz \'päs\, **Octavio** (1914–1998) Mexican poet, writer, and diplomat. After publishing his first book of poetry, *Luna Silvestre* ("Savage Moon"), in 1933, he founded and edited several important literary reviews. Influenced in turn by Marxism, surrealism, existentialism, Buddhism, and Hinduism, his poetry uses rich imagery in dealing with metaphysical questions. His prose works include *The Labyrinth of Solitude* (1950), an influential essay on Mexican history and culture. He was Mexico's ambassador to India 1962–68. He was awarded the Nobel Prize in 1990.

PBS *in full* **Public Broadcasting Service** Private, nonprofit U.S. corporation of public television stations. PBS was founded in 1969 to coordinate and provide its member stations, which now number about 350, with educational, cultural, news, and children's programs, produced by its members and by independent producers worldwide. Its popular programs have included *Sesame Street, Masterpiece Theatre, Great Performances, NewsHour with Jim Lehrer*, and *Nova*. Funding is provided mainly by state governments, viewers' contributions, and grants from private foundations; the U.S. government, through the Corporation for Public Broadcasting, supplies about 15%.

PC See PERSONAL COMPUTER

PCB *in full* **polychlorinated biphenyl** \bī-'fe-n°l, bī-'fē-n°l\ Any of a class of highly stable ORGANIC COMPOUNDS. The commercial product, a mix of several PCB ISOMERS, is a colorless, viscous liquid that hardly dissolves in water. PCBs became widely used as lubricants, heat-transfer fluids, and fire-resistant dielectric fluids in transformers and capacitors in the 1930s and '40s. In the mid-1970s they were found to cause liver dysfunction in humans and came under suspicion as CARCINOGENS; their manufacture and use were consequently restricted. They persist in the environment and have entered the FOOD CHAIN, causing great harm especially to invertebrates and fish.

pea Any of several species, comprising hundreds of varieties, of herbaceous annual plants belonging to the family Leguminosae (or Fabaceae), also known as the pea family (see LEGUME), grown virtually worldwide for their edible seeds. *Pisum sativum* is the common garden pea of the Western world. Some varieties, called sugar peas, have edible pods, which are popular in E. Asian cuisines. See also SWEET PEA.

Peabody \'pē-bə-dē\, **Elizabeth (Palmer)** (1804–1894) U.S. educator. Born in Billerica, Mass., she worked with William Ellery CHANNING (1825–34) and Bronson ALCOTT before opening a Boston bookshop (1839) that became a center for Transcendentalist activities. She published works by Margaret FULLER and Nathaniel HAWTHORNE and also published and wrote for *The Dial*. She opened the first U.S. kindergarten in 1860, and thereafter devoted herself to organizing public and private kindergartens.

Peace Corps U.S. government agency of volunteers, formed in 1961 by Pres. John F. KENNEDY. Its purpose is to assist other countries by providing skilled workers in the fields of education, agriculture, health, trade, technology, and community development. Volunteers are expected to serve for two years in the host country, to speak its language, and to live on a level comparable to that of the local residents. By 2000, over 150,000 volunteers had served in the corps.

Peace of God Movement within the medieval Roman Catholic Church to end private warfare. First heard of in 990 at synods in S and central France, the peace decrees forbade, under pain of excommunication, private warfare or violence against churches, clerics, pilgrims, merchants, women, peasants, and cattle. All those who lived in an area under the Peace of God had to swear to observe and enforce it.

peace pipe See CALUMET

Peace River River, W Canada. Formed in the Canadian Rockies of British Columbia, it flows east into Alberta to join the Slave River just north of Lake ATHABASCA. It is 1,195 mi (1,923 km) long. It was explored by Alexander MACKENZIE in 1792–93 and became a major fur trading route. Today it produces hydroelectric power.

peach Small to medium-sized fruit tree (*Prunus persica*) of the ROSE family, grown in warmer temperate regions, and the fruit it produces. It probably originated in China and spread westward. Peach trees are intolerant of severe cold but require winter chilling to induce spring growth. The long, pointed leaves are glossy green and lance-shaped. Pink or white flowers grow singly or clustered. The fleshy, juicy exterior of the fruit is edible; the seed is called the stone or pit. In freestone types, stones separate easily from ripe flesh; in clingstone types, the flesh adheres firmly to the stone. Thousands of varieties have been developed. Peach skin is downy or fuzzy; smooth-skinned peaches are NECTARINES. Related plants include ALMOND, PLUM, and CHERRY.

peacock Any of three species (family Phasianidae) of resplendent birds of open lowland forests. Blue, or Indian (*Pavo cristatus*), and green, or Javanese (*P. muticus*), peacock males are 35–50 in. (90–130 cm) long and have a 60-in. (150-cm) train of metallic green tail feathers tipped with an iridescent eyespot ringed with blue and bronze. The train is erected, fanned out, and vibrated during courtship. Females (peahens) are duller and have no train. The blue and green male Congo peacock (*Afropavo congensis*) has a short rounded tail.

Peacock, Thomas Love (1785–1866) English novelist and poet. He was a close friend of P. B. SHELLEY, who greatly inspired his writing. His best verse is interspersed in his novels, which are dominated by the conversations of their characters and satirize the intellectual currents of the day. His best-known work, *Nightmare Abbey* (1818), satirizes romantic melancholy.

Peale, Charles Willson (1741–1827) U.S. painter, inventor, and naturalist. Born in Maryland, he began his career by exchanging a saddle for painting lessons. After studying in London with Benjamin WEST, he became the preeminent portrait painter of the middle colonies. In 1786 he founded an institution in Philadelphia for the study of natural law and display of natural history and technological objects; the Peale Museum, the first major U.S. museum, was widely imitated by other museums and later by P. T. BARNUM. He is best remembered for his portraits of the leading figures of the American Revolution.

Peale, Norman Vincent (1898–1993) U.S. Protestant clergyman. Born in Bowersville, Ohio, son of a preacher, he was ordained a pastor in the Methodist Episcopal Church. In 1933 he became pastor of Marble Collegiate Church in New York City, where he remained for the rest of his career. He gained fame through radio and television sermons and through his books, including the best-selling *Power of Positive Thinking* (1952). In 1969 he was elected president of the Reformed Church in America.

Peale, Rembrandt (1778–1860) U.S. painter and writer. A son of C. W. PEALE, he studied with his father and in London. In Paris in 1808–10 he was offered the post of court painter to Napoleon. His early portrait of Thomas JEFFERSON (1805) was his masterpiece. Following his father's example, he opened a museum and portrait gallery in Baltimore, where he established the first illuminating gasworks. He resumed painting with formal subject pieces (e.g., *The Court of Death,* 1820) before returning to portraiture with a series of portraits of George WASHINGTON.

peanut *or* **groundnut** Annual LEGUME (*Arachis hypogaea*) and its edible seeds, which ripen underground in pods. Native to tropical S. America, peanuts were introduced early into the Old World tropics. Each pod contains one to three oblong seeds. Peanuts are a concentrated food; pound for pound they have more protein, minerals, and vitamins than beef liver, more fat than heavy cream, and more calories than sugar. They are pressed for edible oil, ground into peanut butter, eaten as snacks, and used in cooking. The plant is fed to livestock.

pear Any of several species of trees of the genus *Pyrus,* especially *P. communis,* of the ROSE family, or its fruit, cultivated in all temperate-zone countries of both hemispheres. The thousands of varieties include Bartlett (by far the most widely grown), Beurre Bosc, and Beurre d'Anjou. The tree is taller and more upright than the APPLE tree; pear fruits are sweeter and softer than apples. Hard cells (grit, or stone cells) dot the flesh.

pearl Concretion formed by a MOLLUSK consisting of the same material (called nacre, or mother-of-pearl) as the mollusk's shell. Long treasured as gemstones, pearls are valued for their translucence and luster. The more perfect a pearl's shape and the deeper its luster, the greater its value. Jewelers of the 16th–17th cent. often used irregularly shaped "baroque" pearls, formed from muscular tissue, to form the bodies of animals and other figures. In Europe and China, mother-of-pearl has been used as an inlay material for decorating furniture. The discovery that a pearl could be cultivated by insertion of a foreign object inside the mollusk's shell is said to have been made in 13th-cent. China.

Pearl Harbor Inlet, S coast of OAHU island, Hawaii, 6 mi (10 km) west of HONOLULU, forming a harbor connected with the Pacific Ocean. In 1887 Hawaii granted the U.S. the exclusive use of the harbor, and in 1908 a naval station was established, which became the headquarters of the U.S. Pacific Fleet. On Dec. 7, 1941, it was attacked in a major surprise strike by the Japanese air force. Four battleships were sunk, 188 planes were destroyed, and 2,403 people died. The attack precipitated U.S. entry into WORLD WAR II.

Pearl River River, central Mississippi. From JACKSON it flows south into Louisiana and the Gulf of Mexico. About 410 mi (660 km) long, it forms part of the boundary between Mississippi and Louisiana. Its Honey Island Swamp is noted for its wildlife and fishing.

pearlstone See PERLITE

Pearson, Lester B(owles) (1897–1972) Prime minister of Canada (1963–68). Born in Toronto, he joined the Canadian foreign service in 1928. He served in the Canadian House of Commons 1948–68, and was minister of external affairs 1948–56. He led the Canadian delegation to the U.N. 1948–56, and served as president of its General Assembly 1952–53. In 1957 he received the Nobel Peace Price for his help in resolving the SUEZ CRISIS. Head of the Liberal Party from 1958, he rebuilt it to win the 1963 election. As prime minister he confronted the growing Quebec separatist movement and rebuked Charles DE GAULLE for his expressed support. He retired in 1968.

Lester Pearson, 1963

Peary, Robert E(dwin) (1856–1920) U.S. explorer. Born in Cresson, Pa., he joined the U.S. Navy in 1881. He explored Greenland by dog sledge (1886, 1891), finding evidence that it was an island, and returned there (1893–94, 1895, 1896) to transport large meteorites to the U.S. After announcing his intention to reach the North Pole, he made several attempts between 1898 and 1905, sailing on a specially built ship and sledging to within 175 mi (280 km) of the pole. In 1909, accompanied by Matthew Henson (1866–1955) and four Eskimo, he reached what he saw as his goal, and he became widely acknowledged as the first explorer to reach the pole. Evidence now suggests that he may only have reached a point 30–60 mi (50–100 km) short of the pole.

peasant Any member of a class that tills the soil as small landowners or agricultural laborers. The peasant economy generally has a simple technology and a division of labor by age and sex. The basic unit of production is the family or household. Peasant families traditionally consume what they produce, though a portion of their output may be sold in the market or paid to a landlord. Productivity and yields are usually low. Peasants as a class tend to disappear as a society industrializes, though peasantlike social structures may persist. See also EJIDO, FEUDALISM, HACIENDA, SERFDOM.

Peasants' Revolt *or* **Wat Tyler's Rebellion** (1381) First great popular rebellion in English history. It was triggered by the poll tax of 1381, which angered laborers and artisans already resentful of the limits on wages fixed by the Statute of Laborers (1351). The revolt was led by Wat Tyler, who marched into London with a band of Kentish rebels. They captured the Tower of London and beheaded officials responsible for the poll tax. RICHARD II promised reforms, but Tyler was killed in his presence by the mayor of London, and the last of the rebels were soon subdued.

Peasants' War (1524–25) Peasant uprising in Germany. Inspired by reforms brought by the REFORMATION, peasants in W and S Germany invoked divine law to demand freedom from oppression by nobles and landlords. As the uprising spread, some peasant groups organized armies. The revolt was condemned by Martin LUTHER, which contributed to its defeat, principally by the army of the Swabian League. Some 100,000 peasants were killed. Reprisals discouraged further attempts to improve the peasants' plight.

peat Organic fuel consisting of a light, spongy material formed in temperate humid environments by the partial decomposition of vegetable remains under conditions of poor drainage. Vast beds occur in Europe, N. America, and N Asia but are worked only where there is little COAL. Dried peat burns readily, with a smoky flame and a characteristic odor. In Ireland, millions of tons are consumed annually; Russia, Sweden, Germany, and Denmark also use considerable quantities.

peat moss *or* **sphagnum moss** \'sfag-nəm\ Any of more than 160 species of plants that make up the BRYOPHYTE genus *Sphagnum,* which grow in dense clumps in moist areas from tropical to subpolar regions. These pale-green to deep-red plants can hold 20 times their weight in water. As they die and are compressed, they form organic peat, which is harvested and dried for use as fuel for fires, as seedbed cover,

P

and as shipping packaging for plants and live aquatic animals. Gardeners stir peat into soil to increase soil moisture, porosity, and acidity and to reduce erosion.

pecan NUT and tree (*Carya illinoinensis*) of the WALNUT family, native to temperate N. America. Occasionally reaching a height of about 160 ft (50 m), the tree has deeply furrowed bark and feathery leaves. Pecan nut meat, rich and distinctive in flavor and texture, has one of the highest fat contents of any vegetable product and a caloric value close to that of butter.

peccary \'pe-kə-rē\ *or* **javelin** \'ja-və-lən\ Any of three species (family Tayassuidae) of New World even-toed UNGULATES resembling pigs. Found from Texas to Patagonia, peccaries are gray with white markings. They grow to 30–35 in. (75–90 cm) long and weigh 30–65 lbs (15–30 kg). A scent gland that opens on the back and emits a strong, musky odor inspired the belief that peccaries have two navels. Peccaries have spearlike upper canines and eat plants, small animals, and carrion.

Peck, (Eldred) Gregory (b.1916) U.S. film actor. Born in La Jolla, Cal., he acted on Broadway before making his film debut in *Days of Glory* (1944). Known for playing likeable, honest men of high moral quality, he starred in such movies as *Spellbound* (1945), *The Yearling* (1946), *Gentleman's Agreement* (1947), *Twelve O'Clock High* (1949), *Roman Holiday* (1953), *Moby Dick* (1956), *To Kill a Mockingbird* (1962, Academy Award), *MacArthur* (1977), *The Old Gringo* (1989), and *Cape Fear* (1991).

Peckinpah \'pe-kin-ˌpä\, **(David) Sam(uel)** (1925–1984) U.S. film director. Born in Fresno, Cal., he wrote for and directed such programs as *Gunsmoke* and *The Rifleman* before making his debut as a film director with *The Deadly Companions* (1961). It was followed by *Ride the High Country* (1962), *Major Dundee* (1965), *The Wild Bunch* (1969), considered his finest, *Straw Dogs* (1971), *Pat Garrett and Billy the Kid* (1973), and *Cross of Iron* (1977). His films were noted for their magnificent landscapes, embittered characters, and brutal violence.

Pecos River \'pā-kəs\ River, E New Mexico and W Texas. It rises in the SANGRE DE CRISTO MTNS. of New Mexico and flows southeast about 500 mi (800 km) across the Texas border. After many dams it empties into the RIO GRANDE at the Amistad National Recreation Area.

pectin Any of a class of CARBOHYDRATES found in certain plant cell walls and tissues. In fruits, pectin keeps the walls of adjacent cells joined together, helping them remain firm and hold their shape. As fruits become overripe, the pectin breaks down to simple sugars that dissolve more readily, so the fruits become soft and lose their shape. Pectin is used to make jellies, jams, and marmalades. Its thickening properties also make it useful in the confectionery, pharmaceutical, and textile industries.

pedestal In CLASSICAL ARCHITECTURE, a support or base for a column, statue, vase, or OBELISK. It may be square, octagonal, or circular. A single pedestal may also support a colonnade. The classical pedestal, first employed by Roman architects, consists of three parts (from bottom to top): the plinth, the dado (or die), and the cornice (or cap).

pediatrics \ˌpē-dē-'a-triks\ Medical specialty dealing with the development, health, and diseases of children. In the 18th cent., the first children's hospitals were founded. Early pediatricians studied CHILDHOOD DISEASES (see Thomas SYDENHAM) but could do little to cure them. By the mid-20th cent., when ANTIBIOTICS and VACCINES had controlled most of these diseases in the developed world and infant and child mortality had fallen, pediatrics changed its focus to normal growth and child development.

pedigree Record of ancestry or purity of breed (see BREEDING). Pedigrees of domesticated animals are maintained by governmental or private record associations or breed organizations in many countries. In human genetics, pedigree diagrams are used to trace the inheritance of a specific trait, abnormality, or disease. Standard symbols are used to represent males, females, mating (marriage), offspring, possession of the character under study, and its absence.

pediment In geology, any relatively flat surface of bedrock (exposed or lightly covered with soil or gravel) that usually occurs at the base of a mountain. Pediments are most conspicuous in basin-and-range-type desert areas throughout the world, but they also occur in humid areas. Many tropical river towns are situated on pediments, which offer easier building sites than the steep hillsides above or the river marshes below.

pedology \pi-'dä-lə-jē\ *or* **soil science** Scientific discipline concerned with soils, including their physical and chemical properties, the role of organisms in soil production, description and mapping of soil units, and origin and formation of soils. Pedology embraces such subdisciplines as soil chemistry, soil physics, and soil microbiology. Usually, a soil auger is used to obtain core samples, and the soil units are defined, delineated, and mapped by procedures like those used in the mapping of geologic deposits or landforms.

Pedro I \'pā-drō, 'pā-drü\ *known as* **Dom Pedro** (1798–1834) First emperor of Brazil (1822–31) and, briefly, king of Portugal (1826). The son of John VI of Portugal, he became regent of Brazil in 1821, but in 1822 he broke with Lisbon and declared Brazil a constitutional monarchy with himself as emperor. Opposition to his autocratic style induced him to abdicate in favor of his son PEDRO II. When John VI died, Pedro I became Portugal's King Pedro IV, but abdicated in favor of his daughter, the future Queen Maria II. See also José Bonifacio de ANDRADA E SILVA.

Pedro II *orig.* Dom Pedro de Alcântara (1825–1891) Second and last emperor of Brazil (1831–89). He became emperor at age 5 when his father, PEDRO I, abdicated, and was crowned in 1841. His concern for his subjects, skill at arbitrating disputes, and economic leadership brought stability to the country. He led Brazil into the PARAGUAYAN WAR, which brought Brazil prestige and territory. In 1889 Pedro II was removed in a military coup and a republic was established. See also José Bonifacio de ANDRADA E SILVA.

Peel, Sir Robert (1788–1850) British prime minister (1834–35, 1841–46) and principal founder of the CONSERVATIVE PARTY. Peel served as chief secretary for Ireland 1812–18. As home secretary (1822–27, 1828–30) he reorganized England's criminal code, and established London's first disciplined police force, whose members were nicknamed after him "bobbies." After a brief first term as prime minister, Peel led the new Conservative Party to a strong victory in 1841 and became prime minister again. He imposed an income tax and initiated reforms in Ireland. Favoring free trade and reduced tariffs on imports, he repealed the CORN LAWS, which caused his government to fall. He was the chief architect of the mid-Victorian age of stability and prosperity that he did not live to see.

peerage Body of peers or titled nobility in Britain. The five ranks, in descending order, are DUKE, MARQUESS, earl (see COUNT), VISCOUNT, and BARON. Until 1999, peers were entitled to sit in the House of LORDS. Titles may be hereditary or granted for life.

Pegasus \'pe-gə-səs\ In GREEK MYTHOLOGY, a winged horse. It sprang from the blood of MEDUSA as she was beheaded by PERSEUS. BELLEROPHON captured Pegasus and rode him in several of his exploits, but when he tried to ride Pegasus to heaven he was unseated and killed, and Pegasus was placed in the sky as a constellation.

pegmatite \'peg-mə-ˌtīt\ Almost any wholly crystalline IGNEOUS ROCK that is coarse-grained and includes minerals typically found in ordinary igneous rocks (such as granites). Usually found as irregular dikes, lenses, or veins, pegmatite deposits occur in all parts of the world and are the chief source of commercial FELDSPAR and sheet MICA.

Pei \'pā\, **I(eoh) M(ing)** (b.1917) Chinese-U.S. architect. He emigrated to the U.S. in 1935 and studied at MIT and Harvard Univ. His Na-

I. M. Pei, National Center for Atmospheric Research, completed 1967

tional Center for Atmospheric Research, Boulder, Col., mimics the silhouettes of the surrounding peaks. His innovative East Building of the National Gallery of Art (1978) was hailed as one of his finest achievements. Other works include Boston's John Hancock Tower (1973), New York's Jacob Javits Center (1986), a controversial glass pyramid at the LOUVRE MUSEUM (1989), and the acclaimed Miho Museum of Art, Shiga, Japan (1997). Pei received the 1983 Pritzker Architecture Prize.

Peipus \'pī-pəs\, **Lake** *Estonian* **Peipsi Järv** \'pāp-sē-'yarv\ Lake, N central Europe, forming the boundary between Estonia and Russia. It is 60 mi (97 km) long and 31 mi (50 km) wide, and it is frozen for half the year. In 1242 the Russians under ALEXANDER NEVSKY defeated the Teutonic knights (see TEUTONIC ORDER) on the frozen lake in the "Battle on the Ice."

Peirce \'pərs, 'pirs\, **Charles Sanders** (1839–1914) U.S. scientist, logician, and philosopher. Born in Cambridge, Mass., son of the mathematician and astronomer Benjamin Peirce (1809–1880), he spent 30 years as a scientist with the U.S. Coast Guard Survey (1861–91). As a scientist, he is noted for his contributions to the theory of probability, his studies of gravity, and the logic of scientific methodology. He eventually abandoned science for logic and SEMIOTICS. He lectured at Johns Hopkins Univ. 1879–94, then spent the rest of his life writing in seclusion. He is regarded as the founder of PRAGMATISM. Though he made eminent contributions to deductive logic, he was a student primarily of "the logic of science"—of INDUCTION and of "retroduction," or "abduction," the forming and accepting on probation of a hypothesis to explain surprising facts.

Peisistratus \pi-'sis-trə-təs\ (early 6th cent.–527 B.C.) Tyrant of Athens (c.560–559, 556–555, 546–527 B.C.). He first became tyrant in 560 after seizing the Acropolis with the help of a bodyguard. His reign was short-lived, but he gained power again briefly in 556. After several years in exile, he again seized control (546), and remained in power until his death. A patron of the arts, he executed many public works and tried to help small farmers. His unification of Attica and improvement of Athens's prosperity helped make the city preeminent in Greece.

Peking See BEIJING

Pekingese \,pē-kə-'nēz\ Breed of long-haired TOY DOG developed in ancient China, where it was held sacred and was kept in Peking's Imperial Palace. Known as the "lion dog" for its full mane but perhaps also for its courage, it stands 6–9 in. (15–23 cm) and weighs up to 14 lbs (6.5 kg). It has hanging ears, a short, wrinkled muzzle, and a black mask across the face. Chinese royalty carried very small Pekingese, called "sleeve dogs," in their sleeves.

Peking man See ZHOUKOUDIAN

Pelé \'pā-,lā\ *orig.* Edson Arantes do Nascimento (b.1940) Brazilian soccer player, in his time perhaps the most famous athlete in the world. He joined the Santos Football Club in 1956 and helped lead that team to a world club championship in 1962. He led the Brazilian national team to three World Cup victories (1958, 1962, 1970). In 1969 he scored his 1,000th goal. Of average stature, he combined kicking power and accuracy with a remarkable ability to anticipate other players' moves. He is widely regarded as the greatest soccer player of all time.

Pelée \pə-'lā\, **Mt.** Active volcanic mountain, N MARTINIQUE, W. Indies. A gently sloping cone, 4,583 ft (1,397 m) high, it supports luxuriant forests. A violent eruption in 1902 killed about 30,000 people. A minor eruption occurred in 1929.

Pelew See PALAU

Pelham, Henry (1696–1754) British prime minister (1743–54). A supporter of Robert WALPOLE, he became secretary for war in 1724. He succeeded Walpole as prime minister and chancellor of the exchequer in 1743 and led a stable Whig ministry. He resisted attempts to prolong the War of the AUSTRIAN SUCCESSION and signed the Treaty of Aix-la-Chapelle (1748). After the war, he introduced financial reforms, including a reduced land tax and a consolidation of the national debt.

pelican Any of about eight species constituting the genus *Pelecanus* (family Pelecanidae), white or brown birds distinguished by a large, elastic throat pouch. Some species are 70 in. (180 cm) long, have a wingspan of 10 ft (3 m), and weigh up to 30 lbs (13 kg). Pelicans inhabit freshwaters and seacoasts. Most species drive fish into shallow water and, using the pouch as a dip net, scoop them up and immediately swallow them. Chicks thrust their bills down the parent's gullet to obtain regurgitated food.

Pella Ancient capital, MACEDONIA. Located in N Greece northwest of THESSALONIKI, it flourished at the end of the 5th cent. B.C. and developed rapidly under PHILIP II, but declined after the Romans defeated the last Macedonian king. Archaeological excavations begun in 1957 revealed large, well-built houses and rooms with mosaic floors. It was the birthplace of ALEXANDER THE GREAT.

pellagra \pə-'la-grə\ Nutritional disorder caused largely by a deficiency of NIACIN, marked by skin lesions and digestive and neurological disturbances. DERMATITIS usually appears first, resembling severe sunburn, later becoming reddish brown, rough, and scaly. Diarrhea usually alternates with constipation. Later, mental abnormalities may include nervousness, depression, and delirium. Mild cases respond to a well-balanced diet. Pellagra still occurs where diets consist mostly of corn, which is low in both niacin and TRYPTOPHAN (converted to niacin in the body), with little or no protein-rich food. It can also be a side effect of chronic alcoholism.

Peloponnese \'pe-lə-pə-,nēz\ Peninsula, forming S part of mainland Greece. A large, mountainous body of land jutting south into the Mediterranean Sea, it has an area of 8,278 sq mi (21,439 sq km) and is joined to the rest of mainland Greece by the Isthmus of Corinth. The Mycenaean civilization flourished there at MYCENAE and Pylos. Its chief cities during the classical period were CORINTH and SPARTA. Under the Romans it was part of the province of Achaea from 146 B.C. to about the 4th cent. A.D. The modern city of Patras (pop., 1991: 155,000), in the N part, is a commercial center.

Peloponnesian League *or* **Spartan Alliance** Military coalition of Greek city-states led by SPARTA, formed in the 6th cent. B.C. The league was a major force in Greek affairs, forming the core of resistance to the Persian invasions in 490 and 480 and fighting Athens in the PELOPONNESIAN WAR. Its power declined after its defeat at Leuctra in 371, and the league disbanded in 366/365.

Peloponnesian War (431–404 B.C.) War fought between ATHENS and SPARTA, the leading city-states of ancient Greece, along with their allies, which included nearly every other Greek city-state. Its principal cause was a fear of Athenian imperialism. The Athenian alliance relied on its strong navy, the Spartan alliance on its strong army. Fighting broke out in 431, with PERICLES commanding the Athenians. In the first 10 years, Archidamus led the Spartans to defeats. Plague struck Athens in 429, killing Pericles and much of the army. In 421 both states agreed to accept the Peace of Nicias. This lasted six years, until Athens launched its disastrous Sicilian expedition. The war continued until 405, when the Athenian navy was destroyed at the Battle of AEGOSPOTAMI with Persian help. Under blockade, Athens surrendered in 404. Its empire was dismantled, and the Spartans installed the THIRTY TYRANTS.

pelota \pə-'lō-tə\ (Spanish: "little ball") Any of several games in which players take turns, using a glove or implement, hitting a rubber ball either directly at one another or off a wall. The latter version is related to HANDBALL and JAI ALAI, which are played by two or four players on one-, two-, or three-walled courts using gloves, rackets, or bats.

Pelusium \pə-'lü-shē-əm\ Ancient Egyptian city. Located on the easternmost mouth (long silted up) of the NILE RIVER, southeast of modern PORT SAID, it was the main frontier fortress against Palestine in the 6th cent. B.C. In 522 B.C. the Persians, under Cambyses II, defeated the pharaoh Psamtik III there. In Roman times it was a station on the route to the RED SEA.

pelvic girdle *or* **bony pelvis** Basin-shaped complex of BONES that connects the trunk and legs, supports and balances the trunk, and contains and supports internal organs. Each side consists of three bones—the ilium above and to the side, the ischium behind and below, and the pubis in

P

front—which join in front at the pubic symphysis and behind at the sacrum (see VERTEBRAL COLUMN). Women's wider, rounder pelvic girdle allows the birth canal to accommodate the fetal head.

pelvic inflammatory disease (PID) Acute INFLAMMATION of the pelvic cavity in women, caused by bacterial infection (usually GONORRHEA or CHLAMYDIA) of REPRODUCTIVE-SYSTEM structures. Usually a SEXUALLY TRANSMITTED DISEASE, it occurs mainly in sexually active women under 25. PID can resemble gonorrhea, with pain, chills, nausea, fever, and thick, smelly vaginal discharge. Treatment requires antibiotics, bed rest, and sexual abstinence until the infection disappears. Sexual partners must also be treated to prevent reinfection.

Pemex *officially* Petróleos Mexicanos. Mexico's state-owned oil company. In 1938 Pres. Lázaro CÁRDENAS nationalized 17 foreign oil companies to create Pemex, the largest Latin American petroleum company. In the 1970s promising oil discoveries gave rise to a national spending spree, led by the flamboyant Pres. José LÓPEZ PORTILLO and financed by massive borrowing. When the price of oil dropped in 1981, 87% of Pemex's assets were owed to foreign banks; by 1982 the country was virtually bankrupt. By the end of the 1990s Pemex had been reorganized and partially privatized.

penal colony Distant or overseas settlement established to punish criminals with forced labor and isolation from society. Such colonies were developed mostly by the English, French, and Russians. Britain sent criminals to its American colonies until the Revolutionary War; Australia was principally a penal colony from its colonization until the mid-19th cent. FRENCH GUIANA, site of a French penal colony, was infamous for its inhumanity. Russian penal colonies were established in Siberia under the czars but were most widely used during the Stalin era (see GULAG).

Penang \pə-ˈnaŋ\ Island (pop., 1991: 1,100,000), Malaysia, off the NW coast of the MALAY PENINSULA, part of the state of Penang. The capital and chief port is George Town (pop., 1991: 220,000). British colonization began in 1786. From the mid-19th cent. it was a market for tin and rubber. In 1948 it became part of the Federation of Malaya, later Malaysia. In the late 20th cent. it became Malaysia's prime tourist center, with resort hotels mainly on the N coast at Batu Feringgi.

Penates \pə-ˈnā-tēz, pə-ˈnä-tēz\ Roman household gods. They were worshiped privately as protectors of the household and also publicly as protectors of the Roman state. Their name was often used interchangeably with that of the LARES. Each house had a shrine with their images, which were worshiped at the family meal and on special occasions. Offerings were portions of the regular meal or of special cakes, wine, honey, and incense. The number and precise identities of the Penates were a puzzle even to the ancients.

Penderecki \ˌpen-də-ˈret-skē\, **Krzysztof** (b.1933) Polish composer and conductor. His early music (1960–74) involved blocks of sound and ritual, and he developed graphic notation to convey the desired effects, producing vivid works that attracted international attention, including *Threnody for the Victims of Hiroshima* (1960), *Stabat mater* (1962), the *St. Luke Passion* (1965), and the opera *The Devils of Loudun* (1969). After 1975 his music became more traditional, in such works as the opera *Paradise Lost* (1978) and *Lux aeterna* (1983).

Pendergast, Thomas J(oseph) (1872–1945) U.S. politician. Born in St. Joseph, Mo., he was active in municipal politics in Kansas City, Mo., and became the political boss of the city's Democrats by 1916. His political machine dominated city and state politics for almost 25 years, and he helped Harry TRUMAN in his early political career. Attacked for allowing corruption to flourish, he was convicted of income-tax evasion in 1939 and served one year in prison.

Pendleton Civil Service Act (1883) U.S. legislation establishing the modern civil-service system of permanent federal employment based on merit. Public demand for civil-service reform to replace the system based on political party affiliation (the SPOILS SYSTEM) resulted in the bill sponsored by Sen. George Pendleton, which provided for selection of government employees by competitive examination. Only 10% of government jobs were initially covered

by the law, but today over 90% of federal employees are covered.

pendulum Body suspended from a fixed point so that it can swing under the influence of gravity. A simple pendulum consists of a bob (weight) at the end of a string. Its periodic motion is constant, but can be made longer or shorter by changing the length of the string. A change in the mass of the bob alone does not affect the period. Because of their constancy, pendulums were long used to regulate the movement of clocks. See also FOUCAULT PENDULUM.

penguin Any of 18 species (order Sphenisciformes) of flightless seabirds that breed mainly on islands in subantarctic waters and on cool coasts of Africa, Australia, New Zealand, and S. America. A few inhabit temperate and tropical regions. All have a dark back and a white belly. The smallest species, the little blue penguin *(Eudyptula minor)*, is about 16 in. (40 cm) tall; the largest, the emperor penguin *(Aptenodytes forsteri)*, is almost 4 ft (120 cm) tall. At sea for weeks at a time, flocks feed on fish, squid, and crustaceans.

penicillin ANTIBIOTIC derived from the *Penicillium* mold. It was discovered in 1928 by Alexander FLEMING; by 1940, H. W. FLOREY, E. B. CHAIN, and others had produced commercial quantities that proved vital to the treatment of war casualties, making penicillin the first successful antibiotic for human bacterial infections. Many natural and semisynthetic (ampicillin, amoxicillin) variants have since been produced. Among the bacteria susceptible to penicillin are those causing strep throat, spinal MENINGITIS, gas GANGRENE, SYPHILIS, and GONORRHEA. Overuse has led to DRUG RESISTANCE in some strains. Penicillin's chief side effect is ALLERGY, which can be life-threatening.

Peninsular War (1808–14) Part of the NAPOLEONIC WARS, fought on the Iberian Peninsula. After French forces occupied Portugal (1807) and NAPOLEON installed his brother Joseph BONAPARTE as king of Spain (1808), a rebellion began in Madrid and soon erupted in other cities. By 1810 the French had overcome the rebels. Meanwhile, the British under the future duke of WELLINGTON landed in Portugal (1808). After Napoleon withdrew French forces to bolster his invasion of Russia (1812), Wellington began his gradual advance into Spain. The British victory at Vitoria (1813) and their march into SW France forced the French to withdraw from Spain and to reinstall FERDINAND VII as king (1814).

penis Male sex and execretory organ. Three long columns of tissue extend through its length; one expands at the tip into a mushroom-shaped structure (glans penis) and contains the urethra (see URINARY SYSTEM), which ends in a slitlike opening. In sexual arousal, blood fills spaces in the tissue, and blood vessels constrict to hold it there, enlarging and hardening the penis in an erection. The foreskin, a fold of skin covering the glans, is often removed (see CIRCUMCISION). See also IMPOTENCE, REPRODUCTIVE SYSTEM.

Penn, Irving (b.1917) U.S. photographer. Born in Plainfield, N.J., he aspired to be a painter but took a job designing photographic covers for *Vogue* and soon was established as a fashion photographer. After World War II he became much admired as a portraitist of celebrities. His austere images conveyed elegance and sophistication through clarity of line and composition rather than from props or backdrops.

Penn, William (1644–1718) English Quaker leader and founder of Pennsylvania. Expelled from Oxford for his Puritan beliefs, he was sent to manage the family estates in Ireland, where he joined the Society of FRIENDS in 1667. He was imprisoned four times for publishing and speaking in support of Quaker doctrines. In *The Great Case of Liberty of Conscience* (1670) Penn advocated religious toleration and envisioned a colony based on religious and political freedom. On his father's death, he inherited his estates and influence with CHARLES II, who granted him a vast province on the Delaware River. Arriving in Pennsylvania in 1682, he drafted a Frame of Government that established freedom of worship, laid out the city of Philadelphia, and established peaceful relations with the Indians. In 1684 he returned to England to defend his interests against claims by neighboring Maryland. With the accession of his friend JAMES II, he effected the release of imprisoned Quakers and the Declaration of Indulgence (1687), which permitted religious toleration. Back in Pennsylvania (1699–1701), he wrote the Charter of Privileges, which allowed the assembly greater autonomy.

Pennines \\'pe-ˌnīnz\ *or* **Pennine Chain** Mountain range, N England, extending south from the Scottish border to Derbyshire. The highest peak is Cross Fell, at 2,930 ft (893 m) high. Water action has developed underground caverns in the range's limestone, which is extensively quarried. Sheep farming is also important.

Pennsylvania *officially* Commonwealth of Pennsylvania State (pop., 2000: 12,281,000), U.S., middle Atlantic region. It covers 45,333 sq mi (117,412 sq km); its capital is HARRISBURG. The Delaware River forms part of its E boundary. The MONONGAHELA RIVER unites with the ALLEGHENY RIVER at PITTSBURGH to form the OHIO RIVER. The area was inhabited by Indian peoples, including the SHAWNEE and DELAWARE, when Europeans arrived in the 17th cent. In 1664 the English seized control of the region, and in 1681 the English king granted a charter to William PENN, who established a Quaker colony based on religious tolerance in 1682. Much of the fighting of the FRENCH AND INDIAN WAR took place there. The first and second CONTINENTAL CONGRESSES met in PHILADELPHIA, and the DECLARATION OF INDEPENDENCE was signed there in 1776. One of the original states of the Union, it was the second state to ratify the U.S. Constitution in 1787. During the AMERICAN CIVIL WAR it was a center of military activity (see Battle of GETTYSBURG). The postwar period brought great economic, industrial, and population growth, consolidating the state's position as a major commercial power. It is one of the most prosperous states, with an economy based on farming, mining, manufacturing, and high technology. The state continues to produce much of the nation's specialty steel and an abundance of coal. Philadelphia and Pittsburgh are major ports with fine educational, cultural, and musical institutions.

Pennsylvania, University of Private university in Philadelphia, a member of the IVY LEAGUE. Founded in 1740 as a charity school, it became an academy in 1753, with Benjamin FRANKLIN as president of the first board of trustees. With the founding of the first medical school in N. America (1765), it became a university. Today, it includes schools of business (the Wharton School), communication (the Annenberg School), education, engineering, fine arts, law, nursing, dentistry, veterinary medicine, and social work. Total enrollment is about 21,000.

Pennsylvania Railroad Co. Former major U.S. railroad. It was chartered in 1846 for service between Harrisburg and Pittsburgh. In 1856 the company extended its service to Chicago. After the Civil War it expanded to St. Louis and Cincinnati in the west and Norfolk, Va., in the south, with 10,000 mi (16,000 km) of track at its greatest extent. It began to lose money in the mid-20th cent., and in 1968 it merged with its competitor, the New York Central, to form the Penn Central Transportation Co. Penn Central declared bankruptcy in 1970; its passenger service was absorbed by AMTRAK in 1971 and its assets by CONRAIL in 1976.

Pennsylvania State University Public state system of higher education with a main campus in University Park and numerous other campuses and locations. The university originated with the charter of the Farmers' High School in 1855 and was designated the commonwealth's land-grant college in 1862. It took its current name in 1953. Research facilities include the Biotechnology Institute, the Center for Applied Behavioral Science, and the Center for Particle Science and Engineering. Total enrollment is almost 80,000.

Penobscot River \pə-'näb-skət\ River, central Maine, flowing south into Penobscot Bay. The state's longest river, about 350 mi (560 km) long, it is navigable for 60 mi (97 km) to Bangor. Once an important source of salmon, it has become important to the lumber, pulp, and paper industries for hydropower. It was named for the Penobscot Indians.

pension Series of periodic money payments made to a person who retires from employment because of age, disability, or the completion of an agreed span of service. The payments generally continue for the rest of the recipient's life, and they are sometimes extended to a widow or other survivor. Military pensions have existed for many centuries;

private pension plans originated in Europe in the 19th cent. There are two basic types of pension plans: defined contribution and defined benefit. A defined contribution plan invests a defined amount each pay period. The benefit, the amount of the pension, depends on the success of those investments. A defined benefit plan pays a known amount according to some formula, but the amount invested in the fund may vary. Pensions may be funded by making payments into a pension TRUST FUND or by the purchase of ANNUITIES from insurance companies.

Pentagon Huge five-sided building (1941–43) in Arlington, Va., headquarters of the U.S. Department of Defense. Designed by George Edwin Bergstrom, it is the world's largest office building, covering 34 acres (14 hectares) and housing 23,000 workers. Built of structural steel and reinforced concrete with some limestone facing, the five-story structure actually consists of five concentric pentagons, with 10 spokelike corridors connecting the whole. On September 11, 2001, it was struck by an airplane hijacked by AL-QAEDA terrorists, and 189 people died.

Pentagon Papers Secret documents detailing the U.S. role in Indochina from World War II to 1968. The U.S. Defense Department commissioned the study; a project associate, Daniel Ellsberg (b.1931), opposed to U.S. participation in the VIETNAM WAR, leaked details of the documents to the press. In June 1971 the *New York Times* began publishing articles based on the study. The U.S. Justice Department, citing national security, obtained a court order halting publication. The U.S. Supreme Court ruled that the government had failed to justify restraint of publication, and the documents were published widely, fueling dissent over Vietnam policy.

Pentateuch See TORAH

pentathlon Athletic contest entailing five distinct types of competition. In the ancient Olympic Games, the pentathlon included a sprint, LONG JUMP, DISCUS THROW, JAVELIN THROW, and a WRESTLING match. The modern, or military, pentathlon, included in the Olympics from 1912 and made a team event in 1952, includes an equestrian STEEPLECHASE, FENCING, pistol shooting, a freestyle swim, and a cross-country run. Women's pentathlon competition (SHOT PUT, HIGH JUMP, HURDLING race, sprint, and long jump) was replaced in 1981 by the HEPTATHLON.

Pentecost (Greek, *pentecoste:* "fiftieth day") Christian festival commemorating the descent of the HOLY SPIRIT on the disciples of Jesus, after his death, resurrection, and ascension. The disciples began to speak in the many languages of the people assembled there, a sign that they should spread the Christian message throughout the world. Jewish Pentecost was a thanksgiving feast for the first fruits of the wheat harvest. Christian Pentecost is celebrated on the Sunday concluding the 50-day period following Easter.

Pentecostalism Protestant religious movement that originated in the U.S. in the 19th cent. It is characterized by a belief that all Christians should seek a postconversion religious experience called BAPTISM with the HOLY SPIRIT. The experience corresponds to the descent of the Holy Spirit on the twelve APOSTLES (PENTECOST) and is evidenced by speaking in tongues, prophesying, and healing. Pentecostalism grew out of the 19th-cent. HOLINESS MOVEMENT and shares its emphasis on biblical literalism, conversion, and moral rigor. Today there are many Pentecostalist denominations (including the ASSEMBLIES OF GOD) in the U.S. and around the world, especially in the Caribbean, Latin America, and Africa.

Pentium Family of MICROPROCESSORS developed by INTEL CORP. Introduced in 1993, the Pentium contained two processors on a single chip and about 3.3 million TRANSISTORS. Its main features were a 32-bit address BUS, a 64-bit data bus, built-in floating-point units, and two 8KB caches. With processor speeds ranging from 60 to 200 megahertz (MHz), it quickly became the processor of choice for personal computers. It was superseded by the Pentium Pro (1995), then the Pentium II (1997) and the Pentium III (1999). The Pentium 4 (2000) offers clock rates up to 2.20 gigahertz (GHz).

Penutian languages \pə-'nü-tē-ən\ Hypothetical superfamily of N. American Indian languages that unites languages

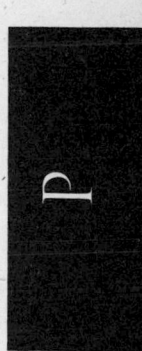

and language families mainly of the far W U.S. and Canada. The Penutian hypothesis, like the Hokan hypothesis (see HOKAN LANGUAGES), attempted to reduce the number of unrelated language families in one of the world's most linguistically diverse areas. At its core was a group of languages spoken along California's central coast and in the CENTRAL VALLEY, to which were added Oregon Penutian (languages once spoken in E Oregon), Chinookan (spoken along the lower Columbia River), Plateau Penutian (languages of PLATEAU INDIAN peoples), Tsimshian (spoken in W British Columbia), and Mexican Penutian (spoken in S Mexico). Aside from the Mexican group, all the languages are nearly or completely extinct.

Penzias \'pent-sē-əs\, **Arno (Allan)** (b.1933) U.S. (German-born) astrophysicist. His family fled Nazi Germany. He worked with Robert WILSON at Bell Laboratories monitoring radio emissions from a ring of gas around the Milky Way galaxy. The two detected an unexpected uniform background static that suggested a thermal energy throughout the universe, which most scientists now agree is COSMIC BACKGROUND RADIATION. They shared a 1978 Nobel Prize with Pyotr Kapitsa (1894–1984) for their work. In 1981 Penzias became vice president of Bell Labs.

peonage \'pē-ə-nij\ Form of involuntary servitude dating from the Spanish conquest of Mexico, when the conquerors forced the poor, especially Indians, to work for Spanish planters and mine operators. In the U.S., "peon" meant a worker compelled to pay a creditor in labor. Though prohibited by U.S. federal law, peonage persisted in some S states. Another form of peonage exists when prisoners are farmed out to labor camps.

peony \'pē-ə-nē\ Any of about 33 species of flowering plants in the widely distributed genus *Paeonia,* sole genus of the family Paenoiaceae. Herbaceous peonies are perennials that grow to about 3 ft (1 m). Their annual stems bear large, glossy, much-divided leaves and produce large single and double flowers of white, pink, rose, and deep crimson. Tree peonies are shrubs about 4–6 ft (1.2–1.8 m) high with permanent rootstocks and woody stems.

People's Liberation Army Unified organization of China's land, sea, and air forces. Its 3 million troops make it one of the largest forces in the world. Initially called the Red Army, it grew under ZHU DE from 5,000 troops in 1929 to 200,000 in 1933. It survived the LONG MARCH in retreat from the Nationalists (see GUOMINDANG), then fought with the Nationalists against the Japanese in N China. After World War II, the Communist forces, renamed the People's Liberation Army, defeated the Nationalists, making possible the formation of the People's Republic of China in 1949.

Peoria City (pop, 2000: 113,000), NW central Illinois, on the Illinois River. A French fort was established on the site in 1680 by R.-R. LA SALLE. Later settlements were by the French, Indians, and other colonists. A major port, trade, and shipping center for a large agricultural area, it is highly industrialized.

Pepin, Donation of See DONATION OF PEPIN

Pepin III \'pe-pən\ *known as* **Pepin the Short** (714?–768) King of the Franks (751–68), the first king of the CAROLINGIAN DYNASTY and the father of CHARLEMAGNE. A son of CHARLES MARTEL, he became de facto ruler of the Franks when his brother entered a monastery in 747. With the backing of the pope, he deposed the last MEROVINGIAN ruler, Childeric III, in 751 and was crowned king. Pepin helped Pope Stephen II combat the Lombards (754, 756) in Italy and also put down revolts in Saxony and Bavaria. See also DONATION OF PEPIN.

pepper *or* **garden pepper** Any of many plants in the genus *Capsicum* of the NIGHTSHADE FAMILY, notably *C. annuum,* *C. frutescens,* and *C. boccatum,* native to Central and S. America and cultivated extensively elsewhere. Red, green, and yellow mild bell or sweet peppers, rich in vitamins A and C, are used in seasoning and as a vegetable. The pungency of hot peppers, including tabasco, chili, and cayenne peppers, comes from the compound capsaicin in the internal partitions of the fruit. The spice BLACK PEPPER comes from an unrelated plant.

pepper, black See BLACK PEPPER

peppermint Strongly aromatic perennial herb (*Mentha piperita,* MINT family), source of a widely used flavoring. Native to Europe and Asia, it has been naturalized in N. America. The oblong clusters of pinkish-lavender flowers are dried for use as a flavoring agent. Oil of peppermint is widely used to flavor confectionery, chewing gum, toothpastes, and medicines. The oil also contains menthol, long used medicinally as a soothing balm.

PepsiCo, Inc. U.S. conglomerate. The SOFT DRINK Pepsi-Cola was created by a pharmacist, Caleb D. Bradham (1867–1934), who gave his tonic its name (from Greek *pepsis,* "digestion") in 1898 and incorporated the Pepsi-Cola Co. in 1902. Its trademark and assets were bought in 1931 by Charles G. Guth (1876–1948), who improved the formula and marketed a 12-ounce bottle for five cents with huge success. In 1940 Pepsi-Cola broadcast the first nationwide radio jingle, "Nickel, Nickel." In 1965 it merged with Frito-Lay, Inc., becoming PepsiCo, Inc. In the 1970s and '80s it bought chains such as Pizza Hut, Taco Bell, and Kentucky Fried Chicken, but in 1997 it spun off its restaurant business.

pepsin Powerful ENZYME in gastric juice (see STOMACH) that partially digests PROTEINS in food. Pepsin is active only in the acid environment of the stomach (PH 1.5–2.5 or less); it is ineffective in the intestine (pH 7). It is used commercially in some cheesemaking, in the leather industry to remove hair and residual tissue from hides, and in the recovery of silver from discarded photographic films by digesting the gelatin layer that holds the silver.

peptic ulcer Sore that develops in the mucous membrane of the STOMACH (more frequent in women) or DUODENUM (accounting for 80% of ulcers, and more frequent in men) when its ability to resist acid in gastric juice is reduced. It causes burning ache and hungerlike pain. Ulcers can bleed, perforate the abdominal wall, or block the gastrointestinal tract. Stress and diet were blamed until *Helicobacter pylori* bacteria and long-term use of ASPIRIN and similar drugs were shown to be the two major causes. The former is treated with combination drug therapy, the latter by stopping the causative drugs if possible or with drugs that reduce acid production.

peptide Organic compound composed of a series of AMINO ACIDS linked by peptide bonds (see COVALENT BOND) between the carbon of one and the nitrogen of the next. Peptide chains longer than a few dozen amino acids are PROTEINS. Biosynthesis of peptides from amino acids takes place on RIBOSOMES and is catalyzed and controlled by ENZYMES. Many HORMONES, ANTIBIOTICS, and other compounds that participate in life processes are peptides.

Pepys \'pēps\, **Samuel** (1633–1703) English diarist and public official. In 1660 he began the diary for which he is chiefly known while working as a clerk. He steadily improved his position, in time becoming president of the Royal Society, trusted confidant of CHARLES II and JAMES II, and friend of the great scholars of his age. His diary (published 1825), which he kept through 1669, presents a fascinating picture of life in Restoration London, with vivid, honest accounts of ordinary as well as great events, including the Plague and the GREAT FIRE OF LONDON.

Pequot \'pē-ˌkwät\ N American Indian peoples who lived in the Thames valley in what is now E Connecticut. Their subsistence was based on corn cultivation, hunting, and fishing. For a brief period they lived amicably with the American colonists, but relations became strained as land pressures grew. In 1636 war broke out, resulting in large losses. Further destruction was caused by a revolt of the MOHEGAN, who had earlier been ruled by a Pequot chief. In 1655 the few remaining Pequot were resettled on the Mystic River. Today they number about 500.

perception Process of registering sensory stimuli as meaningful experience. The dividing line between sensation and perception has varied according to how the terms are defined. A common distinction is that sensations are simple sensory experiences, while percepts are complex constructions of simple elements joined through association. Another is that perception is more subject to the influence of learning. Vision has received the most attention. Structuralists such as E. B. Titchener (1867–1927) focused on the constituent elements of visual perceptions, whereas GESTALT PSYCHOLOGY has stressed examining organized wholes. Visual objects tend to appear stable despite continually changing stimulus features (such as ambient light and perspective). Perceptions may be influenced by expectancies, needs, unconscious ideas, values, and conflicts.

Perceval Hero of ARTHURIAN LEGEND. His childlike innocence protected him from worldly temptation. In CHRÉTIEN DE TROYES's *Le conte du graal,* Perceval visits the castle of the wounded Fisher King and sees the GRAIL, but fails to ask about it and therefore fails to heal the Fisher King. He later sets out in search of the grail and grows spiritually. His story was told in WOLFRAM VON ESCHENBACH's *Parzifal,* which provided the basis for Richard WAGNER's opera *Parsifal* (1882).

perch Either of two species (family Percidae, order Perciformes) of popular food and sport fishes: the Eurasian common perch (*Perca fluviatilis*) or the N. American yellow perch (*P. flavescens*). Some consider the two a single species. Perches are carnivores of quiet ponds, lakes, streams, and rivers. The common perch is greenish, with dark vertical bars on the sides. It grows to 6 lbs (3 kg). The yellow perch, similar but yellower, grows to about 15 in. (40 cm) and weighs up to 2 lbs (1 kg); it is a popular game fish. See also SEA BASS.

percussion instruments Musical instruments that are struck (or sometimes shaken or scraped) to produce sound. They include instruments whose own hard substance is made to vibrate and instruments that include a tight membrane that vibrates. They may produce tones of definite or indefinite pitch. Their primary function is often rhythmic, but many are used as melody instruments. They include the BELL, CARILLON, CYMBAL, DRUM, DULCIMER, GAMELAN, GLOCKENSPIEL, MARIMBA, PIANO, STEEL DRUM, TAMBOURINE, TIMPANI, VIBRAPHONE, and XYLOPHONE.

Percy, Walker (1916–1990) U.S. novelist. Born in Birmingham, Ala., he obtained a medical degree. While recovering from tuberculosis, he decided on a writing career and converted to Roman Catholicism. His first and best-known novel, *The Moviegoer* (1961, National Book Award), introduced his concept of malaise, a sense of spiritual emptiness characteristic of the rootless modern world. His other works, often about the search for faith and love in a New South transformed by industry and technology, include *Love in the Ruins* (1971).

peregrine falcon \'per-ə-grən\ *or* **duck hawk** FALCON species (*Falco peregrinus*) found worldwide but rare today because of bioaccumulation of pesticides. Peregrines are 13–19 in. (33–48 cm) long and gray above, with black-barred whitish underparts. They fly high and dive at tremendous speed (up to 175 mph, or 280 kph—the greatest speeds attained by any bird), striking with clenched talons and killing by impact. They usually nest on a high cliff ledge near water, where bird prey is plentiful. Breeding programs have reintroduced the species into the wild and introduced it into urban areas, but it remains vulnerable.

Perelman \'per-əl-mən\, **S(idney) J(oseph)** (1904–1979) U.S. humorist. Born in Brooklyn, N.Y., Perelman wrote screenplays for such early Marx Brothers films as *Monkey Business* (1931) and *Horse Feathers* (1932). A master of wordplay, he regularly contributed essays to the *New Yorker*; many were collected in such books as *Westward Ha!* (1948) and *The Road to Miltown* (1957). His later screenplays include *Around the World in 80 Days* (1956, Academy Award).

perennial Any plant that persists for several years, usually with new herbaceous growth from a part that survives from season to season. Trees and shrubs are perennial, as are some herbaceous flowers and vegetative ground covers. Perennials have only a limited flowering period, but with maintenance throughout the growing season, they provide a leafy presence and shape to the garden landscape. See also ANNUAL, BIENNIAL.

Peres, Shimon \'per-es\ *orig.* Shimon Perski (b.1923) Israeli (Polish-born) statesman. He emigrated to Palestine with his family in 1934 and joined the HAGANA in 1947. After Israel achieved independence, he held a number of defense positions (1948–65). In 1967 he helped establish the Israel Labour Party. In 1984 he joined a power-sharing arrange-

ment with Yitzhak SHAMIR, the two men alternating as prime minister. Peres's tenure (1984–86) saw Israel's withdrawal from the LEBANESE CIVIL WAR. He was foreign minister under Yitzhak RABIN (1992–95), with whom, along with Yasir ARAFAT, he shared the Nobel Peace Prize in 1994. He became prime minister on Rabin's assassination, and was narrowly defeated by Benjamin Netanyahu (b.1949) in 1996.

perestroika \ˌper-ə-'strȯi-kə\ (Russian: "restructuring") Program instituted in the Soviet Union by Mikhail GORBACHEV in the mid-1980s to restructure political and economic policy. He proposed reducing the Communist Party's leadership in the country's governance and increasing local authority. Seeking to bring the Soviet Union up to economic par with capitalist countries, he encouraged enterprises to become self-financing. The economic bureaucracy, fearing loss of its power and privileges, obstructed much of his program.

Pérez de Cuéllar \'per-es-ˌthā-'kwä-yär\, **Javier** (b.1920) Fifth secretary-general of the UNITED NATIONS (1982–91). Born in Peru, he joined the foreign ministry (1940) and the foreign service (1944), serving in France, Britain, Bolivia, and Brazil. After serving as Peru's first ambassador to the Soviet Union (1969–71), he was appointed ambassador to the U.N. As secretary-general he advocated the use of the UNITED NATIONS SECURITY COUNCIL for keeping the peace. In his second term, he negotiated the cease-fire that ended the IRAN–IRAQ WAR (1988).

Pérez Galdós \'pä-ˌrä͟th-gäl-'dōs\, **Benito** (1843–1920) Spanish novelist. In the 1870s he began a cycle of 46 short historical novels, *Episodios nacionales* (1873–1912). Some of his finest works chronicle contemporary Spain, including *The Disinherited Lady* (1881) and his masterpiece, *Fortunata y Jacinta* (1886–87), a study of two unhappily married women. His earlier works show a reforming zeal and anticlericalism, but after the 1880s he displayed greater sympathy for Spain and its idiosyncrasies, as in *Nazarín* (1895). He was regarded as Spain's greatest novelist since Miguel de CERVANTES.

perfect gas See IDEAL GAS

performance art Nontraditional art form that arose in Europe and the U.S. in the 1960s. Early examples, often called "happenings," created a type of art experience that could not be captured or purchased. Performance art typically employs live performers with props, and may draw on poetry, music, dance, and painting. It may be staged in unconventional venues such as coffeehouses or bars or on the street. Prominent performance artists have included John CAGE, Yoko Ono, N. J. PAIK, and Laurie Anderson.

perfume Fluid preparation used for scenting, composed of natural essences or synthetics and a fixative. Perfumes are concocted by the artful blending of certain fragrant substances in appropriate proportions. The art of perfumery was apparently known to the ancient Chinese, Hindus, and Egyptians; references to perfumes are found in the Bible. Ingredients include natural products, of plant or animal origin, and synthetic materials. Fine perfumes may be blends of more than 100 ingredients.

Pergamum \'pər-gə-məm\ *or* **Pergamus** \'pər-gə-məs\ Ancient Greek city, W ASIA MINOR, near the modern town of Bergama, Turkey. It existed from at least the 5th cent. B.C. but became important in the HELLENISTIC period, when it was the residence of the Attalid dynasty, and reached its height 263–133 B.C. It is an outstanding example of city planning in antiquity, and its library was excelled only by that in ALEXANDRIA, Egypt. Excavations begun in 1878 by the Berlin Museum unearthed many artistic treasures.

pergola \'pər-gə-lə\ Garden walk or terrace typically formed by two rows of columns or posts roofed with an open framework of beams and cross rafters over which plants are trained. Known in ancient Egypt, pergolas were a feature of early Renaissance gardens in Italy and subsequently throughout Europe. They had a marked revival during the ARTS AND CRAFTS MOVEMENT in Britain.

Pergolesi \ˌpər-gə-'lā-zē\, **Giovanni Battista** (1710–1736) Italian composer. In 1732 he was appointed chapel master to a Neapolitan prince. His comic opera *Lo frate 'nnamorato* (1732) was followed in 1733 by a comic intermezzo that be-

P

came his best-known work, *La serva padrona*. His health failing, he moved into a monastery (1736), where he wrote his famous *Stabat mater* and *Salve Regina* before dying at 26. Traveling opera troupes took up *La serva padrona*, and in 1752 its success in Paris set off a major controversy about the superiority of Italian to French opera.

Pericles \'per-ə-ˌklēz\ (c.495–429 B.C.) Athenian general and statesman largely responsible for the full development of Athenian democracy and the Athenian empire. He was elected to power sometime after 461, and he quickly helped adopt essential democratic reforms. He asserted Athenian control over the DELIAN LEAGUE and used the league's treasury to rebuild the Acropolis, sacked by the Persians. Pericles had the Long Walls from Athens to the port at Piraeus strengthened for protection, and when the PELOPONNESIAN WAR broke out in 431, Attica's population was brought inside the walls. When plague broke out, killing one-fourth

Pericles Detail of a marble herm

of the population, Pericles was deposed and fined. Though reelected, he too died of the plague. His funeral oration (c.430) remains one of the greatest defenses of democracy, and his era is remembered as the Golden Age of Athens.

peridot \'per-ə-ˌdät, 'per-ə-ˌdō\ *or* **precious olivine** \'ä-lə-ˌvēn\ Gem-quality, transparent green OLIVINE. Very large crystals are found in Myanmar; peridots from the U.S. are seldom larger than two carats. Yellow-green peridot has been called chrysolite (Greek for "golden stone").

peridotite \pə-'ri-də-ˌtīt\ Coarse-grained, heavy, igneous rock that contains at least 10% OLIVINE, other iron- and magnesium-rich minerals, and not more than 10% FELDSPAR. It is the source of all CHROMIUM ore and naturally occurring DIAMONDS, and of nearly all chrysotile asbestos. Nearly all peridotite is altered to SERPENTINE; in warm, humid climates both have weathered to soils and related deposits that are potential sources of iron, nickel, cobalt, and chromium.

Périgord \ˌpā-rē-'gór\ Historic and cultural region, S France. The counts of Périgord played a part in the troubled affairs of AQUITAINE, and control of Périgord was disputed by the French and the English from 1259. The area was transferred to the house of Albret in 1470. After it was inherited by the crown of NAVARRE, HENRY IV united it with the French crown (1607).

period Basic unit of geologic time, during which specific systems of rocks were formed. Originally, the method for defining the sequence of periods was relative, based on STRATIGRAPHY and PALEONTOLOGY. Now CARBON-14 DATING and similar methods are used to determine absolute ages for various periods (see DATING).

periodic table Organized array of all the chemical ELEMENTS in increasing order of ATOMIC NUMBER. They show a periodic recurrence of certain properties, first discovered in 1869 by Dmitri MENDELEYEV. Those in the same column of the table as usually arranged have similar properties. Members of the same group in the table have the same number of ELECTRONS in the outermost shells of their atoms and form bonds of the same type, usually with the same VALENCE; the NOBLE GASES, with full outer shells, generally do not form bonds. The periodic table has thus greatly deepened understanding of BONDING and chemical behavior.

periodontitis \ˌper-ē-ə-ˌdän-'tī-təs\ INFLAMMATION of soft tissues around the teeth (see TOOTH). Poor dental hygiene leads to deposition of bacterial plaque on the teeth below the GUM line, irritating and eroding nearby tissues. If it is not treated, the gum margin recedes, exposing the roots of the teeth. The process eventually involves the bone anchoring the teeth, which loosen and may fall out. Removal of all

plaque deposits and affected soft tissues can arrest but not reverse bone deterioration.

periscope Optical instrument used in land and sea warfare, submarine NAVIGATION, and elsewhere to enable an observer to see the surroundings while remaining hidden or submerged. A periscope includes two mirrors or reflecting PRISMS to change the direction of the light coming from the scene observed: the first deflects it down through a vertical tube, the second diverts it horizontally so that the scene can be viewed conveniently.

peristalsis \ˌper-ə-'stól-səs\ Progressive wavelike MUSCLE contractions in the ESOPHAGUS, STOMACH, intestines, ureters, and other hollow tubes. In the esophagus, peristaltic waves push food into the stomach. In the stomach, they help mix stomach contents and propel food to the SMALL INTESTINE, where they expose food to the intestinal wall for absorption and move it forward. Peristalsis in the LARGE INTESTINE pushes waste outward and is important in removing gas and dislodging potential bacterial colonies.

peritoneoscopy See LAPAROSCOPY

peritonitis \ˌper-ə-tᵊn-'ī-təs\ INFLAMMATION of the peritoneum (see ABDOMINAL CAVITY), with pus accumulation, abdominal pain and distension, vomiting, and FEVER. It may be acute or chronic, local or generalized. Acute peritonitis usually results from inflammation elsewhere (e.g., by spread of bacterial infection). Primary peritonitis often comes from a perforated gastrointestinal tract, as with rupture in appendicitis.

periwinkle In botany, any of various plants of the genus *Vinca* of the DOGBANE FAMILY. The lesser periwinkle (*V. minor*), which has small lilac-blue flowers, is a dependable, trailing, evergreen perennial that has become widespread over much of E N. America. The greater periwinkle (*V. major*), with larger leaves and larger purplish-blue flowers, is native to continental Europe. ALKALOIDS derived from the periwinkle plant have had some success in inhibiting cancer growth.

periwinkle In zoology, any of some 80 species (family Littorinidae) of widely distributed, chiefly herbivorous shore SNAILS. Periwinkles are usually found on rocks, stones, or pilings between high- and low-tide marks. The common periwinkle (*Littorina littorea*), the largest N species, may grow to 1.5 in. (4 cm) long. It is common on Atlantic coasts. All species are a favorite food of many shorebirds.

perjury In law, the act or crime of knowingly making a false statement while under oath. Perjuries that have the effect of obstructing the adjudication of a case may be given increased punishment for that reason. A person who makes a false statement and later corrects it is usually not considered to have committed perjury.

Perkins, Frances (*orig.* Fannie Coralie) (1882–1965) U.S. public official. Born in Boston, she became a leader in New York organizations to improve women's working conditions. She served as state industrial commissioner 1929–33 under Gov. Franklin ROOSEVELT. As president, Roosevelt appointed her U.S. secretary of labor, the first woman to hold a cabinet post. In her long term (1933–45), she advocated such reforms as a minimum wage, maximum workweek, and unemployment compensation, and helped draft the Social Security Act.

Perkins, Jacob (1766–1849) U.S. inventor. Born in Newburyport, Mass., he built a machine to cut and head nails in one operation around 1790. He developed a method of engraving paper money that made counterfeiting difficult; lack of interest in the U.S. led him to set up a bank-note factory in England (1819). He built a horizontal STEAM ENGINE (1827), designed an improved paddle wheel (1829), and invented a means for the free circulation of water in boilers (1831) that led to the design of modern water-tube boilers.

Perl *in full* Practical Extraction and Reporting Language. High-level computer PROGRAMMING LANGUAGE used for text processing and scripting for interactive Web-site forms. Its syntax is similar to C and it includes several UNIX utilities. It is widely used by system administrators (for writing administrative tasks) and is especially suited for developing prototype versions of programs. Because it is an interpreted language, its programs are highly portable across different operating systems. Originally developed by Larry Wall at NASA's Jet Propulsion Laboratory in 1986, it has since been improved by hundreds of volunteer developers. Like LINUX, it can be obtained free of charge.

perlite *or* **pearlstone** Volcanic glass with concentric cracks such that the rock breaks into small, pearl-like bodies. Perlite is porous and has a waxy to pearly luster and is commonly gray or greenish. Large deposits have been worked in New Mexico, Nevada, California, and other W states. Perlite is used for heat and sound insulation, lightweight ceramic products, and filters. Heat-treated perlite is a substitute for sand in lightweight wall plaster and concrete aggregate.

Perlman, Itzhak (b.1945) Israeli-U.S. violinist. Despite a bout with polio at 4 that left him crippled, he was a prodigy, and he made his U.S. television debut at 13. Since graduating from Juilliard, he has had a highly successful career as orchestral soloist and chamber-music player, with scores of recordings. Blessed with a popular touch, he has appeared on television, played jazz and klezmer music, and involved himself in educating young musicians.

permafrost Perennially frozen earth, with a temperature below 32°F (0°C) for two years or more. Permafrost is estimated to underlie 20% of the earth's land surface and reaches depths of 5,000 ft (1,500 m) in N Siberia. It occurs in 85% of Alaska, more than half of Russia and Canada, and probably all of Antarctica. Permafrost has a significant effect on plant and animal life, and it presents special problems in engineering projects; if the delicate natural balance is not maintained, extensive degradation and ecological damage may result.

Permian period Interval of geologic time, 286–248 million years ago, the last period of the PALEOZOIC ERA. During the Permian, the continents joined to form a single supercontinent, PANGAEA. Hot, dry conditions prevailed almost everywhere, and deserts were widespread. Marine and freshwater fish and amphibians thrived. Reptiles evolved into three distinct groups: the cotylosaurs, the pelycosaurs, and the therapsids. Land plants evolved from ferns to conifers and adapted to drier and well-drained land conditions. Toward the close of the Permian, many forms of life suffered mass extinction, whose causes are unknown. See table at GEOLOGIC TIME.

permutations and combinations Number of ways a subset of objects can be selected from a given set of objects. In a permutation, order is important; in a combination, it is not. Thus, there are six permutations of the letters A, B, C selected two at a time (AB, AC, BC, BA, CA, CB) yet only three combinations (AB, AC, BC). The number of permutations of r objects chosen from a set of n objects, expressed in FACTORIAL notation, is $n! \div (n-r)!$ The number of combinations is $n! \div [r!(n-r)!]$. PROBABILITY THEORY evolved from the study of gambling, including figuring out combinations of playing cards or permutations of win-place-show possibilities in a horse race, and such counting methods played an important role in its development in the 17th cent.

Pernambuco See RECIFE

pernicious anemia Slow-developing disease in which vitamin B_{12} (see VITAMIN B COMPLEX) deficiency impairs red-blood-cell production. It can result from a diet lacking in vitamin B_{12} or when intrinsic factor, needed for intestinal absorption of B_{12}, is absent or inactive. It causes weakness, pallor, and stomach, intestinal, and neurological problems. Its slow development can allow ANEMIA to become very severe before diagnosis. B_{12} injections soon reverse the anemia, but must be continued for life.

Perón \pā-'rōn\, **Eva (Duarte de)** *known as* **Evita** *orig.* María Eva Duarte (1919–1952) Second wife of Argentine president Juan PERÓN. Born into poverty, she was an actress when she married Perón. She was instrumental in the success of his first presidential campaign and won the adulation of the masses. "Evita" acted as de facto minister of health and labor, awarding generous wage increases to workers. With "voluntary" contributions from businesses, labor unions, and the elite, she established thousands of hospitals, schools, and orphanages. After her death of cancer at 33, her grief-stricken followers sought to have her canonized.

Perón, Juan (Domingo) (1895–1974) President of Argentina (1946–55, 1973–74). A military officer, in 1943 he helped overthrow Argentina's ineffective civilian government. As secretary of labor and social welfare he built a loyal following among industrial workers, who helped elect him president in 1946. Perón's political views drew on both the far left and the far right: while he showered workers with benefits, he restricted civil liberties. The charisma of his wife, Eva PERÓN, greatly increased the regime's popular standing. He was reelected in 1951, but economic decline and widespread disaffection led to his overthrow in 1955 by democratically inspired military officers. He lived in exile in Spain for two decades, but continued to influence Argentine affairs. When the PERONIST party was made legal, he was reelected president; he died less than a year after returning to Argentina. His third wife, Isabel (b.1931), succeeded him, but was deposed in 1976.

Juan Perón, 1954

Peronist \pə-'rō-nist\ Member of Argentina's Justicialist Nationalist Movement and adherent of the policies of Juan PERÓN. Perón's political philosophy embraced elements of both left- and right-wing ideology, combining a populist commitment to the redistribution of wealth with authoritarian nationalism and disregard for civil rights. After his death in 1974, the Justicialist movement was weakened by factionalism, but it has retained an important role in Argentine politics.

Perot \pə-'rō\, **H(enry) Ross** (b.1930) U.S. businessman. Born in Texarkana, Texas, he served in the U.S. Navy 1953–57. After working for IBM (1957–62), he formed Electronic Data Systems, and successfully directed it until he sold it in 1984 for $2.5 billion. He became nationally known in 1992 as an independent candidate for U.S. president; appealing to voters dissatisfied with traditional party politics, he won 19% of the popular vote. His Reform Party gradually established its autonomy from Perot himself.

peroxide Any of a class of chemical compounds in which two OXYGEN atoms are linked by a single COVALENT BOND. Several organic (see ORGANIC COMPOUND) and inorganic (see INORGANIC COMPOUND) peroxides are useful as bleaching and oxidizing agents (see OXIDATION-REDUCTION), as initiators of POLYMERIZATION reactions, and in the preparation of hydrogen peroxide (a mild bleach and antiseptic) and other compounds.

Perpendicular style Phase of late GOTHIC ARCHITECTURE in 15th-cent. England. The style was characterized by a predominance of vertical lines in stone window TRACERY, enlargement of windows to great proportions, and conversion of the interior stories into a single unified vertical expanse. Fan VAULTS, springing from slender columns, became popular. The oldest surviving example is probably the choir of Gloucester Cathedral (begun c.1335). Another major monument is King's College Chapel, Cambridge (1446–1515). In the 16th cent., the grafting of Renaissance elements onto the Perpendicular style produced the TUDOR STYLE.

Perpignan \ˌper-pē-'nyäⁿ\ City (pop., 1999: 105,000), S France. Located just north of the Spanish border, it was founded about the 10th cent. It was the capital of ROUSSILLON in the 12th cent., and of the kingdom of MAJORCA 1276–1344. It was heavily fortified during the struggle between France and Spain for the area; it became French in 1659. It is now a market and tourist center.

Perrault \pe-'rō\, **Charles** (1628–1703) French poet, prose writer, and storyteller. He is best remembered for his collection of charming fairy stories written to amuse his children, *Contes de ma mère l'oye,* or *Tales of MOTHER GOOSE* (1697). A leading member of the ACADÉMIE FRANÇAISE, he was involved in a famous controversy on the relative merits of ancient and modern literature; his support for the mod-

P

ern was of landmark significance in the revolt against the confines of prevailing tradition.

Perry, Matthew C(albraith) (1794–1858) U.S. naval officer. Born in S. Kingston, R.I., he followed his brother O. H. PERRY into the navy and commanded the first U.S. navy steamship, the *Fulton* (1837–40). In 1852 Pres. Millard FILL-MORE sent Perry to induce Japan to establish diplomatic relations with the U.S. Concluding that Japan's centuries-old policy of isolation would be ended only by a show of force, Perry led four ships into the fortified harbor of Uraga (1853) and convinced the Japanese to accept his message. In 1854 he entered Edo (now Tokyo) Bay and concluded the first treaty between Japan and the U.S., allowing U.S. trading privileges and opening the Far East to U.S. influence.

Perry, Oliver Hazard (1785–1819) U.S. naval officer. Born in S. Kingston, R.I., the older brother of Matthew PERRY, he entered the navy in 1799. In 1813 he assembled a naval squadron to challenge British control of the Great Lakes in the WAR OF 1812. With 10 small ships, he engaged six British warships in Lake Erie. After his flagship was disabled, he was rowed to the *Niagara,* from which he won the battle by sailing directly into the British line, firing broadside. In reporting the British surrender he wrote, "We have met the enemy and they are ours."

Perse, Saint-John See SAINT-JOHN PERSE

Persephone \pər-'se-fə-nē\ *Latin* **Proserpina** In GREEK MYTHOLOGY, daughter of ZEUS and DEMETER. She was gathering flowers when she was seized by HADES, who carried her off to the underworld to make her his wife. Demeter became so distraught that she allowed barrenness and famine to spread over the earth. Zeus commanded Hades to allow Persephone to return to her mother, but because she had eaten some pomegranate seeds in the underworld, she had to spend one-third of each year with Hades. This myth accounts for the change of the seasons and the annual cycle of growth and decay.

Persepolis \pər-'se-pə-ləs\ Ancient city and capital of PERSIA, northeast of SHIRAZ, in modern SW central Iran. DARIUS I made it the capital of Persia, replacing PASAR-GADAE. In 330 B.C. ALEXAN-DER THE GREAT plundered the city and burned the palace of XERXES I. The city's ruins cover an extensive area and include colossal palaces

Persephone abducted by Hades, sculpture by G. L. Bernini, 1621–22

of Persian kings, a great staircase, an audience hall, and a treasury.

Perseus (212?–c.165 B.C.) Last king of Macedonia (179–168). Son of PHILIP V, he persuaded the king to execute his brother Demetrius. As king, he extended his influence in neighboring states and tried to gain the trust of the Greek world, but alarmed Greece by visiting Delphi with an army. EUMENES II of Pergamum informed Rome of Perseus' allegedly aggressive designs, provoking the Third MACEDONIAN WAR (171–168). The struggle ended in a final defeat of the Macedonians by the Romans, ending the monarchy.

Perseus In GREEK MYTHOLOGY, the slayer of the GORGON MEDUSA. He was the son of ZEUS and DANAË. His grandfather had him thrown into the sea in a chest with his mother as an infant because of a prophecy that Perseus would kill him. As a young man Perseus set out to gain the head of Medusa. On his way home he rescued the Ethiopian princess ANDROMEDA, and she became his wife. Having returned to Argos, he threw a discus that accidentally killed his grandfather, thus fulfilling the prophecy.

Pershing \'pər-zhiŋ, 'pər-shiŋ\, **John J(oseph)** (1860–1948) U.S. Army officer. Born in Laclede, Mo., he served on the W frontier (1886–98), in the Philippines (1899–1903, 1906–13), and as commander of a punitive raid against Pancho VILLA (1916). Named commander in chief of the American Expeditionary Force (AEF) in World War I, he maintained the AEF as an independent army of 2 million men and resisted Allied efforts to use U.S. forces as French and British replacements. He led the assault of the St. Mihiel salient in September 1918 and helped defeat German forces in the

John J. Pershing, 1917

Meuse-Argonne offensive. He became general of the armies in 1919 and was army chief of staff 1921–24. His nickname, "Black Jack," derived from his early service with a black regiment. His memoirs won a Pulitzer Prize (1931).

Persia Historical name for the kingdom of Iran, SW Asia. The name was used for centuries, chiefly in the West, and originated from a region of S Iran formerly known as Persis or Parsa, Parsa being the name of an Indo-European nomadic people who migrated into the area about 1000 B.C. The people of Iran have always called their country Iran.

Persian Gulf Arm of the ARABIAN SEA. It is 550 mi (885 km) long, and connects with the Gulf of OMAN and the Arabian Sea through the Strait of HORMUZ. It contains the island state of Bahrain and is bordered by Iran, the United Arab Emirates, Oman, Saudi Arabia, Qatar, Kuwait, and Iraq. Its economy is dominated by petroleum production. It was the scene of the PERSIAN GULF WAR in 1991.

Persian Gulf War *or* **Gulf War** (1990–91) International conflict triggered by Iraq's invasion of Kuwait in August 1990 to acquire Kuwait's rich oil fields. The U.S. and its NATO allies, supported by an Arab coalition, began massing troops in Saudi Arabia that month. Five months later, a massive U.S.-led air offensive against Iraq began. Saddam HUSSEIN, the Iraqi leader, responded by pumping millions of gallons of Kuwaiti oil into the gulf. A powerful ground offensive (Feb. 24–28, 1991) achieved victory almost immediately, though not before Hussein set scores of oil wells on fire. Estimates for Iraqi military deaths range from 8,000 to over 100,000; the Allies lost about 300 troops. Hussein subsequently faced widespread popular uprisings, which he managed to quell. A U.N.-sanctioned trade embargo remained in effect, pending destruction of Iraq's chemical-and nuclear-weapons research facilities, into the early 21st cent.

Persian language *or* **Farsi language** IRANIAN LANGUAGE spoken by more than 25 million people in Iran as a first language, and by millions more as a second. Modern Persian developed after the introduction of Islam brought a massive infusion of loanwords from ARABIC. Its standardization and literary cultivation took place in NE Persia and Central Asia in the 11th–12th cent. It had a very strong Persian influence on URDU and Ottoman TURKISH. Other TURKIC and INDO-ARYAN languages, CAUCASIAN LANGUAGES, and Iranian languages have also borrowed heavily from Persian. Like other Modern Iranian languages, Persian also shows marked grammatical simplification and changes in sound structure from Old Iranian. It is written in a slightly modified form of the ARABIC ALPHABET.

Persian Wars *or* **Greco-Persian Wars** (492–449 B.C.) Series of wars between Greek states and Persia, particularly two invasions of Greece by Persia (490, 480–479). When DARIUS I came to power in Persia in 522, the Ionian Greek city-states in Anatolia were under Persian control. They rose up unsuccessfully in the Ionian Revolt (499–494). The support lent by Athens provoked Darius to invade Greece (492). His fleet was destroyed in a storm. In 490 he assembled a huge army on a plain near Athens; his devastating defeat at the Battle of MARATHON sent him back to Persia. In 480 the

Persians under XERXES I invaded Greece again, seeking to avenge the defeat. This time all Greece fought together, with Sparta in charge of the army and Athens of the navy. After winning the Battle of THERMOPYLAE, the Persian army reached Athens, which they sacked (480), but the Persian navy was soundly defeated at the Battle of SALAMIS, and Xerxes withdrew it to Persia. His army was defeated at the Battle of PLATAEA in 479, and the navy met a similar fate on the Anatolian coast. Sporadic fighting went on for 30 more years, during which Athens formed the DELIAN LEAGUE to free the Ionians. The Peace of Callias (449) ended the hostilities.

persimmon Either of two trees of the genus *Diospyros* in the EBONY family, and their globular, edible fruits. The native American persimmon *(D. virginiana),* a small tree with dark-red to maroon fruits, grows from the Gulf states north to central Pennsylvania and central Illinois. The widely cultivated Oriental persimmon *(D. kaki)* has larger, more astringent, yellow to red fruit. Persimmons are eaten fresh or stewed or cooked as jam.

personal computer (PC) MICROCOMPUTER designed for use by one person at a time. A typical PC setup contains a CPU; internal MEMORY consisting of RAM and ROM; data storage devices (including a HARD DISK, a FLOPPY DISK, or CD-ROM); and input/output devices (including a display screen, keyboard, MOUSE, and PRINTER). The PC industry began in 1977 when APPLE COMPUTER introduced the Apple II. Radio Shack and Commodore Business Machines also introduced PCs that year. IBM entered the PC market in 1981, and the IBM PC quickly became the industry standard. Apple's Macintosh (1984) was particularly useful for DESKTOP PUBLISHING. MICROSOFT CORP. introduced MS Windows (1985), a GRAPHICAL USER INTERFACE that gave PCs many of the capabilities of the Macintosh. Uses of PCs multiplied as the machines became more powerful and application SOFTWARE proliferated. Today, PCs are used for word processing, Internet access, and many other daily tasks.

personality Totality of an individual's behavioral and emotional characteristics. Personality embraces a person's moods, attitudes, opinions, motivations, and style of thinking, perceiving, speaking, and acting. The ancient Greeks believed that physiology could explain differences in TEMPERAMENT. In the 18th cent., Immanuel KANT, MONTESQUIEU, and Giambattista VICO proposed ways of understanding individual and group differences; in the early 20th cent. Ernst Kretschmer (1888–1964) and the psychoanalysts Sigmund FREUD, Alfred ADLER, and C. G. JUNG offered competing personality theories. Freud's model rested on the power of psychosexual drives as mediated by the structural components of the ID, EGO, and SUPEREGO; the interplay of conscious and unconscious motives; and particularly the array of DEFENSE MECHANISMS an individual employed. Jung, like Freud, emphasized unconscious motives, but he de-emphasized sexuality, classified people as INTROVERTS AND EXTROVERTS, and claimed that an individual personality was a persona (social facade) drawn from the "collective unconscious," a pool of inherited racial memories. Later theories by Erik ERIKSON, Gordon Allport (1897–1967), and Carl ROGERS were also influential. Personality traits are usually seen as the product of both genetic predisposition and experience. See also PERSONALITY DISORDER, PSYCHOLOGICAL TESTING.

personality disorder Maladaptive or abnormal general behavioral pattern that is integral to an individual's PERSONALITY. Rather than being illnesses, personality disorders are pervasive features of the personality that deviate markedly from the cultural norm. They include the dependent, histrionic, narcissistic, obsessive-compulsive, antisocial, avoidant, borderline (unstable), paranoid, and schizoid types. Treatment combines BEHAVIOR THERAPY and PSYCHOTHERAPY.

personal-liberty laws Laws passed by U.S. states in the North to counter the FUGITIVE SLAVE ACTS. Such states as Indiana (1824) and Connecticut (1828) enacted laws giving escaped slaves the right to jury trials on appeal. Vermont and New York (1840) assured fugitives the right of jury trial and provided them with attorneys. After the COMPROMISE OF 1850, most Northern states enacted further guarantees of jury trials and punishment for illegal seizure. These laws were cited by proslavery interests as justification for SECESSION.

personal property See REAL AND PERSONAL PROPERTY

personnel administration See INDUSTRIAL RELATIONS

perspective Depiction of three-dimensional objects and spatial relationships on a two-dimensional plane. In Western art, illusions of volume and space are generally created by use of the linear perspective system, based on the observation that objects appear to shrink and parallel lines to converge at an infinitely distant vanishing point as they recede in space from the viewer. The vanishing point may have been known to the Greeks and Romans but had been lost until Filippo BRUNELLESCHI rediscovered the principles of linear or "mathematical" perspective early in the 15th cent. It dominated Western painting until the late 19th cent., when Paul CÉZANNE flattened the conventional picture plane.

perspiration Fluid given off by the SKIN by simple evaporation or as sweat from SWEAT GLANDS to evaporate and cool the body. When the body temperature rises, the sympathetic nervous system stimulates eccrine sweat glands to secrete water to the skin surface. Human eccrine sweat is essentially a dilute sodium-chloride solution. In extreme conditions, human beings may excrete several quarts of sweat in an hour.

Perth City (metro. area pop., 1996 est.: 1,097,000), and seaport capital of WESTERN AUSTRALIA state, Australia. Located near the mouth of the Swan River, it was settled in 1829. It developed rapidly after the discovery of gold fields in 1890 and the opening of Fremantle Harbor in 1897. It is now a major industrial center, and the seat of the Univ. of Western Australia and Murdoch Univ.

Perth Town (pop., 1995 est.: 42,000), central Scotland. It became a royal burgh in 1210 and was the capital of Scotland until 1437, when King JAMES I of Scotland was murdered there. At the Church of St. John the Baptist in 1559 John KNOX denounced idolatry; one result was the plunder of the town's monasteries and altars. It was a JACOBITE city during the Scottish uprisings of 1715 and 1745. The economy is based on whiskey blending and distilling.

pertussis See WHOOPING COUGH

Peru *officially* **Republic of Peru** Nation, W S. America. Area: 496,225 sq mi (1,285,216 sq km). Population (2000): 25,662,000. Capital: LIMA. Almost half of the people are QUECHUA Indians, and nearly one-third are MESTIZOS; smaller groups include whites and Aymara Indians. Languages: Spanish, Quechua, and Aymara (all official). Religions: Roman Catholicism (official), Protestantism. Currency: new sol. Peru is the third-largest nation in S. America and may be divided into three geographic regions from west to east: the coast, a long, narrow belt of desert lowlands; the highlands, the Peruvian portion of the ANDES; and the vast, forested eastern foothills and plains, consisting mainly of the tropical rain forests of the AMAZON RIVER basin. Peru has a developing mixed economy based largely on manufacturing, services, agriculture, and mining. Most industries, including the petroleum industry, were nationalized in the late 1960s and early 1970s. Many sectors were privatized in the 1990s. It is a republic with one legislative house; its head of state and government is the president. Peru was the center of the INCA empire, which was established around 1230 with its capital at CUZCO. In 1533 it was conquered by Francisco PIZARRO, and was dominated by Spain for almost 300 years as the viceroyalty of PERU. It declared its independence in 1821, and freedom was achieved in 1824. Peru was defeated in the War of the PACIFIC with Chile (1879–84). A boundary dispute with Ecuador lasted for many years and was finally settled in 1942, when the greater part of the Amazon basin was assigned to Peru. The government was overthrown by a military junta in 1968, and civilian rule was restored in 1980. The government of Alberto FUJIMORI suspended the constitution in 1992 in response to severe economic problems and to revolutionary activities by groups including the SHINING PATH and TUPAC AMARÚ. Fujimori and his chief of intelligence fled Peru in 2000 amid charges of corruption and homicide. See map on next page.

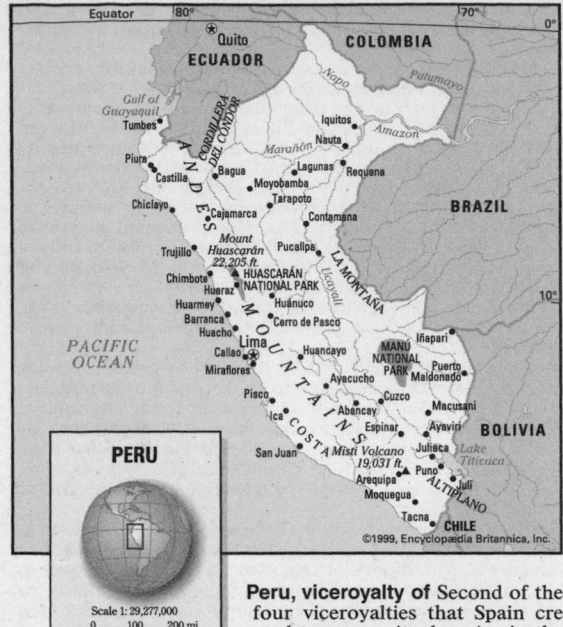

Equator 80° 70° 0°

Quito
★
ECUADOR
COLOMBIA

Gulf of
Guayaquil
Tumbes
Iquitos
Nauta
Piura
Bagua
Castilla
Moyobamba
Chiclayo
Cajamarca
Tarapoto
Contamana
BRAZIL
Mount
Huascarán
22,205 ft.
Trujillo
Chimbote
HUASCARÁN
NATIONAL PARK
Huaraz
Pucallpa
Huarmey
Barranca
Huacho
Huánuco
Cerro de Pasco
PACIFIC
OCEAN
Lima
Callao
Miraflores
Huancayo
MANÚ
NATIONAL
PARK
Íñapari
Puerto
Maldonado
Pisco
Ica
Ayacucho
Cuzco
Abancay
Macusani
Espinar
Ayaviri
San Juan
A Misti Volcano
19,031 ft.
Juliaca Lake
Titicaca
Puno
Juli
Arequipa
Moquegua
BOLIVIA
Tacna
CHILE
©1999, Encyclopædia Britannica, Inc.

PERU

Scale 1: 29,277,000
0   100   200 mi
0   150   300 km

Peru, viceroyalty of Second of the four viceroyalties that Spain created to govern its domains in the Americas. Established in 1543, it initially included most of S. America, but it gradually lost territory to other viceroyalties. Peru, with its silver, was considered Spain's most valuable possession in the Americas. By the late 18th cent., Indian rebellions had destabilized the region, and the viceroyalty was unable to defend itself from José de SAN MARTÍN in 1821. It became part of Peru and Chile in 1824. See also NEW GRANADA, NEW SPAIN, viceroyalty of RÍO DE LA PLATA.

Perugia \pā-'rü-jä\ City (pop., 1998 est.: 154,000), capital of UMBRIA region, central Italy. One of the 12 major cities of the ETRUSCANS, it was ruled by Rome from 310 B.C. It became a Lombard duchy in A.D. 592. It was the center of the great 15th-cent. Umbrian school of painting (see PERUGINO, PINTURICCHIO). It played an active role in the Italian RISORGIMENTO and became part of Italy in 1860. There are notable remains of Etruscan walls, as well as of the well-preserved medieval city. Perugia is noted for its chocolate.

Perugino \per-ə-'jē-nō\ orig. Pietro di Cristoforo Vannucci (c.1450–1523) Italian painter. Born near Perugia, he was probably a pupil of PIERO DELLA FRANCESCA and Andrea del VERROCCHIO. His famous fresco Giving of the Keys to St. Peter (1481–82), in the Sistine Chapel, anticipated High Renaissance ideals in its compositional clarity and sense of spaciousness. He was at the height of his powers (c.1490–1500) when he painted the Crucifixion fresco for the convent of Santa Maria Maddalena dei Pazzi in Florence. His art declined in his later years, but in 1508 he made a brief comeback by painting roundels on the ceiling of the Vatican's Stanza dell'Incendio; the commission for its wall frescoes went to his pupil RAPHAEL.

Pesaro \'pā-zä-ˌrō\ ancient Pisorum. City (pop., 1998 est.: 88,000), MARCHE region, N central Italy. A seaport on the Adriatic, it was destroyed by the OSTROGOTHS in A.D. 536. Rebuilt and fortified, it was sold to the SFORZA FAMILY in 1445 and became part of the PAPAL STATES in 1631. It was the birthplace of composer Gioachino ROSSINI. In World War II, it suffered heavily in the Allied advance of 1944. It is a seaside resort surrounded by an agricultural area. Its museum of MAJOLICA is the richest in Italy.

Peshawar \pə-'shä-wər\ City (metro. area pop., 1998: 988,000), capital of North-West Frontier province, Pakistan. It is located near the KHYBER PASS. Once the capital of the ancient Buddhist kingdom of Gandhara, it was a center of the caravan trade with Afghanistan and central Asia. Captured by the Muslims in 988, by the 16th cent. it was

ruled by the Afghans. It was under British control 1849–1947 and served as an important military base. It is still militarily important; its ancient bazaar remains a meeting place for foreign merchants and traders.

Pessoa \pes-'sō-ə\, Fernando (António Nogueira) (1888–1935) Portuguese poet. While working as a translator, he contributed to avant-garde reviews, especially Orpheu (1915), the organ of Brazilian-Portuguese Modernismo. Only after his death did the rich dream world of his poetry, peopled with fictional alter egos called "heteronyms," become well known. His important volumes include Poesias de Fernando Pessoa (1942), Poesias de Álvaro de Campos (1944), and Poemas de Alberto Caeiro (1946).

pest Any organism, usually an animal, judged as a threat to humans. Most pests either compete with humans for natural resources or transmit disease to humans, their crops, or their livestock. Invertebrate pests include some protozoans, flatworms, nematodes, mollusks, arachnids, and especially insects. Mammals and birds can also be pests. Human activities, such as monocultural farming practices, use of broad-spectrum pesticides, and introduction of exotic species, often result in the proliferation of pest species. Certain fungi, bacteria, and viruses are also considered pests. Plant pests are usually called WEEDS.

Pestalozzi \ˌpes-tə-'lōt-sē\, Johann Heinrich (1746–1827) Swiss educational reformer. Between 1805 and 1825 he directed the Yverdon Institute (near Neuchâtel), which drew pupils and educators (including Friedrich FROEBEL) from all over Europe. His teaching method emphasized such group participatory activities as drawing, writing, singing, physical exercise, model making, collecting, mapmaking, and field trips. His radically innovative ideas included grouping students by ability rather than age and encouraging formal teacher training.

pesticide Any toxic substance used to kill animals or plants regarded as noxious or dangerous. All pesticides act by interfering with the target species' normal metabolism. They are often classified by the type of organisms they are intended to control (e.g., INSECTICIDE, HERBICIDE, FUNGICIDE). Many also inadvertently harm other organisms in the environment, either directly or via consumption of the target organism.

PET See POSITRON EMISSION TOMOGRAPHY

pet Any animal kept by humans for companionship or pleasure rather than for utility. Distinctions between pets and domesticated livestock include the degree of contact between owner and animal and the owner's affection for the animal. Dogs have been kept as pets since prehistoric times; cats, since the 16th cent. B.C.; and horses, since at least 2000 B.C. Other common pets include birds, rabbits, rodents, raccoons, reptiles, and amphibians. Making pets of exotic animals (e.g., monkeys and ocelots) is worrisome because owners can rarely provide for their needs, and the animals' already precarious populations are depleted when members are sold for pets.

Pétain \pā-'taⁿ\, (Henri-) Philippe (1856–1951) French general. His successful defense in the Battle of VERDUN (1916) made him a national hero, and in 1918 he became commander in chief. After the war he served as vice president of the Supreme War Council (1920–30). After the German invasion of France (1940), Pétain was appointed premier at age 84. As head of VICHY FRANCE he attempted to obtain concessions by cooperating with the Germans. In 1942 they forced him to accept Pierre LAVAL as premier and he withdrew to a nominal role as head of state. After the Allied invasion of

Philippe Pétain

France, he fled to Germany. In 1945 he was tried and condemned to death; the sentence was commuted to life in prison, where he died at 95.

Peter I *Russian* Pyotr Alekseyevich *known as* **Peter the Great** (1672–1725) Czar of Russia (1682–1725). Son of Czar ALEXIS, he initially reigned jointly with his half brother Ivan V (1682–96). Interested in progressive influences from Western Europe, he introduced Western technology, modernized the government and military, and transferred the capital to the new city of St. Petersburg (1703). He further increased the power of the monarchy at the expense of the nobles and the Orthodox church. Some of his reforms were implemented brutally, with considerable loss of life. To gain access to the Baltic and Black seas, he fought wars with the Ottoman empire (1695–96) and with Sweden in the Second NORTHERN WAR (1700–21). His campaign against Persia (1722–23) secured for Russia the S and W shores of the Caspian Sea. In 1721 he was proclaimed emperor. For raising Russia to a recognized place among the great European powers, Peter is widely considered one of the outstanding rulers in Russian history, but he has been decried by nationalists for discarding much of what was unique in Russian culture, and his legacy provided a model for Joseph STALIN's brutal transformation of Russian life.

Peter I (1844–1921) King of Serbia (1903–18) and of the Kingdom of Serbs, Croats, and Slovenes (later Yugoslavia) from 1918. From 1858 until 1903 he lived with his family, mostly in exile. He fought with the French army in the FRANCO–PRUSSIAN WAR and with the Serb revolt against the Turks (1875). After the assassination of Alexander Obrenovich (1903), Peter was elected king of Serbia. He advocated a constitutional government and won recognition for his liberal policies. After World War I, he returned to Belgrade and was proclaimed king of the Serbs, Croats, and Slovenes.

Peter III *Russian* Pyotr Fyodorovich *orig.* Karl Peter Ulrich, Herzog (Duke) von Holstein-Gottorp (1728–1762) Czar of Russia (1762). Grandson of PETER I, he was brought to Russia by his aunt ELIZABETH when she became empress (1741). Unpopular for his pro-Prussian attitude, he succeeded Elizabeth and reversed her foreign policy, making peace with Prussia and withdrawing from the SEVEN YEARS' WAR. He offended the Orthodox church by trying to force it to adopt Lutheran practices. After six months he was forced to abdicate by a group of nobles, in collusion with his own wife, Catherine (later CATHERINE II), and Grigory ORLOV, and then murdered.

Peter Damian \'dā-mē-ən\, **St.** (1007–1072) Italian cardinal and doctor of the church. He was prior of Fonte Avellana in the Apennines before being named a cardinal in 1057. He played a leading role in the papal reforms of clerical celibacy and SIMONY and in the promotion of voluntary poverty. He defended Pope Alexander II against the ANTIPOPE Honorius II and reconciled Alexander with the city of Ravenna.

Peterhof See PETRODVORETS

Peter Lombard (c.1100–1160) French bishop and theologian. He was consecrated bishop of Paris in 1159. His *Four Books of Sentences* (1148–51), a systematic collection of teachings of the Church Fathers and opinions of medieval theologians, served as the standard theological text of the Middle Ages. In it, he asserted that sacraments were the cause and not merely the signal of grace and that human actions could be judged good or bad according to their cause and intention.

Petersburg Campaign (1864–65) Series of military operations in S Virginia at the end of the AMERICAN CIVIL WAR. The rail center of Petersburg, Va., was a strategic defense point near Richmond. In June 1864 the Union army began a siege of both cities, and each side built fortifications 35 mi (56 km) long. Confederate troops under Robert E. LEE held the cities, but supplies were scarce and Lee's 50,000 troops were immobilized by lack of horses. In April 1865 the 120,000 Union troops under U. S. GRANT drove the Confederates behind the city's inner defenses, forcing the evacuation of both cities.

Peterson, Oscar (Emmanuel) (b.1925) Canadian pianist and composer, the greatest virtuoso of modern jazz piano. Peterson grew up in Montreal and studied classical piano. His jazz playing is characterized by cascades of notes and an effervescent swing. After a Carnegie Hall debut in 1949 he be-

came one of the busiest pianists in jazz. An outstanding, extroverted improviser and sensitive accompanist, Peterson's playing demonstrates his roots in SWING as well as BEBOP.

Peterson, Roger Tory (1908–1996) U.S. ornithologist. Born in Jamestown, N.Y., he started drawing birds in high school. His *Field Guide to the Birds* (1934), illustrated with paintings that stressed the features that best identified a species in the field, greatly stimulated public interest in bird study. Because of this and many subsequent guides, Peterson was more responsible than any other person for fostering a widespread awareness of birds by the American public.

Peter the Apostle, St. *orig.* Simon (d.c.A.D. 64) Disciple of JESUS, recognized as the leader of the twelve APOSTLES. Jesus called him Cephas (Aramaic for "rock"; rendered in Greek as "Petros") and said "Upon this rock I will build my church." When Jesus was arrested, Peter denied him three times, as Jesus had foretold. Peter worked with St. PAUL in Antioch, did missionary work in Asia Minor, and eventually suffered martyrdom. ST. PETER'S BASILICA is said to have been built on the site of his grave. In Roman Catholicism he is regarded as the first in the unbroken succession of POPES. Jesus' promise to give him the "keys of the kingdom" led to the popular perception of Peter as the gatekeeper of heaven.

Peter the Great See PETER I (RUSSIA)

Peter the Hermit (c.1050–1115) French religious leader. A charismatic ascetic, he preached widely in Europe in support of the First CRUSADE and led his enthusiastic followers to Constantinople in 1096. They advanced to Nicomedia (modern Izmir, Turkey), but Peter was unable to maintain discipline; he returned to Constantinople to ask for help from ALEXIUS I, and in his absence his army was annihilated by the Turks.

Petipa \pä-tē-'på\, **Marius** (1819–1910) French-Russian dancer and choreographer. He received his early training from his ballet-master father and was a principal dancer in France, Belgium, and Spain before joining the Imperial Theater in St. Petersburg in 1847. After creating several ballets, including *The Pharaoh's Daughter,* he became chief choreographer in 1869. By his retirement in 1903, he had produced over 60 ballets, including *Don Quixote* (1869), *Sleeping Beauty* (1890), and *Swan Lake* (1895), which formed the core of the classical Russian repertoire.

petition Written instrument directed to an individual, legislative body, or court in order to seek redress of grievances or request a favor. When brought by a sufficient number of people, a petition can enable a candidate to get on a ballot, cause an issue to be submitted to the electorate (see REFERENDUM AND INITIATIVE), and exert pressure on legislators to vote in a certain way. In the U.S., the right to petition is guaranteed by the 1st Amendment to the Constitution.

Petition of Right (1628) Petition sent by Parliament to King CHARLES I seeking recognition of four principles: no taxation without consent of Parliament, no imprisonment without cause, no quartering of soldiers on subjects, and no martial law in peacetime. To continue receiving subsidies for his policies, Charles was compelled to accept it, but he later ignored its principles.

petit jury \'pe-tē\ *or* **trial jury** Jury of usually 12 people that is impaneled to examine and decide the facts at issue in a trial. It is the standard jury for civil and criminal trials. It has less discretion than is often imagined. The trial judge supervises it, rules on what EVIDENCE it may view and which laws are applicable, and sometimes directs or, at the end of the trial, sets aside its verdict. See also GRAND JURY.

Petöfi \'pet-œ̄-fē\, **Sándor** (1823–1856?) Hungarian poet and revolutionary. He became famous with his first poetry volume, *Versek* (1844). Before the revolution of 1848 he wrote poems that glowed with political passion; one of them, "Talpra magyar" ("Rise, Hungarian"), became an anthem. His works are characterized by realism, humor, descriptive power, and a peculiar vigor and have a direct style adapted from national folk songs. *János vitéz* (1845) is his most popular epic. He became a prisoner of war in 1849 and died in Siberia.

Petra \'pē-trə\ Ruined city, SW Jordan. It was the capital of the Nabataean kingdom from about 312 B.C. until its defeat by the Romans in A.D. 106, when it became part of the province of Arabia. After several centuries as a flourishing

P

trade center, it declined and was captured by the Muslims in the 7th cent. Its ruins were discovered in 1812. Excavations have revealed many rock-cut monuments, including tombs with elaborate facades carved in rose, crimson, and purple sandstone.

Petrarch \'pē-ˌträrk, 'pe-ˌträrk\ *Italian* Francesco Petrarca (1304–1374) Italian scholar, poet, and humanist. Born in Arezzo, he took minor ecclesiastical orders and moved to Avignon, where in 1327 he first saw Laura, the idealized subject of his chaste love and of his celebrated Italian love lyrics; mainly sonnets and odes, most were included in his *Canzoniere* or *Rime* (1360). The greatest scholar of his age, especially of classical Latin, he traveled widely, visiting learned men, searching out manuscripts, and undertaking diplomatic missions. He strongly advocated the continuity between classical culture and the Christian message; in combining the two ideals he is considered the founder and a great representative of HUMANISM. His Latin works include *On Illustrious Men* (begun c.1337), the epic poem *Africa* (begun c.1338), and the autobiographical treatise *Petrarch's Secret* (written 1342–58). His influence on European literature was enormous and lasting, and his deep consciousness of the classical past as a source of literary and philosophical meaning for the present helped pave the way for the RENAISSANCE.

petrel Any of numerous seabirds (order Procellariiformes, particularly family Procellariidae), including 24 species (genera *Pterodroma* and *Bulweria*) called gadfly petrels because of their fluttering flight. Most are dark above and light below, with long wings and a short, wedge-shaped tail. They nest in colonies on tropical and subtropical islands. During the nonbreeding season, petrels roam the open ocean, eating squid and small fishes. See also STORM PETREL.

Petrie \'pē-trē\, (William Matthew) Flinders (*later* Sir Flinders) (1853–1942) British archaeologist who made valuable contributions to the techniques of EXCAVATION and DATING. During excavations in Egypt in the mid-1880s Petrie developed a sequence dating method, based on a comparison of potsherds at various levels, that made possible the reconstruction of ancient history from material remains. His excavations, together with those of Heinrich SCHLIEMANN at Troy, marked the beginning of the examination of successive levels of a site, rather than the previously haphazard digging. His *Methods and Aims in Archaeology* (1904) was the definitive work of its time. Petrie taught at the Univ. of London 1892–1933.

Petrified Forest National Park National park, E Arizona. It has an area of 146 sq mi (378 sq km). Its extensive exhibits include petrified wood in several "forest" areas, fossilized leaves, plants, and broken logs, and the PAINTED DESERT. Other features are petroglyphs and ancient PUEBLO INDIAN ruins.

petrified wood Fossil formed by the infiltration of minerals, usually silica or CALCITE, into natural wood. Often this replacement of organic tissue by mineral deposits is so precise that the internal structure as well as the external shape is retained; sometimes even the cell structure may be determined.

petrochemical Strictly, any of a large class of chemicals (as distinct from fuels) derived from PETROLEUM and NATURAL GAS. The category has been broadened to include a much larger range of organic compounds and a few inorganic compounds. Most petrochemicals consist mainly of carbon and hydrogen and are called HYDROCARBONS. Petrochemicals used as raw materials ("feedstocks") include ETHYLENE (highest volume), propylene, butadiene, benzene, toluene, xylene, and naphthalene. Petrochemical products include PLASTICS (POLYETHYLENE, polypropylene, polystyrene), SOAPS and DETERGENTS, SOLVENTS, DRUGS, FERTILIZERS, PESTICIDES, EXPLOSIVES, synthetic fibers, RUBBERS, paints, EPOXIES, flooring and insulating materials, luggage, and recording disks and tapes.

Petrodvorets \ˌpyi-trə-dvà-'ryets\ *formerly* (*until 1944*) **Peterhof** City (pop., 1995 est.: 82,000), NW Russia. Located near St. Petersburg, it was founded by PETER I THE GREAT as a country estate in 1709. After visiting France in 1717, he decided to create a summer residence to rival the Palace of VERSAILLES. The Baroque Grand Palace (1714–28) was designed by Domenico Trezzini, and its gardens by Alexandre Le Blond (1679–1719). Today the palace and the vast park, with 39 mi (63 km) of canals that connect the intricate system of fountains, are part of a 2,500-acre (1,000-hectare) preserve.

Petrograd See SAINT PETERSBURG

petrol See GASOLINE

petroleum *or* **crude oil** Complex mixture of HYDROCARBONS derived from the geological transformation and decomposition of plants and animals that lived hundreds of millions of years ago. It occurs in the earth in liquid (crude oil), gaseous (NATURAL GAS), or solid (BITUMINOUS COAL, ASPHALT) forms. Petroleum and natural gas are the most important primary FOSSIL FUELS. Asphalt has been used since ancient times to caulk ships and pave roads. In the mid-1800s, oil began to replace whale oil in lamps, and the first well specifically for oil was drilled in 1859. The development of the automobile gave petroleum a new role as the source of GASOLINE. Petroleum and its products are used as fuels for heating, for transport, and for electrical power generation, and as PETROCHEMICAL sources and lubricants. Crude oil and natural gas now account for about 60% of world energy consumption; the U.S. is by far the largest consumer. At present rates of consumption, the known supply will be exhausted by the mid-21st cent. Petroleum is recovered from drilled wells, transported by pipeline or tanker ship to refineries, and there converted to fuels and petrochemicals.

petrology Scientific study of ROCKS, including their composition, texture, and structure; occurrence and distribution; and conditions of origin. Experimental petrology synthesizes rocks in the laboratory to ascertain the physical and chemical conditions under which they form. The subdiscipline of petrography is concerned primarily with the systematic study and description of rocks.

Petronas Towers \pe-'trō-nəs\ Twin stainless-steel-clad skyscrapers in Kuala Lumpur, Malaysia. At 88 stories and 1,483 ft (452 m) high, including their pinnacles, the towers are considered the world's tallest buildings (though, when measured by the roof line, the SEARS TOWER is higher). Designed by Cesar Pelli (b.1926), the circular towers, completed in 1998, house Malaysia's national petroleum company. Their structural frames consist of high-strength, steel-reinforced concrete.

Petronius Arbiter, Gaius *orig.* Titus Petronius Niger (d.A.D. 66) Roman writer. He served as governor of the Asian province of Bithynia and as consul in Rome. After being appointed NERO's authority on taste (hence "Arbiter"), he was accused of plotting to kill the emperor and, though innocent, committed suicide. He is the reputed author of the *Satyricon*, a comic PICARESQUE NOVEL vividly portraying contemporary Roman society through the escapades of a disreputable trio of adventurers.

Petty, Richard (b.1937) U.S. stock-car racer. Born in Level Cross, N.C., in his long professional career he would win 200 races. In 1975 he set the NASCAR record of 13 victories in one season. "King Richard" also won seven Daytona 500 races and seven NASCAR grand national championships. His father, son, and grandson have all been NASCAR racers.

petunia Any of many species of flowering plants in the genus *Petunia*, in the NIGHTSHADE FAMILY, which originated in S. America. The innumerable varieties of showy, trumpet-shaped flowers are immensely popular. From early summer until frost, petunias bloom profusely with single or double blossoms; crisped, fringed, or ruffled flowers; and spectacular variegated hues. Leaves are soft, flabby, and covered with fine, sticky hairs. Technically perennials, petunias are most often grown as annuals.

Peugeot Citroën \pœ̄-'zhō-sē-trō-'en\ *in full* PSA Peugeot Citroën SA. Major French automotive manufacturer and holding company. Peugeot was founded in 1890 by Armand Peugeot (1849–1915), who helped produce the first Peugeot automobile in 1891. Citroën's founder, André-Gustave Citroën (1878–1935), introduced mass-production methods to the French auto industry; soon after introducing the first Citroën car in 1919, it became a major producer of low-priced cars. Citroën was merged with several other automakers before its merger with Peugeot in 1976. In addition to manufacturing cars and trucks, Peugeot is a major producer of bicycles and motorcycles. The holding company owns bank and finance companies throughout Europe.

pewter Tin-based ALLOY used to make domestic utensils. Pewter dates back at least 2,000 years, to Roman times. Ancient pewter contained about 70% TIN and 30% LEAD. It darkened greatly with age, and the lead readily leached out in contact with acidic foods. Pewter with little or no lead is of finer quality, and alloys that include antimony and BISMUTH are more durable and shinier. Modern pewter is about 91% tin, 7.5% antimony, and 1.5% copper. The surface is bluish white with either a bright finish or a soft, satin sheen. It resists tarnish, retaining its color and finish indefinitely.

peyote \pā-'ō-tē\ Either of two species of the genus *Lophophora* in the CACTUS family, native to Mexico. The body of the peyote cactus is spineless, soft, usually blue-green, and only 3 in. (8 cm) wide and 2 in. (5 cm) tall. The more common species, mescal *(L. williamsii)*, has pink to white flowers. *L. diffusa* has white to yellow flowers and a yellow-green body. Well known for its hallucinogenic effects (primarily due to the alkaloid MESCALINE), peyote figures in religious rituals of certain AMERICAN INDIAN peoples. The sale, use, or possession of dried mescal buttons (flowering heads) or live plants is illegal in many places.

pH Quantitative measure of the strength of the ACID (and BASE) in a SOLUTION, defined as the negative common LOGARITHM of the concentration of hydrogen IONS (H^+) in MOLES/liter (written in square brackets): $pH = -\log_{10}[H^+]$. The product of the concentrations in water of H^+ and OH^- (the HYDROXIDE ion) is always about 10^{-14}. The strongest acid solution has about 1 mole/liter of H^+ (and about 10^{-14} of OH^-), for a pH of 1. The strongest basic solution has about 10^{-14} moles/liter of H^+ (and about 1 of OH^-), for a pH of 14. A neutral solution has about 10^{-7} moles/liter of both H^+ and OH^-, for a pH of 7. The pH value, measured by a pH meter, TITRATION, or indicator (e.g., LITMUS) strips, helps inform chemists of the nature, composition, or extent of reaction of substances; biologists of the composition and environment of organisms or their parts or fluids; physicians of the functioning of bodily systems; and agronomists of the suitability of soils for crops and any treatments needed.

Phaedra \'fē-drə\ In Greek legend, the daughter of King MINOS and the second wife of THESEUS after he abandoned her sister ARIADNE. She later fell in love with her stepson Hippolytus; rejected, she accused him of rape. He was killed, and she hanged herself.

Phaedrus \'fē-drəs\ (c.15 B.C.–c.A.D. 50) Roman fabulist. A slave by birth, Phaedrus became a freedman in AUGUSTUS' household. He was the first writer to Latinize whole books of Greek fables, which he did under the name of AESOP. Phaedrus' renderings, noted for their charm, brevity, and didacticism, became very popular in medieval Europe; they include such favorites as "The Fox and the Sour Grapes."

Phaethon \'fā-ə-thən\ In GREEK MYTHOLOGY, the son of HELIOS, the sun god. Taunted as illegitimate, Phaethon asked for permission to drive the chariot of the sun through the heavens for a day in order to prove that Helios was his father. Unable to control the horses, he rode too close to earth and began to scorch it. To prevent further damage, ZEUS hurled a thunderbolt, killing him.

phage See BACTERIOPHAGE

phalarope \'fa-lə-ˌrōp\ Any of three species (genus *Phalaropus*, family Scolopacidae) of slim-necked shorebirds, 6–10 in. (25–25 cm) long, with a straight, slender bill. Females fight for nesting territory and court the males; males do all the nesting duties and lead the young south in autumn. Two species breed around the Arctic Circle and winter on tropical oceans, where they are known as sea snipe. Wilson's phalarope *(P. tricolor)* breeds in W N. America and migrates to the Argentine pampas.

Phanerozoic eon \ˌfa-nə-rə-'zō-ik\ Span of geologic time from 544 million years ago to the present. The Phanerozoic, the eon of visible life, is divided into three major eras: the PALEOZOIC, MESOZOIC, and CENOZOIC. Although life originated in PRECAMBRIAN TIME, it was in the Phanerozoic that many forms arose and evolved. The earth gradually assumed its present configuration and physical features through such processes as PLATE TECTONICS, mountain building, and glaciation. See table at GEOLOGIC TIME.

pharaoh \'fer-ō\ Title applied to Egyptian kings from c.1500 B.C. on. Pharaohs were regarded as gods, retaining their divine status even after death. A pharaoh's will was supreme, and he governed by royal decree, with the assistance of VIZIERS. The common people nevertheless judged a pharaoh by his deeds; many were criticized, plotted against, and even deposed and killed. See also AKHENATON, AMENEMHET I, AMENHOTEP II, AMENHOTEP III, RAMSES II, THUTMOSE III, TUTANKHAMEN.

Pharisee \'far-ə-ˌsē\ Member of a Jewish religious party in Palestine that emerged around 160 B.C. in opposition to the SADDUCEES. The Pharisees held that the Jewish oral tradition was as valid as the TORAH. They struggled to democratize the Jewish religion, fostering the SYNAGOGUE as an institution of worship. Their belief that reason must be applied in the interpretation of the Torah is now basic to Jewish theology.

pharmacology \ˌfär-mə-'käl-ə-jē\ Branch of MEDICINE dealing with the actions of DRUGS in the body—both therapeutic and toxic effects—and development and testing of new drugs and new uses of existing ones. Scientific pharmacology was only possible from the 18th cent. on, when drugs could be purified and standardized. Pharmacologists develop drugs from plant and animal sources and create synthetic versions of these, along with new drugs based on them or their chemical structure. They also test drugs, first in the laboratory for biochemical activity and then on animals, human volunteers, and patients for safety, effectiveness, side effects, and interactions with other drugs and to find the best dose, timing, and route (mouth, injection, etc.). See also FOOD AND DRUG ADMINISTRATION, PHARMACY.

pharmacy Science dealing with collection, preparation, and standardization of DRUGS. Pharmacists, who must earn a qualifying degree, prepare and dispense medications. They are responsible for formulating, storing, and providing correct dosages of medicines, now usually produced by pharmaceutical companies as premeasured tablets or capsules. They also advise patients on the use of drugs. Laws regulating the pharmaceutical industry are based on the national pharmacopoeia (in the U.S., the U.S. Pharmacopoeia or USP), which outlines the purity and dosages of numerous medicinal products.

pharyngeal tonsils See ADENOIDS

pharynx \'far-iŋks\ Inside of the throat, from the MOUTH and NOSE to the TRACHEA and ESOPHAGUS. It has three connected sections: the nasopharynx, at the back of the nasal cavity; the oropharynx, in the back of the oral cavity down to the epiglottis (the flap that closes off the LARYNX during swallowing); and the laryngopharynx, from the epiglottis to the esophagus. The oropharynx contains the palatine TONSILS. The eustachian tubes connect the middle EARS to the pharynx.

phase In THERMODYNAMICS, a chemically and physically uniform quantity of matter that can be separated mechanically from a nonhomogeneous mixture. The three basic phases of matter are SOLID, LIQUID, and GAS; CRYSTALS, COLLOIDS, GLASSES, amorphous materials, and PLASMAS may also be called phases. The different phases of a pure substance are related to each other in terms of TEMPERATURE and PRESSURE. For example, if the temperature of a solid is raised enough, or the pressure is reduced enough, it will become a liquid.

phase In WAVE motion, the fraction of the time required to complete a full cycle that a point completes after last passing through the reference position. Two periodic motions are said to be in phase when corresponding points of each reach maximum or minimum displacements at the same time. If the crests of two waves pass the same point at the same time, they are in phase for that position. Phase differences are important in alternating electric current technology (see ALTERNATING CURRENT).

pheasant Any of about 50 species of mostly long-tailed birds in the family Phasianidae (order Galliformes). Most species inhabit open woodlands and brushy fields. All have a hoarse call. Most males are strikingly colored, some have a fleshy facial ornament. Males sometimes fight to the death for a harem of hens. Male ring-necked or common pheasants *(Phasianus colchicus),* 35 in. (90 cm) long, have a streaming tail, coppery breast, purplish green neck, and ear tufts; they are widespread in the N U.S. Japanese green pheasants *(P. versicolor)* call in concert when an earthquake is imminent.

Pheidias See PHIDIAS

phenol \'fē-ˌnōl, 'fē-ˌnȯl\ Any of a class of organic compounds with a hydroxyl group (–OH; see FUNCTIONAL GROUP) attached to a carbon atom in a ring of an ARO-MATIC COMPOUND. The simplest one is also called phenol. Phenols are similar to ALCOHOLS but dissolve more readily in water and boil at higher temperatures. They may be colorless liquids or white solids; many have a sharp, spicy odor. Some are found in ESSENTIAL OILS. Phenols with higher MOLECULAR WEIGHTS and phenol derivatives have supplanted phenol itself as industrial ANTISEPTICS.

phenomenology Philosophical discipline originated by Edmund HUSSERL to make possible "a descriptive account of the essential structures of the directly given." Phenomenology emphasizes the immediacy of experience, the attempt to isolate it and set it off from all assumptions of existence or causal influence and lay bare its essential structure. Husserl's *Annual for Philosophical and Phenomenological Research* (1913–30) gradually transformed his personal philosophizing into an international movement. Its most notable adherent was Martin HEIDEGGER.

phenotype \'fē-nə-ˌtīp\ All the observable characteristics of an organism, such as shape, size, color, and behavior, that result from the interaction of its GENOTYPE with the environment. The phenotype may change because of environmental changes and changes associated with aging. Different environments can influence the development of inherited traits (e.g., size is affected by available food supply) and can alter expression by similar genotypes (e.g., twins brought up in dissimilar families may mature differently). Furthermore, not all inherited possibilities in the genotype are expressed in the phenotype, because some are the result of inactive, recessive, or inhibited genes. See also VARIATION.

phenylketonuria \ˌfe-nᵊl-ˌkē-tᵊn-'ȯr-ē-ə\ **(PKU)** *or* **phenylpyruvic oligophrenia** \ˌfe-nᵊl-pī-ˌrü-vik-ˌäl-i-gō-'frē-nē-ə\ Inability to normally metabolize the AMINO ACID phenylalanine, whose accumulation interferes with normal childhood development. Central NERVOUS-SYSTEM effects include mental retardation and seizures (see EPILEPSY), with behavioral signs seen at four to six months of age. Newborns are tested for this recessive genetic disorder (see CONGENITAL DISORDER, RECESSIVENESS). Total avoidance of meat, dairy, and high-protein foods, and ASPARTAME until adolescence permits normal development. Protein is supplied in a phenylalanine-free drink. Pregnant women with PKU must resume the diet to prevent severe damage to the unborn child.

pheromone \'fer-ə-ˌmōn\ Any chemical compound secreted in minute amounts to elicit a particular reaction from other organisms of the same species. Pheromones are widespread among insects and vertebrates (except birds) and are present in some fungi, slime molds, and algae. The chemicals may be secreted by special GLANDS or incorporated into other substances (e.g., urine), shed freely or deposited in selected locations. Pheromones are used to bring creatures together (e.g., in termite, bee, and ant colonies), lead them to food (e.g., in scent trails laid by ants), signal danger, attract a mate and elicit sexual behavior, and influence sexual development. Alarm pheromones often last a shorter time and travel a shorter distance than other types. In vertebrates, chemical stimuli often influence parent-young responses. Sex-attractant pheromones are used in certain products to lure and trap unwanted or harmful insects.

Phi Beta Kappa Leading honor society for U.S. college and university students. The oldest Greek-letter society in the U.S., it was founded in 1776 as a secret literary and philosophical society at College of WILLIAM AND MARY. It be-came an honor society in the 19th cent. Membership is now based on general scholarship.

Phibunsongkhram \'pē-bùn-sȯn-ˌkräm\, **Luang** *or* **Luang Pibul Songgram** *orig.* Plaek Khittasangkha (1897–1964) Field marshal and premier of Thailand (1938–44, 1948–57). After military training in France, he helped organize the bloodless coup of 1932 that ended absolute monarchy in Siam. Head of the military government, he changed the country's name to Thailand (1939), and allied himself with Japan; as the war turned against Japan, his government collapsed. The army seized power in 1947 and he was reinstalled as premier in 1948. Opposed to communism, he allied Thailand to the West by helping establish the S.E. ASIA TREATY ORGANIZATION. He was ousted by his military colleagues in 1957 and fled to Japan.

Phidias \'fid-ē-əs\ (c.490–430 B.C.) Greek sculptor. Placed in charge of the great building program initiated by PERI-CLES in Athens, he supervised and probably designed the overall sculptural decoration of the PARTHENON. He also created its most important religious images, including the colossal statue of the Athena Parthenos (438–436). Ancient writers considered his masterpiece to be the statue of Zeus (c.430) at Olympia. He initiated the idealistic classical style that distinguishes Greek art in the later 5th and 4th cent. B.C.

Philadelphia City (pop., 2000: 1,517,000) and port, SE Pennsylvania. The site was occupied by the DELAWARE Indians before William PENN founded the city in 1682. It was the capital of Pennsylvania 1683–1799 and the capital of the U.S. 1790–1800. It was the site of the first and second CONTINENTAL CONGRESSES, the signing of the DECLARATION OF INDEPENDENCE, and the CONSTITUTIONAL CONVEN-TION. With many immigrants from Scotland, Ireland, and Germany, it was the largest and most important city of the U.S. in the 19th cent. and a center of the antislavery movement. In 1876 it was the site of the U.S. Centennial Exposition. It is also the site of the U.S.'s oldest art museum (1805) and the first U.S. hospital (1751). It is a center of commerce, finance, industry, and culture; its numerous educational institutions include the Univ. of PENNSYLVANIA.

philately \fə-'la-tᵊl-ē\ Collection and study of postage stamps. Stamp collectors usually specialize, collecting stamps of one country, one period of time, or one subject (e.g., birds, flowers, art). Value depends on rarity and condition. An issue of stamps that includes a printer's error may have increased value.

Philby, Kim (*orig.* Harold Adrian Russell) (1912–1988) British intelligence officer and Soviet spy. He became a communist while at Cambridge Univ., and in 1933 a Soviet agent. Recruited into British intelligence by Guy BURGESS (1940), he became head of counterespionage operations. In 1949 he was sent to Washington, D.C., as top liaison officer between British and U.S. intelligence services. He revealed top-secret information to the Soviets and in 1951 warned co-spies Burgess and Donald Maclean to escape. Dismissed under suspicion in 1955, he fled in 1963 to the Soviet Union, where he worked for the KGB. The most successful Soviet double agent of the Cold War, he was responsible for the deaths of many Western agents.

Philip, Duke of Edinburgh *known as* **Prince Philip** (b.1921) Husband of Queen ELIZABETH II of Britain. Son of Prince Andrew of Greece and Denmark and Princess Alice, a great-granddaughter of Queen VICTORIA, he was reared in Britain. In World War II he served in combat with the Royal Navy. In 1947 he became a British subject, taking his mother's surname, Mountbatten, and renouncing his right to the Greek and Danish thrones, and married Princess Elizabeth. CHARLES, PRINCE OF WALES, is their son.

Philip, King See METACOM

Philip II *or* **Philip of Macedonia** (382–336 B.C.) 18th king of Macedonia (359–336 B.C.), father of ALEXANDER THE GREAT. Appointed regent for his nephew, he seized the throne. He initially promoted peace with his neighbors, using the time gained in military preparations, but the Greeks formed a coalition against him. He intervened in the Sacred War to free DELPHI from the Phocians, becoming the ally of THEBES and the Thessalian League, whose president he became. DEMOSTHENES turned Athens against him with his

Philippics (346–342), and Thebes also came to view Philip as a threat. He defeated both at the Battle of Chaeronea (338 B.C.), becoming leader of all Greece. He formed the Greek states into the League of CORINTH to attack Persia, but was assassinated by a Macedonian nobleman, possibly in collusion with his wife Olympias and son Alexander.

Philip II *French* Philippe *known as* **Philip Augustus** (1165–1223) French king (1179–1223). The first of the great CAPETIAN kings, he gradually reconquered the French territories held by the kings of England. He joined with RICHARD I on the Third CRUSADE, but the two kings soon quarreled. Philip returned to France (1191) and attacked English possessions. When Richard was killed (1199), his brother JOHN signed a treaty with Philip (1200), but France and England were soon again at war. Philip conquered Normandy (1204) and subdued Maine, Touraine, Anjou, and most of Poitou (1204–5). He later defeated John at the Battle of Bouvines (1214). Philip also expanded his territory into Flanders and Languedoc.

Philip II *Spanish* **Felipe** \fā-ˈlē-pä\ (1527–1598) King of Spain (1556–98) and of Portugal (as Philip I, 1580–98). The son of Emperor CHARLES V, Philip received from his father the duchy of Milan (1540), the kingdoms of Naples and Sicily (1554), the Netherlands (1555), and Spain and its overseas empire (1556). He waged a successful war against France in 1557. He built the palace of EL ESCORIAL and encouraged Spain's literary golden age. He was a champion of the COUNTER-REFORMATION but failed to put down rebellions in the Netherlands (from 1568) and to conquer England, suffering the defeat of the Spanish

Philip II of Spain, painting by Titian

ARMADA (1588). He unified the Iberian Peninsula as king of Portugal from 1580. During his reign the Spanish empire attained its greatest power, extent, and influence.

Philip III *French* Philippe *known as* **Philip the Good** (1396–1467) Duke of BURGUNDY (1419–67). He founded the Burgundian state that rivaled France in the 15th cent. He maintained an alliance with England, breaking it only during his unsuccessful attempt to capture Calais (1435–39). Philip avoided conflict with France and instead attacked his smaller neighbors, conquering Hainaut, Brabant, Holland and Zeeland, and Luxembourg by 1443. A renowned patron of the arts, he presided over one of Europe's most extravagant courts.

Philip IV *French* Philippe *known as* **Philip the Fair** (1268–1314) King of France (1285–1314). He was also king of Navarre (as Philip I, 1284–1305), ruling jointly with his wife, Joan I of Navarre. War with England (1294–1303) ended with a peace treaty and the betrothal of his daughter to the future EDWARD II. Philip forced a harsh treaty on Flanders in 1305. He conducted a long struggle with Boniface VIII (1297–1303) but was pacified by succeeding popes, including CLEMENT V, who began the AVIGNON PAPACY. Philip expelled the Jews from France (1306) and persecuted the Knights TEMPLAR (1307).

Philip IV *Spanish* **Felipe** (1605–1665) King of Spain (1621–65) and of Portugal (as Philip II, 1621–40). He succeeded his father, Philip III, and left the administration of his rule to his chief ministers. Spain's industry and commerce declined, and wars further drained Spain's economy; Portugal regained its independence (1640), and Holland was lost by the Peace of WESTPHALIA (1648). A poet and patron of the arts, Philip was the friend and frequent subject of Diego VELÁZQUEZ.

Philip V (238–179 B.C.) King of Macedonia (221–179). Supporting the Hellenic League, he allied with HANNIBAL in 215 and attacked Roman client states in Illyria. Rome responded in the First MACEDONIAN WAR. Intrigue against Egypt and his unsuccessful sea battle with Rhodes and

Pergamum led Rome to initiate the Second Macedonian War, in which it prevailed at Cynoscephalae (197). Rome's harsh terms eased after Philip made common cause against its Greek foes. Fearing that Rome would turn on him again, he attempted to expand by attacking the Balkans (184, 183, 181); he died on a fourth attempt in 179.

Philip V *Spanish* **Felipe** *orig.* Philippe, duc (Duke) d'Anjou (1683–1746) King of Spain (1700–46). Grandson of LOUIS XIV of France and great-grandson of PHILIP IV of Spain, Philip was named to succeed the childless CHARLES II as king in 1700. Louis's refusal to exclude Philip from the line of succession to the French throne led to the War of the SPANISH SUCCESSION, which resulted in the loss of the SPANISH NETHERLANDS and parts of Italy. Initially influenced by his French advisers through his wife, Maria Luise of Savoy, after her death (1714) he was influenced by his second wife, ELIZABETH FARNESE, and her Italian advisers. Philip later brought Spain into the War of the AUSTRIAN SUCCESSION. His reign marked the beginning of the Bourbon dynasty in Spain (see House of BOURBON).

Philip VI *French* Philippe *known as* **Philip of Valois** (1293–1350) First French king of the Valois dynasty (1328–50). He continued CAPETIAN efforts to centralize the state but made concessions to the nobility, clergy, and bourgeoisie. His disputes with EDWARD III of England led to the outbreak of the HUNDRED YEARS' WAR (1337). French defeats at the battles of Sluys (1340) and CRÉCY (1346) caused crises in France until the spread of the BLACK DEATH (from 1348) overshadowed other considerations.

Philip Augustus See PHILIP II (FRANCE)

Philip Morris Cos. Inc. U.S. HOLDING COMPANY founded in 1985. Philip Morris & Co. was incorporated in New York in 1919. It became a principal maker of cigarettes in the 1930s and '40s, and the popularity of its Marlboro brand grew with its cowboy-themed advertising in the mid-1950s. Its other brands include Benson and Hedges, Virginia Slims, and Merit, and it is now the world's largest tobacco company. By acquiring the Miller Brewing Co. (1969), General Foods (1985), and Kraft Foods (1988), it reduced its dependence on tobacco. In 1998 it agreed to participate with other cigarette manufacturers in paying $206 billion to U.S. states in legal settlements for smoking-related health-care costs. In 2000 it purchased Nabisco.

Philip of Macedonia See PHILIP II

Philipon \fē-lē-ˈpōⁿ\, **Charles** (1802–1862) French caricaturist, lithographer, and journalist. An excellent draftsman with a fertile sense of satire, he published a series of journals of political satire. *La Caricature*, introduced in 1830, was suppressed in 1835; *Le Charivari*, introduced in 1832, became the inspiration for *Punch*, subtitled *The London Charivari*. His best-known drawing shows the transformation of LOUIS-PHILIPPE into a pear. He attracted and inspired the best caricaturists in France, including Honoré DAUMIER and Gustave DORÉ.

Philippe Égalité See duc d'ORLÉANS

Philippi \ˈfi-lə-ˌpī\ Ruined hill town, N central Macedonia, Greece. About 357 B.C. it was fortified by King PHILIP II to control nearby gold mines. In 42 B.C. it was the scene of the decisive Roman battle in which Mark ANTONY and Octavian (later Caesar AUGUSTUS) defeated BRUTUS and CASSIUS, assassins of Julius CAESAR. Many 5th–6th-cent. Christian ruins are spread over the site. St. PAUL preached to Christian converts there.

Philippine–American War *or* **Philippine Insurrection** (1899–1902) War between the U.S. and Filipino revolutionaries, a continuation of the PHILIPPINE REVOLUTION against Spanish rule. The Treaty of Paris (1898) transferred Philippine sovereignty from Spain to the U.S. but was not recognized by Filipino leaders, whose troops continued to wage guerrilla warfare. By 1902 U.S. troops had defeated the insurgency, though sporadic fighting continued until 1906.

Philippine Revolution (1896–98) Filipino independence struggle that failed to end Spanish colonial rule in the Philippines. The late-19th-cent. writings of José RIZAL and others helped stimulate a broad-based movement for Philippine independence. Spain was unwilling to reform its colonial government, and armed rebellion broke out in 1896. Rizal, who had advocated peaceful reform, was shot for

sedition; his martyrdom fueled the revolution. The rebel forces of Emilio AGUINALDO were unable to defeat the Spanish, but in the wake of Spain's defeat in the SPANISH–AMERICAN WAR (1898) the Filipinos proclaimed their independence. The Treaty of Paris ceded the Philippines to the U.S., however, and Aguinaldo was obliged to continue the revolutionary struggle, now against the U.S. (see PHILIPPINE–AMERICAN WAR).

Philippines *officially* **Republic of the Philippines** Nation, an archipelago off the SE coast of Asia. Area: 115,651 sq mi (299,536 sq km). Population (2000): 76,320,000. Capital: MANILA; QUEZON CITY is the designated center of national

PHILIPPINES

Scale 1: 26,283,000

©1999, Encyclopædia Britannica, Inc.

government. Filipinos are predominantly of Malay descent, frequently admixed with Chinese and sometimes with American or Spanish groups. Languages: Pilipino and English (both official); the other main groups are Cebuano, Ilocano, Hiligaynon, and Bicol. Religions: Roman Catholicism, Islam, Protestantism. Currency: Philippine peso. The Philippines consist of about 7,100 islands and islets. The two principal islands are LUZON in the north and MINDANAO in the south. The VISAYAN group is in the central Philippines, MINDORO is directly south of Luzon, and Palawan is isolated in the west. The topography of the archipelago is varied, with inactive volcanoes and mountain ranges the main features of most of the larger islands. The country has a predominantly market economy based largely on agriculture, light industries, and services. It is a republic with two legislative houses; its chief of state and head of government is the president. Discovered by Ferdinand MAGELLAN in 1521, the islands were colonized by the Spanish, who retained control until the Philippines were ceded to the U.S. in 1898 following the SPANISH–AMERICAN WAR. The Commonwealth of the Philippines was established in 1935 to prepare the country for political and economic independence, which was delayed by World War II and the Japanese invasion. The islands were liberated by U.S. forces 1944–45, and the Republic of the Philippines was proclaimed in 1946, with a government patterned on that of the U.S. In 1965 Ferdinand MARCOS was elected president. He declared martial law in 1972, and it lasted until 1981. After 20 years of dictatorial rule, he was driven from power in 1986. Corazon AQUINO became president and instituted a period of democratic rule that continued with the subsequent elections. The government has tried to come to terms with independence fighters in the S islands.

Philips Electronics NV *Dutch* Philips' Gloeilampenfabrieken, NV. Dutch manufacturer of consumer electronics, house-

hold appliances, and lighting equipment. It was founded by Gerard Philips (1858–1942) in 1891 to make incandescent lamps. Its strong research efforts were consolidated in 1914 in a separate organization that became the Philips Research Laboratories. It began manufacturing radios in the 1920s, and after World War II it marketed stereo equipment, televisions, and other products under such brand names as Philips, Magnavox, and Norelco. Philips helped create the cassette tape, the compact disc, and the videocassette recorder.

Philip the Bold See PHILIP II (FRANCE)

Philip the Fair See PHILIP IV (FRANCE)

Philip the Good See PHILIP III (BURGUNDY)

Philistines People of Aegean origin who settled on the S coast of PALESTINE around the 12th cent. B.C., about the time of the Israelites' arrival. They first fought the Israelites in the 11th cent. B.C. In the 10th cent. they were defeated by the Israelite king DAVID; the Bible recounts his slaying of their champion, the giant Goliath. They were later ruled by Assyria, Egypt, Babylonia, Persia, Greece, and Rome. They left no written records.

Phillips, Irna (1901–1973) U.S. radio producer and director. Born in Chicago, she worked as a teacher before creating the first radio SOAP OPERA, *Painted Dreams* (1930). Later known as "Queen of the Soaps," she introduced such techniques as the organ transition and the cliff-hanger ending to each episode. Her daytime radio serials included *Today's Children* (1933–38, 1943–50); *The Guiding Light* (1937–56; television, 1952–); *Road of Life* (1937–59); and *Women in White* (1938–42, 1944–48). She also created the television serials *As the World Turns* (1956) and *Another World* (1964).

philodendron \ˌfi-lə-ˈden-drən\ Any of about 200 species of climbing herbaceous plants that make up the genus *Philodendron* in the ARUM FAMILY, native to the New World tropics. Some are popular indoor foliage plants in colder areas and landscape plants in warmer climates. The common heart-leaf (*Philodendron scandens oxycardium*) is the familiar houseplant. Large varieties include the spade-leaf philodendron (*P. domesticum* or *P. hastatum*), with triangular leaves up to 2 ft (60 cm) long, and the selloum philodendron (*P. selloum*), with deeply cut leaves up to 3 ft (1 m) long.

Philo Judaeus \ˈfī-lō-jü-ˈdē-əs\ *or* **Philo of Alexandria** (15/10 B.C.–A.D. 45/50) Greek-speaking Jewish philosopher. From Alexandria, Egypt, he led a delegation to CALIGULA about A.D. 40 to ask that Jews not be forced to worship the emperor. His philosophy was influenced by PLATO, ARISTOTLE, the Neo-Pythagoreans, the CYNICS, and STOICISM. Philo was original in insisting on an individual Providence able to suspend the laws of nature, in contrast to the prevailing Greek view of a universal Providence who is himself subject to the laws of nature. The first philosopher to seek to synthesize revealed faith and philosophic reason, he is regarded as the most important representative of Hellenistic Judaism and a forerunner of Christian theology.

philosophe \ˌfē-lə-ˈzȯf\ Any of the literary men, scientists, and thinkers of 18th-cent. France who were united, in spite of divergent personal views, in their conviction of the supremacy and efficacy of human reason, and dedicated to the advancement of science and secular thought and to the open-mindedness of the ENLIGHTENMENT. They included VOLTAIRE, MONTESQUIEU, Denis DIDEROT, J. Le R. d'ALEMBERT, and J.-J. ROUSSEAU. The philosophes compiled the *ENCYCLOPÉDIE,* one of the great intellectual achievements of the century.

philosophy Critical examination of the grounds for fundamental beliefs and analysis of the basic concepts employed in the expression of such beliefs. Philosophy may also be defined as reflection on the varieties of human experience, or as the rational, methodical, and systematic consideration of the topics that are of greatest concern to mankind. Philosophers have frequently come to the discipline from different fields and have preferred to reflect on different areas of experience. The world's great religions have all produced allied philosophical schools. Such Western philosophers as THOMAS AQUINAS, George BERKELEY, and Søren KIERKEGAARD saw philosophy as a means to defend religion and dispel the antireligious errors of MATERIALISM and

RATIONALISM. PYTHAGORAS, René DESCARTES, and Bertrand RUSSELL, among others, were primarily mathematicians whose views of reality and knowledge were influenced by mathematics. Such figures as PLATO, Thomas HOBBES, and John Stuart MILL were primarily concerned with POLITICAL PHILOSOPHY. The PRE-SOCRATICS, Francis BACON, and Alfred North WHITEHEAD, among many others, started from an interest in the physical composition of the natural world. Other philosophical fields include AESTHETICS, EPISTEMOLOGY, ETHICS, LOGIC, and METAPHYSICS.

phlebitis \fli-'bī-təs\ INFLAMMATION of the wall of a VEIN. Causes include nearby infection, trauma, surgery, and childbirth. The area over the vein is painful, swollen, red, and hot. It usually occurs in surface veins in the lower leg and can be treated with pain relievers, bed rest, and later mild exercise. Phlebitis can last for years; in such cases, irritation of the vein's inner lining leads to blood-clot formation, (thrombophlebitis; see THROMBOSIS). In deeper veins, this requires anticoagulants to prevent EMBOLISMS.

phlox Any of about 65 species of mostly herbaceous plants (genus *Phlox*), belonging to the family Polemoniaceae. All species but one are native to N. America. Phlox has oval or linear leaves and heads of massed tubular flowers with five flaring lobes. Sizes range from the 5-ft-high (1.5-m) summer phlox (*P. paniculata*) to the 18-in.-high (45-cm) woodland PERENNIAL blue phlox (*P. divaricata*) to the 5-in.-high (13-cm) creeping phlox (*P. subulata*).

Phnom Penh \pə-'nòm-'pen\ City (pop., 1994 est.: 920,000), capital of Cambodia, at the junction of the TONLE SAP and MEKONG RIVER. Founded in 1434 as the capital of the KHMER nation, it became a cultural center, with many institutions of higher learning. When the KHMER ROUGE came to power in Cambodia in 1975, they forced the city's population into the countryside to work in the fields and virtually exterminated the educated class. It was repopulated beginning in 1979, and the city's institutions began a difficult period of recovery. It is a major port of the Mekong River valley, linked to the S. CHINA SEA via Vietnam by a channel of the Mekong delta.

phobia Extreme and irrational fear of a particular object, class of objects, or situation. Phobias are classified as forms of ANXIETY disorder (a NEUROSIS). They are generally believed to result when fear produced by an original threatening situation (such as a near-drowning in childhood) is transferred to other similar situations (such as encounters with bodies of water), the original fear often being repressed or forgotten. BEHAVIOR THERAPY is often successful in overcoming phobias.

Phocaea \fō-'sē-ə\ Ancient city, on the Aegean Sea, northernmost of the IONIAN cities on the W coast of ASIA MINOR. An important maritime state around 1000–550 B.C., it founded a number of colonies, including Massilia (MARSEILLE), but declined after the Persian conquest about 545 B.C. The modern town of Foça attracts tourists to the ancient ruins.

Phocis \'fō-sis\ Ancient territory, central Greece. It extended north from the Gulf of Corinth over the range of Mt. PARNASSUS to the Locrian Mtns. Traditionally, the Phocians controlled the sanctuary and oracle at DELPHI, but they lost control after a war with neighboring Greek states about 590 B.C. Phocis was allied with SPARTA in the PELOPONNESIAN WAR and was conquered by PHILIP II in 346 B.C.

phoebe \'fē-bē\ Any of three species (family Tyrannidae, suborder Tyranni) of suboscine PASSERINES with a habit of twitching the tail when perching. The eastern phoebe (*Sayornis phoebe*) of N. America is 7 in. (18 cm) long and brownish gray. Its call is a brisk "fee-bee" uttered over and over. It makes a mossy nest on a ledge, often under a bridge. Say's phoebe (*S. saya*), a slightly larger bird, occurs in open country in W N. America. The black phoebe (*S. nigricans*) occurs from the SW U.S. to Argentina.

Phoenicia \fi-'nē-shə\ Ancient country, corresponding to modern Lebanon and parts of Syria and Israel. Its chief cities were Sidon and TYRE. The PHOENICIANS were notable merchants and traders in the 1st millennium B.C. The country was conquered successively by the Assyrians, Babylonians, Persians, and ALEXANDER THE GREAT. In 64 B.C. it was incorporated into the Roman province of Syria.

Phoenicians \fi-'nē-shənz\ People of ancient PHOENICIA. They were merchants, traders, and colonizers who probably arrived from the Persian Gulf around 3000 B.C. By the 2nd millennium B.C. they had colonies in the Levant, North Africa, Anatolia, and Cyprus. Ivory and wood carving became their specialties, and their goldsmiths' and metalsmiths' work was well known. Their alphabet became the basis of the Greek alphabet.

Phoenix \'fē-niks\ City (pop., 2000: 1,321,000), capital of Arizona. The area was occupied as early as A.D. 1300 by prehistoric Indians, now known as the HOHOKAM CULTURE. Modern Phoenix was founded in 1870. It became the territorial capital in 1889 and state capital in 1912. Expansion followed World War II, with the population quadrupling between 1950 and 1960. It occupies a semi-arid valley surrounded by mountains and irrigated fields; its economy is based on farming, manufacturing, mining, and tourism.

phoenix In ancient Egypt and in classical antiquity, a fabulous bird associated with the worship of the sun. The Egyptian phoenix was said to be as large as an eagle, with brilliant scarlet and gold plumage and a melodious cry. Only one phoenix existed at a time, and it lived no less than 500 years. As its end approached, it built a nest of aromatic boughs and spices, set it on fire, and was consumed in the flames. From the pyre was born a new phoenix. The phoenix thus symbolized immortality.

phoneme Smallest unit of speech distinguishing one word (or word element) from another (e.g., the sound *p* in *tap*, which differentiates that word from *tab* and *tag*). A phoneme may have variants, called allophones, that differ phonetically without affecting meaning. Phonemes may be recorded with special symbols, such as those of the INTERNATIONAL PHONETIC ALPHABET. In transcription, linguists conventionally place symbols for phonemes between slash marks: /p/.

phonetics Study of SPEECH sounds. It deals with the way they are made (articulatory phonetics), their acoustic properties (acoustic phonetics), and how they combine to make syllables, words, and sentences (linguistic phonetics). The first phoneticians were Indian scholars (c.300 B.C.) who tried to preserve the pronunciation of Sanskrit holy texts. The classical Greeks based a WRITING system on a phonetic alphabet. Modern phonetics began with Alexander Melville Bell (1819–1905), who introduced a system of notation for speech sounds. In the 20th cent., linguists have focused on comparison of all human speech sounds and how speech is perceived.

phonics \'fä-niks\ Method of reading instruction that breaks language down into its simplest components. Children learn the sounds of individual letters first, then the sounds of letters in combination and in simple words. Simple reading exercises with a controlled vocabulary reinforce the process. Phonics-based instruction has declined in favor of "whole-language" instruction, in which children are introduced to whole words at a time, are given real literature rather than reading exercises, and are permitted to spell creatively. A backlash against whole-language teaching has made reading instruction a battlefield.

phonograph *or* **record player** Instrument for reproducing SOUNDS. A phonograph record stores a copy of sound waves as a series of undulations in a wavy groove inscribed on its rotating surface by the recording stylus. When the record is played back, another stylus (needle) responds to the undulations, and its motions are then reconverted into sound. Its invention is generally credited to Thomas EDISON (1877). Stereophonic systems, with two separate channels of information in a single groove, became a commercial reality in 1958. All modern phonograph systems had certain components in common: a turntable that rotated the record; a stylus that tracked a groove in the record; a pickup that converted the movements of the stylus into electrical impulses; an amplifier that intensified these impulses; and a LOUDSPEAKER that converted the amplified signals back into sound. Phonographs and records were the chief means of reproducing recorded sound at home until the 1980s.

phonology \fə-'nä-lə-jē\ Study of sound patterns within languages. Diachronic (historical) phonology traces and ana-

P

lyzes changes in speech sounds and sound systems over time. Synchronic (descriptive) phonology investigates sound patterns at a single stage in a language's development, to identify which ones can occur (in English, for example, *nt* and *rk* appear within or at the end of words but not at the beginning).

phosphate Any of numerous chemical compounds related to phosphoric acid (H_3PO_4). Phosphate SALTS are inorganic compounds containing phosphate IONS. Phosphate ESTERS are organic compounds in which the hydrogens of phosphoric acid are replaced by organic groups (e.g., methyl, ethyl, phenyl). NUCLEIC ACIDS and ATP contain phosphate; bones and teeth contain calcium phosphate. Phosphate rock (mainly calcium phosphate) is one of the four most important basic chemical commodities. Phosphates were formerly used in DETERGENTS, which washed into rivers and lakes, causing EUTROPHICATION; such use is now generally outlawed or regulated. Phosphates are still used in fertilizers, baking powder, and toothpaste.

phospholipid \ˌfäs-fō-ˈli-pəd\ *or* **phosphatide** Any member of a large class of fat-like organic compounds containing PHOSPHATE, as well as carbon, hydrogen, oxygen, and perhaps nitrogen. One end of each molecule is soluble in water and water solutions (including CYTOPLASM), the other end in FATS. They naturally combine to form a two-layer structure (LIPID bilayer) with the fat-soluble ends sandwiched in the middle and the water-soluble ends sticking out. Such lipid bilayers are the structural basis of cell MEMBRANES. Phospholipids are the principal components of the myelin sheaths of NEURONS. See also LECITHIN.

phosphorescence Emission of light from a substance exposed to RADIATION and persisting as an afterglow after the exciting radiation has been removed. Unlike FLUORESCENCE, in phosphorescence the extra energy absorbed is stored in metastable states and reemitted later. Phosphorescence may last from about 10^{-3} second to days or even years. See also LUMINESCENCE.

phosphorus Nonmetallic chemical ELEMENT, chemical symbol P, atomic number 15. The ordinary form, "white phosphorus," is a poisonous, semitransparent, waxy solid that glows in the dark (see PHOSPHORESCENCE) and combusts spontaneously in air, producing dense white fumes of the OXIDE; it is used as a rodenticide and a military smokescreen. Heat or sunlight converts it to "red phosphorus," a violet-red powder that does not phosphoresce or combust. Much less reactive and soluble than white phosphorus, it is used to make other phosphorus compounds and in semiconductors, fertilizers, and safety matches. "Black phosphorus," made by heating the white form under pressure, is flaky like GRAPHITE. Phosphorus seldom occurs uncombined in nature. As the PHOSPHATE ion, it is abundant in many minerals, including APATITE. Phosphorus has VALENCE 3 or 5 in compounds, which have many uses in industry. Phosphine (PH_3) is a chemical raw material and a doping agent for solid-state electronics components. Organic phosphorus compounds are used as plasticizers, gasoline additives, insecticides (e.g., parathion), and nerve gases.

Photius \ˈfō-shē-əs\, **St.** (c.820–891?) Patriarch of Constantinople (858–67, 877–86). A high-ranking civil servant, he was promoted swiftly through the ecclesiastical orders to become patriarch after the deposition of Ignatius, an action that offended Pope Nicholas I. Angry that Nicholas would not recognize him, Photius excommunicated the pope (867), thus beginning the Photian Schism. Photius was deposed the same year but restored in 877 after his successor died. He and Pope John VIII agreed to return Bulgaria to the Roman church but to allow Greek bishops to remain in the Byzantine church.

photocell *or* **photoelectric cell** *or* **electric eye** SOLID-STATE DEVICE with a photosensitive CATHODE that emits ELECTRONS when illuminated, and an ANODE for collecting the emitted electrons. In a photovoltaic cell, light is used to produce voltage. In a photoconductive cell, light is used to regulate the flow of current. Photocells are used in control systems, where interrupting a beam of light opens a circuit, supplying power to a mechanism to bring about a desired operation, such as opening a door or setting off a burglar alarm. Photocells are also used in PHOTOMETRY and SPECTROSCOPY.

photochemical reaction CHEMICAL REACTION initiated by absorption of ENERGY in the form of visible (LIGHT), ULTRAVIOLET, or INFRARED radiation. The most important example is PHOTOSYNTHESIS. Vision depends on photochemical reactions that occur in the eye (see RETINA). In photography, light activates silver nitrate to a state that is easy to reduce to metallic silver grains during development. Bleaching of laundry, tanning of skin, storage of energy in solar batteries, and many industrial reactions are photochemical. Certain air pollutants become more reactive and form noxious compounds in photochemical reactions.

photoelectric effect Phenomenon in which charged particles are released from a material when it absorbs radiant energy (e.g., the ejection of ELECTRONS from the surface of a metal plate when visible light falls on it). It can also occur with ULTRAVIOLET RADIATION, X RAYS, or GAMMA RAYS. The emitting surface may be a solid, liquid, or gas, and the emitted particles may be electrons or ions. The effect was discovered in 1887 by Heinrich HERTZ and explained by Albert EINSTEIN in work for which he received the Nobel Prize.

photography Method of recording permanent images by the action of light projected by a lens in a CAMERA onto a film or other light-sensitive material. It was developed in the 19th cent. through the artistic aspirations of the Frenchmen Nicéphore NIEPCE and L.-J.-M. DAGUERRE, who invented the first commercially successful process, the DAGUERREOTYPE (1837), and the Englishmen Thomas Wedgwood and Fox TALBOT, who patented the negative-positive calotype process that became the forerunner of modern photographic technique. Photography has had a profound impact on society. It was initially used for portraiture and landscapes. In the 1850s and '60s, Mathew BRADY pioneered war photography and photojournalism. Related processes include radiography, TELEVISION, and VIDEOTAPE.

photolysis \fō-ˈtä-lə-səs\ Breakdown of MOLECULES into smaller units via absorption of LIGHT. Flash photolysis, an experimental technique, studies chemical intermediates formed in many PHOTOCHEMICAL REACTIONS. An intense, brief flash of light splits molecules into short-lived fragments, which are analyzed by SPECTROPHOTOMETRY.

photometry \fō-ˈtä-mə-trē\ Precision measurement of the brightness, color, and spectrum of celestial objects to obtain data on their structure, temperature, and composition. About 130 B.C., HIPPARCHUS divided the stars into six MAGNITUDES, from brightest to faintest. On discovery of fainter stars with TELESCOPES, the scale was extended downward. Since the 1940s photographic and photoelectric equipment has vastly extended the sensitivity and wavelength range of astronomical photometry, which can now distinguish giant and dwarf stars, detect metals in stars, and determine surface gravity.

photon *or* **light quantum** Minute energy packet of ELECTROMAGNETIC RADIATION. In 1900 Max PLANCK found that heat radiation is emitted and absorbed in distinct units, which he called quanta (see QUANTUM). In 1905 Albert EINSTEIN explained the PHOTOELECTRIC EFFECT, proposing the existence of discrete energy packets in light. The energies of photons range from high-energy gamma rays and X rays to low-energy infrared and radio waves; all travel at the speed of light. Photons have no ELECTRIC CHARGE or rest mass and are the carriers of the electromagnetic field.

Photorealism Late-20th-cent. painting style based on photography, in which realistic scenes are rendered in meticulous detail. An offshoot of POP ART, it became a trend in U.S. painting in the 1970s. The Photorealists relied on the photograph itself, replicating it in large-scale detail as the reality on which to base an acrylic painting. Subjects often included reflecting surfaces (chrome-plated diners, motorcycles, glass-fronted buildings, etc.). Its awesome technical precision, brilliant color schemes, and visual complexity earned the style wide popularity. Its most notable practitioners were Don Eddy (*New Shoes for H*, 1974), Richard Estes (*Food Shop*, 1967), and Audrey Flack (*Queen*, 1976).

photoreception Biological responses to stimulation by light. In one-celled organisms such as the amoeba, the whole cell may be sensitive to light. Earthworms have photoreceptive cells scattered over their bodies. Most animals have localized photoreceptors of varying complexity. In humans, photoreception relies on the chemical response of a light-sensitive pigment in photoreceptor cells in the RETINA of the EYE. Stimulation of those cells results in a stimulus being conducted toward the NERVOUS SYSTEM. Humans, like other vertebrates, have two types of photosensitive cells: rod cells are responsible for vision when there is little light; cone cells mediate daylight vision and color. Photoreception also refers to PHOTOSYNTHESIS in plants. See also CHEMORECEPTION, SENSE.

Photo-Secession Group of U.S. photographers influenced by the ART NOUVEAU movement. Founded in 1902 by Alfred STIEGLITZ, it sought recognition of photography as an art to be judged on its own terms. Its name reflected that of the SEZESSION movement. Stieglitz did not believe in retouching or manipulating negatives or prints, but others of the group, such as Edward STEICHEN, were adherents of the impressionistic soft-focus school and the new techniques. The record of the Photo-Secession is contained in the quarterly *Camera Work* (1903–17).

photosphere Visible surface of the SUN, about 250 mi (400 km) thick. Temperatures are about 18,000°F (10,000°C) at the bottom and 8,000°F (4,000°C) at the top; its density is about 1/1,000 that of air at sea level. SUNSPOTS are photospheric phenomena. The photosphere consists of grains (cells), masses of hot gas several hundred miles across that rise from inside the sun, radiate energy, and sink back to be replaced by others.

photosynthesis Process by which green plants and certain other organisms transform light into chemical energy. In green plants, light energy is captured by CHLOROPHYLL in the CHLOROPLASTS of the leaves and used to convert water, carbon dioxide, and minerals into oxygen and energy-rich organic compounds (simple and complex sugars) that are the basis of both plant and animal life. Photosynthesis occurs in two stages. During the light-dependent stage (light reaction), chlorophyll absorbs light energy, which excites some electrons in the pigment molecules to higher energy levels; these leave the chlorophyll and pass along a series of molecules, generating NADPH (an enzyme) and high-energy ATP molecules. Oxygen, released as a by-product, passes into the atmosphere through pores in the leaves. NADPH and ATP drive the second stage, the dark reaction, which does not require light. During this stage glucose is

generated using atmospheric carbon dioxide. Photosynthesis is crucial for maintaining life on earth; if it ceased, there would soon be little food or other organic matter on the planet, and most organisms would disappear.

phototube See PHOTOCELL

photovoltaic effect Process in which two dissimilar materials in close contact act as an electric cell when struck by light or other radiant energy. In CRYSTALS of certain elements, the ELECTRONS are not free to move from atom to atom unless light striking the crystal provides the energy needed to free them. These electrons can cross the junction between two dissimilar crystals more easily in one direction, so one side of the junction acquires a negative voltage with respect to the other. While the light shines, the photovoltaic BATTERY can continue to provide voltage and current. See also SOLAR CELL.

Phrachomklao See MONGKUT

Phramongkutklao See VAJIRAVUDH

phrenology \fri-'nä-lə-jē\ Study of the shape of the SKULL as an indication of mental abilities and character traits. Franz Joseph GALL stated that each of the innate mental faculties is based in a specific brain region, whose size reflects the faculty's prominence in a person and is reflected by the skull's surface. He examined the skulls of persons with particular traits (including "criminal" traits) for a feature he could identify with it. His followers divided the scalp into areas they labeled with traits such as combativeness, cautiousness, and form perception. Phrenology has since been wholly discredited.

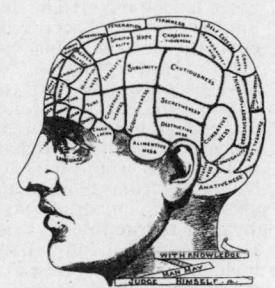

Phrenology Diagram of the skull, 1893

Phrygia \'fri-jē-ə\ Ancient country, W central ASIA MINOR. It was named after the Phryges, who dominated Asia Minor between the HITTITE collapse (12th cent. B.C.) and the ascent of LYDIA (7th cent. B.C.). Their capital was GORDIUM. The kingdom of their legendary king, MIDAS, ended about 700 B.C. with the invasion of the Cimmerians. The Phrygians excelled in metalwork, wood carving, carpet making, and embroidery. Their religious cult of the GREAT MOTHER

Photosynthesis The light reaction of photosynthesis. The light reaction occurs in two photosystems (units of chlorophyll molecules). Light energy (indicated by wavy arrows) absorbed by photosystem II causes the formation of high-energy electrons, which are transferred along a series of acceptor molecules in an electron transport chain to photosystem I. Photosystem II obtains replacement electrons from water molecules, resulting in their split into hydrogen ions (H+) and oxygen atoms. The oxygen atoms combine to form molecular oxygen (O_2), which is released into the atmosphere. The hydrogen ions are released into the lumen. Additional hydrogen ions are pumped into the lumen by electron acceptor molecules. This creates a high concentration of ions inside the lumen. The flow of hydrogen ions back across the photosynthetic membrane provides the energy needed to drive the synthesis of the energy-rich molecule ATP. High-energy electrons released as photosystem I absorbs light energy are used to drive the synthesis of NADPH. Photosystem I obtains replacement electrons from the electron transport chain. ATP provides the energy and NADPH provides the hydrogen atoms needed to drive the subsequent photosynthetic dark reaction, or Calvin cycle.

photosynthetic membrane (thylakoid membrane) $2H^+ + \frac{1}{2}O_2$

H_2O

H^+

lumen

photosystem II 2e⁻

2e⁻

photosystem I

electron carriers

$NADP^+ + 2H^+$

stroma

$NADPH + H^+$

ATP

ATP synthase

$ADP + P$

H^+

H^+

H^+

To Calvin cycle or dark reaction

P

OF THE GODS was passed on to the Greeks. After 1945, U.S. archaeologists discovered carved stone tombs and shrines there.

Phyfe \\'fīf\\, **Duncan** *orig.* Duncan Fife (1768–1854) Scottish-U.S. furniture designer. His family settled in Albany, N.Y., about 1784; there he eventually opened his own shop. In 1792 he moved to New York City, where he changed the spelling of his name and became so successful that he employed 100 carvers and cabinetmakers. One of the first Americans to use the factory method of manufacturing furniture successfully, he interpreted fashionable European styles with such grace that he became a major exponent of Neoclassicism. His furniture, decorated with typical period ornaments such as harps and acanthus leaves, was generally of high-quality mahogany.

phylogeny \\fī-'lä-jə-nē\\ History of the EVOLUTION of a species or group. The fundamental proposition is that plants or animals of different species descended from common ancestors. Modern TAXONOMY is based on phylogeny. Early taxonomic systems had no theoretical basis; organisms were grouped according to apparent similarity. Biologists who propose a phylogeny obtain evidence from the fields of PALEONTOLOGY, comparative ANATOMY, comparative EMBRYOLOGY, BIOCHEMISTRY, and MOLECULAR BIOLOGY. The data and conclusions of phylogeny indicate that today's living creatures are the product of a historical process of evolution and that degrees of resemblance within and between groups correspond to degrees of relationship by descent from common ancestors.

physiatry See PHYSICAL MEDICINE AND REHABILITATION

physical anthropology Branch of ANTHROPOLOGY concerned with the study of HUMAN EVOLUTION and human biological variation. Research on human evolution involves the discovery, analysis, and description of fossilized human remains. Two key goals are the identification of differences between humans and their human and nonhuman ancestors, and the clarification of the biological emergence of humankind. Research on biological variation among contemporary humans once relied heavily on the concept of RACE, but today principles of GENETICS and the analysis of such factors as BLOOD TYPING have largely eliminated race as a scientific category.

physical chemistry Branch of CHEMISTRY concerned with interactions and transformations of materials. Unlike other branches, it deals with the principles of physics underlying all chemical interactions (e.g., GAS LAWS), measuring, correlating, and explaining the quantitative aspects of reactions. QUANTUM MECHANICS has clarified much for physical chemistry by modeling the smallest particles, ATOMS and MOLECULES. Chemical THERMODYNAMICS deals with the relationship between heat and other forms of chemical energy, kinetics with CHEMICAL REACTION rates. Subdisciplines of physical chemistry include ELECTROCHEMISTRY, photochemistry, surface chemistry, and CATALYSIS.

physical medicine and rehabilitation *or* **physiatry** \\,fiz-ē-'a-trē\\ *or* **physical therapy** *or* **rehabilitation medicine** Medical specialty treating chronic disabilities through physical means to help patients return to a comfortable, productive life, despite a medical problem. Its objectives are pain relief, functional improvement or maintenance, training in essential activities, and functional testing of areas such as strength, mobility, breathing capacity, and coordination. Physical medicine may use DIATHERMY, HYDROTHERAPY, MASSAGE, exercise, and functional training. The last can mean learning to work with a guide dog or a PROSTHESIS or learning new ways to carry out everyday activities with a limb missing, sometimes by using assistive devices. See also OCCUPATIONAL THERAPY, ORTHOPEDIC SURGERY.

physics Science that deals with the structure of MATTER and the interactions between the fundamental constituents of the observable universe. Long called natural philosophy, physics covers the behavior of objects under the action of given FORCES and the nature and origin of gravitational, electromagnetic, and nuclear force fields. The goal of physics is to formulate comprehensive principles that bring together and explain all discernible phenomena. See also AERODYNAMICS, ASTROPHYSICS, ATOMIC PHYSICS, BIOPHYSICS, MECHANICS, PARTICLE PHYSICS, QUANTUM MECHANICS, SOLID-STATE PHYSICS.

physiocrat Member of a school of economics, founded in 18th-cent. France, that held that government should not interfere with the operation of natural economic laws and that land is the source of all wealth. Regarded as the first scientific school of economics, the physiocratic school (the name refers to the "rule of nature") was founded by François Quesnay (1694–1774), who demonstrated the economic relation between a workshop and a farm and asserted that the farm alone added to a nation's wealth. The physiocrats pictured an agricultural society in harmony with NATURAL LAW and attacked MERCANTILISM for its emphasis on manufacturing and foreign trade and its mass of regulations. Quesnay's disciples included Victor Riqueti (1715–1789) and Pierre Samuel du Pont de Nemours (1739–1817). In 1776 the leading physiocrats were exiled. Though many of their theories were later demolished, their introduction of SCIENTIFIC METHOD to economics had a permanent effect.

physiology \\,fi-zē-'ä-lə-jē\\ Study of the functioning of living organisms or their constituent tissues or cells. Physiology was usually considered separately from ANATOMY until the development of high-powered microscopes revealed that structure and function were inseparable at the cellular and molecular level. An understanding of BIOCHEMISTRY is fundamental. Physiological processes are dynamic; cells change their function in response to changes in their local environment, and the organism responds to both its internal and external environment. Many physiological reactions are aimed at preserving a constant physical and chemical internal environment (HOMEOSTASIS). See also CYTOLOGY.

phytoplankton \\,fī-tō-'plaŋk-tən\\ Flora of freely floating, often minute organisms that drift with water currents. Like land vegetation, phytoplankton uses carbon dioxide, releases oxygen, and converts minerals to a form animals can use. In fresh water, large numbers of green ALGAE often color lakes and ponds, and CYANOBACTERIA may affect the taste of drinking water. Oceanic phytoplankton is the primary food source, directly or indirectly, of all sea organisms (except in DEEP-SEA VENTS). See also DIATOM, DINOFLAGELLATE.

pi In mathematics, the RATIO of the circumference of a CIRCLE to its diameter. An IRRATIONAL NUMBER (see also TRANSCENDENTAL NUMBER), its approximate value is 3.14159265, but its exact value must be represented by a symbol, the Greek letter π. Pi is used in calculations involving lengths, areas, and volumes of circles, spheres, cylinders, and cones. It also arises in problems dealing with certain periodic phenomena (e.g., motion of pendulums, alternating electric currents).

Piaf, Edith \\'pyȧf *Engl* 'pē-,af\\ *orig.* Edith Giovanna Gassion (1915–1963) French popular singer. She was abandoned at birth by her mother, a café singer, and blinded for four years by meningitis. Her father, a circus acrobat, took her along on tours. She sang for years in the streets of Paris, living a raffish life, until discovered by a cabaret owner. She was soon singing her chansons in the large music halls During World War II she entertained French prisoners of war and aided several in their escapes. She spent the postwar years touring, when her intense perfor-

Edith Piaf, 1948

mances of such songs as "La vie en rose" and "Non, je ne regrette rien" made her the most highly paid performer in the world. Despite her success, her life was marred by illness, accidents, and unhappiness; she died at 47.

Piaget \\pyä-'zhä\\, **Jean** (1896–1980) Swiss psychologist. Trained in zoology and philosophy, Piaget later studied psychology with C. G. JUNG and Eugen Bleuler, and was affiliated with the Univ. of Geneva from 1929 until his death. His theory of "genetic epistemology" proposes a natural timetable for the development of a child's thinking, with four stages—the sensorimotor (ages 0–2), preoperational or symbolic (2–7), concrete operational (7–12), and formal operational (through adulthood)—based on increased cognitive sophistication and ability to use symbols. In 1955 Piaget founded a center for genetic epistemology in Geneva. His books include *The Language and Thought of the Child* (1923), *Judgment and Reasoning in the Child* (1924), and *The Origin of Intelligence in Children* (1948). He is regarded as the foremost developmental psychologist of the 20th cent.

piano *or* **pianoforte** Keyboard instrument with wire strings that sound when struck by hammers activated by the keys. It was invented by Bartolomeo Cristofori (1655–1731) before 1720, with the particular aim of permitting note-to-note dynamic variation (lacking in the HARPSICHORD). Unlike the older CLAVICHORD, it has hammers that are thrown at the strings and bounce back, permitting the struck string to vibrate loudly. A cast-iron frame is needed to withstand the strings' tremendous tension. Pianos have taken various shapes. The original harpsichord (or wing) shape has survived in the modern grand piano; the less-expensive square (actually rectangular) piano, standard in the early 19th cent., was replaced by the upright piano, in which the strings are vertical.

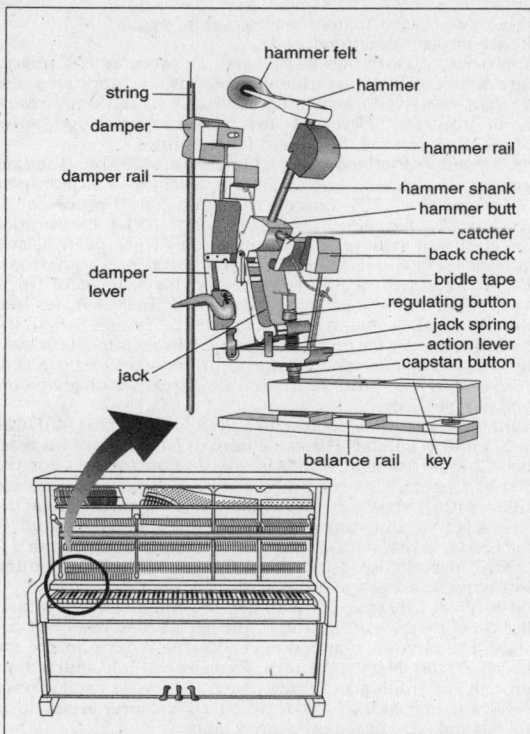

hammer felt
string
damper
hammer
hammer rail
damper rail
hammer shank
hammer butt
catcher
back check
bridle tape
regulating button
jack spring
action lever
capstan button
damper lever
jack
balance rail   key

Piano Each key of a piano actuates a complex mechanical system to strike a taut string and produce a musical tone. Depending on how the keys and pedals are operated, the mechanism may produce a variety of effects on the same note, from muffled to brilliant and from quick to sustained.

Piazzetta \pyät-'tsät-tä\, **Giovanni Battista** (1682–1754) Italian painter and illustrator. Trained as a wood carver by his father, he turned to painting. His art evolved from Italian baroque traditions of the 17th cent. to the Rococo style. He had a strong influence on the young G. B. TIEPOLO about the time he painted the finest of his early religious works, *St. James Led to Martyrdom* (1722). His most popular work is the celebrated *Fortune Teller* (1740). On the founding of

the Venetian Academy in 1750, he was made its first director.

Picabia \pē-kàb-'yà\, **Francis** (1879–1953) French painter and writer. The son of a Cuban diplomat and a Frenchwoman, he was successively involved in Impressionism, Neo-Impressionism, Fauvism, Cubism, and Surrealism. In New York in 1915, he joined Marcel DUCHAMP and Man RAY in founding the U.S. DADA movement. Back in Europe in the 1920s, he plunged into the Surrealist style, then produced abstract and figurative paintings. Notable for his inventiveness as well as his disconcerting changes of style, he founded an avant-garde magazine (1917–24) and published a variety of pamphlets.

Picardy \'pi-kər-dē\ *French* **Picardie** \ˌpē-kàr-'dē\ Historical region, N France. Before 1790 it was bounded by the Strait of Dover, Artois, and Flanders, and by Champagne, Normandy, and the ENGLISH CHANNEL. In the 13th cent. the area included the countships of Amiénois and Vermandois. It was joined to BURGUNDY in 1435 and became a province of France in 1482. It saw heavy fighting in both World Wars, especially in the Battle of the SOMME (1916).

picaresque novel Early form of the NOVEL, usually a first-person narrative, relating the episodic adventures of a rogue or lowborn adventurer (Spanish, *pícaro*) who drifts from place to place and from one social milieu to another in an effort to survive. The genre originated in Spain; it appeared in various European literatures until the mid-18th cent., when the growth of the realistic novel led to its decline. Because of the opportunities for satire they present, picaresque elements enriched many later novels, such as Nikolay GOGOL's *Dead Souls* (1842) and Mark TWAIN's *Huckleberry Finn* (1884).

Picasso, Pablo (Ruiz y) (1881–1973) Spanish-French painter, sculptor, printmaker, and ceramicist. Trained by his father, a professor of drawing, he exhibited his first works at 13. After moving permanently to Paris in 1904, he replaced the predominantly blue tones of his so-called Blue Period (1901–4) with those of pottery and flesh in his Rose Period (1904–6). His first masterpiece, *Les demoiselles d'Avignon* (1907), was controversial for its violent treatment of the female body and the masklike faces derived from his study of African art. In 1908, he and his friend Georges BRAQUE began experimenting with CUBISM, depicting multiple views of an object on the same canvas. Between 1917 and 1924 Picasso designed stage sets for five ballets for the Ballets Russes. In the 1920s and '30s, the Surrealists spurred him to explore new subject matter, particularly the image of the Minotaur. The SPANISH CIVIL WAR inspired perhaps his greatest work, the enormous *Guernica* (1937), whose violent imagery condemned the useless destruction of life. After World War II he joined the Communist Party and devoted his time to sculpture, ceramics, and lithography as well as painting. In his late years he created variations on the works of earlier artists, including 58 pictures based on *Las Meninas* of Diego VELÁZQUEZ. An innovator throughout his 80-year career, Picasso made his influence felt by virtually every 20th-cent. artist.

Piccard \pē-'kär\, **Auguste** (1884–1962) Swiss-Belgian physicist. He taught physics at the Univ. of Brussels (1922–54). In 1930 he designed a balloon with an airtight, pressurized cabin to ascend into the stratosphere to study cosmic rays; in 1932 he ascended over 55,500 ft (16,650 m). The undersea BATHYSCAPHE he designed with his son, Jacques (b.1922), descended in 1953 more than 10,000 ft (3,000 m). His grandson Bernard Piccard (b.1958) made the first round-the-world balloon flight in 1999.

pickerel Any of several N. American PIKES (family Esocidae), distinguished from the northern pike and muskellunge by their smaller size, completely scaled cheeks and gill covers, and banded or chainlike markings. The chain pickerel *(Esox niger)* grows to about 2 ft (0.6 m) and a weight of about 3 lbs (1.4 kg).

Pickering, Timothy (1745–1829) American politician. Born in Salem, Mass., he served in the American Revolution under George WASHINGTON, becoming adjutant general (1777–78) and quartermaster general (1780–85). He later served as U.S. postmaster general (1791–95), secretary of war (1795), and secretary of state (1795–1800). A leader of the FEDER-

P

ALIST PARTY, he served in the U.S. Senate (1803–11) and House of Representatives (1813–17) and opposed the War of 1812.

picketing Posting of employees in front of or near a workplace to call attention to their grievances, discourage patronage, and, during STRIKES, to deter strikebreakers. Picketing is also used in non-work-related protests. The U.S. Norris-LaGuardia Act (1932) facilitated picketing, but the TAFT-HARTLEY ACT (1947) outlawed mass picketing.

Pickett, George E(dward) (1825–1875) U.S. and Confederate army officer. Born in Richmond, Va., he graduated from West Point. He resigned his commission in 1861 to enter the Confederate army and rose to major general. At the Battle of GETTYSBURG, he led the climactic attack known as Pickett's Charge, in which 4,300 men of his division constituted almost half the attacking force under James LONGSTREET. The attempt to breach the Union lines on Cemetery Ridge was repulsed with the loss of about 60% of his men.

Pickford, Mary *orig.* Gladys Mary Smith (1893–1979) U.S. film actress. Born in Toronto, she began acting at age 5. After starring in D. W. GRIFFITH's *The Lonely Villa* (1909), she became one of the first movie stars, known as "America's sweetheart." Her silent films included *Tess of the Storm Country* (1914), *Rebecca of Sunnybrook Farm* (1917), *Poor Little Rich Girl* (1917), and *Pollyanna* (1920). A shrewd businesswoman, she formed UNITED ARTISTS CORP. (1919) with her husband Douglas FAIRBANKS and others. She received an Academy Award for her first sound film, *Coquette* (1929). She retired from acting in 1933 and received a special Academy Award in 1975.

Pico della Mirandola \ˈpē-kō-ˌdäl-lä-mē-ˈrän-dō-ˌlä\, **Giovanni, conte (count) di Concordia** (1463–1494) Italian scholar, philosopher, and humanist. A protégé of Lorenzo de' MEDICI and Marsilio FICINO, in 1486 he posted in Rome a list of 900 theses on logic, mathematics, physics, and other subjects that he proposed to defend against any opponent; the accompanying *Oration on the Dignity of Man* (1486) epitomizes Renaissance HUMANISM. Accused of heresy by the pope, he was cleared, and he was later reconverted to orthodoxy by Girolamo SAVONAROLA. Pico was the first to use Kabbalistic doctrine (see KABBALA) in support of Christian theology. His *Heptaplus* is a seven-point exposition of Genesis; *Of Being and Unity* is part of a synoptic treatment of PLATO and ARISTOTLE. He died at 31.

picornavirus \pē-ˌkȯr-nə-ˈvī-rəs\ Any of a group of the smallest known animal VIRUSES. (*Pico* refers to their small size, *rna* to their core of RNA.) This group of spheroidal viruses includes polioviruses, RHINOVIRUSES, and the virus agent of FOOT-AND-MOUTH DISEASE.

Picts \ˈpikts\ Ancient people of what is now E and NE Scotland. The name (from Latin *picti*, "painted") referred to their body painting or tattooing. They were probably descended from pre-Celtic aborigines. They attacked HADRIAN'S WALL in A.D. 297 and warred constantly with the Romans. They united their two kingdoms by the 7th cent. and converted to Christianity, and in 843 KENNETH I, king of the Scots, included them in the kingdom of Alba, later Scotland.

pidgin \ˈpi-jən\ Language with a very limited vocabulary and a simplified grammar. Pidgins usually arise to permit communication between groups with no language in common; if a pidgin becomes established as the native language of a group, it is known as a CREOLE. Pidgins such as Chinese Pidgin English and Melanesian Pidgin English arose through contact between English-speaking traders and inhabitants of the Far East and the Pacific islands. Most of the small vocabulary of a pidgin language (Melanesian Pidgin has only 2,000 words, Chinese Pidgin English only 700) is usually drawn from a single language.

Piedmont \ˈpēd-ˌmänt\ *Italian* **Piemonte** \pyä-ˈmȯn-tā\ Autonomous region (pop., 1996 est.: 4,289,000), NW Italy. With its capital at TURIN, it borders on France and Switzerland. In the Middle Ages, the House of SAVOY was the region's most important power. It was a center during the 19th-cent. RISORGIMENTO to unite Italy. VICTOR EMMANUEL II, originally king of Piedmont and Sardinia, became modern Italy's first king in 1861. It is centered on the

fertile PO RIVER valley, producing wheat, rice, and wines. Its hydroelectric plants supply energy for much of N Italy.

Piedmont Geographic region, E U.S. Lying between the APPALACHIAN MTNS. and the Atlantic coastal plain, it is a rolling plateau about 600 mi (950 km) long, and stretches between the Hudson River and central Alabama. It is a fertile agricultural region.

Pierce, Franklin (1804–1869) 14th president of the U.S. (1853–57). Born in Hillsboro, N.H., he served in the U.S. House of Representatives (1833–37) and Senate (1837–42). At the deadlocked Democratic convention of 1852, he was nominated as the compromise candidate; though little known, he unexpectedly trounced Winfield SCOTT in the general election. For the sake of harmony and business prosperity, he was inclined to oppose antislavery agitation so as to placate Southern opinion. He promoted U.S. territorial expansion, encouraged plans for a transcontinental railroad, and

Franklin Pierce

approved the GADSDEN PURCHASE. To promote NW migration and conciliate sectional demands, he approved the KANSAS-NEBRASKA ACT but was unable to settle the resultant problems. Defeated for renomination by James BUCHANAN in 1856, he retired from politics.

Piero della Francesca \fran-ˈches-kə\ (c.1420–1492) Italian painter. He became known for his disciplined exploration of perspective. His fresco cycle for San Francesco at Arezzo, *The Legend of the True Cross* (1450s), exemplifies his clarity of structure, controlled use of perspective, and aura of serenity. His famous diptych portrait of his patrons, Count Federico da Montefeltro and his wife (c.1470), is known for its unidealized depiction of their features and the use of landscape in the background. Though he had little influence on his contemporaries, Piero's important contributions to Renaissance painting are now well recognized. Also a writer, he produced theoretical treatises on geometry and perspective.

Piero di Cosimo \kȯ-ˈsē-mō\ *orig.* Piero di Lorenzo (1461/62–1521) Italian painter. His name derives from that of his master, Cosimo Rosselli, whom he assisted on frescoes for the Sistine Chapel. Many of his later mythological paintings are filled with fantastic hybrid human-animal forms engaging in revels (*The Discovery of Honey,* c.1500) or fights (*Battle of the Centaurs and the Lapiths,* c.1500). His art reflects his eccentric personality. He belonged to no school of painting but borrowed from many artists.

Pierre \ˈpir\ City (pop., 2000: 14,000), capital of S. Dakota. It lies on the MISSOURI RIVER, in the geographic center of the state. The city was founded in 1880 as the W terminus of the Chicago and North Western Railway, which spurred its growth as a mining and trade center. The state capital since 1889, it is the hub of a diversified agricultural area with a tourist industry based on nearby lakes.

Pietism \ˈpī-ə-ˌti-zəm\ Reform movement in German LUTHERANISM that arose in the 17th cent. Philipp Jakob Spener (1635–1705), a Lutheran pastor, originated the movement when he organized an "assembly of piety," a regular meeting of Christians for devotional reading and spiritual exchange. Spener advocated greater involvement of the laity in worship, more extensive study of Scripture, and ministerial training that emphasized piety and learning rather than disputation. Pietism influenced the MORAVIAN and Methodist churches (see METHODISM).

Pietro da Cortona *orig.* Pietro Berrettini (1596–1669) Italian painter and architect. The son of a stonemason of Cortona, Tuscany, he was apprenticed to a painter in Florence. His first major work was a series of frescoes in the small church of Santa Bibiana in Rome (1624–26). The rich exuberance of those frescoes was a prelude to his best-known work, the large ceiling fresco *Allegory of Divine Providence and Bar-*

berini Power (1632–39) in the Barberini Palace. Here he demonstrated his mastery of illusion, for the center of the vault appears open to the sky and the figures seem to hover in space. He provided a series of frescoes for the Pitti Palace in Florence. Also a master architect, he designed the church of Sts. Martina e Luca in Rome (1634), the first baroque church built as a unitary whole.

piezoelectricity \pē-ˌā-zō-ə-ˌlek-ˈtri-sə-tē\ Appearance of an ELECTRIC FIELD in certain nonconducting CRYSTALS as a result of the application of mechanical PRESSURE. The converse effect also occurs: an applied electric field produces mechanical deformation in the crystal. Using this effect, a high-frequency ALTERNATING CURRENT can be converted to an ultrasonic wave of the same frequency, or a mechanical vibration, such as sound, can be converted into a corresponding electrical signal. Piezoelectricity is used in microphones, phonograph pickups, and telephone communications systems.

pig Any wild or domestic even-toed UNGULATE (family Suidae) that is a stout-bodied, short-legged omnivore, with thick, sparsely bristled skin, a long mobile snout, and small tail. Pigs are native to European, Asian, and N. African forests. Wild pigs use their tusklike teeth to forage and for defense. Domestic pigs were developed from wild pigs in Europe about 1500 B.C. Pigs are regarded as highly intelligent. Domestic pigs are classified as lard (thick fat, carcass weighing at least 220 lbs, or 100 kg), bacon (carcass about 150 lbs, or 70 kg), and PORK (carcass about 100 lbs, or 45 kg) pigs, depending on the principal product derived from them; they are also a source of leather.

Pigalle \pē-ˈgál\, **Jean-Baptiste** (1714–1785) French sculptor. He trained as a sculptor in Paris and then studied in Rome (1736–40). His famous *Mercury Fastening His Sandals* won him admission to the Royal Academy (1744). The statue became so popular that LOUIS XV commissioned a life-size marble version to present to FREDERICK II of Prussia. He was also noted for his portrait sculptures. His *Nude Voltaire* (1776), an anatomically realistic rendering of the aged philosopher, caused a furor when it was first shown.

pigeon Any species (family Columbidae) of plump, small-billed birds recognizable by their head-bobbing strut. Unlike other birds, pigeons suck liquids and provide the young with regurgitated "pigeon's milk." The 175 species of true pigeons include the Old and New World *Columba* species and the Old World *Streptopelia* species. Common street pigeons are descendants of the Eurasian rock dove *(Columba livia)*. From antiquity pigeons were trained to carry messages over long distances. About 115 species of fruit pigeons occur in Africa, S Asia, Australia, and Pacific islands. The three species of crowned pigeons (genus *Goura*), of New Guinea, are nearly the size of a turkey. See also DOVE, PASSENGER PIGEON.

pigment Any intensely colored compound used to color other materials. Unlike DYES, pigments do not dissolve; they are applied as fine solid particles mixed with a liquid. In general, the same ones are used in oil- and water-based PAINTS, printing INKS, and plastics. They may be inorganic or organic compounds. Natural organic pigments have been used for centuries, but today most are synthetic or inorganic. The primary white pigment is titanium dioxide. Carbon black is the most usual black pigment. Iron oxides give browns, from yellowish through orange to dark brown. Chromium compounds yield chrome yellows, oranges, and greens, cadmium compounds brilliant yellows, oranges, and reds. The most common blues, Prussian blue and ultramarine, are also inorganic. Organic pigments include the nitrogen-containing azo pigments (red, orange, and yellow) and the copper phthalocyanines (blues and greens). CHLOROPHYLL, CAROTENE, and MELANIN are pigments produced by plants and animals for specialized purposes.

pika \ˈpē-kə, ˈpī-kə\ Any of numerous round-eared, tailless members (genus *Ochotona*, family Ochotonidae) of the RABBIT order (Lagomorpha), found in Asia, E Europe, and parts of W N. America. Though not HARES, they are sometimes called mouse hare and little chief hare. The hind legs are less developed than a rabbit's. Their brownish or reddish fur is soft, long, and thick. Pikas are 6–12 in. (15–30 cm) long and weigh 4–14 oz (125–440 g). Most species live in rocky, mountainous areas, but some Asian species inhabit burrows. Pikas "harvest" vegetation, dry it in the sun, and store it for eating in winter.

pike Any of several voracious freshwater fishes (family Esocidae, order Salmoniformes) with a slender body, small scales, long head, shovel-like snout, large mouth, and strong teeth. The northern pike *(Esox lucius)* of N. America, Europe, and N Asia may grow to 4.5 ft (1.4 m) long and weigh 45 lbs (20 kg). It lies motionless then suddenly lunges to seize an approaching fish or invertebrate. Large species also take waterfowl and small mammals. See also PICKEREL.

Pikes Peak Mountain peak, E Colorado, in the ROCKY MTNS. near COLORADO SPRINGS. It was discovered in 1806 by Zebulon Pike (1779–1813). At 14,110 ft (4,301 m), its panoramic view is said to have inspired Katharine Lee Bates to write "America the Beautiful" in 1893.

pilaster \pi-ˈlas-tər\ In CLASSICAL ARCHITECTURE, a shallow rectangular column built into a wall and projecting slightly beyond it. It has a capital and base and conforms to one of the ORDERS. In Roman architecture the pilaster gradually became more decorative than structural.

Pilate \ˈpī-lət\, **Pontius** (d. after A.D. 36) Roman prefect of JUDAEA (A.D. 26–36) who presided at the trial of JESUS. The NEW TESTAMENT represents Pilate as a weak and vacillating man, who found no fault with Jesus but ordered his CRUCIFIXION to please the mob. Known for his severity toward the Jews, he was eventually ordered back to Rome to stand trial for cruelty and oppression. One tradition holds that he killed himself on orders from CALIGULA in A.D. 39; another relates that he converted to Christianity.

Pilcomayo River \ˌpēl-kō-ˈmä-yō\ River, S central S. America. It rises in the E ANDES in Bolivia and flows southeast through the GRAN CHACO of Paraguay to join the PARAGUAY RIVER opposite ASUNCIÓN, after about 1,000 mi (1,600 km). It forms part of the Argentina–Paraguay boundary.

pile See HEMORRHOID

pilgrimage Journey to a shrine or other sacred place undertaken to gain divine aid, as an act of thanksgiving or penance, or to demonstrate devotion. Medieval Christian pilgrims stayed at hospices set up specifically for pilgrims. The chief attractions for pilgrims in the Middle Ages were the Holy Land, SANTIAGO DE COMPOSTELA in Spain, and Rome, but there were hundreds of local pilgrimage sites. More recent pilgrimage sites include the shrine of Our Lady of Guadalupe in Mexico (1531), LOURDES in France (1858), and FÁTIMA in Portugal (1917). Pilgrimage is also important in Buddhism, with sites including Bodh Gaya, where the BUDDHA received enlightenment, and VARANASI, where he delivered his first sermon. All Muslims are enjoined to perform the HAJJ, the pilgrimage to MECCA, at least once in their lifetime.

Pilgrims First settlers of PLYMOUTH (Massachusetts), the first permanent colony in New England (1620). The members of the English Separatist Church, a radical faction of PURITANISM, composed a third of the 102 colonists who sailed aboard the *Mayflower* to N. America, and became the dominant group. The settlers were later collectively referred to as the Forefathers; the term "Pilgrim Fathers" was applied to them by Daniel WEBSTER in 1820.

Pillars of Hercules Two promontories at the E end of Strait of GIBRALTAR, the Rock of GIBRALTAR in Europe and Jebel Musa in CEUTA, N Africa. They are fabled to have been set there by HERACLES as a memorial in his travels to seize the cattle of the giant Geryon.

Pillars of Islam See Pillars of ISLAM

pilot whale Any of one to three species (genus *Globicephala*, family Delphinidae) of toothed WHALE found in all oceans except the Arctic and Antarctic. It is black, usually with a lighter splash on the throat and chest, and has a round, bulging forehead and short beaklike snout. It grows to 13–20 ft (4–6 m) long. Pilot whales live in large schools, sometimes hundreds or thousands, feeding mainly on squid. They have been kept in oceanariums and trained to perform.

Pilsudski \pil-ˈsüt-skē, pil-ˈzüt-skē\, **Jozef (Klemens)** (1867–1935) Polish revolutionary leader. Banished to Siberia for socialist activism (1887–92), he became a leader of the Polish Socialist Party on his return. In 1908 he organized the

secret Union of Military Action, which fought in World War I under Austro-Hungarian command against the Russians. After Poland gained independence in 1918, he served as its first head of state until the constitution was established in 1922. After staging a coup in 1926, he served as premier (1926–28) and minister of defense (1926–35) under handpicked premiers, which allowed him to rule as the dictator of Poland.

Jozef Pilsudski

Piltdown hoax Forgery of human fossil remains that impeded early-20th-cent. progress in the study of HUMAN EVOLUTION. The apparently fossilized skull found at Piltdown Common near Lewes, England, was first proposed as a new species of prehistoric man ("Piltdown man") in 1912. Only in 1954 was the skull shown to consist of a human cranium skillfully joined to the jaw of an orangutan. The hoax may have been perpetrated by the skull's discoverer, Charles Dawson.

Pinatubo \ˌpē-nä-ˈtü-bō\, **Mt.** Mountain, W LUZON, Philippines. Located about 55 mi (90 km) northwest of MANILA, it rose to a height of about 4,800 ft (1,460 m) before its eruption in 1991 (for the first time in 600 years). Its explosions produced a column of smoke and ash more than 20 mi (30 km) high, and left about 100,000 people homeless. Its eruption, which cooled the earth's climate for two years, may have been the largest in the 20th cent.

Pinchot \ˈpin-shō\, **Gifford** (1865–1946) U.S. forestry pioneer. Born in Simsbury, Conn., he graduated from Yale Univ. and studied forestry in Europe. He became the first professional U.S. forester in 1892, and he helped plan the U.S. system of forest reserves (later NATIONAL FORESTS). As chief of the U.S. Forest Service (1898–1910), he established the nation's forest-service system. He founded the Yale School of Forestry and taught there 1903–36. He served as governor of Pennsylvania 1923–27 and 1931–35.

Pinckney, Charles (1757–1824) U.S. political leader. Born in Charleston, S.C., he fought in the American Revolution. He was instrumental in calling for the CONSTITUTIONAL CONVENTION; as a delegate from S. Carolina, he proposed numerous provisions that were incorporated in the final draft of the Constitution. He helped write the S. Carolina constitution and served as governor (1789–92, 1796–98, 1806–8), U.S. Senator (1798–1801), and minister to Spain (1801–5).

Pinckney, Charles Cotesworth (1746–1825) American diplomat. Born in Charleston, S.C., a brother of Thomas PINCKNEY, he was an aide to George WASHINGTON in the American Revolution, commanded at Savannah, and was promoted to brigadier general in 1783. Appointed minister to France (1796), he was involved in negotiations that ended in the XYZ AFFAIR. He was the unsuccessful Federalist candidate for vice president in 1800 and for president in 1804 and 1808.

Pinckney, Eliza *orig.* Elizabeth Lucas (1722–1793) British-American planter. Born in Antigua, W. Indies, she managed her father's S. Carolina plantations from 1739. She experimented with various crops and succeeded in marketing the first American crop of indigo. After her marriage to Charles Pinckney (1744), she revived the cultivation of silkworms and manufacture of silk on his plantation. C. C. PINCKNEY and Thomas PINCKNEY were her sons.

Pinckney, Thomas (1750–1828) U.S. diplomat. Born in Charleston, S.C., the brother of C. C. PINCKNEY, he served as governor of S. Carolina 1787–89 and as minister to Britain 1792–96. As special envoy to Spain (1795), he negotiated the Treaty of San Lorenzo, also called Pinckney's Treaty, which fixed the S border of the U.S. and granted U.S. navigation rights on the Mississippi River. He was a major general in the War of 1812.

Pindar (518/522 B.C.–438? B.C.) Greek poet. Almost all his early poems have been lost, but his reputation was probably established by his later hymns in honor of the gods. He developed into the greatest lyric poet of ancient Greece, respected throughout the Greek world. Of his 17 volumes, only four have survived complete. The extant poems, probably representing his masterpieces, are odes (see PINDARIC ODE) commissioned to celebrate triumphs in various Hellenic athletic games. They are noted for their complexity, rich metaphors, and intensely emotive language.

Pindaric ode Ceremonious poem in the manner of PINDAR, who employed a structure consisting of a strophe (two or more lines repeated as a unit) followed by a metrically harmonious antistrophe and an epode (summary line) in a different meter. The three parts correspond to movements onstage by the CHORUS in Greek drama. After the 16th-cent. publication of Pindar's choral ODES honoring the victors in Greek games, poets writing in various languages created irregular rhymed odes that suggest his style. Such odes in English are among the greatest poems in the language, including John DRYDEN's "Alexander's Feast" and John KEATS's "Ode on a Grecian Urn."

pine Any of 10 genera of coniferous trees (rarely shrubs) of the family Pinaceae (see CONIFER), native to N temperate regions, especially about 90 species of ornamental and timber evergreen conifers of the genus *Pinus.* Needlelike leaves and CONES are solitary or in bunches. Shallow root systems make pines susceptible to wind and surface disturbance. The family includes FIR, DOUGLAS FIR, HEMLOCK, SPRUCE, LARCH, and CEDAR. Many species are sources of softwood timber, paper pulp, oils, and resins.

pineal gland \ˈpī-nē-əl, pī-ˈnē-əl\ *or* **pineal body** *or* **epiphysis cerebri** \ˌi-ˈpif-ə-səs-ˈser-ə-brē\ Endocrine GLAND in the BRAIN that regulates MELATONIN production. It is large in children and shrinks at puberty, to about 0.0035 oz (0.1 g) in adults. It may play a significant role in sexual maturation, CIRCADIAN RHYTHM and SLEEP induction, and SEASONAL AFFECTIVE DISORDER and DEPRESSION. In animals it plays a major role in sexual development, HIBERNATION, METABOLISM, and seasonal breeding.

pineapple Fruit-bearing plant (*Ananas comosus*) of the family Bromeliaceae, native to the New World tropics and subtropics but introduced elsewhere. The plant has a rosette of 30–40 stiff, succulent leaves on a thick, fleshy stem. An inflorescence forms 15–20 months after planting. After fertilization, the many lavender flowers fuse and become fleshy to form the 2–4 lb (1–2 kg) fruit. Ripening takes 5–6 months.

Pinero \pi-ˈnir-ō\, **Arthur Wing** (*later* **Sir Arthur**) (1855–1934) British playwright. His first play was produced in 1877. He wrote a series of successful farces such as *The Magistrate* (1885) before turning to dramas of social issues. *The Second Mrs. Tanqueray* (1893), the first of his plays depicting women confronting their situation in society, established his reputation, and he followed it with such works as *The Notorious Mrs. Ebbsmith* (1895) and *Trelawny of the "Wells"* (1898), becoming the most successful playwright of his time.

Ping Pong See TABLE TENNIS

pinion See GEAR, RACK AND PINION

Pinkerton National Detective Agency U.S. independent police force. Founded in 1850 by Allan Pinkerton (1819–1884), former deputy sheriff of Cook Co., Ill., it initially specialized in railway theft cases, protecting trains and apprehending train robbers. It solved the $700,000 Adams Express Co. theft in 1856 and thwarted a 1861 assassination plot against president-elect Abraham LINCOLN. It later participated in antilabor union activities (see HOMESTEAD STRIKE) and helped break up the MOLLY MAGUIRES.

pink family Family Caryophyllaceae, composed of 2,070 species of flowering plants in 89 genera found mainly in N temperate regions. The approximately 300 species of true pinks belong to the genus *Dianthus;* these are popular in gardens for their fragrant, showy flowers. The family includes CARNATIONS, baby's breath, sweet William, campion, and chickweed.

Pinkham \ˈpiŋk-əm\, **Lydia E(stes)** (1819–1883) U.S. patent-medicine proprietor. Born in Lynn, Mass., Pinkham began making her Vegetable Compound as a home remedy. The compound, a blend of ground herbs, was 18% alcohol. In 1875 her family began selling the medicine, which Pinkham claimed could cure any "female complaint" from nervous prostration to a prolapsed uterus. The business was soon grossing nearly $300,000 a year. Not until the 1920s, with increased regulation, did the Lydia E. Pinkham Medicine Co. reduce both the alcoholic content of the medicine and its claims of efficacy.

Pinochet (Ugarte) \\ˌpē-nə-'shä, *Span* ˌpē-nō-'che\\, **Augusto** (b.1915) Head of Chile's military government (1974–90). A general, he planned and led the coup d'état in which Pres. Salvador ALLENDE died. He crushed liberal opposition and arrested about 130,000 Chileans and foreigners; many were tortured and some 3,000 apparently killed. He led a rapid transition to a free-market economy, which slowed inflation but led to acute hardship for the lower classes. A new constitution in 1981 granted him eight more years as president. He stepped down after free elections installed Patricio Aylwin in 1990. In 1998 he was arrested in England at the request of Spain for crimes against Spanish citizens in Chile during his tenure; he was released 16 months later.

Pinter, Harold (b.1930) British playwright. His early one-act plays *The Room* (1957) and *The Dumbwaiter* (1957) were followed by the full-length *The Birthday Party* (1958; film, 1968), *The Caretaker* (1960), and *The Homecoming* (1965; film, 1973). He uses disjointed small talk and lengthy pauses in dialogue to convey a character's thought (which often contradicts his speech), and has earned a reputation as an innovative and complex dramatist. His later plays include *Old Times* (1971), *No Man's Land* (1975), *Betrayal* (1978; film, 1983), *Mountain Language* (1988), and *Moonlight* (1993). He has also written such screenplays as *The Servant* (1963), *Accident* (1967), and *The Go-Between* (1971), and *The French Lieutenant's Woman* (1981).

pinto Spotted HORSE, also called by such names as paint, piebald, and skewbald to describe variations in color and markings. The American Indian ponies of the W U.S. were often pintos. Most pure-breed associations refuse to register horses with pinto coloring.

Pinturicchio \\ˌpēn-tü-'rēk-kyō\\ *orig.* Bernardino di Betto di Biago (1452?–1513) Italian painter. Born in Perugia, he assisted PERUGINO on the frescoes in the Vatican's SISTINE CHAPEL (1481–82). His most important work, the fresco decoration of six rooms in the Borgia Apartments for Pope ALEXANDER VI (1492–94), features brilliant colors, gilding, and ancient Roman ornamental motifs. His last major works were 10 scenes from the life of PIUS II in the Piccolomini Library of Siena Cathedral.

pinworm Common species (*Enterobius,* or *Oxyuris, vermicularis*) of NEMATODE parasitic to humans, especially children. Female pinworms may be 0.5 in. (13 mm) long; males are much smaller. Pinworms have a very long tail that gives them a pinlike appearance. After mating in the large intestine, the females deposit their fertilized eggs on the skin near the anal opening, and die. The worms' movements cause itching; eggs transferred to the fingernails when the victim scratches may be passed to the mouth. The eggs or larvae make their way to the intestine, and the cycle begins again.

Pio, Padre *orig.* Francesco Forgione (1887–1968) Italian priest. Born into a devout Catholic family, he consecrated himself to Jesus at 5. At 15 he joined the Capuchins and took the name Pio; in 1910 he became a priest. That same year he received the stigmata for the first time. He received them again in 1918; this time they remained with him until his death. This and other signs of his holiness drew growing numbers of pilgrims to him. He was canonized in 2002.

Piombo, Sebastiano del See SEBASTIANO DEL PIOMBO

Pioneer First series of unmanned U.S. deep-space probes. Pioneer 1 was the first spacecraft launched by NASA (1958). Pioneers 1–4 were meant to be lunar missions, but only Pioneer 4 escaped earth's gravity (1964). Pioneers 6–9 orbited the sun (1965–68) to study the solar wind, solar magnetic field, and cosmic rays. Pioneer 10, launched in 1972, was the first space probe to pass the asteroid belt and to fly by JUPITER (1973), whose huge magnetic tail it discovered. It then became the first man-made object to exit the solar system. Pioneer 11's data and photographs (1979) led to the discovery of two more moons and an additional ring around SATURN and radiation belts in its magnetosphere. Pioneer

Venus 1 and 2 began orbiting VENUS in 1978, sending back observations of its atmosphere and surface; Pioneer Venus 2 also released four probes into its atmosphere.

piracy Illegal act of violence, detention, or plunder committed for private ends by the crew of, usually, a private ship against another ship on the high seas. Air piracy (HIJACKING) is a more recent phenomenon. The Phoenicians, Greeks, and Romans engaged in piracy, as did the Vikings, Moors, and other Europeans. It also occurred among Asian peoples. In the late 16th cent., treasure-laden Spanish galleons proceeding from Mexico into the Caribbean were a natural target for pirates. In the 16th–18th cent., pirates from N. Africa's BARBARY COAST threatened commerce in the Mediterranean. The increased size of merchant vessels, improved naval patrolling, and recognition by governments of piracy as an international offense led to its decline in the late 19th cent. See also BLACKBEARD, Francis DRAKE, Jean LAFFITE, Henry MORGAN.

Piraeus \\pī-'rē-əs\\ City (pop., 1991: 182,000), port of ATHENS, Greece. The port and its "long walls," fortified barriers connecting it with Athens, were completed in the mid-5th cent. B.C. The walls were destroyed by SPARTA at the end of the PELOPONNESIAN WAR, rebuilt in 393 B.C., then burned in 86 B.C. by L. C. SULLA. The city regained importance after 1834, when Athens became capital of independent Greece. It remains the largest port in Greece.

Pirandello, Luigi (1867–1936) Italian playwright and novelist. He wrote poetry, short stories, and several novels, including *The Late Mattia Pascal* (1904), before producing his first major play, *Right You Are (If You Think You Are)* (1917), which explored the relativity of truth, a lifelong subject for Pirandello. *Six Characters in Search of an Author* (1921) contrasted art and life; it was followed by the tragedy *Henry IV* (1922). His other plays include *Each in His Own Way* (1924) and *Tonight We Improvise* (1930). Recognized as a major figure in 20th-cent. theater, he was awarded the Nobel Prize in 1934.

Piranesi \\ˌpē-rä-'nä-sē\\, **Giovanni Battista** (1720–1778) Italian printmaker and architect. After settling in Rome in 1747, he developed a highly original etching technique that produced rich textures and bold contrasts of light and shadow. His many prints of classical and postclassical Roman structures contributed to the growth of classical archaeology and the Neoclassical art movement. He is best known today for his extraordinary series of imaginary prisons (*Carceri d'invenzione,* 1745). His prints are among the most impressive architectural representations in Western art.

piranha \\pə-'rä-nə, pə-'rän-yə\\ *or* **caribe** \\kə-'rē-bē\\ Any of several species in the genus *Serrasalmus* (family Characidae), deep-bodied, carnivorous fishes abundant in rivers of E and central S. America and noted for voracity and ferocity. One of the most dangerous species, *S. nattereri,* grows to 2 ft (60 cm) long, but most species are

piranha (*Serrasalmus*)

smaller. Most are either silvery or black. All have saw-edged teeth. Piranhas travel in groups, usually preying on other fishes. They are attracted to the scent of blood and can quickly reduce even a large animal to a skeleton.

Pisa \\'pē-zə, *Italian* 'pē-sä\\ *ancient* Pisae. City (pop., 1998 est.: 93,000), central Italy. Located on the ARNO RIVER, it became a Roman colony about 180 B.C. It flourished during the Middle Ages as the principal urban center of TUSCANY. Pisa's participation in the CRUSADES made it a rival of GENOA and VENICE. The scene of heavy fighting during World War II, it is now an important railway junction; its sites, including its cathedral (with the LEANING TOWER OF PISA), make it a tourist destination. It is home to the Univ. of Pisa (founded 1343) and is the birthplace of GALILEO.

Pisano \\pi-'sä-nō, pi-'zä-nō\\, **Andrea** (c.1295–c.1348) Italian sculptor and architect. He created the earliest of three bronze doors for the Baptistery of the cathedral of Florence (1330–36). In 1337 he succeeded GIOTTO as chief architect of the cathedral's bell tower, to which he added two stories adorned with panel reliefs. In 1347 he was appointed superintending architect of the cathedral of Orvieto. One of the most important Italian sculptors of the 14th cent., he is known for his restrained style and skillful arrangement of figures.

Pisano, Giovanni (c.1250–1319) Italian sculptor and architect. His early work is similar to that of Nicola PISANO, his father and teacher. Around 1285 he began work on the facade of Siena's cathedral, whose lavish and ordered design and ornamentation became the model for future Gothic facade decoration in central Italy. His other great achievement, the Pistoia pulpit (c.1298–1301), is characterized by extreme agitation, its figures, animals, drapery, and landscape being wrenched into physically impossible configurations. His pulpit for the Pisa cathedral (1302–10) is much more classical. He is regarded as Italy's only true Gothic sculptor.

Pisano, Nicola (c.1220–1278?) Italian sculptor. His work, along with that of his son, Giovanni PISANO, created a new sculptural style for the late 13th and 14th cent. in Italy. Little is known of his life. His greatest work, the pulpit in the Baptistery of Pisa Cathedral (1260), is extraordinary in its assertion of a new style. The work draws on many motifs, including Roman reliefs, early Christian frescoes, and French Gothic sculpture, but assimilates them, creating a unified whole that gave a new direction to Tuscan art.

Pishpek See BISHKEK.

Pisidia \pi-'si-dē-ə\ Ancient region, S ASIA MINOR. Most of it was composed of the TAURUS MTNS., which provided refuge for a lawless population that resisted successive conquerors. DIOCLETIAN included Pisidia in the diocese of Asia about A.D. 297. During Byzantine times it continued to be a region of revolt. By 1204 the Byzantines had ceded control of the region to the Turks.

Pissarro \pə-'sär-ō\, **(Jacob-Abraham-) Camille** (1830–1903) French Impressionist painter. Born on the island of St. Thomas, the son of a Jewish merchant, he moved to Paris in 1855. His earliest canvases are broadly painted figure paintings and landscapes that show his characteristically careful observation of nature. In 1871 he took a house in Pontoise, in the countryside outside Paris. These surroundings formed the theme of his art for some 30 years. Despite acute eye trouble, he was most prolific in his later years, producing such Parisian and provincial scenes as *Place du Théâtre Française* (1898) and *Bridge at Bruges* (1903). Pissarro was the only Impressionist painter who participated in all eight of the group's exhibitions (see IMPRESSIONISM).

Camille Pissarro, self-portrait, 1903

pistachio \pə-'sta-shē-ˌō\ Any of nine species of aromatic trees and shrubs, some ornamental, that make up the genus *Pistacia* of the SUMAC (or cashew) family, native to Eurasia, with one species in SW N. America. Commercial pistachio nuts are seeds from the fruit of *P. vera*. They have a pleasing, mild, resinous flavor. The tree bears leaves with thick, wide, leathery, featherlike leaflets and small fruit in clusters.

pistil Female reproductive part of a FLOWER. The pistil typically has a swollen base called the ovary, which contains the potential SEEDS (ovules). The stalk (style) arises from the ovary and has a pollen-receptive tip, the stigma. There may be a single pistil, as in the LILY, or several to many pistils, as in the BUTTERCUP. Differences in the composition and form of the pistil are useful in classifying flowering plants. See also STAMEN.

pistol Hand firearm. The name may derive from Pistoia, Italy, where handguns were made as early as the 15th cent. The two classes of pistol are REVOLVERS and automatics.

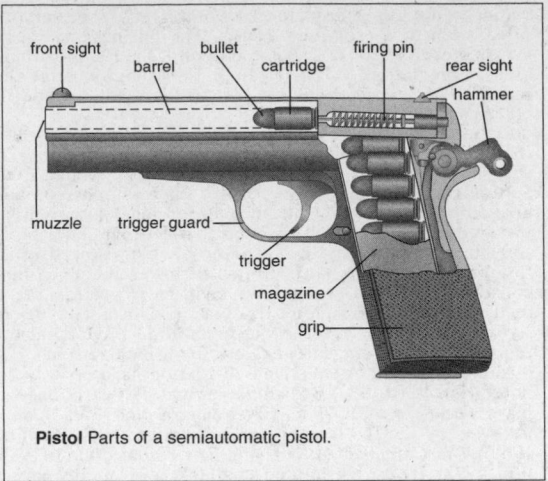

Pistol Parts of a semiautomatic pistol.

Automatics have a mechanism, actuated by the energy of recoil, that feeds cartridges from a magazine in the butt.

piston and cylinder In mechanical engineering, a sliding cylinder with a closed head (the piston) that moves up and down (or back and forth) in a slightly larger cylindrical chamber (the cylinder) by or against pressure of a fluid, as in an engine or pump. The cylinder of a STEAM ENGINE is closed by plates at both ends, with provision for the piston rod, which is rigidly attached to the piston, to pass through one of the end cover plates. The cylinder of an INTERNAL-COMBUSTION ENGINE is closed at one end and open at the other end to permit free oscillation of the connecting rod, which joins the piston to the crankshaft.

pit bull terrier or **Staffordshire terrier** Dog breed developed in 19th-cent. Britain for fighting other dogs in pits. It was created by crossing the BULLDOG (which at the time was longer-legged and more agile) with a terrier. Once known as bull-and-terrier or half-and-half, the pit bull is a stocky, muscular, unusually strong dog with powerful jaws, standing 17–19 in. (43–48 cm) and weighing 30–50 lbs (14–23 kg). See also BULL TERRIER.

Pitcairn Island Island (pop., 1992 est.: 52), S central Pacific Ocean. It is the only inhabited island of the four in the Pitcairn Island group. It has an area of about 2 sq mi (5 sq km). Discovered in 1767 by the British, in 1790 it was settled by mutineers from HMS *Bounty*, led by Fletcher Christian. It was annexed by Britain in 1839. The inhabitants were removed to NORFOLK ISLAND in 1856 because of overpopulation. Some returned to Pitcairn, and their descendants make up the present population.

pitch Quality of a musical tone that varies with the number of vibrations per second (hertz, Hz) of the sounding body and is perceived as highness or lowness. A higher pitch has a higher number of vibrations. The sounds of bodies vibrating in ratios of multiples of two (octaves) are perceived as closely related to each other, so they share a letter designation (like "C" or "F-sharp"). Today the A above middle C is widely standardized as 440 Hz, which implies the pitches of all other notes in the equal-tempered scale. See also INTERVAL, TUNING AND TEMPERAMENT.

pitchblende Amorphous, dense, black, pitchy form of the crystalline uranium oxide mineral uraninite. The primary mineral ore of URANIUM, pitchblende is found in granular masses and has a greasy luster. Three chemical elements were first discovered in pitchblende: uranium, polonium, and RADIUM. Deposits are known in the Czech Republic, Britain, Canada's Northwest Territories and Saskatchewan, and in Arizona, Colorado, Montana, New Mexico, and Utah.

Pitcher, Molly (1753?–1832) American patriot. Thought to have been Irish, in the American Revolution she accompanied her husband, William Hays, a gunner, at the Battle of

Monmouth (1778), where she carried pitchers of water to wounded American soldiers, earning the nickname "Molly Pitcher." According to legend, after her husband collapsed from the heat, she took his place at the cannon and served heroically through the battle. In 1822 she was recognized for her heroism with a state pension. Some historians attribute the act of replacing her husband at the cannon to Margaret Corbin (1751–1800) in the attack on Ft. Washington in 1776.

pitcher plant Any CARNIVOROUS PLANT with pitcher-, trumpet-, or urn-shaped leaves, in several different families: Nepenthaceae (Old World pitcher plants), Cephalotaceae, Asclepiadaceae (MILKWEED FAMILY), and especially Sarraceniaceae (New World pitcher plants, particularly those in the E.N. American genus *Sarracenia*). Pitcher plants grow in wet, acidic, nutrient-poor soil. Their unusual tubular leaves have a series of nectar-secreting glands that extend from the lip down into the interior and attract insects. Once in the plant, the prey tumbles down into a liquid pool and drowns, after which an enzyme secreted within the leaf digests its nutrients. Most pitcher plants produce a crop of pitchered, insect-catching leaves in the spring, and a second crop of tubeless leaves in the fall.

pitot tube \'pē-,tō\ Instrument for measuring the velocity (speed) of a flowing FLUID. Invented by Henri Pitot (1695–1771), it consists of a tube with a short, right-angled bend, which is placed vertically in a moving fluid with the mouth of the bent part directed upstream; the PRESSURE, measured with an attached device, depends on the fluid flow and can be used to calculate the velocity. Pitot tubes are used to measure airspeed in WIND TUNNELS and aboard aircraft in flight; they are also used to measure the flow of liquids (see FLOW METER).

Pitt, William *later* Earl of Chatham *known as* **the Elder Pitt** (1708–1778) British statesman. He entered Parliament in 1735 and became a noted orator. With the outbreak of the SEVEN YEARS' WAR (1756), he was named secretary of state and became virtual prime minister. His leadership brought many British victories that greatly extended the British empire. His wide popular appeal led to the nickname "the Great Commoner," though he was disliked by many in government for his high-handedness. He resigned in 1761 when the cabinet refused to declare war on Spain. Though ill with gout, he became a champion of liberty and spoke in favor of American colonial resistance to the STAMP ACT. He formed another government in 1766, but resigned in 1768 because of ill health.

Pitt, William *known as* **the Younger Pitt** (1759–1806) British statesman and prime minister (1783–1801, 1804–6). The son of William PITT, he entered Parliament in 1781. He was appointed prime minister in 1783 and undertook reforms that reduced the large national debt incurred by the AMERICAN REVOLUTION, reduced tariffs, and restructured the government in India. Forced into conflict with France by the FRENCH REVOLUTIONARY WARS, he formed a series of coalitions with European states against France (1793, 1798, 1805). In 1800 he secured the Act of UNION with Ireland, but he resigned in 1801 when his proposal for Catholic emancipation was denied. His second term as premier (1804–6) was marked by the collapse of the Third Coalition after the Battle of AUSTERLITZ, the news of which weakened his already fragile health.

William Pitt, the Younger
Painting by John Hoppner

Pittsburgh City (pop., 2000: 334,000), SW Pennsylvania. It is situated where the ALLEGHENY and MONONGAHELA rivers unite (known as the "Golden Triangle") to form the OHIO RIVER. In 1758 the French Ft. Duquesne was captured there by the British, and the site was renamed Pitt. In the 19th cent. it developed rapidly as a steel-manufacturing center. The American Federation of Labor began there in 1881 (see AFL-CIO). The second-largest city in the state, it is the center of an urban industrial complex. There are more than 150 industrial research laboratories in the area. It is home to the Univ. of Pittsburgh and CARNEGIE-MELLON UNIV.

pituitary gland \pə-'tü-ə-,ter-ē\ *or* **hypophysis** \hī-'päf-ə-səs\ Endocrine GLAND lying on the underside of the brain. It plays a major part in regulating the ENDOCRINE SYSTEM. Its anterior lobe secretes most of the pituitary hormones, which stimulate growth (see GROWTH HORMONE), egg and sperm development, milk secretion, release of other hormones by various glands, and pigment production. The posterior lobe stores and releases hormones from the HYPOTHALAMUS.

Pius II \'pī-əs\ *orig.* Enea Silvio Piccolomini (1405–1464) Pope (1458–64). An Italian diplomat who became bishop of Trieste (1447) and Siena (1449), he mediated between the German princes and the papacy, arranged the coronation of Frederick III as Holy Roman Emperor (1452), and made peace with Aragon and Naples. As pope he tried unsuccessfully to unite Europe in a crusade against the Turks. Pius was also a noted humanist and a prolific writer on the events of his day.

Pius V, St. *orig.* Antonio or Michele Ghislieri (1504–1572) Pope (1566–72). He joined the Dominican order at 14 and was ordained in 1528. A relentless pursuer of heretics, he was named Commissary General of the INQUISITION in 1551. As pope, he zealously carried out church reforms and succeeded in keeping Protestantism out of Italy, and in 1570 he excommunicated ELIZABETH I. He organized the campaign that led to the victory of the Spanish, Venetian, and papal fleets over the Turks in the Battle of Lepanto in 1571.

Pius IX *orig.* Giovanni Maria Mastai-Ferretti (1792–1878) Pope (1846–78). He became a cardinal in 1840, and pope on the death of Gregory XVI. He set out to make liberal reforms, but the revolutionary fervor of 1848 frightened him into extreme conservatism. He proclaimed the dogma of the IMMACULATE CONCEPTION (1854) and convened the First Vatican Council (1869–70), which promulgated the doctrine of PAPAL INFALLIBILITY. After losing temporal power to VICTOR EMMANUEL II upon Italian unification, he refused any contact with the Italian government. Pius's pontificate was the longest in history.

Pius XII *orig.* Eugenio Maria Giuseppe Giovanni Pacelli (1876–1958) Pope (1939–58). Born in Rome, he served in the papal diplomatic service and as secretary of state to the Holy See before succeeding Pius XI in 1939. He was active in humanitarian work with prisoners and refugees during World War II, but has been criticized for his failure to speak out against the HOLOCAUST. Known for his austere conservatism, he defined the dogma of the bodily assumption of the Virgin in 1950.

pixel *in full* picture element. Smallest unit of a video image with specific luminescence and color. In the most common form of COMPUTER GRAPHICS, the thousands of tiny pixels that make up an individual image are projected onto a display screen as illuminated dots that from a distance appear as a continuous image. An electron beam creates the grid of pixels by tracing each horizontal line from left to right, one pixel at a time, from the top line to the bottom line. A pixel may also be the smallest element of a light-sensitive device, such as a digital or video camera.

Pizarro, Francisco (c.1475–1541) CONQUISTADOR who seized the INCA empire for Spain. In 1513 he joined Vasco Núñez de BALBOA on the expedition that discovered the Pacific. He made two voyages down the Colombian coast (1524–25, 1526–28) and continued southward, naming the new territory Peru. In 1531 he sailed for Peru with 180 men and 37 horses. Having arranged a meeting with the Inca emperor, ATAHUALLPA, he slaughtered his retainers and took him hostage. After accepting a rich ransom for Atahuallpa's release, Pizarro had him garroted. He spent the rest of his life consolidating Spain's hold on Peru. He founded Lima (1535), where he was killed by Spaniards he had betrayed.

pizza Food of Neapolitan origin consisting of a flattened disk of bread dough topped with olive oil, tomatoes, and

cheese, baked quickly and served hot. Pizza came to the U.S. with Italian immigrants; the first U.S. pizzeria opened in 1905, and pizza became one of the nation's favorite foods after World War II.

PKU See PHENYLKETONURIA

placenta \plə-'sen-tə\ Organ in most MAMMALS that develops in the UTERUS along with a FETUS. The umbilical cord attaches it to the fetus at the navel. Nutrients and oxygen in the mother's blood pass across the placenta to the fetus, and metabolic wastes and carbon dioxide from the fetus cross in the other direction; the two blood supplies do not mix. Other substances (e.g., alcohol or drugs) in the mother's blood can also cross the placenta, with effects including CONGENITAL DISORDERS and DRUG ADDICTION in the newborn (see FETAL ALCOHOL SYNDROME); some microorganisms can cross it, but so do the mother's ANTIBODIES. The placenta is expelled at PARTURITION.

placer deposit \'pla-sər\ Natural concentration of heavy minerals caused by the effect of gravity on moving particles. When heavy, stable minerals are freed from their matrix by weathering processes, they are slowly washed downslope into streams, becoming concentrated in stream and beach gravels as workable ore deposits. Minerals that form placer deposits include gold, platinum, cassiterite, magnetite, and various gemstones.

placer mining Oldest method of recovering GOLD from ALLUVIAL and PLACER DEPOSITS. It takes advantage of gold's high density, which causes it to sink more rapidly from moving water than the lighter siliceous materials surrounding it. Panning, used by 19th-cent. miners, employed a pan in which a few handfuls of the gold-bearing soil or gravel and a large amount of water were placed; by swirling the pan's contents, the miner washed the siliceous material over the side, leaving the gold and heavy materials behind. Dredging, the main placer-mining method used today, employs a continuous chain of buckets rotating around a rigid adjustable frame called the ladder. In sluicing, a slightly sloping wooden trough is used as a channel along which gold-bearing gravel is carried by a stream of water; riffles along the bottom of the sluice retard the current so that gold may settle.

Placid, Lake See LAKE PLACID

plagioclase \'plā-jē-ə-,klās\ Any member of the series of abundant FELDSPAR minerals that usually occur as light- to medium-gray-colored, transparent to translucent grains or crystals. It is used in the manufacture of glass and ceramics; iridescent varieties are valued as gemstones. Its primary importance, however, is its role as a rock-forming mineral.

plague \'plāg\ Infectious FEVER caused by the bacterium *Yersinia pestis*, carried by the rat flea. It usually spreads to humans only when the flea runs out of rodent hosts. It takes three forms. Bubonic, the mildest, has characteristic swollen LYMPH NODES (buboes) and is spread only by the flea. It accounts for three-fourths of plague cases. Pneumonic plague has extensive lung involvement and is spread by coughs and sneezes; it is often fatal in three or four days without treatment. In septicemic plague, bacteria overwhelm the bloodstream and often cause death within 24 hours. Measures against fleas and rodents, QUARANTINE, and caution in handling infectious materials help to suppress epidemics. ANTIBIOTICS are effective against plague, and VACCINE can prevent it. See also BLACK DEATH.

plaice Commercially valuable European FLATFISH (*Pleuronectes platessa*). At most 36 in. (90 cm) long, it normally has both eyes on the right side of the head and bony bumps near its eyes. The American plaice (*Hippoglossoides platessoides*) is found in both Europe (where it is called the rough dab) and the U.S. It grows to about 24 in. (60 cm) long.

Plain, the *French* la Plaine. In the FRENCH REVOLUTION, the centrist deputies in the NATIONAL CONVENTION. Their name derived from their place on the floor of the assembly; above them sat the members of the Mountain, or MONTAGNARDS. Led by E.-J. SIEYÈS, the Plain initially voted with the moderate GIRONDINS but later joined the Montagnards in voting for the execution of LOUIS XVI. In 1794 they helped overthrow Maximilien de ROBESPIERRE.

Plain of Esdraelon See Plain of ESDRAELON
Plain of Sharon See Plain of SHARON

Plains Indians Any of various Native American tribes that formerly inhabited the GREAT PLAINS of the U.S. and S Canada. Most of the Plains Indians were nomadic hunters of big game, principally buffalo. They included the ARAPAHO, ASSINIBOIN, BLACKFOOT, CHEYENNE, COMANCHE, Plains CREE, CROW, HIDATSA, KIOWA, MANDAN, OSAGE, PAWNEE, and SIOUX.

Plains of Abraham See Plains of ABRAHAM

planarian \plə-'nar-ē-ən\ Any of about 3,000 species of widely distributed, mostly free-living FLATWORMS of the family Planariidae and related families (class Turbellaria), usually found in freshwater but also in marine and terrestrial environments. The soft, ciliated body is leaf-shaped when elongated. The spade-shaped head has two eyes and sometimes tentacles. Most species are 0.1–0.6 in. (3–15 mm) long; some grow to about 1 ft (30 cm). Planarians swim or creep like slugs. Most feed at night on protozoans, snails, and other worms.

Planck \'pläŋk\, **Max (Karl Ernst Ludwig)** (1858–1947) German physicist. His work on the second law of thermodynamics and blackbody radiation led him to formulate the revolutionary QUANTUM theory of RADIATION, for which he received a Nobel Prize in 1918. He also discovered the quantum of action, now known as Planck's constant, *h*. He championed Albert EINSTEIN's special theory of RELATIVITY, but he opposed the indeterministic, statistical worldview introduced by Niels BOHR, Max BORN, and Werner HEISENBERG after the advent of QUANTUM MECHANICS.

planet Any large body orbiting the SUN or another STAR (see PLANETS OF OTHER STARS), except COMETS, meteoroids (see METEOR), or SATELLITES of a larger body. The nine major planets known to orbit the sun, in order of distance, are MERCURY, VENUS, EARTH, MARS, JUPITER, SATURN, URANUS, NEPTUNE, and PLUTO. The terrestrial planets (the first four) are under 8,000 mi (13,000 km) across and rocky, with relatively thin atmospheres. The sun's heat may have kept more gases from condensing in them. The Jovian planets (the next four), formed where gases were cool enough to condense, grew very massive, and retained huge atmospheres of light gases. These "gas giants" appear similar in structure; none has an accessible surface. Pluto, by far the smallest major planet, resembles the icy satellites of the Jovian planets. There may be planets beyond it. The inner and outer planets are separated by the minor planets of the ASTEROID belt. In ASTROLOGY, great importance is placed on the planets' positions in the ZODIAC. See also PLANETESIMAL, SOLAR SYSTEM.

planetarium Institution for education in ASTRONOMY and related fields, especially space science, where a projector casts images of celestial objects as seen from the earth onto a hemispheric screen. Major planetariums seat over 600 and have extensive exhibit space and collections and projection domes 80 ft (25 m) or more across.

planetary nebula Any of a class of bright nebulae (see NEBULA) that may somewhat resemble planets through a small telescope. A planetary nebula is in fact the outer envelope shed by a red GIANT STAR not massive enough to become a SUPERNOVA. Instead, the intensely hot core becomes exposed (see WHITE DWARF) and ionizes the shell of gas, which expands at tens of miles per second.

planetesimal \,pla-nə-'te-sə-məl\ One of a class of hypothetical bodies that joined to form the PLANETS after condensing from dust and gas early in the solar system's history. According to the nebular hypothesis, as the SOLAR NEBULA formed, clumps of dust left in its midplane as it contracted coalesced into planetesimals the size of pebbles, of boulders, and then of bodies miles across. Pulled together by gravity, these formed protoplanets, precursors of the current planets.

plane tree Any of ten species of large, fast-growing shade trees that make up the genus *Platanus*, sole genus of the family Platanaceae, native to N. America, E Europe, and Asia. Plane trees are planted widely in cities for their resistance to diseases and to air pollution. They are characterized by scaling bark and large, deciduous, usually lobed leaves. Ball-shaped smooth or bristly seed clusters, which dangle singly and often persist after leaf fall, are key identifiers. Winter bark is patchy and picturesque; as the outer bark flakes off, inner bark shows shades of white, gray, green, and yellow. See also SYCAMORE.

planets of other stars *or* **extrasolar planets** Planets of stars other than the sun. Nearly 80 planets ranging from half to 60 times the mass of JUPITER have been detected around over 30 stars, including one similar to the sun. Many have highly elliptical orbits, and most of the rest stay very close to their stars. This raises questions about whether our own solar system is typical, but current methods can detect only massive planets in close orbits, whose gravity has measurable effects on their stars' motion.

plankton Minute marine and freshwater organisms that exist in a drifting, floating state. Plankton is the productive base of both marine and freshwater ecosystems, providing food for larger animals. As a human resource, plankton has only begun to be developed and used. The plantlike community of plankton is called PHYTOPLANKTON, and the animal-like community is called zooplankton, but many planktonic organisms are better described as PROTISTS. Most phytoplankton serves as food for zooplankton, but some of it is carried below the light zone. Zooplankton is used directly as food by fish (including herring) or mammals (including whales).

plant Any organism in the kingdom Plantae, consisting of multicellular, eukaryotic life forms (see EUKARYOTE) with six fundamental characteristics: PHOTOSYNTHESIS as the almost exclusive mode of nutrition; essentially unlimited growth by cell division; cells that contain CELLULOSE in their walls and are therefore somewhat rigid; the absence of organs of movement; the absence of sensory and nervous systems; and life histories that show ALTERNATION OF GENERATIONS. No definition of the kingdom completely excludes all nonplant organisms or even includes all plants. Many plants, for example, do not produce their own food by photosynthesis, being instead parasitic on other living plants (see PARASITISM). Many animals possess plantlike characteristics, such as a lack of mobility (e.g., SPONGES), but in general such animals lack other plant characteristics. PROTOZOANS, BACTERIA, ALGAE, SLIME MOLDS, and fungi (see FUNGUS) are usually not included in the plant kingdom.

Plantagenet \plan-'ta-jə-nət\, **House of** *or* **House of Anjou** \'an-jü\ Royal house of England (1154–1485) that provided 14 kings, including six from its cadet houses of LANCASTER and YORK. The line descended from Geoffrey, count of Anjou (d.1151), and his wife, MATILDA, daughter of the English king HENRY I. Some historians apply the name House of Anjou, or ANGEVIN DYNASTY, to only HENRY II, RICHARD I, and JOHN, and label their successors, including EDWARD I, EDWARD II, and EDWARD III, as Plantagenets. The name may have originated as a nickname (Plante-geneste) for Count Geoffrey, who planted broom shrubs (Latin *genista*) to improve his hunting covers. The Wars of the ROSES saw the defeat of the last Plantagenet king, RICHARD III, in 1485.

plantain Tall plant (*Musa paradisiaca*) of the BANANA family. Believed to have originated in S.E. Asia, the plantain grows 10–33 ft (3–10 m) tall and has a conical false "trunk" formed by the leaf sheaths. The green-colored fruit is larger than a banana and contains more starch. The fruit is not eaten raw but is boiled or fried, often with coconut juice or sugar as flavoring. It may also be dried for later use in cooking or ground for use as meal, which can be further refined to a flour. The plantain is a staple food in E. Africa, the Caribbean, and Latin America.

plantain \'plan-tᵊn\ Any of about 265 species of familiar garden, lawn, and roadside WEEDS in the genus *Plantago* of the family Plantaginaceae. The leaves lack a proper blade, having instead an expanded petiole (leafstalk), with several parallel main veins, emerging at the base of the stalk. Small flowers are borne in spikes or heads atop long leafless stalks. The greater plantain (*P. major*) provides seed spikes for bird food. Ribwort, or English, plantain (*P. lanceolata*) and hoary plantain (*P. media*) are troublesome weeds.

Plante, (Joseph) Jacques (Omer) (1929–1986) Canadian hockey player. Born in Shawinigan Falls, Quebec, he recorded a shutout in the first game of his 18-year NHL career. He was an integral member of the powerful Montreal Canadiens, which won a record five successive STANLEY CUPS (1956–60). He was the first goalie to wear a protective face mask (1959).

plant virus Any of various VIRUSES that can cause plant disease (e.g., the tobacco mosaic virus), some economically important because they infect crop and ornamental plants. Numerous plant viruses are rodlike and can be extracted readily from plant tissue and crystallized. Most lack the fatty membrane found in many animal viruses. Plant viruses are transmitted in various ways, most importantly through the bites of aphids and plant hoppers. Symptoms of virus infection include color changes, dwarfing, and tissue distortion. The appearance of streaks of color in certain tulips is caused by a virus.

plasma \'plaz-mə\ Straw-colored liquid part of BLOOD (including dissolved chemicals but not cells or PLATELETS). It serves as the blood's transport medium, helps maintain BLOOD PRESSURE, distributes body heat, and maintains the body's PH balance. More than 90% consists of water, about 7% proteins, and the rest other substances, including waste products of METABOLISM. Important plasma proteins include ALBUMIN, COAGULATION factors, and GLOBULINS, including GAMMA GLOBULIN and a hormone that stimulates ERYTHROCYTE formation.

plasma Electrically conducting medium in which there are roughly equal numbers of positively and negatively charged particles, produced when the atoms in a gas become ionized (see IONIZATION). Plasma is sometimes called the fourth state of MATTER (the first three being solid, liquid, and gas). A plasma is unique in the way it interacts with itself, with ELECTRIC and MAGNETIC fields, and with its environment. It is estimated that more than 99% of the matter in the universe exists in the plasma state.

plasmid \'plaz-məd\ Genetic element not contained within a CHROMOSOME occurring in many bacterial strains. Plasmids are circular DNA molecules that replicate independently of the bacterial chromosome. They are not essential for the bacterium but may give it a selective advantage. Plasmids are extremely valuable research tools, particularly in GENETIC ENGINEERING.

plasmodium \plaz-'mō-dē-əm\ Any of the parasitic PROTOZOANS of the genus *Plasmodium,* the cause of MALARIA. Infecting mammals, birds, and reptiles, plasmodia occur worldwide, especially in tropical and temperate zones. They are transmitted by the bite of the *Anopheles* MOSQUITO. Their life cycle is complex, proceeding through various stages inside organs and cells of the mosquitoes and vertebrate hosts. Four species give rise to four types of malaria.

plaster of paris Quick-setting GYPSUM plaster consisting of a fine white powder, calcium sulfate hemihydrate, which hardens when moistened and allowed to dry. It is made by heating gypsum to 250–360°F (120–180°C). Its name derives from the abundant gypsum found in Paris. It is used to make molds and casts for ceramics and sculptures, to precast and hold ornamental plasterwork on ceilings and cornices, and for orthopedic bandages (casts). Gesso (plaster of paris mixed with glue) was formerly applied to wood panels, plaster, stone, or canvas to provide the ground for tempera and oil painting.

plasticity Ability of certain SOLIDS to flow or to change shape permanently when subjected to stresses between those that produce temporary deformation, or elastic behavior, and those that cause failure of the material, or rupture. Plasticity allows a solid under the action of outside forces to become permanently deformed without rupturing; ELASTICITY enables a solid to return to its original shape after the load is removed. Plastic deformation occurs in many metal-forming processes (rolling, pressing, FORGING, wire drawing) and in geologic processes (rock folding and rock flow within earth under extremely high pressures and at elevated temperatures).

plastics POLYMERS that can be molded or shaped, usually by heat and pressure. Most are lightweight, transparent, tough organic compounds that do not conduct electricity well. They fall into two classes: Thermoplastics (e.g., POLYETHYLENE, polystyrene) can be melted and formed again and again; thermosetting plastics (e.g., POLYURETHANE, EPOXY), once formed, are destroyed if heated. Few plastics contain only RESIN; many also contain plasticizers (to

P

change the melting point and make them softer), colorants, reinforcements, and fillers (to improve mechanical properties such as stiffness), and stabilizers and antioxidants (to protect against aging, light, or biological agents). Plastics are not biodegradable (see BIODEGRADABILITY), but RECYCLING of plastics has become an important industry. Major industrial uses of plastics include cars, buildings, packaging, textiles, paints, adhesives, pipes, electrical and electronic components, prostheses, toys, brushes, and furniture. Common plastics include polyethylene terephthalate (beverage bottles), PVC (hoses), foamed polystyrene (insulated food containers), and Lucite (shatterproof windows).

plastic surgery SURGERY to correct disfigurement, restore function, or improve appearance. Cosmetic surgery solely to improve appearance is not the main focus of plastic surgery, which is principally utilized after disfigurement by burns or tumor removal, or for reconstructive work. Reconstructive plastic surgery corrects severe functional impairments, fixes physical abnormalities, and compensates for tissue lost to trauma or surgery. MICROSURGERY and computerized DIAGNOSTIC IMAGING techniques have revolutionized the field.

Plata, Río de la Estuary, PARANÁ and URUGUAY rivers, between Uruguay and Argentina. It is about 170 mi (275 km) long, and about 140 mi (220 km) wide at its mouth; at MONTEVIDEO it is about 60 mi (97 km) wide, and opposite BUENOS AIRES 25–28 mi (40–45 km) wide. The endpoint of S. America's second-largest river system, it is of great commercial importance.

Plata, viceroyalty of Río de la See viceroyalty of RÍO DE LA PLATA

Plataea \plə-ˈtē-ə\ Ancient city, BOEOTIA, E central Greece, south of THEBES. It was the scene of the Greek victory over the invading Persians in the Battle of PLATAEA (479 B.C.). Destroyed by the Spartans in 427 B.C., it was rebuilt under the Macedonian kings PHILIP II and ALEXANDER THE GREAT as a symbol of Greek courage in resisting Persia.

Plataea, Battle of (479 B.C.) Battle between Greek and Persian forces near Plataea (modern Plataiaí) in Boeotia. A largely Spartan force, including HELOTS, defeated the Persian army of XERXES I, led by Mardonius; the victory marked the end of Persian attempts to invade mainland Greece.

plateau Extensive area of flat upland, usually bounded by an escarpment on all sides. Together with mountain-enclosed basins, plateaus cover about 45% of the earth's land surface. Low relief distinguishes plateaus from MOUNTAINS, although their origin may be similar. Plateaus, being high, often create their own local climate; the topography of plateaus and their surroundings often produces arid and semiarid conditions.

Plateau Indians Any of various Native American tribes that inhabited the high plateau between the Rocky Mtns. on the east and the Cascade Range on the west. Most spent their summers in the upland hunting grounds, and their winters in permanent villages by rivers. Among this group were the Coeur d'Alene, FLATHEAD, Klamath, Kutenai, Modoc, NEZ PERCÉ, Spokan, Thompson, and Salish.

platelet *or* **thrombocyte** Small, colorless, irregular blood cell crucial in COAGULATION. Produced in BONE MARROW and stored in the SPLEEN, platelets accumulate to block a cut in a blood vessel and provide a surface for fibrin strands to adhere to, contract to pull the strands together, and take part in the conversion sequence of coagulation factors. They also store and transport several chemicals and absorb foreign bodies, including viruses.

plate tectonics Theory that the earth's LITHOSPHERE is divided into about 12 large plates and several small ones that float on and travel independently over the ASTHENOSPHERE. The theory revolutionized the geological sciences in the 1960s by combining the earlier idea of CONTINENTAL DRIFT and the new concept of SEAFLOOR SPREADING. Each plate consists of rigid rock created by upwelling magma at OCEANIC RIDGES, where plates diverge. Where two plates converge, a SUBDUCTION ZONE forms. Most earthquakes and volcanoes occur along the margins of tectonic plates. The interior of a plate moves as a rigid body, with few earthquakes and little volcanic activity.

Plath, Sylvia (1932–1963) U.S. poet. Born in Boston, Plath published her first poem at 8. While attending Cambridge Univ., she married Ted HUGHES. After their separation, she committed suicide at 30. Her reputation grew rapidly thereafter; by the 1970s she was considered a major contemporary poet. Her works, often confessional and preoccupied with alienation, death, and self-destruction, include the volumes *Ariel* (1965) and *The Collected Poems* (1981, Pulitzer

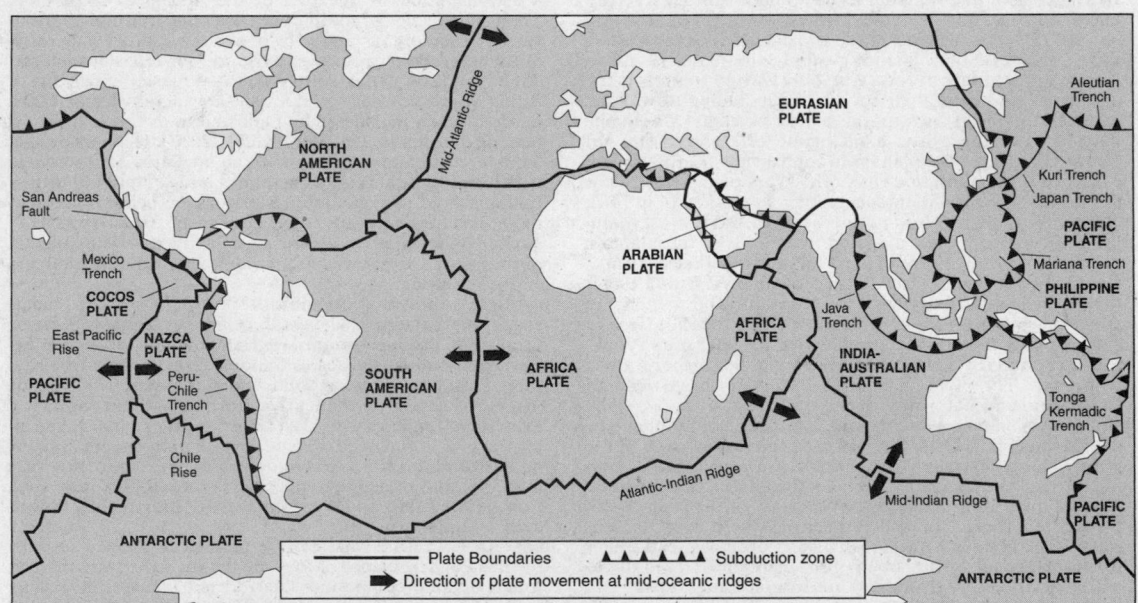

Plate tectonics Major tectonic plates of the earth's lithosphere. New lithosphere is created by upwelling magma at certain plate boundaries, called spreading centers or oceanic ridges, where the plates diverge. At other boundaries, called subduction zones, plates converge until one is forced under the other (subducted) into the earth. The continents are rigidly connected to their respective plates and move as the plates move, a few inches a year.

Prize) and a semiautobiographical novel, *The Bell Jar* (1963).

plating Coating a METAL or other material, such as plastic or china, with a hard, nonporous metallic surface to improve durability and beauty. Early plated goods ("old SHEFFIELD PLATE") consist of a sandwich of copper between two layers of silver. Today surfaces such as gold, silver, stainless steel, palladium, copper, and nickel are applied by dipping an object into a solution containing the desired surface material, which is deposited by chemical or electrochemical action (see ELECTROPLATING). Much plating is done for decorative purposes, but still more is done to increase the durability and CORROSION resistance of softer materials. Most automotive parts, appliances, housewares, and plumbing and electronic equipment are plated for durability. See also GALVANIZING.

platinum One of the TRANSITION ELEMENTS, chemical symbol Pt, atomic number 78. A very heavy, silvery-white precious METAL, it is soft and ductile, with a high melting point and good resistance to corrosion and chemical attack. Small amounts of IRIDIUM are commonly added for a harder, stronger ALLOY that retains platinum's advantages. Platinum is usually found as alloys of 80–90% purity in PLACER DEPOSITS. It is indispensable in high-temperature laboratory work, for electrodes, dishes, and electrical contacts that resist chemical attack even when very hot. Platinum is used in dental alloys and surgical pins. Known as "white gold," it is used in expensive jewelry. An alloy of platinum and cobalt forms the most powerful permanent MAGNETS known. Platinum compounds (VALENCE 2 or 4) include many coordination complexes. It and some compounds are useful CATALYSTS, particularly for HYDROGENATION and in catalytic converters.

Plato \\'plā-tō\\ *orig.* Aristocles (428?–347? B.C.) Greek philosopher whose teachings and writings constitute an essential part of Western philosophy. His father claimed descent from the last king of Athens. Plato must have known SOCRATES from boyhood. After Socrates' death, he fled Athens but returned 12 years later and founded the famous school of philosophy called the Academy, where he taught ARISTOTLE. Building on Socrates' life and thought, he developed a profound, wide-ranging, and immensely influential philosophical system (see PLATONISM). His thought has logical, epistemological, and metaphysical aspects, but much of its underlying motivation is ethical. It is presented in his many dialogues, in most of which Socrates

Plato Roman herm, from a Greek original, 4th cent. B.C.

plays a leading role (e.g., *Apology, Protagoras, Meno, Phaedo, Symposium, Republic, Sophist, Timaeus,* and *Laws*). See also NEOPLATONISM.

Platonism \\'plā-tə-ˌni-zəm\\ Any philosophy that embodies some major idea of PLATO's, especially in taking abstract forms as metaphysically more basic than material things. Platonism is characterized by an intense concern for the quality of human life—always ethical, often religious, and sometimes political, based on a belief in unchanging and eternal realities (the Platonic Forms), independent of the changing things perceived by the senses. This belief in absolute values rooted in an eternal world distinguishes Platonism from the philosophies of Plato's immediate predecessors and successors and from later philosophies inspired by them. See also NEOPLATONISM.

platypus *or* **duckbill** MONOTREME amphibious MAMMAL (*Ornithorhynchus anatinus*) of lakes and streams in E Australia and Tasmania. About 23 in. (60 cm) long, the squat-bodied platypus has a ducklike snout, short legs, webbed feet, and a beaverlike tail. Each day it eats nearly its own weight in crustaceans, fishes, frogs, mollusks, tadpoles, and earthworms; lacking teeth, it crushes its food with ridges in the bill. The male's heel bears a spur connected to a poison-secreting gland. Large fishes and perhaps snakes prey on platypuses. Formerly trapped for their dense, soft fur, they are now protected.

Plautus \\'plȯ-təs\\ (254?–184 B.C.) Roman comic playwright. Little is known about his life. He borrowed plots and dramatic techniques from Greek authors, especially NEW COMEDY playwrights such as MENANDER. His plays, written in verse, were often farces of mistaken identity with opportunities for slapstick, and he popularized such character types as the braggart soldier and the sly servant. His 21 surviving comedies, among the earliest known works in Latin, include *The Pot of Gold, The Captives, The Two Menaechmuses, The Braggart Warrior,* and *Pseudolus.* His work influenced later European comedy, notably William SHAKESPEARE's *Comedy of Errors* and MOLIÈRE's *The Miser*.

playa \\'plī-ə\\ *or* **pan** *or* **flat** *or* **dry lake** Flat-bottomed depression that is periodically covered by water. Playas occur in interior desert basins and adjacent to coasts in arid and semiarid regions. The water that periodically covers the playa slowly filters into the groundwater system, causing the deposition of salt, sand, and mud in the depression.

Player, Gary (Jim) (b.1935) S. African golfer. Born in Johannesburg, he entered the U.S. PGA circuit in 1955. He won the British Open three times (1959, 1968, 1974), the Master's three times (1961, 1974, 1978), the U.S. PGA twice (1962, 1972), and the U.S. Open once (1965).

player piano Piano that mechanically plays music encoded as perforations on a paper roll. An early version (1897) was a cabinet placed in front of an ordinary piano, with wooden "fingers" projecting over the keyboard. A paper roll with perforations corresponding to the notes passed over a tracker bar to activate the release of air by pneumatic devices that set the fingers in motion; the user could control tempo and loudness by levers and pedals. Soon this mechanism was built into the piano itself. The later reproducing player piano could reproduce nuances of tempo and dynamics, the roll being produced by the actual performance. After the 1920s the phonograph led to the instrument's quick decline.

playing cards Small rectangular cards used for playing games, and sometimes for divination and conjuring. Modern cards are divided into four suits: spades, hearts, diamonds, and clubs. A complete pack, or deck, of cards includes 13 cards in each suit (10 numbered cards and three court cards—king, queen, and jack); two extra cards, called jokers (portraying a medieval jester), are often included as well. Their origin is obscure—China and India being the two most likely sources—as is the meaning of their symbols. The earliest reference to cards in Europe occurs in Italy in 1299. The 52-card French deck is now standard throughout the world. See also TAROT.

plea bargaining Negotiation of an agreement between the prosecution and the defense whereby the defendant pleads guilty to a lesser offense or (in the case of multiple offenses) to one or more of the offenses charged, in exchange for more lenient sentencing, recommendations, a specific sentence, or a dismissal of other charges. Supporters claim plea bargaining speeds court proceedings and guarantees a conviction; opponents believe it prevents justice from being served.

plebeian \\ple-'bē-ən\\ (Latin, *plebs*) Member of the general citizenry, as opposed to the PATRICIAN class, in the ancient ROMAN REPUBLIC. Plebeians were originally excluded from all public offices except military TRIBUNE, and they were forbidden to marry patricians. They carried on a campaign for equal rights called Conflict of the Orders, developing a separate political organization and seceding in protest from the state at least five times. Eventually a plebeian dictator (appointed 287 B.C.) made measures passed in the plebeian assembly binding on the whole community.

plebiscite \\'ple-bə-ˌsīt\\ Vote by the people of an entire country or district to decide an issue. Voters are asked to accept or reject a given proposal rather than choose between alternative proposals. By bypassing political parties, plebiscites

offer a way to claim a popular mandate without permitting an opposition party, and totalitarian regimes have used them to legitimize their power. See also REFERENDUM AND INITIATIVE.

Plehve \\'plä-vyi\\, **Vyacheslav (Konstantinovich)** (1846–1904) Russian administrator. In 1881 he was appointed director of the secret police in the ministry of the interior. He became head of the imperial chancellery in 1894 and minister of the interior in 1902. He suppressed revolutionary and liberal movements and harshly pursued Russification policies against minority nationality groups. He was assassinated by a member of the Socialist Revolutionary Party.

Pleiades \\'plē-ə-ˌdēz\\ OPEN CLUSTER of stars in the constellation Taurus, about 400 light-years from earth. It contains a large amount of bright nebulous material and several hundred stars, of which six or seven, visible to the unaided eye, have figured prominently in myth and literature. In the Northern Hemisphere, the motion of the Pleiades in spring and autumn has from ancient times marked the seafaring and farming seasons.

Pleistocene epoch \\'plīs-tə-ˌsēn\\ Earlier and longer of the two epochs of the QUATERNARY PERIOD, 1.8 million to 10,000 years ago. At the height of the Pleistocene glacial ages, more than 30% of the earth's land area was covered by glacial ice; during the interglacial stages, about 10% was. Animals and plants began to resemble those of today. Flowering plants proliferated, and new groups of land mammals, including humans, appeared. At the end of the epoch, mass extinctions occurred; in N. America more than 30 genera of large mammals became extinct within about 2,000 years. Of the many causes proposed for these extinctions, the two most likely are changing environment with changing climate and disruption of the ecological pattern by early humans. See table at GEOLOGIC TIME.

Plekhanov \\pli-'kä-nóf\\, **Georgy (Valentinovich)** (1856–1918) Russian Marxist theorist. Active in the Populist movement and a leader of the Land and Freedom group (1877–80), he fled Russia to avoid arrest and went into a long exile in Geneva (1880–1917). In 1883 he founded the Liberation of Labor, which became the RUSSIAN SOCIAL-DEMOCRATIC WORKERS' PARTY (1898). In *Socialism and Political Struggle* (1883) and *Our Differences* (1885), he described a two-phase revolutionary scheme that influenced Russian Marxist thought and Vladimir LENIN. After the party split (1903), Plekhanov joined the MENSHEVIKS but spent years trying to reunite the party. He opposed the Bolshevik seizure of power, and died in exile in Finland.

Plessy vs. Ferguson U.S. Supreme Court decision (1896) that established the legality of racial SEGREGATION so long as facilities were "separate but equal." The case involved a challenge to Louisiana laws requiring separate rail cars for blacks and whites. Though the laws were upheld, a famous dissent by J. M. HARLAN advanced the idea that the U.S. Constitution is "color-blind." The *Plessy* decision was overturned in 1954 by *BROWN VS. BOARD OF EDUCATION.*

Pleven \\plä-'ven\\, **René** (1901–1993) French politician and premier (1950–51, 1951–52). He served in Charles DE GAULLE's wartime government (1940–45). He cofounded with François MITTERRAND the Democratic and Socialist Union of the Resistance, serving as its president 1946–53. As minister of defense (1949–50, 1952–54), he sponsored the Pleven Plan for a unified European army, but the European Defense Community, based on his plan, collapsed in 1954. He served as minister of justice 1969–73.

Pliny the Elder \\'plin-ē\\ *Latin* Gaius Plinius Secundus (A.D. 23–79) Roman scholar. Pliny pursued a military career, held official positions, and later spent years in semiretirement, studying and writing. His fame rests on his *Naturalis historia,* or *Natural History* (A.D. 77), an encyclopedic work of uneven accuracy that was the European authority on scientific matters up to the Middle Ages.

Pliny the Younger *Latin* Gaius Plinius Caecilius Secundus (A.D. 61/62–113?) Roman author and administrator. The nephew of PLINY THE ELDER, he is known for the nine books of private letters he published in A.D. 100–109. The carefully composed letter, at that time a fashion among the wealthy, was transformed by Pliny into an art. His are charming and meticulous occasional pieces on diverse liter-

ary, social, and domestic themes that intimately illustrate public and private life in the heyday of the Roman empire.

Pliocene epoch \\'plī-ə-ˌsēn\\ Last and shortest epoch of the TERTIARY PERIOD, 5–1.8 million years ago. Pliocene environments were generally cooler and drier than those of preceding Tertiary epochs. A modern aspect is seen in the vertebrate faunas of the Northern Hemisphere. In general, Pliocene mammals grew larger than those of earlier epochs. The more advanced primates continued to evolve, and it is possible that *AUSTRALOPITHECUS,* the first creature that can be termed human, developed late in the Pliocene. See table at GEOLOGIC TIME.

Plisetskaya \\pli-'set-skə-yə\\, **Maya (Mikhaylovna)** (b.1925) Russian prima ballerina, noted for her technical virtuosity and ability to integrate acting with dancing. She joined the BOLSHOI BALLET as a soloist in 1943 and toured worldwide, also appearing as a guest artist with several companies, including the Paris Opera. In the 1980s she was a guest ballet director in Rome and later in Madrid.

Maya Plisetskaya in *Swan Lake,* 1961

PL Kyodan \\'pē-'el-'kyō-dän\\ *in full* Perfect Liberty Kyodan. Religious group founded in Japan by Miki Tokuchika in 1946 as a revival of his father's group, Hito-no-michi. It teaches that the goal of human life is joyful self-expression. The believer may pray that his troubles be transferred to the patriarch, who is strengthened for vicarious suffering by the group's collective prayers. Today PL Kyodan claims more than 2.5 million adherents worldwide.

PLO See PALESTINE LIBERATION ORGANIZATION

Plotinus \\plō-'tī-nəs\\ (A.D. 205–270) Egyptian-Roman philosopher. Probably born in Egypt, he studied in Persia and moved to Rome in A.D. 244, where he became the center of an influential circle of intellectuals. His attempt to form a Platonic republic in Campania about 265 was halted by GALLIENUS. He was the founder of NEOPLATONISM; his collected works, the *Enneads,* compiled by his disciple Porphyry (232?–c.305), are the first and greatest collection of Neoplatonic writings. His works strongly influenced early Christian theology, and his philosophy was widely studied and emulated for many centuries.

Plovdiv \\'plòv-ˌdif\\ City (pop., 1998 est.: 340,000), S central Bulgaria. From A.D. 46 it was called Trimontium and was the capital of the Roman province of THRACE. It changed hands repeatedly during the Middle Ages until 1364, when it was captured by the Turks. It was united with Bulgaria in 1885 and assumed its present name after 1919.

plover \\'plə-vər, 'plō-vər\\ Any of about 36 species (family Charadriidae, order Charadriiformes) of plump-breasted shorebirds. Plovers are 6–12 in. (15–30 cm) long and have long wings, longish legs, a short neck, and a straight, short bill. Many species are plain brown, gray, or sandy above and whitish below. Others are black below in breeding season. Many species run along the shoreline, snapping up small aquatic invertebrates. They have a melodious whistled call. Both parents incubate the eggs and care for the young. See also KILLDEER.

plow *or* **plough** Most important agricultural implement since the beginning of history, used to turn and break up SOIL, to bury crop residues, and to help control WEEDS. The earliest plows were undoubtedly digging sticks with handles for pulling or pushing. By Roman times, plows were pulled by oxen or horses, and today they are drawn by TRACTORS.

plum Any of various widely cultivated trees in the genus *Prunus* of the ROSE family, and their edible fruits. Plums are varied in native and cultivated kinds, and well adapted to a wide range of soils and climatic conditions. The fruits show a wide range of size, flavor, color, and texture. They are widely eaten fresh, dried as prunes, cooked, or baked in pastries. In full bloom, plum trees are covered with densely packed, showy flower clusters. The smooth-skinned fruit has a fleshy, juicy exterior and a hard interior stone or pit. Dried plums are called prunes.

plumbago See GRAPHITE

plumbing System of pipes and fixtures installed in a building to distribute drinkable water and remove waterborne wastes. Virtually no improvement in plumbing systems was made from the time of the ancient Roman AQUEDUCTS and lead pipes until the 19th cent. Present-day water pipes are made of steel, copper, brass, plastic, or other nontoxic material. A building's waste-disposal system has two parts: the drainage system and the venting system. The drainage portion comprises pipes leading from various fixture drains to the central main, which is connected to the sewage system. The venting system consists of pipes leading from an air inlet (usually on the roof) to various points within the drainage system; by providing circulation of air, it protects the trap seals of fixtures from siphonage and back pressure. See also SEWAGE SYSTEM, WATER-SUPPLY SYSTEM.

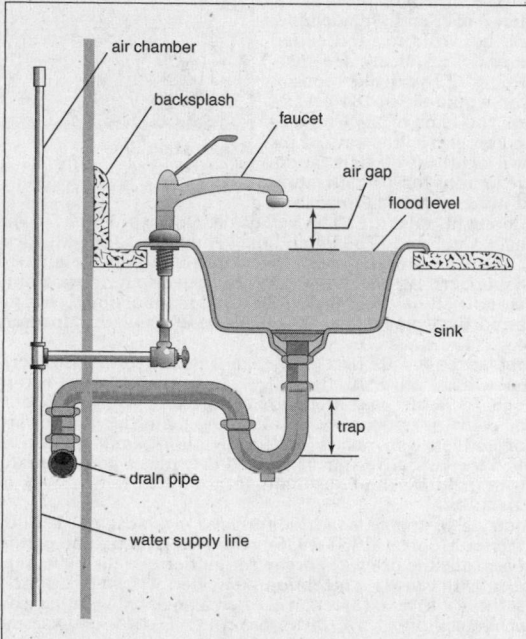

air chamber

backsplash

faucet

air gap

flood level

sink

trap

drain pipe

water supply line

Plumbing The basic components of a plumbing fixture include the water-supply pipes, a valve or faucet for controlling the flow of water, and a drainpipe to carry wastewater away. An air chamber may be added to the supply line to cushion the effects of water hammer. A trap in the drain line leaves a plug of water in the pipe to prevent unwanted sewer gases from entering the room via the drain.

Plunket, St. Oliver (1629–1681) Irish prelate, the last man to suffer martyrdom for the Catholic faith in England. Ordained in Rome, he represented the Irish bishops at the Holy See. In 1669 he was appointed primate of Ireland, and he worked to restore the disorganized church in Ireland. Renewed persecution forced him into hiding in 1673. In the anti-Catholic hysteria caused by the POPISH PLOT (1678), he was betrayed and imprisoned. After a farcical trial, he was convicted of treason and was hanged, drawn, and quartered.

Plutarch \'plü-ˌtärk\ *Greek* Plutarchos *Latin* Plutarchus (A.D. 46?–after 119) Greek biographer and author. His literary output was immense, but his popularity rests primarily on his *Parallel Lives,* a series of pairs of biographies of famous Greeks and Romans. Displaying impressive learning and research, the *Lives* exhibit noble deeds and characters and provide model patterns of behavior. The *Moralia,* or *Ethica,* contains his surviving writings on ethical, religious, physical, political, and literary topics. His works profoundly influenced the evolution of the essay, biography, and historical writing in 16th–19th-cent. Europe.

Pluto Ninth planet from the sun, discovered in 1930 by Clyde W. Tombaugh (1906–1997) and named after the Greek god of the underworld. It is usually the outermost of the known planets, averaging about 3.7 billion mi (5.9 billion km) from the sun, but its eccentric orbit brings it closer than NEPTUNE for 22 years of its 248-year orbit. Pluto appears relatively faint even through a telescope. Its axis is tipped 122°, so it rotates nearly on its side and "backwards," once every 6.387 days. Pluto's diameter is about 1,500 mi (2,400 km), roughly two-thirds that of the moon; it has less than 1% of earth's mass and about 6% of its surface gravity. Observations by INFRARED ASTRONOMY suggest that Pluto has large methane ice polar caps. Its estimated average surface temperature is –380°F (–205°C). Its thin atmosphere contains methane and possibly nitrogen. Pluto has one moon, Charon, discovered in 1978.

plutonium Radioactive (see RADIOACTIVITY) chemical ELEMENT, chemical symbol Pu, atomic number 94. A member of the ACTINIDE series of TRANSITION ELEMENTS, it is used in certain types of nuclear reactors (see NUCLEAR POWER) and in NUCLEAR WEAPONS. It is found in nature only in traces produced by natural NEUTRON irradiation in URANIUM ores. It is produced by neutron irradiation of uranium-238. Plutonium is a silvery METAL that tarnishes in air; it feels warm because of energy released in ALPHA DECAY. Its ISOTOPES, all radioactive, are highly toxic (see RADIATION INJURY) because they give off alpha particles and are specifically absorbed by bone marrow.

Plymouth City (metro. area pop., 1999 est.: 256,000), in DEVON, SW England. It was named Sudstone in the DOMESDAY BOOK of 1086. It was the port from which the English fleet sailed against the Spanish ARMADA in 1588. It was the last port touched by the *Mayflower* before its voyage to America in 1620. During World War II it suffered bomb damage from air raids. The rebuilt city has some of the finest commercial, shopping, and civic centers in Britain and new bridges over the Plym and Tamar rivers.

Plymouth City (pop., 2000: 52,000), SE Massachusetts, on Plymouth Bay. It was the site of the first permanent European settlement in New England, the Colony of New Plymouth, founded by the PILGRIMS in 1620 and governed under the MAYFLOWER COMPACT until 1691, when it became part of MASSACHUSETTS BAY COLONY. Its seaside location and historic associations make Plymouth an outstanding summer resort. Historical attractions include Plimoth Plantation, a re-creation of the original Pilgrim village.

Plymouth Co. (1606–9) Commercial trading company chartered by the English crown to colonize the coast of present-day New England. Also called the Virginia Colony of Plymouth, its shareholders were merchants of Plymouth, Bristol, and Exeter. It established a colony on the coast of Maine in 1607, but soon abandoned it. Inactive after 1609, it was reorganized in 1620 as the Council for New England. See also LONDON CO.

plywood Manufactured panel made up of three or more thin plies (layers) of wood. Each ply is laid down with its grain running perpendicular to the one before it. A strong and inexpensive alternative to solid wood, plywood is widely used both in cabinetmaking (for chests, dressers, wardrobes, and tables) and in house construction (for walls, ceilings, subfloors, and doors).

PMS See PREMENSTRUAL SYNDROME

pneumatic structure Membrane structure that is stabilized by the pressure of compressed air. Air-supported structures are supported by internal air pressure. A network of cables stiffens the fabric, and the assembly is supported by a rigid ring at the edge. The slightly increased air pressure is maintained by compressors or fans; air locks at entrances prevent loss of pressure. Air-supported membranes, first devised by Walter Bird in the late 1940s, found use in temporary warehouses, exhibition buildings, and enclosed stadiums. Air-inflated structures, by contrast, employ double-wall plastic tubes and compartments inflated to provide structural stiffness; the usable part of the structure is not inflated. Pneumatic structures are perhaps the most cost-effective type of building for very long spans.

P

pneumococcus \ˌnü-mə-ˈkä-kəs\ Spheroidal bacterium *(Streptococcus pneumoniae)* that causes human diseases including PNEUMONIA, sinusitis, ear infection, and MENINGITIS. Usually occurring in the upper respiratory tract, this gram-positive (see GRAM STAIN) COCCUS is often found in a chain configuration and surrounded by a POLYSACCHARIDE capsule. Their disease-causing ability resides in the capsule, which delays or prevents their destruction by cells in the bloodstream that normally engulf foreign material.

pneumonia \nu̇-ˈmōn-yə\ INFLAMMATION and solidification of LUNG tissue caused by infection, foreign particle inhalation, or irradiation, but usually by BACTERIA. It is serious but rarely fatal. *Mycoplasma pneumoniae* is the most common cause in healthy individuals. The bronchi and alveoli may be inflamed. Coughing becomes severe and may bring up flecks of blood. *Streptococcus pneumoniae*, more common and generally more severe, usually affects only those with low resistance, especially in hospitals. A highly lethal form caused by *Klebsiella pneumoniae* is almost always confined to hospitalized patients. Other bacterial pneumonias include *Pneumocystis carinii* pneumonia (rare except in AIDS) and LEGIONNAIRES' DISEASE. Most respond to ANTIBIOTICS. VIRUSES set the stage for bacterial pneumonia by weakening the immune system more often than they cause pneumonia directly. Fungal pneumonia usually occurs in hospitalized persons, but contaminated dusts can cause it in healthy individuals. It can develop rapidly and may be fatal.

p-n junction Electric contact in TRANSISTORS and related devices between two different types of material called *p*-type and *n*-type SEMICONDUCTORS. These are pure semiconductor materials, such as SILICON, to which impurities have been added. Materials of *p*-type contain "holes" (vacancies formerly occupied by ELECTRONS) that behave like positively charged particles; *n*-type materials contain free electrons. ELECTRIC CURRENT flows more easily across a *p-n* junction in one direction than in the other. The *p-n* junction forms the basis for COMPUTER CHIPS, SOLAR CELLS, and other electronic devices.

Pobedonostsev \pə-byi-də-ˈnȯst-syif\, **Konstantin (Petrovich)** (1827–1907) Russian administrator. A close adviser to ALEXANDER III, he influenced him to adopt reactionary policies. As director general of the Holy Synod of the Russian Orthodox Church (1880–1905), he assumed great power over domestic policy in education, religion, and censorship. Nicknamed "the Grand Inquisitor," he became the symbol of Russian monarchical absolutism.

Pocahontas \ˌpō-kə-ˈhän-təs\ (1595?–1617) POWHATAN Indian woman who helped maintain peace between English colonists and Native Americans by befriending the settlers at JAMESTOWN, Va. Daughter of the powerful chief POWHATAN, Pocahontas intervened to spare the life of the colony's captive leader, John SMITH. She subsequently converted to Christianity and wedded the colonist John Rolfe (1585–1622), which furthered efforts toward peace. She traveled to England, where she was received at court, but died of smallpox there.

Pocahontas Portrait by an unknown artist, 1615

pocket billiards See POOL
pocket gopher See GOPHER
pocket mouse Any of about 30 species of nocturnal N. American RODENTS constituting the genus *Perognathus* (family Heteromyidae), having fur-lined, external cheek pouches. They are 2.5–5 in. (6–13 cm) long, with a tail of similar length. They usually inhabit dry regions. They carry food (mainly seeds) in their pouches and store it in their burrows. Spiny pocket mice, found from Mexico through Central America, are nocturnal burrowers that inhabit wet, forested regions as well as dry country.

Podgorica \ˈpȯd-ˌgȯr-ēt-sä\ City (pop., 2000 est.: 131,000), capital of MONTENEGRO, S Yugoslavia. As a feudal state capital in the early European Middle Ages, it was known as Ribnica; it was called Podgorica from 1326. It was ruled by the Turks 1474–1878. In 1916 it was occupied by Austria, in 1941 by Italy, and in 1943 by Germany. From 1946 until 1992, it was called Titograd in honor of Marshal TITO.

podiatry \pə-ˈdī-ə-trē\ *or* **chiropody** \kə-ˈräp-əd-ē\ Medical specialty dealing with the FOOT. Podiatrists diagnose and treat foot diseases, disabilities, and deformities by means of PHYSICAL MEDICINE AND REHABILITATION, special shoes and other mechanical devices, drugs, and minor surgery.

Poe, Edgar Allan *orig.* Edgar Poe (1809–1849) U.S. poet, critic, and short-story writer. Born in Boston, Poe was raised by foster parents in Richmond, Va., following his mother's death in 1811. At various times he lived in Boston, Richmond, Baltimore, New York, and Philadelphia, and he wrote for and edited several periodicals. He married a 13-year-old cousin, who would die in 1847. Alcohol, the bane of his irregular and eccentric life, caused his own death at 40. His works are famous for his cultivation of mystery and the macabre.

Edgar Allan Poe
Daguerreotype by S. W. Hartshorn, 1848

Among his tales are "The Fall of the House of Usher," "The Black Cat," and "The Pit and the Pendulum." "The Murders in the Rue Morgue" and "The Purloined Letter" initiated the modern DETECTIVE STORY. His poems are musical and sensuous, as in "The Bells"; they include touching lyrics inspired by women (e.g., "Annabel Lee") and the uncanny (e.g., "The Raven").

poet laureate Title first granted in England for poetic excellence. Begun in 1616, the office was formally established in 1668. Its holder was originally expected to compose poems for court or national occasions; now the office is a reward for eminence in poetry and carries no specific duties. In 1985 the U.S. government created the title of poet laureate, to be held by the consultant in poetry to the Library of CONGRESS.

Poetry U.S. poetry magazine founded in Chicago in 1912 by Harriet Monroe (1860–1936), who was its longtime editor. It remains the principal organ for modern English-language poetry. Because its inception coincided with the CHICAGO LITERARY RENAISSANCE, it is often associated with the raw, local-color poetry of Carl SANDBURG, E. L. MASTERS, and Vachel LINDSAY, but it also championed new formalistic movements, including IMAGISM. Ezra POUND was its original European correspondent. In 2002 it received a gift of $100 million from the heiress Ruth Lilly.

poetry Writing that formulates a concentrated imaginative awareness of experience in language chosen and arranged to create a specific emotional response through its meaning, sound, and rhythm. It may be distinguished from prose by its compression, frequent use of conventions of METER and RHYME, use of the line as a formal unit, heightened vocabulary, and freedom of syntax. Its emotional content is expressed through a variety of techniques, including METAPHOR. See also PROSE POEM, PROSODY.

pogrom \pə-ˈgräm\ (Russian: "devastation, riot") Mob attack, condoned by authorities, against persons and property of a religious, racial, or national minority, especially Jews in Russia. After the assassination of Czar ALEXANDER II (1881), false rumors associating Jews with the murder aroused Russian mobs in over 200 cities and towns to attack Jews and destroy their property. Mob attacks again became common in 1903–6. The government's anti-Semitic policy (1881–1917) and reluctance to stop the attacks led many anti-Semites to believe that their violence was legitimate. Pogroms also occurred in Poland and in Germany during Adolf HITLER's regime.

pogy See MENHADEN
Poincaré \pwaⁿ-kä-ˈrā\, **(Jules-) Henri** (1854–1912) French mathematician, theoretical astronomer, and philosopher of science. He wrote a doctoral dissertation on DIFFERENTIAL EQUATIONS (1879). Working at the Univ. of Paris in celestial

mechanics and mathematical analysis, he independently obtained many of Albert EINSTEIN's results relating to the special theory of relativity, and published them in a paper on the dynamics of the electron (1906). He later wrote books for the general public on the meaning and importance of science and mathematics.

poinsettia \pȯin-'se-tē-ə\ Popular flowering plant *(Euphorbia pulcherrima),* best-known member of the diverse SPURGE family. Native to Mexico and Central America, it grows in moist, wet, wooded ravines and on rocky hillsides. What appear to be flower petals are actually colored leaflike BRACTS that surround a central cluster of tiny yellow flowers. Cultivated varieties are available with red, white, pink, mottled, and striped bracts. Milky latex in the stems and leaves can be irritating to sensitized persons or animals.

Pointe-Noire \ˌpwaⁿt-'nwär\ City (pop., 1992 est.: 576,000) and port, SW Republic of the Congo. It was the capital (1950–58) of the Middle Congo region of FRENCH EQUATORIAL AFRICA. With independence in 1958, it was replaced by BRAZZAVILLE as the national capital, but it remained important for trade. The Congo's second-largest city, it is a principal port and commercial center.

Point Four Program U.S. policy of technical assistance and economic aid to underdeveloped countries, proposed by Pres. Harry TRUMAN as the fourth point of his 1949 inaugural address. It was merged with other foreign-aid programs in 1953. Technical assistance, mainly in agriculture, public health, and education, was provided through contracts with U.S. business and educational organizations.

Poiret \pwä-'re\, **Paul** (1879–1944) French fashion designer. He opened his own shop in Paris in 1902. In 1908 he revived the Empire style, popular in France during the reign of Napoleon. Seeking to restore naturalness to female garb, he was principally responsible for replacing the corset with the girdle. He is best known for the hobble skirt. Fringed and tasseled capes, multicolored feathers, and fox stoles imparted a theatrical look to his designs. His flowing Greek costumes were extremely popular in the prewar era, but his popularity faded in the 1920s and he died in poverty. He is often regarded as the most influential fashion designer of all time.

poison Any substance (natural or synthetic) that damages living tissues and injures or kills. Poisons produced by living organisms are often called TOXINS, or VENOMS if produced by animals. Poisons may be ingested, inhaled, injected, or absorbed through the skin. They do not always have an all-or-none effect; some are far more toxic than others. Poisoning may be acute (a single dose does significant damage) or chronic (repeated or continuous doses produce an eventual effect, as with chemical CARCINOGENS). The effects produced by poisons may be local (hives, blisters, inflammation) or systemic (hemorrhage, convulsions, vomiting, diarrhea, clouding of the senses, paralysis, respiratory or cardiac arrest). Agricultural PESTICIDES are often poisonous to humans. Some industrial chemicals can be very toxic or carcinogenic. Most drugs and health-care products can be poisons if taken inappropriately or in excess. Most forms of RADIATION can be toxic (see RADIATION INJURY). See also ANTIDOTE, FOOD POISONING, LEAD POISONING, MERCURY POISONING, MUSHROOM POISONING.

poison hemlock Any of several poisonous herbaceous plants of the PARSLEY family, especially the common *Conium maculatum,* believed to be the plant that killed SOCRATES. A tall biennial, this plant has green stems spotted with red or purple, large compound leaves, and white flowers. Though the poison is concentrated in the seeds, the entire plant is dangerous to livestock when fresh. It is not related to the HEMLOCK. Water hemlocks *(Cicuta* species) are similar and also dangerous.

poison ivy Either of two species of white-fruited woody vines or shrubs of the SUMAC, or cashew, family, native to N. America. The species found in E N. America *(Toxicodendron,* or *Rhus, radicans)* is abundant; a W species known as poison oak *(T.,* or *R., diversilobum)* is less common. Poisonous to the touch, the plant causes severe inflammation and blistering of the skin. Key identifiers are leaves with three leaflets. The principal toxin (urushiol) may be carried from the plant on clothing, shoes, tools, or soil; by animals; or by smoke from burning plants.

poison sumac Attractive, narrow shrub or small tree *(Rhus,* or *Toxicodendron, vernix)* of the SUMAC, or cashew, family, also called poison elder, native to swampy acidic soils of E N. America. Whitish waxy berries droop loosely from its stalks. The clear sap, which blackens on exposure to air, is extremely toxic and irritating to the skin for many people.

Poitier \'pwä-tē-ˌā\, **Sidney** (b.1924) U.S. actor. Born in Miami and raised in the Bahamas, he acted with the American Negro Theatre before making his film debut in 1950. He played notable roles in *Blackboard Jungle* (1955), *The Defiant Ones* (1958), *Lilies of the Field* (1963, Academy Award), *In the Heat of the Night* (1967), *To Sir with Love* (1967), and *Guess Who's Coming to Dinner* (1967), and he won acclaim on Broadway in *A Raisin in the Sun* (1959; film, 1961). As one of the first black actors to play dignified film roles, he helped break the color barrier in the U.S. film industry. He also directed several films, including *Let's Do It Again* (1975) and *Stir Crazy* (1980).

Poitiers, Battle of (732) See Battle of TOURS/POITIERS

Poitiers \pwä-'tyā\, **Battle of** (Sept. 19, 1356) Catastrophic defeat of the French king John II in the HUNDRED YEARS' WAR. English troops under EDWARD THE BLACK PRINCE were under pursuit from the probably superior French forces. South of Poitiers the English secured themselves in thickets and marshes, where the French knights became bogged down and made easy targets for the English archers. John II, taken prisoner, had to consent to the disadvantageous Treaty of BRÉTIGNY.

Poitou \pwä-'tü\ Historical region, W central France. It was inhabited by the ancient Gallic tribe of Pictones and became part of Roman Aquitania. A meeting place of N and S cultures, its golden age (11th–12th cent.) was characterized by great Romanesque art and architecture. The counts of Poitiers were succeeded by the Angevin kings of England, but by 1375 the French had won the region back. Regional specialties include seafood and white wine.

poker Any of several card games in which a player bets that the value of his or her hand is greater than that of the hands held by others. Each subsequent player must either equal or raise the bet or drop out, and the player holding the highest hand at the end of the betting wins the pot. Two principal forms have developed: straight poker, in which all cards of the standard five-card hand are dealt facedown; and stud poker, in which one or two cards are dealt facedown and the rest faceup (five-card) or the last card down (seven-card). In draw poker, cards may be discarded and additional cards drawn. The traditional ranking of hands is (1) straight flush (five cards of the same suit in sequence), (2) four of a kind, (3) full house (three of a kind, plus a pair), (4) flush (five of a single suit), (5) straight (five in sequence), (6) three of a kind, (7) two pair, (8) one pair. The French game Poque was brought to Louisiana by French settlers in the 18th cent.

pokeweed *or* **pokeberry** *or* **poke** Strong-smelling shrublike plant *(Phytolacca americana)* with a poisonous, fleshy root, native to wet or sandy areas of E N. America. It has white flowers, reddish-black berries, and dark-green, poisonous leaves that often are red-veined or borne on red leafstalks. The berries contain a red dye used to color wine, candies, cloth, and paper.

Pokrovsky Cathedral See SAINT BASIL THE BLESSED

Poland *officially* **Republic of Poland** Nation, central Europe. Area: 120,728 sq mi (312,685 sq km). Population (2000): 38,655,000. Capital: WARSAW. Most of the people are Polish; there are minorities of Ukrainians, Germans, and Belarusans. Language: Polish (official). Religions: Roman Catholicism, Orthodoxy. Currency: zloty. Poland consists almost entirely of lowlands in the N and central regions. The S border is largely formed by the Sudeten and CARPATHIAN MTNS. The VISTULA and ODER, the principal river systems, both drain into the BALTIC SEA. Industries include mining, manufacturing, and public utilities. Poland is a republic with two legislative houses; its chief of state is the president, and its head of government is the prime minister. Established as a kingdom in 922 under Mieszko I, Poland was united with Lithuania in 1386 under the JAGIELLON

P

POLAND

Scale 1: 9,837,000

©1999, Encyclopædia Britannica, Inc.

DYNASTY (1386–1572) to become the dominant power in E central Europe, and enjoyed a prosperous golden age. In 1466 it wrested W and E Prussia from the TEUTONIC ORDER, and its lands eventually stretched to the Black Sea. Wars with Sweden (see Second NORTHERN WAR) and Russia in the later 17th cent. led to the loss of considerable territory. In 1697 the electors of Saxony became kings of Poland, virtually ending Polish independence. In the late 18th cent. Poland was divided between Prussia, Russia, and Austria (see Partitions of POLAND) and ceased to exist. After 1815 the former Polish lands came under Russian domination, and from 1863 Poland was a Russian province, subjected to intensive Russification. After World War I an independent Poland was established by the Allies. The invasion of Poland in 1939 by the U.S.S.R. and Germany precipitated World War II, during which the Nazis sought to purge its culture and its large Jewish population. Reoccupied by Soviet forces in 1945, it was controlled by a Soviet-dominated government from 1947. In the 1980s the SOLIDARITY labor movement, led by Lech WALESA, achieved major political reforms, and free elections were held in 1989. An economic austerity program instituted in 1990 sped the transition to a market economy. Poland became a member of NATO in 1999.

Poland, Partitions of (1772, 1793, 1795) Territorial divisions of Poland by Russia, Prussia, and Austria that reduced its territory until it ceased to exist as a state. In the First Partition (1772), a Poland weakened by civil war and Russian intervention was deprived of almost one-third of its land area. In the Second Partition (1793), it was forced to cede additional lands to Prussia and Russia. To quell a nationalist uprising led by Tadeusz KOSCIUSZKO, Russia and Prussia later invaded and divided its remnants among themselves and Austria in the Third Partition (1795). Only with the establishment of the Polish Republic in 1918 were the results of the partitions reversed.

Polanski \pə-'lan-skē\, **Roman** (b.1933) Polish-French film director. He survived a traumatic wartime childhood under the Nazis. His first feature film, *Knife in the Water* (1962), brought him international fame. He left Poland for Britain, where he made *Repulsion* (1965), and later the U.S., where his *Rosemary's Baby* (1968) had a huge success. In 1969 his new wife, the actress Sharon Tate, was murdered by followers of Charles MANSON. He directed *Macbeth* in 1971, and the acclaimed *Chinatown* in 1974. Arrested for statutory rape in 1977, he fled to France, and there directed *Tess* (1979), *Bitter Moon* (1992), and other films.

polar bear White semiaquatic BEAR *(Ursus maritimus)* found throughout Arctic regions, generally on drifting oceanic ice floes. A swift, wide-ranging traveler and a good swimmer, it stalks and captures its prey. It primarily eats seal but also fish, seaweed, grass, birds, and caribou. The male weighs 900–1,600 lbs (410–720 kg) and is about 5 ft (1.6 m) tall at the shoulder and 7–8 ft (2.2–2.5 m) long. Though shy, it is dangerous when confronted.

Polaris \pə-'lar-əs\ *or* **North Star** Earth's present northern polestar, at the end of the Little Dipper's "handle." Polaris is actually composed of a BINARY STAR and a CEPHEID VARIABLE. Precession of earth's axis made the star Thuban, in the constellation Draco, the North Star in ancient Egyptian times, as Vega, in the constellation Lyra, will be 12,000 years from now.

polarization Property of certain types of ELECTROMAGNETIC RADIATION in which the direction and magnitude of the vibrating ELECTRIC FIELD are related in a specified way. The electric VECTOR representing the magnitude and direction of the electric field in a wave of light is perpendicular to the direction in which the wave is moving. In unpolarized light, the electric vectors point in random orientations about the axis of propagation. Plane-polarized light consists only of waves that vibrate in one direction. In circular polarization the electric vector rotates about the propagation direction. Light may be polarized by REFLECTION or by passing it through polarizing filters, such as certain crystals. Polarized light is used in crystallography, liquid-crystal displays, and optical filters.

Polaroid Corp. Major U.S. manufacturer of photographic equipment and supplies. The company was established as Land-Wheelwright Laboratories in 1932 by Edwin LAND and George Wheelwright (1903–2001) to produce Land's first invention, a plastic-sheet light polarizer (see POLARIZATION). By 1936 Land was using polarized material in sunglasses, and in 1937 the company was incorporated under the Polaroid name. Land invented the first instant camera, marketed in 1947 as the Polaroid Land camera; it delivered a finished sepia-toned print 60 seconds after exposure. The company introduced color film for its Polaroid cameras in the 1960s and instant motion pictures in 1977.

polar wandering Migration of the magnetic poles of the earth through geologic time. Scientific evidence indicates that the magnetic poles have slowly and erratically wandered across the surface of the earth (see GEOMAGNETIC REVERSAL). Pole locations calculated from measurements on rocks younger than about 20 million years are close to the present pole locations, but successively greater distances are revealed for rocks older than 30 million years, indicating that substantial deviations occurred. Calculations of polar wandering formed one of the first important pieces of evidence for CONTINENTAL DRIFT.

Pole, Reginald (1500–1558) English Catholic prelate. Pole was sent by HENRY VIII to study in Italy (1521–27) and given minor offices in the church. Critical of Henry's antipapal policies, he wrote *In Defense of Ecclesiastical Unity* (1536) to defend the pope's spiritual authority, and was sent by Pope PAUL III on missions to persuade Catholic monarchs to depose Henry. In response, Henry executed Pole's brother, Lord Montague (1538), and his mother, Margaret, countess of Salisbury (1541). When the Catholic MARY I acceded in 1553, he was appointed legate for England, where he instituted church reforms and was a strong influence on the queen. He was appointed archbishop of Canterbury (1556), but a conflict between the papacy and England's ally Spain caused the pope to cancel Pole's authority and declare him a heretic. Demoralized, he died hours after Mary herself.

pole construction Method of building that dates back to the Stone Age. Excavations in Europe show rings of stones that may have braced huts made of wooden poles or weighted down the walls of tents made of animal skins supported by central poles. Two types of American Indian pole structures were the WIGWAM and LONGHOUSE. Pole-and-thatch dwellings are common in the Caribbean, Mesoamerica, and the Pacific Islands; bamboo-pole dwellings on piles are found in many wet areas of Asia. A S African method utilizes a ring of poles inserted into the ground and brought together in a crest and expertly thatched.

Polesye \pȯ-ˈlye-sye\ *or* **Pripet Marshes** \ˈpri-ˌpet\ *or* **Pripyat Marshes** \ˈpri-pyət\ Vast marsh region, S Belarus and NW Ukraine. The largest swamp of the European continent, the marshes lie in the thickly forested basin of the PRIPYAT RIVER. They cover a densely wooded and largely uninhabited area of about 104,000 sq mi (270,000 sq km). A vast amount of land reclamation has permitted the development of agricultural areas.

pole vault TRACK-AND-FIELD event consisting of a vault for height over a crossbar with the aid of a long pole. It became a competitive sport in the mid-19th cent. In competition, each vaulter is given three chances to clear a specific height. The bar is raised progressively until a winner emerges.

Polhem \ˈpä-ləm\, **Christopher** (1661–1751) Swedish engineer. From 1693 to 1709 he devised water-powered machinery that mechanized operations at the great Falun copper mine. In 1704 he built a factory in Stjaernsund that used division of labor, hoists, and conveyor belts to minimize manual labor, anticipating mass-production techniques later adopted in America and England. His rolling mill was later adapted by Henry Cort (1740–1800) to the production of wrought iron in England.

police Body of agents organized to maintain civil order and public safety, enforce the law, and investigate crime. Most police forces include a uniformed patrol and traffic-control force, plainclothes divisions for criminal investigations, and a set of enforcement priorities that reflects the community's way of life. Administration may be centralized at the national level downward, or decentralized, with local police forces largely autonomous. Recruits usually receive specialized training and take an exam. The modern metropolitan police force began with Robert PEEL in Britain about 1829. See also SECRET POLICE.

poliomyelitis \ˌpō-lē-ō-ˌmī-ə-ˈlī-təs\ *or* **polio** *or* **infantile paralysis** Acute infectious VIRAL DISEASE that can cause flaccid PARALYSIS of voluntary MUSCLES. Severe epidemics killed or paralyzed many people, mostly children and young adults, until Jonas SALK's and Albert SABIN's VACCINES controlled polio in the developed world. Flulike symptoms may progress to back and limb pain, muscle tenderness, and stiff neck. Destruction of SPINAL-CORD motor cells causes paralysis, ranging from transient weakness to complete permanent paralysis, in fewer than 20% of patients. Patients may need PHYSICAL MEDICINE AND REHABILITATION, mechanical breathing assistance, or tracheal suction to remove secretions.

polis \ˈpä-ləs\ In ancient Greece, an independent city and its surrounding region under a unified government. Usually the town was walled and contained a citadel on raised ground (ACROPOLIS) and a marketplace (AGORA). Government was centered in the town; usually there was an assembly of citizens, a council, and magistrates. Ideally, all citizens participated in the government and in the cults, defense, and economy. Noncitizens included women, minors, metics (resident foreigners), and slaves. See also CITY-STATE.

Polish Corridor Strip of land that gave Poland access to the Baltic Sea. Transferred to Poland by the Treaty of VERSAILLES (1919), the corridor, 20–70 mi (30–110 km) wide, separated E Prussia from the main part of Germany. The Germans resented the transfer, though the region had been historically Polish before the Partitions of POLAND. When Poland refused Adolf HITLER's demands for highways across the corridor and cession of Danzig (GDANSK), Germany seized the pretext to invade Poland (1939), beginning World War II.

Polish language W. SLAVIC LANGUAGE of Poland, spoken by over 41 million people, including 2–3 million in N. America. The standard language was formulated in the 16th cent. Polish is written in the LATIN ALPHABET, and utilizes both digraphs (combinations of letters) and diacritics to distinguish its many consonants. Stress is fixed on the next-to-last syllable.

Polish Succession, War of the (1733–38) European conflict waged ostensibly to determine the successor to Augustus II

of Poland. Austria and Russia supported his son Augustus III, while most Poles, France, and Spain supported STANISLAW I, a former Polish king (1704–9) and father-in-law of France's LOUIS XV. Stanislaw was elected king in 1733, but a Russian threat forced him to flee and Augustus was elected in his place. France declared war on Austria (1733), seeking to reclaim territory in Italy held by Austria. An inconclusive campaign ended in a treaty that redistributed the disputed Italian territory and recognized Augustus as king.

Politburo \ˈpä-lət-ˌbyu̇r-ō\ Supreme policy-making body of the COMMUNIST PARTY OF THE SOVIET UNION, the model for the politburos in other countries. The first Politburo, created in 1917 to provide leadership during the BOLSHEVIK uprising, was dissolved when the coup was accomplished. The party congress of 1919 instructed the Central Committee to elect a new Politburo of five leaders, including Joseph STALIN, which soon overshadowed the Central Committee in power. In 1952 it was replaced by a larger Presidium of the Central Committee. The name Politburo was revived in 1966–91. Its members included the party's general secretary, the minister of defense, the head of the KGB, and the heads of the most important republics or urban party branches.

political convention In U.S. politics, an election-year meeting of POLITICAL-PARTY activists to select candidates for office and decide on party policy. Conventions also serve as morale-boosting rallies for the campaigns that follow. Conventions were instituted in the 1830s to replace the often exclusive and secretive caucus system controlled by party bosses. Today, candidates at the state and local level are nominated by PRIMARY ELECTIONS and the convention merely endorses the nominee. At the national level as well, conventions are now largely limited to ratifying the candidate already selected by the presidential primaries.

political machine In U.S. politics, a political-party organization that controls enough votes to maintain political and administrative control of its community. The rapid growth of cities in the 19th cent. created huge problems for poorly structured city governments. Enterprising politicians were able to create support by doing favors for newcomers in exchange for votes, including giving out patronage jobs and housing. Though machines often helped restructure city governments beneficially, they just as often resulted in poorer service (when jobs were doled out as political rewards), corruption (when contracts were awarded in return for kickbacks), and aggravation of racial or ethnic hostilities (when the machine did not reflect the city's diversity). Reforms, suburban flight, and a more mobile population have weakened machine politics. Famous machines have included those of William Marcy TWEED (New York), James Michael CURLEY (Boston), and Richard DALEY (Chicago).

political party Organized group seeking political power, whether by election or revolution. Parties may be mass-based, appealing for support to the whole electorate, or cadres, with membership confined to an active elite; most parties have features of both types. All parties have an ideology designed to attract supporters (see PARTY SYSTEM). Formal parties arose in Britain and the U.S. in the early 19th cent.; parties are not mentioned in either country's constitution. In the U.S., PRIMARY ELECTIONS at the state level are generally employed to select party candidates.

political philosophy Branch of philosophy that analyzes the state and related concepts such as political obligation, law, social justice, and constitution. The first major work in the Western tradition was PLATO's *Republic*. ARISTOTLE's *Politics* is an empirical study of political institutions. The Roman tradition is exemplified by CICERO. St. AUGUSTINE's *City of God* began the tradition of Christian political thinking, later developed by THOMAS AQUINAS. Niccolò MACHIAVELLI studied the exercise of political power. Thomas HOBBES's *Leviathan* (1651) was followed by Benedict de SPINOZA, John LOCKE, and Jean-Jacques ROUSSEAU in the exposition of a SOCIAL-CONTRACT theory. This was rejected by David HUME and by G. W. F. HEGEL, whose *Philosophy of Right* (1821) was central to 19th-cent. politi-

P

cal thought. Hegel's defense of private property stimulated Karl MARX's critique of it. John Stuart MILL developed Jeremy BENTHAM's utilitarian theory of law and political institutions.

political science Academic discipline concerned with the study of government and politics. It studies such subjects as the nature of states, the functions performed by governments, voter behavior, political parties, and public opinion. Though it has roots in the writings of PLATO and ARISTOTLE, it developed in the modern era with the creation of the SOCIAL SCIENCES. Its scientific character was developed by Henri de SAINT-SIMON and Auguste COMTE; the first institution dedicated to its study, the Free School of Political Science, was founded in Paris in 1871.

Polk, James K(nox) (1795–1849) 11th president of the U.S. (1845–49). Born in Mecklenburg Co., N.C., he became a lawyer in Tennessee and served in the U.S. House of Representatives (1825–39) and as governor of Tennessee (1839–41). At the deadlocked 1844 Democratic convention, Polk was nominated as the compromise candidate; he is considered the first dark-horse presidential candidate. A proponent of W expansion, he campaigned with the slogan "Fifty-four Forty or Fight," to bring a solution to the OREGON QUESTION. He successfully concluded the Oregon border dispute with Britain (1846) and secured passage of the Walker Tariff Act (1846), which lowered import duties and helped foreign trade. He led the prosecution of the MEXICAN WAR, which resulted in large territorial gains. His administration

James K. Polk
Daguerreotype by Mathew Brady, 1849

also established the Department of the INTERIOR, the U.S. NAVAL ACADEMY, and the SMITHSONIAN INSTITUTION, oversaw revision of the treasury system, and proclaimed the validity of the MONROE DOCTRINE. Though efficient and competent, he was exhausted by his efforts and did not seek reelection; he died three months after leaving office.

polka Lively couple dance of Bohemian folk origin (*polka* is Czech for "Polish woman") in duple time, characterized by three quick steps and a hop. Originating in the early 19th cent., it remained popular in the 20th cent. as both a folk dance and a ballroom dance.

Pollaiuolo \ˌpōl-lī-ˈwȯ-lō\, **Antonio del and Piero del** *orig.* Antonio and Piero di Jacopo d'Antonio Benci (c.1432–1498, c.1441–1496) Italian sculptors, painters, engravers, and goldsmiths. The brothers collaborated consistently after 1460, producing their works under a combined signature, and their individual contributions are hard to determine. Antonio is recognized as a superb draftsman and was among the first to practice anatomical dissection in the study of the human form; Piero's individual work is less artistically significant. In Florence they created *The Martyrdom of St. Sebastian* (1475) in the Pucci Chapel of the Church of the Santissima Annunziata. In Rome their works included the tombs of Popes Sixtus IV and Innocent VIII. Antonio's famous *Battle of Nudes* is one of the largest and most important Italian engravings of the 15th cent.

pollen Mass of microscopic SPORES in a SEED PLANT that appears usually as a fine dust. The pollen grains are formed in the STAMENS in seed plants and transported by various means (see POLLINATION) to the PISTIL, where FERTILIZATION occurs. Because the grains often are very distinctive, some species may be identified by their pollen grains alone. Pollen grains in geologic sediments have provided much information on the origin and geologic history of plant life on land. Pollen is produced in such quantities that it is a significant part of the airborne components of earth's atmosphere. The protein-containing substance in many pollen grains (e.g., RAGWEED and many GRASSES) causes HAY FEVER.

pollination Transfer of POLLEN grains in SEED PLANTS from the STAMENS, where they form, to the PISTIL. Pollination is required for FERTILIZATION and the production of SEEDS. On the surface of the pistil the pollen grains germinate (see GERMINATION) and form pollen tubes that grow downward toward the ovules. During fertilization, a sperm cell in a pollen tube fuses with the egg cell of an ovule, giving rise to the plant embryo. The ovule then grows into a seed. Plants commonly rely on external agents for pollen transport. Insects (especially BEES) and wind are the most important pollinators; other agents include birds and bats. An egg may be fertilized by self-pollination (when the sperm comes from pollen produced by the same flower or by another flower on the same plant) or by cross-pollination (when the sperm comes from the pollen of a different plant).

Pollini, Maurizio (b.1942) Italian pianist. He made his debut at 9, and won the Warsaw Chopin Competition in 1960 at 18. His repertoire ranges from J. S. BACH to Karlheinz STOCKHAUSEN, with a specialty in Ludwig van BEETHOVEN. His combination of intellectual grasp and extraordinary technical brilliance have given him a unique standing in the concert world.

Pollock \ˈpä-lək\, **(Paul) Jackson** (1912–1956) U.S. painter. Born in Cody, Wyo., he grew up in California and Arizona. In the early 1930s he studied in New York under T. H. BENTON, and later he was employed on the WPA FEDERAL ART PROJECT. In 1947, after several years of semiabstract work stimulated by psychotherapy, Pollock began to lay his canvas on the floor and pour or drip paint onto it in stages, a style exemplified by *Number Ten, 1949*, the black-and-white *Number Thirty-two, 1950*, and the mural-size *Lavender Mist* (1950). A leading practitioner of ABSTRACT EXPRESSIONISM, particularly the form known as ACTION PAINTING, he was championed by Clement GREENBERG and others and became a celebrity. In 1945 he married the artist Lee Krasner (1908–1984). A turbulent personality, he died in a car crash at 44.

poll tax Tax of a uniform amount levied on each adult. The most famous British poll tax was the one levied in 1380, a main cause of the 1381 PEASANTS' REVOLT. In the U.S., poll taxes were used as a voting prerequisite in the S states, effectively denying impoverished blacks (and often poor whites) the vote. In 1966 the U.S. Supreme Court ruled that states could not levy a poll tax as a requirement for voting in state and local elections.

pollution See AIR POLLUTION, WATER POLLUTION

Polo, Marco (1254?–1324) Venetian merchant and traveler who journeyed from Europe to Asia (1271–95). He joined his father and uncle on a journey to China, traveling along the SILK ROAD and reaching the court of KUBLAI KHAN about 1274. The Polos remained in China for about 17 years, and the Mongol emperor sent Marco on several fact-finding missions to distant lands. Marco may also have governed the city of Yangzhou 1282–87. The Polos returned to Venice in 1295. Captured by the Genoese, Marco was imprisoned along with a writer, Rustichello, who helped him to write the tale of his travels. The book, *Il Milione*, was an instant success, though most medieval readers considered it an extravagant romance rather than a true story.

Marco Polo, from *The Travels of Marco Polo*, 1477

polo Game played on horseback using mallets with long flexible handles to drive a wooden ball through goalposts. It was first played in Persia in the 6th cent. B.C.; from there it spread to Arabia, Tibet, S. Asia, and the Far East. The first British polo clubs were formed in India in the mid-19th cent. Polo has long been primarily played by the wealthy, because of the expense of maintaining a stable of polo "ponies" (actually full-sized adult horses, bred for docility, speed, endurance, and intelligence). The standard team is made up of four players. A game consists of six 7^1/$_2$-minute periods called chukkers or chukkas. The field is 300 yards (274.3 m) long by 160 yards (146.3 m) wide; the indoor game is played on a smaller field.

Pol Pot *orig.* Saloth Sar (c.1925–1998) Totalitarian leader of Cambodia (1975–79). In 1949 he went to France to study radio technology and joined the Communist Party. He returned to Cambodia in 1953 and taught French until he fell under police suspicion in 1963. He spent the next 12 years building up the Cambodian Communist Party. U.S. anticommunist activity in Cambodia, including the toppling of NORODOM SIHANOUK and a bombing campaign in the countryside, drove many to join him. In 1975 his KHMER ROUGE forces captured Phnom Penh, which he ordered entirely evacuated; in the first weeks it is estimated that tens of thousands died. The ruthlessness with which he pursued his intention to return to "year zero" and create an ethnically pure, agrarian, communist state resulted in over 1.5 million deaths. Overthrown by the Vietnamese in 1979, he led an anti-Vietnamese guerrilla war until he was repudiated by the Khmer Rouge and imprisoned (1997); he died the next year.

Polyclitus \,pä-li-'klī-təs\ (fl.5th cent. B.C.) Greek sculptor. His *Doryphorus* (*Spear Bearer,* c.440 B.C.) was known as "the Canon" because it illustrated his book of that name, which proposed the ideal mathematical proportions of the human body and proposed that the sculptor strive for a dramatic counterbalance between the relaxed and tense body parts and the directions in which they move. His balanced and rhythmical bronze statues of young athletes, such as the *Diadumenus* (*Man Tying on a Fillet,* c.420 B.C.), freed Greek sculpture from its tradition of rigid frontal poses. With PHIDIAS, Polyclitus was the most important Greek sculptor of his age.

Polycrates \pə-'lik-rə-,tēz\ (6th cent. B.C.) Tyrant of the Aegean island of SAMOS around 535–522 B.C. He took control during a festival of Hera, eliminating his two brothers, who shared his power. He quickly became notorious for piracy. Initially a supporter of Egypt, he joined the Persians against Egypt in 525 B.C. Attempts to remove him were unsuccessful until the Persian governor of Sardis lured him to the mainland and had him crucified. Polycrates brought wealth and prominence to Samos and was a patron of writers, including ANACREON.

polycystic ovary syndrome *or* **Stein-Leventhal syndrome** Endocrine disorder in women in which high ANDROGEN levels block ovulation (see REPRODUCTIVE SYSTEM). It causes a high proportion of female INFERTILITY cases. Symptoms vary but often include hirsutism, acne, and obesity. MENSTRUATION may be irregular, absent, or excessive. The OVARIES are usually enlarged and contain CYSTS. Treatment attempts to reduce androgen production.

polyester Organic compound, any of a class of POLYMERS formed by ESTER linkages between MONOMERS. Polyesters are strong, colorfast, and resistant to corrosion and chemical attack but tend to build up a static charge. Besides familiar fibers and films (e.g., Dacron, Mylar), polyesters are used to make reinforced plastics, automotive parts, boat hulls, foams, laminates, tapes, piping, bottles, disposable filters, encapsulations, and coatings.

polyethylene (PE) Any of the POLYMERS of ETHYLENE, the largest class of PLASTICS. Its simple basic structure, of ETHYLENE MONOMERS, can be linear (e.g., high-density or HDPE, and ultrahigh molecular weight polyethylene UHMWPE) or branched (low-density or LDPE, and linear low-density polyethylene LLDPE). LDPE and LLDPE have similar properties (high flexibility) and uses (packaging film, plastic bags, mulch, insulation, squeeze bottles, toys, and housewares). HDPE has a dense structure of high strength and moderate stiffness; blow-molded HDPE bottles are accepted by most recycling programs, unlike injection-molded HDPE pails, appliance housings, and toys. UHMWPE can be spun and stretched into fibers with great tensile strength; uses include bulletproof vests.

polygamy \pə-'li-gə-mē\ Marriage to more than one spouse at a time. Polygamy is often used as a synonym for polygyny

(marriage to more than one woman), which is still found widely in non-Western cultures. Polygyny seems to offer the husband increased prestige, economic stability, and sexual companionship while offering cowives a shared labor burden. To preserve harmony in the polygynous family, one wife may be accorded seniority, and each wife and her children may have separate living quarters. Polyandry (marriage to more than one man) is relatively rare; in Tibet and Nepal, where brothers may marry a single woman, the practice serves to limit the number of descendants and keep limited land within the household.

polygon In geometry, any closed CURVE consisting of a set of line segments (sides) connected such that no two segments cross. The simplest polygons are triangles (three sides), quadrilaterals (four sides), and pentagons (five sides). A polygon with all sides equal is equilateral. One with all interior angles equal is equiangular. Any polygon that is both equilateral and equiangular is a regular polygon (e.g., equilateral triangle, square).

polygraph See LIE DETECTOR

polyhedron \,pä-lē-'hē-drən\ In EUCLIDEAN GEOMETRY, a three-dimensional object composed of a finite number of polygonal surfaces (faces). In general, polyhedrons are named according to number of faces. A tetrahedron has four faces, a pentahedron five, and so on. The faces meet at line segments called edges, which meet at points called vertices. See also REGULAR POLYHEDRON

Polykleitos See POLYCLITUS

polymer \'pä-lə-mər\ Any of a class of natural or synthetic substances composed of multiples of MONOMERS. The monomers need not all be the same or have the same structure. Polymers may consist of long chains of unbranched or branched monomers or may be cross-linked networks of monomers in two or three dimensions. Their backbones may be flexible or rigid. Inorganic polymers can be elements or compounds, including DIAMOND, GRAPHITE, FELDSPAR, and GLASS. Many important natural materials are organic polymers, including CELLULOSE, LIGNIN, RUBBER, PROTEINS, and NUCLEIC ACIDS. Synthetic organic polymers include many PLASTICS, including POLYETHYLENES, NYLONS, POLYURETHANES, POLYESTERS, vinyls (e.g., PVC), and synthetic RUBBERS. The SILICONES are the most important mixed organic-inorganic compounds.

polymerase chain reaction \pä-'lə-mə-,rās\ (PCR) Laboratory technique used to make numerous copies of a specific DNA segment quickly and accurately. These are needed for various experiments and procedures in MOLECULAR BIOLOGY, forensic analysis (DNA FINGERPRINTING), evolutionary biology (to amplify DNA fragments found in ancient specimens), and medicine (to diagnose genetic disease or detect low viral counts). Invented by Kary MULLIS, PCR requires a DNA template to copy, NUCLEOTIDES to go into the copies, and the ENZYME DNA polymerase. A three-step cycle lasting a few minutes doubles the number of DNA strands. Repetition of this cycle many times results in an exponential increase in the amount of DNA.

polymerization \pə-,li-mə-rə-'zā-shən\ Any process in which MONOMERS combine chemically to produce a POLYMER. The monomer molecules—usually from at least 100 to many thousands—may or may not all be the same. In nature, ENZYMES carry out polymerization under ordinary conditions to form PROTEINS, NUCLEIC ACIDS, and CARBOHYDRATE polymers; in industry, the reaction is usually done with a CATALYST, often under high pressure or heat.

Polynesia \,pä-lə-'nē-zhə\ Group of islands scattered across a huge triangular area of the E central Pacific. A subdivision of OCEANIA, Polynesia includes New Zealand, Hawaii, Samoa, the Line Islands, FRENCH POLYNESIA, the COOK ISLANDS, the Phoenix Islands, Tuvalu, Tonga, and EASTER ISLAND. Fiji is sometimes included in the group because of its Polynesian population. The islands are mostly small coral atolls, and some are of volcanic origin. Most of the inhabitants are Polynesians. Their languages belong to a subfamily of the AUSTRONESIAN LANGUAGES. In the late 1700s the arrival of Spanish explorers radically altered life in Polynesia. Colonizers, imposing Western belief systems and cultural ways, effectively wiped out most local traditions and customs.

polynomial In algebra, an expression consisting of numbers and variables. Specifically, polynomials are sums of monomials of the form ax^n, where a (the coefficient) can be any real number and n (the degree) must be a whole number. A polynomial's degree is that of its monomial of highest degree. Like whole numbers, polynomials may be prime or factorable into products of primes. They may contain any number of VARIABLES, provided that the power of each variable is a nonnegative integer. Setting a polynomial equal to zero results in a polynomial EQUATION; equating it to a variable results in a polynomial FUNCTION, a particularly useful tool in modeling physical situations. Polynomial equations and functions can be analyzed completely by methods of ALGEBRA and CALCULUS.

polyp \\'pä-ləp\\ Growth projecting from the wall of a cavity lined with a mucous membrane. Shape varies widely; it may have a stalk or many lobes. Polyps most often occur in the nose, urinary bladder, and rectum and colon. Symptoms, if any, result from pressure or from blockage of a passage. Polyps occasionally bleed. Because some become cancerous, it is advisable to have them removed and checked and to undergo routine colonoscopy after age 50.

polyp In zoology, one of two principal CNIDARIAN body forms and, sometimes, an individual in a BRYOZOAN colony. The cnidarian polyp body is a hollow cylindrical structure. The lower end attaches to another surface. The upper, or free, end is directed upward and has a mouth surrounded by extensible tentacles that bear stinging structures called nematocysts. The tentacles capture prey, which is then drawn into the mouth. The polyp may be solitary (see SEA ANEMONE) or colonial (see CORAL). The other cnidarian body form is the MEDUSA.

Polyphemus \\ˌpä-lə-'fē-məs\\ In GREEK MYTHOLOGY, a CYCLOPS. When ODYSSEUS and his companions were cast ashore on the coast of Sicily, Polyphemus imprisoned them in his cave with the intention of eating them. Odysseus got the giant drunk and then blinded him by plunging a burning stake into his single eye. In the morning, Odysseus and the men the giant had not yet devoured made their escape by clinging to the bellies of sheep let out to pasture.

polyphony See COUNTERPOINT

polysaccharide \\ˌpä-lē-'sa-kə-ˌrīd\\ Any of a large class of long-chain SUGARS composed of MONOSACCHARIDES. Because the chains may be unbranched or branched and the monosaccharides may be of one, two, or occasionally more kinds, polysaccharides can be categorized in various ways. CELLULOSE, STARCH, GLYCOGEN, and dextran are all polysaccharides of GLUCOSE, with different CONFIGURATIONS. PECTINS are composed of a galactose derivative, chitin of a glucose derivative.

polysiloxane See SILICONE

polytheism Belief in many gods. Though Judaism, Christianity, and Islam are monotheistic (see MONOTHEISM), most other religions throughout history have been polytheistic. The numerous gods may be dominated by a supreme god or by a small group of powerful gods. The gods originated as abstractions of the forces of nature and of human and social functions such as love, war, marriage, or the arts. In many religions the sky god is powerful and all-knowing and the earth goddess is maternal and associated with fertility. Polytheistic religions generally also include malevolent or benevolent spiritual forces or powers. See also GOD AND GODDESS.

polyurethane Any of a class of very versatile POLYMERS that are made into flexible and rigid foams, fibers, elastomers (elastic polymers), and surface coatings. Foamed polyurethanes are made with a reaction that liberates carbon dioxide bubbles throughout the product. Spandex fibers are highly elastic and have replaced natural and synthetic rubber fibers for many textile purposes. Polyurethane elastomers are made into auto parts, rollers, flexible molds, medical equipment, and shoe soles. Polyurethane surface coatings are applied as sealants to wood, concrete, and machine parts.

polyvinyl chloride See PVC

Pombal \\pə-'bäl\\, **marquês (Marquess) de** *orig.* Sebastião (José) de Carvalho (e Mello) (1699–1782) Portuguese reformer. A diplomat, he became chief minister to King Joseph and came to dominate Portuguese politics (1750–77). He encouraged industry and commerce and stimulated trade with Brazil. After the 1755 earthquake that devastated Lisbon, he organized aid and reconstruction efforts. He restricted the power of the nobility, reorganized Portugal's army, and reformed the university educational system. After Joseph's death (1777), Pombal's power disappeared.

pomegranate \\'pä-mə-ˌgra-nət\\ Fruit of *Punica granatum,* a bush or small tree of Asia, in the family Punicaceae. Native to Iran, it is widely cultivated in warm areas. The orange-sized fruit has smooth, leathery, brownish-yellow to red skin. Several chambers contain many thin, transparent vesicles of reddish, juicy pulp, each containing a seed. The fruit is eaten fresh, and the juice is the source of the grenadine syrup used in flavorings and liqueurs. The plant grows 16–23 ft (5–7 m) tall and has elliptical, bright-green leaves and handsome orange-red flowers. The pomegranate is mentioned in the Bible, by the Prophet Muhammad, and in Greek mythology.

Pomerania \\ˌpä-mə-'rā-nē-ə\\ Historical region, NW central Europe, on the BALTIC SEA between the ODER and VISTULA rivers. It was ruled by Polish princes in the 10th cent. E Pomerania was held by the TEUTONIC ORDER from 1308, until it was reconquered by Poland in 1466. Polish dukes ruled those regions under the HOLY ROMAN EMPIRE until the 17th cent. The elector of BRANDENBURG acquired the duchies in 1637. Prussia united W and central Pomerania in 1815. Most of the area is now in Poland; its westernmost section is in E Germany.

Pomeranian \\ˌpä-mə-'rä-nē-ən\\ Breed of TOY DOG developed from the same sled-dog ancestors as the Keeshond, SAMOYED, and Norwegian elkhound. It is said to have been bred down in size from a 30-lb (14-kg) dog in the duchy of Pomerania in the early 19th cent. Spirited but docile, it has a long coat, foxlike head, and small, erect ears. It stands about 6–7 in. (14–18 cm) and weighs about 3–7 lbs (1.5–3 kg).

Pomo N. American Indian people whose territory was centered in California's Russian River valley. Fish, waterfowl, deer, and wild plant foods were plentiful in this region. Pomo religion involved SECRET SOCIETIES, dances, rituals, and impersonations of spirits. Pomo basketry is often considered the finest in California. Today about 3,000 Pomo live in some 20 communities in their original territory.

Pomona \\pə-'mō-nə\\ Ancient Roman goddess of fruit. Vertumnus, god of the seasons, fell in love with her, but she rejected him, preferring to cultivate her orchards. Refusing to give up, Vertumnus came to her in the form of an old woman and pleaded his case so effectively that Pomona changed her mind and agreed to be his.

Pompadour \\'päm-pə-ˌdȯr\\, **marquise de** *orig.* Jeanne-Antoinette Poisson *known as* **Madame de Pompadour** (1721–1764) French mistress of LOUIS XV. Educated in art and literature, she married a nobleman in 1741 and became admired by Parisian society and by the king, who installed her at Versailles as his mistress in 1745. She, the king, and her brother, appointed director of the king's buildings, planned and built the Place de la Concorde in Paris, the Petit Trianon palace at Versailles, and many other buildings. She and Louis also encouraged painters, sculptors, and craftsmen, making her 20 years in power the height of artistic taste. Her political influence was less astute; the alliance with Austria that she urged led to the disastrous SEVEN YEARS' WAR.

Madame de Pompadour Portrait by François Boucher

Pompeii \\päm-'pā\\ Ancient city, S Italy, southeast of NAPLES. Founded in the 6th cent. B.C. or earlier, it came under Greek and Etruscan influence. It was allied with Rome and colonized by 80 B.C. It was damaged by an earthquake in

A.D. 63 and completely destroyed by the eruption of Mt. VESUVIUS in 79. Volcanic debris buried the town and protected the ruins for years. Archaeological excavations, begun in 1748, have uncovered more than half of the city, including forums, temples, baths, theaters, and hundreds of private homes with extraordinary wall paintings and mosaics. See also HERCULANEUM.

Pompey the Great \\'päm-pē\\ *Latin in full* Gnaeus Pompeius Magnus (106–48 B.C.) Statesman and general of the ROMAN REPUBLIC. His military career was illustrious and included reconquering Spain (76–71), destroying the pirates of the E Mediterranean (from 67), and defeating MITHRADATES (63). In 61 he formed the First TRIUMVIRATE with Julius CAESAR and Marcus Licinius CRASSUS. After Crassus' death (53), Pompey and Caesar fell out. By 52, with Rome in a state of anarchy, he was named sole consul. In 49 Caesar provoked a civil war by crossing the RUBICON in pursuit of Pompey, who fled east with his navy. Defeated at the Battle of Pharsalus (48), Pompey fled with his fleet to Egypt, not realizing the Egyptians would take Caesar's side, and was killed as he prepared to step ashore.

Pompidou \\'päm-pi-ˌdü\\, **Georges (-Jean-Raymond)** (1911–1974) French premier (1962–68) and president (1969–74). After joining the Rothschild bank in Paris, he rose rapidly to become director general (1959). As Charles DE GAULLE's chief aide (1958–59), he helped draft the constitution of the FIFTH REPUBLIC. He secretly negotiated a cease-fire in the ALGERIAN WAR in 1961, and was appointed premier in 1962. In 1968 he skillfully negotiated an end to the French student-worker strikes. Elected president of France in 1969, he continued de Gaulle's policies.

Pompidou Center \\'päm-pi-ˌdü\\ *or* **Beaubourg Center** \\bō-'bür\\ French national cultural center, on the rue Beaubourg in Paris. Its full name, the Georges Pompidou National Art and Cultural Center, recognizes the president of the Republic under whose administration it was commissioned. Opened in 1977, the building attracted notoriety for its brightly colored exterior pipes, ducts, and other exposed architectural elements. Though primarily a museum for 20th-cent. visual arts, it also houses a library, a center for industrial design, a film museum, and a Center for Musical and Acoustical Research.

Ponce de León \\ˌpän-sə-ˌdā-lē-'ōn\\, **Juan** (1460–1521) Spanish explorer. He may have accompanied Christopher COLUMBUS's expedition in 1493, and he later became governor of E Hispaniola. He colonized Puerto Rico (1508–9) and founded a settlement near modern San Juan. Rumors of a fountain of youth in the Bahamas inspired him to lead an expedition in 1513, but he landed instead near modern St. Augustine, Florida, then sailed along Florida's S and W coasts. He sailed again to colonize Florida in 1521, but was wounded in an Indian attack and died in Cuba.

Pondicherry City (pop., 1991: 203,000), seaport, and capital of Pondicherry union territory, SE India. Though the English and Dutch fought to own it, Pondicherry was largely a French possession from 1674 until 1954. A seaside tourist resort, it is well known for its Aurobindo ashram.

Pontchartrain \\'pän-chər-ˌträn\\, **Lake** Lake, SE Louisiana. It is 40 mi (64 km) long and 25 mi (40 km) wide. More a tidal lagoon than a lake, it is brackish and teems with game fish. It is connected through Lake Borgne with the Gulf of MEXICO and by canal with the MISSISSIPPI RIVER. Pontchartrain Causeway, at 23.8 mi (38.4 km) long the world's longest concrete bridge, crosses the lake north of NEW ORLEANS, which lies on the lake.

Pontiac (1720?–1769) Ottawa Indian chief who organized the combined resistance to British power in the Great Lakes area known as Pontiac's War (1763–64). At first friendly with whites, Pontiac realized that his people would lose their ancestral lands if white encroachment were not stopped. He coordinated the attack on 12 fortified British posts by a confederacy of individual tribes, winning a great victory, but in 1766 he agreed to a peace treaty. His murder in 1769 by an Illinois Indian provoked the vengeance of several N Algonquian tribes, resulting in the virtual destruction of the Illinois.

pontifex Member of a council of priests in ancient Rome. The pontifices were responsible for administration of the *jus divinum* (laws concerning religious practices). There were three pontifices under the monarchy, but by the time of Julius CAESAR the number had grown to 16. Among their duties were regulation of the calendar and of expiatory rituals, consecration of temples and sacred objects, superintendence of marriage and the family, and administration of the laws of adoption and succession.

Pontormo \\pōn-'tȯr-mō\\, **Jacopo da** *orig.* Jacopo Carrucci (1494–1556) Florentine painter. He was apprenticed to LEONARDO DA VINCI and later to ANDREA DEL SARTO, who exerted the greatest influence on him. The agitated, almost neurotic emotionalism of his work reflects a departure from the balance and tranquillity of the High Renaissance and is sometimes considered an early manifestation of MANNERISM. Primarily a religious painter, he also did sensitive portraits and was employed by the MEDICI FAMILY to decorate their villa with mythological subjects.

Pontus Ancient district, NE ASIA MINOR adjoining the BLACK SEA. Established as a kingdom in the 4th cent. B.C., it continued expanding until 66 B.C., when its last king, MITHRADATES VI EUPATOR, was defeated by POMPEY THE GREAT. It was incorporated into the Roman empire in 63 B.C.

pony Any of several breeds of small HORSES standing less than 14.2 hands (57 in., 144 cm) high and noted for gentleness and endurance. Among the common pony breeds are the SHETLAND, the stylish and hardy Welsh, the high-stepping Welsh Cob, the Exmoor and Dartmoor, and the Highland.

Pony Express (1860–61) U.S. system of mail delivery by horse and rider relays. The 1,800-mi (2,900-km) route between St. Joseph, Mo., and Sacramento, Cal., included 157 stations. Riders changed horses every 10–15 miles, and it took about 10 days to complete the route. The sponsoring company of Russell, Majors & Wadell employed such riders as William CODY. An important mail link with the West, it became obsolete after 18 months with the completion of the transcontinental telegraph system.

poodle German water retriever. Poodles have a long muzzle, hanging ears, and docked tail. Poodles' wiry hair was traditionally clipped to permit them to swim efficiently when retrieving; today it is usually clipped in ornamental patterns. A dog with unclipped hair, which forms ropelike cords, is called a corded poodle. The standard poodle is more than 15 in. (38 cm) tall and weighs up to 70 lbs (32 kg); the miniature stands 10–15 in. (26–38 cm); the toy is under 10 in. and weighs about 7 lbs (3 kg).

Standard poodle

The national dog of France, the poodle is regarded as the most intelligent of all breeds.

pool *or* **pocket billiards** BILLIARDS game played on an oblong table having six pockets with 15 object balls and a white cue ball. The balls are arranged (racked) in a pyramid formation, and the first player breaks the formation by driving the cue ball into it; to continue play, he or she must pocket a ball. In the popular "8-ball" game, the first player (or team) to sink either the seven solid-colored balls (numbered 1–7) or the seven banded balls (9–15), finishing with the black 8-ball, wins. In "9-ball," only the balls numbered 1–9 are used, and they must be sunk sequentially. Pool probably reached its present form in England and France by 1800; today it is most popular in N. America.

Poona See PUNE.

Poor Laws Body of laws undertaking to provide relief for the poor, developed in 16th-cent. England and maintained, with various changes, until after World War II. The original laws provided relief, including care for the aged, sick, and infant poor as well as work for the able-bodied through local parishes. Their scope was curtailed in the early 19th cent., when poverty among the able-bodied was considered a moral failing. In the 1930s and '40s they were replaced by a comprehensive system of public WELFARE services.

P

Pop art Art in which commonplace objects from the world of popular culture—comic strips, soup cans, road signs, hamburgers, etc.—are used as subject matter. It attempted to achieve an objective, impersonal, and nonelitist art after the highly subjective, personal, and often intimidating ABSTRACT EXPRESSIONISM. It has its origins in DADA and the work of Marcel DUCHAMP; its immediate predecessors were Jasper JOHNS, Larry RIVERS, and Robert RAUSCHENBERG. Largely an American phenomenon of the late 1950s and 1960s, it is exemplified by the work of Roy LICHTENSTEIN, Andy WARHOL, Claes OLDENBURG, Robert INDIANA, and George SEGAL. Its effects—including its decisive destruction of the boundary between "high" and "low" art—have continued to be powerfully felt throughout the visual arts up to the present.

pope Ecclesiastical title of the BISHOP of Rome, head of the Roman Catholic church. Catholic doctrine regards the pope as the successor of St. PETER THE APOSTLE and as the supreme authority in matters of faith and morals, as well as in church discipline and government. Papal infallibility in matters of doctrine was asserted by the First Vatican Council in 1870. See also PAPACY, ROMAN CATHOLICISM.

Popes and Antipopes[1] (antipopes in italics)

Peter	?–c.64
Linus	c.67–76/79
Anacletus	76–88 or 79–91
Clement I	88–97 or 92–101
Evaristus	c.97–c.107
Alexander I	105–115 or 109–119
Sixtus I	c.115–c.125
Telesphorus	c.125–c.136
Hyginus	c.136–c.140
Pius I	c.140–55
Anicetus	c.155–c.166
Soter	c.166–c.175
Eleutherius	c.175–89
Victor I	c.189–99
Zephyrinus	c.199–217
Calixtus I (Callistus)	217?–22
Hippolytus	*217, 18–235*
Urban I	222–30
Pontian	230–35
Anterus	235–36
Fabian	236–50
Cornelius	251–53
Novatian	*251*
Lucius I	253–54
Stephen I	254–57
Sixtus II	257–58
Dionysius	259–68
Felix I	269–74
Eutychian	275–83
Gaius	283–96
Marcellinus	291/96–304
Marcellus I	308–9
Eusebius	309/10
Miltiades (Melchiades)	311–14
Sylvester I	314–35
Mark	336
Julius I	337–52
Liberius	352–66
Felix (II)	*355–58*
Damasus I	366–84
Ursinus	*366–67*
Siricius	384–99
Anastasius I	399–401
Innocent I	401–17
Zosimus	417–18
Boniface I	418–22
Eulalius	*418–19*
Celestine I	422–32
Sixtus III	432–40
Leo I	440–61
Hilary	461–68
Simplicius	468–83
Felix III (or II)[2]	483–92
Gelasius I	492–96
Anastasius II	496–98
Symmachus	498–514
Laurentius	*498, 501–c. 505/507*
Hormisdas	514–23
John I	523–26
Felix IV (or III)[2]	526–30
Dioscorus	*530*
Boniface II	530–32
John II	533–35
Agapetus I	535–36
Silverius	536–37
Vigilius	537–55
Pelagius I	556–61
John III	561–74
Benedict I	575–79
Pelagius II	579–90
Gregory I	590–604
Sabinian	604–6
Boniface III	607
Boniface IV	608–15
Deusdedit (also called Adeodatus I)	615–18
Boniface V	619–25
Honorius I	625–38
Severinus	640
John IV	640–42
Theodore I	642–49
Martin I	649–55
Eugenius I	654–57
Vitalian	657–72
Adeodatus II	672–76
Donus	676–78
Agatho	678–81
Leo II	682–83
Benedict II	684–85
John V	685–86
Conon	686–87
Sergius I	687–701
Theodore	*687*
Paschal	*687*
John VI	701–5
John VII	705–7
Sisinnius	708
Constantine	708–15
Gregory II	715–31
Gregory III	731–41
Zacharias (Zachary)	741–52
Stephen (II)[3]	752
Stephen II (or III)[3]	752–57
Paul I	757–67
Constantine (II)	*767–68*
Philip	*768*
Stephen III (or IV)[3]	768–72
Adrian I	772–95
Leo III	795–816
Stephen IV (or V)[3]	816–17
Paschal I	817–24
Eugenius II	824–27
Valentine	827
Gregory IV	827–44
John	*844*
Sergius II	844–47
Leo IV	847–55
Benedict III	855–58
Anastasius (the Librarian)	*855*
Nicholas I	858–67
Adrian II	867–72
John VIII	872–82
Marinus I	882–84
Adrian III	884–85
Stephen V (or VI)[3]	885–91
Formosus	891–96
Boniface VI	896
Stephen VI (or VII)[3]	896
Romanus	897
Theodore II	897
John IX	898–900
Benedict IV	900
Leo V	903
Christopher	*903–4*
Sergius III	904–11
Anastasius III	911–13
Lando	913–14
John X	914–28
Leo VI	928
Stephen VII (or VIII)[3]	929–31
John XI	931–35
Leo VII	936–39
Stephen VIII (or IX)[3]	939–42
Marinus II	942–46
Agapetus II	946–55
John XII	955–64
Leo VIII[4]	963–65
Benedict V[4]	964–66?
John XIII	965–72
Benedict VI	973–74
Boniface VII (1st time)	*974*
Benedict VII	974–83
John XIV	983–84
Boniface VII (2nd time)	*984–85*
John XV (or XVI)[5]	985–96
Gregory V	996–99
John XVI (or XVII)[5]	*997–98*
Sylvester II	999–1003
John XVII (or XVIII)[5]	1003
John XVIII (or XIX)[5]	1004–9
Sergius IV	1009–12
Gregory (VI)	*1012*
Benedict VIII	1012–24
John XIX (or XX)[5]	1024–32
Benedict IX (1st time)	1032–44
Sylvester III	1045
Benedict IX (2nd time)	1045
Gregory VI	1045–46
Clement II	1046–47
Benedict IX (3rd time)	1047–48
Damasus II	1048
Leo IX	1049–54
Victor II	1055–57
Stephen IX (or X)[3]	1057–58
Benedict X	*1058–59*
Nicholas II	1059–61
Alexander II	1061–73
Honorius (II)	*1061–72*
Gregory VII	1073–85
Clement (III)	*1080–1100*
Victor III	1086–87
Urban II	1088–99
Paschal II	1099–1118
Theodoric	*1100–2*
Albert (Aleric)	*1102*
Sylvester (IV)	*1105–11*
Gelasius II	1118–19
Gregory (VIII)	*1118–21*
Calixtus II (Callistus)	1119–24
Honorius II	1124–30
Celestine (II)	*1124*
Innocent II	1130–43
Anacletus (II)	*1130–38*
Victor (IV)	*1138*
Celestine II	1143–44
Lucius II	1144–45
Eugenius III	1145–53
Anastasius IV	1153–54
Adrian IV	1154–59
Alexander III	1159–81
Victor (IV)	*1159–64*
Paschal (III)	*1164–68*
Calixtus (III)	*1168–78*
Innocent (III)	*1179–80*
Lucius III	1181–85
Urban III	1185–87
Gregory VIII	1187
Clement III	1187–91
Celestine III	1191–98
Innocent III	1198–1216
Honorius III	1216–27
Gregory IX	1227–41
Celestine IV	1241
Innocent IV	1243–54
Alexander IV	1254–61
Urban IV	1261–64
Clement IV	1265–68
Gregory X	1271–76
Innocent V	1276
Adrian V	1276
John XXI[5]	1276–77
Nicholas III	1277–80
Martin IV[5]	1281–85
Honorius IV	1285–87
Nicholas IV	1288–92
Celestine V	1294
Boniface VIII	1294–1303
Benedict XI	1303–4
Clement V (at Avignon, from 1309)	1305–14
John XXII[5] (at Avignon)	1316–34
Nicholas (V) (at Rome)	*1328–30*
Benedict XII (at Avignon)	1334–42
Clement VI (at Avignon)	1342–52
Innocent VI (at Avignon)	1352–62
Urban V (at Avignon)	1362–70
Gregory XI (at Avignon, then Rome from 1377)	1370–78
Urban VI	1378–89
Clement (VII) (at Avignon)	*1378–94*
Boniface IX	1389–1404
Benedict (XIII) (at Avignon)	*1394–1423*
Innocent VII	1404–6
Gregory XII	1406–15
Alexander (V) (at Bologna)	*1409–10*
John (XXIII) (at Bologna)	*1410–15*
Martin V[5]	1417–31
Clement (VIII)	*1423–29*
Eugenius IV	1431–47
Felix (V) (also called Amadeus VIII of Savoy)	*1439–49*

Nicholas V	1447–55	Innocent X	1644–55
Calixtus III (Callistus)	1455–58	Alexander VII	1655–67
		Clement IX	1667–69
Pius II	1458–64	Clement X	1670–76
Paul II	1464–71	Innocent XI	1676–89
Sixtus IV	1471–84	Alexander VIII	1689–91
Innocent VIII	1484–92	Innocent XII	1691–1700
Alexander VI	1492–1503	Clement XI	1700–21
Pius III	1503	Innocent XIII	1721–24
Julius II	1503–13	Benedict XIII	1724–30
Leo X	1513–21	Clement XII	1730–40
Adrian VI	1522–23	Benedict XIV	1740–58
Clement VII	1523–34	Clement XIII	1758–69
Paul III	1534–49	Clement XIV	1769–74
Julius III	1550–55	Pius VI	1775–99
Marcellus II	1555	Pius VII	1800–23
Paul IV	1555–59	Leo XII	1823–29
Pius IV	1559–65	Pius VIII	1829–30
Pius V	1566–72	Gregory XVI	1831–46
Gregory XIII	1572–85	Pius IX	1846–78
Sixtus V	1585–90	Leo XIII	1878–1903
Urban VII	1590	Pius X	1903–14
Gregory XIV	1590–91	Benedict XV	1914–22
Innocent IX	1591	Pius XI	1922–39
Clement VIII	1592–1605	Pius XII	1939–58
Leo XI	1605	John XXIII	1958–63
Paul V	1605–21	Paul VI	1963–78
Gregory XV	1621–23	John Paul I	1978
Urban VIII	1623–44	John Paul II	1978–

[1]Until the 4th cent., the popes were usually known only as bishops of Rome.

[2]The higher number is used if Felix (II), who reigned 355–58 and is ordinarily classed as an antipope, is counted as a pope.

[3]Though elected on March 23, 752, Stephen (II) died two days later before he could be consecrated and thus ordinarily not counted. The issue has made the numbering of subsequent Stephens somewhat irregular.

[4]Either Leo VIII or Benedict V may be considered an antipope.

[5]A confusion in the numbering of popes named John after John XIV (r.983–84) resulted because some 11th-cent. historians mistakenly believed that there had been a pope named John between antipope Boniface VII and the true John XV (r.985–86). Therefore they mistakenly numbered the real popes John XV to XIX as John XVI to XX. These popes have since customarily been renumbered XV to XIX, but John XXI and John XXII continue to bear numbers that they themselves formally adopted on the assumption that there had indeed been 20 Johns before them. In current numbering, there thus exists no pope by the name of John XX. In the 13th cent. the papal chancery misread the names of the two popes Marinus as Martin, and as a result of this error Simon de Brie in 1281 assumed the name of Pope Martin IV instead of Martin II. The enumeration has not been corrected, and thus there exist no Martin II and Martin III.

Pope, Alexander (1688–1744) English poet and satirist. Precluded from formal education by his Catholicism, Pope was mainly self-educated; a deformity limited his physical activities. His first major work was *An Essay on Criticism* (1711), a poem on the art of writing containing brilliant epigrams (e.g., "To err is human, to forgive, divine") that have become proverbs. His witty mock-epic *The Rape of the Lock* (1712, 1714) ridicules fashionable society. The great labor of his life was his verse translations of HOMER's *Iliad* (1720) and *Odyssey* (1726). He became involved in many literary battles, prompting him to write such poems as the scathing mock-epic *The Dunciad* (1728) and *An Epistle to Dr. Arbuthnot* (1735). The philosophical *An Essay on Man* (1733–34) was intended as part of a larger work that he never completed.

Alexander Pope Portrait by Thomas Hudson

Popish Plot (1678) In English history, a widely believed rumor that Jesuits planned to assassinate CHARLES II and replace him with his brother, the Catholic duke of York (later JAMES II). The rumor was fabricated by Titus Oates (1649–1705), an Anglican priest who gave a sworn deposition of his "evidence" to a London justice of the peace. When the latter was found murdered, a panic among the people was followed by accusations and trials, leading to the execution of about 35 innocent people. When Oates was finally discredited, the panic subsided.

poplar Any of at least 35 species and many natural hybrids of trees that make up the genus *Populus* (WILLOW family). Poplars grow throughout N temperate regions. They are rapid-growing but relatively short-lived. Their leaves flutter in the slightest breeze. The relatively soft wood is used to make cardboard boxes, crates, paper, and veneer. N. America has three groups of native poplars: COTTONWOODS, ASPENS, and balsam poplars.

poplar, yellow See TULIP TREE

Popocatépetl \ˌpō-pə-ˈka-tə-ˌpe-tᵊl\ Volcano, SE central Mexico, west of the city of PUEBLA. The perpetually snow-capped, symmetrical cone rises to 17,930 ft (5,465 m). After being inactive for more than 50 years, it erupted in 1994, with recurrences in 1996.

Popol Vuh \ˈpȯ-pōl-ˈvü\ Mayan document that provides valuable information on ancient MAYA mythology and culture. It was written between 1554 and 1558 in the QUICHE language using Spanish letters. It tells of the creation of man, the acts of the gods, and the origin and history of the Quiche people. It was discovered early in the 18th cent. by Francisco Jiménez, a Guatemalan priest, who copied out the original, now lost, and translated it into Spanish.

Popper, Karl (Raimund) (*later* Sir Karl) (1902–1994) Austrian-British philosopher of natural and social science. In *The Logic of Scientific Discovery* (1934), he rejected the traditional conception of INDUCTION, arguing instead that scientific hypotheses can at best only be falsified. His later works include the anti-Marxist *The Open Society and Its Enemies* (1945), *The Poverty of Historicism* (1957), and *Postscript to the Logic of Scientific Discovery* (3 vols., 1981–82).

poppy family Family Papaveraceae, containing about 200 species of mostly herbaceous plants. Most species of this family, which is known for its many garden ornamentals (genus *Papaver*) and for pharmaceutically important plants, are found in the Northern Hemisphere. All have cup-shaped flowers, a capsule fruit, leaves that are usually deeply cut or divided into leaflets, and colored sap. Members include the OPIUM POPPY and the corn, or Flanders, poppy (*P. rhoeas*), the seeds of which may lie dormant for years.

Populares See OPTIMATES AND POPULARES

popular front Coalition of working-class and middle-class political parties that united to defend democracy from an expected fascist assault in the 1930s. The policy of a "united front" against FASCISM was announced at the communist Third International (1935), to include not only communists and socialists but also liberals, moderates, and even conservatives. Popular-front governments were formed in France and Spain in 1936, but they were short-lived. See also Léon BLUM, SPANISH CIVIL WAR.

popular music Historically, any non-FOLK-MUSIC form that acquired mass popularity. After the Industrial Revolution, true folk music began to disappear, and popular music became that of the MUSIC HALL AND VARIETY THEATER, with its upper reaches dominated by waltz music and operettas. In the U.S., MINSTREL SHOWS performed the compositions of such songwriters as Stephen FOSTER. In the 1890s TIN PAN ALLEY emerged, and later the MUSICAL. Beginning with RAGTIME in the 1890s, black Americans had begun combining African rhythms with European harmonic structures, a synthesis that would eventually create JAZZ. The music audience greatly expanded, partly because of technology. By 1930, phonograph records had replaced sheet music as the chief source of music in the home, enabling those without musical training to hear popular songs. The microphone relieved singers of the need for trained voices that could fill large halls. The ability of radio broadcasting to reach rural communities aided the dissemination of new styles, notably COUNTRY MUSIC but also BLUES. U.S. popular music achieved international dominance after World War II. By the 1950s, the black migration to Northern cities had resulted in the cross-fertilization of blues with jazz to create RHYTHM AND BLUES. Rock and roll soon developed as an amalgam of rhythm and blues with country music and other influences (see ROCK MUSIC). In the 1960s, British

P

rock groups became internationally influential. Rock quickly attracted the allegiance of teenagers, who, with new disposable incomes, beame the chief audience for popular music. From the late 1960s black pop gained a huge white audience. The history of pop through the 1990s was basically that of rock and its variants, including DISCO, heavy metal, punk rock, and RAP, which have become the standard musical idiom for young people in many countries.

Popular Party (Italy) See ITALIAN POPULAR PARTY

popular sovereignty Political doctrine that allowed the settlers of U.S. federal territories to decide whether to enter the Union as free or slave states. Applied by Sen. Stephen DOUGLAS as a means to reach a compromise through passage of the KANSAS-NEBRASKA ACT, it was criticized as "squatter sovereignty." The resulting violence between pro- and antislavery factions (see BLEEDING KANSAS) demonstrated its failure.

Populations I and II Two broad classes of stars and stellar groupings, distinguished and named by Walter Baade (1893–1960). Population I consists of younger stars, clusters, and associations in and near the arms of the Milky Way system and other spiral GALAXIES and in irregular galaxies (e.g., the MAGELLANIC CLOUDS). These objects are thought to have originated from interstellar gas that has undergone processes, including SUPERNOVA explosions, that added heavier elements. Population II consists of older (generally 1 billion–15 billion years old) stars and clusters, composed almost entirely of hydrogen and helium, presumably formed from gas clouds that emerged very early in a galaxy's history, found in the GALACTIC HALOS of spiral galaxies, in GLOBULAR CLUSTERS, and, in large numbers, in elliptical galaxies. Astronomers sometimes refer to a Population III, the very first stars to emerge after the BIG BANG.

populism Political philosophy that champions the common person, usually by favorable contrast with an elite. Populism usually combines elements of the left and right, opposing large corporate and financial interests but also frequently targeting ethnic and racial minorities and immigrants for discrimination.

Populist or **Narodnik** \nä-'rȯd-ˌnik\ Member of a socialist movement in Russia in the 1860s and '70s. It attracted intellectuals who believed that political propaganda among the peasants (narod: "people") would lead to their revolt and the liberalization of the czarist regime. Their efforts produced police persecution, which drove the socialists to more radical methods, including terrorism. The revolutionary group Land and Freedom, led by Georgy PLEKHANOV, worked among the peasantry in the 1870s. The populist ideology was later revived by the SOCIALIST REVOLUTIONARY PARTY.

Populist Movement Coalition of U.S. agrarian reformers in the Midwest and South in the 1890s. Farmers' alliances formed in the 1880s in reaction to falling crop prices and poor credit facilities organized the Populist, or People's, Party in 1892; its presidential candidate, James B. Weaver (1833–1912), won over 1 million votes. Many state and local Populist candidates were elected in the Midwest. In 1896 the party joined with the Democratic Party to support the FREE SILVER MOVEMENT and the unsuccessful candidacy of W. J. BRYAN. The movement declined thereafter.

porcelain Vitrified POTTERY with a white, fine-grained body that is usually translucent. It was first made in China during the Tang dynasty (618–907) and in its advanced form during the Yuan dynasty (1279–1368). The three main types are true (or hard-paste) porcelain, artificial (or soft-paste) porcelain, and bone china. Attempts by medieval European potters to imitate true porcelain led to the discovery of soft-paste porcelain. The secret of true porcelain was discovered about 1707 in Saxony (see MEISSEN PORCELAIN). Standard English bone china was produced about 1800 when Josiah Spode II (1754–1827) added calcined bones to the hard-paste porcelain formula. Hard-paste porcelain, though strong, chips more readily than bone china. Well-known English porcelains include Bow and Chelsea porcelain; famous French porcelains include Chantilly, Saint-Cloud, and SÈVRES PORCELAIN. See also STONEWARE.

porch Roofed structure, usually open at front and sides, projecting from the face of a building and used to protect an entrance. If colonnaded, it may be called a PORTICO. A long porch surrounded by a railing, is a veranda. Porches were exceedingly common in the domestic architecture of Britain and the U.S. from the late 18th cent. In Gothic cathedrals the porch was often a small gabled structure projecting from the N or S walls of the NAVE. See also LOGGIA.

porcupine Heavy-bodied, solitary, slow-moving, nocturnal RODENT with quills (modified hairs) along the back, tail, and, on certain species, the neck and shoulders. The quills are easily detached when touched. The New World species (four genera in family Erethizontidae) are arboreal and have barbed quills; the Old World species (four genera in family Hystricidae) are terrestrial and have unbarbed quills. The N. American porcupine (Erethizon dorsatum), about 30 in. (75 cm) long, with a tail about 8 in. (20 cm) long and quills about 3 in. (8 cm) long, drives its powerful tail against an assailant. Crested Old World porcupines run backward, quills erect, into the enemy. The African crested porcupine, the largest terrestrial rodent in Europe and Africa, may weigh 60 lbs (27 kg) and have quills 14 in. (35 cm) long.

porgy \'pȯr-jē\ Any of about 100 species (family Sparidae) of fishes found throughout tropical and temperate seas. Porgies, or sea breams, are typically high-backed, with a single dorsal fin, a small mouth, and strong teeth. Most species do not exceed 1 ft (30 cm) long, but some may grow to 4 ft (120 cm). The S. African musselcrackers, popular sport fishes, grow to 100 lbs (45 kg). In Australia and Japan, several species of Chrysophrys are important food fish (called snappers in Australia). The red sea bream inhabits deep European waters.

Po River ancient Padus. River, N Italy. The country's longest river, it is about 405 mi (652 km) long. It rises in the Cottian Alps on the W frontier and flows northeast to TURIN, then east into the ADRIATIC SEA. Its delta is highly complex, with at least 14 mouths. Industrial cities in its valley include MILAN, PADUA, and VERONA. It brought devastating floods in 589, 1438, 1951, and 1966.

pork Flesh of hogs, usually slaughtered between the ages of six months and one year. It is consumed as cooked fresh meat in various cuts or preparations, including chops and SAUSAGE, or cured or smoked for HAM, bacon, or other products. Because pigs may be infected by the parasitic disease TRICHINOSIS, fresh pork must be cooked to an internal temperature of 160°F (71°C) to destroy the parasite. Pork is forbidden by the dietary laws of Islam and Judaism.

porpoise Any toothed WHALE in the family Phocoenidae (or, per some authorities, part of the DOLPHIN family Delphinidae). The four species (genus Phocoena) of the common, or harbor, porpoise are primarily fish eaters that travel in pairs or large groups. The shy P. phocoena, found throughout the Northern Hemisphere, rarely leaps. The other species of Phocoena are found along Californian and S. American coasts. The active, gregarious Dall porpoise (Phocoenoides dalli) of the N. Pacific and the True porpoise (P. truei) of Japan often swim with ships, usually in groups. Both eat cephalopods and fishes. At most 7 ft (2 m) long, porpoises are shorter and chubbier than dolphins and have a blunt snout. Like dolphins, they are known for their high intelligence.

port Input/output conduit for PERSONAL COMPUTERS. The serial port connects data terminal equipment with devices such as a keyboard or MOUSE. It processes data sequentially, as a series of BITS. The parallel port processes several data bits at once and is used to connect peripherals such as computer PRINTERS and optical SCANNERS. The parallel port is faster, but the serial port is cheaper and requires less power. See also USB.

Port Arthur See LUSHUN

Port-au-Prince \ˌpȯr-tō-'prins\ City (metro. area pop., 1997: 1,556,000), seaport, and capital of Haiti, W. Indies. Founded by the French in 1749, it was destroyed by earthquakes in 1751 and 1770 and has frequently suffered from fires and civil strife. It is the country's principal port and commercial center, producing sugar, flour, cottonseed oil, and textiles. Most of the city suffers from extreme poverty and a lack of the most basic public services.

Port-de-France See NOUMÉA

Porter, Cole (Albert) (1891–1964) U.S. composer and lyricist. Born in Peru, Ind., Porter composed an operetta at 10. At Yale Univ. he composed about 300 songs, including "Bulldog." After making his Broadway debut with *See America First* (1916), he moved to France and became an itinerant playboy. In the 1930s he began writing a series of hit musicals, including *Gay Divorcée* (1932), *Anything Goes* (1934), *Red, Hot and Blue* (1934), the superb *Kiss Me, Kate* (1948), *Can-Can* (1953), and *Silk Stockings* (1955). He also worked

Cole Porter, 1938

on a number of films, including *High Society* (1956). Porter's witty, sophisticated songs, for which he wrote both words and music, include "Night and Day," "Begin the Beguine," and "You're the Top." A riding accident in 1937 left him a semi-invalid; he underwent 30 operations and eventually the amputation of a leg.

Porter, Katherine Anne (1890–1980) U.S. writer. Born in Indian Creek, Texas, she worked as a journalist before moving to Mexico in 1920. Her collections include *Flowering Judas* (1930); *Pale Horse, Pale Rider* (1939), a set of three novellas; and *Collected Short Stories* (1965, Pulitzer Prize). Her stories have a richness of texture and complexity of character delineation usually achieved only in the novel. *Ship of Fools* (1962) is her only novel.

portico Colonnaded PORCH or entrance to a structure, or a covered walkway supported by regularly spaced columns. The portico is a principal feature of Greek TEMPLE architecture and thus a prominent element in Roman and all subsequent Classically inspired structures.

Portillo, José López See José LÓPEZ PORTILLO

Portland Seaport city (pop., 2000: 64,000), SW Maine. First settled in 1632, it was destroyed by Indians in 1676 and 1690. It was incorporated in 1786 and was the state capital 1820–32. A fire destroyed much of the city center in 1866. It is the state's largest city. Industries include pulp and paper and shipbuilding. It was the birthplace of H. W. LONGFELLOW.

Portland City (pop., 2000: 529,000) and port, NW Oregon, on the WILLAMETTE RIVER, southeast of its confluence with the COLUMBIA RIVER. Settled in 1829, it was incorporated in 1851. Early growth was stimulated by gold rushes and the flow of immigrants along the OREGON TRAIL. It is the state's largest city and principal port. Exports include lumber, aluminum, and wheat. Shipbuilding and meat-packing are important. Its many educational institutions include REED COLLEGE.

portland cement Binding agent of present-day CONCRETE. It is a finely ground powder made by burning and grinding a limestone mixed with clay or shale. Patented in 1824, it was named for its resemblance to the limestone of the Isle of Portland, England. The cement combines chemically with the water it is mixed with, then hardens and strengthens.

Port Louis City (pop., 1997 est.: 137,000), capital, and main port of Mauritius. It was founded about 1736 by the French as a port for ships rounding the Cape of GOOD HOPE. With the completion of the SUEZ CANAL in 1869, its importance declined. It is the principal commercial center of the island; its primary export is sugar.

Port Moresby City (pop., 1990: 193,000), capital of Papua New Guinea. Its large, sheltered harbor was explored by British Capt. John Moresby (1830–1922) in 1873. The British annexed the area 1883–84. The town became a main Allied base in World War II. The National Capital District, established in 1974, includes all of Port Moresby. A commercial center, it is also the site of a university.

Porto \'pŏr-tü\ *Portuguese* **Oporto** Seaport city (pop., 1991: 311,000), NW Portugal. Dating from pre-Roman times and held successively by the Alani, Visigoths, Moors, and Christians, it became an important port in the 14th cent. HENRY THE NAVIGATOR was born there in 1394. It was the site of a British victory over the French in the 1809 PENINSULAR

WAR. It is famous for its port wine. Portugal's second-largest city, it undertook major infrastructure investment in 2001 to become a cultural capital.

Porto Alegre \'pŏr-tü-ä-'lä-grē\ Seaport city (metro. area pop., 1996: 3,247,000), S Brazil, near the Atlantic coast. Founded about 1742, it received many German and Italian settlers in the 19th cent. Located on the Guaíba River, it is a center of inland navigation and the most important Brazilian commercial center south of SÃO PAULO. Exports include rice, tobacco, and hides. Industries include shipbuilding, textiles, pharmaceuticals, and chemicals.

Port-of-Spain City (pop., 1996 est.: 43,000), seaport, and capital of Trinidad and Tobago. Formerly the capital of the W. Indies Federation, it is located on Trinidad. It is an air transport center for the Caribbean and has a diversified economy, producing rum, beer, and lumber and exporting oil, sugar, citrus, and asphalt.

Porto-Novo \„pŏr-tō-'nō-vō\ City (pop., 1994 est.: 200,000), seaport, and capital of Benin, on the Gulf of GUINEA, W Africa. It was originally the center of the indigenous kingdom of Porto-Novo. Under the Portuguese from the 17th cent., it developed into a center of the SLAVE TRADE. It became a French protectorate in 1863. In 1904 it became the capital of the French W. African colony of Dahomey. The ruins of old African palaces remain, as does the old Portuguese cathedral.

Port Said \sä-'ēd, 'sīd\ Seaport city (pop., 1996: 470,000), NE Egypt, on the Mediterranean Sea at the N end of the SUEZ CANAL. Founded in 1859, it became the world's most important coaling station. It was the landing point of French and British troops during the SUEZ CRISIS (1956) that followed Egypt's nationalization of the Suez Canal. In the SIX-DAY WAR of 1967, Israeli forces occupied the E bank of the canal, which was closed until 1975. The city was revitalized after 1975.

Portsmouth \'pŏrt-sməth\ City (pop., 1999 est.: 190,000) and seaport, HAMPSHIRE, S England. It was founded in 1194. A naval dockyard was established in 1496 and greatly expanded after 1698; today it is the city's main source of employment. Portsmouth suffered extensive damage from German bombing in World War II. The city was the birthplace of Charles DICKENS.

Portsmouth City (pop., 2000: 101,000) and seaport, SE Virginia, opposite NORFOLK. With Norfolk and NEWPORT NEWS, it constitutes the Port of HAMPTON ROADS. Founded in 1752, it was occupied by both British and American troops during the AMERICAN REVOLUTION. During the AMERICAN CIVIL WAR the U.S. Navy Yard was evacuated by Union troops, allowing Southern troops access to stores of equipment. It is part of a major military complex; shipbuilding and ship repair are the main economic activities.

Portugal *officially* **Portuguese Republic** *ancient* Lusitania. Nation, W coast of the IBERIAN PENINSULA, SW Europe. Area: 35,672 sq mi (92,389 sq km). Population (2000): 10,005,000. Capital: LISBON. Most of the people are Portuguese. Language: Portuguese (official). Religion: Roman Catholicism. Currency: euro. Administratively, the Atlantic islands of the AZORES and MADEIRA are part of Portugal. Portugal is divided roughly in half by the TAGUS RIVER; the highlands rise mostly north of the Tagus and stretch northeast into Spain. It has an industrialized economy in which both the public and private sectors participate. Major industries were nationalized after a military coup in 1974, but many were returned to the private sector in the late 1980s. Light industries predominate, and products include textiles and clothing, paper and wood products, and chemicals. It is a republic with one legislative house; the chief of state is the president, and the head of government is the prime minister. In the 1st millennium B.C., Celtic peoples settled the Iberian peninsula. They were conquered around 140 B.C. by the Romans, who ruled until the 5th cent. A.D., when the area was invaded by Germanic tribes. A Muslim invasion in 711 left only the N part of Portugal in Christian hands. In 1179 it became the kingdom of Portugal and expanded as it reconquered the Muslim-held sectors. The boundaries of modern continental Portugal were completed in 1270 under King Afonso III. In the 15th–16th cent. the monarchy encouraged exploration that took Portuguese

P

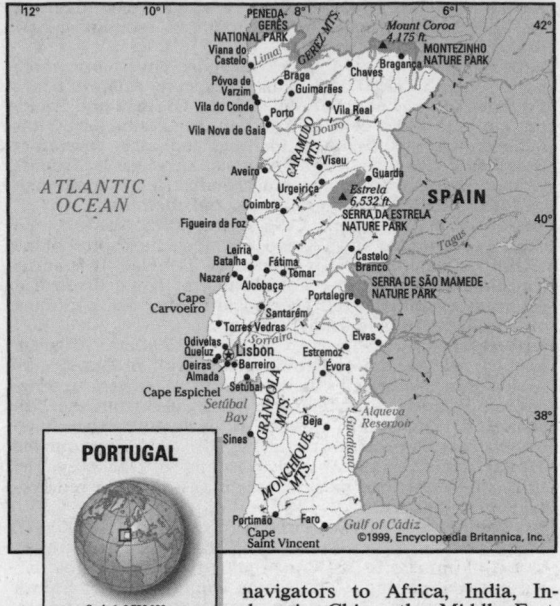

PORTUGAL

Scale 1: 8,756,000
0   40   80 mi
0   60   120 km

©1999, Encyclopædia Britannica, Inc.

navigators to Africa, India, Indonesia, China, the Middle East, and S. America. Though it established several colonies (including Brazil, GOA, Cape Verde Islands, E. TIMOR, Angola, Guinea-Bissau, Mozambique, and MACAO), they achieved independence over the years. Antonio SALAZAR ruled Portugal as a dictator from 1932 until 1968. A new constitution was adopted in 1976 (revised 1982), and civilian rule resumed. It joined the EUROPEAN UNION (1986) and experienced economic prosperity in the 1990s.

Portuguese East Africa See MOZAMBIQUE

Portuguese Guinea See GUINEA-BISSAU

Portuguese language ROMANCE LANGUAGE spoken by about 170 million people in Portugal, Brazil, and other former Portuguese colonies. The first literary works in Portuguese date from the 13th–14th cent. Standard Portuguese is based on the dialect of Lisbon. The differences between Brazilian and European Portuguese are extensive, including changes in PHONOLOGY, verb conjugation, and SYNTAX.

Portuguese man-of-war Any of various floating, warm-water marine CNIDARIANS (genus *Physalia*, class Hydrozoa) found mostly in the Gulf Stream and the Indian and Pacific oceans. The MEDUSA-form body consists of a translucent, jellylike, gas-filled float, which may be 3–12 in. (9–30 cm) long. POLYPS beneath the float bear hanging tentacles up to 165 ft (50 m) long. Nematocysts on some polyps paralyze fish and other prey. Other polyps then attach to, spread over, and digest the victim. A third type of polyp is involved in reproduction. The painful sting of *Physalia* can cause fever, shock, or disruption of heart and lung function.

Portuguese West Africa See ANGOLA

Port-Vila \ˌpȯr-vē-ˈlä\ *or* **Vila** Seaport, capital, and largest town (pop., 1997 est.: 33,000) of Vanuatu, SW Pacific. French in appearance, the town has a population of British, French, and Vietnamese. It was a U.S. base in World War II.

Poseidon \pə-ˈsī-dən\ Greek god of water and the sea. His brothers were ZEUS and HADES. When the three brothers deposed their father, the kingdom of the sea fell by lot to Poseidon. Unpredictable and sometimes violent, he was also god of earthquakes, and he was closely associated with horses. In art he was often shown holding a trident and accompanied by a dolphin and tuna. The Romans identified him with NEPTUNE.

Posen See POZNAN

positivism Any philosophical system that confines itself to the data of experience, excludes A PRIORI or metaphysical speculations, and emphasizes the achievements of science. Positivism is closely connected with EMPIRICISM, PRAGMA-

TISM, and LOGICAL POSITIVISM. More narrowly, the term designates the philosophy of Auguste COMTE, who held that human thought had passed inevitably through a theological stage into a metaphysical stage and was passing into a positive, or scientific, stage.

positron \ˈpä-zə-ˌträn\ SUBATOMIC PARTICLE having the same MASS as an ELECTRON but with a positive electric charge. It constitutes the antiparticle (see ANTIMATTER) of an electron. The existence of the positron was a consequence of the electron theory of Paul DIRAC (1928), and the particle was discovered in COSMIC RAYS by Carl D. Anderson (1905–1991) in 1932. Though they are stable in a vacuum, positrons react quickly with the electrons of ordinary matter, producing GAMMA RAYS in the annihilation. They are emitted in positive BETA DECAY.

positron emission tomography (PET) Imaging technique used in diagnosis and biomedical research. A chemical that emits POSITRONS is injected into the body, and detectors measure their activity as they combine with ELECTRONS and are annihilated. Computers produce images of the organs scanned. PET is particularly useful for studying BRAIN and HEART functions.

possible world In philosophy, the conception of a total way things might have happened. In his *Theodicy* (1710), G. W. LEIBNIZ used the concept of a possible world in attempting to solve the problem of evil, arguing that an all-perfect God would actualize the best of all possible worlds, an idea later satirized by VOLTAIRE in *Candide* (1759). Philosophers have since built many variations on the concept.

Post, C(harles) W(illiam) (1854–1914) U.S. manufacturer of breakfast CEREALS. Post grew up in Springfield, Ill. In the 1880s he became a patient of J. H. KELLOGG at a health sanitarium in Battle Creek, Mich., where he became interested in producing healthful foods like those Kellogg served. In 1895 he founded Postum Cereal Co., the precursor to GENERAL FOODS CORP. His first product, the cereal beverage Postum, was followed by Grape Nuts and Post Toasties.

Post, Emily *orig.* Emily Price (1872–1960) U.S. authority on social behavior. Born in Baltimore to wealth and social position, she was left in straitened circumstances after a divorce and began writing light fiction and magazine articles. In her major work, *Etiquette: The Blue Book of Social Usage*, unlike earlier writers on the subject, she directed her commonsense views to popular audiences. First published in 1922, it appeared in 10 editions in her lifetime. The outpouring of letters it provoked inspired her widely syndicated newspaper column.

postal system System of delivering written or packaged communications to any addressee anywhere in the world. Such systems are usually government-run and are paid for by a combination of user charges and government subsidy. The earliest references to postal services are in Egypt about 2000 B.C. and in China about 1000 B.C. The Roman empire developed various centralized methods of relaying messages. Private postal systems developed with nation-states in the Renaissance, and later became government monopolies. Charging on the basis of weight rather than distance and using prepaid stamps was first proposed in 1837. The General Postal Union (1875; later Universal Postal Union), under which member countries retain postage on outgoing international mail, improved international mail delivery. Airmail and automated mail handling were 20th-cent. developments.

post-and-beam system In building construction, a system in which two upright members, the posts, hold up a third member, the beam, laid horizontally across their top surfaces. The post and beam formed the basis of architecture from prehistoric to Roman times. All structural openings evolved from this system, which is seen in pure form only in colonnades and in FRAMED STRUCTURES, the posts of doors, windows, ceilings, and roofs usually being hidden in walls. Post-and-beam construction has largely been supplanted by the modern steel frame.

poster Eye-catching printed paper announcement or advertisement that is exhibited to promote a product, event, or idea. Posters were popularized by the mid-19th-cent. invention of LITHOGRAPHY, which allowed colored posters to be produced cheaply and easily. Henri de TOULOUSE-LAUTREC created brilliant poster art, and it flourished with the rise of the ART NOUVEAU style, as seen in the work of Alphonse MUCHA. During World War I, posters were used for recruiting and propaganda, and the industrial boom of the early 20th cent. gave rise to advertising posters for every conceivable product and event. Television advertising led to an eclipse in poster art.

Postimpressionism Movement in Western painting that represented both an extension of IMPRESSIONISM and a rejection of its limitations. The term was coined by the British art critic Roger Fry for the works of Paul CÉZANNE, Vincent VAN GOGH, Paul GAUGUIN, Henri de TOULOUSE-LAUTREC, and others. Most of these painters began as Impressionists, yet each abandoned that style to form his own highly personal art. The Postimpressionists often exhibited together but, unlike the Impressionists, a close-knit, convivial group, they painted mainly alone. See also NEO-IMPRESSIONISM.

postmodernism Any of several artistic movements that have challenged the philosophy and practices of modern arts or literature since about the 1960s. In literature this has amounted to a reaction against an ordered view of the world and therefore against fixed ideas about the form and meaning of texts. In its reaction against MODERNISM, postmodern writing, art, and architecture emphasize devices such as pastiche and parody and highly stylized techniques. Postmodernism has also led to a proliferation of critical theories, including DECONSTRUCTION, and the breaking down of the distinction between "high" and pop culture.

postmortem See AUTOPSY.

poststructuralism Movement in LITERARY CRITICISM begun in France in the late 1960s. Based on the theories of Ferdinand de SAUSSURE, Claude LÉVI-STRAUSS, and Jacques DERRIDA, it centers on the idea that language is not a transparency through which we see "truth" or "reality" but rather a structure or code that cannot possess absolute meaning in itself. Poststructuralists believe that all meaning resides in "intertextuality," the relationship of the text to past and nonliterary text and codes, and reject the traditional Western insistence on a single correct reading of a text. Writers associated with the movement include Roland BARTHES, Jacques LACAN, and Michel FOUCAULT. See also DECONSTRUCTION, STRUCTURALISM.

post-traumatic stress disorder Psychological reaction occurring after a highly stressing event, characterized by DEPRESSION, ANXIETY, flashbacks, and recurrent nightmares. The traumatic events can include automobile accidents, rape or assault, military combat, torture, incarceration in a concentration camp, and natural disasters. Long-term effects include family problems, difficulties at work, and abuse of drugs. PSYCHOTHERAPY, including GROUP THERAPY, is used in treatment.

Potala Palace \ˈpō-tə-lə\ Religious and administrative complex, near LHASA, Tibet. It covers 5 sq mi (13 sq km) atop a hill above the Lhasa River. Potrang Karpo (the White Palace, completed 1648) once served as the seat of the Tibetan government and the main residence of the DALAI LAMA. Potrang Marpo (the Red Palace, 1694) houses the tombs of eight Dalai Lamas; it remains a major pilgrimage site for Tibetan Buddhists. The complex, which has a total of 1,000 rooms, was declared a WORLD HERITAGE SITE in 1994.

potash \ˈpät-ˌash\ Name used for various inorganic compounds of POTASSIUM, chiefly a white crystalline CARBONATE formerly obtained from wood ashes. They are used to make special types of glass, pigments, printing inks, and soft soaps; for washing raw wool; and as a lab reagent and general-purpose food additive. Potassium hydroxide is frequently called caustic potash, and in the fertilizer industry, potassium oxide is called potash.

potash mica See MUSCOVITE.

potassium Chemical ELEMENT, one of the ALKALI METALS, chemical symbol K, atomic number 19. It is a soft, silvery-white METAL, not found free in nature. Potassium is essential for life and is present in all soils. Potassium IONS (K^+) and SODIUM ions act at cell membranes in electrochemical impulse transmission and in transport. Potassium compounds (VALENCE 1) are used as fertilizers, and as raw ma-

terials for producing other compounds. The iodide is added to table salt to protect against IODINE DEFICIENCY. See also POTASH, SALTPETER.

potassium-argon dating Method for determining the age of IGNEOUS ROCKS based on the amount of argon-40 in the rock. Radioactive potassium-40 decays to argon-40 with a half-life of about 1.3 billion years, making it useful for dating rocks that are billions of years old. Argon-argon dating provides a more accurate estimate of the original potassium-40 content by means of the ratio of argon-40 to argon-39 in the rock. See also DATING.

potato Herbaceous annual *(Solanum tuberosum)* in the NIGHTSHADE FAMILY. It is the only one of the world's main food crops whose edible portion is a TUBER. Potatoes are a major source of starch as well as amino acids, protein, vitamin C, and B vitamins. The stem grows 20–40 in. (50–100 cm) tall, sprouting spirally arranged compound leaves. Underground, stems enlarge into 1–20 tubers of variable shape and size. The tubers have spirally arranged buds (eyes) that may remain dormant after the tuber is fully grown for up to 10 weeks or more; they grow into plants identical to the parent plant. A native of the Andes, the potato was carried by Spaniards into Europe during the 16th cent. See also SWEET POTATO.

Potemkin \pə-ˈtyem-kin\, **Grigory (Aleksandrovich)** (1739–1791) Russian army officer. He helped bring CATHERINE II to power (1762), fought with distinction in the RUSSO–TURKISH WAR (1768–74), then became Catherine's lover (1774–76) and was made governor-general of "New Russia" (S Ukraine). As a field marshal from 1784, he introduced reforms in the army, built the harbor of Sevastopol, and constructed a fleet in the Black Sea. He attempted unsuccessfully to colonize the Ukrainian steppes, leaving many projects half-complete; his successful disguising of the weak points of his administration led to the claim that

Grigory Potemkin After a portrait by J. B. Lampi, 1789

he erected mere facades—"Potemkin villages"—to show Catherine on her tour of the region.

potential energy Energy stored by an object by virtue of its position. For example, an object raised above the ground acquires potential energy equal to the WORK done against the force of gravity; the energy is released as KINETIC ENERGY when it falls. A stretched spring also has stored potential energy. Other forms of potential energy include electrical potential energy, chemical energy, and NUCLEAR ENERGY.

potlatch Ceremonial distribution of property and gifts practiced among the American Indians of the NW Pacific coast, particularly the KWAKIUTL. A potlatch was given by an heir or successor to assert and validate his newly assumed social position. Ceremonial formalities were observed in inviting guests, in speechmaking, and in distributing goods according to the social rank of the recipients. The ceremony has been much studied for the light it sheds on the nature of property, wealth, prestige, and social status. See also GIFT EXCHANGE.

Potok \ˈpō-täk\, **Chaim** *(orig.* Herman Harold) (1929–2002) U.S. novelist. He was reared in an Orthodox Jewish home and was ordained a Conservative rabbi. He began a career as an editor and writer of scholarly and popular articles and reviews in the 1960s. His novels, which introduced to U.S. fiction the spiritual and cultural life of Orthodox Jews, include *The Chosen* (1967; film, 1981), *The Promise* (1969), and *My Name Is Asher Lev* (1972).

Potomac River \pə-ˈtō-mək\ River, E central U.S. Rising in the APPALACHIAN MTNS. of W. Virginia, it flows southeast about 287 mi (462 km) through the DISTRICT OF COLUMBIA into CHESAPEAKE BAY. It is navigable by large vessels to WASHINGTON, D.C., above which it descends in a series of

rapids and falls. Noted for its beauty, the Potomac is also rich in history. The Chesapeake and Ohio Canal National Historical Park parallels the river.

Potosí \‚pō-tō-'sē\ City (pop., 2000 est.: 147,000), SW Bolivia. Founded in 1545 after the discovery of silver nearby, it grew to be the most populous city in Latin America. After peaking at 160,000 about 1650, its population declined drastically with the slackening of silver production, but expanded in the 19th–20th cent. with the introduction of industries, including tin mining. It is one of the highest cities in the world, at an altitude of 13,700 ft (4,175 m).

Potsdam City (pop., 1998 est.: 136,000) and capital of BRAN-DENBURG state, Germany. It is today a suburb of BERLIN. Chartered in 1317, it became the electoral residence of the margrave of Brandenburg in 1640 under FREDERICK WILLIAM, the Great Elector. It was the Prussian royal residence under FREDERICK II, during whose reign it was a military and intellectual center. It was severely damaged during World War II. In 1945 it was the site of the POTSDAM CONFERENCE. It is home to heavy industry and several scientific and technical institutions. Frederick's magnificent palace, Sans Souci, is an outstanding attraction.

Potsdam Conference (July 17–Aug. 2, 1945) Allied conference held in the Berlin suburb of Potsdam after Germany's surrender in WORLD WAR II. Harry TRUMAN, Joseph STALIN, and Winston CHURCHILL (later replaced by Clement ATT-LEE) met to discuss European peace settlements, occupation of Germany and Austria, reparations, and the continuing war against Japan. France was allowed to share in the occupation, the Polish–German borders were redrawn, and Stalin refused to relinquish control of Eastern Europe.

Potter, (Helen) Beatrix (1866–1943) English author and illustrator of children's books. The illustrated animal stories she sent to a sick child when she was 27 were published as *The Tale of Peter Rabbit* (1902), which became the best-selling children's book of all time. More than 20 sequels followed, featuring such original characters as Jeremy Fisher, Jemima Puddle-Duck, and Mrs. Tiggy-Winkle; each is illustrated with her imaginative and technically superb watercolor drawings.

Beatrix Potter, 1913

pottery One of the oldest and most widespread of the decorative arts, consisting of objects (mostly useful ones, such as vessels, plates, and bowls) made of clay and hardened with heat. It includes EARTHENWARE, the oldest and simplest form, STONEWARE, and PORCELAIN. The Chinese began their sophisticated production of pottery in the Neolithic period, and produced porcelain as early as the 7th cent. A.D. Chinese porcelain, or "china," was widely exported to Europe and had a profound influence on European manufacturers and on taste. Classical Greece and Islamic cultures are also known for their artistic and technical innovations in pottery.

Poulenc \'pü-‚laŋk\, **Francis (Jean Marcel)** (1899–1963) French composer. In his teens he met Erik SATIE, and he soon thereafter became a member of Les SIX. He wrote much piano, chamber, and orchestral music, but is best known for his vocal music, including the operas *Dialogues of the Carmelites* (1956) and *La voix humaine* (1958), such sacred choral works as the *Stabat mater* (1950) and the *Gloria* (1959), reflecting his devout Catholicism, and many admired songs.

Pound, Ezra (Loomis) (1885–1972) U.S. poet and critic. Born in Hailey, Idaho, he spent most of his life in Europe. He became a leader of IMAGISM and a dominant influence in Anglo-American verse, helping promote such writers as W. B. YEATS, James JOYCE, Ernest HEMINGWAY, Robert FROST, and T. S. ELIOT, whose *Waste Land* he brilliantly edited. After World War I he published the important poems "Homage to Sextus Propertius" (1919) and *Hugh Selwyn Mauberley* (1920). He also began publishing *The Can-*

tos, an attempt at an epic sequence of poems, which would remain his major poetic occupation throughout his life. During the Great Depression, he increasingly pursued his interest in history and economics. In World War II he made pro-Fascist radio broadcasts from Italy; detained for treason in 1945, he was initially held at Pisa, where he wrote the moving *Pisan Cantos* (1948, Bollingen Prize). He was held in an American mental hospital until 1958, when he returned to Italy. *The Cantos* (1970) collects his 117 completed cantos.

Pound, Roscoe (1870–1964) U.S. legal educator and botanist. Born in Lincoln, Neb., he studied law and also obtained a PhD in botany (1897). Director of the state botanical survey (1892–1903), he discovered a rare fungus (*Roscopoundia*). He later taught at Harvard Law School (1910–37), where he also served as dean (1916–36), instituting many reforms. He was perhaps the chief U.S. advocate of sociological jurisprudence, which holds that statutes and court decisions are affected by social conditions; his ideas apparently influenced Franklin ROOSEVELT's NEW DEAL programs. After World War II he helped reorganize the Nationalist Chinese judicial system.

pound Unit of weight in the avoirdupois system, the traditional European system of weight (incorporated into the British Imperial system and the U.S. system of weights and measures), equal to 16 oz, 7,000 grains, or 0.4536 kg. It is also a unit of weight in the troy and apothecaries' systems, equal to 12 troy or apothecaries' oz, 5,760 grains, or 0.37 kg. Its Roman ancestor, the *libra,* is the source of the abbreviation *lb.* The troy pound is used for precious metals, the apothecaries' pound for drugs. The British monetary pound is linked historically with the minting of silver coins (sterlings), reckoned in "pounds of sterlings," or "pounds sterling."

Poussin \pü-'san\, **Nicolas** (1594–1665) French painter. Except for two years as court painter to Louis XIII, he spent his entire career in Rome. In early works, he depicted themes from classical mythology in a style reminiscent of TITIAN. Turning to RAPHAEL for inspiration, he developed a style marked by classical clarity and monumentality (e.g., *The Rape of the Sabine Women,* c. 1637, and the *Seven Sacraments* series, 1634–42). His late masterworks, such as *Holy Family on the Steps* (1648), employ a style calculated to express virtue and rectitude, featuring only a few figures painted in harsh colors against a severe background. In his landscapes, such as *Landscape with Polyphemus* (1649), the disorder of nature is reduced to the order of geometry. His austere and highly ordered compositions influenced generations of French painters, including J.-L. DAVID, J.-A.-D. IN-GRES, and Paul CÉZANNE.

Powder River River, N Wyoming and SE Montana. It rises in the foothills of the BIGHORN MTNS. in Wyoming and flows north 375 mi (603 km) to join the YELLOWSTONE RIVER near Terry, Mont.

Powell, Adam Clayton, Jr. (1908–1972) U.S. politician. Born in New Haven, Conn., he succeeded his father as pastor of the Abyssinian Baptist Church in New York's Harlem (1937) and built its membership to 13,000. He was elected to the New York City Council (1941), the first black to serve on that body, and to the U.S. House of Representatives (1945–67, 1969–71), where he effected passage of antipoverty acts and federal aid to education. Known for his flamboyance and unconcern for House decorum, he was investigated for financial misconduct. In 1967 the House voted to exclude him, but the U.S. Supreme Court later overturned its decision.

Powell \'pō-əl, 'paủ(-ə)l\, **Anthony (Dymoke)** (1905–2000) British novelist. He worked in journalism and served in World War II before publishing the first of 12 novels in the autobiographical and satiric series *A Dance to the Music of Time* (1951–75). His best-known work, it reflects his outlook and experiences of English society in the decades before and after the war. His later novels include *The Fisher King* (1986).

Powell, Colin (Luther) (b.1937) U.S. Army officer. Born in New York City, he entered the army after college and served in the Vietnam War. Assistant for national security affairs to Ronald REAGAN (1988), he was promoted to four-star general (1989), then appointed by George BUSH as chairman of the Joint Chiefs of Staff, the first black officer to hold that post. He helped plan the invasion of Panama (1989) and the operations of the PERSIAN GULF WAR. Though immensely popular, he declined to run for president in 1996. He became U.S. secretary of state under Pres. George W. BUSH in 2001.

Powell, John Wesley (1834–1902) U.S. geologist and ethnologist. Born in Mount Morris, N.Y., Powell became director of the U.S. Geological Survey in 1881, where he worked extensively on mapping water sources. He developed the first comprehensive classification of American Indian languages (1877) and was the first director of the SMITHSONIAN INSTITUTION's Bureau of American Ethnology (1879–1902). He described some of his many expeditions down the Colorado River (1871–79) in *Exploration of the Colorado River of the West and Its Tributaries* (1875).

Powell, Lewis F(ranklin), Jr. (1907–1998) U.S. jurist. Born in Suffolk, Va., he practiced law in Virginia, and as chairman of the Richmond school board he oversaw peaceful school integration in 1959. He later served as president of the American Bar Assn. He served on the U.S. Supreme Court from 1972 to 1987, taking moderate-to-liberal stances on civil rights, affirmative action, and separation of church and state, and conservative stands on law enforcement.

Powell, Robert Baden- See Robert BADEN-POWELL

power In science and engineering, the time rate of doing WORK or delivering ENERGY. Power (P) can be expressed as the amount of work done (W), or energy transferred, divided by the time interval (t): $P = W/t$. A given amount of work can be done by a low-powered motor in a long time or by a high-powered motor in a short time. Units of power are those of work (or energy) per unit time, such as foot-pounds per minute, joules per second (called watts), or ergs per second. Power can also be expressed as the product of the FORCE (F) applied to move an object and the speed (v) of the object in the direction of the force: $P = Fv$. See also HORSEPOWER.

Power, Tyrone (Edmund) (1914–1958) U.S. actor. Born in Cincinnati, the descendant of actors, he made his Broadway debut in *Romeo and Juliet* (1935). His first film hit was *Lloyds of London* (1936). He became noted for his action-adventure roles in such movies as *The Rains Came* (1939), *The Mark of Zorro* (1940), *Blood and Sand* (1941), and *Nightmare Alley* (1947), while continuing to act on stage in such plays as *Saint Joan* (1936), *Mister Roberts* (1950), and *Back to Methuselah* (1958).

power of attorney See power of ATTORNEY

Powers, Hiram (1805–1873) U.S.-Italian sculptor. Born in Woodstock, Vt., he worked in a waxworks museum in Cincinnati, then moved to Washington, D.C., where he modeled busts of such figures as Andrew JACKSON (1834). In 1837 he settled permanently in Florence. His marble *Greek Slave* (1843), an image of a nude young woman in chains, caused a sensation at London's Crystal Palace Exposition in 1851. He was one of the most popular sculptors of his time.

Powhatan \ˌpau̇-ə-ˈtan, pau̇-ˈha-tᵊn\ (d.1618) N. American Indian chief, father of POCAHONTAS. At the peak of his power he allegedly controlled 128 villages (about 9,000 inhabitants) of the POWHATAN confederacy. He did not oppose the English settlement at JAMESTOWN, but some of his tribesmen persistently attacked isolated groups of settlers. In 1614 Pocahontas married a settler, and shortly thereafter Powhatan negotiated a peace agreement.

Powhatan Confederacy of at least 30 ALGONQUIAN-speaking N. American Indian tribes that once occupied most of tidewater Virginia and the E shore of Chesapeake Bay. It was named for its powerful chief, POWHATAN. Powhatan women cultivated corn, beans, and squash; the men hunted and waged war, chiefly against the IROQUOIS. The intermittent hostilities with the English settlers, often called the Powhatan War (1622–44), ended with the breaking of the confederacy. Today about 3,000 Powhatan live along the Virginia coast.

powwow American Indian ceremony or gathering of any of various kinds. The term was originally used for healing ceremonies, but it could also refer to exuberant celebrations,

with dancing and singing, of success in hunting or victory in battle. Meetings of tribal councils were also often termed powwows. Today the word is used for large-scale Indian social gatherings with traditional drumming, singing, and dancing. Modern powwows draw tourists as well as participants, and craft items and souvenirs are offered for sale.

poxvirus Any of a group of VIRUSES responsible for a wide range of pox diseases in humans and other animals, including SMALLPOX. (Human CHICKEN POX is caused by herpes varicella-zoster.) It contains DNA, but appears to develop entirely within the CYTOPLASM of affected cells. The virus of rabbit pox has been used with mixed success in Australia to control the wild rabbit population.

Poznań \ˈpȯz-ˌnän\ *German* **Posen** \ˈpōz-ᵊn\ City (pop., 1999 est.: 578,000), W central Poland. One of the oldest cities in Poland, dating from the 9th cent. A.D., it reached the height of prosperity as a trade center from the 15th to the 17th cent., but declined after the Second NORTHERN WAR. In 1793 it was annexed to PRUSSIA, intensifying a Germanization that had begun in the 13th cent. In 1918 it reverted to Poland. During World War II it suffered extensive damage. Rebuilt, it has become the administrative, industrial, academic and cultural center of W Poland.

practical reason Rational capacity by which (rational) agents guide their conduct. In Immanuel KANT's moral philosophy, it is defined as the capacity of a rational being to act according to principles—that is, the conception of laws. Unlike the ethical intuitionists, Kant never held that practical reason intuits the rightness of particular actions or moral principles. For him, practical reason was basically a framework of formative principles rather than a source of specific rules. This is why he put such stress on the CATEGORICAL IMPERATIVE.

Prado Museum \ˈprä-dō\ Spain's national art museum. Founded in Madrid in 1818 by FERDINAND VII, it was opened to the public in 1819. Its holdings were formed over three centuries from the various royal collections of the Habsburg and Bourbon monarchs in Spain. In 1868 it became the National Museum of the Prado. It owns the outstanding collections of the works of El GRECO, Diego VELÁZQUEZ, and Francisco GOYA, and numerous works by such other Spanish masters as José de RIBERA and Francisco de ZURBARÁN. Its other holdings include many Flemish and Italian masterpieces.

Praeneste \prē-ˈnes-tē\ *modern* **Palestrina** Ancient city, LATIUM, in central Italy, northeast of Rome. Founded before the 8th cent. B.C., it saw many battles with Rome before becoming part of the ROMAN EMPIRE. It was a major center for the cult of the goddess Fortuna. It became a favorite resort of wealthy Romans, including Caesar AUGUSTUS, HADRIAN, and PLINY THE YOUNGER. The modern town was the birthplace of G. P. da PALESTRINA.

praetor \ˈprē-tər\ In ancient Rome, an officer who judged cases of equity and who, in the absence of CONSULS, exercised extensive authority in the government. He also produced the public games. After a one-year term, a praetor typically went on to govern a province. Originally open only to PATRICIAN magistrates, the post could be held by PLEBEIANS from around 337 B.C. The number of praetors varied from one to eight.

Praetorian Guard \prē-ˈtȯr-ē-ən\ (Latin, *cohors praetoria*) Household troops of the Roman emperors. In the 2nd cent. B.C. they were bodyguards for Roman generals. During the civil wars, military leaders had personal bodyguards, but in 27 B.C. AUGUSTUS created a permanent corps to guard the emperor and stationed its members around Rome. In A.D. 23, with Sejanus (d. 31) as commander, they gained political influence; from then on, they usually had an important voice in appointing emperors. CONSTANTINE I disbanded the body in 312.

pragmatics Branch of LINGUISTICS and philosophy of language that studies the relationship between linguistic expressions and their users. It is usually defined in contrast to SYNTAX and SEMANTICS as the study of the rules and conventions governing the use of meaningful expressions to perform communicative acts. A distinction between semantics and pragmatics is reflected in the distinction between the strict and literal meaning of the words uttered by a

P

speaker (studied in semantics) and their meaning when uttered on a particular occasion (studied in pragmatics).

Pragmatic Sanction (1713) Decree by Emperor CHARLES VI requiring the undivided descent of his HABSBURG domains. It stipulated that his heritage go to his eldest son or, if none, to his eldest daughter. Much of Charles's later reign was directed toward securing acceptance of the sanction from the other European powers. Since his son died soon after birth (1716), his daughter MARIA THERESA became his heir. On Charles's death (1740), the sanction was contested by Prussia and Bavaria, which led to the War of the AUSTRIAN SUCCESSION.

pragmatism Philosophical movement first given systematic expression by Charles Sanders PEIRCE and William JAMES and later taken up and transformed by John DEWEY. Pragmatists emphasize the practical function of knowledge as an instrument for adapting to reality and controlling it. Pragmatism agrees with EMPIRICISM in emphasizing the priority of experience over A PRIORI reasoning. Pragmatists interpret ideas as instruments and plans of action. In contrast to the conception of ideas as images of reality, pragmatism emphasizes the functional character of ideas: ideas are suggestions and anticipations of possible conduct, hypotheses or forecasts of what will result from a given action, or ways of organizing behavior in the world rather than replicas of the world. See also W. V. O. QUINE, Richard RORTY.

Prague \\'präg\\ City (pop., 1999 est.: 1,193,000), capital of the Czech Republic, on the VLTAVA RIVER. Settled as early as the 9th cent., by the 14th cent. it was one of Europe's leading cultural and trade centers. It was the center of opposition to the HABSBURGS in the early 17th cent. It became the capital of an independent Czechoslovakia in 1918. It was occupied by Germany during World War II and by the U.S.S.R. and other WARSAW PACT military forces in 1968 (see PRAGUE SPRING). In 1989 it was the center of a movement that led to the peaceful overthrow of the Communist government. An outstandingly beautiful city, Prague is the country's major economic and cultural center, famous for its music, literature, and architecture.

Prague Spring (1968) Brief period of liberalization in Czechoslovakia under Alexander DUBCEK. In April 1968 he instituted agricultural and industrial reforms, a revised constitution to guarantee civil rights, autonomy for Slovakia, and democratization of the government. By June, many Czechs were calling for more rapid progress. The Soviet Union and other WARSAW PACT countries, alarmed by the threat of a social-democratic Czechoslovakia, invaded in August, deposed Dubcek, and reinstalled hard-line communists as leaders.

Praia \\'prī-ə\\ City (pop., 1995 est.: 68,000), port, and capital of Cape Verde. It is located on São Tiago (Santiago) Island, about 400 mi (640 km) off the W African bulge. It ships bananas, coffee, and sugarcane, and is a submarine cable station.

prairie Level or rolling grassland, especially that found in central N. America. Decreasing amounts of rainfall, from 40 in. (100 cm) at the forested E edge to less than 12 in. (30 cm) at the desertlike W edge, affect the species composition of the prairie grassland. The vegetation is composed primarily of perennial grasses, with many species of flowering plants of the pea and composite families. The three main types of prairie are the tallgrass prairie; midgrass, or mixed-grass, prairie; and shortgrass prairie, or shortgrass plains.

prairie chicken Either of two species of N. American GROUSE (genus *Tympanuchus*) noted for lek displays (group courtship displays). The greater prairie chicken is about 18 in. (45 cm) long and may weigh almost 2 lbs (1 kg). Its brown plumage is strongly barred below. It occurs from Saskatchewan to coastal Texas and Louisiana. The eastern subspecies, the heath hen, is extinct. The lesser prairie chicken, smaller and paler, inhabits the arid W central Great Plains. The sharp-tailed grouse (*Pedioecetes*) is locally called prairie chicken.

prairie dog Any of five species (genus *Cynomys*) of stout, short-legged, terrestrial SQUIRRELS, named for its barklike call. Once abundant throughout the W U.S. plains, it is now found mostly in protected areas. It is 12–17 in. (30–43 cm) long, including a 1–5-in. (3–12-cm) tail. Their main diet is grass. Colonies consist of well-defined territories defended by a male, several females, and young. Burrows of the black-tailed prairie dog have entry mounds that prevent flooding and serve as lookout posts. The white-tailed prairie dog inhabits higher altitudes, hibernates, and is less colonial.

Prairie school Style of architecture produced in the American Midwest by Frank Lloyd WRIGHT, George Grant Elmslie (1871–1952), Barry Byrne (1883–1967), and others around 1900–17. Prairie houses were generally built of brick, wood, and plaster, with stucco walls and bands of casement windows. The Prairie architects emphasized horizontal lines, using low roofs with wide, projecting eaves; internal spaces flowed around a central fireplace or hearth. The resulting low, spreading structures reach out to nature, not other buildings.

Pramudya Ananta Tur *or* **Pramoedya Ananta Toer** \\prä-'müd-yä-ä-'nän-tä-'tür\\ (b.1925) Javanese writer. While imprisoned by the Dutch (1947–49) for his role in the Indonesian revolt against renewed colonial rule, Pramudya wrote his first published novel, *The Fugitive* (1950). He developed a rich style that incorporates everyday speech and images from classical Javanese culture. Imprisoned 1965–79 for his role in a communist coup attempt, he wrote a series of four novels, including *This Earth of Mankind* (1980) and *Child of All Nations* (1980), that depict Javanese society under Dutch rule. He is the preeminent prose writer of postindependence Indonesia.

Prandtl \\'prän-t⁹l\\, **Ludwig** (1875–1953) German physicist, considered the father of AERODYNAMICS. His 1904 discovery of the BOUNDARY LAYER at the surface of a moving body led to an understanding of skin friction DRAG and of the way streamlining reduces the drag of airplane wings and other moving bodies. His work on wing theory explained the process of airflow over airplane wings.

Pratt Institute Private institution of higher learning in Brooklyn, N.Y. It was founded as a trade school in 1887 by the industrialist Charles Pratt (1830–1891). It comprises schools of architecture, art and design (for which it is especially renowned), liberal arts and sciences, and professional studies. Enrollment is about 3,400.

Pravda \\'präv-də\\ (Russian: "Truth") Former national daily newspaper published in Moscow, the official organ of the Communist Party of the Soviet Union 1918–91. It was founded in St. Petersburg as an underground paper by Vladimir LENIN in 1912. It offered well-written articles and analyses on science, economics, cultural topics, and literature as well as materials to indoctrinate and inform readers on Communist theory and programs. After Communist power ended in 1991, its readership dwindled; it became the voice of the conservative-nationalist opposition and ceased publication in 1996. See also *IZVESTIYA*.

Praxiteles \\prak-'si-t⁹l-ˌēz\\ (fl.c.370–330 B.C.) Greek sculptor. His only known surviving work is the marble *Hermes Carrying the Infant Dionysus*; a few other works survive in Roman copies. PLINY THE ELDER considered his *Aphrodite of Cnidus* the best statue in the world. Through Praxiteles' influence, figures were increasingly shown standing in graceful, sinuous poses, leaning lightly on some support, a pose further developed by sculptors of the HELLENISTIC AGE. Greatest and most original of the 4th-cent. Attic sculptors, he profoundly influenced the later course of Greek sculpture.

Praxiteles, "Aphrodite of Cnidus," Roman copy, c.350 B.C.

prayer Petition made to God or a god. Prayer has been practiced in all religions throughout history. Its characteristic postures (bowing the head, kneeling, prostration) and position of the hands (raised, outstretched, clasped) signify an attitude of submission and devotion. In addition to spontaneous private prayer, most religions have fixed formulas of prayer, often recited in group worship. The four prophetic religions (JUDAISM, CHRISTIANITY, ISLAM, and ZOROASTRIANISM) prescribe a daily set form of individual prayer.

prayer wheel In TIBETAN BUDDHISM, a mechanical device used as an equivalent to the recitation of a MANTRA. It is a hollow metal cylinder, often beautifully embossed, mounted on a rod and containing a consecrated paper bearing a mantra. Each turn of the wheel by hand is considered equivalent to orally reciting the prayer. There are also large cylinders that can be set in motion by hand or attached to windmills or waterwheels and thus kept in continuous motion.

Tibetan prayer wheel

praying mantis See MANTIS

Preakness Stakes One of the three classic U.S. THOROUGHBRED races making up the TRIPLE CROWN. It is held annually in mid-May at Baltimore's Pimlico Race Course. The course distance is 1 3/16 mi. (1.9 km). The field is limited to 3-year-old Thoroughbreds.

Precambrian time Interval of geologic time from 3.8 billion years ago, the age of the oldest known rocks, to 544 million years ago. This interval represents about 80% of the geologic record and provides important evidence of how the continents evolved. The Precambrian includes the ARCHEAN and PROTEROZOIC EONS, and sometimes also the pre-geologic HADEAN EON. It was originally defined as the era that predated the emergence of life in the CAMBRIAN PERIOD; it is now known, however, that life had begun by the early Archean. Soft-bodied organisms without skeletons began to appear toward the end of the Precambrian. See table at GEOLOGIC TIME.

precipitation Water particles that fall from CLOUDS and reach the ground, including drizzle, RAIN, SNOW, ice crystals, and HAIL. Precipitation particles are much larger than cloud particles; an average raindrop is equivalent to about 1 million cloud droplets. Precipitation elements (ice crystals or droplets that form around soluble particles such as salt) form directly from the vapor state, become larger through collision and coalescence, and eventually fall to the ground.

Precisionism Smooth, precise technique used primarily in the 1920s by several U.S. painters in representational canvases depicting sharply defined forms, such as urban skylines, the industrial landscape of factories, and country landscapes with grain elevators and barns or empty desert and sky. The scenes are devoid of people or signs of human activity. Precisionism is a "cool" art, which keeps the viewer at a distance. It had a great influence on Pop art. Though not part of a school or movement, the Precisionist artists, including Charles DEMUTH, Georgia O'KEEFFE, and Charles SHEELER, often exhibited together.

predestination In CHRISTIANITY, the doctrine that God has already determined who will be saved and who will be damned. Three types of predestination doctrine have developed in Christianity. One holds that God singled out the saved because he foresaw their future merits. A second (often identified with John CALVIN) states that from eternity God has determined the saved and the damned, regardless of their merit or lack thereof. A third, set forth by THOMAS AQUINAS and Martin LUTHER, ascribes salvation to the unmerited GRACE of God but links the lack of grace to SIN. In ISLAM, after extensive argumentation, a strict predestination became the mainstream view.

preeclampsia and eclampsia \ˌprē-i-ˈklamp-sē-ə\ Hypertensive conditions induced by PREGNANCY. In preeclampsia,

HYPERTENSION, PROTEIN in the urine, and EDEMA develop late in pregnancy. Persistent hypertension compromises the fetus's blood supply and damages the mother's kidneys. Monitoring of blood pressure and weight gain may detect it before symptoms begin. Eclampsia (with convulsons) follows in about 5% of cases. It can usually be prevented by special diets, drugs, and limited activity or early delivery.

prefabrication Production of standardized building components at a location other than the building site. Units may include doors, stairs, window walls, wall panels, floor panels, roof trusses, room-sized components, and even entire buildings. Prefabrication requires the cooperation of architects, suppliers, and builders regarding the size of basic modular units. In the U.S. building industry, the 4-by-8-ft (1.2-by-2.4-m) panel is a standard unit; architects' plans and prefabricated wall units are based on that module. Advantages of prefabrication include the cost savings of mass production and standardization of parts for quick assembly and erection.

prefect In ancient Rome, any of various high officials primarily with judicial and administrative responsibilities. In the early republic, a prefect of the city took over the CONSULS' duties during their absence from Rome. They lost some importance after the introduction of PRAETORS (mid-4th cent. B.C.), but AUGUSTUS revitalized the office. The prefects supervising the PRAETORIAN GUARD acquired great power and often became virtual prime ministers.

pregnancy Process of gestation that takes place in the female's body as a FETUS develops, from FERTILIZATION to PARTURITION. It begins when a viable SPERM from the male and EGG from the OVARY merge (see FERTILITY). The fertilized egg (zygote) grows by cell division as it moves toward the UTERUS, where it implants in the lining and grows into an EMBRYO and then a fetus. A PLACENTA and umbilical cord develop. A fluid-filled amniotic sac encloses and cushions the fetus. Early in pregnancy, higher ESTROGEN and PROGESTERONE levels halt MENSTRUATION, cause nausea, often with vomiting (morning sickness), and enlarge the breasts and prepare them for LACTATION. Normal weight gain in pregnancy is 20–25 lbs (9–11.5 kg). The fetus's nutritional needs require the mother to take in more calories and especially protein, water, calcium, and iron. FOLIC-ACID supplements help prevent NEURAL TUBE DEFECTS. Smoking, alcohol, and many legal and illegal drugs can cause CONGENITAL DISORDERS and should be avoided. ULTRASOUND imaging is often used to monitor structural and functional progress of the fetus. The due date is estimated as 280 days from the time of last menstruation. See also AMNIOCENTESIS, PREECLAMPSIA AND ECLAMPSIA. See diagram on following page.

premenstrual syndrome (PMS) Variable group of symptoms occurring before MENSTRUATION in 40% of women, severe in about 10% of those. Physical symptoms may include headache, cramps, bloating, and constipation or diarrhea. Emotional symptoms range from irritability, lethargy, and mood swings to hostility, confusion, and depression. Depending on the symptoms, treatment may involve exercise, stress management, nutritional therapy, or drugs. Increasing calcium intake can prevent or reduce cramps, which are best treated with IBUPROFEN.

premier See PRIME MINISTER

Preminger \ˈpre-min-jər\, **Otto (Ludwig)** (1906–1986) Austrian-U.S. film director. Working with Max REINHARDT's theater, he soon became its director. In 1935 he directed *Libel* on Broadway. Invited to Hollywood, he made the thriller *Laura* (1944), which helped establish FILM NOIR. Later landmark films included *The Moon Is Blue* (1953), which challenged Hollywood censorship; the all-black *Carmen Jones* (1954); and *The Man with the Golden Arm* (1955), a tale of drug addiction. His later films included *Anatomy of a Murder* (1959), *Exodus* (1960), and *The Cardinal* (1963).

Prendergast, Maurice (Brazil) (1858–1924) U.S. (Canadianborn) painter. Born in Saint John's, Newfoundland, he moved with his family to Boston in 1868. After study in Paris, he spent much of his career traveling and painting abroad. Influenced by French Impressionism and Postimpressionism, his lively street scenes feature floating geometric areas of brilliant decorative color with a mosaiclike ef-

P

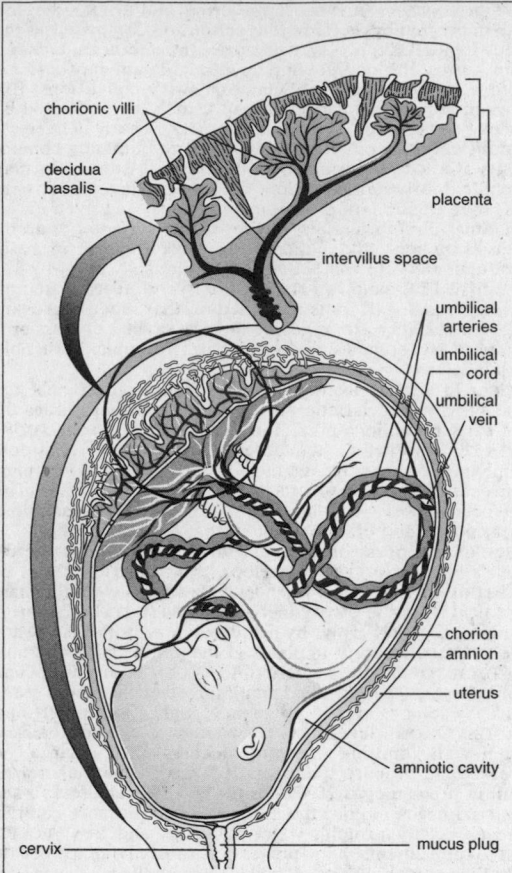

Pregnancy Full-term fetus in the uterus. The amnion, formed from the inner embryonic membrane, encloses the fetus. The space between the amnion and fetus (amniotic cavity) is filled with the watery amniotic fluid. The outermost embryonic membrane, the chorion, has developed fingerlike projections (villi) on its outer surface, which have enlarged and penetrated the decidua basalis layer of the uterus. The chorionic villi and the decidua basalis form the placenta. Maternal blood fills the spaces around the villi (intervillous spaces); oxygen and nutrients diffuse into the villi and pass on to the fetus via the umbilical vein. Waste materials that leave the fetus via the umbilical arteries diffuse out of the villi into the mother's blood.

fect (e.g., *Central Park in 1903*). He produced his most outstanding works in watercolor (*Picnic: Boston Garden*, c.1895; *Venice*, 1899). He later lived in New York and exhibited with The EIGHT.

Prensa \\'pren-sä\\, **La** Argentine daily newspaper, widely regarded as the finest Spanish-language newspaper in the world. Founded in Buenos Aires in 1869, it soon became known for professional, accurate news reporting and independence in editorial opinion. It displayed a concern for human welfare that persisted in the face of government harassment, notably in the 1940s under the regime of Juan PERÓN. From 1951 to 1956 it was a Peronist propaganda organ.

preparatory school School that prepares students for entrance to a higher school. In Europe, where SECONDARY EDUCATION has been selective, preparatory schools cater to pupils wishing to enter the academic secondary schools. In N. America, the term usually refers to private secondary schools that prepare students for college.

Preparedness Movement Pre–World War I campaign to increase U.S. military capabilities and convince the public of the need for U.S. involvement in a European conflict. Such leaders as Theodore ROOSEVELT sought to persuade Pres. Woodrow WILSON to strengthen U.S. national defenses, and organizations sponsored preparedness parades to build public awareness and support. It resulted in passage of the National Defense Act (1916); the U.S. entered the war the next year.

Pre-Raphaelites \\,prē-'rä-fē-ə-,līts\\ Group of young British painters, led by D. G. ROSSETTI, W. H. HUNT, and J. E. MILLAIS, who banded together in 1848 in reaction against what they considered the prevailing unimaginative and artificial historical painting, seeking to express a new moral seriousness and sincerity in their works. Their name, the Pre-Raphaelite Brotherhood, honored the simplicity in depicting nature in Italian art before RAPHAEL, and the symbolism, imagery, and mannered style of their paintings often suggest a faux-medieval world. Later members included E. BURNE-JONES and George Frederic Watts (1817–1904). The group also functioned as a school of writers who often used me-

Pre-Raphaelite painting by D. G. Rossetti, "The Girlhood of Mary Virgin," 1849

dieval settings, as in William MORRIS's *The Defence of Guenevere* (1858). Though active less than 10 years, the group had a profound influence on the arts.

Presbyterianism Form of church government based on rule by elders, or presbyters. The highest court of presbyters is the general assembly. Presbyters are elected by the members of the congregation for fixed terms, in a system intended to affirm the equality of all Christians. The term Presbyterianism also refers to a denomination, the Presbyterian Church. Modern Presbyterian churches trace their origins to the Calvinist churches of the British Isles; in continental Europe such congregations were known as REFORMED CHURCHES. The Presbyterian Church is strongest in Scotland, where it was founded by John KNOX in 1557. See also CALVINISM.

preschool education Childhood education during the period from infancy to age 5 or 6. Institutions and names for preschool education vary (e.g., infant school, day care, maternal school, nursery school, crèche, kindergarten). The first systematic approach was propounded by Friedrich FROEBEL, founder of the KINDERGARTEN. Other theorists include Maria MONTESSORI and Jean PIAGET. Of major concern in preschool education is language development. See also ELEMENTARY EDUCATION.

Prescott, William H(ickling) (1796–1859) U.S. historian. Born in Salem, Mass., he devoted his life to recounting the history of 16th-cent. Spain and its colonies. He is best known for his *History of the Conquest of Mexico* (1843) and *History of the Conquest of Peru* (1847), for which he made rigorous use of original sources, and which earned him a reputation as the first scientific U.S. historian.

preservative Any of numerous chemical additives used to prevent or slow food spoilage caused by chemical changes and maintain a fresh appearance and consistency. Antimycotics (e.g., sodium and calcium propionate, sorbic acid) inhibit mold growth; ANTIOXIDANTS (e.g., butylated hydroxytoluene or BHT) delay rancidity; ANTIBIOTICS (e.g., tetracyclines) prevent bacterial growth; humectants retain moisture; and antistaling agents (e.g., glyceryl monostearate) maintain moisture and softness. Some preservatives also improve the appearance of the product (e.g., sodium nitrate and NITRITE in meats).

president In government, the officer in whom a nation's chief executive power is vested. In some countries, the president is the chief of state but not of the government, in which case the role is primarily ceremonial. Elsewhere, the president is both the leader of the government and the head of state. In the U.S., the president's chief duty is to ensure that the laws of the land are faithfully executed, which he does through various executive agencies and with the aid of his CABINET. He also serves as commander in chief of the armed forces, nominates federal judges, and makes treaties with foreign governments (contingent on Senate approval). See also PRIME MINISTER.

Presley, Elvis (Aaron) (1935–1977) U.S. popular singer, the "King of Rock and Roll."
Born in Tupelo, Miss., Presley was raised in Memphis, where he sang Pentecostal church music. In 1954 he began to record for the producer Sam Phillips, who had been searching for a white singer who sounded like a black man. In 1956 he released "Heartbreak Hotel," the first of numerous million-selling hits, including "Hound Dog" and "All Shook Up," and appeared in *Love Me Tender,* the first of 33 mediocre films. Presley's intensely charismatic style—including his sexy hip shaking, ducktail haircut, and characteristic sneer—excited young fans to wild adulation. After a stint in the army (1958–60), his earlier raucous style was

Elvis Presley, 1968

moderated. In 1968 he introduced a Las Vegas-based touring act with orchestra and gospel-type choir. Battling weight gain and drug dependence, he underwent a personal decline. His death at 42 was mourned by hundreds of thousands at Graceland, his Memphis estate, which became a place of pilgrimage. He remains the most successful solo recording artist in history.

pre-Socratics Earliest Greek philosophers (those who preceded SOCRATES). Their focus on the physical world has led to their being called cosmologists or naturalists. They include the Milesians THALES, ANAXIMANDER, and ANAXIMENES, XENOPHANES OF COLOPHON, PARMENIDES, HERACLEITUS, EMPEDOCLES, ANAXAGORAS, DEMOCRITUS, ZENO OF ELEA, and PYTHAGORAS.

Pressburg See BRATISLAVA

pressure Perpendicular force per unit area, or stress at a point within a confined fluid. A solid object exerts pressure on a floor equal to its WEIGHT divided by the area of contact. The weight of the earth's atmosphere on the earth constitutes ATMOSPHERIC PRESSURE. The pressure exerted by a confined gas results from the average effect of the forces produced on the walls of the container by the continual, numerous collisions by gas molecules. Hydrostatic pressure is the pressure exerted equally in all directions at points within a confined fluid. The standard unit of pressure is the pascal (Pa), which is equal to one newton of force per square meter.

Prester John Legendary Christian ruler of the East. He was believed to be a NESTORIAN and a king-priest (Prester being short for Presbyter, "elder" or "priest") reigning in an unspecified part of the Far East. The legend arose during the CRUSADES in the 12th cent., among European Christians who hoped that Prester John would prove an ally in the effort to regain the Holy Land. In the 13th–14th cent. various missionaries and travelers, including Marco POLO, searched for his kingdom in Asia. After the mid-14th cent., Prester John became identified with the emperor of Ethiopia.

prestressed concrete Concrete reinforced by either pretensioning or posttensioning, allowing it to carry a greater load or span a greater distance than ordinary REINFORCED CONCRETE. In pretensioning, lengths of steel wire or cables are laid in the empty mold and stretched. The concrete is placed and allowed to set, and the cables are released, plac-

ing the concrete into compression as the steel shrinks. In posttensioning, the steel in the concrete is stretched after the curing process. These compressive stresses counteract the tensile bending stresses of an applied load.

Pretoria \pri-'tōr-ē-ə\ City (metro. area pop., 1991: 1,080,000), administrative capital of the Republic of S. Africa. Founded in 1855, it became the capital of the TRANSVAAL in 1860 and the administrative capital of S. Africa in 1910. During the S. AFRICAN WAR in 1899, Winston CHURCHILL escaped from prison there. Primarily a seat of government, Pretoria is also a rail center, with an industrial economy based on iron and steel. It is home to the Univ. of S. Africa and the Univ. of Pretoria. See also BLOEMFONTEIN, CAPE TOWN.

Pretorius \prə-'tü-rē-ūs\, **Andries** (1798–1853) Boer leader in the GREAT TREK who became the dominant figure in Natal and the TRANSVAAL. Pretorius's forces defeated the ZULU at Blood River in 1838 and at Magono in 1840. In 1842 and 1848 he led unsuccessful fights with the British over the annexation of Natal and the Transvaal. In 1852 he participated in the Sand River Convention, where Transvaal independence was recognized. He led negotiations for independence of the Orange River Sovereignty, finally guaranteed in 1854. His son Marthinus Wessel Pretorius (1819–1901) was the first president of the S. African Republic (1857, 1864, 1869) and president of the Orange Free State (1859–63). After British annexation of the Transvaal, Marthinus joined insurgent Boer leaders and helped win recognition of Transvaal independence.

preventive medicine Efforts toward disease prevention in the community and the individual. It covers patient interviews and testing to detect risk factors; sanitary measures in homes, communities, and medical facilities; patient education; and diet and exercise programs as well as preventive drugs and surgery. Important advances in preventive medicine include vaccination (see VACCINE), ANTIBIOTICS, DIAGNOSTIC IMAGING, and recognition of psychological factors. See also EPIDEMIOLOGY, IMMUNOLOGY, PUBLIC HEALTH, QUARANTINE.

Previn \'pre-vin\, **André (George)** *orig.* Andreas (Ludwig) Priwin (b.1929) U.S. (German-born) pianist, composer, and conductor. He fled Nazi persecution with his family for Los Angeles in 1939. He orchestrated and arranged music for MGM in the 1940s and '50s, and thereafter scored films for several studios. A noted classical and jazz pianist, he has served as principal conductor of the London Symphony, Pittsburgh Symphony, Los Angeles Philharmonic, and Royal Philharmonic orchestras. He has also composed a symphony, concertos, and the opera *A Streetcar Named Desire* (1998), as well as popular songs.

Prévost d'Exiles \prā-ˌvō-dāg-'zēl\, **Antoine-François** *known as* **Abbé Prévost** (1697–1763) French novelist. From an early age Prévost alternated between enlistments in the army and entries into the religious life, which he eventually fled in 1728. His fame rests entirely on *Manon Lescaut* (1731), a novel about a young man of good family who ruins his life for a courtesan, which became the basis of two famous operas, Jules MASSENET's *Manon* and Giacomo PUCCINI's *Manon Lescaut.*

PRI See INSTITUTIONAL REVOLUTIONARY PARTY

Priam \'prī-əm\ In GREEK MYTHOLOGY, the last king of TROY. By his wife, HECUBA, he had many children, including HECTOR and PARIS. He reigned during the TROJAN WAR; in its final year he lost 13 sons, three of whom were killed by ACHILLES in a single day. When Troy fell, Achilles' son Neoptolemus killed the elderly Priam on an altar.

Priapus \prī-'ā-pəs\ Greek god of animal and vegetable fertility. He was represented in a caricature of the human form, grotesquely misshapen, with an enormous phallus. His father was DIONYSUS. In Hellenistic times the worship of Priapus spread throughout the ancient world, and he was adopted as the god of gardens.

Pribilof Islands \'pri-bə-ˌlȯf\ Group of four islands, SE BERING SEA, Alaska. They lie about 300 mi (500 km) west of the mainland. The islands passed to the U.S. with the ALASKA PURCHASE (1867). They are known as breeding grounds for most of the world's fur seals. The islands are also home to enormous numbers of birds and blue and white foxes. The indigenous population is made up of ALEUTS.

price Amount of MONEY that has to be paid to acquire a given good, service, or resource. As a measure of value, prices perform a significant economic function, distributing the scarce supply of goods, services, and resources to those who most want them through the adjustments of SUPPLY AND DEMAND. The price mechanism assumes that only by allowing prices to move freely will the supply of any given commodity match demand. If supply is excessive, prices will be low and production will be reduced; this will cause prices to rise until there is a balance of demand and supply. If supply is inadequate, prices will be high, prompting an increase in production that in turn will lead to a reduction in prices. MONOPOLIES or government regulation may limit the efficiency of price as a determinant of supply and demand. In centrally planned economies, the price mechanism may be supplanted by centralized government control. An economy without a price mechanism usually produces surpluses, shortages, BLACK MARKETS, and stunted economic growth.

Price, (Mary Violet) Leontyne (b.1927) U.S. soprano. Born in Laurel, Miss., she was trained at the Juilliard School. She made her name in the international tour of *Porgy and Bess* (1953–55), sang Aïda at La Scala in 1960, and made her Metropolitan Opera debut in 1961. She was one of the Met's most popular stars for more than two decades, and starred in the first production at the new Met at Lincoln Center.

Price, Vincent (Leonard) (1911–1993) U.S. actor. Born in St. Louis, he made his London stage debut as Prince Albert in *Victoria Regina* (1935), then reprised the role on Broadway. In Hollywood, he displayed his cultivated manner and silken voice in such historical roles in *The Private Lives of Elizabeth and Essex* (1939) and *The Three Musketeers* (1948). He is best known as the menacing villain in horror movies such as *House of Wax* (1953) as well as a series of Roger CORMAN movies adapted from E. A. POE stories, including *The Masque of the Red Death* (1964).

price index Measure of change in a set of PRICES, such that a comparison of the values for any two periods or places will show the change in prices between periods or the difference in prices between places. Price indexes were first developed to measure changes in the cost of living in order to determine the wage increases necessary to maintain a constant STANDARD OF LIVING. The best-known price indexes represent the ratio of what a market basket of goods costs today to what it cost in a base period. The most familiar indexes of this type are the CONSUMER PRICE INDEX (CPI) and the producer price index (PPI). The CPI measures changes in retail prices in such component parts as food, clothing, and shelter. The PPI measures changes in the prices charged by manufacturers and wholesalers.

prickly pear Any of a group of flat-stemmed, spiny cacti (see CACTUS) in the genus *Opuntia*, native to the Western Hemisphere, or the edible fruit of certain species. Because their stems have a high water content, prickly pears can be used as forage crops and emergency stock feed during drought. Some species are cultivated as ornamentals and valued for their large flowers.

Priene \prī-'ē-nē\ Ancient city of IONIA, north of the Menderes River, SW Turkey. According to STRABO it was founded by Ionians and Thebans. It prospered under the Romans and Byzantines, then passed into Turkish hands in the 13th cent. A.D. Excavations revealed a Greek town built on terraces; atop a nearby hill is the temple of Athena Polias, dedicated by ALEXANDER THE GREAT in 334 B.C.

priesthood Office of a spiritual leader expert in the ceremonies of worship and the performance of religious rituals. Though chieftains, kings, and heads of households have sometimes performed priestly functions, in most civilizations the priesthood is a specialized office. The priest's duties are concerned less with magic than with the right performance of ritual acts required by the divine powers. Many African societies, for example, differentiated between SHAMANS and the priests responsible for the worship of tribal ancestors. Not every highly developed religion possesses a priesthood, the most notable exception being ISLAM. The idea of the "priesthood of all believers" was also a cardinal doctrine of the REFORMATION.

Priestley, Joseph (1733–1804) English theologian, political theorist, and physical scientist. His early scientific studies resulted in his important *History and Present State of Electricity* (1767). His *Essay on Government* (1768) influenced later UTILITARIANISM. He did important work in chemical reactions and change. He is considered the discoverer of nitrogen, carbon monoxide, ammonia, and several other gases, and in 1774 he became the first to identify OXYGEN; his report led Antoine LAVOISIER to repeat the experiment, deduce oxygen's nature and role, and

Joseph Priestley Portrait by Ellen Sharples, c.1795

name it. He wrote several major theological works. His nonconformist religious views and his political activities made him increasingly controversial in England, and he emigrated to the U.S. in 1794.

primary education See ELEMENTARY EDUCATION

primary election Electoral device for choosing a party's candidates for public office. The formal primary system is peculiar to the U.S., where it came into widespread use in the early 20th cent. Most U.S. states use the primary system both for statewide offices and for president. Delegates supporting a presidential candidate are selected to attend a national convention, where they vote for the candidate. A closed-vote primary is restricted to party members; an open-vote primary is open to all voters in the district.

primate Placental MAMMAL (order Primates) that originated as a forest-dweller perhaps 97.5 million years ago. Primates are typically characterized by a short muzzle, reduced sense of smell, prehensile five-digit hands and feet often with opposable thumbs and big toes, flat nails, depth perception with acute vision that is binocular to some degree, forward-facing eyes, large brain, and prolonged pre- and postnatal development. Most species bear a single young and live in troops headed by a male. The prosimians (suborder Prosimii) include LEMURS (families Lemuridae, Indriidae, Cheirogaleidae, Megaladapidae), the aye-aye (Daubentoniidae), galagos (Galagonidae), LORISES (Lorisidae), and TARSIERS (Tarsiidae). The anthropoids (suborder Anthropoidea) include NEW WORLD MONKEYS (families Callitrichidae and Cebidae), OLD WORLD MONKEYS (Cercopithecidae), GIBBONS (Hylobatidae), the great APES (Pongidae), and humans (Hominidae). The great apes are sometimes classed with humans in Hominidae.

Primaticcio \prē-mə-'tēt-chō\, **Francesco** (1504/5–1570) Italian-French painter, sculptor, and architect. In 1532 FRANCIS I invited him to help redecorate the FONTAINEBLEAU Palace, and Primaticcio became one of the principal artists in France; he remained there the rest of his life. His decorative style in painting and stucco sculpture stressed the human figure, with exaggerated musculature and active, elongated forms. One of the first artists in France to replace religious themes with those of classical mythology, he brought a quiet French elegance to Italian Mannerism.

prime minister *or* **premier** \pri-'mir, pri-'myir\ Head of the executive branch of government in states with a parliamentary system (see PARLIAMENTARY DEMOCRACY). The prime minister is the leader of the POLITICAL PARTY or coalition with a governing majority, and is formally appointed by the head of state. The office was developed in Britain by Robert WALPOLE; its powers were consolidated by William PITT the Younger. The British prime ministry has served as a model for the heads of government in many Commonwealth countries, Europe, and Japan. The prime minister has appointive powers and is responsible for the government's legislative program, budget, and other policies. His term of office lasts until the next scheduled election or until he loses legislative support.

prime number Any positive INTEGER greater than 1 and divisible without remainder only by 1 and itself. Their sequence begins 2, 3, 5, 7, 11, 13, 17, 19, 23, 29 . . . but follows no discernible pattern. The issues of the regularities and irregularities in the distribution of primes are among the most important questions in NUMBER THEORY and the most interesting open questions in mathematics. Primes have been recognized since at least 300 B.C., when they were studied by ERATOSTHENES and by EUCLID, who proved that there are infinitely many primes.

Primo de Rivera, Miguel (1870–1930) Spanish general and dictator of Spain (1923–30). He served as military governor of Cádiz (1915–19), Valencia (1919–22), and Barcelona (1922–23), where he firmly suppressed disorder. Believing the parliamentary system to be corrupt, he took power in a coup in 1923 and dissolved the Cortes. He successfully ended the Moroccan war (1927), settled labor disputes, and undertook public works. Increasing discontent with his repressive government and lack of support from the army forced him to resign in 1930. His son José Antonio (1903–1936) founded the fascist FALANGE party; he was executed when the Popular Front came to power, and was treated as a martyr by the Nationalists.

primogeniture \ˌprī-mō-ˈje-nə-ˌchúr\ Preference in INHERITANCE that is given by law or custom to the eldest son and his issue. The intention has usually been to keep the estate of the deceased, or some part of it, whole and intact, and to acknowledge the importance of age-seniority within the social hierarchy. It is no longer a recognized principle of inheritance in most jurisdictions.

primrose Any flowering plant of the genus *Primula,* one of 28 genera of the family Primulaceae. *Primula* includes more than 500 species, which occur chiefly in the Northern Hemisphere in cool or mountainous regions. The plants are low-growing, usually perennial herbs. Many species are cultivated for their attractive, five-petaled flowers in many colors. Other plants in the primrose family include cyclamens and pimpernels. The evening primrose (family Onagraceae) is not a true primrose.

Prince *orig.* Prince (Rogers) Nelson (b.1958) U.S. singer and songwriter. Born in Minneapolis, the son of a jazz pianist, at 19 he released his first album, on which he played all the instruments. His later albums include *Prince* (1979), *1999* (1982), the soundtrack to the film *Purple Rain* (1983), and *Diamonds and Pearls* (1991). His sexually suggestive lyrics and stage behavior kept him at the center of controversy. From 1993 to 2000 he used an unpronounceable symbol in place of his name.

prince European title of rank, usually denoting a person exercising complete or almost complete sovereignty or a member of a royal family. The wife of a prince is a princess. In Britain, the title was not used until 1301, when EDWARD I invested his eldest son as Prince of WALES.

Prince, Hal (*orig.* Harold Smith) (b.1928) U.S. theatrical producer and director. Born in New York City, he coproduced the successful musical *The Pajama Game* (1954) and went on to produce or coproduce over 30 hit musicals, including *Damn Yankees* (1955), *West Side Story* (1957), and *Fiddler on the Roof* (1964). Frequently working with Stephen SONDHEIM, he won Tony awards for his direction of the musicals *Cabaret* (1966), *Company* (1970), *Follies* (1971), *Candide* (1974), *Sweeney Todd* (1979), *Evita* (1979), *The Phantom of the Opera* (1986), and *Show Boat* (1995).

Prince Edward Island Province (pop., 2000 est.: 139,000), Canada. One of the MARITIME PROVINCES and Canada's smallest province, it is an island in the S Gulf of ST. LAWRENCE, separated from Nova Scotia and New Brunswick by the Northumberland Strait. Its capital is CHARLOTTETOWN. Discovered by Jacques CARTIER in 1534, it was used by MICMAC Indians for fishing and hunting. It was colonized by the French in 1720, then ceded to the British in 1763. Known as the "Cradle of Confederation," it was the site of the Charlottetown Conference of 1864, which led to the federation of Canada. It became a province in 1873. It has good natural harbors on its E and S coasts. There has been little industrial development, and more than half of the island is used for agriculture. Fishing and tourism are also of economic importance.

Princeton, Battle of See Battles of TRENTON AND PRINCETON

Princeton University Private university in Princeton, N.J., a traditional member of the IVY LEAGUE. Founded in 1746, it is the fourth-oldest university in the U.S. and one of the most prestigious. In addition to an undergraduate college and a graduate school, Princeton has a school of engineering and applied science, a school of architecture and urban planning, and the Woodrow Wilson School of Public and International Affairs. Woodrow WILSON served as university president 1902–10. The university has admitted women since 1969. Total enrollment is about 6,500.

Prince William Sound Inlet of the Gulf of ALASKA, S Alaska. It lies east of the Kenai Peninsula and spans 90–100 mi (145–160 km). Its name honors a son of GEORGE III. In 1989 the largest oil spill in history occurred when the tanker *Exxon Valdez* ran aground and lost 10.9 million gallons of crude oil into the relatively pristine sound, with disastrous effects on its ecology.

Príncipe See SÃO TOMÉ AND PRÍNCIPE

printed circuit Electrical device in which the wiring and certain components consist of a thin coat of electrically conductive material applied on an insulating material. Printed circuits replaced conventional wiring after World War II in much electronic equipment, greatly reducing size and weight while improving reliability and uniformity over the hand-soldered circuits formerly used. They are commonly used to mount INTEGRATED CIRCUITS on boards. Mass-produced printed circuit boards allow automated assembly of electronic components, considerably reducing their cost.

printer, computer Electronic device that accepts text or image files from a computer and transfers them to a medium such as paper or film. Printers are classified as impact printers and non-impact printers. Most impact printers are dot-matrix printers, which have a number of pins on the print head that strike the print medium to form a character. Non-impact printers fall into three main categories: laser printers use a laser beam to attract toner to an area of the paper, ink-jet printers spray a jet of liquid ink, and thermal printers use heated pins to imprint an image on special paper. Important printer characteristics include resolution (in dots per inch), speed (in sheets printed per minute), and cache memory (which affects the speed at which a file can be printed).

printing Process for reproducing text and illustrations, traditionally by applying INK to PAPER under pressure. In modern commercial printing, three basic techniques are used. LETTERPRESS PRINTING relies on mechanical pressure to transfer a raised inked image to the surface to be printed. GRAVURE PRINTING transfers ink from recessed cells of varying depths. In OFFSET PRINTING the printing and non-printing areas of the plate differ not in height but in wettability.

printmaking Art form consisting of the production of images, usually on paper, by various techniques of multiplication. Such fine prints are considered original works of art, even though they can exist in multiple copies. Major techniques include relief, intaglio, and surface printing (e.g., LITHOGRAPHY). Early printmaking was influenced by a desire for multiple prints, but artists discovered that when a drawing is translated into a print, it takes on entirely new characteristics, and the metamorphosis became the strongest attraction for artists. See also ENGRAVING, ETCHING, MEZZOTINT, WOODCUT.

prion \ˈprē-ˌän\ Disease-causing agent, discovered by Stanley PRUSINER, responsible for various fatal neurodegenerative diseases called transmissible spongiform encephalopathies. An abnormal form of a normally harmless protein found in mammals and birds, once present in the brain it causes normal proteins to refold into the abnormal shape. As prion proteins multiply, they accumulate within nerve cells, destroying them and eventually causing brain tissue to become riddled with holes. Diseases caused by prions include CREUTZFELDT-JAKOB DISEASE, MAD COW DISEASE, and scrapie. Prions are unlike all other known disease-causing organisms in that they appear to lack NUCLEIC ACID.

Pripyat Marshes See POLESYE

Pripyat River \ˈpri-pyət\ *or* **Pripet River** \ˈpri-ˌpet\ River, NW Ukraine and S Belarus. Rising in NW Ukraine near the Polish border, it flows east through the Pripet Marshes

(POLESYE) to Mazyr, then joins the DNIEPER RIVER after a course of 480 mi (775 km). It is connected by canals with the BUG and NEMAN rivers.

Priscian \\'pri-shən\\ *Latin* Priscianus Caesariensis (fl. c.A.D. 500) Latin grammarian. He used the writings of APOLLONIUS DYSCOLUS on Greek GRAMMAR as a guide in producing his own classic works on Latin grammar. His *Institutiones grammaticae* ("Grammatical Foundations"), with citations from Latin authors, became the standard work for teaching grammar in the Middle Ages.

prism Piece of glass or other transparent material cut with precise angles and plane faces, so that it refracts light (see REFRACTION). A triangular prism can separate white light into its constituent colors by refracting each different WAVELENGTH of light by a different amount. The longer wavelengths are bent the least, the shorter ones the most. The result is the SPECTRUM of visible light, or the rainbow. Prisms are used in certain kinds of SPECTROSCOPY and in various optical systems.

prison Institution for the confinement of people convicted of major crimes. Prisons are distinguished from jails in that jails are usually under local jurisdiction and house inmates sentenced to less than a year. In early U.S. prisons, prisoners were kept in isolation; in the 19th cent., prisoners were permitted to work together, but in silence. At the end of the 19th cent., prison reformers successfully advocated segregation of criminals by type of crime, age, and sex, rewards for good behavior, vocational training, and parole.

Pristina \\'prĕsh-tē-ˌnä\\ City (pop., 2000 est.: 187,000), S Yugoslavia. It is the capital of the KOSOVO autonomous region of the republic of Serbia. It was the capital of the Serbian state before the Turks defeated the Balkan Christian armies in 1389 at the Battle of KOSOVO. It lost many of its ethnic Albanian inhabitants in 1999, when they were driven out by the Serbian campaign of "ethnic cleansing" (see KOSOVO CONFLICT).

Pritzker Architecture Prize World's most prestigious honor in the field of architecture. Established by a prominent Chicago business family, the prize, awarded annually since 1979, bestows $100,000 on an architect whose built contributions are judged worthiest. The international jury has included architects, artists, historians, academicians, critics, and business executives.

privacy, right of Right of a person to be free from intrusion into matters of a personal nature. Although not explicitly mentioned in the U.S. Constitution, it has been held to be implicit in the BILL OF RIGHTS, providing protection from unwarranted government intrusion into areas such as marriage and contraception. It may be overcome by a compelling state interest. In TORT law, privacy is a right not to have one's intimate life and affairs exposed to public view or otherwise invaded. Less broad protections of privacy are afforded public officials and others defined by law as "public figures" (e.g., movie stars).

privateer Privately owned vessel commissioned by a state at war to attack enemy ships, usually merchant vessels, known from the earliest times until the 19th cent. Crews were paid out of the value of any cargo they seized. Limiting privateers to the specified activities was difficult, and the line between privateering and PIRACY was often blurred. In 1856 Britain and other European countries declared privateering illegal; the U.S. finally repudiated it at the end of the 19th cent., and Spain by 1908. See also BUCCANEER, Francis DRAKE, William KIDD, Jean LAFFITE.

privatization Transfer of government services or assets to the private sector. State-owned assets may be sold to private owners, or statutory restrictions on competition between privately and publicly owned enterprises may be lifted. Services formerly provided by government may be contracted out. The objective is often to increase government efficiency. Privatization is the opposite of nationalization, a policy resorted to by governments that want to keep the revenues from major industries, especially those that might otherwise be controlled by foreign interests.

prize cases (1863) Legal dispute in which the U.S. Supreme Court upheld Pres. Abraham LINCOLN's seizure of ships (prizes). In April 1861, three months before Congress declared war, Lincoln authorized a blockade of Confederate ports. In that three-month period, several merchant ships ran the blockade and were captured. When the legality of the seizures was challenged, the Supreme Court upheld presidential use of emergency powers to resist insurrection.

probability theory Branch of mathematics that deals with analysis of random events. Probability is the numerical assessment of likelihood on a scale from 0 (impossibility) to 1 (absolute certainty). Probability is usually expressed as a RATIO. Probability theory grew out of attempts to understand card games and GAMBLING. As science became more rigorous, analogies between certain biological, physical, and social phenomena and games of chance became more evident (e.g., the sexes of newborn infants follow sequences similar to those of coin tosses). As a result, probability became a fundamental tool of modern genetics and many other disciplines. Probability theory is also the basis of the insurance industry, in the form of actuarial statistics.

probate In law, the process of proving in a court (probate court) that an instrument is the valid last WILL and testament of a deceased person. The term also refers broadly to the process of administering an estate. A document purporting to be a will normally requires little authenticating proof. Probate courts also often supervise the administration of estates by executors and oversee the guardianship of minors and others lacking capacity under the law.

probation Conditional suspension of an offender's sentence upon the promise of good behavior and agreement to accept supervision and abide by specified requirements. It differs from PAROLE in that the offender is not required to serve any of his or her sentence. Those convicted of serious offenses and those previously convicted of other offenses are usually not considered for probation.

proboscis monkey \\prə-'bä-səs, prə-'bäs-kəs\\ Species (*Nasalis larvatus,* family Cercopithecidae) of long-tailed arboreal OLD WORLD MONKEY of swampy mangrove forests on Borneo. They live in groups of about 20. They are red-brown with pale underparts; the young monkey has a blue face. The male's nose is long and comically pendulous. Males are 22–28 in. (56–72 cm) long, have a 26–29-in. (66–75-cm) tail, and weigh 26–53 lbs (12–24 kg).

procedural law Law that prescribes the procedures and methods for enforcing rights and duties and for obtaining redress (e.g., in a suit). It is distinguished from substantive law (i.e., law that creates, defines, or regulates rights and duties). Procedural law is a set of established forms for conducting a trial and regulating the events that precede and follow it. It prescribes rules relative to jury selection, evidence, appeal, and representation of counsel, among other matters.

process philosophy 20th-cent. school of philosophy that emphasizes the elements of becoming, change, and novelty in experienced reality and opposes the traditional Western philosophical stress on being, permanence, and uniformity. Reality is seen as essentially historical, emerging from (and bearing) a past and advancing into a novel future. Hence, it cannot be grasped by old static spatial concepts that ignore the temporal and novel. The foremost contributors have been Henri BERGSON and Alfred North WHITEHEAD.

Proclamation of 1763 Proclamation by Britain at the end of the FRENCH AND INDIAN WAR that prohibited settlement by whites on Indian territory. It established a British-administered reservation from west of the Appalachians and south of Hudson Bay to the Floridas and ordered white settlers to withdraw, formalizing Indian land titles. After American colonists and pioneers objected, the proclamation was replaced by the Treaties of FT. STANWIX.

proconsul In the ancient ROMAN REPUBLIC, a CONSUL whose powers had been extended for a definite period beyond his regular one-year term. Such extensions were necessitated by such events as long periods of war. Under the empire (after 27 B.C.), governors of senatorial provinces were called proconsuls.

Procter & Gamble Co. Major U.S. manufacturer of soaps, cleansers, and other household products. It was formed in 1837 when William Procter (1801–1884), a British candle-maker, and James Gamble (1803–1891), an Irish soap-maker, merged their businesses in Cincinnati. The company supplied soap and candles to the Union Army in the Civil

War. Among its later products were Ivory soap (1879); Crisco shortening (1911); Tide, the first synthetic laundry detergent (1946); and Joy, the first liquid synthetic detergent (1949). In 1932 it sponsored the first radio soap opera. A market-research pioneer, the company later made such consumer products as toothpaste, shampoo, deodorant, cake mixes, and coffee, and miscellaneous products such as cellulose pulp and chemicals.

production management *or* **operations management** Planning and control of industrial production processes to ensure smooth and efficient operation. Production-management techniques are used in SERVICE INDUSTRIES as well as manufacturing. Responsibilities include the traditional "five M's": men (and women), machines, methods, materials, and money. Managers are expected to maintain a flexible production process with a versatile workforce. They may use industrial-engineering methods, such as time-study measurements, to design efficient work methods. They are responsible for managing both physical (raw) materials and information materials (data). Inventory control involves tracking component parts, work in process, finished goods, packaging materials, and general supplies. The production cycle requires that sales, financial, engineering, and planning departments continually exchange information such as sales forecasts, inventory levels, and budgets. Managers must also monitor operations to ensure optimum output while meeting cost and quality objectives.

productivity In economics, a measure of productive efficiency calculated as the ratio of what is produced to what is required to produce it. Any of the traditional factors of production—LAND, LABOR, or CAPITAL—can theoretically be used as the denominator of the ratio, but labor is the most commonly and easily quantified—for example, by counting workers engaged on a particular product. In industrial nations, the effects of increasing productivity are shown most clearly in the use of labor. Productivity can be seen not only as a measure of efficiency but also as an indicator of economic development. Productivity increases as an economy becomes more developed. Its pattern of increase typically exhibits long-term stability interrupted by the sudden leaps of major technological advances. Productivity in Europe and the U.S. made great strides following the development of steam power, the railroad, and the gasoline engine. Increases in productivity tend to lead to long-term increases in real wages.

profit In business usage, the excess of total revenue over total COST during a specific period of time. In economics, profit is the excess over the returns to CAPITAL, LAND, and LABOR. It may have various sources: an innovator who introduces a new production technique can earn entrepreneurial profits; changes in consumer tastes may bring some firms windfall profits; or a firm may limit output to prevent prices from falling to the level of costs, thus gaining monopoly profits.

profit sharing System by which employees are paid a share of the PROFITS of the business enterprise in which they are employed, in addition to regular earnings. Profit-sharing plans were probably first developed in France in the early 19th cent. Today such plans are used by businesses in Western Europe, the U.S., and parts of Latin America. Profit shares may be distributed on a current or deferred basis. Under current distribution, profits are paid out to employees immediately in the form of cash or company stock. In deferred-payment plans, profit shares may be paid into a TRUST FUND from which employees can draw ANNUITIES in later years.

progeria \prō-ˈjir-ē-ə\ Disorder with characteristics of premature AGING, decades earlier than normal individuals. Not all systems are affected; there is no senility or aging in the central nervous system. In Hutchinson-Gilford syndrome, children look 60 years old by age 10 and die at an average age of 13. The unrelated Werner's syndrome is a recessive hereditary disease that begins in young adulthood and makes patients look 30 years older than they are; their average lifespan is 47 years.

progesterone \prō-ˈjes-tə-ˌrōn\ STEROID HORMONE secreted by the female REPRODUCTIVE SYSTEM that functions mainly to regulate the condition of the endometrium (see UTERUS),

preparing it to accept a fertilized egg. If the egg is not fertilized, the level of progesterone drops, the uterine lining breaks down, and MENSTRUATION ensues. If the egg is fertilized (see PREGNANCY), the placenta produces progesterone, preparing the MAMMARY GLANDS for LACTATION. Many forms of oral CONTRACEPTION use synthetic progesterone.

program, computer Set of ordered instructions that enable a computer to carry out a specific task. Writers of programs (programmers) may work in MACHINE LANGUAGE or in ASSEMBLY LANGUAGES, but most applications programmers use one of the high-level languages (such as BASIC or C++) that more closely resemble human communication. Other programs then translate the instructions into machine language for the computer to use. Programs are stored on disk and loaded into RAM by the computer's processor, which executes each instruction in the program, one at a time. Programs are often divided into applications and system programs. Applications perform tasks such as WORD PROCESSING, DATABASE functions, or accessing the INTERNET. System programs control the functioning of the computer itself. See also OPERATING SYSTEM.

programmed cell death See APOPTOSIS

programming language Language in which a computer programmer writes instructions for a computer to execute. Some languages, such as COBOL, FORTRAN, PASCAL, and C, are known as procedural languages because they use a sequence of commands to specify how the machine is to solve a problem. Languages that support OBJECT-ORIENTED PROGRAMMING work with whole units of the data to be manipulated. Low-level programming languages address the computer in a way that it can understand directly, but they are very far from human language. High-level languages deal in concepts that humans devise and can understand, but they must be translated by means of a COMPILER into language the computer understands.

Progressive Conservative Party of Canada *known as* **Conservative Party.** Major political party in Canada. It originated with the informal coalition of conservatives and moderate liberals to form the Liberal-Conservative Party led by John MACDONALD (1854). It held power until 1873 and regained dominance as the renamed Conservative Party (1878–96). Later led by Robert BORDEN (1901–20), it regained power in coalition with the Quebec nationalists (1911–20). It was out of power except briefly in 1926 and in 1930–35. When John Bracken, a Progressive, became leader in 1942, it adopted its current name. It regained power under John DIEFENBAKER (1958–63), Joe Clark (1979–80), and Brian MULRONEY (1984–93).

progressive education Movement that took form in Europe and N. America during the late 19th cent. as a reaction to the alleged narrowness of traditional education. A main objective was to educate the "whole child," promoting physical and emotional as well as intellectual growth. Creative and manual arts gained importance in the curriculum, and children were encouraged toward experimentation and independent thinking. Progressive educational ideas were most powerfully advanced in the U.S. by John DEWEY.

Progressive Party U.S. independent political party, short-lived at three periods. The first Progressive Party, known as the BULL MOOSE PARTY, was organized in 1911. The second (1924–25) selected Robert LA FOLLETTE as its presidential candidate. The third, founded in 1947 by Henry WALLACE, focused on changes in foreign policy, favoring a conciliatory policy toward the Soviet Union. Wallace won over 1 million votes in 1948, but the party was never again influential.

progressive systemic sclerosis See SCLERODERMA

progressive tax Tax levied at a rate that increases as the quantity subject to taxation increases. Progressive taxes reflect the view that those who are able to pay more should carry a heavier share of the tax burden. Progressive INCOME TAXES may provide for exemption from tax liability for incomes under a specified amount, or may establish progressively greater rates for larger and larger incomes. Progressive taxes are a stabilizing force in periods of INFLATION or RECESSION because the amount of tax revenue changes more than proportionately with an increase or de-

P

crease in income. For example, in an inflationary economy, a greater percentage of taxpayers' income goes toward taxes, government revenues increase, and the government has more leverage over the economy. Since lower-income taxpayers have an especially difficult time when inflation is high, many economists advocate INDEXATION; several countries adjust their tax rates annually in times of inflation, usually in line with the CONSUMER PRICE INDEX. See also REGRESSIVE TAX.

Prohibition Legal prevention of the manufacture, sale, or transportation of alcoholic beverages. In the U.S., the movement arose out of the religious revivalism of the 1820s. Maine passed the first state Prohibition law in 1846. The drive toward national Prohibition was fueled by the Anti-Saloon League (see TEMPERANCE MOVEMENT). With Prohibition already adopted in 33 states, the 18th Amendment to the U.S. Constitution went into effect in 1920. Prohibition was embraced with varying degrees of enthusiasm in different parts of the country, and enforced accordingly. In urban areas, BOOTLEGGING gave rise to ORGANIZED CRIME, with such gangsters as Al CAPONE. In part because of the rise in crime, its supporters gradually became disenchanted with it. The 21st Amendment repealed the 18th in 1933, and by 1966 all states had also abandoned Prohibition.

prokaryote \prō-'kar-ē-,ōt\ Any cellular organism that lacks a distinct NUCLEUS. BACTERIA (including CYANOBACTERIA) are prokaryotes; all other organisms are EUKARYOTES. Prokaryotic cells lack a nuclear membrane and most of the components of eukaryotic cells. A nuclear region usually consists of circular, double-stranded DNA. Many prokaryotes also contain PLASMIDS. The flagella (see FLAGELLUM) are distinct from those of eukaryotes in design and movement.

Prokofiev \prə-'kȯ-fyif\, **Sergey (Sergeievich)** (1891–1953) Russian composer and pianist. Son of a pianist, he wrote an opera at 9, and he studied with Nikolai RIMSKY-KORSAKOV and others. From 1910 he made a living by performing as a virtuoso. During World War I he wrote his *Scythian Suite* (1915) and First ("Classical") Symphony (1917). His opera *The Love for Three Oranges* premiered in 1921. Paris was his base from 1922, and the 1920s saw three new symphonies and the operas *The Fiery Angel* (1927) and *The Gambler* (1928). In the 1930s, he was drawn back to Russia; there he wrote scores for the ballet *Romeo and Juliet* (1936), *Peter and the Wolf* (1936), the films *Alexander Nevsky* (1938) and *Ivan the Terrible* (1942–45), and the opera *War and Peace* (1943). His health failed after the government's denunciation of his work in 1948.

prolapse Protrusion of an internal organ out of its normal place, usually of the RECTUM or UTERUS outside the body when supporting muscles weaken, especially with age. Chronic rectal prolapse requires surgical repair. The uterus may prolapse into the vagina after gravity adds to weakness from childbirth injuries. Temporary supports and pelvic exercises can relieve mild uterine prolapse, but severe prolapse may require HYSTERECTOMY.

Prometheus \prə-'mē-thē-əs\ In GREEK RELIGION, one of the TITANS and a god of fire. He was a master craftsman and a supreme trickster, and he was sometimes associated with the creation of humans. According to legend, Prometheus stole fire from the gods and gave it to humans. In vengeance, ZEUS created the woman PANDORA, who set loose all the evils of the world. Another tale held that Zeus had Prometheus chained to a mountain and sent an eagle to devour his liver, which regenerated every night so that he could suffer the same torment the next day.

promissory note Short-term credit instrument consisting of a written promise by one person to pay a stated amount of money to another on demand or at a given future date. It is often negotiable and may be secured by the pledge of collateral. During the 20th cent., other specifications came to be added—for example, authorizing the sale of collateral, permitting extensions of time, and allowing acceleration of payment in the event of default. See also BILL OF EXCHANGE.

pronghorn RUMINANT (*Antilocapra americana*) of N. American plains and semideserts, the only living member of the family Antilocapridae. The pronghorn stands 30–40 in.

Pronghorn (*Antilocapra americana*)

(80–100 cm) tall. It is reddish brown with a short, dark-brown mane. Both sexes bear erect, two-pronged horns; the longer prong curves backward, the shorter prong forward. The fastest mammal of N. America, the pronghorn can run 45 mph (70 kph) and can bound up to 20 ft (6 m). Though tens of millions once roamed the West, they were nearly exterminated by hunters in the early 20th cent.

proof In logic and mathematics, an argument that establishes a proposition's validity. Formally, it is a finite sequence of formulas generated according to accepted rules. Each formula either is an AXIOM or is derived from a previously established THEOREM, and the last formula is the statement that is to be proven. The essence of deductive reasoning (see DEDUCTION), this is the basis of EUCLIDEAN GEOMETRY and all scientific methods inspired by it. An alternative form of proof, called mathematical INDUCTION, applies to propositions defined through processes based on the counting numbers. If the proposition holds for $n = 1$, and if the proposition holding for $n = k$ (a constant) means that it also holds for $n = k + 1$, then the proposition holds for all values of n.

propaganda Manipulation of information to influence public opinion. The term comes from *Congregatio de propaganda fide* ("Congregation for Propagation of the Faith"), a missionary organization established by the pope in 1622. Propagandists emphasize information that supports their position and deemphasize or exclude what does not, often employing misleading statements and even lies. LOBBYING, advertising, and missionary activity are all forms of propaganda, but the term is most commonly used in the political arena. Until the 20th cent., pictures and the written media were the principal instruments of propaganda; radio, television, and motion pictures later joined their ranks. Authoritarian and totalitarian regimes use propaganda to keep the support of the populace.

propane Colorless, easily liquefied, HYDROCARBON GAS. Separated from natural gas, light crude oil, and oil-refinery gases, it is available as liquefied propane or as a major constituent of liquefied petroleum gas (LPG). It is an important raw material for the manufacture of ETHYLENE and for the PETROCHEMICAL industry. It is also used as a refrigerant, extractant, solvent, and AEROSOL propellant.

Propertius \prō-'pər-shəs, prō-'pər-shē-əs\, **Sextus** (55/43 B.C.–after 16 B.C.) Roman poet. The first and best known of his four books of ELEGIES, *Cynthia*, was published in 29 B.C., the year he met its heroine (his mistress, whose real name was Hostia). In Book II his main theme is still love, but he also contemplates writing an epic, is preoccupied with thoughts of death, and attacks the materialism of his time. Books III and IV demonstrate a bold command of language and form; among the subjects are Roman mythology and history.

property In law, something that is owned or possessed. Concepts of property vary widely among cultures. In Western society, it is generally regarded as either tangible (e.g., land or goods) or intangible (e.g., STOCKS and BONDS or a PATENT). Individual ownership of property is emphasized in the West, but de-emphasized in many non-Western societies. The use of property is extensively regulated throughout the West. Property may be acquired in various ways. "Occupancy" allows one to become the owner of property formerly not owned by anyone. A far more common means of acquiring property is by transfer from the previous owner, usually by sale, donation, or INHERITANCE. See also EASEMENT, INTELLECTUAL PROPERTY, NUISANCE, REAL AND PERSONAL PROPERTY.

property tax Levy imposed on real estate (land and buildings) and on personal property such as automobiles, jewelry, and furniture. In some countries it may also extend to farm equipment, business equipment, and inventories, as well as intangibles such as stocks and bonds. Property taxes are usually levied by local or state governments rather than national governments and are a major source of tax revenue. Property taxes existed in the ancient world first as land taxes and later as taxes on farmhouses, livestock, and so on. Though sometimes burdensome to the poor, property taxes tend to redistribute the benefits of wealth from higher to lower income groups, since they often pay for schools and other services used by low-income groups.

prophet Person who speaks by divine inspiration, revealing or interpreting the will of a god. The most familiar prophets in the West are such OLD TESTAMENT leaders as MOSES, ISAIAH, and DANIEL, along with the Prophet MUHAMMAD. In contrast to the diviner or interpreter of omens (see DIVINATION), who may answer private questions, prophets often address the destiny and moral life of a whole people. Some prophets seek to create a new society that will realize their message and thus found new religions. Others may look only to reform or purify an existing society and religion.

Prophet, The *orig.* Tenskwatawa (1768–1834) N. American Indian leader. Born in Old Chillicothe, Ohio, the brother of TECUMSEH, he became a religious revivalist among the SHAWNEE based on his 1805 declaration that he had received a message from the "Master of Life." Advocating a return to traditional ways of life, he rejected the white man's alcohol, textile clothing, and individual ownership of property, and worked for an Indian confederacy to resist U.S. encroachment. In Tecumseh's absence he allowed the Shawnee to be drawn into and defeated at the Battle of TIPPECANOE (1811).

proportion In algebra, equality between two RATIOS. In the expression $a/b = c/d$, a and b are in the same proportion as c and d. For example, if one triangle is twice the size of a second, then each side of the first triangle is in the same proportion to the corresponding side of the second as 2 is to 1. A proportion is typically set up to solve a word problem in which one of its four quantities is unknown. It is solved by multiplying one numerator by the opposite denominator and equating the product to that of the other numerator and denominator. The term proportionality describes any relationship that is always in the same ratio.

proprietary colony Type of settlement in British N. America (1660–90). To repay political and financial debts, the British crown, beginning with CHARLES II, awarded supporters vast tracts of land in colonial New York, New Jersey, Pennsylvania, Maryland, and the Carolinas. The proprietors were to supervise and develop the colonies, which became successful enterprises. By 1690 concern about the colonies' growing independence led to the end of proprietary grants.

proprioception \ˌprō-prē-ō-ˈsep-shən\ Perception of stimuli relating to position, posture, equilibrium, or internal condition. Nerve endings in skeletal MUSCLES and on TENDONS provide constant information on limb position and muscle action for coordination of limb movements. In humans, gravity, position, and orientation are registered by tiny grains called otoliths moving within two fluid-filled sacs in the INNER EAR. Rotation is detected by the inertial lag of fluid in the semicircular canals acting on sense hairs. The central NERVOUS SYSTEM integrates signals from the canals to perceive rotation in three dimensions. See also SENSE.

proscenium \prō-ˈsē-nē-əm\ In a THEATER, the frame or arch separating the stage from the AUDITORIUM, through which the action of a play is viewed. The first permanent proscenium in the modern sense was built in 1618 at the Farnese Theater in Parma. Its main purpose was to provide a sense of spectacle and illusion; scene changes were carried out in view of the audience. Not until the 18th cent. was a curtain commonly used to hide scene changes. The proscenium opening was of particular importance to 19th-cent. realistic playwrights, for whom it served as a picture frame through which the audience experienced the illusion of spying on the characters.

prosecutor Government attorney who presents the state's case against the defendant in a criminal prosecution. A prosecutor takes charge of the investigation once a crime has been committed, presents evidence at a hearing before a grand jury, and questions witnesses during the trial. In the U.S., states and counties have their own prosecutors. At the federal level, the U.S. attorney general's office appoints a U.S. attorney for each federal district. In most state and local jurisdictions, prosecutors are elected to office.

prose poem Work in prose that has some of the technical or literary qualities of POETRY (such as regular rhythm, definitely patterned structure, or emotional or imaginative heightening) but that is set on a page as prose. The form took its name from Charles BAUDELAIRE's *Petits poèmes en prose* (1869). Other writers of prose poems include, in the 19th cent., Stéphone MALLARMÉ, Arthur RIMBAUD, and R. M. RILKE, and in the 20th, Amy LOWELL.

Proserpina See PERSEPHONE

prosody \ˈprä-sə-dē\ Study of the elements of language, especially METER, that contribute to rhythmic and acoustic effects in poetry. The basis of "traditional" prosody in English is the classification of verse according to the syllable stress of its lines. Effects such as RHYME scheme, alliteration, and assonance further influence a poem's "sound meaning." Prosody also involves examining the subtleties of a poem's rhythm, its "flow," the historical period to which it belongs, the poetic genre, and the poet's individual style.

Prosser, Gabriel See GABRIEL

prostaglandin \ˌpräs-tə-ˈglan-dən\ Any of a class of organic compounds that occur in many animal tissues and have diverse hormonelike effects in animals (see HORMONE). They have important effects on BLOOD PRESSURE, blood clotting, pain sensation, and reproduction mechanisms. They hold promise for treating heart disease and viral diseases and may be useful in contraception. Some substances that inhibit prostaglandin synthesis (e.g., ASPIRIN) are useful in controlling pain, asthma attacks, or anaphylactic shock.

prostate gland \ˈpräs-ˌtāt\ Chestnut-shaped male reproductive organ, located under the bladder, which adds secretions to the SPERM during ejaculation of SEMEN. It surrounds the urethra (see URINARY SYSTEM). The prostate consists of 30–50 GLANDS, supported by CONNECTIVE TISSUE, that discharge fluids into the urethra and two ejaculatory ducts, contributing 15–30% of the seminal fluid. It reaches its mature size at PUBERTY. Around age 50, it commonly shrinks and decreases its secretions. Enlargement due to inflammation or malignancy, very common after age 60, often leads to difficulty in urinating. Prostate cancer, also very common in older men, usually progresses very slowly.

prosthesis \präs-ˈthē-səs\ Artificial substitute for a missing part of the body, usually an arm or leg. Prostheses have evolved from wooden legs and hooks that replaced hands, to sophisticated plastic, fiberglass, and metal devices. They may have working joints and allow motion either by amplification of electric current generated by muscle contractions or by actual attachment to the patient's muscles. Breast prostheses are used after MASTECTOMY.

prostitution Practice of engaging in sexual activity in exchange for immediate payment in money or other valuables. Prostitutes may be of either sex and may engage in either heterosexual or homosexual activity, but most prostitution has been by females with males as clients. Prostitution is a very old and universal phenomenon; also universal is the disapproval of the prostitute but relative indifference toward the client. In the U.S. most states had banned brothels by 1915 (Nevada being a notable exception). Prostitution is nevertheless tolerated in most U.S. and European cities, where police activity focuses instead on associated crimes. Prostitutes are very often poor and lack skills to support themselves; in many traditional societies, there are few other available money-earning occupations for women without family support. In developing African and Asian nations, prostitution has been largely responsible for the spread of AIDS and the orphaning of hundreds of thousands of children.

Protagoras \prō-ˈtag-ə-rəs\ (c.485–410 B.C.) Greek philosopher, first and most famous of the SOPHISTS. An influential Athenian teacher, he claimed to teach men "virtue" in the conduct of their daily lives. He is best known for his dictum "Man is the measure of all things," an expression of relativism. He expressed his agnosticism in *Concerning the Gods*. He was accused of impiety, his books were publicly burned, and he was exiled from Athens around 415 B.C.

protectionism Policy of protecting domestic industries against foreign competition by means of TARIFFS, SUBSIDIES, import QUOTAS, or other handicaps placed on imports. The chief protectionist measures, government-levied tariffs, raise the price of imported articles. Import quotas limit the quantities of goods that can be imported. Wars and economic depressions historically have resulted in increases in protectionism, while peace and prosperity have tended to encourage FREE TRADE. Protectionist policies were common in Europe in the 17th–18th cent. under MERCANTILISM. Britain abandoned many of its protectionist laws in the 19th cent., and by World War I tariffs were low throughout the Western world. Economic and political dislocation led to rising customs barriers in Europe in the 1920s, and the GREAT DEPRESSION spawned an epidemic of protectionist measures; world trade shrank drastically as a result. The U.S. had a long history of protectionism, but in 1947 it became one of 23 nations to sign the General Agreement on Tariffs and Trade (GATT), which substantially reduced customs tariffs. See also TRADE AGREEMENT, WORLD TRADE ORGANIZATION.

protectorate Relationship in which one country exercises some decisive control over another country or region. The degree of control may vary from merely a guarantee of safety to a disguised form of annexation. Though the relationship is an ancient one, the use of the term dates only from the 19th cent. In modern times most protectorates have been established by treaties requiring the weaker state to surrender management of its international relations, thus losing part of its SOVEREIGNTY.

protein Any of numerous organic compounds, complex POLYMERS of AMINO ACIDS needed for biochemical processes. Twenty different amino acids can occur in proteins, in chains of hundreds to thousands of units. An active protein has three important levels of structure: primary (the amino acid sequence), determined by the GENES; secondary (the geometric shape, often a helix), determined by the angles of the COVALENT BONDS between and within amino acids; and tertiary (the looped and folded overall shape), determined by the HYDROGEN BONDING between amino-acid side chains. The tertiary structure, globular or sheetlike with ridges, crevices, or pockets, holds the key to an ENZYME's activity. Some proteins are simple (amino acids only), some conjugated (e.g., HEMOGLOBIN) to other groups, often VITAMINS or METALS needed in tiny amounts in the diet. Structural proteins include COLLAGEN and KERATIN. Almost all enzymes are proteins. Other biologically active proteins include HORMONES (e.g., INSULIN, ACTH, GROWTH HORMONE); transport proteins, which carry substances across membranes or to different parts of the body; and ANTIBODIES. Proteins have industrial uses in adhesives, plastics, and fibers, but most uses are in foods.

Proterozoic eon \ˌprä-tə-rə-ˈzō-ik, ˌprō-tə-rə-ˈzō-ik\ Geologic division of PRECAMBRIAN TIME, from 2.5 billion to 544 million years ago. Proterozoic rocks have been identified on all the continents and often constitute important sources of metallic ores, notably of iron, gold, copper, uranium, and nickel. Small protocontinents coalesced into one or several large landmasses by the beginning of the Proterozoic. New life forms included BACTERIA and blue-green algae (see CYANOBACTERIA).

Protestant ethic Value attached to hard work, thrift, and self-discipline under certain Protestant doctrines, particularly those of CALVINISM. Max WEBER, in *The Protestant Ethic and the Spirit of Capitalism* (1904–5), held that the Protestant ethic was an important factor in the economic success of Protestant groups in the early stages of European CAPITALISM, in that worldly success came to be interpreted as a sign of the individual's election to eternal salvation. Weber's thesis was variously criticized and expanded throughout the 20th cent.

Protestantism One of the three major branches of CHRISTIANITY, originating in the 16th-cent. REFORMATION. The term applies to the beliefs of Christians who do not adhere to ROMAN CATHOLICISM or EASTERN ORTHODOXY. The followers of Martin LUTHER established the evangelical churches of Germany and Scandinavia; those of John CALVIN and the more radical Huldrych ZWINGLI founded REFORMED CHURCHES in Switzerland and Scotland (PRESBYTERIANISM). The Church of ENGLAND and the EPISCOPAL CHURCH had their origins in 16th-cent. England and are closest to Roman Catholicism in theology and worship. The doctrines of the various Protestant denominations vary considerably, but all emphasize the supremacy of the BIBLE in matters of faith and order, salvation by GRACE through faith and not through works, and the PRIESTHOOD of all believers. See also ADVENTIST, BAPTIST, Society of FRIENDS, MENNONITE, METHODISM.

Proteus \ˈprō-tē-əs\ In GREEK MYTHOLOGY, the prophetic old man of the sea and the shepherd of sea animals. He knew all things—past, present, and future—but disliked telling what he knew. Those who wanted information from him had to catch him sleeping and bind him. He would try to escape by changing his form, but if a captor held him fast he gave the wished-for answer.

protist \ˈprō-təst\ Any member of a kingdom (Protista) of diverse EUKARYOTES, including ALGAE, PROTOZOANS, and lower fungi (see FUNGUS), most of which are single-celled. Many can move, mainly by using flagella (see FLAGELLUM), cilia (see CILIUM), or footlike extensions (pseudopodia). The kingdom was proposed to accommodate intermediate organisms that, even though they possessed some plant or animal characteristics, did not exhibit the specialized features indicative of those groups. Some protists are considered the ancestors of multicellular plants, animals, and fungi. With the development of advanced biochemical, genetic, and imaging techniques, it is now thought that some groups are less closely related to one another than once believed. As a result, the classification of protists, while convenient, is no longer entirely satisfactory.

protoceratops \ˌprō-tə-ˈser-ə-ˌtäps\ Any member of a genus of quadrupedal DINOSAURS found as fossils in Gobi deposits of the CRETACEOUS PERIOD (144–65 million years ago). The hind limbs were strongly developed. Adults were about 7 ft (2 m) long and probably weighed about 400 lbs (180 kg). The skull was about one-fifth the body length. A perforated bony frill rose behind the face. The jaws were beaklike, and there may have been a hornlike structure on the snout. Long spines on the tail suggest that protoceratops was semiaquatic.

protocol In computer science, a set of rules or procedures for transmitting data between electronic devices, such as computers. In order for computers to exchange information, they need rules about how the information will be structured and how each side will send and receive it. Protocols are established by international or industrywide organizations. Perhaps the most important computer protocol is OSI (Open Systems Interconnection), a set of guidelines for implementing networking communications between computers. The most important sets of INTERNET protocols are TCP/IP, HTTP, and FTP.

proton Stable SUBATOMIC PARTICLE (one of the BARYONS) with a unit of positive ELECTRIC CHARGE and a mass 1,836 times that of the ELECTRON. Protons are found in the atomic nucleus along with NEUTRONS. For each ELEMENT, the number of protons in the nucleus is always the same and is its ATOMIC NUMBER. Protons are used as projectiles in PARTICLE ACCELERATORS to produce and study nuclear reactions. They are the chief constituent of primary COSMIC RAYS and are produced in radioactive decay (see RADIOACTIVITY) and nuclear reactions.

protozoan \ˌprō-tə-ˈzō-ən\ Any of a group of small (usually microscopic) single-celled PROTISTS. They are found worldwide in most soils, fresh water, and oceans. While most are solitary individuals, various colonial forms exist. The taxonomic relationships of protozoans to one another and to other protists continue to be revised. The smallest known protozoans are tiny blood parasites less than 2 microns long; the largest may be 16 mm long. Protozoan shapes vary, but all share such eukaryotic features as lipid-protein membranes and membrane-enclosed vacuoles and organelles (see EUKARYOTE). They show wide variation in modes of movement, nutrition, and reproduction. Commonly known protozoans include DINOFLAGELLATES, AMOEBAS, and paramecia (see PARAMECIUM). See diagram on next page.

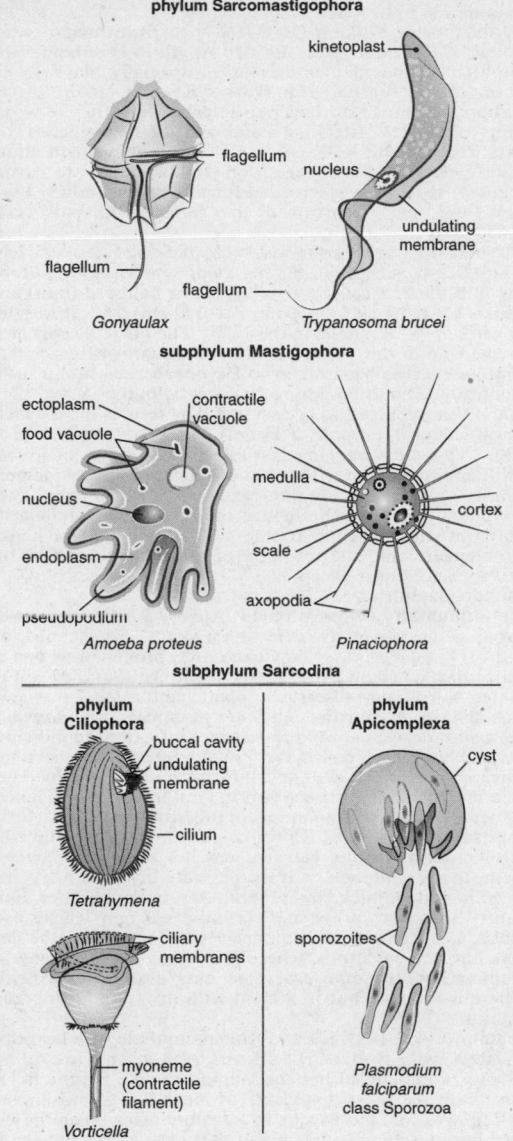

phylum Sarcomastigophora

kinetoplast

flagellum

nucleus

undulating
membrane

flagellum

flagellum

Gonyaulax

Trypanosoma brucei

subphylum Mastigophora

ectoplasm

contractile
vacuole

food vacuole

medulla

nucleus

cortex

scale

endoplasm

axopodia

pseudopodium

Amoeba proteus

Pinaciophora

subphylum Sarcodina

phylum
Ciliophora

phylum
Apicomplexa

buccal cavity
undulating
membrane

cyst

cilium

Tetrahymena

ciliary
membranes

sporozoites

myoneme
(contractile
filament)

*Plasmodium
falciparum*
class Sporozoa

Vorticella

Protozoan Representative protozoans. The zooflagellate *Trypanosoma brucei* is the causative agent of African sleeping sickness. The phytoflagellate *Gonyaulax* is one of the dinoflagellates responsible for the occurrence of red tides. The amoeba is one of the most common sarcodines. Other members of the subphylum Sarcodina, such as the radiolarians, heliozoans, and foraminiferans, usually possess protective coverings. The heliozoan *Pinaciophora* is shown covered with scales. The subphylum Ciliophora, which includes the ciliated *Tetrahymena* and *Vorticella,* contains the greatest number of protozoan species but is the most homogeneous group. The malaria-causing *Plasmodium* is spread by the bite of a mosquito that injects infective spores (sporozoites) into the bloodstream.

Proudhon \prü-ˈdōⁿ\, **Pierre-Joseph** (1809–1865) French journalist and socialist. *What Is Property?* (1840) created a sensation with such phrases as "property is theft." In Lyon (1843–48) he encountered the Mutualists, a weavers' anarchist society whose name he later adopted for his form of ANARCHISM. His *System of Economic Contradictions* (1846) was attacked by Karl MARX and initiated the split between anarchists and Marxists. In Paris in 1848, Proudhon published radical newspapers; imprisoned 1849–52, he was later harassed by the police and fled to Belgium in 1858. On his return in 1862 he gained influence among the workers, including some of the founders of the FIRST INTERNATIONAL.

Proulx \ˈprü\, **(Edna) Annie** (b.1935) U.S. writer. Born in Norwich, Conn., she initially wrote commissioned nonfiction books, founded a rural Vermont newspaper, and published stories in men's outdoor magazines. Her first novel, *Postcards* (1992), depicting the decline of the small farm, received the PEN/Faulkner Award. It was followed by *The Shipping News* (1993, Pulitzer Prize), *Accordion Crimes* (1996), and *That Old Ace in the Hole* (2002). Her story collections *Heart Songs* (1988) and *Close Range* (1999) also won high praise.

Proust \ˈprüst\, **Marcel** (1871–1922) French novelist. Born to a wealthy family, he studied law and literature and became an observant habitué of the most exclusive drawing rooms of the nobility. He published essays and stories, including the story collection *Pleasures and Days* (1896). Around 1897 he began to disengage from social life as his health declined. Half-Jewish himself, he became a major supporter of Alfred DREYFUS in the affair that made French anti-Semitism into a hugely controversial national issue. An incident of involuntary revival of childhood memory through the taste of

Marcel Proust Painting by J.-É. Blanche

a rusk biscuit in 1909 led him to retire almost totally into an eccentric seclusion in his cork-lined bedroom to write *À la recherche du temps perdu* (1913–27; *In Search of Lost Time,* or *Remembrance of Things Past*). The vast seven-part novel is at once a kind of autobiography, a vast social panorama of France, and an immense meditation on love and jealousy and on art and its relation to reality. One of the supreme achievements in fiction of all time, it brought him worldwide fame and affected the entire climate of the 20th-cent. novel.

Provençal language See OCCITAN LANGUAGE

Provence \prō-ˈväⁿs\ Historical and cultural region, SE coastal France. Part of Roman Gallia NARBONENSIS, it was later invaded successively by the Visigoths, Burgundians, and Ostrogoths. It came under the Franks around 536. Its culture was crushed in the ALBIGENSIAN CRUSADE. It was united with the French crown in 1481. Its language, Provençal, was important in the literature of the TROUBADOURS, and its ROMANESQUE ARCHITECTURE was an outstanding cultural achievement of the Middle Ages. It suffered in the 16th-cent. Wars of RELIGION. In 1790, during the FRENCH REVOLUTION, it lost its political institutions.

proverb Succinct and pithy saying that is in general use and expresses commonly held ideas and beliefs. Proverbs are part of every spoken language and folk literature, originating in oral tradition. Literate societies from the ancient Egyptians on have collected their proverbs. In N. America the best-known collection is probably that of *Poor Richard's*, an almanac published 1732–57 by Benjamin FRANKLIN.

Providence City (pop., 2000: 174,000), capital of Rhode Island. It is located at the head of NARRAGANSETT BAY. Founded in 1636 by Roger WILLIAMS as a refuge for religious dissenters, it was partly destroyed in KING PHILIP'S WAR in 1676. It played an important role in the AMERICAN REVOLUTION and was a major port in 18th-cent. W. Indies

P

trade. It became the sole capital of the state in 1900, an honor it had shared with NEWPORT since 1854. It is home to BROWN UNIV. and the RHODE ISLAND SCHOOL OF DESIGN.

Provincetown Town (pop., 2000: 3,400), E Massachusetts, N tip of CAPE COD. It was the first landing place of the PILGRIMS in 1620, and the MAYFLOWER COMPACT was drawn up in its harbor. A whaling and fishing port in the 19th cent., it is now a popular summer resort and noted artists' colony. The PROVINCETOWN PLAYERS theater group originated there.

Provincetown Players U.S. theatrical company (1915–29), founded by a group of writers and artists in Provincetown, Mass., to encourage new and experimental works. One of their first productions was of the first play of Eugene O'NEILL, a founding member. In 1916 the players moved to New York's Greenwich Village. There they introduced several more of O'Neill's plays as well as works by Edna MILLAY, Susan Glaspell, Paul Green, and many others. The company disbanded in 1929, though the Provincetown Playhouse has continued to serve intermittently as a theater.

Provisions of Oxford See Provisions of OXFORD

Provo City (pop., 2000: 105,000), N central Utah. Situated on Utah Lake, it was founded in 1849 by MORMON colonists. Construction of railroads in the 1870s spurred the city's development as a center for the mining of silver, lead, copper, and gold. The founding in 1875 of Brigham Young Academy (now Brigham Young Univ.) also contributed to Provo's growth.

Proxima Centauri See ALPHA CENTAURI

Prozac Trademark for a preparation of the ANTIDEPRESSANT drug fluoxetine. It affects the brain's metabolism of the neurotransmitter SEROTONIN. It is widely used to treat not only depression but also OBSESSIVE-COMPULSIVE DISORDERS, BULIMIA, and chronic HEADACHES. Introduced by Eli Lilly in the late 1980s, it was soon the most widely used antidepressant in the world, and it has spawned many similar drugs.

Prudhoe Bay \'prü-dō\ Small inlet of the BEAUFORT SEA, N Alaska. It has been the center of oil-drilling activities since the discovery of vast petroleum deposits on Alaska's N. Slope in 1968. The TRANS-ALASKA PIPELINE links the area to Valdez on PRINCE WILLIAM SOUND.

Prudhomme, Sully See SULLY PRUDHOMME

Prud'hon \prüe-'dōⁿ\, **Pierre-Paul** (1758–1823) French painter. During his years in Rome (1784–88), the works of CORREGGIO inspired him to introduce a softer effect into French painting. He made drawings for engravers before he came to the attention of Napoleon. His portrait of the empress JOSEPHINE (1805) exhibits the seductive and mysterious quality with which he invested his portraits of women. He achieved fame with his allegorical *Crime Pursued by Divine Vengeance and Justice* (1808). His elegant style served as a bridge from late-18th-cent. Neoclassicism to 19th-cent. Romanticism.

Prusiner \'prü-sə-nər\, **Stanley (Ben)** (b.1942) U.S. neurologist. Born in Des Moines, Iowa, he has taught at UC–Berkeley since 1984. Intrigued by spongiform encephalopathies after a patient died of CREUTZFELDT-JAKOB DISEASE (CJD), he later studied the related sheep disorder scrapie and reported isolation of its causative agent in 1982. Initially criticized, his theory was eventually generally accepted, and it received world attention when MAD COW DISEASE emerged in Britain. The theory may also shed light on disorders such as ALZHEIMER'S DISEASE and PARKINSONISM, which share traits with PRION-based diseases. His work won him a 1997 Nobel Prize.

Prussia *German* **Preussen** Historical region, N Germany. The land of the Prussians on the SE coast of the Baltic Sea came under Polish and German rule in the Middle Ages. In the 17th cent. FREDERICK WILLIAM, elector of BRANDENBURG and scion of the HOHENZOLLERN DYNASTY, conquered the duchy of Prussia and laid the foundations for the kingdom of Prussia, established by FREDERICK I in 1701, with BERLIN as its capital. Under FREDERICK II the Great (1740–86), Prussia built up its formidable army and greatly expanded its territories. As the most powerful German state, under Otto von BISMARCK (from 1862) it threw off Austrian and French influence (see FRANCO–PRUSSIAN

WAR) and united Germany in 1871 under its leadership. After World War I, Prussia existed as a state within the German nation until 1947.

Prynne \'prin\, **William** (1600–1669) English Puritan pamphleteer. His early tracts assailed Anglican ceremonialism. He attacked popular amusements, especially plays, in his book *Histrio Mastix: The Players Scourge* (1633). Archbishop William LAUD had him imprisoned; after he wrote more pamphlets attacking Laud and other Anglicans, his ears were cut off. Released in 1640, Prynne brought about Laud's conviction and execution (1645). Elected to Parliament in 1648, he was expelled for attacks on radical Puritans and later imprisoned for refusing to pay taxes (1650–53).

Przewalski's horse \pshə-'väl-skēz, ˌpər-zhə-'väl-skēz\ Last wild EQUINE subspecies (*Equus caballus przewalskii*) surviving into the 21st cent. It is yellowish or light red (dun) and stands 12–14 hands (48–56 in., 122–142 cm) high. It was discovered in W Mongolia in the 1870s. The horse disappeared in the wild in the 1960s, but the descendants of specimens that had earlier been taken to European zoos began to be reintroduced into the Mongolian steppe in the 1990s.

psalm \'säm\ Sacred song or poem. The term is most widely known from the Book of Psalms in the OLD TESTAMENT. The 150 psalms, ranging in subject from songs of joyous faith and thanksgiving to songs of bitter protest and lamentation, rank among the immortal poetry of all time. They have had a profound influence on the liturgies of Judaism and Christianity. Their dating and authorship are highly problematic, and the tradition of assigning them to King DAVID is no longer accepted.

Pseudo-Demetrius See False DMITRY

pseudomonad \ˌsü-də-'mō-ˌnad\ Any of a large and varied group of gram-negative (see GRAM STAIN), rod-shaped, often curved BACTERIA. Many can move, propelled by one or more flagella (see FLAGELLUM). Most are found in soil or water; some cause diseases in plants, and a few cause serious diseases in humans and other mammals. *Pseudomonas aeruginosa* causes antibiotic-resistant infections in individuals with weakened resistance. Pseudomonads have been implicated in hospital-acquired infections of surgical wounds and severely burned tissue and in fatal infections of cancer patients treated with immunosuppressive drugs.

psoriasis \sə-'rī-ə-səs\ Chronic, recurrent SKIN disorder with reddish, slightly elevated patches or bumps covered with silvery-white scales. If the nails are involved, they may become pitted, thick, and separated from the nail bed. Skin injury, infection, stress, and certain drugs may trigger psoriasis. Skin cells move at an accelerated rate from the dermis into the epidermis, where they slough off, causing inflammation. In some cases, patients also have arthritis. There is no cure, but treatment with drugs and ultraviolet light may help.

Psyche \'sī-kē\ In Greek and Roman mythology, a beautiful princess who won CUPID's love. VENUS, envious of her beauty, commanded her son Cupid to make Psyche fall in love with the most despicable of men. But Cupid himself fell in love, and hid Psyche in a remote place where he visited her secretly under cover of darkness. One night she lit a lamp and discovered his identity. He left angrily, and Psyche wandered the earth searching for him. JUPITER eventually made her immortal and gave her in marriage to Cupid.

psychiatry Branch of medicine concerned with mental disorders. Until the 18th cent., mental-health problems were considered forms of demonic possession; gradually they came to be seen as illnesses requiring treatment. In the 19th cent., research into and classification and treatment of mental illnesses advanced. Sigmund FREUD's psychoanalytic theory dominated the field for many years before it was challenged by behavioral and cognitive therapy and humanistic PSYCHOLOGY in the mid-20th cent. Psychiatrists hold MD degrees and can prescribe drugs and other medical treatments in addition to conducting psychotherapy.

psychoanalysis Method of treating MENTAL DISORDERS that emphasizes the probing of unconscious mental processes. It is based on the psychoanalytic theory devised by Sigmund FREUD in Vienna in the late 19th and early 20th cent. It calls for patients to engage in free ASSOCIATION of ideas. DREAMS are examined as a key to the workings of the unconscious, and the "work" of therapy is to uncover tensions between the instinctual drive of the ID, the perceptions and actions of the EGO, and the censorship imposed by the morality of the SUPEREGO. Careful attention is paid to early childhood experiences (especially those with a sexual dimension); recalling and analyzing these experiences is thought to help free patients from the ANXIETY and neuroses caused by REPRESSION as well as from more serious illnesses known as psychoses (see NEUROSIS, PSYCHOSIS). Some of Freud's early associates, notably C. G. JUNG and Alfred ADLER, rejected his theories on many points and devised alternative methods. Other important figures, including Erik ERIKSON, Karen HORNEY, and Erich FROMM, accepted the basic Freudian framework but contributed their own additions or modifications.

psycholinguistics Study of the mental processes involved in the perception, production, and acquisition of LANGUAGE, with focus on the learning of language by children and on speech processing and comprehension. In the 1960s and '70s, the theories of Noam CHOMSKY stimulated much research; in recent years psycholinguists have employed other models as well. See also LINGUISTICS.

psychological testing Use of tests to measure skill, knowledge, intelligence, capacities, or aptitudes. Best known is the IQ test; other tests include achievement tests and PERSONALITY tests. The latter, used to help diagnose mental disorders and assess clients, include both inventory-type (question-and-response) tests and projective tests such as the Rorschach (inkblot) and thematic apperception (picture-theme) tests. Experimental psychologists routinely devise tests to obtain data on PERCEPTION, LEARNING, and MOTIVATION.

psychology Scientific discipline that studies mental processes and behavior in humans and other animals. Clinical psychology is concerned with the diagnosis and treatment of MENTAL DISORDERS. Other fields include CHILD PSYCHOLOGY, EDUCATIONAL PSYCHOLOGY, and SOCIAL PSYCHOLOGY. The issues studied by psychologists cover a wide spectrum, including LEARNING, cognition, INTELLIGENCE, MOTIVATION, EMOTION, PERCEPTION, PERSONALITY, and the extent to which individual differences are shaped by genetics or environment. Research methods include observation, interviews, psychological testing, laboratory experimentation, and statistical analysis.

psychoneurosis See NEUROSIS

psychopathology See ABNORMAL PSYCHOLOGY

psychopharmacology Study of the effect of drugs on the mind and behavior. Major advances in the 20th cent. include the development of TRANQUILIZERS, ANTIDEPRESSANTS, lithium carbonate (for BIPOLAR DISORDER), certain stimulants (including AMPHETAMINES), and antipsychotic agents such as chlorpromazine (Thorazine), fluphenazine (Prolixin), and haloperidol (Haldol).

psychosis \sī-'kō-səs\ Serious mental derangement characterized by defective or lost contact with reality. The primary psychoses are SCHIZOPHRENIA and the delusional disorders (e.g., megalomania), but extreme DEPRESSION and BIPOLAR DISORDER, substance-induced DELIRIUM, and certain varieties of DEMENTIA share important features with the psychoses. Symptoms include delusions, HALLUCINATIONS, disorganized speech and behavior, and mood disturbances. Treatment usually consists of medication and counseling in an institutional setting.

psychosomatic disorder Bodily ailment or symptom, caused by mental or emotional disturbance, in which psychological stresses adversely affect physiological functioning to the point of distress. Psychosomatic disorders may include HYPERTENSION, respiratory ailments, gastrointestinal disturbances, migraine and tension HEADACHES, sexual dysfunctions, and DERMATITIS. See also HYPOCHONDRIASIS.

psychosurgery Treatment of PSYCHOSIS or other MENTAL DISORDERS by means of brain surgery. The first such technique was the prefrontal LOBOTOMY. Because of its undesirable side effects, it has been largely replaced by the use of tranquilizing and antipsychotic drugs (see PSYCHOPHARMACOLOGY). A more recent technique involves placing tiny le-

sions in specific areas of the brain, and has little effect on intellectual function or quality of life; it has been used to treat OBSESSIVE-COMPULSIVE DISORDER.

psychotherapy Treatment of mental or emotional disturbance through interpersonal communications with a trained counselor or therapist. The goal of many individual and GROUP THERAPIES is to establish a relationship of trust in which the client or patient can feel free to express personal thoughts and emotions and thus gain insight into his or her condition and generally share in the healing power of words. Such therapies include PSYCHOANALYSIS and its variants (see Alfred ADLER, C. G. JUNG), client-centered or nondirective psychotherapy, Gestalt therapy (see GESTALT PSYCHOLOGY), play and art therapy, and general COUNSELING. See also BEHAVIOR THERAPY.

Ptah \'ptä\ In EGYPTIAN RELIGION, the creator god. Ptah was identified by the Greeks with HEPHAESTUS, the divine blacksmith. He was represented as a man in mummy form, wearing a skullcap and a short, straight false beard. He was originally the local deity of MEMPHIS; its political importance caused Ptah's cult to spread across Egypt. With Sekhmet and Nefertem, he was one of the Memphite Triad of deities.

ptarmigan \'tär-mi-gən\ Any of three or four species of GROUSE (genus *Lagopus*) of cold regions. Their plumage changes from white in winter to gray or brown, with barring, in spring and summer. The common ptarmigan (*L. mutus*) occurs throughout the British Isles, Europe, and N. America, where it is called rock ptarmigan. Ptarmigans survive winter in the Arctic by browsing shrubs and scratching up lichens and leaves; they burrow in snow to sleep. Males begin group displays in early spring.

pteranodon \tə-'ra-nə-,dän\ Extinct flying REPTILE (genus *Pteranodon*), descendant of the PTERODACTYL. Fossils are known from Late Cretaceous (98–65 million years ago) deposits of Europe, Asia, and N. America. Pteranodons had a wingspan of 23 ft (7 m) or more, sometimes up to 50 ft (15.5 m). The body was about the size of a modern turkey. Pteranodons had a crest at the back of the skull and long, pelicanlike, toothless jaws. They probably spent much time gliding over the ocean searching for fish.

pterodactyl \,ter-ə-'dak-t°l\ Any member of the PTEROSAUR suborder Pterodactyloidea, known from Late Jurassic and Cretaceous fossils (159–65 million years ago). Members of the typical genus, *Pterodactylus,* ranged from the size of a sparrow to that of an albatross. The teeth were angled forward, possibly for use as straining devices. They were probably able gliders but not efficient as active fliers. Unlike the ARCHAEOPTERYX, the pterodactyl was not an ancestor of the birds.

pterosaur \'ter-ə-,sòr\ Any of several extinct flying REPTILES (order Pterosauria) that flourished during the Jurassic and Cretaceous periods (208–65 million years ago). Pterosaurs hung by their long hind limbs when at rest. They soared and glided on membranous wings attached to the long fourth finger of each forelimb. Pterosaurs had a long beak and a large brain. *Ramphorhynchus* had strong, sharply pointed teeth, a long tail, and a wingspread of about 3 ft (1 m); it probably dived for fish. See also PTERODACTYL.

Ptolemaïs \,tä-lə-'mā-əs\ Ancient coastal city, CYRENAICA, on the NILE RIVER, south of MEMPHIS. It received its name in the 3rd cent. B.C. from PTOLEMY III, who united Cyrenaica with Egypt. It flourished in Hellenistic times, in the early Roman empire, and again from the late 3rd cent. A.D., when DIOCLETIAN made it the metropolis of the Roman province of Upper Libya.

Ptolemy \'tä-lə-mē\ *Latin* Claudius Ptolemaeus (fl.A.D. 127–145) Greek astronomer and mathematician. His great astronomical book, the *Almagest*, contains both his and HIPPARCHUS's findings. The sun, moon, planets, and stars, he believed, were attached to crystalline spheres, centered on the earth, which turned to create day and night, the lunar month, and so on. To explain retrograde planetary motion, he refined a complex model of cycles within cycles that was highly successful at predicting the planets' positions. The earth-centered Ptolemaic system became a dogma of Western Christendom until the COPERNICAN SYSTEM replaced it. Ptolemy's *Geography* contained an estimate of the earth's

P

size, a description of its surface, and a list of places located by latitude and longitude.

Ptolemy I Soter \'tä-lə-mē...'sō-tər\ (c.365–283/282 B.C.) Ruler of Egypt (323–285) and founder of the Ptolemaic dynasty. A Macedonian general of ALEXANDER THE GREAT, Ptolemy became SATRAP of Egypt after Alexander's death. Alexander's successors were soon at war. He earned the name Soter ("Savior") after defeating ANTIGONUS I MONOPHTHALMUS on Rhodes (304), though Antigonus was not finally crushed until 301. Ptolemy secured and expanded his empire through alliances and mar-

Ptolemy I Soter Portrait on a Greek coin

riages. In 286 he and his fellow kings freed Athens from Macedonian occupation. He obtained control of the League of Islanders (including most of the Aegean islands), which formed the basis of Egypt's maritime supremacy. As king he respected Egyptian culture, blended Greek and Egyptian peoples and religions, and founded the Library and Museum of ALEXANDRIA. After his death the Egyptians raised him to the level of a god.

Ptolemy II Philadelphus (308–246 B.C.) King of Egypt (285–246 B.C.), second king of the Ptolemaic dynasty. He reigned as co-ruler (285–282) with his father, PTOLEMY I SOTER, then purged his family of rivals, including his first wife, and married his sister, ARSINOE II. Wars with the rulers of the SELEUCID and Antigonid dynasties weakened his influence in the Aegean and brought near-disaster to his allies Athens and Sparta. He concluded these wars by diplomacy and marriage alliances and managed to regain his influence in the Aegean. A prudent and enlightened ruler, he promoted economic development and made Alexandria into a center for poets and scholars.

Ptolemy III–XV (r.246–30 B.C.) Macedonian kings of the Ptolemaic dynasty in Egypt. Ptolemy III Euergetes ("Benefactor") (fl.246–221) defeated the ruler of the SELEUCID DYNASTY in the Third Syrian War (245–241). Ptolemy IV Philopator ("Father-loving") allowed Egypt to decline under his debauched rule (r.221–205). Ptolemy IX Soter II ruled with his mother (116–110, 109–107), until she expelled him and installed his brother Ptolemy X Alexander (r.107–88). Alexander's unpopularity eventually resulted in his expulsion. Soter II assumed sole rule (88–81), installing his brother's widow, his own daughter, with him. Ptolemy XI Alexander II (r.80 B.C.) was the last fully legitimate Ptolemaic king of Egypt. He took Ptolemy IX Soter II's widow as wife and coruler, on SULLA's command, then murdered her and took sole power, for which the people of Alexandria killed him; his rule lasted 19 days. Ptolemy XIV Theos Philopator II shared power (47–44 B.C.) with his sister CLEOPATRA; it was probably she who had him assassinated, to make way for her son by Julius CAESAR. Ptolemy XV Caesar, or Caesarion, shared power with his mother from 44 B.C.; he was killed by Octavian (later AUGUSTUS) after Cleopatra's suicide in 30 B.C. His death marked the Roman conquest of Egypt and the dynasty's end.

puberty In human physiology, the period of first becoming capable of reproducing sexually. Occurring at about age 12 in girls and age 14 in boys, puberty is characterized by the maturing of the genital organs, development of secondary sex characteristics, swift increase in body size, changes in body shape and composition, and, in girls, onset of MENSTRUATION. See also ADOLESCENCE.

pubic louse See human LOUSE

Public Broadcasting Service See PBS

public debt See NATIONAL DEBT

public health Science and art of preventing disease, prolonging life, and promoting health through organized community efforts. These include sanitation, control of contagious infections, hygiene education, early diagnosis and preventive treatment, and adequate living standards. It requires understanding of EPIDEMIOLOGY, nutrition, antisep-

tic practices, and social science. Historical public-health measures included QUARANTINE of leprosy victims and efforts to improve sanitation following the BLACK DEATH. Population increases in Europe brought with them increased awareness of infant deaths and a proliferation of hospitals. In the U.S. today, public health is studied and coordinated on a national level by the CENTERS FOR DISEASE CONTROL AND PREVENTION; internationally, the WORLD HEALTH ORGANIZATION plays an equivalent role. See also PREVENTIVE MEDICINE.

public house or **pub** Establishment that serves alcoholic beverages for consumption on the premises, especially in Britain. Under English common law, inns and taverns were declared public houses responsible for the well-being of travelers, and expected to receive all travelers in reasonable condition who were willing to pay for food, drink, and lodging. In Tudor England, certain innkeepers were obliged to maintain stables; others served as unofficial postmasters. Their simple signs featured creatures such as lions, dolphins, or swans. In the 18th cent., the word "Arms" added to a pub name indicated protection by a noble family. Though British pubs were traditionally owned by independent licensed proprietors, by the early 20th cent. many were associated with brewery companies.

public relations (PR) Communications that involve promoting a desirable image for a person or group seeking public attention. It originated in the U.S. in the early 20th cent. with pioneers such as Edward BERNAYS and I. L. Lee (1877–1934). Government agencies in Britain and the U.S. soon began hiring publicists to engineer support for their policies and programs, and the public-relations business boomed after World War II. Clients may include individuals such as politicians, performers, and authors, and groups such as business corporations, government agencies, charities, and religious bodies. A publicist's duties include generating favorable publicity and knowing what kind of story is likely to be printed or broadcast. If disaster strikes, the publicist must organize the client's response so as to minimize damage and present credible information to the media.

Public Safety, Committee of See COMMITTEE OF PUBLIC SAFETY

public school or **independent school** In Britain, tuition-charging secondary school that prepares students for university and for public service. The name public school dates from the 18th cent., when the schools began attracting students from beyond their immediate environs, and thus became "public" as opposed to local and are in fact private schools independent of the state system. Important boys' schools include Winchester (1394), ETON (1440), Westminster (1560), and HARROW (1571). Public schools cultivated a class-conscious code of behavior, speech, and appearance that set the standard for British officialdom from the early 19th cent.

public television See PBS

public transportation See MASS TRANSIT

public utility Enterprise that provides certain classes of services to the public, including common-carrier transportation (buses, airlines, railroads); telephone and telegraph services; power, heat and light; and community facilities for water and sanitation. In most countries such enterprises are state-owned and state-operated; in the U.S. they are mainly privately owned, but operate under close regulation to ensure safety and reasonable rates. Given the required technology, they are considered natural MONOPOLIES, since capital costs are large and the existence of competing or parallel systems would be inordinately expensive and wasteful. Some states have recently experimented with deregulation of electricity and natural gas to stimulate price reductions and improved service through competition.

Public Works Administration U.S. government agency (1933–39). Part of the NEW DEAL, the agency was established to reduce unemployment through the construction of highways and public buildings. Authorized by the National Industrial Recovery Act (1933), it was administered by Harold ICKES. It spent about $4 billion to build schools, courthouses, city halls, public-health facilities, and roads, bridges, dams, and subways.

publishing Traditionally, the selection, preparation, and marketing of printed matter—including books, newspapers, magazines, and pamphlets. Contemporary publishing includes the production of materials in electronic formats such as CD-ROMs, as well as materials created or adapted for online distribution. In the modern sense of a copying industry supplying a lay readership, publishing began in Hellenistic Greece, in Rome, and in China. After paper reached the West from China in the 11th cent., the central innovation in Western publishing was Johannes GUTENBERG's invention of movable type. In the 19th–20th cent., technological advances, the rise of literacy and leisure, and ever-increasing information needs contributed to an unprecedented expansion of publishing. Issues that modern publishing must contend with include acquisition of independent publishing concerns by conglomerates, and the growth of broadcast media and especially of the Internet.

Puccini \pü-'chē-nē\, **Giacomo (Antonio Domenico Michele Secondo Maria)** (1858–1924) Italian composer. Born into a musical family, he studied with Amilcare Ponchielli (1834–1886) at the Milan Conservatory. His first opera, *Le villi* (1883), was followed by the unsuccessful *Edgar* (1889), but *Manon Lescaut* (1893) brought him international recognition. *La bohème* (1896), *Tosca* (1900), and *Madam Butterfly* (1904) all achieved huge success worldwide. A domestic scandal distracted him, and it was 1910

Giacomo Puccini

before *The Girl of the Golden West* premiered. The trilogy *Il trittico* (including *Gianni Schicchi*) followed in 1918. He was the most popular opera composer in the world at the time of his death; his unfinished *Turandot* was completed by Franco Alfano (1875–1954).

Puebla State (pop., 2000: 5,070,000), SE central Mexico. It has an area of 13,090 sq mi (33,902 sq km); the capital is PUEBLA city. It lies on a plateau and varies in elevation from 5,000 ft to 8,000 ft (1,500 to 2,400 m), with fertile valleys formed by the SIERRA MADRE Oriental. Pre-Columbian peoples had a highly developed civilization in the area, and there are many archaeological sites. The Spanish made Puebla an economic and religious center, and since the 19th cent. it has been an important agricultural and industrial center.

Puebla (de Zaragoza) City (pop., 1995: 1,158,000), capital of PUEBLA state, SE Mexico. Founded in 1532, it lies on a plain 7,093 ft (2,162 m) above sea level in the SIERRA MADRE Oriental foothills. It was occupied by U.S. forces during the MEXICAN WAR. The national holiday, CINCO DE MAYO, celebrates the defeat of the French at Puebla. Its Spanish colonial architecture is similar to that of the city of TOLEDO, Spain. It is known for its glazed ceramic tiles, glass, and pottery. In 1973 it was badly damaged by an earthquake.

pueblo (Spanish: "town") Community of the PUEBLO INDIANS of the SW U.S., consisting of multistoried apartment houses constructed of large ADOBE blocks, beginning about A.D. 1000. Freestanding structures up to five stories tall were built around a central court. Each floor is set back from the floor under it; the whole structure resembles a zigzag pyramid, with terraces formed by the rooftops of the level below. Movement between levels is by means of ladders through holes in the ceilings. Each pueblo has at least two KIVAS. ACOMA pueblo is believed to be the oldest continuously inhabited place in the U.S. Some of the largest pueblos are at Taos, Isleta, Laguna, and Zuni. See also CLIFF DWELLING.

Pueblo Incident (1968) Capture of the USS *Pueblo* by N. Korea off its coast. Maintaining that the ship, a navy intelligence vessel, had been in international waters, the U.S. negotiated with N. Korea to secure release of its 82 crewmen.

The agreement allowed the U.S. to publicly disavow the confession the crew had signed while admitting the ship's intrusion.

Pueblo Indians Historic descendants of the prehistoric ANASAZI peoples who have for centuries lived in settled PUEBLOS in what is now NE Arizona and NW New Mexico. The contemporary pueblos are divided into eastern and western. The eastern group includes settlements along the Rio Grande in New Mexico (most notably TAOS Pueblo), while the western group includes the HOPI villages of NE Arizona and the ZUNI, Acoma, and Laguna villages of NW New Mexico.

Puente \'pwen-tā\, **Tito** *orig.* Ernesto Antonio Puente, Jr. (1923–2000) U.S. bandleader and percussionist. Born in New York to Puerto Rican parents, Puente studied at Juilliard before forming his own band, and rose to prominence with the mambo and cha-cha-cha fads of the 1950s. Always experimenting, he became a pioneer of Latin-jazz fusion. His compositions include "Oye Como Va." He performed with many artists, especially Celia CRUZ, and recorded well over 100 albums.

puerperal fever \pyü-'ər-pə-rəl\ *or* **childbed fever** Infection of the female REPRODUCTIVE SYSTEM after childbirth or abortion, with FEVER over 100°F (38°C) in the first 10 days. The inner surface of the UTERUS is most often infected, giving BACTERIA access to the bloodstream and lymphatic system to cause SEPTICEMIA and pelvic or generalized PERITONITIS. Severity varies. It has become very rare in developed countries but is still seen after unhygienic abortions.

Puerto Rico *officially* **Commonwealth of Puerto Rico** Self-governing island commonwealth of the w. INDIES, in union with the U.S. Area: 3,515 sq mi (9,104 sq km). Population (2000): 3,916,000. Capital: SAN JUAN. The population is a mixture of diverse ethnic groups, mainly of Spanish and African descent. Languages: Spanish and English (both official). Religion: Roman Catholicism. Currency: U.S. dollar. Puerto Rico is a mountainous island and may be divided into three geographic regions: the mountainous interior, the N plateau, and the coastal plains. It has a developing free-market economy, and manufacturing, financial services, and trade (mostly with the U.S.) are its main components. Tourism is also an important source of income. Its chief of state is the U.S. president, and its head of government is the commonwealth governor. The island was inhabited by Arawak Indians when it was settled by the Spanish in the early 16th cent. It remained largely undeveloped economically until the late 18th cent. After 1830 it gradually developed a plantation economy based on the export crops of sugarcane, coffee, and tobacco. The independence movement began in the late 19th cent., and Spain ceded the island to the U.S. in 1898, after the SPANISH–AMERICAN WAR. In 1917 Puerto Ricans were granted U.S. citizenship, and in 1952 the island became a commonwealth with autonomy in internal affairs. The question of Puerto Rican statehood has been a political issue, with commonwealth status approved by voters in 1967 and again in 1993.

Puerto Vallarta \'pwer-tō-bä-'yär-tä\ City (pop., 1995: 122,000), W central Mexico. It is situated on Banderas Bay. The major port of JALISCO state, it exports bananas, coconut oil, hides, and fine woods. It is also an international tourist resort, known for aquatic sports, fishing (especially for sharks), and hunting.

Pufendorf \'pü-fən-ˌdörf\, **Samuel** *later* Freiherr (Baron) von Pufendorf (1632–1694) German jurist and historian. His most notable works are *Elementorum jurisprudentiae universalis* (1660; "Elements of Universal Jurisprudence") and *De jure naturae et gentium* (1672; "Of the Law and Nature of Nations"), in which he defended the idea of NATURAL LAW and argued that there is no such creature as a natural slave—that all men have a right to equality and freedom.

puffer *or* **blowfish** Any of about 90 species (family Tetraodontidae) of fishes that, when disturbed, inflate themselves into a globular shape with air or water. Most species occur in warm and temperate seas worldwide. Puffers have tough, usually prickly, skin; their fused teeth form a beaklike structure, split in the center of each jaw.

P

The largest grow to 3 ft (90 cm) long, but most are considerably smaller. They contain a lethal toxin.

puffin or **sea parrot** Any of three species (family Alcidae) of stout diving birds with a large, brightly colored beak. Puffins nest in large cliff colonies. Both parents carry up to 10 fish crosswise in the bill to the nest, feeding the single chick for about six weeks. They then leave, and the chick waits alone for its flight feathers to grow and flies out to sea by itself. The common, or Atlantic, puffin (*Fratercula arctica*) is about 12 in. (30 cm) long. The Pacific species are the horned puffin (*F. corniculata*) and the tufted puffin (*Lunda cirrhata*).

Pugachov \ˌpü-gə-ˈchȯf\, **Yemelyan (Ivanovich)** (1742?–1775) Russian COSSACK leader. He fought in the Russian army (1763–70) then wandered among settlements of religious dissidents. Learning of Cossack discontent after their unsuccessful rebellion in 1772, he claimed to be Czar PETER III (murdered in 1762), and decreed the abolition of serfdom. Vowing to depose CATHERINE II, he gathered a large following of Cossacks and peasants in the Ural region. After initial victories against the Russian army, he was captured and executed.

Puget \pü-ˈzhe\, **Pierre** (1620–1694) French sculptor and painter. As a young man he worked under PIETRO DA CORTONA on the ceiling decorations of the Pitti Palace in Florence. Thereafter he worked chiefly in France as painter and sculptor. Such sculptures as *Milo of Crotona* (c.1671–82), in which the athlete is attacked by a lion while his hand is caught in a tree stump, show a strain and anguish that suggest the works of MICHELANGELO.

Puget Sound \ˈpyü-jət\ Arm of the Pacific Ocean. Extending south about 100 mi (160 km) into W Washington state from the Strait of JUAN DE FUCA, it was explored by the English navigator George Vancouver in 1792. It has many islands and many deepwater harbors, including SEATTLE, TACOMA, Everett, and Port Townsend, and provides a sheltered area for recreational boating and salmon fishing.

Puglia \ˈpü-lyä\ or **Apulia** \ä-ˈpü-lyä\ Autonomous region (pop., 1996 est.: 4,083,000), SE Italy. It was ruled in the early Middle Ages by Goths, Lombards, and Byzantines and achieved its greatest glory under the HOHENSTAUFEN DYNASTY, especially FREDERICK II. In 1861 it became part of the Italian kingdom. The wines of the region are the strongest in Italy. Chemical and petrochemical industries are in BARI, the regional capital, and iron and steel plants in TARANTO.

Pugwash Conferences Meetings of eminent scientists to discuss problems of nuclear weapons and world security. The first meeting was held in 1957 at the estate of Cyrus EATON in Pugwash, Nova Scotia. The Pugwash organization was established to convene subsequent conferences to discuss arms control and disarmament; these were held in the Soviet Union, Britain, India, the U.S., and other countries. The organization and its founding president, Joseph Rotblat (b.1908), received the 1995 Nobel Peace Prize.

Pukaskwa National Park \pü-ˈkas-kwə\ National park, central Ontario, on Lake SUPERIOR. Covering 725 sq mi (1,878 sq km), it includes rugged wilderness as well as 50 mi (80 km) of lake shoreline, with rocky islets and coves and spectacular cliffs. Prehistoric Indian remains have been found. Wildlife includes timber wolf, black bear, mink, lynx, white-tailed deer, moose, and woodland caribou. The park has vast forests of white and black spruce, jack pine, poplar, and birch.

Pulitzer \ˈpu̇-lət-sər\, **Joseph** (1847–1911) Hungarian-U.S. newspaper editor and publisher. He emigrated to the U.S. in 1864 to serve in the American Civil War. After the war he became a proprietor of German-language newspapers in St. Louis and entered Missouri politics. In 1878 he merged the *St. Louis Dispatch* (founded 1864) and the *Post* (1875) into the successful *Post-Dispatch*. In New York, he purchased the *World* (1883) and founded the *Evening World* (1887). He helped establish the pattern of the modern newspaper by combining exposés of political corruption and crusading investigative reporting with publicity stunts, self-advertising, and sensationalism. In his will he established the PULITZER PRIZES.

Pulitzer Prize \ˈpu̇-lət-sər, ˈpyü-lət-sər\ Any of a series of annual prizes awarded by Columbia Univ. since 1917 for outstanding public service and achievement in American journalism, letters, and music. Fellowships are also awarded. The prizes, originally endowed by Joseph PULITZER, are highly esteemed and are awarded on the recommendation of judges appointed by the university. Today they include 14 awards in journalism, six in letters, one in music, and four fellowships.

pulley WHEEL that carries a flexible ROPE, cord, cable, chain, or belt on its rim. Pulleys are used singly or in combination to transmit ENERGY and MOTION. In belt drives, pulleys are attached to shafts at their axes, and power is transmitted between the shafts by means of endless belts running over the pulleys. One or more independently rotating pulleys can be used to gain mechanical advantage (force-amplifying effectiveness), especially for lifting weights. The pulley is considered one of the six simple MACHINES.

Pullman, George M(ortimer) (1831–1897) U.S. industrialist. Born in Brocton, N.Y., he became a cabinetmaker in Chicago. In 1858 he remodeled two railroad coaches into sleeping cars; eventually he set up his own firm, and the first true Pullman sleeping car appeared in 1865. In 1867 he founded the Pullman Palace Car Co.; the next year he created the first dining car. In 1880 he built the town of Pullman (now part of Chicago) for its workers; it was a much-discussed social experiment. His factory was the scene of the famous PULLMAN STRIKE of 1894.

Pullman Strike Widespread railroad strike, May 11–July 20, 1894. After financial reverses caused the Pullman Palace Car Co. to cut wages by 25%, local union members called a strike. The company's president, George PULLMAN, refused arbitration, and union president Eugene DEBS called for a nationwide boycott. Sympathy strikes followed in 27 states, and violence broke out in Chicago. The U.S. attorney general obtained an injunction against the strikers for impeding mail service, and federal troops were called in. Debs's conviction for conspiring against interstate commerce established the use of antitrust laws against labor-union activities.

pulmonary alveolus \ˈpu̇l-mə-ˌner-ē-al-ˈvē-ə-ləs\ Any of the 300 million or so small air spaces in the LUNGS where carbon dioxide leaves the blood and oxygen enters it. Alveoli form clusters (alveolar sacs), whose thin walls contain numerous capillaries; gas exchange between them occurs by DIFFUSION. A film of fatty substances (surfactant) over the walls reduces surface tension, keeping the alveoli from collapsing and making it easier to expand the lungs. Alveolar macrophages (see LEUKOCYTE, LYMPHOID TISSUE) act as mobile scavengers, engulfing foreign particles in the lungs.

pulmonary circulation System of blood vessels forming a closed circuit between the HEART and the LUNGS. It carries oxygenated blood in VEINS and deoxygenated blood in ARTERIES. The right ventricle pumps blood into the pulmonary artery, which branches to the right and left lungs. In the CAPILLARIES, blood releases carbon dioxide into the air in the pulmonary alveoli (see PULMONARY ALVEOLUS) and takes up oxygen, which it brings back to the left atrium of the heart through the pulmonary veins. See also CARDIOVASCULAR SYSTEM, CIRCULATION.

pulmonary heart disease Enlargement and eventual failure of the right ventricle of the heart due to disorders of the lungs or their blood vessels or chest-wall abnormalities. Chronic disease is most often caused by chronic BRONCHITIS or EMPHYSEMA. Symptoms include chronic cough, trouble breathing, wheezing, weakness, leg EDEMA, and neck vein distension. The lungs' CAPILLARY network is slowly destroyed; pressure in the pulmonary artery rises and the right ventricle enlarges in response, leading, if uncorrected, to heart failure. Treatment includes a respirator, low-sodium diet, DIURETICS, DIGITALIS, and ANTIBIOTICS for respiratory infection.

pulsar in full **pulsating radio star** Any of a class of cosmic objects that appear to emit very regular pulses of radio waves. A few also give off bursts of visible light, X rays, and gamma radiation. Thought to be rapidly spinning NEUTRON STARS, they were discovered by Antony Hewish (b.1924)

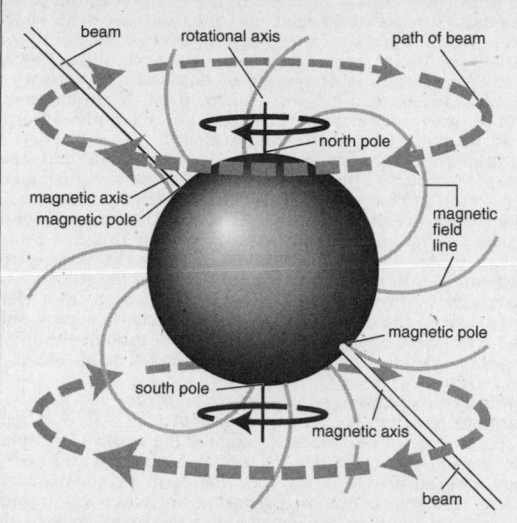

Pulsar A pulsar emits two beams (of radio waves, for instance) along its magnetic axis. If the magnetic axis is offset from the rotational axis, the beams will sweep out circular paths as the star rotates, instead of remaining in one constant position. An observer in the path of such a beam will thus see a periodic pulse of radio waves as the beam sweeps by.

and Jocelyn BELL BURNELL in 1967 with a specially designed radio telescope. More than 500 are known. Intervals between pulses range from one-thousandth of a second to four seconds. Charged particles from the surface enter the star's magnetic field, which accelerates them so that they release radiation as intense beams from the magnetic poles. These differ from the pulsar's axis, so as it spins the beams swing around like a search light and are seen as pulses. Radio pulsars slow down, typically by a millionth of a second per year, and "switch off" after about 10 million years as their magnetic fields weaken.

pulse Pressure wave in the ARTERIES from contraction of the HEART. It can be felt where arteries are near the skin's surface; it is usually read at the carotid artery in the neck or at the wrist. Its rate, strength, and rhythm and the contour of the wave provide valuable information. The average adult pulse rate is 70–80 beats per minute; the rate decreases with age.

puma See COUGAR

pumice \'pə-məs\ Porous, frothlike volcanic glass that has long been used as an abrasive in cleaning, polishing, and scouring compounds. It is also used in precast masonry units, insulation and acoustic tile, and plaster. Pumice is IGNEOUS ROCK that cooled so rapidly there was no time for it to crystallize. When it solidified, the vapors dissolved in it were suddenly released, and the whole mass swelled up into a froth that immediately consolidated.

pump Machine that uses ENERGY to raise, transport, or compress fluids. Pumps are classified by how they transfer energy to the fluid. The basic methods are volume displacement, addition of KINETIC ENERGY, and use of ELECTROMAGNETIC FORCE. Pumps in which displacement is accomplished mechanically are called positive displacement pumps. Kinetic pumps pass kinetic energy to the fluid by means of a rapidly rotating impeller (blade). To use electromagnetic force, the fluid being pumped must be a good electrical conductor. Pumps used to transport or pressurize gases are called COMPRESSORS, blowers, or fans.

pumpkin Fruit of certain varieties of *Cucurbita pepo* or *C. moschata*, of the GOURD family. In the U.S., some pump-

kins are called winter SQUASH. Pumpkins produce very long vines and large (9–18 lb, or 4–8 kg), globe-shaped, usually orange fruits. The lightly furrowed rind is smooth, and the fruit stem is hard and woody. Pumpkins mature in early autumn and can be stored for a few months in a dry, warm place. They are commonly grown in N. America, Britain, and Europe for human food and livestock feed. In the U.S. and Canada pumpkin pie is a traditional Thanksgiving and Christmas dessert. Pumpkins are used in the U.S. for HALLOWEEN decorations.

Punch Hooknosed, humpbacked character in MARIONETTE and puppet shows (see PUPPETRY). Adapted from the COMMEDIA DELL'ARTE, the puppet character was brought to France and England by Italian puppeteers in the 1660s. By 1700 every English puppet show featured Punch and his wife, Judy. Smaller glove puppets were later used in the popular Punch-and-Judy play. The outrageous behavior of the deceitful Punch, established by the 19th cent., continues to delight puppet-show audiences today.

punctuation Standard set of marks used in written and printed texts to clarify meaning and to separate sentences, clauses, words, and parts of words. It may also convey information about a word (e.g., hyphens in compound words) unrelated to speech patterns. In English, the period (.) marks the end of a sentence or abbreviation. The comma (,) usually separates clauses, phrases, or items in a series. The colon (:) often introduces an explanation or series of examples. The semicolon (;) usually separates independent clauses. The dash (—) marks an abrupt transition. The exclamation point (!) signals surprise. The question mark (?) signals a question. The apostrophe (') marks the possessive case or the omission of letters. Quotation marks (" ") set off either quoted words or words used with special significance. Interpolations in a sentence are marked by brackets ([ ]) or parentheses ( ).

Pune \'pü nə\ *formerly* **Poona** City (metro. area pop., 1995: 2,940,000), W India. Called "Queen of the DECCAN," it is the cultural capital of the Maratha peoples. It first gained importance as the capital of the Bhonsle Marathas in the 17th cent. In 1817 it fell to the British. Its mild weather has made it a popular tourist resort. It is a major educational center, and headquarters of the Indian army's S command; it is ringed by a sprawling complex of industrial suburbs.

Punic Wars \'pyü-nik\ *or* **Carthaginian Wars** Three wars (264–241, 218–201, 149–146 B.C.) between Rome and CARTHAGE. The first concerned control of Sicily and of the sea lanes in the W Mediterranean; it ended with Rome victorious. In 218 HANNIBAL attacked Roman territory, starting from Spain and marching overland into Italy with troops and elephants. After an initial Carthaginian victory and another at the Battle of CANNAE, the Romans defeated Hannibal and drove him out of Italy (203). The Third Punic War was essentially the siege of Carthage; it led to the destruction of Carthage, the enslavement of its people, and Roman hegemony in the W Mediterranean. The Carthaginian territory became the Roman province of Africa.

Punjab \ˌpən-'jäb\ State (pop., 1994 est.: 21,695,000), NW India. It occupies 19,448 sq mi (50,370 sq km). The city of CHANDIGARH is the joint administrative capital of Punjab and Haryana. In the 18th cent. the Sikhs (see SIKHISM) built a powerful kingdom in the Punjab, which came under British rule in 1849. In 1947 the area was split between the new nations of India and Pakistan, the smaller E portion going to India. It is the only Indian state with a majority of Sikhs.

Punjabi language *or* **Panjabi language** \ˌpən-jä-bē\ Indo-Aryan language of the Punjab in India and Pakistan. Punjabi has about 26 million speakers in India and perhaps more than 60 million in Pakistan, but linguists have sometimes considered some Pakistani dialects a different language. A significant feature of Punjabi is its development of phonemically distinctive TONE in syllables that have (or originally had) breathy-voiced consonants.

pupa \'pyü-pə\ Inactive, nonfeeding stage in the life of insects that undergo complete METAMORPHOSIS. In a protective covering (cocoon or chrysalis), the LARVA is transformed into an adult. During pupation, larval structures

break down and adult structures form; wings appear for the first time. The adult emerges either by splitting the pupal skin or by secreting a fluid that softens the cocoon.

puppetry Art of creating and manipulating puppets in a theatrical show. Puppets are figures that are moved by one or several puppeteers, who are screened from the spectators. Varieties include glove (or hand) puppets, rod puppets, shadow puppets, and MARIONETTES (or string puppets). By the 18th cent. puppetry was so popular in Europe that permanent theaters were built for the usually itinerant puppeteers. Companies presented favorite stories of the French Guignol, the Italian Arlecchino, the German Kasperle, and the English PUNCH and Judy. By the mid-20th cent. puppetry had reached television with Jim HENSON's Muppets.

Purana \pů-'rä-nə\ In HINDUISM, an encyclopedic collection of myth, legend, and genealogy. A Purana traditionally treats five subjects: primary creation of the universe, secondary creation after periodic annihilation, genealogy of gods and saints, grand epochs, and histories of the royal dynasties. Written in narrative couplets, the Puranas date from about 400 to about 1000. The 18 principal surviving Puranas are grouped according to whether they exalt VISHNU, SHIVA, or BRAHMA.

Purcell \'pər-səl\, Henry (c.1659–1695) British composer. Little is known of his origins, but he was in the Chapel Royal choir from boyhood, and probably studied with Pelham Humfrey (1647–1674) and John Blow (1649–1708). His first known composition was written at age 8. He became organist at Westminster Abbey in 1679 and at the Chapel Royal in 1682. His highly important opera *Dido and Aeneas* (1689) was followed by the "semi-operas" *King Arthur* (1691), *The Fairy Queen* (1692), and *The Indian Queen* (1695). He also wrote much incidental music, some 250 songs, 12 viol fantasias, and many anthems and services. He is regarded as the greatest English composer after William BYRD and before the 20th cent.

purdah Seclusion of women from public observation by means of concealing clothing (including the veil) and walled enclosures as well as screens and curtains within the home. The custom seems to have originated in Persia and was adopted by Muslims during the Arab conquest of what is now Iraq in the 7th cent. The Muslim domination of N India led to its adoption by the Hindu upper classes, who discarded it after the end of British rule in India. Purdah is still practiced in many Islamic countries.

Purdue University State university system with a main campus in W. Lafayette, Ind., and branches in two other locations. Founded in 1869 as a land-grant university, it was named for John Purdue, a founding donor. Three more campuses are operated jointly with INDIANA UNIV. The main campus is a comprehensive research university best known for its scientific and technological disciplines. Enrollment at the main campus is about 35,000.

purgatory In Roman Catholic doctrine, the condition of those who have died in a state of grace but have not been purged of SIN. Souls thus burdened must be purified before entering HEAVEN. The church also teaches that souls in purgatory may be aided by efforts of the living faithful through prayers, almsgiving, INDULGENCES, and other works. The existence of purgatory has been denied by Protestant churches and most Eastern Orthodox churches.

Purge Trials Soviet trials of critics of Joseph STALIN. After the assassination of Sergey KIROV, prominent BOLSHEVIKS were accused of conspiracy to remove Stalin from power. In three widely publicized show trials (1936–38), which presented confessions obtained under torture or fabricated by the secret police, the accused were found guilty and executed or sent to prison. Numerous closed, unpublicized trials of Soviet military leaders resulted in a massive purge throughout the armed forces. The trials eliminated such potential rivals of Stalin as Nikolay BUKHARIN, Lev KAMENEV, Genrikh YAGODA, and Grigory ZINOVYEV.

Purim \'půr-im, pů-'rēm\ Jewish festival celebrating the survival of the Jews marked for death in Persia in the 5th cent B.C. According to the Book of ESTHER, Haman, chief minister of King Ahasuerus, planned a general massacre of the Jews, who were saved by the intercession of Ahasuerus' wife Esther. Purim begins with a day of fasting on the 13th

of Adar (in February or March), the day before the actual holiday. Gifts are exchanged, and donations are made to the poor. Purim is a day of merrymaking and feasting.

purine \'pyůr-ēn\ Any of a class of organic compounds with a two-ring structure composed of CARBON and NITROGEN atoms. The simplest member, purine itself, is not common, but its derivatives with the structure are. Examples are uric acid, CAFFEINE, GUANINE, and ADENINE.

Puritanism Movement in the late 16th and 17th cent. that sought to "purify" the Church of ENGLAND. The movement led to the ENGLISH CIVIL WAR, when Puritans gained considerable power, but after the RESTORATION they were once again a dissenting minority. Some Puritans founded settlements in America (see PILGRIMS), notably the MASSACHUSETTS BAY COLONY. The Puritans of Massachusetts emphasized the conversion experience, by which the elect experienced the descent of GRACE. In their theocracy only the elect were allowed to vote and rule, though the privileges of church membership were extended to all baptized and orthodox persons.

Puritan Revolution See ENGLISH CIVIL WARS

Purkinje \pər-'kin-jē\, Jan Evangelista (1787–1869) Czech experimental physiologist. He created the world's first independent PHYSIOLOGY department and first official physiology laboratory. He introduced the term protoplasm, devised new methods for preparing microscope samples, discovered the skin's sweat glands and the nucleus of the unripe ovum, recognized the uniqueness of fingerprints, and noted that pancreatic extracts digest protein. Several physiological structures or phenomena bear his name.

Purus River \pü-'rüs\ River, NW central S. America. One of the most crooked rivers in the world, it rises in Peru and flows generally northeast through the rain forests of Peru and Brazil. In Brazil, it meanders to join the stretch of the AMAZON RIVER upstream from MANAUS known as the Solimões River. Most of its 1,995-mi (3,211-km) course is navigable. Rubber is gathered from forests along its banks.

Pusan \'pü-,sän\ City (pop., 1995: 3,814,000) and port, S. Korea, at the SE tip of the Korean Peninsula. Pusan was opened to general foreign trade in 1883. It developed into a major port (called Fusan) under Japanese rule 1910–45. It served as the country's temporary capital during the KOREAN WAR. It is the nation's largest port and second-largest city. Industries include shipbuilding and manufacturing. Hot springs are located in the NE suburbs.

Pushkin, Aleksandr (Sergeyevich) (1799–1837) Russian writer. Born into an aristocratic family, he published his first major work, the romantic poem *Ruslan and Ludmila*, in 1820. He became associated with a revolutionary movement that culminated in the unsuccessful DECEMBRIST REVOLT of 1825. Banished to several provincial locations, he produced a cycle of romantic narrative poems that confirmed him as the leading Russian poet of the day and the leader of the Romantic generation of the 1820s. He also worked on his important historical tragedy, *Boris Godunov* (1831), and his central masterpiece, the novel in verse *Eugene Onegin* (1833). After NICHOLAS I allowed him to return to Moscow in 1826, Pushkin abandoned his revolutionary sentiments, turning to the figure of PETER I THE GREAT in poems such as *The Bronze Horseman* (1837). Still the object of suspicion in court circles, he died at 37 after being forced into a duel. He is often considered his country's greatest poet and the founder of modern Russian literature.

Putin \'pü-tyin\, Vladimir (Vladimirovich) (b.1952) Russian president (from 2000). His long career began with the KGB, based in Dresden, ended with his transfer to Leningrad (1990), where by 1993 he was essentially exercising mayoral control. He moved to Moscow in 1996, and in 1997 Boris YELTSIN promoted him to security council head. In 1999 Yeltsin named Putin prime minister, and soon stepped down as president in Putin's favor. In March 2000 Putin won a resounding electoral victory, partly the result of his success in the battle to keep Chechnya from seceding.

putting-out system See DOMESTIC SYSTEM

Putumayo River \,pü-tü-'mä-yō\ River, NW S. America. Rising in SW Colombia, it flows southeast through rain forests, forming much of the Peru–Colombia boundary, crosses into Brazil, where it is known as the Içá, and empties into the AMAZON RIVER after about 980 mi (1,575 km). Navigable for almost its entire length, it is a major transport route.

Puvis de Chavannes \pūē-'vē-də-shà-'vàn\, **Pierre (-Cécile)** (1824–1898) French painter. He is best known for his large canvas paintings for the walls of public buildings in Paris, including the Pantheon (1874–78, 1893–98), the Sorbonne (1889–91), and the Hôtel de Ville (1891–94). He also decorated the staircase of the Boston Public Library (1895–96). His works are usually allegories or idealized depictions of antiquity, in simplified forms and pale frescolike colors. The leading French mural painter of the later 19th cent., he exerted a strong influence on the Postimpressionists.

Puzo, Mario (1920–1999) U.S. novelist. Born in New York City to Italian immigrant parents, in 1969 he published his novel *The Godfather*; the saga of a Mafia family, it remained a huge bestseller for more than five years and was the basis for acclaimed films by F. F. COPPOLA. His later novels included *The Sicilian* (1984), *The Last Don* (1996), and *Omerta* (2000).

PVC *in full* **polyvinyl chloride** Synthetic RESIN, an organic POLYMER. PVC resin mixed with plasticizers, stabilizers, and pigments is made into flexible articles (e.g., raincoats, toys, containers). Nonplasticized resin has been used for rigid products (e.g., water pipes, plumbing fittings, phonograph records). Concern over leaching of vinyl chloride into foods has resulted in restrictions on its use in food containers; its decomposition into hydrogen chloride when burned has also raised concerns. It is produced in larger quantities than any other PLASTIC except polyethylene.

Pygmalion In GREEK MYTHOLOGY, a king of Cyprus who fell in love with a statue of APHRODITE. The goddess took pity on him and brought the statue to life, and he married her. In some versions of the myth Pygmalion was a sculptor who carved the statue himself because he was disgusted with the faults of ordinary women, and when it was brought to life he gave it the name Galatea.

Pygmy Any of a class of people of equatorial Africa ranging under 5 ft (1.5 m) in height. The name is also sometimes loosely applied to the SAN of S Africa and the so-called Negrito peoples of Asia (such as the Philippine Ilongot). Pygmies are also notable in having the highest basal-metabolism rate in the world and a high incidence of SICKLE-CELL ANEMIA. The Mbuti of the Ituri Forest are a well-studied example.

Pygmies of Congo (Zaire)

Pyle \'pīl\, **Ernie** (*orig.* Ernest Taylor) (1900–1945) U.S. journalist. Born near Dana, Ind., Pyle wrote a newspaper column that appeared in as many as 200 newspapers before World War II. His reporting of the campaigns in N. Africa, Sicily, Italy, and France won a Pulitzer Prize in 1944. He was killed at 44 by Japanese machine-gun fire on Okinawa. Compilations of his columns include *Ernie Pyle in England* (1941), *Brave Men* (1944), and *Last Chapter* (1946).

Pynchon \'pin-chən\, **Thomas** (b.1937) U.S. writer. Born in Glen Cove, N.Y., he worked briefly as a technical writer before writing his first novel, *V* (1963). His works have combined black humor and fantasy to depict human alienation in the chaos of modern society. The idea of conspiracy is central to *The Crying of Lot 49* (1966) and to his masterpiece, *Gravity's Rainbow* (1973), an extraordinary novel about the end of World War II, full of paranoid fantasy, grotesque imagery, and esoteric scientific and anthropological material. Later novels include *Vineland* (1990) and *Mason & Dixon* (1997). He has lived in hiding or incognito for decades, refusing to grant interviews or be photographed.

Pyongyang \ˌpyəŋ-'yaŋ\ City (pop., 1996 est.: 2,500,000), capital of N. Korea. Founded in 1122 B.C. according to legend, it is said to be the oldest city in Korea. It was the capital of the KOGURYO kingdom A.D. 427–668. It fell to the Japanese in 1592 and was devastated by the MANCHUS in the early 17th cent. Much of it was destroyed during the SINO–JAPANESE WAR. During the Japanese occupation of Korea 1910–45, it was built up as an industrial city. Captured by U.N. forces during the KOREAN WAR in 1950, it was retaken by Chinese Communist troops. After 1953 it was rebuilt as a heavy industry and transportation center.

pyramid Ancient monumental structure constructed of or faced with stone or brick and having a rectangular base and four sloping triangular sides meeting at an apex. The pyramids of ancient Egypt were royal tombs. Each contained an inner sepulchral chamber that housed the deceased (usually mummified) ruler, members of his entourage, and artifacts. The rest of the pyramid complex consisted of a large enclosure, an adjacent mortuary temple, and a causeway leading down to a pavilion. About 80 royal pyramids survive in Egypt, the greatest being those at GIZA. American pyramids include those at TEOTIHUACÁN and CHICHÉN ITZÁ and various INCA and Chimu structures. These pyramids were generally built of earth and faced with stone; they are typically of stepped form and topped by a platform or temple structure used for rituals, including HUMAN SACRIFICE.

Pyramus and Thisbe \'pir-ə-məs...'thiz-bē\ Hero and heroine of a Babylonian love story related in OVID's *Metamorphoses*. Forbidden to meet, they communicated through a hole in the wall between their two houses before deciding to run away together. Arriving at their meeting place first, Thisbe was scared away by a lion, which shredded the veil she dropped. Pyramus, finding the veil, believed her dead and stabbed himself; she returned and, finding Pyramus dying, killed herself.

Pyrenees \'pir-ə-ˌnēz\ Mountain range, SW Europe. It extends 270 mi (430 km) from the Mediterranean Sea to the Atlantic Ocean. It forms a high wall between France and Spain, its crest generally marking the boundary. Tiny ANDORRA lies among its peaks. The highest point is Aneto Peak, at 11,169 ft (3,404 m). The pass at Roncesvalles was made famous in the 12th-cent. *Chanson de Roland*, based on the Battle of RONCESVALLES (778).

Central Pyrenees

pyridine \'pir-ə-ˌdēn\ Any of a class of AROMATIC COMPOUNDS with a six-member aromatic ring composed of five CARBON atoms and one NITROGEN atom. The simplest one is pyridine itself. Compounds with pyridine rings include NIACIN and pyridoxine (see VITAMIN B COMPLEX), the TUBERCULOSIS drug isoniazid, and other plant products (e.g., NICOTINE). Pyridine is used as a raw material for various drugs, vitamins, and fungicides and as a solvent. It has a nauseating odor and burning taste, so it may be added to ethanol and antifreezes to denature them.

pyrimidine \pə-'rim-ə-ˌdēn\ Any of a class of organic compounds with a ring structure of four CARBON and two NITROGEN atoms. The simplest member, pyrimidine itself, is not common, but derivatives with the structure are. Examples include THIAMINE (vitamin B$_1$), several SULFA DRUGS, BARBITURATES, CYTOSINE, THYMINE, and URACIL.

pyrite *or* **iron pyrite** \'pī-ˌrīt\ *or* **fool's gold** Naturally occurring gold-colored iron disulfide mineral. Pyrite has frequently fooled prospectors into thinking they had discovered gold. It is used commercially as a source of SULFUR, particularly for the production of sulfuric acid. It is mined in Spain, Japan, the U.S., Canada, and Italy.

pyroxene \pī-'räk-ˌsēn\ Group of important rock-forming SILICATE MINERALS of variable composition, among which calcium-, magnesium-, and iron-rich varieties predominate. Pyroxenes are found in most IGNEOUS ROCKS. They vary in color from white to dark green or black. Rare pyroxenes include JADEITE, aegirine, and johannsenite.

Pyrrhus \'pir-əs\ (319–272 B.C.) King of Hellenistic EPIRUS. In 281 he was asked for help against Rome by the Greek enclave of Tarentum (TARANTO), and won costly victories at Heraclea and Ausculum. Crossing to Sicily, he conquered most of the Punic territory, but the Greek Sicilians revolted against his despotism. He suffered serious losses on his return to Italy (275) but defeated Antigonus II Gonatas (319?–239 B.C.) in Macedonia (274) and became king there. He died in a skirmish in Argos trying to help Sparta. His costly victories gave rise to the term "Pyrrhic victory."

Pythagoras \pə-'tha-gə-rəs\ (c.580–c.500 B.C.) Greek philosopher and mathematician. Probably born in Samos, he settled in Croton (S Italy), where he established a community of followers who adhered to a way of life he prescribed. His school of philosophy reduced all meaning to numerical relationships and proposed that all existing objects are fundamentally composed of form and not material substance. The principles of PYTHAGOREANISM influenced the thought of PLATO and ARISTOTLE and contributed to the development of mathematics and Western rational philosophy. The proportions of musical intervals and SCALES were first studied by Pythagoras, and he was the first influential Western practitioner of VEGETARIANISM. None of his writings survive, and it is difficult to distinguish his ideas from those of his disciples. His memory is kept alive partly by the PYTHAGOREAN THEOREM, probably developed by his school after he died.

Pythagoreanism \pə-ˌtha-gə-'rē-ə-ˌni-zəm\ Philosophical school, probably founded by PYTHAGORAS about 525 B.C. It originated as a religious brotherhood for the moral reformation of society; brothers were sworn to loyalty and secrecy. The brotherhood had much in common with the Orphic communities, which sought by rites and abstinence to purify the believer's soul and enable it to escape from the "wheel of birth." Pythagoreanism held that reality, at its deepest level, is mathematical, and that philosophy can be used for spiritual purification. It was the first important Western system of thought to advocate vegetarianism.

Pythagorean theorem \pə-ˌtha-gə-'rē-ən\ Rule relating the lengths of the sides of a right triangle. It says that the sum of the squares of the lengths of the legs is equal to the square of the length of the hypotenuse (the side opposite the right angle). That is, $a^2 + b^2 = c^2$, where c is the length of the hypotenuse. See also law of COSINES, law of SINES.

Pythian Games \'pi-thē-ən\ In ancient Greece, various athletic and musical competitions held in honor of APOLLO, chiefly at DELPHI, from before the 5th cent. B.C. to the 4th cent. A.D. They took place in August of the third year of each four-year period between OLYMPIC GAMES.

python \'pī-ˌthän\ Any of 20–25 species (subfamily Pythoninae, family Boidae) of sluggish, docile, nonvenomous SNAKES found in tropical and temperate regions. Pythons feed on birds and mammals, killing them by constriction. Most species are found near water; some are arboreal. All lay 15–100 eggs, depending on body size. The Asian reticulated python may be the world's longest snake (the ANACONDA is heavier); specimens over 30 ft (9 m) long have been recorded.

Q

Qaddafi \kə-'dä-fē\, **Muammar al-** *or* **Muammar al-Khadafy** (b.1942) Ruler of Libya (from 1969). Son of a BEDOUIN farmer, he graduated from the Univ. of Libya and Libya's military academy as a devout Muslim and ardent nationalist. As a captain in the army, he led the 1969 coup that deposed King IDRIS I. He has espoused his own form of Islamic socialism, and his foreign policy has been anti-Western and anti-Israel. In 1970 he closed U.S. and British military bases and expelled Italians and Jews. In 1973 he nationalized the oil industry. His government was repeatedly linked with terrorist incidents in Europe and elsewhere. After narrowly escaping death in 1986 when U.S. planes bombed sites in Libya, including his own houses, he gradually abandoned his aggressive involvement in foreign affairs.

Qajar dynasty \kä-'jär\ (1794–1925) Ruling dynasty of Iran. It was founded by Agha Mohammad Khan (1742–1797), who reunified Iran and reasserted Iran's rule over territories in Georgia and the Caucasus. His successor (r.1797–1834) lost land to Russia and increased contacts with the West. Nasir al-Din Shah (1831–1896) successfully manipulated Russia and Britain and preserved Persia's independence. Later rulers could not cope with European meddling and the aftermath of World War I, and the dynasty was abolished in 1925. See also Reza Shah PAHLAVI.

Qatar \'kä-tər\ *officially* **State of Qatar** Independent emirate on the W coast of the PERSIAN GULF. Area: 4,412 sq mi

[map: BAHRAIN, Manama, Al Khuwayr, Ra's Rakan, Fuwayrit, Al-Huwaylah, Al-Ghuwayr, Al-Jamaliyah, Ra's Al-Matbakh, Al-Khawr, Al-Wusayl, Dukhān, Ar Rayyān, Doha, Umm Bāb, Al-Kir'ānah, Al-Wakrah, Juh, Musay'id, SAUDI ARABIA, Persian Gulf, Gulf of Bahrain, Dawr al Salwah, Khōr ol-'Udeid, UNITED ARAB EMIRATES, Tropic of Cancer, ©1999, Encyclopædia Britannica, Inc.]

QATAR
Scale 1: 5,305,000
0 20 40 mi
0 30 60 km

(11,427 sq km). Population (2000): 599,000. Capital: DOHA. Most of the population is Arab, with S. Asian and Iranian minorities who are often migrant workers. Languages: Arabic (official), English. Religion: Islam (official). Currency: Qatar riyal. Qatar is mostly stony, sandy, and barren, and consists of salt flats, dune desert, and arid plains. Largely because of oil and natural gas exports, Qatar's gross national product per capita is one of the highest in the world. The government owns all of the agricultural land and generates most of the economic activity. The private sector participates in trade and contracting on a limited scale. It is a monarchy, and its basis of legislation is Islamic law. The head of state and government is the emir assisted by the prime minister. It was partly controlled by Bahrain in the 18th–19th cent. and was nominally part of the OTTOMAN EMPIRE until World War I. In 1916 it became a British protectorate. Oil was discovered in 1940, and the country rapidly modernized. Qatar declared independence in 1971, when the British protectorate ended. In 1991 it served as a base for air strikes against Iraq in the PERSIAN GULF WAR. It is the world's fastest-growing exporter of natural gas. Its Al-Jazeera broadcasts reach 35 million Arabs worldwide.

Qazvin *or* **Kazvin** \kaz-'vēn\ City (pop., 1996: 291,000), NW Iran. Founded as Shad Shahpur in A.D. 250, it flourished under Muslim rule in the 7th cent. GENGHIS KHAN laid waste the city, but it later revived and was made the capital of Persia (1548–98). In the late 18th cent. it became a base for foreign trade. A coup d'état launched from Qazvin in 1921 led to Iran's consolidation under Reza Shah PAHLAVI.

qi *or* **ch'i** \'chē\ In Chinese philosophy, the ethereal substance of which everything is composed. Early Taoist philosophers and alchemists regarded it as a vital force associated with breath and bodily fluids and sought to control its movement within the body in order to achieve longevity and spiritual power. Manipulation of qi is central to Chinese meditation, medicine, and MARTIAL ARTS.

Qianlong emperor *or* **Ch'ien-lung emperor** \chē-'en-'lùn\ *orig.* Hongli (1711–1799) Fourth emperor of the QING DYNASTY in China. His reign (1735–96) was one of the longest in Chinese history. China's boundaries reached their greatest extent, encompassing Mongolia, Tibet, Nepal, Taiwan, and portions of Central Asia. Qianlong sponsored a compilation of the Confucian FIVE CLASSICS; its descriptive catalog is still used today. At the same time, he ordered the expurgation or destruction of all books containing anti-Manchu sentiments. In the first half of his reign, agriculture made great strides and was superior to that in much of Europe. Taxes were light and education was widespread, even among the peasantry. Subsequently, military expeditions and increasing governmental corruption permanently harmed the dynasty.

Qianlong emperor Color on silk, 19th cent.

Qin dynasty *or* **Ch'in dynasty** \'chin\ (221–206 B.C.) Dynasty that established the first great Chinese empire. The Qin (from which the name China is derived), established the approximate boundaries and basic administrative system used by subsequent dynasties. It standardized the CHINESE WRITING SYSTEM and built the GREAT WALL, but it was also notorious for the "Qin bibliocaust," in which all nonutilitarian books were ordered burned. Due to its harshness, the dynasty only outlasted its first emperor, SHI HUANGDI, by four years; it was succeeded by the HAN DYNASTY.

Qing dynasty or **Ch'ing dynasty** \'chiŋ\ or **Manchu dynasty** (1644–1911/12) Last of the imperial dynasties in China. The name Qing was first applied to the dynasty established by the MANCHU in 1636 in Manchuria and by extension to their rule in China. During the Qing dynasty, China's territory and population expanded tremendously. Cultural attitudes were strongly conservative and NEO-CONFUCIANISM was the dominant philosophy. The arts flourished, and BEIJING OPERA originated. Qing porcelain, textiles, tea, paper, sugar, and steel were exported worldwide. In the late 18th cent., military campaigns depleted government finances and corruption grew. Later the TAIPING REBELLION further weakened the dynasty so that it was unable to rebuff the demands of foreign powers in the late 19th cent. The dynasty ended with the Republican Revolution of 1911 and the abdication of the last emperor in 1912.

Qin tomb or **Ch'in tomb** \'chin\ Major Chinese archaeological site near the ancient capital city of Ch'ang-an (now Xi'an), a 20-sq-mi (50-sq-km) funerary compound built by the emperor SHI HUANGDI. In 1974 workers drilling a well discovered a subterranean chamber that contained some 6,000 life-size terra-cotta soldiers with individually detailed faces, horses, weapons, and other objects. Three nearby chambers containing more than 1,400 figures have also been unearthed; the tomb itself has not yet been excavated.

Qishon River or **Kishon River** \'kī-ˌshän\ River, N Israel. It rises near Mt. Gilboa and flows about 25 mi (40 km) to the Mediterranean Sea just north of HAIFA. It was the scene of biblical events, including the Israelite victory of DEBORAH over the Canaanites, and of ELIJAH's slaying of the prophets of BAAL. Its mouth is the main base of Israel's fishing fleet.

Qom \'kùm\ City (pop., 1996: 778,000), N central Iran. Located 92 mi (147 km) south of Tehran, it is an industrial center for textiles and petroleum products. A SHIITE center in the 8th cent., it became a pilgrimage site in the 17th cent. Some 10 kings and 400 Islamic saints are buried in and around Qom. It is the site of the largest *madrasah* (theological college) in Iran.

quadratic equation Algebraic EQUATION of particular importance in OPTIMIZATION. Its standard form is $ax^2 + bx + c = 0$, and its solution is given by the quadratic formula

$$x = \frac{-b \pm \sqrt{b^2 - 4ac}}{2a}$$

which guarantees two REAL-NUMBER solutions, one real-number solution, or two COMPLEX-NUMBER solutions, depending on whether $b^2 - 4ac$ is greater than, equal to, or less than 0.

Quadruple Alliance (1815) Alliance between Britain, Russia, Austria, and Prussia first formed in 1813 to oppose France in the final phase of the NAPOLEONIC WARS. It was officially renewed in 1815 to enforce the peace settlement concluded at the Congress of VIENNA. The allies then met occasionally (1818-22) to keep European political development within terms of the 1815 settlement.

quaestor \'kwe-stər, 'kwē-stər\ (Latin: "investigator") In ancient Rome, an officer appointed by a CONSUL as his deputy. Around 450 B.C. they became magistrates, a class of high-level government administrators that included the consuls, PRAETORS, and PREFECTS. Quaestors, the lowest level of this class, were elected by the people, and ranged in number from four to 20.

quail Any of several species of short-tailed game birds (family Phasianidae), some with a

California quail (*Callipepla californica*)

head plume. Species range from 5 to 13 in. (13–33 cm) long. Some of the 95 Old World species have leg spurs, but the 36 New World species never do. Quails prefer open country and brushy borders. The male may help incubate the 12 eggs. The common quail (*Coturnix coturnix*) of Eurasia and Africa is the only migratory bird in the order Galliformes. Quails are generally smaller than PARTRIDGES. See also BOBWHITE.

Quakers See Society of FRIENDS

Quantrill \'kwän-trəl\, **William C(larke)** (1837–1865) U.S. outlaw and Confederate guerrilla. Born in Canal Dover, Ohio, he moved to Kansas, where by 1860 he was a horse thief and murderer. In the Civil War he gathered a gang of guerrillas to raid and rob Union towns and farms; Quantrill's Raiders were given official status by the Confederates in 1862. In 1863 his group of about 450 men sacked the free-state town of Lawrence, Kan., killing 150 people. They later surprised a Union detachment and killed 90 captured soldiers. Quantrill was mortally wounded in a raid into Kentucky.

quantum In physics, a discrete natural unit, or packet, of energy, charge, angular momentum, or other physical property. Light, for example, which appears in some respects as a continuous electromagnetic wave, on the submicroscopic level is emitted and absorbed in quanta, called PHOTONS; for light of a given wavelength, all the quanta have the same energy and momentum. Other forms of electromagnetic energy, such as X RAYS and GAMMA RAYS, also consist of photons. Submicroscopic mechanical vibrations in the layers of atoms comprising CRYSTALS also give up or take on energy and momentum in quanta called phonons. See also QUANTUM MECHANICS.

quantum chromodynamics (QCD) Theory that describes the action of the STRONG FORCE. The strong force acts only on certain particles, principally QUARKS that are bound together in the PROTONS and NEUTRONS of the atomic NUCLEUS, as well as in less stable, more exotic forms of matter. Quarks interact via the strong force because they carry a form of "strong charge," which has been given the name "color," though there is no connection with the usual sense of color. See also STANDARD MODEL.

quantum computing Experimental method of computing that makes use of QUANTUM MECHANICS and the UNCERTAINTY PRINCIPLE. Quantum computers would allow a BIT to store a value of 0 and 1 simultaneously. They pursue multiple lines of inquiry simultaneously, with the final output dependent on the interference pattern generated by the various calculations.

quantum electrodynamics (QED) QUANTUM theory of the interactions of charged particles with the electromagnetic field. It describes the interactions of LIGHT with MATTER as well as those of charged particles with each other. Its foundations were laid by Paul DIRAC when he discovered an equation describing the motion and spin of electrons that incorporated both QUANTUM MECHANICS and the theory of special RELATIVITY. The theory rests on the idea that charged particles interact by emitting and absorbing PHOTONS. It has become a model for other QUANTUM FIELD THEORIES.

quantum field theory Theory that brings QUANTUM MECHANICS and special RELATIVITY together to account for subatomic phenomena (see QUANTUM CHROMODYNAMICS, QUANTUM ELECTRODYNAMICS). In particular, the interactions of SUBATOMIC PARTICLES are described in terms of their interactions with fields, such as the electromagnetic field. However, the fields are quantized and represented by particles, such as PHOTONS for the electromagnetic field. The ELECTROWEAK THEORY, a unified theory of ELECTROMAGNETIC and WEAK FORCES, has considerable experimental support, and can likely be extended to include the strong force. Theories that include the gravitational force (see GRAVITATION) are more speculative. See also GRAND UNIFIED THEORY, STANDARD MODEL, UNIFIED FIELD THEORY.

quantum mechanics Branch of mathematical physics that deals with atomic and subatomic systems. It is concerned with phenomena that are so small-scale that they cannot be described in classical terms, and is formulated entirely in terms of statistical probabilities. Considered one of the great ideas of the 20th cent., quantum mechanics was developed mainly by Niels BOHR, Erwin SCHRÖDINGER, Werner HEISENBERG, and Max BORN. It explained the structure of ATOMS, atomic nuclei (see NUCLEUS), and MOLECULES; the behavior of SUBATOMIC PARTICLES; the nature of chemical bonds (see BONDING); the properties of crystalline solids (see CRYSTAL); NUCLEAR ENERGY; and the forces that stabilize collapsed STARS. It also led directly to the development of the LASER, the electron microscope, and the TRANSISTOR.

quarantine Detention of humans or animals suspected to have communicable disease until they are proved free of INFECTION, or separation of a known infected individual from healthy ones until the danger of transmission passes. Though appropriate in some cases (e.g., DIPHTHERIA), it is ineffective for diseases that are spread by other means (e.g., plague) or are contagious before symptoms appear. In some cases, contacts (e.g., the family of a hepatitis patient) are notified, educated on precautions, and monitored for development of illness. Quarantine is more often applied to animals (e.g., for RABIES).

quark Any of a group of SUBATOMIC PARTICLES thought to be among the fundamental constituents of MATTER, more specifically, of PROTONS and NEUTRONS. The concept was first proposed by Murray GELL-MANN and George Zweig (b.1937). Quarks include all particles that interact by means of the STRONG FORCE. They have MASS and SPIN, and obey the PAULI EXCLUSION PRINCIPLE. They have not been resolved into smaller components. Their behavior is explained by the theory of QUANTUM CHROMODYNAMICS. There are six types of quark, called up, down, strange, charmed, bottom, and top. Only the up and down quarks are needed to make protons and neutrons; the others occur in heavier, unstable particles.

quartz Second most abundant mineral (after FELDSPAR) in the earth's crust, present in many rocks. Quartz, which consists of silica, or silicon dioxide, has great economic importance. Many varieties are gemstones, including AMETHYST, CITRINE, smoky quartz, and rose quartz. SANDSTONE, composed mainly of quartz, is an important building stone. Large amounts of quartz sand (or silica sand) are used in the manufacture of glass and ceramics and for molds in metal casting. Silica glass (or fused quartz) is used in optics to transmit ultraviolet light. Tubing and various vessels of fused quartz have important laboratory applications, and quartz fibers are employed in extremely sensitive weighing devices.

quartzite SANDSTONE that has been converted into a solid QUARTZ rock, usually by recrystallization (METAMORPHISM). Quartzites are usually white; they fracture smoothly and break up into rubble under frost action. Because they weather slowly, they tend to project as hills or mountain masses; many prominent ridges in the Appalachian Mtns. are composed of quartzite. Pure quartzites are a source of silica for the manufacture of silica brick. Quartzite is also quarried for paving and roofing materials.

quasar \'kwā-ˌzär\ in full **quasi-stellar radio source** Any of a class of rare cosmic objects of high luminosity and strong radio emission. Closely related objects with the same optical appearance that do not emit radio waves are the so-called QSOs (quasi-stellar objects). Most quasars exhibit very large RED SHIFTS, suggesting that they are moving away at speeds approaching that of light and are some of the most distant known objects in the universe. Only a light-year or two across, they are up to 1,000 times brighter than galaxies 100,000 times as large, so they can be observed from over 10 billion light-years away. Many investigators attribute such energy generation to high-speed spiraling of gas into a supermassive BLACK HOLE at the center of an otherwise normal GALAXY. See also ACTIVE GALACTIC NUCLEUS.

Quasimodo \ˌkwä-zē-'mō-dō\, **Salvatore** (1901–1968) Italian poet, critic, and translator. A government engineer, he became a leader of HERMETICISM after the publication of his first poetry collection, *Acque e terre* (1930; "Waters and Land"). After World War II his social convictions shaped his work, beginning with *Giorno dopo giorno* (1947; "Day After Day"). He published an astonishing range of translations and wrote many essays, including those in *The Poet and the Politician* (1960). He received the Nobel Prize in 1959.

Quaternary period \'kwä-tər-ˌner-ē, kwə-'tər-nə-rē\ Interval of geologic time, 1.8 million years ago to the present, in the CENOZOIC ERA. The Quaternary is subdivided into the PLEISTOCENE EPOCH and the HOLOCENE EPOCH. Characterized by major cyclical changes of climate that produced vast ice sheets, the period is frequently called the Great Ice Age. Its major biologic feature was the evolution and dispersion of humans. The extinction of many large mammals toward the end of the last ice age may be related to the rapid territorial expansion of humans. See table at GEOLOGIC TIME.

Quayle, (James) Dan(forth) (b.1947) U.S. politician. Born in Indianapolis, he served as associate publisher of his family's *Huntington Herald-Press* (1974–76) before serving in the U.S. House of Representatives (1976–80) and Senate (1980–88). As the Republican candidate for vice president, he was elected with George BUSH in 1988. During his term, Quayle traveled widely on goodwill missions but was ridiculed for various gaffes.

Quebec Province (pop., 1999 est.: 7,363,000), E Canada. It is bounded by the Hudson Strait, Newfoundland, the Gulf of ST. LAWRENCE, New Brunswick, the U.S., Ontario, and HUDSON BAY. Its capital is QUEBEC city. The original inhabitants were Inuits (see ESKIMO) and members of the Algonquian, Cree, and other Indian tribes. Settled by the French in the early 17th cent., it was lost to the British in the FRENCH AND INDIAN WAR, but the struggle for authority between the French and British groups led to a rebellion by French Canadians in 1837. The rebellion was quelled, and in 1867 Quebec (CANADA EAST) united with New Brunswick and Nova Scotia to form the Dominion of Canada. Most of the population is of French descent. Various movements for independence have continued during the 20th cent.; the PARTI QUÉBÉCOIS won provincial elections in 1976, but its independence referendum was defeated in 1980. A second independence referendum was narrowly defeated in 1995. Principal industries include mining, hydroelectric power, and forestry.

Quebec or **Quebec City** City (metro. area pop., 1996: 672,000), port, and capital of QUEBEC province. It lies at the confluence of the ST. LAWRENCE and St. Charles rivers, about 150 mi (240 km) northeast of MONTREAL, on a rocky promontory. Canada's oldest city, it was settled by the French in 1608 as a trading post. It was the capital of NEW FRANCE 1663–1763, of Lower Canada 1791–1841, and of CANADA EAST 1841–67. Most of the population is French-speaking and Roman Catholic. The Old World charm of its architecture and winding streets attracts numerous tourists. It is the site of LAVAL UNIV. Shipbuilding is an important industry.

Quebec, Battle of (Sept. 13, 1759) Decisive battle of the FRENCH AND INDIAN WAR. In June, James WOLFE led a British force of 250 ships with 8,500 soldiers to take up positions in the St. Lawrence River around Quebec. French forces under the Marquis de MONTCALM withstood a two-month siege of the city. In September the British secretly landed 4,000 men and forced a confrontation with French troops on the Plains of ABRAHAM. The French were routed, and both Wolfe and Montcalm were mortally wounded.

Quebec Act (1774) British statute establishing Quebec's government and extending its borders. By providing for a governor and appointed council, religious freedom for Roman Catholics, and use of the French civil code, it attempted to resolve the problem of making the colony a province of British N. America and win French-Canadian loyalty. It also extended the borders of Quebec to include the land between the Ohio and Mississippi rivers, claimed by American colonists. It was considered one of the INTOLERABLE ACTS, which led to the AMERICAN REVOLUTION.

Québécois, Parti See PARTI QUÉBÉCOIS

Quechua \'ke-chə-wə\ S. American Indian population of the Andes from Ecuador to Bolivia. In the early 15th cent. the Quechuas were conquered by the Chancas, who in turn were subdued by the INCAS. Much of Quechua tradition endured under the Incas, but it was drastically altered by the 16th-cent. Spanish conquest. Traditional Quechuas now lead isolated lives as marginal farmers in the high Andes. See also QUECHUAN LANGUAGES.

Quechuan languages \'ke-chə-wən\ Family of closely related S. American Indian languages spoken by some 12 million people in S Colombia and Ecuador, Bolivia, and N Argentina. Southern Peruvian Quechua, one language of the family, was an administrative language within the INCA empire and was spread by Inca colonization.

Queen, Ellery *pseudonym of* Frederic Dannay (*orig.* Daniel Nathan) *and* Manfred Bennington Lee (*orig.* Manford Lepofsky) (1905–1982; 1905–1971) U.S. writers. The two cousins, born respectively in Brooklyn and White Plains, N.Y., collaborated on more than 35 best-selling novels featuring the detective Ellery Queen, beginning with *The Roman Hat Mystery* (1929). As Barnaby Ross, they wrote about a second detective, Drury Lane. They cofounded *Ellery Queen's Mystery Magazine* (1941) and Mystery Writers of America.

Queen Anne's lace *or* **wild carrot** Bristly biennial (*Daucus carota*) of the PARSLEY family, native to Eurasia but now found almost worldwide. An ancestor of the cultivated CARROT, it grows 5 ft (1.5 m) tall and has divided, long, feathery leaves. Flat-topped clusters (umbels) of white or pink flowers resemble lace. The enlarged root is edible but very bitter.

Queen Anne's War (1702–13) Second in a series of wars between Britain and France for control of N. America, the American phase of the War of the SPANISH SUCCESSION. American colonial settlements along the New York and New England borders with Canada were raided by French forces and their Indian allies. The British capture of Port Royal (1710) resulted in French-held Acadia's becoming the British province of Nova Scotia. Under the Treaty of Utrecht (1713), Britain also acquired Newfoundland and the Hudson Bay region from France.

Queen Charlotte Islands Group of about 150 islands (pop., 1991: 5,000) off W British Columbia. They have an area of 3,705 sq mi (9,596 sq km). The two largest islands, Graham and Moresby, rise to nearly 4,000 ft (1,200 m). The inhabitants, including HAIDA Indians, engage in fishing and ranching.

Queen Elizabeth Islands Island group, N Canada. Part of the Canadian Arctic archipelago, it includes all the islands north of latitude 74°30′ N, such as the Parry and Sverdrup groups. The largest islands are ELLESMERE and Melville. Total land area is over 150,000 sq mi (390,000 sq km). Probably first visited by the Vikings around A.D. 1000, the islands were partially explored (1615–16) by William Baffin (c.1584–1622) and Robert Bylot (fl.1610–1616). Split between the NORTHWEST TERRITORIES and NUNAVUT, they were named in 1953 to honor Queen ELIZABETH II.

Queens Borough (pop., 2000: 2,229,000) of NEW YORK CITY, coextensive with Queens county, SE New York. The largest of the five boroughs, it lies on W LONG ISLAND. The first settlements, made by the Dutch 1636–56, came under English control in 1664. It became a borough in 1898. Queens was primarily rural during the 19th cent., but some of its shore communities began attracting summer vacationers. Development was spurred by the construction of the Queensboro Bridge and the Long Island Railroad tunnel. It is mostly residential, with manufacturing around Long Island City, and storage and shipping facilities lining the East River. It is the site of New York City's major airports, Kennedy and La Guardia.

Queensland State (pop., 1998 est.: 3,456,000), NE Australia. Bounded on the north by the Pacific Ocean and the GREAT BARRIER REEF, it has an area of 667,000 sq mi (1,727,530 sq km); the capital is BRISBANE. Its topical coastal region attracts many tourists. Inland from the GREAT DIVIDING RANGE, which runs the entire length of the state, mining and cattle ranching are important. Capt. James COOK charted the coast in 1770. In the 19th cent. the state housed several penal colonies, and drew settlers to mine its gold.

Quercia, Jacopo della See JACOPO DELLA QUERCIA

Querétaro City (pop., 1995: 469,000), capital of QUERÉTARO state, Mexico. Situated 6,119 ft (1,865 m) above sea level, it is considered an excellent example of a Spanish colonial city. It was made part of the AZTEC empire in 1446. Under Spanish control from 1531, it became a supply center for the rich mining districts of GUANAJUATO and ZACATECAS.

Emperor MAXIMILIAN was executed there in 1867, and the Mexican Constitution of 1917 was written there. It is the site of one of Mexico's oldest and largest cotton factories.

Querétaro \kä-'rä-tä-ˌrō\ State (pop., 2000: 1,402,000), central Mexico. It has an area of 4,420 sq mi (11,449 sq km), and its capital is QUERÉTARO city. Situated on the central plateau, in 1531 the area was conquered by Spain, which began colonization in the 1550s. It was administered with Guanajuato before it became a state in 1824. Chief mineral products are opals and mercury. Medicinal plants, sweet potatoes, fruits, and grains are among the many crops cultivated.

quetzal \ket-'säl\ Any of several tropical arboreal, short-billed, fruit-eating birds (genus *Pharomachrus*) in the trogon family (Trogonidae). It was the sacred bird of the ancient MAYAS and AZTECS. Found in remote cloud forests from S Mexico to Bolivia, it is the national emblem of Guatemala. The resplendent, or Guatemalan, quetzal is about 50 in. (125 cm) long. Long blue-green plumes cover the tail; the breast and head, with a rounded hairlike crest, are gold-green; the blue back has a curly gold-tinged mantle; and the belly is red. The quetzal is now listed as endangered.

Quetzalcóatl \ˌkät-säl-'kō-ä-təl, ˌkät-säl-kō-'ä-təl\ Feathered Serpent, a major deity of ancient Mexico. Quetzalcóatl began as a god of vegetation in the TEOTIHUACÁN civilization. For the TOLTECS he was the god of the morning and evening star. The AZTECS revered him as the patron of priests, the inventor of the calendar and of books, and the protector of craftsmen. He was also a symbol of death and resurrection. MONTEZUMA II regarded Hernán CORTÉS as the fulfillment of a prophecy that Quetzalcóatl, conceived as a white priest-king, would return from the east.

Quezon (y Molina) \'kä-sòn\, **Manuel (Luis)** (1878–1944) Filipino statesman. Convinced that the only way to Philippine independence was through cooperation with the U.S., he served as the Philippines' representative in the U.S. House of Representatives (1909–16) and played a major role in obtaining Congress's pledge of independence for the Philippines (1916). President of the Philippine Senate 1916–35, he became president of the Commonwealth (a precursor to the independent republic) in 1935; when Japan occupied the Philippines in 1942, he formed a government-in-exile in the U.S. Quezon City is named in his honor.

Quezon City \'kä-ˌsòn\ City (pop., 2000.: 2,160,000), Luzon Island, Philippines, abutting MANILA. Pres. Manuel QUEZON selected the site in 1939, and it replaced Manila as the capital in 1948, but the seat of government moved back to Manila in 1976. The city is home to two universities.

Quiche *or* **K'iche** *or* **Kiche** \kē-'chā\ Indian population of the Guatemalan highlands, largest ethnic group speaking a MAYAN LANGUAGE. The Quiche Mayas had an advanced civilization in pre-Columbian times. Records of their history and mythology are preserved in the *Popol Vuh*. Traditional Quiche are agricultural, live in thatched huts, and practice weaving and pottery. Many were killed or displaced by the Guatemalan military in the early 1980s; they now number about 700,000.

quicklime See LIME

quicksand State in which water-saturated sand loses its supporting capacity. It is usually found in a hollow at the mouth of a large river or along a stream or beach where pools of water become partly filled with sand and an underlying layer of stiff clay or other dense material prevents drainage. Any sand may become "quick" if its effective weight is being carried by water between the grains. The sand-water suspension is denser than an animal or human body, so the body cannot sink below the surface, but struggling may lead to loss of balance and drowning.

quicksilver See MERCURY

Quiller-Couch, Arthur (Thomas) (*later* **Sir Arthur**) (1863–1944) English poet, novelist, and anthologist. A professor at Cambridge Univ. from 1912, he is noted for compiling *The Oxford Book of English Verse 1250–1900* (1900) and *The Oxford Book of Ballads* (1910). His works, written in a clear and apparently effortless style, include many novels and short stories, verse, and criticism, including *On the Art of Writing* (1916) and *On the Art of Reading* (1920).

quilombo \kē-'lòm-bō\ *or* **mocambo** In colonial Brazil, a community organized by fugitive slaves. Quilombos were located in inaccessible areas and usually consisted of fewer than 100 people, who survived by farming and raiding. The largest and most famous was Palmares, which by the 1690s had 20,000 inhabitants. It owed its prosperity to abundant irrigated land and abducted slaves from Portuguese plantations, who were kept in bondage.

quilting Process of stitching together two layers of fabric, usually with a soft, thick substance placed between them. The layer of wool, cotton, or other stuffing provides insulation; the stitching keeps the stuffing evenly distributed and also provides opportunity for artistic expression. Quilting has long been used for clothing in many parts of the world. It reached its fullest development in the U.S., where it was popularly used for petticoats and comforters. By 1800 the U.S. quilt had distinctive features, such as colored fabric sewn on the outer layers (appliqué) and stitching that echoed the appliqué pattern.

quince Any of the fruit shrubs and small trees that make up the genus *Cydonia*, in the ROSE family. Common quince (*C. oblonga*) is native to the Mediterranean. The raw golden-yellow fruit has a strong fragrant aroma and astringent taste; it takes on a pink color when cooked and makes an excellent preserve. The Japanese quince (*Chaenomeles* species) is an ornamental shrub widely used for its flowers, which open fully before the leaves in late winter and early spring.

Quincey, Thomas De See Thomas DE QUINCEY

Quine, W(illard) V(an) O(rman) (1908–2000) U.S. logician and philosopher. Born in Akron, Ohio, he was trained in mathematics and later studied under Rudolf CARNAP, then taught at Harvard Univ. 1936–78. He advocated systematic constructivist analysis of philosophy. His early career emphasized technical aspects of logic; his later work investigated more general philosophical issues within a systematic linguistic framework. He is known as a proponent of philosophical NATURALISM. His works include *A System of Logistic* (1934), *Word and Object* (1960), *Philosophy of Logic* (1970), and *Theories and Things* (1981).

quinine \'kwī-,nīn\ ALKALOID found in the bark of cinchona trees and shrubs. Its chemical structure is large and complex, with several rings. Until the 1940s, when newer antimalarials were developed, quinine was the only drug known to Western medicine for the prevention and treatment of MALARIA. It has benefited more people than any other drug used against infectious disease in history. Quinine is also occasionally used to treat pain and fever and is a flavoring agent in some carbonated beverages, including tonic water.

Quinn, Anthony (1915–2001) U.S. (Mexican-born) film actor. Of mixed Irish-Mexican parentage, he began appearing in bit parts in movies in 1936. After appearing on Broadway in *A Streetcar Named Desire*, he won Academy Awards in *Viva Zapata!* (1952) and *Lust for Life* (1956). Noted for his earthy masculinity, he acted in over 100 other films, notably *La Strada* (1954), *Requiem for a Heavyweight* (1962), and *Zorba the Greek* (1964).

Quintana Roo \kē-'tä-nä-'rō\ State (pop., 2000: 874,000), E YUCATÁN PENINSULA, SE Mexico. Bounded by the Caribbean Sea and Belize, it has an area of 19,397 sq mi (50,212 sq km). The capital is Chetumal. The region was long used as a place of exile for political prisoners. It became a state in 1974. It is the site of many MAYA ruins, many beautiful beaches, and such resorts as CANCÚN and Cozumel island, where Hernán CORTÉS landed in 1519. Its main product is chicle.

Quintero \kēn-'ter-ō\, **José (Benjamín)** (1924–1999) U.S. (Panamanian-born) theatrical director. After directing his first play in 1949, he cofounded the off-Broadway theater Circle in the Square, where he directed regularly from 1950, establishing it as a major center for serious theater. His direction of Tennessee WILLIAMS's *Summer and Smoke* (1952) confirmed his reputation. He was best known for his productions of Williams and Eugene O'NEILL, including *The Iceman Cometh* (1956), *Long Day's Journey Into Night* (1956), and *A Moon for the Misbegotten* (1973, Tony Award).

Quintilian *Latin* Marcus Fabius Quintilianus (A.D. 35?–after 96) Latin teacher and writer. From about 68 to 88 he taught rhetoric, becoming Rome's leading teacher. His *Institutio*

oratoria is a practical survey of rhetoric in 12 books and a major contribution to educational theory and literary criticism. His dual emphasis on intellectual and moral training appealed to humanists of the 15th–16th cent. and through them influenced the modern view of education as all-around character training to equip a student for life.

Quirinus \kwə-'rī-nəs\ Major Roman deity ranking close to JUPITER and MARS. Despite his importance, little is known about Quirinus, who was originally a god of the SABINES. He may have been another form of Mars. By the late republic he was identified with ROMULUS. His festival was the Quirinalia.

Quisling, Vidkun (Abraham Lauritz Jonsson) (1887–1945) Norwegian politician and German collaborator in World War II. Norway's minister of defense, he resigned in 1933 to form the fascist National Union party. He actively collaborated in the German conquest of Norway (1940) and served in the occupation government. His attempts to convert Norwegians to NATIONAL SOCIALISM aroused strong opposition. In 1945 he was found guilty of treason and executed. His name became a synonym for "traitor."

Quito \'kē-tō\ City (pop., 2000: 1,616,000), capital of Ecuador. It lies on the lower slopes of a dormant volcano, at an altitude of 9,350 ft (2,850 m). A pre-Columbian town, it was captured by the INCAS in 1487 and taken by the Spanish in 1534. It is the oldest of all S. American capitals and preserves much of its colonial atmosphere. In 1535 the Franciscans established the first art school in S. America there. One of Ecuador's two major industrial centers, it produces textiles and light consumer goods. It is the site of two universities.

quiz show See GAME SHOW

Qumran \kum-'rän\ Site on the NW shore of the DEAD SEA, where the DEAD SEA SCROLLS were discovered in 1947. Ruins of buildings less than a mile from the sea may have been occupied by ESSENES, the probable authors of the scrolls. The buildings include a scriptorium, a potter's workshop, and a flour mill; water was supplied through an aqueduct. The Essenes are thought to have founded a monastic community at Qumran in the mid-2nd cent. B.C. It was destroyed by Roman legions in A.D. 68.

quota In international trade, a government-imposed limit on the quantity of goods and services that may be exported or imported over a specified period of time. By limiting the availability of foreign goods, a quota aims to allow domestic goods to compete more successfully, though the price of the goods may also rise. Quotas restricting trade were first imposed on a large scale during World War I. In the 1920s, quotas were progressively abolished and replaced by tariffs, but their use was revived in the wave of PROTECTIONISM set off by the GREAT DEPRESSION. After World War II, the Western European countries gradually dismantled quantitative import restrictions, but the U.S. was slower to discard them. See also FREE TRADE.

Quqon \kə-'kòn\ *or* **Kokand** \kə-'känt\ *ancient* Fergana Region, E Uzbekistan. A powerful khanate by the 18th cent., it recognized Chinese sovereignty about 1760. Conquered by Russia in 1876, it became part of the new Uzbek S.S.R. in 1924, and of independent Uzbekistan in 1991. Its chief city, also called Quqon (pop., 1993 est.: 184,000), was founded in 1732.

Quran \ku-'rän\ *or* **Koran** \kə-'ran, kə'rän\ Sacred SCRIPTURE of ISLAM, regarded by Muslims as the infallible word of God, revealed to the Prophet MUHAMMAD. The book, first compiled in its authoritative form in the 7th cent., consists of 114 chapters (suras) written in Arabic. The earliest suras call for moral and religious obedience; the ones written later provide directives for the creation of a social structure that will support the moral life called for by God. The Quran also describes the joys of paradise and the terrors of hell; emphasis on God's stern judgment is tempered by references to his mercy. Muslims believe the God who spoke to Muhammad is the God worshiped by Jews and Christians, but that the revelations received by those religions are incomplete. The Quran is also the primary source of Islamic law (SHARIA). Traditionally translation was forbidden; modern translations are regarded as paraphrases to facilitate understanding of the actual scripture.

R

Ra See RE

Rabanus Maurus *or* **Hrabanus Maurus** \rä-ˈbä-nu̇s-ˈmau̇-ru̇s\ (c.780–856) German theologian. A Benedictine monk, he became director of the school at the Fulda monastery near Frankfurt am Main in 803. He built Fulda into a leading European center of learning and, after he became abbot in 822, a base for Christian missions throughout Europe. His encyclopedia *On the Nature of Things* (842–47) drew on all past knowledge; he also wrote treatises on education and grammar and commentaries on the Bible. His work contributed so much to the development of German literature that he received the title Praeceptor Germaniae ("Teacher of Germany").

Rabat \rə-ˈbät\ *Arabic* **Ribat** \ri-ˈbät\ City (metro. area pop., with SALÉ, 1994: 1,386,000), capital of Morocco, on the Atlantic coast opposite Salé. One of Morocco's four imperial cities, it was founded in the 12th cent. by the ALMOHAD ruler ABD AL-MUMIN. After 1609 Rabat-Salé became the home of many Andalusian MOORS who had been driven from Spain and, later, of the Sallee Corsairs, the most dreaded of BARBARY COAST pirates. Under the French, it was made the administrative capital of a French protectorate after 1912. Now a center of the textile industry, it is noted for its carpets, blankets, and leather handicrafts.

rabbi \ˈra-ˌbī\ *or* **rebbe** \ˈre-bə\ In Judaism, a person qualified by study of the Hebrew scriptures and the TALMUD to serve as spiritual leader of a Jewish community or congregation. Ordination can be conferred by any rabbi, but it usually depends on a written statement issued by the candidate's teacher. Though rabbis are considered teachers rather than priests, they conduct religious services, assist at BAR MITZVAHS, perform marriages, and are present at funerals. The rabbi also counsels and consoles members of his congregation and oversees the religious education of the young.

rabbinic Judaism \rə-ˈbi-nik\ Principal form of JUDAISM that developed after the fall of the Second Temple of JERUSALEM (A.D. 70). It originated in the teachings of the PHARISEES, who emphasized the need for critical interpretation of the TORAH. It is centered on study of the TALMUD. Its mode of worship and life discipline continue to be practiced by Jews worldwide.

rabbit Any small, bounding, gnawing mammal of the family Leporidae. Rabbits have long ears, a short tail, long hind legs, and two pairs of upper incisors—one pair behind a larger, functional pair. They grow to 10–18 in. (25–45 cm) long and weigh 1–4 lbs (0.5–2 kg). Their reproductive rate is very high; unlike HARES, rabbits are born naked, blind, and helpless. Most species are nocturnal and live alone in burrows, but the European, or Old World, rabbit (*Oryctolagus cuniculus*) lives in warrens of many burrows. The 13 species of N. American cottontail rabbits (genus *Sylvilagus*) have white on the underside of the tail.

Rabelais \rà-ˈble, *Engl* ˈra-bə-ˌlā\, **François** (1494?–1553) French writer and priest. He took holy orders as a Franciscan, later moved to a Benedictine house, and in 1530 left the Benedictines to study medicine, a profession he would follow the rest of his life. His fame rests on the five comic novels (one of doubtful authenticity) known collectively as *Gargantua and Pantagruel*, including the masterpieces *Pantagruel* (1532) and *Gargantua* (1534) as well as *Le tiers livre* (1546; "The Third Book"), his most profound work. These works display a delight in words, a mastery of storytelling, and deep humanist learning in a mosaic of scholarly, literary, and scientific parody that is unlike any previous work in French. Though banned by civil and church authorities for their satirical content and earthy humor, they were read throughout Europe.

François Rabelais Painting by an unknown artist, 17th cent.

Rabi \ˈrä-bē\, **I(sidor) I(saac)** (1898–1988) U.S. (Polish-born) physicist. In 1940–45 at MIT he led a group of scientists who helped develop RADAR. He was the first to propose the joint European laboratory CERN, and he helped found New York's Brookhaven National Laboratory. His method for measuring the magnetic properties of atoms, atomic nuclei, and molecules (1937) led to the atomic clock, the maser, the laser, magnetic resonance imaging, and the central technique for molecular and atomic beam experimentation, and won him a 1944 Nobel Prize.

rabies \ˈrā-ˌbēz\ Acute, usually fatal infectious disease of warm-blooded animals that attacks the central NERVOUS SYSTEM. It is spread by contact with an infected animal's saliva, usually from a bite. The RHABDOVIRUS that causes it spreads along nerve tissue from the wound to the brain. Symptoms usually appear four to six weeks later, often beginning with irritability and aggressiveness. Wild animals lose their fear of humans but are easily provoked to bite, as are pets. Death usually comes three to five days after symptoms begin. In humans, death can result from a seizure in the early phase. If not treated within a day or two with a serum containing antibodies and then a series of vaccinations, rabies in humans is almost always fatal. Immediate cleansing of animal bites with soap and water can remove much of the virus.

Rabin \rə-ˈbēn\, **Yitzhak** (1922–1995) Israeli statesman. He fought in the Israeli war of independence and became chief of staff in 1964. His strategies helped win the SIX-DAY WAR. After retiring from the army (1968), he served as ambassador to the U.S. (1968–73). As head of Israel's Labour Party, he twice served as prime minister (1974–77, 1992–95). During his first tenure, he secured a cease-fire with Syria and ordered the raid on Entebbe (see ENTEBBE INCIDENT). As defense minister (1984–90), he responded forcefully to the first Palestinian INTIFADA. In 1993 he negotiated a political settlement calling for limited Palestinian self-rule, for which he shared the 1994 Nobel Peace Prize with Shimon PERES and Yasir ARAFAT. He was assassinated by a right-wing Jewish extremist.

raccoon *or* **ringtail** Any member of several species of omnivorous, nocturnal CARNIVORES (genus *Procyon*, family Procyonidae) characterized by a bushy, ringed tail and a black mask. The N. American raccoon (*P. lotor*) has a stout body, short legs, and small erect ears. It is 30–36 in. (75–90 cm) long and has a 10-in. (25-cm) tail, and weighs over 20 lbs (10 kg). The feet resemble slender human hands. Raccoons eat arthropods, rodents, frogs, berries, fruit, and plants; in towns and cities they thrive on garbage. They prefer woods near water. The crab-eating raccoon (*P. cancrivorus*) of S. America is similar.

race Term once commonly used in PHYSICAL ANTHROPOLOGY to denote a division of humankind possessing traits that characterize it as a distinct human type (e.g., Caucasoid, Mongoloid, Negroid). Today the term has little scientific standing, as older methods of differentiation, including hair form and body measurement, have given way to the comparative analysis of DNA and gene frequencies relating to such factors as BLOOD TYPING, the excretion of AMINO ACIDS, and inherited ENZYME deficiencies. Because all human populations are extremely similar genetically, most researchers have abandoned the concept of race for the concept of the cline, a graded series of differences occurring along a line of environmental or geographical transition. This reflects the recognition that human populations have never been stable; genes have constantly flowed from one gene pool to another, impeded only by physical or ecological boundaries, though relative isolation has preserved genetic differences and allowed populations to maximally adapt to climatic and disease factors over long periods of time. "Race" is today primarily a sociological designation, identifying a class sharing some outward physical characteristics and some commonalities of culture and history. See also human CLIMATIC ADAPTATION, RACISM.

racer Any of several slender, swift SNAKES (subspecies of *Coluber constrictor,* family Colubridae) of N. and Central America and Asia. Some grow to 6 ft (1.8 m) long. Among the fastest of snakes, racers can move at 3.5 mph (5.6 kpm). They hold down their prey, usually a small warm-blooded animal, by the weight of their coils and then swallow it. If cornered, they strike repeatedly with a sideways motion that tears a victim's skin.

Rachel In the Book of GENESIS, one of JACOB's two wives. Jacob was forced to serve her father Laban for seven years to win her, but at the end of that time he was tricked into marrying her sister Leah. He was allowed to marry Rachel as well after seven more years of labor. She eventually gave birth to JOSEPH, and she died giving birth to Benjamin.

Rachmaninoff \räk-ˈmä-nə-ˌnȯf\, **Sergei (Vassilievich)** (1873–1943) Russian-U.S. composer and pianist. He studied at the St. Petersburg and Moscow conservatories, writing his first opera, *Aleko* (1892), in 17 days. His first symphony (1897) was such a disaster that he could not compose for three years. Known for his titanic virtuosity as a pianist, he toured widely while returning to composing prolifically. He moved to the U.S. after the 1917 revolution. His works, most of them in a lush late-Romantic style, include three symphonies, four piano concertos, the opera *Francesca da Rimini* (1906), the tone poem *From the Isle of the Dead* (1909), and *Symphonic Dances* (1940).

Racine \rå-ˈsēn\, **Jean (-Baptiste)** (1639–1699) French playwright and master of French classical tragedy. His first play was produced by MOLIÈRE in 1664. Their friendship ended when Racine took his next play, *Alexandre le grand* (1665), to a competing theater and seduced Molière's mistress and leading actress. She starred in Racine's successful *Andromaque* (1667), which explored his theme of the tragic folly of passionate love. His only comedy, *The Litigants* (1668), was followed by his great tragedies *Britannicus* (1669), *Bérénice* (1670), and *Bajazet* (1672). After writing his masterpiece, *Phèdre* (1677), he retired to become

Jean Racine

official historian to LOUIS XIV. His final plays, *Esther* (1689) and *Athalie* (1691), were commissioned by the king's wife, Mme. de MAINTENON.

racism Belief that RACE is the primary determinant of human traits and capacities and that some races are inherently superior to others. More broadly, the term refers to any racial prejudice or discrimination. Racism was prevalent in the era of European COLONIALISM; the British viewed imperialism as a noble activity ("the white man's burden") destined to bring civilization to the benighted races, while the French invoked the notion of the *mission civilisatrice,* their duty to bring civilization to backward peoples. An influential modern proponent was the comte de Gobineau, who held that the so-called ARYAN was the supreme race. Adolf HITLER used this view to justify the persecution of Jews and other non-Aryans. S. African society was built on the principle of APARTHEID, or racial "separateness." Today the general trend is away from racism, though the problem of racist thinking remains intractable.

rack and pinion Mechanical device consisting of a bar of rectangular cross section (the rack), having teeth on one side that mesh with teeth on a small GEAR (the pinion). If the pinion rotates about a fixed axis, the rack will move in a straight path. Some AUTOMOBILE steering mechanisms have rack-and-pinion drives that use this principle. If the rack is fixed and the pinion is carried in bearings on a table guided on tracks parallel to the rack, rotation of the pinion shaft will move the table parallel to the rack.

racketeering See ORGANIZED CRIME

Rackham, Arthur (1867–1939) British artist and illustrator. While a staff artist for a London newspaper, he also began illustrating books. His highly detailed drawings revealed a unique imagination. He achieved renown with a 1900 edition of *Grimm's Fairy Tales*, and his illustrations for *Rip Van Winkle* (1905) brought him recognition in America as well. Altogether he illustrated more than 60 books of classic fiction, poetry, drama, and children's literature.

racquetball Game similar to HANDBALL, played on a four-walled court with a short-handled racquet and a ball larger than that used in handball. The game was invented in 1950 by Joseph G. Sobek (1918–1998). By the late 1990s there were 8.5 million racquetball players in 91 countries.

radar System that uses electromagnetic echoes to detect and locate objects in space. It can also measure the distance to an object and the speed at which the object is moving toward or away from the observing unit. Radar originated in the experimental work of Heinrich HERTZ in the late 1880s. During World War II, British and U.S. researchers developed a high-powered MICROWAVE radar system. Radar is used today in identification and monitoring of satellites in earth orbit, as a navigational aid for airplanes and marine vessels, and for air-traffic control around major airports.

radar astronomy See RADIO AND RADAR ASTRONOMY

Radcliffe, Ann *orig*. Ann Ward (1764–1823) English gothic novelist. She achieved fame with her third novel, *The Romance of the Forest* (1791). With *The Mysteries of Udolpho* (1794), she became the most popular novelist in England. *The Italian* (1797), which displays rare psychological insight, reveals her full powers. In her tales, scenes of terror and suspense are infused with an aura of romantic sensibility.

Radcliffe-Brown, A(lfred) R(eginald) (1881–1955) British social anthropologist. He taught at the Univs. of Cape Town, Sydney, Chicago, and Oxford. In his version of FUNCTIONALISM, the component parts of society (e.g., the kinship system, the legal system) have an indispensable function for one another and are interdependent for their continued existence. He also developed a systematic framework of concepts relating to the social structures of small-scale societies. Such major works as *The Andaman Islanders* (1922) and *Structure and Function in Primitive Society* (1952) had a profound impact on British and American social anthropology.

Radetzky \rä-ˈdet-skē\, **Joseph, Graf (Count)** (1766–1858) Austrian army officer. He fought with distinction against the French in the Napoleonic Wars. As commander in chief of the Austrian army in N Italy (1831–57), he suppressed the revolt in the Austrian-ruled provinces of Lombardy and Venetia in 1848, then served as their governor-general 1849–57. He was regarded by conservatives as a national hero.

Radha \ˈrä-dä\ In Hindu mythology, mistress of the god KRISHNA when he lived among the cowherds of Vrndavana. Though Radha was the wife of another cowherd, she was Krishna's most beloved consort. The allegorical love of

Radha (the human soul) and Krishna (the divine) has been celebrated in the poetry of many Indian languages, and Radha is often worshiped along with Krishna, especially in N and E India.

radiant heating HEATING system in which heat is transmitted by radiation from a heated surface using electric-resistance wiring or hot-water heating pipes embedded in the floor, ceiling, or walls. Panel heating employs very large surfaces (typically an entire ceiling or floor) containing electrical conductors, hot-water pipes, or hot-air ducts. Often there is no visible heating equipment in the room.

radiation Process by which ENERGY is emitted from a source and propagated through the surrounding medium, or the energy involved in this process. Radiation consists of a flow of atomic or subatomic particles or of WAVES. Familiar examples are LIGHT (a form of ELECTROMAGNETIC RADIATION) and SOUND (a form of acoustic radiation), both with a range of frequencies and intensities. Electromagnetic radiation is also often treated as discrete packets of energy, called PHOTONS. All matter is constantly bombarded by radiation from cosmic and terrestrial sources, and radioactive elements emit several types of radiation (see RADIOACTIVITY). See also INFRARED RADIATION, THERMAL RADIATION, ULTRAVIOLET RADIATION.

radiation injury Tissue damage caused by exposure to ionizing RADIATION. Structures with rapid cell turnover (e.g., skin, stomach or intestinal lining, and bone marrow) are most susceptible. High-dose irradiation of the last two causes radiation sickness. Nausea and vomiting subside in a few hours. They are followed in intestinal cases by abdominal pain, fever, and diarrhea leading to dehydration and a fatal shocklike state, and in bone-marrow cases (two to three weeks later) by fever, weakness, hair loss, infection, and hemorrhage. Lower radiation doses can cause cancer (notably LEUKEMIA and BREAST CANCER). Radiation exposure in early pregnancy can produce abnormalities in the EMBRYO.

radiation therapy *or* **radiotherapy** *or* **therapeutic radiology** Use of RADIATION sources to treat or relieve diseases, usually fast-growing CANCER (including LEUKEMIA). However, radiation can also cause cancer (see RADIATION INJURY); other complications include nausea, hair loss, weight loss, and weakness. Radioactive substances may be implanted in tumors (see NUCLEAR MEDICINE). External radiation involves 10–20 sessions either after surgical removal of the growth or when surgery is impossible; it can deliver higher doses to deep tumors than implantation. INFRARED and ULTRAVIOLET RADIATION is applied with lamps to relieve INFLAMMATION.

Radical Republican Member of the REPUBLICAN PARTY in the 1860s committed to emancipation of the slaves and racial justice. Zealous antislavery advocates in Congress pressed Pres. Abraham LINCOLN to include emancipation as a war aim. They later opposed his process of lenient RECONSTRUCTION of the South under presidential control and countered with the harsh WADE-DAVIS BILL. Pres. Andrew JOHNSON's attempt to break the Radicals' power led them to pass the TENURE OF OFFICE ACT; his challenge of the act led to impeachment proceedings. Radical Republican influence waned as white control over Southern governments gradually returned in the 1870s.

Radical-Socialist Party French political party. The oldest of France's political parties, it was founded in 1901 but had its origins in the 1870s when the reformist wing of the French Republican Party, led by Georges CLEMENCEAU, became known as the Radicals. Traditionally a centrist party, it was prominent in the THIRD and FOURTH REPUBLICS. In the 1920s and '30s it joined coalition governments with the FRENCH SOCIALIST PARTY. After 1945 it led other centrist groups in important coalitions.

radio ELECTROMAGNETIC RADIATION of lower frequency (hence longer wavelength) than visible light or INFRARED RADIATION, and consisting of the range of frequencies used for navigation signals, AM and FM broadcasting, TELEVISION transmissions, CELL-PHONE communications, and various forms of RADAR. For radio transmission, information is imparted to a carrier wave by varying (modulating) its amplitude, frequency, or duration. The technology of radio arose from the work of Heinrich HERTZ, Guglielmo MARCONI, and others, and improvement followed the development of the VACUUM TUBE, the electronic-tube OSCILLATOR, and the replacement of tubes by TRANSISTORS and of wires by PRINTED CIRCUITS.

radioactivity Property exhibited by certain types of matter of emitting RADIATION spontaneously. It was first reported in 1896 by Henri BECQUEREL for a URANIUM salt; in 1898 Marie CURIE and her husband discovered two other naturally occurring, strongly radioactive elements, RADIUM and polonium. The radiation is emitted by unstable atomic nuclei (see NUCLEUS) as they attempt to become more stable. The main processes of radioactivity are ALPHA DECAY, BETA DECAY, and gamma decay. In 1934 it was discovered that radioactivity could be induced in ordinary matter by artificial transmutation.

radio and radar astronomy Study of celestial bodies by measuring the radio energy they emit or reflect. It began in 1931 with Karl JANSKY's discovery of radio waves from an extraterrestrial source. After 1945, huge radar-dish antennas and other technological advances let astronomers study fainter sources in greater detail. Radio waves penetrate much of the gas and dust in space, giving a much clearer picture of the Milky Way's center and structure than optical observation can. This has allowed detailed studies of the INTERSTELLAR MEDIUM and the discovery of such objects as PULSARS and QUASARS. In radar astronomy, radio signals are sent to near-earth bodies or phenomena (e.g., meteor trails, the moon, asteroids, nearby planets) and the reflections measured, providing precise data on distance and surface structure. Radar waves can penetrate even dense clouds, allowing the surface mapping of VENUS.

radio broadcasting See BROADCASTING

radiocarbon dating See CARBON-14 DATING

radiology Branch of medicine that uses RADIATION for diagnosis (DIAGNOSTIC IMAGING) and treatment (RADIATION THERAPY) of disease. Originally, it involved X RAYS for diagnosis and GAMMA RAYS, X rays, and other ionizing radiation for treatment. Diagnostic methods now include isotope scanning (see NUCLEAR MEDICINE), use of nonionizing radiation, as in ULTRASOUND and magnetic resonance imaging, and radioimmunoassay. Radiotherapy now includes, in cancer treatment, radioactive hormones and chemotherapeutic drugs.

radio telescope Combination of RADIO receiver and ANTENNA, used for observation in radio astronomy (see RADIO AND RADAR ASTRONOMY). Because some astronomical radio sources are extremely faint on earth, radio telescopes are usually very large, and only the most sensitive radio receivers are used. The first large fully steerable radio telescope was completed in 1957 at Jodrell Bank, England. The world's largest fully steerable radio telescope is the 100-m (328-ft) antenna operated by the Max Planck Institute in Germany. The largest single radio telescope is the 1,000-ft (305-m) fixed spherical reflector at the ARECIBO OBSERVATORY in Puerto Rico. Radio telescopes enabled investigators to discover intense radio emissions from Jupiter and have been used to measure the temperatures of all the planets. See also VERY LARGE ARRAY.

radiotherapy See RADIATION THERAPY

radio wave WAVE from the portion of the ELECTROMAGNETIC SPECTRUM at lower frequencies than INFRARED RADIATION. The wavelengths of radio waves vary from around 1 millimeter to thousands of meters. Radio waves are used in the transmission of communications signals that travel through the air in a straight line or by reflection from the ionosphere, or to and from a communications satellite. They are used in television, navigation, telecommunications, radar, and for many other purposes. See diagram on next page.

radish Annual or biennial plant *(Raphanus sativus)* of the MUSTARD FAMILY, probably of Oriental origin, grown for its large, succulent root. Radishes have a sharp taste and are usually eaten raw. The shape of the edible portion of the root varies greatly, as does the color. Radishes may weigh only a few ounces (U.S. and European varieties) or, in the case of the Japanese daikon, more than 2 lbs (1 kg).

Radishchev \rə-'dyēsh-chif\, **Aleksandr (Nikolayevich)** (1749–1802) Russian political writer. Though a nobleman, he pursued a career as a civil servant. Influenced by such writers as J.-J. ROUSSEAU, he wrote *A Journey from St. Petersburg to Moscow* (1790), in which he described examples of social injustice, hoping to enlighten CATHERINE II. Instead, he was arrested and exiled to Siberia. He inspired later revolutionaries, including those who instigated the DECEMBRIST REVOLT.

radium Chemical ELEMENT, heaviest ALKALINE EARTH METAL, chemical symbol Ra, atomic number 88. It was discovered by Marie and Pierre CURIE in 1898 and isolated by 1910. All its ISOTOPES are radioactive (see RADIOACTIVITY). Radium occurs in ores such as PITCHBLENDE as a product of radioactive decay of heavier elements, including URANIUM. Its use in medicine (see RADIATION THERAPY, RADIOLOGY, NUCLEAR MEDICINE) has declined because of its cost, and its use in consumer goods was halted because it can cause RADIATION INJURY. It is still used for some radiography and as a source of NEUTRONS.

radon \ˈrā-ˌdän\ Chemical ELEMENT, chemical symbol Rn, atomic number 86. The heaviest NOBLE GAS, it is colorless, odorless, tasteless, radioactive (see RADIOACTIVITY), and relatively unreactive (forming compounds only with FLUORINE). It is rare because all its ISOTOPES are short-lived and because RADIUM, its source, is scarce. It seeps from certain soils and rocks (such as granite) into the atmosphere and can accumulate in poorly ventilated spaces, including house basements; using such spaces is now known to increase the risk of LUNG CANCER. Radon is used in radiotherapy, radiography, and in research.

Raeburn, Henry (*later* **Sir Henry**) (1756–1823) Scottish portrait painter. Though apprenticed early to a goldsmith, he lacked formal training as a painter. He worked principally as a miniaturist and evolved a distinctive style of oil por-

traiture, painting directly on the canvas without preliminary drawings. His portraits are characterized by a vigorous handling of paint and vivid and experimental lighting effects, usually from behind the sitters' heads. He was elected president of the Edinburgh Society of Artists in 1812 and knighted in 1822.

Raetia *or* **Rhaetia** \ˈrē-shē-ə\ Ancient Roman province south of the DANUBE RIVER, consisting of parts of present-day Austria, Switzerland, and Germany. Conquered by Rome in 15 B.C., it became important for its position on the highways between Italy and the Danube and between Gaul and the Balkans. Because it was a frontier province, its boundaries shifted when German tribes encroached; in the 1st cent. A.D., the N boundary extended to the NECKAR RIVER, but in the 3rd cent. it was pulled back. By 450, Rome controlled only the alpine regions.

RAF \ˈär-ˈā-ˈef\ *in full* **Royal Air Force** Armed service charged with the air defense of Britain and other defense obligations. It originated in 1911, with one balloon and one airplane company. In 1918 the naval and military wings of the British air forces were merged into the RAF. An RAF cadet college was established in 1920, and an RAF staff college in 1922. At the outbreak of World War II, the RAF's first-line strength was about 2,000 aircraft. RAF fighter pilots distinguished themselves in the Battle of BRITAIN against the numerically superior German Luftwaffe.

Raffles, (Thomas) Stamford (*later* **Sir Stamford**) (1781–1826) British colonial administrator and founder of Singapore. He joined the British E. INDIA CO. at 14, and his hard work won him an appointment at 23 to the government of Penang (in present-day Malaysia). There he undertook an intensive study of the Malayan peoples, and his knowledge allowed him to play a key role in the British defeat of Dutch-French forces in Java, where he became lieutenant governor in 1811. He inaugurated a mass of reforms aimed at transforming the Dutch colonial system and improving the condition of the native population. He was recalled by the company (1816), which deemed his reforms too costly; though he was popular in London and was knighted, his authority when he resumed his Eastern service was severely restricted. Undeterred, he went on to found the port city of Singapore in 1819 to ensure British access to the China seas. Raffles is credited with the creation of Britain's Far Eastern empire.

raga In classical Indian music, a principle akin to MODE. A raga can be regarded as a vocabulary of melodic figures that tend, as a group, to emphasize certain tones of a scale, giving the raga a specific emotional character and implying the kind of music to be improvised. The emphasis on certain pitches effectively divides the scale into primary and secondary tones; the secondary tones serve to ornament the primary tones. Each scale can have several different ragas, depending on which of its tones are made primary. The division of tones between primary and secondary is not always hard and fast, and a tertiary level (ornaments of the ornaments) is often available.

Ragae See RHAGAE

Raglan (of Raglan), Baron *orig.* FitzRoy James Henry Somerset (1788–1855) English army officer. Military secretary to the duke of WELLINGTON, he was appointed commander in chief of British forces in the CRIMEAN WAR (1854). He gave an ambiguous order in the Battle of BALAKLAVA that led to the disastrous charge of the Light Cavalry Brigade, and became the scapegoat for the campaign's lack of progress and the inadequate supplies to the troops in the winter of 1854–55. The raglan sleeve was probably designed to adapt his coat to the arm he had amputated after the Battle of WATERLOO.

Ragnarok \ˈräg-nə-ˌrœk, ˈräg-nə-ˌräk\ In Scandinavian mythology, the end of the divine and human worlds. As described in the 10th-cent. Icelandic poem *Völuspá* and other sources, giants and demons will attack the gods, the sun will be darkened, the stars will vanish, and the earth will sink into the sea. Afterward the earth will rise again, the innocent will return from the dead, and the just will live in a hall roofed with gold.

ragtime U.S. popular music of the late 19th and early 20th cent. distinguished by its heavily syncopated rhythm. Rag-

Radio wave Radio waves lie at the low-frequency end of the electromagnetic spectrum. They are primarily used in various types of communications signals. Also of importance is the detection of natural radio sources in radio and radar astronomy. A few applications are shown at their approximate positions in the spectrum (on a logarithmic scale). Microwaves are a subset of the radio spectrum, ranging from about 1 to 1000 mm in wavelength, or a frequency between about 1 and 100 GHz. The microwave region is used especially in various forms of radar, in communications with spacecraft and satellites (as in the Global Positioning System), and in microwave ovens. Amateur communications, such as CB (citizens' band) and shortwave radio occur around 10 MHz. Marine navigation and communications systems operate especially below 1 MHz. Other devices or systems using radio waves include metal detectors, loran, and magnetic resonance imaging.

Chart labels (top to bottom): 100 GHz; radar — 10 GHz; microwave satellites — 1 GHz; cell phones; TV; FM radio; TV — 100 MHz; CB radio — 10 MHz; AM radio — 1 MHz; marine — 100 kHz; — 10 kHz

time music usually took the form of piano pieces, in which the accented left-hand beat was opposed in the right hand by a fast, bouncing melody that gave the music its powerful forward impetus. They typically featured three or four discrete 16-bar strains performed at a moderate tempo. The most celebrated ragtime composer was Scott JOPLIN. Ragtime's rhythm and structure were important influences on the development of JAZZ.

ragweed Any of about 15 species of weedy plants (see WEED) that make up the genus *Ambrosia* in the COMPOSITE FAMILY, most of which are native to N. America. They have rough hairy stems, mostly lobed or divided leaves, and inconspicuous greenish flowers. Common ragweed *(A. artemisiifolia)* is found across N. America. POLLEN shed by ragweeds in great abundance in late summer is the principal cause of HAY FEVER in E and middle N. America.

rail Any of about 100 species (family Rallidae) of slender marsh birds. Rails have short rounded wings, a short tail, large feet, and long toes. Their loud call, especially at night, reveals their presence in dense vegetation. Species vary from 4 to 18 in. (11–45 cm) long. Short-billed species are often called crakes. The king *(Rallus elegans),* clapper *(R. longirostris),* and Virginia *(R. limicola)* rails and the sora, or Carolina rail *(Porzana carolina),* have been hunted in the U.S.; several are now endangered or extinct.

railroad Mode of land transportation in which flange-wheeled vehicles move over two parallel steel rails or tracks, drawn by a LOCOMOTIVE or propelled by self-contained motors. The earliest railroads were built in European mines in the 16th cent., using cars pulled on tracks by men or horses. With the advent of the steam locomotive and construction of the first railway in 1825, the modern railroad developed quickly. The first U.S. railroad, the Baltimore and Ohio, began operation in 1827. Specialized railroad cars were built to transport freight and passengers, including the sleeping cars developed by George PULLMAN. In the U.S. the transcontinental railroad, completed in 1869, began an era of railroad expansion and consolidation that involved such financial empire builders as Cornelius VANDERBILT, Jay GOULD, Edward HARRIMAN, and Leland STANFORD. The railroad's importance in the U.S. began to diminish from the early 20th cent., but in Europe, Asia, and Africa it continues to provide vital transportation links.

rain PRECIPITATION of liquid water drops with diameters greater than 0.02 in. (0.5 mm). Smaller drops are usually called drizzle. Raindrops may form by the coalescence of colliding small water droplets or from the melting of snowflakes and other ice particles as they fall into warm air near the ground. Hawaii's Mt. Waialeale, with an annual average of 460 in. (11,700 mm), is the earth's wettest point. Less than 10 in. (250 mm) and more than 60 in. (1,500 mm) per year represent approximate extremes of rainfall for all the continents.

rainbow Series of concentric colored arcs that may be seen when light from the sun falls on a collection of water drops such as in rain, spray, or fog. The colored rays of the rainbow are caused by the REFRACTION and internal REFLECTION of light rays that enter the drop, each color being bent through a slightly different angle. Hence, the combined colors are separated upon emerging from the drop. The most brilliant and most common rainbow results from light that emerges after one internal reflection. The colors of the arc (from outside to inside) are red, orange, yellow, green, blue, indigo, and violet. Occasionally a less-intense secondary bow may be observed; it has its color sequence reversed.

rain dance Ceremonial dance performed to bring rain needed to water crops. Rain dances have been customary in many cultures, from the ancient Egyptians and MAYAS to the peoples of the 20th-cent. Balkans. Rain dances often include dancing in a circle, the participation of young girls, decoration with green vegetation, nudity, the pouring of water, and whirling.

Rainey, Ma *orig.* Gertrude Malissa Nix Pridgett (1886–1939) U.S. singer. Born in Columbus, Ga., Rainey began touring southern tent shows, levee camps, and cabarets at 17 in a song-and-dance team with her husband. She performed through the 1920s, leading her own troupes. An earthy stage presence, known for her flamboyant dress, Rainey recorded

more than 90 songs (including "See See Rider" and "Ma Rainey's Black Bottom") from 1923 to 1928. The first great professional blues vocalist, she earned the sobriquet "Mother of the Blues."

rain forest Lush FOREST, generally composed of tall, broad-leaved trees and usually found in wet tropical regions around the equator, mainly in S. and Central America, W. and Central Africa, Indonesia, parts of S.E. Asia, and tropical Australia. Depending on the amount of annual rainfall, the trees may be evergreens or mainly deciduous. The former require more water. Temperatures remain high, usually about 85°F (30°C) during the day and 70°F (20°C) at night. Most rain-forest soils tend to be permanently moist and not very fertile, because the hot, humid weather causes organic matter to decompose rapidly and to be absorbed quickly by tree roots and fungi. Rain forests have many vertical layers of plant and animal development. The highest plant layer, the tree canopy, extends to heights of 100–160 ft (30–50 m). The next-highest layer is filled with small trees, LIANAS, and EPIPHYTES. Above the ground surface the space is occupied by tree branches, twigs, and foliage. Many species of animals live in the undergrowth. The rain forest floor is bare except for a thin layer of HUMUS and fallen leaves. Animals inhabiting this layer (e.g., rhinoceroses, gorillas, elephants, leopards, and bears) are adapted to walking and climbing short distances. Burrowing animals are found below the soil surface, as are microorganisms that help decompose and free much of the organic litter accumulated by other plants and animals from all layers. The climate of the ground layer is unusually stable because the upper stories of tree canopies and the lower branches filter sunlight and heat radiation and reduce wind speeds, keeping the temperatures fairly even.

Rainier \rə-'nir\, **Mt.** Mountain, Washington state, southeast of TACOMA. At 14,410 ft (4,392 m), it is the highest point in the CASCADE RANGE and in the state. It covers 100 sq mi (260 sq km) and is surrounded by the largest single-mountain glacier system in the U.S. outside Alaska, with 41 glaciers radiating from the summit. A dormant volcano that last erupted 2,000 years ago, it is the major part of the popular Mt. Rainier National Park.

Rainier III \ren-'yā, *Engl* rā-'nir\ *orig.* Rainier-Louis-Henri-Maxence-Bertrand de Grimaldi (b.1923) Prince of Monaco (from 1949), 31st in a line of hereditary rulers. He expanded and diversified Monaco's enterprises, expanded the national territory by one-fifth through land retrieval from the seas, and promulgated a new constitution, blending modern principles with tradition. His wedding to Grace KELLY in 1956 attracted worldwide attention.

Rainy Lake Narrow lake astride the Canadian–U.S. border, between Minnesota and SW Ontario. It is about 50 mi (80 km) long. Its shores are irregular, and it contains more than 500 islands. The region is the site of several Indian reservations and, though extremely cold in winter, is popular for hunting, fishing, and canoeing.

Rajneesh \'rəj-ˌnēsh, räj-'nēsh\, **Bhagwan Shree** *orig.* Chandra Mohan Jain (1931–1990) Indian spiritual leader. A teacher of philosophy, he lectured throughout India and established an ashram in Pune (Poona). He preached an eclectic doctrine of Eastern mysticism, individual devotion, and a notorious sexual freedom while amassing vast personal wealth. By the early 1970s he had attracted 200,000 devotees. He was deported from the U.S. for immigration fraud in 1985, and spent his last years in Pune.

Rajputana \ˌräj-pə-'tä-nə\ Region of NW India that now includes Rajasthan state and small sections of Madhya Pradesh and Gujarat. The NW part is largely the Thar Desert, but the southeast is very fertile. The Rajput states came under British protection by treaties in 1818; most of the area was formed into Rajasthan state in 1948.

Rajputs \'räj-ˌpu̇ts\ Caste of landowners located mainly in central and N India, numbering about 12 million. The Rajputs regard themselves as descendants or members of the Kshattriya (warrior ruling) class, though in fact they vary greatly in status. After the fall of the GUPTA DYNASTY, invaders and indigenous peoples in NW India were probably integrated, the leaders in both groups becoming Kshattriyas. In the 9th–10th cent. the Rajputs became important politically, and for centuries they prevented complete Muslim domination of Hindu India. See also RAJPUTANA.

Raleigh \ˈrȯ-lē, ˈrä-lē\ City (pop., 2000: 276,000), capital of N. Carolina. It was selected as the state capital in 1788. Manufactures include textiles, electronic equipment, and processed foods. An educational center, it is part of N. Carolina's Research Triangle, along with Durham and Chapel Hill, an area of cultural, scientific, and educational institutions, including DUKE UNIV. and the Univ. of N. CAROLINA.

Raleigh, Walter (*later* **Sir Walter**) (1554?–1618) English adventurer. He joined his half-brother Humphrey GILBERT on a piratical expedition against the Spanish (1578), then fought against the Irish rebels in Munster (1580). He caught the attention of ELIZABETH I, who made him her favorite at court. In 1584 he sent an expedition to explore the coast north of Florida, and to establish an unsuccessful colony at ROANOKE ISLAND. Out of favor at court from about 1592, he led an unsuccessful expedition up the Orinoco River in search of gold. When Elizabeth died (1603), he was accused of plotting to depose JAMES I

Sir Walter Raleigh Engraving by Simon Pass, 1614

and imprisoned. Released in 1616, he led another unsuccessful expedition to search for gold in Guyana. When his men burned a Spanish settlement, he was rearrested and executed, at the demand of the Spanish ambassador.

RAM \ˈram\ *in full* **random-access memory** Computer main MEMORY whose contents can be accessed (read or written) directly by the CPU in a very short time regardless of the sequence in which they were recorded. Two types of memory are possible with random-access circuits, static RAM (SRAM) and dynamic RAM (DRAM). A single memory chip is made up of several million memory cells. In a SRAM chip, each memory cell stores a binary digit (1 or 0) for as long as power is supplied. In a DRAM chip, the charge on cells must be refreshed periodically in order to retain data. Because it has fewer components, DRAM requires less chip area than SRAM; hence a DRAM chip can hold more memory, though its access time is slower.

Rama Major Hindu deity. The name became associated with Ramacandra, the seventh incarnation of VISHNU, whose story is told in the *RAMAYANA*. Conceived as a model of reason, virtue, and right action, Rama was one of the chief objects of the BHAKTI cults. In temples his image is attended by the figures of his wife, SITA; his half-brother, Laksmana; and the monkey general, HANUMAN.

Rama IV See MONGKUT

Rama VI See VAJIRAVUDH

Ramadan \ra-mä-ˈdän\ In ISLAM, a holy month of fasting, the ninth month of the Muslim year, commemorating the revelation of the QURAN to MUHAMMAD. Muslims are required to fast and abstain from sexual activity during daylight hours. Because Islam uses a lunar calendar, Ramadan can fall in any season of the year. The Ramadan fast is considered one of the Five Pillars of ISLAM.

Ramakrishna (Paramahamsa) *orig.* Gadadhar Chatopadhyaya (1836–1886) Indian mystic. Born into a poor Brahman family, he worked as a priest in Calcutta, where he had a vision and commenced spiritual practices in a number of religious tradi-

Ramakrishna, c.1881

tions. He denounced sexual desire and money as the twin evils that put spiritual enlightenment beyond reach, rejected the caste system, and held that all religions are in essence the same and that all are true. A religious order bearing his name sends missionaries throughout the world.

Ramanuja \rä-ˈmä-nu̇-jə\ (1017?–1137) Indian theologian and philosopher, the most influential thinker of devotional HINDUISM. After a long pilgrimage through India, he founded centers to spread devotion to VISHNU and LAKSHMI. He provided an intellectual basis for the practice of BHAKTI in major commentaries on Hindu religious texts. His chief philosophical contributions follow from his conviction that the phenomenal world is real and provides real knowledge, and that the exigencies of daily life are not contrary to the life of the spirit.

Ramayana \rä-ˈmä-yə-nə\ Indian epic poem, composed in Sanskrit around 300 B.C. With the *MAHABHARATA,* it is one of the two great epic poems of India. Consisting of 24,000 couplets in seven books, it describes the royal birth of RAMA and the loss of his throne. He is banished to the forest with his wife, SITA, and his half-brother, Laksmana. When a demon king carries off Sita, HANUMAN, the monkey general, helps Rana rescue her. Rama regains his kingdom, but Sita is banished when her chastity is questioned, although she proves her innocence.

Rambert \räm-ˈber\ **Marie** (*later* **Dame Marie**) *orig.* Cyvia Rambam (1888–1982) Polish-English ballet producer and director. She studied with Émile Jaques-Dalcroze, and taught eurythmics to the BALLETS RUSSES, where it influenced Vaslav NIJINSKY's avant-garde choreography. She founded a ballet school in 1920, and established the Ballet Club (later Ballet Rambert) in 1935. By encouraging new choreographers such as Frederick ASHTON and supporting young dancers, she helped foster the rise of English ballet. Her troupe, renamed the Rambert Dance Co., has continued to perform.

Rameau \ra-ˈmō\ **Jean-Philippe** (1683–1764) French composer and music theorist. He held organist posts until he was 49. From 1733 he wrote a series of highly successful operas, including *Hippolyte et Aricie* (1733), assuring his place as the most important French opera composer since J.-B. LULLY. The *querelles des bouffons* (1752–53), a famous artistic controversy over French and Italian opera, was settled in favor of the French style by Rameau's music. He also won renown for his many harpsichord pieces. His highly influential *Treatise on Harmony* (1722) asserted that harmony is the basis of music, and that chords, then understood principally as collections of intervals above a bass, should instead be seen as representing inversions of more fundamental harmonic entities.

ramjet Air-breathing JET ENGINE that operates with no major moving parts. It relies on the craft's forward motion (optimally at more than twice the speed of sound) to draw in air and on a specially shaped intake passage to compress the air for combustion. After fuel sprayed into the engine has been ignited, combustion is self-sustaining.

rammed earth *or* **pisé de terre** \ˌpē-ˌzā-də-ˈter\ Building material made by compacting and drying a stiff mixture of clay, sand or other aggregate, and water. The most durable of the earth-building forms, it is formed into building blocks (see ADOBE) or rammed within removable wooden forms in layers or lifts to construct walls. China's Erligang (c.1600 B.C.), a rammed-earth fortification, covers 1.2 sq mi (3.2 sq km) and may have taken 10,000 people more than 12 years to build.

Rampal \räm-ˈpäl\ **Jean-Pierre (Louis)** (1922–2000) French flutist. From 1947 he appeared widely in chamber music and solo recitals, and in the 1950s he founded his own chamber groups. His sweetness of tone and virtuosity in a largely baroque repertoire, as evidenced on a great many admired recordings, made him the first flutist to attain major international stardom.

Ramses II \ˈram-ˌsēz\ *known as* **Ramses the Great** (d.1213 B.C.) King of ancient Egypt, 1279–1213 B.C. His family came to power decades after AKHENATON. He set about restoring Egypt's power, subduing rebellion in S Syria and fighting the HITTITES. He captured towns in Galilee and Amor, but, unable to defeat the Hittites, he assented to a

peace treaty in 1258 B.C., marrying one and perhaps two of the Hittite king's daughters. Early on he built himself a residence city in the Nile delta as a base for military campaigns and resumed construction of the temple of Osiris. He added to the temple at KARNAK and completed a funerary temple for his father at LUXOR. In Nubia he built six temples, most famously those at ABU SIMBEL.

Ramses III (d.1156 B.C.) King of ancient Egypt, 1187–1156 B.C. Son of Setnakht, the founder of Egypt's 20th dynasty, he fought off Libyan invaders in the fifth year of his reign and the SEA PEOPLES two years later, eventually achieving a lasting peace. He then reorganized society into classes grouped by occupation and resumed temple building. He encouraged trade and industry, and the nation prospered. A delay in sending monthly rations to temple builders in Thebes around 1158 B.C. resulted in the first recorded labor dispute.

Rand, Ayn *orig.* Alissa Rosenbaum (1905–1982) Russian-U.S. writer. She emigrated to the U.S. in 1926 and worked as a screenwriter. She won a cult following with two best-selling novels presenting her belief that all real achievement comes from individual ability and effort, that laissez-faire capitalism is most congenial to the exercise of talent, and that selfishness is a virtue, altruism a vice. In *The Fountainhead* (1943), a superior individual transcends traditionalism and conformism. *Atlas Shrugged* (1957) combines science fiction and a political message. She expounded her "objectivist" philosophy in nonfiction works and as editor of two journals, and became an icon of radical libertarianism.

Randolph, A(sa) Philip (1889–1979) U.S. civil rights leader. Born in Crescent City, Fla., he moved to New York in 1911. In 1917 he cofounded the journal *The Messenger* (later *Black Worker*) and called for more positions for blacks in the war industry and the armed forces. He founded the Brotherhood of Sleeping Car Porters, the first successful black trade union, in 1925, and remained its president until 1968. In 1941 he lobbied Pres. Franklin ROOSEVELT to ban discrimination in defense industries and federal bureaus. In 1948 he influenced Pres. Harry TRUMAN to bar segregation in the armed forces. In 1955 he was made a vice president of the new AFL-CIO, and in 1960 he helped form the Negro American Labor Council to fight discrimination within the AFL-CIO.

Randolph, Edmund Jennings (1753–1813) U.S. politician. Born in Williamsburg, Va., he helped draft the state's constitution (1776), and served in the Continental Congress 1779–82. As a delegate to the CONSTITUTIONAL CONVENTION, he presented the Virginia Plan that influenced the final draft of the U.S. Constitution. As governor of Virginia (1786–88), he effected the state's ratification of the Constitution. He served as U.S. attorney general (1789–94) and secretary of state (1794–95). He served as chief counsel for Aaron BURR in his 1807 trial.

random-access memory See RAM

Random House U.S. publishing company. It was founded by Bennett CERF and Donald S. Klopfer in 1925. As it grew it published many successful and prestigious writers and gathered under its corporate roof many other firms, including Alfred A. Knopf (acquired 1960), Pantheon Books (1961), Ballantine (1973), and Crown (1988). In 1998 it became a part of one of the world's largest media companies, Bertelsmann AG.

range finder Instrument used to measure the distance from the instrument to a selected point or object. The optical range finder, used chiefly in CAMERAS, consists of an arrangement of LENSES and PRISMS set at each end of a tube. The object's range is determined by measuring the angles formed by a line of sight at each end of the tube; the smaller the angles, the greater the distance, and vice versa. Since the mid-1940s, radar has replaced optical range finders for most military targeting, and the laser range finder (1965) has largely replaced optical range finders for SURVEYING.

Rangoon See YANGON

Ranjit Singh \'rən-jit-'siⁿ-hə\ (1780–1839) Founder of the Sikh kingdom of the PUNJAB. He became chief of the Shukerchakias (a Sikh group) on the death of his father in 1792. In 1799 he seized Lahore and in 1801 he proclaimed himself maharaja of the Punjab. In 1802 he captured Amritsar, a city sacred to the Sikhs, and by 1820 he had consolidated his rule over the whole Punjab. The Sikh state he created, with Sikhs, Muslims, and Hindus in both the army and the cabinet, collapsed soon after his death. See also SIKHISM, SIKH WARS.

Ranke \'rän-kə\, **Leopold von** *orig.* Leopold Ranke (1795–1886) German historian. Teaching at the Univ. of Berlin (1825–71), he championed objective writing based on textual criticism of source materials. His scholarly technique and way of teaching (he was the first to establish a historical seminar) had great influence on Western historiography. His many works typically are subtle accounts of particular limited periods in European political history that take comparatively little notice of social and economic forces.

Rankin, Jeannette (1880–1973) U.S. reformer, first woman member of the U.S. Congress (1917–19, 1941–43). Born in Missoula, Mont., she became active in women's-suffrage work. Elected to the U.S. House of Representatives in 1916, she introduced the first bill to give women independent citizenship. A pacifist, she voted against declaring war on Germany (1917). Reelected in 1940, she became the only legislator to vote against declaration of war on Japan. Declining to seek reelection, she continued to lecture on social reform. In 1968, at 87, she led 5,000 women, the "Jeannette Rankin Brigade," to protest the Vietnam War.

Rankine \'raŋ-kən\, **William J(ohn) M(acquorn)** (1820–1872) Scottish engineer and physicist, one of the founders of THERMODYNAMICS. His classic *Manual of the Steam Engine and Other Prime Movers* (1859) was the first attempt at a systematic treatment of the theory of STEAM ENGINES. He worked out a thermodynamic cycle of events (the Rankine cycle) that was used as a standard for the performance of steam-power installations in which a condensable vapor provides the working fluid.

Ransom, John Crowe (1888–1974) U.S. poet and critic. Born in Pulaski, Tenn., at Vanderbilt Univ. he became the leader of the Fugitives, a group of poets who shared a belief in the South and its regional traditions and published the influential journal *The Fugitive* (1922–25). At Kenyon College, he founded and edited (1939–59) the *Kenyon Review*. His literary studies include *The New Criticism* (1941), which gave its name to an important critical movement (see NEW CRITICISM). His *Selected Poems* (1945; rev. ed., 1969) won the National Book Award.

rap Musical style in which rhymed verse is chanted ("rapped") to a musical accompaniment, whose primary element is usually beats. Rap, which first appeared in New York's black and Latino neighborhoods, came to prominence with the Sugar Hill Gang's "Rapper's Delight" (1979), which featured light verse rhymed over the bass and beats of Chic's disco hit "Good Times." In the early 1980s the breakdance fad fueled rap's growth; stars included Kurtis Blow, Run-DMC, LL Cool J, and Public Enemy. The late 1980s saw the advent of "gangsta rap," with misogynistic lyrics glamorizing violence and drug dealing. Having gained a huge white audience, rap has continued to thrive and evolve.

Rapa Nui See EASTER ISLAND

rape Annual plant (*Brassica napus*) of the MUSTARD FAMILY, native to Europe. This 1-ft-tall (30-cm) plant has a long, thin taproot; smooth, bluish-green, deeply scalloped leaves; and clusters of yellow flowers. Each round, elongated seedpod has a short beak and contains many seeds. The seeds yield an oil (rapeseed oil, or canola) that is the lowest in saturated fat of any edible oil, making it popular for use in cooking.

rape Unlawful sexual activity, usually sexual intercourse, carried out forcibly or under threat of injury and against the will of the victim. Though traditionally limited to attacks on women by men, in recent years the definition of rape has been broadened to cover same-sex attacks and attacks against those who, because of mental illness, intoxication, or other reasons, are incapable of valid consent. Statutory rape, or intercourse with a person younger than a certain age (from 14 to 18 years), has long been a serious crime in most jurisdictions. Rape is generally considered an expression of anger or aggression and a pathological assertion of power by the rapist. Many rape victims fail to report the crime, deterred by the prospect of a distressing cross-examination in court and the difficulty in proving a crime for which there usually are no witnesses.

Raphael In the BIBLE and the QURAN, one of the archangels. In the apocryphal *Book of Tobit* he appears in human disguise and conquers the demon Asmodeus. His name in Hebrew means "God has healed," and in Tobit his business is to heal the earth. Raphael is reckoned among the saints in both Eastern and Western churches.

Raphael \'ra-fē-əl, 'rä-fē-əl\ *orig.* Raffaello Sanzio (1483–1520) Italian painter and architect. As a member of PERUGINO's workshop, he established his mastery by 17. In 1504 he moved to Florence, where he executed many of his famous Madonnas, including *The Madonna of the Goldfinch* (c.1506). Though influenced by LEONARDO DA VINCI, his figure types were his own creation, with round, gentle faces that reveal human sentiments raised to a sublime serenity. In 1508 he was summoned to Rome to decorate a suite of papal chambers in the Vatican. The frescoes in the Stanza della Segnatura are probably his greatest work; the most famous, *The School of Athens* (1510–11), is a complex and magnificently ordered allegory of secular knowledge showing Greek philosophers in an architectural setting. The Madonnas he painted in Rome emphasize movement and grandeur, partly under MICHELANGELO's influence. The *Sistine Madonna* (1513) shows the richness of color and new boldness of compositional invention typical of his Roman period. He became the most important portraitist in Rome, designed 10 large tapestries to hang in the SISTINE CHAPEL, assumed the direction of work on ST. PETER'S BASILICA at the death of Donato BRAMANTE, and took charge of virtually all the papacy's projects in architecture, painting, and the preservation of antiquities. When he died on his 37th birthday, his last masterpiece, the *Transfiguration* altarpiece, was placed at the head of his bier.

raptures of the deep See NITROGEN NARCOSIS

rare earth metal Any of a large class of chemical ELEMENTS including scandium (atomic number 21), yttrium (39), and the 15 elements from 57 (lanthanum) to 71 (see LANTHANIDES). The rare earths themselves are pure or mixed OXIDES of these METALS, originally thought to be quite scarce; CERIUM is the most plentiful. The metals never occur free. These metals are similar chemically because their atomic structures are generally similar; all form compounds of VALENCE 3.

Rask \'räsk\, **Rasmus (Kristian)** (1787–1832) Danish linguist. A scholar of INDO-EUROPEAN LANGUAGES, he was a principal founder of the science of comparative LINGUISTICS. His observation that sound shifts between corresponding words in Indo-European languages followed predictable patterns was the basis of a fundamental law of linguistics later enunciated by Jacob GRIMM (Grimm's law). Rask also carried out extensive research on Old Norse. By the end of his life he had mastered 25 languages and dialects.

raspberry Any of many species of fruit-bearing bushes of the genus *Rubus* in the ROSE family. When picked, the juicy red, purple, or black berry separates from its core. Red raspberries are propagated by suckers from the roots of the parent plant or from root cuttings. Raspberries contain iron and vitamin C. They are eaten fresh and are also very popular in jams, as a pastry filling, and as a flavoring for liqueurs.

Rasputin \ra-'spyü-t°n\, **Grigory (Yefimovich)** *orig.* Grigory (Yefimovich) Novykh (1872?–1916) Russian mystic influential at the court of Czar NICHOLAS II and ALEXANDRA. An illiterate peasant, he earned the name *rasputin* ("debauched one") for his early licentious behavior. After undergoing a religious experience, he gained a reputation as a holy man, able to heal the sick. He became

Grigory Rasputin

known to Nicholas and the susceptible Alexandra, and proved capable of stopping the bleeding of their hemophiliac son, probably by hypnotism. He became a favorite at court, despite his flagrant debauchery. When Nicholas left Alexandra in charge of Russia's internal affairs in 1915, Rasputin influenced her appointment of incompetent cabinet ministers. Alarmed by Russia's drift toward disaster, a group of noblemen assassinated him by poisoning him, shooting him, and finally throwing him into the ice-filled Neva River. The RUSSIAN REVOLUTION OF 1917 followed weeks later.

Rastafarian \ˌras-tə-'fer-ē-ən\ Member of a political and religious movement among blacks especially in Jamaica. Rastafarians worship HAILE SELASSIE as the MESSIAH. They believe that blacks are the Israelites reincarnated, who have suffered at the hands of the white race in punishment for their sins; they will eventually be redeemed by repatriation to Africa and will compel the whites to serve them. These beliefs, first enunciated in 1953, can be traced to several independent prophets, particularly Marcus GARVEY. Ideas of repatriation have tended to give way to either black militancy or mysticism. The Rastafarian life usually includes vegetarianism, the wearing of dreadlocks, and the smoking of marijuana.

Rastenburg Assassination Plot See JULY PLOT

rat Any of more than 500 forms of RODENT (genus *Rattus,* family Muridae). The black rat (*Rattus rattus*) and the Norway rat (*R. norvegicus*) are the aggressive, omnivorous animals commonly associated with the name. They prefer areas of human habitation, where they can easily find food. They have keen senses and can climb, jump, burrow, or gnaw their way into seemingly inaccessible places. They reproduce extremely rapidly (up to 150 offspring a year) and have few natural predators. Rats transmit numerous human diseases and have often destroyed grain supplies. The black rat is about 8 in. (20 cm) long, excluding the slightly longer tail. Laboratory rats are strains of the Norway rat (also called the brown, barn, sewer, or wharf rat).

ratchet Mechanical device that transmits intermittent MOTION or permits a shaft to rotate in only one direction. Reversible ratchets are used on socket WRENCH handles and are convenient for tightening or loosening bolts in positions where a complete revolution of a wrench handle is impossible. They are used in mechanical jacks to lock the jack rod after each successive lift.

Rathbone, Basil (1892–1967) British actor. He made his stage debut in 1911; from 1924 he appeared in Hollywood movies, often in romantic roles. With his distinctive voice and gaunt appearance, he was cast as a villain in several swashbuckling movies. He won praise in *Romeo and Juliet* (1936) and *If I Were King* (1938), but became best known for portraying Sherlock Holmes in a series of films that began with *The Hound of the Baskervilles* (1939).

ratio Quotient of two values. The ratio of *a* to *b* can be written *a:b* or as the fraction *a/b*. Ratios arise whenever comparisons are made. They are usually reduced to lowest terms for simplicity. Thus, a school with 1,000 students and 50 teachers has a student/teacher ratio of 20 to 1. When two ratios are set equal to each other, the resulting equation is called a PROPORTION. See also GOLDEN RATIO.

rationalism Philosophical view that regards reason as the chief source and test of knowledge. Long the rival of EMPIRICISM, the doctrine that all knowledge ultimately comes from sense experience, rationalism holds reason to be a faculty that can lay hold of truths beyond the reach of sense perception. In stressing the existence of a "natural light," rationalism has also been the rival of systems claiming esoteric knowledge, and has opposed approaches that stress the biological, volitional, unconscious, or existential at the expense of the rational.

rational number Any number that can be represented as the quotient of two INTEGERS (i.e., the denominator cannot equal zero). The set of rational numbers includes all integers as well as all FRACTIONS. In decimal form, rational numbers are either terminating or repeating decimals.

rationing Government allocation of scarce resources and consumer goods, usually adopted during wars, famines, or other national emergencies. Rationing by use prohibits the

less important uses of a commodity (e.g., the use of gasoline for pleasure trips). Rationing by quantity limits the amounts of a commodity available to each claimant (e.g., a pound of butter per month). Rationing by value limits the amount of money consumers can spend on commodities that are difficult to standardize (e.g., clothing). Point rationing assigns a point value to each commodity and allocates a certain number of points to each consumer. These can be tracked through coupons, which are issued to consumers and must be exchanged for the approved amounts of rationed goods.

ratite \\'ra-ˌtīt\\ Any bird species that cannot fly because its smooth, or raftlike, sternum (breastbone) lacks a keel to which flight muscles can be anchored. The group includes some of the largest birds of all time. Two extinct types, the slow-moving, heavy-bodied elephant bird of Madagascar and the MOA of New Zealand, grew to 10 ft (3 m) tall. Extant ratites include the CASSOWARY, EMU, KIWI, OSTRICH, and RHEA.

Rattigan, Terence (Mervyn) (*later* **Sir Terence**) (1911–1977) British playwright. After writing two successful comedies, he won acclaim for the drama *The Winslow Boy* (1946; film, 1948). His best-known work, *Separate Tables* (1955; film, 1958), explored the isolation created by rigidly imposed social conventions. His other plays included *The Browning Version* (1948), *Ross* (1960), and *A Bequest to the Nation* (1970). He also wrote many screenplays.

rattlesnake Any of about 30 species in two genera of New World pit vipers having a tail rattle that produces a buzzing sound when vibrated. The rattle is composed of horny, loosely connected segments added one at a time with each molt. Species range from 1 to 8 ft (30–250 cm) long. Most eat small animals. All bear live young. In hot areas rattlesnakes become nocturnal; in cold areas they hibernate in groups. Heat-sensitive organs on the sides of the head help them locate and strike their prey. A rattlesnake bite, though painful, is not fatal if treated. See also SIDEWINDER.

Rauschenberg \\'rau̇-shən-ˌberg\\, **Robert** (*orig.* Milton) (b.1925) U.S. painter and graphic artist. Born in Port Arthur, Tex., he studied under Josef ALBERS. His "combine" paintings of the 1950s, incorporating such objects as soda bottles, traffic barricades, and stuffed birds, anticipated the Pop art movement. In later work, he used silkscreen and other techniques to transfer images from the commercial print media and his own photographs to canvas, reinforcing and unifying the images with bold strokes of paint.

Ravana \\'rä-və-nə\\ In Hinduism, king of the demons. Ravana had 10 heads and 20 arms. He ruled in the kingdom of Lanka. His abduction of SITA and defeat by her husband, RAMA, are the central events of the epic *RAMAYANA*. The demon king is also remembered for shaking Mt. Kailasa until SHIVA intervened and imprisoned him beneath it for 1,000 years.

Ravel \\rȧ-'vel\\, **(Joseph) Maurice** (1875–1937) French composer. At 14 he entered the Paris Conservatoire, where he studied with Gabriel FAURÉ, writing the important piano piece *Jeux d'eau* and a string quartet. In the next decade he produced some of his best-known music, including *Gaspard de la nuit* for piano (1908) and *Rapsodie espagnole* (1908). Later works include the ballet *Daphnis et Chloé* (1912), the operas *L'heure espagnole* (1911) and *L'enfant et les sortilèges* (1925), the orchestral works *La valse* (1920) and *Bolero* (1928), two piano concertos, and many beautiful songs. Ravel's works are admired for their superb craftsmanship and orchestration, and he remains the most popular of all French composers.

raven Any of several species (genus *Corvus*, CROW family Corvidae) of heavy-billed, usually solitary, songbirds, now restricted to undisturbed areas. The common raven (*C. corax*), the biggest PASSERINE, grows to 26 in. (66 cm) long and has a wingspan of more than 4 ft (1.3 m). Ravens eat rodents, insects, grain, birds' eggs, and, in winter, carrion and refuse. Captive nestlings may learn to mimic a few words. The large nest, a crude structure of sticks, is built high on a cliff or treetop.

Ravenna \\rə-'ve-nə\\ City (metro. area pop., 1998 est.: 138,000), NE Italy, near the Adriatic Sea. It was the capital of the W Roman empire in the 5th cent. A.D. and of the Os-

trogothic kingdom and Byzantine Italy in the 6th–8th cent. Its art and architecture reflect a fusion of Roman forms with Byzantine mosaics and other decoration; sites include the 6th-cent. basilica of Sant'Apollinare Nuovo and the octagonal church of San Vitale.

Ravi River \\'rä-vē\\ River, NW India and NE Pakistan, one of the five rivers of the PUNJAB. It rises in the HIMALAYAS in India and flows past Chamba, turning southwest at the boundary of KASHMIR. It then flows along the Pakistani border and past LAHORE, emptying into the Chenab River after a course of about 450 mi (725 km).

Rawalpindi \\ˌrä-wəl-'pin-dē\\ City (pop., 1998: 1,406,000), PUNJAB province, N Pakistan, southwest of ISLAMABAD. The ancient city of TAXILA has been identified with nearby ruins. Strategically located, it controls the routes to Kashmir and was the site of an important British military station. The capital of Pakistan 1959–69, it is the headquarters of the Pakistan army. Mankial, south of the city, is a 3rd-cent.-B.C. Buddhist STUPA site.

Rawlings, Jerry J(ohn) (b.1947) Ghanaian leader who twice (1979, 1981) seized power in coups. After the first coup Rawlings, a junior air-force officer, yielded power to an elected civilian president, Hilla Limann, but ousted him two years later. He initially created workers' councils and established production and price controls, but later abandoned them. His policies afforded Ghana relative political and economic stability. He was returned to office by election in 1996; he stepped down as president in 2001.

Rawls, John (1921–2002) U.S. philosopher. Born in Baltimore, he taught at Cornell (1962–79) and later Harvard (from 1979). In his *Theory of Justice* (1971), he offered an alternative to UTILITARIANISM. He asserted that if people had to choose principles of justice from behind a "veil of ignorance" that restricted what they could know of their own position in society, they would not seek to maximize overall utility but would instead both protect their liberty and safeguard themselves against the worst possible outcome. They would thus sanction only the kinds of inequalities (e.g., in wealth) that would benefit the worst off.

ray Any of 300–350 mostly marine species of cartilaginous fish (order Batoidei) classified as ELECTRIC RAYS, SAWFISHES, SKATES, and STINGRAYS. Many species are slow-moving bottom-dwellers. The gill openings and mouth are on the underside of the flattened body. Winglike pectoral fins extend along the sides of the head. All but electric rays have a long, slender tail, often with saw-edged, venomous spines. See also MANTA RAY.

Ray, James Earl (1928–1998) U.S. assassin. Born in Alton, Ill., he became a small-time crook. He escaped from the Missouri state prison in 1967. In Memphis on April 4, 1968, he shot M. L. KING from a rooming house as King emerged from his motel room across the street. Ray fled to Toronto, Lisbon, and London, where he was arrested. Pleading guilty, he was sentenced to 99 years in prison; several months later he recanted his confession, to no effect. He tried to reopen his case several months before he died.

Ray, John (1627–1705) British naturalist and botanist. With Francis Willughby (1635–1672) he undertook a complete catalog of living things, of which he published numerous volumes. His enduring legacy to botany was the establishment of species as the ultimate unit of taxonomy. He attempted to base his systems of classification on all the structural characteristics of organisms, including internal anatomy, rather than on a single feature. He effectively established the class of mammals, and he divided insects according to the presence or absence of multiple metamorphoses. Ray's work helped make possible Carolus LINNAEUS's later contributions.

Ray, Man *orig.* Emmanuel Radnitsky (1890–1976) U.S. photographer, painter, and filmmaker. Born in Philadelphia, he grew up in New York. With Marcel DUCHAMP he formed the New York DADA group in 1917 and produced READY-MADES. In 1921 he moved to Paris and became associated with the Surrealists. He rediscovered the technique for making photograms, which he called "rayographs," by placing objects on light-sensitive paper. He turned to portrait photography and made a virtually complete record of the celebrities of Parisian cultural life of the 1920s and '30s. He also made important contributions as an avant-garde film-maker in the 1920s.

Ray, Nicholas orig. Raymond Nicholas Kienzle (1911–1979) U.S. film director. Born in Galesville, Wis., he began directing plays in the mid-1930s. After working in New York with John HOUSEMAN and Elia KAZAN, he followed them to Hollywood, where he directed *They Live by Night* (1948). Much admired by believers in the AUTEUR THEORY, Ray was praised for *In a Lonely Place* (1950), *The Lusty Men* (1952), *Johnny Guitar* (1954), the landmark film of youthful rebellion *Rebel Without a Cause* (1955), *Bitter Victory* (1958), and *55 Days at Peking* (1963).

Ray, Satyajit (1921–1992) Indian film director. He studied with Rabindranath TAGORE, and sold all his possessions to make his first film, *Pather Panchali* (1955), which was extremely successful at the Cannes Film Festival. With *Aparajito* (1956) and *The World of Apu* (1959), he completed the brilliant Apu Trilogy and brought Indian cinema to world attention. He later won acclaim for *Devi* (1960), *Two Daughters* (1961), and *The Home and the World* (1984). He wrote all his own screenplays, noted for their humanism and poetry, though his short stories and novellas became his main source of income. In 1992 he received an honorary Academy Award.

Satyajit Ray

Rayburn, Sam(uel) (Taliaferro) (1882–1961) U.S. politician. Born in Roane Co., Tenn., he taught school before becoming a lawyer in Texas. He was elected as a Democrat to the U.S. House of Representatives in 1912, where he served for 48 years, including 17 years as speaker (1940–46, 1949–53, 1955–61). A skillful tactician, he influenced the passage of much NEW DEAL legislation. He was the long-time mentor to Lyndon JOHNSON and a trusted adviser to presidents from Franklin ROOSEVELT to John F. KENNEDY.

ray flower See COMPOSITE FAMILY

Rayleigh scattering Dispersion of ELECTROMAGNETIC RADIATION by particles with radii less than 1/10 the WAVELENGTH of the radiation. It is named for Baron Rayleigh (1842–1919), who described it in 1871. Since blue light is at the short wavelength end of the visible SPECTRUM, it is scattered in the atmosphere much more than the longer-wavelength red light. This causes the blue color of the sky, since the observer sees only the scattered light.

Raymond, Antonin (1888–1976) Czech-U.S. architect. He assisted Frank Lloyd WRIGHT in building the Imperial Hotel, Tokyo (1916). Remaining in Japan, he became one of the few modernist architects working there and he influenced Junzo Yoshimura (1908–1997) and Kunio MAEKAWA. Among his works were the Reader's Digest Building, Tokyo (1951) and the Nagoya International School (opened 1967), a circular structure serving a flexible educational program.

Raymond of Peñafort \ˌpän-yə-ˈfȯrt\, **St.** *Spanish* Raimundo (c.1185–1275) Catalan Dominican friar. He studied and taught CANON LAW at Bologna, then returned to Barcelona, where he joined the Dominicans and wrote a manual for confessors widely used in the late Middle Ages. Appointed papal chaplain by Pope GREGORY IX (1230), he was commissioned to codify the papal statues and rulings on canon law; these *Decretals* (1234) remained part of church law until 1917.

Rayonnant style \re-yən-ˈän\ French style (13th cent.) that represents the height of GOTHIC ARCHITECTURE. Turning their attention to decoration, architects focused on pinnacles, moldings, and especially window TRACERY. The style's name reflects the radiating character of the ROSE WINDOW. Other features include the thinning of vertical supporting members, the enlargement of windows, and the combination of the triforium gallery and CLERESTORY into one large glazed area, until walls became largely undifferentiated screens of tracery, mullions, and glass. Amiens Cathedral (1220–70) is cited as its earliest manifestation. Especially fine achievements include NOTRE-DAME DE PARIS and the extraordinary Sainte-Chapelle, Paris (consecrated 1248).

Razi \ˈrä-zē\, **al-** *in full* Abu Bakr Muhammad ibn Zakariya al-Razi *Latin* **Rhazes** (865?–925?) Persian alchemist and philosopher. He saw himself as the Islamic version of SOCRATES in philosophy and of HIPPOCRATES in medicine. In *Kitab al-hawi* ("The Comprehensive Book") he surveyed Greek, Syrian, early Arabic, and some Indian medical knowledge, adding his own comments. His philosophical writings include *The Spiritual Physick of Rhazes*, a popular ethical treatise and major alchemical study. He was considered the greatest physician of the Islamic world.

Razin \ˈrä-zyin\, **Stenka** (orig. Stepan Timofeyevich) (c.1630–1671) Russian COSSACK rebel. In 1667 he led a band of runaway serfs to establish an outpost on the upper Don River. They raided Russian and Persian settlements on the Caspian Sea (1667–70), acquiring great fame and wealth. He then led his Cossack anarchists into the Volga River region, where he was joined by disaffected peasants. After seizing Tsaritsyn (now Volgograd), Astrakhan, and Saratov, his force of 20,000 was defeated by the Russian army at Simbirsk. Razin was captured, tortured, and executed. He became a popular Russian folk hero, immortalized in songs and legends.

razorback whale See FIN WHALE

RCA Corp. U.S. electronics and entertainment delivery firm. It was founded as the Radio Corp. of America by GENERAL ELECTRIC CO. in 1919 to acquire Marconi Wireless Telegraph Co. of America for commercial transatlantic radio communications. RCA founded NBC in 1926. GE shed RCA in 1930 for antitrust considerations. In 1939 RCA developed the first experimental television set and began selling black-and-white sets in 1946. General Electric re-acquired RCA in 1986, but sold it in 1987 to Thomson-Brandt, SA, now Thomson Multimedia.

Re \ˈrä\ *or* **Ra** \ˈrä\ In ancient EGYPTIAN RELIGION, the creator god and god of the sun. He was believed to sail across the sky in his solar bark and at night to travel in another bark through the underworld, where he had to vanquish a serpent before he could be born again. From the 4th dynasty, kings held the title Son of Re. Re later became part of the throne name they adopted at accession and was appended to the names of such gods as AMON and Sebek.

reactance Measure of the opposition that an electrical CIRCUIT or a part of a circuit presents to ELECTRIC CURRENT insofar as the current is varying or alternating. Steady electric currents flowing along conductors in one direction undergo opposition called electrical RESISTANCE, but no reactance. Reactance is present when conductors carry ALTERNATING CURRENT, and is of two types, inductive and capacitive. Inductive reactance is associated with the varying magnetic field that surrounds a wire or a coil carrying a current. Capacitive reactance is associated with the changing electric field between two conducting surfaces (plates) separated from each other by an insulating medium. The ohm (Ω) is the unit of reactance.

reaction rate Speed at which a CHEMICAL REACTION proceeds, in terms of amount of product formed or amount of reactant consumed per unit of time. The reaction rate depends on the nature of the reacting substances and the type of chemical change, as well as temperature and pressure, especially if GASES are involved. CATALYSTS usually accelerate reaction rates. The prediction, measurement, and interpretation of reaction rates are subjects of the branch of chemistry known as chemical kinetics.

Reade, Charles (1814–1884) English novelist and dramatist. An officer at Oxford Univ., he put much of his time and resources into writing and staging his melodramatic plays. His novels indignantly expose the social injustices of his times. He is best remembered for the historical romance *The Cloister and the Hearth* (1861); his other novels include *It Is Never Too Late to Mend* (1856), attacking prison conditions; and *Hard Cash* (1863), on the abuse of mental patients.

Reader's Digest U.S.-based monthly magazine. It was founded by DeWitt and Lila WALLACE in 1922 as a digest of condensed articles of topical interest and entertainment

value taken from other periodicals. From 1934 it published condensed versions of current books. It probably has the largest circulation of any periodical in the world, appearing in 48 editions and 19 languages worldwide.

Reading \'re-diŋ\ City (pop., 1999 est.: 143,000), England, west of LONDON. A Danish encampment as early as A.D. 871, it was given a town charter by King HENRY III in 1253. It suffered severely in the ENGLISH CIVIL WARS of the mid-17th cent. Oscar WILDE was imprisoned in Reading Gaol in 1897. It is noted for the bulbs produced in its nurseries, and is the site of a university.

read-only memory See ROM

ready-made Everyday object selected and designated as art. The name was coined by Marcel DUCHAMP, whose first ready-mades included a snow shovel that he picked up on a snowy day in New York, and a wheel mounted on a stool (1913). They represented a protest against the excessive importance attached to works of art. The ready-made concept, though widely regarded for decades as an insult to art, was adapted by such later artists as Robert RAUSCHENBERG, Andy WARHOL, and Jasper JOHNS.

Reagan \'rā-gən\, **Ronald W(ilson)** (b.1911) 40th president of the U.S. (1981–89). Born in Tampico, Ill., he attended Eureka College and worked as a sports announcer before going to Hollywood in 1937. He had roles in 50 films and was twice president of the Screen Actors Guild (1947–52, 1959–60). Having gradually changed from liberal Democrat to conservative Republican, he served as governor of California 1967–74. In 1980 he defeated Pres. Jimmy CARTER to become president. Shortly after taking office, he was wounded in an assassination attempt. He adopted

Ronald Reagan, 1981

SUPPLY-SIDE ECONOMICS to promote rapid economic growth; Congress approved most of his proposals (1981), which succeeded in lowering inflation but nearly tripled the national debt. He began the largest peacetime military buildup in U.S. history and in 1983 proposed construction of the STRATEGIC DEFENSE INITIATIVE. His foreign policy included the INF Treaty to restrict INTERMEDIATE-RANGE NUCLEAR WEAPONS and the invasion of GRENADA. In 1984 he defeated Walter MONDALE in a landslide for reelection. The IRAN-CONTRA AFFAIR significantly weakened his popularity. His artful communication skills enabled him to pursue numerous conservative policies with conspicuous success. In 1994 he revealed that he had Alzheimer's disease.

real and personal property Basic types of property in English COMMON LAW, roughly corresponding to the division between immovables and movables in CIVIL LAW. Real property consists of land, buildings, crops, and other resources, improvements, or fixtures still attached to the land. Personal property is essentially all property other than real property, including goods, animals, money, and vehicles.

realism In the visual arts, an aesthetic that promotes accurate, detailed, unembellished depiction of nature or of contemporary life over imaginative idealization. In the early 1830s, the painters of the BARBIZON SCHOOL school espoused realism in their faithful reproduction of the landscape near their village. Gustave COURBET was the first artist to proclaim and practice the realist aesthetic; his *Burial at Ornans* and *The Stone Breakers* (1849) shocked the public and critics with their frank depiction of peasants and laborers. Honoré DAUMIER used an energetic linear style and bold detail to caricature the immorality he saw in French society. Realism emerged in the U.S. in the work of Winslow HOMER and Thomas EAKINS. German artists associated with the NEUE SACHLICHKEIT worked in a realist style to express their disillusionment after World War I. The Depression-era movement known as SOCIAL REALISM adopted a similarly harsh realism to depict the injustices of U.S. society. See also NATURALISM.

realism In literature, the theory or practice of fidelity to nature or to real life and to accurate representation without idealization of everyday life. The 18th-cent. works of Daniel DEFOE, Henry FIELDING, and Tobias SMOLLETT are among the earliest examples of realism in English literature. It was consciously adopted as an aesthetic program in the mid-19th cent. in France; Gustave FLAUBERT's *Madame Bovary* (1857) established the movement in European literature. The realist emphasis on detachment and objectivity, along with lucid but restrained social criticism, became integral to the novel in the late 19th cent. See also NATURALISM.

realism In philosophy, any viewpoint that accords to the objects of human knowledge an existence independent of whether they are being perceived. Against nominalism, which denies that UNIVERSALS have any reality at all, and conceptualism, which grants universals reality only as concepts within the mind, realism asserts that universals exist independently. Against IDEALISM and PHENOMENALISM, it asserts that the existence of material objects and their qualities is independent of their being perceived. Moral realism asserts that moral qualities of actions (such as being morally good or bad, or ethically right or wrong) belong to the actions themselves and are not mere products of a mind. In opposition to conventionalism, realism holds that scientific theories are objectively true (or false) based on their correspondence (or lack of it) to an independently existing reality.

real number In mathematics, a quantity that can be expressed as a finite or infinite decimal expansion. The counting NUMBERS, INTEGERS, RATIONAL NUMBERS, and IRRATIONAL NUMBERS are all real numbers. Real numbers are used in measuring continuously varying quantities (e.g., size, time), in contrast to measurements that result from counting. See also IMAGINARY NUMBER.

Réaumur \rā-ō-'mᵫr, *Engl* ˌrā-ō-'myúr\, **René-Antoine Ferchault de** (1683–1757) French physicist and entomologist. He invented the Réaumur thermometric scale, on which 0° marks the freezing point of water and 80° marks the boiling point. He invented the opaque white glass known as Réaumur porcelain, improved techniques for making iron and steel, and isolated gastric juice. His *Memoirs Serving as a Natural History of Insects* (1734–42), though unfinished, was a milestone in entomological history.

rebate Retroactive refund or credit given to a buyer of a product or service. Rebates are used as purchase incentives. So-called deferred (or exclusive-patronage) rebates are used by large vendors of perishables and consumer durable goods. To receive one, the purchaser must use a particular vendor for a fixed period of time. Rebating was a common pricing tactic in the 19th cent., often used by large industrialists to undercut competition. The U.S. railroad industry granted secret rebates; those given to STANDARD OIL CO. helped it acquire a monopoly over the oil industry.

rebbe See RABBI

Recent epoch See HOLOCENE EPOCH

recession Downward trend in the BUSINESS CYCLE characterized by a decline in production and employment, which in turn causes a decline in household incomes and spending. Even though not all households and businesses experience actual declines in income, their expectations about the future become less certain and cause them to delay making large purchases or investments. This drop in demand leads to a corresponding fall in output and thus worsens the economic situation. Whether a recession develops into a DEPRESSION depends on such factors as the extent and quality of CREDIT extended during the previous period of prosperity, the amount of speculation permitted, the ability of government MONETARY and FISCAL policies to reverse the downward trend, and the amount of excess productive capacity in existence.

recessiveness Failure of one of a pair of genes (ALLELES) present in an individual to express itself in an observable manner because of the greater influence, or DOMINANCE, of its opposite-acting partner. Both alleles affect the same inherited characteristic, but the presence of the recessive gene cannot be determined by observation of the organism: Though present in the organism's GENOTYPE (gene makeup), the recessive trait is not evident in its PHENOTYPE (observable characteristics).

Recife \ri-ˈsē-fē\ *formerly* **Pernambuco** \ˌper-nəm-ˈbü-kü\ Seaport (pop., 1996: 1,346,000), NE Brazil. Founded by the Portuguese in the early 16th cent., it was sacked by British privateers in 1595 and occupied by the Dutch 1630–54. It has been called the Venice of Brazil because it is crossed by waterways and its component parts are linked by numerous bridges. Situated near Point Plata, the easternmost point of S. America, it is one of the leading ports of Brazil. It is home to several universities.

recitative \ˌre-sə-tə-ˈtēv\ Style of accompanied solo singing that imitates speech rhythms and tones. Representing an attempt at an ideally expressive musical text setting, which the ancient Greeks were thought to have mastered, it appeared in tandem with OPERA around 1600, the first operas being largely written in recitative. Recitative style soon began to separate from lyrical ARIA style, and regular alternation of recitative with aria became the rule for both opera and CANTATA. The presence of recitative (as opposed to spoken dialogue) most clearly distinguishes opera from the MUSICAL and related genres.

recombination In genetics, regrouping of the maternal and paternal GENES during the formation of sex cells (gametes). Recombination occurs randomly in nature as a normal event of MEIOSIS, enhanced by crossing-over. Because of recombination, no two daughter cells are identical, nor are any identical to the parent cell. Recombination has become a powerful tool to increase understanding of genetic mechanisms and manipulate recombination itself by transplanting genes from one CHROMOSOME to another. See also GENETIC ENGINEERING, MOLECULAR BIOLOGY.

recompression chamber See HYPERBARIC CHAMBER

Reconstruction (1865–77) Period after the AMERICAN CIVIL WAR affecting former Confederate states. Problems associated with readmitting the 11 Southern states were confronted first by Pres. Abraham LINCOLN, who planned to readmit states in which at least 10% of the voters had pledged loyalty to the Union. This lenient approach was opposed by the RADICAL REPUBLICANS. Pres. Andrew JOHNSON continued Lincoln's moderate policies, but demand for stricter legislation resulted in the Reconstruction Acts of 1867. These established military districts in the South and required the Southern states' acceptance of the 14th and 15th Amendments to the Constitution to ensure the freedmen's civil rights. Southern resentment of the imposed government, which included Republicans, CARPETBAGGERS, and SCALAWAGS, and of the activities of the FREEDMEN'S BUREAU led to the formation of the KU KLUX KLAN. By the 1870s conservative Democrats again controlled most state governments in the South. While Reconstruction was often seen as a period of corruption, many constructive legal and educational reforms were introduced.

Reconstruction Finance Corporation (RFC) U.S. government agency established (1932) to provide loans to railroads, banks, and businesses. The RFC was an attempt by Pres. Herbert HOOVER to counter the early effects of the GREAT DEPRESSION by rescuing institutions from default. It was widely used by Pres. Franklin ROOSEVELT in the NEW DEAL and to finance defense plants in World War II. After the war, its functions were gradually transferred to other agencies.

recorder Cylindrical, usually wooden, wind instrument with fingerholes. Its rather soft tones are produced by air blown against the sharp edge of an opening in the tube. Recorders range in size from the sopranino to the contrabass. They emerged in the 14th cent. and were widely used in ensembles and orchestras until the Classical era. Displaced by the transverse FLUTE, it was revived in the 20th cent.

record player See PHONOGRAPH

rectum End segment of the LARGE INTESTINE (see DIGESTION) in which FECES accumulate just prior to discharge. It is 5–6 in. (13–15 cm) long and lined with mucous membrane. One set of muscles separates it from the anal canal; another shortens it to expel feces. The rectal walls distend as feces enter, which stimulates the urge for DEFECATION.

recycling *or* **materials salvage** Recovery and reuse of materials from consumed products. The main motives for recycling have been the increasing scarcity and cost of natural resources (including oil, gas, coal, mineral ores, and trees) and the pollution of air (see AIR POLLUTION), water (see WATER POLLUTION), and land by waste materials. Internal recycling is the reuse in a manufacturing process of materials that are a waste product of that process, and is common in the metals industry. External recycling is the reclaiming of materials from a product that is worn out or no longer useful; an example is the collection of old newspapers and magazines for the manufacture of paper products.

Red Army Army of the Soviet Union. Formed in the aftermath of the RUSSIAN REVOLUTION OF 1917, it was brilliantly headed by Leon TROTSKY. Formed of workers and peasants, it initially lacked an officers' corps, and Trotsky was forced to mobilize officers of the former imperial army. The COMMUNIST PARTY placed commissars in all army units to ensure political orthodoxy. Joseph STALIN purged the military leadership in 1937, leaving the army unprepared for the German surprise attack in 1941. It had recovered enough by 1945 to be surpassed in strength only by the U.S. Army, with forces numbering over 11 million. In 1946 the word Red was dropped; in 1960 the commissars' duties were transferred to its officers.

Red Army Faction See BAADER-MEINHOF GANG

redbird See CARDINAL

red blood cell See ERYTHROCYTE

Red Brigades *Italian* Brigate Rosse. Extreme left-wing terrorist organization in Italy. Its self-proclaimed aim was to cause a Marxist upheaval led by a "revolutionary proletariat." Reputedly founded by Renato Curcio (b.1945), it began carrying out violent acts with firebombings (1970), escalating to kidnappings (1971) and murders (1974), most notably that of Aldo MORO (1978). At its height, it probably had 400–500 full-time members and a few thousand supporters. Arrests and imprisonments weakened the organization in the 1980s.

Red Cloud *orig.* Mahpiua Luta (1822–1909) American Indian leader. Born in present-day Nebraska, Red Cloud, as principal chief of the Oglala Teton Dakota (SIOUX), led the opposition of both Sioux and Cheyenne to the U.S. government's development of the Bozeman Trail to goldfields in Montana Territory (1865–67). Relentlessly attacking workers along the route, he refused to negotiate until the U.S. agreed to halt the project, whereupon he allowed himself to be settled on the Red Cloud Agency in Nebraska.

Red Cross *officially* **International Movement of the Red Cross and Red Crescent** *formerly* **International Red Cross** Humanitarian agency with national affiliates worldwide. Established for the care of victims of battle, it now aids in the prevention and relief of human suffering generally. It arose out of the work of Henri DUNANT, who proposed the formation of voluntary relief societies in all countries, the first of which came into being in 1864. The name Red Crescent, adopted in 1906 at the insistence of the Ottoman empire, is used in Muslim countries. In peacetime, the Red Cross aids victims of natural disasters and maintains blood banks. In wartime, it serves as an intermediary between belligerents and visits prisoner-of-war camps. Its operating principles are humanity, impartiality, and neutrality. Its headquarters are in Geneva. The American Red Cross was founded by Clara BARTON in 1881 and first chartered by Congress in 1900; it runs the world's largest blood donor service and coordinates natural-disaster relief efforts. The Red Cross received the Nobel Peace Prize in 1917, 1944, and 1963.

red-figure pottery Type of Greek pottery that flourished from the late 6th to the late 4th cent. B.C. Developed in Athens, it quickly overtook the older BLACK-FIGURE POTTERY as the preferred style of vase painting. The background was painted black, and the outline details on the figures were also painted (rather than incised) in black, but the rest of each figure was unpainted and so retained the orange-red color of the natural vase. By comparison with incising, the painting of the details allowed more flexibility in rendering human form, movements, expressions, and perspective.

Redford, (Charles) Robert (b.1937) U.S. film actor and director. Born in Santa Monica, Cal., he made his Broadway debut in 1959 and won acclaim in *Barefoot in the Park*

(1963; film, 1967). The blond, appealing Redford later appeared on film with Paul NEWMAN in the hits *Butch Cassidy and the Sundance Kid* (1969) and *The Sting* (1973), as well as in *The Candidate* (1972), *All the President's Men* (1976), and *The Natural* (1984). He has directed such films as *Ordinary People* (1980, Academy Award), *The Milagro Beanfield War* (1988), *A River Runs Through It* (1992), and *Quiz Show* (1994). In 1980 he founded the Sundance Institute to sponsor young filmmakers' works, and its film festival became the major showcase for U.S. independent films.

Redgrave, Vanessa (b.1937) British actress. Daughter of the actor Michael Redgrave, she made her London stage debut in 1958 and won praise as Rosalind in *As You Like It* (1961). Her performances in such movies as *Morgan!* (1966), *Blow-Up* (1966), *Camelot* (1967), *Isadora* (1968), *Mary, Queen of Scots* (1971), and *Julia* (1977, Academy Award) won her adulation as one of the world's greatest actresses, though she was criticized for her left-wing activism, especially on behalf of Palestinians. Her later films included *The Bostonians* (1984), *Howards End* (1992), and *Mrs. Dalloway* (1998). Her sister Lynn (b.1943) has had a distinguished stage career in London and New York. Her film career includes roles in *Georgy Girl* (1966), *Shine* (1996), and *Gods and Monsters* (1998).

Red Guards Radical university and high-school students formed into paramilitary units of the Chinese CULTURAL REVOLUTION. They responded in 1966 to MAO ZEDONG's call to revitalize the revolutionary spirit of the Chinese Communist Party. Numbering in the millions, they attacked and persecuted local party leaders, schoolteachers, and other intellectuals, attempting to purge the country of its pre-Communist culture. Internal strife ensued as units argued over which best represented MAOISM. Their disruptions of industrial production and urban life led the government to redirect them to the countryside in 1968, where the movement gradually subsided.

Redi \\'re-dē\\, **Francesco** (1626–1697) Italian physician and poet. He demonstrated in 1668, in one of the first biological experiments with proper controls, that the presence of maggots in rotting meat does not result from spontaneous generation. Redi set up a series of flasks containing different meats; half were sealed, half open. Though the meat in all the flasks rotted, Redi found that only in the uncovered flasks, which flies had entered freely, did the meat contain maggots. As a poet, he is known chiefly for his *Bacco in Toscana* (1685).

Redon \\rə-'dōⁿ\\, **Odilon** (1840–1916) French printmaker and painter. He studied under J.-L. GÉRÔME and learned lithography under Henri FANTIN-LATOUR. He came to be associated with the Symbolist painters (see SYMBOLISM). His oils and pastels, chiefly still lifes with flowers, won him admiration as a colorist from Henri MATISSE. His prints (nearly 200 in all), which explore fantastic, often macabre themes, foreshadowed Surrealism and Dada.

Redouté \\rə-dü-'tā\\, **Pierre Joseph** (1759–1840) French painter. Born in Belgium, he became a favored artist at the court of France, patronized by kings from LOUIS XVI

Odilon Redon, self-portrait, 1904

to LOUIS-PHILIPPE. His delicate botanical prints were not only framed as pictures but also used for china. His *Les Liliacées* (1802–15) contained 500 plates of lilies. *Les Roses* (1817–21) is considered his finest series, and its classic images are still widely reproduced.

redox See OXIDATION-REDUCTION

Red River *Chinese* **Yuan Chiang** \\'ywän-'jyän\\ *Vietnamese* **Song Hong** \\'sȯŋ-'hȯŋ\\ River, S.E. Asia. It rises in Yunnan province, S China, and flows past HANOI into the Gulf of TONKIN. The principal river of N Vietnam, it is about 500 mi (805 km) long and has a wide, fertile delta.

Red River River, S central U.S. It rises in the high plains of E New Mexico and flows southeast across Texas and Louisiana to the MISSISSIPPI RIVER, forming part of the Texas–Oklahoma border. It is 1,290 mi (2,080 km) long. In Texas it was the site of the RED RIVER INDIAN WAR (1874).

Red River Indian War (1874–75) Uprising of Indian warriors from reservation tribes. After settlement of SW tribes on reservations in Oklahoma and Texas (1867), discontented braves broke out repeatedly to raid white travelers and settlers. An attack in 1874 killed 60 Texans. Federal troops under William T. SHERMAN converged on Indians concentrated in the Red River valley of Texas. Indian resistance forced 14 pitched battles before eventually surrendering and returning to the reservations.

Red River of the North River, N U.S. and S Manitoba. It flows north, forming the Minnesota–N. Dakota boundary, before emptying into Lake WINNIPEG after a course of 545 mi (877 km). Explored 1732–33, the river, named after the reddish-brown silt it carries, became a transportation link between Lake Winnipeg and the MISSISSIPPI RIVER system. Its fertile valley produces cereals, potatoes, and sugar beets, and supports cattle raising.

Red Sea Narrow inland sea between the ARABIAN PENINSULA and NE Africa. It extends southeast from Suez, Egypt, for about 1,200 mi (1,930 km), and separates the coasts of Egypt, the Sudan, and Eritrea from those of Saudi Arabia and Yemen. It contains some of the world's warmest and saltiest seawater. With its connection to the Mediterranean Sea via the SUEZ CANAL, it is one of the most heavily traveled waterways in the world. Its name is derived from color changes observed in its waters.

red shift Displacement of the SPECTRUM of an astronomical object toward longer wavelengths (visible light shifts toward red). In 1929 Edwin HUBBLE reported that distant galaxies had red shifts proportionate to their distances (see HUBBLE'S CONSTANT). Based on the DOPPLER EFFECT, Hubble concluded that galaxies are receding from the Milky Way, leading to expanding-universe theories. Modern cosmological theories explain the red shift as arising from stretching of the photon's wavelength as it travels through expanding space.

Red Square Open square, central MOSCOW. It covers almost 800,000 sq ft (73,000 sq m). Dating from the late 15th cent., it has long been a busy market area as well as a focal point in Russian history, the scene of executions, demonstrations, riots, and parades. The KREMLIN, Cathedral of ST. BASIL THE BLESSED (1555–60) and LENIN's tomb are situated on the square.

red tide Discoloration of seawater caused by DINOFLAGELLATES during periodic blooms (population increases). Toxic substances released by these organisms into the water may be lethal to fish and other marine life, and they irritate the human respiratory system. The causes of red tide (which often is not red) are uncertain; it may require the confluence of several natural phenomena, in which human influence may or may not play a part.

Red Turbans Peasant rebel movement that flourished in N China at the end of the YUAN DYNASTY. The Red Turbans, whose leader was regarded as an incarnation of the BODHISATTVA Maitreya, were opposed to alien MONGOL rule; their movement gained momentum from the famine that followed crop failures in the 1330s. Their marauding, which began in the 1350s, took them as far as Korea. Though their rebellion was put down, rival rebel forces under Zhu Yuanzhang (1328–1398) toppled the Yuan dynasty and founded the MING.

reduction Any of a class of CHEMICAL REACTIONS in which the number of ELECTRONS associated with an ATOM or group of atoms is increased. The electrons taken up by the substance reduced are supplied by another substance, often hydrogen (H_2), which is thereby oxidized. See also OXIDATION-REDUCTION.

reduction division See MEIOSIS

redwood *or* **sequoia** Coniferous evergreen timber tree (*Sequoia sempervirens*) of the family Taxodiaceae, found in the fog belt of the coastal range from SW Oregon to central California at elevations up to 3,300 ft (1,000 m). The genus name commemorates the Cherokee Indian SEQUOYAH.

Redwoods are the tallest living trees, often exceeding 300 ft (90 m) in height; one has reached 368 ft (112 m). Typical trunk diameters are 10–20 ft (3–6 m) or more. The redwood tree takes 400–500 years to reach maturity; some are known to be more than 1,500 years old. As the tree ages, the lower limbs fall away, leaving a clear, columnar trunk. Redwood timber is weather-durable and has many uses. Today many of the remaining redwood stands are protected. See also BIG TREE, DAWN REDWOOD.

reed In botany, any of several species of large aquatic GRASSES, especially in the genus *Phragmites* (family Gramineae or Poaceae). The common, or water, reed *(P. australis)* occurs along the margins of lakes, fens, marshes, and streams from the Arctic to the tropics. It is a broad-leaved grass, about 5–15 ft (1.5–5 m) tall, with feathery flower clusters and stiff, smooth stems. Dried reed stems have been used for millennia as thatching and construction material, in basketry, and in REED INSTRUMENTS.

Reed, Carol (*later* **Sir Carol**) (1906–1976) British film director. Initially a stage director, he began directing films in 1935, winning praise for *The Stars Look Down* (1939) and *Night Train* (1940). His greatest successes included the thrillers *Odd Man Out* (1947), *The Fallen Idol* (1948), and the classic *The Third Man* (1949). His later films include *Our Man in Havana* (1959) and *Oliver!* (1968, Academy Award).

Reed, John (1887–1920) U.S. journalist. Born to a wealthy family in Portland, Ore., he began writing for the radical socialist journal *The Masses* in 1913. A war correspondent during World War I, he became a friend of Vladimir LENIN and witnessed the RUSSIAN REVOLUTION OF 1917, described in his book *Ten Days That Shook the World* (1919). He became head of the U.S. Communist Labor Party; indicted for sedition, he escaped to the Soviet Union, where he died of typhus and was buried beside the Kremlin wall.

Reed, Thomas B(rackett) (1839–1902) U.S. politician. Born in Portland, Me., he served in the U.S. House of Representatives 1877–99. As speaker (1889–91, 1895–99) he introduced procedural changes that strengthened majority control and increased the power of the speaker and the rules committee. "Czar Reed" and his rules were attacked by opponents, and ten years later the speaker's powers were reduced.

Reed, Walter (1851–1902) U.S. pathologist and bacteriologist. Born in Belroi, Va., he investigated the spread of TYPHOID fever in military camps during the Spanish-American War and was later curator of the Army Medical Museum in Washington, D.C. YELLOW FEVER was believed to be spread by bedding and other articles, but Carlos Finlay (1833–1915) had theorized that it was carried by insects. Reed's team ruled out a bacterium suspected as the cause and found patterns of spread that supported the insect theory. Controlled experiments proved transmission by mosquito bite, and in 1901 an outbreak in Havana was controlled within 90 days.

Reed College Private liberal-arts college in Portland, Ore. Founded in 1909, it is named after Simeon Reed, a Portland businessman. It offers undergraduate programs in 22 major fields. It is known for its rigorous standards and its emphasis is on independent learning. Enrollment is about 1,400.

reed instruments Any wind instrument whose sound results from air that causes a thin blade, or reed, of cane or metal to vibrate, thereby setting up a sound wave in an enclosed air column or in the open air. A single reed may hit against a frame (beating reeds), as in the CLARINET or SAXOPHONE, or may vibrate freely through a closely fitting frame (free reeds), as in a HARMONICA or ACCORDION. Beating reeds in WOODWIND INSTRUMENTS depend on the pipe's sounding length (as determined by the fingering) to determine the pitch. Free reeds have their own single pitch, determined by their thickness and length. A double reed, as in the OBOE or BASSOON, consists of two cane blades tied together that beat against each other.

reed organ See HARMONIUM

reef, coral See CORAL REEF

reference frame *or* **frame of reference** Coordinate system that allows description of time and position of points relative to a body. The axes, or lines, emanate from a position called the origin. As a point moves, its VELOCITY can be described in terms of changes in displacement and direction. Reference frames are arbitrary: for a man sitting in a moving train, the description of his motion depends on the chosen frame of reference; he is not moving relative to the train, but is moving relative to the earth.

referendum and initiative Electoral devices by which voters may express their wishes regarding government policy or proposed legislation. Optional referenda are put on the ballot when a sufficient number of voters sign a PETITION demanding that a law passed by the legislature be ratified by the people. Obligatory referenda are those required by law; voluntary referenda are submitted by the legislature to voters to decide an issue or test public opinion. Initiatives are used to invoke a popular vote on a proposed law or constitutional amendment. Referenda and initiatives are most commonly used in the U.S. and Switzerland.

reflection Change in the direction of propagation of a WAVE that strikes a boundary through which it cannot pass and bounces back. The angle of incidence is the angle between the path of the wave and a line perpendicular to the boundary. The angle of reflection is the angle between the same line and the path of the reflected wave. All reflected waves obey the law of reflection: the angle of reflection equals the angle of incidence. The reflectivity of a material is the fraction of energy of the oncoming wave that is reflected by it.

reflex In biology, an inborn response to a stimulus that involves an impulse passing from a sensory nerve cell to a muscle or gland without reaching consciousness. Simple reflexes include sucking, swallowing, blinking, scratching, and the knee jerk. Most reflexes consist of complex patterns of many unconsciously coordinated muscular actions, such as walking, that form the basis of much instinctive behavior in animals.

Reformation *or* **Protestant Reformation** Break with ROMAN CATHOLICISM and the establishment of Protestant churches in the 16th cent. Though reformers such as Jan HUS and John WYCLIFFE attacked abuses in the Roman Catholic church in the late medieval period, the Reformation is usually dated from 1517, when Martin LUTHER posted his NINETY-FIVE THESES. Various Protestant denominations were soon founded by more radical reformers, such as Huldrych ZWINGLI and the ANABAPTISTS. John CALVIN established a theocracy in Geneva after his conversion to the Protestant cause. The Reformation took firm hold in N Europe; Spain and Italy remained resistant and became centers of the COUNTER-REFORMATION. In England, the Reformation's roots were primarily political rather than religious, motivated by the pope's refusal to grant HENRY VIII a divorce. In Scotland, the Calvinist John KNOX founded the Presbyterian church (see PRESBYTERIANISM).

Reform Bill of 1832 British parliamentary act that expanded the electorate. It transferred voting privileges from the small rural boroughs controlled by the nobility and gentry to the heavily populated but underrepresented industrial towns. Conceived by Prime Minister Charles GREY and introduced by John RUSSELL, the act redistributed seats in the House of Commons and lowered the electoral qualifications to allow voting by small property owners (much of the middle class).

Reformed church Any of several Protestant groups strongly influenced by CALVINISM. They are often called by national names (Swiss Reformed, Dutch Reformed, etc.). The name was originally used by all the Protestant churches that arose out of the 16th-cent. REFORMATION, but was later confined to the Calvinistic churches of continental Europe. See also PRESBYTERIANISM.

Reform Judaism Religious movement that has modified or abandoned many traditional Jewish beliefs and practices in an effort to adapt JUDAISM to the modern world. It originated in Germany in 1809 and spread to the U.S. in the 1840s under the leadership of Rabbi I. M. WISE. Reform Judaism permits men and women to sit together in the synagogue, holds a confirmation ceremony for girls parallel to the boys' BAR MITZVAH, and does not observe daily public worship, strict dietary laws, or the restriction of normal activities on the SABBATH. Its principles, enunciated in the Pittsburgh Platform (1885), were revised in the more con-

QR

servative Columbus Platform (1937). See also CONSERVATIVE JUDAISM, ORTHODOX JUDAISM.

Reform Party Political movement in Canada in the 1830s and '40s. Reformers in Upper Canada (later Ontario) urged that provincial governments be made accountable to elected legislative assemblies ("responsible government"). Reformers in Lower Canada (later Quebec) joined Louis PAPINEAU and his Patriote Party. Reform Party candidates served as premier in 1842–43 and 1848–54 in the province of Canada (union of Upper and Lower Canada). In the 1850s the party split between a moderate group, which allied with John MACDONALD's PROGRESSIVE CONSERVATIVE PARTY, and a radical faction, the CLEAR GRITS, from which the LIBERAL PARTY emerged.

refraction Change in direction of a WAVE as it leaves one medium and enters another. Waves, such as sound and light waves, travel at different speeds in different media. When a wave enters a new medium at an angle of less than 90°, the change in speed occurs sooner on one side of the wave than on the other, causing the wave to bend, or refract. Refraction explains the apparent bending of a pencil when it is partly immersed in water and viewed from above the surface. It also causes the optical illusion of the MIRAGE.

refrigeration Process of removing HEAT from an enclosed space or from a substance in order to lower the temperature. Refrigeration is used chiefly to store foodstuffs at low temperatures, thus inhibiting the destructive action of bacteria, yeasts, and molds. Many perishable products can be frozen, permitting them to be kept for months and even years with little loss in nutrition or flavor. See also AIR-CONDITIONING, HEAT EXCHANGER.

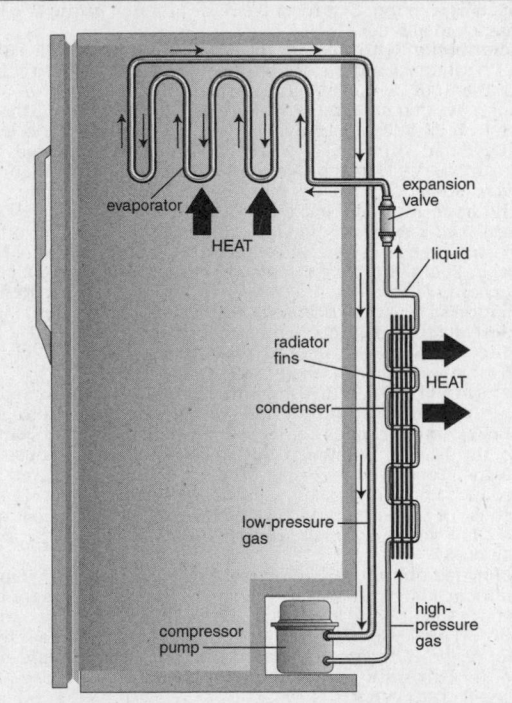

Refrigeration A compressor pressurizes the refrigerant gas, heating it and forcing it through the system. The gas cools and liquefies in the condenser, giving up its heat to the room. The liquid's temperature and pressure are lowered when it passes through an expansion valve. The cold liquid passes into the evaporator coils, where heat drawn from the warmer refrigerator compartment causes it to vaporize. The gas is then returned to the compressor to repeat the cycle.

refugee Person involuntarily displaced from his or her homeland. Until the late 19th cent. and the emergence of fixed and closed national boundaries, waves of refugees were always absorbed by neighboring countries. Immigration restrictions and increasing numbers of refugees necessitated special action to aid them. In 1921 Fridtjof NANSEN created a League of Nations Passport to allow refugees to move freely across national boundaries. Refugee status at that time was accorded to migrants only if their departure was involuntary and asylum was sought in another country. In 1938 its definition was expanded to include a fear of persecution because of ethnicity, religion, nationality, group membership, or political opinion. Later the criteria were expanded again to include flight from home within one's own country. Today most of the world's refugees are in Africa, the Middle East, and the Balkans.

Reger \'rā-gər\, (Johann Baptist Joseph) Max(imilian) (1873–1916) German composer and organist. Initially a student and assistant of Hugo Riemann (1849–1919), Reger became a prolific composer of songs, piano pieces, and especially organ music. His music, combining progressive and conservative elements and often highly chromatic, has always been more popular in Germany than elsewhere.

reggae \'re-gā\ Jamaican popular music and dance style. It originated in the mid-1960s as a music of the Jamaican poor, reflecting social discontent and the RASTAFARIAN movement. Its instrumentation features a loud electric bass, around which an ensemble of organ, piano, drums, and lead and rhythm electric guitars plays short ostinato phrases with regular accents on the offbeats. Reggae was popularized in the U.S. by the film *The Harder They Come* (1973) and through tours by Bob MARLEY and by Toots (Hibbert) and the Maytals.

Reggio di Calabria \'red-jō-dē-kä-'lä-brē-ə\ *ancient* Rhegium. City (metro. area pop., 1998 est.: 180,000), S Italy, on the Strait of MESSINA. Founded as a Greek colony in the 8th cent. B.C., it was allied with Athens in the 5th cent. B.C. and with Rome around 280 B.C. From the 5th cent. A.D. it was ruled successively by the Visigoths, Ostrogoths, Byzantines, and Arabs. It was conquered by the Normans about 1060 and became part of the kingdom of The Two SICILIES. Destroyed many times by Saracen invaders and by earthquakes, it has been repeatedly rebuilt. It is a tourist resort and seaport.

Regina \ri-'jī-nə\ City (pop., 1996: 180,000), capital of Saskatchewan. It lies in the S central part of the province. It was the administrative headquarters of the Northwest Territories 1882–1905, and headquarters of the ROYAL CANADIAN MOUNTED POLICE until 1920. After World War II it expanded rapidly to become the transportation, manufacturing, and distributing center for a vast agricultural area.

regression In STATISTICS, a process for determining a line or curve that best represents the general trend of a data set. Linear regression results in a line of best fit, for which the sum of the squares of the vertical distances between the proposed line and the points of the data set are minimized. Other types of regression may be based on higher-degree POLYNOMIAL functions or EXPONENTIAL FUNCTIONS.

regressive tax Tax levied at a rate that decreases as its base increases. The base is often considered to be the taxpayer's total income. Regressivity is considered undesirable because poorer people pay a greater percentage of their income in tax than wealthier people. Consumption taxes and SALES TAXES are usually considered regressive because of their set rate structures. Tobacco, gasoline, and liquor sales taxes, because they are so high, are the most regressive taxes. To limit regressivity, some U.S. states have exempted medicine and grocery items from sales tax. PROPERTY TAX is often judged regressive because poorer people spend a larger percentage of their income on housing than wealthier people. See also PROGRESSIVE TAX.

regular polyhedron Geometric solid all of whose faces are identical regular POLYGONS and all of whose angles are equal. There are only five such POLYHEDRONS. The cube is constructed from the square, the dodecahedron from the regular pentagon, and the tetrahedron, octahedron, and icosahedron (with 20 faces) from the equilateral triangle.

Though described by EUCLID, they are often called the Platonic solids.

regulatory agency Independent government commission charged by the legislature with setting and enforcing standards for specific industries in the private sector. The concept was invented by the U.S. government in 1887, and regulatory agencies exist almost exclusively in the U.S. The theory is that a commission of experts on an industry is better equipped to regulate it than the legislature or executive departments. Designed to operate with a minimum of executive or legislative supervision, agencies have executive, legislative, and judicial functions, and their regulations have the force of law. Important regulatory agencies include the FOOD AND DRUG ADMINISTRATION, FEDERAL COMMUNICATIONS COMMISSION, and SECURITIES AND EXCHANGE COMMISSION.

Rehnquist \'ren-ˌkwist\, **William H(ubbs)** (b.1924) U.S. jurist. Born in Milwaukee, he practiced law in Phoenix (1953–69), where he became active in the conservative wing of the Republican Party. At the U.S. Justice Department (1969–71), he opposed civil-rights legislation and advocated greatly enlarged police powers. Nominated for the Supreme Court in 1972, he became chief justice in 1986. He has led the Court along a conservative path. In 1999 he presided over the Senate impeachment trial of Pres. William CLINTON.

Reich \'rīsh\, **Steve** (orig. Stephen Michael) (b.1936) U.S. composer. Born in New York City, he majored in philosophy before pursuing interests in Balinese music and learning drumming in Ghana. His early music explored the process of simultaneous repeated patterns gradually slipping out of phase ("process music"), and he was prominent among the early "minimalists" of the 1970s. His early works include *Drumming* (1971) and *Music for 18 Musicians* (1976); later works such as *Different Trains* (1988) show an expanded compositional vocabulary.

Reich \'rīk\, **Wilhelm** (1897–1957) Austrian-U.S. psychologist. He joined the faculty of the Vienna Psychoanalytic Institute in 1924. In *The Function of the Orgasm* (1927), he argued that the failure to achieve orgasm could produce neurosis. An advocate of sexual education and freedom as well as of radical left-wing politics, he left Germany in 1933 and settled in the U.S. in 1939. After breaking with the psychoanalytic movement in 1934, he developed a pseudoscientific system called orgonomy. Conceiving of mental illness as deficiency of cosmic energy, measured in "orgone" units, he treated it by placing the patient in an "orgone box." Reich's views brought him into conflict with U.S. authorities in the early 1950s; convicted of contempt of court, he died in prison.

Reichstadt, Duke of See NAPOLEON II

Reichstag fire \'rīks-ˌtäk\ (Feb. 27, 1933) Burning of the German parliament building (Reichstag) in Berlin. Allegedly set by a Dutch communist, the fire was used by Adolf HITLER to turn public opinion against his opponents. He enacted a decree suspending constitutional protection of personal rights, which effectively began the NAZI PARTY dictatorship. The fire was widely believed to have been set by the Nazis themselves, but it remains the subject of debate and research.

Reign of Terror *French* la Terreur (1793–94) Period in the FRENCH REVOLUTION. Established to take harsh measures against those suspected of being enemies of the Revolution (including nobles, priests, and hoarders), it was controlled by the radical COMMITTEE OF PUBLIC SAFETY and Maximilen de ROBESPIERRE. The Terror eliminated enemies on both the left (Jacques HÉBERT) and the right (Georges DANTON). A law passed in June 1794 that suspended a suspect's right to public trial or legal defense caused the THERMIDORIAN REACTION and Robespierre's overthrow. About 300,000 suspects were arrested during the period; about 17,000 were executed and many others died in prison.

Reims or **Rheims** \'rēmz, *French* 'reⁿs\ City (pop., 1999: 187,000), NE France. In the 5th cent. the Frankish king CLOVIS I was baptized there; in honor of this occasion most later French kings were crowned there. Badly damaged in World Wars I and II, it was the scene of Germany's unconditional surrender in May 1945. It is a major champagne producing center. Its 13th-cent. cathedral of Notre-Dame, though damaged by bombing, is one of the most notable Gothic cathedrals in France.

reincarnation or **transmigration of souls** or **metempsychosis** Doctrine of the rebirth of the SOUL in one or more successive existences, which may be human, animal, or vegetable. Belief in reincarnation is characteristic of Asian religions, especially HINDUISM, JAINISM, BUDDHISM, and SIKHISM. All hold to the doctrine of KARMA, the belief that actions in this life will have their effect in the next. Escape from the cycle of birth and rebirth through enlightenment is a primary spiritual goal. MANICHAEISM and GNOSTICISM also accepted the concept of reincarnation, as do such modern spiritual movements as THEOSOPHY.

reindeer Any species of Arctic DEER in the genus *Rangifer* (family Cervidae), especially Old World species. New World species are usually called CARIBOU. The reindeer herded by the Sami (Lapps) are used as draft and pack animals and as a source of meat and milk; their skins are used for tents, boots, and other clothing.

Reiner, Carl (b.1922) U.S. actor, writer, director, and producer. Born in the Bronx, N.Y., he acted with Sid CAESAR in the television comedy series *Your Show of Shows* (1950–54). He created and produced *The Dick Van Dyke Show* (1961–66), for which he won several Emmy awards. His novel *Enter Laughing* (1958) was adapted as a play (1963) and a movie (1967). He directed such films as *Where's Poppa* (1970) and *Oh, God!* (1977). His son Rob Reiner (b.1947) became famous as "Meathead" in television's *All in the Family* (1971–78). Rob's film-directing career has included *This Is Spinal Tap* (1984), *Stand By Me* (1986), *The Princess Bride* (1987), *When Harry Met Sally . . .* (1989), *Misery* (1990), and *A Few Good Men* (1992).

reinforced concrete Concrete in which steel is embedded for added strength. The reinforcing steel—rods, bars, or mesh—absorbs the tensile, shear, and sometimes the compressive stresses in a concrete structure. Plain concrete does not easily withstand tensile and shear stresses caused by wind, earthquakes, vibrations, and other forces and is therefore unsuitable in most structural applications. In reinforced concrete, the tensile strength of steel and the compressive strength of concrete work together. The invention of reinforced concrete in the 19th cent. revolutionized the construction industry, and concrete became one of the world's most common building materials.

Reinhardt, Ad(olf Frederick) (1913–1967) U.S. painter. Born in Buffalo, N.Y., he studied art after graduating from Columbia Univ. He employed several abstract styles, but by the early 1950s he had restricted his works to monochrome paintings incorporating squares and oblong shapes against backgrounds of similar color, in which line, brushwork, and most other visual elements were suppressed. He explained his style as an art that would be entirely separate from life. He influenced the MINIMALISM of the 1960s.

Reinhardt, Django (orig. Jean-Baptiste) (1910–1953) French guitarist, the first great European jazz soloist. Of Gypsy parentage, Reinhardt adapted his guitar technique to accommodate the loss of the use of two fingers burned in a caravan fire in 1928. With jazz violinist Stéphane Grappelli (1908–1997), he formed the Quintette du Hot Club de France in 1934. One of the first important guitar soloists in jazz, his blend of SWING and the Gypsy tradition as well as his unconventional technique made him a legendary figure.

Reinhardt, Max orig. Max Goldmann (1873–1943) German (Austrian-born) theatrical director. An actor in Berlin from 1894, he directed his first play in 1902 and managed a small theater from 1903; he became famous for his creative staging of *A Midsummer Night's Dream*. He

Max Reinhardt

bought Berlin's Deutsches Theater and remodeled it with the latest innovations in scenic design and lighting. Known for his stunning visual effects, he won acclaim for his staging of the religious spectacle *The Miracle* (1911). He co-founded the Salzburg Festival in 1920, where he staged *Jedermann* (an adaptation of *Everyman*). He left Germany in 1933 and eventually settled in the U.S. A major influence on 20th-cent. drama, he helped increase the creative authority of the director.

relapsing fever Infectious disease with recurring FEVER, caused by several SPIROCHETES of the genus *Borrelia,* transmitted by lice, ticks, and bedbugs. Onset is sudden, with high fever, which breaks within a week with profuse sweating. Symptoms return about a week later. There may be two to 10 relapses, usually decreasing in severity. Mortality usually ranges from 0 to 6%, up to 30% in rare epidemics. The first microorganisms clearly associated with serious human disease (1867–68), the spirochetes mutate repeatedly, so that the host's IMMUNITY no longer is effective, which produces the relapses. Antibiotics can be effective, but inadequate therapy may leave spirochetes alive to reinvade the bloodstream.

relational database DATABASE in which all data are stored in tables. The description of an item is provided by the set of its attribute values, stored as one row or record of the table. Similar items from different records can appear in a table column. The relational approach allows queries that involve several tables by providing automatic links across tables. Payroll data, for example, can be stored in one table and personnel-benefits data in another; complete information on an employee can be obtained by joining the tables on the employee's identification number. The relational approach is currently the most popular model for DATABASE MANAGEMENT SYSTEMS.

relative density See SPECIFIC GRAVITY

relativity Concept in PHYSICS that measurements change when considered by observers in various states of motion. In classical physics, it was assumed that all observers anywhere in the universe would obtain identical measurements of space and time intervals. According to relativity theory, this is not so. There are two distinct theories of relativity, both proposed by Albert EINSTEIN. The special theory (1905) developed from Einstein's acceptance that the speed of LIGHT is the same in all REFERENCE FRAMES. It is concerned primarily with electric and magnetic phenomena and their propagation in space and time. The general theory (1916) was developed primarily to deal with GRAVITATION and involves accelerating reference frames. Both theories are major milestones in the history of modern physics. See also SPACE-TIME.

relief (Italian *rilievo*, from *rilevare:* "to raise") In sculpture, any work in which the figures project from a supporting background, usually a plane surface. Bas-reliefs ("low reliefs"), in which the design projects only slightly, were common on the walls of stone buildings in ancient Egypt, Assyria, and elsewhere in the Middle East. High reliefs, in which the forms project at least half or more of their natural circumference, were first employed by the ancient Greeks. Italian Renaissance sculptors combined high and low relief in strikingly illusionistic compositions, as in Lorenzo GHIBERTI's bronze doors in Florence. The dramatic possibilities of the Renaissance concept of relief were later notably employed by François RUDE (*The Marseillaise,* 1833–36) and Auguste RODIN (*The Gates of Hell*).

relief Public or private aid to people in economic need because of natural disasters, wars, economic upheaval, chronic unemployment, or other conditions that prevent self-sufficiency. Relief of chronic social conditions is now usually referred to as WELFARE. In 17th-cent. China the government maintained granaries for use in times of famine. Through the 19th cent., disaster relief in Europe consisted largely of emergency grants of food, clothing, and medical care through hastily organized local committees. In the 20th cent., disaster relief became one of the chief activities of the International RED CROSS and other international agencies. In England, the Poor Law Reform Act of 1834 required people able to work to enter a workhouse in order to receive public assistance. The U.S. government responded to the Great Depression with the NEW DEAL, which emphasized work relief programs such as the WORKS PROGRESS ADMINISTRATION. In the later 20th cent., the work requirement was abandoned in most countries, but the U.S. enacted "workfare" laws in 1996 cutting off relief for most able-bodied welfare recipients who fail to take government-sponsored jobs.

relief printing See LETTERPRESS PRINTING

religion Relation of human beings to God or the gods or to whatever they consider sacred or, in some cases, merely supernatural. Archaeological evidence suggests that religious beliefs have existed since the first human communities. They are generally shared by a community, and they express the communal culture and values through myth, doctrine, and ritual. Worship is probably the most basic element of religion, but moral conduct, right belief, and participation in religious institutions are also important. Broadly speaking, some religions (e.g., JUDAISM, CHRISTIANITY, and ISLAM) are outwardly focused, and others (e.g., JAINISM, BUDDHISM) are inwardly focused.

Religion, Wars of (1562–98) Conflicts in France between Protestants and Catholics. The spread of French CALVINISM persuaded the French ruler CATHERINE DE MÉDICIS to show tolerance for the HUGUENOTS, which angered the powerful Catholic GUISE family. Its partisans massacred a Huguenot congregation at Vassy (1562), causing an uprising in the provinces. Many inconclusive skirmishes followed, and compromises were reached in 1563, 1568, and 1570. After the SAINT BARTHOLOMEW'S DAY Massacre (1572), the civil war resumed. A peace compromise in 1576 allowed the Huguenots freedom of worship. In 1584 the Huguenot leader Henry of Navarre (later HENRY IV) became heir to the French throne. This led to the War of the Three Henrys (1587-89) and later brought Spain to aid the Catholics. The wars ended with Henry's embrace of Catholicism and the religious toleration of the Huguenots guaranteed by the Edict of NANTES (1598).

Remagen \\'rā-ˌmäg-ᵊn\\ Town (pop., 1992 est.: 15,000), W Germany. Located on the RHINE RIVER, southeast of BONN, it still has Roman remains. In World War II its railroad bridge was the site where Allied troops forced a crossing of the Rhine (1945) for the first time in the war.

Remak \\'rā-ˌmäk\\, **Robert** (1815–1865) German embryologist and neurologist. He discovered and named the three germ layers of cells that develop in the early EMBRYO: the ectoderm, mesoderm, and endoderm. He also discovered various other structures and was a pioneer in electrotherapy for nervous diseases. He achieved enough eminence to become a university lecturer despite Prussian laws barring Jews from teaching.

remanent magnetism See PALEOMAGNETISM

Remarque \\rə-ˈmärk\\, **Erich Maria** *orig.* Erich Paul Remark (1898–1970) German-Swiss novelist. Drafted into the army at 18, he was wounded in World War I. He is chiefly remembered for *All Quiet on the Western Front* (1929), a brutally realistic account of the daily routine of ordinary soldiers and perhaps the best-known novel about that war. He came to the U.S. in 1939, but settled in Switzerland after World War II. His other works include *Arc de Triomphe* (1946; film, 1948).

Rembrandt (Harmenszoon) van Rijn \\rīn\\ (1606–1669) Dutch painter and etcher. The son of a prosperous miller in Leiden, he was apprenticed to masters there and in Amsterdam. After moving to Amsterdam in 1631, he quickly became the city's most fashionable portrait painter, and in 1632 he was commissioned to paint the celebrated *Anatomy Lesson of Dr. Nicolaes Tulp.* Yearning for recognition as a biblical and mythological painter, he produced his *Sacrifice of Isaac* (1635) and the unconventional masterpiece *Danaë* (1636). He painted many tender pictures of his wife, Saskia, between 1634 and her death in 1642. In 1642 he completed his largest painting, the extraordinary but controversial *Militia Company of Captain Frans Banning Cocq* (known as *The Night Watch*), a watershed in his life and art. He later turned increasingly to etchings and biblical subjects; his *Christ at Emmaus* (1648) exemplifies the quiet dignity and vulnerability of his later spirituality. In his last decade he treated biblical subjects like portraits, and also did a wealth of self-portraits; many of these paintings evoke a timeless world of quiet, deep emotion. His paintings are characterized by luxuriant brushwork, rich color, and a mastery of chiaroscuro. The silent human figure, Rembrandt's central subject, contributes to the sense of a shared dialogue between viewer and picture, the foundation of Rembrandt's greatness and of his popularity today.

Remington, Eliphalet (1793–1861) U.S. firearms manufacturer and inventor. Son of a blacksmith in Suffield, Conn., he grew up near Utica, N.Y., where he made his first flintlock rifle (1816). In 1828 he built a large arms factory. He and his son Philo improved arms manufacturing methods and produced the first cast-steel, drilled rifle barrel made in the U.S. In 1847 he supplied the U.S. Navy with its first breech-loading rifle. His Remington Arms Co. made small arms for the U.S. government during the American Civil War and World Wars I and II.

Remington, Frederic (1861–1909) U.S. painter, illustrator, and sculptor. Born in Canton, N.Y., he studied at Yale Univ. He traveled widely and specialized in depicting Indians, cowboys, soldiers, horses, and other aspects of life on the Plains. His work is notable for its rendering of swift action and its accuracy of detail. He covered the Spanish-American War (1898) as a correspondent. His bronze sculptures and the countless reproductions of his works as newspaper engravings brought him wealth and fame.

remora \'re-mə-rə\ *or* **sharksucker** *or* **suckerfish** Any of 8–10 species of marine fishes (family Echeneidae) noted for attaching themselves to SHARKS, other marine animals, and oceangoing ships by means of a flat, oval sucking disk on top of the head. They are thin and dark, 1–3 ft (30–90 cm) long. They live in warm waters worldwide, feeding on the leavings or the external parasites of their hosts.

Renaissance \'re-nə-ˌsäns\ (French: "rebirth") Late-medieval cultural movement in European civilization that brought renewed interest in classical learning and values. The Renaissance began in Italy during the late 13th cent. and spread throughout Europe in the 15th cent., ending in the 16th–17th cent. Inspired by ancient Greece and Rome, Renaissance artists produced painting and sculpture based on the observation of the visible world and practiced according to mathematical principles of balance, harmony, and perspective. The new aesthetic tenets found expression in the works of such Italian artists as LEONARDO DA VINCI, Sandro BOTTICELLI, RAPHAEL, TITIAN, and MICHELANGELO, and the city of Florence became the center of Renaissance art. In the world of letters, humanists such as Desiderius ERASMUS rejected religious orthodoxy in favor of the study of human nature, and such writers as PETRARCH and Giovanni BOCCACCIO in Italy, François RABELAIS in France, and William SHAKESPEARE in England produced works that emphasized the intricacies of human character.

Renaissance architecture Style of architecture, reflecting the rebirth of Classical culture, that originated in Florence in the early 15th cent. and spread throughout Europe, replacing the medieval Gothic style. Ancient Roman forms, including the column and round arch, the tunnel VAULT, and the dome, were revived. The basic design element was the ORDER. Knowledge of CLASSICAL ARCHITECTURE came from the ruins of ancient buildings and the writings of VITRUVIUS. As in the Classical period, proportion was the most important factor of beauty; this concern resulted in clear, easily comprehended space and mass, distinguishing the Renaissance style from the more complex Gothic. Filippo BRUNELLESCHI is considered the first Renaissance architect. Leon Battista ALBERTI's *Ten Books on Architecture*, inspired by Vitruvius, became a bible of Renaissance architecture. From Florence the early Renaissance style spread through Italy. Donato BRAMANTE's move to Rome ushered in the High Renaissance (c.1500–20). Mannerism, the style of the Late Renaissance (1520–1600), was characterized by sophistication, complexity, and novelty rather than the harmony, clarity, and repose of the High Renaissance, and Sebastiano Serlio (1475–1554), Giacomo da Vignola (1507–1573), and Andrea PALLADIO published influential books.

renal calculus See KIDNEY STONE
renal failure See KIDNEY FAILURE
renal system See URINARY SYSTEM
renal transplant See KIDNEY TRANSPLANT

Renan \rə-ˈnäⁿ\, **(Joseph-) Ernest** (1823–1892) French philosopher, historian, and scholar of religion. He trained for the priesthood but left the Catholic church in 1845, feeling that its teachings were incompatible with the findings of historical criticism. His *Life of Jesus* (1863) was an attempt to reconstruct the mind of Jesus as a wholly human person. It was virulently denounced by the church but widely read by the general public. His later works include the series *History of the People of Israel* (1888–96).

Reni \'rä-nē\, **Guido** (1575–1642) Italian painter. Apprenticed at 10, he was later influenced by the novel naturalism of the CARRACCI FAMILY of his native Bologna, the frescoes of RAPHAEL, and ancient Greco-Roman sculpture. He executed many important commissions in Rome, including the celebrated ceiling fresco *Aurora* (1613–14). In his religious and mythological works, he tempered baroque exuberance and complexity with classical restraint, tender emotion, and delicate coloring.

Rennes \'ren\ City (pop., 1999: 206,000), W France. It was the capital of BRITTANY in the Middle Ages, and a rival of NANTES. It was the seat of the Brittany parliament 1561–1675. It was almost completely destroyed by fire in 1720, and heavily bombed in World War II. An industrial city, it is also the cultural center of Brittany.

Reno \'rē-nō\ City (pop., 2000: 180,000), W Nevada. It lies near the California border and Lake TAHOE. From around 1920, after several well-known people were granted divorces or quickly married there under liberal state laws, it became famous as a busy divorce and marriage center. It is also a year-round vacation site. When gambling was legalized in Nevada in 1931, Reno began to attract tourists to its many casinos.

Renoir \rən-ˈwär\, **(Pierre-) Auguste** (1841–1919) French painter. Renoir began working as a decorator of porcelain at 13 and studied painting at night. He formed a close friendship with his fellow student Claude MONET and became a leading member of the Paris Impressionists. His early works were typically Impressionist snapshots of real life, full of sparkling color and light, and included *Le Moulin de la Galette* (1876) and *The Luncheon of the Boating Party* (1881). A visit to Italy (1881–82) introduced him to RAPHAEL, and by the mid-1880s he had broken with IMPRESSIONISM to employ a more disciplined, formal technique. In works such as *Bathers* (1884–87), he emphasized volume, form, contours, and line. In his later works, he departed from strict Classicism to paint colorful still lifes, portraits, nudes, and landscapes of S France, where he settled in 1907. Rheumatism confined him to a wheelchair by 1912, but he never ceased to paint, often with his brush attached to his hand. Jean RENOIR was his son.

Renoir, Jean (1894–1979) French film director. The son of Auguste RENOIR, he directed his first film, *La fille de l'eau*, in 1924. His films were marked by a keen pictorial sense and a deep appreciation for the unpredictability of human character. He cowrote the screenplays for many of his films, including *Madame Bovary* (1934), *The Crime of Monsieur Lange* (1936), and *La bête humaine* (1938) as well as his two masterpieces, *Grand Illusion* (1937) and *The Rules of the Game* (1939), among the greatest films ever made. In the U.S. (1940–51) he directed *The Diary of a Chambermaid* (1946) and *The River* (1951). He received an honorary Academy Award in 1975.

Rensselaer Polytechnic Institute \ˌren-sə-ˈlēr\ Private technological university in Troy, N.Y. Founded in 1824 by Stephen Van Rensselaer, it was one of the first U.S. colleges dedicated to science and civil engineering. It comprises schools of architecture, engineering, humanities and social sciences, management, and science. Facilities include a technology park, a communications center, and a center for industrial innovation. Total enrollment is about 6,500.

rent In common usage, payment made in return for the right to use property belonging to another. In CLASSICAL ECONOMICS, rent was the income gained from cultivated or improved land after the deduction of all production costs. In modern economic usage, rent is the difference between the total return to a factor of production (LAND, LABOR, CAPI-

TAL) and its supply PRICE, the minimum amount necessary to attain its services.

reparations Payment in money or materials by a nation defeated in war. After WORLD WAR I, reparations to the ALLIED POWERS were required of Germany by the Treaty of VERSAILLES. Though the original amount of $33 billion was later reduced and finally canceled, German resentment over reparations was used by ultranationalists to foment political unrest.

Repin \\'ryā-pyin, *Engl* 'rā-pin\\, **Ilya (Yefimovich)** (1844–1930) Russian painter. After training at the St. Petersburg Academy of Fine Arts, he visited France and Italy. On his return he began painting subjects from Russian history. In 1873 he achieved international fame with *Volga Boatmen*, a grim, powerful image that became the model for Soviet SOCIALIST REALISM. Among his best-known works is *Ivan the Terrible and His Son Ivan* (1895). He also painted vigorous portraits (including Leo TOLSTOY and Modest MUSSORGSKY). In 1894 he became professor of historical painting at the St. Petersburg Academy.

representationalism Theory of knowledge based on the assertion that the mind perceives only mental representations of material objects, not the objects themselves. Human knowledge is thus challenged to show that such images correspond to the external objects. The doctrine has roots in CARTESIANISM, the EMPIRICISM of John LOCKE and David HUME, and the IDEALISM of Immanuel KANT.

repression In metabolism, a control mechanism by which a protein molecule, called a repressor, prevents the synthesis of an ENZYME by binding to (and thus hindering the action of) the DNA that controls the enzyme's synthesis. See also INHIBITION.

repression In psychoanalytic theory, the exclusion of distressing memories, thoughts, or feelings, often sexual or aggressive urges or painful childhood memories, from the unconscious mind. Repression is thought to give rise to ANXIETY and to neurotic symptoms, which begin when a forbidden impulse threatens to become conscious. PSYCHOANALYSIS seeks to uncover repressed memories and feelings through free ASSOCIATION as well as to examine the repressed wishes released in DREAMS.

reproduction Process by which organisms replicate themselves, assuring continuation of their species. The two basic forms are asexual and sexual. Asexual reproduction (e.g., fission, spore formation, regeneration, and vegetative reproduction) produces an offspring genetically identical to its single parent (see CLONE). Sexual reproduction produces a new individual through the union of special sex cells (gametes), usually from different parents (see MEIOSIS). With sexual reproduction, each offspring is genetically unique (except in cases of multiple offspring derived from divisions of one zygote). Most animals reproduce sexually.

reproductive system, human Organ system by which humans reproduce. In females, the OVARIES sit near the openings of the fallopian (uterine) tubes, which carry EGGS from the ovaries to the UTERUS. The cervix extends from the lower end of the uterus into the VAGINA, whose opening, as well as that of the urethra (see URINARY SYSTEM), is covered by four folds of skin (the labia); the clitoris is located where the labia join in front. The activity of the ovaries and uterus goes through a monthly cycle (see MENSTRUATION) except during PREGNANCY and nursing. In males, the TESTES lie in a sac of skin (the scrotum). A long duct (the vas deferens) leads from each testis and carries SPERM to the ejaculatory ducts in the PROSTATE GLAND; these join the urethra, which continues through the PENIS. In the urethra, sperm mixes with other secretions to form SEMEN. In early embryos, the reproductive systems are undetermined. By birth the organs appropriate to each sex have typically developed. At PUBERTY their activity increases and maturation occurs. See diagram, right.

reptile Any of some 6,000 species of the class Reptilia, air-breathing VERTEBRATES that have internal fertilization and a scaly body and are cold-blooded. Most species have short legs (or none) and long tails. Living reptiles include SNAKES and LIZARDS (order Squamata), CROCODILES (Crocodilia), and TURTLES (Chelonia). Being cold-blooded, reptiles are not found in very cold regions, and in regions with cold

winters they usually hibernate. They range in size from GECKOS of about 1 in. (3 cm) long to the PYTHON, which grows to 30 ft (9 m); the largest turtle weighs about 1,500 lbs (680 kg). Extinct reptiles include the DINOSAURS and PTEROSAURS.

republic Form of government in which the leader is periodically appointed under a constitution. It was originally contrasted with governments in which leadership was heredi-

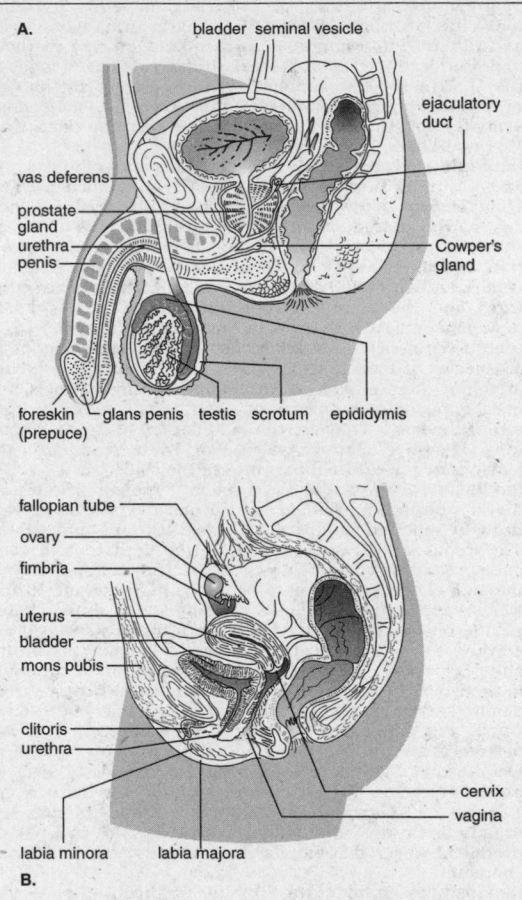

Reproductive system A. Male reproductive system. The scrotum, a pouch of skin, is divided into two sacs, each containing a testis and its associated epididymis. Tubules within the testes contain sperm cells at different stages of development. As sperm leaves the testes, it passes into the epididymis, a highly coiled tube that serves as a reservoir for sperm. The vas deferens, a duct leading out from the epididymis, joins with the duct of the seminal vesicles as it passes through the prostate gland to form a single tube (ejaculatory duct) which opens into the urethra, the tube that conveys both sperm and urine out through the penis. B. Female reproductive system. In a menstruating woman, a follicle containing an egg matures each month in either of two ovaries. Ovulation occurs as the mature follicle ruptures and releases an egg, which is drawn into the ovary's associated fallopian (uterine) tube, which contains a fringe of fingerlike projections (fimbriae). Fertilization usually occurs in the fallopian tube as the egg travels to the uterus. Successful implantation of a fertilized egg in the uterus results in development of an embryo. The vagina, a muscular tube that leads to the uterus, allows sperm to pass into the uterus and serves as a passageway for the fetus during childbirth.

tary, but is now understood to mean a state ruled by representatives elected by its populace, all of which is enfranchised. See also DEMOCRACY.

Republican, Radical See RADICAL REPUBLICAN

Republican Party *or* **GOP (Grand Old Party)** One of two major U.S. political parties. Formed in 1854 by former members of the WHIG, DEMOCRATIC, and FREE SOIL parties who chose the party's name to recall the Jeffersonian Republicans' concern with the national interest above sectional interests and states' rights, it opposed slavery and its extension into the territories (see KANSAS-NEBRASKA ACT). Its first presidential candidate, J. C. FRÉMONT, won 11 states in 1856; its second, Abraham LINCOLN, won the 1860 election. Its association with the Union victory in the AMERICAN CIVIL WAR allowed it a long period of dominance; Republican candidates won 14 of 18 presidential elections between 1860 and 1932, through support from an alliance of farmers and big-business interests. The presidency of Theodore ROOSEVELT produced a progressive wing of the party, which divided it and gave control to the Democrats 1913–21. The party's inability to deal with the GREAT DEPRESSION led to its ouster from power (1933–53) until Dwight EISENHOWER's presidency brought a moderate wing to prominence. But the party's platform remained conservative, calling for a strong anti-Communist stance, a reduction of government regulation of the economy, lower taxes, and resistance to civil rights legislation. The GOP gained new support from suburbanites and white Southerners disturbed by integration. Richard NIXON won narrowly in 1968 and by a landslide in 1972, but resigned in 1974. Conservatives regained control of the party with the elections of Ronald REAGAN (1980, 1984) and George BUSH (1988). The 1992 election of Democrat William CLINTON was offset by the Republicans' regaining control of Congress (1994) for the first time in 40 years. The election of George W. BUSH in 2000 again brought the party's conservative wing to power.

Republican River River, central U.S. Rising in E Colorado, it flows 422 mi (679 km) through S Nebraska and NE Kansas to unite with the Smoky Hill River at Junction City and form the Kansas River. It is part of the Missouri River Basin flood-control and land-reclamation project.

requiem Musical setting of the MASS for the dead. (*Requiem*, Latin for "rest," is the first word of the mass.) The requiem's text omits the standard mass Ordinary's joyous sections and keeps only the Kyrie, Sanctus, and Agnus Dei, which are combined with other sections including the Dies Irae ("Day of Wrath"). Famous requiems include those of W. A. MOZART, Giuseppe VERDI, and Johannes BRAHMS.

resin \ˈre-zᵊn\ Any natural or synthetic ORGANIC COMPOUND consisting of a noncrystalline (amorphous) solid or viscous liquid substance or mixture. Natural resins are usually transparent or translucent yellow to brown and can melt and burn. Most are exuded from trees when the bark is injured. The fluid secretion usually dries out and hardens (and is thus a "drying oil"). Natural resins may be spirit-soluble (e.g., BALSAMS, TURPENTINE, mastics, and shellac) or oil-soluble (e.g., amber, Oriental lacquer). Synthetic resins are not clearly differentiated from PLASTICS; the term resin is often used for the raw plastic product or the POLYMER fluid to be processed into it. See also ION-EXCHANGE RESIN.

Resistance *or* **Underground** Clandestine groups opposed to Nazi rule in German-occupied Europe in World War II. The groups included unarmed civilians as well as armed bands of partisans or guerrilla fighters. Activities ranged from assisting the escape of Jews and Allied airmen shot down over enemy territory to committing sabotage, ambushing German patrols, and sending intelligence information to the Allies. Resistance groups were not always unified; some rival groups divided along communist and noncommunist lines. However, in France the National Council of the Resistance coordinated all French groups, which gave support to the NORMANDY CAMPAIGN and helped liberate Paris. Resistance groups in other N European countries also undertook military actions to help the Allied forces in 1944–45.

resistance Opposition that a material or electrical CIRCUIT offers to the flow of ELECTRIC CURRENT. It is the property of a circuit that transforms electrical energy into HEAT energy as it opposes the flow of current. The resistance of an electrical CONDUCTOR generally increases with increasing temperature and is utilized in devices such as lamps and heaters. The ohm (Ω) is the common unit of electrical resistance; one ohm is equal to one volt (see ELECTROMOTIVE FORCE) per ampere. See also OHM'S LAW, REACTANCE.

Resnais \rə-ˈnā\, **Alain** (b.1922) French film director. He initially made short films on the visual arts (*Van Gogh*, 1948) and documentaries (*Night and Fog*, 1956). His first feature film, *Hiroshima mon amour* (1959), one of the earliest and best films of the NEW WAVE, created a sensation with its alternation between past and present. He continued his exploration of time and memory in *Last Year at Marienbad* (1961). His later films include *Stavisky* (1974) and *My American Uncle* (1980).

resonance In physics, the relatively large selective response of an object or a system that vibrates in step with an externally applied VIBRATION. Acoustical resonance is the vibration induced in a string of a given pitch when a note of the same pitch is produced nearby, or in the sound box of an instrument such as a guitar. Mechanical resonance, such as that produced in a bridge by wind or by marching soldiers, can eventually produce wide swings great enough to cause the bridge's destruction. Resonance in frequency-sensitive electrical CIRCUITS makes it possible for certain communication devices to accept signals of some frequencies but reject others. See also MAGNETIC RESONANCE, NUCLEAR MAGNETIC RESONANCE.

Respighi \re-ˈspē-gē\, **Ottorino** (1879–1936) Italian composer. Trained in Bologna, he played viola in a Russian orchestra and studied with Nikolai RIMSKY-KORSAKOV. His best-known works are the colorful tone poems *The Fountains of Rome* (1916), *The Pines of Rome* (1924), and *Feste Romane* (1929). Interested in earlier music, he also produced such works as *Ancient Airs and Dances* (1917–32).

respiration Process of taking in air for OXYGEN and releasing it to dispose of CARBON DIOXIDE. Nerve centers in the brain regulate the movements of muscles of respiration (DIAPHRAGM and chest-wall muscles). Blood in the PULMONARY CIRCULATION brings carbon dioxide from the tissues to be exhaled and takes up oxygen from the air in the PULMONARY ALVEOLI to carry it to the heart and the rest of the body. Because the body stores almost no oxygen, interruption of respiration—by asphyxiation, drowning, or chest-muscle paralysis—for more than a few minutes brings death. Disorders affecting respiration include ALLERGY, ASTHMA, BRONCHITIS, EMPHYSEMA, PNEUMONIA, and TUBERCULOSIS. See also RESPIRATORY SYSTEM.

respiratory distress syndrome *or* **idiopathic respiratory distress syndrome** Common complication in newborns. Symptoms include very labored breathing, bluish skin tinge, and low blood oxygen levels. Insufficient surfactant in the PULMONARY ALVEOLI raises surface tension, hampering lung expansion. The alveoli collapse and a membrane develops in the alveolar ducts. Once the leading cause of death in premature infants, the syndrome is now usually treated for a few days with positive-pressure ventilation with no aftereffects.

respiratory system Organ system involved in RESPIRATION. In humans, the DIAPHRAGM and the muscles between the ribs generate a pumping action, moving air through a system of conducting airways. The upper airway system comprises the NOSE, SINUSES, and PHARYNX; the lower airway system consists of the LARYNX, TRACHEA, bronchi, bronchioles, and alveolar ducts (see PULMONARY ALVEOLUS). The blood and CARDIOVASCULAR SYSTEM can be considered part of the respiratory system. See also THORACIC CAVITY. See diagram on following page.

restaurant Establishment where refreshments or meals are served to paying guests. Though inns and taverns served simple fare to travelers for centuries, the first modern restaurant with a varied menu is said to have belonged to A. Boulanger, a soup vendor who opened his business in Paris in 1765. The sign above his door supposedly advertised restoratives, or *restaurants*, referring to his soups and broths. By 1804 Paris had more than 500 restaurants, and France soon became internationally famous for its cuisine. Other European restaurants include the Italian *trattorie*, the

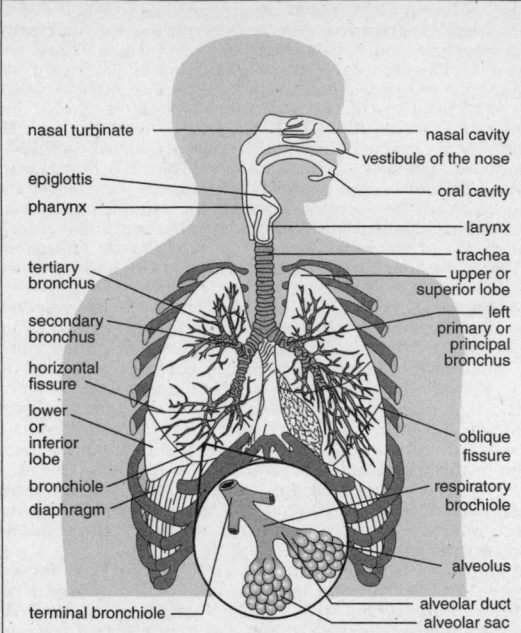

nasal turbinate

nasal cavity

vestibule of the nose

epiglottis

oral cavity

pharynx

larynx

trachea

tertiary bronchus

upper or superior lobe

left primary or principal bronchus

secondary bronchus

horizontal fissure

lower or inferior lobe

oblique fissure

bronchiole

respiratory brochiole

diaphragm

alveolus

terminal bronchiole

alveolar duct
alveolar sac

Respiratory system As air enters the nasal cavity through the nostrils, it is warmed and moistened by mucous membranes of the nasal turbinates before entering the pharynx. Stiff hairs lining the vestibule inside the nostrils help filter the entering air. The air-filled sinuses adjacent to the nasal cavity produce mucus. The larynx connects the pharynx with the trachea or windpipe. The cartilaginous epiglottis prevents food from entering the larynx during swallowing. A left and right primary bronchus supply each lung with air from the trachea. They divide into smaller secondary and tertiary bronchi; the smallest divisions, bronchioles, lead to the cup-shaped, thin-walled alveoli, which occur in clusters (alveolar sacs). Oxygen and carbon dioxide are exchanged between the alveoli and surrounding capillaries. Oblique fissures or grooves of each lung separate the upper lobe from the lower lobe. The horizontal, or transverse, fissure of the right lung forms a middle lobe. Movement of the diaphragm along with the ribs and rib muscles causes expansion and contraction of the lungs during breathing.

German *Weinstuben,* the Spanish tapas bars, and the PUBLIC HOUSES of England. Asian restaurants include the Japanese sushi bars and teahouses serving formal Kaiseki cuisine as well as the noodle shops of China. In the U.S., the cafeteria originated in San Francisco during the 1849 gold rush; it displays a variety of foods and features self-service. The U.S. also pioneered fast-food restaurants such as Horn & Hardart's mechanized Automats (1902–91), White Castle (founded 1921), and McDonald's (see Ray KROC).

Restoration Restoration of the monarchy in England in 1660. It marked the return of CHARLES II as king (1660–85) following the period of Oliver CROMWELL's Commonwealth. The bishops were restored to Parliament, which established a strict Anglican orthodoxy. The period, which also included the reign of JAMES II (1685–88), was marked by an expansion in colonial trade and a revival of drama and literature (see RESTORATION LITERATURE).

Restoration literature English literature written after the RESTORATION of the monarchy in 1660. Some equate its era with the reign of CHARLES II (1660–85), while others add the reign of JAMES II (1685–88). Such literary forms as the novel, biography, history, travel writing, and journalism began to develop with sureness during the period. Pamphlets and poetry (notably by John DRYDEN) flourished, but the

age is chiefly remembered for its glittering, critical, and often bawdy stage comedies by George ETHEREGE, Thomas SHADWELL, William WYCHERLEY, John VANBRUGH, William CONGREVE, and George FARQUHAR.

retailing Selling of merchandise directly to the consumer. Retailing began several thousand years ago with peddlers hawking their wares at the earliest marketplaces. Modern retailing is extremely competitive, with high failure rates. Price is the most important arena of competition, but other factors include convenience of location, selection and display of merchandise, attractiveness of the establishment, and reputation. Retailing today includes vending machines, telephone sales, direct-mail marketing, discount houses, specialty stores, DEPARTMENT STORES, supermarkets, e-commerce, and consumer COOPERATIVES.

reticuloendothelial system \re-ˌtik-yə-lō-ˌen-də-ˈthē-lē-əl\ *or* **macrophage system** \ˈmak-rə-ˌfāj\ Part of the body's defenses consisting of a class of cells widely distributed in the body. Reticuloendothelial cells filter out and destroy BACTERIA, VIRUSES, and foreign substances, and destroy worn-out or abnormal cells and tissues. Precursor cells in bone marrow develop into monocytes (see LEUKOCYTE), which are released into the bloodstream. Most enter body tissues, developing into much larger cells called macrophages. Some roam through the circulation and between cells and can coalesce into a single cell around a foreign object to engulf it. Reticuloendothelial cells also interact with LYMPHOCYTES in immune reactions. Cells in the SPLEEN destroy old red blood cells and recycle their HEMOGLOBIN. See also LYMPHATIC SYSTEM.

retina \ˈre-tᵊn-ə\ Layer of nerve tissue covering the back two-thirds of the eyeball. Light focused onto the retina by the lens of the EYE stimulates two types of light-sensitive cells: rods, which are sensitive to low light levels, and cones, which provide detailed vision and color perception. Chemical changes in these cells trigger nerve impulses, which are carried through the optic nerve to the brain. Disorders decrease vision and can cause BLINDNESS (see DETACHED RETINA, MACULAR DEGENERATION).

retrograde motion In astronomy, the actual or apparent motion of a body in a direction opposite to that of the "direct" motion of most similar bodies. The term originally referred to the apparent reversal of the planets' motion through the stars for several months in each SYNODIC PERIOD. This made earth-centered models of the universe (see PTOLEMY) overly complex, but was naturally explained in heliocentric models (see COPERNICAN SYSTEM) by earth's motion relative to other planets. Nearly all bodies in the SOLAR SYSTEM revolve and rotate in the same counterclockwise direction, which probably arose as the SOLAR NEBULA formed. The few objects moving the other way (e.g., Venus, Uranus, and Pluto for rotation) are also described as retrograde.

retrovirus \ˌre-trō-ˈvī-rəs\ Any of a group of VIRUSES that, unlike most viruses and all cellular organisms, carry their genetic blueprint as RNA. Retroviruses cause some cancers and viral infections of animals, and at least one type of human cancer. The retrovirus HIV is the cause of AIDS in humans. They use RNA to synthesize DNA, the reverse of the usual cell process; this makes it possible for genetic material from a retrovirus to enter and become a permanent part of the GENES of an infected cell.

Réunion \rē-ˈyün-yən\ Island (pop., 2000: 727,000) and French overseas department, Mascarene Islands, W Indian Ocean. Located 425 mi (684 km) east of Madagascar, it is about 39 mi (63 km) long and 28 mi (45 km) wide. Its capital is ST.-DENIS. It consists mainly of rugged mountains dissected by torrential rivers. It was settled in the 17th cent. by the French, who brought slaves from E Africa to work on coffee and sugar plantations. In 1946 it became an overseas department of France. Its economy is based almost entirely on sugar for export.

Reuters \ˈroi-tərz\ British cooperative NEWS AGENCY. Founded in 1851 by P. J. Reuter (1816–1899), it was initially concerned with commercial news but soon began to serve a newspaper clientele. Reuters and two rival agencies eventually agreed on a division of territory and for many years held a virtual monopoly on world press services. In 1925 its structure began moving toward a cooperative of British and

Australasian press interests. As a cooperative, it draws on an extensive range of resources and provides services in most countries.

Reuther \\'rü-thər\\, **Walter (Philip)** (1907–1970) U.S. labor leader. Born in Wheeling, W.V., he traveled around the world in the 1930s, developing a lifelong distaste for communism after spending two years in a Soviet auto factory. He became a local union leader in Detroit and helped organize sit-down strikes—during which he suffered brutal physical attacks—that made the UNITED AUTOMOBILE WORKERS (UAW) a power in the auto industry. As president of the UAW from 1946 until his death, he was an effective negotiator of wages-and-hours gains. He became president of the Congress of Industrial Organizations (CIO) in 1952 and was an architect of the AFL-CIO merger in 1955. He was second in power to George MEANY at the AFL-CIO; however, their repeated clashes resulted in Reuther's leading the UAW out of the AFL-CIO in 1968. He died in a plane crash.

revelation Transmission of knowledge from a god or the gods to humans. In the Western monotheistic religions of Judaism, Christianity, and Islam, revelation is the basis of religious knowledge. God may communicate with his chosen servants through dreams, visions, or physical manifestations. His will may also be translated directly into writing through the handing down of divine law (e.g., the TEN COMMANDMENTS) or SCRIPTURE (e.g., the BIBLE and the QURAN). Other religions emphasize "cosmic" revelation, in which any and all aspects of the world may reveal the nature of a single underlying divine power (e.g., BRAHMAN in the VEDAS).

Revelation, Book of or **Revelations** or **Apocalypse of John** Last book of the NEW TESTAMENT. It consists of two main parts, the first containing moral admonitions to several Christian churches in Asia Minor, and the second composed of extraordinary visions, allegories, and symbols that have been the subject of varying interpretations throughout history. The book may reflect a contemporary crisis of faith, possibly the result of Roman persecutions. References to "a thousand years" have led some to expect that the final victory over evil will come after the completion of a millennium (see MILLENNIALISM). Modern scholarship accepts that the book was written not by St. JOHN THE APOSTLE but by various unknown authors in the late 1st cent. A.D. See also APOCALYPSE.

Revels, Hiram R(hoades) (1822–1901) U.S. clergyman and politician. Born to free blacks in Fayetteville, N.C., he became a pastor and principal of a Baltimore school for blacks. In the Civil War he helped organize black volunteer regiments for the Union army. After the war he moved to Natchez, Miss., and in 1870 was elected to the U.S. Senate to fill the unexpired term of Jefferson DAVIS, becoming the first black elected to the Senate. He later served as president of Alcorn A&M College for blacks (1871–74, 1876–83).

revenue bond or **limited obligation bond** BOND issued by a municipality, state, or public agency authorized to build, acquire, or improve a revenue-producing property such as a waterworks, electric generating plant, or railroad. Unlike general-obligation bonds, which are repaid through a variety of tax sources, revenue bonds are payable from specified revenues only, usually the revenues from the facility for which the bond was originally issued. Revenue bonds typically pay interest rates higher than those of general-obligation bonds.

revenue sharing Funding arrangement in which one government unit grants a portion of its tax income to another government unit. For example, provinces or states may share revenue with local governments, or national governments with provinces or states. Laws determine the formulas by which revenue is shared, limiting the controls of the supplier over the receiver and specifying whether the receiver must provide matching funds. Such countries as Canada, India, and Switzerland have used revenue sharing. The U.S. pursued a revenue-sharing program (1972–86) in which state and local governments received federal funds to spend as they saw fit.

Revere, Paul (1735–1818) American patriot and silversmith. Born in Boston, he entered his father's trade as a silversmith and engraver. An ardent patriot, he took part in the BOSTON TEA PARTY. As the principal rider for Boston's Committee of Safety, he arranged to signal the British approach by having lanterns placed in Boston's Old North Church steeple: "One if by land and two if by sea." On April 18, 1775, he set off to ride to Lexington to alert colonists that British troops were on the march and to warn Samuel ADAMS and John HANCOCK to flee. Though stopped by a British patrol, he was able to alert the patriot leaders. In the AMERICAN REVOLUTION, Revere constructed a powder mill to supply colonial arms. After the war he discovered a process for rolling sheet copper and opened a rolling mill that produced sheathing for such ships as the USS *CONSTITUTION*. His handsome silver bowls, flatware, and utensils are museum pieces today.

Revillagigedo \\rä-'vē-yä-hē-'hä-thō\\ Group of islands, Mexico, in the Pacific Ocean, about 300 mi (500 km) south of the BAJA CALIFORNIA peninsula. It consists of numerous volcanic islands; the largest, Socorro, rises to an elevation of 3,707 ft (1,130 m). The islands are rich in sulfur, fish, and guano.

revivalism Reawakening of Christian values and commitment. The spiritual fervor of revival-style preaching, typically performed by itinerant, charismatic preachers before large gatherings, is thought to have a restorative effect on those who have been led away from the right path. Many Protestant sects came into being during revivalist periods, notably METHODISM. Common themes are a literal interpretation of the BIBLE, emphasis on the conversion experience, and a call to live devoutly. Revivalism can be interpreted as a precursor of 20th-cent. Christian FUNDAMENTALISM. See also GREAT AWAKENING, Dwight MOODY.

revolution Fundamental, rapid, and often irreversible change in the established order. In the political sense, revolution is a radical change in government, usually accomplished through violence, that may also result in changes to the economic system, social structure, and cultural values. The Greeks saw revolution as a result of societal breakdown. Renaissance humanism led to the belief that changes in government might sometimes be necessary and good. John MILTON saw revolution as the means of achieving freedom; Immanuel KANT believed it was a force for the advancement of mankind; and G. W. F. HEGEL's view of revolution as the fulfillment of human destiny influenced Karl MARX.

Revolutionary War See AMERICAN REVOLUTION
Revolution of 1688 See GLORIOUS REVOLUTION
Revolutions of 1848 Series of republican revolts against European monarchies. They began in Sicily and spread to France, the German and Italian states, and the Austrian empire. In France the revolution established the SECOND REPUBLIC, and in Central Europe liberal political reform appeared likely. However, the armies loyal to the monarchies soon reestablished their power and rescinded most of the promised reforms. The revolts eventually ended in failure and repression.

revolver PISTOL with a revolving cylinder that provides multishot action. As early as the 17th cent. pistols were being made with a revolving cylinder to load cartridges into a single barrel. In 1835 Samuel COLT established the standard of a cylinder with multiple chambers, each of which successively locked in position behind the barrel and was discharged by pressure on the trigger. In Colt's single-action revolvers, the cylinder revolved as the hammer was cocked manually. Double-action revolvers, in which the cylinder revolves as the trigger is pulled, were developed soon afterward.

Rexroth, Kenneth (1905–1982) U.S. poet, translator, essayist, and painter. Born in South Bend, Ind., he spent much of his youth traveling in the West, organizing and speaking for unions. His early poems were experimental, influenced by Surrealism; his later work was praised for its tight form and its wit and humanistic passion. He was an early champion of the BEAT MOVEMENT. His works include many translations of Japanese, Chinese, Greek, Latin, and Spanish poetry.

Rey See RHAGAE
Reye's syndrome \\'rīz, 'rāz\\ Acute neurological illness in children following INFLUENZA, CHICKEN POX, or other vi-

QR

ral infections. Vomiting, lethargy, and confusion begin as the child appears to be recovering, followed hours or days later by drowsiness, disorientation, seizures, respiratory arrest, and coma. At worst, it causes fatty liver degeneration and potentially fatal brain swelling. There is no specific cure, but treatment helps over 70% of patients survive (some with brain damage). Its incidence has decreased since the recognition that it often follows use of ASPIRIN or other SALICYLIC-ACID derivatives in children during a viral illness; parents are now warned.

Reykjavík \'rā-kyä-ˌvēk\ City (pop., 1999: 105,000), capital of Iceland. According to tradition, it was founded in 874 by the Norseman Ingólfur Arnarson. Long a small Danish fishing village, it became the capital of a self-governing Iceland under the Danish king in 1918 and of the independent Republic of Iceland in 1944. In World War II it was a U.S. naval and air base. It is the commercial, industrial, and cultural center of the island, its major fishing port, and the site of nearly half of the nation's industries.

Reynolds, Joshua (*later* **Sir Joshua**) (1723–1792) British portrait painter. Son of a clergyman-schoolmaster, he was apprenticed to a London portraitist in 1740. His large group portrait *The Eliot Family* (c.1746) reveals the influence of Anthony VAN DYCK. The impressions gained in Italy (1750–52), particularly in Venice, inspired his painting for the rest of his life. He established a portrait studio in London in 1753; immediately successful, he introduced new vigor into English portraiture. He was elected the first president of the Royal Academy in 1768. Through his art and teaching, Reynolds led British painting away from the anecdotal pictures of the early 18th cent. toward the formal rhetoric of continental academic painting. His lectures, *Discourses Delivered at the Royal Academy* (1769–90), advocating rigorous academic training and study of the old masters, rank among the most important art criticism of the time.

Reynolds, Osborne (1842–1912) British engineer and physicist. The first professor of engineering at the Univ. of Manchester (1868), best known for his work in HYDRAULICS and hydrodynamics, he formulated the law of resistance in parallel channels (1883), the theory of LUBRICATION (1886), and the standard mathematical framework used in TURBULENCE work (1889). He made pioneering contributions to the concept of group velocity. The Reynolds stress in fluids with turbulent motion and the Reynolds number, indicating steadiness of flow, are named for him.

Rg Veda See RIG VEDA

rhabdovirus \ˌrab-dō-'vī-rəs\ Any of a group of VIRUSES responsible for RABIES and vesicular stomatitis (an acute disease of cattle and horses). The bullet-shaped virus particle is encased in a fatty membrane and contains RNA.

Rhaetia See RAETIA

Rhaetian Alps \'rē-tēən\ Segment of the central ALPS extending along the Italian–Swiss and Austrian–Swiss borders but mainly in E Switzerland. Bernina Peak, on the Italian border, is the highest point at 13,284 ft (4,049 m). Swiss National Park is known for its rugged alpine scenery and its wildlife.

Rhagae *or* **Ragae** \'rä-ˌjē\ *Persian* **Rey** Ancient city, MEDIA. It was formerly one of the great cities of Iran; its ruins are at modern Rey, near TEHRAN. Under the SASANIANS (3rd–7th cent. A.D.), it was a center of ZOROASTRIANISM. It was captured by the Muslims in A.D. 641. It grew in importance until the 12th cent.; in 1220 it was destroyed by the MONGOLS, and its inhabitants were massacred. It was famous for its decorated silks and for ceramics. HARUN AL-RASHID was born here around 765.

Rhazes See al-RAZI

Rh blood-group system System for classifying BLOOD according to presence or absence of the Rh ANTIGEN (factor) in ERYTHROCYTES. Rh-negative persons who receive Rh-positive BLOOD TRANSFUSIONS produce ANTIBODIES to Rh factor, which attack red blood cells with the factor if they are ever received again, causing serious illness. The antibodies also attack the red cells of an Rh-positive fetus carried by an Rh-negative woman if she has had a previous Rh-positive transfusion or pregnancy. See also BLOOD TYPING.

Rhea \'rē-ə\ Greek goddess, one of the TITANS. She married her brother CRONUS, who swallowed all their children except ZEUS, whom Rhea concealed. Zeus then overcame Cronus and restored his siblings.

rhea \'rē-ə\ Either of two ostrich-like species of S. American three-toed RATITE birds (family Rheidae). The common rhea (*Rhea americana*) is about 4 ft (120 cm) tall and weighs about 50 lbs (20 kg). It has luxuriant plumage, brown or gray above and whitish below. Darwin's rhea (*Pterocnemia pennata*) is smaller. Rheas live in open country, often among grazing animals. Both species are endangered.

Rhee, Syngman (1875–1965) First president of the Republic of Korea (S. Korea). After earning a PhD at Princeton, he returned to Korea in 1910, the year Japan annexed Korea. Hostile toward Japanese rule, he left again for the U.S. in 1912. For the next 30 years he spoke out for Korean independence; in 1919 he was elected president of a provisional government in exile. Rhee returned to Korea at the end of World War II and was elected president in 1948. He held that post until 1960, when opposition to his authoritarian policies (which included outlawing the opposition Progressive Party) forced his resignation and exile.

Rheims See REIMS

rhesus monkey \'rē-səs\ Sand-colored MACAQUE (*Macaca mulatta*), widespread in S and SE Asian forests. Rhesus monkeys are 17–25 in. (47–64 cm) long, excluding the furry 8–12-in. (20–30-cm) tail, and weigh 10–24 lbs (4.5–11 kg). They are held sacred in some parts of India. Hardy in captivity and highly intelligent, they have been used frequently in medical research. The determination of the Rh (from rhesus) factor in human blood involves reaction with the blood of this species. See also RH BLOOD-GROUP SYSTEM.

rhetoric Art of speaking or writing effectively. It may entail the study of principles and rules of composition formulated by critics of ancient times, and can also involve the study of writing or speaking as a means of communication or persuasion. Classical rhetoric probably developed in Syracuse in the 5th cent. B.C., when dispossessed landowners argued claims before their fellow citizens. Shrewd speakers sought help from teachers of oratory, called rhetors. This use of language was of interest to philosophers such as PLATO and ARISTOTLE because the oratorical arguments called into question the relationships among language, truth, and morality. Renaissance scholars and poets studied rhetoric closely, but by the 19th cent. the term had come to mean empty political discourse.

rheumatic fever \rù-'ma-tik\ Generalized disease caused by certain types of STREPTOCOCCUS bacteria. It occurs mostly in children and young adults. Symptoms may be mild, or sudden fever, joint pain, and inflammation may begin days to weeks after a streptococcal infection, usually of the throat. HEART inflammation can lead to valve scarring, markedly shortening life. After recovery, survivors are prone to future attacks. PENICILLIN given when the initial infection (strep throat) is diagnosed can prevent it. Otherwise, SALICYLIC-ACID derivatives or STEROIDS help the symptoms.

rheumatoid arthritis \'rü-mə-ˌtȯid\ Chronic, progressive AUTOIMMUNE DISEASE causing CONNECTIVE-TISSUE INFLAMMATION, mostly in synovial JOINTS. It can occur at any age, is more common in women, and has an unpredictable course. It usually starts gradually, with pain and stiffness in one or more joints, then swelling and heat. Membrane inflammation and thickening scars joint structures and destroys CARTILAGE. In severe cases, adhesions immobilize and deform the joints, and adjacent skin, bones, and muscles atrophy. If high-dose aspirin, ibuprofen, and other NSAIDS do not relieve pain and disability, low-dose STEROIDS may be tried. Physical medicine and rehabilitation reduce pain and swelling with heat and exercises. Surgery can replace destroyed hip, knee, or finger joints. There is also a juvenile form.

Rhineland *German* **Rheinland** Region of Germany west of the RHINE RIVER, with an area of about 9,000 sq mi (23,000 sq km). The chief city is COLOGNE. In the 19th cent. it became the most prosperous area of Germany. After World War I, Allied troops occupied portions of the area on the border with France, and it was the scene of recurrent crises and controversies during the 1920s. In 1936 Adolf HITLER ordered German troops to enter its demilitarized zone; weak objections by the Allies foreshadowed Hitler's later annexation of the SUDETENLAND.

Rhine River *German* **Rhein** River, W Europe. Rising in the Swiss ALPS, it flows north and west through W Germany to drain through the delta region of the Netherlands into the North Sea. The most important river of W Europe, it is 820 mi (1,319 km) long and navigable for 540 mi (870 km). Its many canals connect it with the RHÔNE, MARNE, and DANUBE river systems. The Rhine carries more traffic than any other river in the world. It has played a prominent part in German history and legend. In World War II its course was a major line of defense. Major cities along its banks include BASEL, MANNHEIM, KOBLENZ, COLOGNE, DUISBURG, and ROTTERDAM.

rhinoceros Any of five extant African and Asian species (family Rhinocerotidae) of three-toed UNGULATES. One of the largest of all land animals (the white rhinoceros is second only to the elephant), it is distinguished by one or two horns on its upper snout. All have thick, virtually hairless skin that forms platelike folds at the shoulders and thighs. Rhinos grow to 8–14 ft (2.5–4.3 m) long and 3–6.5 ft (1.5–2 m) tall; adults weigh 3–5 tons. Most inhabit open grassland, scrub forest, or marsh, but the Sumatran rhino lives in deep forest. All species—which include the African black rhino, the great Indian rhino, and the Java rhino—either browse or graze for food. The rhinoc-

African black rhinoceros (*Diceros bicornis*)

eros was brought to the brink of extinction by hunters, mostly seeking the horn, which is valued in Asia as an aphrodisiac. Only a few thousand survive, almost all on reserves.

rhinovirus \ˌrī-nō-ˈvī-rəs\ Any of a group of PICORNAVIRUSES capable of causing common COLDS in humans. The virus is thought to be transmitted by airborne droplets. Because of the great number of cold viruses, VACCINES against them are virtually impossible to develop. See also ADENOVIRUS.

rhizome Horizontal underground plant stem capable of producing the upward shoot and downward root systems of a new plant. This capability allows vegetative (asexual) propagation and enables plants to survive an annual unfavorable season underground. In some plants (e.g., WATER LILIES, many FERNS, and forest herbs), the rhizome is the only stem of the plant.

Rhode Island *officially* **Rhode Island and Providence Plantations** State (pop., 2000: 1,048,000), NE U.S. One of the NEW ENGLAND states and the smallest U.S. state, it covers 1,212 sq mi (3,139 sq km); its capital is PROVIDENCE. It borders the Atlantic Ocean. The original inhabitants were Narragansett Indians. The first European settlement was in 1636 by Roger WILLIAMS and his followers, who were banished from Massachusetts; in 1663 King CHARLES II granted a charter to Williams. Though it never officially joined the New England colonies in KING PHILIP'S WAR, it suffered greatly when many settlements were burned. It was in the forefront fighting British customs laws leading up to the AMERICAN REVOLUTION. An original state of the Union, it was the 13th to ratify the Constitution, in 1790, only after the BILL OF RIGHTS was included. The cotton-textile mill built by Samuel SLATER in Pawtucket in 1790 initiated the INDUSTRIAL REVOLUTION in the U.S. Its original charter remained in effect until Dorr's Rebellion in 1842 led to extension of suffrage. Manufacturing is important to the economy, and products include jewelry and silverware, textiles and clothing, and electrical machinery and electronics. The

resort town of NEWPORT is known for its music festivals and yachting.

Rhode Island School of Design (RISD) One of the most eminent fine-arts colleges in the U.S., located in Providence, R.I. It was founded in 1877 but did not offer college-level instruction until 1932. It combines professional arts training with a broad liberal-arts curriculum. Enrollment is about 2,000.

Rhodes *Greek* **Ródhos** \ˈrō-ˌthōs\ Island of Greece, the largest of the Dodecanese group and the most easterly in the Aegean Sea. The main city is Rhodes (pop., 1995 est.: 45,000). The earliest known settlers were the Dorians about 1000 B.C. In the classical period, it vacillated between Athens, Sparta, and Persia. A devastating earthquake around 225 B.C. destroyed the Colossus of RHODES. In the medieval period it was occupied by the Byzantines and Saracens before the Knights of St. John (see KNIGHTS OF MALTA) converted the island into a fortress and held it until 1523, when the Turks took control. From 1912 it was ruled by Italy, and in 1947 it was awarded to Greece. Year-round tourism has brought it prosperity.

Rhodes, Cecil (John) (1853–1902) Financier, statesman, and empire builder of British S. Africa. Born in England, in 1871 Rhodes joined his brother in S. Africa, where he became interested in diamond mining. He founded DE BEERS CONSOLIDATED MINES (1888), and by 1891 was mining 90% of the world's diamonds. He persuaded Britain to establish a protectorate over Bechuanaland (1884), clashing with Boer president Paul KRUGER. He obtained digging concessions from Lobengula (1889), but later overran him militarily (1893). At his instigation, Britain chartered the British S. Africa Co. (1889) and put Rhodes in charge. He extended its control to two N provinces, which were eventually named after him, Southern Rhodesia (now Zimbabwe) and Northern Rhodesia (now Zambia). His interest in the mineral-rich TRANSVAAL led to his plotting to overthrow Kruger (1895), but the attempt failed and Rhodes was forced to resign as prime minister of Cape Colony and head of the British S. Africa Co. His will bequeathed most of his fortune to establishing the Rhodes Scholarships.

Rhodes, Colossus of Enormous bronze statue of the sun god Helios that towered more than 100 ft (30 m) over the harbor of Rhodes in Greece. The work of Chares of Lindos, the statue (built c.294–282 B.C.) commemorated the raising of Demetrios I Poliorcetes' long siege of Rhodes (305–304 B.C). One of the SEVEN WONDERS OF THE WORLD, it was toppled by an earthquake about 225 B.C. In A.D. 653 raiding Arabs broke up its remains and sold the bronze for scrap.

Colossus of Rhodes Wood engraving reconstruction by Sidney Barclay, c.1875

Rhodesia Region, S central Africa, now divided into Zimbabwe in the south and Zambia in the north. Named after Cecil RHODES, it was administered by the British S. Africa Co. in the 19th cent. and exploited for its gold, copper, and coal deposits. Southern Rhodesia became a self-governing British colony (1923), and Northern Rhodesia a British protectorate (1924). They joined in the Federation of Rhodesia and Nyasaland 1953–63.

Rhodesia See ZIMBABWE

Rhodes scholarship Grant to attend the Univ. of OXFORD. The program was established in 1902 by the will of Cecil RHODES. Until 1976, when women were accepted, candidates had to be unmarried males resident in a Commonwealth country, the U.S., or S. Africa. The highly competitive scholarships, which take into account moral character and physical fitness, are usually for two years.

rhododendron \ˌrō-də-ˈden-drən\ Any of about 800 diverse species of trees and shrubs that make up the genus *Rhodo-*

dendron in the HEATH FAMILY, notable for their attractive flowers and handsome foliage. They are native chiefly in the N temperate zone, especially in SE Asia and Malaysia. Some are evergreens, others deciduous. Flowers are usually tubular to funnel-shaped and occur in a wide range of colors. See also AZALEA.

Rhodope Mountains \'rä-də-pē\ Mountain range, BALKAN PENINSULA, SE Europe. Extending southeast along the border between Bulgaria and Macedonia, Greece, the range forms an important climatic barrier, protecting the Aegean lowlands from cold northerly winds. The mountains were a refuge for Slavic peoples during the period of Turkish rule (15th–19th cent.). The lakes, river valleys, and extensive forests attract tourism.

Rhone River River, Switzerland and France. An historic S gateway, and the only major river of the continent that flows directly to the Mediterranean Sea, it is 505 mi (813 km) long. Rising in the Swiss ALPS, it flows into Lake GENEVA, then crosses into France through the JURA Mtns. It continues south through LYON, AVIGNON, and Tarascon to ARLES and enters the Mediterranean west of MARSEILLE.

rhubarb Any of several species of the genus *Rheum* (family Polygonaceae), especially *R. rhaponticum* (or *R. rhabarbarum*), a hardy perennial of cool temperate climates grown for its large, succulent, edible leafstalks. The fleshy, tart, and highly acid leafstalks are used in pies, compotes and preserves. The huge leaves that unfold in early spring are toxic to cattle and humans; later in the season a large central flower stalk may bear numerous small, greenish-white flowers and angular, winged fruits.

rhyme Type of echoing produced by the close placement of two or more words with similar-sounding final syllables. Rhyme is used in poetry to produce sounds that appeal to the ear and to unify and establish a poem's stanzaic form. End rhyme (i.e., rhyme used at the end of a line to echo the end of another line) is most common, but internal rhyme (occurring within the end of a line) is frequently used as an embellishment. Types of "true rhyme" include masculine rhyme, in which the two words end with the same vowel-consonant combination (stand/land); and feminine rhyme (or double rhyme), in which two syllables rhyme (profession/discretion).

rhythm and blues (R&B) Any of several closely related musical styles developed in the U.S. by black artists. All made use of JAZZ syncopations and the flatted blues chords. They grew out of the BLUES of the rural South and were greatly influenced by GOSPEL MUSIC. The earliest style, called "race," was the style of the "jump" band, which emphasized strong rhythm, solo instrumental work, and vocals in a shout-blues manner. A second style, often called "Chicago blues" and exemplified by Muddy WATERS, was typically played by a small group with amplified instruments. The third style featured close, gospel-influenced vocal harmonies often backed by an orchestra. In the mid-1950s the term was adopted by the music industry for music intended for the black audience; with the gradual disappearance of racial barriers, the Chicago blues style began to seem a folk tradition, while the gospel style was transformed into SOUL MUSIC. Rhythm and blues was the chief antecedent of ROCK MUSIC.

rhythm and meter Two aspects of the organization of time in Western music. Rhythm consists of the complete pattern of longer and shorter notes, measured from the beginning of each note to that of the next, and is frequently irregular and complex. Meter, like poetical METER, is usually a regular pattern of accented and unaccented beats, and provides the context in which rhythm is understood. In notated music, meter is indicated by a time signature—in which the lower number specifies the basic unit or subunit of the beat (e.g., 8 usually indicates that eighth-notes are the basic subunit) and the upper number specifies the number of units or subunits in a measure.

Ribalta \rē-'bäl-tä\, **Francisco** (1565–1628) Spanish painter. After settling in Valencia in 1598, he abandoned Mannerism for a darker and more naturalistic style (e.g., his *Santiago* altarpiece, 1603), under the influence of CARAVAGGIO. After 1612 he achieved originality and grandeur in such paintings

as *Christ Embracing St. Bernard*, marked by powerfully modeled forms, simplicity of composition, and naturalistic lighting, which influenced Francisco de ZURBARÁN and José de RIBERA.

Ribbentrop \'ri-bən-ˌträp\, **Joachim von** (1893–1946) German diplomat and foreign minister under the Nazi regime. A wine merchant, he met Adolf HITLER in 1932 and became his chief adviser on foreign affairs. As ambassador to Britain (1936–38), he advised Hitler that Britain could not aid Poland effectively. As foreign minister (1938–45), he negotiated the Pact of Steel with Italy (1939), the GERMAN–SOVIET NONAGGRESSION PACT, and the Tripartite Pact with Japan and Italy. He was found guilty at the NUREMBERG TRIALS and hanged.

Ribera \rē-'ber-ə\, **José de** (1591–1652) Spanish painter and printmaker. Though born in Spain, he spent most of his life in Naples (then a Spanish possession). Most of his works are of religious subjects. Dramatic light and shadow and sometimes horrific detail emphasize the suffering of the saints, as in *The Martyrdom of St. Bartholomew* (c.1630). In later works his modeling is softer, and he demonstrates strong human sympathy, as in *The Clubfooted Boy* (1642). His etchings are among the finest produced in the baroque period.

riboflavin \ˌrī-bə-'flā-vən\ *or* **vitamin B₂** Yellow, water-soluble organic compound, abundant in whey, egg white, and other foods. It has a complex structure incorporating three rings. Green plants and most microorganisms can synthesize it; animals need to acquire it in their diet. A syndrome resembling PELLAGRA is thought to result from riboflavin deficiency.

ribose \'rī-ˌbōs\ Five-carbon SUGAR found in RNA. (In DNA the corresponding sugar is the closely related deoxyribose.) A ribose molecule combined with ADENINE, GUANINE, CYTOSINE, or URACIL forms a NUCLEOSIDE; adding a PHOSPHATE group forms a NUCLEOTIDE. The ribose of one nucleotide joins with the phosphate of the next to form the RNA backbone.

ribosome \'rī-bə-ˌsōm\ Tiny particle, the site of PROTEIN synthesis, that is present in large numbers in living cells. Ribosomes occur both free within cells and attached to the ENDOPLASMIC RETICULUM. They are 40% protein and 60% RNA, and account for a large proportion of the total RNA of a cell.

Ricardo, David (1772–1823) British economist. He made a fortune in the London stock exchange before turning to the study of political economy. Inspired by the writings of Adam SMITH, his writings in support of a metal currency standard were influential. In his major work, *The Principles of Political Economy and Taxation* (1817), he asserted that the domestic values of commodities were largely determined by the labor required for their production. His Iron Law of Wages stated that attempts to improve the real income of workers were futile and that wages tended to stabilize at subsistence level. Though many of his ideas are obsolete, he was a major figure in the development of CLASSICAL ECONOMICS, and is credited as the first person to systematize economics.

Ricci \'rēt-chē\, **Matteo** (1552–1610) Italian Jesuit missionary who introduced Christianity into China. From a noble family, he joined the Jesuits and volunteered for missionary work overseas. He arrived in Goa in 1578, and proceeded to China in 1582. Though China's interior was closed to foreigners, his willingness to adopt the Chinese language and culture gave him entry. In 1597 he was appointed director of Jesuit activities in China. In 1601 he was finally admitted to Beijing, where he preached the Gospel, taught science to scholars, and translated Christian works into Chinese.

rice Edible starchy CEREAL grain and the annual GRASS (*Oryza sativa*, family Gramineae, or Poaceae) that produces it. Roughly one-half the world's population, including almost all of E. and S.E. Asia, depends on rice as its principal staple food. First cultivated in India more than 4,000 years ago, rice gradually spread westward and is now cultivated widely in flooded fields (paddies) and river deltas of tropical, semitropical, and temperate regions. Growing to about 4 ft (1.2 m) in height, rice has long, flattened leaves and an inflorescence made up of spikelets bearing flowers that produce the fruit, or grain. Removal of just the husk produces nutritious brown rice. Removal of the bran layer leaves white rice, greatly diminished in nutrients. See also WILD RICE.

Rice, Jerry (Lee) (b.1962) U.S. football player. Born in Starkville, Miss., he won All-America honors at Mississippi Valley State Univ. A member of the San Francisco 49ers (1985–2000) and the Oakland Raiders (from 2001), he holds several all-time career records, including those for receptions (1,455+), yardage (21,595+), and touchdowns (190+). He is considered by many the greatest wide receiver of all time.

Rice (*Oryza sativa*)

Rice University Private university in Houston. It was founded in 1891 and endowed by William Marsh Rice. It has schools of humanities, social sciences, architecture, music, natural sciences, and engineering and a graduate school of administration. Total enrollment is about 4,500.

Rich, Adrienne (Cecile) (b.1929) U.S. poet, scholar, and critic. Born in Baltimore, she displayed her formal mastery in her first volume, *A Change of World* (1951). A highly personal and powerful style emerged in her subsequent work. Her increasing commitment to a lesbian-feminist aesthetic came to politicize much of her work. Among her collections are *Diving into the Wreck* (1973, National Book Award) and *The Dream of a Common Language* (1978). Her nonfiction *Of Woman Born* (1976, National Book Award) was widely read.

Richard, (Joseph Henri) Maurice (1921–2000) Canadian ice-hockey player. Born in Montreal, he played right wing for the Montreal Canadiens (1942–60). He was the first National Hockey League player to score 50 goals in a regular (50-game) season (1943–44). His nickname, "Rocket," acknowledged his speed and aggressive play.

Richard I *known as* **Richard the Lionheart(ed)** *French* Richard Coeur de Lion (1157–1199) King of England, duke of Normandy, and count of Anjou (1189–99). He inherited Aquitaine from his mother, ELEANOR OF AQUITAINE. Denied real authority there, he rebelled against his father, HENRY II (1173–74), and later enlisted PHILIP II of France in a successful campaign against Henry (1189). Crowned king of England on Henry's death that year, Richard embarked on the Third CRUSADE (1190). He won victories in the Holy Land, but after failing to gain Jerusalem he signed a truce (1192) with SALADIN. On his way home Richard was captured by Leopold of Austria and held by Henry VI of Germany until a ransom was paid (1194). Back in England, he reclaimed the throne from his brother JOHN, then spent the rest of his life in Normandy fighting against Philip II.

Richard II (1367–1400) King of England (1377–99). He inherited the throne as a boy, and his uncle JOHN OF GAUNT and other nobles dominated the government. The BLACK DEATH brought on economic problems, leading to the PEASANTS' REVOLT (1381), which Richard quelled with false promises. His noble enemies placed limits on his royal power (1386–89), but he later took revenge on them; he banished John of Gaunt's son, Henry, and confiscated his vast estates. While Richard was absent in Ireland, Henry invaded England (1399) and seized power as HENRY IV. Richard abdicated the throne and died in prison.

Richard III (1452–1485) Duke of Gloucester (1461–83) and last Yorkist king of England (1483–85). With his brother King EDWARD IV, Richard was driven into exile in 1470 but returned and defeated the Lancastrians in 1471 (see Wars of the ROSES). On Edward's death (1483), Richard became protector for Edward's son, the 12-year-old King Edward V, but he usurped the throne and confined Edward and his little brother to the Tower of London, where they were murdered. Henry Tudor (later HENRY VII) raised an army

against Richard, who was defeated and killed at the Battle of BOSWORTH FIELD. Later Tudor histories painting Richard as a monster may have been exaggerated.

Richards, I(vor) A(rmstrong) (1893–1979) English-U.S. critic and poet. In *Principles of Literary Criticism* (1924) he introduced a new way of reading poetry that led to the NEW CRITICISM. A student of psychology, he concluded that poetry performs a therapeutic function by coordinating various human impulses into an aesthetic whole. In the 1930s he developed a language system of 850 basic words, known as Basic English, that he believed would promote international understanding.

Richardson, Henry Handel (*orig.* Ethel Florence Lindesay) (1870–1946) Australian-English novelist. She spent most of her life abroad, settling in England in 1904. *Maurice Guest* (1908), her antiromantic first novel, concerns a music student's disastrous love affair. Her masterpiece, *The Fortunes of Richard Mahony* (3 vols., 1917–29), combining description of an Australian immigrant's life and work in the goldfields with a powerful character study, is considered the greatest Australian novel to that time.

Richardson, Henry Hobson (1838–1886) U.S. architect. Born in Priestley Plantation, La., he won a national reputation with his designs for Boston's Brattle Square (1870–72) and Trinity (1872–77) churches. He designed houses, libraries, suburban railroad stations, educational buildings, and commercial and civic structures. In place of the prevailing Neo-Gothic style, he favored horizontal lines, simple silhouettes, and large-scale Romanesque or Byzantine-inspired details. The Crane Memorial Library in Quincy, Mass. (1880–82) stands with his finest mature works. The functionalism of Richardson's designs foreshadowed the work of Louis SULLIVAN.

Richardson, Ralph (David) (*later* **Sir Ralph**) (1902–1983) British actor. He gained prominence at the OLD VIC in such roles as Peer Gynt, Petruchio, Falstaff, and Volpone, winning a reputation as one of the greatest actors of his time. From 1933 he appeared onscreen, playing urbane, witty characters and later eccentric old men in such films as *The Fugitive* (1939), *The Fallen Idol* (1948), *The Heiress* (1949), *Long Day's Journey into Night* (1962), and *Doctor Zhivago* (1965).

Richardson, Samuel (1689–1761) English novelist. A prosperous printer by trade, he conceived the idea of writing a book using a series of letters on the same subject. His major novels were the EPISTOLARY NOVEL *Pamela* (1740), about a servant who avoids seduction and is rewarded by marriage; and his huge masterpiece *Clarissa* (7 vols., 1747–48), a tragedy with multiple narrators that develops a profoundly suggestive interplay of opposed voices. *The History of Sir Charles Grandison* (1753–54), which blends moral discussion and a comic ending, influenced later writers, especially Jane AUSTEN.

Richardson, Tony (*orig.* Cecil Antonio) (1928–1991) British director. Directing the English Stage Co., he won acclaim with John OSBORNE's *Look Back in Anger* (1956), and led the company in reinterpreting classic plays and in productions of Eugène IONESCO and Samuel BECKETT. He directed *The Entertainer* (1958) and *A Taste of Honey* (1960) on Broadway. He made screen versions of Osborne's plays as well as *The Loneliness of the Long Distance Runner* (1962), *Tom Jones* (1963, Academy Award), *Ned Kelly* (1970), and *Blue Sky* (1993). He was married to Vanessa REDGRAVE (1962–67); their daughters Miranda and Joely Richardson are both film actresses.

Richelieu \\'ri-shə-ˌlü, *French* rē-shə-'lyœ̄\\, **cardinal et duc (Duke) de** *orig.* Armand-Jean du Plessis (1585–1642) French statesman and chief minister to LOUIS XIII. As bishop of Luçon, he was the first bishop in France to implement reforms decreed by the Council of TRENT and brought order to a diocese ruined by the Wars of RELIGION. He became an adviser to MARIE DE MÉDICIS in 1616, and later councillor to her son, Louis XIII. Named a cardinal in 1622, he served as chief minister from 1624 and became the controlling influence in France's policies. He established royal absolutism by suppressing the political power of the HUGUENOTS and reducing the influence of the nobles. Seeking to

weaken the Habsburgs, he entered the THIRTY YEARS' WAR. Devious and brilliant, he increased the power of the BOURBON dynasty and established orderly government in France. He also founded the ACADÉMIE FRANÇAISE and rebuilt the Sorbonne.

Cardinal de Richelieu
Portrait by Philippe de Champaigne

Richler, Mordecai (1931–2001) Canadian novelist. Born in Montreal, he grew up in a Jewish working-class neighborhood in which many of his novels are set. He spent the years 1954–72 in England. *The Apprenticeship of Duddy Kravitz* (1959; film, 1974) is a bawdy account of a Jewish boy in Montreal and his transformation into a ruthless businessman. *Cocksure* (1968) and *St. Urbain's Horseman* (1971) examine N. Americans in England. His later novels include *Joshua Then and Now* (1980; film, 1985) and *Solomon Gursky Was Here* (1989).

Richmond City (pop., 2000: 198,000), capital of Virginia. It is located in the E central part of the state. It became the state capital in 1779 and played an important role in the AMERICAN REVOLUTION. During the AMERICAN CIVIL WAR it was the capital of the CONFEDERATE STATES OF AMERICA. It was taken by Gen. U. S. GRANT in 1865, and much of the business district was burned. Now a major tobacco market and government center, it is home to Virginia Commonwealth Univ. (1838).

Richter scale \\'rik-tər\\ Widely used measure of the magnitude of an EARTHQUAKE, introduced in 1935 by U.S. seismologists Beno Gutenberg (1889–1960) and Charles F. Richter (1900–1985). The scale is logarithmic, so that each increase of one unit represents a 10-fold increase in magnitude (amplitude of SEISMIC WAVES). The magnitude is then translated into energy released. Though the scale has no theoretical upper limit, the most severe earthquakes have not exceeded a scale value of 9. The moment magnitude scale, in use since 1993, is more accurate for large earthquakes; it takes into account the amount of fault slippage, the size of the area ruptured, and the nature of the materials that faulted.

Richthofen \\'rikt-ˌhō-fən\\, **Manfred, Freiherr (Baron) von** *known as* **The Red Baron** (1892–1918) German World War I ace. Born to a famous and wealthy family, in 1915 he joined the air force and in 1916 took command of a fighter group that came to be known as "Richthofen's Flying Circus" for its decorated scarlet planes. He had been acclaimed Germany's greatest aviation ace, credited with shooting down 80 enemy airplanes, before he was shot down at the age of 25.

Manfred von Richthofen

Rickenbacker, Eddie (*orig.* Edward Vernon) (1890–1973) U.S. World War I ace and industrialist. Born in Columbus, Ohio, he was a top racing driver by 1917, when he entered the army and became a fighter pilot. For shooting down 26 enemy airplanes in World War I, he was awarded the Medal of Honor. He later directed his own automobile company. As president of EASTERN AIR LINES 1938–59, he oversaw its growth into a major corporation.

rickets *or* **vitamin D deficiency** Disease of infancy and childhood characterized by defective BONE growth due to lack of VITAMIN D. Calcium phosphate is not properly deposited in the bones, which become soft, curved, and stunted. Early symptoms include restlessness, profuse sweating, lack of muscle tone, soft skull bones, and developmental delays. Muscles may cramp and twitch. Effects may include bowlegs and knock-knees. A narrow chest and pelvis can later increase susceptibility to lung diseases and impede childbirth. Treatment is with vitamin D, sunlight, and a balanced diet. Adding vitamin D to milk has reduced rickets in high-latitude areas where the skin cannot produce enough.

rickettsia \\ri-'ket-sē-ə\\ Any of the rod-shaped BACTERIA of the family Rickettsiaceae (named for Howard Ricketts, 1871–1910). They are rod-shaped or variably spherical, and most are gram-negative (see GRAM STAIN). Natural parasites of certain ARTHROPODS, they can cause serious diseases in humans and other animals after a bite from an arthropod carrier. Certain species can also be transmitted when arthropod feces are inhaled or enter broken skin. TYPHUS, trench fever, and ROCKY MTN. SPOTTED FEVER are rickettsial infections. Treatment includes ANTIBIOTICS.

Rickey, Branch (Wesley) (1881–1965) U.S. baseball executive. Born in Stockdale, Ohio, he played professional baseball before beginning a long association with the St. Louis Cardinals (president, 1917–19; field manager, 1919–25; general manager, 1925–42). In 1919 he devised the farm system of training ballplayers. As president and general manager of the Brooklyn Dodgers (1943–50), in 1945 he hired the first two black players in non-NEGRO LEAGUE baseball (1945), including Jackie ROBINSON, defying strong resistance. He was later associated with the Pittsburgh Pirates (1950–59).

Rickover, Hyman G(eorge) (1900–1986) U.S. (Russian-born) naval nuclear engineer. His family emigrated to the U.S. in 1906. After graduating from Annapolis, he served on submarines and other ships, then headed the electrical section of the Navy's Bureau of Ships in World War II. From 1947 he led the Navy's nuclear-propulsion program; his team developed the first atomic-powered submarine, the USS *Nautilus*, launched in 1954. He later headed research on reactor development for the Atomic Energy Commission. Promoted to admiral in 1973, he was noted for his outspoken views and singleminded advocacy of nuclear power development.

riddle Deliberately enigmatic or ambiguous question requiring a thoughtful and often witty answer, part of the folklore of most cultures from ancient times. The descriptive riddle usually describes something in an intentionally enigmatic manner (thus an egg is "a little white house without door or window"). The shrewd or witty question type is illustrated by a classical Greek example: "What is the strongest of all things?"—"Love: iron is strong, but the blacksmith is stronger, and love can subdue the blacksmith."

Ride, Sally (Kristen) (b.1951) U.S. astronaut. Born in Los Angeles, she received a PhD in physics from Stanford Univ. and joined NASA in 1977. In 1983 she was flight engineer on the seventh space-shuttle mission, becoming the first American woman and the third woman ever in space. She went on to pursue science education, especially for young people.

Ridgway, Matthew B(unker) (1895–1993) U.S. Army officer. Born in Ft. Monroe, Va., he graduated from West Point. In World War II he commanded an airborne division in the invasion of Sicily (1943), the first airborne assault in U.S. history, and in the NORMANDY CAMPAIGN. In the KOREAN WAR he led the U.S. 8th Army, rallying U.N. forces and forcing the Chinese out of S. Korea. He succeeded Douglas MACARTHUR as Allied commander in the Far East (1951). He later served as supreme commander of NATO forces (1952) and army chief of staff (1953–55).

Riefenstahl \\'rē-fən-ˌshtäl\\, **Leni** (*orig.* Berta Helene Amalie) (b.1902) German film director. An actress in German nature films, she made and starred in the mystical *The Blue Light* (1932). For Adolf HITLER she directed the propaganda film *Triumph of the Will* (1935), a documentary glorifying the NUREMBERG RALLIES. She was praised for the technical brilliance of *Olympia* (1938), on the 1936 Berlin Olympics. After World War II she was eventually cleared of complicity in Nazi war crimes, but her film career never recovered, and she worked principally as a photographer.

Riel \\rē-'el\\, **Louis** (1844–1885) Canadian leader of the MÉTIS people in W Canada. Born in St. Boniface, Manitoba, he headed a revolt against Canadian expansion in the west that resulted in the establishment of the province of Manitoba (1870). In 1885 he led a Métis uprising in Saskatchewan that was crushed by the Canadians. Riel was found guilty of treason and hanged. His death led to ethnic conflicts in Quebec and Ontario and marked the beginning of the nationalist movement.

Riemann \'rē-,män\, **(Georg Friedrich) Bernhard** (1826–1866) German mathematician. His dissertation (1851) was on function theory. He became convinced that mathematical theory could link magnetism, light, gravitation, and electricity and suggested FIELD THEORIES, in which the space surrounding electrical charges may be mathematically described. While continuing to develop unifying mathematical themes in the laws of physics, he created Riemannian geometry (or elliptic geometry; see NON-EUCLIDEAN GEOMETRY), which proved essential to Albert EINSTEIN's model of SPACE-TIME in RELATIVITY theory. Riemann surfaces, Riemann integrals, and Riemann curvature, among other concepts, contributed to the understanding of curves and surfaces, as well as of CALCULUS.

Riemenschneider \'rē-mən-,shnī-dər\, **Tilman** (c.1460–1531) German sculptor. He settled in Würzburg in 1483 and opened a highly successful workshop. He was a city councillor (1504–20) and burgomeister (1520–25), but his sympathies with the revolutionaries in the PEASANTS' WAR led to a brief imprisonment. His wood and stone sculpture, characterized by sharply folded, flowing drapery, included monumental tombs and altarpieces, and made him one of the major masters of late Gothic art in Germany.

Rienzo, Cola di See COLA DI RIENZO

Riesman, David (1909–2002) U.S. sociologist. Born in Philadelphia and educated at Harvard Univ., he taught at the Univ. of Chicago (1946–58) and Harvard (1958–80). He studied primarily the social character of the urban middle class and is noted for *The Lonely Crowd* (1950), whose title became a catchphrase for the alienation of the individual in modern urban society.

Rietveld \'rēt-,velt\, **Gerrit (Thomas)** (1888–1964) Dutch architect and furniture designer. In 1918 he created his famous red-and-blue armchair, which, with its emphasis on geometry and use of primary colors, became a symbol of De STIJL. His masterpiece is the Schroeder House in Utrecht (1924), remarkable for its interplay of right-angle forms, planes, and lines.

rifle Firearm whose barrel is rifled (i.e., has spiral grooves cut inside it to give a spin to the projectile). Rifled firearms date to at least the 15th cent., when it was discovered that imparting a spin to the projectile improved its range and accuracy. Early muzzle-loading rifles were more difficult to load than smoothbore MUSKETS, but the invention of metallic cartridges led to breech-loading mechanisms. Bolt-action rifles, using a manually operated cylinder to drive the cartridge into the rifle's chamber, are the most common type for hunting. See also ASSAULT RIFLE.

rift valley Elongated trough formed by the depression of the earth's crust between two FAULTS. Rift valleys are usually narrow and long, with a relatively flat floor and steep sides. Rift valleys are found on the continents and along the crests of OCEANIC RIDGES. They occur where two plates that make up the earth's surface are separating (see PLATE TECTONICS). Submarine rift valleys are usually centers of SEAFLOOR SPREADING, where magma wells up from the MANTLE. The most extensive continental rift valleys are those of the E. African Rift System (see GREAT RIFT VALLEY).

Rift Valley See GREAT RIFT VALLEY

Riga \'rē-gə\ City (pop., 1999: 796,000), capital of Latvia. It lies on the Dvina River, near the Gulf of Riga. Founded in 1201, it joined the HANSEATIC LEAGUE in 1282. In the Middle Ages it was dominated by the TEUTONIC ORDER, and it was fought over by Poles and Russians in the 16th cent. It was captured by Sweden in 1621 and granted self-government but was ceded to Russia in 1721. It was the capital of an independent Latvia 1918–40, and again from 1991. It is a principal Baltic port and a major administrative, cultural, and industrial center. Its medieval remains include a 13th-cent. church and a 14th-cent. castle.

right Portion of the political spectrum associated with CONSERVATISM. The term derives from the seating arrangement of the French revolutionary parliament in the 1790s, in which the conservative representatives sat to the presiding officer's right. In the 19th cent., the term applied to conservatives who supported authority, tradition, and property. In the 20th cent. a divergent, radical form developed that was associated with FASCISM. See also LEFT.

right-to-work law In the U.S., any state law prohibiting labor agreements that require all employees to be union members. Supporters of such laws maintain that they are more equitable because they allow a person to choose whether or not to join a LABOR UNION. Opponents maintain that they reduce workers' job security by weakening the bargaining power of unions.

right whale Any of three species (genera *Balaena* and *Caperea*) of BALEEN WHALES (family Balaenidae) with a stout body and an enormous head. (The name refers to two species considered the "right" whales to hunt because of their value, slowness, and buoyancy after death.) The upper jaw is strongly arched, and the lower lip curves upward along the side, giving the lower jaw a scooplike form. The bowhead whale *(Balaena mysticetus),* inhabiting Arctic and N temperate waters, grows to about 65 ft (20 m). The black right whale *(B. glacialis)* grows to 60 ft (18 m); it may have a "bonnet," a horny growth infested with parasites, on its snout. Both species have been protected since 1946.

Rig Veda \rig-'vā-də\ Oldest religious SCRIPTURE in the world and most revered of the VEDAS, dating from the second millennium B.C. or earlier. Consisting of more than 1,000 hymns addressed to devas (gods), it is mainly concerned with the propitiation of divinities associated with the sky and atmosphere. It makes reference to such rituals as marriage and funeral rites, which differ little from those practiced today in Hinduism. It is the source of much Indian thought.

Riis \'rēs\, **Jacob A(ugust)** (1849–1914) Danish-U.S. social reformer. He emigrated to New York at 21 and became a police reporter for the *Tribune* (1877–88) and *Evening Sun* (1888–99). He publicized the deplorable living conditions in the slums of New York's Lower East Side, photographing the rooms and hallways of tenements. His book *How the Other Half Lives* (1890) stirred the nation's social conscience and spurred the first significant legislation to improve tenements.

Rijn, Rembrandt van See REMBRANDT VAN RIJN

Riley, James Whitcomb (1849–1916) U.S. poet. Born in Greenfield, Ind., he became known for his verse contributions to the *Indianapolis Daily Journal*, written in Hoosier dialect ostensibly by a farmer, which established his reputation as "the poet of the common people." His best-known poems include "When the Frost Is on the Punkin" and "The Raggedy Man." Among his many collections are *The Old Swimmin' Hole* (1883) and *Home Folks* (1900).

rilievo See RELIEF

Rilke \'ril-kə\, **Rainer Maria** (*orig.* René Maria) (1875–1926) Austrian-German poet. After an unhappy childhood, Rilke began a life of wandering that took him across Europe. His visits to Russia inspired his long poem cycle *The Book of Hours* (1905). In 1902–14 his geographic center was Paris, where he developed a new lyrical style that attempted to capture the plastic essence of a physical object; the results were *New Poems* (1907–8) and its prose counterpart, the novel *The Notebook of Malte Laurids Brigge* (1910). After 13 years of writing very little, in 1922 he completed the 10 poems of the *Duino Elegies* (1923), a profound meditation on the paradoxes of human existence and one of the century's poetic masterpieces. With astonishing speed, he then composed *Sonnets to Orpheus* (1923), a superb 55-poem cycle. The two works brought him international fame.

Rimbaud \raⁿ-'bō\, **(Jean-Nicolas-) Arthur** (1854–1891) French poet. The son of an army captain, he had begun by age 16 to write violent, blasphemous poems, and he formulated an aesthetic doctrine stating that a poet must become a seer, break down the restraints and controls on personality, and thus become the instrument for the voice of the eternal. Invited to Paris by Paul VERLAINE, he engaged in a wild and dissipated life. *The Drunken Boat* (written 1871)

displays his astonishing verbal virtuosity and a daring choice of images and metaphors. In *Les illuminations* (written 1872–74), he tried to abolish the distinction between reality and hallucination. *A Season in Hell* (1873), which alternates prose passages with dazzling lyrics, became his farewell to poetry at age 19. After a falling-out, Verlaine shot and wounded Rimbaud. Rimbaud abandoned literature and from 1875 led a vagabond life as a trader, mainly in Ethiopia; he died after his leg was amputated at 37. The Dionysian power of his verse and his liberation of language from the constraints of form greatly influenced the SYMBOLIST MOVEMENT and 20th-cent. poetry.

Rimsky-Korsakov, Nikolai (Andreyevich) (1844–1908) Russian composer. While a naval cadet he met other composers, and from 1867 he was included among the MIGHTY FIVE. In 1873 he took the new post of Inspector of Naval Bands. He helped Aleksandr BORODIN orchestrate *Prince Igor* and revised several of Modest MUSSORGSKY's works. He wrote many colorful operas, much loved in Russia, including *Sadko* (1896), *The Tale of Tsar Saltan* (1903), *The Legend of the Invisible City of Kitezh* (1905), and *The Golden Cockerel* (1908); other works include three symphonies, the suite *Scheherazade* (1888), and the *Russian Easter Festival* overture. All his works are distinguished by brilliant orchestration. His many students included Sergey PROKOFIEV and Igor STRAVINSKY.

Nikolai Rimsky-Korsakov
Portrait by V. A. Serov

rinderpest Acute, highly contagious viral disease of RUMINANTS (including wild cloven-hoofed ones), common in Africa, the Indian subcontinent, and the Middle East. The virus spreads by close direct or indirect contact. It is the most severe infectious disease of cattle, with sudden onset and high mortality. Local eradication depends on controlling it in wild animals and eliminating infected domestic animals; vaccination combined with quarantine is effective.

ring Circular band of gold, silver, or other precious or decorative material, usually worn on the finger. The earliest examples were found in the tombs of ancient Egypt. In addition to being worn as adornment, rings have functioned as symbols of authority, fidelity, or social status. In the early Roman republic, most were made of iron, gold being reserved for persons of high status; but by the 3rd cent. B.C. anyone except a slave could wear a gold ring. The Romans are thought to have originated engagement rings, symbolizing a promise of marriage. In the Middle Ages, signet rings were important in religious, legal, and commercial transactions; memorial, posy, and keepsake rings served sentimental purposes; occult rings supposedly had magical powers; and poison rings could be filled with poison for the purpose of suicide or homicide.

Ringgold, Faith (b.1930) U.S. artist and writer. Born in New York City, she taught art in New York's public schools. In 1963 she began her "American People" series of paintings, which dealt with the civil-rights movement from a female perspective. In the 1970s she became active in promoting feminist art and the racial integration of the New York art world. Her famous "story quilts" depict stories set in the context of African-American history. She adapted one of her quilts, *Tar Beach,* as a children's book, and went on to publish other books for children.

Ringling Brothers U.S. circus owners. After five of the seven brothers formed a song-and-dance troupe, in 1884 they organized their first circus in their hometown, Baraboo, Wis., and began to tour the Midwest in circus wagons. They acquired smaller circuses, and in 1907 bought the Barnum & Bailey Circus to form the leading U.S. circus. The guiding managers were Charles Ringling (1863–1926) and later John Ringling (1866–1936), whose acquisition of American Circus Corp. in 1929 brought 11 major circuses under Ringling control. The Ringling Brothers and Barnum & Bailey Circus passed out of Ringling family hands in 1967.

Ring of Fire Belt of seismic and volcanic activity roughly surrounding the Pacific Ocean. It includes the ANDES, coastal Central and N. America, the ALEUTIAN and KURIL islands, KAMCHATKA, Taiwan, E Indonesia, New Zealand, the Japanese and Philippine islands, and the island arcs of the W Pacific. About 70% of all historically recorded active volcanoes have occurred in this belt. See also PLATE TECTONICS.

ringworm Superficial skin changes caused by certain fungi (see FUNGUS) that live on the skin, feeding on KERATIN. Skin responses vary from slight scaling to blistering and marked disruption of the keratin layer (depending on body area and type of fungus), usually in a ring shape. It includes ATHLETE'S FOOT, jock itch, and fungal infections of the body, hands, nails, beard, and scalp. Spread usually depends on susceptibility and predisposing factors (e.g., excessive perspiration). Ringworm is treated with medications applied to the skin or taken orally. Limited ultraviolet-light exposure may also help.

Rio de Janeiro City (pop., 1996: 5,551,000) and port, SE Brazil. The site became important in the 18th cent. as an outlet for mineral exports from gold and diamond mines. Located on one of the largest harbors in the world and known for its scenic views, it was the capital of Brazil from 1822 to 1960, when the national capital was moved to BRASILIA. It is the country's second-largest manufacturing center after SÃO PAULO. Noted for its wide streets, superb beaches (see COPACABANA), and public parks and gardens, it is a leading tourist and resort center. Its opulent and riotous CARNIVAL is world-famous.

Río de la Plata, viceroyalty of Last of the four viceroyalties that Spain created to govern its New World colonies. Established in 1776, it controlled an area previously under the viceroyalty of PERU and included what is now Argentina, Uruguay, Paraguay, and Bolivia. Successive viceroys defended the territory against Portugal and Britain and helped Buenos Aires become a flourishing outpost of the Spanish empire. Salted meat from the cattle ranches of the interior, exported as cheap food for slaves, brought unprecedented wealth to the colony. In 1810 the Creoles sent the viceroy into exile. See also NEW GRANADA, NEW SPAIN.

Río de la Plata See Río de la PLATA

Rio Grande \'rē-ō-'grand\ *in Mexico* **Río Bravo** River, N. America. One of the longest rivers of N. America, it flows 1,900 mi (3,000 km) from its sources in the S ROCKY MTNS. of SW Colorado to the Gulf of MEXICO. It flows generally south, passing southeast between Texas and Mexico, marking the entire border. The earliest European settlements were along the lower course of the river in the 16th cent., but many of the PUEBLO INDIAN settlements of New Mexico date from before the Spanish conquest. With normal rainfall, it is a major source of irrigation. It flows through BIG BEND NATIONAL PARK.

Riopelle \rē-ò-'pel\, **Jean-Paul** (1923–2002) Canadian painter. Born in Montreal, he moved to Paris in 1947. His early lyrical, abstract paintings evolved into a denser, more powerful impasto style; he is renowned for his use of various media (including watercolor, ink, oils, crayon, and chalk) and he also produced large collage murals. He achieved international acclaim with the huge triptych *Pavane* (1954). He is the leading Canadian abstract painter of his generation.

rip current *or* **riptide** Narrow strong current of water that flows sporadically seaward in a direction perpendicular to a beach. The currents are unrelated to tides. Rip currents form at long coasts that are approached by wave trains that are nearly parallel to the shoreline. During periods of large waves, water builds up at the beach and cannot escape as longshore currents, which require oblique wave approach. The buildup continues until water can escape by surging for several minutes through a low point in a breaker, creating an undertow that can be dangerous for swimmers.

Ripken, Cal(vin Edwin), Jr. (b.1960) U.S. baseball player. He was born in Havre de Grace, Md.; his father and brother both played professional baseball. He played shortstop for the Baltimore Orioles from 1981, and broke several single-season records. In 1995 he broke Lou GEHRIG's long-standing record of consecutive games played (2,130), eventually running his streak to 2,632 games before taking a day off in 1998. He retired in 2001.

Ripley, George (1802–1880) U.S. journalist and reformer. Born in Greenfield, Mass., he became a Unitarian minister. A member of the Transcendental Club and an editor of *The Dial,* its literary magazine, he founded the utopian community BROOK FARM in 1841. When it closed in 1847, he worked as literary critic for the *New York Tribune* to pay off its debts. His *Cyclopedia* (1862) became a popular reference book.

risk In economics and finance, an allowance for the possibility of loss in a loan or investment. Default risk refers to the chance that a borrower will not repay a loan; a lender may charge the true INTEREST plus a premium for the default risk. All stock investment carries implicit risk since there is no guarantee of return on investment (ROI). Trading or variability risk is the amount that the return may vary, up or down, from the expected ROI.

Risorgimento \rē-ˌzȯr-ji-ˈmen-tō\ (Italian: "Resurgence") 19th-cent. movement for Italian unification. Reforms introduced by France into its Italian states 1800–15 provided an impetus for the movement. Secret groups such as YOUNG ITALY advocated Italian unity, and such leaders as Camillo CAVOUR, who founded the journal *Il Risorgimento* (1847), Giuseppe GARIBALDI, and Giuseppe MAZZINI called for liberal reforms and a united Italy. After the failure of the REVOLUTIONS OF 1848, leadership passed to Cavour and Piedmont, which formed an alliance with France against Austria (1859). The unification of most of Italy in 1861, followed by the annexation of Venetia (1866) and papal Rome (1870), marked the end of the Risorgimento.

rite of passage See rite of PASSAGE

Ritsos \ˈrēt-sȯs\, **Yannis** (1909–1990) Greek poet. His first two collections mixed socialist philosophy with images of his personal suffering. His third collection, *Funeral Procession* (1936), provided the words for the anthem of the Greek Left. He fought as a Communist during the Nazi occupation and Greek civil war, and spent four years in prison camps. Exiled in 1967, he was prohibited from publishing until 1972. Despite those obstacles, he wrote 117 books, including plays and essays.

Rivadavia \ˌrē-vä-ˈthä-vē-ə\, **Bernardino** (1780–1845) First president of the Argentine republic (1826–27). Active in the 1810 movement for independence from Spain, he came to dominate the ruling revolutionary triumvirate in 1811. He disbanded the Spanish courts, abolished censorship, and ended the slave trade. As president, he continued to advance reforms but was unable to end a fruitless war with Brazil. Unable to win acceptance for a centralist constitution, he resigned. His cultural initiatives, such as founding the Univ. of Buenos Aires, were among his greatest achievements.

river Natural stream of water that flows in a channel with defined banks. Rivers are a fundamental link in the HYDROLOGIC CYCLE, and they play a major role in shaping the surface features of the earth. Even apparently arid desert regions are greatly influenced by river action when periodic floodwaters surge down usually dry watercourses. Rivers are fed by overland runoff, groundwater seepage, and meltwater from the edges of snowfields and glaciers; direct precipitation contributes only slightly. Losses of river water result from percolation into rock, gravel, or sand; evaporation; and ultimately outflow into the ocean.

Rivera, Diego (1886–1957) Mexican muralist. After study in Spain, he settled in Paris in 1909. He briefly espoused Cubism but abandoned it for a visual language of simplified forms and bold areas of color. Returning to Mexico in 1921, he sought to create a new national art on revolutionary themes in the wake of the MEXICAN REVOLUTION. He painted many public murals, the most ambitious of which is in the National Palace. He worked in the U.S. 1930–34, where his mural for New York's Rockefeller Center aroused a storm of controversy and was ultimately replaced because it contained the figure of Vladimir LENIN; he later reproduced it at the Palace of Fine Arts in Mexico City. With J. C. OROZCO and D. A. SIQUEIROS, he created a re-

vival of FRESCO PAINTING that became Mexico's most significant contribution to 20th-cent. art. His large-scale, didactic murals contain scenes of Mexican history, culture, and industry, with Indians, peasants, conquistadores, and factory workers drawn as simplified figures in crowded, shallow spaces. Rivera was married to Frida KAHLO.

Rivera, Luis Muñoz See Luis MUÑOZ RIVERA

river blindness *or* **onchocerciasis** \ˌäŋ-kō-ˌsər-ˈkī-ə-səs\ Human disease caused by a filarial worm native to Africa and transmitted by several BLACKFLIES. It is so called because the flies breed on rivers and mostly affect riverine populations. Blindness is caused by dead microfilariae—the larvae that can be produced for some 15–18 years by adult worms—inside the eye. River blindness is common in savannah areas of Africa and in Guatemala and Mexico. In 1987 the World Health Organization began to distribute the drug ivermectin, which eliminates the microfilariae.

Rivers, Larry *orig.* Yitzroch Loiza Grossberg (1923–2002) U.S. painter associated with ABSTRACT EXPRESSIONISM and POP ART. Born in New York, he was a professional jazz saxophonist before turning to painting. His early works are characterized by complex, fragmentary, and multiple views; best known is the harshly realistic *Double Portrait of Berdie* (1955). From the 1960s he introduced commercial images into his work, as well as elements of collage, construction, and sculpture; an elaborate example is his huge *History of the Russian Revolution* (1965).

Riverside City (pop., 2000: 255,000), S California. With SAN BERNARDINO and Ontario, it forms a metropolitan complex east of LOS ANGELES. Settled in the 1870s, it became a citrus-growing area. It is home to a campus of the Univ. of CALIFORNIA.

Riviera \ˌri-vē-ˈer-ə\ Coastal region bordering on the Mediterranean Sea in SE France and NW Italy. It extends from CANNES, France, to La Spezia, Italy. The French Riviera is also called the CÔTE D'AZUR. Noted for its scenery and pleasant climate, it is one of the major tourist centers of Europe. Because of its mild winters, many delicate plants flourish there, and flowers are grown out of season for export to N markets. See also MONTE CARLO, NICE.

Riyadh \rē-ˈyäd\ City (metro. area pop., 1999 est.: 3,183,000), capital of Saudi Arabia, in the E central part of the country. Chosen as the capital of the SAUD DYNASTY in 1824, after 1902 it became the center for IBN SAUD's conquest of the ARABIAN PENINSULA, and in 1932 the capital of the new kingdom of Saudi Arabia. Discovery of immense petroleum deposits in the 1930s transformed the old town into a showplace of modern technology. It is the kingdom's administrative, commercial, education, and transportation center.

Rizal (y Alonso) \rē-ˈsäl\, **José** *in full* José Protasio Rizal Mercado y Alonso Realonda (1861–1896) Filipino patriot and writer. Committed to the reform of Spanish rule in his home country, Rizal lived in Europe 1882–92, where he published novels exposing the evils of Spanish rule and became the leader of the Propaganda Movement, which produced reform-oriented articles, magazines, and poetry. He returned to the Philippines to found a nonviolent-reform society, but was deported to Mindanao. When the Katipunan nationalist secret society revolted in 1896, the Spanish arrested and executed Rizal, though he had taken no part in the insurrection (see PHILIPPINE REVOLUTION). His martyrdom convinced Filipinos that there was no alternative to independence from Spain.

RKO Radio Pictures U.S. film studio. Created in 1928 as Radio-Keith-Orpheum when the Radio Corp. of America (RCA CORP.) acquired the Keith-Albee-Orpheum theater chain and a production firm, RKO became noted for its Fred ASTAIRE–Ginger ROGERS musicals and Katharine HEPBURN's early movies, as well as such films as *Cimarron* (1931), *The Informer* (1935), and *Citizen Kane* (1941). It was bought by Howard HUGHES in 1948; his inattention doomed the company, and it ceased production in 1953 and was sold to Desilu Productions (1957). Today, as RKO General, it operates radio and television stations and theaters.

RNA *in full* **ribonucleic acid** \ˌrī-bō-nü-ˈklē-ik, ˌrī-bō-nü-ˈklā-ik\ One of the two main types of NUCLEIC ACID (the other being DNA), which functions in cellular PROTEIN synthesis in all living cells and replaces DNA as the carrier of

genetic information in some viruses. Like DNA, it consists of strands of NUCLEOTIDES joined along their length, but the strands are single and it has URACIL (U) where DNA has THYMINE. Messenger RNA (mRNA) carries the message of the genetic code from DNA (in CHROMOSOMES) to the site of protein synthesis (on RIBOSOMES). Ribosomal RNA (rRNA), part of the building material of ribosomes, participates in protein synthesis. Transfer RNA (tRNA) is the smallest type. Each nucleotide triplet on mRNA specifies which AMINO ACID comes next on the protein being synthesized, and a tRNA molecule with that triplet's complement on its protruding end brings the specified amino acid to the site to be linked into the protein.

roach See COCKROACH

Roach, Hal (*orig.* Harold Eugene) (1892–1992) U.S. film producer. Born in Elmira, N.Y., he was a bit player in Hollywood when he befriended Harold LLOYD; he directed and produced Lloyd's *Just Nuts* (1915), then formed the Hal Roach Studio (1919) and produced such other Lloyd comedies as *Safety Last* (1923) and thousands of comedy shorts, winning Academy Awards for *The Music Box* (1932) and *Bored of Education* (1936). In addition to producing the Will ROGERS films and the "Our Gang" shorts, he teamed LAUREL AND HARDY and produced their films, as well as such other successes as *Topper* (1937) and *Of Mice and Men* (1939). In 1984 he received an Academy Award for lifetime achievement.

road Traveled way on which people, animals, or wheeled vehicles move. The earliest roads developed from paths and trails and appeared with the invention of wheeled vehicles, around 3000 B.C.; the first major road extended 1,775 mi (2,850 km) from the Persian Gulf to the Aegean Sea. The Romans used roads to maintain control of their empire, building over 53,000 mi (85,000 km) of roadways; Roman construction techniques remained the most advanced until the late 1700s. The invention of MACADAM (c.1820) provided a quick and durable method for building roads, and asphalt and concrete also began to be used. Motorized traffic in the 20th cent. led to the limited-access highway; the first was a parkway in New York City (1925). Superhighways also appeared in Italy and Germany in the 1930s. In the 1950s the U.S. interstate highway system began to link the country's major cities.

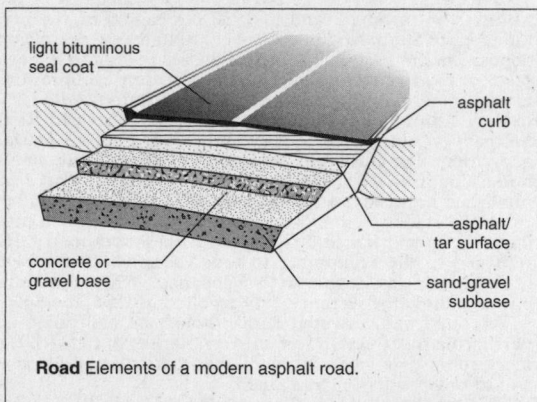

light bituminous seal coat

asphalt curb

asphalt/ tar surface

concrete or gravel base

sand-gravel subbase

Road Elements of a modern asphalt road.

roadrunner *or* **chaparral cock** \ˌsha-pə-ˈral\ Either of two species of terrestrial CUCKOO, especially *Geococcyx californianus* (family Cuculidae), of Mexican and SW U.S. deserts. About 22 in. (56 cm) long, it has streaked brown-and-white plumage, a short shaggy crest, stout bluish legs, and a long tail carried at an angle. A weak flier, it prefers to run. Using its stout bill, it pounds insects, lizards, and snakes to death, then swallows them head first. The lesser roadrunner (*G. velox*), of Mexico and Central America, is smaller.

Roanoke Island Island, off N. Carolina coast, inside the OUTER BANKS. It is about 12 mi (19 km) long and 3 mi (5 km) wide. It was the site of the first English settlement in N. America; its original colonists, led by Walter RALEIGH, re-

mained for only 10 months in 1585. A second group arrived in 1587. When a supply ship arrived in 1590 all the colonists had vanished; their fate was never known. It is now a resort and residential area.

Roanoke River River, S Virginia and NE N. Carolina. Formed by the confluence of forks in W. Virginia, it flows southeast for 380 mi (612 km) into Albemarle Sound, on the Atlantic coast of N. Carolina. It is navigable by small craft from its mouth to Weldon, N.C.

Robbe-Grillet \rȯb-grē-ˈyä\, **Alain** (b.1922) French writer. He became the leading theoretician of the *nouveau roman* ("new novel"), the French ANTINOVEL that emerged in the 1950s. His narratives lack conventional elements such as chronological plot and are composed largely of recurring images and repeated fragments of dialogue. Among his works are fiction, including *The Erasers* (1953) and *Jealousy* (1957); the essay *Towards a New Novel* (1963); and the memoir *Ghosts in the Mirror* (1984). He is also a screenwriter and film director, best known for his screenplay for *Last Year at Marienbad* (1961).

robbery See THEFT

Robbia family, Della See DELLA ROBBIA FAMILY

Robbins, Jerome (1918–1998) U.S. dancer, choreographer, and director. Born in New York City, he joined the Ballet Theatre (later AMERICAN BALLET THEATRE) in 1940, creating roles in several ballets. His first choreographic success was Leonard BERNSTEIN's *Fancy Free*, which became the musical *On the Town* (1944); this was followed by many successful Broadway musicals and films, including *West Side Story* (1957), *Gypsy* (1959), and *Fiddler on the Roof* (1964). He joined the NEW YORK CITY BALLET in 1949, and was associate director (1950–59), resident choreographer and ballet master (1969–83), and codirector with Peter MARTINS until retiring in 1990. His choreography blended modern, academic, and popular dance styles in a variety of American idioms.

Robert I *known as* **Robert the Bruce** (1274–1329) King of Scotland (1306–29). He sided with the Scots against England and fought under William WALLACE. He gained the Scottish throne in 1306 after stabbing a rival to death in a quarrel. Twice defeated by EDWARD I (1306), he became a fugitive, hiding on a remote island off the Irish coast. He returned to Scotland in 1307 and began gathering supporters, and in 1314 he defeated EDWARD II at the Battle of BANNOCKBURN. EDWARD III finally recognized him and confirmed Scottish independence in 1328.

Robert II *known as* **Robert Curthose** \ˈkùr-tōz\ (1054?–1134) Duke of Normandy (1087–1106). The eldest son of WILLIAM I, he was named heir to Normandy but rebelled twice (c.1077, c.1082) and was exiled to Italy until his father's death (1087). He joined the First CRUSADE, in which he fought bravely and helped to capture Jerusalem (1099). He led an unsuccessful invasion of England after HENRY I became king (1100); Henry then invaded Normandy (1105–6) and captured Robert, who spent the rest of his life as a prisoner.

Robert II (1316–1390) King of Scotland (1371–90). Grandson of ROBERT I the Bruce, he served as regent during the periods of exile and imprisonment of his uncle, DAVID II, and took the throne on David's death in 1371. The first king of the House of STUART, he had little effect on political and military affairs, taking no active part in the renewed war with England (1378–88). Succession after his death was disputed by his numerous children and their descendants.

Robert Guiscard \gēs-ˈkàr\ (c.1015–1085) Norman adventurer and duke of Apulia (1059–85). Born into a family of Norman knights, he fought in S Italy, defeating the Byzantines, Lombards, and papacy (1053) and taking over Apulia. His brother Roger (later count of Sicily) helped him to conquer Sicily and Calabria, and he gained control of Salerno in 1076, making it the capital of his duchy. Robert made an abortive attempt to gain the Byzantine throne (1083) but returned to Italy to defend Pope GREGORY VII from his enemies.

Robert-Houdin \rȯ-ber-ü-ˈdaⁿ\, **Jean-Eugène** *orig.* Jean-Eugène Robert (1805–1871) French magician, considered the father of modern CONJURING. At the Palais-Royal (1845–55), he performed on a bare stage in evening dress rather than the usual wizardlike costume. He used familiar objects to create his illusions, and was the first magician to use electricity. He exposed magicians who relied on supernatural explanations for their feats; sent to Algeria by the French government, he countered the influence of the dervishes by duplicating their feats.

Roberts, Charles G(eorge) D(ouglas) (*later* **Sir Charles**) (1860–1943) Canadian poet. His best-known poems are simple descriptive lyrics about the scenery and rural life of his native New Brunswick and Nova Scotia. He published some 12 verse volumes, including *In Divers Tones* (1887) and *The Vagrant of Time* (1927). His prose includes short stories that display his intimate knowledge of the Canadian woods, including *Earth's Enigmas* (1896) and *Red Fox* (1905).

Roberts, Oral (b.1918) U.S. evangelist. Born near Ada, Okla., the son of a Pentecostal preacher, he spent 12 years as a pastor in the South and built up his own organization, the Pentecostal Holiness Church. He studied at Oklahoma Baptist College (1943–45), emerging as a Methodist. Claiming direct communications from God, he began an itinerant ministry of faith healing in the late 1940s. The Oral Roberts Evangelistic Assn., based in Tulsa, became the parent organization for other endeavors, including a publishing firm. From the 1950s he reached wide audiences through radio and television. In 1963 he founded Oral Roberts Univ. in Tulsa.

Roberts, Richard (1789–1864) British inventor. He was an uneducated Welsh quarryman before he took a position with Henry MAUDSLAY and then established his own machine-tool factory. He was one of the inventors of the metal planer, and he made important improvements to the LATHE. His multiple-spindle spinning mule (1779) marked an important advance in spinning technology. He developed a screw-cutting lathe and built railway locomotives with interchangeable parts, automatic machinery for punching holes in plate, and the first successful gas meter. Not a shrewd businessman, he died in poverty.

Robertson, Oscar (Palmer) (b.1938) U.S. basketball player. Born in Charlotte, Tenn., he played with the Cincinnati Royals 1960–69. "The Big O" twice led the league in combined average for points, rebounds, and assists (1961–62, 1963–64). He played for the Milwaukee Bucks 1970–74. He ended his career with 26,710 points, 7,804 rebounds, and 9,887 assists.

Robertson, Pat (*orig.* Marion Gordon) (b.1930) U.S. evangelist. Born in Lexington, Va., he attended Washington and Lee Univ., served in the Marine Corps, and earned a law degree from Yale Univ. A religious conversion led to his becoming a Southern Baptist minister in 1959. In 1960 he started the nation's first Christian television station, which he built into the Christian Broadcasting Network. In 1988 he campaigned for the Republican presidential nomination. In 1989 he founded the Christian Coalition, a conservative political organization that went on to exercise wide influence.

Robeson \'rōb-sən\, **Paul (Bustill)** (1898–1976) U.S. singer, actor, and activist. Born in Princeton, N.J., to a former slave and a Quaker mother, Robeson attended Rutgers Univ., where he was an All-America football player and graduated at the head of his class. He earned a law degree at Columbia Univ., but later turned to theater, joining a group that included Eugene O'NEILL and appearing in his *The Emperor Jones* (1924; film, 1933), a huge success in New York and London. Robeson's superb bass-baritone brought him worldwide renown with his performance of "Ol' Man River" in *Show Boat* (1928). His lead role in *Othello* won high praise in London (1930) and on Broadway (1943). He visited the Soviet Union in 1934, and became identified with strong left-wing commitments. In 1950 his passport was withdrawn. Viciously harassed, Robeson left the U.S. to live in Europe and travel in Soviet-bloc countries, but returned in 1963 because of ill health.

Robespierre \,rō-bes-'pyer\, **Maximilien (François-Marie-Isidore) de** (1758–1794) French revolutionary. Elected to the National Assembly (1789), where he became notorious as an outspoken radical in favor of individual rights, he became a leading member of the MONTAGNARDS in the National Convention. After calling for the death of LOUIS XVI,

he led the Jacobins (see JACOBIN CLUB) and the COMMITTEE OF PUBLIC SAFETY (1793) in establishing the REIGN OF TERROR. Despite earlier support from the people of Paris, who called him "the Incorruptible," he lost his dominating authority and was overthrown and guillotined in the THERMIDORIAN REACTION. Often regarded as a bloodthirsty dictator, he was later valued for his social ideals of reducing inequality.

Maximilien de Robespierre
Portrait by an unknown artist

robin Either of two THRUSH species (family Turdidae). The American robin *(Turdus migratorius)*, 10 in. (25 cm) long, with a rusty breast, lives in deciduous forests and sometimes towns. The European robin, or robin redbreast *(Erithacus rubecula)*, breeds throughout Europe, W Asia, and part of N. Africa. It is 5.5 in. (14 cm) long, with a rusty-orange face and breast.

Robin Hood Legendary English outlaw. The hero of ballads dating from as early as the 14th cent., Robin Hood was a rebel who robbed and killed landowners and government officials and gave his gains to the poor. His greatest enemy was the sheriff of Nottingham. The ballads emerged during a time of agrarian unrest that culminated in the PEASANTS' REVOLT of 1381. There is no evidence of Robin Hood's historical existence. In postmedieval ballads and stories he was a nobleman in the reign of King JOHN who took refuge in Sherwood Forest after losing his lands. His men included Little John and Friar Tuck; his beloved was Maid Marion.

Robinson, Bill (*orig.* Luther) *known as* **Bojangles** (1878–1949) U.S. tap dancer. Born in Richmond, Va., he developed extraordinary tap-dancing skills, and was the first black to appear in white vaudeville shows, and later the first black in Florenz ZIEGFELD's Follies. He danced in theaters and nightclubs nationwide and appeared in films, notably in four with Shirley TEMPLE and in the all-black *Stormy Weather* (1943), becoming a beloved American institution.

Robinson, Edward G. *orig.* Emmanuel Goldenberg (1893–1973) U.S. (Romanian-born) film actor. He grew up poor in New York and was largely a stage actor until the advent of sound movies. After winning fame as a gangster boss in *Little Caesar* (1931), he often played tough guys and criminals. His later films include *Barbary Coast* (1935), *Double Indemnity* (1944), *All My Sons* (1948), *Key Largo* (1948), and *The Cincinnati Kid* (1965). In 1973 he was posthumously awarded an honorary Academy Award.

Robinson, Edwin Arlington (1869–1935) U.S. poet. Raised in Head Tide, Me., he endured years of poverty before his poetry began to attract attention. He is best known for short dramatic lyrics about the people in a small New England village, including "Richard Cory" and "Miniver Cheevy." His collections include *The Children of the Night* (1897), *The Man Against the Sky* (1916), and *Collected Poems* (1921, Pulitzer Prize). He also wrote long narrative poems, including *The Man Who Died Twice* (1924, Pulitzer Prize) and *Tristram* (1927, Pulitzer Prize).

Robinson, Frank (b.1935) U.S. baseball player and the first black manager in major-league baseball. Born in Beaumont, Texas, he played principally for the Cincinnati Reds (1956–65) and Baltimore Orioles (1966–71). In 1966 he won the triple crown, leading the league in home runs (49), runs batted in (122), and batting average (.316). He later managed the Cleveland Indians (1975–77), San Francisco Giants (1981–84), Baltimore Orioles (1988–91), and Montreal Expos (from 2002).

Robinson, Jackie (*orig.* Jack Roosevelt) (1919–1972) U.S. baseball player, the first black player in the major leagues. Born in Cairo, Ga., Robinson became an outstanding performer in several sports at Pasadena Junior College and UCLA, and served in the army in World War II. He played in the NEGRO LEAGUES before being signed by Branch RICKEY to a Brooklyn Dodgers farm team (1945–46). On

being advanced to the majors in 1947, he endured with notable dignity the early opposition to his presence. In his first year he led the league in stolen bases and was chosen rookie of the year. In 1949 he won the batting championship with a .342 average and was voted the league's Most Valuable Player. He retired in 1956 with a career batting average of .311. In his later years he strongly supported the cause of civil rights.

Jackie Robinson, 1946

Robinson, Mary *orig.* Mary Bourke (b.1944) Irish politician, first woman president of Ireland (1990–97). A professor of law (1969–75), she served in the Irish senate 1969–89 as a Labour Party member. In 1990 she was a coalition candidate for president, and narrowly won. She served as U.N. high commissioner for human rights 1997–2002.

Robinson, Smokey (*orig.* William) (b.1940) U.S. singer and songwriter. Born in Detroit, Robinson formed a group while still in high school. As the Miracles, they released their first single, produced by Berry Gordy, Jr., who shortly thereafter founded the MOTOWN label. "Shop Around" (1961) became Motown's first hit; it was followed by such hits as "The Tracks of My Tears," and Robinson wrote such hits for other artists as "My Girl" and "My Guy." He became president of Motown in 1972.

Robinson, Sugar Ray *orig.* Walker Smith, Jr. (1921–1989) U.S. boxer. Born in Detroit, he began boxing in high school in New York City and won all of his 89 amateur fights. He was six times a world champion, once (1946–51) as a welterweight (147 lbs) and five times (1951–60) as a middleweight (160 lbs). In 201 professional bouts, he made 109 knockouts. His outstanding ability and flamboyant personality made him a hero of boxing fans worldwide, and he is sometimes considered the best fighter in history.

robotics Design, construction, and use of machines (robots) to perform tasks traditionally done by human beings. Robots include any automatically operated machine that replaces human effort, though it may not look much like a human being or function in a humanlike manner. Robots are widely used in such industries as automobile manufacture to perform simple repetitive tasks, and in industries where work must be performed in hazardous environments. Many aspects of robotics involve ARTIFICIAL INTELLIGENCE; robots may be equipped with the equivalent of human senses such as vision, touch, and the ability to sense temperature. Some are capable of simple decision making. A robot in human form is called an android.

Rob Roy *orig.* Robert MacGregor (1671–1734) Scottish Highland outlaw. Nephew of the chief of the MacGregor clan, he became a freebooter, apparently engaging in cattle stealing and blackmail. After the penal laws against the MacGregors were reintroduced (1693), he took the surname Campbell and frequently signed himself Rob Roy ("Red Rob"), in reference to his red hair. He became a brigand after his financial ruin in 1712 and exacted tribute for protection against thieves. He was portrayed as a Scottish Robin Hood in Walter SCOTT's novel *Rob Roy*.

Rochambeau \ˌrō-ˌsham-ˈbō\, **comte (Count) de** *orig.* Jean-Baptiste-Donatien de Vimeur (1725–1807) French army officer. He was put in command of a French army of 6,000 to join the Continental Army in the American Revolution (1780). After waiting in vain for French naval support, he joined forces with George WASHINGTON at White Plains, N.Y., in 1781. They marched to YORKTOWN, where they besieged British forces and forced their surrender. Returned to France, he commanded the Army of the North in the French Revolution and was made a marshal of France.

Roche \ˈrōsh\, **(Eamonn) Kevin** (b.1922) Irish-U.S. architect. After studying under Ludwig MIES VAN DER ROHE, he became Eero SAARINEN's principal design associate (1954–61), working with John Dinkeloo (1918–81) on such projects as the Dulles International Airport Terminal Building (1962) and St. Louis's Gateway Arch (1965). The two launched their own firm in 1966. Well-known works include the Ford Foundation headquarters in New York City (1968) and the General Foods headquarters in Rye, N.Y. (1977). Roche won the Pritzker Architecture Prize in 1982.

Rochefoucauld, duc de La See duc de LA ROCHEFOUCAULD

Roche limit \ˈrōsh\ Minimum distance, calculated by Édouard Roche in 1850, at which a large SATELLITE can orbit a body without being torn apart by tidal forces. If their composition is similar, the theoretical limit is about 2.5 times the larger body's radius. The rings of SATURN lie inside its Roche limit and may be debris from a moon.

Rochester City (pop., 2000: 220,000) and port, NW New York. Founded in 1811, it became a boom town with construction of the ERIE CANAL and rail connections. Margaret and Kate Fox attracted world attention in the 1840s with their seances known as the "Rochester rappings." The city was a terminus of the UNDERGROUND RAILROAD. S. B. ANTHONY lived there 1866–1906. In the 1890s George EASTMAN developed photographic equipment there and founded EASTMAN KODAK CO. It is the home of the Univ. of ROCHESTER, Eastman School of Music, and Rochester Institute of Technology.

Rochester, Earl of *orig.* **John Wilmot** (1647–1680) English poet and wit. The most notorious debauchee of the RESTORATION court, Rochester was also its best poet and one of the most original and powerful English satirists. *A Satyr Against Mankind* (1675) is a scathing denunciation of rationalism and optimism that contrasts human perfidy with animal wisdom. In 1680 he became ill, experienced a religious conversion, and recanted his past, ordering "all his profane and lewd writings" burned.

Rochester, University of Private university in Rochester, N.Y., founded in 1850. It includes a college of engineering and applied science, and schools of music (the renowned Eastman School), business administration, and education and human development, as well as a medical center. Total enrollment is about 8,400.

rock Naturally occurring aggregate of MINERALS. The three major classes of rock—IGNEOUS, SEDIMENTARY, and METAMORPHIC—are based on the processes that formed them. These three classes are further subdivided on the basis of various factors, especially chemical, mineralogical, and textural attributes (see ACID AND BASIC ROCKS, CRYSTALLINE ROCK, EXTRUSIVE ROCK). See also INTRUSIVE ROCK.

rock art Ancient or prehistoric drawing, painting, or similar work on or of stone. Rock art includes pictographs (drawings or paintings), petroglyphs (carvings or inscriptions), petroforms (rocks laid out in patterns), and geoglyphs (ground drawings). The ancient animals, tools, and human activities depicted often help shed light on daily life in the distant past, though the images are frequently symbolic. Sometimes the art at a single site may extend over several centuries. Rock art may have played a role in prehistoric religion. See also ALTAMIRA, LASCAUX GROTTO.

rock crystal Transparent variety of QUARTZ that is valued for its clarity and total lack of color or flaws. Formerly used extensively as a gemstone, it has been replaced by glass and plastic; rhinestones originally were quartz pebbles from the Rhine River. Its optical properties led to its use in lenses and prisms; its piezoelectric properties (see PIEZOELECTRICITY) are used to control the oscillation of electrical circuits.

Rockefeller, John D(avison) (1839–1937) U.S. industrialist and philanthropist. Born in Richford, N.Y., he moved with his family to Cleveland in 1853. In 1859 he established a commission business dealing in hay, grain, meats, and other goods. In 1863 he built an oil refinery that soon was the largest in the area. With a few associates he incorporated STANDARD OIL CO. (Ohio) in 1870. He bought out competitors to control the oil-refinery business in Cleveland (1872) and in the U.S. (1882). As a result of antitrust proceedings, he later converted his trust, the first major U.S. business trust company, into a holding company. In the 1890s he turned his attention to philanthropy. He founded the Univ. of CHICAGO in 1892, the Rockefeller Institute for Medical Research (later ROCKEFELLER UNIV.) in 1901, and the Rockefeller Foundation in 1913. His son John D. Rockefeller, Jr. (1874–1960), built ROCKEFELLER CENTER in New York and restored colonial Williamsburg, Va.

Rockefeller, Nelson (Aldrich) (1908–1979) U.S. politician. Born in Bar Harbor, Me., a grandson of John D. ROCKEFELLER, he worked for several family enterprises, including Creole Petroleum in Venezuela (1935–40), before serving as coordinator of inter-American affairs at the U.S. State Department (1940–44). As governor of New York (1959–73), he oversaw expansion of the state's fiscal, cultural, and educational systems. He sought the Republican presidential nomination in 1964 and 1968, but conservatives opposed his liberal views. He served as U.S. vice president (1974–77) under Gerald FORD. A major art patron, he founded the Museum of Primitive Art (later incorporated into the METROPOLITAN MUSEUM OF ART).

Rockefeller Center Complex of 14 limestone skyscrapers on a 12-acre (5-hectare) site, built 1929–40 in midtown Manhattan. It was designed by a team headed by Henry Hofmeister, H. W. Corbett, Raymond M. HOOD, and Wallace K. Harrison. Wood veneering, mural painting, mosaics, and sculpture were integrated with the architecture. Radio City Music Hall (1932) is noted for its ART DECO interior.

Rockefeller University Private graduate research university in New York City devoted to the biomedical sciences. Founded by John D. ROCKEFELLER in 1901, it became affiliated with the State Univ. of NEW YORK in 1954. It offers tuition-free advanced instruction and research opportunities to about 150 gifted students. A number of major biomedical advances have been achieved at Rockefeller, and its faculty have included more than 15 Nobel Prize laureates.

Rockefeller Center, New York City

rocket Jet-propulsion device that uses either solid or liquid propellants to provide the fuel and oxidizer needed for combustion. The term is also commonly applied to any of various vehicles, including FIREWORKS, skyrockets, guided missiles, and SPACECRAFT launch vehicles, that are driven by such a propulsive device. Typically, thrust (forward motion) is produced by reaction to a rearward expulsion of hot gases at extremely high speed. The most common types of rockets burn chemical propellants. Combustion provides the hot gases that are ejected in a jet through a nozzle at the rear of the rocket.

rocket See ARUGULA

Rockingham, Marquess of *orig.* Charles Watson-Wentworth (1730–1782) British politician. He served at the courts of GEORGE II. Under GEORGE III he served as prime minister in 1765–66, and obtained repeal of the unpopular STAMP ACT. He and Edmund BURKE later led the parliamentary opposition and spoke in favor of independence for the American colonies. In his brief second ministry (1782), he began peace negotiations with the U.S. and obtained legislative independence for the Irish parliament.

rock music *or* **rock and roll** Musical style that arose in the U.S. in the mid-1950s and became the dominant form of popular music in the world. Its basic elements were one or several vocalists, heavily amplified electric guitars, and drums. It began as a simple style, relying on heavy, dance-oriented rhythms, uncomplicated melodies and harmonies, and lyrics sympathetic to its audience's concerns—young love, adolescence, and cars. Its roots lay principally in RHYTHM AND BLUES and to a lesser extent in COUNTRY MUSIC and other styles, which lay outside the popular mainstream in the early 1950s, when the Cleveland disc jockey Alan Freed (1921–1965) began programming rhythm and blues for his white audience. The highly rhythmic, sensual music of Chuck BERRY, Bill Haley, and particularly Elvis PRESLEY in 1955–56 struck a responsive chord in the newly affluent postwar teenage audience, creating a huge industry. In the 1960s, several influences combined to lift rock out of a swift decline into blandness. In England, the BEATLES and the ROLLING STONES were found to have retained the freshness of its very early years. At the same time, Bob DYLAN and others were developing "folk rock," a blending of traditional ballad and verse forms with rock, often exploring social and political themes. Such groups as the Byrds, Jefferson Airplane, and the Doors combined imaginative lyrics with instrumental virtuosity and solo improvisation, and Janis JOPLIN and Jimi HENDRIX made exotic elaborations on traditional rhythm and blues. The 1970s saw the rise of singer-songwriters such as Elton JOHN and Bruce SPRINGSTEEN, and rock assimilated other forms to produce pop rock, jazz-rock, and punk rock. From the 1980s, rock was complemented by music videos, short video programs built around individual popular songs.

Rockne \'räk-nē\, **Knute (Kenneth)** (1888–1931) U.S. (Norwegian-born) football coach. He emigrated with his family to Chicago in 1893. He ran track and played end on the NOTRE DAME football team, becoming part of a passing combination that established the forward pass as a major weapon. After playing end for numerous professional teams, he became head coach (1919–32) at Notre Dame. In Rockne's 13 seasons, his "Fighting Irish" won 105 games, lost 12, and tied five. He trained such famous players as George "The Gipper" Gipp and the FOUR HORSEMEN, and his colorful personality captured the public's imagination.

Rockwell, Norman (1894–1978) U.S. illustrator. Born in New York City, he studied at the Art Students League. From 1916 to 1963 he produced 317 covers for *The Saturday Evening Post*. Most of his works are humorous treatments of idealized small town and family life. During World War II, posters of his *Four Freedoms* were distributed by the Office of War Information. Though loved by the public, Rockwell's work was often dismissed by critics. Late in his career, he turned to more serious subjects (e.g., a series on racism for *Look* magazine), and in the 1990s his critical reputation enjoyed a positive reassessment.

Rocky Mountain goat See MOUNTAIN GOAT

Rocky Mountains *or* **Rockies** Mountain system, W N. America. It extends some 3,000 mi (4,800 km) from the Mexican frontier to the Arctic Ocean, through the W U.S. and Canada. The highest peak in the U.S. Rockies is Mt. Elbert in Colorado, at 14,433 ft (4,399 m); in the Canadian Rockies, it is Mt. Robson in British Columbia, at 12,972 ft (3,954 m). The CONTINENTAL DIVIDE, located in the mountains, separates rivers flowing to the east and to the west. Wildlife includes grizzly bear, brown bear, elk, bighorn sheep, and cougar. The area is rich in diverse mineral deposits. Rocky Mtn., YELLOWSTONE, GLACIER, and GRAND TETON national parks in the U.S. are major recreational facilities.

Rocky Mountain spotted fever TYPHUS-like disease first seen in the Rocky Mtn. region, caused by the bacterium *Rickettsia rickettsii* (see RICKETTSIA) and transmitted by various TICKS. Central-nervous-system involvement causes restlessness, insomnia, and delirium. Prostration may progress to coma, with death possible in a week or more. Mortality increases with age. Recovery is slow but usually complete as visual disturbances, deafness, and mental confusion pass. Prompt antibiotic treatment hastens it and reduces mortality. Prevention depends on avoiding tick bites. A vaccine reduces the risk of infection somewhat and of death greatly.

Rococo style \rə-'kō-ˌkō, rō-kə-'kō\ *or* **Late Baroque** Style in interior design, the decorative arts, painting, architecture, and sculpture that originated in Paris in the early 18th cent. Reacting against the ponderous official baroque style of LOUIS XIV's reign, Rococo was light, elegant, and elaborately ornamented. Walls, ceilings, and moldings feature interlacings of curves and countercurves based on S and C shapes, shell forms and other natural shapes, and Chinese motifs. Painting was characterized by easygoing treatments of mythological and courtship themes, delicate brushwork, and sensuous coloring; notable practitioners include An-

toine WATTEAU, François BOUCHER, and Jean-Honoré FRA-
GONARD. Rococo style spread throughout France and such
other countries as Germany and Austria. Among the finest
German examples is the church at Vierzehnheiligen, designed by Balthasar NEUMANN.

Rodchenko \räd-'cheṇ-kō\, **Aleksandr (Mikhailovich)**
(1891–1956) Russian painter, sculptor, designer, and photographer. He initially embraced a completely abstract,
highly geometric style, using a ruler and compass. His series
of black-on-black geometric paintings (1918) was a direct
response to Kazimir MALEVICH's *White on White.* As leader
of a wing of CONSTRUCTIVISM that sought to produce works
appropriate to workers' daily lives, he renounced easel
painting and took up photography and book, furniture, and
set design. His innovations in lighting in his photography influenced Sergei EISENSTEIN. He later returned to easel
painting.

Roddenberry, Gene (*orig.* Eugene Wesley) (1921–1991) U.S.
television and film producer. Born in El Paso, Tex., he
worked as a police officer (1949–53) before becoming a
writer for such television series as *Dragnet* and *Dr. Kildare.*
He created and produced the *Star Trek* series (1966–69); re-
run in syndication, it developed a durable cult following.
He produced six *Star Trek* movies, and from 1987 produced
the TV series *Star Trek: The Next Generation.*

rodent Any member of the order Rodentia, which contains
half of all living MAMMAL species. Rodents are gnawing,
mostly herbivorous, placental mammals. They have one
pair of upper and one pair of lower, continuously growing,
incisors. Rodent families include SQUIRRELS (Sciuridae);
Old World mice (see MOUSE) and RATS (Muridae); deer
mice (see DEER MOUSE), GERBILS, HAMSTERS, LEMMINGS,
MUSKRATS, wood rats, and VOLES (Cricetidae); BEAVER
(Castoridae); GOPHERS (Geomyidae); GUINEA PIGS (Caviidae); pocket mice (see POCKET MOUSE) and KANGAROO
RATS and mice (Heteromyidae); New and Old World POR-
CUPINES (Erethizontidae and Hystricidae); and hutia
(Capromyidae).

rodeo Public performance featuring competitive or exhibition bronco riding, calf roping, steer wrestling, and Brahma
bull riding. Rodeo developed from informal competitions
among COWBOYS held from the mid-19th cent. The oldest
surviving annual show is the one at Cheyenne, Wy. (established 1897). In calf roping and steer wrestling, the contestant seeks to bring down the animal in the shortest possible
time. In riding events, contestants seek to stay on their
mounts as long as possible.

Rodgers, Jimmie (*orig.* James Charles) (1897–1933) U.S.
COUNTRY-MUSIC singer. Born in Meridian, Miss., he left
school at 14 to work on the railroad. There he learned guitar and banjo, absorbed BLUES techniques from black
coworkers, and created his characteristic sound and blend
of traditional work, blues, hobo, and cowboy songs. By
1924, disabled from work by tuberculosis, he began to perform, and "the Singing Brakeman" soon became the first
solo star of country music. His recordings include "Blue
Yodel No. 1" and "Mississippi River Blues." He died at 35.
He was one of the original inductees into the Country Music Hall of Fame.

Rodgers, Richard (1902–1979) U.S. composer. A New York
City native, Rodgers studied
at Columbia Univ., where he
met Lorenz HART. His first
success with Hart was *The
Garrick Gaieties* (1925). *On
Your Toes* (1936), with the ballet *Slaughter on Tenth Avenue,*
established serious dance as a
permanent part of musical
comedy. Among their other
collaborations were *Babes in
Arms* (1937), *The Boys from
Syracuse* (1938), and *Pal Joey*
(1940). After Hart's death,
Rodgers worked with Oscar
HAMMERSTEIN. Their *Okla-
homa!* (1943, Pulitzer Prize)
enjoyed a record-breaking

Richard Rodgers

Broadway run, and their 17-year partnership made them the
foremost team in the history of the American musical.

Rodin \rō-'daⁿ\, **(François-) Auguste (-René)** (1840–1917)
French sculptor. Insolvent and repeatedly rejected by the
École des Beaux-Arts, he earned his living by doing decorative stonework. Not until his late thirties, after a trip to
Italy, did he develop a personal style free of academic restraints and establish his reputation with *The Age of Bronze*
(exhibited 1878), whose realism was so great that he was accused of forming its mold on a living person. His *Gates of
Hell,* a bronze door commissioned in 1880 for a proposed
Musée des Arts Décoratifs, remained unfinished at his
death, but two of its many figures were the bases of his most
famous images, *The Thinker* (1880) and *The Kiss* (1886). His
portraits include monumental figures of Victor HUGO and
Honoré de BALZAC. Though his works caused controversy
for their unconventionality, he was successful enough that
he could establish a large workshop. He revitalized sculpture as an art of personal expression and has been considered one of its greatest portraitists.

Roebling \'rœb-liṇ, *Engl* 'rō-bliṇ\, **John Augustus** (1806–
1869) German-U.S. civil engineer. He emigrated to the U.S.
in 1831. In the 1850s and '60s Roebling and his son Washington (1837–1926) built four suspension bridges: two at
Pittsburgh, one at Niagara Falls (1855), and one at Cincinnati (1866). When his design for the BROOKLYN BRIDGE was
accepted, he was appointed chief engineer. He died from an
injury he received as construction began. Washington completed the project in 1883; himself incapacitated from 1872
by decompression sickness, his completion of the work depended heavily on his wife, Emily Warren Roebling (1843–
1903).

Roentgen \'rœnt-gən\, **Abraham** (1711–1793) German furniture designer and cabinetmaker. In 1750 he established a
shop near Cologne. The outstanding Rococo-style furniture
he produced there was often decorated with inlay work of
ivory and other semiprecious materials. Much of his work
was created for various German courts. His son David
(1743–1807), who succeeded him as head of the firm in
1772, was appointed cabinetmaker to MARIE-ANTOINETTE
of France. Under his direction, the family workshop became famous also for music boxes, clocks, and mechanical
toys.

Roentgen, Wilhelm Conrad See W. C. RÖNTGEN

Roethke \'ret-kē\, **Theodore** (1908–1963) U.S. poet. Born in
Saginaw, Mich., he wrote poetry characterized by introspection and intense lyricism. His verse collections include
The Waking (1953, Pulitzer Prize), *Words for the Wind* (1957,
Bollingen Prize, National Book Award), and *The Far Field*
(1964, National Book Award). His later career was interrupted by hospitalizations for manic depression.

Roe vs. Wade U.S. Supreme Court decision (1973) that established a woman's right to have an ABORTION without
undue restrictive interference from the government. A
Texas law prohibiting abortions was challenged by an unmarried pregnant woman ("Jane Roe"), and the Court
found that the state had violated her right to privacy. Harry
BLACKMUN wrote for the seven-member majority that the
state's legitimate concern for the protection of prenatal life
increased as a pregnancy advanced. While allowing that the
state might forbid abortions during the third trimester, he
held that a woman was entitled to obtain an abortion freely,
after medical consultation, during the first trimester and in
an authorized clinic during the second. The *Roe* decision,
perhaps the most controversial in the Court's history, remains at the center of the issue of abortion rights.

Roger II (1095–1154) Grand count of Sicily (1105–30) and
king of Sicily (1130–54). A capable and energetic ruler, he
incorporated the mainland territories of Calabria (1122)
and Apulia (1127). He was crowned king by the antipope
Anacletus II, and he forced Pope Innocent II to confirm
him in 1139. He refused to join the Second CRUSADE, preferring as the ruler of a largely Arab population to show tolerance toward Muslims. His court was an intellectual center
for both Arab and Western scholars.

Rogers, Carl R(ansom) (1902–1987) U.S. psychologist. Born
in Oak Park, Ill., in 1963 he helped found an institute for
the study of the person in La Jolla, Cal. He is known as the

originator of client-centered, or nondirective, psychotherapy and helped establish HUMANISTIC PSYCHOLOGY. His writings include *Counseling and Psychotherapy* (1942), *Client-Centered Therapy* (1951), and *On Becoming a Person* (1961).

Rogers, Fred (McFeely) (1928–2003) U.S. television host and producer. Born in Latrobe, Pa., he produced the local public-television show *The Children's Corner* (1954–61) before developing *Mister Rogers' Neighborhood* in 1968. Known for his gentleness and his desire to educate, Rogers, a Presbyterian minister, used puppets, music, and guests to teach his viewers about various subjects and emotions. He retired in 2001; his much-honored show was the longest-running U.S. children's television program of all time.

Rogers, Ginger *orig.* Virginia Katherine McMath (1911–1995) U.S. film actress. Born in Independence, Mo., she made her Broadway debut in 1929. After starring in *Girl Crazy* (1930–31), she moved to Hollywood. Her first performance with Fred ASTAIRE, in *Flying Down to Rio* (1933), was so popular that they continued the partnership in nine more movies, including *The Gay Divorcee* (1934), *Top Hat* (1935), and *Swing Time* (1936). She later acted in the drama *Kitty Foyle* (1940, Academy Award) and in light comedies.

Rogers, Roy *orig.* Leonard Franklin Slye (1911–1998) U.S. actor and singer. Born in Cincinnati, he moved to California and formed the singing group Sons of the Pioneers, which performed on radio and later in movies. He acted in westerns with Gene AUTRY, whom he soon replaced as "King of the Cowboys." His films include *Tumbling Tumbleweeds* (1935) and *Yellow Rose of Texas* (1944). He acted in several with his wife, Dale Evans, usually riding his famous horse, Trigger. He also starred in *The Roy Rogers Show* on radio (1944–55) and television (1951–57).

Rogers, Will(iam Penn Adair) (1879–1935) U.S. humorist. Raised in Cherokee Territory (now Oklahoma), he demonstrated his rope-twirling skills in Wild West shows and vaudeville and gradually wove homespun wit into his act. He performed in the Ziegfeld Follies from 1915. Noted for his good-natured but sharp criticism of current affairs, he wrote a column in the *New York Times* from 1922. He performed on radio and in movies such as *State Fair* (1933). His death in a plane crash in Alaska with the aviator Wiley Post (1899–1935) was widely mourned.

Roget \rō-ˈzhā\, **Peter Mark** (1779–1869) English physician and philologist. In 1814 he invented a slide rule for calculating the roots and powers of numbers. He was instrumental in founding the Univ. of London (1828). He is best known for his *Thesaurus of English Words and Phrases* (1852), a comprehensive classification of synonyms or verbal equivalents.

Rohan \rō-ˈäⁿ\, **Henri, duc (Duke) de** (1579–1638) French HUGUENOT leader. At 16 he entered the army of HENRY IV, who made him a peer of France in 1603. After Henry's death (1610), Rohan led the Huguenots in revolt against the government of MARIE DE MÉDICIS (1615–16) and became the Huguenots' foremost general in the civil wars of the 1620s, a subject of his celebrated *Mémoires*. He later successfully commanded a French expedition against the Habsburgs in Lombardy. In 1637 he went to Switzerland, where he died in the THIRTY YEARS' WAR battle at Rheinfelden.

Rohe, Ludwig Mies van der See Ludwig MIES VAN DER ROHE

Röhm \ˈrœm\, **Ernst** (1887–1934) German leader of the SA. He helped found the NAZI PARTY, and offered Adolf HITLER the use of his private strong-arm force (later the SA). After brief imprisonment for his part in the BEER HALL PUTSCH, Röhm went to Bolivia as a military instructor (1925–30), then was recalled by Hitler to reorganize and command the SA. When Röhm's ambition that the SA supplant or absorb the regular army came to be opposed by Hitler and his advisers, Hitler had Röhm murdered during the Night of the Long Knives.

Rokitansky \ˌrō-kē-ˈtän-skē\, **Karl, Freiherr (Baron) von** (1804–1878) Austrian pathologist. He inspired Ignaz SEMMELWEIS to study medicine and supported his efforts to eliminate PUERPERAL FEVER by antiseptic procedures. He differentiated pneumonias originating in lobes of the lung and in bronchioles, made a fundamental study of acute yellow atrophy of the liver, and established the micropathol-

ogy of emphysema. His *Treatise of Pathological Anatomy* (3 vols., 1842–46) elevated PATHOLOGY to an established science. During his career he performed more than 30,000 autopsies.

Roland, Chanson de See CHANSON DE ROLAND

Rolland \rȯ-ˈläⁿ\, **Romain** (1866–1944) French novelist, dramatist, and essayist. His life and writings reflected his concern with major social, political, and spiritual events. His best-known novel is *Jean-Christophe* (1904–12), a 10-volume epic whose protagonist is modeled half on Ludwig van BEETHOVEN and half on himself. His pamphlet *Above the Battle* (1915) called on France and Germany to respect truth and humanity during World War I. In the 1920s he turned to interpreting Asian mystical philosophy in such works as *Mahatma Gandhi* (1924). He wrote several other major biographies, including *Beethoven* (1910). He was awarded the Nobel Prize in 1915.

roller bearing One of the two types of rolling, or antifriction, BEARINGS, the other being the BALL BEARING. Like a ball bearing, a roller bearing has two grooved tracks, but the balls are replaced by rollers. The rollers may be cylinders or shortened cones. If the rollers are cylindrical, only radial loads (perpendicular to the axis of rotation) can be carried, but with conical rollers both radial and thrust, or axial, loads (parallel to the axis of rotation) can be carried.

roller-skating Sport in which the participants use roller skates (shoes with sets of wheels attached) to move about on special rinks or paved surfaces. Their invention may date to the 1760s, but the first practical four-wheel skate was designed in the U.S. in 1863. Roller-skating speed events became popular in the early 20th cent. Later, team competitions in "roller derbies" on banked tracks became a spectator sport. In the late 20th cent., roller skates gave way to in-line (Rollerblade) skates, in which a single row of wheels is used in place of the standard rectangular configuration.

Rolling Stones British musical group. Its original members were singer Mick Jagger (b.1943), guitarists Keith Richards (b.1943) and Brian Jones (1944–1969), bassist Bill Wyman (b.1936), and drummer Charlie Watts (b.1941). Jones was succeeded by Mick Taylor (b.1948) in 1969, who was replaced by Ron Wood (b.1947) in 1976. The band was formed in 1962. By 1966 a series of outstanding songs had made it second in popularity only to the BEATLES. Jagger and Richards wrote most of its songs, which are marked by a driving backbeat and biting and satirical lyrics. The group's popularity peaked with such albums as *Beggar's Banquet* (1968) and *Exile on Main Street* (1972). They have continued to perform long after the other classic rock bands of the 1960s disbanded.

Rollins, Sonny (*orig.* Theodore Walter) (b.1930) U.S. saxophonist and composer, one of the greatest improvisers in jazz. Born in New York City, Rollins performed with many musicians in the late 1940s, including Miles DAVIS. A member of the Clifford Brown–Max Roach quintet in 1955–57, he has since worked as leader of his own groups. Rollins's robust tone and technical dexterity are matched with athletic endurance in the service of the logical evolution of ideas in his solos.

Rolls-Royce PLC British manufacturer of luxury automobiles and aviation engines. Charles S. Rolls (1877–1910), a pioneer motorist and aviator, and Henry Royce (1863–1933), an engineer, incorporated Rolls-Royce Ltd. in 1906. Their handsome and immaculately engineered cars included the Silver Ghost model (1906), a series of Phantoms, the Silver Dawn, Silver Cloud, Silver Shadow, and Silver Wraith. In 1931 Rolls-Royce acquired Bentley Motors Ltd. From 1914 Rolls-Royce also produced airplane engines. A fixed-price contract with Lockheed Aircraft drove the company into bankruptcy in 1971. Split into two companies, its jet-engine division became Rolls-Royce PLC, while Rolls-Royce Motor Holdings Ltd. merged with Vickers Ltd. in 1980 and was purchased by VOLKSWAGEN in 1998.

Rølvaag \ˈrœl-ˌväg\, **Ole (Edvart)** (1876–1931) Norwegian-U.S. novelist. He emigrated to the U.S. in 1896 and spent most of his life teaching at St. Olaf College (Northfield, Minn.). His works, written in Norwegian, are noted for their realistic portrayals of Norwegian settlers on the

Dakota prairies and of the clash between transplanted and native cultures in the U.S. His best-known work is *Giants in the Earth* (1927), a translation of two of his novels.

ROM \\'räm\\ *in full* **read-only memory** Form of computer MEMORY that does not lose its contents when the power supply is cut off and that is not rewritable once it is manufactured or written. It is generally employed for programs designed for repeated use without modification, such as the start-up procedures of a PERSONAL COMPUTER. See also CD-ROM, COMPACT DISC.

Rom See GYPSIES

Romains \\rȯ-'man\\, **Jules** *orig.* Louis-Henri-Jean Farigoule (1885–1972) French novelist, dramatist, and poet. Romains first became known as a poet and as founder (c.1908–11), with Georges Chennevière, of the literary movement Unanimisme, which combined belief in universal brotherhood with the psychological concept of group consciousness. His most popular work was the comedy *Knock* (1923). His masterpiece, *Men of Good Will* (27 vols., 1932–46), is a vast novel cycle exemplifying his interest in collective life.

roman à clef \\rȯ-män-à-'klā\\ (French: "novel with a key") Novel that has the extraliterary interest of portraying identifiable people more or less thinly disguised as fictional characters. The tradition dates to 17th-cent. France, when aristocratic writers included in their historical romances representations of well-known figures in the court of LOUIS XIV. A more recent example is W. Somerset MAUGHAM's *Cakes and Ale* (1930), widely held to portray Thomas HARDY and Horace WALPOLE.

Roman Africa See Roman AFRICA

Roman alphabet See LATIN ALPHABET

Roman Catholicism Largest single Christian denomination in the world, with nearly one billion members, or 18% of the world's population. The Roman Catholic church has been responsible for introducing Christianity in many parts of the world. It regards itself as the only legitimate inheritor of the ministry of JESUS, by virtue of an unbroken succession of leaders beginning with St. PETER THE APOSTLE. Church organization is strictly hierarchical. The POPE appoints and presides over about 150 CARDINALS. Each of the church's 500 ARCHBISHOPS heads an archdiocese, beneath which are about 1,800 dioceses, each headed by a BISHOP. Within dioceses are parishes, each served by a church and a priest. Only men can enter the priesthood; women can become nuns. The basic form of worship is the MASS. Theologically, Roman Catholicism differs from PROTESTANTISM with regard to its understanding of the sources of REVELATION and the channels of GRACE. With EASTERN ORTHODOXY it asserts that both SCRIPTURE and church tradition reveal the basis of Christian belief and church polity. It sets the number of SACRAMENTS at seven (BAPTISM, penance, EUCHARIST, matrimony, ordination, CONFIRMATION, and anointing of the sick). It encourages devotion to MARY and the SAINTS. The Second VATICAN COUNCIL (1962–65) liberalized many aspects of the church, but the rle of women in the church, clerical celibacy, church opposition to divorce, most contraception, and abortion remain contentious issues.

romance Literary form that developed in the courts of mid-12th-cent. France and had its heyday in France and Germany between the mid-12th and mid-13th cent. in the works of such masters as CHRÉTIEN DE TROYES and GOTTFRIED VON STRASSBURG. The staple subject matter is chivalric adventure (see CHIVALRY). Most romances draw their plots from classical history and legend, ARTHURIAN LEGEND, and the adventures of CHARLEMAGNE. They share a taste for the exotic, the remote, and the miraculous. Lingering echoes can be found in the ROMANTICISM of the 18th–19th cent. and today's popular romantic novels.

Romance languages Group of related languages derived from LATIN, with nearly 400 million native speakers. The major Romance languages—FRENCH, SPANISH, PORTUGUESE, ITALIAN, and ROMANIAN—are national languages. Spanish, the official language of 18 American countries and Spain, has the most speakers. Languages spoken in smaller areas include Catalan, OCCITAN, Sardinian, and Rhaeto-Romance. The Romance languages began as DIALECTS of Vulgar Latin, which spread during the Roman occupation of Europe and developed into separate languages in the 5th–9th cent. Later, European colonialism and trading spread them to the Americas, Africa, and Asia.

Roman Curia Group of Vatican bureaus that assist the pope in exercising his jurisdiction over the Roman Catholic Church. It is traditionally associated with the College of CARDINALS. A cardinal named as secretary of state coordinates the activities of the Curia, and various sacred congregations handle administrative matters—for example, the Sacred Congregation for the Causes of Saints is concerned with beatification and canonization and with the preservation of relics.

Roman de la Rose \\rō-'män-də-lä-'rōs\\ ("Romance of the Rose") One of the most popular medieval French poems. Modeled on OVID's *Art of Love*, its first 4,058 lines were written around 1230 by Guillaume de Lorris; they form a charming dream allegory drawing on COURTLY-LOVE traditions. About 1280 Jean de Meun wrote the rest of the more than 21,000 lines, incorporating a vast mass of encyclopedic information and opinions on many contemporary topics, which secured the poem's fame. Translated by Geoffrey CHAUCER, it was an important influence on his writings.

Romanesque architecture Architecture current in Europe from about the mid-11th cent. to the advent of GOTHIC ARCHITECTURE. A fusion of Roman, Carolingian and Ottonian, Byzantine, and local Germanic traditions, it was a product of the great expansion of MONASTICISM in the 10th–11th cent., larger churches being needed to accommodate the numerous monks and priests, as well as pilgrims. For the sake of fire resistance, masonry vaulting began to replace timber construction. Romanesque churches incorporated semicircular arches for windows, doors, and arcades; barrel or groin VAULTS; massive piers and walls, with few windows, to contain the outward thrust of the vaults; and side aisles with galleries above them. French churches commonly expanded on the early Christian BASILICA plan, incorporating radiating chapels to accommodate more priests, and ambulatories around the sanctuary APSE for visiting pilgrims.

Romanesque art Sculpture and painting that reached its height in Western Europe about 1075–1125, a fusion of Roman, Carolingian and Byzantine art with local Germanic traditions. The expansion of monasticism in the 10th–11th cent. revived the art of monumental sculpture after almost 600 years of dormancy. RELIEF sculpture depicted biblical history and church doctrine on column capitals and around the massive doors of churches. Romanesque art was concerned with transcendental values, in sharp contrast to the naturalism and humanism of the earlier classical and later GOTHIC ART traditions. Monumental painting that imitated the sculptural style covered the interior walls of churches. Both sculpture and painting incorporated a broad range of subject matter, including theological works, reflecting the revival of learning. See also ROMANESQUE ARCHITECTURE.

Romania *or* **Rumania** Nation, SE Europe. Area: 91,699 sq mi (237,500 sq km). Population (2000): 22,435,000. Capital: BUCHAREST. Most of the people are Romanian, with Hungarians a minority. Language: Romanian (official). Religion: Romanian Orthodoxy. Currency: leu. The land is dominated by the great arc of the CARPATHIAN MTNS., whose highest peak, Moldoveanu, is 8,346 ft (2,544 m). The DANUBE RIVER forms the S boundary with Bulgaria. Under communist rule 1948–89, Romania had a centrally planned economy that was transformed from an agricultural into an industrial economy. From 1991, the post-communist government began returning industrial and commercial enterprises to the private sector. Romania is a republic with two legislative houses; its chief of state is the president, and the head of government is the prime minister. Romania was formed in 1862 by the unification of Moldavia and WALACHIA (for the earlier history, see DACIA). During World War I, it sided with the Allies and doubled its territory in 1918 with the addition of TRANSYLVANIA, Bukovina, and BESSARABIA. Allied with Germany in World War II, it was occupied by Soviet troops in 1944 and became a satellite country of the U.S.S.R. in 1948. During the 1960s Romania's foreign policy was frequently independent of the

©1999, Encyclopædia Britannica, Inc.

Soviet Union's. The communist regime of Nicolae CEAUSESCU was overthrown in 1989, and free elections were held in 1990. Throughout the 1990s Romania struggled with rampant corruption and organized crime as it tried to stabilize its economy; in 2000 it confronted its worst drought in 50 years.

Romanian language \rü-'mä-nē-ən, rō-'mä-nē-ən\ ROMANCE LANGUAGE spoken mainly in ROMANIA and MOLDOVA. It is one of the four major dialects of Balkan Romance. The others are spoken in scattered communities. The earliest known continuous text in Romanian dates from 1521. Romanian's phonology, grammar, and vocabulary reflect its relative isolation from other Romance languages and its close contact with the SLAVIC LANGUAGES. Written in the CYRILLIC ALPHABET until the 19th cent., Romanian now uses the LATIN ALPHABET.

Roman mythology Oral and literary traditions of the ancient Romans concerning their gods and heroes and the nature and history of the cosmos. Much of what became Roman mythology was borrowed from GREEK MYTHOLOGY at a later date, as Greek gods were associated with their Roman counterparts. As in Greek mythology, legendary Roman heroes were given semidivine status. See also ROMAN RELIGION.

Roman numerals System of representing numbers devised by the ancient Romans. The symbols I, V, X, L, C, D, and M stand, respectively, for 1, 5, 10, 50, 100, 500, and 1,000 in the HINDU-ARABIC NUMERAL system. A symbol placed after another of equal or greater value adds its value; for example, II = 2 and LX = 60. A symbol placed before one of greater value subtracts its value; for example, IV = 4 and XL = 40.

1	I	8	VIII	40	XL	900	CM
2	II	9	IX	50	L	1,000	M
3	III	10	X	60	LX	5,000	$\overline{\text{V}}$
4	IV	11	XI	90	XC	10,000	$\overline{\text{X}}$
5	V	19	XIX	100	C	50,000	$\overline{\text{L}}$
6	VI	20	XX	200	CC	100,000	$\overline{\text{C}}$
7	VII	30	XXX	500	D	500,000	$\overline{\text{D}}$

Romano, Giulio See GIULIO ROMANO
Romanov, Michael See MICHAEL
Romanov dynasty \rō-'mä-nóf, 'rō-mə-ˌnóf\ Rulers of Russia from 1613 to 1917. The name derived from Roman Yurev (d.1543), whose daughter was the first wife of IVAN

IV; her nephews assumed the surname Romanov, and the dynasty began with the election of MICHAEL Romanov as czar in 1613. He was succeeded by his son ALEXIS and grandsons Fyodor III (r.1676–82), Ivan V, and PETER I. The crown passed to Peter's wife Catherine I, (r.1725–27), his grandson Peter II (r.1727–30), and Ivan V's daughter ANNA. The line of descent returned to Peter's daughter ELIZABETH, her nephew PETER III and his wife CATHERINE II the Great, and their son PAUL I. Paul established a definite order of succession and was followed by his sons ALEXANDER I and NICHOLAS I then by Nicholas's son ALEXANDER II, grandson ALEXANDER III, and great-grandson NICHOLAS II, the last ruler of the Russian monarchy.

Roman religion Religious beliefs of the Romans from ancient times until official acceptance of Christianity in the 4th cent. A.D. The Romans believed that everything was subordinate to the rule of the gods, and the object of their religion was to secure divine cooperation and benevolence. Prayer and sacrifice at temples were used to propitiate the gods. The chief Roman priest, head of the state religion, was known as the PONTIFEX maximus; priests known as *augures* practiced divination to determine whether the gods approved of an action. The earliest Roman gods were the sky god JUPITER, the war god MARS, and QUIRINUS. Many other deities were borrowed from GREEK RELIGION, and the stories woven into ROMAN MYTHOLOGY were often taken directly from GREEK MYTHOLOGY. Domestic shrines were devoted to divine ancestors or protectors, the LARES and PENATES. During the Roman empire, dead emperors were also raised to the status of divinities.

Roman Gods and Goddesses

Apollo	god of sunlight, music, poetry, and, prophecy	Minerva	goddess of wisdom, the arts, and trades
Aurora	goddess of the dawn	Mithras	god of light
Bacchus	god of wine	Neptune	god of the sea
Bellona	goddess of war	Ops	goddess of fertility
Ceres	goddess of agriculture	Pales	goddess of flocks and shepherds
Cupid	god of love		
Diana	goddess of fertility, hunting, and the moon	Pluto	god of the underworld
Faunus	god of prophecy	Pomona	goddess of fruit trees and fruit
Flora	goddess of flowers		
Janus	god of gates and doors	Proserpine	goddess of the underworld
Juno	goddess of marriage and women	Saturn	god of seed time and harvest
Jupiter	supreme god and god of the sky and weather	Venus	goddess of beauty and love
Libitina	goddess of funerals	Vertumnus	god of the seasons
Maia	goddess of growth and increase	Vesta	goddess of the hearth
Mars	god of war	Vulcan	god of fire
Mercury	messenger god and god of commerce		

Roman republic and empire Ancient state that once ruled the Western world. It centered on the city of ROME from the founding of the republic (509 B.C.) through the establishment of the empire (27 B.C.) to the final eclipse of the empire of the West (5th cent. A.D.). The republic's government consisted of two CONSULS, the SENATE, and magistrates, originally all PATRICIANS, and two popular PLEBEIAN assemblies. A written code, the Law of the Twelve Tables (451 B.C.), became the basis of Roman private law. By 200 B.C., Roman territory included all of Italy; by the late republican period it encompassed most of W Europe, N Africa, and the Near East, organized into provinces. After a period of civil war, Julius CAESAR took power as DICTATOR. Following his assassination (44 B.C.), conflict among Mark ANTONY, LEPIDUS, and Octavian resulted in Octavian's victory (31) and his accession as emperor AUGUSTUS (r.27 B.C.–A.D. 14). The imperial government combined aspects of the republic and a monarchy. In A.D. 395 the empire split into E and W halves, with the west under severe pressure from barbarians. Rome was sacked by the VISIGOTHS in 410; it fell to German invaders in 476; the East continued as the BYZANTINE EMPIRE through the Middle Ages. See table on following page.

Roman Emperors*

Augustus	27 BC–AD 14	Carus	282–83
Tiberius	14–37	Carinus	283–85
Caligula	37–41	Numerian	283–84
Claudius	41–54	Constantine I	312–37
Nero	54–68	Constantine II	337–40
Galba	68–69	Constans I	337–50
Otho	69	Constantius II	337–61
Vitellius	69	Magnentius	350–53
Vespasian	69–79	Julian	361–63
Titus	79–81	Jovian	363–64
Domitian	81–96	Theodosius I	379–95
Nerva	96–98	*East only*	
Trajan	98–117	Diocletian	284–305
Hadrian	117–38	Galerius	305–11
Antoninus Pius	138–61	Licinius	308–24
Marcus Aurelius	161–80	Valens	364–78
Lucius Verus	161–69	Procopius	365–66
Commodus	177–92	Arcadius	395–408
Pertinax	193	Theodosius II	408–50
Didius Julianus	193	Marcian	450–57
Septimius Severus	193–211	Leo I	457–74
Caracalla	198–217	Leo II	474
Geta	209–12	Zeno	474–91
Macrinus	217–18	*West only*	
Elagabalus	218–22	Maximian	286–305
Alexander Severus	222–35	??	306–8
Maximin	235–38	Constantius I Chlorus	305–6
Gordian I	238	Severus	306–7
Gordian II	238	Maxentius	306–12
Maximus	238	Valentinian I	364–75
Balbinus	238	Gratian	375–83
Gordian III	238–44	Valentinian II	375–92
Philip	244–49	Honorius	395–423
Decius	249–51	Constantius III	421
Hostilian	251	Valentinian III	425–55
Gallus	251–53	Petronius Maximus	455
Aemilian	253	Avitus	455–56
Valerian	253–60	Majorian	457–61
Gallienus	253–68	Libius Severus	461–67
Claudius II Gothicus	268–70	Anthemius	467–72
Quintillus	269–70	Olybrius	472
Aurelian	270–75	Glycerius	473–74
Tacitus	275–76	Julius Nepos	474–75
Florian	276	Romulus Augustulus	475–76
Probus	276–82		

*For Eastern emperors after the fall of Rome, see BYZANTINE EMPIRE.

Romanticism Literary, artistic, and philosophical movement that began in Europe in the 18th cent. and lasted until the mid-19th cent. In its intense focus on the individual consciousness, it was both a continuation of and a reaction against the ENLIGHTENMENT. Romanticism emphasized the individual, the irrational, the imaginative, the spontaneous, the emotional, the visionary, and the transcendental. Among its attitudes were a deepened appreciation of the beauties of nature; a general exaltation of emotion over reason and of the senses over intellect; a heightened examination of human personality; a preoccupation with the genius and the hero; a new view of the artist as a supremely individual creator; an emphasis on imagination as a gateway to transcendent experience; a consuming interest in folk culture and the medieval era; and a predilection for the exotic, the remote, the mysterious, the occult, the monstrous, the diseased, and even the satanic. See also CLASSICISM and TRANSCENDENTALISM.

Romany language \'rŏ-mə-nē\ Indo-Aryan language of the Roma (see GYPSIES), spoken in many countries of the world, with its greatest concentration of speakers in E Europe. Romany is believed to have separated from the N Indian languages about A.D. 1000. Its DIALECTS, which include many loanwords from languages where the Roma have lived, are classified according to the many languages that influenced them. Romany has no tradition of writing but a rich oral tradition. In the 20th cent. some collections of Romany poems and folktales were published in E Europe.

Romberg, Sigmund (1887–1951) Hungarian-U.S. composer. Trained in Vienna in composition, violin, and organ, in 1909 he moved to New York, where, as staff composer for the impresario Jacob Shubert, he prepared scores for about 40 musical shows. His first notable operetta, *Maytime* (1917), was followed by *Blossom Time* (1921), *The Student Prince* (1924), *The Desert Song* (1926), and *The New Moon* (1928). His last success was *Up in Central Park* (1945). In all he wrote almost 80 stage shows.

Rome *Italian* **Roma** City (pop., 2000: 2,643,000), capital of Italy. It is situated in the central part of the country, on the TIBER RIVER. The historical site of Rome on its seven hills was occupied as early as the Bronze Age (c.1500 B.C.). It became the capital of the ROMAN REPUBLIC AND EMPIRE. The Romans gradually conquered the Italian peninsula (see ETRUSCANS), extended their dominion over the entire Mediterranean basin (see PUNIC WARS), and expanded their empire into continental Europe. Under POMPEY THE GREAT and Julius CAESAR, Rome's influence was extended over Syria, Jerusalem, Cyprus, and Gaul. After the battle of ACTIUM, all Roman lands were controlled by Octavian (Caesar AUGUSTUS), the first Roman emperor. As the imperial capital, Rome became the site of magnificent palaces, temples, public baths, theaters, and stadiums. It remained the imperial capital until Emperor CONSTANTINE THE GREAT dedicated Constantinople (now ISTANBUL) in A.D. 330. It was sacked by the VISIGOTHS in 410. By the end of the 6th cent., the protection of the city was in the hands of the Roman Catholic church (see HOLY ROMAN EMPIRE). The city flourished during the RENAISSANCE and was the seat of the PAPACY and the PAPAL STATES. In 1870 it became the capital of a united Italy. Modern Rome, with its extraordinary ancient ruins, Renaissance and Baroque architecture, and vibrant cultural life, is one of the great cities of the world. See also VATICAN CITY.

Rome, March on (Oct. 1922) Insurrection that brought Benito MUSSOLINI to power in Italy. Emboldened by social discontent, Fascist Party leaders, assisted by the armed BLACKSHIRTS, planned to march on Rome and force King VICTOR EMMANUEL III to call on Mussolini to form a government. Since the king was unwilling to use the Italian army to defend Rome, the government capitulated to the Fascists' demands. The March on Rome turned into a parade to show the Fascist Party's support for Mussolini as the new prime minister.

Rommel \'rȯ-məl\, **Erwin (Johannes Eugen)** (1891–1944) German army commander in WORLD WAR II. A teacher at military academies, he wrote the acclaimed textbook *Infantry Attacks* (1937). He led his Afrika Korps troops in early successes in the N. AFRICA CAMPAIGN. Known as the "Desert Fox" for his audacious surprise attacks, he was promoted to field marshal. After his defeat in the Battles of EL ALAMEIN, he returned to Germany and in 1944 was given command of the defense of the NW French coast. His tactical suggestions were ignored, and after the Allied NORMANDY CAMPAIGN began, he became convinced that the war could not be won. Implicated in the JULY PLOT to kill Adolf HITLER, he was ordered to take poison so that Hitler could avoid a trial of the esteemed "people's marshal."

Romney, George (1734–1802) British portrait painter. He began his career by touring the N counties, painting portraits for a few guineas each. In 1762 he established himself as a portraitist in London and quickly won favor among society patrons by the flattery of his likenesses. Infatuated with Emma Hart (later Lady HAMILTON) about 1781–82, he went on to paint more than 50 images of her. Line rather than color dominates his work, and the flowing rhythms and easy poses of Roman classical sculpture underlie its smooth patterns.

Romulus and Remus Twins who were the legendary founders of ROME. The offspring of MARS and Rhea Silvia, a VESTAL VIRGIN and princess, as infants they were thrown into the TIBER RIVER by their great-uncle Amulius, who feared they would lay claim to his title. Suckled by a she-wolf and raised by a shepherd, the twins founded a city on the site where they had been saved from the river. When Romulus built a city wall, Remus jumped over it and was killed by his brother. The city was named for Romulus, who ruled until his disappearance in a storm. Believing that he had become a deity, the Romans worshiped him as QUIRINUS.

rondeau \'rän-dō, *French* rōⁿ-'dō\ One of several FORMES FIXES (fixed forms) in French lyric poetry and song of the 14th–15th cent., later popular with many English poets. It has only two rhymes and consists of 13 or 15 lines of 8 or 10 syllables divided into three stanzas. The beginning of the first line of the first stanza serves as the refrain of the second and third stanzas.

rondo Musical form characterized by the initial statement and periodic restatement of a melody alternately with contrasting material. It originated in the French baroque harpsichord rondeau. Most rondos fall into either a five part *(abaca)* or a seven-part *(abacaba)* form. In the late 18th and 19th cent., rondo form was often used for the romping final movements of sonatas, quartets, symphonies, and concertos.

ronin \'rō-nin\ Japanese masterless SAMURAI. He was essentially a vagabond unless he could enter the service of another lord. Disruptive to society, in the early 17th cent. ronin led unsuccessful revolts against the TOKUGAWA SHOGUNATE. The most famous ronin were the 47 whose actions were celebrated in CHIKAMATSU MONZAEMON's play *Chushingura.* By avenging their lord's death in defiance of a shogunal order forbidding the vendetta, the 47 ronin, who were subsequently forced to commit suicide, embodied the ideals of BUSHIDO, the warrior's code.

Ronsard \rōn-'sàr\, **Pierre de** (1524–1585) French poet. Of a noble family, he became the foremost poet of La Pléiade, a literary group that used classical and Italian models to elevate the French language as a medium for literary expression. Among his diverse works were *Odes* (1550), inspired by HORACE; *Les amours* (1552); and *Sonnets pour Hélène,* now perhaps his most famous collection. He perfected and established the ALEXANDRINE as the classic form in French for scathing satire, elegiac tenderness, and tragic passion.

Röntgen \'rent-gən, 'rent-jən\, **Wilhelm Conrad** *or* **Wilhelm Conrad Roentgen** (1845–1923) German physicist. In 1895 he discovered mysterious rays that did not exhibit properties such as reflection or refraction, which he called X RAYS. He later produced the first X-ray photographs, showing the interiors of metal objects and the bones in his wife's hand. He also did important research in a wide variety of other fields. In 1901 he was awarded the first Nobel Prize for Physics.

roof Covering of the top of a building. Roofs have been constructed in a wide variety of forms—flat, pitched, vaulted, domed, or in combinations. Thatched roofs, usually sloping, were the earliest type and are still used in rural Africa and elsewhere. Flat roofs have historically been used in arid climates where drainage of water off the roof is not important. They became more widespread in the 19th cent., when new waterproof roofing materials made them more practical. The simplest sloping roof is the lean-to (or shed) roof, which has only one slope. A roof with two slopes that form a triangle at each end is called a gable roof. A hipped (or hip) roof has sloping sides and ends meeting at inclined projecting angles called hips. The gambrel roof has two slopes on each of its two sides, the upper being less steep than the lower. The mansard roof has two slopes on all four sides.

Roon \'rōn\, **Albrecht (Theodor Emil), Graf (Count) von** (1803–1879) Prussian army officer. He aided Prince William (later WILLIAM I) in suppressing the insurrection in Baden (1848). As minister of war (1859–73), he improved the Prussian army by requiring universal military service and a permanent reserve. His reforms contributed to decisive victories in the SEVEN WEEKS' WAR (1866) and the FRANCO–PRUSSIAN WAR (1870–71).

Rooney, Mickey *orig.* Joe Yule, Jr. (b.1920) U.S. film actor. Born in Brooklyn, N.Y., he joined his family's vaudeville act from age 2. He starred in 50 RKO short film comedies as Mickey McGuire (1927–33) and won praise in *A Midsummer Night's Dream* (1935) and *Boys Town* (1938). From 1937 he played the cocky, energetic Andy Hardy in a series of popular films, often teamed with Judy GARLAND. His later films include *National Velvet* (1944) and *The Black Stallion* (1979). He made a successful Broadway debut in *Sugar Babies* in 1979, and received an honorary Academy Award in 1983.

Roosevelt \'rō-zə-ˌvelt, 'rō-zə-vəlt\, **(Anna) Eleanor** (1884–1962) U.S. first lady and diplomat. Born in New York City, the niece of Theodore ROOSEVELT, she married her distant cousin, Franklin ROOSEVELT, in 1905. She raised their five children and became active in politics after her husband's polio attack (1921). As first lady (1933–45), she traveled around the U.S. to report on living conditions and public opinion for her husband, and supported such humanitarian causes as child welfare and civil rights. She wrote the syndicated column "My Day" and several books. After her husband's death, she was appointed a delegate to the U.N. (1945, 1949–52, 1961), whose founding she had strongly advocated. As chair of its Commission on Human Rights (1946–51), she helped draft the UNIVERSAL DECLARATION OF HUMAN RIGHTS (1948). In the 1950s she traveled around the world for the U.N. and remained active in the Democratic Party.

Roosevelt, Franklin D(elano) (1882–1945) 32nd president of the U.S. (1933–45). Born in Hyde Park, N.Y., he was attracted to politics as an admirer of his cousin Theodore ROOSEVELT, and became active in the Democratic Party. In 1905 he married Eleanor ROOSEVELT, who would become a valued adviser. He served as U.S. assistant secretary of the navy (1913–20). In 1921 he was stricken with polio; though unable to walk, he remained active in politics. As governor of New

Franklin D. Roosevelt

York (1929–33), he set up the first state relief agency in the U.S. In 1932 he won the presidential nomination and easily defeated Pres. Herbert HOOVER. In his inaugural address to a nation of more than 13 million unemployed, he pronounced that "the only thing we have to fear is fear itself." Congress passed most of the changes he sought in his ambitious NEW DEAL program in the first hundred days of his term. He was overwhelmingly reelected in 1936 over Alfred LANDON. To overcome legal challenges to the New Deal, he proposed enlarging the U.S. Supreme Court, but his "court-packing" plan aroused angry opposition. By the late 1930s economic recovery had slowed, but Roosevelt was more concerned with the growing threat of war. In 1940 he was reelected to an unprecedented third term, defeating Wendell WILLKIE. He maintained U.S. neutrality toward the war in Europe, but approved the principle of LEND-LEASE and in 1941 met with Winston CHURCHILL to draft the Atlantic Charter. With U.S. entry into WORLD WAR II, he mobilized industry for military production and formed an alliance with Britain and the Soviet Union. Despite declining health, he won reelection for a fourth term against Thomas DEWEY (1944), but died a few months later. His presidency is regarded as one of the greatest in U.S. history.

Roosevelt, Theodore (1858–1919) 26th president of the U.S. (1901–9). Born in New York City, he became a Republican leader in the New York legislature opposed to the Democratic political machine. After political defeats and the death of his wife, he went to the Dakota Territory to ranch. He returned to serve on the U.S. Civil Service Commission (1889–95). A supporter of William MCKINLEY, he served as assistant secretary of the navy (1897–98). When the SPANISH–AMERICAN WAR was declared, he resigned to organize a cavalry unit, the ROUGH RIDERS. He returned to New York a hero and was elected governor in 1899. Elected vice-president with McKinley, he became president on McKin-

Theodore Roosevelt

ley's assassination in 1901. One of his early initiatives was to urge enforcement of the SHERMAN ANTITRUST ACT against business monopolies. He won election in his own right in 1904. At his urging, Congress regulated railroad rates and passed the Pure Food and Drug Act (1906) to provide new consumer protections. He set aside national forests, parks, and mineral, oil, and coal lands for conservation. He and secretary of state Elihu ROOT announced the Roosevelt corollary to the MONROE DOCTRINE, which reinforced the U.S. position as defender of the Western Hemisphere. For mediating an end to the RUSSO–JAPANESE WAR, he received the 1906 Nobel Peace Prize. He secured a treaty with Panama for construction of a canal. Declining to seek re-election, he secured the nomination for W. H. TAFT. After traveling in Africa and Europe, he tried to defeat Taft for the nomination in 1912; rejected, he organized the BULL MOOSE PARTY but failed to win the election. Throughout his life he continued to write, publishing extensively on history, politics, travel, and nature.

root In botany, the underground anchoring part of a plant. It grows downward in response to gravity, absorbs water and dissolved minerals, and stores reserve food. Primary root systems have a deep sturdy taproot plus secondary or lateral smaller roots, and root hairs. Additional support (e.g., in CORN and ORCHIDS) comes from stem offshoots called adventitious, or prop, roots. Fleshy roots that store food may be modified taproots (e.g., CARROTS, TURNIPS, and BEETS) or modified adventitious roots (e.g. CASSAVA). TUBERS such as the POTATO are modified, fleshy, underground stems. Aerial roots arise from the stem and either pass through the air before reaching the soil or remain hanging in the air.

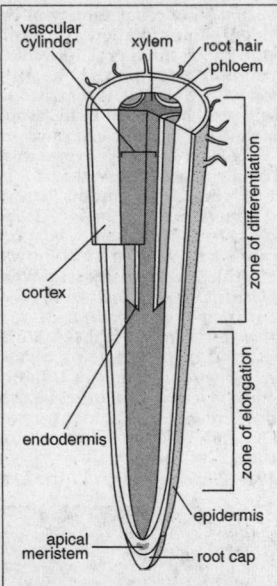

Root Structure of a root. The apical meristem is an area of actively dividing cells that forms all the root's cells. The root cap provides a protective covering that facilitates passage of the root through soil. Cells become specialized for specific functions in the zone of differentiation, or maturation zone. The epidermal layer allows passage of water and dissolved materials into the interior. Cells of the cortex store food and transport water and substances to the endodermis, which regulates their entry into the vascular cylinder, containing the xylem and phloem.

Root, Elihu (1845–1937) U.S. lawyer and diplomat. Born in Clinton, N.Y., he became a U.S. attorney in 1883 and served as secretary of war 1899–1904. As secretary of state (1905–9) under Theodore ROOSEVELT, he concluded treaties with Japan and S. American countries to improve relations with the U.S. He was awarded the Nobel Peace Prize in 1912. He served in the U.S. Senate 1909–15. A supporter of the League of Nations, he helped frame the statute establishing the World Court.

Root, Elisha King (1808–1865) U.S. engineer. Born in Ludlow, Mass., he worked in a cotton mill from age 10 and later as a machinist. He became superintendent of Samuel COLT's firearms company in 1849, and later succeeded Colt as president. In 1853 he designed a drop hammer, which was soon being used in every forge in the world. His numerous inno-

vations were principally responsible for Colt's preeminence in small arms.

rope Assemblage of fibers, filaments, or wires compacted by twisting or braiding into a long, flexible line. Wire rope is often referred to as cable. The basic requirement for service is that the rope remain firmly compacted and structurally stable, even while being bent, twisted, and pulled. Rope's most important property is its TENSILE STRENGTH. Because even short fibers can be spun into long flexible YARNS, practically any fiber can be made into a rope. Braided ropes deteriorate more slowly than twisted ropes.

Rorik See RURIK

Rorschach \'rŏr-ˌshäk\, **Hermann** (1884–1922) Swiss psychiatrist. Nicknamed Kleck ("inkblot") as a schoolboy because of his skill in sketching, he earned his MD from the Univ. of Zurich and became vice president of the Swiss Psychoanalytic Society in 1919. He devised the Rorschach inkblot test to gauge the perceptions, intelligence, and emotional traits of his patients, and summarized his findings in *Psychodiagnostics* (1921).

Rorty, Richard (McKay) (b.1931) U.S. philosopher. Born in New York City, he has taught at Princeton Univ. (1961–82) and the Univ. of Virginia (from 1982). He is noted for promoting a reconciliation between ANALYTIC PHILOSOPHY and CONTINENTAL PHILOSOPHY. His *Philosophy and the Mirror of Nature* (1979) is a critique of REPRESENTATIONALISM, in place of which he advocates a position inspired by PRAGMATISM. His later books include *Contingency, Irony and Solidarity* (1988).

Rosario City (pop., 1999: 1,000,000) and river port, E central Argentina, on the PARANÁ RIVER. Founded in 1725, in 1819 the city was burned by revolutionaries. In 1860 it was able to welcome oceangoing ships to its natural harbor, which became a major port. The city exports grain, meat, and lumber, and produces steel, automobiles, and agricultural machinery. It is Argentina's third-largest city.

rosary Religious exercise in which prayers are recited and counted on a string of beads or knotted cord, which is also called a rosary. Many of these devices are highly ornamental and incorporate jewels. The practice of using a rosary occurs in such world religions as Christianity, Hinduism, Buddhism, and Islam. In Christianity, the most common rosary is that of the Virgin MARY. Its origin is uncertain, but it reached its definitive form in the 15th cent.

rose Any of about 100 species in the genus *Rosa* (family Rosaceae) characterized by their beautiful, fragrant flowers. *Rosa* species are probably the most widely recognized and appreciated ornamental flowering plants. Hundreds of varieties and hybrids are cultivated. Roses are susceptible to numerous fungal diseases. The rose family contains about 3,000 species and accounts for 45% of the species in the rose order (Rosales). Other popular garden plants and ornamentals in the rose family include HAWTHORN, mountain ash, and flowering CHERRY. The family also is home to many important fruits, including APPLES, PEACHES, STRAWBERRIES, PEARS, PLUMS, APRICOTS, ALMONDS, QUINCES, BLACKBERRIES, and RASPBERRIES. Many members have thorns or prickles.

Rose, Pete(r Edward) (b.1942) U.S. baseball player. Born in Cincinnati, he played for the Cincinnati Reds (1963–79, 1984–86), the Philadelphia Phillies (1980–83), and the Montreal Expos (1984). His 4,256 career hits and 3,562 games played both remain all-time records, and he ranks fifth in career runs (2,165). In 1989, after being investigated for allegedly betting on baseball games, including those of his own Reds, Rose was banned from the sport for life.

Roseau \rō-'zō\ Town (pop., 1991: 16,000), capital of Dominica, W. INDIES. Its port exports limes, tropical vegetables, and spices. There are botanical gardens and nearby waterfalls and thermal springs. The town was burned by the French in 1805 and suffered nearly total destruction by a hurricane in 1979.

Rose Bowl *formally* **Pasadena Tournament of Roses** Oldest U.S. postseason college football contest, held in Pasadena, Cal., on New Year's Day. Each game is preceded by a "Rose Parade" featuring floats of elaborate floral design. The first festival was held in 1890, and the first football game in 1902. From 1947 to 2001 participation was limited to the winning teams of the Big Ten and Pacific Coast (now Pacific Ten) conferences.

Rosecrans \\'rō-zə-ˌkranz\\, **William S(tarke)** (1819–1898) U.S. general. Born in Kingston Township, Ohio, he served in the army before resigning to become an architect and civil engineer. In the AMERICAN CIVIL WAR he led Union forces to early victories. In 1863 he advanced on Confederate troops at Chattanooga, forcing them out of the city. An ill-planned move precipitated the Battle of CHICKAMAUGA and forced his troops to retreat into Chattanooga, where they were besieged; Rosecrans's error led to his being removed from command.

rosemary Small perennial evergreen shrub (*Rosmarinus officinalis*) of the MINT family whose leaves are used to flavor food. The bush grows 3–7.5 ft (1–2.3 m) tall and has short needlelike leaves, dark green and shiny above, white beneath. Bluish flowers grow in small clusters. Bees are particularly fond of rosemary. Native to the Mediterranean, it has been naturalized throughout Europe and temperate America.

Rosenberg, Julius and Ethel *orig.* Ethel Greenglass (1918–1953, 1915–1953) U.S. spies. Born in New York City, both joined the Communist Party. In 1940 Julius became an engineer with the U.S. Army Signal Corps. The two apparently gave military secrets to the Soviet military in a conspiracy with Ethel's brother, Sgt. David Greenglass, a machinist on the atomic-bomb project at Los Alamos, and Harry Gold, a courier for the U.S. espionage ring. They were all arrested in mid-1950. Greenglass and Gold received prison terms, but the Rosenbergs were sentenced to death. Despite a worldwide campaign for mercy, they were executed in 1953, the only U.S. civilians ever executed for espionage.

Rosenquist, James (b.1933) U.S. painter. Born in Grand Forks, N.D., he began his career as an abstract painter but was later drawn to POP ART. Such features of his large canvases as pop-culture iconography, advertising logos, and superimposed images may stem from his early work as a billboard painter. He has also created large works combining lithography, screenprinting, etching, and collage.

Rose of Lima, St. *orig.* Isabel de Flores (1586–1617) Patron saint of S. America, the first person born in the Western Hemisphere to be canonized by the Roman Catholic church (1671). Born to a wealthy family in Lima, in 1606 she joined a Dominican order. She lived in seclusion in a hut in the family garden, fasting, wearing a crown of thorns, and sleeping on broken glass, and experienced many visions, particularly of the devil. Many miracles were reported after her death.

rose quartz Translucent, coarse-grained variety of QUARTZ found in PEGMATITES. Rose quartz is valued for its pale to rich pink color; it has been carved since early times and has been faceted to provide gems of good brilliance. Its milky aspect is attributed to tiny needlelike inclusions of RUTILE, which can give the polished stone a star-shaped figure like that found in sapphire, but not as sharp or intense. Rose quartz occurs in Brazil, Madagascar, Sweden, Namibia, California, and Maine.

Roses, Wars of the (1455–85) Series of dynastic civil wars between the Houses of LANCASTER and YORK for the English throne. The wars were named for the emblems of the two houses, the white rose of York and the red of Lancaster. Both claimed the throne through descent from EDWARD III. Lancastrians held the throne from 1399, but during one of HENRY VI's bouts with madness in 1453 the duke of York was declared protector of the realm. Henry reestablished his authority in 1455, and the battle was joined. The Yorkists succeeded in putting EDWARD IV on the throne in 1461, but the wars continued, and in 1471 they murdered Henry. In 1483 RICHARD III overrode the claims of his nephew Edward V to seize the throne, alienating many Yorkists. The Lancastrian Henry Tudor (HENRY VII) defeated and killed Richard at the Battle of BOSWORTH FIELD, ending the wars. He united the houses by marriage and defeated a Yorkist rising in 1487. See also Earl of WARWICK.

Rosetta Stone \\rō-'ze-tə\\ Inscribed stone slab, now in the British Museum, that provided an important key to interpreting Egyptian HIEROGLYPHS. An irregularly shaped block of black basalt with inscriptions in hieroglyphs, demotic EGYPTIAN, and Greek, it was discovered by Napoleon's troops near the town of Rosetta (Rashid), northeast of Alexandria, in 1799. The text concerns the deeds of Ptolemy V Epiphanes (205–180 B.C.). Thomas YOUNG isolated the proper names in the demotic version, and J.-F. CHAMPOLLION completed the decipherment after grasping that some hieroglyphs were phonetic.

rose window In GOTHIC ARCHITECTURE, a decorated circular window, often glazed with stained glass, that first appeared in mid-12th-cent. cathedrals. It was used mainly at the W end of the NAVE and the ends of the transept. The bar TRACERY of a High Gothic rose window consisted of a series of radiating forms, each tipped by a pointed arch at the outside of the circle. The rose windows of NOTRE-DAME DE PARIS are particularly noteworthy.

Rosh Hashanah \\ˌräsh-hə-'shä-nə\\ Jewish New Year. Sometimes called the Day of Judgment or Day of Remembrance, Rosh Hashanah falls on Tishri 1 (in September or October) and ushers in a 10-day period of self-examination and penitence that ends with YOM KIPPUR. It celebrates the creation of the world and the responsibilities of the Jews as God's chosen people. The liturgy includes the blowing of the ram's horn, or shofar, a call for spiritual awakening. Bread and fruit dipped in honey are eaten as omens of sweetness for the year ahead.

Rosicrucian \\ˌrō-zə-'krü-shən\\ Member of a secret worldwide brotherhood claiming to possess esoteric wisdom handed down from ancient times. Its symbol combines a rose and a cross. Its earliest known document, *Account of the Brotherhood* (1614), tells the story of the supposed founder, Christian Rosenkreuz ("Rose Cross"), allegedly born in 1378, who is said to have acquired wisdom on trips to the Middle East that he imparted to followers in Germany. He is now generally considered a symbolic rather than a real character. Some say Rosicrucianism is only the accumulated wisdom passed down from PLATO, JESUS, PHILO JUDAEUS, PLOTINUS, and others. No reliable evidence dates its history earlier than the 17th cent. The "Ancient Mystical Order Rosae Crucis" (1915) and other Rosicrucian groups continue to operate today.

Ross, Betsy *orig.* Elizabeth Griscom (1752–1836) American patriot. Born in Philadelphia, she worked as a seamstress and upholsterer. According to legend, in 1776 she was visited by George WASHINGTON and Robert MORRIS, who asked her to make a flag for the new nation based on a sketch by Washington. Though Ross made flags for the navy, no firm evidence supports this legend of the national flag. In 1777 the Continental Congress adopted the Stars and Stripes as the U.S. flag.

Ross, Diana See SUPREMES

Ross, Harold W(allace) (1892–1951) U.S. editor. Born in Aspen, Col., he worked as a reporter and editor before launching *The NEW YORKER* in 1925. The new magazine soon attracted established writers and artists as well as young talent drawn by its innovative style and Ross's encouragement. His famously unvarnished speech and bluster masked extraordinary editorial instincts and capacities. Ross remained the guiding force behind *The New Yorker* until his death.

Ross, John *Indian name* Tsan-Usdi ("Little John") (1790–1866) American Indian chief. Born near Lookout Mtn., N.C., the son of a Scottish father and part-Cherokee mother, he grew up as a CHEROKEE. As president of the National Council of Cherokees (1819–26) and principal chief of the Cherokee Nation (1828–39), he resisted attempts to seize Cherokee farms and lands in Georgia and unsuccessfully petitioned Andrew JACKSON to defend the Indians' rights. In 1838 he was forced to lead his people on the infamous TRAIL OF TEARS to the Oklahoma Territory. There he became chief of the new United Cherokee Nation (1839–66).

Ross, Ronald (*later* **Sir Ronald**) (1857–1932) British bacteriologist. While working in India, he discovered the PLASMODIUM parasite (cause of MALARIA) in the gastrointestinal tract of the *Anopheles* mosquito in 1897. He used infected and healthy birds to learn its entire life cycle, including its presence in the mosquito's salivary glands, showing how it is transmitted by a bite. In 1902 he received the second Nobel Prize for physiology or medicine.

Rosse, Earl of *orig.* **William Parsons** (1800–1867) Irish astronomer. His "Leviathan," 54 ft (16.2 m) long, was the largest reflecting TELESCOPE of the 19th cent. With it Rosse discovered the spiral shape of many GALAXIES, and he studied and named the CRAB NEBULA. He was also the first to discover binary and triple stars. He served in the House of Commons 1821–34; on inheriting his father's earldom in 1841, he joined the House of Lords.

Rossellini \ˌrōs-säl-ˈlē-nē\, **Roberto** (1906–1977) Italian film director. He directed his first feature film, *White Ship*, in 1941. His *Open City* (1945), acclaimed as one of the first examples of Italian NEOREALISM, was written with Federico FELLINI, who also collaborated on *Paisan* (1946). He made several films starring Ingrid BERGMAN, beginning with *Stromboli* (1949), but the scandal of their adulterous affair and marriage damaged their careers. He later directed *General della Rovere* (1959) and a series of didactic historical works. His daughter Isabella Rossellini (b.1952) has appeared in such films as *Blue Velvet* (1986) and *Big Night* (1996).

Rossellino \ˌrōs-säl-ˈlē-nō\, **Bernardo** (1409–1464) Italian architect and sculptor. His tomb for Leonardo Bruni (1444–50) in Santa Croce, Florence, was one of the greatest achievements of early Renaissance sculpture, marked by a fine balance between sculpture and architecture, figure and decoration. He also designed the apse of ST. PETER'S BASILICA and the cathedral and Piccolomini Palace in Pienza (1460–64). His brother Antonio (1427–1479), who regularly assisted him, was a master of portraiture in sculpture, achieving extremely detailed and realistic likenesses. His greatest work is the Chapel of the Cardinal of Portugal, an elaborate combination of architecture and figurative sculpture in San Miniato al Monte, outside Florence.

Rossetti \rō-ˈze-tē\, **Christina (Georgina)** (1830–1894) English poet. The sister of D. G. ROSSETTI, she found her highest inspiration in her deep religious faith. The collections *Goblin Market* (1862) and *The Prince's Progress* (1866) contain most of her finest work. Her best poetry is strong, personal, and unforced, uniting the devotional and passionate sides of her nature. Her *Sing-Song* (1872), a collection of nursery rhymes, is among the finest children's books of the 19th cent.

Rossetti \rō-ˈzet-ē, rō-ˈset-ē\, **Dante Gabriel** (*orig.* Gabriel Charles Dante) (1828–1882) British painter and poet. Brother of Christina ROS-

Christina Rossetti Drawing by D. G. Rossetti, 1866

SETTI, he trained at the Royal Academy, but vacillated between painting and poetry. As an informal pupil of F. M. BROWN, he absorbed Brown's admiration for the German NAZARENES, and in 1848, with several friends, he formed the PRE-RAPHAELITES. Rossetti expanded the Brotherhood's aims by linking poetry, painting, and social idealism and by treating "Pre-Raphaelite" as synonymous with a romanticized medieval past. When his oil paintings were severely criticized, he turned to watercolors based on literary works and became very successful. After the death of his long-ailing wife in 1862, possibly by suicide, literary themes gave way to pictures of women, particularly William MORRIS's wife, Jane. His poetry, including the sonnet sequence "The House of Life," was widely admired. He broke with Morris in 1875 over his love for Jane, and spent his later years as an alcoholic recluse.

Ross Ice Shelf World's largest body of floating ice, lying at the head of Ross Sea, an enormous indentation in Antarctica. Its area is estimated to be about the size of France. The great white barrier wall of the shelf's front, first seen in 1841 by Capt. James C. Ross (1800–1862), rises in places to 200 ft (60 m). The ice shelf was a gateway for expeditions by Roald AMUNDSEN and R. F. SCOTT (1911–12) and R. E. Byrd (1928–41). It is the site of several research stations.

Rossini, Gioacchino (Antonio) (1792–1868) Italian composer. At 14 he entered Bologna's conservatory, where he wrote mostly sacred music. From 1812 he produced theater works at a terrific rate, and for 15 years he was the dominant voice of Italian opera; his major successes included *L'Italiana in Algeri* (1813), *Otello* (1816), *The Barber of Seville* (1816), *La Cenerentola* (1817), *Mosè in Egitto* (1818), *The Siege of Corinth* (1826), and *Semiramide* (1823). The musical formulas he devised would shape Italian opera until Giuseppe VERDI, but his wit and invention using them was unparalleled. From 1824 he spent much time in Paris, where he wrote his masterpiece, *William Tell* (1829). After 1832 his health was poor and he composed little.

Rosso \ˈrōs-sō\, **Giovanni Battista** known as **Rosso Fiorentino** (1494–1540) Italian painter and decorator. He trained under ANDREA DEL SARTO, alongside Jacopo da PONTORMO, with whom he became a leading figure in the development of MANNERISM. The highly charged emotionalism of his early works (e.g., the *Assumption* fresco, 1513–14, in Florence's Santissima Annunziata) is more subdued in such later works as *Dead Christ with Angels* (1525–26). In 1530 he went to France at the invitation of FRANCIS I; there he became a founder of the FONTAINEBLEAU SCHOOL, and the ornamental style he developed influenced decorative arts across N Europe.

Rostand \rȯs-ˈtäⁿ\, **Edmond (-Eugène)** (1868–1918) French playwright. His most popular work is the heroic comedy *Cyrano de Bergerac* (1898), the story of an ugly, long-nosed soldier who despairs of winning the lady he loves and helps a friend woo her instead. The final example of French Romantic drama, it was enormously successful internationally. He also wrote *L'aiglon* (1900) for Sarah BERNHARDT.

Rostock \ˈrȯ-ˌstȯk\ City (pop., 1998 est.: 213,000) and seaport, NE Germany, 8 mi (13 km) from the BALTIC SEA. Founded in 1218, it was a powerful member of the HANSEATIC LEAGUE in the 14th cent. Wooden ships were built in its shipyards until 1851, when the first German steam-propelled vessel was built there. It was heavily damaged in World War II. After the war it was developed as E. Germany's principal ocean port. It is an important fishing and shipbuilding center.

Rostov \rə-ˈstȯf\ City (pop., 1991 est.: 36,000), W central Russia. Founded before A.D. 862, Rostov was an outstanding center of early medieval Russia as the capital of the Rostov-Suzdal principality from 1207 until it came under the control of MOSCOW in 1474. Its immense kremlin and beautifully decorated medieval churches have been preserved. It still produces traditional handmade enamelware.

Rostov-na-Donu \rə-ˈstȯf-nä-ˈdȯ-nü\ *English* **Rostov-on-Don** City (pop., 1997 est.: 1,023,000), S Russia in Europe. Located on the DON RIVER about 28 mi (45 km) from the Sea of AZOV, it was founded in 1749 and grew steadily with 19th-cent. Russian colonization. It suffered extensive damage in World War II, but was rebuilt. It is a transportation center; the nearby DONETS BASIN led to major industrialization in recent decades.

Rostropovich \ˌrȯs-trə-ˈpō-vich\, **Mstislav (Leopoldovich)** (b.1927) Russian-U.S. cellist and conductor. Born in Azerbaijan, he studied composition (with Dmitri SHOSTAKOVICH), piano, and cello at the Moscow Conservatory. He had pieces written for him by such composers as Shostakovich, Sergey PROKOFIEV, and Benjamin BRITTEN. A political dissident, he left the Soviet Union in 1974. Settling in the U.S., he served as music director of the National Symphony Orchestra (1977–96), while becoming perhaps the world's most famous cellist.

rotary engine INTERNAL-COMBUSTION ENGINE in which the combustion chambers and cylinders rotate with the driven shaft around a fixed control shaft to which pistons are attached. The gas pressures of combustion are used to rotate the shaft. In the widely used Wankel engine, a triangular rotor rotates with an orbital motion in a specially shaped casing, and forms rotating crescent-shaped combustion chambers between its sides and the curved wall of the casing.

rotary press PRINTING press that prints on PAPER passing between a supporting cylinder and a cylinder containing the printing plates. In contrast, the flatbed press has a flat printing surface. The rotary press is used mainly in high-speed operations in which the press takes paper from a roll, as in newspaper printing. It may not only print as many as four colors but also cut and fold and bind in a cover, all in one continuous automatic process. Large presses can print up to 60,000 copies of 128 standard-size pages in an hour.

Roth, Philip (Milton) (b.1933) U.S. writer. A native of Newark, N.J., he first achieved fame with *Goodbye Columbus* (1959), whose title story candidly depicts the boorish materialism of a suburban family. His works are characterized by an acute ear for dialogue, a concern with Jewish middle-class life, and the painful entanglements of sexual and familial love. Among his subsequent novels are the comic and scandalous *Portnoy's Complaint* (1969) and an admired series centering on a writer named Nathan Zuckerman, including *The Ghost Writer* (1979). Later works include *Sabbath's Theater* (1995, National Book Award) and *American Pastoral* (1997, Pulitzer Prize).

Rothko, Mark *orig.* Marcus Rothkowitz (1903–1970) U.S. (Russian-born) painter. His family settled in Portland, Ore., in 1913, and he took up painting after moving to New York in 1925. His early realistic style culminated in the *Subway* series (late 1930s). The semiabstract forms of *Baptismal Scene* (1945) developed into a highly personal contemplative form of ABSTRACT EXPRESSIONISM by 1948. He spent the rest of his career refining a basic style featuring two or three soft-edged rectangles that nearly filled his wall-sized canvases. In 1965–66 he completed 14 immense canvases, whose somber intensity reveals his deepening mysticism; they are now housed in a chapel in Houston, which was named the Rothko Chapel after his suicide.

Rothschild family European banking dynasty. Mayer A. Rothschild (1744–1812), whose family name derived from the red shield (*rote Schild*) on its house in the Jewish ghetto, started out in a Frankfurt banking house. The financial transactions of the Napoleonic Wars of 1792–1815 were the foundation of the Rothschild fortune. Mayer and his oldest son, Amschel (1773–1855), supervised the growing business, while Nathan (1777–1836) established a branch in London in 1804. James (or Jakob, 1792–1868) settled in Paris in 1811, and Salomon (1774–1855) and Karl (1788–1855) opened offices in Vienna and Naples in the 1820s. The Rothschild

Mayer Amschel Rothschild

business later focused on government securities and industrial companies, including railway, coal, ironworking, oil, and metallurgical investments. By the late 19th cent. their position had been eroded by the new commercial banks. Mayer's five sons were made barons of the Austrian empire, a Rothschild was the first Jew to enter the British Parliament, and another was the first to be elevated to the British peerage. The Austrian house was seized by the Nazis. The British and French families distinguished themselves as scientists and philanthropists. Baron Philippe de Rothschild (1902–1988) became a premier winemaker.

rotifer \ˈrō-tə-fər\ Any of about 2,000 species of microscopic, multicellular, water-dwelling INVERTEBRATES constituting the class Rotifera, or Rotaria (phylum Aschelminthes; see WORM). Currents created by the rotifer's corona (moving cilia arranged in a circle at the head) sweep bacteria, protozoans, and detritus into the mouth. Body shape varies greatly among species. Rotifers are common in freshwater on all continents, but some live in saltwater. The species may be free-living or parasitic, solitary or colonial, and free-swimming, crawling, or sedentary.

Rotterdam City (pop., 1999 est.: 593,000) and seaport, W Netherlands. It lies near the NORTH SEA. Founded in the 13th cent., it developed into a major port and commercial city. Heavily damaged in World War II, it was extensively rebuilt on a new plan. One of the world's busiest cargo-handling ports, it is a major transshipment port, with tens of thousands of RHINE RIVER barges using its facilities. The second-largest city in the Netherlands, it has large oil refineries and produces chemicals, paper, and clothing. It is also a cultural and educational center.

Rottweiler \ˈrät-ˌwī-lər, ˈrȯt-ˌvī-lər\ Breed of dog descended from a breed of cattle dog in ancient Rottweil, Germany. From the Middle Ages to about 1900, it accompanied butchers on buying expeditions, carrying money in a neck pouch. It has also served as a guard dog, drover's dog, draft dog, and police dog. Stocky and muscular, and black with tan markings, it stands 22–27 in. (56–69 cm) and weighs 90–110 lbs (41–50 kg).

rotunda In Classical and Neoclassical architecture, a building or room that is circular in plan and covered with a dome. The PANTHEON is a Classical Roman rotunda. The Villa Rotonda at Vicenza, designed by Andrea PALLADIO, is an Italian Renaissance example. The U.S. CAPITOL displays the rotunda in its familiar role as part of a monumental public building.

Rouault \rü-ˈō\, **Georges (-Henri)** (1871–1958) French painter. His apprenticeship in a glazier's shop restoring medieval stained glass (1885–90) influenced his mature style as a painter. His style evolved toward FAUVISM before he established a highly personal form of EXPRESSIONISM. An ardent Roman Catholic, he painted subjects apparently fallen from grace—prostitutes, tragic clowns, and pitiless judges. After 1914 his subject matter became more specifically religious, and he shifted from watercolor to oil. His layers of paint became thick and rich, his forms simplified, and his colors and black lines reminiscent of stained glass. In the

Georges Rouault, "The Workman's Apprentice (Self-Portrait)," 1925

1930s he produced a splendid series on Christ's Passion. His series of clowns in the 1940s are virtual self-portraits.

Rouen \rü-ˈäⁿ\ City (pop., 1999: 106,000), NW France, on the SEINE RIVER. It became important in the 3rd cent. A.D., with the arrival of Christianity with St. Mellon. Sacked by the Normans in 876, it became the medieval capital of NORMANDY. It came under English rule in 1066 and again in 1419. JOAN OF ARC was executed there in 1431. Historic buildings include the 14th-cent. abbey of St. Ouen and the great Gothic cathedral. It was the birthplace of Pierre CORNEILLE and Gustave FLAUBERT.

Rough Riders 1st Volunteer Cavalry regiment in the SPANISH–AMERICAN WAR. Organized and led by Theodore ROOSEVELT and Leonard Wood (1860–1927), it included cowboys, miners, policemen, and college athletes. The most famous of its exploits in Cuba was an uphill charge in the Battle of Santiago (July 1, 1898) in which the group helped capture Kettle Hill and then charged across a valley to assist in seizing San Juan Ridge and its high point, San Juan Hill. Wide press coverage helped establish Roosevelt's reputation.

roulette \rü-ˈlet\ Gambling game in which players bet on which red or black numbered compartment of a revolving wheel a small ball will come to rest in. Roulette emerged in the late 18th cent. in the casinos of Europe. All bets are placed against the "house," or casino bank. Bets may be on a single number or various combinations of numbers that pay off at lesser odds if the winner is among them. Betting that a red or black or odd or even number will come up are other options.

roundworm See NEMATODE

Rousseau \rü-ˈsō\, **Henri** *known as* **Le Douanier Rousseau** (1844–1910) French painter. He worked as a toll collector (not as a *douanier*, or customs officer, the epithet his friends later used), but found time to paint and draw. Completely self-taught, he exhibited some early paintings, including *Carnival Evening*, in 1886. It is typical of naive art;

everything is drawn literally, the clouds look solid, and the costumes receive more attention than the figures themselves—but it achieves a striking mood and mystery. In 1894 his *War* won him recognition by the avant-garde. His best-known works are richly colored images of lush jungles, wild beasts, and exotic figures (e.g., *The Sleeping Gypsy*, 1897). He died a pauper; only after his death was his greatness recognized.

Rousseau, Jean-Jacques (1712–1778) Swiss-French philosopher. He wrote on music and economics for Denis DIDEROT's *Encyclopédie*. His *Discourse on the Arts and Sciences* (1750) asserted that humans had been corrupted and enslaved by society and civilization, an idea to which he returned throughout his life and which set him apart from both conservatives and radicals. His light opera *Le devin du village* (1752) had a long-running success, despite its naive music, and made him famous. His *Discourse on the Origin and Foundations of Inequality Among Men* (1754) attacked private property. His *Social Contract* (1762) argued that if a civil society, or state, could be based on a genuine SOCIAL CONTRACT, people would receive in exchange for their natural independence a better kind of freedom. The work became the basic text of the French Revolution, though it has long been seen to support totalitarian regimes as well as radical democracy. His novel *Émile* expressed his ideas on education, and became widely influential over the following century. His *Confessions* (published 1781–88) is one of the most famous of all autobiographies.

Rousseau \rü-'sō\, **(Pierre-Etienne-) Théodore** (1812–1867) French painter. He began to paint at 14 and soon was painting outdoors directly from nature, a novel practice at the time. From the 1830s he painted regularly in the village of Barbizon, where he became a leader of the BARBIZON SCHOOL of landscape painters. His paintings, which show nature as a wild, undisciplined force, counter the calmly idealized landscapes of Neoclassicism, and his small, highly textured brush strokes presage those of the Impressionists.

Roussel \rü-'sel\, **Albert (Charles Paul Marie)** (1869–1937) French composer. After serving as a midshipman, he studied 10 years at Paris's Schola Cantorum. His opera-ballet *Padmavati* (1918), with its Indian scales, won enthusiasm from younger composers; his other works include the ballets *The Spider's Feast* (1913) and *Bacchus et Ariane* (1930) and four symphonies.

Roussillon \ˌrü-sē-'yōⁿ\ Historical and cultural region, S France, bordering Spain and the Mediterranean Sea. Conquered by Rome in the 2nd cent. B.C., it was later held by the VISIGOTHS, the Arabs, and the Carolingian Franks. Monasticism flourished from the 10th cent., and the area has rich remains of ROMANESQUE ARCHITECTURE. It belonged to ARAGON and Spain from the 12th cent. until 1659. The chief city is PERPIGNAN. There are numerous families of Catalan gypsies, and Catalan is widely spoken.

Rowe \'rō\, **Nicholas** (1674–1718) English writer. His plays, which did much to assist the rise of domestic tragedy (in which the protagonists are middle-class rather than aristocratic), include *Tamerlane* (1702), *The Fair Penitent* (1703), and *The Tragedy of Jane Shore* (1714). He is also remembered as the first to attempt a critical edition of William SHAKESPEARE (1709, 1714). He became poet laureate in 1715. Rowe is regarded as the foremost 18th-cent. English tragic dramatist.

rowing Propulsion of a boat by means of oars. As a sport, it involves one of two kinds of boat: (1) the shell, a narrow, light racing boat propelled by eight rowers pulling single oars under the direction of a coxswain; and (2) the scull, a racing shell propelled by one or two rowers using sculls (pairs of oars). Organized racing began at the Univs. of Oxford and Cambridge in the 1820s, culminating in 1839 in the Henley Regatta. Rowing events in the Olympic Games have been held for men since 1900 and for women since 1976.

Rowlandson, Thomas (1756–1827) British caricaturist. After establishing a portrait studio, he began to draw caricatures to supplement his income, and found such success with them that caricature became his major occupation. The comic images he created lampooned familiar social types of his day—the antiquarian, the blowsy barmaid, the hack writer. He also illustrated editions of the novels of

Tobias SMOLLETT, Oliver GOLDSMITH, and Lawrence STERNE.

Rowling \'rō-liŋ\, **J(oanne) K(athleen)** (b.1965) British author. After graduating from Univ. of Exeter, she worked as a language teacher and began writing as a single mother. Her first book, *Harry Potter and the Philosopher's* (or *Sorcerer's*) *Stone* (1997; film, 2001), was an immediate and enormous success. It follows the adventures of a lonely orphan who discovers that he is actually a wizard and enrolls at the Hogwarts School of Wizardry. Its sequels, beginning with *Harry Potter and the Chamber of Secrets* (1998; film, 2002), also became huge worldwide best-sellers.

Roxas (y Acuna) \ 'rō-k̲äs\, **Manuel** (1892–1948) First president (1946–48) of the Republic of the Philippines. A lawyer, he began his political career in 1917 and served as speaker of the legislature 1922–34. An advocate for Philippine independence from the U.S., he helped draw up a constitution in 1935. He collaborated with the pro-Japanese administration during World War II but was defended in postwar trials by Gen. Douglas MACARTHUR. He became president when independence was achieved (1946), and obtained rehabilitation funds from the U.S., but was forced to permit U.S. military bases and make other concessions. His government's corruption and brutality led to the HUKBALAHAP REBELLION.

Royal Air Force See RAF

Royal Ballet English ballet company and school. In 1931 Ninette DE VALOIS and Lilian Baylis (1874–1937) organized the Vic-Wells Ballet, naming it for the two theaters (Old Vic and Sadler's Wells) where it performed. In the 1940s the group was renamed the Sadler's Wells Ballet; it moved to Covent Garden in 1946. Alicia MARKOVA, Margot FONTEYN, and Robert HELPMANN were among its early members. In 1956 it received a royal charter to become the Royal Ballet. Such artists as Rudolf NUREYEV, Frederick ASHTON, Kenneth MACMILLAN, and Bronislava NIJINSKA have been associated with the company.**Saint Denis** \ˌsänt-'den-əs\, **Ruth** *orig.* Ruth Dennis (1877–1968) U.S. modern-dance innovator. Born in Newark, N.J., she was a vaudeville performer before developing her dramatic dance act based on Asian dance forms. She toured in Europe (1906–9) to wide acclaim, returning to tour in the U.S. In 1915 she and her husband, Ted SHAWN, established the Denishawn dance company and school to develop a new choreographic style of abstract "music visualization." She toured with the company until it disbanded in 1931 when she and Shawn separated. She continued to perform, teach, and lecture into the 1960s.

Royal Botanic Gardens, Kew See KEW GARDENS

Royal Canadian Mounted Police *or* **Mounties** Federal police force of Canada. It is also the only force in the Yukon, Northwest, and Nunavut territories. It was founded as the North West Mounted Police (1873) with a force of 300 men to bring order to W Canada, where U.S. traders were creating havoc by trading whiskey to the Indians for furs. That success was followed by peacekeeping in the KLONDIKE GOLD RUSH (1898) and later settlement of the west. In 1920 it became a federal force and its headquarters moved to Ottawa.

Royal Dutch/Shell Group Multinational corporate group owned by Royal Dutch Petroleum Co. Ltd. of The Hague and Shell Transport and Trading Co., PLC, of London. Marcus Samuel (1853–1927) took over his father's import-export business (which included oriental shells) in London in 1878, entered the oil business in the Far East, and in 1897 founded Shell Transport and Trading Co., Ltd. Meanwhile, in 1890 a group of Dutch businessmen founded the Royal Dutch Co., which built its first refinery in Sumatra in 1892. In 1907 the two companies merged and began acquiring producing concerns worldwide. The group's principal U.S. subsidiary is Shell Oil Co. (founded 1922). Today Royal Dutch/Shell is one of the 10 largest corporate groups in the world.

Royal Greenwich Observatory \'gre-nich\ Astronomical OBSERVATORY, oldest science institution in Britain, founded for navigational purposes in 1675 by Charles II at GREENWICH, England. Its other main contributions have been in timekeeping, star location, and almanac publication. Its popular *Nautical Almanac* (first published in 1767), based on the time at the Greenwich meridian, led in part to the latter's being made earth's prime meridian and the starting point for international time zones in 1884 (see GREENWICH MEAN TIME).

Royall \'rȯi-əl\, **Anne Newport** *orig.* Anne Newport (1769–1854) U.S. writer, considered the nation's first newspaperwoman. Born in Baltimore, she was widowed in her 50s. She journeyed across the country and during 1826–31 published 10 accounts of her travels, which remain valuable sources of social history. Eccentric and acerbic, she was convicted in 1829 of being a "common scold." She published her outspoken and controversial views on various subjects in her muckraking Washington newspapers, *Paul Pry* (1831–36) and *The Huntress* (1836–54).

Royal Navy Naval military organization of Britain. Organized sea power was first used in England by ALFRED the Great, who launched ships to repel a Viking invasion. In the 16th cent., HENRY VIII built a fleet of fighting ships armed with large guns and created a naval administration. Under ELIZABETH I the navy became the means for extending the British Empire worldwide. In the 18th cent., the Royal Navy engaged in a long struggle with the French for maritime supremacy, and it later played a key role in Britain's stand against NAPOLEON. For the rest of the 19th cent., it helped enforce what became known as the Pax Britannica, the long period of relative peace in Europe that depended on British maritime supremacy. It protected shipping in World Wars I and II and remained the world's most powerful navy until the mid-20th cent.

Royal Shakespeare Co. (RSC) Major British theatrical company. Originally attached to the Shakespeare Memorial Theatre in Stratford-upon-Avon, which opened in 1879 as the site of an annual festival of William SHAKESPEARE's plays, it was called the Shakespeare Memorial Co. until 1961. It was renamed and reorganized into two units; the Stratford unit performs plays by Shakespeare and other Elizabethan and Jacobean playwrights, while the London unit also performs modern plays and classics of other eras.

Royal Society (of London for the Promotion of Natural Knowledge) Oldest scientific society in Britain. Founded in 1660, its early members included Christopher WREN, Isaac NEWTON, and Edmond HALLEY. It provided an impetus to scientific thought in England, and its achievements became internationally famous. *Philosophical Transactions,* one of the earliest periodicals in the West (1665), publishes scientific papers. Today the society has more than 1,000 fellows and 90 foreign members.

Royce, Josiah (1855–1916) U.S. philosopher. Born in Grass Valley, Cal., he taught at Harvard Univ. from 1882 to his death. An idealist in the Hegelian tradition, he taught a monistic IDEALISM. He also made contributions to psychology, social ethics, literary criticism, history, and metaphysics. His books include *The Religious Aspect of Philosophy* (1885), *The Spirit of Modern Philosophy* (1892), *Studies of Good and Evil* (1898), *The World and the Individual* (1900–1), and *The Philosophy of Loyalty* (1908). His emphasis on individuality and will over intellect strongly influenced later U.S. philosophy.

Royko, Mike (*orig.* Michael) (1932–1997) U.S. columnist. A native of Chicago, Royko joined the *Chicago Daily News* in 1959, becoming a full-time columnist in 1964. His acerbic and insightful essays reflected his working-class ethnic origins, often exposing injustices visited on ordinary people. He later moved to the *Chicago Sun-Times* and then to the *Chicago Tribune*. His widely syndicated column earned him a Pulitzer Prize in 1972. Richard J. DALEY was the subject of his best-selling book *Boss* (1971).

Rozelle, Pete (*orig.* Alvin Ray) (1926–1996) U.S. commissioner of the NATIONAL FOOTBALL LEAGUE. Born in South Gate, Cal., he was named commissioner in 1960. He doubled the league's size, helped create the SUPER BOWL, and negotiated lucrative television deals with the networks. In 1966 Rozelle succeeded in merging the NFL with the rival American Football League. In 1970 he persuaded ABC to broadcast "Monday Night Football," which proved a huge success. NFL attendance more than tripled during his tenure, which lasted until 1989.

Rub al-Khali \'rüb-ȧl-'ḵȧ-lē\ Vast desert, S ARABIAN PENINSULA. It covers about 250,000 sq mi (650,000 sq km) in SE Saudi Arabia, Yemen, Oman, and the United Arab Emirates. The largest area of continuous sand in the world, it is virtually uninhabited and largely unexplored. In 1948 Al-Ghawar, the world's largest oilfield, was discovered there.

rubber *or* **natural rubber** Organic compound, an elastic POLYMER made from the LATEX of various RUBBER TREES and RUBBER PLANTS. Natural rubber now competes with synthetic alternatives. Rubber's usefulness is based on its unique elasticity, which allows it to be stretched and to recover its shape; it is made possible by VULCANIZATION. Fillers and other additives allow tailoring of properties to the desired use. More than half of all rubber goes into making tires; the rest is used principally in belts, hoses, gaskets, shoes, clothing, furniture, and toys.

rubber plant *or* **India rubber plant** Tropical tree (*Ficus elastica*) of the MULBERRY FAMILY. It has large, thick, oblong leaves and figlike fruits in pairs along its branches. The milky sap, or LATEX, was once an important source of an inferior natural RUBBER. Young potted plants are durable and grow well under less-than-ideal indoor conditions. See also RUBBER TREE.

rubber tree S. American tropical tree (*Hevea brasiliensis*) of the SPURGE family. Cultivated in the tropics and subtropics, especially in S.E. Asia and W Africa, it has replaced the RUBBER PLANT as the chief source of natural RUBBER. The milky liquid (LATEX) that oozes from any wound to the tree bark is concentrated to 60% rubber content for making dipped goods (surgical gloves, prophylactics, toys, bottles, shoes, and balls).

rubella \rü-'be-lə\ *or* **German measles** VIRAL DISEASE with a usually mild course, except in women in the first 20 weeks of pregnancy, in whom it can cause major fetal birth defects or death. Sore throat and fever are followed by swollen glands and a rash. Up to 30% of infections may have no symptoms. Lifelong immunity follows infection. Rubella was not known to be dangerous until 1941. The virus was isolated in 1962, and a vaccine became available in 1969.

Rubens, Peter Paul (1577–1640) Flemish painter. After apprenticeships in Antwerp, he was admitted to its painters' guild in 1598. He went to Italy in 1600 and until 1608 worked for the duke of Mantua, who in 1603 sent him to Spain to present paintings and other gifts to Philip III, the first of many diplomatic missions he would perform for various courts over three decades. Returning to the Spanish Netherlands (now Belgium) in 1608, he was appointed court painter to the Spanish Habsburg regents, and over the next decade produced numerous altarpieces. In 1620 he contracted to design 39 ceiling paintings for the Jesuit church, to be completed by assistants, including the young Anthony VAN DYCK. In France he did 21 large canvases for MARIE DE MÉDICIS and a tapestry cycle for LOUIS XIII; for Britain his *Allegory of Peace and War* (1629–30) commemorated the success of his own diplomatic efforts to end hostilities between Britain and Spain, and he decorated the royal Banqueting House for CHARLES I; in Spain he did more than 60 oil sketches for PHILIP IV's hunting lodge. Both Charles and Philip knighted him. His output was prodigious. His style was a fusion of Flemish realism, Italian Renaissance classicism, and his own astounding invention. The opulent figures in his paintings generate a pervasive sense of movement in vivid, dynamic compositions. His profound stylistic influence extended over three centuries.

Rubicon \'rü-bi-ˌkän\ Small stream that separated Cisalpine GAUL from Italy in the era of the Roman republic. The movement of Julius CAESAR's forces over the Rubicon into Italy in 49 B.C. violated the law that forbade a general to lead an army out of the province to which he was assigned. Caesar's act thus amounted to a declaration of war against the Roman Senate. "Crossing the Rubicon" came to describe a step irrevocably committing a person to a given course of action.

rubidium-strontium dating \rü-'bi-dē-əm-'strän-shē-əm\ Method of estimating the age of rocks, minerals, and meteorites by measuring the amount of the stable isotope strontium-87 formed by the decay of the unstable isotope rubidium-87. The method is applicable to very old rocks because

QR

the transformation is extremely slow: the half-life of rubidium-87 is 48.8 billion years. See also DATING.

Rubinstein, Anton (Grigor'yevich) (1829–1894) Russian composer and pianist. After touring as a piano virtuoso, in 1862 he founded the St. Petersburg Conservatory, and he thereafter devoted much energy to improving the quality of Russian musical education. His once popular compositions, including six symphonies and five piano concertos, have largely disappeared from the repertoire. His brother Nicolai (1835–1881), also a famous pianist and teacher, founded the Moscow Conservatory in the 1860s.

Rubinstein, Arthur (1887–1982) Polish-U.S. pianist. He studied with Joseph Joachim (1831–1907) and I. J. PADEREWSKI and accompanied the violinist Eugène Ysaye (1858–1931) before stopping performing for five years (1932–37) to improve his technique, and reemerging as a giant of 20th-cent. music. Moving to the U.S., he became equally noted as soloist and chamber musician, with such partners as Jascha HEIFETZ and Gregor Piatigorsky (1903–1976). Active through his eighties, his repertoire ranged widely, his playing of Frédéric CHOPIN and Johannes BRAHMS being particularly admired.

Rubinstein, Helena (1870–1965) Polish-U.S. cosmetician. She went to Australia in 1902, where she opened a beauty salon, offering free consultation along with a special cream. An immediate success, she opened a salon in London in 1908 and another in Paris in 1912. In 1914 she emigrated to the U.S. She began wholesale distribution of her products in 1917. After World War II she built factories on five continents. In 1953 she established the Helena Rubinstein Foundation to coordinate her gifts to museums, colleges, and institutions for the needy.

Rublev \rəb-'lyȯf\, **Andrei** *or* **Andrei Rublyov** (c.1360–1430) Russian painter. He was trained in the stylized tradition of Byzantine art, but to its more humanistic 14th-cent. approach he added a truly Russian element, a complete unworldliness that distinguishes his work. He assisted Theophanes the Greek in decorating the Cathedral of the Annunciation in Moscow. The greatest of medieval Russian ICON painters, he is best known for *The Old Testament Trinity* (c.1410).

ruby Gemstone composed of transparent red CORUNDUM. Its color varies from deep to pale red, depending on its chromium and iron content; the most valued is a pigeon-blood red. Ruby is a mineral of very limited distribution. Its best-known source is in Myanmar, and rubies have also been found in Thailand, and Sri Lanka. Rubies have been produced synthtetically with much success; those containing 2.5% chromic oxide have the prized pigeon-blood red color. Ruby is the birthstone for July.

Rude \'rüd\, **François** (1784–1855) French sculptor. His early work was in the Neoclassical tradition, but he was uncomfortable within its restrictions and soon adopted a dynamic, emotional style. An ardent Bonapartist, he is best known for *Departure of the Volunteers of 1792* (1833–36), on the ARC DE TRIOMPHE; popularly called *La Marseillaise*, it catches the martial spirit of the Napoleonic era.

Rudolf (1858–1889) Archduke and crown prince of Austria. The son of Emperor FRANCIS JOSEPH, he received a broad education and traveled widely. As heir to the throne of Austria-Hungary, he hoped to bring reform to the empire, but his liberal views alienated his father and he was excluded from the business of government. He became despondent and allegedly formed a suicide pact with his mistress, Maria Vetsera; the two were found shot dead in the hunting lodge at Mayerling. Efforts to disguise the facts provoked many rumors, while romantic writers found inspiration in the story.

Rudolf I *or* **Rudolf of Habsburg** (1218–1291) First German king (1273–91) of the HABSBURG DYNASTY. To his inherited lands (c.1239), he added territory by marriage and through negotiation. Crowned German king (1273), he was recognized by Pope Gregory X only after promising to lead a new crusade and to renounce imperial rights in Rome, the papal territories, and Italy. He worked to combat the expansionist policies of France, but French influence at the papal court kept him from being crowned Holy Roman Emperor.

Rudolph, Wilma (Glodean) (1940–1994) U.S. sprinter. Born in St. Bethlehem, Tenn., she was a sickly child who wore an orthopedic shoe until she was 11. After setting a world record in the 200-m dash (22.9 sec), she won the 100-m and 200-m dashes and was a member of the winning 4×100-m relay team at the 1960 Olympic Games.

rue family *or* **citrus family** Family Rutaceae, made up of about 1,700 species of mostly woody shrubs and trees in 160 genera. Valuable for timber, edible fruits, and as ornamentals, members are found worldwide in warm temperate and tropical regions. The flowers are fragrant and usually white. Economically important fruits in the family include LEMONS, LIMES, ORANGES, GRAPEFRUIT, CITRONS, and KUMQUATS. Among the ornamentals are common rue *(Ruta graveolens)* and the unusual burning bush *(Dictamnus albus)*, whose aromatic leaves contain a flammable gas.

rug and carpet Any decorative textile normally made of a thick material and intended as a floor covering. Floor coverings made of plaited rushes date from the 5th or 4th millennium B.C. Carpets were first made in central and W Asia as coverings for earthen floors; they were also used as blankets, saddle covers, storage bags, tent doorways, and tomb covers. The prayer rug was designed to be carried everywhere. Oriental carpets imported into Europe in the 16th–17th cent. were often used as wall decoration. Carpet weaving reached its peak of artistry in 16th-cent. Persia. In the West, outstanding carpets were produced at factories in 17th-cent. France and 18th-cent. England. Most handmade carpets were made from sheep's wool, which was colored with natural dyes, until the 19th cent., when chemical dyes were introduced.

rugby Game similar to SOCCER and FOOTBALL, played by teams of 13 (professional) or 15 (amateur) members each, using an inflated oval ball. Play is continuous, with no timeouts or substitutions. The ball may be kicked, carried, or passed laterally or backward (but not forward). The object is to score goals (worth three points) by kicking the ball between the uprights of the opponent's goal, or tries (touchdowns, worth four points), by carrying the ball behind the opponent's goal line. The scrum, or scrummage (scrimmage), is a play in which the forwards of each side come together in a tight formation and struggle to gain possession of the ball when it is tossed in among them. Rugby originated at England's Rugby School in 1823. Professional rugby was organized in 1895. It remains most popular in England, Australia, and New Zealand.

Ruhr occupation (1923–25) Occupation of the industrial RUHR RIVER valley region in Germany by French and Belgian troops. The action was provoked by German deficiencies in the coal and coke deliveries to France required by the reparations agreement after World War I. French-Belgian occupation of the entire region in 1923 was met by passive resistance by German workers, which paralyzed the Ruhr's economy and precipitated the collapse of the German currency. The dispute was settled by reducing reparations, and the occupation ended in 1925.

Ruhr River \'rür\ River, W Germany. A tributary of the lower RHINE RIVER, it rises on the N side of Winterberg and flows 146 mi (235 km) west. The Ruhr valley is a major mining and manufacturing region; it includes the industrial cities of ESSEN, DÜSSELDORF, and DORTMUND. The Ruhr coalfield is one of the world's largest. Industries begun by the Krupp and Thyssen families flourished in the 19th–20th cent. (see THYSSEN-KRUPP STAHL). The river was militarily important in World War I, and its valley was occupied 1923–25 by France and Belgium (see RUHR OCCUPATION). As the industrial heart of Nazi Germany, it was severely bombed in World War II. It is now a center of steel production and chemical manufacturing.

Ruisdael \'rȯis-ˌdäl\, **Jacob (Isaakszoon) van** (1628/29–1682) Dutch landscape painter. He was enrolled in the Haarlem painters' guild in 1648 and settled in Amsterdam about 1656. He was a remarkably versatile artist, and some 700 paintings have been attributed to him. Whereas earlier Dutch artists used trees merely as decorative devices, Ruisdael made them the subject of his paintings and imbued them with forceful personalities through vigorous brushwork and strong colors, evident in his famous *Jewish Ceme-*

tery (c.1660), where three tombstones crumble to ruin amid an ever-renewing nature. His late works include numerous panoramas of the flat Dutch countryside, dominated by a vast, clouded sky.

rules of order See PARLIAMENTARY PROCEDURE

rum DISTILLED LIQUOR made from SUGARCANE products, primarily molasses. It is first mentioned in records from Barbados around 1650. Rum figured in the slave trade: slaves from Africa were traded in the W. Indies for molasses, the molasses was made into rum in New England, and the rum was then traded to Africa for more slaves. Two major types are marketed. The light-bodied rums, traditionally of Puerto Rico and Cuba, employ cultivated yeast and are blended and aged 1–4 years. The heavier dark rums, traditionally of Jamaica, use yeast spores from the air and are distilled in simple pot stills before being blended and aged 5–7 years. Rum is drunk straight or mixed, and is used in cooking.

Rumania See ROMANIA

Rumi \'rü-ˌmē\, **Jalal al-Din al-** *or* **Mawlana** (1207?–1273) Anatolian-Persian mystic and poet. He was a theologian and teacher when he met Shams al-Din, a holy man; their intimate relationship scandalized Rumi's followers, who had Shams murdered. *The Collected Poetry of Shams* contains Rumi's verses on his love for Shams. His didactic epic *Masnavi-ye Manavi* ("Spiritual Couplets") widely influenced Muslim mystical thought and literature. After his death, his disciples were organized as the Mawlawiyah order, or whirling DERVISHES. Rumi is regarded as the greatest Sufi mystic and poet in the Persian language. In English translation, his work has become widely popular.

ruminant \'rü-mə-nənt\ Any UNGULATE of the suborder Ruminantia or Tylopoda (order Artiodactyla), including ANTELOPE, CAMELS, CATTLE, DEER, GIRAFFES, GOATS, OKAPIS, PRONGHORN, and SHEEP. Most ruminants have a four-chambered stomach, two-toed feet, and small or absent upper incisors. Camels and CHEVROTAINS have three-chambered stomachs. Ruminants store masses of grass (grazers) or foliage (browsers) in the first stomach chamber, the rumen, where it softens. They later regurgitate the material, called cud, and chew it again to further break down the cellulose. The chewed cud goes directly to the other chambers, where various microorganisms help in its digestion.

Rundstedt \'rùnt-ˌshtet\, **(Karl Rudolf) Gerd von** (1875–1953) German general in World War II. Chief of staff of an army corps in World War I, he was active after the war in Germany's secret rearmament. Promoted to field marshal (1940), he commanded armies in the invasions of Poland, France, and the Soviet Union. As commander in chief on the Western Front (1942–45), he fortified France against the expected Allied invasion, and directed the Battle of the BULGE.

Runeberg \'rü-nə-ˌberʸ\, **Johan Ludvig** (1804–1877) Finnish poet who wrote in Swedish. His works, combining classicism with Romantic feeling and an understanding of peasant life and character, include the epic poems *The Moose Hunters* (1832) and *Hanna* (1836), which won him a place in Swedish letters; and *Kung Fjalar*, a cycle of romances derived from old legends. His patriotic poem "Our Country," from *Tales of Ensign Stål* (1848, 1860), became the Finnish national anthem. Runeberg is considered Finland's national poet.

runic writing *or* **futhark** \'fü-ˌthärk\ Writing system used by Germanic peoples of N Europe, Britain, Scandinavia, and Iceland from roughly the 3rd to the 16th or 17th cent. A.D. Three main varieties were used in different regions and time periods: Early, or Common Germanic (Teutonic); Anglo-Saxon, or Anglian; and Nordic, or Scandinavian. Of uncertain origins, it is clearly derived from one of the alphabets of the Mediterranean area. More than 4,000 runic inscriptions are extant.

Runyon, (Alfred) Damon (1884–1946) U.S. journalist and short-story writer. Born in Manhattan, Kan., he served in the Spanish–American War as a teenager. In 1911 he moved to New York, where he wrote sports journalism and later a syndicated column. He is best known for *Guys and Dolls* (1931), stories about a racy section of Broadway written in

the uniquely rendered slang that became his trademark, which became a famous musical by Frank LOESSER (1950).

Rupert, Prince (1619–1682) Royalist commander in the ENGLISH CIVIL WARS. Born in Germany, Rupert became a favorite of his uncle, CHARLES I, whom he joined in England in 1642. In the English Civil Wars, he was given command of the cavalry and became known for his daring tactics in winning early victories. He met defeat at the Battle of MARSTON MOOR but was appointed commander of the king's army. When he surrendered Bristol (1645), he was dismissed and then banished from England. With the RESTORATION (1660), he was given naval commands in the ANGLO–DUTCH WARS. He was a founder and first governor of the HUDSON'S BAY CO.

rural electrification Project of the U.S. government in the 1930s. As part of the NEW DEAL, the Rural Electrification Administration (REA) was established (1935) to bring electric power to farms, thereby raising the standard of rural living and slowing the migration of farm workers to cities. Through providing low-interest construction loans, the project eventually equipped over 98% of U.S. farms with electricity.

Rurik *or* **Rorik** (d.879?) Semilegendary founder of the Rurik dynasty of KIEVAN RUS. He was a Varangian prince, and according to one 12th-cent. Russian chronicle, the people of Novgorod invited him to take over their strife-ridden government (c.862). Other historians think that he conquered Novgorod or that he and his army were rebellious mercenaries. Igor (c.877–945), probably his son, is held to be the real founder of the Russian princely house, which ruled Russia until 1598.

Rus See KIEVAN RUS

rush Any of several flowering plants distinguished by cylindrical stalks or hollow, stemlike leaves. They are found in temperate regions, particularly in moist or shady locations. The rush family (Juncaceae) includes the genera *Juncus,* the common rushes, and *Luzula,* the wood rushes. Common rushes are used in basket weaving, while rush pith serves as wicks in open oil lamps and tallow candles (rushlights). Other rushes include the CATTAIL, HORSETAIL, flowering rush (*Butomus umbellatus,* family Butomaceae), and sweet flag (*Acorus calamus,* ARUM FAMILY).

Rush, Benjamin (1746–1813) U.S. physician and political leader. Born near Philadelphia, he was a dogmatic theorist who proposed that all diseases are fevers caused by overstimulation of blood vessels, with a simple remedy—bloodletting and purges. He advocated humane treatment for insane patients; his idea that insanity often had physical causes marked a significant advance. He wrote the first chemistry textbook and the first psychiatry treatise in the U.S. An early and active American patriot and a member of the Continental Congress, Rush signed the Declaration of Independence.

Rushdie \'rùsh-dē, *commonly* 'rəsh-dē\, **(Ahmed) Salman** (b.1947) Indian-British novelist. Educated in England, he won international recognition with *Midnight's Children* (1981), an allegorical novel about modern India; in 1993 it was named the finest novel in the history of the Booker Prize. *Shame* (1983) is a scathing portrait of politics and sexual morality in Pakistan. *The Satanic Verses* (1988), which includes among its bizarre happenings some episodes based on the life of MUHAMMAD, was denounced as blasphemous, and in 1989 Rushdie was condemned to death by Iran's Ruhollah KHOMEINI. He became the focus of enormous international attention and was compelled to remain in hiding for years. His later novels include *The Moor's Last Sigh* (1995) and *The Ground Beneath Her Feet* (1999).

Rushing, Jimmy (*orig.* James Andrew) (1903–1972) U.S. singer, one of the great voices of the BLUES during the swing era. Born in Oklahoma City, Rushing joined Count BASIE's first group in 1935 and remained with Basie until 1950, thereafter leading his own small groups or singing with other bands. Rushing's full tenor voice, although associated with Basie's blues-based repertoire, was also well suited to popular songs and ballads.

Rushmore, Mt. Peak and national memorial, BLACK HILLS, SW S. Dakota. Sculptures of the heads of presidents George WASHINGTON, Thomas JEFFERSON, Abraham LINCOLN, and

QR

Theodore ROOSEVELT are carved on the granite face of the mountain, which is 6,000 ft (1,829 m) high. The four heads, each about 60 ft (18 m) high, represent, respectively, the nation's founding, political philosophy, preservation, and expansion and conservation. Work on it was carried out 1927–41 under Gutzon BORGLUM.

Ruskin, John (1819–1900) English art critic. Born to wealth, he was such a facile writer that he became the preeminent art critic of 19th-cent. Britain. His multivolume *Modern Painters* (1843–60), planned as a defense of J. M. W. TURNER, expanded to become a general survey of art. In Turner he saw "truth to nature" in landscape painting, the same truth he would find in Gothic architecture. His voluminous writings include *The Seven Lamps of Architecture* (1849) and *The Stones of Venice* (1851–53). He was a defender of the PRE-RAPHAELITES. In 1869 he was elected Oxford's first Slade professor of fine art; he resigned in 1879 after J. M. WHISTLER won a libel suit against him. His opinions on art were considered all but infallible, but his idiosyncrasies made his personal life as wretched as he made the lives of the modern painters he denounced. His marriage was never consummated, and his wife obtained an annulment to marry J. E. MILLAIS. He suffered a series of episodes of acute mania from 1878 until his death.

Russell, Bertrand (Arthur William), 3rd Earl Russell (1872–1970) British logician and philosopher. Born into the British nobility, he studied at Cambridge Univ. and was a fellow there from 1895. In *The Principles of Mathematics* (1903) and (with Alfred North WHITEHEAD) *Principia Mathematica* (3 vols., 1910–13), the epochal work for which he is best known, he sought to demonstrate that the whole of mathematics derives from logic. In *The Theory and Practice of Bolshevism* (1919), he criticized early Soviet communism. In 1927 he and his wife founded a progressive school, and he wrote books on education.

Bertrand Russell, 1960

He analyzed language down to its minimum requirements in order to avoid unnecessarily postulating the existence of the objects denoted by descriptive phrases. This effort led to a theory of descriptions, a philosophy of logical atomism. In *An Inquiry into Meaning and Truth* (1940) and *Human Knowledge* (1948), he aimed at reducing to a minimum the pretensions of human knowledge. His books for a general public include *A History of Western Philosophy* (1945). After World War II he became a leader in the campaign for nuclear disarmament, and he vehemently opposed U.S. involvement in the Vietnam War. He received the Nobel Prize for Literature in 1950.

Russell, Bill (*orig.* William Felton) (b.1934) U.S. basketball player. Born in Monroe, La., the 6-ft 10-in. center led the Univ. of San Francisco to two NCAA championships (1955–56). Playing for the Boston Celtics (1956–69), Russell led his team to 11 NBA championships in 13 seasons—the last two as coach, having become in 1967 the first black coach of a major professional sports team. Russell's career mark for rebounds (21,620) is second only to that of Wilt CHAMBERLAIN. The Associated Press selected him as the outstanding professional basketball player of the 1960s. He later coached the Seattle SuperSonics (1973–77).

Russell, Charles T(aze) (1852–1916) U.S. religious leader. Born in Pittsburgh, he was raised in the Congregational church but was unable to reconcile God's mercy with the idea of hell. Influenced by the ADVENTISTS, he adopted a doctrine of MILLENNIALISM. He founded the International Bible Students Assn. in 1872 (renamed JEHOVAH'S WITNESSES in 1931) and taught that the final days would come in 1914, after which Christ's kingdom on earth would begin. In 1884 he founded the Watch Tower Bible and Tract Society, today one of the world's largest publishers. He won

many converts despite the apparent failure of his apocalyptic prediction.

Russell, John, Lord *later* **Earl Russell (of Kingston Russell)** (1792–1878) British prime minister (1846–52, 1865–66). A member of the prominent Russell family, he entered Parliament in 1813. He made reform a cause of the WHIG PARTY, leading the effort to pass the REFORM BILL OF 1832. As home secretary (1835), he reduced the number of capital crimes and began state support of education. In the 1840s he advocated free trade and forced Robert PEEL out of office. As prime minister he established the 10-hour day in factories (1847) and a board of public health (1848), but party disunity defeated his attempts at wider social and economic reform.

Russell, Lillian *orig.* Helen Louise Leonard (1861–1922) U.S. singer and actress. Born in Clinton, Iowa, she achieved stardom in *Grand Mogul* (1881), and later won acclaim in *La Grande-Duchesse de Gérolstein* (1890). Representing the feminine ideal of her generation, she was as famous for her flamboyant personal life as for her hourglass figure, her beauty, and her voice. After 1912 she wrote a syndicated column on health, beauty, and love and lectured before vaudeville audiences.

Russia *officially* **Russian Federation** Nation, E Europe and N Asia, former republic of the U.S.S.R. Area: 6,592,812 sq mi (17,075,383 sq km). Population (2000): 146,001,000. Capital: MOSCOW. Most of the people are Russian; minorities include Tatars and Ukrainians. Languages: Russian (official), various Turkic and Uralic languages. Religion: Russian Orthodox Christianity, Islam, but most of the people are nonreligious. Currency: ruble. The land and its environments are varied, including the URAL MTNS. and ranges in E SIBERIA, with the highest peaks in KAMCHATKA. The Russian plain contains the great VOLGA and Northern Dvina rivers, and in the Siberian plain are the valleys of the OB, YENISEY, LENA, and AMUR rivers. Tundra covers extensive portions in the north, and in the south there are forests, steppes, and fertile areas. The economy was industrialized from 1917 to 1945 but was in serious decline by the 1980s. In 1992 the government decreed radical reforms to convert the centrally planned economy into a market economy based on private enterprise. Russia is a republic with a bicameral legislative body; its head of state is the president,

Leaders of Muscovy, Russia, and the Russian Empire

Princes of Muscovy: Danilovich dynasty*		Czars and Empresses of Russia: Romanov dynasty**	
Daniel	c.1276–1303	Michael III	1613–45
Yury	1303–25	Alexis	1645–76
Ivan I	1325–40	Fyodor III	1676–82
Semyon (Simeon)	1340–53	Peter I (Ivan V	
Ivan II	1353–59	coruler 1682–96)	1682–1725
Dmitry Donskoy	1359–89	Catherine I	1725–27
Vasily I	1389–1425	Peter II	1727–30
Vasily II	1425–62	Anna	1730–40
Ivan III	1462–1505	Ivan VI	1740–41
Vasily III	1505–33	Elizabeth	1741–61 (O.S.)
Ivan IV	1533–47		
Czars of Russia: Danilovich dynasty		Peter III***	1761–62 (O.S.)
Ivan IV	1547–84	Catherine II	1762–96
Fyodor I	1584–98	Paul	1796–1801
Czars of Russia: Time of Troubles		Alexander I	1801–25
Boris Godunov	1598–1605	Nicholas I	1825–55
Fyodor II	1605	Alexander II	1855–81
False Dmitry	1605–6	Alexander III	1881–94
Vasily (IV)	1606–10	Nicholas II	1894–1917
Interregnum	1610–12		

*The Danilovich dynasty is a late branch of the Rurik dynasty, named after its progenitor, Daniel, son of Alexander Nevsky.

**In 1721 Peter I the Great took the title of "emperor" (Russian: *imperator*), considering it a larger, more European title than the Russian "czar." However, every male sovereign continued usually to be called czar (and his consort czarina, or czaritsa), though every female sovereign was conventionally called empress (*imperatritsa*).

***The direct line of the Romanov dynasty came to an end in 1761 with the death of Elizabeth, daughter of Peter I, but subsequent rulers of the "Holstein–Gottorp dynasty" (the first, Peter III, was son of Charles Frederick, duke of Holstein–Gottorp, and Anna, daughter of Peter I) took the family name of Romanov.

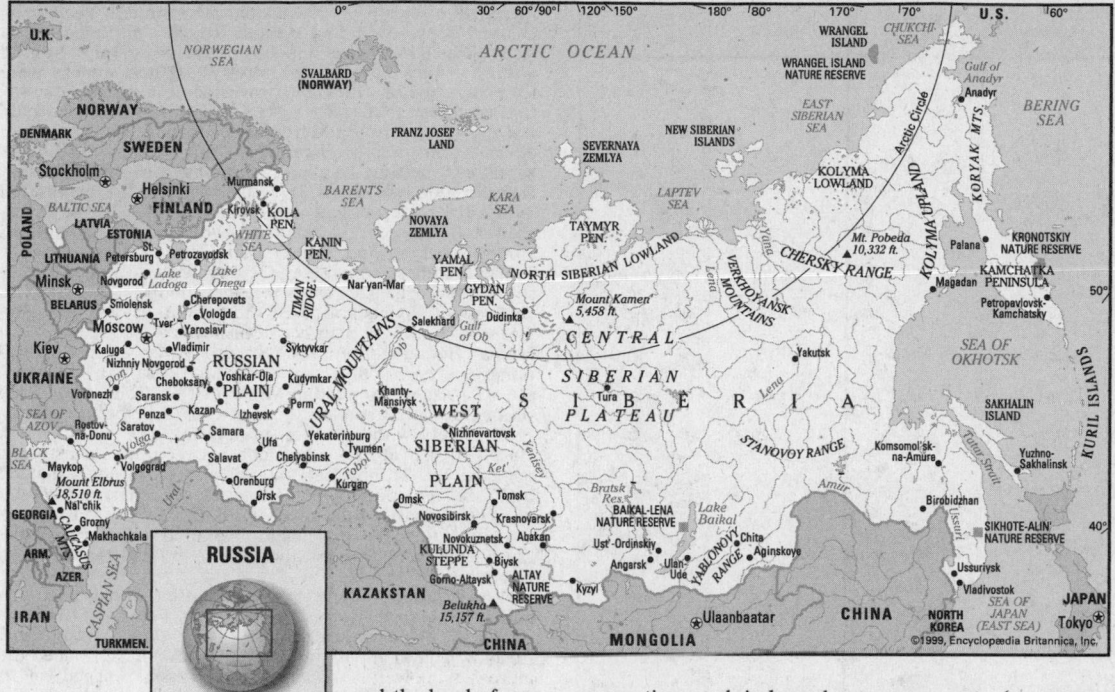

RUSSIA

Scale 1: 55,746,000

0   300   600 mi

0   400   800 km

©1999, Encyclopædia Britannica, Inc.

and the head of government is the prime minister. The region between the DNIESTER and the Volga rivers was inhabited from ancient times by various peoples, including the SLAVS. The area was overrun in the 8th cent. B.C.–6th cent. A.D. by successive nomadic peoples, including the Sythians, Sarmatians, Goths, Huns, and Avars. KIEVAN RUS, a confederation of principalities ruling from KIEV, emerged around the 10th cent. It lost supremacy in the 11th–12th cent. to independent principalities such as NOVGOROD and Vladimir. Novgorod ascended in the north and was the only Russian principality to escape the domination of the Mongol GOLDEN HORDE in the 13th cent. In the 14th–15th cent. the princes of MOSCOW gradually overthrew the Mongols. Under IVAN IV, Russia began to expand. The ROMANOV DYNASTY arose in 1613. Expansion continued under PETER I (the Great) and CATHERINE II (the Great). The area was invaded by NAPOLEON in 1812; after his defeat, Russia received most of the grand duchy of WARSAW (1815). Russia annexed Georgia, Armenia, and Caucasus territories in the 19th cent. The Russian southward advance against the OTTOMAN EMPIRE was of key importance to Europe (see CRIMEA). Russia was defeated in the CRIMEAN WAR. Chinese cession of the Amur River's left bank in 1858 marked Russia's expansion in the Far East. It sold Alaska to the U.S. in 1867 (see ALASKA PURCHASE). Its defeat in the RUSSO–JAPANESE WAR led to an unsuccessful uprising in 1905 (see RUSSIAN REVOLUTION OF 1905). In World War I it fought against the CENTRAL POWERS. The popular overthrow of the Czarist regime in 1917 marked the beginning of a government of soviets (see RUSSIAN REVOLUTION OF 1917). The BOLSHEVIKS brought the main part of the former empire under Communist control and organized it as the Russian Soviet Federated Socialist Republic (coextensive with present-day Russia). The Russian S.F.S.R. joined other soviet republics in 1922 to form the U.S.S.R. (see UNION OF SOVIET SOCIALIST REPUBLICS for history 1922–91). Upon the dissolution of the U.S.S.R. in 1991, the Russian S.F.S.R. was renamed and became the leading member of the COMMONWEALTH OF INDEPENDENT STATES. It adopted a new constitution in 1993. It has since struggled on several fronts, beset with economic difficulties, political

corruption, and independence movements (see CHECHNYA).

Russian Civil War (1918–20) Conflict between the newly formed BOLSHEVIK government and its RED ARMY against the anti-Bolshevik forces in Russia. The unfavorable treaty with Germany (1918) caused the anti-Lenin socialists to break with the Bolsheviks and join the right-wing Whites and their volunteer army under Anton DENIKIN. In an attempt to create another front in WORLD WAR I, the Allies gave limited support to the Whites. The Moscow government responded by expelling non-Bolshevik deputies from the government and giving increased powers to the secret police (Cheka) to arrest and execute anti-Bolshevik suspects. Anti-Bolsheviks gained power in the Ukraine and Omsk, where Aleksandr KOLCHAK and other dissident groups joined together to fight the Red Army. Confused by the struggles between communists, Russian Whites, and Ukrainian nationalists, the Allies withdrew their support by 1919. After early military successes, the White forces under Kolchak were defeated by early 1920. The last White stronghold in the Crimea under Pyotr WRANGEL was defeated in November 1920, ending the war.

Russian Formalism See FORMALISM

Russian language E. SLAVIC LANGUAGE spoken by about 170 million people in Russia, former republics of the Soviet Union, and emigré communities. For many non-Russian ethnic groups, it is a common second language and LINGUA FRANCA. Russian-speakers penetrated Siberia in the 16th cent. and reached the Pacific in the 17th cent. Russian became a full-fledged literary language in the 18th cent., when it finally displaced Church Slavic (see OLD CHURCH SLAVIC LANGUAGE). Russian is typical of most Slavic languages in having an elaborate case system and a distinction between perfective and imperfective verb forms, expressed by a combination of prefixes and suffixes. It employs the CYRILLIC ALPHABET. See diagram on next page.

Russian Orthodox Church Eastern Orthodox church of Russia, its de facto national church. In 988 Prince Vladimir of Kiev (later St. VLADIMIR) embraced Byzantine Orthodoxy and ordered the baptism of his population. By the 14th cent., the metropolitan of Kiev and all Russia (head of the Russian church) was residing in Moscow. Moscow came to see itself as the "third Rome" and the last bulwark of true Orthodoxy; in 1589 the head of the Russian church ob-

QR

Letters	English Spelling	Letters	English Spelling
А а	a	С с	s
Б б	b	Т т	t
В в	v	У у	u
Г г	g	Ф ф	f
Д д	d	Х х	kh
Е е	e	Ц ц	ts
Ж ж	zh	Ч ч	ch
З з	z	Ш ш	sh
И и Й й	i, y	Щ щ	shch
К к	k	Ъ ъ	"
Л л	l	Ы ы	y
М м	m	Ь ь	'
Н н	n	Э э	e
О о	o	Ю ю	yu
П п	p	Я я	ya
Р р	r		

Russian language The Russian Cyrillic alphabet, with English sound equivalents. Originally used for writing Old Church Slavic, the alphabet in its various modern forms is used in writing several Slavic languages as well as some non-Slavic languages of the former Soviet Union.

tained the title patriarch, putting him on a level with the patriarchs of Constantinople, Alexandria, Antioch, and Jerusalem. The reforms of NIKON caused a schism within the church, and PETER I abolished the patriarchate in 1721, making church administration a department of the state. The patriarchate was reestablished in 1917, two months before the Bolshevik revolution, but under the Soviets the church was deprived of its legal rights and practically suppressed. It saw a great resurgence following the collapse of the Soviet Union (1991). The Russian Orthodox Church in the U.S. became independent from Moscow in 1970.

Russian Revolution of 1905 Unsuccessful uprising in Russia against the czarist regime. After several years of mounting discontent, a peaceful demonstration was crushed in the Bloody Sunday massacre (Jan. 1905). General strikes followed in St. Petersburg and other industrial cities, and the revolt spread to Poland, Finland, and Georgia. By October general strikes had spread to all the large cities, and the workers' councils or SOVIETS, often led by the MENSHEVIKS, became revolutionary governments. The strikes' magnitude convinced NICHOLAS II, advised by Sergey WITTE, to issue the OCTOBER MANIFESTO, promising an elected legislature. The concessions satisfied most moderates, though the more ardent revolutionaries refused to yield, and pockets of resistance were harshly suppressed as the regime restored its authority. While most of the revolutionary leaders, including Leon TROTSKY, were arrested, the revolution forced the czar to institute a new constitution and a DUMA, though he failed to implement various promised reforms.

Russian Revolution of 1917 Revolution that overthrew the czar and placed the BOLSHEVIKS in power. Governmental corruption, the reactionary policies of NICHOLAS II, and Russian losses in WORLD WAR I contributed to widespread dissatisfaction and economic hardship. In February 1917, riots over food scarcity broke out in Petrograd (St. Petersburg). When the army joined the rebels, Nicholas was

forced to abdicate. A provisional government, headed by Georgy LVOV, tried to continue Russia's participation in World War I, but it was opposed by the powerful Petrograd SOVIET, which favored withdrawal. Other soviets were formed in major cities and towns, dominated by the SOCIALIST REVOLUTIONARY PARTY, the MENSHEVIKS, and the BOLSHEVIKS. Between March and October, the Provisional Government was reorganized four times; Aleksandr KERENSKY became its head in July, but was unable to halt Russia's slide into chaos. By September the Bolsheviks, led by Vladimir LENIN, had achieved majorities in the Petrograd and Moscow soviets and won increasing support among workers and soldiers. In October they staged a nearly bloodless coup (the "October Revolution"). Kerensky tried to organize resistance, then fled the country. The congress of soviets approved the formation of a new government composed mainly of Bolsheviks.

Russian Social-Democratic Workers' Party Marxist revolutionary party that preceded the COMMUNIST PARTY OF THE SOVIET UNION. Founded in Minsk in 1898, it held that Russia could achieve socialism only after developing a bourgeois society with an urban proletariat. The party split in 1903 because of the argument between the BOLSHEVIK wing, led by Vladimir LENIN, and the MENSHEVIK wing, led by L. MARTOV, over Lenin's proposals for a party composed of professional revolutionaries. In the RUSSIAN REVOLUTION OF 1917, the Bolsheviks broke completely with the Mensheviks and changed their name to "Russian Communist Party (Bolshevik)."

Russo–Japanese War (1904–5) Conflict between Russia and Japan over territorial expansion in E. Asia. After Russia leased the strategically important Port Arthur (now Lüshun, China) and expanded into Manchuria, it faced the increasing power of Japan. When Russia reneged on its agreement with Japan to withdraw troops from Manchuria, the Japanese fleet attacked the Russia naval squadron at Port Arthur and began a siege of the city in February 1904. Japanese land forces cut the Russian army off from coming to aid Port Arthur and pushed it back to Mukden (now Shenyang). In January 1905 the corrupt Russian commander surrendered the garrison at Port Arthur, despite adequate stores and ammunition for its continued defense. Heavy fighting around Mukden ended in March 1905 with the withdrawal of Russian troops. Russia abandoned its expansionist policy in E. Asia and Japan gained effective control of Korea and much of Manchuria.

Russo–Turkish Wars Series of 12 wars (1676–1878) fought between Russia and the OTTOMAN EMPIRE. Russia waged the early wars in an attempt to establish a port on the Black Sea. In the war of 1695–96, PETER I captured the fortress of Azov, but attempts to seize the Balkans failed. In CATHERINE II's reign, the first major Russo–Turkish war (1768–74) pushed Russian borders south. Catherine annexed the Crimean Peninsula (1783) and in 1792 Russia gained the entire W Ukrainian Black Sea coast. In the 19th cent. wars were fought over the Dardanelles and Bosporus straits, the Caucasus, and Crimea (see CRIMEAN WAR). The 1877–78 Russo–Turkish War pitted Russia and Serbia against Turkey over Bosnia and Herzegovina. Russia won, but Britain and Austria-Hungary limited its gains.

rutabaga \ˌrü-tə-ˈbā-gə\ Swedish TURNIP (*Brassica napus*) in the MUSTARD FAMILY. A hardy biennial, the rutabaga is a cool-season plant cultivated for its fleshy roots and tender leaves. Its white or yellow flesh is firmer and more nutritious than ordinary turnips and its roots keep much better during winter. Rutabagas are extensively cultivated as a vegetable and as a cattle fodder crop in Canada, Britain, and N Europe, and to a lesser extent in the U.S.

Rutgers, The State University of New Jersey State university system with its main campus at New Brunswick and smaller campuses at Newark and Camden. It was founded as Queens College in 1766 and renamed in 1825 for the philanthropist Henry Rutgers. It became a land-grant institution in 1864. At the New Brunswick campus are the original college and three other residential colleges, one (Douglass) enrolling only women, as well as several graduate and professional schools. The Newark and Camden campuses each have a college of arts and sciences, a graduate school, and schools of law, business management, and other professional subjects. Total enrollment is about 48,000.

Ruth, Babe (*orig.* George Herman) (1895–1948) U.S. baseball player, one of the greatest hitters and most popular figures in the sport's history. Born in Baltimore and raised in poverty, he joined the Boston Red Sox in 1914. He started as a pitcher, compiling an outstanding record (94 wins, 46 losses), but switched to the outfield because of his powerful hitting. Sold to the New York Yankees in 1920, he remained with the team until 1934. He coached the Brooklyn Dodgers in 1938, but his reputation for irresponsibility prevented his obtaining a permanent coaching or manager's job. In 1927 he set the most famous of all baseball records when he hit 60 home runs in a single season, a mark that stood until 1961. He hit at least 50 home

Babe Ruth

runs in four separate seasons and at least 40 in each of 11 seasons. His career slugging percentage (.690) remains an all-time record; he ranks second in runs (2,174) and runs batted in (2,213), and third in career home runs (714) and extra-base hits (1,356).

Ruthenian language See UKRAINIAN LANGUAGE

Rutherford, Ernest *later* Baron Rutherford (of Nelson) (1871–1937) New Zealand-British physicist. In 1895–97 he discovered two types of RADIOACTIVITY, ALPHA DECAY and BETA DECAY. He later identified the alpha particle as a helium NUCLEUS, and used it in his discovery of the atomic nucleus. With Frederick SODDY he formulated the transformation theory of radioactivity (1902). He served as chair of Cambridge Univ.'s Cavendish Laboratory from 1919. In 1919 he became the first person to artificially disintegrate an element, and in 1920 he hypothesized the existence of the NEUTRON. His work contributed greatly to understanding the disintegration and transmutation of radioactive elements and became fundamental to much of 20th-cent. physics. In 1908 he was awarded the Nobel Prize. He was ennobled in 1931. Element 104, rutherfordium, is named in his honor.

rutile \'rü-ˌtīl\ Commercially important TITANIUM mineral. It forms red to reddish brown, hard, brilliant metallic, slender crystals. Rutile has minor uses in porcelain and glass manufacture as a coloring agent. It is also used as a gem, but synthetic rutile is actually superior; it has fire (flashes of color) and brilliance (light deflection) like those of diamond. Rutile is mined in Norway and is widespread in the Alps, the S U.S., and Mexico.

Ruysdael, Jacob van See Jacob van RUISDAEL

Rwanda \rə-ˈwän-də\ *officially* **Republic of Rwanda** Nation, E central Africa. Area: 9,757 sq mi (25,271 sq km). Population (2000): 7,229,000. Capital: KIGALI. The population is mostly HUTU, with a TUTSI minority. Languages: Rwanda, French, English (all official). Religions: Roman Catholicism, Protestantism, Islam, indigenous beliefs. Currency: Rwanda franc. Rwanda is a mountainous, landlocked country. Most of it is at an elevation of more than 5,000 ft (1,500 m). There are bamboo forests, wooded regions, and grassy savannas with rich and varied wildlife. It is a developing country with a mainly free-enterprise economy based on agriculture. It is ruled by a transitional regime with one legislative body; its head of state and government is the president, assisted by the prime minister. Originally inhabited by the Twa, a PYGMY people, it then became home to the Hutu, who were well established there when the Tutsi appeared in the 14th cent. The Tutsi conquered the Hutu and in the 15th cent. founded a kingdom near Kigali. The kingdom expanded steadily, and by the early 20th cent. Rwanda was a unified state with a military structure. The Belgians

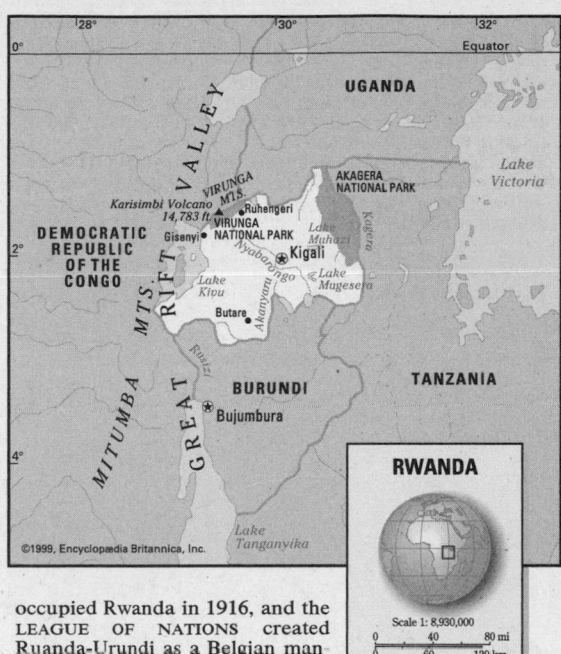

RWANDA

Scale 1: 8,930,000

©1999, Encyclopædia Britannica, Inc.

occupied Rwanda in 1916, and the LEAGUE OF NATIONS created Ruanda-Urundi as a Belgian mandate in 1923. The Tutsi retained their dominance until shortly before Rwanda reached independence in 1962, when the Hutu took control of the government and stripped the Tutsi of much of their land. Many Tutsis fled Rwanda, and the Hutu dominated the country's political system, waging sporadic civil wars until mid-1994, when the death of the country's leader in a plane crash led to massive violence. The Tutsi-led Rwandan Patriotic Front (RPF) took over the country by force after the massacre of almost 500,000 Tutsis by Hutus. Two million refugees, mostly Hutu, fled to neighboring Congo (Zaire) after the RPF's victory. Rwanda became deeply involved in the Congo militarily, and gradually forced the return of almost all its refugees.

Ryan, (Lynn) Nolan, Jr. (b.1947) U.S. baseball player. Born in Refugio, Texas, he played for the New York Mets (1968–71), California Angels (1972–79), Houston Astros (1980–88), and Texas Rangers (1989–93). In 1983 he became the first pitcher to surpass Walter JOHNSON's 1927 record of 3,508 career strikeouts, and he retired in 1993 at the advanced age of 46 with an astonishing 5,714. He also set a record for most no-hit games (7).

Ryder, Albert Pinkham (1847–1917) U.S. painter. Born in New Bedford, Mass., a fishing port, he never lost his obsession with the sea. He settled in New York about 1870. His highly personal seascapes, including *Toilers of the Sea,* reflect his feeling of human helplessness against the forces of nature. Thick yellow light (usually moonlight) heightens the mood of mystery in such paintings as *The Race Track* and *Death on a Pale Horse.*

Ryder Cup Biennial team golf event first held in 1927. It was originally played between teams of golfers from the U.S. and Britain; since 1979 players opposing the U.S. have been chosen from all of Europe. The trophy was donated by the British seed merchant Samuel Ryder.

rye CEREAL GRASS (*Secale cereale*) and its edible grain, used to make rye bread and rye whiskey, as livestock feed, and as a pasture plant. Native to SW Asia, today it is grown extensively in Europe, Asia, and N. America. Rye thrives where climate and soil are relatively unfavorable and at high altitudes and is the most winter-hardy of all small grains. It is high in carbohydrates and provides small quantities of protein, potassium, and B vitamins. Rye flour lacks the elasticity of wheat flour and thus is frequently blended with it for baking. The tough fibrous STRAW of rye is used for animal bedding, thatching, mattresses, hats, and paper.

Ryle, Gilbert (1900–1976) British philosopher. He taught at Oxford Univ. (1945–68), where he became a leading figure in the "Oxford philosophy," or "ordinary language," movement, which attempted to dissipate confusion arising from the misapplication of language. His classic *The Concept of Mind* (1949) challenged René DESCARTES's traditional distinction between body and mind. In *Dilemmas* (1954) he analyzed propositions that appear irreconcilable. His other books include *Philosophical Arguments* (1945), *A Rational Animal* (1962), *Plato's Progress* (1966), and *The Thinking of Thoughts* (1968).

Ryukyu Islands \rē-'yü-ˌkyü\ Island chain (pop., 1999 est.: 1,311,000), Japan. It extends in an arc 600 mi (970 km) long from S Japan to N Taiwan. The 55 islands and islets have a total land area of 870 sq mi (2,254 sq km). Chinese and Japanese sovereignty were successively imposed on the archipelago from the 14th to the 19th cent. In 1879 the Ryukyus became an integral part of Japan. After Japan's defeat in World War II, the U.S. took control of the islands; it returned them all by 1972 but maintains military bases on OKINAWA.

S

SA *in full* Sturmabteilung (German: "Assault Division") *known as* **Storm Troopers** *or* **Brownshirts** Nazi paramilitary organization that aided Adolf HITLER's rise to power. Founded in Munich in 1921, it drew its early membership from the nationalistic Freikorps. Outfitted in brown uniforms after the fashion of the Italian Fascist BLACKSHIRTS, the SA protected NAZI PARTY meetings and assaulted political opponents. Headed by Ernst RÖHM, by 1932 it had grown to a force of over 400,000. Röhm wanted to merge the regular army into the SA, but Hitler had become wary of its growing power. In 1934 he ordered a "blood purge" of the SA (see NIGHT OF THE LONG KNIVES). Thereafter it was reduced to a minor political role.

Saale River \'zä-lə, *Engl* 'sä-lə\ River, E central Germany. It flows north from Bavaria 265 mi (426 km) to join the ELBE RIVER just above Barby. As it crosses THURINGIA, it enters a deep valley dominated by castles.

Saarbrücken \zär-'brü̇-kən\ City (pop., 1996: 186,000), capital of SAARLAND state, SW Germany, on the SAAR RIVER. Chartered in 1321, it passed to Prussia in 1815, and became the capital of the Saar region in 1919. The present city was formed in 1909. In 1959 it was made capital of Saarland. Historic buildings include the 18th-cent. baroque Ludwigskirche, the Gothic abbey church of St. Arnual (c.1270–1330), and the Old Bridge over the Saar (1546).

Saarinen \'sär-ə-nən\, **Eero** (1910–1961) U.S. (Finnish-born) architect. His father, Eliel Saarinen (1873–1950), was the foremost Finnish architect of his time; his major works include the Helsinki railway station (1904–14). Eero joined his father's practice after studying at Yale. His vast General Motors Technical Center in Warren, Mich. (1948–56), was followed in 1948 by his design for St. Louis's Gateway Arch (completed 1965). Other works include the Kresge Auditorium and chapel at MIT (1955), and Morse and Stiles Colleges at Yale (1962). His TWA terminal at Kennedy International Airport (1956–62) employs two cantilevered concrete shells that extend dramatically outward, suggesting wings.

Eero Saarinen, on a chair he designed, photo by Arnold Newman, 1948

Saarland \'zär-ˌlänt, *Engl* 'sär-ˌland\ *or* **Saargebiet** \'zär-gə-ˌbēt\ State, SW Germany. It has an area of 992 sq mi (2,569 sq km). The capital, SAARBRÜCKEN, lies along the SAAR RIVER. The region was contested by France and Germany from the 17th cent. until 1815, when it was divided between Bavaria and Prussia. When ALSACE-LORRAINE was added to the German empire in 1871, the Saar developed rapidly as a coal-mining and industrial area, producing iron and steel. It was controlled by France 1919-35 before reverting to Germany. French forces occupied it after World War II, but it was eventually restored to Germany and became a state in 1957.

Saar River \'sär, 'zär\ *French* **Sarre** \'sär\ River, France and Germany. It flows 153 mi (246 km) across NE France and enters the MOSELLE RIVER above Trier, Germany. The N part of the valley is a wine-growing district; the middle area north of SAARBRÜCKEN is a center of heavy industry.

Saba Island (pop., 1998 est.: 1,500) of the NETHERLANDS ANTILLES in the Caribbean Sea. It lies 16 mi (26 km) northwest of St. Eustatius, with which it forms the Lesser ANTILLES. It has an area of 5 sq mi (13 sq km) and is the peak of an extinct volcano. It was settled by the Dutch in 1632, but its inaccessibility and ruggedness made it a buccaneers' stronghold. The economy depends on tourism.

Sabah dynasty Ruling family of Kuwait since 1756. In that year a group of families living in what is now Kuwait appointed a member of the Sabah family, Sabah bin Jaber (r.c.1752–64), to be their ruler. The present emir rules with the assistance of a prime minister, a council of ministers, and a national assembly, but the family may choose succeeding emirs from its own ranks.

Sabbath Day of the week set aside for worship and observance of religious duties in Judaism and Christianity. The Jewish Sabbath begins at sunset on Friday and lasts until sunset the next day, during which time no ordinary work or act of labor is performed. For most Christian denominations, the Sabbath is on Sunday; prescribed conduct varies considerably. In Islam, Friday is the day of worship.

saber-toothed tiger *or* **saber-toothed cat** Any of the extinct CAT species forming the subfamily Machairodontinae. They had two long, bladelike canine teeth in the upper jaw. They lived from 36.6 million years ago to about 10,000 years ago. The best-known, the short-limbed *Smilodon* of the Americas, was bigger than the modern lion. Its "sabers," which grew to 8 in. (20 cm) long, were used to stab and slash prey, including the MASTODON, whose pattern of extinction paralleled its own.

Sabin \'sā-bin\, **Albert B(ruce)** (1906–1993) U.S. (Polish-born) microbiologist. He grew polio virus in human nerve tissue outside the body, and proved that POLIOMYELITIS is primarily an infection of the digestive tract. He postulated that an oral VACCINE would work longer than Jonas SALK's injections of killed virus, and isolated weakened strains of each of the three types of polio virus that would stimulate antibody production but not produce disease. The Sabin oral polio vaccine, approved for use in the U.S. in 1960, became the main defense against polio throughout the world.

Sabine River \sə-'bēn\ River, E Texas and W Louisiana. Rising in NE Texas, it flows southeast and south to enter the Gulf of Mexico after 578 mi (930 km). The river, which includes Toledo Bend Reservoir, forms the S section of the Texas–Louisiana boundary and is a link in the GULF INTRACOASTAL WATERWAY.

Sabines \'sā-ˌbīnz\ Ancient Italic tribe located east of the Tiber River. According to legend, ROMULUS invited them to a festival and then carried off ("raped") their women to provide wives for his men. The second king of Rome, Numa Pompilius, probably a Sabine, supposedly created virtually all the Romans' religious institutions and practices. Later groups displaced the Sabines from Rome and the Romans conquered them in 290.

sable Arboreal CARNIVORE (*Martes zibellina*, family Mustelidae) that inhabits forests of N Asia and is highly valued for its dark fur. The name is sometimes applied to related European and Asian species and to the American MARTEN. The sable is 13–20 in. (32–51 cm) long, excluding the 5–7-in. (13–18-cm) tail, and weighs 2–4 lbs (0.9–1.8 kg).

Sac See SAUK

Sacagawea \ˌsa-kə-jə-ˈwē-ə\ (1786?–1812) SHOSHONE Indian woman who, carrying her infant son on her back, traveled thousands of wilderness miles with the LEWIS AND CLARK EXPEDITION (1804–6). Sacagawea was instrumental in obtaining horses and guides from a band of Shoshone at a point when the expedition might otherwise have ended. Her fortitude in the face of hazards and deprivations became legendary.

saccharin \ˈsa-kə-rən\ Synthetic organic compound that is 200–700 times as sweet as cane sugar. The sodium or calcium salt of saccharin is widely used as a diet sweetener. Its safety is controversial because it appears to be a weak CARCINOGEN. See also ASPARTAME.

Sacchi \ˈsäk-kē\, **Andrea** (1599–1661) Italian painter active in Rome. Employed with PIETRO DA CORTONA to decorate the Barberini Palace, he produced the ceiling fresco *Allegory of Divine Wisdom* (1629–31). His two altarpieces in the church of Santa Maria della Concezione (1631–38) are distinguished by their Classicism. Other notable works include eight canvases in the cupola of the Baptistery of St. John in Rome (1639–45). He was the leading exponent of the Classical tradition in 17th-cent. Roman painting.

Sacco-Vanzetti case Murder trial in Massachusetts (1920–27). After the murder of a paymaster and a guard at a shoe factory (1920), the immigrant anarchists Nicola Sacco (1891–1927), a shoemaker, and Bartolomeo Vanzetti (1888–1927), a fish peddler, were tried and found guilty. Radicals and socialists protested the men's innocence, and many others felt they had been convicted for their beliefs. In 1925 a convicted murderer confessed to participating in the crime, but attempts to obtain a retrial failed. Protest meetings were held throughout the U.S. An advisory panel agreed with the governor's refusal to grant clemency, and the men were executed. They became martyrs to radicals' belief that the legal system was biased. Though opinion remained divided on the men's guilt, most agreed that defects in the trial warranted a retrial.

Sachs, Nelly (Leonie) (1891–1970) German-Swedish poet and dramatist. Sachs wrote poems mainly for her own entertainment until the advent of Nazism forced her to flee to Sweden. Her lyrics from those years combine lean simplicity with imagery variously tender, searing, or mystical. In the famous title poem from *O the Chimneys* (1967), Israel's body drifts upward as smoke from the Nazi death camps. Her best-known play is *Eli* (1951). She shared the 1966 Nobel Prize with S. Y. AGNON.

Sachsen See SAXONY

Sackler, Arthur M(itchell) (1913–1987) U.S. physician, medical publisher, and art collector. Born in New York City, in 1949 he founded the Creedmore Institute of Psychobiological Studies in New York, and did pioneering research in the field of psychobiology. He founded the biweekly *Medical Tribune* newspaper, funded research at several universities, and endowed art galleries at universities and museums, donating art from his own vast collection, including the world's largest collection of ancient Chinese art, to the Metropolitan Museum of Art.

Sackville, Thomas *later* **Earl of Dorset** (1536–1608) English politician and poet. A member of the Privy Council (1585), he conveyed the death sentence to MARY, QUEEN OF SCOTS, in 1586. He later served as lord high treasurer 1599–1608 and presided at the trial of the 2nd Earl of ESSEX. He was coauthor of *The Tragedie of Gorboduc* (1561), the earliest English drama in blank verse.

Sackville-West, Vita (*orig.* Victoria Mary) (1892–1962) British writer. The daughter of a baron, she married the diplomat and author Harold Nicolson (1886–1968) in 1913; her journal was the basis of *Portrait of a Marriage* (1973) by their son Nigel, which described a happy marriage in which both partners were principally homosexual. Her best-known novels are *The Edwardians* (1930) and *All Passion Spent* (1931). She also wrote poetry (including *The Land*, 1926), biographies, and gardening books. She inspired the title character in Virginia WOOLF's novel *Orlando*.

sacrament Religious action or symbol in which spiritual power is believed to be transmitted through material elements or the performance of ritual. The concept is ancient; prehistoric people believed that they could advantageously influence events in the natural world through ritual. In modern religions, sacraments are primarily associated with CHRISTIANITY and are said to derive from practices instituted by JESUS. As codified by St. THOMAS AQUINAS and promulgated by the Council of TRENT, the sacraments of ROMAN CATHOLICISM are seven in number: BAPTISM, CONFIRMATION, the EUCHARIST, penance, anointing of the sick, ordination, and matrimony.

Sacramento City (pop., 2000: 407,000), capital of California. It is located in the CENTRAL VALLEY, where the SACRAMENTO and American rivers meet. First settled in 1839 as New Helvetia by John SUTTER, it became an important trading center during the GOLD RUSH. The present city was laid out in 1848 and named for the river. It became the state capital in 1854, terminus of the first California railroad in 1856, and the W terminus of the PONY EXPRESS in 1860. A ship canal completed in 1963 made the city a deepwater port. The city's industries include food processing, printing, and aerospace products.

Sacramento River River, N California. Rising near Mt. SHASTA, it flows 382 mi (615 km) southwest between the Cascade and Sierra Nevada ranges, through the N CENTRAL VALLEY to SAN FRANCISCO BAY. It was the scene of the GOLD RUSH of 1849. California's largest river, it accommodates oceangoing vessels as far as SACRAMENTO, and flows through one of the world's richest agricultural regions.

sacrifice Act of offering objects to a divinity, thereby making them holy. The intention is to perpetuate, intensify, or reestablish a connection between the human and the divine, particularly to gain the favor of the god or to placate divine wrath. The term often applies specifically to blood sacrifice, which entails the death or destruction of the thing sacrificed (see HUMAN SACRIFICE). The sacrifice of fruits, flowers, or crops is more often referred to as an offering.

sacrifice, human See HUMAN SACRIFICE

Sadat \sə-ˈdat\, **(Muhammad) Anwar al-** (1918–1981) President of Egypt (1970–81). He joined G. A. NASSER's conspiracy to depose the monarchy in 1950, and later served as vice president (1964–66, 1969–70). He became president when Nasser died in 1970. In 1973 he joined with Syria in a surprise attack on Israel, losing militarily but gaining politically. In 1979 he concluded a peace treaty with Menachem BEGIN. The two men shared the 1978 Nobel Peace Prize. Faced with a worsening domestic economy, Sadat suppressed public dissent. His assassination by a Muslim extremist elicited shock and grief worldwide. See also ARAB-ISRAELI WARS, CAMP DAVID ACCORDS, Hosni MUBARAK.

saddle Seat for a rider on the back of an animal, usually a horse. The leather saddle was developed after the 3rd cent. B.C., probably by peoples of the Asian steppes, where the stirrup and the horse collar also originated. It greatly improved a rider's ability to control a moving horse, especially in combat. Improvements made in medieval Europe were related to feudal battles among knights. Modern saddles include the light, flat English or Hungarian style used for sport and recreation, and the sturdy Western style used originally for cattle roping and now also for recreation.

Sadducee \ˈsa-jə-ˌsē\ Member of a Jewish priestly sect that flourished for about two centuries, until the destruction (A.D. 70) of the Second Temple of JERUSALEM. Sadducees were generally wealthier and more conservative than their rivals, the PHARISEES. They believed in strict interpretation of the TORAH and thus rejected such ideas as immortality of the soul and bodily resurrection after death. They probably played some part in JESUS' death. Their wealth and complicity with Roman rulers made them unpopular with the common people.

Sade \ˈsåd\, **Marquis de** *orig.* Donatien-Alphonse-François, comte (count) de Sade (1740–1814) French novelist and philosopher. After abandoning a military career, he became involved in a life of debauchery and outrageous scandal with prostitutes and with local young people he abducted, for which he was repeatedly imprisoned, once narrowly escaping execution. Despite his noble birth, he supported the French Revolution, which he saw as representing political and sexual liberation. He was twice sent to the insane asylum at Charenton (1789–90, 1801–14), where he would eventually die. He overcame boredom and anger in prison and the asylum by writing sexually graphic plays and novels, including *The 120 Days of Sodom* (written 1785) and *Justine* (1791). His other works include *Philosophy in the Bedroom* (1793).

sadhu and swami In India, a religious ascetic or holy person. Sadhus are typically wandering ascetics who subsist on alms. They may follow the tenets of a belief system such as HINDUISM or JAINISM, but are more typically regarded as saintly in their own right. The term swami refers to a sadhu ordained in a specific order and is associated particularly with VEDANTA. Sadhus and swamis typically possess little, eschew conventional dress, and have shaven heads or matted, unkempt hair.

Sadhu

sadism \'sā-ˌdi-zəm, 'sa-ˌdi-zəm\ Psychosexual disorder in which sexual urges are gratified by inflicting pain on another person. The term is derived from the name of the Marquis de SADE. The level and extent of sadistic violence may vary from mild pain to extreme brutality, sometimes leading to serious injury or death. Sadism is often linked to MASOCHISM, and many individuals who have one tendency also have the other, though some sadists seek out nonmasochists and derive excitement from their unwillingness.

Safaqis See SFAX

Safavid dynasty \sä-'fä-vəd\ (1502–1736) Persian dynasty. It was founded by ISMAIL I, who converted his people from Sunni to Shiite Islam. He captured Tabriz and became shah of Azerbaijan (1501) and Persia (1502). ABBAS I (r.1588–1629) brought the dynasty to its peak; his capital, ESFAHAN, was the center of Safavid architectural achievement. The dynasty declined in the century following his reign and eventually fell to the tyrant Nadir Shah (1688–1747).

Safdie \'saf-dē\, **Moshe** (b.1938) Israeli-Canadian architect. He began his career in the offices of Louis KAHN. His Habitat '67, a prefabricated concrete complex of modular apartment units stacked irregularly along a zigzagged framework evocative of an Italian hill town or a PUEBLO, aroused intense international interest but failed to catch on as a low-cost housing option. Later works include Yeshivat Porat Joseph Rabbinical College in Jerusalem (1971–79) and Coldspring New Town near Baltimore (1971).

safe sex Practices that reduce the risk of contracting SEXUALLY TRANSMITTED DISEASES, especially AIDS, during SEXUAL INTERCOURSE and similar activities. The term usually refers to use of condoms, which greatly reduce the chance of infection but are not 100% effective. Abstinence and staying monogamous with an uninfected and monogamous partner are completely safe.

safflower Flowering annual plant *(Carthamus tinctorius)* of the COMPOSITE FAMILY. Native to parts of Asia and Africa, it is now widely grown as an oil crop. Oil obtained from the seeds is valued for its high proportion of polyunsaturated fats. Since the oil does not yellow with age, it is also a useful base for varnish and paint. The plant, which grows 1–4 ft (0.3–1.2 m) high, has flowers that were formerly a source of textile dyes.

saffron Golden-colored seasoning and dye obtained from the dried stigmas of flowers of the saffron CROCUS *(Crocus sativus)*. Because 1 lb (0.45 kg) of saffron represents 75,000 blossoms, it is the world's most expensive spice. The color and flavor are essential ingredients for certain Mediterranean and Asian dishes, and saffron is the official color for the robes of Buddhist priests. Greeks and Romans scattered saffron as a perfume in halls, courts, theaters, and baths.

saga Genre of prose narrative typically dealing with prominent figures and events of the heroic age in Norway and Iceland, especially as recorded in Icelandic manuscripts of the late 12th and 13th cent. Once thought to be orally transmitted history that had finally been written down, sagas are now usually regarded as reconstructions of the past, imaginative in varying degrees and created according to aesthetic principles. Important ideals in sagas are heroism and loyalty; revenge often plays a part. Action is preferred to reflection, and description of the inner motives and point of view of protagonists is minimized. See also GRETTIS SAGA, ICELANDERS' SAGAS, NJÁLS SAGA.

Sagan \'sā-gən\, **Carl (Edward)** (1934–1996) U.S. astronomer and science writer. Born in Brooklyn, N.Y., he worked on planetary astronomy and on the SETI project at the Smithsonian Astrophysical Observatory (1962–68). Known for his clear writing and enthusiasm as a popular science writer and commentator, he won a Pulitzer Prize for *Dragons of Eden* (1977). The companion book to his television series *Cosmos* (1980) became the all-time best-selling science book in English. In the 1980s he warned of "nuclear winter" as an environmental effect of nuclear war.

sage Aromatic perennial herb *(Salvia officinalis)* of the MINT family, native to the Mediterranean. Its leaves are used fresh or dried as a flavoring in many foods, and are also brewed as a tea. The stems have rough or wrinkled, downy, gray-green or whitish-green oval leaves. The flowers may be purple, pink, white, or red.

Sage, Russell (1816–1906) U.S. financier. Born in Shenandoah, N.Y., he worked as an errand boy before starting a wholesale grocery business (1839), then a Hudson River shipping trade. He served in Congress 1853–57. A brilliant investor, he eventually acquired an interest in more than 40 railroads, serving as director or president of 20. He helped organize the Atlantic & Pacific Telegraph Co. In 1872 he originated stock-market puts and calls (options to buy or sell a set amount of stock at a set price and within a given time limit). His wife, Margaret Olivia Sage (1828–1918), established the Russell Sage Foundation and Russell Sage College (Troy, N.Y.) after his death.

sagebrush Any of various shrubby species of the genus *Artemisia* of the COMPOSITE FAMILY. Native to semiarid plains and mountain slopes in W N. America, these shrubs are adapted both to dry, hot summers and to moist, mild winters. Common sagebrush *(A. tridentata)* is a many-branched shrub, usually about 3–6.5 ft (1–2 m) high, with silvery gray, bitter-aromatic foliage.

Sagittarius A Strongest source of cosmic RADIO WAVES, lying in the direction of the constellation Sagittarius, discovered by Karl JANSKY in 1931. The nucleus of the MILKY WAY GALAXY, it is relatively small and an intense source of INFRARED RADIATION. Observations indicate it is an ACTIVE GALACTIC NUCLEUS containing a BLACK HOLE with a mass 10,000–1 million times the sun's and properties like those of other active galactic nuclei but on a much smaller scale.

sago \'sā-gō\ Food STARCH derived from several sago PALMS, chiefly *Metroxylon rumphii* and *M. sagu*, native to Indonesia. Sago is a basic food of the SW Pacific, where it is used in meal form to prepare soups, cakes, and puddings. Elsewhere it is used as a pudding and sauce thickener and as a textile stiffener. The thick trunk grows to 30 ft (9 m) tall in low marshy areas. At 15 years the core of the mature trunk is engorged with starchy material. Cultivated plants are cut down when the flower spike appears, and the starchy pith is extracted from the stems.

saguaro \sə-'wär-ə, sə-'gwär-ō\ Large, candelabra-shaped, branched CACTUS *(Cereus giganteus*, or *Carnegiea gigantea)* native to SW N. America. Mature saguaros may reach 50 ft (15 m) in height. They bloom for the first time when 50–75 years old. They may die at 150–200 years (at a weight of up to 10 tons, or 9,000 kg), most commonly by being uprooted by wind or washouts. The white, night-blooming flowers, which remain open into the next day, are the Arizona state flower. The red fruits have been an important food of American Indians.

Saguenay River \ˌsa-gə-'nā\ River, S central Quebec. It drains Lac St.-Jean into the ST. LAWRENCE RIVER northeast of QUEBEC city. Flowing east, it descends about 300 ft (90 m) in the first third of its 105-mi (169-km) course, providing hydroelectric power. Its fjordlike shores include cliffs 1,000–1,800 ft (300–550m) high. It is a scenic recreational area.

Sahara Largest tropical desert in the world, encompassing almost all of N Africa. Covering about 3,500,000 sq mi (9,065,000 sq km), it is bounded by the ATLANTIC OCEAN, the ATLAS MTNS., the MEDITERRANEAN SEA, the RED SEA, and the SAHEL. It includes portions of Morocco, Algeria, Tunisia, Libya, Egypt, Mauritania, Mali, Niger, Chad, and Sudan. Features include large oasis depressions, extensive stony plains, rock-strewn plateaus, abrupt mountains, sand sheets and dunes, and sand seas. Scattered clusters of inhabitants survive in fragile ecological balance wherever vegetation or water sources occur. See also LIBYAN DESERT.

Sahel \sä-'hel\ Semiarid region, W and N central Africa. Extending from Senegal eastward to the Sudan, it forms a transitional zone between the arid SAHARA to the north and the humid savannas to the south. From the late 20th cent. it has been afflicted by desertification and soil erosion due to overgrazing and overfarming. It suffered a devastating drought and famine in the early 1970s, and by 1973 sections of the Sahara had advanced southward as much as 60 mi (100 km). Severe drought and famine struck again in 1983–85, and the desert continued to expand southward.

Said \sä-'ēd\, **Edward W(illiam)** (b.1935) Egyptian-U.S. literary critic. Born to an affluent Christian family, he attended school in the U.S. In *Orientalism* (1978), perhaps his best-known work, he examines Western stereotypes of the Islamic world and argues that Orientalist scholarship is based on Western imperialism. An outspoken proponent of Palestinian issues, he has written on the Middle East in such works as *The Question of Palestine* (1979) and *The Politics of Dispossession* (1994). He treats the complex interaction of literature and politics in such works as *Culture and Imperialism* (1993).

Said ibn Sultan \sä-'ēd-,ib-ən-sùl-'tän\ *or* **Said Sayyid** \sä-'ēd-'sī-əd\ (1791–1856) Ruler of Muscat and Oman and of ZANZIBAR (1806–56), who made Zanzibar the principal power in E Africa and the commercial capital of the W Indian Ocean. Under Said, Zanzibar caravans were sent into central Africa to extract ivory and slaves. In 1822 he forbade his subjects to sell slaves to European traders. From 1828 he developed Zanzibar and Pemba into the world's largest clove producers, and he built up a large navy to extend his commercial interests.

Saigon See HO CHI MINH CITY

sailfish Valued food and game fish in the genus *Istiophorus* (family Istiophoridae). It has a long, rounded spear extending from its snout but is distinguished from MARLINS and related species especially by its large, sail-like dorsal fin, which is bright blue and spotted. Deep blue above and silvery below, sailfish grow to about 11 ft (3.4 m) long and 200 lbs (90 kg) or more. Some scientists recognize more than a single species (*I. platypterus*).

sailing *or* **yachting** Sport or pastime of racing or cruising a sailboat or yacht. A modern yacht is a sailboat used for racing. In the 17th cent. Dutch royalty sailed early yachts for pleasure; CHARLES II brought the sport to England. Organized yacht racing on the Thames began in the mid-18th cent.; in N. America yachting began with the Dutch in New York in the 17th cent. Sailboat races are held over two kinds of courses, point-to-point and closed. Yacht racing has been part of the OLYMPIC GAMES since 1900. The AMERICA'S CUP is the preeminent prize in yachting. See diagram, right.

sailplane See GLIDER

saint Holy person. St. PAUL used the term to mean a member of the Christian community, but more commonly it refers to those noted for their holiness and venerated during their lifetimes or after death. In Roman Catholicism and Eastern Orthodoxy, saints are publicly recognized by the church and are considered intercessors with God for the living. Often Christian saints perform miracles in their lifetime, or miracles occur in their names after their death. In Islam, *wali* ("friend of God") is often translated as saint; in Buddhism, ARHATS and BODHISATTVAS are roughly equivalent to saints. See also CANONIZATION.

Saint Andrews City (pop., 1995 est.: 15,000) and seaport, E Scotland. It was formerly the ecclesiastical capital of Scotland; in the 6th cent. A.D., St. Kenneth is believed to have formed a Celtic religious community there. It was one of the principal towns in Scotland in the Middle Ages. In 1472 its archbishop was recognized as the primate of Scotland. A popular seaside resort, it is noted for its golf courses and for the Univ. of ST. ANDREWS.

Saint Andrews, University of Oldest university in Scotland, founded in 1411 on the outskirts of St. Andrews. Its buildings include St. Salvator's College (1450), St. Leonard's College (1512; merged with St. Salvator's in 1747), and the Univ. Library (1612). A third college, St. Mary's (1537), has always taught theology exclusively. Total enrollment is about 5,000.

Saint Augustine \'ò-gə-,stēn\ City (pop., 2000: 12,000), NE Florida. It is the oldest continuously settled U.S. city. In 1513 Juan PONCE DE LEÓN landed there and claimed the territory for Spain. It became part of the U.S. in 1821. The Castillo de San Marcos, now a national monument, is a symbol of the era of Spanish control. During the AMERICAN REVOLUTION the city was a refuge for LOYALISTS. A winter and summer resort, it is a port on the ATLANTIC INTRACOASTAL WATERWAY.

Saint Bartholomew's Day, Massacre of (Aug. 24–25, 1572) Murder of French HUGUENOTS in Paris by Catholics. As part of the ongoing Wars of RELIGION, CATHERINE DE MÉDICIS agreed to a plot to assassinate the Huguenot Gaspar de COLIGNY. When he was only wounded, Catherine

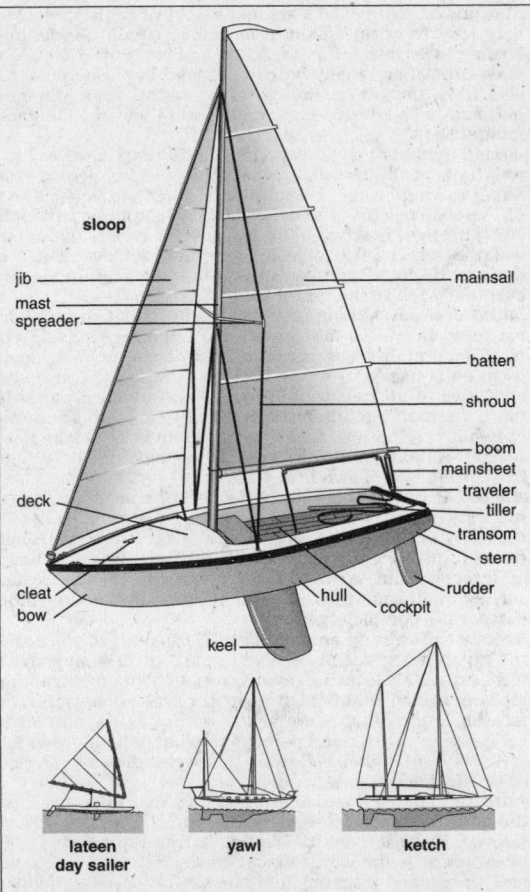

sloop

jib — mast — spreader

deck

cleat — bow

keel

mainsail

batten

shroud

boom — mainsheet — traveler — tiller — transom — stern — rudder

hull — cockpit

lateen day sailer   yawl   ketch

Sailing Principal parts of a simple sailboat. The weight of the keel helps the boat remain upright; the rudder provides steering control. The principal sail is called the mainsail; the jib is a smaller headsail. The shrouds are ropes that provide lateral support to the mast.

feared discovery of her complicity and secretly urged faithful nobles to murder all the Huguenot leaders, who were in Paris for the wedding of the future HENRY IV. The massacre began on August 24; after the leaders had been murdered, Huguenot homes and shops were pillaged and their occupants murdered and thrown into the Seine. Even after the royal order on August 25 to stop the killing, it spread widely. By October, about 3,000 Huguenots had been murdered in Paris and probably tens of thousands more in the provinces.

Saint Basil the Blessed *or* **Pokrovsky Cathedral** \pǝ-'króf-skē\ Church constructed at the S end of Red Square in Moscow (1554–60) by IVAN IV as a votive offering for his victories over the Tatars. Built of brick and stone, it is a unique and magnificent architectural fantasy exhibiting Byzantine influences. Eight chapels topped by onion domes, each one distinctively painted, surround a central church with a tower topped by a tent-shaped roof and a small golden cupola.

Saint Basil the Blessed

Saint Bernard Breed of rescue dog that saved about 2,500 people over 300 years of service at a hospice in Great St. Bernard pass in the Pennine Alps. Probably descended from mastiff-like dogs, it was brought to the hospice in the late 17th cent. A powerful dog with a massive head and drooping ears, it stands at least 25 in. (65 cm) and weighs 110–200 lbs (50–90 kg). The long-haired variety was produced by crosses with the Newfoundland.

Saint Christopher and Nevis See SAINT KITTS-NEVIS

Saint Clair, Lake Lake, forming part of the boundary between Michigan and Ontario. Roughly circular, with an area of 467 sq mi (1,210 sq km), it connects by river with Lake HURON to the north and Lake ERIE to the south. It is in a popular summer recreation area. Suburbs of DETROIT lie on its W shore.

Saint Croix \'krói\ Largest island (pop., 1995 est.: 51,000) of the U.S. VIRGIN ISLANDS, with an area of 84 sq mi (218 sq km). Its capital is Christiansted; Frederiksted is the commercial center. In 1493 it was visited by Christopher COLUMBUS. It was colonized in turn by the Dutch, English, Spanish, and French, purchased by Denmark in 1733, and sold to the U.S. in 1917. In 1989 it was devastated by a hurricane. Tourism is the main industry; rum is distilled and exported.

Saint-Denis \ˌseⁿ-dǝ-'nē\ City (pop., 1999: 86,000), N France, now a suburb of PARIS. King DAGOBERT I founded its famous abbey church in the 7th cent. and built it over the tomb of St. DENIS, patron saint of France. Abbot SUGER built a new basilica which later transformed Western architecture from the ROMANESQUE to the GOTHIC: most late-12th-cent. French cathedrals, including CHARTRES, are based on that of St.-Denis. It was historically the burial place of French monarchs, including LOUIS XII, HENRY II, and CATHERINE DE MÉDICIS.

Saint-Denis \ˌsaⁿ-dǝ-'nē\ City (pop., 1999: 131,000), capital of the French overseas department of RÉUNION. It lies on the N coast, wedged between the ocean and a mountain rising abruptly behind it. An artificial harbor at Le Port replaced it as the main port in the 1880s.

Saint Denis \ˌsānt-'den-ǝs\, **Ruth** *orig.* Ruth Dennis (1877–1968) U.S. modern-dance innovator. Born in Newark, N.J., she was a vaudeville performer before developing her dramatic dance act based on Asian dance forms. She toured in Europe (1906–9) to wide acclaim, returning to tour in the U.S. In 1915 she and her husband, Ted SHAWN, established the Denishawn dance company and school to develop a new choreographic style of abstract "music visualization." She toured with the company until it disbanded in 1931 when

she and Shawn separated. She continued to perform, teach, and lecture into the 1960s.

Sainte-Beuve \saⁿt-'bœv\, **Charles-Augustin** (1804–1869) French literary historian and critic. He wrote essays in which he developed a new approach to critiquing living writers that involved extensive biographical research to understand their mental attitudes. His famous *Causeries du lundi* ("Monday Chats"), published in newspapers 1849–69, were detailed, well-rounded literary studies in which he applied historical frames of reference to contemporary writing. His methods revolutionized French criticism by freeing it from personal prejudice and partisan passions. His *Port-Royal* (1840–48) is a scholarly history of an abbey and of 17th-cent. France.

Saint Elias Mountains \ǝ-'lī-ǝs\ Segment of the Pacific COAST RANGES, SW Yukon Territory and E Alaska. The mountains extend southeast about 250 mi (400 km) along the Canada–U.S. border. Many peaks exceed 17,000 ft (5,200 km), including Mt. LOGAN. In 1741 Vitus BERING sighted Mt. St. Elias (18,008 ft, or 5,489 km) and became the European discoverer of NW America. The mountains contain the world's most extensive ice fields outside the polar ice caps. Part of the range is in GLACIER BAY NATIONAL PARK.

Saint Elmo's fire Glow accompanying the brushlike discharges of atmospheric electricity that usually appears as a crackling tip of light on such pointed objects as church towers or the masts of ships during stormy weather. It is also commonly observed on the prominent points of aircraft flying near thunderstorms. St. Elmo is an Italian corruption of St. Erasmus, patron saint of sailors, who traditionally regarded St. Elmo's fire as a sign of his guardianship over them.

Saint-Exupéry \saⁿ-tãg-zǖe-pā-'rē\, **Antoine (-Marie-Roger) de** (1900–1944) French aviator and writer. He flew as a commercial, test, and military reconnaissance pilot; he died when he was shot down on a wartime Air Force mission over the Mediterranean. His writings exalt perilous adventure and aviation, as in the classic novel *Night Flight* (1931). *Wind, Sand, and Stars* (1939) is a lyrical memoir; *The Little Prince* (1943) is a child's fable for adults.

Saint-Gaudens \sānt-'gó-dⁿnz\, **Augustus** (1848–1907) U.S. (Irish-born) sculptor. He was brought to the U.S. in infancy and at 13 was apprenticed to a cameo cutter. He studied sculpture in New York and Paris, then settled in New York in 1872. Between 1880 and 1897 he executed most of the works that earned him his reputation as the foremost American sculptor of the late 19th cent. His first important commission was the monument to David FARRAGUT (1878–81) in New York. For Boston he produced his great relief monument to Col. Robert G. Shaw and his black Civil War regiment (1884–97). The memorial to the wife of Henry ADAMS (1886–91) in Washington, D.C., a mysterious draped figure with a shadowed face, is often considered his greatest work.

Saint George's Town (pop., 1991 est.: 5,000), capital of Grenada, in the W. INDIES. Founded by the French in 1650, it became the capital of the WINDWARD ISLANDS (1885–1958). It exports cacao, nutmeg, mace, and bananas. It saw fighting during the 1983 military intervention in Grenada by U.S. and Caribbean forces.

Saint Gotthard Pass \'gä-tǝrd\ Mountain pass, Lepontine Alps, S Switzerland. An auto and railway route between central Europe and Italy, it lies at an elevation of 6,916 ft (2,108 m) and is 16 mi (26 km) long. A long, winding auto route leads across the pass, and the St. Gotthard Tunnel extends for more than 9 mi (14 km) beneath it. The railway through the tunnel connects LUCERNE with MILAN.

Saint Helena \'he-lǝ-nǝ, hǝ-'lē-nǝ\ Island (pop., 2000: 7,200), S Atlantic Ocean. Located 1,200 mi (1,950 km) west of Africa, it has an area of 47 sq mi (122 sq km). The capital and port is Jamestown. With Ascension Island and Tristan da Cunha Islands, it constitutes a British crown colony. Discovered in 1502, it became a port of call for ships sailing between Europe and the E. Indies. Because of its remoteness, it was used as the final place of exile for NAPOLEON (1815–21). It declined in importance after the SUEZ CANAL was opened in 1869.

Saint Helens, Mt. Volcanic peak in the CASCADE RANGE, SW Washington. Dormant since 1857, it erupted in 1980 in one of the greatest volcanic explosions ever recorded in N. America. The earthquake, eruption, and avalanche killed 60 people and thousands of animals, and 10 million trees were blown down by the lateral air blast. The peak, over 9,600 ft (2,925 m) high, was reduced to 8,366 ft (2,550 m). Mt. St. Helens National Volcanic Monument was established in 1982.

Saint John City (pop., 1991: 75,000), S New Brunswick. It is situated on the Bay of FUNDY. The site, visited by Samuel de CHAMPLAIN in 1604, was occupied by the British in 1758. It was chartered as the first city in Canada in 1785. The city recovered from a disastrous fire in 1877. Its year-round ice-free harbor fostered shipping, shipbuilding, and fishing. It is the province's largest city and principal port.

Saint John, Henry See Viscount BOLINGBROKE

Saint-John Perse \san-dzhón-'pers\ orig. Marie-René-Auguste-Aléxis Saint-Léger Léger (1887–1975) French poet. He served in various diplomatic posts from 1914 until his dismissal by the collaborationist Vichy government in 1940. He spent the years 1940–57 in exile in the U.S. His difficult poetry, admired by poets for its precision and purity, made little appeal to the general public. His works include *Anabasis* (1924; translated by T. S. ELIOT), *Winds* (1946), and *Birds* (1962). He was awarded the Nobel Prize in 1960.

Saint John's City (pop., 1991 est.: 22,000), capital of Antigua and Barbuda, W. Indies. It lies on Antigua's NW coast. It is a resort and the island's main port, handling sugar, cotton, machinery, and lumber.

Saint John's City (pop., 2000: 99,000), port, and capital of Newfoundland, on the SE Atlantic coast. Colonized by the British in 1583, and attacked several times by the French, it was securely British from 1762 and prospered as a fishing port, despite several disastrous fires in the 19th cent. It is a major ocean port and the base for the province's fishing fleet. The annual regatta is one of the oldest sports events in N. America. Signal Hill Historic Park memorializes Guglielmo MARCONI's reception of the first transatlantic wireless message from Europe (1901).

Saint-John's-wort Common name for plants in the family Hypericaceae, which contains 350 species of herbs or low shrubs in eight genera. Most species (about 300) belong to the genus *Hypericum*. Several species are cultivated in temperate regions for their handsome flowers. *H. perforatum*, a showy golden flower grown in both the Old and New Worlds whose buds contain a red oil, has long been credited with magical and medicinal powers; today it is widely used for its possible efficacy against depression.

Saint-Just \san-'zhᵫst\, **Louis (-Antoine-Léon) de** (1767–1794) French Revolutionary leader. In support of the French Revolution, he wrote the radical treatise *Esprit de la révolution* (1791). A close associate of Maximilien ROBESPIERRE and a member of the COMMITTEE OF PUBLIC SAFETY, he was elected president of the National Convention in 1793 and sponsored decrees that confiscated property of the Revolution's enemies and redistributed it to the poor. A fanatical leader of the REIGN OF TERROR, he was arrested in the THERMIDORIAN REACTION and guillotined at 26.

Saint Kitts-Nevis *officially* **Federation of Saint Kitts and Nevis** *or* **Saint Christopher and Nevis** Independent nation of the LEEWARD ISLANDS in the E Caribbean. Area: 104 sq mi (269 sq km). Population (2000): 39,000. Capital: BASSETERRE (on St. Kitts). Most of the population is of African descent. Language: English (official). Religion: Protestantism. Currency: Eastern Caribbean dollar. The islands—Saint Kitts, Nevis, and Sombrero—are of volcanic origin, with mountain ranges rising to 3,793 ft (1,156 m). The climate is tropical, and heavy vegetation covers most of the mountainous interior. The economy is based on agriculture. Sugar has long been the mainstay, and tourism is also important. It is a constitutional monarchy with one legislative house; its chief of state is the British monarch represented by the governor-general, and the head of government is the prime minister. St. Kitts became the first British colony in the W. Indies in 1623. Anglo–French rivalry grew in the 17th cent. and lasted more than a century. In 1783, by

SAINT KITTS-NEVIS

Scale 1: 610,000

©1999, Encyclopædia Britannica, Inc.

the Treaty of Versailles, the islands became wholly British possessions. They were united with Anguilla 1882–1980 but became an independent federation within the British Commonwealth in 1983. In 1997 Nevis considered becoming independent.

Saint Laurent \'san-ló-'rän\, **Louis (Stephen)** (1882–1973) Prime minister of Canada (1948–57). Born in Compton, Quebec, he served in the House of Commons 1942–58 and in W. L. M. KING's cabinet. As leader of the Liberal Party (1948), he succeeded King as prime minister. He promoted Canadian unity by equalizing provincial revenues and expanded social security and university education. He supported Canadian membership in NATO and helped establish the St. Lawrence Seaway.

Saint Laurent \san-ló-'rän\, **Yves (-Henri-Donat-Mathieu)** (b.1936) Algerian-French fashion designer. He left Algeria for Paris to pursue a fashion career and at 17 was hired as Christian DIOR's assistant. When Dior died four years later, he was named head of the House of Dior. In 1962 he opened his own fashion house and quickly emerged as one of the world's most influential designers, noted especially for his popularization of women's trousers for all occasions and his extensive ready-to-wear line.

Saint Lawrence, Gulf of Deep gulf of the Atlantic Ocean, off E Canada. It has an area of about 60,000 sq mi (155,000 sq km). It is enclosed by Nova Scotia, Newfoundland, New Brunswick, and Quebec; its outlets are the ST. LAWRENCE RIVER, the Strait of Belle Isle between Newfoundland and the mainland, and Cabot Strait. It has many islands, including PRINCE EDWARD ISLAND and the MAGDALEN ISLANDS.

Saint Lawrence River River, S Quebec and SE Ontario. It flows northeast out of Lake ONTARIO into the Gulf of ST. LAWRENCE and is about 760 mi (1,225 km) long. It passes through the THOUSAND ISLANDS and for about 120 mi (195 km) forms the boundary between New York and Ontario. MONTREAL lies on the river; below QUEBEC city it widens to 90 mi (145 km). Major tributaries include the Ottawa, SAGUENAY, Richelieu, and Manicouagan rivers, all in Canada. It links the Atlantic Ocean with the GREAT LAKES through the ST. LAWRENCE SEAWAY.

Saint Lawrence Seaway U.S.–Canadian waterway and lock system linking the Atlantic Ocean with the GREAT LAKES. Its construction (1954–59) involved clearing a 186-mi (299-km) stretch of the ST. LAWRENCE RIVER between MONTREAL and Lake ONTARIO. It includes 2,340 mi (3,766 km) of lakes, rivers, locks, and canals that connect Duluth, Minn., with the Gulf of ST. LAWRENCE. With the Great

Lakes, it provides 9,500 mi (15,300 km) of navigable water-ways, allowing deep-draft ocean vessels access to the Great Lakes' rich industrial and agricultural regions.

Saint Louis City (pop., 2000: 348,000), E central Missouri. Located on the MISSISSIPPI RIVER, below its confluence with the MISSOURI RIVER, it was founded in 1764 as a trad-ing post (see Auguste CHOUTEAU) and became the cross-roads of westward expansion for exploring parties, fur-trad-ing expeditions, and pioneers traveling the SANTA FE and OREGON trails. Since the 19th-cent. steamboat era and the arrival of the railroads in the 1850s, it has been a major transportation hub. The largest city in the state, it is home to WASHINGTON UNIV. and St. Louis Univ. Its Gateway Arch was designed by Eero SAARINEN.

Saint Lucia \'lü-shə\ Island nation, WINDWARD ISLANDS, E Caribbean Sea. Area: 238 sq mi (616 sq km). Population (2000): 157,000. Capital: CASTRIES. Most of the population

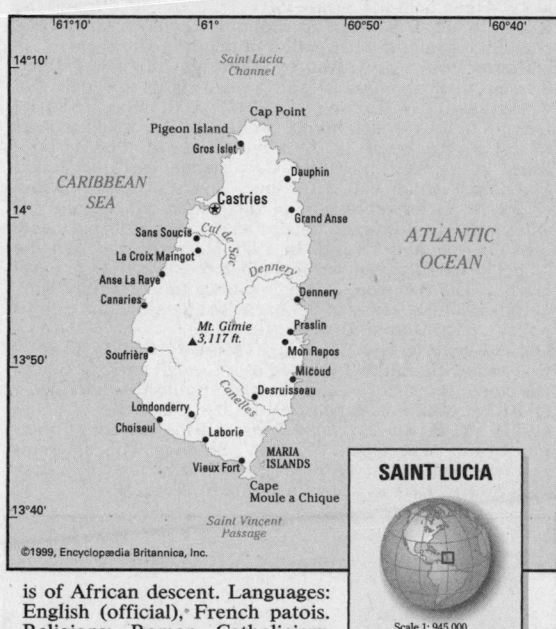

Saint Lucia Channel

Cap Point

Pigeon Island
Gros Islet
Dauphin

CARIBBEAN SEA

Castries

Grand Anse

Sans Soucis
La Croix Maingot
Anse La Raye
Canaries

Dennery

Mt. Gimie
▲3,117 ft.
Praslin
Mon Repos
Micoud

Soufrière
Desruisseau

Londonderry
Choiseul
Laborie

Vieux Fort
MARIA ISLANDS

Cape Moule a Chique

Saint Vincent Passage

ATLANTIC OCEAN

©1999, Encyclopædia Britannica, Inc.

SAINT LUCIA

Scale 1: 945,000

0   4   8 mi
0   6   12 km

is of African descent. Languages: English (official), French patois. Religions: Roman Catholicism, Protestantism. Currency: Eastern Caribbean dollar. St. Lucia is of volcanic origin, and its Qualibou volcano, which continues to emit steam and gases, is a prime tourist sight. Wooded mountains run north–south, culminating in Mt. Gimie (3,117 ft, or 950 m). It is a consti-tutional monarchy with a parliament of two legislative houses; its chief of state is the British monarch represented by the governor-general, and the head of government is the prime minister. CARIBS replaced early ARAWAK inhabitants around A.D. 800–1300. Settled by the French in 1650, it was ceded to Great Britain in 1814 and became one of the Wind-ward Islands in 1871. It became fully independent in 1979. The economy is based on agriculture and tourism.

Saint Mark's Basilica or **San Marco Basilica** Church in Venice built to house the remains of St. Mark. The first BASILICA, begun in 829, was burned during a revolt in 976; the present structure, one of the most beautiful buildings in Europe, was completed in 1071. The plan is an Eastern sym-metrical Greek cross (see CHURCH) surmounted by five domes. The design is distinctly Byzantine. The interior is decorated with mosaics on gold background; the floor is of inlaid marble and glass. In the restricted light their colors glow fantastically.

Saint Martin or Dutch **Sint Maarten** Island, LEEWARD IS-LANDS, E W. Indies. Northwest of ST. KITTS-NEVIS, it covers an area of 33 sq mi (85 sq km). Discovered by Christopher COLUMBUS, it was divided in 1648 between the French and the Dutch. The N section of the island (20 sq mi or 52 sq

km) is a dependency of the French overseas department of GUADELOUPE. The island's S section (13 sq mi or 34 sq km) is administratively part of the NETHERLANDS ANTILLES. The island's economy is based on tourism.

Saint Paul City (pop., 2000: 287,000), capital of Minnesota. It is in the E part of the state, on the MISSISSIPPI RIVER just east of MINNEAPOLIS, with which it forms the Twin Cities. In 1805 Zebulon Pike made an unofficial treaty there with the Dakota (Sioux) for possession of the region. First settled in 1838, it became the capital of the Minnesota Territory in 1849 and of the state in 1858. Its location on the Mississippi and its rail links helped develop the upper Midwest and pro-moted its livestock market. It is a major transportation, commercial, and industrial center. Educational institutions include Macalaster and Concordia colleges.

Saint Paul's Cathedral Cathedral of the Church of England in London. The present building is a domed church of great openness designed in a restrained but superbly detailed classical baroque style by Christopher WREN and con-structed (1675–1710) of Portland stone. It replaced Old St. Paul's, destroyed in the Great Fire of 1666. The interior is characterized by ironwork and woodcarving by master craftsworkers. The majestic dome, set on a colonnaded drum, rises 365 ft (111 m).

Saint Peter's Basilica Present church of St. Peter's in Rome, begun by Pope JULIUS II in 1506 and completed in 1615. It is the church of the popes and the world's largest cathedral. It replaced Old St. Peter's, erected by Constantine over Pe-ter's traditional burial place. In the original plan of Donato BRAMANTE, it took the form of a Greek cross around a cen-tral dome; Antonio DA SANGALLO THE YOUNGER adapted Bramante's symmetrical plan. MICHELANGELO nearly com-pleted the drum for the massive dome before his death. Pope Paul V (r.1605–21) then insisted on a longitudinal plan for liturgical reasons, and adopted the plan of Carlo Maderno (1556–1629), which extended the nave. Gian Lorenzo BERNINI added the vast elliptical piazza, lined by colonnades. The interior contains such masterpieces as Michelangelo's Pietà and Bernini's baldachin and bronze Throne of St. Peter.

Saint Petersburg City (pop., 2000: 248,000), W central Florida. It is near the tip of Pinellas Peninsula, adjacent to TAMPA BAY. Settled in 1876, it became in the late 1940s one of the first Florida cities to encourage tourists to spend their retirement years there. It is a winter resort and a cen-ter for yachting and sport fishing. It is connected by bridges to TAMPA.

Saint Petersburg Russian **Sankt-Peterburg** \'sȧnkt-ˌpʸə-tʸər-ˈbu̇rk\ formerly (1914–24) **Petrograd** or (1924–91) **Lenin-grad** City (pop., 1997 est.: 4,216,000) and port, NW Russia. It is Russia's second-largest city after MOSCOW. Founded by PETER I (Peter the Great) in 1703, it was the capital of the Russian empire 1712–1917. It was the scene of the DECEM-BRIST REVOLT in 1825 and the BLOODY SUNDAY attack on workers in the RUSSIAN REVOLUTION OF 1905, and the original center of the BOLSHEVIK revolution (see RUSSIAN REVOLUTION OF 1917). In World War II it underwent a seige by German forces (Sept. 1941–Jan. 1944), during which as many as one million people died (see Siege of LENINGRAD). From 1990 it helped swing the country from Communist control. It is a cultural, educational, and indus-trial center and Russia's largest seaport. One of Europe's most beautiful cities, it is intersected by many canals, crossed by more than 600 bridges; it is the site of many palaces, cathedrals, and museums (see HERMITAGE).

Saint-Pierre and Miquelon \ˌsänt-ˈpir...ˈmi-kə-ˌlän French seⁿ-ˈpyer-ā-mē-ˈklȯⁿ\ French overseas territorial collectivity (pop., 1993 est.: 6,000). It consists of two islands south of Newfoundland. Miquelon has an area of 83 sq mi (215 sq km). St.-Pierre, with an area of 10 sq mi (26 sq km), is the administrative and commercial center. First settled by sea-farers from W France early in the 17th cent., the islands changed hands several times between France and Britain until an 1814 treaty made French possession final. The economy is based on cod fishing.

Saint-Saëns \saⁿ-ˈsäⁿs\, (Charles) Camille (1835–1921) French composer. Astonishingly gifted from childhood, with a phenomenal musical memory, he became a darling

S

of the salons and a celebrated improviser. To promote new French music, he founded the Société Nationale de Musique in 1871. His compositions, often brilliant in their effects, include the opera *Samson et Dalila* (1877), five piano concertos, three symphonies, two cello concertos, three violin concertos, the tone poem *Danse macabre* (1874), and the suite *Carnival of the Animals* (1886).

Saintsbury, George (Edward Bateman) (1845–1933) English literary historian and critic. He produced several successful volumes of criticism of French literature and extensive writings on English literature. His works were influential because they combined authoritative scholarship with the popular appeal of entertaining prose. They include *A History of Criticism and Literary Taste in Europe from the Earliest Texts to the Present Day* (1900–4), one of the first surveys of critical literary theory and practice.

Saint-Simon \saⁿ-sē-ˈmōⁿ\, **(Claude-) Henri (de Rouvroy, comte) de** (1760–1825) French social theorist. Having made a fortune in land speculation but gradually dissipated it, he turned to the study of science and technology as the solution to society's problems, and wrote *On the Reorganization of European Society* (1814) and (with Auguste COMTE) *Industry* (1816–18), in which he envisioned an industrialized state directed by modern science. In *The New Christianity* (1825), he stated that religion should guide society toward improving life for the poor. His disciples helped influence the rise of Christian Socialism.

Saint Thomas Chief island (pop., 2000: 51,000), U.S. VIRGIN ISLANDS. Located east of Puerto Rico, it covers 32 sq mi (83 sq km). Its capital is CHARLOTTE AMALIE. Sighted in 1493 by Christopher COLUMBUS, St. Thomas was colonized first by the Dutch (1657), then the Danish (1666). It became one of the chief Caribbean sugar producers and a major slaving center. Sugar prices fell after 1820, and slavery was abolished in 1848. The U.S. bought St. Thomas in 1917 as a naval base. The chief industry is tourism.

Saint Vincent, Cape Cape, southwesternmost point of Portugal. To the Greeks and Romans it was known as Promontorium Sacrum (Sacred Point) because of a shrine site. Pastoralism and fishing are the economic mainstays of the region. About 1420 Prince HENRY THE NAVIGATOR established a naval observatory and school for navigators here. Many naval battles have taken place off the cape.

Saint Vincent and the Grenadines \ˈgre-nə-ˌdēnz\ Island nation, WINDWARD ISLANDS in the E Caribbean. It includes St. Vincent island and the N GRENADINES. Area: 150 sq mi (388 sq km). Pop. (2000): 113,000. Capital: KINGSTOWN. Most of the population is of African descent. Languages: English (official), French patois. Religion: Protestantism. Currency: Eastern Caribbean dollar. The islands are composed of volcanic rock. Thickly wooded volcanic mountains run north-south and are cut by many swift streams. Mt. Soufrière (4,048 ft, or 1,234 m), the highest of the mountains, has had devastating volcanic eruptions. Agriculture is the mainstay of the economy, and export crops include bananas and arrowroot. Tourism is also important. It is a constitutional monarchy with one legislative house; its chief of state is the British monarch represented by the governor-general, and the head of government is the prime minister. The French and the British contested for control of St. Vincent until 1763, when it was ceded to England by the Treaty of PARIS. The original inhabitants, the CARIBS, recognized British sovereignty but revolted in 1795. Most of the Caribs were deported; many who remained were killed in volcanic eruptions in 1812 and 1902. In 1969 St. Vincent became a self-governing state in association with the United Kingdom, and in 1979 it achieved full independence. See map, right.

Saipan \sī-ˈpan, sī-ˈpän\ Island (pop., 2000: 62,000), NORTHERN MARIANA ISLANDS, in the W Pacific Ocean. It has an area of 47 sq mi (122 sq km). Ruled by Spain 1565–1899, it then passed to Germany 1899–1914. A Japanese mandate from 1920, it was captured in 1944 after fierce fighting by U.S. forces in World War II; some 30,000 Japanese soldiers died, and thousands of civilians leapt to their deaths from cliffs instead of surrendering. It was the headquarters of the U.S.-administered U.N. Trust Territory of the PACIFIC ISLANDS (terminated 1990). Copra is the island's chief product.

Saivism See SHAIVISM

sake \ˈsä-kē\ Japanese ALCOHOLIC BEVERAGE made from fermented RICE. It dates to at least the 3rd cent. A.D. Sake is light in color, with a sweet flavor; its alcohol content is about 18% by volume. Often mistakenly called a wine, sake is closer in its method of manufacture to BEER. Steamed rice is combined with a mold that converts the rice STARCH to fermentable sugars; the mix is kneaded into a paste, twice fermented (with fresh rice and water added), filtered, and bottled. In Japan it is the national beverage and the traditional drink of the SHINTO gods.

Sakha See YAKUT

Sakhalin \ˌsä-kä-ˈlēn\ Island, extreme E Russia. With the KURIL ISLANDS, it forms an administrative region (pop., 1996 est.: 648,000) of Russia. It covers an area of 28,597 sq mi (74,066 sq km). Sakhalin was first settled by Russians in 1853; in 1875 Japan ceded it in exchange for the Kuril Islands. Japan held the S part 1905–45, then ceded it and the Kurils to the U.S.S.R. The economy includes lumbering, coal mining, and the extraction of oil and natural gas.

Sakharov \ˈsä-kə-ˌrȯf\, **Andrey (Dmitriyevich)** (1921–1989) Russian nuclear physicist and human-rights advocate. He worked with I. Y. Tamm (1895–1971) to develop the Soviet Union's first hydrogen bomb, but in 1961 he opposed plans to test a large bomb in the atmosphere. In 1968 he published in the West "Progress, Coexistence, and Intellectual Freedom," which called for nuclear-arms reduction and criticized Soviet repression of dissidents, and he and his wife, Yelena G. Bonner, thereafter continued to advocate civil liberties and reform. In 1975 Sakharov received the Nobel Peace Price but was forbidden to travel to Oslo to receive it. The two were exiled to Gorky (now Nizhniy Novgorod) 1980–86. Many of Sakharov's causes became official policy under Mikhail GORBACHEV.

Saki \ˈsä-kē\ *orig.* H(ector) H(ugh) Munro (1870–1916) Scottish writer. He initially worked as a foreign correspondent. His comic short stories and sketches, published in *Reginald* (1904), *Reginald in Russia* (1910), *The Chronicles of Clovis* (1911), and *Beasts and Super-Beasts* (1914), include "Tobermory" and "The Open Window." Studded with epigrams and with well-contrived plots, they satirize the Edwardian social scene. He was killed in action in World War I.

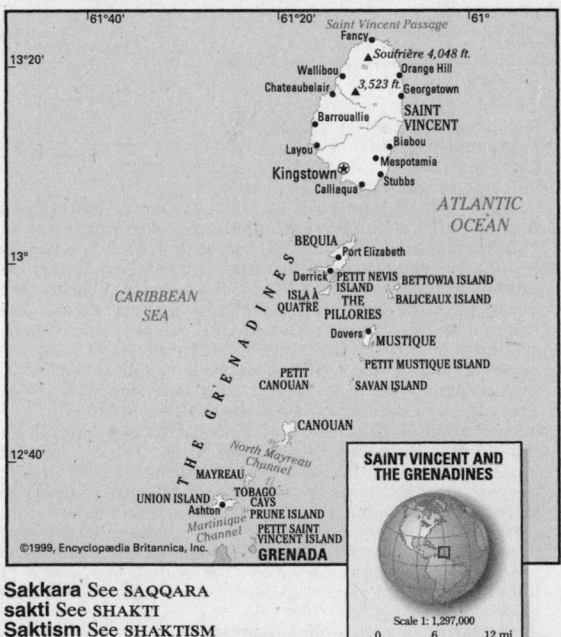

©1999, Encyclopædia Britannica, Inc.

SAINT VINCENT AND THE GRENADINES

Scale 1: 1,297,000

0   6   12 mi
0   6   12   18 km

Sakkara See SAQQARA
sakti See SHAKTI
Saktism See SHAKTISM
Saladin \ˈsa-lə-dⁿn\ *in full* Salah al-Din Yusuf ibn Ayyub (1137/8–1193) Kurdish sultan of Egypt, Syria, Yemen, and Palestine and founder of the Ayyubid dynasty (1173–1250). He began

his military career under his uncle. On his uncle's death Saladin ordered Shawar, vizier of the FATIMID DYNASTY, assassinated, and became vizier of Egypt. In 1171 he abolished the Shiite Fatimid caliphate and announced a return to Sunni Islam. From 1174, as sultan, he succeeded in uniting Egypt, Syria, N Mesopotamia, and Palestine. His excellent leadership rekindled Muslim resistance to the crusaders. In 1187 he retook Jerusalem from the crusaders after 88 years. The Christian conquest had been marked by slaughter, but Saladin's troops demonstrated courteous and civilized behavior. His victory deeply shocked the West and led to the call for the Third CRUSADE (1189–92), led by RICHARD I; their stalemate resulted in a peace treaty favorable to Saladin. He is considered one of the greatest of Muslim heroes.

Salamanca *ancient* Salmantica *or* Helmantica. City (pop., 1998 est.: 158,000), W Spain. Sacked by HANNIBAL in 217 B.C., it later became a Roman station. Captured by Moors in the 8th cent., it was reconquered by Christians 1087–1102. It was occupied by the French in the PENINSULAR WAR. It is a cultural as well as commercial center, and the site of a 12th-cent. Romanesque cathedral and a Gothic-style cathedral (begun 1513). The Univ. of Salamanca (founded 1218) is one of the oldest in the world.

salamander Any member of about 400 species in 10 AMPHIBIAN families (order Caudata), commonly found in freshwater and damp woodlands of the Northern Hemisphere. Salamanders are generally nocturnal, 4–6 in. (10–15 cm) long, and brightly colored. They have a tail, two pairs of limbs, and teeth on the jaws and roof of the mouth. The largest species, the Chinese giant salamander (*Andrias davidianus*), is 5 ft (1.5 m) long. Salamanders eat insects, worms, snails, and other small animals, including members of their own species. See also NEWT.

Salamis \'sa-lə-məs\ Ancient city, Cyprus. Located on Cyprus's E coast, it had an active trade with PHOENICIA, Egypt, and CILICIA. A major Hellenic center during the struggles between Greece and Persia, it was the scene of a Greek naval victory in 449 B.C., and again in 306 B.C. when Demetrius I Poliorcetes defeated PTOLEMY I SOTER of Egypt. Under the Byzantine empire it was known as Constantia after Constantius II rebuilt it A.D. 337–61. It was destroyed by the Arabs in 647–48.

Salamis, Battle of (480 B.C.) Battle in the PERSIAN WARS, the first great naval battle ever recorded. The Greeks, with about 370 TRIREMES led by THEMISTOCLES, lured the Persian fleet of about 800 GALLEYS into the narrow strait between the island of Salamis and the Athenian port of Piraeus, where they sank about 300 vessels while losing only about 40 of their own. The setback to XERXES gave the Greek city-states time to unite against him.

Salazar \ˌsa-lə-'zär\, **António** **(de Oliveira)** (1889–1970) Portuguese prime minister (1932–68). Appointed by António CARMONA as prime minister (1932), he established the authoritarian New State, curtailing political freedom and concentrating on economic recovery, and ruled as a virtual dictator. Sympathetic to Francisco FRANCO and the Axis Powers, he maintained Portugal's neutrality in World War II. He greatly improved the country's transportation, utilities, and education systems. He fought to preserve Portugal's African colonies after the general decolonization.

Salé \sa-'lā\ *Arabic* **Sla** \'slä\ City (metro. area pop. with RABAT, 1994: 1,386,000), NW Morocco. Located at the mouth of the Bou Regreg River, opposite Rabat, it was founded in the 10th cent. and reached its peak as a medieval merchant port. After 1627 Salé, with Rabat as its vassal, became the corsair republic of Bou Regreg and the base for the Sallee Corsairs, the most dreaded of the BARBARY COAST pirates. It has many mosques and mausoleums; its greatest shrine is the tomb of Sidi Abd Allah ibn Hasan, the city's patron saint.

Salem City (pop., 2000: 137,000), capital of Oregon. It lies along the WILLAMETTE RIVER, southwest of PORTLAND. Founded in 1840, the town prospered as migration increased over the OREGON TRAIL. It became the state capital in 1859. It was an early river port whose growth was stimulated by rail connections in the 1870s. It is a food-processing center for a dairy and fruit-growing area.

Salem witch trials (May–Oct. 1692) American colonial persecutions for witchcraft. In the town of Salem, Massachusetts Bay Colony, several young girls, stimulated by supernatural tales told by a W. Indian slave, claimed to be possessed by the devil and accused three women of witchcraft. Under pressure, the accused women named others in false confessions. Trials before a special three-judge court resulted in the conviction and hanging of 19 "witches" and the imprisonment of nearly 150 others. As public zeal abated, the trials were stopped and then condemned.

Salerno City (pop., 1998 est.: 143,000), S Italy. Founded by the Romans in 197 B.C., it was the capital of an independent Lombard principality from 839 to about 1076. Conquered by the Norman ROBERT GUISCARD, it became his capital. In World War II, its coast was the scene of a major battle (Sept. 1943) between Allied landing forces and the Germans. It is an active seaport in an industrial area; its landmarks include the oldest medical school in Europe (probably founded in the 9th cent.) and a cathedral (845, rebuilt 1076–85) with the tombs of St. MATTHEW and Pope GREGORY VII.

sales tax Levy imposed on the sale of goods and services. A sales tax on the manufacture, purchase, sale, or consumption of a specific commodity is known as an excise tax. Though excise taxes have been used since ancient times, the general sales tax is a comparatively recent innovation. Sales taxes are ad valorem taxes, imposed "according to the value" (i.e., monetary value) of the taxable commodity. They are classified according to the levels of business activity at which they are imposed—production, wholesale, or retail. In Western Europe a variation of the sales tax, the VALUE-ADDED TAX, is widely used. Most sales taxes are ultimately borne by the consumer. Because sales taxes at the retail level are REGRESSIVE TAXES, essential goods such as food, clothing, or drugs are sometimes exempted. See also INCOME TAX.

salicylic acid White, crystalline solid ORGANIC COMPOUND used chiefly to make ASPIRIN and other pharmaceutical products, including methyl salicylate (oil of WINTERGREEN), phenyl salicylate (for sunburn creams and pill coatings), and salicylanilide (a cutaneous FUNGICIDE. It occurs in species of *Spirea* and *Salix* (WILLOW).

Salieri \säl-'yer-ē\, **Antonio** (1750–1825) Italian composer. He moved to Vienna in 1766, becoming composer and conductor of the Italian opera at the imperial court (1774) and later court kapellmeister (1788). Vienna's most popular opera composer for many years, he had such important students as Ludwig van BEETHOVEN, Franz SCHUBERT, and Franz LISZT. In addition to his more than 40 operas, he wrote much other secular and sacred music. Though he and W. A. MOZART were rivals, there is no basis to the story that he poisoned Mozart, and he probably never claimed to have done so.

Salinas (de Gortari) \sä-'lē-näs\, **Carlos** (b.1948) President of Mexico (1988–94). Son of a senator, Salinas earned a PhD in economics at Harvard Univ. and held various governmental posts until he was elected president in 1988 by a slim margin; vote fraud was widely charged. He pursued a program of economic retrenchment and privatization of inefficient state-owned corporations. In 1991–92 his government conegotiated the N. AMERICAN FREE TRADE AGREEMENT. The economic collapse immediately following his term made him the target of bitter criticism. The assassination of his party's nominee as his successor was linked to his associates, and Salinas fled into exile. His brother Raúl, suspected of extensive corruption, was convicted in 1999 of complicity in another assassination.

Salinger \'sa-lin-jər\, **J(erome) D(avid)** (b.1919) U.S. writer. Born in New York City, he began to publish short stories in periodicals in 1940. After World War II his stories, some based on his army experiences, appeared increasingly in the *New Yorker*. His entire literary output comprises 13 stories and novellas, including *Nine Stories* (1953), *Franny and Zooey* (1961), and *The Catcher in the Rye* (1951), a novel of adolescent anguish that won great critical and popular admiration, especially among college students. He retreated into a mysterious seclusion in New Hampshire and ceased to publish.

Salisbury See HARARE

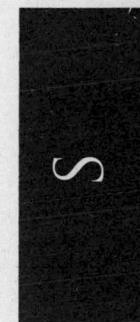

Salisbury, Earl of See Robert CECIL

Salisbury, Marquess of *orig.* Robert Arthur Talbot Gascoyne-Cecil (1830–1903) British prime minister (1885–86, 1886–92, 1895–1902). After serving as secretary for India (1874–78) and foreign secretary (1878–80), he led the Conservative opposition in the House of Lords. As prime minister on three occasions beginning in 1885, he opposed alliances, maintained strong national interests, and presided over an expansion of Britain's colonial empire, especially in Africa. He retired in 1902 in favor of his nephew, A. J. BALFOUR.

saliva Thick, colorless fluid constantly present in the mouth, composed of water, mucus, proteins, mineral salts, and amylase, an enzyme that breaks down starches. One to two liters are produced daily by the SALIVARY GLANDS. Small amounts are continually produced, but the presence or smell of food increases flow. Saliva's main function is to keep the inside of the mouth moist, dissolving food molecules for taste and easing swallowing. It also helps control the body's water balance, since lack of it stimulates thirst. Saliva reduces dental CARIES and infection by removing food debris, dead cells, bacteria, and white blood cells.

salivary gland \'sal-ə-ˌver-ē\ Any of the organs that secrete SALIVA. Three pairs of major glands secrete saliva into the mouth through distinct ducts: the parotid glands, between the ear and lower JAW; the submaxillary glands, along the side of the lower jaw; and the sublingual glands, in the floor of the mouth. There are also numerous small glands in the tongue, palate, lips, and cheeks.

Saljuq dynasty See SELJUQ DYNASTY

Salk \'sȯk\, **Jonas (Edward)** (1914–1995) U.S. physician and researcher. Born in New York City, he worked with other scientists to classify POLIOMYELITIS VIRUS, confirming earlier studies that identified three strains. He showed that killed virus of each strain could induce antibody formation without producing disease. Salk's VACCINE was released for use in the U.S. in 1955. From 1963 he directed the Salk Institute in La Jolla, Cal. He was awarded the Presidential Medal of Freedom in 1977. See also Albert SABIN.

Sallé \sȧ-'lā\, **Marie** (1707–1756) French dancer and choreographer. She made her debut at the Paris Opera in 1721. In London and Paris, she performed in a new expressive, dramatic style that later was championed as the *ballet d'action* by Jean-Georges NOVERRE. With *Pygmalion* (1734), she became the first woman to choreograph a ballet in which she danced, and the first to discard the traditional restrictive costume for a muslin dress. Her rivalry with Marie CAMARGO was celebrated.

Sallust \'sa-ləst\ *Latin* Gaius Sallustius Crispus (86?–35/34 B.C.) Roman historian. One of the great Latin literary stylists, he is notable for his narrative writings about political personalities, corruption, and party rivalry. His works, whose influence pervades later Roman historiography, are *Catiline's War* (43–42 B.C.), dealing with corruption in Roman politics; *The Jugurthine War* (41–40), exploring party struggles in Rome in the late 2nd cent. B.C.; and *Histories*, of which only fragments remain.

salmon Any member of eight species: the Atlantic salmon (*Salmo salar*), and six species of Pacific salmon (genus *Oncorhynchus,* family Salmonidae)—the chum, chinook, pink, and sockeye salmon, the coho, and the cherry salmon (*O. masu*) of Japan. Adult salmon live at sea, then migrate, fighting rapids and leaping high falls, to the stream where they hatched to spawn. See also TROUT.

salmonella \ˌsal-mə-'ne-lə\ Any of the rod-shaped, gram-negative (see GRAM STAIN), non-oxygen-requiring BACTERIA of the genus *Salmonella*. Their main habitat is the intestinal tract of humans and other animals. Some of the 2,200 known species exist without causing disease; others are serious pathogens. Infections caused by salmonellae are called salmonelloses, including TYPHOID and paratyphoid fever in humans. Refrigeration prevents their reproduction but does not kill them; as a result, many salmonellae can develop in foods such as chicken, eggs, unpasteurized milk, ground meat, and fish. GASTROENTERITIS from salmonellae involves diarrhea, vomiting, chills, and painful headaches.

salmonellosis \ˌsal-mə-ˌne-'lō-səs\ Any of several bacterial infections caused by SALMONELLA, including TYPHOID and

GASTROENTERITIS (see FOOD POISONING). Meat from diseased animals carries the BACTERIA, and any food can pick it up from infected feces in the field or during storage, or from contaminated food or utensils during food preparation. Eggs from infected hens can carry it within. Onset is sudden and sometimes severe, with nausea, vomiting, diarrhea, prostration, and low fever. Most patients recover within days, with some degree of immunity. It is destroyed by thorough cooking.

Salmon River River, central Idaho. It flows northeast past the town of Salmon, then west to join the SNAKE RIVER south of the Idaho–Oregon–Washington border. It is about 420 mi (676 km) long. It is the largest tributary of the Snake and flows through an extensive area of national forests.

Salome \sə-'lō-mē, 'sa-lə-(ˌ)mā\ Stepdaughter of HEROD ANTIPAS, who caused the death of JOHN THE BAPTIST. The event is recounted in the gospels of Matthew and Mark, though her name is given only by the historian JOSEPHUS. John had been imprisoned for denouncing Herod's adulterous marriage to Herodias. When Salome, daughter of Herodias, danced before the king, he promised to give her anything she asked as a reward, and she requested John's head on a platter.

Salomon \'sa-lə-mən\, **Haym** (1740–1785) Polish-American patriot and financier. He arrived in New York in 1772 and soon became a successful merchant and financier. A supporter of the colonists, he was imprisoned by the British. In 1778 he escaped to Philadelphia, where he opened a brokerage office. He made major loans to help finance the new government, gave interest-free private loans to James MADISON, Thomas JEFFERSON, and others, and obtained French loans to the American government.

Salon \sȧ-'lōⁿ\ Official exhibition of art sponsored by the French government. It originated in 1667 when LOUIS XIV sponsored an exhibit of the works of the members of the Royal Academy of Painting and Sculpture, held in the Salon d'Apollon of the Louvre Palace. After 1737 it became an annual event, and in 1748 the jury system of selection was introduced. Academicians maintained near-total control over the teaching and exhibition of art through most of the 19th cent. In 1881 the new Société des Artistes Français began to oversee the Salon, and with the growing importance of independent exhibitions of the works of avant-garde artists, it gradually lost its influence and prestige.

Salonika See THESSALONÍKI

salsa (Spanish: "sauce") Contemporary Latin-American dance music. Salsa developed in Cuba in the 1940s, drawing on local musical styles such as *charanga* (featuring primarily strings and flute) and the dance music of the *conjuntos* (bands), which included vocals, trumpet, and African percussion instruments, and blending in elements of jazz. In New York in the 1950s, it incorporated traditional Puerto Rican rhythms, and later elements from RHYTHM AND BLUES as well. Its stars have included Celia CRUZ and Tito PUENTE.

SALT *in full* **Strategic Arms Limitation Talks** Negotiations between the U.S. and the Soviet Union aimed at curtailing the manufacture of strategic nuclear missiles. The first round of negotiations (1969–72) resulted in a treaty regulating ANTIBALLISTIC MISSILES and freezing the number of ICBMs and submarine-launched ballistic missiles. A second round of talks (SALT II, 1972–79) ended with an agreement to limit strategic launchers (see MIRV). Though never formally ratified by the U.S. Senate, its terms were observed by both sides. See also NUCLEAR TEST-BAN TREATY, START.

salt Chemical COMPOUND formed when the hydrogen of an ACID is replaced by a METAL or its equivalent. Typically, an acid and a BASE react to form a salt and water. Most inorganic salts ionize (see ION) in water solution. SODIUM CHLORIDE is common table salt.

Salta City (pop., 1999 est.: 457,000), NW Argentina. It lies in the irrigated Andean valley of Lerma. Founded in 1582, it was the scene of the defeat of the Spanish royal forces in 1813 during the Argentine war of independence. The economy is based on lumbering, stock raising, and mining. It is a tourist center with nearby thermal springs, and a center of archaeological investigations of pre-Columbian cultures.

salt dome Largely subsurface geologic structure that consists of a vertical cylinder of SALT and its surrounding horizontal or inclined strata. Major accumulations of oil and NATURAL GAS are associated with salt domes in the U.S., Mexico, the North Sea, Germany, and Romania; domes along the Gulf Coast contain large quantities of SULFUR. Salt domes are also major sources of salt and potash on the Gulf Coast and in Germany. Used for underground storage of liquefied propane gas, salt domes also have been considered as sites for disposal of radioactive wastes.

Saltillo \säl-'tē-yō\ City (pop., 1995: 510,000), capital of COAHUILA state, NE Mexico. Founded in 1575, it was the first Spanish settlement in the area. In 1824–36 it was the capital of a vast province that included what is now Texas. Gold, silver, lead, and coal are mined in nearby mountains. At an elevation of 5,246 ft (1,599 m), it has a cool, dry climate that has made it a summer resort.

Salt Lake City City (pop., 2000: 182,000), capital of Utah. Located near the SE end of GREAT SALT LAKE, it was founded in 1847 by Brigham YOUNG and a group of 148 MORMONS as a refuge from religious persecution. It prospered from rail connections and became the state capital in 1896. The largest city in the state, it lies at an altitude of 4,390 ft (1,338 m). It is a commercial center for nearby mining operations. As the headquarters of the Church of Jesus Christ of Latter-day Saints, it influences the social, economic, political, and cultural life of the state and region. It is the site of the Mormon Temple and Tabernacle.

Salton Sea Saline lake, SE California. The area that is now the lake was a salt-covered sink or depression about 280 ft (85 m) below sea level until 1905–6, when diversion controls on the COLORADO RIVER broke below the California–Mexico border and floodwaters rushed north, filling the depression. In 1907 levees were built to prevent further deepening of the depression. The lake has an area of 344 sq mi (890 sq km). Its surface is now about 235 ft (72 m) below sea level; its steadily increasing salinity is now greater than that of seawater, endangering its fish populations. It has swimming, boating, and camping facilities.

saltpeter or **niter** Transparent, colorless, or white powder or crystals of POTASSIUM NITRATE, found native in deposits. It is a strong oxidizing agent (see OXIDATION-REDUCTION), used in fireworks, EXPLOSIVES, matches, fertilizers, glassmaking, steel TEMPERING, and food curing; as a reagent; and as an oxidizer in solid rocket propellants. The term is also used for sodium nitrate (Chile saltpeter), calcium nitrate (lime saltpeter), and the explosive and fertilizer ammonium nitrate (Norway saltpeter).

Salvador or **Bahia** City (pop., 1996: 2,209,000), port, and capital of BAHIA state, E Brazil. One of Brazil's oldest cities, it was founded in 1549 as the Portuguese colonial capital. At the center of the regional sugar trade, it became a prize for pirates. The Portuguese made it a major center for the African slave trade. It has grown continuously since 1940, and its port is one of the nation's finest.

salvation In religion, deliverance from fundamentally negative conditions, such as suffering, evil, death, or SAMSARA, or the restoration or elevation of the natural world to a higher, better state. Eastern religions tend to stress self-help through individual discipline and practice, sometimes over the course of many lifetimes. In Christianity, JESUS is the source of salvation and faith in his saving power is stressed. Islam emphasizes submission to God. Judaism posits collective salvation for the people of Israel.

Salvation Army International Christian charitable movement. It was founded in 1865 by William BOOTH to help the poor of London. He adopted the name Salvation Army in 1878 and established the organization on a military pattern. Members are called soldiers, and officers earn ranks that range from lieutenant to brigadier. Doctrines are similar to those of other evangelical Protestant denominations, though there are no SACRAMENTS. The meetings are characterized by singing, instrumental music, personal testimony, free prayer, and an open invitation to repentance. The Salvation Army now provides a wide variety of social services in more than 100 countries.

Salween River \'sal-ˌwĕn\ Chinese **Nu** River, S.E. Asia. Rising in E Tibet, it flows generally south for about 1,500 mi (2,400 km) through Yunnan province, China, and E Myanmar, emptying into the Andaman Sea at Moulmein. It forms the frontier between Myanmar and Thailand for about 80 mi (130 km). It is the longest river in Myanmar, but dangerous rapids hinder its use as a major waterway.

Salzburg ancient Juvavum. City (pop., 1999 est.: 144,000), N central Austria. It was made a bishopric by St. BONIFACE in 739 and was raised to an archbishopric in 798. Its archbishops became princes of the HOLY ROMAN EMPIRE in 1278; it became the seat of their powerful ecclesiastical principality. A music center for centuries, it was the birthplace of W. A. MOZART; the annual Salzburg Festival is held there. Notable buildings include the archepiscopal palaces and a 17th-cent. cathedral.

sama \sä-'ma\ In SUFISM, the practice of listening to music, chanting, and dancing as a means of producing a state of religious ecstasy and mystical trance. Practitioners hold that music prepares the soul for a deeper comprehension of divine realities. God, as the source of beauty, is taken to be approachable through these activities because they contain or exemplify beauty. Strong ascetic training is required to ensure that music so employed does not arouse base instincts.

samadhi \sə-'mä-dē\ State of intense concentration or absorption of consciousness, the product of meditation. In Hinduism, it is achieved through YOGA, in which the consciousness is absorbed in the object of meditation. In ZEN Buddhism, samadhi allows the meditator to overcome dualistic subject-object awareness through unity with the object of meditation.

Samar \'sä-ˌmär\ Island (pop., 2000: 1,517,000), E central part of the Philippines. The third-largest after LUZON and MINDANAO, it is one of the VISAYAN ISLANDS and has an area of 5,050 sq mi (13,080 sq km). Occupied by the Japanese in 1942, it was retaken by the U.S. in 1944. The rugged interior is sparsely settled. Coconuts and abaca are the main cash crops, with logging and sawmill operations on the E coast.

Samara \sə-'mä-rə\ formerly (1935–91) **Kuybyshev** \'kü-ē-bə-shəf\ City (pop., 1997 est.: 1,170,000) and river port, E Russia. Located on the VOLGA RIVER, it was founded in 1586 to protect the Volga trade route. It was the scene of the rebellion of Yemelyan PUGACHOV against CATHERINE II in 1773–74. It later became a major trade center. Its growth was stimulated during World War II by the relocation there of numerous government functions when MOSCOW was threatened. It is the center of a network of pipelines; oil and petrochemicals are the major industries.

Samaria \sə-'mar-ē-ə\ Central region, ancient Palestine. Extending for about 40 mi (65 km) north–south and 35 mi (56 km) east–west, it was bounded by GALILEE, JUDAEA, the Mediterranean Sea, and the JORDAN RIVER. Ancient Shechem (near modern Nablus) was the region's crossroads and political center until the 8th cent. B.C. The town of Samaria, its capital, was built by King Omri about 880 B.C. It was taken by SARGON II around 724–721 B.C. and its inhabitants were transported into captivity. It was rebuilt by King HEROD. In A.D. 6 the region became part of the Roman province of Judaea.

Samaritans Inhabitants of ancient SAMARIA. Samaria was home to Jews who were not deported in 722 B.C. when the Assyrians conquered Israel, and Jews who later returned refused the help of the Samaritans in rebuilding the Temple of JERUSALEM. In the 4th cent. B.C., the Samaritans built their own temple in Nablus (now in Jordan), where a small remnant of the community lives today. They speak Arabic but pray in Hebrew. The dislike of Jews for Samaritans was the background of the parable of the Good Samaritan (Luke 10:25–37).

Samarqand or **Samarkand** \ˌsä-mər-'känd\ City (pop., 1996 est.: 362,000), E central Uzbekistan. One of the oldest cities in central Asia, it was captured by ALEXANDER THE GREAT in 329 B.C. From the 6th cent. A.D. it was ruled successively by the Turks, Arabs, and Samanids of Iran and was an important point on the SILK ROAD until its destruction by GENGHIS KHAN in 1220. It became the capital of the empire of TIMUR (Tamerlane) about 1370. It expanded considerably during the Soviet period.

Samhain See HALLOWEEN

samizdat \'sä-mēz-ˌdät\ System whereby literature suppressed by the Soviet government was clandestinely written, printed, and distributed; also, the literature itself. Samizdat began appearing in the 1950s. It typically took the form of carbon copies of typewritten sheets that were passed from reader to reader. The subjects included dissident activities, protests addressed to the regime, transcripts of political trials, analyses of socioeconomic and cultural themes, and even pornography. Samizdat disappeared with the fall of the Soviet government.

Samoa *officially* **Independent State of Samoa** *formerly* **Western Samoa** Independent state, S central Pacific Ocean, northeast of New Zealand. Area: 1,093 sq mi (2,831 sq km). Population (2000): 179,000. Capital: APIA (on Upolu Island). The people are mainly Polynesian, closely akin to Tongans and to New Zealand's MAORIS. Languages: Samoan and English (both official). Religion: Christianity. Currency: tala. Samoa is part of the Samoan archipelago and consists of two major islands, Upolu and Savai'i, both of which are volcanic. There are also seven small islands, two of which, Apolima and Manono, are inhabited. It has a developing economy based mainly on agriculture, with some light manufacturing, fishing, lumbering, and tourism. It is a constitutional monarchy with one legislative house; the chief of state is the head of state, and the head of government is the prime minister. Polynesians inhabited the islands for thousands of years before they were visited by Europeans in the 18th cent. The islands were contested by the U.S., Britain, and Germany until 1899, when they were divided between the U.S. and Germany. In 1914 Western Samoa was occupied by New Zealand, which received it as a League of Nations mandate in 1920. After World War II, it became a U.N. trust territory administered by New Zealand and achieved independence in 1962. In 1997 the word Western was dropped from the country's name. See also map at OCEANIA.

Samoa, American See AMERICAN SAMOA

Samori Ture *or* **Samory Touré** \sä-'mȯr-ē-tü-'rā\ (c.1830–1900) Muslim reformer and military adventurer. A member of the MALINKE people, Samori in 1868 established a religious chiefdom in the Kankan region of Guinea. He fought the French in 1883, 1886, and 1891, managing to expand into the Sudan, but was ultimately forced to transfer his kingdom to the upper Ivory Coast.

Sámos \'sä-ˌmōs\ Island (pop., 1991: 42,000) in the Aegean Sea, Greece. It is located just off the W coast of Turkey, and has an area of 184 sq mi (476 sq km). It was a leading commercial center of Greece by the 7th cent. B.C., and was noted for its cultural achievements, especially in sculpture, during the reign of POLYCRATES. Ruled successively by Persia, Athens, Sparta, Rome, Byzantium, and Turkey, it was annexed to Greece in 1912. The island produces wine, olives, fruit, cotton, and tobacco.

Samoyed \'sa-mə-ˌyed\ Breed of sturdily built, huskylike dog developed in Siberia, where SIBERIAN PEOPLES kept it as a sled dog and herd dog for their reindeer. It has erect ears, dark almond-shaped eyes, and a characteristic "smile." It stands 19–24 in. (48–60 cm) and weighs 50–65 lbs (23–30 kg), and has a long, heavy, whitish coat. Gentle, loyal, and intelligent, it makes a capable guard and a good companion.

Sampras, Pete (b.1971) U.S. tennis player. Born in Washington, D.C., he learned tennis after moving to S California. A five-time U.S. Open champion (1990, 1993, 1995–96, 2002), seven-time Wimbledon champion (1993–95, 1997–2000), and two-time Australian Open champion (1994, 1997), he holds a world record of 14 Grand Slam victories. He is known for his high-powered serves, accurate volleys, and unassuming demeanor.

samsara \səm-'sär-ə, səŋ-'sär-ə\ In BUDDHISM and HINDUISM, the endless round of birth, death, and rebirth to which all conditioned beings are subject. Samsara is conceived as having no perceptible beginning or end. The particulars of an individual's wanderings in samsara are determined by KARMA. In Hinduism, MOKSHA is release from samsara. In Buddhism, samsara is transcended by the attainment of NIRVANA.

samskara \səm-'skär-ə, səŋ-'skär-ə\ In HINDUISM, any of the personal sacraments traditionally observed at every stage of life, from the moment of conception to the scattering of one's funeral ashes. The observance of the samskaras differs considerably according to region, CASTE, or family. The most generally accepted list of 16 traditional samskaras includes ceremonies for conception, a male birth, name-giving, entrance into the religious community, and marriage.

Samson Israelite warrior hero of the OLD TESTAMENT Book of Judges. Samson performed many powerful acts, including slaying a lion and moving the gates of GAZA. When he revealed to a Philistine woman, Delilah, that his hair was the source of his strength, she shaved his head while he was sleeping, leaving him powerless. He was blinded and enslaved by the PHILISTINES, but later his strength was restored and he pulled down the pillars of a temple where 3,000 Philistines had gathered, killing them and himself.

Samuel (c.11th cent. B.C.) OLD TESTAMENT prophet, the first after MOSES and the last of the judges of ancient Israel. His story is told in two biblical books that relate the history of Israel in the 11th–10th cent. B.C., when the first monarchy of Israel was established and the tribes of Israel united under a single kingdom with its capital at Jerusalem. Samuel received a revelation that led to the installation of SAUL as king, but later announced an oracle rejecting Saul and secretly anointed DAVID as king.

Samuel, Herbert Louis *later* Viscount Samuel (of Mount Carmel and of Toxteth) (1870–1963) British politician. A social worker in the London slums, he entered the House of Commons in 1902, where he effected legislation that established juvenile courts and the Borstal system for youthful offenders. Appointed the first British high commissioner for Palestine (1920–25), he improved the region's economy and promoted harmony among its religious communities. He led the Liberal Party 1931–35. As president of the British (later Royal) Institute of Philosophy (1931–59), he wrote such popular works as *Practical Ethics* (1935) and *Belief and Action* (1937).

Samuelson, Paul (Anthony) (b.1915) U.S. economist. Born in Gary, Ind., he received his PhD from Harvard. He taught at MIT 1940–86. His *Foundations of Economic Analysis* (1947) outlines a basic theme of his work, the universal nature of consumer behavior as the key to economic theory. His studies included the dynamics of economic systems, analyses of public goods, welfare economics, and public expenditure. His classic *Economics* (1948) is the best-selling U.S. economics textbook of all time. For his fundamental contributions to nearly all branches of economics, he became in 1970 the third person to be awarded the Nobel Prize in Economics.

samurai Member of the Japanese warrior class. The samurai became important with the rise in private estates (SHOEN), which needed samurai protection, and when MINAMOTO YORITOMO established the KAMAKURA SHOGUNATE (1192–1333) they became the ruling class. Characterized by discipline, stoicism, and service (see BUSHIDO), samurai culture developed further during the ASHIKAGA SHOGUNATE (1338–1573). During two centuries of peace under the TOKUGAWA SHOGUNATE (1603–1867), they were largely transformed into civil bureaucrats. By the mid-19th cent., lower-ranking samurai, eager for societal change and anxious to create a strong Japan in the face of Western encroachment, overthrew the shogunal government in the MEIJI RESTORATION of 1868. Feudal distinctions were abolished in 1871. Some samurai rebelled but most supported the modernization of Japan.

San *formerly* **Bushmen** Group of peoples living in and around the KALAHARI DESERT region of S Africa. Two well-known San groups are the !Kung and the G/wi. San shelters are semicircular structures of branches, twigs, and grass; their equipment is portable, their possessions few and light. They have traditionally hunted using bows and snares, and gathered wild vegetables, fruits, and nuts. Numbering about 50,000, most are today restricted to harsh, semiarid areas, and work on European farms or serve other Africans, notably the Tswana.

Sanaa \sä-'nä\ City (pop., 1995 est.: 972,000), capital of Yemen. It was built on the site of the ancient pre-Islamic stronghold of Ghumdan. It was converted to Islam in 632. Nominally under Ottoman sovereignty from 1516, it was effectively controlled by the Zaydi imams from the early 17th cent. to 1872. It became the capital of an independent Yemen after the Ottoman defeat in World War I. In 1990, after Yemen's merger with the People's Democratic Republic of Yemen, it became the capital of the unified nation.

San Andreas Fault \‚san-an-'drā-əs\ Zone at the boundary between two tectonic plates, running along the coast of N California for 650 mi (1,050 km) and passing seaward in the vicinity of SAN FRANCISCO. Movement along the FAULT is characterized by frequent EARTHQUAKES, including the major San Francisco quake of 1906, when parts of the fault line moved as much as 21 ft (6.4 m), and the less serious earthquake of 1989.

San Antonio City (pop., 2000: 1,145,000), S central Texas. It was founded in 1718 by the Spanish, at the headwaters of the San Antonio River, as a mission on the site of an Indian village. The mission, called the ALAMO, became a military post in 1794; it was the site of the historic siege in 1836. In the late 19th cent., San Antonio became a major cattle center as the starting point of the CHISHOLM TRAIL. Military installations spurred its rapid growth after 1940.

San Bernardino City (pop., 2000: 185,000), S California. It lies about 60 mi (100 km) east of LOS ANGELES. It was laid out by MORMONS in 1852 and developed as a trade center for the surrounding citrus groves and vineyards. Other industries, including aerospace, electronics, and steel, are now the economic mainstays.

Sancho I *known as* **Sancho the Founder** (1154–1211) Second king of Portugal (1185–1211). The son of AFONSO I, he resettled depopulated areas of Portugal, established new towns, and rebuilt frontier strongholds and castles. He encouraged foreign settlers and granted large tracts to military orders. When Portugal was invaded by the Almohad Moors, he sent a crusader fleet against them (1189), but he lost control of lands S of the Tagus River (1191).

sand Mineral, rock, or soil particles that are 0.0008–0.08 in. (0.02–2 mm) in diameter. Most rock-forming minerals are found in sand, but QUARTZ is by far the most common. Most sands also contain a small quantity of FELDSPAR, as well as white MICA. In the pottery and glassmaking industries, very pure quartz sands are used as a source of silica. Similar sands are used for lining the hearths of steel furnaces. Quartz and garnet sands are used extensively as abrasives. Among ordinary sand's many uses, it is a basic ingredient of mortar, cement, and concrete.

Sand \'sä\[n]d, *Engl* 'sand\, **George** *orig.* Amandine-Aurore-Lucile Lucie Dupin (1804–1876) French writer. Married in 1822, she soon tired of her husband, Casimir Dudevant, and began a series of liaisons; her noted lovers included Frédéric CHOPIN. She became famous (under her pseudonym) with her novel *Indiana* (1832), a protest against conventions that bind an unhappy wife to her husband. *Lélia* (1833) extended her iconoclastic views on social and class associations. Her finest works are the so-called rustic novels, including *The Devil's Pool* (1846) and *Little Fadette* (1849).

George Sand

sandbar *or* **offshore bar** Submerged or partly exposed ridge of sand or coarse sediment that is built by waves offshore from a beach. As the breaking waves excavate a trough in the sandy bottom, some of this sand is carried forward onto the beach and the rest is deposited on the offshore flank of the trough. Sand suspended in the backwash and in rip currents adds to the bar. The bar's top is kept below still-water level by the waves breaking over it.

Sandburg, Carl (1878–1967) U.S. poet, historian, novelist, and folklorist. Born in Galesburg, Ill., in 1913 he moved to Chicago, where he worked in journalism. He won recogni-

tion in 1914 with poems, including "Chicago," in *POETRY* magazine. His Whitmanesque free verse eulogizing American workers appeared in such volumes as *Smoke and Steel* (1920) and *The People, Yes* (1936). *The American Songbag* (1927) and *New American Songbag* (1950) collect folksongs he performed. His other works include *Abraham Lincoln: The War Years* (1939, Pulitzer Prize); *Remembrance Rock* (1948); and the children's book *Rootabaga Stories* (1922).

Sand Creek Massacre *or* **Chivington Massacre** (Nov. 29, 1864) Surprise attack by U.S. troops on a Cheyenne camp. A force of 1,200 men under Col. John M. Chivington attacked several hundred Cheyenne camped on Sand Creek near Ft. Lyon in SE Colorado Territory. The Indians, who had been conducting peace negotiations with the fort's commander, raised a white flag, but the troops continued to attack, massacring over 200 Indians. The slayings led to the PLAINS INDIAN wars.

sand dollar Any ECHINODERM (order Clypeastroida, class Echinoidea) that has a coinlike, thin-edged body. It burrows in sand, feeding on organic particles wafted to the central mouth. Small spines covering the body are used for digging and crawling. Tests (external skeletons) of the common sand dollar *(Echinarachnius parma),* which often wash up on beaches in N. America and Japan, are 2–4 in. (5–10 cm) in diameter.

sand fly Any of several species in the DIPTERAN family Phlebotomidae (sometimes considered part of the family Psychodidae) with aquatic larvae that live on beaches, in mud, or in wet organic debris. The genus *Phlebotomus* transmits the pappataci fever virus and can carry the protozoan parasites that cause kala azar, Oriental sore, espundia, and bartonellosis. The name is also used for species of the BLACKFLY and biting MIDGE families.

sandhill crane CRANE species (*Grus canadensis,* family Gruidae), 35–43 in. (90–110 cm) long, with a red crown, a grayish body tinged with sandy yellow, and a long, harsh, penetrating call. It is one of the oldest of all bird species. It breeds from Alaska to Hudson Bay. A smaller, nonmigratory subspecies breeds in Florida and S Georgia; others are classified as rare or critically endangered. Sandhill cranes have been used as surrogate parents in efforts to save the WHOOPING CRANE from extinction.

San Diego City (pop., 2000: 1,223,000) and port, SW California. It is located on San Diego Bay, the site of major naval and military bases. In 1769 the Spanish established a military post on the site and Junípero SERRA dedicated the first California mission there. It was captured from Mexico in 1846, and a new city was laid out in 1867. The arrival of the Santa Fe railroad in 1884 stimulated the city's growth. Industrial development is dominated by aerospace, electronics, and shipbuilding, and the city is the main commercial outlet for the farm produce of S California. Balboa Park and its SAN DIEGO ZOO are renowned.

San Diego Zoo World's largest collection of mammals, birds, and reptiles, located in San Diego, Cal. The 100-acre (40.5-hectare) zoo, founded in 1916, has some 800 animal species and some 6,500 plant species. The nearby 1,800-acre (729-hectare) San Diego Wild Animal Park allows over 250 species of animals to roam through Asian, African, and Australian habitats. A research department, the Center for Reproduction of Endangered Species (1975), has contributed to the zoo's success in managing and breeding endangered species.

Sandinistas Members of Nicaragua's Sandinista National Liberation Front (FSLN). The group, named for the guerrilla leader Augusto Sandino (1895–1934), was founded in 1962 to oppose the SOMOZA FAMILY's dictatorship and gained support among students, workers, and peasants for their guerrilla war. They split into factions in the mid-1970s but reunited in 1978–79 to finally overthrow Pres. Anastasio Somoza. Daniel ORTEGA led the Sandinista government (1979–90), which implemented literacy and health programs. To topple the government, the U.S. imposed a trade embargo, pressured international lending institutions to withhold aid, and supported the CONTRAS. The FSLN lost the presidency in 1990 to Violeta CHAMORRO.

sandpainting Type of art practiced among the NAVAJO and PUEBLO INDIANS and among Tibetan Buddhists. Sandpaint-

S

ings are stylized, symbolic pictures (in Tibet, MANDALAS) prepared by trickling small quantities of crushed, colored sandstone, charcoal, or pollen on a background of clean smoothed sand. The pictures may include representations of deities, cosmic worlds, and various SYMBOLS described in chants that accompany various religious and healing rites.

sandpiper Any of numerous shorebirds (family Scolopacidae) found nearly worldwide. Sandpipers, 6–12 in. (15–30 cm) long, have a moderately long bill and long, narrow wings. Their plumage has a complicated "dead-grass" pattern. They run along ocean and inland beaches and mudflats, picking up insects, crustaceans, and worms and uttering thin, piping cries. Many species migrate in great flocks.

sand shark Any of about six species of shallow-water, bottom-dwelling SHARKS in the genus *Odontaspis* (family Odontaspididae). They are 10–20 ft (3–6 m) long. Voracious but generally sluggish, they have long, slim, pointed teeth and prey on fishes and INVERTEBRATES. The sand tiger *(O. taurus)* of the Atlantic and the gray nurse *(O. arenarius)* of Australia are potentially dangerous.

sandstone Sedimentary rock formed from sand-sized grains (0.0025–0.08 in., or 0.06–2 mm, in diameter). The spaces between grains may be empty or filled with either a chemical cement of silica or calcium carbonate or a fine-grained matrix of silt and clay particles. The principal mineral constituents are QUARTZ, FELDSPAR, and rock fragments. Sandstones are quarried for use as building stone; they are important to geologists as indicators of erosional and depositional processes.

Sandwich, Earl of *orig.* John Montagu (1718–1792) British statesman. As first lord of the admiralty (1748–51, 1771–82) during the American Revolution, he was criticized for keeping much of the British fleet in European waters to avoid French attack. His promotion of exploration led Capt. James COOK to name the Sandwich Islands (later Hawaii) after him in 1778. The sandwich was named after him in 1762 when he spent 24 hours at a gaming table without other food.

San Fernando Valley Valley, S California, northwest of central LOS ANGELES. It is bounded by the SAN GABRIEL, Santa Susana, and Santa Monica mountains and the Simi Hills. Originally an agricultural area, it now contains suburbs including Encino, N. Hollywood, Studio City, and Van Nuys.

San Francisco City (pop., 2000: 777,000) and port, N California. It lies on the W side of SAN FRANCISCO BAY, with an exceptionally good harbor. It grew rapidly after the discovery of gold nearby around 1849 (see GOLD RUSH). In 1869 it became the terminus of the first transcontinental railroad. It suffered extensive damage from the earthquake and fire of 1906. It was prominent in the American cultural revolution of the 1960s. It suffered heavy earthquake damage in 1989. It is a commercial, cultural, and financial center and one of the country's most cosmopolitan cities. A noted educational center, it is a popular tourist destination and the site of the GOLDEN GATE BRIDGE.

San Francisco Bay Inlet of the Pacific Ocean, W central California. A drowned river valley, it is connected with the Pacific by the Golden Gate Strait, which is spanned by the GOLDEN GATE BRIDGE. The bay is one of the world's finest natural harbors. The cities of SAN FRANCISCO, OAKLAND, and BERKELEY lie on the bay; its islands include ALCATRAZ.

San Gabriel Mountains Segment of the Pacific COAST RANGES, S California. Many peaks exceed 9,000 ft (2,700 m); the highest is San Antonio Peak, or "Old Baldy," at 10,080 ft (3,072 m). The range also includes Mt. Wilson Observatory, northeast of PASADENA.

Sangallo the Younger, Antonio da See Antonio DA SANGALLO THE YOUNGER

Sanger, Frederick (b.1918) British biochemist. He elucidated the structure of the INSULIN molecule, determining the exact order of all its amino acids. His techniques made it possible to discover the structure of many other complex proteins. In 1958 he won a Nobel Prize for this work. In 1980 Sanger became the fourth person ever to be awarded a second Nobel Prize, which he shared with Paul BERG and Walter Gilbert (b.1932), for determining the sequences of nucleotides in the DNA molecule of a small virus.

Sanger, Margaret *orig.* Margaret Louisa Higgins (1879–1966) U.S. BIRTH CONTROL pioneer. Born in Corning, N.Y., she practiced obstetrical nursing in New York's Lower East Side, where she noticed a relationship between poverty, uncontrolled fertility, and infant and maternal mortality. In 1914 she published *The Woman Rebel* (later *Birth Control Review*), which was banned as obscene. She was arrested in 1916 when she opened the nation's first birth-control clinic. Her legal appeals brought publicity and support, and the federal courts soon granted physicians the right to prescribe contraceptives. In 1921 she founded the American Birth Control League. She organized the first World Population Conference (1927) and became the founding president of the International Planned Parenthood Federation (1953).

sangha \ˈseŋ-gə\ Buddhist monastic order, traditionally composed of four groups: monks, nuns, laymen, and laywomen. Established by the BUDDHA, it is the world's oldest body of celibate clerics. Together with the Buddha and the DHARMA, it is one of the "three jewels" of Buddhism. Members depend on alms from the community, since they are discouraged from engaging in commerce or agriculture.

Sangre de Cristo Mountains \ˈsaŋ-grē-də-ˈkris-tō\ Segment of the S ROCKY MTNS. It extends southeast for about 250 mi (400 km) from S central Colorado to N central New Mexico. Many of the peaks exceed 14,000 ft (4,300 m).

Sanhedrin \san-ˈhē-drən, san-ˈhe-drən\ Jewish council that operated in Roman Palestine from the time of the MACCABEES (c.165 B.C.) to the end of the patriarchate (A.D. 425). While the term refers to the supreme Jewish court, the Sanhedrin's exact composition and powers are reported variously in different sources. It is mentioned in the New Testament as having played a role in the trials of JESUS, St. PETER THE APOSTLE, and St. JOHN THE BAPTIST. According to Talmudic sources, the Great Sanhedrin was a court of 71 sages that met on fixed occasions in the Temple of JERUSALEM, acting as a religious legislative body, trial court, and administrator of rituals.

San Jacinto Mountains \ˌsan-jə-ˈsin-tō\ Segment of the Pacific COAST RANGES, SW California. San Jacinto Peak is the highest point, at 10,804 ft (3,293 m); PALM SPRINGS lies at its E base. The range is largely within conservation areas. The mountains attract tourists, provide outdoor recreation, and are an important watershed for the surrounding area.

San Joaquin River \ˌsan-wä-ˈkēn\ River, central California. Formed in the SIERRA NEVADA, it flows past STOCKTON to join the SACRAMENTO RIVER. It is 350 mi (560 km) long and is dammed for hydroelectric power. Its valley is the S part of the CENTRAL VALLEY, one of the most productive agricultural regions in the world.

San Jose \ˌsan-hō-ˈzā\ City (pop., 2000: 895,000), W central California. It is located southeast of SAN FRANCISCO. Founded in 1777, it was the state's first capital (1849–51). In 1850 it became the first chartered city in California. It was a trade depot for the California gold fields. The railroad from San Francisco made the city a distribution center for a rich agricultural area producing fruit and wine. San Jose is also part of SILICON VALLEY, manufacturing electronic, computer, and aerospace components.

San José \ˌsän-hō-ˈsā\ City (metro. area pop., 1998: 1,015,000), capital of Costa Rica. Founded around 1738, it developed as a tobacco center in the Spanish colonial era. In 1823 it became the capital and in the 1840s a major center for coffee production. The political, social, and economic hub of Costa Rica, it grew rapidly in the 20th cent. in both population and area.

San Juan \sän-ˈhwän\ City (metro. area pop., 1999 est.: 440,000), seaport, and capital of Puerto Rico. Visited in 1508 by Juan PONCE DE LEON, it became a frequent starting point for voyages of discovery. Several times it was attacked by the British, including Francis DRAKE in 1595. During the SPANISH–AMERICAN WAR, it fell to the U.S. in 1898. It expanded rapidly in the 20th cent. and is one of the major ports and tourist resorts of the W. Indies. Industries include petroleum and sugar refining, brewing, and distilling. Many U.S. banks and corporations maintain offices there.

San Luis Potosí City (pop., 1995: 586,000), capital of SAN LUIS POTOSÍ state, Mexico. It lies 6,158 ft (1,877 m) above sea level. Founded as a Franciscan mission in 1583 and made a city in 1658, it was the site of Benito JUÁREZ's government in 1863. In 1910 Francisco MADERO drew up the basic social and political program of the MEXICAN REVOLUTION in the city. It is the hub of a rich silver mining and agricultural region, with metal smelting and refining.

San Luis Potosí \sän-'lwēs-pō-tō-'sē\ State (pop., 2000: 2,296,000), NE Mexico. It has an area of 24,351 sq mi (63,068 sq km). The capital is SAN LUIS POTOSÍ. It is a fertile agricultural area; livestock-raising is important, and hides, tallow, and wool are exported. Some of the richest silver mines in Mexico are located in the state.

San Marco Basilica See SAINT MARK'S BASILICA

San Marino *officially* **Republic of San Marino** Nation, central Italian Peninsula, S Europe. It is located near the ADRIATIC SEA and is surrounded by Italy. Area: 24 sq mi (62 sq

km). Population (2000): 27,000. Capital: San Marino. Most of the people are Italian. Language: Italian (official). Religion: Roman Catholicism. Currency: Italian lira. The territory has an irregular rectangular form with a maximum length of 8 mi (13 km). It is crossed by streams that flow into the Adriatic Sea. It is dominated by Mt. Titano, 2,424 ft (739 m) high, on which the capital, the town of San Marino (pop., 1997: 2,300), is located, surrounded by triple walls. The economy is based on private enterprise and includes tourism, commerce, agriculture, crafts, and fine printing; its postage stamps and coins are prized. It is a republic with one legislative house; its heads of state and government are two captains-regent. According to tradition, it was founded in the early 4th cent. A.D. by St. Marinus. By the 12th cent. it had developed into a commune and remained independent despite challenges from neighboring rulers, including the Malatesta family in nearby Rimini, Italy. San Marino survived the Renaissance as a relic of the self-governing Italian city-state and remained an independent republic after the unification of Italy in 1861. It is one of the smallest republics in the world, and may be the oldest state in Europe.

San Martín \sän-mär-'tēn\, **José de** (1778–1850) National hero of Argentina who helped lead the revolutions against Spanish rule in Argentina (1812), Chile (1818), and Peru (1821). Educated in Spain, initially he fought loyally for Spain against the Moors (1791), the British (1798), and the Portuguese (1801), but in 1812 he returned to the New World to help the revolutionaries. His greatest campaign was the liberation of Lima, critical to the independence of the Argentine provinces. His bold strategy was to lead an army over the forbidding Andes. In 1817 he liberated Chile,

which he turned over to Bernardo O'HIGGINS, and proceeded to Peru by ship, where he blockaded the chief port until the royalists withdrew. He then entered Lima and declared the independence of Peru. The following year, after a meeting with Simón BOLÍVAR, he retired to France, leaving Bolívar to complete the liberation of Peru.

sannyasi \san-'yä-sē\ In HINDUISM, one who renounces all ties with family and society and pursues spiritual liberation. Sannyasis are a class of SADHU that do not live in communities, instead leading a mendicant, itinerant life. Those recognized as having achieved full self-knowledge are considered free of all worldly rules and duties. After death, their bodies, rather than being cremated, are buried in a seated, meditative posture.

San Pedro Sula \sän-'pā-thrō-'sü-lä\ City (pop., 1999 est.: 452,000), NW Honduras. It lies about 100 mi (160 km) northwest of TEGUCIGALPA. Founded by the Spanish in 1536, it is the country's second-largest city and chief industrial center, producing textiles, foodstuffs, clothing, beverages, and furniture.

San Salvador City (metro. area pop., 1992 est.: 1,522,000), capital of El Salvador. Moved to its present site in 1528, it became the capital in 1839. During the late 1970s it became the focus of political violence. It is the country's financial, commercial, and industrial center, producing textiles and clothing, leather goods, and wood products. It is also the site of the Univ. of El Salvador. Ruined by earthquakes in 1854, 1873, 1917, and 1986 and by heavy floods in 1934, it has been rebuilt often.

San Salvador See BAHAMAS

sansculotte \sän-kǖ-'lŏt, *Engl* sanz-kü-'lät\ (French, *sansculotte:* "without breeches") In the FRENCH REVOLUTION, one of the ill-clad volunteers of the Revolutionary army; also a Parisian ultrademocrat of the Revolution. The working-class sansculottes wore long trousers to distinguish themselves from the upper classes, who wore knee-breeches (*culotte*). Allied with the JACOBIN CLUB in the REIGN OF TERROR, sansculottes included extremists of all classes. Their influence waned after 1794.

San Sebastián \sän-sä-bäs-'tyän\ *Basque* **Donostia** \thō-nō-'stē-ä\ Seaport (pop., 1998 est.: 178,000), N Spain. It lies on the Bay of BISCAY, near the French border. First mentioned in 1014, it was chartered about 1175. The town was burned in 1813 during the PENINSULAR WAR. Formerly the summer residence of the Spanish royal court, it is now a fashionable seaside resort. Nearby is Mt. Urgull, with the 16th-cent. Mota Castle at its summit.

San Simeon Former estate of William Randolph HEARST, S California. It was built on a vast private estate of 245,000 acres (99,000 hectares), developed in the 1860s by Hearst's father. In 1919–20, with the architect Julia MORGAN, Hearst began construction of a complex of luxurious buildings and gardens. The main residence, later called Hearst Castle, is a Spanish Renaissance building with 150 rooms, a cathedral-like façade, and two bell towers. The site's embellishment continued (1919–48) with numerous subsidiary buildings, Mediterranean gardens, statuary, pools, fountains, a pergola, and priceless art treasures.

Sanskrit language Old INDO-ARYAN LANGUAGE, the classical literary language of HINDUISM. The most ancient form is Vedic, attested in its earliest form in parts of the RIG VEDA. Literary activity in so-called Classical Sanskrit flourished roughly between 500 B.C. and A.D. 1000. Today Sanskrit (now usually written in the Devanagari script) serves as a learned language and LINGUA FRANCA for Brahman scholars. It is an archaic INDO-EUROPEAN LANGUAGE with an elaborate system of nominal and verbal inflection.

Sansovino \sän-so-'vē-nō\, **Andrea** *orig.* Andrea Contucci (c.1467–1529) Italian sculptor. The fine detail and high emotional pitch of his marble Altar of the Sacrament in Florence's Santo Spirito (1485–90) typify his early work; his marble *Baptism of Christ* (1502), above one of the Baptistery doors in Florence, marks a shift to High Renaissance style with its dignified poses and strong but controlled emotion. His tombs for two cardinals in Rome's Santa Maria del Popolo (completed 1509) were his most influential innovation, with their triumphal-arch form and the novel sleeping

---

ITALY

12°25′   12°30′   12°35′ 44°

Ausa

Serravalle

Re

Acquaviva   Domagnano   Fiumicello

San Marino ⊛   Borgo Maggiore

▲ Monte Titano

San Giovanni

Faetano   43°55′

San Marino   **ITALY**

Chiesanuova   Fiorentino

Montegiardino

©1999, Encyclopædia Britannica, Inc.

SAN MARINO

Scale 1: 175,500

0   1   2 mi
0   1   2   3 km

attitude of the deceased cardinals. His works display the transition from early to High Renaissance.

Sansovino \ˌsän-sō-'vē-nō\, **Jacopo** *orig.* Jacopo Tatti (1486–1570) Italian sculptor and architect. He trained in Florence under Andrea SANSOVINO, whose name he adopted. In 1505–6 he moved to Rome to study architecture and later worked on the restoration of ancient sculpture. After the sack of Rome in 1527 he fled to Venice, where he was appointed state architect (1529). His Library of St. Mark's (begun 1537) is one of the major architectural works of the 16th cent. His vivid sculptures were often important decorative elements of his buildings, and he was more successful than any other Renaissance architect in fusing architecture and sculpture.

Santa Ana City (pop., 2000: 338,000), SW California. Located east of LONG BEACH, it developed as a center for the farm produce of the Santa Ana valley after the Southern Pacific Railroad connected it to LOS ANGELES in 1878. Military installations and freeway construction spurred its growth after World War II.

Santa Anna, Antonio (López de) (1794–1876) Soldier and president of Mexico (1833–36, 1844–45, 1847, 1853–55). He fought on both sides of nearly every issue of the day. He is famous for his glorious victories, including his thwarting of Spain's attempt to reconquer Mexico (1829), and his ignominious failures, including his capture by Sam HOUSTON at San Jacinto in the Texas revolt (1836). When the MEXICAN WAR broke out, he contacted Pres. James K. POLK to broker a peace, but on arriving in Mexico he led Mexican forces against the U.S. (1846–47) and was driven into exile. When MAXIMILIAN was made emperor, Santa Anna offered his services both to Maximilian and to his opponents; neither side accepted. See also ALAMO.

Antonio Santa Anna
Daguerreotype
by F. W. Seiders

Santa Barbara City (pop., 2000: 92,000), S California, on the Pacific coast. Named in 1602 for the patron saint of mariners, it became the site of a mission in 1786; it is the W headquarters of the FRANCISCAN Order, in continuous use since its founding. The city developed into a busy port. After the arrival (1887) of the Southern Pacific Railroad, it became a popular seaside resort. Its economy is bolstered by livestock farms and petroleum production. It is home to a campus of the Univ. of California (1891).

Santa Barbara Islands See CHANNEL ISLANDS (CALIFORNIA)

Santa Claus See St. NICHOLAS

Santa Cruz \ˌsän-tä-'krüs\ City (pop., 2000 est.: 1,016,000), E central Bolivia. Founded by Spaniards from Paraguay in 1561, it was attacked repeatedly by Indians until 1595, when it was moved to its present location. In 1811 its inhabitants declared their independence from Spain. By some measures Bolivia's largest city, it is a trade center for sugarcane and rice. It has an oil refinery and is the seat of a university.

Santa Fe City (pop., 2000: 62,000), capital of New Mexico. It lies at the foot of the SANGRE DE CRISTO MTNS. Founded by the Spanish in 1610, it was the administrative, military, and missionary headquarters of a vast Spanish colonial province during the 18th cent. After New Mexico was ceded to the U.S., Santa Fe became the capital of the territory in 1851. In 1912 it became the state capital. It was the W terminus of the SANTA FE TRAIL. It is a popular resort and tourist center noted for Indian and Mexican handicrafts, and the cultural capital of the southwest.

Santa Fe Railway See ATCHISON, TOPEKA AND SANTA FE RAILROAD CO.

Santa Fe Trail Historic wagon trail from INDEPENDENCE, Mo., to SANTA FE, N.M. An important commercial route from 1821 to 1880, it was opened by William BECKNELL and

used by merchant wagon caravans. From the MISSOURI RIVER, it proceeded to and along the Arkansas River. At the W end, three routes turned south to Santa Fe, the shortest being the Cimarron Cutoff through the valley of the Cimarron River. When the Santa Fe railroad was completed in 1880, use of the trail ceased.

Santa Isabel See MALABO

Santander \ˌsän-ˌtän-'der\ Port city (pop., 1998 est.: 184,000), capital of Cantabria, N Spain. A major seaport and summer resort, it is situated on a rocky peninsula on the Bay of BISCAY. The city was rebuilt after a disastrous fire in 1941. In addition to tourism, the economy is based on fishing, iron refining, and shipbuilding. The caves of ALTAMIRA and Castillo are nearby.

Santayana \ˌsän-tä-'yä-nä\, **George** *orig.* Jorge Augustín Nicolás Ruiz de Santillana (1863–1952) Spanish-U.S. philosopher, poet, and humanist. He moved to the U.S. as a boy in 1872, and he taught philosophy at Harvard Univ. from 1889 to 1912, when he returned to Europe. He made important contributions to aesthetics, speculative philosophy, and literary criticism, including *The Sense of Beauty* (1896) and *Interpretations of Poetry and Religion* (1900). *The Life of Reason* (1905–6) is a major theoretical work. He also wrote a novel, *The Last Puritan* (1935), and an autobiography, *Persons and Places* (3 vols., 1944–53).

Santería \ˌsän-te-'rē-ə\ Religious movement that originated in Cuba. It combines elements of W. African YORUBA religion with ROMAN CATHOLICISM. Worship centers on *orishas,* deities or patron saints (with parallels among the Roman Catholic saints) that combine a force of nature and humanlike characteristics. Practices may include trance dancing, rhythmic drumming, spirit possession, and animal sacrifice. Santería has a considerable following in the U.S. in areas with large African and Hispanic populations. See also CANDOMBLÉ, MACUMBA, VODUN.

Santiago (de Chile) \ˌsan-tē-'ä-gō\ City (metro. area pop., 1999 est.: 4,640,000), capital of Chile. It is located in central Chile. Founded in 1541 by the Spanish, the city has suffered repeatedly from earthquakes, floods, and civil disorders. It became the capital of an independent Chile in 1818. The country's economic center and principal industrial city, it also boasts a cosmopolitan cultural life and is the home of the Univ. of Chile.

Santiago (de Compostela) City (pop., 1991: 88,000), capital of GALICIA autonomous community, NW Spain. It contains a Romanesque cathedral completed in 1211 that was built on the tomb of the apostle St. JAMES. The tomb, discovered in the 9th cent., became the most important Christian pilgrimage site in Europe after that of Rome. Chief economic activities include silverwork and wood engraving.

Santiago (de los Caballeros) City (pop., 1993: 365,000), N central Dominican Republic. Founded about 1500, it was destroyed by an earthquake in 1562 and rebuilt a few miles away; ruins of the old city are still visible. The country's second-largest city, it produces pharmaceuticals, cigarettes, rum, and coffee.

Santiago de Cuba Seaport city (pop., 1994 est.: 440,000), E Cuba. The second-largest city in Cuba, it was founded in 1514 and was the capital of Cuba until 1589. It was a focal point of the SPANISH–AMERICAN WAR, and in 1898 the entire Spanish fleet was destroyed near its coast. In 1953 it was the scene of Fidel CASTRO's attack against the Moncada army barracks. It is the center of an agricultural and mining region and exports copper, manganese, sugar, and fruit.

Santo Domingo City (metro. area pop., 1993: 1,610,000), capital of the Dominican Republic. Founded in 1496 by Christopher COLUMBUS's brother Bartolomeo as the capital of the first Spanish colony in the New World, it became the oldest permanent city established by Europeans in the W hemisphere. Annexed to Spain in 1861, it became the capital of the independent Dominican Republic in 1865. The city was renamed Ciudad Trujillo in 1936 for Pres. Rafael TRUJILLO but reverted to its original name after his assassination in 1961. It is the commercial and cultural center of the republic and its principal seaport.

Santorini See THÍRA

Santorio, Santorio *Latin* Sanctorius (1561–1636) Italian physician. He adapted several of GALILEO's inventions to develop a medical thermometer and a pulse clock. To test GALEN's assertion that respiration also occurs through the skin as "insensible perspiration," Santorio built a large scale on which he frequently ate, worked, and slept, so he could study his body-weight changes in relation to his solid and liquid intake and output. After 30 years, he found the total of visible excreta was less than the amount ingested; his study marked the introduction of quantitative procedure into medical research.

São Francisco River \ˌsau̇ⁿm-frăⁿ-ˈsēs-kü\ River, E Brazil. The largest river wholly within Brazil, it flows north and east across the great central plateau for about 1,811 mi (2,914 km) to the Atlantic Ocean. The fish of the river are an important food source. Hydroelectric dams provide power throughout NE Brazil.

Saône River \ˈsōn\ *ancient* Arar. River, E France. It flows generally south to join the RHONE RIVER at LYON. It is navigable upstream from Lyon for 233 mi (373 km) and has 30 locks along its course, which is almost completely canalized. It is connected by canal to both the RHINE and SEINE rivers.

São Paulo \ˌsau̇ⁿm-ˈpau̇-lü\ City (metro. area pop., 1996: 16,583,000), SE Brazil. It is located 30 mi (48 km) from its Atlantic port of Santos. Founded by Portuguese Jesuits in 1554, it became a base for exploration in the 17th cent. In 1822 it was the scene of the declaration of Brazilian independence by Emperor PEDRO I. It developed rapidly from the late 19th cent. It is the foremost industrial center in LATIN AMERICA, producing steel, motor vehicles, machine tools, textiles, and appliances, as well as an important cultural and publishing center. It is the third-largest city in the world.

São Tomé \ˌsau̇ⁿ-tü-ˈmä\ City (pop., 1991: 43,000), capital of São Tomé and Príncipe. It is on the island of São Tomé. It is the country's largest city and its major port.

São Tomé and Príncipe \ˌsau̇ⁿ-tü-ˈmä...ˈprēn-sē-pē\ *officially* **Democratic Republic of São Tomé and Príncipe** Island nation, central Africa. It is situated near the equator in the

Gulf of GUINEA, west of the African mainland. Area: 386 sq mi (1,000 sq km). Population (2000): 144,000. Capital: SÃO TOMÉ. Most of the people are African. Languages: Portuguese (official), Creole dialects. Religion: Christianity. Currency: dobra. The country consists of the two main islands, São Tomé and Príncipe, which are separated by about 90 mi (145 km), and a number of islets. The two main islands each have NE lowlands, central volcanic highlands, and swift-flowing streams. The economy is partly government-controlled and partly private and is based on agriculture and fishing. It is a republic with one legislative house; its chief of state is the president, and the head of government is the prime minister. First visited by European navigators in the 1470s, the islands were colonized by the Portuguese in the 16th cent. and were used in the trade and transshipment of slaves. Sugar and cocoa were the main cash crops. The islands became an overseas province of Portugal in 1951 and achieved independence in 1975. During recent decades its economy was heavily dependent on international assistance, but deepwater oil exploration is continuing offshore.

Sapir \sə-ˈpir\, **Edward** (1884–1939) U.S. (Polish-born) linguist and anthropologist. He was a founder of ethnolinguistics, which considers the relationship of culture to language, and a principal developer of the American (descriptive) school of structural LINGUISTICS. He became widely known for his contributions to the study of N. AMERICAN INDIAN LANGUAGES. His best-known work is *Language* (1921).

sapphire Transparent to translucent natural or synthetic variety of CORUNDUM that is highly prized as a gemstone. Its color, due mainly to small amounts of iron and titanium, varies widely but normally ranges from very pale blue to deep indigo. Red varieties are called RUBY. Synthetic sapphire has been produced commercially since 1902. Much is used in jewelry, but most is used in the manufacture of jewel bearings, gauges, dies, and other specialized components. It is found in Sri Lanka, Myanmar, India, and Montana. Sapphire is the birthstone for September.

Sappho \ˈsa-fō\ (fl.c.610–c.580 B.C.) Greek lyric poet. Born on the island of Lesbos, she became the leading spirit of an informal women's society, of a type common among women of good family in her era. Her principal themes are the loves, jealousies, and hates that flourished in that atmosphere. Her writing, though not formally literary, is concise, direct, and picturesque and expresses a range of feelings, including her love for other women, which produced the word "lesbian" (from the island's name). Though much admired in antiquity, most of her work was lost by the early Middle Ages.

Sapporo \sä-ˈpō-rō\ City (pop., 1995 est.: 1,757,000), HOKKAIDO, Japan. Laid out in 1871 with wide, tree-lined streets, it became the capital in 1886. It is a major commercial center. Chief industries are lumbering, printing, and publishing. A center for skiing and winter sports, it was the site of the Winter OLYMPIC GAMES in 1972. The annual Snow Festival features giant sculptures carved from packed snow. It is the site of two universities.

sapsucker Either of two species of N. American WOODPECKERS that drill holes in neat, close rows to obtain sap and insects. The yellow-bellied sapsucker (*Sphyrapicus varius*), about 8 in. (20 cm) long, breeds in N regions and S mountains and migrates as far as the W. Indies and Central America. Both sexes have bold head markings. Williamson's sapsucker (*S. thyroideus*), which lives in high pine forests of the W U.S., is uncommon.

Saqqara *or* **Sakkara** \sə-ˈkär-ə\ Site of ancient ruins, Lower Egypt. Part of the necropolis of the ancient city of MEMPHIS, it is located southwest of CAIRO. Large mud-brick tombs, or mastabas, have been found that date to the beginning of Egyptian history. South of the Archaic-period cemetery lies the Step Pyramid, the oldest PYRAMID in Egypt. It was built by Djoser, second king (c.2650–c.2575 B.C.) of the 3rd dynasty.

Saragossa \ˌsar-ə-ˈgä-sə\ *Spanish* **Zaragoza** \ˌzä-rä-ˈgō-sä\ City (metro. area pop., 1998: 603,000), capital of ARAGON autonomous community, NE Spain. It is located on the EBRO RIVER. It became an episcopal see in the 3rd cent. A.D. and was taken by the Moors about 714. It was the capital of Aragon in the 12th–15th cent. It underwent two sieges (1808–9) by the French, which were commemorated in Lord BYRON's *Childe Harold*. It is an industrial center and the site of the annual National Trade Fair. Notable buildings include Romanesque and Gothic churches and palaces. Its university was founded in 1474.

Sarah (fl. early 2nd millennium B.C.) In the Old Testament, the wife of ABRAHAM and mother of ISAAC. In GENESIS, God promised Abraham that she would be "a mother of nations," but Sarah refused to believe, and had already given Abraham her maidservant Hagar, with whom he fathered Ishmael. Nevertheless, Sarah did conceive and bear Isaac at 90.

Sarajevo \'sä-rä-ye-ˌvò, *Engl* ˌsar-ə-'yā-vō\ City (pop., 1997 est.: 360,000), capital of Bosnia and Herzegovina. After the Turks invaded in the late 15th cent., it developed as a trading center and stronghold of Muslim culture. From 1878 it was part of the Austro-Hungarian empire (see AUSTRIA-HUNGARY). In 1914 Archduke FRANCIS FERDINAND was assassinated by a Serbian nationalist there, which action precipitated World War I. After Bosnia and Herzegovina declared independence in 1992, it became a focal point of fierce civil war as Serb militias drove thousands of Bosnian Muslims from the countryside to take refuge in the city (see BOSNIAN CONFLICT). It was the host of the 1984 Winter OLYMPIC GAMES. It retains a strong Muslim character, with many mosques and an ancient marketplace.

Saramago \ˌsä-rä-'mä-gü\, **Jose** (b.1922) Portuguese novelist. From a poor family, he worked as a mechanic before becoming a journalist. In his 50s he began writing the novels that would establish his international reputation. His breakthrough work was *Baltasar and Blimunda* (1982). His later novels, in which magic realism is mixed with political commentary, include *The Stone Raft* (1986) and *Blindness* (1995). He was awarded the Nobel Prize in 1998.

Saranac Lakes \'sar-ə-ˌnak\ Three lakes, NE New York. Located in the ADIRONDACK MTNS. region, they range in size from about 2.5 mi (4 km) wide to about 8 mi (13 km) long. The village of Saranac Lake (pop., 2000: 5,000) is a summer and winter sports resort.

Sarandon \sə-'ran-dən\, **Susan** *orig.* Susan Abigail Tomalin (b.1946) U.S. film actress. Born in New York City, she made her screen debut in 1970. After winning fans in the campy *Rocky Horror Picture Show* (1975), she proved her talent in films such as *Pretty Baby* (1978) and *Atlantic City* (1981). While working on *Bull Durham* (1988), she began a long relationship with the actor Tim Robbins (b.1958). Her later films include *Thelma and Louise* (1991) and *Dead Man Walking* (1996, Academy Award).

Saratoga, Battles of (1777) Engagements in the AMERICAN REVOLUTION. British troops under John Burgoyne marching from Canada engaged the Continental Army under Horatio GATES at the Battle of Freeman's Farm, or First Battle of Saratoga (Sept. 19). Failing to break the American lines, the British met a counterattack led by Benedict ARNOLD at the Battle of Bemis Heights, or Second Battle of Saratoga (Oct. 7). Burgoyne began to retreat, but Gates, with 20,000 men, surrounded the British and forced their surrender (Oct. 17). The victory induced the French to offer open recognition and aid.

Saratov \sə-'rä-təf\ City (pop., 1997 est.: 892,000), W Russia. Located on the VOLGA RIVER, it was founded in 1590 as a fortress to protect the trade route along the Volga. Linked to MOSCOW by railroad in the 1870s, Saratov became a major commercial center. Its road bridge across the Volga (opened 1965) is the largest in Europe. It produces industrial, electrical, and petrochemical equipment. Its educational institutions include a university (founded 1919) and a music conservatory.

sardine Any of certain species of small (6–12 in., or 15–30 cm, long) food fishes of the HERRING family (Clupeidae), especially in the genera *Sardina, Sardinops,* and *Sardinella.* The common herring *(Clupea harengus)* is found throughout the N. Atlantic. The five species of *Sardinops* live in the Pacific and Indian oceans. Sardines are small, silvery, slender fishes that live in dense schools, migrating along the coast. They are usually caught with an encircling net, particularly the purse seine, and mainly at night.

Sardinia *Italian* **Sardegna** \sär-'dän-yä\ Island and Italian autonomous region (pop., 1996 est.: 1,661,000), off the S Italian coast. It has an area of 9,194 sq mi (23,813 sq km); its capital is CAGLIARI. Thousands of structures made of basalt blocks, called nuraghi, are a dominating feature of the island; some date to about 1500–400 B.C. Phoenicians were its first recorded settlers about 800 B.C. Roman rule began in 238 B.C. In the early Middle Ages, PISA and GENOA struggled over its domination. The kingdom of Sardinia, which

included the lands of Piedmont, was ruled by the House of SAVOY from 1720 until the unification of Italy in 1861. Agriculture, fishing, and mining are economic mainstays.

Sardis \'sär-dəs\ *or* **Sardes** \'sär-dēz\ Ancient city, ASIA MINOR, east of IZMIR (Smyrna). It was the capital of the kingdom of LYDIA from the 7th cent. B.C. and the first city to mint gold and silver coins. It fell to the Persians about 546 B.C. and to the Romans in 133 B.C. Destroyed by an earthquake in A.D. 17, it was rebuilt and remained one of the great cities of Asia Minor until the later Byzantine period. It was obliterated by TIMUR in 1402. Its ruins include the ancient Lydian citadel and remains of the Hellenistic and Byzantine city.

Sardou \sär-'dü\, **Victorien** (1831–1908) French playwright. He owed his initial success to the actress Pauline Déjazet, for whom he wrote several of his 70 works. Several later works, including *Fédora* (1882), were written for Sarah BERNHARDT. His *La Tosca* (1887) was adapted by Giacomo PUCCINI as an opera. His last success was *Madame Sans-Gêne* (1893). Relying heavily on theatrical devices and plot contrivances, he is remembered as a craftsman of the bourgeois drama that G. B. SHAW belittled as "Sardoodledom."

Sargasso Sea Body of still water in the N. Atlantic Ocean. Elliptical in shape and strewn with a brown floating seaweed of the genus *Sargassum,* it lies between the parallels 20° N and 35° N and the meridians 30° W and 70° W and encompasses the BERMUDA islands. It was first mentioned by Christopher COLUMBUS, who crossed it in 1492; the seaweed suggested the proximity of land and encouraged him to sail on.

sargassum \sär-'ga-süm\ Any of the brown ALGAE of the genus *Sargassum.* They are adapted for a free-floating tropical environment, even though many species grow attached to rocks along the coast. The SARGASSO SEA covers a sizable part of the central North Atlantic Ocean. Sargassums are used as fertilizer in New Zealand and as a component of soups and soy sauce in Japan.

Sargent, John Singer (1856–1925) U.S.-British painter. Son of wealthy American parents, he was born in Italy and grew up in Europe, not seeing the U.S. until 1876. Having studied painting in Paris, in 1879 he traveled to Madrid and Haarlem to study the works of Diego VELÁZQUEZ and Frans HALS; his finest works were painted soon afterward. Best known is his *Madame X,* which created a scandal at the 1884 Salon; critics found it eccentric and erotic. Discouraged, he moved permanently to London, though he often visited the U.S. Not until 1887 did he achieve the acclaim he was to enjoy in the U.S. and England the rest of his life. His elegant portraits created an enduring image of high society of the Edwardian age; the best, painted with his slashing brush strokes, capture his subjects in revealing, off-guard moments. He largely gave up portraiture in 1907 and devoted the rest of his life to murals and landscapes.

Sargon \'sär-gän\ (r.2334–2279? B.C.) Ancient Mesopotamian ruler. What is known of him comes from legends and tales; his capital city, Agade, has never been located. He came to prominence by defeating a Sumerian king, thereby attaining an empire in S Mesopotamia. He enlarged the empire from Iraq to Anatolia, and trade flourished with the Indus valley, Oman, the Persian Gulf coast, Cappadocia, and the Mediterranean.

Sargon II (d.705 B.C.) Assyrian king (721–705 B.C.). He continued the empire-building work of his father, TIGLATH-PILESER III. His conquests ranged from S Babylonia to Armenia to the Mediterranean. He probably died in battle in NW Persia. His son, SENNACHERIB, succeeded him.

Sarnoff, David (1891–1971) U.S. (Russian-born) communications executive. After emigrating with his family to New York in 1900, he became a radio operator for the Marconi telegraph company; in 1912 he heard the distress signal from the *Titanic* and remained at his instrument for 72 hours relaying news. Rapidly promoted, he became general manager of the newly formed Radio Corp. of America (RCA CORP.) in 1921. He had proposed the first commercially marketed radio receiver in 1916. He formed the radio network NBC in 1926. Perceiving television's potential, he set up an experimental television station (1928) and demonstrated the new medium at the New York World's Fair (1939). President of RCA 1930–47, he served as chairman of the board until 1970.

Saronic Gulf \sə-'rä-nik\ Gulf of the AEGEAN SEA, SE coast of Greece. Some 50 mi (80 km) long and 30 mi (50 km) wide, it separates ATTICA and the PELOPONNESE and is linked to the Gulf of Corinth. It was the site of the Battle of SALAMIS (480 B.C.). Its ports include PIRAEUS and MEGARA.

Saroyan \sə-'ròi-ən\, **William** (1908–1981) U.S. writer. Born in Fresno, Cal., he made his initial impact during the Depression with brash, original, and irreverent stories celebrating the joy of living in spite of poverty, hunger, and insecurity. His story collections include *The Daring Young Man on the Flying Trapeze* (1934) and *My Name is Aram* (1940). His other works include the play *The Time of Your Life* (1939, Pulitzer Prize) and *The Human Comedy* (1943).

Sarraute \sà-'rōt\, **Nathalie** *orig.* Nathalie Ilyanova Tcherniak (1900–1999) French novelist and essayist. *Tropismes* (1939), a collection of sketches, introduced her idea of tropisms, the "things that are not said and the movements that cross our consciousness very rapidly." A leading theorist of the *nouveau roman* ("new novel"), the French ANTINOVEL, she discarded conventions of plot, chronology, characterization, and point of view. Her novels—including *Portrait of a Man Unknown* (1948) and *Le planétarium* (1959)—and her plays focus on the unspoken "subconversations" in human interactions.

sarsaparilla \ˌsas-pə-'ri-lə\ Aromatic flavoring agent originally made from the dried roots of several tropical vines of the family Smilacaceae. Once a popular tonic, sarsaparilla now is blended with WINTERGREEN and other flavors and used in carbonated beverages, or to flavor and mask the taste of medicines. In N. America, the strongly aromatic roots of the wild sarsaparilla (*Aralia nudicaulis*) and false, or bristly, sarsaparilla (*A. hispida*), of the GINSENG family, are sometimes substituted for true sarsaparilla.

Sarto, Andrea del See ANDREA DEL SARTO

Sartre \'sàrtrə\, **Jean-Paul** (1905–1980) French philosopher, novelist, and playwright. He studied at the Sorbonne, where he met Simone de BEAUVOIR, his lifelong companion and intellectual collaborator. His first novel, *Nausea* (1938), narrates the revulsion of a young man confronted with the contingency of existence. *Huis-clos* (1944, *No Exit*) became the most celebrated of his plays. In *Being and Nothingness* (1943) he places human consciousness, or nothingness (*néant*), in opposition to being, or thingness (*être*). With *Existentialism and Humanism* (1946), these works

Jean-Paul Sartre Photo by Gisèle Freund, 1968

formed the foundations of postwar EXISTENTIALISM. He used the PHENOMENOLOGY of Edmund HUSSERL in *Imagination* (1936) and *Sketch for a Theory of the Emotions* (1939). His final works included an autobiography, *The Words* (1963), and the huge study *Flaubert* (4 vols., 1971–72). A central figure of the French left, he opposed the Vietnam War and supported the 1968 revolutionaries. He declined the 1964 Nobel Prize for Literature.

Sasanian dynasty *or* **Sassanian dynasty** \sa-'sā-nē-ən\ (A.D. 224–651) Last Persian dynasty before the Arab conquest. Founded by Ardashir I (r.224–41) and named for his ancestor Sasan (c.1st cent. A.D.), it replaced the Parthian empire (see PARTHIA). Its capital was CTESIPHON. The dynasty battled neighbors in the west and east throughout much of its existence. In the 3rd cent. its empire stretched from Georgia to N Arabia, and from the Indus River to the Tigris and Euphrates. Traditions of the ACHAEMENIAN DYNASTY were revived, including Zoroastrianism, and art and architecture flourished. Its important rulers included Shapur I (d.272), Shapur II (309–379), KHOSROW I, and KHOSROW II.

Saskatchewan \sas-'ka-chə-ˌwän\ Province (pop., 1999 est.: 1,028,000), W Canada. It is bounded by Alberta, Manitoba, the Northwest Territories, and the U.S. The capital is REGINA. A plains region, with prairie to the south and wooded country to the north, it supports rich and varied wildlife. The Cree Indians inhabited the region for some 5,000 years before it was claimed by the HUDSON'S BAY CO., which controlled the area from 1670 until it surrendered the land to the British in 1868. It was part of the Northwest Territory until 1869, and in 1870 became part of the Dominion of Canada. From 1882 the extension of the railroad brought large numbers of European settlers. The province was created in 1905. Its economy is based on oil, gas, and potash production, grains, and livestock. The largest city is SASKATOON.

Saskatchewan River River, SW and S central Canada. The largest river system of Alberta and Saskatchewan, it rises in the Canadian Rockies as the N. and S. Saskatchewan rivers, which are 800 mi (1,287 km) and 865 mi (1,392 km) long, respectively. The combined streams continue east 340 mi (550 km) to enter Lake WINNIPEG.

Saskatoon \ˌsas-kə-'tün\ City (pop., 1996: 194,000), S central Saskatchewan. It was founded on the S. SASKATCHEWAN RIVER in 1883 as the proposed capital of a temperance colony. It grew rapidly following the arrival of the railroad in 1890. Saskatchewan's largest city, it is a cultural and educational center and a major distribution hub. It is home to the Univ. of Saskatchewan (founded 1907).

Sasquatch See BIGFOOT

sassafras \'sa-sə-ˌfras\ N. American tree (*Sassafras albidum*) of the LAUREL FAMILY. The aromatic leaf, bark, and root are used as a flavoring, as a traditional home medicine, and as a tea. The aromatic roots yield oil of sassafras, once the characteristic ingredient of root beer. The tree is native to E N. America. It is usually small but may attain a height of 65 ft (20 m) or more. It has furrowed bark, bright-green twigs, small clusters of yellow flowers followed by dark-blue berries, and three distinctive forms of leaves, often on the same twig: three-lobed, two-lobed (mitten-shaped), and entire.

Sassanian dynasty See SASANIAN DYNASTY

SAT Standardized test taken by U.S. students applying to colleges. It is divided into verbal and mathematical sections. Promulgated largely through the efforts of James B. CONANT to promote merit-based (rather than class-based) college admissions, it is now taken by millions each year. Scores declined as the test came to be widely administered, and in 1995 the score of 500 for each section (midway between the extremes of 200 and 800) was reestablished as the actual mean score of those tested. The test has been insistently criticized for a claimed bias in favor of the white middle class, and for its multiple-choice format, which critics claim is inadequate to test important capacities.

satanism Worship of Satan, or the DEVIL, the personality or principle regarded in the Judeo-Christian tradition as embodying absolute evil. Satanist cults have been documented, however sketchily, back to the 17th cent. Their central feature is the black MASS, a corrupted and inverted rendition of the Christian EUCHARIST. Practices are said to include animal SACRIFICE and deviant sexual activity. Practitioners believe that Satan is more powerful than the forces of good.

satellite Object orbiting a larger astronomical object, usually a planet. The MOON was the only one known until the discovery of the GALILEAN SATELLITES. All the sun's planets except Mercury and Venus have natural satellites, which vary greatly in size and composition. The first artificial satellite was SPUTNIK 1 (1957). Since then, hundreds have been sent into orbit around earth, Venus, Mars, Jupiter, and the sun and moon for scientific research, communication (see COMMUNICATIONS SATELLITE), weather forecasting, earth resources management, and military intelligence. See also LANDSAT.

satellite, communications See COMMUNICATIONS SATELLITE

sati See SUTTEE

Satie \sà-'tē\, **Erik** (*orig.* Eric Alfred Leslie) (1866–1925) French composer. His Scottish mother died when he was 7, and he was reared by his grandparents in Normandy. He at-

S

tended the Paris Conservatoire, and from 1888 he played piano at Le Chat Noir, a bohemian hangout. Living in austere poverty, he gained prominence in 1911 when Maurice RAVEL played his *Three Sarabandes* (1887), and was acknowledged as a forerunner of modern music by Claude DEBUSSY, Jean COCTEAU, and Les SIX. His mostly short piano works are as odd, witty, and charming as he was, and often sport such bizarre titles as *Three Pieces in the Form of a Pear*.

satin Fabric constructed by the satin WEAVING method, one of the three basic TEXTILE weaves. Satin weave superficially resembles twill, but lacks the regular step in each successive weft that characterizes twills. Thus, there is no strong diagonal line, and the fabric is smooth-faced, with an unbroken surface made up of long floating warp yarns. Because satins are susceptible to wear, they are considered luxury fabrics. Satin is made in different weights for various uses, including evening dresses, linings, bedspreads, and upholstery. Though originally of silk, it may be made of yarns of other fibers.

satire Artistic form in which human or individual vices, folly, abuses, or shortcomings are held up to censure by means of ridicule, irony, or other methods. Literature and drama are its chief vehicles, but it is also found in such mediums as film and political cartoons. Satire generally follows the example of either of two Romans, HORACE or JUVENAL. To Horace the satirist is an urbane man of the world who sees folly everywhere but is moved to gentle laughter rather than to rage. Juvenal's satirist is an upright man who is horrified and angered by corruption. Their different perspectives produced the subgenres of satire identified by John DRYDEN as comic satire and tragic satire.

Sato \\'sä-tō\\, **Eisaku** (1901–1975) Prime minister of Japan (1964–1972). He served in cabinet posts from 1958. As prime minister, he presided over Japan's post-World War II reemergence as a major world power. He improved relations with other Asian countries and oversaw the return of the Ryukyu Islands from the U.S. to Japan. For his policies on nuclear weapons, which led to Japan's signing the nuclear nonproliferation treaty, he shared the 1974 Nobel Peace Prize.

satrap Provincial governor under the ACHAEMENIAN DYNASTY. DARIUS I (r.522–486 B.C.) established 20 satrapies. Usually of the royal family or Persian nobility, satraps held office indefinitely. They collected taxes, were the highest judicial authority, and were responsible for internal security and raising and maintaining an army. After the mid-5th cent. B.C., with central authority weakened, satrapies became virtually independent.

Satsuma \\'sät-sü-ˌmä\\ Japanese feudal domain in S Kyushu. It was ruled by the Shimazu family from the late 12th cent. until the MEIJI RESTORATION in 1868. In 1609 the family conquered the RYUKYU ISLANDS, and trade with the Ryukyus continued during the TOKUGAWA SHOGUNATE, when the rest of the country was forbidden contact with the outside world. This trade enriched Satsuma and provided experience with foreign affairs that became useful in the 19th cent. when Western powers started pressuring Japan to end its isolation. Satsuma leaders included Shimazu Shigehide (1745–1833), who founded schools of medicine, mathematics, and astronomy, and Shimazu Nariakira (1809–1858), who adopted Western-style military techniques and armaments. These advantages, along with a traditional enmity toward the Tokugawa family, enabled Satsuma to help overthrow the shogunal government.

saturation State of an ORGANIC COMPOUND in which all its CARBON atoms are linked by single bonds. Saturation also means the state of a SOLUTION or vapor (see VAPORIZATION) in which it has the highest possible concentration of the dissolved or vaporized material at a given pressure and temperature. See also FATTY ACID, HYDROGENATION.

Saturn Roman god of agriculture, equated with the Greek deity CRONUS. His children included JUNO, NEPTUNE, and CERES. His festival, Saturnalia (beginning Dec. 17), became the most popular Roman festival; its influence is still felt in the celebration of CHRISTMAS and the Western New Year. During Saturnalia, all business transactions were suspended, presents were exchanged, and slaves were given token freedom. Saturday is named for Saturn.

Saturn Sixth PLANET from the sun, second-largest after Jupiter, named after the Roman god of sowing and seed. It has about 95 times earth's mass and over 700 times its volume. Its outer layers are gaseous, mainly hydrogen. Models of its interior suggest a rocky core within a shallow layer of liquid metallic hydrogen and an envelope of molecular hydrogen. Saturn has at least 18 icy satellites (including Titan, the biggest) and an extensive ring system, with seven main sections visible from earth by telescope. The rings, first observed in 1610 by GALILEO, are made up of countless particles, thought to range from grains of fine dust to a few possibly tens of miles across; they are probably mostly water ice. Saturn's day is about 10.5 hours; its year is 29.5 earth years. Its rapid rotation generates a strong magnetic field and large magnetosphere. Its gravity at the top of its atmosphere is 16% greater than earth's. Its average distance from the sun is 887 million mi (1,427 billion km).

Saturn Any of a series of large U.S. two- and three-stage vehicles for launching spacecraft, first fired in 1961. Saturn I, the first U.S. rocket specifically developed for spaceflight, placed test versions of APOLLO spacecraft into orbit and launched unmanned spacecraft. Saturn V, the largest rocket booster ever built by the U.S., was used for Apollo lunar missions and to launch SKYLAB.

satyagraha \\ˌsət-'yä-grə-hə\\ Philosophy of nonviolent protest, or passive resistance. Mohandas GANDHI introduced it in S. Africa (1906) and, from 1917, developed it in India in the period leading up to independence from Britain. Satyagraha involves refusing to submit to or cooperate with anything perceived as wrong, while adhering to the principle of nonviolence in order to maintain the tranquillity of mind required for insight and understanding. The principle played a significant role in the civil rights activism of M. L. KING. See also CIVIL DISOBRDIENCE.

satyr and silenus \\'sā-tər...sī-'lē-nəs\\ In GREEK MYTHOLOGY, wild woodland creatures that are part man and part beast, the bestial part being represented as the legs of a goat or horse. From the 5th cent. B.C., the name Silenus was applied to the foster father and tutor of DIONYSUS. Satyrs and sileni are depicted in art and literature in the company of NYMPHS, whom they constantly pursue.

Saud dynasty \\sä-'üd\\ Rulers of present-day Saudi Arabia. In the 18th cent. Muhammad ibn Saud (d.1765), chief of an Arabian village, rose to power together with the WAHHABI movement. He and his son Abd al-Aziz I (r.1764–1803) conquered much of Arabia; Saud I (r.1803–14) conquered Medina in 1804 and Mecca in 1806. The Ottomans and Egyptians had crushed the Saudis and Wahhabis by 1818. A second Saudi state rose in 1824 under Muhammad ibn Saud's grandson Turki (r.1823–34), who made Riyadh his capital. When Turki's son Faisal (r.1843–65) died, succession disputes led to civil war. Saudis regained power in 1902, when IBN SAUD recaptured Riyadh. He established the kingdom of Saudi Arabia in 1932. One of his sons, Fahd (b.1923), is the country's current ruler.

Saudi Arabia \\'saü-dē, 'sȯ-dē\\ *officially* **Kingdom of Saudi Arabia** Country, SW Asia. It occupies four-fifths of the ARABIAN PENINSULA and is bounded by the Red Sea and the Persian Gulf. Area: 865,000 sq mi (2.24 million sq km). Population (2000): 22,024,000. Capital: RIYADH. The people are predominantly Arab. Language: Arabic (official). Religion: Islam (official) (Sunnite). Currency: Saudi riyal. The country is a plateau region, with bands of imposing highlands rising from the narrow Red Sea coast. More than 95% is desert, including the world's largest continuous sand area, the RUB AL-KHALI (Empty Quarter). The largest petroleum producer of the ORGANIZATION OF PETROLEUM EXPORTING COUNTRIES (OPEC) and the third-largest producer in the world, it holds reserves representing one-fourth of the world total. Other products include natural gas, gypsum, dates, wheat, and desalinated water. It is a monarchy; its head of state and government is the king. Saudi Arabia is the historical home of ISLAM, founded by MUHAMMAD in MEDINA in 622. During medieval times, local and foreign rulers fought for control of the peninsula; in 1517 the Ottomans prevailed. In the 18th–19th cent. Islamic leaders supporting religious reform struggled to regain Saudi territory, all of which was restored by 1904. The British held

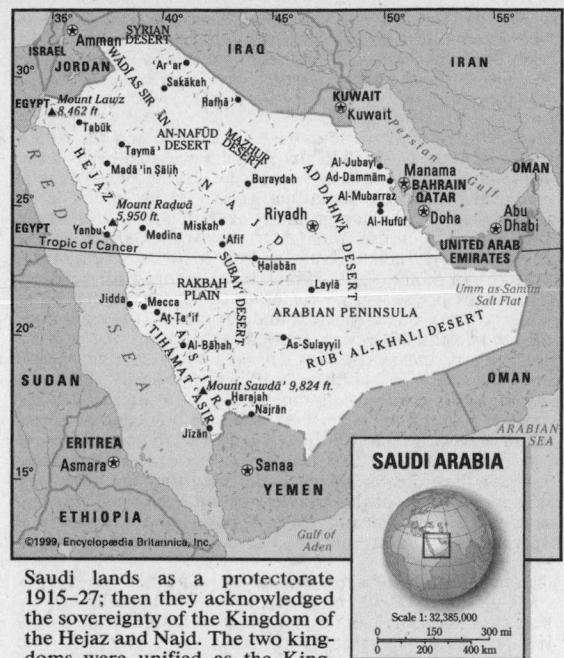

Saudi lands as a protectorate 1915–27; then they acknowledged the sovereignty of the Kingdom of the Hejaz and Najd. The two kingdoms were unified as the Kingdom of Saudi Arabia in 1932. Since World War II, it has supported the Palestinian cause in the Middle East and maintained close ties wth the U.S. In 2000 Saudi Arabia and Yemen settled their longstanding border dispute.

Sauk \'sȯk\ *or* **Sac** N. American Indian people who traditionally inhabited the region of what is now Green Bay, Wis. They raised corn and other crops and hunted bison. By about 1800 the Sauk had settled along the Mississippi River in central Illinois, but they were forced to cede these lands to the U.S. In 1832 a group of Sauk and Fox led by BLACK HAWK made a tragically unsuccessful attempt to return to their Illinois lands. Today about 1,000 Sauk live in Oklahoma.

Saul *Hebrew* Shaul. First king of Israel (r.1021–1000 B.C.). According to the biblical books of Samuel I and II, he was anointed king by the prophet SAMUEL, who later rejected him in favor of

Sauk chief Keokuk, painted by J. O. Lewis, 1825

DAVID, of whom Saul was intensely jealous. He died battling the Philistines at Mt. Gilboa; David delivered the Israelites and paid tribute to the fallen Saul.

Sault Sainte Marie \ˌsü-ˌsänt-mə-ˈrē\ City (pop., 2000: 17,000), E Upper Peninsula, Michigan. Located between Lakes SUPERIOR and HURON, it is linked to its Canadian twin city, Sault Sainte Marie, Ontario (pop., 1996: 80,000), by road and rail bridges. The U.S. and Canada both operate a part of the Sault Sainte Marie Canals, or Soo Canals, a hub of the ST. LAWRENCE SEAWAY. The first U.S. canal went into operation in 1855. The Canadian canal, which has one lock, was completed in 1895.

sauna Bath in steam from water thrown on heated stones. Known in ancient times in various places, saunas are most closely identified with the Finnish people. Traditionally, a wooden hut is built near the edge of a lake, with rows of flat stones inside. These are heated by burning wood in a space under the floor. Cold water is then thrown on them to create steam. The unclothed users sit on wooden benches in the steam-filled hut, then beat themselves with branches until their skin is red and tingling and dive into the cold water, or in winter roll in the snow. This is thought to be good for the circulation.

saurischian \sȯ-ˈris-kē-ən\ Any "lizard-hipped" DINOSAUR species (order Saurischia), with hip bones arranged like those of modern REPTILES, the pubis bone pointed forward and down. The order includes all carnivorous and some giant herbivorous dinosaurs. Saurischians first appeared in the Late TRIASSIC PERIOD (227–208 million years ago). The order consists of three suborders: THEROPODS, SAUROPODS, and staurikosaurs (suborder Staurikosauria). Staurikosaurs seem to have been medium-sized flesh-eaters similar to the theropods. See also ORNITHISCHIAN.

sauropod \'sȯr-ə-ˌpäd\ Any species of four-legged, herbivorous SAURISCHIANS in the suborder Sauropoda. The largest of all DINOSAURS, they existed from the Late Triassic through the Cretaceous period (230–65 million years ago). All species had a small head on an extremely long neck; a long, massive body; thick, pillarlike legs; and a very long, tapering, whiplike tail. Sauropods ranged from 50 ft (15 m) long to the 100-ft (30-m) *Brachiosaurus*, which weighed 90 tons (80 metric tons). See also BRONTOSAURUS, DIPLODOCUS, THEROPOD.

sausage Highly seasoned minced meat, usually PORK or BEEF, traditionally stuffed into animal intestines. Sausage has been known since ancient times. Some varieties are known by their city of origin (the frankfurter from Frankfurt am Main, romano from Rome, etc.). Sausage meat may be fresh, smoked, or pickled. It may be mixed with other meats and additives such as cereals, preservatives, and various spices. Casings may be intestine, fabric bags, or synthetic materials. All but dry (smoked) sausages require refrigeration. Cooked and dry sausages are ready to eat; fresh (and fresh-frozen) sausages must be cooked.

Saussure \sō-ˈsᵫr\, **Ferdinand de** (1857–1913) Swiss linguist. Though his only written work appeared while he was still a university student, Saussure became very influential as a teacher, principally at the Univ. of Geneva (1901–13). Two students reconstructed his notes as *Course in General Linguistics* (1916), often considered the starting point of 20th-cent. LINGUISTICS. He saw language as a structured system that may be approached both as it exists at a particular time and as it changes over time. His concepts may be regarded as the beginning of STRUCTURALISM.

Sauveur \sō-ˈvœr\, **Albert** (1863–1939) Belgian-U.S. metallurgist. He taught at Harvard Univ. 1899–1939. His microscopic and photomicroscopic studies of metal structures make him one of the founders of physical METALLURGY. His work in heat treating of metals is regarded as a scientific landmark.

Savannah City (pop., 2000: 131,000), SE Georgia. It is the oldest city in Georgia and its principal seaport. Established in 1733 by James OGLETHORPE, it was the birthplace of the Georgia colony, the colonial government seat, and capital of the state until 1786. A major Confederate supply port during the AMERICAN CIVIL WAR, the city was the objective of Union Gen. W. T. SHERMAN's march to the sea in 1864. Noted for its beautiful historic buildings, it is a leading tourist center.

Savigny \'zä-vin-yē\, **Friedrich Karl von** (1779–1861) German legal historian. He helped found the influential "historical school" of jurisprudence. His *History of Roman Law in the Middle Ages* (6 vols., 1815–31) laid the foundation for the modern study of medieval law. He founded a system for establishing a modern German CIVIL LAW with his *System of Modern Roman Law* (8 vols., 1840–49). A product of Romanticism, he regarded law as a reflection of a people's customs and spirit that could not be imposed artificially by means of rational, formal legislation.

Savimbi \sə-ˈvim-bē\, **Jonas (Malheiro)** (1934–2002) Angolan guerrilla leader and politician. He founded the National Union for the Total Independence of Angola (UNITA) in 1966. Independence was finally achieved in 1975, but with aid from China, S. Africa, and the U.S., UNITA's guerrilla army waged an extended war against the

new Soviet-backed government. In 1991 Savimbi agreed to participate in free multiparty elections, but after losing he resumed military action. A peace accord (1994) and later agreements (1996) permitted UNITA to join a coalition government, but Savimbi declined to become vice president and violence continued. He died fighting government troops.

saving Process of setting aside a portion of current income for future use, or the resources accumulated in this way. Savings may take the form of bank deposits and cash holdings or securities. If individuals consume more than the value of their income, then their saving is negative and they are said to be dissaving. Individual saving may be measured by estimating disposable income and subtracting current CONSUMPTION expenditures. A measure of business saving is the increase in net worth shown on a BALANCE SHEET. Total national saving is the excess of national income over consumption and taxes. An increase in productive wealth requires that some individuals must abstain from consuming their entire income and make their savings available for INVESTMENT.

savings and loan association Financial institution that accepts savings from depositors and uses those funds primarily to make loans to home buyers. Savings and loan associations (S&Ls) originated with 18th-cent. British building societies, in which workmen banded together to finance the building of their homes. The first U.S. S&L was established in Philadelphia in 1831. S&Ls were initially cooperative institutions in which savers were shareholders. Today they are mutual organizations that are not obliged to rely on individual deposits for funds but are permitted to borrow from other financial institutions and to market mortgage-backed SECURITIES, money-market certificates, and STOCK. Because high INFLATION and rising interest rates in the 1970s made fixed-rate mortgages unprofitable, regulations were altered to permit S&Ls to renegotiate mortgages. In the late 1980s, a growing number of S&Ls failed because inadequate regulation had allowed risky investments and fraud to flourish. The government was obliged to cover vast losses in excess of $200 billion. A new organization supervised by the FEDERAL DEPOSIT INSURANCE CORP. was formed to take over insurance functions, and the Resolution Trust Corp. was established to handle the bailout of the failed S&Ls.

savings bank Financial institution that gathers savings and pays INTEREST or DIVIDENDS to savers. It channels the savings of individuals who wish to consume less than their incomes to borrowers who wish to spend more. This function is performed by mutual savings banks, SAVINGS AND LOAN ASSOCIATIONS, CREDIT UNIONS, postal savings systems, and municipal savings banks. Unlike COMMERCIAL BANKS, these institutions do not permit deposits on demand. The earliest savings banks developed from the municipal pawnshops of Italy (see PAWNBROKING). Others were founded in Germany in 1778 and The Netherlands in 1817. The first U.S. savings banks were nonprofit institutions established in the early 1800s for charitable purposes.

Savonarola \ˌsa-və-nə-ˈrō-lə, *Italian* ˌsä-vō-nä-ˈrô-lä\, **Girolamo** (1452–1498) Italian religious reformer. He joined the DOMINICAN order in 1475 and was sent to Florence to lecture at the convent of San Marco, where he became known for his learning and asceticism. He preached that the church needed reforming and would be scourged. After the overthrow of the MEDICI FAMILY (1494), Savonarola became leader of Florence, setting up a democratic but severely puritanical government and seeking to establish a Christian republic as a base for reforming Italy and the church. He was opposed by the Arrabiati, supporters of the Medici, and by Pope ALEXANDER VI. Convicted of heresy (1498), he was hanged and burned. Despite popular veneration, attempts to bring about his canonization have been unsuccessful.

Savoy *French* **Savoie** \sà-ˈvwä\ *Italian* **Savoia** \sä-ˈvô-yä\ Historical region, SE France and NW Italy. From the 11th cent. the counts of Savoy ruled it as part of the kingdom of ARLES. In the 18th cent. Savoy and PIEDMONT in Italy were incorporated into the kingdom of SARDINIA, and the dukes of Savoy became kings of Sardinia. Savoy and Piedmont were ceded to France in 1792, but Savoy was restored to its traditional rulers in 1815, with the addition of GENOA. In 1860 Sardinia, Genoa, and Piedmont joined other Italian states to form the kingdom of Italy. The House of SAVOY was the ruling house of Italy until 1946, when the Italian Republic was established.

Savoy, House of Historic dynasty of Europe and the ruling house of Italy 1861–1946. Its founder was Umberto I the Whitehanded (d.1048?), who held the county of Savoy. His medieval successors, including AMADEUS VI, added territory in the W Alps. Though under French domination in the 17th cent., the house under VICTOR AMADEUS II acquired territory in NE Italy and attained the royal title, first of the kingdom of Sicily (1713), which he exchanged for Sardinia (1720). The house was powerful in the RISORGIMENTO, and under VICTOR EMMANUEL II and CHARLES ALBERT it contributed to the 19th-cent. unification of Italy. UMBERTO I and VICTOR EMMANUEL III served mainly as figureheads until the vote for a republic in 1946 ended Savoy rule.

saw Tool for cutting solid materials. Most saws take the form of a thin metal strip with teeth on one edge or a thin metal disk with teeth on the edge. The teeth are usually set to alternate sides so that the kerf (groove) cut by the saw is wider than the thickness of the saw; the saw blade can thus move freely in the groove without binding. Thin-strip saws are used in various ways in both hand and machine operations; circular, or disk, saws are always machine-powered.

Sawatch Range \sə-ˈwäch\ Range of the ROCKY MTNS., central Colorado. It is 100 mi (160 km) long. It includes Mt. Elbert (14,433 ft, or 4,399 m), the highest point in the Rockies. Its middle portion, with Mts. Yale, Harvard, and Princeton, is usually called the Collegiate Range. The discovery of gold attracted settlers in 1860; ranching, dairying, and tourism are the main industries today.

Sawchuk \ˈsȯw-chək\, **Terry** (*orig.* Terrence Gordon) (1929–1970) Canadian-U.S. hockey goalie. Born in Winnipeg, Manitoba, he joined the National Hockey League in 1949, playing for the Detroit Red Wings (1949–54, 1957–64), Boston Bruins (1955–56), Toronto Maple Leafs (1964–67), and other teams. His career record of 103 shutouts still stands, as does his record of most games (971); he ranks second in career wins (435).

sawfish Any of about six species (genus *Pristis,* family Pristidae) of sharklike RAY. Sawfishes have a long head, long body, and a long, toothed, bladelike snout. The largest attain lengths of 23 ft (7 m) or more. These bottom-dwellers inhabit shallow waters of subtropical and tropical bays and estuaries and sometimes swim up rivers. Their saws are used either to dig out bottom animals or, when lashed about, to kill or maim schooling fishes. Sawfishes are fished in some areas for food, oil, and skins.

sawfly Any of numerous, widely distributed insect species in five families (superfamily Tenthredinoidea, order Hymenoptera). Typical sawflies (family Tenthredinidae), often brightly colored, are found on flowers; the N. American pear slug eats pear, cherry, and plum leaves. Argid sawflies (family Argidae) feed on rose bushes and willow, oak, and birch trees. The N. American elm sawfly (family Cimbicidae) feeds on elm and willow. The N. American conifer sawflies (family Diprionidae) are common pests of coniferous trees. The pergid sawflies (family Pergidae) inhabit S. America and Australia.

sawmill Machine or plant with power-driven machines for sawing logs into rough-squared sections or into planks and boards. A sawmill may be equipped with planing, molding, tenoning, and other machines for finishing processes. Cutting is performed on various large machines; reciprocating saws, band saws, or circular saws cut the log into various thicknesses as it moves past the saw on a feeder table. The biggest mills are usually located where timber can be brought by river or rail.

Sax, Adolphe (*orig.* Antoine Joseph) (1814–1894) Belgian instrument maker. Son of an accomplished instrument maker, he worked for his father until 1842, making improvements on the clarinet and bass clarinet. He then set up shop in Paris, and invented several new families of instruments, including the saxhorns, the saxtrombas, and most successfully, the SAXOPHONES. He taught saxophone at the Paris Conservatory 1857–71.

Saxe, (Hermann-) Maurice, comte (Count) de (1696–1750) German-French general. He served under EUGENE OF SAVOY in Flanders and was made Count of Saxony (Saxe) in 1711. He commanded a German regiment in the French service (1719) and made innovations in military training, especially in musketry. He served with distinction in the French army in the War of the POLISH SUCCESSION and successfully led French forces in the War of the AUSTRIAN SUCCESSION, capturing Prague (1741) and invading the Austrian Netherlands. Appointed marshal-general of France by LOUIS XV, Saxe led the successful invasion of Holland in 1747.

Saxe-Coburg-Gotha, House of See House of WINDSOR

saxifrage \'sak-sə-frij\ Any of about 300 species of the genus *Saxifraga,* of the family Saxifragaceae, which is composed of 36 genera of mostly perennial herbaceous plants. Saxifrages are known for their ability to thrive on exposed rocky crags and in fissures of rocks, although most grow in moist, shaded woodlands in N cold and temperate regions. Leaves characteristically alternate along the stem and sometimes are deeply lobed or form rosettes. Flowers generally are borne in branched clusters and range widely in color. The fruit is a capsule. *Saxifraga* species are prized for their small, bright flowers, fine-textured foliage, and early spring flowering.

Saxo Grammaticus \'sak-sō-grə-'ma-ti-kəs\ *orig.* Saxo (fl.mid-12th cent.–early 13th cent.) Danish historian. His 16-volume *Gesta Danorum* ("Story of the Danes") is the first important work on the history of Denmark and the first Danish contribution to world literature. A panorama of his country's antiquity and traditions, it inspired many 19th-cent. Danish Romantic poets and was the original source of the story of William SHAKESPEARE's *Hamlet.* Saxo's brilliant, ornate Latin earned him the name "Grammaticus" in the 14th cent.

Saxons Germanic people who lived along the Baltic coast in ancient times and later migrated west as far as the British Isles. The Saxons became pirates in the North Sea during the decline of the Roman empire, and in the early 5th cent. they spread through N Germany and along the coasts of Gaul and Britain. They fought CHARLEMAGNE (772–804) before being incorporated into the Frankish kingdom, and they settled Britain along with other Germanic invaders, including the ANGLES and the Jutes.

Saxony *German* **Sachsen** \'zäk-sən\ Historical region, former state, and re-created state, Germany. Before 1180 the name was applied to the territory conquered around A.D. 200–700 by the SAXONS, who were later conquered and Christianized by CHARLEMAGNE. In the mid-9th cent. it became part of the German kingdom of the FRANKS. The territory was broken up in 1180. From 1422 the name was applied to a large region, including the country from THURINGIA to Lusatia, bordering Bohemia. It was part of the German empire 1871–1918, and a free state in the WEIMAR REPUBLIC 1919–33. The state was abolished in 1952. Upon German reunification in 1990, a new state of Saxony was created.

saxophone Single-reed wind instrument with a conical metal tube and finger keys. Though made of brass, it is classified as a WOODWIND INSTRUMENT. The saxophone family includes instruments with at least eight different ranges, the tenor and alto instruments being the most common. The smallest (highest-range) saxophones are straight; the rest have curved necks and their bells are bent up and out. All are transposing instruments in B-flat and E-flat, with the same written 3½-octave range. Patented in 1846 by Adolphe SAX, saxophones became centrally important in military, dance, and jazz bands.

Say \'se, *Engl* 'sā\, **J(ean)-B(aptiste)** (1767–1832) French economist. He edited a magazine and started a spinning mill before joining the faculty of the Conservatory of Arts and Crafts (1817–30). In *A Treatise on Political Economy* (1803), he advanced his law of markets, which claims that supply creates its own demand. He attributed economic DEPRESSION to temporary overproduction for some markets and underproduction for others, an imbalance that must automatically adjust itself as overproducers redirect their production to conform with consumer preferences. Say's law remained central to orthodox economics until the GREAT DEPRESSION.

Sayers, Dorothy L(eigh) (1893–1957) English scholar and writer. In *Whose Body?* (1923), she created the detective Lord Peter Wimsey, a witty, dashing young gentleman-scholar who would be featured in such later short-story collections and novels as *Strong Poison* (1930) and *Busman's Honeymoon* (1937). After the 1930s she concentrated on theological dramas and books, radio plays, and scholarly translations, notably of DANTE's *Divine Comedy.*

Sayles, John (b.1950) U.S. film director. Born in Schenectady, N.Y., he wrote short stories and novels, including *Union Dues* (1977), before becoming a screenwriter for Roger CORMAN. He made his directorial debut with the acclaimed *Return of the Secaucus Seven* (1980). Usually writing his own screenplays, he has explored social and political issues in *Lianna* (1982), *Matewan* (1987), *Eight Men Out* (1988), *Lone Star* (1996), and *Sunshine State* (2002). He also directed the children's movie *The Secret of Roan Inish* (1994).

Sazonov \sə-'zȯ-nəf\, **Sergey (Dmitriyevich)** (1860–1927) Russian diplomat. As minister of foreign affairs 1910–16, he promoted close relations with Britain and France and supported the Balkan League against Turkey. He contributed to the precipitating events of World War I by insisting that NICHOLAS II mobilize the Russian army (July 30, 1914); two days later, Germany declared war on Russia. He set Russia's war aim as the annexation of Constantinople and the Turkish straits, but was dismissed when he urged the czar to grant Poland autonomy. In 1917 he moved to France.

scalawag U.S. Southerner who supported RECONSTRUCTION. Opponents also applied the pejorative term to those who joined with CARPETBAGGERS and freedmen to support REPUBLICAN PARTY policies. Scalawags included former Whigs and hill-country farmers with Unionist sympathies and comprised almost 20% of the white electorate after the AMERICAN CIVIL WAR. Many held government positions in the South and advocated moderate reforms.

scale Primary pitches of a KEY or MODE arranged within an octave. Scales are distinguished by the pattern of the INTERVALS between adjacent notes. A scale can be seen as an abstraction from MELODY—that is, the pitches of a melody arranged in stepwise order.

Scale Examples of the chromatic, major, and minor scales.

scale insect Any member of several families of sap-sucking INSECTS (order Homoptera) whose bodies are covered by a waxy shell (the scale). Scale insects may attack any part of a plant, but each species is host-specific. Many species are serious plant pests; the cottony-cushion scale (*Icerya purchasi*) has threatened the California citrus industry. Others have commercial value; the lac insect is used in a red dye and in shellac, and cochineal, a red dyestuff, consists of the pulverized bodies of *Dactylopius coccus.*.

Scalia \skə-'lē-ə\, **Antonin** (b.1936) U.S. jurist. Born in Trenton, N.J., he served as an assistant U.S. attorney general (1974–77), and taught at the Univ. of Chicago (1977–82). A staunch conservative, he was appointed to the U.S. Court of Appeals (1982) and then to the U.S. Supreme Court (1986). There Scalia has opposed judicial activism and applied narrow interpretations to acts of Congress while granting some leniency to state and local laws, provided they do not conflict with federal law or with conservative constitutional principles.

scallop Any of more than 400 species (family Pectinidae) of marine BIVALVES. The two halves of the shell (valves) are usually fan-shaped. The shells are 1–6 in. (2.5–15 cm) long. They may be smooth or ribbed and red, purple, orange, yellow, or white. Cilia filter microscopic plants and animals from the water and move them toward the mouth. Scallops swim by clapping the valves, propelling themselves forward. The muscle that closes the valves is a popular food item.

scalping Removal of all or part of the scalp, with hair attached, from an enemy's head. It is best known as a practice of N. American Indian warfare. At first confined to eastern tribes, it spread as a result of bounties offered by the French, English, Dutch, and Spanish for the scalps of enemy Indians and sometimes of enemy whites. Many American frontiersmen and soldiers adopted the custom. Among PLAINS INDIANS, scalps were taken for war honors, usually from dead enemies. For live victims, the operation was not necessarily fatal.

scaly anteater See PANGOLIN

scampi or **Dublin Bay prawn** or **Norway lobster** Edible LOBSTER (*Nephrops norvegicus*), widespread in the Mediterranean and NE Atlantic. It is sold as a delicacy. Scampi live in burrows on soft sea bottoms at depths of 30 to 820 ft (10–250 m). They grow to about 8 in. (20 cm) long and weigh about 7 oz (200 g).

Scandinavia Region of N Europe, usually defined as comprising Norway, Sweden, and Denmark, and sometimes also Finland and Iceland. Norway and Sweden occupy the Scandinavian Peninsula. The Scandinavian peoples are culturally similar, and speak a closely related group of GERMANIC LANGUAGES.

scanner, optical Computer input device that uses a light beam to scan codes, text, or graphics directly into a computer or computer system. BAR-CODE scanners are used widely in retail stores, and in manufacturing for inventory control. Optical scanners are also used in FAX machines and to input text and graphics directly into PERSONAL COMPUTERS for further manipulation using software applications. See also OCR.

Scapa Flow Sea basin, ORKNEY ISLANDS, off N Scotland. It is about 15 mi (24 km) long and 8 mi (13 km) wide. Its sheltered waters served as a major British naval base during World Wars I and II. The Germans scuttled their fleet there after World War I. The base was fortified in World War II following German attacks and the sinking of the battleship *Royal Oak* in 1939. The base closed in 1956.

scapegoat In the Old Testament, a goat that was symbolically burdened with the SINS of the people and then killed on YOM KIPPUR to rid Jerusalem of its iniquities. Similar rituals were held elsewhere in the ancient world, where individuals were sometimes allowed or made to take on the sins or penalties of others. CHRISTIANITY reflects this notion in its belief that JESUS died to atone for the sins of mankind.

scar Mark left on the skin after a wound heals. Cells called fibroblasts produce COLLAGEN fibers, which form bundles that make up the bulk of scar tissue. Scars have a blood supply but no oil glands or elastic tissue. Hypertrophic scars grow overly thick and fibrous but remain within the original wound site; tumorlike growths called keloids may extend beyond the wound's limits. Both can inhibit movement, especially around a joint. All scars, especially those from unaided healing of third-degree burns, can become malignant. Treatment of serious scars is one of the most important problems in PLASTIC SURGERY.

scarab \ˈskar-əb\ In EGYPTIAN RELIGION, a symbol of immortality much used in funerary art. It was inspired by the life cycle of the SCARAB BEETLE. The dung balls that the beetles consume, lay their eggs in, and use to feed their young were associated with immortality and with the passage of the sun across the heavens. First appearing around 2575–2130 B.C.,

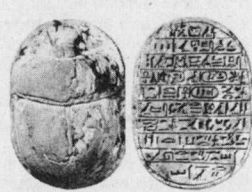

Scarab commemorating the marriage of Amenhotep III and Queen Tiy, 18th dynasty

scarabs were fashioned in great numbers during the Middle Kingdom and New Kingdom.

scarab beetle Any of about 30,000 BEETLE species (family Scarabaeidae), found worldwide, that are compact, heavy-bodied, and oval. Species range from about 0.2 to 5 in. (5–120 mm) long and include one of the heaviest known insects. One species of DUNG BEETLE, *Scarabaeus sacer*, was sacred to the ancient Egyptians. Many species are agricultural pests (e.g., JAPANESE BEETLE, JUNE BEETLE); many are popular with insect collectors because they are large and have beautifully colored, hard, highly polished forewings.

Scarborough City (pop., 1994 est.: 109,000), N Yorkshire, England. Located on the North Sea coast, it originated as a 10th-cent. Viking fishing settlement at the site of a 4th-cent. Roman signal station. After 1626, spa development made it a fashionable destination. It remains a popular seaside resort.

Scarborough City (pop., 1996: 559,000), SE Ontario. It is part of the municipality of Metropolitan Toronto. Its coastal bluffs reminded settlers of SCARBOROUGH, England. Originally a farming community, it later became an industrial and residential urban compound.

Scarlatti, (Pietro) Alessandro (Gaspare) (1660–1725) Italian composer. By 1680 he was chapel master in Rome for Queen CHRISTINA of Sweden. He left this secure position to become chapel master of the viceroy of Naples (1684–1702). Most of the operas produced in the city during this period were his own, and they were increasingly heard in other cities as well, including Leipzig and London. He wrote at least 70 operas and some 600 secular cantatas; his opera overtures (*sinfonie*) were important forerunners of the symphony. Domenico SCARLATTI was his son.

Scarlatti \skär-ˈlät-ē\, **(Giuseppe) Domenico** (1685–1757) Italian composer and keyboard player. Son of Alessandro SCARLATTI, he worked as his father's assistant in Naples. By 1723 he was tutor to the Spanish infanta (later crown princess) Maria Barbara, in whose service he remained for much of his life. Though he wrote operas, oratorios, cantatas, and other works, his reputation rests on the 555 brilliant one-movement keyboard sonatas he wrote for her, one of the greatest bodies of work by any baroque composer.

scarlet fever Acute infectious disease caused by some types of STREPTOCOCCUS bacteria. Fever, sore throat, headache, and, in children, vomiting are followed in two to three days by a rash. The skin peels in about one-third of cases. Glands are usually swollen. Complications frequently involve the sinuses, ears, and neck. NEPHRITIS, ARTHRITIS, or RHEUMATIC FEVER may occur later. Treatment involves PENICILLIN or GAMMA GLOBULIN, bed rest, and adequate fluid intake. Scarlet fever has become uncommon and much milder since the mid-20th cent.

scaup Any of three species (genus *Aythya*, family Anatidae) of DIVING DUCKS. The greater scaup, or big bluebill (*A. marila*), breeds across Eurasia and most of the Nearctic region. The lesser scaup, or little bluebill (*A. affinis*), breeds in NW N. America. Both are popular game birds, 15–20 in. (38–51 cm) long, that winter along the U.S. coasts. . The third species is the New Zealand scaup (*A. novaeseelandiae*). Scaups eat mainly clams.

Scheherazade or **Sheherazade** \shə-ˌher-ə-ˈzäd\ Fictional sultan's wife who narrates *The THOUSAND AND ONE NIGHTS*. According to the story that serves as the collection's framework, the Sultan Shahrya found his first wife unfaithful, and thereafter decided to marry and kill a new wife each day. Scheherazade, in an effort to avoid his previous wives' fate, related to him a fascinating story every night, promising to finish it on the following night. The sultan enjoyed the stories so much that he put off her execution indefinitely and finally abandoned the idea altogether.

Schelde River \ˈskel-də\ or **Scheldt River** \ˈskelt\ *French* **Escaut** \es-ˈkō\ River, W Europe. It rises in N France, flows to the Belgian city of ANTWERP, and empties into the NORTH SEA after a course of 270 mi (435 km). Along with the Lower RHINE and MEUSE rivers, it drains one of the world's most densely populated areas. A channel allows deep-draft vessels to reach Antwerp at full tide.

scherzo \'skert-ˌsō\ (Italian: "joke") Musical movement in rapid triple time, which replaced the minuet in such genres as the SYMPHONY and SONATA in the 19th cent. It formally often resembles the minuet, being in rounded binary form and having a contrasting trio section between two statements of the scherzo proper, but its tempo is often much faster and its style may range from playful to vehement or grotesque.

Schiaparelli \ˌskyä-pä-'rel-lē\, **Elsa** (1890–1973) Italian-French fashion designer. After working as a screenwriter in the U.S., she settled in Paris and opened her first shop in the late 1920s. By 1935 she was a leader in haute couture. Her designs combined eccentricity with simplicity and a trim neatness with flamboyant color. Her "shocking pink," the sensation of the 1947 season, is still regularly revived. With Christian DIOR, she was instrumental in the worldwide commercialization of Parisian fashion.

Schiele \'shē-lə\, **Egon** (1890–1918) Austrian painter and printmaker. He was strongly influenced by the JUGENDSTIL movement, and the linearity and subtlety of his work owe much to Gustav KLIMT's decorative elegance; yet he always emphasized expression over decoration, heightening the emotive power of line with a feverish intensity. His candid, agitated, erotic images caused a sensation, and in 1912 he was briefly imprisoned for indecency. His landscapes exhibit the same febrile quality of color and line. He died at 29 in an influenza epidemic.

Schiller \'shil-ər\, **(Johann Christoph) Friedrich (von)** (1759–1805) German dramatist, poet, and literary theorist, one of the greatest figures in his nation's literature. With his successful first play, *The Robbers* (1781), he took up the exploration of freedom, a central theme throughout his works. *Don Carlos* (1787), his first major poetic drama, helped establish BLANK VERSE as the recognized medium of German poetic drama. His jubilant "Ode to Joy" was later used in Ludwig van BEETHOVEN's Symphony No. 9. The historical drama *Wallenstein* (1800) was his epic masterpiece. During a period spent formulating his views on aesthetic activity, he produced major historical works, philosophical essays, exquisite reflective poems, and popular ballads. He spent his last years in ill health in Weimar, near his friend J. W. von GOETHE. His mature plays, including *Maria Stuart* (performed 1800) and *Wilhelm Tell* (1804), examine the inward freedom that ennobles the soul.

Schinkel \'shiŋ-kəl\, **Karl Friedrich** (1781–1841) German architect and painter. As state architect of Prussia (from 1815), he executed many commissions for FREDERICK WILLIAM III and other royal family members. His mausoleum for Queen Louise (1810) and the Werdersche Kirche, Berlin (1821–30), are among the earliest GOTHIC REVIVAL designs in Europe. Other works included the GREEK REVIVAL Schauspielhaus (1818) and Altes Museum (1822–30), both in Berlin. His later work as a city planner resulted in new boulevards and squares in Berlin. He is also known for his stage sets and ironwork designs.

schipperke \'ski-pər-kē, 'shi-pər-kē\ Dog breed that originated in Flanders and was used as a guard on barges. The schipperke ("little captain") is short, thickset, and tailless, with a dense black coat and a foxlike head. It stands 12–13 in. (31–33 cm) and weighs up to 18 lbs (8 kg). It has a lively, inquisitive expression and is generally hardy and energetic, an able vermin hunter, and a good watchdog.

Schism \'si-zəm\, **Western** *or* **Great Schism** (1378–1417) Period when there were two, and later three, rival popes, each with his own College of CARDINALS. The schism began soon after the papal residence was returned to Rome from Avignon (see AVIGNON PAPACY). URBAN VI was elected amid local demands for an Italian pope, but a group of cardinals with French sympathies elected an antipope, Clement VII, who took up residence at Avignon. Cardinals from both sides met at Pisa in 1409 and elected a third pope in an effort to end the schism. The rift was not healed until the Council of Constance vacated all three seats and elected MARTIN V as pope in 1417.

Schism of 1054 *or* **East–West Schism** Event that separated the Byzantine and Roman churches. The Eastern and Western churches had long been estranged over doctrinal issues (see EASTERN ORTHODOXY, ROMAN CATHOLICISM). The

Eastern Church resented the Roman enforcement of clerical celibacy and the limitation of the right of confirmation to the bishop. There were also jurisdictional disputes between Rome and Constantinople. In 1054 Pope LEO IX and the patriarch of Constantinople, Michael Cerularius, excommunicated each other, an event that marked the final break between the two churches. The rift widened in subsequent centuries, and the churches have remained separate, though the excommunications were lifted in the 20th cent.

schist \'shist\ Crystalline METAMORPHIC ROCK that can be easily split into layers. Most schists are composed largely of platy minerals such as MUSCOVITE, chlorite, TALC, biotite, and GRAPHITE. Many schists are green. Schists are usually classified by their mineralogy, with varietal names that indicate the characteristic mineral present.

schistosomiasis \ˌshis-tə-sə-'mī-ə-səs\ *or* **bilharziasis** \ˌbil-ˌhär-'zī-ə-səs\ Group of chronic disorders caused by parasitic FLATWORMS of the genus *Schistosoma* (blood FLUKES). Depending on the infecting species, eggs released by the females reach either the intestine or the bladder of the victim, are excreted in feces or urine, and hatch on contact with fresh water. The larvae invade snails, develop to the next stage, emerge into the water, and invade mammals, including humans. An initial reaction (inflammation, cough, fever, hives) and blood in the stools and urine give way to a chronic stage, in which eggs impacted in the walls of organs cause fibrous thickening. This can lead to serious damage to internal organs. Early diagnosis and persistent treatment to kill the adult worms usually succeed. Some 200 million people today suffer from active schistosomiasis.

schizophrenia \ˌskit-sə-'frē-nē-ə\ Any of a group of severe mental disorders that share such symptoms as HALLUCINATIONS, delusions, blunted emotions, disorganized thinking, and withdrawal from reality. Four main types are recognized: the paranoid, characterized by delusions of persecution or grandeur with unrealistic, illogical thinking and auditory hallucinations; the disorganized (hebephrenic), characterized by disordered speech and behavior and shallow or inappropriate emotional responses; the catatonic, characterized by motor inflexibility, stupor, or stereotyped movements along with mutism, echolalia, or other speech abnormalities; and the undifferentiated, a nonspecific type. Schizophrenia seems to occur in 0.5–1% of the population. There is strong evidence that genetic inheritance plays a role. Treatment consists of drug therapy and counseling. About one-third of all patients make a full recovery, and one-third deteriorate into a chronic condition.

Schlegel \'shlā-gəl\, **August Wilhelm von** (1767–1845) German scholar and critic. With his brother Friedrich von SCHLEGEL he founded the periodical *Athenäum* (1798–1800), which became the organ of German ROMANTICISM. His translations of the works of William SHAKESPEARE (1797–1810) are among the finest of all German literary translations. His *Lectures on Dramatic Art and Literature* (1809–11) was widely translated and helped spread fundamental Romantic ideas throughout Europe.

Schlegel, Friedrich von (1772–1829) German writer and critic. He contributed many of his projects and theories to journals such as *Athenäum* (1798–1800), which he and his brother A. W. von SCHLEGEL founded. His study of Sanskrit led him to publish *Concerning the Language and Wisdom of India* (1808), a pioneering attempt at comparative Indo-European linguistics. His conception of a universal, historical, and comparative literary scholarship has been profoundly influential, and he originated many philosophical ideas that inspired early German ROMANTICISM.

Schleicher \'shlī-kər\, **August** (1821–1868) German linguist. He began his career studying classical and Slavic languages. Influenced by G. W. F. HEGEL and Charles DARWIN, he formed the theory that a language is an organism, with periods of development, maturity, and decline. He invented a system of language classification that traces groups of related languages and arranges them in a genealogical tree. His model was a major development in the study of INDO-EUROPEAN LANGUAGES.

Schleicher, Kurt von (1882–1934) German politician. A career army officer, he became a key figure in the WEIMAR REPUBLIC. His intrigues won him the posts of defense min-

ister (1932) and chancellor (1932–33). Seeking to keep the Nazis under the army's control, he offered to participate in a government with Adolf HITLER, but Hitler refused and thereafter regarded him as his chief enemy. Dismissed by Paul von HINDENBURG in favor of Hitler, Schleicher was murdered during the NIGHT OF THE LONG KNIVES.

Schleiden \'shlī-dən\, **Matthias Jakob** (1804–1881) German botanist. He and Theodor SCHWANN developed the CELL theory, which states that organisms are composed of cells or substances made by cells; they were thus the first to formulate what was then an informal belief as a principle of biology equal in importance to the atomic theory of chemistry. He also recognized the importance of the cell nucleus and sensed its connection with cell division.

Schleiermacher \'shlī-ər-ˌmäḵ-ər\, **Friedrich (Ernst Daniel)** (1768–1834) German theologian, preacher, and classical philologist. He joined the clergy in 1796. His *On Religion* (1799) declared that the Romantics were not as far from religion as they thought. From 1810 to his death, he taught at the Univ. of Berlin. He helped unite Prussia's Lutheran and Reformed churches in 1817. His major work, *The Christian Faith* (1821–22), is a systematic and influential interpretation of Christian dogma. He is generally recognized as the founder of modern Protestant theology.

Schlesinger \'shlā-ziŋ-ər, 'shle-sin-jər\, **Arthur M(eier) and Arthur M(eier), Jr.** (1888–1965, b.1917) U.S. historians. Born in Xenia, Ohio, the elder Schlesinger taught at Harvard Univ. for three decades. He helped to broaden the study of U.S. history by emphasizing social and urban developments. His books include *The Colonial Merchants and the American Revolution, 1763–1776* (1917) and he coedited the series *A History of American Life* (1928–43). His son, born in Columbus, Ohio, taught at Harvard (1946–61) and the City Univ. of New York (1966–95). Long active in liberal politics, he served as John F. KENNEDY's special assistant. His books include *The Age of Jackson* (1946, Pulitzer Prize), *The Age of Roosevelt* (3 vols., 1957–60), *A Thousand Days* (1965, Pulitzer Prize), and *The Cycles of American History* (1986).

Schlesinger, John (Richard) (b.1926) British film and theater director. He became a documentary director for BBC television, where he won praise for his *Terminus* (1960). His feature films *A Kind of Loving* (1962) and *Billy Liar* (1963), caustic depictions of English urban life, were followed by the successful *Darling* (1965) and *Far From the Madding Crowd* (1967). His first U.S. film, *Midnight Cowboy* (1969), won him an Academy Award. His later films include *Sunday Bloody Sunday* (1971), *Marathon Man* (1976), and *Cold Comfort Farm* (1995).

Schleswig-Holstein \'shläs-ˌviḵ-'hōl-ˌshtīn\ Historical area and state (pop., 1997 est.: 2,749,000), NW Germany. It occupies the S half of the JUTLAND Peninsula and includes Fehmarn Island and various islands in the N. FRISIAN group. Its capital is KIEL. From the 15th cent. the former duchies of Schleswig and Holstein were subject to the claims of Denmark, Sweden, the Holy Roman Empire, Prussia, and Austria. In 1866 both areas became part of Prussia (see SCHLESWIG-HOLSTEIN QUESTION). The N part of Schleswig was awarded to Denmark in 1920. The rest of Schleswig-Holstein became a state of W. Germany after World War II.

Schleswig-Holstein Question \'shles-ˌwig-'hōl-ˌstīn\ Conflict between Denmark and Prussia over SCHLESWIG-HOLSTEIN. In the 1840s the Danish-speaking population of N Schleswig wanted to incorporate Schleswig with Denmark, whereas the German-speaking majority of the two duchies wanted to combine them as a state within the GERMAN CONFEDERATION. An 1848 uprising by Germans in the region, aided by the Prussian army, ousted Denmark's troops. In 1863 a renewed attempt by Denmark to annex Schleswig caused Prussia and Austria to declare war in 1864. Defeated, Denmark was forced to surrender all of Schleswig-Holstein to Prussia and Austria.

Schlieffen Plan \'shlē-fən\ Plan of attack used by the German armies at the outbreak of WORLD WAR I. It was named after its developer, Count Alfred von Schlieffen (1833–1913), former chief of the German general staff. To meet the possibility of Germany's facing a war against France in the west and Russia in the east, Schlieffen proposed that Germany should first aim a rapid, decisive blow with a large force at France's flank through Belgium, then sweep around and crush the French armies against a smaller German force in the south. In 1914 the plan was modified by Gen. von Moltke, who reduced the size of the attacking army and was blamed for Germany's failure to win a quick victory.

Schliemann \'shlē-män\, **Heinrich** (1822–1890) German archaeologist and excavator of TROY, MYCENAE, and TIRYNS. As a boy he loved the Homeric poems, and he eventually learned ancient and modern Greek and many other languages. As a military contractor in the Crimean War he made a sufficient fortune to retire (at 36) and devote himself to archaeology. In 1873, at Hissarlik, Turkey, he discovered the remains of ancient Troy (verifying the historical event of the TROJAN WAR) and a treasure of gold jewelry ("Priam's Treasure"), which he smuggled out of the country. Because the Ottoman government prevented his return, he began excavating Mycenae, where he found more invaluable remains and treasures. He and Wilhelm Dörpfeld (1853–1940) resumed work at Hissarlik in 1878, advancing archaeological technique. In 1884 they excavated the great fortified site at Tiryns. Schliemann's excavations helped lengthen considerably the perspective of history and popularize archaeology.

Heinrich Schliemann
Engraving by A. Weger

Schmidt \'shmit\, **Helmut** (b.1918) Chancellor of W. Germany (1974–82). A member of the Social Democratic Party, he was minister of defense (1969–72) and finance (1972–74) before succeeding Willy BRANDT as chancellor in 1974. A popular and capable chancellor, he continued the policy of OSTPOLITIK while maintaining W. Germany's key position in NATO and the European Community. He wrote numerous books on German politics and international relations.

Schnabel \'shnä-bəl\, **Artur** (1882–1951) Austrian pianist and composer. After studying with the great Theodor Leschetizky in Vienna, he settled in Berlin (1900–33), where he composed, taught, and gave legendary performances of the complete sonatas of Ludwig van BEETHOVEN and Franz SCHUBERT, becoming the first to record the complete Beethoven cycle. During the Nazi period, he moved to London, then to the U.S. Though he mostly played the works of the past, his own compositions were ultramodern. Today he is uniquely revered by serious pianists.

Schnabel \'shnä-bəl\, **Julian** (b.1951) U.S. painter. Born in New York City, he studied at the Univ. of Houston and in New York. In the 1980s he was a leading exponent of NEO-EXPRESSIONISM. His works exhibit jarring color harmonies and a primitive style; his best-known works incorporate shards of broken plates. Though he has enjoyed considerable success, there has been controversy regarding both the quality of his work and his aggressive self-promotion. He has also directed films, including *Basquiat* (1996) and *Before Night Falls* (2000).

schnauzer \'shnaùt-sər, 'shnaù-zər\ Any of three German dog breeds having a wiry black, salt-and-pepper, or black-and-tan coat. The standard, 17–20 in. (43–51 cm) high and weighing 26–37 lbs (12–17 kg), dates to the 15th cent. The miniature, 12–14 in. (30–36 cm) high and weighing 13–15 lbs (6–7 kg), was developed in the 19th cent. The giant schnauzer stands 21–26 in. (53–66 cm) and weighs 66–77 lbs (30–35 kg).

Schnittke \'shnit-kə\, **Alfred (Garrievich)** (1934–1998) Russian composer. He scored more than 60 films, and was one of the first Soviet composers to experiment with serialism. After the death of Dmitri SHOSTAKOVICH, he became the leading Soviet composer, and gained a major international reputation as he evolved a highly eclectic style ("polystylistics"). He wrote nine symphonies, six concerti grossi, many concertos, four string quartets, and the operas *Life with an Idiot* (1992), *Gesualdo* (1995), and *Historia von D. Johann Fausten* (1995).

Schnitzler \'shnits-lər\, **Arthur** (1862–1931) Austrian playwright and novelist. While practicing medicine in Vienna, he became known for his psychological dramas that fearlessly depicted the erotic lives of his characters, beginning with the early play *Anatol* (1893). His best-known play, *Reigen* (*Merry-Go-Round*, 1897), tracing the links connecting the partners in a series of sexual encounters, was considered scandalous when first performed in 1920. His drama *Playing with Love* (1896) and his most successful novel, *None but the Brave* (1901), revealed the hollowness of the Austrian military code of honor.

Schoenberg \'shœn-ˌberk, *Engl* 'shərn-ˌbərg\, **Arnold (Franz Walter)** (1874–1951) Austrian-U.S. composer. Raised Catholic by his Jewish-born parents, he learned violin and cello and studied composition with Alexander Zemlinsky (1871–1942). With Richard STRAUSS's help he obtained a teaching post in Berlin, but soon returned to Vienna, having composed his huge *Gurrelieder* (1901). In 1904 Alban BERG and Anton WEBERN began their studies with him, which would profoundly shape their later artistic careers. Around 1906 Schoenberg came to believe that tonality had to be abandoned. His period of "free ATONALITY" (1907–16) produced such works as *Erwartung*, the *Five Orchestral Pieces* (both 1909), and the notorious *Pierrot lunaire* (1912). He devoted the years 1916–23 to teaching and conducting and to seeking a way to organize atonality, which led to his development of the twelve-tone method (see SERIALISM). In 1930 he began work on a three-act twelve-tone opera; *Moses und Aron* remained unfinished at his death. The rise of Nazism forced him to flee to the U.S., where he taught at UCLA 1936–44. Though his music was never embraced by a broad public, he may have exercised a greater influence on 20th-cent. music than any other composer.

Scholasticism Theological and philosophical movement, beginning in the 11th cent., that sought to integrate the secular understanding of the ancient world, as exemplified by ARISTOTLE, with the dogma implicit in the revelations of Christianity. Its aim was a synthesis of learning in which theology surmounted the hierarchy of knowledge. Principal figures were Peter ABELARD, St. ANSELM OF CANTERBURY, St. ALBERTUS MAGNUS, and Roger BACON. The movement flourished in the 13th cent., drawing on the writings of St. THOMAS AQUINAS. By the 14th cent. Scholasticism was in decline, but it had laid the foundations for many revivals and revisitations in later centuries. Modern philosophers influenced by Scholasticism include Jacques MARITAIN.

schooner \'skü-nər\ Sailing ship rigged with fore-and-aft sails on its two or more masts. The first schooner was built in 1713, probably at Gloucester, Mass., by Andrew Robinson. Compared to a square-rigged ship, it was ideal for coastal sailing; it handled better in varying coastal winds, had shallower drafts, and required a smaller crew in proportion to its size. By 1800 it was the most important N. American ship, used in the coastal trade and fishing. After 1800 it became popular in Europe and worldwide. CLIPPER SHIPS married the schooner design to that of the three-masted merchantman.

Schopenhauer \'shō-pən-ˌhau̇-ər\, **Arthur** (1788–1860) German philosopher. He founded his philosophical system on the UPANISHADS and the works of PLATO and Immanuel KANT. His magnum opus, *The World as Will and Idea* (1819), consists of reflections on the theory of knowledge and the philosophy of nature, aesthetics, and ethics, and proposes a metaphysical doctrine of the will

Arthur Schopenhauer, 1855

in immediate reaction against the idealism of G. W. F. HEGEL. His turning from spirit and reason to the powers of intuition, creativity, and the irrational affected the ideas and methods of vitalism, life philosophy, EXISTENTIALISM, and ANTHROPOLOGY. His other works include *On the Will in Nature* (1836), *The Two Main Problems of Ethics* (1841), and *Parerga und Paralipomena* (1851). His works earned him the sobriquet "the philosopher of pessimism."

Schreiner \'shrī-nər\, **Olive (Emilie Albertina)** (1855–1920) S. African writer. She had no formal education but read widely, developing a powerful intellect and militantly feminist and liberal views. In 1883 she published (as Ralph Iron) the semiautobiographical *Story of an African Farm*. The first great S. African novel, it concerns a girl living on an isolated farm who struggles for independence in the face of rigid Boer social conventions. Her later works include *Woman and Labour* (1911), a bible of the women's movement.

Schröder \'shrœ-dər\, **Gerhard** (b.1944) Chancellor of Germany from 1998. A member of the Social Democratic Party, he served in the Bundestag 1980–86, and became premier of the state of Lower Saxony in 1990. His election as federal chancellor in 1998 ended 16 years of conservative rule under Helmut KOHL.

Schrödinger \'shrœ-diŋ-ər\, **Erwin** (1887–1961) Austrian physicist. He left Nazi Germany in 1933 and eventually settled in Ireland, where he joined the Dublin Institute for Advanced Studies (1940–56). He made fundamental contributions to QUANTUM MECHANICS, and shared a 1933 Nobel Prize with Paul DIRAC for his development of the wave equation now called the SCHRÖDINGER EQUATION. In addition to his scientific research, he made contributions to philosophy and the history of science.

Schrödinger equation \'shrœ-diŋ-ər\ Fundamental equation developed in 1926 by Erwin SCHRÖDINGER that established the mathematics of QUANTUM MECHANICS. It determines the behavior of the WAVE FUNCTION that describes the wavelike properties of a subatomic system. It relates KINETIC ENERGY and POTENTIAL ENERGY to the total energy, and is solved to find the different energy levels of the system. The equation is used extensively in ATOMIC, nuclear, and SOLID-STATE PHYSICS. See also WAVE-PARTICLE DUALITY.

Schubert \'shü-ˌbert\, **Franz (Peter)** (1797–1828) Austrian composer. He learned violin, organ, and piano at home, sang with the choir of the imperial chapel, and studied several years with Antonio SALIERI. From 1814 to 1818 he taught unhappily at his father's school. He wrote his first symphony in 1813; by age 21 he had written five more. His extraordinary early song "Gretchen am Spinnrade" (1814) heralded a genius that would transform the German lied. Always living in near poverty, he became the center of a close-knit Bohemian circle that regularly gathered for "Schubertiades," evenings of music and sociability. In 1822 he suffered the first symptoms of the disease (probably syphilis) that would eventually kill him. His nine symphonies included the "Unfinished" (1822) and the "Great C Major" (1827). His chamber works included 15 string quartets, two piano trios, and the "Trout" Quintet (1819), and he wrote over 20 piano sonatas. He also wrote almost 15 stage works (some unfinished) and five masses. Though his last years were made miserable by illness, his phenomenal musical production rarely flagged, and his greatness became widely recognized. His 600 songs, including the song cycles *Die schöne Müllerin* (1823) and *Winterreise* (1827), made the lied a serious genre and sparked its great development in later decades. He died at 31, having produced more masterpieces by that age than almost any other composer in history.

Schuller \'shu̇l-ər\, **Gunther (Alexander)** (b.1925) U.S. composer, conductor, and educator. Born in New York City, he played French horn at the Metropolitan Opera 1945–59, as well as with such jazz musicians as Miles DAVIS and the Modern Jazz Quartet. His "third stream" music (combining classical and jazz styles) has included such compositions as *Seven Studies on Themes of Paul Klee* (1959). He was president of the New England Conservatory of Music 1967–77, and directed the Berkshire Music Center 1974–84. A pre-

eminent authority on jazz, he is the author of the acclaimed *Early Jazz* (1968) and *The Swing Era* (1988).

Schultz \'shŭlts\, **Dutch** *orig.* Arthur Flegenheimer (1902–1935) U.S. gangster. Born in the Bronx, N.Y., Schultz advanced from burglaries to bootlegging and ownership of breweries and speakeasies in the Bronx and Manhattan. When the murderous "Dutchman" made plans to assassinate the prosecutor Thomas DEWEY, he himself was murdered by N.Y. crime bosses, who feared his plan would result in a crackdown on organized crime.

Schulz \'shŭlts\, **Charles** (1922–2000) U.S. cartoonist. Born in Minneapolis, he took a correspondence course in cartooning and worked as a freelance cartoonist before creating *Peanuts* (originally *Li'l Folks*, 1950), which would become the most widely syndicated comic strip of all time. The strip, whose characters are boys and girls aged 3–5 and a beagle with a grandiose imagination, deals with the frustrations of everyday life, often with philosophical and psychological overtones. Just before his death, after 50 years of continuous production, Schulz announced the end of his strip.

Schumacher \'shü-ˌmäk-ər, *Engl* 'shü-ˌmäk-ər\, **E(rnst) F(riedrich)** (1911–1977) German-British economist. He settled in England in 1937. During World War II he worked on theories for full-employment policies and plans for Britain's postwar welfare state. In 1950–70 he was an adviser to Britain's nationalized coal industry. After a visit to Burma in 1955, he decided that poor countries needed an "intermediate technology" adapted to the unique needs of each in order to develop. In the influential *Small Is Beautiful* (1973) he argued that capitalism brought higher living standards at the cost of deteriorating culture and that bigness—especially large industries and large cities—was unaffordable.

Schuman \'shü-ˌmän\, **Robert** (1886–1963) French statesman. He was a member of the French National Assembly from 1919. After working in the French Resistance in World War II, he served as premier (1947–48), foreign minister (1948–52), and minister of justice (1955–56). In 1950 he proposed the Schuman Plan to promote European economic and military unity, which led to the EUROPEAN ECONOMIC COMMUNITY (EEC). He served as president of the EEC's consultative assembly (1958–60).

Schuman \'shü-mən\, **William (Howard)** (1910–1992) U.S. composer and administrator. Born in New York City, he wrote songs in high school with his friend Frank LOESSER, and he later studied composition with Roy Harris. His *Secular Cantata No. 2: A Free Song* won the first Pulitzer Prize for music (1943). Other works include ballets for Martha GRAHAM, *New England Triptych* (1956), and 10 symphonies. As president of the Juilliard School (1945–62), he modernized its curriculum. He served as the first president of Lincoln Center (1962–68).

Schumann, Robert (Alexander) (1810–1856) German composer. Son of a bookseller, he took up law studies to please his mother, but skipped classes to study piano with Friedrich Wieck, and soon moved in with the Wiecks. In 1831 he began composing. Several reverses led to a suicide attempt in 1833. He emerged from it by starting an important music journal, *Neue Zeitschrift für Musik*, in 1834. He fell in love with Wieck's 16-year-old daughter Clara (1819–1896), and Wieck's strenuous efforts failed to prevent their marriage in 1840. The first phase of Schumann's compositional life ended with the publication (1837–39) of much piano music, including *Davidsbündlertänze*, *Carnaval*, *Kinderszenen*, and *Kreisleriana*. The "year of song," 1840, resulted in the song cycles *Dichterliebe* and *Frauenliebe und -leben* and over 100 other songs. In 1841 he produced two of his four symphonies

Robert and Clara Schumann Lithograph by J. Hofelich

and his piano concerto; in 1842 he concentrated on chamber music. His mental deterioration accelerated; he was placed in a sanatorium and died there two years later. Clara Schumann, a gifted composer herself, gained far greater renown as a virtuoso pianist.

Schumpeter \'shŭm-ˌpā-tər\, **Joseph A(lois)** (1883–1950) Moravian-U.S. economist and sociologist. He taught at several European universities before joining the faculty of Harvard Univ. (1932–50). His popular book *Capitalism, Socialism, and Democracy* (1942) argued that capitalism would eventually perish of its own success. His posthumous *History of Economic Analysis* (1954) is an exhaustive study of the development of analytic methods in economics.

Schuschnigg \'shŭsh-nik\, **Kurt von** (1897–1977) Austrian chancellor (1934–38). He served in the cabinet of Engelbert DOLLFUSS; after Dollfuss was assassinated, Schuschnigg was named chancellor. He disbanded the paramilitary Heimwehr in 1936 and tried to prevent the German takeover of Austria. After making concessions to Adolf HITLER in February 1938, he sought to reassert national independence through a plebiscite to be held on March 13. However, on March 11 Germany invaded Austria and carried out the ANSCHLUSS, and Schuschnigg was imprisoned until 1945. He later lived and taught in the U.S. (1948–67).

Schütz \'shēts\, **Heinrich** (1585–1672) German composer. An innkeeper's son, he was heard singing by a nobleman staying at the inn, who underwrote his university education. In 1609 he began study with Giovanni GABRIELI in Venice. From 1614 he worked for the elector of Saxony in Dresden. As kapellmeister in Dresden from 1619, he published his first collection of sacred music, *Psalms of David*. His lost opera *Dafne* (1627) was the first German opera. He traveled to Italy in 1628, where Claudio MONTEVERDI acquainted him with new musical developments, and he adopted aspects of the Italian style in his three great collections of *Symphoniae sacrae* (1629, 1647, 1650) for chorus and instruments. He is regarded as the most important German composer of the 17th cent.

Schwab, Charles M(ichael) (1862–1939) U.S. entrepreneur and steel-industry pioneer. Born in Williamsburg, Pa., he joined Andrew CARNEGIE's steelworks at Braddock, Pa., as a laborer and rose swiftly. He returned the plant in Homestead to normal production after the bloody HOMESTEAD STRIKE. Named president of Carnegie Steel Co. at the age of 35, Schwab proposed the merger that would create the U.S. STEEL CORP., and became its first president in 1901. He resigned in 1903 to devote himself to the BETHLEHEM STEEL CORP., which he built into one of the nation's largest steel producers.

Schwann \'shvän\, **Theodor** (1810–1882) German physiologist. He founded modern HISTOLOGY by recognizing the CELL as the basic unit of animal structure. A year after Mathias SCHLEIDEN advanced the cell theory for plants, Schwann extended it to animals. He isolated a substance responsible for digestion in the stomach, the first enzyme prepared from animal tissue, and named it pepsin. He coined the term metabolism, identified the role played by microorganisms in the decomposition of organic matter, and formulated the basic principles of embryology.

Schwartz \'shwȯrts\, **Delmore** (1913–1966) U.S. poet, short-story writer, and critic. Born in Brooklyn, N.Y., he became an editor of *Partisan Review* (1943–55). His works include *In Dreams Begin Responsibilities* (1939), consisting of a short story and poetry; and *Successful Love* (1961), a collection of short stories primarily about middle-class Jewish family life. His work is noted for its lyrical descriptions of cultural alienation and the search for identity. Brilliant but unstable, he became alcoholic and declined into insanity.

Schwarzenegger \'shwȯrts-ə-ˌneg-ər\, **Arnold (Alois)** (b.1947) Austrian-U.S. film actor. Having moved to the U.S. in 1968, he won the title of Mr. Universe five times. After appearing in the documentary *Pumping Iron* (1977), he starred in the hit *Conan the Barbarian* (1982) and its sequel (1984). Noted for his extraordinary physique and heavy accent, he became a huge international star with *The Terminator* (1984). His other films include *Twins* (1988), *Total Recall* (1990), and *True Lies* (1994).

Schwarzkopf \'shwȯrts-ˌkȯf\, **(Olga Maria) Elisabeth (Fredericke)** (*later* **Dame Elisabeth**) (b.1915) German-British soprano. She debuted in 1938, and a 1942 recital in Berlin caused Karl Böhm to invite her to the Vienna State Opera. She sang at Covent Garden 1947–52; her voice bloomed, and she began her long associations with the Salzburg Festival (1949–64) and La Scala (1949–63). Her annual lieder recitals were legendary. Her opera farewell (1972) was in her famous role as the Marschallin in *Der Rosenkavalier.*

Schwarzkopf, H(erbert) Norman (b.1934) U.S. Army commander. Born in Trenton, N.J., he graduated from West Point and fought in the Vietnam War. In 1983 he directed the invasion of Grenada. In 1988 he became commander of the U.S. Central Command, which included operations in the Middle East. To confront Iraq's invasion of Kuwait in 1990, he directed the buildup of 700,000 U.S. and allied troops in Saudi Arabia, and he commanded the Desert Storm operations in the PERSIAN GULF WAR (1991).

Schwarzschild \'shwȯrt-ˌshilt\, **Karl** (1873–1916) German astronomer. He published his first paper (on celestial orbits) at 16. He gave the first exact solution of Albert EINSTEIN's general equations of gravitation, which led to a description of how mass curves space. He also used those equations to lay the foundation of black-hole theory showing that bodies of sufficient mass would have an escape velocity greater than the speed of light and therefore would not be directly observable. See also SCHWARZSCHILD RADIUS.

Schwarzschild radius *or* **gravitational radius** Radius below which the gravitational attraction between a body's particles must cause its irreversible collapse, named for Karl SCHWARZSCHILD. This is thought to be how massive stars become BLACK HOLES. The gravitational radius (R_g) of an object of mass M is given by $R_g = 2GM/c^2$, where G is the universal gravitational constant and c the speed of light. The sun's Schwarzschild radius would be about 1.8 mi (3.0 km).

Schweitzer \'shwīt-sər\, **Albert** (1875–1965) Alsatian-German theologian, philosopher, organist, and mission doctor. In his early years he took a degree in philosophy and became an accomplished organist. In his huge biography of J. S. BACH (1905), he viewed Bach as a religious mystic. He also wrote on organ construction and produced an edition of Bach's organ works. His books on religion include several on St. Paul; his *Quest of the Historical Jesus* (1910) became widely influential. In 1905 he decided to become a mission doctor. He and his wife moved in 1913 to Lambaréné

Albert Schweitzer Photo by Yousuf Karsh

in present-day Gabon, and with local helpers built a hospital on the banks of the Ogooué River, to which they later added a leper colony. In 1952 he received the Nobel Peace Prize. His philosophical books discuss his famous principle of "reverence for life."

Schwitters \'shvit-ərz\, **Kurt** (1887–1948) German DADA artist and poet. Associated with the Berlin Dadaists from 1918, he moved to Hannover in 1924. He assembled collages and other constructions from everyday objects (train tickets, wooden spools, postage stamps); his poems were composites of newspaper headlines, advertising slogans, and other printed ephemera. He referred to all his artistic activities—and later even to himself—as *Merz,* the syllable left when he snipped letters from *Kommerz* ("commerce"). When the Nazis declared his art "degenerate" in 1937, he moved to Norway and later to England.

sciatica \sī-'a-ti-kə\ Pain along the course of the sciatic nerve, from the lower back down each leg. It often begins after lower-back strain and is associated with spinal-disk herniation (see HERNIA). Pain is increased by coughing, sneezing, or bending the neck forward. Muscle relaxants, painkillers, and nerve stimulation are among the treatments, but surgery to relieve pressure on the nerve may be needed. Rarely, sciatica arises from other causes.

science fiction Fiction dealing principally with the impact of actual or imagined science on society or individuals, or more generally, literary fantasy including a scientific factor as an essential orienting component. From beginnings in the works of Jules VERNE and H. G. WELLS, it emerged as a genre in the pulp magazine *Amazing Stories,* founded in 1926. It came into its own as serious fiction in the magazine *Astounding Science Fiction* in the late 1930s and in works by such writers as Isaac ASIMOV, Arthur C. CLARKE, and Robert HEINLEIN. A great boom in popularity followed World War II. Much recent fiction deals with the effects of artificial intelligence on anarchic future societies.

Scientific American U.S. monthly magazine interpreting scientific developments to lay readers. It was founded in 1845 as a newspaper describing new inventions. By 1853 its circulation had reached 30,000 and it was reporting on various sciences, such as astronomy and medicine, apart from inventions. In 1921 it became a monthly. Its articles—solidly based on scholarly research, well written, and accompanied by definitions and illustrations—have made it the most highly regarded magazine of its genre.

Scientology, Church of Religious and pseudoscientific movement established in the U.S. by L. Ron HUBBARD in 1954. It uses a system of psychotherapy, known as Dianetics, that seeks to free subjects from the destructive imprints of past experiences, called engrams. Scientology also includes a highly structured system of belief dealing with the origins of life and the universe and involving the human soul, or thetan. The organization has been criticized for allegedly exerting unreasonable control over its followers and has faced charges of fraud, tax evasion, and financial mismanagement.

Scilly \'si-lē\, **Isles of** *or* **Scilly Isles** Group of about 50 tiny islands and many more islets (pop., 1999 est.: 2,100), off LAND'S END, SW England. During the ENGLISH CIVIL WARS, Prince Charles sheltered there until his escape to JERSEY in 1646. The islands were a haunt of pirates and notorious for smuggling activities. Most of their inhabitants live on St. Mary's.

Scipio Africanus the Elder \'si-pē-ō, 'ski-pē-ō\ *in full* Publius Cornelius Scipio Africanus (236–184/183 B.C.) Roman general in the Second PUNIC WAR. As a military TRIBUNE, he fought at the Battle of CANNAE (216), managing to escape from the defeat. While still young, he secured Spain for Rome by 206, driving the Carthaginians out and avenging his father's death. As CONSUL in 205 he won the right to attack the Carthaginians in Africa. In 202 he won a major victory over HANNIBAL at the Battle of Zama, ending the Second Punic War and winning the name Africanus. Assailed by political opponents, Scipio withdrew from public life and died a virtual exile.

Scipio Africanus the Younger *or* **Scipio Aemilianus** \i-ˌmil-ē-'ā-nəs\ *in full* Publius Cornelius Scipio Aemilianus Africanus Numantinus (185/184–129 B.C.) Roman general credited with the final subjugation of CARTHAGE. The adoptive son of Publius Scipio, son of SCIPIO AFRICANUS THE ELDER, he first distinguished himself in the Third MACEDONIAN WAR (168). He displayed great military skill against Carthage while serving as military TRIBUNE. Though underage, he was elected CONSUL in 147 and returned to Africa. He besieged and destroyed Carthage (146), ending the Third PUNIC WAR and establishing the province of Africa. Again made consul (134), he was given command of the Celtiberian War, and he secured Spain by besieging and destroying Numantia (133).

scirocco See SIROCCO

SCLC See SOUTHERN CHRISTIAN LEADERSHIP CONFERENCE

scleroderma \ˌskler-ə-'dər-mə\ *or* **progressive systemic sclerosis** \sis-'tem-ik-sklə-'rō-səs\ Chronic disease that hardens the SKIN and fixes it to underlying structures. Swelling and COLLAGEN buildup lead to loss of elasticity. It usually begins at age 25–55, more often in women, with severe inflammation of underlying tissue and stiffness, pain, and skin tautness and thickening. Systemic problems that may arise years later include fever, trouble breathing, inflammation of heart muscle or membranes, gastrointestinal

disorders, and kidney malfunction. The disease may finally stabilize or gradually regress. STEROIDS may help, and physical medicine and rehabilitation with heat, massage, and passive exercise help prevent limb fixation and deformity.

Scofield, (David) Paul (b.1922) British actor. He joined the ROYAL SHAKESPEARE CO. in 1946, winning acclaim as Henry V and Hamlet. He had his greatest success in *A Man for All Seasons* (1960) and reprised the role on film (1966, Academy Award). He continued to excel in stage productions, notably *Uncle Vanya* (1970) and *Amadeus* (1979), and onscreen in *King Lear* (1971), *A Delicate Balance* (1973), *Quiz Show* (1994), and *The Crucible* (1996).

Scone \'skün\, **Stone of** Rectangular block of yellow sandstone decorated with a Celtic cross, associated with the crowning of Scottish kings since medieval times. Legend says it was Jacob's pillow in the Holy Land, and it was taken to Ireland and then carried off by invading Scots. KENNETH I MacAlpin brought it to the Scottish village of Scone about 840. EDWARD I took it to England (1296), where it was later placed under the Coronation Chair in Westminster Abbey as a symbol of the authority of English kings over Scotland. It was finally returned to Scotland in 1996.

Scopes trial (July 10–21, 1925) Widely publicized trial in Dayton, Tenn. John T. Scopes (1900–1970), a high-school teacher, was charged with teaching Charles DARWIN's theory of EVOLUTION, which violated a state law prohibiting teaching that denied the divine creation of humans. The "Monkey Trial" was broadcast live on radio and attracted worldwide interest. The prosecutor was W. J. BRYAN; the defense attorney was Clarence DARROW. The judge limited arguments to the basic charge to avoid a discussion of Darwin's theory. Scopes was found guilty and fined $100; he was later acquitted on a technicality.

score In music, the parts of all the instruments or singers of an ensemble notated with simultaneous sounds aligned vertically, on a system of parallel staffs arranged one above another. Polyphonic music was being composed for some 600 years before scores came into regular use in the 16th–17th cent., and they have since become essential for conductors.

Scorel \'skȯr-əl\, **Jan van** (1495–1562) Dutch humanist, architect, engineer, and painter. After five years of work and study in Europe, including Rome, he returned to Holland (1524) and introduced such Italian Renaissance elements as nudes, classical draperies and architecture, and spacious imaginary landscapes into his paintings. His greatest works are his portraits, which show his gift for characterization. He successfully combined the idealism of Renaissance Italy with the naturalism of N European art in his paintings, and influenced successive generations of Dutch artists.

scorpion Any of some 1,300 nocturnal ARACHNID species (order Scorpionida, subphylum Chelicerata) having a segmented tail tipped with a venomous stinger. One pair of appendages tear apart insect and spider prey; strong, clawlike pincers on the large second pair are used as feelers and for grasping prey while sucking the tissue fluids. The venom is either a hemotoxin that, in humans, causes swelling, redness, and pain or a neurotoxin that may cause convulsions, paralysis, cardiac irregularities, and death. Most scorpions will sting a human only if provoked. Nocturnal hunters, most species are tropical or subtropical.

scorpion fish Any of the numerous species of carnivorous marine fish of the family Scorpaenidae, especially those in the genus *Scorpaena*. They have large, spiny heads and strong, sometimes venomous, fin spines. Some species are brightly colored, often red. The largest species grow to about 40 in. (1 m) long. Scorpion fish lie quietly on the bottom, often among rocks. See also LIONFISH, ZEBRA FISH.

Scorsese \skȯr-'sä-zē\, **Martin** (b.1942) U.S. film director. Born in New York City, he won critical attention for his feature film *Mean Streets* (1973) and was widely praised for *Taxi Driver* (1976), which starred his frequent lead actor Robert DE NIRO. Noted for his realistic portrayals of New York street life and his use of graphic violence, he rose to the top rank of American directors with such films as *New York, New York* (1977), the acclaimed *Raging Bull* (1980), *The King of Comedy* (1983), *The Color of Money* (1986), the controversial *Last Temptation of Christ* (1988), *GoodFellas* (1990), and *The Age of Innocence* (1993).

scotch See WHISKEY

Scotland Northernmost country of the United Kingdom. Area: 30,418 sq mi (78,783 sq km). Population (1998 est.): 5,120,000. Capital: EDINBURGH. The population is a blend of Celtic, Angle, and Norman ancestry. Languages: English (official), SCOTTISH GAELIC, Scots. Religion: Church of Scotland (Presbyterian) (established). Currency: pound sterling. The Highlands, in the north, are occupied by a series of lakes and the Grampian Mtns.; the Lowlands include some of Scotland's best farmland; and the Southern Uplands feature narrow, flat valleys separating table mountains. Important industries are coal and oil production, electronics, forestry, and marine fishing. PICTS inhabited the region when it was invaded by the Romans about A.D. 80. In the 5th cent. it split into four kingdoms under the Picts, Scots, Britons, and Angles. Scottish unification began in the 9th cent. and the Scottish ruler was forced to pay homage to the English crown in 1174, leading to numerous future disputes. The Scottish and English kingdoms were united in 1603 when James VI, son of MARY, QUEEN OF SCOTS, ascended the English throne as JAMES I. Scotland became part of the United Kingdom of Great Britain in 1707, when the parliaments of both governments passed the Act of Union. Despite two rebellions, after 1745, the history of Scotland became part of the history of Great Britain. In 1999 the Scots established their own parliament to vote on wide-ranging political issues, while remaining part of the United Kingdom.

Scotland Yard *officially* **New Scotland Yard** Headquarters of the London Metropolitan Police, and, by extension, the force itself. The London police force was created in 1829 by Robert PEEL and housed at 4 Whitehall Place, which had an entrance in Great Scotland Yard. In 1890 it moved to a new building; that location became New Scotland Yard, a name that was kept when it moved again in 1967. In addition to duties common to all metropolitan police forces (including crime detection and prevention and traffic management), it is entrusted with civil defense in times of emergency. It keeps records on all known criminals in Britain, and other British police forces often seek its assistance.

Scott, George C(ampbell) (1927–1999) U.S. actor. Born in Wise, Va., he won praise for his early film roles in *Anatomy of a Murder* (1959), *The Hustler* (1961), and *Petulia* (1968). A strong screen personality, he was noted for his bull neck and barking voice. He refused an Academy Award for *Patton* (1970), calling the competition a "meat parade." Among his later films were *The Hospital* (1972) and *Hardcore* (1979). His television work included *The Price* (1970, Emmy award, also refused).

Scott, Peter Markham (*later* **Sir Peter**) (1909–1989) British conservationist and artist. Son of R. F. SCOTT, he gained early renown as a wildlife painter. In 1946 he founded the Severn Wildfowl Trust (now the Wildfowl and Wetlands Trust). Through a captive breeding program, he saved the nene from extinction in the 1950s. In 1961 he founded the World Wildlife Fund (World Wide Fund for Nature). He helped create the *Red Data Book* (see ENDANGERED SPECIES).

Scott, Ridley (b.1937) British film director. He worked in British television, then formed his own production company in 1967 to make television commercials. His first feature film, *The Duellists* (1977), was followed by the science-fiction thrillers *Alien* (1979) and *Blade Runner* (1982), a box-office hit that became a cult classic for its vividly dark images. His later films include *Black Rain* (1989), the widely acclaimed *Thelma and Louise* (1991), and *Gladiator* (2000).

Scott, Robert Falcon (1868–1912) British explorer. He joined the Royal Navy in 1880, and led an Antarctic expedition (1901–4). Leading a second expedition, in Octo-

Robert Falcon Scott

ber 1911 he and 11 others started overland for the South Pole. After their motor sledges broke down and seven men returned to base camp, Scott and four others trekked for 81 days to reach the pole in January 1912, only to find that Roald AMUNDSEN had preceded them. Beset by bad weather and insufficient supplies, the men died on the return trip, Scott and the last two survivors only 11 miles from their base camp. In England Scott was celebrated as a national hero, though his judgment has been questioned.

Scott, Walter (*later* **Sir Walter**) (1771–1832) Scottish writer, often considered both the inventor and the greatest practitioner of the historical novel. From childhood Scott was familiar with stories of the Border region of Scotland. Though trained in law, his interest in border ballads led to the collection *Minstrelsy of the Scottish Border* (1802–3). His first original poetic romance, *The Lay of the Last Minstrel* (1805), established his reputation; *The Lady of the Lake* (1810) was his most successful contribution to the genre. He tired of narrative poetry and turned to prose romances. The extremely popular series of "Waverley novels" consists of more than two dozen works dealing with Scottish history, including the masterpieces *Old Mortality* (1816), *Rob Roy* (1817), and *The Heart of Midlothian* (1818). He drew on English history and other themes for *Ivanhoe* (1819), *Kenilworth* (1821), and *Quentin Durward* (1823).

Scott, Winfield (1786–1866) U.S. Army officer. Born in Petersburg, Va., he fought in the War of 1812. Promoted to major general, he traveled to Europe to study tactics. He advocated a well-trained and disciplined army and earned the nickname "Old Fuss and Feathers" for his emphasis on formalities. In 1841 he became commanding general of the U.S. Army. He directed operations during the MEXICAN WAR and led the U.S. invasion at Veracruz. He was the Whig Party's presidential nominee in 1852, but lost to Franklin PIERCE.

Scottish Gaelic language CELTIC LANGUAGE of N Scotland, a descendant of the Irish speech introduced into N Britain by invaders in the 4th–5th cent. By the Middle Ages, it was the language of all of the Scottish Highlands and part of the Lowlands. Only after the collapse of Classical Modern Irish (see IRISH LANGUAGE) did writers regularly begin to use features that distinguish Scottish Gaelic dialects from Irish dialects. Increasing Anglicization, suppression of traditional culture, and the 19th-cent. land clearances precipitated a marked decline; today it is probably a true community language for fewer than 80,000 people, most on the NW coast and the Hebrides.

Scotts Bluff National Monument National monument, W Nebraska. Established in 1919, it has an area of 5 sq mi (13 sq km). Its focus is a large bluff that rises 800 ft (244 m) above the N. PLATTE RIVER and was a landmark on the OREGON TRAIL.

Scottsboro case U.S. civil rights controversy. In 1931, in Scottsboro, Ala., nine black youths were charged with the rape of two white women. Despite testimony by doctors that no rape had occurred, the all-white jury convicted them and sentenced all but one to death. In 1932, following public outcry, the U.S. Supreme Court overturned the convictions on grounds of inadequate legal counsel. A subsequent conviction of one of the youths was overturned by the Supreme Court since blacks had systematically been excluded from the state's juries. Alabama retried and reconvicted the defendants individually, but yielded to public pressure and freed or paroled all but one, who later escaped.

Scott vs. Stanford See DRED SCOTT DECISION

Scotus, John Duns See John DUNS SCOTUS

scouting Activities of various national and worldwide organizations for youth aimed at developing character, citizenship, and individual skills. Scouting began when Robert BADEN-POWELL published *Scouting for Boys* (1908), in which he described the games and contests he used to train cavalry troops in scouting, envisioning small groups of boys who would learn tracking, reconnaissance, mapping, and other outdoor skills under a peer leader. The Boy Scouts, as established by Baden-Powell, was for boys 11–15 years old. The concept became so popular that separate organizations for girls (Girl Guides or Girl Scouts, 1910) and for younger boys (Wolf Cubs or Cub Scouts, 1916) and older boys (Explorers) were also formed.

Scrabble Game in which two to four players compete in forming words with lettered wooden tiles on a 225-square board. Words spelled out by the tiles interlock as in a crossword puzzle. Words are scored by adding up the point values of their letters. The game was developed by Alfred Butts, an unemployed architect, in 1931, and redesigned by Butts and James Brunot in 1948. Tens of millions of sets have been sold in many languages worldwide.

screw In machine construction, a usually circular cylindrical member with a continuous spiral rib or thread, used either as a fastener or as a FORCE and MOTION modifier. Various types of screws are used to clamp machine parts together. Wood screws are made in a wide variety of diameters and lengths. Screws that modify force and motion are known as power screws. The screw is considered one of the six simple MACHINES.

Scriabin \ˈskryä-bin\, Alexander (Nikolaevich) (1872–1915) Russian composer and pianist. He enjoyed a successful concert career, and his early compositions were mostly for piano. Obsessed with Richard WAGNER and Friedrich NIETZSCHE, he began composing in an entirely new nontonal style based on his "mystic chord," producing a third symphony and the *Divine Poem* (1904). Influenced by theosophy, he wrote the tone poem *Poem of Ecstasy* (1908). He experimented with "light shows" in his *Prometheus* (1910) in preparation for a huge operatic ritual, *Mysterium*, which was never composed. A lip tumor led to his death at 43.

Alexander Scriabin

Scribe \ˈskrēb\, (**Augustin**) **Eugène** (1791–1861) French playwright and librettist. Most of his 350 dramas proved extremely successful, and he became the most popular opera librettist of his time. His librettos include Vincenzo BELLINI's *La sonnambula* (1831), Gaetano DONIZETTI's *L'elisir d'amore* (1832), Giacomo MEYERBEER's *Les Huguenots* (1836), and Giuseppe VERDI's *Les vêpres siciliennes* (1855).

Scribner, Charles *orig.* Charles Scrivener (1821–1871) U.S. publisher. In 1846, in partnership with Isaac D. Baker (d.1850), Scribner established the publishing firm of Baker & Scribner in his native New York City. In 1878 the firm was renamed Charles Scribner's Sons. Its list initially consisted of philosophical and theological books, but later included British and continental European literature. After his death it was headed principally by his son Charles (1854–1930), during whose long presidency (1879–1928) the firm published such authors as Henry JAMES, Edith WHARTON, and Ernest HEMINGWAY. Later presidents were his son Charles (1890–1952) and grandson Charles, Jr. (1921–1995). The firm was purchased in 1984 by Macmillan, Inc.

scrimshaw Decoration of bone or ivory objects, such as whale's teeth and walrus tusks, with fanciful designs, traditionally carved by N. American whale fishermen with a jackknife or sail needle and emphasized with black pigments (e.g., lampblack). Among the traditional subjects are whaling scenes, ships, naval battles, flower bouquets, and the Irish harp. Examples date from the late 17th cent., but the craft reached its peak in 1830–50. It is still practiced by whalers in Siberia and Alaska.

Scripps, Edward W(yllis) (1854–1926) U.S. newspaper publisher. Born near Rushville, Ill., he began publishing his own papers in 1878 and eventually owned 34 in 15 states. He was a partner in forming the first major U.S. newspaper chain, the Scripps-McRae League of Newspapers (1894). In 1907 he consolidated regional Scripps news services as United Press (after 1958, United Press International). In 1922 he transferred his interests to his son, Robert Paine Scripps (1895–1938), who with Roy W. Howard (1883–

1964) formed the Scripps-Howard chain. Today's the E.W. Scripps Co. includes varied media holdings.

scripture Sacred writings of religions, comprising a large portion of the literature of the world. Nearly all scriptures were originally oral and were initially passed down as memorized texts. In some religions, notably ISLAM, HINDUISM, and BUDDHISM, there is still strong emphasis on the value of reciting or chanting the scriptures aloud. The Hebrew Bible (OLD TESTAMENT) is the scripture of JUDAISM; the BIBLE (Old and NEW TESTAMENTS together) is the scripture of CHRISTIANITY; and the QURAN is the scripture of Islam. Scriptures of Hinduism include the VEDAS and UPANISHADS. See also ADI GRANTH, AVESTA, Book of MORMON, SUTRA, TRIPITAKA.

Scruggs, Earl See Lester FLATT

scuba diving Swimming done under water with a self-contained underwater-breathing apparatus (SCUBA), as opposed to skin diving, which requires only a snorkel, goggles, and flippers. Scuba gear was invented by Jacques-Yves COUSTEAU and Émile Gagnan in 1943. Diving clubs formed quickly as the new technology became widely available. Scuba diving is used in oceanography, in underwater exploration and salvage work, in the study of water pollution, and for recreation.

sculpin *or* **bullhead** *or* **sea scorpion** Any of about 300 species (family Cottidae) of inactive, bottom-dwelling fishes found principally in N regions. Sculpins have one or more spines on the gill covers, large fanlike pectoral fins, and naked or spiny skin. The head is usually wide and heavy. The largest species grow to 2 ft (60 cm) long; the miller's-thumb *(Cottus gobio),* common in European lakes and rivers, is only about 4 in. (10 cm) long. Other species are found in Asia and N. America.

sculpture Three-dimensional art produced especially by forming hard or plastic materials into three-dimensional objects, usually by carving or modeling. The designs may be produced in freestanding objects (i.e., in the round), in relief, or in environments, and a variety of media may be used, including clay, wax, stone, metal, fabric, wood, plaster, rubber, and found objects. Materials may be carved, modeled, molded, cast, wrought, welded, sewn, or assembled and combined. Until the 20th cent., sculpture was considered a representational art, but since the early 1900s nonrepresentational works have been produced.

scurvy *or* **vitamin C deficiency** Nutritional disorder caused by deficiency of VITAMIN C, interfering with tissue synthesis and causing bleeding gums, loose teeth, stiff joints and legs, slow wound healing, and anemia. Scurvy among sailors was recognized as diet-related in 1753, when James LIND showed that drinking citrus juice could cure and prevent it. Full-blown scurvy is now rare, and adequate vitamin C usually cures even severe cases in days.

Scylla and Charybdis \'si-lə...kə-'rib-dis\ In GREEK MYTHOLOGY, two monsters that guarded opposite sides of a narrow passage through which ODYSSEUS had to sail in his wanderings. These waters are now identified with the Strait of MESSINA. Scylla, a monster with six snaky heads, seized and devoured six of Odysseus' companions; Charybdis, the personification of a whirlpool, drank down and belched forth the waters three times a day. The shipwrecked Odysseus saved himself by clinging to a tree on the shore.

Scythians \'si-thē-ənz\ Nomadic people of Iranian stock who migrated from Central Asia to S Russia in the 8th–7th cent. B.C. Fierce warriors, they were among the first expert horsemen, which enabled them to establish an empire from W Persia through Syria and Judaea to Egypt. They repelled an invasion by the Persian DARIUS I around 513 B.C. Their civilization produced wealthy aristocrats ("Royal Scyths"), whose graves held richly worked articles of gold and other precious materials. They fought with double-curved bows, trefoil-shaped arrows, and Persian swords. Burial called for the sacrifice of the dead man's wife and servants. In the 5th cent. B.C., the royal family intermarried with Greeks. The community fell to the Sarmatians in the 2nd cent. B.C.

SDI See STRATEGIC DEFENSE INITIATIVE

SDS See STUDENTS FOR A DEMOCRATIC SOCIETY

Sea, Law of the International law codified in a treaty signed in 1982 by 117 nations and covering the status and use of TERRITORIAL WATERS, sea lanes, and ocean resources. It was not initially signed by the U.S., England, W. Germany, Israel, Italy, and several other industrialized nations, but by 1998 the U.S. had accepted most of its provisions. The code defines territorial waters as those extending 12 nautical mi (22 km) beyond a nation's coast and gives to each nation exclusive fishing and mining rights in waters extending to 200 nautical mi (370 km) from its coast.

sea anemone \ə-,ne-mə-,nē\ Any of more than 1,000 CNIDARIAN species in the order Actiniaria, found from the tidal zone of all oceans to depths of more than 30,000 ft (10,000 m). Species vary from less than 1 in. (3 cm) to about 5 ft (1.5 m) in diameter. The mouth, at one end of the cylindrical body, is surrounded by petal-like, usually colorful, tentacles that bear stinging nematocysts. Most species remain permanently attached to a hard surface such as a rock or the back of a crab.

sea bass Any of about 400 species (family Serranidae) of carnivorous fishes, most of which inhabit shallow regions of warm and tropical seas. Species range from about 1 in. (3 cm) to 6 ft (1.8 m) long and may weigh 500 lbs (225 kg). About 12 species in the family Moronidae (sometimes considered a subfamily of Serranidae) inhabit temperate waters. The Chilean sea bass, a popular food fish, is not a true sea bass. The Chilean sea bass, a popular food fish, is not a true sea bass. See also BASS.

Seaborg \'sē-,bòrg\, **Glenn (Theodore)** (1912–1999) U.S. nuclear chemist. Born in Ishpeming, Mich., he worked with others to discover some 100 isotopes, including many of major importance. In 1941 he and his colleagues discovered PLUTONIUM, then discovered and isolated the elements americium, curium, berkelium, californium, einsteinium, fermium, mendelevium, and nobelium (atomic numbers 95–102). He joined the MANHATTAN PROJECT in 1942 and was instrumental in the development of the ATOMIC BOMB, though he pleaded unsuccessfully with Pres. Truman not to use it on civilian targets. He shared a 1951 Nobel Prize. Prediction of new elements' chemical properties and placement in the PERIODIC TABLE was helped greatly by Seaborg's "actinide concept." Head of the Atomic Energy Commission 1961–71, he led the negotiations that eventuated in the Limited Nuclear Test-Ban Treaty (1963) and later played a leading role in the passage of the NUCLEAR NONPROLIFERATION TREATY. In 1997 his name was given to the new element seaborgium, the first time a living person had been so honored.

sea cucumber Any of 1,100 species of ECHINODERMS constituting the class Holothurioidea, found in all oceans, mostly in shallow water. The soft, cylindrical body is 0.75 in. (2 cm) to 6.5 ft (2 m) long and 0.4–8 in. (1–20 cm) thick. Most species' bodies are covered with hundreds of tube feet, and 10 or more tentacles surround the mouth. Many can expel their internal organs and grow new ones. Several exude a toxin lethal to fish and small animals. Locomotion is sluglike. See also SHELLFISH.

seafloor spreading Theory that oceanic crust forms along submarine mountain zones, or OCEANIC RIDGES, and spreads out laterally. In 1960 U.S. geophysicist Harry H. Hess (1906–1969) postulated that molten material from the earth's MANTLE continuously wells up along the crests of the midocean ridges. As the MAGMA cools, it is pushed away from the flanks of the ridges. This spreading is thought to cause the migration, or drifting apart, of the continents; for example, those bordering the Atlantic Ocean are moving away from the MID-ATLANTIC RIDGE at about 1–2 cm (0.4–0.8 in.) per year. Hess's theory was pivotal in the development of the theory of PLATE TECTONICS.

seafood Edible freshwater and ocean creatures, excluding mammals. Seafood includes FISHES, CRUSTACEANS, MOLLUSKS, edible JELLYFISH, sea TURTLES, FROGS, SEA URCHINS, and SEA CUCUMBERS. The eggs of some species are eaten as CAVIAR. Seafood furnishes about 15% of the world's protein intake. Lean fish is equivalent to beef or poultry in its protein yield (18–25% by weight), but much lower in calories. Much seafood is eaten raw, dried, smoked, salted, pickled, or fermented. Otherwise it is cooked, often in stews or soups.

Seagram Building High-rise office building in New York City (1958). Designed by Ludwig MIES VAN DER ROHE and Philip JOHNSON, this sleek skyscraper is a pure example of a rectilinear prism sheathed in glass and bronze; it took the INTERNATIONAL STYLE to its zenith, while displaying Mies's exceptional sense of proportion and concern for detail.

sea horse Any of about 24 species (family Syngnathidae) of fishes that usually live along warm seashores, clinging to plants with a forward-curled, prehensile tail. Species range from 1.5 to 12 in. (4–30 cm) long. Sea horses have bony rings instead of scales, and their eyes can move independently. They swim upright, sucking small organisms into their mouths. The female deposits her eggs into a brood pouch beneath the male's tail, and the male expels the newly hatched young.

seal Aquatic carnivore with webbed flippers and streamlined body. Earless seals (of the family Phocidae, with 18 species) propel themselves in water by side-to-side strokes of the hind limbs. On land, they wriggle on their belly or pull themselves with their forelimbs. Earless species include the ELEPHANT SEAL, HARBOR SEAL, HARP SEAL, and leopard seal. The eared seals (family Otariidae, with five species of SEA LION and nine of fur seal) propel themselves in water by a rowing motion of their front limbs; on land, they use all four limbs.

sea level Position of the air–sea boundary, to which all terrestrial elevations and submarine depths are referred. The sea level at any location changes constantly with changes in tides, atmospheric pressure, and wind conditions. Consequently, the level is better defined as mean sea level, the height of the sea surface averaged over time and over all stages of the tide.

sea lion Any of five species (family Otariidae) of eared SEALS found along coasts on both sides of the Pacific, from Alaska to Australia. The males of all but the California sea lion have a mane. Males range from 8 to 11 ft (2.5–3.3 m) long and weigh 600–2,200 lbs (270–1,000 kg). They breed in large herds; males establish a harem of 3–20 females. The California sea lion (*Zalophus californianus*) is the trained seal of circuses and zoos.

seamount Large submarine volcanic mountain rising about 0.6 mi (1 km) or more above the surrounding seafloor; smaller submarine volcanoes are called sea knolls, and flat-topped seamounts are called guyots. Seamounts are abundant and occur in all major ocean basins. Virtually every oceanographic expedition discovers new seamounts, and it is estimated that about 20,000 exist worldwide.

sea otter *or* **great sea otter** Marine OTTER (*Enhydra lutris*) of the N Pacific, usually found in kelp beds. Floating on its back, it opens mollusks by smashing them on a stone balanced on its chest. The large hind feet are broad and flipperlike. It is 40–65 in. (100–160 cm) long and weighs 35–90 lbs (16–40 kg). Hunted almost to extinction for its thick lustrous fur, it is now fully protected.

sea parrot See PUFFIN

Sea Peoples Any of the groups of aggressive seafarers who invaded eastern Anatolia, Syria, Palestine, Cyprus, and Egypt toward the end of the BRONZE AGE. They were especially active in the 13th cent. B.C. Though the extent and origin of the upheavals remain uncertain, Sea Peoples are believed responsible for the destruction of old powers such as the HITTITE empire. The only major tribe to settle permanently in Palestine were the PHILISTINES.

seaplane Aircraft that can land, float, and take off on water. The first practical seaplanes were built and flown in 1911–12 by Glenn CURTISS, who developed both the float seaplane, essentially a land plane with pontoons instead of landing wheels, and the flying boat, a boatlike plane that combined a main float and fuselage in a single body. A retractable landing wheel was later added to create an amphibian aircraft. By the late 1920s seaplanes held the speed and range records for aircraft. Their utility diminished with the building of long-range land-based airplanes and aircraft carriers.

search and seizure In law enforcement, an exploratory investigation of a premises or a person and the taking into custody of property or an individual in the interest of gaining evidence of unlawful activity or guilt. In the U.S., the 4th Amendment to the Constitution prohibits unreasonable searches and seizures and requires that a warrant specifying the place to be searched and the persons and things to be seized be issued following a finding of probable cause.

search engine Tool for finding information, especially on the INTERNET or WORLD WIDE WEB. Search engines are essentially massive DATABASES. Most consist of three parts: at least one program, called a spider, crawler, or bot, that "crawls" through the Internet gathering information; a database, which stores the gathered information; and a search tool, with which users search through the database by typing in keywords describing the information desired (usually at a Web site dedicated to the search engine). Metasearch engines search a subset (usually 10 or so) of the huge number of search-engine databases and then compile and index the results.

Searle, Ronald (William Fordham) (b.1920) British cartoonist, painter, and author. He published his first cartoons in the late 1930s. In 1941 he created cartoons of the bizarre schoolgirls who later became the subject of four films, beginning with *The Belles of St. Trinian's* (1954). He joined the staff of *Punch* in 1956 before moving to Paris in 1961. He has published more than 50 books.

Sears, Roebuck and Co. U.S. merchandising company, one of the world's largest retailers. It was founded in 1893 by Richard W. Sears (1863–1914) and Alvah C. Roebuck (1864–1948). The company grew rapidly, using mail-order catalogs to sell merchandise at low prices to farms and small towns that lacked access to retail outlets or were overcharged at existing stores. Under Robert E. Wood (1928–54), Sears built retail stores across the U.S., and by 1931 its retail sales had topped its mail-order sales. It diversified into financial services in the 1980s and introduced the Discover credit card in 1985, but in 1992 it began selling off its financial-services subsidiaries. It discontinued its famous catalog in 1993 and spun off its Allstate insurance firm (founded 1931) in 1995.

Sears Tower Skyscraper office building in Chicago. With 110 floors and a height of 1,454 ft (443 m), it became the world's tallest building at its completion in 1974. Its architect, Fazlur Khan (1928–1982), designed it as a bundled-tube (see SKYSCRAPER) structure to resist lateral forces. The exterior is sheathed in black aluminum and bronze-tinted glass.

sea scorpion See SCULPIN

sea slug See NUDIBRANCH

season Any of four divisions of the year according to consistent annual changes in the weather. In the Northern Hemisphere, winter formally begins on the winter SOLSTICE, December 21 or 22; spring on the vernal EQUINOX, March 20 or 21; summer on the summer solstice, June 21 or 22; and fall or autumn on the autumnal equinox, September 22 or 23. In the Southern Hemisphere, the dates of onset of summer and winter are reversed, as are those of spring and fall. See diagram on following page.

seasonal affective disorder (SAD) Cyclical DEPRESSION occurring in winter, apparently caused by insufficient sunlight. Symptoms can include all those of major depression, and there is a risk of suicide. The cause may be related to regulation of the body's temperature and hormones and may involve the PINEAL GLAND and MELATONIN. Exposure to intense full-spectrum light from fluorescent bulbs has proved effective as treatment. Dawn simulation (exposure to low light levels in the final sleep period) and negative-ion therapy can also help.

sea star See STARFISH

Seastrom, Victor See Victor SJÖSTRÖM

SEATO See SOUTHEAST ASIA TREATY ORGANIZATION

Seattle City (pop., 2000: 563,000) and seaport, Washington state. It is the largest city in the state and the commercial, industrial, and financial center of the Pacific Northwest. It is flanked by the OLYMPIC MTNS. and CASCADE RANGE. Laid out in 1853, it withstood an Indian attack (1856), anti-Chinese riots (1880s), and a disastrous fire (1889) to emerge

S

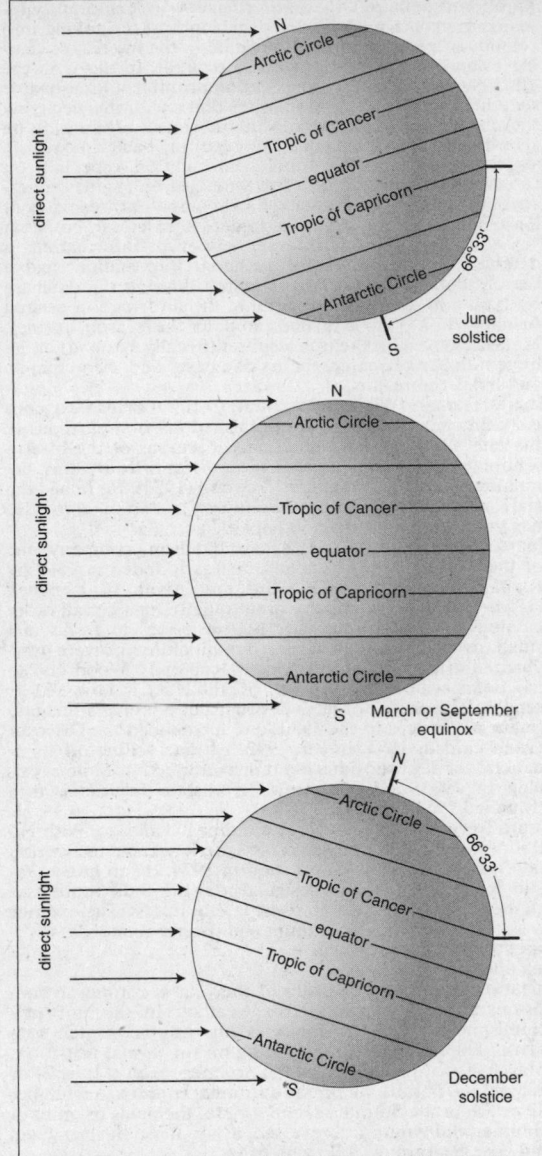

Season Because the earth is tilted on its axis with respect to the plane of its orbit around the sun, different parts of its surface are in direct (overhead) sunlight at different times of the year. The change in the amount of sunlight reaching the surface at various latitudes is the primary cause of the seasons.

as the gateway to the Orient and Alaska. It supplied the Yukon and Alaskan gold rushes in the 1890s. World War II brought a great boom to the city. Seattle Center, site of the 1962 World's Fair, contains the 607-ft (185-m) Space Needle. It is home to the BOEING CO. (1916) and the Univ. of WASHINGTON (1861).

Seattle Slew (1974–2002) U.S. Thoroughbred racehorse. He was the first unbeaten racer ever to win the TRIPLE CROWN (1977). In his racing career of 17 races, he won 14, was second twice, and fourth once.

sea urchin Any of about 700 species (class Echinoidea) of ECHINODERMS found worldwide. Sea urchins have a globular body covered with movable, sometimes poisonous, spines up to 12 in. (30 cm) long. Pores along the internal skeleton accommodate often sucker-tipped tube feet. Sea urchins live on the seafloor. The mouth is on the body's underside; teeth are extruded to scrape algae and other food from rocks. Some species excavate hiding places in coral or rock.

seawater WATER that makes up the oceans and seas. Seawater is a complex mixture of 96.5% water, 2.5% salts, and small amounts of other substances. Much of the world's magnesium is recovered from seawater, as are large quantities of bromine. In some regions, table salt is obtained by evaporating seawater. Despite the high processing costs, large DESALINATION plants have been built in dry areas along seacoasts in the Middle East and elsewhere to supply drinking water.

seaweed Any of certain species of red, green, and brown marine ALGAE that generally are anchored to the sea bottom or to a solid structure by rootlike holdfasts that do not extract nutrients. The most obvious seaweeds are brown algae; mosslike carpets of red algae are seen at low tides. Brown algae commonly found as seaweeds include KELP, which include the largest algae, and SARGASSUM. Some seaweeds have hollow, gas-filled floats that keep their fronds at the surface of the water. *Ulva* species, commonly called sea lettuce, are among the relatively few green algae that are seaweeds. Seaweeds are used as food, and brown algae are used in FERTILIZERS.

sebaceous gland \si-'bā-shəs\ Small OIL-producing gland in the SKIN, usually connected to a HAIR follicle by a duct into which it releases sebum, a component of the slightly greasy film on the skin. The glands are distributed over the entire body except the palms and soles, most abundantly on the scalp and face. Well developed at birth, they shrink during childhood but enlarge again and increase their output at puberty, often leading to ACNE.

Sebastian, St. (d.c.288) Christian martyr who died during the persecutions of DIOCLETIAN. According to legend, he was born in Gaul and went to Rome to serve in the army. When officials learned that he was a Christian seeking converts, they ordered his execution by archers. Left for dead, he was nursed back to health by a Christian widow. He presented himself before the emperor, who condemned him to death. In Renaissance art he was often depicted as a handsome youth pierced by arrows.

Sebastiano del Piombo \se-bäs-'tyä-nō-del-'pyȯm-bō\ *orig.* Sebastiano Luciani (1485/86–1547) Italian painter. Highly influenced by his teacher, GIORGIONE, in 1511 he moved to Rome and became a member of MICHELANGELO's circle. His *Pietà* (1513), *Flagellation* (1516–24), and *Raising of Lazarus* (1516–18), all based on Michelangelo's sketches, combined the warm coloring of the Venetian school with Michelangelo's anatomical clarity and firm sculptural drawing. After Raphael's death, Sebastiano's reputation as a portraitist was unparalleled. In 1531 Pope Clement VII, the subject of one of his finest portraits (1526), appointed him keeper of the papal seal; his nickname derives from the fact that the seal was of lead (Italian, *piombo*).

Sebastopol See SEVASTOPOL

secession (1860–61) Withdrawal of 11 Southern states from the U.S. The precipitating event was the election of Abraham LINCOLN as president (1860). Most slaveholding states had vowed to secede if the Republican candidate won, since the party strongly opposed slavery and its extension into the new territories. Earlier threats of secession were made by states'-rights advocates in the NULLIFICATION crisis (1832), and in the 1850s before the MISSOURI COMPROMISE. Secession was first approved by S. Carolina (1860); six other states followed in the period before Lincoln's inauguration. After Lincoln resisted the South's attack on FORT SUMTER, four other slaveholding states voted to secede, joining the newly formed CONFEDERATE STATES OF AMERICA.

secondary education Traditional second stage in formal education, beginning at age 11–13 and ending usually at age 15–18. In the U.S., over 80% of students of secondary-school age attend a HIGH SCHOOL. In the British system, most students (90% in Britain) attend comprehensive schools similar to American high schools; the rest attend either grammar schools (publicly funded PREPARATORY

SCHOOLS), technical schools, or PUBLIC SCHOOLS, which are actually private. In France, students 15–18 years of age who have completed the first part of their secondary education attend either a general (academic) or a vocational lycée. In Germany, students who have completed grade 9 may enter a *Hauptschule* leading to apprenticeship training, a *Realschule* leading to either vocational school or apprenticeship training, or an academically oriented GYMNASIUM.

Second Empire (1852–70) Period in France under the rule of Emperor NAPOLEON III (the original empire having been that of NAPOLEON). In its early years (1852–59), the empire was authoritarian but enjoyed economic growth. Liberal reforms were gradually introduced after 1859, but political liberalization led to increased opposition to the government. In 1870 a new constitution establishing a quasi-parliamentary regime was widely approved, but France's defeat in the FRANCO–PRUSSIAN WAR resulted in the overthrow of the government and the end of the Second Empire.

Second Empire style See BEAUX-ARTS STYLE

Second International *or* **Socialist International** (1889–1914) Federation of socialist political parties and trade unions. Unlike the centralized FIRST INTERNATIONAL, it was a loose federation that met at various intervals. By 1912 it represented the socialist parties of all European countries, the U.S., Canada, and Japan, with a membership of about 9 million. It reaffirmed Marxist doctrine while supporting parliamentary democracy, but its main concern became the prevention of a European war. When that failed, the International ended in 1914.

Second Republic (1848–52) French republic established after the REVOLUTIONS OF 1848 (following the original republic during the FRENCH REVOLUTION). The liberal republicans' hope of establishing an enduring democratic regime was soon frustrated. In 1848 Louis-Napoléon (later NAPOLEON III) was elected president and a monarchist majority was elected to the legislative assembly, which passed conservative measures restricting voting rights and freedom of the press. Realizing that his power and future reelection were limited by the assembly's actions, Louis-Napoléon organized a coup d'état in 1851. A new constitution reduced the assembly's power, and a plebiscite to approve the change was accompanied by officially inspired petitions for the empire's restoration. In 1852 the SECOND EMPIRE was born.

Secretariat (1971–1989) U.S. Thoroughbred racehorse. In 1973 he became the first TRIPLE CROWN winner since Citation in 1948. In his two-year career, he came in first 16 times, second three times, and third once. He is often regarded as the greatest Thoroughbred in history.

secretary bird African raptor (*Sagittarius serpentarius,* family Sagittaridae), the only living BIRD OF PREY that hunts on foot. It has long scaly legs and is 4 ft (1.2 m) long with a 7-ft (2.1-m) wingspread. Twenty black crest feathers make it appear to be carrying quill pens behind its ears. Secretary birds kill snakes (their main prey) by stamping on them, flailing them against the ground, or dropping them from aloft. They are protected in most African nations.

secret police Police established by national governments to maintain political and social control. Generally clandestine, secret police have operated independently of the civil police. Notorious 20th-cent. examples were the Nazi GESTAPO and the Russian KGB. Secret-police tactics include arrest, imprisonment, torture, and execution of political enemies and intimidation of potential opposition members.

secret society Any of various oath-bound societies devoted to brotherhood (or sisterhood), moral discipline, and mutual assistance. Such societies usually conduct rituals of initiation to instruct new members (see rite of PASSAGE). Greek and Roman MYSTERY RELIGIONS had their secular counterparts in clandestine social clubs. In W Africa, secret societies such as Poro (for men) and Sande (for women) served to translate slight advantages of wealth and prestige into political authority. Fraternal orders such as FREEMASONRY may be considered secret societies, as may criminal groups such as the MAFIA and the Chinese TRIADS and hate groups such as the KU KLUX KLAN.

Secular Games *Latin* Ludi saeculares. Celebrations held in ancient Rome at the beginning of a new *saeculum,* or generation, usually at intervals of several decades. Similar games were originally held by the ETRUSCANS as offerings to the underworld gods. The Romans at first also worshiped the underworld gods, but later introduced APOLLO, DIANA, and LETO in a festival that lasted several days and nights and included sports, music, theater, and circuses. The first known Roman games were held in 249 B.C.; they ceased in the 4th cent. A.D. under CONSTANTINE I, who converted to Christianity.

Securities and Exchange Commission (SEC) U.S. regulatory commission established in 1934 to restore investor confidence by ending the misleading sales practices and stock manipulations that had led to the stock market's 1929 collapse. It prohibited the buying of stock without adequate funds, initiated registration and supervision of securities markets and stockbrokers, established rules regarding proxies, prohibited insider trading, and required that companies offering securities make full public disclosure of all relevant information.

security In finance, written evidence of ownership conferring the right to receive property not currently in the holder's possession. The most common securities are STOCKS and BONDS. Governments, companies, and financial institutions use securities to raise money. Stocks are securities issued in the form of equity ownership. Bonds are securities that take the form of debt. They constitute promises to pay a specified amount at a specified date and to pay interest at a specified rate in the interim. Most government securities are bonds that pay a fixed amount of interest per year; unlike commercial securities, their repayment is guaranteed. Both stocks and bonds are traded publicly on organized STOCK EXCHANGES. External forces affect security prices, and for individual stocks the company's current and prospective financial performance play an important role.

Security Council, U.N. See UNITED NATIONS SECURITY COUNCIL

Seder \'sā-dər\ Ritual meal served on the first night of PASSOVER, commemorating the flight of the Jews from Egypt. Presided over by the head of the family, the Seder follows a liturgy, the HAGGADAH, that reminds participants of the story of the EXODUS. The ritual includes blessings, the pouring of wine, and ritual questions about the meaning of the event asked by the youngest child present. The meal includes unleavened bread and bitter herbs, the bread symbolizing the haste with which the Israelites left Egypt and the herbs symbolizing the bitterness of slavery.

sedge family Family Cyperaceae, one of the 10 largest families of flowering plants, composed of about 5,000 species of grasslike herbs that inhabit wet regions worldwide. Sedges are monocots (see COTYLEDON) of extraordinary ecological importance; forming the base of food webs, they provide food and shelter for aquatic and wetland animals. They are also important as ornamentals and weeds, and are used in woven products. Key characteristics that distinguish sedges from GRASSES are solid stems that are often triangular in cross section; leaves, when present, that clasp the stem with a sheath; and small spikes of minute flowers that are not enclosed in bracts. The genus *Carex* represents the true sedges. PAPYRUS and bulrushes are also included in this family.

sedimentary rock Rock formed at or near the earth's surface by the accumulation and LITHIFICATION of fragments of preexisting rocks. Sedimentary rocks can be formed only where sediments are deposited long enough to become compacted and cemented into hard beds or strata (see STRATIFICATION). They are the most common rocks exposed on the earth's surface; their defining characteristic is that they are formed in layers. Each layer has features that reflect the conditions during deposition, the nature of the source material (and, often, the organisms present), and the means of transport. See also SHALE.

sedimentation In geology, the process of deposition of a solid material from a state of suspension or solution in a fluid (usually air or water). It also includes deposits from glacial ice and materials collected under the effect of gravity alone, as in accumulations of rock debris at the base of cliffs.

S

sedition Crime of creating a revolt, disturbance, or violence against lawful civil authority with the intent to cause its overthrow or destruction. Limited to organizing and encouraging opposition to government rather than directly participating in its overthrow, sedition is regarded as falling one step short of TREASON. In the U.S., the display of a certain flag or the advocacy of a particular movement, such as SYNDICALISM, ANARCHISM, or COMMUNISM, has periodically been declared seditious. In recent decades the courts have applied a more stringent test to ensure that constitutional freedoms are not abridged.

seed Reproductive structure in plants that consists of a plant embryo, usually accompanied by a supply of food (endosperm, which is produced during fertilization) and enclosed in a protective coat. Seed embryos contain one or more COTYLEDONS. In typical FLOWERING PLANTS, seed production follows POLLINATION and fertilization. As seeds mature, the ovary that enclosed the ovules develops into a fruit containing the seeds. Most seeds are small, weighing less than a gram; the smallest contain no food reserve. Seeds are highly adapted to transportation by animals, wind, and water. When circumstances are favorable, water and oxygen penetrate the seed coat, and GERMINATION occurs. Some remain viable for only about a week; others have germinated after thousands of years.

seed plant *or* **spermatophyte** \spər-ˈma-tə-ˌfīt\ Any of the FLOWERING PLANTS (angiosperms) and the CONIFERS and related plants (GYMNOSPERMS). Seed plants share many features with FERNS, including the presence of vascular tissue, but unlike ferns they have stems that branch sideways. Seed plants have generally more complex plant bodies and reproduce via SEEDS. The seed represents a significant improvement over the SPORE, with its limited capacity for survival. Seed plants also differ from ferns in having GAMETOPHYTES that are reduced in size and are embedded in the SPOROPHYTES (and thus are less vulnerable to environmental stress). Another land-based adaptation of seed plants is POLLEN, which promotes genetic RECOMBINATION and distribution of the species over a wide geographic area.

Seeger, Pete(r) (b.1919) U.S. folk singer and songwriter. Born in New York City, son of the ethnomusicologist Charles Seeger (1886–1979) and stepson of the composer Ruth Crawford Seeger (1901–1953), he studied at Harvard but left to travel the country by hopping freight trains, gathering tunes, and learning the banjo. In 1940 he organized the Almanac Singers with Woody GUTHRIE, and performed widely at union halls and farm meetings, In 1948 he joined three other musicians to form the Weavers. Shortly after the group became successful, it was blacklisted because of Seeger's previous left-wing activities. They broke up in 1952, but reunited three years later and proved highly influential in the "folk revival." Seeger continued to suffer from blacklisting. He fostered the growth of the hootenanny, and he wrote such folk standards as "Where Have All the Flowers Gone" and "If I Had a Hammer."

Sefarim, Mendele Moykher See MENDELE MOYKHER SEFARIM.

Seferis \se-ˈfer-ēs\, **George** *orig.* Giorgios Stylianou Seferiades *or* Yeoryios Stilianou Sepheriades (1900–1971) Greek poet. He held various diplomatic posts 1926–62. His first poetry collection was *I strofi* (1931; "The Turning Point"). He is considered the leading Greek poet of "the generation of the '30s," which introduced Symbolism to modern Greek literature. He was awarded the Nobel Prize in 1963.

Segal \ˈsē-gəl\, **George** (1924–2000) U.S. sculptor. Born in New York City, he began his career as a figurative painter. In the early 1960s he was associated with the POP ART movement. His distinctive sculptures, consisting of monochromatic life-size plaster figures cast from live models, situated in mundane environments, capture a mood of anonymity and alienation. Notable works include *The Gas Station* (1963), *The Truck* (1966), and *The Hot Dog Stand* (1978).

Segesta \sē-ˈjes-tə\ Ancient city, NW Sicily. Culturally, it was Greek, but it generally took the Carthaginian side against its Greek neighbors. Early in the First PUNIC WAR, it was allied with Rome. Its ruins include a 3rd-cent.-B.C. theater and a 5th-cent.-B.C. temple to Artemis.

Segovia, Andrés (1893–1987) Spanish guitarist. Almost entirely self-taught, by the 1920s he was touring internationally; he would continue to perform into his nineties. He was by far the most important force in making the guitar a concert instrument. He commissioned works by prominent composers and arranged music ranging from the Renaissance to the 19th cent. for solo guitar.

Andrés Segovia

segregation Separation of individuals or groups. Racial segregation provides a means of maintaining the economic advantages and higher social status of the politically dominant group. In recent times it has been used primarily by white populations to maintain their ascendancy over other groups through legal and social color bars. In the U.S. South, public facilities were segregated from the late 19th cent. into the 1950s (see JIM CROW LAWS). The CIVIL RIGHTS MOVEMENT and the CIVIL RIGHTS ACT OF 1964 helped end segregation in education and public facilities. See also APARTHEID.

seignorialism See MANORIALISM

Seine River \ˈsen\ *ancient* Sequana. Second-longest river in France. It rises northwest of DIJON and flows through PARIS before emptying into the ENGLISH CHANNEL at LE HAVRE after a course of 485 mi (780 km). It drains an area of about 36,400 sq mi (78,700 sq km) in N France; its network carries most of France's inland waterway traffic.

seismic wave \ˈsīz-mik\ Earth vibration generated by an EARTHQUAKE, explosion, or similar phenomenon. Earthquakes produce both body waves, which travel within the earth, and surface waves, which travel along the surface. Seismograms (recorded traces of the amplitude and frequency of seismic waves) yield information about the earth and its subsurface structure; artificially generated seismic waves are used in oil and gas prospecting.

seismology \sīz-ˈmä-lə-jē\ Scientific discipline concerned with the study of EARTHQUAKES and SEISMIC WAVES. A branch of GEOPHYSICS, it has provided much information about the composition of the earth's interior. Recent work has focused on predicting earthquakes in hopes of minimizing the risk to humans. Seismologists have also studied artificially induced quakes in an effort to find ways of controlling natural earthquakes.

Seistan See SISTAN

Selassie, Haile See HAILE SELASSIE

Seldes \ˈsel-dəs\, **George** (1890–1995) U.S. journalist. Born in Alliance, N.J., he worked for the *Chicago Tribune* 1918–1928. In *You Can't Print That* (1928) he criticized censorship and strictures on journalists, a continuing theme in his career. He reported on the rise of fascism in Italy and Spain in the 1930s, and he and his wife founded *In Fact*, a journal devoted to press criticism (1940–50). His other targets included the tobacco industry and J. Edgar HOOVER. His brother, Gilbert Seldes (1893–1970), wrote such books as *The Seven Lively Arts* (1924) and was a columnist for the *New York Evening Journal* and the *Saturday Evening Post*, film critic for *The New Republic*, and the first director of television for CBS News.

selection In biology, the preferential survival and reproduction or preferential elimination of individuals with certain GENOTYPES, by means of natural or artificial controlling factors. The theory of EVOLUTION by NATURAL SELECTION was proposed by Charles DARWIN and Alfred Russel WALLACE in 1858. Artificial selection differs from natural selection in that inherited variations in a species are manipulated through controlled BREEDING in order to create qualities economically or aesthetically desirable to humans.

Selene \sə-ˈlē-nē\ *Latin* **Luna** In GREEK and ROMAN religion, the goddess that personified the moon. Her siblings were HELIOS and Eos, the goddess of dawn. Selene fell in love with Endymion, a handsome young shepherd; her husband ZEUS cast Endymion into eternal sleep, but she visited him in the cave where he slept, and he fathered her 50 daughters.

selenium \sə-'lē-nē-əm\ Semimetallic chemical ELEMENT, chemical symbol Se, atomic number 34. It is widely distributed, usually in small amounts, occasionally uncombined but more often as selenides of iron, lead, silver, or copper. Of selenium's several forms, the gray metallic crystalline one is the most stable at room temperature. Its electrical conductivity increases when LIGHT strikes it and it can convert light directly into ELECTRICITY, so selenium is used in PHOTOCELLS, SOLAR CELLS, and light meters. It serves as a red colorant for glass and glazes. Many selenium compounds (VALENCE 2, 4, or 6) are toxic, though the element is not. Vital to living cells, it works as an ANTIOXIDANT; it is used in nutritional supplements and animal feeds.

Seles \'se-ləs\, **Monica** (b.1973) Yugoslav-U.S. tennis player. Born in Novi Sad, she came to the U.S. to train in 1985. She became one of the dominant women stars of the 1990s, achieving multiple wins in the French Open (1990–92), Australian Open (1991–93, 1996), and U.S. Open (1991–92). In 1993 she stopped competing temporarily after being stabbed on a court in Hamburg. She returned to win the Australian Open in 1996 and a bronze medal at the 2000 Olympics.

Seleucia (on the Tigris) \sə-'lü-shə\ Ancient city, on the TIGRIS RIVER, central Iraq. Founded by SELEUCUS I NICATOR in the late 4th cent. B.C. as his E capital, it replaced BABYLON as MESOPOTAMIA's leading city. PLINY THE ELDER estimated its population at 600,000. During the Parthian domination of the Tigris-Euphrates valley that began in the 2nd cent. B.C., it maintained its position and trade. In A.D. 165 the Romans burned the city, marking the end of Hellenism in Mesopotamia. See also SELEUCID DYNASTY.

Seleucid dynasty \sə-'lü-səd\ Macedonian Greek dynasty (312–64 B.C.) founded by SELEUCUS I NICATOR. Carved from ALEXANDER THE GREAT's empire, the Seleucid domain stretched from Thrace to the border of India and included Babylonia, Syria, and Anatolia. Seleucus was succeeded in 281 by ANTIOCHUS I SOTER, who reigned until 261. He was followed by Antiochus II (r.261–246), Seleucus II Callinicus (r.246–225), and Seleucus III (r.225–223). The empire was at its height under ANTIOCHUS III the Great (r.223–187), but it began a slow decline at the end of his reign. The decline accelerated after the death of ANTIOCHUS IV (r.175–164), and the dynasty met its end at the hands of the Roman POMPEY THE GREAT in 64 B.C.

Seleucus I Nicator \sə-'lü-kəs...ni-'kā-tər\ (359/354–281 B.C.) Macedonian army officer, founder of the SELEUCID DYNASTY. Following the death of ALEXANDER THE GREAT, under whom he served, Seleucus won an empire centered on Syria and Iran. In 312, after being ousted by ANTIGONUS I MONOPHTHALMUS and serving PTOLEMY I SOTER, he reconquered Babylon. By 303 he had extended his empire to India. In 301 he helped defeat Antigonus at the Battle of Ipsus and received Syria,

Seleucus I Nicator Coin, late 4th–early 3rd cent. B.C.

later taking S Syria from Ptolemy. In 294, when his son became sick with love for Seleucus' wife (the son's stepmother), he gave her to him and made the son coregent. Hoping to reestablish Alexander's empire, Seleucus defeated Lysimachus (281), another of Alexander's former generals who had become a satrap in Asia Minor.

self-defense In CRIMINAL LAW, an affirmative defense (e.g., to a murder charge) alleging that the defendant used serious force necessarily for self-protection. The claim of self-defense must normally rely on a reasonable belief that the other party intended to inflict great bodily harm or death and that avoidance by retreating was impossible. See also HOMICIDE.

self-determination Process by which a group of people, usually possessing a degree of political consciousness, form their own state and government. The idea evolved as a byproduct of NATIONALISM. According to the U.N. charter, a people has the right to form itself into a state or to otherwise determine the form of its association with another state, and every state has the right to choose its own political, economic, social, and cultural systems.

self-esteem Fundamental sense of personal worth and ability. Parents may foster self-esteem by expressing affection and support for the child as well as by helping the child set realistic (rather than unreachably high) goals for achievement. Karen HORNEY asserted that low self-esteem produces a personality that excessively craves approval and affection and exhibits an extreme desire for personal achievement. Alfred ADLER claimed that it leads people to strive to overcome their perceived inferiorities and to develop strengths or talents in compensation.

self-incrimination In CRIMINAL LAW, incrimination of and by oneself, particularly through testimony. The 5th Amendment to the U.S. Constitution protects a person from being compelled to make self-incriminating statements, one intention being to prevent coercion of testimony. Though people may be required to testify, they are permitted to refuse to answer questions if an answer would be potentially self-incriminating. See also EXCLUSIONARY RULE.

Seljuq dynasty \'sel-jük\ or **Saljuq dynasty** \'sal-jük\ (c.11th–13th cent.) Muslim TURKMEN dynasty that ruled Persia, Iraq, Syria, and Anatolia. Seljuq was the chief of a nomadic Turkish tribe. His grandsons Chaghri Beg and TOGHRIL BEG conquered realms in Iran. Under ALP-ARSLAN and Malik-shah, the empire came to include all of Iran, Mesopotamia, Syria, and Palestine; Alp-Arslan's victory over the Byzantine emperor led to several CRUSADES. The Seljuqs adopted the Persian culture and language. By 1200 Seljuq power remained only in Anatolia, which collapsed in a war against vassals in 1230. See also NIZAM AL-MULK.

Sellers, Peter (*orig.* Richard Henry) (1925–1980) British film actor. The son of vaudeville performers, in the 1950s he performed on radio in the popular comedy series *The Goon Show*. His film performances in *The Mouse That Roared* (1959), *I'm All Right, Jack* (1959), *Lolita* (1962), and *Dr. Strangelove* (1964), in which he played three characters, were especially well received. He was enormously popular as the bumbling Inspector Clouseau in *The Pink Panther* (1964) and its sequels, and later won praise as a simple-minded gardener in *Being There* (1979).

Sellers, William (1824–1905) U.S. engineer and manufacturer. Born in Delaware Co., Pa., he founded his first firm to manufacture machinists' tools and mill gearing. His formulas for matching screw threads and nuts (1864) became the U.S. standards. In 1868 he founded Edge Moor Iron Co., which became the largest plant in the world for supplying and building iron bridges (including the BROOKLYN BRIDGE) and other large structures. He was president from 1873 of Midvale Steel Co. (Nicetown, Pa.), which became the major metal supplier for U.S. government ordnance and small arms.

Selye \'zel-yə\, **Hans (Hugo Bruno)** (1907–1982) Austro-Hungarian-Canadian endocrinologist. In early work on the effects of STRESS, he injected ovarian hormones into rats; this stimulated the adrenal glands, causing deterioration of the thymus gland, ulcers, and finally death. He later showed that physical injury, environmental stress, and toxins could have similar effects. Extending his theory to humans, he proved that a stress-induced hormonal-system breakdown could lead to heart disease and hypertension.

Selznick, David O(liver) (1902–1965) U.S. film producer. Born in Pittsburgh, he worked for MGM, RKO, and other studios, producing such films as *Dinner at Eight* (1933), *King Kong* (1933), *David Copperfield* (1935), and *A Tale of Two Cities* (1935) before forming Selznick International in 1936 and producing such hits as *A Star Is Born* (1937). He was essential to the enormous success of *Gone with the Wind* (1939), overseeing every aspect with detailed memos. He brought Alfred HITCHCOCK to the U.S. and produced *Rebecca* (1940) and *Spellbound* (1945). He also produced *Duel*

in the Sun (1946), *The Third Man* (1949), and *A Farewell to Arms* (1957).

semantics Study of meaning, one of the major areas of linguistic study (see LINGUISTICS). Members of the school of interpretive semantics study the structures of language independent of their conditions of use. In contrast, generative semantics holds that the meaning of sentences is a function of their use. Still another group maintains that theorists must take into account the psychological questions of how people form concepts and how these relate to word meanings.

semaphore \'se-mə-ˌfōr\ Method of visual signaling, usually with flags or lights. Before radio, a semaphore system was widely used to send messages between ships. A person would stand with arms extended, moving two flags to specific angles to indicate letters or numbers. Before the telegraph, semaphore signaling with lights on high towers was used to transmit messages between distant points; messages were read by telescope.

Semarang \sə-'mär-ˌaŋ\ City (pop., 1995 est.: 1,367,000), JAVA, Indonesia. Despite being one of the largest ports in Java, its harbor is unprotected against monsoons, which can cause suspension of port operations.

Sembène \sem-'ben\, **Ousmane** (b.1923) Senegalese writer and film director. He fought with the Free French in World War II. His writings, often on historical-political themes, include *The Black Docker* (1956) and *God's Bits of Wood* (1960). Around 1960 he became interested in film; after studying in Moscow, he made films reflecting a strong social commitment, including *Black Girl* (1966), the first feature produced in sub-Saharan Africa. With *Mandabi* (1968), he began to film in the Wolof language.

Semele \'se-mə-ˌlē\ In GREEK MYTHOLOGY, the mother of DIONYSUS. When Semele became the lover of ZEUS, the enraged HERA tricked Semele into asking to see the god in all his splendor. Having promised to grant Semele's every wish, Zeus was forced to comply, and the firebolts emanating from him destroyed her. Zeus rescued the unborn Dionysus, who some stories say later descended into HADES to bring Semele back to take her place among the immortals.

semen \'sē-mən\ *or* **seminal fluid** Whitish thick fluid emitted from the male reproductive tract that contains SPERM. Sperm cells, produced by the TESTES in humans, represent 2–5% of semen volume; fluids from tubules, glands, and storage areas of the REPRODUCTIVE SYSTEM bathe them as they travel down. During ejaculation, liquids from the PROSTATE GLAND and seminal vesicles dilute the sperm and provide a suitable environment. An average ejaculation of a human male expels 0.1–0.3 cu inches (2–5 ml), containing 200–300 million sperm.

semiconductor Class of crystalline solids with electrical conductivity midway between that of a CONDUCTOR and an INSULATOR. Such materials can be treated chemically to allow transmission and control of an ELECTRIC CURRENT. Semiconductors are used in electronic devices such as DIODES, TRANSISTORS, and INTEGRATED CIRCUITS. Intrinsic semiconductors, such as SILICON, GERMANIUM, and gallium arsenide, have a high degree of chemical purity, but their conductivity is poor. Extrinsic semiconductors contain impurities that produce much greater conductivity. Intrinsic semiconductors can be converted into extrinsic semiconductors by adding small amounts of impurities, a process called doping.

seminary Educational institution, usually for training in theology. In the U.S. the term was formerly also used to refer to institutions of higher learning for women. Since at least the 4th cent. there have been seminaries for the training of clergy. The first known group of seminarians was gathered by St. Basil of Ancyra. In the Middle Ages, most theological training was in monasteries, and later in the universities. After the REFORMATION, seminaries again came into use, especially in the U.S.

Seminole \'se-mə-ˌnōl\ N. American Indian people who split off from the CREEK in the later 18th cent. and settled in N Florida, where they were joined by runaway slaves, Indian and black, from Georgia. The Seminoles lived more by hunting and fishing than by agriculture. They constructed shelters of thatched roofs supported by poles. In an effort to stem white encroachment, they fought a succession of wars (the SEMINOLE WARS). Today about 2,000 Seminole live in Florida and 5,000 in Oklahoma.

Seminole Wars (1817–18, 1835–42, 1855–58) Three conflicts between the U.S. and the SEMINOLE Indians of Florida. The first began when U.S. authorities tried to recapture runaway black slaves living among Seminole bands. After U.S. forces seized Spanish-held Pensacola and St. Marks, Spain ceded its Florida territory under the Transcontinental Treaty (1819). The second conflict followed the refusal of most Seminoles to relocate under the INDIAN REMOVAL ACT. Led by OSCEOLA, warriors hid in the Everglades and used guerrilla tactics to defend their land; about 2,000 U.S. soldiers were killed in the prolonged fighting. After Osceola was captured, most Seminoles agreed to emigrate west. The third conflict arose from efforts to oust the remaining Seminoles.

semiotics \ˌsē-mē-'ä-tiks, ˌse-mē-'ä-tiks\ *or* **semiology** Study of signs and sign-using behavior, especially in language. In the late 19th and early 20th cent., the work of Ferdinand de SAUSSURE and C. S. PEIRCE led to semiotics' emergence as a mode for examining phenomena in different fields, today including aesthetics, anthropology, communications, psychology, and semantics. See also POSTSTRUCTURALISM, STRUCTURALISM.

Semite Person speaking one of the SEMITIC LANGUAGES. The term came to include ARABS, Akkadians, Canaanites, some Ethiopians, and ARAMAEAN tribes including Hebrews. Semitic tribes migrated from the ARABIAN PENINSULA, beginning around 2500 B.C., to the Mediterranean coast, MESOPOTAMIA, and the Nile delta. The Hebrews settled with other Semites in PALESTINE, founding a new religion and nation. See also JUDAISM.

Semitic languages \sə-'mi-tik\ Family of AFROASIATIC LANGUAGES spoken in N Africa and SW Asia. No other language family has been attested in writing over a greater time span—from the late 3rd millennium B.C. to the present. Traditional classifications divide the family into an E and W group. E. Semitic languages include AKKADIAN and Eblaite, the language of a CUNEIFORM archive found at the ancient city of EBLA. W. Semitic contains as one major subgroup N.W. Semitic, which includes Ugaritic, known from texts of around 1400–1190 B.C.; the closely related Canaanite languages (including Moabite, Phoenician, and Ancient HEBREW); and ARAMAIC. Further subgrouping is controversial; traditionally, ARABIC was placed in a distinct S. Semitic subgroup of W. Semitic, though a more recent classification puts it together with N.W. Semitic. The S. Semitic languages include all forms of Arabic and Ethiopic.

Semmelweis \'ze-məl-ˌvīs\, **Ignaz (Philipp)** *Hungarian* Ignac Fulop Semmelweis (1818–1865) Hungarian-Austrian physician. At Vienna's obstetric clinic, at a time when European maternity hospitals saw death rates from PUERPERAL FEVER of up to 30%, Semmelweis noticed that far fewer women died in the midwives' division of the clinic than in the division where students were taught, often after coming from the dissecting room. Concluding that students carried the infection, he had them wash their hands in chlorinated lime before each exam, and mortality dropped from 18% to 1%. His *Etiology, Understanding, and Preventing of Childbed Fever* (1861) was nevertheless widely rejected abroad.

Senate, Roman Governing and advisory council that was the most permanent element in the constitution of ancient Rome. Under the monarchy, it served as an advisory council, with undefined powers. During the republic, it advised the CONSULS and supposedly stood second to them in power. Senators were appointed by the consuls, and later by censors, who were lesser magistrates; in 81 B.C., former QUAESTORS automatically became senators. It became the chief governing body, and controlled the republic's finances. The emperor AUGUSTUS reduced the Senate's power, while giving it new judicial and legislative functions. The Senate's power continued to fade until it disappeared in the 6th cent. A.D.

Sendak, Maurice (Bernard) (b.1928) U.S. artist and writer. Born in New York City, he illustrated more than 80 children's books by other writers before writing one himself. His *Kenny's Window* (1956) was followed by the innovative trilogy *Where the Wild Things Are* (1963), *In the Night*

Kitchen (1970), and *Outside Over There* (1981). He collaborated with Carole King on the musical *Really Rosie* (1978) and designed stage productions of *The Magic Flute* (1980) and *The Nutcracker* (1983).

Sendero Luminoso See SHINING PATH

Seneca \'se-ni-kə\ N. American Indian people who lived in what is now W New York and E Ohio. Families linked by maternal kinship occupied LONGHOUSES; they lived by hunting, fishing, and agriculture. The Seneca was the largest nation of the IROQUOIS CONFEDERACY; warfare with other Indian nations was frequent. In the American Revolution the Seneca were British allies, resulting in the destruction of their villages. In 1797 they secured land for 12 reservations in W New York, four of which still exist. Today the Seneca number about 4,500. See also CORNPLANTER, HANDSOME LAKE.

Seneca \'se-ni-kə\, **Lucius Annaeus** (4 B.C.?–A.D. 65). Roman philosopher, statesman, and playwright. He began a career in politics and law about A.D. 31. While banished to Corsica for adultery (41–49), he wrote the philosophical treatises *Consolationes*. He became tutor and later adviser to NERO, and from 54 to 62 was a leading intellectual figure in Rome. An adherent of STOICISM, he wrote *Epistilae morales,* a collection of essays on moral problems. He also left a series of verse tragedies marked by violence and bloodshed, including *Thyestes, Hercules,* and *Medea.* His plays influenced Elizabethan drama, notably William SHAKESPEARE's *Titus Andronicus* and John WEBSTER's *Duchess of Malfi.*

Seneca Falls Convention (July 19–20, 1848) Assembly held at Seneca Falls, N.Y., that launched the U.S. WOMEN'S SUFFRAGE MOVEMENT. It was initiated by E. C. STANTON (who lived in Seneca Falls) and Lucretia MOTT. Over 200 people attended, including 40 men. The group passed the Declaration of Sentiments, a list of grievances and demands that called on women to organize and petition for their rights. A controversial demand for the right to vote passed by a narrow margin.

Senegal \ˌse-ni-'gȯl\ *officially* **Republic of Senegal** Nation, W Africa. Area: 75,955 sq mi (196,722 sq km). Population (2000): 9,987,000. Capital: DAKAR. There are seven major

©1999, Encyclopædia Britannica, Inc.

SENEGAL

Scale 1: 14,627,000
0   60   120 mi
0   80   160 km

ethnic groups in Senegal, including the WOLOF, Serer, FULANI, and MALINKE, each speaking a separate language, and a number of smaller groups. Language: French (official). Religion: Islam (more than 90% of the population). Currency: CFA franc. The climate varies from dry desert to moist tropics. Forests cover

about 31% of the total area, about 27% is arable, and approximately 30% is pasture or rangeland. Fish, crustaceans, and peanuts are the most important cash and export produce. Other important industries are chemical manufacturing, mining, and tourism. Senegal has large reserves of phosphates and iron ore. It is a republic with two legislative houses; its head of state and government is the president assisted by the prime minister. Links between the peoples of Senegal and N. Africa were established in the 10th cent. A.D. Islam was introduced in the 11th cent., although ANIMISM retained a hold on the country into the 19th cent. The Portuguese explored the coast in 1445, and in 1638 the French established a trading post at the mouth of the SENEGAL RIVER. Throughout the 17th–18th cent., Europeans exported slaves, ivory, and gold from Senegal. The French gained control over the coast in the early 19th cent. and moved inland, halting the expansion of the Tukulor empire; in 1895 Senegal became part of FRENCH W. AFRICA. Its inhabitants were made French citizens in 1946, and it became an overseas territory of France. It became an autonomous republic in 1958 and an independent state in 1960. In 1982 it entered a confederation with Gambia, called Senegambia, which was dissolved in 1989. In recent years uprisings in part of the country have caused political disorder.

Senegal River River, W Africa. It rises in Guinea and flows northwest across Mali, then west to the Atlantic Ocean, forming the N border of Senegal. It is 1,020 mi (1,641 km) long. Dams control floodwaters and prevent the encroachment of saltwater during the dry season.

Senghor \seŋ-'gȯr\, **Léopold (Sédar)** (1906–2001) Poet, president of Senegal (1960–80), and cofounder of the NEGRITUDE movement. He completed his studies in Paris and became a teacher there. Captured by the Germans, he spent two years in concentration camps, where he wrote some of his finest poems. He was elected to the French National Assembly in 1945. In 1948 he edited *Hosties noires,* a seminal anthology of French-language African poetry. That same year he founded the Senegalese Progressive Union, which, as the Socialist Party (since 1976), remains Senegal's governing party. When Senegal gained independence in 1960, he was unanimously elected president. Advocating a moderate "African socialism," he became an internationally respected spokesman for Africa. In 1984 he became the first black inducted into the Académie Française.

Léopold Senghor addressing the U.N. General Assembly, 1961

senile dementia \'sē-ˌnīl-di-'men-chə\ DEMENTIA of old age (mostly after age 75), with loss of NEURONS and BRAIN-tissue shrinkage. Onset is usually gradual. Memory loss may progress until the patient cannot function independently. Language skills, spatial or temporal orientation, judgment, and other cognitive capacities may also decline, and there may be personality changes. ALZHEIMER'S DISEASE accounts for about 50% of cases. Next most common is multi-infarct dementia, in which a series of small STROKES destroy more and more of the brain.

Sennacherib \sə-'na-kə-rəb\ (d.681 B.C.) King of Assyria (r.705/4–681 B.C.), son and successor of SARGON II. Between 703 and 689 he undertook six campaigns against ELAM, which was stirring up insurrection in Babylonia; the last campaign saw the sack of BABYLON. He dealt firmly with an Egyptian-backed rebellion in Palestine in 701, but spared Jerusalem. He rebuilt the city of NINEVEH and planted fruit trees and exotic plants, including cotton, building extensive canals for irrigation. He devised better methods of bronze casting and improved well technology. He was assassinated by a son.

S

Sennett, Mack *orig.* Michael Sinnott (1880–1960) U.S. (Canadian-born) film director. Born in Quebec, he joined the Biograph studio in 1908, and soon was directing comedies under D. W. GRIFFITH's tutelage. He formed his own Keystone Co. in 1912 and produced the first U.S. feature-length comedy, *Tillie's Punctured Romance* (1914), but became most famous for over 1,000 comedy shorts, often featuring the slapstick comedy of the Keystone Kops. He hired such stars as Mabel Normand, Fatty Arbuckle, and Charlie CHAPLIN. He excelled in comic timing and improvisation, and used trick camera work to produce his famous comic chase scenes. In 1937 he received a special Academy Award.

sense *or* **sensory reception** *or* **sense perception** Mechanism by which information is received about one's external or internal environment. Stimuli received by nerves, in some cases through specialized organs with receptor cells sensitive to one type of stimulus, are converted into impulses that travel to the brain, where they are analyzed. In addition to the "five senses"—sight, hearing, smell, taste, and touch—humans have senses of motion (kinesthetic sense), heat, cold, pressure, pain, and balance. See also CHEMORECEPTION, EAR, EYE, INNER EAR, NOSE, PHOTORECEPTION, PROPRIOCEPTION, TASTE, TONGUE.

Seoul \'sōl\ City (pop., 1995: 10,229,000), capital of the Republic of Korea (S. Korea) since 1946. Located near the center of the undivided Korean peninsula, Seoul was the capital of the Korean CHOSON DYNASTY 1394–1910, and the center of Japanese rule of Korea 1910–45. During the KOREAN WAR it was the capital of the U.S. military government and suffered extensive damage. In 1988 it was the site of the Summer OLYMPIC GAMES. One of the world's largest cities, it is the commercial, cultural, educational, and industrial center of S. Korea.

Sephardi \sə-'fär-dē\ Descendant of the Jews who lived in Spain and Portugal from the Middle Ages until their expulsion in the late 15th cent. They fled first to the Ottoman empire and eventually settled in W Europe and the Balkan states. They differ from the ASHKENAZI Jews in their traditional language, Ladino, and in their preservation of Babylonian rather than Palestinian Jewish ritual traditions. Of today's estimated 700,000 Sephardic Jews, many live in Israel.

Sepoy Mutiny See INDIAN MUTINY

seppuku \'se-pə-ˌkü\ *or* **hara-kiri** Japanese ritual suicide by disembowelment, practiced by the SAMURAI. It was favored because it was slow and painful, and therefore demonstrated courage and strong resolve. Voluntary seppuku was performed to avoid the dishonor of capture, show loyalty to one's lord by following him into death, or atone for failure. Obligatory seppuku was a method of capital punishment for a samurai, who would be beheaded by a second once he had made an initial stab wound himself. Obligatory seppuku was abolished in 1873, but voluntary seppuku continued to occur; a notable 20th-cent. example was Yukio MISHIMA.

September 11 attacks (2001) Terrorist attacks on the WORLD TRADE CENTER and the PENTAGON. Using four hijacked commercial airliners in a coordinated assault, suicide terrorists affiliated with AL-QAEDA crashed two of them into the World Trade Center and one into the Pentagon; the fourth plane, apparently intended to hit the White House or the U.S. Capitol, crashed in W Pennsylvania when passengers overpowered the hijackers. The combined death toll exceeded 3,000 people in the buildings, planes, and nearby areas, making this the deadliest terrorist attack on U.S. soil in history. In response, the U.S. declared a "war on TERRORISM," invaded Afghanistan in pursuit of Al-Qaeda and Osama BIN LADEN, and established a Department of HOMELAND SECURITY.

septicemia \ˌsep-ti-'sē-mē-ə\ *or* **blood poisoning** Invasion of the bloodstream after surgery or infectious disease by microorganisms—typically gram-negative (see GRAM STAIN) BACTERIA—and the TOXINS they release. The latter trigger immune responses and widespread COAGULATION in blood vessels. High fever, chills, weakness, and sweating are followed by a drop in blood pressure. Multiple INFECTIONS are often present, requiring broad-spectrum ANTIBIOTICS as well as drainage of foci of infection. Without immediate treatment, septic shock follows, with a mortality rate over 50%.

Septimania \ˌsep-tə-'mā-nē-ə\ Ancient territory, S France. Located between the GARONNE and RHÔNE rivers and the PYRENEES and Cevennes mountains, it was settled during the reign of the Roman emperor Caesar AUGUSTUS by veterans of the Seventh Legion (Septimani). The region was subsumed under the counts of TOULOUSE in the 9th cent.

Septuagint \sep-'tü-ə-jənt\ Earliest extant Greek translation of the OLD TESTAMENT, presumably made for the use of the Jewish community in Egypt when Greek was the lingua franca. It dates from the 3rd–2nd cent. B.C. The name Septuagint was derived from a legend that 72 translators worked on it. The Septuagint rather than the original Hebrew Bible was the main basis for the Old Latin, Coptic, Ethiopic, Armenian, Georgian, Slavonic, and some Arabic translations of the BIBLE.

sequencing Determining of the order of AMINO acids in a PROTEIN or of NUCLEOTIDES in a NUCLEIC ACID. The results have increased understanding of the mechanisms of life processes and have numerous applications. Whereas Frederick SANGER required 10 years to sequence INSULIN and about as long to sequence the DNA of a small VIRUS, automated instruments and techniques can now do either task in days or hours. See also GENETIC CODE, POLYMERASE CHAIN REACTION.

sequoia See REDWOOD

sequoia, giant See BIG TREE

Sequoia National Park National park, SIERRA NEVADA range, California. The 629-sq-mi (1,629-sq-km) area was set aside in 1890 to protect groves of huge trees (*Sequoiadendron giganteum*) which are among the world's largest and oldest living things. The largest tree in the park is thought to be 3,000–4,000 years old.

Sequoyah *or* **Sequoya** *or* **Sequoia** \si-'kwȯi-ə\ (c.1760–1843) Creator of the CHEROKEE writing system. Convinced that the secret of the white people's power was written language, Sequoyah set about developing a Cherokee system. Adapting letters from English, Greek, and Hebrew, he created a system of 86 symbols representing all the syllables of the Cherokee language. Most Cherokee quickly became literate as a result.

Seram See CERAM

seraph \'ser-əf\ In Jewish, Christian, and Islamic literature, a celestial being with two or three pairs of wings who guards the throne of God. In Christian angelology, seraphim are the highest-ranking of the ANGELS. They appear in the Old Testament in a vision of ISAIAH as six-winged creatures praising God. See also CHERUB.

Serbia *Serbo-Croatian* **Srbija** \'sər-bē-ˌyä\ Constituent republic of Yugoslavia, comprising 80% of its area. The formerly autonomous provinces of VOJVODINA and KOSOVO are within its borders. Area: 34,116 sq mi (88,361 sq km). Population (1997 est.): 5,763,000. Capital: BELGRADE. Ethnic Serbs, Croats, Bosnians, and Albanians live in the republic. Language: Serbo-Croatian (official). Religions: Serbian Orthodox, Islam, Roman Catholic. Currency: Yugoslav new dinar. Serbia is mountainous, with forests in the central area and low-lying plains in the north. The fertile plains of Vojvodina supply much of the nation's grain, tobacco, and sugar beets, while the hilly central areas specialize in dairy, fruit, and livestock. Mining and manufacturing were the economic mainstays before the 1990s civil war. Serbs settled the region in the 6th–7th cent. A.D. In the 9th cent. they converted to Eastern Orthodox Christianity. The Ottoman Turks triumphed at the Battle of KOSOVO in 1389. It became completely independent of Turkey in 1878. After World War I, it became part of the Kingdom of Serbs, Croats, and Slovenes, which was renamed Yugoslavia in 1929. In 1946 Serbia was made one of six federated republics of Yugoslavia. After an unsuccessful attempt to prevent Slovenia's secession in 1991, Serb elements of the Yugoslav armed forces began assisting Bosnian Serbs to sweep Muslims and Croats from E and N Bosnia and Herzegovina. After Yugoslavia's breakup, Serbia joined with Montenegro to form a new Yugoslav federation. The area remained in turmoil (see BOSNIAN CONFLICT). The 1995 Dayton peace accords brought little relief. Slobodan MILOSEVIC retained power, and the push for more autonomy by Albanian Kosovars provoked another round of fighting in 1998–99 (see KOSOVO CONFLICT). A change in the Yugoslav government late in 2000 brought reinstatement in the United Nations and the Council of Europe.

Serbian and Croatian language *or* **Serbo-Croatian language** \krō-'ā-shən\ S. SLAVIC LANGUAGE spoken by some 21 million people in Croatia, Bosnia-Herzegovina, Serbia, Montenegro, and Kosovo. As the dominant language of pre-1991 Yugoslavia, it was used or understood by most ethnic groups of the federation. Historically, Serbia's literary language was the Serbian adaptation of Church Slavic (see OLD CHURCH SLAVIC LANGUAGE). In the 19th cent. a new literary language based on colloquial Serbian was successfully developed. In the 19th cent., the Zagreb-based Illyrian political movement turned a central dialect in hopes of uniting Croatians and bringing them closer to their Slavic brethren. The move toward a unified "Serbo-Croatian" was supported by the Yugoslav kingdom (1918–41) and communist Yugoslavia (1945–91). Yugoslavia's political disintegration has led to declarations of distinct Serbian, Croatian, and Bosnian languages.

Serengeti National Park \ˌser-ən-'ge-tē\ Wildlife refuge, N central Tanzania. The park covers 5,700 sq mi (14,750 sq km). An international tourist attraction, it is the only place in Africa where vast land animal migrations still take place. Some 200 species of birds as well as lions, leopards, elephants, rhinoceroses, hippopotamuses, giraffes, and baboons inhabit the park.

serfdom Condition in medieval Europe in which a tenant farmer was bound to a hereditary plot of land and to the will of his landlord. Unlike slaves, serfs only changed lords when the land they worked changed hands. From about the 2nd cent. A.D., large privately owned estates in the Roman empire were broken up and given to peasant farmers, who came to depend on larger landowners for protection in turbulent times. In 332 CONSTANTINE I established serfdom legally by requiring the tenant farmers to pay labor services to their lords. As serfs, they could not marry, change occupations, or move without their lord's permission, and they had to give a major portion of their harvest to their lord. The development of centralized political power, the labor shortage brought about by the BLACK DEATH, and endemic peasant uprisings in the 14th–15th cent. led to the gradual emancipation of serfs in Western Europe. In Eastern Europe serfdom became more entrenched during that period; Russia's serfs were not freed until 1861. See also FEUDALISM.

serialism Use of an ordered set of pitches as the basis of a musical composition. The terms twelve-tone music and serialism, though not entirely synonymous, are often used interchangeably. The serial method was worked out by Arnold SCHOENBERG in the years 1916–23. To Schoenberg, it represented the culmination of the growth of CHROMATICISM. Concerned to erase the system of TONALITY, which he regarded as outworn but which he realized tended to assert itself even against a composer's will, Schoenberg's original method stipulated (among several other requirements) that no note could be repeated before all 11 other notes of the chromatic scale had been used. Serialism, a broader term than twelve-tone music, can apply to use of fewer than 12 tones. In the later "total serialism," not only pitch but also rhythm, dynamics, register, and instrumentation are organized into ordered sets.

serigraphy See SILK SCREEN

Serkin, Rudolf (1903–1991) Austro-Hungarian-U.S. pianist. He made his debut at 12. He emigrated to the U.S. in 1939 and began teaching at the Curtis Institute, which he served as director 1968–75. In 1950 he helped found the Marlboro Music Festival in Vermont, which under Serkin would become the principal center for chamber music in the U.S. He was known for his highly intelligent and expressive but self-effacing playing of the German-Austrian classics. His son, Peter (b.1947), is a well-known pianist, with a wide repertoire.

Serling, Rod(man) (1924–1975) U.S. television writer and producer. Born in Syracuse, N.Y., he became a freelance television screenwriter in 1953. He wrote teleplays for such series as *Kraft Television Theater* and *Playhouse 90,* including *Requiem for a Heavyweight* (1956, Emmy award). He created and narrated the famous supernatural series *The Twilight Zone* (1959–65), and narrated the similar series *Night Gallery* (1970–73).

Sermon on the Mount Biblical collection of religious teachings and ethical sayings attributed to JESUS, as reported in the Gospel of St. MATTHEW. The sermon was addressed to disciples and a large crowd of listeners to guide them in a life of discipline based on a new law of love, even of enemies. It is the source of many familiar Christian homilies and oft-quoted passages, including the Beatitudes and the LORD'S PRAYER.

serotonin \ˌser-ə-'tō-nən\ Organic compount derived from the amino acid TRYPTOPHAN. It occurs in brain and intestinal tissue, platelets, and certain connective-tissue cells and is a component of many animal VENOMS (e.g., wasp, toad). A strong stimulator of blood-vessel constriction and a NEUROTRANSMITTER, serotonin concentrates in certain brain areas, especially the midbrain and HYPOTHALAMUS. Some cases of DEPRESSION are apparently caused by reduced amounts or activity of serotonin in the brain; many ANTIDEPRESSANTS counteract that condition.

serpentine \'sər-pən-ˌtēn\ Any of a group of magnesium-rich silicate minerals. Serpentine generally occurs as chrysotile, the most common variety of ASBESTOS, and as antigorite or lizardite, both of which are commonly massive and fine-grained. Named for its resemblance to a snake's skin, serpentine is usually grayish, white, or green. It takes a high polish and is sometimes used as an ornamental stone.

Serra \'ser-ə\, **Junípero** (1713–1784) Spanish missionary. A Franciscan priest, he worked as a missionary in Mexico 1750–67. When Spain began its occupation of Alta California (now California), he joined the expedition and in 1769 founded Mission San Diego. From 1770 to 1782 he founded eight more Californian missions, strengthening Spain's control of the area. His work earned him the title of Apostle of California.

Serra, Richard (b.1939) U.S. sculptor. Born in San Francisco, he paid for his college education by working in steel factories. From 1961 he studied with Josef ALBERS at Yale Univ., then settled in New York. In 1969–70 gravity became a major element of his work; the *Prop* series consisted of huge plates of lead or steel leaning against each other, supported only by their opposing weights. He is best known for his enormous, sometimes controversial outdoor pieces that interact with the environment, particularly *Tilted Arc,* installed in New York's Federal Plaza in 1981 but removed in 1989.

Sert, José Luis *Catalan* Josep Lluís Sert i Lopéz (1902–1983) Spanish-U.S. architect. He initially worked with LE CORBUSIER in Paris. On his own, he designed the Spanish pavilion at the Paris World's Fair (1937). Moving to the U.S. in 1939, he worked in urban development for Bogotá and Havana, among other cities. He served as dean of the Graduate School of Design at Harvard Univ. (1953–59). His work is exemplified by his Peabody Terrace married-students' housing at Harvard (1963–65). His outstanding museum designs include the Maeght Foundation in St.-Paul-de-Vence, France (1968), and the Joan Miró Foundation in Barcelona (1975).

serval \'sər-vəl\ Long-limbed CAT (*Felis serval*) of grass and bush country in sub-Saharan Africa. It has a long neck and large, cupped ears. It is 32–40 in. (80–100 cm) long, has an 8–12-in. (20–30-cm) tail, stands about 20 in. (50 cm), and may weigh over 30 lbs (15 kg). Its long coat is usually brownish with black spots or stripes.

Serval *(Felis serval)*

server Network computer, computer program, or device that processes requests from a client (see CLIENT-SERVER ARCHITECTURE). A Web server is a computer that uses the HTTP protocol to send Web pages to a requesting client's computer. On a LOCAL AREA

NETWORK, a print server manages one or more printers, and prints files sent to it by client computers. Network servers (which manage network traffic) and file servers (which store and retrieve files for clients) are two more examples of servers.

Servetus \sər-'vē-təs\, **Michael** (1511?–1553) Spanish physician and theologian. His views alienated both Roman Catholics and Protestants, beginning with his first book, *De Trinitatis erroribus* (1531), in which he denied the Holy Trinity. His *Biblia sacra ex Santis Pagnini translatione* (1542) was notable for its theory of prophecy. Elsewhere he questioned the usefulness of baptism and criticized the NICENE CREED. Persecuted by John CALVIN, he was convicted of heresy in Geneva and burned. He was the first to accurately describe cardiopulmonary circulation of the blood (1553).

Service, Robert (William) (1874–1958) English-Canadian poet. He emigrated to Canada in 1894 and lived eight years in the Yukon. His *Songs of a Sourdough* (1907) and *Ballads of a Cheechako* (1909) were enormously popular. He became known as "the Canadian Kipling" with such rollicking ballads as "The Shooting of Dan McGrew." His other works include the novel *The Trail of '98* (1910).

service academies, U.S. See UNITED STATES SERVICE ACADEMIES

service industry Enterprise that produces useful labor rather than goods. Industries that produce goods (tangible objects) include agriculture, mining, manufacturing, and construction. Service industries include everything else: banking, communications, wholesale and retail trade, all professional services such as engineering and medicine, all consumer services, and all government services. In the U.S., the service sector accounted for more than half the gross domestic product in 1929, two-thirds in 1978, and more than three-quarters in 1993. With increasing mechanization, a smaller workforce is able to produce more goods, and the service functions of distribution, management, FINANCE, and sales become relatively more important.

servomechanism Device used to correct the performance of a mechanism automatically, by means of feedback. The term properly applies only to systems in which the feedback and error-correction signals control mechanical position or velocity. Servomechanisms were first used in military and marine navigation equipment. Today they are used in automatic machine tools, satellite-tracking antennas, automatic navigation systems, and antiaircraft-gun control systems; their design is considered to be a branch of both ROBOTICS and CYBERNETICS.

sesame Erect, annual plant (*Sesamum indicum*) of numerous types and varieties in the family Pedaliaceae. It has been cultivated since antiquity for its seeds, which are used as food and flavoring and yield a prized oil. The hulled seeds have a mild, nutlike aroma and taste. The whole seed is used extensively in the cuisines of the Middle East and Asia. Sesame oil is used as a salad or cooking oil, in shortening and margarine, and in the manufacture of soaps, pharmaceuticals, cosmetics, and lubricants.

Sessions, Roger (Huntington) (1896–1985) U.S. composer. Born in Brooklyn, N.Y., he taught principally at Princeton Univ. His early neoclassicism preceded his adoption of serialism around 1953. His works include the operas *The Trial of Lucullus* (1947) and *Montezuma* (1963), eight symphonies, a *Concerto for Orchestra* (1982, Pulitzer Prize), and *When Lilacs Last in the Door-yard Bloom'd* (1970). His seriousness has kept his works from a wide audience.

set In mathematics and logic, any collection of objects (elements), which may be mathematical (e.g., NUMBERS, FUNCTIONS) or not. The intuitive idea of a set is probably even older than that of number. Members of a herd of animals, for example, could be matched with stones in a sack without members of either set actually being counted. The notion extends into the infinite. For example, the set of integers from 1 to 100 is finite, whereas the set of all integers is infinite. A set is commonly represented as a list of all its members enclosed in braces. A set with no members is called an empty, or null, set.

setback In architecture, a steplike recession in the profile of a high-rise building. Usually dictated by BUILDING CODES to allow sunlight to reach streets and lower floors, the building must take another step back from the street for every specified added height interval. In the 1920s, architects drew attention to their setbacks with decorative devices—mosaics; Chinese, Mayan, or Greek motifs; or Cubistic blocks. The INTERNATIONAL STYLE glass-wall skyscraper typically met zoning requirements with one huge setback at ground level that created a plaza. The late 20th cent. saw a return to decorative setbacks.

Seth *or* **Set** Ancient Egyptian god. A trickster, he was a sky god, lord of the desert, and master of storms, disorder, and warfare. He was the brother of OSIRIS, whom he killed, and he was antagonistic to HORUS. Seth's cult largely died out in the 1st millennium B.C. He was later regarded as entirely evil and identified as a god of the Persians and other invaders of Egypt.

SETI *in full* **Search for Extraterrestrial Intelligence** Ongoing project designed to search for extraterrestrial life. Based in the U.S., SETI focuses on receiving and analyzing signals from space, mostly RADIO WAVES, looking for patterns likely to have been sent by intelligent beings. Approaches include examining sunlike stars and making systematic sweeps in all directions. SETI remains controversial; Congress ended NASA's SETI project in 1992. It is now funded privately. A recent effort uses hundreds of thousands of home computers to analyze recorded data. See also DRAKE EQUATION.

Seti I (d.2379 B.C.) Egyptian king of the 19th dynasty (r.2390–2379 B.C.). His father, Ramses I, had reigned only two years. It was Seti who was the real founder of the greatness of the Ramessids, though his son RAMSES II is more famous. Seti did much to promote Egypt's prosperity. He fortified the frontier, opened mines and quarries, dug wells, rebuilt temples and shrines, and built the great temple at ABYDOS.

Seton \'sē-tᵊn\, **Ernest Thompson** *orig.* Ernest Evan Thompson (1860–1946) Canadian-U.S. naturalist and writer. Seton's family emigrated to Canada from England in 1866. Initially a wild-animal artist, in 1898 he published his most popular book, the story collection *Wild Animals I Have Known*. He fought to establish reservations for American Indians and parks for endangered prairie animals. In 1902 he founded the Woodcraft Indians to give children opportunities for nature study. He chaired the committee that established the Boy Scouts of America.

Seton \sē-tᵊn\, **St. Elizabeth Ann** *orig.* Elizabeth Ann Bayley *known as* **Mother Seton** (1774–1821) U.S. religious leader and educator, the first native-born U.S. citizen canonized by the Roman Catholic church. Born in New York City, in 1797 she founded the Society for the Relief of Poor Widows with Small Children, and in 1803 she was herself left a widow with five children. After converting to Roman Catholicism in 1805, she opened a free Catholic elementary school in Baltimore in 1809. In 1813 she founded the Sisters of Charity, the first U.S. religious order. She is often considered the mother of the U.S. parochial-school system. She was canonized in 1975.

set theory Branch of mathematics that deals with the properties of SETS. It is most valuable as applied to other areas of mathematics, which borrow from and adapt its terminology and concepts. These include the operations of union (∪) and intersection (∩). The union of two sets is a set containing all the elements of both sets, each listed once. The intersection is the set of all elements common to both original sets. Set theory is useful in analyzing difficult concepts in mathematics and LOGIC. It was placed on a firm theoretical footing by Georg CANTOR.

Settignano, Desiderio da See DESIDERIO DA SETTIGNANO

settlement In law, a compromise or agreement between litigants to settle the matters in dispute between them in order to dispose of and conclude their litigation. Generally, as a result of the settlement, prosecution of the action is withdrawn or dismissed without any judgment being entered. The parties may, however, incorporate the terms of the settlement into a consent decree, recorded by the court. Most suits brought today are either withdrawn or settled.

Settlement, Act of (June 12, 1701) Act of Parliament that thereafter regulated the succession to the English throne. It decreed that if King WILLIAM III or Princess (later Queen) ANNE died without issue, the crown was to pass to JAMES I's granddaughter Sophie of Hanover (1630–1714) and her Protestant heirs (see House of HANOVER). It also decreed that future monarchs must belong to the Church of England and that judges could not be dismissed on the sovereign's whim.

settlement house *or* **social settlement** *or* **community center** Neighborhood social-welfare agency. The staff of a settlement house may sponsor clubs, classes, athletic teams, and interest groups; they may employ such specialists as vocational counselors and caseworkers. The settlement movement began with the founding of Toynbee Hall in London in 1884 by Samuel Augustus Barnett (1844–1913). It soon spread to the U.S. with the establishment of such institutions as Hull House in Chicago (founded by Jane ADDAMS). Most countries now have similar institutions. In the late 19th and early 20th cent, U.S. settlement houses were active among the masses of new immigrants and worked for reform legislation such as workers' compensation and child-labor laws.

settling In building construction, the gradual subsiding of a structure as the soil beneath its foundation consolidates under loading. This may continue for several years after the structure's completion. Primary consolidation occurs as water is squeezed out from the soil; secondary consolidation results from adjustments in its internal structure under a sustained load. Whereas fixed-end beams are incapable of rotating under uneven settlement loads and bend in response to the stress, simply supported beams, the ends of which act as hinges, will rotate slightly and remain straight. Special columns with jacking devices may then be used to level the beams. Floating foundations and piles are often used as well.

Seurat \sœ̄-'rà\, **Georges (-Pierre)** (1859–1891) French painter. He entered the École des Beaux-Arts in 1878 and exhibited at the 1883 Salon, though he had already lost sympathy with its conservative policies. To achieve scientifically the color effects that the Impressionists had pursued, he developed pointillism, the technique of juxtaposing tiny brush strokes of contrasting colors to portray the play of light. His huge compositions included *Une Baignade, Asnières* (1883–84) and his masterpiece, *Sunday Afternoon on the Island of La Grande Jatte* (1884–86). As an aesthetic theorist, he explored the effects that could be achieved with the three primary colors and their complements.

Seuss, Dr. See T. S. GEISEL

Sevastopol *formerly* **Sebastopol** \sə-'vas-tə-ˌpōl\ Seaport city (pop., 1998 est.: 356,000) in the CRIMEA, S Ukraine. In 1783 the Russians began construction of a naval base on the BLACK SEA. A commercial port in the early 19th cent., it was besieged and devestated by Anglo-French forces for 11 months (1854–55) during the CRIMEAN WAR. It was the anti-Bolshevik White Army headquarters in the RUSSIAN CIVIL WAR (1918–20). In World War II it was destroyed after a long siege but again reconstructed. The chief base of the Russian Black Sea fleet since the early 19th cent., it has extensive dockyard facilities and arsenals.

Seven Cities of Cíbola See Seven Cities of CÍBOLA

Seven Days' Battles (June 25–July 1, 1862) AMERICAN CIVIL WAR battles that prevented Union capture of Richmond, Va. In a series of attacks and counterattacks by both sides, the Confederate army under Robert E. LEE forced Union troops under George MCCLELLAN to retreat from a position 4 mi (6 km) east of the Confederate capital to a new base on the James River. The withdrawal of the Army of the Potomac ended the Peninsular Campaign. Casualties were estimated at 16,000 for the Union and 20,000 for the Confederates.

Seven Oaks Massacre (1816) Destruction of a Canadian fur-trading settlement. Sixty MÉTIS directed by an agent of the NORTH WEST CO. set out to run provisions past the rival HUDSON'S BAY CO. settlement on the Red River. They were intercepted by the colony's governor and 25 soldiers at nearby Seven Oaks. An argument grew into a fight in which the Métis killed 20 men, including the governor, and forced the rest to abandon the colony, which was restored the next year.

Seventh-day Adventist See ADVENTIST

Seven Weeks' War *or* **Austro–Prussian War** (June–August 1866) Conflict between Prussia on one side and Austria, Bavaria, Saxony, Hanover, and minor German states on the other. A contrived dispute by Prussia's Otto von BISMARCK over the SCHLESWIG-HOLSTEIN QUESTION resulted in a Prussian attack on Austrian forces in Bohemia. The Prussian army, modernized and reorganized, decisively defeated Austria at the Battle of Königgrätz. The war was formally concluded by the Treaty of Prague, which assigned Schleswig-Holstein and other territories to Prussia.

Seven Wonders of the World Preeminent architectural and sculptural achievements of antiquity, as listed by various Greco-Roman observers. Included on the best known list were the Pyramids of GIZA (the oldest of the wonders and the only one substantially in existence today), the Hanging Gardens of Babylon (landscaped rooftop terraces on a ZIGGURAT, ascribed to either NEBUCHADNEZZAR II or the semilegendary Queen Sammu-ramat), the Statue of Zeus at Olympia (a large gold-and-ivory figure by PHIDIAS), the Temple of Artemis at Ephesus (built in 356 B.C., famous for its size and works of art), the Mausoleum of HALICARNASSUS, the Colossus of RHODES, and the Pharos of Alexandria (a 350-ft lighthouse built about 280 B.C. on an island off Alexandria).

Seven Years' War (1756–63) Major European conflict between Austria and its allies France, Saxony, Sweden, and Russia on one side against Prussia and its allies Hanover and Britain on the other. The war arose out of Austria's attempt to win back the rich province of SILESIA, taken by Prussia in the War of the AUSTRIAN SUCCESSION. Early victories by FREDERICK II the Great were offset by a decisive Prussian deteat near Frankfurt (1759). After inconclusive fighting in 1760–61, Frederick concluded a peace with Russia (1762) and drove the Austrians from Silesia. The war also involved the overseas colonial struggles between Britain and France in N. America (see FRENCH AND INDIAN WAR) and in India. The Treaty of Hubertusburg (1763) confirmed Prussia's stature as a major European power.

Severn River \'se-vərn\ *Welsh* **Hafren** \'hä-vren\ *ancient* Sabrina. River, E Wales and W England. Britain's longest river, it is 180 mi (290 km) long from its source to tidal waters. It rises in E central Wales and flows south to the BRISTOL CHANNEL and the Atlantic Ocean.

Severus \sə-'vir-əs\, **Septimius** *in full* Lucius Septimius Severus Pertinax (A.D. 146–211) Roman emperor (193–211). Named emperor by his troops after the murder of emperor Publius Helvius Pertinax, he marched on Rome and took the throne. He effectively made Rome a military monarchy, giving the army a dominant role in government. He annexed Mesopotamia, and he died attempting to subdue non-Roman Britain, having named his son CARACALLA his successor, thereby founding a personal dynasty.

Severus Alexander *in full* Marcus Aurelius Severus Alexander *orig.* Gessius Bassianus Alexianus (A.D. 208–235) Roman emperor (222–35). At 14 he succeeded ELAGABALUS, who had been murdered at the prompting of Severus' mother and grandmother, both of whom held real power during his rule. Civil lawlessness reigned, and Severus' military incompetence led to defeat by the Persians. When he bought peace from the Alemanni tribes, his indignant soldiers murdered him and his mother.

Sévigné \sā-vēn-'yā\, **Marquise de** *orig.* Marie de Rabutin-Chantal (1626–1696) French writer. Of old Burgundian nobility, she was well educated and moved in court society in Paris. After her daughter moved to Provence, she began writing letters to her that recounted events and described people and details of daily life. The stories and gossip in the 1,700 letters of this correspondence, related in a natural, spontaneous tone, provide a vivid picture of the 17th-cent. French aristocracy.

Seville \sə-'vil\ *Spanish* **Sevilla** \sā-'bē-yä\ *ancient* Hispalis. City (pop., 1998 est.: 702,000), capital of ANDALUSIA autonomous community, Spain. Located on the GUADALQUIVIR RIVER, it is Spain's leading inland port. Originally an Iberian town, it prospered under the Romans, and later the Vandals and the Visigoths. In 711 it came under the Moors and was a cultural and commercial center until the 13th

cent., when Spanish Christians under Ferdinand III captured it. After 1492 it became the center of Spanish colonial trade with the Americas. Famous for its beauty, it is one of Spain's main tourist magnets, with historic mosques, cathedrals, and the 12th-cent. Alcázar Palace. It was the site of the Spanish-American Exposition in 1929 and the World Exposition in 1992. The Univ. of Seville was founded in 1502.

Sèvres porcelain \'sev-rə\ French PORCELAIN made at the royal (now national) factory of Sèvres from 1756 until the present. Sèvres became the leading porcelain factory in Europe under the patronage of Madame de POMPADOUR, who involved the foremost artists of the day (e.g., François BOUCHER and E.-M. FALCONET) in the enterprise. Sèvres porcelain is famous for many styles and techniques, including white figures representing cupids, shepherdesses, or nymphs and the embellishment of grounds with minute patterns in gold.

Sèvres soft-paste porcelain jardiniere, 1761

sewage system Collection of pipes and mains, treatment works, and discharge lines (sewers) for wastewater. Early civilizations often built drainage systems in urban areas to handle storm runoff. The Romans constructed elaborate systems that also drained wastewater from the public baths. In the Middle Ages these systems fell into disrepair. As the populations of cities grew, disastrous epidemics of cholera and typhoid fever broke out, the result of ineffective separation of sewage and drinking water. The concentration of population and the addition to sewage of manufacturing waste that occurred during the INDUSTRIAL REVOLUTION increased the need for effective sewage treatment. Sewer pipe is laid following street patterns, and access holes allow periodic inspection and cleaning. Catch basins along street gutters direct storm water to the storm sewers. Civil engineers determine the volume of sewage likely, the route of the system, and the slope of the pipe to ensure an even flow by gravity that will not leave solids behind. In flat regions, pumping stations are sometimes needed. Modern sewage systems include domestic and industrial sewers and storm sewers. Sewage treatment plants remove organic matter from waste water. As sewage enters the plant, large objects are screened out; grit and sand are then removed by settling or screening with finer mesh. Suspended solids (sludge) settle out in primary sedimentation tanks. The remaining sewage is aerated and mixed with microorganisms to decompose organic matter. A secondary sedimentation tank allows any remaining solids to settle out; the remaining liquid effluent is discharged into a body of water. Sludge may be disposed of in landfills, dumped at sea, used as fertilizer, or decomposed further in heated digestion tanks to produce methane gas to power the plant.

Sewall \'sü-əl\, **Samuel** (1652–1730) American (British-born) colonial merchant and jurist. A member of the governor's council (1684–1725), in 1692 he was appointed to preside at the SALEM WITCH TRIALS. He later admitted the error of the court's decision to execute the 19 people convicted and stood alone to hear his confession read aloud. His three-volume *Diary* (published 1878–82) provides a view of New England Puritan life.

Sewanee See Univ. of the SOUTH

Seward \'sü-ərd\, **William H(enry)** (1801–1872) U.S. politician. Born in Florida, N.Y., he served as governor 1839–43. In the U.S. Senate (1849–61), he was an antislavery leader. A close adviser to Pres. Abraham LINCOLN, he served as U.S. secretary of state 1861–69. He helped prevent foreign recognition of the Confederacy and obtained settlement in the TRENT AFFAIR. In 1865 he was stabbed by a coconspirator of J. W. BOOTH, but recovered. He is best remembered for successfully negotiating the ALASKA PURCHASE (1867), which critics called Seward's Folly.

Sewell \'sü-əl\, **Anna** (1820–1878) British writer. Her concern for the humane treatment of horses began early in life. Confined to her house as an invalid, she spent her last years writing the children's classic *Black Beauty* (1877), a fictional autobiography of a gentle, highbred horse. It had a strong moral purpose and is said to have been instrumental in abolishing the cruel use of the checkrein.

sewing machine Machine for stitching material (such as cloth or leather), usually having a needle and shuttle to carry THREAD. Invented by Elias HOWE in 1846 and successfully manufactured by Howe and I. M. SINGER, it became the first widely distributed mechanical home appliance and has also been an important industrial machine. Modern sewing machines are usually powered by an electric motor, but the foot-treadle machine is still in wide use in much of the world.

sex Sum of features by which a member of a plant or animal species can be placed into one of two complementary reproductive groups, male or female. Males and females may or may not have apparent structural differences, but they always have functional, hormonal, and chromosomal differences. Patterns of behavior, sometimes elaborate, may also distinguish the sexes in some species. See also REPRODUCTION.

sex chromosome Either of a pair of CHROMOSOMES that determine whether an individual is male or female. The sex chromosomes of mammals are designated X and Y; in humans, they constitute one pair of the total 23. Individuals with two X chromosomes (XX) are female; those having one X and one Y (XY) are male. Traits controlled only by genes found on the X chromosome (e.g., hemophilia, red-green color blindness) are said to be sex-linked, and occur far more frequently in males than in females, since a male inheriting a gene for a recessive (see RECESSIVENESS) trait on the X chromosome lacks a corresponding gene on the Y chromosome that might counteract its effects.

sex hormone Organic compound produced by the sex glands (OVARIES and TESTES) or other organ that has an effect on the sexual features of an organism. Like many other kinds of HORMONES, sex hormones may be artificially synthesized. See also ANDROGEN, ESTROGEN, PROGESTERONE.

sextant Instrument for determining the ANGLE between the horizon and a celestial body, used to determine LATITUDE AND LONGITUDE. It consists of a metal arc, marked in degrees, and a movable radial arm. A TELESCOPE, mounted to the framework, is lined up with the horizon. The radial arm is moved until the star is reflected into a half-silvered mirror (mounted on the arm) in line with the telescope and appears, through the telescope, to coincide with the horizon. The angular distance of the star above the horizon is then read from the graduated arc. From this angle and the exact time of day as registered by a CHRONOMETER, the latitude can be determined by means of published tables. Invented in 1731, the sextant replaced the octant and became an essential tool of navigation.

Sexton, Anne *orig.* Anne Gray Harvey (1928–1974) U.S. poet. Born in Newton, Mass., she devoted her first book of poetry, *To Bedlam and Part Way Back* (1960), to examining her mental breakdowns and subsequent recoveries with confessional intensity. She continued probing her personal life in *All My Pretty Ones* (1962) and *Live or Die* (1966, Pulitzer Prize). She died a suicide. Several volumes of poetry were published posthumously.

sexual harassment Unsolicited verbal or physical behavior of a sexual nature. Sexual harassment today may embrace any sexually motivated behavior considered offensive by the recipient. Legal recourse is available in cases that occur in the workplace. In 1994 the U.S. Supreme Court ruled that behavior can be considered sexual harassment and an abridgment of an individual's civil rights if it creates a hostile and abusive environment.

sexual intercourse *or* **coitus** *or* **copulation** Act in which the male reproductive organ enters the female reproductive tract (see REPRODUCTIVE SYSTEM). Various sexual activities (foreplay) lead to physiological changes that progress to orgasm (climax) and resolution. If it is completed, SEMEN passes from the male's into the female's body. If conditions favor FERTILIZATION, a SPERM joins with an EGG and PREG-

NANCY begins (see FERTILITY, REPRODUCTION); CONTRA-CEPTION can prevent this. Intercourse with an unwilling partner is RAPE. See also SAFE SEX, SEXUALLY TRANSMITTED DISEASE.

sexually transmitted disease (STD) Disease transmitted primarily by direct sexual contact. STDs usually affect the genitals and REPRODUCTIVE and URINARY systems but can be spread to the mouth or rectum by oral or anal sex. In later stages they may attack other organs and systems. The best known are SYPHILIS, GONORRHEA, AIDS, and HERPES SIMPLEX type II. Yeast infections (see CANDIDA) produce a thick, whitish vaginal discharge and genital irritation and itch in women and sometimes irritation of the penis in men. See also CHLAMYDIA, HEPATITIS, PELVIC INFLAMMATORY DISEASE, TRICHOMONAD, WART.

Seychelles \sā-'shel, sā-'shelz\ *officially* **Republic of Seychelles** Island republic, W Indian Ocean. Area: 175 sq mi (453 sq km). Population (2000): 82,000. Capital: VICTORIA.

INDIAN OCEAN

ARIDE I.

PRASLIN I.

NORTH I.

LA DIGUE I.

SILHOUETTE I.

MAHÉ I.   Victoria

55°15'   55°30'   55°45'

4°15'

4°30'

4°45'

©1999, Encyclopædia Britannica, Inc.

SEYCHELLES

Scale 1: 1,380,000
0   5   10   15 mi
0   10   20 km

The mixed population is of French, black, and Asian ancestry. Languages: Creole, English, French. Religion: Roman Catholicism. Currency: Seychelles rupee. Located E of Tanzania, the Seychelles are composed of two main island groups: the Mahé group of 40 central mountainous islands, and a second group of over 70 outlying, flat, coralline islands. The country's developing economy is heavily dependent on tourism. Exports include fish and petroleum products. It is a republic with one legislative house; its head of state and government is the president. The first recorded landing on the uninhabited Seychelles was made in 1609 by the British E. INDIA CO. The archipelago was claimed by the French in 1756 and surrendered to the British in 1810. It became a British crown colony in 1903, and a republic within the COMMONWEALTH in 1976. A one-party socialist state since 1979, the Seychelles began moving toward democracy in the 1990s; it adopted a new constitution in 1993.

Seymour, Jane (1509?–1537) Third wife of HENRY VIII of England. A lady-in-waiting to CATHERINE OF ARAGON and Anne BOLEYN, she first attracted Henry's attention about 1535 but refused to be his mistress. This probably hastened Boleyn's downfall (1536), after which Seymour and Henry were married privately. She gave birth to his only male heir, the future EDWARD VI, but died 12 days later, to Henry's genuine sorrow.

Seyss-Inquart \'zīs-'iŋk-,värt\, **Arthur** (1892–1946) Austrian Nazi leader. Named Austrian minister of interior and security, he replaced Kurt von SCHUSCHNIGG as chancellor in 1938. He welcomed the ANSCHLUSS by Germany and became governor of the Austrian administration (1938–39). In World War II he was German high commissioner of the Netherlands (1940–45) and carried out the Nazi policy against Dutch Jews. He was tried at the NUREMBERG TRIALS and executed as a war criminal.

Sezession \zā-tses-'yōn\ Name for several groups of progressive artists that broke away from established and conservative artists' organizations in Austria and Germany. The first secession group was formed in Munich in 1892. It was followed by the Berlin Sezession movement, formed by Max Liebermann (1847–1935) in 1892. The most famous of the groups, formed in Vienna in 1897 by Gustav KLIMT, favored a highly ornamental ART NOUVEAU style over the prevailing academicism. The Sezession movement influenced such artists and architects as Egon SCHIELE and Josef HOFFMANN. See also PHOTO-SECESSION.

Sfax \'sfaks\ *or* **Safaqis** \sə-'fä-kis\ Port city (pop., 1994: 231,000), E central Tunisia. An Islamic trading center, it was occupied by the Normans in the 12th cent. and the Spanish in the 16th cent., and later served as a stronghold of the BARBARY COAST pirates. In World War II it was a base for German forces until taken by the British in 1943. Tunisia's second-largest city, it is a transportation hub and major fishing port.

Sforim, Mendele Moykher See MENDELE MOYKHER SFORIM

Sforza, Ludovico (1452–1508) Regent (1480–94) and duke of Milan (1494–98). A member of the SFORZA FAMILY, he plotted to take over as regent for his young nephew. He made Milan supreme among the Italian states, and his patronage of scholars and artists such as LEONARDO DA VINCI made his court renowned in Europe. He bribed MAXIMILIAN I to declare him duke of Milan. He fought to expel the French from Italy. After LOUIS XII conquered Milan (1498), Ludovico tried unsuccessfully to retake it (1500); captured, he died in prison.

Sforza family Italian family that ruled Milan 1450–1535. The family began with the condottiere leader Muzio Attendolo (1369–1424), who was given the nickname Sforza ("Force"). His illegitimate son Francesco Sforza became duke of Milan in 1450. Galeazzo Maria Sforza (1444–1476) succeeded his father in 1466 and, though a despotic ruler, he introduced the cultivation of rice, built canals and encouraged commerce, and was a patron of the arts. Gian Galeazzo Sforza (1469–1494) succeeded his assassinated father in 1476 under the regency of his mother and uncle, Ludovico SFORZA, who usurped the government in 1481 and established Milan's supremacy. After Ludovico was driven from power by LOUIS XII of France in 1499, his son Massimiliano (1493–1530) returned to rule briefly (1513–16) before yielding the duchy to France. Another son and Francesco Maria (1495–1535), returned after the French defeat to rule from 1522, until his death without heirs ended the ducal line in 1535. The duchy then passed to CHARLES V and the Habsburgs.

SGML *in full* Standard Generalized Markup Language. MARKUP LANGUAGE for organizing and tagging elements of a document, including headings, paragraphs, tables, and graphics. The elements are marked according to their meaning and relationship to other elements. The tagged elements can then be formatted in different ways for different presentations. SGML is usable in a wide range of applications, including print publishing, CD-ROMs, and database systems. Generic coding of electronic manuscripts was first proposed in the late 1960s; in 1969 an IBM team developed GML. SGML was created by the American National Standards Institute (ANSI) from GML, and accepted internationally in 1986. See also HTML, XML.

Shabeelle River \sha-'be-lĕ\ *in Ethiopia* **Shebele River** \she-'be-lĕ\ River, E Africa. It rises in the Ethiopian Highlands and flows southeast through the arid OGADEN Plateau. In Somalia it approaches the coast near MOGADISHU, then flows southwest 200 mi (320 km) parallel with the coast. Its total length is 1,250 mi (2,011 km). During rainy periods in Ethiopia, it joins the Jubba River; in drier years it disappears in marshes and sand flats northeast of the Jubba confluence.

Shackleton, Ernest Henry (*later* **Sir Ernest**) (1874–1922) British explorer. In 1901 he joined R. F. SCOTT's expedition

to the Antarctic. In 1908 he led a sledging party to within 97 mi (156 km) of the pole. In 1914 he planned to cross Antarctica via the South Pole. His ship *Endurance* was caught in pack ice and drifted for 10 months before being crushed. Shackleton and his crew drifted on ice floes for another five months until they reached Elephant Island. He and five others sailed 800 mi (1,300 km) to S. Georgia Island to get help, then he led four relief expeditions to rescue his men. He died at the outset of another expedition.

shad Any of several saltwater food fishes of the HERRING family (Clupeidae) that swim up rivers to spawn. Shad eggs (roe) are a delicacy in the U.S. The American shad *(Alosa sapidissima)*, an Atlantic fish introduced into the Pacific, is a migratory plankton eater and a good game fish. The Allis (or Allice) shad *(A. alosa)* of Europe is about 30 in. (75 cm) long and weighs about 8 lbs (3.6 kg). See also WHITEFISH.

Shadwell, Thomas (1642?–1692) English dramatist. One of the court wits after the RESTORATION (1660), he wrote 18 plays, of which his broad comedies of manners are the best remembered. *Epsom-Wells* (1672) was a phenomenal success. After his friendship with John DRYDEN ended over differences in politics and dramatic techniques, both men produced satires attacking the other. In 1688 Shadwell succeeded Dryden as poet laureate and historiographer royal.

Shaffer \'shaf-ər\, **Peter (Levin)** (b.1926) British playwright. He first won notice for his comedy *Five Finger Exercise* (1958) and his epic tragedy *The Royal Hunt of the Sun* (1964). His *Equus* (1973, Tony Award; film, 1977) was a hit in London and New York. He was also acclaimed for *Amadeus* (1979; film, 1984, Academy Award), which treated Antonio SALIERI's rivalry with W. A. MOZART. His later plays include *Lettice and Lovage* (1988).

Shaftesbury, 1st Earl of *orig.* Anthony Ashley Cooper (1621–1683) English politician. He was appointed by Oliver CROMWELL to the council of state (1653–54, 1659). One of 12 commissioners sent to invite CHARLES II to return to England, he was appointed to Charles's privy council (1660) and served as chancellor of the exchequer (1661–72) and lord chancellor (1672–73). Dismissed by Charles for supporting the anti-Catholic TEST ACT and opposing the marriage of Charles's brother James (later JAMES II) to another Catholic, Shaftesbury became a leader of the WHIG opposition. He tried unsuccessfully to pass the Exclusion Bill to keep James from the throne. In 1681 Charles dissolved the Parliament; Shaftesbury was arrested and tried for treason but acquitted. In 1682 he fled to Holland.

Shaftesbury, 7th Earl of *orig.* Anthony Ashley Cooper (1801–1885) English politician and social reformer. As a member of Parliament (1826–51), he supported Catholic emancipation and repeal of the CORN LAWS. From 1833 he led the factory reform movement in Parliament and effected passage of the Mines Act (1842) and the Ten Hours Act (1847), which shortened the working day in textile mills. As president of the Ragged Schools Union (1843–83), he promoted the free education of destitute children. One of the most effective social reformers of 19th-cent. England, he also led the evangelical movement within the Church of England and financially supported several missionary societies.

Shah Jahan \'shä-jə-'hän\ (1592–1666) Mughal emperor of India (1628–58). During his father Jahangir's reign (1605–27), he was part of the clique that dominated MUGHAL-DYNASTY politics. His own reign was notable for its successes against the Deccan states. Though attempts to reconquer lost territory almost bankrupted the empire, his reign marked the zenith of Mughal court splendor. Of his great architectural undertakings (including a fortress-palace built when he transferred the capital from Agra to Delhi), the most famous is the TAJ MAHAL. Though a more orthodox Muslim than his father, he was less orthodox than his son AURANGZEB, who deposed him in 1658.

Shahn, Ben(jamin) (1898–1969) U.S. (Lithuanian-born) painter and graphic artist. His family emigrated to New York in 1906. He worked as a lithographer's apprentice and later studied painting. In 1931–33 he achieved fame with a series of gouache paintings inspired by the Sacco-Vanzetti case, combining realism and abstraction in the service of sharp sociopolitical comment (see SOCIAL REALISM). In 1933 he assisted Diego RIVERA with his Rockefeller Center mural. In 1935–38 he depicted rural poverty as an artist and photographer for the Farm Security Administration. After World War II he concentrated on easel painting, poster design, and book illustration.

Shah of Iran See M. R. Shah PAHLAVI, R. Shah PAHLAVI

Shaivism *or* **Saivism** \'shī-ˌvi-zəm\ One of three main forms of modern HINDUISM, centered on the worship of SHIVA. The earliest of the cults devoted to Shiva date from the 4th cent. B.C. Today Shaivism includes diverse movements, both religious and secular, all of which take Shiva as the supreme and all-powerful deity and teacher, and view gaining the nature of Shiva as the ultimate goal of existence. This is believed to be brought about by the performance of complex ritual. See also SHAKTISM, VAISHNAVISM.

Shaka \'shä-kə\ (1787?–1828) ZULU chief (1816–28), founder of S Africa's Zulu Empire. Raised as an outcast, Shaka proved himself a brilliant warrior and by 1816 had become head of the Zulu. He improved weapons systems, instituted a regimental system, and developed standard tactics. He subjugated tribes of coastal ZULULAND, contributing to the Mfecane disturbances of the 1820s. After his mother's death in 1827, he became psychotic and began killing his own people; he was murdered by his half brothers.

Shaker Member of the United Society of Believers in Christ's Second Appearing, a celibate millenarian sect that established communal settlements in the U.S. in the 18th cent. The movement was brought to the U.S. in 1774 by Ann LEE, whose followers accepted her as the second incarnation of Christ. It spread throughout New England from its base near Albany, N.Y., and later into Kentucky, Ohio, and Indiana, eventually establishing 19 communities. Communities held property in common, observed celibacy, and pursued a life of productive labor. Though sometimes persecuted for their pacifism, Shakers won admiration for their model farms and prosperous communities. Their talent for simple, functional design led to numerous innovations (see SHAKER FURNITURE). After the 1840s the movement gradually declined; today the lone remaining community is at Sabbathday Lake, Me.

Shaker furniture Furniture designed for the religious colonies of SHAKERS founded in the U.S. in the late 18th cent. The Shakers' designs reflected their beliefs that good craftsmanship was in itself an act of prayer and that form should follow function. Constructed of pine or other inexpensive wood, each item was fashioned solely to serve its intended use and was devoid of decoration. Interest in Shaker furniture and other Shaker crafts revived in the 20th cent., after most Shaker colonies had dissolved, and imitations are now widely produced.

Shakespeare, William (1564–1616) British poet and playwright, often considered the greatest writer in world literature. He spent his early life in Stratford-upon-Avon. By 1594 he was apparently a rising playwright in London and an actor in a leading theater company, the Lord CHAMBERLAIN'S MEN, which performed at the GLOBE THEATRE from 1599. His earliest plays include the comedies *Love's Labour's Lost, The Comedy of Errors, The Taming of the Shrew,* and *A Midsummer Night's Dream;* history plays including *Henry VI, Richard III,* and *Richard II;* and the tragedy *Romeo and Juliet.* The plays apparently written in the late 1590s are mostly comedies, including *The Merchant of Venice, The Merry Wives of Windsor, Much Ado About Nothing,* and *As You Like It,* and histories, including *Henry IV, Henry V,* and *Julius Caesar.* Between 1600 and 1606 he may have written the comedies *Twelfth Night, All's Well That Ends Well,* and *Measure for Measure,* as well as the great tragedies *Hamlet, Othello, Macbeth,* and *King Lear;* the tragedies *Antony and Cleopatra, Coriolanus,* and *Timon of Athens* may also be included among his late works, as may the fantastical romances *The Winter's Tale* and *The Tempest.* His plays, written largely in iambic pentameter verse, are marked by extraordinary poetry, vivid and complex characterizations, and a highly inventive use of English. His 154 sonnets were published in 1609. Shakespeare retired to Stratford by 1610. The first collected edition of his plays, or First Folio, was published in 1623. Considerable mystery surrounds his life and work, and other writers, particularly the 17th Earl of OXFORD, have frequently been proposed as the actual authors of his plays and poems.

shakti *or* **sakti** \\'shǝk-tē\ In HINDUISM, the creative energy inherent in and proceeding from God. It is exemplified by the female principle, the female reproductive organs, or the female goddess Shakti, wife of SHIVA. In tantric Hinduism, shakti is associated with the lowest of the CHAKRAS, lying dormant within the body as a coiled serpent (KUNDALINI) that must be aroused to reach spiritual liberation by uniting with Shiva at the top of the head. See also SHAKTISM.

Shaktism *or* **Saktism** \\'shǝk-,ti-zǝm\ Worship of the supreme Hindu goddess Shakti (see SHAKTI). Together with VAISH-NAVISM and SHAIVISM, it is one of the major forms of HIN-DUISM practiced today. Particularly prominent in the Bengal and Assam, Shaktism takes various forms depending on conceptions of Shakti, who has many names. (Some scholars consider most female deities in Hinduism to be various manifestations of her.) Shaktism is inseparably related to the system of practices for the purification of mind and body that are grouped under tantric Hinduism (see TANTRA).

shale Any of a group of fine-grained, laminated SEDIMEN-TARY ROCKS consisting of silt- and clay-sized particles. Shale constitutes roughly 60% of the sedimentary rock in the earth's crust. Shales are a valuable raw material for tile, brick, and pottery and constitute a major source of alumina for portland cement. See also OIL SHALE.

shale oil Synthetic crude oil that is extracted from OIL SHALE by pyrolysis, or destructive distillation. It cannot be refined by the methods that have been developed for PE-TROLEUM, however, because shale oil is low in hydrogen and contains large amounts of nitrogen and sulfur compounds. To be made usable, it must be hydrogenated and then chemically treated to remove the nitrogen and sulfur, a process still too expensive to be commercially competitive.

shallot Mildly aromatic herbaceous plant (*Allium ascalonicum*) of the LILY FAMILY, probably of Asiatic origin, used to flavor foods. Closely related to the ONION and GARLIC, the shallot is a hardy perennial with short, small, cylindrical, and hollow leaves; lavender to red flowers in a compact umbel; and small, elongated, angular BULBS. The bulbs develop in clusters on a common base. The leaves are sometimes eaten when green.

shaman \\'shä-mǝn\ Person who uses MAGIC to cure the sick, divine the unknown, or control events. The shaman is classically associated with certain Arctic and Central Asian peoples, but today the term is applied to shamanistic systems throughout the world. As MEDICINE MAN and priest, the shaman cures illnesses, directs communal sacrifices, and escorts the SOULS of the dead to the other world. He operates by using techniques of ecstasy, the power to leave his body at will during a trancelike state. A person becomes a shaman either by inheritance or by self-election. See also ANIMISM.

Shamir \shǝ-'mēr\, **Yitzhak** *orig.* Yitzhak Jazernicki (b.1915) Polish-Israeli statesman. He emigrated in 1935 to Palestine, where he helped found the Stern Gang of freedom fighters. Twice arrested by British authorities (1941, 1946), he twice escaped and eventually found asylum in France. After Israel achieved independence, he served as a secret-service operative until 1965. He was speaker of the Knesset (1977–80) and later foreign minister under Menachem BEGIN (1980–83). He served as prime minister almost continuously from 1983 to 1992, often sharing power with the Labour Party.

Shan *Shan* **Tai** S.E. Asian people who live primarily in E and NW Myanmar, numbering more than 4 million. They live mainly in the valleys and plains on the Shan Plateau, where they grow rice or practice slash-and-burn agriculture. They are THERAVADA Buddhists and have their own written language and literature. They dominated much of Myanmar in the 13th–16th cent.; in recent decades they have been at odds with the national government over the issue of local autonomy. See also TAI.

Shang dynasty *or* **Yin dynasty** Traditionally, the second of China's dynasties, following the XIA DYNASTY. Its rule was said to have spanned 1766–1122 B.C. Shang society included a king, local governors, nobles, and the masses, who engaged in agriculture. The Shang developed a 12-month, 360-day calendar with intercalary months added as necessary. The CHINESE WRITING SYSTEM began to develop; numerous records and ceremonial inscriptions survive. Surviving artifacts include musical instruments, superb bronze vessels, pottery for ceremonial and daily use, and jade and ivory ornaments.

Shanghai \\'shaŋ-'hī\ Municipality with provincial status (pop., 1999 est.: 14,740,000), E central China. It is located on the Huangpu River, which allows oceangoing vessels access during high tide. Under the MING DYNASTY it was an area of intense cotton production. It was the first Chinese port opened to trade with the West after the OPIUM WARS (1842) and came to dominate the nation's commerce. The site of the CHINESE COMMUNIST PARTY's founding in 1921, it saw severe fighting in the SINO–JAPANESE WAR and was occupied by Japan during World War II. Now China's chief industrial and commercial center, and one of its leading research centers, it is the focus of China's special economic zones, established to foster foreign trade.

Shankar \\'shän-,kär\, **Ravi** (b.1920) Indian sitar player. He studied music and dance, touring with his brother Uday's dance troupe. After serving as music director of All-India Radio (1948–56), he began a series of European and U.S. tours. A founder of the National Orchestra of India, he founded the Kinnara School of Music in Bombay and later in Los Angeles. His performances with Yehudi MENUHIN and his association with the BEATLES' George Harrison were primarily responsible for bringing Indian music to a broad Western audience.

Shannon, Claude (Elwood) (1916–2001) U.S. electrical engineer. Born in Petoskey, Mich., he received his PhD from MIT. He had a long career at Bell Laboratories (1941–72) and as a professor at MIT (1957–78). On the basis of his 1948 paper "The Mathematical Theory of Communication," he is considered the founder of communication theory. He was awarded the National Medal of Science in 1966 and the Kyoto Prize in 1985.

Shannon River River, Ireland. The country's longest river, it rises near the border of Northern Ireland and flows for about 230 mi (370 km) to enter the Atlantic Ocean below Limerick. Surrounded by marshes and bogs, it widens at various points into lakes. Formerly important commercially, today it is used by pleasure craft.

Shapley, Harlow (1885–1972) U.S. astronomer. Born in Nashville, Mo., in 1911 he began analyzing the light variation of numerous binary stars when they eclipse one another, and proposed that Cepheid variables are pulsating variable stars. His study of the distribution of globular clusters in the galaxy led him to deduce that the sun was 50,000 (now estimated at about 28,000) light-years from the center of the galaxy, leading to the first realistic estimate of the galaxy's size. Shapley also studied neighboring galaxies, especially the Magellanic Clouds, and found that galaxies tend to occur in clusters.

Sharansky, Natan See Anatoly SHCHARANSKY

sharecropping See TENANT FARMING

Sharia \\'shä-'rē-ä\ Legal and moral code of ISLAM, systematized in the early centuries of the Muslim era (8th–9th cent. A.D.). It rests on four bases: the QURAN; the SUNNA, as recorded in the HADITH; *ijma,* or universal agreement; and *qiya,* or analogical reasoning. Unlike Western law, Sharia purports to be grounded in divine revelation. Among modern Muslim countries, Saudi Arabia and Iran retain Sharia as the law of the land, secular as well as religious. Most Islamic fundamentalist groups insist that Muslim countries should be governed by Sharia.

shark Any of more than 300 species of predatory cartilaginous fish (order Selachii). An ancient animal, it has changed little in 100 million years. The skin typically has toothlike scales. Most sharks have a muscular, asymmetrical, upturned tail; pointed fins; a pointed snout; and sharp triangular teeth. Sharks have no swim bladder and must swim perpetually to keep from sinking. Most species bear living young. Several species can be dangerous to humans (e.g., GREAT WHITE SHARK, HAMMERHEAD SHARK, SAND SHARK,

MAKO SHARK, tiger shark); smaller ones, called topes, hounds, and DOGFISHES, are fished commercially.

sharksucker See REMORA

Sharon \shə-'rōn\, **Ariel** (b.1928) Israeli general and politician. Born in Palestine, he did intelligence and reconnaissance work after Israel achieved independence. During the SUEZ CRISIS he captured the Mitla Pass, which he recaptured during the SIX-DAY WAR. He led the Israelis in the 1973 Yom Kippur War. As minister of agriculture in charge of settlements (1977), he advocated Jewish settlement of occupied Arab territory. As minister of defense (1981–83) he oversaw Israel's invasion of Lebanon (see LEBANESE CIVIL WAR). Held indirectly responsible for massacres at the Sabra and Shatila refugee camps, he was forced to resign in 1983. He became prime minister in 2001 after Yasir ARAFAT's rejection of an Israeli peace plan and the start of a wave of Palestinian suicide bombings.

Sharon, Plain of Mediterranean coastal plain, W Israel. Extending 55 mi (89 km) from Mt. Carmel to TEL AVIV-JAFFA, and roughly triangular in shape, it has been inhabited since remote antiquity. Modern resettlement of the agricultural lands of Palestine by Jews began in the late 19th cent., and by the early 1930s it had become the most densely settled area of Jewish Palestine. It produces citrus fruits, vegetables, and cotton, and is a popular tourist destination.

shar-pei \'shär-'pā\ Ancient breed of dog that originated in China. Shar-peis are notable for their loose, wrinkled skin, especially when young. They have a short bristly coat, wide blunt muzzle, blue-black tongue, and unusual black gums.

Shasta, Mt. Peak, CASCADE RANGE, N California. A double-peaked extinct volcano, 14,162 ft (4,317 m) high, it dominates the landscape for a hundred miles. Its glaciers are popular with skiers and climbers. The first ascent was made in 1854.

Shatt al Arab \'shät-ál-'ár-əb\ Channel, SE Iraq, formed by the confluence of the TIGRIS and EUPHRATES rivers. It flows southeastward for 120 mi (193 km), passing BASRA before emptying into the Persian Gulf. Its S portion borders Iran. In the 1980s it was the scene of prolonged fighting in the IRAN–IRAQ WAR.

Shaw, Anna Howard (1847–1919) U.S. (British-born) suffragist. By age 15 she was a frontier schoolteacher, and in 1880 she became the first woman minister of the Methodist Protestant Church. She took up the causes of temperance and women's suffrage in 1885 and became an important spokesperson for both. She earned a medical degree the next year. She served as president of the National American Woman Suffrage Assn. 1904–15.

Shaw, George Bernard (1856–1950) British playwright and critic. After moving from Dublin to London in 1876, he worked as a music, art, and drama critic and was active in the socialist FABIAN SOCIETY. In his first play, *Widowers' Houses* (1892), he emphasized social and economic issues, adopting the ironic comedic tone that would characterize all his work. He described his first plays as "unpleasant" because they forced the spectator to face unpleasant facts; these included *Mrs. Warren's Profession* (1893), which concerned prostitution and was banned until 1902. His four "pleasant" plays include the comedies *Arms and the Man* (1894) and *Candida* (1895). His next plays included *Caesar and Cleopatra* (1899) and *Man and Superman* (1905). He used high comedy to explore society's foibles in *Major Barbara* (1905) and *Pygmalion* (1913), his comedic masterpiece. Other notable plays include *Androcles and the Lion* (1912), *Heartbreak House* (1919), and *Saint Joan* (1923). He received the Nobel Prize in 1925.

George Bernard Shaw Photo by Yousuf Karsh

Shawn, Ted (orig. Edwin Myers) (1891–1972) U.S. modern dancer and choreographer. Born in Kansas City, Mo., he married Ruth SAINT DENIS in 1914. They cofounded the Denishawn school and company in 1915; their tours brought MODERN DANCE to many parts of the U.S. for the first time. After they separated in 1931, Shawn established a company of male dancers and choreographed works that embodied a vigorous, masculine style. In 1933 he founded the Jacob's Pillow Dance Festival in Becket, Mass.

Shawnee \shó-'nē\ N. American Indian people from the central Ohio River Valley. They lived by hunting and corn agriculture. In the 17th cent. the Shawnee were driven from their home by the IROQUOIS, scattering into widely separated areas. After 1725 the tribe reunited in Ohio. Following their defeat by Gen. Anthony WAYNE (1794), they broke into three independent branches that eventually settled in Oklahoma. Today they number about 4,000.

shaykh See SHEIKH

Shays' Rebellion Uprising in W Massachusetts, 1786–87. In a period of economic depression and land seizures for debt collection, several hundred farmers led by Daniel Shays (1747?–1825) marched on the state supreme court in Springfield, which they prevented from carrying out foreclosures and debt collection. Shays then led a force of about 1,200 men in attacking the nearby federal arsenal, but they were repulsed. The state soon enacted laws easing the economic condition of debtors.

Shcharansky \shə-'ran-skē\, **Anatoly (Borisovich)** *later* **Natan Sharansky** (b.1948) Soviet dissident. Born in Ukraine, he worked as a computer specialist and interpreter for Andrey SAKHAROV. A Jew, he applied to emigrate to Israel in 1973 but was refused and discharged from his job. He became an advocate for dissidents, contacting Western journalists to publicize their cause. In 1977 he was arrested for treason and sentenced to 13 years in prison. His wife, Avital, championed his cause from Israel. Released in 1986, he settled in Israel, where he founded a party stressing immigrants' concerns.

Sheba, Queen of (fl.10th cent. B.C.) In Jewish and Islamic traditions, ruler of the Kingdom of Saba in SW Arabia. In an Old Testament story, she visited King SOLOMON to test his wisdom. In Islamic tradition she is known as Bilqis and is converted from worship of the sun to worship of God, marrying either Solomon himself or a Hamdani tribesman. She also exists in Persian and Ethiopian folk traditions.

Shebele River See SHABEELLE RIVER

Sheeler, Charles (1883–1965) U.S. painter and photographer. Born in Philadelphia, he initially earned a living as a photographer. His acclaimed series of photographs of the Ford automobile plant at River Rouge, Mich. (1927), was followed by a series on Chartres Cathedral (1929). In his paintings, early Cubist influence led to the PRECISIONISM of his maturity. He treated industrial and architectural subjects in an abstract-realist style, as in his painting *Rolling Power* (1939), which revealed the abstract power of a locomotive's driving wheels.

Sheen, Fulton J(ohn) (1895–1979) U.S. religious leader. Born in El Paso, Ill., he was ordained in 1919 and taught at Catholic Univ. from 1926 to 1950. In 1930 he began his 22-year radio career on the program *The Catholic Hour,* which reached an estimated 4 million listeners. In the 1950s he began a weekly television series, *Life Is Worth Living;* it was followed by two more series. At his death he was one of the best-known clerics in the U.S.

sheep RUMINANTS (BOVID genus *Ovis*) that have scent glands in the face and hind feet. Species range from 80 to 400 lbs (35–180 kg). The coat of wild species consists of outer hair underlain by WOOL. Sheep graze in flocks, preferably on short, fine grasses and legumes. They have been domesticated from at least 5000 B.C. in the Middle East, Europe, and central Asia. Most domesticated breeds produce fine wool; others are raised for meat. The flesh of mature sheep is called mutton; that of immature sheep is called lamb.

Sheffield City (pop., 1999 est.: 501,000), S. Yorkshire, England. Set at the foot of the PENNINES, it was the site of a castle and parish church early in the 12th cent. Known for its cutlery since medieval times, it remains the center of the industry today. It developed a steel industry from the mid-19th cent.; such innovations as the process for making STAINLESS STEEL originated there. In 1568 MARY, QUEEN

OF SCOTS, was imprisoned in its Norman castle (now in ruins).

Sheffield plate Articles made of copper coated with silver by fusion. The technique was discovered about 1742 by the Sheffield (Yorkshire) cutler Thomas Boulsover, who noted that the combination of fused silver and copper retained the ductility of both metals. Workshops in Britain, Europe, and N. America produced cooking and eating utensils of Sheffield plate. After the introduction of ELECTROPLATING in 1840, production of Sheffield plate declined. Admired for its soft, glowing gray luster, Sheffield-plate ware soon came to be prized and collected.

Sheherazade See SCHEHERAZADE

shell ARTILLERY projectile, cartridge case, or shotgun cartridge. It originated in the 15th cent. as a container for metal or stone shot, dispersed when the container burst after leaving the GUN. Explosive shells, in the 16th–18th cent., were cast-iron balls filled with GUNPOWDER and lit by a fuse, used in high-angle fire (including MORTARS). In the 19th cent., shells were adopted for direct-fire artillery as SHRAPNEL. Modern artillery shells consist of a casing (usually steel), a propelling charge, and a bursting charge. In RIFLE, PISTOL, and MACHINE-GUN ammunition, the word usually signifies the brass casing that contains the propulsive charge. In shotgun ammunition, the shell is the entire cartridge, including shot, powder, primer, and case.

Shell See ROYAL DUTCH/SHELL GROUP

Shelley, Mary Wollstonecraft *orig.* Mary Wollstonecraft Godwin (1797–1851) English Romantic novelist. Daughter of William GODWIN and Mary WOLLSTONECRAFT, she eloped with P. B. SHELLEY in 1814. Her best-known work is *Frankenstein* (1818), a narrative of the dreadful consequences of a scientist's artificially creating a human being. After her husband's death in 1822, she devoted herself to publicizing his writings. *The Last Man* (1826), an account of the destruction of the human race by a plague, is considered her best novel.

Shelley, Percy Bysshe (1792–1822) English Romantic poet. The heir to rich estates, Shelley was a rebellious youth who was expelled from Oxford in 1811 for refusing to admit authorship of *The Necessity of Atheism*. Later that year he eloped with Harriet Westbrook, the daughter of a tavern owner. He gradually channeled his passionate pursuit of personal love and social justice into poetry. His first major poem, *Queen Mab* (1813), is a utopian political epic. In 1814 he eloped to France with Mary Wollstonecraft Godwin (see M. W. SHELLEY); in 1816, after

Percy Bysshe Shelley
Painting by A. Curran, 1819

Harriet drowned herself, they were married. In 1818 the Shelleys moved to Italy, where he composed his masterpiece, the lyric drama *Prometheus Unbound* (1820), which was published with such shorter poems as "Ode to the West Wind" and "To a Skylark." *Epipsychidion* (1821) is a Dantesque fable about the relationship of sexual desire to spiritual love and artistic creation. Shelley drowned at 29 while sailing in a storm off the Italian coast, leaving unfinished his great visionary poem *The Triumph of Life*.

shellfish Any aquatic MOLLUSK, CRUSTACEAN, or ECHINODERM that has a shell. OYSTERS, MUSSELS, SCALLOPS, and CLAMS rank among the most commercially important. Certain gastropod mollusks, such as ABALONE, WHELK, and CONCH, are also marketed. The main crustaceans are SHRIMP, LOBSTER, and CRAB. Among echinoderms, SEA URCHINS and SEA CUCUMBERS are locally popular. Being highly perishable, many shellfish are cooked live to protect against the effects of spoilage.

sheltie See SHETLAND SHEEPDOG

Shenandoah National Park National park, BLUE RIDGE MTNS., N Virginia. Formed in 1935, it consists of 193,537 acres (78,322 hectares). Heavily forested, it is noted for its scenery, which affords some of the widest views in the E states.

Shenandoah Valley Valley, chiefly in Virginia. It extends about 150 mi (240 km) southwest from Harpers Ferry, W.V., between the BLUE RIDGE MTNS. and the ALLEGHENIES. It is drained by the Shenandoah River. The Valley Pike, used by Tuscarora and Shawnee Indians, later become a main artery for westward expansion. It saw military operations throughout the AMERICAN CIVIL WAR; today its many parks, caverns, and scenic drives are tourist attractions.

Shenyang *or* **Shen-yang** \'shən-'yän\ *formerly* **Mukden** \'mùk-dən\ City (pop., 1999 est.: 3,876,000), capital of Liaoning province, NE China. An ancient city, it was the capital of the MANCHU empire 1625–44. After 1895 it was fought over by Russia and Japan in the struggle for MANCHURIA. It was occupied by the Japanese 1931–45. From 1948 it was a base for the Communist conquest of the Chinese mainland. It is one of China's leading industrial cities as well as a cultural and educational center.

Shepard, Alan B(artlett), Jr. (1923–1998) U.S. astronaut. Born in E. Derry, N.H., he became one of the original seven MERCURY program astronauts in 1959. In May 1961, 23 days after Yury GAGARIN became the first human to orbit earth, Shepard's 15-minute suborbital flight reached an altitude of 115 mi (185 km). In 1971 he commanded the Apollo 14 flight, the first to land in the lunar highlands.

Shepard, Sam *orig.* Samuel Shepard Rogers (b.1943) U.S. playwright and actor. Born in Ft. Sheridan, Ill., he wrote one-act dramas and experimental plays that were performed off-Broadway in the 1960s. His successful full-length plays, noted for their often surreal images drawn from the American West, science fiction, and popular culture, include *The Tooth of Crime* (1972), *Curse of the Starving Class* (1976), *Buried Child* (1979, Pulitzer Prize), *True West* (1980), *Fool for Love* (1983; film, 1985), *A Lie of the Mind* (1985), and *Simpatico* (1996). He acted in numerous movies, including *The Right Stuff* (1983).

Sheraton, Thomas (1751?–1806) British cabinetmaker. Little is known of his life. He gave his name to a Neoclassic style of furniture characterized by a firm feminine refinement of late Georgian. His four-part *Cabinet-Maker and Upholsterers' Drawing Book* (1791–93) greatly influenced British and U.S. design. His natural approach to contemporary design used wood for its own sake, rather than covering it with gilt or excessive ormolu.

Sheridan, Philip H(enry) (1831–1888) U.S. Army officer. Born in Albany, N.Y., he graduated from West Point. In the Civil War he led a Union division in Tennessee and helped win the Battle of CHATTANOOGA with his cavalry charge up Missionary Ridge. As commander of the Army of the Shenandoah, he drove Confederate forces under Jubal EARLY from the Shenandoah Valley. He joined U. S. GRANT to help secure Union victories in the PETERSBURG CAMPAIGN. After the war he became general of the army (1883).

Sheridan, Richard Brinsley (Butler) (1751–1816) British playwright. Born in Dublin, he settled in London. His comedy *The Rivals* (1775) introduced the popular character Mrs. Malaprop and established him as a leading dramatist. He became manager and later owner of the DRURY LANE THEATRE (1776–1809), where his plays were produced. He won wide acclaim for his COMEDY OF MANNERS *The School for Scandal* (1777) and showed his flair for satirical wit again in *The Critic* (1779). In 1780 he became a member of Parliament, where he was a noted orator for the minority Whig party.

Sherman, Roger (1721–1793) American jurist and politician. Born in Newton, Mass., he served as judge of the Connecticut superior court (1766–85) and mayor of New Haven (1784–93). A delegate to the Continental Congress, he signed the Declaration of Independence and helped draft the Articles of Confederation. At the Constitutional Convention, he proposed a compromise on congressional representation that combined facets of the two opposing plans by the large and small states. His Connecticut (or Great) Compromise provided for the bicameral federal legislature.

Sherman, William Tecumseh (1820–1891) U.S. Army general. Born in Lancaster, Ohio, he graduated from West Point, but pursued a banking career. In the American Civil

S

War he served under U. S. GRANT at Shiloh. With Grant he helped win the VICKSBURG CAMPAIGN and the Battle of CHATTANOOGA. As commander of the division of the Mississippi, he assembled 100,000 troops for the invasion of Georgia (1864). After engagements with Confederate troops under Joseph Johnston, he captured and burned Atlanta and began his devastating March to the Sea to capture Savannah, leaving a trail of near-total destruction. In 1865 he marched north, destroying Confederate railroads and sources of supply in N. and S. Carolina. He succeeded Grant as commander of the army (1869–84). Often credited with the saying "War is hell," he was a major architect of modern total war.

Sherman Antitrust Act (1890) First U.S. legislation enacted to curb concentrations of power that restrict trade and reduce economic competition. Proposed by Sen. John Sherman, it made illegal all attempts to monopolize any part of trade or commerce in the U.S. Initially used against trade unions, it was more widely enforced under Pres. Theodore ROOSEVELT. In 1914 Congress strengthened the act with the Clayton Antitrust Act (see ANTITRUST LAW). In 1920 the U.S. Supreme Court ruled that only "unreasonable" restraint of trade constituted a violation. Later cases reinforced the prohibition against MONOPOLY control, including the 1984 break-up of AT&T.

Sherpas Mountain-dwelling people of Nepal and of Sikkim state, India, numbering about 120,000. Sherpas are of Tibetan culture and descent and speak a Tibetan dialect. Along with farming and cattle breeding, they make a living spinning and weaving wool. They have won fame as porters in the high Himalayas.

Sherrington, Charles Scott (later **Sir Charles**) (1857–1952) English physiologist. By studying animals whose cerebral cortexes had been removed, he showed that REFLEXES are integrated activities of the total organism, not based on isolated "reflex arcs." Sherrington's law states that when one set of muscles is stimulated, muscles opposing their action are inhibited. He showed that the role of proprioception in reflexes that maintain upright posture against gravity is independent of cerebral function and skin sensation. His work influenced the development of brain surgery and treatment of nervous disorders, and he coined the terms neuron and synapse. In 1932 he shared a Nobel Prize.

sherry Fortified WINE of Spanish origin. Essential to its taste is the action of flor, a mildewlike growth encouraged by a slight exposure to air after FERMENTATION. Also unique is a system of blending wines of many vintage years. Sherry is fortified after fermentation with high-proof BRANDY to 16–18% alcohol. It is served primarily as an aperitif or a dessert wine.

Sherwood, Robert E(mmet) (1896–1955) U.S. playwright. Born in New Rochelle, N.Y., he became a New York magazine editor. He examined the pointlessness of war in his first play, *The Road to Rome* (1927), and won wide acclaim for *The Petrified Forest* (1935). *Idiot's Delight* (1936), *Abe Lincoln in Illinois* (1938), and *There Shall Be No Night* (1940) won Pulitzer Prizes. In 1938 he cofounded the influential Playwrights' Company. During World War II he wrote speeches for Pres. Franklin ROOSEVELT; his book *Roosevelt and Hopkins* (1948) won a Pulitzer Prize. Many of his plays were adapted for film; his original screenplays include *The Best Years of Our Lives* (1946, Academy Award).

Sherwood Forest Woodland and former royal hunting ground, NOTTINGHAMSHIRE, England. Known for its association with the legendary ROBIN HOOD, it formerly extended into Derbyshire. Today some woodland remains, near NOTTINGHAM.

Shetland Islands or **Zetland Islands** Group of about 100 islands, Scotland. They lie 130 mi (210 km) north of the Scottish mainland and about 400 mi (640 km) south of the ARCTIC CIRCLE. Fewer than 20 are inhabited. The northernmost point of Britain, they have fjordlike coasts and a climate warmed by the N. Atlantic Current. Ruled by the Norse from the 8th cent., in 1472 they were annexed by Scotland. They are famous for the SHETLAND PONY, the SHETLAND SHEEPDOG, and the Shetland sheep, whose fine wool is used in the distinctive Shetland and Fair Isle knitted patterns. The North Sea oil industry has contributed to the economy.

Shetland pony Breed of PONY that originated in Scotland's SHETLAND ISLANDS. Well adapted to the islands' harsh climate and scant food supply, Shetlands were used as pack horses. Around 1850 they were taken to England to work in coal mines and to the U.S., where a more refined pony suitable for children was developed. Except for certain dwarf ponies, the Shetland is the smallest breed of HORSE; its average height is about 40 in. (102 cm).

Shetland sheepdog or **sheltie** Breed of sheepdog developed from a Scottish WORKING DOG to herd the small sheep of the Shetland Islands. The sheltie resembles the rough-coated COLLIE but in miniature; it stands 13–16 in. (33–41 cm). Sturdy and agile, it is noted for its herding ability, intelligence, and affectionate nature.

Shevardnadze \ˌshe-vərd-ˈnäd-zə\, **Eduard (Amvrosiyevich)** (b.1928) Soviet-Georgian politician. As foreign minister under Mikhail GORBACHEV (1985–90, 1991), he implemented the Soviet withdrawal from Afghanistan in 1988, new arms treaties with the U.S., and Russia's tacit acquiescence in the fall of the communist regimes of Eastern Europe (1989–90), while promoting the reform policies of GLASNOST and PERESTROIKA. After the Soviet Union's collapse, he returned to the newly independent republic of Georgia, where he served as the elected head of state from 1992.

Shia See SHIITE

shiatsu See ACUPRESSURE

shigella \shi-ˈgel-ə\ Any of the rod-shaped BACTERIA of the genus *Shigella,* which are normal inhabitants of the intestinal tract and can cause DYSENTERY. Shigellae are gram-negative (see GRAM STAIN), non-spore-forming and stationary. *S. dysenteriae,* spread by contaminated water and food, causes the most severe dysentery because of its potent toxin.

shih tzu \ˈshē-ˈdzü\ Breed of TOY DOG developed in Tibet from the PEKINGESE and LHASA APSO. Sturdily built and short-legged, it stands about 10 in. (26 cm) and weighs 18 lbs (8 kg) or less. It has a short muzzle, hanging ears, and heavily haired tail, which it carries over its back. Its long coat falls over the eyes, forming a beard.

Shi Huangdi or **Shih Huang-ti** \ˈshir-ˈhwäŋ-ˈdē\ orig. Zhao Zheng (c.260–210/9 B.C.) Chinese ruler and founder of the QIN DYNASTY. His father was king of Qin, which was regarded as barbarous but had developed a strong bureaucratic government under the philosophy of legalism (see HANFEIZI). Zheng eliminated the other Chinese states until in 221 B.C. Qin ruled supreme. He proclaimed himself Qin Shi Huangdi ("First Sovereign Emperor of Qin") and initiated reforms to create a fully centralized administration. He was interested in magic and alchemy, hoping for an elixir of immortality; his reliance on magicians was strongly condemned by Confucian scholars, many of whom he executed. The scholars also advocated a return to old feudal ways; their obstinacy led him to order the burning of all nonutilitarian books. Traditional histories regarded him as the ultimate villain. Though the Qin dynasty collapsed after his death, future dynasties adopted his administrative structure. He was buried in a massive tomb with an army of more than 6,000 terra-cotta soldiers and horses (see QIN TOMB).

Shiite \ˈshē-ˌīt\ Member of the Shia branch of ISLAM, which resulted from the first FITNAH, or split, within the religion. The Shiites supported ALI, MUHAMMAD's son-in-law, as the Prophet's heir; when the majority of Muslims (who constitute SUNNI Islam) rejected him, Shia became a religious movement. Ali's followers insisted that a CALIPH, or IMAM, be a lineal descendant of Ali and his wife, FATIMA. Shia's legal tradition is generally regarded as the most conservative in Islam. Though Shiites represent only about 10% of Muslims in the world, they are a majority in Iran and Iraq, and there are sizable populations in Yemen, Syria, Lebanon, E. Africa, Pakistan, and N India.

shikhara See SIKHARA

Shiloh \ˈshī-lō\, **Battle of** (Apr. 6–7, 1862) Second major engagement of the AMERICAN CIVIL WAR. Union forces under U. S. GRANT, including William T. SHERMAN, camped at Pittsburg Landing, Tenn. (near Shiloh Church), in preparation for an offensive. Confederate forces under A. S. Johnston and P. G. T. BEAUREGARD attacked, surprising the Union troops and forcing their retreat, but Johnston was mortally wounded. A Union counterattack regained the lost ground, and the Confederates withdrew to Corinth, Miss. The battle was considered a Confederate defeat. Heavy casualties, about 10,000 for each side, immobilized the armies for several weeks.

shingle Thin piece of building material made of wood, asphaltic material, slate, metal, or concrete, laid in overlapping rows to shed water. Shingles are widely used as roof covering and sometimes also for SIDING (see SHINGLE STYLE). Wood shingles are usually made of cypress, redwood, or Western red cedar.

shingles *or* **herpes zoster** \'hər-ˌpēz-'zäs-tər\ Acute viral skin and nerve infection. Groups of small blisters appear along certain nerve segments, most often on the back, sometimes after a dull ache at the site; pain becomes more severe when the blisters break out. Caused by the same virus as CHICKEN POX, it probably results from reactivation of seemingly inactive virus in a partially immune person. Recovery from the infection usually occurs within two weeks, but NEURALGIA may last months or even years longer.

Shingle style In the U.S., a style of wood-shingle-covered domestic architecture of the 1870s and '80s. Among the finest examples are Henry Hobson RICHARDSON's Sherman House (1874–75), Newport, R.I., and Stoughton House (1882–83), Cambridge, Mass. The style was stimulated by a revived interest in colonial American architecture. The small size of the shingle made it easy to cover a variety of shapes. The Shingle style is characterized by a free-flowing plan; open porches and irregular roof lines add to the picturesque or rustic effect.

Shining Path *Spanish* **Sendero Luminoso** Maoist movement in Peru dedicated to violent revolution. It was founded in 1970 by a philosophy professor, Abimael Guzmán Reynoso (b.1934), as a result of a split in Peru's Communist Party. The *senderistas* began their campaign among the poor Indians of the high Andes, promoting Indian empowerment at the expense of Peru's traditional elite. They gained control of large areas of Peru through violence and intimidation. By 1992, when Guzmán was captured, they had caused an estimated 25,000 deaths and seriously disrupted the Peruvian economy.

Shinto Indigenous religion of Japan, based on the worship of spirits known as *kami*. The term Shinto came into use to distinguish indigenous Japanese beliefs from Buddhism, which had been introduced into Japan in the 6th cent. A.D. Shinto has no founder and no official SCRIPTURE, though its mythology is collected in the *Kojiki* ("Records of Ancient Matters") and *Nihon shoki* ("Chronicles of Japan"), written in the 8th cent. At its core are beliefs in the mysterious creating and harmonizing power of *kami*. According to Shinto myths, in the beginning a certain number of *kami* simply emerged, and one pair, Izanagi and Izanami, gave birth to the Japanese islands, as well as to the *kami* who became ancestors of the various clans. The Japanese imperial family claims descent from Izanagi's daughter, the sun goddess AMATERASU. Life lived in accordance with the will of the *kami* is believed to produce a mystical power that gains their protection, cooperation, and approval.

Shipka Pass Pass in the BALKAN MTNS., central Bulgaria. It is 4,376 ft (1,334 m) high. A main route between Bulgaria and Turkey, the pass was the site of fierce fighting during the RUSSO–TURKISH WARS; in one battle (1878) the Turks lost so many soldiers that their leader Suleyman earned the name the "Shipka butcher."

Shippen, William, Jr. (1736–1808) U.S. physician. Born in Philadelphia, he earned his MD in Edinburgh. In 1762 he established the first American maternity hospital, and in 1765, with John MORGAN, he organized the first medical school in the American colonics, where he became the first systematic teacher of anatomy, surgery, and obstetrics. He was one of the first to use dissected human bodies to teach anatomy.

shipping Act or business of transporting passengers and goods by water. The Egyptians were probably the first to use seagoing vessels (c.1500 B.C.); the Phoenicians, Cretans, Greeks, and Romans also all relied on waterways. In Asia, Chinese ships equipped with multiple masts and a rudder were making sea voyages by A.D. 200; from as early as the 4th cent. B.C. the Chinese also relied heavily on inland waterways to transport food to their large cities (see GRAND CANAL). Japan, too mountainous to rely on roads for mass transport, also relied on waterways for shipping from early in its history. The spice trade was a great stimulus to shipping; the tea trade had a similar effect, as did the discovery of gold in the New World. From the 17th to the 19th cent., the slave trade was a major source of Atlantic shipping. The U.S. and England were the ascendant shipping nations in the 19th cent.; Germany, Norway, Japan, The Netherlands, and France joined them in the early 20th cent. Today shipping remains vital to the world economy. Many U.S. merchant ships are registered elsewhere to avoid heavy taxes. See also British E. INDIA CO., Dutch E. INDIA CO., French E. INDIA CO.

Shiraz \shē-'räz\ City (pop., 1996: 1,053,000), S central Iran. It was important during the Seleucid (312–175 B.C.), Parthian (247 B.C.–A.D. 224), and Sasanid (c.A.D. 224–651) periods, and reached its peak in the 10th–11th cent. In the 14th cent. TIMUR occupied Shiraz, which had become a Muslim center rivaling BAGHDAD. Famous for its wine, gardens, shrines, and mosques, it was the birthplace of the poets Sa'di and HAFEZ.

Shirer \'shīr-ər\, **William L(awrence)** (1904–1993) U.S. journalist, historian, and novelist. Born in Chicago, he served as a foreign correspondent in Europe and India from the 1920s. *Berlin Diary* (1941) collects his impressions of European political events. He was blacklisted in the 1950s as a leftist sympathizer. He is best known for *The Rise and Fall of the Third Reich* (1969, National Book Award), a massive study of Nazi Germany. His other major work is *The Collapse of the Third Republic* (1969), a study of France.

Shiva *or* **Siva** \'shi-və, 'shē-və\ Major deity of HINDUISM, believed to have many manifestations. Like VISHNU, he is the subject of an elaborate and sometimes contradictory mythology. He is both the destroyer and the restorer, the great ascetic and the symbol of sensuality, the benevolent herdsman of souls and the wrathful avenger. His female consort is known under such manifestations as Parvati, DURGA, and KALI. In SHAIVISM he is worshiped as the paramount lord.

Shiva Bronze statue, c.A.D. 900

shock State in which the circulation fails to supply enough blood to body tissues to meet basic requirements. Symptoms—weak, rapid PULSE; low BLOOD PRESSURE; and cold, sweaty skin—are not all present in every case. Causes include low blood volume, caused by bleeding or fluid loss from BURNS or DEHYDRATION; inability of the heart to pump enough blood, due to MYOCARDIAL INFARCTION or pulmonary EMBOLISM; and blood-vessel dilation as a result of SEPTICEMIA, allergy (including ANAPHYLAXIS), or drugs. All result in reduced capillary blood flow; reflexes increase heart rate and constrict small blood vessels to protect the blood supply to essential organs. Without treatment of the underlying cause, these mechanisms fail; cases tend to require different and occasionally contradictory treatment (e.g., intravenous fluids are good for a patient with massive blood loss but bad for a weakened heart).

shock absorber Device for controlling unwanted motion of a spring-mounted vehicle. On an automobile, the springs act as a cushion between the axles and the body and reduce the shocks produced by a rough road surface. Since some combinations of road surface and car speed may result in excessive up-and-down motion, shock absorbers—which today are hydraulic devices that oppose both compression and stretching of the springs—slow down and reduce its magnitude.

S

Shockley, William B(radford) (1910–1989) U.S. engineer and teacher. Born in Palo Alto, Cal., he received his PhD from Harvard. He joined Bell Laboratories in 1936, where his work led to the development of the TRANSISTOR. During World War II he directed research for the navy in antisubmarine warfare. In 1956 he shared a Nobel Prize with John BARDEEN and Walter Brattain (1902–1987) for his work on the transistor. He taught at Stanford Univ. 1958–74. From the late 1960s he earned notoriety for his controversial views on the intellectual capacity of blacks.

shock therapy Method of treating psychiatric disorders by inducing shock through drugs or electric current. Insulin-shock therapy, in which large doses of insulin would throw the patient into a brief coma, was formerly used for the treatment of SCHIZOPHRENIA. Electroconvulsive, or electroshock, therapy involves passing an electric current through the patient's head between two electrodes placed over the temples, causing a convulsive seizure; it was used for BIPOLAR DISORDER and other types of DEPRESSION. Both were developed in the 1930s; their use has declined since the introduction of tranquilizing drugs and antidepressants.

shoe Outer covering for the foot, usually of leather, with a stiff or thick sole and heel. Early examples from Mesopotamia were moccasinlike wraparounds of leather; not until the Hellenistic Age did shoes become luxurious. The Romans developed shoes fitted for the left and right feet, and differentiated according to sex and rank. In the 14th–15th cent., shoes became extremely long and pointed. In the 16th cent., the toes became extremely broad. In the 17th cent., shoes had moderately high heels and were often decorated with large rosettes of lace and ribbons, which gave way to gold or silver buckles in the 18th cent. The first shoe factory opened in 1760, in Massachusetts, but not until the 19th cent. were shoes manufactured quickly and inexpensively.

Shoemaker, Bill or **Willie Shoemaker** (*orig.* William Lee) (b.1931) U.S. jockey. Born in Fabens, Texas, he won the Kentucky Derby four times, the Belmont Stakes five times, and the Preakness twice. He rode more than 8,800 winners in his 41-year career, which ended in 1989, and is considered the greatest American jockey of his time.

Shoemaker-Levy 9 COMET that collided with JUPITER in July 1994, discovered by Carolyn and Eugene Shoemaker and David Levy 16 months earlier. It broke into over 20 fragments when it passed near Jupiter in July 1992; these collided sequentially with Jupiter two years later within a week, leaving dark spots larger than the earth at their impact sites in its atmosphere.

shoen \'shō-'en\ In Japan (c.8th–15th cent.), private, tax-free, often autonomous estates. Landowners would commend their parcels of land to powerful families or religious institutions with tax-free status, thereby obtaining that status for themselves. The increasing number of shoen undermined the political and economic power of the central government and contributed to the growth of powerful local clans. Under the KAMAKURA SHOGUNATE, the government asserted authority over the shoen by inserting its own stewards into each estate to collect taxes. During Japan's WARRING STATES PERIOD, the shoen gave way to consolidated landholdings in the control of DAIMYO.

shogun \'shō-gən\ (Japanese: "barbarian-quelling generalissimo") In Japan during the HEIAN PERIOD, a title bestowed on occasion on a general after a successful campaign, and later applied to all shogunate leaders. MINAMOTO YORITOMO received the title in 1192 after gaining control of Japan and formed the KAMAKURA SHOGUNATE. Later Kamakura shoguns lost actual power to the HOJO FAMILY while remaining rulers in name. Ashikaga Takauji received the title of shogun in 1338 and established the ASHIKAGA SHOGUNATE, but his successors enjoyed even less control over Japan and the country fell into civil war. In 1603 TOKUGAWA IEYASU established the TOKUGAWA SHOGUNATE, which proved the most durable. Since the title of shogun ultimately came from the emperor, he became a rallying point for those who in 1868 brought down the shogunate in the MEIJI RESTORATION.

shoji \'shō-jē\ In Japanese architecture, sliding partition doors and windows made of a latticework wooden frame and covered with a tough, translucent white paper. When closed, they softly diffuse light throughout the house. In summer they can be slid back or removed, opening the house to the outside.

Sholem Aleichem \'shȯ-ləm-ə-'lā-ḵəm\ *orig.* Sholem Yakov Rabinowitz (1859–1916) Russian writer. Beginning in 1883 he published more than 40 widely translated volumes of novels, stories, and plays in Yiddish. English translations include *Jewish Children* and *The Old Country*. His stories about his best-known character, Tevye the dairyman, were the basis for the musical *Fiddler on the Roof* (1964).

Sholokhov \'shȯl-ə-ḵəf\, **Mikhail (Aleksandrovich)** (1905–1984) Russian novelist. A native of the Don river region, he is best known for the huge novel *The Quiet Don,* translated in two parts as *And Quiet Flows the Don* (1934) and *The Don Flows Home to the Sea* (1940). A portrayal of the struggle between the Cossacks and Bolsheviks, it became the most widely read novel in Russia. It became controversial when Aleksandr SOLZHENITSYN alleged that it was plagiarized from the Cossack writer Fyodor Kryukov (d.1920). Sholokhov received the Nobel Prize in 1965.

shooting star See METEOR

shopping mall or **shopping center** Collection of independent retail stores, services, and parking areas constructed and maintained by a management firm as a unit. In the U.S., postwar migration from cities to suburbs and increased automobile use created a perceived need for centralized shopping facilities. The largest type, the regional center with vast parking lots, grew from the smaller, urban shopping arcade. The arcade developed out of the need for shelter from the weather; Buffalo, N.Y., and Cleveland have charming trussed and glass-roofed examples. In recent years large shopping malls have attempted to revive an arcadelike atmosphere. The world's largest malls are the W. Edmonton Mall in Alberta, Canada, and the Mall of America in Bloomington, Minn.

shore See COAST

Shorter, Frank (b.1947) U.S. runner. Born in Munich of American parents, he won his first marathon in 1970. At the 1972 Olympic Games, Shorter became the first American in 64 years to win a gold medal in the marathon, and sparked a running boom in the U.S. At the 1976 Olympics he won the silver medal.

shorthair cat Breed of DOMESTIC CAT. Show standards call for a sturdily built cat with strong-boned legs, a round head, round eyes, and ears that are rounded at the tips. The coat must be short and may be of almost any color or pattern. Tabby (stripes and mottled patterns in silver, brown, blue, and red), is common.

shorthand or **stenography** \stə-'nä-grə-fē\ System for rapid WRITING that uses symbols or abbreviations for letters, words, or phrases. Employed since antiquity, shorthand has been used in England since the 16th cent. Popular modern systems include Pitman, Gregg, and Speedwriting. Many are phonetic and call for writing words as they sound. Shorthand has been used in reporting proceedings of legislative bodies and courts and in taking dictated business correspondence.

Short Parliament See LONG PARLIAMENT

short story Brief fictional prose narrative. It usually presents a single significant episode or scene involving a limited number of characters. The form encourages economy of setting and concise narration; character is disclosed in action and dramatic encounter but seldom fully developed. A short story may concentrate on the creation of mood rather than the telling of a story. Despite numerous precedents, it emerged only in the 19th cent. as a distinct literary genre.

Shoshone \shə-'shō-nē\ Group of closely related N. American Indian peoples that traditionally occupied the Great Basin region of the U.S. The Shoshone are usually divided into four groups: Western (unmounted) Shoshone, centered in E Nevada; Northern (mounted) Shoshone of NW Utah and S Idaho; Wind River Shoshone in W Wyoming; and COMANCHE in W Texas. The Western Shoshone subsisted through hunting and gathering. The Northern Shoshone and Wind River Shoshone probably acquired horses by 1680, and adopted much of PLAINS INDIAN culture; they hunted buffalo, used TEPEES and skin clothing, and warred on other tribes. After splitting from the Wind River group, the Comanche moved south. Today the Shoshone number about 10,000.

Shostakovich \ˌshäs-tə-ˈkō-vich\, **Dmitri (Dmitrievich)** (1906–1975) Russian composer. He entered the St. Petersburg Conservatory at 13. His Symphony No. 1 (1925) attracted international attention, displaying his command of a large scale and an expressive palette ranging from unaffected lyricism to bitter satire to grand heroics. His next symphonies and such theater works as *The Nose* (1928), *The Age of Gold* (1930), and *Lady Macbeth of Mtsensk* (1932) were his most "modernistic" works. The government's denunciation of *Lady Macbeth* in *Pravda* (1936) led to his adopting a very different style. His wartime Sym-

Dmitri Shostakovich, early 1940s

phony No. 7 became a symbol of patriotism. Devastated after his music was again denounced in 1948, he began putting his most personal feelings into chamber works, particularly the remarkable 15 string quartets, but also composed two outspokenly personal symphonies, including no. 13, "Babi Yar" (1962). He is remembered as the greatest Russian composer to follow Igor STRAVINSKY.

shotgun Smoothbore shoulder weapon designed to fire a number of pellets, or shot, that scatter after they leave the muzzle. It is used mainly against small moving targets, especially birds. Fowling pieces appeared in 16th-cent. Europe; repeating shotguns became available in the 1880s. The range of a modern shotgun is about 50 yards (45 m).

Shotoku Taishi \shō-ˈtō-kù-ˈtä-ē-shē\ (574–622) Japanese regent. Named (593) crown prince and regent for his aunt, Empress Suiko, he was the de facto ruler of Japan. He promoted Buddhism and Confucianism and adopted the Chinese calendar and court ranks. He built the Horyu Temple, including the oldest known wood building in the world, and is credited with writing the "Seventeen-Article Constitution," which describes Confucian ethics and the Chinese bureaucratic system. Since his death he has been regarded as a Buddhist saint.

shot put Field event in which a metal ball is heaved for distance. It derives from the ancient event of "putting the stone"; later a shot (cannonball) was substituted. A 16-lb (7.3-kg) shot was adopted for men in the first modern Olympic Games (1896); an 8.8-lb (4-kg) weight is used by women.

Showa emperor See HIROHITO

Showa period \ˈshō-ə\ (1926–1989) Period of Japanese history corresponding to the reign of HIROHITO, the Showa emperor. It included the militarism of the 1930s and Japan's disastrous participation in World War II. The postwar era was one of rehabilitation, marked by Japan's joining the U.N. in 1956, hosting the 1964 and 1972 Olympics, and holding the Osaka World Exposition in 1970. Japan experienced a so-called "economic miracle," with annual growth averaging 10% in 1955–60 and higher in the years following. In the 1980s, the Japanese economy became one of the world's largest, with per capita income surpassing that of the U.S. Japanese society became increasingly urban. U.S. influence on popular culture was very strong. The Showa period also saw more people living in nuclear families than in extended families, love marriages rather than arranged marriages, fewer children, and more opportunities for women. See also OCCUPATION (OF JAPAN).

shrapnel \ˈshrap-nᵊl\ Originally, a projectile invented by the British artillery officer Henry Shrapnel (1761–1842), containing small spherical bullets and an explosive charge to scatter the shot and fragments of the shell casing. A time fuse set off the charge late in the shell's flight. The resulting hail of high-velocity debris was often lethal; it caused most

of the artillery-inflicted wounds in World War I. In World War II a high-explosive bursting charge that fragmented the shell's iron casing made shrapnel balls unnecessary.

Shreve, Henry Miller (1785–1851) U.S. inventor and explorer. Born in New Jersey, he grew up on the W Pennsylvania frontier. In the War of 1812 he was skipper of the *Enterprise*, the second steamboat on the Mississippi, carrying supplies for Andrew JACKSON's army. The trip convinced Shreve of the need for improved design. His design for the *Washington*—with a flat shallow hull, a steam engine on the main deck, and a second deck—established the Mississippi steamboat type. To clear rivers of debris, he later designed the first snag boat. His camp in Louisiana became the city of Shreveport.

Shreveport City (pop., 2000: 200,000), NW Louisiana. Founded in 1837 on the RED RIVER, it became a Confederate state capital during the AMERICAN CIVIL WAR. It developed rapidly after oil was discovered in 1906, and is now a commercial and industrial center.

shrew Any of 290 small INSECTIVORE species (family Soricidae) of the Northern Hemisphere and the Andes. They resemble moles, and have tiny eyes and ears, a hanging snout, and long, hook-tipped incisors. Species are 1.5–11 in. (3.5–27 cm) long, excluding the 1–4-in. (2.5–10-cm) tail and weigh as little as 0.07 oz (2 g). The smallest shrews are the smallest of all mammals. Most species live in ground litter, but some live in burrows or trees and a few are semiaquatic. Shrews have the highest metabolic rates of any mammal (with pulses as high as 800 beats per minute). Their normal prey is invertebrates. Some species have toxic saliva (painful to humans).

Shrewsbury, Duke of *orig.* Charles Talbot (1660–1718) English statesman. Raised as a Catholic, he became a Protestant in 1679 and in 1688 was one of seven men who invited William of Orange to seize power from JAMES II. After aiding the successful rebellion, Shrewsbury served WILLIAM III as secretary of state (1689–90, 1694–99). He later served as lord lieutenant of Ireland (1710–14) and was appointed by Queen ANNE as lord high treasurer (1714). He obtained recognition of GEORGE I as the legitimate royal heir and assured the peaceful succession of the House of HANOVER.

shrike Any of about 64 species of solitary, predatory songbirds (family Laniidae), especially any of the 25 species of the genus *Lanius*. Shrikes kill insects, lizards, mice, and birds with their bill or may impale their prey on a thorn (earning them the name butcher bird). The great gray shrike (*L. excubitor*), or northern shrike, is about 10 in. (25 cm) long and has a black mask. The only other New World species is the smaller loggerhead shrike (*L. ludovicianus*) of N. America.

shrimp Any of approximately 2,000 DECAPOD species (suborder Natantia) having a semitransparent body flattened from side to side and a flexible abdomen terminating in a fanlike tail. Shrimps occur in shallow and deep ocean waters and in lakes and streams. Species range from less than an inch to about 8 in. (20 cm) long. Larger species are often called prawns. Shrimps swim backward by rapidly flexing the abdomen and tail. Many species are commercially important as food.

Shropshire \ˈshräp-shir\ County (pop., 2000: 284,000), W England. It is divided by the SEVERN RIVER; its county seat is Shrewsbury. Remnants of Neolithic, Bronze Age, and early Iron Age inhabitants have been found. The SAXON conquest brought the construction of OFFA'S DYKE, marking the England–Wales border. After the NORMAN CONQUEST of 1066, a double line of castles was established as fortification against the Welsh. In the 13th cent. the high quality of Shropshire wool brought prosperity to the region. In the early 18th cent. it became the greatest iron-producing area in England.

Shroud of Turin See Shroud of TURIN

shrub Any woody plant that has several stems, none of which is dominant, and is usually less than 10 ft (3 m) tall. When much-branched and dense, it may be called a bush. TREES not only are taller but have a dominant stem, or trunk, and a definite crown shape. Some shrubs may grow to the size of a small tree.

Shubert Brothers U.S. theatrical managers and producers. After emigrating from Russia in 1882, brothers Lee (1872?–1953) and Sam (c.1875–1905) leased theaters and presented plays in Syracuse, N.Y. By 1900 Jacob (1880–1963) had joined the business, and the brothers leased their first theaters in New York City. They led an independent movement against the Theatrical Syndicate, which controlled U.S. theatrical bookings, and prevailed after a long legal battle. Lee and Jacob later built theaters across the U.S. and came to own over 60 legitimate houses and many movie theaters. They produced over 1,000 different shows, including 600 plays, revues, and musicals. Theatrical unions such as Actors' Equity were formed in response to their often sharp business practices. Charged with monopoly practices in 1950, they sold a number of theaters but retained many prestigious houses.

Shula, Don(ald Francis) (b.1930) U.S. football coach. Born in Grand River, Ohio, he played football for the Baltimore Colts and other NFL clubs. Under Shula as head coach (1963–69), the Colts won 71 games, lost 23, and tied four. As coach of the Miami Dolphins (1970–96), he became the first NFL coach to win 100 games in 10 seasons; in 1972–73 the Dolphins became the first team to go undefeated through an entire season and the play-offs. Shula holds the all-time NFL record for victories, with 347.

Shu Maung See U NE WIN

Shun \'shùn\ In Chinese mythology, one of the three legendary emperors, along with Yao and Da Yu, of the golden age of antiquity (c.23rd cent. B.C.), singled out by CONFUCIUS as models of integrity and virtue. Though his father repeatedly tried to murder him, Shun remained loyal to him. Because heaven and earth knew of his virtue, animals assisted him in all his labors. Shun is credited with standardizing weights and measures, regulating waterways, and organizing the kingdom into provinces.

Shute, Nevil *orig.* Nevil Shute Norway (1899–1960) English-Australian novelist. Trained as an aeronautical engineer, Shute drew on technical detail in his fiction. His early works include *What Happened to the Corbetts* (1939), a foretaste of the bombing of civilians in World War II. He settled in Australia, and his later novels reflect a growing despair about the future; they include *A Town Like Alice* (1950; film, 1956) and *On The Beach* (1957; film, 1959), about the nuclear annihilation of the human race.

Siad Barre \'sē-ˌäd-'bär-ā\, **Mohamed** (1919?–1995) President of Somalia (1969–91). When Somalia achieved independence in 1960 he was made a colonel. He seized power after the president's assassination in 1969. Under Siad Barre, Somali forces invaded SE Ethiopia in 1977, but were eventually repelled. His government was charged with human-rights abuses, and from 1988 government forces repeatedly clashed with rebels. He fled in 1991, leaving Somalia in a state of civil war and on the brink of mass starvation.

Siam See THAILAND

Siamese cat Breed of slender, short-haired DOMESTIC CAT that originated in Thailand (Siam). The Siamese has a pale fawn or gray body with dark points on the ears, face, legs, and tail. The points may be dark brown (seal point), blue-gray (blue point), milk-chocolate brown (chocolate point), pinkish gray (lilac point), or reddish orange (red point). The head is wedge-shaped. The blue eyes are slanted. Siamese are considered highly intelligent and are very vocal, with a distinctive yowling mew.

Siamese fighting fish Freshwater tropical fish (*Betta splendens;* family Belontiidae, or Anabantidae), noted for the males' mutual pugnacity. Native to Thailand, it was domesticated for use in contests. Combat consists mainly of fin nipping and is accompanied by a display of extended gill covers, spread fins, and intensified coloring. It grows to about 2.5 in. (6.5 cm) long. Domesticated, it has been bred with long, flowing fins and in such colors as red, green, blue, and lavender.

Siamese twins *or* **conjoined twins** Identical twins whose EMBRYOS did not separate completely. Siamese twins are physically joined (typically along the trunk or the head) and often share some organs. Symmetrical Siamese twins, relatively normal except for the areas of fusion, can sometimes be separated by surgery. In asymmetrical Siamese twins,

one (the host) is fairly normal, but the other, severely underdeveloped and dependent on the host for nutrition, may have to be surgically separated to save the host. The term originally referred to Chang and Eng, born in 1811 in Siam, who were joined by a ligament from breastbone to navel.

Sian See XI'AN

Sibelius \si-'bāl-yəs\, **Jean** (*orig.* Johan Julius Christian) (1865–1957) Finnish composer. He studied with Karl Goldmark (1830–1915), and rapidly developed into an orchestral composer. His support for national independence from Russia resulted in such works based on Finnish folklore as *Kullervo* (1892), the *Karelia* suite (1893), *Legends from the Kalevala* (1893), and *Finlandia* (1900). His major achievements were his seven symphonies (1899–1924), the violin concerto (1903), and *Tapiola* (1926). His works, marked by a sweeping but melancholy Romanticism, achieved huge international popularity. Out of sympathy with prevalent musical trends, he wrote nothing in his last 30 years.

Siberia Vast region, N central Asia, largely in Russia. It extends from the URAL MTNS. to the Pacific Ocean and from the Arctic Ocean to central Kazakstan and the boundaries of China and Mongolia; it covers about 5,000,000 sq mi (13,000,000 sq km), or almost one-tenth of the earth's land mass. It is notorious for the length and severity of its almost snowless winters. Temperatures of –90°F (–68°C) have been recorded. The area was under Chinese influence from about 1000 B.C., followed by the Turkic-Mongols in the 3rd cent. B.C. Russian trappers and COSSACKS colonized it in the late 16th cent. It was connected to other parts of Russia by the Trans-Siberian Railroad in 1904. E Siberia was the scene of the anti-Bolshevik government of Aleksandr KOLCHAK 1918–20. It was made part of the Russian S.F.S.R. in 1922. Russia exiled criminals and political prisoners there, and in the 1930s Joseph STALIN set up forced-labor camps that fueled industrial growth. It has deposits of coal, petroleum, natural gas, diamonds, iron ore, and gold, and it produces steel, aluminum, and machinery, as well as wheat, rye, oats, and sunflowers. Its main cities include NOVOSIBIRSK, OMSK, KRASNOYARSK, and IRKUTSK.

Siberian husky Breed of dog developed in Siberia by the Chukchi people, who used it as a sled dog, companion, and guard. It was brought to Alaska in 1909 for sled-dog races. It stands 20–24 in. (51–60 cm) and weighs 35–60 lbs (16–27 kg). It is usually gray, tan, or black and white; head markings may resemble a cap, mask, or spectacles. The breed, kept pure for hundreds of years in Siberia, is noted for intelligence and a gentle temperament.

Siberian peoples Any of a large number of small ethnic groups living in SIBERIA. Most engage in reindeer herding or fishing. In the past, many had separate dwellings for winter (partially or entirely underground) and summer (various styles of tent). Shamanism was common, and the family was the basic societal unit. The Soviet government attempted to settle Siberian peoples on collective farms and to introduce new occupations, but some groups, such as the Koryak and the Nenets, still engage in their traditional pursuits. Other Siberian peoples include the Chuckchi, Evenki, Ket, Khanty, Mansi, YAKUT, and Yukaghir.

Sibyl Prophetess of Greek legend. She was a figure of the mythical past whose prophecies, phrased in Greek hexameters, were handed down in writing. In the late 4th cent. B.C., the number of sibyls multiplied. Sibyls were associated with various ORACLES, especially those of APOLLO, who was said to be their inspiration. They were typically depicted as extremely old women living in caves, who delivered their prophecies in an ecstatic frenzy. A famous collection of prophecies, the Sibylline Books, was traditionally consulted only in emergencies.

Sicilian Vespers (1282) Massacre of the French that began a Sicilian revolt, backed by Peter III of Aragon, against the Angevin king CHARLES I. The rising broke out when Sicilians killed some insulting French soldiers at vespers in the church of Santo Spirito in Palermo. The people of the city followed suit and massacred 2,000 of its French inhabitants. All of Sicily soon revolted, and the war became a French–Aragonese struggle for possession of Sicily. The conflict was finally resolved when the Sicilians chose Frederick III, brother of the king of Aragon, as their ruler in 1302.

Sicilies, The Two Former kingdom, Italy. It united the S part of the Italian peninsula with the island of SICILY. The region was conquered by the Normans but was divided in 1282 between the French on the mainland and the Spanish on the island, both with rulers claiming the title of king of Sicily. In 1442 ALFONSO V of Aragon reunited the two areas and took the title of king of The Two Sicilies. This title became official in 1816. Conquered by Giuseppe GARIBALDI in 1860, The Two Sicilies became part of the kingdom of Italy.

Sicily \'si-sə-lē\ *Italian* **Sicilia** \sē-'chēl-yä\ Island and autonomous region (pop., 1996 est.: 5,095,000), Italy. It is separated from the mainland by the Strait of MESSINA. The largest island (9,830 sq mi, or 25,460 sq km) in the Mediterranean Sea, it is also the site of Europe's highest active volcano, Mt. ETNA. The capital is PALERMO. It has been a crossroads of history. The Greeks colonized it in the 8th–6th cent. B.C., and in the 3rd cent. B.C. it became the first Roman province. It came under Byzantine rule in the 6th cent. A.D., and in 965 fell to Arab conquest from N. Africa. It was taken in 1060 by the NORMANS. In the 12th–13th cent. and again in the 18th cent., it formed part of the kingdom of The Two SICILIES. In 1861 it was incorporated into the kingdom of Italy. Olive, almond, lemon, and orange trees thrive on its arid but fertile soil.

sickle-cell anemia Serious HEMOGLOBIN disorder. About one in 400 blacks worldwide has the disease, caused by inheriting two copies of a recessive gene that makes those with one copy of it (about one in 12 blacks worldwide) resistant to MALARIA. The gene specifies an abnormal hemoglobin that distorts ERYTHROCYTES into a rigid sickle shape. The cells become clogged in capillaries, damaging or destroying various tissues. Symptoms include chronic ANEMIA, shortness of breath, fever, and episodic "crises" (severe pain in the abdomen, bones, or muscles). Hydroxyurea treatment greatly lessens severity of crises and increases life expectancy, previously about 45 years.

Sicyon \'si-sē-ən\ Ancient city, N PELOPONNESE, S Greece. Located just northwest of CORINTH, it attained its greatest power in the 6th cent. B.C. under Cleisthenes, grandfather of CLEISTHENES OF ATHENS. During the 4th cent. B.C. it was celebrated for its school of painters and sculptors, which included LYSIPPUS. In the 3rd cent. B.C. it gained prominence in the ACHAEAN LEAGUE.

Siddons, Sarah *orig.* Sarah Kemble (1755–1831) British actress. After acting with her father's traveling company, she made her London debut in *Fatal Marriage* at the DRURY LANE THEATRE in 1782 and was instantly acclaimed the leading tragedienne of the time. She played Shakespearean parts, notably Lady Macbeth, from 1785 until she retired in 1812.

Side \'sē-də\ Ancient city, SW Turkey. The most important port of ancient Pamphylia, it originally lay on the Mediterranean coast; it now lies inland. ALEXANDER THE GREAT occupied it; ANTIOCHUS III was defeated there in 190 B.C. In the 1st cent. B.C. pirates made it their chief slave market. The ruins include the remains of a colossal theater, built on arches and considered one of the finest in ASIA MINOR.

sidereal period \sī-'dir-ē-əl\ Time a celestial body in the solar system takes to complete one revolution with respect to the stars (as seen from a fixed point outside the system). For a planet, it can be calculated from the SYNODIC PERIOD. For the moon or an artificial satellite of earth, it is the time required to return to the same position against the background of stars. See also DAY.

sidewinder Species (*Crotalus cerastes*) of small, nocturnal RATTLESNAKE, found in sandy deserts of Mexico and the SW U.S. It is 18–30 in. (45–75 cm) long, with hornlike scales above its eyes. It moves by looping itself obliquely across the sand, leaving a characteristic J-shaped trail. Its venomous bite is usually not fatal to humans.

siding Material used to surface the exterior of a building to protect against exposure to the elements, prevent heat loss, and visually unify the facade. The word siding implies wood units, or products imitative of wood, used on houses. Types of siding include clapboard, horizontal lap siding, vertical board siding, and SHINGLE. Board-and-batten siding, sometimes found in CARPENTER GOTHIC houses and very modest structures, consists of vertical wood boards with their butt joints covered by battens (narrow strips). Both aluminum and polyvinyl-fluoride-coated siding ("vinyl siding") were developed as maintenance-free alternatives to wood clapboard, which they mimic. Fiberboard, a pressed-wood-pulp product, is sometimes used, though its long-term durability is limited.

Sidney, Sir Philip (1554–1586) English poet. He was born into an aristocratic family. *Astrophel and Stella* (1591), inspired by Sidney's passion for his aunt's married ward, is considered the finest Elizabethan SONNET cycle after William SHAKESPEARE's sonnets. *The Defence of Poesie* (1595), an urbane and eloquent plea for imaginative literature, introduced the critical ideas of Renaissance theorists to England. His heroic romance *Arcadia,* though unfinished, is the most important work of English prose fiction of the 16th cent. None of his works was published in his lifetime. He died from a battle-wound infection at 31, and was widely mourned as the ideal gentleman of his day.

Sidon \'sīd-ᵊn\ Seaport (metro. area pop., 1994 est.: 150,000), SW Lebanon. It was a principal city of PHOENICIA from the 2nd millennium B.C. and a parent city of TYRE. Ruled successively by the Assyrians, Babylonians, and Persians, it was conquered by ALEXANDER THE GREAT about 330 B.C. Under Roman rule it was a center for the manufacture of glass and purple dyes. It changed hands several times during the CRUSADES and fell to the Muslims in 1291 and to the Ottoman Turks in 1517.

SIDS See SUDDEN INFANT DEATH SYNDROME

Siegel \'sē-gəl\, **Bugsy** (*orig.* Benjamin) (1906–1947) U.S. gangster. Born in Brooklyn, N.Y., he began his career extorting money from Jewish peddlers on New York's Lower East Side. He joined with Meyer LANSKY and began operating bootlegging and gambling rackets; they later formed the forerunner of MURDER, INC. In 1937 he was sent to the West Coast, and soon set up gambling, narcotics smuggling, and blackmail operations. In 1945 he built the Flamingo Hotel and Casino in Las Vegas. Originally budgeted at $1.5 million, its cost was driven to $6 million through his skimming. This angered Lansky and other bosses, and Siegel was shot down in his mansion.

Siegfried \'sig-ˌfrēd, *German* 'zēk-ˌfrēt\ *Old Norse* **Sigurd** Hero of German and Old Norse mythology noted for his outstanding strength and courage. He is one of the heroes of the Poetic EDDA and the NIBELUNGENLIED, and he figures in many sometimes inconsistent legends. In the earliest stories, he is presented as a boy of noble lineage who grew up without parental care, but other accounts provide elaborate detail of a courtly upbringing. He plays a part in the story of BRUNHILD, in which he meets his death. He is the hero of Richard WAGNER's *Ring of the Nibelung.*

Siemens \'sē-mənz\, **(Charles) William** (*orig.* Karl Wilhelm) (*later* **Sir William**) (1823–1883) German-British engineer and inventor. He emigrated to Britain in 1844. In 1861 he patented the open-hearth furnace; the open-hearth process was soon being widely used in steelmaking and eventually replaced the BESSEMER PROCESS. He was a principal in the company that laid the first successful transatlantic TELEGRAPH cable (1866). His three brothers were also eminent engineers and industrialists (see SIEMENS AG).

Siemens AG \'sē-mənz\ German electrical-equipment manufacturer. Siemens & Halske was founded in Berlin in 1847 to build telegraph installations. Under Werner Siemens (1816–1892) and his three brothers (including William SIEMENS), it expanded to produce dynamos, cables, telephones, electric power, and electric lighting. In 1903 its power-engineering activities were transferred to the new Siemens-Schuckertwerke GmbH, and in 1932 Siemens-Reiniger-Werke AG was established to produce medical equipment. The Siemens companies expanded greatly during the Third Reich, during which they employed slave labor and helped build and operate the AUSCHWITZ and BUCHENWALD camps. They flourished again in the 1950s, and by 1966, when the three Siemens companies merged to form Siemens AG, were among the world's largest electrical suppliers. Today, with employees in over 190 countries, they promote industrial solutions and produce computer systems, power plants, microwave devices, and large-scale medical equipment.

Siena \sē-'e-nä\ *ancient* Saena Julia. City (pop., 1995 est.: 65,000), W Italy. It is located south of FLORENCE. Founded by the ETRUSCANS, it passed to the Romans and later the Lombards. Rivalry with Florence made Siena the center of pro-imperial Ghibellinism in TUSCANY. It was conquered by Charles of Anjou in 1270 and joined the Guelph confederation (see GUELPHS AND GHIBELLINES). Conquered by the Holy Roman emperor CHARLES V in 1555, it was ceded to Florence. Historic sites include the Gothic-Romanesque cathedral, the Univ. of Siena (founded 1240), and the Piazza del Campo, where horse races originating in medieval times are still held.

Sienkiewicz \shʸen-'kʸe-vʸēch\, **Henryk (Adam Alexander Pius)** (1846–1916) Polish novelist. In 1869 he began to publish critical works showing the influence of POSITIVISM. He published successful short stories before producing the great trilogy consisting of *With Fire and Sword* (1884), *The Deluge* (1886), and *Pan Michael* (1887–88), historical novels that vividly recount Poland's struggles against Cossacks, Tatars, Swedes, and Turks. *Quo Vadis?* (1896), set in Rome under Nero, established his international reputation. He received the Nobel Prize in 1905.

Sierra Club U.S. conservation organization. It was founded in 1892 by a group of Californians, including John MUIR, to sponsor wilderness outings in Pacific Coast mountain regions. As its first president, Muir initiated the club's involvement in political action on behalf of conservation. With branches in all 50 states, it works to educate the public on environmental issues and lobbies for environmental legislation.

Sierra Leone \sē-,er-ə-lē-'ōn\ *officially* **Republic of Sierra Leone** Nation, W Africa. Area: 27,699 sq mi (71,740 sq km). Population (2000.): 5,233,000. Capital: FREETOWN. The

©1999, Encyclopædia Britannica, Inc.

SIERRA LEONE
Scale 1: 75,789,000
0 25 50 75 mi
0 50 100 km

Mende and Temne are the largest of about 18 ethnic groups. Languages: English (official), Krio (an English-African creole). Religions: Islam, traditional animist beliefs, Christianity. Currency: leone. Sierra Leone has four physical regions: the coastal swamp; the Sierra Leone Peninsula, with thickly wooded mountains that rise from the swamps; the interior plains, consisting of grasslands and rolling wooded country; and the E plateau region, encompassing several mountains. More than one-fourth of the country is forest. Wildlife includes chimpanzees, tigers, and crocodiles. The economy is based largely on agriculture and mining; rice, cassava, coffee, cacao, and oil palm are major crops, and diamonds, iron ore, and bauxite are mined. It is ruled by a military regime which suspended the constitu-

tion in 1997; its usual head of state and government is the president. Its earliest inhabitants were probably the Buloms; the Mende and Temne peoples arrived in the 15th cent. The coastal region was visited by the Portuguese in the 15th cent., and by 1495 there was a Portuguese fort on the site of modern Freetown. European ships visited the coast regularly to trade for slaves and ivory, and the English built trading posts on offshore islands in the 17th cent. British abolitionists and philanthropists founded Freetown in 1787 as a private venture for freed and runaway slaves. In 1808 the coastal settlement became a British colony. The region became a British protectorate in 1896. It achieved independence in 1961 and became a republic in 1971. It was marked by political and economic turmoil as successive military regimes tried to assume power. U.N. peacekeeping forces were ineffectual in preventing bloodletting and atrocities until a decade of civil war ended in 2002.

Sierra Madre Principal mountain system, Mexico. It includes the ranges of the Sierra Madre Occidental (west), the Sierra Madre Oriental (east), and the Sierra Madre del Sur (south). The Sierra Madre Occidental extends for about 700 mi (1,120 km), parallel with the Gulf of California and the Pacific Ocean. The Sierra Madre Oriental originates in the barren hills of the RÍO GRANDE to the north and extends about 700 mi (1,120 km), roughly parallel with the Gulf of Mexico. It rises to 12,008 ft (3,660 m) at the peak of Mt. Peña Nevada. The sparsely inhabited Sierra Madre del Sur stretches through the S Mexican states of GUERRERO and OAXACA.

Sierra Nevada Mountain range, E California. It extends more than 250 mi (400 km) from the MOJAVE DESERT to the CASCADE RANGE. Its peaks are 11,000–14,000 ft (3,350–4,300 m) high; Mt. WHITNEY is the highest. It is a year-round recreation center.

Sierra redwood See BIG TREE

Sieyès \syā-'yes\, **Emmanuel-Joseph** (1748–1836) French political theorist. An influential Catholic priest in sympathy with the reform movement before the French Revolution, he won great popularity with his pamphlet "What Is the Third Estate?" (1789) and was elected to represent the THIRD ESTATE in the Estates General. He led the movement to establish the NATIONAL ASSEMBLY, then served in the National Convention until the radical Jacobins seized control (1793). During the DIRECTORY, he served as a legislator (1795–99) and on the Directory itself (1799). He helped organize the coup that brought him into conflict with his power. After the monarchy's restoration (1815), he lived in exile until 1830.

Sigismund \'si-jəs-mənd\ (1368–1437) German king (1411–37) and Holy Roman Emperor (1433–37). He became king of Hungary by marriage (1387) and pawned his German lands to raise funds for defense (1388). He pursued an expansionist policy that brought him into conflict with his brother Wenceslas, whom he imprisoned (1402–3) in an abortive effort to seize Bohemia. He was twice defeated by the Turks (1396, 1428). He inherited the Bohemian crown in 1419, but wars against the HUSSITES delayed his coronation until 1436. In 1433 he became the last emperor of the House of Luxembourg.

Sigismund III Vasa *Polish* Zygmunt Waza (1566–1632) King of Poland (1587–1632) and of Sweden (1592–99). Son of King John III of Sweden (1537–1592) and grandson of Sigismund I of Poland, he was elected king of Poland in 1587. On his father's death (1592), he accepted the Swedish throne. He left his paternal uncle Charles (later CHARLES IX) as regent in Sweden and returned to Poland, but Charles later rose in rebellion and deposed Sigismund (1599). He waged war intermittently from 1600 to regain the Swedish throne. He invaded Russia in the Time of TROUBLES and held Moscow 1610–12. In the Polish–Swedish conflict of 1621, he lost most of Polish Livonia to GUSTAV II ADOLF of Sweden.

Signac \sē-'nyȧk\, **Paul** (1863–1935) French painter. At 18 he gave up architecture to pursue painting in the Impressionist manner. With Georges SEURAT he developed an exact mathematical system of applying dots of color, which they called pointillism (see NEO-IMPRESSIONISM). He traveled extensively along the European coast painting landscapes and seascapes; in his later years he painted street scenes of Paris and other cities. He was a master of watercolor, in which he achieved great brilliance of color and a free, spontaneous style.

sign language Communication through bodily movements, especially of the hands and arms, rather than through speech. It has long been used by speakers of mutually unintelligible languages and is widely used for communication by the deaf. Charles-Michel, abbé de l'Épée (1712–1789), developed the first sign language for the deaf; his system developed into French Sign Language (FSL), still used in France. Brought to the U.S. in 1816 by Thomas Gallaudet (1787–1851), it evolved into American Sign Language (ASL, or Ameslan), now used by more than half a million people. Most sign languages express concepts rather than elements of words and thus have more in common with each other than with their countries' spoken languages.

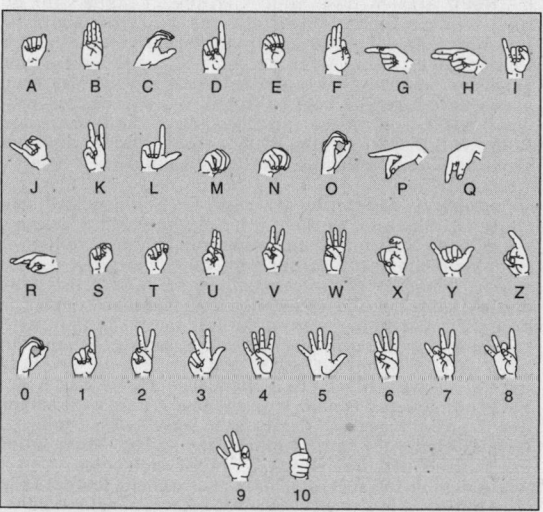

Sign language The alphabet and the numbers 0–10 in American Sign Language.

Signorelli \ˌsēn-yō-ˈrel-lē\, **Luca (d'Egidio di Ventura de')** (c.1445/50–1523) Italian painter. Probably a student of PIERO DELLA FRANCESCA, he went to Rome about 1483, where he produced the *Testament of Moses* fresco in the Sistine Chapel. The dramatic action and depiction of great muscular effort in this and similar works mark him as essentially a Florentine naturalist. His masterpiece, the *End of the World* and *Last Judgment* frescoes in Orvieto Cathedral, with their many muscular nudes, greatly influenced MICHELANGELO.

Sigurd See SIEGFRIED

Sihanouk, Norodom See NORODOM SIHANOUK

sikhara *or* **shikhara** \ˈshi-kə-rə\ Tower characteristic of Hindu temples of N India. The sikhara over the sanctuary of a temple is usually tapered convexly, consisting of piled-up roof slabs of diminishing size. The surface is covered with vinelike ogee arch tracery; at the top is a cushion-shaped grooved disk, and above that a pot with a

Sikhara Udayesvara temple, Madhya Pradesh, India, 1059–82

crowning finial. The sikhara developed during the Gupta period (4th–6th cent. A.D.) and steadily grew taller and more elaborate. Half spires may be added on either side of the sikhara. A smaller, rectilinear sikhara is frequently used above the temple halls.

Sikhism \ˈsē-ˌkiz-əm\ Indian monotheistic religion founded in the late 15th cent. by GURU NANAK. Most of its 18 million members live in the PUNJAB, the site of their holiest shrine, the GOLDEN TEMPLE, and the center of Sikh authority, the Akal Takht. The ADI GRANTH is the canonical SCRIPTURE of Sikhism. Its theology is based on a supreme God who governs with justice and grace. Human beings, irrespective of CASTE and gender distinctions, have the opportunity to become one with God. The basic human flaw of self-centeredness can be overcome through proper reverence for God, commitment to hard work, service to humanity, and sharing the fruits of one's labor. Sikhs accept the Hindu ideas of SAMSARA and KARMA, and they view themselves as the Khalsa, a chosen race of soldier-saints committed to a Spartan code of conduct and a crusade for righteousness.

Sikh Wars \ˈsēk\ (1845–46, 1848–49) Two wars fought between the Sikhs and the British. In the first war Sikhs invaded British India under the pretext of forestalling a British attack on the Sikh state in the PUNJAB. They were defeated, and the British annexed some of their lands. The second war was a Sikh national revolt that ended in a British victory and full annexation of the Punjab.

Sikkim \ˈsi-kəm\ State (pop., 1994 est.: 444,000), E HIMALAYAS, NE India. Mt. KANCHENJUNGA, third-highest peak in the world, forms its W border. It has an area of 2,744 sq mi (7,107 sq km); the capital, GANGTOK, is the only urban center. As an independent country, it fought prolonged wars in the 18th and 19th cent. with Bhutan and Nepal. In 1950 it became an Indian protectorate, and in 1975, a state of India. It exports agricultural products, especially cardamom. Its mineral resources include copper, lead, zinc, coal, iron ore, and garnets.

Sikorski, Wladyslaw (Eugeniusz) (1881–1943) Polish general and politician. Born in Austrian Poland, in World War I he was head of the Polish Legion, which joined with Austria against Russia. He served as prime minister of Poland 1923–24. From 1928 he joined the opposition to the government controlled by Jozef PILSUDSKI. After 1939, he became prime minister of the Polish government-in-exile. When he asked Joseph STALIN to allow investigation of the KATYN MASSACRE, Stalin broke off Soviet–Polish diplomatic contact. Sikorski died in an airplane crash several months later.

Sikorsky, Igor (Ivan) (1889–1972) Russian-U.S. pioneer in aircraft design. After studying engineering in Kiev, he set up his own shop to develop the HELICOPTER. Failing to build a workable model, he turned to fixed-wing airplane design and in 1913 built the first four-engine airplane, with an innovative enclosed cabin. He emigrated to the U.S. in 1919. In 1931 he produced a twin-engine amphibian aircraft, and in 1939 he finally realized a viable helicopter design. He directed his company, a division of United Aircraft Corp., from 1929 to 1957.

Igor Sikorsky

silenus See SATYR AND SILENUS

Silesia \sī-ˈlē-zhə\ *Polish* **Shlask** \ˈshläsk\ *German* **Schlesien** \ˈshlä-zē-on\ Historic region, E central Europe. It now lies mainly in SW Poland, with parts in Germany and the Czech Republic. It became a possession of the Bohemian crown, and thus part of the HOLY ROMAN EMPIRE, in 1335. Having splintered into many principalities, it passed to the Austrian HABSBURGS in 1526; it was taken by Prussia in 1742. After World War I it was divided between Poland, Czechoslovakia, and Germany. During World War II Polish

Silesia was the site of atrocities by Nazi and, later, Soviet forces. In 1945 the Allied powers assigned virtually all of Silesia to Poland; today it contains almost one-fourth of Poland's population.

silhouette \ˌsi-lü-'et\ Profile portrait in black against white (or vice versa), either painted or cut from paper, especially popular around 1750–1850 as the least expensive method of portraiture. The name derives from Étienne de Silhouette, Louis XV's finance minister, notorious for his frugality and his hobby of making cut-paper shadow portraits. Early portraits and scenes were produced by drawing the outline cast by candlelight or lamplight; when paper became widely available, they were often cut out freehand directly from life. Photography rendered silhouettes nearly obsolete, and they became a type of itinerant folk art.

silicate mineral Any of a large group of silicon-oxygen compounds widely distributed throughout the solar system. The silicates make up about 95% of the earth's crust and upper mantle, occurring as the major constituents of most IGNEOUS ROCKS. They are important constituents of lunar samples, meteorites, and most asteroids; planetary probes have detected them on Mercury, Venus, and Mars. Of the approximately 600 known silicate minerals, only the FELDSPARS, amphiboles, PYROXENES, MICAS, OLIVINES, feldspathoids, and ZEOLITES are significant in rock formation.

siliceous rock \sə-'li-shəs\ Any of a group of SEDIMENTARY ROCKS that consist largely of silicon dioxide, either as QUARTZ or as CHERT, the most common siliceous rock. Bedded cherts may be an original organic or inorganic precipitate. Nodular cherts appear to be produced by the alteration of preexisting sedimentary rock; silica distributed throughout the rock dissolves and reprecipitates to form nodules.

silicon Nonmetallic to semimetallic chemical ELEMENT, chemical symbol Si, atomic number 14. Second only to oxygen in abundance in the earth's crust, it never occurs free but is found in almost all rocks and in sand, clay, and soils. Pure silicon is a hard, dark gray solid with a metallic luster. It is an important SEMICONDUCTOR; doped with boron, phosphorus, or arsenic, it is used in various electronic circuit and switching devices, including computer chips, transistors, and diodes. Silicon is also used in metallurgy as a reducing (see REDUCTION) agent and in steel, brass, and bronze. Its usual VALENCE in compounds is 4. Silica (silicon dioxide) is used as sand and clay for many purposes; as QUARTZ, it forms special GLASSES. Silicates are used in making glass, enamels, and ceramics, and in soaps, wood treatment, cements, and dyeing. See also SILICATE MINERALS, SILICONE.

silicone or **polysiloxane** Any of a diverse class of POLYMERS manufactured as fluids, RESINS, or elastomers. They are partially organic compounds, but composed of alternating SILICON and OXYGEN atoms. In most silicones, two organic groups, usually methyl or phenyl, are attached to each silicon atom. Silicones in general are exceptionally stable and inert. Silicone fluids are used in hydraulic fluids and emulsion-breaking compositions and as adhesives, lubricants, water repellents, and protective coatings. Silicone rubbers are used in electrical insulators, gaskets, specialized tubing, automobile engine components, flexible windows, and surgical membranes and implants.

Silicon Valley Industrial strip, W central California. Located between SAN JOSE and Palo Alto in the San Jose and Santa Clara valleys, it came into prominence in the early 1980s as the country's principal center of high-technology industries, including electronics and computer corporations. Its (unofficial) name derives from the extensive use of SILICON in electronics.

silicosis \ˌsi-lə-'kō-səs\ Common LUNG disease caused by long-term inhalation of silica mineral dust. Known since the 18th cent., it usually occurs after 10–20 years of exposure in jobs such as mining, stonecutting, grinding, or polishing. The smallest particles do the most damage, killing macrophages (see RETICULOENDOTHELIAL SYSTEM) that engulf them in the pulmonary alveoli. Dead cells accumulate, forming fibrous masses that reduce lung elasticity. Patients

are vulnerable to TUBERCULOSIS, EMPHYSEMA, and PNEUMONIA. Control of silicosis depends on prevention with face masks, proper ventilation, and X-ray monitoring of workers' lungs.

silk Animal fiber produced by certain insects as building material for cocoons and webs. In commercial use it refers to the filaments produced by the caterpillars of several moth species of the genus *Bombyx* (silkworms). Silk is a continuous filament around each cocoon. It is freed by softening the cocoon in water and then locating the filament end; the filaments from several cocoons are unwound at the same time to form a single strand. Several very thin strands are twisted together to make thicker, stronger YARN. Since World War II the substitution of synthetic fibers has greatly reduced the silk industry, but silk remains an important luxury material and is a major product of Japan, S. Korea, and Thailand.

Silk Road Ancient trade route that linked China with Europe. Originally a CARAVAN route and used from about 100 B.C., the 4,000-mi (6,400-km) road started in XI'AN, China, followed the GREAT WALL to the northwest, crossed Afghanistan, and went on to the E Mediterranean Sea, where goods were taken by boat to Rome. Silk was carried westward, while wool, gold, and silver were carried eastward. With the fall of Rome, the route became unsafe; it was revived under the Mongols, and Marco POLO used it in the 13th cent.

silk screen or **serigraphy** \sə-'ri-grə-fē\ Sophisticated stenciling technique for surface printing, in which a design is cut out of paper and then printed by rubbing, rolling, or spraying paint or ink through the cutout areas. It was developed about 1900 and originally used in advertising and display work. In the 1950s fine artists began to use the process. It got its name from the fine-mesh silk that, when tacked to a wooden frame, serves as a support for the cut-paper stencil, which is glued to it. The wooden frame holding the screen is hinged to a slightly larger wooden board, the printing paper is placed on the board under the screen, and the paint is pressed through the screen with a squeegee (rubber blade) the same width as the screen. Many colors can be used, with a separate screen for each color.

Silla Kingdom of ancient Korea that unified Korea under the Unified Silla dynasty (668–935). Traditionally believed to have been founded by Hyokkose in 57 B.C., Silla emerged as a full-fledged kingdom in the 6th cent. A unique military corps, the *hwarang*, was organized; later allied with TANG-DYNASTY China, it defeated the Korean states of PAEKCHE in 660 and KOGURYO in 668, then expelled the Tang forces to create an independent Korean nation-state. It adopted a Chinese bureaucratic structure, but its aristocracy was never replaced by a bureaucratic class based on merit.

Sills, Beverly orig. Belle Silverman (b.1929) U.S. soprano. Born in Brooklyn, N.Y., she sang on radio as a child and made her operatic debut in 1946. From 1955 she sang with the New York City Opera. Her coloratura performance in *Julius Caesar* (1966) made her one of the most celebrated opera stars in the world. After 25 years singing with the company, she served as its director 1979–89. An effervescent personality, she became widely popular hosting broadcast concerts and opera performances.

Silone \sē-'lō-nā\, **Ignazio** orig. Secondo Tranquilli (1900–1978) Italian writer and political leader. A founder of the Italian Communist Party in 1921, he was driven into exile by the fascists. In 1930 he settled in Switzerland. He became internationally famous with his first novel, *Fontamara* (1930), which was followed by *Bread and Wine* (1937). *The School for Dictators* (1938) is a powerful antifascist satire. After World War II he returned to Italian politics before retiring to write such works as *A Handful of Blackberries* (1952).

silt Sediment particles 0.00016–0.0024 in. (0.004–0.06 mm) in diameter, regardless of mineral type. Silt is easily transported by moving currents but settles in still water. A consolidated aggregate of silt particles is called siltstone. Silt deposits formed by wind are known as LOESS. Sediments are seldom composed entirely of silt but rather are a mixture of clay, silt, and sand. Clay-rich silt, upon consolidation, frequently develops parting along bedding surfaces and is then called SHALE.

Silurian period \sī-'lu̇r-ē-ən\ Interval of geologic time, 438–410 million years ago, in the PALEOZOIC ERA. It marks the first appearance of land plants and jawed fishes. Land masses were probably distributed as follows: Arctic Canada, Scandinavia, and Australia were in the tropics; Japan and the Philippines were inside the Arctic Circle; S. America and Africa were near the S. Pole. The land surface was buried by an ice sheet, possibly as deep as that covering Antarctica today.

silver Chemical ELEMENT, one of the TRANSITION ELEMENTS, chemical symbol Ag, atomic number 47. It is a white, lustrous precious METAL, valued for its beauty and its electrical conductivity, which is the highest of any metal. Widely distributed in nature in small amounts, it is usually recovered as a by-product of copper and lead production. Its use in bullion and coins was overtaken in the 1960s by demand for industrial purposes, especially photography (see PHOTOCHEMICAL REACTION). It is also used in printed electrical circuits, electronic conductors, and contacts. It is the CATALYST for converting ethylene to ethylene oxide. Its use in ALLOYS in sterling and plated silverware, ornaments, and jewelry remains important; yellow gold used in jewelry is 25% silver, and gold dental alloys are about 10% silver. Silver dental fillings are an AMALGAM of silver and MERCURY. Silver compounds have VALENCE 1. The chloride, bromide, and iodide are used in photography and the iodide in cloud seeding. See also SILVER NITRATE.

Silver Age In Latin literature, the period from around A.D. 18 to 133, second only to the preceding Golden Age (c.70 B.C.–A.D. 18) in literary achievement. SATIRE was the most vigorous literary form, exemplified by JUVENAL, MARTIAL, and PETRONIUS. Other figures included TACITUS and SUETONIUS in history, PLINY THE ELDER and PLINY THE YOUNGER in letter writing, and QUINTILIAN in literary criticism. Prose was characteristically elaborate and poetical in style. See also AUGUSTAN AGE.

silverfish Species (*Lepisma saccharina*) of quick-moving, slender, flat, wingless insect having three tail bristles and silvery scales. Females deposit fertilized eggs in cracks and hidden places. Silverfish normally live indoors and, because they eat starchy materials (e.g., paste, bookbindings, and wallpaper), can cause much damage. They live two to three years and molt throughout life.

silver nitrate Inorganic compound, colorless, transparent crystals. The most important SILVER compound, it is used to prepare other silver salts and as a reagent in ANALYSIS. Dilute solutions may be applied to newborns' eyes to prevent blindness from GONORRHEA. Eating silver nitrate causes violent abdominal pain and GASTROENTERITIS.

silverpoint See METAL POINT

Silvers, Phil *orig.* Philip Silversmith (1912–1985) U.S. actor and comedian. Born in Brooklyn, N.Y., he began his career in vaudeville and burlesque. After making his film debut in 1940, he appeared as comic relief in many feature films. He starred on Broadway in *Top Banana* (1951–52, Tony Award; film, 1954). He is best remembered as Sgt. Bilko in television's *Phil Silvers Show* (1955–59). He appeared in the film *A Funny Thing Happened on the Way to the Forum* (1966) and its Broadway revival (1972, Tony Award).

silver standard Monetary standard under which the basic unit of CURRENCY is defined as a stated quantity of silver. No country now operates under a silver standard. In the 1870s most European countries adopted the GOLD STANDARD, and by the early 1900s only China, Mexico, and a few small countries still used the silver standard. In 1873 the U.S. Treasury stopped coining silver, which led to the FREE SILVER MOVEMENT, but the defeat of W. J. BRYAN ended agitation for free silver in the U.S.

Simenon \sē-mə-'nōⁿ\, **Georges (Joseph Chrétien)** (1903–1989) Belgian-French novelist. His first novel under his own name was *The Case of Peter the Lett* (1931), in which he introduced the Parisian police official Inspector Maigret. He wrote some 80 more Maigret novels, as well as about 130 psychological novels, among other works, and was one of

the most prolific and widely published authors of the 20th cent. The central theme running through his fiction is the isolated existence of the neurotic, abnormal individual.

Georges Simenon

Simeon Stylites \stī-'līt-ēz\, **St.** *or* **Simeon the Elder** (c.A.D. 390–459) Syrian ascetic. Expelled from a monastic community for excessive austerity, he became a hermit. His miracle working drew such crowds that he took to living atop a 6-ft (2-m) pillar (Greek, *stylos*) around 420, becoming the first of the stylites (pillar hermits). He remained atop a second, 50-ft (15-m) pillar until his death; a railing prevented his falling, and disciples brought him food. He inspired other ascetics, and stylites were documented as late as the 19th cent. in Russia.

simile \'si-mə-lē\ FIGURE OF SPEECH involving a comparison between two unlike entities. In a simile, unlike a METAPHOR, the resemblance is indicated by the words "like" or "as." Similes in everyday speech reflect simple comparisons, as in "He eats like a bird." Similes in literature may be specific and direct or more lengthy and complex. The Homeric, or epic, simile, which is typically used in epic poetry, often extends to several lines.

Simla *or* **Shimla** City (pop., 1991: 82,000), capital of Himachal Pradesh state, NW India. It was built by the British on a ridge of the Himalayan foothills some 7,100 ft (2,200 m) high. It served as the British summer capital 1865–1939, and as the headquarters of PUNJAB 1947–53. Its cool climate and scenic setting make it one of India's most popular hill resorts.

Simmel \'zim-əl\, **Georg** (1858–1918) German sociologist and philosopher. From teaching posts at the Univs. of Berlin (1885–1914) and Strassburg (1914–18), Simmel did much to establish SOCIOLOGY as a basic social science in Germany. He sought to isolate the general forms or recurrent regularities of social interaction from the specific content of definite kinds of activity (e.g., political, economic, or aesthetic), giving special attention to the problem of authority and obedience. In *The Philosophy of Money* (1900) he stressed the role of a money economy in specializing social activity and depersonalizing individual and social relationships. See also INTERACTIONISM.

Simon \sē-'mōⁿ\, **Claude (-Eugène-Henri)** (b.1913) French writer. Captured during World War II, he escaped to join the French Resistance. His works, mixing narration and STREAM OF CONSCIOUSNESS in densely constructed prose, are representative of the *nouveau roman* ("new novel"), or French ANTINOVEL, that emerged in the 1950s. Perhaps most important is the cycle comprising *The Grass* (1958), *The Flanders Road* (1960), *The Palace* (1962), and *Histoire* (1967), with its recurring characters and events. He received the Nobel Prize in 1985.

Simon \'sī-mən\, **Herbert A(lexander)** (1916–2001) U.S. social scientist. Born in Milwaukee, he received his PhD from the Univ. of Chicago in 1943. At Carnegie-Mellon Univ. (from 1949), he taught psychology and later computer science. In *Administrative Behavior* (1947) Simon argued for recognizing multiple factors (including psychological ones) beyond the desire for maximum profits in corporate decision-making. He later tried to simulate decision-making by means of ARTIFICIAL INTELLIGENCE. He was awarded the Nobel Prize in Economics in 1978.

Simon, (Marvin) Neil (b.1927) U.S. playwright. Born in New York City, he worked as a comedy writer for Sid CAESAR in the 1950s. *Come Blow Your Horn* (1961) was the first of a long series of hit comedies, which included *Barefoot in the Park* (1963), *The Odd Couple* (1965), *Plaza Suite* (1968), *The Sunshine Boys* (1972), and *California Suite* (1976). His later plays include the autobiographical trilogy *Brighton Beach*

Memoirs (1983), *Biloxi Blues* (1985, Tony Award), and *Broadway Bound* (1986). His plays, most of which became successful films, dealt humorously with the everyday conflicts of ordinary middle-class people, often in New York. For *Lost in Yonkers* (1991), he received a Tony Award and a Pulitzer Prize. Simon also wrote the books for several musicals, including *Sweet Charity* (1966) and *Promises, Promises* (1968). He is regarded as the most successful playwright in U.S. history.

Simon, Paul (Frederic) (b.1941) U.S. pop singer and songwriter. Born in Newark, N.J., Simon began performing with Art Garfunkel (b.1941) in the 1950s. Simon and Garfunkel's first hit single was "Sounds of Silence" (1966); others over the next six years included "Mrs. Robinson" (for the film *The Graduate*) and "Bridge over Troubled Water." After the two parted company, Simon released several hit albums. His *Graceland* (1986), recorded with African musicians, became the most successful and influential album of the new genre of "world music." African and Brazilian musics informed *Rhythm of the Saints* (1990).

Simon & Schuster \'shü-stər\ U.S. publishing company. It was founded in 1924 by Richard L. Simon (1899–1960) and M. Lincoln Schuster (1897–1970), whose initial project, the original crossword-puzzle book, was a best-seller. Among their other innovations was Pocket Books, the first U.S. paperback line, launched in 1939. The company came to publish a wide variety of books. Owned by Viacom Inc. since 1994, Simon & Schuster now concentrates on fiction and nonfiction for the general reader.

Simonde de Sismondi, J.-C.-L. See J.-C.-L. Simonde de SISMONDI

Simon de Montfort See Simon de MONTFORT

simony \'si-mə-nē, 'sī-mə-nē\ Buying or selling of church offices or powers. Simony became widespread in Europe in the 9th–10th cent., as promotions to the priesthood or episcopate were bestowed by the wealthy and influential in return for money. Rigorously attacked by Pope GREGORY VII, the practice recurred in the 15th cent., but after the 16th cent. its more flagrant forms disappeared.

Simplon Pass \'sim-,plän\ Alpine pass and tunnel, S Switzerland. It is situated between the Pennine and Lepontine Alps at 6,581 ft (2,006 m). Important since the mid-13th cent., it became a major link between central and S Europe when NAPOLEON had a carriage road built there 1800–1807. An AUGUSTINIAN hospice dating from 1235 is near the summit. In winter, cars are moved by train through a 12.5-mi (20-km) tunnel connecting Switzerland and Italy.

Simpson, James Young (*later* **Sir James**) (1811–1870) Scottish obstetrician. After news of the use of ether in surgery in Boston reached Scotland, Simpson employed it to relieve labor pains (1847) and later substituted chloroform, which he continued to use despite opposition from obstetricians and the clergy. He also introduced iron-wire sutures, the use of pressure to stop bleeding, and long obstetrical forceps.

Simpson, O(renthal) J(ames) (b.1947) U.S. football player. Born in San Francisco, Simpson set rushing records at USC (1965–68), was named All-American, and won the HEISMAN TROPHY (1968). He joined the Buffalo Bills in 1969, with whom he continued to set records and became a great box-office draw. Knee injuries led to his retirement in 1979. Handsome and genial, he became a popular film and television actor, advertising spokesman, and sports commentator. In 1994 his estranged wife, Nicole Brown Simpson, and her friend Ronald Goldman were stabbed to death outside her house. Charged with the murders, Simpson became the defendant in a long televised trial that attracted unprecedented public attention. A jury acquitted him in 1995, but in a separate civil trial in 1997 he was found guilty in the wrongful-death suit brought by the Brown and Goldman families.

simulation, computer Use of a computer to represent the dynamic responses and behavior of a real or proposed system. A mathematical description of a system is developed as a computer program that uses equations to represent relationships within the system. When the program is run it forms an analog, usually represented graphically, of the behavior of the modeled system. Variables in the program can be adjusted to simulate varying conditions in the system. Computer simulations are used to study things that cannot be easily or safely tested in real life, such as weather patterns or a nuclear blast.

simultaneous equations See SYSTEM OF EQUATIONS

sin Wrongdoing, particularly the breaking of moral or religious rules. In the OLD TESTAMENT, sin is viewed as a hatred of God or defiance of his commandments. The NEW TESTAMENT regards sinfulness as the inherent state of humanity, which JESUS came into the world to heal. Christian theologians divide sin into actual and ORIGINAL SIN. Actual sin, consisting of evil acts, words, and deeds, is in turn divided into mortal sin, in which one deliberately turns away from God, and venial sin, a less serious transgression committed without full awareness of wrongdoing. In Islam, sin is a straying from God's path. In Hinduism and Buddhism, the good and evil deeds of one lifetime affect one's rebirth in the next.

Sinai \'sī-,nī\ Peninsula, NE Egypt. Located between the gulfs of SUEZ and AQABA at the N end of the Red Sea, it covers 23,500 sq mi (61,000 sq km). Its S region is mountainous and includes Mt. SINAI, while its N two-thirds is an arid plateau known as the Sinai Desert. It is famous as the route of the Israelite exodus from Egypt. Part of the Roman empire, and later of the empire's successors and the Ottoman Turks, it was turned over to Egypt at the end of World War I. It was the scene of the principal campaign of the ARAB–ISRAELI WAR (1967) and was occupied by Israel from 1967 until 1982, when it was then returned to Egypt.

Sinai, Mt. *or* **Mt. Horeb** Peak, S central SINAI, Egypt. It rises 7,497 ft (2,285 m). It is renowned as the site where MOSES received the TEN COMMANDMENTS. Sacred in the Jewish, Christian, and Islamic traditions, it is an important pilgrimage site. St. Catherine's, probably the world's oldest continuously inhabited Christian monastery, is at its N base.

Sinaloa \,sē-nä-'lō-ä\ State (pop., 2000: 2,535,000), NW Mexico. Located on the Gulf of CALIFORNIA, the 22,521-sq-mi (58,328-sq-km) territory consists of a tropical coastal plain that rises inland to the SIERRA MADRE Occidental. MAZATLÁN is on its coast. It produces wheat, cotton, tobacco, and sugarcane. Salt, graphite, manganese, and gold are mined.

Sinatra, Frank (*orig.* Francis Albert) (1915–1998) U.S. singer and actor. Born in Hoboken, N.J., Sinatra began his singing career in the mid-1930s and was discovered by Harry JAMES. He achieved sweeping national popularity in 1940–42 while singing with the Tommy DORSEY Orchestra. After 1953 he reached his peak in such albums as *In the Wee Small Hours* (1955), *Songs for Swingin' Lovers* (1956), *Come Fly with Me* (1958), and *Only the Lonely* (1958). He appeared in about 80 films; after his performance in *From Here to Eternity* (1953, Academy Award) revived his flagging career,

Frank Sinatra, 1963

he starred in such films as *The Man with the Golden Arm* (1955), *High Society* (1956), *Pal Joey* (1957), and *The Manchurian Candidate* (1962). In 1961 he founded Reprise Records. His masterly performances, alternately swinging and affectingly melancholic, brought him a success almost unparalleled in the history of American popular music.

Sinclair, Upton (Beall) (1878–1968) U.S. novelist. Born in Baltimore, in 1906 he wrote *The Jungle*, a best-selling exposé of conditions in the Chicago stockyards. A landmark among proletarian novels, it aroused great public indignation and led to passage of the U.S. Pure Food and Drug Act. Many other topical novels followed, as well as the successful Lanny Budd series of 11 contemporary historical novels, including *Dragon's Teeth* (1942, Pulitzer Prize). In the 1930s Sinclair organized a socialist movement and won the Democratic nomination for governor of California.

sine See TRIGONOMETRIC FUNCTION

sines, law of Principle of TRIGONOMETRY stating that the lengths of the sides of any triangle are proportional to the sines of the opposite angles. That is,

$$\frac{a}{\sin A} = \frac{b}{\sin B} = \frac{c}{\sin C}$$

when *a*, *b* and *c* are the sides and *A*, *B* and *C* are the opposite angles.

Singapore *officially* **Republic of Singapore** Island republic, S.E. Asia. Situated off the S tip of the MALAY PENINSULA, it includes Singapore island and 60 other islets. Area: 240 sq

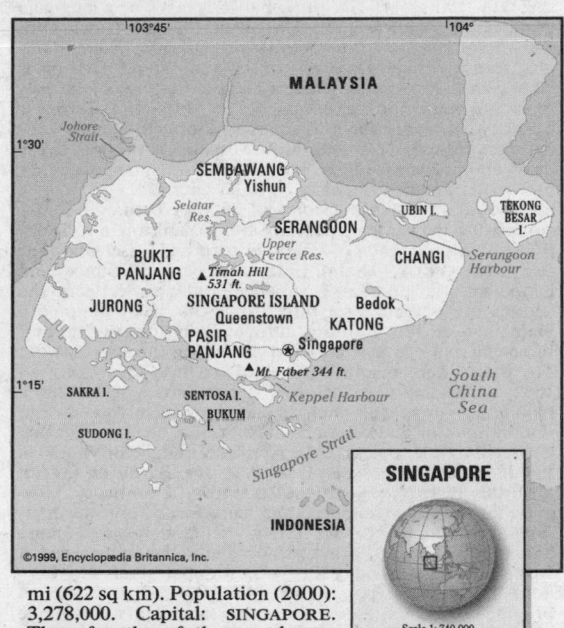

SINGAPORE
Scale 1: 740,000
0   8 mi
0   6   12 km

©1999, Encyclopædia Britannica, Inc.

mi (622 sq km). Population (2000): 3,278,000. Capital: SINGAPORE. Three-fourths of the people are Chinese; most of the rest are Malays and Indians. Languages: English, Mandarin, Malay, Tamil (all official). Religions: Buddhism, Taoism, Islam, Christianity, Hinduism. Currency: Singapore dollar. Nearly two-thirds of the island's hilly landscape lies less than 50 ft (15 m) above sea level; it has a hot, humid climate. Although only about 2% of its land is arable, it is among the most productive fruit and vegetable cropland in the world. The economy is based largely on international trade and finance. It has more than 100 commercial banks, most of which are foreign, and is the headquarters of the Asian Dollar Market. Its port is one of the largest in the world, and it is one of the world's leading petroleum refiners. It has the highest per capita income of any country in S.E. Asia. It is a republic with one legislative house; its chief of state is the president, and the head of government is the prime minister. Long inhabited by fishermen and pirates, it was an outpost of the Sumatran empire of Shrivijaya until the 14th cent., when it passed to JAVA and then Siam. It became part of the MALACCA empire in the 15th cent. In the 16th cent. the Portuguese controlled the area; they were followed by the Dutch in the 17th cent. In 1819 it was ceded to the British E. INDIA CO., becoming part of the Straits Settlements and the center of British colonial activity in S.E. Asia. The Japanese occupied the island 1942–45. In 1946 it becae a crown colony. It achieved full internal self-government in 1959, became a part of Malaysia in 1963, and became independent in 1965. It is influential in the affairs of the ASSN. OF S.E. ASIAN NATIONS. The country's dominant voice in politics for 30 years after independence was LEE KUAN YEW. Its economy was affected during the 1990s Asian economic crises, but it recovered more easily than did many of its neighbors.

Singapore City (metro. area pop., 1992 est.: 2,792,000), capital of the Republic of Singapore. It so dominates the island that the republic is often called a city-state. Known for its many parks and tree-lined streets, it offers glimpses into the cultures brought to it by immigrants from all parts of Asia. An important Malay city in the 13th cent., it was refounded by Stamford RAFFLES of the British E. INDIA CO. in 1819. It developed as a port and naval base, and today is one of the world's great commercial centers. Its thriving banking, insurance, and brokerage firms make it the chief trading and financial center of S.E. Asia. It is home to the National Univ. of Singapore (1980).

Singer, Isaac Bashevis *Yiddish* Yitskhok Bashevis Zinger (1904–1991) Polish-U.S. writer. After publishing his first novel, *Satan in Goray* (1932), he emigrated to the U.S. in 1935. Though he wrote mostly in Yiddish, he personally supervised the English translations of his work. Depicting Jewish life in Poland and the U.S., his works are a rich blend of irony, wit, and wisdom, flavored distinctively with the occult and the grotesque. His works include the novels *The Family Moskat* (1950), *The Magician of Lublin* (1960), and *Enemies: A Love Story* (1972; film, 1989), and the story collections *Gimpel the Fool* (1957), *The Spinoza of Market Street* (1961), and *A Crown of Feathers* (1973). He was awarded the Nobel Prize in 1978.

Singer, Isaac Merritt (1811–1875) U.S. inventor and manufacturer. Born in Pittstown, N.Y., he patented a rock-drilling machine (1839) and a metal- and wood-carving machine (1849) before producing an improved version of Elias HOWE's SEWING MACHINE in 1851 and soon thereafter founding I. M. Singer & Co. to manufacture it. Howe's successful patent-infringement suit against him in 1854 did not prevent Singer's company from becoming the world's largest sewing-machine producer. He also pioneered the use of installment credit plans.

single tax Tax on land values intended as the sole source of government revenues. Proposed by Henry GEORGE in *Progress and Poverty* (1879), the plan gained considerable support in subsequent decades but was never implemented. Advocates argued that since land is a fixed resource, the income it yields is a product of the economy's growth and not individual effort, so it can fairly be taxed to support the government. Critics protested that the single tax would take no account of an individual's actual ability to pay.

Sinhalese \ˌsin-gə-ˈlēz\ Largest ethnic group of Sri Lanka, numbering over 12 million. Their ancestors are believed to have come from N India. Most Sinhalese are agriculturalists and most adhere to THERAVADA Buddhism. Like other peoples of Sri Lanka, the Sinhalese have a caste society with a complex structure based largely on occupation.

Sinitic languages See CHINESE LANGUAGES

sinkhole *or* **sink** *or* **doline** \də-ˈlē-nə\ Depression formed as underlying LIMESTONE bedrock is dissolved by GROUNDWATER. Sinkholes vary greatly in area and depth and may be very large. Those caused by the collapse of a cavern roof generally have steep rock sides and may receive streams that then flow underground. Those caused by the gradual dissolving of rock under a soil mantle are generally shallower; they may become clogged with clay and hold a small lake.

Sinn Féin \ˈshin-ˈfān\ (Irish: "We Alone") Nationalist political party in Ireland. It was founded by Arthur GRIFFITH and others in 1902, and its policy involved passive resistance to the British. After the EASTER RISING, the demand of its leader Eamon DE VALERA for a united, republican Ireland won the party 73 out of 105 seats in the 1918 election. Its power diminished after 1926, when de Valera founded FIANNA FÁIL, which absorbed most of Sinn Féin's membership. Now the political arm of the IRISH REPUBLICAN ARMY, it actively supports Irish unification; under Gerry ADAMS, it has participated in the peace talks on Northern Ireland.

Sino–French War (1883–85) Conflict between China and France over Vietnam. In 1880, when France began to extend its presence in Vietnam northward, China sent troops and engaged in limited battles. The governor-general, LI HONGZHANG, negotiated an agreement whereby N. Vietnam would be a joint protectorate, but a faction in China

rejected it. The French defeated Chinese reinforcements in 1883, and the new settlement was more strongly in France's favor. This too was rejected in China; further hostilities resulted in its fleet of 11 steamers being destroyed. In 1885 China signed a peace treaty accepting the settlement of 1883.

Sino–Japanese War (1894–95) Conflict between China and Japan over Korea. Though Korea had long been China's most important client state, Japan became interested in it for its natural resources and its strategic location. Tensions between radical, pro-Japanese Koreans, who favored modernization, and conservative Korean government officials supported by China brought China and Japan into conflict (see TONGHAK UPRISING). Foreign observers predicted an easy victory for the more massive Chinese forces, but Japan scored overwhelming victories on both land and sea. In the peace treaty, China recognized the independence of Korea and ceded Taiwan and its nearby islands to Japan. China's resistance to Japan's aggression in Chinese territory from 1937 to 1945 is also referred to as the Sino–Japanese War (see MANCHUGUO, NANJING MASSACRE).

Sino-Tibetan languages \ˌsī-nō-tə-ˈbe-tən\ Superfamily of languages whose two branches are the Sinitic or CHINESE LANGUAGES and the Tibeto-Burman family, a group of several hundred very diverse languages spoken by about 65 million people from N Pakistan east to Vietnam, and from the Tibetan plateau south to the Malay Peninsula. W Tibeto-Burman languages include TIBETAN and Nepal's Bodish and Himalayan languages. Tibeto-Burman languages of NE India include the Bodo-Garo languages (spoken in ASSAM) and the N Naga languages of Nagaland. Central Tibeto-Burman languages are spoken mainly in Arunachal Pradesh in India and in adjacent parts of China and Myanmar. NE Tibeto-Burman consists of languages spoken in W Sichuan and NW Yunnan in China. The Burmese-Lolo subgroup includes Burmese, the national language of Myanmar (Burma), and the Loloish languages, spread over Yunnan and other parts of S.E. Asia. Karen, spoken by the Karen of Myanmar and Thailand, forms a distinct subgroup. Tibetan and Burmese are the only Tibeto-Burman languages with long literary traditions. Burmese is written in an adaptation of the Mon script (see MON-KHMER LANGUAGES).

sinus Body cavity or hollow. The paranasal sinuses (known commonly simply as the sinuses), are the four sets of cavities in the bones adjoining the NOSE: maxillary, between the eye socket and the PALATE and upper jaw; frontal, just above and between the eye sockets; ethmoidal, consisting of 3–18 thin-walled cavities between the nasal cavities and the eye sockets; and sphenoidal, behind the nasal cavity. All are absent or small at birth, enlarge gradually until puberty, and then grow rapidly. They affect the sound of the voice and may help to warm inhaled air. Their lining produces mucus, which drains into the nasal cavity. Blockage of their outlets by swelling (from allergy or infection; see SINUSITIS) or POLYPS hampers breathing through the nose and can lead to serious infection. Severe obstruction may require surgery.

Sinus The paranasal sinuses.

sinusitis \ˌsī-nə-ˈsī-təs\ INFLAMMATION of the SINUSES. Acute sinusitis, usually due to infections such as the common COLD, causes pain and tenderness, nasal obstruction and discharge, and malaise. Nose drops or inhalations containing drugs that contract blood vessels help drain the sinuses. Antibiotics may be used for bacterial infections. Chronic sinusitis involves frequent colds, pus, obstructed breathing, loss of sense of smell, and sometimes headache. If antibiotics or repeated rinsing out do not help, surgery may be needed.

Siouan languages \ˈsü-ən\ Family of N. American Indian languages, located mainly west of the Mississippi River in the 17th–18th cent. The principal languages and language groups were Winnebago in Wisconsin, Chiwere (Iowa, Oto, and Missouri) in Iowa and N Missouri, Dhegiha (Ponca, Omaha, Kansa, Osage, Quapaw) in an area extending from E Nebraska to Arkansas, Sioux or Dakota (a range of dialects including Santee or Dakota proper in Minnesota, Teton or Lakota in N. and S. Dakota, and Assiniboine in Canada), Hidatsa and Mandan on the middle Missouri River, and Crow in Wyoming and Montana. The extant Siouan languages are now spoken mainly or solely by older adults.

Sioux \ˈsü\ or **Dakota** Group of PLAINS INDIAN peoples comprising the Santee (Eastern Sioux), Yankton, and Teton (Western Sioux), each of which in turn had lesser divisions (e.g., BLACKFOOT, Oglala). In the 17th cent. the Sioux lived in the area around Lake Superior, but attacks from the OJIBWA drove them west into Minnesota. They adopted a Plains way of life, hunting buffalo, living in TEPEES, emphasizing valor in warfare, and practicing the SUN DANCE. The Sioux were resolute in resisting white incursions. In 1862, white treaty violations led the Santee to mount a bloody uprising; after their defeat, they were forced onto reservations in S. Dakota and Nebraska. Serious fighting between U.S. troops and the Yankton and Teton Sioux in the 1860s and 1870s culminated in the Battle of LITTLE BIGHORN in 1876, a great Indian victory. Eventually, however, the Sioux surrendered and were forced onto reservations. In 1890 the GHOST DANCE religion inspired many Sioux to take up arms, leading to the massacre at WOUNDED KNEE. Today the Sioux number about 75,000.

Sioux Falls City (pop., 2000: 124,000), SE S. Dakota. Founded in 1857 and now the state's largest city, it has one of the largest livestock markets in the U.S. and is home to the Earth Resource Observation Systems (EROS) Data Center. Nearby is one of the world's first commercial nuclear power plants.

Sippar \si-ˈpär\ Ancient city, BABYLONIA, southwest of present-day BAGHDAD on the EUPHRATES RIVER. From the 3rd millennium B.C. it was a center of worship of the Sumerian sun-god Shamash. It was subject to the 1st dynasty of Babylon and was sacked by the Elamites in 1174 B.C. It recovered and was later captured by the Assyrians. Excavations have uncovered parts of a large temple and thousands of clay tablets.

Siqueiros \sē-ˈkā-rōs\, **David Alfaro** (1896–1975) Mexican painter. A Marxist activist from his youth, he fought in the Mexican Revolution. After studies in Europe, he returned to Mexico (1922) and began his lifework of decorating public buildings with murals and organizing unions of artists and workers. With Diego RIVERA and J. C. OROZCO, he cofounded the renowned school of Mexican mural painting. His murals are marked by great dynamism, monumental size and vigor, and a limited color range subordinated to dramatic effects of light and shadow. His easel paintings (e.g., *Echo of a Scream*, 1937) helped establish his international reputation.

Siracusa See SYRACUSE

siren In GREEK MYTHOLOGY, a creature, half bird and half woman, who lures sailors to their doom with her sweet singing. HOMER placed sirens near the rocks of Scylla; in the *Odyssey*, Odysseus has his men plug their ears with wax and has himself tied to his ship's mast in order to hear their singing without endangering the ship. In one tale of JASON and the ARGONAUTS, ORPHEUS sings so sweetly that the crew do not listen to the sirens.

Sirius \ˈsir-ē-əs\ or **Dog Star** Brightest star in the night sky (apparent MAGNITUDE −1.5), a BINARY STAR about 8.6

light-years away in the constellation Canis Major. The bright component is a blue-white star 23 times as luminous as the sun; its companion was the first known WHITE DWARF STAR. The ancient Egyptians used its predawn rising to predict the Nile's annual flooding. The ancient Romans associated the Dog Star's rising at dawn with the hottest part of the year, called the "dog days."

sirocco *or* **scirocco** \sə-'rä-kō, shi-'rä-kō\ Warm, humid wind over the Mediterranean Sea and S Europe, where it blows from the south or southeast and brings rain and fog. Produced by low-pressure centers, it originates over N. Africa as a dry wind and picks up moisture as it crosses the Mediterranean.

sisal \'sī-səl\ Plant (*Agave sisalana*) of the AGAVE FAMILY, and the fiber from its leaves. The fiber is made into ropes and twine, as well as into matting, rugs, hats, and brushes. Growing to a height of about 3 ft (1 m) and a diameter of about 15 in. (38 cm), the stalk bears fleshy, rigid, gray to dark-green, lance-shaped leaves in a dense rosette. Tanzania and Brazil are the main producers.

Sisley \'siz-lē, sēs-'lā\, **Alfred** (1839–1899) British-French landscape painter. Born in Paris of English parents, he began painting as an amateur. His early style was much influenced by Camille COROT. He became associated with Claude MONET and Auguste RENOIR, and with them became one of the founders of IMPRESSIONISM. His works are distinguished from those of his colleagues by their softly harmonious values. His life was a constant struggle against poverty; not until after his death did his talent begin to be widely recognized.

Sismondi \sēs-mōⁿ-'dē, *Engl* sis-'män-dē\, **J(ean-) C(harles-) L(éonard) Simonde de** (1773–1842) Swiss economist and historian. His *History of the Italian Republics in the Middle Ages* (1809–18) inspired the leaders of the RISORGIMENTO. In his influential *New Principles of Political Economy* (1819), he criticized capitalism and argued for regulation of economic competition and for a balance between production and consumption. He urged social reforms to improve working-class living conditions. His theories influenced such later economists as Karl MARX and J. M. KEYNES.

Sissle, Noble See Eubie BLAKE

Sistan *or* **Seistan** \sē-'stän\ Extensive border region, E Iran and SW Afghanistan. It comprises a large marshland depression with a true desert climate. It is the reputed homeland of the legendary Kayanian dynasty of Persia and played an important part in Persian history, especially under the SAFAVIDS (1502–1736). In the 19th cent. it was the center of a dispute between Persia and Afghanistan that led to the modern delimitation of their frontier.

Sistine Chapel \'sis-,tēn\ Papal chapel in the VATICAN PALACE, Rome. Constructed 1473–81 by Giovanni dei Dolci for Pope SIXTUS IV (for whom it is named), it is the site of the principal papal ceremonies. Its exterior is drab and unadorned, but its interior walls and ceiling are decorated with frescoes by Florentine Renaissance masters, including PERUGINO, PINTURICCHIO, Sandro BOTTICELLI, Domenico GHIRLANDAIO, and Luca SIGNORELLI. The most important works are the magnificent frescoes by MICHELANGELO on the ceiling and the W wall behind the altar. The ceiling frescoes, depicting Old Testament scenes, were commissioned by Pope JULIUS II and painted 1508–12; the *Last Judgment* fresco on the W wall was painted 1536–41 for Pope Paul III. A controversial 10-year cleaning and restoration of the ceiling was completed in 1989, and of the W wall in 1994.

Sisyphus \'si-sə-fəs\ In GREEK MYTHOLOGY, the king of Corinth who was punished in Hades by having to roll a huge stone up a hill over and over again. When Death came to fetch him, Sisyphus had him chained up so that no one died until ARES came to free Death. Before being taken to the underworld, Sisyphus asked his wife to leave his body unburied. When he reached Hades he was permitted to go back to earth to punish his wife, and he lived to a ripe old age before dying a second time. These actions were the reason for his punishment.

SI system See INTERNATIONAL SYSTEM OF UNITS

Sita \'sē-,tä\ In Hindu mythology, the consort of RAMA. Rama won her as his bride by bending SHIVA's bow. Her abduction by the demon king RAVANA and subsequent rescue are described in the *RAMAYANA*. She kept herself chaste during her long imprisonment, and on her return she proved her purity by undergoing an ordeal by fire. She is one of the most revered figures in the Hindu pantheon.

sitar \si-'tär, 'si-,tär\ Long-necked STRINGED INSTRUMENT of N India, the dominant instrument in Hindustani music. It is often played with the tamboura (drone-lute) and tabla (small drums). It has a deep pear-shaped gourd body, a wide neck, and movable frets. It normally has four or five melody strings, which are plucked with a plectrum; several drone strings; and numerous sympathetic strings (caused to vibrate by the other strings' vibrations). A gourd resonator is attached to the top of the neck.

Sitting Bull (1831?–1890) Teton SIOUX chief under whom the Sioux peoples united in their struggle for survival. Frequent skirmishes between the U.S. Army and Sitting Bull's warriors occurred in 1863–68, at the end of which the Sioux agreed to accept a reservation in SW S. Dakota. When gold was discovered in the Black Hills in the mid-1870s, further outbreaks occurred. At the Battle of the Rosebud, troops under Gen. George Crook were forced to retreat; and at the Battle of LITTLE BIGHORN, Col. G. A. CUSTER and his men were killed. In 1877 Sitting Bull led his followers into Canada, but, with the buffalo reduced to near-extinction, starvation eventually drove the Sioux to surrender. From 1883 Sitting Bull lived on Indian Agency lands. During the GHOST DANCE movement, he was arrested; he was killed when his warriors tried to rescue him.

Sitwell family British family of writers. Edith Sitwell (1887–1964) attracted attention when she joined her brothers in a revolt against GEORGIAN POETRY. Her early work, which emphasizes the value of sound, includes *Façade* (1923), set to music by William WALTON. Beginning with *Gold Coast Customs* (1929), her style became less artificial and experimental, and during World War II she emerged as a poet of some emotional depth. Her later poetry is informed by religious symbolism. She was famous for her formidable personality, Elizabethan dress, and eccentric opinions. Her brother Osbert (1892–1969) became famous, with his siblings, as a tilter at establishment windmills in literature and the arts. His memoirs, including *Left Hand! Right Hand!* (1944) and *Noble Essences* (1950), create with conscious nostalgia the portrait of a vanished aristocratic age. Their brother Sacheverell (1897–1988) is best known for his books on art, architecture, and travel. His *Southern Baroque Art* (1924) was the forerunner of much academic research.

Siva See SHIVA

Six \'sēs\, **Les** (French: "The Six") Group of young French composers in the 1920s. Named by the critic Henri Collet (1885–1951), the composers were Arthur HONEGGER, Darius MILHAUD, Francis POULENC, Georges Auric (1899–1983), Louis Durey (1888–1979), and Germaine Tailleferre (1892–1983). Most of its members were attracted by the iconoclastic music of Erik SATIE, and they benefited from the promotion of Jean COCTEAU.

Six-Day War *or* **Arab–Israeli War of 1967** War between Israel and its Arab neighbors. It was precipitated by Pres. G. A. NASSER of Egypt, who demanded withdrawal of U.N. peacekeeping forces from the SINAI Peninsula and then began massing troops there. Convinced that a joint Arab attack was imminent, Israel launched a preemptive strike on June 5 that destroyed the Egyptian air force on the ground and captured the Sinai and the GAZA STRIP, the WEST BANK of the Jordan River and the Old City of Jerusalem, and the GOLAN HEIGHTS. See also ARAB–ISRAELI WARS.

Six Dynasties (A.D. 220–589) In China, the period between the end of the HAN DYNASTY and the foundation of the SUI. The name is derived from the six successive dynasties that had their capital at NANJING: the Wu (222–80), Eastern JIN (317–420), Liusong (420–79), Southern Qi (479–502), Southern Liang (502–57), and Southern Chen (557–89). During this period N China was ruled by a succession of kingdoms; most important was that of the NORTHERN WEI DYNASTY. Despite the chaos of the age, great advances were made in medicine, astronomy, botany, and chemistry. Buddhism and Taoism became great popular religions, and the translation of Buddhist texts focused Chinese attention on literature, calligraphy, and painting.

S

Sixtus IV *orig.* Francesco della Rovere (1414–1484) Pope (1471–84). A Franciscan from Genoa, he enriched his family and the Papal States through SIMONY and heavy taxation. He failed in his effort to unite the Russian and Roman churches. He endorsed the unsuccessful Pazzi conspiracy to overthrow Lorenzo de' MEDICI. He also incited Venice to attack Ferrara, then, in a turnabout, placed Venice under interdict (1483) as a rival to the Papal States. A patron of arts and letters, he built the SISTINE CHAPEL, which takes its name from him.

Sixtus V *orig.* Felice Peretti (1520–1590) Pope (1585–90). Elected pope at a time when the Papal States were in chaos, he restored order using harsh measures. He raised vast sums and carried out an extensive building program in Rome. He defined the Sacred College of CARDINALS (1586), reformed the ROMAN CURIA (1588), and became a founder of the COUNTER-REFORMATION. His foreign policy was aimed at combatting Protestantism; he excommunicated the Protestant Henry of Navarre (later HENRY IV of France) and promised subsidies in return for a Spanish invasion of England.

Sjaelland \'she-ˌlän\ *English* **Zealand** Largest and most populous island (pop., 1989 est.: 1,972,000), of Denmark, between the KATTEGAT and the BALTIC SEA. It covers 2,715 sq mi (7,031 sq km); COPENHAGEN is its major city. It has many Stone Age and Viking relics, including the Viking fortress of Trælleborg (c.1000), as well as medieval churches, castles, and manor houses.

Sjöström \'shœ-strœm\, **Victor** *or* **Victor Seastrom** (1879–1960) Swedish film actor and director. Trained as a stage actor, he directed and starred in his first movie, *The Gardener,* in 1912. With such notable films as *Ingeborg Holm* (1913), *The Outlaw and His Wife* (1918), and *The Phantom Carriage* (1921), he established the artistic excellence of the Swedish silent film. In Hollywood he directed movies such as *The Scarlet Letter* (1926) and *The Wind* (1928). He returned to Sweden in 1930 and acted in numerous films, notably Ingmar BERGMAN's *Wild Strawberries* (1957).

skaldic poetry \'skól-dik\ Oral court poetry originating in Norway but developed chiefly by Icelandic poets (skalds) from the 9th to the 13th cent. It was contemporary with Eddic poetry (see EDDA), but differed from it in meter, diction, and style. Skalds were identified by name. Their poems were descriptive, occasional, and subjective, their meters strictly syllabic, and their language ornamented with similes and metaphors. Formal subjects were the mythical stories engraved on shields, praise of kings, epitaphs, and genealogies.

Skanderbeg \'skän-dər-ˌbeg\ *orig.* George Kastrioti (1405–1468) Albanian leader and national hero. Son of a prince, he was given early as a hostage to the Turkish sultan. He served in the Turkish army and was given the name Iskander and the rank of bey. In 1444 he joined his Albanian countrymen against the Turks; organizing a league of Albanian princes, he was elected commander in chief. From 1444 to 1466 he repulsed 13 Turkish invasions; his defeat of Murad II's armies in 1450 made him a hero in the Western world. After his death, however, Albania soon became part of the Ottoman empire.

skandha \'skən-də\ In BUDDHISM, the five elements that constitute an individual's mental and physical existence. They are *rupa* (physical matter), *vedana* (feeling), *sanna* (perception), *sankharas* (mental formations), and *vinnana* (consciousness). At death the four mental skandhas dissociate from the *rupa* and find a new physical base, resulting in a new birth.

Skara Brae \'skä-rä-'brä\ One of the most perfectly preserved STONE AGE villages in Europe, built around 2000–1500 B.C., on Scotland's Orkney Islands. Its excavation began in the 1860s. Huts were of undressed, mortarless stone slabs, with stone furniture. They were linked by paved alleys; some had been covered by banking them with mixed sand, peat ash, and refuse, becoming stone-roofed tunnels. A sewer drained the whole. Inhabitants lived on the flesh and milk of their cattle and on shellfish; they probably wore skins. For tools they used local stone, beach pebbles, and animal bones. Pottery vessels show incised and relief designs, including the only example of a true spiral known from prehistoric Britain.

skate Any of nine genera (suborder Rajoidea) of rounded to diamond-shaped RAYS. These bottom-dwellers are found from tropical to near-Arctic waters and from the shallows to depths of more than 9,000 ft (2,700 m). Most have spines on the upper surface, and some have weak electrical organs in their long, slender tails. Skates lay oblong, leathery eggs. Species vary from 20 in. (50 cm) to 8 ft (2.5 m) long. They swim with an undulating movement of their pectoral fins. They trap active prey by dropping down on them from above.

skateboarding Form of recreation in which a person rides standing balanced on a small board mounted on wheels. The skateboard first appeared in the early 1960s on paved areas along California beaches as a makeshift diversion for surfers when the ocean was flat. Skateboard parks now provide a variety of slopes and banked surfaces for sudden turns and flamboyant stunts. The skateboarding craze contributed to the emergence of SNOWBOARDING.

skating Sport in which bladelike runners or sets of wheels attached to shoes are used for gliding on ice or on surfaces other than ice. See FIGURE SKATING, ICE HOCKEY, ROLLER-SKATING, SPEED SKATING.

skeet shooting Sport in which marksmen use shotguns to shoot at clay targets (pigeons) hurled into the air by spring devices called traps. It differs from trapshooting in that skeet traps are set at two points on the field and targets may be thrown diagonally across the shooter's field of vision. Skeet shooting has been an Olympic event since 1968.

skeleton Bony framework of the body. It includes the SKULL, VERTEBRAL COLUMN, collarbone, shoulder blades, rib cage, and PELVIC GIRDLE and the BONES of the hands, arms, feet, and legs. The skeleton supports the body and protects its internal organs. It is held together by LIGAMENTS and moved at the JOINTS by the MUSCLES, which are attached to it. See also CARTILAGE. See diagram on following page.

skeleton dance See DANCE OF DEATH

Skelton, John (c.1460–1529) English poet. Appointed court poet to Henry VII in 1489, Skelton became a tutor and eventually an adviser to Henry VIII. In 1498 he took holy orders. He wrote political and religious satires in an individual poetic style of short rhyming lines, called Skeltonics. Among his poems are *Bowge of Courte,* satirizing life at court, and *Phyllyp Sparowe,* lampooning the liturgical office for the dead. He wrote the first secular MORALITY PLAY in English, *Magnyfycence* (1516), followed by three political satires directed against Cardinal WOLSEY and humanist learning.

skepticism Philosophical attitude of doubting knowledge claims. Since ancient times, skeptics have challenged accepted views in science, morals, and religion. Pyrrhon of Elis (c.360–272 B.C.) sought mental peace by avoiding commitment to any particular view; from the 1st cent. B.C., Pyrrhonism's proponents sought to achieve suspension of judgment by systematically opposing various kinds of knowledge claims. One of its later leaders was Sextus Empiricus (2nd or 3rd cent. B.C.). Prominent among modern skeptical philosophers are Michel de MONTAIGNE, Pierre BAYLE, and David HUME.

skiing Sport involving moving over snow on a pair of long flat runners (skis) attached to shoes or boots. Skiing was born in Scandinavia; the oldest skis, found in Swedish and Finnish bogs, are 4,000–5,000 years old. The earliest skis were often short and broad. Skiing had reached N China by the 7th cent. A.D. Used in warfare in Scandinavia from the 13th cent. or earlier, skis have continued to be used for transport and travel to the present day. The earliest mode of skiing developed into the sport now called CROSS-COUNTRY SKIING. Competitive cross-country skiing began in Norway in the 1840s. Improvements on primitive bindings around 1860 led to far wider recreational skiing. SKI-JUMPING competitions date from the 1870s. Downhill skiing was limited (in the absence of mountain railways or cable cars) by the need to climb the hill after skiing down; the building of ski lifts began in the 1930s. Skis were originally made of wood, usually hickory, but no wood has been used in downhill skis for many decades. The business of skiing began its serious growth in the 1930s and became

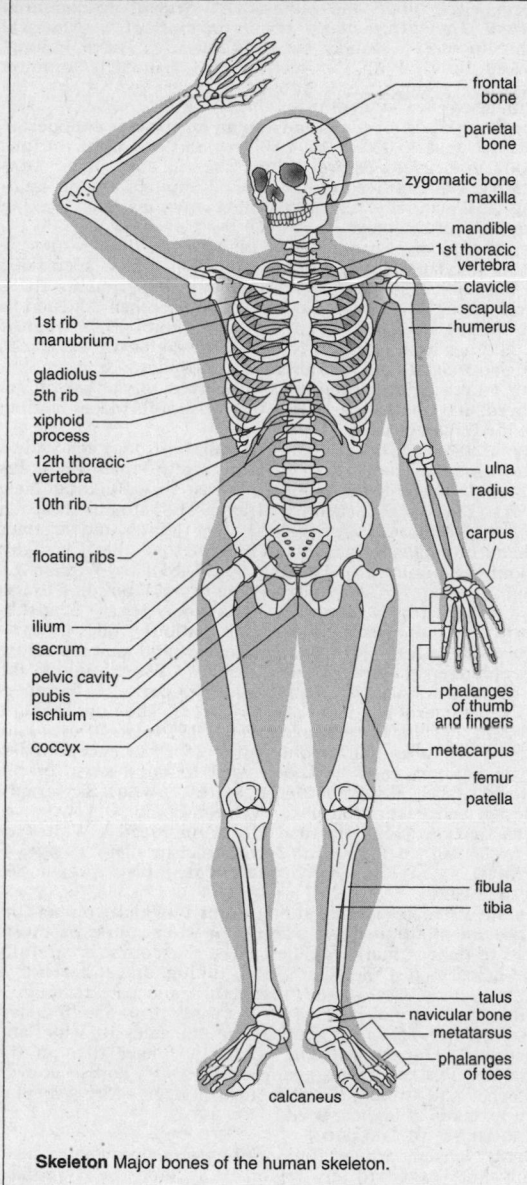

Skeleton Major bones of the human skeleton.

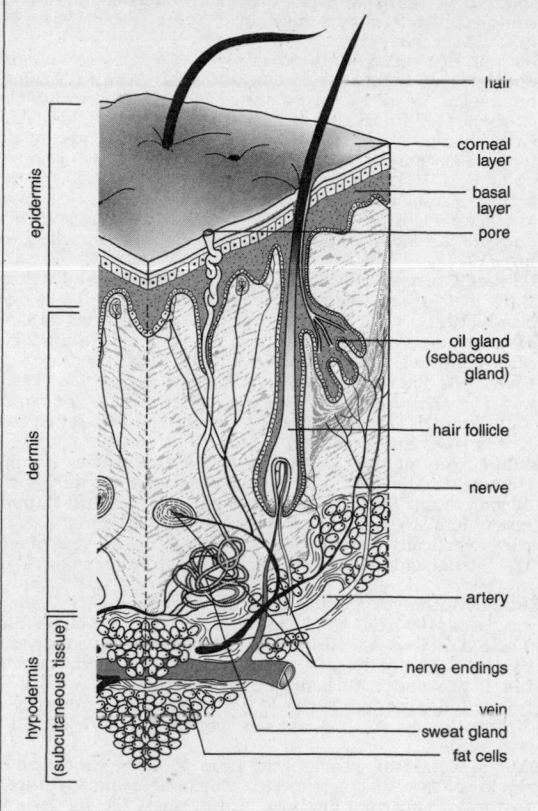

Skin A section through the skin. The tough, dead cells of the outer epidermal surface (corneal layer) serve as a physical barrier and are continually replaced by cells produced in the basal layer. The thick supportive layer of dermis contains nerve endings, blood vessels, sweat glands, hair follicles, and oil glands. The hair follicle encloses the root of the hair. Oil glands associated with hair follicles secrete an oily substance (sebum) which lubricates the skin surface. The watery secretions of the tubular sweat glands are released onto the skin's surface through small pores. A layer of fat cells lies below the dermis.

explosive in the 1950s and '60s; huge resorts now dot the Alps and the Rocky Mtns.

ski jumping Skiing event in which contestants ski down a steep ramp curved upward at the end and launch themselves into the air for distance. Using a crouch position, skiers can achieve ramp speeds of 75 mi (120 km) per hour. After takeoff, they lean far forward from the ankles with skis held open to form a V, minimizing wind resistance and maximizing lift. Scoring is based partly on distance and partly on form.

skin Surface covering of the body that protects it and receives external sensory stimuli, consisting of an epidermis over a thicker dermis. The epidermis contains cells involved in immune defenses, sensory receptors, pigment cells, and KERATIN-producing cells. The last harden and migrate to the surface to form a dead, relatively dry outer layer of tissue that constantly sloughs away. The dermis contains sensory nerves and blood vessels within CONNECTIVE TISSUE. COLLAGEN and elastin fibers give skin its tough, elastic quality. Certain cells take part in immune responses. A FAT layer under the dermis provides nutritional storage, cushioning, and insulation. Skin disorders range from DERMATITIS and ACNE to SKIN CANCER. Changes in color (e.g., JAUNDICE) or texture may be clues to systemic disorders. See also DERMATOLOGY, HAIR, NAIL, PERSPIRATION, SEBACEOUS GLAND, SWEAT GLAND.

skin cancer Malignant tumor of the SKIN, including some of the most common cancers. Light-skinned people have the highest risk but can reduce it by limiting exposure to sunlight. The most common types arise in the epidermis and have become more frequent with the thinning of the atmosphere's OZONE LAYER. The most serious is MELANOMA, which is frequently fatal if not treated early with surgery. Cancers arising from the dermis are rare; the best known is KAPOSI'S SARCOMA.

skink Any of about 1,275 species (family Scincidae) of LIZARDS found throughout the tropics and in temperate regions of N. America. Skinks have a cylindrical body, a conical head, and a long, tapering tail. Some species are 26 in. (66 cm) long, but most are under 8 in. (20 cm). Some have

S

small or no limbs. Most are ground-dwellers or burrowers; some are arboreal or semiaquatic. Some species lay eggs; others bear live young.

Skinner, B(urrhus) F(rederic) (1904–1990) U.S. psychologist and influential theorist of BEHAVIORISM. Born in Susquehanna, Pa., he first achieved notice with *The Behavior of Organisms* (1938). In the mid-1940s he presented his "Air-Crib," a soundproof, germ-free, air-conditioned box meant to serve as an optimal environment for the first two years of childhood. In the controversial *Walden Two* (1948), he described a utopia based on behavioral engineering. He taught at Harvard Univ. 1948–74. His other works include *Science and Human Behavior* (1953) and *Beyond Freedom and Dignity* (1971).

Skinner, Cornelia Otis (1901–1979) U.S. actress and writer. Born in Chicago, she made her stage debut in *Blood and Sand* (1921) with her actor-father, Otis Skinner (1858–1942). In the 1930s she wrote and staged her own monodramas, including *The Wives of Henry VIII* and *The Loves of Charles II*. She won acclaim in such plays as *Candida* (1939) and *The Pleasure of His Company* (1958), which she wrote with Samuel Taylor. She also cowrote the best-seller *Our Hearts Were Young and Gay* (1942).

skipper Any of some 3,000 LEPIDOPTERAN species (family Hesperiidae) named for their fast (up to 20 mph, or 30 kph), darting flight. The head and stout body of the adult skipper resemble a MOTH's, but most skippers hold the first pair of wings vertically at rest, as BUTTERFLIES do. Most skippers are diurnal and lack the wing-coupling structures typical of moths.

Skopje \'skôp-ye\ *Serbian* **Skoplje** \'skôp-lye\ City (metro. area pop., 1994: 541,000), capital of Republic of Macedonia. The old city is located on a terraced riverbank dominated by an ancient fortress. Skopje was a capital of medieval Serbia. It was under Turkish rule 1392–1913, then was incorporated into modern Serbia. After an earthquake destroyed 80% of the city in 1963, aid was sent by 78 countries and it was rebuilt.

skull Skeletal framework of the head. With the exception of the lower JAW, its bones meet in immovable joints (sutures) to form a unit that encloses and protects the BRAIN and SENSE organs and gives shape to the face. The cranium, the upper part enclosing the brain, is globular and relatively large compared to the facial portion. Its base has an opening through which the SPINAL CORD connects to the brain. The skull sits on the top vertebra (atlas).

Skull Front and side views of the human skull.

skunk Any of several black-and-white New World species in the CARNIVORE family Mustelidae that eject an odoriferous liquid (as far as 12 ft, or 3.7 m) when threatened. The liquid becomes a fine mist which causes tearing of the eyes and choking. Most are 18–37 in. (46–93 cm) long, including the bushy tail, and weigh 2–13 lbs (1–6 kg); the spotted skunks (genus *Spilogale*) are much smaller. Skunks eat rodents, in-

sects, eggs, birds, and plants. The striped, or common, skunk *(Mephitis mephitis)* occurs in most of N. America. The hog-nosed skunks (genus *Conepatus*) have a long, naked snout. With the scent glands removed, common skunks are sometimes kept as pets.

skunk bear See WOLVERINE

skydiving Sport of jumping from an airplane at a moderate altitude (e.g., 6,000 ft, or 1,800 m) and executing various body maneuvers before pulling the rip cord of a PARACHUTE. Competitive events include jumping for style, landing with accuracy, and performing in teams (e.g., making free-fall formations).

Skylab U.S. space program that launched its first SPACE STATION (Skylab) into earth orbit in 1973. Three successive teams of astronauts did research and experiments there over the next 171 days. Skylab's orbit was then adjusted to an altitude meant to keep it in space until 1983, when it would again be adjusted for use with the SPACE SHUTTLE. High SUNSPOT activity increased atmospheric drag on Skylab, and the shuttle program was delayed. Skylab's orbit decayed, and it fell to earth in 1979, most of its pieces landing in the Indian Ocean.

skyscraper Very tall multistoried building, today generally a HIGH-RISE of more than 40–50 stories. James Bogardus (1800–1874) built the pioneering Cast Iron Building, New York (1848), with a rigid iron frame. The refinement of the BESSEMER PROCESS for making steel (lighter and stronger than iron) made extremely tall buildings possible. Chicago's Home Insurance Co. Building (1884–85), by William Le Baron Jenney (1832–1907), was the first tall building to use a steel skeleton. Structurally, skyscrapers consist of a substructure supported by a deep foundation of piles or CAISSONS beneath the ground, an aboveground superstructure of columns and girders, and a CURTAIN WALL hung on the structural framework. Tube structures permit skyscrapers to resist lateral wind and seismic forces. The bundled-tube system, developed by Fazlur Khan (1928–1982), uses narrow steel tubes clustered together to form exceptionally rigid columns, and has been used to build some of the world's tallest skyscrapers (e.g., SEARS TOWER). Skyscraper design and decoration have evolved: Louis SULLIVAN emphasized verticality; the firm of McKim, Mead & White (see Charles MCKIM) stressed Neoclassicism. The INTERNATIONAL STYLE was ideally suited to skyscraper design. See also SETBACK.

slalom \'slä-ləm\ Alpine skiing event in which competitors race one at a time down a zigzag or wavy course past a series of flags or markers called gates. The course is carefully designed to test the skier's skill, timing, and judgment. A skier who misses a gate must return and pass through it from the proper side. Men's events use 55–75 gates, women's 45–65. In the giant slalom, the gates are wider and set farther apart, and the course is longer than in the slalom. The supergiant slalom ("super-G") course is even steeper and straighter and features longer, more sweeping turns taken at higher speed.

slander See DEFAMATION

slang Nonstandard vocabulary of extreme informality, usually not limited to any region. It includes newly coined words, shortened forms, and standard words used playfully out of their usual context. Slang is drawn from the vocabularies of limited groups: cant, the words or expressions coined or adopted by an age, ethnic, occupational, or other group (e.g., college students, jazz musicians); jargon, the shoptalk or technical terminology specific to an occupation; and argot, the secret cant and jargon used by thieves or other criminals. Slang often serves as a testing ground for new words. Some prove useful enough to become accepted as standard. For example, *blizzard, okay,* and *gas* have become standard, while *conbobberation* ("disturbance") and *tomato* ("girl") have been discarded. Some words and expressions have a lasting place in slang; for instance, *beat it* ("go away"), first used in the 16th cent., has neither become standard English nor vanished.

slapstick Comedy characterized by broad humor, absurd situations, and vigorous, often violent action. It took its name from a paddlelike device, probably introduced by 16th-cent. COMMEDIA DELL'ARTE troupes, that produced a resounding whack when one comic actor used it to strike another. Slapstick comedy became popular in music halls and vaudeville theaters and was carried into films by Charlie CHAPLIN, Mack SENNETT's Keystone Kops, LAUREL AND HARDY, the MARX BROTHERS, and the Three STOOGES.

slate Fine-grained, clayey METAMORPHIC ROCK that splits readily into thin slabs that have great tensile strength and durability. Some other rocks that occur in thin beds are improperly called slate because they can be used for roofing. True slates generally split not along the bedding plane but along planes of CLEAVAGE that may intersect the bedding plane at high angles. Slates may be black, blue, purple, red, green, or gray. Slate is used for electrical panels, laboratory tabletops, roofing, and flooring; crushed slate is used on composition roofing, in aggregates, and as a filler.

Slater, Samuel (1768–1835) British-U.S. industrialist. He emigrated to the U.S. in 1789, where he reproduced versions of Richard ARKWRIGHT's spinning and carding machines from memory and in 1793 established the first successful American cotton mill at Pawtucket, R.I., the first of several plants. He is regarded as the founder of the U.S. cotton textile industry.

Slave Acts, Fugitive See FUGITIVE SLAVE ACTS

slave codes In U.S. history, laws governing the status of slaves, enacted by those colonies or states that permitted SLAVERY. Slaves were considered property rather than persons. Their testimony was inadmissible in court cases involving whites; they could make no contract nor own any property; even if attacked, they could not strike a white person; they could not leave their owner's premises without permission; they could not assemble unless a white person was present; they could not be taught to read or write; and they were not permitted to marry. Offenders were subject to punishment, including whipping, branding, imprisonment, and death. See also BLACK CODES.

slave narrative American literary genre consisting of slave memoirs of daily plantation life, including the sufferings and humiliations borne and the eventual escape to freedom. The major period of slave narratives was 1830–60. Some were factual autobiographies, while others were influenced or sensationalized by the writer's desire to arouse sympathy for the abolitionist cause. The genre reached its height with the autobiography of Frederick DOUGLASS (1845). In the 20th cent., documentary narratives were compiled from recorded interviews with former slaves.

slavery Condition in which one human being is owned by another. A slave was considered in law as property, or chattel, and was deprived of most rights ordinarily held by free persons. Slavery has existed on nearly every continent and throughout recorded history, typically in societies whose economy is of a market type capable of producing surpluses, where the slave becomes a commodity who is bought and sold for profit. The Greeks and Romans accepted the institution of slavery, as did the Maya, Inca, and Aztecs. Europeans in the New World began importing slaves from Africa in the 16th cent. (see SLAVE TRADE); most were taken to the Caribbean and Brazil. By the mid-19th cent., the slave population in the U.S. had risen to more than 4 million. Most worked on plantations in the South, their status governed by SLAVE CODES. Britain abolished slavery in its colonies in 1833; France did the same in 1848. In the U.S. slavery was formally abolished by the EMANCIPATION PROCLAMATION (1863). Today slavery is not legally recognized by any government in the world. See also ABOLITIONISM, DRED SCOTT DECISION, FUGITIVE SLAVE ACTS, SERFDOM, UNDERGROUND RAILROAD.

slave trade Capturing, selling, and buying of slaves. SLAVERY has existed throughout the world throughout history; trading in slaves has been equally universal. Slaves were taken from great population reservoirs: the Slavs and contiguous Iranians from antiquity to the 19th cent., the sub-Saharan Africans during the Christian era, and the Germanic, Celtic, and Romance peoples during the Viking era. Elaborate trade networks developed: in the 9th–10th cent., Vikings might take E. Slavic slaves to Arab and Jewish traders, who would take them to Verdun and León, whence they might be sold throughout Moorish Spain and N. Africa. The transatlantic slave trade is the best known. In Africa, women and children but not men were wanted locally as slaves for labor and for lineage incorporation; from about 1500, captive men were taken to the coast and sold to Europeans, then transported to the Caribbean or Brazil, where they were sold at auction and taken throughout the New World. In the 17th–18th cent., African slaves were traded in the Caribbean for molasses, which was made in the American colonies into rum and traded back to Africa for more slaves.

Slavic languages \'slä-vik, 'sla-vik\ *or* **Slavonic languages** Branch of the Indo-European language family spoken by more than 315 million people in central and E Europe and N Asia. The Slavic family is usually divided into three subgroups: W. Slavic, comprising POLISH, Slovak, CZECH, and Sorbian (Lusatian, Wendish); E. Slavic, comprising RUSSIAN, UKRAINIAN, and Belarusian; and S. Slavic, comprising Slovene, SERBIAN AND CROATIAN, BULGARIAN, and Macedonian. Polish belongs to the Lechitic (Lekhitic) subgroup of W. Slavic languages. A much greater Slavic speech area in central Europe was gradually Germanized from about the 9th cent. Among INDO-EUROPEAN LANGUAGES, Slavic is closest to the family of BALTIC LANGUAGES.

Slavonia Historical region, CROATIA. It lay between the Sava River on the south and the DRAVA and DANUBE rivers on the north and east. It was included in the kingdom of Croatia in the 10th cent. As Slavonia-Croatia, it joins DALMATIA and Istria as one of the three traditional regions of Croatia.

Slavophiles and Westernizers Opposing groups of intellectuals in 19th-cent. Russia. Prominent in the 1840s and '50s, the Slavophiles believed that Russia should rely on its unique character and history to determine its future development. They hoped to restore the autocracy and the church to their ideal forms before PETER I the Great introduced Western reforms. The Slavophile movement declined in the 1860s, but its principles were used by extreme nationalists, advocates of PAN-SLAVISM, and revolutionary POPULISTS. It was opposed by the Westernizers, who viewed Western Europe as a model for Russian modernization.

Slavs \'slävz\ Most numerous ethnic and linguistic body of peoples in Europe. They live chiefly in E and SE Europe but also extend across N Asia to the Pacific. Slavs are customarily subdivided into E Slavs (Russians, Ukrainians, and Belarusians), W Slavs (Poles, Czechs, Slovaks, and Wends, or Sorbs) and S Slavs (Serbs, Croats, Bulgarians, Slovenes, and Macedonians). Historically, W Slavs were integrated into Western Europe. E and S Slavs suffered Mongol and Turkish invasions and evolved more autocratic, state-centered forms of government. Religion (mainly Eastern Orthodoxy and Roman Catholicism) divides Slavs, as does the use of the CYRILLIC and LATIN ALPHABETS. Medieval Slavic polities that left a rich cultural heritage developed in Bohemia, Poland, Croatia, Bosnia, Serbia, and Bulgaria, but by the 19th cent. all these states had been absorbed by powerful neighbors (the Ottoman empire, Austria, Hungary, Prussia, Russia). In the 16th cent., Muscovy (later Russia) embarked on a course of expansion that eventually made it the most powerful Slavic state. PAN-SLAVISM in the 19th cent. influenced the formation of the new Slavic states after World War I, though by the end of the 20th cent. Czechoslovakia and Yugoslavia—the two attempts to integrate different Slavic peoples into single polities—had both disintegrated.

sleep Natural periodic suspension of CONSCIOUSNESS during which the powers of the body are restored. The average human sleep requirement is about 7.5 hours. Sleep is divided into two main types, REM (rapid-eye-movement) and NREM (non-REM); each recurs cyclically several times during a normal period of sleep. REM sleep is characterized by increased neuronal activity of the forebrain and midbrain, depressed muscle tone, dreaming (see DREAM), and rapid eye movements. NREM sleep is divided into four stages, the last of which is the deep, restorative, quiet sleep commonly associated with "a good night's rest."

sleeping sickness Protozoal disease transmitted by the bite of the TSETSE FLY. Two forms, caused by different species of the genus *Trypanosoma*, occur in separate regions in Africa. The PROTOZOAN enters the bloodstream and invades the LYMPH NODES and SPLEEN. Irregular fever and delayed pain sensation develop. In the Rhodesian form, the

S

patient soon dies of massive blood infection. The Gambian type progresses to brain and spinal-cord invasion, causing severe headache, fatigue, PARALYSIS, CHOREA, and sleepiness, followed over two or three years by emaciation, coma, and death. Early drug treatment improves the chance of recovery. Sleeping sickness is still prevalent in parts of Africa despite heroic efforts to control it.

slime mold Any of about 500 species of primitive organisms that contain true nuclei and resemble both PROTISTS and fungi (see FUNGUS). They typically thrive in dark, cool, moist conditions such as on forest floors. BACTERIA, YEAST, MOLDS, and fungi provide the main source of slime-mold nutrition. The complex life cycle of slime molds, exhibiting complete ALTERNATION OF GENERATIONS, may clarify the early evolution of both plant and animal cells. In the presence of water a tiny SPORE releases a mass of cytoplasm called a swarm cell, which later develops into an amoeba-like creeping cell called a myxamoeba. Both swarm cells and myxamoebas can fuse in sexual union; the resulting fertilized cell, or plasmodium, forms a spore case, which, when it dries, disintegrates and releases spores to begin the cycle again.

Sloan, Alfred P(ritchard), Jr. (1875–1966) U.S. corporate executive. Born in New Haven, Conn., he became its president of Hyatt Roller Bearing Co. at age 26. Hyatt was acquired by GENERAL MOTORS CORP., and Sloan rose to become president of GM in 1923. Under his leadership it surpassed FORD MOTOR CO. and became the largest corporation in the world. He served as chairman of the board 1937–56. He endowed the Alfred P. Sloan Foundation and contributed to the Sloan-Kettering Cancer Center in New York and to the school of management at MIT.

Sloan, John (French) (1871–1951) U.S. artist. Born in Lock Haven, Pa., he worked as a commercial newspaper artist in Philadelphia, where he studied with Robert HENRI. He followed Henri to New York, where with six others they exhibited as The EIGHT. Sloan's realistic urban paintings gave rise to the epithet ASH CAN SCHOOL. Such works as *Sunday, Women Drying Their Hair* (1912), *McSorley's Bar* (1912), and *Backyards, Greenwich Village* (1914) are sympathetic portrayals of working men and women.

Slocum, Joshua (1844–1909?) Canadian seaman and adventurer. Born in Wilmot Township, Nova Scotia, he became captain of a trading vessel by 1869. Wrecked on the Brazilian coast in 1886, he built a canoe and paddled back to New York. He set sail from Boston in 1895 in a 36-ft, 9-in. (11.1-m) fishing boat. In three years, two months, and two days, he sailed 46,000 mi (74,000 km) in a circuitous route ending in Newport, R.I., becoming the first man to sail around the world singlehandedly. He wrote the classic *Sailing Alone Around the World*.

slope Numerical measure of a line's inclination relative to the horizontal. In ANALYTIC GEOMETRY, the slope of any line, ray, or line segment is the ratio of the vertical to the horizontal distance between any two points on it ("slope equals rise over run"). In DIFFERENTIAL CALCULUS, the slope of a line tangent to the graph of a function is given by that function's DERIVATIVE and represents the instantaneous rate of change of the function with respect to change in the independent variable.

sloth Nocturnal, solitary, tree-dwelling MAMMAL (family Bradypodidae), found in S. and Central America. About 2 ft (60 cm) long, sloths have long curved claws and long forelimbs. A green alga grows in the shaggy fur. The four species of three-toed sloths, or ais, eat only leaves of the trumpet tree. The two species of two-toed sloths, or unaus *(Choloepus)*, eat various plants. Sloths cannot walk. They cling upright to trunks, hang upside down (in which position they sleep some 15 hours a day), or move, extremely slowly, by pulling hand over hand. Their natural green camouflage is their chief protection.

Slovakia *officially* **Slovak Republic** Nation, central Europe. Area: 18,933 sq mi (49,035 sq km). Population (2000): 5,403,000. Capital: BRATISLAVA. About nine-tenths of the population are Slovak; Hungarians form the largest minority. Language: Slovak (official). Religion: Roman Catholicism, Protestantism, Orthodoxy. Currency: Slovak koruna. The CARPATHIAN MTNS. dominate Slovakia, with lowlands

©1999, Encyclopædia Britannica, Inc.

SLOVAKIA

Scale 1: 6,249,000

in the SW and SE regions. The MORAVA and DANUBE rivers form parts of the S border. The country grows grain, sugar beets, and vegetable crops and raises pigs, sheep, and cattle, but the economy is based on mining and manufacturing; it has substantial deposits of iron ore, copper, magnesite, lead, and zinc. It is a republic with one legislative house; its chief of state is the president, and the head of government is the prime minister. Slovakia was inhabited in the first centuries A.D. by Illyrian, Celtic, and Germanic tribes. Slovaks settled there around the 6th cent. It became part of Great MORAVIA in the 9th cent. but was conquered by the MAGYARS about 907. It remained in the kingdom of Hungary until the end of World War I, when the Slovaks joined the Czechs to form the new state of Czechoslovakia in 1918. In 1938 Slovakia was declared an autonomous unit within Czechoslovakia; it was nominally independent under German protection 1939–45. After the expulsion of the Germans, Slovakia joined a reconstituted Czechoslovakia, which came under Soviet domination in 1948. In 1969 a partnership between the Czechs and Slovaks established the Slovak Socialist Republic. The fall of the Communist regime in 1989 led to a revival of interest in autonomy, and Slovakia became an independent nation in 1993

Slovenia *officially* **Republic of Slovenia** Country, NW Balkans. Area: 7,821 sq mi (20,256 sq km). Population (2000): 1,963,000. Capital: LJUBLJANA. The vast majority of the population is Slovene. Language: Slovene (official). Religion: Roman Catholicism (83%). Currency: Slovene tolar. Slovenia is predominantly mountainous and wooded, with deep, fertile valleys and numerous rivers. One of the more prosperous regions of the Balkans, it has an economy largely based on manufacturing. It extracts coal, ferrosilicon, and petroleum; forestry, livestock, and crops, including potatoes, grains, and fruits, are also important. It is a republic with two legislative houses; its head of state is the president, and the head of government is the prime minister. The Slovenes settled the region in the 6th cent. A.D. In the 8th cent. it was incorporated into the Frankish empire of CHARLEMAGNE, and in the 9th cent. it came under Germany as part of the HOLY ROMAN EMPIRE. Except for 1809–13, when NAPOLEON ruled the area, most of the lands belonged to Austria until the formation of the kingdom of Serbs, Croats, and Slovenes in 1918. It became a constituent republic of Yugoslavia in 1946, and received a section of the former Italian Adriatic coastline in 1947. In 1990 Slovenia held the first contested multiparty elections in Yugoslavia since before World War II. In 1991 it seceded from Yu-

Map showing AUSTRIA, HUNGARY, KARAWANKEN MOUNTAINS, JULIAN ALPS, ITALY, Jesenice, Lake Bled, Maribor, Mursko Sobota, Mura, Drava, Ptuj, Velenje, Celje, Triglav Mountain 9,395 ft., Kranj, Javornik, Trbovlje, Hrastnik, Zagorje, Idrija, Ljubljana, Nova Gorica, Krško, Novo Mesto, Soča, KRAS PLATEAU, Postojna, Zagreb, Sava, Gulf of Venice, Koper, Kočevje, CROATIA

©1999, Encyclopædia Britannica, Inc.

SLOVENIA

Scale 1: 4,314,000

0   20   40 mi
0   30   60 km

goslavia; its independence was internationally recognized in 1992.

slug Any species of GASTROPOD that glides along on a broad tapered foot and has no shell or one that is merely an internal plate or a series of granules. Most slugs use the mantle cavity (see MOLLUSK) as a lung. Slugs have a soft, slimy body and live in moist habitats on land. All are hermaphroditic. In temperate regions, the common slugs eat fungi and decaying leaves. Other species eat plants, snails, and earthworms. See also NUDIBRANCH.

slum Densely populated area of substandard housing, usually in a city, characterized by unsanitary conditions and social disorganization. Rapid INDUSTRIALIZATION in 19th-cent. Europe was accompanied by rapid population growth and the concentration of working-class people in overcrowded, poorly built housing. England passed the first legislation for building low-income housing to certain minimum standards in 1851, and laws for slum clearance in 1868. In the U.S., slum development coincided with the arrival of large numbers of immigrants in the late 19th and early 20th cent.; laws concerning adequate ventilation, fire protection, and sanitation were soon passed. In the 20th cent., government and private organizations built low-income housing and appropriated funds for urban renewal. Shantytowns, which often grow up around urban centers in developing countries as rural populations migrate to the cities in search of employment, are one sort of slum for which alleviating measures have yet to be successfully introduced. See also URBAN PLANNING.

Sluter \'slū-tər\, **Claus** (c.1340/60–c.1405) Early Netherlandish sculptor. He entered the service of Philip II the Bold in 1385 and became his chief sculptor in 1389. All his surviving sculptures were made for the Carthusian monastery of Champmol at Dijon, which Philip founded. Sluter moved beyond the prevailing French taste for graceful figures toward highly individual naturalistic forms. His works infuse realism with spirituality and monumental grandeur. His influence was extensive among both painters and sculptors of 15th-cent. N Europe.

small intestine Long, narrow tube in which most DIGESTION takes place. It extends 22–25 ft (6.7–7.6 m), from the STOMACH to the LARGE INTESTINE. The mesentery, a membrane structure, supports it and contains its blood supply, lymphatics, and insulating fat. The AUTONOMIC NERVOUS SYSTEM supplies it with nerves to start and stop PERISTALSIS. It is lined with minute fingerlike projections (villi) that greatly increase its surface area for ENZYME secretion and food absorption. Its three sections, the DUODENUM, jejunum, and

ILEUM, have distinct characteristics. Normally, food takes three to six hours to pass through it. See also GASTROENTERITIS, DIVERTICULUM.

smallpox *or* **variola** \və-'rī-ə-lə\ One of the world's most dreaded plagues before 1977. An infectious VIRAL DISEASE only of humans, it causes fever and then a rash of variable severity that blisters and dries up, leaving scars. It is not spread easily, but the virus can survive for long periods outside the body (e.g., in bedding). Edward JENNER developed a VACCINE from cowpox. The World Health Organization's eradication project reduced smallpox deaths from 2 million in 1967 to zero in 1977–1980. The virus now exists only in laboratories; it may be under development for purposes of BIOLOGICAL WARFARE.

Smalls, Robert (1839–1915) U.S. naval hero. Born to plantation slaves in Beaufort, S.C., he was taken to Charleston, where, in the American Civil War, he was forced into the Confederate navy to serve on the armed frigate *Planter*. In 1862 he and 12 other slaves seized control of the ship and turned it over to the Union navy. He became its captain in 1863. After the war he served in the U.S. House of Representatives (1875–79, 1881–87).

Smallwood, Joey (*orig.* Joseph Roberts) (1900–1991) Canadian politician. Born in Gambo, Newfoundland, he worked for socialist publications in New York (1921–25), then returned to Newfoundland to become a union organizer and radio broadcaster. He was elected to a convention to decide Newfoundland's future (1946), and his vigorous campaign helped effect its admission to Canada as a province (1948). He served as its first premier 1949–71.

smart bomb Bomb with a guidance system that directs its path toward a target, steered by fins or wings. Guidance systems may be electro-optical, laser, or infrared. Electro-optical sensors send pictures of the target area to aircrew, who lock the weapon onto the target or guide it to impact. Laser-guided weapons follow the reflections of a laser beam trained on the target from another source. Infrared guidance responds to heat generated by the target. Smart bombs and missiles were extensively used in the Vietnam War.

Smeaton, John (1724–1792) British civil engineer. In 1756–59 he rebuilt the Eddystone Lighthouse (off Plymouth), during which he rediscovered hydraulic cement (lost since the fall of Rome) as the best mortar for underwater construction. He constructed the great Forth and Clyde Canal in Scotland; built bridges at Perth, Banff, and Coldstream; and completed the harbor at Ramsgate, Kent. He was a leader in the transition from wind-and-water to steam power; with his improvements, Thomas NEWCOMEN's atmospheric STEAM ENGINE achieved its maximum performance. He is regarded as the founder of the CIVIL-ENGINEERING profession in Britain.

smell Special SENSE concerned with the perception of odor. Smell, like TASTE, is regarded as a type of CHEMORECEPTION. The concept of smell as experienced by humans becomes less distinct when invertebrates and lower vertebrates (fish and amphibians) are considered, because many lower animals detect chemicals in the environment by means of receptors in various locations on the body, and no invertebrate possesses a chemoreceptive structure resembling the vertebrate nasal cavity (see NOSE). Smell contributes greatly to what is normally perceived as taste. For many animals, smell is involved in locating food and identifying other animals, including mating partners and enemies. Many vertebrates, especially carnivores, possess a far more acute sense of smell than do humans, as do many invertebrates, including insects.

smelt Any of certain slender, silvery, carnivorous, food fishes (family Osmeridae) having a small fleshy fin. Smelts live in cold N seas. The American smelt (*Osmerus mordax*), introduced from the Atlantic to the Great Lakes, is the largest smelt, about 15 in. (38 cm) long. The European smelt (*O. eperlanus*) is similar. Among Pacific species are the rainbow herring, capelin, and eulachon, or candlefish, which is so oily at spawning time that it can be dried and burned as a candle.

smelting Process by which a METAL is obtained from its ORE, either as the element or as a simple compound, usually by heating beyond the melting point, ordinarily in the pres-

ence of reducing agents such as COKE or oxidizing agents such as air (see OXIDATION-REDUCTION). A metal whose ore is an oxygen compound (e.g., iron, zinc, or lead OXIDE) is heated in a BLAST FURNACE; the oxide combines with the carbon in the coke, escaping as carbon monoxide or carbon dioxide. Other impurities are removed by adding FLUX, with which they combine to form slag. If the ore is a sulfide mineral (e.g., copper, nickel, lead, or cobalt), air or oxygen is blasted through to oxidize the sulfide to sulfur dioxide and any iron to oxide slag, leaving the metal. See also MET-ALLURGY.

Smetana \\'sme-t³n-ə\\, **Bedrich** (1824–1884) Czech (Bohemian) composer. Having failed as a concert pianist, he opened two schools of music. He became conductor of the national theater in 1866. His second opera was the highly successful *The Bartered Bride* (1866). *Dalibor* (1868) followed and also became popular; he would complete five more operas. Though deaf by 1874, in his last decade he wrote some of his most beloved music, including *Má vlast* (1875), with the famous "The Moldau." The strongly Czech character of his music made Smetana the preeminent Czech nationalist composer.

smew See MERGANSER

Smith, Adam (1723–1790) Scottish social philosopher and political economist. A series of public lectures in Edinburgh (from 1748) led to a lifelong friendship with David HUME and his appointment to the Glasgow faculty in 1751. His *Theory of Moral Sentiments* was published in 1759. In 1776, after nine years of work, Smith published *An Inquiry into the Nature and Causes of the Wealth of Nations,* the first comprehensive system of political economy. In it he argued for an economic system based on individual self-interest that would be led, as if by an "invisible hand," to achieve the greatest good for all, and posited the DIVISION OF LABOR as the chief factor in economic growth. A reaction to the system of MERCANTILISM then current, it stands as the beginning of CLASSICAL ECONOMICS. *The Wealth of Nations* in time won him an enormous reputation, and would become virtually the most influential work on economics ever published. Though often regarded as the bible of CAPITALISM, it is harshly critical of the shortcomings of unrestrained free enterprise and monopoly.

Smith, Alfred E(manuel) (1873–1944) U.S. politician. Born in New York City, he began his political career with a job from Tammany Hall (1895). After serving as speaker of the state assembly, he twice served as governor of New York (1919–20, 1923–28) and fought for improved housing, child welfare, and efficient government. In 1928 he won the Democratic nomination for president, the first Roman Catholic to be nominated, but lost to Herbert HOOVER.

Smith, Bessie (*orig.* Elizabeth) (1894–1937) U.S. blues and jazz singer, the most successful black entertainer of her time. Born in Chattanooga, Tenn., Smith sang popular songs as well as blues on the minstrel and vaudeville stage, and began recording in 1923. Her interpretations represent the fully realized transition of the rural folk tradition of the blues to its urbane structure and expressiveness. A bold, supremely confident artist with a powerful voice, she became known as "Empress of the Blues." She died following a car crash, having apparently been refused treatment for reasons of racial prejudice.

Bessie Smith

Smith, Cyril Stanley (1903–1992) British-U.S. metallurgist. As a member of the MANHATTAN PROJECT, he determined the properties and technology of PLUTONIUM and URANIUM, the essential materials of the ATOMIC BOMB. He published many books on the history of metallurgy, including *A History of Metallography* (1960).

Smith, David (Roland) (1906–1965) U.S. sculptor. Born in Decatur, Ill., he learned to work with metal at an automo-

bile plant. In 1926 he went to New York to study painting. His sculptures grew out of his abstract paintings, to which he attached so many bits of wood, metal, and found objects that they became virtual sculptures. He became the first U.S. artist to make welded metal sculpture. In 1940 he moved to Bolton Landing, N.Y., and

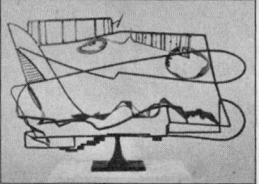
David Smith, "Hudson River Landscape," 1951

there made his large yet seemingly weightless metal sculptures until his death in a car crash. His abstract biomorphic and geometric forms are remarkable for their erratic inventiveness, stylistic diversity, and high aesthetic quality.

Smith, Gerrit (1797–1874) U.S. reformer. Born into a wealthy family in Utica, N.Y., he became active in the temperance movement (1828) and built one of the first U.S. temperance hotels at Peterboro, N.Y. An active abolitionist, he made it a stop on the UNDERGROUND RAILROAD. He was the presidential candidate of the Liberty Party in 1848 and 1852. He paid the legal expenses of many slaves arrested under the FUGITIVE SLAVE ACTS, and he gave a farm to his friend John BROWN.

Smith, Hamilton O(thanel) (b.1931) U.S. microbiologist. Born in New York City, he received his MD from Johns Hopkins Univ. While studying the mechanism whereby *Haemophilus influenzae* takes up DNA from a particular bacteriophage, Smith, Werner ARBER, and Daniel Nathans (1928–1997) discovered the first of what came to be called type II restriction enzymes. Unlike previously studied restriction enzymes, the type II enzymes allowed the scientists to cut DNA at a particular point, and have become valuable tools in the study of DNA structure and in recombinant-DNA technology. The three shared a 1978 Nobel Prize.

Smith, Ian (Douglas) (b.1919) First native-born prime minister of the British colony of S. Rhodesia (1964–65). An ardent advocate of white rule, in 1965 he declared Rhodesia's independence from the Commonwealth. He faced guerrilla attacks from Robert MUGABE and Joshua NKOMO through most of the 1970s. In 1979 he completed a transfer of power to the black majority.

Smith, John (1580–1631) English colonist. After a period as a military adventurer, he joined an English group preparing to establish a colony in N. America. The group arrived at Chesapeake Bay in 1607 and established the first permanent English settlement in N. America at JAMESTOWN; Smith became its leader. On an exploratory river voyage he was captured by Indians of the POWHATAN Confederacy and saved from death by POCAHONTAS. An injury forced his return to England in 1609. Supported by the PLYMOUTH CO., he sailed in 1614 to the area he named New England. He mapped the coast and wrote descriptions of Virginia and New England that encouraged others to colonize.

Smith, Joseph (1805–1844) Founder of the MORMON Church. Born in Sharon, Vt., he began experiencing visions as a teenager in Palmyra, N.Y. In 1827 he claimed that an angel had directed him to buried golden plates containing God's revelation; these he translated into the *Book of Mormon* (1830). He led converts eventually to Illinois, where he established the town of Nauvoo (1839), which soon became the state's largest town. Imprisoned for treason after his efforts to silence Mormon dissenters led to mob violence, he was murdered at 38 by a lynch mob. His work was continued by Brigham YOUNG.

Smith, Maggie (*orig.* Margaret Natalie) (*later* **Dame Maggie**) (b.1934) British ac-

Joseph Smith Painting by an unknown artist

tress. After winning praise in *The Rehearsal* (1961) and *Mary, Mary* (1963), she joined the National Theatre, where she starred opposite Laurence OLIVIER in *Othello* (1964; film, 1965). Her later films include *The Prime of Miss Jean Brodie* (1969, Academy Award), *Travels with My Aunt* (1972), *California Suite* (1978, Academy Award), and *The Lonely Passion of Judith Hearne* (1987). Known for her nervous intensity, acid wit, and flawless timing, she has many great stage performances to her credit.

Smith, Margaret Chase *orig.* Margaret Madeline Chase (1897–1995) U.S. politician. Born in Skowhegan, Me., she served as secretary to her husband, Clyde Smith, after he was elected to Congress as a Republican in 1936. Disabled in 1940, he urged voters to elect her in his stead. She became the first woman to win election to both houses of Congress, serving in the House of Representatives (1940–49) and Senate (1949–73). Though a staunch anticommunist, she was the first of her party to condemn Joseph MCCARTHY's tactics, and she won respect for her rocklike integrity.

Smith, Red (*orig.* Walter Wellesley) (1905–1982) U.S. sports columnist. Born in Green Bay, Wis., he began writing his column, "Views of Sport," in the *New York Herald Tribune* in 1945; it was syndicated soon thereafter. He joined the *Times* in 1971. His writing shunned jargon and displayed literary craftsmanship, wry humor, and deep knowledge. He won a Pulitzer Prize in 1976. His columns were collected in five books.

Smith, Stevie (*orig.* Florence Margaret) (1902–1971) British poet. She lived much of her life with an aunt, working as a secretary. Her poetry, an unsentimental combination of the ludicrous and the pathetic, expresses an original and visionary personality. In the 1960s her poetry readings became popular, and she made radio broadcasts and recordings. Her collections include *A Good Time Was Had by All* (1937), and *Not Waving but Drowning* (1957), whose title poem appears in many anthologies.

Smith, W(illiam) Eugene (1918–1978) U.S. photojournalist. Born in Wichita, Kan., he worked as a magazine photographer in New York. As a war correspondent for *Life* magazine, he covered many of the important battles of the Pacific theater. He produced a number of photo essays for *Life*, such as *Spanish Village* (1951), a study of villagers' daily struggle to draw life from exhausted soil. His most famous picture, *The Walk to Paradise Garden* (1947), showing his own children entering a forest clearing, concluded the landmark exhibition *The Family of Man.*

Smith, William (1769–1839) English geologist, known as the founder of the science of STRATIGRAPHY. He produced the first geologic map of England and Wales (1815), setting the style for modern geologic maps. He introduced many techniques still used, including the use of fossils for the dating of layers. Current geologic maps of England differ from his primarily in detail, and many of the colorful names he applied to the strata are also used today.

Smith College Private liberal-arts college for women in Northampton, Mass. It was founded in 1871 through the bequest of Sophia Smith (1796–1870). Master's degrees are granted in several fields, and the PhD in social work. Smith belongs to a consortium with AMHERST, Hampshire, and MOUNT HOLYOKE colleges and the Univ. of Massachusetts. Enrollment is about 2,800.

Smithsonian Institution U.S. research institution. Enabled by the bequest of the English chemist James Smithson (1765–1829), it was established in Washington, D.C., by an 1846 act of Congress. The Smithsonian administers numerous bureaus, including the John F. Kennedy Center for the Performing Arts, the National Air and Space Museum, the National Gallery of Art, the National Zoological Park, and the Smithsonian Astrophysical Observatory.

smog Polluted air over a community. The term, a combination of "smoke" and "fog," was popularized in the early 20th cent. and now commonly refers to the pall of automotive or industrial origin that lies over many cities. Sulfurous smog results from the use of sulfur-bearing fossil fuels, particularly coal, and is aggravated by dampness. Photochemical smog occurs when nitrogen oxides and hydrocarbon vapors emitted mainly from automobiles react in the presence of sunlight to produce a light brownish coloration of the atmosphere, reduced visibility, plant damage, irritation of the eyes, and respiratory distress.

smoking Breathing the fumes of burning plant material, especially TOBACCO, from a cigarette, cigar, or pipe. Despite social and medical arguments against tobacco use, the habit has spread worldwide. NICOTINE and related ALKALOIDS furnish the psychoactive effects and, along with tar (a residue containing resins and other by-products), the negative health effects. Those effects include LUNG CANCER, oral and throat cancers, HEART DISEASE, STROKE, EMPHYSEMA, chronic BRONCHITIS, and MACULAR DEGENERATION. Passive smoking (breathing the smoke from others' cigarettes) increases nonsmokers' risk of lung cancer and the risk of SUDDEN INFANT DEATH SYNDROME. Antismoking campaigns have greatly reduced smoking in the U.S. even as it rises in many other countries.

Smoky Mountains See GREAT SMOKY MTNS.

Smolensk \smō-'lensk\ City (pop., 1997 est.: 356,000), W Russia. One of the oldest and most historic of Russian cities, it was a key stronghold on the DNIEPER RIVER by the 9th cent. and became a commercial center on the trade route between the BALTIC SEA and the BYZANTINE EMPIRE. Sacked by the TATARS around 1240, it was fought over several times, then taken by Russia in 1654. It was burned during NAPOLEON's invasion of Russia in 1812. The scene of heavy fighting in World War II, it was occupied by the Germans 1941–43. It is now a light-industry and educational center.

Smollett \'smä-lət\, **Tobias (George)** (1721–1771) English satirical novelist. Throughout his life Smollett combined the roles of medical man and writer. He is best known for his novels, including the PICARESQUE NOVELS *Roderick Random* (1748) and *Peregrine Pickle* (1751). In an active publishing career he did translations, edited periodicals, and compiled a 58-volume *Universal History*. In 1766 he published the irascible *Travels Through France and Italy*. His finest work, *Humphry Clinker* (1771), is a humorous EPISTOLARY NOVEL.

Smoot-Hawley Tariff Act (1930) U.S. edict. It raised import duties by as much as 50%, deepening the worldwide GREAT DEPRESSION. Despite a petition from 1,000 economists urging Pres. Herbert HOOVER to veto the act, it was passed as a protective measure for domestic industries. Other countries retaliated with similarly high protective tariffs, and overseas banks began to collapse. In 1934 Pres. Franklin ROOSEVELT signed the Trade Agreements Act, which reduced such tariffs.

smuggling Act of importing and exporting secretly and illegally to avoid paying duties or to evade enforcement of laws (e.g., drug- or firearms-control laws). Smuggling is probably as old as the first tax or regulation on trade. Two main methods exist: the undetected running of cargoes across frontiers, and the concealment of goods in unlikely places on ships or cars, in baggage or cargo, or on the person.

Smuts \'smüts\, **Jan (Christian)** (1870–1950) S. African statesman, soldier, and prime minister (1919–24, 1939–48). An AFRIKANER, Smuts studied law at Cambridge Univ. He fought the British in the S. AFRICAN WAR, and joined with Louis Botha (1862–1919) to oppose implementation of the peace terms. By 1905 Smuts was reconciled to British control. In World War I he joined again with Botha to suppress rebellion, conquer S.W. Africa, and launch a campaign in E. Africa. At Versailles he helped promote the LEAGUE OF NATIONS. When Botha died, he became prime minister. Defeated in 1924 by a NATIONAL PARTY coalition, in 1933 he helped J. B. M. HERTZOG force out the extreme nationalists, and in 1939 he replaced Hertzog as prime minister. His efforts

Jan Smuts

helped prevent Germany and Italy from conquering N Africa. Defeated by Daniel MALAN's Nationalists in 1948, he became chancellor of Cambridge Univ.

Smyrna See IZMIR

Smyth, Ethel (Mary) (*later* **Dame Ethel**) (1858–1944) British composer. After studying in Leipzig, she first gained notice with her sweeping Mass in D (1893). *The Wreckers* (1906) was the most admired English opera of its time. Her *March of the Women* (1911) reflected her strong involvement in the women's suffrage movement. Her comic opera *The Boatswain's Mate* (1916) enjoyed considerable success. Her notably eclectic work ranges from conventional to experimental.

snail Any species of GASTROPOD that glides along on a broad tapered foot and has a high coiled shell into which it can withdraw. Snails are found in the ocean, in fresh waters, and on land. Most marine snails have gills in the mantle cavity (see MOLLUSK); most land and freshwater snails use the mantle cavity itself as a lung. Snails may be either scavengers or predators. Some species are used as food. See also LIMPET, PERIWINKLE, SLUG, WHELK.

snake Any member of about 11 REPTILE families (suborder Serpentes, order Squamata) that has a long, slender body with no limbs, external ears, or eyelids. About 2,700 snake species are known to exist, most numerously in the tropics. Their skin is covered with scales. They have good eyesight, and they continually taste the air with their tongues. Though they lack a voice, they are capable of hissing. Most live on the ground, but some are arboreal or aquatic, and some are burrowers. They move by muscular contraction, aided by elongated scales on their abdomen. The construction of their jaws and bodies enables them to swallow large prey whole. They lay eggs or bear live young. About one-fifth of snake species are venomous; some can kill humans with their bite. Others kill their prey by constriction or simply ingesting. Species range from less than 5 in. (12 cm) to over 30 ft (9 m) long. Snakes grow continuously throughout their life, shedding their outgrown skin at each growth increment.

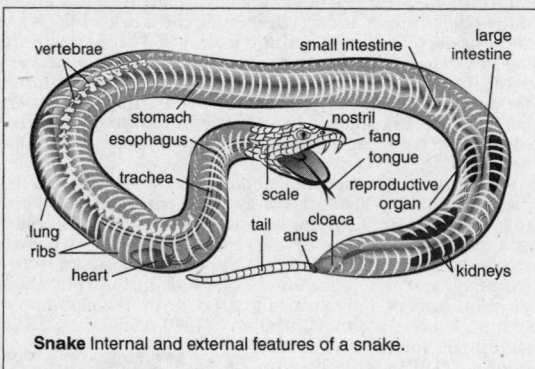

Snake Internal and external features of a snake.

snakebird See ANHINGA

snakebite Wound from the bite of a SNAKE, especially a venomous one. A person bitten by a venomous snake needs immediate medical care. Antivenin must be specific to the type of VENOM, so the snake should be identified or accurately described. Different kinds of venom break down red blood cells or attack the nervous system. Local tissue destruction may lead to GANGRENE. First aid seeks to keep the venom from spreading to the rest of the body. The bitten limb should be kept still below heart level with a broad, firm (not tight) bandage around it above the bite. Cutting, suction, tourniquets, and applying ice are not advised.

Snake River River, NW U.S. The largest tributary of the CO-LUMBIA RIVER, it rises in the mountains of YELLOWSTONE NATIONAL PARK in Wyoming and flows south through Idaho 1,040 mi (1,670 km) to enter the Columbia in SE Washington. The lower Snake flows through HELLS CANYON.

snapdragon family Family Scrophulariaceae, containing about 4,000 species of flowering plants in 190 genera, found worldwide. The family is notable for its many ornamental garden plants, including snapdragon (*Antirrhinum* species) and FOXGLOVE. *Antirrhinum* contains about 40 species native to W N. America and the W Mediterranean. Flowers of the family are tubular and bilaterally symmetrical (two-lipped).

snapper Any of about 250 species of valuable food fishes (family Lutjanidae), found throughout the tropics. These active schooling fishes have large mouths, sharp canine teeth, and blunt or forked tails. Many species grow to 2–3 ft (60–90 cm) long. Snappers eat crustaceans and other fishes. Some species, such as the Atlantic dog snapper, contain a toxin. The red snapper, a bright red fish, inhabits deep Atlantic waters. The emperor snapper is a red-and-white Indo-Pacific fish.

snapping turtle Either of two species (family Chelydridae) of edible, omnivorous, freshwater TURTLES found in N. and Central America. Known for fierceness, they lunge at aggressors and prey and bite them with their powerful jaws. The common snapping turtle (*Chelydra serpentina*) has a shell 8–12 in. (20–30 cm) long and weighs 10–35 lbs (4.5–16 kg). The alligator snapping turtle (*Macrochelys*, or *Macroclemys, temmincki*), the largest freshwater turtle in the U.S., has a shell 16–28 in. (40–70 cm) long and weighs 40–155 lbs (18–70 kg), and lures fishes by means of a wormlike appendage on the floor of its open mouth.

Snead, Sam(uel Jackson) (1912–2002) U.S. golfer. Born near Hot Springs, Va., he reportedly never took a golf lesson. Known for his straw hat and his flowing, powerful swing, "Slammin' Sammy" won the PGA championship three times (1942, 1949, 1951), the British Open (1946), and the Masters three times (1949, 1952, 1954). He won more PGA tournaments (81) than any other player in history.

Snell's law Mathematical relationship between the path taken by a ray of light as it moves from one medium to another and the refractive indices of the two media. Discovered in 1621 by Willebrord Snell (1580–1626), the law went unpublished until its mention by Christiaan HUYGENS. See also REFRACTION.

snipe Any of about 20 species of birds (family Scolopacidae) that frequent wet meadows and marshes in temperate and warm regions worldwide. They are short-legged and chunky, with brown, black, and white stripes and bars. The wings are pointed. The long, flexible bill is used to probe mud for worms. The common snipe (*Gallinago*, or *Capella, gallinago*) is about 12 in. (30 cm) long, including the bill.

Common snipe (*Gallinago gallinago*)

Snorri Sturluson \'snōr-ē-'stūer-lŭe-sòn\ (1179–1241) Icelandic poet, historian, and chieftain. Snorri served as president of the Icelandic high court and was a vassal of King Haakon IV of Norway. He was the author of the *Prose EDDA* and the *Heimskringla,* a history of Norwegian kings. His writings are remarkable for their scope and formal assurance; his genius lay in his power to present history with the immediacy of drama. His relations with Haakon deteriorated, and he was assassinated on the king's order.

snout beetle See WEEVIL

Snow, C(harles) P(ercy) *later* Baron Snow (of the City of Leicester) (1905–1980) British novelist and scientist. A molecular physicist at Cambridge Univ., he served as a scientific adviser to the government. His 11-novel sequence *Strangers and Brothers* (1940–70) analyzes bureaucratic man and the corrupting influence of power. *The Two Cultures and the Scientific Revolution* (1959) and later nonfiction works deal with the cultural separation between practitioners of science and literature.

snow Solid form of water that crystallizes in the atmosphere and falls to the earth, covering about 23% of the earth's surface either permanently or temporarily. Snowflakes are formed by crystals of ice that generally have a hexagonal pattern. Snow cover has a significant effect on climate and on plant, animal, and human life. By increasing the reflection of solar radiation and interfering with the conduction of heat from the ground, it induces a cold climate. The low heat conduction protects small plants from the effects of the lowest winter temperatures; on the other hand, late disappearance of snow in the spring delays the growth of plants.

snowboarding Sport of sliding downhill over snow on a snowboard, a wide ski ridden in a surfing position. Derived from SURFING and SKATEBOARDING, snowboarding began to burgeon among young people in the U.S. in the mid-1980s. The first Olympic competition was held in 1998. The two main events are giant slalom (similar to Alpine giant SLALOM) and halfpipe, in which riders use a large, snow-covered trench (halfpipe) to repeatedly launch themselves into the air and perform acrobatic feats.

Snowdonia National Park Park, N Wales. Covering 838 sq mi (2,171 sq km), it is best known for its mountains, composed largely of volcanic rock and cut by valleys that show the influence of Ice Age glaciers. Mt. Snowdon, 3,560 ft (1,085 m) high, is the highest peak in England and Wales.

snow leopard *or* **ounce** Endangered species (*Panthera uncia*) of nocturnal, long-haired big CAT that inhabits the high mountains of central Asia and India. It is about 6 ft (1.8 m) long, including the 3-ft (1-m) tail, stands about 2 ft (0.5 m) high, and weighs 60–120 lbs (27–55 kg). Its dense, soft coat is pale grayish with dark rosettes and a dark streak along the spine. It preys on marmots, wild sheep and goats, birds, and other animals. It is hunted for the market in goods used in Asian traditional medicine.

snowshoe hare *or* **snowshoe rabbit** *or* **varying hare** N. American species (*Lepus americanus*) of HARE that turns to pure white in winter. All four feet are large in proportion to body size, a snowshoe-like adaptation that enables the hare to travel over snow.

Snyder, Gary (Sherman) (b.1930) U.S. poet. Born in San Francisco, Snyder worked as a forest ranger, logger, and seaman and studied Zen Buddhism in Japan 1958–66. His poetry, early identified with the BEAT MOVEMENT, initially contained images drawn from his outdoor work in the Pacific Northwest and later reflected his interest in Eastern philosophies. His volumes include *Turtle Island* (1974, Pulitzer Prize). He has been a spokesman for communal living and ecological activism.

Soane, John (*later* **Sir John**) (1753–1837) British architect. He was appointed architect to the Bank of England in 1788, and in 1806 he succeeded his mentor, George Dance (1741–1837), at the Royal Academy. His work is characterized by a tendency to reduce classical elements to their structural essentials; use of linear ornamentation, shallow domes, and top lighting; and ingenious handling of interior space.

soap Organic compound, SALT of a FATTY ACID. Soaps are emulsifying agents commonly used for cleaning; they have long been made from LYE and any vegetable OIL or animal FAT. DETERGENTS are entirely synthetic and may or may not be soaps. Soaps of METALS heavier than sodium are not very soluble; the curdy precipitate made by soap in HARD WATER is the calcium or magnesium salt of the fatty acid in the soap. Heavy-metal soaps are used in lubricating greases, as gel thickeners, and in paints.

soap opera Broadcast serial drama, characterized by a permanent cast of actors, a continuing story, tangled interpersonal situations, and a melodramatic or sentimental style. Its name derived from the soap manufacturers who originally sponsored such programs. Soap operas began in the early 1930s as 15-minute daytime radio episodes and continued on television as 30-minute and later hour-long episodes. Aimed at housewives, they initially focused on middle-class family life, but by the 1970s their content included a wider variety of situations and greater sexual explicitness. In the 1980s similar series began to be aired in prime-time evening hours (e.g., *Dallas* and *Dynasty*). See also Anne and Frank HUMMERT, Irna PHILLIPS.

soaring *or* **gliding** Sport of flying a GLIDER or sailplane. The craft is towed behind a powered airplane to an altitude of about 2,000 ft (600 m) and then released. The glider pilot makes use of rising currents of warm air, such as those above a sunlit field, to maintain or gain altitude. National soaring contests include events for altitude, speed, distance, and accuracy in returning to a starting point.

soccer *or* **association football** Game in which two 11-member teams try to propel a ball into the opposing team's goal, using any part of the body except the hands and arms. Only the goalkeeper, who must remain near the goal, may use hands and arms. The first uniform set of soccer rules was put in place in 1863 by England's Football Assn. Professional leagues began appearing in the late 1880s. The Fédération Internationale de Football Association (FIFA), founded in 1904, has hosted the WORLD CUP every four years since 1930. Now played in over 150 nations, with over 40 million registered players, it is the world's most popular ball game.

social class See social CLASS

social contract Actual or hypothetical compact between the ruled and their rulers. It is most closely associated with the writings of Thomas HOBBES, John LOCKE, and Jean-Jacques ROUSSEAU. Hobbes argued for a social contract that gave the rulers absolute power, in return for which they would protect the people from their natural state of warfare. Locke believed that rulers were obliged to protect not only the people but also their private property. Rousseau believed that, in surrendering individual freedom, people acquired a sense of moral and civic obligation, and that government must rest on the general will of the governed. The idea of the social contract influenced the shapers of the

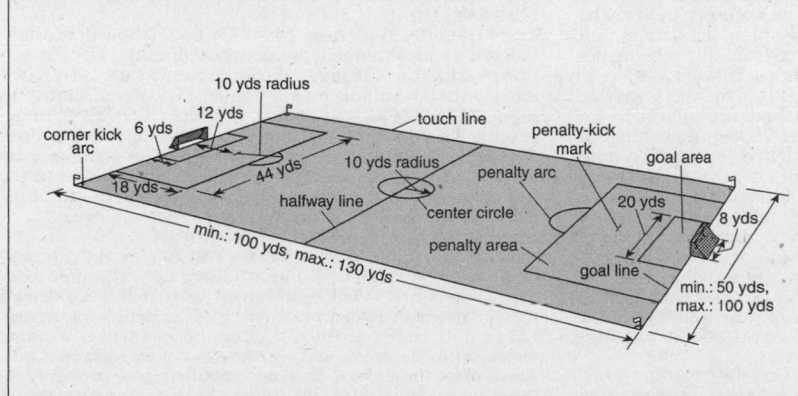

Soccer A professional soccer field. International rules allow for variations in the overall field dimensions (goal lines: 50–100 yards; touch lines: 100–130 yards), but the touch lines must be longer than the goal lines. Play begins with a kickoff at the center line. When the ball is driven across the touch line, it is put back in play by a throw-in by the opposing side. A ball driven over the goal line but not into the goal by the attacking team is returned to play with a goal kick by the opposing goalkeeper. A player fouled in the penalty area is awarded a penalty kick at the goal, which is defended only by the goalkeeper. Within the goal area the goalkeeper may use his hands to stop and hold the ball.

AMERICAN and FRENCH REVOLUTIONS and the constitutions that followed them.

social Darwinism Theory that persons, groups, and races are subject to the same laws of NATURAL SELECTION as Charles DARWIN had proposed for plants and animals in nature. Social Darwinists, such as Herbert SPENCER, held that the life of humans in society was a struggle for existence ruled by "survival of the fittest," in Spencer's words. Wealth was said to be a sign of natural superiority, its absence a sign of unfitness. The theory was used to support LAISSEZ-FAIRE capitalism and political conservatism. Social Darwinism declined as scientific knowledge expanded.

social democracy Political ideology that advocates a peaceful, evolutionary transition of society from CAPITALISM to SOCIALISM, using established political processes. It rejects MARXISM's advocacy of social revolution. Social democracy began as a political movement in Germany in the 1870s. Eduard Bernstein (1850–1932) argued (1899) that capitalism was overcoming many of the weaknesses Karl MARX had seen in it (including unemployment and overproduction) and that universal suffrage would lead peacefully to a socialist government. After 1945, social-democratic governments came to power first in W. Germany (see SOCIAL DEMOCRATIC PARTY), Sweden, and Britain (under the LABOUR PARTY), and later in many other countries. State regulation gradually came to be regarded as an adequate substitute for state ownership.

Social Democratic Party of Germany (SPD) German political party. Formed in 1875 as the Socialist Workers' Party and renamed in 1890, it is Germany's oldest and largest single party. Its influence grew until World War I, when centrists led by Karl KAUTSKY formed the Independent Social Democrats and leftists led by Rosa LUXEMBURG and Karl LIEBKNECHT formed the Spartacists. Its right wing under Friedrich EBERT helped crush the Soviet-style uprisings in Germany in 1918. Germany's severe economic problems caused a drop in support in the 1920s. Outlawed by the Nazis in 1933, the party revived after World War II in W. Germany and grew steadily. It formed coalition governments with the CHRISTIAN DEMOCRATIC UNION (1966–69) and the Free Democratic Party (1969–82). In 1990 it reunited with a newly independent SPD from the former E. Germany.

social insurance Compulsory public-insurance program that protects against various economic risks (e.g., loss of income due to sickness, old age, or unemployment). Social insurance is considered one type of SOCIAL SECURITY. The first compulsory national social-insurance programs were established in Germany under Otto von BISMARCK: HEALTH INSURANCE in 1883, WORKERS' COMPENSATION in 1884, and old-age and disability PENSIONS in 1889. After 1920, social insurance was rapidly adopted throughout Europe and the Western Hemisphere. The U.S. lagged behind until the passage of the SOCIAL SECURITY ACT in 1935. Social Security in the U.S. now provides retirement benefits, health care for persons over 65, and disability insurance. Social-insurance contributions are normally compulsory and may be made by the insured person's employer and the state as well as by the individual. Social insurance is usually self-financing. See also UNEMPLOYMENT INSURANCE, WELFARE.

socialism System of social organization in which private property and the distribution of income are subject to social control. Socialist thought ranges widely from statist to libertarian, from Marxist to liberal. The term was first used to describe the doctrines of Charles FOURIER, Henri de SAINT-SIMON, and Robert OWEN (see UTOPIAN SOCIALISM). Karl MARX and Friedrich ENGELS, seeing socialism as a transition state between CAPITALISM and COMMUNISM, appropriated what they found useful in socialist movements to develop their "scientific socialism." In the 20th cent., the Soviet Union was the principal model of strictly centralized socialism, while Sweden and Denmark were well known for their noncommunist socialism. See also SOCIAL DEMOCRACY.

Socialist International See SECOND INTERNATIONAL

Socialist Realism Officially sanctioned theory and method of artistic and literary composition in the Soviet Union from 1932 to the mid-1980s. Unlike 19th-cent. Russian REALISM, it took as its primary theme the struggle to build socialism and a classless society and called for the didactic use of art to develop social consciousness. Artists were expected to take a positive view of socialist society and to keep in mind its historical relevance, requisites that seldom coincided with their real experiences and frequently undermined the artistic credibility of their works.

Socialist Revolutionary Party (SR) Russian political party. The ideological heir to the 19th-cent. POPULISTS, it was founded in 1901 by agrarian socialists and appealed mainly to the peasantry. The principal alternative to the RUSSIAN SOCIAL-DEMOCRATIC WORKERS' PARTY, it relied on terrorist tactics and carried out hundreds of political assassinations. By 1917 it was Russia's largest socialist group; its members included Aleksandr KERENSKY and Viktor CHERNOV. After the RUSSIAN REVOLUTION OF 1917, its radical wing joined the BOLSHEVIK government. It was suppressed by Vladimir LENIN after the RUSSIAN CIVIL WAR.

social psychology Branch of PSYCHOLOGY concerned with the individual or group in the context of social interaction. The field emerged in the U.S. in the 1920s. Topics include the attribution of social status based on perceptual cues, the influence of social factors (such as peers) on a person's attitudes and beliefs, the functioning of small groups and large organizations, and the dynamics of face-to-face interactions.

Social Realism Trend in U.S. art, originating about 1930, toward treating themes of social protest—poverty, political corruption, labor-management conflict—in a naturalistic manner. The movement was stimulated in part by the ASH CAN SCHOOL, the GREAT DEPRESSION, and the WPA FEDERAL ART PROJECT. Works in this vein include Ben SHAHN's *Passion of Sacco and Vanzetti* (1931–32) and William Gropper's *The Senate* (1935).

social science Any discipline or branch of science that deals with the sociocultural aspects of human behavior. The social sciences generally include CULTURAL ANTHROPOLOGY, ECONOMICS, POLITICAL SCIENCE, SOCIOLOGY, and SOCIAL PSYCHOLOGY. Comparative law and comparative religion (the comparative study of diverse legal systems and religions) are also sometimes regarded as social sciences.

social security Public provision for the economic security and social welfare of all individuals. Social-security programs are designed to protect individuals and their families from income losses due to unemployment, work injury, maternity, sickness, old age, and death and to improve their welfare through public services. The term encompasses not only SOCIAL INSURANCE but also health and welfare services and various income-maintenance programs. The first organized cooperative efforts to provide for the economic security of individuals were instituted by workingmen's associations, mutual-benefit societies, and LABOR UNIONS; social security was not widely established by law until the 19th and 20th cent. Almost all the developed nations now have social-security programs. See also SOCIAL SECURITY ACT, UNEMPLOYMENT INSURANCE, WELFARE, WORKERS' COMPENSATION.

Social Security Act (Aug. 14, 1935) Legislation that established a national old-age pension system in the U.S. Dissatisfied with the government response to the GREAT DEPRESSION, about 5 million people joined "Townsend clubs" to support the plan of Francis E. Townsend (1867–1960) to demand a $200 monthly pension for everyone over 60. Pres. Franklin ROOSEVELT set up a committee on economic security (1934), which recommended legislative action to the U.S. Congress. The act provided old-age benefits to be financed by a payroll tax on employers and employees.

social settlement See SETTLEMENT HOUSE

Social War *or* **Italic War** *or* **Marsic War** (90–89 B.C.) Rebellion waged by ancient Rome's Italian allies (Latin, *Socii*). The Italians had aided Rome in its wars, but were denied the privileges of Roman citizenship. The people of central Italy's hills began an uprising for independence, winning victories in the north and south. After Rome granted citizenship to those who had not revolted and probably to those who would immediately lay down their arms, SULLA defeated the weakened rebels in the south, and legislation was passed to unify Italy south of the Po River.

social welfare See WELFARE

social work Any of various professional activities or methods concerned with providing social services (such as investigatory and treatment services or material aid) to disadvantaged, distressed, or vulnerable persons or groups. The field originated in the charity organizations in Europe and the U.S. in the late 19th cent. The training of volunteer workers by these organizations led directly to the founding of the first schools of social work and indirectly to increased government responsibility for the welfare of the disadvantaged. Social workers may serve the needs of children and families, the poor or homeless, immigrants, veterans, the mentally ill, the handicapped, victims of rape or domestic violence, and persons dependent on alcohol or drugs. See also WELFARE.

Society Islands Archipelago (pop., 1988: 163,000), W FRENCH POLYNESIA. Its capital is PAPEETE, on its chief island, TAHITI. The islands are volcanic in origin and mountainous. They were visited in 1769 by Capt. James COOK with a scientific expedition of the ROYAL SOCIETY (hence their name). They were claimed by France in 1768. Their chief products are copra and pearls. Made famous by Paul GAUGUIN, they are known for their spellbinding beauty and perfect weather.

sociobiology Systematic study of the biological basis of social behavior. The concept was popularized by Edward O. WILSON in his *Sociobiology* (1975) and by Richard Dawkins (b.1941) in *The Selfish Gene* (1976). Sociobiology attempts to understand and explain animal (and human) social behavior in the light of NATURAL SELECTION. The transmission of GENES through successful reproduction is seen as the central motivator in animals' struggle for survival. Though sociobiology has contributed insights into animal behavior (such as altruism in social insects), it remains controversial when applied to human social behavior.

sociocultural evolution Development of culture and society from simple to complex forms. In the late 19th cent., E. B. TYLOR and L. H. MORGAN elaborated the theory of cultural evolution from "primitive" to "civilized" societies, specifying criteria for categorizing cultures within a fixed system of growth of humanity. A widespread reaction followed; Franz BOAS introduced the "culture history" approach, which concentrated on fieldwork among native peoples to identify actual cultural and historical processes rather than speculative stages of growth. Others used aspects of sociocultural evolution to show a progression from bands and TRIBES at one end to chiefdoms and STATES at the other. More recently some anthropologists have adopted a general systems approach, examining cultures as emergent systems. Others continue to reject evolutionary thinking and look instead at historical contingencies, contacts with other cultures, and the operation of cultural SYMBOL systems. See also SOCIAL DARWINISM.

sociology Science of society, social institutions, and social relationships, and specifically the systematic study of the development, structure, interaction, and collective behavior of organized human groups. It emerged at the end of the 19th cent. through the work of Émile DURKHEIM in France, Max WEBER and Georg SIMMEL in Germany, and Robert E. Park (1864–1944) in the U.S. Today sociologists use observational techniques, surveys and interviews, statistical analysis, and controlled experiments to study such subjects as the FAMILY, ethnic relations, schooling, social CLASS, bureaucracy, religious movements, deviance, the elderly, and social change.

Socotra \sə-ʹkō-trə\ Island, Yemen, in the Indian Ocean. Located about 210 mi (340 km) southeast of Yemen, it is about 1,400 sq mi (3,600 sq km) in area. Its flora includes myrrh, frankincense, and the dragon's blood tree. Mentioned in various legends, it was long ruled by the Mahra sultans of SE Yemen. In 1886 it came under British protection, and in 1967 became part of independent Yemen.

Socrates (c.470–399 B.C.) Greek philosopher, first of the great trio (with PLATO and ARISTOTLE) who laid the philosophical foundations of Western culture. Since Socrates wrote nothing, information about his personality and doctrine is found chiefly in PLATO's dialogues and XENOPHON's *Memorabilia*. Living during the chaos of the PELOPON-

NESIAN WAR, with its erosion of moral values, Socrates urged followers to "know thyself" and explore the essence of virtue. He lived in poverty, exemplifying his own moral teachings. His teaching method (the "Socratic method") consisted largely of asking probing questions, which cumulatively revealed the students' unsupported assumptions and misconceptions. His many students included Plato, ALCIBIADES, and Critias (c.480–403 B.C.). When Alcibiades became a traitor and Critias joined the

Socrates

Sparta-imposed THIRTY TYRANTS, Socrates was accused of impiety and of corrupting the Athenian youth, and was condemned to death in 399 B.C.; Plato's *Phaedo* recounts the dignity with which he submitted to his sentence. Socrates influenced the CYNICS, the Cyrenaics, and the Megarian school, but it was mainly through Plato that his efforts bore their full fruit.

soda, caustic See CAUSTIC SODA

Soddy, Frederick (1877–1956) British chemist. He worked with Ernest RUTHERFORD to develop a theory of the disintegration of radioactive elements. In 1912 he was among the first to conclude that elements might exist in forms (ISOTOPES) of different ATOMIC WEIGHTS but indistinguishable chemically. His researches led to CARBON-14 DATING. He received a 1921 Nobel Prize.

sodium Chemical ELEMENT, one of the ALKALI METALS, chemical symbol Na, atomic number 11. A very soft, silvery-white METAL, the sixth most abundant element on earth, it occurs mainly as HALITE, never free. Extremely reactive, it is used as a reagent and raw material, in metallurgy, as a heat exchanger, and in sodium-vapor lamps. Sodium is essential for life but rarely deficient in diets; high intake is linked to HYPERTENSION. Sodium in compounds, many of great industrial importance (including BICARBONATE OF SODA, CAUSTIC SODA, SALTPETER, and SODIUM CHLORIDE), has VALENCE 1. Sodium CARBONATE, one of the four most important basic chemical commodities, is used in making glass, detergents, and cleansers. Sodium hypochlorite (household BLEACH) is also used to bleach paper pulp and textiles and to chlorinate water. The SULFATE is used in the KRAFT PROCESS and also used to make paperboard, glass, and detergents. The thiosulfate ("hypo") is used in developing photographs.

sodium bicarbonate See BICARBONATE OF SODA

sodium chloride *or* **table salt** Inorganic compound of SODIUM and CHLORINE, a SALT in which IONIC BONDS hold the two components in the familiar white crystals. Salt is essential to health; blood and all other physiological fluids are dilute salt solutions. It is used in manufacturing CHLORINE, CAUSTIC SODA, sodium CARBONATE, BICARBONATE OF SODA, SOAP, and chlorine BLEACH, as well as in ceramic glazes, metallurgy, food preservation, curing of hides, road de-icing, water softening, photography, and in many consumer products. It is mined, extracted from sea water, and obtained from dry salt lakes. See also HALITE.

Sodom and Gomorrah \ʹsä-dəm...gə-ʹmȯr-ə\ Legendary cities of ancient Palestine. According to the Old Testament book of Genesis, they were destroyed by "brimstone and fire" because of their wickedness. Their site is unknown, but may be in an area now beneath the DEAD SEA. The area may once have been fertile, and could have drawn the biblical LOT to graze his flock. The cities' legendary wickedness has inspired many writers.

Sofia \ʹsō-fē-ə, sō-ʹfē-ə,\ *ancient* Serdica. City (pop., 1998: 1,122,000), capital of Bulgaria. Established as a Thracian settlement about the 8th cent. B.C., it flourished under the Romans. Plundered by the Huns in the 5th cent. A.D., it was rebuilt under the Byzantine empire. The Turks held it from 1382 until it was liberated by the Russians in 1878. In 1879 it was made the Bulgarian capital. The Univ. of Sofia (1888)

is Bulgaria's oldest. Its historical monuments include the 6th-cent. Church of St. Sofia.

softball Game resembling BASEBALL but played on a smaller diamond with a larger ball (12 in., or 30.5 cm, in circumference), which is pitched underhand. Since the first standard set of rules was published in the 1920s, the game has been popular as an amateur sport in the U.S., and since the 1960s it has grown considerably in popularity outside of N. America. In U.S. high schools and colleges it is a popular women's sport; a women's softball competition was added to the Olympic Games in 1996.

soft coal See BITUMINOUS COAL

soft drink Nonalcoholic beverage, usually carbonated, consisting of water, CARBON DIOXIDE, flavoring, and a sweet syrup. Attempts to reproduce the natural effervescence of certain spring waters for presumed health benefits began before 1700. The 1790s saw the successful preparation of carbonated "mineral water" by Jacob Schweppe of Geneva; by the early 1800s it was being bottled and sold commercially. Today there are hundreds of varieties of flavored soft drink.

software Entire set of programs and commands associated with the operation of a computer system, including the OPERATING SYSTEM. The term differentiates these from HARDWARE. Two main types of software are system software, which controls a computer's internal functioning, and application software, which directs the computer to execute commands that solve practical problems. A third category is network software, which coordinates communication between networked computers. Software is written by programmers in any number of PROGRAMMING LANGUAGES. This information, the source code, is translated by a COMPILER into MACHINE LANGUAGE, which the computer can understand and act on.

softwood Timber obtained from coniferous trees (mainly of the PINE and FIR families). Softwood is mostly obtained from the Baltic, Scandinavia, and N. America and is the source of about 80% of the world's production of timber. Softwoods of longleaf pine, DOUGLAS FIR, and YEW are much harder in the mechanical sense than several HARDWOODS.

Sogdiana \ˌsäg-dē-'a-nə\ Province of the ancient Persian empire. It was centered in the fertile valley of the Zeravshan River, in modern Uzbekistan. Ruled by DARIUS I in the 6th cent. B.C., it was conquered by ALEXANDER THE GREAT in the 4th cent. B.C. It asserted its independence from the SELEUCID DYNASTY about 250 B.C. as part of the Bactrian kingdom (see BACTRIA). Under the Samanid dynasty (9th–10th cent. A.D.), it was a focal point of Islamic civilization. See also BUKHARA.

Sogne Fjord \'sȯŋ-nə\ *or* **Sognefjorden** \'sȯŋ-nə-ˌfyȯr-dən\ Longest and deepest fjord in Norway. It extends 127 mi (204 km) inland from the Norwegian Sea and has a maximum depth of 4,291 ft (1,308 m). It provides some of the most picturesque scenery in Norway.

soil Earthen material that covers land surfaces and is formed by the action of natural forces on the residue of rocks and minerals on the earth's surface. The most important constituents of soil are crystalline CLAY and organic matter. Soil is produced primarily by WEATHERING and LEACHING. Environmental factors such as rainfall, topography, and vegetation influence soil formation and properties, as do the activities of some animals, so that very different soils may be formed from the same parent material.

soil science See PEDOLOGY

Soka-gakkai \'sō-kä-'gäk-kī\ Lay religious and political group associated with the Buddhist sect Nichiren-sho-shu (see NICHIREN BUDDHISM). It is the most successful of Japan's new religious movements of the 20th cent. Founded in 1930, Soka-gakkai came to prominence in the later 20th cent., eventually developing a membership of over 6 million. In 1964 it established the Komeito (Clean Government Party), which by the 1980s was Japan's third-largest political party. It also conducts educational and cultural activities.

Sokhumi *formerly* **Sukhumi** \sù-'ku̇-mē\ *ancient* Dioscurias. Seaport (pop., 1991 est.: 120,000), Republic of Georgia. Located on the BLACK SEA, it was the site of an ancient Greek colony that was later held successively by the Romans, Byzantines, Turks, and Russians. It has long been a popular resort.

Sokolow \'sȯ-kȯ-lȯv\, **Anna** (1910–2000) U.S. modern dancer, choreographer, and teacher. Born in Hartford, Conn., she studied with Martha GRAHAM and formed her own dance group in 1934, with which she performed until retiring in 1954. From 1939 to 1949 she spent part of each year in Mexico City, where she formed Mexico's first modern-dance group. Her choreography has often treated subjects of social concern.

Sokoto \sō-'kō-tō\ City (pop., 1996 est.: 205,000), NW Nigeria. It lies along the Sokoto River on a traditional caravan route that leads north across the SAHARA. It was the capital of the FULANI empire. Modern Sokoto is a major trade center. A pilgrimage destination, it is the site of mosques, a sultan's palace, and USMAN DAN FODIO's tomb.

Sol \'säl\ In ROMAN RELIGION, the name of two distinct sun gods at Rome. The original Sol, or Sol Indiges, had an annual sacrifice and shrines on the Quirinal and in the Circus Maximus. After the importation of various Syrian sun cults, ELAGABALUS built a temple to Sol Invictus on the Palatine and attempted to make his worship the principal religion at Rome. The worship of Sol remained the chief imperial cult until the rise of CHRISTIANITY.

solar cell Any device that directly converts the ENERGY in LIGHT into electrical energy through the process of photovoltaics (see PHOTOVOLTAIC EFFECT). Solar cells do not use chemical reactions to produce electric power, and they have no moving parts. Most are designed for converting sunlight into ELECTRICITY. In large arrays, they can function as central electric power stations analogous to nuclear

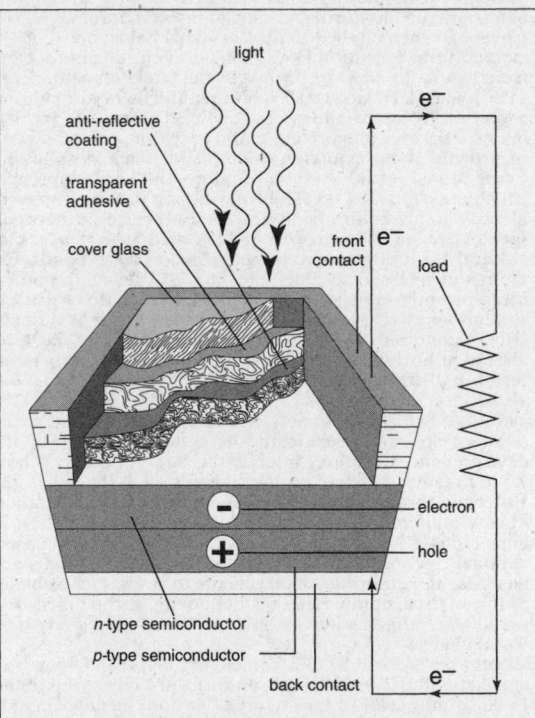

light

e⁻

anti-reflective coating

transparent adhesive

cover glass

front contact

e⁻

load

electron

hole

n-type semiconductor

p-type semiconductor

back contact

e⁻

Solar cell When sunlight strikes the solar cell, an electron is freed by the photoelectric effect. The two dissimilar semiconductors possess a natural difference in electric potential (voltage), which causes the electrons to flow through the external circuit, supplying power to the load. The flow of electricity results from the characteristics of the semiconductors, and is powered entirely by light striking the cell.

or coal- or oil-fired power plants. Because they have no moving parts that could require service or fuels that would require replenishment, they are used to provide power in remote locations, including space satellites.

solar cycle Period in which several important kinds of solar activity repeat, discovered in 1843 by Samuel Heinrich Schwabe (1789–1875). Lasting about 22 years on average, it includes two 11-year cycles of SUNSPOTS, in which the magnetic polarities of spots in the SUN's northern and southern hemispheres switch, and two peaks and two declines in the phenomena (e.g., solar prominences, auroras) that vary in the same period. Attempts have been made to connect the cycle to various solar and terrestrial phenomena.

solar flare Sudden intense brightening of a small part of the SUN's surface, often near SUNSPOTS. Flares develop in a few minutes and may last hours, releasing intense X rays and streams of energetic particles. They appear connected with magnetic field fluxes during the SOLAR CYCLE. The ejected particles reach earth in a day or two and can disrupt radio communications and cause auroras, and may pose a radiation hazard to astronauts.

solar heating Use of solar radiation to heat water or air in buildings. There are two types: passive and active. Passive heating relies on architectural design; the building's location, orientation, layout, materials, and construction are utilized to maximize the heating effect of sunlight. A well-insulated building with a large south-facing window can trap heat on sunny days. Brick, stone, or tile capacity walls can absorb the sun's energy and radiate it into the interior, usually after a time lag of several hours. In active solar heating, mechanical means are used. In liquid-based systems, a blackened metal plate on the exterior absorbs sunlight and traps heat, which is transferred to a carrier fluid. Alternatively, fluid may be pumped through a glass tube or volume of space onto which sunlight has been focused by mirrors. The warmed fluid is pumped to an insulated storage tank and can supply a home with hot water or provide space heating through tubes in floors and ceilings.

solar nebula Gaseous cloud from which, in the nebular hypothesis of the origin of the SOLAR SYSTEM, the sun and planets formed by condensation. In 1755 Immanuel KANT suggested that a NEBULA in slow rotation, gradually pulled together by its own gravity into a disk, became the sun and planets. Pierre-Simon LAPLACE proposed a similar model in 1796. But J. C. MAXWELL showed that shearing forces acting on the disk would have prevented condensation into individual planets. In addition, the sun has less ANGULAR MOMENTUM than the theory seems to require. For decades the collision theory—that the planets formed after another star passed close to the sun—was more popular. Since objections to this theory grew more convincing than those to the nebular hypothesis, a modified version of the latter has become the prevailing theory of the solar system's origin.

solar system EARTH's SUN, its PLANETS and their natural SATELLITES, and the ASTEROIDS, COMETS, meteoroids (see METEOR), and interplanetary dust and gas held by the sun's gravity. The sun contains more than 99% of the solar system's mass; most of the rest is in the planets, about 70% in JUPITER. The SOLAR WIND is also part of the solar system. The prevailing theory holds that the solar system originated from the SOLAR NEBULA. See also MARS, MERCURY, NEPTUNE, PLUTO, SATURN, URANUS, VENUS.

solar wind Flux of particles, chiefly PROTONS and ELECTRONS with some nuclei of heavier elements, accelerated by the solar CORONA's high temperatures to speeds that propel them out of the sun's gravitational field. SOLAR FLARES increase its intensity. The solar wind deflects planets' MAGNETOSPHERES and comets' tails away from the sun. The portion not blocked by a planet travels to about 20 ASTRONOMICAL UNITS out, where it cools and eventually diffuses into interstellar space.

soldering \'sä-dər-iŋ\ Process that uses METAL ALLOYS with low melting points to join metallic surfaces without melting them. Tin-lead solders, once widely used, have been replaced by lead-free alloys. Solders are supplied in wire, bar, or premixed-paste form, depending on the application. Soldering can be carried out using a torch, a soldering iron, a flame heater, or an induction heater.

sole Any of several FLATFISHES, especially about 100 species in the family Soleidae. Those found from Europe to Australia and Japan are marine; some New World species live in freshwater. The eyes are on the right side of the head. The Dover sole *(Solea solea)*, found from estuaries to offshore waters in the E Atlantic and Mediterranean, grows to 20 in. (50 cm) long. The hogchoker *(Trinectes maculatus)*, is seldom over 10 in. (25 cm) long.

Solent \'sō-lənt\, **The** Strait of the ENGLISH CHANNEL. It extends 15 mi (24 km) between mainland England and the Isle of WIGHT and varies in width from 2 to 5 mi (3 to 8 km). It is the scene of yacht races and is famous for the naval reviews off Spithead.

Soleri \sō-'ler-ē\, **Paolo** (b.1919) Italian-U.S. architect. He worked under Frank Lloyd WRIGHT in Arizona (1947–49). Beginning in 1959, he drew up plans for a series of compact urban centers that would extend vertically into space. These megastructures were designed to conserve energy and resources, preserve natural surroundings, and condense human activities within integrated total environments. In 1970 he began constructing a prototype town called Arcosanti, for a population of 7,000, between Phoenix and Flagstaff, Ariz. The work, by students and volunteers, is still in progress.

solid One of the three basic states of MATTER (see PHASE). A solid forms from either a LIQUID or a GAS (the other two states), because the energy of atoms is less when the atoms take up the relatively ordered, three-dimensional structure of a solid. All solids have the ability to support loads applied either perpendicular (normal) or parallel (shear) to a surface. Solids can be crystalline (as in metals), noncrystalline (as in plastics), or quasicrystalline (as in metal alloys).

Solidarity *Polish* Solidarność. Polish trade union. Workers' strikes in 1980 at the shipyards in Gdansk and elsewhere compelled the government to allow independent unions. Solidarity was founded to unite the regional trade unions, and Lech WALESA was elected chairman. It won economic reforms and free elections before the Soviet Union forced the Polish government to suppress the union in 1981. The focus of worldwide attention, it continued as an underground organization until 1989, when the government recognized its legality. In the free elections of 1989, Solidarity candidates won most of the assembly seats and formed a coalition government. In the 1990s the union's role diminished as new political parties emerged.

solid-state device Electronic device that uses the electric, magnetic, or optical properties of a solid CRYSTAL. Synthetic crystals of elements such as SILICON, gallium arsenide, and GERMANIUM are used in TRANSISTORS, rectifiers, and INTEGRATED CIRCUITS. The first solid-state device was the "cat's whisker" (1906), in which a fine wire was moved across a solid crystal to detect a radio signal. See also SEMICONDUCTOR.

solid-state physics Branch of PHYSICS concerned with the physical properties of solid materials. It deals with the properties of CRYSTAL-LATTICE arrangements of ATOMS, and dislocations and defects in the arrangements. These structures are especially important in the study of the conductance of heat and electricity through solid materials.

soliloquy \sə-'li-lə-,kwē\ Dramatic monologue that gives the illusion of being a series of unspoken reflections. An accepted dramatic convention in the 16th–17th cent., it was used artfully by William SHAKESPEARE to reveal the minds of his characters. Pierre CORNEILLE emphasized its lyricism, while Jean RACINE favored it for dramatic effect. Overused in English Restoration plays (1660–85), it fell into disfavor. In the 20th cent., Tennessee WILLIAMS and Arthur MILLER, among others, adapted it by introducing narrators who alternately mused on and took part in the action, and it has been used by contemporary playwrights such as John GUARE and Brian FRIEL.

Solomon (fl. mid-10th cent. B.C.) Son and successor of DAVID. Through the efforts of his mother, Bathsheba, and the prophet Nathan, Solomon was anointed king while David was still alive. He liquidated his opponents ruthlessly and installed friends in key posts. He established Israelite colonies outside his kingdom's borders, cooperating with such friendly rulers as the Queen of SHEBA to increase com-

merce. The crowning achievement of his vast building program was the Temple of JERUSALEM. He reorganized the nation into 12 tribes with 12 administrative districts. After the ascension to the throne of his son Rehoboam, the N tribes seceded and formed their own kingdom of Israel. His legendary wisdom is recorded in the Book of Proverbs, and he is traditionally named as the author of the biblical Song of Solomon. He was regarded as the greatest king of Israel.

Solomon Islands Island nation, SW Pacific Ocean. It includes the islands of GUADALCANAL, Malaita, San Cristobal, Choiseul, Santa Isabel, Florida, and Rennell; the Russell, Shortland, Santa Cruz, and New Georgia island groups; and small islands and reefs (see map at OCEANIA). Area: 10,954 sq mi (28,370 sq km). Population (2000): 466,000. Capital: HONIARA. The population is largely Melanesian. Languages: English (official), Pijin (an English-based pidgin), and more than 60 indigenous Melanesian languages. Religion: Christianity (mostly Protestantism). Currency: Solomon Islands dollar. The Solomons group consists of seven large volcanic islands arranged in two parallel chains that converge in the southeast. They consist mostly of heavily wooded, mountainous terrain drained by short, swift-flowing rivers. The climate is tropical. The economy is based on agriculture, fishing, and lumbering. Tourism is increasing as cruise ships and visitors to World War II battlefields stop at the islands. The nation is a constitutional monarchy with one legislative house; its chief of state is the British monarch represented by the governor-general, and the head of government is the prime minister. The Solomon Islands were probably settled around 2000 B.C. by Austronesian people. Visited by the Spanish in 1568, they were subsequently explored and charted by the Dutch, French, and British. They were under British protection 1893–1900 and became the British Solomon Islands. The Japanese invasion of 1942 ignited three years of the most bitter fighting in the Pacific, particularly on Guadalcanal. The protectorate became self-governing in 1975 and fully independent in 1978. A peace accord in 2000 ended two years of ethnic conflict. Another island group named Solomon Islands, which includes BOUGAINVILLE, is part of Papua New Guinea.

Solon \'sō-lən\ (c.630–c.560 B.C.) Athenian statesman, reformer, and poet, known as one of the Seven Wise Men of Greece. Though he held the office of ARCHON around 594, he did not gain full power as a reformer and legislator until about 20 years later. He ended aristocratic rule and permitted participation by all citizens who had achieved a measure of wealth, eliminating any bloodline requirement. He replaced DRACO's code with more humane laws, freed citizens enslaved for debt and redeemed their land, encouraged professions, and reformed coinage and weights and measures.

Solow \'sō-lō\, **Robert M(erton)** (b.1924) U.S. economist. Born in Brooklyn, N.Y., he received his PhD from Harvard Univ., and he began teaching at MIT in 1949. Solow developed a mathematical model that could show the relative contributions of various factors to sustained national economic growth, and demonstrated that the rate of technological progress is more important to growth than capital accumulation or increases in labor. From the 1960s on, his studies were influential in persuading governments to invest in research and development. In 1987 he was awarded the Nobel Prize.

solstice \'sòl-stis\ Either of the two moments in the year when the sun's apparent path is farthest north or south from earth's equator; also, either of the two points along the ECLIPTIC that the sun passes through at these times. In the Northern Hemisphere the summer solstice occurs on June 21 or 22, the winter solstice on December 21 or 22. In the Southern Hemisphere, the seasons are reversed. See also EQUINOX.

Solti \'shòl-tē\, **Georg** (later **Sir Georg**) (1912–1997) Hungarian-British conductor. After making his piano debut at 12, he studied with Bela BARTOK and Zoltan KODALY, and later served as Arturo TOSCANINI's assistant. After the war he took over the Bavarian State Opera (1945–52), then moved to the Frankfurt Opera (1952–61). As director of Covent Garden (1961–71), he made the first complete recording of Richard WAGNER's *Ring* cycle (1958–65), still one of the most celebrated recordings of all time. Under Solti (1969–91), the Chicago Symphony Orchestra won extraordinary praise and success.

solubility Degree to which a substance dissolves in a SOLVENT to make a SOLUTION (usually expressed as grams of solute per liter of solvent). Solubility of one fluid in another may be complete (e.g., methanol and water) or partial (oil and water dissolve only slightly). In general, "like dissolves like" (e.g., aromatic hydrocarbons dissolve in each other but not in water). Generally, solubilities of solids increase with temperature and those of gases decrease with temperature and increase with pressure.

solution In chemistry, a homogeneous mixture of two or more substances in relative amounts that can vary continuously up to the limit of solubility (SATURATION), if any, of one in the other. Most solutions are LIQUIDS, but solutions of GASES and SOLIDS are possible—for example, AIR (composed primarily of oxygen and nitrogen) or BRASS (composed chiefly of copper and zinc). The liquid in a solution is the SOLVENT, and the substance added is the solute; if both are liquids, the one present in a smaller amount is usually considered the solute. Materials with IONIC BONDS (e.g., SALTS) and many with COVALENT BONDS (e.g., ACIDS, BASES, ALCOHOLS) dissociate into IONS on dissolving and are called ELECTROLYTES. Their solutions can conduct ELECTRICITY and have other properties that differ from those of nonelectrolytes. Solutions are involved in most chemical reactions, refining and purification, industrial processing, and biological phenomena.

Solvay process \'säl-,vā\ or **ammonia-soda process** Method of manufacturing sodium carbonate (soda ash), devised by Ernest Solvay (1838–1922). Common salt (sodium chloride) is treated with ammonia and then carbon dioxide to form sodium bicarbonate and ammonium chloride. When heated, the bicarbonate yields sodium carbonate; the ammonium chloride is treated with lime to produce ammonia (for reuse) and calcium chloride. The process proved of great commercial value, since large quantities of soda ash are used in making glass, detergents, and cleansers.

solvent Substance, ordinarily a LIQUID, in which other materials dissolve to form a SOLUTION. Polar solvents (e.g., WATER) favor formation of IONS; nonpolar ones (e.g., HYDROCARBONS) do not. Many organic compounds are used as solvents, including AROMATIC COMPOUNDS and other hydrocarbons, ALCOHOLS, ESTERS, ETHERS, KETONES and AMINES. Their chief uses are as industrial cleaners and in extractive processes, pharmaceuticals, inks, paints, varnishes, and lacquers.

Solway Firth Inlet of the IRISH SEA. On the border between England and Scotland, it extends inland for 38 mi (61 km). HADRIAN'S WALL terminates on its S shore.

Solzhenitsyn \,sōl-zhə-'nēt-sin\, **Aleksandr (Isayevich)** (b.1918) Russian novelist and historian. Arrested in 1945 for criticizing Joseph STALIN, he spent eight years in prisons and labor camps. With *One Day in the Life of Ivan Denisovich* (1962), based on his labor-camp experiences, he emerged as an eloquent opponent of government repression. He was forced to publish later works abroad, including *The First Circle* (1968), *Cancer Ward* (1968), and *August 1914* (1971). The first volume of *The Gulag Archipelago* (1973), one of the greatest works in Russian prose, led to his being charged with treason. Exiled in 1974, he lived in the U.S., enjoying worldwide fame, until 1994. In the late 1980s glasnost brought renewed access to his work in Russia, but also a loss of interest in it. He was awarded the 1970 Nobel Prize.

Somalia Country, NE Africa. Located in the Horn of Africa, it stretches from the equator to the Red Sea. Area: 246,000 sq mi (637,000 sq km). Population (2000): 7,253,000 (excluding an estimated 450,000 refugees in other countries). Capital: MOGADISHU. Most of the people are nomadic or seminomadic Somalis. Language: Somali, Arabic (both official). Religion: Islam (official). Currency: Somali shilling. Much of Somalia is semidesert. The central and S regions are flat, while the N region rises to form rugged mountain ranges. Only about 2% of its land is arable, though more than half is grazeable. Somalia has a developing, mixed economy largely based on livestock and agriculture. It is

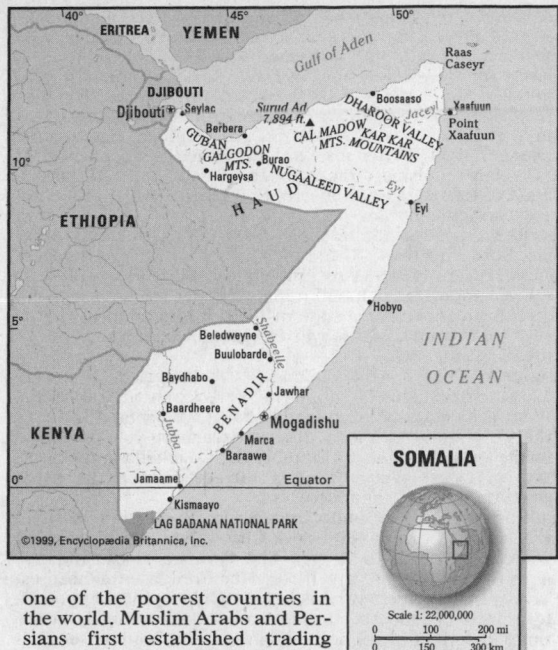

SOMALIA

Scale 1: 22,000,000
0   100   200 mi
0   150   300 km

one of the poorest countries in the world. Muslim Arabs and Persians first established trading posts along the coasts in the 7th–10th cent. By the 10th cent. Somali nomads occupied the area inland from the Gulf of ADEN, and the south and west were inhabited by various groups of pastoral OROMO peoples. Intensive European exploration began after the British occupation of ADEN in 1839, and in the late 19th cent. Britain and Italy set up protectorates in the region. During World War II the Italians invaded British Somaliland (1940); a year later British troops retook the area, and Britain administered the region until 1950, when ITALIAN SOMALILAND became a U.N. trust territory. In 1960 it was united with the former British Somaliland, and the two became the independent Republic of Somalia. Since then it has suffered political and civil strife, including military dictatorship, civil wars, drought, and famine. From the 1990s no effective central government has existed. In 1991, a proclamation of a Republic of Somaliland, on territory corresponding to the former British Somaliland, was issued by a breakaway group. It did not receive international recognition, but it operated more smoothly than the area of traditional Somalia. A U.N. peacekeeping force intervened in 1992 to secure food supplies; fighting continued and the peacekeeping force left in 1995. The country remained in turmoil. Severe floods devastated the S region in 1999.

Somaliland \sə-'mä-lē-ˌland\ Historical name for the region of E Africa between the equator and the Gulf of Aden that includes Somalia, Djibouti, and SE Ethiopia. It has an area of about 300,000 sq mi (775,000 sq km). In the 7th–12th cent. A.D. Muslim traders settled on the coast and formed sultanates. The nomadic Somalis, who occupied the N part of the country in the 10th–15th cent., adopted Islam and eventually came to control the sultanates themselves. In the late 19th cent., France, Italy, and Britain partitioned the region. In 1960 British Somaliland and ITALIAN SOMALILAND united to form the Republic of Somalia. French Somaliland became the Republic of Djibouti in 1977.

Somalis \sə-'mä-lēz\ People occupying all of Somalia and parts of Djibouti, Ethiopia, and Kenya. All have been Muslims since at least the 14th cent. Numbering about 7 million, they are primarily nomadic herdsmen. Intense competition for scarce resources has led to many blood feuds and wars with neighboring peoples. Other Somalis live in the urban centers, especially along the coast of the Horn of Africa; many act as commercial middlemen between the Arab world and the nomads of the interior.

somatotropin See GROWTH HORMONE

Somerset County (pop., 1998 est.: 489,000), SW England. Its county seat is Taunton. The remains of prehistoric villages are found in the region. From the 7th cent. A.D., Somerset formed the westernmost part of the kingdom of WESSEX. It is mainly an agricultural county and is known for its cider. Tourists visit its BRISTOL CHANNEL resorts and historic mansions.

Somerset, Duke of orig. Edward Seymour (c.1500–1552) English politician. After his sister, Jane SEYMOUR, married HENRY VIII in 1536, Somerset rose rapidly in royal favor. His forces invaded Scotland and sacked Edinburgh in 1544, and decisively defeated the French at Boulogne in 1545. After Henry's death (1547), he was named Protector of England during the minority of EDWARD VI. When the Scots rejected his appeal for a voluntary union with England, he invaded Scotland and won the Battle of Pinkie (1547). He introduced moderate Protestant reforms, but these provoked Catholic uprisings in W England. Opposed by the duke of NORTHUMBERLAND, he was deposed in 1549 and later imprisoned and executed.

Somme \'sóm, 'säm, 'səm\, **Battle of the** (July 1–Nov. 13, 1916) Allied offensive in WORLD WAR I. British and French forces launched a frontal attack against an entrenched German army north of the Somme River in France. A weeklong artillery bombardment was followed by a British infantry assault; some 20,000 British troops died on the first day. The offensive deteriorated into a battle of attrition, hampered by torrential rains in October that made the muddy battlefield impassable. By the time it was abandoned, the Allies had advanced only 5 mi (8 km). With 650,000 German casualties, 420,000 British, and 195,000 French, the battle became a metaphor for futile and indiscriminate slaughter.

Somme River \'səm\ River, N France. It rises near St.-Quentin and flows westward 152 mi (245 km) to the ENGLISH CHANNEL. Canals connect it with navigable waterways that link PARIS and FLANDERS. Its upper basin saw heavy fighting in World War I, particularly in the Battle of the SOMME (1916).

Somoza family \sō-'mō-sə\ Family that controlled Nicaragua for over 40 years. The dynasty's founder, Anastasio Somoza García (1896–1956), became head of Nicaragua's army in 1933 and, after deposing the elected president in 1936, ruled the country despotically until his assassination. He was succeeded by his elder son, Luis Somoza Debayle (1922–1967), and later by his younger son, Anastasio Somoza Debayle (1925–1980), whose corrupt and brutal rule (1963–79) led to his overthrow by the SANDINISTAS.

sonar Technique for detecting and determining the distance and direction of underwater objects by tracking echoes. In active sonar a sound wave is generated that spreads outward and is reflected back by a target object. Passive systems simply pick up the noise produced by the target (such as a submarine or torpedo). A third kind of sonar, used in communication systems, requires a projector and receiver at both ends. Sonar was first used to detect submarines in 1916. Modern nonmilitary uses include fish and wreck finding, depth sounding, mapping of the ocean floor, and Doppler navigation (see DOPPLER EFFECT).

sonata Musical form for one or more instruments, usually consisting of three or four movements. The name originally simply indicated nonvocal music. In the 1650s two types of ensemble sonatas began to be codified, the sonata da chiesa (church sonata) and sonata da camera (chamber sonata). The former, intended for church performance, was generally in four movements, two of them slow; the latter was usually a SUITE of dances. The so-called solo sonata (for soloist—usually violin—and CONTINUO) and the trio sonata (for two soloists and continuo) became standard. In the 1740s solo keyboard sonatas began to be written. C. P. E. BACH established the three-movement keyboard sonata as the norm. Duo sonatas, usually for violin and keyboard, simultaneously became highly popular. From Bach's time onward, the first movement was generally in allegro tempo and in SONATA FORM. The second movement was usually slow. The last movement was generally a minuet, RONDO, or THEME AND VARIATIONS. In a four-movement sonata, the third was usually a minuet or SCHERZO.

sonata form *or* **sonata-allegro form** Form of most first movements, and often other movements, in such musical genres as the SYMPHONY, STRING QUARTET, and SONATA. It evolved from two-part forms such as the dances of the baroque SUITE. The first part, or exposition, presents the movement's basic thematic material, which is often divided into two thematic groups, the second being in the dominant key or (if the movement is in a minor key) in the relative major key. The second section, or development, generally treats the earlier themes freely, often moving to various keys. In the final section, or recapitulation, all the themes are repeated in the tonic. Sonata form was the most common form for instrumental works in Western art music from about 1760 to the 20th cent.

Sondheim \'sänd-ˌhīm\, **Stephen (Joshua)** (b.1930) U.S. composer and lyricist. Born in New York City, he wrote his first musical at 15 under Oscar HAMMERSTEIN. He made his first mark on Broadway as lyricist for *West Side Story* (1957) and later *Gypsy* (1959). He wrote both music and lyrics for *A Funny Thing Happened on the Way to the Forum* (1962, Tony Award), *Company* (1970, Tony Award), *Follies* (1971), *A Little Night Music* (1973, Tony Award), *Sweeney Todd* (1979, Tony Award), *Sunday in the Park with George* (1984, Pulitzer Prize), and *Into the Woods* (1987), among other works. His works are known for their intellectuality, musical complexity, and frequently dark tone.

song Short piece of music for voice, with or without instrumental accompaniment. Folk songs—traditional songs without a known composer, transmitted orally rather than in written form—have existed for millennia, but have left few traces in ancient sources. Virtually all known preliterate societies have a repertory of songs. Folk songs often accompany religious ceremonies, dancing, labor, or courting; they may tell stories or express emotions; the music follows obvious conventions and is often repetitive. Songs written by a particular composer and poet generally are more sophisticated and are not attached to activities. In the West, the continuous tradition of secular art songs begins with the TROUBADOURS and TROUVÈRES of the 12th–13th cent. The 14th cent. produced a great body of polyphonic songs in the FORMES FIXES. Later the Italian MADRIGAL becomes the most distinguished genre. The 19th cent. was a golden age for the art song, notably the German LIED. In the 20th cent. the popular song displaced the more cultivated art song, and popular music is today synonymous with popular song.

Song dynasty *or* **Sung dynasty** \'suṅ\ (960–1279) Chinese dynasty, founded by TAIZU, that united the entire country until 1127 and the S portion until 1279 (when N China was controlled by the JUCHEN). Commerce flourished, paper currency came into increasing use, and several cities grew to over a million people. WANG ANSHI worked for more equitable taxation and other reforms. Widespread printing brought increased literacy; private academies and state schools sent more candidates through the CHINESE EXAMINATION SYSTEM. In the 12th cent., ZHU XI systemized NEO-CONFUCIANISM. The Song was also an era of scholarship: groundbreaking treatises on architecture and botany were published, as was the famous history *Zizhi tongjian* of Sima Guang. Landscape painting, decorative arts, and architecture all reached a high point during the Song.

Songhai empire *or* **Songhay empire** \'sȯn̈-ˌhī\ Ancient Muslim trading state, W. Africa. Centered on the middle NIGER RIVER in what is now central Mali, it eventually extended into Niger and Nigeria. Established about A.D. 800, it reached its greatest extent in the 16th cent. before falling to Moroccan forces in 1591. Its important cities were Gao and TOMBOUCTOU.

Song Hong See RED RIVER

sonnet Fixed verse form having 14 lines that are typically five-foot iambics rhyming according to a prescribed scheme. It seems to have originated in the 13th cent. among the Sicilian school of court poets. In the 14th cent., PETRARCH established the most widely used sonnet form. The Petrarchan (or Italian) sonnet characteristically consists of an eight-line octave, rhyming *abbaabba*, that states a problem, asks a question, or expresses an emotional tension, followed by a six-line sestet, of varying rhyme schemes, that resolves the problem, answers the question, or resolves the tension. From the Italian form, Elizabethan poets gradually developed the Shakespearean (or English) sonnet. It consists of three quatrains, each with an independent rhyme scheme, and ends with a rhymed couplet.

Sonni Ali \sȯn-'ē-ä-'lē\ (d.1492) W. African monarch who initiated the expansion of the SONGHAI EMPIRE. His first major conquest (1468) was the great city of TOMBOUCTOU in the declining MALI EMPIRE. He subdued Jenné (now Djenné) in 1473 after a seven-year siege. He spent most of his reign repulsing attacks by the Dendi, FULANI, MOSSI, and TUAREG. Arab chroniclers characterized him as a cruel and capricious tyrant.

Sonora \sə-'nȯr-ə\ State (pop., 2000: 2,213,000), NW Mexico. Bordering the U.S. and the Gulf of California, it covers 71,403 sq mi (184,934 sq km); its capital is Hermosillo. It was an important colonial mining district for copper, gold, and silver. It became a state in 1830. It is generally arid; irrigation is used to grow winter vegetables, cereals, cotton, tobacco, and corn.

Sonoran Desert Arid region, W N. America. It covers 120,000 sq mi (310,000 sq km) in SW Arizona, SE California, W SONORA state, Mexico, and N Baja California; it includes the Colorado and Yuma deserts. Irrigation has produced fertile agricultural areas, notably the Coachella and IMPERIAL VALLEYS. Warm winters attract tourists to PALM SPRINGS, TUCSON, and PHOENIX.

Sontag \'sän-ˌtag\, **Susan** *orig.* Susan Rosenblatt (b.1933) U.S. writer. Born in New York City, she taught philosophy while contributing to the *New York Review of Books* and *Partisan Review* in the early 1960s. Her French-influenced essays are characterized by a serious philosophical approach to aspects of modern culture rarely taken seriously at the time, including films, popular music, and "camp" sensibility. Collections include the influential *Against Interpretation* (1968) and *Styles of Radical Will* (1969). Her later critical works include *On Photography* (1977) and *Illness as Metaphor* (1977). Her novels include *The Volcano Lover* (1992) and *In America* (1999, National Book Award).

Sony Corp. Major Japanese manufacturer of consumer electronics. Founded by Ibuka Masaru (1908–1997) and Akio Morita (1921–1999) in 1946, it adopted its present name in 1958. Its first major consumer item was an audio tape recorder, introduced in 1950. Since then it has pioneered new technology for consumer products marketed worldwide, including the first pocket-sized transistor radio (1957) and a color video cassette recorder (1969), and the Walkman portable radio. Sony purchased CBS Records Group, the world's largest record company, in 1987–88 and Columbia Pictures Entertainment in 1989.

Soong family \'sun̈\ Influential 20th-cent. Chinese family. Charlie Soong (1866–1918) made his fortune as a publisher, initially of Bibles, and became a supporter of SUN YAT-SEN, whose Nationalist Party (see GUOMINDANG) he helped finance. His first daughter married a businessman who also provided financial support to the Nationalists; his second daughter, Soong Ch'ing-ling (1892–1981), married Sun Yat-sen; his third daughter, Soong Mei-ling (b.1897) became CHIANG KAI-SHEK's second wife. A son, T. V. Soong (1894–1971), established the Central Bank of China and served in the Nationalist government. The 1949 Communist takeover divided the family: Ch'ing-ling, who had earlier denounced the Nationalists for betraying Sun Yat-sen's ideals, remained on the mainland. Mei-ling accompanied Chiang Kai-shek to Taiwan and publicized his cause in the West; as Madam Chiang, she became extremely popular in the U.S. T. V. Soong, once reputed the richest man in the world, moved to the U.S.

Sophia \'sȯ-fyə\ *Russian* Sofya Alekseyevna (1657–1704) Regent of Russia (1682–89). Daughter of Czar ALEXIS, she objected to the succession of her half brother PETER I the

Sophia Engraving by A. Bloteling

Great as czar (1682) and arranged to have her brother Ivan V proclaimed coruler; she assumed the role of regent. With help from her lover, Vasily GOLITSYN, she promoted the development of industry and concluded peace treaties with Poland (1686) and China (1689). After sponsoring two disastrous military campaigns against the Crimean Tatars (1687, 1689), she tried to regain her influence by ousting Peter. She was instead overthrown by Peter in 1689 and forced to enter a convent.

sophists \\'sä-fists\\ Group of itinerant professional teachers and writers prominent in Greece in the later 5th cent. B.C. The sophistic movement arose at a time when there was much questioning of the absolute nature of familiar values and ways of life. An antithesis arose between nature and custom, tradition, or law, in which custom could be regarded either as a hindrance to natural freedom or as a beneficial and civilizing restraint on natural anarchy. Both views were represented among the sophists. Their most eminent representative was PROTAGORAS; others include Prodicus, Hippias, Antiphon, and Critias. A later "second sophistic school" existed in the 2nd cent. A.D.

Sophocles \\'sä-fə-ˌklēz\\ (496?–406 B.C.) Greek playwright. With AESCHYLUS and EURIPIDES, he was one of the three great tragic playwrights of classical Athens. He served successively in important Athenian posts as a treasurer, commander, and adviser. He competed in dramatic festivals, defeating Aeschylus to win his first victory in 468 B.C. He went on to write 123 dramas for dramatic competitions, winning over 20 victories. Only seven tragedies survive in their entirety, including *Antigone, Ajax, Electra, The Trachinian Women, Philoctetes, Oedipus at Colonus,* and *Oedipus the King,* his best-known work. He was the first to introduce a third actor onstage. His plays are noted for their supple language, vivid characterization, and formal perfection.

soprano Highest vocal register, ranging from about middle C to the second A above. Sopranos are normally female but may also include boy sopranos. Soprano voices are traditionally classified as dramatic (rich and powerful), lyric (lighter), and coloratura (high and very agile). The mezzo-soprano range is about a 3rd lower.

Sopwith, Thomas (Octave Murdoch) (*later* **Sir Thomas**) (1888–1989) British aircraft designer. He taught himself to fly in 1910 and won a prize for the longest flight to the European continent. In 1912 he founded his own aircraft company, which in World War I built such planes as the Camel, the Pup, and the Triplane. His firm produced the Hurricane fighter and the Lancaster bomber in World War II, and later the Harrier, a vertical-takeoff jet fighter.

Soranus of Ephesus \\sō-'rā-nəs...'e-fə-səs\\ (fl.2nd cent. A.D.) Greek gynecologist, obstetrician, and pediatrician. A keen observer and unusually competent practitioner, he wrote works that influenced medical opinion for 1,500 years. His remarkable *On Midwifery and the Diseases of Women* describes innovative contraceptive methods and obstetric techniques, as well as rickets. His suggested treatments for nervous disorders resemble aspects of modern psychotherapy.

Sorby, Henry Clifton (1826–1908) British amateur scientist. Convinced of the value of the microscope to geology, Sorby began in 1849 to prepare thin sections of rocks for microscopic study. He developed a new type of spectrum microscope for analyzing the light of organic pigments (1865). Later research was devoted to meteors, the origin of layered rocks, weathering, and marine biology. He published works dealing with the physical geography of geologic periods and rock breakdown and buildup. Sorby is considered the father of microscopical petrography and metallography.

sorcery See WITCHCRAFT AND SORCERY

sorghum \\'sòr-gəm\\ CEREAL grain plant of the family Gramineae (Poaceae), probably native to Africa, widely grown for its edible starchy seeds. All types raised for grain belong to the species *Sorghum vulgare,* which includes varieties of grain sorghums and grass sorghums (grown for hay and fodder), and broomcorn (used in making brooms and brushes). The strong grass usually grows 2–8 ft (0.5–2.5 m) or higher. The seeds are smaller than those of wheat. Resistant to drought and heat, sorghum is one of Africa's major cereal grains. It is also grown in the U.S., India, Pakistan,

China, and elsewhere. The grain is usually ground into meal for porridge, flatbreads, and cakes.

sorority See FRATERNITY AND SORORITY

Soros \\'sòr-ōs\\, **George** (b.1930) Hungarian-U.S. financier. He left his native Hungary in 1944 and settled in London in 1947, where he joined a merchant bank. He moved to New York in 1956 and initially worked as an analyst of European securities. By 1979 his daring investments and currency speculation had brought large profits, some of which he used to found his influential Soros Foundations, dedicated to creating open societies in many Eastern European countries and Russia. Other Soros programs aim to enlarge public debate on a wide range of controversial issues.

sorrel Any of several hardy perennial herbs of the BUCKWHEAT family, widespread in temperate regions. Sheep sorrel (*Rumex acetosella*) is an attractive but troublesome weed. It has slender, triangular leaves and tiny yellow or reddish flowers. The pungent, sour leaves are used as a vegetable, as a flavoring in omelets and sauces, in soups, and, when young, in salads. Wood sorrels, unrelated plants, belong to the genus *Oxalis* (see OXALIS).

Sosa (Peralta), Sammy (*orig.* Samuel) (b.1968) U.S. (Dominican-born) baseball player. He came to the U.S. as a child. After brief stints with the Texas Rangers and Chicago White Sox, he joined the Chicago Cubs in 1992. In 1993 the right fielder became the Cubs' first player to hit 30 home runs and steal 30 bases in one season. In 1998 he dramatically battled Mark MCGWIRE for the all-time season home-run record; he finished the year with 66 home runs, earning him the National League's Most Valuable Player award. In 1999 he hit 63 homers.

Sotho \\'sō-ˌtō\\ Bantu-speaking peoples (numbering 10 million) occupying the high grasslands of S Africa. The main Sotho groups are the Pedi and Lovedu in the north, the Tswana in the west, and the Basuto of Lesotho. Most farm and raise livestock.

Soto, Hernando de See Hernando DE SOTO

soul Immaterial aspect or essence of a person, conjoined with the body during life and separable at death. The concept of a soul is found in nearly all cultures and religions, though the interpretations of its nature vary considerably. The early Hebrews did not consider the soul as distinct from the body, but later Jewish writers perceived the two as separate. Christian theology adopted the Greek concept of an immortal soul, adding the notion that God created the soul and infused it into the body at conception. In HINDUISM, each soul, or ATMAN, was created at the beginning of time and imprisoned in an earthly body; at death, the soul passes to a new body according to the laws of KARMA. BUDDHISM asserts that any sense of an individual self is illusory.

soul music Style of U.S. popular music sung primarily by black musicians, having its roots in GOSPEL MUSIC and RHYTHM AND BLUES. The term, first used in the 1960s, was an allusion to the music's intensity of feeling and earthiness. In its earliest stages, soul music was found most commonly in the South, but many of the young singers who were to popularize it migrated to cities in the North. The founding of MOTOWN in Detroit and Stax-Volt in Memphis did much to encourage the style. Its most popular performers include James BROWN, Ray CHARLES, and Aretha FRANKLIN.

sound Mechanical disturbance that propagates as a longitudinal WAVE through a solid, liquid, or gas. A sound wave is generated by a vibrating object. The vibrations cause alternating compressions (regions of crowding) and rarefactions (regions of scarcity) in the particles of the medium. The speed of sound through a medium depends on the medium's ELASTICITY, DENSITY, and TEMPERATURE. The FREQUENCY of a sound wave, perceived as PITCH, is the number of compressions (or rarefactions) that pass a fixed point per unit time. The audible frequencies range from approximately 20 hertz to 20 kilohertz. See also ACOUSTICS, EAR, HEARING, ULTRASONICS.

Sound, The See ORESUND

sound barrier Sharp rise in aerodynamic DRAG that occurs as an aircraft approaches the speed of SOUND. The sound barrier was formerly an obstacle to supersonic flight. If an aircraft flies at somewhat less than sonic speed, the pressure waves (sound waves) it creates outspeed their sources and

spread out ahead of it. Once the aircraft reaches sonic speed the waves are unable to get out of its way. Strong local shock waves form on the wings and body; airflow around the craft becomes unsteady, and severe and dangerous buffeting may result. Generally, aircraft properly designed for supersonic flight have little difficulty in passing through the sound barrier. The first pilot to break the sound barrier was Chuck YEAGER (1947).

sound card or **audio card** INTEGRATED CIRCUIT that generates an audio signal and sends it to a computer's speakers. The sound card can accept an analog sound (as from a microphone) and convert it to digital data that can be stored in an audio file, or accept digitized audio signals (as from an audio file) and convert them to analog signals that can be played on the computer's speakers.

sound reception See HEARING

Souphanouvong \sü-ʹpä-nü-ˌvȯŋ\ (1909–1995) Leader of the revolutionary Pathet Lao movement and president of Laos (1975–86). Half brother of SOUVANNA PHOUMA, he was trained in civil engineering in France and built bridges and roads in Vietnam 1938–45. After World War II he broke with the Free Laos government-in-exile to ally with the VIET MINH, founding the communist-oriented Pathet Lao (1950). When it came to power in 1974–75, he became Laos's ceremonial head of state.

Souris River \ʹsu̇r-əs\ River, Saskatchewan, Manitoba, and N. Dakota. It rises in SE Saskatchewan, then flows southeast into N. Dakota, where it turns north, joining the ASSINIBOINE RIVER in Manitoba after a course of 600 mi (966 km).

Sousa \ʹsü-zə\, **John Philip** (1854–1932) U.S. bandmaster and composer, known as "The March King." Sousa grew up in Washington, D.C., and enlisted in the Marine Corps in 1868. He directed the Marine Band (1880–92), building it into a virtuoso ensemble. In 1892 he formed his own band, with which he toured internationally to great acclaim. He composed 136 military marches, including "Semper Fidelis" (the official march of the Marines), "The Washington Post," and "The Stars and Stripes Forever." He also wrote successful operettas, including *El Capitan* (1896). In the 1890s he developed the SOUSAPHONE.

sousaphone or **helicon** Spiral circular bass or contrabass TUBA. Traditionally made of brass, it is now often made of fiberglass for lightness. The helicon was perfected in Vienna in 1849 by Ignaz Stowasser, who manufactured it in various sizes. J. P. SOUSA designed a removable and rotatable bell for it in 1892. Designed for portability, the instruments have become standard in marching bands.

Souter \ʹsü-tər\, **David H(ackett)** (b.1939) U.S. jurist. Born in Melrose, Mass., he studied at Harvard and Oxford. In New Hampshire he was promoted to state attorney general in 1976, and joined its supreme court in 1983. In 1990 he was named to the First U.S. Circuit Court of Appeals, and later that year to the U.S. Supreme Court. His decisions, conservative at the outset, have become moderate or liberal on most issues.

South, University of the *known as* **Sewanee** Private university in Sewanee, Tenn., founded in 1857. Affiliated with the Episcopal church, it has a college of arts and sciences and a school of theology. Its literary journal, *The Sewanee Review,* was founded in 1892. Current enrollment is about 1,300.

South Africa, Republic of *formerly* **Union of South Africa** Southernmost country on the African continent. The kingdom of LESOTHO lies within its boundaries. Area: 470,689 sq mi (1,219,080 sq km). Population (2000): 43,421,000. Capitals: PRETORIA, executive; CAPE TOWN, legislative; BLOEMFONTEIN, judicial. Three-fourths of the population are black Africans: they include the ZULU, XHOSA, SOTHO, and Tswana; one-eighth are whites, and most of the remainder are of mixed race or Indian descent. Languages: Afrikaans, English, and nine BANTU LANGUAGES (all official). Religions: Christianity, traditional beliefs. Currency: rand. S. Africa has three major zones: the broad interior plateau, the surrounding mountainous Great Escarpment, and a narrow belt of coastal plain. It has a temperate subtropical climate. It is the world's largest producer of gold and a leading producer and exporter of coal, diamonds, platinum, and vanadium. It is a republic with two legislative houses; its head of

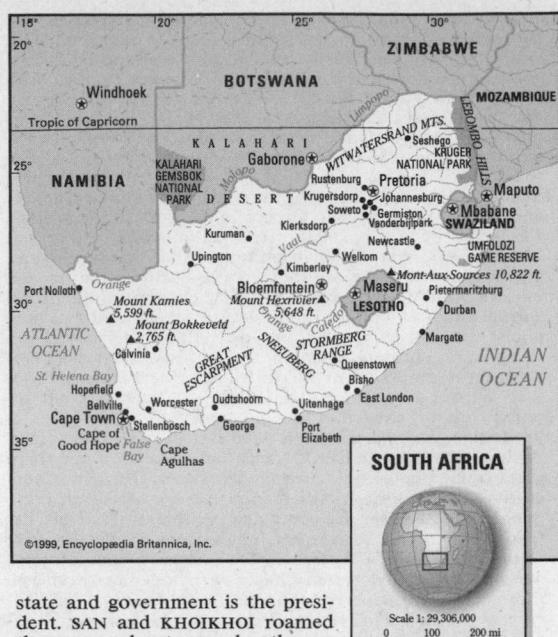

©1999, Encyclopædia Britannica, Inc.

SOUTH AFRICA

Scale 1: 29,306,000
0   100   200 mi
0   150   300 km

state and government is the president. SAN and KHOIKHOI roamed the area as hunters and gatherers in the Stone Age, and the latter had developed a pastoralist culture by the time of European contact. By the 14th cent., BANTU PEOPLES had settled in the area and developed gold and copper mining and an active E. African trade. In 1652 the Dutch established a colony at the Cape of GOOD HOPE; the Dutch settlers became known as Boers and later as AFRIKANERS, after their AFRIKAANS LAGUAGE. In 1795 British forces captured the Cape, and in 1830, to escape British rule, Dutch settlers made the GREAT TREK northward and established the independent Boer republics of ORANGE FREE STATE and the S. African Republic (later the TRANSVAAL region), which the British annexed as colonies by 1902 (see S. AFRICAN WAR). In 1910 the British colonies of Cape Colony, Transvaal, NATAL, and Orange River were unified into the new Union of S. Africa. It became independent and withdrew from the COMMONWEALTH in 1961. Throughout the 20th cent. S. African politics were dominated by the question of maintaining white supremacy over the country's black majority, and in 1948 S. Africa formally instituted APARTHEID. Faced by increasing worldwide condemnation, it began dismantling the policy in the 1980s and ended it in 1989. In free elections in 1994, Nelson MANDELA became the country's first black president. High rates of AIDS and violent crime beset the nation's new leadership.

South African War or **Boer War** War between Great Britain and the two Boer (AFRIKANER) republics, the S. African Republic (TRANSVAAL) and the ORANGE FREE STATE, from 1899 to 1902. It was caused when the Boer leader Paul KRUGER refused to grant political rights to the English in the interior, and the British high commissioner responded aggressively. Initially the Boers defeated the British in major engagements and besieged the key towns of Ladysmith, Mafikeng, and Kimberley; but British reinforcements under H. H. KITCHENER and Frederick S. Roberts dispersed the Boer armies and occupied Bloemfontein, Johannesburg, and Pretoria (1900). Boer commando attacks led Kitchener to destroy Boer farms and herd Boer civilians into concentration camps. More than 20,000 civilians died as a result, causing international outrage. The Boers accepted defeat at the Peace of Vereeniging.

South America Continent, Western Hemisphere. The world's fourth-largest continent, it is bounded by the Caribbean Sea, the Atlantic Ocean, and the Pacific Ocean. It is separated from Antarctica by the DRAKE PASSAGE and is joined to N. America by the Isthmus of Panama. Area: 6,878,000 sq

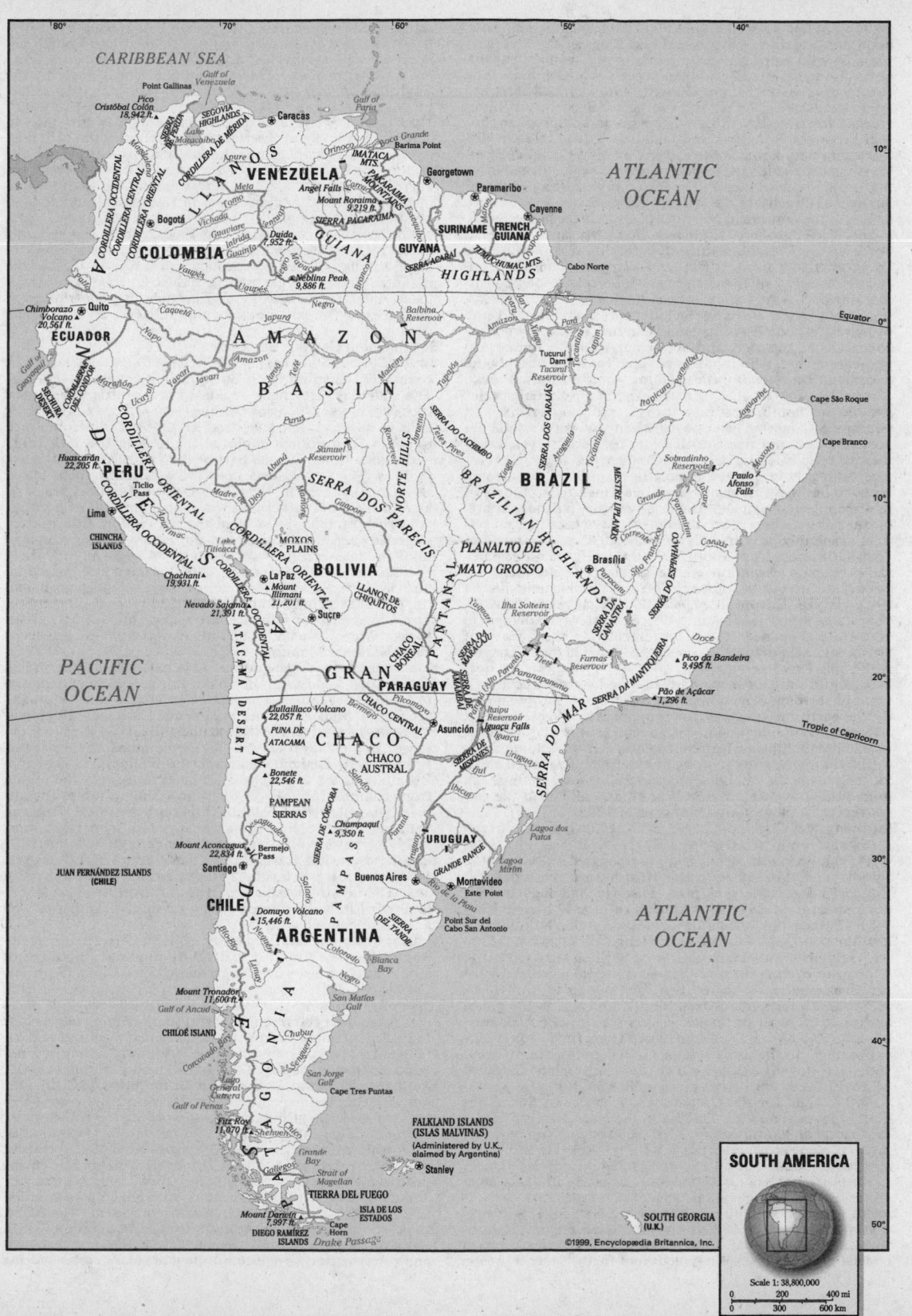

CARIBBEAN SEA

Point Gallinas

Pico
Cristóbal Colón
18,942 ft.

Gulf of
Venezuela

SEGOVIA
HIGHLANDS

Caracas

Gulf of
Paria

Barima Point

ATLANTIC
OCEAN

LLANOS

VENEZUELA

Angel Falls

Mount Roraima
9,219 ft.

SIERRA PACARAIMA

MATACA
MTS.

PACARAIMA
MOUNTAINS

Georgetown

Paramaribo

Cayenne

Bogotá

COLOMBIA

Duida
7,952 ft.

GUIANA

GUYANA

SURINAME

FRENCH
GUIANA

Neblina Peak
9,886 ft.

SERRA ACARAI

TUMUCUMAC MTS.

HIGHLANDS

Cabo Norte

Chimborazo
Volcano
20,561 ft.

Quito

ECUADOR

A M A Z O N

Balbina
Reservoir

Equator

0°

Tucuruí
Dam

Tucuruí
Reservoir

Cape São Roque

Cape Branco

Huascarán
22,205 ft.

PERU

Ticlio
Pass

Lima

CHINCHA
ISLANDS

B A S I N

SERRA DOS PARECIS

NORTE HILLS

SERRA DO CACHIMBO

SERRA DOS CARAJAS

BRAZIL

MESTRE LIPLANDS

Sobradinho
Reservoir

Paulo
Afonso
Falls

Chachani
19,931 ft.

Nevado Sajama
21,391 ft.

CORDILLERA OCCIDENTAL

CORDILLERA ORIENTAL

MOXOS
PLAINS

La Paz

Mount
Illimani
21,201 ft.

Sucre

BOLIVIA

LLANOS DE
CHIQUITOS

PLANALTO DE
MATO GROSSO

BRAZILIAN HIGHLANDS

Brasília

Ilha Solteira
Reservoir

Doce

Pico da Bandeira
9,495 ft.

PACIFIC
OCEAN

ATACAMA DESERT

PANTANAL

CHACO
BOREAL

GRAN

PARAGUAY

SERRA DA MANTIQUEIRA

SERRA DA CANASTRA

Pão de Açúcar
1,296 ft.

Tropic of Capricorn

Llullaillaco Volcano
22,057 ft.

PUNA DE
ATACAMA

CHACO

CHACO CENTRAL

CHACO
AUSTRAL

Asunción

Iguaçu Reservoir

Iguaçu Falls

SERRA DO MAR

Bonete
22,546 ft.

PAMPEAN
SIERRAS

Champaquí
9,350 ft.

URUGUAY

GRANDE RANGE

Lagoa dos
Patos

Mount Aconcagua
22,834 ft.

Santiago

Bermejo
Pass

Buenos Aires

Montevideo

Este Point

ATLANTIC
OCEAN

JUAN FERNÁNDEZ ISLANDS
(CHILE)

CHILE

Domuyo Volcano
15,446 ft.

ARGENTINA

PAMPAS

SIERRA
DEL TANDIL

Point Sur del
Cabo San Antonio

Mount Tronador
11,600 ft.

CHILOÉ ISLAND

Blanca
Bay

San Matías
Gulf

Lago
General
Carrera

Gulf of Penas

Fitz Roy
11,070 ft.

PATAGONIA

San Jorge
Gulf

Cape Tres Puntas

FALKLAND ISLANDS
(ISLAS MALVINAS)
(Administered by U.K.,
claimed by Argentina)

Stanley

Grande
Bay

Strait of
Magellan

TIERRA DEL FUEGO

ISLA DE LOS
ESTADOS

SOUTH GEORGIA
(U.K.)

Mount Darwin
7,997 ft.

DIEGO RAMÍREZ
ISLANDS

Cape
Horn

Drake Passage

©1999, Encyclopædia Britannica, Inc.

S

SOUTH AMERICA

Scale 1: 38,800,000

0   200   400 mi
0 300   600 km

mi (17,814,000 sq km). Pop., 2000 est.: 341,624,000. Four main ethnic groups have populated S. America: American Indians, who were the continent's pre-Columbian inhabitants; Iberians, Spanish, and Portuguese who dominated the continent from the 16th to the early 19th cent.; the Africans imported as their slaves; and the post-independence immigrants from overseas, mostly Germans and S Europeans but also Lebanese, S. Asians, and Japanese. The people are 90% Christian, with about 85% of those Roman Catholic. Spanish is the official language everywhere except in Brazil (Portuguese), French Guiana (French), Guyana (English), and Suriname (Dutch). In the west, the ANDES stretch the entire length of the continent; Mt. ACONCAGUA is the highest peak in the W Hemisphere. Highlands lie in the north and east, bordered by lowland sedimentary basins that include the AMAZON RIVER basin, the world's largest drainage basin, and the PAMPAS of E Argentina, whose fertile soils constitute one of S. America's most productive agricultural areas. Important river systems include the Amazon and the ORINOCO. About 7% of its land is arable, producing mainly corn, wheat, and rice, and about one-fourth is under permanent pasture. About half is covered by forest, mainly the enormous but steadily diminishing Amazon Rain Forest. Almost one-fourth of all the world's known animal species live in the continent's rain forests, plateaus, rivers, and swamps. S. America has one-eighth of the world's total deposits of iron and one-fourth of its copper reserves. Commercial crops include bananas, citrus fruits, sugar, and coffee; fishing is important along the Pacific coast. Income tends to be unevenly distributed between large numbers of poor people and a small number of wealthy families. Asiatic hunters and gatherers are thought to have been its first settlers, probably arriving less than 12,000 years ago. The growth of agriculture about 2600 B.C. initiated a period of rapid cultural evolution whose greatest development occurred in the central Andes region and culminated with the INCA empire. European exploration began when Christopher COLUMBUS landed in 1498; Spanish and Portuguese adventurers opened it for settlement. By the Treaty of TORDESILLAS, Portugal received the E part of the continent, while Spain received the rest. The native peoples were decimated and most of those who survived were reduced to a form of serfdom. The continent was free of European rule by the early 1800s except for the Guianas. Most countries adopted a republican form of government; social and economic inequalities or border disputes led to periodic revolutions in many, and the army has consistently played a major role even in nominally democratic governments. All joined the U.N. after World War II, and all joined the ORGANIZATION OF AMERICAN STATES in 1948.

Southampton City (pop., 1999 est.: 215,000) and ENGLISH CHANNEL port, HAMPSHIRE, England. It was chartered (c.1155) by King HENRY II and incorporated in 1445. In the Middle Ages it became a major British port, and today it is England's second-largest port. Historic buildings include the 11th-cent. St. Michael's Church and the 12th-cent. King John's Palace, one of Britain's oldest domestic buildings.

Southampton, 3rd Earl of *orig.* Henry Wriothesley (1573–1624) English nobleman, patron of William SHAKESPEARE. A favorite of ELIZABETH I, he was a liberal patron of writers. Shakespeare dedicated two long poems to him (1593, 1594), and he has often been identified as the noble youth addressed in most of Shakespeare's sonnets. He accompanied the 2nd earl of ESSEX on expeditions (1596, 1597). For supporting the Essex rebellion (1601), he was imprisoned 1601–3; following JAMES I's accession, he regained his place at court becoming a privy councillor in 1619. He volunteered to fight for the United Provinces against Spain, but died of fever soon after landing in the Netherlands.

Southampton Island Island, Keewatin region, Nunavut. Lying at the entrance to HUDSON BAY, it is roughly triangular and has an area of 15,913 sq mi (41,214 sq km). Its plateau in the northeast has 1,000-ft (300-m) coastal cliffs. Its waters are noted for Arctic char fishing.

South Carolina State (pop., 2000: 4,012,000), SE U.S. It covers 31,113 sq mi (80,583 sq km) and is an original state of the Union; its capital is COLUMBIA. It comprises a broad coastal plain, with a rolling piedmont farther inland. At the time of European contact the area was inhabited by SIOUX, IROQUOIS, and Muskogean Indians. Spanish and French settlements were established and abandoned in the 16th cent.; the first permanent European settlement was made by the English in 1670 at Charles Town, moved to the present site of CHARLESTON in 1680. During the AMERICAN REVOLUTION there were several military campaigns in the state. In 1788 S. Carolina was the eighth state to ratify the U.S. constitution. In 1860 it became the first state to secede from the Union. The initial action of the AMERICAN CIVIL WAR occurred there at FT. SUMTER. It was readmitted to the Union in 1868. Constitutional revisions in 1895 disenfranchised almost all the state's blacks, and a rigid policy of racial segregation persisted until the mid-1960s, when the national CIVIL RIGHTS MOVEMENT began to have some effect in ameliorating policies. S. Carolina is a leader in U.S. textile manufacturing and has a large industrial base. Tourism is its second-largest industry. Agriculture also contributes to the economy; major crops include tobacco, soybeans, and cotton.

South China Sea See CHINA SEA

South Dakota State (pop., 2000: 755,000), N central U.S. It covers 77,116 sq mi (199,730 sq km); its capital is PIERRE. The state has three main regions: the E prairie; the central GREAT PLAINS, which contain the BADLANDS; and the Black Hills to the west. The MISSOURI RIVER bisects it from north to south. The French explored the area in the 18th cent., and sold it to the U.S. as part of the LOUISIANA PURCHASE in 1803. The LEWIS AND CLARK EXPEDITION spent about seven weeks there in 1804. The Dakota Territory was created in 1861, but settlement was sparse until the Black Hills gold rush of 1875–76 swelled the population. Intermittent wars between the Indians and immigrant whites occurred until the massacre at WOUNDED KNEE in 1890. S. Dakota became the 40th U.S. state in 1889. Farming and related industries form the state's economic base. It is a leader in cattle and hog production, and its main crops are grains. Tourism is a major industry; attractions include Mt. RUSHMORE, Wind Cave and Badlands national parks, and Jewel Cave National Monument.

Southeast Asia Vast region of Asia lying east of the Indian subcontinent and south of China. It is generally understood to include Myanmar, Thailand, Cambodia, Laos, Vietnam, Singapore, Malaysia, Indonesia, Brunei, and the Philippines.

Southeast Asia Treaty Organization (SEATO) Regional defense organization (1955–77) encompassing Australia, France, New Zealand, Pakistan, the Philippines, Thailand, Britain, and the U.S. It was founded to protect the region from communism. SEATO had no standing forces, but its members engaged in combined military exercises. Pakistan withdrew in 1968, and France suspended financial support in 1975. The organization was disbanded officially in 1977.

Southend-on-Sea Resort (pop., 1999 est.: 172,000), Essex, SE England. It lies on the THAMES estuary and the NORTH SEA. The nearest seaside resort to LONDON, it attracts millions of visitors. It is noted for its 1.5-mi (2-km) pier as well as its beaches and gardens.

Southern California, University of (USC) Private university in Los Angeles, founded in 1880. It comprises a college of letters, arts, and sciences, a graduate school, and 18 professional schools. It is especially known for programs in film, law, music, business, engineering, and social work. It operates more than 100 research institutes, including centers for the study of earthquakes, marine science, robotics and intelligent systems, and population. Its library contains a notable cinema collection. Total enrollment is about 28,000.

Southern Christian Leadership Conference (SCLC) U.S. nonsectarian agency founded by M. L. KING and others in 1957 to assist local organizations working for full equality of blacks. Operating primarily in the South, it conducted leadership-training programs, citizen-education projects, and voter-registration drives. It played a major role in the campaigns to urge passage of the 1964 CIVIL RIGHTS ACT and the 1965 VOTING RIGHTS ACT. After King's assassination in 1968, Ralph ABERNATHY became president. The SCLC split in 1971 when Jesse JACKSON founded Operation PUSH.

Southey \'saů-thē, 'sə-thē\, **Robert** (1774–1843) English poet and prose writer. In youth Southey ardently embraced the ideals of the French Revolution, as did S. T. COLERIDGE, with whom he was associated from 1794. Around 1799 he devoted himself to writing; later he was obliged to produce unremittingly to support both his and Coleridge's family. In 1813 he was appointed poet laureate. His poetry is now little read, but his masterly prose style is seen in such works as *Life of Nelson* (1813), *Life of Wesley* (1820), and *The Doctor* (1834–47).

South Island Island (pop., 1998 est.: 925,000), larger and southernmost of the two principal islands of New Zealand. Separated from NORTH ISLAND by Cook Strait, it has an area of 58,676 sq mi (151,971 sq km). Mountains occupy most of the island. Its main cities are CHRISTCHURCH and Dunedin. Fiordland National Park contains numerous coastal fjords.

South Korea See S. KOREA

South Pole S extremity of the earth's axis, located at 90°S latitude. It is the S point from which all meridians of longitude start. The area around it is a lofty plateau in W central ANTARCTICA, with ice as much as 8,850 ft (2,700 m) thick. It has six months of complete daylight and six months of total darkness each year. It was first reached by Roald AMUNDSEN in 1911, one month before R. F. SCOTT; Richard BYRD flew to the pole in 1929. The magnetic South Pole lies about 66°00′ S, 139°06′ E; it moves about 8 mi (13 km) northwest each year. The geomagnetic South Pole also moves; during the early 1990s it was located at about 79°13′ S, 108°44′ E.

South-West Africa See NAMIBIA

South-West Africa People's Organization (SWAPO) Party in S.-W. Africa (now Namibia) that advocated independence from S. Africa. Founded in 1960, it used diplomacy to attain its goals until 1966, when, led by Sam Nujoma and backed by the Soviet Union, SWAPO began using Angola as a guerrilla base. From 1978, S. Africa made periodic retaliatory strikes into Angola. That same year the U.N. recognized SWAPO as the Namibian people's sole representative. S. Africa finally accepted a U.N. resolution requiring the withdrawal of its own troops and the holding of free elections in 1988.

Soutine \sü-ˈtēn\, **Chaim** (1893–1943) Russian-French painter. Born near Minsk, he studied art in Vilnius, then moved to Paris in 1913. An art dealer enabled him to paint for three years in S France, where his highly individualistic style emerged. A form of Expressionism, it is characterized by thick impasto, agitated brushwork, convulsive compositional rhythms, and disturbing psychological content. Best known are his studies of choirboys and cooks, his series of pageboys, and his paintings of hung poultry and beef carcasses, which vividly convey the color and luminosity of putrescence.

Souvanna Phouma \sü-ˈvä-nä-ˈpü-mä\ (1901–1984) Premier of Laos (1951–54, 1960, 1962, 1974–75). Nephew of King Sisavangvong of Laos, he did not support his uncle's decision to welcome back French rule after World War II. With his half brother SOUPHANOUVONG, he joined the Free Laos movement and went into exile. As the French began to concede authority, he returned (1949) and in 1951 was elected premier. Civil war broke out between the communist Pathet Lao and rightist members of government; Souvanna served as premier sporadically during that period. He tried to maintain Laotian neutrality during the VIETNAM WAR, but came to depend on U.S. military aid. From 1975 he remained an adviser to the Pathet Lao–dominated government.

sovereignty In political theory, the ultimate authority in the decision-making process of the state and in the maintenance of order. In 16th-cent. France, Jean Bodin (1530–1596) used the concept of sovereignty to bolster the power of the king over his feudal lords, heralding the transition from feudalism to nationalism. By the end of the 18th cent., the concept of the SOCIAL CONTRACT led to the idea of popular sovereignty, sovereignty by the people through an organized government. International conventions and the UNITED NATIONS put restrictions on the powers of sovereign nations in the international arena, as does INTERNATIONAL LAW.

soviet Council that represented the primary unit of government in the Soviet Union. The first soviet was formed during the RUSSIAN REVOLUTION OF 1905 to coordinate revolutionary activities. Socialist leaders formed the second soviet in early 1917, with one deputy for every 1,000 workers and every military company. After the RUSSIAN REVOLUTION OF 1917, the BOLSHEVIKS became dominant in all soviets. In 1918 a new constitution established soviets as the formal unit of local and regional government. The 1936 constitution created a directly elected bicameral Supreme Soviet, but the single candidate per district was chosen by the Communist Party.

Soviet Union See UNION OF SOVIET SOCIALIST REPUBLICS

Soweto \sə-ˈwä-tō\ Township (pop., 1991: 597,000), NE Republic of S. Africa. It adjoins JOHANNESBURG on the southwest, and its name is an acronym derived from South-Western Townships. The townships grew out of shantytowns that arose with the arrival of black laborers from rural areas, especially between the World Wars. Most of Soweto's residents commute to Johannesburg for employment. It is the country's largest black urban complex, and its residents were active in the protests that helped bring an end to APARTHEID by 1991.

soybean Annual LEGUME *(Glycine max,* or *G. soja)* of the pea family and its edible seed. The soybean plant has an erect, branching stem, white to purple flowers, and one to four seeds per pod. It has been cultivated for some 5,000 years in E Asia. Introduced into the U.S. in 1804, it began to be farmed widely as a livestock feed in the 1930s, and the U.S. is now the world's foremost soybean producer. Economically the world's most important BEAN, the soybean provides vegetable protein for millions of people and ingredients for hundreds of chemical products, including paints, adhesives, and fertilizers. Because soybeans contain no starch, they are a good source of protein for diabetics. Soybean oil is made into margarine, shortening, and vegetarian cheeses and meats. Other food products include soy meats, soy milk, TOFU, salad sprouts, and soy sauce.

Soyinka \shō-ˈyiŋ-kä\, **Wole** (*orig.* Akinwande Oluwole) (b.1934) Nigerian playwright. His plays, written in English and drawing on W. African folk traditions, often focus on the tensions between tradition and progress. They include *A Dance of the Forests* (1960), *The Lion and the Jewel* (1963), *Madmen and Specialists* (1970), and *Death and the King's Horseman* (1975). He has written several volumes of poetry; his best-known novel is *The Interpreters* (1965). A champion of Nigerian democracy, he has been repeatedly jailed and exiled. In 1986 he became the first African to be awarded the Nobel Prize for Literature.

Wole Soyinka

Spaak \ˈspäk\, **Paul-Henri** (1899–1972) Belgian statesman. For most of the period 1936–66 he served as Belgium's foreign minister, and twice as its premier (1938–39, 1947–50). An advocate of European cooperation, he helped form the Benelux Economic Union (1944) and helped draft the U.N. charter; in 1946 he served as the U.N. General Assembly's first president. He helped form NATO and served as its secretary-general 1957–61. He also helped create the EUROPEAN ECONOMIC COMMUNITY.

spacecraft Vehicle designed to operate, with or without a crew, in a controlled flight pattern in earth orbit or outer space. Since streamlining is not needed, its shape is tailored to its mission (see SPACE EXPLORATION). Spacecraft are accelerated to ESCAPE VELOCITY by staged rockets, which are then jettisoned. The spacecraft goes on to earth orbit or a destination in space. It may have its own small liquid-fuel rocket engines for maneuvering and solar cells, storage batteries, and/or fuel cells for internal power. Unmanned spacecraft can have their programming adjusted by radio signals from earth.

S

space exploration Investigation of the universe beyond earth's atmosphere via manned and unmanned SPACE-CRAFT. Study of ROCKETS began early in the 20th cent.; in Germany, it led to development of the V-2 MISSILE in the 1930s. After World War II the "space race" between the U.S. and the Soviet Union advanced high-altitude rocket technology. Both launched their first SATELLITES (see SPUTNIK, EXPLORER) in the late 1950s and their first manned space vehicles (Vostok and MERCURY) in 1961. Longer and more complex manned missions followed, most notably the U.S. APOLLO program, including the first manned lunar landing in 1969, and the Soviet Soyuz and Salyut missions. In the 1960s and '70s, U.S. and Soviet scientists also sent unmanned probes to the planets (e.g., PIONEER, Venera, Viking, VOYAGER). Orbiting observatories permit study of distant objects from above earth's atmosphere. Scientific research has also been done on manned experimental SPACE STATIONS (SKYLAB, Salyut, MIR). Since the mid-1970s, the U.S. has devoted most of its resources to the SPACE SHUTTLE and the INTERNATIONAL SPACE STATION. Russia has continued the Soviet Union's space program on a reduced basis.

space shuttle *formally* Space Transportation System (STS) Reusable rocket-launched vehicle developed by NASA to transport people and cargo between earth and orbiting spacecraft and return to earth. Its first launch was that of *Columbia* in 1981. Designed to reduce spaceflight costs, the shuttle has a winged orbiter that carries crew and cargo; two large, solid-fuel booster rockets; and an external tank of liquid fuel and oxidizer for the orbiter's three main rocket engines. The orbiter is launched vertically and makes an unpowered descent similar to a glider. Each can be used up to 100 times. Astronauts use a remote-controlled robot arm or make space walks to handle equipment outside the orbiter. The shuttle sometimes carries a special facility (Spacelab) for experiments. The first five orbiters were *Enterprise* (used only for testing), *COLUMBIA, CHALLENGER, Discovery,* and *Atlantis; Challenger* and *Columbia* both exploded in midair.

space station Manned artificial SATELLITE in fixed orbit used as a base for scientific observation and experiment, refueling spacecraft, or launching satellites and missiles. The Soviet Union's attempt to orbit Salyut 1 in 1971 was unsuccessful. The U.S. successfully launched SKYLAB in 1973. From 1974 to 1982 the Soviet's succeeded in orbiting the smaller Salyuts 3–7, and in 1986 they launched the core module of MIR. The INTERNATIONAL SPACE STATION is scheduled for completion in 2004. See diagram, right.

space-time Single entity that relates space and time in a four-dimensional structure, postulated by Albert EINSTEIN in his theories of RELATIVITY. In the Newtonian universe there was no connection between space and time: space was a flat, three-dimensional arrangement of all possible point locations, and time was an independent one-dimensional concept. Einstein showed that a complete description of relative motion requires equations that include time as well as the three spatial dimensions. He also showed that space-time is curved, which allowed him to account for GRAVITATION in his general theory of relativity.

Spagnuolo, Pietro See Pietro BERRUGUETE

Spahn, Warren (Edward) (b.1921) U.S. baseball pitcher. Born in Buffalo, N.Y., he spent most of his career with the Boston (later Milwaukee) Braves (1942, 1946–64). He amassed 2,583 career strikeouts, the third-highest total in history to that time. His feat of winning 20 or more games in each of 13 seasons was also a record. His total of 363 wins established a record for left-handers.

Spain *officially* Kingdom of Spain *Spanish* España Nation, SW Europe. One of Europe's largest countries, it is located on the IBERIAN PENINSULA; it also includes the BALEARIC and CANARY ISLANDS. Area: 194,898 sq mi (504,783 sq km). Population (2000): 40,128,000. Capital: MADRID. The people are predominantly Spanish, with a minority of BASQUES and GYPSIES. Languages: Castilian Spanish (official), Catalan, Galician, and Basque. Religions: Roman Catholicism (67%). Currency: euro. Spain's large central plateau is surrounded by the EBRO RIVER valley, the mountainous CATALONIA region, the Mediterranean coastal region of VALENCIA, the

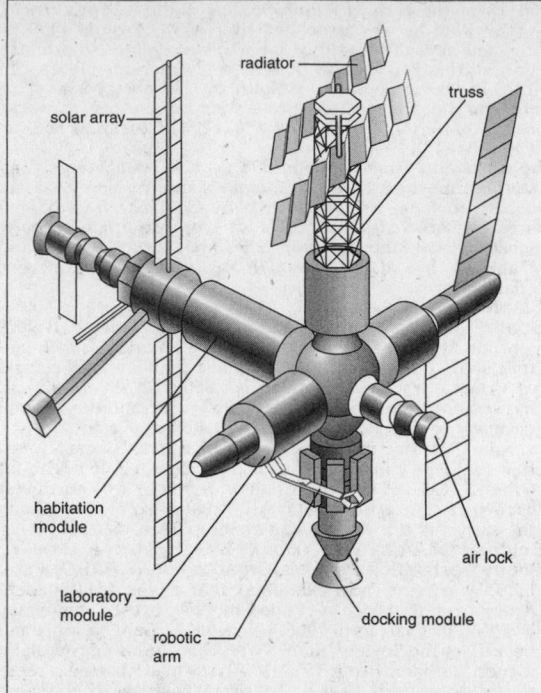

radiator

solar array

truss

habitation module

air lock

laboratory module

docking module

robotic arm

Space station The basic modules and components of a space station. The docking module connects other modules together and allows spacecraft to dock with the station. The air lock allows spacecraft to exit the station to work outside. The solar arrays provide power, and the radiators emit excess heat into space.

GUADALQUIVIR RIVER valley, and the mountainous region extending from the PYRENEES to the Atlantic coast. It has a developed market economy based on services, light and heavy industries, and agriculture. Mineral resources include iron ore, mercury, and coal; agricultural products include grains and livestock. Spain is one of the world's major producers of wine. Tourism is also a major industry. It is a constitutional monarchy with two legislative houses; its chief of state is the king, and the head of government is the prime minister. Remains of Stone Age populations dating back some 35,000 years have been found throughout Spain. Celtic peoples arrived in the 9th cent. B.C., followed by the Romans, who dominated Spain from about 200 B.C. until the Visigoth invasion. In the early 8th cent. most of the peninsula fell to Muslims (Moors) from N. Africa, and remained under their control until it was gradually reconquered by the Christian kingdoms of CASTILE, ARAGON, and Portugal. Spain was reunited in 1479 following the marriage of FERDINAND V (of Aragon) and ISABELLA I (of Castile). The last Muslim kingdom, GRANADA, was reconquered in 1492, and around this time, Spain was also established as a colonial power in the Americas. In 1516 the throne passed to the HABSBURGS, whose rule ended in 1700 when PHILIP V became the first BOURBON king of Spain. His ascendancy caused the War of the SPANISH SUCCESSION, which resulted in the loss of numerous European possessions and sparked revolution within most of Spain's American colonies. It lost its remaining overseas possessions, including Cuba, GUAM, Philippines, and PUERTO RICO, to the U.S. in the SPANISH–AMERICAN WAR (1898). Spain elected to become a republic in 1931. The SPANISH CIVIL WAR followed in 1936, ending in 1939 with victory for the Nationalists under Gen. Francisco FRANCO. He became chief of state and remained in power until his death in 1975. His

©1999, Encyclopædia Britannica, Inc.

SPAIN

Scale 1: 16,741,000

successor, JUAN CARLOS I, became king and restored the monarchy; a new constitution in 1978 established a parliamentary monarchy. Spain joined the EUROPEAN COMMUNITY in 1986. For the 1992 quincentennial of Christopher COLUMBUS's first voyage from Spain to the Americas, it celebrated with a fair in SEVILLE and the OLYMPIC GAMES in BARCELONA. From the 1990s it grew closer in its foreign relations with other European countries, but continued to suffer internally as Basque separatists pressed their claims for independence and returned to terrorism.

spaniel Any of several breeds of dogs used to flush game. Spaniels originated in Spain, but most modern breeds were developed in Britain. Breeds range from 14 to 20 in. (36–51 cm) and from 22 to 55 lbs (10–25 kg). The larger breeds are called springers, the smaller ones cockers. Breeds include the cocker spaniel, a round-headed, floppy-eared dog; the English and Welsh springer spaniels; the American water spaniel, a curly-coated, dark brown dog; the Brittany spaniel, a short-tailed French dog and the only spaniel that points; and the English toy spaniel.

Spanish–American War (1898) Conflict between the U.S. and Spain that ended Spanish colonial rule in the New World. The war originated in Cuba's struggle for independence. The newspapers of William Randolph HEARST fanned U.S. sympathy for the rebels, which grew after the unexplained destruction of the *MAINE*. After Congress declared Cuba's right to independence, Spain declared war on the U.S. in 1898. Commodore George DEWEY defeated the Spanish fleet in the Philippines (see Battle of MANILA BAY), and Gen. William Shafter led regular troops and volunteers (including Theodore ROOSEVELT and his ROUGH RIDERS) in the destruction of Spain's Caribbean fleet near Santiago, Cuba (July 17, 1898). In the Treaty of Paris, Spain renounced all claim to Cuba and ceded Guam, Puerto Rico, and the Philippines to the U.S., marking the U.S.'s emergence as a world power.

Spanish Armada See Spanish ARMADA

Spanish Civil War (1936–39) Military revolt against the government of Spain. After the 1936 elections produced a Popular Front government supported mainly by left-wing parties, a military uprising was led by the rebel Nationalists and supported by conservative elements in the clergy, military, and landowners as well as the fascist FALANGE. The ruling Republican government was supported by workers and many in the educated middle class as well as militant anarchists and communists. Government forces put down the uprising in most regions except parts of NW and SW Spain, where the Nationalists named Francisco FRANCO head of state. Both sides repressed opposition; together, they executed or assassinated over 50,000 suspected enemies. The Nationalists received troops, tanks, and planes from Nazi Germany and Fascist Italy, which used Spain as a warfare testing ground. The Republicans (also called Loyalists) were sent matériel mainly by the Soviet Union; the volunteer INTERNATIONAL BRIGADES also joined the Republicans. The two sides fought fierce and bloody skirmishes in a war of attrition. The Nationalist side gradually gained territory and by April 1938 succeeded in splitting Spain from east to west, causing 250,000 Republican forces to flee into France. In March 1939 the remaining Republican forces surrendered. About 500,000 people died in the war, and all Spaniards were deeply scarred by the trauma.

Spanish Guinea See EQUATORIAL GUINEA

Spanish Influenza Epidemic See INFLUENZA EPIDEMIC OF 1918–19

Spanish Inquisition See INQUISITION

Spanish language ROMANCE LANGUAGE spoken in Spain and in large parts of the New World. It has more than 332 million speakers, including over 23 million in the U.S. Its earliest written materials date from the 10th cent., its first literary works from about 1150. The Castilian dialect, the source of modern standard Spanish, arose in the 9th cent. in N central Spain (Old Castile). In the late 15th cent. the kingdoms of Castile, León, and Aragon merged, and Castilian became the official language of all Spain. Latin-American regional dialects are derived from Castilian but differ from it in PHONOLOGY. Spanish has almost completely lost the case system of Latin. Nouns and adjectives show masculine or feminine gender, and the verb system is generally regular, but complex.

Spanish Main N coast of S. America roughly between the Isthmus of PANAMA and the delta of the ORINOCO RIVER when it was under Spanish control. The term also refers to the Caribbean Sea and adjacent waters, especially at the time the region was infested by pirates.

Spanish Mission style See MISSION STYLE

Spanish moss EPIPHYTE (*Tillandsia usneoides*) in the PINEAPPLE family, found in S N. America, the W. Indies, and Central and S. America. It often hangs in large, beard-like, silvery-gray masses from trees and other plants and even on telephone poles. It takes in carbon dioxide and rainwater or dew for PHOTOSYNTHESIS through tiny, hair-like scales that cover its threadlike leaves and long, thread-like stems. It absorbs nutrients from dust and solvents in rainwater, or from decaying organic matter around its aerial roots. Stalkless yellow flowers appear rarely. Spanish moss is sometimes used as a filler in packing, and around potted plants or floral arrangements.

Spanish Netherlands Spanish-held provinces in the S Low Countries (modern Belgium and Luxembourg). Alessandro FARNESE was sent to represent Spain in the Netherlands, and by 1585 he had reestablished Spanish control over the S provinces, ending the union with the N provinces that followed the Pacification of GHENT. In the 17th cent. the region saw a resurgence of economic and intellectual growth. As a buffer between Protestant and Catholic states, it was the scene of constant warfare; areas were ceded to the Dutch Republic (1648) and France (1659). After the War of the SPANISH SUCCESSION, it passed to Emperor CHARLES VI and became the Austrian Netherlands.

Spanish Sahara See WESTERN SAHARA

Spanish Succession, War of the (1701–14) Conflict arising from the disputed succession to the throne of Spain after the death of the childless CHARLES II. The Habsburg Charles had named the Bourbon Philip, duc d'Anjou, as his successor; when Philip took the Spanish throne as PHILIP V, his grandfather LOUIS XIV invaded the SPANISH NETHERLANDS. The former anti-French alliance from the War of the GRAND ALLIANCE was revived in 1701 by Britain, the Dutch Republic, and the Holy Roman emperor. The English forces, led by the duke of MARLBOROUGH, won a series of victories (1704–9), including the Battle of Blenheim, that forced the French and Spanish out of the Low Countries and Italy. The imperial general, EUGENE OF SAVOY,

S

also won notable victories. The Peace of UTRECHT marked the rising power of Britain at the expense of both France and Spain.

Spark, Muriel (Sarah) *orig.* Muriel Camberg (b.1918) British writer. Until 1957 she published only poetry and criticism. Her fiction uses satire and wit to present serious themes, often questions about good and evil. *Memento Mori* (1959) is her most widely praised novel; the best known is *The Prime of Miss Jean Brodie* (1961; film, 1969). Her later novels, often more sinister in tone, include *The Abbess of Crewe* (1974) and *Reality and Dreams* (1997).

spark plug Device that fits into the cylinder head of an INTERNAL-COMBUSTION ENGINE and carries two ELECTRODES separated by an air gap, across which current from a high-tension IGNITION SYSTEM discharges, creating a spark and igniting the fuel. The electrodes and the insulator separating them must withstand high temperatures, as well as an electric stress of up to several thousand volts.

sparrow Any of numerous species of small songbirds having a conical bill, particularly members of the Old World family Ploceidae, the HOUSE SPARROW, and most members of the New World family Fringillidae. The trim-looking chipping and tree sparrows have a reddish brown cap. The finely streaked savanna and vesper sparrows inhabit grassy fields. The heavily streaked song and fox sparrows are woodland dwellers. The white-crowned and white-throated sparrows are larger than most species.

sparrow hawk Small HAWK (usually genus *Accipiter,* family Accipitridae), found in Africa, Europe, and Asia. They are gray above, barred-white below, and sometimes have white tail bars. The American KESTREL is also called sparrow hawk.

Sparta *or* **Lacedaemon** \,la-sə-'dē-mən\ Ancient Greek city-state, capital of Laconia and chief city of the PELOPONNESE. Of DORIAN origin, it was founded in the 9th cent. B.C. and developed as a strictly militaristic society. In the 8th–5th cent. B.C., it subdued neighboring Messenia. From the 5th cent. B.C., the ruling class of Sparta devoted itself to war. After a long contest with ATHENS in the PELOPONNESIAN WAR (460–404 B.C.), it attained hegemony over all of Greece. Sparta's power was broken by THEBES in 371 B.C. It lost its independence around 192 B.C. when it was forced to join the ACHAEAN LEAGUE. The Visigoths captured and destroyed the city in A.D. 396. The ruins of its acropolis, agora, theater, and temples remain.

Spartacus \'spär-tə-kəs\ (d.71 B.C.) Leader in the Gladiatorial War against Rome (73–71). A Thracian, he served in the Roman army. He became a bandit, and was sold as a slave when caught. He escaped a gladiatorial school and set up camp on Mt. Vesuvius, where he was joined by other runaway slaves and some peasants. With a force of 90,000, he overran most of S Italy, defeating two consuls (72). He led his army north to Cisalpine Gaul, where he hoped to release them to find freedom, but they refused to leave, preferring to continue the struggle, and he returned south. Marcus Licinius CRASSUS' legions caught the slave army in Lucania and defeated it; Spartacus fell in pitched battle. Pompey's army killed many of those escaping north, and Crassus crucified 6,000 prisoners along the Appian Way.

Spartan Alliance See PELOPONNESIAN LEAGUE

Spassky, Boris (Vasilyevich) (b.1937) Soviet chess master. He attained the rank of international grand master in 1955. After a period of intermittent involvement with chess, he beat Tigran Petrosyan for the world title in 1969. In 1972 he lost it to Bobby FISCHER in a highly publicized match.

speaker See LOUDSPEAKER

spearmint Aromatic herb *(Mentha spicata)* of the MINT family, the common garden mint widely used for culinary purposes. It has lax, tapering spikes of reddish-lilac flowers and sharply serrated leaves that are used fresh or dried to flavor many foods. Native to Europe and Asia, spearmint has been naturalized in N. America.

special education Education for students (such as the physically disabled or mentally retarded) with special needs. An early proponent of education for the blind was Valentin Haüy, who opened a school in Paris in 1784; his efforts were followed by those of Louis BRAILLE. Not until Friedrich Moritz Hill (1805–1874) developed an oral method of instruction did teaching to the deaf become established; it was advanced by the development of standardized SIGN LANGUAGES. Scientific attempts to educate mentally retarded children began with the efforts of Jean-Marc-Gaspard Itard (1775–1838) to train a feral child known as the Wild Boy of Aveyron; later theorists included Édouard Séguin (1812–1880) and M. MONTESSORI. Children with motor disabilities are today usually integrated into the standard classroom. Children with LEARNING DISABILITIES and speech problems usually require specialized techniques. For children with social and emotional problems, special therapeutic and clinical services may be provided.

Special Forces See GREEN BERETS

Special Olympics International program to provide people with mental retardation year-round training and athletic competition in Olympic-type sports. Inaugurated in 1968 through the efforts of Eunice Kennedy Shriver, the Special Olympics was officially recognized by the International Olympic Committee in 1988. Games are held every two years, alternating between winter and summer sports.

speciation \,spē-shē-'ā-shən\ Formation of new and distinct SPECIES, whereby a single evolutionary line splits into two or more genetically independent ones. One of the fundamental processes of EVOLUTION, speciation may occur in many ways, but in the vast majority of cases, the initiating factor is geographic separation. At least three factors then come into play: GENETIC DRIFT, often coupled with the FOUNDER PRINCIPLE; different MUTATIONS; and different SELECTION pressures.

Specie Circular \'spē-,shē\ (July 11, 1836) Executive order issued by Pres. Andrew JACKSON. To reduce the amount of paper money in circulation and limit land speculation, it required payment for purchases of public lands in gold or silver (specie means "money in coin"). The result was deflationary and contributed to the Panic of 1837. It was repealed by Congress in 1838.

species \'spē-,shēz, 'spē-,sēz\ Subdivision of biological classification composed of related organisms. Organisms are grouped into species according to their outer similarities, but more important in classifying those that reproduce sexually is their ability to interbreed successfully, producing viable offspring. Because genetic variations originate in individuals which then pass on their variations only within the species, it is at the species level that EVOLUTION takes place (see SPECIATION). The international system of BINOMIAL NOMENCLATURE assigns new species a two-part name.

specific gravity *or* **relative density** Ratio of the DENSITY of a substance to that of a standard substance. For solids and liquids, the standard substance is usually water at 39.2°F (4.0°C), which has a density of 1.00 kg/liter. Gases are usually compared to dry air, which has a density of 1.29 g/liter at 32°F (0°C) and 1 atmosphere pressure. Because it is a ratio of two quantities that have the same dimensions (mass per unit volume), specific gravity has no dimension.

spectrometer \spek-'trä-mə-tər\ Device for detecting and analyzing RADIATION, used for molecular SPECTROSCOPY. It includes a radiation source, a sample, and a detection and analysis device. Emission spectrographs excite MOLECULES of a sample to higher ENERGY states and analyze the radiation emitted when they decay to the original energy state. Absorption spectrometers pass radiation of known WAVELENGTH through a sample, varying the wavelengths to produce a spectrum of results; the detector system reveals to what extent each wavelength is absorbed. Different designs allow study of various kinds of samples over many frequencies and under different conditions.

spectrophotometry \,spek-trō-fə-'tä-mə-trē\ Branch of SPECTROSCOPY dealing with measurement of radiant ENERGY transmitted or reflected by a body as a function of WAVELENGTH. Different types of spectrophotometers cover wide ranges of the ELECTROMAGNETIC SPECTRUM: ULTRAVIOLET (UV), visible LIGHT, INFRARED (IR), or MICROWAVE. UV spectrophotometry is useful in quantifying colorless substances in SOLUTION. IR spectrophotometry is used to study complex molecular structures. See also COLORIMETRY.

spectroscopy \spek-'trä-skə-pē\ Branch of ANALYSIS devoted to identifying elements and compounds and elucidating atomic and molecular structure by measuring the radiant ENERGY absorbed or emitted by a substance at characteristic WAVELENGTHS of the ELECTROMAGNETIC SPECTRUM (including GAMMA RAY, X RAY, ULTRAVIOLET, visible LIGHT, INFRARED, MICROWAVE, and RADIO-frequency radiation) on excitation by an external energy source. Experiments involve a light source, a PRISM or grating to form the SPECTRUM, detectors for observing or recording, devices for measuring wavelengths and intensities, and interpretation of the measured quantities to identify chemicals or give clues to the structure of atoms and molecules. HELIUM, CESIUM, and rubidium were discovered by spectroscopy of the sun's spectrum. Specialized techniques include Raman spectroscopy, NUCLEAR MAGNETIC RESONANCE, nuclear quadrupole resonance, dynamic reflectance spectroscopy, microwave and gamma ray spectroscopy, and electron spin resonance. See also MASS SPECTROMETRY, SPECTROPHOTOMETRY.

spectrum Arrangement according to WAVELENGTH (or FREQUENCY) of ELECTROMAGNETIC RADIATION. The visible, "rainbow" spectrum is the portion of the ELECTROMAGNETIC SPECTRUM that is visible as light to the human eye. Some sources emit only certain wavelengths and produce an emission spectrum of bright lines with dark spaces between. Such line spectra are characteristic of the emitting elements. Atoms and molecules absorb certain wavelengths and so remove them from a complete spectrum; the resulting absorption spectrum contains dark lines or bands at these wavelengths.

speech Human communication through audible LANGUAGE. Speech sounds are made with air exhaled from the lungs, which passes between the vocal cords in the LARYNX and out through the vocal tract (PHARYNX and oral and nasal cavities). This airstream is shaped into different sounds by the articulators, mainly the TONGUE, PALATE, and lips. Articulatory PHONETICS describes each sound in terms of how the articulators make it. Speech is also described in terms of SYNTAX, lexicon (inventory of words or MORPHEMES), and PHONOLOGY (sounds).

speech, figure of See FIGURE OF SPEECH

speech recognition *or* **voice recognition** Ability of COMPUTER systems to accept speech commands or transcribe speech into text. In automatic speech recognition (ASR), the goal is to transform the content of speech into the basis for linguistic or cognitive tasks, such as translation into another language. Practical applications include DATABASE-query systems, INFORMATION RETRIEVAL systems, and security systems. Speech recognition has promising applications in ROBOTICS, particularly development of robots that can "hear." See also PATTERN RECOGNITION.

speech synthesis Generation of speech by artificial means, usually by COMPUTER. Simulating human speech is referred to as low-level synthesis. High-level synthesis deals with the conversion of text to a form that can drive a low-level synthesis system. Among other applications, this technology provides speaking aid to the speech-impaired and reading aid to the sight-impaired.

speech therapy Therapeutic treatment to correct defects in speaking. Such defects may originate in the brain, the ear (see DEAFNESS), or anywhere along the vocal tract. Therapy begins with diagnosis of underlying physical, physiological, or emotional dysfunction. It may involve training in breathing, use of the voice, and/or speaking habits. See also APHASIA, STUTTERING.

speed skating Sport of racing on ice skates. The blade of the speed skate is longer and thinner than that of the hockey or figure skate. Two types of track are used in international competition. The long track is a 400-m oval on which two skaters race simultaneously. The short track is a 111-m oval on which four to six skaters race during each heat.

Speer \'shpär\, **Albert** (1905–1981) German Nazi official. An architect and active member of the Nazi Party, he impressed Adolf HITLER and was appointed chief architect of the Third Reich in 1933. He designed the parade grounds and banners of the NUREMBERG RALLIES including the one filmed by Leni RIEFENSTAHL. In 1942 he became minister for war production and expanded the system of conscript and slave labor that maintained Germany's wartime productivity. Convicted at the Nuremberg Trials, he served 20 years in prison. He wrote the memoirs *Inside the Third Reich* (1969) and *Spandau* (1975).

Speke \'spēk\, **John Hanning** (1827–1864) British explorer, the first European to reach Lake VICTORIA. He was a member of Richard BURTON's expedition, and in 1858 the two became the first Europeans to reach Lake TANGANYIKA. On the return trip Speke struck out northward alone. In July 1858 he reached the great lake, which he named for the queen. On a second expedition in 1860 he proved that it was the source of the Nile.

Spelman College Private, historically black, women's liberal-arts college in Atlanta. Its history is traced to 1881, when two Boston women began teaching 11 black women in a church basement. Donations from John D. ROCKEFELLER, beginning in 1884, assured the school's growth; it is named for his wife's mother. It is one of six African-American institutions in the Atlanta area that share students, faculty, facilities, and curricula. Enrollment is about 2,000.

spelt Subspecies (*Triticum aestivum spelta*) of WHEAT that has lax spikes and spikelets containing two light-red kernels. It was cultivated by the ancient Babylonians and the ancient Swiss lake dwellers; it is now grown for livestock forage and used in baked goods and cereals.

Spencer, Christopher M(iner) (1833–1922) U.S. inventor and manufacturer. Born in Manchester, Conn., in 1860 he patented a repeating carbine whose seven cartridges could be fired in 18 seconds. It was quickly adopted by the U.S. government, and Spencer's factory produced 200,000 Spencer carbines and rifles during the Civil War. He also patented a breechloader and a magazine gun. His innovative screw-making lathes enabled the huge success of his Hartford Machine Screw Co. (established 1876).

Spencer, Herbert (1820–1903) British sociologist and philosopher, advocate of the theory of SOCIAL DARWINISM. His *System of Synthetic Philosophy* (9 vols., 1855–96) held that the physical, organic, and social realms are interconnected and develop according to identical evolutionary principles. He saw human societies as evolving by means of increasing division of labor from undifferentiated hordes into complex civilizations according to a form of SOCIOCULTURAL EVOLUTION. Spencer's speculative sociology was soon superseded by the findings of CULTURAL ANTHROPOLOGY and a more empirically based SOCIOLOGY. He was one of the most argumentative and most discussed Victorian thinkers.

Spender, Stephen (Harold) (*later* **Sir Stephen**) (1909–1995) English poet and critic. In the 1930s he and his friends W. H. AUDEN and Cecil DAY-LEWIS became identified with leftist "new writing." His poems express a self-critical, compassionate personality. He was better known for his perceptive criticism, as in *The Destructive Element* (1935) and *The Struggle of the Modern* (1963), and for his association with the influential review *Encounter* (1953–67). He also wrote short stories, essays, and an autobiography.

Spengler \'shpeŋ-glər\, **Oswald** (1880–1936) German philosopher. He is remembered for his influential *The Decline of the West* (2 vols., 1918–22), which contends that civilizations pass through a life cycle, blossoming and decaying like natural organisms, and that Western culture is irreversibly past its creative stage and headed into eclipse. Though acclaimed by a public disillusioned in the wake of World War I, his work was criticized by both scholars and the Nazi Party.

Spenser, Edmund (1552/53–1599) English poet. His first important publication, *The Shepheardes Calender* (1579), can be called the first work of the English literary Renaissance. In 1580 he became secretary to the lord deputy of Ireland, where he spent much of his remaining life; in

Edmund Spenser Painting by an unknown artist

1588 or 1589 he took over a large property at Kilcolman, near Cork. In 1590 he published the first part of the long allegorical poem *The Faerie Queene* (first folio ed., 1609), an imaginative vindication of Protestantism and Puritanism and a glorification of England and Elizabeth I. One of the greatest poems in English, it was composed in a revolutionary nine-line stanzaic pattern, the "Spenserian stanza," that was used by many later poets. He completed just over half of its intended 12 books. In the Irish uprising of 1598, Kilcolman was burned; Spenser, probably in despair, died shortly after.

Speransky \spyi-'rȧn-skē\, **Mikhail (Mikhaylovich)** *later* **Count Speransky** (1772–1839) Russian politician. He served as an assistant to Czar ALEXANDER I (1807–12), but his proposed financial and administrative reforms angered the nobles, who had him exiled (1812–16). A member of the state council from 1821 under NICHOLAS I, he compiled the first complete collection of Russian law (1830).

sperm *or* **spermatozoon** \spər-ˌma-tə-'zō-ən\ Male reproductive CELL. In mammals, sperm are produced in the TESTES and travel through the REPRODUCTIVE SYSTEM. At FERTILIZATION, one sperm of the roughly 300 million in an average ejaculation (see SEMEN) fertilizes an EGG. A mature human sperm has a flat, almond-shaped head, 4–5 by 2–3 microns, with a cap (acrosome) containing chemicals that help it penetrate the egg. It is essentially a cell NUCLEUS, with 23 CHROMOSOMES (including either the X or Y that determines the child's sex). A 50-micron FLAGELLUM propels the sperm, which may live in a woman's reproductive tract for two to three days after SEXUAL INTERCOURSE, to the egg. Sperm may be frozen and stored for ARTIFICIAL INSEMINATION.

spermatophyte See SEED PLANT

sperm whale Thickset, blunt-snouted toothed WHALE (*Physeter catodon,* family Physeteridae) with small, paddlelike flippers and rounded humps on the back. Sperm whales have an enormous head, squarish in profile, and a narrow, underslung lower jaw with large conical teeth. They are dark blue-gray or brownish. (Herman MELVILLE's Moby-Dick was presumably an albino.) The male grows to 60 ft (18 m). Herds of 15–20 live in temperate and tropical waters worldwide. They commonly dive to 1,200 ft (350 m), feeding primarily on cephalopods. The whales have been hunted for their spermaceti (a waxy substance in the snout, used in ointments and cosmetics) and for AMBERGRIS.

Sperry, Elmer (Ambrose) (1860–1930) U.S. inventor and industrialist. Born in Cortland, N.Y., the precociously gifted youth opened his own factory in Chicago at 20 to make dynamos and arc lamps. He designed an electrical industrial locomotive and motor transmission machinery for streetcars, and later made electric automobiles powered by his patented battery. He invented processes for salvaging tin and producing white lead. His greatest inventions, beginning with the gyrocompass, sprang from the GYROSCOPE (till then considered only a toy). He extended the gyro principle to guidance of torpedoes, to gyropilots for the steering of ships and for stabilizing airplanes, and finally to a ship stabilizer. In all, he founded eight manufacturing companies and took out more than 400 patents.

Sperry, Roger (1913–1994) U.S. neurobiologist. Born in Hartford, Conn., he studied functional specialization in the hemispheres of the cerebral cortex, examining animals and then humans with EPILEPSY in whose BRAINS the corpus callosum had been severed. He showed that the left side of the brain is normally dominant for analytical and verbal tasks and the right for spatial tasks, music, and certain other areas. His techniques laid the groundwork for much more specialized explorations. He shared a 1981 Nobel Prize.

sphagnum See PEAT MOSS

sphere In geometry, the set of all points in three-dimensional space lying the same distance (the radius) from a given point (the center), or the result of rotating a circle about one of its diameters. The components and properties of a sphere are analogous to those of a circle. A diameter is any line segment connecting two points of a sphere and passing through its center. The circumference is the length of any great circle, the intersection of the sphere with any plane passing through its center. The formula for determining a sphere's surface area is $4\pi r^2$; its volume is determined by $(4/3)\pi r^3$. The study of spheres is basic to terrestrial geography and is one of the principal areas of EUCLIDEAN GEOMETRY and elliptic geometry.

sphere, celestial See CELESTIAL SPHERE

spherical coordinate system In geometry, a COORDINATE SYSTEM in which any point in three-dimensional space is specified by its angle with respect to a polar axis and angle of rotation with respect to a prime meridian on a sphere of a given radius. A point is specified by the triplet (r, θ, φ), where r is the point's distance from the origin (the radius), θ is the angle of rotation from the initial meridian plane, and φ is the angle from the polar axis (analogous to a ray from the origin through the North Pole).

sphinx Mythological creature with a lion's body and a human's head. It figures prominently in Egyptian and Greek art and legend. The winged sphinx of Thebes was said to have terrorized people by demanding the answer to a riddle: What is it that has one voice and yet becomes successively four-footed, then two-footed, then three-footed? She devoured every person who answered incorrectly. When OEDIPUS correctly answered "man"—who crawls on all fours in infancy, walks on two feet when grown, and leans on a staff in old age—the sphinx killed herself. The earliest example in art is the Great Sphinx at Giza in Egypt, built around 2500 B.C.

sphinx moth See HAWK MOTH

sphynx cat \'sfiŋks\ Breed of hairless DOMESTIC CAT, founded on two spontaneous mutations in shorthaired cats, in 1975 and 1978. Sphynx cats must be bathed regularly to keep the skin free of the oils that the coat on a normal cat absorbs, and the very large ears must be cleaned regularly.

spice and herb Dried parts of various plants cultivated for their aromatic, savory, or medicinal substances. Spices are the fragrant or pungent products of such tropical or subtropical species as CARDAMOM, CINNAMON, CLOVES, GINGER, and PEPPER; spice seeds include ANISE, CARAWAY, FENNEL, and SESAME. Herbs are the fragrant leaves of such plants as MARJORAM, MINT, ROSEMARY, and THYME. Historically the most notable uses of spices and herbs were in medicine and in the making of holy oils and unguents; they were also used to flavor food and beverages and to inhibit or hide spoilage. Important early trade routes, including those between Asia, the Middle East, and Europe, were initially forged to obtain exotic spices and herbs. The 15th-cent. voyages of discovery resulted largely from the spice trade, and in the 17th cent. the British E. INDIA CO., Dutch E. INDIA CO., and French E. INDIA CO. battled furiously for dominance.

spider Any of some 34,000 predatory, mostly terrestrial, ARACHNID species in the order Araneida, abundant worldwide except in Antarctica. Spiders have two main body parts, eight legs, two pincerlike venomous appendages, and two spinnerets. Species range from less than an inch (2.5 mm) to about 3.5 in. (9 cm) long. The venom of a few species (e.g., BROWN RECLUSE) is harmful to humans. Most species catch insect prey in a web of silk extruded from the spinnerets. Species are classified largely by arrangement of eyes and type of web. See also BLACK WIDOW, TARANTULA.

spider monkey Any of four species (family Cebidae) of diurnal, arboreal NEW WORLD MONKEYS found from Mexico to Brazil. Long-limbed and somewhat potbellied, they are 14–26 in. (35–66 cm) long and have thumbless hands and a heavily furred, prehensile 24–36-in. (60–92-cm) tail. They swing through branches, using their tails and hands, or leap or drop spread-eagled from tree to tree. They eat fruit, nuts, flowers, and buds. They are used in laboratory studies of malaria, to which they are susceptible.

spider plant African plant of genus *Chlorophytum* (LILY FAMILY). This popular houseplant has long, narrow, grassy green-and-white-striped leaves. Periodically a flower stem emerges, and tiny white flowers (not always produced) are replaced by young plantlets, which can then be detached and rooted.

Spielberg, Steven (b.1947) U.S. film director and producer. Born in Cincinnati, he became a director of television movies for Universal Pictures. In 1974 he directed the feature film *The Sugarland Express.* After his box-office smash *Jaws* (1975), he went on to direct such other huge successes as *Close Encounters of the Third Kind* (1977), *Raiders of the Lost Ark* (1981), and *E.T.* (1982). His later movies include *Jurassic Park* (1993), *Schindler's List* (1993, Academy Award), *The Color Purple* (1985), *Empire of the Sun* (1987), *Amistad* (1997), and *Saving Private Ryan* (1998, Academy Award). His brisk editing, rich color cinematography, memorable sound tracks, and inventive special effects have made him the most successful filmmaker in the world. In 1994 he cofounded DreamWorks SKG, a film, animation, and television production company.

Spillane, Mickey (*orig.* Frank Morrison) (b.1918) U.S. writer. Born in Brooklyn, N.Y., he initially wrote for pulp magazines to pay for his schooling. His first novel, *I, The Jury* (1947), introduced the detective Mike Hammer, who later appeared in works from *My Gun Is Quick* (1950) to *Black Alley* (1996). His other novels, all characterized by violence and sexual licentiousness, include a series with the agent Tiger Mann. At his height Spillane was perhaps the best-selling writer in the world.

spin Amount of ANGULAR MOMENTUM associated with a SUBATOMIC PARTICLE or NUCLEUS. ELECTRONS, NEUTRONS, and PROTONS have a spin of $1/2$; pions and helium nuclei have zero spin. The spin of a complex nucleus is the vector sum of the orbital angular momentum and intrinsic spins of the constituent nucleons. For nuclei of even mass number, the multiple is an integral; for those of odd mass number, it is a half-integer.

spinach Hardy, leafy annual *(Spinacia oleracea)* of the goosefoot family (Chenopodiaceae), used as a vegetable. The edible leaves, somewhat triangular and either flat or puckered, are arranged in a rosette, from which a seedstalk emerges. Spinach requires cool weather and deep, rich, well-limed soil to give quick growth and maximum leaf area. A nutritious vegetable, spinach is rich in iron and vitamins A and C.

spinal column See VERTEBRAL COLUMN.

spinal cord Body's major nerve tract, about 18 in. (45 cm) long, running from the base of the BRAIN through the VERTEBRAL COLUMN. It is covered by the fibrous membranes called meninges and cushioned by cerebrospinal fluid. It connects the peripheral nervous system to the brain, and it and the brain constitute the central NERVOUS SYSTEM. Sensory impulses reach the brain via the spinal cord, and impulses from the brain travel down the spinal cord to motor neurons, which reach the body's muscles and glands via spinal nerves, which branch into peripheral nerves. In humans there are 31 pairs of spinal nerves containing both sensory and motor fibers, which originate in the spinal cord and pass out between the vertebrae to all parts of the body. Injury to the spinal cord may result in loss of communication between the brain and outlying parts and cause paralysis, loss of sensation, or weakness in areas below the injured region. Because nerve cells and fibers cannot regenerate themselves, the effects are usually permanent. See diagram, right

spinel \spə-'nel\ Mineral composed of magnesium aluminum oxide. Its color, due to various impurities, ranges from blood-red to blue, green, brown, and colorless. Synthetic spinel is manufactured for use as imitation gemstones. Spinel may also refer more broadly to any of various mineral oxides of magnesium, iron, zinc, or manganese in combination with aluminum, chromium, or iron.

spinning jenny Early multiple-spindle machine for spinning WOOL or COTTON. The hand-powered spinning jenny was patented by James HARGREAVES in 1770. The development of the SPINNING WHEEL into the spinning jenny was a significant factor in the industrialization of the TEXTILE industry.

spinning wheel Early machine for turning TEXTILE fiber into THREAD or YARN. Probably invented in India, it reached Europe in the Middle Ages. The improvement of the loom in 18th-cent. England created a yarn shortage and a demand for mechanical spinning. The result was a series of inventions—including the drawing frame, SPINNING JENNY, spinning mule, and water frame—that converted

the spinning wheel into a powered, mechanized component of the INDUSTRIAL REVOLUTION.

Spinoza \spi-'nō-zə\, **Benedict de** *Hebrew* **Baruch Spinoza** (1632–1677) Dutch Jewish philosopher, a major exponent of 17th-cent. RATIONALISM. He was born in Amsterdam to Portuguese parents. His early interest in new scientific and philosophical ideas led to his expulsion from the synagogue in 1656, and he thereafter made his living as a lens grinder and polisher. His philosophy represents a development of and reaction to that of René DESCARTES. He found three unsatisfactory features in the Cartesian metaphysics: the transcendence of God, mind–body dualism, and the ascription of free will both to God and to human beings. To Spinoza, those doctrines made the world unintelligible, since it was impossible to explain the relation between God and the world or between mind and body or to account for events

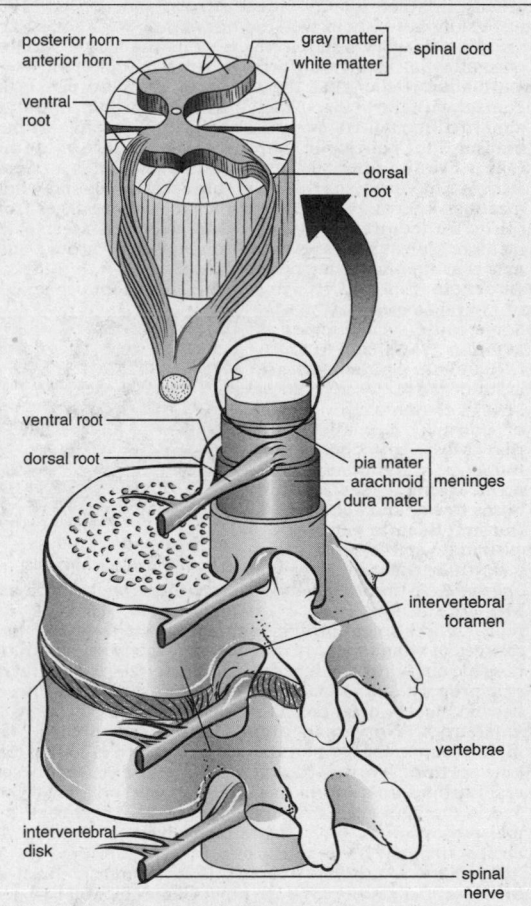

Spinal cord Section of a spinal cord. The anterior horn of the gray matter contains cell bodies from which the motor fibers of the spinal nerves arise. Its posterior horn contains cell bodies from which fibers pass to the brain carrying impulses brought by sensory fibers entering from the spinal nerves. Interneurons in the gray matter connect impulses within the cord. The white matter contains tracts of fibers which ascend to the brain with sensory impulses and descend from the brain carrying motor impulses. Nerve fibers emerge from the spinal cord through the foramina and form a dorsal root (containing fibers of sensory neurons) and a ventral root (containing fibers of motor neurons), which merge to form the spinal nerves.

occasioned by free will. In his masterpiece, *Ethics* (1677), he tried to construct a monistic system of metaphysics that would definitively solve these problems. His other major works are the *Tractatus Theologico-Politicus* (1670) and the unfinished *Tractatus Politicus.*

spiny anteater See ECHIDNA

spirits See DISTILLED LIQUOR

spiritual N. American folk hymn. White spirituals derived especially from the setting of psalm and hymn texts to familiar folk tunes, particularly useful for congregations that could not read music. Camp meetings and revivals were marked by spontaneous mass singing, often involving call-and-response patterns and free ornamentation of the melodies by the singers. Themes included going home to the promised land and the defeat of Satan; typical refrains were "Roll, Jordan" and "Glory Hallelujah." Black spirituals developed in part from white rural folk hymnody, but differ greatly in voice quality, vocal effects, and rhythm. They were sung not only in worship but also as work songs, and the text imagery often reflects concrete tasks. Modern GOSPEL MUSIC derives principally from the spiritual.

spiritualism Belief that the SOULS of the dead can make contact with the living, usually through a medium or during abnormal mental states such as trances. The basis of spiritualism is the conviction that spirit is the essence of life and that it lives on after the body dies. A medium is a person sensitive to vibrations from the spirit world, who may hold meetings known as séances in order to seek messages from spirits. A "control" is a spirit that gives messages to the medium. Spirits may also manifest themselves through such means as rapping or levitating objects.

spirochete \\'spī-rə-ˌkēt\\ Any of an order (Spirochaetales) of spiral-shaped BACTERIA. Some cause such diseases as SYPHILIS, YAWS, and RELAPSING FEVER. Spirochetes are gram-negative (see GRAM STAIN); they move by means of unusual flagella-like fibrils. Most spirochetes are found in a liquid environment. Several species are borne by lice and ticks, which transmit them to humans.

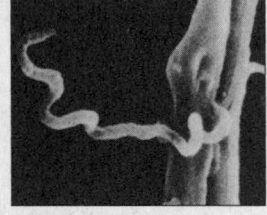

Spirochete attached to testicular cell membranes

spirulina \\ˌspir-ü-'lē-nə\\ Any CYANOBACTERIA in the genus *Spirulina.* A traditional food source in parts of Africa and Mexico, spirulina is an exceptionally rich source of vitamins, minerals, and protein, and one of the few nonanimal sources of vitamin B_{12}. It is now being widely studied for its possible antiviral, anticancer, antibacterial, and antiparasitic properties, and has been used against allergies, ulcers, anemia, heavy-metal poisoning, and radiation poisoning.

Spitsbergen Norwegian archipelago, Arctic Ocean. The main group in the SVALBARD archipelago, it lies 360 mi (580 km) north of Norway. Its possession was disputed by several European nations in the 17th cent. over whaling rights, and in the 20th cent. over mining rights. Norway took formal possession in 1925. It has extensive coal deposits. Its chief settlement is Green Harbor.

Spitz, Mark (Andrew) (b.1950) U.S. swimmer. Born in Modesto, Cal., at the 1968 Olympic Games he won two gold medals in team relay races. In the 1972 Olympics he won four individual men's events (setting four world records) and three team events; Spitz's feat of winning seven gold medals in a single Olympic Games remains unmatched.

spleen Lymphoid organ in the left side of the abdomen behind the stomach. It is one of four places where reticuloendothelial cells are found (see RETICULOENDOTHELIAL SYSTEM). Two types of tissue are intermixed: white pulp is LYMPHOID TISSUE containing LYMPHOCYTE production centers; red pulp is a network of channels filled with blood where most blood filtration occurs, and is the major site of destruction of deteriorating ERYTHROCYTES and recycling of their HEMOGLOBIN. Both contain cells (see LEUKOCYTE) that remove foreign material and initiate an ANTIBODY-producing process. The spleen becomes enlarged in some infections. Its rupture in high-impact injuries may require

surgical removal, which leaves the patient more susceptible to overwhelming infection.

Split *ancient* Spalatum. Seaport (pop., 1991: 200,000), DALMATIA, Croatia. The Roman emperor DIOCLETIAN lived at Split until his death in A.D. 313. After the Avars sacked the town in 615, the inhabitants built a new town within Diocletian's palace. It came under Byzantine rule in the 9th cent., passed to Venice in 1420, and was held by Austria in the 18th and 19th cent. It came under Yugoslavia in 1918, and became part of independent Croatia in 1992. The port facilities were destroyed in World War II, but the old city was little damaged.

Spock, Benjamin (McLane) (1903–1998) U.S. pediatrician. Born in New Haven, Conn., he taught psychiatry and child development. His *Common Sense Book of Baby and Child Care* (1946), which urged parental flexibility and reliance on common sense and discouraged corporal punishment, has influenced generations of parents and has sold over 50 million copies. In 1967 he ceased his practice to devote himself to the anti–Vietnam War movement. His advocacy late in life of a vegan (see VEGETARIANISM) diet for children aroused great controversy.

Spohr \\'shpōr\\, **Louis** (*orig.* **Ludwig**) (1784–1859) German composer and violinist. He was kapellmeister in Kassel from 1822, and eventually became director of all the city's music. Highly prolific, he wrote 15 violin concertos, four clarinet concertos, many operas (including *Jessonda,* 1823), nine symphonies, and over 30 string quartets. Considered a giant as a performer and composer in the 19th cent., he has since been largely neglected.

spoils system *or* **patronage system** In U.S. politics, the practice by political parties of rewarding partisans and workers after winning an election. Proponents claim it helps maintain an active party organization, while critics charge that it awards appointments to the unqualified and is inefficient because all jobs change hands after an election. In the U.S., the PENDLETON CIVIL SERVICE ACT (1883) was the first step in introducing the merit system in government hiring. It has almost completely replaced the spoils system. See also CIVIL SERVICE.

Spokane \\spō-'kan\\ City (pop., 2000.: 196,000), E Washington. Situated at the falls of the Spokane River, it was incorporated in 1881 after the arrival of the Northern Pacific Railway. After a fire in 1889, it was rebuilt and developed into a trade and shipping hub. Completion of the Grand Coulee Dam Project (1941) assured industrial growth. It is home to Gonzaga Univ. (1887) and is a gateway to the resorts of Mt. Spokane and several national forests.

sponge Any of some 5,000 species (phylum Porifera) of permanently affixed (sessile), mostly marine INVERTEBRATES, found from shallow to deep waters. Simple sponges are hollow cylinders with a large opening at the top through which water and wastes are expelled. A thin, perforated outer epidermal layer covers a porous skeleton composed of interlocking spicules of calcium carbonate, silica, or spongin, a proteinaceous material. The body, ranging in diameter or length from 1 in. (2.5 cm) to several yards, may be fingerlike, treelike, or a shapeless mass. Sponges lack organs and specialized tissue; flagellated cells move water into the central cavity through the perforations, and individual cells digest microscocpic food, excrete waste, and absorb oxygen. Sponges can reproduce asexually or sexually. Since antiquity, sponges have been harvested for use in bathing and scrubbing; most sponges sold today are synthetic. See diagram on following page.

spoonbill Any of six species (family Threskiornithidae) of long-necked, long-legged wading birds, inhabitants of Old and New World estuaries, saltwater bayous, and lakes. They are 24–32 in. (60–80 cm) long and have a long, straight bill that is spatulate at the tip. Most species are white, sometimes rose-tinged; the roseate spoonbill (*Ajaia ajaja*) of N. and S. America is deep pink and strikingly beautiful. With a side-to-side motion of the bill, they sweep mud and shallow water for fishes and crustaceans. Some species, including the black-billed spoonbill, are endangered. See also IBIS.

spore Reproductive cell capable of developing into a new individual without fusing with another reproductive cell. Spores thus differ from gametes. Spores are agents of non-

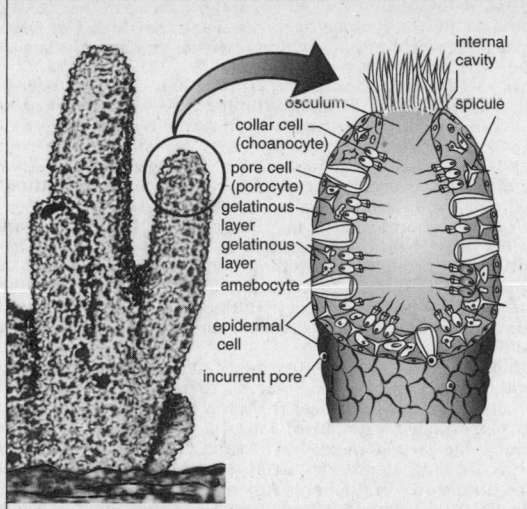

internal cavity

osculum

spicule

collar cell (choanocyte)

pore cell (porocyte)

gelatinous layer

gelatinous layer

amebocyte

epidermal cell

incurrent pore

Sponge A simple saclike sponge. Its surface is perforated by small openings (incurrent pores) formed by tubelike cells (porocytes), which open into the internal cavity. A gelatinous middle layer contains the skeletal elements (spicules and spongin fibers) as well as amebocytes active in digestion, waste removal, and spicule and spongin formation. Flagellated collar cells (choanocytes) line the internal cavity, create currents to move water containing oxygen and food into the sponge, and engulf and digest food particles. Water and wastes are expelled through the ostium opening, whose size can be altered to regulate water flow through the sponge.

sexual reproduction; gametes are agents of sexual reproduction. Spores are produced by BACTERIA, fungi (see FUNGUS), and green plants. Bacterial spores serve largely as a dormant stage in the life cycle, preserving the bacterium through periods of unfavorable conditions. Fungal spores serve a function similar to that of SEEDS in plants; they germinate and grow into new individuals under suitable conditions. Among green plants (all of which have a life cycle characterized by ALTERNATION OF GENERATIONS), spores are the reproductive agents of the nonsexual generation (SPOROPHYTE), giving rise to the sexual generation (GAMETOPHYTE).

sporophyte \'spōr-ə-ˌfīt\ In many plants and algae, the nonsexual phase in the ALTERNATION OF GENERATIONS, or an individual representing the phase. The alternate, sexual phase is the GAMETOPHYTE. In the sporophyte phase, a plant body grows and eventually produces SPORES through MEIOSIS. These spores divide by MITOSIS to produce gametophytes, which then can carry out sexual reproduction.

sports medicine Medical and paramedical supervision and treatment of athletes. It has four aspects. Preparation (conditioning) uses diet, exercises, and monitoring of practice sessions to improve performance. Prevention identifies any predisposition to injury or illness and covers warmup, stretching, and design and use of protective equipment. Care includes many surgical techniques developed in sports medicine (e.g., for knee injuries) that are now used for the general population. Rehabilitation (see PHYSICAL MEDICINE AND REHABILITATION) prepares an injured or ill athlete to return to activity.

spotted fever See ROCKY MTN. SPOTTED FEVER

spreadsheet Computer SOFTWARE that allows the user to enter columns and rows of numbers. Any cell of the ledger may contain either data or a formula that describes the value that should be inserted there based on the values in other cells. When a change is made in one cell, the program recalculates the contents of all cells affected by the change.

Spreadsheets are widely used for performing business calculations.

spring Opening at or near the earth's surface where water from underground sources is discharged. Springs discharge either at ground level or directly into the bed of a stream, lake, or sea. Water that emerges at the surface without a perceptible current is called a seep.

spring Elastic machine component able to deflect under load in a prescribed manner and to recover its initial shape when unloaded. The combination of force and displacement in a deflected spring is ENERGY, which may be stored when moving loads are being stopped or when the spring is wound up for use as a power source (e.g., in a watch). Though most springs are mechanical, hydraulic (liquid) and air springs exist.

Spring and Autumn Annals See CHUNQIU

Spring and Autumn period (770–476 B.C.) Period of the Chinese ZHOU DYNASTY named for the Confucian Classic *CHUNQIU* ("Spring and Autumn Annals"). During this period the imperial house's authority diminished as local nobles struggled for power. States formed political and economic coalitions for military purposes as well as for drainage projects, canals, and other civil-engineering projects. Merchants and artisans emerged as social groups. Classical Chinese thought began in this period (see CONFUCIUS).

springbok *or* **springbuck** Species of ANTELOPE (*Antidorcas marsupialis*), native to treeless plains of S Africa. It stands about 30 in. (80 cm) high at the shoulder, and both sexes have ringed, lyre-shaped horns. A fold of skin from mid-back to rump can be opened to display a crest of white hair. The body has a broad horizontal dark-brown band. When excited, the springbok makes a series of vertical leaps up to 12 ft (3.5 m) high, an action called pronking.

Springfield City (pop., 2000: 111,000), capital of Illinois. It lies in the central part of the state. Through the efforts of Abraham LINCOLN and other members of the Illinois legislature, the state capital was transferred there in 1837. Lincoln lived there until he became president in 1861; he is buried there. It is a market center for a rich farming area.

Springfield City (pop., 2000: 152,000), SW Massachusetts, on the CONNECTICUT RIVER. It was settled in 1636. During the AMERICAN REVOLUTION, it was the site of an arsenal which was a target of SHAYS' REBELLION in 1786. The SPRINGFIELD ARMORY was of major importance in several wars. Springfield is home to the Basketball Hall of Fame. It was the birthplace of Theodor GEISEL (Dr. Seuss).

Springfield Armory Weapons factory established at SPRINGFIELD, Mass., by the U.S. Congress in 1794. It grew out of an arsenal established by the revolutionary government in 1777, the site being chosen partly for its inaccessibility to British forces. The armory pioneered mass-production manufacturing techniques, and produced weapons ranging from smoothbore muskets in its earliest days to the famous SPRINGFIELD RIFLE and the M1 rifle of World War II, designed by John GARAND. It closed in 1968 and is now a national historic site.

Springfield rifle Any of several RIFLES used by the U.S. Army 1873–1936, all taking their name from the SPRINGFIELD ARMORY. The most famous began as the Model 1903 Springfield, an adaptation of the German Mauser. Modified for Model 1906 ammunition, it entered history as the Springfield .30-06, one of the most reliable and accurate military firearms in history. It was replaced by the Garand (M1) rifle of World War II, also designed at the Springfield Armory. The retired Springfield .30-06 was widely modified into a sporting rifle. See also M16 RIFLE.

Springsteen, Bruce (Frederick Joseph) (b.1949) U.S. singer and songwriter. Born in Freehold, N.J., he formed his own 10-piece band in the early 1970s. His third album, *Born to Run* (1975), became a huge success, as did *The River* (1980) and *Born in the USA* (1984). Springsteen's sensitive lyrics, often voicing his working-class sympathies, gave him vast appeal, and his generous concerts have been among the best-attended of those of any rock musician.

spruce Any of about 40 species of evergreen trees that make up the genus *Picea* (PINE family), native to temperate and cold regions of the Northern Hemisphere. These

pyramid-shaped trees have whorled branches and needle-like, spirally arranged leaves that connect to their stems via a peglike woody base. Tough, finely grained, resonant, and pliable, spruce wood is used for sounding boards in pianos and bodies of violins, as well as in construction, for boats and barrels, and as pulpwood. Common N. American species are black spruce *(P. mariana),* a source of spruce GUM, and white spruce *(P. glauca),* a source of timber. Blue, or Colorado spruce *(P. pungens)* is used as an ornamental because of its bluish leaves and symmetrical growth habit.

spurge One of the largest flowering-plant genera *(Euphorbia),* with more than 1,600 species. It takes its common name from a group of annual herbs used as purgatives, or spurges. Many spurges are important as ornamentals or as sources of drugs; many others are weeds. One of the best-known is the POINSETTIA. *Euphorbia* is part of the family Euphorbiaceae, which contains about 7,500 species of flowering annual and perennial herbs and woody shrubs or trees. Euphorbia flowers usually lack petals and are borne in cup-shaped clusters. The stems of many species contain a milky latex. Economically important spurge family members include the castor-oil plant, croton, CASSAVA, and RUBBER TREE.

Sputnik \'spŭt-nik\ Any of a series of satellites whose launching by the Soviet Union began the Space Age. Sputnik 1, the first satellite launched by humans (Oct. 1957), orbited until early 1958. Sputnik 2 carried a dog, Laika, the first living creature in space; since Sputnik 2 was not designed to sustain life, Laika did not survive. Eight more Sputnik missions tested life-support systems and reentry procedures on various animals and furnished data on space temperatures, pressures, particles, radiation, and magnetic fields.

Squanto (d.1622) Pawtuxet Indian interpreter and guide. Squanto learned English after escaping an attempt to sell him into slavery and joining the Newfoundland Co. At Plymouth colony, he was made Gov. William BRADFORD's Indian emissary; he also served as interpreter during negotiations between the Pilgrims and the Wampanoag Indians.

square dance Dance for sets of four couples standing in square formation. The most popular type of U.S. folk dance, it derived from the quadrille. It progresses through specific patterns called or sung out to the dancers by a caller and accompanied by lively music played on instruments such as fiddle, banjo, accordion, guitar, and piano.

squash Any of various fruits of the genus *Cucurbita* in the GOURD family, widely cultivated as vegetables and for livestock feed. The principal species are *C. maxima, C. moschata,* and certain varieties of *C. pepo.* Summer squash is a quick-growing, small-fruited, nontrailing or bush type of *C. pepo.* The fruits do not store well and must be used soon after harvest (see ZUCCHINI). Winter varieties of squash are long-vining, tough-skinned, generally large-fruited, long-season types. Harvested fruits can be stored many months if kept dry and well above freezing. Examples include acorn squash and PUMPKIN. Native to the Americas, squash was widely cultivated by American Indians before Europeans arrived.

squash (rackets) Singles or doubles game played in a four-walled court with a long-handled racket and a rubber ball that can be hit off any number of walls. It probably originated in the mid-19th cent. at England's HARROW SCHOOL. The standard international game uses a relatively soft, slow ball; hardball squash, played in the U.S., is played on a narrower court with a harder, faster ball. The object is to bounce the ball off the front wall in such a way as to defeat an opponent's attempt to return it.

squash bug *or* **leaf-footed bug** Any of more than 2,000 widely distributed insect species (family Coreidae), including many important plant pests. Most species are more than 0.4 in. (10 mm) long. Many have enlarged, flattened extensions on the legs. The N. American squash bug *(Anasa tristis)* is an important pest of squash, melon, and pumpkin (plants in the GOURD family). Piercing and sucking mouthparts enable them to attack the parts of plants that insecticides rarely penetrate.

squatter sovereignty See POPULAR SOVEREIGNTY

Squaw Valley Valley, E California. It is located in the SIERRA NEVADA on the E slope of Squaw Peak, northwest of Lake TAHOE. A world-famous winter sports area, it was the site of the 1960 Winter OLYMPIC GAMES.

Squibb, E(dward) R(obinson) (1819–1900) U.S. pharmaceutical manufacturer. Born in Wilmington, Del., he worked as a doctor on navy ships and was dismayed by the poor quality of the medicines. At the Brooklyn Naval Hospital (from 1851) he devised a safe method for making anesthetic ether and also discovered processes for making chloroform, fluid extracts, and bismuth salts. In 1858 he set up his own Brooklyn laboratory. During the Civil War the Union Army relied heavily on his drugs, and by 1883 he was manufacturing 324 products and selling them around the world. A Quaker idealist, he refused to patent his medicines, and he crusaded for purity in drug manufacture. He did not live to see the culmination of his work in the Pure Food and Drug Act of 1906.

squid Any of numerous 10-armed CEPHALOPODS, found in both coastal and oceanic waters, that prey on fishes and crustaceans. Species range from less than 0.75 in. (1.5 cm) to more than 65 ft (20 m) long (in the case of the giant squid, the largest of all INVERTEBRATES). Two of the 10 arms are long, slender tentacles; each has an expanded end and four rows of suckers. An internal shell supports the slender tubular body of most species. Squids may be swift swimmers (propelling themselves by contracting and relaxing their mantle) or mere drifters; water expelled from a funnel below the head can propel the squid backward. Like the OCTOPUS, it may emit an inky cloud from its ink sac when in danger.

squint See STRABISMUS

squirrel Any of about 260 species in 50 genera (family Sciuridae) of mostly diurnal RODENTS. Many species are arboreal; some are terrestrial. All have strong hind legs and a hairy tail. They range in total length from the 4-in. (10-cm) African pygmy squirrel to the giant squirrels of Asia, about 35 in. (90 cm) long. Tree dwellers live in a tree hollow or nest. Ground dwellers live in burrows, and many become dormant in winter (hibernate) or summer (estivate). Most species are primarily vegetarian and are fond of seeds and nuts. See also CHIPMUNK, FLYING SQUIRREL, GROUND SQUIRREL, MARMOT, PRAIRIE DOG.

Sri Lanka \ˌsrē-'län-kə\ *officially* **Democratic Socialist Republic of Sri Lanka** *formerly* **Ceylon** Island country in the Indian Ocean, off the SE coast of India. Area: 25,332 sq mi (65,610 sq km). Population (2000): 19,246,000. Capitals: COLOMBO (executive), Sri Jayewardenepura Kotte (legislative and judicial). About 75% of the population is SINHALESE; other ethnic groups include TAMILS and Muslims. Languages: Sinhalese and Tamil (both official), English. Religions: Buddhism, Hinduism, Islam, Christianity. Currency: Sri Lanka rupee. Highlands make up Sri Lanka's S central region and heart, with narrow gorges and deep river valleys. The surrounding lowlands include hills and fertile plains. It has a developing mixed economy, largely based on agriculture, services, and light industries. Tea, rubber, and coconuts are exported. The island is world-famous for its gemstones, which include sapphires, rubies, and topaz. It leads the world in the production of high-grade graphite. It is a republic with one legislative house; its head of state and government is the president, assisted by the prime minister. The Sinhalese people of Sri Lanka probably originated with aboriginal inhabitants blending with migrating Indo-Aryans from India around the 5th cent. B.C. The Tamils were later immigrants from Dravidian India, migrating over a period from the early centuries A.D. to about 1200. Buddhism was introduced during the 3rd cent. B.C. As Buddhism spread, the Sinhalese kingdom extended its political control over Ceylon, but lost it to invaders from S India in the 10th cent. A.D. Between 1200 and 1505 Sinhalese power gravitated to SW Ceylon, while a S Indian dynasty seized power in the north and established the Tamil kingdom in the 14th cent. Foreign invasions from India, China, and Malaya occurred in the 13th–15th cent. In 1505 the Portuguese arrived, and by 1619 they controlled most of the island. The Sinhalese enlisted the Dutch to help oust the Portuguese, and it eventually came under the control of the Dutch E. INDIA CO.,

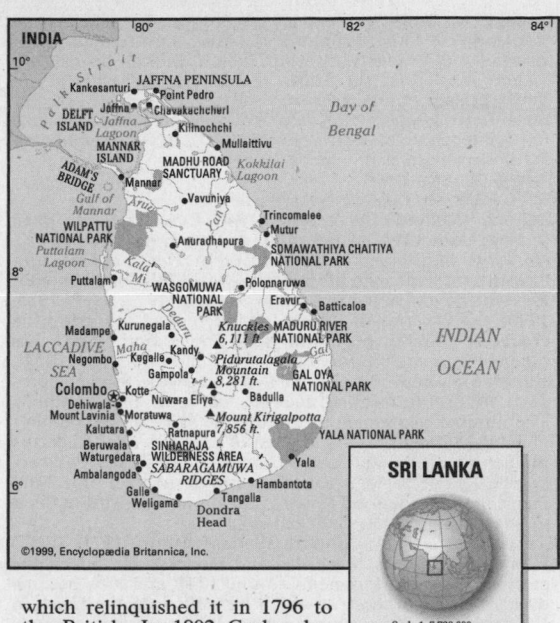

INDIA
SRI LANKA

Scale 1: 7,798,000
0   30   60 mi
0   50   100 km

©1999, Encyclopædia Britannica, Inc.

Germaine de Staël Portrait by J.-B. Isabey, 1810

cal propagandist, and salon hostess. Born in Paris, she first became known for a book on J.-J. ROUSSEAU (1788). The most brilliant period of her career began in 1794, when she returned to Paris after the Reign of Terror; her salon, known for its literary and intellectual figures, flourished, and she published political and literary essays, notably *A Treatise on the Influence of the Passions upon the Happiness of Individuals and of Nations* (1796), an important document of European ROMANTICISM. In 1803 Napoleon had her banished from Paris, and she made Switzerland her home. Probably her most important work is *Germany* (1810), a serious study of German culture and society.

Stafford Town (pop., 1994 est.: 123,000), county seat of STAFFORDSHIRE, W central England. Founded by the daughter of ALFRED the Great, the town had its own mint from the reign of Aethelstan to that of HENRY II. Chartered in 1206, it grew as a market town. Parliamentarians demolished its 11th-cent. walls and castle in 1643 during the ENGLISH CIVIL WARS. It was the birthplace of Izaak WALTON, and its Swan Hotel was associated with Charles DICKENS.

Staffordshire \'sta-fərd-ˌshir\ County (pop., 1998 est.: 810,000), central England. Its county seat is STAFFORD. Its N moorlands form the S tip of the PENNINES. Traces of Neolithic, Bronze Age, and Iron Age settlements remain. The area was the center of the kingdom of MERCIA in the 7th–9th cent. Staffordshire has mined coal and iron since the 13th cent. Its pottery industry became famous in the 18th cent. with the innovations of Josiah WEDGWOOD.

Staffordshire terrier See PIT BULL TERRIER

stagecoach Public COACH pulled by horses regularly traveling a fixed route between stations or stages. Stagecoaches appeared in London by 1640 and in Paris by 1660. In the 19th cent. they were most widely used in the U.S. and in England. In the U.S. they were the only means of travel for long distances overland, carrying passengers and mail to locations especially in the West. As railroad travel became more common, stagecoach travel diminished except to remote locations.

Stagg, Amos Alonzo (1862–1965) U.S. college football coach. Born in W. Orange, N.J., he played end for Yale and was chosen for the first All-America team in 1889. During his 41-year tenure at the Univ. of Chicago (1892–1932), he devised the end-around play, the man in motion, the huddle, the shift play, and the tackling dummy. He later coached at three other colleges, retiring in 1960 after the longest coaching career in football history.

Stahl, Franklin W(illiam) (b.1929) U.S. geneticist. Born in Boston, he worked primarily at the Univ. of Oregon. With Matthew MESELSON he discovered and described (1958) the mode of replication of DNA. They found that the double-stranded helix separates into two strands, each of which directs the construction of a new sister strand.

stained glass Colored glass used to make decorative windows and other objects through which light passes. Stained glass is often made in large, richly detailed panels that are set together in a framework of lead. It acquires its color by the addition of metallic oxides to molten glass. A purely Western phenomenon, it originated as a fine art of the Christian church, beginning in the 12th–13th cent., when it was combined with GOTHIC ARCHITECTURE to create brilliant, moving effects. A decline set in after the 13th cent., when stained-glass artists began to seek the realistic effects sought by Renaissance painters, effects to which the technique was less suited and which diverted artists from exploiting the all-important light-refracting quality of glass. Stained-glass artists later achieved high quality during the 19th-cent. GOTHIC REVIVAL, in the Art Nouveau designs of

which relinquished it in 1796 to the British. In 1802 Ceylon became a crown colony, gaining independence in 1948. It became the Republic of Sri Lanka in 1972, and was renamed the Democratic Socialist Republic of Sri Lanka in 1978. Civil strife between Tamil and Sinhalese groups has beset the country in recent years, with the Tamils demanding a separate autonomous state in N Sri Lanka.

Srinagar \srē-'nə-gər\ City (pop., 1990 est.: 850,000), summer capital of KASHMIR state, NW India. It lies on the banks of the JHELUM RIVER in the Vale of Kashmir. Situated amid clear lakes and lofty mountains, it has long had a considerable tourist economy. Gondolas ply the canals and waterways, and the floating gardens of Dal Lake are a famous attraction.

SS *in full* Schutzstaffel (German: "Protective Echelon") Paramilitary corps of the NAZI PARTY. Founded in 1925 by Adolf HITLER as a personal bodyguard, it was directed from 1929 by Heinrich HIMMLER, who enlarged its membership to over 250,000. Wearing black uniforms and special insignia (lightning-like runic S's, death's-head badges, and silver daggers), the SS purged the SA on Hitler's orders in 1934. The corps was divided into the General SS (*Allgemeine-SS)*, which dealt with police matters and included the GESTAPO, and the Armed SS (*Waffen-SS)*, which included the concentration-camp guards and the 39 elite combat regiments. Schooled in racial hatred and absolute obedience to Hitler, the SS carried out massive executions of political opponents, Gypsies, Jews, communists, partisans, and Russian prisoners.

stadium Enclosure that provides a broad space for sports events and tiers of seats for a large number of spectators. Some stadiums are rectangular with curved corners; others are elliptical or U-shaped. As a type of long-span structure, the stadium played a significant role in 20th-cent. construction technology. The building of large stadiums has been greatly facilitated by the use of reinforced concrete, steel, and membrane structures, which have made possible daring new designs. The Houston Astrodome (1965) was the first major fully roofed stadium. Cables contributed significantly to speed of construction, lightness of roof, and economy in covered stadiums. The enormous Hubert H. Humphrey Metrodome in Minneapolis (opened 1982) was built using a cable system.

Staël \'stäl\, **Germaine de** *orig.* baronne (baroness) Anne-Louise-Germaine Necker de Staël-Holstein *known as* **Madame de Staël** (1766–1817) French-Swiss writer, politi-

S

L. C. TIFFANY, and in the work of such 20th-cent. artists as Marc CHAGALL.

stainless steel Any of a family of ALLOY STEELS usually containing 10–30% CHROMIUM, which, together with low carbon content, gives remarkable resistance to corrosion and heat. Other elements, such as nickel, molybdenum, titanium, aluminum, niobium, copper, and nitrogen, may be added to increase corrosion resistance to specific environments, enhance resistance to oxidation (see OXIDATION-REDUCTION), and impart special characteristics.

Staked Plain See LLANO ESTACADO

stalactite and stalagmite \stə-ˈlak-ˌtīt...stə-ˈlag-ˌmīt\ Elongated forms of various minerals deposited from solution by slowly dripping water. A stalactite hangs like an icicle from the ceiling or side of a cavern. A stalagmite rises from the floor of a cavern. The two are not necessarily paired. The dominant mineral in such deposits is CALCITE (calcium carbonate), and the largest displays are formed in caves of LIMESTONE and DOLOMITE.

Stalin, Joseph *orig.* Iosif Vissarionovich Dzhugashvili (1879–1953) Soviet politician and dictator. The son of a cobbler, he studied at a seminary but was expelled for revolutionary activity in 1899. He joined the BOLSHEVIK faction of the RUSSIAN SOCIAL-DEMOCRATIC WORKERS' PARTY in 1903. A disciple of Vladimir LENIN, he remained active behind the scenes and in exile (1913–17) until the RUSSIAN REVOLUTION OF 1917 brought the Bolsheviks to power. Having adopted the name Stalin (from Russian *stal*: "steel"), he served as commissar for nationalities in the Bolshevik

Joseph Stalin

government (1917–23). He became secretary-general of the party's Central Committee from 1922, the post that later provided the power base for his dictatorship. After Lenin's death (1924), Stalin overcame his rivals, including Leon TROTSKY, Grigory ZINOVYEV, and Lev KAMENEV and took control of Soviet politics. In 1928 he inaugurated the FIVE-YEAR PLANS that radically altered Soviet economic and social structures and resulted in the deaths of many millions. In the 1930s he eliminated threats to his power through the PURGE TRIALS and through widespread secret executions. In WORLD WAR II he signed the GERMAN-SOVIET NONAGGRESSION PACT (1939) and annexed parts of Eastern Europe to strengthen his W frontiers. When Germany invaded Russia (1941), Stalin took control of military operations. He allied Russia with Britain and the U.S. at the TEHRAN, YALTA, and POTSDAM conferences, where he demonstrated his negotiating skill. After the war he consolidated Soviet power in Eastern Europe and continued his suppression of internal dissent; increasingly paranoid, he was preparing to mount another purge when he died. Noted for bringing the Soviet Union into world prominence, at terrible cost to his own people, he left a legacy of repression and fear as well as industrial and military power.

Stalinabad See DUSHANBE

Stalingrad See VOLGOGRAD

Stalingrad, Battle of (1942–43) Unsuccessful German assault on the Soviet city in World War II. German forces invaded the Soviet Union in 1941, and had advanced to the suburbs of Stalingrad (now Volgograd) by the summer of 1942. Met by a determined RED ARMY defense commanded by Vasily CHUIKOV, they reached the city's center after fierce street fighting. In November the Soviets counterattacked and encircled the German army, which surrendered in February 1943 with 91,000 troops. The Axis forces lost 800,000 dead; Soviet forces lost over 1 million dead.

Stalinism Policies of Joseph STALIN and his imitators elsewhere in the Soviet bloc. On taking power, Stalin brooked no dissent from Communist Party policies, of which he assumed the role of sole infallible interpreter. Postponing the struggle for world proletarian revolution, he decreed the wholesale collectivization of Russian agriculture and a program of rapid industrialization, which, though broadly effective, resulted in the deaths of many millions. Purges in the 1930s (see PURGE TRIALS) resulted in the deaths of millions more, as opponents were executed or sent to the GULAG. After Stalin's death, Nikita KHRUSHCHEV repudiated Stalinism (1956) as an aberration.

Stalino See DONETSK

Stalin Peak See COMMUNISM PEAK

Stallone, (Michael) Sylvester (b.1946) U.S. film actor. Born in New York City, he began appearing in movies in 1970. He wrote and starred in the surprise hit *Rocky* (1976), winning instant fame with his portrayal of a Philadelphia boxer. He cowrote and acted in its four sequels (1979, 1982, 1985, 1990) and a series of violent action movies featuring the character Rambo, beginning with *First Blood* (1982). His other films include *Cliffhanger* (1993) and *Cop Land* (1997).

stamen Male reproductive part of a FLOWER. Stamens produce POLLEN in terminal saclike structures called anthers. The number of stamens is usually the same as the number of petals. Stamens usually consist of a long slender stalk, the filament, with the anthers at the tip. Small secretory structures called nectaries are often found at the base of the stamens and provide food rewards for insect and bird pollinators (see POLLINATION). See also PISTIL.

Stamitz \ˈshtä-mits\, **Johann (Wenzel Anton)** (1717–1757) Hungarian-German composer and violinist. He joined the elector's court in Mannheim around 1741, and soon became director of its orchestra, which he built into the finest in Europe. In his 75 symphonies he helped establish the four-movement form as standard and introduced the orchestral crescendo to Germany from Italy. He and his students made up the "Mannheim School." His son Carl (1745–1801) toured widely as a violin soloist and wrote more than 50 symphonies.

stammering See STUTTERING

Stamp Act (1765) British parliamentary measure to tax the American colonies. To pay for costs resulting from the FRENCH AND INDIAN WAR, the British imposed a stamp tax on printed matter. It was vigorously opposed by the colonists, whose representatives had not been consulted. Colonists refused to use the stamps, and mobs intimidated stamp agents. The Stamp Act Congress, with representatives from nine colonies, petitioned Parliament for repeal, as did British merchants suffering from colonial boycotts. Parliament repealed the act in 1766.

stamp collecting See PHILATELY

standardbred Breed of light HORSE developed in the U.S., primarily for harness racing. The foundation sire was an English THOROUGHBRED imported in 1788; his progeny were bred especially with the Morgan. The standardbred's height is 15–16 hands (60–64 in., 152–163 cm); its weight is 900–1,000 lbs (410–450 kg). "Standard" refers to a requirement imposed in 1871 that, to be registered, a horse must meet certain standards of speed (e.g., trotting a mile in 2.5 minutes).

Standard Generalized Markup Language See SGML

standardization In industry, the development and application of standards that make it possible to manufacture a large volume of interchangeable parts. Standardization may focus on engineering standards, such as properties of materials, fits and tolerances, and drafting practices; or on product standards, which are embodied in formulas, descriptions, drawings, or models. Standards make it easier for firms to communicate with their suppliers and help prevent conflict and duplication of effort. Governmental departments and trade and technical associations help to set standards within industries; these are coordinated by organizations such as the American National Standards Institute (ANSI) and the INTERNATIONAL ORGANIZATION FOR STANDARDIZATION (ISO).

standard model In physics, the combination of two theories of PARTICLE PHYSICS into a single framework to describe all interactions of SUBATOMIC PARTICLES except those due to gravity (see GRAVITATION). The two theories, the ELECTROWEAK THEORY and the theory of QUANTUM CHROMODYNAMICS, describe the interactions between particles in terms of the exchange of intermediary particles. The model has proved highly accurate in predicting certain interactions, but it does not explain all aspects of subatomic particles. The search goes on for a more complete theory, and in particular a UNIFIED FIELD THEORY.

standard of living Level of material comfort that an individual or group aspires to or may achieve. This includes not only privately purchased goods and services but collectively consumed goods and services. A standard of living determined for a group such as a country must be examined critically. If the mean values increase over time but the rich become richer and the poor poorer, the group may not be collectively better off. Useful indicators include life expectancy, access to nutritious food and a safe water supply, and availability of medical care.

Standard Oil Co. and Trust U.S. company and corporate trust that held a near monopoly over the U.S. oil industry 1870–11. The company originated in 1863, when John D. ROCKEFELLER started a Cleveland refining firm, which, with other facilities, was incorporated as the Standard Oil Co. in 1870. By 1880 it controlled the refining of 90–95% of all oil produced in the U.S. In 1882 Standard Oil and affiliated oil companies were combined in the Standard Oil Trust, which eventually included some 40 corporations. In 1892 the Ohio Supreme Court ordered the trust dissolved, but it continued to operate elsewhere. Its monopolistic practices were exposed in Ida TARBELL's *History of the Standard Oil Company* (1904), and after a lengthy antitrust suit it was broken up in 1911. Standard Oil Co. (New Jersey) changed its name to Exxon Corp. in 1972; other corporations such as Mobil, Amoco, and Chevron include companies that once belonged to the trust (see EXXON MOBIL CORP.).

Standards and Technology, National Institute of See BUREAU OF STANDARDS

standard time Official local time of a region or country. Local mean solar time depends on longitude; it advances by four minutes per degree eastward. The earth can thus be divided into 24 standard time zones, each approximately 15° in longitude. The actual boundaries of each time zone are determined by local authorities and in many places deviate considerably from 15°. See also GREENWICH MEAN TIME.

Standish, Myles (1584?–1656) British-American colonist. He fought in the Netherlands, where he met the Pilgrims, with whom he later sailed to N. America on the *Mayflower* (1620). As the PLYMOUTH colony's military leader, he led several expeditions against hostile Indian tribes. He was mythologized in H. W. LONGFELLOW's poem *The Courtship of Miles Standish* (1858); the story that he asked John ALDEN to propose marriage for him has no historical basis.

Stanford, (Amasa) Leland (1824–1893) U.S. entrepreneur, a builder of the first transcontinental railroad. Born in Watervliet, N.Y., he practiced law in Wisconsin before settling in Sacramento, Cal. He served as governor of California (1861–63). He invested heavily in the plan to build a transcontinental railroad, and was the founding president of the Central Pacific Railroad (1861–93). During his tenure its track was built eastward to join that of the UNION PACIFIC at Promontory, Utah (1869), and he played a major role in further railroad development. He served in the U.S. Senate 1885–93. He and his wife, Jane, founded STANFORD UNIV. in 1885.

Stanford University Private university in Stanford, Cal., near Palo Alto. It was founded in 1885 by Leland STANFORD and his wife, Jane. The buildings, designed by Frederick Law OLMSTED, imitate old mission architecture. The university is consistently ranked as one of the finest in the U.S. Research facilities include the Food Research Institute, the Hoover Institution on War, Revolution, and Peace, the Stanford Linear Accelerator Center (SLAC), and the Hopkins Marine Station. The university libraries hold over six million volumes. Total enrollment is about 14,000.

Stanhope, 3rd Earl *orig.* Charles Stanhope (1753–1816) English politician and inventor. A member of Parliament (1780–86), he became chairman of the Revolution Society, favoring parliamentary reform. An experimental scientist, he invented calculating machines, a printing press and a mi-

croscope lens named for him, a stereotyping machine, and a steam carriage.

Stanislavsky \ˌsta-ni-ˈsläf-skē\, **Konstantin (Sergeyevich)** *orig.* Konstantin Sergeyevich Alekseyev (1863–1938) Russian director and actor. An actor from age 14, in 1888 he cofounded the Society of Art and Literature, with its permanent dramatic company. He won praise in 1891 for his first independent production, *The Fruits of Enlightenment*. In 1898 he cofounded the MOSCOW ART THEATRE; it restaged Anton CHEKHOV's *The Seagull* to great acclaim, and he continued to direct and act in many Russian plays, including Chekhov's *Uncle Vanya* (1899) and *The Cherry Orchard* (1904). He began training his actors using an innovative technique (see STANISLAVSKY METHOD). His company toured Europe and the U.S. (1922–24), where his method, described in *My Life in Art* (1924) and *An Actor Prepares* (1926), became highly influential.

Stanislavsky method *or* **Method acting** Influential system of dramatic training developed by Konstantin STANISLAVSKY. Developed in reaction to the histrionic acting styles of the 19th cent., it requires that an actor use his emotion memory (i.e., his recall of past experiences and emotions) to identify with the character's inner motivation. Noted U.S. practitioners have included Lee STRASBERG, Marlon BRANDO, and Dustin HOFFMAN.

Stanislaw I \stä-ˈnē-släf\ *orig.* Stanislaw Leszczynski (1677–1766) King of Poland (1704–9, 1733). He became king when CHARLES XII of Sweden invaded Poland (1702), deposed King Augustus II, and placed Stanislaw on the throne (1704). When Sweden was defeated by the Russians in 1709, Augustus regained the throne and Stanislaw settled in France, where his daughter Marie married LOUIS XV. After Augustus's death (1733), Stanislaw was elected king of Poland, but Russia invaded, causing the War of the POLISH SUCCESSION. Deposed again, Stanislaw was granted the provinces of Lorraine and Bar.

Stanley, Francis Edgar and Freelan O. (1849–1918, 1849–1940) U.S. inventors of the steam-driven AUTOMOBILE. Born in Kingfield, Me., in 1883 the twin brothers invented a dry-plate photographic process and began experiments with steam engines. In 1897 they built a steam-powered car, and in 1902 they established a company to manufacture their "Stanley Steamers." In 1906 they set a world record for the fastest mile, in 28.2 seconds. They retired in 1917; their company continued to manufacture cars until 1924.

Stanley, Henry Morton (*later* **Sir Henry**) *orig.* John Rowlands (1841–1904) British-U.S. explorer of central Africa. Stanley sailed to the U.S. as a cabin boy in 1859. After becoming a journalist for the *New York Herald* in 1867, he embarked (1871) on a journey to locate David LIVINGSTONE, of whom little had been heard since his departure for Africa in 1866. On finding him at Ujiji on Lake TANGANYIKA, Stanley uttered the famous words "Dr. Livingstone, I presume?" He explored central Africa for extended periods between 1874 and 1884, often for LEOPOLD II of Belgium, for whom he paved the way for the creation of the Congo

Henry Morton Stanley, Portrait by Hubert von Herkomer

Free State. His last expedition (1888) was for the relief of Mehmed EMIN PASHA and his men. His highly popular books included *Through the Dark Continent* (1878) and *In Darkest Africa* (1890).

Stanley Cup Trophy awarded annually for the NATIONAL HOCKEY LEAGUE championship. Named for its donor, the Canadian governor-general Frederick Arthur Stanley (1841–1908), it was first awarded in the 1893–94 season.

Stanleyville See KISANGANI

Stanton, Edwin M(cMasters) (1814–1869) U.S. secretary of war (1862–68). Born in Steubenville, Ohio, he became a

lawyer and abolitionist. He was appointed U.S. attorney general in 1861 and secretary of war in 1862. He ably administered the Union effort in the Civil War. Conflict with Pres. Andrew JOHNSON over Reconstruction policy and his alliance with the Radical Republicans led to Stanton's dismissal by Johnson, in deliberate violation of the TENURE OF OFFICE ACT. Stanton refused to leave office, but he resigned after Johnson was acquitted in the impeachment trial.

Stanton, Elizabeth Cady *orig.* Elizabeth Cady (1815–1902) U.S. women's suffrage leader. Born in Johnstown, N.Y., she married the abolitionist Henry B. Stanton in 1840 and began working to secure passage of a New York law giving property rights to married women. She and Lucretia MOTT organized the 1848 SENECA FALLS CONVENTION. She joined forces in 1850 with Susan B. ANTHONY in the WOMEN'S SUFFRAGE MOVEMENT. In 1869 she became the founding president of the National Woman Suffrage Association.

Stanwyck, Barbara *orig.* Ruby Stevens (1907–1990) U.S. film actress. Born in Brooklyn, N.Y., she won notice with her Broadway role in *The Noose* (1926). She made her screen debut in 1927 and went on to appear in over 80 films, often portraying strong-willed, independent women. Her movies include *Stella Dallas* (1937), *Double Indemnity* (1944), and *Sorry, Wrong Number* (1948). She later starred in the television series *The Big Valley* (1965–69). She received an honorary Academy Award in 1981.

staphylococcus \ˌsta-fə-lō-ˈkä-kəs\ Any of the spherical BACTERIA of the genus *Staphylococcus*, present in great numbers on the mucous membranes and skin of all humans and other warm-blooded animals. The cells characteristically group together in grapelike clusters. Staphylococci are gram-positive (see GRAM STAIN) and stationary and do not require oxygen. *S. aureus* is an important agent of wound infections, boils, TOXIC SHOCK SYNDROME, and one of the most common types of FOOD POISONING. The largest cause of hospital infections (accounting for almost 15%), "staph" is often difficult to treat because of its increasing resistance to ANTIBIOTICS.

star Any massive, celestial body of gas that shines by radiant energy it generates. Of the MILKY WAY's hundreds of billions of stars, a tiny fraction are visible to the unaided eye. The closest star is about 4.3 light-years away; the most distant are in GALAXIES billions of light-years away. Single stars are the minority; most stars occur in BINARY STARS, GLOBULAR CLUSTERS, or OPEN CLUSTERS. The stars in CONSTELLATIONS are not close but lie in the same direction from earth. Stars vary greatly in brightness (MAGNITUDE), color, temperature, mass, size, chemical composition, and age. In nearly all, HYDROGEN is the most abundant element. Stars are classified by SPECTRUM, from blue-white to red, as O, B, A, F, G, K, or M; the SUN is a G-type star. A star forms when part of a dense interstellar cloud of hydrogen and dust collapses from its gravity, raising its density and internal temperature until it is hot enough to trigger NUCLEAR FUSION in its core (if not, it becomes a BROWN DWARF). Once its hydrogen is exhausted, the core shrinks and heats up while the star's outer layers expand greatly and cool, making the star a red giant. What happens when a star no longer produces enough energy to counter its gravity depends largely on its mass and whether it is part of a close binary system (see BLACK HOLE, NEUTRON STAR, NOVA, SUPERNOVA, WHITE DWARF STAR). See also CEPHEID VARIABLE, DWARF STAR, ECLIPSING VARIABLE STAR, GIANT STAR, HERTZSPRUNG-RUSSELL DIAGRAM, SUPERGIANT STAR, T TAURI STAR, VARIABLE STAR, POPULATIONS I AND II.

starch Any of several white, granular organic compounds produced by all green plants. They are POLYSACCHARIDES; the constituent MONOSACCHARIDES are GLUCOSE units made in PHOTOSYNTHESIS. The glucose chains are unbranched in amylose and branched in amylopectin, which occur mixed in starches. Starch consumed by animals is broken down into glucose by ENZYMES during DIGESTION. Commercial starch is made mainly from corn, though wheat, tapioca, rice, and potato starch are also used. Starch has many uses in foods, as well as in the paper, textile, and personal-care products industries and in adhesives and explosives. See also CARBOHYDRATE, GLYCOGEN.

Star Chamber British prerogative court, or court through which sovereign authority was exercised, with wide civil and criminal jurisdiction that was marked by secrecy, the absence of juries, and an inquisitorial rather than accusatorial system of justice. It met in a room in the palace of Westminster whose ceiling was decorated with stars. It was employed extensively under HENRY VIII because of its ability to enforce the law when other courts were unable to do so because of corruption and influence. When CHARLES I used it to enforce unpopular political and ecclesiastical policies, it became a symbol of oppression to his and Archbishop William LAUD's parliamentary and Puritan opponents, and it was abolished by the Long Parliament in 1641.

starfish *or* **sea star** Any of 1,800 ECHINODERM species (class Asteroidea) that have regenerable arms surrounding an indistinct disk and that inhabit all oceans. Species range from 0.4 to 25 in. (1–65 cm) across, but most are 8–12 in. (20–30 cm) across. Their arms, usually five, are hollow; on the lower side are tube feet, sometimes sucker-tipped. Some species sweep organic particles into the mouth on the underside of the disk. Others either evert the stomach upon their prey for external digestion or swallow the prey whole.

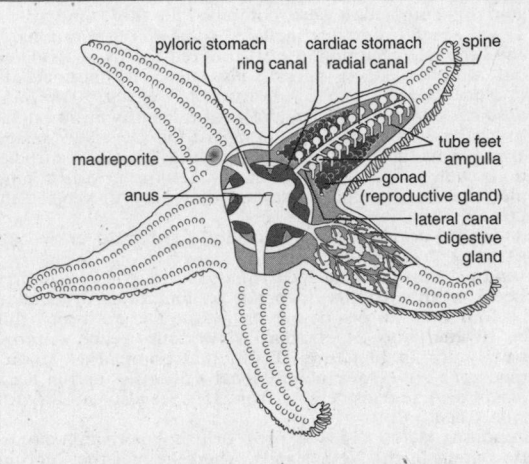

Starfish Principal features of a starfish. Water for the water vascular system enters through the madreporite and passes into a ring canal and on to radial and lateral canals, from which it enters the tube feet, which are connected to saclike ampullae on top. Contraction of the tube feet forces water into the ampullae, creating suction that allows suckers at the ends of the feet to hold to a surface. When the ampullae contract, water is forced into the feet, extending them and releasing the suction. These coordinated actions permit movement, attachment, and capture of prey. In many starfish, the cardiac stomach is everted through the mouth on the body's undersurface to envelop prey, and digestion may begin outside the body before the stomach is drawn back in.

Stark, John (1728–1822) American Revolutionary officer. Born in Londonderry, N.H., he served in the French and Indian War. In the AMERICAN REVOLUTION, he fought at the Battle of BUNKER HILL, commanded the militia that defeated the British at the Battle of Bennington, Vt., and helped force the British surrender at the Battle of SARATOGA.

starling Any of about 168 species (family Sturnidae) of songbirds of temperate Eurasia, Africa, and Australia. The best-known is *Sturnus vulgaris,* an 8-in. (20-cm), chunky, iridescent black bird with a long sharp bill. It has been introduced to most parts of the world, except S. America. The millions in N. America are descendants of 100 birds released in New York City in 1890. They often damage fruit and grain crops and usurp nests of native songbirds. They are vocal year-round.

Starling, Ernest Henry (1866–1927) British physiologist. His studies of lymph secretion clarified the roles of different pressures in fluid exchanges between vessels and tissues.

Starling and William BAYLISS showed how nerve impulses control peristalsis and coined the term hormone. Starling also found that water and necessary chemicals filtered out by the kidneys are returned lower down the nephron. His *Principles of Human Physiology* (1912), continually revised, remains a standard international text.

Star of David See Star of DAVID

Starr, Belle *orig.* Myra Belle Shirley (1848–1889) U.S. outlaw. Born in Washington Co., Md., she lived in Texas from 1863. She bore a child by the outlaw Cole Younger (1844–1916) and another by Jim Reed, with whom she rustled cattle and horses. She fashioned herself the "bandit queen," often dressing in velvet and feathers. In 1880 she married Sam Starr, and their Oklahoma ranch became an outlaws' hideout. Sam was killed in a gunfight in 1887, and Belle herself was later shot down near her ranch.

START *in full* **Strategic Arms Reduction Talks** Negotiations between the U.S. and the Soviet Union aimed at reducing those countries' nuclear arsenals and delivery systems. Two sets of negotiations (1982–83, 1985–91) concluded in an agreement committing the Soviet Union to a reduction from 11,000 to 8,000 nuclear weapons, and the U.S. to a reduction from 12,000 to 10,000. After the Soviet Union's collapse (1991), a supplementary agreement (1992) obligated Ukraine, Belarus, and Kazakhstan to either destroy the nuclear weapons on their soil or give them to Russia. See also SALT.

Star Wars See STRATEGIC DEFENSE INITIATIVE

state Political organization of society or, more narrowly, the institutions of government. It is distinguished from other social groups by its purpose (establishment of order and security), methods (its laws and their enforcement), territory (its area of jurisdiction), and sovereignty. In some countries (e.g., the U.S.), the term also refers to nonsovereign political units subject to the authority of the larger state, or federal union.

State, U.S. Department of Federal executive division responsible for carrying out U.S. foreign policy. Established in 1789, and the oldest of the federal departments, it is the president's principal means of conducting treaty negotiations and forging agreements with foreign nations. It includes the U.S. Foreign Service and various offices of diplomatic security, foreign intelligence, policy analysis, international narcotics control, and protocol.

Staten Island Island in New York Harbor, a borough (pop., 2000: 444,000) of NEW YORK CITY. It has an area of almost 60 sq mi (155 sq km) and is connected with BROOKLYN by the Verrazano-Narrows Bridge and with New Jersey by several bridges; it is accessible to MANHATTAN by the venerable Staten Island Ferry. The Dutch attempted to colonize the island in 1630 but were thwarted by the Delaware Indians. In 1661 the Dutch W. India Co. granted the island to the French and settlements were established. Following the acquisition of New Netherland in 1664 by Britain, English and Welsh farmers established homes and farms on the island. Mostly residential, it has some industry, including shipbuilding yards, printing plants, and oil storage tanks and refineries.

States General See ESTATES GENERAL

states' rights All government rights or powers held by the individual states of a federal union under the provisions of a federal constitution. In some federally organized countries, these powers are those that remain after the powers of the central government are enumerated in the constitution. In others, the powers of both levels of government are defined in their constitutions. In the U.S., some states claimed the right to nullify federal authority and secede, which led to the AMERICAN CIVIL WAR. In the civil-rights era, the concept of states' rights was invoked by opponents of racial integration in public schools. The federal government can influence state policy even in areas that are constitutionally the purview of the states (e.g., education, local road construction) through withholding funds from states that fail to comply with its wishes.

statistics Branch of mathematics dealing with gathering, analyzing, and making inferences from data in all the sciences. Statistical tools not only summarize past data through such indicators as the mean (see MEAN, MEDIAN, AND MODE) and the standard deviation but can predict future events using FREQUENCY DISTRIBUTION functions. Statistics provides ways to design efficient experiments that eliminate time-consuming trial and error. Double-blind tests for polls, intelligence and aptitude tests, and medical, biological, and industrial experiments all benefit from statistical methods and theories. See also ESTIMATION, PROBABILITY THEORY, REGRESSION.

Statue of Liberty National Monument National monument, Liberty Island (formerly Bedloe's Island), New York Harbor, New York. Covering 58 acres (23 hectares), it includes the colossal statue "Liberty Enlightening the World," sculpted by F.-A. BARTHOLDI and dedicated in 1886. The 302-ft (92-m) statue of a woman holding a tablet and upraised torch was given to the U.S. by France and commemorates the friendship of the two countries. It was extensively restored for its spectacular centennial on July 4, 1986. In 1965 nearby ELLIS ISLAND was added to the monument.

stave church Type of medieval Norwegian wooden church. The stone foundation supports four horizontal wooden members, from which rise four corner posts, or staves, which are joined together by four upper crossbeams. From this boxlike frame, timbers extend outward, supporting a series of uprights, or masts. The church at Borgund (c.1150), one of about 24 surviving examples, has six tiers of double-sloped roofs, shell-like exterior shingles, and elaborate carvings of dragons and other motifs.

Stavisky Affair (1934) French financial and political scandal. When bonds sold to working-class citizens by a credit organization run by the Russian-born swindler Serge A. Stavisky (1886–1934) were found to be worthless, Stavisky fled to Chamonix and allegedly committed suicide. Members of the right believed he had been murdered to cover up complicity with corrupt government officials. Demonstrations against the government by antirepublican groups culminated in a riot that killed 15 people. Two successive prime ministers were forced to resign.

STD See SEXUALLY TRANSMITTED DISEASE

steady-state theory Concept of an EXPANDING UNIVERSE whose average density remains constant, matter being created throughout it to form new stars and galaxies at the same rate that old ones recede from sight. A steady-state universe has no beginning or end. Its average density and arrangement of galaxies of all ages are the same as seen from every point. Put forward by William Macmillan (1861–1948) in the 1920s, the theory was modified by Fred HOYLE to deal with problems raised by the BIG-BANG model, supported by much evidence obtained since the 1950s.

stealth Any military technology intended to make vehicles or missiles nearly invisible to enemy RADAR or other electronic detection. In World War II, the Germans coated their U-boat snorkels with radar-absorbent material. The postwar era saw research into radar echoes, and by the 1980s the U.S. had developed models of stealth technology, including a bomber with surface materials and coatings that can absorb radar transmissions and smooth, rounded shapes that reduce radar echoes. Aircraft are less detectable when its weapons are recessed, and shielding engine exhaust makes infrared detection more difficult.

steam Invisible GAS consisting of vaporized WATER. When mixed with minute droplets of water, it has a white, cloudy appearance. In nature, steam is produced by the heating of underground water by volcanic processes and is emitted from HOT SPRINGS, GEYSERS, and FUMAROLES. Modern industrial society relies on steam power; water is heated to steam in power plants, and the pressurized steam drives TURBINES that produce ELECTRIC CURRENT: thermal energy is converted to mechanical energy, which is converted into electricity.

steamboat *or* **steamship** Watercraft propelled by steam; more narrowly, a shallow-draft paddle-wheel steamboat widely used on rivers in the 19th cent., particularly the Mississippi River. The first regular steamboat service, operating on the Mississippi, was established in 1812. Until about 1870 the steamboat dominated the economy, agriculture, and commerce of the middle U.S. The first ocean voyage of a steamboat occurred along the E coast of the U.S. in 1809, and Europeans soon developed steamboats capable of crossing Europe's stormy, narrow seas. The first transat-

lantic steamboat journey was made by the *Savannah* in 1819, and the first commercial shipping line, the Cunard Line (see Samuel CUNARD), was established in 1840. The screw propeller replaced the paddle wheel in oceanic steamers in the later 19th cent. See also OCEAN LINER.

steam engine Machine that uses steam power to perform mechanical work through the agency of heat. In a steam engine, hot STEAM, usually supplied by a BOILER, expands under pressure, and part of the heat energy is converted into work. The rest of the heat may be allowed to escape, or, for maximum engine efficiency, the steam may be condensed in a separate apparatus, a CONDENSER, at comparatively low temperature and pressure. For high efficiency, the steam must decrease substantially in temperature as it expands within the engine. The greatest output of work in relation to the heat supplied is obtained by using a low condenser temperature and a high boiler pressure. See also Thomas NEWCOMEN, James WATT.

Stebbins, G(eorge) Ledyard (1906–2000) U.S. botanist. Born in Lawrence, N.Y., he taught in the Univ. of California system. In *Variation and Evolution in Plants* (1950) he became the first biologist to apply the modern synthetic theory of EVOLUTION to higher organisms. Working with polyploid plants (new species that originated by a spontaneous doubling of the CHROMOSOMES of an existing species), he employed a technique for doubling a plant's chromosomal number artificially to produce successful artificial polyploids from wild-grass species, becoming the first person to artificially synthesize a plant species that could thrive under natural conditions.

steel ALLOY of IRON and about 2% or less CARBON. Pure iron is soft, but carbon greatly hardens it. Several iron-carbon constituents with different compositions and/or crystal structures exist; each microstructure differs in hardness, strength, toughness, corrosion resistance, and electrical resistivity, so adjusting the carbon content changes the properties. HEAT TREATING, mechanical working at cold or hot temperatures, or addition of alloying elements may also give superior properties. The three major classes are CARBON STEELS, low-alloy steels, and high-alloy steels. Low-alloy steels (with up to 8% alloying elements) are exceptionally strong and are used for machine parts, aircraft landing gear, shafts, hand tools, and gears, and in buildings and bridges. High-alloy steels, with more than 8% alloying elements (e.g., STAINLESS STEELS) offer unusual properties. Making steel involves melting, purifying (refining), and alloying, carried out at about 2,900°F (1,600°C). Steel is obtained by refining iron (from a BLAST FURNACE) or scrap steel, then removing excess carbon and impurities and adding alloying elements. Molten steel can be poured into ingot MOLDS; ingots are reheated and rolled into semifinished shapes which are worked into finished products. Some steps can be saved by continuous CASTING. Forming semifinished steel into finished shapes may be done by two major methods: hot-working consists primarily of hammering and pressing (together called FORGING), EXTRUSION, and rolling the steel under high heat; cold-working, which includes rolling, extrusion, and drawing, is generally used to make bars, wire, tubes, sheets, and strips. Molten steel can also be cast directly into products. Certain products are protected from CORROSION by ELECTROPLATING, GALVANIZING, or tinplating.

steel drum Tuned gong made from the end, and part of the wall, of an oil barrel. The barrel's end surface is hammered into a concave shape, and several areas are outlined by chiseled grooves. It is heated and tempered, and bosses or domes are hammered into the outlined areas; the depth, curvature, and size of each boss determines its pitch. Melodies, complex accompaniments, and counterpoint can be played with mallets on a single drum. The steel drum originated in Trinidad in the 1940s.

Steele, Richard (*later* **Sir Richard**) (1672–1729) English journalist, dramatist, essayist, and politician. He began his long friendship with Joseph ADDISON at school. He launched and was the principal author of the essay periodical *The Tatler* (Apr. 1709–Jan. 1711), in which he created the mixture of entertainment and instruction in manners and morals that he and Addison would perfect in *The Spec-*

tator (1711–12, 1714). He made many later ventures into journalism and held several government posts. In 1714 he became governor of DRURY LANE THEATRE, where he produced *The Conscious Lovers* (1723), one of the century's most popular plays and perhaps the best example of English sentimental comedy.

Steen \'stān\, **Jan (Havickszoon)** (1626–1679) Dutch painter. In 1648 he became a founding member of the Leiden painters' guild. One of the greatest Dutch genre painters, he is known for his humor and ability to capture subtle facial expressions, especially of children. His figures, which became larger and more individually characterized in his later works, were often shown playing cards or skittles, or carousing in inns and taverns. His paintings show great technical skill, particularly with color.

steeplechase Either of two distinct sporting events: (1) a horse race over a closed course with obstacles, including hedges and walls; or (2) a footrace of 3,000 m over hurdles and a water jump. The name derives from impromptu races by fox hunters in 18th-cent. Ireland over natural country in which church steeples served as course landmarks. Equestrian steeplechase is most popular in England, France, and Ireland; the most famous equestrian steeplechase is the Grand National in Liverpool. Track-and-field steeplechase dates back to 1850 at Oxford. The course and distance were standardized at the 1920 Olympic Games.

Stefan Dusan \'dü-shän\ *or* **Stefan Uros IV** (1308–1355) King of Serbia (1331–46) and emperor of the Serbs and Greeks (1346–55). He deposed his father, Stefan Decansky, in 1331. The greatest ruler of medieval Serbia, he began a war of conquest against Byzantium in 1334, gaining control of Albania and Macedonia by 1346 and Epirus and Thessaly by 1348. Dusan reformed the Serbian administration on the Byzantine model and introduced a law code. His empire broke apart soon after his death.

Steffens, (Joseph) Lincoln (1866–1936) U.S. journalist and reformer. Born in San Francisco, he worked for New York newspapers before becoming managing editor of *McClure's Magazine* (1901–6), where he began his famous muckraking articles, later published as *The Shame of the Cities* (1904), exposing corruption in politics and big business. He lectured widely and aroused public interest in seeking solutions. He later supported revolutionary activities in Mexico and Russia. The success of his *Autobiography* (1931) returned him to the lecture circuit.

Stegner, Wallace (Earle) (1909–1993) U.S. writer. Born in Lake Mills, Iowa, Stegner had a distinguished career teaching writing, notably at Stanford Univ. *The Big Rock Candy Mountain* (1943) was his first critical and popular success. His later novels include *Angle of Repose* (1971, Pulitzer Prize) and *The Spectator Bird* (1976, National Book Award). His nonfiction includes two histories of the settlement of Utah and a biography of J. W. POWELL (1954).

stegosaur Any member of the genus *Stegosaurus*, herbivorous, four-legged DINOSAURS of the Late JURASSIC PERIOD (159–144 million years ago). Stegosaurs reached a length of about 20 ft (6.5 m). The skull and brain were very small, and the forelimbs were much shorter than the hind limbs. Stegosaurs had double rows of large, triangular bony plates along their backs and tail (possibly a temperature-regulating system) and several long pointed bony spikes on the end of the tail.

Steichen \'stī-kən\, **Edward (Jean)** (*orig.* Édouard Jean) (1879–1973) U.S. (Luxembourg-born) photographer. Training in painting influenced his photography; he frequently used chemicals to achieve prints that resembled soft, fuzzy mezzotints or wash drawings. In 1902 he joined Alfred STIEGLITZ in forming the PHOTO-SECESSION group. His style evolved from painterly impressionism to sharp realism after World War I. His portraits of artists and celebrities from

Edward Steichen, 1960

the 1920s and '30s are remarkable evocations of character. In 1955 he organized the *Family of Man* exhibition of 503 photographs (selected from over 2 million), which was seen by more than 9 million people worldwide.

Stein, Gertrude (1874–1946) U.S. avant-garde writer. Born in Allegheny, Pa., from 1909 she lived with her companion Alice B. Toklas (1877–1967) in Paris. Their home was a salon for leading artists and writers, including Pablo PICASSO, Henri MATISSE, and Ernest HEMINGWAY. An early supporter of Cubism, she tried to parallel its theories in her work. Her prose displayed a unique style employing repetition and fragmentation, especially in the immense novel *The Making of Americans* (written 1906–11). Her only book to reach a wide public was *The Autobiography of Alice B. Toklas* (1933), actually Stein's own autobiography. Her other works include *Four Saints in Three Acts* (1934) and *The Mother of Us All* (1947), opera librettos scored by Virgil THOMSON.

Stein \'shtīn\, **(Heinrich Friedrich) Karl, Reichsfreiherr (Imperial Baron) vom und zum** (1757–1831) Prussian statesman. As minister of economic affairs (1804–7) and chief minister (1807–8) to FREDERICK WILLIAM III, he introduced wide-ranging reforms that modernized the Prussian government. He abolished serfdom, reformed the laws on land ownership, and helped reorganize the military. Anticipating war with France, he was forced to resign under pressure from NAPOLEON (1808). As an adviser to Czar ALEXANDER I (1812–15), he negotiated the Russo–Prussian treaty that formed the last European coalition against Napoleon.

Steinbeck, John (Ernst) (1902–1968) U.S. novelist. Born in Salinas, Cal., he earned his reputation mostly with the naturalistic novels on proletarian themes that he wrote in the 1930s, including *Tortilla Flat* (1935; film, 1942), *Of Mice and Men* (1937; film 1939), and the acclaimed *The Grapes of Wrath* (1939, Pulitzer Prize; film, 1940), which aroused widespread sympathy for the plight of migrant farm workers. In World War II he served as a war correspondent. His later novels include *Cannery Row* (1945; film, 1982), *The Pearl* (1947; film, 1948), and *East of Eden* (1952; film, 1955). He received the Nobel Prize in 1962.

Steinberg, Saul *orig.* Saul Jacobson (1914–1999) Romanian-U.S. cartoonist and illustrator. He studied architecture in Milan, meanwhile publishing cartoons in Italian magazines. Settling in New York in 1942, he worked as a freelance artist and cartoonist, mainly for *The New Yorker*. His instantly recognizable works are often surrealistic or whimsically nightmarish visions of contemporary America and frequently employ odd versions of pop-culture icons.

Steinem, Gloria (b.1934) U.S. political activist, feminist, and editor. Born in Toledo, Ohio, she began her career as a writer and journalist. She was a founder of the National Women's Political Caucus (1971), and in 1972 she founded *Ms.,* a trendsetting magazine that treated contemporary issues from a feminist perspective. In 1966 she helped found the NATIONAL ORGANIZATION FOR WOMEN. Her books include *Outrageous Acts and Everyday Rebellions* (1983) and *Revolution from Within* (1992).

Steiner \'shtī-nər\, **Rudolf** (1861–1925) Austrian-Swiss social and spiritual philosopher, founder of ANTHROPOSOPHY. He edited J. W. von GOETHE's scientific works. Having helped found the German Theosophic Assn. (see THEOSOPHY), in 1912 he founded the Anthroposophical Society. A progressive school he founded in 1919 for the workers at the Waldorf Astoria factory led to the international Waldorf School movement. Steiner's writings include *The Philosophy of Spiritual Activity* (1894), *Occult Science* (1913), and *Story of My Life* (1924).

Stein-Leventhal syndrome See POLYCYSTIC OVARY SYNDROME.

Steinmetz \'shtīn-ˌmets, *Engl* 'stīn-ˌmets\, **Charles Proteus** (*orig.* Karl August Rudolf) (1865–1923) German-U.S. electrical engineer. He emi-

Charles Proteus Steinmetz

grated to the U.S. in 1889 and began working for General Electric Co. in 1893. He taught at Union College from 1902. His experiments led to the law of hysteresis, which deals with power loss in electrical machinery when magnetic action is converted to unusable heat; the constant he calculated has remained a part of electrical engineering. In 1893 he developed a simplified symbolic method of calculating alternating-current phenomena. His theory of traveling waves led to development of devices to protect high-power transmission lines from lightning. He patented over 200 inventions.

Steinway German-U.S. piano-manufacturing firm. Henry E. Steinway, born Heinrich Engelhard Steinweg (1797–1871), was trained as an organ builder in his native Germany, and began building pianos in 1836. He and most of his family followed one of his sons to the U.S. in 1850, and in 1853 father and sons founded their own company in New York City, which came to dominate the market. Steinway's improvements set the standard for the modern grand piano.

stele \'stē-lē, 'stēl\ *or* **stela** \'stē-lə\ Standing stone tablet used in the ancient world primarily as a grave marker but also for dedication, commemoration, and demarcation. They were used in Egypt, Greece, Asia, and the Mayan empire. In Babylon, the Code of HAMMURABI was engraved on a tall stele. The largest number of stelae were produced in ATTICA, chiefly as grave markers. On the stelae men were shown as warriors or athletes, women surrounded by their children, children with their pets or toys.

Stella, Frank (Philip) (b.1936) U.S. painter. Born in Malden, Mass., he moved to New York after studying history at Princeton Univ., and there began his innovative "black paintings" (1958–60), incorporating symmetrical series of thin white stripes that replicated the canvas shape when seen against their black backgrounds. As a leading figure of MINIMALISM, in the mid-1960s he began an influential series marked by intersecting geometric shapes and plays of vivid colors. In the 1970s he began producing sensuously colored, mixed-media reliefs featuring more organic shapes.

stem cell Unspecialized CELL that gives rise to differentiated cells. Stem cells in embryos have the capacity to develop into any kind of tissue in the body and are thus essential to fetal development. Stem cells in adults are involved in the renewal of tissue; less flexible than embryonic stem cells, they can typically develop only into the type of tissue in which they arise (e.g., a blood-forming stem cell can develop into any of various kinds of blood cells). Stem-cell research holds promise for the treatment of numerous diseases and conditions in which tissues have been damaged (such as diabetes, Parkinson's disease, and cirrhosis) and even the growing of replacement organs.

Stendhal \staⁿ-'dȧl, *Engl* sten-'däl\ *orig.* Marie-Henri Beyle (1783–1842) French novelist. From 1806 he served in Napoleon's army; after the French empire fell in 1814, he settled in Italy but later returned to Paris. During 1821–30, while leading an active social life, he wrote works including the masterpiece *Rouge et noir* (1830; *The Red and the Black*), a powerful character study of an ambitious young man that is also an acute picture of Restoration France. His other major work, *The Charterhouse of Parma* (1839), is remarkable for its sophisticated rendering of human psychology and its subtly drawn portraits. His unfinished autobiographical works, *Memoirs of an Egotist* (1892) and *The Life of Henry Brulard* (1890), are among his most original achievements.

Stengel, Casey (*orig.* Charles Dillon) (1891–1975) U.S. baseball player and manager. Born in Kansas City, he played outfield with the Brooklyn Dodgers (1912–17) and other teams. He became a coach and manager of the Dodgers and Boston Braves, but achieved his greatest success with the New York Yankees (1949–61), leading the team to 10 pennants and seven World Series championships in 12 years. He later served as vice president and manager of the new New York Mets (1962–65). He was known for his showmanship and his idiosyncratic use and misuse of English.

Stenmark, Ingemar (b.1956) Swedish Alpine skier. He won his first World Cup race in 1974. In 1976, 1977, and 1978 he was the overall victor in the World Cup (slalom, giant slalom, and downhill). In the 1980 Olympic Games he won gold medals in slalom and giant slalom. His lifetime total of

86 World Cup victories still stands as a record, and he is perhaps the greatest slalom and giant slalom skier of all time.

Steno \'stä-nō\, **Nicolaus** *Danish* Niels Steensen *or* Niels Stensen (1638–1686) Danish geologist and anatomist. An eminent physician, in 1660 he discovered the parotid salivary duct (Stensen's duct). He was also the first to realize that the earth's geologic history might be deciphered by careful study of rock strata and FOSSILS, which he identified as the remains of ancient living organisms. In 1669 he made the fundamental crystallographic discovery that all quartz crystals have the same angles between corresponding faces.

stenography See SHORTHAND

stenosis See AORTIC STENOSIS

Stephen *or* **Stephen of Blois** \'blwä\ (1097?–1154) King of England (1135–54). The nephew of HENRY I, he pledged to support MATILDA but claimed the throne himself. In the civil strife that followed he was unable to win the loyalty of all the barons. Matilda invaded (1139), and in a display of chivalry Stephen had her escorted to Bristol. Soon in control of most of W England, she captured Stephen in battle (1141), but her arrogance provoked a rebellion, and he was released (1141). He continued his weak rule; by agreement, Matilda's son Henry (later HENRY II) was named as Stephen's successor.

Stephen *known as* **Stephen the Great** (1435–1504) Prince of MOLDAVIA (1457–1504). With the help of the Walachian prince VLAD III TEPES, Stephen secured the throne of Moldavia. He repelled a Hungarian invasion (1467) and later defeated invading Turks (1475, 1476), winning renown for his resistance. In 1503 Stephen signed a treaty preserving Moldavian independence at the cost of an annual tribute to the Turks.

Stephen, St. (1st cent.) First Christian martyr. As told in the Acts of the Apostles, he was a foreign-born Jew who lived in Jerusalem and joined the church at an early date. He was one of seven deacons appointed by the Apostles to care for elderly women, widows, and orphans. His defense of Christianity so outraged the SANHEDRIN that he was condemned to be stoned to death. One of those who assented to the execution was Saul of Tarsus (later St. PAUL).

Stephen I *or* **St. Stephen** *orig.* Vajk (c.970–1038) First king of Hungary (1000–38) and founder of the Hungarian state. The son of a Magyar chieftain, he was born a pagan but was later baptized as a Christian. After defeating his cousin to claim the throne, Stephen was crowned; his royal crown, a national treasure, was a gift of Pope SYLVESTER II. His rule was mainly peaceful, and he organized Hungarian government and church administration on German models. He is the patron saint of Hungary.

Stephen Bathory \'bä-tȯr-ē\ *Hungarian* Istvan Bathory *Polish* Stefan Batory (1533–1586) King of Poland (1575–86). In 1571 he was elected prince of Transylvania by the Hungarians, and in 1575, as son-in-law of the late Sigismund I, he was elected king of Poland by the Polish nobility. A forceful and ambitious monarch, he successfully defended Poland's E Baltic provinces against Russian incursion and forced the cession of Livonia to Poland in 1582.

Stephen Dusan See STEFAN DUSAN

Stephens, Alexander H(amilton) (1812–1883) U.S. politician. Born in Wilkes Co., Ga., he served in the U.S. House of Representatives 1843–59, where he defended slavery but opposed dissolution of the Union. When Georgia seceded, he was elected vice president of the Confederacy. He supported constitutional government, opposed attempts by Jefferson DAVIS to infringe on individuals' rights, and advocated a program of prisoner exchanges. He later served again in the House (1873–82) and as governor of Georgia (1882–83).

Stephenson, George (1781–1848) British engineer, principal inventor of the LOCOMOTIVE. He worked initially as chief mechanic at a coal mine, where his interest in steam engines led to experiments on a machine to pull coal-filled cars out of the mines. In 1815 he devised a powerful "steam blast" system that made the locomotive practical. In 1825 he built a steam locomotive for the first passenger railway, from Stockton to Darlington, which could carry 450 people at 15 mph (24 kph). In 1829, assisted by his son Robert

STEPHENSON, he built his improved locomotive, the *Rocket,* which won a speed competition at 36 mph (58 kph) and became the model for later locomotives.

Stephenson, Robert (1803–1859) British civil engineer. The son of George STEPHENSON, he assisted his father in constructing the "Rocket" and several railways. He spanned the Tyne River with a six-arch iron bridge. Called on to build a secure railroad bridge over the Menai Strait to the Welsh mainland, Stephenson conceived a unique tubular design, which proved highly successful.

George Stephenson
Engraving after H. P. Briggs

Steptoe, Patrick (Christopher) and Robert (Geoffrey) Edwards (1913–1988, b.1925) British medical researchers. They perfected human in vitro fertilization, leading to the birth of the first "test-tube baby" in 1978. Steptoe had conducted research on STERILIZATION and INFERTILITY, and Edwards had succeeded in 1968 in fertilizing human ova outside the uterus. Their partnership resulted in the birth of more than 1,000 babies.

stereochemistry Study of stereoisomers (see ISOMER). Louis PASTEUR showed that tartaric acid had OPTICAL ACTIVITY that depended on molecular asymmetry, and Jacobus VAN'T HOFF and Joseph-Achille Le Bel (1847–1930) independently explained how a molecule with a carbon atom bonded to four different groups has two mirror-image forms. Stereochemistry deals with stereoisomers and their synthesis. John Cornforth (b.1917) and Vladimir Prelog (1906–1998) shared a 1975 Nobel Prize for work on stereoisomerism of alkaloids, enzymes, and antibiotics.

sterilization Any surgical procedure intended to end FERTILITY permanently (see CONTRACEPTION). Such operations remove or interrupt the anatomical pathways through which the cells involved in FERTILIZATION travel (see REPRODUCTIVE SYSTEM). The operations used in humans are VASECTOMY in men and tubal ligation (tying off and blocking or cutting of the fallopian tubes) in women. Animals are sterilized by CASTRATION in males and spaying (removal of the OVARIES) in females.

Stern, Isaac (1920–2001) U.S. (Ukrainian-born) violinist. His family came to the U.S. when he was an infant. He first performed with the San Francisco Symphony at 14. After the war, he began to tour extensively (including the Soviet Union in 1956). In 1960 he formed a famous trio with pianist Eugene Istomin (b.1925) and cellist Leonard Rose (1918–1984). He was instrumental in saving Carnegie Hall from demolition, and was a key presence in the musical life of Israel.

Sternberg, Josef von *orig.* Jonas Stern (1894–1969) U.S. (Austrian-born) film director. Emigrating to New York as a boy, by 1923 he was a scriptwriter and cameraman in Hollywood. In 1927 he made the first serious gangster movie, *Underworld.* His films became noted for their striking visual effects and atmospheric use of light and dark. In Germany he made *The Blue Angel* (1930), starring Marlene DIETRICH; returning to Hollywood, he directed her in *Morocco* (1930), *Shanghai Express* (1932), *Blonde Venus* (1932), *The Scarlet Empress* (1934), and *The Devil Is a Woman* (1935). His career thereafter declined; his late films include *Macao* (1952).

Sterne, Laurence (1713–1768) English novelist and humorist. Sterne was a clergyman in York for many years before his writing talents became apparent. Turning his parishes over to a curate, he began *Tristram Shandy* (1759–67), an experimental novel issued in nine parts in which the story is subordinate to its narrator's free associations and digressions. It is considered one of the most important ancestors of psychological and STREAM-OF-CONSCIOUSNESS fiction. He later undertook the travels that inspired his unfinished *Sentimental Journey Through France and Italy*

(1768), a comic novel that defies conventional expectations of a travel book.

steroid Any of a class of natural or synthetic organic compounds with 17 carbon atoms in a three-dimensional arrangement of four rings. The CONFIGURATION of the nucleus, the nature of the groups attached to it, and their positions distinguish different steroids. Hundreds have been found in plants and animals and thousands more synthesized or made by modifying natural steroids. Examples include many HORMONES (including the SEX HORMONES), BILE acids, sterols (including CHOLESTEROL), and oral contraceptives. See also ANABOLIC STEROIDS, CORTISONE, DIGITALIS.

Stettin See SZCZECIN

Steuben \\'stü-bən\\, **Frederick William (Augustus)** (1730–1794) German-American Revolutionary officer. He joined the Prussian army at 16 and was a captain in the Seven Years' War. Recommended to George WASHINGTON, he arrived in America in 1777. Appointed to train the Continental forces at Valley Forge, Pa., he produced a disciplined fighting force that became the model for the entire Continental Army. Appointed inspector general of the army and promoted to major general (1778), he helped command at the Siege of YORKTOWN.

Stevens, George (1904–1975) U.S. film director. Born in Oakland, Cal., he became a Hollywood cameraman and photographed many of LAUREL AND HARDY's comedies before turning to directing in 1933. Noted for his brilliant camera techniques, he achieved fame with *Alice Adams* (1935) and *Swing Time* (1936). His later films include *Woman of the Year* (1942), *A Place in the Sun* (1951, Academy Award), the classic western *Shane* (1953), and *Giant* (1956, Academy Award).

Stevens, John (1749–1838) U.S. engineer and inventor. Born in New York City, he served as a colonel in the American Revolution. His outline for a PATENT law formed the basis of the U.S. patent system (1790). In 1802 he became the first person to employ a powered screw to propel a ship. In 1809 his steamship *Phoenix* became the world's first seagoing steamboat. In Philadelphia in 1811 he inaugurated the world's first steam-ferry service. In 1825, at age 76, he built the first American steam LOCOMOTIVE. He was the father of R. L. STEVENS. Another son, Edwin Augustus Stevens (1795–1868), was the inventor of the Stevens plow and a pioneer builder of ironclad warships. A third son, John Cox Stevens (1785–1857), headed the group that sent the yacht *America* to Britain and established the AMERICA'S CUP.

Stevens, John Paul (b.1920) U.S. jurist. Born in Chicago, he was appointed to the U.S. Circuit Court of Appeals in 1970, and to the U.S. Supreme Court in 1975. An independent-minded justice, Stevens has become, with the departure of several colleagues, perhaps the Court's most liberal member.

Stevens, Robert Livingston (1787–1856) U.S. engineer. Born in Hoboken, N.J., the son of John STEVENS, he designed the railway T-rail in 1830, and later the railroad spike. He found that rails laid on wooden ties, with crushed stone or gravel beneath, provided a roadbed superior to any known before; his construction remains in universal use.

Stevens, Thaddeus (1792–1868) U.S. politician. Born in Danville, Vt., he practiced law in Pennsylvania, defending fugitive slaves without fee. In the U.S. House of Representatives (1849–53, 1859–68), he opposed the extension of slavery into the W territories. After the Civil War he was a leader of the RADICAL REPUBLICANS and demanded strict criteria, including justice for blacks, for readmission of the seceded states. He opposed the moderate Reconstruction policies of Pres. Andrew JOHNSON and introduced the resolution for his impeachment.

Stevens, Wallace (1879–1955) U.S. poet. Born in Reading, Pa., Stevens joined an insurance firm in Hartford as a lawyer in 1916; he rose to vice president, a position he held until his death. His poems began appearing in 1914. In *Harmonium* (1923), his first and most verbally brilliant book, he introduced the theme that occupied his creative lifetime: the relationship between imagination and reality. His later poetry, in such collections as *Ideas of Order* (1936) and *The*

Man with the Blue Guitar (1937) continued to explore this theme with greater depth and rigor. Not until his late years was he recognized as a major poet by more than a few; he received a Pulitzer Prize only with his *Collected Poems* in 1955. He is now often considered America's greatest 20th-cent. poet.

Stevenson, Adlai E(wing) (1900–1965) U.S. politician and diplomat. Born in Christian Co., Ky., the grandson of a vice president, he practiced law in Chicago from 1926. He was assistant to the secretary of the navy (1941–44) and later a delegate to the U.N. (1946–47). As governor of Illinois (1949–53), he introduced liberal reforms. Noted for his eloquence and wit, he was twice the Democratic candidate for president (1952, 1956) but lost both times to Dwight EISENHOWER. He later served as chief U.S. representative to the U.N. (1961–65).

Stevenson, Robert Louis (Balfour) (1850–1894) Scottish writer. He traveled frequently, partly in search of better climates for his tuberculosis, which would cause his death at 44. He became known for accounts such as *Travels with a Donkey in the Cévennes* (1879) and essays in periodicals. His immensely popular novels *Treasure Island* (1883), *Kidnapped* (1886), *Dr. Jekyll and Mr. Hyde* (1886), and *The Master of Ballantrae* (1889) were written over the course of a few years. *A Child's Garden of Verses* (1885) is one of the most influential children's works of the 19th cent. In his last years he lived in Samoa and produced works moving toward a new maturity, including the novel *Weir of Hermiston* (1896), his unfinished masterpiece.

Robert Louis Stevenson

Stewart See House of STUART

Stewart, James (Maitland) (1908–1997) U.S. film actor. Born in Indiana, Pa., he studied architecture at Princeton Univ. and made his film debut in 1935. He played endearingly simple and idealistic characters in Frank CAPRA's *You Can't Take It with You* (1938) and *Mr. Smith Goes to Washington* (1939). After serving as a bomber pilot in World War II, he starred in the Christmas classic *It's a Wonderful Life* (1946). His other movies include *Destry Rides Again* (1939), *The Philadelphia Story* (1940, Academy Award), *Harvey* (1950), *The Glenn Miller Story* (1954), *Anatomy of a Murder* (1959), and Alfred HITCHCOCK's *Rope* (1948), *Rear Window* (1954), and *Vertigo* (1958).

Stewart, Potter (1915–1985) U.S. jurist. Born in Jackson, Mich., he was appointed to the U.S. Court of Appeals in 1954 and to the U.S. Supreme Court in 1958; he served until 1981. A moderate, he wrote the majority opinion in the *Shelton vs. Tucker* case, which held unconstitutional the requirement that teachers list all the associations to which they belong, and wrote a memorable dissent in *Miranda vs. Arizona*.

stickleback Any of about 12 species (family Gasterosteidae) of scaleless fishes inhabiting temperate fresh- and saltwaters. Sticklebacks grow to 6 in. (15 cm) long. They have a row of spines on the back, a sharp spine in each of the pelvic fins, and hard armor plates on their sides. The male builds a nest, coaxes one or more females in to lay eggs, fertilizes the eggs, and aggressively defends eggs and young.

Stickley, Gustav (1858–1942) U.S. furniture designer. Born in Osceola, Wis., he worked at a chair factory owned by an uncle. After taking over the factory, he moved it to Binghamton and then Syracuse, New York. Influenced by the ARTS AND CRAFTS MOVEMENT and by visits to old missions in the American Southwest, he introduced (c.1900) a highly original line of sturdy oak furniture. To spread his ideas and designs, he published the influential magazine *The Craftsman* 1901–16. In 1916 two younger brothers established a firm to produce furniture from his designs and gave the style the name Mission, by which name it is still popular today.

Stieglitz \'stĕg-lits\, **Alfred** (1864–1946) U.S. photographer. Born in Hoboken, N.J., he was taken to Europe by his wealthy family to further his education. In 1883 he abandoned engineering studies in Berlin for a photographic career. Returning to the U.S. in 1890, he made the first successful photographs in snow, in rain, and at night. In 1902 he founded the PHOTO-SECESSION group to establish photography as an art. His own best photographs are perhaps two series (1917–27), one of portraits of his wife, Georgia O'KEEFFE, and the other of cloud shapes corresponding to emotional experiences. His photographs were the first to be exhibited in major U.S. museums. He also was the first to exhibit, at his "291" gallery in New York, works of modern European and U.S. painters, five years before the ARMORY SHOW.

stigmata \stig-'mä-tə\ In Christian MYSTICISM, bodily marks, scars, or pains suffered in places corresponding to those of the crucified JESUS—on the hands and feet, near the heart, and sometimes on the head, shoulders, and back. They are taken as signs of holiness. The first to experience the stigmata was St. FRANCIS OF ASSISI (1224). Of the more than 330 persons identified with stigmata since the 14th cent., 60 were declared saints or the blessed by the Roman Catholic church.

Stijl \'stīl, 'stāl\, **De** (Dutch: "The Style") Group of Dutch artists founded in 1917, including Theo van DOESBURG and Piet MONDRIAN. Its members, working in an abstract style, sought laws of equilibrium and harmony applicable both to art and to life, an ideal reflecting their Calvinist background. Through its journal, *De Stijl* (1917–31), it influenced painting, the decorative arts (including furniture design), typography, and especially architecture, where its aesthetic found expression at the BAUHAUS and in the INTERNATIONAL STYLE.

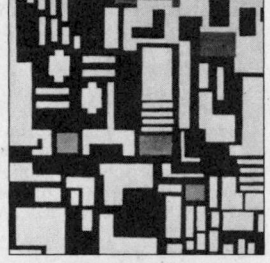

De Stijl "Card Players" by Theo van Doesburg, 1917

Stikine River \sti-'kēn\ River, NW British Columbia and SE Alaska. It flows from the Stikine Ranges of British Columbia to the Pacific Ocean in a course of 335 mi (540 km). A major access route during the KLONDIKE GOLD RUSH of 1896, it is a chief route to the Cassiar Mtns. mining region.

Still, Clyfford (1904–1980) U.S. painter. Born in Grandin, N.D., he studied and later taught at Washington State College. After experimenting with several styles he became involved in ABSTRACT EXPRESSIONISM and was a pioneer of the very large, monochromatic painting. Forgoing the thin, unmodulated pigments of his colleagues Barnett NEWMAN and Mark ROTHKO, he used thickly applied opaque paint (impasto) in expressively modulated, jagged forms to portray raw, aggressive power.

still-life painting Depiction of inanimate objects for the sake of their qualities of form, color, texture, composition, and sometimes allegorical or symbolical significance. Still lifes were painted in ancient Greece and Rome, but the modern still life emerged as an independent genre in the Renaissance. Netherlandish still lifes often depicted skulls, candles, and hourglasses as allegories of mortality, or flowers and fruits to symbolize nature's cycle. Several factors contributed to the rise of still life in the 16th–17th cent.: an interest in realistic representation, a wealthy middle class that wanted artworks to decorate its homes, and increased demand for paintings of secular subjects other than portraits. Dutch and Flemish painters were the masters of still life in the 17th cent. From the 18th cent. until the rise of nonobjective painting after World War II, France was the center of still-life painting.

Stilwell, Joseph W(arren) (1883–1946) U.S. Army officer. Born in Palatka, Fla., he graduated from West Point and served in World War I. A military attaché in Beijing (1935–39), he became chief of staff to Gen. CHIANG KAI-SHEK and commanded Chinese armies in Burma (1939–42). As commander of U.S. forces in China, Burma, and India, he oversaw construction of the Ledo or STILWELL ROAD, a strategic military link with the Burma Road. He later commanded the U.S. 10th Army in the Pacific (1945–46).

Stilwell Road *formerly* **Ledo Road** Former military highway, Asia. It was 478 mi (769 km) long and linked NE India with the BURMA ROAD. In World War II, U.S. Army engineers and Chinese troops constructed it to link the railheads of Ledo, India, and Mogaung, Burma. Named for Gen. Joseph STILWELL, it crossed the difficult Pangsau Pass of the Patkai Range.

Stimson, Henry L(ewis) (1867–1950) U.S. statesman. Born in New York City, he practiced law and served as U.S. secretary of war (1911–13) and later secretary of state (1929–33). After the Japanese occupation of Manchuria (1931), he sent a diplomatic note to Japan reaffirming U.S. treaty rights; this became known as the Stimson Doctrine. Again secretary of war (1940–45), he oversaw the expansion and training of U.S. forces in World War II. As chief adviser on atomic policy to Franklin ROOSEVELT and Harry TRUMAN, he recommended use of the atomic bomb on Hiroshima and Nagasaki.

stimulant Any drug that excites any bodily function, usually one that stimulates the central NERVOUS SYSTEM, inducing alertness, elevated mood, wakefulness, increased speech and motor activity, and decreased appetite. Their mood-elevating effects make some stimulants (e.g., AMPHETAMINES, CAFFEINE and its relatives, COCAINE, NICOTINE) drugs of abuse (see DRUG ADDICTION).

stingray *or* **whip-tailed ray** Any of various species (family Dasyatidae) of RAYS noted for their slender, whiplike tail with barbed, usually venomous spines. Most species inhabit warm seas; a few live in the rivers of S. America. Species range in width from 10 in. (25 cm) to 7 ft (2 m). They may lie partially buried in the shallows, lashing their tail when disturbed. Large stingrays can drive their tail spines into a wooden boat. The spines cause serious, extremely painful wounds.

Stirling Burgh (pop., 1991: 27,984), S central Scotland, on the River FORTH. Made a royal burgh about 1130 and a royal residence in 1226, it was the birthplace of JAMES II of Scotland and site of the coronations of MARY, QUEEN OF SCOTS, and James VI of Scotland (later JAMES I of England). Two battles were fought nearby: the Battle of Stirling Bridge (1297), where Scottish troops routed the English, and the Battle of BANNOCKBURN (1314). It flourished until the mid-16th cent. and shared with EDINBURGH the privileges of a capital city.

Stirling, Earl of See William ALEXANDER

Stirling, James (Frazer) (*later* **Sir James**) (1926–1992) Scottish architect. He began working (1956–63) in the New Brutalist style. The engineering building at Leicester Univ. (1963) brought him early fame. In the 1970s Stirling developed his own brand of POSTMODERNISM that made use of complex geometric abstraction, bold colors, and classical elements. The Neue Staatsgalerie (1977–84) in Stuttgart is among his finest statements. Stirling won the 1981 Pritzker Architecture Prize.

stochastic process \stə-'kas-tik\ In PROBABILITY THEORY, a family of random variables indexed to some other set and having the property that for each finite subset of the index set, the collection of random variables indexed to it has a joint probability distribution. Examples include Markov processes (in which the present value of the variable depends only upon the immediate past and not upon the whole sequence of past events), such as stock-market fluctuations, and time series (in which temperature or rainfall measurements, for example, are taken at the same time each day).

stock In finance, the subscribed capital of a corporation or limited-liability company, usually divided into shares and represented by transferable certificates. Many companies have only one class of stock, called common stock. Common stock, as a share of ownership in the company, entitles the holder to an interest in the company's earnings and assets. It usually carries voting rights enabling participation in the running of the company. DIVIDENDS paid on common stock are often unstable because they vary with earnings;

they are also usually less than earnings, the difference being used by the management to expand the firm. To appeal to investors who want assured dividends, some companies issue preferred stock, which has a prior claim to dividends paid by the company and, in most cases, to the company's assets in case of its dissolution. See also SECURITY, STOCK EXCHANGE.

stock-car racing Form of automobile racing, popular in the U.S., in which cars that conform externally to standard U.S. commercial models are raced, usually on oval, paved tracks. The National Assn. for Stock Car Auto Racing (NASCAR), founded in 1947, gave the sport its first formal organization. The Daytona 500 is its premier race.

stock exchange or **stock market** or *(in continental Europe)* **Bourse** Organized market for the sale and purchase of SECURITIES such as STOCKS and BONDS. Trading is done by members of the exchange, who serve as brokers, buying and selling for others and charging commissions. Stock exchanges differ in eligibility requirements and in the degree to which the government participates in their management. The LONDON STOCK EXCHANGE, for example, is an independent institution, free from government regulation. In the U.S., the NEW YORK STOCK EXCHANGE and the NASDAQ-Amex Market Group are not directly run by the government but are regulated by law. In Europe, members of the exchanges are often appointed by government officials and have semigovernmental status.

Stockhausen \\'shtȯk-ˌhau̇-zən\\, **Karlheinz** (b.1928) German composer. He began pursuing "total serialism" after hearing Olivier MESSIAEN's music at Darmstadt in 1951, and studied with Messiaen. His early works included *Kontrapunkte* and *Klavierstücke I–IV* (1952–53). His important *Gesang der Jünglinge* (1956) used a highly processed recording of a boy soprano mixed with electronic sounds. His extensions of serialism continued in such pieces as *Zeitmasse* (1956) and *Gruppen* (1957), and he became a leading avant-garde spokesman. His *Momente* (1964) influentially applied serialism to groups of sounds rather than single pitches. From the late 1960s he conceived ever grander schemes, some incorporating literature, dance, and ritual, as in the *Licht* series (from 1978).

Stockholm City (pop., 1999 est.: 736,000), capital of Sweden. It is built on numerous islands and peninsulas connected by old bridges and modern overpasses. According to tradition, Swedish ruler Birger Jarl founded Stockholm about 1250. In the Middle Ages it became Sweden's chief trade port, and in 1436 the capital. GUSTAV I VASA liberated it from Danish rule in 1523. It developed rapidly in the mid-17th cent. as Sweden became a great power. It was redeveloped in the 19th cent. It is the country's leading cultural, commercial, financial, and educational center, and is regarded as one of the most beautiful capitals in the world.

Stock Market Crash of 1929 Economic event in the U.S. that precipitated the GREAT DEPRESSION. The U.S. stock market expanded rapidly in the late 1920s and reached a peak in August 1929, when prices began to decline while speculation increased. On October 24, "Black Thursday," the market fell sharply. Banks and investment companies bought large blocks of stock to stem the PANIC, but on October 29, "Black Tuesday," prices collapsed. The crash began a 10-year economic slump that affected all the Western industrialized countries.

stock option Contractual agreement entitling the holder to buy or sell a share of STOCK at a designated price for a specified period of time. The various kinds of stock options include put and call options, which may be purchased in anticipation of changes in stock prices, as a means of speculation or HEDGING. A put gives its holder an option to sell, or put, shares to another party at a fixed price even if the market price declines. A call gives the holder an option to buy, or call for, shares at a fixed price even if the market price rises. U.S. corporations often issue stock options to executives as a form of incentive in addition to salary.

Stockton City (pop., 2000: 244,000), central California, on the SAN JOAQUIN RIVER. Connected to SAN FRANCISCO BAY by a 78-mi (126-km) deepwater channel, it is one of the state's two inland ports. It was founded in 1847 and grew rapidly during the 1849 GOLD RUSH, then became a market

for farm produce and wines. The completion of the channel in 1933 made it a major port as well as a supply depot for U.S. Pacific military operations.

stoichiometry \\ˌstȯi-kē-'ä-mə-trē\\ Determination of the proportions (by weight or number of MOLECULES) in which ELEMENTS or COMPOUNDS react with one another. The rules for determining stoichiometric relationships are based on the laws of conservation of MASS and ENERGY (see CONSERVATION LAW) and the law of combining weights or volumes. The tools used are CHEMICAL FORMULAS, CHEMICAL EQUATIONS, ATOMIC WEIGHTS, and MOLECULAR or FORMULA weights.

Stoicism \\'stō-ə-ˌsi-zəm\\ School of philosophy in Greco-Roman antiquity. Inspired by SOCRATES and DIOGENES OF SINOPE, Stoicism was founded at Athens by Zeno of Citium around 300 B.C. and flourished until at least A.D. 200. It stressed duty and held that, through reason, one can come to regard the universe as rational and governed by fate and, in regulating one's life, one can emulate the grandeur of the calm and order of the universe by learning to accept events with a stern and tranquil mind and to achieve a lofty moral worth. Its teachings have been transmitted through CICERO, SENECA, EPICTETUS, and MARCUS AURELIUS.

Stoker, Bram *(orig.* Abraham) (1847–1912) Irish writer. Though bedridden until he was 7, Stoker later became an outstanding athlete. He was the manager of actor Henry Irving (1838–1905) for 27 years, during which he began writing fiction; his masterpiece was the immensely successful gothic novel *Dracula* (1897). Derived from vampire legends, the tale became the basis for a whole genre of literature and film. None of his other works, including *The Lair of the White Worm* (1911), approached its popularity or quality.

Stokes, William (1804–1878) Irish physician. He received his MD from the Univ. of Edinburgh and returned to Dublin, where he continued Robert J. GRAVES's educational reforms, encouraging students to work, under faculty supervision, in hospital wards and to acquire a general as well as a medical education. His publications included *A Treatise on the Diagnosis and Treatment of Diseases of the Chest* (1837), *The Diseases of the Heart and Aorta* (1854), and one of the first English works on the stethoscope.

Stokowski, Leopold (Antoni Stanislaw Boleslawowich) (1882–1977) British-U.S. conductor and organist. After holding organist positions, he became conductor of the Cincinnati Symphony (1909–12), with great success. From there he moved to the Philadelphia Orchestra, and in the years 1912–38 made it a world-class ensemble, creating the lush "Philadelphia sound." He grasped very early the importance of recording. He made himself a star, appearing in *Fantasia* (1940) and other films, and used his fame to help foster fledgling music organizations, including the American Symphony Orchestra, which he formed in 1962. His strong advocacy of new music did much to end the provinciality of American musical taste.

Stoller, Mike See Jerry LEIBER

Stolypin \\stȯ-'lē-pyin\\, **Pyotr (Arkadyevich)** (1862–1911) Russian politician. As governor of two Russian provinces (1902–3), he improved the welfare of the peasants while also subduing their rebellions. Appointed minister of the interior and prime minister in 1906, he initiated agrarian reforms that gave the peasants greater freedom to choose representatives to the ZEMSTVO councils and to acquire land, but his repressive measures against rebels earned him the enmity of liberals. He dissolved the DUMA when it opposed his reforms, but later won support from moderates. He was assassinated by a revolutionary in 1911.

stomach Digestive sac in the left upper ABDOMINAL CAVITY. It has four regions: the cardia leads down from the ESOPHAGUS; the fundus curves above it; the body is the largest part; and the antrum narrows to join the DUODENUM at the pyloric valve. Iron and very fat-soluble substances (e.g., alcohol, some drugs) are absorbed in the stomach. PERISTALSIS mixes food with ENZYMES and HYDROCHLORIC ACID from glands in its lining and moves the resulting chyme toward the SMALL INTESTINE. The vagus nerve and sympathetic nervous system control the stomach's secretions and movements. Emotional stress affects its function. Common

disorders include gastritis, PEPTIC ULCER, hiatal HERNIA, and cancer. See also DIGESTION.

Stone, Edward Durell (1902–1978) U.S. architect. Born in Fayetteville, Ark., he joined the New York firm that designed Radio City Music Hall, then organized his own firm in 1936. A champion of the INTERNATIONAL STYLE, he designed El Panamá Hotel in Panama City (1946), the U.S. embassy in New Delhi (1954), the U.S. pavilion at the Brussels World's Fair (1958), the KENNEDY CENTER FOR THE PERFORMING ARTS in Washington, D.C. (1964), and the Amoco Building in Chicago (1969). He also taught at NYU (1927–42) and Yale Univ. (1946–52).

Stone, Harlan Fiske (1872–1946) U.S. jurist. Born in Chesterfield, N.H., he served as dean of Columbia Law School (1910–23) before becoming U.S. attorney general in 1924. During his tenure he reorganized the FEDERAL BUREAU OF INVESTIGATION after its reputation had been tarnished by the TEAPOT DOME and other scandals. In 1925 he was appointed to the U.S. Supreme Court, and in 1941 he became chief justice. Generally liberal, he wrote more than 600 opinions, many on important constitutional questions.

Stone, I. F. orig. Isidor Feinstein (1907–1989) U.S. journalist. Born in Philadelphia, he started his own investigative newsletter in New York. From the outset, *I. F. Stone's Weekly* (1953–67; *I. F. Stone's Bi-Weekly,* 1967–71) had an influence far greater than the size of its readership, which included some of the nation's most prominent politicians, academicians, and journalists. The sole author, Stone created a unique blend of wit, erudition, and pointed political commentary, and became known for his espousal of unpopular causes long before they were taken up by the liberal establishment.

Stone, Lucy (1818–1893) U.S. WOMEN'S SUFFRAGE leader. Born in W. Brookfield, Mass., she became a lecturer for the Massachusetts Anti-Slavery Society and soon began speaking for women's rights. She retained her own name after marriage to Henry Blackwell (1825–1909), as a protest against the unequal laws applicable to married women; other women who later chose to do the same called themselves "Lucy Stoners." In 1869 they helped establish the American Woman Suffrage Assn. and founded the influential suffrage magazine *Woman's Journal*, which they edited until their deaths, assisted by their daughter Alice Stone Blackwell (1857–1950).

Stone, Oliver (b.1946) U.S. film director. Born in New York City, he made his directorial debut with *Seizure* (1974) and wrote screenplays for films marked by their rapid pace and violence, including *Midnight Express* (1978). He wrote and directed *Platoon* (1986, Academy Award), drawing on his Vietnam military experience, *Wall Street* (1987), *Born on the Fourth of July* (1989, Academy Award), *JFK* (1991), and *Natural Born Killers* (1994), some of them noted for their anti-establishment and even paranoiac interpretations.

Stone Age First known period of prehistoric human culture, characterized by the use of stone tools. It is divided into three periods: PALEOLITHIC, MESOLITHIC, and NEOLITHIC. The term is little used by specialists today. See also BRONZE AGE, IRON AGE, STONE-TOOL INDUSTRY.

Stonehenge Monumental circular arrangement of standing stones located near Salisbury, Wiltshire, England. The stones are believed to have been put in place in three main phases between about 3100 and 1550 B.C. Stonehenge is believed to have been a place of worship and ritual. Many theories have been advanced as to its specific purpose, but none have been proven. Stones erected during the second phase of construction (c.2100 B.C.) were aligned with the sunrise at the summer SOLSTICE, suggesting some ritual connection with that event.

Stone of Scone See Stone of SCONE

stone-tool industry Any of several assemblages of artifacts displaying humankind's earliest technology. These stone tools serve as the major means of determining HOMINID activities. Archaeologists have classified distinct stone-tool industries on the basis of style and use, and named them after the site of their original identification. The major industries include (in chronological order) the OLDOWAN, Acheulian, MOUSTERIAN, AURIGNACIAN, Solutrean, and MAGDALENIAN.

Stonewall rebellion (June 28, 1969) Action by homosexuals in New York City. In response to police raids on the Stonewall Inn, a homosexual bar in Greenwich Village, about 1,000 homosexuals and others taunted police and threw debris; police responded with violence. Similar riots on succeeding nights were followed by protest rallies. The event marked the awakening of gay rights organizations throughout the U.S.; it is commemorated annually in Gay and Lesbian Pride Week.

stoneware POTTERY fired at a high temperature (about 2,200°F, or 1,200°C) until vitrified (made glasslike and impervious to liquid). Because stoneware is nonporous, glaze is applied only for decoration. Stoneware originated in China about 1400 B.C. and was exported to Europe in the 17th cent. Red to dark-brown in color, it was copied in Germany, England, and the Netherlands. See also PORCELAIN.

Stono rebellion (1739) Largest slave uprising in early America. On September 9, near the Stono River 20 mi (30 km) from Charleston, S.C., slaves gathered, raided a firearms shop, and headed south, killing more than 20 whites as they went. Other slaves joined the rebellion until the group was about 60 strong. Whites set out in armed pursuit, and by dusk half the slaves were dead and half had escaped; most were eventually captured and executed. White colonists quickly passed a Negro Act that limited slave privileges even more seriously.

Stooges, Three U.S. comedy team. Formed as a vaudeville team by brothers Moe and Shemp Howard (1897–1975, 1900–1955), who performed with "Ted Healy and His Stooges," in 1928 the brothers added Larry Fine (1911–1974) to the act, which appeared in Broadway revues. In 1930 Shemp was replaced by his brother Curly (1906–1952). In 1934 they began a series of comedy shorts that numbered over 200 before ending in 1958, consisting largely of violent slapstick.

stools See FECES

Stoppard, Tom (*later* Sir Tom) orig. Tomas Straussler (b.1937) British (Czech-born) playwright. His first play, *A Walk on the Water,* was televised in 1963, and he won fame with the absurdist *Rosencrantz and Guildenstern Are Dead* (1967; film, 1991). His later plays, marked by verbal brilliance and a playful interest in pivotal historical moments, include *Jumpers* (1972), *Travesties* (1974), *Every Good Boy Deserves Favour* (1977), *The Real Thing* (1982), *Arcadia* (1993), and *The Invention of Love* (1997). He has also written screenplays for such films as *Empire of the Sun* (1987) and *Shakespeare in Love* (1998, Academy Award).

stork Any of 17 species (family Ciconiidae) of voiceless, long-necked, mainly Old World birds. Storks are 2–5 ft (60–150 cm) tall, often with a brightly colored head and upper neck. They fly by alternately flapping and soaring, with neck outstretched and legs trailing. Usually found in flocks, storks pair off during the breeding season, and both parents incubate the eggs. Typical storks have a straight bill; the four species of wood stork have a curved bill. The only U.S. stork, the wood ibis (*Mycteria americana*), is white, with black wings and tail and a curved bill. See also IBIS, MARABOU.

storm petrel Any of about 20 species (family Hydrobatidae) of PETRELS that vary from 5 to 10 in. (13–25 cm) long. All are dark gray or brown, often with a white rump. Most species breeding in S oceans "walk" over the water with wings spread, picking up minute marine organisms. Most N species swoop over the water like tiny terns, occasionally alighting on the surface.

Storm Troopers See SA

Story, Joseph (1779–1845) U.S. jurist. Born in Marblehead, Mass., he served in the U.S. Congress 1805–11. In 1811, at 32, he was appointed to the U.S. Supreme Court. There he joined John MARSHALL in construing the U.S. Constitution in favor of expanding federal power. His opinion in *Martin vs. Hunter's Lessee* (1816) established the Court's appellate authority over the highest state courts. He wrote an influential series of commentaries, including *Commentaries on the Constitution of the United States* (1833), *The Conflict of Laws* (1834), and *On Equity Jurisprudence* (1836). He and James Kent (1763–1847) are considered the founders of U.S. equity jurisprudence.

Stoss \\'shtōs\\, **Veit** (1445/50–1533) German sculptor and wood carver. He worked mainly in Poland 1477–96; among his principal works is the majestic high altar in the Church of the Virgin Mary in Krakow (1477–89). After his return to Germany, he settled in Nuremberg and produced important wood and stone sculptures in churches there and in Bamberg. His nervous, angular forms, realistic detail, and virtuoso wood carving exercised great influence on German late-Gothic sculpture.

Veit Stoss, "The Archangel Raphael," 1516–18

Stout, Rex (Todhunter) (1886–1975) U.S. writer. Born in Noblesville, Ind., he is remembered for 46 genteel mystery novels and novelettes, beginning with *Fer-de-Lance* (1934), that revolve around Nero Wolfe, a brilliant, obese aesthete who solves crimes without leaving his New York City apartment. Stout endowed his detective with his own passions for haute cuisine and the growing of orchids.

Stowe \\'stō\\, **Harriet Beecher** *orig.* Harriet Elizabeth Beecher (1811–1896) U.S. writer and philanthropist. Born in Litchfield, Conn., the sister of H. W. BEECHER and Catharine BEECHER, she taught school in Hartford and in Cincinnati, where she came into contact with fugitive slaves and learned about life in the South. She later settled in Maine. Her antislavery novel *Uncle Tom's Cabin* (1852) had so great an impact that it has often been cited (by Abraham LINCOLN, among others) among the causes of the American Civil War. Her other works include the novels *Dred* (1856), also against slavery, and *The Minister's Wooing* (1859).

strabismus \\strə-'biz-məs\\ *or* **squint** Failure of the EYES to align properly to focus on an object. The affected eye may deviate in any direction, including inward (cross-eye) or outward (walleye). Problems may lie in PHOTORECEPTION or the nerves that relay images to the brain, or defects in the nerves that control the muscles that move the eyes. The development of a child's ability to focus the eyes and merge images from the two RETINAS into one is impeded. The brain suppresses the image from the deviant eye, which may become functionally blind. Treatment may involve exercises to strengthen the weak eye or surgery or both.

Strabo \\'strā-bō\\ (64/63 B.C.–after A.D. 23?) Greek geographer and historian. He studied under Aristodemus before moving to Rome (44 B.C.) to study with the Aristotelian school, then became a Stoic. Of his 47-volume *Historical Sketches*, covering the years 145–31 B.C. (published c.20 B.C.), only a few quotations remain. His *Geographical Sketches* (after c.A.D. 14) is the only extant work on the range of peoples and countries known to Greeks and Romans during the reign of Caesar AUGUSTUS.

Strachey \\'strā-chē\\, **(Giles) Lytton** (1880–1932) English biographer and critic. After studying at Cambridge, he became a leader in the BLOOMSBURY GROUP. Adopting an irreverent attitude to the past, he opened a new era of biographical writing with his *Eminent Victorians* (1918), consisting of four sketches of Victorian idols whom he portrayed as multifaceted, flawed human beings. Fascinated by personality and motive, he treated his subjects idiosyncratically and somewhat cynically. He also published *Queen Victoria* (1921), *Elizabeth and Essex* (1928), and *Portraits in Miniature* (1931).

Stradivari \\strä-dē-'vär-ē\\, **Antonio** (1644–1737) Italian musical-instrument maker. An apprentice of Nicola Amati (1596–1684), he established his own business in Cremona, eventually working with his sons Francesco (1671–1743) and Omobono (1679–1742). Though he made other stringed instruments, after 1680 he concentrated on violins. Moving away from the Amati style, he developed (c.1690) the "long Strad." His later, smaller cellos have served as the model for most modern instruments. The period 1700–20 is considered the peak of his productivity and quality.

Strafford, Earl of See Thomas WENTWORTH

strain In the physical sciences and engineering, a number that describes the relative deformation of elastic, plastic, and fluid materials under applied forces. Normal strain is caused by forces perpendicular to planes or cross sections of the material, such as in a volume that is under pressure on all sides. Shear strain is caused by forces that are parallel to, and lie in, planes or cross sections, such as in a short metal tube that is twisted about its longitudinal axis.

Straits Question Recurrent controversy in the 19th–20th cent. over the passage of warships through the BOSPORUS and DARDANELLES straits. Both straits were in Turkish territory, but when Russia gained control of the N shore of the Black Sea its ships were given free passage. Russia sought to control the passage of non-Turkish ships by treaty in 1833, but it was reversed in 1841. The Treaty of Lausanne (1923) allowed free passage to all warships, until it was revised by the Montreux Convention (1936) to reestablish Turkey's right to restrict access by navies of non–Black Sea states.

Strand, Paul (1890–1976) U.S. photographer. Born in New York City, he studied photography with Lewis HINE. At Hine's urging, he frequented Alfred STIEGLITZ's "291" gallery; the avant-garde paintings he saw there led him to emphasize abstract form and pattern in his photographs, such as *Wall Street* (1915). He rejected soft-focus pictorialism in favor of the minute detail and rich tonal range afforded by the use of large-format cameras. Much of his later work was devoted to N. American and European scenes and landscapes. He collaborated on documentary films with Charles Sheeler and Pare Lorentz.

Strasberg, Lee *orig.* Israel Strassberg (1901–1982) U.S. (Russian-born) theater director and teacher. He emigrated to New York with his family at age 7. After acting lessons with teachers trained by Konstantin STANISLAVSKY, he joined the THEATRE GUILD. In 1931 he cofounded the Group Theatre, where he directed such successful plays as *Men in White* (1933). After working in Hollywood (1941–48), he became artistic director of New York's ACTORS STUDIO, where he developed his form of the STANISLAVSKY METHOD and trained such students as Marlon BRANDO, Marilyn MONROE, Dustin HOFFMAN, and Julie HARRIS.

Strasbourg \\'sträs-ˌbùrg\\ *German* **Strassburg** \\'shträs-ˌbùrk\\ City (pop., 1999: 264,000), E France, on the Franco–German border. The FRANKS captured it in the 5th cent., and in 842 the Oath of Strasbourg, uniting the W. and E. Franks, was concluded there. It became a free city within the HOLY ROMAN EMPIRE in 1262. Seized by the French in 1681 and captured by Germany in the FRANCO–PRUSSIAN WAR, it reverted to France after World War I and was occupied by Germany again during World War II. A major river port and industrial center, it is the seat of the Council of Europe. Famous buildings include the restored medieval cathedral with its 14th-cent. astronomical clock. The EUROPEAN UNION's parliament has met there since 1979.

Strasser \\'shträ-sər\\, **Gregor and Otto** (1892–1934, 1897–1974) German politicians. The brothers joined the Nazi Party in the early 1920s. Gregor became its leader in the north and built a mass movement with the help of Otto and the young Joseph GOEBBELS, advocating a socialism couched in nationalist and racist terminology. Otto resigned in 1930, disillusioned by Adolf HITLER's nonsocialist goals. Gregor became head of the Nazi political organization, second only to Hitler in power, but came to share his brother's disillusionment and resigned in 1932. Gregor was murdered on Hitler's orders in 1934; Otto escaped into exile.

Strategic Arms Limitation Talks See SALT

Strategic Arms Reduction Talks See START

Strategic Defense Initiative (SDI) *or* **Star Wars** Proposed U.S. strategic defense system against nuclear attacks. Announced by Pres. Ronald REAGAN in 1983, SDI was intended to defend the U.S. from Soviet attack by intercepting ICBMs in flight with technology then not yet developed,

including space- and earth-based laser stations and air- and ground-based ANTIBALLISTIC MISSILES. The space component of SDI led to its being derisively dubbed "Star Wars" after the popular film. Widely criticized as unworkable, it was also decried for accelerating the arms race and undermining arms-control agreements. After the fall of the Soviet Union the project was scaled back to focus on protecting the U.S. from a small attack by a rogue nation or an accidentally launched missile. In 2001 Pres. George W. Bush moved to implement a new antimissile defense program.

Stratemeyer \\'stra-tə-ˌmī-ər\\, **Edward** (1862–1930) U.S. writer of popular juvenile fiction. He began writing adventure stories and later edited several publications and began writing series of books. In 1906 he founded the Stratemeyer Literary Syndicate, which would publish the Rover Boys, Hardy Boys, Tom Swift, Bobbsey Twins, and Nancy Drew series, written by himself and a stable of hack writers under a variety of names.

Stratford Festival Annual summer theatrical festival in Stratford, Ontario. Cofounded by Tyrone GUTHRIE in 1953, it features productions of William SHAKESPEARE's plays (Stratford was chosen because its name matched that of Shakespeare's birthplace). It also performs other classic dramatic works in its innovative open-stage Festival Theatre.

Stratford-upon-Avon Town (pop., 1995 est.: 28,000), WARWICKSHIRE, central England, on the Upper AVON RIVER. The first royal charter was granted in 1553. For centuries a country market town, it became a tourist center because of its association with William SHAKESPEARE, who was born and died there. The Shakespeare Centre includes a library and art gallery (opened 1881) and the Royal Shakespeare Theatre (opened 1932).

Strathclyde Medieval Celtic kingdom, Scotland. Located south of the CLYDE RIVER, it was established in the 6th cent. The Picts and Vikings ravaged the kingdom in the 8th–9th cent., and the English took it over in the early 10th cent. The Anglo-Saxon king Edmund I leased it in 945 to the Scots king Malcolm I. It became a province of Scotland in the 11th cent.

stratification Layering that occurs in most SEDIMENTARY ROCKS and in IGNEOUS ROCKS that are formed at the earth's surface, such as from lava flows and volcanic deposits. The layers (strata) may range from thin sheets that cover many square miles to thick lenslike bodies that are only a few feet wide.

stratigraphy \\strə-'ti-grə-fē\\ Scientific discipline concerned with describing rock successions and interpreting them in terms of a general time scale. It provides a basis for historical geology, and its methods are applied in such fields as petroleum geology and archaeology. It deals primarily with SEDIMENTARY ROCKS but may also encompass layered igneous rocks (e.g., those resulting from successive lava flows).

Stratofortress See B-52

stratosphere Layer of the ATMOSPHERE located above the TROPOSPHERE. It extends from a lower boundary of about 7 mi (11 km) altitude to an upper boundary (the stratopause) at about 30 mi (50 km). The OZONE LAYER is a part of the stratosphere.

Straus family \\'straůs\\ German-U.S. merchandising family that distinguished itself in public service and philanthropy. Lazarus Straus emigrated to the U.S. in 1852, followed by his wife and three sons: Isidor (1845–1912), Nathan (1848–1931), and Oscar Solomon (1850–1926). They established a crockery firm that led to their gaining ownership of R. H. MACY AND CO. in 1896. Isidor established the department store chain of Abraham & Straus and engaged in philanthropic works; he and his wife perished aboard the *Titanic* after giving Mrs. Straus's place in a lifeboat to their maid. Nathan was noted for his philanthropy; he distributed food, coal, and milk during the 1892 depression; built the first tuberculosis preventorium for children (1909); provided food for New York's poor during the harsh winter of 1914–15; and devoted many years to public-health work in Palestine. Oscar was appointed Secretary of Commerce and Labor by Theodore ROOSEVELT, becoming the first Jewish Cabinet

member (1906–9); he also served as emissary to Ottoman Turkey and as an adviser to Pres. Woodrow WILSON.

Strauss \\'shtraůs, *Engl* 'straůs\\, **Johann (Baptist), Jr.** (1825–1899) Austrian composer. His father, Johann Strauss, Sr. (1804–1849), became conductor of a dance orchestra in 1824, for which he began to write waltzes, galops, polkas, and quadrilles, eventually publishing more than 250 works. As bandmaster of a local regiment, he also wrote marches, including the *Radetzky March*. Johann Jr. soon surpassed his father's popularity and productivity, becoming known as the "Waltz King." By inducing his brothers, Josef (1827–1870) and Eduard (1835–1916), to take over his conducting duties, he gained more time to compose the symphonic waltzes for which he is best known, including *The Beautiful Blue Danube* (1867) and *Tales from the Vienna Woods* (1868). His operettas include the popular *Die Fledermaus* (1874) and *The Gypsy Baron* (1885).

Strauss, Richard (Georg) (1864–1949) German composer and conductor. He began composing at 6, and before he was 20 he had had major orchestral premieres. A convert to Wagnerism, he began to write orchestral tone poems, including *Don Juan* (1889), *Death and Transfiguration* (1890), *Till Eulenspiegel's Merry Pranks* (1895), *Thus Spake Zarathustra* (1896), *Don Quixote* (1897), and *Ein Heldenleben* (1898). From 1894 on, he held major conducting posts. After 1900 he turned to opera. His third opera, *Salome* (1905), caused a sensation, and with *Elektra* (1908) he began a productive collaboration with the poet

Richard Strauss Portrait by Max Liebermann, 1918

Hugo von HOFMANNSTHAL, with whom he wrote his greatest operas, including *Der Rosenkavalier* (1910), *Ariadne auf Naxos* (1912), and *Die Frau ohne Schatten* (1918). He later wrote eight more operas, mostly lesser works, but produced several remarkable late pieces, including *Metamorphosen* (1945) and the *Four Last Songs* (1948).

Stravinsky, Igor (Fyodorovich) (1882–1971) Russian-French-U.S. composer. Son of an operatic bass, he studied privately with Nikolai RIMSKY-KORSAKOV (1902–8). Sergey DIAGHILEV commissioned him to write the *Firebird* ballet (1910), which made him Russia's leading young composer. The great ballet *Petrushka* (1911) followed. His next ballet, the viscerally exciting and brutalist *Rite of Spring* (1913), was a landmark in music history; its Paris premiere caused a virtual riot, and Stravinsky's international notoriety was assured. He turned to smaller forces for *Les noces* (1923), and adopted a radically different style of restrained neoclassicism with his Octet (1923). His major neoclassical works included *Oedipus rex* (1927), the ballet *Apollo* (1928), the *Symphony of Psalms* (1930), the *Symphony in C* (1940), and the *Symphony in Three Movements* (1945), and culminated in the opera *The Rake's Progress* (1951). From 1954 he employed his own version of serialism. His later works include *Agon* (1957)—the last of his many ballets choreographed by George BALANCHINE—and *Requiem Canticles* (1966).

straw Stalks of GRASSES, particularly CEREAL grasses that have been dried and threshed. Since ancient times, humans have used straw as litter and fodder for cattle, as a covering for floors, for coarse bedding, and even as clothing. It can also be woven into baskets, hats, and floor mats. Thatched roofs consist of straw laid down approximately 1 ft (30 cm) thick and secured by strong cords. Chemically pulped straw is used for coarse paper and cheap cardboard.

strawberry Fruit plant of the genus *Fragaria* (ROSE family), the chief cultivated varieties of which are *F. virginiana* and *F. chiloensis*, native to the Americas. The low-growing, herbaceous plant has a fibrous root system and a crown from which basal leaves arise. The leaves are compound, with three leaflets, sawtooth-edged and hairy. Small clusters of white flowers grow on slender stalks. The plant propagates by horizontal stems as it ages. Rich in vitamin C and iron, strawberries are very perishable and require cool, dry storage.

Strayhorn, Billy (*orig.* William) (1915–1967) U.S. pianist, composer, and arranger. Born in Dayton, Ohio, Strayhorn approached Duke ELLINGTON with a composition in 1938, and was soon contributing arrangements and original works to the band. His "Take the 'A' Train" (1941) became its theme. Strayhorn became noted for the structural and harmonic sophistication of pieces such as "Lush Life" and "Day Dream." Over three decades, his work so complemented Ellington's that it is often impossible to distinguish their contributions.

streaming Method of transmitting a media file in a continuous stream of data that can be processed before the entire file has been completely received. Streaming is especially effective for downloading large multimedia files from the INTERNET; it permits, for example, a video clip to begin playing on a user's computer as soon as it begins to be downloaded. To accept streaming data, the receiving computer needs to be running a player that decompresses the incoming data and sends the resulting signals to the display and speakers. The audio and video files may be prerecorded, but streaming can also accommodate a live feed over the Internet.

stream of consciousness Narrative technique in nondramatic fiction intended to render the flow of myriad impressions that impinge on an individual consciousness. To represent the mind at work, a writer may incorporate snatches of thought and grammatical constructions that do not seem coherent because they are based on the free association of ideas and images. In the 20th cent., writers attempting to capture the total flow of their characters' consciousness commonly used the techniques of interior monologue, which represents a sequence of thought and feeling. Novelists who have employed the technique include James JOYCE, William FAULKNER, and Virginia WOOLF.

Streep, Meryl (*orig.* Mary Louise) (b.1949) U.S. film actress. Born in Summit, N.J., she appeared on Broadway and in such television films as *The Holocaust* (1978, Emmy award). An unusually versatile and expressive actress, she won stardom in *The Deer Hunter* (1978), *Manhattan* (1979), and *Kramer vs. Kramer* (1979, Academy Award). Her later films include *The French Lieutenant's Woman* (1981), *Sophie's Choice* (1982, Academy Award), *Silkwood* (1983), *Out of Africa* (1985), *Ironweed* (1987), *A Cry in the Dark* (1988), and *The Bridges of Madison County* (1995).

streetcar *or* **trolley car** Passenger-carrying vehicle that runs on rails laid in city streets. Streetcars in the 1830s were pulled by horses. Electric motors later supplied the power, with electricity transmitted by a trolley from overhead electric lines. From the 1890s to the 1940s, streetcars were widely used in cities around the world; they were gradually replaced by the AUTOMOBILE, the BUS, and the SUBWAY. A variant, the cable car, invented in 1873 for use on San Francisco's steep hills, is drawn by a continuous cable set in a slot between the tracks.

Streicher \\'shtrī-kər\\, **Julius** (1885–1946) German Nazi demogogue. A friend of Adolf HITLER, in 1923 he founded the anti-Semitic weekly *Der Stürmer,* which provided a focus for Hitler's racial policies. A virulent advocate of persecution of the Jews, Streicher initiated the campaign that led to the NUREMBERG LAWS in 1935. He was appointed gauleiter (district leader) of Franconia, but his sadistic excesses alienated party officials. Stripped of his posts in 1940, he remained editor of *Der Stürmer.* He was tried at Nuremberg and hanged as a war criminal.

Streisand, Barbra (*orig.* Barbara Joan) (b.1942) U.S. singer and actress. Born in Brooklyn, N.Y., she appeared on Broadway in *I Can Get It for You Wholesale* (1962), and became a major star with *Funny Girl* (1964; film, 1968, Academy Award). Her richly beautiful voice made her one of the world's most popular singers in the 1970s and '80s. She starred in such movies as *Hello, Dolly!* (1969), *What's Up Doc?* (1972), and *The Way We Were* (1973), and later directed and starred in *Yentl* (1983) and *The Prince of Tides* (1991).

streptococcus \\,strep-tə-'kä-kəs\\ Any of the spheroidal BACTERIA of the genus *Streptococcus.* The cells characteristically group together in chains resembling a string of beads. Streptococci are gram-positive (see GRAM STAIN) and stationary and do not require oxygen. Some species cause infections, including RHEUMATIC FEVER, SCARLET FEVER, strep throat, and TONSILLITIS. Others are used in commercial starters for the production of butter, cultured buttermilk, and certain cheeses. See also PNEUMOCOCCUS.

streptomyces \\,strep-tə-'mī-sēz\\ Any of the threadlike ACTINOMYCETES, BACTERIA of the genus *Streptomyces,* occurring in soil and water. These gram-positive (see GRAM STAIN), oxygen-requiring bacteria form a branching net called a mycelium that bears chains of SPORES at maturity. Many species are important in the decomposition of organic matter in soil. Certain species produce broad-spectrum ANTIBIOTICS such as TETRACYCLINE and streptomycin.

Stresemann \\'shtrā-zə-,män\\, **Gustav** (1878–1929) German statesman of the WEIMAR REPUBLIC. Noted as an expert on municipal affairs and a writer on economics, in 1918 he founded the German People's Party and sought to form coalitions with other democratic parties. As chancellor (1923) and foreign minister (1923–29), he worked to restore Germany's international status, pursuing a conciliatory policy with the Allied Powers. He negotiated the Pact of Locarno (1925), an attempt to ensure peace in Europe, and secured Germany's admission to the League of Nations. He shared the 1926 Nobel Peace Prize with Aristide BRIAND.

stress In psychology, a state of bodily or mental tension. Stress is an unavoidable effect of living and is an especially complex phenomenon in modern technological society. It has been linked to CORONARY HEART DISEASE and PSYCHOSOMATIC DISORDERS. Treatment usually combines COUNSELING or PSYCHOTHERAPY and medication.

strike Collective refusal by employees to work under the conditions set by employers. Strikes may arise from disputes over wages and working conditions; they may also be conducted in sympathy with other striking workers. Many are organized by LABOR UNIONS; strikes not authorized by the union (wildcat strikes) may be directed against union leadership as well as the employer. The right to strike is granted in principle to workers in nearly all industrialized countries, and its use has paralleled the rise of unions since the 19th cent. Most strikes are intended to inflict a cost on employers. In Western Europe and elsewhere, workers have carried out general strikes aimed at winning changes in the political system rather than concessions from employers. See also BOYCOTT.

Strindberg \\'strin-,berʸ, *Engl* 'strind-,bərg\\, **(Johan) August** (1849–1912) Swedish playwright and novelist. While working as a journalist, he wrote the historical drama *Mäster Olof* (1872), now considered the first modern Swedish drama. He won fame with his novel *The Red Room* (1879), which satirized the Stockholm art world. He moved restlessly around Europe for six years, writing his three major plays, *The Father* (1887), *Miss Julie* (1888), and *The Creditors* (1890)—works marked by bitterness and iconoclasm, which combined dramatic naturalism and psychology in portraying the battle of the sexes—as well as three novels. After a mental breakdown he experienced a religious conversion that inspired such symbolic dramas as *The Dance of Death* (1901), *A Dream Play* (1902), and five "chamber plays," including *The Ghost Sonata* (1907).

August Strindberg
Lithograph by Edvard Munch, 1896

stringed instruments Musical instruments that produce sound by the vibrations of strings. The strings may be of gut, metal, fiber, or plastic, and may be plucked, bowed, or struck. The orchestral stringed instruments include the VI-OLIN, VIOLA, CELLO, DOUBLE BASS, and HARP. See also BALALAIKA, CLAVICHORD, DULCIMER, GUITAR, HARPSI-CHORD, KITHARA, KOTO, LUTE, LYRE, MANDOLIN, PIANO, SITAR, UKULELE, VIOL.

string quartet Ensemble consisting of two violins, viola, and cello, or a work written for such an ensemble. Since about 1775 the string quartet has been perhaps the predominant genre of CHAMBER MUSIC. It was principally developed by F. J. HAYDN, who wrote some 70 quartets between 1757 and 1803. W. A. MOZART, Ludwig van BEETHOVEN, Franz SCHU-BERT, Bela BARTOK, and Dmitri SHOSTAKOVICH are the pre-eminent subsequent quartet composers. Quartets have tra-ditionally observed the four-movement design of the SONATA and SYMPHONY.

string theory See SUPERSTRING THEORY

strip mining or **surface mining** Removal of the soil and rock (overburden) above a seam of COAL or other mineral and extraction of the exposed mineral. The method is most effective where the mineral is not deeply buried, though many modern strip mines employ equipment capable of re-moving overburden nearly 200 ft (60 m) thick. In Europe the technique is widely used for brown-coal deposits, while in the U.S. a large proportion of both ANTHRACITE and BI-TUMINOUS COAL is so mined. Strip mining is most econom-ical where flat terrain and horizontal seams permit a large area to be stripped; in rolling or mountainous terrain, a contour method is used. Strip mining has been criticized, especially in the U.S., for its damage to the local environ-ment. See also PLACER MINING.

strobilus See CONE

stroboscope Instrument that repeatedly illuminates a rotat-ing or vibrating object in order to study its motion, speed, or vibration frequency. By producing light in very short bursts timed to occur when the moving part is in the same phase of its motion, a machine part, for example, may be made to appear to slow down or stop.

Stroessner \'stres-nər\, **Alfredo** (b.1912) Military leader and president of Paraguay (1954–89). Stroessner joined the army in 1932 and rose to become commander in chief in 1951. He deposed Pres. Federico Chávez (1881?–1978) and was the sole candidate in the 1954 presidential elections. He stabilized the currency, moderated inflation, and provided some new schools and health facilities, but spent half the national revenues on the military and harshly suppressed his opponents. After election to his eighth term, he was de-posed in a coup.

Stroheim \'shtrō-ˌhīm, *Engl* 'strō-ˌhīm\, **Erich von** *orig.* Erich Oswald Stroheim (1885–1957) Austrian-U.S. film di-rector. He emigrated to the U.S. in 1909. In Hollywood from 1914, he worked for D. W. GRIFFITH and acted in his trademark role as a Prussian officer. His directorial debut, *Blind Husbands* (1919), was followed by *Foolish Wives* (1922). *Greed* (1924), his masterpiece, was damagingly cut; it was followed by *The Merry Widow* (1925), *The Wedding March* (1928), and *Queen Kelly* (1928). His extravagance and demand for artistic control scuttled his career, and he re-turned to acting, notably in *Grand Illusion* (1937).

stroke *or* **cerebrovascular accident (CVA)** Sudden impair-ment of BRAIN function due to HYPOXIA, which may cause death of brain tissue. HYPERTENSION, ARTERIOSCLEROSIS, SMOKING, high CHOLESTEROL, DIABETES MELLITUS, old age, ATRIAL FIBRILLATION, and genetic defects are risk fac-tors. Strokes due to THROMBOSIS (the most common cause), EMBOLISM, or arterial spasm, which cause reduced blood supply, must be distinguished from those due to HEMOR-RHAGE which are usually severe and often fatal. Depending on its site in the brain, a stroke's effects may include APHA-SIA, ataxia, local PARALYSIS, and/or disorders of one or more senses. A massive stroke can produce one-sided paral-ysis, inability to speak, coma, or death within hours or days. ANTICOAGULANTS can arrest strokes caused by clots but worsen those caused by bleeding. Transient ischemic at-tacks ("mini-strokes"), with short-term loss of function, re-sult from blockage of blood flow to small areas. They tend to recur and may worsen, leading to multi-infarct dementia (see SENILE DEMENTIA) or stroke.

Stromboli \'sträm-bō-ˌlē\ Volcano, Stromboli Island, off NE SICILY, Italy. One of Europe's most active volcanoes, it is 3,038 ft (926 m) high. Though the last serious eruption was in 1921, lava flows continuously from its crater to the sea.

strong force *or* **strong nuclear force** Fundamental force acting between elementary particles of matter, mainly QUARKS. The strong force binds quarks together in clusters to form PROTONS and NEUTRONS and heavier short-lived particles. It holds together the atomic NUCLEUS and under-lies interactions among all particles containing quarks. Within its short range (about 10–15 m), the strong force ap-pears to become stronger with distance. At such distances, the strong interaction between quarks is about 100 times greater than the ELECTROMAGNETIC FORCE.

strontium \'strän(t)-shē-əm, 'strän-tē-əm\ Chemical ELE-MENT, one of the ALKALINE EARTH METALS, chemical sym-bol Sr, atomic number 38. A soft METAL, it has a silvery lus-ter when freshly cut but reacts rapidly with air. Both strontium and its compounds (VALENCE 2) resemble CAL-CIUM and BARIUM so closely that strontium has few uses of its own. The nitrate and chlorate, very volatile, give off bril-liant crimson flames and are used in flares, fireworks, and tracer bullets. The radioactive ISOTOPE strontium-90 (see RADIOACTIVITY) is the principal health hazard in FALLOUT.

structuralism European critical movement of the mid-20th cent. It is based on the linguistic theories of Ferdinand de SAUSSURE, which hold that language is a self-contained sys-tem of signs, and the cultural theories of Claude LÉVI-STRAUSS, which hold that cultures, like languages, can be viewed as systems of signs and analyzed in terms of the structural relations among their elements. Binary opposi-tions (e.g., male/female, public/private, cooked/raw) are believed to reveal the unconscious logic or "grammar" of a system. Literary structuralism views literary texts as sys-tems of interlocking signs and seeks to make explicit the hidden logic governing the form and content of a work. The works of Michel FOUCAULT, Jacques LACAN, Roman JAKOBSON, and Roland BARTHES have been prominent. See also DECONSTRUCTION, SEMIOTICS.

Struve \'shtrü-və\, **Friedrich (Georg Wilhelm von)** (1793–1864) German-Russian astronomer. He left Germany for Russia in 1808 to avoid Napoleon's draft. As director of the observatory at the Univ. of Dorpat, he founded the modern study of binary stars, measuring over 3,000 in his survey of over 120,000 stars. He was among the first to measure stel-lar parallax. He supervised construction of a new observa-tory at Pulkovo and became its director in 1839. His son, Otto Struve (1819–1905), was director of Pulkovo Observa-tory (1862–89); his grandson Gustav Wilhelm Ludwig Struve (1858–1920) was director of Univ. of Kharkov Ob-servatory; Otto STRUVE was his great-grandson.

Struve *Engl* 'strü-vē\, **Otto** (1897–1963) Russian-U.S. as-tronomer. Born in Ukraine, the great-grandson of Friedrich STRUVE, he served in the Russian army in World War I be-fore emigrating to the U.S. At the Yerkes Observatory, he made important contributions to stellar spectroscopy and astrophysics, including discovering the widespread distribu-tion of hydrogen and other elements in space. He was di-rector of Yerkes and later of McDonald Observatory in Texas, which he organized, and directed the National Radio Astronomy Observatory in Green Bank, W.V., 1959–62. Struve published about 700 papers and several books.

Struve \'strü-və\, **Pyotr (Berngardovich)** (1870–1944) Russ-ian economist and journalist. In 1898 he wrote a manifesto for the newly formed RUSSIAN SOCIAL-DEMOCRATIC WORK-ERS' PARTY. After his exile in 1901, he broke with revolu-tionary Marxism; he edited the illegal but widely read jour-nal *Osvobozhdeniy* ("Liberation") (1902–5), calling for a constitutional monarchy. He returned to Russia in 1905, joined the CONSTITUTIONAL DEMOCRATIC PARTY, and edited the moderate journal *Russkaya mysly* ("Russian Thought"). In 1917 he left Russia for Paris.

strychnine \'strik-ˌnīn\ Organic chemical, a poisonous AL-KALOID obtained from seeds of the nux vomica tree and re-lated plants. It does not dissolve in water and not well in al-cohol, and it has an intense bitter taste. It has been used in rodent POISONS. Within 20 minutes it causes painful muscle contractions and convulsions; death usually results from respiratory muscle spasms. Small doses are used by veterinarians as a stimulant.

Stuart, Charles Edward (Louis Philip Casimir) *known as* **Bonnie Prince Charlie** (1720–1788) Claimant to the British throne. Son of the royal pretender J. E. STUART, in 1745 the "Young Pretender" landed in Scotland, where he raised an army of 2,400 among the clans. After taking Edinburgh, he crossed the English border and reached Derby, but a lack of strong support from the JACOBITES and the French forced his retreat. He was decisively defeated at Culloden (1746) and, aided by Flora Macdonald (1722–1790) and disguised as her maid, escaped to France. He wandered about Europe trying to revive his cause, but his debauched behavior alienated his friends. He later became romanticized in ballads and legends.

Stuart, Gilbert (Charles) (1755–1828) U.S. painter. Born in N. Kingston, R.I., he went to London in 1775 and worked with Benjamin WEST. He opened his own London studio in 1782 and enjoyed great success, but fled to Dublin in 1787 to escape his creditors. After six years there, he returned to the U.S. and quickly established himself as the nation's leading portraitist. Critics have praised his painterly brushwork, luminous color, and psychological penetration. Of his nearly 1,000 portraits, the most famous is an unfinished head of George WASHINGTON (1796).

Stuart *or* **Stewart** *or* **Steuart, House of** Royal house of Scotland (1371–1714) and of England (1603–49, 1660–1714). Its earliest members were stewards in 11th-cent. Brittany, and one who entered the service of DAVID I in Scotland received the title of steward. The 6th steward married the daughter of ROBERT I the Bruce, and in 1371 their son became ROBERT II, the first Stewart king of Scotland. His descendants included the Scottish monarchs JAMES I, JAMES II, JAMES III, JAMES IV, MARY, QUEEN OF SCOTS, and James VI (who inherited the English throne as JAMES I). The Stuarts (who eventually adopted the French-influenced spelling of their name) were excluded from the English throne after CHARLES I until the restoration of CHARLES II in 1660. He was followed by JAMES II, WILLIAM III and MARY II, and ANNE. In 1714 the British crown passed to the House of HANOVER, despite later claims by J. E. STUART and C. E. STUART.

Stuart, James (Francis) Edward (1688–1766) Claimant to the British throne. Son of the exiled JAMES II, he was raised in France as a Catholic. On the death of his father (1701), he was proclaimed king of England by the French king LOUIS XIV, but the English parliament passed a bill of attainder against him. In the JACOBITE uprising (1715), James landed in Scotland, but within two months the uprising collapsed. He lived thereafter in Rome under the pope's patronage. He became known as the "Old Pretender" to distinguish him from his son, C. E. STUART.

Stuart, Jeb (*orig.* James Ewell Brown) (1833–1864) U.S. army officer. Born in Patrick Co., Va., he was an aide to Col. Robert E. LEE in the defeat of John BROWN's raid on Harpers Ferry. In 1861 he became brigadier general of a Confederate cavalry brigade. On scouting raids he obtained information on Union troop movements that contributed to victories, including at the Second Battle of BULL RUN; Lee called Stuart the "eyes of the army." He helped win the battles of Fredericksburg and Chancellorsville. Before the Battle of GETTYSBURG, he was asked to gather information on Union troop movements; delayed, he arrived after the battle had begun. Though criticized, he continued to provide intelligence to Confederate forces. He was mortally wounded in the Battle of Spotsylvania Court House.

Stubbs, George (1724–1806) British animal painter. Son of a prosperous tanner, he was a self-taught painter. His masterly portraits of hunters and racehorses brought him innumerable commissions. Perhaps most impressive are his pictures of informal groups of horses, such as *Mares and Foals in a Landscape* (c.1760–70). He also painted lions, tigers, giraffes, monkeys, and rhinoceroses, which he was able to observe in private menageries. His book *The Anatomy of the Horse* (1762), containing 18 masterfully engraved plates, was widely acclaimed.

stucco Exterior or interior plasterwork used as three-dimensional ornamentation, as a smooth paintable surface, or as a wet ground for fresco painting. Today the term is most often restricted to the rough plaster coating of exterior walls. Stucco was applied to Greek temple walls as early as 1400 B.C. Roman architects stuccoed the rough stone or brick walls of monuments. Stucco was widely used in baroque and Renaissance architecture. In the warmer regions of the U.S., the 1920s stucco bungalow became virtually ubiquitous. Because of the many ways in which it can be treated, stuccowork has remained popular.

Studebaker family U.S. manufacturers whose firm became the world's largest producer of horse-drawn vehicles and a leader in automobile manufacturing. In 1852 Clement Studebaker (1831–1901) started a blacksmith and wagon shop in South Bend, Ind., with his brother Henry (1826–1895). Later joined by other brothers, the family business supplied vehicles to the U.S. government during the American Civil War and helped outfit settlers moving west. By 1902 it had built its first electric cars, and by 1904 gasoline-powered cars. In 1954 the Studebaker Corp. merged with the Packard Motor Car Co.; in 1966 it ceased production.

Students for a Democratic Society (SDS) Activist student organization. Founded at the Univ. of Michigan in 1960, its chapters were involved in the CIVIL RIGHTS MOVEMENT. Its "Port Huron Statement" of principles (1962) called for a new "participatory democracy." After organizing a national march in 1965 to protest the VIETNAM WAR, it became more militant, organizing sit-ins to protest universities' participation in defense-related research. By 1969 it had split into factions; the most notorious was the terrorist-oriented Weathermen. By the mid-1970s the group was defunct.

studio system System whereby U.S. movie companies controlled all aspects of production, distribution, and exhibition. In the 1920s PARAMOUNT and MGM acquired theater chains to strengthen their vertical control of the industry, and WARNER BROTHERS, RKO, and TWENTIETH CENTURY-FOX soon built similar empires. Studio heads controlled the types of movies to be made and the directors and actors to be hired. Under the "star system," certain actors and actresses were groomed for stardom, with studio executives choosing their roles, publicizing their glamorized offscreen lives, and controlling them through long contracts. The system declined after a 1948 Supreme Court decision forced the large studios to sell their theater chains; with increasing competition from television, by the 1960s it had effectively ended.

stupa Monument erected in memory of the BUDDHA or a Buddhist saint, often marking a sacred spot, commemorating an event, or housing a relic. A simple stupa may consist of a circular earthenware base supporting a massive solid dome, from which projects an umbrella, symbolizing protection. This basic design is the inspiration for other types of Buddhist monuments, including PAGODAS. Many important stupas have become places of pilgrimage.

Stupa III and its single gateway, Sanchi, Madhya Pradesh, India

sturgeon Any of about 20 species (family Acipenseridae) of large fishes abundant in S Russia, Ukraine, and N. America. Most species live in the sea and ascend rivers to spawn; a few live permanently in freshwaters. Four tactile barbels near the toothless mouth detect prey on the mud bottom. Sturgeon flesh and eggs, or roe (CAVIAR), are sold for food. The common Old World sturgeon (*Acipenser sturio*) and *A. oxyrhynchus*, found along E N. America, are generally about 10 ft (3 m) long and weigh about 500 lbs (225 kg). See also BELUGA.

Sturges \ˈstər-jəs\, **Preston** *orig.* Edmond Preston Biden (1898–1959) U.S. film director. Born in Chicago, he wrote the Broadway hits *Strictly Dishonorable* (1929) and *Child of Manhattan* (1931). Moving to Hollywood, he became a noted screenwriter, winning an Academy Award for *The Great McGinty* (1940), the first film he directed. He went on to write and direct such distinctive satirical comedies as *The Lady Eve* (1941), *Sullivan's Travels* (1941), *The Palm Beach*

Story (1941), *The Miracle of Morgan's Creek* (1944), and *Hail the Conquering Hero* (1944), characterized by their witty dialogue, rapid pace, and memorable minor characters.

Sturluson See SNORRI STURLUSON

Sturm und Drang \ˌshtùrm-ùnt-ˈdräŋ\ (German: "storm and stress") German literary movement of the later 18th cent. characterized by a revolt against the ENLIGHTENMENT cult of rationalism and the sterile imitation of French literature. It exalted nature, intuition, impulse, emotion, fancy, and inborn genius as the wellsprings of literature. Influenced by J.-J. ROUSSEAU and others, it took its name from a play by Friedrich von Klinger (1752–1831). Dramatic works were its most characteristic product. Its most gifted representatives were Friedrich SCHILLER and J. W. von GOETHE.

stuttering *or* **stammering** *or* **dysphemia** \dis-ˈfē-mē-ə\ Speech defect affecting the rhythm and fluency of speech, with involuntary repetition of sounds or syllables and intermittent blocking or prolongation of sounds, syllables, and words. Stutterers consistently have trouble with words starting with CONSONANTS, first words in sentences, and multisyllable words. Stuttering has a psychological, not a physiological, basis, tending to appear in children pressured to speak fluently in public. About 80% recover without treatment, usually by early adulthood. This probably results from increased self-esteem, acceptance of the problem, and consequent relaxation. See also SPEECH THERAPY.

Stuttgart \ˈshtùt-ˌgärt\ City (pop., 1996 est.: 586,000), SW Germany, on the NECKAR RIVER. It became a town in the 13th cent. and passed to the counts of WÜRTTEMBERG, serving as their capital until the 19th cent. The THIRTY YEARS' WAR, French invasions in the 17th cent., and heavy bombing during World War II took a toll on the city. It has revived as a cultural, industrial, and publishing center and home to Stuttgart Univ.

Stuyvesant \ˈstī-və-sənt\, **Peter** (1592?–1672) Dutch colonial governor. In 1645 he became director general of all Dutch possessions in N. America, including New Netherland. He arrived in New Amsterdam (later New York City) in 1647 and soon faced conflict with the burghers' demands for self-government. He established a municipal government but continued to control it. He settled the boundary with Connecticut (1650) and expelled the Swedes from Delaware, incorporating the colony into Dutch territory (1655). Incursions from the New England colonies and a British squadron forced him to surrender New Netherland to the British (1664).

sty *or* **hordeolum** \hȯr-ˈdē-ə-ləm\ Infection of an eyelid gland. An external sty results from infection of a SEBACEOUS GLAND at the edge of the eyelid. The sty reddens and swells. Warm compresses help it break sooner. An internal sty is caused by infection of a gland under the eyelid lining. More painful than an external sty, it usually breaks through the inner lining of the lid when it discharges. See also BOIL.

Style Moderne See ART DECO

Stylites See SIMEON STYLITES

Styne, Jule *orig.* Julius Kerwin Stein (1905–1994) U.S. (British-born) songwriter. Born to Ukrainian Jewish parents in London, he and his family settled in Chicago in 1912. He moved to Hollywood in 1937, and in the 1940s he worked with lyricist Sammy Cahn (1919–1993), writing ballads for Frank SINATRA, the film musical *Anchors Aweigh* (1945), and the Broadway musical *High Button Shoes* (1947). He collaborated with other lyricists on *Gentlemen Prefer Blondes* (1949; film, 1953), *Bells Are Ringing* (1956; film, 1960), *Gypsy* (1959; film, 1962), and *Funny Girl* (1964; film, 1968). His songs include "Let It Snow," "The Party's Over," and "People."

Styria \ˈstir-ē-ə\ *German* **Steiermark** \ˈshtī-ər-ˌmärk\ State (pop., 1999 est.: 1,205,000), SE Austria. It has an area of 6,327 sq mi (16,387 sq km); its capital is GRAZ. Inhabited since the Stone Age, the region came under the Romans as part of the Celtic kingdom of NORICUM. It became a duchy in 1180 and a HABSBURG crown land in 1282. After World War I, a S portion was ceded to Yugoslavia.

Styron, William (b.1925) U.S. novelist. A native of Newport News, Va., Styron became part of the American expatriate community in Paris in the 1950s. His first novel, *Lie Down in Darkness* (1951), tells of a disturbed young woman who commits suicide. The controversial *Confessions of Nat Turner* (1967, Pulitzer Prize) vividly evokes the slavery era. His later work includes *Sophie's Choice* (1979; film, 1982). His works often treat violent themes in a rich, Faulknerian style.

Styx \ˈstiks\ In GREEK MYTHOLOGY, a river of the underworld. The name comes from a Greek word that denotes both hatred and extreme cold, and it expresses loathing of death. In the epics of HOMER, the gods swore by the water of Styx as their most binding oath. The ancients believed that its poisonous water would dissolve any vessel except one made of the hoof of a horse or an ass.

subatomic particle *or* **elementary particle** Any of various self-contained units of matter or energy. Discovery of the ELECTRON in 1897 and of the atomic NUCLEUS in 1911 established that the ATOM is actually a composite of a cloud of electrons surrounding a tiny but heavy core. By the early 1930s it was found that the nucleus is composed of PROTONS and NEUTRONS. In the early 1970s it was discovered that these particles are made up of several types of QUARKS, which, together with several types of LEPTONS, constitute the fundamental building blocks of all matter. A third major group of subatomic particles consists of BOSONS, which transmit the forces of the universe. More than 200 subatomic particles have been detected so far, and most appear to have a corresponding antiparticle (see ANTIMATTER).

subconscious See UNCONSCIOUS

subduction zone Oceanic trench area in which, according to the theory of PLATE TECTONICS, the seafloor underthrusts an adjacent plate, dragging the accumulated trench sediments downward into the earth's upper mantle. Earthquakes occur along the angle of the descending plate. See also DEEP-SEA TRENCH.

Subic Bay Inlet of the S. CHINA SEA, SW LUZON, Philippines. From 1901 the U.S. maintained at Subic Bay the largest naval installation in the Philippines. The area suffered heavy damage in World War II and was occupied by the Japanese 1942–44. The base played a prominent role in the VIETNAM WAR (1955–75). It was transferred to the Philippines in 1992.

submachine gun Lightweight automatic small-arms weapon chambered for relatively low-energy pistol cartridges and fired from the hip or shoulder. It usually has a box-type magazine for 10–50 cartridges. It weighs 6–10 lbs (2.5–4.5 kg), can fire 650 or more rounds per minute, and is effective up to 200 yards (180 m). Important types include the Thompson submachine gun, or tommy gun (patented 1920), the British Sten gun of World War II, and the later Israeli UZI.

submarine Naval vessel capable of operating under water for sustained periods. In the 18th–19th cent., American inventors such as David Bushnell (1742?–1824) and Robert FULTON experimented with submarines. In 1898 John P. Holland (1840–1914) launched the *Holland,* which had both internal-combustion engines (for surface locomotion) and electric motors (for submerged cruising). By the eve of World War I, all major navies had submarines; the German U-BOAT was an especially potent threat. World War II saw extensive submarine campaigns. The snorkel, adopted by the Germans in 1940, supplied fresh air to the diesel engine of the submerged craft, thus making it unnecessary to surface to recharge batteries. The shift to nuclear power with the USS *Nautilus* in 1954 meant that submarines could remain submerged and operate at high speed indefinitely. SONAR is widely used. Subs may be armed with missiles fitted with nuclear warheads. Because they are so difficult to locate, they have been of great importance in the forces of nuclear-armed nations. See also DEPTH CHARGE, TRIDENT MISSILE.

submarine canyon Narrow, steep-sided underwater valley cut into a CONTINENTAL SLOPE. Submarine canyons resemble river canyons on land, usually having steep, rocky walls. Those of the Grand Bahama Canyon, which are thought to be the deepest, cut nearly 3 mi (5 km) into the continental slope. Most submarine canyons extend only about 30 mi (50 km) or less, but a few are more than 200 mi (300 km) long.

submarine fan Accumulation of land-derived sediment on the seafloor. A fan is shaped like the section of a cone, with its apex at the mouth of a SUBMARINE CANYON. The sediments consist largely of sandy material that drops from the canyon current in successively finer layers (see TURBIDITY CURRENT). Submarine fan valleys, with low relief and natural levees, often occur on submarine fans.

submarine fracture zone Long, narrow, and mountainous submarine lineation that generally separates ocean-floor ridges of different depths. The largest fracture zones, in the E Pacific, are more than 1,000 mi (1,600 km) long and 60–125 mi (100–200 km) wide. Numerous shorter fracture zones in the Atlantic are associated with the MID-ATLANTIC RIDGE.

submarine mine Stationary explosive device placed in the water and designed to destroy ships that touch or approach it. In use since the mid-19th cent., it consists of an explosive charge fitted with a device that detonates the charge when a ship or submarine is nearby. It is anchored to the sea floor by a cable and may be detonated by contact, by an approaching ship's magnetic field, by changes in water pressure, or by the sound of a ship's propellers. Effective in World War I, its role was even greater in World War II, when mines sank 1,118 Allied ships and 1,316 Axis ships. See also LAND MINE.

submarine plateau See OCEANIC PLATEAU

subpoena \sə-'pē-nə\ In law, a WRIT commanding the person upon whom it has been served to appear in court or before a congressional committee, GRAND JURY, or some other body, under a penalty for failure to comply. Unlike a summons, a subpoena may command the recipient to produce evidence necessary to the resolution of a legal matter or controversy.

subsidy Governmental assistance, either through direct payments or through indirect means such as price cuts and favorable contracts, to a person or group in order to promote a public objective. Subsidies to transportation, housing, agriculture, mining, and other industries have been instituted on the grounds that they serve the public interest. Subsidies to the arts, sciences, humanities, and religion also exist in many nations. Subsidies may be implemented through direct payments in cash or kind, through governmental provision of goods or services at low prices, through governmental purchase of goods or services at high prices, or through tax concessions. Since subsidies result in either higher taxes or higher prices for consumer goods and may help sustain inefficient producers, subsidy is desirable only if its effects increase total benefits more than total costs (see COST-BENEFIT ANALYSIS).

subsistence farming Form of farming in which nearly all the crops or livestock raised are used to maintain the farmer and his family, leaving little surplus for sale or trade. Preindustrial agricultural peoples throughout the world practiced subsistence farming. As urban centers grew, agricultural production became more specialized and farmers began producing surpluses of certain crops to trade for manufactured goods or sell for cash. Subsistence farming persists today in sub-Saharan Africa and other developing areas.

subsoil Layer (stratum) of earth immediately below the surface soil, consisting predominantly of minerals and leached materials such as iron and aluminum compounds. HUMUS remains and clay accumulate in subsoil, but the teeming macroscopic and microscopic organisms that make the topsoil rich with organic matter spend little time in the subsoil layer. Stripping topsoil while clearing land for crop growth or commercial development exposes the subsoil and increases EROSION.

substantive law See PROCEDURAL LAW

subsurface water See GROUNDWATER

subway Underground railway system used to transport passengers within urban and suburban areas. The first subway line, 3.75 mi (6 km) long, opened in London in 1863; the first electrified subway opened there in 1890. Subways later opened in Budapest (1896), Boston (1897), Paris (1900), Berlin (1902), New York (1904), Madrid (1919), Tokyo (1927), and Moscow (1935). Improvements in systems built from the 1970s on (including San Francisco, Washington, D.C., and Los Angeles) include computer technology to run subway trains by remote control.

succubus See INCUBUS AND SUCCUBUS

succulent Any plant with fleshy, thick tissues adapted to water storage. Some succulents (e.g., the CACTUS) store water only in the stem and have no leaves or very small leaves; others (e.g., AGAVES) store water mainly in the leaves. Most have deep or broad root systems and are native to either deserts or regions that have a semiarid season. Succulents exchange gases with the atmosphere at night in order to minimize TRANSPIRATION.

suckerfish See REMORA

Suckling, Sir John (1609–1642) English CAVALIER POET, dramatist, and courtier. He became prominent at court as a gallant and a gamester; he is credited with inventing cribbage. After participating in a foiled plot to rescue the Earl of Strafford from the Tower of London, he fled to France and is believed to have committed suicide. He wrote four plays, the best being the lively comedy *The Goblins* (1638). His reputation as a poet rests on his lyrics; his masterpiece is "A Ballad upon a Wedding."

Sucre \'sü-krä\ Constitutional capital (pop., 2000: 192,000), Bolivia. Founded by the Spanish about 1539, it became the capital of the Charcas territory of Upper Peru in 1561, and in 1609 the seat of an archdiocese. The Bolivian declaration of independence was signed there in 1825, and it became the capital in 1839. An effort to move the capital to LA PAZ in 1898 resulted in a civil war, which left the two cities sharing capital status. Sucre is also the nation's judicial center. The Univ. of San Francisco Xavier, one of the oldest in S. America, was founded there in 1624.

Sucre \'sü-krä\, **Antonio José de** (1795–1830) Liberator of Ecuador and first president of Bolivia (1826–28). A close ally of Simón BOLÍVAR, Sucre fought in the revolutionary struggles of Venezuela, Colombia, Gran Colombia (now Ecuador), Peru, and Upper Peru (now Bolivia), defeating royalist forces throughout the region. In 1826 he set up a Bolivian government and briefly served as president. Assassinated in 1830 at 35, he remains one of the most respected leaders of the Latin-American wars for independence.

sucrose \'sü-ˌkrōs\ *or* **table sugar** Organic compound, colorless, sweet-tasting crystals that dissolve in water. Sucrose is a disaccharide; HYDROLYSIS yields "invert sugar," a 50:50 mixture of FRUCTOSE and GLUCOSE, its two constituent MONOSACCHARIDES. Sucrose occurs naturally in sugarcane, sugar beets, sugar-maple sap, dates, and honey. It is produced commercially in large amounts and is used almost entirely as food. See also SUGAR.

Sudan \sü-'dan\ *or* **The Sudan** *officially* **Republic of the Sudan** Nation, NE Africa. Area: 966,757 sq mi (2,503,890 sq km). Population (2000): 35,080,000. Capital: KHARTOUM. Muslim Arab ethnic groups live in the northern and central two-thirds of the country, while Nilotic and Sudanic peoples live in the south. Languages: Arabic (official); 100 others spoken. Religions: Islam, animism, Christianity. Currency: Sudanese dinar. The largest country in Africa, the Sudan encompasses an immense plain with the SAHARA desert in the north, sand dunes in the west, semiarid shrub lands in the S central belt, and enormous swamps and tropical rain forests in the south. The NILE RIVER flows the entire length of the country. Wildlife includes lion, leopard, elephant, giraffe, and zebra. It has a developing mixed economy based largely on agriculture. One of the largest irrigation projects in the world provides water to farms between the White and Blue Niles. Chief cash crops are sugarcane, sorghum, peanuts, and sesame; petroleum and livestock are also important. It is ruled by an Islamic military regime. Evidence of inhabitation in the Sudan dates back tens of thousands of years. From the end of the 4th millennium B.C., NUBIA (now N Sudan) periodically came under Egyptian rule, and it was part of the kingdom of CUSH from the 11th cent. B.C. to the 4th cent. A.D. Christian missionaries converted the Sudan's three principal kingdoms during the 6th cent. A.D.; these black Christian kingdoms coexisted with their Muslim Arab neighbors in Egypt for centuries, until the influx of Arab immigrants brought about their collapse in the 13th–15th cent. Egypt had conquered all of the Sudan by 1874, and encouraged British interference in the region; this aroused Muslim opposition and led to the MAHDIST MOVEMENT, which captured Khartoum in 1885 and established a Muslim theocracy in the Sudan that lasted

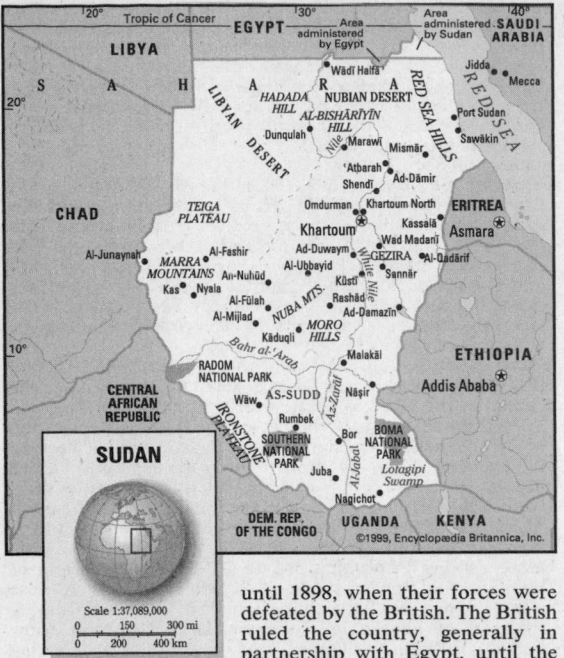

SUDAN

Scale 1:37,089,000

0   150   300 mi

0   200   400 km

©1999, Encyclopædia Britannica, Inc.

until 1898, when their forces were defeated by the British. The British ruled the country, generally in partnership with Egypt, until the Sudan achieved independence in 1956. Since then the country has fluctuated between ineffective parliamentary government and unstable military rule. The non-Muslim population of the south has engaged in ongoing rebellion against the Muslim-controlled government of the north, leading to the deaths of over 1.5 million people from violence and war-related famine in recent years.

Sudan *or* **the Sudan** Vast tract of open savanna plains, N central Africa. Extending across 2 million sq mi (5 million sq km), it lies between the S limits of the SAHARA and LIBYAN DESERTS and the N limits of the equatorial rain forests. It extends from the W coast more than 3,500 mi (5,500 km) to the mountains of Ethiopia and the Red Sea. The SAHEL makes up its N reaches.

sudden infant death syndrome (SIDS) *or* **crib death** Unexpected death of an apparently well infant. It occurs worldwide, almost always during sleep at night and usually at 2–4 months of age. Sleeping face down and exposure to cigarette smoke have been implicated. It is more common in cases of premature birth, low birth weight, and poor prenatal care. Some babies who die of SIDS have been found to have brain-stem abnormalities that interfere with their response to high carbon-dioxide levels in the blood.

Sudetenland \sü-'dā-t°n-₁land\ Sections of Bohemia and Moravia around the Sudeten mountain ranges. Formerly part of Austria, the predominantly German-speaking area was incorporated into Czechoslovakia after World War I. Discontent among the Sudeten Germans was exploited by the NAZI PARTY. The inflammatory situation convinced Britain and France that, to avoid war, Czechoslovakia must be persuaded to give the region autonomy. Adolf HITLER's demand that it be ceded to Germany was eventually accomplished by the MUNICH AGREEMENT. After World War II the region was restored to Czechoslovakia, which expelled its German inhabitants.

Suetonius \swē-'tō-nē-əs, ₁sü-ə-'tō-nē-əs\ *Latin* Gaius Suetonius Tranquillus (A.D. 69?–after 122) Roman biographer and antiquarian. His writings include *De viris illustribus* ("Concerning Illustrious Men"), short biographies of literary figures that were the ultimate source of nearly all that is known about the lives of eminent Roman authors. *Lives of the Caesars*, his other major work, is largely responsible for the vivid picture of Roman society that dominated historical thought until modified in modern times.

Suez, Gulf of NW arm of the Red Sea, between Africa proper and the SINAI Peninsula. It is 195 mi (314 km) long and 12–20 mi (19–32 km) wide. Linked to the Mediterranean Sea by the SUEZ CANAL, it is an important shipping route. In the 1970s and '80s, oil was discovered at numerous locations in the gulf.

Suez Canal Ship canal, Isthmus of Suez, Egypt. Connecting the Red Sea with the E Mediterranean Sea, it extends 100 mi (160 km) from PORT SAID to the Gulf of SUEZ, and allows ships to sail directly between the Mediterranean and the Indian Ocean. It was completed in 1869 after 11 years of construction. Its ownership remained largely in French and British hands until its nationalization by Egypt in 1956 sparked the SUEZ CRISIS. It has a minimum width of 179 ft (55 m) and a depth of about 40 ft (12 m) at low tide. It is one of the world's most heavily used shipping lanes.

Suez Crisis (1956) International crisis that arose from Egyptian Pres. G. A. NASSER's nationalization of the SUEZ CANAL. The French and British, who had strong interests in the canal, sent troops to occupy the canal zone. Their ally Israel seized the Sinai Peninsula. International opposition quickly forced the French and British out, and Israel withdrew in 1957. The incident was widely perceived as heralding the end of Britain as a major international power. Nasser's prestige, by contrast, soared within the developing world. See also ARAB–ISRAELI WARS, Anthony EDEN.

Suffolk County (pop., 1998 est.: 671,000), E England. It lies on the North Sea; the county seat is Ipswich. During Anglo-Saxon times it formed part of the kingdom of E. ANGLIA; the SUTTON HOO ship burial dates from this time. Its medieval prosperity was based largely on the wool industry. Since then, agriculture has been the major economic activity. Newmarket is famous for its racing stables, and the coast is dotted with holiday resorts.

Sufism \'sü-₁fi-zəm\ Mystical movement within ISLAM that seeks to find divine love and knowledge through direct personal experience of God. Sufism arose as an organized movement after the death of MUHAMMAD (A.D. 632) among different groups who found orthodox Islam to be spiritually stifling. The practices of contemporary Sufi orders and suborders vary, but most include the recitation of the name of God or of certain phrases from the QURAN as a way to enable the soul to experience the higher reality toward which it naturally aspires. Though Sufi practitioners have often been at odds with the mainstream of Islamic theology and law, the importance of Sufism in the history of Islam is incalculable. Sufi literature, especially love poetry, represents a golden age in Arabic, Persian, Turkish, and Urdu languages. See also AHMADIYA, DERVISH.

sugar Any of numerous sweet, colorless organic compounds that dissolve readily in water and occur in the sap of seed plants and the milk of mammals. Sugars (whose names end in "-ose") are the simplest CARBOHYDRATES. Commercial production of sugar is almost entirely for food. See also FRUCTOSE, GLUCOSE, LACTOSE, SUCROSE.

Sugar Act (1764) British legislation to raise revenue from N. American colonies. A revision of the unenforced Molasses Act of 1733, it imposed new duties on sugar and molasses imported into the colonies from non-British Caribbean sources. The act was the first attempt to recoup from the colonies the expenses of the FRENCH AND INDIAN WAR and the cost of maintaining British troops in N. America. The colonists objected to the act as taxation without representation, and protests increased with passage of the STAMP ACT.

sugar beet Variety of BEET (*Beta vulgaris*) that accounts for about two-fifths of global sugar production, making it second only to SUGARCANE as a source of the world's sugar. Unlike sugarcane, sugar beets can be grown in temperate or cold climates in Europe, N. America, and Asia. The sugar beet was grown as a garden vegetable and for fodder long before it was valued for its sugar content.

sugarcane Giant, thick, perennial GRASS (*Saccharum officinarum;* family Gramineae or Poaceae), cultivated in tropical and subtropical regions worldwide for its sweet sap, a major source of sugar and molasses. The plant grows in clumps of solid stalks with regularly spaced nodes or joints. Graceful, sword-shaped leaves fold in a sheath around the stem. Mature canes may be 10–20 ft (3–6 m) tall and 1–3 in.

(2.5–7.5 cm) in diameter. Molasses, the syrup remaining after sugar is crystallized, is used in cooking, in making rum, and as feed for farm animals. Cane fiber is burned as fuel or used as filler for paper and particleboard.

Sugawara Michizane \sù-'gä-wä-rä-ˌmē-chə-'zä-nä\ (845–903) Japanese scholar of Chinese literature, later deified as Tenjin, patron of scholarship and literature. He was given important government posts by the emperor Uda, but when Uda's son took the throne Michizane's fortunes were reversed, and he was sent into exile. Following his death in exile, calamities in the capital were attributed to his vengeful spirit, and he was posthumously reinstated. At shrines dedicated to Tenjin, schoolchildren often buy amulets for good luck on exams.

Suger \sü-'zher\ (1081–1151) Abbot of St.-Denis and adviser to Louis VI and Louis VII. A peasant boy educated at the abbey of St.-Denis, he was a schoolmate and close friend of Louis VI. In 1122 he was elected abbot, and he used popular veneration for the saint to rally military support for the king. Suger's work on the abbey church of ST.-DENIS was instrumental in the development of GOTHIC ARCHITECTURE. He arranged a treaty ending the civil war between Louis VII and his vassal Thibaut, and he served as regent (1147–49) during the king's absence on the Second CRUSADE.

Suharto (b.1921) Second president of Indonesia (1967–98). He began his military career with the Dutch colonial army, switched to a Japanese-sponsored defense corps (1942–45), then joined the guerrilla forces seeking independence from the Dutch. When Indonesia became independent (1950), he was a lieutenant colonel; he rose to general in 1960. A strong anticommunist, he crushed an attempted communist coup d'état in 1965 with a brutal purge that left some 500,000 dead. He deposed the sitting president, SUKARNO, and became president in 1967. He established authoritarian rule, stabilized the economy, and was repeatedly elected without opposition. In 1975 he annexed E. TIMOR, killing over 100,000 E. Timorese. In 1998 a severe economic downturn focused attention on his government's corruption; massive demonstrations forced his resignation after 31 years in power.

suicide Act of intentionally taking one's own life. Suicide may have psychological origins such as the difficulty of coping with DEPRESSION or other MENTAL DISORDERS; it may be motivated by the desire to test the affection of friends and relations or to punish them for lack of support. It may also stem from social and cultural pressures, especially those that tend to increase isolation, and it has been correlated with factors such as widowhood, childlessness, and urban life. Convicted criminals in ancient Greece were permitted to take their own lives; the Japanese custom of SEPPUKU allowed samurai to commit ritual suicide, and Buddhists have burned themselves alive in social protest. Suicide is condemned by Islam, Judaism, and Christianity, and suicide attempts are still often punishable by law. In modern society, however, suicide attempts are often seen as appeals for help, and since the 1950s suicide-prevention groups have been established, with telephone hot-lines serving as a source of counseling.

Sui dynasty \'swē\ (581–618) Short-lived Chinese dynasty that unified N and S China after centuries of division. The first Sui emperor, WENDI, established uniform institutions of government throughout the country, promulgated a new legal system, conducted a census, recruited officials through examinations, and reestablished Confucian rituals. The Sui capital at Changan was greatly expanded. The cultural and artistic renaissance that was to reach its height under the succeeding TANG DYNASTY was set in motion.

suite Set of instrumental dances or dancelike movements. The suite originated in the paired dances of the 14th–16th cent. (pavane–galliard, basse danse–saltarello, etc.). In the 16th–17th cent., German composers began to write sets of three or four dances. In the late 17th cent., a basic ordering of four dances—allemande, courante, sarabande, and gigue—became established as standard; other dances came to be interpolated between the sarabande and gigue.

Sukarno (1901–1970) First president of Indonesia (1949–66). He excelled in languages, and did much to create mod-

ern Indonesian. He emerged as a charismatic leader in the country's independence movement, despite imprisonment (1929–31) and exile (1933–42) by the Dutch. He served the Japanese invaders as a chief adviser, seeking independence from them. Following Japan's defeat, he declared independence; the Dutch did not transfer sovereignty until 1949. Once he became president, Indonesia made gains in health, education, and cultural self-awareness, but democracy and the economy foundered. His government was corrupt, inflation soared, and the country experienced a continuous state of crisis. An attempted coup by communists in 1965 led to a military takeover by SUHARTO.

Sukhothai kingdom \'sù-kə-'tī\ Former kingdom, N central Thailand. It was founded in the mid-13th cent. when a local Tai ruler led a revolt against the KHMER. Its third ruler, Ramkhamhaeng, began about 1279 to extend its power to the south onto the MALAY PENINSULA, to the west into what is now Myanmar, and to the northeast into modern Laos. In 1438 it was absorbed into the kingdom of Ayutthaya.

Sulawesi \ˌsü-lə-'wä-sē\ *or* **Celebes** \'se-lə-ˌbēz\ Island (pop., 1995 est.: 13,772,000), Indonesia. One of the Greater SUNDA ISLES, it lies in the MALAY ARCHIPELAGO east of BORNEO and has an area of 72,775 sq mi (188,487 sq km). The island is extremely mountainous. Muslims arrived in the 15th cent.; the Portuguese first visited in 1512. The first foreign settlement in 1607 by the Dutch at Makasar (now UJUNG PANDANG) initiated a power rivalry with the native sultans that lasted into the 20th cent. Communist rebellions against the Indonesian government have marked recent years.

Suleyman I \sē-lä-'män\ *known as* **Suleyman the Magnificent** (1495?–1566) Ottoman sultan (r.1520–66). He became sultan after his grandfather, BAYEZID II, and his father, Selim I. He led campaigns against the Christians, taking Belgrade (1521) and Rhodes (1522). Campaigns in Hungary (1541, 1543) divided the nation between Habsburg-dominated and Ottoman-dominated areas. His first campaign against the Persian empire (1534–35) captured Iraq and Asia Minor; his second (1548–49) brought conquests in SE Asia Minor around Lake Van. His navy, under BARBAROSSA, controlled the Mediterranean. In his realm he built mosques, bridges, and aqueducts, and he surrounded himself with great poets and legal scholars. His reign is considered a high point of the OTTOMAN EMPIRE.

sulfa drug Common term for sulfonamide drug, any member of a class of synthetic antibacterial drugs (e.g., sulfadiazine) with a particular chemical structure including both SULFUR and NITROGEN atoms. Their effectiveness against BACTERIA was discovered in 1932 by Gerhard DOMAGK, and they became the first chemical substances systematically used against human bacterial infections. Because of their toxicity and growing bacterial resistance, sulfa drugs are no longer in common use (except for urinary-tract infections), having been largely superseded by ANTIBIOTICS.

sulfate Any of numerous chemical compounds related to SULFURIC ACID. The SALTS are inorganic compounds containing the sulfate ION, in IONIC BONDS with any of various CATIONS. The ESTERS are organic compounds in which the acid's hydrogen atoms are replaced by organic groups. See also BONDING.

sulfur Nonmetallic chemical ELEMENT, chemical symbol S, atomic number 16. It is very reactive but occurs native in deposits, as well as combined in various ORES (e.g., PYRITE, GALENA); in COAL, PETROLEUM, and NATURAL GAS; and in the water in sulfur springs. Sulfur is the third most abundant constituent of MINERALS and one of the four most important basic chemical commodities. Pure sulfur, a tasteless, odorless, brittle yellow solid, occurs in several crystalline and amorphous forms, including brimstone and flowers of sulfur. It combines (VALENCE 2, 4, or 6) with nearly all other elements. Its most familiar compound is hydrogen sulfide, the poisonous gas that smells like rotten eggs. Sodium sulfite is a reducing agent used to pulp paper and in photography. Organic compounds with sulfur include several AMINO ACIDS, the SULFA DRUGS, and many insecticides, solvents, and substances used in making rubber and rayon. See also SULFATE, SULFUR DIOXIDE, SULFURIC ACID.

sulfur dioxide Inorganic compound, heavy, colorless, poisonous GAS (SO_2). It has the pungent, irritating smell of a just-struck match. Huge quantities are made industrially for use as a bleach, reducing agent, and as sulfites (food preservatives). It is a precursor of the trioxide (SO_3), used to make SULFURIC ACID. Sulfur dioxide is formed on burning sulfur-containing fuels; measures to control sulfur dioxide AIR POLLUTION have been widely adopted.

sulfuric acid \ˌsəl-ˈfyùr-ik\ *or* **oil of vitriol** Dense, colorless, oily, corrosive liquid inorganic compound. A very strong ACID, it is also an oxidizing (see OXIDATION-REDUCTION) and dehydrating agent and chars many organic materials. It is one of the most important industrial chemicals, used in manufacturing fertilizers, pigments, dyes, drugs, explosives, detergents, and inorganic salts and acids, in petroleum refining and metallurgical processes, and as the acid in lead-acid storage batteries. It is made industrially by dissolving sulfur trioxide in water. See also SULFATE.

Sulla (Felix), Lucius Cornelius (138–78 B.C.) Victor in the Roman civil war (88–82) and DICTATOR (82–79). He fought alongside Gaius MARIUS against JUGURTHA, whose capture through Sulla's trickery led to a break with Marius. After being made CONSUL, he was given command in the war against MITHRADATES VI; when Marius was named to replace him, he marched on Rome, and Marius fled. Though he succeeded in subduing Mithradates, the reigning popular party declared him a public enemy. From S Italy he marched again successfully on Rome (83). Proclaimed DICTATOR with no time limit, he became chiefly known for his ruthlessness. He resigned in 79.

Sullivan, Arthur (Seymour) (*later* **Sir Arthur**) (1842–1900) British composer. Having attended the Royal Academy and the Leipzig Conservatory, he seemed destined to be an important composer, and his music for *The Tempest* (1861), *Irish Symphony* (1866), and songs (including "Onward, Christian Soldiers" and "The Lost Chord") were widely performed. In 1871 he first collaborated in comic opera with W. S. GILBERT, and in 1875 their *Trial by Jury* became a hit. Their collaboration continued with *H.M.S. Pinafore* (1878), *The Pirates of Penzance* (1879), *Patience* (1881), *Iolanthe* (1882), *The Mikado* (1885), *The Yeomen of the Guard* (1888), *The Gondoliers* (1889), and others, many of which would delight international audiences for more than a century.

Sullivan, Ed(ward Vincent) (1901–1974) U.S. television host. Born in New York City, he wrote a Broadway gossip column for the *Daily News* from 1932. Known for discovering interesting new performers, he was hired by CBS to host its variety program *Toast of the Town* (1948–55), later called *The Ed Sullivan Show* (1955–71), where he presented highly diverse entertainment in a program that became a national institution.

Sullivan, Harry Stack (1892–1949) U.S. psychiatrist. Born in Norwich, N.Y., he became an innovator in the use of psychotherapy to treat SCHIZOPHRENIA, which he viewed as stemming from disturbed interpersonal relationships in early childhood. He helped establish the William Alanson White Psychiatric Foundation (1933) and the Washington School of Psychiatry (1936), and he founded (1938) the journal *Psychiatry*. His works include *The Interpersonal Theory of Psychiatry* (1953) and *The Fusion of Psychiatry and Social Science* (1964).

Sullivan, John L(awrence) (1858–1918) U.S. bareknuckle boxer. Born in Roxbury, Mass., he became heavyweight champion in 1882 by knocking out Paddy Ryan. His 75-round knockout of Jake Kilrain in 1889 was the last title bout under London Prize Ring (bareknuckle) rules. In his only

John L. Sullivan

championship defense under the Queensberry rules, he was knocked out by Jim Corbett (1866–1933) in 21 rounds in 1892. From 1878 to 1905 Sullivan had 35 bouts, of which he won 31, 16 by knockouts. Some regard him as a U.S. champion only, because he had only one international match of consequence.

Sullivan, Louis H(enry) (1856–1924) U.S. architect, the father of modern U.S. architecture. Born in Boston, he joined the office of Dankmar Adler (1844–1900) in 1879, becoming Adler's partner at age 24. Their 14-year association produced more than 100 buildings, many of them landmarks. Their first important work was the 17-story Auditorium Building (1889), unadorned on the arcaded exterior and dazzlingly rich on the interior. Their most important skyscraper is the 10-story steel-framed Wainwright Building, St. Louis (1890–91); above its two-story base, the vertical elements are stressed and horizontals recessed, and it is capped by a decorative frieze and cornice. In 1895 the partnership dissolved, and Sullivan's practice began a steady decline. One of his few major commissions was Chicago's Carson Pirie Scott store (1899–1904). Sullivan's ornamentation was based not on precedent but on geometry and natural forms. He considered that a building's design should indicate its functions, hence his dictum "form follows function."

Sully \sū̄-ˈlē\, **duc (Duke) de** *orig.* Maximilien de Béthune (1560–1641) French statesman. Son of a French Huguenot noble, he was sent to the court of Henry of Navarre (later HENRY IV). As superintendent of finances from 1598, he instituted reforms in taxation and administration. A trusted agent to Henry, he promoted a system of national improvements, encouraged agriculture, and strengthened the military. His political role ended with Henry's assassination (1610).

Sully Prudhomme \sū̄-lē-prǖ-ˈdȯm\ *orig.* René-François-Armand Prudhomme (1839–1907) French poet. Early on he published fluent and melancholic verse in volumes beginning with *Stances et poèmes* (1865). He later adopted the more objective approach of the PARNASSIAN POETS and attempted to represent philosophical concepts in verse. Among his best-known later works are *La justice* (1878) and *Le bonheur* (1888). In 1901 he was awarded the first Nobel Prize for Literature.

Sulu Archipelago Volcanic and coral archipelago, SW Philippines, between MINDANAO and BORNEO. A double island chain, it extends 170 mi (270 km) and includes about 400 named islands and more than 500 unnamed ones. The islanders were converted to Islam by ABU BAKR in the mid-15th cent. The islands and its inhabitants, whom the Spanish called MOROS, fell to Spain in the 19th cent. and in 1899 came under U.S. authority. The archipelago was ceded to the Philippines in 1940. The islands provide a haven for smugglers and pirates.

Sulzberger, Arthur Ochs (b.1926) U.S. newspaper publisher. Grandson of Adolph S. OCHS, he spent a dozen years in various newspaper posts before succeeding his father, Arthur Hays Sulzberger (1891–1968), as publisher of *The NEW YORK TIMES* in 1963. During his tenure he introduced many innovations that strengthened the paper's reputation, including an increase in coverage of such fields as economics, the environment, medicine, law, and science. In 1992 he was succeeded by his son, Arthur Sulzberger, Jr. (b.1951).

sumac \ˈshü-ˌmak, ˈsü-ˌmak\ Any of certain species of shrubs and small trees in the genus *Rhus* of the family Anacardiaceae (the sumac, or cashew, family), native to temperate and subtropical zones. All sumacs have a milky or resinous sap, which in some species (e.g., POISON SUMAC) can irritate the skin. Used in the past as a source of dyes, medicines, and beverages, sumacs are now valued as ornamentals, soil binders, and cover plants. The smooth, or scarlet, sumac (*R. glabra*), native to the E and central U.S., is the most common.

Sumatra \sù-ˈmä-trə\ Island (pop., 1995 est.: 40,344,000), W Indonesia. It is one of the SUNDA ISLES and the second-largest island of Indonesia. It is 1,060 mi (1,706 km) long; a chief city is PALEMBANG. It was ruled by the Srivijaya empire from the 7th cent. and the Majapahit empire in the 14th–16th cent. First the Portuguese, then the Dutch and English established forts there. In 1950 it became part of the

Republic of Indonesia. Its exports include rubber, tobacco, coffee, pepper, and timber products; mineral reserves include petroleum and coal.

Sumbawa \süm-'bä-wä\ Island (pop., 1990 est: 373,000), Lesser SUNDA ISLES, Indonesia. Its Bima Bay is one of the best harbors in Indonesia. Its highest point is volcanic Mt. Tambora (9,354 ft, or 2,851 m), whose eruption in 1815 killed 50,000 people. From 1674 the Dutch E. INDIA CO. held some power over the island; the Dutch gained direct control in the early 20th cent. It became part of independent Indonesia in 1950. It has been known for its small, sturdy horses since the 14th cent.

Sumer \'sü-mər\ S division of ancient BABYLONIA, S MESOPOTAMIA, Tigris-Euphrates Valley, in what is now S Iraq. It was first settled about 4500–4000 B.C. by the Ubaidians, who drained the marshes for agriculture and developed trade. The Sumerians, arrived around 3300 B.C. and developed the world's first known cities, which evolved into city-states. As rivalry among them increased, each adopted the institution of kingship, and eventually they were loosely united under one city or another, beginning with KISH about 2800 B.C. Thereafter, Kish, ERECH, UR, NIPPUR, and LAGASH vied for ascendancy for hundreds of years. The area came under the ELAM (c.2530–2450 B.C.) and later the AKKAD, led by SARGON (r.2334–2279 B.C.). The city-states were largely independent after the Akkadian empire collapsed until they were reunified under the Third Dynasty of Ur (21st–20th cent. B.C.). This kingdom disappeared into the Babylonian empire of the 18th cent. B.C. The Sumerian legacy includes the first known wheeled vehicles and potter's wheels, a system of writing (see CUNEIFORM), and codes of law.

Summerhill School Experimental primary and secondary boarding school in Leiston, Suffolk, England. Founded in 1921 by A. S. Neill (1883–1973), the school is self-governing and emphasizes the student's own motivation to learn (class attendance is optional). Neill's controversial book *Summerhill* (1960) sparked much debate about alternatives to conventional schooling, particularly in the U.S.

sumo \'sü-mō\ Japanese form of wrestling in which a contestant loses if he is forced out of the ring (a 15-ft circle) or if any part of his body except the soles of his feet touches the ground. Weight and strength are of the greatest importance, though speed of attack is also useful. The wrestlers, who are fed a special protein diet and may weigh over 300 lbs (136 kg), wear only loincloths and grip each other by the belt. Sumo is an ancient sport with a complex system of ranking; lengthy rituals and elaborate posturings accompany the bouts, which often last only a few seconds.

sun STAR around which the SOLAR SYSTEM revolves. About 5 billion years old, it is the dominant body of the system, with more than 99% of its mass. It converts 5 million tons of matter into energy every second by NUCLEAR FUSION, producing NEUTRINOS and radiation. A small amount of this energy penetrates earth's ATMOSPHERE, providing the light and heat that support life. Solar radiation can also supply electricity (see SOLAR CELL). A sphere of luminous gas 864,950 mi (1.392 million km) in diameter, the sun has 330,000 times earth's mass. Its temperature is close to 27,000,000°F (15,000,000°C) at the core and about 10,000°F (6,000°C) at the surface. A G-type (yellow) star, it is fairly average for a main-sequence star (see HERTZSPRUNG-RUSSELL DIAGRAM). The PHOTOSPHERE is in constant motion; the number and positions of SUNSPOTS change in a regular SOLAR CYCLE (see CHROMOSPHERE, CORONA, SOLAR FLARE, SOLAR WIND). Effects on earth include AURORAS and disruption of radio communications and power transmission. The sun appears to have remained relatively unchanged for billions of years.

sun bear *or* **honey bear** Smallest member (*Helarctos,* or *Ursus, malayanus*) of the bear family (Ursidae), found in SE Asian forests. Nocturnal and tree-climbing, it weighs 60–140 lbs (27–64 kg) and is 3–4 ft (1–1.2 m) long, with an orange-yellow crescent on the chest, said to represent the sun. Shy and intelligent, it uses its long, curved claws to tear or dig for bee and termite nests, and also eats fruit, honey, and small vertebrates.

Sunbelt Region, south and SW U.S. It is characterized by a warm climate, rapid population growth since 1970, and relatively conservative voting patterns. Composed of 15 states, it extends from Virginia and Florida in the southeast through Nevada in the southwest, and includes S California.

sunburn Acute skin INFLAMMATION caused by overexposure to ULTRAVIOLET RADIATION from sunlight or other sources. More common and more severe in light-skinned people, it ranges from mild redness and tenderness to intense pain, EDEMA, and blistering, sometimes with shock, fever, and nausea. The process begins after 15 minutes in the sun, but redness starts 6–12 hours later. Pigment cells in the skin increase MELANIN production ("tan"). Cold compresses and ANALGESICS reduce pain. Long-term sun exposure can eventually cause SKIN CANCER, as well as skin wrinkling and thickening.

Sunda Isles Archipelago extending from the MALAY PENINSULA to the MOLUCCAS. The islands make up most of the land area of Indonesia. They include the Greater Sunda Islands (SUMATRA, JAVA, BORNEO, SULAWESI, and adjacent smaller islands), and the Lesser Sunda Islands (BALI, LOMBOK, SUMBAWA, Sumba, Flores, TIMOR, Alor, and adjacent smaller islands). Most of the islands are part of a geologically unstable and volcanically active ISLAND ARC.

sun dance Most spectacular and important religious ceremony of the 19th-cent. PLAINS INDIANS. Ordinarily held in early summer (hence the name), it was an occasion to reaffirm basic beliefs about the universe and the supernatural through rituals. The ceremony was most highly developed among the ARAPAHO, CHEYENNE, and Oglala SIOUX. The central rite involved dancers who, to fulfill a vow or seek "power" (spiritual energy and insight), danced for several days without food or drink, their ordeal ending in frenzy and exhaustion. Among some tribes self-torture and mutilation were practiced.

Sundanese Ethnic group of the island of JAVA, Indonesia, numbering about 26 million. They are a highland people of W Java, distinguished from the JAVANESE mainly by their language and their strict adherence to Islam. Once followers of Mahayana Buddhism, they converted to Islam in the 16th cent. Sundanese villages are ruled by a headman and a council of elders. Marriage, birth, and death ceremonies incorporate Hindu elements. Modern developments have tended to erase differences between the Sundanese and other peoples of Java.

Sunday, Billy (*orig.* William Ashley) (1862/63–1935) U.S. revivalist. Born in Ames, Iowa, he became a professional baseball player with the Chicago White Sox in 1883. In 1887 he underwent a conversion experience; he began preaching in 1897 and was ordained in the Presbyterian church in 1903. A flamboyant preacher of fundamentalist theology, he advocated a strict morality and campaigned effectively for Prohibition. He conducted hundreds of revival meetings and reached an estimated 100 million people. His popularity faded in the 1920s.

Sunderland Seaport (pop.: 1999 est.: 289,000), N England, at the mouth of the Wear River on the North Sea. It formerly included Monkwearmouth, site of a monastery built in 674 where the Venerable BEDE studied. Sunderland itself was chartered in the late 12th cent. The port grew rapidly as the coal trade developed in the 17th cent., and by the mid-18th cent. it was a major shipbuilding center.

Sunderland, Earl of *orig.* Robert Spencer (1641–1702) English statesman, chief adviser to CHARLES II, JAMES II, and WILLIAM III. As secretary of state (1679–81, 1683), he became the chief architect of Charles's pro-French foreign policy. He converted to Roman Catholicism to maintain his influence in James's reign. After William became king, Sunderland renounced his Catholicism and became the principal intermediary between the king and Parliament.

sundew Any of about 100 species of annual and perennial flowering CARNIVOROUS PLANTS that make up the family Droseraceae (sundew family). Sundews are found throughout tropical and temperate regions. Both leaf surfaces are generally covered with sticky, gland-tipped hairs and sensitive tentacles that trap insects. After the trapped prey has been digested by enzymes secreted by the tentacles, the leaf

S

reopens, resetting the trap. The best-known sundew is the VENUS'S-FLYTRAP. See also PITCHER PLANT.

sunfish Any of numerous species of brightly colored N. American carnivorous freshwater fishes placed with the CRAPPIES and black basses in the family Centrarchidae. Usually less than 8 in. (20 cm) long, sunfishes are fine food and game fishes. The best known are the black-banded sunfish (*Enneacanthus chaetodon*) of the E U.S. and the bluegill (*Lepomis macrochirus*), which has an orange belly and blue markings. The longear sunfish has orange spots and wavy, bright blue streaks.

sunflower Any of 60 species of annual herbaceous plants in the genus *Helianthus* (COMPOSITE FAMILY), native mostly to N. and S. America. The common sunflower (*H. annuus*) has a rough, hairy stem 3–15 ft (1–4.5 m) high; broad, coarsely toothed, rough leaves; and large, flat, platelike compound flowers. Disk flowers swirl in a tight brown, yellow, or purple spiral; ray flowers are yellow to red. The leaves are used as fodder, the flowers yield a yellow dye, and the seeds contain oil and are used for food. The oil is used for cooking, in soaps and paints, and as a lubricant.

Sung dynasty See SONG DYNASTY

sunna \'sù-nə\ Body of traditional social and legal custom and practice that constitutes proper observance of ISLAM. Early Muslims disagreed over what constituted sunna, owing to the wide variety of pre-Islamic practices among converted peoples. In the 8th cent., the sunna of MUHAMMAD, as preserved in eyewitness records, was codified as the HADITH by al-Shafii (767–820). Later Muslim scholars devised a system for attesting the authenticity of various practices claimed as descending from Muhammad. See also SHARIA.

Sunni \'sù-nē\ Larger of the two major divisions of ISLAM, comprising 90% of the world's Muslims. Sunnis regard theirs as the mainstream and traditionalist branch of Islam, as distinguished from the SHIITES. Sunnis recognize the first four Umayyad caliphs (see UMAYYAD DYNASTY) as MUHAMMAD's rightful successors. Because Muhammad's theocratic state was seen as an earthly, temporal dominion, Sunnis were willing to accept unexceptional and even foreign caliphs, provided order and religious orthodoxy were maintained. Sunni orthodoxy emphasizes consensus based on the views and customs of the majority of the community, thereby enabling them to incorporate customs that arose historically but that had no roots in the QURAN. Today Sunni Muslims number about 1 billion.

sunspot Cooler-than-average region of gas on the SUN's surface associated with strong local magnetic activity. Sunspots appear dark in contrast with the surrounding PHOTOSPHERE, thousands of degrees hotter. Spots several times earth's size are visible through a filter to the unaided eye: small ones are hard to see with a telescope. They come and go as part of the SOLAR CYCLE, usually in pairs or groups, and may last for months; their cause appears to be related to the sun's magnetic field reversals. High sunspot activity is associated on earth with brighter AURORAS and interference with radio signals.

sun worship Veneration of the sun or its representation as a deity. It appears in several early cultures, notably in ancient Egypt, Indo-Europe, and Mesoamerica, where kings ruled by the power of the sun and claimed descent from it. The sun was often seen as the ruler of both the upper and the lower world, which he visits daily. Sun heroes and deities also figure in Indo-Iranian, Greco-Roman, and Scandinavian mythologies. See also AMATERASU, RE, SOL, SURYA.

SUNY See State Univ. of NEW YORK

Sun Yat-sen \'sùn-'yät-'sen\ *pinyin* **Sun Yixian** \'sùn-'ē-shē-'ən\ (1866–1925) Leader of the GUOMINDANG (Chinese Nationalist Party), known as the father of modern China. Sun began a medical career in 1892, but, troubled by the conservative

Sun Yat-sen

QING DYNASTY's inability to prevent repeated humiliations at the hands of Western nations, he soon switched to politics. A letter to LI HONGZHANG in which Sun detailed ways in which China could gain strength was ignored, and he went abroad to organize expatriate Chinese; in 1905 he became head of a revolutionary coalition. The revolts he helped plot failed, but in 1911 a rebellion in Wuhan unexpectedly overthrew the provincial government. Other provincial secessions followed, and Sun returned to be elected provisional president of a new government. The emperor abdicated in 1912, and Sun turned over the government to YUAN SHIKAI. The two men split in 1913; Sun headed a separatist regime in the south. In 1924, aided by Soviet advisers, he reorganized his Nationalist Party and established a military academy, headed by CHIANG KAI-SHEK. He delivered lectures on his doctrine, the Three Principles of the People (nationalism, democracy, and people's livelihood), but died before he could put it into practice.

Sunzi *or* **Sun-tzu** \'sün-'dzü\ (fl. 6th cent. B.C.) Chinese military strategist. A general who served the state of Wu late in the SPRING AND AUTUMN PERIOD (770–476 B.C.), he is traditionally regarded as the author of the earliest treatise on war and military science, *The Art of War,* though it was more likely written somewhat later. A systematic guide to strategy and tactics, it emphasizes the unpredictability of battle and the need for flexible responses. Its insistence on the close relationship between political considerations and military policy influenced modern strategists, notably MAO ZEDONG.

Super Bowl Annual championship game of the NATIONAL FOOTBALL LEAGUE, played by the winners of the American and National Football Conferences. The first was held in 1967. It normally falls on the last Sunday in January, and is watched by more Americans than any other sporting event.

supercomputer Class of the fastest high-performance DIGITAL COMPUTERS available at a given time. Current PERSONAL COMPUTERS are more powerful than the supercomputers of two decades ago. Supercomputers are used primarily for scientific and engineering work. Unlike conventional computers, they usually have more than one CPU; higher-performance supercomputers may have thousands of individual processors. Supercomputers also have huge storage capacity and very fast input/output capability, and can operate on corresponding elements of arrays of numbers rather than on one pair of elements at a time.

superconductivity Almost total lack of electrical RESISTANCE in certain materials when they are cooled to a temperature near ABSOLUTE ZERO. Superconducting materials allow low power dissipation, high-speed operation, and high sensitivity. Since it was first discovered in mercury by Heike Kamerlingh Onnes (1853–1926) in 1911, similar behavior has been found in some 25 other chemical elements and in thousands of alloys and compounds. Superconductors are used in medical imaging, magnetic energy-storage systems, motors, generators, transformers, computer components, and sensitive magnetic-field measuring devices.

superego In Freudian psychoanalytic theory, one of the three aspects of the human personality, along with the ID and the EGO. The last of these to develop, the superego is the ethical component of the personality, providing the moral standards by which the ego operates. The superego is formed during the first five years of life in response to parental punishment and approval; the developing superego serves to control aggressive or other socially unacceptable impulses. Violation of its standards gives rise to feelings of guilt or anxiety.

superfluidity Unusual property of liquid HELIUM cooled below –455.75°F (–270.97°C) (near ABSOLUTE ZERO). At such low temperatures, helium exhibits an enormous rise in heat conductivity and rapid flow through capillaries or over the rim of its container. To explain such behavior, the substance is described in terms of a "two-fluid" mixture model consisting of normal and superfluid helium. In normal helium the atoms are in excited states, whereas in superfluid helium they are in their ground state. It is assumed that the superfluid component can move through the container without FRICTION, thereby explaining the unusual behavior.

supergiant star STAR whose luminosity is typically several MAGNITUDES brighter and its size several times larger than those of a GIANT STAR. Like other stars, they are distinguished in practice by SPECTROSCOPY. A supergiant's diameter may be several hundred times the sun's and nearly a million times its luminosity. Supergiants probably last only a few million years.

Superior, Lake Lake, U.S. and Canada. The largest of the five GREAT LAKES, it is the world's largest freshwater lake. It has an area of 31,800 sq mi (82,362 sq km) and depths reaching 1,330 ft (405 m). It is known for its picturesque coastline and its numerous shipwrecks. The head of the Great Lakes–ST. LAWRENCE SEAWAY system, it is connected to Lake HURON at its SE end via the SAULT STE. MARIE locks. Ships transport grain, flour, and iron ore during the eight-month navigation season. The French missionary Claude-Jean Allouez charted the lake in 1667. The region came under British control 1763–83 and remained in British hands until 1817.

supermarket Large retail store operated on a self-service basis, selling groceries, produce, meat, bakery and dairy products, and sometimes nonfood goods. Supermarkets were first established in the U.S. during the 1930s as no-frills retail stores offering low prices. By the 1950s they were the major food marketing channel in the U.S. and had spread through much of Europe, as part of a trend in developed countries toward reducing costs and simplifying MARKETING. In the 1960s they appeared in the Middle East, Asia, and Latin America, where they are patronized largely by the upper middle class.

supernova Any of a class of violently exploding stars whose luminosity suddenly increases to millions or even billions of times its normal level. Like NOVAS, supernovas undergo a tremendous, rapid brightening lasting a few weeks, then dim slowly, and show blue-shifted emission lines on SPECTROSCOPY, implying that hot gases are blown outward. In such an explosion, a star collapses into a NEUTRON STAR or BLACK HOLE. Vast amounts of its matter may be blasted into space with such energy that the exploding star outshines its entire galaxy. Only seven supernovas are known of before the 17th cent.; the remnants of the most famous, in A.D. 1054, are visible as the CRAB NEBULA. Supernova explosions release tremendous amounts of RADIO energy, X RAYS, COSMIC RAYS, and many of the heavier ELEMENTS that make up planets.

superstring theory Any of a number of theories in PARTICLE PHYSICS that treat SUBATOMIC PARTICLES as infinitesimal one-dimensional "stringlike" objects rather than dimensionless points in SPACE-TIME. Different vibrations of the strings correspond to different particles. Introduced in attempts to describe the STRONG FORCE, superstring theories might provide a fully self-consistent QUANTUM FIELD THEORY that could describe gravity as well as the WEAK, strong, and ELECTROMAGNETIC FORCES. The most promising superstring theories propose 10 dimensions; four correspond to the three ordinary spatial dimensions and time; the rest are curled up and not perceptible.

supply and demand Relationship between the quantity of a commodity available for sale and the quantity that consumers are willing and able to buy. Demand depends on the PRICE of the commodity and competing items, and on consumers' incomes, needs, and tastes. Supply depends not only on the price obtainable for the commodity but also on the prices of similar products, the techniques of production, and the availability and costs of inputs. If buyers want to purchase more of a commodity than is available, they will tend to bid the price up. If more is available than buyers care to purchase, suppliers will bid prices down. The function of the MARKET is to equalize demand and supply through the price mechanism.

supply-side economics Theory that focuses on influencing the supply of labor and goods, using tax cuts and benefit cuts as incentives to work and produce goods. It was expounded by Arthur Laffer (b.1940) and implemented by Pres. Ronald REAGAN in the 1980s. Supporters point to the economic growth of the 1980s as proof of its efficacy; detractors point to the massive federal deficits and speculation that accompanied that growth.

suprarenal gland See ADRENAL GLAND

Suprematism First movement of pure geometrical abstraction in art, introduced in Russia about 1913. Originated by Kazimir MALEVICH and disseminated by El LISSITZKY and the BAUHAUS school, it had far-reaching influence on Western art and design. Malevich aimed to convey the "supremacy of feeling in art," which he believed could be expressed through the simplest of visual forms. He exhibited the first Suprematist compositions in 1915, the year he issued the Suprematist manifesto.

Supreme Court of the United States Final court of APPEAL in the U.S. judicial system and final interpreter of the U.S. CONSTITUTION. Instituted by the Constitution in 1787, it was granted authority to act in cases arising under the Constitution, laws, or treaties of the U.S.; in controversies to which the U.S. is a party; in controversies between states or between citizens of different states; in cases of admiralty and maritime jurisdiction; and in cases affecting diplomats. Its size, which is set by Congress, varied somewhat before stabilizing at nine in 1869. Appointments to the Court are made by the president with the advice and consent of the Senate. The Court has from an early date exercised the power of JUDICIAL REVIEW. Relatively few cases are brought in its original jurisdiction. The usual route to the Court is by appeal. Much of its work consists of clarifying, refining, and testing the Constitution's philosophic ideals and translating them into working principles.

Supremes U.S. vocal trio, one of the most successful female groups in history. The original Supremes—Diana Ross (b.1944), Mary Wilson (b.1944), and Florence Ballard (1939–1976)—began recording for Motown (as The Primettes) on graduating from high school in Detroit. Their long string of MOTOWN hits in the mid-1960s began with "Where Did Our Love Go?" In 1966 Ballard was replaced with Cindy Birdsong (b.1939). Ross left the Supremes in 1969 to pursue a highly successful solo career, and Wilson left in 1977.

Sur See TYRE

Surabaya \ˌsu̇r-ə-ˈbī-ə\ Seaport city (pop., 1995 est.: 2,701,000), NE coast of JAVA, Indonesia. It is Indonesia's second-largest city and main naval base. It has been E Java's chief trading center since the 14th cent. The Dutch gained control in the 18th cent. Occupied by the Japanese in World War II, it suffered heavy damage; it was damaged again during Indonesia's war for independence (1945–49).

Surat \ˈsu̇r-ət, sə-ˈrat\ City (metro. area pop., 2001: 2,811,000), SE Gujarat state, W central India. A major seaport from the 16th cent., it was conquered by the Mughals in 1573 and was twice sacked by the Marathas in the 17th cent. It became a center for textile manufacturing and shipbuilding. The British established their first Indian trading station there about 1612, marking the beginning of the British empire in India. It served as the seat of the British Indian government until the late 17th cent., when the seat was moved to BOMBAY. Surat's cottons, silks, brocades, and objects of gold and silver are still famous.

surface In geometry, a two-dimensional collection of points (flat surface), a three-dimensional collection of points whose cross section is a CURVE (curved surface), or the boundary of any three-dimensional solid. In general, a surface is a continuous boundary dividing a three-dimensional space into two regions. Surfaces are often called by the names of the regions they enclose, but a surface is essentially two-dimensional and has an area, and the region it encloses is three-dimensional and has a volume.

surface mining See STRIP MINING

surface tension Property of a liquid surface that causes it to act like a stretched elastic membrane (see ELASTICITY). Its strength depends on the forces of attraction among the particles of the liquid itself and with the gas, solid, or liquid with which it comes in contact. Surface tension allows certain insects to stand on the surface of water and can support a razor blade placed horizontally on the liquid's surface. Surface tension results in spherical drops of liquid, as the liquid tends to minimize its surface area. See also CAPILLARITY.

surfing Sport of riding breaking waves toward the shore, especially with a surfboard. The sport originated prehistorically in the South Seas. In 1821 surfing was banned by mis-

sionaries who thought it immoral. It was revived in the 1920s by the famous Hawaiian swimmer Duke Kahanamoku (1890–1968). Today surfing is enjoyed throughout the world. The goal is to maneuver on the unbroken face of the wave, preferably as far back toward the curl ("tube") as possible. In addition to surfboards, surfers can use belly- and kneeboards or kayaks, or they can bodysurf using no vehicle at all.

surgery Branch of medicine concerned with treatment by physical means. In addition to operations requiring access to the inside of the body (open surgery), it includes manipulation from outside the body (e.g., setting of a broken bone, skin grafts). Modern surgery began in the mid-19th cent. with use of ANESTHETICS and ANTISEPTICS. Other important advances have included DIAGNOSTIC IMAGING, BLOOD TYPING, intubation to support breathing, intravenous administration of fluids and drugs, heart-lung machines (see ARTIFICIAL HEART), ENDOSCOPY, and devices that monitor body functions. See also MICROSURGERY, OPEN-HEART SURGERY, ORTHOPEDICS, PLASTIC SURGERY, TRANSPLANT.

Suriname \ˌsu̇-rə-ˈnä-mə\ *officially* **Republic of Suriname** *formerly* **Dutch Guiana** Nation, N central coast of S. America. Area: 63,251 sq mi (163,820 sq km). Population (2000): 431,000. Capital: PARAMARIBO. The population includes E. Indians, Creoles, Javanese, and smaller groups of blacks,

SURINAME

Scale 1: 8,710,000
0   40   80 mi
0   60   120 km

©1999, Encyclopædia Britannica, Inc.

Chinese, S. American Indians, and Dutch. Languages: Dutch (official), English, Sranan (a creole), Hindi. Religions: Christianity; also Hinduism and Islam. Currency: Suriname guilder. The country has a low, narrow coastal plain, with inland savannas, a forested plateau region, and mountain ranges. Seven major rivers, including the Courantyne, MARONI, and Suriname, cross it to empty into the Atlantic. Bauxite mining, aluminum production, and agriculture are the largest sectors of the economy. Exports include rice, bananas, sugarcane, oranges, and shrimp. It is a republic with one legislative house; its head of state and government is the president. Suriname was inhabited by various native peoples prior to European settlement. Spanish explorers claimed it in 1593, but the Dutch began to settle there in 1602, followed by the English in 1651. It was ceded to the Dutch in 1667, and in 1682 the Dutch W. India Co. introduced coffee and sugarcane plantations and African slaves to cultivate them. Slavery was abolished in 1863, and indentured servants were brought from China, Java, and India to work the plantations, adding to the population mix. Except for brief interludes of British rule (1799–1802,

1804–15), it remained a Dutch colony. It gained internal autonomy in 1954 and independence in 1975. A military coup in 1980 ended civilian control until the electorate approved a new constitution in 1987. Military control resumed after a coup in 1990. Elections were held in 1992, followed by a resumption of democratic government.

Surrealism Movement in the visual arts and literature that flourished in Europe between World Wars I and II. A reaction against the "rationalism" that had led to World War I, it was founded in 1924 by André BRETON as a means of joining dream and fantasy to everyday reality to form "an absolute reality, a surreality." Drawing on the theories of Sigmund FREUD, he concluded that the unconscious was the wellspring of the imagination. Surrealism's major achievements were in painting. Some artists practiced organic, emblematic, or absolute Surrealism, expressing the unconscious through suggestive yet indefinite biomorphic images (Jean ARP, Max ERNST, André MASSON, Joan MIRÓ). Others created realistically painted images, removed from their context and reassembled within a paradoxical or shocking framework (Salvador DALÍ, René MAGRITTE).

Surrey County (pop., 1998 est.: 1,060,000), S England. It is located southwest of LONDON. Sheep raising was an important medieval activity, and by the 16th cent. a cloth trade was also growing. Transport of local timber was facilitated in 1801 when the Surrey Iron Railway was established as the first public railway. During the 19th cent., the world's densest network of suburban railways developed in N Surrey. Suburban growth continued after World War II.

Surrey, Earl of *orig.* **Henry Howard** (1517–1547) English poet. Because of his aristocratic birth and connections, Surrey was involved in the jockeying for place that accompanied HENRY VIII's policies. Accused of treason and Roman Catholicism, he was executed at age 30. Most of his poetry was published 10 years later. With Thomas WYATT, he introduced into England the styles and meters of the Italian humanist poets, laying the foundation of a great age in English poetry. He translated two books of VIRGIL's *Aeneid,* marking the first use in English of BLANK VERSE; and was the first to develop the SONNET form used by William SHAKESPEARE.

Surtees, Robert Smith (1803–1864) English novelist. Passionately addicted to riding to hounds from his youth, Surtees devoted nearly all his writings to horses and riding. In 1831 he launched *New Sporting Magazine.* His famous comic character Mr. Jorrocks, a blunt Cockney grocer entirely given over to fox hunting, appeared in *Jorrocks's Jaunts and Jollities* (1838), *Handley Cross* (1843), and *Hillingdon Hall* (1845). These and later novels portray the boredom, ill manners, discomfort, and coarse food of English provincial life.

surveying Method of making accurate measurements of the earth's surfaces. Its principal uses are in transportation, building, land use, and communications. The Romans are said to have used the plane table, which consists of a drawing board mounted on a tripod and a straightedge along which lines are drawn. The publication of logarithmic tables (1620) led to portable angle-measuring "topographic" instruments; they included pivoted arms for sighting and could be used for measuring both horizontal and vertical angles. Two revolutionary 20th-cent. innovations were photogrammetry (mapping from aerial photographs) and electronic distance measurement, including use of the laser.

Surveyor Any of seven unmanned U.S. space probes sent to the MOON 1966–68. Surveyor 2 crashed on the moon, and radio contact with Surveyor 4 was lost minutes before landing, but the rest sent back thousands of pictures; some sampled and tested lunar soil. Surveyor 6 made the first liftoff from an extraterrestrial body; Surveyor 7 landed in the lunar highlands, which showed differences from lower areas. See also LUNA, PIONEER.

Surya In HINDUISM, the sun and the sun god. Though once ranking with the major Hindu deities, he is now worshiped as the supreme deity only by the small Savra sect. Nevertheless, he is still invoked by all orthodox Hindus in daily prayer, and his temples are found throughout India. The PURANAS record that the weapons of the gods were forged from pieces trimmed from Surya.

Suryavarman II \ˌsùr-yə-ˈvär-mən\ (d.c.1150) Cambodian king (c.1113–50) under whom ANGKOR WAT was built. He established sole rule over Cambodia about 1113, and expanded it to include much of modern Thailand, portions of Vietnam, and part of the Malay Peninsula. He promulgated VAISHNAVISM, rather than the Buddhism of his predecessors, as the official religion. Construction of Angkor Wat, the world's largest religious structure, began under Suryavarman, and he figures prominently in its decorations. He died during a campaign against the kingdom of Champa.

Susanna Figure in an apocryphal book of the Bible. Set in Babylon during the Jewish exile, it tells of a woman falsely accused of adultery by two elders who had earlier tried to seduce her. She is saved from death by DANIEL's intervention. The tale is one of a cycle of traditions added to the Book of Daniel when it was translated into Greek.

Suslov \ˈsüs-ˌlȯf\, **Mikhail (Andreyevich)** (1902–1982) Soviet ideologue. After teaching economics, in the 1930s he helped supervise the Stalinist purges in the Urals and the Ukraine. Later a leading official in the Caucasus, he supervised the deportation of ethnic minorities in World War II. From 1955 he held a pivotal position in the ruling clique. A political conservative, he helped Nikita KHRUSHCHEV quell a conspiracy in the Politburo in 1957, but organized the bloodless coup in 1964 that ousted Khrushchev and substituted Leonid BREZHNEV.

suspension, automobile Elastic members designed to cushion the impact of road irregularities on a portion of an automotive vehicle. The members link the vehicle's tires with its suspended portion, and usually consist of springs and SHOCK ABSORBERS. Spring elements used for automobile suspension members include leaf springs, coil springs, torsion bars, and air springs. The springs absorb the energy of impacts of the tires along the road surface, and the shocks damp or dissipate that energy. See diagram, right.

Susquehanna River \ˌsəs-kwə-ˈha-nə\ River, central New York, Pennsylvania, and Maryland. One of the longest rivers in the E U.S., it is about 444 mi (715 km) long. It rises in Otsego Lake, central New York, and winds through the APPALACHIAN MTNS. before flowing into N CHESAPEAKE BAY. Its valley was a significant land route to the OHIO RIVER, and later a coal mining region.

Sutherland, Graham (Vivian) (1903–1980) British painter. After studying art in London, he taught and practiced printmaking (1926–40). His early representationalism evolved into Surrealism. Turning to painting, he served as an official war artist 1940–45; his war paintings are an evocative record of desolation. His "thorn period" began with his important *Crucifixion* (1946); he later incorporated insect and plant forms, particularly thorns, which he transformed into powerful totemic images. He designed the enormous tapestry (c.1955–61) for the new Coventry Cathedral.

Sutherland, Joan (*later* **Dame Joan**) (b.1926) Australian soprano. After debuting in Sydney in 1947, she moved to London. Having sung minor roles at Covent Garden from 1952, she rose to major stardom in 1959 in *Lucia di Lammermoor*. She made her Metropolitan Opera debut in 1961, and her gloriously beautiful voice made her a favorite there and worldwide in bel canto roles until her retirement in 1991.

Sutlej River \ˈsət-ˌlej\ River, Asia. The longest of the "Five Rivers" that give PUNJAB its name, it is 900 mi (1,450 km) long. It rises in SW Tibet and flows west through the HIMALAYAS and southwest across Punjab province of Pakistan. It forms 65 mi (105 km) of the Indo–Pakistani border. It joins the Chenab River in Pakistan to become the Panjnad, the link between the Five Rivers and the INDUS.

sutra \ˈsü-trə\ *Pali* **sutta** In HINDUISM, a brief aphoristic composition; in BUDDHISM, a more extended exposition of a subject and the basic form of the SCRIPTURE of both THERAVADA and MAHAYANA traditions. Early Indian philosophers did not work with written texts, and later philosophers often disdained them, so there was a need for very brief works that could be committed to memory. Eventually nearly all Indian philosophical systems had their own sutras. See also DIAMOND SUTRA, LOTUS SUTRA, TRIPITAKA.

suttee *or* **sati** \ˈsə-ˌtē, ˌsə-ˈtē\ Indian practice whereby a widow burns herself to death either on the funeral pyre of

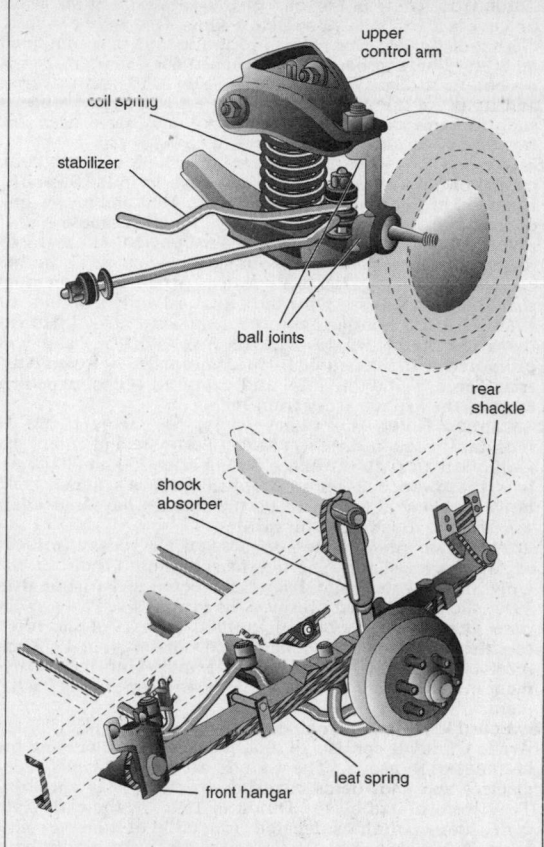

Suspension, automobile A vehicle is suspended over its wheels by springs, usually either coil or leaf springs. Irregularities in the road surface are transmitted mechanically to the springs. The energy in the compressed springs is dissipated by shock absorbers mounted inside coil springs or beside leaf springs.

her husband or soon after his death. The custom may be rooted in ancient beliefs that a husband needed his companions in the afterlife. Developed by the 4th cent. B.C., it became widespread in the 17th–18th cent. but was banned in British India in 1829. Frequent instances continued to occur for many years thereafter, and occasional instances are still reported today.

Sutter, John (Augustus) *orig.* Johann August Suter (1803–1880) Swiss-U.S. (German-born) pioneer. He arrived in the U.S. in 1834. Having obtained a land grant from the Mexican governor, he established the colony of Nueva Helvetia (later SACRAMENTO, Cal.). On the American River he built Sutter's Fort, a trading post, in 1841. When gold was found there in 1848, he tried to keep it a secret. In the resulting GOLD RUSH, squatters and gold seekers invaded his land and stole his goods and livestock. U.S. courts denied his claim to his Mexican land grant, and Sutter was bankrupt by 1852.

Sutton, Walter S(tanborough) (1877–1916) U.S. geneticist. Born in Utica, N.Y., he became a surgeon. In 1902 he provided the earliest detailed demonstration that somatic chromosomes (those in cells other than sex cells) occur in distinct pairs of like chromosomes, hypothesizing that chromosomes carry the units of inheritance (genes) and that their behavior during meiosis is the physical basis of Gregor MENDEL's law of HEREDITY. His work formed the foundation for the chromosomal theory of heredity.

Sutton Hoo Estate in Suffolk, England, the site of the grave or cenotaph of an Anglo-Saxon king. One of the richest Germanic burials ever found in Europe (1939), it contained an 80-ft (24-m) wooden ship equipped for the afterlife (but no body). It displayed both pagan and Christian features, and its grave goods included solid gold and silver objects such as cups and bowls. The burial may have been for Raedwald (d.624?) or Aethelhere (d.654).

Suva Seaport town (metro. area pop., 1996 est.: 167,000), capital of Fiji. It has one of the best harbors in the S Pacific. Founded in 1849, it was made a city in 1952 and is now one of the largest urban centers in the S. Pacific islands.

Suvorov \sü-'vȯ-rȯf\, **Aleksandr (Vasilyevich)** (1729–1800) Russian army commander. Joining the army at 15, he became an officer in 1754. He wrote a battle-training manual that helped Russia win the Russo–Polish conflict of 1768–72 and a conflict with the Turks in 1773–74. He led the army in the Russo–Turkish War (1787–92) and was promoted to field marshal. He commanded a Russo-Austrian force in Italy in 1799 and captured Milan, expelling most of the French army from Italy.

Suwannee River \sə-'wä-nē\ River, SE Georgia and N Florida. It rises in the OKEFENOKEE SWAMP and enters the Gulf of MEXICO at Suwannee Sound after 250 mi (400 km). It is the Swanee River of Stephen FOSTER's famed "Old Folks at Home." In the 1780s the sound's bays and inlets were rendezvous points for pirates.

Suzman \'súz-mən\, **Helen** orig. Helen Gavronsky (b.1917) S. African legislator. She taught economic history at the Univ. of Witwatersrand 1945–52. Elected to Parliament in 1953, she and 11 others formed the Progressive Party to oppose APARTHEID. Reelected in 1961, until 1974 she often cast the lone vote against apartheid measures. In 1978 she received the U.N. Human Rights award. Until her retirement in 1989, she remained a significant voice in the Parliament.

Svalbard \'sfäl-,bär\ Archipelago, Arctic Ocean, north of the Arctic Circle. It consists of nine main islands, including the SPITSBERGEN group. The islands are mountainous, with glaciers and snowfields covering nearly 60% of the area. They were visited by the Dutch in 1596. In the early 20th cent., many countries debated ownership of mineral rights there. A Norwegian possession since 1925, the islands have been the site of many scientific polar expeditions (beginning in 1773). The population numbers about 3,000.

Sverdlov \'sv^yerd-lȯf\, **Yakov (Mikhaylovich)** (1885–1919) Soviet politician. A Bolshevik organizer in the Urals, he was often arrested and exiled. In the RUSSIAN REVOLUTION OF 1917, he headed the Bolshevik secretariat and helped plan the October coup that brought the Bolsheviks to power. As titular head of state, he worked closely with Vladimir LENIN to consolidate power. His death at 33 from an infectious illness left a void in the hierarchy that was filled by Joseph STALIN in 1922.

Sverdlovsk See YEKATERINBURG

Svyatoslav I \'svyȧ-tə-sləf\ (d.972) Grand prince of Kiev (945–72). The greatest of the Varangian (Viking) princes of early Russian history, he defeated the Khazars and other peoples in the N Caucasus (963–65) and conquered the Bulgars (967). He refused to cede his conquest to the Byzantines until their army defeated him and forced the surrender of Balkan territory (971). He was killed in an ambush on his way back to Kiev.

Swabia German **Schwaben** \'shväb-ᵊn\ Duchy, medieval Germany, nearly coextensive with modern Baden-Württemberg, Hesse, and W Bavaria states, as well as parts of E Switzerland and Alsace. The Suevi and Alemanni tribes occupied the area from the 3rd cent. A.D. From about the 10th cent., it became one of the five great tribal duchies of early medieval Germany. It was ruled by the HOHENSTAUFEN DYNASTY 1077–1268. Several alliances of Swabian cities, known as the Swabian Leagues, were formed in the 14th–16th cent. The region made up a division of the HOLY ROMAN EMPIRE in the 16th–19th cent. Its chief cities included AUGSBURG, FREIBURG, Konstanz, and Ulm.

Swahili language \swä-'hē-lē\ BANTU LANGUAGE spoken in Tanzania, Kenya, Uganda, and Congo (Zaire) as a first language by more than 2 million people and as a second lan-guage by about 60 million. Standard Swahili is based on a dialect of Zanzibar, which was spread far inland in the 19th cent. by ivory and slave traders. European colonial governments that occupied E. Africa toward the end of the century also used it. Modern Swahili is usually written in the LATIN ALPHABET. Among Bantu languages, Swahili is remarkable for the number of Arabic loanwords it has absorbed.

swallow Any of 74 species (family Hirundinidae) of songbirds found nearly worldwide. Swallows are 4–9 in. (10–23 cm) long, with long, pointed, narrow wings. The dark upper plumage may have a metallic sheen. Swallows capture insects on the wing. They nest in tree holes, burrow into sandbank, or plaster mud nests to walls. Some species (e.g., the common swallow, *Hirundo rustica*) are long-distance migrants; all have a strong homing instinct. The swallows of California's San Juan Capistrano Mission are cliff swallows (*Petrochelidon pyrrhonota*). See also MARTIN.

swallowing Act that moves food from the mouth to the STOMACH. The TONGUE pushes liquid or chewed food mixed with SALIVA into the PHARYNX. REFLEX takes over as the soft PALATE rises to close off the nasal cavity; the LARYNX rises and the epiglottis covers the TRACHEA, interrupting breathing. Pressure in the mouth and pharynx pushes food toward the ESOPHAGUS, whose upper sphincter opens to let food in. Breathing resumes as the larynx lowers. As PERISTALSIS pushes food to the stomach, the lower esophageal sphincter opens. Painful swallowing is usually caused by INFLAMMATION.

swami See SADHU AND SWAMI

Swammerdam \'sväm-ər-,däm\, **Jan** (1637–1680) Dutch naturalist. An adept microscopist, in 1658 he became the first person to observe and describe red blood cells. In his *General History of Insects* he accurately described and illustrated the life histories and anatomy of many insect species. He studied tadpole and adult frog anatomy and described the ovarian follicles of mammals. His improved techniques for injecting wax and dyes into cadavers had important consequences for the study of human anatomy. His ingenious experiments showed that muscles alter in shape but not in size during contraction.

swamp Freshwater wetland ecosystem characterized by poorly drained mineral soils and plant life dominated by trees. Swamps have a sufficient water supply to keep the ground waterlogged, and the water has a high-enough mineral content to stimulate decay of organisms and to prevent the accumulation of organic materials. See also MARSH.

swan Long-necked, heavy-bodied, big-footed WATERFOWL (genus *Cygnus,* family Anatidae). Among waterfowl, swans are the largest and fastest, both swimming and flying; at about 50 lbs (23 kg), the mute swan (*C. olor*) is the heaviest flying bird. Swans dabble in shallows for aquatic plants. Five all-white, black-legged species live in the Northern Hemisphere; a black and a black-necked species live in the Southern Hemisphere. Males (cobs) and females (pens) look alike. Swans mate for life.

Mute swan (*Cygnus olor*)

Their graceful form when swimming has made swans emblems of beauty for centuries.

Swansea \'swän-zē\ Welsh **Abertawe** \,a-bər-'taú-ə\ Seaport (pop., 1999 est.: 230,000), S Wales. Lying along the BRISTOL CHANNEL, it is the second-largest city in Wales. It dates from the 12th cent. Up to the early 18th cent. it was a small market town, but by the mid-19th cent. it was the center of the world copper trade. Though badly damaged by German bombing in 1941 it has been redeveloped. The poet Dylan THOMAS was born here.

Swanson, Gloria orig. Gloria May Josephine Svensson (1899–1983) U.S. film actress. Born in Chicago, she achieved stardom in a series of C. B. DEMILLE farces, including *Male and Female* (1919), *Zaza* (1923), and *Madame*

Sans-Gêne (1925). The glamorous queen of silent movies, she formed her own production company with backing from her lover Joseph KENNEDY, making *Sadie Thompson* (1928) and the disastrous *Queen Kelly* (1928). She made an acclaimed comeback as an aging silent-film star in *Sunset Boulevard* (1950).

SWAPO See SOUTH-WEST AFRICA PEOPLE'S ORGANIZATION

Swarthmore College Private liberal-arts college in Swarthmore, Pa., near Philadelphia. It was founded by a group of Quakers in 1864. Consistently ranked as one of the best colleges in the U.S., it participates in an exchange program with BRYN MAWR and HAVERFORD colleges and the Univ. of PENNSYLVANIA. Enrollment is about 1,500.

swastika Equilateral cross with its arms bent at right angles, all in the same rotary direction, usually clockwise. It is used widely throughout the world as a symbol of prosperity and good fortune. In India, it continues to be the most common auspicious symbol of Hindus and Jains, as well as for Buddhists, for whom it symbolizes the Buddha's feet or footprints. In China and Japan, it has been used to denote plurality, prosperity, and long life. It occurs as a motif in early Christian and Byzantine art, as well as in Maya and Navajo art. The counterclockwise swastika, suggested as a general anti-Semitic symbol in 1910 by Guido von List, was adopted as the symbol of the NAZI PARTY at its founding in 1919–20.

Swazi \'swä-zē\ *or* **Swati** \'swä-tē\ Bantu-speaking people inhabiting the grasslands of Swaziland and neighboring regions. The Swazi (numbering 2 million) are chiefly agriculturalists and herders. Political, economic, and ritual power is shared by a hereditary male ruler and his mother, and the king's wives and children are settled in dispersed royal villages.

Swaziland *officially* **Kingdom of Swaziland** Nation, S Africa. Area: 6,704 sq mi (17,364 sq km). Population (2000): 1,083,000. Capitals: MBABANE (administrative); LOBAMBA

prime minister. Stone tools and rock paintings indicate prehistoric habitation in the region, but it was not settled until the BANTU-speaking Swazi people migrated there in the 18th cent. and established the nucleus of the Swazi nation. The British gained control in the 19th cent. after the Swazi king sought their aid against the Zulus. Following the S. AFRICAN WAR, the British governor of TRANSVAAL administered Swaziland; his powers were transferred to the British high commissioner in 1906. In 1949 the British rejected the Union of S. Africa's request to control Swaziland. The country gained limited self-government in 1963 and achieved independence in 1968. In the 1970s new constitutions were framed based on the supreme authority of the king and traditional tribal government. During the 1990s forces demanding democracy arose, but the kingdom remained in place as a new constitution was being drafted.

sweat gland Either of two types of PERSPIRATION GLANDS in the SKIN. Eccrine sweat glands use evaporation to cool the skin by secreting water when body temperature rises. Apocrine sweat glands, usually associated with hair follicles, are concentrated in the underarms and genital region. Starting at puberty, hormones stimulate them to continuously secrete a fatty sweat.

sweat lodge Hut or lodge used by American Indian peoples for ritual or therapeutic sweating. It is usually made of bent saplings and skin or blanket coverings and is heated by steam from water poured on hot stones. Some groups believe the lodge becomes a symbolic center in which the six cardinal directions, the past and present, and the human and spiritual worlds are connected.

Sweden *officially* **Kingdom of Sweden** *Swedish* **Sverige** \'sve-rē-yə\ Nation, N Europe, located on the Scandinavian Peninsula. Area: 173,732 sq mi (449,964 sq km). Population (2000): 8,864,000. Capital: STOCKHOLM. The population is largely homogeneous, although there are Finnish and Lap-

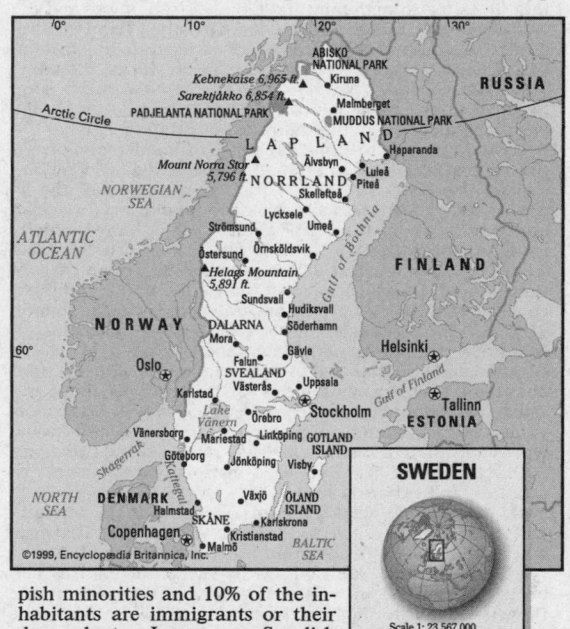

SWAZILAND
Scale 1: 2,956,000
0   10   20   30 mi
0   20   40 km

SWEDEN
Scale 1: 23,567,000
0   100   200 mi
0   100   200   300 km

©1999, Encyclopædia Britannica, Inc.

(legislative). About nine-tenths of the population is SWAZI and about one-tenth ZULU, with a small number of other minorities. Languages: Swazi, English (both official). Religions: Christianity, animism. Currency: lilangeni. The landlocked country is composed of high, middle, and low velds, culminating in the Lubombo escarpment in the east. Fauna includes hippopotamus, antelope, zebra, and crocodile. Four major rivers, including the Komati, flow through the country and irrigate citrus and sugarcane estates. Mineral resources include asbestos and diamonds. It is a monarchy with two legislative houses; its head of state and government is the king, assisted by the

pish minorities and 10% of the inhabitants are immigrants or their descendents. Language: Swedish (official). Religion: Church of Sweden (Lutheranism). Currency: Swedish krona. Sweden has three regions. Mountainous Norrland covers about three-fifths of the country and has vast forests and large ore deposits. Svealand has undulating glacial ridges and contains most of the country's 90,000 lakes. Gotaland comprises the stony Småland highlands and the rich Skåne plains. About 15% of Sweden lies north of the ARCTIC CIRCLE. Its economy is largely based on services, heavy industries, and international trade. It has large deposits of iron ore; industries include mining, lumbering, steel manufacturing, and tourism. It raises grains, sugar beets, potatoes, and livestock. One of the world's richest countries, it is known for its comprehensive social welfare system. It is a constitutional monarchy with one legislative house; its chief of state is the king, and the head of government is the prime minister. The first inhabitants were apparently hunters who crossed the land bridge from Europe around 12,000 B.C. During the Viking era (9th–10th cent.), the Swedes controlled river trade in E Europe between the Baltic Sea and Black Sea and also raided W European lands. Sweden was loosely united and Christianized in the 11th–12th cent. It conquered the Finns in the 12th cent. and in the 14th united with Norway and Denmark under a single monarhy. It broke away in 1523 under GUSTAV I VASA. In the 17th cent. it emerged as a great European power in the Baltic region, but its dominance declined after its defeat in the Second NORTHERN WAR (1700–21). It became a constitutional monarchy in 1809 and united with Norway 1815–1905; it acknowledged Norwegian independence in 1905. It maintained its neutrality during both World Wars. It was a charter member of the U.N., but abstained from membership in NATO and the EUROPEAN UNION until the 1990s. A new constitution drafted in 1975 reduced the monarch's powers to ceremonial head of state. In 1997 it decided to begin the controversial shutdown of its NUCLEAR POWER industry.

Swedenborg, Emanuel (1688–1772) Swedish scientist, theologian, and mystic. After graduating from the Univ. of Uppsala, he spent five years abroad studying the natural sciences. On his return he began publication of Sweden's first scientific journal, *Daedelus Hyperboreas*. His writing gradually shifted toward philosophy of nature and metaphysics, as he became convinced that the universe had a basically spiritual structure. In 1744 he had a vision of Christ, and in 1745 he received a call to abandon worldly learning. After that, he came to maintain that God was the power and life within all creatures, and that the Christian Trinity represented the three essential qualities of God: love, wisdom, and activity. He published more than 30 works, including *The True Christian Religion* (1771). Societies were soon founded to propagate his pantheistic teaching, notably the New Jerusalem Church, established in London in 1787.

Swedish language National language of Sweden and one of two official languages of Finland, spoken by about 9 million people. It belongs to the E. Scandinavian group of the N. GERMANIC LANGUAGES and is closely related to Norwegian and Danish. Its history until about 1225 is known chiefly from RUNIC WRITING. Modern Swedish is usually dated from 1526, when a translation of the New Testament was first printed. Standard Swedish has no noun inflections except for the possessive and has only neuter and common genders. Like Norwegian, it has two tonal word accents.

Sweelinck \\'swā-liŋk\\, **Jan Pieterszoon** (1562–1621) Dutch composer. As organist at Amsterdam's Old Church from about 1580, he became famous for his improvisations, and taught important composers of the N. German school of organists (which would culminate in J. S. BACH). His vocal works appeared in *Psalms of David* (1604–14) and *Cantiones sacrae* (1619); he also published many keyboard fantasias, toccatas, and variation sets.

sweet pea Annual plant (*Lathyrus odoratus*) of the pea family (see LEGUME), native to Italy and widely cultivated elsewhere for its beautiful, fragrant flowers. The long (4–6 ft, or 1.2–2 m), vinelike stem climbs by means of tendrils and bears featherlike leaves. White, pink, red, violet, or purple flowers are borne singly or in clusters of two to four. The fruit is a hairy pod about 2 in. (5 cm) long. Hundreds of varieties of sweet pea have been developed.

sweet potato Food plant (*Ipomoea batatas*; MORNING-GLORY FAMILY) native to tropical America and widely cultivated. Botanically unrelated to the white POTATO or the YAM, sweet potatoes are oblong or pointed oval, tuberous roots. Skin color ranges from light buff to brown to purplish-red; the pulp may be white (highest in starch) to orange (also high in CAROTENE) to purple. Long, trailing plant stems bear funnel-shaped flowers.

Sweyn I *or* **Sweyn Forkbeard** \\'svän\\ (d.1014) King of Denmark (c.987–1014) and VIKING conqueror of Norway and England. He rebelled against his father, Harald Bluetooth (987), chasing him from Denmark. With Swedish and Norwegian allies he defeated OLAF I (c.1000), becoming virtual ruler of Norway. Sweyn led raids on England in 1003–4 and became king after a successful military campaign in 1013, forcing ETHELRED II into exile; the Anglo-Danish empire continued under his son CANUTE THE GREAT.

swift Any of about 75 species (family Apodidae) of birds found almost worldwide. The fastest of small birds, swifts can fly at 70 mph (110 kph). They are 4–9 in. (9–23 cm) long and have long wings and a chunky dark body. Swifts capture insects, drink, bathe, and sometimes mate on the wing. The feet, incapable of perching, are used to cling to vertical surfaces. Swifts use their sticky saliva to glue the nest to a cave wall, the inside of a chimney, or a tree hollow.

Swift, Jonathan (1667–1745) Irish author, the foremost prose satirist in English. He was ordained an Anglican priest in 1695. His first major work, *A Tale of a Tub* (1704), comprises three satiric sketches on religion and learning; he also became known for religious and political essays and impish pamphlets written under the name "Isaac Bickerstaff." Reluctantly setting aside his loyalty to the Whigs, in 1710 he became the leading writer for the Tories because of their support for the established church. *Journal to Stella* (written 1710–13) consists of letters recording his reactions to the changing world. As a re-

Jonathan Swift Painting by Charles Jervas

ward for writing and editing Tory publications, in 1713 he was awarded the deanery of St. Patrick's Cathedral, Dublin. He spent nearly all the rest of his life in Ireland, where he devoted himself to exposing English wrongheaded and unfair treatment of Ireland. His ironic tract "A Modest Proposal" (1729) proposes ameliorating Irish poverty by butchering children and selling them as food to wealthy English landlords. His famously brilliant and bitter satire *Gulliver's Travels* (1726) reflects Swift's vision of humanity's ambiguous position between bestiality and rationality.

swimming Propulsion of the body through water by combined arm and leg motions. Swimming is popular as an all-around body developer and as competitive sport. Events include freestyle (crawl-stroke) races at distances of 50, 100, 200, 400, 800, and 1,500 m; backstroke, breaststroke, and butterfly races at 100 and 200 m; individual medley races at 200 and 400 m; freestyle relays, 4×100 m and 4×200 m; and the medley relay, 4×100 m. Long-distance competitions, usually of 15–37 mi (24–59 km), are generally held on lakes and inland waters.

Swinburne, Algernon Charles (1837–1909) English poet and critic. His verse drama *Atalanta in Calydon* (1865) first showed his lyric powers. *Poems and Ballads* (1866), containing some of his best work, displays his paganism and masochism and provoked controversy. His verse is marked by emphatic rhythms, much alliteration and internal rhyme, and lush subject matter. His health collapsed in 1879 and he spent his last 30 years under a friend's guardianship. Among his outstanding critical writings are his monographs on William SHAKESPEARE (1880), Victor HUGO (1886), and Ben JONSON (1889).

swine fever See HOG CHOLERA

swing JAZZ played with a steady beat using the harmonic structure of popular songs and the BLUES as the basis for improvisations and arrangements. The popular music of the U.S. from about 1930 to 1945, swing is characterized by syncopated rhythmic momentum with equal stress on all four beats of a measure. Larger jazz bands required some arranged material, and the arrangements of Fletcher HENDERSON, Duke ELLINGTON, and Count BASIE made them the primary innovators of big-band swing. See also SWING DANCE.

swing dance Social dance form dating from the 1940s. Danced in the U.S. to SWING music, the dance steps have distinct regional variations, including such forms as the West Coast swing, the East's jitterbug-lindy, and the South's shag. Performance versions include extreme athletic moves. Though swing dance had largely disappeared by 1960, a revival began in the late 1980s and has since spread widely.

Swiss chard See CHARD

Switzerland *officially* **Swiss Confederation** *French* **Suisse** \'swēs\ *German* **Schweiz** \'shvīts\ *Italian* **Svizzera** \'zvēt-tsä-rä\ *Romansh* **Helvetica** Landlocked country, central Europe. Area: 15,940 sq mi (41,284 sq km). Population (2000): 7,177,000. Capital: BERN. The population is German,

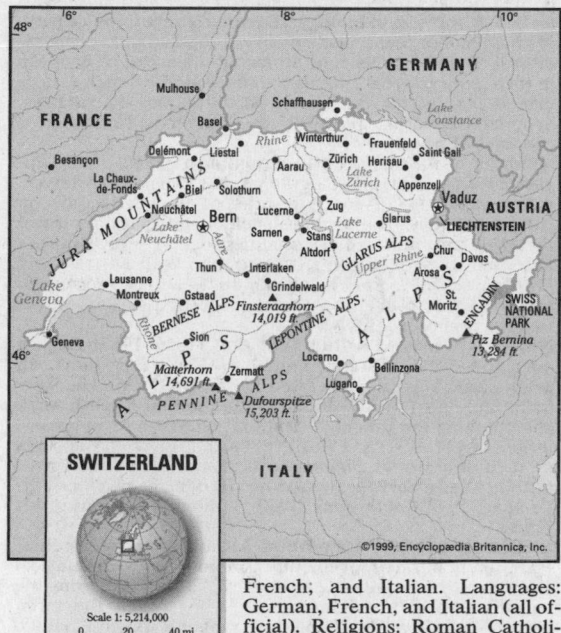

SWITZERLAND

©1999, Encyclopædia Britannica, Inc.

Scale 1: 5,214,000

French, and Italian. Languages: German, French, and Italian (all official). Religions: Roman Catholicism (about 45%), Protestantism (40%). Currency: Swiss franc. Switzerland is divided into three regions: the meadow-covered JURA Mtns.; the central Mittelland, a rich agricultural and urbanized area; and the lofty crags of the ALPS. It is one of the world's major financial centers; its economy is based largely on international trade and banking, as well as light and heavy industries. Its manufactures include watches, precision instruments, machinery, and chemicals. Tourism and agriculture are also important; products include grains, sugar beets, fruits and vegetables, dairy products, chocolate, and wine. Despite diverse races, religions, and languages, Switzerland has maintained the world's oldest democracy for some 700 years. It is a federal state with two legislative houses; its head of state and government is the president. The original inhabitants were the Helvetians, who were conquered by the Romans in the 1st cent. B.C. Germanic tribes penetrated the region from the 3rd–6th cent. A.D., and Muslim and Magyar raiders ventured in during the 10th cent. It came under the FRANKS in the 9th cent. and the HOLY ROMAN EMPIRE in the 11th cnt. In 1291 three cantons formed an anti-Habsburg league that became the nucleus of the Swiss Confederation. It was a center of the REFORMATION, which divided the confederation and led to a period of political and religious conflict. The French organized Switzerland as the Helvetic Republic in 1798. In 1815 the Congress of VIENNA recognized Swiss independence and guaranteed its neutrality. A new federal state was formed in 1848 with Bern as the capital. It remained neutral in both World Wars, and continued to guard this stance. With the formation of the EUROPEAN UNION, it began the effort to achieve provisional association with the European economic area.

sword Hand weapon consisting of a long metal blade fitted with a handle or hilt. Roman swords had a short, flat blade and a hilt distinct from the blade. Medieval European swords were heavy and equipped with a large hilt and a protective guard, or pommel. The blade was straight and pointed. The introduction of firearms and the consequent discarding of body armor required the swordsman to be able to parry, and the rapier, with its narrow, pointed blade, came into use. Swords with curved blades were introduced into Europe by the Turks, whose curved scimitar was modified in the West to the cavalry saber. Japanese swords, renowned for hardness and extreme sharpness, were the weapon of the SAMURAI. Repeating firearms ended the sword's military value, though its continued use in duels led to the modern sport of FENCING.

sword dance Folk dance by men holding swords or two-handled blades, expressing themes such as human and animal sacrifice for fertility, battle mime, and defense against evil spirits. It originated in Greek and Roman times. A sword dance appeared in Germany in 1350 and later was part of the court ballet when mock battles were staged. The MORRIS DANCE retains remnants of the sword dance.

swordfish Species (*Xiphias gladius*) of prized food and game fish, found in warm and temperate oceans worldwide. A slender, scaleless fish, it has a tall dorsal fin and a long sword, used for slashing at prey fishes, extending from its snout. The sword is flat, rather than rounded as in MARLINS. The swordfish lacks teeth and pelvic fins. It is purplish or bluish above, silvery below, and grows as large as 15 ft (4.5 m) and 1,000 lbs (450 kg).

Sybaris \'si-bə-rəs\ Ancient Greek city, S Italy, on the Gulf of Tarentum. Founded about 720 B.C. by Achaeans and known for its wealth and luxury (hence the term *sybarite*), it was one of the oldest cities of MAGNA GRAECIA. It was twice razed by the Crotoniates (510 B.C., c.448 B.C.).

sycamore \'si-kə-ˌmȯr\ Any of several distinct trees called by the same name though in different genera and families. In the U.S. the term refers to the American PLANE TREE or buttonwood (*Platanus occidentalis*), a hardy street tree. The sycamore MAPLE (*Acer pseudoplatanus*) is sometimes also called simply sycamore. The biblical sycamore, actually the sycamore FIG (*Ficus sycomorus*), was used by the ancient Egyptians to make mummy cases.

Sydenham \'si-dᵊn-əm\, **Thomas** (1624–1689) British physician. His *Observationes medicae* (1676) was a standard textbook for two centuries. His treatise on gout (1683) is considered his masterpiece. He was among the first to explain the nature of hysteria and St. Vitus' dance (Sydenham's chorea) and to use iron to treat iron-deficiency anemia. Sydenham also named scarlet fever and differentiated it from measles, and helped popularize the use of quinine for malaria.

Sydney City (metro. area pop., 1998 est.: 3,986,000), capital of NEW SOUTH WALES, Australia. Located on Australia's SE coast, it is the oldest and largest city in Australia and a major commercial and manufacturing center. It was founded in 1788 as a penal colony (see BOTANY BAY) and quickly became a major trading center. It is built on one of the world's finest natural harbors. It is dominated by Sydney Harbour Bridge, one of the biggest single-span bridges in the world, and the SYDNEY OPERA HOUSE. It is widely known for its water sports, recreational facilities, cultural life, and universities.

Sydney Opera House Performing-arts center in Sydney, Australia. Its dynamic, imaginative design, by the Danish architect Jørn Utzon (b.1918), placed first in a 1956 competition and brought him international fame. Many problems resulted from the bold design, a series of glittering white shell-shaped roofs. After years of research, he gave the vaults a more spherical geometry, making them easier and more economical to build. The center finally opened in 1973.

Sydow \'sē-dō, *Swed* 'sœ-dȯv\, **Max von** (*orig.* Carl Adolf von) (b.1929) Swedish actor. A noted stage actor in Sweden, he became best known for his dour, brooding characterizations in Ingmar BERGMAN's films, notably *The Seventh Seal* (1957), *The Magician* (1958), *The Virgin Spring* (1960), *Winter Light* (1963), and *The Passion of Anna*

S

(1969). His numerous other movies include *The Greatest Story Ever Told* (1965), *The Exorcist* (1973), and *Pelle the Conqueror* (1988).

syllogism \'si-lə-ˌji-zəm\ Form of argument that, in its most commonly discussed instances, has two categorical propositions as premises and one categorical proposition as conclusion. For example: Every human is mortal (every M is P); every philosopher is human (every S is M); therefore, every philosopher is mortal (every S is P). Such arguments have exactly three terms (human, philosopher, mortal). An argument with three categorical (as opposed to hypothetical) propositions is a categorical syllogism. The term that occurs in both premises but not in the conclusion (human) is the middle term; the predicate term in the conclusion is called the major term, the conclusion the minor term. The pattern in which the terms S, M, and P (minor, middle, major) are arranged is called the figure of the syllogism.

Sylvester II *orig.* Gerbert of Aurillac (c.945–1003) First French pope (999–1003). Renowned as a scholar of logic and mathematics, he became archbishop of Reims (991) and of Ravenna (c.998). As pope he worked closely with Emperor OTTO III, strengthening papal authority in distant states such as Kiev and Norway as well as in Italy. He denounced SIMONY, demanded clerical celibacy, and limited the power of the bishops. He wrote textbooks and other works on mathematics, the sciences, music, and philosophy.

Sylvius \'sil-vē-əs\, **Franciscus** *orig.* **Franz de le Boë** \ˌdä-lä-ˈbō-ä\ *French* **François du Bois** \dǖē-ˈbō-ä\ (1614–1672) German-Dutch physician, physiologist, anatomist, and chemist. He based his medical system on William HARVEY's discovery of the circulation of the blood and felt that the most important life processes, both normal and pathological, took place in the blood. An outstanding teacher, Sylvius had students instructed on hospital wards. He was the first to distinguish glands made up of smaller units with converging ducts from those forming a rounded mass. Several anatomical structures are named after him.

symbiosis Any of several living arrangements between members of two different species, including commensalism, mutualism, and PARASITISM. In commensalism, one species obtains nutrients, shelter, support, or locomotion from the host species, which is substantially unaffected (e.g., REMORAS obtain locomotion and food from sharks). In mutualism, both species benefit; in many mutualistic relationships, neither species can live without the other (e.g., protozoans in the gut of TERMITES digest the wood ingested by the termites).

symbol Communication element intended to represent or stand for a person, object, group, process, or idea. Symbols may be presented graphically (e.g., the CROSS for Christianity) or representationally (e.g., Uncle Sam standing for the U.S.). They may involve associated letters (e.g., C for the chemical element carbon), or they may be assigned arbitrarily (e.g., the dollar symbol). Symbols are not a LANGUAGE of and by themselves; rather they are devices by which ideas often too complex to articulate in ordinary language are transmitted between people sharing a common CULTURE. Every society has evolved a symbol system that reflects a specific cultural logic. Though a symbol may take the discrete form of a wedding ring or a totem pole, symbols tend to appear in clusters and depend on one another for their accretion of meaning and value. See also SEMIOTICS.

symbolic interactionism See INTERACTIONISM

Symbolism In art, a loosely organized movement that flourished in the 1880s and '90s and was closely related to the SYMBOLIST MOVEMENT in literature. In reaction against both REALISM and IMPRESSIONISM, Symbolist painters stressed art's subjective, symbolic, and decorative functions, and turned to the mystical and occult in an attempt to evoke subjective states of mind by visual means. Its leading exponents were Gustave MOREAU, Odilon REDON, and Pierre PUVIS DE CHAVANNES. Though associated primarily with France, it flourished all over Europe and had great international impact.

Symbolist movement Literary movement that originated with a group of French poets in the late 19th cent., spread to painting and the theater, and influenced Russian, European, and American literature of the 20th cent. Reacting against the rigid conventions of traditional French poetry, Symbolist poets sought to convey individual emotional experience through the subtle, suggestive use of highly metaphorical language. Principal Symbolist poets included Stéphane MALLARMÉ, Paul VERLAINE, Arthur RIMBAUD, and Émile VERHAEREN. Many Symbolists were also identified with the DECADENTS. Just as Symbolist painters (see SYMBOLISM) avoided concrete representation in favor of fantasy and imagination, Symbolist dramatists relied on myth, mood, and atmosphere to reveal only indirectly the deeper truths of existence.

symmetry In geometry, the property by which the sides of a figure or object reflect each other across a line (axis of symmetry) or surface; in biology, the orderly repetition of parts of an animal or plant; in chemistry, a fundamental property of orderly arrangements of atoms in molecules or crystals; in physics, a concept of balance illustrated by such fundamental laws as the third of NEWTON'S LAWS OF MOTION. Symmetry in nature underlies one of the most fundamental concepts of beauty.

Symonds \'si-məndz\, **John Addington** (1840–1893) English essayist, poet, and biographer. His chief work, *Renaissance in Italy* (1875–86), is a series of extended essays on cultural history. His writings include translations, travel sketches, and studies of personalities such as Percy B. SHELLEY, Ben JONSON, MICHELANGELO, and Walt WHITMAN. *A Problem in Greek Ethics* (written 1871) and *A Problem in Modern Ethics* (1881) were among the first serious works treating homosexuality.

Symons \'si-mənz\, **Arthur (William)** (1865–1945) English poet and critic. He contributed to *The Yellow Book*, an avant-garde journal, and edited *The Savoy* (1896). His *Symbolist Movement in Literature* (1899), the first English work championing the French SYMBOLIST MOVEMENT in poetry, influenced W. B. YEATS and T. S. ELIOT. His poetry appears in such volumes as *Silhouettes* (1892) and *London Nights* (1895). After a nervous breakdown in 1908, he produced little apart from *Confessions* (1930), a moving account of his illness.

symphonic poem *or* **tone poem** Musical work for orchestra, usually in one movement, inspired by an extramusical story or idea, usually a literary text. It evolved from the concert OVERTURE. Franz LISZT, who coined the term, wrote 13 such works. Famous symphonic poems include Bedrich SMETANA's *Moldau* (1879), Paul DUKAS's *Sorceror's Apprentice* (1897), and Jean SIBELIUS's *Finlandia* (1900).

symphony Long musical composition for orchestra, usually in several movements. The term was used for overtures in early Italian opera. The late-17th-cent. Neapolitan opera overture, or *sinfonia*, had three movements, their tempos being fast-slow-fast. Soon such overtures began to be performed by themselves in concert settings, like another forerunner of the symphony, the CONCERTO GROSSO. The two merged in the symphonies of G. B. Sammartini (1700–1775). Around 1750, German and Viennese composers began to add a minuet movement. F. J. HAYDN wrote over 100 symphonies of remarkable originality in the years 1755–95; since Haydn, it has been regarded as the most important orchestral genre. W. A. MOZART wrote about 35 original symphonies. Ludwig van BEETHOVEN's nine symphonies endowed the genre with enormous weight and ambition. Later symphonists include Franz SCHUBERT, Anton BRUCKNER, Johannes BRAHMS, P. I. TCHAIKOVSKY, and Gustav MAHLER.

symposium In ancient Greece, an aristocratic banquet at which men met to discuss philosophical and political issues and recite poetry. The participants, all male aristocrats, wore garlands and leaned on the left elbow on couches, and there was much drinking of wine. In PLATO's famous *Symposium*, an imaginary dialogue takes place between SOCRATES, ARISTOPHANES, ALCIBIADES, and others on the subject of love. ARISTOTLE, XENOPHON, and EPICURUS wrote symposium literature on other subjects.

synagogue In Judaism, a community house of worship that also serves as a place for assembly and study. Synagogues flourished alongside the ancient Temple cult and existed long before Titus's destruction of the Second Temple (A.D. 70). Thereafter, synagogues took on even greater importance as the focal point of Jewish life. There is no standard synagogue architecture. A typical synagogue contains an ark (where the scrolls of the Law are kept), an "eternal light" burning before the ark, two candelabra, pews, a *bimah* (dais), and sometimes a ritual bath *(mikvah)*.

synapse \'si-,naps\ Site of transmission of electric nerve impulses between two NEURONS or between a neuron and a gland or muscle cell. At chemical synapses, impulses are transmitted across microscopic spaces by chemical substances called NEUROTRANSMITTERS. In electric synapses, direct communication between nerve cells whose membranes are fused is possible because IONS flow between the cells. Electric synapses are found mainly in invertebrates and lower vertebrates; they transmit messages faster than chemical synapses. Chemical transmission seems to have evolved in large, complex vertebrate nervous systems, in which multiple messages must be transmitted over long distances.

synchronized swimming Swimming in which the movements of one or more swimmers are synchronized with a musical accompaniment so as to form changing patterns in the water. The sport developed in the U.S. in the 1930s and was admitted as an Olympic event in 1984; in 1996 the rules were changed to allow only teams of eight women.

syncope \'sin-kə-pē\ Effect of temporary impairment of blood circulation to a part of the body. It is often used as a synonym for fainting, which is loss of consciousness due to inadequate blood flow to the brain. Paleness, nausea, sweating, and then pupil dilation, yawning, deep rapid breathing, and rapid heartbeat usually precede it. It lasts from under a minute to several minutes and may be followed by headache, confusion, and a weak feeling. The cause may be physical (e.g., HEART FAILURE, low blood sugar) or emotional (e.g., fear, anxiety). Local syncope is coldness and numbness in a small area, especially the fingers, from diminished blood flow.

syndicalism \'sin-di-kə-,li-zəm\ Movement that advocated direct action by the working class to abolish the capitalist order, including the state, and replace it with a social order based on workers organized in self-governing production units, or syndicates. It evolved from French trade-union ANARCHISM at the end of the 19th cent. At the peak of its influence, before World War I, the movement had over a million members in Europe, Latin America, and the U.S. After the war, syndicalists tended to drift toward the Soviet model of COMMUNISM or be lured by the prospects for working-class gains offered by LABOR UNIONS and democratic reforms.

Synge \'sin\, **John Millington** (1871–1909) Irish playwright. Inspired by W. B. YEATS with enthusiasm for the Irish language and people, he spent his summers 1899–1902 on the Aran Islands, and he based his first plays, *In the Shadow of the Glen* (1903) and *Riders to the Sea* (1904), on islanders' stories. His most famous play, *The Playboy of the Western World* (1907), with its unsentimental treatment of Irish character traits, caused riots at its opening at the ABBEY THEATRE. His unfinished *Deirdre of the Sorrows* was performed in 1910. Synge was a leading figure of the IRISH LITERARY RENAISSANCE.

synodic period \sə-'nä-dik\ Time required for a body in the SOLAR SYSTEM to return to the same position relative to the sun as seen from earth. The moon's synodic period is the time in which it returns to the same phase (e.g., between one full moon and the next). A planet's synodic period is the time it takes earth to overtake it, or vice versa, as both go around the sun. See also SIDEREAL PERIOD.

syntax Arrangement of words in sentences, clauses, and phrases, and the study of the formation of sentences. In English, syntax is based on word order; for example, "The girl loves the boy" follows standard subject-verb-object word order, and switching the order of such a sentence would change the meaning or make the sentence meaningless. Word order is much more flexible in languages like Latin, in which word endings make it unnecessary to rely on word order to know a word's function in the sentence.

synthesizer Machine that electronically generates and modifies sounds, frequently with the use of a digital computer, for use in the composition of electronic music and in live performance. It generates wave forms and then subjects them to alteration in intensity, duration, frequency, and timbre. It may use subtractive synthesis (removing unwanted components from a signal containing a fundamental and all related overtones), additive synthesis (building tones from signals for pure sine-wave tones), or such other techniques as whole-sound sampling (digital recording of sounds). The first synthesizer was developed around 1955 by RCA. Compact, commercially viable synthesizers with pianolike keyboards were produced in the 1960s by Robert Moog (b.1934) and Donald Buchla (b.1937). With transistor technology, these soon became practical for performance use and became fixtures in rock bands.

synthetic ammonia process See HABER-BOSCH PROCESS

syphilis \'si-fə-ləs\ SEXUALLY TRANSMITTED DISEASE caused by the SPIROCHETE *Treponema pallidum*. Without treatment, it may progress through three stages: primary, characterized by a chancre (sore) and low fever; secondary (weeks to months later; only half of those infected display symptoms), with a rash, LYMPH-NODE swelling, and bone, joint, eye, and nervous-system involvement; and tertiary, after a latency period that can last years. Only one-fourth of those infected display tertiary symptoms, which can be benign or incapacitating and even fatal; almost any part of the body may be attacked. Syphilis can be passed to a fetus from an infected mother. PENICILLIN is effective. See also YAWS.

Syracuse *Italian* **Siracusa** *ancient* Syracusae Seaport city (pop., 1998 est.: 127,000), E coast of Sicily, Italy. Founded in 734 B.C. by Greeks from CORINTH, it was seized by Hippocrates of Gela in 485 B.C. and ruled by tyrants until about 465 B.C. In 413 B.C., during the PELOPONNESIAN WAR, it defeated an Athenian invasion force. Under DIONYSIUS I the Elder 405–367 B.C., it became the most powerful of the Greek cities, fighting three wars against rival CARTHAGE. It fell to Rome in 211 B.C. It was sacked by Frankish invaders in A.D. 280 and captured by Arabs in 878. Now a fishing port and tourist center, it has many examples of medieval and Renaissance architecture as well as Greek and Roman ruins. It was the birthplace of THEOCRITUS and ARCHIMEDES.

Syracuse City (pop., 2000: 147,000), central New York. The site, at the S end of Lake Oneida, was once the headquarters of the IROQUOIS CONFEDERACY. It was visited by the French in the 17th cent. Indian hostility and the swampy location precluded settlement until 1786. Soon a saltworks based on its brine springs began operation; it supplied most of the nation's salt until 1870. Set on the ERIE CANAL, it is a distribution center for the central New York agricultural region. It is the site of SYRACUSE UNIV. (1870).

Syracuse University Private university in Syracuse, N.Y., founded in 1870. It has colleges of arts and sciences, visual and performing arts, and human development, and schools of architecture, engineering, nursing, communications (the S. I. Newhouse School), social work, information studies, management, and public affairs (the Maxwell School). Enrollment is about 14,500.

Syria *officially* **Syrian Arab Republic** Country, SW Asia, E coast of the Mediterranean Sea. Area: 71,498 sq mi (185,180 sq km). Population (2000): 16,306,000. Capital: DAMASCUS. Arabs are the main ethnic group, with Kurds the largest minority. Languages: Arabic (official), French, Kurdish, Armenian, English. Religions: Islam (Sunni, Alawite, Druze), Christianity (minority). Currency: Syrian pound. Syria consists of a coastal zone, with abundant water supplies; a mountain zone that includes the Anti-Lebanon Mtns.; and a portion of the SYRIAN DESERT. The EUPHRATES RIVER is its most important water source and only navigable river. It has a mixed economy based on agriculture, trade, and mining and manufacturing. Crops include cotton, cereals, fruits, tobacco, and livestock. Mineral resources include petroleum, natural gas, and iron ore; manufactures include textiles, cement, and shoes. It is a republic with one legislative house; its head of state and government is the president, whose religion is required to be Islam. Islam is the basis of the legal system. Syria has been inhabited for several thousand years. From the 3rd millennium B.C., it has been under the control variously of

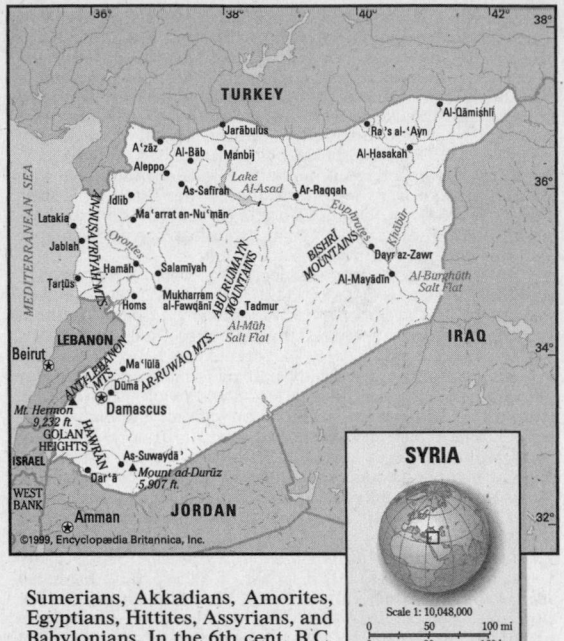

Sumerians, Akkadians, Amorites, Egyptians, Hittites, Assyrians, and Babylonians. In the 6th cent. B.C. it became part of the Persian empire, which fell to ALEXANDER THE GREAT in 333 B.C. SELEUCID rulers governed it from 301 to about 164 B.C.; then Parthians and Nabataean Arabs divided the region. It flourished as a Roman province (64 B.C.–A.D. 300) and as part of Byzantium (300–634), until Muslims invaded and established control. It came under the Ottoman Turks in 1516, who held it, except for brief rules by the Egyptians, until the British invaded in World War I. After the war it became a French mandate; it achieved independence in 1944. It united with Egypt in the United Arab Republic (1958–61) and formed a short-lived federation with Egypt and Libya in 1971. During the ARAB–ISRAELI WAR (1967), it lost the GOLAN HEIGHTS to Israel. Syrian troops have frequently clashed with Israeli troops and the Syrian government has been implicated in acts of international terrorism. Hafiz al-ASSAD's long and harsh regime was marked also by antagonism toward Syria's neighbors Turkey and Iraq.

Syrian Desert Arid wasteland, SW Asia. It extends over much of N Saudi Arabia, E Jordan, S Syria, and W Iraq. Largely covered by lava flows, it formed a nearly impenetrable barrier between the populated areas of the LEVANT and MESOPOTAMIA until modern times.

syrinx See PANPIPE

system of equations *or* **simultaneous equations** In algebra, two or more equations to be solved together (i.e., the solution must satisfy all the equations in the system). For a system to have a unique solution, the number of equations must equal the number of unknowns. Even then a solution is not guaranteed. A system of linear equations can be represented by a MATRIX whose elements are the coefficients of the equations. Though simple systems of two equations in two unknowns can be solved by substitution, larger systems are best handled with matrix techniques.

systems engineering Technique employing engineering and science in the planning and development stages of a system. Systems engineering was first applied to the organization of telephone systems in the 1920s and '30s. Many systems-engineering techniques were developed during World War II for deploying military equipment. Postwar growth in the field was spurred by the development of electronic systems, computers, and information theory. Systems engineering usually involves incorporating new technology into complex systems, in which a change in one part affects many others. One tool used is the flowchart, which shows the system in graphic form, with geometric figures representing various subsystems and arrows representing their interactions. Other tools include mathematical models, probability theory, statistical analysis, and computer simulations.

Szczecin \'shchet-ₑshēn\ *German* **Stettin** \shte-'tēn\ Seaport (pop., 1999 est.: 417,000), NW Poland, near the mouth of the ODER RIVER. A Slavic fishing and commercial center for centuries, it was annexed to Poland in the 10th cent. It joined the HANSEATIC LEAGUE in 1360. It passed to Sweden in 1648, Prussia in 1720, and Poland after World War II. During the war its port was completely destroyed and the city greatly depopulated. Both were rebuilt, and Szczecin is now part of Poland's largest port complex. It is a cultural center of W Poland.

Szell \'sel, 'zel\, **George** (1897–1970) Hungarian-U.S. conductor. He made his debut as a pianist at 11, and before his 20th birthday had appeared with the Berlin Philharmonic as pianist, conductor, and composer. He established himself as an opera conductor in Berlin (1924–30) and Prague (1930–36) before emigrating to the U.S. At the helm of the Cleveland Orchestra (1946–70), he imposed stern discipline to achieve the legendary precision that made the orchestra one of the world's finest.

Szent-Györgyi \sänt-'jórj, sänt-'jór-jē\, **Albert** (1893–1986) Hungarian-U.S. biochemist. His discoveries about the roles played by certain organic compounds, especially VITAMIN C, in the oxidation (see OXIDATION-REDUCTION) of nutrients by cells brought him a 1937 Nobel Prize. His work on intermediates in the cell laid the foundation for the elucidation of the TRICARBOXYLIC ACID CYCLE by Hans KREBS, and he worked on the biochemistry of muscular action (demonstrating the role of ATP) and of CELL division.

Szilard \'zi-ₑlärd\, **Leo** (1898–1964) Hungarian-U.S. physicist. He fled Nazi Germany in 1934, and worked at the Univ. of Chicago from 1942. In 1929 he established the relation between ENTROPY and transfer of information, and in 1934 he helped develop the first method of separating isotopes of artificial radioactive elements. He helped Enrico FERMI conduct the first sustained nuclear CHAIN REACTION and construct the first NUCLEAR REACTOR. He was instrumental in establishing the MANHATTAN PROJECT, in which he helped develop the atomic bomb. After the first use of the bomb, he promoted the peaceful uses of atomic energy and the control of nuclear weapons.

Szymanowski \ₑshi-mä-'nóf-skē\, **Karol (Maciej)** (1882–1937) Polish composer. Born to a cultivated family, he studied music in Warsaw. Finding opportunities in Poland limited for new music, he traveled in Europe, Africa, and the Middle East. After losing all his possessions in World War I, he became a fervent nationalist, studying native Polish music and incorporating it into his own, including the opera *King Roger* (1924). He wrote four symphonies, three concertos, a *Stabat mater* (1926), the ballet *Harnasie* (1931), many songs, and much fine piano music.

Szymborska \shim-'bòr-ska\, **Wislawa** (b.1923) Polish poet. Her first two volumes of poetry were attempts to conform to SOCIALIST REALISM. Later poems, notable for their precise and concrete language and ironic detachment, express her dissatisfaction with communism and explore philosophical, moral, and ethical issues. She received the Nobel Prize in 1996.

T

Taal \tä-'äl, 'täl\, **Lake** *formerly* **Lake Bombon** Lake, SW LU-ZON, Philippines. It covers 94 sq mi (244 sq km) and occupies a volcanic crater less than 10 ft (3 m) above sea level. Volcano Island, or Taal Volcano, which rises from the lake, contains another small crater (Yellow Lake). The volcano has erupted 25 times since 1572, most recently in 1970. The lake is a major tourist attraction.

Tabasco \tə-'bas-kō\ State (pop., 2000: 1,889,000), SE Mexico. It covers 9,522 sq mi (24,662 sq km). Pre-Columbian Indian cultures included those of the QUICHÉ, OLMEC, Tabasca, and NAHUA. In 1519 Hernán CORTÉS first clashed with the Indians. It became a state in 1824. Agriculture, forestry, beekeeping, fishing, and cattle-raising provided much of the state's income before petroleum exploitation began in the 1960s. The state now has over 30 oil fields.

Tabernacle In Jewish history, the portable sanctuary constructed by MOSES as a place of worship for the Hebrew tribes during their period of wandering. Elaborately described in EXODUS, it was divided into an outer room and an inner room, the Holy of Holies, which housed the ARK OF THE COVENANT. With the erection of the Temple of JERUSALEM, the Tabernacle no longer served a purpose. In modern ROMAN CATHOLICISM and EASTERN ORTHODOXY, the tabernacle is the receptacle on the church altar in which the consecrated elements of the EUCHARIST are stored.

table tennis *or* **Ping-Pong** Game based on tennis that is played on a tabletop with wooden paddles and a small hollow plastic ball. The object is to hit the ball so that it goes over the net and bounces in such a way as to defeat the opponent's attempt to return it. Both singles and doubles games are played. Each game is won by the player or team that first reaches 21 points. Invented in England in the early 20th cent., it soon spread throughout the world; E. Asian countries now dominate the sport. It has been an Olympic sport since 1988.

taboo Prohibition against touching, saying, or doing something for fear of immediate harm from a supernatural force. The term is of Polynesian origin and was first noted by Capt. James COOK during his 1771 visit to Tonga, but taboos have been present in virtually all cultures. They may include prohibitions on fishing or hunting at certain seasons, eating certain foods, interacting with members of other social classes, coming into contact with corpses, and (for women) performing certain activities during menstruation. Most taboos relate to objects and actions that are significant for the maintenance of social order.

Tabriz \ta-'brēz\ City (pop., 1996: 1,191,000), NW Iran. Earthquakes and invasions by Arabs, Turks, and Mongols have destroyed the city numerous times. The Turkish ruler TIMUR conquered it in 1392. For 200 years control passed several times between Iran and Turkey, and later, between the Turks and Russians. In the 1850s the Bab and 40,000 of his followers were executed there (see BABISM). It suffered bombing damage in the IRAN–IRAQ WAR (1980s). Notable ancient sites include the splendid Blue Mosque (1465–66) and the remains of the 12-sided tomb of Mahmud GHAZAN.

tachycardia \ˌta-ki-'kär-dē-ə\ HEART rate over 100 beats per minute. If in response to exercise or stress, it is no danger to healthy people, but when it originates elsewhere than the heart's natural PACEMAKER, it is a CARDIAC ARRHYTHMIA. Symptoms include fatigue, faintness, shortness of breath, and feeling the heart thumping. It may subside within minutes or hours, but in serious heart, lung, or circulatory dis-ease it can precede ATRIAL FIBRILLATION or MYOCARDIAL INFARCTION and demands immediate medical attention. Tachycardias can be treated by an electric shock to the heart, drugs, and pacemakers.

Tacitus \'ta-sə-təs\ *Latin* Publius Cornelius Tacitus (A.D. 56?–120?) Roman orator and public official. He began his career with a minor magistracy, eventually advancing to the proconsulate of Asia, the top provincial governorship (A.D. 112–113). His works include *De vita Julii Agricolae,* a biographical account of his father-in-law, governor of Britain; the *Germania* (*De origine et situ Germanorum*), describing the people of the Roman frontier on the Rhine; the *Histories*, concerning the Roman empire from A.D. 69 to 96; and the later *Annals*, dealing with the empire from A.D. 14 to 68. Only parts of each are extant. Tacitus is regarded as perhaps the greatest historian and one of the greatest prose stylists to write in Latin.

Tacoma Seaport (pop., 2000: 193,000), W Washington, on PUGET SOUND. Settled in 1864, it grew to become a lumbering and port city. A boat-building center, it also has smelters and foundries. It is a gateway to Mt. RAINIER National Park.

Taconic Range Part of the APPALACHIAN MOUNTAIN system, NE U.S. It extends 150 mi (240 km) from S Vermont to N New York. In Massachusetts the mountains form the W section of the BERKSHIRE HILLS. Taconic State Park, in New York, is a popular mountain recreation area.

Tadema, Lawrence Alma- See Lawrence ALMA-TADEMA

Tadmor See PALMYRA

Taegu \'ta-'gü\ City (pop., 1995: 2,449,000), SE S. Korea. For centuries the administrative, economic, and cultural center of SE Korea, it developed during the CHOSON DYNASTY (1392–1910) into one of the country's three big market cities. It has important textile industries, but is best known for the apples grown nearby. The area attracts visitors to its parks, ancient pagodas, and the 9th-cent. Buddhist temple containing the TRIPITAKA.

T'aejo See YI SONG-GYE

Taejon \'ta-'jŏn\ Special city (province) (pop., 1995: 1,272,000) and capital of Ch'ungch'ong province, SE S. Korea. It was a poor village until rail connections spurred development in the early 1900s. During the KOREAN WAR (1950–53), it was a temporary capital of the Republic of Korea, and 70% of the city was destroyed; it has since been rebuilt. It is home to Chungnam National Univ.

tae kwon do \'tī-'kwän-'dō\ Korean MARTIAL ART resembling KARATE. It is characterized by the use of high standing and jump kicks as well as punches and is practiced for sport, self-defense, and spiritual development. In sparring, blows are stopped just short of contact. Tae kwon do was formalized and named in 1955; it became an Olympic sport in 2000.

Taft, Robert A(lphonso) (1889–1953) U.S. politician. Born in Cincinnati, the son of W. H. TAFT, he served in the U.S. Senate 1939–53, where his traditional conservativism earned him the nickname "Mr. Republican." He opposed centralizing power in the federal government and cosponsored the TAFT-HARTLEY ACT to restrict organized labor. An isolationist, he opposed U.S. involvement in postwar international organizations. He was a favorite-son candidate at Republican national conventions, especially in 1948 and 1952, but internationalists in the party opposed his conservative views.

Taft, William Howard (1857–1930) 27th president of the U.S. (1909–13). Born in Cincinnati, he served as U.S. solicitor general (1890–92) and U.S. appellate judge (1892–1900). He headed the Philippine Commission to set up a civilian government in the islands and was its first civilian governor (1901–4). He served as U.S. secretary of war (1904–8) under Pres. Theodore ROOSEVELT, who supported Taft's nomination for president in 1908. He won the election but became allied with the conservative Republicans, causing a rift with party progressives. He was again the nominee in 1912, but the split with Roosevelt and the BULL MOOSE PARTY resulted in his defeat by Woodrow WILSON. Taft later taught law at Yale Univ. (1913–21). As chief justice of the U.S. Supreme Court (1921–30), he secured passage of the Judges Act of 1925, which gave the Court wider discretion in accepting cases. His opinion in *Myers vs. U.S.* (1926) upheld the president's authority to remove federal officials.

William Howard Taft, 1909

Taft-Hartley Act *officially* Labor-Management Relations Act (1947) U.S. legislation that restricted labor unions. Sponsored by Sen. Robert TAFT and Rep. Fred A. Hartley, Jr., the act amended much of the pro-union WAGNER ACT and was passed by a Republican-controlled Congress over the veto of Pres. Harry TRUMAN. It allowed employees the right not to join unions, required advance notice of a labor strike, authorized an 80-day federal injunction when a strike threatened national health or safety, restricted union political contributions, and required union officials to take an oath pledging they were not communists.

Tagalog language AUSTRONESIAN language of the Philippines, spoken as a first language by about 17 million people on the island of Luzon. With vocabulary enrichment from other Philippine languages, it is the basis of Pilipino, the national language, which is now understood by more than 60% of the Philippine population. Though a script ultimately of S. Asian origin was in use for Tagalog in the 16th cent., all recent literature in the language has utilized adaptations of the LATIN ALPHABET.

Taglioni \täl-'yō-nē\, **Marie** (1804–1884) Italian ballet dancer whose delicate dancing typified the early-19th-cent. Romantic style. She trained with her dancer-choreographer father, Filippo Taglioni (1777–1871), making her debut in Vienna in 1822. She danced in his *La sylphide* at the Paris Opera in 1832 to great acclaim. She toured throughout Europe and danced with the Imperial Ballet in St. Petersburg 1837–42; she retired in 1847. She was one of the first to dance on pointe, execute floating leaps, and dress in the full, light skirt that would evolve into the tutu.

Tagore \'tä-ˌgòr, *Engl* tə-'gòr\, **Debendranath** (1817–1905) Hindu philosopher and religious reformer. Born into a wealthy family, he studied both Eastern and Western philosophy. Striving to purge Hinduism of abuses, he spoke vehemently against SUTTEE and tried to bring education within the reach of all. In his zeal to erase idolatry and undemocratic practices, he rejected the VEDAS but, unable to find a middle path between radical rationalism and Brahman conservatism, he retired from public life. He was known as the Great Sage. Rabindranath TAGORE was his son.

Tagore, Rabindranath (1861–1941) Bengali poet, composer, and painter. The son of Debendranath TAGORE, he published several books of poetry in his twenties. His later religious poetry was introduced to the West in *Gitanjali* (1912). Through international travel and lecturing, he acted as an agent of cultural exchange both in the West and in India. He ardently supported Indian independence; as a protest against the Massacre of AMRITSAR, he repudiated the knighthood he had received in 1915. The experimental school he founded to blend Eastern and Western philosophies became Vishva-Bharati Univ. (1921). He was awarded the 1913 Nobel Prize for Literature.

Rabindranath Tagore

Tagus River \'tä-gəs\ *Spanish* **Rio Tajo** \'tä-hō\ *Portuguese* **Rio Tejo** \'rē-ü-'tä-zhü\ Longest waterway of the IBERIAN PENINSULA. It rises in E central Spain and flows west across Spain and Portugal for 626 mi (1,007 km) to empty into the Atlantic Ocean near LISBON. It is of vital economic importance. Dams harness it for irrigation and hydroelectric power, and large artificial lakes have been created. Navigable for about 100 mi (160 km), it supplies a fine natural harbor at Lisbon.

Tahiti Island (pop., 1995 est.: 155,000), SOCIETY ISLANDS, FRENCH POLYNESIA. The largest of the Society's E group, it occupies an area of 402 sq mi (1,042 sq km). PAPEETE is the capital. The island's interior is mountainous, rising to 7,339 ft (2,237 m) at Mt. Orohena. Long inhabited by Polynesians, it was claimed for France in 1768 by L.-A. de BOUGAINVILLE. It became a French colony in 1880 and is now part of self-governing French Polynesia. Its great beauty was celebrated by Paul GAUGUIN. French nuclear testing in the area brought calls for independence in recent years. Tourism is economically important.

Tahoe, Lake Lake on the California–Nevada border. It occupies a fault basin in the N SIERRA NEVADA. It is 22 mi (35 km) long by 10 mi (16 km) wide and lies at an elevation of 6,229 ft (1,899 m). Fed by numerous small streams, the intensely blue lake and the surrounding national forests have been developed as popular tourist resorts, leading to a dismaying decline in the water's clarity.

Tai \'tī\ Peoples of mainland S.E. Asia, including the Thai or Siamese (in Thailand), the Lao (in Laos and Thailand), the SHAN (in Myanmar), the Lü (primarily in Yunnan province, China), the Yunnan Tai (in Yunnan), and the tribal Tai (in Vietnam). All speak TAI LANGUAGES, and most are THERAVADA Buddhists. None of the Tai peoples has a caste system, and the status of Tai women is high. Today the Tai number about 76 million.

Tai See SHAN

t'ai chi ch'uan *pinyin* **taijiquan** \'tī-'jē-'chwän\ Ancient Chinese form of exercise or of attack and defense. As exercise, it is designed to relax and condition the body, which it accomplishes partly by harmonizing the principles of YIN-YANG. It employs flowing, deliberate movements with carefully prescribed stances and positions. As a mode of attack and defense, it resembles KUNG FU. It dates to the 3rd cent. A.D.

T'ai-chung \'tī-'chùŋ\ City (pop., 2000 est.: 940,000), W central Taiwan. Most of the old town was torn down under the Japanese occupation (1895–1945) and replaced by a planned modern city. Since the early 19th cent. it has been a major market for rice, sugar, and bananas. In the 1970s, an international seaport was developed west of the city, and T'ai-chung was designated an export-processing zone to encourage foreign investment. In 1999 it suffered one of Taiwan's worst earthquakes.

taiga \'tī-gə\ *or* **boreal forest** Open coniferous forest (see CONIFER) growing on swampy ground that is commonly covered with LICHENS. It is the characteristic vegetation of the subpolar region of N Eurasia and N N. America, bounded by the colder TUNDRA to the north and the warmer temperate zone to the south. SPRUCES and PINES are the dominant trees. Soil organisms are PROTOZOANS, NEMATODES, and ROTIFERS; insects that decompose plant litter are lacking, so HUMUS accumulates very slowly. The taiga is rich in fur-bearing animals (e.g., sable, fox, and ermine) and is home to deer, bears, and wolves. Siberian taiga alone accounts for 19% of the world's forested area and possibly 25% of total forest volume. It is a major source of lumber for construction, and huge expanses have been clear-cut.

taijiquan See T'AI CHI CH'UAN

tail Extension of the VERTEBRAL COLUMN beyond the trunk, or any slender projection resembling such a structure. In fishes and other animals living in water, it is very important to movement. Many tree-dwelling animals (e.g., squirrels) use the tail for balance and as a rudder when leaping; in some (e.g., certain monkeys), it is adapted for grasping. Birds' tail feathers aid in flight maneuverability. Other animals use their tails for defense (e.g., porcupines), social signals (e.g., dogs and cats), warning signals (e.g., deer and rattlesnakes), and hunting (e.g., alligators).

Tai languages Family of closely related languages spoken in S.E. Asia and S China by more than 80 million people. According to a widely used classification, Tai comprises three branches. The Southwestern group includes Thai, the national language of Thailand; NE Thai (Isan) and Lao, spoken in E Thailand and Laos; and other languages spoken in Thailand, Myanmar, and Vietnam. The Central group includes Nung, Tay (Thô), and S. Zhuang, spoken in N Vietnam and China. The Northern group includes Buyi (Bouyei) and Northern Zhuang, spoken in China. All Tai languages are TONE languages, and as in Chinese and Vietnamese, most MORPHEMES in the native vocabulary consist of single syllables. Most scholars believe the Tai family is related to a number of other languages spoken by minority peoples of S China and N Vietnam, making up the Kadai or Tai-Kadai family.

T'ai-nan \'tī-'nän\ *formerly* **Dainan** City (pop., 2000 est.: 728,000), SW Taiwan. The Han Chinese settled there as early as 1590. The Dutch ruled from 1623 until they were driven out in 1662 by ZHENG CHENGGONG, who made it his capital. It remained the island's capital under the QING DYNASTY (from 1683), and grew into Taiwan's commercial and educational center. The capital was transferred to TAIPEI in 1891. Today T'ai-nan is a major market and tourism center.

Taine \'ten\, **Hippolyte (-Adolphe)** (1828–1893) French thinker, critic, and historian. He earned a reputation as one of the most esteemed exponents of 19th-cent. French POSITIVISM with his attempts to apply the scientific method to the study of the humanities. His works include a *History of English Literature* (1863–64), containing an explanation of his approach to cultural and literary history and his scientific attitude toward criticism; *On Intelligence* (1871), a study in psychology; and his monumental historical analysis *Les origines de la France contemporaine* (3 vols., 1876–99).

Taino \'tī-nō\ ARAWAK Indians of the island of HISPANIOLA, Puerto Rico, and E Cuba. They grew cassava and corn, hunted birds and small animals, fished, and worked stone and wood. Their society consisted of nobles, commoners, and slaves ruled by hereditary chiefs and subchiefs. They became extinct within 100 years of the Spanish conquest.

Taipei \'tī-'pā\ City (pop., 2000 est.: 2,641,000), capital of Taiwan. Founded in 1708, it became an important center of the tea trade in the mid-19th cent. Taiwan was proclaimed a province of China in 1886, and Taipei was later made the capital, retaining that designation under Japanese rule (1895–1945). In 1949 it became the capital of the Chinese Nationalist government. Its many educational institutions include the National Taiwan Univ. (1928). The National Palace Museum houses one of the world's largest collections of Chinese artifacts.

Taiping Rebellion \'tī-'pin\ (1850–64) Large-scale rebellion against the QING DYNASTY in China. The peasants, having suffered floods and famines in the late 1840s, were ripe for rebellion, which came under the leadership of the religious visionary HONG XIUQUAN. He preached the brotherhood and sisterhood of all people under God; property was to be held in common. His followers' militant faith unified a fiercely disciplined army of more than a million men and women. They captured Nanjing in 1853 and renamed it Tianjing ("Heavenly Capital"). Their attempts to capture Beijing failed, but an expedition into the Upper Chang (Yangtze) River valley scored many victories. Hong's idiosyncratic Christianity alienated the Chinese scholar-gentry, without whom the Taiping forces were unable to govern the countryside or supply their cities effectively. In 1860 an at-

tempt to take Shanghai was repelled by U.S.- and British-led forces, and by 1862 Chinese forces under ZENG GUOFAN had surrounded Nanjing. The city fell in 1864, but almost 100,000 of the Taiping followers preferred death to capture. Sporadic resistance continued elsewhere until 1868. More than 20 million people may have died in the rebellion.

Taisho period (1912–26) Period in Japanese history corresponding to the reign of the Taisho emperor, Yoshihito (1879–1926). It followed the MEIJI PERIOD and saw a continuation of Japan's rise on the international scene and liberalism at home. Japan continued to push China for economic and political concessions and entered into treaties with Western nations that acknowledged its interests in Korea, Manchuria, and the rest of China. Rural Japan did not fare as well as urban Japan, and a domestic depression led to much suffering.

Taiwan *officially* **Republic of China** *formerly* **Formosa** Island, off SE China. Both the Republic of China (Taiwan) and the People's Republic of China (mainland China) claim jurisdiction over it. Area: 13,969 sq mi (36,179 sq km), including its outlying islands. Population (2000): 22,186,000.

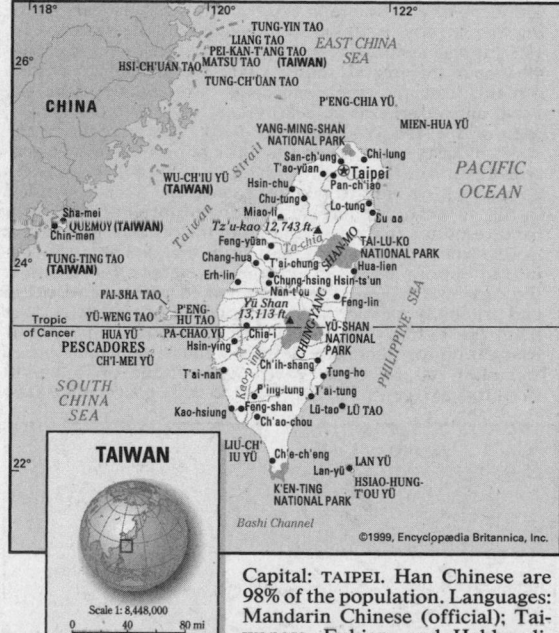

Capital: TAIPEI. Han Chinese are 98% of the population. Languages: Mandarin Chinese (official); Taiwanese, Fukien, and Hakka dialects also spoken. Religions: Buddhism, Taoism, Confucianism; small minority, Christianity. Currency: new Taiwan dollar. Lying 100 mi (160 km) off the Chinese mainland, it is composed mainly of mountains and hills, with densely populated coastal plains in the west. It has one of the highest population densities in the world. It is a leading industrial power of the Pacific Rim, with an economy based on manufacturing industries, international trade, and services. Leading exports include electronic equipment, garments, and textiles. Agricultural exports include frozen pork, sugar, canned mushrooms, bananas, and tea. It is a major producer of Chinese-language motion pictures. It is a republic with one legislative branch; its chief of state is the president, and the head of government is the premier. Known to the Chinese as early as the 7th cent., it was widely settled by them early in the 17th cent. In 1646 the Dutch seized control of the island, only to be ousted in 1661 by a large influx of Chinese MING-DYNASTY refugees. It fell to the MANCHUS in 1683 and was not open to Europeans again until 1858. In 1895 it was ceded to Japan following the SINO–JAPANESE WAR. A Japanese military center in World War II, it was frequently bombed by U.S. planes. After Japan's defeat, it was returned to China, which was then governed by the Nationalists. When the Communists took

over mainland China in 1949, the Nationalist government (see GUOMINDANG) fled to Taiwan and made it their seat of government, with Gen. CHIANG KAI-SHEK as president. In 1954 he and the U.S. signed a mutual defense treaty, and Taiwan received U.S. support for almost three decades, developing its economy in spectacular fashion. It was recognized by many non-Communist countries as the representative of all China until 1971, when it was replaced in the U.N. by the People's Republic of China. Martial law was lifted in Taiwan in 1987, and travel restrictions with mainland China in 1988. In 1989 opposition parties were legalized. The 1990s saw an increasingly close, though still informal, relationship with the mainland: many Taiwanese continue polarized over the issue.

Taiwan Strait or **Formosa Strait** Arm of the NW Pacific Ocean. Lying between China and TAIWAN, it is about 115 mi (185 km) wide. The strait connects the S. CHINA SEA and E. China Sea.

Taiyuan or **T'ai-yüan** \'tī-'ywän\ City (pop., 1999 est.: 1,768,000), capital of Shanxi province, China. Known since the time of the ZHOU DYNASTY, it was an administrative capital in the time of the MONGOLS (12th–14th cent.). It was the scene of a massacre in 1900 of foreign missionaries during the BOXER REBELLION. Invaded by the Japanese in 1937, it was again besieged by Communist forces in 1948–49. One of the greatest industrial cities in China, it produces cement, iron and steel, and coal. Cave temples from the TANG and YUAN eras lie nearby.

Taizu or **T'ai-tsu** \'tī-'dzü\ (927–976) First emperor of the SONG dynasty, who began the unification of China. A general under the Later Zhou dynasty (951–60), he was induced by his troops to take over when the dynasty was left in the hands of a child successor. An upright man, Taizu forgave minor faults while holding his officials to account in important matters. He frequently traveled about incognito to observe conditions among his people. He reformed the CHINESE EXAMINATION SYSTEM to prevent favoritism and gradually moved the administration of the prefectures from the military to civil officials. He provided a stable foundation for the future development of the dynasty.

Tajikistan \tä-ˌji-ki-'stan\ officially **Republic of Tajikistan** Country, SW central Asia. Area: 55,300 sq mi (143,100 sq

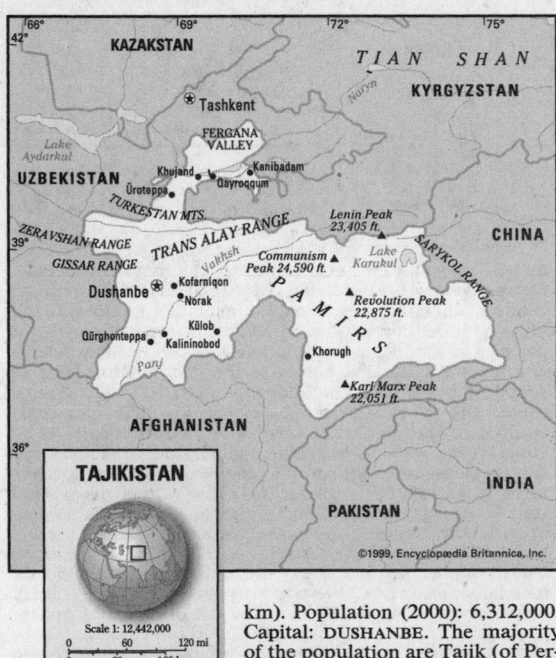

©1999, Encyclopædia Britannica, Inc.

TAJIKISTAN

Scale 1: 12,442,000
0   60   120 mi
0   80   160 km

km). Population (2000): 6,312,000. Capital: DUSHANBE. The majority of the population are Tajik (of Persian descent); Uzbeks make up a large minority. Language: Tajik (official). Religion: Islam (Sunni). Currency: Tajik ruble. An earthquake-prone, mountainous country, about half of

its territory lies above elevations of 10,000 ft (3,000 m), with the PAMIRS dominating the east. The AMU DARYA and Syr Darya rivers cross it and are used for irrigation. Cotton, cattle, fruits, vegetables, and grain are raised. Heavy industries include coal mining, petroleum and natural-gas extraction, metalworking, and nitrogen fertilizer production. Light industries include cotton milling, food processing, and textiles. Tajikistan is a republic with two legislative houses; its chief of state is the president, and the head of government is the prime minister. Settled by the Persians around the 6th cent. B.C., Tajikistan was part of the empires of the Persians and of ALEXANDER THE GREAT and his successors. In the 7th–8th cent. A.D., it was conquered by the Arabs, who introduced Islam. The Uzbeks controlled the region in the 15th–18th cent. In the 1860s Russia took over much of Tajikistan. In 1924 it became an autonomous republic under the administration of the Uzbek Soviet Socialist Republic, and it gained republic status in 1929. It achieved independence with the collapse of the Soviet Union in 1991. Civil war raged through much of the 1990s between government forces and an opposition of mostly Islamic forces. Peace was reached in 1997, but random criminal and political violence continues to impede progress.

Taj Mahal \'täzh-mə-'häl\ Mausoleum outside Agra, India, built by the Mughal emperor SHAH JAHAN in memory of his wife, Mumtaz Mahal. The Taj complex, begun around 1632, took 22 years to complete. At its center lies a square garden area bounded by two oblong sections, one comprising the mausoleum and the other an entrance gateway. The mausoleum, of pure-white marble inlaid with semiprecious stones, stands on a high marble plinth with a minaret at each corner. It has four identical facades, each with a massive central arch, and is surmounted by a bulbous double dome and four domed kiosks. Its interior centers on an octagonal chamber containing the marble tombs, enclosed by a perforated marble screen, with sarcophagi below. It is regarded as one of the world's most beautiful buildings.

Takemitsu \tä-ke-'mit-sù\, **Toru** (1930–1996) Japanese composer. In 1951 he founded Tokyo's Experimental Laboratory to promote an integration of Japanese music with contemporary European developments. Soon acknowledged as Japan's leading composer, he explored serialism, aleatory, graphic notation, and electronic music combined with traditional Japanese motives and instruments (e.g., November Steps 1967), creating an individual sound world in which silence plays a large part.

Taklimakan or **Takla Makan** \ˌtä-klə-mə-'kän\ Desert, forming the greater part of the Tarim River basin, W central China. One of the world's largest sandy wastes, it is about 600 mi (965 km) across, with an area of 105,000 sq mi (272,000 sq km). It is flanked by high mountain ranges, including the KUNLUN MTNS. Its wind-blown sand cover is as much as 1,000 ft (300 m) thick; pyramidal dunes can reach 1,000 ft (300 m) in height.

Talbot, (William Henry) Fox (1800–1877) English chemist and pioneer photographer. In 1840 he developed the calotype; an early photographic process that improved on the daguerreotype, it involved the use of a photographic negative, from which multiple prints could be made. His The Pencil of Nature (1844–46) was the first book with photographic illustrations. Talbot also was also one of the first to decipher the cuneiform inscriptions of Nineveh.

talc Common SILICATE MINERAL that is distinguished from almost all other minerals by its extreme softness. Its soapy or greasy feel accounts for the name soapstone, given to compact aggregates of talc with other rock-forming minerals. Soapstones have been used since ancient times for carvings, ornaments, and utensils. Talc is also used in lubricants and dusting powders; as a filler in ceramics, paint, paper, roofing materials, plastic, and rubber; as a carrier in insecticides; and as a mild abrasive in the polishing of cereal grains.

Taliban \ˌtä-lē-'bȧn\ Afghan Islamic fundamentalist group. In the chaos following the Soviet Union's withdrawal from Afghanistan in 1989 (see AFGHAN WARS), a group of Islamic fundamentalist students came to the forefront as a military power. In 1996 they captured Kabul and instituted an Islamic fundamentalist regime, doling out harsh punishments (based on SHARIA law) and forbidding the education of women while harboring the terrorist Osama BIN LADEN. After the SEPTEMBER 11 ATTACKS, the U.S. invaded Afghanistan, and the regime was overthrown in Dec. 2001, though its leader, Mullah Mohammed Omar, remained at large.

Ta-lien See DALIAN

Taliesin \ˌta-lē-ˈe-sin\ Home and architectural school of Frank Lloyd WRIGHT. Located near Spring Green, Wis., it was begun in 1911 and was rebuilt after fires in 1914 and 1925. Taliesin West, near Scottsdale, Ariz., was begun in 1938 as a winter home for Wright and his students. Wright, of Welsh descent, named them after the renowned Welsh poet (fl.6th cent. A.D.) Both structures were continually renovated until Wright's death in 1959.

Tallahassee City (2000: 151,000), capital of Florida. Spanish settlers arrived after Hernando DE SOTO's visit in 1539. It became the capital of the state of Florida in 1845. In the AMERICAN CIVIL WAR, the secession resolution was adopted there in 1861; it was the only capital of a Confederate state east of the Mississippi not captured by Union forces. It is home to Florida State Univ. (founded 1851).

Tallahatchie River River, N Mississippi. It rises in Tippah Co. and flows southwest 230 mi (370 km) to join the Yalobusha River and form the Yazoo River. It is navigable for about 100 mi (160 km).

Tallapoosa River River, Georgia and Alabama. Rising in NW Georgia, it flows southwest for about 268 mi (431 km), joining the Coosa River to form the ALABAMA RIVER. Three private power dams have created reservoirs, including Lake Martin, for river control, power, and recreation.

Tallchief, Maria (b.1925) U.S. ballet dancer of American Indian descent. Born in Fairfax, Okla., she danced with the Ballet Russe de Monte Carlo (1942–47), then joined the NEW YORK CITY BALLET in 1948 and became its prima ballerina, creating leading roles in many ballets choreographed for her by George BALANCHINE, her husband from 1946 to 1952. She left the company in 1965, became artistic director of the Lyric Opera Ballet in Chicago, and founded the Chicago City Ballet in 1980.

Talleyrand (-Périgord) \tä-le-ˈräⁿ\, **Charles-Maurice de** (1754–1838) French statesman. He became bishop of Autun in 1788. Elected to represent the clergy at the Estates General (1789), he became the "bishop of the Revolution" by calling for confiscation of church property to fund the new government; he was excommunicated by the pope in 1790. He was expelled from France during the REIGN OF TERROR, lived in the U.S. 1794–96, then returned to serve in the DIRECTORY as foreign minister (1797–99). Adept at political survival, he supported NAPOLEON and again became foreign minister (1799–1807) and later grand chamberlain (1804–7). As Napoleon faced defeat, Talleyrand secretly worked to restore the monarchy; in 1814 he was appointed foreign minister to LOUIS XVIII and represented France at the Congress of VIENNA. Forced by ultraroyalists to resign (1815), he later became minister in the July Revolution of 1830 and served as ambassador to Britain 1830–34.

Tallinn \ˈta-lən\ *formerly (until 1918)* **Revel** \ˈrä-vəl\ Seaport city (pop., 1999 est.: 411,000), capital of Estonia. A fortified settlement existed there from the late 1st millennium B.C. In 1219 it was captured by the Danes, who built a new fortress. Trade flourished after it joined the HANSEATIC LEAGUE in 1285. In 1346 it was sold to the TEUTONIC ORDER, and in 1561 it passed to Sweden. Russia captured it in 1710. It was the capital of independent Estonia from 1918 to 1940, when Estonia was annexed to the U.S.S.R. (1940–91). In World War II it was occupied by German forces 1941–44 and was severely damaged. Rebuilt, it again became the capital of independent Estonia in 1991. It is a major commercial and fishing port, an industrial center, and the cultural center of Estonia.

Tallis \ˈta-ləs\, **Thomas** (c.1505–1585) British composer. By 1543 he was a Gentleman of the Chapel Royal, as both organist and composer. Though a Catholic, he was one of the first to write hymns in English for the Anglican church, and he remained in favor after ELIZABETH I's accession. His powerful *Lamentations of Jeremiah* are regarded as his greatest body of work; his 40-part motet *Spem in alium* is his most famous piece. He also wrote three masses and about 40 other motets. William BYRD was one of his students.

Talmud \täl-ˈmüd, ˈtal-məd\ In JUDAISM, the systematic amplification and analysis of passages of the MISHNA, the Gemara (a commentary on the Mishna), and other oral law. Two Talmuds exist, produced by two different groups of Jewish scholars: the Palestinian Talmud (c.A.D. 400) and the Babylonian Talmud (c.A.D. 600). The Babylonian Talmud is more extensive and thus more highly esteemed. The Talmud remains a text of central importance, particularly in ORTHODOX JUDAISM. Intensive modern Talmudic scholarship is pursued in Israel and the U.S. See also HALAKHAH.

tamarin Any of about 25 species of long-tusked MARMOSETS in the genera *Leontopithecus* (or *Leontideus*) and *Saguinus*. Tamarins are 8–12 in. (20–30 cm) long, excluding the 12–16-in. (30–40-cm) tail. The emperor tamarin *(Saguinus imperator)* has long grizzled gray fur, a reddish tail, and long white moustaches. The three species of *Leontopithecus* are endangered.

tamarind \ˈta-mə-rənd\ Evergreen tree *(Tamarindus indica)* of the pea family (see LEGUME), native to tropical Africa and cultivated elsewhere. The tree grows about 80 ft (24 m) tall and has featherlike leaves. It bears small clusters of yellow flowers and plump pods that do not split open. The seeds in the soft, brownish edible pulp are used in foods, beverages, and medicines.

Tamaulipas \ˌtä-mau̇-ˈlē-päs\ State (pop., 2000: 2,747,000), NE Mexico. Located on the Gulf of Mexico, it covers 30,822 sq mi (79,829 sq km). The capital is Ciudad Victoria. Large areas are irrigated. Agriculture is the main industry; products include sorghum, soybeans, sugarcane, cotton, coffee, and fruit. Fisheries and copper mining also are important. It produces a third of Mexico's natural gas and increasing quantities of petroleum.

Tamayo \tə-ˈmī-ō\, **Rufino** (1899–1991) Mexican-U.S. painter and graphic artist. He studied at Mexico City's School of Fine Arts and then taught at the National Museum of Archaeology (1921–26). He preferred easel painting to the monumental proportions and political rhetoric of J. C. OROZCO, Diego RIVERA, and D. A. SIQUEIROS. His distinctive style blended Cubism and Surrealism with Mexican folk-art subjects involving semiabstract figures, still lifes, and animals in vibrant colors. From 1936 he lived principally in New York. He designed murals for Mexico City's Palace of Fine Arts (1952–53) and UNESCO's Paris headquarters (1958).

tambourine Small frame drum with one skin nailed or glued to a shallow circular frame, into which jingles or pellet bells are set. It is struck with the hand or simply shaken. Tambourines were played in ancient Mesopotamia, Greece, and Rome, especially in religious contexts, and have long been prominent in the Middle East. Crusaders brought them to Europe in the 13th cent.

Tamburlaine See TIMUR

Tamerlane See TIMUR

Tamil language DRAVIDIAN language spoken by more than 63 million people. It is an official language of Tamil Nadu state in India and of Sri Lanka. The earliest Tamil inscriptions date from about 200 B.C.; literature in the language has a 2,000-year history. Tamil script is descended from the S Indian Pallava script (see INDIC WRITING SYSTEMS). Tamil has several regional dialects, Brahman and non-Brahman caste dialects, and a marked division between literary and colloquial forms.

Tamils \ˈtä-məlz, ˈta-məlz\ People originally of S India who speak the TAMIL LANGUAGE. The Tamils have a long history of sea travel and commerce; they traded with the ancient Greeks and Romans. They have a rich literary tradition and helped transmit Indian culture to S. E. Asia. They are mostly Hindus (the Tamil area in India is a center of traditional Hinduism). In Sri Lanka tensions between the Ceylon Tamils (one of two separate Tamil populations) and the Sinhalese Buddhist majority prompted a Tamil guerrilla insurgency in the 1980s that continues today. The Tamils number about 57 million, with 3.2 million living in Sri Lanka.

Tamiris \tə-ˈmir-əs\, **Helen** *orig.* Helen Becker (1905–1966) U.S. choreographer and dancer. Born in New York City, in 1930 she founded her own company and the School of American Dance, which she directed until 1945. Many of her own works, such as *Pioneer Memories* and *Walt Whit-*

TUV

mun Suite, drew on American themes. From 1945 to 1957 she choreographed such Broadway musicals as *Show Boat, Annie Get Your Gun,* and *Fanny.*

Tammany Hall \'ta-mə-nē\ Democratic Party's executive committee in New York City. The group was organized in 1789 in opposition to the FEDERALIST PARTY's ruling "aristocrats"; its name derived from a pre-Revolutionary association named after the benevolent Indian chief Tammanend. The Society of Tammany, incorporated in 1805 as a benevolent body, became identified with the city's Democratic Party. By advocating extending the franchise to propertyless white males, it became popular with Irish immigrants and the working class. Gifts to the poor and political favors resulted in support for Tammany candidates at the polls. The rise of such bosses as W. M. TWEED associated the group with political corruption. Its power was strongest in the late 19th and early 20th cent.; it declined in the 1930s under the reforms of Pres. Franklin ROOSEVELT and Mayor Fiorello LA GUARDIA.

Tammuz \'tä-ˌmüz\ Mesopotamian god of fertility. Worship of Tammuz was centered around two yearly festivals, one in the early spring in which his marriage to the goddess Inanna symbolized the fertilization of nature for the coming year, and one in summer when his death at the hands of demons was lamented. He is thought to be the precursor of several later deities associated with agriculture and fertility.

tamoxifen \ta-'mäk-si-ˌfen\ Synthetic HORMONE, marketed as Nolvadex, that prevents the binding of ESTROGEN to estrogen-sensitive BREAST CANCER cells. The most serious side effect is an increased risk of THROMBOSIS, which may require patients to take an ANTICOAGULANT as well. Studies on its effectiveness continue.

Tampa City (pop., 2002: 303,000), W central Florida, on the NE end of TAMPA BAY. The U.S. Army established Ft. Brooke on the site in 1824 to oversee the removal of the SEMINOLE Indians. The town developed as a cigar-making center after 1886. It is a winter and fishing resort, home to the Univ. of S. Florida, and a major tourist center; attractions include Busch Gardens and Cypress Gardens.

Tampa Bay Inlet, Gulf of Mexico, W Florida. It is 25 mi (40 km) long and 7–12 mi (11–19 km) wide. ST. PETERSBURG lies on the W shore and TAMPA on the northeast. Hernando DE SOTO began his travels through the SE U.S. from Tampa Bay in 1539. It is spanned by the 15-mi (25-km) Sunshine Skyway Bridge.

Tampico \täm-'pē-kō\ Seaport (pop., 1995: 279,000), SE TAMAULIPAS state, NE Mexico. It grew around a Franciscan monastery founded about 1532. Destroyed by pirates in 1683, it was not resettled until 1823. Until 1901 it was an unsanitary and second-rate port. With the exploitation of surrounding petroleum resources, it became the most modern port in Mexico and one of the country's leading seaports. It is also a seaside resort.

Tanagra \'ta-nə-grə, tə-'na-grə\ Ancient town, BOEOTIA, E central Greece. The chief town of the E Boeotians, it was the scene of the Athenian defeat by the Spartans in 457 B.C. during the first PELOPONNESIAN WAR. Finely modeled terra-cotta statuettes, known as Tanagra figures, were made there around 340–150 B.C. for export.

Tananarive See ANTANANARIVO

Tanana River \'ta-nə-ˌnȯ\ River, E central Alaska. Rising in the Wrangell Mtns., it flows northwest 550 mi (885 km) to join the YUKON RIVER. It was first explored by Russian traders in the mid-19th cent. Its valley was an important gold-producing area in the 1904 GOLD RUSH; it is also a lumbering district and one of Alaska's major farming regions. The Alaska Highway follows it for nearly its entire course.

Tancred \'taŋ-krəd\ (d.1194) King of Sicily (1190–94), the last of the Norman rulers. He rebelled twice (1155, 1161) against his uncle William I of Sicily, and he gained the Sicilian throne after the death of William II. He gave in to the financial demands of RICHARD I the Lionheart (1191) after Richard occupied Messina. Emperor Henry VI sought to wrest the Sicilian throne from Tancred, unsuccessfully besieging Naples in 1191 and marching on Sicily again in 1194. Tancred died before his arrival, and Henry was crowned king.

Tandy, Jessica See Hume CRONYN AND JESSICA TANDY

Taney, Roger B(rooke) (1777–1864) U.S. jurist. Born in Calvert Co., Md., he was appointed U.S. attorney general in 1831; he achieved national prominence by opposing the BANK OF THE U.S. In 1835 he was named to succeed Chief Justice John MARSHALL and was confirmed despite powerful resistance. He is remembered principally for the DRED SCOTT decision. Though he considered slavery an evil, he believed its elimination should be brought about gradually and chiefly by the states where it existed.

Roger B. Taney Photo by Mathew Brady

Tanganyika \ˌtan-gən-'yē-kə\ **Lake** Lake, central Africa. Located on the boundary between Tanzania and Congo (Zaire), it is the longest freshwater lake in the world, at 410 mi (660 km) long, and the second-deepest, at 4,710 ft (1,436 m) deep. Oil palms and rice grow along its steep shores; hippopotamuses and crocodiles abound. It was first visited by Europeans in 1858.

Tang dynasty *or* **T'ang dynasty** \'täŋ\ (618–907) Chinese dynasty that became a golden age for poetry, sculpture, and Buddhism. The Tang capital of Changan became a great international metropolis, with traders from Central Asia, Arabia, Persia, Korea, and Japan passing through. The economy flourished in the 8th–9th cent., as rural market towns grew to join the metropolitan markets of Changan and Luoyang. Buddhism enjoyed great favor; there were new translations of the Buddhist scriptures and growth of indigenous sects, including Chan (see ZEN). Poetry was the greatest glory of the period; nearly 50,000 works by 2,000 poets survive. The Tang government never completely controlled the N Chinese border, where nomad tribes made constant incursions; periodic rebellions from the mid-8th cent. onward also weakened its power.

Tange \'tän-gä\, **Kenzo** (b.1913) Japanese architect. Tange initially worked in the office of Kunio MAEKAWA. His best-known early work was the Peace Center, Hiroshima (1946–56). The Kagawa prefectural offices in Takamatsu (1955–58) notably blended the modern and traditional. In 1959 he and his students published the Boston Harbor project, launching the Metabolist school. He became a master of complex geometries; his National Gymnasium for Tokyo's 1964 Olympic Games exemplifies his later style, boldly dramatic and complexly geometrical. More recent works include the New Tokyo City Hall complex (1991). Tange won the Pritzker Architecture Prize in 1987.

tangent See TRIGONOMETRIC FUNCTION

tangent line \'tan-jənt\ In geometry, a line that intersects a circle exactly once; in calculus, a line that touches a curve at one point and whose SLOPE is equal to that of the curve at that point. Particularly useful as approximations of curves in the immediate vicinity of the point of tangency, tangent lines are the basis of many ESTIMATION techniques. The numerical value of the slope of the tangent line to the graph of a function at any point equals that of the function's DERIVATIVE at that point.

tangerine Small, thin-skinned variety of the mandarin ORANGE species (*Citrus reticulata deliciosa*). Probably native to S.E. Asia, today it is cultivated in subtropical regions worldwide. The tree is smaller than other orange trees, with slender twigs and lance-shaped leaves. The fruit is slightly flattened at each end and has a loose peel. Easily separated segments are abundant in vitamin C. Oil from the fragrant skin is used in flavorings and liqueurs. Tangerines crossed with GRAPEFRUIT produce hybrids known as tangelos.

Tangier \tan-'jir\ *French* **Tanger** \tän-'zhā\ *Arabic* **Tanjah** \'tän-jə\ *ancient* Tingis. Seaport (metro. area pop., 1994: 522,000), N Morocco. Located on the Strait of GIBRALTAR, it was an ancient Phoenician trading post, and later a Roman settlement. It was later captured successively by the

Vandals, Byzantines, and Arabs. It fell to the Portuguese in 1471; it later passed to the British, who gave it up to Morocco in 1684. When Morocco became a French protectorate in 1912, Tangier was granted special status; in 1923 it officially became an international city, governed by an international commission. In 1956 it was integrated with the kingdom of Morocco. It became a free port and royal summer residence in the 1960s. The old town is dominated by a Casbah and the Great Mosque.

tango S. American BALLROOM DANCE. Originally a spirited Spanish flamenco dance, it evolved into a ballroom dance in Buenos Aires, possibly influenced by the Cuban habanera. It was made popular in the U.S. by Vernon and Irene CASTLE. Early versions were fast and exuberant; these were later modified to the smoother ballroom step, characterized by long pauses and stylized body positions and danced to music in 4/4 time.

Tanguy \tän-'gē\, **Yves** (1900–1955) French-U.S. painter. In 1923, after serving in the merchant marine, he was inspired to start painting when he saw the works of Giorgio de CHIRICO. He joined the Surrealists in 1925 and participated in all their major exhibitions. In a unique style, he depicted strange, amorphous creatures and unidentifiable objects set in barren, brightly lit landscapes with infinite horizons. Despite their smooth, painstaking detail, his pictures have a timeless, dreamlike quality (e.g., *The Invisibles*, 1951). He emigrated to the U.S. in 1939.

tank Heavily armed and armored combat vehicle that moves on two continuous metal chains (tracks). It is usually equipped with a CANNON mounted in a revolving turret as well as lighter automatic weapons. The British developed tanks during World War I for the muddy, uneven terrain of the trench battle zone. They first saw combat at the Battle of the SOMME (1916). In World War II, Germany's tank force was proved effective in fast-moving massed formations with great striking power. Most modern battle tanks weigh more than 50 tons yet attain speeds of 30–40 mph (50–70 kph). The standard main armament is a 120-mm gun, which fires armor-piercing projectiles; laser rangefinders and infrared imaging devices aid in sighting.

Tanner, Henry Ossawa (1859–1937) U.S.-French painter. Born in Pittsburgh, he studied under Thomas EAKINS at the Pennsylvania Academy of Fine Arts, where he was the only black student. He moved to Paris in 1891, and by 1894 his work was being exhibited at the annual Salons, where he was awarded honorable mention in 1896 for *Daniel in the Lions' Den* and won a medal in 1897 for his *Raising of Lazarus*. He gained international acclaim for his landscapes and his treatments of biblical themes. In 1927 he became the first African-American granted full membership in the National Academy of Design.

Tannhäuser \'tän-ˌhȯi-zər\ (c.1200–c.1270) German lyric poet and legendary hero. He was a professional minnesinger, or poet-musician, and a few of his works are extant. In the legend preserved in a popular ballad, *Danhauser*, he lives a life of pleasure but, torn by remorse, goes to Rome to seek remission of his sins. The pope tells him that, as his pilgrim's staff would never put on leaf again, so his sins can never be forgiven. Shortly afterward his discarded staff puts forth green leaves. The pope sends messengers after him, but he is never seen again.

tannin *or* **tannic acid** Any of a group of pale yellow to light brown amorphous substances widely distributed in plants and used chiefly in TANNING leather, dyeing fabric, and making ink. Their solutions are acid and have an astringent taste (see TEA). Tannins are used industrially to clarify wine and beer.

tanning Chemical treatment of raw animal hides or skins to convert them into LEATHER. Vegetable tanning (using bark, wood, roots, or berries) is very ancient. The tanning agent (e.g., vegetable TANNIN, SALTS such as chromium sulfate, or fish or animal oil) displaces water from the interstices between the PROTEIN (mostly COLLAGEN) fibers in the skin and cements the fibers together. The tanning of fair skin by sunlight is completely different: Ultraviolet light causes production and redistribution of MELANIN in epidermal cells.

tantalum \'tan-tə-ləm\ Chemical ELEMENT, one of the TRANSITION elements, chemical symbol Ta, atomic number

73. It is a dense, hard, unreactive, silvery-gray METAL with an extremely high melting point. Relatively rare, it is difficult to separate from niobium, the element above it in the PERIODIC TABLE, with which it shares many properties. Its chief uses are in electrolytic capacitors, corrosion-resistant chemical equipment, dental and surgical instruments, tools, catalysts, and components of electron tubes.

Tantalus \'tan-tᵊl-əs\ In GREEK MYTHOLOGY, the king of Sipylus (or Phrygia). A friend of the gods, he offended them by repeating their secrets on earth. Another version of the myth held that he killed his son Pelops and served him to the gods. In the underworld he was placed up to his neck in water, which flowed away every time he tried to drink, just as the branches overhead swung out of reach whenever he tried to pick the fruit from them.

tantra \'tən-trə\ In some Indian religions, a text that deals with esoteric aspects of religious teaching. There is considerable tantric literature and practice in HINDUISM and BUDDHISM. Typically representing teachings of relatively late development and incorporating elements of different traditions, they are often eschewed by orthodox practitioners. In Hinduism, tantras deal with popular aspects of the religion, such as spells, rituals, and symbols. Buddhist tantric literature has reference to numerous practices, some involving sexual activity, that have no basis in canonical literature.

Tanzania \ˌtan-zə-'nē-ə\ *officially* **United Republic of Tanzania** Country, E Africa. It includes the islands of ZANZIBAR, Pemba, and Mafia in the Indian Ocean. Area: 364,881 sq mi (945,037 sq km). Population (2000): 35,306,000. Capital:

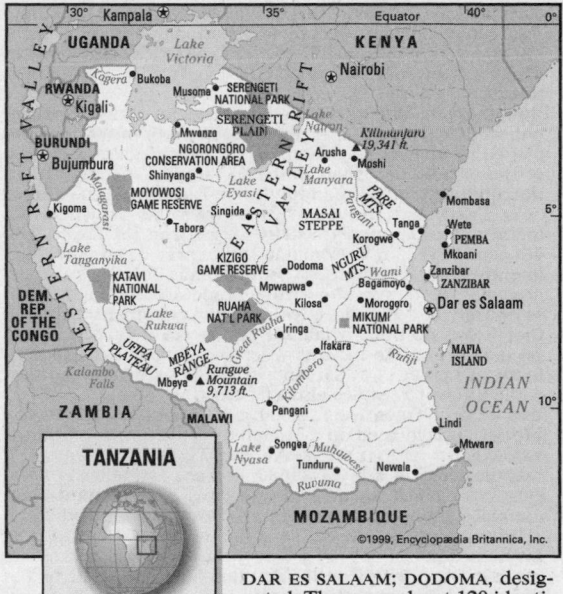

DAR ES SALAAM; DODOMA, designated. There are about 120 identifiable ethnic groups; the largest, the Sukuma, are about one-fifth of the population. Languages: Swahili, English (both official). Religions: Islam, animism, Christianity. Currency: Tanzanian shilling. Although most of Tanzania consists of plain and plateau, it has some spectacular relief features, including Mt. KILIMANJARO and Mt. Lengai, an active volcano. All or portions of Lakes MALAWI, TANGANYIKA, VICTORIA, and Rukwa lie within it, as do the headwaters of the NILE, CONGO, and ZAMBEZI rivers. SERENGETI NATIONAL PARK is the most famous of its extensive game reserves. Important mineral deposits include gold, diamonds, gemstones, iron ore, coal, and natural gas; it is the only known source of the gemstone Tanzanite. The centrally planned economy is based largely on agriculture; major crops include corn, sugarcane, bananas, rice, coffee, and cloves. Industries include food processing, textiles, cement, and brewing. It is a republic with one legislative

TUV

house; its head of state and government is the president. In-habited from the 1st millennium B.C., it was occupied by Arab and Indian traders and BANTU PEOPLES by the 10th cent. A.D. The Portuguese gained control of the coastline in the late 15th cent., but they were driven out by the Arabs of Oman and ZANZIBAR in the late 18th cent. German colonists entered the area in the 1880s, and in 1891 the Germans declared the region a protectorate as GERMAN E. AFRICA. In World War I Britain captured the German holdings, which became a British mandate (1920) under the name Tanganyika. Britain retained control of the region after World War II when it became a U.N. trust territory (1946). Tanganyika gained independence in 1961 and became a republic in 1962. In 1964 it united with Zanzibar under the name Tanzania. It has experienced both political and economic struggles in recent years.

Tanzimat \ˌtän-zē-ˈmät\ (Turkish: "reorganization") (1839–76) Reforms undertaken in Ottoman Turkey to modernize society and reduce the influence of the Muslim clergy. The first set of reforms (1839) sought to secularize the government and to reform taxation and military conscription. Later reforms (1856) established a secular school system and a new law code. Efforts to centralize government administration ended by concentrating all authority in the sultan. See also ABDULHAMID II, YOUNG TURKS.

tao *pinyin* **dao** \ˈdau̇\ In Chinese philosophy, a fundamental concept signifying the correct or divine way. In CONFUCIANISM, tao signifies a morally correct path of behavior. In TAOISM, the concept encompasses the visible process of nature, by which all things change, as well as the principle underlying this process. This principle, known as Absolute Tao, can be only imperfectly understood by the practitioner but is the guiding principle in life. Taoists advocate a way of life that brings one closer to conformity with essential nature.

Taoism *pinyin* **Daoism** \ˈdau̇-ˌiz-əm\ Major Chinese religio-philosophical tradition. Though the concept of TAO was employed by all Chinese schools of thought, Taoism arose out of the promotion of tao as the social ideal. LAOZI is traditionally regarded as the founder of Taoism and the author of its classic text, the *TAO-TE CHING*. Other Taoist classics include the *Zhuangzi* (see ZHUANGZI) and the *Liezi* (3rd–4th cent. A.D.). In Taoism, tao is the force or principle that latently contains the forms, entities, and forces of all phenomena. DE, or superior virtue, is acquired through action so entirely in accordance with the natural order that its author leaves no trace of himself in his work. Taoism's focus on nature and the natural order complements the societal focus of CONFUCIANISM, and its synthesis with BUDDHISM is the basis of ZEN. See also YIN-YANG.

Taos \ˈtau̇s\ Town (pop. 5,000) and resort, N New Mexico. It is located on a branch of the RIO GRANDE in the SANGRE DE CRISTO MTNS. An early Spanish settlement, it was the scene of a revolt (1680) of Taos and other PUEBLO INDIANS against Spain, and later was an important commercial center on the SANTA FE TRAIL. In the 20th cent. artists and writers moved there, including D. H. LAWRENCE; his home and that of Kit CARSON are historic sites.

Tao-te ching *pinyin* **Daode jing** \ˈdau̇-ˈdə-ˈjiŋ\ Classic text of Chinese philosophy. Written between the 6th and 3rd cent. B.C., it was once called the *Laozi* after its traditional author LAOZI. It presents a way of life intended to restore harmony and tranquillity to a kingdom racked by disorder. It promotes a course of nonaction, understood as restraint from any unnatural action rather than complete passivity, thereby allowing the TAO to resolve things naturally. It was designed as a handbook for rulers, who should rule by inaction, imposing no restrictions or prohibitions on their subjects. It has had a tremendous influence on all later schools of Chinese philosophy and religion.

Tapajos River \ˌtä-pä-ˈzhȯs\ River, N Brazil. Formed by the Teles Pires and Juruena rivers, it flows northeast to empty into the AMAZON RIVER just above Santarém after a course of 807 mi (1,298 km). Though interrupted by rapids, its entire length is navigable. Several important rubber plantations lie along its banks.

tapas \ˈtə-pəs\ Ascetic practice carried out to achieve spiritual power or purification. In HINDUISM, it is associated with YOGA as a way of purifying the body in preparation for the more exacting spiritual exercises leading to liberation. In JAINISM, its practice is a central means of breaking the cycle of rebirths by preventing new KARMA from forming and by eliminating the old. Tapas can take many forms, including fasting, controlling the breath, and holding difficult and painful body postures.

tap dance Style of American theatrical dance using precise rhythmical patterns of foot movement and audible foot tapping. It is derived from the clog dances, jigs, and reels of the British Isles and the rhythmic foot stamping of Africa. Popular in 19th-cent. minstrel shows, the "buck-and-wing" (danced vigorously in wooden-soled shoes) and "soft-shoe" (danced smoothly in soft-soled shoes) versions developed as separate techniques; by 1925 they had merged, and metal taps were attached to shoe heels and toes to produce a sharper sound. The dance was also popular in variety shows and early musicals.

tape recorder Recording system that makes use of electro-magnetic phenomena to record and reproduce SOUND waves. The tape consists of a plastic backing coated with a thin layer of tiny particles of magnetic powder. The recording head of the tape deck consists of a tiny C-shaped magnet with its gap adjacent to the moving tape. The incoming sound wave, having been converted by a microphone into an electrical signal, produces a time-varying magnetic field in the gap of the magnet. As the tape moves past the recording head, the powder is magnetized in such a way that the tape carries a record of the shape of the wave being recorded.

tapestry Heavy, reversible, patterned hand-woven textile, usually in the form of a hanging or upholstery fabric. Tapestries are often designed as sets of panels intended to be hung together. The earliest known tapestries were made from linen by the ancient Egyptians. Tapestry weaving was well established in Peru by the 6th cent. A.D., and outstanding silk tapestries were made in China from the 7th cent. on. In Western Europe, tapestry making flourished from the 13th cent. Among the greatest European tapestries are the 15th-cent. *Lady with the Unicorn* set and the 16th-cent. *Acts of the Apostles* set, based on cartoons by RAPHAEL. Tapestry art was revitalized in late-19th-cent. Britain with the ARTS AND CRAFTS MOVEMENT. In the 20th cent., abstract tapestries were produced at the BAUHAUS, and many painters allowed their paintings to provide the basis for tapestry art.

tapeworm Any of about 3,000 species (class Cestoda, phylum Platyhelminthes) of parasitic FLATWORMS. Tapeworms range from 0.04 in. (1 mm) to more than 50 ft (15 m) long. The head bears suckers and often hooks for attaching to the liver or digestive tract of the host. Once attached, tapeworms absorb food through their body wall. The body consists largely of a series of proglottids (units containing both male and female reproductive organs) which continually form at the base of the neck. Following fertilization, each mature proglottid containing thousands of embryos breaks off and is eliminated in the host's feces. The life cycle may require more than one host. For species that infest humans, the intermediate host is implied by the name (e.g., beef tapeworm). Human infestation is common in the SE U.S.; humans usually acquire tapeworms through fecal contamination of soil or water or inadequate cooking of meat or fish. See diagram on next page.

tapir \ˈtā-pər\ Any of four extant members (genus *Tapirus*) of the family Tapiridae, heavy-bodied, odd-toed UNGULATES, 6–8 ft (1.8–2.5 m) long and up to 3 ft (1 m) high. They have short ears and legs and a fleshy snout overhanging the upper lip. Two species have a short, bristly mane. The Malayan tapir (*T. indicus*) is black and white; the single Central American and two S. American species are plain brown or gray. Tapirs inhabit the deep forest or swamp.

Tappan \ˈtap-ən\, **Arthur** (1786–1865) U.S. merchant and philanthropist. Born in Northampton, Mass., he operated a silk-importing firm in New York (1826–37) with his brother Lewis (1788–1873); they also founded the first commercial credit-rating service (1841). He used his wealth to support missionary societies and the abolitionist crusade, helping found the AMERICAN ANTI-SLAVERY SOCIETY and serving as

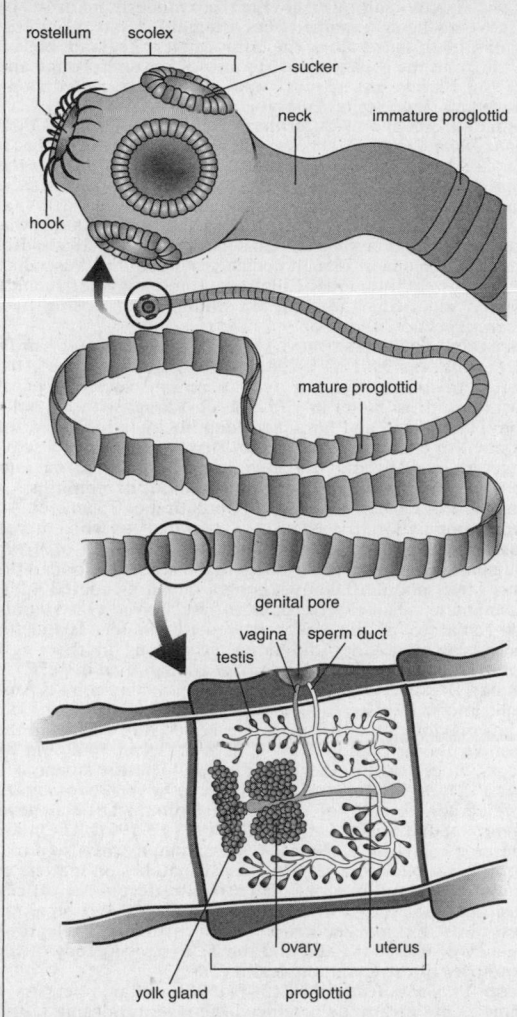

Tapeworm Principal features of the beef tapeworm. The head or scolex contains suckers and hooks for attaching to the human host. A series of reproductive organs (proglottids) continually form at the base of the neck, and following fertilization they mature and break off. Each proglottid, eliminated in the host's feces, contains thousands of embryos. If these are ingested by cattle (the intermediate host) grazing on food contaminated with feces, they develop into larvae, which bore through the intestinal wall into the circulatory system and are carried to muscle tissues, which they burrow into, forming a dormant cyst. When meat is inadequately cooked, humans become infected with the larvae, which attach to the intestinal wall.

its first president (1833–40). After breaking with W. L. GARRISON, he created the American and Foreign Anti-Slavery Society (1840).

Tara \'tä-rä\ In BUDDHISM, a savior-goddess with numerous forms. Her worship is popular in Nepal, Tibet, and Mongolia. She is the feminine counterpart of AVALOKITESVARA. She came into existence when his tear fell to the ground and formed a lake; out of its waters rose a lotus, which, on opening, revealed the goddess. She is the protector of navigation and earthly travel, as well as of spiritual travel along the path to Enlightenment.

Taranto \'tä-rän-ˌtō\ *ancient* Tarentum. Seaport (metro. area pop., 1996 est.: 212,000), PUGLIA region, SE Italy. The old city is on a small island, with newer areas on the mainland. Founded by Greeks from SPARTA in the 8th cent. B.C., it became one of the leading cities of MAGNA GRAECIA. It reached its zenith in the 4th cent. B.C. under ARCHYTAS. It came under Rome in 272 B.C., and later, successively, the Goths, Byzantines, Lombards, Arabs, and Normans. By the 15th cent. it was part of the kingdom of Naples. Part of the kingdom of the Two SICILIES from 1815, it joined the kingdom of Italy in 1861. It was an important stronghold of the Italian Navy in both world wars and is today the site of a naval base and extensive shipyards.

tarantula \tə-ran-chə-lə\ Any SPIDER in the family Theraphosidae. It is found from the SW U.S. to S. America. Most species have a hairy body and long, hairy legs. They are nocturnal predators, principally of insects. In the SW U.S., tarantulas of the genus *Aphonopelma* may have a body 2 in. (5 cm) long and a leg spread of nearly 5 in. (12 cm). They may inflict a painful bite if provoked. The most common U.S. species, *Eurypelma californicum,* may live up to 30 years.

Tarawa \tə-'rä-wə, 'ta-rə-wä\ Coral atoll (pop., 1995: 32,000), GILBERT ISLANDS, Kiribati. It is made up of 15 islets along a reef 22 mi (35 km) long. Occupied by the Japanese during World War II, it was seized by U.S. Marines in 1943 after a costly battle. It was the capital of Gilbert and Ellice Islands until 1975.

Tarbell \'tär-bəl\, **Ida M(inerva)** (1857–1944) U.S. investigative journalist. Born in Erie Co., Pa., she became best known for *The History of the Standard Oil Company* (1904), an account of the rise of a business monopoly that led to the government's epochal antitrust suit against the company. One of the journalists Theodore ROOSEVELT dubbed MUCKRAKERS, she also wrote for *American Magazine* (1906–15) and was its co-owner and coeditor for several years. Among her other works are popular biographies and an autobiography.

tariff *or* **customs duty** Tax levied on a commodity traded across international borders. Usually assessed on imports, tariffs may apply to all foreign goods or only to goods produced outside the borders of a CUSTOMS UNION. A tariff may be assessed directly, at the border, or indirectly, by requiring the prior purchase of a license or permit. Tariffs provide a source of revenue and protect local industry. By driving up the price of the imported item, they allow domestic competitors either to charge higher prices or to take advantage of their own lighter taxes to charge lower prices. Tariffs are often used to protect "infant industries" or to safeguard older industries that are in decline. They are sometimes criticized for imposing hidden costs on domestic consumers and encouraging inefficiency in domestic industries. Tariffs are subject to negotiation and treaty among nations (see TRADE AGREEMENT, WORLD TRADE ORGANIZATION).

Tarkington, (Newton) Booth (1869–1946) U.S. novelist and dramatist. A native of Indianapolis, he became known for satirical and sometimes romanticized pictures of American Midwesterners. *Penrod* (1914) and *Seventeen* (1916) are young-people's classics. *The Magnificent Ambersons* (1918, Pulitzer Prize; film, 1942) traces the decline of a prominent family. *Alice Adams* (1921) is perhaps his most finished novel. His many plays include an adaptation of his *Monsieur Beaucaire* (1901).

Tarn River River, SW France. Rising in the Lozère Mtns., it flows west and southwest for 233 mi (375 km) into the GARONNE RIVER. Its magnificent gorges, which extend for more than 30 mi (48 km), are popular tourist attractions.

taro \'tär-ō\ Herbaceous plant (*Colocasia esculenta*) of the ARUM FAMILY, probably native to S.E. Asia, that spread to the Pacific islands. It is a staple crop cultivated for its large, starchy, spherical underground TUBERS, which, though poisonous raw, become edible with heating. It is consumed as a cooked vegetable or made into puddings, breads, or Polynesian poi (a pasty mass of fermented taro starch). The large leaves (also poisonous raw) are commonly eaten stewed.

tarot \'tar-ˌō\ Sets of cards used in fortune-telling. Cards approximating their present form first appeared in the late

TUV

14th cent. Modern tarot decks consist of 78 cards, of which 22 have pictures representing forces, characters, virtues, and vices. The remaining cards are divided into four suits—(1) wands, batons, or rods, (2) cups, (3) swords, and (4) coins, pentacles, or disks—of 14 cards each. Each suit has 10 numbered cards and four court cards (king, queen, knight, and page). Modern PLAYING CARDS evolved from the latter. Initially used as playing cards, tarot cards were imbued with esoteric associations in the 18th cent. In fortune-telling, each card's basic meaning is altered by the card's position in the spread of cards laid out by the fortune-teller, its orientation, and the cards that are near it.

Tarquinia \tär-'kwēn-yä\ *formerly (until 1922)* **Corneto** Town (pop., 1991: 14,000), N LAZIO region, central Italy. It developed from Tárchuna, a chief city of the Etruscan confederation. It became a Roman colony (as Tarquinii) in the 1st cent. B.C. and was moved to its present site after Lombard and Saracen invasions in the 6th–8th cent. A.D. Remains of a great temple include a group of terra-cotta winged horses that is considered a masterpiece of Etruscan art. The famous necropolis contains the most important painted tombs in Etruscan Italy.

tarragon \'tar-ə-gən\ Bushy aromatic herb (*Artemisia dracunculus*) of the COMPOSITE FAMILY. Dried tarragon is a common ingredient in seasoning blends, such as fines herbes. The fresh leaves are used in salads, and vinegar in which fresh tarragon has been steeped is a distinctive condiment. The plant is probably native to Siberia.

tarsier \'tär-sē-ər, 'tär-sē-,ā\ Any of three species (genus *Tarsius*, family Tarsiidae) of nocturnal prosimian PRIMATES found on several SE Asian islands. Tarsiers have large, goggling eyes and a round head that can be rotated 180°. The ears are large, membranous, and almost constantly in motion. Tarsiers are 4–6 in. (9–16 cm) long; the thin, tufted tail is about twice that length. Tarsiers cling vertically to trees and leap from trunk to trunk. They have greatly elongated hind limbs and disklike adhesive pads on the digit tips.

Tarsus City (pop., 1997: 190,000), S central Turkey, near the Mediterranean coast. Settled from Neolithic times, it was razed and rebuilt around 700 B.C. by the Assyrian king SENNACHERIB. In 67 B.C. it was absorbed into the new Roman province of CILICIA, becoming its principal city. It was the site of the first meeting between Mark ANTONY and CLEOPATRA and was the birthplace of St. PAUL. It remained a leading cultural center through the early Byzantine period. It passed to the Ottoman Turks in the early 16th cent. Modern Tarsus is a prosperous agricultural and cotton-milling center.

tartan Plaid pattern of bands, stripes, or lines of various colors and of definite width and sequence, woven into woolen cloth. Such patterns have existed for centuries in many cultures, but have come to be regarded as fundamentally Scottish and as a quasi-heraldic Scottish family or clan emblem, though few seem to predate the 17th or even 18th cent. as clan emblems. The Scottish Tartans Society (founded 1963) maintains a register of all known tartans, numbering about 1,300.

Tartars See TATARS

Tartarus \'tär-tə-rəs\ In GREEK MYTHOLOGY, the lowest depths of the underworld. It was a region of eternal darkness where the evil were punished after death for having offended the gods. Later classical authors sometimes used Tartarus interchangeably with HADES to designate the entire underworld.

Tashkent \tash-'kent, tash-'kend\ City (pop., 1998 est.: 2,137,000), capital of Uzbekistan. Dating from about the 1st cent. B.C., it was an important trade center on the caravan routes to Europe and the Orient. Held successively by the Arabs, the Mongols, and the Turks, it was taken by the Russians in 1865 and made the administrative center of Turkistan in 1867. The city was heavily damaged by an earthquake in 1966. Today it is the main economic and cultural center of central Asia. Its many institutions of higher education include the Uzbek Academy of Sciences (1943).

Tasman \'tàs-män\, **Abel Janszoon** (1603?–1659?) Dutch explorer. In the service of the Dutch E. INDIA CO., he made voyages to E. and S.E. Asia 1634–39. In 1642 he was sent by Anthony van DIEMEN to find the hypothetical S continent of the Pacific. Sailing from Batavia (modern Jakarta), he discovered land he named Van Diemen's Land (now Tasmania), then sailed along the coast of New Zealand, believing it to be the S continent. He also discovered Tonga and the Fiji Islands. On his next voyage (1644) he sailed along the N and W coasts of Australia.

Tasmania \taz-'mā-nē-ə\ *formerly* **Van Diemen's Land** \'dē-mənz\ Island (pop., 1998 est.: 472,000), state of Australia. It is located off the SE corner of the continent. HOBART is the capital. Originally inhabited by AUSTRALIAN ABORIGINES, it was explored and named Van Diemen's Land by A. J. TASMAN in 1642. Taken by the British in the early 1800s, it was used as an auxiliary penal settlement until the 1850s. Renamed Tasmania in 1856, it became a state of the Australian Commonwealth in 1901. Chief economic activities include copper, zinc, tin, and tungsten mining, and raising livestock, especially for wool.

Tasmanian devil MARSUPIAL species (*Sarcophilus harrisii* or *S. ursinus*, family Dasyuridae), now extinct on the Australian mainland, that survives in remote rocky areas of Tasmania. It is 30–40 in. (75–100 cm) long, with a stocky body, large head and jaws, and long bushy tail. Named for its devilish expression and husky snarl, it is mainly a scavenger of wallaby and sheep carcasses. Its three or four young remain in the mother's pouch about five months.

Tasmanians Extinct Australoid population of Tasmania. An isolate population of AUSTRALIAN ABORIGINES who entered Tasmania 25,000–40,000 years ago, they were cut off from the mainland when a general rise in the sea level flooded the Bass Strait about 10,000 years ago. Of an estimated 4,000 Tasmanians when the Europeans first arrived (1803), only 200 remained by the 1830s; moved to Flinders Island for their protection, they did not survive long in their new home, and the last full-blooded Tasmanian died in 1876.

Tasman Sea Part of the SW Pacific Ocean, between SE Australia and W New Zealand. About 1,400 mi (2,250 km) wide, it has maximum depths exceeding 17,000 ft (5,200 m) in the Tasman Basin. Explored by A. J. TASMAN in 1642 and by Capt. James COOK in the 1770s, it is notoriously stormy.

Tass \'tàs\ *in full* Telegrafnoe Agentsvo Sovetskovo Soyuza ("Telegraph Agency of the Soviet Union") Official news agency of the Soviet Union from 1925 to 1991. The main source of news for all Soviet news media, it was also a major international wire service. Tass dispatches on matters of public policy and international affairs reflected the official position of the state. After the Soviet Union's 1991 breakup, Tass was reorganized into the Information Telegraph Agency of Russia (ITAR) and the Telegraph Agency of the Countries of the Commonwealth (Tass).

Tasso \'täs-sō\, **Torquato** (1544–1595) Italian poet. As a courtier in Ferrara, he produced the pastoral drama *L'Aminta* (1581; performed 1573), a lyrical idealization of court life. In 1575 he completed his celebrated and influential masterpiece on the First Crusade, *Gerusalemme liberata* (1581; *Jerusalem Delivered*), a heroic epic in OTTAVA RIMA that blends historical events with imaginary romantic and idyllic episodes. He developed a persecution mania and from 1579 to 1586 was incarcerated in a hospital. The subject of literary legend for centuries, he is regarded as the greatest Italian poet of the late Renaissance.

taste *or* **taste perception** Special SENSE for perceiving and distinguishing the sweet, sour, bitter, or salty quality of a dissolved substance, mediated by more than 9,000 taste buds on the TONGUE and some on the roof of the mouth and throat. The CHEMORECEPTION of taste is only capable of distinguishing these four qualities; the rest of what is usually perceived as taste is attributable to SMELL. See diagram on next page.

Tatar language \'tä-tər\ *formerly* **Volga Tatar language** TURKIC LANGUAGE with some 8 million speakers. Its speakers include less than half the population of Tatarstan in Russia, with the remainder scattered across W Russian, Siberia, and the Central Asian republics. Tatar is characterized by a remarkable series of vowel shifts that distinguish it from all other Turkic languages. Crimean Tatar and Chulym Tatar are not closely related to Tatar.

Tatars \'tä-tərz\ *or* **Tartars** Turkic-speaking peoples who today live mainly in W central Russia, Kazakhstan, and W

Taste A. Taste centers on the tongue's surface. Taste buds on the tip of the tongue are most sensitive to sweet tastes, those on the sides to sour, those at the back to bitter, and those on the tip and sides to salty. B. Close-up of a papilla showing location of the taste buds. C. Structure of a taste bud. Each is composed of narrow modified epithelial taste cells with specialized hairs (microvilli) that project into a pore opening onto the tongue's surface and broader supporting cells. Impulses from the taste cells are carried by nerve pathways to the brain.

Siberia. They first appeared as nomadic tribes in NE Mongolia in the 5th cent. Some joined the armies of GENGHIS KHAN. Especially identified with the GOLDEN HORDE, they were converted to Islam in the 14th cent. The Golden Horde soon became independent Tatar khanates (see KHAN). Their economy has long been based on mixed farming and herding, and they developed craftsmanship in wood, ceramics, leather, cloth, and metal. Today there are about 6 million Tatars; they are most numerous in the Russian republic of Tatarstan.

Tate, (John Orley) Allen (1899–1979) U.S. poet and novelist. Born in Winchester, Ky., he attended Vanderbilt Univ., where he helped found *The Fugitive* (1922–25), a poetry magazine concentrating largely on the South, and contributed to *I'll Take My Stand* (1930), a Fugitive manifesto defending the region's conservative agrarian society. A leading exponent of the NEW CRITICISM, he emphasized the writer's need for tradition, which he found in Southern culture and later in Roman Catholicism, to which he converted in 1950. His best-known poem is "Ode to the Confederate Dead" (1926).

Tate, Nahum (1652–1715) Irish-English poet and playwright. Though he wrote plays of his own, he is best known for his adaptations of Elizabethan works, notably William SHAKESPEARE's *King Lear*, with a happy ending. He wrote the libretto for Henry PURCELL's *Dido and Aeneas* (1689?) and collaborated with Nicholas Brady in *A New Version of the Psalms of David* (1696). The best of his own poems is "Panacea: A Poem upon Tea" (1700). He became England's poet laureate in 1692.

Tate Gallery Art museum in London housing the national collection of British painting and sculpture and of modern British and European art. Named after the sugar tycoon Sir Henry Tate (1819–1899), who donated his collection of Victorian art to the nation in 1890, the Neoclassical building opened in 1897. In 1987 the Clore Gallery was added to house the principal collection of J. M. W. TURNER's works. The Tate Modern, a converted power plant housing the modern collections, opened in 2000.

Tati \tà-ʹtē\, **Jacques** *orig.* Jacques Tatischeff (1908–1982) French film actor and director. A popular music-hall entertainer in the 1930s, he appeared in comedy shorts before writing, directing, and starring in a series of comic feature films—*Jour de fête* (1949), *Monsieur Hulot's Holiday* (1953), *Mon oncle* (1958), *Playtime* (1968), *Traffic* (1971), and *Parade* (1974)—in which he became known for his inspired physical comedy and his accident-prone alter ego, Monsieur Hulot.

Tatlin \ʹtàt-lyin\, **Vladimir (Yevgrafovich)** (1885–1953) Ukrainian sculptor and painter. After a visit to Paris (1914), he became the leader of a group of Moscow artists who sought to apply engineering techniques to sculpture, a movement that developed into CONSTRUCTIVISM. He pioneered the use of iron, glass, wood, and wire in nonrepresentational constructions. His *Monument to the Third International*, commissioned by the Soviet government in 1919, was one of the first buildings conceived entirely in abstract terms, and was intended to be, at more than 1,300 ft (400 m), the world's tallest structure, but the government disapproved of nonfigurative art and it was never built. After 1933 Tatlin worked largely as a stage designer.

tattoo Permanent mark or design made on the body by pigment introduced through ruptures in the skin. Tattooing has been practiced in most parts of the world, and examples have been found on Egyptian and Nubian mummies dating from 2000 B.C. Decoration is perhaps the most common motive, though designs may also serve to identify rank, status, or membership and are thought by some to provide magical protection against sickness or misfortune. The word comes from Tahiti, where it was recorded by James COOK's expedition in 1769. The first electric tattooing implement was patented in the U.S. in 1891.

Tatum \ʹtā-təm\, **Art(hur)** (1909–1956) U.S. jazz pianist. Born in Toledo, Ohio, he was blind from birth. Influenced by Fats WALLER and Earl HINES, his playing achieved a synthesis of stride and SWING piano traditions. He developed an unprecedented technical and harmonic control, capable of astonishing speed and intricate elaborations of melody, and by 1937 he was recognized as the outstanding pianist in jazz.

Tatum, Edward L(awrie) (1909–1975) U.S. biochemist. Born in Boulder, Col., he worked with George BEADLE at Stanford Univ., where they confirmed that all biochemical processes in organisms are ultimately controlled by genes, that these processes can be broken down into a series of individual sequential chemical reactions, each controlled by a single gene, and that mutation of a single gene changes the cell's ability to carry out only a single chemical reaction. Each gene was found to determine the structure of a specific ENZYME (the "one gene, one enzyme" hypothesis). With Joshua LEDERBERG, Tatum discovered the occurrence of genetic RECOMBINATION, or "sex," between certain bacteria. Tatum, Beadle, and Lederberg shared a Nobel Prize in 1958.

Taurus Mountains Mountain chain, S Turkey, parallel to the Mediterranean coast. It extends to the upper reaches of the

TUV

EUPHRATES RIVER in the east. It has many peaks 10,000–12,000 ft (3,000–3,700 m) high. The Cilician Gates pass, 38 mi (61 km) long and used by caravans and armies since antiquity, crosses the range north of TARSUS.

Taussig \'taú-sig\, **Helen Brooke** (1898–1986) U.S. physician. Born in Cambridge, Mass., as head of a Baltimore heart clinic (1930–63) she studied "blue babies" (babies whose heart malformations cause low blood oxygen content) and pioneered use of fluoroscopy and X rays to pinpoint the defect responsible for each set of symptoms. The surgical treatment she devised with Alfred Blalock (1899–1964) saved thousands of such infants, and her research spurred development of other surgical treatments for heart disorders, comprehensively described in her *Congenital Malformations of the Heart* (2 vols., 1947). She also helped alert U.S. physicians to the dangers of THALIDOMIDE.

tautog See WRASSE

tax Government levy on persons, groups, or businesses. Taxes have existed since ancient times—PROPERTY TAXES and SALES TAXES were known in Rome—but TARIFFS were favored over internal taxes as a source of revenue. Modern economies have increasingly favored internal taxes. Taxes are meant to cover government spending, promote stable economic growth, and lessen inequalities in the distribution of income and wealth. They have also been used for nonfiscal reasons, such as to encourage or discourage certain activities (e.g., cigarette consumption). Taxes may be direct or indirect. Direct taxes are those that the taxpayer cannot shift onto someone else; they are mainly taxes on persons and are based on an individual's ability to pay. They include INCOME TAXES, taxes on net worth, INHERITANCE and ESTATE TAXES, and gift taxes. Indirect taxes are those that can be shifted to someone other than the person legally responsible for payment. These include excise taxes, sales taxes, and VALUE-ADDED TAXES. Taxes may also be classified according to the effect they have on the distribution of wealth. A proportional tax is one that imposes the same relative burden on all taxpayers, unlike PROGRESSIVE TAXES and REGRESSIVE TAXES.

Taxco (de Alarcón) \'täs-kō\ City (pop., 1990: 87,000), GUERRERO state, S central Mexico. A silver-mining site in pre-Columbian times, it prospered in the Spanish colonial period and is still renowned for its silver. Because of its colonial character, with its cobblestone streets and the baroque Church of Santa Prisca, it has been declared a national monument.

Taxila \'tak-sə-lə\ Ancient city, NW India. Its ruins, including temples and a fortress, lie west of RAWALPINDI, Pakistan. It was the capital of the Buddhist kingdom of Gandhara and a center of learning. Founded by Bharata, the younger brother of Rama, it came under Persian rule, and in 326 B.C. was surrendered to ALEXANDER THE GREAT. It became an important Buddhist center under King ASHOKA around 261 B.C. Its prosperity resulted from its position at the junction of three great trade routes, which eventually declined. It was finally destroyed by the Huns in the 5th cent.

taxol \'taks-ȯl\ Organic compound with a complex multiring molecule that occurs in the bark of Pacific YEWS. It appears to be active against certain cancers, disrupting cell division and interfering with separation of the nuclear CHROMOSOMES. Semisynthetic and synthetic processes to make it have averted total destruction of yew forests.

taxonomy \tak-'sä-nə-mē\ In biology, the classification of organisms into a hierarchy of groupings, from the general to the particular: kingdom, phylum, class, order, family, genus, SPECIES. The black-capped chickadee, for example, is an animal (kingdom Animalia) with a dorsal nerve cord (phylum Chordata) and feathers (class Aves: birds) that perches (order Passeriformes: perching birds) and is small with a short bill (family Paridae), a song that sounds like "chik-a-dee" (genus *Parus*), and a black-capped head (species *atricapillus*). Most authorities recognize five kingdoms: monerans (PROKARYOTES), PROTISTS, fungi (see FUNGUS), PLANTS, and ANIMALS. Carolus LINNAEUS established the scheme of using Latin generic and specific names in the mid-18th cent.

Taylor, Elizabeth (Rosemond) (b.1932) U.S. film actress. Born in London, she left with her American parents in 1939. Noted for her exceptional beauty from childhood, she became a star with *National Velvet* in 1944. She was a glamorous adult star in *Father of the Bride* (1950), *A Place in the Sun* (1951), *Giant* (1956), *Cat on a Hot Tin Roof* (1958), *Suddenly Last Summer* (1959), *Butterfield 8* (1960, Academy Award), and *Cleopatra* (1963). In *Who's Afraid of Virginia Woolf* (1966, Academy Award) and other films, she starred opposite her husband, Richard BURTON. Her personal life and eight marriages were avidly followed in the popular press. In later years she campaigned energetically for AIDS research. In 2000 she was created a Dame of the British Empire.

Taylor, Frederick W(inslow) (1856–1915) U.S. inventor and engineer. Born in Germantown, Pa., he worked at Midvale Steel Co. (1878–90), where he introduced TIME-AND-MOTION STUDY to reduce manufacturing costs. Though his system provoked opposition from labor when carried to extremes, it had an immense impact on the development of MASS PRODUCTION techniques and has influenced the development of virtually every modern industrial country.

Taylor, Maxwell (Davenport) (1901–1987) U.S. Army officer. Born in Keytesville, Mo., he helped organize the army's first airborne division early in World War II. He commanded a parachute assault in the NORMANDY CAMPAIGN and in the Battle of the BULGE (1944). He served as commanding general of U.N. forces in Korea (1953), Army chief of staff (1955–59), chairman of the Joint Chiefs of Staff (1962–64), ambassador to S. Vietnam (1964–65), and special consultant to Pres. Lyndon JOHNSON (1965–69). He advocated the maintenance of conventional infantry as a prudent alternative to nuclear weapons in war.

Taylor, Paul (Belville) (b.1930) U.S. modern dancer, choreographer, and director. Born in Pittsburgh, he joined Martha GRAHAM's company in 1953, where he was a leading soloist until 1960. In 1957 he established the Paul Taylor Dance Co., which was soon touring frequently in the U.S. and abroad. He choreographed over 100 works in a variety of styles, including *Duet* (1957), *Orbs* (1966), and *Nightshade* (1979). He retired from performing in the 1970s but continues to direct his company.

Taylor, Zachary (1784–1850) 12th president of the U.S. (1849–50). Born in Montebello, Va., he grew up on the Kentucky frontier. He fought in the War of 1812, the Black Hawk War (1832), and the Seminole Wars (1835–42), earning the nickname "Old Rough-and-Ready" for his indifference to hardship. Sent to Texas in anticipation of war with Mexico, he defeated the Mexican invaders at Palo Alto and Resaca de la Palma (1846). After the MEXICAN WAR formally began, he captured Monterrey. Ignoring orders to remain there, he marched south to defeat a large Mexican force at Buena

Zachary Taylor

Vista (1847). A national hero, he was nominated as the Whig candidate for president (1848) and defeated Lewis CASS to win the election. His brief term was marked by a controversy over the new territories that produced the COMPROMISE OF 1850 and by a scandal involving members of his cabinet. He died, probably of cholera, after only 16 months in office and was succeeded by Millard FILLMORE.

Tay River Longest river in Scotland. It rises on the N slopes of Ben Lui and flows through Loch Tay to enter the NORTH SEA below DUNDEE after 120 mi (193 km). It drains 2,400 sq mi (6,200 sq km), the largest drainage area in Scotland.

Tay-Sachs disease \'tā-'saks\ Recessive hereditary metabolic disorder, mostly in ASHKENAZI Jews, causing progressive mental and neurologic deterioration and death by age 5. Infants appear normal at birth but soon become listless and inattentive, lose motor abilities, and develop seizures. Blindness and general paralysis usually precede death. Tests can detect the disease in fetuses and the Tay-Sachs gene in carriers. There is no treatment.

Tbilisi \tə-bi-ˈlē-sē\ *formerly* **Tiflis** City (pop., 1998 est.: 1,399,000), capital of the Republic of Georgia. Founded about A.D. 458, it held a strategic position on trade routes between Europe and Asia. After successive Persian, Byzantine, Arab, Mongol, and Turkish rule, it came under the Russians around 1801. It was made the capital of the Transcaucasian Federation in 1921, the Georgian S.S.R. in 1936, and the independent Republic of Georgia in 1991. The Soviet military massacred civilians during an independence demonstration there in 1989. It is now a major cultural, research, and industrial center and the site of a university (1918).

T cell With the B CELL, one of the two main types of LYMPHOCYTE, essential parts of the IMMUNE SYSTEM. T cells originate in the bone marrow, mature in the thymus, and travel in the blood to other LYMPHOID TISSUES. T cells directly attack invaders (ANTIGENS) by binding to them and helping remove them from the body. Because the body contains millions of T and B cells, many of which carry unique receptors, it can respond to virtually any antigen. See also ANTIBODY, IMMUNOLOGY.

Tchaikovsky \chə-ˈkȯf-skē, chī-ˈkȯf-skē\, **Piotr Ilyich** (1840–1893) Russian composer. His mother's death when he was 14 turned the sensitive boy to composition. From 1866 he taught at the Moscow Conservatory. His Piano Concerto No. 1 (1875) became immensely popular. In 1875 he wrote *Swan Lake* for the Bolshoi Ballet. In 1877 came a commission from the wealthy Nadezhda von Meck (1831–1894), who became his patron and correspondent, though they never met. The opera *Eugene Onegin* (1878) soon followed. Though homosexual, he proposed to a woman out of politeness; after three disastrous months of marriage, he attempted suicide. His composition was overshadowed by his personal crisis for years. His *Sleeping Beauty* ballet (1889) was followed by the opera *The Queen of Spades* (1890) and the great ballet *The Nutcracker* (1892). His "Pathétique" Symphony (1893) premiered four days before his death from cholera. His ballets were the greatest written in the 19th cent., and his six symphonies have never lost their popularity.

TCP/IP *in full* Transmission Control Protocol/Internet Protocol. Standard INTERNET communications PROTOCOLS. The Internet is a packet-switched network, in which information is broken down into small packets, sent individually over many different routes at the same time, and then reassembled. TCP is the component that collects and reassembles the packets of data, while IP makes sure the packets are sent to the right destination. TCP/IP was developed in the 1970s and adopted as the protocol standard for ARPANET (the predecessor to the Internet) in 1983.

tea Beverage produced by steeping in freshly boiled water the young leaves and leaf buds of the tea plant, *Camellia sinensis,* a member of the family Theaceae, which contains 40 genera of trees and shrubs. According to legend, it has been known in China since about 2700 B.C. It was established in Japan by the 13th cent. and was spread to India by the English in the 19th cent. Today tea is the most widely consumed drink in the world. Major tea types are classified by processing method: fermented, or black, tea produces an amber-colored, full-flavored beverage; semifermented, or oolong, tea yields a slightly bitter, light brownish-green liquid; and unfermented, or green, tea, results in a mild, slightly bitter, pale greenish-yellow beverage. CAFFEINE is responsible for tea's stimulating effect. Green tea has in recent years attracted much favorable attention for a wide range of possible beneficial effects. Infusions and decoctions of the leaves, bark, and roots of many other, unrelated plants are commonly drunk as herbal or medicinal teas.

Tea Act (1773) British legislation giving a tea monopoly in the American colonies to the British E. India Co. It adjusted the duty regulations to allow the failing company to sell its large tea surplus below the prices charged by colonial competitors. The act, opposed by colonists as another example of taxation without representation, led to the BOSTON TEA PARTY.

tea ceremony Ritualized preparation and drinking of TEA developed in Japan. It involves a host and one or more guests; the tea, utensils, and movements of preparation, serving, and drinking the tea are all prescribed. Introduced from China in the 12th cent., tea was drunk by Zen monks to help them stay awake. Tea-tasting competitions developed into a meditative form among the warrior aristocracy in the 15th cent. The most famous exponent of the tea ceremony was Sen no Rikyu (1522–1591), who codified a style known as *wabi,* which favored rustic, rough-shaped tea bowls and spare, simple surroundings. Three popular schools of the tea ceremony trace their roots to Rikyu; in the 20th cent. mastery of the tea ceremony was one accomplishment of a well-bred young woman.

Teach, Edward See BLACKBEARD

teak Large deciduous tree *(Tectona grandis)* of the verbena family, and its wood, one of the most valuable and durable timbers. The tree has a straight stem, a spreading crown, and four-sided branchlets. The branches end in many small white flowers. The unseasoned heartwood has a pleasant, strong aromatic fragrance and a beautiful golden-yellow color. Seasoned wood is brown, mottled with darker streaks. Resistant to the effects of water, teakwood is used for shipbuilding, fine furniture, door and window frames, wharves, bridges, flooring, and paneling. Its desirability has led to severe overcutting in tropical forests.

teal Any of about 15 species (genus *Anas,* family Anatidae) of small DABBLING DUCKS found on the major continents and many islands. Many are popular game birds. The Holarctic green-winged teal, usually found in a dense flock, is 13–15 in. (33–38 cm) long. The small blue-winged teal breeds across Canada and the N U.S. and winters south of the U.S. Flocks of many species take off and change direction in unison.

Teamsters Union *officially* **International Brotherhood of Teamsters, Chauffeurs, Warehousemen and Helpers of America (IBT)** Largest labor union in the U.S., representing truck drivers and workers in related industries such as aviation. It was formed in 1903 with the merger of two team-drivers' unions; by the 1930s, intercity truck drivers were predominant. From 1907 to 1952 the union was headed by Daniel J. Tobin (1875–1955), who built it up from 40,000 members to more than one million. The Teamsters were expelled from the AFL-CIO in 1957 for corruption. Between 1957 and 1988 three Teamsters presidents—Dave Beck, Jimmy HOFFA, and Roy Williams—were sentenced to prison terms. The union was readmitted to the AFL-CIO in 1987, but its image remained tarnished.

Teapot Dome scandal Secret leasing of U.S. government land to private interests. In 1922 oil reserves at Teapot Dome, Wyo., and Elk Hills, Cal., were improperly leased to private oil companies by Secretary of the Interior Albert FALL, who accepted cash gifts in return. When the leases became known, Congress directed Pres. Warren HARDING to cancel them. A later investigation revealed illegal actions by several government officials. The scandal became a symbol of government corruption.

tear duct and gland *or* **lachrymal duct and gland** \ˈlak-rə-məl\ Structures that produce, distribute, and carry away tears. A gland above the outer corner of each EYE secretes tears between the membrane (conjunctiva) lining the upper eyelid and that over the eyeball. Tears moisten and lubricate the conjunctiva and then flow into the minute openings (near the inner corners of the eyelids) of the tear ducts, which lead to the nasal cavity.

tear gas Any of a group of substances, most often synthetic organic HALOGEN compounds, that irritate the mucous membranes of the eyes, causing a stinging sensation and tears. They may also cause coughing, choking, and general debility. Tear gas was first used in warfare in World War I. Today it is mainly used by law-enforcement agencies to disperse mobs, disable rioters, and flush out armed suspects without deadly force.

Teasdale, Sara *orig.* Sara Trevor (1884–1933) U.S. poet. Born in St. Louis, she settled in Chicago. *Rivers to the Sea* (1915) established her as a popular poet, and *Love Songs* (1917) won the first Pulitzer Prize for poetry. Over time her verse became simpler and more austere. After her divorce in 1929,

TUV

she moved to New York City, where she lived in virtual retirement. Many poems in her last book, *Strange Victory* (1933), foreshadow her death by her own hand at 48.

Tebaldi \tä-'bäl-dē\, **Renata** (b.1922) Italian soprano. She sang at La Scala under Arturo TOSCANINI for its 1946 reopening and over the next decade. She debuted at the Metropolitan Opera in 1955 and sang there for 17 years in such roles as Desdemona, Tosca, Manon Lescaut, Mimi, and Violetta. Her voice was known for its great beauty and warmth.

technetium \tek-'nē-shē-əm\ Metallic chemical ELEMENT, one of the TRANSITION elements, chemical symbol Tc, atomic number 43. All its ISOTOPES are radioactive (see RADIOACTIVITY); some occur in trace amounts as NUCLEAR FISSION products of URANIUM. Its isotope technetium-97 was the first element artificially produced (see CYCLOTRON). Technetium-99 is the most-used isotope in NUCLEAR MEDICINE. Technetium resembles platinum in appearance and manganese in chemical behavior.

tectonics Scientific study of the deformation of the rocks that make up the earth's crust and the forces that produce such deformation. It deals with the folding and faulting associated with mountain building, the large-scale movements of the crust, and sudden horizontal displacements along faults. The chief working principle of tectonics is the concept of PLATE TECTONICS.

Tecumseh \tə-'kəm-sə\ (1768–1813) SHAWNEE Indian chief. He established a confederation made up of members of the CREEK and other nations. In 1811 his brother's attack on W. H. HARRISON's troops at TIPPECANOE ended in defeat. Tecumseh and his followers fought for the British in the War of 1812 and captured Detroit; several lesser successes followed. His death in battle marked the end of Indian resistance in the Old Northwest.

Tedder, Arthur William *later* Baron Tedder (of Glenguin) (1890–1967) British air marshal. As head of the RAF Middle East Command in World War II, he commanded Allied air operations in N. Africa and Italy, and in 1944 he was appointed head of Allied air operations in Western Europe. His policy of bombing German communications and providing close air support of ground operations contributed significantly to the success of the NORMANDY CAMPAIGN and the Allied advance into Germany.

Teflon Trademark name for POLYMERS of tetrafluoroethylene fluorocarbon (polytetrafluoroethylene, or PTFE) or fluorinated ethylene-propylene (FEP). Teflon is a tough, waxy, nonflammable organic compound with a slippery surface, attacked by very few chemicals and stable over a wide temperature range. It is used in gaskets, bearings, container and pipe linings, electrical insulation, parts for valves and pumps, and protective coatings on cooking utensils and saw blades.

Tegucigalpa \tā-ˌgü-sē-'gäl-pä\ City (metro. area pop., 1999: 988,000), capital of Honduras. It was founded in 1578 as a gold- and silver-mining center and made the permanent capital of Honduras in 1880. It is home to the National Univ. of Honduras (1847) and an 18th-cent. cathedral.

Tehran *or* **Teheran** \tä-(ə-)'rän\ City (pop., 1996: 6,759,000), capital of Iran. It is situated on the S slopes of the ELBURZ MTNS. Originally a suburb of ancient Rey (RHAGAE), it became the Iranian capital in A.D. 1220. It was the home of several SAFAVID rulers of Persia (16th–18th cent.). It became prominent after its capture by the AGA KHAN, who made it his capital in 1788. It underwent rapid modernization after 1925 and especially after World War II. In 1943 it was the site of the TEHRAN CONFERENCE. In 1979 the U.S. embassy was seized by militants (see IRAN HOSTAGE CRISIS). Tehran produces more than half of Iran's manufactured goods. It is the seat of several universities.

Tehran Conference (Nov. 28–Dec. 1, 1943) Meeting of Franklin ROOSEVELT, Winston CHURCHILL, and Joseph STALIN in Tehran during World War II. Stalin agreed to launch a military offensive from the east to coincide with a planned invasion of German-occupied France from the west. Also discussed but not settled were Eastern Europe's postwar borders and a postwar international organization.

Teilhard de Chardin \ˌtā-yàr-də-shàr-'daⁿ\, **(Marie-Joseph-) Pierre** (1881–1955) French philosopher and paleontologist.

Ordained a Jesuit priest in 1911, he taught geology from 1918 at the Institut Catholique, and in 1929 he directed the Peking Man excavations at ZHOUKOUDIAN. His geological work won him high honors but was disapproved by the Jesuit order. His philosophy was strongly informed by his scientific work, which he believed helped prove the existence of God. He is known for his theory that mankind is evolving toward a final spiritual unity that he called the Omega point. Though he wrote his major philosophical works, *The Divine Milieu* (1957) and *The Phenomenon of Man* (1955), in the 1920s and '30s, the Jesuits forbade publication in his lifetime.

Tekakwitha \ˌtek-ə-'kwith-ə\, **Kateri** (1656–1680) First N. American Indian considered for canonization. The daughter of an Algonquin Christian mother and a non-Christian Mohawk father, she was born in what is now Auriesville, N.Y. Partially blinded by smallpox, she was deeply impressed by the lives and words of three Jesuit missionaries she met at age 11, and at 20 she was baptized. Harassed in her home village, she fled to a Christian Indian mission near Montreal, where she became known as the "Lily of the Mohawks" for her kindness, faith, and heroic suffering before her early death. She was beatified in 1980.

Te Kanawa \te-'kä-nə-wə\, **Kiri (Janette)** (*later* **Dame Kiri**) (b.1944) New Zealand soprano. Daughter of a Maori, she went to London for study in 1966 and made her Covent Garden debut in 1970. She became especially admired as the Countess in *The Marriage of Figaro*. In 1974 she made a triumphal debut at the Metropolitan Opera, substituting at the last moment in *Otello*. A glamorous and regally imperturbable presence with a rich voice, she sang at the 1981 wedding of Prince Charles.

tektite Any of a class of small, natural glassy objects found on the earth's surface and associated with METEORITE impacts. When a large meteorite, comet, or asteroid hits the earth, it melts the rocks at the site, producing masses of molten droplets that are blasted into and out of the earth's atmosphere. The droplets cool quickly to a glassy form and then fall back to the earth.

Tel Aviv-Jaffa \ˌtel-ə-'vēv-'jä-fə\ *or* **Tel Aviv-Yafo** \ˌtel-ə-'vēv-'yä-fō\ City (pop., 1999 est.: 348,000), Israel, on the Mediterranean Sea. The hub of Israel's largest urban center, it combines the ancient port of Jaffa with Tel Aviv, its former suburb. Tel Aviv was founded in 1909 and was the capital of Israel 1948–50. By 1936 it was the largest and most important city in Palestine. Jaffa was an old Canaanite city that was taken by Egypt in the 15th cent. B.C. and occupied by the Israelite kings DAVID and SOLOMON. Over the centuries it was ruled by the Ptolemies, Syrians, and Romans, captured by the Crusaders, and razed by the Mamluks. The British surrendered it to Jewish military forces during the first ARAB–ISRAELI WAR (1948). It is Israel's main business and cultural center, the site of more than half of Israel's industrial plants, and home to Tel Aviv Univ. (1953) and Bar-Ilan Univ. (1953).

telecommunications Communication between parties at a distance from one another. Modern telecommunication systems include TELEPHONE, FAX, DATA TRANSMISSION, RADIO, and TELEVISION. Digital transmission is used to achieve high reliability without noise or interference and because digital switching systems are cheaper than analog systems. In order to use digital transmission, analog signals must be converted to digital. In data transmission the signals are already in digital form; most television, radio, and voice communications are analog and must be converted. Transmission may occur over cables or wireless radio relay systems, or via satellite links.

telegraph Electromagnetic communication device. In 1832 Samuel MORSE made sketches of ideas for a system of electric telegraphy, and in 1835 he developed a code to represent letters and numbers (MORSE CODE). In 1837 he was granted a patent on an electromagnetic telegraph that transmitted signals along a wire. That same year British inventors patented a telegraph system that activated five needle pointers that could be made to point to specific letters and numbers on their mounting plate. Public use of Morse's telegraph system began in 1844 and lasted more than 100 years.

Teleki \\'te-le-ki\\, **Pal, Grof (Count)** (1879–1941) Hungarian politician. An eminent geographer, he taught at Budapest Univ., then returned to politics as minister of education (1938–39) and premier (1939–41). Hoping to use Germany's power to win back Hungarian territories lost after World War I, he initially cooperated with Adolf HITLER. In 1941, caught between German demands for support after it invaded Yugoslavia (with which Hungary had signed a friendship treaty) and British threats against helping Germany, he committed suicide.

Telemann \\'tä-lə-,män\\, **Georg Philipp** (1681–1767) German composer. He had learned several instruments by age 10, and composed an opera at 12. While studying law at Leipzig Univ., he became music director of the Opera (1702) and kapellmeister to a count (1705). Moving to Eisenach (c.1708), where he befriended J. S. BACH, he composed French-style instrumental music and German-style sacred music. In Hamburg he served as musical director of the Opera (1722–38), for which he wrote several dozen Italian-influenced works. He wrote some 600 cantatas, and a total of some 2,000 pieces, many of high quality.

telemetry \\tə-'le-mə-trē\\ Collection of data from instruments located at remote or inaccessible points for measurement, monitoring, display, and recording of objects there. Transmission of the information may be over wires or, more commonly, by RADIO. The technique is used extensively for oil-pipeline monitoring and control systems and in oceanography and meteorology. Telemetry for rockets and satellites has continued to grow in complexity and in breadth of application since the 1950s. Data can be transmitted from inside internal-combustion engines during tests or from manned and unmanned spacecraft. Other applications include biomedical research and remote observation of operations with highly radioactive material.

teleological ethics Theory that derives duty from what is valuable as an end, in opposition to deontological ethics. Teleological ethics holds that the basic standard of duty is the contribution that an action makes to the realization of nonmoral values. Teleological theories differ on the nature of the nonmoral goods that actions ought to promote. Eudaemonism emphasizes the cultivation of VIRTUE as the end of all action. UTILITARIANISM holds that the end consists in the aggregate balance of pleasure to pain. Other teleological theories claim that the end of action is survival and growth, as in evolutionary ethics (Herbert SPENCER); power over others (Niccolò MACHIAVELLI and Friedrich NIETZSCHE); satisfaction and adjustment, as in PRAGMATISM (John DEWEY); and freedom, as in EXISTENTIALISM (Jean-Paul SARTRE).

teleology \\,tē-lē-'ä-lə-jē\\ Causality in which the effect is explained by an end (Greek, *telos*) to be realized. Teleology thus differs from efficient causality, in which an effect is dependent on prior events. Aristotle's account of teleology declared that a full explanation of anything must consider its final cause—the purpose for which the thing exists or was produced. Though many philosophers have conceived of biological processes as involving a guiding end, modern science appeals only to efficient causes.

telephone Instrument designed for simultaneous transmission and reception of the human voice. It converts the sound waves of the human voice to pulses of electrical current, transmits the current, and then retranslates the current back to sound. The U.S. patent granted to A. G. BELL in 1876 for the telephone is often called the most valuable ever issued. Within 20 years, the telephone acquired a form that has remained fundamentally unchanged. The advent of the TRANSISTOR (1947) led to lightweight, compact circuitry (see CELL PHONE). Advances in electronics have led to "smart" features such as automatic redialing, caller identification, call waiting, and call forwarding. Telephone systems are also a primary access route for the INTERNET.

telescope Device that collects light from and magnifies images of distant objects, the most important tool in ASTRONOMY. The first telescopes focused visible light by REFRACTION through LENSES; later ones used REFLECTION from curved mirrors (see OPTICS). Their invention is traditionally credited to Hans Lippershey (1570?–1619?), who adapted Antonie van LEEUWENHOEK's use of lenses in MICROSCOPES.

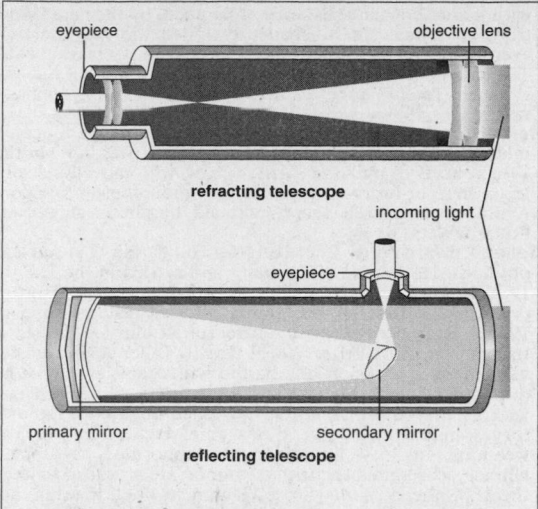

refracting telescope

reflecting telescope

Telescope A refracting telescope forms an image by focusing light from a distant object using lenses. A reflecting telescope uses mirrors to focus the light. Both types use lenses in the eyepiece to magnify the image formed.

Among the earliest were those modeled after GALILEO's simple telescopes. Johannes KEPLER'S improved version (1611) became the basis for modern refracting instruments. The reflecting telescope came into its own after William HERSCHEL used one to discover URANUS in 1781. Radio telescopes (see RADIO AND RADAR ASTRONOMY) and telescopes that detect other parts of the ELECTROMAGNETIC SPECTRUM have been used (see GAMMA-RAY ASTRONOMY, INFRARED ASTRONOMY, ULTRAVIOLET ASTRONOMY, X-RAY ASTRONOMY). Spaceflight has allowed telescopes to orbit earth to avoid distortion by the atmosphere (e.g., the HUBBLE SPACE TELESCOPE).

Teletype Telegraphic instrument that sends and receives printed messages and data via telephone cables or radio relay systems. Teletypewriters (or teleprinters) became common for commercial use in the 1920s. The trademark Teletype became synonymous with teleprinters in the U.S. Coding schemes used for teleprinters included a variation of the BAUDOT code (1920s) and ASCII (1960s). Since the advent of high-speed DATA TRANSMISSION in the 1980s, teletype has given way to E-MAIL and FAX.

television (TV) Electronic system for transmitting still or moving images and sound to receivers that recreate the picture and sound. Early versions (1900–20) of the CATHODE-RAY TUBE, methods of amplifying an electronic signal, and theoretical formulation of the electronic-scanning principle later became the basis of modern TV. RCA demonstrated the first all-electronic TV in 1932. Color TV (in the 1950s), CABLE TV systems (introduced in the 1960s), and recording or playback machines (in the 1980s; see VCR) followed. HIGH-DEFINITION TELEVISION is the newest television technology. See also John L. BAIRD, Lee DE FOREST, P. C. GOLDMARK, Vladimir ZWORYKIN.

television, cable See CABLE TELEVISION

telex International telegraphic message-transfer service consisting of a network of teleprinters. Subscribers can exchange textual communications and data directly with one another. Telex systems originated in Europe in the early 1930s and were widely used for several decades. Telex is still used for applications in which high transmission speeds are not necessary and in areas where more modern data equipment is not available.

Tell, William *German* Wilhelm Tell. Swiss national hero whose historical existence is disputed. According to tradition, in the 13th or early 14th cent. he defied Austrian authority and was forced to shoot an apple from his son's head

T U V

with a crossbow at a distance of 80 paces by the hated Austrian governor. He subsequently killed the governor, an event that supposedly led to rebellion against Austrian rule. The marksman's test is widely found in folklore, and the story has resemblances to the founding myths of other nations.

Tell el-Amarna Ancient city, NILE RIVER, Egypt. Located midway between THEBES and MEMPHIS, it was built in the 14th cent. B.C. by King AKHENATON, who moved his subjects there in order to found a new monotheistic religion. Artifacts discovered there included hundreds of CUNEIFORM tablets.

Teller, Edward (*orig.* Ede) (b.1908) Hungarian-U.S. nuclear physicist. He left Nazi Germany and settled in the U.S. in 1935. In 1941 he joined Enrico FERMI's team in the effort to produce the first self-sustaining nuclear reaction, and in 1943 J. Robert OPPENHEIMER recruited him for the MANHATTAN PROJECT. After World War II, Teller advocated development of a fusion bomb, and with Stanislaw ULAM he developed a workable HYDROGEN BOMB in 1952. The same year he helped establish the Lawrence Livermore Laboratory, which became the U.S.'s chief factory for nuclear weapons. In 1954 he joined the opposition to Oppenheimer's continued security clearance. He crusaded to keep the U.S. ahead of the Soviet Union in nuclear arms, opposed arms treaties, and convinced Pres. Ronald Reagan of the need for the STRATEGIC DEFENSE INITIATIVE.

Tell Mardikh See EBLA

Telloh See LAGASH

Telugu language \\'te-lə-ˌgü\\ DRAVIDIAN language spoken by more than 66 million people, mostly in S. India. It is the official language of the state of Andhra Pradesh. The earliest inscription entirely in Telugu is from the 6th cent.; literary texts begin in the 11th cent. The Telugu script is closely akin to Kannada script (see INDIC WRITING SYSTEMS). Like other major Dravidian languages, Telugu has very marked distinctions between literary and colloquial registers and between social dialects.

Tempe \\'tem-pē, tem-'pē\\ City (pop., 2000: 159,000), SW central Arizona, near Phoenix. First settled in 1872, it was renamed in 1880 for the Vale of TEMPE. After World War II it experienced rapid growth. It is home to Arizona State Univ. (founded 1885).

Tempe \\'tem-pē\\, **Vale of** *Greek* **Témbi** Narrow 6-mi (10-km) valley between Mt. OLYMPUS and Mt. Ossa, NE THESSALY, Greece. The ancient Greeks dedicated Tempe to the cult of APOLLO. Legends attribute its formation to a blow from POSEIDON's trident; geologists believe it was carved by stream action. Providing access from the coast to the Thessalian plain, it has been a traditional invasion route. Ruins of castles and fortifications, from the Roman period to the Middle Ages, mark its strong points.

temperament In the study of PERSONALITY, an individual's characteristic inclination or mode of emotional response. The notion originated with GALEN, who developed it from an earlier theory regarding the four "humors": blood, phlegm, and black and yellow bile. Today researchers emphasize physiological processes (including the ENDOCRINE and autonomic NERVOUS systems) and CULTURE and LEARNING.

temperament See TUNING AND TEMPERAMENT

temperance movement International social movement dedicated to the control of alcohol consumption through the promotion of moderation and abstinence. It began as a church-sponsored movement in the early 19th cent. in the U.S. and attracted the efforts of many women; by 1833 the U.S. had 6,000 local temperance societies. The first European temperance society was formed in Ireland in 1826. An international temperance movement began in Utica, N.Y., in 1851, and spread worldwide. See also PROHIBITION.

tempera painting Painting executed with ground pigment mixed with a water-soluble material, such as egg yolk, gum, or wax. Tempera paint is resistant to water and allows overpainting with more color; the thin, transparent layers of paint produce a clear, luminous effect. The exclusive medium for panel painting in the Middle Ages and early Renaissance, it was largely superseded in the 15th cent. by OIL PAINTING.

temperature Measure of hotness expressed in terms of any of several arbitrary scales, such as Fahrenheit, Celsius, or Kelvin. HEAT flows from a hotter body to a colder one and continues to do so until both are at the same temperature. Temperature is a measure of the average ENERGY of the molecules of a body, whereas heat is a measure of the total amount of thermal energy in a body. The most common temperature scales are based on arbitrarily defined fixed points. On the Fahrenheit scale, 32° is the freezing point of water and 212° the boiling point (at standard atmospheric pressure). The Celsius scale defines the triple point of water (at which all three phases, solid, liquid, and gas, coexist in equilibrium) at 0.01° and the boiling point at 100°. The Kelvin scale sets the zero point at ABSOLUTE ZERO and uses a degree (called the kelvin) the same size as that of the Celsius scale.

temperature inversion An increase of air temperature with altitude. Reversing the normal temperature condition of the TROPOSPHERE, where temperature decreases with altitude, inversions can determine cloud forms, precipitation, and visibility. A pronounced inversion acts as a lid, preventing the upward movement of the air below it; clouds cannot grow high enough to produce showers and, at the same time, visibility may be greatly reduced by trapped pollutants (see SMOG). Because the air near the base of the inversion is cool, fog is frequently present there.

tempering Heat treating of metal ALLOYS, particularly STEEL, to yield specific properties. For instance, raising the temperature of hardened steel to 752°F (400°C) and holding it for a time before quenching in oil decreases its hardness and brittleness and produces a strong and tough steel. Quench-and-temper HEAT TREATING is applied at many different cooling rates, holding times, and temperatures, and is a very important means of controlling the properties of steel.

Templar *or* **Knight Templar** \\'tem-plər\\ Member of a religious military order of knighthood established during the CRUSADES. At its beginning (c.1119), the group consisted of eight or nine French knights who devoted themselves to protecting pilgrims to Jerusalem from Muslim warriors. They were given quarters near the site of the former Temple of JERUSALEM, from which they derived their name. Their numbers increased rapidly, partly because of the propagandistic writing of St. BERNARD DE CLAIRVAUX, who also wrote their rule of life. They flourished for two centuries, expanding to other countries, growing in number to 20,000, and acquiring vast wealth and property. By 1304 rumors, probably false, of irreligious practices and blasphemies had made them the target of persecution. The Templars were suppressed in 1312, their property was confiscated, and many members were imprisoned or executed. Their last leader, Jacques de Molay (1243–1314), was burned at the stake.

temple Edifice constructed for the worship of a deity. Features commonly include a sanctuary and an ALTAR. Ancient Egypt had mortuary temples for the cults of dead kings, and cult temples that held images of deities. The cult temple typically included a massive gateway with a court leading to an imposing hall and a shrine. Most Classical Greek temples had a gable roof supported by columns, with a portico at each end (amphiprostyle temple), a colonnade extending all around (peripteral temple), or a double line of columns all around (dipteral temple). An inner enclosure housed the image of a deity, and an altar stood outside. Roman temples kept the altar inside, and the colonnade was often reduced to a row of columns. Hindu temples generally consist of a towering shrine and a columned hall surrounded by an elaborate wall. Buddhist temples range from half-buried sanctuaries with richly carved entrances to single carved towers or statues. The Chinese and Japanese Buddhist temple is typically a one-story building of richly carved, painted, or tiled timber constructed around an atrium used for worship, though towering PAGODAS were sometimes built as temples over a shrine. In the Americas, Inca and Mayan temples were constructed of stone, often richly carved; they were generally stair-stepped pyramids, with the shrine at the top. See also SYNAGOGUE.

Temple, Shirley *later* **Shirley Temple Black** (b.1928) U.S. child actress. Born in Santa Monica, Cal., she made her film debut at 4. A precocious performer known for her dimples and golden curls, she became the country's most popular female star in the Depression era in such films as *Little Miss Marker* (1934), *Bright Eyes* (1934), in which she sang "On the Good Ship Lollipop," *The Little Colonel* (1935), and *Wee Willie Winkie* (1937). She received a special Academy Award in 1934. As an adult she served as U.S. ambassador to Ghana (1974–76) and Czechoslovakia (1989–92).

Shirley Temple

Temple of Heaven Large religious complex in the old outer city of Beijing, considered the supreme achievement of traditional Chinese architecture. Its layout symbolizes the belief that heaven is round and earth square. The Hall of Prayer for Good Harvests (1420) has three concentric circles of massive wood columns; in a remarkable feat of engineering, they support the three roof levels and, in succession, a huge square brace (earth), circular architrave (heaven), and vast interior cupola. The Imperial Vault of Heaven (1530; rebuilt 1572) is a circular domed building constructed without crossbeams. The Circular Mound Altar (1530; rebuilt 1749) is a triple-tiered white stone terrace enclosed by two sets of walls that are square outside and round inside.

tenant See LANDLORD AND TENANT

tenant farming Agricultural system in which landowners rent their land to farmers and receive either cash or a share of the product in return. Landowners may also contribute operating CAPITAL and management. Under one arrangement, known as sharecropping, the landowner furnishes all the capital and sometimes the food, clothing, and medical expenses of the tenant and may also supervise the work. The sharecropper then pays the landowner with a portion of the output grown on the land. In other forms of tenant farming, the tenant may furnish all the equipment and have substantial autonomy in the farm's operation. Tenants and their families probably constitute two-fifths of the world's population engaged in agriculture.

Ten Commandments List of religious precepts sacred in JUDAISM and CHRISTIANITY. They include injunctions to honor God, the SABBATH, and one's parents, as well as bans on idolatry, blasphemy, murder, adultery, theft, false witness, and covetousness. In the Old Testament Book of EXODUS, they are divinely revealed to MOSES on Mt. SINAI and engraved on two stone tablets. Most scholars propose a date between the 16th and 13th cent. B.C. for the commandments.

tendinitis or **tendonitis** \ˌten-dᵊn-ˈī-təs\ INFLAMMATION of a TENDON sheath, due to irritation by overuse of the tendons, which slide within them, or to bacterial infection. It is often an OCCUPATIONAL DISEASE, affecting tendons used in repetitive motions. The tendon becomes swollen and red, with pain that increases on motion. Treatment involves immobilization, and gradually increasing motion after inflammation subsides, which may happen sooner with STEROID injections. Repeated episodes can permanently thicken the sheath, limiting motion.

tendon Tissue attaching a muscle to other body parts, usually bones, to transmit the mechanical force of muscle contraction to the other part. Much like LIGAMENTS, tendons are composed of dense, fibrous CONNECTIVE TISSUE with a high COLLAGEN content, which makes them remarkably tough and strong.

tendril Plant organ specialized to anchor and support vining stems. A tendril is a slender strand, produced usually from the node of a stem, by which a VINE or other plant may climb. Sensitive to contact, it turns toward any object it brushes against, wraps about it, and clings to it. Later, strong mechanical tissue develops in the tendrils, making them strong enough to support the weight of the plant.

Some tendrils have enlargements at the ends that flatten and produce an adhesive that firmly cements them to their support. Tendril plants include GRAPE, English IVY, SWEET PEA, GOURDS, and PASSIONFLOWERS.

Teng Hsiao-p'ing See DENG XIAOPING

Teniers \tə-ˈnirs, tä-ˈnyä\, **David** Name of two Flemish painters. Little is known about the work of the elder Teniers (1582–1649) except that he painted primarily religious subjects. His more famous, highly prolific son, David the Younger (1610–1690), is best known for his genre scenes of peasant life. He was brilliant at handling crowd scenes in an open landscape, characterizing his figures with a warm and often humorous touch. As court painter to the archduke Leopold William, he also made many small-scale copies of paintings in the archduke's collection; published as *Theatrum Pictorium* (1660), they constitute a valuable inventory of a great 17th-cent. collection.

Tennessee State (pop., 2000: 5,689,000), SE central U.S. It occupies 42,144 sq mi (109,153 sq km); its capital is NASHVILLE. The GREAT SMOKY MTNS. edge the E part of the state, while the MISSISSIPPI RIVER is on its W boundary. The TENNESSEE RIVER valley dominates much of the state. It has a moderate climate; about half is forested. American Indians, including CHICKASAW, CHEROKEE, and SHAWNEE, inhabited the region when Spanish, French, and English explorers visited it in the 16th–17th cent. It was included in the British charter of Carolina and in the French Louisiana claim, and was ceded to Great Britain after the FRENCH AND INDIAN WAR. The first permanent settlement was made about 1770. It was part of N. Carolina until 1785, when the area's settlers broke away and formed the free state of Franklin. N. Carolina relinquished its claim in 1789, and Tennessee became the 16th U.S. state in 1796. In 1861 it seceded from the Union; the hard-fought AMERICAN CIVIL WAR battles of SHILOH, CHATTANOOGA, Stones River, and Nashville occurred there. In 1866 it was the first state readmitted to the Union. During the RECONSTRUCTION era, blacks lost what little power they had gained. After World War II, it became a testing ground for those involved in the CIVIL RIGHTS MOVEMENT. The state's economy is based on manufacturing. The TENNESSEE VALLEY AUTHORITY is the nation's largest electric-power generating system.

Tennessee River Navigable river, Tennessee, N Alabama, and W Kentucky. Formed by the Holston and French Broad rivers in E Tennessee, it flows 652 mi (1,049 km) before joining the OHIO RIVER in Kentucky. During the AMERICAN CIVIL WAR it served as a strategic invasion route into the W Confederacy. Its development as one of the world's greatest irrigation and hydropower systems began in 1933 with the TENNESSEE VALLEY AUTHORITY. It is linked by waterway to the TOMBIGBEE RIVER.

Tennessee Valley Authority (TVA) U.S. government agency established in 1933 to control floods, improve navigation, and generate electrical power along the TENNESSEE RIVER and its tributaries. The TVA is a public corporation governed by a board of directors. It has jurisdiction over the entire basin of the river, which covers parts of seven states, principally Tennessee and Alabama. A creation of the NEW DEAL, the TVA built a system of dams, deepened the channel, and encouraged the development of port facilities. The projects greatly increased traffic on the river and provided cheap electricity, spurring the industrial development of what had been a chronically depressed regional economy. See also PUBLIC WORKS ADMINISTRATION.

Tenniel \ˈten-yəl\, **John** (*later* *Sir John*) (1820–1914) British illustrator and satirical artist. After attracting attention with his mural decorations, he began drawing for *Punch* magazine in 1850, and in time became its chief cartoonist. His drawings lent new dignity to the political cartoon. Of his many book illustrations, best known are those for Lewis CARROLL's *Alice's Adventures in Wonderland* (1865) and *Through the Looking-Glass* (1872), remarkable for their subtlety and cleverness.

tennis Game played with rackets and a light, elastic ball by two players or pairs of players on a rectangular court divided by a low net. Tennis is played indoors and outdoors, on hard-surface, clay, and grass courts. The object is to hit the ball over the net and into the opponent's half of the

TUV

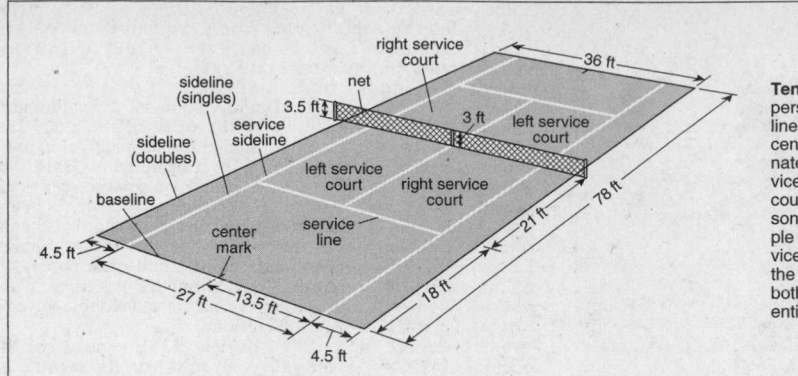

Labels on diagram: right service court, sideline (singles), net, 36 ft, sideline (doubles), service sideline, 3.5 ft, 3 ft, left service court, baseline, left service court, right service court, center mark, service line, 78 ft, 21 ft, 4.5 ft, 27 ft, 13.5 ft, 18 ft, 4.5 ft

Tennis A professional tennis court. The person serving stands behind the baseline, alternately to the right and left of the center mark, and must land the ball alternately in the opposite left and right service court. A narrower portion of the court is used in singles tennis (one person on a side) than in doubles (two people on a side), though the size of the service court does not change. In doubles, the two partners alternate in serving, but both may otherwise roam freely over the entire court.

court in such a way as to defeat the opponent's attempt to return it. Each player serves for an entire game. Points are scored as 15, 30, 40, and game (the term "love" is used for 0). A tied score ("deuce") requires continued play until a two-point margin is achieved. The first player to win six games, with a lead of two games, takes the set. A match consists of the best two out of three (or three out of five) sets. Tennis developed in the 1870s in Britain from earlier racket-and-ball games. The first world lawn-tennis championship was held in 1877 at WIMBLEDON; clay- and hard-court competitions emerged later. The major tournaments for individual players constitute the "Grand Slam" of tennis: the national championships of Britain (Wimbledon), the U.S., Australia, and France.

Tennis Court Oath (June 20, 1789) Oath taken by deputies of the THIRD ESTATE in the FRENCH REVOLUTION. Believing that their new NATIONAL ASSEMBLY was to be disbanded, they met at a nearby tennis court when they were locked out of their usual meeting hall at Versailles. They vowed never to separate until a written constitution was established for France. Their solidarity forced LOUIS XVI to order the clergy and the nobility to join with the Third Estate in the National Assembly.

Tennyson \'te-nə-sən\, **Alfred** *later* Baron Tennyson (of Aldworth and Freshwater) *known as* **Alfred, Lord Tennyson** (1809–1892) English poet, the leading poet of the Victorian Age. While attending Cambridge Univ., Tennyson published *Poems, Chiefly Lyrical* (1830). Another volume, including "The Lotos-Eaters," was published in 1832. When his close friend Arthur Hallam died suddenly in 1833, the severe shock prompted Tennyson to write poems that eventually became part of the vast *In Memoriam* (1850) and lyrics that later appeared in the brooding *Maud* (1855). *Poems* (1842), including "Ulysses," followed, then *The Princess* (1847), a long antifeminist fantasia. In 1850 he was named poet laureate of England. Among his subsequent works are "The Charge of the Light Brigade" (1855); *Idylls of the King* (1859), treating the ARTHURIAN LEGEND; and *Enoch Arden* (1864). A consummate poet, Tennyson was also regarded as a spokesman for the educated English middle class. His works often dealt with the difficulties of an age when traditional assumptions were increasingly called into question by science and modern progress.

Tenochtitlán \tä-ˌnȯch-tēt-ˈlän\ Ancient capital of the AZTEC empire. Located at the site of modern MEXICO CITY, it was founded about 1325 and was the Aztec capital by the late 15th cent. Originally located on two small islands in Lake Texcoco, it spread on artificial islands to cover more than 5 sq mi (13 sq km). The population in 1519 was around 400,000 people, the largest concentration in Mesoamerican history. It contained the palace of MONTEZUMA II, said to consist of 300 rooms, as well as hundreds of temples. It was destroyed by Hernán CORTÉS in 1521.

tenor High male voice range, extending from about the second B below middle C to the G above. In the polyphony of the 13th–16th cent., the tenor was the part that held (Latin,

tenere: "to hold") the CANTUS FIRMUS. Tenor voices are often classified as dramatic, lyric, or heroic (heldentenor).

tenor tuba See EUPHONIUM

tense In GRAMMAR, an inflected form of a verb indicating the time of a narrated event in relation to the time of speaking. Time is often perceived as having three main divisions, past, present, and future, defined in relation to the time when the event is described. Other categories, including MOOD and aspect, may further specify the action as definite or indefinite, completed or not completed, lasting or non-lasting, and recurring or occurring once.

tensile strength \'ten-səl\ Ratio of the maximum load a material can support without fracture when being stretched to the original area of a cross section of the material. When stresses less than the tensile strength are removed, a material completely or partially returns to its original size and shape (see ELASTICITY). As the stress approaches the tensile strength, the material constricts and is easily fractured. Tensile strengths are measured in units of force per unit area.

Tenskwatawa See The PROPHET

tent caterpillar Any MOTH larvae (see LARVA) of the genus *Malacosoma* (family Lasiocampidae). Tent caterpillars are often brightly colored. After hatching from eggs, the eastern tent caterpillar *(M. americanum),* of E N. America, spins huge, tent-shaped communal nests in tree crotches. They leave their silken tent each day throughout the summer to feed on the surrounding leaves. The forest tent caterpillar *(M. disstria)* is common in the S U.S.

Ten Thousand Smokes, Valley of Volcanic region, SW Alaska. Located in KATMAI NATIONAL PARK, it covers 56 sq mi (145 sq km). It was created when the eruption of the Novarupta and Mt. Katmai volcanoes in 1912, the largest in the world in the 20th cent., covered the valley in a flow of lava. An expedition in 1915 discovered tens of thousands of fissures spouting smoke, gas, and steam in the valley floor; some had temperatures as high as 1,200°F (649°C). About 60 years later, there were fewer than 12 fumaroles.

Tenure of Office Act (1867) Law forbidding the U.S. president to remove civil officers without Senate consent. Passed by the RADICAL REPUBLICANS over Pres. Andrew JOHNSON's veto, it sought to prevent Johnson from removing cabinet members who supported Congress's harsh RECONSTRUCTION policies. When Johnson tried to dismiss his secretary of war, Edwin STANTON, an ally of the Radical Republicans, they began IMPEACHMENT proceedings. The law was later repealed; in 1926 it was found unconstitutional.

Tenzing Norgay \'ten-ˌziŋ-ˈnȯr-gē\ (1914–1986) Nepalese SHERPA mountaineer. He served on numerous expeditions before joining Edmund HILLARY as sirdar, or organizer of porters. In 1953 he and Hillary became the first two people to reach the summit of Mt. EVEREST.

Teotihuacán \ˌtā-ō-ˌtē-wä-ˈkän\ Largest (though not most populous) city of pre-Columbian central Mexico, about 30 mi (50 km) northeast of Mexico City. It wielded its greatest influence in the first 900 years A.D., after which it was sacked by the TOLTECS. At its height, some 150,000 people lived in the city, which covered 8 sq mi (21 sq km). Its plazas, temples, and palaces are dominated by the Pyramid of the Moon and the Pyramid of the Sun. Capital of one of the earliest MESOAMERICAN CIVILIZATIONS, it may have been the center of the Toltec civilization. See also TULA.

tepee Tall tent dwelling used by the PLAINS INDIANS. It was suited to a nomadic life of buffalo hunting, being easily folded and dragged by a horse. It was made by stretching dressed and fitted buffalo skins over a skeleton of 20–30 wooden poles, all slanted in toward a central point and tied together near the top. A flap at the top allowed smoke to escape. The tepee became a popular symbol of all Indians, although the WIGWAM, wickiup, hogan, IGLOO, and LONGHOUSE were at least as important.

tequila \tə-ˈkē-lə\ DISTILLED liquor, usually clear in color and unaged, made from the fermented juice of the Mexican AGAVE plant. It contains 40–50% alcohol. It was developed soon after the Spaniards brought distillation to Mexico, and is named for the town of Tequila. Mescal, a stronger-flavored liquor, is made from a wild agave from Oaxaca.

Terborch \tər-ˈbȯrk, *Engl* tər-ˈbȯrk\, **Gerard** (1617–1681) Dutch painter. After travels in England, Italy, Westphalia, and Spain, he returned to Holland in 1648. His works consist almost equally of portraits and genre paintings. He achieved extraordinarily rich effects with the clothing in his portraits. His superb color sense is seen to advantage in his interior genre pieces, in which he depicted with grace and fidelity the atmosphere of well-to-do middle-class life in 17th-cent. Holland.

Terbrugghen \tər-ˈbrü-gən\, **Hendrik** (c.1588–1629) Dutch painter. He reportedly spent 10 years in Italy; on his return to Utrecht in 1615, his work, including his two versions of *The Calling of St. Matthew* (c.1617, 1621), showed the strong influence of CARAVAGGIO. He is most indebted to Caravaggio for his chiaroscuro, though his own light is more atmospheric and silvery, as in *The Flute Player* (1621). His masterpiece is *St. Sebastian Attended by Irene and Her Maid* (1625). He was a leader of the UTRECHT SCHOOL.

Terence *orig.* Publius Terentius Afer (c.195–159? B.C.) Roman comic dramatist. Born a slave, he was taken to Rome, educated, and later freed. His six extant verse plays, *The Woman of Andros, The Mother-in-Law, The Self-Tormentor, The Eunuch, Phormio,* and *The Brothers,* were based on Greek originals (including four by MENANDER), but use contemporary colloquial Latin and introduce a measure of realism. He influenced such later dramatists as MOLIÈRE and William SHAKESPEARE.

Teresa (of Calcutta), Mother *orig.* Agnes Gonxha Bojaxhiu (1910–1997) Albanian-born nun, founder of the Order of the Missionaries of Charity. She became a nun and went to India as a young woman. After studying nursing, she moved to Calcutta's slums; in 1948 she founded her order, which served the blind, the aged, lepers, the disabled, and the dying. In 1971 Pope Paul VI awarded her the first Pope John XXIII Peace Prize. In 1979 she received the Nobel Peace Prize. Her order grew to include hundreds of centers in more than 90 countries.

Teresa of Ávila, St. *orig.* Teresa de Cepeda y Ahumada (1515–1582) Spanish mystic. After entering a convent around the age of 20, she fell seriously ill. She underwent a religious awakening in 1555 and, despite her frail health, initiated the Carmelite Reform, leading the order's return to its original austere practices, including poverty and seclusion from the world. St. JOHN OF THE CROSS joined her in her efforts, establishing reformed Carmelite monasteries. Her spiritual writings, accepted as the classical exposition of the contemplative life, are still widely read today, among them *The Interior Castle* (1588). In 1970 she became the first woman elevated to the status of Doctor of the Church.

Terkel \ˈtər-kəl\, **Studs** *orig.* Louis Turkel (b.1912) U.S. radio host and author. Born in New York City, he moved to Chicago at 8. He gave up a legal career to become a radio disk jockey and interviewer, exposure that led to his own television show in 1950. In 1953, blacklisted from television for his leftist leanings, he returned to radio. His best-selling books include *Hard Times* (1970), about the Depression;

Working (1974), on Americans and their jobs; *The Good War,* on World War II (1984, Pulitzer Prize); and *Race* (1992), on American feelings about race.

termite Any of 1,900 species (order Isoptera) of mostly tropical, social, cellulose-eating insects that are usually soft-bodied and wingless. Intestinal microorganisms enable them to digest cellulose. Termite colonies consist of a fertile queen and king (reproductives), workers (the most numerous), and soldiers. Kings are less than an inch long (1–2 cm), but a queen may grow to more than 4 in. (11 cm). Workers and soldiers are sterile and blind. They survive two to five years; reproductives may live for 60–70 years. Termites live in a sealed, humid nest in wood or underground. Underground nests may be built up into a mound. Periodically, alates (winged, sighted forms) develop and leave the nest to start a new colony. Termites eat chiefly wood.

tern Any of about 40 species (subfamily Sterninae, family Laridae) of slender, web-footed, migratory water birds. Species vary from 8 to 22 in. (20–55 cm) long. The plumage is white, black-and-white, or black; the bill is sharply pointed. Most species have long, pointed wings and a forked tail. Terns plunge into the water to catch crustaceans and fishes. See also ARCTIC TERN.

Sooty tern *(Sterna fuscata)*

terpene See ISOPRENOID

terra-cotta (Italian: "baked earth") Fairly coarse, porous clay that, when fired, assumes a color ranging from dull ochre to red. Terra-cotta objects are usually left unglazed and are often utilitarian, because of their cheapness, versatility, and durability. Small terra-cotta figures from 3000 B.C. have been found in Greece and others throughout the Roman empire from the 4th cent. B.C. Its use died out when the Roman empire collapsed, but was revived in Italy and Germany in the 15th cent.

terrapin Any omnivorous aquatic TURTLE of the family Emydidae, especially the diamondback terrapin (*Malaclemys terrapin*). The diamondback inhabits salt marshes and coasts from New England to the Gulf of Mexico. It has raised diamond-shaped patterns on its upper shell. The female attains a shell length of about 9 in. (23 cm); the male grows to about 6 in. (14 cm). The eight species of the turtle genus *Pseudemys* (or *Chrysemys*) are sometimes referred to as terrapins. They inhabit freshwaters from the NE U.S. to Argentina.

terrier Any of several dog breeds developed, mostly in England, to find and kill vermin and for use in the sports of foxhunting and dog fighting. Bred to fight and kill, they often were pugnacious but are now bred for a friendlier temperament. Most breeds are small and lean, with a rough wiry coat, long head, square jaw, and deep-set eyes. All terriers are vocal and inclined to chase and confront. Most breeds were named for the place where they were developed. See also AIREDALE TERRIER, BULL TERRIER, IRISH TERRIER, PIT BULL TERRIER.

territorial waters Waters under the sovereign jurisdiction of a nation or state, including both marginal sea and inland waters. The concept originated in the 17th cent. Though the doctrine that the sea must be free to all was upheld, a nation's jurisdiction over its coastal waters was also recognized. Nations subscribing to the Law of the SEA observe a territorial limit of 12 nautical mi (10.5 mi, 22 km) from shore. Territorial rights include the airspace above those waters and the seabed below them.

Terror, Reign of See REIGN OF TERROR

terrorism Systematic threat or use of unpredicted violence by organized groups to achieve a political objective. Definitions of terrorism have been hotly disputed. The term—which is generally rejected by those it is applied to—usually

refers to acts against civilians, and is sometimes distinguished from guerrilla warfare, which principally targets armed forces. Terrorists' victims may be chosen either randomly or symbolically. Terrorism has been used throughout history and throughout the world by nationalist and ethnic groups and by revolutionaries of both the left and the right. Though usually thought of as an instrument for destabilizing or overthrowing existing political institutions, terror has also been employed internally by a government against its own subjects to create a climate of fear and encourage adherence to the national ideology; examples include the French Revolution (see REIGN OF TERROR), Nazi Germany, and the Soviet Union in the Stalinist era. Terrorism's impact has been magnified by the deadliness of modern-day weapons and the ability of mass communications to inform the world of such acts. The deadliest terrorist attacks ever occurred in September 2001, when AL QUAEDA terrorists hijacked four commercial airplanes and crashed two into the WORLD TRADE CENTER and one into the PENTAGON, killing over 3,000 people.

Tertiary period \'tər-shē-ˌer-ē\ Interval of geologic time, 65–1.8 million years ago, in the CENOZOIC ERA. The Tertiary has five subdivisions: the PALEOCENE (the earliest), EOCENE, OLIGOCENE, MIOCENE, and PLIOCENE EPOCHS. During most of the Tertiary, the major continents were largely similar to those of today. Emergence and submergence of land bridges between continents critically affected the migration of animals and plants. Virtually all the existing major mountain ranges were formed during the Tertiary. See table at GEOLOGIC TIME.

terza rima \'tert-sə-'rē-mə\ Verse form consisting of tercets, or three-line stanzas, in which the second line of each rhymes with the first and third lines of the next: *aba, bcb, cdc,* . . .. DANTE, in *The Divine Comedy* (c.1310–14), was the first to use terza rima in a long poem. A demanding form, it has not been widely adopted in languages less rich in rhymes than Italian. Poets who have experimented with terza rima include P. B. SHELLEY, Robert BROWNING, and W. H. AUDEN.

Teschen \'te-shən\ Former E European duchy. It was originally a principality linked to the Polish duchy of SILESIA, and passed in 1526 to the HABSBURGS. In 1920 Poland and Czechoslovakia contested and then divided the region; Poland received the E district, including the city of Teschen (now Cieszyn), while Czechoslovakia received the rest. The Czechs were forced to cede their section to Poland in 1938. Germany occupied the entire region until after World War II, when the 1920 borders were restored.

Tesla, Nikola (1856–1943) Croatian-U.S. inventor and researcher. He studied in Austria and Bohemia and worked in Paris before coming to the U.S. in 1884. He worked for Thomas EDISON and George WESTINGHOUSE, but preferred independent research. His inventions made production and distribution of alternating-current electric power possible. He invented an induction coil that is still widely used in radio technology, the Tesla coil (c.1890). He established an electric-power station at Niagara Falls in 1893. He discovered terrestrial stationary waves (1899–1900), proving that the earth is a conductor. Many of his ideas remained in his notebooks, which are still examined by engineers for inventive clues.

Nikola Tesla

Test Act (1673) Act passed by the British Parliament that required holders of civil and military offices to profess the religion of the Church of ENGLAND. Though directed primarily against Roman Catholics, it extended to all non-Anglicans; it was modified in 1689 to enable most non-Catholics to qualify. An act adopted in 1828 removed the test. The U.S. CONSTITUTION, prescribes that "no religious test" shall be required for any officeholder.

testes *or* **testicles** Male reproductive organs (see REPRODUCTIVE SYSTEM). Humans have two oval-shaped testes 1.5–2 in. (4–5 cm) long that produce SPERM and ANDROGENS (mainly TESTOSTERONE), contained in a sac (scrotum) behind the PENIS. Each testis is divided into 200–400 lobes containing 3–10 very thin coiled tubes each, which produce the sperm and contract to expel them through a network of canals to another structure in the scrotum, the epididymis, for storage. At PUBERTY the cells in the testes are stimulated by hormones to develop into fertile sperm cells.

testosterone \tes-'tä-stər-ˌōn\ Masculinizing SEX HORMONE produced by the TESTES. It is responsible for the development of the male sex organs and secondary sex characteristics (e.g., facial hair, masculine musculature, deep voice, and male-pattern baldness), as well as such psychological traits as aggression and confidence. Testosterone can be manufactured by modifying other STEROIDS. It has various uses in medicine.

tetanus \'te-tə-nəs\ *or* **lockjaw** Acute BACTERIAL DISEASE caused by *Clostridium tetani* (see CLOSTRIDIUM). Spores of this organism are common, especially in soil; it thrives away from oxygen in deep wounds, especially punctures. Its toxin causes muscle rigidity with frequent spasms, around the site of the wound or throughout the body. The jaw muscles are almost always involved (lockjaw). Vaccination every ten years is the best protection; ANTITOXIN prevents or delays symptoms but has limited value once they develop. Treatment usually includes antibiotics. Recovered patients are not immune.

Teton Range \'tē-ˌtän\ Range of the N ROCKY MTNS., NW Wyoming. It extends 40 mi (64 km) across from the S boundary of YELLOWSTONE NATIONAL PARK to Teton Pass. Many peaks exceed 12,000 ft (3,700 m); the highest is Grand Teton (13,766 ft, or 4,196 m). Much of the range lies within GRAND TETON NATIONAL PARK.

tetracycline Any of a class of broad-spectrum ANTIBIOTICS with a common basic structure. They may be isolated directly from several species of ACTINOMYCETES or modified from the compounds isolated. They are effective against BACTERIA, RICKETTSIA, CHLAMYDIA, and MYCOPLASMA. Overuse of these and other antibiotics has led to DRUG RESISTANCE in microorganisms.

tetrarch (Greek: "ruler of a quarter") In Greco-Roman antiquity, the ruler of a principality, originally the ruler of one-quarter of a region or province. The first tetrarchs ruled the four tetrarchies of Thessaly under PHILIP II of Macedonia. Tetrarchs ruled in Galatia (in Asia Minor) before the Roman conquest (169 B.C.), and still later in Hellenized Syria and Palestine, where the title denoted the semi-independent ruler of a divided kingdom or minor district.

Teutonic Order *or* **Teutonic Knights** \tü-'tä-nik\ *officially* House of the Hospitallers of St. Mary of the Teutons. Religious order important in E Europe in the late Middle Ages. Founded in 1189–90 to nurse the sick in Palestine during the Third CRUSADE, it was militarized in 1198 and given land in Jerusalem and Germany. Gaining control of Prussia by 1283, it made Marienburg the center of a military principality (1309–1525). The order extended its influence until defeated at the Battle of Tannenberg (1410). Another Polish victory in 1466 forced the knights to become vassals of the Polish king. NAPOLEON declared the order dissolved in 1809 and redistributed most of its remaining lands. In 1834 the Austrian emperor refounded it as a charitable religious order, and it is now headquartered in Vienna.

Tewodros II \tä-'wò-dròs\ *or* **Theodore II** (1818?–1868) Emperor of Ethiopia (1855–68), often called Ethiopia's first modern ruler. He reunified the Ethiopian kingdoms into one empire, attempted to focus loyalty around the government rather than the Ethiopian church, and worked to abolish the feudal system. Though he failed in his aims, his example was followed by his successors. His reign ended when a British force attacked in response to the imprisonment of several British citizens.

Texas State (pop., 2000: 20,852,000), SW U.S. Occupying 266,807 sq mi (691,030 sq km), it is the second-largest state in both area and population. Its capital is AUSTIN. Plains and hills make up the terrain, which ranges from the fertile prairie of the Coastal Plains on the Gulf of MEXICO through the central GREAT PLAINS grasslands to the arid High Plains of the Panhandle. The forerunners of W. Texas Indians inhabited the area as much as 37,000 years ago. Some of the tribes later formed the Caddo confederacy. Indians, including APACHES, lived in the region when the Spanish arrived in 1528. The first settlement was attempted in 1685 by the French, who claimed the region as part of Louisiana. In 1803 the U.S. acquired the French claim in the LOUISIANA PURCHASE, but relinquished it to Spain by treaty in 1819. It became part of Mexico at Mexican independence in 1821. In 1836 Texans declared independence from Mexico as the Republic of Texas (see Stephen AUSTIN, Sam HOUSTON). After a 10-year struggle to remain independent, Texas became the 28th U.S. state in 1845. Its boundary with Mexico was fixed after the MEXICAN WAR (1848). In the AMERICAN CIVIL WAR, it seceded from the Union (1861); it was readmitted in 1870. After the war, railroad building and increased shipping helped expand the economy, and the discovery of oil in 1901 transformed it. While Texas still leads all other states in oil and natural-gas production and in petroleum-refining capacity, its manufacture of electronics, aerospace components, and other high-technology items is increasingly important. It is also the U.S.'s leading cotton, beef-cattle, and sheep producer.

Texas, University of State university system with 13 campuses. It was founded in 1883. The main campus, at Austin, is the second most populous campus in the U.S. (enrollment 48,000). It is a comprehensive research and teaching institution, offering about 100 undergraduate programs and about 190 graduate degree programs. The Lyndon B. JOHNSON Library and Museum is located there. Total enrollment for the Univ. of Texas system is about 142,000.

Texas A&M University State university system based in College Station. The outgrowth of the Agricultural and Mechanical College of Texas (founded 1876), the system includes nine campuses. The College Station campus comprises 10 colleges; enrollment at College Station is about 42,000. The Galveston campus specializes in marine science and maritime studies.

Texas Rangers Loosely organized police force in Texas. The first members were "minutemen" hired by U.S. settlers as protection against Indian attacks in the 1830s. Though they did not wear uniforms, they were highly disciplined and known for their marksmanship, making the Colt six-shooter the weapon of the West. At their peak in the 1870s, the Rangers brought law and order to hundreds of miles of Texas frontier. In 1935 they were merged with the state highway patrol.

textile Any filament, fiber, or YARN that can be made into fabric or cloth, and the resulting material itself. The word includes woven, knitted, bonded, felted, and tufted fabrics. The basic raw materials used in textile production are fibers, either obtained from natural sources (e.g., WOOL) or produced from chemical substances (e.g., POLYESTER). Textiles are used for wearing apparel, household linens, upholstery, draperies, and carpets, in addition to being used widely in industry.

Tezcatlipoca \ˌtäs-kät-lē-ˈpō-kə\ Omnipotent god of the AZTEC pantheon. The protector of slaves, he severely punished masters who ill-treated them. He is said to have put an end to the TOLTECS' golden age. Each year his worshipers selected a handsome prisoner of war who was allowed to live in princely luxury for a year before being sacrificed. Tezcatlipoca is represented in art with an obsidian mirror, in which he sees all.

Thackeray, William Makepeace (1811–1863) English novelist. His early writings appear in such volumes as *The Book of Snobs* (1848), a collection of his articles from *Punch;* and *Miscellanies* (1855–57), which includes the historical novel *Barry Lyndon* (1844). His fame rests chiefly on the novels *Vanity Fair* (1847–48), a panoramic survey of English manners and human frailties set in the Napoleonic era, and *Henry Esmond* (1852), set in the early 18th cent. *Pendennis* (1848–50) is a partly fictionalized autobiography. His huge popularity declined in the 20th cent.

Thailand \ˈtī-ˌland\ *officially* **Kingdom of Thailand** *formerly* **Siam** Kingdom, S.E. Asia. Area: 198,115 sq mi (513,115 sq km). Population (2000): 62,423,000. Capital: BANGKOK. The population is predominantly Thai, with Chinese, KHMER,

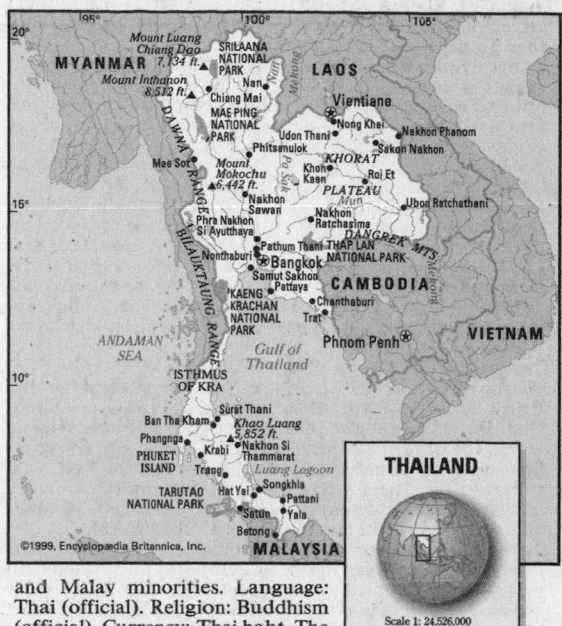

and Malay minorities. Language: Thai (official). Religion: Buddhism (official). Currency: Thai baht. The country encompasses forested hills and mountains, a central plain containing the Chao Phraya River delta, and a plateau in the northeast. Its market economy is based largely on services, light industries, and agriculture. It is a large producer of tungsten and tin. Among its chief agricultural products are sugarcane, rice, cassava, corn, rubber, and pineapples; manufactures include electrical machinery, clothing, and canned goods. Tourism is also important. It is a constitutional monarchy with two legislative houses; its chief of state is the king, and the head of government is the prime minister. The region of Thailand has been continuously occupied for 20,000 years. It was part of the MON and Khmer kingdoms from the 9th cent. A.D. Thai-speaking peoples emigrated from China around the 10th cent. During the 13th cent. two Thai states emerged: the SUKHOTHAI KINGDOM, founded about 1220 after a successful revolt against the Khmer, and Chiang Mai, founded in 1296 after the Mon were defeated. In 1351 the Thai kingdom of Ayutthaya succeeded Sukhothai. The Burmese were its most powerful rival, occupying it briefly in the 16th cent. and destroying it in 1767. The CHAKRI DYNASTY came to power in 1782, moving the capital to Bangkok and extending the empire along the MALAY PENINSULA and into Laos and Cambodia. It was named Siam in 1856. Though Western influence increased during the 19th cent., Siam's rulers avoided colonization by granting concessions to European countries; it was the only S.E. Asian nation able to do so. In 1917 it entered World War I on the side of the Allies. It became a constitutional monarchy following a military coup in 1932 and was officially renamed Thailand in 1939. It was occupied by Japan in World War II. It participated in the KOREAN WAR as a U.N. forces member. It was allied with S. Vietnam in the VIETNAM WAR. Along with other S.E. Asian nations, it suffered from the 1990s regional financial crisis.

Thalberg, Irving G(rant) (1899–1936) U.S. film executive. Born in New York City, he skipped college (knowing that a rheumatic heart condition might kill him before age 30) and soon became a studio manager in Hollywood. Hired by MGM as head of production in 1925, he became known as the "boy wonder of Hollywood." Supervising script selection and final film editing, he was responsible for the high

quality of such MGM movies as *Grand Hotel* (1932), *The Barretts of Wimpole Street* (1934), *Mutiny on the Bounty* (1935), *Naughty Marietta* (1935), and *Romeo and Juliet* (1936). He died of pneumonia at 37.

Thales of Miletus \'thā-lēz...mī-'lē-təs\ (fl.6th cent. B.C.) Greek philosopher. None of his writings survive. The claim that Thales was the founder of Western philosophy rests primarily on ARISTOTLE, who wrote that he was the first to suggest a single material basis for the universe, namely water. Thales' significance lies in his attempt to explain nature by the simplification of phenomena and in his search for causes within nature itself rather than in the caprices of gods.

thalidomide \thə-'li-də-,mīd\ Drug formerly used as a sedative and to prevent morning sickness during pregnancy. Synthesized in 1954, it was introduced in almost 50 countries. In 1961 it was found to cause CONGENITAL DISORDERS when taken in early pregnancy; 5,000–10,000 deformed babies were born. It was never distributed for clinical use in the U.S. (see H. B. TAUSSIG). Thalidomide appears effective against LEPROSY and certain late-stage AIDS symptoms.

Thames \'temz\, **Battle of the** (Oct. 5, 1813) Decisive U.S. victory over the British in the WAR OF 1812. After the British defeat in the Battle of Lake Erie, U.S. troops under Gen. W. H. HARRISON pursued retreating British soldiers across the Ontario peninsula. The British force of 600 regulars and 1,000 Indians under TECUMSEH met the 3,500 U.S. troops at the Thames River near Moraviantown, Ontario, and were quickly defeated; Tecumseh was killed. The U.S. victory ended the Indian alliance with the British.

Thames River *ancient* Tamesis. Principal river of England. It rises in the Cotswolds in GLOUCESTERSHIRE and winds 210 mi (338 km) eastward across S central England into a great estuary, emptying into the North Sea. It has been celebrated by bards throughout history. One of the world's most important commercial waterways, it is navigable by large vessels to LONDON.

Thanatos \'tha-nə-,täs\ Ancient Greek personification of death. He appeared to humans to carry them off to the underworld when the time allotted to them by the FATES had expired. Thanatos was once defeated by HERACLES, who wrestled him to save the life of ALCESTIS, and he was tricked by SISYPHUS, who wanted a second chance at life.

Thanksgiving Day U.S. holiday. In the autumn of 1621 Plymouth governor William BRADFORD invited neighboring Indians to join the Pilgrims for a three-day festival of recreation and feasting in gratitude for the bounty of the season, which had been partly enabled by the Indians' advice. A national holiday since 1863, it is celebrated on the fourth Thursday in November; the traditional meal consists of New World foods. Canada adopted Thanksgiving as a national holiday in 1879; it is celebrated on the second Monday in October.

Thant, U (1909–1974) Third secretary-general of the UNITED NATIONS (1961–71), the first Asian to hold the post. Born in Myanmar (Burma), he taught high school before entering government service. Posted to the U.N. in 1952, he became Burma's U.N. ambassador in 1957. In 1961 he became acting secretary-general after Dag HAMMARSKJÖLD's death; he became permanent secretary-general in 1962. He played a diplomatic role in the CUBAN MISSILE CRISIS, devised a plan to end the Congolese civil war (1962), and sent peacekeeping forces to Cyprus (1964).

Tharp, Twyla (b.1941) U.S. dancer, director, and choreographer. Born in Portland, Ind., she danced with Paul TAYLOR's company before beginning to choreograph for various companies, creating such works as *Push Comes to Shove* (1976), *Baker's Dozen* (1979), and *Nine Sinatra Songs* (1982). In 1965 she formed her own group, the Twyla Tharp Dance Co.; it disbanded in 1988. She has also choreographed for the Broadway theater and several films (including *Amadeus*, 1984). Notable for her humor, Tharp was one of the first American choreographers to use popular music.

Thatcher, Margaret *later* Baroness Thatcher (of Kesteven) *orig.* Margaret Hilda Roberts (b.1925) British prime minister (1979–90). She earned degrees at Oxford Univ., worked as a research chemist, and later read for the bar and spe-

cialized in tax law. Elected to Parliament in 1959, she served as secretary of state for education and science 1970–74. She succeeded Edward HEATH as Conservative Party leader in 1975. In 1979 she became Britain's first woman prime minister. She energetically advocated individual initiative, confronted the labor unions, privatized national industries and utilities, pursued a strong monetarist policy, and endorsed a firm commitment to NATO. Her landslide victory in 1983 owed partly to her decisive

Margaret Thatcher, 1983

leadership in the FALKLAND ISLANDS WAR. A split over European monetary and political integration led to her resignation in 1990.

theater Building or space in which performances are given before an audience. It contains an AUDITORIUM and stage. In ancient Greece, where Western theater began (5th cent. B.C.), theaters were constructed in natural hollows between hills. The audience sat in a tiered semicircle facing a flat circular space where the action took place. The theaters of Elizabethan England were open to the sky, with the audience looking on from tiered galleries or a courtyard. The main innovation was the rectangular thrust stage, surrounded on three sides by spectators. The first permanent indoor theater was Andrea PALLADIO's Olimpico Theater in Vicenza, Italy (1585). The Farnese Theater in Parma (1618) was designed with a horseshoe-shaped auditorium and the first permanent PROSCENIUM arch. Baroque European court theaters added tiered boxes for royalty. Richard WAGNER's Festspielhaus in Bayreuth, Germany (1876), with its fan-shaped seating plan, deep orchestra pit, and darkened auditorium, reintroduced classical principles that are still in use. The proscenium theater prevailed in the 17th–20th cent.; in the 20th cent., it was supplemented by other types of theaters, such as the thrust stage and theater-in-the-round. In Asia, stage arrangements have remained simple, with the audience usually grouped informally around an open space; notable exceptions are the NO drama and KABUKI of Japan. See also AMPHITHEATER.

theater Live performance of dramatic actions in order to tell a story or create a spectacle. One of the oldest and most important art forms in cultures worldwide, theater is thought to have its earliest origins in religious ritual; it often enacts myths or stories central to the belief structure of a culture, or creates comedy through travesty of such narratives. In Western civilization, theater began in ancient Greece and was adapted in Roman times; revived in the medieval liturgical dramas, it flourished in the Renaissance with the Italian COMMEDIA DELL'ARTE and in the 17th–18th cent. with such established companies as the COMÉDIE-FRANÇAISE. Varying theatrical forms may evolve to suit the tastes of different audiences (e.g., in Japan, the KABUKI of the townspeople and the NO DRAMA of the court). In Europe and the U.S. in the 19th and early 20th cent., theater was a major source of entertainment for all social classes, with forms ranging from BURLESQUE and VAUDEVILLE to serious dramas. Though the MUSICALS of BROADWAY and the FARCES of London's West End retain their popular appeal, the rise of television and movies has eroded audiences for live theater.

theater of fact See theater of FACT

theater of the absurd See theater of the ABSURD

Theatre Guild U.S. theatrical society. Founded in New York in 1918 by Lawrence Langner (1890–1962) and others, it proposed to produce high-quality, noncommercial plays. After the premiere of G. B. SHAW's *Heartbreak House* in 1920, the Guild became his U.S. agent and staged 15 of his plays. It also produced successful plays by Eugene O'NEILL, Maxwell ANDERSON, and Robert SHERWOOD and featured such actors as the LUNTS and Helen HAYES. It helped develop the American MUSICAL by staging *Porgy and Bess*

(1935), *Oklahoma!* (1943), and *Carousel* (1945), and produced the radio and television series *Theatre Guild on the Air* (1945–63). In 1950 it became part of the American National Theatre and Academy (ANTA).

Thebes \'thēbz\ *biblical* No. Famed ancient city, N Egypt, on the banks of the NILE RIVER. In early times it also included KARNAK and LUXOR; the Valley of the KINGS was nearby. The earliest monuments in the city itself date from the 11th dynasty, around the 21st cent. B.C., when the rulers of Thebes united Egypt and made Thebes the capital of Upper Egypt. It remained the capital until the end of the Middle Kingdom (c.18th cent. B.C.). After two centuries of obscurity, it flourished as Egypt's political and religious center throughout the New Kingdom period, well known for achievements in sculpture and architecture. It began to decline in the 12th cent. B.C. under RAMSES III. It was sacked by Assyrians in the mid-7th cent. B.C., by Persians in the 6th–4th cent. B.C., and by Romans about 30 B.C. Its ruins include the Temple of Amon at Karnak, the tomb of TUTANKHAMEN, and the great mortuary temples of RAMSES II and HATSHEPSUT.

Thebes *Greek* **Thívai** \'thē-ve\ Ancient city, BOEOTIA, E central Greece, one of the chief Greek city-states. Traditionally said to have been founded by CADMUS, it was the seat of the legendary OEDIPUS and the setting for many classic Greek tragedies. Its celebrated seven-gated wall is usually attributed to AMPHION. It was a center of MYCENAEAN power in the Bronze Age (c.1500–1200 B.C.). Hostility to ATHENS led it to side with the Persians in the PERSIAN WARS and with SPARTA in the PELOPONNESIAN WAR. Thebes and Sparta subsequently clashed, and the victorious Sparta occupied it. It revolted about 380 B.C. and Thebes defeated Sparta at the battles of Tegyra (375 B.C.) and Leuctra (371 B.C.). It joined Athens against PHILIP II and shared the defeat at the Battle of Chaeronea in 338 B.C. It was sacked by ALEXANDER THE GREAT in 336. Its remains include remnants of the city walls and the Mycenaean palace (c.1450–1350 B.C.).

theft In law, the crime of taking the property or services of another without consent. Under most statutes, theft encompasses the crimes of larceny, robbery, and BURGLARY. Larceny is the crime of taking and carrying away the goods of another with intent to steal. Grand larceny, or larceny of property of substantial value, is a felony, whereas petty larceny is a misdemeanor. The same principle applies to grand theft and petty theft. See also EMBEZZLEMENT, FRAUD.

theism View that all observable phenomena are dependent on but distinct from one supreme being. The view usually entails the idea that God is beyond human comprehension, perfect and self-sustained, but also peculiarly involved in the world and its events. Theists seek support for their view in rational argument and appeals to experience. A central issue is reconciling an omnipotent and perfect God with the existence of evil. See also AGNOSTICISM, ATHEISM, DEISM, MONOTHEISM, POLYTHEISM, THEODICY.

theme and variations Musical form in which a statement of a theme or harmonic pattern is followed by a series of altered versions of the theme. The practice, originally involving use of a repeated bass line (basso ostinato, or ground bass), began in early-16th-cent. dance music in Italy and Spain; the chaconne and passacaglia both usually employ a brief bass line repeated many times. English keyboard composers were soon developing melodic variations extensively. In the 17th cent., organ and harpsichord variations became a standard form in Germany. Piano variations in the 19th cent. often employed popular tunes or opera melodies; variation form was also commonly used in symphonies, quartets, and sonatas.

Themistocles \the-'mis-tə-,klēz\ (524?–c.460 B.C.) Athenian politician and naval strategist. As ARCHON (493) he built defensible harbors at Piraeus, and in 483, concerned about Persia's intentions, he persuaded the assembly to increase the navy. When XERXES I invaded, Themistocles lured his ships to their destruction at the Battle of SALAMIS (480). Despite his victory, Athens later ostracized the strongly democratic Themistocles (472) as the city's politics turned reactionary. He eventually fled the Peloponnese, and served as governor of some Asian Greek cities still under Persian rule until his death.

theocracy \thē-'ä-krə-sē\ Government by those regarded as divinely guided. The government's leaders may be clergy, or the state's legal system may be based on religious law. Theocratic rule was a constant of early civilizations. The ENLIGHTENMENT marked the end of theocracy in most Western countries. Present-day examples include Saudi Arabia, Iran, Afghanistan, and the Vatican.

Theocritus \thē-'ä-krə-təs\ (c.310–250 B.C.) Greek poet. Little is known of his life. His surviving poems consist of bucolics and mimes, set in the country, and epics, lyrics, and epigrams, set in towns. The bucolics, his most influential works, introduced the PASTORAL convention into poetry and were the sources of VIRGIL's *Eclogues* and much Renaissance poetry and drama. His best-known idylls include *Thalysia* ("Harvest Festival"), which presents the poet's friends and rivals in the guise of rustics.

theodicy \thē-'ä-də-sē\ Argument for the justification of God, concerned with reconciling God's goodness with the observable facts of evil and suffering. Under POLYTHEISM, evil is attributed to a conflict of wills between deities. The solution is less simple in MONOTHEISM. In some approaches, the perfect world created by God was spoiled by human disobedience or SIN. In others, God withdrew after creating the world, which then fell into decay. In general, however, God is understood to be the author of all that is good in the world and humans the source of evil.

Theodora (497?–548) Byzantine empress, wife of JUSTINIAN I. An actress, she became the mistress of Justinian, who married her in 525, and she was proclaimed empress when he became emperor in 527. Probably the most powerful woman in Byzantine history, she was her husband's most trusted adviser, sponsoring legal reforms and wielding great influence in diplomacy and internal politics. Her advice quelled the Nika revolt (532). She recognized the rights of women and ended persecution of Monophysite Christians, with whom she sympathized.

Theodora Byzantine mosaic, Ravenna, Italy

Theodorakis \,thē-ə-də-'räkis\, **Mikis** (*orig.* Michalis) (b.1925) Greek composer. A member of the wartime resistance, he later served in the Greek parliament. As a member of the Communist Party, he was arrested during the 1967 military coup and released only in 1970 under international pressure. Best known for his film scores, including *Zorba the Greek* (1964), *Z* (1969), and *State of Siege* (1972), he has also composed seven symphonies, four operas, ballets, and over 1,000 songs. He is esteemed in his homeland as a national hero.

Theodore I Lascaris \'las-kə-rəs\ (1174?–1221) First emperor of NICAEA, the Byzantine government-in-exile during the crusaders' occupation of Constantinople. He distinguished himself during the sieges of Constantinople in the Fourth CRUSADE (1203–4). After the Byzantine capital fell, he formed a new Byzantine state. He took the title emperor in 1208 and successfully defended Nicaea against the crusaders, the Turks, and his rival emperor David Comnenus. He signed a treaty (c.1214) with the Latin emperor of Constantinople defining Nicaea's boundaries, and betrothed his daughter to the heir to the Latin imperial throne.

Theodore II See TEWODROS II

Theodore of Canterbury, St. (602?–690) Seventh archbishop of Canterbury (668–90), the first to unify the English church. Sent from Rome to Canterbury, he helped establish a famous school at the monastery later known as St. Augustine's. Theodore centralized the English church, calling its first general synod (672) to end Celtic practices, affirm church doctrine, and divide dioceses. He made peace be-

tween King Aethelred of Mercia and King Ecgfrith of Northumbria.

Theodoric *known as* **Theodoric the Great** (454?–526) King of the OSTROGOTHS and founder of the Ostrogothic kingdom in Italy. Sent by the Byzantine emperor Zeno to invade Italy in 488, he made himself sole ruler by 493 and murdered ODOACER by treachery. With Ravenna as his capital, he held sway over a kingdom that included Sicily, Dalmatia, and some German lands. An Arian (see ARIANISM), he tolerated Catholicism and promoted peace between GOTHS and Romans.

Theodosius I \ˌthē-ə-'dō-shē-əs\ *or* **Theodosius the Great** *in full* Flavius Theodosius (A.D. 347–395) Roman emperor of the East (379–92) and of East and West (392–95). Born in Spain of Christian parents, he distinguished himself in the military and was proclaimed coemperor by GRATIAN to rule in the E empire (379). To settle the contentious debate over true Christianity, he adopted the NICENE CREED as the Christian norm (380). He reached a treaty with the VISIGOTHS (382). When the Spanish general Maximus overthrew the new coemperor in the W empire (387), Theodosius defeated the usurper (388) and claimed supreme authority over the whole empire (392). In 392 forces advocating paganism led by Arbogast and Eugenius took power in Rome. In 394 Theodosius defeated them, and claimed the Christian God victorious over the pagan gods.

Theodosius II (A.D. 401–450) Eastern Roman emperor (408–50). Grandson of THEODOSIUS I, he became sole ruler of the East when he was 7, initially under a regency. A gentle, scholarly man, he allowed relatives and ministers to dominate his government. His generals twice repelled the Persians (422, 447) but failed to evict the VANDALS from Roman Africa (429) and to prevent ATTILA's invasions (441–43, 447). The NESTORIAN heresy caused internal upheaval. Theodosius was credited with building the wall around Constantinople (413) and promulgating the Theodosian Code (438).

theology Study of the nature of God and the relationship of the human and divine. In CHRISTIANITY and other theistic religions (see THEISM), it examines doctrines concerning such subjects as SIN, faith, and GRACE and considers the terms of God's COVENANT with humankind. Theology typically takes for granted the authority of a religious teacher or the validity of a religious experience. It is distinguished from PHILOSOPHY in being concerned with justifying and explicating a faith, rather than questioning the underlying assumptions of such faith.

theorem In mathematics or logic, a statement whose validity has been established or proved (see PROOF). It consists of a hypothesis and a conclusion, beginning with certain assumptions that are necessary and sufficient to establish a result. A system of theorems that build on and augment each other constitutes a theory. Within any theory, however, only statements that are essential, important, or of special interest are called theorems. A statement proved as a direct consequence of a theorem is a corollary of the theorem. Some theorems are singled out and given titles (e.g., GÖDEL'S THEOREM, PYTHAGOREAN THEOREM).

theosophy \thē-'ä-sə-fē\ Religious philosophy with mystical concerns that can be traced to the ancient world. It holds that God must be experienced directly in mystical experience. It is characterized by esoteric doctrine and an interest in occult phenomena. Theosophical beliefs are found in NEOPLATONISM, GNOSTICISM, and among students of the KABBALA, but Jakob BÖHME is often called the father of modern theosophy. The Theosophical Society was founded by Helena BLAVATSKY in 1875. See also Annie BESANT.

Thera See THIRA

therapeutic radiology See RADIATION THERAPY

Theravada \ˌter-ə-'vä-də\ Major form of BUDDHISM, prevalent in Myanmar, Sri Lanka, Thailand, Cambodia, and Laos. It is the only survivor among the HINAYANA schools of Buddhism, and is generally regarded as the oldest, most orthodox, and most conservative form of Buddhism. It is believed to have survived intact from the 500 Elders, who followed in the tradition of the monks of the first Buddhist SANGHA. Theravada accepts the Pali canon (see TRIPITAKA) as authoritative scripture. Theravadins revere the historical

BUDDHA but do not recognize the various celestial buddhas and ancillary gods associated with MAHAYANA BUDDHISM.

Theresa of Lisieux \lēz-'yœ\, **St.** *orig.* Marie-Françoise-Thérèse Martin (1873–1897) French Carmelite nun, doctor of the Roman Catholic church. She entered the convent at Lisieux at 15. At the insistence of the prioress, she wrote an account of her spiritual development, in which she called for an absolute and childlike surrender to God, which she called the Little Way. After her death from tuberculosis at 24, the book was published as *Story of a Soul* (1898) and became widely popular, and Theresa's burial site at Lisieux became a place of pilgrimage.

thermae \'thər-mē\ Public bathing complex of ancient Rome, designed for relaxation and social activity as well as bathing. The baths consisted of a large open garden surrounded by subsidiary club rooms and a main block with hot room, steam room, and warm room, along with smaller bathrooms, cold room, and courts for exercise. Imperial thermae, such as the Baths of Caracalla (A.D. 216), were immense and opulently furnished. Service was supplied by slaves moving through underground passageways. Heated air was circulated from a fire under the floor; lighting was provided by an ingenious system of CLERESTORY windows.

thermal conduction Transfer of HEAT energy resulting from differences in temperature between adjacent bodies or adjacent parts of a body. In the absence of a HEAT PUMP, energy flows from warmer regions to cooler regions. The transfer of energy occurs as a result of collision among the particles of the matter involved. The rate of transfer of energy is proportional to the cross-sectional area of contact and to the difference in temperature between the two regions. See also CONDUCTOR, CONVECTION, RADIATION.

thermal radiation Process by which ENERGY is emitted by a warm surface. The energy is ELECTROMAGNETIC RADIATION and so travels at the speed of light and does not require a medium to carry it. Thermal radiation ranges in FREQUENCY from low-frequency infrared rays to high-frequency ultraviolet rays (see ELECTROMAGNETIC SPECTRUM). The intensity and frequency distribution of the emitted rays are determined by the nature and temperature of the emitting surface. An example of thermal radiation is the heating of the earth by the sun.

thermal spring See HOT SPRING

Thermidorian Reaction (1794) Revolt in the FRENCH REVOLUTION against the REIGN OF TERROR that was initiated on 9 Thermidor (July 27). Weary of the mounting executions (1,300 in June alone), the NATIONAL CONVENTION decreed the arrest of Maximilien de ROBESPIERRE, Louis de SAINT-JUST, and other members of the COMMITTEE OF PUBLIC SAFETY. They and others were guillotined, inaugurating a brief "White Terror" against the radical JACOBIN CLUB and ushering in the DIRECTORY.

thermocouple *or* **thermal junction** *or* **thermoelectric thermometer** Temperature-measuring instrument consisting of two wires of different metals joined at each end. One junction is placed where the temperature is to be measured, and the other is kept at a constant lower (reference) temperature. A measuring instrument is connected in the electrical circuit. The temperature difference causes the development of an ELECTROMOTIVE FORCE that is approximately proportional to the difference between the temperatures.

thermodynamics Study of the relationships among HEAT, WORK, TEMPERATURE, and ENERGY. Any physical system will spontaneously approach an EQUILIBRIUM that can be described by specifying its properties, such as PRESSURE, temperature, or chemical composition. If external constraints change, these properties generally change. The three laws of thermodynamics describe these changes and predict the equilibrium state of the system. The first law states that whenever energy is converted from one form to another, the total quantity of energy remains the same. The second states that, in a closed system, the ENTROPY of the system does not decrease. The third states that, as a system approaches ABSOLUTE ZERO, further extraction of energy becomes more difficult and eventually theoretically impossible.

thermonuclear bomb See HYDROGEN BOMB

thermonuclear weapon See NUCLEAR WEAPON

Thermopylae \thər-'mä-pə-lē\, **Battle of** Battle in N Greece (480 B.C.) in the PERSIAN WARS, celebrated in literature as an example of heroic resistance against great odds. The Greek forces, mostly Spartan, were led by LEONIDAS. After three days of holding their own against the Persian king XERXES I and his vast southward-advancing army, the Greeks were betrayed, and the Persians were able to out-flank them. Sending the main army in retreat, Leonidas and a small contingent remained behind to resist the advance and were killed to the last man.

thermostat Device that detects TEMPERATURE changes so as to maintain the temperature of an enclosed area essentially constant. It generates signals, usually electrical, to activate relays, valves, or switches when the temperature rises above or falls below the desired value. Thermostats are used to control the flow of fuel to a burner, of electric current to a heating or cooling unit, or of a heated or cooled gas or liq-uid into the area it serves. They are also used in fire-detec-tion warning systems.

theropod \'thir-ə-,päd\ Any species of bipedal, carnivorous SAURISCHIAN in the suborder Theropoda. The chicken-sized *Compsognathus,* the smallest known adult DINOSAUR, probably weighed 2–4 lbs (1–2 kg); the TYRANNOSAURS weighed tons. The theropods also included ALLOSAURUS, DEINONYCHUS, megalosaurus, oviraptor, and VELOCIRAP-TOR. Theropod remains have been recovered from the Late TRIASSIC PERIOD through the Late CRETACEOUS PERIOD (227–65 million years ago) from all continents except Antarctica. Their well-developed hind legs provided sup-port and locomotion; their short forelimbs had mobile hands. Modern birds probably descended from one line of small theropods.

Theseum \thi-'sē-əm\ Temple in Athens dedicated to HE-PHAESTUS and ATHENA as patrons of the arts and crafts. Built around 450 B.C., it is slightly older than the PAR-THENON. Some of its sculptures represent the exploits of THESEUS, but its overall theme was actually the apotheosis of HERACLES. It is surrounded by a single row of Doric columns. It is the world's best-preserved ancient Greek tem-ple, largely because of its medieval conversion to a Christ-ian church.

Theseus \'thē-sē-əs, 'thes-,yüs\ Hero of ancient Greek leg-end. On his journey to Athens, he slew many legendary vil-lains, including Procrustes. In Athens he found his father, King Aegeus, married to MEDEA; she tried to poison him but failed, and Aegeus declared him heir to the throne. In Crete Theseus met ARIADNE and slew the MINOTAUR; on re-turning to Athens he forgot to replace the ship's black sail with a white one signaling his victory, and Aegeus threw himself from the Acropolis in grief. Theseus went on to unite and extend the borders of ATTICA. He captured the AMAZON princess Antiope (Hippolyte), and the Amazons at-tacked Athens, which Antiope died defending. Theseus ab-ducted the child HELEN and attempted to steal PERSE-PHONE from Hades, but was confined in the underworld until his rescue by HERACLES. He died when the king of Scyros threw him from a cliff.

Thespis \'thes-pəs\ (fl.6th cent. B.C.) Greek poet, often con-sidered the "inventor of TRAGEDY." He is the first recorded winner of a prize for tragedy at the Great Dionysia, a drama festival, around 534 B.C. According to the rhetorician Themistius, ARISTOTLE said that tragedy in its earliest stage was entirely choral until the prologue and speeches were first introduced by Thespis. Thespis, according to Themistius' account, was thus the first "actor," and tragic dialogue began when he exchanged words with the leader of the chorus.

Thessaloniki \,the-sä-lō-'nē-kē\ *formerly* **Salonika** \sə-'lä-ni-kə\ Seaport (pop., 1991: 378,000), Macedonia, Greece. Founded in 316 B.C., it became the capital of the Roman province of Macedonia in 146 B.C. and grew to great im-portance. The apostle PAUL visited around A.D. 49–50 and later addressed epistles to converts there. It prospered dur-ing the Byzantine empire. It was part of the Ottoman em-pire 1430–1912. Headquarters of the YOUNG TURKS in 1908, it was returned to Greece in 1913. It is Greece's second-largest city and seaport.

Thessaly \'the-sə-lē\ Historical region and current adminis-trative region, E central Greece. It was the site of many cul-tures in the 3rd–2nd millennia B.C.; by around 1000 B.C. Greeks had established power there. It was made a separate Roman province in the 4th cent. A.D. In the 7th–13th cent. it was controlled by Slavs, Saracens, Bulgars, and Normans. In the late 14th cent. it passed to the Turks; it was returned to Greece in 1881. It saw heavy fighting between Allied and Axis forces in 1941. It is the site of Mt. OLYMPUS.

Thetis \'thē-təs\ In GREEK MYTHOLOGY, a NEREID loved by both ZEUS and POSEIDON. When it was revealed that Thetis was destined to bear a son who would be mightier than his father, the two gods gave her to Peleus, king of the Myrmidons. She resisted the union by changing into various shapes, but eventually bore Peleus' son ACHILLES. Some legends relate that she bore seven children, all of whom perished either when she tried to render them im-mortal or when she killed them as the offspring of a forced marriage.

thiamine \'thī-ə-mən\ *or* **vitamin B₁** Organic compound, part of the VITAMIN B COMPLEX, necessary in the diet. It plays an important role in CARBOHYDRATE METABOLISM. Its complex molecular structure includes two substituted rings. Thiamine is found most abundantly in whole cereal grains and certain other seeds. It is removed in the refining process; deficiency leads to BERIBERI.

Thiers \tē-'er\, **(Louis-) Adolphe** (1797–1877) French politi-cian and historian. A journalist, he cofounded the opposi-tion newspaper *National* in 1830. He supported LOUIS-PHILIPPE and served as minister of the interior (1832, 1834–36) and premier and foreign minister (1836, 1840). Follow-ing the FEBRUARY REVOLUTION, he helped elect Louis-Napoléon (later NAPOLEON III) president of the SECOND REPUBLIC; he later attacked Napoleon III's imperial poli-cies. As president of the THIRD REPUBLIC 1871–73, he ne-gotiated the end of the FRANCO–PRUSSIAN WAR and crushed the PARIS COMMUNE. He also wrote such major his-torical works as *History of the French Revolution* (10 vols., 1823–27) and *History of the Consulate and the Empire* (20 vols., 1845–62).

Thimphu \thim-'pü\ Town (pop., 1993 est.: 30,000), capital of Bhutan. It lies on the Raidak River. The Tashi Chho cas-tle, a traditional fortified monastery and one of the finest examples of traditional Bhutanese architecture, houses the offices of the royal government. The local economy relies on agriculture and lumbering.

think tank Institute, corporation, or group organized for in-terdisciplinary research, usually conducted for governmen-tal and commercial clients. Projects for government clients often involve social-policy planning and national defense. Commercial projects include developing and testing new technologies and new products. Funding sources include endowments, contracts, private donations, and sales of re-ports.

thin-layer chromatography (TLC) Type of CHROMATOGRA-PHY using as the stationary phase a thin layer (0.01 inch, or 0.25 mm) of a finely ground matrix coated on a glass plate or incorporated in a plastic film. Solutions of the mixtures to be analyzed, and of reference materials, are spotted near one edge. The edge of the plate is then dipped in a SOLVENT. The solvent travels up the matrix by CAPILLARITY, moving the components of the samples at various rates. The com-ponents, visible as separated spots, are identified by com-paring the distances they have traveled with those of the known reference materials. TLC is useful for biological mixtures, especially LIPIDS in animal or vegetable tissues and ISOPRENOIDS and ESSENTIAL OILS found in flowers and plants.

Thíra \'thē-rä\ *ancient* **Thera** \'thir-ə\ *formerly* **Santorini** Is-land, S CYCLADES, Greece. The remaining half of an ex-ploded volcano, it surrounds a lagoon with volcanic cliffs rising to almost 1,000 ft (300 m). MINOAN remains date to before 2000 B.C. One of the largest known volcanic erup-tions occurred on the island about 1500 B.C., depositing ash and pumice as far away as Egypt and Israel. The eruption has been linked to such phenomena as the miracles of the EXODUS and the sinking of ATLANTIS. Excavations have re-vealed a rich Minoan city.

TUV

Third Estate *French* Tiers État. In French history, one of the three orders (with the nobility and the clergy) of the ES-TATES GENERAL before the FRENCH REVOLUTION. The unprivileged order, it represented the great majority of the people. Its transformation with the TENNIS COURT OATH into a NATIONAL ASSEMBLY in 1789 marked the beginning of the Revolution.

Third International See COMINTERN

Third Reich \'rīk\ Official designation for the NAZI PARTY's regime in Germany from January 1933 to May 1945. The name reflects Adolf HITLER's conception of his expansionist regime as the presumed successor of the HOLY ROMAN EMPIRE (800–1806, the First Reich) and the German empire of 1871–1918 (the Second Reich).

Third Republic French government 1870–1940. After the fall of the SECOND EMPIRE and the suppression of the PARIS COMMUNE, a new constitution established a regime based on parliamentary supremacy. Despite its series of short-lived governments, the Third Republic was marked by social stability (except for the Alfred DREYFUS affair), industrialization, and establishment of a professional civil service. It ended with the fall of France to the Germans in 1940. Notable leaders included Leon BLUM, Georges BOULANGER, Aristide BRIAND, Georges CLEMENCEAU, Edouard DALADIER, Félix FAURE, Jules FERRY, Leon GAM-BETTA, Jules GRÉVY, Edouard HERRIOT, Jean JAURÈS, Pierre LAVAL, Albert LEBRUN, Maurice MAC-MAHON, Philippe PÉTAIN, and Adolphe THIERS.

Third Section *or* **Third Department** Office created in 1826 by Czar NICHOLAS I to conduct secret police operations. It gathered information on political dissidents and banished suspected political criminals to remote regions. It collaborated with the Corps of Gendarmes (formed in 1836), a military force that operated throughout Russia, and with a network of spies and informers. Having grown increasingly repressive, it was abolished in 1880; its functions were transferred to the police of the interior ministry.

third world Political designation originally used (1963) to describe those states not part of the first world (capitalist, economically developed states led by the U.S.) or the second world (communist states led by the Soviet Union). The third, or developing, world consists of former colonies in Africa, Asia, and Latin America. With the end of the Cold War and the increased economic competitiveness of some developing countries, the term has lost its analytic clarity.

Thirty Tyrants (404–403 B.C.) Spartan-imposed oligarchy that ruled Athens after the PELOPONNESIAN WAR. Thirty commissioners were appointed to the oligarchy, which had an extremist conservative core. Their oppressive regime fostered a bloody purge, in which perhaps 1,500 residents were killed. Many moderates fled the city; gathering a force, they returned to defeat the tyrants' forces in 403.

Thirty Years' War (1618–48) Series of intermittent conflicts in Europe fought for various reasons, including religious, dynastic, territorial, and commercial rivalries. Mainly a struggle between the Habsburg-controlled Holy Roman Empire and the Protestant principalities that relied on the chief anti-Catholic powers of Sweden and the Netherlands, it also involved the rivalry of France with the Habsburg powers. The conflicts began in 1618 when the future emperor FERDINAND II tried to impose Roman Catholicism on his domains and the Protestant nobles rebelled. The battlefield centered on the principalities in Germany, which suffered severely from plundering armies. Early successes by the CATHOLIC LEAGUE were countered by military gains by Sweden. When the bloodshed ended with the Peace of WESTPHALIA (1648), the balance of power in Europe had been radically changed. France emerged as the chief Western power and states of the Holy Roman Empire were granted full sovereignty.

thistle Weedy species of *Cirsium, Carduus, Echinops, Sonchus*, and other plant genera of the COMPOSITE FAMILY. The term usually refers to prickly leaved species of *Carduus* and *Cirsium*, which have dense heads of small, usually pink or purple flowers. Canadian thistle *(Cirsium arvense)* is a troublesome weed in agricultural areas of N. America. The thistle is the national emblem of Scotland.

Thocmectony See S. W. HOPKINS

Thomas, Clarence (b.1948) U.S. jurist. Born in Pin Point, Ga., he graduated from Yale Law School and served as assistant attorney general in Missouri (1974–77) and chairman of the Equal Employment Opportunity Commission (1982–90). Appointed to the U.S. Court of Appeals in 1990 and to the U.S. Supreme Court in 1991, he is the Court's second black justice. His confirmation hearings were complicated by accusations of SEXUAL HARASSMENT by Anita Hill, a law professor (b.1956), which produced enormous public controversy. He denied the charges, and the Senate narrowly voted to confirm him. Though a quiet presence on the Court, he has never swerved from a strong conservatism.

Thomas, Dylan (Marlais) (1914–1953) Welsh poet and prose writer. His early verse, with its rich language and emotional intensity, made him famous. In *Deaths and Entrances* (1946), with "Fern Hill," he often adopts a bardic, oracular voice. *In Country Sleep* (1952), containing "Do Not Go Gentle into That Good Night," and *Collected Poems* (1952) followed. Thomas's prose includes the comic *Portrait of the Artist as a Young Dog* (1940); a play, *Under Milk Wood* (1954); and the reminiscence *A Child's Christmas in Wales* (1955). His sonorous recitations contributed greatly to his fame. He died at 39 of an alcohol overdose in New York while on tour.

Thomas, George H(enry) (1816–1870) U.S. general. Born in Southampton Co., Va., he graduated from West Point. He remained loyal to the Union when the Civil War broke out. In E Kentucky, he won the first important Union victory in the west in 1862. At the Battle of CHICKAMAUGA he organized an unyielding defense, earning the nickname "the Rock of Chickamauga." In 1864 he defeated Confederate forces at Nashville, earning the thanks of Congress.

Thomas, Lewis (1913–1993) U.S. physician and author. Born in Queens, N.Y., he served as dean of NYU's medical school and president of Memorial Sloan-Kettering Cancer Center. He translated his passionate interest in and wonder at the intricate mysteries of biology into lucid meditations and reflections on biology in award-winning essays. The best known of his widely read books is *The Lives of a Cell* (1974, National Book Award).

Thomas, Lowell (Jackson) (1892–1981) U.S. radio commentator, journalist, and author. A war correspondent while in his 20s, Thomas helped make T. E. LAWRENCE famous with his exclusive coverage and later with the book *With Lawrence in Arabia* (1924). He was a preeminent broadcaster with CBS from 1930; his radio nightly news was an American institution for nearly two generations, and he appeared on television from its earliest days. He wrote more than 50 books of adventure and comment.

Thomas, Norman (Mattoon) (1884–1968) U.S. social reformer and politician. Born in Marion, Ohio, he was ordained a Presbyterian minister. He joined the Socialist Party in 1918 and left his parish post in New York to become secretary of the pacifist Fellowship of Reconciliation. He helped found the AMERICAN CIVIL LIBERTIES UNION, and served as codirector of the League for Industrial Democracy 1922–37. He was repeatedly the Socialist Party's candidate for president (1928–48), and headed the party from 1926. After World War II he pressed for nuclear disarmament as chairman of the Postwar World Council.

Thomas, St. (d.A.D. 53?) One of the 12 Disciples of JESUS. He is best known for requiring physical proof of Jesus' resurrection before he could believe it; hence the phrase "doubting Thomas." When Jesus reappeared and had Thomas touch his wounds, Thomas became the first person to explicitly acknowledge Jesus' divinity, saying "My Lord and my God."

Thomas à Becket See St. Thomas BECKET

Thomas à Kempis *orig.* Thomas Hemerken (1379/80–1471) German monk and theologian. He moved to Deventer, the Netherlands, around 1392 and joined a community devoted to the care and education of the poor. In 1387 he entered the Augustinian monastery at Agnietenberg. He is credited with writing *The Imitation of Christ*, the most influential devotional work in Christian literature after the Bible. Noted for its simple language and style, it emphasizes spiritual over materialistic life and affirms the rewards of a life centered on Christ.

Thomas Aquinas \ə-'kwī-nəs\, **St.** (1224/25–1274) Foremost philosopher and theologian of the Roman Catholic church. Born of noble parents at Roccasecca, Italy, he studied at the Univ. of Naples, joined the Dominicans, and taught at the Univ. of Paris. His time in Paris coincided with the rediscovery of Aristotelian science; his great achievement was to integrate into Christian thought the rigors of ARISTOTLE's philosophy. He held that reason can operate within faith; while the philosopher relies solely on reason, the theologian accepts faith as his starting point and then proceeds to conclusion through the use of reason. This point of view was controversial, as was his belief in the religious value of nature, for which he argued that to detract from the perfection of creation was to detract from the creator. He was opposed by St. BONAVENTURE. He was canonized in 1323, named a Doctor of the Church in 1567, and declared the champion of orthodoxy during the modernist crisis at the end of the 19th cent. A prolific writer, he produced more than 80 works, including *Summa theologica* (1265–73). See also THOMISM.

Thomism \'tō-,mi-zəm\ Philosophical and theological system developed by St. THOMAS AQUINAS. It holds that the human SOUL is real and immortal, that human knowledge is based both on sensory experience and on the mind's reflective capacity, and that all creatures have a natural tendency to love God that can be perfected and elevated by GRACE and application. In the 20th cent., Thomism was developed by Étienne Gilson (1884–1978) and Jacques MARITAIN.

Thompson, Dorothy (1894–1961) U.S. journalist. Born in Lancaster, N.Y., she became a freelance correspondent in Europe. Her reporting on the Nazis so infuriated Adolf HITLER that in 1934 she became the first U.S. correspondent expelled from Germany. Her column "On the Record" became hugely popular and was syndicated from 1941 to 1958 in as many as 170 newspapers. Her many books include *New Russia* (1928), *I Saw Hitler!* (1932), and *The Courage to Be Happy* (1957). She was married to Sinclair LEWIS 1928–42.

Thompson, Emma (b.1959) British actress. Initially a stage and television actress, she was married to Kenneth BRANAGH 1989–94, and appeared in several of his films, including *Henry V* (1989) and *Much Ado About Nothing* (1993). She later starred in *Howards End* (1992, Academy Award), *The Remains of the Day* (1993), *Sense and Sensibility* (1995), for which she won an Academy Award for best screenplay, and *Primary Colors* (1998).

Thomson, J(oseph) J(ohn) (*later* **Sir Joseph**) (1856–1940) English physicist. He taught at Cambridge Univ.'s Cavendish Laboratory (1884–1918), which he developed into a world-renowned institution. In 1897 he showed that CATHODE RAYS are rapidly moving particles, and by measuring their displacement by electric and magnetic fields determined that these particles were nearly 2,000 times less massive than the lightest known atomic particle; they are now known as ELECTRONS. His discovery helped revolutionize the knowledge of atomic structure. In 1903 he suggested a discontinuous theory of LIGHT, foreshadowing Albert EINSTEIN's later theory of photons. He later discovered ISOTOPES and invented MASS SPECTROMETRY. In 1906 Thomson received a Nobel Prize for his research into the electrical conductivity of gases.

Thomson, Roy (Herbert) *later* Baron Thomson of Fleet (1894–1976) Canadian-British publisher. A native of Ontario, Thomson began acquiring radio stations and newspapers there in the 1930s; later he expanded his interests to Britain and the U.S. In 1959 he purchased the Kemsley group of newspapers, the largest in Britain. In 1967 he made his most important purchase, *The TIMES* of London, and his major investment in it provided it financial stability. International Thomson is today one of the largest publishing conglomerates in the world.

Thomson, Virgil (1896–1989) U.S. composer and critic. Born in Kansas City, he studied piano and organ at Harvard Univ. Studying in Paris with Nadia BOULANGER (1921), he began to compose. Resident in Paris 1925–40, he wrote the operas *Four Saints in Three Acts* (1928) and *The Mother of Us All* (1946) with Gertrude STEIN, affecting a charmingly naïve style. Other works include the film scores *The Plow That Broke the Plains* (1936) and *The Louisiana Story* (1949, Pulitzer Prize). His gracefully written music criticism for the *New York Herald Tribune* (1940–54) was respected for its concern with music rather than performers.

Thor Germanic deity who appeared as a great, red-bearded warrior of tremendous strength. He was the implacable foe of the harmful race of giants but was benevolent toward humans. His name is the Germanic word for thunder. His great weapon was his hammer. His greatest enemy was the world serpent Jörmungand, which he was destined to kill, and be killed by, in the RAGNAROK. Thursday is named for Thor.

thoracic cavity \thə-'ra-sik\ *or* **chest cavity** Second-largest hollow space of the body, enclosed by the ribs, VERTEBRAL COLUMN, and breastbone and separated from the ABDOMINAL CAVITY by the DIAPHRAGM. It contains the LUNGS and bronchi, part of the ESOPHAGUS and TRACHEA, and the HEART and major blood vessels. A membrane called the pleura lines the cavity and continues over the lung and the rest of the cavity's contents. Disorders include blood (hemothorax) or air (pneumothorax) in the pleural cavity, and inflammation of the pleura (pleurisy).

Thoreau \thə-'rō\, **Henry David** (1817–1862) U.S. thinker, essayist, and naturalist. Born in Concord, Mass., Thoreau taught school before deciding to become a poet of nature. He came under the influence of R. W. EMERSON and began to publish pieces in the Transcendentalist magazine *The Dial*. In 1845–47, to demonstrate how satisfying a simple life could be, he lived in a hut beside Concord's Walden Pond, an experience that produced his masterwork, *Walden* (1854). His protest against the Mexican–American War led to the essay "Civil Disobedience" (1849), which would later influence Mohandas GANDHI and M. L. KING. In later years his interest in TRANSCENDENTALISM waned and he became a dedicated abolitionist. His many nature writings and records of his wanderings (including *A Week on the Concord and Merrimack Rivers*, 1849) display the mind of a brilliant naturalist. After his death his collected writings were published in 20 volumes.

Thorez \tò-'rez\, **Maurice** (1900–1964) French communist politician. A coal miner from age 12, he joined the FRENCH COMMUNIST PARTY, was arrested several times for agitation, and rose to secretary-general of the party (1930). He served in the Chamber of Deputies (1932–39, 1945–60), and helped form the POPULAR FRONT government in 1936. He later served as a minister of state (1945) and deputy premier (1946, 1947). He remained a dedicated Stalinist even after Nikita KHRUSHCHEV's denunciation in 1956.

Thoroughbred Light breed of racing and jumping HORSE descended from three desert stallions brought to England between 1689 and 1724. Thoroughbreds have a delicate head, slim body, broad chest, and short back. They stand about 16 hands (64 in., 163 cm) high and weigh about 1,000 lbs (450 kg). They are sensitive and high-spirited.

Thorpe, Jim (*orig.* James Francis) (1888–1953) U.S. athlete. Born on an Indian reservation near Pargue, Okla., he was of predominantly American Indian (Sauk and Fox) descent. He trained as a foot-

Jim Thorpe demonstrating the drop kick

TUV

ball halfback under Pop WARNER at vocational school, where he also excelled at baseball, basketball, boxing, lacrosse, swimming, and hockey. In 1912 he won the Olympic decathlon and pentathlon by wide margins. After playing outfield for several National League baseball teams (1913–19), he went on to become an early star of professional football (1919–26). In 1920–21 he served as first president of what would become the NATIONAL FOOTBALL LEAGUE. He had difficulty adjusting to his retirement and suffered near-poverty and bouts of alcoholism. Thorpe is generally regarded as the greatest American athlete of the entire 20th cent.

Thoth \\'tōth, 'thōth, 'tōt\\ Egyptian god of the moon and of reckoning, learning, and writing. He was the inventor of writing, the creator of languages, the representative of RE, and the scribe, interpreter, and adviser of the gods. In the myth of OSIRIS, Thoth protected the pregnant ISIS and healed the eye of her son HORUS. He judged the deceased and reported the results to Osiris. He was often represented with the head of an ibis. The Greeks identified Thoth with HERMES; as Hermes Trismegistos he was regarded as the author of the HERMETIC WRITINGS.

Thousand and One Nights, The *or **Arabian Nights' Entertainment*** *Arabic Alf laylah wa laylah.* Collection of Oriental stories. The frame story, in which the vengeful King Shahryar's plan to marry and execute a new wife each day is foiled by the resourceful Scheherazade, is probably Indian; the tales with which Scheherazade beguiles Shahryar, postponing her execution, come from India, Iran, Iraq, Egypt, and Turkey. It is now believed that the collection is a composite work originally transmitted orally and developed over several centuries. Sir Richard BURTON's translation (1885–88) has become the best-known English version.

Thousand Islands Group of about 1,500 small islands extending 80 mi (128 km) in the ST. LAWRENCE RIVER between New York state and Ontario, Canada. Some belong to Canada and some to the U.S. They include summer resort facilities. The 8.5-mi (13.7-km) Thousand Islands International Bridge connects New York and Ontario.

Thrace Ancient and modern region, SE BALKAN PENINSULA. Its borders have varied. In ancient Greek times it was bounded by the DANUBE RIVER, the AEGEAN SEA, and the BLACK SEA. Modern Thrace corresponds to S Bulgaria, the Greek province of Thrace, and European Turkey, including the GALLIPOLI peninsula. The Thracians settled the region in the 2nd millennium B.C.; their culture was noted for its poetry and music, and their soldiers were known as superior fighters. Colonized by Greeks and subject successively to Persia, Macedon, and Rome, it later became part of the Byzantine empire, and in 1453 part of the Ottoman empire. The N part was annexed by Bulgaria in 1885; the E part passed to Turkey in 1923. The region harvests corn, grapes, oysters, and eels; the chief cash crop is Turkish tobacco.

thrasher Any of 17 species (family Mimidae) of New World songbirds having a downcurved bill and noted for noisily foraging in dense thickets and for loud varied songs. Thrashers occur from N Canada to central Mexico and the Caribbean. The brown thrasher *(Toxostoma rufum),* of N. America east of the Rocky Mtns., is about 12 in. (30 cm) long and has red-brown plumage with streaked underparts.

thread Tightly twisted YARN consisting of several strands that has a circular cross-section and is used for sewing. Thread is usually wound on spools, with thread size (degree of fineness) indicated on the spool end. COTTON thread can be used with fabrics made from yarn of plant origin, such as cotton and linen, and with rayon (made from cellulose, a plant substance). SILK thread is suitable for silks and wools, both of animal origin. NYLON and POLYESTER threads are appropriate for synthetics and for knits with a high degree of stretch.

Three Gorges Dam Project Dam designed to span China's CHANG (Yangtze) RIVER. On completion, scheduled for 2009, it would be the largest dam in the world, generating as much hydroelectricity as 15 coal-burning power stations. It would also create an immense deep-water reservoir that would allow 10,000-ton freighters to navigate 1,400 mi (2,250 km) inland from the E China Sea. The extremely controversial project will require displacement of over a

million people and destruction of magnificent scenery and archaeological sites. Though construction began in 1993, a third of the National People's Congress failed to support it and the WORLD BANK would not advance funds. Critics contend that smaller dams on Chang tributaries could accomplish the same purpose.

Three Kingdoms (A.D. 220–80) Trio of warring Chinese states that followed the demise of the HAN DYNASTY. The kingdom of Wei, ruled by CAO CAO's son, controlled N China; the kingdom of Shu-Han was established in present-day Sichuan by Liu Bei and his adviser ZHUGE LIANG; and the kingdom of Wu was established in the south, with its capital at Nanjing. They were all subsumed into the JIN DYNASTY by 280. The Three Kingdoms era of warfare and intrigue has inspired Chinese historical fiction ever since.

3M See MINNESOTA MINING & MANUFACTURING CO.

Three Mile Island Nuclear power station near Harrisburg, Pa., site of the most serious accident of the U.S. nuclear power industry (Mar. 28, 1979). Mechanical failures and human errors caused a partial meltdown of the nuclear core and the release of radioactive gases. The accident increased public fears about nuclear safety and effectively stopped construction of nuclear reactors and further development of U.S. nuclear power plants.

thrombocyte See PLATELET

thrombosis \\thräm-'bō-səs\\ Formation of a blood clot (thrombus) in the heart or a blood vessel. Contributing factors include injury to a blood vessel's lining from INFLAMMATION or atherosclerosis (see ARTERIOSCLEROSIS), blood flow that is turbulent (e.g., from an ANEURYSM) or sluggish (e.g., from prolonged bed rest), or COAGULATION abnormalities. Thrombosis is a particular danger after major surgery. A thrombus can block blood flow at the point of clot formation or break free to block it elsewhere (EMBOLISM).

throne Chair of state set on a dais and often surmounted by a canopy, representing the power of the dignitary who sits on it. In Greek history, thrones were identified as seats of the gods; soon the word included the symbolic seats of those who held religious or secular power, a meaning common to virtually all cultures. The oldest surviving throne was built into the walls of Knossos (c.1800 B.C.). Probably the most magnificent was the jewel-studded Peacock Throne of the rulers of Delhi, stolen from India by Persia in 1739 and thereafter the symbol of the Persian/Iranian monarchy. In the late 17th and 18th cent., thrones were often made of silver, but later versions tend to be of gilded wood.

throttle VALVE for regulating the supply of a fluid (as steam) to an engine, especially vaporized fuel delivered to the cylinders of an INTERNAL-COMBUSTION ENGINE. In an automobile engine, air flows down through the throat of the CARBURETOR, past the throttle valve, and into the intake manifold. A throat is formed by the reduced diameter, and acceleration of the air through this smaller passage causes a decrease in pressure related to the amount of air flowing. This decrease results in gasoline flow from the jet into the airstream. Any increase in airflow caused by change in engine speed or throttle position increases the pressure differential acting on the fuel and causes more fuel to flow.

thrush Any of about 300 species of songbirds (family Turdidae) that usually have a slender bill and "booted" lower legs (i.e., covered in front with one long scale instead of many short ones). Thrushes are 5–12 in. (13–30 cm) long. Most have dull plumage, often with patches of bright yellow, red, or blue. Found virtually worldwide, they are most diverse in the Old World, especially in Africa. The N species are strong migrants. Some, including the hermit thrush and WOOD THRUSH, have notably beautiful songs. See also BLACKBIRD, BLUEBIRD, ROBIN.

Thuan Thien See LE LOI

Thucydides \\thü-'si-də-ˌdēz\\ (c.460–404? B.C.) Greatest of ancient Greek historians. An Athenian who commanded a fleet in the Peloponnesian War, Thucydides failed to prevent the capture of the important city of Amphipolis and was exiled for 20 years. In exile he wrote his *History of the Peloponnesian War;* evidently he did not live to complete it, for it stops abruptly in 411 B.C. A carefully drawn, strictly chronological narrative of events, it presents the first recorded political and moral analysis of a nation's war policies.

Thunder Bay City (pop., 1996: 114,000), W central Ontario. It is located on the NW shore of Lake SUPERIOR. Its first settlement was a French fur-trading post about 1678. In the 1870s and 1880s silver strikes and the arrival of the Canadian Pacific Railway brought prosperity to the twin towns of Port Arthur and Fort William that had grown up there. They merged in 1970 as Thunder Bay. It is one of Canada's busiest ports, with grain storage and transshipment depots.

thunderbird In N. American Indian mythology, a powerful spirit in the form of a bird that watered the earth and made vegetation grow. Lightning was believed to flash from its eyes or beak, and the beating of its wings was thought to represent rolling thunder. Similar figures have been found throughout Africa, Asia, and Europe.

thunderstorm Violent, short-lived atmospheric disturbance, almost always associated with cumulonimbus clouds (very tall, dense rain clouds) and accompanied by thunder and LIGHTNING. Such storms usually generate strong, gusty winds and heavy rain, and occasionally HAIL or TORNADOES. Thunderstorms occur almost worldwide, although rarely in the polar regions. In the U.S. the areas of maximum thunderstorm activity are the Florida peninsula and the coast of the Gulf of Mexico (70–80 days per year).

Thurber, James (Grover) (1894–1961) U.S. writer and cartoonist. Born in Columbus, Ohio, he was on the *New Yorker*'s staff 1927–33 and thereafter remained a leading contributor. His cartoons became some of the most popular and recognizable in America. His writings include *My Life and Hard Times* (1933), *Fables for Our Time* (1940), the *New Yorker* memoir *The Years with Ross* (1959), and the children's book *The 13 Clocks* (1950); his best-known story is "The Secret Life of Walter Mitty" (1939; film, 1946).

Thuringia \thù-'rin-jē-ə\ *German* **Thüringen** \'tü̇-riṅ-ən\ Historic region and state (pop., 1997 est.: 2,485,000), Germany. It includes the land around the Thuringian Forest in what was formerly SW E. GERMANY. The capital is ERFURT. The Germanic Thuringians appeared after A.D. 350. In 1485 the area became part of SAXONY. Following the partition of Germany in 1945, the state became part of E. Germany; it became a state of the unified Germany in 1990. The economy is largely industrial.

Thurmond, (James) Strom (b.1902) U.S. politician. Born in Edgefield, S.C., he served as governor 1947–51. At the 1948 Democratic convention he led a faction of Southern delegates opposed to the party's civil rights policy; the so-called DIXIECRATS nominated Thurmond for president. Elected to the U.S. Senate, he would become its longest-serving member in history (1955–2003). Highly conservative, he advocated states' rights, opposed civil rights legislation, and supported increases in military spending.

Thutmose III \thüt-'mō-sə\ (d.1426 B.C.) Egyptian king of the 18th dynasty (r.1479–1426 B.C.), often regarded as the greatest PHARAOH. He ascended the throne around the age of 10, but did not rule in his own right until the death of his aunt, HATSHEPSUT. He began military campaigns to reestablish Egyptian rule in Syria and Palestine and later to conquer Mesopotamia. He subdued the Nubian tribes to the south and employed them in the gold mines that became the basis of Egypt's wealth. He established a system whereby native rulers would pay yearly tribute to Egypt and send their heirs to Egypt, where they would be educated at court. At home he enlarged the temple of Amon at Karnak. His mummy was discovered in 1889 and his mortuary temple in 1962.

thyme \'tīm\ Pungent herb (*Thymus vulgaris*) of the MINT family. A small, low-growing shrub, it has small, curled leaves that give off a fragrant odor when crushed. The dried leaves and flowering tops are used to flavor a wide range of foods. The essential oil has antiseptic and anesthetic properties and is used as an internal medicine, and in perfumes and toothpastes.

thymine \'thī-ˌmēn\ Organic compound of the PYRIMIDINE family, consisting of a ring containing both nitrogen and carbon atoms, and a methyl group. It occurs in combined form in many important biological molecules, particularly

DNA (where its complementary base is ADENINE). It or its corresponding NUCLEOSIDE or NUCLEOTIDE is made from DNA by HYDROLYSIS.

thymus \'thī-məs\ Lymphoid organ (see LYMPHOID TISSUE) between the breastbone and the heart. Stem cells in its outer cortex develop into different kinds of T CELLS (for "thymus"; see LYMPHOCYTE). Some migrate to the inner medulla and enter the bloodstream; those that do not may be destroyed to prevent autoimmune reactions. This process is most active during infancy. If a newborn's thymus is removed, not enough T cells are produced, the SPLEEN and LYMPH NODES have little tissue, and the immune system fails, causing a gradual, fatal wasting disease. Thymus removal in adults has little effect.

thyroid gland Endocrine gland in the throat that secretes HORMONES vital to metabolism and growth. Secretion of thyroid hormones is controlled by thyroid-stimulating hormone (TSH), released by the PITUITARY GLAND (see ENDOCRINE SYSTEM). These hormones' primary action in adults is to regulate cellular oxygen consumption (metabolic rate). They also lower blood CHOLESTEROL and are necessary for normal growth and development of children, in whom deficiency causes CRETINISM. The thyroid also produces calcitonin, a hormone that stimulates deposition of calcium from the blood into the bones. See also GOITER, GRAVES' DISEASE, IODINE DEFICIENCY.

Thyssen Krupp Stahl \'tü̇-sən-'krủp-'shtäl\ German steel company. The Krupp firm began in 1811 when Friedrich Krupp (1787–1826) founded a steel plant in Essen. Known for its high-quality steel and its cannons and other armaments, Krupp prospered with the rise of the German navy. It enjoyed a monopoly on arms manufacturing during World War I; one of its most potent weapons was "BIG BERTHA." After the war, Germany was forbidden to manufacture arms, but Krupp remained a vast industrial empire. Its factories were central to Germany's illegal rearmament under Adolf HITLER in the 1930s. After World War II, Alfried Krupp (1907–1967) was convicted of war crimes for using slave labor and ordered to forfeit all his property, but with the outbreak of the Korean War he was granted amnesty and his property restored. In 1968, after his son renounced the Krupp name and fortune, the company went public. In 1992 it merged with Hoesch AG. Thyssen AG originated as a steel rolling mill founded by August Thyssen (1842–1926). In 1999 the rival companies merged to become Thyssen Krupp Stahl.

Tiahuanaco \ˌtē-ä-wä-'nä-kō\ *or* **Tiwanaku** \ˌtē-wä-'nä-kü\ Major pre-Columbian ANDEAN CIVILIZATION known from ruins near the S shore of Lake Titicaca in Bolivia. The great and enduring empire at its height encompassed parts of Bolivia, Argentina, Chile, and Peru. Its earliest remains may date from about 200 B.C.; Tiahuanaco influence may be visible in artifacts from the 2nd millennium B.C. The site's major buildings date from A.D. 600 to 1000. Much of the culture's success was due to its raised-field farming technique: raised planting surfaces were separated by canals that retained the sun's heat during the cold nights and kept the crops from freezing. Tiahuanaco culture vanished by 1200.

Tiananmen Square \'tyản-'ản-'men\ Largest public square in the world, built in Beijing in 1651 and enlarged in 1958. Named for the massive stone "Gate of Heavenly Peace" (Tiananmen) at its N end, it contains and is surrounded by halls, museums, and monuments, including the Mao Zedong Memorial Hall, where Mao's body rests in state. It had been the rallying point for student demonstrations since 1919. In 1989 massive pro-democracy demonstrations attracted more than a million protesters, who occupied large sections of Beijing. Tanks were called in to disperse the crowds; hundreds were killed and thousands arrested, and the movement was effectively crushed.

Tianjin *or* **T'ien-chen** *or* **Tientsin** \'tyen-'jin\ Seaport and municipality with provincial status (pop., 1999 est.: 9,590,000), on the Hai River, NE China. Connected to the CHANG RIVER by the GRAND CANAL, it is China's fourth-largest city. It has been a major transportation and trading center since MONGOL times. It was a garrison town during the MING DYNASTY dynasty (1368–1644). The British and French occupied it during the Second OPIUM WAR (1856–60); a treaty

TUV

signed there in 1858 opened 11 Chinese ports to foreign trade. It was the scene of heavy fighting during the BOXER REBELLION (1900), after which its walls were razed. It is the country's second-largest manufacturing center. Educational institutions include Tianjin Univ. (1895) and Nankai Univ. (1919).

Tian Shan *or* **Tien Shan** \'tyen-'shän\ Mountain chain (*shan*), Kyrgyzstan and W China. Its ranges and valleys stretch east–west for about 1,500 mi (2,500 km). Its highest point is Pobeda Peak, at 24,406 ft (7,439 m). Most of the area's population lives in the FERGANA VALLEY.

Tianshi Dao See FIVE PECKS OF RICE

Tiberias \tī-'bir-ē-əs\ *Hebrew* **Teverya** \tə-'ver-yə\ Town (pop., 2000 est.: 37,000) and resort, Sea of GALILEE, NE Israel. At 689 ft (210 m) below sea level, it is one of the lowest-lying cities in the world. Founded about A.D. 20 by HEROD ANTIPAS, it was named for TIBERIUS. It became the seat of the SANHEDRIN, and the TALMUD was edited there in the 3rd–6th cent. SALADIN took the town from the Crusaders in 1187. The modern town became part of independent Israel in 1948. Historic sites include the tomb of Moses MAIMONIDES. It is one of the four holy cities of JUDAISM, along with HEBRON, JERUSALEM, and Zefat.

Tiberias, Lake See Sea of GALILEE

Tiberius *in full* Tiberius (Julius) Caesar Augustus *orig.* Tiberius Claudius Nero (42 B.C.–A.D. 37) Second Roman emperor (A.D. 14–37). He was raised by his stepfather AUGUSTUS, and he became a successful military commander early in life. Forced to give up his beloved wife to marry Augustus' daughter JULIA (12 B.C.), he went into self-imposed exile on Rhodes (6 B.C.). By 4 B.C. Julia was exiled for promiscuity by Augustus, who recalled Tiberius and named him his heir. As emperor he initially ran the state efficiently and instituted some reforms, with only occasional severity. When his son Drusus died mysteriously, he gave his trust to his chief administrator Sejanus, and was persuaded to move to Capri (27). He became increasingly violent, killing and torturing at whim. He executed Sejanus in 31, then named CALIGULA his heir. In 37 the commander of the PRAETORIAN GUARD killed him in his bed.

Tiber River \'tī-bər\ *Italian* **Tevere** \'tā-vā-rā\ River, Italy. The country's second-longest river, it rises in the Tuscan APENNINES and flows south for 252 mi (405 km), ultimately passing through ROME before entering the Mediterranean at OSTIA. It was an important route for trade in Roman times; silting has limited its use in modern times.

Tibet \ti-'bet\ *Tibetan* **Bod** \'bōd\ *Chinese* **Xizang** *or* **Hsitsang** \'shē-'dzän\ Former country, now autonomous region (pop., 1999 est: 2,560,000), W China. The capital is LHASA. Before the 1950s it was a unique entity, with its own Buddhist customs and religion, that sought isolation from the rest of the world. Situated on a plateau averaging 16,000 ft (4,900 m) above sea level, it is the highest region in the world. Its surrounding mountain ranges include the KUNLUN MTNS. and the HIMALAYAS; Mt. EVEREST rises on its border with Nepal. Tibet emerged as a powerful Buddhist kingdom in the 7th–8th cent A.D. It came under the MONGOLS in the 13th cent. and under the MANCHUS in the 18th cent. After the 1911–12 Chinese revolution, it became independent under British influence. The Communist Chinese occupied the region in 1950 and harshly suppressed an anti-Chinese rebellion in 1959. In 1965 it was made a nominally autonomous region within Communist China. Its Buddhist culture was nearly destroyed during the Chinese CULTURAL REVOLUTION. Tibet's spiritual leader, the DALAI LAMA, set up a government-in-exile in India in 1959 and continued his attempt to rally world opinion for Tibetan independence.

Tibetan Buddhism Form of MAHAYANA BUDDHISM that evolved from the 7th cent. in Tibet. It incorporates the rituals of VAJRAYANA, the monastic disciplines of early THERAVADA, and the shamanistic features of Bon, Tibet's indigenous religion. The predominant Tibetan sect for the past three centuries has been DGE-LUGS-PA, headed by the DALAI LAMA. The Tibetan canon is divided into canonical texts translated mostly from Sanskrit and commentaries by Indian masters. After the Chinese Communist takeover in 1959, Tibetans began a massive emigration that has spread Tibetan Buddhism around the globe.

Tibetan language SINO-TIBETAN LANGUAGE spoken by more than 5 million people in Tibet, China, Bhutan, Nepal, India, and Pakistan. Since the occupation of Tibet by China in 1959, enclaves of Tibetan-speakers have dispersed to India and other parts of the world. Spoken Tibetan comprises a very diverse range of dialects. Most Tibetans share a common literary language, written in a distinctive script since the 8th cent. A.D.

tic Sudden rapid, recurring MUSCLE contraction—usually a blink, sniff, twitch, or shrug—always brief, irresistible, and localized. Frequency decreases from head to foot. Unlike a spasm, a CRAMP, or the movements of CHOREA or EPILEPSY, it does not interfere with other movement and can be held off for a time. It can become ingrained as a habit of which the person is unaware. Most tics are probably psychological, but similar movements occur in some physical disorders (e.g., late-stage ENCEPHALITIS). Psychotherapy, relaxation training, and biofeedback training have had some success in treating tics.

tick Any of some 825 parasitic ARACHNID species (suborder Ixodida, order Parasitiformes). The largest may be slightly more than an inch (30 mm) long. Hard ticks start and end each developmental stage—egg, larva, nymph, adult—on the ground; at the completion of each stage, they attach to a host (usually a MAMMAL), engorge on blood, then drop to the ground. Soft ticks feed intermittently, and live in the host's den or nest. Hard ticks may secrete paralyzing or lethal neurotoxins and transmit diseases. Soft ticks may also carry diseases. The deer tick is the principal vector of LYME DISEASE.

tidal power Electricity produced by TURBINES operated by TIDE flow. Large amounts of power are potentially available from the tides in certain locations, such as Canada's Bay of FUNDY, but this potential power is not continuous and varies with the seasons. The first working modern tidal power plant was built in France in 1961–67 and has 24 power units of 10,000 kilowatts each.

tidal wave See TSUNAMI

tide Regular, periodic rise and fall of the surface of the sea, occurring in most places twice a day. Tides result from differences in the gravitational forces exerted at different points on the earth's surface by either the sun (because of its enormous mass) or the moon (because of its proximity to earth). Tidal forces from the moon are about twice as strong as those from the sun. The largest tides (spring tides, exhibiting very large change in sea level between high and low tides) occur at the new and full moon, when the earth, moon, and sun are aligned and the sun's tidal forces are added to those of the moon. The smallest tides (neap tides) occur when the sun and moon are at right angles (from earth), and the tidal forces from the sun partially cancel those from the moon.

Tieck \'tyek\, **(Johann) Ludwig** (1773–1853) German writer and critic. His first works are associated with early Romanticism. *Volksmärchen* (1797) includes one of his best short novels, *Blond Eckbert*. This period culminated in the grotesque, lyrical plays *Life and Death of St. Genevieve* (1800) and *Emperor Octavian* (1804). Later his writing moved toward realism. While he was an adviser and critic at the Dresden theater (1825–42), he became a great literary authority and wrote 40 short novels.

T'ien-chin See TIANJIN

Tien Shan See TIAN SHAN

T'ien-shih Tao See FIVE PECKS OF RICE

Tientsin See TIANJIN

Tiepolo \tē-'ā-pə-lō\, **Giovanni Battista** (1696–1770) Italian painter and etcher. By the 1730s his fame had gone beyond his native Venice, and he accepted commissions to decorate two palaces in Milan (1731), the Cappella Colleoni in Bergamo (1731–32), and the Villa Loschi at Biron (1734). In 1750 he went to Würzburg with his sons and collaborators, G. D. TIEPOLO and Lorenzo Tiepolo (1736–1776), to decorate the prince-archbishop's palace. His Würzburg frescoes and canvases are his most boldly luminous work. In 1762 he accepted an invitation to paint ceilings in the royal palace in Madrid, again with his sons, his last great undertaking. Though he was initially drawn to a melancholic chiaroscuro style, his later work is full of bright color and bold brush play; his luminous, poetic frescoes both extend the tradition of baroque ceiling decoration and epitomize Rococo lightness and elegance. Tiepolo is now ranked with the greatest painters of all time.

Tiepolo \'tye-pō-lō\, **Giovanni Domenico** (1727–1804) Italian painter and printmaker. He was apprenticed to his father, G. B. TIEPOLO, in Venice in the early 1740s and worked with him in Madrid from 1762 until the elder's death. His most notable early works are the chinoiserie decorations of the Villa Valmarana in Vicenza (1757). Back in Venice, he executed several frescoes and paintings of scenes from the commedia dell'arte. A talented genre painter and caricaturist, he produced many engravings and etchings after his own and his father's designs.

Tierra del Fuego \tē-,er-ə-thel-'fwä-gō\ Archipelago off the S tip of S. America. It is separated from the Antarctic Archipelago by the DRAKE PASSAGE. About two-thirds of the mountainous islands are Chilean and one-third Argentine. The main island, Tierra del Fuego, is divided between Chile and Argentina; the Argentine city of Ushuaia there is the southernmost city in the world. From 1880 colonization by Chilean and Argentine nations was sparked by the discovery of gold. Chile's only oil field is there. The region's name (meaning "Land of Fire") refers to its many volcanoes.

Tiffany, Louis Comfort (1848–1933) U.S. painter, craftsman, philanthropist, and designer. Born in New York City, the son of the famous jeweler Charles Louis Tiffany (1812–1902), he studied with George INNESS and was a recognized painter before he began to experiment with stained glass in 1875. He founded a glassmaking factory in Queens, N.Y., in 1878. There he developed an iridescent glass he called Favrile, which achieved widespread popularity in Europe. After 1900 Tiffany's firm ventured into lamps, jewelry, and pottery. He is internationally recognized as one of the greatest forces of the ART NOUVEAU style.

tiger Reddish tan, striped, great CAT of forests, grasslands, and swamps in E Russia, parts of China, India, and SE Asia. Tigers are solitary, nocturnal hunters. Locality and subspecies determine size, color, and stripes. S tigers, such as the Bengal *(Panthera tigris tigris),* are smaller and more brightly colored than N ones, such as the rare Siberian tiger *(P. t. altaica).* Males grow to over 3 ft (1 m) high and 7 ft (2.2 m) long, excluding the 3-ft (1-m) tail, and may weigh 350–640 lbs (160–290 kg). Tigers live about 11 years. Tigers are seriously endangered; three subspecies are now extinct.

Tiglath-pileser III \'tig-,lath-pī-'lē-zər\ (r.745–727 B.C.) King of Assyria who led the last and greatest phase of Assyrian expansion. Bent on strengthening Assyria, he subdivided large provinces to quash independence movements and resettled tens of thousands of people to ensure loyalty. He defeated his N neighbor, Uratu (743 B.C.), then subjected Syria and Palestine (734) and took over the throne of Babylon. See also ASHURBANIPAL, SARGON II.

Tigray \'ti-,grā\ Historic region of N Ethiopia. Its dramatic landscape includes plateau regions over 10,000 ft (3,000 m) high and plains below sea level. Tigray contains the core of the ancient AKSUM kingdom and Ethiopia's oldest town, the 3,000-year-old Yeha. It formerly controlled trade routes from the Red Sea to the empire in the south, but after losing control of the coast in the 16th cent. it was dominated by the south and later threatened by the Egyptian, Sudanese, British, and Italian armies. A rebellion begun in 1975 against the Ethiopian government worsened the effects of a disastrous drought and famine in 1984–85. The rebels' victory in 1991 resulted in the installing of their leader as Ethiopia's prime minister. In 1999 Ethiopia's border war with Eritrea led to the displacement of over 300,000 people in Tigray.

Tigris River \'tī-grəs\ *Arabic* **Shatt Dijla** \,shät-'dij-lə\ *biblical* Hiddekel. River, SE Turkey and Iraq. It is 1,180 mi (1,900 km) long. It originates in the TAURUS MTNS. and flows southeast through Turkey and past BAGHDAD to join the EUPHRATES RIVER in SE Iraq; there it forms the SHATT AL ARAB. With the Euphrates it defined ancient MESOPOTAMIA. Important for its irrigation capacity, it gave rise to sustained civilization. The ruins of NINEVEH, ASHUR, CTESIPHON, and SELEUCIA lie on its banks.

Tijuana \tē-'hwä-nä\ City (pop., 2000: 1,212,000), NW BAJA CALIFORNIA, Mexico. It lies just south of SAN DIEGO, Cal. Settled in 1862, it developed as a border resort with gambling casinos, and later became the main entry point to Mexico for U.S. tourists, while retaining its dubious reputation. It has the largest concentration of maquiladora firms in the country and is the world's largest television manufacturing center.

Tikal \tē-'käl\ Ancient MAYA city, N Guatemala. First occupied as a small village in a tropical rain forest about 900–300 B.C., it grew into an important ceremonial center. It flourished around A.D. 600–900, with the building of great plazas, pyramids, and palaces and with the flowering of Maya art in monumental sculpture. At its height, the core city had a population of 10,000, with an outlying population of about 50,000. Major excavation began in 1956.

tilapia \tə-'lä-pē-ə\ Any of numerous, mostly freshwater, fish species (genus *Tilapia,* family Cichlidae), native to Africa. They resemble N. American sunfishes; one species grows to 20 lbs (9 kg). *Tilapia* are easy to raise and harvest for food; they grow rapidly and resist disease. They have been used in warm-water aquaculture systems since the early Egyptian civilization. See also CICHLID.

Tilden, Bill (*orig.* William Tatem) (1893–1953) U.S. tennis player. Born to a wealthy family in Philadelphia, he was slow to develop his game but eventually won seven U.S. singles championships (1920–25, 1929) and three Wimbledon singles championships (1920–21, 1930). He also won many doubles titles and 21 of 28 Davis Cup matches. His overpowering play and temperamental personality made him one of the most colorful sports figures of his time.

Tilden, Samuel J(ones) (1814–1886) U.S. politician. Born in New Lebanon, N.Y., he became a leader in New York's Democratic Party; as state party chairman (1865–75), he effected the overthrow of the Tammany Hall boss W. M. TWEED. As governor (1875–76) he continued his reforms. In 1876 he was the Democratic nominee for president. The bitterly fought campaign ended in a popular-vote victory for Tilden, but Republicans contested the results in four states. The specially appointed ELECTORAL COMMISSION awarded the election to Rutherford B. HAYES. Unwilling to cause further conflict, Tilden accepted the decision and returned to his prosperous law practice. He left his large fortune to establish a free public library for New York City.

tile Thin, flat slab or block used structurally or decoratively in building. Traditionally, tiles have been made of glazed or unglazed fired clay, but modern tiles are also made of plastic, glass, or asphalt. Ceramic tiles, used for walls, floors, and countertops, are usually machine-pressed, made of fine clays, and very hard. Quarry tiles (used for flooring) and terra-cotta, made of natural clays, are less hard and more porous but very popular for economic and aesthetic reasons. Structural tile, of fired clay, is a hollow tile used for building partitions. Roof tiles of baked clay and of marble were used in ancient Greece. Tiles came to be widely used in Islamic architecture. Colored glazed tiles spread from Spain to Latin America. By the 15th cent. tilework was used widely in N Europe; blue-painted tiles from Delft were especially renowned. Modern clay roofing tiles may be flat or curved; around the Mediterranean, S-shaped tiles (pantiles), laid with alternate convex and concave surfaces uppermost, are common.

Tillich \'ti-lik, *Engl* 'ti-lik\, **Paul (Johannes)** (1886–1965) German-U.S. Protestant theologian. He taught at Marburg, Dresden, and Frankfurt am Main before the Nazi takeover in 1933 prompted him to emigrate to the U.S. He joined the faculty of Union Theological Seminary, and became respected for his lucid preaching and his *Systematic Theology* (3 vols., 1951–63). He moved to Harvard Univ. in 1955. His theological system combined biblical, existentialist, and metaphysical elements, and he tried to convey an understanding of God that depended neither on revelation nor on science. His other works include *The Courage to Be* (1952) and *Dynamics of Faith* (1957).

till-less agriculture See NO-TILL FARMING

Tilly, Graf (Count) von *orig.* Johann Tserclaes (1559–1632) Flemish-Bavarian general in the THIRTY YEARS' WAR. Born in the Spanish Netherlands, in 1594 he joined the emperor

Rudolf II's army against the Turks. Appointed by Maximilian I of Bavaria to reorganize the Bavarian army (1610), Tilly created an efficient force that became the spearhead of the CATHOLIC LEAGUE in the Thirty Years' War. In 1630 he added the imperial forces to his command. In 1631 he besieged the Protestant city of Magdeburg, but failed to stop the Swedish advance into Germany; he was defeated at Breitenfeld and later fatally wounded.

Tilsit \'til-zit\, **Treaties of** (1807) Agreements that France signed separately with Russia and Prussia at Tilsit, N Prussia (now Sovetsk, Russia), following NAPOLEON's victories in the NAPOLEONIC WARS. France and Russia became allies and divided Europe between them, reducing Prussia and Austria to helplessness. In secret provisions, Russia joined the CONTINENTAL SYSTEM against British trade, but it later opened Russian ports to neutral ships, causing the alliance to fail and paving the way for Napoleon's invasion of Russia in 1812.

timbre \'tam-bər\ Quality of sound that distinguishes one instrument or voice from another. Timbre largely results from the relative strength of the OVERTONES produced by different instruments; usually varying across the range of pitches, it is what principally permits a listener to distinguish a clarinet from a saxophone, or an alto from a tenor, when both are sounding the same pitch. One element of timbre results from the differing methods of producing the sounds (blowing, bowing, striking, etc.), especially audible at the moment a note begins.

Timbuktu See TOMBOUCTOU

Time Major U.S. weekly newsmagazine. It was founded in 1923 by Henry LUCE and Briton Hadden (1898–1929). It became the most influential newsmagazine in the U.S., with a format of short articles arranged in subject "departments," which became the standard for later newsmagazines. Luce was long the magazine's guiding force, and it reflected his moderately conservative political viewpoint. By the 1970s it assumed a more centrist stance. It now appears in several foreign-language editions.

time-and-motion study Analysis of the time spent in performing a job or series of jobs. Such studies, first instituted in offices and factories in the U.S. in the early 20th cent., were widely adopted as a means of improving work methods by subdividing the different operations of a job into measurable elements, and were in turn used as aids in STANDARDIZATION of work, improving work methods, and checking the efficiency of people and equipment.

Time of Troubles See Time of TROUBLES

Times, The Daily newspaper published in London, one of Britain's oldest and most influential. Founded by John Walter (1739–1812) in 1785 as *The Daily Universal Register*, it became *The Times* in 1788, publishing commercial news and notices along with some scandal. By the mid-1800s it had developed into a widely respected national journal and

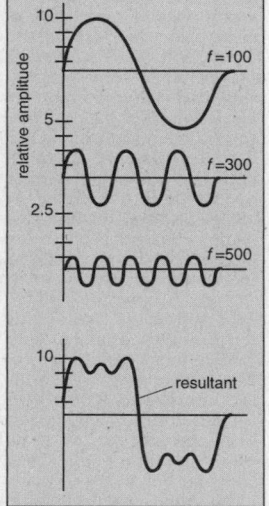

Timbre A mixture of three pure tones (top) yields a complex resultant tone (bottom), such as might be produced by an actual instrument, whose perceived quality or "color" is its timbre. The strong fundamental tone (top)—which would be perceived by the listener as the only tone played—has a frequency of 100. The other tones shown, with frequencies of 300 and 500, are weaker overtones of the fundamental; their relative loudness (amplitude), reflected in the complex resultant wave form, constitutes an essential aspect of the unique timbre the wave form represents.

daily historical record. Late in the 19th cent. its reputation declined, but it regained its preeminence under the editorship of William Haley (1952–67). In 1981 it was bought by Rupert MURDOCH.

Times Literary Supplement (TLS) Weekly literary journal long famous for its coverage of all aspects of literature. Founded in 1902 as a supplement to *The Sunday Times* of London, the TLS sets the tone and standards of excellence in the field of literary criticism. It presents reviews of fiction and nonfiction published in several languages, and its essays are written with sophistication and scholarly authority and in a lively style. See also *The TIMES*.

Time Warner Largest worldwide media and entertainment conglomerate, created first by the 1989 merger of Time Inc. and Warner Communications. Time Inc. was founded in 1922 to publish *TIME* magazine, and grew with the founding of *Fortune* (1930), *LIFE* (1936), *Sports Illustrated* (1954), *Money* (1972), and *People* (1974). The company acquired the publisher Little, Brown & Co., the Book-of-the-Month Club, and American Television and Communications, founding Home Box Office (HBO) in 1972. The 1989 merger included WARNER BROTHERS movie studio, a recording company, and a cable-television operator. In 1996 Time Warner acquired Ted TURNER's Turner Broadcasting System. Its merger with AMERICA ONLINE in 2001 was the largest corporate merger to that date.

Timisoara \,tē-mē-'shwä-rä\ City (pop., 1997 est.: 334,000), W Romania. First settled in Neolithic and Roman times, it was sacked by the Tatars in the 13th cent. Rebuilt, for a few years it was the residence of CHARLES I of Hungary. The Turks held it 1552–1716. Occupied by Serbia in 1919, it was allotted to Romania in 1920 by treaty. Demonstrations there in 1989 led to the execution of Pres. Nicolae CEAUSESCU and the end of Communist rule in Romania. It is a manufacturing, commercial, and cultural center.

Timor \'tē-,mór, tē-'mór\ Island, S MALAY ARCHIPELAGO. It is the easternmost of the Lesser SUNDA ISLES. Indonesian-Malay peoples live along the coast and Melanesian aboriginals in the mountains. The Portuguese began trading with Timor about 1520. In 1613 the Dutch settled at the island's SW tip. Treaties in 1860 and 1914 divided the island between them. In 1950 the Dutch transferred W Timor to Indonesia. E Timor was held by the Portuguese until 1975, when Indonesian troops invaded and annexed the area, the incursion resulted in over 100,000 E Timorese deaths. Continued agitation eventually resulted in recognition of E. TIMOR as a nation in 2002.

timpani \'tim-pə-nē\ *or* **kettledrums** Large bowl-shaped drums with pedal mechanisms for altering their pitch by changing the membrane's tension. The timpani are the principal orchestral percussion instruments. Each drum usually has a range of a 5th; they are normally used in pairs. Until about 1800 each drum was tuned to a single pitch (usually tonic or dominant) that could not be altered in performance.

Timur \tē-'mür\ *or* **Tamerlane** \'ta-mər-,lān\ *or* **Tamburlaine** (1336–1405) Turkic conqueror. Born near SAMARQAND, he settled in Transoxania (modern Uzbekistan) after fighting there under GENGHIS KHAN's son. (Timur Lenk, or Tamerlane, means "Timur the Lame," re-

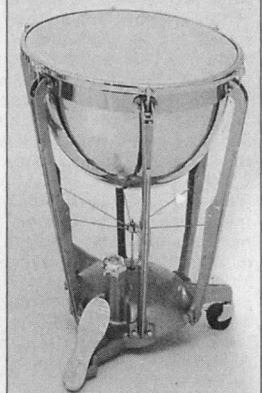

Timpani

flecting the battle wounds he received.) Through machinations and treachery he took over Transoxania, then began his conquest of Persia, taking Khorasan and E Persia in 1383–85 and W Persia in 1386–94. He occupied Moscow for a year. When revolts broke out in Persia, he ruthlessly suppressed them, massacring the populations of whole cities. In 1398 he invaded India, leaving a trail of carnage. Next he marched on Damascus, deporting its artisans to Samarkand, and on Baghdad, destroying its monuments. In 1404 he prepared to invade China but died early in the march. Though Timur strove to make Samarkand the most splendid city in Asia, he himself preferred to be always on the move. His most lasting memorials are the architectural monuments of Samarkand and the dynasty he established.

tin Chemical ELEMENT, chemical symbol Sn, atomic number 50. It is a soft, silvery-white METAL with a bluish tinge, employed since antiquity in BRONZE. It occurs chiefly as the OXIDE. Since it is nontoxic, ductile, malleable, and easily worked, it is used to plate steel cans ("tin cans") for food and to coat and plate other items. Pure tin is too weak to be used alone, but its many alloys include soft solder, PEWTER, bronze, and low-temperature casting alloys. Its compounds (VALENCE 2 or 4) are used in tin GALVANIZING and manufacturing polymers and dyes, in toothpastes, as stabilizers for perfumes, and as a catalyst and a polishing powder for steel. Tin bonds with carbon to form organotin compounds, used to stabilize PVC and in biocides and fungicides.

Tinbergen, Nikolaas (1907–1988) Dutch-British zoologist, a founder (with Konrad LORENZ) of the science of ETHOLOGY. Teaching at the Univ. of Leiden and later at Oxford Univ., he emphasized the importance of both instinctive and learned behavior to survival and used animal behavior as a basis for speculation on human violence and aggression. His observations of seagulls led to important generalizations on courtship and mating behavior. With his wife, Elizabeth, he also studied human behavioral disorders, particularly AUTISM. With Lorenz and Karl von FRISCH he shared a Nobel Prize in 1973.

tincal See BORAX

Ting Ling See DING LING

Tinguely \taⁿ-ˈglē\, **Jean** (1925–1991) Swiss sculptor and experimental artist. As a student in Basel, he showed interest in movement as an artistic medium, and in 1953 he moved to Paris and began to construct sophisticated KINETIC SCULPTURES. He created a sensation when his *Homage to New York* (1960) failed to self-destruct at the Museum of Modern Art, but his *Study for an End of the World* (1961) detonated successfully. Tinguely's art satirized the mindless overproduction of material goods and expressed his conviction that the essence of both life and art consists of continuous change, movement, and instability.

Tin Pan Alley Genre of U.S. POPULAR MUSIC that arose in New York in the late 19th cent. The name referred to the street on which the industry was based—28th Street between Fifth Avenue and Broadway in the early 20th cent., around Broadway and 32nd Street in the 1920s, and ultimately on Broadway between 42nd and 50th Streets. "Tin pan" referred to the sound of pianos furiously pounded by "song pluggers" demonstrating tunes to publishers. The genre included commercial ballads, dance music, and vaudeville songs, and its name eventually became synonymous with U.S. popular music. The rise of film, audio recording, radio, and TV eventually created a demand for a wider range of music, and songwriting centers grew up in Hollywood and Nashville.

Tintoretto orig. Jacopo Robusti (1519–1594) Italian painter active in Venice. His father was a silk dyer (*tintore*); hence the nickname Tintoretto ("Little Dyer"). His early influences include MICHELANGELO and TITIAN. In *Christ and the Adulteress* (c.1545) figures are set in vast spaces in fanciful perspectives, in distinctly Mannerist style. In 1548 he won critical attention with his *St. Mark Freeing the Slave*, rich in structural elements of post-Michelangelo art. By 1555 he was a famous painter, with a style marked by quickness of execution, great vivacity of color, variegated perspective, and a dynamic conception of space. In his most important undertaking, the decoration of Venice's Scuola Grande di San Rocco (1564–88), he exhibited his passionate style and profound religious faith. His technique and vision were wholly personal and constantly evolving. He is recognized as the greatest representative of MANNERISM, interpreted in accordance with the great tradition of Venice.

Tipitaka See TRIPITAKA

Tippecanoe \ˌti-pə-kə-ˈnü\, **Battle of** (Nov. 7, 1811) Victory by U.S. troops over the SHAWNEE. Gen. W. H. HARRISON led a U.S. force in pursuit of the Shawnee to destroy an intertribal alliance promoted by TECUMSEH and his brother, The PROPHET. At the Indian capital of Prophetstown on the Tippecanoe River, Ind., the Indians attacked the troops but were repulsed. Both sides suffered equal losses, but the battle was considered a victory for Harrison.

Tippett \ˈtip-ət\, **Michael (Kemp)** (*later* **Sir Michael**) (1905–1998) British composer. Despite thorough musical training, he gave the impression of being self-taught because his music was so original. He is best known for his settings of his own texts, including the cantatas *A Child of Our Time* (1941) and *The Mask of Time* (1984), and the operas *The Midsummer Marriage* (1952), *The Knot Garden* (1969), and *The Ice Break* (1976). His other works include four symphonies and five string quartets.

Tiranë or **Tirana** \ti-ˈrä-nə\ City (pop., 1999 est.: 279,000), capital of Albania. Founded in the early 17th cent., it became a trading center and, in 1920, the capital of Albania. In World War II, it was occupied by Axis forces (1939–44). It is the nation's largest city and main industrial and cultural center, home to the national library and theater, and site of the Univ. of Tiranë (1957).

tire Rubber cushion that fits around a wheel and usually contains compressed air. Solid-rubber tires were used on road vehicles until they were replaced by air-filled pneumatic tires, which came into common use when John Dunlop (1840–1921) put them on bicycles in 1888 and the French manufacturer MICHELIN began to produce them for motor vehicles. The tire consisted of an inner tube containing compressed air that was covered by an outer rubber casing to provide traction. In the 1950s tubeless tires became standard on most automobiles.

Tiresias \tī-ˈrē-sē-əs\ In GREEK MYTHOLOGY, a blind Theban seer. In HOMER's *Odyssey* he retained his prophetic gifts even in the underworld, where ODYSSEUS was sent to consult him. It was said that he was once turned into a woman for killing the female of two mating snakes; upon thereafter killing the male, he became a man again. According to one legend, he was blinded by HERA for arguing, on the basis of his unique experience, that women derive greater pleasure from sex than men do; his gift of prophecy was a compensatory gesture from ZEUS.

Tirol or **Tyrol** \tə-ˈrōl, ˈtī-ˌrōl\ State (pop., 1999 est.: 662,000), W Austria. It consists of N. Tirol and E. Tirol, separated by the state of Salzburg and the Italian region of TRENTINO–ALTO ADIGE. It is a mountainous region bordered by the Bavarian Alps and the Ötztaler Alps; its capital is INNSBRUCK. It was acquired by the HABSBURGS in 1363. It was the scene of revolts in 1525 during the REFORMATION, and again in 1809 against French and Bavarian rule. The S Tirol was transferred to Italy in 1919. Renowned for its skiing, it attracts many tourists.

Tirso de Molina \ˈtir-sō-dä-mə-ˈlē-nə\ orig. Gabriel Téllez (1584–1648) Spanish playwright. A friar from 1601, he became inspired by Lope de VEGA and wrote a vast number of works; about 80 have survived. His best-known play, the tragedy *The Seducer of Seville* (1630), introduced the legendary DON JUAN. He was noted for portraying the psychological conflicts of his characters. Though he also excelled in comedy, he was the greatest Spanish tragedian of his time.

Tiryns \ˈtir-ənz, ˈtīr-ənz\ Ancient city, E PELOPONNESE, S Greece. It developed as an important MYCENAEAN center, reaching its height about 1400 B.C. It declined as ARGOS grew in power after 1100 B.C.; the Argives destroyed it around 468 B.C. Ruins of its palace and massive walls date from the 15th–12th cent. B.C. The term "Cyclopean masonry" derives from the huge stones used in its construction, supposedly the work of the CYCLOPS for PROTEUS. The city is also connected with PERSEUS and HERACLES.

tissue culture Biological research method in which tissue fragments are sustained in an artificial environment for examination and manipulation of cell behavior. It has been used to study normal and abnormal cell structure; biochemical, genetic, and reproductive activity; metabolism, functions, and aging and healing processes; and reactions to physical, chemical, and biological agents (e.g., drugs, viruses). A tiny sample of the tissue is spread on or in a cul-

T U V

ture medium of biological (e.g., blood serum or tissue extract), synthetic, or mixed origin having the appropriate nutrients, temperature, and pH for the cells being incubated. The results are observed with a microscope, sometimes after treatment (e.g., staining) to highlight particular features. Some viruses also grow in tissue cultures.

Tisza, Kalman (1830–1902) Hungarian premier (1875–90). He took part in the struggle for Hungarian national autonomy that produced the COMPROMISE OF 1867. He formed a coalition of the nobility, business interests, and small landowners into the new Liberal Party (1875) and became prime minister; his reforms helped Hungary develop into a modern state. He resigned over interference from the Austrian emperor but continued as leader of the Liberal Party, with his son, Istvan (1861–1918). Istvan served as prime minister (1903–5, 1913–17), but opposed voting franchise reform and resigned over the king's 1917 decree for such reform. Held responsible for his country's suffering as Germany's ally in World War I, he was assassinated by leftists.

Tisza River *or* **Tisa River** \'ti-sä\ River, W Ukraine, E Hungary, and N Yugoslavia. Rising in the CARPATHIAN MTNS. of W Ukraine, it flows west, forming part of the Ukraine–Romania border, then continues southwest across Hungary and into Yugoslavia to empty into the DANUBE RIVER above BELGRADE. It is 619 mi (996 km) long. The Tiszalök Dam (1954) forms the largest reservoir in Hungary.

Titan \'tī-tən\ In GREEK MYTHOLOGY, any of the children of URANUS and GAEA and their descendants. There were 12 original Titans, including CRONUS and RHEA. Encouraged by Gaea, the Titans rebelled against their father. Cronus deposed Uranus by castrating him, and became king himself. Cronus' son ZEUS rebelled against his father, launching a struggle in which most of the Titans sided with Cronus. Zeus and his siblings won, and Zeus imprisoned the Titans in a cavity below TARTARUS.

Titanic British luxury passenger liner that sank on April 15, 1912, en route to New York from Southampton, England, on its maiden voyage. Over 1,500 of its 2,200 passengers were lost. The largest and most luxurious ship afloat, was considered unsinkable. On April 14, it collided with an iceberg southeast of Newfoundland; five of its watertight compartments ruptured and the ship sank. As a result, new rules were drawn up requiring adequate lifeboat capacity (the *Titanic* had only 1,178 lifeboat places) and a 24-hour radio watch for distress signals on all ships (a nearby ship had not heard its signal because no one had been on duty). The International Ice Patrol was established to monitor icebergs in shipping lanes. In 1985 the wreck was found lying upright in two pieces at a depth of 13,000 ft (4,000 m).

titanium \tī-'tā-nē-əm\ Chemical ELEMENT, one of the TRANSITION ELEMENTS, chemical symbol Ti, atomic number 22. A silvery gray, lightweight, high-strength, low-corrosion structural METAL, it is found combined in almost all rocks and soils and in plants and animals. Its chief commercial ores are ilmenite and RUTILE. Its alloys are used for parts for high-speed aircraft, spacecraft, missiles, and ships; in electrodes; in chemical, desalination, and food-handling equipment; and in prostheses. Its compounds (VALENCE 2, 3, or 4) include titanium trichloride (used as a catalyst in polypropylene production) and titanium dioxide (the PIGMENT with the greatest hiding power of all white pigments).

Titan rocket Any of a series of U.S. rockets developed as intercontinental ballistic missiles (ICBMs) but also used for space launches. Titan I missiles (used 1962–65), designed to deliver a four-megaton nuclear warhead over 5,000 mi (8,000 km) to targets in the Soviet Union, were stored in underground silos but had to be launched from ground level; fueling took at least 15 minutes. The much larger Titan II (1965) could be launched directly from its silo. With a nine-megaton warhead (the most powerful ever mounted on a U.S. missile), it was the principal weapon in the land-based U.S. nuclear arsenal until the 1980s, when more accurate solid-fueled ICBMs (e.g., MINUTEMAN) replaced it. NASA used it to launch Gemini spacecraft in the 1960s. The Titan IV (late 1980s), has larger engines for heavy cargo like that carried by the SPACE SHUTTLE. At nearly 200 ft (60 m), it is the largest nonreusable U.S. launch vehicle.

tithe Contribution of a tenth of one's income for religious purposes. Tithing dates to the Old Testament. It was enjoined by ecclesiastical law from the 6th cent. and enforced in Europe by secular law from the 8th cent. After the Reformation, tithes were imposed for the benefit of both the Protestant and Roman Catholic churches. They were generally repealed in the 18th–20th cent.; in Germany citizens must pay a church tax unless they formally renounce membership in a church. Certain U.S. sects (e.g., the MORMONS) require it, and members of other churches may tithe voluntarily. Tithing was never accepted by the Eastern Orthodox churches.

Titian \'ti-shən\ *orig.* Tiziano Vecellio (c.1485/90–1576) Italian painter active in Venice. As a young man he was taught by Giovanni BELLINI and worked closely with GIORGIONE. After Giorgione's early death (1510), Titian established himself as the leading painter of the Republic of Venice. Among his most important religious paintings is the revolutionary and monumental *Assumption* (1516–18) for Santa Maria dei Frari, in which the Virgin ascends to heaven in a blaze of color. Titian was also interested in mythological themes, and his many depictions of Venus display his work's sheer beauty and inherent eroticism. *Bacchus and Ariadne* (1520–23), with its pagan abandon, is one of the greatest works of Renaissance art. His psychologically penetrating portraits include portrayals of leading Italian aristocrats, religious figures, and Emperor Charles V. He reached the height of his powers in *The Rape of Europa* (c.1559–62), one of several paintings done for PHILIP II of Spain. He was recognized as supremely gifted in his lifetime, and his reputation has never declined.

Titicaca \ˌtē-tē-'kä-kä\, **Lake** Lake, Peru–Bolivia border. The world's highest navigable lake, it lies at 12,500 ft (3,810 m) in the ANDES. The second-largest lake of S. America, it is 120 mi (190 km) long by 50 mi (80 km) wide. It contains 41 islands, some densely populated. The remains of one of the oldest known American civilizations have been found in the area. Temple ruins mark the spot where the legendary founders of the INCA were sent down to earth by the sun.

Tito \'tē-tō\ *orig.* Josip Broz (1892–1980) Yugoslav premier (1945–53), and president (1953–80). Born in Croatia, he fought in the Austro-Hungarian army in World War I and was captured by the Russians. While in Russia, he joined the BOLSHEVIKS. In 1920 he returned to Croatia, where he became a local leader of the Communist Party of Yugoslavia. He rose in the party hierarchy, interrupted by a prison term (1928–34), to become its secretary-general in 1939. In World War II, Tito (a pseudonym he adopted around 1935) proved an effective leader of Yugoslav partisans. As marshal from 1943, he strengthened communist control of Yugoslavia. As premier and president, he developed an independent form of socialist rule in defiance of the Soviet Union, pursued a policy of nonalignment, and improved relations with the Western powers. His system of "symmetrical federalism" (1974) established equality among the six republics and Serbia's autonomous provinces (including Kosovo), while maintaining tight control to prevent separatist movements.

Titograd See PODGORICA

titration \tī-'trā-shən\ Process of chemical ANALYSIS in which the quantity of some constituent of a sample is determined by adding an exactly known quantity of another substance with which it reacts in a definite, known proportion. The solution of known concentration is gradually added to the unknown solution until the equivalence point is reached. The equivalence point is determined by a change of color in an indicator (e.g., LITMUS) or in an electrical property. See also PH.

Titus *in full* Titus Vespasianus Augustus *orig.* Titus Flavius Vespasianus (A.D. 39–81) Roman emperor (79–81). When his father, VESPASIAN, became emperor (69), he gave Titus full command in Judaea, whereupon Titus captured and destroyed Jerusalem (70). He later took charge of the empire's general military operations. As emperor he developed goodwill in Rome for his extravagant spending; his projects included the completion of the Colosseum. He died suddenly, perhaps killed by DOMITIAN.

Tivoli \ˈtē-vō-lē\ *ancient* Tibur. Town (pop., 1991: 51,000), LAZIO, central Italy. Originally an independent member of the Latin League and a rival of nearby ROME, it received Roman citizenship in 90 B.C. and attained prosperity as a summer resort. Many wealthy Romans built villas and erected temples in the vicinity, and the remains are among the most impressive to survive from antiquity. They include HADRIAN'S VILLA and the poet HORACE's Sabine farm. It is also the site of the Villa d'Este (begun 1550), with its magnificent gardens and unrivaled Renaissance fountains.

Tlaloc \ˈtlä-lōk\ Aztec rain god, highly revered and feared for his ability to bestow or withhold prosperity. Five of the 18 months of the ritual year were dedicated to him, and children were sacrificed to him during two of the months. He could send out rain, provoke drought and hunger, and cause lightning and hurricanes. Dropsy, leprosy, and rheumatism were said to be caused by Tlaloc and his fellow deities.

Tlaxcala \tlä-ˈskä-lä\ State (pop., 2000: 962,000), central Mexico. The smallest Mexican state, it consists largely of plateau, covering 1,551 sq mi (4,016 sq km). The Indian principality of Tlaxcala was Hernán CORTÉS's principal Indian ally in the conquest of Mexico. Today's state produces cereals, raises dairy cows and fighting bulls, and is known for the weaving of serapes and woolen cloth.

Tlazoltéotl \ˌtlä-sōl-ˈtē-ō-tᵊl\ Important and complex Aztec earth-mother goddess who had four manifestations. First, she was a carefree young temptress, then a destructive goddess of gambling and uncertainty. In middle age, she was able to absorb human wrongdoing. In her final form, she was a terrifying hag preying on youths. She provoked carnal lust and illicit sexual activity, but she also granted absolution and removed corruption from the world.

Tlingit \ˈtliŋ gət\ Northernmost Indians of the N Pacific Coast of N. America, inhabiting the islands and coast of S Alaska. The traditional Tlingit economy was based on salmon fishing, though sea and land mammals were also hunted. Wood, often decorated with stylized designs, was used for houses, TOTEM POLES, canoes, dishes, and other objects. POTLATCHES marked a cycle of rituals mourning the death of a chief. Today the Tlingit number about 15,000.

TM See TRANSCENDENTAL MEDITATION

TNT *in full* **trinitrotoluene** \ˌtrī-ˌnī-trō-ˈtäl-yə-ˌwēn\ Pale yellow, solid organic compound. Because TNT melts below the boiling point of water but explodes only above 464°F (240°C), it can safely be melted and poured into casings. It is relatively insensitive to shock and cannot be exploded without a detonator, making it the preferred chemical explosive, used in munitions and for demolition.

toad Any member of 26 genera (order Anura) of mainly terrestrial, nocturnal, tailless AMPHIBIANS. Toads have a squat body, short legs, and teeth in the upper jaw. They eat insects or small animals. The more than 300 species of true toads (*Bufo*) are found almost worldwide. They are 1–10 in. (2–25 cm) long and have thick, dry, often warty skin. Some species' poison, secreted by glands on the back, can paralyze or kill animals as large as dogs, but toads do not cause warts. Toads reproduce by laying in water two long jelly tubes containing 600–30,000 eggs. See also FROG, HORNED TOAD.

toadstool See MUSHROOM

tobacco Any of numerous species of plants in the genus *Nicotiana*, of the NIGHTSHADE FAMILY; or the cured leaves of several of the species, used after processing for smoking, snuffing, chewing, and extracting of NICOTINE. Native to the New

Cultivated tobacco (*Nicotiana tabacum*)

World, common tobacco (*N. tabacum*) grows 4–6 ft (1–2 m) high and bears usually pink flowers and huge leaves, as long as 2–3 ft (0.6–1 m). When Christopher COLUMBUS reached the Americas, he reported natives using tobacco as it is used today, as well as in religious ceremonies. Believed to have medicinal properties, tobacco was introduced into Europe and the rest of the world, becoming the chief commodity traded by the British colonists. Awareness of the numerous serious health risks posed by tobacco, including various cancers and a range of respiratory diseases, has led to campaigns against its use, but the number of tobacco users worldwide continues to rise. The World Health Organization estimates that within two decades smoking will cause more deaths than any single disease.

Toba dynasty See NORTHERN WEI DYNASTY

Tobago See TRINIDAD AND TOBAGO

Tobey, Mark (1890–1976) U.S. painter. Born in Centerville, Wis., he studied at the Art Institute of Chicago. In 1918 he converted to the Baha'i religion and his work became inspired by Oriental art and thought. In the 1930s he achieved notoriety with his "white writing" paintings, consisting of a web of calligraphic marks painted in white on a gray or colored ground (e.g., *Broadway*, 1936), which soon displaced his representational work. His style is distinguished by his use of the small format and a refined execution in watercolor, tempera, or pastel.

Tobit \ˈtō-bət\ Main character in the Bible's apocryphal *Book of Tobit*. Tobit, a pious Jew living in exile in NINEVEH, is struck blind in spite of performing numerous good works. Sarah, daughter of a close relative, has had seven husbands, each of whom was killed by a demon on their wedding night. The two pray for deliverance, and the angel RAPHAEL intercedes for them. Tobit regains his sight, and Sarah marries Tobit's son Tobias.

tobogganing Sport of sliding down a snow-covered hill on a toboggan, a long, flat-bottomed sled made of thin boards curved up at the front end. The sport appears to have originated on the slopes of Mt. Royal in Montreal in the late 19th cent. In the early 20th cent. many tobogganing chutes (3-ft-wide wood- or ice-sided channels) were built.

Tobruk *ancient* Antipyrgos. Port city (pop., 1988 est.: 110,000), NE Libya. For centuries it served as a way station on the coastal caravan route. An Italian military post by 1911, it was the scene of prolonged fighting during World War II (see N. AFRICA CAMPAIGNS). The British captured it in 1941; it fell to a German siege in 1942 and was recaptured by the British the same year. Rebuilt, it was expanded in the 1960s to include a port terminal linked by pipeline to the Sarir oil field.

Tocantins River \ˌtō-kän-ˈtēⁿs\ River, E central and NE Brazil. It rises in several headstreams, including the PARANÁ RIVER, and flows north and west to join the ARAGUAIA RIVER. It again turns north and flows into the Pará River after a course of 1,677 mi (2,699 km). Its rapids and waterfalls make it largely unnavigable.

tocopherol See VITAMIN E

Tocqueville \ˈtōk-ˌvil, tȯk-ˈvēl\, **Alexis (-Charles-Henri-Maurice Clérel) de** (1805–1859) French political scientist. Born into an aristocratic family with ties to the king, he entered government service, but after the 1830 Revolution his position became precarious, and he undertook a nine-month study trip to the U.S. Out of it came *Democracy in America* (4 vols., 1835–40), a highly perceptive and prescient analysis of the political and social system of the U.S. and of the vitality, excesses, and potential future of democracy. He held various political offices from 1839 on. *The Old*

Alexis de Tocqueville Painting by T. Chassériau

TUV

Regime and the Revolution (1856), a pessimistic analysis of French political tendencies, was part of an unfinished study of the French Revolution.

Todai Temple \'tō-,dī\ *Japanese* **Todai-ji** Monumental Buddhist temple located in Nara, Japan. The main buildings were constructed (745–52) under the emperor Shomu, marking the adoption of Buddhism as a state religion. The Great Buddha Hall, built within a 2-sq-mi (5-sq-km) enclosure, measured about 288 by 169 ft (88 by 52 m) and, as restored today, is the largest wooden building in the world. The 53-ft (16-m) Great Sun Buddha was installed in 752. The Shosoin is a repository for more than 9,000 works of art from the NARA period.

tofu Soft, bland food product made from SOYBEANS. Believed to date from China's Han dynasty (206 B.C.–A.D. 220), tofu is today an important source of protein in E. and S.E. Asia. Dried soybeans are soaked in water, crushed, and boiled to produce a solid pulp and liquid soy "milk." Coagulants are then added to the milk to separate the curds from the whey. The resulting soft cakes are cut into squares and stored in water.

toga Loose, draped outer garment adopted by the Romans from the Etruscans. Originally worn by both sexes of all classes, it was gradually abandoned by women, then by laborers, and finally by patricians, but it remained the state dress, the garment of the emperor and high officials. Made from an oval-shaped piece of material, the toga had voluminous folds that made activity difficult, and thus became the distinctive garment of the upper classes. The color of the toga worn depended on class, age, and the character of such special events as mourning and triumphs.

Toghril Beg \tȯg-'rēl-'beg\ (c.990–1063) Founder of the SELJUQ dynasty. He and his brother Chagri took refuge in Central Asia after being defeated by MAHMUD OF GHAZNA. Later they built up a power base in NE Iran, defeating Mahmud's son in 1040. Chagri took over Khorasan, and Toghril prepared to conquer the rest of Iran. In the 1040s he extended his authority to Rayy, Hamadan, and Esfahan, and in 1055 he entered Baghdad with a mission to overthrow the Shiite FATIMID dynasty. A rebellion delayed his conquest, but in 1060 Toghril crushed the revolt and regained Baghdad.

Togliatti \tȯl-'yä-tē\, **Palmiro** (1893–1964) Italian communist leader. In 1919 he helped found the left-wing weekly *L'Ordine Nuovo* ("New Order"); from 1921, he edited the Communist Party newspaper. In Moscow when the party was banned in Italy (1926), he remained in exile and became a member of the COMINTERN secretariat (1935). He returned in 1944, and served in a coalition government as vice premier (1945). He advocated a democratic form of communism and made the Italian Communist Party (see DEMOCRATIC PARTY OF THE LEFT) the largest in Western Europe.

Togo *officially* **Republic of Togo** Republic, W Africa. Area: 21,925 sq mi (56,785 sq km). Population (2000): 5,019,000. Capital: LOMÉ. It has some 30 ethnic groups; the EWE are the largest. Languages: French (official), Ewe, other ethnic languages. Religions: animism, Christianity, Islam. Currency: CFA franc. Togo occupies a strip of land about 70 mi (113 km) wide that extends about 340 mi (545 km) inland from the Gulf of GUINEA. Regions include a swampy coastal plain, a N savanna, and a central mountain range. The developing economy is based largely on agriculture. Chief crops are cotton, coffee, cocoa, cassava, and copra. It is one of the world's leading producers of phosphates. Cement and petroleum refining are also important. It is a republic with one legislative house; its chief of state is the president, supported by the military, and the head of government is the prime minister. Until 1884 what is now Togo was an intermediate zone between the black African military states of ASHANTI and DAHOMEY, and its various ethnic groups lived in general isolation from each other. In 1884 it became part of the TOGOLAND German protectorate, which was occupied by British and French forces in 1914. In 1922 the League of Nations assigned E Togoland to France and the W portion to Britain. In 1946 the British and French governments placed the territories under U.N. trusteeship. Ten years later British Togoland was incorporated into the GOLD COAST and French Togoland became an autonomous

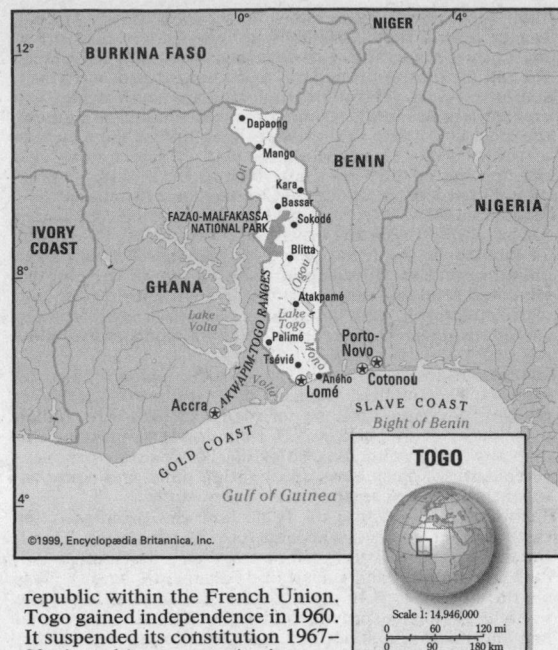

©1999, Encyclopædia Britannica, Inc.

TOGO

Scale 1: 14,946,000
0   60   120 mi
0   90   180 km

republic within the French Union. Togo gained independence in 1960. It suspended its constitution 1967–80. A multiparty constitution was approved in 1992, but the political situation remains unstable.

Togoland Former German protectorate, W Africa. Now divided between Togo and Ghana, it covered an area between the British GOLD COAST colony and French Dahomey (now Benin). It was inhabited by a mixture of EWE and other peoples. Its coast became a unit of Germany in 1884. In 1914 it was captured by Anglo-French forces and divided into two zones. The British zone was placed under control of the Gold Coast (now Ghana), with which it merged in 1956. The French zone became the independent Republic of Togo in 1960. Support for the reunification of Togoland still exists, especially among Ewe people in Ghana.

Tojo Hideki \'tō-jō-hē-'dā-kē\ (1884–1948) Japanese army general and prime minister (1941–44) during World War II. Under his direction, PEARL HARBOR was attacked and great victories were initially scored throughout S.E. Asia and the Pacific, but prolonged reverses in the Pacific and the successful U.S. invasion of the Marianas resulted in his removal from office. After an unsuccessful suicide attempt, he was tried and executed as a war criminal.

Tokugawa Ieyasu \,tō-kù-'gä-wä-yä-'yä-sù\ (1543–1616) Founder of the TOKUGAWA SHOGUNATE and ruler of Japan 1603–16. Ieyasu allied himself initially with the powerful general Oda Nobunaga, which enabled Ieyasu to slowly build up his territory; by the 1580s he had become an important DAIMYO. When Nobunaga died, Ieyasu offered a vow of fealty to TOYOTOMI HIDEYOSHI, who was extending his control over SW Japan; Ieyasu, meanwhile, enlarged his vassal force and increased his domain's productivity. When Hideyoshi died, Ieyasu had the largest army and the best-organized domain in all Japan; he emerged as victor from the ensuing power struggle. He confiscated his enemies' lands and gave them new domains away from Japan's heartland, much of which became Tokugawa property. He received the title of SHOGUN and later passed the title to his son, thereby establishing it as hereditary among the Tokugawa.

Tokugawa shogunate (1603–1867) Military government of Japan established by TOKUGAWA IEYASU as SHOGUN in 1603. He established his capital at Edo (Tokyo) and assigned DAIMYO domains according to their friendliness or hostility toward the Tokugawa; allies were given domains nearer to Edo. To protect Japan from outside influences, particularly Christian missionaries, he forbade Japanese to travel abroad and forbade foreigners to visit Japan (except for Chinese and Dutch traders, who could trade only at Nagasaki). TOYOTOMI HIDEYOSHI's division of society into four fixed classes was preserved; the SAMURAI class became the civil bureaucrats. Increased travel to Edo and other cities led to urban development and urban culture (see EDO PERIOD, GENROKU PERIOD). By the mid-18th cent. the shogunate began to suffer financially; fiscal reform proved largely unsuccessful. During its last 30 years there were numerous peasant uprisings and evidence of samurai unrest. It was overthrown by the domains of SATSUMA and Choshu in 1867.

Tokyo *formerly (until 1868)* **Edo** City (pop., 1999 est.: 11,837,000; metro. area pop., 2000 est.: 33,400,000), capital of Japan, SE HONSHU. The small fishing village of Edo existed for centuries before it became the capital of the TOKUGAWA SHOGUNATE in 1603. By the 19th cent. it was one of the largest cities in the world. Under the MEIJI RESTORATION, in 1868 it replaced KYOTO as the imperial capital, and Edo was renamed Tokyo. A devastating earthquake in 1923 destroyed most of the city and killed more than 100,000 people, but it was largely rebuilt by 1930. Much of it also had to be reconstructed after 1945, when U.S. fire bombing devastated the city. It is the administrative, cultural, financial, commercial, and educational center of Japan, and the center of an extensive complex of industrial suburbs. Attractions include the Imperial Palace with its broad gardens, and numerous temples and shrines. There are some 150 institutions of higher learning, including the Univ. of TOKYO (1877).

Tokyo, University of State-financed university in Tokyo, the largest and most prestigious university in Japan. Founded in 1877, it was destroyed in the earthquake and fire of 1923, and reorganized after World War II. It has graduate faculties of agriculture, economics, education, engineering, law, letters, medicine, pharmacology, and science. Among its many research units are centers for the study of molecular and cellular biology, earthquakes, solid-state physics, cosmic radiation, oceanography, and Asian culture. Total enrollment is about 27,000.

Tokyo Bay Inlet, W Pacific Ocean. Located off SE Honshu, Japan, it is about 30 mi (48 km) long and 23 mi (37 km) wide. It provides a spacious harbor for TOKYO, YOKOHAMA, and KAWASAKI. A highway connecting Kawasaki with Kisarazu across the bay uses an undersea tunnel 31,000 ft (9,300 m) long.

Tokyo Rose *orig.* Iva Ikuko Toguri (b.1916) U.S. broadcaster. Born in Los Angeles, she was visiting Japan when World War II broke out. In 1943 she began radio announcing for a propaganda program beamed at U.S. troops, and eventually became one of 13 U.S.-born women announcers collectively known as Tokyo Rose. Convicted of treason, she served six years in prison. Mitigating information later came to light, and she was pardoned in 1977.

Toledo City (pop., 2000: 314,000), NW Ohio. It is the principal GREAT LAKES port, located at the SW end of Lake ERIE. The area was opened to white settlement after the 1794 Battle of FALLEN TIMBERS. It figured in the so-called Toledo War of 1835–36, a bloodless boundary dispute between Michigan Territory and Ohio. Industrial development was spurred in the 1830s and '40s by the arrival of canals and railroads. Glassmaking, now a major industry, was introduced in the late 1880s. Its port is one of the world's largest shippers of bituminous coal. It is home to the Univ. of Toledo (1872).

Toledo \tə-ˈlē-dō, *Span* tō-ˈlä-thō\ *ancient* Toletum. City (pop., 1991: 60,000), capital of CASTILLA–LA MANCHA, S central Spain, on the TAGUS RIVER. Conquered by Rome in 193 B.C., in the 6th cent. A.D. it became the Visigoths' capital in Spain. Under the Moors (712–1085), it became a center of Hebrew and Arabic culture and was noted for the manufacture of swords. Taken by ALFONSO VI in 1085, it became the capital of New Castile and, in 1230, of the united kingdom of CASTILLA Y LEÓN. It was noted for its religious tolerance toward Jews and Arabs during the 11th–15th cent. It lost importance after MADRID became the capital in 1560. Known for its great wealth of notable architecture, the entire urban area is a national monument. It was the home of El GRECO.

Tolkien \ˈtäl-ˌkēn, *commonly* ˈtōl-ˌkin\, J(ohn) R(onald) R(euel) (1892–1973) English (S. African-born) novelist and scholar. A professor of Anglo-Saxon and English at Oxford (1925–59), Tolkien achieved fame for his epic trilogy *The Lord of the Rings* (1954–56), consisting of *The Fellowship of the Ring*, *The Two Towers*, and *The Return of the King*. *The Hobbit* (1937) serves as an introduction to the series. Set in the mythical past, the richly inventive trilogy chronicles the struggle between good and evil kingdoms to possess a magic ring that controls the balance of power in the world.

toll Sum levied on users of certain roads, canals, bridges, and tunnels, primarily to pay for construction and maintenance. Tolls were known in the ancient world and were widely used in medieval Europe to support bridge construction. Canal building, which became extensive in Europe in the 18th–19th cent., was financed chiefly by tolls, and many major roads were built by private companies with the right to collect tolls. The National Road, built in the U.S. beginning in 1806, was financed through the sale of public land, but maintenance costs soon led Congress to authorize tolls. Toll roads passed out of fashion for a time but were revived with the Pennsylvania Turnpike in the 1930s, and after World War II many states built toll expressways. In the U.S., tolls are also used to finance long-span bridges and major tunnels.

Tolly, Mikhail Barclay de See Mikhail BARCLAY DE TOLLY

Tolstoy, Leo *Russian* Lev Nikolayevich, Count Tolstoy (1828–1910) Russian writer, one of the world's greatest novelists. A prominent aristocrat, Tolstoy spent much of his life at his family estate of Yasnaya Polyana. He was already known as a brilliant writer for the short stories in *Sevastopol Sketches* (1855–56) and the novel *The Cossacks* (1863) when *War and Peace* (1865–69) established him as Russia's preeminent novelist. Set during the Napoleonic Wars, it examines the lives of a large group of characters,

Leo Tolstoy (left)

centering around the figure of the spiritually questing Pierre. Its structure, with its flawless placement of complex characters in a turbulent historical setting, is regarded as one of the great technical achievements of the Western novel. His other great novel, *Anna Karenina* (1875–77), centers on an aristocratic woman who deserts her husband for a lover, and on the search for meaning by the autobiographical character Levin. After its publication Tolstoy underwent a spiritual crisis and turned to a form of Christian anarchism. Advocating simplicity and nonviolence, he devoted himself to social reform. His later works include *The Death of Ivan Ilich* (1886), considered the greatest novella in Russian literature. He lived like a peasant on his great estate, practicing a radical asceticism. Finding his marriage unbearable, he departed suddenly for the local railway station, where he contracted a fatal pneumonia in the cold.

Toltecs Nahuatl-speaking people who held sway over central Mexico from the 10th to the 12th cent. Whether their urban center was TULA or TEOTIHUACÁN is a matter of dispute. In the 10th cent. they formed a number of small states into an empire. They introduced the cult of QUETZALCÓATL, and Toltec religious and military influences were absorbed by the MAYA. They were noted as builders and craftsmen; artifacts include fine metalwork and gigantic statues. They were succeeded by the AZTECS. See also MESOAMERICAN CIVILIZATION.

Toluca (de Lerdo) \tō-ˈlü-kä\ City (pop., 1995: 368,000), capital of MEXICO state, central Mexico. At an elevation of 8,793 ft (2,680 m), it is one of the highest cities in N. America. The site of the modern city, founded in 1530, was inhabited by the Otomi Indians by the 13th cent. It is a commercial center in an agriculture and livestock region. Its archaeological sites include some influenced by AZTECS and TOLTECS.

TUV

tomato Any fruit of the numerous cultivated varieties of *Lycopersicon esculentum*, a plant of the NIGHTSHADE FAMILY. The plant has many branches and hairy, strongly odorous, feathery leaves. The drooping, clustered, yellow flowers are followed by red, scarlet, or yellow fruits. The tomato fruit varies in shape from spherical to elongate and in size from 0.6 in. (1.5 cm) across to more than 3 in. (7.5 cm) across. The Spanish brought tomatoes from S. America to Europe in the early 16th cent.; they were introduced to N. America from Europe by the 1780s. Tomatoes are used raw, cooked as a vegetable or puree, and pickled, canned, and sun-dried.

tomb Home or house for the dead. The term is applied loosely to all kinds of graves, funerary monuments, and memorials. Prehistoric tomb burial mounds were usually built around a hut containing personal effects for use in the afterlife. Spectacularly huge mounds surrounded by moats were a prominent feature of the Tumulus period in Japan (3rd–6th cent.). Burial mounds, sometimes shaped like animals, were characteristic also of Indian cultures of E central N. America around 1000 B.C.–A.D. 700. In Egypt tombs assumed great importance, especially in the form of PYRAMIDS. In medieval Christian thought, the tomb became a symbol of a heavenly home; in the Roman CATACOMBS, the walls display scenes of paradise. Since the Renaissance, the idea of the tomb as a home has survived only faintly in the MAUSOLEUMS or vaults of modern cemeteries. See also STELE.

Tombigbee River \täm-'big-bē\ River, Alabama. Formed by the confluence of its E and W forks near Amory, Miss., it flows south into Alabama nearly 400 mi (650 km) to join the ALABAMA RIVER and form the Mobile and Tensaw rivers.

Tombouctou \ˌtōⁿ-bük-'tü\ *or* **Timbuktu** Town (pop., 1987: 32,000), Mali, on the S edge of the SAHARA near the NIGER RIVER. Founded around A.D. 1100 by TUAREG nomads, it became an important post on the trans-Saharan caravan routes in the 12th cent. After it was incorporated within the MALI EMPIRE, it became a great center of Islamic culture and education (c.1400–1600), reaching its height as a commercial and cultural center under SONGHAI rule about 1500, but it declined rapidly after European ships began to render the trans-Saharan trade routes obsolescent. The French captured it in 1893. It became part of independent Mali in 1960.

Tombstone City (pop., 2000: 1,500), SE Arizona. The site was named by Ed Schieffelin (1847–1897), who discovered silver there in 1877 after being told that all he would find would be his tombstone. By 1881 a silver rush had drawn such prospectors and gunmen as Doc HOLLIDAY and Johnny Ringo. Feuds were common, including the 1881 gun battle at the OK Corral between the Earp (see Wyatt EARP) and Clanton families.

tomography \tō-'mä-grə-fē\ Radiological technique for obtaining clear X-RAY images of internal structures by focusing on a specific plane within the body to produce a cross-sectional image. It allows the examination of structures that do not show up clearly on conventional X-ray images. See also COMPUTED AXIAL TOMOGRAPHY.

tonality Organization of music around a single pitch, especially the Western system of KEYS that grew out of the modal music of the Renaissance in the 17th cent. The term is often used to refer to the network of relationships implicit in the seven principal tones of a given key, each of which has the potential to become the tonic temporarily by means of MODULATION, whereby a new network of relationships arises. Because of its capacity to extend pitch relationships to remote lengths in an audibly comprehensible way, the tonal system permits the composition of music of enormous complexity.

Tonatiuh \tō-'nä-tē-ü\ Sun deity of the AZTECS and NAHUAS. According to most myths, there were four eras that preceded the era of Tonatiuh, each of which ended by cataclysm. He was viewed as a god constantly threatened by the awesome tasks of his daily birth at sunrise, arduous journey across the sky, and death at each sunset. He was the object of human sacrifice, which was thought necessary to sustain him. He was depicted in the center of the Aztec calendar.

tone In LINGUISTICS, a variation in the pitch of the voice while speaking languages (called tone languages) in which pitch differentiates words with an identical sequences of consonants and vowels. For example, *man* in Mandarin Chinese may mean either "deceive" or "slow," depending on its pitch. In tone languages, what matters is not absolute pitch but the pitch of one word relative to another or how pitch changes within a word.

tone See PITCH, TIMBRE

tone poem See SYMPHONIC POEM

Tonga *officially* **Kingdom of Tonga** Nation, SW Pacific Ocean. Area: 290 sq mi (750 sq km). Population (2000): 100,000. Capital: NUKU'ALOFA. The people are of Polynesian ancestry. Languages: Tongan, English (both official). Religions: Free Wesleyanism, Roman Catholicism, Mormonism. Currency: pa'anga. Tonga includes an archipelago of about 169 islands that extends north to south in two parallel chains for about 500 mi (800 km). Only 36 are permanently inhabited. The E islands are low and formed of coral limestone; those in the west are mountainous and of volcanic origin, and four of the W islands have active volcanoes. The country has a developing free-market economy based mainly on agriculture. Chief products include fish, coconuts, sweet potatoes, and bananas. Tourism also is important. Tonga is a constitutional monarchy with one legislative house; the head of state and government is the king, assisted by the privy council. Tonga was inhabited at least 3,000 years ago by people of the Lapita culture. The Tongans developed a stratified social system headed by a paramount ruler whose dominion by the 13th cent. extended as far as the Hawaiian Islands. The Dutch visited the islands in the 17th cent., but effective contact dates from 1773, when Capt. James COOK arrived and named the archipelago the Friendly Islands. The modern kingdom was established during the reign (1845–93) of King George Tupou I. It became a British protectorate in 1900. This was dissolved in 1970, when Tonga, the only ancient kingdom surviving from the pre-European period in Polynesia, achieved complete independence within the COMMONWEALTH. See also map at OCEANIA.

Tonghak See CH'ONDOGYO

Tonghak Uprising (1894) Korean peasant rebellion that sparked the SINO–JAPANESE WAR. Despite persecution, impoverished peasants turned increasingly to Tonghak ("Eastern Learning"; see CH'ONDOGYO), a religion that opposed Western culture and espoused equality before Heaven. When staged demonstrations were repressed, the peasants rebelled, defeating government troops in S Korea. The government called on China for aid; Japan sent in troops without being asked, and China and Japan clashed. The rebels laid down their arms to defuse tensions, but the Sino–Japanese War ensued nevertheless.

tongue Muscular organ on the floor of the MOUTH. It is important in motions of eating, drinking, and SWALLOWING, and its complex movements shape the sounds of SPEECH. Its top surface consists of thousands of raised projections (papillae), in which the receptors of TASTE (taste buds) are embedded. The tongue's appearance (e.g., coated or red) can give clues to disease elsewhere. Disorders of the tongue include cancer (often caused by smokeless tobacco), leukoplakia (white patches), fungal infection, and CONGENITAL DISORDERS. Animals use the tongue to serve varied functions: frogs' tongues are adapted to capturing prey, snakes' tongues collect and transfer odors to a specialized sensory structure, and cats use their tongues for grooming and cleaning.

tongues, gift of *or* **glossolalia** Utterances approximating words and speech but generally unintelligible, usually produced during states of trance or delirium. The religious interpretation of the phenomenon is that the speaker is possessed by a supernatural spirit, is in conversation with divine beings, or is the channel of a divine proclamation. Among followers of JESUS, it occurred first at PENTECOST. Today it is mainly associated with charismatic Protestant movements such as PENTECOSTALISM.

Tonkin Former French protectorate, S.E. Asia, now constituting the greater part of N Vietnam. It was part of China from the 2nd cent. B.C. until the Vietnamese won independence in the 10th cent. A.D. The French seized the area in 1883, and in 1887 it became part of FRENCH INDOCHINA.

Tonkin, Gulf of Arm of the S. CHINA SEA, between N Vietnam and Hainan island, China. In 1964 the Vietnamese reportedly fired on U.S. ships there, leading the U.S. Congress to adopt the GULF OF TONKIN RESOLUTION supporting increased U.S. involvement in the VIETNAM WAR.

Tonkin Gulf Resolution See GULF OF TONKIN RESOLUTION

Tonle Sap \tŏn-'lä-'sap\ Lake, W Cambodia. The largest freshwater body in S.E. Asia, it receives several tributaries as well as the floodwaters of the MEKONG RIVER. Though only a swamp in the dry season, during the rainy season its area increases from 1,000 sq mi (2,600 sq km) to about 9,500 sq mi (25,000 sq km). A large carp industry supports numerous floating fishing villages. The ruins of ANGKOR lie near its NW shore.

tonsil Small mass of LYMPHOID TISSUE in the wall of the PHARYNX. The term usually refers to the palatine tonsils on each side of the throat. They are thought to produce antibodies to help prevent respiratory and digestive-tract infection but often become infected themselves (see TONSILLITIS), mostly in children. There are also pharyngeal tonsils, better known as ADENOIDS, and lingual tonsils, at the base of the TONGUE.

tonsillitis Inflammatory INFECTION of the TONSILS, usually with hemolytic streptococci (see STREPTOCOCCUS) or VIRUSES. The symptoms are sore throat, trouble in swallowing, fever, and enlarged LYMPH NODES on the neck. SULFA DRUGS or other antibiotics are prescribed in severe bacterial infections to prevent complications (e.g., ABSCESS, NEPHRITIS, RHEUMATIC FEVER). Streptococcal infection can spread to nearby structures. Tonsils that become chronically inflamed and enlarged require surgical removal (tonsillectomy).

Tony awards Annual awards for distinguished achievement in the U.S. theater. Named for the actress-producer Antoinette (Tony) Perry (1888–1946), the annual awards were established in 1947 by the American Theatre Wing to recognize excellence in plays and musicals staged on BROADWAY. Awards are given in a wide range of categories.

tool and die making Manufacturing of stamping DIES, plastics MOLDS, and jigs and fixtures to be used in the mass production of solid objects. The making of dies for punch presses constitutes most of the work done in tool and die shops, and most such pressworking dies are used in the manufacture of sheet-metal parts. See also MACHINE TOOL.

Toomer, Jean (*orig.* Nathan Eugene) (1894–1967) U.S. poet and novelist of the HARLEM RENAISSANCE. Born in Washington, D.C., he taught briefly before turning to writing. *Cane* (1923), considered his best work, is an experimental novel about being black in the U.S.; it had a strong influence on younger black writers. Ambivalent about his mixed racial background and preoccupied with spiritual matters, he avoided race issues in subsequent works.

tooth Any of the hard structures in the MOUTH used for biting and chewing and in speech. Each consists of a crown above the GUM and one or more roots below it, embedded in the JAW. Its inner pulp contains the blood and nerve supply for the bonelike dentin, covered in the crown by enamel. Twenty primary (baby) teeth come in by age 2 1/2 and fall out between ages 5 and 13 to be replaced by 32 permanent teeth. The incisors, in front, are shaped mostly for biting, the pointed canines for tearing, and the premolars and molars for grinding food. The teeth are subject to CARIES (decay), caused by acid from bacteria in plaque, a yellowish film that builds up on teeth. See also DENTISTRY. See diagram, right.

tooth decay See CARIES

Topa See NORTHERN WEI DYNASTY

topaz Aluminum silicate mineral, valued as a gemstone. It is formed by fluorine-bearing vapors given off during the last stages of the crystallization of IGNEOUS ROCKS. Pure topaz may be colorless, yellow, blue, or brown. Imperial topaz, with vivid reddish orange color, from Minas Gerais, Brazil, is very highly valued. Topaz is the birthstone for November.

Topeka \tə-'pē-kə\ City (pop., 2000: 122,000), capital of Kansas. It was founded in 1854 by antislavery colonists and was a center of the antislavery FREE SOIL PARTY. In 1859 it was the headquarters for the building of the ATCHISON, TOPEKA, AND SANTA FE RAIL CO. The MENNINGER FAMILY established its clinics there, making Topeka a national center for the treatment of mental illness.

Topeka Constitution (1855) Resolution to establish an antislavery territorial government in Kansas. To counter the proslavery government established after passage of the KANSAS-NEBRASKA ACT, antislavery settlers met in Topeka to draft a constitution that banned slavery. In 1856 they elected a free-state governor and legislature, which created two governments. The U.S. House of Representatives voted to admit Kansas under the Topeka Constitution, but the Senate blocked the move. The unresolved situation led to the conflict known as BLEEDING KANSAS.

topiary Art of training living trees and shrubs into artificial, decorative shapes. Topiary was practiced by the 1st cent. A.D. The earliest topiary probably took the form of edgings, cones, columns, and spires. This architectural use gave way to elaborate shapes such as ships, hunters, and hounds. The fashion reached its height in Britain around 1700 but was displaced by the so-called natural garden.

topology \tə-'pä-lə-jē\ In mathematics, the study of the properties of a geometric object that remains unchanged by deformations such as bending, stretching, or squeezing but not breaking. A sphere is topologically equivalent to a cube because, without breaking them, each can be deformed into the other as if they were made of modeling clay. A sphere is not equivalent to a doughnut, because the former would have to be broken to put a hole in it. Topological concepts and methods underlie much of modern mathematics.

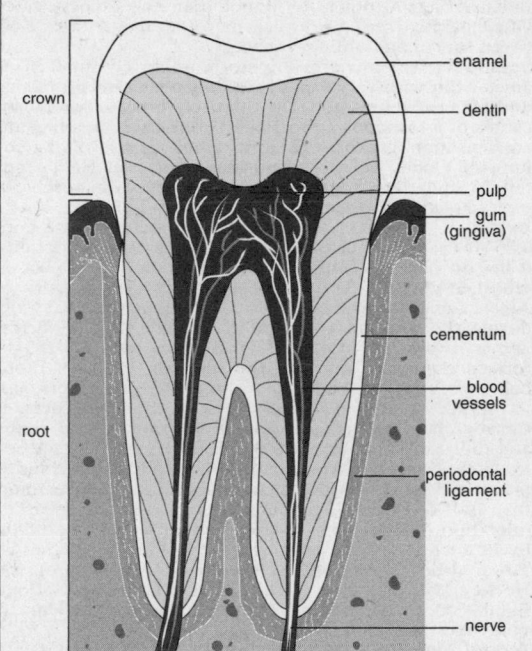

Tooth Cross section of an adult molar. The crown (the part of the tooth above the gum) is protected by a hard outer layer of enamel. The roots sit in a socket in the jawbone and are covered with cementum, a bonelike material. The periodontal ligament anchors the cementum in the jaw and cushions the tooth from the pressures of chewing. The tooth's main portion, the dentin, surrounds the soft pulp, which carries the blood vessels and nerves. Specialized cells of the pulp project threadlike extensions into the dentin through narrow channels and serve to form new dentin from minerals in the blood.

TUV

Torah \tō-'rä, 'tō-rə, 'tòr-ə\ *or* **Pentateuch** \'pen-tə-,tük\ In JUDAISM, the divine revelations to Israel; specifically, the first five books of the BIBLE: GENESIS, EXODUS, Leviticus, Numbers, and Deuteronomy. Although traditionally ascribed to MOSES, they were probably written and compiled in the 9th–5th cent. B.C., though drawing on much older traditions. The term Torah (but not Pentateuch) is often applied to the whole Hebrew Scripture or, even more generally, to that and other Jewish sacred literature and oral tradition.

torana \'tòr-ə-nə\ Indian gateway, usually of stone, marking the entrance to a Buddhist shrine or STUPA or to a Hindu temple. Toranas typically consist of two pillars carrying two or three transverse beams that extend beyond the pillars on either side. Strongly reminiscent of wooden construction, toranas are often covered from top to bottom with exquisite sculpture. See also TORII.

Tordesillas \,tòr-dä-'sēl-yäs\, **Treaty of** (1494) Agreement between Spain and Portugal over lands in the New World. In 1493 Pope ALEXANDER VI had granted Spain all the lands west of a line 100 leagues west of the Cape Verde Islands, in return for an agreement to Christianize the peoples of the New World; Portuguese expeditions were to keep to the east. At Tordesillas, Spain, negotiators moved that line west, allowing Portugal to claim Brazil when it was discovered in 1500.

torii \'tòr-ē-,ē\ Symbolic gateway marking the entrance to Shinto shrines or other sacred spots in Japan. It usually consists of two cylindrical posts topped by a crosswise upward-curving rectangular beam, with a second crosswise beam a short distance below. Some authorities relate the torii to the Indian TORANA, others to Manchurian and Chinese gates. Often painted red, the torii demarcates the boundary between sacred and ordinary space.

tornado Violent low-pressure storm, relatively small in diameter but with very rapidly rotating winds and an intense updraft near the center. The relatively low pressure at the center of a tornado's funnel-like vortex causes cooling and condensation, making the storm visible as a revolving column of cloud. Tornadoes normally travel at 30–40 mph (50–65 kph). The winds around the vortex can reach 500 mph (800 kph). Tornadoes often occur in groups.

Toronto City (pop., 1996: 654,000; metro. area pop.: 4,264,000), capital of ONTARIO. Canada's third-largest city, it lies on Lake ONTARIO. Site of a French trading post established about 1750, it was founded in 1793 as York by Americans loyal to the British. U.S. troops sacked it twice during the WAR OF 1812. In 1834 it received its current name; it became capital of Ontario in 1867. In 1954 it formed a municipality with the adjoining towns of Etobicoke, E. York, N. YORK, SCARBOROUGH, and York that has made it the most populous metropolitan area in Canada. It is Canada's financial and commercial center and the seat of the Toronto Stock Exchange. It has access to Atlantic shipping via the ST. LAWRENCE SEAWAY and to major U.S. ports via the GREAT LAKES. It produces more than half of Canada's manufactured goods. Extensive immigration during 1950–90 transformed it into one of the liveliest cities on the continent. It is the site of the CN Tower (the world's tallest freestanding structure), the Hockey Hall of Fame, and the annual Canadian National Exhibition. Its educational institutions include the Univ. of TORONTO (1827).

Toronto, University of Public university in Toronto. It was founded in 1843 and reorganized in 1853 and 1887. It comprises nine undergraduate colleges, three federated universities, four affiliated theological colleges, and numerous other units. Notable among its research units are centers for the study of medieval culture and society, religion, Russia and E. Europe, international relations, drama, biomedical engineering, history of science and technology, and aerospace science. Total enrollment is about 55,000.

torpedo Cigar-shaped, self-propelled underwater MISSILE, launched from a SUBMARINE, surface vessel, or airplane and designed to explode on contact with surface vessels and submarines. It contains devices to control depth and direction as well as a detonator for the warhead. The first modern torpedo (1866) carried an 18-lb (8-kg) charge of dynamite in its nose and was powered by a compressed-air engine; its range was 200–700 yards (180–640 m). Torpedoes were used by submarines in both world wars, when many merchant ships were sunk, mostly by German U-BOATS. Torpedoes are now propelled by battery-powered electric motors.

torque *or* **moment** In PHYSICS, the tendency of a FORCE to rotate the body to which it is applied. Torque is always specified with regard to the axis of rotation. It is equal to the magnitude of the component of the force perpendicular to the axis of rotation, multiplied by the shortest distance between the axis and the direction of the force component.

Torquemada \,tòr-kā-'mä-thä\, **Tomás de** (1420–1498) First grand inquisitor in Spain (1487–98). A Dominican prior, he became confessor and adviser to FERDINAND V and ISABELLA I. He guided the Spanish INQUISITION, directing its fierce persecution of Jews, Moors, and others identified as heretics, sorcerers, or criminals. He probably influenced Ferdinand and Isabella in their decision to expel the Jews from Spain (1492). His name has become synonymous with the cruel fanaticism of the Inquisition.

Tomás de Torquemada

Torrijos (Herrera) \tòr-'ē-hōs\, **Omar** (1929–1981) Virtual dictator of Panama (1968–78). He rose to the rank of general and came to power in 1968 in a coup d'état. A nationalist and populist, he was one of the few Latin American heads of state to visit Fidel CASTRO in Cuba, though he suppressed leftist labor agitators and students at home. In 1977 he achieved his supreme goal when Pres. Jimmy CARTER signed two treaties transferring the PANAMA CANAL and CANAL ZONE to Panamanian sovereignty in 1999. He died in a plane crash.

torsion bar Rod or bar that resists twisting (see TORQUE) and has a strong tendency to return to its original position when twisted. In an AUTOMOBILE, a torsion bar is a long spring-steel element with one end held rigidly to the frame and the other end twisted by a lever connected to the axle. It thus provides a SPRING action for the vehicle.

tort Wrongful act, other than a breach of contract, that injures another and for which the law permits a civil (noncriminal) action to be brought. Relief may be obtained in the form of damages or an injunction. ASSAULT, DEFAMATION, MALPRACTICE, NEGLIGENCE, NUISANCE, product liability, property damage, and trespass are all (apart from their potentially criminal and contractual aspects) torts.

tortoise Any of some 40 species (family Testudinidae) of slow-moving, terrestrial, herbivorous TURTLES, found in the Old and New Worlds but chiefly in Africa and Madagascar. Tortoises have a high, domed shell, heavy elephant-like hind legs, and hard-scaled forelegs. The four N. American species (genus *Gopherus*) have a shell 8–14 in. (20–35 cm) long and flattened forelimbs adapted for burrowing. Most giant tortoises are now rare or extinct. One captive Galápagos tortoise had a shell 4.25 ft (1.3 m) long and weighed 300 lbs (140 kg).

torture Infliction of intolerable physical or psychological pain. Torture has been used by those in power for punishment, coercion, and intimidation, especially of enemies, and for extracting confessions and information. It was widely used by the Greeks and Romans. Its use in Europe increased in the 12th cent. as a means of obtaining confessions. It was common and sanctioned in the 14th–18th cent.; the Roman Catholic Church supported its use during the INQUISITION. Common instruments were the strappado (for repeatedly hoisting the body by the wrists behind the back and dropping it), the rack (for stretching the limbs and body), and the thumbscrew (for crushing the thumbs). By 1800 torture was illegal in most European countries, but it became common again in the 20th cent., notably in Nazi

Germany and the Soviet Union, and is still widely practiced in Latin America, Africa, and the Middle East.

Tory Member of a political group in England, especially in the 18th cent. Originally an Irish term for an outlaw, the name was applied as a term of abuse to those who supported James, the Catholic duke of York (later JAMES II); they were opposed by the WHIGS in that struggle (1679). They came to represent the resistance, mainly by the country gentry, to religious toleration and foreign entanglements. The Tories' political power diminished after Viscount BOLINGBROKE, a leading Tory, fled to France in 1715; Tory sentiment survived in the unsuccessful JACOBITE movement. After 1784, William PITT the Younger emerged as the leader of a new Tory party, representing the country gentry, merchants, and administrators. After 1815 the party gradually evolved into the CONSERVATIVE PARTY, whose members are still called Tories.

Toscanini \ˌtäs-kə-ˈnē-nē\, **Arturo** (1867–1957) Italian conductor. He entered a conservatory at 9. A professional cellist, he stepped in to conduct *Aïda* in Buenos Aires in 1886. Conducting in various Italian houses, he gave the premieres of *I Pagliacci* (1892) and *La Bohème* (1896) and he later served as music director of La Scala (1898–1903, 1906–8, 1920–29) and the Metropolitan Opera (1908–15). In 1930 he became the first non-German to conduct at Bayreuth, but he stopped performing in Germany to protest Nazi policies. The NBC Orchestra was formed for him in 1937, and he conducted it until his retirement in 1954. Admired for his dictatorial perfectionism, he was the most famous conductor of his time.

totalitarianism Form of government that subordinates all aspects of its citizens' lives to the authority of the state, with a single charismatic leader as the ultimate authority. The term was coined in the early 1920s by Benito MUSSOLINI, but totalitarianism has existed throughout history. It is distinguished from DICTATORSHIP and AUTHORITARIANISM by its supplanting of all political institutions and all old legal and social traditions with new ones to meet the state's needs. Organized violence may be legitimized. The police operate without the constraint of laws. Where pursuit of the state's goal is the only ideological foundation for such a government, achievement of the goal can never be acknowledged.

Total Quality Control (TQC) System for optimizing production based on ideas developed by Japanese industries from the 1950s on. The system began with the concept of Quality Circles, in which groups of 10–20 workers were given responsibility for the quality of the products they produced. It gradually evolved into various techniques for maximizing productivity and quality, including close monitoring of staff and excellent customer service. The concept of *kaizen*, the notion that improvement must involve all members of a company, is central to TQC.

totemism Complex of ideas and practices based on the belief in kinship or mystical relationship between a group (or individual) and a natural object, such as an animal or plant. A society exhibits totemism if it is divided into an apparently fixed number of clans, each of which has a specific relationship to a totem, which may be a feared or respected hunted animal or an edible plant. Very commonly connected with origin MYTHS and with instituted morality, the totem is almost always accompanied by TABOOS of avoidance or of strictly ritualized contact.

totem pole Carved and painted vertical log, constructed by many NORTHWEST COAST INDIAN peoples. The poles display mythological images, usually animal spirits, whose significance is their association with the lineage. Each figure represents a type of family crest. Some poles relate a family legend in the form of pictographs.

Totem poles with reconstructed Tlingit longhouse, Alaska

Poles are usually erected to identify the owner of a house or property, welcome visitors, indicate a portal or passageway, or mark a gravesite.

toucan \ˈtü-ˌkan\ Any of about 40 species (family Ramphastidae) of large-billed, long-tailed Central and S. American birds. Many species are black with a bold breast color; their thick, saw-edged bills are brightly and distinctively colored. Bands of toucans emit loud barks, bugling calls, and harsh croaks. They eat fruit, insects, lizards, and nestling birds. *Ramphastos* species are up to 24 in. (60 cm) long, a third of which may be the bill. Smaller species (toucanets) are 10–14 in. (25–35 cm) long.

Toulouse \tü-ˈlüz\ *ancient* Tolosa. City (pop., 1999: 390,000), S France, on the GARONNE RIVER. Founded in ancient times, it was taken from its Celtic inhabitants by the Romans in 106 B.C. Protestants were massacred there during the 16th-cent. Wars of RELIGION. In 1814 it was the scene of the last battle of the PENINSULAR WAR. It is a center of the French aviation industry. It has a Gothic cathedral, a Romanesque basilica, and the tomb of St. THOMAS AQUINAS. Its university, founded in 1224, is one of the oldest in the world.

Toulouse-Lautrec (-Monfa) \tü-ˈlüz-lō-ˈtrek\, **Henri (-Marie-Raymond) de** (1864–1901) French painter and graphic artist. Born to an old aristocratic family, he developed his interest in art during lengthy convalescence after both his legs were fractured in separate accidents that left them permanently stunted. In 1881 he resolved to become an artist; he established a studio in the Montmartre district of Paris in 1884 and began his lifelong association with the area's cafés, cabarets, entertainers, and artists. He captured the effect of the movement of dancers, circus performers, and other entertainers by simplifying outlines and juxtaposing intense colors. His lithographs were among his most powerful works, and his memorable posters helped define the possibilities of the genre. His pieces are often sharply satirical, but he was also capable of great sympathy, as in his studies of prostitutes (e.g., *At the Salon*, 1896). His extraordinary style helped set the course of avant-garde art for decades to come. A heavy drinker, he died at 36.

Toungoo dynasty \ˈtau̇n-ˌgü\ Ruling house in Myanmar in the 15th/16th–18th cent. The founder of the empire is considered to be either King Minkyinyo (r.1486–1531) or his son Tabinshwehti (r.1531–50), who expanded and unified the empire from its capital, Toungoo. Tabinshwehti's brother-in-law Bayinnaung (r.1551–81) extended the dynasty's reach to include much of Laos and Siam. No ruler ever managed to conquer Arakan (in S Myanmar), though many tried. The empire slowly disintegrated after Bayinnaung's death, but the dynasty continued until 1752.

Tour, Georges de La See Georges de LA TOUR

Touraine \tü-ˈren\ Historical region, NW central France. It encompassed the former province of Touraine; its capital was at TOURS. Conquered by Rome, in the 5th cent. A.D. it was incorporated in the Visigothic kingdom, and it passed to the FRANKS in 507. It came under French influence in the early 13th cent. The province was abolished in 1789 during the FRENCH REVOLUTION. The region, which includes the LOIRE RIVER valley, known for its magnificent chateaus, is sometimes called the Garden of France.

Tour de France \ˌtür-də-ˈfrä⁸s\ Bicycle race held annually since 1903 on a 4,000-km (2,484-mi) course principally through France and Belgium. The world's preeminent cycling event, it admits 120 or more male contestants. The race is divided into about 21 daily stages; each stage is timed, and the rider with the lowest aggregate time for all stages is the winner. See also Lance ARMSTRONG.

Touré \tü-ˈrä\, **(Ahmed) Sékou** (1922–1984) First president of Guinea (1958–84). Touré, who claimed to be descended from SAMORI TURE, helped lead Guinea's campaign for independence in 1958. He actively supported Kwame NKRUMAH's program for African unity, and gave Nkrumah asylum when he was deposed in 1966. He was initially viewed as a moderate Islamic leader, but after an attempted invasion from Portuguese Guinea (now Guinea-Bissau) in 1971, his regime became harshly authoritarian.

Tourette's syndrome \tü-ˈrets\ Rare neurological disease that causes repetitive motor and vocal TICS. It occurs world-

wide, is usually inherited, generally begins at age 2–15, and is three times more common in males. Motor tics occur first in about 80% of cases, compulsions to utter abnormal sounds in the rest. Repetition of words heard and spontaneous repetition of one's own words are two distinctive symptoms. Other vocal tics may include meaningless sounds. Motor tics may be virtually unnoticeable; more complex ones may appear intentional (e.g., hopping, clapping). Sleep, intense concentration, and exertion tend to suppress the tics; emotional stress worsens them. Unlike psychiatric compulsive disorders, Tourette's syndrome has a neurological origin and may improve with antipsychotic drugs.

tourmaline \'tər-mə-lən, 'tər-mə-ˌlēn\ Complex SILICATE MINERAL that is often used as a gemstone. Three types of tourmaline, distinguished by the presence of certain elements, include black iron tourmaline (schorl), brown magnesium tourmaline (dravite), and alkali tourmalines, which may be pink, green, blue, or colorless. Gem-quality stones are found especially in the U.S., Brazil, Russia, and Madagascar.

Tours \'tür\ City (pop., 1999: 133,000), NW central France. In the 3rd cent. A.D. it was made an episcopal see, and St. MARTIN became bishop in the 4th cent.; a magnificent basilica was raised above his tomb in the late 5th cent., attracting pilgrims for hundreds of years. In the 5th cent. it became part of the Frankish dominion; CHARLES MARTEL defeated Moorish invaders nearby at the Battle of TOURS/POITIERS in 732. Under ALCUIN it developed as a center of learning. It was the seat of French government during the siege of Paris (1870) in the FRANCO–PRUSSIAN WAR. It is now the chief tourist center for the LOIRE valley.

Tours/Poitiers \pwä-'työ\, **Battle of** (Oct. 732) Victory won by the Frankish leader CHARLES MARTEL over Muslim invaders from Spain. Charles led Frankish troops against a Muslim army seeking to gain control of Aquitaine. The Arab leader was killed, and the Arabs retreated. The decisive battle marked the end of the Muslim invasions of Frankish territory.

Toussaint-Louverture \'tü-ˌsaⁿ-'lü-vər-ˌtür\ *orig.* François Dominique Toussaint (1743?–1803) Leader of the Haitian independence movement during the French Revolution. A freed slave, in 1791 he joined a slave rebellion, and soon assembled an army of his own. When France and Spain went to war in 1793, he joined the Spaniards, but in 1794 he switched his allegiance because France had recently abolished slavery. His revolt created the first independent nation in Latin America. He rose to governor-general of Saint-Domingue (i.e., Haiti). Treaties with the British secured French withdrawal. In 1801 he turned his attention to Santo Domingo, the Spanish-controlled portion of Hispaniola, driving out the Spanish and freeing the slaves there. He made himself governor-general for life, but was deposed by the French in 1802 and died in custody in France. See also Jean-Jacques DESSALINES.

tower Any freestanding or attached structure that is relatively tall in proportion to its base. The Romans, Byzantines, and medieval Europeans built defensive towers as part of their city walls (e.g., the TOWER OF LONDON). Indian temple architecture uses towers of various types (e.g., the SIKHARA). Towers were an important feature of churches and cathedrals built in the Romanesque and Gothic periods. The Italian CAMPANILE could either be attached to a church or freestanding. The use of towers declined somewhat during the Renaissance but reappeared in baroque architecture. The EIFFEL TOWER was the first structure to reveal the true vertical potential of steel construction.

Tower of London Royal fortress on the N bank of the River Thames. The central keep, or DONJON, known as the White Tower because of its limestone, was begun about 1078 by WILLIAM I the Conqueror inside the Roman city wall. In the 12th–13th cent. it became the nucleus of a series of concentric defenses. The Tower was long used as a state prison; many were murdered or executed there.

town meeting Legislative assembly of a U.S. town. Dating from the colonial era, it is still largely a New England phenomenon, partly because the region's towns tend to hold powers that are granted to counties elsewhere. Executive authority is usually held by a three- or five-member board

of selectmen. Open town meetings, normally held annually, allow all registered voters to vote on the articles listed on the agenda, and are regarded as an exceptionally pure form of democracy; representative town meetings allow only elected members to vote.

Townshend (of Rainham) \'taün-zənd\, **Viscount** *orig.* Charles Townshend (1675–1738) British politician. He married the sister of Robert WALPOLE, and served as secretary of state 1714–16. With Walpole, he led the Whig Party. Again secretary of state 1721–30, he formed the League of Hanover (with France and Prussia) against Austria and Spain. He resigned when Walpole opposed an aggressive policy against Austria. Also interested in agricultural reform, Townshend developed the use of turnips in crop rotation, earning the nickname Turnip Townshend.

Townshend Acts (1767) Four British parliamentary measures to tax the American colonists. The acts imposed duties on imports of lead, paint, glass, paper, and tea. Colonial quartering of British troops was also revived. The colonists protested the new measures as taxation without representation. Nonimportation agreements among colonial merchants cut British imports in half by 1769. In 1770 all the duties except the tax on tea were repealed.

toxic diffuse goiter See GRAVES' DISEASE

toxicology Study of POISONS and their effects, particularly on living systems. It overlaps with BIOCHEMISTRY, HISTOLOGY, PHARMACOLOGY, PATHOLOGY, and other fields. Its functions have expanded from identifying poisons and searching for treatments to include forensic toxicology (see FORENSIC MEDICINE); testing and detection of new potentially toxic substances used in workplaces, in agriculture, in COSMETICS, as food additives, and as DRUGS; and the study of toxic waste in the air, water, and soil, including CHLOROFLUOROCARBONS, ACID RAIN, DIOXIN, and radioactive ISOTOPES.

toxic shock syndrome BACTERIAL DISEASE caused by a TOXIN produced by *Staphylococcus aureus* (see STAPHYLOCOCCUS). It was first recognized in 1978 in women using superabsorbent tampons (no longer made). High fever, diarrhea, vomiting, and rash may progress to abdominal tenderness, drop in BLOOD PRESSURE, SHOCK, respiratory distress, and KIDNEY FAILURE. ANTIBIOTICS are not effective. With intensive supportive therapy, most patients recover in 7–10 days, but 10–15% die.

toxin Any substance poisonous to an organism; often restricted to POISONS produced by living organisms. There are toxins in BACTERIA (see BACTERIAL DISEASES), DINOFLAGELLATES, ALGAE, fungi (mycotoxins; see MUSHROOM POISONING), higher plants (phytotoxins), and animals (zootoxins, or VENOMS). Poisonous plants include nightshade (see NIGHTSHADE FAMILY), POISON HEMLOCK, FOXGLOVE, MISTLETOE, and POISON IVY. Many plant toxins apparently protect their producers against certain animals (especially insects) or fungi. Similar defensive secretions in animals may be widely distributed or concentrated in certain tissues, often with some sort of delivery system (e.g., spines, fangs). Many normally edible fishes and shellfishes become poisonous after feeding on toxic plants or algae. See also ANTIDOTE, FOOD POISONING.

toy dog Any of several breeds of DOGS bred to be small, portable, and good-natured. Toy dogs were traditionally pampered and treasured by aristocracy around the world, and several breeds are ancient. They range from hairless (the Chinese crested dog) to profusely coated (the SHIH TZU). Some breeds, such as the PEKINGESE, could be owned only by royalty. The Cavalier King Charles spaniel was a favorite of English royalty. Toy POODLES are popular in the U.S. Other toy dogs include the affenpinscher, MALTESE, PAPILLON, POMERANIAN, and Yorkshire terrier.

Toynbee, Arnold (Joseph) (1889–1975) English historian. He is best known for his 12-volume *A Study of History* (1934–61), which put forward a philosophy of history, based on an analysis of the development and decline of 26 civilizations. Criticisms of his *Study* include his use of myths and metaphors as being of comparable value to factual data and his reliance on a view of religion as a regenerative force. His other works include *Civilization on Trial* (1948), *East to West* (1958), and *Hellenism* (1959).

Toyota Motor Corp. Largest Japanese automobile manufacturer. It began in 1933 as a division of the Toyoda Automatic Loom Works, Ltd. In the 1960s and '70s the company expanded rapidly, exporting large numbers of cars. It introduced its luxurious Lexus line in 1989. Today one of the world's largest corporations, Toyota has assembly plants and distributors worldwide, and its subsidiaries produce cars and car parts, rubber and cork materials, steel, synthetic resins, automatic looms, and cotton and woolen goods.

Toyotomi Hideyoshi \ˌhē-de-ˈyō-shē\ (1536/7–1598) Japanese warrior and statesman. He began life as a peasant but was raised to the rank of SAMURAI while a soldier for Oda Nobunaga. After Nobunaga's death, he was appointed *kampaku* (chancellor to the emperor). Having concluded an alliance with his former rival TOKUGAWA IEYASU, he became in 1590 the head of an alliance of DAIMYO that constituted a government of national unification. To stabilize society, he imposed the division of society into samurai, farmers, artisans, and tradesmen (an adaptation of ancient Chinese social divisions). With visions of empire, he made two unsuccessful attempts to invade Korea (1592, 1597). After his death, power passed to Tokugawa Ieyasu.

TQC See TOTAL QUALITY CONTROL

tracery In architecture, bars or ribs used decoratively in windows, especially the ornamental openwork in Gothic windows. In the earliest phase, two or three narrow, arched windows were placed close together under a single large arch, with the section of wall between the small and large arches pierced by a circular or four-lobed opening. The complexity of this plate tracery increased, reaching a climax in the magnificent windows of CHARTRES CATHEDRAL. After about 1220 windows began to be subdivided by mullions, or upright bars, that continued at the head of the window to branch and form the patterns of bar

Gothic tracery Rose window (1350) in the church of St. Lorenz, Nuremberg, Germany

tracery. Elaborate bar tracery soon became an important element of GOTHIC ARCHITECTURE and one of its finest achievements, as in the ROSE WINDOWS of the French RAYONNANT STYLE.

trachea \ˈtrā-kē-ə\ *or* **windpipe** Tube in the throat and upper THORACIC CAVITY through which air passes in RESPIRATION. It begins at the LARYNX and splits just above heart level into the two main bronchi, which enter the LUNGS. In adults it is about 6 in. (15 cm) long and 1 in. (2.5 cm) in diameter. Its structure—a membrane strengthened by 16–20 CARTILAGE rings open in the back, with their free ends connected by muscle bands—allows the trachea to stretch and contract in breathing. An inner mucous membrane has cilia (see CILIUM) that project inward to trap particles. Such diseases as DIPHTHERIA, SYPHILIS, TUBERCULOSIS, and TYPHOID often involve the trachea.

tracheophyte See VASCULAR PLANT

track and field *British* **athletics** Variety of sport competitions held on a running track and on the adjacent field. It is the oldest form of organized sports, having been a part of the ancient OLYMPIC GAMES from about 776 B.C. to A.D. 393. Modern events include various runs (100-m dash, MARATHON, etc.), relay races, HURDLING, STEEPLECHASE, HIGH JUMP, POLE VAULT, LONG JUMP, SHOT PUT, DISCUS THROW, HAMMER THROW, JAVELIN THROW, DECATHLON, PENTATHLON, and HEPTATHLON. Cross-country running and speed walking are usually considered adjuncts of track-and-field athletics. Events are held indoors and outdoors; some events are modified or eliminated for indoor competition.

Tractarian movement See OXFORD MOVEMENT

tractor High-power, low-speed traction vehicle. The two main types are wheeled and continuous-track. Most modern tractors are powered by internal combustion engines running on gasoline or diesel fuel. Tractors are used for pulling equipment such as plows and cultivators, for pushing implements such as bulldozers and diggers, and for operating stationary devices such as saws and winches. The first tractors grew out of the STEAM ENGINES used on farms; in 1892 an Iowa blacksmith, John Froehlich, built the first farm vehicle powered by a gasoline engine. The tractor revolutionized farming, displacing draft animals and many farm workers.

Tracy, Spencer (1900–1967) U.S. film actor. Born in Milwaukee, he first starred on Broadway in *The Last Mile* (1930) and on film in *Up the River* (1930). With his craggy features and his sincere, expert acting, he won Academy Awards for roles in *Captains Courageous* (1937) and *Boys Town* (1938); his other films include *Inherit the Wind* (1960) and *Judgment at Nuremberg* (1961). He had a long relationship with Katharine HEPBURN, with whom he costarred in nine films, including *Woman of the Year* (1942), *Adam's Rib* (1949), and *Guess Who's Coming to Dinner* (1967).

trade, balance of See BALANCE OF TRADE

Trade, Board of Organized market for the exchange of commodity contracts. The first grain-futures exchange in the U.S. was organized in Chicago in 1848. The Board of Trade began as a voluntary association of prominent Chicago grain merchants. Initially it sold grain by sample; later it introduced a system of inspection and grading to standardize the market and facilitate trading. By 1858 the trading floor was limited to members with seats on the exchange. It is today the world's largest commodity exchange.

trade agreement Any contractual arrangement between states concerning their trade relations. Trade agreements may be bilateral or multilateral, that is, between two states or more than two. For most countries international trade is regulated by unilateral barriers, including TARIFFS, nontariff barriers, and government prohibitions. Trade agreements aim to reduce such barriers in order to increase trade. Reciprocity is a necessary feature of trade agreements, since no state would sign an agreement unless it expected to gain at least as much as it lost. Another common feature is a most-favored-nation clause, which provides against the possibility that one of the parties to the agreement will later offer lower tariffs to another country. Agreements often provide for "national treatment of nontariff restrictions" to prohibit discriminatory regulations, selective excise taxes, quotas, and special licensing requirements. General multilateral agreements are sometimes easier to reach than separate bilateral agreements, since the gains to efficient producers from worldwide tariff reductions are large enough to warrant substantial concessions. The 1947 General Agreement on Tariffs and Trade (GATT) reduced world tariff levels and greatly expanded world trade. See also N. AMERICAN FREE TRADE AGREEMENT, WORLD TRADE ORGANIZATION.

trade fair *or* **trade show** Temporary market organized to promote trade, where buyers and sellers gather to transact business. Trade fairs are organized at regular intervals, generally at the same location and time of year. They are especially common in Europe and Asia. Though they may feature general exhibits of goods and merchandise, fairs confined to a single industry or even to a specialized segment of an industry have become increasingly common.

trademark Mark used by a manufacturer or merchant to identify the origin or ownership of goods and distinguish them from others. Trademarks may be words or groups of words, letters, numerals, devices, names, the shape or other presentation of products or their packages, or combinations of colors. A trademark (indicated by ™ or, when registered, by the symbol ®) is considered the property of the holder and is protected by law from unauthorized use by others. It need not be registered with the U.S. Patent and Trademark Office or a state bureau, though registration often proves legally advantageous. See also COPYRIGHT.

Trafalgar \trə-ˈfal-gər\, **Battle of** (Oct. 21, 1805) Naval engagement in the NAPOLEONIC WARS that established British naval supremacy in Europe. It was fought west of Cape Trafalgar, Spain, between a Franco-Spanish fleet of 33 ships and a British fleet of 27 ships under Horatio NELSON. The

T U V

French ships formed a single line and were attacked by the English at two points. After sending the famous signal "England expects that every man will do his duty," Nelson broke through the center and in the pell-mell battle captured 20 ships. Near the end of the battle, Nelson was mortally wounded by a sniper. No British ships were lost and NAPOLEON abandoned his plan to invade England.

tragedy Drama of a serious and dignified character that typically describes the development of a conflict between the protagonist and a superior force (such as destiny, circumstance, or society) and reaches a sorrowful or disastrous conclusion. Tragedy of a high order has been created in three periods and locales, each with a characteristic emphasis and style: Attica, in Greece, in the 5th cent. B.C.; Elizabethan and Jacobean England (1558–1625); and 17th-cent. France. See also COMEDY.

Traherne \trə-'hərn\, **Thomas** (1637–1674) English mystical poet and religious writer. Most of his works were unknown for centuries. The discovery in 1896 in a London street bookstall of the manuscripts of *Poetical Works* (1903) and the prose *Centuries of Meditations* (1908) created a literary sensation. Later the manuscript of *Poems of Felicity* (1910) was discovered in the British Museum. His poetry is overshadowed by his vivid prose.

Trail of Tears Forced migration of the CHEROKEE Indians in 1838–39. In 1835, when gold was discovered on Cherokee land in Georgia, a small minority of Cherokee ceded all tribal land east of the Mississippi for $5 million. The U.S. Supreme Court invalidated the deal, but the ruling was ignored by state officials, and Pres. Andrew JACKSON refused to enforce it. The subsequent eviction and 116-day forced march of thousands of Cherokee to Oklahoma was badly mismanaged, and inadequate food supply, frigid weather, and the cruelty of escorting troops led to the death of about 4,000 Cherokees.

Trajan \'trā-jən\ *in full* Caesar Nerva Traianus Germanicus *orig.* Marcus Ulpius Traianus (A.D. 53–117) Roman emperor (98–117), the first born outside Italy. A military commander who was named CONSUL in 91, he was adopted by NERVA as his successor in 97. After Nerva's death in 98, he deified the former emperor and named himself Jupiter's representative on earth. He weakened the PRAETORIAN GUARD at Rome, gave the SENATE new authority, supported the poor with government welfare, and built public works, including a forum with Trajan's Column, a

Trajan

structure commemorating his Dacian Wars. He added Dacia, Mesopotamia, and Parthia to the empire.

trampoline Resilient sheet or web (often of nylon) supported by springs in a metal frame and used as a springboard and landing area in tumbling. Trampolining is an individual sport of acrobatic movements performed after rebounding into the air from the trampoline. A world championship was established in 1964; competitors are scored on difficulty, execution, and form.

tranquilizer DRUG used to reduce anxiety, fear, tension, agitation, and related disturbed mental states. Major tranquilizers (antipsychotic agents, or neuroleptics) are used to treat SCHIZOPHRENIA and other PSYCHOSES. They are thought to block the activity of DOPAMINE in the brain. Minor tranquilizers (antianxiety agents, or anxiolytics) are usually benzodiazepines, including diazepam (Valium) and chlordiazepoxide (Librium). They reduce both physical and psychological effects of anxiety, fear, and stress by enhancing the action of the NEUROTRANSMITTER gamma-aminobutyric acid (GABA).

Trans-Alaska Pipeline *or* **Alaska Pipeline** Oil pipeline running 800 mi (1,300 km) north–south across Alaska. Completed in 1977, it transports crude oil from the oil fields of PRUDHOE BAY on the Arctic Ocean to an ice-free port at Valdez. To avoid thawing the adjacent PERMAFROST, about half of the line is elevated.

Trans-Canada Highway World's longest national road, extending east-west for 4,860 mi (7,821 km) between Victoria, British Columbia, and St. John's, Newfoundland. Completed in 1965, it links many major Canadian cities and provides access to important national and provincial parks.

transcendental argument In philosophy, a form of argument that is supposed to proceed from a fact to the necessary conditions of its possibility. A transcendental argument is simply a form of deduction, with the typical pattern: Only if p then q; q is true; therefore, p is true. The interest and the difficulty usually reside in the setting up of the major premises. For example, Immanuel KANT tried to prove the principle of causality by showing that it is a necessary condition of the possibility of making empirically verifiable statements in natural science.

Transcendentalism Movement of 19th-cent. New England philosophers and writers who were loosely bound together by an idealistic belief in the essential unity of all creation, the innate goodness of humankind, and the supremacy of vision over logic and experience for the revelation of the deepest truths. Part of ROMANTICISM, it developed around Concord, Mass., attracting such individualistic figures as R. W. EMERSON, H. D. THOREAU, Margaret FULLER, and Bronson ALCOTT. Transcendentalist writers represent the first flowering of American artistic genius and introduced the AMERICAN RENAISSANCE in literature.

Transcendental Meditation (TM) Spiritual development technique developed by MAHARISHI MAHESH YOGI, a former Hindu ascetic. It became popular in the West in the 1960s. It is based on specific MEDITATION techniques, and the perspective behind it has roots in VEDANTA. Practice entails the mental repetition of a MANTRA in order to still the mind and experience a deeper level of consciousness; the result is deep relaxation, which can lead to inner joy, vitality, and creativity.

transcendental number Number that is not algebraic, in the sense that it is not the solution of an ALGEBRAIC EQUATION with rational-number coefficients. The numbers e (the base of natural LOGARITHMS, about 2.718) and π (see PI), as well as any algebraic number raised to the power of an IRRATIONAL NUMBER, are transcendental numbers.

transducer Device that converts one form of ENERGY to another. A MICROPHONE is an acoustic transducer, converting sound waves into electrical signals. Different types of transducers act on heat, radiation, sound, strain, vibrations, pressure, and acceleration; they may emit mechanical, electrical, pneumatic, or hydraulic signals. Examples include LOUDSPEAKERS, PHOTOCELLS, THERMOCOUPLES, and TRANSFORMERS.

transformation In mathematics, a rule for changing a geometric figure or algebraic expression into another, usually accompanied by a rule for transforming it back. In geometry and TOPOLOGY, a transformation (e.g., flipping, rotating, or stretching) moves each point in a figure or graph to another position. A graph also undergoes a transformation when its COORDINATE SYSTEM is changed. In analysis, a transformation is a procedure that changes one function into another. Of special interest are transformations forming a group, in which any two transformations applied successively produce the same result as another transformation in the group and each transformation has an inverse transformation (which undoes it) in the group. See also GROUP THEORY.

transformer Device that transfers electric energy from one ALTERNATING-CURRENT CIRCUIT to one or more other circuits, either increasing (stepping up) or reducing (stepping down) the voltage. Uses include reducing the line voltage to operate low-voltage devices (e.g., doorbells) and raising the voltage from electric GENERATORS so that electric power can be transmitted over long distances. Transformers act through ELECTROMAGNETIC INDUCTION; current in the primary coil induces current in the secondary coil. The secondary voltage is calculated by multiplying the primary voltage by the ratio of the number of turns in the secondary coil to that in the primary.

transfusion See BLOOD TRANSFUSION

transistor SOLID-STATE SEMICONDUCTOR device for amplifying, controlling, and generating electrical signals. Invented at Bell Labs (1947) by John BARDEEN, Walter Brattain (1902–1987), and William SHOCKLEY, it displaced the VACUUM TUBE in many applications. Transistors consist of layers of different semiconductors produced by addition of impurities (such as arsenic or boron) to SILICON. These impurities affect the way electric current moves through the silicon. Transistors were pivotal in the advancement of electronics because of their small size, low power requirements, low heat generation, modest cost, reliability, and speed of operation. Single transistors were superseded by INTEGRATED CIRCUITS in the 1960s and '70s; present-day COMPUTER CHIPS contain millions of transistors.

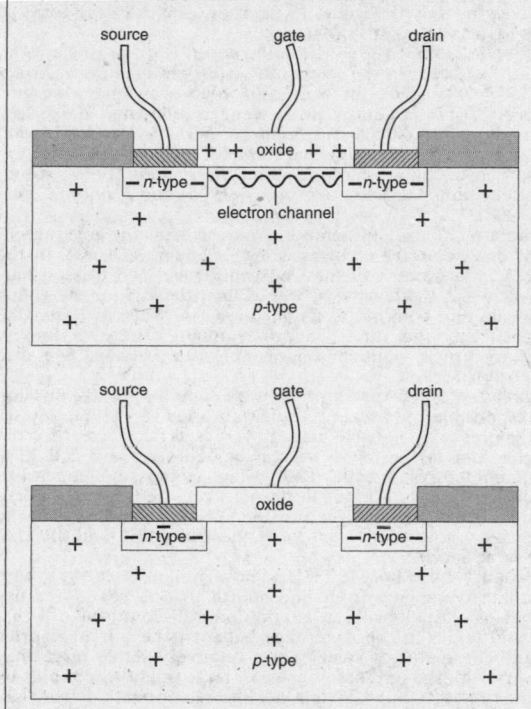

Transistor A transistor is a sandwich of dissimilar semiconductors to which are attached three electrodes. Because of the unique electrical properties that occur at p-n junctions, current between two of the electrodes may be turned on or off like a switch by varying the voltage applied to the third electrode. In the metal-oxide semiconductor field-effect transistor (MOSFET) shown, current flows between the source and drain electrodes and is regulated by the gate electrode. The n-type semiconductor regions have an excess of electrons, but are separated from each other by the p-type region, which has an excess of positive charge, called "holes." If a positive voltage is applied to the gate (top), electrons in the p-region will be attracted to the area under the oxide, forming a channel of negative charge between the source and drain. If a positive voltage is then applied to the drain, a current of electrons flows through the device and the transistor is on. If the gate voltage is removed (bottom), the electron channel is broken and the transistor is off.

transition element Any chemical ELEMENT with valence ELECTRONS in two shells instead of only one. This structure gives them their outstanding ability to form complex IONS, or coordination compounds, with a central atom or ion surrounded by LIGANDS in a regular arrangement. The elements in the PERIODIC TABLE from scandium to COPPER (atomic numbers 21–29), yttrium to SILVER (39–47), and lanthanum to GOLD (57–79, including the LANTHANIDE series) are frequently designated the three main transition series. (Those in the ACTINIDE series and beyond, 89–111, also qualify.) All are METALS, many of major economic or industrial importance (e.g., IRON, NICKEL, TITANIUM). Most are dense, hard, and brittle, conduct heat and electricity well, have high melting points, and form ALLOYS with each other and other metals. They form compounds (of various VALENCES), many of which are colored and paramagnetic (see PARAMAGNETISM) and often act as CATALYSTS. See also BONDING.

transitive law Property of relationship that states that if A is in a given relation to B and B is in the same relation to C, then A is also in that relation to C. Equality, for example, is a transitive relation (if A = B and B = C, then A = C).

Transkei \'trans-ˈkā, 'trans-ˈkī\ administrative region, Republic of S. Africa. It borders on the Indian Ocean and Lesotho. It was created by S. Africa in 1959 as the first Bantu homeland, a non-independent black state designated (together with CISKEI) for the XHOSA. It was made a nominally independent republic in 1976, and all black Africans with language ties to Transkei lost their S. African citizenship and became citizens of the new country, which, however, existed only as an element of the APARTHEID system. The region was reincorporated into S. Africa in 1994.

transmigration of souls See REINCARNATION

transmission System in an engine that transmits power generated by the engine to the point where it is to be used. Most mechanical transmissions function as rotary speed changers; the ratio of the output speed to the input speed may be either constant (as in a gearbox) or variable. On variable-speed transmissions, the speeds may be variable in individual steps (as on an automobile) or continuously variable. Step-variable transmissions usually use either GEARS or chains; stepless transmissions use belts, chains, or rolling-contact bodies.

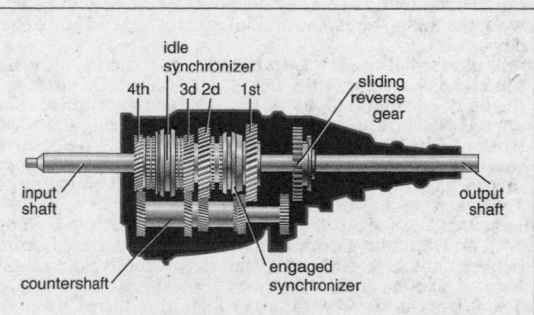

Transmission A four-speed manual transmission. Power from the rotating input shaft turns the countershaft (or layshaft), which meshes with all four gears on the output shaft. Which gear drives the output shaft is determined by the positions of the synchronizer assemblies, which are controlled by the gearshift stick (here, first gear is engaged). The unengaged gears simply revolve around the output shaft without transmitting power.

transpiration Loss of water from a plant, mainly through the stomata (leaf pores). Darkness, internal water deficit, and extremes of temperature tend to close stomata and decrease transpiration; illumination, ample water supply, and optimum temperature cause stomata to open and increase transpiration. Since stomatal openings are necessary for the exchange of gases, transpiration is considered by some to be merely an unavoidable phenomenon that accompanies the real functions of the stomata.

transplant *or* **graft** Partial or complete organ or other body part removed from one site and attached at another. It may come from the same or a different person or an animal. One from the same person (e.g., a skin graft) is not rejected.

Transplants from another person or, especially, an animal are rejected unless they are unusually compatible or have no blood vessels (e.g., the cornea), or if the recipient's immune reaction is suppressed by lifelong drug treatment (see IMMUNOSUPPRESSION). Transplanted tissues must match more closely than BLOOD TRANSFUSIONS. Rejection matters less in skin grafts, which may need to last only weeks, and bone grafts, whose structure remains after the cells die. In BONE-MARROW transplants, the donor's marrow cells may attack the recipient's tissues, often fatally. Lung transplants have greater chance of success as part of a heart-and-lung transplant. See also HEART TRANSPLANT, KIDNEY TRANSPLANT.

Transportation, U.S. Department of Federal executive agency responsible for programs and policies relating to transportation. Established in 1966, it includes the Federal Aviation Administration, Federal Highway Administration, Federal Railroad Administration, U.S. COAST GUARD, and National Highway Traffic Safety Administration.

transsexualism Self-identification with one sex by a person who has the external genitalia and secondary sexual characteristics of the other. Early in life, such a person adopts the behavior characteristic of the opposite sex. Surgery and hormone therapy now allow permanent sex change. The male-to-female operation is more common. The penis and testes are removed and an artificial vagina created; breasts are created with implants or female sex hormones. Female transsexuals may undergo mastectomy and hormone treatments to produce male secondary sexual characteristics, but attempts to create an artificial penis have not been satisfactory.

Trans-Siberian Railroad Longest single rail system in Russia, running from Moscow to Vladivostok, a distance of 5,778 mi (9,198 km). Conceived by Czar ALEXANDER III, its construction began in 1891. It was completed in 1904; a parallel section skirting Manchuria was completed in 1916. The railroad opened large areas of Siberia to settlement and industrialization by means of spur lines linking outlying areas with the main line. The complete trip takes about eight days.

transubstantiation In CHRISTIANITY, the change by which the bread and wine of the EUCHARIST become in substance the body and blood of JESUS, though their appearance is not altered. This transformation is thought to bring the literal truth of Christ's presence to the participants. The doctrine was first elaborated by theologians in the 13th cent. and was incorporated into documents of the Council of TRENT. In 1965 PAUL VI reaffirmed the dogma.

Transvaal \trans-ˈväl\ *formerly (1856–77, 1881–1902)* **South African Republic** Former province, NE S. Africa. Located between the LIMPOPO and Vaal rivers, the region was inhabited around 1800 chiefly by various BANTU PEOPLES. The Boers (AFRIKANERS) began migrating there during the GREAT TREK of the 1830s. They established the short-lived S. African Republic in 1856. Discoveries of diamonds and gold deposits (1868–74) heightened British interest, and the British annexed the republic in 1877. A Boer rebellion restored it in 1881. In 1895 L. S. JAMESON attempted to incite new foreign settlers to overthrow the Boer government. In 1899 Transvaal joined with ORANGE FREE STATE against Britain in the S. AFRICAN (BOER) WAR. In 1902, following the British victory, it became a crown colony. It joined the Union of S. Africa in 1910. In 1994 it was split into four provinces. The region is extremely rich in mineral and agricultural resources.

Trans World Airlines, Inc. (TWA) Major U.S. airline. Formed in 1930 as Transcontinental & Western Air, Inc., the company established the first coast-to-coast service that same year. In 1946 TWA began flights between New York and Paris, and it expanded by the 1950s to Europe, the Middle East, Africa, and Asia. It adopted its present name in 1950. Howard HUGHES was its principal stockholder and guiding genius from 1939 to 1960–61. Financially troubled since the 1980s, TWA twice landed in bankruptcy court in the 1990s. It was acquired by American Airlines in 2001.

Transylvania Historic region, NW and central Romania. It consists of a plateau surrounded by the CARPATHIAN MTNS. and the Transylvanian Alps. It was included in the Roman province of DACIA in the 2nd cent. A.D. The MAGYARS (Hungarians) conquered the area in the 9th cent. When Hungary was divided between the HABSBURGS and the Turks in the 16th cent., Transylvania became an autonomous principality within the Ottoman empire. When Austria-Hungary was defeated in World War I, the Romanians of Transylvania proclaimed the land united with Romania. Hungary regained the N portion during World War II, but the entire region was ceded to Romania in 1947.

travertine \ˈtra-vər-ˌtēn\ Dense, banded rock composed of calcium carbonate. Formed by rapid evaporation of river and spring waters, especially HOT SPRINGS, it is a variety of LIMESTONE that has a light color and takes a good polish. It is often used for walls and interior decorations in public buildings and as a paving stone. Travertine is mined extensively in Italy. It occurs in limestone caves in the form of STALACTITES AND STALAGMITES.

Travolta, John (b.1954) U.S. film actor. Born in Englewood, N.J., he acted in the television series *Welcome Back, Kotter* (1975–78), where his cleft chin, blue eyes, and wide grin brought him an enthusiastic teenage following. He starred in the wildly successful *Saturday Night Fever* (1977), and later in *Grease* (1978) and *Urban Cowboy* (1980). He returned to major stardom with *Pulp Fiction* (1994); subsequent films included *Get Shorty* (1995) and *Primary Colors* (1998).

treason Offense of attempting to overthrow the government of one's country or of assisting its enemies in war. In the U.S., the framers of the Constitution defined treason narrowly—as the levying of war against the U.S. or the giving of aid and comfort to its enemies—in order to lessen the possibility that those in power might falsely or loosely charge their political opponents with treason. See also SEDITION.

Treasury, U.S. Department of the Federal executive division responsible for fiscal policy. Established in 1789, it advises the president on fiscal matters, serves as fiscal agent for the government, performs certain law-enforcement activities, manufactures currency and postage stamps, and supervises national banks. Among its agencies are the Bureau of Alcohol, Tobacco and Firearms, the U.S. Customs Service, the INTERNAL REVENUE SERVICE, the U.S. Mint, and the U.S. Secret Service.

treasury bill Short-term U.S. government SECURITY with maturity ranging from one month to one year. Treasury bills are usually sold at auction on a discount basis with a yield equal to the difference between the purchase price and the maturity value. Their relatively stable price may vary with the purchase or sale of large quantities of bills by the CENTRAL BANK. Their yield rate is normally lower than that of longer-term securities. First used extensively during World War I, treasury bills became a permanent element in the NATIONAL DEBT, attractive to the government for their flexibility and relatively low interest. The minimum order for treasury bills is now $1,000.

treaty Written instrument binding two or more states under INTERNATIONAL LAW. The term is generally reserved for important agreements, usually requiring, in addition to the signatures of authorized persons, ratification by the governments involved. A treaty usually contains an enumeration of the issues agreed on and clauses that discuss its ratification procedures, lifespan, and terms for termination. Treaties may be political, commercial, constitutional, or administrative, or they may relate to criminal and civil justice or codify international law.

Treblinka \tre-ˈbliŋ-kä\ German Nazi CONCENTRATION camp. Located near the village of Treblinka, Poland, it opened in 1941 as a forced-labor camp. A larger and ultrasecret second camp a mile away, called T.II, opened in 1942 as an extermination camp for Jews. Victims were stripped and marched into "bathhouses," where they were gassed with carbon monoxide from ceiling pipes. Ukrainian guards and up to 1,500 Jewish prisoner-workers performed the executions, estimated at 700,000–900,000. The T.II camp was closed in October 1943, the labor camp in July 1944.

tree Woody perennial plant. Most trees have a single self-supporting trunk containing woody tissues, and in most species the trunk produces branches. Trees provide many valuable products, especially WOOD, one of the world's chief building materials, and wood pulp, used in papermaking. Wood is also a major fuel source. Trees also supply edible FRUITS and NUTS. They help clean the air by taking in carbon dioxide and releasing oxygen during PHOTOSYNTHESIS. Their root systems help conserve water and prevent floods and soil erosion. Trees provide homes and food for a wide variety of animals. The tallest trees are the Pacific coast REDWOODS; the oldest are the bristlecone pines, some of which are over 4,000 years old. See also CONIFER, DECIDUOUS tree, EVERGREEN, FOREST.

Trek, Great See GREAT TREK

trematode See FLUKE

trench warfare Warfare in which the opposing sides attack, counterattack, and defend from sets of trenches dug into the ground. It was developed by Sébastien de VAUBAN in the 17th cent. for laying siege to fortresses. Its defensive use was established during the American Civil War. It reached its highest development in World War I. A typical construction was a series of two to four parallel trenches, dug in a zigzag, sandbagged, and floored with wooden planks. A perpendicular trench connected them. The first row was fronted by barbed wire and contained machine-gun emplacements. The rear trenches housed most of the troops. Increased use of tanks marked the end of trench warfare.

Trent, Council of (1545–63) 19th ecumenical council of the Roman Catholic church, which made sweeping reforms and laid down dogma clarifying nearly all doctrines contested by the Protestants. Convened by Pope PAUL III at Trento in N Italy, it revitalized ROMAN CATHOLICISM in many parts of Europe. In its first period (1545–47) it accepted the NICENE CREED as the basis of Catholic faith, fixed the canon of the OLD and NEW TESTAMENTS, set the number of SACRAMENTS at seven, and defined the nature and consequences of ORIGINAL SIN; it also ruled against Martin LUTHER's doctrine of justification by faith. In its second period (1551–52) it confirmed the doctrine of TRANSUBSTANTIATION. In the final period (1562–63) it defined the MASS as a true sacrifice. By the end of the 16th cent., the church had reclaimed many of its European followers.

Trent Affair (1861) Incident in the AMERICAN CIVIL WAR involving freedom of the seas. The Union frigate *San Jacinto* stopped the neutral British steamer *Trent* to seize two Confederate commissioners who were en route to England and France to seek support for the Confederacy. Protests in Britain denounced the action and called for war. William SEWARD admitted the Union's error in not bringing the ship into a U.S. port for adjudication, and the two men were soon released.

Trent Canal Canal, SE Ontario, linking Lake HURON with Lake ONTARIO. It extends from Georgian Bay up the Severn River to Lake Simcoe, connects several lakes to Rice Lake, and passes down the Trent River to Lake Ontario. Its 242-mi (387-km) main course includes 33 mi (53 km) of manmade channels and 42 locks. Construction began in 1833. Once valued by the lumber trade, it is now a tourist attraction.

Trentino–Alto adige \tren-ˈtē-nō-ˌäl-tō-ˈä-dē-jā\ *formerly (until 1947)* **Venezia Tridentina** Autonomous region (pop., 1996 est.: 913,000), NE Italy. Its capital is TRENTO. A mountainous area, it has some of the highest peaks in Europe. Historically it included the medieval ecclesiastical principalities of Trento and Bressanone. Austria annexed it in 1815; it was ceded to Italy at the end of World War I. The population is a mix of German and Italian speakers; the regional parliament alternates German-speaking and Italian-speaking chairmen. The region grows grain and grapes, raises cattle, and mines zinc and lead. Tourism is a major industry.

Trento *English* **Trent** *ancient* Tridentum. City (pop., 1998 est.: 104,000), capital of TRENTINO–ALTO ADIGE region, N Italy, on the ADIGE RIVER. A Roman colony on the road to the Brenner Pass in the ALPS, in the Christian era it came under the Ostrogoths, Lombards, and Franks. It was the site of the Council of TRENT (1545–63). Part of the Napoleonic kingdom of Italy in the early 19th cent., it passed to Austria in 1814 and to Italy in 1918.

Trenton City (pop., 2000: 85,000), capital of New Jersey. It was settled about 1679 by English Quakers. On Christmas night, 1776, George WASHINGTON led his army across the ice-choked Delaware River to attack Hessian troops quartered at Trenton (see battles of TRENTON AND PRINCETON). It served as temporary capital of the U.S. in 1784 and 1799, and was made the state capital in 1790. A canal and railroad line in the 1830s spurred manufacturing, and Trenton remains an industrial city.

Trenton and Princeton, Battles of (1776–77) Engagements in the AMERICAN REVOLUTION. Defeats in New York forced the army under George WASHINGTON to retreat through New Jersey into Pennsylvania. On Dec. 25, 1776, he led a force of 6,000 across the ice-filled Delaware River to surprise the 1,400-man British-Hessian force at Trenton, capturing 900 men. A British force of 7,000 under Charles CORNWALLIS arrived to force the American army into retreat. At night Washington led his men around the British to defeat an outpost at Princeton, causing Cornwallis to retreat and enabling Washington to lead his troops into winter quarters near Morristown. The victories restored American morale.

Trevelyan \tri-ˈvel-yən\, **G(eorge) M(acauley)** (1876–1962) English historian. He is known for books accessible to general readers that often reflect the Whig tradition in English thought and a keen interest in the Anglo-Saxon element in the English constitution. They include *Under Queen Anne* (3 vols., 1930–34), *British History in the Nineteenth Century (1782–1901)* (1922), *History of England* (1926), and *English Social History* (1942).

Trevithick \trə-ˈvi-thik\, **Richard** (1771–1833) British inventor. An engineer for several ore mines in Cornwall, in 1797 he developed a small, light high-pressure steam engine to replace the large, low-pressure mine engines then used for hoisting ore. In 1801 he built the first steam carriage, which he later drove in London. In 1803 he built the first steam railway LOCOMOTIVE for an ironworks in Wales. He abandoned his locomotive projects in 1808 because the iron rails were too fragile to carry their weight. He adapted his engine to produce the first steam dredger in 1806. In 1816 he traveled to Peru to deliver engines to silver mines, hoping to become wealthy, but returned in 1827 penniless.

Trevor, William *orig.* William Trevor Cox (b.1928) Irish-English writer. His works focus largely on the psychology of eccentrics, outcasts, and the elderly. His novels include *The Old Boys* (1964), *Other People's Worlds* (1980) and *Felicia's Journey* (1994). He is best known for his many acclaimed short stories.

Triad Term used variously for secret societies in QING-DYNASTY China, for modern Chinese crime gangs, and for crime gangs of other Asian nationals. A secret society with the name Triad started operating in the early 19th cent. in S China, where it took root and spread. In the 1850s Triad rebellions threatened Shanghai and Xiamen (Amoy) and contributed to the revolution of 1911. Chinese secret societies have in common sworn brotherhood, strict rules, a family relationship among members, a hierarchy of functions, and hereditary membership.

triage \ˈtrē-ˌäzh, trē-ˈäzh\ Division of patients for priority of care, usually into three categories: those who will not survive even with treatment; those who will survive without treatment; and those whose survival depends on treatment. If triage is applied, the treatment of patients requiring it is not delayed by useless or unnecessary treatment of those in the other groups. Triage originated in military medicine, when limited resources faced many wounded soldiers. It is used in civilian settings during disasters or epidemics, and in emergency rooms.

trial In law, a judicial examination of issues of fact or law for the purpose of determining the rights of the parties involved. Attorneys for the plaintiff and the defendant make opening statements to a judge or jury, then the attorney for the plaintiff calls witnesses, whom the defense attorney may cross-examine. Unless the case is then dismissed for lack of sufficient evidence, the defense attorney next takes a turn calling witnesses, whom the plaintiff's attorney cross-examines. Both sides make closing arguments. In a trial before a jury, the judge instructs the jury on the applicable laws, and the jury retires to reach a verdict. If the defendant is found guilty, the judge then hands down a sentence.

TUV

trial by ordeal See ORDEAL

triangle Geometric figure with three sides and three angles. Each two sides meet at a point called a vertex, and the three angles sum to 180°. A triangle with one 90° (right) angle is a right triangle. A triangle with all sides (and thus all angles) equal is equilateral, one with two sides equal is isosceles, and one with no two sides equal is scalene. Triangles are particularly useful in surveying, astronomy, and navigation. See also TRIGONOMETRY.

Triangle Shirtwaist Co. fire (Mar. 25, 1911) Disaster that led to the enactment of many safety and labor laws. The fire in a New York City garment factory resulted in the deaths of 146 people, mostly young immigrant women. The sweatshop had few fire escapes and its doors were locked to prevent theft, forcing panicked workers to leap from upperfloor windows. Public outcry led to new fire codes and child-labor laws and greater union influence.

Triassic period \trī-'a-sik\ Interval of geologic time, 248–208 million years ago, in the MESOZOIC ERA. Many new terrestrial and marine vertebrates emerged. The seas became inhabited by large marine reptiles. On land, ancestral forms of various modern amphibians arose, as did reptiles such as turtles and crocodilians. By the late Triassic, ARCHOSAURS were dominant, and the first true mammals, small shrewlike omnivores, evolved. Seed ferns probably dominated the flora of S GONDWANA, and GYMNOSPERMS, including conifers, were common throughout much of PANGAEA. See table at GEOLOGIC TIME.

triathlon Athletic long-distance race in three phases. The usual event includes an ocean swim of 3.8 km (2.4 mi), a bicycle tour of 180 km (112 mi), and a marathon run of 42.2 km (26.2 mi).

tribe Social group defined by traditions of common DESCENT and having temporary or permanent political integration above the FAMILY and clan levels as well as a shared language, CULTURE, and IDEOLOGY. Tribes are usually composed of a number of smaller local communities (e.g., bands or villages) and may be combined into larger clusters, sometimes called nations. Members typically share a tribal name and a contiguous territory; they work together in such joint endeavors as trade, agriculture, house construction, warfare, and ceremonial activities.

tribune In ancient Rome, any of various military and civil officials. Military tribunes were originally infantry commanders. In the early republic some were appointed by CONSULS, others elected by the people. During the Roman empire (from 27 B.C.), the emperor nominated military tribunes, the office of which was considered preliminary to a senatorial or equestrian career (see EQUES). Of the civil tribunes, the most important were the tribunes of the plebs (see PLEBEIAN), who were elected in the plebeian assembly. By 450 B.C. there were 10 plebeian tribunes, who had the right to intervene in cases of unjust acts of consuls or magistrates. Under the empire, the plebeian tribunes' power passed to the emperor.

tricarboxylic acid cycle \ˌtrī-ˌkär-bäk-'sil-ik\ *or* **Krebs cycle** *or* **citric-acid cycle** Final stage of the chemical processes by which living cells obtain energy from foodstuffs. Described by Hans KREBS in 1937, the cycle has been shown in animals, plants, microorganisms, and fungi, and is thus a feature of cell chemistry shared by all types of life. It is a complex series of reactions beginning and ending with the compound oxaloacetate. In addition to re-forming oxaloacetate, the cycle produces CARBON DIOXIDE and ATP. The enzymes that catalyze each step are located in mitochondria (see MITOCHONDRION) in animals, in CHLOROPLASTS in plants, and in the cell MEMBRANE in microorganisms.

triceratops \trī-'ser-ə-ˌtäps\ Any member of the ORNITHISCHIAN genus *Triceratops*, large plant-eating DINOSAURS of the Late CRETACEOUS PERIOD (98–65 million years ago). Triceratopses had a very long skull (some more than 6 ft, or 2 m, long); a large bony frill about the neck; a beaklike mouth; and two pointed horns, more than 3 ft (1 m) long, above the eyes. Adults weighed 4–5 tons (3.6–4.5 metric tons) and grew up to 30 ft (9 m) long.

trichinosis \ˌtri-kə-'nō-səs\ Disorder caused by the roundworm trichina, commonly acquired from undercooked infested PORK. Larval worms invade the small intestine, ma-

turing within a week. Fertilized females deposit new larvae, which are carried by the blood, notably to the muscles, where they encapsulate and may remain alive for years. Though trichinosis usually eventually subsides, it may be fatal if the heart and brain are involved. In the U.S. the incidence detected at autopsy is perhaps 15–20%. Few infected persons have sufficient parasites to produce symptoms. Drugs can relieve symptoms and destroy parasites in the intestine. There is no practical way to detect trichinous pork; the surest safeguard remains thorough cooking.

trichomonad \ˌtri-kə-'mō-ˌnad\ Any PROTOZOAN of the zooflagellate order Trichomonadida. Trichomonads have three to six flagella, and may have one or multiple nuclei. Most inhabit the digestive systems of animals. Three species occur in humans.

trickster tale In oral traditions worldwide, a story of deceit, magic, and violence perpetrated by a mythical animal-human (trickster). The trickster-hero is both creator god and innocent fool, evil destroyer and childlike prankster. Coyote is the trickster of tales from American Indian peoples in California and the Southwest. In the Pacific Northwest, the trickster is Raven. Many African peoples also have tales about tricksters (hare, spider, tortoise, etc.), which slaves brought to the New World. Tales involving the trickster Br'er Rabbit were given literary form by Joel Chandler HARRIS.

Trident missile U.S.-made SUBMARINE-launched ballistic missile. It succeeded the Poseidon and Polaris missiles. Their accuracy made Tridents a threat to missile silos in the former Soviet Union. Their range allows the submarines that carry them to patrol widely in the Atlantic and Pacific oceans, making detection extremely difficult.

Trieste *ancient* Tergeste. Seaport city (pop., 1998 est.: 220,000), capital of the FRIULI–VENEZIA GIULIA region, NE Italy. It lies at the head of the ADRIATIC SEA. It placed itself in 1382 under HABSBURG protection and became the prosperous main port of the Austro-Hungarian empire. After World War I it was ceded to Italy. Occupied by Germany in World War II, it was seized by Yugoslavia in 1945. Returned to Italy in 1954, it became the regional capital in 1963.

triggerfish Any of about 30 species (family Balistidae) of tropical shallow-water marine fishes. Triggerfishes are deep-bodied, usually colorful fishes with large scales, highset eyes, and three dorsal-fin spines. When the fish is threatened, it darts into a coral crevice and erects its large and strong first spine, which it locks in place by the second (the "trigger"); when the trigger is later withdrawn, the first snaps back down. The largest grow to 2 ft (60 cm) long.

triglyceride \trī-'gli-sə-ˌrīd\ Any of an important class of naturally occurring LIPIDS. They are ESTERS in which three molecules of FATTY ACIDS (all the same, or different kinds) are linked to GLYCEROL The types of triglycerides in animals vary with the species and the fats in their food. In mammals they are stored in ADIPOSE TISSUE until needed. Many vegetable triglycerides (OILS) are liquid at room temperature and tend to contain a greater variety of fatty acids. ALKALI breaks triglycerides down into glycerol and three molecules of SOAP (saponification).

trigonometric function \ˌtri-gə-nə-'me-trik\ In mathematics, one of six functions (sine, cosine, tangent, cotangent, secant, and cosecant) that represent ratios of sides of right TRIANGLES. They are also known as the circular functions, since their values can be defined as ratios of the x and y coordinates (see COORDINATE SYSTEM) of points on a circle of radius 1 that correspond to ANGLES in standard positions. Such values have been tabulated and programmed into scientific calculators and computers. This allows TRIGONOMETRY to be easily applied to surveying, engineering, and navigation problems in which one of a right triangle's acute angles and the length of a side are known and the lengths of the other sides are to be found. The functions' DERIVATIVES are useful for solving DIFFERENTIAL EQUATIONS.

trigonometry Mathematical discipline dealing with the relationships between the sides and ANGLES of TRIANGLES. It emerged as a rigorous discipline in the 15th cent., when the demand for accurate surveying techniques and navigational methods led to its use for the "solution" of right triangles, which can be found by using ratios in the form of the TRIGONOMETRIC FUNCTIONS.

Trilling, Lionel (1905–1975) U.S. literary critic and teacher. Born in New York City, he taught at Columbia Univ. from 1931 until his death. His collections of literary essays include *The Liberal Imagination* (1950), *The Opposing Self* (1955), and *Beyond Culture* (1965). His other works include *Freud and the Crisis of Our Culture* (1955) and the novel *The Middle of the Journey* (1947). He was perhaps the most famous American literary critic of the 1950s and '60s.

trilobite \'trī-lə-ˌbīt\ Any of a group of ovate ARTHROPODS (subphylum Trilobita) that came to dominate the seas about 540 million years ago and became extinct about 245 million years ago. Trilobites had a chitinous exoskeleton. The head, thorax, and tail were segmented; each segment bore two appendages. The forwardmost appendages were sense and feeding organs. Most species had two compound eyes, though some were eyeless. Some were predators, others were scavengers, and still others probably ate plankton. The largest may have weighed 10 lbs (4.5 kg).

trimurti \tri-'mùr-tē\ In HINDUISM, the triad of the three great gods: BRAHMA, VISHNU, and SHIVA. Scholars consider the trimurti doctrine an attempt to reconcile different monotheistic approaches with one another and with the philosophic doctrine of ultimate reality. The three gods are collapsed into a single form with three faces. Each god is in charge of an aspect of creation, with Brahma as creator, Vishnu as preserver, and Shiva as destroyer; however, some sects ascribe all aspects of creation to their deity of choice.

Trinidad and Tobago \'tri-nə-ˌdad...tə-'bā-gō\ *officially* **Republic of Trinidad and Tobago** Nation, consisting of the islands of Trinidad and Tobago, in the CARIBBEAN SEA off Venezuela. Area: 1,980 sq mi (5,128 sq km). Population (2000): 1,292,000. Capital: PORT OF SPAIN. The people are

Map of Trinidad and Tobago showing: 62°, 61°, CARIBBEAN SEA, TOBAGO, Charlotteville, Plymouth, MAIN RIDGE, Roxborough, Scarborough, 11°, VENEZUELA, Chupara Point, Mount Aripo 3,083 ft, RANGE, Galera Point, NORTHERN, VALENCIA WILDLIFE SANCTUARY, ATLANTIC OCEAN, Dragon's Mouths, Tunapuna, Arima, Arouca, Port of Spain, Caroni, Sangre Grande, Chaguanas, Couva, Mount Tamana 1,010 ft, Gulf of Paria, Couva, Navet, Rio Claro, TRINIDAD, San Fernando, Point Radix, Princes Town, Ortoire, Point Fortin, Oropouche, Siparia, Serpent's Mouth, 10°, TRINITY HILLS WILDLIFE SANCTUARY, VENEZUELA. ©1999, Encyclopædia Britannica, Inc. Inset: TRINIDAD AND TOBAGO globe, Scale 1: 2,652,000, 0 10 20 mi, 0 10 20 30 km.

mainly of E. Indian and African ancestry. Language: English (official). Religions: Roman Catholicism, Protestantism, Hinduism, Islam. Currency: Trinidad and Tobago dollar. The islands are mostly flat or rolling, with narrow belts of mountainous highlands and luxuriant rain forests. The Caroni Swamp, an important bird sanctuary on Trinidad, supports flamingo, egret, and scarlet ibis. The country has large reserves of petroleum and natural gas, as well as the world's largest supply of natural asphalt. Other industries include agriculture, fishing, and tourism. Chief crops include sugarcane, citrus fruits, cocoa, and coffee. It is a republic with two legislative houses; its chief of state is

the president, and the head of government is the prime minister. When Christopher COLUMBUS visited Trinidad in 1498, it was inhabited by the ARAWAK Indians; CARIBS inhabited Tobago. The islands were settled by the Spanish in the 16th cent. In the 17th–18th cent. African slaves were imported for plantation labor to replace the original Indian population, which had been worked to death by the Spanish. Trinidad was surrendered to the British in 1797. The British attempted to settle Tobago in 1721, but the French captured the island in 1781 and transformed it into a sugar-producing colony. The British acquired it in 1802. After slavery ended in the islands 1834–38, immigrants from India were brought in to work the plantations. Trinidad and Tobago were administratively combined in 1889. Granted limited self-government in 1925, the islands became an independent state within the COMMONWEALTH in 1962, and a republic in 1976. Political unrest was followed in 1990 by an attempted Muslim-fundamentalist coup against the government.

Trinity, Holy In Christian doctrine, the unity of the Father, Son and HOLY SPIRIT as one God in three Persons. The doctrine of the Trinity is not biblical, but was formulated in the early church to interpret the way God revealed himself: first to Israel, then in JESUS as Savior, and finally as Holy Spirit, preserver of the church. It was explicitly stated at the Council of Nicaea in A.D. 325.

Trinity College See Univ. of DUBLIN

Tripitaka \tri-'pi-tə-kə\ *Pali* **Tipitaka** Collective term for the three major divisions of the Pali canon, the canon of THERAVADA Buddhism. (The term means "Triple Basket.") It consists of the Abhidhamma Pitaka, the Sutta Pitaka, and the Vinaya Pitaka, which were transmitted orally by the SANGHA before being committed to writing about 500 years after the Buddha's death. The texts appeared in two languages, Sanskrit and Pali.

Triple Alliance, War of the See PARAGUAYAN WAR

Triple Crown In U.S. horse racing, an unofficial championship attributed to a Thoroughbred horse that in a single season wins the KENTUCKY DERBY, the PREAKNESS STAKES, and the BELMONT STAKES. First won in 1919 by Sir Barton, it has since been won 10 times, most recently by Affirmed (1978).

Tripoli \'tri-pə-lē\ *Arabic* **Tarabulus al-Sham** \tə-'rä-bə-ləs-al-'sham\ ("The Eastern Tripoli") Seaport (pop., 1994 est.: 240,000), NW Lebanon. Founded about 700 B.C., it became the capital of a federation of three city-states of PHOENICIA: SIDON, TYRE, and Arvad. It was taken by the Muslims in the mid-7th cent. A.D., and partially destroyed and rebuilt by crusaders. It was occupied by the Egyptians in the 1830s, the British in 1918, and the British and Free French in 1941. It became part of the Republic of Lebanon in 1946. It was the scene of a siege in 1983 by Palestinian rebels against Yasir ARAFAT. It is a major port with important oil storage and refining operations, and a popular beach resort.

Tripoli *Arabic* **Tarabulus al-Gharb** \tə-'rä-bə-ləs-al-'gärb\ ("The Western Tripoli") City (metro. area pop., 1995 est.: 1,682,000), capital of Libya. Located on the Mediterranean Sea, it is the nation's largest city and chief seaport. Founded by the PHOENICIANS around the 7th cent. B.C., it was one of the three cities of the region of TRIPOLITANIA. It was controlled by the Romans from the 1st cent. B.C., and later by the Byzantines. It was conquered by the Arabs in 645. Taken by the Turks in 1551, it was made a colonial capital of the Ottoman empire. It was under Italy's control 1911–43, after which it was occupied by the British until Libya's independence in 1951. Historic structures include numerous mosques and a Roman triumphal arch.

Tripolitania \tri-ˌpä-lə-'tā-nē-ə\ Historical region, N. Africa, now NW Libya. Colonized by the PHOENICIANS in the 7th cent. B.C., it was named for its three chief cities—Leptis Magna, Oea (TRIPOLI), and Sabrata. It made up the E part of Carthaginian territory by the 3rd cent. B.C. It was later part of Roman AFRICA, then ruled by successive Arab and Berber dynasties before becoming part of the Ottoman empire in 1551. As one of the BARBARY COAST states, it plundered shipping in the Mediterranean, leading to the Tripolitan War with the U.S. (1801–5). The Italians acquired the region in 1912. It was the scene of fierce fighting between

TUV

British and German forces in 1942. In 1951, with the provinces of CYRENAICA and Fezzan, it formed the independent kingdom of Libya.

trireme \\'trī-ˌrēm\\ Light, fast, and maneuverable oar-powered warship. Persia, Phoenicia, and the Greek city-states used it to vie for mastery of the Mediterranean from the Battle of SALAMIS (480 B.C.) through the end of the PELOPONNESIAN WAR (404). The Athenian trireme was about 120 ft (37 m) long and was rowed by 170 oarsmen seated in three tiers along each side. Square-rigged sails were used when the ship was not engaged in battle. Armed with a bronze-clad ram, it carried spearmen and bowmen to attack enemy crews. By the late 4th cent. B.C., it was replaced by heavier ships. See also GALLEY.

Tristan and Isolde Lovers in a medieval romance based on Celtic legend. The hero Tristan goes to Ireland to ask the hand of the princess Isolde for his uncle, King Mark of Cornwall. On their return the two mistakenly drink a love potion and fall deeply in love. After many adventures, they make peace with Mark, who marries Isolde. In Brittany Tristan marries another noble Isolde. Wounded by a poisoned arrow, he sends for the first Isolde. His jealous wife tells him she has refused to come; he dies just before she arrives, and she dies in his arms. The original poem has not survived, but it exists in many later versions. GOTTFRIED VON STRASSBURG's 13th-cent. masterpiece was the basis for Richard WAGNER's 1865 opera.

triticale \\ˌtri-tə-'kā-lē\\ WHEAT-RYE hybrid that has a high yield and rich protein content. The first cross was reported in 1875, the first fertile cross in 1888. In favorable environmental circumstances its yield equals that of wheat; under poor conditions its yield exceeds that of wheat. Its flour can be blended with wheat flour for breadmaking.

tritium \\'tri-tē-əm, 'tri-shē-əm\\ Isotope of HYDROGEN, chemical symbol written as ^{3}H or T, with atomic number 1 but ATOMIC WEIGHT approximately 3. Its nucleus contains one PROTON and two NEUTRONS. Tritium is radioactive (see RADIOACTIVITY), with a half-life of 12.32 years. Its occurrence in natural water at 10^{-18} the amount of ordinary hydrogen is probably due to the action of COSMIC RAYS. Some tritium is used in self-luminous phosphors and dials and as a radioactive tracer in chemical and biochemical studies. See also DEUTERIUM, HEAVY WATER, NUCLEAR FUSION, NUCLEAR WEAPON.

Triton \\'trī-tᵊn\\ In GREEK MYTHOLOGY, a merman and a demigod of the sea. He was the son of POSEIDON and Amphitrite. He was represented as human to the waist, with the tail of a fish, and he had a spiral conch shell that he blew either to calm or raise the waves. Some traditions stated that there were many tritons.

Triton \\'trī-tᵊn\\ Largest of Neptune's known moons. It is about 1,700 mi (2,700 km) across, somewhat smaller than earth's moon, and orbits opposite the direction of Neptune's rotation. It both rotates and revolves about once every six earth days. It has a very thin nitrogen/methane atmosphere and a surface temperature of −400°F (−240°C). Ice covers it, pitted by what may be a few meteorite craters. Plumes of gas observed by Voyager may be venting through fissures.

triumph Ancient Roman ritual procession honoring a general who had won a major battle and killed at least 5,000 of the enemy. Senators and magistrates were followed by sacrificial animals, captured loot, and captives in chains. The general, in a purple-and-gold tunic, rode in a chariot, holding a laurel branch in his right hand and an ivory scepter in his left, while a slave held a golden crown over his head. Lastly came the soldiers, singing songs.

triumphal arch Monumental structure, originating in Rome, pierced by at least one arched passageway and erected to honor a person or commemorate an event. It usually spanned a street or roadway and was built for the triumphal procession of a victorious army. The basic form consisted of two piers connected by an arch and crowned by a superstructure, or attic, that served as a base for statues and bore inscriptions. The Roman triumphal arch had a facade of marble columns, and the archway and sides were adorned with relief sculpture. Among those built since the Renaissance is the ARC DE TRIOMPHE in Paris.

triumvirate \\trī-'əm-vir-ət\\ In ancient Rome, usually a board of three officials who assisted higher magistrates in judicial functions, oversaw festival banquets, or ran the mint. The First Triumvirate (60 B.C.) of POMPEY, Julius CAESAR, and Marcus Licinius CRASSUS was an informal group of three strong leaders with no sanctioned powers. The Second Triumvirate (43 B.C.), consisting of Mark ANTONY, LEPIDUS, and Octavian (later AUGUSTUS), held absolute dictatorial power.

Trobrianders Melanesian people of the TROBRIAND ISLANDS. Subsistence is based on yams and other vegetables, pigs, and fish. Trobrianders are noted for their elaborate intertribal trading system, the *kula,* by which red shell necklaces are traded between permanent trading partners in a clockwise direction around a ring of islands; white shell bracelets are traded counterclockwise. Wealth is extremely important as a sign of power. They were the subject of highly influential studies by Bronislaw MALINOWSKI.

Trobriand Islands \\'trō-brē-ˌand\\ *or* **Kiriwina Islands** \\ˌkir-ə-'wē-nə\\ Group of small coral islands, Solomon Sea, Papua New Guinea. The islands are low-lying, with coral reefs. The group has a total land area of about 170 sq mi (440 sq km). The largest, Kiriwina, served as a base for the Allies in 1943. The anthropologist Bronislaw MALINOWSKI conducted groundbreaking research among the Trobriand Islanders 1915–18.

Troilus and Cressida \\'troi-ləs...'kre-si-də\\ Lovers in medieval romance. In the *Iliad,* Troilus, son of PRIAM and HECUBA, is dead before the TROJAN WAR starts. In non-Homeric legends he was said to have been killed during the war. He became a romantic figure in the Middle Ages, when he was portrayed as a young lover betrayed by the faithless Cressida, who abandoned him for the Greek warrior Diomedes. The first version of the story was written by the 12th-cent. trouvère Benoît de Sainte-Maure; more-famous versions were written by Giovanni BOCCACCIO, Geoffrey CHAUCER, and William SHAKESPEARE.

Trojan War Mostly legendary conflict between the Greeks and the people of TROY in W Asia Minor. It was dated by later Greeks to the 12th or 13th cent. B.C. It is celebrated in HOMER's *Iliad,* in Greek tragedy, and in Roman literature. In Homer's account, the Trojan prince PARIS ran off with the beautiful HELEN, wife of MENELAUS of Sparta, whose brother AGAMEMNON then led a Greek expedition to retrieve her. The war lasted 10 years; its participants included HECTOR, ACHILLES, PRIAM, ODYSSEUS, and AJAX. Its end resulted from a ruse: The Greeks built a large wooden horse; the Trojans brought the horse into the walled city and a raiding party of Greeks swarmed out, opening the gates to their comrades and sacking Troy. The extent of the legend's actual historical content is not known; excavations at Troy have revealed human habitation from 3000 B.C. to A.D. 1200, and there is evidence of violent destruction about 1250 B.C.

trolley car See STREETCAR

Trollope \\'trä-ləp\\, **Anthony** (1815–1882) English novelist. He worked for the post office 1834–67. Beginning in 1844 he produced 47 novels, writing mainly before breakfast at a fixed rate of 1,000 words an hour. His most famous works are the six "Barsetshire novels," including *Barchester Towers* (1857). Depicting the social scene in an imaginary English county, they abound in memorable characters and atmosphere. The Palliser novels, which deal with political issues, include the sharply satirical *The Eustace Diamonds* (1872). Other works include the highly regarded

Anthony Trollope Painting by S. Laurence, 1865

The Way We Live Now (1875). His mother, Frances Trollope (1780–1863), won fame with her controversial *Domestic Manners of the Americans* (1832).

trombone BRASS INSTRUMENT with an extendable slide with which the length of its tubing can be increased. The slide performs the same function as the valves in other brass instruments. Valve trombones were developed in the early 19th cent.; they provide increased agility but diminished tone quality. Trombones exist in several sizes; the tenor trombone in B-flat is the standard instrument. The trombone developed in the 15th cent. and has changed little over 400 years. By the 16th cent. it had been adopted by town, court, church, and military bands; it began to be used in the symphony orchestra around 1800. In the 20th cent. it became important in dance and jazz bands.

trompe l'oeil \trōⁿp-ˈlœ̄i, *Engl* ˌtrómp-ˈlói\ (French: "deceive the eye") Style of representation in which a painted object is intended to deceive the viewer into believing it is the object itself. First employed by the ancient Greeks, trompe l'oeil was also popular with Roman muralists. Since the early Renaissance, European painters have used trompe l'oeil to create false frames from which the contents of still lifes or portraits seemed to spill, and to paint windowlike images that appeared to be actual openings in a wall or ceiling.

Trondheim \ˈtrȯn-ˌhām\ City and seaport (pop., 1999: 147,000), central Norway, on Trondheim Fjord. It was founded by King OLAF I TRYGGVASON in 997 and was Norway's capital until the 14th cent. It prospered as a trade center until the HANSEATIC LEAGUE made BERGEN its chief port. It revived in the late 19th cent. when linked by rail to OSLO, and is now Norway's third-largest city.

tropical cyclone Severe atmospheric disturbance in tropical oceans. Tropical cyclones have very low atmospheric pressures in the calm, clear center (the eye) of a circular structure of rain, cloud, and very high winds. In the Atlantic and Caribbean they are called hurricanes; in the Pacific, typhoons. Tropical cyclones rotate clockwise in the Southern Hemisphere and counterclockwise in the Northern. They may be 50–500 mi (80–800 km) in diameter, and sustained winds in excess of 100 mph (160 kph) are common.

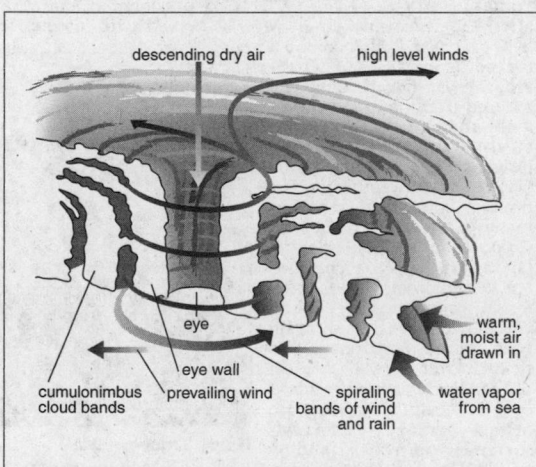

descending dry air   high level winds

eye

warm, moist air drawn in

cumulonimbus cloud bands   eye wall   prevailing wind   spiraling bands of wind and rain   water vapor from sea

Tropical cyclone Cross section of a cyclonic storm. A cyclone derives its power from the warm air and water found at tropical latitudes. Its winds rotate around the low-pressure center, or "eye," where relative calm prevails. Wind and rain are usually most severe in or near the eye wall.

tropical medicine Science of diseases seen primarily in tropical or subtropical climates. It arose in the 19th cent. when colonial doctors encountered infectious diseases unknown in Europe. The discovery that many tropical diseases (e.g., MALARIA, YELLOW FEVER) were spread by mosquitoes led to discovery of other vectors' roles (see SLEEPING SICKNESS, PLAGUE, TYPHUS) and to efforts to destroy vector breeding grounds (e.g., by draining swamps). Research in-

stitutes and national and international commissions were organized to control common tropical illnesses. Newly independent governments have taken over most of these efforts, with help from the WORLD HEALTH ORGANIZATION and the former colonizing countries.

Tropic of Cancer Parallel of latitude approximately 23°27′ north of the EQUATOR. It is the N boundary of the tropics, and it marks the northernmost latitude at which the sun can be seen directly overhead at noon.

Tropic of Capricorn Parallel of latitude approximately 23°27′ south of the EQUATOR. It is the S boundary of the tropics, and it marks the southernmost latitude at which the sun can be seen directly overhead at noon.

troposphere \ˈtrō-pə-ˌsfir\ Lowest region of the ATMOSPHERE, between the earth and the STRATOSPHERE. The upper boundary is about 6–8 mi (10–13 km) above the earth's surface. The troposphere is marked by decreasing temperature with altitude, which distinguishes it from the constant-temperature stratosphere. Most clouds and weather systems occur in the troposphere.

Trotsky, Leon *orig.* Lev Davidovich Bronshtein (1879–1940) Russian communist leader. Exiled to Siberia in 1898 for his revolutionary activities, he escaped in 1902 with a forged passport using the name Trotsky and fled to London, where he met Vladimir LENIN. In 1903 Trotsky became a MENSHEVIK; he returned to St. Petersburg to help lead the RUSSIAN REVOLUTION OF 1905. Arrested and again exiled to Siberia, he wrote *Results and Prospects*, setting forth his theory of "permanent revolution." He escaped to Vienna in 1907 and moved around Europe and the U.S. until the RUSSIAN REVOLUTION OF 1917 brought him back to St. Petersburg (then Petrograd), where he became a BOLSHEVIK and was elected leader of the workers' soviet. He played a major role in the establishment of Lenin's communist regime. As commissar of war (1918–24), Trotsky rebuilt and brilliantly commanded the RED ARMY during the RUSSIAN CIVIL WAR. Though favored by Lenin to succeed him, he lost support after Lenin's death (1924) and was forced out of power by Joseph STALIN. After a campaign of denunciation, he was banished from Russia (1929). In Turkey and France, he wrote his memoirs and a history of the revolution. Under Soviet pressure, he was forced to move around Europe and eventually found asylum in 1936 in Mexico, where, falsely accused in the PURGE TRIALS as the chief conspirator against Stalin, he was murdered by a Spanish communist.

Trotskyism Marxist ideology based on the theory of permanent revolution first expounded by Leon TROTSKY. He believed that because all national economic development was affected by the laws of the world market, a revolution depended on revolutions in other countries for permanent success, a position that put him at odds with Joseph STALIN's "socialism in one country." He attacked the Stalinist bureaucracy as "Bonapartist" (based on the dictatorship of one man). In the 1930s Trotskyists advocated a united front with trade unions against FASCISM. After Trotsky's murder (1940), Trotskyism became a generic term for various revolutionary doctrines that opposed the Soviet form of COMMUNISM.

troubadour \ˈtrü-bə-ˌdȯr, ˈtrü-bə-ˌdu̇r\ One of a class of lyric poets and poet-musicians that flourished from the 11th through the 13th cent., chiefly in S France, N Spain, and N Italy. They wrote in the *langue d'oc* of S France (see LANGUEDOC) and cultivated a lyric poetry intricate in meter and rhyme and usually reflecting the ideals of COURTLY LOVE. Favored at courts, troubadours were charged with creating around the court ladies an aura of pleasant cultivation. Their poetry, often set to music, was to influence all later European lyrical poetry. The troubadour tradition was annihilated by the ALBIGENSIAN CRUSADE. See also TROUVÈRE.

Troubles, Time of (1606–13) Period of political crisis in Russia. The BOYARS opposed the rule of Boris GODUNOV and after his death placed the nobleman Vasily Shuysky (1552–1612) on the throne in 1606. Shuysky's rule was weakened by revolts, challenges by the second False DMITRY, and the invasion of Russia by the Polish king SIGISMUND III VASA in 1610. The Russians finally ousted the Poles from Moscow in

T
U
V

1612. A new representative assembly met in 1613 and elected Michael Romanov as czar.

Troughton \'trō-tən\, **Edward** (1753–1835) British maker of scientific instruments. At 17 he joined his brother's mechanician's shop, where he applied himself singlemindedly to inventing. His new mode of graduating arcs of circles (1778) represented one of the greatest improvements ever made in the art of instrument-making. He constructed the first modern transit-circle in 1805, and in 1812 he erected a mural circle (for measuring polar distances) at the Greenwich Observatory. His sextants came to be used by navigators to the virtual exclusion of all others.

trout Any of several prized game and food fishes of the family Salmonidae, native to the Northern Hemisphere but widely introduced elsewhere. Though most species inhabit cool freshwaters, a few (called sea trout) migrate to the sea between spawnings. The genus *Oncorhynchus* includes SALMON and several trout species; *Salvelinus* contains trout regarded as chars. Most species live among submerged objects or in riffles and deep pools, eating insects, small fishes and their eggs, and crustaceans.

trouvère \trü-'ver\ One of a school of poets that flourished in N France from the 11th to the 14th cent. Trouvères were the counterparts in the language of N France (the *langue d'oïl*) to the Provençal TROUBADOURS. Of both aristocratic and humble origins, they were originally connected with feudal courts but later found middle-class patrons. Their works, including the CHANSONS DE GESTE, are generally narratives; their basic subject was COURTLY LOVE. Their lyrics were intended to be sung, by the poet alone or accompanied by a hired musician.

Troy *or* **Ilium** Ancient city in Troas, NW ASIA MINOR. It holds an enduring place in both literature and archaeology. The archaeological site at modern Hissarlik, Turkey, was first excavated by Heinrich SCHLIEMANN 1870–90. It consists of nine layers dating from the Neolithic period to Roman times (c.3000 B.C.–4th cent. A.D.). Whether it is the actual city of HOMER is still debated. In Greek legend, Troy was destroyed by the Greeks in the 10-year TROJAN WAR. The heroes of Troy were identified by Schliemann with the MYCENAEANS of the Greek Bronze Age, placing the war about 1200 B.C.

Truce of God Measure by the medieval Roman Catholic Church to suspend warfare on certain days of the week and for certain church festivals and Lent. It was instituted in France as early as 1027, and elsewhere in Europe during the next several decades. The popes later undertook its direction, and at the Council of Clermont (1095) proclaimed a weekly truce for all Christendom. The truce was most powerful in the 12th cent. but never entirely effective.

Trucial States See UNITED ARAB EMIRATES

truck Motor vehicle designed to carry freight or heavy articles. The first truck was built in Germany in 1896 by Gottlieb DAIMLER. By the 1920s trucks had become a major means of freight transportation. Gasoline engines for trucks were common until the 1940s, when DIESEL ENGINES generally replaced them. Trucks may be either straight (all axles attached to the frame) or articulated (two or more frames connected by couplings). Air brakes were added to trucks in 1918 and four-wheel brakes in 1925; later improvements included power steering.

Trudeau \trü-'dō\, **Garry** (*orig.* Garretson Beekman) (b.1948) U.S. cartoonist. Born in New York City, he studied art at Yale Univ., where his comic strip *Bull Tales* in the *Yale Daily News* acquired a loyal following. Syndicated in 1970 as *Doonesbury*, the strip's subtle humor, complex characterizations, and literate sophistication represented a departure from the traditional fare of simple jokes and punch lines, and it has often lampooned public figures and addressed highly charged issues. In 1975 it won Trudeau a Pulitzer Prize.

Trudeau, Pierre (Elliott) (1919–2000) Prime minister of Canada (1968–79, 1980–84). Born in Montreal, he practiced law before being elected to the Canadian House of Commons (1966–84). He became leader of the Liberal Party and prime minister in 1968. He advocated a strong federal government and oversaw the defeat of the Quebec separatist

movement. After nine months out of office, he returned in 1980 to initiate reforms that effected passage of the CANADA ACT. His term saw the adoption of official bilingualism. Trudeau increasingly played a major role internationally, becoming an advocate for underdeveloped nations and a peacemaker between the Soviet bloc and the West.

Truffaut \trü-'fō, *Engl* trü-'fō\, **François** (1932–1984) French film director. A film critic for the avant-garde *Cahiers du Cinéma*, he helped establish the NEW WAVE movement. His first feature film was the semi-autobiographical *The 400 Blows* (1959), a portrait of a delinquent boy that won him international acclaim. Influenced by Jean RENOIR and Alfred HITCHCOCK, he made such varied and admired movies as *Shoot the Piano Player* (1960), *Jules and Jim* (1961), *Fahrenheit 451* (1966), *The Wild Child* (1969), *Day for Night* (1973, Academy Award), *The Story of Adele H.* (1975), and *The Last Metro* (1980).

truffle Edible, underground FUNGUS in the genus *Tuber* (class Ascomycetes, division Mycota), prized as a food delicacy. Truffles flourish in temperate open woodlands on calcium-rich soil. The different species range from pea-sized to orange-sized. Truffles usually are associated with tree roots and are found up to about 1 ft (30 cm) below the soil surface. Gatherers usually detect mature truffles with the help of trained pigs or dogs. The truffle is important in French cookery and is among the most highly valued foods in the world. False truffles (genus *Rhizopogon*) form small, underground, potato-like structures under coniferous trees in parts of N. America.

Trujillo (Molina) \trü-'hē-yō\, **Rafael (Leónidas)** (1891–1961) Dictator of the Dominican Republic (1930–61). He became a general in 1927. In 1930 he seized power from Pres. Horacio Vásquez, and from then until his assassination he remained in absolute control of the country. Though he introduced some economic modernization, its benefits were distributed inequitably, corruption was rife, and Dominicans suffered a loss of civil liberties under his regime.

Truman, Harry S. (1884–1972) 33rd president of the U.S. (1945–53). Born in Lamar, Mo., he served with distinction in World War I. He became a partner in a Kansas City haberdashery; when it failed, he entered Democratic politics with the help of Thomas PENDERGAST. As presiding judge of the county court (1926–34), his reputation for honesty and good management gained him bipartisan support. In the U.S. Senate (1935–45), he led a committee that exposed fraud in defense production. In 1944 he was elected vice president on Pres. Franklin ROOSEVELT's ticket. After only 82 days in office, he became president on Roosevelt's death. He helped arrange Germany's surrender on May 8, ending

Harry Truman, 1945

World War II in Europe, and in July attended the POTSDAM CONFERENCE. The Pacific war ended officially on Sept. 2, after he ordered atomic bombs dropped on HIROSHIMA and NAGASAKI; his justification was a report that 500,000 U.S. troops would be lost in a conventional invasion of Japan. He announced the TRUMAN DOCTRINE (1947), established the CENTRAL INTELLIGENCE AGENCY, and pressed for passage of the MARSHALL PLAN to aid European countries. In 1948 he defeated Thomas DEWEY despite widespread expectation of his own defeat. He initiated a policy of CONTAINMENT of the Soviet Union, pursued his POINT FOUR PROGRAM, and initiated the Berlin airlift (see BERLIN BLOCKADE AND AIRLIFT) and the NATO pact of 1949. In the KOREAN WAR he sent troops under Gen. Douglas MACARTHUR to head the U.N. forces. The war, including his removal of MacArthur, occupied his administration until he retired.

Though he was often criticized during his presidency, Truman's reputation grew steadily in later years.

Truman Doctrine Pronouncement by Pres. Harry TRUMAN. On March 12, 1947, he called for immediate economic and military aid to Greece, threatened by a communist insurrection, and to Turkey, under pressure from Soviet expansion in the Mediterranean. Engaged in the COLD WAR with the Soviet Union, the U.S. sought to protect those governments after Britain announced that it could no longer give them aid. In response, Congress appropriated $400 million in aid.

Trumbull, John (1756–1843) U.S. painter. Born in Lebanon, Conn., son of Gov. Jonathan Trumbull (1710–1785), he served as an aide to George WASHINGTON during the American Revolution and later as secretary to John JAY in London. In 1784 he studied painting in London with Benjamin WEST, and he soon began the celebrated series of historical paintings and engravings he would work on throughout his life. In 1817 he was commissioned by Congress to paint the four large pictures that decorate the Capitol rotunda; most of the figures in the often-reproduced *Declaration of Independence* were painted from life.

trumpet BRASS INSTRUMENT with tubing twice-folded in an elongated shape. The modern trumpet has a mostly cylindrical bore, three valves, and a cup-shaped mouthpiece. The trumpet had taken its basic modern shape, with its ovoid loop, by 1500. In the 17th–18th cent. it employed crooks (removable lengths of tubing) to enable playing in different keys. The valved trumpet was developed in the 1820s. The trumpet has been associated with ceremonial and military uses since the 16th cent. Its brilliant sound has since made it indispensable in a wide variety of ensembles. See also CORNET, FLUGELHORN.

Truong Chinh \trü-ˈȯṇ-ˈchin\ *orig.* Dang Xuan Khu (1907–1988) Vietnamese politician and communist intellectual. An anticolonialist activist as a youth, he joined HO CHI MINH in 1928. He eventually became the Indochinese Communist Party's leading propagandist and, in 1941, its secretary-general. With VO NGUYEN GIAP he developed the strategy that led to a Vietnamese victory over the Japanese occupation forces in 1945. With Le Duan (1908–1986) and Pham Van Dong (1906–2000), he ruled N. Vietnam after Ho's death in 1969.

truss In building construction, a structural frame usually fabricated from pieces of metal or timber to form a series of triangles lying in a single plane. The linear members are subject only to compression or tension. The horizontal pieces forming the top and bottom of the truss are called the chords, and the sloping and vertical pieces connecting the chords are collectively called the web. Unlike a VAULT, the truss exerts no thrust but only downward pressure; supporting walls require no buttressing or extra thickening. Trusses have been used extensively in roofing and bridges.

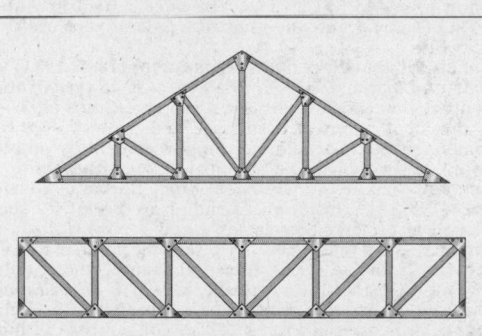

Truss A truss's outer members are called the chords, its interior members are called the web members, and each triangular section is called a panel. A pitched truss (top) has inclined top chords; a flat truss (bottom) has parallel top and bottom chords.

trust In law, a relationship between parties in which one, the trustee or FIDUCIARY, has the power to manage property, and the other, the BENEFICIARY, has the privilege of receiving the benefits from that property. Trusts are used in a variety of contexts, most notably in family settlements and in charitable gifts. Trusts are often created for the sake of advantageous tax treatment (including exemption). A charitable trust, unlike most trusts, does not require definite beneficiaries and may exist in perpetuity. See also TRUST COMPANY.

trust company Company, often a COMMERCIAL BANK, acting as trustee for individuals and businesses and providing related financial or estate-planning services. Trust services for individuals commonly include the administration of estates, living trusts (trusts that become effective during the lifetime of its maker, or settlor), and testamentary trusts (trusts originating in a will). Services for businesses include the administration of corporate bond indentures and corporate pension funds.

trust fund Property (e.g, money or securities) held in a trust; that is, property held legally by one party for the benefit of another. The legal owner, or trustee, has the right to use the property, but must do so to the benefit of the equitable owner, or beneficiary. In Anglo-American law, trust funds are set up principally for family settlements and for charitable giving or, in the commercial sector, to provide for employee pensions and profit-sharing programs.

Truth, Sojourner *orig.* Isabella (1797?–1883) U.S. evangelist and reformer. She was born into slavery in Ulster Co., N.Y., where she bore five children. After being freed, she worked as a domestic in New York City (1829–43) and began preaching on street corners. Adopting the name Sojourner Truth, she left New York to obey a "call" to travel and preach. Adding abolitionism and women's rights to her religious messages, she traveled in the Midwest, where her magnetism drew large crowds. In the Civil War she gathered supplies for black volunteer regiments. After the war she worked for the freedmen's relief organization.

Sojourner Truth

tryptophan \ˈtrip-tə-ˌfan\ One of the essential AMINO ACIDS, found in small amounts in most PROTEINS. It plays an important role in growth and development and in the biosynthesis of SEROTONIN and NIACIN (thus, deficiency of both niacin and tryptophan causes PELLAGRA). Its occurrence in milk is the reason milk helps people sleep. It is used in medicine and nutrition research, in enriched foods, and as a dietary supplement.

Ts'ao Chan See CAO ZHAN

Ts'ao Ts'ao See CAO CAO

tsar See CZAR

Tsaritsyn See VOLGOGRAD

Tschermak von Seysenegg \ˈcher-ˌmäk-fȯn-ˈzī-zə-ˌnek\, **Erich** (1871–1962) Austrian botanist. He was one of the codiscoverers of Gregor MENDEL's classic papers on heredity and the garden pea. Before finding Mendel's papers he had conducted his own breeding experiments with the garden pea, but found that Mendel's work duplicated and in some ways surpassed his own. See also William BATESON, Carl Erich CORRENS, Hugo DE VRIES.

Tselinograd See ASTANA

Tseng Kuo-fan See ZENG GUOFAN

tsetse fly \ˈtset-sē, ˈtsē-tsē\ Any of about 21 species (genus *Glossina*, family Muscidae) of African bloodsucking DIPTERANS usually larger than a HOUSEFLY. They have stiff, piercing mouthparts. Only two species commonly transmit the protozoan parasites (trypanosomes) that cause human

SLEEPING SICKNESS: *G. palpalis,* found primarily in dense streamside vegetation, and *G. morsitans,* found in more open woodlands. Both sexes suck blood almost daily.

Tshombe \'chòm-bā\, **Moise (-Kapenda)** (1919–1969) Congolese leader. After losing national elections to Patrice LUMUMBA in 1960, Tshombe declared his Katanga province independent. When the U.N. intervened in 1963, he was exiled; he returned as premier under Joseph KASAVUBU in 1964 but was dismissed in 1965.

Tsimshian \'chim-shē-ən\ NORTHWEST COAST INDIAN people from W central British Columbia and S Alaska. The Tsimshian economy was based on fishing, with some hunting in winter. Large winter houses, made of wood and often carved and painted,

Moise Tshombe

symbolized family wealth. POTLATCHES marked various important events. Today the Tsimshian number about 10,000.

Tsinan See JINAN

Ts'u-hsi See CIXI

tsunami \tsü-'nä-mē\ *or* **seismic sea wave** *or* **tidal wave** Catastrophic ocean WAVE, usually caused by a submarine EARTHQUAKE with a magnitude greater than 6.5 on the RICHTER SCALE. Underwater or coastal landslides or volcanic eruptions also may cause tsunamis. The "tidal wave" (actually a series of waves) has no connection with the tides. Perhaps the most destructive tsunami ever occurred in 1703 at Awa, Japan, killing more than 100,000 people. The volcanic explosions of KRAKATAU island in 1883 created waves as high as 100 ft (30 m) and killed more than 36,000 people.

Tsvet \'tsvet\, **Mikhail (Semyonovich)** (1872–1919) Italian-Russian botanist and chemist. He is credited with the discovery and application of CHROMATOGRAPHY. He extracted plant pigments with ether and alcohol and percolated the solution through columns of calcium carbonate or powdered sugar; the different pigments appeared as separate colored bands. Tsvet also discovered several new CHLOROPHYLLS. His work was not discovered by mainstream Western scientists for nearly 30 years.

Tsvetayeva \tsvʸi-'tà-yə-və\, **Marina (Ivanovna)** (1892–1941) Russian poet. She published her first poetry collection in 1910. Her verses on the Russian Revolution glorify the anti-Bolshevik resistance. She lived abroad 1922–39, mostly in Paris, writing varied works including poetry that increasingly reflected nostalgia for her homeland. Many of her best poetic qualities are displayed in the long verse fairy tale *Tsar-devitsa* (1922; "Tsar-Maiden"). Though little known outside Russia, she is considered one of the finest 20th-cent. poets in Russian.

T Tauri star \'tē-'tòr-ī\ Any of a class of very young STARS, with masses less than twice the sun's, at an early stage in stellar evolution. Only recently formed from condensing interstellar gas and dust and now contracting more slowly, they remain relatively unstable, with unpredictable changes in brightness, until their interior temperatures rise enough to support NUCLEAR FUSION. More than 500 have been observed.

Tuareg \'twä-ˌreg\ Nomadic Berber-speaking people of the SW Sahara. Their feudal, matrilineal culture divides society into nobles, clergy, vassals, artisans, and slavelike laborers. N Tuareg live mainly in true desert; S Tuareg live in steppe and savanna. They have traditionally engaged in herding, agriculture, convoying caravans, and raiding neighboring tribes. They combine many pre-Islamic rituals and customs with Sunni Islam. Droughts in the 1970s and '80s reduced their numbers and eroded their traditional way of life.

tuba Deep-pitched valved BRASS INSTRUMENT with a widely expanding conical bore. Tubas vary in size and pitch. The tubing is coiled in an oblong shape, and the bell points upward or forward. Patented in 1835, the tuba soon became the foundation of the brass section in the orchestra and in military and brass bands.

tuber Short, thickened, mostly underground stem that constitutes the resting stage of certain seed plants. It is often an organ of food storage, reproduction, or both. It bears minute scale leaves, each with a bud that has the potential for developing into a new plant. The common POTATO is a typical tuber. The term is also used imprecisely but widely for fleshy roots or RHIZOMES that resemble tubers.

tuberculosis (TB) \tü-ˌbər-kyə-'lō-səs\ *formerly* **consumption** BACTERIAL DISEASE caused by some species of MYCOBACTERIUM. It has occurred throughout history worldwide. In the 18th–19th cent. it reached near-epidemic proportions in the rapidly industrializing and urbanizing West, where it was the leading cause of death until the early 20th cent. TB resurged in the 1980s, transmitted from AIDS patients to others, especially in enclosed settings that promote spread. It is still a major cause of death in many countries. The body isolates the bacteria by forming tiny tubercles (nodules) around them. This often arrests TB's progress, but if not treated, it may become active—and contagious—later. The primary form (mostly in children) is often mild but may spread through the body, producing tubercles in many organs; it can be fatal. The secondary form (mainly in young adults) starts with loss of energy and weight and persistent cough, progressing to heavy sweating, and possibly pleurisy (see THORACIC CAVITY) and spitting up blood. Growing tubercle masses may destroy so much lung tissue that RESPIRATION cannot supply the body with enough oxygen. A VACCINE with weakened bacteria has helped control infection, but preventing exposure by recognizing and treating active TB early is more effective. Because many strains are resistant to drugs, treatment requires at least two drugs to which the patient's strain is sensitive for at least six months.

tube worm Any of numerous species of sedentary, solitary or colonial, marine WORMS that spend their entire life in a tube made from special secretions or from sand grains glued together. They range from less than an inch (25 mm) to more than 20 ft (6 m) long. The bottom of the tube is attached to the seafloor; the mouth and tentacles are at the upper, open end. The worm breathes through gills, the tentacles, or the body wall. Tube worms occur in the ANNELID class Polychaeta and in the phyla Phoronida and Pogonophora. Many live in deep-ocean vent areas.

Tubman, Harriet (c.1820–1913) U.S. abolitionist. Born into slavery in Dorchester Co., Md., she escaped north by the UNDERGROUND RAILROAD in 1849. She made frequent trips into the South to lead over 300 slaves to freedom, despite large rewards offered for her arrest, and became known to abolitionists as the "Moses of her people." In the Civil War, she served as a nurse, laundress, and spy for Union forces in S. Carolina. She later settled in Auburn, N.Y., and was eventually granted a federal pension for her war work.

Tubman, William V(acanarat) S(hadrach) (1895–1971) President of Liberia, 1944–71. Trained as a lawyer, Tubman eventually ascended to Liberia's Supreme Court (1937–44). As president he enacted suffrage and property rights for women, enabled participation in government by all ethnic groups, and established a nationwide school system.

Tuchman \'tək-mən\, **Barbara** *orig.* Barbara Wertheim (1912–1989) U.S. historian. Born in New York City, she developed a masterly literary style and a powerful grasp of complex issues that made her a leading popular historian. Her works include *The Guns of August* (1962, Pulitzer Prize), on the first month of World War I; *Stilwell and the American Experience in China, 1911–45* (1970, Pulitzer Prize); *A Distant Mirror* (1978), concerning 14th-cent. France; and *The March of Folly* (1984).

Tucson \'tü-ˌsän\ City (pop., 2000: 487,000), SE Arizona. It lies along the Santa Cruz River on a SONORAN DESERT plateau rimmed by mountains. In 1776 the small pueblo of Tucson was made a Spanish presidio (fort). The U.S. acquired the territory through the 1853 GADSDEN PURCHASE. It was the territorial capital 1867–77. It grew with the arrival of the railroad in 1880 and the discovery of silver at nearby TOMBSTONE. Its dry, sunny climate and unique desert locale have made it a popular tourist and health resort and retirement community. It is the seat of the Univ. of Arizona (1885).

Tudjman \'tuj-mən\, **Franjo** (1922–1999) President of Croatia (1990–99). He taught at the Univ. of Zagreb 1963–67, and later wrote numerous books on history and politics. Expelled from the Yugoslav Communist Party in 1967 for his nationalist writings, he became leader of the right-wing Croatian Democratic Union in 1989. Elected president of Croatia, he proclaimed its independence from Yugoslavia in 1991, precipitating an armed conflict with Serbia. His excesses in the BOSNIAN CONFLICT and his autocratic rule earned Tudjman a reputation for brutality.

Tudor, Henry See HENRY VII (ENGLAND)

Tudor, House of English royal dynasty that gave five sovereigns to England (1485–1603). The Tudors originated in the 13th cent. but the dynasty's fortunes were established by Owen Tudor (c.1400–1461), a Welsh adventurer who took service with HENRY V and married Henry's widow, Catherine of Valois (1401–1437). Owen and Catherine's son Edmund Tudor (c.1430–1456) married a descendant of the House of LANCASTER. Their son Henry Tudor claimed the English throne as HENRY VII in 1485 and cemented his claim with his marriage to Elizabeth of the House of YORK, daughter of EDWARD IV. The Tudor dynasty continued with the reigns of HENRY VIII and his children EDWARD VI, MARY I, and ELIZABETH I. In 1603 it was succeeded by the House of STUART.

Tudor, Margaret See MARGARET TUDOR

Tudor, Mary See MARY I

Tudor style Architectural style in England (1485–1558) that made lavish use of half-timbering, oriels, GABLES, decorative brickwork, and rich plasterwork. Exposed diagonal bracing usually occurs at building corners, with the second story often sporting a picturesque cantilevered overhang to counterbalance the load carried by the spanning portions of the beams.

tuff Relatively soft, porous rock usually formed by the cementation of volcanic ash. Tuff may vary greatly in texture and in chemical and mineralogical composition. In some eruptions, foaming MAGMA wells to the surface as an emulsion of hot gases and incandescent particles; the shredded pumice-like material spreads swiftly as a glowing avalanche (NUÉE ARDENTE).

Tufts University Private university in Medford, Mass., near Boston. It was established in 1852 and named after its founding benefactor, Charles Tufts. It has schools of medicine, veterinary medicine, biomedicine, law, international relations (the Fletcher School), nutrition, and dentistry, along with many research units. Total enrollment is about 8,500.

Tu Fu See DU FU

Tuileries Palace \'twē-lə-ˌrēz\ French royal residence, adjacent to the LOUVRE in Paris, destroyed by arson in 1871. Commissioned by CATHERINE DE MÉDICIS, it was begun in 1564 by Philibert Delorme (c.1515–1570); the next 200 years saw numerous additions and alterations by Jacques du Cerceau (c.1520–1585), Louis Le Vau (1612–1670), and others. The Tuileries Gardens have changed little since André LE NÔTRE redesigned them in 1664 and extended the central walkway far beyond the gardens to where the ARC DE TRIOMPHE now stands.

Tula Ancient city in Mexico, the capital of the TOLTECS, which flourished in the 10th–12th cent. Its exact location is uncertain; the archaeological site now designated Tula in Hidalgo state has been the choice of historians, but other scholars identify Tula with TEOTIHUACÁN. The Tula site suggests a city that had a population in the tens of thousands. Its art and architecture are strikingly similar to those of the AZTEC capital, TENOCHTITLÁN, and its artistic themes suggest that the Aztecs' self-concept as warrior-priests of the sun god was borrowed directly from Tula.

Tulane University Private university in New Orleans. It was founded in 1834 and later named for a major donor, Paul Tulane. It has schools of architecture, engineering, law, medicine, social work, and public health, among other divisions, as well as various institutes. Total enrollment is about 12,000.

tulip Any of almost 4,000 varieties of about 100 species of cultivated bulbous herbaceous plants making up the genus *Tulipa* in the LILY FAMILY, native to Eurasia. Among the most popular of all garden flowers, the tulip produces two or three thick, bluish-green leaves clustered at the base of the plant. The bell-shaped flowers have three petals and three sepals. Colors range widely. Streaked blossoms get their streaks from a harmless virus infection that causes the color to disappear in patterns.

tulip tree N. American ornamental and timber tree *(Liriodendron tulipifera)* of the MAGNOLIA family. It occurs in mixed hardwood stands in E N. America. It is taller than all other E broad-leaved trees (up to 200 ft, or 60 m), and its trunk often has a diameter greater than 7 ft (2 m). Long-stemmed, bright-green leaves have two to four side lobes. Yellowish-green tuliplike flowers have six petals, orange at their bases, and three bright-green sepals. The wood is used to manufacture furniture parts, plywood panels, paper, and boxes.

Tull, Jethro (1674–1741) British agronomist and inventor. Around 1701 he perfected a horse-drawn seed drill that economically sowed the seeds in neat rows, and later a horse-drawn hoe. He stressed the use of manure and the importance of breaking up the soil into small particles. Tull's methods, though initially attacked, helped form the basis of modern agriculture.

Tulsa City (pop., 2000: 393,000), NE Oklahoma, on the ARKANSAS RIVER. It originated in 1836 as a settlement of Creek Indian immigrants; white settlement began in 1882 after the arrival of the railway. The discovery of oil nearby in the early 20th cent. launched phenomenal growth. Most major oil companies now have plants and offices in the city. It is the head of the Arkansas River Navigation System, a waterway stretching 440 mi (708 km) to the MISSISSIPPI RIVER. A commercial and financial center, it is the seat of the Univ. of Tulsa (1894) and Oral Roberts Univ. (1965).

tumbleweed Plant that breaks away from its roots and is driven about by the wind as a light rolling mass, scattering seeds as it goes. Examples include pigweed *(Amaranth retroflexus,* a widespread weed in the W U.S.) and other AMARANTHS, tumbling mustard, and Russian thistle.

tumor *or* **neoplasm** Mass of abnormal tissue that arises from normal cells, has no useful function, and tends to grow. Cell abnormalities may include increased size or number, or loss of characteristics that differentiate their tissue of origin. Cells in malignant tumors (see CANCER) have a distorted size, shape, and/or structure. Malignant tumors invade tissues locally and spread (metastasize) in blood or lymph. Tumors may not cause pain until they press on or invade nerves. Both benign and malignant tumors can press on nearby structures, block vessels, or produce excess hormones, all of which can cause death. Benign tumors remain as a solid mass that can be removed by surgery if accessible; they may become malignant. Malignant tumors, though they may remain quiescent for a time, never become benign.

tuna Any of seven species (genus *Thunnus,* family Scombridae) of commercially valuable food fishes. Species range from the 80-lb (36-kg) ALBACORE to the bluefin tuna *(T. thynnus),* which grows to 14 ft (4.3 m) long and weighs up to 1,800 lbs (800 kg). Tunas have a slender, streamlined body and a forked or crescent-shaped tail. They are unique among fishes in maintaining a body temperature above the water temperature. They migrate long distances over all the world's oceans.

tundra Treeless, level or rolling ground above the TAIGA in polar regions (Arctic tundra) or on high mountains (alpine tundra), characterized by bare ground and rock or by such vegetation as mosses, lichens, small herbs, and low shrubs. Animal species in the Arctic tundra include lemmings, the Arctic fox, the Arctic wolf, caribou, reindeer, and musk-oxen. In the alpine tundra many animals, including mountain sheep and wildcats, descend to warmer zones during winter. Alpine tundra is more moderate and has more rainfall than does Arctic tundra. The freezing climate of the Arctic produces a layer of PERMAFROST. An overlying layer of soil alternates between freezing and thawing. Alpine tundras have a freeze-thaw layer but no permafrost. Arctic tun-

TUV

dra covers about one-tenth of the earth's surface. Alpine tundras begin above the timberline of spruce and firs. Because of the few plant and animal species and the fragility of the food chains in tundra regions, damage to any element of the habitat affects the whole ecosystem.

Tung-Pei See MANCHURIA

tungsten *or* **wolfram** \'wùl-frəm\ Chemical ELEMENT, one of the TRANSITION ELEMENTS, chemical symbol W, atomic number 74. Exceptionally strong, white to grayish, and brittle, it has the highest melting point of any METAL. Its chief uses are in STEELS to increase hardness and strength and in lightbulb filaments. It is also used in electrical contacts, rocket nozzles, chemical apparatus, high-speed rotors, and solar-energy devices. Tungsten is relatively inert. Its most important compound, tungsten CARBIDE, noted for its hardness, is used to increase the wear-resistance of cast iron and of tools' cutting edges.

tungsten-halogen lamp See HALOGEN LAMP

Tunguska event \tùŋ-'gü-skə\ (June 30, 1908) Enormous aerial explosion that flattened about 500,000 acres (2,000 sq km) of pine forest near Siberia's Stony Tunguska River. Its energy was equal to that of 10–15 megatons of TNT. A large COMET fragment may have disintegrated high in the atmosphere, creating a fireball and blast wave but no crater. Witnesses saw a fireball lighting the horizon, initially visible about 500 mi (800 km) away; then the ground trembled and hot winds threw people down and shook buildings. Dust scattered high in the atmosphere caused abnormally bright night skies in Siberia and Europe for some time afterward.

tuning and temperament Two aspects of assuring that musical tones sound well together. Tuning assures a good sound for a given pair of tones; temperament adjusts the tuning to assure a good sound for any and all pairs of tones. Two vibrating strings sound best together if the ratio between their lengths can be expressed by two small whole numbers. If two strings vibrate in a ratio of 2:1, the vibrations will always coincide and so reinforce each other. But if they vibrate in a ratio of 197:100 (very close to 2:1), they will cancel each other out three times per second, creating audible "beats" which make the interval sound "out of tune." Since a tone produced by one ratio will not necessarily agree with the same tone created by repeatedly applying another ratio, either some intervals must be mistuned to allow for the perfect tuning of others or all intervals must be slightly mistuned. Before 1700, several systems of temperament were used; since then, "equal temperament," in which the ratios represented by each pair of adjacent notes are identical, has prevailed.

Tunis \'tü-nəs\ City (pop., 1994: 674,000), capital of Tunisia. Only a small town under CARTHAGE, it became important after the Muslim conquest in the 7th cent. A.D. It became the capital city under the ABBASID DYNASTY (9th cent.), and one of the leading cities of the Muslim world under the HAFSID DYNASTY (13th cent.). The Spanish and Turks held it during the 16th cent. It was made the national capital when Tunisia gained independence from France in 1956. It produces textiles, carpets, and olive oil, and has metallurgical industries. Tourism is also important.

Tunisia \tü-'nē-zhə\ *officially* **Republic of Tunisia** Nation, N. Africa. Area: 59,664 sq mi (154,530 sq km). Population (2000): 9,593,000. Capital: TUNIS. The population is of Arab and Berber ancestry. Languages: Arabic (official), French. Religion: Islam (official). Currency: Tunisian dinar. Tunisia is made up of a coastal region, mountains, an extensive plateau, a marshy area with shallow salt lakes, and a tract of the SAHARA desert. The Medjerda is its largest (286 mi, or 460 km long) and only perennial river. Tunisia contains some of the largest phosphate and natural gas reserves in Africa, as well as substantial oil reserves. Major economic sectors are services, agriculture, light industries, and the production and export of petroleum and phosphates. Tourism, focusing on Tunisia's beaches and Roman ruins, is also important. Tunisia is a republic with one legislative house; its chief of state is the president, and the head of government is the prime minister. From the 12th cent. B.C. the Phoenicians had a series of trading posts on the N. African coast. By the 6th cent. B.C. the Carthaginian kingdom encompassed most of present-day Tunisia. The Romans ruled

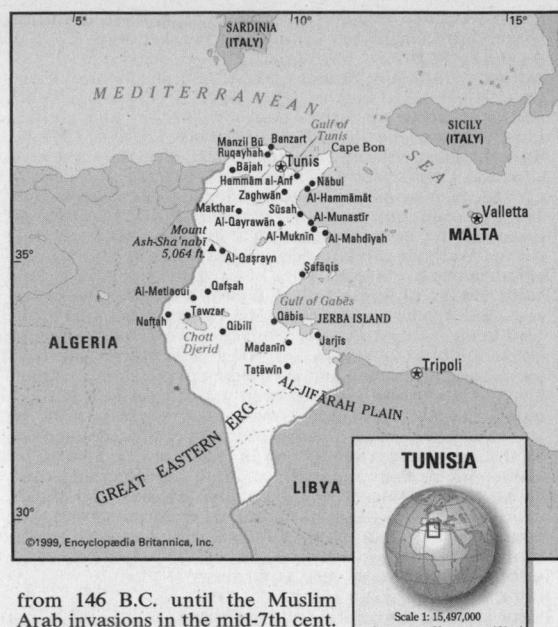

TUNISIA

Scale 1: 15,497,000

©1999, Encyclopædia Britannica, Inc.

from 146 B.C. until the Muslim Arab invasions in the mid-7th cent. A.D. The area was fought over, won, and lost by many, including the ABBASIDS, the ALMOHADS, and Spain. The Ottoman Turks finally conquered it in 1574 and held it until the late 19th cent. For a time it maintained autonomy as the French, British, and Italians contended for the region. In 1881 it became a French protectorate. In World War II U.S. and British forces captured it in 1943 to end a brief German occupation. In 1956 France granted it full independence; Habib BOURGUIBA assumed power and remained in office until 1987.

tunnel Horizontal or nearly horizontal underground or underwater passageway. Tunnels are used mainly for mining, as passageways for trains and motor vehicles, and for conducting water. Ancient civilizations used tunnels to carry water for irrigation and drinking, and in the 22nd cent. B.C. the Babylonians built a tunnel for pedestrian traffic under the Euphrates River. The Romans built AQUEDUCT tunnels through mountains. The introduction of gunpowder blasting in the 17th cent. marked a great advance in solid-rock excavation. For softer soils, excavation is accomplished using devices such as the tunneling mole, with its rotating wheel that continuously excavates material and loads it onto a conveyor belt. Railroad transportation in the 19th–20th cent. led to a tremendous expansion in the number and length of tunnels. In modern tunneling, steel is generally used for support until a concrete lining can be installed.

tunneling *or* **barrier penetration** In physics, the passage of a particle through a seemingly impassable energy barrier as a consequence of its quantum-mechanical wave properties, though its energy may be too low to surmount the barrier, according to classical physics. The scanning tunneling microscope represents one application of tunneling.

Tunney, Gene (*orig.* James Joseph) (1898–1978) U.S. boxer. Born in New York City, "the Fighting Marine" defeated Jack DEMPSEY in 1926 to become the world heavyweight champion. In Chicago in 1927, Dempsey knocked Tunney to the canvas in the seventh round but failed to retire immediately to a neutral corner; the resulting "long count" allowed Tunney to rise and win the fight. He retired the next year.

Tupac Amarú \tü-'päk-ä-mär-'ü\ Revolutionary group in Peru, founded in 1983. It held 490 people hostage in the Japanese embassy in Lima (1996) to gain release of jailed comrades. After several weeks, soldiers stormed the embassy and killed all the guerrillas. The group takes its name from the Indian revolutionary Tupac Amarú II (born José

Gabriel Condorcanqui, 1742?–1781), who in 1780 led Peruvian Indian peasants in the last widespread. rebellion against Spain. The Indians identified him with his ancestor Tupac Amarú (d.1572), ATAHUALLPA's second successor as leader of the INCA.

Tupamaro \ˌtü-pə-ˈmä-rō\ Member of the National Liberation Movement, an Uruguayan leftist urban guerrilla organization founded about 1963 and named for TUPAC AMARÚ. At first the Tupamaros robbed banks and businesses and distributed the goods to the poor, but later they mounted a wave of violence aimed at the authorities. The government that seized power in 1973 killed some 300 and imprisoned 3,000 others. When democratic rule returned in 1985, the Tupamaros were reorganized as a political party.

tupelo \ˈtü-pə-ˌlō\ Any of about seven species of trees that make up the genus *Nyssa* in the sour gum family (Nyssaceae). Five, including the black gum *(N. sylvatica),* are found in moist or swampy areas of E N. America. They all have horizontal or hanging branches, broad leaves, and male and female flowers on different plants. N. American species bear greenish-white flowers and small bluish-black or purple berries. Tupelo wood, most of which comes from the water tupelo *(N. aquatica),* is used for crates and boxes, flooring, wooden utensils, and veneers.

Tupolev \ˈtü-pə-yif\, **Andrei (Nikolayevich)** (1888–1972) Russian aircraft designer. In 1918 he cofounded the Central Aerohydrodynamics Institute, and in 1922 he became head of its design bureau, producing airplanes of all-metal construction. Later assigned to design military aircraft, he produced the Tu-2 twin-engine bomber, which was widely used in World War II. He also designed a copy of the U.S. B-29; the resulting Tu-4 became the Soviet Union's principal bomber. He later adapted jet propulsion to several piston-engine aircraft, which led to the Tu-104 (1955), one of the first jets to provide regular passenger service.

turbidity current Underwater current of abrasive sediments. Such currents appear to be relatively short-lived phenomena that occur at great depths. They are thought to be caused by the slumping of sediment that has piled up at the heads of SUBMARINE CANYONS; a dense slurry then flows down the canyon to spread out over the ocean floor and deposit a layer of sand in deep water. Repeated deposition forms SUBMARINE FANS.

turbine \ˈtər-bən, ˈtər-ˌbīn\ Any of various devices that convert the ENERGY in a stream of fluid into mechanical energy by passing the stream through a system of fixed and moving fanlike blades and causing the latter to rotate. A turbine looks like a large wheel with many small radiating blades around its rim. There are four broad classes of turbine: water (hydraulic), steam, wind, and gas. The most important application of the first three is the generation of electricity; gas turbines are most often used in aircraft.

turbojet JET ENGINE in which a TURBINE-driven COMPRESSOR draws in and compresses air, forcing it into a combustion chamber into which fuel is injected. Ignition causes the gases to expand and to rush first through the turbine and then through a nozzle at the rear. Forward thrust is generated by the rearward momentum of the exhaust gases. In the more powerful and economical turbofan or fanjet, some of the incoming air is bypassed around the combustion chamber and is accelerated to the rear by a turbine-operated fan. See also RAMJET.

turboprop Hybrid engine that provides jet thrust and also drives a propeller. It is similar to the TURBOJET except that an added TURBINE, behind the combustion chamber, works through a shaft and speed-reducing gears to turn a propeller at the front of the engine. Less efficient than the modern turbojet at high speeds, it is now used only for relatively short-range aircraft.

turbulence In FLUID MECHANICS, a flow condition in which local speed and pressure change unpredictably as an average flow is maintained. Common examples are wind and water swirling around obstructions, or fast flow of any sort. Eddies, vortices, and a reduction in DRAG are characteristics of turbulence. The dimpled surface of golf balls encourages turbulence in the BOUNDARY LAYER, and swimsuits with rough surfaces may help swimmers to move faster.

Turcoman See TURKMEN

Turenne \tü-ˈren\, **vicomte (Viscount) de** *orig.* Henri de La Tour d'Auvergne (1611–1675) French military leader. He earned his reputation as a military leader in the Thirty Years' War, especially with the capture of Turin (1640). Made a marshal of France (1643), he joined the aristocrats in the FRONDE (1649), but later he skillfully commanded the royal army to defeat the forces led by the prince de CONDÉ, ending France's war with Spain. Appointed marshal-general (1660), Turenne marched alongside LOUIS XIV in joint command of the French armies against Spain to victory in the War of Devolution (1667–68). His bold strategies won numerous victories against the imperial army in Germany (1672–75), but he was killed in action at Sasbach. NAPOLEON esteemed Turenne as the greatest military leader in history.

turf In horticulture, the surface layer of soil with its matted, dense vegetation, usually GRASSES grown for ornamental or recreational use. Such turf grasses include Kentucky BLUEGRASS and creeping BENT GRASS. Turf grasses are often grown on turf, or sod, farms. Plugs, blocks, squares, or strips are cut and transplanted to areas where they quickly establish and grow. Lawns are fine-textured turfs that are mowed regularly and closely to develop into dense, uniformly green coverings.

Turgenev \tür-ˈgyā-nᵊyif\, **Ivan (Sergeyevich)** (1818–1883) Russian novelist, poet, and playwright. His years at the Univ. of Berlin convinced him of the need for Russia to Westernize. He lived in Europe after about 1862. He is known for realistic, affectionate portrayals of the Russian peasantry and for penetrating studies of the Russian intelligentsia who were attempting to move the country into a new age. He gained fame with the short-story cycle *A Sportsman's Sketches* (1852), which criticizes serfdom. His dramatic masterpiece, *A Month in the Country*

Ivan Turgenev

(1855), and the novel *Rudin* (1856) followed. His interest in change and intergenerational differences is reflected in the controversial *Fathers and Sons* (1862), his greatest novel. *Smoke* (1867) caricatures the intelligentsia. The late *A Lear of the Steppes* (1870) and *Torrents of Spring* (1872) combine eloquent nostalgia with quasi-fantasy.

Turgot \tür-ˈgō\, **Anne-Robert-Jacques** *later* **baron de l'Aulne** (1727–1781) French administrator and economist. As intendant (governor) of Limoges (1761–74), he instituted economic and administrative reforms. A PHYSIOCRAT, in 1766 he wrote *Reflections on the Formation and Distribution of Wealth.* In 1774 he was appointed comptroller general by LOUIS XVI and introduced his Six Edicts to expand economic reforms. His effort to abolish the corvée (unpaid forced labor by peasants) was opposed by the privileged classes, and he was dismissed in 1776.

Turin *Italian* **Torino** City (pop., 1998 est.: 915,000), PIEDMONT region, Italy. Partly destroyed by HANNIBAL in 218 B.C., it was made a Roman military colony under Caesar AUGUSTUS. It became the seat of government under CHARLEMAGNE (742–814). Capital of the kingdom of SARDINIA in 1720, it was occupied by the French during the NAPOLEONIC WARS. Center of the RISORGIMENTO movement, it served as the first capital of a united Italy 1861–65. During World War II it sustained heavy damage from Allied air raids, but was rebuilt. It is the hub of Italy's automotive industry and an international fashion center. The Shroud of TURIN resides in its 15th-cent. cathedral.

Turin, Shroud of Linen fragment long said to be the burial garment of JESUS. It has been preserved since 1578 in the Cathedral of San Giovanni Battista in Turin, Italy. Measuring 14 ft 3 in. by 3 ft 7 in. (4.3 m by 1.1 m), it appears to portray images of the back and front of a gaunt man and contain markings that correspond to the STIGMATA. It emerged

TUV

historically in 1354 and went on exhibition in 1389. In 1988 independent tests determined that the cloth was made around 1260–1390.

Turing \\'tür-iŋ\\, **Alan (Mathison)** (1912–1954) English mathematician and logician. He studied at Cambridge Univ. and at Princeton's Institute for Advanced Study. In a 1936 paper, he proved that there cannot exist any universal algorithmic method of determining truth in mathematics and that mathematics will always contain undecidable propositions. That paper also introduced the TURING MACHINE. He believed that computers eventually would be capable of thought indistinguishable from that of a human and proposed the TURING TEST to assess this. His papers on the subject became the foundation of research in ARTIFICIAL INTELLIGENCE. He did valuable work in CRYPTOGRAPHY during World War II, then taught at the Univ. of Manchester. His suicide at 41 followed an arrest for homosexual acts and extreme medical treatments aimed at changing his sexual orientation.

Turing machine Hypothetical computing device proposed by Alan TURING (1936). Not actually a machine, it is an idealized mathematical model that reduces the logical structure of any computing device to its essentials. It consists of a tape, a tape head that can read and write, and a control mechanism in the head that can store instructions. It would perform its functions in a sequence of discrete steps. Turing's extrapolation of the essential features of data processing was instrumental in the development of modern DIGITAL COMPUTERS, which use his basic scheme of an input/output device (tape and tape reader), central processing unit (CPU, or control mechanism), and stored MEMORY.

Turing test Test proposed by Alan TURING to determine whether a computer can be said to "think." Turing suggested the "imitation game," wherein a person, within a fixed time frame, must distinguish between a computer and a human subject based on their replies to questions. The computer's success at "thinking" is measured by how often it is misidentified as the human subject. The test is performed today in competitions that test the success of ARTIFICIAL INTELLIGENCE.

Turkana remains See LAKE TURKANA REMAINS

Turkey *officially* **Republic of Turkey** Nation, SW Asia and SE Europe. Area: 300,948 sq mi (779,452 sq km); about 97% lies

©1999, Encyclopædia Britannica, Inc.

TURKEY

Scale 1: 24,576,000
0   100   200 mi
0   150   300 km

in Asia. Population (2000): 65,667,000. Capital: ANKARA. Ethnic groups include the Turks and Kurds. Languages: Turkish (official), Kurdish, Arabic. Religion: Islam (mostly Sunnite). Currency: Turkish lira. Turkey is a mountainous country with an extensive plateau covering

central ASIA MINOR. The highest peak is Mt. ARARAT. The TAURUS MTNS. lie in the south. Its rivers include the TIGRIS, EUPHRATES, Kizil Irmak, and Menderes. It is a major exporter of chromite, and also mines boron, iron ore, coal, lignite, and bauxite. It is the Middle East's leading steel producer. Chief agricultural products include wheat, sugar beets, fruits, and tobacco. Tourism also is important. It is a republic with one legislative house; its chief of state is the president, and the head of government is the prime minister. Turkey's early history corresponds to that of ASIA MINOR, the BYZANTINE EMPIRE, and the OTTOMAN EMPIRE. Byzantine rule emerged when CONSTANTINE I the Great made Constantinople (now ISTANBUL) his capital. The Ottoman empire, begun in the 12th cent., dominated for more than 600 years; it ended in 1918 after the YOUNG TURKS precipitated its demise. Under M. K. ATATURK, a republic was proclaimed in 1923, and the caliphate abolished in 1924. Turkey remained neutral throughout most of World War II, siding with the Allies in 1945. Since the war it has alternated between civil and military governments and has had several conflicts with Greece over Cyprus. The 1990s saw political and civic turmoil between Islamicists and secularists.

turkey Either of two species of birds in the family Meleagrididae. The N. American common turkey (*Meleagris gallopavo*) has been domesticated since pre-Columbian times. The adult male has a naked, bright-red head, a fleshy red ornament (snood) growing over the bill, and a fleshy wattle on the throat. The male (gobbler or tom) may be 50 in. (1.3 m) long and weigh over 20 lbs (10 kg). The wild turkey inhabits woodlands near water, eating seeds and insects. An excellent source of meat and easily shot, it was practically exterminated by European settlers; conservation efforts have reestablished it. The ocellated turkey (*Agriocharis,* or *Meleagris, ocellata*) of Central America has never been domesticated.

turkey vulture *or* **turkey buzzard** Species (*Cathartes aura*) of long-winged, long-tailed VULTURE (family Cathartidae), about 30 in. (75 cm) long, with dark plumage, whitish beak and legs, bare red head covered with whitish bumps, and a 6-ft (1.8-m) wingspread. It uses its keen sense of smell to find carrion. It occurs throughout most of the Americas.

Turkic languages Family of more than 20 ALTAIC languages spoken by some 135 million people from the Balkans to central Siberia. They divide Turkic into four groups. The SE or Uighur group comprises Uighur, spoken mainly in Xinjiang, China; and Uzbek, spoken mainly in Uzbekistan and surrounding countries. The SW or Oguz (Oghuz) group includes TURKISH; Azerbaijani (Azeri), spoken in Azerbaijan and NW Iran; Crimean Tatar (Crimean Turkish), spoken mostly in Ukraine and Uzbekistan; and Turkmen, used in Turkmenistan, N Iran, and N Afghanistan. The NW or Kipchak group includes Kazak, spoken in Kazakhstan and surrounding areas; Kyrgyz (Kirghiz), spoken in Kyrgyzstan and adjacent areas; TATAR; and Bashkir, spoken in Bashkortostan and adjacent areas in Russia. The NE or Altai group comprises a group of languages and dialects spoken in Siberia northeast of the Irtysh River and in adjacent parts of Mongolia, and Yakut (Sakha), spoken in Yakutia and adjacent areas. The earliest attestations of Turkic are a group of 8th-cent. inscriptions of N Mongolia, in a distinctive writing system called Turkic runes. With the Islamicization of nearly all Turkic peoples southwest of the Irtysh beginning around 900, Turkic languages began to adopt the ARABIC ALPHABET. Today the LATIN and CYRILLIC alphabets are more extensively used.

Turkic peoples See TURKS

Turkish bath Bath originating in the Middle East, combining exposure to warm air, steam immersion, massage, and a cold bath or shower. The Turkish bath (*hammām*) combines the massage and cosmetic aspects of the Eastern bath tradition with Roman plumbing and heating techniques. Turkish baths were smaller than the Roman THERMAE and more sparsely lit, and often richly decorated with marble or mosaics. Used for socializing and relaxation, they were popular throughout the Islamic world; some are still in use. In the 19th cent., the Turkish bath was imported to Europe and the U.S.

Turkish language TURKIC language of Turkey, spoken by about 90% of its population. Turkish has about 59 million speakers, with many enclaves around Europe. Anatolian Turkish, written in the ARABIC ALPHABET, is first attested in the 13th cent. Ottoman Turkish was so heavily influenced by Persian and Arabic that it became incomprehensible to lower social strata. Efforts to re-Turkicize the language made serious gains in the 20th cent. with the founding of the Turkish republic. Much Perso-Arabic vocabulary was removed, and the LATIN ALPHABET was adopted with the addition of diacritics for sounds peculiar to Turkish.

Turkistan *or* **Turkestan** Historical region, central Asia. The total area of more than 1,000,000 sq mi (2,600,000 sq km) was divided by the PAMIRS and TIAN SHAN range into W. and E. Turkistan. W. Turkistan, or Russian Turkestan, came under Russian rule in the 19th cent.; it included present-day Turkmenistan, Uzbekistan, Tajikistan, Kyrgyzstan, and S Kazakstan. E. Turkistan, or Chinese Turkestan, was annexed by China in the 8th cent.; it included the former province of Sinkiang (now Xinjiang Uygur).

Turkmen *or* **Turkoman** *or* **Turcoman** Muslim people belonging to the SW branch of the Turkic linguistic group. They number more than six million; most live in Turkmenistan and adjacent Central Asian countries. Initially a nomadic pastoral people living in tent villages, some later took up agriculture. They have traditionally divided themselves by economic function, each division being headed by a KHAN.

Turkmenistan Republic, W central Asia. Area: 188,500 sq mi (488,100 sq km). Population (2000): 4,885,000. Capital: ASHGABAT. Turkmen make up more than 75% of the population, followed by Uzbeks, Russians, Kazaks, Tatars,

[Map of Turkmenistan showing surrounding countries: KAZAKSTAN, UZBEKISTAN, IRAN, AFGHANISTAN, CASPIAN SEA, ARAL SEA, KARAKUM DESERT, Ashgabat, and other cities and features. Inset labeled TURKMENISTAN with globe. Scale 1: 19,553,000, 0–80–160 mi, 0–120–240 km. ©1999, Encyclopædia Britannica, Inc.]

Ukrainians, and Armenians. Language: Turkmen (official). Religions: Sunni Islam, Russian Orthodoxy. Currency: Turkmen manat. Though there are some hills and low mountains, about nine-tenths of Turkmenistan is desert, chiefly the KARAKUM. The main rivers are the AMU DARYA and Murgab. Many irrigation canals and reservoirs have been built, including the Karakum Canal, which runs 870 mi (1,400 km) between the Amu Darya and the CASPIAN SEA. The country's chief products are oil and natural gas, cotton, silk, carpets, fish, and fruit. It is a republic with one legislative house; its head of state and government is the president, assisted by the People's Council. The earliest traces of human settlement in central Asia, dating back to Paleolithic times, have been found in Turkmenistan. The nomadic, tribal Turkmen probably entered the area in the 11th cent. A.D. They were conquered by the Russians in the early 1880s and the region became part of Russian Turke-

stan. It was organized as the Turkmen Soviet Socialist Republic in 1924 and became a constituent republic of the U.S.S.R. in 1925. The country gained full independence from the Soviet Union in 1991 under the name Turkmenistan. The next decade was marked by economic struggles, as an eccentric dictatorship imposed a far-reaching nationalist and racialist "Turkmenization" on its institutions and everyday life.

Turks *or* **Turkic peoples** Various peoples who speak TURKIC LANGUAGES. They are connected with the T'u-chüeh, nomadic people who in the 6th cent. founded an empire stretching from Mongolia to the Black Sea. In the 11th cent. the SELJUQS created an extensive empire after defeating the Byzantines at the Battle of Manzikert (1071); the Turks then took Anatolia, base of the later OTTOMAN EMPIRE. Though overrun by the MONGOLS, the Turks succeeded in absorbing them after GENGHIS KHAN's death (1227). In the 14th cent. TIMUR held SW Central Asia, but in the 15th cent. Russian expansion drove the Turks eastward. Today the Turkic peoples live mostly in Turkey, Uzbekistan, Afghanistan, Kazakhstan, and Turkmenistan.

Turks and Caicos Islands \ˈkä-ˌkōs, ˈkä-kəs\ British dependency (pop., 1993 est.: 13,000), W INDIES. It is made up of two small island groups at the SE end of the BAHAMAS. The Turks group includes Grand Turk and Salt Cay; the Caicos group includes S. Caicos, E. Caicos, Middle (or Grand) Caicos, N. Caicos, Providenciales, and W. Caicos. When Juan PONCE DE LEÓN visited in 1512, the islands were inhabited by Indians. British colonists from BERMUDA arrived in 1678. The islands became a crown colony in 1962 and shared a governor with the Bahamas 1965–73. A new constitution was adopted in 1988. The chief industries are tourism and offshore financial services.

Turner, Frederick Jackson (1861–1932) U.S. historian. Born in Portage, Wisc., he rejected the doctrine that U.S. institutions could be traced mainly to European origins, and demonstrated his theories in a series of essays. In "The Significance of the Frontier in American History" (1893), he asserted that the American character had been shaped by frontier life and the end of the frontier era. His essays were collected in *The Frontier in American History* (1920) and *The Significance of Sections in American History* (1932, Pulitzer Prize).

Turner, J(oseph) M(allord) W(illiam) (1775–1851) British landscape painter. He entered the Royal Academy school in 1789. In 1802 he became a full academician and in 1807 was appointed professor of perspective. His early work was concerned with accurate depictions of places, but *The Shipwreck* (1805) shows his new emphasis on luminosity, atmosphere, and romantic, dramatic subjects. In later paintings, such as *Sunrise, with a Boat Between Headlands* (1845), architectural and natural details are sacrificed to effects of color and light. His compositions became more fluid, suggesting

J. M. W. Turner, self-portrait, 1798

movement and space. In breaking down conventional formulas of representation, he anticipated French IMPRESSIONISM. His immense reputation in the 19th cent. was due largely to John RUSKIN's enthusiasm for his early works; 20th-cent. critics celebrated the abstract qualities of his late color compositions.

Turner, Lana (*orig.* Julia Jean Mildred Frances) (1920–1995) U.S. film actress. Born in Wallace, Idaho, she made her screen debut in 1937. A sultry, shapely blonde, publicized by MGM as the "Sweater Girl," she became a popular World War II pinup while starring in such movies as *Ziegfeld Girl* (1941), *Honky Tonk* (1941), and *Johnny Eager* (1942), and later *The Postman Always Rings Twice* (1946), *Peyton Place* (1957), and *Imitation of Life* (1959). Her tumultuous private life included eight marriages and the sensational 1958 stabbing to death of her gangster boyfriend by her 14-year-old daughter.

T U V

Turner, Nat (1800–1831) U.S. insurrectionist. Born into slavery in Southampton Co., Va., he became convinced of his mission to lead American slaves out of bondage and developed a scheme to capture the armory at Jerusalem, Va. He began his insurrection by killing his master's family, then led 75 slaves as they killed about 60 whites on a two-day march to Jerusalem. State militia and local whites defeated the insurrectionists, who were captured or killed. Turner eluded arrest for six weeks but was found, tried, and hanged. Alarmed, Southern states passed legislation forbidding the education, movement, or assembly of slaves.

Turner, Ted (*orig.* Robert Edward, III) (b.1938) U.S. broadcasting entrepreneur. Born in Cincinnati, he took over his father's Atlanta-based advertising firm in 1963 and restored it to profitability. In 1970 he bought an Atlanta television station, which in 1975 became the superstation of the Turner Broadcasting System, broadcasting via satellite to cable systems nationwide. In 1976 he bought the Atlanta Braves baseball team and in 1977 the Atlanta Hawks basketball team. In 1977 he piloted his yacht, *Courageous*, to victory in the AMERICA'S CUP race. He expanded his broadcasting empire with the 1980 launch of CNN and the 1986 purchase of MGM and its library of over 4,000 old movies. In 1996 he merged his broadcasting system with Time Warner and became its vice-chairman. In 1999 he pledged $1 billion to the United Nations.

turnip Hardy biennial plant in the MUSTARD FAMILY, cultivated for its fleshy roots and tender leaves. There are two species, the turnip proper (*Brassica rapa*) and the RUTABAGA. The true turnip probably originated in middle and E Asia and spread throughout the temperate zone. Both species are fast-growing, cool-season crops.

turpentine Any resinous exudate or extract from CONIFERS, especially PINES. Semifluid mixtures of organic compounds consisting of RESINS dissolved in a volatile OIL, turpentines can be distilled (see DISTILLATION) into the volatile oil of turpentine and the nonvolatile rosin. A mixture of ISOPRENOIDS, chiefly pinene, turpentine is a colorless, odorous, flammable liquid that does not mix with water but is a good SOLVENT for many substances, including paints and varnishes. It is used as a raw material for resins, insecticides, oil additives, synthetic pine oil, and CAMPHOR.

turquoise Hydrated copper and aluminum phosphate mineral that is used extensively as a gemstone. The color of turquoise ranges from blue through various shades of green to yellowish gray; a delicate sky-blue is most valued for gem purposes. Numerous deposits of turquoise in the SW U.S. have been worked for centuries by American Indians. The mineral also occurs in Iran, N Africa, Australia, and Siberia.

turtle Any of more than 250 species (order Chelonia) of REPTILES having a bony shell overlaid with horny shields. Turtles have existed for 200 million years, making them the oldest surviving reptiles. Most species are aquatic or semiaquatic; some are terrestrial. Turtles eat plants, animals, or both. They are toothless, have a horny beak, and range from less than 4 in. (10 cm) to more than 7 ft (2 m) long. They have sturdy, sprawling limbs with short feet or paddlelike flippers (marine turtles). Most pull the head backward into the shell. Almost half the known turtle species are rare, threatened, or endangered. See also SNAPPING TURTLE, TERRAPIN, TORTOISE.

Tuscany *Italian* **Toscana** Autonomous region (pop., 1996 est.: 3,523,000), W central Italy. Its capital is FLORENCE. It came under Roman rule in the 3d cent. B.C. Its several independent city-states in the 12th–13th cent. were subsequently united under the MEDICI dukes of Florence. It passed to SARDINIA and the kingdom of Italy in the 1860s. The region suffered severe damage in World War II and extensive floods in 1966. Its mineral resources include the world-famous Carrara MARBLE, while its agricultural products include olives, olive oil, wines, and livestock. Tourism is important, especially in Florence, PISA, and SIENA.

Tusculum \'təs-kyə-ləm\ Ancient town, LATIUM, Italy. Located near ROME, it was a Latin settlement as early as the 1st millennium B.C. It was a favorite resort of wealthy Romans from the 1st to the 4th cent. A.D., and the home of M. T. CICERO. Ruins include a forum, a 2nd-cent. amphitheater, and a medieval castle.

Tuskegee Airmen \tə-'skē-gē\ Black servicemen of the U.S. Army Air Forces (USAAF) who trained at Alabama's Tuskegee Army Air Field in World War II, the first African-American military flying unit. The first class in 1941 became the 99th Pursuit Squadron, commanded by Benjamin DAVIS. In 1944 it was joined by three more squadrons to constitute the 332nd Fighter Group, which was the USAAF's only escort group that did not lose a bomber to enemy planes. A second black flying group, the 477th Bombardment Group, was established later in the war. In all, the Tuskegee Airmen flew 1,578 missions, destroyed 261 enemy aircraft, and won over 850 medals.

Tuskegee University Private university in Tuskegee, Ala. Booker T. WASHINGTON founded the school in 1881 as a teachers college for blacks. George Washington CARVER conducted most of his research at Tuskegee (1896–1943). Today the university includes schools of arts and sciences, education, engineering and architecture, nursing, and veterinary medicine. Total enrollment is about 3,000.

Tussaud \tü-'sō\, **Marie** *orig.* Marie Grosholtz (1761–1850) French-British founder of Madame Tussaud's museum of wax figures in London. From 1780 until the French Revolution, she served as art tutor to Louis XVI's sister. During the Reign of Terror she made death masks from heads (frequently those of her friends) freshly severed by the guillotine. In 1802 she moved to Britain with her collection of wax models. Her museum contains a variety of historical figures, including the original models she made of such contemporaries as VOLTAIRE and Benjamin FRANKLIN.

Tutankhamen \ˌtü-ˌtän-'kä-mən\ *orig.* Tutankhaten (r.1333–1323 B.C.) Egyptian PHARAOH of the 18th dynasty. About 8 when he took the throne, he was advised to move back to Memphis from Akhetaton, the city of his father-in-law and predecessor, AKHENATON. During his reign traditional religion was restored after the changes made by Akhenaton. Shortly before he died, still in his teens, he sent troops to Syria to aid an ally against HITTITE vassals. His tomb's location was forgotten and his burial chamber was not opened until 1922. Its treasures made Tutankhamen perhaps the best-known of the pharaohs despite his early death and few accomplishments.

Tutsi \'tüt-sē\ African group, numbering 1.5 million, who live in Rwanda and Burundi. They represent an aristocratic minority, which has dominated the more populous HUTU. Originally warrior-herders, the Tutsi entered the area in the 14th or 15th cent. Assisted by German and Belgian colonial regimes, they cultivated a lord–vassal relationship with the Hutu. Today Hutu and Tutsi cultures have become integrated; both speak Rwanda and Rundi and adhere to similar religious beliefs. The Tutsi retained their dominant position over the Hutu in Rwanda until 1961, when the monarch was overthrown. An unsuccessful Hutu revolt in Burundi in 1972 led to 100,000 deaths, mostly Hutu. In Burundi (1993) and Rwanda (1994), further clashes occurred, the latter including a Hutu genocidal campaign in which over a million people died and 1–2 million Hutu were forced into refugee camps.

Tutu, Desmond (Mpilo) (*later* **Sir Desmond**) (b.1931) S. African Anglican cleric. He studied theology at King's College, London, then became an Anglican priest in 1961, and bishop of Lesotho in 1976. Named general secretary of the S. African Council of Churches in 1978, he became an eloquent and outspoken advocate for the rights of black S. Africans, advocating nonviolent protest and international economic sanctions. In 1984 he received the Nobel Peace Prize. In 1986 he was elected the first black archbishop of Cape Town and head of S. Africa's 1.6-million-member Anglican Church. He retired from the primacy in 1996 and became chairman of the Truth and Reconciliation Commission.

Tuvalu \tü-'vä-lü\ *formerly* **Ellice Islands** \'e-lis\ Nation, W central Pacific Ocean. Area: 9.25 sq mi (23.96 sq km). Population (2000): 11,000. Capital: Fongafale (on the FUNAFUTI atoll). Most of the people are Polynesian. Language: Tuvalu, English. Religion: Church of Tuvalu (evolved from Congregational missions). Currency: Tuvalu dollar (equivalent to Australian dollar). Tuvalu is an island group made up of five atolls and four coral islands, all of them low-lying and covered mainly with coconut palms, breadfruit trees, and grasses. The economy is based on subsistence agriculture and fishing. It is a constitutional monarchy with one legislative house; its chief of state is the British monarch represented by the governor-general, and the head of government is the prime minister. The original Polynesian settlers probably came mainly from Samoa or Tonga. The islands were sighted by the Spanish in the 16th cent. Europeans settled there in the 19th cent. and intermarried with Tuvaluans. During this period Peruvian slave traders, known as "blackbirders," devastated the population. In 1856 the U.S. claimed the four S islands for guano mining. Missionaries from Europe arrived in 1865 and rapidly converted the islanders to Christianity. In 1892 Tuvalu joined the British GILBERT ISLANDS, a protectorate that became the Gilbert and Ellice Islands colony in 1916. Tuvaluans voted in 1974 for separation from the Gilberts (now Kiribati). Tuvalu gained independence in 1978. Elections were held in 1981, and a revised constitution was adopted in 1986. See also map at OCEANIA.

Tuxtla (Gutiérrez) \'tüst-lä\ City (pop., 1995: 378,000), capital of CHIAPAS state, SE Mexico. The Spanish who arrived there in the 16th cent. were frequently beset by native Indians, and the town grew slowly. In 1892 it was made the state capital. The region has archaeological remains of pre-Columbian culture.

Tuzla \'tüz-lä\ Town (pop., 1991: 132,000), NE Bosnia and Herzegovina. Deposits of rock salt are located nearby, and its name is from the Turkish *tuz*, "salt." It was a Turkish garrison town from 1510 until it passed to the Austro-Hungarian empire in the 19th cent. It was incorporated into Yugoslavia in 1918. It was a target during the BOSNIAN CONFLICT.

TVA See TENNESSEE VALLEY AUTHORITY

TWA See TRANS WORLD AIRLINES, INC.

Twain, Mark *orig.* Samuel Langhorne Clemens (1835–1910) U.S. writer. Born in Florida, Mo., he grew up in nearby Hannibal, on the Mississippi River. In 1856 he signed on as an apprentice to a steamboat pilot. He plied the Mississippi for almost four years before heading west, where he wrote the story that made him famous, "The Celebrated Jumping Frog of Calaveras County" (1865). He traveled widely as a successful lecturer and to obtain material for his writing, including *The Innocents Abroad* (1869) and *Roughing It* (1872). He won a worldwide audience for his stories of youthful adventures, especially *Tom Sawyer* (1876), *The Prince and the Pauper* (1881), *Life on the Mississippi* (1883), and *Huckleberry Finn* (1884), one of the masterpieces of American fiction. The satirical *A Connecticut Yankee in King Arthur's Court* (1889) and increasingly grim works including *Pudd'nhead Wilson* (1894) followed. In the 1890s financial speculations bankrupted him and his eldest daughter died. After his wife's death (1904), he expressed his pessimism in such late works as *Letters from the Earth* (published 1962).

Tweed, William Marcy *known as* **Boss Tweed** (1823–1878) U.S. politician. Born in New York City, he was initially a bookkeeper. As city alderman (1851–56), he gained influence in TAMMANY HALL. He appointed political cronies to key city posts and built a group later called the Tweed ring. As head of Tammany's general committee (from 1860), he controlled the Democratic Party's nominations to all city positions, while receiving payments from contractors and corporations. Elected to the state senate (1868), he also became Tammany's grand sachem

William Marcy Tweed

(leader) and controlled city and state political patronage. He gained control of the city treasury and plundered sums estimated at $30–200 million. Reformers and exposure by the press, including Thomas NAST's cartoons in *Harper's*

Weekly, brought prosecution, led by Samuel TILDEN, that sent Tweed to prison (1873–75, 1876–78).

Twentieth Century–Fox Film Corp. U.S. movie studio. It was formed in 1935 by the merger of Twentieth Century Pictures (founded in 1933 by Joseph Schenck and Darryl ZANUCK) and the Fox Film Corp. (founded in 1915 by William Fox). The new studio produced mainly westerns and musicals, as well as such notable films as *The Grapes of Wrath* (1940) and *The Snake Pit* (1948). In 1953 it introduced CinemaScope with *The Robe,* and later it made such hits as *The King and I* (1956), *South Pacific* (1958), *The Sound of Music* (1965), *Patton* (1970), and *Star Wars* (1977), the film industry's most profitable movie to that time. In 1985 the company was sold to Rupert MURDOCH.

Twentieth Congress of the Communist Party of the Soviet Union (Feb. 14–25, 1956) Meeting at which Nikita KHRUSHCHEV repudiated Joseph STALIN and STALINISM. Khrushchev's secret speech denouncing the former Soviet leader was accompanied by his Report announcing a new foreign policy, based on "the Leninist principle of coexistence of states with different social systems." Khrushchev also used the Congress to take control of the party from the Stalinist old guard.

twenty-one See BLACKJACK

Two Sicilies See Two SICILIES

Tycho Brahe See Tycho BRAHE

Tyler, Anne (b.1941) U.S. writer. Born in Minneapolis, she settled in Baltimore in 1967. Her novels, comedies of manner marked by compassionate wit and precise details of domestic life, include *Dinner at the Homesick Restaurant* (1982), *The Accidental Tourist* (1985; film, 1988), *Breathing Lessons* (1988, Pulitzer Prize), and *Saint Maybe* (1991). Several focus on eccentric middle-class people living in chaotic, disunited families in Baltimore.

Tyler, John (1790–1862) 10th president of the U.S. (1841–45). Born in Charles City Co., Va., he served in the U.S. House of Representatives (1817–21), as governor of Virginia (1825–27), and in the Senate (1827–36), as a states'-rights supporter. After breaking with the Democratic Party, he was nominated by the WHIG PARTY for vice president under W. H. HARRISON. They won the 1840 election, stressing party loyalty and the slogan "Tippecanoe and Tyler too!" Harrison died a month after taking office, and Tyler became the first to attain the presidency "by accident." He vetoed a national bank bill

John Tyler Portrait by George Healy, 1858

supported by the Whigs, and all but one member of the cabinet resigned, leaving him without party support. Nonetheless, he reorganized the navy, settled the second of the SEMINOLE WARS in Florida, and oversaw the annexation of Texas. Nominated for reelection, he withdrew in favor of James K. POLK and retired to his Virginia plantation. He organized the Washington Peace Conference (1861) to resolve sectional differences, but when the Senate rejected a proposed compromise, Tyler urged Virginia to secede.

Tyler, Wat See PEASANTS' REVOLT

Tylor, Edward Burnett (*later* **Sir Edward**) (1832–1917) British anthropologist, often called the founder of CULTURAL ANTHROPOLOGY. He taught at Oxford Univ. (1884–1909), where he became the first professor of anthropology. His *Primitive Culture* (2 vols., 1871) developed the theory of an evolutionary relationship between primitive and modern cultures, stressing the cultural achievements that marked the progression of all humanity from a "savage" to a "civilized" state. At a time when there was still controversy over whether all human races belonged to a single species, Tylor was a powerful advocate of the unity of all humankind. He was instrumental in establishing anthropology as an academic discipline.

typeface See FONT

typesetting Setting of type for use in any of various PRINTING processes. Type for printing, using woodblocks, was invented in China in the 11th cent, and movable type using metal molds had appeared in Korea by the 13th cent. It was reinvented in Europe in the 1450s by Johannes GUTENBERG. For much of its history, typesetting and printing were often performed by the same person, who arranged movable type, one character at a time, in rows corresponding to the individual lines in the publication, and operated the hand press to imprint the image on paper. Typesetting was revolutionized in the 1880s with the invention of the "hot-metal" processes: Linotype (1884), in which each line of type was assembled by use of a typewriter-like keyboard and cast as a single slug of molten metal, and Monotype (1887), which also used a keyboard but cast each character separately. Photocomposition—the composition of text directly on film or photosensitive paper, using a rotating drum or disk with cutout type characters through which light could be directed onto the receiving surface—appeared in the early 20th cent. Today characters are generated by computer; systems include a keyboard that produces magnetic tape for input, a computer for making hyphenation, layout, and other page-makeup decisions, and a unit that transfers the images to light-sensitive paper or film by pulses from a laser beam, which forms each character in response to computer-generated electric pulses. Increasingly, typesetting projects are sent to the printer as electronic files rather than on paper or film.

typewriter Writing machine in which the characters are produced by steel types activated by keys on a keyboard striking the paper through an inked ribbon, the paper being held by a roller that moves along with a carriage when a key is struck. The first practical typewriter was patented in 1868 by Christopher Latham Sholes (1819–1890); commercial production began at the Remington firearms company in 1874. By the end of the century the typewriter had come to dominate the American office. The first electric typewriter for office use was introduced in 1920. From the 1970s typewriters began to be replaced by PERSONAL COMPUTERS and their associated printers.

typhoid or **typhoid fever** Acute BACTERIAL DISEASE. *Salmonella typhi,* usually ingested in food or water, multiplies in the intestinal wall and then enters the bloodstream, causing SEPTICEMIA. Headache, aching, and restlessness are followed by high fever with delirium, and a rash on the trunk. The sites where the bacteria multiplied become inflamed and may ulcerate, leading to intestinal bleeding or PERITONITIS. Patients become exhausted and emaciated; up to 25% die if not treated. ANTIBIOTIC treatment is effective. Patients can become carriers, who can contaminate the food they handle. Prevention depends mainly on water and sewage treatment and excluding carriers from food-handling jobs.

Typhoid Mary *orig.* Mary Mallon (1870?–1938) U.S. carrier of TYPHOID. A 1904 typhoid epidemic on Long Island was traced to households where she had been a cook. She fled, but authorities finally caught up with her and isolated her on an island off the Bronx. In 1910 she was released after agreeing not to take a food-handling job again, but she did, causing more outbreaks. She was again isolated, for the rest of her life. Three deaths and 51 cases were directly attributed to her.

typhoon See TROPICAL CYCLONE

typhus Any of a group of related diseases caused by different species of RICKETTSIA that release TOXINS into the blood. Headache, chills, fever, and general pains begin suddenly and a rash soon after. The different bacteria are transmitted by lice, fleas, mites, and ticks. Epidemic typhus, spread by the body louse, is one of the great scourges of history, associated with crowded, filthy conditions. Improved hygiene has nearly eliminated it from the Western world, but it persists in many countries, despite modern vaccines and pesticides. See also ROCKY MTN. SPOTTED FEVER.

typographic printing See LETTERPRESS PRINTING

typography Design or selection of letter forms to be organized into words and sentences and printed on a page. Typography originated after the invention of printing from movable type in the mid-15th cent. The three major type families in the history of Western printing are roman, italic, and black letter (Gothic). All had their origin in the scripts of the calligraphers whose work was ultimately replaced by printing. In the succeeding centuries typographers have created some 10,000 typefaces (a complete set of letter forms of a particular design). Commonly used typefaces include Caslon, Baskerville, Bodoni, Garamond, and Times Roman.

tyrannosaur Any THEROPOD in the genus *Tyrannosaurus,* the largest carnivorous DINOSAURS, found as fossils in Late Cretaceous (98–65 million years ago) deposits in N. America and E Asia. Adults were more than 40 ft (12 m) long and 16–18 ft (over 5 m) tall and weighed 6 tons (5.4 metric tons) or more. Tyrannosaurs walked with the long tail off the ground. They had a short, thick neck, a very large skull, and pointed teeth, up to 6 in. (15 cm) long, with serrated edges. Each small forelimb had two claws, perhaps for holding struggling prey. The best-known species is *Tyrannosaurus rex,* the largest terrestrial carnivore that ever lived.

Tyre \'tīr\ *Arabic* **Sur** \'sür\ Town (metro. area pop., 1994: 80,000), S Lebanon. In the 11th–6th cent. B.C., it was a major commercial city, center of PHOENICIAN civilization, and a dominant sea power. It was noted for its silken garments and Tyrian purple dye. It is frequently mentioned in the Bible. It fell to ALEXANDER THE GREAT in 332 B.C. Later under the SELEUCIDS, then the Romans, it passed to the Muslims in the 7th cent. A.D. After its capture by the Crusaders in 1124, it became a chief city of the kingdom of Jerusalem. It fell again to the Muslims in 1291 and was destroyed. The modern town was included in Lebanon in 1920.

Tyrol See TIROL

Tyrone \'tī-rən\, **Earl of** *orig.* Hugh O'Neill (c.1540–1616) Irish rebel. As chieftain of the powerful O'Neill family of Ulster from 1593, he led skirmishes against the English and won a battle in Ulster that sparked a countrywide revolt (1598). He received aid and troops from Spain (1601) but was defeated by the English at Kinsale and forced to surrender (1603). In 1607 he fled with about 100 chieftains; the so-called "flight of the earls" brought an end to Gaelic Ulster, and the province was rapidly anglicized.

Tyson, Mike (*orig.* Michael Gerald) (b.1966) U.S. boxer. Born in New York City, he was a street-gang member who began boxing in reform school. In 1986 he defeated Trevor Berbick, becoming at 20 the youngest heavyweight champion in history. He defended the title against 10 challengers before losing to James "Buster" Douglas in 1990. In 1992 he was convicted of rape and sentenced to six years in prison; he was released on parole in 1995. In 1996 he challenged but lost to Evander Holyfield; in a 1997 rematch he was disqualified for biting off a piece of Holyfield's ear, and his license was revoked.

U

U-2 Affair (1960) Confrontation between the U.S. and the Soviet Union. After the Soviet Union shot down a U.S. U-2 reconnaissance plane and claimed that the pilot, F. Gary Powers (1929–1977), had stated that his mission was to collect Soviet intelligence data, Nikita KHRUSHCHEV declared that he would not take part in a scheduled summit conference with the U.S., Britain, and France unless the U.S. immediately stopped such flights, apologized, and punished those responsible. Pres. Dwight EISENHOWER agreed only to the first stipulation, and the summit was adjourned. Powers was sentenced to 10 years in prison; in 1962 he was exchanged for the Soviet spy Rudolf Abel.

Ubangi River \ü-'baŋ-gē\ River, central Africa. Formed by the Bomu and Uele rivers on the N central border of Congo (Zaire), it flows west and south, forming most of the boundary with Republic of the Congo and the Central African Republic, then empties into the CONGO RIVER. It is 700 mi (1126 km) long.

Ubangi-Shari See CENTRAL AFRICAN REPUBLIC

Ubasti See BASTET

U-boat *German* Unterseeboot. German SUBMARINE ("undersea boat"). The first German submarine, the U-1, was built in 1905. By the eve of World War I, Germany possessed merchant U-boats over 300 ft (90 m) long and able to carry 700 tons (635 metric tons) of cargo; fitted with TORPEDO tubes and deck guns, they became the first submarines used in war. U-boat warfare against merchant ships was largely responsible for U.S. entry into the war. In World War II the U-boat initially enjoyed great success, but Allied tactics eventually prevailed. Of the 1,162 U-boats built during World War II, 785 were destroyed.

UC See Univ. of CALIFORNIA

Ucayali River \ü-kä-'yä-lē\ River, central and N Peru. Formed by the Apurimac and Urubamba rivers, it meanders north to unite with the Marañón and become the chief headstream of the AMAZON RIVER. It is navigable for most of its 1,000-mi (1,600-km) length.

Uccello \ü-'che-lō\, **Paolo** *orig.* Paolo di Dono (1397–1475) Italian painter. Apprenticed to the workshop of Lorenzo GHIBERTI, at 18 he was admitted to the painters' guild in Florence. *The Deluge,* one of his frescoes in the Chiostro Verde of Santa Maria Novella, demonstrates his intense study of perspective. His three panels depicting the Battle of San Romano, like all the extant works of his mature years, combine the decorative late Gothic style with the new heroic style of the early Renaissance.

UCLA See Univ. of CALIFORNIA

Udall \'yü-dəl, 'yü-ˌdȯl\, **Nicholas** (1505?–1556) English playwright. The headmaster of Eton College from 1534 and of Westminster from 1555, Udall was well known as a translator. Of his many plays, only one is extant, *Ralph Roister Doister* (performed c.1553), the first known English comedy. About a braggart soldier-hero who is exposed as an arrant coward, it marks the emergence of comedy from the medieval morality plays, interludes, and farces.

Ufa \ü-'fä\ City (pop., 1997 est.: 1,082,000), W Russia. It was founded as a fortress in 1574 to protect the trade route across the URAL MTNS. from KAZAN to Tyumen. It developed as an industrial center from the late 19th cent., and especially after World War II. Chief industries include electrical equipment, lumber and veneer, and oil refining.

Uffizi Gallery \ü-'fēt-sē\ Art museum in Florence, housing the world's finest collection of Italian Renaissance painting.

The core collection derives from the MEDICI FAMILY. In 1559 Cosimo I de' MEDICI hired Giorgio VASARI to design the Uffizi Palace (1560–80), originally for use as government offices *(uffizi).* In 1737 Maria Ludovica, last of the Medici, bequeathed the family collections to Tuscany; the collection was opened to the public in 1769. The building was restored and enlarged after bomb damage in World War II and flooding in 1966. The museum's outstanding collections include 100,000 prints and drawings.

UFO See UNIDENTIFIED FLYING OBJECT

Uganda \yü-'gan-də, yü-'gän-də\ *officially* **Republic of Uganda** Nation, E Africa. Area: 93,070 sq mi (241,040 sq km). Population (2000): 23,318,000. Capital: KAMPALA. There are dozens of African ethnic groups, as well as a small but influential Asian community. Languages: English

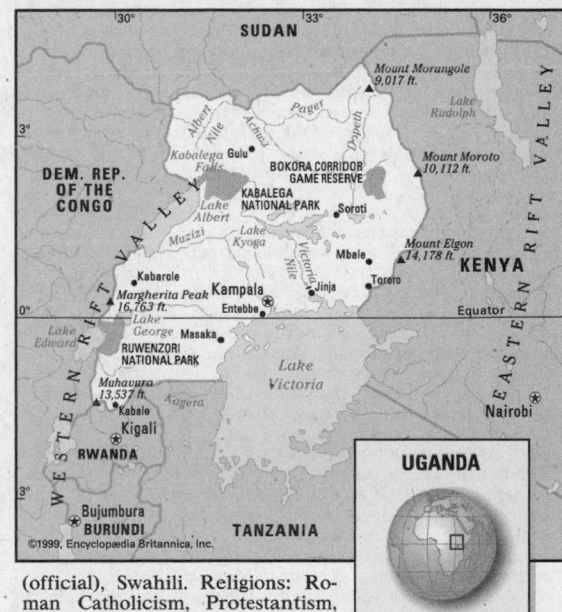

(official), Swahili. Religions: Roman Catholicism, Protestantism, Islam, and indigenous beliefs. Currency: Ugandan shilling. A landlocked country on the equator, Uganda is largely situated on a plateau, with volcanic mountains edging its E and W borders; Mt Elgon (14,178 ft, or 4,322 m) is the highest peak. Part of Lake VICTORIA occupies virtually all of SE Uganda; other major lakes are Lakes ALBERT, Kyoga, EDWARD, George, and Bisina. The NILE RIVER traverses it. Huge tracts of land are devoted to national parks and game reserves. The economy is based largely on agriculture and food processing. Livestock raising and fishing are also important, and there is some manufacturing and mining. It is a republic with one legislative house; its head of state and government is the president. By the 19th cent. the region was composed of several separate kingdoms inhabited by various peoples, including Bantu- and Nilotic-speaking tribes. Arab traders reached the area in the 1840s. The native kingdom of Buganda was visited by the first European explorers in 1862. Protestant and Catholic missionaries arrived in the 1870s, and the development of religious factions led to persecution and civil strife. In 1894 Buganda was formally proclaimed a British protectorate. As Uganda, it gained its independence in 1962, and in 1967 it adopted a republican constitution. The civilian government was overthrown in 1971 and replaced by the brutal regime of Idi AMIN. His invasion of Tanzania in late 1978 resulted in the collapse of his regime. The civilian government was again deposed by the military in 1985; under Yoweri Museveni (from 1986) the country regained stability.

Uighurs *or* **Uygurs** \'wē-ˌgŭrz\ Turkic-speaking people of Central Asia. More than 7.7 million Uighurs live in NW China today, and some 300,000 in Uzbekistan, Kazakstan, and Kyrgyzstan. They are mentioned in Chinese records from the 3rd cent. A.D. They established a kingdom in the 8th cent., which was overrun in 840, then established another around the Tian Mtns.; it was overthrown in 1209 by the MONGOLS. Most are Muslims, and they have often agitated for independence.

Ujung Pandang \'ü-ˌjŭŋ-'pän-ˌdäŋ\ *formerly* **Macassar** \mə-'ka-sər\ City (pop., 1995 est.: 1,092,000), SULAWESI, Indonesia. Already a thriving port when the Portuguese arrived in the 16th cent., it came under control of the Dutch, who finally deposed the sultan in 1667. It was made a free port in 1848 and the capital of the Dutch-sponsored state of Indonesia Timur (E. Indonesia) in 1946. In 1949 it became part of the Republic of Indonesia.

ukiyo-e \ü-ˌkē-ō-'ā\ (Japanese: "pictures of the floating world") Dominant art movement of the EDO PERIOD (1603–1867) in Japan. Screen paintings were the first works to be done in the style, which depicted aspects of the entertainment quarters ("floating world") of Edo (modern Tokyo) and other cities. The medium was most fully exploited by wood-block printmakers and such celebrated artists as HIROSHIGE ANDO, HOKUSAI, and UTAMARO. Favorite subjects included famous courtesans and prostitutes, kabuki actors in famous roles, and erotica; they were executed in flat, decorative colors and expressive patterns. *Ukiyo-e* prints designed for mass consumption attracted much attention in Europe in the 19th cent. and had a great influence on avant-garde French artists.

Ukraine \yü-'krān\ Republic, SE Europe. Area: 233,100 sq mi (603,700 sq km). Population (2000): 49,242,000. Capital: KIEV. Ethnic Ukrainians make up 65% of the population; minorities are principally Russians. Languages: Ukrainian (official), Russian, Romanian, Polish, Hungarian. Religion: Ukrainian Orthodoxy. Currency: hryvny. Ukraine consists of level plains and the CARPATHIAN MTNS., which extend through the W region for more than 150 mi (240 km). The BUG, DNIEPER, DONETS, and DNIESTER are its major rivers. The DONETS BASIN in the E central region is one of the major heavy-industrial and mining-metallurgical complexes of Europe. It mines iron ore and coal, and produces natural gas, petroleum, iron, and steel. It is a major producer of winter wheat and sugar beets. Ukraine is a republic with one legislative body; its head of state is the president, and the head of government is the prime minister. Different parts of the area were invaded and occupied in the first millennium B.C. by the Cimmerians, Scythians, and Sarmatians, and in the first millennium A.D. by the Goths, Huns, Bulgars, Avars, Khazars, and Magyars. Slavic tribes settled there after the 4th cent. Kiev was its chief town. The Mongol conquest in the mid-13th century decisively ended Kievan power. Ruled by Lithuania in the 14th cent. and Poland in the 16th cent., it fell to Russian rule in the 18th cent. The Ukrainian National Republic, established in 1917, declared its independence from Soviet Russia in 1918 but was reconquered in 1919; it was made the Ukrainian Soviet Socialist Republic of the U.S.S.R. in 1923. The NW region was held by Poland 1919–39. The Ukraine suffered a severe famine in 1932–33 under Soviet leader Joseph STALIN; over 5 million Ukrainians died of starvation in an unprecedented peacetime catastrophe. Overrun by Axis armies in 1941 in World War II, it was further devastated before being retaken by the Soviets in 1944. In 1986 it was the site of the

UKRAINE

Scale 1: 19,690,000

©1999, Encyclopædia Britannica, Inc.

CHERNOBYL ACCIDENT. It declared independence in 1991. In recent years it has struggled both politically and economically. Its declining population reflects severe environmental degradation.

Ukrainian language \yü-'krā-nē-ən\ E. SLAVIC LANGUAGE spoken by about 41 million people mainly in Ukraine, Poland, Slovakia, and Russia. Only about three-quarters of Ukrainians are first-language speakers of Ukrainian, but there are millions of first-language speakers in Russia, Belarus, and the Central Asian republics. Ukraine's premodern literary language was Church Slavic (see OLD CHURCH SLAVIC LANGUAGE). With the fall of the Zaporizhzhya COSSACKS in the 18th cent., Ukrainian-speakers were stateless and the status of the language, thought of as peasant speech by the nobility, was low. The language and orthography (using a form of the CYRILLIC ALPHABET) were gradually standardized in the 19th cent.

ukulele \ˌyü-kə-'lä-lē\ Small Hawaiian four-stringed guitar. It developed out of a Portuguese instrument introduced to Hawaii by sailors in the 1870s. It became highly popular in the U.S. after World War I, used in jazz and bluegrass ensembles and as an amateur solo instrument.

Ulaanbaatar *or* **Ulan Bator** \ˌü-ˌlän-'bä-ˌtór\ City (pop., 1999: 691,000), capital of Mongolia. It was founded in the mid-17th cent. as the residence of the high priest of Tibetan Buddhism. A century later it had become a trading center on caravan routes between Russia and China. It became the capital when the Mongolian People's Republic was established in 1924, and remained the capital when in 1992 the country's name was changed to Mongolia. It is Mongolia's main industrial center and home to a university and academy of sciences.

Ulaid cycle See ULSTER CYCLE

Ulam \'ü-ləm\, **Stanislaw M(arcin)** (1909–1984) Polish-U.S. mathematician and atomic physicist. He was invited by John VON NEUMANN to Princeton's Institute for Advanced Study in 1936. In 1943 he moved to LOS ALAMOS, where his work included development of the Monte Carlo method of finding approximate solutions to problems. Later, he and Edward TELLER developed a two-stage radiation implosion design (the "Teller-Ulam configuration") that could generate an explosion capable of initiating nuclear fusion, which led to the HYDROGEN BOMB.

Ulan Bator See ULAANBAATAR

Ulanova \ü-'lä-nə-və\, **Galina (Sergeyevna)** (1910–1998) Russian ballet dancer, the first prima ballerina assoluta of the Soviet Union. She trained with Agrippina VAGANOVA in

Leningrad and joined the Kirov Theater company in 1928, where she began to develop the unique lyrical, dramatic style that won her wide acclaim. In 1944 she moved to the BOLSHOI BALLET and during the 1950s enjoyed great success touring with the company. She retired from dancing in 1962 but continued as ballet mistress and coach at the Bolshoi.

Ulbricht \\'ul-ˌbrikt, *Engl* 'ul-ˌbrikt\\, **Walter** (1893–1973) German communist head of E. Germany (1960–73). He led the German Communist party in Berlin 1929–33, then fled abroad after the Nazi takeover. As an agent for the COMINTERN, he persecuted Trotskyites and other deviationists. In 1945 he helped form the Socialist Unity Party in E. Germany, and served as its general secretary 1950–71. He was deputy premier of E. Germany 1949–60, and chairman of its council of state 1960–73. A constant foe of W. Germany, he built the BERLIN WALL in 1961. He exercised rigid control over E. Germany while developing its industrial strength.

ulcer Concave sore on the skin or lining of an organ, with well-defined, sometimes raised edges. The main symptom is pain. The term most often refers to PEPTIC ULCER but also includes skin ulcer, common on legs with VARICOSE VEINS and the feet of people with DIABETES MELLITUS, and decubitus ulcer (bedsore or pressure sore). Other causes include INFECTION, trauma (e.g., BURN, FROSTBITE), and CANCER (likely in ulcers hard to the touch). Skin ulcers over a month old should be checked for cancer, especially after middle age.

Ullmann, Liv (b.1939) Norwegian-Swedish film actress. After her stage debut in Oslo, she became internationally famous in the films of Ingmar BERGMAN, including *Persona* (1966), *Cries and Whispers* (1972), *Scenes from a Marriage* (1973), and *Autumn Sonata* (1978). Noted for her expressive face and subtle acting, she also starred in other Swedish and international films, including *The Emigrants* (1971) and *The New Land* (1973), and appeared on stage in the U.S. and Europe. She directed *Private Confessions* (1999) from Bergman's screenplay.

Ulmanis \\'ul-mä-nis\\, **Karlis** (1877–1942) Latvian independence leader and premier (1918, 1919–21, 1925–26, 1931–32, 1934–40). An agronomist, he was active in the Latvian independence movement. Forced into exile, he taught at the Univ. of Nebraska 1905–13. Returning to Latvia, he founded the Latvian Farmers' Union (1917) to press for independence from Russia. In 1918 he became premier of the newly independent republic. In his various terms of office he worked to resist internal dissension and military threats from Russia. Soviet occupation forced his resignation in 1940, and he was deported to Russia, where he died.

Ulster Historical province, N IRELAND. It now forms northern Ireland and three counties in the republic of Ireland. The ancient province was home to the Roman Catholic O'Neills (earls of TYRONE), who rebelled against English rule about 1600. After they fled, most of the land was confiscated by the British king JAMES I and settled with Protestants. In the early 20th cent. its opposition to Irish HOME RULE led to the formation of Northern Ireland.

Ulster cycle *or* **Ulaid cycle** \\'ü-lᵊthʸ, 'ü-ləgʸ\\ In early Irish literature, a group of legends and tales dealing with the heroic age of the Ulaid, a people of NE Ireland. The stories, set in the 1st cent. B.C., were recorded from oral tradition between the 8th and 11th cent. and are preserved in the 12th-cent. *Book of the Dun Cow*, *Book of Leinster*, and later compilations. Reflecting the customs of a free pre-Christian aristocracy, they combine mythological and legendary elements. Among the stories is *The Tragic Death of the Sons of Usnech*, later dramatized by W. B. YEATS and J. M. SYNGE.

ultrasonics Vibrational or stress waves in elastic media that have a FREQUENCY above 20 kilohertz, the highest that can be detected by the human ear. The waves can be generated or detected by piezoelectric transducers (see PIEZOELECTRICITY). High-power ultrasonics produce distortion in the medium; applications include ultrasonic welding, drilling, cleaning of surfaces (such as jewelry), and disruption of biological structures. Low-power ultrasonic waves do not cause distortions; uses include SONAR, structure testing, and medical imaging. Some animals, including bats, employ ultrasonic ECHOLOCATION for navigation.

ultrasound *or* **ultrasonography** Use of ultrasonic waves to produce images of body structures. The waves travel through tissues and are reflected back; the reflected echoes are received and analyzed by an electronic apparatus. The results can be displayed as still images or as a moving picture of the inside of the body. Unlike X RAYS or other ionizing radiation, ultrasound carries minimal if any risk. Most often used during pregnancy to examine the fetus, ultrasound is also used on internal organs, the eye, breast, and major blood vessels. It can often show whether a growth is benign or malignant. See also DIAGNOSTIC IMAGING.

ultraviolet astronomy Study of the ultraviolet (UV) spectra of astronomical objects. It became feasible once instruments could orbit above earth's atmosphere, which absorbs most ELECTROMAGNETIC RADIATION of UV WAVELENGTHS. Since the early 1960s, satellite observatories carrying UV telescopes, including the HUBBLE SPACE TELESCOPE, have collected UV-wavelength data on chemical abundances and processes in interstellar matter, the sun, white dwarf stars, comets, quasars, nebulae, and distant star clusters. See also SPECTRUM.

ultraviolet radiation Portion of the ELECTROMAGNETIC SPECTRUM extending from the violet end of the visible light region to the X-RAY region. Ultraviolet (UV) radiation is divided into three bands: UVA (also called black light), UVB (responsible for most effects on organisms), and UVC (which does not reach the earth's surface). Most UV rays from the sun are absorbed by the earth's OZONE LAYER. UV has low penetrating power, so its effects on humans are limited to the skin, and include stimulation of production of VITAMIN D, SUNBURN, aging signs, and carcinogenic changes.

Ulysses See ODYSSEUS

Umar ibn al-Khattab \\'ü-mär-ˌib-nül-ḵät-'täb\\ (586?–644) Second CALIPH (634–44). He became a Muslim about 615, and his daughter Hafsa married MUHAMMAD in 625. He was nominated by ABU BAKR as his successor. As caliph he spread Islam to Egypt, Syria, and Persia. His innovations affected taxation, social welfare, and administrative methods; he was noted for his justice, social ideals, and statesmanship.

Umayyad dynasty \\ü-'mä-yəd\\ (661–750) First great Muslim dynasty. It was founded by MUAWIYAH I when he became the fifth caliph. He moved the capital to DAMASCUS and used the Syrian army to extend the Arab empire. Under ABD AL-MALIK (r.685–705) the Umayyad empire extended from Spain to Central Asia and India. Their decline began with a defeat by the Byzantines in 717; intertribal feuding and the failure of financial reforms eventually led to their unseating by the ABBASID DYNASTY, though a branch ruled Spain until 1051. See also ABD AL-RAHMAN III, ABU MUSLIM, HUSAYN IBN ALI.

Umberto I (1844–1900) King of Italy (1878–1900). The son of VICTOR EMMANUEL II, he led his country out of its isolation and into the Triple Alliance (1882), with Germany and Austria-Hungary. However, a tariff war with France led to economic difficulties (1888), and Umberto's colonial policy in Africa was ended by Italy's defeat by Ethiopia (1896). Facing increasing social unrest, he imposed martial law (1898), and the ensuing period of turmoil culminated in his assassination by an anarchist.

Umbria Autonomous region (pop., 1996 est.: 826,000), central Italy. It is located in the APENNINES; its capital is PERUGIA. Originally inhabited by the ancient Italic Umbrian tribe, it came under Rome about 300 B.C. During the Christian era it became part of the PAPAL STATES. The 15th–16th-cent. Umbrian school of painting included PERUGINO and PINTURICCHIO. Umbria was the home of St. FRANCIS OF ASSISI. Agriculture is its principal economic mainstay.

U.N. See UNITED NATIONS

Unabomber See Theodore KACZYNSKI

Un-American Activities Committee, House See HOUSE UN-AMERICAN ACTIVITIES COMMITTEE

Unamuno (y Jugo) \\ˌü-nä-'mü-nō\\, **Miguel de** (1864–1936) Spanish philosopher and writer. Rector of the Univ. of Salamanca 1901–14 and 1931–36, he was dismissed first for espousing the Allied cause in World War I and later for denouncing Francisco FRANCO's Falangists. Though he also wrote poetry (including *The Christ of Velázquez*, 1920) and

T U V

plays, he was most influential as an essayist and novelist. In *The Tragic Sense of Life in Men and Peoples* (1913), he stressed the role spiritual anxiety plays in driving one to live the fullest possible life. His most famous novel is *Abel Sánchez* (1917).

uncertainty principle *or* **Heisenberg uncertainty principle** *or* **indeterminacy principle** Principle that states that the position and velocity of an object cannot both be measured exactly at the same time, and that the concepts of exact position and exact velocity together have no meaning in nature. Articulated by Werner HEISENBERG in 1927, it applies only at the small scales of ATOMS and SUBATOMIC PARTICLES. Any attempt to measure the velocity of a subatomic particle precisely will displace the particle in an unpredictable way, thus invalidating any simultaneous measurement of its position. The principle also applies to other related pairs of variables, such as energy and time.

Uncle Sam Popular U.S. symbol, usually associated with a cartoon figure having long white hair and chin whiskers and dressed in a swallow-tailed coat, vest, tall hat, and striped trousers. The name probably originated with "Uncle Sam" Wilson, a businessman who provided beef to the army during the War of 1812. The "U.S." government stamp on his barrels came to be associated with his nickname. The Uncle Sam figure evolved in the hands of cartoonists; its most familiar treatment appeared on wartime recruiting posters with the caption "I want you."

unconscious *or* **subconscious** In PSYCHOANALYSIS, the part of the psychic apparatus that does not ordinarily enter the individual's awareness but may be manifested by slips of the tongue, DREAMS, or neurotic symptoms. The existence of unconscious mental activities, first elaborated by Sigmund FREUD, is now a well-established principle of PSYCHIATRY. The origin of many neurotic symptoms is said to depend on conflicts that have been removed from CONSCIOUSNESS by REPRESSION and maintained in the unconscious through various DEFENSE MECHANISMS. Recent research has shed light on the relationship between brain physiology and the levels of consciousness at which people retain memories.

Underground See RESISTANCE

underground See SUBWAY

Underground Railroad Secret system in N U.S. states to help escaping slaves. Its name derived from the need for secrecy and the railway terms used in the conduct of the system. Various routes in 14 states, called lines, provided safe stopping places (stations) for the leaders (conductors) and their charges (packages) while fleeing north, sometimes to Canada. The system developed in defiance of the FUGITIVE SLAVE ACTS and was active mainly from 1830 to 1860. An estimated 40,000–100,000 slaves used the network. Assistance was provided mainly by free blacks, philanthropists, church leaders, and abolitionists.

Undset \\'ün-set\\, **Sigrid** (1882–1949) Norwegian novelist. Her early novels deal with the position of women in the contemporary lower middle class. Her masterpiece, the trilogy *Kristin Lavransdatter* (1920–22), is set in medieval Norway and depicts the spiritual growth of a strong woman. Her later works, including the historical *The Master of Hestviken* (1925–27), reflect her interest in religion. She received the Nobel Prize in 1928.

Sigrid Undset

unemployment Condition of a person who is able to work, is actively seeking work, but is unable to find any. Statistics on unemployment are considered an important indicator of a country's economic health. Since World War II full employment has been a goal of many governments. Full employment does not necessarily mean a zero unemployment rate, since at any given time the unemployment rate will include some people who are simply between jobs. In the U.S. 2% is often cited as a base rate. "Underemployment" refers to workers who are able to find employment only for shorter than normal periods—for example, part-time workers and seasonal workers—or to those whose education or training makes them overqualified for their jobs.

unemployment insurance Form of SOCIAL INSURANCE designed to compensate workers for short-term, involuntary unemployment. In most countries, workers who are permanently disabled or who have been unemployed for a long period of time are covered under other plans. In countries such as Canada and Britain, workers in any occupation may qualify for unemployment insurance; the U.S. denies coverage to certain workers, such as government employees and the self-employed. In most countries, benefits are related to earnings and are paid for a limited period of time. Funding may come out of general government revenues or from specific taxes placed on employers or employees.

UNESCO *in full* **United Nations Educational, Scientific, and Cultural Organization** Specialized agency of the U.N. created in 1946 to aid peace by promoting international collaboration in education, science, and culture. It supports member states' efforts to eliminate illiteracy, encouraging the extension of free education, and acts as a clearinghouse for the exchange of ideas and knowledge. In 1984 the U.S. (later followed by several other countries) withdrew from UNESCO to protest what it saw as UNESCO's politicization; it has not rejoined.

Ungaretti \\,üŋ-gä-'rät-tē\\, **Giuseppe** (1888–1970) Egyptian-Italian poet. He lived in Alexandria until he was 24; the desert regions of Egypt provide recurring images in his work. He was the founder of HERMETICISM, which began with his *Il porto sepolto* (1916; "The Buried Port") and brought about a reorientation in modern Italian poetry. Though experimental, his poetry developed in a coherent direction in *Allegria di naufragi* (1919; "Gay Shipwrecks") and later collections. After World War II his works became more structured and straightforward in tone.

ungulate \\'əŋ-gyə-lət\\ Any hoofed, herbivorous, quadruped, placental mammal in three or four orders: Artiodactyla, the even-toed ungulates (including PIGS, CAMELS, DEER, and bovines); Perissodactyla, the odd-toed ungulates (including HORSES, TAPIRS, and RHINOCEROSES); Proboscidea (ELEPHANTS); and, by some authorities, Hyracoidea. There are ten orders of extinct ungulates. See also RUMINANT.

UNICEF *in full* **United Nations Children's Fund** Special U.N. program devoted to the health, nutrition, education, and general welfare of children. It originally provided relief to children in need following World War II. After 1950 its efforts turned to general programs for improvement of children's welfare. It was awarded the Nobel Peace Prize in 1965. It depends on fundraising and card sales for much of its support.

unicorn Mythological animal resembling a white horse with a single horn on its forehead. The unicorn was depicted in Mesopotamian art and was referred to in the ancient myths of India and China. Its earliest description in Greek literature dates from about 400 B.C. and probably refers to the Indian rhinoceros. The unicorn was believed to be fierce and difficult to capture, but if a virgin were brought before it, it would lay its head in the virgin's lap. Medieval writers associated the unicorn with JESUS.

unidentified flying object (UFO) Aerial object or optical phenomenon not readily explainable. Interest in UFOs increased with aeronautic and astronautic advances after World War II. A government panel investigating sightings in the 1950s reported that 90% coincided with astronomical or meteorological phenomena or sightings of aircraft, birds, or hot gases, sometimes in unusual weather. In the mid-1960s a few scientists concluded that the small remaining percentage indicated extraterrestrial visitors but were met with prompt resistance from other scientists. A U.S. Air Force study begun in 1968 firmly rejected this sensational hypothesis, but many in the U.S. public, and a few scientists, still supported it. UFO reports vary widely in reliability. The unaided eye is easily fooled; radar sightings may fail to distinguish physical objects from meteor trails or rain and are subject to radio interference. See also SETI.

Unification Church *officially* Holy Spirit Assn. for the Unification of World Christianity. Religious movement founded (1954) in S. Korea by Sun Myung MOON. Influenced by YIN-YANG principles and Korean shamanism, it seeks to establish divine rule on earth through the fulfillment of the uncompleted mission of JESUS procreative marriage—and the restoration of the family. The church has been criticized for its recruitment policies (said to include BRAINWASHING) and business practices. Its mass marriage ceremonies have gained press attention. Its worldwide membership is about 200,000 in more than 100 countries.

unified field theory Attempt to describe all fundamental interactions between elementary particles in terms of a single theoretical framework based on QUANTUM FIELD THEORY. So far, the WEAK FORCE and the ELECTROMAGNETIC FORCE have been united in ELECTROWEAK THEORY, and the STRONG FORCE is described by QUANTUM CHROMODYNAMICS. However, attempts to unite the strong and electroweak theories in a GRAND UNIFIED THEORY have failed, as have attempts at a self-consistent quantum field theory of GRAVITATION. See also STANDARD MODEL.

uniformitarianism Doctrine in geology that physical, chemical, and biologic processes now at work on and within the earth have operated with general uniformity through immensely long periods of time and are sufficient to account for all geologic change. In other words, the present is the key to the past. The principle, originated by John Hutton in 1788 and advanced by Charles LYELL, is fundamental to geologic thinking and underlies the development of the science of geology.

Uniform Resource Locator See URL

union See LABOR UNION

Union, Act of (May 1, 1707) Treaty that effected the union of England (and Wales) and Scotland under the name of Great Britain. It benefited England's need for political safeguards against a possible JACOBITE restoration through Scotland, and it gave Scotland freedom of trade with England. The two kingdoms adopted the Protestant succession, preserved Scots law and the law courts, and agreed to uniform taxation.

Union, Act of (Jan. 1, 1801) Legislative agreement uniting Great Britain and Ireland under the name of the United Kingdom of Great Britain and Ireland. As prime minister, William PITT decided that the best solution to the Irish problem was a union to strengthen the connection between the two countries. The Irish parliament resisted the proposal, which called for its abolition, but votes bought by cash or honors ensured passage of the agreement in 1800.

Union of Soviet Socialist Republics (U.S.S.R.) *or* **Soviet Union** Former republic, E Europe and N and central Asia. It consisted, in its final years, of 15 soviet socialist republics that gained independence at its dissolution: Armenia, Azerbaijan, Belorussia (now Belarus), Estonia, Georgia, Kazakstan, Kirgiziya (now Kyrgyzstan), Latvia, Lithuania, Moldova, Russia, Tajikistan, Turkmenistan, Ukraine, and Uzbekistan. It also contained 20 autonomous soviet socialist republics. It had an area of 8,649,512 sq mi (22,402,235 sq km). Its capital was MOSCOW. Stretching from the Baltic and Black seas to the Pacific Ocean, the Soviet Union was the largest country on the globe, having a maximum east–west extent of about 6,800 mi (11,000 km) and a maximum north–south extent of about 2,800 mi (4,500 km). It encompassed 11 time zones. Its regions contained fertile lands, deserts, tundra, high mountains, some of the world's largest rivers, and large inland waters, including most of the CASPIAN SEA. The coastline on the Arctic Ocean extended 3,000 mi (4,800 km), while that on the Pacific was 1,000 mi (1,600 km) long. It was an agricultural, mining, and industrial power. Following the RUSSIAN REVOLUTION OF 1917, four socialist republics were established; in 1922 they formed the Union of Soviet Socialist Republics, to which other republics were later added. A power struggle begun in 1924 ended in 1927 when Joseph STALIN prevailed over Leon TROTSKY. Implementation of the first of the FIVE-YEAR PLANS in 1928 centralized industry and collectivized agriculture. A purge in the late 1930s resulted in the imprisonment or execution of millions of persons considered dangerous to the state (see PURGE TRIALS). After World War II, the U.S.S.R. and the U.S. with their respective allies engaged in the COLD WAR. In the late 1940s the U.S.S.R. brought about the establishment of Communist regimes throughout E Europe. It exploded its first atomic bomb in 1949. Following Stalin's death, it experienced limited liberalization under Nikita KHRUSHCHEV. It launched the first manned orbital space flight in 1961. Under Leonid BREZHNEV there was a reversal of the move towards liberalization. In the mid-1980s Mikhail GORBACHEV instituted a liberal policy of PERESTROIKA. The Communist government toppled in 1990, and a program to create a market economy was implemented. The U.S.S.R. was officially dissolved on Dec. 25, 1991.

Union Pacific Railroad Co. Company that extended the U.S. railway system to the Pacific Coast. Incorporated in 1862, it was built westward 1,006 mi (1,620 km) from Omaha, Neb., to meet the Central Pacific. The two railroads were joined at Promontory, Utah, in 1869. The Union Pacific was financed largely by federal loans and land grants, but involvement in the Crédit Mobilier scandal left it badly in debt. It was reorganized in 1897 by Edward HARRIMAN, under whose leadership the railroad took part in the economic development of the West. In 1982 it merged with the Missouri Pacific and the Western Pacific railroads; its acquisition of the Southern Pacific in 1996 made it the largest railroad in the U.S., with control of almost all rail-based shipping in the W two-thirds of the U.S.

union shop Arrangement whereby workers are required to join a particular union soon after beginning employment. It differs from the so-called closed shop (declared illegal in 1947) in that the employer's choice of new employees is not restricted to union members. Advocates of the union shop argue that it prevents workers from enjoying the benefits of unionism without bearing their share of the costs. Union shops are uncommon in most countries. They are both legal and common in the U.S. and Japan, but in some U.S. states RIGHT-TO-WORK LAWS prohibit requiring union membership as a condition of employment, thus forbidding both the union shop and the closed shop.

Unitarianism Religious movement that stresses free use of reason in religion, holds that God exists in only one person, and denies the divinity of JESUS and the doctrine of the Holy TRINITY. Its modern roots are traced to several thinkers of the Protestant REFORMATION. The mainstream of British and American Unitarianism grew out of Calvinist PURITANISM. The scientist Joseph PRIESTLEY was a founder of the English Unitarians, who became a force in Parliament and were noted advocates of social reform. In the U.S., Unitarianism developed out of New England CONGREGATIONALISM that rejected the 18th-cent. revival movement. See also CALVINISM, UNIVERSALISM.

Unitas \yü-ˈnī-təs\, **Johnny** (*orig.* John Constantine) (1933–2002) U.S. football quarterback. Born in Pittsburgh, he played for the Univ. of Louisville; though selected in the NFL draft, he played semiprofessionally before signing with the Baltimore Colts. Playing with the Colts from 1957 to 1971, he led them to five league championship games (1958, 1959, 1964, 1968, 1970) and two Super Bowl games (1969, 1971). He later played for the San Diego Chargers (1971–73) before retiring. His career total for touchdown passes (290) is the fifth-highest on record.

United Airlines, Inc. U.S. international airline. It first operated transcontinental passenger flights in 1929. It became the first airline to introduce stewardesses in 1930. United expanded rapidly after World War II and became the largest air carrier in the Western world when it merged with Capital Airlines in 1961. United acquired PAN AMERICAN WORLD AIRWAYS routes in 1986 and 1991. United employees purchased a controlling share of the airline in 1994, making it the largest employee-owned company in the U.S. In 2002 it filed for bankruptcy protection.

United Arab Emirates *formerly* **Trucial States** \ˈtrü-shəl\ Federation of seven states, E ARABIAN PENINSULA. They are the emirates of ABU DHABI, DUBAYY, Ajman, Al-Shariqah, Umm al-Qaywayn, Ras al-Khaimah, and Al-Fujayrah. Area: 32,280 sq mi (83,600 sq km). Population (2000): 3,022,000. Capital: ABU DHABI. Indigenous inhabitants are Arabs, but a large part of the population is made

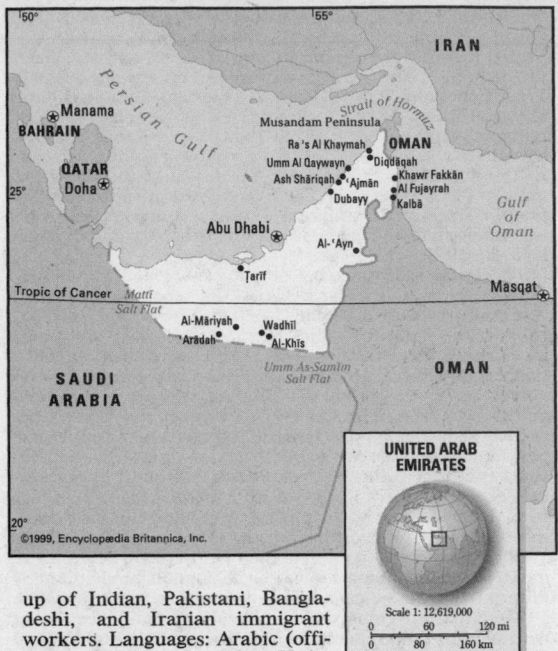

UNITED ARAB
EMIRATES

Scale 1: 12,619,000
0   60   120 mi
0   80   160 km

©1999, Encyclopædia Britannica, Inc.

up of Indian, Pakistani, Bangladeshi, and Iranian immigrant workers. Languages: Arabic (official), English, Persian, Urdu, Hindi. Religions: Islam (official), Christianity, Hinduism. Currency: U.A.E. dirham. The United Arab Emirates' low-lying desert plain is broken by the Al-Hajar Mtns. along the Musandam Peninsula. Three natural deepwater harbors are located along the Gulf of OMAN. It has 10% of the world's petroleum reserves and 5% of its natural-gas reserves; their production makes up the principal industries. Other important economic activities include fishing, herding, and growing of dates. The federation has one appointive advisory body; its chief of state is the president and the head of government is the prime minister. In 1820 the British exacted a peace treaty with local rulers along the coast. The area formerly called the Pirate Coast became known as the Trucial Coast. In 1892 the rulers agreed to restrict foreign relations to Britain. Though the British administered the region from 1843, they never assumed sovereignty; each state maintained full internal control. The states formed the Trucial States Council in 1960. In 1971 the sheiks terminated defense treaties with Britain and established a six-member federation. Ras al-Khaimah joined in 1972. The U.A.E. aided coalition forces against Iraq in the PERSIAN GULF WAR (1991).

United Arab Republic See EGYPT

United Artists Corp. Former U.S. film company. It was founded in 1919 by Charlie CHAPLIN, Mary PICKFORD, Douglas FAIRBANKS, and D. W. GRIFFITH in order to gain complete freedom to produce and distribute their own movies. The first major production company controlled by its artists, it prospered with the films of its founders, including *The Gold Rush* (1925), and those of such producers as Samuel GOLDWYN. After 1951 it became mainly a distributor, releasing such successful movies as *High Noon* (1952), *Some Like It Hot* (1959), and *West Side Story* (1961). It was sold to TransAmerica Corp. in 1967 and resold to MGM in 1981; its name disappeared when it was reorganized in 1992.

United Automobile Workers *in full* **United Automobile, Aerospace, and Agricultural Implement Workers of America (UAW)** U.S. industrial union. The UAW was founded in 1935, when the Committee for Industrial Organization (see AFL-CIO) began to organize automotive workers. The union successfully countered automakers' initial resistance with sit-down strikes and a 1937 Supreme Court decision upholding the right to organize as declared in the WAGNER ACT. GENERAL MOTORS CORP. was the first to recognize the

UAW (1937). Under Walter REUTHER, the union won contracts providing for cost-of-living adjustments, health plans, and vacations. Reuther's friction with George MEANY led the UAW to withdraw from the AFL-CIO 1968–81. Competition from foreign imports eroded the union's benefits in the 1980s and '90s.

United Fruit Co. U.S.-based fruit company. It was founded in 1899 in the merger of the Boston Fruit Co. and other companies that sold bananas grown in Central America, Colombia, and the Caribbean. United Fruit became the largest employer in Central America, developing vast tracts of jungle and building one of the largest private navies in the world. Attacked in the Latin American press as *el pulpo* ("the octopus"), the company was widely accused of exploiting workers and influencing governments during the era of "dollar diplomacy" in the early to mid-20th cent. It later transferred some of its landholdings to individual growers. In 1970 United Fruit merged with AMK Corp. to form United Brands Co., which changed its name in 1990 to Chiquita Brands International, Inc.

United Kingdom of Great Britain and Northern Ireland *commonly shortened to* **United Kingdom** *or* **Great Britain** Kingdom, W Europe, comprising GREAT BRITAIN (ENGLAND, SCOTLAND, and WALES) and Northern IRELAND. Area: 94,251 sq mi (244,110 sq km). Population (2000): 59,714,000. Capital: LONDON. The population is composed of English (major ethnic group), Scots, Irish, and Welsh and immigrants from India, the W. Indies, Pakistan, and

British Sovereigns

Kings of Wessex		
Egbert (S)	802–39	
Aethelwulf (S)	839–56/58	
Aethelbald (S)	855/56–60	
Aethelberht (S)	860–65/66	
Aethelred I (S)	865/66–71	
Alfred the Great (S)	871–99	
Edward the Elder (S)	899–924	
Sovereigns of England		
Athelstan[1] (S)	925–39	
Edmund I (S)	939–46	
Eadred (S)	946–55	
Eadwig (S)	955–59	
Edgar (S)	959–75	
Edward the Martyr (S)	975–78	
Ethelred II the Unready (S)	978–1013	
Sweyn Forkbeard (D)	1013–14	
Ethelred II the Unready[2] (S)	1014–16	
Edmund II Ironside (S)	1016	
Canute (D)	1016–35	
Harold I Harefoot (D)	1035–40	
Hardecanute (D)	1040–42	
Edward the Confessor (S)	1042–66	
Harold II (S)	1066	
William I the Conqueror (N)	1066–87	
William II (N)	1087–1100	
Henry I (N)	1100–35	
Stephen (B)	1135–54	
Henry II (P)	1154–89	
Richard I (P)	1189–99	
John (P)	1199–1216	
Henry III (P)	1216–72	
Edward I (P)	1272–1307	

Edward II (P)	1307–27	
Edward III (P)	1327–77	
Richard II (P)	1377–99	
Henry IV (P:L)	1399–1413	
Henry V (P:L)	1413–22	
Henry VI (P:L)	1422–61	
Edward IV (P:Y)	1461–70	
Henry VI[2]	1470–71	
Edward IV[2]	1471–83	
Edward V (P:Y)	1483	
Richard III (P:Y)	1483–85	
Henry VII (T)	1483–1509	
Henry VIII (T)	1509–1547	
Edward VI (T)	1547–53	
Mary I (T)	1553–58	
Elizabeth I (T)	1558–1603	
Sovereigns of Great Britain and the United Kingdom		
James I (VI of Scotland) (St)	1603–25	
Charles I (St)	1625–49	
Commonwealth		
Oliver Cromwell	1653–58	
Richard Cromwell	1658–59	
Charles II (St)	1660–85	
James II (St)	1685–88	
William III & Mary II (O/St)	1689–1702[3]	
Anne (St)	1702–14	
George I (H)	1714–27	
George II (H)	1727–60	
George III (H)	1760–1820	
George IV (H)	1820–30	
William IV (H)	1830–37	
Victoria (H)	1837–1901	
Edward VII (SCG)	1901–10	
George V (W)	1910–36	
Edward VIII (W)	1936[4]	
George VI (W)	1936–52	
Elizabeth II (W)	1952–	

Dynasty or house: S=Saxon, D=Danish, N=Norman, B=Blois, P=Plantagenet, L=Lancaster, Y=York, T=Tudor, St=Stuart, O=Orange, H=Hanover, SCG=Saxe-Coburg-Gotha, W=Windsor

[1]Athelstan was king of Wessex and the first king of all England.
[2]restored
[3]William and Mary, as husband and wife, reigned jointly until Mary's death in 1694.
[4]Edward VIII succeeded on the death of his father on January 20, 1936, but abdicated on December 11 before his coronation.

UNITED KINGDOM

Scale 1: 10,288,000

0   50   100 mi
0   80   160 km

©1999, Encyclopædia Britannica, Inc.

Bangladesh. Languages: English (official), also Welsh and Scottish Gaelic. Religions: Churches of England and Scotland (established); no established church in Northern Ireland or Wales; Roman Catholicism, Protestant denominations, Islam, Judaism, Hinduism, Sikhism. Currency: pound sterling. The country has hill, lowland, upland, highland, and mountain regions. Tin and iron ore deposits, once central to the economy, have become exhausted or uneconomical to work. The coal industry, despite its steady decline since the early 1950s, remains one of the largest and most technologically advanced in Europe. Offshore petroleum and natural gas reserves are significant. Chief crops are wheat, sugar beets, potatoes, and barley. Major manufactures include motor vehicles, aerospace equipment, electronic data-processing, telecommunication equipment, and petrochemicals. Fishing and publishing also are important economic activities. It is a constitutional monarchy with two legislative houses; its chief of state is the sovereign, and the head of government is the prime minister. The early (see STONEHENGE) pre-Roman inhabitants of Britain were Celtic-speaking peoples, including the Brythonic people of Wales, the Picts of Scotland, and the Britons of Britain. Celts also settled in Ireland around 500 B.C. Julius CAESAR invaded and took control of the area 55–54 B.C. The Roman province of Britannia endured until the 5th cent. and included present-day England and Wales. In the 5th cent. Nordic tribes of Angles, Saxons, and Jutes invaded Britain. The invasions had little effect on the Celtic peoples of Wales and Scotland. Christianity began to flourish in the 6th cent. During the 8th–9th cent., Vikings, particularly Danes, raided the coasts of Britain. In the late 9th

cent. ALFRED the Great repelled a Danish invasion, which helped bring about the unification of England under Athelstan. The Scots attained dominance in Scotland, and MALCOLM II (1005–34) completed the unification of Scotland. William of Normandy (see WILLIAM I) the Conqueror took England in 1066. The Norman kings established a strong central government and feudal state. The French language of the Norman rulers eventually merged with the Anglo-Saxon of the common people to form the English language. From the 11th cent., Scotland came under the influence of the English throne. HENRY II conquered Ireland in the late 12th cent. His sons RICHARD I and JOHN had conflicts with the clergy and nobles, and eventually John was forced to grant the nobles concessions in the MAGNA CARTA (1215). The concept of community of the realm developed during the 13th cent., providing the foundation for parliamentary government. During the reign of EDWARD I, statute law developed to supplement English COMMON LAW, and the first PARLIAMENT was convened. In 1314 Robert Bruce (see ROBERT I) won independence for Scotland. The TUDORS became the ruling family of England following the Wars of the ROSES (1455–85). HENRY VIII established the Church of England and incorporated Wales as part of England. The reign of ELIZABETH I began a period of colonial expansion; 1588 brought the defeat of the SPANISH ARMADA. In 1603 James VI of Scotland ascended to the English throne, becoming JAMES I, and established a personal union of the two kingdoms. The ENGLISH CIVIL WARS erupted in 1642 between Royalists and Parliamentarians, ending in the execution of CHARLES I (1649). After eleven years of Puritan rule under Oliver CROMWELL and his son (1649–60), the monarchy was restored with CHARLES II. In 1707 England and Scotland assented to the Act of UNION, forming the kingdom of Great Britain. The Hanoverians ascended to the English throne in 1714, when George Louis, elector of HANOVER, became GEORGE I of Great Britain. During the reign of GEORGE III, Great Britain's American colonies won independence (1783). This was followed by a period of war with revolutionary France and later with the empire of NAPOLEON (1789–1815). In 1801 legislation united Great Britain with Ireland to create the United Kingdom of Great Britain and Ireland. Britain was the birthplace of the INDUSTRIAL REVOLUTION in the late 18th cent., and it remained the world's foremost economic power until the late 19th cent. During the reign of Queen VICTORIA, Britain's colonial expansion reached its zenith, though the older dominions, including Canada and Australia, were granted independence (1867 and 1901, respectively). The United Kingdom entered WORLD WAR I allied with France and Russia in 1914. Following the war, revolutionary disorder erupted in Ireland, and in 1921 the Irish Free State (see IRELAND) was granted dominion status. The six counties of ULSTER, however, remained in the United Kingdom as Northern IRELAND. The United Kingdom entered WORLD WAR II in 1939. Following the war the Irish Free State became the Irish Republic and left the COMMONWEALTH. India also gained independence from the United Kingdom. Throughout the postwar period and into the 1970s, the United Kingdom continued to grant independence to its overseas colonies and dependencies. With U.N. forces, it participated in the KOREAN WAR (1950–53). In 1956 it intervened militarily in Egypt during the SUEZ CRISIS. In 1982 it defeated Argentina to retain sovereignty of the FALKLAND ISLANDS. As a result of continuing social strife in Northern Ireland, it joined with Ireland in several peace initiatives during recent decades. In 1997 it recognized referendums in Scotland and Wales establishing parliaments in each country, though both remained part of the United Kingdom.

United Mine Workers of America (UMWA) U.S. labor union. Founded in 1890, the UMWA grew rapidly under the leadership of John Mitchell (president 1898–1908) despite determined opposition from coal-mine operators. By 1920, when John L. LEWIS took over, the union had half a million members. Lewis capitalized on the pro-labor climate of the NEW DEAL and led numerous strikes to win fair pay, safe working conditions, and benefits. The UMWA was a mainstay of the Congress of Industrial Organizations (see AFL-CIO) in its early years, but withdrew in 1942. It finally joined

TUV

the AFL-CIO in 1989, but its membership and importance declined in the later 20th cent.

United Nations (U.N.) International organization founded in 1945 to maintain international peace and security, develop friendly relations among nations on equal terms, and encourage international cooperation in solving intractable human problems. An international organization to succeed the LEAGUE OF NATIONS was discussed at the YALTA CONFERENCE, and the U.N. charter was drawn up at the U.N. Conference on International Organization (1945). It has six principal organs: the Economic and Social Council, the U.N. GENERAL ASSEMBLY, the INTERNATIONAL COURT OF JUSTICE, the Secretariat, the U.N. SECURITY COUNCIL, and the U.N. Trusteeship Council. It also has 14 specialized agen-

U.N. Member States

1945	Argentina, Belarus, Brazil, Chile, China, Cuba, Denmark, Dominican Republic, Egypt, El Salvador, France, Haiti, Iran, Lebanon, Luxembourg, New Zealand, Nicaragua, Paraguay, Philippines, Poland, Russian Federation[3], Saudi Arabia, Syria, Turkey, Ukraine, United Kingdom, United States of America, Yugoslavia, Greece, India, Peru, Australia, Costa Rica, Liberia, Colombia, Mexico, S. Africa, Canada, Ethiopia, Panama, Bolivia, Venezuela, Guatemala, Norway, Netherlands, Honduras, Uruguay, Ecuador, Iraq, Belgium
1946	Afghanistan, Iceland, Sweden, Thailand
1947	Pakistan, Yemen[6]
1948	Burma (Myanmar)
1949	Israel
1950	Indonesia
1955	Albania, Austria, Bulgaria, Cambodia, Finland, Hungary, Ireland, Italy, Jordan, Laos, Libya, Nepal, Portugal, Romania, Spain, Sri Lanka
1956	Morocco, Sudan, Tunisia, Japan
1957	Ghana, Malaysia
1958	Guinea
1960	Dahomey (Benin), Upper Volta (Burkina Faso), Cameroon, Central African Republic, Chad, Congo, Democratic Republic of the Congo, Ivory Coast, Cyprus, Gabon, Madagascar, Niger, Somalia, Togo, Mali, Senegal, Nigeria
1961	Sierra Leone, Mauritania, Mongolia, Tanzania[5]
1962	Burundi, Jamaica, Rwanda, Trinidad and Tobago, Algeria, Uganda
1963	Kuwait, Kenya
1964	Malawi, Malta, Zambia
1965	Gambia, Maldives, Singapore
1966	Guyana, Botswana, Lesotho, Barbados
1968	Mauritius, Swaziland, Equatorial Guinea
1970	Fiji
1971	Bahrain, Bhutan, Qatar, Oman, United Arab Emirates
1973	Bahamas, Germany[2]
1974	Bangladesh, Grenada, Guinea-Bissau
1975	Cape Verde, Mozambique, São Tome and Principe, Papua New Guinea, Comoros, Suriname
1976	Seychelles, Angola, Samoa
1977	Djibouti, Vietnam
1978	Solomon Islands, Dominica
1979	Saint Lucia
1980	Zimbabwe, Saint Vincent and the Grenadines
1981	Vanuatu, Belize, Antigua and Barbuda
1983	Saint Kitts and Nevis
1984	Brunei Darussalam
1990	Namibia, Liechtenstein
1991	Estonia, N. Korea, S. Korea, Latvia, Lithuania, Marshall Islands, Micronesia
1992	Armenia, Kazakstan, Kyrgyzstan, Moldova, San Marino, Tajikistan, Turkmenistan, Uzbekistan, Azerbaijan, Bosnia and Herzegovina, Croatia, Slovenia, Georgia
1993	Czech Republic[1], Slovakia[1], Macedonia[4], Eritrea, Monaco, Andorra
1994	Palau
1999	Kiribati, Nauru, Tonga
2000	Tuvalu
2002	East Timor, Switzerland

[1]Czechoslovakia was an original member from 1945. The Czech Republic and the Slovak Republic obtained separate memberships in 1992.

[2]E. Germany and W. Germany were admitted as separate members in 1973; the two countries reunified in 1990.

[3]The seat held by the Soviet Union, a member from 1945, was assumed by Russia in 1991.

[4]Macedonia is referred to in the U.N. as "The former Yugoslav Republic of Macedonia" pending settlement of a dispute over its name.

[5]Tanganyika, a member from 1961, merged in 1964 with Zanzibar, a member from 1963, to form the new country of Tanzania.

[6]N. Yemen, a member from 1947, merged in 1990 with S. Yemen, a member from 1967.

cies (e.g., UNESCO) and a number of special offices, programs, and funds (e.g., UNICEF). The U.N. is involved with economic, cultural, and humanitarian activities and the coordination or regulation of international postal services, civil aviation, telecommunications, and shipping. Its peacekeeping troops may be deployed for the long term or for limited stays. Its world headquarters are in New York City; its European headquarters are in Geneva. In 2000 the U.N. had 189 member nations. Its principal administrative officer is the secretary-general, who is elected to a five-year renewable term by the General Assembly on the recommendation of the Security Council. Since the U.N.'s founding the secretaries-general have been Trygve LIE (1946–53), Dag HAMMARSKJÖLD (1953–61), U. THANT (1961–71), Kurt WALDHEIM (1972–81), Javier PÉREZ DE CUÉLLAR (1982–91), Boutros BOUTROS-GHALI (1992–96), and Kofi ANNAN (from 1997). The U.N. received the Nobel Peace Prize in 2001.

United Nations Children's Fund See UNICEF

United Nations General Assembly One of six principal components of the UNITED NATIONS and the only one in which all U.N. members are represented. It meets annually or in special sessions. Primarily a deliberative body, it may discuss and make recommendations about any issue within the scope of the U.N. charter. Its president is elected annually on a rotating basis from five geographic groups of members.

United Nations Security Council Division of the U.N. whose primary responsibility is to maintain international peace and security. It originally had five permanent members—Taiwan (succeeded in 1971 by China), France, England, the U.S., and the Soviet Union (succeeded in 1991 by Russia)—and six rotating members elected by the UNITED NATIONS GENERAL ASSEMBLY for two-year terms. In 1965 the nonpermanent membership was enlarged to 10 members. U.N. members agree to abide by the Security Council's resolutions. To prevent or stop aggression, it may impose diplomatic or economic sanctions or authorize the use of military force. Since any of the five permanent members may veto a decision on substantive matters, the body has been rendered toothless on innumerable occasions.

United Netherlands, Republic of the See DUTCH REPUBLIC

United States *officially* **United States of America** Federal republic, N. America. It is made up of 48 contiguous states occupying the mid continent, Alaska at the NW extreme of N. America, and the island state of Hawaii in the mid-Pacific Ocean. Area, including the U.S. share of the GREAT LAKES: 3,679,192 sq mi (9,529,063 sq km). Population (2000): 281,422,000. Capital: WASHINGTON, D.C. The population is composed of whites, blacks, Hispanics, Asians, Pacific Islanders, American Indians, Eskimos, and Aleuts. Languages: English (predominant), Spanish. Religions: Protestantism, Roman Catholicism, Judaism, Islam. Currency: U.S. dollar. The country's regions encompass mountains, plains, lowlands, and deserts. Mountain ranges include the APPALACHIANS, OZARKS, ROCKY MTNS., CASCADES, and SIERRA NEVADAS. The lowest point is DEATH VALLEY, Cal. The highest point is Alaska's Mt. MCKINLEY; within the coterminous U.S., it is Mt. WHITNEY. Chief rivers are the MISSISSIPPI system, COLORADO, COLUMBIA, and RIO GRANDE. The GREAT LAKES, GREAT SALT LAKE, and OKEECHOBEE are the largest lakes. The U.S. is among the world's leading producers of several minerals, including copper, silver, zinc, gold, coal, petroleum, and natural gas; it is the world's chief exporter of food. Its manufactures include iron and steel, chemicals, electronic equipment, and textiles. Other important industries are tourism, dairying, livestock raising, fishing, and lumbering. It is a republic with two legislative houses; its head of state and government is the president. The territory was originally inhabited for several thousand years by numerous AMERICAN INDIAN peoples who had probably emigrated from Asia. European exploration and settlement from the 16th cent. began displacement of the Indians. The first permanent European settlement, by the Spanish, was at ST. AUGUSTINE, Fla., in 1565; the British settled JAMESTOWN, Va. (1607); PLYMOUTH, Mass. (1620); Maryland (1634); and Pennsylvania (1681). They took New York, New Jersey, and Delaware from the Dutch in 1664, a year after the Carolinas had been granted to British noblemen. The British defeat of the French in 1763 (see FRENCH AND INDIAN WAR) assured British political control over its 13 colonies. Political unrest caused by British colonial policy culminated in the AMERICAN REVOLUTION (1775–83) and the DECLARATION OF INDEPENDENCE (1776). The U.S. was first organized under the ARTICLES OF CONFEDERATION (1781), then finally under the CONSTITUTION OF THE U.S. (1787) as a federal republic. Boundaries extended west to the Mississippi River, excluding Spanish Florida. Land acquired from France by the LOUISIANA PURCHASE (1803) nearly doubled the country's territory. The U.S. fought the WAR OF 1812 with the British and acquired Florida from Spain in 1819. In 1830 it legalized removal of American Indians to lands west of the Mississippi River. Settlement expanded into the Far West in the mid-19th cent., especially after the discovery of gold in California in 1848 (see GOLD RUSH). Victory in the MEXICAN WAR (1846–48) brought the territory of seven more future states (including California and Texas) into U.S. hands. The NW boundary was established by treaty with Great Britain in 1846. The U.S. acquired S Arizona by the GADSDEN PURCHASE (1853). It suffered disunity during the con-

U.S. Presidents and Vice Presidents

President	Term	Vice president	Term
George Washington	1789–97	John Adams	1789–97
John Adams	1797–1801	Thomas Jefferson	1797–1801
Thomas Jefferson	1801–9	Aaron Burr	1801–5
		George Clinton	1805–9
James Madison	1809–17	George Clinton	1809–12*
		Elbridge Gerry	1813–14*
James Monroe	1817–25	Daniel D. Tompkins	1817–25
John Quincy Adams	1825–29	John C. Calhoun	1825–29
Andrew Jackson	1829–37	John C. Calhoun	1829–32**
		Martin Van Buren	1833–37
Martin Van Buren	1837–41	Richard M. Johnson	1837–41
William Henry Harrison	1841*	John Tyler	1841
John Tyler	1841–45		
James K. Polk	1845–49	George M. Dallas	1845–49
Zachary Taylor	1849–50*	Millard Fillmore	1849–50
Millard Fillmore	1850–53		
Franklin Pierce	1853–57	William Rufus de V. King	1853*
James Buchanan	1857–61	John C. Breckinridge	1857–61
Abraham Lincoln	1861–65*	Hannibal Hamlin	1861–65
		Andrew Johnson	1865
Andrew Johnson	1865–69		
Ulysses S. Grant	1869–77	Schuyler Colfax	1869–73
		Henry Wilson	1873–75*
Rutherford B. Hayes	1877–81	William A. Wheeler	1877–81
James A. Garfield	1881*	Chester A. Arthur	1881
Chester A. Arthur	1881–85		
Grover Cleveland	1885–89	Thomas A. Hendricks	1885*
Benjamin Harrison	1889–93	Levi P. Morton	1889–93
Grover Cleveland	1893–97	Adlai E. Stevenson	1893–97
William McKinley	1897–1901*	Garret A. Hobart	1897–99*
		Theodore Roosevelt	1901
Theodore Roosevelt	1901–9	Charles W. Fairbanks	1905–9
William Howard Taft	1909–13	James S. Sherman	1909–12*
Woodrow Wilson	1913–21	Thomas R. Marshall	1913–21
Warren G. Harding	1921–23*	Calvin Coolidge	1921–23
Calvin Coolidge	1923–29	Charles G. Dawes	1925–29
Herbert Hoover	1929–33	Charles Curtis	1929–33
Franklin D. Roosevelt	1933–45*	John Nance Garner	1933–41
		Henry A. Wallace	1941–45
		Harry S. Truman	1945
Harry S. Truman	1945–53	Alben W. Barkley	1949–53
Dwight D. Eisenhower	1953–61	Richard M. Nixon	1953–61
John F. Kennedy	1961–63*	Lyndon B. Johnson	1961–63
Lyndon B. Johnson	1963–69	Hubert H. Humphrey	1965–69
Richard M. Nixon	1969–74**	Spiro T. Agnew	1969–73**
		Gerald R. Ford	1973–74
Gerald R. Ford	1974–77	Nelson A. Rockefeller	1974–77
Jimmy Carter	1977–81	Walter F. Mondale	1977–81
Ronald Reagan	1981–89	George Bush	1981–89
George Bush	1989–93	Dan Quayle	1989–93
William J. Clinton	1993–2001	Albert Gore	1993–2001
George W. Bush	2001–	Richard B. Cheney	2001–

*Died in office. **Resigned from office.

flict between the slavery-based plantation economy in the South and the free industrial and agricultural economy in the North, culminating in the AMERICAN CIVIL WAR, and the abolition of slavery under the 13th Amendment. After RECONSTRUCTION (1865–77), the U.S. experienced rapid growth, urbanization, industrial development, and European immigration. In 1877 it authorized allotment of Indian reservation land to individual tribesmen, resulting in widespread loss of land to whites. By the end of the 19th cent., it had developed foreign trade and acquired outlying territories, including Alaska, Midway island, the Hawaiian Islands, the Philippines, Puerto Rico, Guam, Wake Island, American Samoa, the Panama Canal Zone, and the Virgin Islands. The U.S. participated in WORLD WAR I 1917–18. It granted suffrage to women in 1920 and citizenship to American Indians in 1924. The stock market crash of 1929 led to the GREAT DEPRESSION. The U.S. entered WORLD WAR II after the Japanese bombing of PEARL HARBOR (Dec. 7, 1941). Its explosion of the first ATOMIC BOMB on HIROSHIMA, Japan (Aug. 6, 1945), brought about the end of the war, and made it the leader of the Western world, involved it in the reconstruction of Europe and Japan, and embroiled it in a COLD WAR with the Soviet Union. It participated in the KOREAN WAR. In 1952 it granted autonomous commonwealth status to Puerto Rico. Racial segregation in schools was declared unconstitutional in 1954. Alaska and Hawaii were made states in 1959. In 1964 Congress passed the CIVIL RIGHTS ACT and authorized full-scale intervention in the VIETNAM WAR. The mid- to late-1960s were marked by widespread civil disorders, including race riots and antiwar demonstrations. The U.S. accomplished the first manned lunar landing in 1969. All U.S. troops were withdrawn from Vietnam in 1973. The U.S. led a coalition of forces against Iraq in the PERSIAN GULF WAR (1991), and participated in NATO air strikes against Serb forces in the former Yugoslavia in 1995 and 1999. Administration of the PANAMA CANAL was turned over to Panama in 1999. Terrorist attacks against the WORLD TRADE CENTER and the PENTAGON in Sept. 2001 provoked the U.S. to invade Afghanistan and commence a general "war on terrorism." See map on following pages.

United States, Bank of the See BANK OF THE U.S.

United States Air Force (USAF) Major component of the U.S. military organization, with primary responsibility for AIR WARFARE, air defense, and military space research. U.S. military activities in the air began with army use of balloons for reconnaissance during the Civil War and the Spanish-American War; in 1907 the Aeronautical Division of the Signal Corps was created. In 1920 the Air Service (after 1926, Air Corps) was created as a unit of the Army; in 1941 it became the Army Air Forces. In 1947 the independent U.S. Air Force was created. The Department of the Air Force is headquartered at the PENTAGON. Separate agencies include the Air Force Reserve, the Air Force Intelligence Service, and the UNITED STATES AIR FORCE ACADEMY. In 2000 there were over 350,000 Air Force personnel on active duty.

United States Air Force Academy Institution for the training of commissioned officers for the U.S. AIR FORCE, located in Colorado Springs, Col. It opened in 1955. Graduates receive a bachelor's degree and a second-lieutenant's commission. Candidates may come from the armed services, be children of deceased veterans, or be nominated by U.S. senators or representatives or by the president or vice president, and must take a competitive entrance examination. Enrollment is about 4,000.

United States Army Major branch of the U.S. military forces, charged with preserving peace and security and defending the nation. The first regular U.S. fighting force, the Continental Army, was organized by the CONTINENTAL CONGRESS on June 14, 1775, to supplement local MILITIAS in the American Revolution, under civilian control. The U.S. Constitution named the president as commander in chief, and in 1789 the civilian Department of War was established. The Continental Army was officially disbanded in 1783, and a small regular army was established. Thereafter, the army's size grew in crises, swelled by CONSCRIPTION, and shrank in peacetime. The Department of the Army is headed by the secretary of the army. The Army Staff ad-

TUV

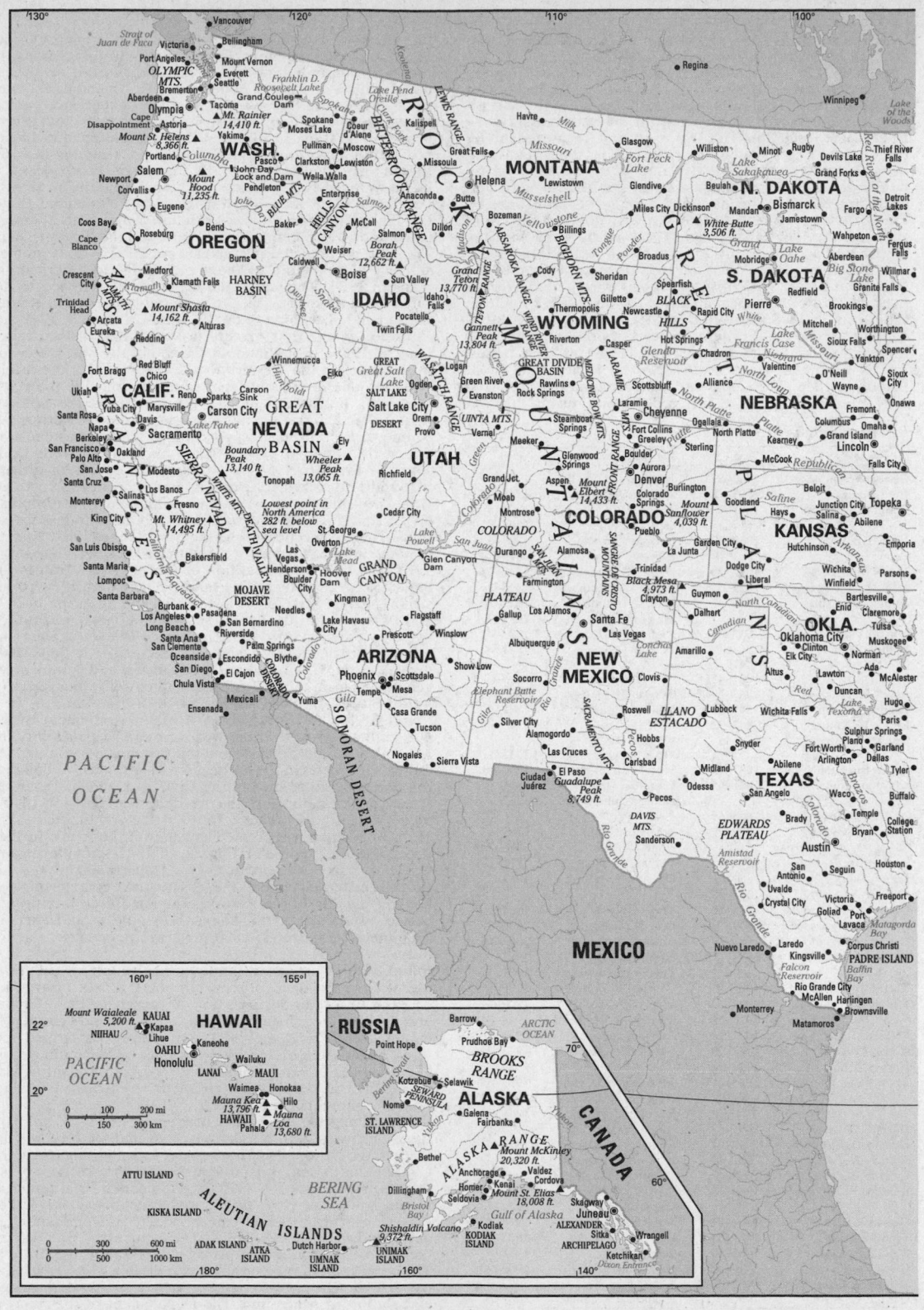

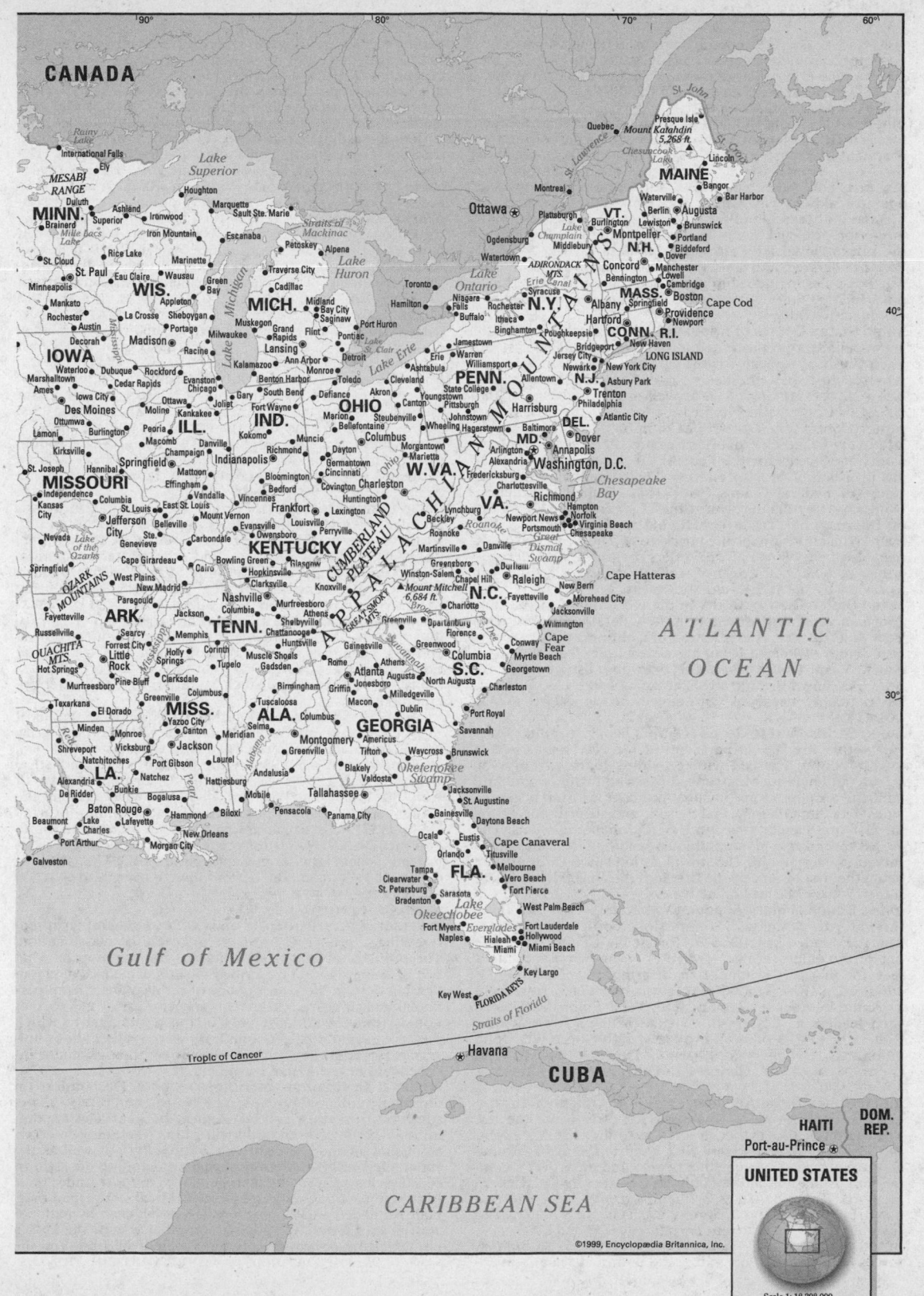

vises and assists the secretary and administers civil functions, including the civil-works program of the Corps of Engineers. The army also administers the UNITED STATES MILITARY ACADEMY at West Point. In 2000 there were about 400,000 soldiers on active duty.

United States Coast Guard U.S. military service that enforces maritime laws. During peacetime it is part of the Department of Transportation, in wartime the Department of the Navy. The Coast Guard enforces federal laws on the high seas and waters within U.S. jurisdiction, develops and operates aids to navigation, and maintains a network of lifeboat and search-and-rescue stations. It assists in the interdiction of illegal narcotics bound for the U.S. It operates the International Ice Patrol, gathers data for the National Weather Service, and assists distressed ships and planes. Its wartime roles include ship escort, port security, and transport. In 2000 there were some 35,000 Coast Guard personnel on active duty.

United States Courts of Appeals In the U.S., the intermediate appellate courts included in the federal judicial system. Each Court of Appeals for the 11 numbered circuits is empowered to review the decisions of federal district courts (see U.S. DISTRICT COURT), as well as the divisions of the U.S. Tax Court within its jurisdiction and the U.S. Bankruptcy Courts. The District of Columbia has its own appellate court because so many cases are filed there. The U.S. Court of Appeals for the Federal Circuit (created in 1982) has jurisdiction over specialized courts, including the U.S. Court of Federal Claims (which has original jurisdiction over non-TORT claims against the U.S.) and the U.S. Court of International Trade (which has exclusive jurisdiction over civil actions under the tariff laws). The Federal Circuit may also review and enforce orders of various federal regulatory agencies. All Court of Appeals decisions are subject to review by the U.S. SUPREME COURT.

United States District Court In the U.S., any of the 90 trial courts of general jurisdiction in the federal judicial system. Each state, as well as the District of Columbia and the Commonwealth of Puerto Rico, has at least one federal district court. A court may have more than one district judge; its other personnel include a U.S. attorney and a U.S. marshal. District-court decisions are subject to appeal to a U.S. COURT OF APPEALS.

United States Marine Corps (USMC) Separate military service within the U.S. Department of the Navy (see UNITED STATES NAVY), charged with providing marine troops for seizure and defense of advanced bases and with conducting land and air operations during naval campaigns. It also provides detachments for naval vessels, and security forces for naval shore installations and U.S. diplomatic missions. The corps specializes in amphibious landings. Marines have served in every major U.S. naval action since 1775, usually being the first or among the first to fight. In 2000 there were some 175,000 Marines on active duty.

United States Military Academy *known as* **West Point** Institution for the training of commissioned officers for the U.S. ARMY. Founded in 1802 at the fort at West Point, N.Y., it is one of the oldest service academies in the world and, in effect, the first U.S. school of engineering. Women were first admitted in 1976. Graduates receive a bachelor's degree and a second-lieutenant's commission. West Point has trained such leaders as Ulysses S. GRANT, William T. SHERMAN, Robert E. LEE, Stonewall JACKSON, Jefferson DAVIS, John PERSHING, Dwight EISENHOWER, Douglas MACARTHUR, Omar BRADLEY, and George PATTON. Current enrollment is about 4,000.

United States Naval Academy *known as* **Annapolis** Institution for the training of commissioned officers for the U.S. NAVY and U.S. MARINE CORPS. It was founded at Annapolis, Md., in 1845. Women were first admitted in 1976. Graduates are awarded a bachelor's degree and an officer's commission. Annapolis alumni include George DEWEY, Richard E. BYRD, Chester NIMITZ, William HALSEY, A. A. MICHELSON, Hyman RICKOVER, Jimmy CARTER, Ross PEROT, and several astronauts. Current enrollment is about 4,000.

United States Navy Major branch of the U.S. military forces, charged with defending the nation at sea and maintaining security on the seas wherever U.S. interests extend. The Continental Navy was established by the CONTINENTAL CONGRESS in 1775. It was disbanded in 1784, but reconstituted as the Department of the Navy in 1798. The navy took part in the WAR OF 1812 and the American Civil War. Sea victories during the Spanish-American War (1898) led to a period of steady growth. In World War I, it provided troop transport, minelaying, and escort of merchant ships. The Japanese attack on the naval base at Pearl Harbor (1941) led to U.S. entry into World War II, in which, in addition to antisubmarine and troop transport duties, the navy conducted amphibious assaults in the Pacific theater and along the European coast. AIRCRAFT CARRIERS proved decisive in battles with Japanese forces. Since World War II it has remained the largest and most powerful navy in the world. The Department of the Navy is headed by the secretary of the navy. The navy includes the UNITED STATES MARINE CORPS and, during wartime, the UNITED STATES COAST GUARD. In 2000 there were almost 400,000 Navy personnel on active duty, excluding the Marine Corps and Coast Guard. See also UNITED STATES NAVAL ACADEMY.

United States service academies Group of institutions of higher education for the training of military and merchant marine officers: the U.S. MILITARY ACADEMY, the U.S. NAVAL ACADEMY, the U.S. AIR FORCE ACADEMY, the U.S. Coast Guard Academy (established 1876 near New London, Conn.; enrollment 800), and the U.S. Merchant Marine Academy (established 1943 at Kings Point, Long Island, N.Y.; enrollment 900).

United States Steel Corp. Former U.S. corporation. It was founded in 1901 by Charles SCHWAB, Elbert GARY, and J. P. MORGAN to consolidate Andrew CARNEGIE's Carnegie Steel Co., Gary's Federal Steel Co., and other metal companies. Gary dominated the corporation in its early years, organizing price agreements among steel producers and opposing unions. The corporation recognized the UNITED STEELWORKERS OF AMERICA in 1936. The largest U.S. steel producer, in the later 20th cent. U.S. Steel diversified into oil and gas, chemicals, mining, construction, and transportation. In 1986, the HOLDING COMPANY USX Corp. was established to oversee U.S. Steel, Marathon Oil, and other operating units.

United Steelworkers of America (USWA) U.S. union of steel, aluminum, and other metallurgical workers. It grew out of the Steel Workers Organizing Committee (SWOC), established jointly in 1936 by the Committee for Industrial Organization (see AFL-CIO) and the Amalgamated Assn. of Iron, Steel, and Tin Workers. In 1942 SWOC became the United Steelworkers of America. Under Philip Murray (1886–1952) it developed into a powerful union with a million members. It won unprecedented benefits in the postwar period but saw its power decline as the U.S. steel industry shrank from the 1970s onward. See also UNITED STATES STEEL CORP.

unit trust See MUTUAL FUND

universal In EPISTEMOLOGY and LOGIC, a general term representing a property, form, or principle of classification. The problem of universals concerns the question of what sort of being should be ascribed to such principles of classification (e.g., is there an essence of redness apart from particular red things?). ARISTOTLE argued against PLATO that FORMS (universals) exist only in the particulars in which they are exemplified. Though both were realists about universals (see REALISM), they differed over their existence independent of particular exemplars.

Universal Declaration of Human Rights Declaration on universal human rights adopted by the UNITED NATIONS GENERAL ASSEMBLY in 1948. Among its 30 articles are definitions of the civil and political rights (including freedom from slavery and the right to a nationality), as well as the economic, social, and cultural rights (including the right to social security), owed by member states to those under their jurisdiction. It has acquired more juridical status than originally intended and has been widely used, even by national courts, as a means of judging compliance with the U.N.'s human-rights obligations. It has formed the basis for the work of such organizations as AMNESTY INTERNATIONAL.

Universalism Belief in the SALVATION of all SOULS. Arising at various times in Christian history, the concept became an organized movement in America in the mid-18th cent. It maintains the impossibility that a loving God would bestow salvation on only a portion of humankind while dooming the rest to eternal punishment. It stresses the use of reason in religion. The miraculous elements of traditional CHRISTIANITY are rejected and JESUS is not held to be divine. Universalist and Unitarian churches (see UNITARIANISM) in the U.S. merged in 1961.

Universal Pictures U.S. film studio. Formed by Carl LAEMMLE in 1912, it became a top producer of popular, low-budget serials in the 1920s and of horror movies in the 1930s; its later films included the ABBOTT AND COSTELLO comedies. In 1966 it became a division of Universal City Studios, the largest packager of television series. It turned part of its Hollywood movie lot into the Universal Studios theme park, and later opened a second theme park in Orlando, Fla.

Universal Resource Locator See URL

Universal Serial Bus See USB

Universal Time Mean (solar) time of the Greenwich meridian (0° longitude). Universal Time replaced GREENWICH MEAN TIME in 1928; since 1972 it has been based on international atomic time, a uniform time derived from the frequencies of certain atomic transitions and measured by an atomic clock.

universe Whole cosmic system of matter and energy of which the earth is a part, governed by the STRONG FORCE, the WEAK FORCE, the ELECTROMAGNETIC FORCE, and GRAVITATION. Its main constituents are the GALAXIES, containing STARS and stellar groupings and nebulae (see NEBULA). All atoms, subatomic particles, and everything they compose are also part of the universe. Numerous theories have been proposed for its origin and structure. See also BIG BANG, COSMOLOGY, EXPANDING UNIVERSE, STEADY-STATE THEORY.

university Institution of higher education, usually comprising a liberal-arts-and-sciences college and various graduate and professional schools. A university differs from a COLLEGE in having a broader curriculum and offering advanced degrees. The first true university was the Univ. of BOLOGNA (11th cent.); the first in N Europe was the Univ. of PARIS, which served as a model for the universities of OXFORD, CAMBRIDGE, HEIDELBERG, and others. One of the first modern universities, in which secular rationalism replaced religious orthodoxy, was the Univ. of Halle (founded 1694 in Halle, Germany); its liberalism was adopted by GÖTTINGEN, BERLIN, and other German universities. The German model of the university as a complex of schools and research institutes also exerted worldwide influence. The growth of universities in the U.S., where most colleges had been established by religious denominations, was greatly spurred by the MORRILL ACT OF 1862.

UNIX \'yü-niks\ OPERATING SYSTEM for DIGITAL COMPUTERS, developed by Ken Thompson of Bell Laboratories in 1969. The C language was subsequently developed specifically for UNIX, and the system was rewritten almost entirely in C. UNIX is very popular in universities, where it is used mostly on scientific and engineering workstations, and it is used on most of the SERVERS of INTERNET SERVICE PROVIDERS. Because its modular construction allows it to be easily modified, it has been improved in many ways by academic and industrial institutions (see LINUX).

Unser, Bobby (*orig.* Robert William) **and Al(fred)** (b.1934, b.1939) U.S. racing drivers. The Unser brothers were born in Albuquerque, N.M., to a family of drivers. Both won the Pikes Peak hill climb before racing in the INDIANAPOLIS 500, which Bobby won in 1968, 1975, and 1981, and Al in 1970, 1971, 1978, and 1987. Al's son Al Unser, Jr. (b.1962), won it in 1992 and 1994.

untouchable Former classification of various low-status persons and those outside the Hindu CASTE system in Indian society. The term Dalit is now used for such people (in preference to Mohandas GANDHI's term, *harijan*), and their plight is recognized by the Indian constitution and by legislation. The groups traditionally considered untouchable included people such as fishermen (who killed fish) and sweepers (whose work put them in contact with human excretions), and those who ate animal flesh. Many untouchables converted to other religions to escape discrimination.

Upanishad \ü-'pä-ni-ˌshäd\ Any of 108 speculative texts of the VEDAS that contain elaborations in poetry and verse. They are believed to have been composed after 500 B.C. Teaching based on them is called VEDANTA. Generally the Upanishads are concerned with the nature of reality, the individual soul (ATMAN) and the universal soul (BRAHMAN), and with the theory of the transmigration of souls and the nature of morality.

UPC See UNIVERSAL PRODUCT CODE

Updike, John (Hoyer) (b.1932) U.S. writer. Born in Shillington, Pa., in 1955 he began a long association with the *New Yorker*. His works are known for their careful craftsmanship and subtle depiction of American middle-class life. His famous "Rabbit" tetralogy—*Rabbit, Run* (1960), *Rabbit Redux* (1971), *Rabbit Is Rich* (1981, Pulitzer Prize), and *Rabbit at Rest* (1990, Pulitzer Prize)—follows a very ordinary American man through the later 20th cent. A Jewish novelist named Bech is the subject of three other novels. Updike's other fiction includes *The Centaur* (1963), *Couples* (1968), and *The Witches of Eastwick* (1984; film, 1987). He has also published short-story collections, reviews, essays, and light verse.

Upper Canada See CANADA WEST

Upper Volta See BURKINA FASO

Uppsala \'üp-ˌsä-ˌlä\ City (metro. area pop., 1999 est.: 187,000), Sweden. Located north of STOCKHOLM, by the 13th cent. it was an important commercial center. Relinquishing its early political primacy to Stockholm, it remained the seat of the archbishop of Sweden; its Gothic cathedral is Sweden's largest. Uppsala University (1477) is Sweden's oldest university. Uppsala was the home of Carolus LINNAEUS.

Ur \'ər, ûr\ Ancient city and district, SUMER, S BABYLONIA. It was situated on a former channel of the EUPHRATES RIVER. One of the oldest cities of MESOPOTAMIA, it was settled sometime in the 4th millennium B.C. In the 25th cent. B.C., it was the capital of S Mesopotamia under its first dynasty; it again became important around the 22nd cent. B.C. It is mentioned in the Bible as the early home of the Hebrew patriarch ABRAHAM in the 18th cent. B.C. It was later repeatedly captured and destroyed. NEBUCHADNEZZAR II restored it in the 6th cent. B.C. Excavations have uncovered remains of great archaeological value.

Ur NE facade of the ziggurat

uracil \'yùr-ə-ˌsil\ Organic compound of the PYRIMIDINE family, consisting of a ring containing both nitrogen and carbon atoms. It occurs in combined form in many important biological molecules, including RNA and several coenzymes active in CARBOHYDRATE METABOLISM. During synthesis of an RNA strand from DNA, uracil pairs with ADENINE. It or its corresponding NUCLEOSIDE or NUCLEOTIDE may be prepared from RNA by HYDROLYSIS.

Uralic languages \yù-'ra-lik\ Family of more than 30 languages spoken by some 25 million people in central and N Eurasia. A primary division is between the FINNO-UGRIC LANGUAGES, which account for most of the languages and speakers, and the Samoyedic languages. Samoyedic languages have historically been spoken in the forest region of N Siberia and in the tundra and coastal zones from the Ob to the White Sea and east into the Taymyr Peninsula. Of

T U V

these, Nenets, which has 25,000 speakers and is still being learned by children, is the most viable.

Ural Mountains \ˈyu̇r-əl\ Mountain range, Russia and Kazakstan. Constituting the boundary between Europe and Asia, the range extends south for 1,640 mi (2,640 km) from the Kara Sea to the URAL RIVER. The mountains average 3,000–4,000 ft (900–1,200 m) in height; the highest peak is Mt. Narodnaya, at 6,217 ft (1,895 m). Since World War II, the Middle Urals has contained one of the largest industrial regions of the COMMONWEALTH OF INDEPENDENT STATES, producing metal goods, chemicals, and machinery.

Ural River River, Russia and Kazakstan. Rising in the S URAL MTNS., it flows through W Kazakstan to the CASPIAN SEA at Atyrau. It is 1,509 mi (2,428 km) long and drains an area of 91,500 sq mi (237,000 sq km).

uranium Chemical ELEMENT, RARE EARTH METAL of the ACTINIDE series (with many TRANSITION ELEMENT properties), chemical symbol U, atomic number 92. A dense, hard, silvery-white METAL that tarnishes in air, it is isolated from such ores as PITCHBLENDE. Until the discovery of the first transuranium element in 1940, uranium was believed to be the heaviest element. RADIOACTIVITY was discovered in uranium by Henri BECQUEREL. All its ISOTOPES are radioactive. Some uranium compounds have been used as colors in ceramic glazes, in lightbulb filaments, in photography, and as dyes and mordants. See also ATOMIC BOMB, CHAIN REACTION, NUCLEAR FISSION, NUCLEAR POWER, URANIUM-234–URANIUM-238 DATING, URANIUM-THORIUM-LEAD DATING.

uranium-thorium-lead dating *or* **common-lead dating** Method of dating very old rocks by means of the amount of common LEAD they contain. Common lead is any lead from a rock or mineral that contains a small amount of the radioactive precursors of lead (i.e., the isotopes URANIUM-235, uranium-238, and thorium-232). By this method, the age of the earth has been estimated to be about 4.6 billion years. See also DATING.

uranium-234–uranium-238 dating Method of DATING that makes use of the radioactive decay of URANIUM-238 to uranium-234; the method can be used for dating sediments from either a marine or a PLAYA lake environment. This method is useful for the period 100,000–1.2 million years before the present.

Uranus *or* **Ouranus** \ˈyu̇r-ə-nəs, yu̇-ˈrā-nəs\ Ancient Greek personification of HEAVEN. When GAEA emerged from CHAOS, she produced Uranus, the mountains, and the sea. Her subsequent union with Uranus produced the TITANS and the Cyclopes (see CYCLOPS). Uranus despised his offspring and hid them in Gaea's body. In response to her appeal for vengeance, CRONUS castrated Uranus. From the drops of blood that fell on Earth were born other minor deities. His severed genitals floated on the sea, producing a white foam from which sprang APHRODITE.

Uranus Seventh planet from the sun, named for the Greek god personifying heaven. A blue-green gas giant, discovered in 1781 by William HERSCHEL, it has almost 15 times earth's mass and over 50 times its volume. The gravity at the top of its atmosphere is 11% weaker than earth's. It is 31,800 mi (51,100 km) across; Uranus has 10 narrow, dark rings, separated by broad dust bands consisting mainly of boulder-sized chunks of dark material; 15 moons; and a magnetic field about as strong as earth's. With a horizontal axis, it appears to spin on its side, about once every 17 hours. It takes 84 years to orbit the sun, at a mean distance of 1.78 billion mi (2.87 billion km). Its interior is thought to be ice and gas, perhaps with a small rocky core. Its atmosphere appears to be thousands of miles deep and contains methane, hydrogen, and helium.

Urartu \u̇-ˈrär-ˌtü\ Ancient kingdom around Lake Van, E. Turkey. Today the region is divided among Armenia, E Turkey, and NW Iran. The kingdom flourished from the 13th to the 7th cent. B.C., enjoying considerable power in the 9th–8th cent. B.C. Archaeological finds date from the time of King Shalmaneser I (c.1274–1245) of Assyria. Repeatedly attacked by Assyrian kings, it ceased to exist after invasions in the 7th cent. B.C.

Urban II *orig.* Odo of Châtillon-sur-Marne (c.1035–1099) Pope (1088–99). He was made cardinal by GREGORY VII,

whose reforms he furthered. Elected pope in 1088, Urban strengthened the role of the papacy in the reform movement. He called for the First CRUSADE at the Council of Clermont (1095) in response to the appeal of ALEXIUS I COMNENUS, promoted the union of the Eastern and Western churches, and supported the Christian reconquest of Spain from the Moors.

Urban VI *orig.* Bartolomeo Prignano (1318?–1389) Pope (1378–89). He served as papal chancellor for Gregory XI, whom he was chosen to succeed. This election of an Italian appeased the Romans, who wanted to end the French-dominated AVIGNON PAPACY, but his harsh reforms soon angered the French cardinals, prompting them to elect the antipope Clement VII and beginning the Western SCHISM (1378). Urban warred with Naples when its queen backed Clement. Strife over the schism reduced the Papal States to anarchy, and Urban's death may have been from poisoning.

urban planning Programs pursued in most industrialized countries in an attempt to improve the urban environment. Evidence of urban planning can be found in the ruins of ancient cities, including orderly street systems and conduits for water and sewage. During the Renaissance, European cities were consciously planned to achieve practical traffic movement and provide fortification against invasion. Such concepts were exported to the New World, where William PENN developed the standard gridiron plan in street layout. The modern urban planning movement arose in response to the squalor of the SLUMS created by the Industrial Revolution. City planners imposed regulatory laws establishing standards for housing and public health conditions, and introduced parks and playgrounds into congested city neighborhoods. In the 20th cent., ZONING to regulate building activity became a key tool for city planners.

Urdu language \ˈu̇r-dü\ INDO-ARYAN LANGUAGE used by Muslims in India and Pakistan. In the sociopolitical realm, Urdu and HINDI are different languages, but the colloquial basis of both is identical, and as a written language Urdu differs from Hindi principally in its greater acceptance of Perso-Arabic vocabulary and in some syntactic features. It is written in the ARABIC ALPHABET with modification of some letters. As Pakistan's official language, Urdu has been promoted as a token of national unity, though less than 8% of Pakistanis speak it as a first language.

urea \yu̇-ˈrē-ə\ *or* **carbamide** One of the simplest organic compounds and the first synthesized from inorganic raw materials (see INORGANIC COMPOUND), in 1828. The chief nitrogenous end product of PROTEIN breakdown in mammals and some fishes, it occurs not only in URINE but also in blood, bile, milk, and perspiration. It is one of the industrial chemicals produced in largest quantities; it is a major agricultural fertilizer and animal-feed ingredient. It is also used to make urea-formaldehyde PLASTICS (including foamed plastics; see POLYURETHANES), as well as to synthesize barbiturates, as a stabilizer in explosives, and in adhesives, hydrocarbon processing, and flameproofing.

uremia \yu̇-ˈrē-mē-ə\ Excess nitrogenous waste products in the blood and their toxic effects. Kidney impairment (see BRIGHT'S DISEASE, DIABETES MELLITUS, HYPERTENSION, KIDNEY FAILURE, NEPHRITIS) or disorders that hinder urine excretion allow UREA and other wastes to accumulate. Symptoms may include fatigue; itching and muscle twitches; dry, flaky, yellowish skin; dry mouth, metallic taste, and ammonia breath; and nausea, vomiting, diarrhea, and constipation. Advanced stages can lead to HYPERTENSION, seizures, HEART FAILURE, and death. If the underlying disorder cannot be treated, DIALYSIS or KIDNEY TRANSPLANT may be required.

Urey \ˈyu̇r-ē\, **Harold C(layton)** (1893–1981) U.S. scientist. Born in Walkerton, Ind., he was awarded a Nobel Prize in 1934 for discovering DEUTERIUM and HEAVY WATER. He was a key figure in the development of the ATOMIC BOMB. He also devised methods for estimating the temperature of ancient oceans, theorized on the compositions of primordial atmospheres, and studied the relative abundances of the elements, making fundamental contributions to a widely accepted theory of the origin of the earth and other planets.

urinalysis \ˌyu̇r-ə-ˈna-lə-səs\ Laboratory examination of a URINE sample. Abnormal concentrations of substances normally found in urine or presence of those that are not may indicate a disorder. Color, specific gravity, or volume changes may reveal a specific disease or injury. Significant findings include high glucose and acetone in DIABETES MELLITUS; uric acid in GOUT; and UREA, ALBUMINS, and GLOBULINS in kidney disease. Hormones may be evidence of pregnancy or endocrine imbalance. Urinalysis can also detect poisons and drugs.

urinary system *or* **renal system** \'rē-nəl\ System that produces and discharges URINE to rid the body of waste products. It consists of the KIDNEYS; the ureters, two thin muscular tubes 10–12 in. (25–30 cm) long that move the urine by PERISTALSIS; the hollow, muscular bladder, which receives and stores it; and the urethra, through which it leaves the body. In women the urethra is an inch or two long. In men it is longer (since it passes through the PENIS) and carries SEMEN as well as urine. See also DEHYDRATION, EDEMA, KIDNEY FAILURE, KIDNEY STONE.

urination Process of excreting URINE from the bladder (see URINARY SYSTEM). Nerve centers in the spinal cord and brain control it through involuntary and voluntary muscles. The need to void is felt when the bladder holds 3.5–5 oz (100–150 ml) of urine and becomes uncomfortable at a volume of 14–15 oz (350–400 ml). The detrusor contracts and the sphincter (muscular constriction) of the urethra relaxes to empty the bladder. Normally it empties completely, but bladder stones or prostatic disorders can block outflow. See also ENURESIS, INCONTINENCE.

urine Liquid solution of metabolic wastes and other, often toxic, substances filtered from PLASMA. The fluid in the Bowman's capsule at the start of each NEPHRON is essentially plasma without the large molecules (e.g., proteins). The final urine that exits the KIDNEY consists of water, UREA, inorganic SALTS, uric acid, creatinine, AMMONIA, and broken-down blood pigments, including urochrome, which makes urine yellow. See also URINALYSIS, URINARY SYSTEM, URINATION.

URL *in full* Uniform Resource Locator *or* Universal Resource Locator. Address of a resource on the INTERNET. The resource can be any type of file stored on a server, even an application program. The address contains three elements: the type of PROTOCOL used to access the file (e.g., HTTP for a Web page, ftp for an FTP site); the DOMAIN NAME or IP address of the server where the file resides; and, optionally, the description of the file's location. For example, the URL *http://www.m-w.com/cool/cool.htm* instructs the browser to use the HTTP protocol, go to the www.m-w.com Web server, and access the file named *cool.htm* (which is in the *cool* directory).

Urmia, Lake *Persian* **Daryacheh-ye Orumiyeh** \ˌdär-yä-ˈche-ye-ù-ˌrü-ˈmē-yə\ Shallow saline lake, NW Iran. The largest lake in the Middle East, it covers an area that varies from 2,000 to 2,300 sq mi (5,200–6,000 sq km). It is about 87 mi (140 km) long and 25–35 mi (40–55 km) wide, with a maximum depth of 53 ft (16 m). Fed by three rivers, it has no outlet.

Urnfield culture Late BRONZE AGE culture of Europe, so called because its people placed their cremated dead in urns. It spread from E central Europe and N Italy in the 12th cent. B.C. and later to Ukraine, Sicily, Scandinavia, France, and Spain. In some areas barrows marked the graves. The culture was warlike, with fortified settlements and bronze weapons. The uniformity of the culture and the persistence of certain pottery and metal forms apparently had great influence on Early IRON AGE culture.

urology \yù-ˈrä-lə-jē\ Medical specialty dealing with the URINARY SYSTEM and male REPRODUCTIVE SYSTEM. Most modern urological procedures originated in the 19th cent. Today, urologists use bladder catheters (see CATHETERIZATION), the cystoscope (to view the inside of the bladder), and various DIAGNOSTIC IMAGING techniques; treat prostatic disorders; perform VASECTOMIES; and may surgically remove stones in the urinary tract and cancers of the kidneys, bladder, and testicles. Urology deals mostly with male patients; the urinary tract in females may be treated by gynecologists (see OBSTETRICS AND GYNECOLOGY).

Uruguay \ˌü-rü-ˈgwī, *Engl* ˈyùr-ə-ˌgwā\ *officially* **Oriental Republic of Uruguay** Country, SE S. America. Area: 68,037 sq

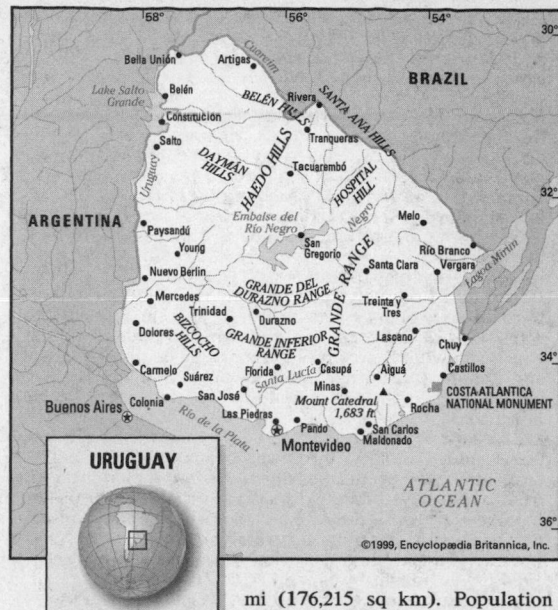

URUGUAY

Scale 1: 10,810,000
0   50   100 mi
0   80   160 km

©1999, Encyclopædia Britannica, Inc.

mi (176,215 sq km). Population (2000): 3,278,000. Capital: MONTEVIDEO. Caucasians, mostly of Spanish and Italian origin, are the predominant ethnic group; the remainder are mestizos, mulattos, and blacks. Few Indians remain. Language: Spanish (official). Religions: Roman Catholicism, Protestantism, Judaism. Currency: Uruguayan peso. The only S. American country lying entirely outside the tropics, its topography consists mainly of low plateaus and low hilly regions. The principal river is the Negro; the URUGUAY RIVER forms the country's entire W border with Argentina. Mineral and energy resources are limited. Pastures, covering almost four-fifths of the land area, support large herds of livestock for meat, leather goods, and wool. Chief crops include wheat, corn, oats, and barley. Other important industries are tourism, fishing, and the manufacturing of textiles, chemicals, and transportation equipment. It is a republic with two legislative houses; its head of state and government is the president. Prior to European settlement, Uruguay was inhabited mainly by the Charrúa Indians. The Spanish navigator Juan Díaz de Solís (1470?–1516) sailed into the Río de la PLATA in 1516. The Portuguese established Colonia in 1680. Subsequently, the Spanish established Montevideo in 1726, driving the Portuguese from their settlement; 50 years later Uruguay became part of the viceroyalty of RÍO DE LA PLATA. It gained independence from Spain in 1811. The Portuguese regained it in 182, incorporating it into Brazil as a province. A revolt against Brazil in 1825 led to its being recognized as an independent state in 1828. It battled Paraguay 1865–70. For much of World War II it remained neutral. The presidential office was abolished in 1951 and replaced with a nine-member council. The country adopted a new constitution and restored the presidential system in 1966. The military held power from 1973 to 1985. The 1990s brought a general upturn in the economy.

Uruguay River River, SE S. America. Rising in S Brazil, it forms the Argentina–S Brazil and Uruguay–Argentina borders. Above BUENOS AIRES, it combines with the PARANÁ RIVER to form the great estuary of the Río de la PLATA. Its 990-mi (1,593-km) course is navigable by ocean vessels for about 130 mi (210 km).

Uruk See ERECH

U.S. See UNITED STATES

USA Today National U.S. daily newspaper, the first of its kind. Launched in 1982 by Allen Neuharth, head of the GANNETT CO. chain, it soon achieved the largest circulation of any American newspaper. Initially considered gimmicky

T U V

and insubstantial, it gradually developed a reputation for higher quality. The features that originally set it apart—abundant colorful graphics, very brief stories, and a concentration on sports and celebrity—have influenced other newspapers.

USB *in full* Universal Serial Bus. Type of serial BUS that allows peripheral devices (disks, digital cameras, printers, etc.) to be easily connected to a computer. A "plug-and-play" interface, it allows a device to be added without an adapter card and without rebooting the computer. The USB 2.0 standard supports data-transfer speeds up to 480 megabits per second, multiple data streams, and up to 127 peripherals.

USC See Univ. of SOUTHERN CALIFORNIA

Usman dan Fodio \ü-'smän-'dän-fō-'dē-ō\ (1754–1817) FULANI mystic, philosopher, and reformer. In a JIHAD (holy war), 1804–8, he created a new Muslim state, the Fulani empire, in what is now N Nigeria, where he promoted Islam and founded the important Sokoto caliphate. His large body of writings in Arabic and Fula continues to enjoy wide influence.

U.S. News & World Report Weekly newsmagazine. *U.S. News* was founded in 1933 by David Lawrence (1888–1973) to cover domestic events; he founded *World Report* in 1945 to treat world news. The two merged in 1948. From its start, *U.S. News & World Report* had a somewhat more conservative viewpoint than its larger rivals, *TIME* and *NEWSWEEK*, and paid less attention to sports and the arts. In 1984 it was bought by Mortimer B. Zuckerman.

U.S.S.R. See UNION OF SOVIET SOCIALIST REPUBLICS

Ustinov \'yüs-tə-ˌnòf\, **Peter (Alexander)** (*later* **Sir Peter**) (b.1921) British actor and playwright. He made his film debut in 1941 and later appeared in *Lola Montez* (1955), *Spartacus* (1960, Academy Award), and *Topkapi* (1964, Academy Award), and as Hercule Poirot in movies based on Agatha CHRISTIE's mysteries, beginning with *Death on the Nile* (1978). He both starred in and directed *Billy Budd* (1962), among other films. He has written successful plays such as *The Love of Four Colonels* (1951) and *Romanoff and Juliet* (1956). He won Emmy awards for several television performances.

Usumbura See BUJUMBURA

usury \'yü-zhə-rē\ In law, the crime of charging an unlawfully high rate of INTEREST. In Old English law, the taking of any compensation whatsoever was termed usury. With the expansion of trade in the 13th cent., the demand for credit increased, necessitating a modification in the definition of the term. In 1545 England fixed a legal maximum interest; a practice later followed by other Western nations.

Utah State, (pop., 2000: 2,233,000), W U.S. It covers 84,899 sq mi (219,888 sq km); its capital is SALT LAKE CITY. Utah contains the GREAT SALT LAKE and parts of the middle ROCKY MTNS. and Uinta Mtns. The W third of the state is a broad desert-like area. About 70% of the land is owned by either the federal or the state government. The region was inhabited as early as 10,000 B.C. Around A.D. 400 the PUEBLO INDIANS lived throughout Utah; they were followed by other groups, including the SHOSHONE, UTE, and PAIUTE Indians. Spanish missionaries visited there in the late 18th cent. It passed to Mexico in 1821. While Jim BRIDGER discovered the Great Salt Lake in 1824, the area's first permanent settlers were MORMONS, who were led to the valley of the Great Salt Lake in 1847 by Brigham YOUNG. The U.S. acquired the region after the MEXICAN WAR, and in 1850 organized the Utah Territory; it was reduced to the area of the present state by 1868. A conflict between Mormon authorities and the U.S. government known as the Utah War occurred in 1857–58, and statehood was denied until the Mormons renounced POLYGAMY. When they did, it entered the Union in 1896 as the 45th state. The Mormon Church has officially been politically neutral since the early 20th cent. and the influence of economic blocs has become more important. Utah has large reserves of coal and petroleum, and is the world's largest producer of beryllium. Major industries include agriculture and tourism.

Utamaro \ù-tä-'mä-rō\ *orig.* Kitagawa Nebsuyoshi (1753–1806) Japanese printmaker and painter. He moved from a provincial town to Edo (now Tokyo) in his youth; his early work included many illustrated books. One of the greatest UKIYO-E artists, he is known especially for his masterfully composed portraits of sensuous female beauties. Unlike other *ukiyo-e* artists, who favored prints of women in groups, Utamaro concentrated on half-length single portraits.

Ute \'yüt\ American Indians traditionally inhabiting W Colorado and E Utah (whose name derives from Ute). Until the 19th cent., the Ute had no horses and subsisted by food collecting. They were virtually indistinguishable from the Southern PAIUTE. After acquiring horses they became organized as loose bands of hunters, often targeting livestock. After the Indian wars of 1864–70 most Ute were settled on reservations. Today they number about 5,000.

uterus *or* **womb** Inverted-pear-shaped organ of the female REPRODUCTIVE SYSTEM, in which the EMBRYO and FETUS develop during PREGNANCY. It lies over and behind the bladder; the uterine (fallopian) tubes enter it at the top; at the other end, the cervix extends down into the VAGINA. The uterine lining (endometrium), a moist mucous membrane, changes in thickness during the menstrual cycle (see MENSTRUATION), being thickest at ovulation (see OVARY) in readiness for a fertilized EGG. Disorders of the uterus include infections, benign and malignant tumors, PROLAPSE, ENDOMETRIOSIS, and fibroids (leiomyomas).

Utica \'yü-ti-kə\ Ancient Phoenician settlement, N African coast. Traditionally considered the oldest settlement of PHOENICIA, it was located in what is now Tunisia. After its founding about the 8th cent. B.C., it grew rapidly and became second in importance only to CARTHAGE. Made the capital of the Roman province of Africa after the Third PUNIC WAR (149–146 B.C.), it later declined. Excavations have uncovered Phoenician and Roman remains.

utilitarianism Ethical principle that an action is right if it tends to maximize happiness, not only that of the agent but of all affected by the action. Thus, utilitarians focus on the consequences of an act rather than on its intrinsic nature or the motives of the agent. Classical utilitarianism is hedonist, but values other than pleasure (ideal utilitarianism) can be employed; anything can be regarded as valuable that appears as an object of rational or informed desire (preference utilitarianism). Jeremy BENTHAM's *Introduction to the Principles of Morals and Legislation* (1789) and John Stuart MILL's *Utilitarianism* (1863) are major statements of utilitarianism.

Uto-Aztecan languages \ˌyü-tō-'az-ˌte-kən\ Family of more than 30 American Indian languages spoken in pre-Columbian N. and Central America. Uto-Aztecan can be divided into a N and a S branch. The N branch includes the languages of the Northern and Southern PAIUTES, UTES, SHOSHONES, COMANCHES, and HOPI. The S branch includes some languages of Arizona and Mexican Indian peoples, including the Tarahumara of Chihuahua, the Yaqui of NW Mexico and Arizona, and the Cora and Huichol of Nayarit and Jalisco; its southernmost extension includes NAHUATL.

utopian socialism Political and social idea of the mid-19th cent. Utopian socialists drew from such reformers as Robert OWEN and Charles FOURIER and from early communist and socialist ideas. Advocates included Louis BLANC and the founders of the ONEIDA COMMUNITY and BROOK FARM. Utopian settlements were also attempted by such religious groups as the MENNONITES, SHAKERS, and MORMONS.

Utrecht \'ü-ˌtrekt, 'yü-ˌtrekt\ City (pop., 1999 est.: 233,000), central Netherlands. The site of successive Roman, Frisian, and Frankish fortresses, it became an episcopal see in 696 under St. Willibrord. Its greatest prosperity was in the 11th–12th cent. In 1527 it was transferred to Holy Roman Emperor CHARLES V and became part of the HABSBURG dominions. It was ruled by Spain until the 1570s. It was the site of the signing of the Union of Utrecht (1579), which established a league of N Netherlands provinces against Spain. Occupied by the French 1795–1813, it was the residence of Louis BONAPARTE, king of Holland 1806–10. The only Dutch pope, Adrian VI, was born there. It is a financial and insurance center.

Utrecht, Peace of (1713–14) Series of treaties concluding the War of the SPANISH SUCCESSION. France concluded treaties with Britain, the Dutch Republic, Prussia, Portugal, and

Savoy, in which it ceded various territories, including regions in Canada, to Britain. France also recognized Queen ANNE as the British sovereign, acknowledged FREDERICK I's royal title, and recognized VICTOR AMADEUS II as king of Sicily. Spain ceded Gibraltar to Britain and gave Britain the exclusive right to supply the Spanish colonies with African slaves for 30 years. The Spanish succession was settled in favor of the Bourbon PHILIP V. The treaties gave Britain the largest portion of colonial and commercial spoils and made it the leader in world trade.

Utrecht school Principally a group of three Dutch painters from UTRECHT—Dirck van Baburen (c.1590–1624), Gerrit van HONTHORST, and Hendrik TERBRUGGHEN—who were greatly influenced by CARAVAGGIO's art during travels to Rome. They used their newly learned technique in artwork with primarily religious subject matter, but also produced brothel scenes and pictures in sets, such as five works devoted to the senses. The numerous candles, lanterns, and other sources of artificial light in their paintings also differentiate them from Caravaggio, who never used such devices.

Utrillo \ū-trē-ˈyō, *Engl* yü-ˈtri-lō\, **Maurice** (1883–1955) French painter. When he became an alcoholic in his teens, his mother, the painter and artist's model Suzanne Valadon (1865–1938), encouraged him to take up painting as therapy; it soon became his obsession. Interested in reproducing what he saw as faithfully as possible, he depicted the old, deteriorating houses and streets of the Montmartre district of Paris. His best work is that of his "white period" (c.1908–14), so called for his lavish use of zinc white in heavy layers to show aging, cracked walls.

Uxmal \üz-ˈmäl, üsh-ˈmäl\ Ancient city, YUCATÁN state, SE Mexico. It was the chief city of the later MAYA empire (600–c.900 A.D.). After about 1000, major construction ceased, although Uxmal continued to participate in the political League of Mayapan. When the league dissolved, Uxmal was abandoned (c.1450). The superb Maya ruins include a pyramid, palace, and quadrangle.

Uygurs See UIGHURS

Uzbekistan \üz-ˌbe-ki-ˈstan\ *officially* **Republic of Uzbekistan** Nation, W central Asia. The Karakalpakstan Autonomous Republic is within its borders. Area: 172,700 sq mi (447,400 sq km). Population (2000): 24,756,000. Capital: TASHKENT. The Uzbeks make up more than 75% of the population; Russians, Tajiks, Kazaks, Tatars, and Karakalpaks make up the remainder. Languages: Uzbek (official), Russian, Tajik. Religions: Islam (Sunni), Russian Orthodoxy. Currency: sum. Uzbekistan lies in the heart of central Asia, largely between the AMU DARYA and the Syr Darya rivers. Although it contains fertile oases and high mountain ranges in the south and east, almost four-fifths of the country consists of flat, sun-baked lowlands. Two-thirds of the ARAL SEA extends into Uzbekistan. It is a major producer and exporter of natural gas and has sizable reserves of petroleum, coal, and various metallic ores. It is one of central Asia's major cotton growers; it also grows fruits and vegetables and raises karakul sheep. It is the main producer of

machinery and heavy equipment in central Asia. It is a republic with one legislative body; its head of state is the president, and the head of government is the prime minister. GENGHIS KHAN's grandson Shibaqan received the territory as his inheritance in the 13th cent. A.D. His Mongols ruled over nearly 100 mainly Turkic tribes, who would eventually intermarry with the Mongols to form the Uzbeks and other Turkic peoples of central Asia. In the early 16th cent., a federation of Mongol-Uzbeks invaded and occupied settled regions, including an area called Transoxania that would become the Uzbeks' permanent homeland. By the early 19th cent., the region was dominated by the khanates of Khiva, BUKHRA, and QUQON, all of which eventually succumbed to Russian domination. The Uzbek Soviet Socialist Republic was created in 1924. In June 1990 Uzbekistan became the first central Asian republic to declare sovereignty. It achieved full independence from the Soviet Union in 1991. During the 1990s, its declining economy remained strictly controlled, and its political system was deemed harsh.

Uzi submachine gun \ˈü-zē\ Compact automatic weapon used worldwide by police and special forces. It was designed by the Israeli Uziel Gal after the Arab–Israeli War of 1948. It is 26 in. (650 mm) long with its folding metal butt fully extended; the barrel is only 10 in. (260 mm) long. When loaded with a magazine of 9-mm pistol ammunition, it weighs about 9 lbs (4 kg).

TUV

V

V-1 missile *or* **flying bomb** *or* **buzz bomb** German MISSILE of World War II. The forerunner of modern CRUISE MISSILES, it was about 25 ft (8 m) long and had a wingspan of about 18 ft (5.5 m). It carried an explosive warhead of almost 1,900 lbs (850 kg) and had an average range of 150 mi (240 km). More than 8,000 V-1s were launched against London in 1944–45. See also V-2 MISSILE.

V-2 missile World War II German ballistic MISSILE, forerunner of space ROCKETS and long-range missiles. Developed starting in 1936 under Wernher von BRAUN, V-2s were fired against Paris, Britain, and Belgium (1944–45). After the war, the U.S. and the Soviet Union captured many; research on them led to their missile and space-exploration programs. See also V-1 MISSILE.

vaccine Preparation containing either killed or weakened live microorganisms, or a toxoid, introduced by mouth, by injection, or by nasal spray to stimulate production of ANTIBODIES against an infectious agent. This confers IMMUNITY to that agent. The first vaccine, against SMALLPOX, was introduced by Edward JENNER in 1798. Vaccines have been developed against diseases caused by BACTERIA (e.g., TYPHOID, WHOOPING COUGH, TUBERCULOSIS) and by VIRUSES (e.g., MEASLES, INFLUENZA, RABIES, POLIOMYELITIS). Effectiveness varies, and a small percentage of people have adverse reactions. Those with IMMUNODEFICIENCY should not receive live vaccines.

vacuole \\'vak-yə-ˌwōl\\ Space within a cell that is empty of CYTOPLASM, lined with a membrane, and filled with fluid. Especially in PROTOZOANS, vacuoles perform functions such as storage, ingestion, digestion, excretion, and expulsion of excess water. Plant cells often have large central vacuoles.

vacuum Space in which there is no MATTER or in which the PRESSURE is so low that any particles in the space do not affect any processes being carried on there. It is a condition well below normal ATMOSPHERIC PRESSURE. A vacuum can be created using a vacuum pump or by reducing the pressure using a fast flow of fluid (see BERNOULLI'S PRINCIPLE).

vacuum tube Electron tube consisting of a sealed glass or metal container enclosing a vacuum. It was used in early electronic circuitry to control a flow of electrons. In the first half of the 20th cent., vacuum tubes allowed the development of radio broadcasting, long-distance telephone service, television, and the first electronic digital computers, which were the largest vacuum-tube systems ever built. TRANSISTORS have replaced them in virtually all applications, but they are still occasionally used in display devices for television sets and computers (CATHODE-RAY TUBES), in microwave ovens, and space satellites.

Vadim \\və-'dēm\\, **Roger** *orig.* Roger Vladimir Plemiannikov (1928–2000) French film director. He directed and cowrote the highly successful erotic film *And God Created Woman* (1956), which established his wife, Briget BARDOT, as a sex symbol. He duplicated this winning formula with two later wives, Annette Stroyberg in *Dangerous Liaisons* (1959) and Jane FONDA in *Barbarella* (1968), and his lover, Catherine DENEUVE, in *Vice and Virtue* (1962).

Vaduz \\fä-'düts\\ City (pop., 1998 est.: 5,000), capital of Liechtenstein. Located on the RHINE RIVER, it was greatly damaged in 1499 in a war between the Swiss and MAXIMILIAN I, but later rebuilt. The Liechtenstein family gained possession in the early 18th cent. It is a flourishing tourist center; the ruling prince's castle overlooks the town.

Vaganova \\və-'gà-nə-və\\, **Agrippina (Yakovlevna)** (1879–1951) Russian ballet dancer and teacher whose system of instruction combined classic technique with an athletic, acrobatic post-Revolution style. She danced with the MARIINSKY THEATER company 1897–1917. She began teaching at the Leningrad Choreographic (formerly Imperial Ballet) school in 1921, and became its director in 1934; there she trained many of Russia's future leading dancers and teachers. Her textbook *Fundamentals of the Classic Dance* (1934) has been used worldwide.

vagina \\və-'jī-nə\\ Genital canal in females. Together with the cavity of the UTERUS, it forms the birth canal. In most virgins, its external opening is partially closed by a thin fold of tissue (hymen). The vagina's lining thickens and thins during the menstrual cycle (see MENSTRUATION) in response to ESTROGEN from the OVARIES, being thickest and most elastic during ovulation and pregnancy. Elastic muscle walls accommodate movement of the penis during intercourse and passage of a child during delivery. A mucuslike fluid seeps through them for lubrication during sexual arousal. Vaginal disorders include bacterial and fungal infections (e.g., SEXUALLY TRANSMITTED DISEASES, CANDIDA), vaginitis, sores (see ULCER), and PROLAPSE.

vagrancy Act of wandering about without employment or identifiable means of support. In the U.S., laws against vagrancy were used by police and prosecutors as a tool for proscribing a wide range of behavior. Most such laws have been struck down as unconstitutionally vague, and vagrancy has thus been largely decriminalized.

Vail Town (pop., 2000: 4,500), W central Colorado. Located in the ROCKY MTNS. west of DENVER, it was founded as a resort town in 1962, and built in the style of an Alpine village. The skiable terrain around Vail Mtn. extends for 15 sq mi (39 sq km), making Vail the largest ski resort in N. America.

Vaishnavism \\'vīsh-nə-ˌvi-zəm\\ Worship of VISHNU as the supreme deity, as well as of his incarnations, mainly RAMA and KRISHNA. Vaishnavism is one of the major forms of modern HINDUISM, along with SHAIVISM and SHAKTISM, and is probably the most popular and most widely practiced. Characterized by an emphasis on BHAKTI, its goal is to escape from the cycle of birth and death in order to enjoy the presence of Vishnu.

Vaishya \\'vīsh-yə\\ Third-highest of the four VARNAS of India. Traditionally described as commoners, Vaishyas are connected with such productive labor as trade, agriculture, and pastoralism. They rank below the BRAHMANS and the Kshatriyas but above the Sudras. They are credited historically with favoring the rise of the reformist religious beliefs of BUDDHISM and JAINISM. They have become a symbol of middle-class prestige, and many rise to higher classes.

Vajiravudh \\ˌvä-jē-rä-'vüd\\ *or* **Phramongkutklao** \\ˌprä-ˌmóŋ-kùt-'klaù\\ *or* **Rama VI** (1881–1925) King of Siam (1910–25). Educated at Oxford, he undertook numerous social reforms as king, including making monogamy the only legal form of marriage. In 1921 he made primary education free and compulsory. He was successful in foreign policy, restoring full fiscal autonomy to Siam. A prolific writer, he introduced Western forms to Thai literature, translated William SHAKESPEARE's works, and composed about 50 original plays.

vajra \\'vəj-rə\\ Five-pronged ritual object extensively employed in the ceremonies of TIBETAN BUDDHISM. It is made of brass or bronze, the four prongs at each end curving around the central fifth to form a lotus-bud shape. In Sanskrit the word means both thunderbolt and diamond: like a thunderbolt it cuts through ignorance, and like a diamond it destroys but is itself indestructible. In ritual use, it is often employed in conjunction with a bell in the execution of MUDRAS.

Vajrayana \ˌvəj-rə-ˈyä-nə\ Form of tantric BUDDHISM (see TANTRA) that emerged in India in the first millennium A.D. and spread to Tibet, where it is the predominant tradition in TIBETAN BUDDHISM. Vajrayana aims to recapture the enlightenment experience of the BUDDHA Gautama, and it places special emphasis on the notion that enlightenment arises from the realization that seemingly opposite principles are in truth one. It introduced innovations involving the use of MANTRAS and MANDALAS as aids to meditation.

Valdemar I \ˈväl-də-mär\ *known as* **Valdemar the Great** (1131–1182) King of Denmark (1157–82). He ended more than 25 years of civil wars and defeated the Wends (Slavs) by 1169, freeing Danish ships from piracy. He acknowledged the overlordship of FREDERICK I Barbarossa and accepted his antipope Victor IV; he later acknowledged Pope ALEXANDER III (c.1165) and rejected Frederick. He gained church approval for hereditary rule by his dynasty, the Valdemars, and in 1181 he allied with Frederick as an equal, aided by the marriage of their children.

Valdemar IV Atterdag \ˈät-tər-ˌdåg\ (c.1320–1375) King of Denmark (1340–75). A son of King Christopher II, he sold Estonia (1346), gained control of Zealand (1349), and subdued a revolt in Jutland (1350). By regaining Skåne from Sweden, he completed the reunification of his father's kingdom (1360). His aggressive foreign policy led to conflict with the HANSEATIC LEAGUE, which defeated him in 1368, forcing him to concede trading privileges but allowing his kingdom to remain intact. The marriage of his daughter Margaret to the Norwegian king Haakon VI made possible the unification of Denmark and Norway.

valence \ˈvā-ləns\ Number of bonds (see BONDING) an ATOM can form. Hydrogen (H) always has valence 1, so other ELEMENTS' valences equal the number of hydrogen atoms they combine with. Thus, oxygen (O) has valence 2, as in water (H_2O); nitrogen (N) has valence 3, as in ammonia (NH_3); and chlorine (Cl) has valence 1, as in hydrochloric acid (HCl). The valence depends on the number of unpaired ELECTRONS in the outermost (and, in TRANSITION ELEMENTS, the next) shell of the atom's structure. The sharing of the unpaired (valence) electrons in a bond mimics the stable configuration of the NOBLE GASES. Elements that can achieve stable configurations by various combinations have more than one valence.

Valencia Autonomous community (pop., 1998: 4,023,000), E Spain. Encompassing the provinces of Alicante, Castellón, and Valencia, it covers 8,998 sq mi (23,305 sq km); its capital is VALENCIA. It is a generally mountainous region, with salt lagoons on the coast. Part of the caliphate of CÓRDOBA (11th cent.), it subsequently became an independent Moorish kingdom. It was held by the Spanish commander El CID 1094–99; after his death it again was lost to the Moors, until King James I of ARAGON took it in 1238. One of the richest farming regions in the Mediterranean basin, it produces oranges, rice, grapes, and olives.

Valencia City and seaport (pop., 1998: 739,000), capital of VALENCIA, E Spain. A Roman settlement by 138 B.C., it was taken by the Visigoths in A.D. 413 and the Moors in 714. It became the seat of the independent Moorish kingdom of Valencia in 1021. After 1238 it was ruled by the Aragonese kings. The first Spanish printing press was established there in 1474, and the city was the seat of the Valencian school of painting. It was severely damaged in the PENINSULAR WAR, during the SPANISH CIVIL WAR, and by flood in 1957.

Valencia City (pop., 1992 est.: 1,034,000), NW Venezuela. Founded in 1555, it rivaled CARACAS as the region's major city well into the 19th cent. In 1814, during the struggle for Venezuela's independence, it was the site of a bloody battle. It served as national capital in 1812, 1830, and 1858. It is a principal industrial and transportation center.

Valentine's Day Lovers' holiday celebrated on February 14, the feast day of St. Valentine, one of two 3rd-cent. Roman martyrs of the same name. St. Valentine is considered the patron of lovers and especially of those unhappily in love. The feast day became a lovers' festival in the 14th cent. Today it is marked by the exchange of romantic cards (valentines), flowers, and other gifts.

Valentinian I \ˌva-lən-ˈti-nē-ən\ *in full* Flavius Valentinianus (A.D. 321–375). Roman emperor (364–75). He served in the military in Africa under his father. Proclaimed emperor by the army, he made his brother Valens (A.D. 328–378) ruler in the East while he ruled the West. Both showed religious toleration. Valentinian defeated the Alemanni in Gaul in 365, then moved to support the defense of Britain. He named his 9-year-old son GRATIAN coemperor (367) to ensure the succession. Despite his achievements, he was known for his cruelty and poor choice of ministers.

Valentino, Rudolph *orig.* Rodolfo Guglielmi di Valentina d'Antonguolla (1895–1926) Italian-U.S. film actor. He emigrated to the U.S. in 1913, and played small parts in movies until his role in *The Four Horsemen of the Apocalypse* (1921) made him a star. Skillfully promoted, his popularity soared among women as he played the sultry lover in such romantic dramas as *The Sheik* (1921), *Blood and Sand* (1922), *The Eagle* (1925), and *The Son of the Sheik* (1926). His sudden death at 31 from a ruptured ulcer caused worldwide hysteria, several suicides, and riots at his funeral.

Rudolph Valentino in *The Sheik,* with Agnes Ayres, 1921

Vale of Tempe See Vale of TEMPE
Vale of the White Horse See Vale of the WHITE HORSE
Valera, Eamon de See Eamon DE VALERA
Valerian *Latin* Publius Licinius Valerianus (d.260 A.D.) Roman emperor (253–260). A military commander elected emperor by his soldiers (253), Valerian renewed the persecution of the Christians and executed Pope Sixtus II in 258. He appointed his son Publius Licinius GALLIENUS to rule the W part of the empire, then marched east to repel the Persian invasion. At first successful, he was later defeated by the Persian king Shapur I and died in captivity.

valerian Any of the more than 400 species of annual and perennial herbaceous plants in about 10 genera that make up the family Valerianaceae. The true valerians (native to the temperate zones, the Andes Mtns., and Africa) have tubular flowers, often spurred at the base and clustered in tight heads. The largest genus, *Valeriana,* contains about 200 species and is best known for common valerian (*V. officinalis*), used by modern herbalists to calm the nerves and induce sleep.

Valéry \ˌva-lə-ˈrē\, (Ambroise-) **Paul** (-Toussaint-Jules) (1871–1945) French poet, essayist, and critic. Valéry's early poems were published in magazines of the SYMBOLIST MOVEMENT. After 1894 he wrote daily in his notebooks, later published as the famous *Cahiers*. He revised his early work to create his greatest poem, *La jeune parque* (1917). It was followed by *Album de vers anciens, 1890–1900* (1920) and *Charmes ou poèmes* (1922), containing "Le cimetière marin," which established him as the outstanding French poet of his time. He later became a prominent public personage.

Valhalla \val-ˈha-lə, väl-ˈhä-lə\ In GERMANIC RELIGION, the hall of slain warriors who live blissfully under the leadership of ODIN. In the splendid palace, roofed with shields, the warriors feast on the flesh of a boar slaughtered daily and made whole again each evening. Their sport is to fight one another every day, with the slain being revived in the evening. Thus they will live until the RAGNAROK, when they will fight at the side of Odin against the Giants. See also ASGARD, FREYJA, VALKYRIE.

validity In LOGIC, the property of an argument consisting in the fact that the truth of the premises logically guarantees the truth of the conclusion. Whenever the premises are true, the conclusion must be true, because of the form of

T U V

the argument. Some arguments that fail to be valid are acceptable on grounds other than formal logic (e.g., inductively strong arguments), and their conclusions are supported with less than logical necessity. Defective forms of argument in which the premises provide no rational grounds for accepting the conclusion are called fallacies (see formal and informal FALLACY).

Valium Trademark for a preparation of diazepam; a tranquillizing drug used to treat anxiety and tension states and as an aid in sedation, first introduced in 1963. Side effects include drowsiness and muscular incoordination; physical dependence can result after prolonged use. The discovery of Valium and similar drugs led to a new era in psychopharmacology.

Valkyrie \val-'kir-ē, 'val-kə-rē\ In GERMANIC RELIGION, any of a group of maidens who are sent by ODIN to select slain warriors worthy of a place in VALHALLA. They rode to the battlefield on horses or, in some accounts, flew through the air and sea. According to various myths, they were either purely supernatural or human with supernatural powers; they were associated with fairness, brightness, and gold as well as with bloodshed.

Valla \'väl-lä\, **Lorenzo** (1407–1457) Italian humanist, philosopher, and literary critic. He was royal secretary and historian for ALFONSO V of Aragon 1435–48. In his polemical style, he criticized the works of BOETHIUS, ARISTOTLE, and CICERO. Found heretical by the INQUISITION for his refusal to believe that the Apostles' Creed was composed by the 12 Apostles, he narrowly avoided being burned at the stake. His *Elegantiae linguae Latinae* (printed 1471) was the first Renaissance textbook of Latin grammar. His *Annotations on the New Testament* (printed 1505) was his last major work.

Valladolid \ˌva-lə-də-'lid, *Span* ˌbäl-yä-thō-'lēth\ City (pop., 1998 est.: 320,000), capital of the autonomous community of CASTILLA Y LEÓN, Spain. It was the seat of the Castilian court until about 1600. The Catholic monarchs ISABELLA of Castile and FERDINAND of Aragon were married there in 1469. It suffered heavy damage by fire in 1561 and by the French during the PENINSULAR WAR. It has many medieval buildings, and its university (founded 1346) is one of Spain's oldest.

Vallandigham \və-'lan-di-gəm\, **Clement L(aird)** (1820–1871) U.S. politician. Born in Lisbon, Ohio, he served in the U.S. House of Representatives (1857–63), where he became a leader of the antiwar COPPERHEADS. As a result of his vociferous criticism of Pres. Abraham LINCOLN's administration and its pursuit of the Civil War, he was found guilty of treasonable sentiments (1863) and sentenced to exile in the South. He soon made his way to Canada, then illegally to Ohio, where he continued his antigovernment speeches.

Valle d'Aosta \ˌvä-lā-dä-'ós-tə\ Autonomous region (pop., 1996 est.: 119,000), NW Italy. It is enclosed on three sides by the ALPS. After the fall of the W Roman empire, it formed part of the Burgundian and Frankish kingdoms. It was acquired in the 11th cent. by the House of SAVOY. The autonomous region of Valle d'Aosta was created in 1945, in recognition of the French cultural orientation of the area. Its economy rests on its dairy products and tourism.

Valle-Inclán \'bäl-yä-ēŋ-'klän\, **Ramón María del** *orig.* Ramón Valle y Villanueva de Arosa (1866–1936) Spanish novelist, playwright, and poet. His first four works, collectively called the *Sonatas* (1902–5), are evocatively written in a tone of refined and elegant decadence. Some later plays and novels take an intentionally absurdist and cruelly satiric tone to express what he saw as the Spanish deformation of European civilization.

Valletta \və-'le-tə\ Seaport city (pop., 1999 est.: 7,100), capital of Malta. Built on a rocky promontory after the Great Siege of Malta in 1565, which checked the advance of OTTOMAN power in S Europe, it became the Maltese capital in 1570. After 1814 it was made the principal base of the British Mediterranean naval fleet and remained important through World War II, during which it suffered heavy damage from bombing raids. Several 16th-cent. buildings still exist. The city's economy relies mainly on trade and tourism.

valley Elongate depression of the earth's surface. Valleys are commonly drained by rivers and may be in a relatively flat plain or between ranges of hills or mountains. Valleys formed by rivers are typically V-shaped; those formed by glaciers, U-shaped. Valley evolution is controlled mainly by climate and rock type. Very narrow, deep valleys with steep sides are called CANYONS; smaller valleys of similar appearance are called gorges.

Valley Forge National Historical Park Preserve, SE Pennsylvania. The 3,468-acre (1,404-hectare) park commemorates the site where Gen. George WASHINGTON camped with his Continental Army in the winter of 1777–78 during the AMERICAN REVOLUTION. Though the bitterly harsh winter and lack of provisions could have devastated the American war effort, the army, under Washington's leadership and that of the Marquis de LAFAYETTE and Baron von STEUBEN, emerged as a disciplined and efficient force.

Valley of Ten Thousand Smokes See Valley of TEN THOUSAND SMOKES

Valley of the Kings See Valley of the KINGS

Valois \väl-'wä\ Medieval county and duchy, N France. It was under the Merovingian kings (c.500–751) and their successors, the Carolingians, until it became a hereditary countship. In 1214 King PHILIP II Augustus annexed it. The duchy's last representative, Henry III, was succeeded in 1589 by the House of BOURBON. In 1790 the duchy was abolished.

Valois, Ninette de See Ninette DE VALOIS

Valparaiso \ˌval-pə-'rī-zō\ City (pop., 1999: 283,000) and seaport, central Chile. It was founded by the Spanish in 1536; few of its colonial buildings have survived a succession of pirate raids, severe storms, fires, and earthquakes (recently, 1906 and 1971). After Chilean independence in 1818, the city's port developed with the growth of the Chilean navy. As Chile's principal seaport, it handles the bulk of the country's imports. Still a naval facility, it also produces chemicals and textiles.

value-added tax Government levy on the amount a firm adds to the price of a commodity during production and distribution. In the most common method of calculation, the seller totals the taxes he has collected on goods sold and paid on goods purchased; his net tax liability is the difference between the tax collected and the tax paid. The burden of the value-added tax, like that of other SALES TAXES, tends to be passed on to the consumer. To limit its regressiveness, most countries set lower rates for consumer necessities than for luxury items. In 1954 France became the first country to adopt the value-added tax on a large scale. It has since been adopted throughout most of Western Europe and in many countries in S. America, Asia, and Africa. See also REGRESSIVE TAX.

valve Device for controlling the flow of fluids (liquids, gases, slurries) in a pipe or other enclosure. It exerts control by means of a movable element that opens, shuts, or partially blocks an opening in a passageway. Some valves operate automatically; check (or nonreturn) valves, for example, are self-acting valves that permit flow in only one direction.

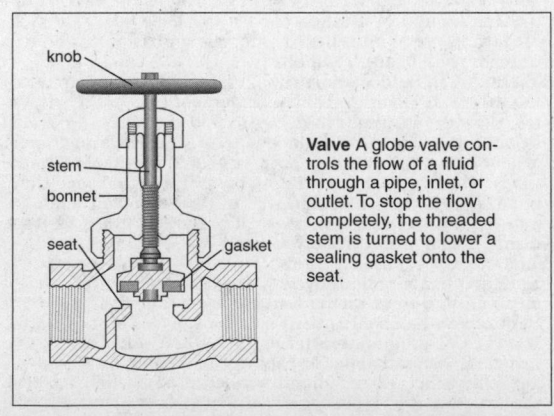

Valve A globe valve controls the flow of a fluid through a pipe, inlet, or outlet. To stop the flow completely, the threaded stem is turned to lower a sealing gasket onto the seat.

Safety valves open at a predetermined pressure; the movable element usually has a weighted lever or a spring strong enough to hold the valve closed until a particular pressure is reached.

vampire In popular legend, a bloodsucking creature that rises from its burial place at night to drink the blood of humans, sometimes in the form of a bat. By daybreak it must return to its grave or to a coffin filled with its native earth. Vampires figure in the folklore of many Eurasian countries, notably in Hungary and other Slavic regions. The disinterment in Serbia in 1725 and 1732 of several fluid-filled corpses that villagers claimed were vampires led to widespread interest in vampirism. Vampires are supposedly dead humans who maintain a kind of life by biting the necks of living humans and sucking their blood; their victims become vampires after death. These "undead" creatures can be warded off by crucifixes or wreaths of garlic and can be killed by exposure to the sun or by an oak stake driven through the heart. The most famous vampire was created by Bram STOKER in his *Dracula* (1897).

vampire bat Any of three species (family Desmodontidae) of blood-eating BATS native to the New World tropics. They grow to 2–3.5 in. (6–9 cm) long. They live in colonies in caves, hollow trees, and culverts, leaving after dark to forage close to the ground. They feed on quietly resting birds and mammals, including the occasional human, making a small cut with their sharp incisor teeth, often without disturbing the prey, and lapping the blood. The wounds are not serious but may transmit diseases.

vanadium \və-'nā-dē-əm\ Chemical ELEMENT, one of the TRANSITION ELEMENTS, chemical symbol V, atomic number 23. A silvery-white, soft METAL found (always combined) in various minerals, coal, and petroleum, it is used in alloys with steel and iron. Unalloyed, it is used in high-temperature applications, as a target for X rays, and as a catalyst. Its compounds (of various VALENCES) have many beautiful colors in solution and are used as catalysts and mordants (see DYE).

Van Allen radiation belts Two doughnut-shaped zones of high-energy charged particles (see ELECTRIC CHARGE) trapped at high altitudes in earth's MAGNETIC FIELD, discovered (1958) by James A. Van Allen (b.1914). Most intense over the equator and nearly absent above the poles, they merge gradually. The flux of charged particles is densest in two regions— one, mostly PROTONS thought to be produced by primary COSMIC RAYS striking the atmosphere, centered about 3,700 mi (6,000 km) above the earth's surface, and the other, including some helium ions from the SOLAR WIND, about 12,500 mi (20,000 km) above the earth's surface. Intense solar activity (see SOLAR CYCLE) causes disruptions of the belts, linked in turn with AURORAS and magnetic storms.

Vanbrugh \'van-ˌbrük, van-'brü\, **John** (*later* **Sir John**) (1664–1726) English dramatist and architect. His successful Restoration comedies of manners include *The Relapse* (1696) and *The Provok'd Wife* (1697). He also wrote lively adaptations from the French, including *The Country House* (performed 1703) and *The Confederacy* (1705). His architectural masterpiece, designed with Nicholas Hawksmoor (1661–1736), was BLENHEIM PALACE (1705–16), which brought the English baroque style to its culmination.

Van Buren, Martin (1782–1862) Eighth president of the U.S. (1837–41). Born in Kinderhook, N.Y., he served in the state senate (1812–20), becoming the leader of an informal group called the Albany Regency because they dominated state politics even after Van Buren went to Washington. In the U.S. Senate (1821–28), he supported states' rights and opposed a strong central government. After J. Q. ADAMS became

Martin Van Buren
Daguerreotype, c.1845–50

president, he joined with Andrew JACKSON and others to form a group that later became the DEMOCRATIC PARTY. Secretary of state 1829–31, he was nominated for vice president at the first Democratic convention (1832) and served under Jackson (1833–37). As Jackson's chosen successor, he defeated W. H. HARRISON in 1836. His presidency was marked by an economic depression, the Maine–Canada border dispute, the SEMINOLE WAR in Florida, and debate over the annexation of Texas. Defeated in his bid for reelection, he failed to win the Democratic nomination in 1844 because of his antislavery views. In 1848 he was nominated by the FREE SOIL PARTY but failed to win the election and retired.

Vance, Cyrus (Roberts) (1917–2002) U.S. public official. Born in Clarksburg, W.V., he served as general counsel for the U.S. Defense Department (1960–62) and secretary of the army (1962); as deputy secretary of defense (1963–67) he actively supported the VIETNAM WAR. He later urged Pres. Lyndon JOHNSON to stop the bombing of N. Vietnam, and was sent to Paris in 1968 with Averell HARRIMAN to negotiate peace. As secretary of state (1977–80) under Pres. Jimmy CARTER, he worked to obtain the SALT II arms-control treaty and was instrumental in the CAMP DAVID ACCORDS. He resigned in 1980 over Carter's management of the IRAN HOSTAGE CRISIS.

Vancouver City (metro. area pop., 1996: 1,832,000), SW British Columbia. Originating as a lumber processing settlement on a fine natural harbor, it recovered from a disastrous fire (1886) to become Canada's principal seaport. Its development was aided by completion of the transcontinental railroad in 1887 and the opening of the PANAMA CANAL in 1914. Economic activities include lumber production, oil refining, fishing, and shipbuilding.

Vancouver Island \'van-'kü-vər\ Island (pop., 2000: 700,000) off SW British Columbia. It is the largest island (12,079 sq mi, or 31,285 sq km) on the Pacific coast of N. America. It has several peaks of more than 7,000 ft (2,100 m), as well as several fine harbors. The chief city is VICTORIA. Inhabited by coastal Indians for millennia, it was visited by Capt. James COOK in 1778. It was surveyed in 1792 by George Vancouver (1757–1798) and was held by the HUDSON'S BAY CO. until it was made a British crown colony in 1849. It united with British Columbia in 1866.

Vandals Germanic people who ruled a kingdom in N. Africa 429–534 and who sacked Rome in 455. Fleeing westward from the HUNS, they invaded Gaul before settling in Spain (409). Under King Gaiseric (r.428–77) they migrated to N. Africa (429) and captured Carthage (439). The Vandals later annexed Sardinia, Corsica, and Sicily, and their pirate fleets controlled much of the W Mediterranean. When they invaded Italy and captured Rome (455), they plundered the city and its artworks, and their name has remained a synonym for willful desecration and destruction. The Vandals were Arian Christians (see ARIANISM) who persecuted Roman Catholics in Africa. They were conquered when the Byzantines invaded N. Africa (533–34).

Van de Graaff, Robert J(emison) (1901–1967) U.S. physicist. Born in Tuscaloosa, Ala., he served on the faculty at MIT 1934–60. He developed a high-voltage electrostatic generator (the Van de Graaff generator) that serves as a type of PARTICLE ACCELERATOR. In 1946 he cofounded the High Voltage Engineering Corp. to manufacture his accelerator. Widely used in atomic research, the device was also adapted to produce high-energy X rays for medical and industrial uses.

Vandenberg, Arthur H(endrick) (1884–1951) U.S. politician. Born in Grand Rapids, Mich., he served as editor of the *Grand Rapids Herald* 1906–28. As a Republican in the U.S. Senate (1928–51), he was a critic of Pres. Franklin ROOSEVELT's foreign policy but revised his isolationist position after the attack on Pearl Harbor. In 1945 he advocated U.S. participation in international alliances, which gave valuable Republican support to the U.N. He led Republican congressional support for measures introduced by Pres. Harry TRUMAN, including the Marshall Plan, the Truman Doctrine, and NATO.

Vanderbilt, Cornelius (1794–1877) U.S. shipping and railroad magnate. Born on Staten Island, N.Y., he began a pas-

T U V

senger ferry business in New
York harbor in 1810 with
one boat, which he expanded
to a small fleet in the War of
1812. He sold his boats to
work as a steamship captain
(1818–29), then started his
own steamship company on
the Hudson River. He was
soon providing transportation along the E seacoast. He
formed the Accessory Transit Co. to provide transport
to the California gold fields
via Nicaragua, undercutting
his competitors, and sold out
at a high price (1858). Turning to railroads, he acquired
controlling stock in the New
York and Harlem Railroad.

Cornelius Vanderbilt

After losing a battle for the Erie Railroad (1868), he bought
and consolidated the Hudson River and the New York Central railroads (1869), and later bought the Lake Shore and
Michigan Southern Railroad (1873). At his death, he left a
fortune of over $100 million, the largest in the U.S. to that
date. He gave $1 million to Central (later VANDERBILT)
UNIV., and left almost all the rest to his son William H. Vanderbilt (1821–1885), who greatly expanded the New York
Central network, acquired other railroads, and doubled the
family fortune.

Vanderbilt University Private university in Nashville, Tenn.
It was founded in 1873 and named after Cornelius VANDER-
BILT. About 40 master's, 40 doctoral, and several professional degree programs are offered through its graduate
school, divinity school, and schools of law, engineering,
music, management, medicine, and nursing. Research institutes are devoted to education and human development,
public policy, and the humanities. Its campus was designated a national arboretum in 1988. Total enrollment is
about 10,000.

van der Goes, Hugo See Hugo van der GOES

van der Rohe, Ludwig Mies See Ludwig MIES VAN DER
ROHE

van der Waals \\'van-dər-ˌwȯlz\\, **Johannes Diederik** (1837–
1923) Dutch physicist. He extended the classical IDEAL-GAS
law (see GAS LAWS) to describe the behavior of real gases,
deriving the van der Waals equation of state in 1881. His
work led to the liquefying of several common gases and
made possible the study of temperatures near absolute zero.
The VAN DER WAALS FORCES were named in his honor. He
received a 1910 Nobel Prize.

van der Waals forces Relatively weak electrical FORCES that
attract neutral (uncharged) MOLECULES to each other in
GASES, liquefied and solidified gases, and almost all organic
LIQUIDS and SOLIDS. Solids held together by van der Waals
forces typically have lower MELTING POINTS and are softer
than those held together by IONIC, COVALENT, and metallic
bonds (see BONDING). They are somewhat weaker than hydrogen bonds. See also J. D. VAN DER WAALS.

van der Weyden, Rogier See Rogier van der WEYDEN

Van Der Zee, James (Augustus Joseph) (1886–1983) U.S.
photographer. Born in Lenox, Mass., he moved in 1906 with
his family to Harlem in New York City. After working in a
portrait studio, he set up his own studio. The portraits he
took from 1918 to 1945 chronicled the HARLEM RENAIS-
SANCE; among his many renowned subjects were Countee
CULLEN, Bill ROBINSON, and Marcus GARVEY. After World
War II his fortunes declined along with Harlem's, until the
Metropolitan Museum of Art exhibited his photographs in
1969.

van de Velde, Henri See Henri van de VELDE

van Doesburg, Theo See Theo van DOESBURG

Van Doren, Carl (Clinton) and Mark (1885–1950, 1894–
1972) U.S. writers and teachers. The brothers were born in
Hope, Ill. Carl edited the *Cambridge History of American
Literature* (1917–21). His many critical works include the
biography *Benjamin Franklin* (1938, Pulitzer Prize). Mark
published more than 20 volumes of verse, including *Spring

Thunder (1924) and *Collected Poems* (1922–38) (1939,
Pulitzer Prize), as well as three novels, several volumes of
short stories, and numerous critical works.

Van Dyck \\van-'dīk\\, **Anthony** (*later* **Sir Anthony**) (1599–
1641) Flemish painter. Apprenticed to an Antwerp painter
at 10, he soon came under the influence of P. P. RUBENS,
for his early works are painted in Rubens's melodramatic
style, though with darker and warmer color and more angular figures. He was a master in the Antwerp artists' guild
by 19, at which time he was also working with Rubens. He
spent over five years in Italy (1621–27); on his return, he received many commissions for altarpieces and portraits. He
is chiefly known for his portraits, in which he idealized his
models without sacrificing their individuality. In Britain in
1632, he was appointed court painter by CHARLES I. With a
comfortable income from his many portraits, his life
matched his clients' in luxury. His influence was pervasive
and lasting; Flemish, Dutch, and German portraitists imitated his style and technique, and the 18th-cent. English
portraitists, especially Thomas GAINSBOROUGH and Joshua
REYNOLDS, were deeply indebted to him.

Van Dyke, Dick (*orig.* Richard Wayne) (b.1925) U.S. actor
and comedian. Born in West Plains, Mo., he made his
Broadway debut in 1959 and starred in the musical *Bye Bye
Birdie* (1960–61, Tony Award; film, 1963). His successful
television comedy series *The Dick Van Dyke Show* (1961–66)
won several Emmy awards; it was followed by *The New Dick
Van Dyke Show* (1971–74) and later the mystery series *Diagnosis Murder* (1993–2001). He has starred in such movies as
Mary Poppins (1964) and *Chitty, Chitty, Bang, Bang* (1968).

Vane, Henry (*later* **Sir Henry**) (1613–1662) English politician. Son of the royal adviser Henry Vane the Elder (1589–
1655), he was converted to Puritanism and in 1635 sailed to
New England, where he served as governor of Massachusetts 1636–37. After returning to England, he served with
his father in the LONG PARLIAMENT, where they helped secure the impeachment of Thomas WENTWORTH. He led the
House of Commons from 1643 and was a member of the
Commonwealth's Council of State 1649–53. After the
RESTORATION, he was executed for treason.

van Eyck, Jan See Jan van EYCK

van Gogh \\vän-'kōk, *Engl* van-'gō\\, **Vincent (Willem)** (1853–
1890) Dutch painter. Ap-
prenticed to art dealers in The
Hague, he worked in their
London and Paris branches
1873–76. After much per-
sonal turmoil, he began to
draw and paint in watercolor
(1880). In 1886 he joined his
brother Theo, an art dealer,
in Paris, where he became acquainted with Impressionism
and Postimpressionism. In
1888 he moved to Arles, in S
France; there he painted

**Vincent van Gogh, "The
Starry Night," 1889**

more than 200 canvases in 15 months. His favorite subjects
were still lifes, landscapes, and peasant figures; among his
most famous paintings are *The Potato Eaters* (1885), *Starry
Night* (1889), and *Self-Portrait with Pipe and Bandaged Ear*
(1888; he had sliced off his ear after a quarrel with Paul
GAUGUIN). Living in poverty and suffering from depression,
he entered an asylum but continued to paint; during his 12-
month stay (1889) he completed 150 paintings and drawings. A move to Auvers-sur-Oise in 1890 was followed by
another burst of activity, but he soon suffered a relapse and
shot himself at 37. His 10-year artistic career produced
more than 800 paintings and 700 drawings, of which he sold
only one in his lifetime. His work became powerfully influential, and he is considered the greatest Dutch painter since
REMBRANDT.

vanilla Any member of a group of tropical climbing OR-
CHIDS that make up the genus *Vanilla*, and the flavoring
agent extracted from its seedpods. The plant has a long,
fleshy climbing stem that attaches itself by aerial rootlets
to trees; roots also penetrate the soil. Numerous flowers
open a few at a time and last only a day. The fruit is a bean
pod about 8 in. (20 cm) long at maturity. Vanilla is used in

a variety of sweet foods and beverages as well as in perfumery.

Vanir \\'vä-ˌnir\ In GERMANIC RELIGION, the race of gods responsible for wealth, fertility, and commerce. They included Njörd and his children FREYR and FREYJA, among others. They were originally subordinate to the warlike AESIR, but after defeating the Aesir in battle they were granted equal status.

van Ostade, Adriaen See Adriaen van OSTADE

van't Hoff \vänt-'hòf\, **Jacobus H(enricus)** (1852–1911) Dutch physical chemist. His early work was on stereochemistry. His later work outlined the principles of chemical kinetics, applied the laws of THERMODYNAMICS to chemical equilibria, introduced modern concepts of chemical affinity, and advanced understanding of ELECTROLYTES. Equations relating osmotic pressure (see OSMOSIS) to mole fraction of solute and relating the equilibrium constant to temperature bear his name. In 1901 he was awarded the first Nobel Prize for Chemistry.

Vanuatu \ˌvan-wä-'tü\ officially **Republic of Vanuatu** formerly **New Hebrides** \'he-brə-ˌdēz\ Republic, consisting of a chain of 10 principal and 60 smaller islands, SW Pacific Ocean. Area: 4,707 sq mi (12,190 sq km). Population (2000): 199,000. Capital: PORT-VILA. The population is mainly indigenous Melanesian; there are also small numbers of French, Chinese, Vietnamese, and Pacific Islanders. Languages: Bislama, English, French (all official); Melanesian languages and dialects. Religion: Christianity, including Presbyterianism, Anglicanism, and Roman Catholicism. Currency: vatu. Extending for 400 mi (650 km), it includes the islands of Espíritu Santo, Malekula, Efate, Ambrim, Erromango, Tanna, Epi, Aneityum, Maéwo, and Pentecost. The larger islands are volcanic in origin and mountainous; several have active volcanoes. Some, especially Efate and Malekula, have good harbors. The highest point is Mt. Tabwémasana (6,165 ft or 1,879 m) on Espíritu Santo. The developing free-market economy is based mainly on agriculture, cattle raising, and fishing. Tourism is increasingly important. It is a republic with a single legislative house; its head of state is the president, and the head of government is the prime minister. The islands were inhabited for at least 3,000 years by Melanesian peoples before being discovered in 1606 by the Portuguese. They were rediscovered by French navigator L.-A. de BOUGAINVILLE in 1768, then explored by English mariner Capt. James COOK in 1744 and named New Hebrides. Sandalwood merchants and European missionaries arrived in the mid-19th cent.; they were followed by British and French cotton planters. Control of the group was sought by both the French and British; in 1906 they agreed to joint sovereignty. During World War II a major Allied naval base was on Espíritu Santo; the island group escaped Japanese invasion. New Hebrides became the independent Republic of Vanuatu in 1980. Much of the nation's housing was ravaged by a hurricane in 1987. See also map at OCEANIA.

vaporization Conversion of a substance from the LIQUID or SOLID phase into the gaseous (see GAS), or vapor, phase. It includes boiling, in which vapor bubbles form in a liquid, and sublimation, in which a solid is converted directly to vapor. Vaporization requires that HEAT be supplied to the liquid or solid; the same amount of heat is released in CONDENSATION. If the surroundings do not supply enough heat, the temperature of the remaining substance vaporizing drops. See also EVAPORATION, LATENT HEAT.

vapor lamp See ELECTRIC DISCHARGE LAMP

Varanasi \vä-'rä-nə-sē,\ or **Benares** \'bə-'när-əs\ City (pop., 2002 est.: 1,100,000), Uttar Pradesh, India. Settled before the 2nd millennium B.C. on the GANGES RIVER, it is one of the oldest continuously inhabited cities in the world. It is one of the seven sacred cities of Hinduism and has numerous shrines, temples, and palaces, and miles of steps for ritual bathing. In nearby Sarnath the BUDDHA delivered his first sermon.

Vardon, Harry (1870–1937) British golfer. A technical innovator, he won the British Open six times (1896, 1898, 1899, 1903, 1911, 1914) and the U.S. Open once (1900). The Vardon Trophy is awarded annually to the professional with the best scoring average.

Varèse \vä-'rez\, **Edgard (Victor Achille Charles)** (1883–1965) French-U.S. composer. After studies in Paris, he moved to Berlin, where he met musicians in tune with his forward-looking ideas. His *Bourgogne* (1907) caused a scandal because of its dissonance. His budding conducting career was interrupted by World War I, and he moved to the U.S. In 1921 he cofounded the International Composers Guild. His output was small, but every piece became a classic, including *Offrandes, Amériques* (both 1921), *Hyperprism, Octandre* (both 1923), *Arcana* (1927), and *Ionisation* (1931), works remarkable for the way they used instruments, especially percussion, to create blocks of sound. With his later *Déserts* (1954) and *Poème électronique* (1958), it became evident that he had been waiting for technology to catch up with his imagination.

Vargas \'vär-gəs\, **Getúlio (Dorneles)** (1883–1954) President of Brazil (1930–45, 1951–54). He was elected governor of Rio Grande do Sul in 1928 and ran unsuccessfully for president in 1930, but later that year overthrew the national government. In 1937 he abolished the constitutional government and set up the totalitarian New State, reducing the autonomy of the states. He enacted labor reforms and social-security laws, introduced educational reforms, enfranchised women, and granted the secret ballot. Deposed by a coup in 1945, he was elected president again in 1951; unable to hold support, and faced with forced retirement, he took his own life.

Vargas Llosa \'bär-gäs-'yō-sä\, **(Jorge) Mario (Pedro)** (b.1936) Peruvian writer. His widely acclaimed first novel, *The Time of the Hero* (1963), describes adolescents striving for survival in a military school and reflects the malaise afflicting Peru. His commitment to social change is evident in his early novels, essays, and plays. He turned increasingly conservative in the face of the SHINING PATH insurgency, and in 1990 he ran for president of Peru. His best-known works include *Aunt Julia and the Scriptwriter* (1977) and *The War of the End of the World* (1981). He won the Cervantes Prize in 1994.

variable In ALGEBRA, a symbol (usually a letter) standing in for an unknown numerical value in an EQUATION. Commonly used variables include x and y (real-number unknowns), z (complex-number unknowns), t (time), r (radius), and s (arc length). Variables should be distinguished from coefficients, fixed values that multiply powers of variables in POLYNOMIALS and ALGEBRAIC EQUATIONS. In the QUADRATIC EQUATION $ax^2 + bx + c = 0$, x is the variable and $a, b,$ and c are coefficients whose values must be specified to solve the equation.

variable, complex See COMPLEX VARIABLE

variable star STAR whose brightness varies visibly. Pulsating variables have rhythmic increases and decreases in brightness and size. Explosive variables include NOVAS and SUPERNOVAS, which briefly brighten rapidly and then dim more slowly. Flare stars' sporadic brightening is probably due to events similar to SOLAR FLARES. ECLIPSING VARIABLE STARS appear variable because light from one star is blocked by another. See also BINARY STAR, CEPHEID VARIABLE, PULSAR, T TAURI STAR.

variation In biology, any difference between cells, individual organisms, or groups of organisms within a species caused either by genetic differences (variation in GENOTYPE) or by the effect of environmental factors on the expression of genetic potentials (variation in PHENOTYPE). Variation may be shown in physical appearance, metabolism, fertility, mode of reproduction, behavior, learning and mental ability, and other obvious or measurable characters. Genotypic variations are caused by differences in number or structure of CHROMOSOMES or by differences in the GENES carried by the chromosomes. Eye color, body form, and disease resistance are genotypic variations. Phenotypic variations may result from internal factors, and also include stages in an organism's life cycle and seasonal variations.

variations See THEME AND VARIATIONS

varicella See CHICKEN POX

varicose vein \'var-ə-ˌkōs\ or **varix** Twisted and distended VEIN, ARTERY, or lymphatic vessel. Varicose veins occur mostly in the legs, when malfunctioning valves let blood pool in veins near the skin. Causes include hereditary valve

TUV

and vein wall weakness, and internal or external pressure on veins. Varices are common in pregnancy. Symptoms include a heavy feeling, with leg cramps and swelling after standing a long time. Complications include skin ULCERS and THROMBOSIS. Treatment involves strong support hose, injection therapy, or surgery. Varices in the ESOPHAGUS, common in liver disease, can ulcerate and bleed. See also HEMORRHOID.

variety theater See MUSIC HALL AND VARIETY THEATER

varing hare See SNOWSHOE HARE

variola See SMALLPOX

Varmus, Harold (Elliot) (b.1939) U.S. virologist. Born in Oceanside, N.Y., he joined the faculty of UC–San Francisco in 1970. With J. Michael Bishop (b.1936), he discovered that, under certain circumstances, normal genes in healthy body cells can cause cancer. These oncogenes ordinarily control cell division and growth, but viruses or carcinogens can activate them. The two shared a 1989 Nobel Prize. Varmus later served as director of the National Institutes of Health 1993–99 and president of Memorial Sloan-Kettering Cancer Center (from 1999).

Varna Seaport city (pop., 1998: 300,000), Bulgaria, on the Black Sea coast. Founded by Greeks in the 6th cent. B.C., it later was Thracian, Macedonian, and Roman. In A.D. 681 it became part of the first Bulgarian empire (c.679–1018). It came under OTTOMAN domination in 1391. It was ceded to Bulgaria in 1878. It is an important administrative, economic, cultural, and resort center. Industries include exporting, shipbuilding, and manufacturing.

varna \'vər-nə\ Any of the four traditional social classes of Hindu India. Mentioned in the RIG VEDA, the four are the BRAHMAN, the Kshatriya, the VAISHYA, and the Sudra. Traditional lawmakers specified a set of obligations, observed mainly in theory only, to each varna: the Brahman, to study and advise; the Kshatriya, to protect; the Vaishya, to cultivate; and the Sudra, to serve. An unofficial fifth class, the *pancama*, was created to include certain UNTOUCHABLES and tribal groups falling outside this system. Individual CASTES, of which there are dozens, sometimes seek to raise their social rank by identifying with a particular varna.

Vasarely \,va-zə-'re-lē\, **Victor** orig. Viktor Vásárhelyi (1908–1997) Hungarian-French painter. Trained in Budapest in the Bauhaus tradition, he moved to Paris in 1930. By the 1940s he was painting animated surfaces of geometric forms and interacting colors. His style reached maturity in the mid-1950s and 1960s, with the use of more vibrant colors to increase the sense of movement through optical illusion, as in *Sirius II* (1954), and he became one of the leading figures of the OP ART movement.

Vasari \vä-'zä-rē\, **Giorgio** (1511–1574) Italian painter, architect, and writer. Though a prolific painter in the Mannerist style, he is more highly regarded as an architect (see UFFIZI GALLERY), but even his architecture is overshadowed by his writings. His *Lives of the Most Eminent Architects, Painters, and Sculptors* (1550) offers biographies of Renaissance artists. His style is eminently readable and his material is well researched, though when facts were scarce he did not hesitate to fill in the gaps. The work's enlarged second edition (1568) has proved an invaluable resource for art historians.

Vasco da Gama See Vasco da GAMA

vascular plant or **tracheophyte** \'trā-kē-ə-ˌfīt\ Any plant that has a specialized conducting system consisting mostly of phloem (food-conducting tissue) and xylem (water-conducting tissue), collectively called vascular tissue. FERNS, GYMNOSPERMS, and FLOWERING PLANTS are all vascular plants. Because they have vascular tissues, these plants have true stems, LEAVES, and ROOTS, modifications of which enable species of vascular plants to survive in a variety of habitats under diverse conditions. This ability to flourish in so many different habitats has made vascular plants dominant among terrestrial plants. See also BRYOPHYTE.

vasectomy \və-'sek-tə-mē\ Severing of the vas deferens, which carries SPERM from the TESTES to the PROSTATE GLAND, to cause sterility or prevent infection. This relatively simple procedure, which can be performed in a doctor's office with local anesthetics, removes the ability to fa-

ther children without affecting ability to achieve erection or orgasm. The vas is cut near its beginning, in the scrotum.

Vasily I \'va-sə-lē\ *Russian* Vasily Dmitriyevich (1371–1425) Grand prince of Moscow (1389–1425). Succeeding his father as grand prince of Moscow and Vladimir, he enlarged his realm to include Nizhniy Novgorod and Murom in the central Volga region, but his efforts to expand westward brought him into conflict with Lithuania and Novgorod. He prepared to fight TIMUR in 1395, but the Mongol leader withdrew from Russian lands without a battle. Vasily kept his state independent until the Tatars reasserted control in 1408.

Vasily II *Russian* Vasily Vasilyevich *known as* **Vasily the Blind** (1415–1462) Grand Prince of Moscow (1425–62). At age 10 he was named to succeed his father VASILY I, but for many years his uncle and cousins struggled to wrest the throne from him. Despite being blinded by his cousin Dmitry Shemyaka (1446), he regained power in 1447, quelled internal strife in his realm by 1452, and enlarged his state's territory by absorbing nearby principalities. During his reign the Russian Church asserted its independence from the patriarch at Constantinople.

vassal See FEUDALISM

Vassar College Private liberal-arts college in Poughkeepsie, N.Y. It was founded as a college for women by Matthew Vassar (1792–1868) in 1861. It became coeducational in 1968. The F. L. Loeb Art Center houses one of the oldest art collections in the U.S. Enrollment is about 2,500.

VAT See VALUE-ADDED TAX

Vatican City *in full* **State of the Vatican City** Independent papal state, S Europe, within the commune of ROME, Italy. Area: 108.7 acres (44 hectares). Population (2000): 800. Its medieval and Renaissance walls form its boundaries except on the southeast at St. Peter's Square. Within the walls is a miniature nation, with its own diplomatic missions, newspaper, post office, radio station, banking system, army of more than 100 Swiss Guards, and publishing house. Extraterritoriality of the state extends to Castel Gandolfo (the pope's residence) and to several churches and palaces in Rome proper. Its independent sovereignty was recognized in the LATERAN TREATY of 1929. The POPE has absolute executive, legislative, and judicial powers within the city. He appoints the members of the Vatican's government organs, which are separate from those of the Holy See. Its many imposing buildings include ST. PETER'S BASILICA, VATICAN PALACE, and the VATICAN MUSEUMS AND GALLERIES. Frescoes by MICHELANGELO (in the SISTINE CHAPEL) and by PINTURICCHIO, and RAPHAEL's Stanze are also there. The Vatican Library contains a priceless collection of manuscripts from the pre-Christian and Christian eras.

Vatican Council, Second (1962–65) 21st ecumenical council of the Roman Catholic church, announced by Pope JOHN XXIII. Among the most notable of the 16 documents enacted were the "Dogmatic Constitution on the Church," which provides for greater involvement of laypeople in the church; the "Dogmatic Constitution of Divine Revelation," which maintains an open attitude toward scholarly study of the BIBLE; the "Constitution on the Sacred Liturgy," which provides for the use of vernacular languages in the MASS in place of Latin; and the "Pastoral Constitution on the Church in the World of Today," which attempts to relate the church to contemporary culture. Observers from other Christian churches were invited to the council in a gesture of ECUMENISM.

Vatican Museums and Galleries Institutions and palaces in VATICAN CITY housing the art collections of the popes since the early 15th cent. Among the many separate museums are the 18th-cent. Pio-Clementino Museum, which exhibits classical sculpture; the exhibition rooms in the Vatican Library; and the SISTINE CHAPEL. The Vatican collections are most famous for their classical statues (including *Apollo Belvedere, Belvedere Torso, Laocoön*) but also contain important examples of Egyptian and Early Christian art. The Pinacoteca ("Picture Gallery"), founded by Pius VI in 1797, contains Italian religious paintings and Russian and Byzantine art. In 1956 a modern-art collection was begun with secular works by such artists as Vincent VAN GOGH and

Pablo PICASSO. The Vatican collections are among the largest and most important in the world.

Vatican Palace Pope's residence since the late 14th cent., located north of ST. PETER'S BASILICA in the Vatican. First enclosed in 850, the compound contains gardens (begun by NERO), courtyards, living quarters, galleries, and the VATICAN MUSEUMS and Library. The residence, with more than 1,400 rooms, was begun in the 13th cent. by Pope Nicholas III. NICHOLAS V founded the Vatican Library. Under JULIUS II, Giovanni dei Dolci built the SISTINE CHAPEL, noted for MICHELANGELO's ceiling. Donato BRAMANTE completed the palace's N facade and planned the immense Belvedere court, and RAPHAEL painted his masterpieces in the palace. Antonio DA SANGALLO, employed by PAUL III, designed the Sala Regia (Royal Hall) and Pauline Chapel, decorated by Michelangelo. Domenico Fontana added the present library building under SIXTUS V. Urban VIII built the Matilda Chapel and, under Alexander VII, Gian Lorenzo BERNINI built the Scala Regia (Royal Stairway).

Vauban \vō-ˈbäⁿ\, **Sébastien Le Prestre de** (1633–1707) French military engineer. In 1653 he joined the newly formed engineer corps. He designed fortifications for numerous French towns and devised siege tactics that led to many successes in the French wars of LOUIS XIV's reign; his innovations revolutionized the art of siege tactics and defensive fortification. He also introduced the tactic of ricochet gunfire and invented the socket bayonet. His treatises on fortification and siege-craft were studied for over 100 years.

Vaucanson \vō-kaü-ˈsōⁿ\, **Jacques de** (1709–1782) French inventor. In 1739 he constructed an automaton that imitated the motions of a live duck, including eating and "digesting." He automated the LOOM by means of perforated cards that guided hooks connected to the warp yarns (see WEAVING). His innovation was ignored for decades until J.-M. JACQUARD reconstructed and improved on it; the JACQUARD LOOM became one of the most important inventions of the INDUSTRIAL REVOLUTION.

vaudeville \ˈvȯd-ˌvil\ Light entertainment popular in the U.S. in the late 19th and early 20th cent. It consisted of 10–15 unrelated acts featuring magicians, acrobats, comedians, trained animals, singers, and dancers. From the coarse variety shows held in beer halls for a primarily male audience, Tony Pastor developed a successful "clean variety show" at his New York theater in 1881 and influenced other managers to follow suit. By 1900 chains of vaudeville theaters around the country included Martin Beck's Orpheum Circuit, of which New York's Palace Theater was the most famous (1913–32). Entertainers who began in vaudeville included Mae WEST, W. C. FIELDS, Will ROGERS, Buster KEATON, Charlie CHAPLIN, the MARX BROTHERS, ABBOTT AND COSTELLO, Milton BERLE, and Bob HOPE.

Vaughan \ˈvȯn, ˈvän\, **Henry** (1622–1695) Anglo-Welsh poet and mystic. A doctor, he wrote two volumes of secular poems before reading the religious poet George HERBERT and giving up "idle verse." He is chiefly remembered for the spiritual imagination evident in his fresh and convincing religious verse, and is considered one of the major practitioners of METAPHYSICAL POETRY. Works that reveal the depth of his convictions include *Silex Scintillans* (1650; "The Glittering Flint") and the prose *Mount of Olives* (1652).

Vaughan, Sarah (Lois) (1924–1990) U.S. jazz singer. Born in Newark, N.J., Vaughan won an amateur contest in 1942 and joined Earl HINES's big band as vocalist and second pianist the following year. Joining Billy Eckstine in 1944, she gained exposure to the new music of BEBOP,

Sarah Vaughan

and later recorded with Dizzy GILLESPIE and Charlie PARKER. She thereafter alternated between popular song and jazz. A vast range and wide vibrato in the service of her harmonic sensitivity enabled Vaughan to employ a seemingly instrumental approach in her singing.

Vaughan Williams \vȯn-ˈwil-yəms\, **Ralph** (1872–1958) British composer. He earned a doctorate from Cambridge Univ. and studied with Max BRUCH and Maurice RAVEL. Having collected English folk song for his academic work, he combined folk melody with modern harmonies to forge a personal style that came to represent the core of 20th-cent. English music. His nine symphonies, including his *Sea Symphony* (1909), *London Symphony* (1913), *Pastoral Symphony* (1921), and *Sinfonia Antarctica* (1952), were his most exploratory works. Other popular pieces include *The Lark Ascending* (1914) and *Serenade to Music* (1938). He also wrote five operas, including *Riders to the Sea* (1936), and he edited *The English Hymnal* (1906).

vault In building construction, an arched structure forming a ceiling or roof. The masonry vault exerts the same kind of thrust as the ARCH, and must be supported along its entire length by heavy walls. The basic barrel vault, in effect a continuous series of arches, first appeared in ancient Egypt and the Middle East. Roman architects discovered that two barrel vaults intersecting at right angles (a groin vault) could, when repeated in series, span rectangular areas of unlimited length. Medieval European builders developed the rib vault, a skeleton of arches or ribs on which the masonry could be laid. The fan vault, popular in the English PERPENDICULAR STYLE, used fan-shaped clusters of tracery-like ribs springing from pendants or columns. The 19th cent. saw the use of large iron skeletons for vaults of lightweight materials (see CRYSTAL PALACE). An important modern innovation is the reinforced-concrete shell vault, which can often behave as a deep beam and exert no lateral thrust.

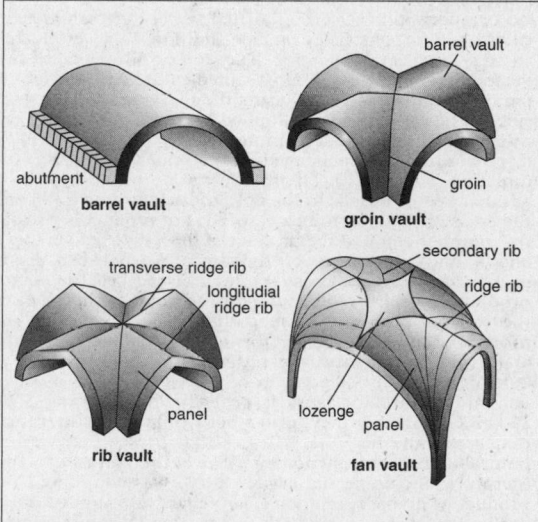

Vault Four common types of vault. A barrel vault (also called a cradle vault, tunnel vault, or wagon vault) has a semicircular cross section. A groin (or cross) vault is formed by the perpendicular intersection of two barrel vaults. A rib (or ribbed) vault is supported by a series of arched diagonal ribs that divide the vault's surface into panels. A fan vault is composed of concave sections with ribs spreading out like a fan.

vaulting Gymnastics exercise in which the athlete leaps over a cylindrical form similar to the side horse except that the pommels are absent. In men's vaulting, the horse is placed lengthwise; in women's vaulting, sideways. In both events the athlete runs toward the horse, rebounds off a springboard, and vaults over the horse. A variety of acrobatic movements may be performed while airborne. Vaulting has been an Olympic event since 1896.

VCR *in full* **videocassette recorder** Electromechanical device that records, stores on a VIDEOTAPE cassette, and plays back on a TV set recorded images and sound. The first commercial VCRs were marketed by Sony Corp. in 1969. They have from two to seven tape heads that read and write video and audio tracks on magnetic tape. Home movies can be made with a camcorder system, a VCR connected to a simple video camera.

Veblen \\'veb-lən\, **Thorstein (Bunde)** (1857–1929) U.S. economist. Born in Manitowoc County, Wis., he grew up in Minnesota and earned a PhD in philosophy from Yale Univ. He taught economics at the Univ. of Chicago and other universities. In 1899 he published his classic *Theory of the Leisure Class*, applying Darwin's evolutionary theories to modern economic life, highlighting the competitive and predatory nature of the business world. With dry humor he identified the markers of American social class, and he coined the term "conspicuous consumption" to describe the display of wealth. His reputation was highest in the 1930s, when the GREAT DEPRESSION was seen as a vindication of his criticism of the business system.

vector In mathematics, a quantity characterized by magnitude and direction. Some physical and geometric quantities, called scalars, can be fully defined by a single number specifying their magnitude in suitable units of measure (e.g., mass in grams, time in seconds). Vector quantities like velocity, force, and displacement must be specified by a magnitude and a direction. A two-dimensional vector is specified by two coordinates, a three-dimensional vector by three coordinates, and so on. Vector analysis is a branch of mathematics that explores the utility of this type of representation and defines the ways such quantities may be combined. See also VECTOR OPERATIONS.

vector operations Extension of the laws of elementary ALGEBRA to VECTORS. They include addition, subtraction, and three types of multiplication. The sum or difference of two vectors is a third vector, represented as the diagonal of the parallelogram constructed using the two original vectors as sides. When a vector is multiplied by a positive scalar (i.e., number), its magnitude is multiplied by the scalar and its direction remains unchanged (if the scalar is negative, the direction is reversed). The multiplication of a vector $\mathbf{a}$ by another vector $\mathbf{b}$ leads to the dot product, written $\mathbf{a} \cdot \mathbf{b}$, and the cross product, written $\mathbf{a} \times \mathbf{b}$. The dot product is a scalar real number equal to the product of the lengths of vectors $\mathbf{a}$ and $\mathbf{b}$ and the cosine of the angle (θ) between them: $\mathbf{a} \cdot \mathbf{b} = ab\cos\theta$. The cross product, also called the vector product, is a third vector ($\mathbf{c}$), perpendicular to the plane of the original vectors. The magnitude of $\mathbf{c}$ is equal to the product of the lengths of vectors $\mathbf{a}$ and $\mathbf{b}$ and the sine of the angle (θ) between them: $\mathbf{c} = ab\sin\theta$.

Veda \\'vā-də\ Any of a group of sacred hymns and verses composed in archaic Sanskrit, probably in the period 1500–1200 B.C. Together they form a body of liturgical literature that extols the hereditary deities that personified various natural and cosmic phenomena. The entire corpus of Vedic literature, including the UPANISHADS, was considered the product of divine revelation. The Vedas were handed down orally for many generations before being committed to writing. See also RIG VEDA, VEDANTA.

Vedanta \vā-'dän-tə\ System (DARSHAN) of Indian philosophy that forms the basis of most modern schools of HINDUISM. Its three fundamental texts are the UPANISHADS, the BHAGAVADGITA, and the Brahma Sutras, which are very brief interpretations of the Upanishads. Several schools of Vedanta have developed, differentiated by their conception of the relationship between the self (ATMAN) and the absolute (BRAHMAN). They share beliefs in SAMSARA and the authority of the VEDAS, recognize Brahman as both the material and instrumental cause of the world, and believe the atman is responsible for its actions and their consequences (see KARMA).

Vedic religion \\'vā-dik\ *or* **Vedism** Ancient religion of India that was contemporary with the composition of the VEDAS.

It was the precursor of HINDUISM. The religion of the Indo-European-speaking peoples who entered India around 1500 B.C. from the region of present-day Iran, it was a polytheistic system in which INDRA was the highest-ranked god. It involved the worship of numerous male divinities connected with the sky and natural phenomena. Ceremonies centered on ritual sacrifice of animals and on the use of soma (a special drink) to achieve trancelike states. Out of Vedism developed the philosophical concepts of ATMAN and BRAHMAN. The spread (8th–5th cent. B.C.) of the related concepts of reincarnation, KARMA, and release from the cycle of rebirth through meditation rather than sacrifice marked the end of the Vedic period and the rise of Hinduism.

Veeck \\'vek\ (*orig.* William Louis) (1914–1986) U.S. baseball-club executive. Born in Hinsdale, Ill., the son of the president of the Chicago Cubs, he became co-owner of the Cleveland Indians (1946–48), St. Louis Browns (1949–53), and Chicago White Sox (1959–68, 1976–81). Believing that baseball was a form of entertainment and should not be treated like a business, he introduced many innovations in promotion and was almost always able to improve a team's attendance and usually its performance.

Vega \\'vä-gə\, **Garcilaso de la** *known as* **El Inca** (1539–1616) Peruvian historian. Son of a CONQUISTADOR and an INCA noblewoman, raised in wealth in Peru, he absorbed the traditions of both cultures. Going to Spain in 1560, he served as captain in the Spanish army against the Moors, then entered the priesthood. He is best known for *La Florida del Ynca* (an account of Hernando DE SOTO's expeditions north of Mexico) and his history of Peru. He was related to his namesake, the Spanish Golden Age poet Garcilaso de la Vega (1503–1536).

Vega \\'vä-gə\, **Lope de** *in full* Lope Félix de Vega Carpio (1562–1635) Spanish playwright. Called the "Phoenix of Spain," the phenomenally prolific Vega wrote as many as 1,800 plays, of which 431 survive, and established the *comedia* (tragicomic social drama) that typified the Spanish Golden Age. His dramas, Spanish in setting, included historical plays based on a national legend (e.g., *Peribáñez* and *El mejor alcalde, el rey*), and "cloak-and-sword" dramas of contemporary manners and intrigue, which turned on some point of honor (e.g., *El acero de Madrid*). He established the comic character, or *gracioso,* as a commentator on the follies of his social superiors. *All Citizens Are Soldiers* is his best-known work outside Spain. He also wrote 21 volumes of nondramatic works in verse and prose, including *The New Art of Writing Plays* (1609).

vegetable In the broadest sense, all plant life and plant products (vegetable matter); in common, narrow usage, the fresh edible portion of herbaceous plants (roots, stems, leaves, flowers, or fruit), either eaten fresh or prepared in some way. Almost all known vegetables were first cultivated in ancient Old or New World civilizations. Vegetables are good sources of minerals, VITAMINS (especially A and C), and dietary FIBER. All the amino acids needed to synthesize PROTEIN are available in vegetables. Aging and spoiling can be prevented by such preservation methods as dehydration, canning, freezing, fermenting, and pickling.

vegetarianism Theory or practice of eating only plants. The vegetarian diet includes grains, vegetables, fruits, and nuts; it excludes meat, poultry, and fish, but some vegetarians eat dairy products (lactovegetarians), egg products (ovovegetarians), or both (ovolactovegetarians). Those who eat no animal products (including honey) are called vegans. Motivations vary and include ethics, self-denial or religious taboo, ecology, and health. Vegetarians point to the many health benefits of their diet, including low rates of heart disease, diabetes, colon cancer, and overweight. Vegetarians must be careful to consume enough iron and, especially for vegans, calcium and vitamins D and B_{12}. Many Hindu sects and most Buddhists are vegetarian, and much of the world eats hardly any meat because it is unavailable.

vein Vessel that carries blood to the heart. Except for pulmonary veins (see PULMONARY CIRCULATION), veins bear deoxygenated blood from CAPILLARIES, which converge into venules and then veins, finally emptying into the venae cavae (see CARDIOVASCULAR SYSTEM, VENA CAVA). Blood moves through veins by contraction of the surrounding muscles. Backflow is prevented by valves in most veins' inner layer. The thin middle layer is mostly COLLAGEN fibers and the thick outer layer mostly CONNECTIVE TISSUE. See also CIRCULATION, VARICOSE VEIN.

Velázquez \və-ˈlas-kəs, *Span* bā-ˈlath-kāth\, **Diego (Rodríguez de Silva)** (1599–1660) Spanish painter. Born in Seville, he was trained in the naturalistic style. His early works were mostly religious or genre scenes. After arriving in Madrid in 1623, he painted a portrait of PHILIP IV that won him an appointment as court painter. His position gave him access to the royal collections, including works by TITIAN, the greatest influence on his style. After a visit to Italy (1629–31), he entered his most productive period. He created a new type of informal royal portrait for Philip's hunting lodge, and his portraits of court dwarfs display the same discerning eye as those of his royal subjects. On a second visit to Rome (1649–51), he painted his fine portrait of Pope Innocent X. In his masterpiece, *Las Meninas* (*The Maids of Honor,* 1656), the artist is shown painting the king and queen in the presence of the infanta Margarita and her attendants; the nearly life-size figures create an illusion of reality unsurpassed by any other artist of his age. He is universally acknowledged as one of the giants of Western art.

Velde, Henri van de (1863–1957) Belgian architect, designer, and teacher. He made vital contributions as a teacher in Germany, where he became known through the interiors he exhibited at Dresden in 1897. Sharing the philosophy of William MORRIS and the ARTS AND CRAFTS MOVEMENT in England, he directed and taught at the Weimar School of Arts and Crafts, which gave rise to the BAUHAUS. His architectural works included the Werkbund Theatre in Cologne (1914) and the Belgian pavilions at the international exhibitions in Paris (1937) and New York (1939).

velociraptor \və-ˈlä-sə-ˌrap-tər\ Any THEROPOD in the genus *Velociraptor* (family Dromaeosauridae) that flourished in central and E Asia during the Late CRETACEOUS PERIOD (98–65 million years ago). It was related to the earlier N. American genus *Deinonychus* (see DEINONYCHUS). Both had a sickle-shaped claw on each foot. Swift, agile predators of small herbivores, they grew up to 6 ft (1.8 m) long and weighed up to 100 lbs (45 kg).

velocity VECTOR quantity that designates the speed and direction in which a body moves. It can be represented graphically by an arrow (pointing in the direction of the MOTION), the length of which is proportional to the magnitude, or speed. For an object in circular motion, the direction at any instant is tangential to the circle at that point, and so is perpendicular to the radius at that point.

velvet Fabric having a short, dense pile, used in clothing and upholstery. Velvet is made in the pile weave (see WEAVING), of SILK, COTTON, or synthetic fibers, and is characterized by a soft, downy surface formed by clipped YARNS. Velvets can be made water-repellent and crush-resistant.

vena cava \ˌvē-nə-ˈkā-və\ Either of two major VEINS that deliver oxygen-depleted blood to the right side of the heart. The superior vena cava drains the upper body, and the inferior vena cava drains the lower body. See also CARDIOVASCULAR SYSTEM, CIRCULATION.

Venda Bantu-speakers who inhabit the NE corner of S. Africa. Numbering over 700,000, the Venda were the last of the peoples in this area to come under European control. Agriculture and cattle-raising are their predominant economic activities.

Vendée \vän-ˈdā\, **Wars of the** (1793–96) Insurrections in the west of France during the FRENCH REVOLUTION. In the religious and impoverished Vendée region, discontent with the new government grew after it instituted strict controls over the Catholic church (1790). An uprising in opposition to the conscription acts (1793) spread throughout the region, where peasants were joined by royalists to form the Catholic and Royal Army. Led by François Charette de La Contrie (1763–1796), the Vendéan army of 65,000 was defeated at Cholet, Le Mans (about 15,000 rebels killed), and Savenay. Vicious reprisals by the government provoked further resistance, until an amnesty was announced (1794) and the Vendée was granted freedom from conscription (1795). La Charette joined a British-backed landing of exiled French nobles in Brittany (1795), but after their defeat and

his execution (1796) the counterrevolutionary struggle ended.

veneer Extremely thin sheet of rich-colored wood (such as mahogany, ebony, or rosewood) or precious materials (such as ivory or tortoiseshell) cut in decorative patterns and applied to the surface of a piece of furniture. Though veneering was practiced in classical antiquity, its use lapsed in the Middle Ages. It was revived in 17th cent. France and spread to other European countries. Artistic veneering is most evident in the 18th and early 19th cent., when Thomas CHIPPENDALE, George HEPPLEWHITE, and Thomas SHERATON used mahogany and satinwood veneers. By the mid-19th cent., mechanical saws allowed veneering to be used in mass production to cover defects in cheap furniture.

Venetian glass Variety of glassware made in Venice from the 13th cent. to the present. In the 15th cent., efforts were concentrated on the perfection of *cristallo* (clear glass that approximated rock crystal in appearance). By the 16th cent., Venetian glassmakers mastered techniques of adding color and of removing the smoky tint produced by metal in the glass material. These and other secrets were guarded closely, but eventually many Venetian glassmakers defected, and the techniques became known in France, Germany, the Netherlands, and England.

Venetian school Renaissance art and artists of VENICE, characterized by a love of light and color. Jacopo Bellini (see BELLINI FAMILY) was the first in this influential line, followed by his son Giovanni, the instructor of Venice's great High Renaissance painters, including GIORGIONE and TITIAN. Titian became the dominant force in Venetian painting, and his rich colors and painterly technique were widely imitated. Other 16th-cent. masters included VERONESE, known for his vast, brilliantly colored canvases, and TINTORETTO, who combined Mannerist elements with the Venetian love of light as a means of defining form and heightening drama. G. B. TIEPOLO was the last important Venetian figure painter and one of the greatest artists of the Rococo period.

Veneto \ˈve-nə-ˌtō\ Autonomous region (pop., 1996 est.: 4,433,000), N Italy. The capital is VENICE. Bordered by Austria, the Adriatic Sea, and Lake GARDA, the N part is mountainous, while the S part consists of a fertile plain. Parts were under Roman rule by the 2nd–1st cent. B.C. (see PADUA, VERONA) and later were subject to the Lombards. In the Middle Ages, several city-states gained importance, but most subsequently were subject to Venice. In the early 19th cent. the area came under Austrian rule. It was returned and joined to Italy in the 1860s.

Venezia Tridentina See TRENTINO-ALTO ADIGE

Venezuela *officially* **Bolivarian Republic of Venezuela** Country, N S. America. Area: 352,144 sq mi (912,050 sq km). Population (2000): 24,170,000. Capital: CARACAS. Nearly 70% of the population is of mulatto-mestizo ancestry, followed by whites (about 20%), blacks (9%), and American Indians. Languages: Spanish (official), some 25 Indian dialects, English. Religions: Roman Catholicism; small percentage Protestantism. Currency: bolívar. Mountain ranges and plains dominate Venezuela's topography. In the west, a NE spur of the ANDES peaks at Pico Bolívar. The llanos (plains) occupy one-third of the country's central region. The ORINOCO RIVER system covers practically the entire country and has an extensive and thickly wooded delta. The highest waterfall in the world, ANGEL FALLS, is in Venezuela. Lakes include Maracaibo and Valencia. Principal mineral resources are petroleum and natural gas. Other mineral reserves include iron, bauxite, gold, and diamonds. Industries include steel, chemicals, textiles, and oil refining. Agricultural products, including sugar, coffee, corn, bananas, and cacao, are important. It is a republic with a unicameral legislature; its head of state and government is the president. Venezuela was inhabited by indigenous peoples perhaps as early as the 2nd millennium B.C. In 1498 Christopher COLUMBUS sighted it; in 1499 the navigators Alonso de Ojeda, Amerigo VESPUCCI, and Juan de la Cosa traced the coast. A Spanish missionary established the first European settlement at Cumana about 1520. In 1718 it was included in the viceroyalty of NEW GRANADA, and it was made a captaincy general in 131. Venezuelan Creoles led by Francisco

TUV

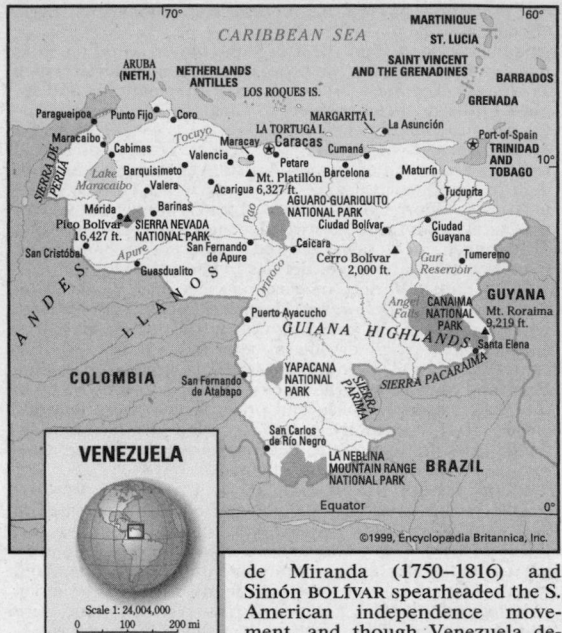

CARIBBEAN SEA

VENEZUELA

Scale 1: 24,004,000

de Miranda (1750–1816) and
Simón BOLÍVAR spearheaded the S.
American independence movement, and though Venezuela declared independence from Spain in
1811, it was not assured until 1821.
Military dictators generally ruled the country from 1830
until the overthrow of Marcos Pérez Jiménez (1914–2001)
in 1958. A new constitution adopted in 1961 marked the beginning of democracy. As a founding member of OPEC
(ORGANIZATION OF PETROLEUM EXPORTING COUNTRIES),
it enjoyed relative economic prosperity from oil production
during the 1970s. It later suffered economic decline; political unrest led to election of an audaciously leftist president,
Hugo Chávez, in 1999.

Venice *Italian* **Venezia** \vā-'nēt-syä\ City (pop., 2000 est.:
277,000), capital of VENETO region, N Italy. Built on the Lagoon of Venice, it encompasses some 118 islands, the whole
90-mi (145-km) perimeter of the lagoon, and two industrial
mainland boroughs. Settlements in the 5th cent. A.D. were
built uniquely on islands as protection against raids. It was
a vassal of the Byzantine empire until the 10th cent. Beginning with control of a trading route to the Levant, it
emerged from the Fourth CRUSADE (1202–4) as ruler of a
colonial empire that included CRETE, EUBOEA, CYCLADES,
the IONIAN ISLANDS, and footholds in Morea and EPIRUS.
In 1381 it defeated GENOA after a century-long struggle for
commercial supremacy in the Levant and E Mediterranean.
In the 15th cent. the Venetian Republic became an extensive Italian state. It gradually lost its E possessions to Ottoman Turks, and gave up its last hold in the Aegean in
1715. The republic dissolved and the territory was ceded to
Austria in 1797. Incorporated into NAPOLEON's kingdom of
Italy in 1805, it was restored to Austria in 1815, then ceded
to Italy in 1866. Flooding along its many miles of canals
caused severe damage in 1966. In the late 20th cent., widespread efforts were made to control inundation of the city
and to preserve its architecture, which includes representations of Italian, Arabic, Byzantine, and Renaissance styles.
There are some 450 palaces and homes of major historic importance. Notable among its 400 bridges is the Bridge of
Sighs, built about 800, and among its churches, ST. MARK's
BASILICA. Tourism is the main economic activity.

Venizélos \ˌven-yə-'ze-lós\, **Eleuthérios (Kyriakos)** (1864–
1936) Greek revolutionary leader. In 1905 he led an insurrection that forced the autocratic high commissioner to
leave Crete (1905), and he later effected the union of Crete
with Greece. As premier of Greece (1910–15) he helped
form the anti-Ottoman Balkan League. During the BALKAN
WARS, his policies doubled Greece's area and population. In

World War I he resigned when opposed by the pro-German
king CONSTANTINE I, led the opposition that forced the king
into exile, and again became premier (1917–20), aligning
Greece with the Allies. He served three more stints as premier (1924, 1928–32, 1933), but was forced into exile when
the monarchy was restored in 1935.

venom POISON secreted by an animal, produced by specialized GLANDS often associated with spines, teeth, or stings. It
may be primarily for paralyzing or killing prey or may be
purely defensive. Some venoms also function as digestive
fluids. Their effects can range from localized skin inflammation to almost immediate death; they include NERVOUS-
SYSTEM excitation (CRAMPS, VOMITING, convulsions) or depression (PARALYSIS, respiratory or cardiac depression or
arrest), HEMORRHAGE, red-blood-cell breakdown, circulatory collapse, and allergic reactions (including HIVES and
inflammation). Many major groups of animals contain venomous species: snakes (COBRAS, MAMBAS, VIPERS); fish
(STINGRAYS, spiny SHARKS, certain CATFISH, puffers);
lizards (GILA MONSTERS, beaded lizards); SCORPIONS; spiders (BLACK WIDOW spiders, BROWN RECLUSE SPIDERS); social insects (BEES, WASPS, some ANTS); and marine invertebrates (SEA ANEMONES, fire CORALS, JELLYFISH, SEA
URCHINS). See also ANTIDOTE.

Venturi, Robert (Charles) (b.1925) U.S. architect. Born in
Philadelphia, he worked with Eero SAARINEN and Louis
KAHN. His postmodernist philosophy, set forth in *Complexity and Contradiction in Architecture* (1966) and *Learning
from Las Vegas* (1972), called for openness to the multiple
influences of historical tradition, ordinary commercial architecture, and Pop art. His buildings often exhibit ironic
humor. Important commissions include the Seattle Art Museum (1985–91) and the Sainsbury Wing of London's National Gallery (1986–91). He won the 1991 Pritzker Architecture Prize.

venturi tube \ven-'tùr-ē\ Short pipe with a constricted inner
surface, used to measure fluid flows and as a pump. The effects of constricted channels on fluid flow were first investigated by Giovanni Battista Venturi (1746–1822), but it was
Clemens Herschel (1842–1930) who devised the instrument
in 1888. Fluid passing through the tube speeds up as it enters the tube's narrow throat, and the pressure drops. There
are countless applications for the principle, including the
automobile CARBURETOR. The pressure differential can
also be used to measure fluid flow (see FLOW METER).

Venus Roman goddess of cultivated fields and gardens, later
associated with APHRODITE. She was the daughter of JUPI-
TER and Dione, the wife of VULCAN, and the mother of CU-
PID. She was famous for her affairs with both gods and mortals, and she became associated with many aspects of
femininity. She was identified with ISHTAR. She has been a
favorite subject in art since ancient times.

Venus Second PLANET from the sun. Named for the Roman
goddess of love, Venus is, after the MOON, the brightest natural object in the night sky. It comes closer to earth—about
26 million mi (42 million km)—than any other planet. Its
nearly circular orbit, at 67 million mi (108 million km) from
the sun, takes 225 days; its rotation, in RETROGRADE MO-
TION, takes even longer (244 days). As viewed from earth,
Venus has phases like the moon's, completing a cycle in 584
days; nearly the same face is toward earth at each closest
approach. Seen only near sunrise or sunset, it is known as
both the morning and the evening star. Venus is a near twin
of earth in size and mass but is completely enveloped by
thick clouds of concentrated sulfuric-acid droplets. Its surface gravity is about 90% that of earth. Its atmosphere is
over 96% carbon dioxide, with an atmospheric pressure
about 90 times earth's. This and the thick cloud cover trap
incoming solar energy so efficiently that Venus has the
highest surface temperature of any of the sun's planets,
about 860°F (460°C).

Venus's-flytrap *or* **Venus flytrap** CARNIVOROUS PLANT (*Di-
onaea muscipula),* sole member of its genus, in the SUNDEW
family. Native to N. and S. Carolina, it is a perennial common in damp, mossy areas. It bears hinged leaves with spiny
teeth along their margins and a round cluster of small white
flowers at the tip of an erect stem 8–12 in. (20–30 cm) tall.
When an insect alights on a leaf and stimulates its sensitive

hairs, the leaf snaps shut in about half a second. Leaf glands secrete a red sap that digests the insect's body. After 10 days of digestion, the leaf reopens. The trap dies after capturing three or four insects.

Veracruz (Llave) \ˌver-ə-'krüz\ City (pop., 1995: 381,000) and port on the Gulf of MEXICO, E central Mexico. Hernán CORTÉS founded La Villa Rica de la Veracruz as the first Mexican municipality in 1519, but the site was twice abandoned because of its unhealthy conditions; the present city dates from about 1600. As the chief link between colonial Mexico and Spain, Veracruz prospered as a port and became the most "Spanish" of Mexican cities. Both the 1857 and 1917 Mexican constitutions were proclaimed there. A revolt against Pres. Francisco MADERO occurred there in 1912. It is one of Mexico's chief seaports and a commercial center for the Gulf coast.

Veracruz State (pop., 2000: 6,901,000), E central Mexico. Bordering the Gulf of MEXICO, it occupies 28,114 sq mi (72,815 sq km); its capital is JALAPA. The state's low, sandy gulf area rises inland to a central plateau, where CITLALTÉPETL, Mexico's highest peak, is located. The area was inhabited by pre-Columbian cultures, including the OLMECS. It has more than 25% of Mexico's petroleum reserves.

Vercingetorix \ˌvər-sən-'je-tə-ˌriks\ (d.46 B.C.) Chieftain of the Gallic tribe of the Arverni. Julius CAESAR had almost subjugated Gaul (see GALLIC WARS) when Vercingetorix led the Gauls against him (52 B.C.), employing guerrilla tactics. After winning a major victory at Gergovia, his later attack on the Roman army failed, and he was forced to surrender. Taken to Rome in chains, he was displayed in Caesar's TRIUMPH and executed six years later.

Verdi \'ver-dē\, **Giuseppe (Fortunato Francesco)** (1813–1901) Italian composer. An innkeeper's son, he began to write operas in Milan while working as an organist. In 1839 his *Oberto* was successfully performed at La Scala. *Un giorno di regno* (1840) was a failure; much worse, Verdi's two young daughters and his wife died. Ready to give up, he was convinced to compose *Nabucco* (1842), his first big success, it was followed by the equally successful *I lombardi* (1843). For the rest of the decade he wrote a hit opera every year. Rejecting the prevailing patchwork structure of Italian opera, he sought ways of maintaining momentum, and began conceiving of an opera as a series of integrated scenes, then as unified acts. Attracted to stories in which the private and public come into conflict, he produced a series of masterworks, including *Rigoletto* (1851), *La traviata* (1853), *Simon Boccanegra* (1857), *Un ballo in mascara* (1859), *Don Carlos* (1867), and *Aïda* (1871). A fervent nationalist, Verdi became a great national figure. After he composed his great *Requiem* (1874), he teamed with the librettist Arrigo Boito (1842–1918) to write the two great operas of his old age, *Otello* (1886) and *Falstaff* (1890).

Verdun \vər-'dən\, **Battle of** (Feb. 21–July 1916) Major engagement of World War I. As part of its strategy of war by attrition, Germany selected the fortress of Verdun as the site it believed France would defend to the last man. After a massive bombardment, the Germans advanced with little opposition before the reinforced French army under Philippe PÉTAIN slowed them. For two months the hills around Verdun were bombarded, attacked, and counterattacked. By July, Germany, which was also engaged in the Battle of the SOMME, had abandoned its strategy, and France gradually regained its territory. The devastating losses included over 400,000 French casualties and nearly as many German casualties.

Verdun, Treaty of (843) Treaty partitioning the Carolingian empire among the three surviving sons of LOUIS I the Pious. It began the dissolution of CHARLEMAGNE's empire and the formation of the modern countries of Western Europe. Lothair I received the imperial title and Francia Media, which included much of present-day Italy. Louis the German received Francia Orientalis, the land east of the Rhine River, and Charles II the Bald received Francia Occidentalis, the remainder of modern France.

Vérendrye, Pierre Gaultier de Varennes, sieur de la See Pierre G. de V. de LA VÉRENDRYE.

Verga \'vār-gä\, **Giovanni** (1840–1922) Italian writer. Verga was the most important of the Italian *verismo* (realist)

school of novelists. His best works include the short stories of *Little Novels of Sicily* (1883), the novels *The House by the Medlar Tree* (1881; filmed by Luchino VISCONTI as *La terra trema*, 1948) and *Mastro-Don Gesualdo* (1889), and the play *Cavalleria rusticana* (1884; "Rustic Chivalry"), the basis for a famous opera. His influence on the post–World War II generation of Italian writers was particularly marked.

Vergennes \ver-'zhen\, **comte (Count) de** *orig.* Charles Gravier (1719–1787) French statesman. As ambassador to Ottoman Turkey (1754–68), he ably defended French policies during the Seven Years' War. As LOUIS XVI's minister of foreign affairs (1774–87), he advocated French financial and military support for the colonists in the American Revolution and helped negotiate the Treaty of Paris (1783).

Vergil See VIRGIL

Verhaeren \ver-'hä-ren, ver-ä-'ren\, **Émile** (1855–1916) Belgian poet. He produced more than 30 collections of poetry in French outstanding for its strength and range. *Les Flamandes* (1883) contains violently naturalistic poems; his later work shows a growing concern for social problems. His major works include *The Sunlit Hours* (1896) and *Belgium's Agony* (1915). His three main themes are Flanders, human energy, and his tender love for his wife. He was one of the group in Brussels who brought about the literary and artistic renaissance of the 1890s.

Verlaine \ver-'len\, **Paul (-Marie)** (1844–1896) French lyric poet. After entering the civil service, he became associated with the PARNASSIAN POETS. His early collections, including *Poèmes saturniens* (1866), *Fêtes galantes* (1869), and *La bonne chanson* (1870), show the intense lyricism and musicality that would mark all his verse. His marriage was shattered by his infatuation with Arthur RIMBAUD, and the two scandalized Paris with their behavior in 1872–73. While in prison (1873–75) for shooting Rimbaud when the latter threatened to leave him, he converted to Catholicism. His "Art poétique" was adopted in 1882 by the poets of the SYMBOLIST MOVEMENT. *Les poètes maudits* (1884; "The Accursed Poets") consists of short biographical studies of six poets. He spent his late years in poverty. He is regarded as the third great member (after Charles BAUDELAIRE and Stéphane MALLARMÉ) of the so-called DECADENTS.

Vermeer \vər-'mer, vər-'mir\, **Jan** or **Johannes Vermeer** (1632–1675) Dutch painter. He was born in Delft, where his parents kept a tavern, and spent his entire life there. He twice served as head of the Delft artists' guild, but seems to have depended on art dealing to support his family. He painted mainly interior genre subjects, often showing solitary figures of women absorbed in some ordinary, everyday activity. His interiors combine a microscopic observation of objects with a meticulous depiction of the gradations of daylight on varied shapes and surfaces. His masterpieces (none dated) include *View of Delft, Young Woman Reading a Letter*, and *Allegory of Painting*, his most symbolically complex work. He manages to be unique within a typically Dutch genre. His work was not widely appreciated in his own time, and he remained in obscurity until 1866, when Théophile Thoré celebrated his work and attributed 76 paintings to him; later authorities have reduced the number to between 30 and 35, while proclaiming him one of the greatest painters of all time.

Vermont State (pop., 2000: 609,000), NE U.S. One of the NEW ENGLAND states, it covers 9,614 sq mi (24,900 sq km); its capital is MONTPELIER. The GREEN MTNS. extend through the center of Vermont; the highest is Mt. Mansfield, at 4,393 ft (1,339 m). Most of the rivers drain into Lake CHAMPLAIN. Settled originally by Abenaki Indians, the region was explored by Samuel de CHAMPLAIN, who in 1609 discovered the lake that now bears his name. The French made the first permanent European settlement in 1666 on Isle La Motte. Both the Dutch and the British established settlements in the 18th cent., but the area fell exclusively to the British in 1763. Disputes arose between New York and New Hampshire concerning jurisdiction of the area: New Hampshire had awarded grants to settlers. In 1770 Ethan ALLEN organized the Green Mountain Boys to repel encroachers from W New York. When the AMERICAN REVOLUTION intervened, Allen and his group, fighting for the colonies, captured Ft. Ticonderoga from the British in

TUV

1775. Vermonters created an independent republic in 1777, and in 1791 it became the 14th U.S. state. In 1864 it was the site of the only AMERICAN CIVIL WAR action north of Pennsylvania when a band of Confederates raided St. Albans from Canada. Dairying and the mining of granite and marble contribute to the economy. In the 1930s the first ski runs were built, and by the 1960s a winter tourist industry had developed.

Verne, Jules (1828–1905) French writer. The success of his *Five Weeks in a Balloon* (1863) led to further remarkable voyage adventures, with their increasingly fantastic but carefully conceived scientific wonders that often anticipated 20th-cent. technology, including *A Journey to the Center of the Earth* (1864), *Twenty Thousand Leagues Under the Sea* (1870), and *Around the World in Eighty Days* (1873). Verne's work shaped the entire development of science fiction.

Vernet \ver-ˈnā\, **(Claude-) Joseph** (1714–1789) French painter. He catered to a new taste for idealized, somewhat sentimentalized landscapes. His shipwrecks, sunsets, and conflagrations reveal a subtle observation of light and atmosphere. His series of 15 *Ports of France* (1754–65) constitute a remarkable record of 18th-cent. life. His son Carle (1758–1836) produced vast battle scenes for Napoleon, but his real talent was for intimate genre scenes and drawing. Carle's long series of fashionable studies, often satirizing contemporary manners and costume, were widely reproduced as engravings. Carle's son Horace (1789–1863) became one of France's most important military painters, also known for his sporting subjects. A Bonapartist, he glorified the Napoleonic era. He was later commissioned by Louis-Philippe and Napoleon III to produce the battle pieces at Versailles.

Verona City (pop., 1998 est.: 254,000), N Italy. Located on the ADIGE RIVER, it became a Roman colony in 89 B.C. and was the birthplace of the poet CATULLUS. It was the site of ODOACER's defeat by the Ostrogothic king THEODORIC in 489. It was occupied by CHARLEMAGNE in 774. Verona came under the della Scala family 1260–1387, then passed in 1405 to VENICE, which held it almost continuously until 1797, when it was ceded to Austria. It became part of the kingdom of Italy in 1866. It is noted for its ancient Roman amphitheater, now used for opera, and for Romanesque and Gothic buildings.

Veronese \ˌver-ə-ˈnä-sē\, **Paolo** *orig.* Paolo Caliari (1528–1588) Italian painter. Son of a stonecutter from Verona (the source of his nickname), he was apprenticed at 13 to a painter. After 1553, when he received the first of many commissions in Venice, he became a major painter of the 16th-cent. VENETIAN SCHOOL, known for his splendid use of color and pageantlike compositions. His ceiling paintings for the Doges' Palace employ skillful foreshortenings that make figures appear to be floating in space. He decorated the villas and palaces of the Venetian nobility and received many commissions for frescoes, altarpieces, and devotional paintings, including numerous "suppers" (e.g., *The Pilgrims of Emmaus* and *Feast in the House of the Pharisees*) depicting large groups of figures in architectural settings. For a villa built by Andrea PALLADIO at Maser (c.1561), he brilliantly interpreted its architectural structure, painting the walls with illusionistic landscapes and the ceilings with blue skies and figures from classical mythology. Whimsical details in his *Last Supper* (commissioned 1573) caused him to be summoned before the Inquisition. Painters from the 16th cent. on were inspired by his use of color.

Verrazzano \ˌver-ə-ˈzä-nō\, **Giovanni da** (1485–1528) Italian-French explorer. Educated in Florence, he moved to Dieppe, France, where he entered the maritime service. In 1524 he was sent to find a westward passage to Asia and reached N. America. He explored the E coast, becoming the first European to explore present-day New York harbor and Narragansett Bay, and continued north to Newfoundland. He later led expeditions to Brazil (1527) and to the Caribbean, where he was killed by cannibals.

Verrocchio \və-ˈrò-kē-ˌō\, **Andrea del** (1435–1488) Italian sculptor and painter. Little is certain about his early life. His most important works were executed under the patronage of the Medici in his native Florence. Many well-known artists studied at his studio, including LEONARDO DA VINCI and PERUGINO; the young Leonardo probably painted part of Verrocchio's *Baptism of Christ* (c.1470). Verrocchio's reputation as one of the great relief sculptors of the 15th cent. was established with his cenotaph in the cathedral at Pistoia; the relief's arrangement of figures into a dramatically unified composition anticipates the baroque sculpture of the 17th cent. His bronze statue of Bartolomeo Colleoni (erected in Venice 1496) is one of the greatest equestrian statues of the Renaissance.

Versailles \ver-ˈsī\, **Palace of** Baroque palace southwest of Paris built chiefly under LOUIS XIV. It was the principal residence of the French kings and the seat of government 1682–1789, housing some 1,000 courtiers and 4,000 attendants. Originally a hunting lodge, it was enlarged by LOUIS XIII and Louis XIV. Louis Le Vau (1612–1670), with Charles LE BRUN and André LE NÔTRE, began work on the palace in the 1660s. A masterpiece of formal grandeur intended as the visible expression of the glory of France, Versailles became the palatial ideal throughout Europe and the Americas. Le Nôtre's inventive arrangements created vistas, terraces, formal gardens, and wooded areas that celebrated the delights of both open and intimate space. After Le Vau's death, Jules Hardouin-Mansart (1646–1708) built the N and S wings, the Orangerie, and the Grand Trianon. Later additions include the classically restrained Petit Trianon, built 1761–64 for Madame de POMPADOUR. In the French Revolution, Versailles was identified as a symbol of royal extravagance. In 1837 LOUIS-PHILIPPE restored the palace and turned it into a museum.

Versailles, Treaty of International agreement, signed in 1919 at the Palace of Versailles, that concluded WORLD WAR I. It was negotiated primarily by the U.S., Britain, and France, without participation by the war's losers. Germany was forced to accept blame for Allied losses and to pay major reparations. Its European territory was reduced by about 10%, its overseas possessions were confiscated, and its military establishment was reduced. Though some of the treaty's terms were eased in the 1920s, the bitterness it created led to the rise of the NAZI PARTY. The treaty also established the LEAGUE OF NATIONS.

vertebral column \vər-ˈtē-brəl, ˈvərt-ə-brəl\ *or* **spinal column** *or* **spine** *or* **backbone** Flexible bony column extending the length of the torso. In humans, it consists of 32–34 vertebrae, with different shapes and functions in each of five regions: seven cervical, in the neck (including the atlas and axis, modified for free movement of the SKULL); twelve thoracic, in the chest; five lumbar, in the lower back; five sacral (fused into the sacrum, part of the PELVIC GIRDLE); and three to five coccygeal (vestigial tailbones fused into the coccyx). The body of each vertebra is separated from its neighbors by intervertebral disks of CARTILAGE. Behind the body is a Y-shaped vertebral (neural) arch with structures extending up and down to form JOINTS with the adjacent vertebrae and to the back and sides to provide attachment points for MUSCLES and LIGAMENTS. The spine supports the torso and protects the SPINAL CORD.

vertebrate Any animal of the CHORDATE subphylum Vertebrata, which includes the FISHES, AMPHIBIANS, REPTILES, BIRDS, and MAMMALS. Vertebrates have an internal SKELETON formed of cartilage, bone, or both. The skeleton consists of a backbone, which partly encloses a spinal cord; a SKULL, which encloses the brain; and usually two pairs of limbs. Nerves extending from the SPINAL CORD and brain permeate the skin, muscles, and internal organs. The muscular system consists primarily of bilaterally paired masses attached to bones or cartilage. Skin and scales, feathers, fur, or hair cover the outer surface. See also INVERTEBRATE.

vertical integration Form of business organization in which all stages of production of a good, from the acquisition of raw materials to the retailing of the final product, are controlled by one company. A current example is the oil industry, in which a single firm commonly owns the oil wells, refines the oil, and sells gasoline at roadside stations. In horizontal integration, by contrast, a company attempts to control a single stage of production or a single industry completely, which allows economies of scale but reduces competition.

vertigo \ˈvər-tə-ˌgō\ Feeling that one is spinning or that one's surroundings are spinning around one, causing confusion and difficulty keeping one's balance, sometimes accompanied by NAUSEA and VOMITING. Vertigo is normal after actual spinning, since INNER-EAR fluid continues to move once the body has stopped, producing a mismatch between visual and internal sensations. Other causes include CONCUSSION and abnormalities of the inner ear (e.g., labyrinthitis; see OTITIS), of the nerves that carry signals from it, or of the brain centers that receive them (e.g., STROKE). See also MOTION SICKNESS, PROPRIOCEPTION.

Verwoerd \fər-ˈvürt\, **Hendrik (Frensch)** (1901–1966) S. African (Dutch-born) prime minister (1958–66). A professor at the Univ. of Stellenbosch, in 1937 he became editor of the AFRIKANER nationalist daily in Johannesburg. As minister of native affairs (from 1950), he was responsible for much of the country's new APARTHEID legislation. As prime minister from 1958, he pushed through legislation resettling blacks in reservations. His policies provoked demonstrations, sometimes violent. In 1960 white voters approved his recommendation that S. Africa leave the British Commonwealth, realizing his dream of a republic. He was stabbed to death in the parliamentary chamber by a mixed-race parliamentary messenger.

Very Large Array (VLA) Array of 27 RADIO TELESCOPES operated on the plains of San Agustin near Socorro, N.M., by the National Radio Astronomy Observatory since 1980. Each telescope is 81 ft (25 m) across and can be moved along rails in a huge Y pattern whose arms are about 13 mi (21 km) long. The signals recorded are integrated by computer, so the entire array acts as a single radio antenna; its resolving power equals that of the best ground-based optical telescopes. The VLA has produced many of the most detailed radio images of quasars, galaxies, supernovas, and the Milky Way's nucleus.

Vesalius \və-ˈsā-lē-əs\, **Andreas** *Flemish* Andries van Wesel (1514–1564) Flemish physician. As a lecturer in surgery, he insisted on dissecting corpses himself, instead of relying on untrained assistants, to learn ANATOMY. Comparing his observations to ancient texts led him to question the theories of GALEN, at that time still considered authoritative. Vesalius' own complete textbook of human anatomy, *De humani corporis fabrica libri septem* (1543; "Seven Books on the Structure of the Human Body"), commonly called the *Fabrica*, was the most extensive and accurate description of the human body that had ever been published.

Vesey \ˈvē-zē\, **Denmark** (1767?–1822) U.S. insurrectionist. Born in the W. Indies, he was sold to a Bermuda slaver captain, with whom he sailed on numerous voyages. They settled in Charleston, S.C., and Vesey was allowed to purchase his freedom for $600 in 1800. Determined to relieve the oppression of slaves, he organized blacks (up to 9,000 by some estimates) for an uprising in which they would seize arsenals, kill all whites, and burn Charleston. After a house servant warned the authorities, 130 blacks were arrested; Vesey was tried and hanged with 35 others.

Vespasian \ves-ˈpā-zhən\ *in full* Caesar Vespasianus Augustus *orig.* Titus Flavius Vespasianus (A.D. 9–79) Roman emperor (69–79), founder of the FLAVIAN DYNASTY. Though of humble birth, he won military glory in Britain and was awarded a TRIUMPH by CLAUDIUS. In 63 he became PROCONSUL of Africa. After the emperor GALBA's murder (69), he was proclaimed emperor by the legions, while Vitellius (A.D. 15-69) claimed the title in Cologne; his forces soon defeated Vitellius in Italy. Though he claimed absolute power, he was a popular emperor and lived simply. He built the Temple of Peace and began the COLOSSEUM, and he reformed the army and PRAETORIAN GUARD. He ended the Jewish war (70) and the Rhineland revolt, adding lands in Germany and Britain and pacifying Wales. He was succeeded by his son TITUS.

Vespucci \ves-ˈpü-chē\, **Amerigo** (1454–1512) Italian-Spanish navigator and cartographer. He entered the Medici family business and in 1491 was sent to Seville, where he helped outfit the ships for Christopher COLUMBUS's expeditions. He took part in two (or four—the number is disputed) voyages to the New World; he was navigator on a Spanish ex-

pedition (1499–1500) that probably discovered the mouth of the Amazon River, and he led a Portuguese expedition (1501–2) that discovered Guanabara Bay (Rio de Janeiro) and the Río de la Plata. In the accounts of the voyages (published 1507), the terms America (from his first name) and New World were first used to describe the lands he visited.

Amerigo Vespucci Portrait by an unknown artist

Vesta In ROMAN RELIGION, the goddess of the hearth, identified with the Greek HESTIA. Because maintaining a hearth fire was important in ancient times, she was worshiped in every household. Her temple in Rome had a perpetual fire that was attended by the VESTAL VIRGINS. The fire was extinguished and renewed annually on March 1st; its extinction at any other time portended disaster for Rome.

Vestal Virgin In ROMAN RELIGION, any of six priestesses, representing the daughters of the royal house, who tended the state cult of VESTA. Chosen between the ages of 6 and 10, they served for 30 years, during which time they had to remain virgins; unchastity was punishable by burial alive. Their duties included tending the perpetual fire in the Temple of Vesta, fetching water from a sacred spring, preparing ritual food, caring for sacred objects, and officiating at the public worship of Vesta.

Vesuvius Active volcano, E side of the Bay of NAPLES, S Italy. It originated about 200,000 years ago; its current height of 4,198 ft (1,280 m) has varied considerably after each of its major eruptions; in 1900 it was 4,275 ft (1,303 m) high; in 1906, 3,668 ft (1,118 m) high; in the 1960s, 4,203 ft (1,281 m) high. Destructive eruptions occurred in A.D. 79, when POMPEII and HERCULANEUM were destroyed, and in 1631, when about 3,000 people were killed. More than 2 million people live in the area of Vesuvius, whose fertile slopes are covered with vineyards and orchards.

vetch Any of about 150 species of herbaceous plants in the genus *Vicia* of the pea family (see LEGUME). A few species are cultivated as important fodder and COVER CROPS and as green manure. Trailing or climbing stems grow 1–4 ft (0.3–1.2 m) tall, bearing compound leaves with several pairs of leaflets. Variously colored flowers are borne singly or in clusters. Like other legumes, vetches add nitrogen to the soil. See also CROWN VETCH.

Veterans Affairs, U.S. Department of (VA) Federal executive division responsible for programs and policies relating to veterans and their families. Established in 1989, it succeeded the Veterans Administration (formed in 1930). The VA administers benefits for medical care, educational assistance and vocational rehabilitation, pensions and life insurance, and payments for disability or death related to military service.

Veterans Day U.S. holiday celebrated on November 11, honoring veterans of the U.S. armed forces and those killed in battle. Originally, as Armistice Day, it commemorated the ending of WORLD WAR I on November 11, 1918. In 1954 it was renamed Veterans Day. It is typically observed with parades, speeches, and flowers placed on military graves and memorials. It is called Remembrance Day in Canada and Remembrance Sunday (on the Sunday nearest to Nov. 11) in Britain.

veterinary science Medical field dealing with animals and with diseases that are contagious between animals and humans. It was a medical specialty in ancient Egypt and Babylonia but went through a period of virtual nonexistence in medieval Europe before reappearing in the mid-18th cent. with the founding of the first veterinary schools. Veterinarians practice internal medicine, surgery, and preventive medicine, using the same techniques used on humans. Many specialize in either small animals (pets) or large ones (livestock); a few specialize in wild animals.

TUV

Viagra Trademark for the first oral drug for male IMPO-TENCE, generic name sildenafil. Before the FDA approved Viagra in 1998, impotence was treated with surgical implants, suppositories, pumps, and drugs injected into the PENIS. Taken as a pill shortly before SEXUAL INTERCOURSE, Viagra dilates blood vessels in the penis, allowing a natural sexual response. It works in about 70% of cases; it should not be used by anyone taking nitroglycerin or with heart problems, hypotension, hypertension, recent stroke, or certain eye disorders.

vibraphone *or* **vibraharp** Percussion instrument with tuned metal bars, arranged keyboard-style like the XYLOPHONE, which are struck with mallets. Each bar has a resonating tube suspended vertically below it to sustain the tone; small electrically powered spinning disks at the tops of the resonators produce a vibrato effect. Invented around 1920, it became a popular jazz instrument.

vibration Periodic back-and-forth motion of the particles of an elastic body or medium. It is usually a result of the displacement of a body from an EQUILIBRIUM condition, followed by the body's response to the forces that tend to restore equilibrium. Free vibrations occur when a system is disturbed but immediately allowed to move without restraint. One example is the motion of a weight suspended by a spring. If the weight is pulled down and then released, it continues to bounce up and down, the amplitude of the vibrations decreasing until it comes to rest. See also RESONANCE.

vibrio \'vib-rē-ō\ Any of a group of aquatic, comma-shaped BACTERIA in the family Vibrionaceae. They are gram-negative (see GRAM STAIN), highly capable of movement (with one to three flagella at one end), and do not require oxygen. Their cells are curved rods, single or strung together in S-shapes or spirals. Two species are of significance to humans: one causes CHOLERA, the other acute bacterial DIARRHEA.

Vicente \vē-'sān-tə\, **Gil** (1465?–1536?) Portuguese playwright, the founder of Portuguese drama. His first plays were produced in 1502, and for the next 34 years he acted as court dramatist and poet laureate, staging his plays to celebrate great events and religious occasions. His 44 extant plays—tragicomedies, farces, and *autos sacramentales* (short biblical plays)—include *Exhortation to War* (1513), *The Forge of Love* (1524), and *The Pilgrimage of the Aggrieved* (1533).

Vichy France \'vē-shē\ *officially* French State *French* État français (July 1940–Sept. 1944) French regime in WORLD WAR II after the German defeat of France. The Franco–German armistice (June 1940) divided France into two zones: one under German military occupation and one under nominal French control (the SE two-fifths of the country). The National Assembly, summoned at Vichy to ratify the armistice, was persuaded by Pierre LAVAL to grant Philippe PÉTAIN full powers in the "French State." The antirepublican Vichy government collaborated with the Germans and became a tool of German policy, especially after the Germans occupied all of France in 1942. By early 1944 the RÉSISTANCE movement against the GESTAPO and Vichy militias created a period of civil war in France, and after the liberation of Paris the Vichy regime was abolished.

Vicksburg Campaign (1862–63) Engagements fought at Vicksburg, Miss., in the AMERICAN CIVIL WAR. Confederate forces held the fortified city against Union naval bombardment from the Mississippi River (1862) and land attacks. In April 1863 U. S. GRANT ferried troops across the river at night and quickly took nearby Port Gibson and Grand Gulf to prevent Confederate forces from aiding those in the city, then besieged the city for six weeks. On July 4 Gen. John Pemberton surrendered his force of 30,000, leaving the Mississippi River completely under Union control and splitting the Confederacy in half.

Vico \'vē-kō\, **Giambattista** (1668–1744) Italian philosopher of cultural history and law. In his major work *New Science* (1725), Vico attempted to bring about the convergence of history and the more systematic social sciences in a single science of humanity. He affirmed that Providence must right the course of history so that humanity would not be engulfed in successive cataclysms. Increasingly recognized as one of the important figures in European intellectual history, Vico is seen today as a forerunner of the founders of CULTURAL ANTHROPOLOGY.

Victor Amadeus II \,äm-ə-'dā-əs\ *Italian* Vittorio Amedeo (1666–1732) King of Sicily (1713–20) and of Sardinia (1720–30). As duke of Savoy (from 1675), he grew up under a pro-French regency headed by his mother. In the War of the SPANISH SUCCESSION he shifted to the Habsburg side; with the French defeat at Turin (1706) he secured his position in Italy. The Treaty of UTRECHT (1713) gave him the title of king of Sicily, which he was obliged to exchange for Sardinia in 1720. As the first king of Sardinia, which also included Piedmont and Savoy, he established the foundation for the future Italian national state.

Victor Emmanuel II *Italian* Vittorio Emanuele (1820–1878) King of Sardinia (1849–61) and first king of a united Italy (1861–78). The son of CHARLES ALBERT, he became king of Sardinia when his father abdicated in 1849. Assisted by his minister Camillo CAVOUR, he strengthened the kingdom and supported the RISORGIMENTO movement for unity. In the war with Austria (1859–61), he commanded troops to victories in major battles. He secretly encouraged Giuseppe GARIBALDI in the conquest of Sicily and Naples and led the invasion of the Papal States. He assumed the title of king of Italy in 1861 and later acquired Venetia (1866) and Rome (1870).

Victor Emmanuel III *Italian* Vittorio Emanuele (1869–1947) King of Italy (1900–1946). Son of UMBERTO I, he came to the throne on his father's assassination (1900). He accepted a Liberal cabinet and later agreed to Italy's entry into World War I. He failed to prevent the rise of Benito MUSSOLINI and the Fascist seizure of power, which turned him into a figurehead sovereign. In 1943, after disastrous Italian military losses, he had Mussolini arrested and replaced by Pietro BADOGLIO as premier. In an attempt to preserve the monarchy, he abdicated to his son Umberto in 1946. When the Italian republic was declared in 1946, father and son went into exile.

Victoria City (metro. area pop., 1996 est.: 304,000), capital of British Columbia. It is located on the SE tip of VANCOUVER ISLAND, overlooking JUAN DE FUCA STRAIT. It was founded in 1843 by the HUDSON'S BAY CO. It became the capital in 1866 when Vancouver Island united with British Columbia. It is now one of the province's largest business centers, a tourist resort, and a retirement community. A major port, it is the Pacific headquarters of the Canadian navy.

Victoria Seaport city, HONG KONG, China. It lies on the N shore of Hong Kong island (pop., 1996: 1,313,000). It is connected to the Chinese mainland by ferry and by tunnels. Historically regarded as the capital, it is the chief administrative, commercial, and cultural center of Hong Kong.

Victoria *orig.* Alexandrina Victoria (1819–1901) Queen of the United Kingdom (1837–1901) and Empress of India (from 1876). She succeeded her uncle, WILLIAM IV, in 1837. She was first guided as queen by the Whig prime minister Lord MELBOURNE and (from 1840) by her husband, Prince ALBERT. Devoted to him, she accepted his decisions on all issues in the period sometimes called the "Albertine monarchy." They had nine children, through whose marriages descended many of the royal families of Europe. From 1861 Victoria deeply mourned Albert's death and thereafter made royal decisions as she believed he would have advised. She was frequently at

Queen Victoria

odds with Prime Minister William GLADSTONE and welcomed his replacement by Benjamin DISRAELI in 1874. The Victorian age was marked by British expansion. She remains the longest-reigning monarch in British history.

Victoria Town (pop., 1999: 28,000), capital of the Republic of Seychelles. Located on Mahé Island, it is the only port of the archipelago and the country's business and cultural center.

Victoria State (pop., 1998 est.: 4,661,000), SE Australia. It covers an area of 87,900 sq mi (227,600 sq km); its capital is MELBOURNE. The state's W and NW parts are sandy desert and lowland, while the central and E parts form the S end of the AUSTRALIAN ALPS. The SW coastal region is known as GIPPSLAND. The MURRAY RIVER forms most of the boundary with NEW S. WALES. AUSTRALIAN ABORIGINES had lived in the region for at least 40,000 years before contact with Europeans. Some 60 years after Capt. James COOK first sighted its coastline (1770), the area was settled by immigrants from TASMANIA, and disease devasted the aborigines. In 1901 Victoria became a state of the Commonwealth of Australia. It is very productive agriculturally.

Victoria, Lake *or* **Victoria Nyanza** Largest lake in Africa and chief reservoir of the NILE RIVER. The S half lies in Tanzania, the N half in Uganda; it borders Kenya in the northeast. The second-largest freshwater lake in the world (after Lake SUPERIOR), it is about 210 mi (337 km) long, 150 mi (240 km) wide, and up to 270 ft (82 m) deep. The Kagera River is its largest tributary; its only outlet is the Victoria Nile. J. H. SPEKE, searching for the source of the Nile in 1858, was the first European to sight it; he named it for Queen VICTORIA. H. M. STANLEY circumnavigated it in 1875. It became a reservoir after completion of Owen Falls Dam in 1954.

Victoria, Tomás Luis de (1548–1611) Spanish composer. He went to Rome around 1565 as an organist and singer, eventually becoming chapel master for a Jesuit congregation (1573–77) and being ordained a priest (1575). In 1587 he returned to Spain as chaplain to the king's sister, in whose convent he served as organist and choirmaster until his death. He wrote 20 masses, 18 Magnificats, and 52 motets (including *O magnum mysterium*). His music is mystical, impressive, and moving, and he was renowned as the greatest Spanish composer of the Renaissance.

Victoria and Albert Museum Museum of decorative arts in London. It was conceived by Prince ALBERT as a way to improve the standards of British design by making the finest models available for study. The core collection, consisting of objects purchased at the 1851 CRYSTAL PALACE exhibition, was opened by Queen VICTORIA in 1857. It was moved to a new building designed by Sir Aston Webb, which opened to the public in 1909. It houses vast collections of European sculpture, ceramics, furniture, metalwork, jewelry, textiles, and musical instruments from medieval times to the present; remarkable Chinese ceramics, jade, and sculpture; the premier collection of Italian Renaissance sculpture outside Italy; and the outstanding national collection of British watercolors, miniatures, prints, and drawings. It is regarded as the world's greatest decorative-arts museum.

Victoria Desert See GREAT VICTORIA DESERT

Victoria Falls Waterfall, at the border between Zambia and Zimbabwe. Approximately twice as wide and twice as deep as NIAGARA FALLS, the falls span the entire breadth of the ZAMBEZI RIVER at one of its widest points (more than 5,500 ft, or 1,700 m). There, the river plunges over a precipice to a drop of 355 ft (108 m). Victoria Falls was designated a WORLD HERITAGE SITE in 1989. The first European sighting of the falls was in 1855 by David LIVINGSTONE, who named them after Queen VICTORIA.

Victoria Falls See IGUAZÚ FALLS

Victoria Island Third-largest island of the ARCTIC ARCHIPELAGO, Canada. It is about 320 mi (515 km) long and 170–370 mi (270–600 km) wide. Discovered in 1838 by Thomas Simpson (1808–1840), it was named for Queen VICTORIA. It was formerly part of the NORTHWEST TERRITORIES; a portion was transferred to NUNAVUT in 1999.

vicuña \vi-'kün-yə, vī-'kü-nə\ S. American lamoid (see ALPACA), the smallest species (*Lama*, or *Vicugna, vicugna*) in the CAMEL family, found in semiarid grasslands of the central Andes at altitudes of 12,000–16,000 ft (3,600–4,800 m). The remarkably long, soft, lustrous coat is cinnamon to white; a dense, silky, white fleece hangs from the flanks and base of the neck. Vicuñas are about 36 in. (90 cm) high and weigh over 100 lbs (50 kg). Vicuñas are untamable but have been hunted for centuries for their fur; they are now protected as an endangered species.

Vidal \'vē-,däl, vē-'däl\, **Gore** (*orig.* Eugene Luther) (b.1925) U.S. writer. Born in West Point, N.Y., Vidal began publishing his writings soon after his wartime army service. Though he has written plays, screenplays, and political essays, he is best known for his irreverent and intellectually adroit novels. *The City and the Pillar* (1948) became notorious for its homoerotic subject matter. *Myra Breckenridge* (1968) was acclaimed for its wild satire. His other successful novels, many of them historical, include *Julian* (1964), *Washington, D.C.* (1967), *Burr* (1974), and *Lincoln* (1984). Known for his iconoclastic political views, he has twice run for Congressional office.

video card INTEGRATED CIRCUIT that generates the video signal sent to a computer display. The card is usually located on the computer motherboard or is a separate circuit board, but is sometimes built into the computer display unit. It contains a digital-to-analog module, as well as MEMORY chips that store display data. All video cards (also known as video adapters, video boards, and video controllers) adhere to a display standard, such as SVGA or XGA.

videocassette recorder See VCR

videodisc Rigid circular plate of either metal or plastic used to record video and audio signals for playback on a conventional television receiver. There are two major classes of videodiscs, magnetic and nonmagnetic. Magnetic videodiscs have an oxide-coated surface onto which input signals are recorded as magnetic patterns. Nonmagnetic videodiscs use either a mechanical recording system analogous to that used in phonograph records, or optical technology that uses a laser to read data coded as a sequence of pits on the disc. The most common type of videodisc today is the DVD.

videotape Magnetic tape used to record visual images and sound, or the recording itself. There are two types of videotape recorders, the transverse (or quad) and the helical. In a transverse unit, the tape passes over four rotating heads. It achieves 1,500-in.-per-minute head-to-tape speed, necessary for high picture quality. The helical unit uses tape traveling around a drum in the form of a helix. VCRs use the VHS (Video Home System) format, consisting of two helical bands and tape 1/2 in. (1 cm) wide.

Vidor \'vē-dȯr\, **King (Wallis)** (1894–1982) U.S. film director. Born in Galveston, Texas, he directed his first feature film in 1919 and won acclaim for *The Big Parade* (1925) and *The Crowd* (1928), considered a silent-movie classic. Noted for his realistic portrayals of contemporary life, he directed the first all-black film, *Hallelujah!* (1929), as well as *Our Daily Bread* (1934) and *The Citadel* (1938). His later movies included the western epic *Duel in the Sun* (1946), *The Fountainhead* (1949), and *War and Peace* (1956).

Vienna City (pop., 1999 est.: 1,609,000), capital of Austria. Located on the DANUBE RIVER, it was founded by the Celts. It was an important trade center during the CRUSADES. It was the seat of the HOLY ROMAN EMPIRE 1558–1806, of the Austrian (and HABSBURG) empire 1806–67, and of the Austro-Hungarian empire until 1918. In 1814–15 it was the seat of the Congress of VIENNA. The administrative center of German Austria 1938–45, it was frequently bombed during World War II. It was under joint Soviet-Western Allied occupation 1945–55. The commercial and industrial center of Austria, it also is a cultural center renowned for its architecture and music; it was the birthplace of the composers Franz SCHUBERT, Johann STRAUSS, and Arnold SCHOENBERG, and home to W. A. MOZART, Ludwig van BEETHOVEN, Johannes BRAHMS, and Gustav MAHLER. It also was the home of such major cultural figures as Sigmund FREUD and Oskar KOKOSCHKA.

Vienna, Congress of (1814–15) Assembly that reorganized Europe after the NAPOLEONIC WARS. The powers of the QUADRUPLE ALLIANCE were joined in Vienna by Bourbon France as a major participant and by Sweden and Portugal; many minor states also sent representatives. The principal negotiators were Klemens von METTERNICH (Austria); Alexander I (Russia); FREDERICK WILLIAM III and Karl von HARDENBERG (Prussia); Viscount CASTLEREAGH (Britain);

and C.-M. de TALLEYRAND (France). The Congress reduced France to its 1789 borders. A new kingdom of Poland was established, under Russian sovereignty. To check future aggression by France, its neighbors were strengthened: the Netherlands acquired Belgium, Prussia gained territory along the Rhine River, and the Italian kingdom acquired Genoa. The German states were joined as the GERMAN CONFEDERATION, subject to Austria's influence. For its part in the defeat of Napoleon, Britain acquired valuable colonies, including Malta, the Cape of Good Hope, and Ceylon. The settlement was the most comprehensive treaty that Europe had ever seen.

Vienna, University of State-financed university at Vienna. Founded in 1365 on the model of the Univ. of PARIS, it is the oldest university in the German-speaking world. Reorganized in 1384, it became noted for medicine, law, and theology, and was a center for the Revolution of 1848. The modern university includes faculties of theology, social sciences and economics, medicine, sciences, mathematics, and natural sciences. Total enrollment is about 72,000.

Vienna Circle *German* **Wiener Kreis** \'vē-nər-'krīs\ Group of philosophers, scientists, and mathematicians formed in the 1920s that met regularly in Vienna to investigate scientific language and scientific method. It formed around Moritz Schlick (1882–1936), who taught at the Univ. of Vienna; its members included Rudolf CARNAP, Kurt GÖDEL, and Otto Neurath (1882–1945). The movement associated with the Circle has been called LOGICAL POSITIVISM. Its members focused on the form of scientific theories, formulation of a verifiability principle of meaning, and a doctrine of unified science. The group dissolved after the Nazis invaded Austria in 1938.

Vientiane \,vyen-'tyän\ *Laotian* **Viangchan** \,vyeŋ-'chän\ City (metro. area pop., 1995 est.: 532,000), capital of Laos. It is located north of the MEKONG RIVER. Founded in the late 13th cent., it was made the administrative center of an early Laotian kingdom in the mid-16th cent. In 1778 it came under Siamese control. The French made it the capital of their colony in the 1890s; it remained the administrative center after Laos gained independence in 1953. It is Laos's principal port of entry.

Viet Cong *in full* Viet Nam Cong San. Guerrilla force that sought to reunify N. and S. Vietnam under communist leadership from the late 1950s through 1975. Originally a collection of various groups opposed to S. Vietnam's Pres. NGO DINH DIEM, it became the military arm of the National Liberation Front (1960) and later of the Provisional Revolutionary Government (PRG; 1969). Members were originally recruited from S. Vietnam, but they received guidance, weapons, and later reinforcements from the north. The Viet Cong's guerrilla war against the S. Vietnamese government was successful (see VIETNAM WAR), and following a full-scale invasion, the PRG assumed power in S. Vietnam in 1975.

Viet Minh \'vyet-'min\ *in full* Viet Nam Doc Lap Dong Minh Hoi. Organization that led the struggle for Vietnamese independence from French rule. Formed in 1941 by HO CHI MINH as a broad-based nationalist organization, it was led by communists. In 1943 the Viet Minh, under VO NGUYEN GIAP, began guerrilla operations against the occupying Japanese; when the Japanese surrendered to the Allies, the Viet Minh seized Hanoi and proclaimed Vietnam's independence. In the First INDOCHINA WAR that followed, the Viet Minh (and its successor groups) defeated the French. Elements of the Viet Minh also joined the VIET CONG.

Vietnam *officially* **Socialist Republic of Vietnam** Nation, SE Asia. Area: 127,816 sq mi (331,041 sq km). Population (2000): 78,774,000. Capital: HANOI. Almost 90% of the total population is Vietnamese; minorities include Chinese, Hmong, Thai, Khmer, and Chan. Languages: Vietnamese (official), French, Chinese, English, Khmer. Religions: Buddhism, Taoism, Confucianism, Roman Catholicism, Islam, Protestantism. Currency: dong. Vietnam is about 1,025 mi (1,650 km) long, 210–340 mi (340–550 km) wide at its widest parts, and 35 mi (56 km) wide at its narrowest part. N Vietnam is mountainous; Fan-si-pan, the country's highest peak, rises to 10,306 ft (3,141 m). The RED RIVER is the principal river. S Vietnam is dominated by the MEKONG RIVER delta. A

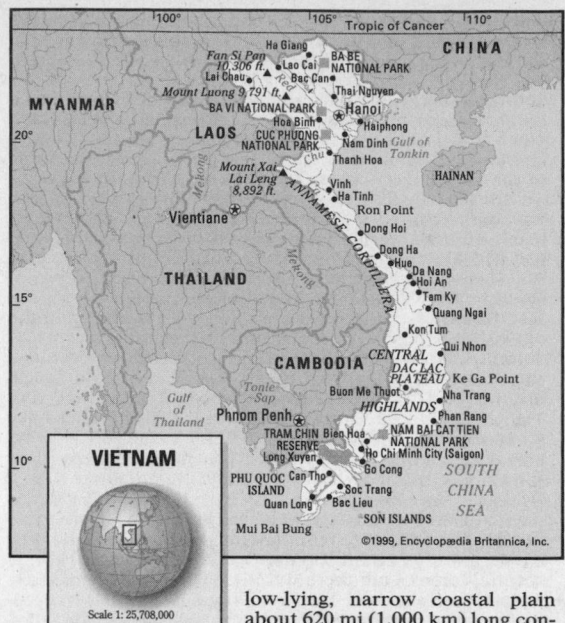

©1999, Encyclopædia Britannica, Inc.

VIETNAM

Scale 1: 25,708,000

low-lying, narrow coastal plain about 620 mi (1,000 km) long connects the two major river deltas. The densely forested Annamese Cordillera extends through W central Vietnam and covers two-thirds of the total land area. N Vietnam is rich in mineral resources, especially anthracite and lignite coal. Some petroleum deposits exist off the S coast. Significant food crops include rice, sugarcane, coffee, tea, and bananas. Food processing and fishing are important industries, as is the manufacture of steel and phosphates. It is a socialist republic with one legislative house; its chief of state is the president, and its head of government is the prime minister. A distinct Vietnamese group began to emerge about 200 B.C. in the independent kingdom of Nam Viet, which was later annexed to China in the 1st cent. B.C. The Vietnamese were under continuous Chinese control until the 10th cent. A.D. The S region was gradually overrun by Vietnamese from the north in the late 15th cent. The area was divided into two parts in the early 17th cent., with the N part knwn as TONKIN, and the S part as COCHIN CHINA. In 1802 the N and S parts of Vietnam were unified under a single dynasty. Following several years of attempted French colonial expansion in the region, the French captured Saigon in 1859 and later the rest of the area, controlling it until World War II (see FRENCH INDOCHINA). The Japanese occupied Vietnam 1940–45, and declared it independent at the end of World War II, a move the French opposed. They fought the First INDOCHINA WAR until French forces with U.S. financial backing were defeated at DIEN BIEN PHU in 1954; evacuation of French troops ensued. Following an international conference at Geneva, Vietnam was partitioned along the 17th parallel, with the N part under HO CHI MINH, and the S part under BAO DAI; the partition was to be temporary, but the reunification elections scheduled for 1956 were never held. Bao Dai declared the independence of S. Vietnam (Republic of Vietnam), while the Communists established N. Vietnam (Democratic Republic of Vietnam). The activities of N. Vietnamese guerrillas and pro-communist rebels in S. Vietnam led to U.S. intervention and the VIETNAM WAR. A cease-fire agreement was signed in 1973, and U.S. troops were withdrawn. The civil war soon resumed, and in 1975 N. Vietnam invaded S. Vietnam and the S. Vietnamese government collapsed. In 1976 the two Vietnams were united as the Socialist Republic of Vietnam. From the mid-1980s, the government enacted a series of economic reforms and began to open up to Asian and W nations. In 1995 the U.S. officially normalized relations with Vietnam.

Vietnamese language MON-KHMER LANGUAGE, the native language of 60–65 million people in Vietnam and a second language for many of Vietnam's minority ethnic groups. For much of Vietnam's history, Classical CHINESE was the dominant literary language, and Chinese vocabulary given a Vietnamese pronunciation ("Sino-Vietnamese") remains a significant part of the language's lexicon. By the 13th cent., Chinese characters were adapted to write native Vietnamese words. Today Vietnamese uses the LATIN ALPHABET with diacritics distinguishing vowel qualities and tones.

Vietnam Veterans Memorial Monument in Washington, D.C., designed by Maya LIN. It consists of two low, black granite walls that meet to form a wide V shape, engraved with the names of the more than 58,000 U.S. dead and missing-in-action who served in the VIETNAM WAR, listed by date of casualty. In response to protests, a traditional statue was commissioned for the entrance to the site. Since its dedication in 1982, the wall has become one of the city's most visited and most affecting tourist attractions.

Vietnam War (1955–75) Protracted effort by S. Vietnam and the U.S. to prevent N. and S. Vietnam from being united under communist leadership. After the First INDOCHINA WAR, Vietnam was partitioned to separate the warring parties until free elections could be held in 1956. Under HO CHI MINH, the North was expected to win the elections, which the leader in the South, NGO DINH DIEM, refused to hold. In the war that ensued, the VIET CONG fought a guerrilla war against U.S.-supported S. Vietnamese forces. At the height of U.S. involvement, there were over 500,000 U.S. military personnel in Vietnam. The Tet Offensive of 1968, in which the Viet Cong attacked 36 major S. Vietnamese cities and towns, marked a turning point in the war. Many in the U.S. had come to oppose the war on moral and practical grounds, and Pres. Lyndon JOHNSON decided to shift to a policy of "de-escalation." Peace talks were begun in Paris. Between 1969 and 1973 U.S. troops were withdrawn from Vietnam, but the war was expanded to Cambodia and Laos in 1970. Peace talks, which had reached a stalemate in 1971, started again in 1973, producing a cease-fire agreement. Fighting continued, and both sides denounced the other for numerous truce violations. In 1975 the N. Vietnamese launched a full-scale invasion of the South, which soon surrendered, and in 1976 the country was reunited as the Socialist Republic of Vietnam. More than 2 million people (including 58,000 Americans) died over the course of the war, half of them civilians.

Viganò \vē-'gä-nō\, **Salvatore** (1769–1821) Italian dancer and choreographer. He studied dance with his father and toured in Spain and Vienna, where he began to choreograph works in a style synthesizing dance and mime, which he called "coreodramma." He created over 40 works, including Beethoven's *Creatures of Prometheus* (1801) and *I titani* (1819). In 1811 he became ballet master at La Scala in Milan, where he promoted the development of ballet in Italy.

Vigée-Lebrun \vē-'zhā-lä-'broeⁿ\, **(Marie-Louise-) Élisabeth** (1755–1842) French painter. Taught first by her father, she was also advised by Joseph VERNET. In 1779 she was summoned to Versailles to paint MARIE-ANTOINETTE, whom she would paint at least 25 more times. At the outbreak of the French Revolution, she left France and traveled abroad, painting portraits of such notables as Lord BYRON and Germaine de STAËL and playing a leading role in society. Her paintings are notable for their freshness, charm, and sensitivity.

Vigny \vē-'nyē\, **Alfred-Victor, comte (count) de** (1797–1863) French poet, dramatist, and novelist. His *Cinq-Mars* (1826) was the first important historical novel in French. Growing disillusioned politically, he wrote *Stello* (1832), on separating the poetic and political life. *Chatterton* (1835), one of the finest Romantic dramas, glorifies the anguish of the misunderstood artist. His pessimism was manifest also in *The Military Necessity* (1835), whose first and third stories are his prose masterpieces. His later writings include poetry collected posthumously in *Les destinées* (1864).

Vikings *or* **Norsemen** Scandinavian seafaring warriors who raided and colonized areas of Europe in the 9th–11th cent. Overpopulation at home, ease of conquest abroad, and their extraordinary capacity as shipbuilders and sailors in-

spired their adventures. In 865 Vikings conquered E. Anglia, Northumbria, and much of Mercia. Wessex under ALFRED the Great made a truce in 878 that led to Danish control of much of England. This was fiercely contested until 1042, when native rule was restored. The Scandinavians permanently affected English social structure, dialect, and names. In the W seas, Scandinavians had settled in Iceland by 900, whence they traveled to Greenland and N. America. They invaded Ireland in 795, establishing kingdoms at Dublin, Limerick, and Waterford. The Battle of Clontarf (1014) ended the threat of Scandinavian rule. France suffered periodic Viking raids but no domination. In Russia Vikings briefly dominated Novgorod, Kiev, and other centers, but were quickly absorbed by the Slav population. Viking activity ended in the 11th cent.

Viking ship See LONGSHIP

Vila See PORT-VILA

villa Country estate, complete with house, grounds, and subsidiary buildings. The term particularly applies to the suburban summer residences of the ancient Romans and their later Italian imitators. Roman villas often included elaborate terracing, long colonnades, towers, gardens with reflecting pools and fountains, and extensive reservoirs. In Britain the term has come to mean a small detached or semidetached suburban home. See also HADRIAN'S VILLA, Andrea PALLADIO.

Villa \'vē-yə\, **Pancho** *orig.* Doroteo Arango (1878–1923) Mexican guerrilla leader. An advocate of radical LAND REFORM, he joined Francisco MADERO's uprising against Porfirio DÍAZ. His *División del Norte* later joined forces with Venustiano CARRANZA to overthrow Victoriano HUERTA, but he soon broke with the moderate Carranza and in 1914 was forced to flee with Emiliano ZAPATA. In 1916, to show that Carranza did not control the north, he raided a town in New Mexico. A U.S. force led by Gen. John PERSHING was sent against him, but he proved impossible to capture. Granted a pardon after Carranza's overthrow (1920), he was later assassinated. See also MEXICAN REVOLUTION.

Villa-Lobos \,vē-lə-'lō-bōsh\, **Heitor** (1887–1959) Brazilian composer. He was exposed to folk music as a child, and his later extensive ethnomusicological studies (1905–12) had great influence on his own works. Self-taught as a composer, he enjoyed the support of Arthur RUBINSTEIN. In 1922 his music came to national attention, and he was given a grant to live in Paris (1923–30), where his music was received enthusiastically. On his return, he founded the Ministry of Education conservatory (1942) and the Brazilian Academy of Music (1945) and became Brazil's semiofficial ambassador to the world. His many works include his nine *Bachianas brasileiras* for various ensembles, and his 14 *Chôros*, based on a popular form of street music.

Villanovan culture \,vi-lə-'nō-vən\ Early IRON AGE culture in Italy, named after the village where the first site was found in 1853. It appeared in the 10th or 9th cent. B.C. as a branch of the URNFIELD CULTURE. Its dead were cremated and the ashes put in a decorated pottery two-story urn or in a terra-cotta hut urn. Expert metalworkers, the Villanovans controlled Tuscany's copper and iron mines. Their culture began to fade in the 7th cent.

Villard \və-'lärd\, **Henry** *orig.* Ferdinand Heinrich Gustav Hilgard (1835–1900) German-U.S. journalist and financier. In 1853 he emigrated to the U.S. During the Civil War he was a correspondent for two New York newspapers. In 1881 he purchased the *Nation* magazine and the *New York Evening Post*. In the 1870s Villard organized several railroads in Oregon, and he served as president (1881–84) and chairman of the board (1888–93) of the Northern Pacific, a transcontinental railroad completed under his management. He created the Edison General Electric Co. in 1889, serving as president until its reorganization in 1892 as the GENERAL ELECTRIC CO.

Villars \vī-'lär\, **Claude-Louis-Hector, duc (Duke) de** (1653–1734) French soldier. After leading French forces to early victories in the War of the Spanish Succession, he was made a marshal of France (1702). He continued successful military campaigns in Germany (1705–8) and inflicted heavy losses on the duke of MARLBOROUGH's forces at Malplaquet. He served on the regency council for the young LOUIS

TUV

xv. At the outbreak of the War of the Polish Succession, he was named marshal-general of France (1733).

Villella \vi-'le-lə\, **Edward** (b.1936) U.S. ballet dancer, choreographer, and director. Born in New York City, he joined the NEW YORK CITY BALLET in 1957, becoming a principal dancer in 1960. He danced leading roles in many of George BALANCHINE's ballets, notably *The Prodigal Son* (1960), displaying a powerful technique, and helped attract many new fans to ballet. He retired from dancing in 1983. In 1986 he founded the Miami City Ballet, where he continues as artistic director.

Villiers, George See 1st Duke of BUCKINGHAM

Villon \vē-'yōⁿ, vē-'lón\, **François** *orig.* François de Montcorbier *or* François des Loges (1431–after 1463) French lyric poet. Villon was a rigorously trained scholar who led a life of criminal excess; he killed a priest in 1455, then became involved in robbery, theft, and brawling. Incarcerated several times, in 1462 he received a death sentence that was commuted to banishment. He was never heard from again. His works include *Le petit testament* (published 1489), ironic bequests to friends and acquaintances; and *Le testament* (1489), which reviews his life with great emotional and poetic depth. His verse, which often reflects his tumultuous life, makes a direct, unsentimental appeal to the emotions but also displays remarkable control of rhyme and composition.

Vilnius \'vil-nē-əs\ City (pop., 2000: 578,000), capital of Lithuania. Founded in the 10th cent., it became the capital of Lithuania in 1323. It was destroyed in 1377 by the Teutonic Knights, but was rebuilt. It passed to Russia in 1795, and for several centuries was a noted European center for Jewish learning. It was occupied by the Germans in World Wars I and II and suffered heavy damage and extermination of its Jewish population. In 1939 it was restored to Lithuania, which the Soviets annexed in 1940. In 1991 it became the capital of the newly independent Lithuania. It has many historic Gothic, Renaissance, and baroque buildings.

Vincent de Paul, St. (1581–1660) French religious leader. In 1625 he founded the Congregation of the Mission (also called Lazarists or Vincentians) in Paris as a preaching and teaching order. He also established Confraternities of Charity, associations of laywomen who nursed the sick. With St. Louise de Marillac he cofounded the Daughters of Charity (Sisters of Charity of St. Vincent de Paul).

Vincent of Beauvais \bō-'vä\ (c.1190–1264) French scholar. A Dominican priest (c.1220), he became lector and chaplain to the court of King LOUIS IX. By 1244 he had compiled *Speculum majus* ("Great Mirror"), an 80-book compendium that included human history and natural history and science known to the West, as well as European literature, law, politics, and economics. His work influenced scholars and poets up to the 18th cent.

Vinci, Leonardo da See LEONARDO DA VINCI

vine Plant whose stem requires support and that climbs by TENDRILS or twining or creeps along the ground, or the stem of such a plant. Examples include BITTERSWEET, most GRAPES, some HONEYSUCKLES, IVY, LIANAS, and MELONS.

vinegar Sour liquid obtained by FERMENTATION of weak alcoholic liquids. Probably first made from WINE (French *vinaigre* means "sour wine"), vinegar may also be made from malted BARLEY, RICE, or other substances. The source substance, which must contain sugar, is fermented by YEAST to produce alcohol. When aerated, bacteria cause it to convert to acetic acid, water, and various other compounds. Vinegar is used in pickling and in creating marinades, dressings, and other sauces.

Vinland Wooded land in N. America visited and named by LEIF ERIKSSON THE LUCKY in or about A.D. 1000. It was probably located along the Atlantic coast of what is now E or NE Canada. The Vikings' visits to Vinland (named "wine land" for its wild grapes) are recorded in the Norse SAGAS. Leif Eriksson is said to have led the first expedition. A final expedition was led about 1013 by ERIK THE RED's daughter Freydis. In 1963 the remains of a Norse settlement were discovered at L'ANSE AUX MEADOWS, at the northernmost tip of NEWFOUNDLAND.

Vinson, Fred(erick Moore) (1890–1953) U.S. jurist. Born in Louisa, Ky., he served in Congress before joining the U.S.

Court of Appeals (1938–1943), after which he held high executive positions, including secretary of the treasury under Pres. Harry TRUMAN. He helped establish the International Bank for Reconstruction and Development and the INTERNATIONAL MONETARY FUND. As chief justice of the U.S. Supreme Court (1946–53), he favored Truman's internal-security policies and upheld the rights of minorities to equal protection.

viol \'vī-əl, 'vī-ˌōl\ *or* **viola da gamba** \vē-ˌō-lə-də-'gäm-bə\ Bowed STRINGED INSTRUMENT of the 16th–18th cent. The viols are distinguished from the VIOLIN family by a fretted fingerboard, sloping shoulders, flat back, six strings, and milder tone. They exist in four sizes: treble, tenor, bass, and double bass (violone). They are played vertically, the body being held between the legs or rested on the knee. The viol family appeared in the late 15th cent. and soon became widely popular. The violin family, with their more penetrating tone, gradually displaced the viols in the 18th cent.

viola \vī-'ō-lə, vē-'ō-lə\ STRINGED INSTRUMENT, the tenor member of the VIOLIN family. It closely resembles the violin but is slightly larger; its strings are tuned a 5th lower and its tone is darker, warmer, and less powerful. The modern orchestra uses six to 10 violas. The viola d'amore is an 18th-cent. instrument with six or seven melody strings and several sympathetic (resonating) strings strung under them.

violet Any of the approximately 500 species of herbaceous plants or low shrubs that make up the genus *Viola*, which includes the small, solid-colored violets and the larger-flowered, often multicolored violas and PANSIES. Many *Viola* species have two types of flowers: the showy spring flower is infertile; the less conspicuous summer flower is self-fertilizing. The best-known species of *Viola* have heart-shaped leaves. The family Violaceae, to which *Viola* belongs, has members worldwide; they are typically small trees and shrubs. See also AFRICAN VIOLET.

violin Family of bowed STRINGED INSTRUMENTS consisting of the violin, VIOLA, CELLO, and DOUBLE BASS. The instrument called the violin is its highest-pitched member. It has a fretless fingerboard, four strings, and a distinctively shaped wooden body whose "waist" permits freedom of bowing. It is held on the shoulder and bowed with the right hand. It evolved in Italy in the 16th-17th cent. from the medieval fiddle and other instruments; later innovations increased its tonal power. With its brilliance, agility, and singing tone, the violin has been immensely important in Western art music, and it has the largest repertoire of any stringed instrument, including thousands of concertos. It is the foundation of the symphony orchestra, which today usually includes 20–26 violins. It is played as a folk instrument in many countries, folk violins being often called fiddles.

Viollet-le-Duc \ˌvē-ə-'lä-lə-'dük\, **Eugène-Emmanuel** (1814–1879) French GOTHIC REVIVAL architect, restorer, and writer. Placed in charge of restoring the abbey church at Vézelay (1840), he also assisted in restoring the Sainte-Chapelle (1840) and NOTRE-DAME DE PARIS (1845), and supervised the restoration of many other medieval buildings, including Amiens Cathedral (1849) and the fortifications of Carcassonne (1852). He is most distinguished for his writings, which include the *Descriptive Dictionary of French Architecture from the 11th to the 16th Century* (10 vols., 1854–68) and *Discourses on Architecture* (1858–72). His theories of rational architectural design linked the revivalism of the Romantic period to 20th-cent. FUNCTIONALISM and influenced the architects of the CHICAGO SCHOOL.

violoncello See CELLO

viper Any of about 200 species (family Viperidae) of venomous snakes in two subfamilies: Viperinae (Old World vipers of Europe, Asia, and Africa) and Crotalinae (pit vipers). Two long, hollow, venom-injecting fangs attached to the viper's upper jaw can be folded back in the mouth when not in use. Vipers range in length from less than 12 in. (30 cm) to more than 10 ft (3 m). Many Old World vipers are terrestrial; a few are arboreal or burrowers.

viral diseases \'vī-rəl\ Diseases caused by VIRUSES. Long-term IMMUNITY usually follows viral CHILDHOOD DISEASES. The common COLD recurs because many different viruses cause it and immunity against one does not protect against others. Some viruses mutate fast enough to reinfect people after recovery (see INFLUENZA) or to keep the IMMUNE SYSTEM from fighting them off (see AIDS). Certain CANCERS are caused by viruses. VACCINES can prevent some viral diseases. Most antiviral drugs work only against specific viruses; ANTIBIOTICS are never effective. See also POLIOMYELITIS, SMALLPOX.

Virchow \\'fir-kō\\, **Rudolf (Carl)** (1821–1902) German pathologist, anthropologist, and statesman. In 1847 he cofounded the PATHOLOGY journal now named for him (*Virchows Archiv*). He held university chairs of pathological anatomy for 53 years. He was elected to the Prussian Diet and founded the Progressive Party. He coined the terms thrombosis and embolism while disproving the theory that PHLEBITIS causes most diseases. His work supported emerging ideas on cell division and metabolism. His rejection of the theory that bacteria cause disease and of Ignaz SEMMELWEIS's advocacy of antisepsis delayed the use of antiseptics. Virchow founded two anthropological societies and accompanied Heinrich SCHLIEMANN to Troy (1879) and Egypt (1888).

vireo \\'vir-ē-ˌō\\ Any of 42 species (family Vireonidae) of New World songbirds with a stout, slightly notched, hooktipped bill. Vireos are 4–7 in. (10–18 cm) long and are plain gray or greenish, with white or yellow touches. They glean insects from foliage, repeating loud short phrases over and over. The red-eyed vireo (*Vireo olivaceus*), which breeds from S Canada to Argentina, is 6 in. (15 cm) long and has a black-outlined, white eye stripe that contrasts with its gray crown.

Virgil *or* **Vergil** \\'vər-jil\\ *Latin* Publius Vergilius Maro (70–19 B.C.) Greatest of Roman poets. Son of a prosperous farmer, Virgil eventually became a member of the circle around Octavian (later Caesar AUGUSTUS) and was patronized by MAECENAS. His poetry reflects the turbulence in Italy during a period of civil war and the subsequent trend toward stability. His 10 pastoral *Eclogues* (42–37 B.C.) may be read as a prophecy of tranquility. The *Georgics* (37–30 B.C.) point toward a Golden Age in the form of the repopulation of rural Italy and the rehabilitation of agriculture. His great epic, the *Aeneid* (begun c.29 B.C., but unfinished at his death), is a celebration of the founding of Rome by the legendary AENEAS; it is one of the masterpieces of world literature. In later centuries his works were regarded in the Roman empire as virtually sacred, and he was taken up reverently by Christians as well, including DANTE. Virgil's influence on European literature is perhaps second only to HOMER's.

Virgin Birth Fundamental doctrine of orthodox Christianity that JESUS had no natural father but was conceived by MARY through the power of the HOLY SPIRIT. The doctrine was universally accepted in the Christian church by the 2nd cent. It remains a basic article of belief in Roman Catholicism, Eastern Orthodoxy, most Protestant churches, and Islam. The doctrine of Mary's perpetual virginity is accepted by the Orthodox and Roman Catholic churches. See also IMMACULATE CONCEPTION.

Virginia *officially* **Commonwealth of Virginia** State (pop., 2000: 7,078,000), E U.S. Located on the central Atlantic seaboard, it covers an area of 40,767 sq mi (105,586 sq km); its capital is RICHMOND. The coastal plain, also known as the Tidewater, lies in the east, the Piedmont, in mid-state, and the BLUE RIDGE and APPALACHIAN MOUNTAINS in the west. The POTOMAC, Shenandoah, James, and ROANOKE rivers flow through the state. It was inhabited by American Indians when futile attempts were made by Sir Walter RALEIGH to found settlements 1584–87. Britain's first American colony was founded there in 1607 at JAMESTOWN. On the eve of the AMERICAN REVOLUTION, it was the largest of the 13 colonies and one of the first to resist the British STAMP ACT. Its citizens were among the leaders of the Revolutionary period and later contributed four of the country's first five presidents. In 1788 it became the 10th state to ratify the U.S. Constitution. Though slavery was outlawed, it continued to be an important part of Virginia's economy, and helped precipitate Nat TURNER's insurrection (1831). It passed an ordinance of secession in 1861, but

the W part of the state refused to secede: it split off to become W. Virginia in 1863. Virginia, whose capital of Richmond was also the capital of the Confederacy, bore the brunt of military action during the AMERICAN CIVIL WAR. It was readmitted to the Union in 1870. Strife over state debt took over political life for the next decades, but after World War I the state's prosperity increased. World War II brought thousands to its military camps and caused the NORFOLK area to boom. The federal government is Virginia's largest employer, while manufacturing is the second largest. Its port of HAMPTON ROADS is one of the nation's leading ports. Tourism is important; its many historical sites include Colonial WILLIAMSBURG, George WASHINGTON's MOUNT VERNON, Thomas JEFFERSON's MONTICELLO, the Civil War battlefields, and Gen. R. E. LEE's house, now in Arlington National Cemetery. The College of WILLIAM AND MARY (founded 1693) is the country's second-oldest college; the Univ. of VIRGINIA was largely the creation of Thomas Jefferson.

Virginia, University of Public university founded in Charlottesville by Thomas JEFFERSON. It was chartered in 1819 and opened in 1825. Jefferson designed its famously beautiful campus and buildings, planned the curriculum, and selected the faculty. By the time of the Civil War, the university was second only to Harvard in size of faculty and student body. It first admitted women in 1970. It has highly regarded schools of law, medicine, architecture, and other disciplines. Total enrollment is about 22,000.

Virginia and Kentucky Resolutions Measures passed by the legislatures of Virginia and Kentucky in 1798–99 as a protest against the ALIEN AND SEDITION ACTS. Drafted anonymously by James MADISON and Thomas JEFFERSON, they protested limitations on civil liberties and declared the right of states to decide on the constitutionality of federal legislation. Southern states later used the measures to support the theories of NULLIFICATION and SECESSION.

Virginia Beach City (pop., 2000: 425,000), SE Virginia. It is situated on the Atlantic Ocean and CHESAPEAKE BAY. Founded in 1887, it developed as a resort after a railroad was built linking it with NORFOLK. After World War I it became an important base in the national coastal defense system. Its economy is based on tourism and military installations. The Cape Henry Lighthouse (1791) is nearby.

Virginia deer See WHITE-TAILED DEER

Virgin Islands, British Dependent territory (pop., 1993 est.: 18,000) of the United Kingdom, E Caribbean Sea. Part of the island chain of the Virgin Islands, which are divided between the U.K. and the U.S., it consists of four larger islands (Tortola, Anegada, Virgin Gorda, and Jost Van Dyke) and many smaller uninhabited islands. The chief town and port is Road Town on Tortola. Most islanders are black or mulatto, the descendants of African slaves. English is the chief language and Protestantism is the chief religion. The islands are generally hilly, and many have lagoons with coral reefs and barrier beaches. Tourism is the mainstay of the economy. The islands were an early haunt for pirates, and Tortola was held by Dutch buccaneers until it was taken by English sugarcane planters in 1666; it was annexed by the British-administered LEEWARD ISLANDS in 1672. See also VIRGIN ISLANDS OF THE U.S..

Virgin Islands of the U.S. Unincorporated U.S. island territory, at the E end of the Greater ANTILLES, NE CARIBBEAN SEA. It consists of the islands of ST. CROIX, St. John, and ST. THOMAS and about 50 small islets. Area: 136 sq mi (352 sq km). Population, 2000: 121,000. Capital: CHARLOTTE AMALIE. About 80% of the population is black or mulatto. The people are U.S. citizens and elect a nonvoting representative to the U.S. House of Representatives, but they do not vote in U.S. national elections. Languages: English (official), French, Spanish. Religions: Protestantism, Roman Catholicism. Tourism dominates the economy. The hilly islands were inhabited by the CARIBS when Christopher COLUMBUS landed on St. Croix in 1493. St. Croix was later occupied by the Dutch, English, French, and Spanish. Denmark occupied St. Thomas, St. John, and St. Croix and established them as a Danish colony in 1754. The U.S. purchased the Danish W. Indies in 1917 for $25 million and changed the name to the Virgin Islands. In 1954 the current

T
U
V

governmental structure was adopted, and in 1970 the first popularly elected governor took office. The area suffered extensive damage by hurricane in 1995.

Virgo cluster Closest large cluster of galaxies about 50 million light-years away toward the constellation Virgo. Its gravity has slowed the Milky Way's motion away from it by about 125 mi/second (200 km/second) since the BIG BANG. About 200 bright galaxies and thousands of faint ones reside in it. The giant elliptical galaxy M87 (Virgo A), near its center, is one of the strongest radio sources in the sky and a powerful X-ray source. Images of M87's ACTIVE GALACTIC NUCLEUS (1994) showed that a supermassive BLACK HOLE is likely present.

virion \'vī-rē-ˌän\ Entire VIRUS particle, consisting of an outer protein shell (called a capsid) and an inner core of NUCLEIC ACID (either RNA or DNA). The core gives the virus infectivity, and the capsid provides specificity (i.e., determines which organisms the virus can infect). If the capsid is further encased by a fatty membrane, the virion can be inactivated by exposure to a solvent such as ether or chloroform. Virions of most PLANT VIRUSES are rod-shaped.

viroid \'vī-ˌroid\ Infectious particle that is smaller than any known VIRUS. The particle consists of an extremely small circular RNA molecule that lacks the protein coat of a virus. Viroids appear to be transmitted mechanically from one cell to another. They are of much interest because of their subviral nature and their unknown mode of action. Viroids are agents of certain plant diseases; whether they occur in animal cells is uncertain.

virology \vī-'rä-lə-jē\ Branch of microbiology that deals with the study of VIRUSES. In 1892 a Russian bacteriologist observed that the agent of tobacco mosaic disease could pass through a filter that did not permit the passage of BACTERIA. Modern virology began in the early 20th cent., when BACTERIOPHAGES were discovered. Direct visualization of viruses became possible after the electron microscope was introduced (c.1940).

virtual reality Use of computer modeling and SIMULATION to enable a person to interact with an artificial sensory environment. A computer-generated environment simulates reality by means of interactive devices that send and receive information and are worn as goggles, headsets, gloves, or body suits. The illusion of being in the created environment (telepresence) is accomplished by motion sensors that pick up the user's movements and adjust his or her view accordingly. The basis of the technology emerged in the 1960s in flight simulators. It came of age in the 1980s and is now used in games, exhibits, and aerospace simulators, while development goes forward in medicine and biotechnology, engineering, design, and marketing.

virtue Practical dispositions in conformity with standards of excellence or with principles of PRACTICAL REASON. The seven cardinal virtues of the Christian tradition include the four "natural," or cardinal, virtues inculcated in the old pagan world, and the three "theological" virtues specifically prescribed in Christianity. The natural virtues, which are listed by Plato, are prudence, temperance, fortitude, and justice. To these St. PAUL added the theological virtues of faith, hope, and love—virtues which, in Christian teaching, do not originate naturally in humanity but are instead imparted by God through Christ.

virus Microscopic, simple infectious agent that can multiply only in living cells of animals, plants, or bacteria. Viruses are much smaller than BACTERIA, and consist of single- or double-stranded NUCLEIC ACID (DNA or RNA) surrounded by a PROTEIN shell called a capsid; some viruses also have an outer envelope composed of LIPIDS and proteins. They vary in shape. The two main classes are RNA viruses (including RETROVIRUSES, PICORNAVIRUSES, and RHABDOVIRUSES) and DNA viruses (including ADENOVIRUSES and POXVIRUSES). Outside of a living cell, a virus is inactive, but within a host cell it becomes active, capable of taking over the cell's metabolic machinery for the production of new virus particles (VIRIONS). Some animal viruses produce latent infections, (compare LYSOGENY), becoming periodically active in acute episodes, as in the case of the HERPES SIMPLEX viruses. Many human diseases, including INFLUENZA, the common COLD, and AIDS, as well as many

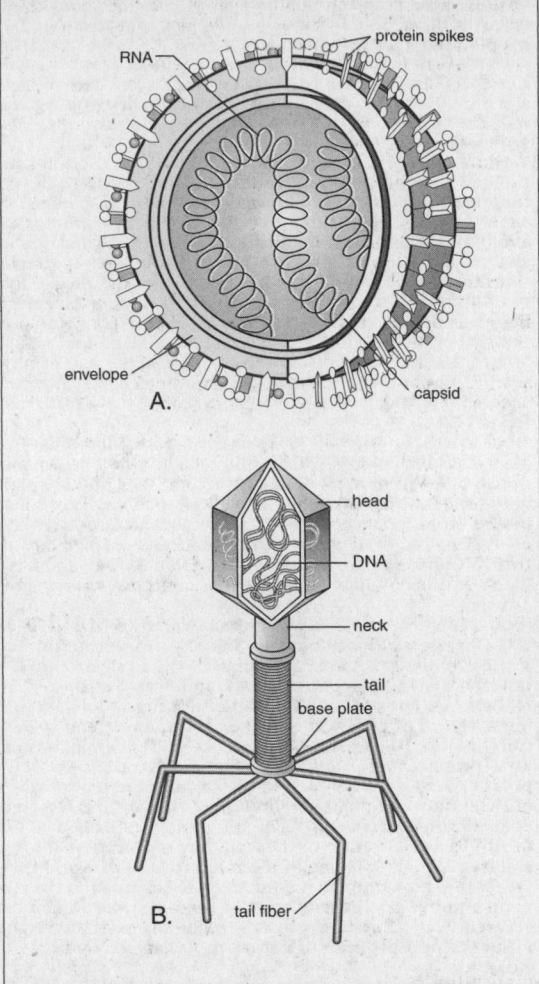

Virus A. Influenza virus. The influenza virus possesses both a protein shell (capsid) and a lipid and protein envelope. The protein spikes of the envelope facilitate adherence and entry into the host cell. The capsid proteins determine the influenza type (A, B, C), and the highly variable proteins of the spikes and envelope determine the different strains within each type. B. Bacteriophage (bacterial virus). This bacteriophage has a capsid shaped like an icosahedron (with 20 sides). The tail fibers attach the virus to the bacterium, bringing the base plate into contact with the surface. The tail contracts and DNA from the head is injected into the host.

economically important plant and animal diseases, are caused by viruses. Successful VACCINES have been developed to combat such viral diseases as MEASLES, MUMPS, POLIOMYELITIS, SMALLPOX, and RUBELLA. Drug therapy is generally not useful in controlling established viral infections. See also ARBOVIRUS, BACTERIOPHAGE, CYTOMEGALOVIRUS, EPSTEIN-BARR VIRUS, HANTAVIRUS, MYXOVIRUS, PAPILLOMAVIRUS, PLANT VIRUS, RHINOVIRUS.

virus, computer See COMPUTER VIRUS

Visayan Islands \vi-'sī-ən\ Group of islands, central Philippines. Covering 23,944 sq mi (62,015 sq km), they make up the central group of the Philippine archipelago. The main islands are Bohol, CEBU, LEYTE, Masbate, NEGROS, Panay, and SAMAR. Agriculture and fishing are important. The major urban center is CEBU city.

Visconti \vēs-'kōn-tē\, **Gian Galeazzo** *known as* **Count of Valor** (1351–1402) Leader of Milan who brought the Visconti dynasty to its height. The son of the coruler of Milan, he united all the Visconti lands, added the March of Treviso (1387), and became a prince of the Holy Roman Empire through bribery. By 1402 he held Pisa, Siena, Umbria, and Bologna. He was close to becoming ruler of all N Italy and was planning an attack on Florence when he died of the plague.

Visconti, Luchino *orig.* Don Luchino Visconti, conte (Count) di Modrone (1906–1976) Italian film and theater director. An assistant to Jean RENOIR from 1935, he directed his first film, *Ossessione* (1942), in a neorealistic style. His later films included the documentary-style drama *La terra trema* (1948), *Rocco and His Brothers* (1960), *The Leopard* (1963), *The Damned* (1969), and *Death in Venice* (1971). As a stage director, he introduced to Italy works by Jean COCTEAU, Arthur MILLER, and Tennessee WILLIAMS, and he staged operas starring Maria CALLAS.

viscosity \vis-'kä-sə-tē\ Resistance of a fluid to a change in shape or to movement of neighboring portions relative to one another, in opposition to flow. It may also be thought of as internal FRICTION between molecules. Viscosity must be taken into account when fluids are used in lubrication or transported in pipelines. It also determines the liquid flow in spraying, injection molding, and surface coating. The viscosity of liquids decreases rapidly with an increase in temperature, but that of gases increases with an increase in temperature.

viscount \'vī-ˌkaůnt\ European title of nobility, ranking immediately below a COUNT, or earl. The wife of a viscount is a viscountess. In the Carolingian period, the *vicecomes* were deputies of the counts *(comes)*. In the 11th cent. most of Normandy was divided into *vicomtés*, but the viscountcy was not introduced into England until the 15th cent.

Vishnu \'vish-nü\ Principal Hindu deity worshiped as the protector and preserver of the world and restorer of DHARMA. He is known chiefly through his AVATARS, particularly RAMA and KRISHNA. In theory, he manifests himself whenever he is needed to fight evil. His various names, numbering about 1,000, are repeated as acts of devotion by his worshipers.

Visigoths \'vi-zə-ˌgäths\ W division of the GOTHS. Separated from the OSTROGOTHS (E Goths) in the 4th cent. A.D., they crossed the Danube into the Roman empire. Oppressed by Roman taxation, they revolted and plundered the Balkan provinces, defeating the Romans at the Battle of ADRIANOPLE (378). THEODOSIUS I settled them in Moesia (382) to defend the frontier. Converted to Arian Christianity, they left Moesia in 395 under ALARIC I and invaded Greece and Italy, sacking Rome (410) and settling in S Gaul and Spain (415). Recalled from Spain by Constantius III, they lost their first king, Theodoric I, in a battle against ATTILA (451). They were federates of Rome until King Euric declared independence (475). He extended their kingdom to include modern SW France and most of Spain. In 507 they were defeated by the FRANKS under CLOVIS I; retaining only SEPTIMANIA, they held it and much of Spain until defeated by the Muslims in 711.

vision See PHOTORECEPTION

Vistula River \'vis-chə-lə\ *Polish* **Wisla** \'vē-swä\ River, Poland. It rises in the CARPATHIAN MTNS. of SW Poland, flows through WARSAW and Torun, then empties into the BALTIC SEA at GDANSK. At 651 mi (1,047 km) it is the nation's longest river; its tributaries include the BUG.

vitamin ORGANIC COMPOUND required in small amounts in the diet to maintain normal metabolic functions. Many vitamins act as or are converted to coenzymes. They neither provide energy nor are incorporated into tissues. Water-soluble vitamins (VITAMIN B COMPLEX, VITAMIN C) are excreted quickly. Fat-soluble vitamins (VITAMIN A, VITAMIN D, VITAMIN E, and VITAMIN K) require BILE salts for absorption and are stored in the body. Deficiency of specific vitamins can lead to diseases (including BERIBERI, NEURAL TUBE DEFECT, PERNICIOUS ANEMIA, RICKETS, and SCURVY). Excess amounts, especially of fat-soluble vitamins, can also be dangerous. Several vitamins are now known to support the IMMUNE SYSTEM. Most vitamins are adequately supplied by a balanced diet, but people with higher requirements may need supplements.

vitamin A Fat-soluble ALCOHOL, most abundant in fish and especially in fish-liver oils. It is not found in plants, but many vegetables and fruits contain CAROTENES, which are readily converted in the body to vitamin A. It functions directly in vision, especially night vision. Humans require vitamin A in very small amounts (1 mg a day is recommended for adults). Unlike carotenes, it is toxic to the liver in large amounts and is readily destroyed by exposure to heat, light, or air.

vitamin B complex Water-soluble organic compounds with loosely similar properties, distribution in natural sources, and physiological functions. Most are coenzymes, and all appear essential to the metabolic processes of all animal life. They include THIAMINE (B_1), RIBOFLAVIN (B_2), NIACIN (B_3), pyridoxine (B_6), pantothenic acid, FOLIC ACID, BIOTIN, and cyanocobalamin (B_{12}); some authorities also include CHOLINE, carnitine, lipoic acid, myoinositol, and *para*-aminobenzoic acid. Good sources of vitamin B_6 are vegetable fats, whole-grain cereals, legumes, yeast, muscle meats, liver, and fish. Pantothenic acid is synthesized by bacteria normally occurring in the intestine. Vitamin B_{12} prevents PERNICIOUS ANEMIA; sources are milk, meat, liver, eggs, and fish.

vitamin C *or* **ascorbic acid** Water-soluble organic compound, important in many aspects of animal METABOLISM. Most animals produce it in their bodies, but humans, other primates, and guinea pigs need it in the diet to prevent SCURVY. It is essential in COLLAGEN synthesis, wound healing, and other processes. It can shorten and reduce the symptoms of the COMMON COLD and is now widely recognized to prevent colds as well. It works as an ANTIOXIDANT in the body and is used as a preservative. It is easily destroyed by heat or oxygen. Excellent sources are citrus fruits and dark-green vegetables.

vitamin D Any of a group of fat-soluble ALCOHOLS important in CALCIUM METABOLISM in animals to form strong bones and teeth and prevent RICKETS and OSTEOPOROSIS. In humans, vitamin D is formed by action of sunlight on sterols (see STEROID) in the skin. It occurs in fish-liver oils and is added to margarine, milk, and cereals for the benefit of those who may not get enough sunlight. Because the body cannot excrete it, prolonged high intake can cause a toxic reaction.

vitamin E *or* **tocopherol** \tō-'kä-fə-ˌrȯl\ Any of a group of related fat-soluble organic compounds with two rings and 26–29 carbon atoms. Alpha, the most potent, occurs in certain plant oils and leaves of green vegetables. Vitamin E acts as an ANTIOXIDANT in body tissues and may prolong life by slowing oxidative destruction of membranes. Besides uses in foods, nutritional research, and supplements, tocopherols are used to retard rancidity in FATS.

vitamin K Any of several fat-soluble compounds essential for the clotting of blood. A deficiency of vitamin K in the body leads to an increase in clotting time. In 1929 a fat-soluble substance present in green leafy vegetables was found to be required for coagulation of blood. Several related compounds having vitamin-K activity have been isolated and synthesized. Vitamin K_1 is synthesized by plants; vitamin K_2 is of microbial origin and is the important form in mammalian tissue. All other forms of vitamin K are converted to vitamin K_2 in the body.

vitiligo \ˌvit-ᵊl-'ī-ˌgō\ *or* **leukoderma** SKIN disorder manifested by smooth, white spots. Though the pigment-making cells of the skin are structurally intact, they have lost the ability to synthesize the pigment MELANIN. Those with vitiligo (about 1% of adults) are usually in good general health, but vitiligo presents a cosmetic problem that can be serious in dark-skinned people. Normal skin color rarely returns, and there is no known cure.

Vitoria \vē-'tōr-ē-ə\ City (pop., 1998 est.: 216,000), capital of BASQUE COUNTRY autonomous community, NE Spain. Founded by the Visigothic king Leovigild in 581, it was captured by Alfonso VIII in 1200 and incorporated into his kingdom. In 1813 the future duke of WELLINGTON defeated the French there, driving them from Spain and effectively ending the PENINSULAR WAR. A rapidly growing manufacturing center, it retains several medieval buildings.

TUV

vitriol, oil of See SULFURIC ACID

Vitruvius \və-ˈtrü-vē-əs\ *in full* Marcus Vitruvius Pollio (fl.1st cent. B.C.) Roman architect, engineer, and author of the celebrated treatise *De architectura,* a handbook for Roman architects covering almost every aspect of architecture and city planning. His prefaces promote his desire to preserve the Classical Greek tradition in the design of temples and public buildings. His work was the chief authority on ancient CLASSICAL ARCHITECTURE throughout the antique revival of the Renaissance, the classical phase of the baroque, and the Neoclassical period.

Vitsyebsk \ˈvēt-syipsk\ *or* **Vitebsk** \ˈvē-tipsk\ City (pop., 1998 est.: 364,000), NE Belarus. First mentioned in 1021, it was the chief town of an independent principality for some 200 years. It passed to Lithuania in 1320, later to Poland, and then to Russia in 1772. Over the years it suffered destruction by the Poles, the Swedes, Napoleon in 1812, and the Germans in World War II. It is now a major industrial center.

Vivaldi \vi-ˈväl-dē\, **Antonio (Lucio)** (1678–1741) Italian composer. Taught violin by his father, he was ordained a priest in 1703. He spent most of his career teaching violin and leading the orchestra at a Venetian girls' orphanage. By 1720 he had become involved in opera as both composer (he would write more than 40) and impresario. His concertos were highly influential in setting the genre's three-movement form and its characteristic treatment of thematic material, and he popularized such effects as pizzicato and muting. His *L'estro armonico* (1711), a collection of concerti grossi, attracted international attention. The violin concertos of *La stravaganza* (c.1714) were eagerly awaited, as were its successors, including *The Four Seasons* (1725). In all he wrote over 500 concertos. Vivaldi's highly imaginative works exercised a strong influence on J. S. BACH.

Vivarini family \ˌvē-vä-ˈrē-nē\ Family of 15th-cent. Venetian painters. Antonio Vivarini (c.1415–c.1480) collaborated from 1441 with his brother-in-law, Giovanni d'Alemagna (d.1450), on altarpieces, four of which survive in the churches of San Zaccaria (1443) and San Pantalon (1444), and on a large three-part canvas in the Accademia (1446). Antonio's younger brother and pupil Bartolomeo (1432?–after 1500) collaborated with Antonio after 1450. His work was imitative of Andrea MANTEGNA. His most distinguished independent works include the altarpieces in the churches of Sts. Giovanni e Paolo (1473), Santa Maria dei Frari (1474), and San Giovanni Bragora (1478) and in the Accademia (1477). Antonio's son Alvise (c.1445–c.1505) came under the influence of Giovanni BELLINI, with whom he worked on paintings (now lost) for the Doges' Palace (1488). The overlapping careers of Antonio, Bartolomeo, and Alvise recapitulate the overall development of Venetian painting from the late Gothic period to the threshold of the High Renaissance.

vivisection Operation on a living animal for experimental rather than healing purposes; more broadly, all experimentation on live animals. It is opposed by many as cruelty and supported by others on the ground that it advances medicine; a middle position is to oppose unnecessarily cruel practices, use alternatives when possible, and restrict experiments to necessary medical research. Testing chemicals on animals to find the lethal dose still occurs despite alternative methods (computer simulations, TISSUE CULTURE tests). An antivivisection movement in the late 19th cent. broadened its scope to include prevention of all cruelty to animals and later gave rise to the ANIMAL-RIGHTS MOVEMENT.

vizier \və-ˈzir\ *Arabic* wazir. Chief minister of the ABBASID caliphs, and later a high government official in various Muslim countries. In the OTTOMAN EMPIRE, the title could be held by several people at once; under MEHMED II the position of grand vizier, the absolute representative of the sultan, was created. In pharaonic Egypt, a vizier was a civil officer who held viceregal power.

Vlad III Tepes \ˈvläd...ˈtse-pesh\ *or* **Vlad the Impaler** (1431?–1476) Ruler of WALACHIA (1448, 1456–62, 1476). He succeeded his father, Vlad II Dracul ("dragon"). He gained the throne decisively in 1456 with the help of Janos HUNYADI. He fought the Turkish invasions of Walachia and built many fortifications to hold them back, including the fortress of Poenari with its stairway of 1,400 steps. Though an effective administrator and military leader, he was notorious for cruel depravities. In establishing his domination over the Walachian nobility, he tortured to death many thousands of men, women, and children by impaling them upright on thin stakes. His epithet Dracula ("son of the dragon") was used by Bram STOKER for the Romanian vampire count in his famous novel.

Vladimir I \ˈvla-də-mər, vlə-ˈdē-mir\, **St.** *Russian* Vladimir Svyatoslavich (956?–1015) Grand prince of Kiev (980–1015). He became prince of Novgorod in 970, and later seized Kiev from his brother. He consolidated the Kievan realm from Ukraine to the Baltic Sea by 980. Originally a pagan, Vladimir made a pact (c.987) with BASIL II, providing him with military aid in exchange for marriage to Basil's sister and promising to convert to Christianity. He adopted the Byzantine rite for his realm, determining the course of Russian Christianity.

Vladivostok \ˌvla-də-və-ˈstäk, ˌvla-də-ˈväs-ˌtäk\ Seaport city (pop., 1997 est.: 623,000), SE Russia in Asia. Founded in 1860, it became the main Russian Pacific naval base in 1872 and grew rapidly as a military base after the RUSSIAN REVOLUTION OF 1917. Its military importance was such that it was closed to foreign shipping from the late 1950s. After the collapse of the U.S.S.R. in 1991, it reemerged as a commercial port. It is the E terminus of the TRANS-SIBERIAN RAILROAD, and the cultural center of the Russian Far East.

Vlaminck \vlə-ˈmaŋk\, **Maurice de** (1876–1958) French painter. Noted for his brash temperament as well as his flair for landscapes, he began in 1900 to share a studio with André DERAIN, a friend from childhood. His experiments with pure, intense color applied in thick daubs earned him association with FAUVISM, but by 1908 he had turned to painting landscapes of thickly applied whites, grays, and deep blues, and his style moved closer to that of Paul CÉZANNE. About 1915 he began to develop a personal, strongly stated style that placed him solidly in the realm of French EXPRESSIONISM.

Vltava River \ˈvəl-tə-və\ *German* **Moldau** River, Czech Republic. It rises in SW BOHEMIA and flows southeast, then north across Bohemia to empty into the ELBE RIVER. At 270 mi (435 km), it is the nation's longest river.

vocal cord Either of two folds of mucous membrane that extend across the interior cavity of the LARYNX and are primarily responsible for voice production. Sound is produced by their vibration in response to the passage between them of air from the lungs. The pitch of sound varies with the degree of vocal-cord tension. Sounds are then modified by the tongue, palate, and lips to produce SPEECH. When at rest, the vocal cords lie apart, forming a V-shaped opening (glottis) through which air is breathed. Inflammation (as from excessive use) affects the contraction of the vocal cords, resulting in hoarseness.

vodka Colorless DISTILLED LIQUOR usually made from a grain mash (generally RYE or WHEAT). Potato vodka originated in Russia in the 14th cent. Vodka is highly neutral, most flavoring substances being eliminated during distillation and filtration. Distilled water is usually added before bottling in order to lower alcohol content to 40–43% by volume (80–86 proof). Vodka is not aged. It is traditionally consumed unmixed and chilled, in small glasses; in the U.S. and elsewhere it is often used in mixed drinks.

vodun \vō-ˈdün\ *or* **voodoo** National folk religion of Haiti. It combines theological and magical elements of AFRICAN RELIGIONS and ritual elements of ROMAN CATHOLICISM. Practitioners profess belief in a supreme God but give more attention to a large number of spirits called the *loa,* which can be identified as local or African gods, deified ancestors, or Catholic saints. The *loa* attach themselves to individuals or families, for whom they act as helpers, protectors, and guides in return for ritual services. A priest or priestess leads devotees in ritual ceremonies involving song, drumming, dance, prayer, food preparation, and animal sacrifice. The *loa* possess worshipers during services. A well-known aspect of vodun is the ZOMBIE. See also MACUMBA, SANTERÍA.

voice In GRAMMAR, the form of a verb indicating the relation between the participants (subject, object) in a narrated event and the event itself. English grammar distinguishes between the active voice ("The hunter killed the bear") and the passive voice ("The bear was killed by the hunter"). In the active voice, the emphasis is on the agent performing the action named, whereas the passive voice indicates that the subject receives the action.

voice box See LARYNX

voice mail Electronic system for recording telephone messages. Typically, the caller hears a prerecorded message and then has an opportunity to leave a message in return. The person called can retrieve the message at a later time by entering a code. Voice mail is distinguished from an answering machine by its ability to provide service to multiple phone lines and by the more sophisticated functions that it offers.

voice recognition See SPEECH RECOGNITION

Vojvodina \ˈvȯi-vȯ-ˌdē-nä\ Province (pop., 1997 est.: 1,954,000), Yugoslavia, within the republic of SERBIA. Its chief city is NOVI SAD. Slavs settled there in the 6th–7th cent., followed by Hungarian nomads. Ottoman Turks controlled the region from the early 16th cent. to the late 18th cent., when it became part of the Austrian HABSBURG empire. By then it was a center of Serbian Orthodox culture. In 1849 portions of the historical regions of Backa and Banat were united as Vojvodina under Croatia-Slavonia. In 1867 it reverted to Hungary, and in 1918 it was made part of the kingdom of Serbs, Croats, and Slovenes (later Yugoslavia). In 1945 it became an autonomous province of the Serb republic, but in 1989 Slobodan MILOSEVIC rescinded this status. In 1999, after receiving tens of thousands of Serbian refugees from KOSOVO, it demanded restoration of its autonomy, and in 2002 partial autonomy was granted.

volcanic glass Any glassy rock formed from LAVA or MAGMA that has cooled suddenly. Its chemical composition is close to that of GRANITE. Such molten material may reach very low temperatures without crystallizing; its high viscosity also inhibits crystallization.

volcanism \ˈväl-kə-ˌni-zəm\ *or* **vulcanism** Any of various processes and phenomena associated with the surface discharge of molten rock or hot water and steam, including VOLCANOES, GEYSERS, and FUMAROLES. Most active volcanoes occur where two plates converge and one overrides the other (see PLATE TECTONICS). Volcanism can also occur along an OCEANIC RIDGE. A few volcanoes occur within plates, far from margins, as a plate moves over a HOT SPOT.

volcano Vent in the crust of the earth from which molten rock, debris, and steam issue. Fissure volcanoes occur along fractures in the crust and may extend for many miles; LAVA is ejected relatively quietly and forms enormous plains or plateaus of volcanic rock. Central volcanoes have a single vertical lava pipe and develop a conical profile; lava flows from the throat and follows the easiest path downhill. Often highly viscous lava clogs the throat, causing a pressure buildup followed by a violent eruption, which may completely remove the top of the cone. See diagram, right.

volcanology *or* **vulcanology** Scientific discipline concerned with volcanic phenomena. It deals with the formation, distribution, and classification of VOLCANOES, as well as the LAVA, dust, ash, and gas ejected during an eruption, and the relationships between volcanic eruptions and other large-scale geologic processes, such as mountain building and earthquakes. One of its chief aims is to determine the causes of volcanic eruptions in order to predict them. Another aim is to obtain data that may aid in locating commercially valuable deposits of ores.

vole Any burrowing RODENT (family Cricetidae) with a blunt snout, small ears, and short limbs. Most species are herbivorous and are found throughout N. America and Eurasia. The approximately 45 species of the genus *Microtus,* also called meadow mice, are 4–10 in. (10–26 cm) long, including the tail. About 10 species of pine voles inhabit swamps, fields, and hardwood forests. Water voles are found only in Eurasia and usually live near a stream, ditch, or lake.

Volga-Baltic Waterway Series of rivers and canals, W Russia. Linking the VOLGA RIVER with the BALTIC SEA, it includes the NEVA RIVER, a canal along Lake LADOGA, and the Sheksna River past Cherepovets through the Rybinsk Reservoir.

Its total length is about 700 mi (1,100 km). Seven automatic locks were installed in 1964.

Volga River River, W Russia. Europe's longest river and the principal waterway of W Russia, it rises northwest of MOSCOW and flows 2,193 mi (3,530 km) southeastward to the CASPIAN SEA. It is used for power production, irrigation, flood control, and transportation. The river has played a sustaining role in the life of the Russian people; in Russian folklore it is called "Mother Volga."

Volga Tatar language See TATAR LANGUAGE

Volgograd *formerly (until 1925)* **Tsaritsyn** *(1925–61)* **Stalingrad** City (pop., 1997 est.: 1,005,000), SW Russia. Located on the VOLGA RIVER, it was founded as Tsaritsyn in 1589. During the RUSSIAN CIVIL WAR (1918–20), Joseph STALIN organized the city's defense against the White Russian armies, and it was later renamed in his honor. During World War II it was reduced to rubble in the Battle of STALINGRAD. Rebuilt as a manufacturing center, it is a major railroad junction and the E terminus of the Volga-Don Ship Canal.

Volkswagen AG Major German automobile manufacturer. It was founded in 1937 by the Nazi government to mass-produce a low-priced "people's car" *(Volkswagen).* After World War II it was rebuilt and within a decade it was producing half of W. Germany's motor vehicles. Marketing the small, rounded car as the Beetle massively increased sales in the 1960s, making it the leading auto import in the U.S. Competition brought Volkswagen near bankruptcy by 1974, but it rebounded with sportier models such as the Rabbit. In 1998 it introduced a new version of the Beetle. Volkswagen owns several other auto companies, including Audi and ROLLS-ROYCE.

volleyball Game played by two teams of six players each, in which an inflated ball is volleyed over a high net. Each team tries to make the ball touch the court within the opposing side's playing areas. A team may touch the ball three times before returning it. The team that first scores 15 points wins the game. Invented in 1895 by William G. Morgan in Holyoke, Mass., it soon proved to have wide appeal for both sexes in schools, playgrounds, and the armed forces. Inter-

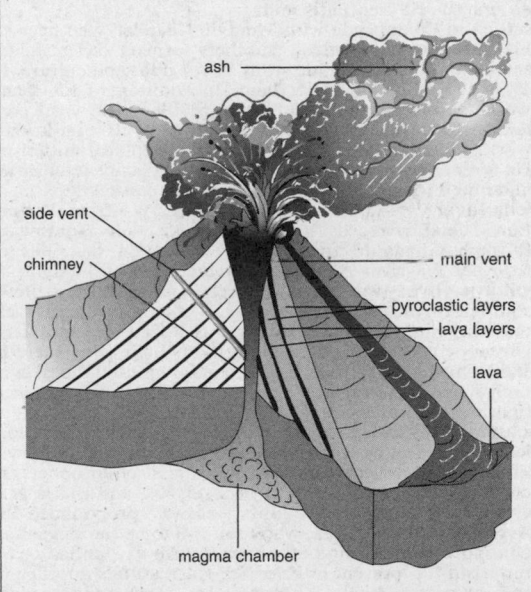

Volcano A volcano forms when magma beneath the earth's crust forces its way to the surface. Alternating layers of solidified lava and pyroclastic materials (ash and cinders) build up the typical cone-shaped volcano as they are ejected through the central vent during eruptions.

TUV

national competition began in 1913, and volleyball became an Olympic sport in 1964. Beach volleyball, with two players on a side, became an Olympic sport in 1996.

Volstead Act See PROHIBITION

Völsunga saga \ˈvœl-sůṇ-ə, ˈvōl-sůṇ-ə\ ("Saga of the Volsungs") Best of the Icelandic sagas known as *fornaldar sögur* ("sagas of antiquity"). Dating from roughly 1270, it was the first to be written down. It contains the Northern version of the story told in the *NIBELUNGENLIED*. Based on the heroic poems in the *Poetic EDDA*, it is especially valuable because it preserves in prose form some of the poems from the Edda that were lost.

Volta \ˈvōl-tə\, **Alessandro (Giuseppe Antonio Anastasio)** (1745–1827) Italian scientist. In 1775 he invented the electrophorus, a device used to generate static electricity. After Luigi GALVANI in 1780 produced an electric current by connecting two different metals with the muscle of a frog, Volta began experimenting with metals alone and found that animal tissue was not needed to produce current. He demonstrated the first electric BATTERY in 1800. The volt was named in his honor.

Voltaire \vōl-ˈter\ *orig.* François-Marie Arouet (1694–1778) French writer, one of the greatest 18th-cent. European authors. He made his name with classical tragedies and continued to write for the theater all his life. He was twice sent to the Bastille for his remarks and in 1726 was exiled to England; he returned to France in 1728 or 1729. His epic poem *La Henriade* (1728) was well received, but his lampoons of the Regency and his liberal religious opinions caused offense. *Lettres philosophiques* (1734), in which he spoke out against established religious and political systems, caused an uproar. He fled Paris and

Voltaire

settled in Champagne with Mme du Châtelet, who became his patroness and mistress, and there turned to scientific research and the systematic study of religions and culture. In 1754 he settled in Switzerland. In addition to his many works on philosophical and moral problems, he wrote *contes* ("tales") including *Zadig* (1747) and his best-known work, *Candide* (1759), a satire on philosophical optimism. He is remembered as a crusader against tyranny and bigotry and noted for his wit, satire, and critical capacity.

Volta River \ˈväl-tə, ˈvōl-tə\ River, Ghana, W Africa. The nation's chief river, it flows from Lake Volta southward through Ghana to the Bight of BENIN in the Gulf of GUINEA. The river system is 1,000 mi (1,600 km) long.

Volturno River \väl-ˈtůr-nō\ River, S central Italy. It flows southeast from the Abruzzese APENNINES, then turns west to empty into the Gulf of Gaeta. It is 109 mi (175 km) long. Giuseppe GARIBALDI defeated a Neapolitan army there in 1860. During World War II, German forces used the river as their line of defense after the fall of NAPLES; after arduous fighting, the Allies crossed it in October 1943.

voluntarism \ˈvä-lən-tə-ˌri-zəm\ Metaphysical or psychological system that assigns a more predominant role to the will than to the intellect. Christian voluntarist philosophers include St. AUGUSTINE, John DUNS SCOTUS, and Blaise PASCAL. A metaphysical voluntarism was propounded by Arthur SCHOPENHAUER, who took will to be the single, unconscious force behind all of reality. An existentialist voluntarism was present in Friedrich NIETZSCHE's doctrine of the overriding "will to power." And a pragmatic voluntarism is evident in William JAMES's reference of belief, knowledge, and truth to practical ends.

vomiting Forcible ejection of the stomach contents from the mouth, usually following NAUSEA. Causes include illness, MOTION SICKNESS, certain drugs, INNER-EAR disorders, and head injury. Two centers in the brain are believed to con-

trol it; the vomiting center initiates and controls a series of muscle contractions beginning at the small intestine and moving upward. This reaction may be set off by the chemoreceptor trigger zone, stimulated by many toxins and drugs, to rid the body of them, or by stimuli from parts of the body that may be stressed or diseased. Severe vomiting may cause dehydration, malnutrition, or esophageal wall rupture. Vomiting of blood may be a sign of bleeding ULCER or other upper digestive tract disorders. See also BULIMIA.

Vo Nguyen Giap \ˈvȯ-ˈŋūē-ən-ˈzyàp, *Engl* ˈvō-en-gī-ˈen-jē-ˈap\ (b.1912) Vietnamese military leader. A high-school friend of HO CHI MINH, he became a professor of history, and converted many colleagues and students to his political views. He fled to China in 1939 when the French banned the Indochinese Communist Party, but returned in 1941. In 1945 he led the VIET MINH forces that defeated the Japanese occupation forces. A master of guerrilla tactics, he brought French colonial rule to an end at the Battle of DIEN BIEN PHU (1954), and he led the forces of the North that defeated the U.S. and S. Vietnam in the VIETNAM WAR. He served in various roles in the postwar government of Vietnam.

Vonnegut \ˈvä-nə-ˌgət\, **Kurt, Jr.** (b.1922) U.S. novelist. Born in Indianapolis, he was captured by the Germans during World War II and survived the Allied firebombing of Dresden, an experience he made part of *Slaughterhouse-Five* (1969; film, 1972). His pessimistic and satirical novels use fantasy and science fiction to highlight the horrors and ironies of 20th-cent. civilization. They include *Player Piano* (1952), *Cat's Cradle* (1963), *Breakfast of Champions* (1973), and *Hocus Pocus* (1990). He also has written plays and collections of short stories, including *Welcome to the Monkey House* (1968).

von Neumann \vän-ˈnȯi-män\, **John** (*orig.* **Johann**) (1903–1957) Hungarian-U.S. mathematician. One of the original faculty of Princeton's Institute for Advanced Study (from 1933), he solved one of David HILBERT's 23 theoretical problems and collaborated on developing an algebraic ring with profound applications in quantum physics. During World War II he participated in the development of the ATOMIC BOMB. After the war he made major contributions to the development of high-speed computers; one of his computers was essential to the creation of the HYDROGEN BOMB. As

John von Neumann

coauthor of *Theory of Games and Economic Behavior* (1944), he was one of the founders of GAME THEORY.

voodoo See VODUN

Voronezh \və-ˈrȯ-nish\ City (pop., 1997 est.: 910,000), W Russia. It was founded in 1586 as a fortress. PETER I the Great built a naval flotilla in Voronezh for use in his campaigns against the Turks. It later became a center for the grain trade. Occupied by the Germans and largely destroyed in World War II, it was rebuilt in the postwar era. It has a range of engineering, chemical, and food-processing industries.

Voroshilov \ˌvȯr-ə-ˈshē-ˌlȯf\, **Kliment (Yefremovich)** (1881–1969) Soviet military leader. A notable commander in World War I and in the Russian Civil War, he became a close associate of Joseph STALIN and was appointed people's commissar for defense (1925). Named a marshal of the Soviet Union (1935), he reorganized the Soviet general staff, mechanized the army, and developed the air force. After the initial Soviet defeats in World War II, he was removed as defense commissar. He later chaired the Presidium of the Supreme Soviet (1953–57).

Vorster \ˈfȯr-stər\, **John** (*orig.* Balthazar Johannes) (1915–1983) S. African prime minister (1966–78). Vorster was arrested in 1942 for supporting Germany in World War II. In the 1948 elections he was rejected by the NATIONAL PARTY as too extreme, but his support grew in the 1950s. As minister of justice (1961–66) under Hendrik VERWOERD he rigidly enforced APARTHEID. When Verwoerd was assassinated, Vorster was chosen to replace him. In the 1970s he sent troops against Angola's Soviet- and Cuban-supported government. He resigned in 1978.

Vorticism \'vȯr-ti-ˌsi-zəm\ Literary and artistic movement that flourished in England 1912–15. Founded by Wyndham LEWIS, it attempted to relate art to industrialization. It opposed 19th-cent. sentimentality and extolled the energy of the machine and machine-made products, and it promoted something of a cult of sheer violence. In the visual arts, Vorticist compositions were abstract and sharp-planed. Artists involved in the movement included the poet Ezra POUND and the sculptor Jacob EPSTEIN.

Voting Rights Act Act passed by the U.S. Congress in 1965 to ensure the voting rights of African-Americans. While the Constitution's 15th Amendment had guaranteed the right to vote regardless of race since 1870, blacks in the South faced efforts to disenfranchise them (including poll taxes and literacy tests) as late as the 1960s. The act prohibited many Southern states from using literacy tests to determine eligibility to vote. Later laws prohibited literacy tests in all states and made poll taxes illegal in state and local elections.

Vouet \'vwe, *Engl* vü-'ā\, **Simon** (1590–1649) French painter. He formed his style in Italy, where he lived 1614–27. His early work was influenced by CARAVAGGIO, but works done after 1620 display more idealized figures and use more evenly diffused white light. He returned to Paris in 1627 to become first painter to Louis XIII. He dominated the city artistically for the next 15 years, introducing the Italian baroque style in France with such paintings as *St. Charles Borromeo* (c.1640). His late works display the soft, idealized modeling, sensuous forms, and bright colors for which he is best known.

vowel SPEECH sound in which air from the lungs passes through the mouth with minimal obstruction and without audible friction, like the *i* in *fit*. The word also refers to a letter representing such a sound (*a, e, i, o, u*, and sometimes *y*). In articulatory PHONETICS, vowels are classified by tongue and lip position. Single vowel sounds are monophthongs; two vowel sounds pronounced as one syllable, like the *ou* in *round*, are diphthongs.

Voyager Either of two unmanned U.S. probes launched in 1977 to study the sun's outer planets. Voyager 1 flew by JUPITER in 1979 and SATURN in 1980. Voyager 2's slower flight took it past Jupiter, Saturn, and URANUS to reach NEPTUNE in 1989. Data and images from both revealed new details about these planets and their moons and rings. They will pass beyond the solar system; Voyager 2 should operate until about 2020.

Voyageurs National Park \ˌvwä-yä-'zhər\ National park, N Minnesota. Located along the Canadian border, it was named for the area's only French-Canadian fur-trading frontiersmen. It occupies 217,892 acres (88,178 hectares) and consists of a network of streams and lakes, the largest of which is RAINY LAKE.

Vuillard \vwē-'yär\, **(Jean-) Édouard** (1868–1940) French painter, printmaker, and decorator. With Pierre BONNARD he developed the Intimist style, characterized by small paintings of daily home life, such as *Woman Sweeping* (c.1892). He was an original member of the NABIS; his *Jardins de Paris* (*Public Gardens,* 1894), a series of decorative panels, used pale light and neutral colors to create a mood of restful calm. His numerous commissions for public buildings included murals in the Palais de Chaillot (1937) and in the League of Nations building in Geneva (1939), and he also designed for the BALLETS RUSSES.

Vulcan Ancient Roman god of fire. He was the counterpart of the Greek HEPHAESTUS. Vulcan was especially associated with the destructive aspects of fire, such as volcanoes or conflagrations, and for this reason his temples were usually located outside the city. Often invoked to avert fire, he was addressed with epithets such as Mulciber ("Fire Allayer").

vulcanism See VOLCANISM

vulcanization Chemical process, discovered by Charles GOODYEAR (1839), by which the physical properties of natural or synthetic RUBBER are improved. It consists principally of heating rubber with sulfur; other substances are also added. The sulfur combines chemically with the rubber, mostly in the form of cross-links (bridges) between the long-chain molecules; however, the reactions are not fully understood. Vulcanized rubber has higher tensile strength and resistance to swelling and abrasion, and is elastic over a greater range of temperatures.

vulcanology See VOLCANOLOGY

vulture Any of 20 species of bare-headed, keen-sighted BIRDS OF PREY found in temperate and tropical regions. New World vultures (family Cathartidae) are 24–28 in. (60–70 cm) long. Old World vultures (family Accipitridae) include the smallest (20 in., or 50 cm, long) and the largest vulture species. The cinereous, or black, vulture (*Aegypius monachus*) weighs almost 30 lbs (13 kg) and has a 9-ft (2.7-m) wingspread. Most species eat carrion, garbage, and excrement. See also CONDOR, MARABOU, TURKEY VULTURE.

Vyshinsky \və-'shin-skē\, **Andrey (Yanuaryevich)** (1883–1954) Soviet politician. Appointed chief prosecutor of the Soviet Union (1935), he gained worldwide notoriety for his zeal in prosecuting the PURGE TRIALS. He supervised the annexation of Latvia (1940) and established a communist regime in Romania (1945). He later served as Soviet foreign minister (1949–53) and representative to the U.N. (1949–54), where he frequently launched bitter attacks on the U.S.

Vytautas the Great \vē-'taủ-täs\ *Lithuanian* Vytautas Didysis (1350–1430) Lithuanian ruler. Continuing a family struggle for control of Lithuania, he fought his cousin WLADYSLAW II JAGIELLO but made peace in 1384. His popularity grew until Wladyslaw was obliged to make him vice regent (1392), which allowed him to become effective ruler of Lithuania. He subdued rebellious nobles but was defeated by Mongols in the east (1399). He and Wladyslaw united Lithuania and Poland (1401) and waged war on the TEUTONIC ORDER, defeating them at the Battle of Tannenberg (1410).

W

Waals, Johannes Diederik van der See J. D. VAN DER WAALS

Wabash River \\'wȯ-ˌbash\\ River, Indiana and Illinois. Rising in W Ohio, it flows southwest across Indiana, then forms the S section of the Indiana–Illinois boundary. It empties into the OHIO RIVER after 475 mi (764 km). During the 18th cent. it was a transportation link between Louisiana and Quebec. After the WAR OF 1812, its basin was rapidly developed by settlers. After the coming of the railroads in the 1850s, navigation almost disappeared.

WAC See WOMEN'S ARMY CORPS

Wace \\'wās, 'wäs\\ (c.1100–after 1174) Anglo-Norman poet. He is known for his two verse chronicles, the *Roman de Brut* (1155) and the *Roman de Rou* (1160–74), named respectively after the reputed founders of the Britons and Normans. The *Brut* is a romanticized account of GEOFFREY OF MONMOUTH's *Historia regum Britanniae*. It was important in the development of the ARTHURIAN LEGEND, and its literary style influenced later verse romances. The *Rou* is a history of the Norman dukes.

Waco \\'wā-kō\\ City (pop., 2000: 114,000), N central Texas. Located on the BRAZOS RIVER, it was founded in 1849. After 1865 it became a river-bridge crossing on cattle trails; later its economy was based on cotton. Its diversified economy now includes manufacturing and tourism. A tornado devastated Waco in 1953. In 1993, after a 51-day standoff with federal agents, more than 70 BRANCH DAVIDIANS perished in a fire at their compound near Waco.

Wade-Davis Bill (1864) Measure passed by Congress to set RECONSTRUCTION policy, cosponsored by Sen. Benjamin Wade and Rep. Henry W. Davis to counter Pres. Abraham LINCOLN's lenient plans for readmitting Southern states after the Civil War. Supported by the RADICAL REPUBLICANS, it called for provisional military government of the seceded states, an oath of allegiance from a majority of the state's whites, and new state constitutions that would disqualify Confederate officials from holding office. Lincoln considered the bill too harsh and by pocket veto allowed it to expire.

wage-price control Setting of government guidelines to limit increases in wages and PRICES. By the extreme approach of controlling wages and prices, governments hope to control INFLATION and prevent extremes in the BUSINESS CYCLE. Regulation is strongest in countries with highly centralized methods of setting wages (e.g., The Netherlands, where wage settlements must be approved by the government and price increases are investigated). Other countries, including the U.S., have also made efforts at restraining wage and price increases, usually seeking the voluntary cooperation of management and labor. In the U.S., wage-price controls were instituted by Pres. Franklin D. ROOSEVELT during World War II and by Pres. Richard NIXON in the early 1970s, when high inflation combined with rising unemployment to create instability.

Wagner \\'wag-nər\\, **Honus** (*orig.* John Peter) (1874–1955) U.S. baseball player. Born in Mansfield (now Carnegie), Pa., he played shortstop principally for the Pittsburgh Pirates (1900–17), and coached the team from 1933 to 1951. He led the National League in batting average in eight seasons and in stolen bases five seasons. His total of 252 three-base hits remains a National League record. The "Flying Dutchman" is considered one of the greatest all-around players in baseball history.

Wagner \\'väg-nər\\, **Otto** (1841–1918) Austrian architect and teacher. In 1893 his plan for Vienna (not executed) won a major competition. Among his notable works are a number of stations for the City Railway of Vienna (1894–97). His Postal Savings Bank (1904–6), which had little decoration, is recognized as a milestone in the history of modern architecture, particularly for the curving glass roof of its central hall.

Wagner \\'väg-nər\\, **(Wilhelm) Richard** (1813–1883) German composer. His childhood was divided between Dresden and Leipzig, where he had his first composition lessons. The success of his opera *Rienzi* (1840) led him to be more adventurous in *The Flying Dutchman* (1843), and even more so in *Tannhäuser* (1845). Caught up in the political turmoil of 1848, he was forced to flee Dresden for Zurich. There he wrote influential essays, asserting that music had reached a limit after Ludwig van BEETHOVEN, and that the "artwork of the future" would unite music and theater in a *Gesamtkunstwerk* ("total artwork"). In 1850 he saw his *Lohengrin* produced. He had begun his most ambitious work, *The Ring of the Nibelung*, a four-opera cycle based on the myths of the ancient Norse sagas. The need for large-scale unity brought him to the concept of the leitmotiv, a short musical fragment that symbolizes a character, thing, or idea. He ceased work on the *Ring*'s third opera, *Siegfried,* in the throes of an adulterous love, and wrote an extraordinary opera of forbidden love, *Tristan und Isolde* (1859), which also seemed to break the bonds of tonality. He sought a German prince to support his immense artistic dreams, and LUDWIG II of Bavaria responded. Shortly thereafter, Cosima Liszt von Bülow became the mother of the first of his children; they married in 1870, after his own wife's death. He completed work on *Die Meistersinger*, the *Ring* cycle, and *Parsifal*, as he also oversaw the building of the great theater at BAYREUTH (1872–76) dedicated to his operas. His astonishing works made Wagner one of the most influential figures in the history of Western music, and indeed of Western culture.

Wagner Act *or* **National Labor Relations Act** (1935) Labor legislation passed by the U.S. Congress. Sponsored by Sen. Robert Wagner, the act protected workers' rights to form unions and to bargain collectively. A three-member National Labor Relations Board was established to supervise union elections and prohibit employers from engaging in unfair labor practices. The act is considered the most important piece of labor legislation in the 20th cent.

Wahhabi \\wȧ-'hȧb-ē\\ Member of a Muslim puritan movement founded in the 18th cent. by Muhammad ibn Abd al-Wahhab (1703–1792). Members emphasize the absolute oneness of God. They reject all acts implying POLYTHEISM and advocate a return to the original teachings of Islam as found in the QURAN and the HADITH. They stress literal belief in the canonical texts of Islam and the establishment of a Muslim state based on Islamic law. Adopted by the ruling Saudi family in 1744, the movement was assured of dominance on the Arabian Peninsula with the creation of the kingdom of Saudi Arabia in 1932.

Waikiki \\ˌwī-kə-'kē\\ Resort area, S OAHU island, Hawaii. Its famous beach, located in SE HONOLULU near Diamond Head, is lined with luxury hotels; it has water-sports facilities as well as an aquarium, a zoo, gardens, and the International Market Place. The area was once a favorite resort of island monarchs.

Wailing Wall See WESTERN WALL

Waite, Morrison (Remick) (1816–1888) U.S. jurist. Born in Lyme, Conn., he practiced law in Ohio. In his most notable case he prosecuted the *Alabama* claims. In 1874 he was appointed chief justice of the U.S. Supreme Court. The Waite Court hindered civil rights with such decisions as *U.S. vs. Cruikshank,* in which he stated that the 15th Amendment did not give blacks the vote because "the right to vote comes from the states." In *Munn vs. Illinois* (1877), he upheld legislation fixing maximum rates chargeable by grain elevators and railroads, saying that a business or private property "affected with a public interest" was subject to governmental regulation.

waiting-line theory See QUEUING THEORY

Wakefield City (metro. area pop., 1999 est.: 311,000), administrative center for W. Yorkshire, ENGLAND. During the Wars of the ROSES, Richard, duke of York, was captured there and beheaded by Lancastrians. In the 15th cent. the Wakefield Plays, one of the collections of English MIRACLE PLAYS, were presented there. The town was attacked and taken by the Parliamentarian general Baron FAIRFAX in 1643 during the ENGLISH CIVIL WARS. It has been known as a textile center since the 16th cent.

Wakefield, Edward Gibbon (1796–1862) British colonizer of S. Australia and New Zealand. After viewing the problems of the penal system, including the forcible removal of convicts to British colonies, he proposed colonization by the sale of small landholdings to ordinary citizens, and influenced the founding of S. Australia as a nonconvict settlement. As organizer and manager of the New Zealand Land Co. (1838–49), he sent colonists to settle New Zealand and forced the British government to recognize the colony. He founded a Church of England settlement at Canterbury, New Zealand (1847).

Wake Forest University Private university in Winston-Salem, N.C. Founded in 1834, it is affiliated with the Baptist church. It includes schools of business, law, management, and medicine. Research facilities include a primate center and a laser physics laboratory. Total enrollment is about 6,000.

Wake Island Atoll, central Pacific Ocean. An unincorporated territory of the U.S., it is composed of three low-lying coral islets that surround a lagoon and occupy a total land area of 2.5 sq mi (6.5 sq km). The site of an uncompleted U.S. air and submarine base, Wake was attacked and occupied by Japanese forces in December 1941 after a 15-day resistance by a small contingent of U.S. marines. Now administered by the U.S. Air Force, it is used for weather research and as a commercial aircraft emergency stopover.

Waksman, Selman (Abraham) (1888–1973) Ukrainian-U.S. biochemist. After the discovery of penicillin, he played a major role in initiating a calculated, systematic search for ANTIBIOTICS (a term he coined in 1941) among microorganisms. His 1943 discovery of streptomycin, the first specific agent effective in the treatment of tuberculosis, brought him a 1952 Nobel Prize. Waksman also isolated and developed several other antibiotics, including neomycin.

Walachia \wä-'lā-kē-ə\ Former principality, S central Europe, between the DANUBE RIVER and Transylvania Alps, Romania. It was founded in 1290 by Radu Negru, a vassal of Hungary, and achieved independence from Hungary in 1330. Walachia was under the Turks in the 15th cent., though some princes resisted, notably Vlad Dracul (1436–47) and VLAD III TEPES. Walachia annexed MOLDAVIA and TRANSYLVANIA in the late 16th cent. In 1774 it came under Russia's protection, which ended after the CRIMEAN WAR. In 1859 Walachia united with Moldavia to form Romania.

Walcott \'wȯl-ˌkät\, **Derek (Alton)** (b.1930) Saint Lucian poet and playwright. Most of his works explore the Caribbean cultural experience. He is best known for his poetry; in volumes such as *In a Green Night* (1962), *Another Life* (1973), *The Star-Apple Kingdom* (1979), and *The Bounty* (1997), Walcott's erudition is submerged in sweeping rhythmic and sensuous sonorities. His epic *Omeros* (1990) is a retelling of the *Odyssey* in Caribbean terms. His best-known plays are *Dream on Monkey Mountain* (produced 1967) and *Ti-Jean and His Brothers* (1958). In 1992 he became the first Caribbean writer to be awarded the Nobel Prize.

Waldheim \'vält-ˌhīm\, **Kurt** (b.1918) Fourth secretary-general of the UNITED NATIONS (1972–81). Born in Austria, he served in the German army during World War II. He entered the Austrian foreign service and served as ambassador to the U.N. (1964–68, 1970–71) and as foreign minister (1968–70). Elected U.N. secretary-general, he oversaw disaster relief in Bangladesh, Nicaragua, and Guatemala and peacekeeping missions in Cyprus, the Middle East, Angola, and Guinea. He returned to Austria and ran for president in 1986. His candidacy became controversial when it was learned that he had lied about the nature of his military service and his Nazi connections. Elected nonetheless, he was diplomatically isolated throughout his term (1986–92).

Wales *Welsh* **Cymru** \'kəm-rē\ Principality, part of the United Kingdom. It occupies a peninsula on the W side of GREAT BRITAIN. Area: 8,019 sq mi (20,768 sq km). Population (1998 est.): 2,933,000. Capital: CARDIFF. The population is of Mediterranean, Celtic, Anglo-Saxon, and Anglo-Norman ancestry. Languages: English, Welsh. Wales is almost entirely an upland area generally known as the Cambrian Mtns. The highest peak in England and Wales, Mt. Snowdon, is found in SNOWDONIA NATIONAL PARK. The SEVERN, WYE and Dee are the longest rivers. The country mines coal, slate, and lead; imports and refines petroleum; and manufactures consumer electronics. Tourism is important. In prehistoric times, British Celtic-speakers dominated the region. The Romans ruled from the 1st cent. A.D. until the 4th–5th cent. Welsh Celts fought off incursions from the Anglo-Saxons but failed to unite. The Norman conquerors of England brought S Wales under their rule in 1093. EDWARD I conquered N Wales and made it a principality in 1284. Since 1301 the heir to the English throne has carried the title Prince of Wales. It was incorporated with England in the reign of HENRY VIII. It became a leading international coal-mining center during the 19th cent. The Welsh Nationalist Party, founded in 1925, gathered force in the 1960s, when Welsh nationalist aspirations rose. In 1999 Wales convened its new National Assembly, with limited self-governing powers.

Wales, Prince of Title of the heir apparent to the British throne. In 1301 EDWARD I of England granted it to his son Edward after conquering Wales and executing the last native Welsh prince (1283). Most of the eldest sons of English sovereigns have since been given the title, which ceases to exist when a Prince of Wales becomes king, until a monarch bestows it on a son.

Walesa \vä-'len-sə, *Polish* vä-'weⁿ-sə\, **Lech** (b.1943) Polish labor leader and president of Poland (1990–95). An electrician, he worked in the Lenin Shipyard at Gdansk 1967–76 but was fired for his antigovernment activities. In 1980 he joined workers in a strike and soon became leader of the SOLIDARITY trade union; it was banned in 1981, and he was detained into 1982. In 1983 he was awarded the Nobel Peace Prize. He continued to direct the outlawed union until it received legal recognition in 1988. He won Poland's first direct presidential election by a landslide in 1990, and helped guide Poland into a free-market economy. His confrontational style eroded his popularity, and he lost his bid for reelection.

Walker, Alice (Malsenior) (b.1944) U.S. writer. Born in Eatonton, Ga., she worked in the civil rights movement in the 1960s. Her works are noted for their insightful treatment of African-American culture. Her third and most popular novel, *The Color Purple* (1982, Pulitzer Prize; film, 1985), depicts a black woman's struggle for racial and sexual equality. Her later novels include *The Temple of My Familiar* (1989). She has also written essays, several books of poetry, short stories, and children's books.

Walker, Sarah Breedlove *orig.* Sarah Breedlove (1867–1919) U.S. businesswoman and philanthropist, the first black female millionaire in the U.S. Born near Delta, La., she was a widowed washerwoman in 1905 when she developed a method for straightening curly hair. She founded the Madame C. J. Walker Manufacturing Co. to sell her treatment, and her door-to-door saleswomen became familiar figures in the black communities of the U.S. and the Caribbean. She augmented her earnings with shrewd real-

estate investments, and she donated two-thirds of her fortune to charitable and educational institutions.

Walker, William (1824–1860) U.S. military adventurer. Born in Nashville, Tenn., he moved to California in 1850. His interest in colonizing Baja California developed into a filibustering (insurrection) scheme. He landed at La Paz (1853) and proclaimed Lower California and Sonora an independent republic, but Mexican resistance forced him back to the U.S. In 1855 he sailed to Nicaragua, where he effectively established himself as leader, becoming president in 1856. After he helped company officers seize Cornelius VANDERBILT's Accessory Transit Co., Vanderbilt induced five Central American republics to drive Walker out in 1857. In 1860 he attempted a filibuster in Honduras, where he was captured and executed at 36.

walking catfish Species (*Clarias batrachus*) of Asian and African CATFISH that can progress remarkable distances over dry land. It uses its pectoral-fin spines as anchors to prevent jackknifing as its body musculature produces snakelike movements. Treelike respiratory structures extending above the gill chambers enable it to breathe. Introduced into S Florida, it poses a serious threat to native fauna.

wallaby \'wä-lə-bē\ Any of about 25 species of medium-sized KANGAROOS, found chiefly in Australia. Brush wallabies (11 species) are built like the big kangaroos. Rock wallabies live among rocks, usually near water. Nail-tailed wallabies, named for a horny growth on the tail tip, rotate their forelimbs while hopping. The small hare wallabies resemble HARES in movement and some habits. The small, stocky scrub wallabies, hunted for meat and fur, have short hind limbs and pointy noses. Several wallaby species have been exterminated, and several others are endangered.

Wallace, Alfred Russel (1823–1913) British naturalist. A surveyor and architect, he became interested in botany and traveled to the Amazon in 1848 to collect specimens. In 1854–62 he toured the Malay Archipelago, augmenting his collection. His observations of the islands led to his developing a theory of the origin of species through natural selection independently of, and simultaneously with, Charles DARWIN, though Darwin developed his own theory in much greater detail, provided far more evidence for it, and was mainly responsible for its acceptance. Unlike Darwin, Wallace insisted that the higher mental capacities of humans could not have arisen by natural selection but that some nonbiological agency must have been responsible. In the realm of public policy he supported socialism, pacifism, land nationalization, and women's suffrage. His works include *Contributions to the Theory of Natural Selection* (1870), *Geographical Distribution of Animals* (2 vols., 1876), and *Darwinism* (1889).

Wallace, (William Roy) DeWitt and Lila Acheson *orig.* Lila Bell Acheson (1889–1981, 1889–1984) U.S. publishers. Born in St. Paul, Minn., DeWitt Wallace developed the idea of a pocket-sized digest of popular articles while recuperating from wounds suffered in World War I. Lila Acheson, born in Virden, Manitoba, worked in social services during the war. The two were married in 1921. After various publishers rejected the digest idea, they began publishing *READER'S DIGEST* themselves on a low budget, and had rapid success. DeWitt served as editor until 1965. They supported numerous philanthropic causes; the Lila Wallace–Reader's Digest Fund has been a major benefactor of the arts and culture.

Wallace, (Richard Horatio) Edgar (1875–1932) British novelist and playwright. He published his first novel, *The Four Just Men*, in 1905. With works such as *Sanders of the River* (1911), *The Crimson Circle* (1922), and *The Terror* (1930), he virtually invented the modern "thriller"; the plots of his detective and suspense stories are complex but clearly developed and end in exciting climaxes. His output (including 175 books) was prodigious and his rate of production so great as to be the subject of humor.

Wallace, George C(orley) (1919–1998) U.S. politician. Born in Clio, Ala., he became a circuit court judge (1953–59), known for his resistance to federal investigation of racial discrimination. Campaigning as a segregationist, he was

elected governor in 1963 and kept his pledge "to stand in the schoolhouse door" to prevent enrollment of black students at the Univ. of Alabama, yielding only in the face of the federalized National Guard. He formed the American Independent Party and was its presidential candidate in 1968, winning 13% of the popular vote. He again served as governor 1971–79. While campaigning for the 1972 Democratic presidential nomination, he was shot and left partly paralyzed. In the 1980s he renounced his segregationist views, and he won his last term as governor (1983–87) with support from black voters.

Wallace, Henry A(gard) (1888–1965) U.S. vice president (1941–45). Born in Adair Co., Iowa, he became an agricultural expert and succeeded his father as editor of *Wallace's Farmer* (1924–33). As U.S. secretary of agriculture (1933–40), he shaped Franklin ROOSEVELT's farm policy. He served as vice president in Roosevelt's third term but was replaced by Harry TRUMAN. He was later secretary of commerce (1945–46). Very liberal in his views, he helped form the PROGRESSIVE PARTY in 1947 and was its candidate against Truman in the 1948 presidential election, winning over 1 million votes.

Wallace, Lew(is) (1827–1905) U.S. writer. Born in Brookville, Ind., he served in the Mexican War and in the American Civil War, in which he rose to major general. His reputation rests on three novels: *The Fair God* (1873), on the Spanish conquest of Mexico; *The Prince of India* (1893), on the Byzantine empire; and the enormously popular *Ben-Hur* (1880; films, 1925, 1959), set in the Roman empire during the time of Christ.

Wallace, Mike (*orig.* Myron Leon) (b.1918) U.S. television journalist. Born in Brookline, Mass., he worked as an announcer and newscaster on radio from 1939 and on television from 1946. He joined CBS as a reporter in 1963 and was coeditor of the long-running *60 Minutes* from its first program in 1968. Noted for his aggressive interviewing style, he has won numerous Emmy awards.

Wallace, William (*later Sir William*) (c.1270–1305) Scottish national hero. Son of a small landowner, he began his attacks on English settlements and garrisons in 1297, after EDWARD I declared himself ruler of Scotland. His army defeated a much larger English force at Stirling Bridge, captured Stirling Castle, and then ravaged N England, for which Wallace was knighted and proclaimed guardian of the Scottish kingdom. In 1298 Edward I invaded Scotland and defeated Wallace at the Battle of Falkirk. Disgraced, Wallace resigned his guardianship but continued to fight a guerrilla war. In 1305 he was arrested by the English and hanged. The next year, the future ROBERT I raised the rebellion that eventually won independence.

wallaroo \,wä-lə-'rü\ *or* **euro** \'yù̇r-ˌō\ One of the three largest species of KANGAROO. The wallaroo (*Macropus robustus*) is smaller and stockier than the other two species (also in the genus *Macropus*). It lives in rocky country throughout Australia except in Victoria.

Wallenberg \'wä-lən-ˌbərg, *Swed* 'wä-lən-ˌber-ē\, **Raoul** (1912–1947?) Swedish humanitarian. In 1936 he became the foreign representative of a Hungarian trading company whose president was Jewish. When the Nazis sent troops to round up Jews in Hungary (1944), Wallenberg asked to be sent to Budapest as a diplomat. There he rescued thousands of Jews by sheltering them in "protected houses" under the Swedish flag or securing their escape. Soon after Soviet troops occupied Budapest (1945), he was arrested on suspicion of espionage. He allegedly died of a heart attack in prison in Moscow in 1947. Freed Soviet prisoners reported him alive in 1951, 1959, and 1975.

Wallenda \vä-'len-dä, *Engl* wȯ-'len-də\, **Karl** (1905–1978) German-U.S. circus acrobat. His Great Wallendas acrobatic troupe achieved fame in Europe for cycling on the high wire without a safety net. His wife, Helen Kreis (1910–1996), joined the troupe in 1926 and later was balanced at the peak of the seven-person pyramid, its most famous act. The troupe traveled with the RINGLING BROS. and Barnum & Bailey Circus 1928–46, then performed as freelancers. Karl's nephew Gunther (1927–1996) trained on the wire from age 5; when a pyramid collapsed in 1962, Gunther was the only member left standing and rescued three who were clinging to the wire; two others were killed and one was paralyzed. Karl died in a fall from a wind-whipped wire 123 ft (37 m) above a street in Puerto Rico.

Wallenstein \\'vä-lən-ˌshtīn, *Engl* 'wä-lən-ˌstīn\\, **Albrecht Wenzel Eusebius von** *later* Herzog (Duke) von Mecklenburg (1583–1634) Austrian general. A noble of Bohemia, he served with the future emperor FERDINAND II in the campaign against Venice in 1617, remained loyal to Ferdinand when other nobles revolted (1618–23), and was made governor of Bohemia. He commanded the imperial armies in the Thirty Years' War. After successes in the war against Denmark (1625–29), he was awarded the principality of Sagan (1627) and the duchy of Mecklenburg (1629). In 1631 he drove the Swedish army from Bavaria and Franconia but was defeated at Lützen (1632). Believing he had the support of his generals, he mounted a revolt against the emperor (1634) and was assassinated.

Waller, Edmund (1606–1687) English poet. As a member of Parliament in the 1640s, he was arrested for his part in a plot to establish London as a stronghold of the king; he narrowly avoided death. He later wrote poetic tributes to both Oliver CROMWELL (1655) and CHARLES II (1660). Rejecting the dense verse of METAPHYSICAL POETRY, he adopted smooth, regular versification, preparing the way for the heroic couplet's emergence as the dominant form of English poetry. His lyrics include "Go, lovely Rose!"

Waller, Fats (*orig.* Thomas Wright) (1904–1943) U.S. jazz pianist, singer, and composer. Born in New York City, Waller was influenced early by James P. JOHNSON and became a major stride pianist. From 1934 he recorded with a small ensemble, Fats Waller and His Rhythm, integrating his vocals and unique comic timing with instrumental finesse. His contagious performances of his own songs, such as "Ain't Misbehavin'" and "Honeysuckle Rose," are classics. A notorious bon vivant, Waller died of pneumonia following a heavy touring schedule.

Wallis, Barnes (Neville) (*later* **Sir Barnes**) (1887–1979) British aeronautical designer and military engineer. He invented the "dambuster" bombs used in World War II by the RAF to destroy dams in Germany's industrial Ruhr area. He also produced the 22,000-lb (10,000 kg) "Grand Slam" bomb and was responsible for the bombs that destroyed the German V-rocket sites and much of Germany's railway system. In 1971 he designed an aircraft that could fly five times the speed of sound.

Wallis and Futuna Islands Island group, SW Pacific Ocean, northeast of Fiji. It is a self-governing overseas territory (pop., 1993 est.: 14,000) of France. Of the 11 islands and islets, only Uvéa and Futuna are populated. The administrative seat is Matautu, on Uvéa.

Wall Street Street in New York City where many major U.S. financial institutions are located. It was named for an earthen wall built by Dutch settlers in 1653 to repel an expected English invasion. Even before the Civil War it was recognized as the nation's financial capital, and it remains a worldwide symbol of high finance. The Wall Street, or financial, district contains the NEW YORK STOCK EXCHANGE, the AMERICAN STOCK EXCHANGE, and the Federal Reserve Bank of New York. The district is also the headquarters for many INVESTMENT BANKS, securities dealers, insurance companies, and brokerage firms.

Wall Street Journal, The Daily business newspaper, the most influential U.S. business-oriented paper. Founded in 1889 by Charles H. Dow (1851–1902), it quickly won success. Beginning in the Great Depression, it began to feature more articles, reviews, and opinion on nonbusiness subjects. Published in New York and in four regional editions, it has the second-highest daily circulation of any U.S. newspaper. It is also published in Asian, European, and other special editions.

Wal-Mart Stores, Inc. U.S. retail-sales chain. It was founded by Sam WALTON, who opened the first store in Rogers, Ark., in 1962. The company expanded by combining volume buying and a low-cost delivery system that enabled its stores to offer goods at discount prices in locations where there was little competition from other retail chains. In 1983 it opened

Sam's Clubs, a chain of deep-discount wholesale warehouse outlets, and in 1987 its first hypermarket, combining a grocery supermarket and general merchandise store. Today it is the largest corporation in the world, with over 3,000 stores in the U.S. alone.

walnut Any of about 20 species of DECIDUOUS TREES in the genus *Juglans,* family Juglandaceae. Black walnut (*J. nigra*) of E N. America and English, or Persian, walnut (*J. regia*), native to Iran, are valuable timber trees that produce edible NUTS. The butternut (*J. cinerea*) of E N. America also produces an edible nut. The walnut family also contains seven genera of N temperate flowering plants. PECAN and HICKORY are among the many family members that are prized for both their edible nuts and their strong, attractive woods. Tiny, resinous scales that look like yellow dots on the undersurface of the leaflets give *Juglans* species a pungent aroma.

Walpole, Horace (*orig.* Horatio) *later* Earl of Orford (1717–1797) English writer, connoisseur, and collector. The son of Robert WALPOLE, he had an undistinguished career in Parliament. He transformed his villa at Twickenham into a pseudo-Gothic showplace called Strawberry Hill. He became famous for *The Castle of Otranto* (1765), the first GOTHIC NOVEL in English. His private correspondence of more than 3,000 letters, intended for posthumous publication, constitute a survey of the history, manners, and taste of his age.

Walpole, Hugh (Seymour) (*later* **Sir Hugh**) (1884–1941) British novelist, critic, and dramatist. Among his important novels is the semiautobiographical series that includes *Jeremy* (1919), *Jeremy and Hamlet* (1923), and *Jeremy at Crale* (1927). The "Herries Chronicle," about an English country family, comprises *Rogue Herries* (1930), *Judith Paris* (1931), *The Fortress* (1932), and *Vanessa* (1933).

Walpole, Robert *later* Earl of Orford (1676–1745) English statesman generally regarded as the first British prime minister. Elected to the House of Commons in 1701, he became an active Whig. He served as secretary at war 1708–10 and treasurer of the navy 1710–11. The Tory government sought to remove his influence by impeaching him for corruption, and he was expelled from the Commons in 1712. With the accession of GEORGE I (1714), he rose rapidly to become first lord of the treasury and chancellor of the exchequer (1715–17, 1721–42). He cultivated the support of GEORGE II from 1727 and used royal patronage for political ends, skillfully managing the House of Commons to win support for his trade and fiscal programs.

Robert Walpole Painting by Godfrey Kneller c.1710–15

With his consolidation of power, he effectively became the first British prime minister. He avoided foreign entanglements and kept England neutral until 1739. He resigned under pressure in 1742. His acclaimed art collection, sold to Russia in 1779, became part of the Hermitage Museum collection.

Walpurgis Night Night before May 1. The name comes from the 8th-cent. St. Walburga (or Walpurgis), an English missionary who ran an important early convent in Germany, May 1 being one of her feast days. In Sweden it is celebrated with bonfires as the beginning of spring. In Germany, as Walpurgisnacht, it was the night witches were supposed to meet in the Harz Mtns. (see BROCKEN.)

walrus Only living species (*Odobenus rosmarus*) of the pinniped family Odobenidae. Larger than the related SEALS, walrus males grow up to 12 ft (3.7 m) long and weigh up to 2,800 lbs (1,270 kg). Both sexes have long, downward-pointing tusks that may grow to 3 ft (1 m) long and weigh 12 lbs (5.4 kg) each. They live on ice floes, in groups of up to 100, on relatively shallow water in arctic seas. They may dive to great depths for shellfish. On land and ice, they move on all four limbs. They generally follow the ice line south in winter and north in summer. Traditionally important to humans as sources of food and clothing, they have also been hunted commercially for centuries, which has resulted in serious depletion of their numbers.

Walsh, Raoul (1887–1980) U.S. film director. Born in New York City, he became an assistant to D. W. GRIFFITH in 1912. In his 50-year career, he directed over 200 films, including many outdoor action movies noted for their brisk pacing; they included *What Price Glory?* (1926), *The Roaring Twenties* (1939), *They Drive by Night* (1940), *They Died with Their Boots On* (1941), *High Sierra* (1941), and *White Heat* (1949).

Walsingham, Francis (*later* **Sir Francis**) (1532?–1590) English statesman and adviser to Queen ELIZABETH I. A member of Parliament from 1563, he became ambassador to the French court (1570–73) and established friendly relations between France and England. Admitted to the Privy Council in 1573, he became secretary of state to Elizabeth and faithfully executed her foreign policy. He proved invaluable in uncovering conspiracies by Catholics against Elizabeth's life, including the plots to free MARY, QUEEN OF SCOTS.

Walter, Bruno *orig.* Bruno Walter Schlesinger (1876–1962) German-U.S. conductor. An associate of Gustav MAHLER, he was long a faithful proponent of Mahler's music, giving the world premieres of *Das Lied von der Erde* and the Symphony No. 9. He headed the opera houses in Munich (1913–22), Berlin (1925–33), and elsewhere. After moving to the U.S. in 1939, he often conducted the New York Philharmonic, Metropolitan Opera, and Philadelphia Orchestra, and was admired for the warmth of his interpretations.

Walters, Barbara (b.1931) U.S. television journalist. Born in Boston, she worked as an interviewer (1964–74) and cohost (1974–76) of NBC's *Today* show. In 1976–78, with an unprecedented salary, she was coanchor of the *ABC Evening News*, the first woman to anchor a network newscast. From 1976 she hosted a series of specials, interviewing celebrities and world leaders. From 1984 she also cohosted ABC's *20/20* news magazine program.

Walther von der Vogelweide \\'väl-tər-fòn-der-'fō-gəl-ˌvī-də\\ (c.1170–c.1230) Greatest German lyric poet of the Middle Ages. Of knightly birth, he served masters in several courts. His poetry goes far beyond the artificial conventions followed by other minnesingers, or poet-musicians, of his time, by introducing an element of realism. More than half of his approximately 200 extant poems are political, moral, or religious; the rest are love poems, among them the popular "Unter der Linden."

Walton, Izaak (1593–1683) English biographer and author. A prosperous ironmonger with only a few years of schooling, he read widely, developed scholarly tastes, and associated with men of learning. A friend and fishing companion of John DONNE and George HERBERT, he wrote biographies of both men. His classic *The Compleat Angler* (1653), a pastoral discourse on the joys and stratagems of fishing, is one of the most frequently reprinted works in English literature.

Walton, Sam(uel Moore) (1918–1992) U.S. retail magnate, founder of WAL-MART STORES, INC. Born in Kingfisher, Okla., he trained with the J. C. Penney Co. In 1945 he started a chain of variety stores in Arkansas, and in 1962 he opened his first Wal-Mart discount store. Whereas other discount-store chains were usually situated in or near large cities, Walton chose small towns where there was little competition. In 1983 he opened the first Sam's Wholesale Club. Walton remained Wal-Mart's chairman until his death, by which time there were over 1,700 stores and Walton's family was the wealthiest in the U.S.

Walton, William (Turner) (*later* **Sir William**) (1902–1983) British composer. The son of musicians, he made a splash at age 19 by setting Edith SITWELL's whimsical verse in the jazzy *Façade* (1923). Such later works as *Belshazzar's Feast* (1931), two symphonies, and concertos for viola, violin, and cello marked him as Edward ELGAR's successor. His scores for the films *Henry V* (1944), *Hamlet* (1947), and *Richard III* (1955) became well known.

waltz Ballroom turning dance, characterized by a step, slide, and step in 3/4 time. It was highly popular in the 19th and early 20th cent. Variations include the rapid, whirling Viennese waltz and the slower, dipping Boston waltz, modified by Vernon and Irene CASTLE as the hesitation waltz. Many 19th-cent. composers wrote waltz music, most notably Franz SCHUBERT, Frédéric CHOPIN, Johannes BRAHMS, and Johann STRAUSS.

wampum Tubular shell beads assembled into strings or woven into belts or embroidered ornaments. Before contact with white settlers, Indians used wampum primarily ceremonially or in GIFT EXCHANGES. In the early 17th cent. it came to be used as money in trade with whites because of a shortage of European currency.

Wang Anshi *or* **Wang An-shih** \\'wän-'än-'shir\\ (1021–1086) Chinese writer and government reformer of the SONG DYNASTY. A provincial official from 1042, he entered the imperial government in 1060 and initiated his "New Policies" of 1069–76. He created a fund for agricultural loans to farmers to spare them the exorbitant demands of moneylenders; he also levied a graduated tax on all families. He enabled officials to purchase supplies at the cheapest price in the most convenient market. He established a village militia system and restructured the CHINESE EXAMINATION SYSTEM. His reforms were unpopular with conservatives, and Wang was forced to resign in 1074, returning in 1075 with less political power. After the emperor's death an antireform clique came to power and dismantled Wang's reforms. Wang also was a noted prose stylist.

Wang Jingwei *or* **Wang Ching-wei** \\'wän-'jin-'wā\\ (1883–1944) Chinese politician. A leading polemicist for SUN YAT-SEN's revolutionary group, in 1910 he tried to assassinate the imperial regent and was caught; his courage in the face of execution resulted in his sentence being reduced. He was released in 1911 after the Republican Revolution. In the 1920s he served as a major official in the Nationalist Party (see GUOMINDANG). After Sun's death, he chaired the party while CHIANG KAI-SHEK led the NORTHERN EXPEDITION against China's WARLORDS. Chiang and Wang vied for party control; in a compromise in 1932, Wang became president and Chiang headed the military. After war erupted with Japan, Wang called on the Chinese to work out a peaceful settlement. In 1940 he became head of a puppet regime that governed the Japanese-occupied areas centered on Nanjing.

Wang Yangming *or* **Wang Yang-ming** \\'wän-'yän-'min\\ (1472–1529) Chinese scholar and official whose idealistic interpretation of NEO-CONFUCIANISM influenced philosophical thinking in E. Asia for centuries. Son of a high government official, he was banished in 1506 to a post in remote Guizhou, where hardship and solitude led him to focus on philosophy. He concluded that investigation of the principles of things should occur within the mind rather than through actual objects. Named governor of S Jiangxi in 1516, he suppressed several rebellions and implemented governmental, social, and educational reform. He was appointed war minister in 1521. His philosophy spread across China for 150 years and greatly influenced Japanese thought during that time.

Wankel \\'vän-kəl\\, **Felix** (1902–1988) German inventor. In 1954 he completed the design of his distinctive engine, with an orbiting rotor in the shape of a curved equilateral triangle, which does the work done by the moving pistons in other internal-combustion engines. Its advantages include light weight, few moving parts, compactness, and low initial cost. The first unit was tested in 1957, and the Japanese automobile company Mazda produced and developed the engine commercially.

Wankie National Park See HWANGE NATIONAL PARK

Wannsee Conference \\'vän-ˌzä\\ (Jan. 20, 1942) Meeting of Nazi officials in the Berlin suburb of Grossen-Wannsee to plan the "final solution" to the "Jewish question." The meeting of 15 Nazi bureaucrats, including Adolf EICHMANN, was led by Reinhard HEYDRICH, who had been ordered in 1941 to prepare such a plan. All Jews were to be rounded up, transported eastward, and organized into labor gangs. The expected harsh living conditions would produce a "natural diminution" of Jews, and those that survived would be "treated accordingly." The conference report did not explicitly mention extermination, but within months the first gas chambers were installed at AUSCHWITZ and TREBLINKA. See also HOLOCAUST.

wapiti \'wä-pə-tē\ Species *(Cervus canadensis)* of N. American DEER, often considered the same species as the red deer. It is now confined to the Rocky Mtns. and S Canada. It is the second-largest living deer species (the MOOSE is first). Males may stand taller than 5 ft (1.5 m) at the shoulder and weigh up to 1,100 lbs (500 kg). The male's five-tined antlers tower almost 4 ft (1.2 m) above his head. Wapiti live in large bands in winter and in small groups in summer. See also ELK.

war State of armed conflict between two or more entities. It is characterized by intentional violence on the part of large bodies of individuals organized and trained for that purpose. Some wars are fought internally between rival political factions (civil war); others are fought against an external enemy. Wars have been fought in the name of religion, in self-defense, to acquire territory or resources, and to further the political aims of the aggressor state's leadership.

Warbeck, Perkin (1474?–1499) Flemish impostor, pretender to the throne of HENRY VII. While working as a servant in Ireland in 1491, he was misidentified as royalty while dressed in his master's rich silks, and was soon persuaded to impersonate Richard, duke of York, who was presumed to have been murdered with his brother in the Tower of London in 1483. Encouraged by European monarchs, he gathered forces on the continent for an invasion. After abortive attempts in 1495 and 1496, he landed in Cornwall in 1497 but was captured and hanged.

warble fly Any of several DIPTERAN species (BOTFLY family Oestridae or the family Hypodermatidae), widespread in Europe and N. America. The warble flies *Hypoderma lineatum* and *H. bovis,* also called cattle grubs, deposit their eggs on cattle legs. The larvae penetrate the skin, migrate through the body, and produce a lump, or warble, on the animal's back. Warbles contain breathing holes, which reduce the hide's commercial value. One species *(Oedemagena tarandi)* is a reindeer pest.

warbler Any songbird of almost 350 Old World species (family Sylviidae) or about 120 New World species (family Parulidae, see WOOD WARBLER). Old World warblers, found in gardens, woodlands, and marshes, have a slender bill adapted for gleaning insects from foliage. They are drab greenish, brownish, or black and 3.5–10 in. (9–26 cm) long.

Warburg \'vär-ˌbûrk, *Engl* 'wȯr-ˌbərg\, **Otto (Heinrich)** (1883–1970) German biochemist. In the 1920s, he investigated the process by which living organisms consume oxygen, introducing the technique of measuring changes in gas pressure for studying rates of oxygen uptake. His search for the cell components involved in oxygen consumption led to identification of the role of CYTOCHROMES. He was awarded a 1931 Nobel Prize. He was the first to observe that the growth of cancer cells requires much less oxygen than that of normal cells.

war crime Any violation of the laws of war, as laid down by international customary law and certain international treaties. War crimes were categorized following World War II as (1) conventional war crimes (including murder, ill treatment, or deportation of a civilian population), (2) crimes against peace, or (3) crimes against humanity (political, racial, or religious persecution against any civilian population). The London Agreement of 1945 provided for an international military tribunal to try major Axis war criminals (see NUREMBERG TRIALS), stating that a defendant's position as head of state would not free him from accountability, nor would having acted on orders or out of military necessity. See also GENEVA CONVENTIONS, HAGUE CONVENTIONS.

Ward, Barbara (Mary) *later* Baroness Jackson (of Lodsworth) (1914–1981) British economist and writer. A writer and editor at *The Economist* (from 1939), she was an influential adviser to the Vatican, the U.N., and the World Bank. Her books on the worldwide threat from poverty among third-world nations and the importance of conservation, which reached a wide audience, included *The Rich Nations and the Poor Nations* (1962), *Spaceship Earth* (1966), *Only One Earth* (with René DUBOS, 1972), and *Progress for a Small Planet* (1980).

warfare See AIR WARFARE, AMPHIBIOUS WARFARE, BIOLOGICAL WARFARE, CHEMICAL WARFARE, TRENCH WARFARE

War Hawks Members of the U.S. Congress who advocated war with Britain (1811). The term was applied to Southern and Western congressmen who strongly promoted U.S. expansion into the Northwest and Canada and vigorously protested British aid to Indians. The fervor of the War Hawks, who included Henry CLAY and John C. CALHOUN, helped cause the WAR OF 1812.

Warhol, Andy *orig.* Andrew Warhola (1928–1987) U.S. artist, filmmaker, and leading exponent of the POP ART movement. Born in Pittsburgh, he studied pictorial design at the Carnegie Institute of Technology, then worked in New York as a commercial illustrator. An adroit self-publicist, he conceived the idea of the artist as celebrity. In 1962 he achieved notoriety when he exhibited paintings of Campbell's Soup cans and replicas of Brillo soap-pad boxes. In later work he used the photographic silk-screen technique to print numerous variations of garishly colored celebrity portraits. In the 1960s he made underground films known for their plotlessness, inventive eroticism, and inordinate length. He also involved himself in a range of advertising and other commercial projects. His death resulted from a botched operation. He was one of the most famous and important American cultural figures of the later 20th cent., and the effects of his work on conceptions of art continue to be felt.

warlord In China, an independent military commander in the early 20th cent. Warlords ruled various parts of China following the death (1916) of YUAN SHIKAI, first president of the Republic of China. In SE China, SUN YAT-SEN and the Nationalist Party gained the backing of a warlord based in Guangzhou. In N China three leading warlords emerged: ZHANG ZUOLIN, a Japanese-backed bandit in Manchuria; Wu Peifu, a traditionally educated officer in central China; and Feng Yuxiang, who seized Beijing in 1924. The Nationalist Party consolidated its control in the south and, under CHIANG KAI-SHEK, swept northward (see NORTHERN EXPEDITION), reuniting the country in 1928. Numerous local warlords continued to exert de facto power over their own domains until the Japanese invasion.

Warner, Pop (*orig.* Glenn Scobey) (1871–1954) U.S. college football coach. Born in Springfield, N.Y., he excelled in several sports at Cornell Univ. He coached at the Carlisle (Pa.) Indian School (1898–1904, 1906–15), where he trained Jim THORPE; the Univ. of Pittsburgh (1915–23); and Stanford Univ. (1924–32). Warner's innovations helped refine the modern game. In 46 seasons (1895–1940) his teams won 312 games, lost 104, and tied 32. The Pop Warner Organization is the country's largest youth football league.

Warner Brothers U.S. film studio. Beginning in Pennsylvania as theater owners, the four Warner brothers started producing their own films in 1913 and moved to Hollywood in 1917. They founded Warner Brothers Pictures in 1923, with Harry (1881–1958) as president in New York, Albert (1884–1967) as treasurer, and Sam (1888–1927) and Jack (1892–1978) as studio managers in Hollywood. They helped develop the important Vitaphone sound process, and produced *The Jazz Singer* (1927), the first feature film with synchronized music and dialogue. The studio went on to produce gangster films starring James CAGNEY and E. G. ROBINSON, adventure movies with Errol FLYNN, and mystery dramas with Humphrey BOGART. After his brothers retired, Jack became president (1956–72). In 1989 the studio was merged into Time Warner.

War of 1812 U.S.–British conflict arising from U.S. grievances over oppressive British maritime practices in the NAPOLEONIC WARS. To enforce its blockade of French ports, the British boarded U.S. and other neutral ships to check cargo they suspected was being sent to France. The U.S. reacted by passing the EMBARGO ACT (1807); Congress's WAR HAWKS called for expulsion of the British from Canada to ensure frontier security. When the U.S. demanded an end to the interference, Britain refused, and the U.S. declared war on June 18, 1812. Despite early U.S. naval victories, notably that of the *CONSTITUTION,* Britain maintained its blockade of E U.S. ports. A British force burned public buildings in Washington, D.C., including the WHITE HOUSE, in retali-

W X Y Z

ation for similar U.S. acts in York (Toronto), Canada. The war became increasingly unpopular, especially in New England (see HARTFORD CONVENTION). The Treaty of Ghent (Dec. 24, 1814) essentially restored territories captured by each side. Before news of the treaty reached the U.S., it won a major victory in the Battle of NEW ORLEANS. See also Battle of the THAMES, Isaac HULL, F. S. KEY, O. H. PERRY.

War of Independence, U.S. See AMERICAN REVOLUTION

warrant In law, authorization in writing empowering a person to perform an act or execute an office. Arrest warrants are necessary (except in certain circumstances) for an arrest to be considered legal. Search warrants entitle the holder to enter and search a property. Both are classes of judicial warrants. Nonjudicial warrants include tax warrants (which provide the authority to collect taxes) and land warrants (which entitle the holder to a specific tract of public land).

Warren, Earl (1891–1974) U.S. jurist and politician. Born in Los Angeles, he served as state attorney general (1939–43) before winning three terms as governor (1943–53). He was criticized for interning Japanese citizens in concentration camps during World War II. In 1948 he ran for vice president on the Republican ticket with Thomas DEWEY. He was appointed chief justice of the U.S. Supreme Court in 1953, in which post he would remain until 1969. The Warren Court proved to be strongly liberal, and the era saw sweeping changes in U.S. constitutional law. Among Warren's

Earl Warren, 1953

notable opinions are those in *BROWN VS. BOARD OF EDUCATION*; *Reynolds vs. Sims*, the "one man, one vote" decision that required state legislative reapportionment (1964); and *MIRANDA VS. ARIZONA*. After the assassination of Pres. John KENNEDY he chaired the so-called WARREN COMMISSION.

Warren, Harry *orig.* Salvatore Guaragna (1893–1981) U.S. songwriter. The youngest of 12 children, the Brooklyn-born Warren toured with brass bands and carnivals from age 15. In the 1920s he began contributing tunes to Broadway musicals. In 1932 he moved to Hollywood, where he scored such films as *Gold Diggers of 1933, 42nd Street* (1933), *Down Argentine Way* (1940), and *Sun Valley Serenade* (1941), and received Academy Awards for "Lullaby of Broadway," "You'll Never Know," and "On the Atchison, Topeka and the Santa Fe." Between 1935 and 1950 he wrote more top-10 hit songs than any other songwriter.

Warren, Mercy Otis *orig.* Mercy Otis (1728–1814) U.S. writer. Born in Barnstable, Mass., the sister of James OTIS, she became a friend and correspondent of the leading political figures of her day. She commented on contemporary issues in political satires, plays, and pamphlets. Though a defender of the American Revolution, she opposed the Constitution, arguing that power should rest with the states. Her *History of the Rise, Progress, and Termination of the American Revolution* (3 vols., 1805) covered the period 1765–1800.

Warren, Robert Penn (1905–1989) U.S. novelist, poet, and critic. Born in Guthrie, Ky., Warren attended Vanderbilt Univ., where he joined the Fugitives, a group of poets who advocated the agrarian way of life in the South. Later he helped found and edit *The Southern Review* (1935–42). His writings often treat moral dilemmas in a South beset by the erosion of its traditional rural values. His best-known novel is *All the King's Men* (1946, Pulitzer Prize; film, 1949). He won Pulitzer Prizes for poetry in 1958 and 1979 and became the first U.S. poet laureate in 1986.

Warren Commission (1963–64) *officially* President's Commission on the Assassination of President John F. Kennedy. Group appointed by Pres. Lyndon JOHNSON to investigate the circumstances surrounding John F. KENNEDY's slaying and the shooting of his assassin, L. H. OSWALD. The seven-member commission was chaired by Earl WARREN. After months of investigation, it reported that Kennedy was killed by Oswald's firing of a rifle from the Texas School-Book Depository and that Oswald's murder by Jack Ruby two days later was not part of a conspiracy. Its findings have been repeatedly questioned, but no conclusive contradictory evidence has been found.

Warring States period In China and later in Japan, a period in which small feuding kingdoms or fiefdoms struggled for supremacy. The Chinese Warring States period (475–221 B.C.) was dominated by six or seven feuding kingdoms; it was also the age of the Confucian thinkers MENCIUS and Xunzi. In Japan's Warring States period (1482–1558), rival DAIMYO sought to consolidate and increase their landholdings.

Warsaw City (pop., 1999 est.: 1,618,000), capital of Poland, on the VISTULA RIVER. Founded about 1300, it became the capital in 1596. It was destroyed in 1794 by the Russians. In 1807 it was made the capital of the Grand Duchy of WARSAW by NAPOLEON. Taken by the Russians in 1813, it was the center of Polish insurrection in 1830–31 and 1860. It was occupied by the Germans in WORLD WAR I and again in WORLD WAR II, when its large Jewish population revolted in the WARSAW GHETTO UPRISING (1943). After the unsuccessful WARSAW UPRISING in 1944, the Germans virtually destroyed the city. Rebuilt, it is now an industrial and educational center. Among its historic buildings are a 14th-cent. Gothic cathedral and a medieval castle.

Warsaw, Grand Duchy of Independent Polish state (1807–15), created by NAPOLEON. Established in 1807 after the Poles had helped Napoleon defeat Prussia, it consisted originally of most of the Polish lands that Prussia had taken in the 1790s. For Napoleon's second war against Russia (1812), it supplied nearly 98,000 men, but with Napoleon's defeat the Russians assumed control. Later, the Congress of VIENNA divided it into three parts: the Grand Duchy of POZNAN; the free Republic of KRAKOW; and the Congress Kingdom of Poland, which was joined to Russia.

Warsaw Ghetto Uprising (Apr. 19–May 16, 1943) Revolt by Polish Jews under Nazi occupation. By July 1942 the Nazis had herded 500,000 Jews into the ghetto in Warsaw. Though starvation killed many thousands, the Nazis began deporting 5,000 Jews a day to rural "labor camps." When word reached the ghetto in early 1943 that the destination was actually the gas chambers at TREBLINKA, the underground Jewish combat group ZOB attacked the Nazis, killing 50. On April 19 Heinrich HIMMLER sent 2,000 SS troops to clear the ghetto of its remaining 56,000 Jews. For four weeks the Jewish ZOB, including Itzhak ZUCKERMAN, fought with pistols and homemade bombs until their ammunition ran out. Nearly all the Jews were either killed or deported.

Warsaw Pact *or* **Warsaw Treaty Organization** Military alliance of the Soviet Union, Albania (until 1968), Bulgaria, Czechoslovakia, E. Germany, Hungary, Poland, and Romania, formed in 1955 in response to W. Germany's entry into NATO. Its terms included a unified military command and the stationing of Soviet troops in the other member states. Though its ostensible goal was to protect against NATO attack, Warsaw Pact troops were used only to suppress uprisings in Poland (1956), Hungary (1956), and Czechoslovakia (1968). The alliance was dissolved in 1991 after the collapse of the Soviet bloc.

Warsaw Uprising (Aug.–Oct. 1944) Insurrection in Warsaw in WORLD WAR II that failed to prevent the pro-Soviet takeover of Poland. In July 1944, as Soviet troops approached Warsaw, the Polish underground was encouraged to stage an uprising against the Germans; its 50,000 troops attacked the weakened German force and gained control of most of Warsaw. German reinforcements then bombarded the city for 63 days. The approaching Red Army halted, and the Soviets refused to allow aid from the Allies to the beleaguered Poles, who were forced to surrender in October; the Germans then deported the city's population and destroyed most of the city itself. By allowing the Polish underground to be eliminated, the Soviets diminished resistance to their political domination of Poland in 1945.

Wars of the Roses See Wars of the ROSES

wart *or* **verruca** \və-'rü-kə\ Well-defined small growth on the skin, usually caused by a PAPILLOMAVIRUS, which triggers overproduction of epidermal cells. The most common type is a round bump with a dry, rough surface. Warts are usually painless except in pressure areas, such as the sole of the foot (plantar wart). Genital warts are merely a nuisance unless they become large or numerous enough to interfere with urination, defecation, or childbirth, but some viral strains are associated with cancer. Warts are considered contagious. Treatment to remove warts includes applying acids or subfreezing chemicals (cryotherapy), or surgery; they sometimes disappear spontaneously.

warthog Large-headed species *(Phacochoerus aethiopicus)* of PIG (UNGULATE family Suidae), inhabiting open and lightly forested areas of Africa. Warthogs have a coarse mane. The male has two pairs of bumps (warts) on the face. Both sexes have tusks. The tusks on the lower jaw are weapons; those on the upper jaw curve upward and inward in a semicircle, growing to more than 24 in. (60 cm) in some males. Warthogs live in groups, feeding on vegetation.

Warwick \'wär-ik\ Town (metro. area pop., 1994 est.: 120,000), county seat of WARWICKSHIRE, central England. Known for its historic castle, it grew up at a crossing place on the River AVON. By 1086 it was a royal borough, and WILLIAM I ordered the castle to be enlarged. The present-day castle dates mainly from the 14th–15th cent. With its virtually intact structure and its fine collections of paintings and armor, it has become a major tourist attraction.

Warwick \'wär-ik\, **Earl of** *orig.* **Richard Neville** (1428–1471) English nobleman influential in the Wars of the ROSES. With his father, the earl of Salisbury, he helped the Yorkists win the Battle of St. Albans (1455). Appointed captain of Calais, in 1460 he crossed to England to defeat and capture HENRY VI at Northampton. In 1461 he marched on London with the duke of York's son Edward, soon crowned EDWARD IV. Warwick was the virtual ruler during Edward's early reign, but tensions between the two mounted, and in 1469 Warwick engineered a revolt that forced Edward to flee to Flanders in 1470. Warwick joined the Lancastrians and restored Henry VI to the throne, earning his later nickname "the Kingmaker." He was killed by Edward's forces at the Battle of Barnet.

Warwickshire \'wär-ik-ˌshir\ County (pop., 1998 est.: 507,000), central England. Its county seat is WARWICK. In Saxon times it formed a border zone between the kingdoms of WESSEX and MERCIA. The Battle of Edgehill (1642), the first serious clash of the ENGLISH CIVIL WARS, was fought here. Historical structures include Norman and early English churches, and buildings at STRATFORD-UPON-AVON associated with William SHAKESPEARE. Dairy farming, fruit growing, and coal mining are important economic activities.

Wasatch Mountains \'wȯ-ˌsach\ Range of the S central ROCKY MTNS. They extend about 250 mi (400 km) from SE Idaho to central Utah. Mt. Timpanogos (12,008 ft, or 3,660 m) is the highest peak.

Washington State (pop., 2000: 5,894,000), NW U.S. It covers an area of 68,139 sq mi (176,479 sq km); its capital is OLYMPIA. The state contains the CASCADE RANGE, which includes Mt. RAINIER and Mt. ST. HELENS, and the OLYMPIC MTNS. JUAN DE FUCA STRAIT and PUGET SOUND extend inland from the Pacific Ocean. Cape Alva, the most westerly point of the coterminous U.S., is in Washington, as is the COLUMBIA RIVER. The area was inhabited by Pacific Coast Indians, including the CHINOOK and NEZ PERCÉ, when the region was visited by Spanish, Russian, British, and French explorers 1543–1792. Claimed by the Spanish and British, it was crossed by the LEWIS AND CLARK EXPEDITION in 1805. Spain surrendered to the U.S. its territories north of California in 1819. Until the 1840s, international agreement permitted citizens of both the U.S. and Britain to settle in what was known as Oregon Country. An 1846 treaty with Great Britain set the present Washington–Canada boundary; the Oregon Country was added to the U.S., and renamed the Territory of Oregon in 1848. Washington received territorial status in 1853 and was reduced to its present size in 1863. It was admitted to the Union as the 42nd state in 1889. In the late 1890s it was the main staging point for gold miners

going to the Alaskan and Yukon strikes. The greatest stimulus to its 20th-cent. progress came with the development of hydroelectric power and the work on the Bonneville and Grand Coulee dams. Its important manufactures include aircraft and shipbuilding. Expanding trade with Pacific Rim countries, high technology, and tourism add to the economy.

Washington, Booker T(aliaferro) (1856–1915) U.S. educator. Born into slavery in Franklin Co., Va., he moved with his family to W. Virginia after emancipation. He worked from age 9, then attended (1872–75) and taught at the Hampton (Va.) Institute. In 1881 he was selected to head the Tuskegee Normal and Industrial Institute, a new teacher-training school for blacks, and he successfully transformed it into a thriving institution (later TUSKEGEE UNIV.). The most prominent black leader of his time, he held the controversial conviction that blacks could best gain equality by improving their economic situation through education rather than by demanding equal rights. His books include *Up from Slavery* (1901).

Washington, D.C. City (pop., 2000: 572,000), capital of the U.S. It is coextensive with the DISTRICT OF COLUMBIA. Situated at the navigational head of the POTOMAC RIVER, between Maryland and Virginia, it has an area of 69 sq mi (179 sq km). The site was chosen by George WASHINGTON in 1790, as a political compromise that satisfied both Northern and Southern states. Designed by P.-C. L'ENFANT, it is one of the few cities in the world planned expressly as a national capital. The federal government occupied it in 1800. British troops burned the city (1814) during the WAR OF 1812. Significant buildings include the Capitol, WHITE HOUSE, and Library of CONGRESS. The WASHINGTON MONUMENT, Lincoln Memorial, Jefferson Memorial, and VIETNAM VETERANS MEMORIAL are among the most famous of the city's more than 300 memorials and statues. The SMITHSONIAN INSTITUTION is in Washington, as are numerous other cultural and educational institutions.

Washington, Denzel (b.1954) U.S. film actor. Born in Mt. Vernon, N.Y., he acted in the television series *St. Elsewhere* 1982–88. In movies from 1981, he won acclaim for his roles in *Cry Freedom* (1987), *Glory* (1989, Academy Award), and *Mississippi Masala* (1991). Praised for his performance in Spike LEE's *Malcolm X* (1992), he also starred in such films as *The Pelican Brief* (1993), *Philadelphia* (1993), and *Training Day* (2001, Academy Award).

Washington, Dinah *orig.* **Ruth Lee Jones** (1924–1963) U.S. singer. Born in Tuscaloosa, Ala., Washington sang in church choirs as a child. She joined Lionel HAMPTON's band in 1943, embarking on a solo career in 1946. Her recordings encompassed rhythm-and-blues, jazz, and country music; her 1959 "What a Difference a Day Makes" was a pop hit. Known as "Queen of the Blues," her voice, alternately gentle and brassy, was remarkable for its clarity and projection. She died from an accidental overdose of sleeping pills.

Washington, George (1732–1799) American Revolutionary commander-in-chief (1775–83) and first president of the U.S. (1789–97). Born in Westmoreland Co., Va., he was educated privately and worked as a surveyor from age 16. In 1752 he inherited his brother's estate at MOUNT VERNON. In the FRENCH AND INDIAN WAR he was commissioned a colonel and sent to the Ohio Territory. After Edward BRADDOCK was killed, Washington became commander of all Virginia forces, entrusted with defending the W frontier (1755–58). He resigned to manage his estate and in 1759 married Martha Dandridge Custis (1731–1802), a widow. He served in the House of BURGESSES 1759–74, where he supported the colonists' cause, and in the Continental

George Washington Painting by Gilbert Stuart

W X Y Z

Congress 1774–75. In 1775 he was elected to command the Continental Army. In the ensuing AMERICAN REVOLUTION, he proved a brilliant commander and stalwart leader despite several defeats. With the war effectively ended by the capture of YORKTOWN (1781), he resigned his commission and returned to Mount Vernon (1783). Presiding officer of the CONSTITUTIONAL CONVENTION (1787), he helped secure ratification of the Constitution in Virginia. When the state electors met to select the first president (1789), Washington was the unanimous choice. He formed a cabinet to balance sectional and political differences but was committed to a strong central government. Elected to a second term, he followed a middle course between the political factions that became the FEDERALIST PARTY and DEMOCRATIC PARTY. He proclaimed a policy of neutrality in the war between Britain and France (1793). He declined to serve a third term, setting a 144-year precedent. Known as the "father of his country," he is universally regarded as one of the greatest figures in U.S. history.

Washington, Mt. Peak in the Presidential Range of the WHITE MTNS., N New Hampshire. At 6,288 ft (1,917 m), it is the highest point in the NE U.S. It is noted for its extreme weather conditions; the world's highest wind velocity (231 mph, or 372 kph) was recorded there in 1934.

Washington, University of Public university in Seattle, founded in 1861. It is a comprehensive research university with sea-grant status. It consists of colleges of architecture and urban planning, arts and sciences, education, engineering, forestry, and oceanography as well as schools of business, dentistry, drama, communications, international studies, law, library science, music, medicine, nursing, pharmacy, public affairs, and social work. Total enrollment is about 35,000.

Washington and Lee University Private university in Lexington, Va. Founded as an academy in 1749, it is one of the oldest institutions of higher learning in the U.S. It is named after George WASHINGTON, who donated $50,000 in 1796, and Robert E. LEE, who served as its president 1865–70. It became coeducational in 1984. It has a law school and a school of commerce, economics, and politics. Enrollment is about 2,000.

Washington Monument Memorial to George WASHINGTON, in Washington, D.C. Built 1848–84, it is a granite OBELISK over 555 ft (169 m) high, faced with Maryland marble. It is located on a westward extension of the Mall. The top can be reached by elevator or an interior iron stairway.

Washington Post, The Daily newspaper published in Washington, D.C., one of the nation's great newspapers. Established in 1877 as a Democratic Party organ, it changed orientation and ownership several times and faced constant economic problems until Eugene Meyer (1875–1959) purchased it in 1933. Under Meyer (to 1946), Philip L. Graham (1946–63), Katharine GRAHAM (1963–79), and Donald E. Graham (from 1979), it acquired international prestige, becoming known for its independent editorial stance and accurate reporting.

Washington University Private university in St. Louis. Founded as a seminary in 1853, it became a university in 1857. It is a comprehensive research and teaching institution, with one of the leading medical schools in the U.S. It has schools of architecture, business (the Olin School), engineering and applied science, fine arts, law, and social work, as well as a space science center, a center for the study of Islamic culture and society, and an institute for the deaf. Total enrollment is about 11,000.

Washita River \'wä-shi-ˌtò\ River, W and S central Oklahoma. It rises in NW Texas and flows east then southeast to S central Oklahoma, and south into the RED RIVER. It is 626 mi (1,007 km) long. In the Battle of the Washita (1868), Gen. G. A. CUSTER attacked a CHEYENNE Indian encampment.

Washita River See OUACHITA RIVER

wasp Any of more than 20,000, usually winged, insect species in the order Hymenoptera. The abdomen is attached to the thorax by a slender petiole, or "waist," and the female has a formidable stinger. Most species are solitary, a few are highly social, and some may be either. Adults feed primarily on nectar. Most solitary wasps nest in tunnels in the ground

and feed larvae with paralyzed insects or spiders. The paperlike nest of social wasps (family Vespidae) consists of chewed plant material mixed with saliva and arranged in adjacent hexagonal cells. The female lays one egg in each cell and provisions it with a macerated caterpillar.

Wassermann \'vä-sər-ˌmän, *Engl* 'wä-sər-mən\, **August von** (1866–1925) German bacteriologist. With Albert Neisser (1855–1916) he developed a test for the antibody to the SPIROCHETE that causes SYPHILIS. That test is still used to diagnose syphilis. He is also noted for developing tests for tuberculosis.

Wasserstein \'wä-sər-ˌstīn\, **Wendy** (b.1950) U.S. playwright. Born in Brooklyn, N.Y., she wrote her first play in 1973. She won favorable notice for *Uncommon Women and Others* (1977), which was followed by *Isn't It Romantic* (1981) and *The Heidi Chronicles* (1988, Tony Award, Pulitzer Prize), and became noted for her comic gift and her portrayals of single women. Her later plays include *The Sisters Rosensweig* (1992) and *An American Daughter* (1997).

water Inorganic compound composed of HYDROGEN and OXYGEN (H_2O), existing in LIQUID, GAS (STEAM, water vapor), and SOLID (ICE) states. At room temperature, water is a colorless, odorless, tasteless liquid. One of the most abundant compounds, water covers about 75% of the earth's surface. Its ability to dissolve many other substances is an outstanding quality. Life is believed to have originated in the world's oceans, and living organisms rely on aqueous solutions (including blood and digestive juices) for virtually every process. Because water molecules are asymmetric and therefore ELECTRIC DIPOLES, HYDROGEN BONDING between molecules in liquid water and in ice is important in holding them together. Many of water's complex physical and chemical properties arise from this extensive hydrogen bonding. Water undergoes dissociation to the IONS H^+ (or H_3O^+) and OH^-, particularly in the presence of salts and other solutes; it may act as an ACID or as a BASE. It has myriad industrial uses, including as a suspending agent (papermaking, coal slurrying), solvent, diluting agent, coolant, and source of hydrogen; it is used in filtration, washing, steam generation, hydration of lime and cement, textile processing, sulfur mining, HYDROLYSIS, HYDRAULICS, as well as in beverages and foods. See also HARD WATER, HEAVY WATER.

water buffalo *or* **Indian buffalo** Either of two types of oxlike BOVID (species *Bubalus bubalis*) domesticated in Asia from earliest recorded times. Its name derives from its suitability for work on waterlogged land. It stands 5–6 ft (1.5–1.8 m) and may weigh over 2,000 lbs (1,000 kg). The horns measure up to 7 ft (2 m) across. One type, the swamp buffalo, is the principal draft animal of S China and SE Asia. The other, the river buffalo, is used for dairy and meat production and draft work in S and SW Asia and Egypt.

water clock *or* **clepsydra** \'klep-sə-drə\ Ancient device for measuring time by the gradual flow of water. One form, used by Africans and N. American Indians, consisted of a floating vessel that shipped water through a hole until it sank. In another form, water escaped through a hole in a vessel marked with graduated lines; specimens from Egypt date from the 14th cent. B.C. The Roman clepsydra consisted of a cylinder into which water dripped; a float provided readings against a scale on the cylinder wall.

watercolor Painting made with a pigment ground in gum, usually gum arabic, and applied with brush and water to a surface, usually paper. The pigment is ordinarily transparent but can be made opaque by mixing with a whiting to produce GOUACHE. Transparent watercolor allows for freshness and luminosity. Whereas oil paintings achieve their effects by a building up of color, watercolors rely on what is left out, with empty, unpainted spaces being an integral part of the work.

watercress Perennial plant (*Nasturtium officinale*) of the MUSTARD FAMILY, native to Eurasia and naturalized throughout N. America. It grows submerged, floating on the water, or spread over mud surfaces in cool flowing streams. White flowers are followed by small, beanlike seedpods. Cress is often cultivated in tanks for its young shoots, which are used in salads. The delicate, light-green, peppery-flavored leaves are rich in vitamin C.

Waterford glass Glassware produced in Waterford, Ireland, from the 1720s to the present, characterized by thick walls, deeply incised geometric cutting, and brilliant polish. Characteristic Waterford products include Rococo chandeliers, wall lamps, bowls, and vases. After 1770 Waterford glassmakers gradually abandoned the Rococo style in favor of the more restrained Neoclassical style popular in England.

waterfowl Any member of the family Anatidae, web-footed birds with a broad bill containing fine plates, or lamellae; usually stocky and often long-necked, including DUCKS, geese (see GOOSE), and SWANS. Waterfowl feed by dabbling, diving, or grazing. Most species are social and have an array of formal displays and group cohesion signals. The female usually builds the nest and incubates the 3–12 eggs. Many species are migratory.

Watergate scandal (1972–74) Political scandal involving Pres. Richard NIXON's administration. In June 1972 five burglars were arrested after breaking into the Democratic Party's national headquarters at the Watergate complex in Washington, D.C. The White House denied any connection to the burglary, and Nixon was reelected. In January 1973 the trial of the burglars revealed details of a cover-up by Nixon's aides. In April Attorney General Elliot Richardson appointed Archibald Cox as special prosecutor. A Senate committee under Sam Ervin held televised hearings and learned of the existence of tapes of conversations in the president's office. Nixon refused to relinquish the tapes and ordered Cox fired (Oct. 20). Richardson resigned in protest, and the public outcry and the new special prosecutor, Leon Jaworski, forced Nixon to surrender the tapes, which revealed clear signs of his involvement. In July 1974 the judiciary committee of the House of Representatives passed three articles of impeachment. On Aug. 5 Nixon supplied three tapes that clearly implicated him in the cover-up. Maintaining his innocence, he resigned on Aug. 8. He was pardoned a month later by his successor, Gerald FORD.

water hyacinth Any of about five species that make up the genus *Eichhornia* of the pickerelweed family (Pontederiaceae), native mainly to the New World tropics. Some species float in shallow water; others are rooted in muddy stream banks and lakeshores. All have rosettes of stalked leaves and flowers arranged in spikes or clusters. The common water hyacinth (*E. crassipes*) is the most widespread species. Its purple flowers have blue and yellow markings. It reproduces quickly, often clogging slow-flowing streams. It is used as an ornamental in outdoor pools and aquariums.

water lily Any of the mostly perennial freshwater plants in eight genera that make up the family Nymphaeaceae, native to temperate and tropical regions. Most have rounded, floating, waxy-coated leaves growing atop long stalks. Thick, fleshy, creeping underwater stems are buried in the mud. Showy, solitary, cuplike flowers with numerous spirally arranged petals are borne at or above the water surface on long stalks. The genus *Nymphaea* includes the water lilies proper (or water nymphs). The common N. American white water lily is *N. odorata*. The lotus of ancient Egyptian art was usually the blue lotus (*N. caerulea*). The largest water lilies are two species that make up the tropical S. American genus *Victoria*. Water lilies provide food for fish and wildlife but sometimes cause drainage problems because of their rapid growth. Many varieties have been developed for ornamental use.

Waterloo, Battle of (June 18, 1815) Final defeat of NAPOLEON in the NAPOLEONIC WARS. The battle was fought near Waterloo village, south of Brussels, by Napoleon's 72,000 troops against the duke of WELLINGTON's Allied army of 68,000 aided by 45,000 Prussians under Gebhard von BLÜCHER. After the French defeated the Prussians at Ligny and held Wellington at Quatre-Bras on June 16, Napoleon's marshals, including Michel NEY, failed to eliminate either enemy while they were separated. Napoleon delayed his attack at Waterloo until midday, to allow the ground to dry, which enabled Blücher's force to join Wellington. Four attacks on the Allied center failed to break through, and Napoleon had to move troops to meet the Prussian flanking attack. When Ney captured a farmhouse at the center of the Allied line, his call for reinforcements was refused. Wellington's forces, despite heavy losses, forced the French into a disorganized retreat. The French suffered 25,000 casualties, Wellington's army 15,000, and Blücher's 8,000.

watermelon Succulent fruit of *Citrullus lanatus*, in the GOURD family, native to tropical Africa and widely cultivated. The vines spread across the ground with branched tendrils, deeply cut leaves, and light-yellow flowers. Each vine bears 2–15 large, sweet, very juicy fruits with flat black seeds. Varieties differ in flesh color, shape, and rind thickness.

water moccasin *or* **cottonmouth moccasin** Species (*Agkistrodon piscivorus*) of pit viper that inhabits marshy lowlands of the SE U.S. It threatens with the mouth open, showing the cottony-white interior. It is up to 5 ft (1.5 m) long and is completely black or brown with darker crossbands. A dangerous snake with a potentially lethal bite, it will eat almost any small animal. See also COPPERHEAD.

water pollution State resulting when substances are released into a body of water, where they become dissolved or suspended in the water or deposited on the bottom, accumulating to the extent that they overwhelm its capacity to absorb, break down, or recycle them. Contributions to water pollution include substances drawn from the air (see ACID RAIN), silt from soil erosion, chemical FERTILIZERS and PESTICIDES, runoff from septic tanks, outflow from livestock feedlots, chemical wastes (some toxic) from industries, and sewage and other urban wastes from cities and towns. When organic matter exceeds the capacity of microorganisms in the water to break it down and recycle it, the excess of nutrients encourages algal water blooms. When these algae die, their remains add further to the organic wastes already in the water, and eventually the water becomes deficient in oxygen. Organisms that do not require oxygen then attack the organic wastes, releasing harmful gases such as methane and hydrogen sulfide. The result is a foul-smelling, waste-filled body of water. See also EUTROPHICATION.

water polo Goal game, similar to soccer, that is played in water by teams of swimmers (seven per side) using a ball resembling a soccer ball. The name derives from a mid-19th-cent. version of the sport in which players rode barrels and struck the ball with sticks. A rough and demanding game, it is played by both men and women. Modern water polo was introduced as an Olympic sport in 1900.

waterpower POWER produced by a stream of water as it turns a wheel or similar device. The WATERWHEEL, probably invented in the 1st cent. B.C., was widely used throughout the Middle Ages and into modern times for grinding grain, operating bellows for furnaces, and other purposes. The more compact water TURBINE, which passes water through a series of fixed and rotating blades, was introduced in 1827. Water turbines, used originally for direct mechanical drive for irrigation, now are used almost exclusively to generate HYDROELECTRIC POWER.

Waters, Ethel (1896?–1977) U.S. blues and jazz singer and actress. Born in Chester, Pa., she was a professional singer by 17, and later recorded with Duke ELLINGTON and Benny GOODMAN. She made her Broadway debut in 1927, and starred in *Blackbirds* (1930). In 1933 she appeared in Irving BERLIN's *As Thousands Cheer,* in which she sang "Heat Wave." Later stage successes included *Cabin in the Sky* (1940; film, 1943) and *The Member of the Wedding* (1950; film, 1952). Her other films included *Pinky* (1949).

Waters, Muddy *orig.* McKinley Morganfield (1915–1983) U.S. BLUES guitarist and singer. Born in Rolling Fork in the Mississippi Delta, he taught himself harmonica and guitar, eagerly absorbing the styles of Robert JOHNSON and Son House. He was first recorded in 1941 by Alan Lomax. In 1943 he moved to Chicago; there he broke with the country blues style by playing over a heavy dance rhythm, adopting the electric guitar and adding piano and drums while retaining a moan-and-shout vocal style. The result, which came to be known as urban blues, was a major forerunner of ROCK MUSIC and SOUL MUSIC. The 1960s brought Waters international fame.

waterskiing Sport of planing and jumping on water skis, broad skilike runners that a rider wears while being towed by a motorboat. The sport originated in the U.S. in the 1920s. International competitions have been held since

WXYZ

1946. Single-ski slalom competition is held on a course consisting of a specified number of buoys around which the skier must negotiate. Jumping competitions employ a ramp.

water snake Any of 65–80 SNAKE species of genus *Natrix*, family Colubridae, and members of several New World genera, especially *Nerodia*. They kill fishes and amphibians with a nonvenomous bite. The New World species live in or near water and bear live young; European species are less water-dependent and lay eggs. All are bad-tempered; in defense, they inflate the head, strike, and release a foul secretion. They average about 3 ft (1 m) long; some Old World species reach 6 ft (1.8 m).

water-supply system Facilities for the collection, treatment, storage, and distribution of water. Ancient systems included wells, storage reservoirs, CANALS and AQUEDUCTS, and water-distribution systems. Highly advanced systems appeared around 2500 B.C. and reached their peak in the Roman aqueduct system. The Middle Ages saw epidemics caused by waterborne organisms because of neglect of water supplies. In the 17th–18th cent., distribution systems utilizing cast-iron pipes, aqueducts, and pumps began to be installed. The link between polluted water and disease came to be understood in the 19th cent., and treatment methods were introduced. Modern reservoirs are formed usually by constructing DAMS. Treated water is pumped either directly into a city or town's distribution system or to an elevated storage location, such as a water tank. See also PLUMBING.

water table *or* **groundwater table** Surface of a body of underground water below which the soil or rocks are permanently saturated with water. The water table separates the zone of saturation from the zone of aeration above it. The water table fluctuates with the seasons and from year to year because it is affected by climatic variations. It also is affected by withdrawing excessive amounts of water from wells or by recharging them artificially. See also AQUIFER.

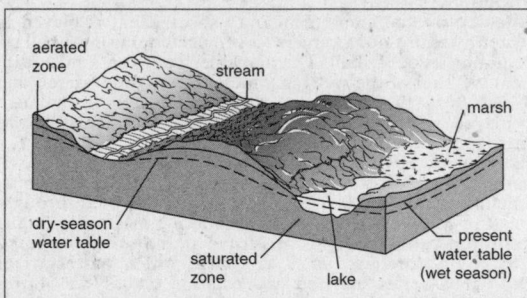

Water table Diagram showing seasonal variations in groundwater levels, which rise and fall with precipitation and drought.

waterwheel Machine for tapping the energy of running or falling water by means of a set of paddles or buckets mounted around a wheel. The force of the water against the paddles, or its weight poured into the buckets, rotates the wheel. The resulting power is transmitted to machinery via the shaft of the wheel. The waterwheel, perhaps the earliest source of mechanical energy to replace that of humans and animals, was first used for such tasks as raising water and grinding grain.

Watie \'wä-tē\, **Stand** *orig.* De Gata Ga (1806–1871) American Indian leader. Born in Rome, Ga., he learned English at a mission school and helped publish a tribal newspaper. In 1835 he joined three other CHEROKEE chiefs to sign the Treaty of New Echota, which surrendered Cherokee lands in Georgia and forced the tribe to move to Indian Territory in present-day Oklahoma. In the Civil War he raised a Cherokee rifle regiment for the Confederacy and directed cavalry raids on property of Indians who backed the Union.

Watson, Doc (*orig.* Arthel Lane) (b.1923) U.S. COUNTRY-MUSIC singer, banjoist, and guitarist. Blind from birth, Watson grew up on a farm in N. Carolina, learning guitar, banjo, and harmonica. He began recording professionally in his late thirties and quickly rose to prominence with his renditions of traditional and popular tunes backed by his virtuoso flat-picking guitar style, and has toured successfully for four decades.

Watson, James D(ewey) (b.1928) U.S. geneticist and biophysicist. Born in Chicago, he earned his PhD at Indiana Univ. in 1950. Using X-ray diffraction techniques, he began work in Britain with Francis CRICK on the problem of DNA structure. In 1952 he determined the structure of the protein coat surrounding the tobacco mosaic virus. In early 1953 he suddenly saw that the essential DNA components, four organic bases, must be linked in definite pairs, a discovery that enabled Watson and Crick to formulate a double-helix molecular model for DNA. In 1962 they and Maurice WILKINS shared the Nobel Prize. Watson's *The Double Helix* (1968) was a best-selling personal account of the DNA discovery.

Watson, Thomas J(ohn), Sr. (1874–1956) U.S. industrialist. Born in Campbell, N.Y., he went to work for the National Cash Register Co. in 1899. In 1914 he became president of the company that in 1924 became IBM, which he built into the world's largest manufacturer of electric typewriters and data-processing equipment. He assembled a highly motivated, well-trained, and well-paid research-and-development staff, gave pep talks, enforced a strict dress code, and posted the famous "Think" sign in company offices. He was noted for his efforts on behalf of the arts and world peace. His son Thomas John Watson, Jr. (1914–1993), succeeded him as president (1952) and CEO (1956). By the time of his retirement, IBM was the world's largest computer company and one of the world's largest corporations.

Watt, James (1736–1819) Scottish engineer and inventor. Though largely self-taught, he began work early as an instrument maker and later as a civil engineer. Watt's major improvement to Thomas NEWCOMEN's steam engine was the use of a separate CONDENSER (1769), which reduced the loss of LATENT HEAT and greatly increased its efficiency. With Matthew BOULTON he began manufacture of his new engine in 1775. In 1781 he added rotary motion to replace the up-and-down action of the original engine. In 1782 he patented the double-acting engine, in which the piston pushed as well as pulled. His

James Watt Painting by H. Howard

application of the centrifugal governor for automatic control of the speed of the engine (1788) and his invention of a pressure gauge (1790) virtually completed the Watt engine, which had immense consequences for the INDUSTRIAL REVOLUTION. He introduced the concept of HORSEPOWER; the watt, a unit of power, is named for him.

Watteau \vȧ-'tō, *Engl* wä-'tō\, **(Jean-) Antoine** (1684–1721) French painter. At 18 he moved to Paris, where he worked for a series of painters; one of them was a theatrical set designer, and much of Watteau's work consequently embraced the artifice of the theater, particularly the COMMEDIA DELL'ARTE and the ballet. His works typified the lyrically charming and graceful Rococo style. The greatest, his *Pilgrimage to the Island of Cythera,* was his presentation piece when he was inducted into the Academy in 1717. The academicians, unable to fit him into any of the recognized categories, welcomed him as a painter of "elegant festivities," or *fêtes galantes,* an important new genre of painting to which countless later Rococo pictures belong.

wattle See ACACIA.

Watts, André (b.1946) U.S. (German-born) pianist. The son of an African-American soldier and a Hungarian mother, he made his debut at 9 with the Philadelphia Orchestra, and he attracted wide attention when at 16 he performed on television under Leonard BERNSTEIN. He toured the world under

State Department auspices in 1967, and a 1976 concert was the first live television broadcast of a solo recital in history.

Watts, Isaac (1674–1748) English Nonconformist minister, regarded as the father of English hymnody. Watts studied at the Dissenting Academy in London and later became pastor of an important Congregational church. His hymns, numbering more than 600, became known throughout Protestant Christendom; they include "O God, Our Help in Ages Past" and "Joy to the World." A man of great erudition, he published books on a range of subjects.

Wat Tyler's Rebellion See PEASANTS' REVOLT

Watusi See TUTSI

Waugh \'wȯ\, **Evelyn (Arthur St. John)** (1903–1966) English novelist. His finest satirical novels, which display his sardonic wit and technical brilliance, include *Decline and Fall* (1928), *Vile Bodies* (1930), *Black Mischief* (1932), *A Handful of Dust* (1934), *Scoop* (1938), and *The Loved One* (1948). He converted to Roman Catholicism in 1930, and his Catholicism is insistently reflected in his novels from then on. After service in World War II he led a retired life; his later works, intended to be more serious but written with less élan, include *Brideshead Revisited* (1945) and the *Sword of Honour* trilogy (1952–61).

wave Propagation of disturbances from place to place in a regular and organized way. Most familiar are surface WAVES that travel on water, but sound, light, and the motion of SUBATOMIC PARTICLES all exhibit wavelike properties. In the simplest waves, the disturbance oscillates periodically with a fixed FREQUENCY and WAVELENGTH. Mechanical waves, such as sound, require a medium through which to travel, but electromagnetic waves (see ELECTROMAGNETIC RADIATION) do not require a medium and can be propagated through a vacuum. See also SEISMIC WAVE.

wave In oceanography, a moving ridge or swell on the surface of a body of water, normally having a forward motion distinct from the motions of the particles that compose it. Ocean waves are fairly regular, with an identifiable WAVELENGTH between adjacent crests. Waves result when a generating force (usually the wind) displaces surface water and a restoring force returns it to its undisturbed position. SURFACE TENSION alone is the restoring force for small waves; for large waves, gravity is more important.

wave function Variable quantity that mathematically describes the WAVE characteristics of a particle. It is related to the likelihood of the particle being at a given point in space at a given time, and may be thought of as an expression for the amplitude of the particle wave. See also WAVE-PARTICLE DUALITY.

wavelength Distance between corresponding points of two consecutive waves. "Corresponding points" refers to two points or particles that have completed identical fractions of their periodic motion. In transverse waves, wavelength is measured from crest to crest. In longitudinal waves, it is measured from compression to compression. Wavelength, λ, is equal to the speed v of a wave in a medium divided by its FREQUENCY f, or $\lambda = v/f$.

wave-particle duality Principle that SUBATOMIC PARTICLES possess some wavelike characteristics, and that electromagnetic WAVES, such as light, possess some particlelike characteristics. In 1905, by demonstrating the PHOTOELECTRIC EFFECT, Albert EINSTEIN showed that light, which had been thought of as a form of electromagnetic wave, must also be thought of as localized in packets of discrete energy (see PHOTON). In 1924 Louis de BROGLIE proposed that ELECTRONS have wave properties; this was experimentally established in 1927 by the demonstration of their DIFFRACTION. The theory of QUANTUM ELECTRODYNAMICS combines the wave theory and the particle theory of ELECTROMAGNETIC RADIATION.

wax Any of a class of pliable substances, ORGANIC COMPOUNDS of animal, plant, mineral, or synthetic origin, less greasy, harder, and more brittle than FATS. Waxes contain mostly compounds of high MOLECULAR WEIGHT. Many melt at moderate temperatures and form hard films that can take a high polish. Animal and plant waxes are ESTERS of FATTY ACIDS and either a sterol (see STEROID) or a straight-chain higher ALCOHOL. Animal waxes include beeswax; wool wax (lanolin); and sperm oil and spermaceti (from SPERM WHALES). Plant waxes include carnauba wax, candelilla wax, and sugarcane wax. About 90% of the waxes in commerce are recovered by dewaxing PETROLEUM. There are three main types: paraffin (used in candles, crayons, paper coating, and industrial polishes), microcrystalline wax (used in paper coating), and petrolatum (used in ointments and cosmetics). Synthetic waxes (carbowaxes) are commonly blended with petroleum waxes.

waxwing Any of three species (family Bombycillidae) of elegant-looking songbirds named for shiny red beads on the tips of the secondary wing feathers. All species are gray-brown. The common, or Bohemian, waxwing (*Bombycilla garrulus*) is 8 in. (20 cm) long and has yellow, white, and red wing markings. It breeds in N forests of Eurasia and America. The cedar waxwing (*B. cedrorum*), smaller and less colorful, breeds in Canada and the N U.S. The Japanese waxwing (*B. japonica*) is restricted to NE Asia.

Wayne, Anthony (1745–1796) American Revolutionary officer. Born near Paoli, Pa., he joined the Continental Army and was given command of Ft. Ticonderoga (1776). He led troops in the battles of the Brandywine, Paoli, and Germantown. For his boldness in storming the British fort at Stony Point, N.Y. (1779), he earned the nickname "Mad Anthony." He served in the siege of Yorktown and later defeated the Indians allied with the British in Georgia. In 1792 Pres. George WASHINGTON sent Wayne to fight the Indians in the Ohio Territory, and he decisively ended Indian resistance at the Battle of FALLEN TIMBERS (1794).

Wayne, John *orig.* Marion Michael Morrison (1907–1979) U.S. film actor. Born in Winterset, Iowa, he won his first leading role in *The Big Trail* (1930), then played in more than 80 low-budget movies before winning acclaim for his role in John FORD's *Stagecoach* (1939). Noted for his image as the strong, silent man, Wayne, nicknamed "Duke," became one of the top box-office attractions in movie history. He starred in such other westerns (many directed by Ford) as *Red River* (1948), *She Wore a Yellow Ribbon* (1949), *The Searchers* (1956), *Rio Bravo* (1959), and *True Grit* (1969, Academy Award), as well as in *The Quiet Man* (1952), *The Alamo* (1960), which he also directed, and *The Green Berets* (1968), which he codirected.

WCTU See WOMAN'S CHRISTIAN TEMPERANCE UNION

weak force *or* **weak nuclear force** Fundamental interaction that underlies some forms of RADIOACTIVITY and certain interactions between SUBATOMIC PARTICLES. It acts on all elementary particles that have a SPIN of $^1/_2$. The particles interact weakly by exchanging particles that have integer spins. These particles have masses about 100 times that of a PROTON, and it is this relative massiveness that makes the weak force appear weak at low energies. It is now known that the weak force has intrinsically the same strength as the ELECTROMAGNETIC FORCE, and the two are believed to be different manifestations of a single electroweak force (see ELECTROWEAK THEORY).

weasel Any of several genera (CARNIVORE family Mustelidae) of voracious nocturnal predators. Weasels have slender bodies and necks, small flat heads, short legs, clawed toes, and dense short fur. Their total length is 7–20 in. (17–50 cm), and they may weigh 1–12 oz (30–350 g). The approximately 10 New World and Eurasian species of *Mustela* are reddish brown; in cold regions, their winter coat turns white, and the pelt, especially of the stoat (*M. erminea*), is called ERMINE. Weasels generally feed on rodents, fish, frogs, and birds' eggs.

weather State of the atmosphere at a particular place during a short period of time. It involves day-to-day changes in temperature, humidity, precipitation, air pressure, wind, and cloud cover. Most weather occurs in the TROPOSPHERE, but phenomena of the higher regions of the atmosphere, such as JET STREAMS, and geographic features, most notably mountains and large bodies of water, also affect it. See also CLIMATE.

weathering Physical disintegration and chemical decomposition of rocks, minerals, and immature soils at or near the earth's surface. Physical, chemical, and biological processes induced or modified by wind, water, and climate cause the changes. Weathering is distinguished from EROSION in that no transportation of material is involved.

WXYZ

weather modification Alteration of atmospheric conditions by human activity, sufficient to modify the weather on a local or regional scale. Deliberate alterations include seeding clouds to induce or augment precipitation, and firing silver-iodide particles into clouds to suppress hail and to reduce fog at airports. Inadvertent alterations are the result of industrialization and urbanization (see ACID RAIN, GLOBAL WARMING, GREENHOUSE EFFECT).

weaving Production of fabric by interlacing two sets of YARNS so that they cross each other, normally at right angles, usually accomplished with a hand- or power-operated LOOM. In weaving, lengthwise yarns are called warp and crosswise yarns are called weft, or filling. Most woven fabrics are made with their outer edges finished in a manner that avoids raveling. The three basic weaves are plain or tabby (weft threads go over one warp thread, then under one), twill (distinguished by diagonal lines), and SATIN. Fancy weaves, such as pile, Jacquard, dobby, and leno, require more complicated looms or attachments.

Web See WORLD WIDE WEB

Webb, Sidney (James) and Beatrice (1858–1943, 1859–1947) British socialist reformers. Sidney joined the FABIAN SOCIETY in 1885 and wrote the first Fabian tract, *Facts for Socialists* (1887). He met Beatrice (born Martha Beatrice Potter), author of *The Cooperative Movement in Great Britain* (1891), and they were married in 1892. Together they wrote the influential *History of Trade Unionism* (1894) and *Industrial Democracy* (1897). On the London County Council (1892–1910), Sidney effected extensive reforms in public education. The Webbs cofounded the London School of Economics and helped reorganize the Univ. of London. As a member of the Poor Laws commission (1905–9), Beatrice wrote a report that anticipated the WELFARE STATE. In 1914 they joined the Labour Party, and Sidney wrote its influential policy statement, *Labour and the New Social Order* (1918). Impressed by the Soviet Union after their trip in 1932, the Webbs wrote *Soviet Communism: A New Civilisation?* (1935).

Webber, Andrew Lloyd See Andrew LLOYD WEBBER

Weber \'vā-bər\, **Carl Maria (Friedrich Ernst) von** (1786–1826) German composer. Son of a musician and theater manager, he was born with a deformed hip and was never strong. After his early operas began to have success, he took over direction of the Prague Opera (1813–16), which he saved from ruin. Showing signs of the tuberculosis that would kill him, he began to compose prolifically. Appointed kapellmeister for life in Dresden, he began work on his operatic masterpiece, *Der Freischütz* (1821), which made him an international star. *Euryanthe* (1823) was crippled by a poor libretto, and his final opera, *Oberon* (1826), was a success only in London. He died at 39, and is remembered as one of the creators of musical Romanticism.

Weber \'vā-bər\, **Max** (1864–1920) German sociologist and political economist. Son of a wealthy liberal politician and a Calvinist mother, Weber was a compulsively diligent scholar who suffered occasional nervous collapses. Insights derived from his own experience inform his most famous and controversial work, *The Protestant Ethic and the Spirit of Capitalism* (1904–5), which examines the relationship between Calvinist (or Puritan) morality, compulsive labor, bureaucracy, and economic success under capitalism (see PROTESTANT ETHIC). Weber also wrote penetratingly on social phenomena such as charisma and mysticism. His efforts helped establish SOCIOLOGY as an academic discipline in Germany. Through his insistence on the need for objectivity and his analysis of human action in terms of motivation, he profoundly influenced sociological theory. His voluminous writings, mostly published posthumously, include *Economy and Society* (2 vols., 1922–25) and *General Economic History* (1923).

Webern \'vā-bərn\, **Anton (Friedrich Wilhelm von)** (1883–1945) Austrian composer. He learned piano and cello, and earned a doctorate with a thesis on Heinrich ISAAC. In 1904 he and Alban BERG began composition lessons with Arnold SCHOENBERG, and he was soon combining atonality with complex counterpoint in the manner of Isaac, producing works distinctive for their extreme brevity and delicacy. Af-

ter Schoenberg laid out his twelve-tone system for him in 1923, Webern embarked on such longer pieces as the *Symphony* (1928), *Concerto* (1934), and *Variations for Piano* (1936), but their character remained radically different from those of any contemporary. He worked most of his life as a conductor. During Austria's postwar occupation, he stepped outside during a curfew and was shot by an American soldier. Though he was little appreciated during his lifetime, his works soon became hugely influential internationally.

Web site Collection of files and related resources accessible through the WORLD WIDE WEB. Typical files found at a Web site are HTML documents with their associated graphic image files (GIF, JPEG, etc.), scripted programs (in PERL, JAVA, etc.), and similar resources. A Web site may contain hundreds or thousands of related files. A Web site's usual starting point, called a home page, usually functions as a table of contents, with hyperlinks to other sections of the site. Web sites are hosted on one or more Web SERVERS, which transfer requested files using the HTTP protocol. Although the term "site" implies a single physical location, the files and resources of a Web site may actually be spread among several servers in different places. The particular file desired by a client is specified by a URL that is either typed into a BROWSER or accessed by selecting a hyperlink.

Webster, Ben(jamin Francis) (1909–1973) U.S. tenor saxophonist. Born in Kansas City, he played in several important swing bands before joining Duke ELLINGTON in 1940. After 1943 he worked mostly with small ensembles. His sensual, breathy tone and wide vibrato were his trademarks, and he became one of the master interpreters of ballads in jazz.

Webster, Daniel (1782–1852) U.S. lawyer and politician. Born in Salisbury, N.H., he served in the U.S. House of Representatives (1813–17) before moving to Boston (1816) where he built a prosperous law practice and returned to the House (1823–27). He argued several precedent-setting cases before the U.S. Supreme Court, including the DARTMOUTH COLLEGE CASE and *MCCULLOCH VS. MARYLAND*. In the U.S. Senate (1827–41, 1845–50), he became famous as an orator in supporting the Union and opposing the nullification movement and its advocate John C. CALHOUN. As U.S. secretary of state (1841–43, 1850–52) he negotiated the Webster-Ashburton Treaty to settle the Canada–Maine border dispute.

Webster, John (c.1580–c.1625) English playwright. Little is known of his life, but he may have started out as an actor. He is best remembered for the revenge tragedies *The White Devil* (1612) and *The Duchess of Malfi* (1623), both of which concern the bloody deeds that arise out of family quarrels among the Italian nobility. They are often considered the greatest 17th-cent. English tragedies apart from those of William SHAKESPEARE.

Webster, Noah (1758–1843) U.S. lexicographer and writer. Born in W. Hartford, Conn., he spent many years lecturing and agitating for educational reform along American lines. His *Grammatical Institute of the English Language* included *The American Spelling Book* (1783), the famed "Blue-Backed Speller" that went on to sell some 100 million copies. An ardent and influential Federalist, he founded two pro-Federalist newspapers (1793) and wrote numerous articles on politics and many other subjects. In 1807 he began work on his landmark *American Dictionary of the English Language* (1828; 2nd ed. 1840), which became the most comprehensive dictionary of English in the world. Reflecting his principle that spelling, grammar, and usage should be based on the living, spoken language, it was instrumental in establishing the dignity and vitality of American English. In 1821 he cofounded Amherst College. Webster also wrote pioneering works on medicine and meterology.

Wedekind \'vā-də-ˌkint\, **Frank** (*orig.* Benjamin Franklin) (1864–1918) German actor and playwright. In 1891 his tragedy *The Awakening of Spring* created a scandal with its theme of awakening adolescent sexuality. In his "Lulu" cycle, *Earth Spirit* (1895) and *Pandora's Box* (1904), he extended the theme of sex to the underworld of society and introduced the amoral Lulu. His plays used episodic scenes, fragmented dialogue, distortion, and caricature, prefiguring the theater of the ABSURD and forming a transition from realism to expressionism.

wedge In mechanics, a device that tapers to a thin edge, usually made of metal or wood, and used for splitting, lifting, or tightening, such as to secure a hammer head onto its handle. The wedge is considered one of the six simple MACHINES. Wedges have been used since prehistoric times to split logs and rocks; for rocks, wooden wedges, caused to swell by wetting, have been used.

Wedgwood, Josiah (1730–1795) British pottery designer and manufacturer. His family had been potters since the 17th cent., and after forming a partnership with another potter he went into business for himself. He took a scientific approach to pottery making and was so successful that the makers of even MEISSEN and SÈVRES PORCELAIN found their trade affected. His many innovations include development of a green glaze still popular today, the perfection of creamware, and the invention of the pyrometer to measure high temperatures. Charles DARWIN was his grandson. See also WEDGWOOD WARE, WOOD FAMILY.

Wedgwood ware English STONEWARE made by Staffordshire factories originally established by Josiah WEDGWOOD. Creamware appealed to the middle class because of its high quality, durability, and affordability. Black basalts (from 1768), unglazed stoneware of fine texture ideal for imitating antique objects, appealed to antiquarians. Also in the Neoclassical tradition was jasperware (from 1775), a white, matte, unglazed stoneware that could be stained; white ornaments were then applied, achieving the look of an antique cameo. With the help of such artists as John FLAXMAN, Wedgwood copied many antique designs. Production of fine Wedgwood ware continues to the present day.

weed Any plant growing where it is not wanted. On cultivated land, weeds compete with crops for water, light, and nutrients. On rangelands and in pastures, weeds are those plants that grazing animals dislike or that are poisonous. Many weeds are hosts of plant disease organisms or of insect pests. Some originally unwanted plants later were found useful and came under cultivation, while some cultivated plants, when transplanted to new climates, escaped cultivation and became weeds.

weevil *or* **snout beetle** Any of about 40,000 BEETLE species in the largest family of beetles, Curculionidae, also the largest family in the animal kingdom. Most weevils have long, elbowed antennae that may fold into special grooves on the prominent snout. Many species are wingless. Most species feed exclusively on plants and are less than 0.25 in. (6 mm) long; some are more than 3 in. (80 mm) long. The family includes many destructive pests, including the BOLL WEEVIL.

Wegener \ˈvā-gə-nər\, **Alfred (Lothar)** (1880–1930) German meteorologist and geophysicist. After earning a PhD in astronomy (1905), he became interested in paleoclimatology and traveled to Greenland to research polar air circulation. In 1912 he formulated the first complete statement of the CONTINENTAL DRIFT hypothesis, which he published in *The Origin of Continents and Oceans* (1915). Most geologists rejected his theory, but it was resurrected in the 1960s as part of the theory of PLATE TECTONICS. Wegener died during his fourth expedition to Greenland.

weight Gravitational force of attraction on an object, caused by the presence of a massive second object, such as the earth or moon. It is a consequence of the universal law of GRAVITATION. At the same location, more massive (see MASS) objects weigh more. The farther an object is from the earth, the less it weighs. Weight W is the product of an object's mass m and the acceleration of gravity g at the location of the object, or $W = mg$. Since weight is a measure of force rather than of mass, the units of weight are newtons (N).

weight lifting Sport in which barbells are lifted competitively or as an exercise. The two main events are (1) the snatch, in which the barbell is lifted from the floor to arm's length overhead in a single motion; and (2) the clean and jerk, in which it is lifted first to the shoulders and then, after a pause, to arm's length overhead. Contestants are divided into 10 body-weight categories ranging from flyweight to superheavyweight. Lifts may range to over 1,000

lbs (455 kg) in the heavyweight divisions. The origins of modern competition are to be found in 18th- and 19th-cent. strongman contests.

weights and measures Standard quantities by which comparisons are made between an object to be measured and a known quantity of the same kind. Weights and measures are fundamental to the sciences, to engineering, building, and other technical matters, and to much everyday activity. See also FOOT, GRAM, INTERNATIONAL SYSTEM OF UNITS, METER, METRIC SYSTEM, POUND.

weight training System of conditioning involving lifting weights, especially for strength and endurance. It may include the use of barbells and dumbbells, Nautilus or similar machines, or a combination of these. Athletes use it to improve their performance, nonathletes use it for general conditioning or bodybuilding, and those recovering from an injury may use it as part of an overall rehabilitation program.

Weil \ˈvey\, **Simone** (1909–1943) French mystic and social philosopher. She taught philosophy in secondary schools and labored in factories, sharing her wages with the poor and living in poverty. She worked in the French Resistance in World War II. Though born Jewish, she became a Roman Catholic in the 1940s. She died at 34 of tuberculosis and self-imposed starvation in sympathy for those suffering in occupied France. Her posthumously published works, including *Gravity and Grace* (1947), *The Need for Roots* (1949), *Waiting for God* (1950), and *Notebooks* (3 vols., 1951–56), which particularly influenced French and English social thought, explore the spiritual shortcomings of modern industrial society and the horrors of totalitarianism.

Weill \ˈvīl\, **Kurt (Julian)** (1900–1950) German-U.S. composer. Son of a cantor, by 15 he was working as a theater accompanist. For a master class with Ferruccio BUSONI (1920), he wrote his first symphony. The sparse and spiky style of his one-act opera *Der Protagonist* (1925) prefigured that of his greatest works. In 1927 he teamed with Bertolt BRECHT to write *The Threepenny Opera* (1928) in a new "cabaret" style; the musical had enormous success in Berlin and elsewhere. In 1929 the two produced *Happy End*, and in 1930 *The Rise and Fall of the City of Mahagonny*. When the Nazis took power in 1933, he fled to Paris with his wife, Lotte LENYA, where he wrote *The Seven Deadly Sins* (1933). In the U.S. (from 1935) he collaborated on such musicals as *Knickerbocker Holiday* (1938), *Lady in the Dark* (1941), *One Touch of Venus* (1943), and *Lost in the Stars* (1949).

weimaraner \ˌvī-mə-ˈrä-nər, ˈwī-mə-ˌrä-nər\ Dog breed developed in the early 19th cent. by German nobles of the court of Weimar. A graceful dog, it has hanging ears and a short, sleek, mouse- or silver-gray coat. It stands 23–27 in. (58–69 cm) and weighs 70–85 lbs (32–39 kg). It has an alert, well-balanced stance and is valued as an aggressive hunter and a good companion and watchdog.

Weimar Republic \ˈvī-ˌmär\ Government of Germany 1919–33. The assembly that adopted its constitution met at Weimar in 1919. In its early years, the government was troubled by postwar economic and financial problems and political instability, but it had recovered considerably by the late 1920s. Its leaders included presidents Friedrich EBERT (1919–25) and Paul von HINDENBURG (1925–34). Its collapse in the GREAT DEPRESSION enabled Adolf HITLER to rise to power and become chancellor (1933), after which he suspended the Weimar constitution.

Wei Mengbian *or* **Wei Meng-Pien** \ˈwā-ˈmən-ˈpyen\ (fl. A.D. 340) Chinese mechanical engineer. He devised numerous wheeled vehicles, including a hodometer (for measuring distance) and a south-pointing carriage. He also built a wagon mill in which rotation of the wheels drove a set of millstones and hammers that automatically processed grain.

Wei River \ˈwā\ River, N central China. It rises in the mountains of SE Gansu province and flows east 537 mi (864 km) to join the HUANG RIVER. Its valley was the earliest center of Chinese civilization and the site of a succession of capital cities. In the 3rd cent. B.C., its junction with the Ching River was the site of the first ambitious irrigation works in China.

Weir \ˈwir\, **Peter (Lindsay)** (b.1944) Australian film director. He won an international audience with the haunting

WXYZ

Picnic at Hanging Rock (1975), which was followed by *The Last Wave* (1977), *Gallipoli* (1981), and *The Year of Living Dangerously* (1982). His later movies, made in Hollywood, include *Witness* (1985), *The Mosquito Coast* (1986), *Dead Poets Society* (1989), and *The Truman Show* (1998).

Weiss \'vīs\, **Peter (Ulrich)** (1916–1982) German playwright. After fleeing Germany in 1934, he settled in Sweden. He made avant-garde films, then turned to fiction, with his novel *Exile* (1962), and drama. Preoccupied with revolution and violence, he won international acclaim for his play *The Persecution and Assassination of Jean-Paul Marat as Performed by the Inmates of the Asylum of Charenton Under the Direction of the Marquis de Sade* (1964). Associated with the "theater of fact" movement, he also wrote the documentary dramas *The Investigation* (1965) and *Discourse on Vietnam* (1968).

Weissmuller \'wīs-ˌməl-ər\, **Johnny** (*orig.* Peter John) (1904–1984) U.S. freestyle swimmer and actor. Born in Pennsylvania, he attended the Univ. of Chicago. He won five Olympic gold medals (three in 1924, two in 1928) and set 67 world records. He later became even more famous as an actor, starring as Tarzan of the Apes in 12 films (1932–48) and later creating the role of Jungle Jim for film and television.

Weizmann \'vīts-män\, **Chaim (Azriel)** (1874–1952) Russian-Palestinian chemist and first president of Israel (1949–52). Born in present-day Belarus, he earned a doctorate in chemistry and patented several dyestuffs before moving to England to teach in 1904. His 1912 discovery of a bacterium that could convert carbohydrate to acetone, valuable for British armaments, won him favor that aided his negotiations for the BALFOUR DECLARATION (1917). In 1919 he obtained an agreement on Jewish-Arab coexistence in Palestine, and in 1920 he became president of the World Zionist Organization, a post from which he was ousted in 1931. He was sent to the U.S. to secure support for Israel in 1948, and in 1949 he was elected Israel's first president.

Welch, William Henry (1850–1934) U.S. pathologist. Born in Norfolk, Conn., he opened the nation's first PATHOLOGY laboratory at Bellevue Hospital Medical College (1879). From 1893 he directed the rise of Johns Hopkins Univ., where he developed the country's first true university department of pathology, recruiting William OSLER and William HALSTED for the faculty. His curriculum revolutionized U.S. medicine by having students study physical sciences and be actively involved in clinical duties and laboratory work. Welch also demonstrated the effects of diphtheria toxin and discovered bacteria involved in wound fever and gas gangrene.

Weld, Theodore Dwight (1803–1895) U.S. reformer. Born in Hampton, Conn., he left his divinity studies to become an agent for the AMERICAN ANTI-SLAVERY SOCIETY (1834). His pamphlets *The Bible Against Slavery* (1837) and *Slavery as It Is* (1839) helped convert such figures as James BIRNEY, H. W. BEECHER, and H. B. STOWE to the antislavery cause. He married his coworker Angelina GRIMKÉ (1838), and they directed schools and taught in New Jersey and Massachusetts.

welding Technique for joining metallic parts, usually through the application of heat. Discovered in the 1st millennium A.D. during attempts to manipulate IRON into useful shapes, it produced a strong, tough blade. Welding traditionally involved interlayering relatively soft and tough iron with high-carbon material, followed by hammer FORGING. Modern processes include gas, arc, and resistance welding. More recently, electron-beam welding, laser welding, and several solid-phase processes have been developed. See also BRAZING, SOLDERING.

welfare *or* **social welfare** Any of a variety of governmental programs that provide assistance to those in need. Programs include PENSIONS, disability and UNEMPLOYMENT INSURANCE, family allowances, survivor benefits, and national health insurance. The earliest modern welfare laws were enacted in Germany in the 1880s (see SOCIAL INSURANCE), and by the 1920s and '30s most Western nations had adopted similar programs. Most industrialized countries require firms to insure workers for disability (see WORKERS' COMPENSATION). Many countries pay a family allowance to reduce the poverty of large families or to increase the

birthrate. Survivor benefits, provided for widows below pension age left with a dependent child, vary considerably among nations. Of the wealthier nations, only the U.S. fails to provide national health insurance other than for the aged and the poor (see MEDICARE AND MEDICAID).

welfare economics Branch of economics that seeks to evaluate economic policies in terms of their effects on the community's well-being. It was first established in the 20th cent. Early writers defined welfare as the sum of the satisfactions accruing to an individual through an economic system, and argued that a poor man would derive more satisfaction than a rich man from an increase in income. Later writers objected that making such comparisons with any precision was impossible. A more limited criterion was later developed: one economic situation was deemed superior to another if at least one person had been made better off without anyone else being made worse off.

welfare state Concept of government in which the state plays a key role in protecting and promoting the economic and social well-being of its citizens. The term may be applied to a variety of forms of economic and social organization. A basic feature of the welfare state is SOCIAL INSURANCE, intended to provide benefits during periods of greatest need (e.g., old age, illness, UNEMPLOYMENT). The welfare state also usually includes public provision of education, health services, and housing. Such provisions are less extensive in the U.S. than in Western Europe, where comprehensive health coverage and state-subsidized university-level education are common. In socialist countries the welfare state also covers employment and administration of consumer prices. With the decline of LAISSEZ-FAIRE economics in the 20th cent., most nations instituted at least some measures associated with the welfare state. Britain adopted comprehensive social insurance in 1948, and in the U.S., welfare-state principles guided programs such as the NEW DEAL and the Fair Deal. Scandinavian countries provide state aid for the individual in almost all phases of life.

Weller, Thomas H(uckle) (b.1915) U.S. physician and virologist. Born in Ann Arbor, Mich., he studied at Harvard Medical School. For culturing POLIOMYELITIS VIRUS, which led to the development of polio vaccines, he shared a 1954 Nobel Prize with John Enders (1879–1985) and Frederick Robbins (b.1916). He was the first (with Franklin Neva) to culture rubella virus and to isolate chicken-pox virus from human cell cultures.

Welles \'welz\, **Gideon** (1802–1878) U.S. politician. Born in Glastonbury, Conn., he cofounded the *Hartford Times* (1826–36). In 1856 he founded one of the first Republican Party newspapers in New England, the *Hartford Evening Press*. As U.S. secretary of the navy (1861–69), in the Civil War he built a large Union navy from a few ships and helped form the strategic naval blockade. His diary (published 1911) gives valuable insights into the Civil War.

Welles, (George) Orson (1915–1985) U.S. film director, actor, and producer. Born in Kenosha, Wis., he made his Broadway debut in 1934. He directed an all-black cast in *Macbeth* for the Federal Theater Project. In 1937 he and John HOUSEMAN formed the Mercury Theatre, creating a series of radio dramas and winning notoriety with their panic-producing broadcast of *War of the Worlds* (1938). Welles then moved to Hollywood, where he cowrote, directed, produced, and acted in the classic *Citizen Kane* (1941), noted for its innovative narrative technique and atmospheric cinematography and considered the most influential movie in film history. His other films include *The Magnificent Ambersons* (1942), *Journey into Fear* (1943), *The Lady from Shanghai* (1948), *Othello* (1952), *Touch of Evil* (1958), and *Chimes at Midnight* (1966). His problems with Hollywood studios curtailed future productions. He was also notable as an actor in *Jane Eyre* (1944), *The Third Man* (1949), and *Compulsion* (1959).

Wellesley (of Norragh), Marquess *orig.* Richard Colley Wellesley (1760–1842) British statesman. He inherited his father's Irish title as earl of Mornington but served in the British House of Commons 1784–97. As governor of Madras and governor-general of Bengal (1797–1805), he used military force and annexation to greatly enlarge the British empire in India, but was recalled for his vast expenditures. He served as foreign secretary 1809–12. As lord lieutenant of Ireland (1821–28, 1833–34) he tried to reconcile Protestants and Catholics. Despite his own achievements, he became increasingly jealous of his younger brother, the duke of WELLINGTON.

Wellesley College Private women's college in Wellesley, Mass., chartered in 1870. Long one of the most eminent women's colleges in the U.S., it was the first to provide scientific laboratories. Among its facilities are an advanced science center and an observatory. Enrollment is about 2,300.

Wellington City (pop., 1996: 160,000), port, and capital of New Zealand. It is located in S NORTH ISLAND. Founded in 1840, it became the capital in 1865. It is the financial, commercial, and transportation center of New Zealand, and the headquarters of many cultural, scientific, and agricultural organizations.

Wellington, Duke of *orig.* Arthur Wellesley (1769–1852) British general. Son of the Irish earl of Mornington, he entered the army in 1787. Sent to India in 1796, he commanded troops to victories in the Maratha War (1803). Commanding British troops in the PENINSULAR WAR, he defeated the French in 1814, for which he was promoted to field marshal and created a duke. After NAPOLEON renewed the war against the European powers, the "Iron Duke" commanded the Allied armies to victory at WATERLOO (1815). Richly rewarded by English and foreign sovereigns, he became one of the most honored men in Europe. After serving in the Tory cabinet as master general of ordnance (1818–27), he served as prime minister 1828–30, but lost his office for opposing parliamentary reform. He was honored on his death by a monumental funeral and burial alongside Horatio NELSON.

well-made play *French* pièce bien faite. Play constructed according to strict technical principles that produce neatness of plot and theatrical effectiveness. The form was developed about 1825 by Eugène SCRIBE; it called for complex, artificial plotting, a buildup of suspense, a climactic scene in which all problems are resolved, and a happy ending. Scribe's hundreds of successful plays were imitated all over Europe; other such playwrights included Victorien SARDOU, Georges FEYDEAU, and A. W. PINERO.

Wellman, William (Augustus) (1896–1975) U.S. film director. Born in Brookline, Mass., he was a flying ace in World War I and later a barnstorming stunt pilot. Known as "Wild Bill," he made the aerial dogfight classic *Wings* (1929, Academy Award), setting standards for documentary realism, and launched a gangster movie trend with *Public Enemy* (1931), starring James CAGNEY. His other films include *A Star Is Born* (1937), *Beau Geste* (1939), *The Ox-Bow Incident* (1942), *The Story of GI Joe* (1945), and *The High and the Mighty* (1954).

Wells, H(erbert) G(eorge) (1866–1946) English novelist, journalist, sociologist, and historian. While studying science under T. H. HUXLEY, Wells formulated a romantic conception of the subject that would inspire the inventive and influential science-fiction and fantasy novels for which he is best known, including the epochal *The Time Machine* (1895), *The Invisible Man* (1897), and *The War of the Worlds* (1898). He simultaneously took on a public role as an agitator for progressive causes, including the League of Nations. He drew on memories of his lower-middle-class early life in works including the novel *Tono-Bungay* (1908). After World War I he undertook nonfiction works, including *The Outline of History* (1920). *The Shape of Things to Come* (1933) was an antifascist warning. Most of his late works reveal a pessimistic, even bitter outlook.

Wells, Ida B(ell) *or* **Ida Bell Wells-Barnett** (1862–1931) U.S. advocate for blacks' and women's rights. Born to slaves in Holly Springs, Miss., she was a teacher until she turned to journalism in the late 1880s, writing articles for black-owned newspapers. In 1892, after she denounced the lynching of three of her friends, her newspaper office was destroyed by whites. She lectured and founded antilynching societies and black women's clubs throughout the U.S. In 1895 she married Ferdinand Barnett and began writing for his newspaper, the *Chicago Conservator*. She founded the Chicago Negro Fellowship League and Chicago's Alpha Suffrage Club, perhaps the first black women's-suffrage group.

Wells Fargo & Co. U.S. company formerly involved in both express transport and banking. Founded in 1852, Wells, Fargo transported gold between the W. and E. coasts in the wake of the California GOLD RUSH. By 1866 it had gained control of almost all stagecoach business in the West. In 1905 its banking operations were separated from its express operations. The express carrier disappeared by the mid-1920s, but its security services still exist as Wells Fargo Armored Service Corp., a subsidiary of Baker Industries. The Wells Fargo Bank's holding company, Wells Fargo & Co., was established in 1968. The bank has subsidiaries and affiliates worldwide. In 1998 Wells Fargo & Co. merged with Norwest Corp.

Welsh language CELTIC LANGUAGE of Wales. Welsh is spoken by 18–20% of the population of Wales, or more than half a million people, though the number of first-language speakers is uncertain. Welsh is traditionally divided into three periods: Old Welsh (c.800–1150); Middle Welsh (c.1150–1500), with a rich medieval literature including poetic texts; and Modern Welsh (from c.1500). Vernacular Welsh, split along dialectal lines, has long been diverging from literary Welsh; many modern speakers cannot write or easily understand the traditional written language. The issue of an acceptable modern standard remains unresolved.

Welty, Eudora (1909–2001) U.S. short-story writer and novelist. A native of Jackson, Miss., Welty focused her work on a small town that resembled her birthplace and the Delta country. Her main subject is the intricacies of human relationships. She first gained attention for the story collection *A Curtain of Green* (1941), containing "Why I Live at the P.O." Other stories appear in *The Wide Net* (1943), *The Golden Apples* (1949), and *The Bride of the Innisfallen* (1955). Her novels include *Delta Wedding* (1946), *The Ponder Heart* (1954), *Losing Battles* (1970), and *The Optimist's Daughter* (1972, Pulitzer Prize).

Wenceslas II (1271–1305) King of BOHEMIA (1278–1305). He inherited the throne from his father at age 7, but his cousin Otto IV of Brandenburg served as his regent until 1283. Wenceslas gained full control of the country only after suppressing a dissident faction in 1290. A capable ruler who enlarged his kingdom, he annexed most of Upper Silesia and occupied Kraków (1291). He became king of Poland in 1300 and placed his son Wenceslas on the Hungarian throne (1301–4).

Wenders \'ven-dərs\, **Wim** (*orig.* Ernst Wilhelm) (b.1945) German film director. He directed feature films from 1973, including *Alice in the Cities* (1974), *Kings of the Road* (1976), and *The American Friend* (1977). He won acclaim in the U.S. for *Paris, Texas* (1984) and *Wings of Desire* (1987), similarly concerned with alienation and anxiety. He later directed the documentary *Buena Vista Social Club* (1999).

Wendi *or* **Wen-ti** \'wən-'dē\ *orig.* Liu Heng (d.157 B.C.) Fourth emperor of the Chinese HAN DYNASTY. His long reign (180/179–157 B.C.) was one of good government and peaceful consolidation of power; China's economy prospered and its population expanded. To later ages Wendi epitomized the virtues of frugality and benevolence.

Wendi *or* **Wen-ti** *orig.* Yang Jian (541–604) Founder of the Chinese SUI DYNASTY. He was born into a powerful family in N China, an area controlled by the non-Chinese Northern Zhou dynasty (557–81). When the Zhou emperor died, Wendi seized the throne and in 581 proclaimed the Sui dynasty. Intending to build a strong, centralized state, he designed a huge new capital at Changan and attacked entrenched local interests. He conquered the dynasties of S China, reuniting China, and broke the power of the Turkish empires in Turkistan and Mongolia. He produced a new legal code, and his government brought in tax revenues and maintained price-regulating granaries. He later became deeply involved with BUDDHISM, building shrines and dedicating relics.

Wen-ti See WENDI

Wentworth, Thomas *later* **Earl of Strafford** (1593–1641). English politician and leading adviser to CHARLES I. As lord president of the north (1628–33), he quelled defiance to the crown. As lord deputy of Ireland (1633–39), he consoli-

WXYZ

dated the royal authority, extended English settlement, and reformed the administration. He was recalled to command Charles's army against a Scottish revolt, but the costly war was opposed by the LONG PARLIAMENT; as a target representing the king's authority, he was impeached and executed.

Wenwang *or* **Wen-wang** \'wən-'wäŋ\ (c.12th cent. B.C.) Chinese king. Ruler of Zhou, one of the semibarbaric states on the W frontier of China, he was regarded by Confucian historians as a model king. He is traditionally said to have written the *YI JING (I ching)* during his imprisonment by the last ruler of the SHANG DYNASTY. His son was WUWANG, founder of the ZHOU DYNASTY.

werewolf In European folklore, a man who changes into a wolf at night and devours animals, people, or corpses, returning to human form by day. Some werewolves are thought to change shape at will; others, who inherited the condition or acquired it by being bitten by a werewolf, are transformed involuntarily under the influence of a full moon. Belief in werewolves is found throughout the world.

Wertmüller \'vert-ˌmü-lər\, **Lina** *orig.* Arcangela Wertmüller von Elgg (b.1928) Italian film director. An assistant to Federico FELLINI, she began writing and directing her own films in 1963. She achieved international fame with *The Seduction of Mimi* (1972), a satire on sexual hypocrisy, and *Love and Anarchy* (1972). Her most controversial works were the witty *Swept Away* (1974) and the morally ambiguous *Seven Beauties* (1976), about a man scrabbling to survive in a Nazi concentration camp. Her later movies included *Ciao Professore* (1994).

Weser River \'vā-zər\ River, W Germany. Formed by the Fulda and Werra rivers at Münden, it flows northward 273 mi (440 km) into the NORTH SEA through a large estuary. It has several hydroelectric dams and is linked with numerous canals.

Wesley, John (1703–1791) Anglican clergyman, evangelist, and cofounder of METHODISM. He graduated from Oxford Univ. and became a priest in the Church of England in 1728. From 1729 he participated in a religious study group in Oxford organized by his brother Charles (1707–1788). Members were called the "Methodists" for their emphasis on methodical study and devotion. In the late 1730s they came under the influence of the MORAVIAN CHURCH. In 1738, inspired by Martin LUTHER, both men had religious experiences that convinced them that salvation was possible through faith alone. They had great success in preaching to the masses in the succeeding decades. In 1784 John began ordaining ministers himself when the bishop of London refused to do so and declared his independence from the Church of England. The two wrote several thousand hymn texts, including "Hark, the Herald Angels Sing."

Wesleyan University Private university in Middletown, Conn. It was founded in 1831 by Methodists. It offers 50 fields of undergraduate and graduate study, with 11 master's programs and doctoral programs in music and sciences. Facilities include centers for African-American and E. Asian studies, an observatory, and a Center for Humanities and Arts. Enrollment is about 3,300.

Wessex Ancient Anglo-Saxon kingdom, S Britain. Its area approximated that of the modern counties of HAMPSHIRE, DORSET, WILTSHIRE, SOMERSET, Berkshire, and Avon; its capital was WINCHESTER. It is thought to have been founded by Saxon invaders around 494. Wessex conquered Kent and Sussex and, in the 9th cent., under King ALFRED the Great, kept the Danes from conquering England south of the Danelaw. By 927 it had reconquered the Danelaw, and Alfred's grandson, Athelstan, became the king of all England; thereafter all kings of Wessex were kings of England. The region figures prominently in ARTHURIAN LEGEND; Thomas HARDY set his works of fiction in "Wessex."

West, Benjamin (1738–1820) American-British painter. After studying painting in his native Philadelphia, he established himself as a portraitist in New York. He studied in Italy (1760–63) before settling in London. The patronage of GEORGE III freed him of the need to paint portraits for a living, and he became known for historical, religious, and mythological subjects. His *Death of General Wolfe* (1771) aroused controversy for its depiction of modern dress

rather than the flowing robes expected in a history painting, but was one of his most popular works. He never returned to America, but through such pupils or followers as Gilbert STUART, C. W. PEALE, and J. S. COPLEY he exerted considerable influence on the development of U.S. art.

West, Jerry (*orig.* Jerome Alan) (b.1938) U.S. basketball player and coach. Born in Cheylan, W.V., he became a two-time All-American at the Univ. of W. Virginia. As a guard for the Los Angeles Lakers (1960–74), he compiled a career scoring average of 27 points (fourth in all-time standings); his jump shot was particularly well known. As the Lakers' head coach (1976–79), he led them to 145 wins and 101 losses.

West, Mae (1892–1980) U.S. film actress. Born in Brooklyn, N.Y., she made her Broadway debut as a singer and dancer in 1911. In 1926 she began to write, produce, and star in her own Broadway plays, including the sensation-creating *Sex* (1926), *Diamond Lil* (1928), and *The Constant Sinner* (1931). Her frank sensuality, regal postures, and suggestive wisecracks became her trademarks in such popular movies as *She Done Him Wrong* (1933), *Belle of the Nineties* (1934), *I'm No Angel* (1933), and *My Little Chickadee* (1940).

West, Nathanael *orig.* Nathan Weinstein (1903–1940) U.S. writer. Born in New York City, he was supporting himself as a hotel manager when he wrote the novella *Miss Lonelyhearts* (1933), about an advice columnist whose attempts to solace his correspondents end in ironic defeat. *A Cool Million* (1934) mocks the American success dream; *The Day of the Locust* (1939) depicts the savagery lurking beneath the Hollywood dream. Since his death in an auto accident at 37, West has come to be considered a major American novelist.

West, Rebecca (*later* **Dame Rebecca**) *orig.* Cicily Isabel Fairfield (1892–1983) British journalist, novelist, and critic. From 1911 West contributed to the left-wing press and made a name as a fighter for woman suffrage. Her novels, including *The Birds Fall Down* (1966), attracted less attention than her social and cultural writings. Her history of Yugoslavia, *Black Lamb and Grey Falcon* (1942), is regarded as one of the century's finest nonfiction works. Later books include *The Meaning of Treason* (1949). Her admired reports on the NUREMBERG TRIALS were collected in *A Train of Powder* (1955).

West Bank Area (pop., 2000 est.: 2,020,000), Palestine, west of the JORDAN RIVER. The territory, about 2,270 sq mi (5,900 sq km) excluding E. Jerusalem, is also known within Israel as Judaea and Samaria. Settlements include Nabulus, HEBRON, BETHLEHEM, and JERICHO. Under a 1947 U.N. agreement it was to become Palestinian when the State of Israel was formed. Arabs denounced the partition plan and attacked Israel (see ARAB–ISRAELI WARS). Following a truce, Jordan annexed it in 1950 and governed it until Israel occupied it in 1967 (see SIX-DAY WAR). During the 1970s and '80s, Israel established settlements there, provoking Arab resentment. Arab uprisings began in 1987 in Gaza and spread to the W. Bank (see INTIFADA). In 1991 peace talks began; agreement was reached to gradually return parts of the area to the Palestinians. Israeli troops withdrew from most of Hebron in 1997. A new wave of suicide bombings in 2001 led to Israeli raids on Palestinian cities.

western Genre of novels and short stories, motion pictures, and television and radio shows set in the American West, usually during 1850–1900, when the area was opened to white settlers. The dime novels of E. Z. C. Judson (1823–1886) began to appear in the 1860s and led to a flood of mostly formulaic and highly romanticized fiction over the next hundred years. Conflicts between white pioneers and Indians and between cattle ranchers and fence-building farmers form two basic themes. Cowboys, the town sheriff, and the U.S. marshal are staple figures, and lawlessness and gun violence are standard.

Western Australia State (pop., 1998 est.: 1,831,000), W Australia. Covering 975,100 sq mi (2,525,500 sq km), it constitutes one-third of the continent, but has less than one-tenth of Australia's population; its capital is PERTH. The extensive interior region has three deserts: Great Sandy, Gibson, and GREAT VICTORIA. The coast has few good harbors. AUSTRALIAN ABORIGINES have occupied Western Australia for about 40,000 years. The W coast, visited in 1616 by the

Dutch, was explored by William DAMPIER in 1688 and 1699. In 1829 Capt. James Stirling (1791–1865) led the first group of settlers there to establish Australia's first nonconvict colony. The discovery of gold in 1886 prompted a movement for constitutional autonomy, which was granted in 1890. Initially the state suffered from slow growth, but in recent decades its economy, fueled by agriculture and mining, has been expanding.

Western Electric Co. Inc. Former U.S. telecommunications company. Founded in 1869, the firm was incorporated in Chicago in 1872. It offered a series of new products, including the world's first commercial typewriters and incandescent lamps. In 1882 it was reincorporated, becoming part of the Bell system (see AT&T CORP.). It became a major manufacturer of telephone equipment and communications satellites, in addition to producing radar and missile systems. In 1983, with the breakup of AT&T, its factories were taken over by the new entity that became AT&T Laboratories.

Western Isles See HEBRIDES ISLANDS

Westernizers See SLAVOPHILES AND WESTERNIZERS

Western Sahara *formerly* **Spanish Sahara** Territory, NW Africa. Area: 102,703 sq mi (265,867 sq km). Population (2000 est.): 245,000. Capital: EL AAIÚN. In the 4th cent. B.C. there was trade between it and Europe; later there was little European contact until the 19th cent. In 1884 Spain claimed a protectorate over the Rio de Oro region. Boundary agreements with France were concluded in 1900 and 1912. Spain formally united the area's N and S parts into the overseas province of the Spanish Sahara in 1958. In 1976 Spain relinquished its claim and the region was divided between Mauritania and Morocco; Morocco occupied the whole territory in 1979. Separatists based in Algeria declared a government-in-exile in 1976; the issue of Western Sahara's status was still unresolved in 2002. Western Sahara has vast phosphate deposits, and some potash and iron ore deposits.

Western Samoa See SAMOA

Western Schism See Western SCHISM

Western Union Corp. Former U.S. telecommunications company. It was founded in 1851 to build a TELEGRAPH line from Buffalo, N.Y., to St. Louis. By the end of 1861 Western Union had built the first transcontinental telegraph line. Western Union diversified into teletypewriter services, money orders, and mailgrams. In 1988 the company was reorganized as Western Union Corp. to handle money transfers and related services. After declaring bankruptcy in 1993, it sold its financial-services arm to First Financial Management Corp., which merged with First Data in 1995.

Western Wall *or* **Wailing Wall** Place of prayer in JERUSALEM sacred to the Jewish people. It is the only remnant of the Second Temple of JERUSALEM. Because it now forms part of a larger wall surrounding the DOME OF THE ROCK and al-Aqsa Mosque, Jews and Muslims have long fought over its control. When Israel captured the Old City in 1967, the Jews once more gained control of the site.

West Indies Islands enclosing the CARIBBEAN SEA. They may be divided into the following groups: the Greater ANTILLES, including Cuba, Jamaica, HISPANIOLA (Haiti and the Dominican Republic), and PUERTO RICO; the Lesser Antilles, including the VIRGIN ISLANDS, WINDWARD ISLANDS, LEEWARD ISLANDS, Barbados, and the islands in the S Caribbean north of Venezuela (generally considered to include Trinidad and Tobago); and the Bahamas.

Westinghouse, George (1846–1914) U.S. inventor and industrialist. Born in Central Bridge, N.Y., his first major invention was an air brake (patented 1869), which was eventually made compulsory on all American trains. His major achievement was the adoption by the U.S. of alternating current for electric power transmission. The electrical system being developed in the 1880s used direct current (DC), though alternating-current (AC) systems were being developed in Europe. Westinghouse purchased the patents for Nikola TESLA's AC motor and hired Tesla to modify it for use in his power system. In 1886 he incorporated the predecessor of WESTINGHOUSE ELECTRIC CORP. He eventually prevailed over powerful opposition from advocates of DC power, and in 1893 his company was hired to light the Chicago world's fair. He also obtained the rights to develop Niagara Falls with AC generators.

Westinghouse Electric Corp. U.S. television and radio broadcasting company, formerly an electrical-equipment manufacturer. It was founded in 1886 by George WESTINGHOUSE to make and sell alternating-current electrical systems. The company became a major supplier to the electric-utility industry. After World War II Westinghouse also manufactured nuclear reactors and defense electronics. In the 1990s it bought television and radio stations throughout the U.S., and in 1995 it acquired the television network CBS Inc. It sold its defense-electronics unit in 1996, changed its name to CBS Corp. in 1997, and sold Westinghouse Electric Co. and its nuclear operations to British Nuclear Fuels in 1999.

Westminster, Statute of (1931) Parliamentary statute that effected the equality of Britain and the then-dominions of Canada, Australia, New Zealand, S. Africa, Ireland, and Newfoundland. The self-governing dominions were to be regarded as "autonomous communities within the BRITISH EMPIRE." United in their allegiance to the crown, the nations individually controlled their own domestic and foreign affairs as equal members of the British COMMONWEALTH of Nations.

Westminster Abbey Church in London. A Norman-style church (consecrated 1065) on the site was pulled down in 1245 by Henry III (except for the nave) and replaced with the present Gothic-style abbey church. The chapel of Henry VII (begun c.1503) is noted for its exquisite fan vaulting. ELIZABETH I refounded the church as the Collegiate Church of St. Peter in Westminster (1560). The W towers (1745), by Nicholas Hawksmoor and John James, were the last addition. Every British sovereign since William the Conqueror has been crowned in the abbey except Edward V and Edward VIII. Many are also buried there, and it is crowded with the tombs and memorials to other famous Britons. Part of the S transept is known as the Poets' Corner.

Westminster Abbey

Westminster Confession Confession of faith of English-speaking Presbyterians, representing a theological consensus of international CALVINISM. It was completed in 1646 and approved by Parliament in 1648. When the monarchy was restored in 1660, the Confession lost official status in England, but it had already been adopted by the Church of Scotland (1647) and various other churches. The Confession states that the sole doctrinal authority is scripture and gives reformed views of the SACRAMENTS, the ministry, and GRACE. See also PRESBYTERIANISM.

West Nile virus Mosquito-borne viral infection. It causes an illness marked by fever, headache, muscle ache, skin rash, and sometimes encephalitis or meningitis. It normally circulates between birds and mosquitoes and is capable of infecting humans and other mammals. Originally occurring in Africa and the Mideast, it first appeared in the NE U.S. in 1999. Outbreaks spread across the country, but the effects on humans became milder. By 2003 over 250 deaths had resulted in the U.S., mostly among the elderly.

Weston, Edward (1886–1958) U.S. photographer. Born in Highland Park, Ill., he was a camera enthusiast from boyhood. In his early work he imitated Impressionist paintings, but in 1915 an exhibition of modern art inspired him to emphasize abstract form and sharp resolution of detail. His realistic pictures convey the beauty of natural objects through skillful composition and subtleties of tone, light, and texture. He is best known for his photographs of nudes and nature taken in California.

Westphalia Former province of PRUSSIA, now part of Germany. Settled by Saxons called Westphalians around A.D. 700, it was created a duchy in 1180 and for several centuries was administered for the archbishop of COLOGNE. The Peace of WESTPHALIA (1648) was signed at MÜNSTER. In 1807 NAPOLEON created the kingdom of Westphalia. Reor-

W X Y Z

ganized by the Congress of VIENNA in 1815, it became a province of Prussia in 1816, with its capital at Münster. Its cities suffered severe bombings in World War II. In 1946 it was divided among three states of W. Germany.

Westphalia, Peace of (1648) European settlements that ended the THIRTY YEARS' WAR, negotiated in the Westphalian towns of Münster and Osnabrück. Two assemblies produced one treaty between Spain and the Dutch and another between Emperor FERDINAND III, the other German princes, France, and Sweden. Territorial changes gave Sweden control of the Baltic Sea and ensured France a firm frontier west of the Rhine River. Independence was confirmed for the United Provinces of the Netherlands and for the Swiss Confederation. The treaties also confirmed the Peace of AUGSBURG and extended religious toleration to include the Reformed (Calvinist) Church. The Holy Roman Empire was forced to recognize its German princes as absolute sovereigns in their own dominions, which greatly weakened its central authority.

West Point See UNITED STATES MILITARY ACADEMY

West River See XI RIVER

West Virginia State (pop., 2000: 1,808,000), E central U.S. It covers an area of 24,232 sq mi (62,760 sq km); its capital is CHARLESTON. The OHIO RIVER forms a large section of the upper W boundary, while the POTOMAC forms a section of the N boundary. Other rivers are the Great Kanawha, Little Kanawha, MONONGAHELA, and Shenandoah. "The Mountain State," it includes part of the APPALACHIAN MTNS. and is generally rugged land; the highest elevation is Spruce Knob (4,861 ft, or 1,482 m). Long occupied by Indian hunters, it was home to the Adena, or Mound Builders, who left archaeological traces. They were succeeded by the IROQUOIS and the CHEROKEE. The first permanent white settlement was in the 1730s. The English controlled the region during the 1750s and 1760s. Though E Virginia was rapidly settled, the area's W rugged terrain restricted settlement there. After the AMERICAN REVOLUTION, largely nonslaving settlers moved west, where they grew dissatisfied with the Virginia government. With the outbreak of the AMERICAN CIVIL WAR, residents from W Virginia voted against the ordinance of secession in 1861. In 1863 it was admitted to the Union as the 35th state. Its industrial emergence, encouraged by railroad expansion, began in the 1870s when its natural resources, including coal and gas, contributed to the growth of the U.S. In the 20th cent., recreation and tourism became economically important.

Weyden \'vī-dᵊn, 'vā-dᵊn\, **Rogier van der** (1399/1400–1464) Flemish painter. At the rather advanced age of 27 he entered the studio of Robert CAMPIN. In early paintings, he combined Campin's bold style with the elegance and subtle visual refinements he admired in the art of Jan van EYCK. By 1435 he moved to Brussels and soon was appointed city painter. During that period (c.1435–40) he executed the celebrated panel of the *Descent from the Cross* for the chapel of the Archers' Guild of Louvain. Though most of his work was religious, he produced secular paintings (now lost) and some sensitive portraits. His art affected generations of Flemish artists and introduced the Flemish style throughout Europe.

whale Any of several species of aquatic MAMMALS found in oceans, seas, rivers, and estuaries worldwide but especially in the Antarctic Ocean. They evolved from land mammals, possibly the hippopotamus. They have two flippers, and the tail is horizontally flattened into two flukes; they breathe through one or two blowholes on top of the large head. Whales are regarded as highly intelligent. The BLUE WHALE is apparently the largest animal that ever lived. Whales are divided into two groups: toothed whales (Odontoceti), which use their teeth to feed on fish and squid, and BALEEN WHALES. Whales are commonly distinguished from the smaller PORPOISES and mammalian DOLPHINS and sometimes from NARWHALS, but all are CETACEANS. Overfishing has greatly depleted whale populations worldwide. See also BELUGA, BLUE WHALE, PILOT WHALE, SPERM WHALE.

whaling Hunting of WHALES for food, oil, or both. Whaling dates to prehistoric times, when Arctic peoples used stone tools to hunt whales. The Basque were the first Europeans to hunt whales commercially in the 14th–16th cent. They were followed by the Dutch and the Germans in the 17th cent. and the British and their colonists in the 18th cent. In 1712 the first SPERM WHALE was killed; its oil proved more valuable than that of the RIGHT WHALE. Whaling expeditions in pursuit of the sperm whale could last for four years. Overfishing, vegetable oil, steel-boned corsets, and the discovery of petroleum (1859) led to a steep decline in whaling in the later 19th cent., but Norwegian innovations made hunting the BLUE WHALE and the sei whale commercially feasible, and the number of whales killed rose from under 2,000 to over 20,000 between 1900 and 1911. The Norwegians and British dominated whaling into the mid-20th cent., when overfishing again made it unprofitable for most nations, though not Japan and the Soviet Union. Concern over the near-extinction of many species led to the establishment in 1946 of the International Whaling Commission. Commercial whaling was prohibited altogether in 1986, but several nations, notably Japan, Norway, and the Soviet Union, initially refused to comply.

Wharton, Edith *orig.* Edith Newbold Jones (1862–1937) U.S. writer. Born in New York City into upper-class society, Wharton began writing a few years after her marriage in 1885. Her works examine the barriers of social convention, especially in the upper class, that stand in the way of individual happiness. Her novel *The House of Mirth* (1905) established her as a leading writer. *Ethan Frome* (1911) exploits the grimmer possibilities of New England farm life. Her other books, of which she wrote almost 50, include the novels *The Custom of the Country* (1913) and *The Age of Innocence* (1920, Pulitzer Prize).

wheat Any of various CEREAL GRASSES in the genus *Triticum* of the Gramineae (or Poaceae) family, one of the oldest and most important of the cereal crops. More farmland is devoted to wheat than to any other food crop; China is the largest wheat producer. The plant has long, slender leaves, hollow stems in most varieties, and flowers in spikelets. Of the thousands of varieties known, the most important are *T. aestivum,* used to make bread; *T. durum,* used in making pasta; and *T. compactum* (club wheat), used for cake, crackers, cookies, pastries, and household flours. Winter wheat (sown in fall) and spring wheat (usually sown in spring) are the two major types. Most wheat flour is used for breadmaking. Small quantities are used in the production of starch, malt, gluten, alcohol, and other products.

Wheatley, Phillis (1753?–1784) First U.S. black woman poet. Probably born in Senegal, she was sold from a slave ship in 1761 to John Wheatley, a Boston merchant. The Wheatleys taught her to read and write English and Latin. At about 14 she began writing poetry modeled on Alexander POPE and other Neoclassical writers. Her verse attracted much attention. *Poems on Various Subjects, Religious and Moral* (1773), published in England, spread her fame to Europe. Freed in 1773, she married, worked as a servant, and died in poverty.

wheel Circular frame of hard material capable of turning on an axle. The oldest known wheel was a wooden disk of planks held together by crosspieces. A pottery wheel or turntable was developed about 3500 B.C. in Mesopotamia. The spoked wheel appeared about 2000 B.C. on CHARIOTS. Later developments included iron hubs that turned on greased axles. Perhaps the most important invention in human history, the wheel was essential to developing civilizations, and has remained essential to power generation, transportation, industrial manufacturing, and countless other applications.

whelk Any marine SNAIL of the family Buccinidae, or a snail having a similar shell. Some whelks are called CONCHS. The sturdy shell of most species in the family is slender and has a wide opening in the first whorl. The animal feeds on other mollusks through its long proboscis; some species also kill fishes and crustaceans caught in commercial traps. Most are cold-water species; tropical species are smaller and more colorful.

Whig Member of a political faction in England, particularly in the 18th cent. Originally a term for Scottish Presbyterians, it came to imply nonconformity and rebellion and was applied in 1679 to those who wanted to exclude James, the Catholic duke of York (later JAMES II), from succession to the throne of England. Opposed by the TORY faction in that struggle, the Whigs later represented the aristocratic, landowning families and the wealthy middle classes. They maintained power through patronage and connections in Parliament, but there was no distinct party until 1784, when C. J. FOX represented those who sought parliamentary reform. After 1815 and following various party realignments, the political group became the LIBERAL PARTY. See also WHIG PARTY.

Whig Party (1834–54) U.S. political party. Organized by opponents to Pres. Andrew JACKSON ("King Andrew"), it took its name from the British antimonarchist party. It favored a program of national development and supported the Second BANK OF THE U.S., espoused by Henry CLAY. Its candidate, W. H. HARRISON, won the 1840 presidential election, but his death halted enactment of the Whig nationalistic program. Clay was the party's unsuccessful candidate in 1844. In 1848 it nominated Zachary TAYLOR, who won the election. The party began to split into the "conscience" (antislavery) and "cotton" (proslavery) Whigs and was further divided by the COMPROMISE OF 1850. Its nominee in 1852, Winfield SCOTT, failed to win wide support as most Southern Whigs joined the DEMOCRATIC PARTY. In 1854 most Northern Whigs joined the new REPUBLICAN PARTY.

whippet Breed of HOUND dog developed in 19th-cent. Britain to chase rabbits in an arena. It was developed from TERRIERS and English and Italian GREYHOUNDS, which it resembles. It stands 18–22 in. (46–56 cm) and weighs about 28 lbs (13 kg). Capable of speeds up to 35 mph (56 kph), it is typically quiet and even-tempered.

Whippet

whippoorwill Species (Caprimulgus vociferus) of nocturnal N. American bird, similar to the NIGHTJAR, named for its resonant "whip-poor-will" call, which it may repeat 400 times without stopping. It lives in woods near open country, where it catches insects on the wing of dusk and dawn. By day it sleeps on the forest floor or perches lengthwise on a branch. About 10 in. (25 cm) long, it has mottled brownish plumage.

whip-tailed ray See STINGRAY

whiskey Any of several DISTILLED LIQUORS made from a fermented mash of CEREAL grains, aged in wooden containers. The earliest direct account of whiskey making is found in Scottish records from 1494. Scotch whisky has a distinctive smoky malt flavor; it is made primarily from malted BARLEY that is heated and then fermented, distilled, and blended with similar whiskeys. Irish whiskeys lack any smoky flavor and may be mixed with neutral grain spirits. Canadian whisky is a blend of highly flavored and neutral grain whiskeys. In the U.S., the largest producer and consumer of whiskey, both straight and blended whiskeys are produced. Bourbon, first produced in Bourbon Co., Ky., is a full-bodied unblended whiskey derived from corn grain. Whiskeys are consumed both unmixed and mixed in cocktails, punches, and other beverages.

Whiskey Rebellion (1794) American uprising to protest a federal liquor tax. Farmers in W Pennsylvania rebelled against paying a tax on their locally distilled whiskey and attacked federal revenue collectors. After 500 armed men burned the home of a tax inspector, Pres. George WASHINGTON ordered 13,000 federal troops to the area. The event established the authority of federal law within the states and strengthened support for a strong central government.

Whiskey Ring (1875) Group of U.S. whiskey distillers who defrauded the government of taxes. The ring operated mainly in St. Louis, Milwaukee, and Chicago and kept liquor taxes after bribing Internal Revenue officials. An investigation resulted in 238 indictments and 110 convictions. While not involved, Pres. U. S. GRANT was tarnished by the scandal. The Republican Party allegedly received some of the illegally held tax money.

Whistler, James (Abbott) McNeill (1834–1903) U.S.-British painter, etcher, and lithographer. Born in Lowell, Mass., he attended West Point but soon abandoned the army for art. In 1855 he arrived in Paris to study painting. In 1863 he

moved to London, where he had considerable success, becoming widely famous for his wit. An articulate theorist, he expounded on the "correspondences" between the arts, especially painting and music, and helped introduce Britain to modern French painting and Japanese art. From the 1870s on he concentrated on portraits. His most famous work is *Arrangement in Grey and Black, No. 1* (1871–72), known as *Whistler's Mother*. In 1877 he brought a libel suit against John RUSKIN for attacking his *Nocturne in Black and Gold: The Falling Rocket* (1875); he won his case but the costs of the suit bankrupted him. A commission for etchings took him to Venice in 1880, and the 50-odd works he produced there won him success again in London on his return.

Whitby, Synod of Meeting of the Christian Church of the Anglo-Saxon kingdom of Northumbria in 663–64 to decide whether to follow Celtic or Roman usages. Though Northumbria had been mainly converted by Celtic missionaries, the king decided for Rome, believing that Rome followed the teaching of St. PETER, holder of the keys to heaven. The decision led to the acceptance of Roman usage elsewhere in England.

White, E(lwyn) B(rooks) (1899–1985) U.S. essayist and literary stylist. Born in Mount Vernon, N.Y., White joined the fledgling *New Yorker*'s staff in 1927, and would contribute to it and later to *Harper's* magazine over several decades. His *Stuart Little* (1945), *Charlotte's Web* (1952), and *The Trumpet of the Swan* (1970) are classics of children's literature. His revision of *The Elements of Style* (1959), by his professor William Strunk, became a standard style manual for writers. He received a Pulitzer Prize special citation in 1978.

White, James S(pringer) and Ellen G(ould) *orig.* Ellen Gould Harmon (1821–1881, 1827–1915) Cofounders of the Seventh-Day Adventists. James, born in Palmyra, Me., was a schoolteacher and then a minister who accepted the ADVENTIST views of William Miller (1782–1849). He married Ellen Harmon, born in Gorham, Me., in 1846; she had become a Millerite at 13. Ellen had over 2,000 visions before she died; these helped guide the Seventh-Day Adventist Church, which was formed in 1863. Ellen continued preaching after James's death, coming to be regarded by some as a prophet. Of her many books, the best known is *Steps to Christ*.

White, John (d.1593?) British artist, explorer, and N. American colonist. He returned from an expedition to Greenland in 1577 with sketches of the land and its people. His 1585 trip to colonize Roanoke was sponsored by Sir Walter RALEIGH. White's paintings and sketches illustrated a report of the region after the colony was abandoned (1586). Appointed governor of a second colony, he arrived at Roanoke with 100 colonists (1587), then returned to England for supplies. A relief expedition to Roanoke in 1590 found no trace of the colonists.

White, Minor (1908–1976) U.S. photographer and editor. Born in Minneapolis, he began to photograph seriously in 1938 for the WORKS PROGRESS ADMINISTRATION. In 1946 he worked with Edward WESTON and Alfred STIEGLITZ before moving to San Francisco, where he worked closely with Ansel ADAMS. He succeeded Adams as head of the Calif. School of Fine Arts photography department, and later taught at MIT. He cofounded and edited (1952–76) the photography magazine *Aperture*. His efforts to extend photography's range of expression made him one of the century's most influential photographers.

White, Patrick (Victor Martindale) (1912–1990) Australian (English-born) writer. As a youth White moved between Australia and England. He saw Australia as a country in a volatile process of growth and self-definition; his somewhat misanthropic novels, which often explore the possibilities of savagery in that context, include *Voss* (1957), *Riders in the Chariot* (1961), and *The Twyborn Affair* (1979). His other works include plays and short stories. In 1973 he became the first Australian to receive the Nobel Prize for Literature.

White, Stanford (1853–1906) U.S. architect. Born in New York City, he trained with Henry Hobson RICHARDSON. In 1880 he formed a firm with Charles MCKIM and William R. Mead that soon became the most famous in the country, known especially for its Shingle-style country and seaside mansions, and later its Neoclassical structures. White's de-

WXYZ

sign for the Casino (1881) at Newport, R.I., exhibited the graceful proportions and Italian Renaissance ornamentation at which he excelled. His New York commissions included Madison Square Garden (1891) and the Washington Arch (1891). He also designed jewelry, furniture, and interiors. An extrovert noted for his lavish entertainments, he was shot to death by the husband of a showgirl with whom he had had a love affair.

White, T(erence) H(anbury) (1906–1964) English (Indian-born) novelist, social historian, and satirist. Originally a teacher, he attained his first critical success with the autobiographical *England Have My Bones* (1936). He later devoted himself to writing, studying subjects such as ARTHURIAN LEGEND while living a largely reclusive life. He is best known for his adaptation of Thomas MALORY's *Le Morte Darthur* in the four-novel epic *The Once and Future King* (1958).

White, Theodore H(arold) (1915–1986) U.S. writer. Born in Boston, White became one of *Time*'s first foreign correspondents, serving in East Asia 1939–45 and later in Europe. He is best known for his astute, suspenseful accounts of two presidential elections, *The Making of the President, 1960* (1961, Pulitzer Prize) and *The Making of the President, 1964* (1965), which were followed by similar analyses of the 1968 and 1972 campaigns.

white blood cell See LEUKOCYTE

white dwarf star Any of a class of small, faint STARS at the end of their evolution without the mass to become NEUTRON STARS or BLACK HOLES. The first ones found were white, but various colors occur, depending on temperature. Extremely dense, they typically have the sun's mass in the earth's volume. With its nuclear fuel used up, a white dwarf cannot produce heat by NUCLEAR FUSION to counteract its own gravity, which compresses the electrons and nuclei of its atoms to the limit. Its residual thermal energy lasts billions of years; it then becomes a cold, inert stellar remnant, sometimes called a black dwarf. White dwarf stars play a crucial role in NOVA outbursts, and if mass transfer increases their mass beyond the Chandrasekhar limit, they collapse and generate a SUPERNOVA explosion.

whitefish Any of several silvery food fishes (family Salmonidae, or Coregonidae), inhabiting cold N lakes. Whitefish weigh about 2–5 lbs (1–2 kg); they eat insect larvae and other small animals. The Lake Superior whitefish *(Coregonus clupeaformis),* also called whiting or shad, is the largest of the lake whitefishes. The best sport fishes of the family are the Rocky Mtn. whitefish *(Prosopium williamsoni)* and other round whitefishes.

white-footed mouse See DEER MOUSE

Whitehead, Alfred North (1861–1947) British mathematician and philosopher. He taught principally at Cambridge Univ. (1885–1911) and Harvard (1924–37). His *Treatise on Universal Algebra* (1898) extended Boolean symbolic logic. He collaborated with Bertrand RUSSELL on the epochal *Principia Mathematica* (1910–13). He later developed a comprehensive metaphysical theory. In *Process and Reality* (1929), he proposed that the universe consists entirely of becomings. Other works include "On Mathematical Concepts of the Material World" (1905), *An Introduction to Mathematics* (1911), "The Aims of Education" (1916), *The Concept of Nature* (1920), and *Religion in the Making* (1926).

Alfred North Whitehead

Whitehorse City (pop., 2000 est.: 21,000), capital of Yukon Territory. Located on the YUKON RIVER, it was founded during the KLONDIKE GOLD RUSH (1897–98). Robert SERVICE got inspiration for his ballads while working there. The territorial capital since 1952, it is an important transportation center on the Alaska Highway, as well as an outfitting base.

White Horse, Vale of the Valley, OXFORDSHIRE, England. It is named for the White Horse, a gigantic (374 ft or 114 m long) prehistoric figure of a horse formed by cutting away the turf on the side of a chalk hill. A number of other prehistoric remains are in the vicinity, including the megalith known as Wayland's Smithy.

White House Official residence, in Washington, D.C., for every U.S. president since John ADAMS. In 1791 James Hoban (1762–1831) won the commission to build the presidential residence with his plan for a Georgian mansion in the style of Andrea PALLADIO. The British burned the structure in 1814, but it was rebuilt and enlarged under Hoban's direction. In the 1820s, Hoban added E and W terraces as well as a semicircular S portico and a colonnaded N portico. The later addition of the West Wing (1902) and East Wing (1942) provided additional office space. Theodore ROOSEVELT adopted "White House" as the building's official name in 1902.

White Lotus Dissident Chinese society. In the 12th cent., it was a pious vegetarian group dedicated to the worship of the Buddha Amitabha. It developed into a millenarian organization active in rebellions (c.1300) in the YUAN DYNASTY. The White Lotus Rebellion (1796–1804), in the mountains of central China, consisted of uncoordinated guerrilla bands that were hard to combat; it was eventually put down by peasants organized into local militias. Later Chinese governments used the term White Lotus for all illegal millenarian groups. The Nian Rebellion of 1852 may have been a new manifestation, as was the secret society behind the BOXER REBELLION.

White Monk See CISTERCIAN

White Mountains Segment of the APPALACHIAN MTNS. It extends 87 mi (140 km) across N New Hampshire and into W Maine. Containing the highest elevations in the NE U.S., its loftiest peaks, mostly 5,000–6,000 ft (1,500–1,800 m), occur in the Presidential Range, a series of summits named for U.S. presidents. The highest is Mt. WASHINGTON. Most of the White Mtns. lie within the White Mtn. National Forest. It is a popular resort area.

White Nile See NILE RIVER

White River River, Arkansas. It rises in NW Arkansas, flows north into S Missouri, then bends southeast and south to join the ARKANSAS RIVER near its confluence with the MISSISSIPPI RIVER. It is 685 mi (1,102 km) long.

White Sea Sea, extension of the ARCTIC OCEAN, NW Russia. It resembles a huge inlet; its shape is defined by the Kola Peninsula. Rivers, including the Northern Dvina and Onega, flow into it. An important transportation route, it remains navigable year-round with the help of icebreakers in winter. ARKHANGELSK is its principal port.

white shark See GREAT WHITE SHARK

white-tailed deer *or* **Virginia deer** Common reddish brown DEER *(Odocoileus virginianus),* an important game animal from S Canada to S. America. The tail, white on the underside, is held aloft when the deer is alarmed or running. The male has forwardly curved antlers with several unbranched tines. Northern white-tailed deer grow up to 3.5 ft (107 cm) tall and weigh up to 400 lbs (180 kg). The white-tailed deer lives in open woodlands and eats leaves, twigs, fruits, nuts, lichen, and fungi.

Whitman, Marcus (1802–1847) U.S. missionary and pioneer. Born in Rushville, N.Y., he became a physician and Congregational missionary and was sent to the Oregon region. In 1836 he and his wife founded a mission among the Cayuse Indians near present-day Walla Walla, Wash. In 1842 he traveled east to encourage settlement of the Oregon country; he returned in a caravan of 1,000 immigrants. Caring for Indian children in a measles epidemic, he was accused of sorcery when many died while white children survived. The Indians attacked the whites and massacred 14, including the Whitmans. Their deaths led Congress to organize the Oregon Territory in 1848.

Whitman, Walt(er) (1819–1892) U.S. poet, journalist, and essayist. Born in West Hills, Long Island, N.Y., Whitman left school at 12 and went on to hold a great variety of jobs, including writing and editing for periodicals. His revolutionary poetry dealt with extremely private experiences while celebrating the collective experience of an idealized democratic American life. His *Leaves of Grass* (first ed., 1855), revised and much expanded in successively larger editions, was too frank and unconventional to win wide acceptance in its day, but exerted a strong influence on American and foreign literature. Written without rhyme or traditional meter, such poems as "I Sing the Body Electric" and "Song of Myself" assert the beauty of the human body, physical health, and sexuality; later editions included "Crossing Brooklyn Ferry," "Out of the Cradle Endlessly Rocking," and

Walt Whitman Photo by Mathew Brady

"When Lilacs Last in the Dooryard Bloom'd." The prose *Democratic Vistas* (1871) and *Specimen Days & Collect* (1882–83) drew on wartime and later experiences. Whitman exerted a powerful influence on 20th-cent. poetry.

Whitney, Eli (1765–1825) U.S. inventor and manufacturer. Born in Westboro, Mass., he is best remembered as the inventor of the COTTON GIN (1793), which led to greatly increased production of the short-staple cotton grown in the South, making the region prosperous. The most important innovation credited to Whitney may be the concept of MASS PRODUCTION of interchangeable parts. His idea of manufacturing quantities of identical parts for assembly into muskets, after undertaking in 1797 to supply the U.S. government with 10,000 muskets, helped inaugurate the vastly important AMERICAN SYSTEM OF MANUFACTURE.

Whitney, Gertrude Vanderbilt *orig.* Gertrude Vanderbilt (1875–1942) U.S. sculptor and art patron. Great-granddaughter of Cornelius VANDERBILT, she was born to great wealth in New York City, and studied sculpture there and in Paris. Among her major works were the *Titanic Memorial* in Washington, D.C. (1914–31), and *Washington Heights War Memorial* in New York (1922). All her works were simple, direct, and traditional. In 1929 she offered to donate her collection of modern American artworks to the Metropolitan Museum of Art, but was refused. The next year she founded the Whitney Museum of American Art; today it is the foremost museum of American art.

Whitney, John Hay (1904–1982) U.S. multimillionaire and sportsman. Born in Ellsworth, Me., the son of Harry Payne Whitney and Gertrude Vanderbilt WHITNEY, "Jock" Whitney attended Yale Univ. and later Oxford. He became a champion polo player, his stables produced notable racehorses, he invested in successful films and Broadway plays, and he boasted one of the finest art collections in the U.S. For his service in World War II, he was awarded the Legion of Merit. Whitney served as ambassador to Britain 1956–61. He was publisher and editor in chief of the *New York Herald Tribune* in its last years. He founded the John Hay Whitney Foundation in 1946.

Whitney, Mt. Peak in the SIERRA NEVADA, SE central California. Located in SEQUOIA NATIONAL PARK, it is 14,494 ft (4,418 m) high, the highest point in the contiguous U.S.

Whittier, John Greenleaf (1807–1892) U.S. poet and reformer. A Quaker born on a farm near Haverhill, Mass., Whittier published his first volume of poems in 1831. During 1833–42 he became a prominent antislavery crusader, and he thereafter continued to support humanitarian causes. After the Civil War he was noted for his vivid portrayals of rural New England life. His best-known poem is the nostalgic pastoral "Snow-Bound" (1866).

Whittington, Richard *known as* **Dick Whittington** (d.1423) Lord mayor of London (1397–99, 1406–7, 1419–20). The son of a knight, he earned a vast fortune as a merchant and made loans to HENRY IV and HENRY V before serving as lord mayor. In legend he is portrayed as an orphan who ventures his only possession, a cat, to be sold on one of his master's trading ships. Ill-treated by the cook, he runs away, but at the edge of the city he hears the city bells say, "Turn again, Whittington, lord mayor of great London." He re-

turns to find that his cat has been sold for a great sum to a Moorish ruler plagued by rats. He becomes a wealthy merchant and later lord mayor.

Whittle, Frank (*later* **Sir Frank**) (1907–1996) British inventor of the JET ENGINE. He obtained his first patent for a TURBOJET engine in 1930, and in 1936 he cofounded Power Jets Ltd. The outbreak of World War II spurred the British government to support Whittle's work, and the first jet-powered aircraft took off in 1941. He received the Order of Merit in 1986.

WHO See WORLD HEALTH ORGANIZATION

wholesaling Selling of merchandise to anyone other than a retail customer, usually in quantity. Wholesaling became especially necessary after the introduction of MASS PRODUCTION and mass marketing. Without wholesalers, large manufacturers would have to market their products directly to a huge number of retailers or consumers at high unit costs, and retailers or consumers would have to deal with an inconveniently large number of manufacturers. There are three major categories of wholesalers. Merchant wholesalers, the most important category, are independent businesses that buy merchandise in great quantities from manufacturers and resell it to retailers. Manufacturers' sales branches are businesses founded by manufacturers to sell directly to retailers. Merchandise agents and brokers represent various manufacturers; they usually do not buy the merchandise they handle but instead arrange for its shelf space and display. See also RETAILING.

whooping cough *or* **pertussis** Acute, very contagious CHILDHOOD DISEASE, typically with bouts of coughing followed by a long, loud inhalation (whoop) and ending with mucus expulsion and often vomiting. Caused by the bacterium *Bordetella pertussis,* it initially resembles a cold with a short dry cough. After one or two weeks, coughing bouts begin and last four to six weeks. Serious complications include bronchopneumonia (PNEUMONIA involving the bronchi), asphyxia, and rarely, seizures and signs of brain damage. Treatment is supportive. Antibiotics are ineffective but can combat additional infections; children are routinely vaccinated against it.

whooping crane Migratory N. American bird (*Grus americana*), one of the world's rarest birds. The tallest N. American bird, it is almost 5 ft (150 cm) tall and has a wingspread of about 7 ft (210 cm). It is white with black-tipped wings, black legs, and a bare red face and crown. Its shrill, whooping call can be heard for 2 miles (3 km). It was almost exterminated in the early 20th cent.; by century's end there were fewer than 300 alive. See also SANDHILL CRANE.

Whorf \'wòrf\, **Benjamin Lee** (1897–1941) U.S. linguist. Born in Winthrop, Mass., he worked professionally as a fire-prevention authority. The concept he developed (under Edward SAPIR's influence) of the equation of culture and language became known as the Whorf (or Sapir-Whorf) hypothesis. He maintained that a language's structure tends to condition the ways its speakers think—for example, that the way a people views time and punctuality may be influenced by the types of verb TENSES in its language.

Wicca Modern Western witchcraft movement. Some practitioners consider Wicca the religion of pre-Christian Europe, forced underground by the Christian church. Modern Wicca is usually dated to the work of Gerald B. Gardner (1884–1964) and Doreen Valiente (1922–1999), who, after the repeal of the last Witchcraft Act in England (1951), went public with their cult, centered on a horned god of fertility and a great earth goddess. Wiccans share a belief in the importance of the feminine principle, a deep respect for nature, and a pantheistic and polytheistic worldview. They practice some form of ritual magic, almost always considered good or constructive.

Wichita \'wi-chə-ˌtò\ City (pop., 2000: 344,000), S central Kansas, on the ARKANSAS RIVER. Founded in 1864, it developed with the Texas cattle trade along the CHISHOLM TRAIL and the rapid spread of agricultural settlement along the ATCHISON, TOPEKA AND SANTA FE RAILROAD. In the 1870s it was a major cattle-shipping center. It developed as a center of the aircraft industry in the 1920s; oil refining, grain processing, and livestock marketing are also important.

W X Y Z

Wideman, John Edgar (b.1941) U.S. writer. Born in Washington, D.C., he grew up in Homewood, Pa. The second African-American to receive a Rhodes scholarship to Oxford Univ., he published his first novel, *A Glance Away*, in 1967. He won PEN/Faulkner Awards for *Sent for You Yesterday* (1983) and *Philadelphia Fire* (1990), a fictional account of the bombing of the militant black group MOVE. The nonfiction *Fatheralong* examines his relationship with his son, now in prison. A recent novel is *The Cattle Killing* (1996).

Wieland \\'vē-ˌlänt\\, **Heinrich Otto** (1877–1957) German chemist. He won a 1927 Nobel Prize for research on BILE acids that showed that the three then isolated had similar structures and were structurally related to CHOLESTEROL. He also found that different forms of nitrogen in organic compounds can be detected and distinguished from each other. Wieland's theory that oxidation in living tissues occurs through removal of hydrogen atoms (see OXIDATION-REDUCTION) was of great importance to physiology, biochemistry, and medicine.

Wiener \\'wē-nər\\, **Norbert** (1894–1964) U.S. mathematician. Born in Columbia, Mo., he earned a PhD from Harvard at 18. He joined the faculty of MIT in 1919. His work on generalized harmonic analysis won the American Mathematical Society's Bôcher Prize in 1933. The origin of CYBERNETICS as an independent science is generally dated from the 1948 publication of his *Cybernetics*. He made contributions to quantum theory and, during World War II, to gunfire control. Crater Wiener on the Moon is named for him.

Wiener Werkstätte \\'vē-nər-'verk-ˌshtet-ə\\ *English* Vienna Workshops. Cooperative enterprise for crafts and design founded in Vienna in 1903. Inspired by William MORRIS and the English ARTS AND CRAFTS MOVEMENT, it was founded by Koloman Moser (1868–1918) and Josef HOFFMANN with the goal of restoring the values of hand craftsmanship. It had close ties to the Vienna SEZESSION and ART NOUVEAU movements. In jewelry, furnishings, interior design, and fashion, it often celebrated the beauty of geometry and became widely known for elegance and innovation; this "square style" influenced the work of the BAUHAUS craftsmen in the 1920s as well as the work of F. L. WRIGHT.

Wiesbaden \\'vēs-ˌbä-dən\\ City (pop., 1998 est.: 268,000), capital of HESSE, S Germany, on the RHINE RIVER. Since Roman times it has been noted for its hot saline springs. Made an imperial city in 1241, it passed to the counts of Nassau in 1255. It became part of Prussia in 1866. In 1946 it became the capital of the newly created state of Hesse. Noted for its spa in the 18th–19th cent., it was frequented by J. W. von GOETHE, Johannes BRAHMS, and Fyodor DOSTOYEVSKY. It continues to be a popular resort. It has printing firms, publishing houses, and film studios; it is noted for its Sekt (German champagne).

Wiesel \\vē-'zel\\, **Elie** (*orig.* Elizer) (b.1928) Romanian-U.S. novelist. Living in a small Hasidic community, he was deported in 1944 to Auschwitz and then to Buchenwald; his parents and sister were killed. All his works reflect his experiences as a survivor of the Holocaust. They include *Night* (1958), *A Beggar in Jerusalem* (1968), and *The Forgotten* (1989). He was awarded the 1986 Nobel Peace Prize for his universal condemnation of violence, hatred, and oppression.

Wiesel \\'vē-səl\\, **Torsten (Nils)** (b.1924) Swedish-U.S. neurobiologist. He and David Hubel (b.1926) investigated brain function. By analyzing nerve impulses from the eye in laboratory animals, they detected many structural and functional details of the visual cortex. Their studies of the effects of visual impairments in young animals lent strong support to the view that prompt surgery is crucial to correct certain eye defects in newborn children. The two shared a 1981 Nobel Prize with Roger SPERRY.

wig Manufactured head covering of real or artificial hair worn in the theater, as personal adornment, disguise, or symbol of office, or for religious reasons. Ancient Egyptians, Greeks, and Romans used wigs, often as protection from the sun. In the West, the wig first became an acceptable form of adornment or corrective for nature's defects in the 16th cent., and men's perukes, or periwigs, came into widespread use in the 17th and 18th cent. Women wore wigs surreptitiously in the 18th–19th cent.; after the development of inexpensive synthetic wigs in the 20th cent., women's wigs increased in popularity.

Wight, Isle of Island and county (pop., 1998 est.: 127,000) off the S coast of England, in the ENGLISH CHANNEL. Separated from the mainland by The SOLENT, the island has an area of 147 sq mi (381 sq km). Its backbone is a chalk ridge that extends across its entire breadth, the thickest bed of chalk in the British Isles. The Needles are three detached masses of chalk that lie off its westernmost point. The island's warm, sunny climate has made it a popular vacation spot.

Wigner, Eugene (Paul) (*orig.* Jeno Pal) (1902–1995) Hungarian-U.S. physicist. Having emigrated to the U.S. in 1930, he was instrumental in getting the MANHATTAN PROJECT started and was present when Enrico FERMI initiated the first chain reaction. He determined that the nuclear force is short-range and does not involve an ELECTRIC CHARGE, using GROUP THEORY to investigate atomic structure. His name was given to several formulations, including the Breit-Wigner formula, which describes resonant nuclear reactions. He shared a 1963 Nobel Prize for his insights into QUANTUM MECHANICS, especially principles governing interaction of protons and neutrons in the nucleus and his formulation of the law of conservation of PARITY (see CONSERVATION LAW). He also received numerous awards for his work for peace.

wigwam American Indian dwelling, characteristic of the ALGONQUIAN-speaking nomadic tribes of what is now the NE U.S. It is constructed of saplings driven into the ground in a circle and tied together at the top, then covered with mats of woven rushes or sewn bark.

Wilberforce, William (1759–1833) British politician. He entered the House of Commons in 1780. Converted to evangelical Christianity (1785), he agitated against the slave trade; his sponsorship of antislavery legislation led to abolition of the slave trade in the British W. Indies (1807). From 1821 he agitated for emancipation of all slaves and was joined by Thomas F. Buxton (1786–1845), who continued to sponsor legislation after Wilberforce retired (1825); the Slavery Abolition Act was passed one month after Wilberforce's death.

Wilbur, Richard (Purdy) (b.1921) U.S. poet, critic, editor, and translator. Born in New York City, he won an early reputation with the collections *The Beautiful Changes* (1947) and *Ceremony* (1950). His urbane, well-crafted verse later appeared in such volumes as *Things of This World* (1956, Pulitzer Prize), *Walking to Sleep* (1969, Bollingen Prize), and *New and Collected Poems* (1988, Pulitzer Prize). He also has translated the plays of MOLIÈRE and written children's books. He served as the country's second poet laureate in 1987–88.

wild boar See BOAR

wild carrot See QUEEN ANNE'S LACE

wildcat Wild species (*Felis silvestris*) of CAT (family Felidae) native to Eurasian forests. Very similar to the domestic yellowish tabby, it will interbreed with DOMESTIC CATS, of which it is presumably an ancestor. It preys on birds and small animals at night. In N. America the name is used for the BOBCAT and LYNX; in Africa it refers to the Caffre cat.

Wilde, Oscar (Fingal O'Flahertie Wills) (1854–1900) Irish wit, poet, and dramatist. A spokesman for AESTHETICISM, in the early 1880s he gave a lecture tour in the U.S. and established himself in London circles by his wit and flamboyance. His only novel, *The Picture of Dorian Gray* (1891), combines gothic elements with mockery of bourgeois morality. His macabre play *Salomé* (1893) became the basis for Richard STRAUSS's opera; his other plays, all successes, include *Lady Windermere's Fan*

Oscar Wilde, 1882

(1893), *A Woman of No Importance* (1893), and *An Ideal Husband* (1895). His greatest work was the comedy *The Importance of Being Earnest* (1899), a satire of Victorian social hypocrisy. Though happily married, in 1891 he began an intimate relationship with the young Lord Alfred Douglas, son of the Marquess of Queensberry. Accused by the latter as a sodomite, Wilde sued him and lost, then was arrested and convicted in a trial that became internationally celebrated. Imprisoned 1895–97, he wrote a recriminatory letter to his lover that was published as *De Profundis* (1905). After his release, he moved to Paris; his only later work was *The Ballad of Reading Gaol* (1898). He died at 46.

wildebeest See GNU

Wilder, Billy (*orig.* Samuel) (1906–2002) Austrian-U.S. film director. A reporter and screenwriter, he fled Germany in 1933 and arrived in Hollywood a year later. He cowrote screenplays with Charles Brackett and established his reputation as a director with *Double Indemnity* (1944). Noted for his humorous treatment of controversial subjects and his biting indictments of hypocrisy, he also directed *The Lost Weekend* (1945, Academy Award), *Sunset Boulevard* (1950, Academy Award for best screenplay), *Stalag 17* (1953), and *The Apartment* (1960, Academy Award). His acclaimed comedies include *Sabrina* (1954), *The Seven Year Itch* (1955), and *Some Like It Hot* (1959).

Wilder, Laura Ingalls *orig.* Laura Ingalls (1867–1957) U.S. children's author. Born in Lake Pepin, Wis., she led the pioneer life with her family, living in Kansas, Minnesota, Iowa, S. Dakota (where she married), and Missouri. Encouraged by her daughter to write down her childhood memories, she wrote the internationally popular *Little House* books (1932–1943), eight (or nine) in all.

Wilder, Thornton (Niven) (1897–1975) U.S. playwright and novelist. Born in Madison, Wis., he earned wide acclaim for his second novel, *The Bridge of San Luis Rey* (1927, Pulitzer Prize). His *Our Town* (1938, Pulitzer Prize), which became one of the most enduringly popular of all American plays, was followed by the successful *The Skin of Our Teeth* (1942, Pulitzer Prize). In them he rejected naturalism, often discarding props and scenery and having the characters address the audience directly. His *The Matchmaker* (1954) was adapted into the musical *Hello, Dolly!* (1964).

wild pig See BOAR

wild rice Coarse annual GRASS (*Zizania aquatica*) of the family Gramineae (or Poaceae) whose grain has long been an important food of American Indians. Not related to RICE, wild rice grows naturally in shallow water in marshes and along the shores of streams and lakes in N central N. America. The plant, about 3–10 ft (1–3 m) tall, is topped with a large, open flower cluster. The ripened grains, dark brown to purplish-black, are slender rods 0.4–0.8 in. (1–2 cm) long.

Wild West Show Theatrical extravaganza produced by W. F. (Buffalo Bill) CODY. First performed in 1883, the show reached New York's Madison Square Garden in 1887 with a cast of 100 Indians, the sharpshooter Annie OAKLEY, and such wild animals as buffalo, elk, bear, and deer. The four-hour spectacle, including an attack on a stagecoach, toured Europe to great success in the 1890s, and continued touring the U.S. until 1916.

Wilfrid, St. *or* **Wilfrid of York** (634–709?) English bishop who established close relations between the Anglo-Saxon Church and the papacy. At the Synod of WHITBY he successfully advocated the adoption of Roman over Celtic usages. As bishop of York, he introduced the BENEDICTINE Rule to the kingdom. A quarrel over the division of his diocese obliged Wilfrid to take refuge in Sussex, where he Christianized the people and founded a monastery at Selsey.

Wilhelmina (Helena Pauline Maria) (1880–1962) Queen of the Netherlands (1890–1948). Daughter of King William III, she became queen on his death, under her mother's regency until 1898, and soon gained wide popular approval. After Germany invaded the Netherlands in 1940, she left with her family for London. Throughout World War II her radio broadcasts to the Dutch people were a symbol of resistance to the German occupation. In 1948 she abdicated in favor of her daughter, JULIANA.

Wilkes, John (1725–1797) English politician. His early life was profligate, and he bribed voters to win election to the House of Commons (1757). For an attack on the government in his journal the *North Briton* (1763), he was prosecuted for libel and expelled from Parliament. Reelected, he continued to print his attacks and was twice again expelled (1764, 1769). Regarded as a victim of persecution and a champion of liberty, he gained widespread popular support. He become lord mayor of London in 1774. Back in the House of Commons 1774–90, he supported parliamentary reform and freedom of the press.

Wilkins, Maurice (Hugh Frederick) (b.1916) New Zealand-British biophysicist. He participated in the MANHATTAN PROJECT. On his return to Britain, he began investigations that led to studies of DNA. His X-ray diffraction studies of DNA proved crucial to the determination of DNA's molecular structure by James WATSON and Francis CRICK, for which the three were awarded a 1962 Nobel Prize. He later used X-ray diffraction to study RNA.

Wilkins, Roy (1901–1981) U.S. civil rights leader. Born in St. Louis, he became managing editor of the black-owned *Kansas City Call*. In 1931 he joined the staff of the NAACP and was editor (1934–49) of its official publication, *The Crisis*. As executive director of the NAACP (1955–77), he set it on a course to seek equal rights through legal redress. He helped organize the 1963 March on Washington, and chaired the U.S. delegation to the International Conference on Human Rights in 1968.

Wilkinson, David (1771–1852) U.S. inventor. Born in Smithfield, R.I., in 1797 he invented a gauge and sliding lathe for turning iron and brass, which proved valuable in constructing machines for U.S. armories. He produced much of the machinery used by Samuel SLATER, and apparently built the first American steamboat 16 years before Robert FULTON.

Wilkinson, James (1757–1825) American army officer and double agent. Born in Calvert Co., Md., he served in the AMERICAN REVOLUTION under Horatio GATES and was involved in the Thomas CONWAY cabal. He settled in Kentucky in 1784 and schemed to ally the Kentucky region with Spain, while in fact working against Spain. He allegedly planned to conquer the Mexican provinces of Spain and conspired with Aaron BURR to establish an independent government; when he betrayed Burr's plan, he was investigated but cleared.

will In law, a formal declaration, usually in the form of an executed document, of a person's wishes regarding the disposal of his or her property after death. It is valid if it meets the laws of the law, which usually requires that it be witnessed. It may be considered invalid if, among other instances, the testator was mentally incapable of disposing of his or her property, if it imposes unreasonable or cruel demands as a condition of inheritance, or if the testator did not have clear title to the bequeathed assets. See also PROBATE.

Willamette River \wə-'la-mət\ River, NW Oregon. It flows north for 300 mi (485 km) into the COLUMBIA RIVER near PORTLAND. Oregon's most populous cities, including SALEM and EUGENE, are in its valley.

Willemstad \'vi-ləm-ˌstät\ City (pop., 1999: 123,000), capital of the NETHERLANDS ANTILLES, W. INDIES. Located on CURAÇAO, it was founded in 1634. It has many Dutch-Colonial buildings and the oldest (1732) synagogue in the W Hemisphere. Its chief industries are oil refining, banking, and tourism.

William I *known as* **William the Conqueror** (1028?–1087) Duke of Normandy (1035–87) and king of England (1066–87). He succeeded his father as duke of Normandy, subduing rebellions and becoming the mightiest feudal lord in France. In 1051 EDWARD THE CONFESSOR promised to make him heir to the English throne, but on Edward's death in 1066, HAROLD II became king. Determined to assert his right to the throne, William sailed from Normandy with an invasion force, defeated Harold at the Battle of HASTINGS, and was crowned king (see NORMAN CONQUEST). To secure England's frontiers, he invaded Scotland (1072) and Wales (1081). In 1086 he ordered the survey summarized in the DOMESDAY BOOK. He divided his lands among his sons, giv-

ing Normandy and Maine to ROBERT II and England to WILLIAM II.

William I *known as* **William the Lion** (1143–1214) King of Scotland (1165–1214). Forced to relinquish the earldom of Northumberland to England's HENRY II in 1157, he succeeded his brother, Malcolm IV, as king of Scotland and in 1173 joined a revolt of Henry's sons in an attempt to regain Northumberland. Captured in 1174, he was released after submitting to Henry's overlordship; he bought his release from subjection in 1189. He was forced to renounce his claim to Northumberland by King JOHN in 1209. William created many of the major burghs of modern Scotland.

William I *Dutch* Willem Frederik (1772–1843) King of the Netherlands (1815–40). Son of William V, prince of Orange, he emigrated to England after the French invasion of the Dutch Republic (1795). He sided with Prussia against NAPO-LEON and lived in exile at the Prussian court until 1812. After the Dutch revolt against French rule, he became king of the United Netherlands (1815), which included Belgium, Liège, and Luxembourg. He led an economic recovery program, but his autocratic methods and imposition of Dutch as the official language provoked a revolt by Belgium (1830) that led to its independence. In 1840 he abdicated in favor of his son, WILLIAM II.

William I *German* Wilhelm Friedrich Ludwig (1797–1888) King of Prussia (1861–88) and German emperor (1871–88). Son of FREDERICK WILLIAM III of Prussia, he was military governor of Rhineland province from 1849, and succeeded his brother on the Prussian throne in 1861. A supporter of military reform, he appointed Otto von BISMARCK prime minister (1862). Though conservative, he cautiously supported Bismarck's policies in the SEVEN WEEKS' WAR and the FRANCO–PRUSSIAN WAR. Proclaimed German emperor in 1871, he oversaw the continued rise of Germany as a European power.

William I *Dutch* Willem *known as* **William the Silent** (1533–1584) First stadtholder of the United Provinces of the Netherlands (1572–84). He inherited the principality of Orange and other vast estates from his cousin in 1544. Appointed by PHILIP II to the council of state (1555), he helped negotiate a pro-Habsburg treaty, earning his byname for keeping silent about secret policy decisions, and was named stadtholder (governor) in Holland, Zeeland, and Utrecht in 1559. Opposed to Philip's strict ordinances against Protestants, he led an unsuccessful revolt in 1568, but in 1572 succeeded in uniting the N provinces. He was proclaimed their stadtholder, and his position was solidified by the Pacification of GHENT (1576). He sought help from France in the revolt against Spain, and in 1579 he was outlawed by Philip. In 1584 he was shot by a fanatical Catholic.

William II *or* **William Rufus** (1056?–1100) King of England (1087–1100). He inherited England from his father, WILLIAM I, and quelled a rebellion by barons loyal to his brother ROBERT II (1088). A tyrannical ruler, he brutally punished the leaders of a second revolt (1095). He reduced the Scottish kings to vassals (1093), subjugated Wales (1097), and waged war on Normandy (1089–96), gaining control when Robert mortgaged the duchy. His death in a hunting accident may have been ordered by his brother Henry (later HENRY I).

William II *Dutch* Willem Frederik George Lodewijk (1792–1849) King of the Netherlands (1840–49). Son of WILLIAM I, he commanded Dutch troops in the Battle of WATERLOO (1815). Sent by his father to Belgium in 1830 to appease the rebels, he failed to stop the independence movement. In 1840 he became king of the Netherlands on his father's abdication. As king, he helped stabilize the economy. In 1848 he oversaw passage of a new liberal constitution that established direct elections and secured basic civil liberties.

William II *German* Friedrich Wilhelm Viktor Albert *known as* **Kaiser Wilhelm** (1859–1941) German emperor (kaiser) (1888–1918). Grandson of WILLIAM I and also of Queen VIC-TORIA, William succeeded his father to the throne in 1888. Two years later, he forced the resignation of Otto von BIS-MARCK. He was characterized by his frequently militaristic manner and by his vacillating policies that undermined those of his chancellors. From 1897 he encouraged the strengthening of the German fleet and challenged France's

position (see the MOROCCAN CRISES). He sided with Austria-Hungary against Serbia (1914), and in World War I encouraged the grandiose war aims of the generals and politicians. After Germany's defeat, he fled to the Netherlands, ending the monarchy in Germany.

William III *Dutch* Willem Hendrik (1650–1702) Stadtholder of the United Provinces of the Netherlands (1672–1702) and king of England (1689–1702). Son of William II, Prince of Orange, and Mary, daughter of CHARLES I of England, he was born soon after his father's death. Named stadtholder by popular acclaim in 1672, he successfully defended his country against CHARLES II of England and LOUIS XIV of France. In 1677 he married Mary (later MARY II), daughter of the future English king JAMES II. In 1688 William was invited by James's opponents to intervene against the Catholic ruler, and he landed with a Dutch army, to carry out the GLORIOUS REVOLUTION. He and Mary were proclaimed joint rulers of England in 1689; he ruled alone after Mary's death in 1694. He directed the European opposition to Louis XIV, which led to the War of the GRAND ALLIANCE. In Britain he secured religious toleration, strengthened Parliament, and oversaw the Act of SETTLEMENT.

William IV (1765–1837) King of Great Britain and Ireland and of Hanover (1830–37). The son of GEORGE III, he entered the royal navy at 13 and fought in the American Revolution, leaving the navy as a rear admiral in 1790. After numerous love affairs and fathering 10 illegitimate children by the actress Dorothea Jordan (1761–1816), he succeeded his brother GEORGE IV as king. Opposed to parliamentary reform, William delayed consideration of the REFORM BILL OF 1832, but his prime minister, Earl GREY, persuaded him to force its passage. On William's death, the British crown passed to his niece, VICTORIA, and the Hanoverian crown to his brother Ernest Augustus, duke of Cumberland (1771–1851).

William and Mary, College of State-supported college in Williamsburg, Va. The second-oldest institution of higher education in the U.S. (after HARVARD UNIV.), it was chartered in 1693 by King WILLIAM III and Queen MARY II. Its alumni include Thomas JEFFERSON, John MARSHALL, James MONROE, and John TYLER. George WASHINGTON was the college's first American chancellor, from 1788 to 1799. PHI BETA KAPPA was organized there in 1776. Enrollment is about 8,000.

William of Ockham See William of OCKHAM

William Rufus See WILLIAM II (ENGLAND)

Williams, Daniel Hale (1858–1931) U.S. surgeon. Born in Hollidaysburg, Pa., in 1891 he founded Provident Hospital in Chicago, the first interracial hospital in the U.S., to provide training for black interns and nurses. There in 1893 he performed the first successful heart surgery; the patient lived at least 20 years after Williams sutured a wound of the pericardium (the sac around the heart). In 1913 he became the only black charter member of the American College of Surgeons.

Williams, Eric (Eustace) (1911–1981) First and longtime prime minister of independent Trinidad and Tobago (1962–81). He received a doctorate from Oxford Univ. and taught at Howard Univ. in the U.S. before founding the People's National Movement (PNM) in 1956 and taking his nation into the Federation of the W. Indies in 1958, only to withdraw in favor of independence in 1962. He stressed social services and education and stimulated development by cautiously attracting foreign investment. He served as prime minister until his death.

Williams, Hank (*orig.* Hiram King) (1923–1953) U.S. singer and guitarist. Born into poverty in Georgiana, Ala., Williams began playing guitar at 8, made his radio debut at 13, and formed his first band at 14. His "Lovesick Blues" became a smash hit in 1949, and he joined the GRAND OLE OPRY that year after an extraordinary debut appearance. He wrote almost all his own songs, including "Jambalaya," "Your Cheatin' Heart," and "Hey, Good Lookin'." His death at 29 may have resulted from drug and alcohol abuse. He remains perhaps the most revered figure in the history of COUNTRY MUSIC.

Williams, John (Towner) (b.1932) U.S. composer and conductor. Born in Queens, N.Y., Williams began his career as a jazz pianist, but began to compose for TV and film in 1958. The most successful film composer in history, he has scored over 100 films, including *Jaws* (1975), the *Star Wars* trilogy, the *Indiana Jones* films, *E.T.* (1982), and *Schindler's List* (1993), and has won five Academy Awards. He has also written many concert works. He was conductor of the Boston Pops 1980–93.

Williams, Mary Lou (1910–1981) U.S. pianist, composer, arranger, and bandleader. Born in Atlanta, Williams wrote arrangements for many swing bands, including Duke ELLINGTON, beginning in 1929. Her *Zodiac Suite* was performed by the New York Philharmonic in 1946. A pianist with strong roots in the BLUES and early jazz, Williams embraced the innovations of BEBOP and later free jazz, performing with musicians as diverse as Dizzy GILLESPIE and Cecil Taylor.

Williams, Ralph Vaughan See Ralph VAUGHAN WILLIAMS

Williams, Robin (b.1952) U.S. film actor and comedian. Born in Chicago, he worked as a stand-up comedian before winning favorable notice in the television series *Mork and Mindy* (1978–82). A nervous, creative comic with a gift for rapid-fire improvisation, he has played comic and serious roles in such movies as *Good Morning Vietnam* (1987), *Dead Poets Society* (1989), *The Fisher King* (1991), *Mrs. Doubtfire* (1993), and *Good Will Hunting* (1997, Academy Award).

Williams, Roger (1603?–1683) British-American clergyman and founder of Rhode Island. He arrived in Boston in 1631 and became pastor of the separatist Plymouth Colony (1632–33). Banned from the MASSACHUSETTS BAY COLONY for his beliefs, including support for religious toleration and the rights of Indians, he founded the colony of Rhode Island and the town of Providence (1636). The colony established a democratic government and separation of church and state, and became a haven for Quakers and others seeking religious liberty. He obtained a charter for the colony (1643) and served as its first president, maintaining friendly relations with the Indians and acting as peacemaker for nearby colonies.

Williams, Ted (*orig.* Theodore Samuel) (1918–2002) U.S. baseball player, one of the great hitters of all time. Born in San Diego, he began playing professionally at 17. He was an outfielder with the Boston Red Sox from 1939 until his retirement in 1960. Tall and thin, he was dubbed "the Splendid Splinter," or more simply "the Kid." He compiled a lifetime batting average of .344, the fifth-highest on record. He batted .406 in 1941, becoming the last .400 hitter of the century. His career slugging percentage (.634) is second only to that of Babe RUTH. He is the only player besides Rogers HORNSBY to have twice won the batting triple crown. Despite losing five years of his career to service as a wartime flyer, he hit a total of 521 home runs (twelfth-highest in history). He later managed the Washington Senators (1969–72).

Williams, Tennessee (*orig.* Thomas Lanier) (1911–1983) U.S. playwright. Born in Columbus, Miss., he won recognition for his one-act plays *American Blues* (1939). Much wider success came with *The Glass Menagerie* (1944; film, 1950), *Summer and Smoke* (1948; film, 1961), *A Streetcar Named Desire* (1947, Pulitzer Prize; film, 1951), *Camino Real* (1953), and *Cat on a Hot Tin Roof* (1955, Pulitzer Prize; film, 1958). His plays, which also included *Suddenly Last Summer* (1958; film, 1959), *Sweet Bird of Youth* (1959; film, 1962), and *The Night of the Iguana* (1961; film, 1964), described a world of repressed sexuality and violence thinly veiled by gentility. He also wrote the novel *The Roman Spring of Mrs. Stone* (1950; film, 1961) and the screenplays for *The Rose Tattoo* (1955, adapted from his 1951 play) and *Baby Doll* (1956). A clear-sighted chronicler of fragile illusions, he is regarded as one of the greatest American playwrights.

Williams, Venus and Serena (b.1980, 1981) U.S. tennis players. Born in Lynwood, Cal., and Saginaw, Mich., respectively, the sisters were trained in tennis from age 4 by their father. They won several major titles in 1997. Venus won the singles championship at Wimbledon in 2000, becoming the first black woman to do so since Althea GIBSON, and won both the U.S. Open and Wimbledon championships in 2001. Serena won the U.S. Open in 1999 and in 2002 de-

feated her sister in the finals of the French Open, Wimbledon, and the U.S. Open. In 2000 the sisters won an Olympic gold medal in doubles, and they have captured doubles titles at all four Grand Slam tournaments.

Williams, William Carlos (1883–1963) U.S. poet. Williams spent a lifetime writing poetry and practicing pediatrics in his hometown of Rutherford, N.J. He is noted for making the ordinary appear extraordinary through a powerful evocation of the world of common objects, in such collections as *Spring and All* (1923). *Paterson* (1946–58) grew into a five-volume epic vision of modern American life. His other poetry includes *Pictures from Brueghel* (1962, Pulitzer Prize). His numerous prose works include essays, a trilogy of novels, short stories, drama, and autobiography.

Williamsburg City (pop., 2000: 12,000), SE Virginia. Located on a tidewater peninsula, it was settled in 1633 as Middle Plantation and served as a refuge from Indian attacks. The College of WILLIAM AND MARY was founded there in 1693. After the burning of nearby JAMESTOWN in 1699, it served as the capital of Virginia until 1780. During the AMERICAN CIVIL WAR, Confederate forces were defeated at the Battle of Williamsburg in 1862. Colonial Williamsburg is an extensive restoration of several hundred colonial buildings.

Williams College Private liberal-arts college in Williamstown, Mass. Established in 1793 by the Congregational Church, it is consistently rated as one of the best colleges in the U.S. Campus facilities include notable collections of art and materials relating to U.S. history. Enrollment is about 2,200.

William's War, King See KING WILLIAM'S WAR

William Tell See William TELL

William the Conqueror See WILLIAM I (THE CONQUERER)

William the Silent See WILLIAM I (NETHERLANDS)

Willkie, Wendell L(ewis) (1892–1944) U.S. politician. Born in Elwood, Ind., he moved to New York in 1929 as an attorney for the Commonwealth and Southern Corp., of which he was president 1933–40. He led the opposition of utilities companies to competition from the federally funded Tennessee Valley Authority. His criticism of Pres. Franklin ROOSEVELT led to his dark-horse victory at the 1940 Republican presidential convention. After a vigorous campaign, he won only 10 states but received more votes than any other Republican to that time. His *One World* (1943) was a best-selling plea for postwar international cooperation.

willow Any shrub or tree of the genus *Salix*, family Salicaceae, native mostly to N temperate regions, and common in lowland and marshy areas. Willows are valued as ornamentals and for their shade, erosion control, and timber. Certain species yield salicin, the source of SALICYLIC ACID. All species have alternate, usually narrow leaves, catkins, and seeds with long, silky hairs. Pussy willows, the male form of several shrubby species, have woolly catkins that form before the leaves appear. Weeping willows have long drooping branches and leaves.

Wills, Helen (Newington) *later* **Helen Wills Moody** (1905–1998) U.S. tennis player. Born in Centerville, Cal., she won the first of seven U.S. singles titles in 1923. She took the gold medal in both singles and doubles at the 1924 Olympic Games. So overpowering was her game that from 1927 to 1932 she won every set she played in U.S. singles play. She took the Wimbledon title eight times (1927–30, 1932, 1933, 1935, 1938).

Wilmington City (pop., 2000: 73,000), N Delaware. It is the state's largest city and its industrial, financial, and commercial center and main port. Settled by Swedes in 1638 and called Ft. Christina, it was captured by Peter STUYVESANT's Dutch forces in 1655; they were ousted by the English in 1664. It became a prosperous port after the Quakers moved there in the 1730s. The Battle of the BRANDYWINE was fought nearby. In 1802 E. I. du Pont de Nemours established a gunpowder mill there (see DU PONT CO.).

Wilmot Proviso \prə-ˈvī-ˌzō\ (1846) Proposal in the U.S. Congress to prohibit the extension of slavery to the territories. Offered by Rep. David Wilmot as an amendment to a bill that purchased territory from Mexico, it prohibited slavery in the new territory. It provoked a national debate that reflected the growing discord between North and

W X Y Z

South. Though never approved by Congress, it became a basic tenet of the REPUBLICAN PARTY.

Wilson, Alexander (1766–1813) Scottish-U.S. ornithologist. In Scotland his satirical poetry led to a fine and imprisonment, and in 1794 he emigrated to the U.S. Influenced by William BARTRAM, he decided about 1804 to write on N. American birds, and began studying art and ornithology. His pioneering *American Ornithology* (9 vols., 1808–14) established him as a founder of the field.

Wilson, August (b.1945) U.S. playwright. Born in Pittsburgh, he cofounded the Black Horizons Theater (1968), published poetry in black journals, and produced several plays, including *Jitney* (1982), before his *Ma Rainey's Black Bottom* opened on Broadway in 1984. Inspired by the colloquial language, music, folklore, and storytelling tradition of black Americans, he continued his cycle of plays, each set in a different decade of the 20th cent., with *Fences* (1986, Pulitzer Prize), *Joe Turner's Come and Gone* (1988), *The Piano Lesson* (1990, Pulitzer Prize), *Two Trains Running* (1992), and *Seven Guitars* (1996).

Wilson, Edmund (1895–1972) U.S. writer. Born in Red Bank, N.J., he worked as a reporter and magazine editor before his writings, in which he probed diverse subjects with scholarship and common sense in lucid prose, began appearing in the *New Republic* and later the *New Yorker*. Among his influential critical works are *Axel's Castle* (1931), a survey of the Symbolist poets; *To the Finland Station* (1940), a study of the thinkers who set the stage for the Russian Revolution; and *Patriotic Gore* (1962) analyzing American Civil War literature. His other writings include short stories, and journals. He was widely regarded as the leading man of letters of his time.

Wilson, Edward O(sborne) (b.1929) U.S. biologist. Born in Birmingham, Ala., he taught at Harvard from 1956. Recognized as the world's leading authority on ants, he discovered their use of pheromones for communication. His *The Insect Societies* (1971) was the definitive treatment of the subject. In 1975 he published *Sociobiology*, a highly controversial and influential study of the genetic basis of social behavior in which he claimed that even a characteristic such as unselfish generosity may be genetically based and that preservation of the gene rather than the individual is the focus of evolutionary strategy. In *On Human Nature* (1978, Pulitzer Prize) he explored SOCIOBIOLOGY's implications in regard to human aggression, sexuality, and ethics. With Bert Hölldobler he wrote the major study *The Ants* (1991, Pulitzer Prize). He has been a strong advocate for global conservation.

Wilson, (James) Harold *later* Baron Wilson (of Rievaulx) (1916–1995) British prime minister (1964–70, 1974–76). While at Oxford Univ., he collaborated with William BEVERIDGE on work that led to the latter's 1942 report. Drafted into the civil service, he produced a study of the mining industry; his book *New Deal for Coal* (1945) was the basis for the Labour Party's plan to nationalize the coal mines. He became leader of the Labour Party in 1963. As prime minister, he widened the party's voting majority in 1966 but faced economic problems after the devaluation of the pound in 1967. In his second term, he confirmed Britain's membership in the EUROPEAN ECONOMIC COMMUNITY (1975). He resigned unexpectedly in 1976.

Wilson, Harriet E. *orig.* Harriet Adams (1828?–1863?) U.S. writer, probably the first African-American to publish a novel in English in the U.S. Little is known of her early life, but she probably worked as a servant in New Hampshire and later Massachusetts. Her one book, written to make money to reclaim her son from foster care, is *Our Nig* (1859), a largely autobiographical novel that treats racism in the pre–Civil War North.

Wilson, James (1742–1798) Scottish-American lawyer and politician. He arrived in Philadelphia in 1765, where he practiced law. In 1774 he published a widely read treatise proposing a commonwealth of British colonies. A delegate to the Continental Congress (1775–77), he signed the Declaration of Independence. He helped draft the U.S. Constitution and the Pennsylvania state constitution, delivering lectures that became landmarks in American jurisprudence. He served on the U.S. Supreme Court 1789–98.

Wilson, J(ohn) Tuzo (1908–1993) Canadian geologist and geophysicist. Born in Ottawa, he became a professor of geophysics at the Univ. of Toronto. He established global patterns of faulting and the structure of the continents, and in the 1960s he became the world's leading spokesman for the theory of CONTINENTAL DRIFT. His studies also were important for the SEAFLOOR SPREADING hypothesis and the theory of convection currents within the earth.

Wilson, Robert W(oodrow) (b.1936) U.S. radio astronomer. Born in Houston, he headed Bell Labs' Radio Physics Research Department 1976–94. With Arno PENZIAS, he detected the COSMIC BACKGROUND RADIATION, for which the two shared a 1978 Nobel Prize with Pyotr Kapitsa (1894–1984).

Wilson, (Thomas) Woodrow (1856–1924) 28th president of the U.S. (1913–21). Born in Staunton, Va., he earned a law degree and later a doctorate. He taught political science at Princeton Univ. 1890–1902 before becoming its president (1902–10). Elected governor of New Jersey, his reform measures attracted national attention, and he became the Democratic presidential nominee in 1912. Emphasizing the progressive measures of his New Freedom policy, he defeated Theodore ROOSEVELT and W. H. TAFT to win the presidency. As president, he

Woodrow Wilson

approved legislation that created the FEDERAL RESERVE SYSTEM, established the FEDERAL TRADE COMMISSION, and strengthened labor unions. In foreign affairs, he maintained U.S. neutrality in WORLD WAR I, offering to mediate a settlement and initiate peace negotiations, even after the sinking of the LUSITANIA (1915). Having "kept us out of war," he was narrowly re-elected in 1916, defeating C. E. HUGHES. Germany's renewed submarine attacks on passenger ships caused Wilson to ask for a declaration of war in April 1917. In a continuing effort to negotiate a peace agreement, he presented the FOURTEEN POINTS (1918). At the PARIS PEACE CONFERENCE, he attempted to stand on his original principles but was forced to compromise. The Treaty of VERSAILLES faced opposition in the Senate from the Republican majority led by H. C. LODGE. In search of support for the treaty and its LEAGUE OF NATIONS, Wilson began a cross-country speaking tour, but he collapsed and returned to Washington, D.C. (Sept. 1919), where a stroke left him partially paralyzed. He rejected any attempts to compromise his version of the League of Nations and urged his Senate followers to reject the treaty, which was defeated in 1920. He was awarded the 1919 Nobel Peace Prize.

Wilson's disease *or* **hepatolenticular degeneration** \ˈhi-ˌpat-ə-lən-ˌtik-yə-lər\ Recessive hereditary defect (see RECESSIVENESS) that impairs ability to metabolize copper, which accumulates in the basal ganglia of the brain (involved in control of movement), causing progressive degeneration; forms a brownish ring at the margin of the cornea of the eye; and is deposited in the liver, gradually leading to CIRRHOSIS. It usually appears in the teens or twenties. Early diagnosis and treatment with diet and a substance to chelate copper can reverse the effects and prevent permanent damage.

Wiltshire \ˈwilt-ˌshir\ County (pop., 1998 est.: 426,000), S England. It lies in a watershed separating the basins of the BRISTOL CHANNEL, the ENGLISH CHANNEL, and the River THAMES. In prehistoric times its chalk uplands were the most heavily populated parts of England; its prehistoric monuments include STONEHENGE and Iron Age hill forts. The town of Salisbury has long been an ecclesiastical center and is renowned for its cathedral.

Wimbledon Municipal center in the Greater London borough of Merton, site of the annual lawn-tennis All-England Championships. The oldest (founded 1877) and most prestigious tennis tournament in the world, it is one of four that make up the Grand Slam of tennis, and the only one still played on natural grass.

Winchell, Walter *orig.* Walter Winchel (1897–1972) U.S. journalist and broadcaster. Born in New York, he entered vaudeville at 13. He later became a full-time gossip columnist at the *New York Daily Mirror*, where his widely syndicated column appeared until 1963. He had a weekly radio program from 1932 until the early 1950s. A prolific phrasemaker, he was noted for his slangy Broadway idiom. His opinionated news reports brought him a massive audience and great influence from the 1930s through the 1950s.

Winchester City (pop., 1995 est.: 39,000), county seat of HAMPSHIRE, England. It was the capital of WESSEX and a center of learning under ALFRED the Great; later it was the seat of the Danish king CANUTE's government. It remained important under the Norman kings until the late 12th cent. It is known for its cathedral (11th–14th cent.) and for Winchester College, founded in 1382.

Winchester, Oliver (Fisher) (1810–1880) U.S. manufacturer of guns and ammunition. Born in Boston, in 1857 he purchased the Volcanic Repeating Arms Co., which became the Winchester Repeating Arms Co. (1867). His chief gun designer, B. T. Henry, designed the lever-action Henry repeating rifle (patented 1860). Widely used in the American Civil War, it inaugurated a long line of Winchester guns, including the Model 73, a favorite weapon of settlers in the U.S. West.

Winckelmann \'viŋ-kəl-ˌmän, *Engl* 'wiŋ-kəl-mən\, **Johann (Joachim)** (1717–1768) German archaeologist and art historian. He studied theology and medicine before he discovered Greek art. His essay *Reflections on the Painting and Sculpture of the Greeks* (1755) became a manifesto of the Greek ideal in education and art. After converting to Catholicism he moved to Rome (1755) and held important posts in the Vatican. His *History of the Art of Antiquity* (1764) inaugurated the study of art history as a discipline and of archaeology as a humane science. His writings reawakened the popular taste for classical art and helped generate the Neoclassical movement in the arts.

wind Movement of air relative to the surface of the earth. Wind is an important factor in climate and weather. It is also the generating force of most ocean and freshwater waves. Wind occurs because of horizontal and vertical differences in atmospheric pressure. The general pattern of winds over the earth is known as the general circulation, and specific winds are named for the direction from which they originate (e.g., a wind blowing from west to east is a westerly). Wind speeds are often classified according to the Beaufort scale.

Beaufort Scale

No.	Name	Wind speed, mph (kph)	Description
0	Calm	<1 (<1)	Calm; smoke rises vertically
1	Light air	1–3 (1–5)	Direction of wind shown by smoke but not by wind vanes
2	Light breeze	4–7 (6–11)	Wind felt on face; leaves rustle; wind vane moves
3	Gentle breeze	8–12 (12–19)	Leaves and small twigs in constant motion; wind extends light flag
4	Moderate breeze	13–18 (20–29)	Wind raises dust and loose paper; small branches move
5	Fresh breeze	19–24 (30–39)	Small-leaved trees begin to sway; crested wavelets form on inland waters
6	Strong breeze	25–31 (40–50)	Large branches move; overhead wires whistle; umbrellas difficult to control
7	Moderate gale or near gale	32–38 (51–61)	Whole trees sway; walking against wind is difficult
8	Fresh gale or gale	39–46 (62–74)	Twigs break off trees; moving cars veer
9	Strong gale	47–54 (75–87)	Slight structural damage occurs; shingles may blow away
10	Whole gale or storm	55–63 (88–102)	Trees uprooted; considerable structural damage occurs
11	Storm or violent storm	64–72 (103–117)	Widespread damage occurs
12	Hurricane	>73 (>118)	Widespread damage occurs

windchill Still-air temperature that would have the same cooling effect on exposed skin as a given combination of temperature and wind speed. As the wind speed increases, the windchill equivalent temperature decreases; e.g., an air temperature of 30°F (–1.1°C) with a wind speed of 20 mph (32.2 kph) produces a windchill of 17°F (–8°C). It is not an exact measure, since other variables that affect heat loss, such as humidity, are not considered. However, windchill is often given in weather reports to describe how cold it feels.

	temperature (°F)												
wind speed (mph)	35	30	25	20	15	10	5	0	–5	–10	–15	–20	–25
5	31	25	19	13	7	1	–5	–11	–16	–22	–28	–34	–40
10	27	21	15	9	3	–4	–10	–16	–22	–28	–35	–41	–47
15	25	19	13	6	0	–7	–13	–19	–26	–32	–39	–45	–51
20	24	17	11	4	–2	–9	–15	–22	–29	–35	–42	–48	–55
25	23	16	9	3	–4	–11	–17	–24	–31	–37	–44	–51	–58
30	22	15	8	1	–5	–12	–19	–26	–33	–39	–46	–53	–60
35	21	14	7	0	–7	–14	–21	–27	–34	–41	–48	–55	–62
40	20	13	6	–1	–8	–15	–22	–29	–36	–43	–50	–57	–64
45	19	12	5	–2	–9	–16	–23	–30	–37	–44	–51	–58	–65

Windermere Lake, NW England. Located in the SE LAKE DISTRICT, it is the country's largest lake, 10.5 mi (17 km) long and 1 mi (1.6 km) wide, with a maximum depth of 219 ft (67 m). Part of a national park, it is a popular tourist center.

Windhoek \'vint-ˌhük\ Town (pop., 1997 est.: 169,000), capital of Namibia. Originally settled by African peoples, in 1890 the site of the present town was claimed for the German government. In 1915 S. African forces occupied the area, then known as S.W. Africa. When Namibia became independent in 1990, Windhoek became its capital. It is the country's main commercial center.

windmill Machine for harnessing the energy of the wind using sails mounted on a rotating shaft. The sails are mounted at an angle or are given a slight twist, so that the force of wind against them has two components, one of which, in the plane of the sails, causes rotation. Their most important traditional use was for grinding grain, though in certain areas their use in land drainage and water pumping was equally important. Windmill use became increasingly widespread in Europe (particularly the Netherlands) from the 12th cent. to the early 19th cent., but thereafter slowly declined. See also WIND POWER.

window Opening in the wall of a building for light and air, and sometimes to frame a view. Since early times, the openings have been filled with stone, wooden, or iron grilles, with panes of glass, or with other translucent material such as mica or, in the Far East, paper. A window in a vertically sliding frame is called a sash window: a single-hung sash has only one half that moves; in a double-hung sash, both parts slide. A casement window swings open on hinges attached to the upright side of the frame. Awning windows swing outward on hinges attached to the top of the frame; hopper windows swing inward on hinges attached to the bottom of the frame. Large, fixed (nonoperating) areas of glass are commonly called picture windows. See also ROSE WINDOW, SHOJI.

windpipe See TRACHEA

wind power Use of the energy in winds to produce power. Though wind is irregular and spread out, it contains tremendous amounts of energy. Sophisticated wind TURBINES have been developed to convert this energy to electric power. The use of wind-energy systems grew considerably in the 1980s and '90s. Germany today produces more wind energy than any other country. Nearly 15,000 wind turbines are now in operation in California. See also WINDMILL.

wind shear Rapid change of wind speed and direction over a very short distance. A narrow zone of abrupt velocity change is known as a shear line. Wind shear is observed near the ground, often during thunderstorms, and in JET STREAMS, where it may be associated with clear-air turbulence. Wind shear has been a factor in many airplane crashes.

Windsor, Duchess of *orig.* Bessie Wallis Warfield (1896–1986) U.S.-British wife of the duke of Windsor (formerly

W X Y Z

EDWARD VIII). Born in Blue Ridge Summit, Pa., she married Earl Spencer in 1916. After their divorce (1927), she married Ernest Simpson (1928) and moved with him to London. As a member of fashionable British society, she met Edward, Prince of Wales, and the two gradually fell in love. She filed for divorce in 1936, intending to marry Edward (by then King Edward), but as a woman twice divorced, she was unacceptable as a prospective British queen. Edward renounced the throne, and they were married in 1937. The two thereafter lived a well-publicized international social life.

Windsor, House of *formerly (1901–17)* **House of Saxe-Coburg-Gotha** Royal house of Britain, which succeeded the House of HANOVER on the death of Queen VICTORIA. The dynastic name of Saxe-Coburg-Gotha was that of Victoria's German-born husband, Prince ALBERT. The dynasty included EDWARD VII, GEORGE V, EDWARD VIII, GEORGE VI, and ELIZABETH II. In the anti-German atmosphere of World War I, George V proclaimed that all British male descendants of Victoria would adopt the surname of Windsor.

Windsor City (pop., 1996: 198,000), S Ontario. Located opposite DETROIT, Mich., it was settled by French farmers shortly after 1701, when a fort was established at Detroit. With its strategic location, it became an industrial center, an important railway terminus, and a busy port in GREAT LAKES shipping. It is Canada's leading port of entry from the U.S.

Windsor Castle Principal British royal residence, on the River Thames in Windsor, Berkshire, S England. It comprises two quadrilateral building courts, or upper and lower wards, separated by the massive Round Tower (erected by HENRY II). The present-day complex has been reworked repeatedly since WILLIAM I the Conqueror first constructed a stockade on the site. The lower ward includes the Albert Memorial Chapel and St. George's Chapel, the burial place of 10 sovereigns. The upper ward includes the monarch's private apartments and the royal library.

windsurfing Sport of riding a sailboard, a modified surfboard with a movable mast that is sailed by one person standing up. Capable of moderately high speeds, sailboards are usually used on lakes, or close to shore on the ocean. The sport originated in the U.S. in the late 1960s; it was introduced at the Olympic Games in 1984.

wind tunnel Device for producing a controlled stream of air to study the effects on objects such as aircraft moving through air or the effects of moving air on models of stationary objects. Applications range from testing of airframes (the structures of aircraft and spacecraft) to research on BOUNDARY LAYER, TURBULENCE, DRAG, and LIFT. Measurements of air pressure and other characteristics at many points on the model yield information about how the total wind load is distributed. Wind tunnels have been used to solve design problems in automobiles, boats, trains, bridges, and buildings.

Windward Islands Island group, Lesser ANTILLES, W. Indies. Located at the E end of the CARIBBEAN SEA, they include Dominica (sometimes classified as part of the LEEWARD ISLANDS), MARTINIQUE, St. Lucia, St. Vincent, Grenada, and GRENADINES.

wine ALCOHOLIC BEVERAGE made from the fermented juice of GRAPES. Though known by the ancients, wine was not drunk in its matured form until the development of the bottle and cork in the late 17th cent. In wine manufacture, grapes are crushed and strained and the juice (called must) is sealed in vats along with YEAST and often sulfur dioxide, which suppresses other organisms. FERMENTATION continues for several weeks, then the wine is poured into wooden barrels or other containers for a second fermentation (aging). It is clarified and bottled before undergoing final maturation. Wines may be classified according to color as red, rosé (pink), or white; color depends on whether the skins of red grapes are allowed to ferment with the juice. Wine taste is described as sweet (high in sugar content) or dry (containing little or no sugar). Sparkling wines, such as CHAMPAGNE, contain suspended carbon dioxide, the result of bottling the wine before fermentation is complete. Fortified wines, such as port and SHERRY, contain added brandy. The leading wine-producing countries are France, Italy, Germany, the U.S., Spain, Portugal, and Chile.

Winfrey, Oprah (Gail) (b.1954) U.S. television talk-show host. Born in Kosciusko, Miss., she worked in television in Baltimore, where she cohosted her first talk show (1977–83), then hosted *A.M. Chicago* (1984), which became the city's highest-rated morning show. The renamed *Oprah Winfrey Show* was syndicated in 1986, making her the first black woman to host a successful national daytime talk show. The enormously popular show has earned her several Emmy awards. In 1996 she introduced "Oprah's Book Club" to foster reading. She appeared in the movies *The Color Purple* (1985) and *Beloved* (1998), which she also produced. In 2000 she launched a magazine, *O.*

wing In zoology, one of the paired structures certain animals use for flying. Bat and bird wings are modifications of the VERTEBRATE forelimb. In birds, the fingers are reduced and the forearm is lengthened. The primary flight feathers propel the bird forward, and the secondaries (on the upper wing) provide lift. Bat wings consist of a membrane stretched over elongated arm and hand bones. Insect wings are folds of integument ("skin"). Most insects have two pairs of wings; DIPTERANS (flies) have only one developed pair, and BEETLES have two but use only one for flying. The two wings on a side usually move together, but DRAGONFLY wings work independently.

Winnebago \ˌwi-nə-ˈbā-gō\ N. American Indian people who before the 17th cent. lived in what is now E Wisconsin and later expanded into SW Wisconsin and NW Illinois. They lived in villages of dome-shaped wigwams, cultivated corn, squash, beans, and tobacco, and hunted bison. Their major ceremony was the Medicine Dance, in which both men and women participated. The Winnebago were involved in the BLACK HAWK War of 1832, after which most of the tribe was removed to other Midwestern states. Today they number about 7,500.

Winnemucca, Sarah Hopkins See S. W. HOPKINS

Winnipeg City (pop., 2000: 630,000), capital of Manitoba. It lies at the confluence of the RED RIVER OF THE NORTH and ASSINIBOINE RIVER. In the early 19th cent. Tommy DOUGLAS founded a Scottish settlement there. Development ensued with the arrival of Canada's first transcontinental railroad in 1881. Following disastrous floods in 1950, much of the city was rebuilt. It is a cultural, financial, commercial, industrial, and government center.

Winnipeg, Lake Lake, S central Manitoba. Fed by many rivers, including the SASKATCHEWAN, RED RIVER OF THE NORTH, and Winnipeg, it is drained by the NELSON RIVER. It is 264 mi (425 km) long. Pierre de LA VÉRENDRYE visited the lake in 1733. With an average depth of 50 ft (15 m), it is important for shipping, commercial fishing, and recreation.

Winslow, Josiah (1629?–1680) American colonist. Born in Plymouth colony, Mass., he succeeded Myles STANDISH as commander of its military forces in 1656. As assistant governor of the colony (1657–73), he served on the NEW ENGLAND CONFEDERATION's directorate. He was elected governor of PLYMOUTH colony (1673–80), the first native-born colonial governor, and established its first public school. In KING PHILIP'S WAR he commanded the confederation's military forces.

Winston-Salem City (pop., 2000: 186,000), N central N. Carolina. With High Point and GREENSBORO it forms a tri-city industrial area. Salem was laid out by Moravian colonists in 1766. Winston was founded in 1849 and named for an American Revolutionary soldier. The two towns were consolidated as Winston-Salem in 1913. R. J. Reynolds founded his tobacco company in Salem in 1875, and tobacco still dominates the city's economy.

wintergreen Any of several evergreen plants in the HEATH order (Ericales). They grow as woodland wildflowers and are cultivated as garden ground cover. They are also a source of oil of wintergreen, which is used to flavor candies and chewing gum and to soothe muscular aches. Wintergreen is an alternative common name for several woodland herbs: *Pyrola* (shinleaf), about 12 species of creeping PERENNIALS; and *Gaultheria procumbens* (also called teaberry), with white flowers and spicy red berries.

Winthrop, John (1588–1649) British-American governor of the MASSACHUSETTS BAY COLONY. In 1629 he joined the Massachusetts Bay Co., and he was elected governor of the colony that was to be established in New England. An ardent Puritan, he guided the colonists on his arrival in N. America in 1630, and was elected governor 12 times during 1631–48. Though widely respected, he was criticized for opposing the formation of a representative assembly (1634), and Roger WILLIAMS and Anne HUTCHINSON decried the colony's limitations on religious expression. His son, John Winthrop (1606–1676), was an influential governor of Connecticut (1659–76).

wireless communications System using radio-frequency, infrared, microwave, or other types of electromagnetic or acoustic waves to transmit signals or data. Wireless devices include CELL PHONES, two-way radios, remote garage-door openers, and television remote controls. Wireless modems, microwave transmitters, and satellites make it possible to access the Internet from anywhere in the world. A Wireless Markup Language (WML) based on XML is used in such narrow-band devices as cell phones and pagers, for the transfer and display of text.

wire service See NEWS AGENCY

Wisconsin State (pop., 2000: 5,364,000), N Midwest, U.S. It covers an area of 56,153 sq mi (145,436 sq km), including part of Lake MICHIGAN; its capital is MADISON. With many unique landforms, such as the Door Peninsula between Lake Michigan and GREEN BAY, its N area has one of the greatest concentrations of lakes in the world. The WISCONSIN and Chippewa rivers cross the state to flow into the MISSISSIPPI. Forests cover about 45% of it. Originally inhabited by the Adena, or Mound Builders, the region was home to several different Indian tribes, including the OJIBWA, Menominee, and WINNEBAGO, when Europeans arrived. The French explorer Jean Nicolet (1598–1642) visited Wisconsin in 1634; the first permanent European settlement was established in 1717. The area remained under French control until 1763, when France ceded it to Great Britain after the FRENCH AND INDIAN WAR. After the AMERICAN REVOLUTION the region was ceded to the U.S. The Europeans dispossessed the Indians of their land (see BLACK HAWK), and settled the region. It became the Wisconsin Territory in 1836. It was admitted to the Union as the 30th state in 1848. The Progressive movement (see PROGRESSIVE PARTY) began in Wisconsin about 1900, resulting in the passage of legislation that made the state a leader in social reform. It is the major milk, butter, and cheese producer in the U.S. Tourism and recreation also are economically important. Wisconsin ports handle much of the GREAT LAKES domestic freight shipping.

Wisconsin, University of State system of higher education comprising 13 four-year campuses, 13 two-year campuses, and statewide extension services. The main campus was founded at Madison in 1849. In 1971 it was merged with the Wisconsin State Universities system, creating one of the largest such systems in the nation (total enrollment 150,000). The Madison campus is a comprehensive research and academic center, with many highly regarded departments, colleges, and schools that have consistently produced leaders in their disciplines. Enrollment at Madison is about 40,000.

Wisconsin River River, central and SW Wisconsin. It rises near the Michigan border and flows south through central Wisconsin, then turns west and enters the MISSISSIPPI RIVER after 430 mi (690 km). Lake Wisconsin is formed by a dam near Prairie du Sac.

Wise, Isaac Mayer (1819–1900) Czech-U.S. rabbi and organizer of REFORM JUDAISM in the U.S. Emigrating from Bohemia, in 1854 he accepted a pulpit in Cincinnati, a post he held the rest of his life. He was instrumental in the formation of the Union of American Hebrew Congregations and of the Central Conference of American Rabbis, both of which he presided over. Though he failed to unite all American Jews, he did bring about unanimity among Reform Jews.

Wister, Owen (1860–1938) U.S. novelist. Born in Philadelphia, he spent his summers in the West from 1885. His novel

The Virginian (1902) was a great popular success, now regarded as the first western of high quality. His other major work was *Roosevelt* (1930), detailing his long acquaintance with his Harvard classmate Theodore ROOSEVELT.

wisteria \wis-'tir-ē-ə\ Any of the twining, usually woody vines that make up the genus *Wisteria*, of the pea family (see LEGUME), native mostly to Asia and N. America. They are widely cultivated for their attractive feathery leaves, spreading growth, and beautiful, profuse flowers (blue, purple, rose, or white), which grow in large, drooping clusters.

witan \'wi-tän\ *or* **witenagemot** \'wi-tᵊn-ə-gə-ˌmōt\ Council of the Anglo-Saxon kings in medieval England. Usually attended by high-ranking nobles and bishops, the witan was expected to advise the king on all matters on which he chose to ask its opinion. It attested his grants of land to churches or laymen, consented to his issue of new laws, and helped him deal with rebels and disaffected subjects.

witchcraft and sorcery Use of alleged supernatural powers, usually for antisocial or evil purposes. Sorcery is sometimes distinguished from witchcraft in that it may be practiced by anyone with the appropriate knowledge, using charms, spells, or potions; whereas witchcraft is considered to result from inherent mystical power and to be practiced by invisible means. Both are especially prevalent in close-knit communities experiencing decline or misfortune and embroiled in petty social conflict. In ancient Greece witchcraft is mentioned as early as Homer (see CIRCE). The best-known sorceress in classical times was the legendary MEDEA. The Bible contains several references to witches. The early Church Fathers held that witchcraft was a delusion and denounced its practice. In the Middle Ages, witchcraft was believed to involve demonic possession and so came within the scope of the INQUISITION. In the witch-hunts of the 16th–17th cent., European courts frequently regarded witches and sorcerers alike as candidates for burning, and some 50,000 were executed; many more were tortured and imprisoned. See also MAGIC, SALEM WITCH TRIALS.

witch-hazel family Family Hamamelidaceae, composed of 23 genera of shrubs and trees, native to tropical and warm temperate regions. The six species of the genus *Hamamelis* include such ornamentals as witch hazel, winter hazel, and *Fothergilla*. Members have flowers with four or five petals and sepals each. Common witch hazel (*H. virginiana*) flowers in fall and retains yellow, cuplike calyxes (collections of sepals) through the winter. Its forked twigs were sometimes used for DOWSING. The fragrant liniment witch hazel is made from the dried leaves and sometimes from twigs and bark. Brilliant autumn leaf color is an outstanding trait of *Parrotia persica*. Another genus, *Altingia*, has seven species, all Asian and all valued for their timber. *A. excelsa* is one of the largest trees of the Asian tropics.

Witherspoon, John (1723–1794) Scottish-American clergyman. Ordained a Presbyterian minister, in 1768 he was sent to become president of the College of New Jersey (later Princeton Univ.), where he expanded the curriculum and increased enrollment. An advocate for colonists' rights, he was a member of the Continental Congress (1776–79, 1780–82), and was the only clergyman to sign the DECLARATION OF INDEPENDENCE. He helped organize the Presbyterian Church in the U.S. as a national body (1785–89).

Witte \'vi-tə\, **Sergey (Yulyevich), Count** (1849–1915) Russian statesman. As minister of finance 1892–1903, he improved communications and promoted construction of the TRANS-SIBERIAN RAILWAY. He negotiated the end of the RUSSO–JAPANESE WAR. Though opposed to constitutionalism, he persuaded Czar NICHOLAS II to issue the OCTOBER MANIFESTO in 1905 and was appointed the first constitutional premier. He repressed further civil disruption and restored Russian finances with European loans. In 1906 the czar, favoring a more conservative regime, replaced him with Piotr STOLYPIN.

Wittelsbach \'vi-təls-ˌbäk\, **House of** German noble family that ruled in Bavaria from the 12th to the 20th cent. In 1124 Otto V, count of Scheyern (d.1155), moved the family residence to the castle of Wittelsbach. In 1180 his son Otto VI became Otto I, duke of Bavaria. In 1214 Otto II obtained the Palatinate of the Rhine. A descendant, LOUIS IV, as Holy

W X Y Z

Roman emperor divided the lands. The Bavarian dukes became electors from 1623, and the last direct line died out in 1777. The Palatine branch united with Bavaria in 1799 under MAXIMILIAN I as king of Bavaria (1806). His descendants (including LUDWIG I and LUDWIG II) were kings until the abdication of Ludwig III in 1918.

Wittgenstein \\'vit-gən-,shtīn\\, **Ludwig (Josef Johann)** (1889–1951) Austrian-British philosopher, one of the most influential figures in 20th-cent. philosophy. The son of an immensely wealthy industrialist, he studied mechanical engineering in Berlin and Manchester. The works of Bertrand RUSSELL led him into mathematics, and he later studied under Russell at Cambridge (1912–13). He produced two original and influential systems of philosophical thought, his logical theories and later his philosophy of language. His great *Tractatus Logico-Philosophicus*, completed in a prisoner-of-war camp during World War I, dealt with the question of how language expresses meaning. It exerted great influence on the VIENNA CIRCLE and the school of LOGICAL POSITIVISM. Thereafter, he gave away all of his fortune and worked in an odd variety of jobs, before returning to Cambridge as a fellow in 1929, where he came to exert a powerful influence on English-language philosophy. In *Philosophical Investigations* (1953) he strove to show how language is linked to actions and reactions, with the aim of demonstrating that its significance is due not to an intangible realm of mind but to the human forms of life in which it plays a role. See also ANALYTIC PHILOSOPHY.

Witz \\'vits\\, **Konrad** (c.1400–1445/46) German-Swiss painter. Born in Germany, in 1434 he entered the painters' guild in Basel, where he worked most of his life. His masterpiece, *The Miraculous Draft of Fishes* (1444), from an altarpiece for the cathedral of Geneva, exemplifies such precise realism that the light reflected off the water's surface is carefully distinguished from the light reflected off the stones beneath the shallow water. He was one of the first European artists to incorporate realistic landscapes into religious paintings.

Wladyslaw II Jagiello \\vlȧ-'dis-lȧf...yȧg-'yel-lō\\ (1351?–1434) Grand duke of Lithuania (1377–1401) and king of Poland (1386–1434), founder of the JAGIELLON DYNASTY. He had to defeat rivals, including his cousin VYTAUTAS, in order to secure his rule in Lithuania. He married the Polish queen Jadwiga (1386) after agreeing to Christianize Lithuania and unite it with Poland. He signed a treaty (1401) recognizing Vytautas as duke on the condition that Poland and Lithuania pursue a common foreign policy, and together they broke the power of the TEUTONIC ORDER.

Wobblies See INDUSTRIAL WORKERS OF THE WORLD

Wodehouse \\'wu̇d-,hau̇s\\, **P(elham) G(renville)** (*later* **Sir Pelham**) (1881–1975) English-U.S. writer. Of the many beloved fictional characters he created, he is best known for Bertie Wooster and his supreme "gentleman's gentleman," Jeeves, who appeared in comic stories and novels from "Extricating Young Gussie" (1915) to *Much Obliged, Jeeves* (1971). He wrote more than 90 books and 20 film scripts and collaborated on many plays as well as musical comedies by Jerome KERN, George GERSHWIN, and others.

wolf Any of three extant species of wild DOG. The gray, or timber, wolf (*Canis lupus*) is probably the ancestor of all domestic dogs. It is now found primarily in Canada, Alaska, the Balkans, and Russia. Wolves are intelligent and social. Their primary prey are deer, moose, and caribou. Because wolves have killed livestock, they have been persecuted by farmers and ranchers. A male gray wolf may be 7 ft (2 m) long and weigh up to 175 lbs (80 kg); it is the largest living wild canid. Gray wolves live in hierarchical packs whose territories cover at least 38 sq mi (100 sq km) and hunt mostly at night. The much smaller red wolf (*C. rufus*) is now extinct in the wild. The Ethiopian or Abyssinian wolf (*C. simensis*) was formerly considered a jackal. See also DIRE WOLF.

Wolf \\'vȯlf\\, **Hugo (Filipp Jakob)** (1860–1903) Austrian composer. He entered the Vienna Conservatory at 15, but lost patience with his teachers' conservatism and soon left. By 18 he probably already had the syphilis that would kill him, making him mentally unstable. As a critic (1884–87), he attracted attention for his vituperation. In 1888–89 he produced the remarkable songs of the *Mörike Lieder*, the *Eichendorff Lieder*, the *Goethe Lieder*, and much of the *Spanish Songbook*—more than half his total output. He wrote nothing from 1891 to 1894, then quickly composed the opera *Der Corregidor* (1896) and finished the *Italian Songbook* (1896). In 1897 he suffered a complete breakdown, and he thereafter lived largely in an asylum.

Wolfe \\'wu̇lf\\, **James** (1727–1759) British army commander. After a distinguished military career in Europe, in 1758 he helped lead Gen. Jeffery AMHERST's successful expedition against the French on Cape Breton Island. In 1759 he was appointed commander of the British army on its mission to capture Quebec. In the ensuing Battle of QUEBEC, he defeated the French in less than an hour, but died of his third wound received in the battle.

Wolfe \\'wu̇lf\\, **Thomas (Clayton)** (1900–1938) U.S. writer. Born in Asheville, N.C., Wolfe moved to New York City and taught at NYU while working at writing plays. *Look Homeward, Angel* (1929), his first and best-known novel, and *Of Time and the River* (1935) are thinly veiled autobiography, written in an extravagant and energetic style. His short stories were collected in *From Death to Morning* (1935). After his death at 37 from tuberculosis, the novels *The Web and the Rock* (1939) and *You Can't Go Home Again* (1940) were among the works extracted by his editor from the manuscripts he left.

Wolfe, Tom *orig.* Thomas Kennerly Wolfe, Jr. (b.1930) U.S. journalist and novelist. Born in Richmond, Va., he earned a doctorate from Yale Univ. and soon became known as a proponent of New Journalism, the application of fiction-writing techniques to journalism. *The Electric Kool-Aid Acid Test* (1968) chronicled the life of a traveling group of hippies. *The Right Stuff* (1979; film, 1983) examined the astronaut program. Other controversial nonfiction books attacked fashionable 1960s leftism, modern abstract art, and international architectural styles. His satirical novel *The Bonfire of the Vanities* (1987) was a huge best-seller.

Wölfflin \\'vœlf-lin\\, **Heinrich** (1864–1945) Swiss art historian. He studied and later taught at the Univs. of Basel, Berlin, and Munich. His chief work, *Principles of Art History* (1915), synthesized his ideas into a complete aesthetic system that was to become of great importance in art criticism. He avoided the popular anecdotal approach and emphasized the formal stylistic analysis of drawing, composition, light, color, subject matter, and other pictorial elements as they were handled similarly by the painters of a particular period or national school.

wolfram See TUNGSTEN

Wolfram von Eschenbach \\'vȯlf-räm-fȯn-'esh-ən-,bäk\\ (c.1170–c.1220) German poet. An impoverished Bavarian knight, Wolfram apparently served a succession of lords. The epic *Parzival*, one of his eight surviving lyric poems, introduced the theme of the Holy Grail into German literature and is one of the masterpieces of the Middle Ages. Wolfram's influence on later poets was profound; he is considered one of the greatest Middle High German epic poets.

Wollstonecraft \\'wȯl-stən-,kraft\\, **Mary** (1759–1797) English writer. She taught school and worked as a governess and for a London publisher. Her early *Thoughts on the Education of Daughters* (1787) foreshadowed her mature work, *A Vindication of the Rights of Woman* (1792), whose core is a plea for equality of education for men and women. The *Vindication* is widely regarded as the founding document of modern feminism. In 1797 she married William GODWIN; she died days after the birth of their daughter, the future Mary SHELLEY.

Wolof \\'wō-lȯf\\ Muslim people of Senegal and Gambia. In the 14th–16th cent. the Wolof maintained a powerful empire. Traditional Wolof society was highly stratified, consisting of royalty, an aristocracy, a warrior class, commoners, slaves, and members of despised artisan castes. Today most Wolof (numbering 4.5 million) are farmers, but many live and work in Dakar and Banjul. Wolof women are renowned for their elaborate hair styles, gold ornaments, and voluminous dresses.

Wolsey \\'wu̇l-zē\\, **Thomas, Cardinal** (1475?–1530) English prelate and statesman. He served as chaplain to HENRY VII and later HENRY VIII, for whom he organized the successful campaign against the French (1513). On Henry's recommendation, the pope made Wolsey archbishop of York (1514), cardinal (1515), and papal legate (1518). In 1515 Henry appointed him lord chancellor of England, which added to his power and wealth. Though he introduced judicial and monastic reforms, Wolsey became unpopular for raising taxes. In 1529 he failed to persuade the pope to grant Henry an annulment of his marriage to CATHERINE OF ARAGON, for which he soon lost most of his offices. In 1530 he was arrested for treason for corresponding with the French court, and he died on his way to face the king.

wolverine or **skunk bear** Solitary, voracious, nocturnal carnivore (*Gulo gulo*) of N timberlands worldwide. Wolverines are 26–36 in. (65–90 cm) long and 14–18 in. (36–45 cm) high, and weigh 20–65 lbs (9–30 kg). They have short bowed legs, hairy soles, and long, sharp claws. Their long, coarse hair is used to trim parkas. The anal glands secrete an unpleasant-smelling fluid. A cunning, fearless predator, the wolverine will attack almost any animal.

Woman's Christian Temperance Union (WCTU) U.S. TEMPERANCE MOVEMENT organization. Founded in Cleveland, Ohio, in 1874, it used educational, social, and political means to promote legislation. Its president (1879–98) was Frances Willard (1839–1898), an effective speaker and lobbyist who also led the World's Woman's Christian Temperance Union from its founding in 1883. The WCTU was instrumental in the eventual adoption of PROHIBITION.

womb See UTERUS

wombat Either of two species (family Phascolomyidae, or Vombatidae) of nocturnal Australian MARSUPIALS that are heavily built, 28–47 in. (70–120 cm) long, and tailless. The single newborn develops in the mother's pouch for about five months. Wombats eat grasses and shrub roots. The common wombat (*Phascolomis*, or *Vombatus, ursinus*), considered a pest, has coarse dark hair and short ears. The rare Queensland hairy-nosed wombat (*Lasiorhinus barnardi*) has fine fur and longer ears; the population lives principally in a national park.

Common wombat (*Vombatus ursinus*)

Women's Army Corps (WAC) U.S. Army unit. It was established by Congress to enlist women for auxiliary noncombat duty in WORLD WAR II. Its first head was O. C. HOBBY. By 1945 nearly 100,000 women had served. After the war the government requested reenlistment to meet employment needs of army hospitals and administrative centers. The WAC became part of the regular army in 1948; in 1978 it was dissolved as a separate unit.

women's liberation movement Revival of FEMINISM in the 1960s by U.S. women. A coalition of American women's groups, including the NATIONAL ORGANIZATION FOR WOMEN, sought to overturn laws that enforced discrimination in matters such as contract and property rights and employment and pay. The movement also sought to broaden women's self-awareness and challenge traditional stereotypes of women. An effort in the 1970s to pass the EQUAL RIGHTS AMENDMENT failed, but its aims were later largely achieved by other means.

women's suffrage movement Movement to grant women the right by law to vote. Women's voting rights became an issue in the 19th cent., especially in Britain and the U.S. In the U.S. the women's suffrage movement arose from the antislavery movement; such leaders as Lucretia MOTT and E. C. STANTON believed that equality should extend to women as well as blacks and organized the SENECA FALLS CONVENTION (1848). In 1850 Lucy STONE established the movement's first national convention. Stanton and S. B. ANTHONY formed the National Woman Suffrage Assn. in 1869 to secure an amendment to the Constitution, while Stone founded the American Woman Suffrage Assn. to seek similar amendments to state constitutions; in 1890 the two organizations merged. Following Wyoming's lead in 1890,

states began adopting such amendments; by 1918 women had acquired suffrage in 15 states. After a suffrage amendment was passed by Congress, a vigorous campaign brought ratification, and in 1919 the 19th Amendment became part of the Constitution. In Britain, the first women's suffrage committee was formed in Manchester in 1865. Despite growing support, suffrage bills were continually defeated; in frustration, some suffragists became militant activists under the leadership of Emmeline and Christabel PANKHURST. Parliament finally passed a suffrage bill in 1918. Women had already won voting rights in New Zealand (1893), Australia (1902), Finland (1906), Norway (1913), and the Soviet Union (1917). These were followed by Poland (1918), Sweden (1919), Germany (1919), and Ireland (1922); France, Italy, India, and Japan passed such laws after World War II.

Wonder, Stevie *orig.* Steveland Judkins (b.1950) U.S. SOUL-MUSIC singer and songwriter. Born in Saginaw, Mich., he was blind virtually from birth. He was a skillful performer on the piano and other instruments by age 8. At 10 he signed with the fledgling MOTOWN label. His first hit, "Fingertips, Part 2" (1963), was followed by many top-selling singles, including "Up-Tight." After studying composition at USC, he enjoyed enormous success with such albums as *Songs in the Key of Life* (1976) and such hits as "Superstition" and "Ebony and Ivory." He has spoken out against nuclear war and apartheid and raised funds for his eye-disease facility, Wonderland.

Wonders of the World, Seven See SEVEN WONDERS OF THE WORLD

wood Hard, fibrous material formed by the accumulation of vascular tissue in some plants. It is the principal strengthening tissue found in the stems and roots of TREES and SHRUBS. Wood forms around a central core (pith) in a series of concentric layers called growth rings. Heartwood, the central portion, is darker and composed of cells that are no

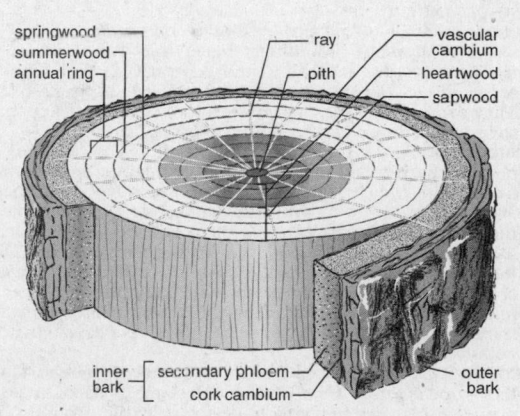

Wood Cross section of a tree trunk. Wood is formed by the accumulation of secondary xylem produced by growth of the vascular cambium tissue. Each growth layer is distinguished by early or springwood, composed of large thin-walled cells produced during the spring when water is usually abundant, and the denser late or summerwood, composed of small cells with thick walls. Growth rings vary in width as a result of differing climatic conditions; in temperate climates, a ring is equivalent to one year's growth. The dark heartwood consists of xylem that has been infiltrated by gums and resins and has lost its ability to conduct water, unlike the actively functioning sapwood. Certain conducting cells form rays that conduct water and dissolved substances laterally across the xylem. Bark is composed of the tissues outside the vascular cambium, incl. secondary phloem, cork cells, and cork-producing cells (cork cambium). The outer bark, composed of dead tissue, protects the inner region from injury, disease, and desiccation.

longer active. Sapwood, the lighter area surrounding it, contains actively conducting xylem cells. Wood is one of the most abundant and versatile natural materials on earth, and unlike coal, ores, and petroleum, is renewable with proper care. The most widely used woods come from two groups of trees: the CONIFERS, or SOFTWOODS, and the broadleaves, or HARDWOODS. Density and moisture content affect the strength of wood; in addition to load-bearing strength, other variable factors include elasticity and toughness. Wood is insulating to heat and electricity and has desirable acoustical properties. Some identifying physical characteristics of wood include color, odor, texture, and grain. Some 10,000 different wood products are commercially available, ranging from lumber and plywood to paper, from fine furniture to toothpicks. Chemically derived products from wood and wood residues include cellophane, charcoal, dyestuffs, explosives, lacquers, and turpentine. Wood is also widely used for fuel.

Wood, Grant (1891–1942) U.S. painter. Born near Anamosa, Iowa, he was trained as a craftsman and designer as well as a painter. On a visit to Germany in 1928, he was strongly influenced by 15th-cent. German and Flemish paintings and soon abandoned his Impressionist manner for the detailed, realistic manner he is known for. His *American Gothic* caused a sensation when exhibited in 1930. A telling portrait of the sober, hardworking Midwestern farmer, it has become one of the best-known icons of U.S. art, though it is often misinterpreted: the woman is not the man's wife but his unmarried daughter.

wood alcohol See METHANOL

Wood Buffalo National Park Park, W Canada. It is set between ATHABASCA and GREAT SLAVE lakes. The world's largest park, it occupies 17,300 sq mi (44,807 sq km). It is a vast region of forests and plains, crossed by the PEACE RIVER and dotted with lakes. It is the habitat of the world's largest remaining herd of wood buffalo (BISON), as well as of bear, caribou, and moose, and a nesting ground for the WHOOPING CRANE.

woodchuck *or* **groundhog** Species *(Marmota monax)* of solitary MARMOT inhabiting fields and forest edges in Alaska, Canada, and the E and central U.S. Woodchucks are 17–20 in. (42–52 cm) long and weigh 4–14 lbs (2–6 kg). They are good diggers, swimmers, and climbers. Their burrows have a main entrance and an escape tunnel.

woodcock Any of five species (family Scolopacidae) of plump, sharp-billed migratory birds of damp, dense woodlands. With eyes set far back on the head, a woodcock has a 360° field of vision. It drums its feet to coax earthworms to the surface and then extracts them with its long, forceps-like bill; it may eat twice its weight in worms each day. The female American woodcock *(Scolopax, or Philohela, minor)* is about 11 in. (28 cm) long; the male is slightly smaller. The male's striking courtship display includes a long, repeated spiraling and dropping sequence. Woodcocks have been popular game birds.

woodcut Design printed from a wood block incised along the wood's grain. One of the oldest methods of making prints, it was used in China to decorate textiles from the 5th cent. Printing from wood blocks on textiles was known in Europe from the early 14th cent., but developed little until paper began to be manufactured in the late 14th cent. In the early 15th cent., religious images and playing cards were first made from wood blocks. Black-line woodcut reached its greatest perfection in the 16th cent. with Albrecht DÜRER and his followers. In the late 19th and early 20th cent., artists such as Edvard MUNCH, Paul GAUGUIN, and the German Expressionists rediscovered the expressive potential of woodcuts. Woodcuts have played an important role in the history of Japanese art (see UKIYO-E).

Wood family English family of Staffordshire potters, a major force in the development of Staffordshire wares from peasant pottery to an organized industry. Its most prominent members were Ralph Wood (1715–1772), his brother Aaron (1717–1785), and his son Ralph Jr. (1748–1795). The elder Ralph became famous for his extremely well-modeled figures with colored glazes, and he is credited with introducing the Toby mug. Ralph Jr. was related to Josiah WEDGWOOD, and the two names were often linked professionally.

He produced a variety of figures, coloring them with enamel rather than glazes, and supplied some of them to Wedgwood. Aaron's son Enoch (1759–1840) apprenticed with Wedgwood but by 1783 was established as an independent potter in partnership with his cousin Ralph Jr. Much of his earthenware was exported to the U.S. The firm closed in 1846.

Woodhull, Victoria *orig.* Victoria Claflin (1838–1927) U.S. social reformer. Born in Homer, Ohio, she was raised in a family of traveling spiritualists with her sister Tennessee Claflin (1845–1923). After Victoria's marriage ended in 1864, the sisters founded *Woodhull and Claflin's Weekly* (1870), which advocated equal rights for women, a single standard of morality for both sexes, and free love. In 1872 a splinter group of radical suffragists nominated Woodhull for president with Frederick DOUGLASS as vice president. For printing news of an alleged adulterous affair by H. W. BEECHER, they were charged with libel but acquitted (1873). They moved to England (1877), where they lectured, worked for charities, and married wealthy Englishmen. Woodhull and her daughter published the eugenics journal *Humanitarian* (1892–1910).

Victoria Woodhull, c.1872

Woodland cultures Prehistoric cultures of E N. America dating from the 1st millennium B.C. They included the Adena and HOPEWELL cultures, and were characterized by the raising of corn, beans, and squash, the fashioning of distinctive pottery, and the building of burial mounds. Most of these cultures were replaced by the MISSISSIPPIAN CULTURE in the 1st millennium A.D.

wood mouse See FIELD MOUSE

woodpecker Any of about 180 species (family Picidae) of mostly nonmigratory, solitary birds found nearly worldwide. Woodpeckers spiral up tree trunks, probing for insects, and chisel nest holes in dead wood by means of rapidly repeating blows of the beak. Some species eat fruits and berries or tree sap. Woodpeckers are usually silent, except in spring, when males call loudly and drum on hollow wood. Species range from 6 to 18 in. (15–47 cm) long. Most are patterned in black, white, or yellow and bright colors. See also FLICKER, IVORY-BILLED WOODPECKER, SAPSUCKER.

Woods, Lake of the Lake astride the Canadian–U.S. boundary, SW Ontario, SE Manitoba, and N Minnesota. Irregular in shape, it is 70 mi (110 km) long and up to 60 mi (95 km) wide. It has an estimated 25,000 mi (40,000 km) of shoreline and more than 14,000 islands. It drains north through the Winnipeg River into Lake WINNIPEG. Visited by French explorers in 1688, it became an important fur-trading route between the GREAT LAKES and W Canada. The Northwest Angle, the northernmost point of the coterminous U.S., is separated from the rest of Minnesota by a part of the lake.

Woods, Tiger *(orig.* Eldrick) (b.1975) U.S. golfer. Born in Cypress, Cal., to a Thai mother and a black U.S. Army officer, he won the first of three consecutive U.S. Junior Amateur Championships (1991–93) at 15. In 1994 he became the youngest winner (at 18) of the U.S. Amateur competition, which he also won in 1995 and 1996. After two years at Stanford Univ., in 1997 Woods became the youngest player (at 21) ever to win the Masters Tournament, winning by a record margin of 12 strokes, and the youngest player ever ranked no. 1 in world golf competition. In 2000 he became, at 24, the youngest player ever to win a career Grand Slam.

Woodson, Carter G(odwin) (1875–1950) U.S. historian. Born in New Canton, Va., he supported himself as a coal miner and was unable to enroll in high school until he was 20. He went on to receive a PhD from Harvard Univ. In 1915 he founded the Assn. for the Study of Negro Life and

History to encourage the study of the black past. In the early 1920s he founded Associated Publishers to bring out books on black life and culture. His many books include the college text *The Negro in Our History* (1922).

Woodstock (Art and Music Fair) ROCK festival held near Bethel, N.Y. (its site was to have been nearby Woodstock), on Aug. 15–17, 1969. About 450,000 young rock fans listened to such performers as the GRATEFUL DEAD, Jimi HENDRIX, and Janis JOPLIN. The festival, whose participants exhibited extraordinary good feeling in the face of rain and organizational chaos, marked the high point of U.S. youth counterculture in the 1960s. It was documented in the film *Woodstock* (1970).

wood thrush One of the 11 species of THRUSHES (in the genus *Hylocichla,* or *Catharus*) called nightingale thrushes because of their rich songs. *H. mustelina* is common in E U.S. broadleaf forests; it is 8 in. (20 cm) long and has drab, spotted plumage.

wood warbler Any of about 120 species of lively N. and Central American songbirds in the family Parulidae. Wood warblers superficially resemble the true WARBLERS of the Old World but are usually more brightly colored (at least in the breeding season) and smaller (about 5 in., or 13 cm, long). They commonly inhabit woodlands and sometimes marshes and dry scrub. Their songs are buzzy and monotonous.

Woodward, C(omer) Vann (1908–1999) U.S. historian. Born in Vanndale, Ark., he became known for his writings on the American South and the Civil War, including *The Strange Career of Jim Crow* (1955). He edited *Mary Chesnut's Civil War* (1981; Pulitzer Prize) and *The Oxford History of the United States.* Woodward's writings transformed the nation's understanding of the South.

Woodward, Robert B(urns) (1917–1979) U.S. chemist. Born in Boston, he developed "Woodward's rules" for determining structure by ultraviolet SPECTROSCOPY. In 1945 his methods finally clarified the structure of penicillin and of many more complex natural products. He proposed the correct biosynthetic pathway of steroid hormones. He was the most accomplished synthesist of complex ORGANIC COMPOUNDS, including quinine and vitamin B_{12} (in over 100 reactions), a task that led to the fundamental concept of conservation of orbital symmetry. He received a 1965 Nobel Prize.

woodwind instruments Wind instruments that produce sound by either directing a stream of air against the edge of a hole or by making a reed or a double reed vibrate (see REED INSTRUMENTS). In BRASS INSTRUMENTS, by contrast, the airstream passes directly from the player's vibrating lips into the air column. See also BASSOON, CLARINET, ENGLISH HORN, FLUTE, OBOE, PANPIPE, RECORDER, and SAXOPHONE.

wool Animal fiber that is the protective covering, or fleece, of SHEEP or such other hairy mammals as goats and camels. Wool is readied by washing, CARDING, sometimes combing, then spinning. Coarser than such fibers as cotton, linen, silk, and rayon, wool is resilient, so wool fabrics and garments tend to retain shape, drape well, and resist wrinkling. Wool is warm and lightweight and takes dyes well. Woolen YARNS are thick and full and are used for such items as tweed fabrics and blankets. Worsteds usually are made from longer fibers.

Woolf \'wu̇lf\, **Virginia** orig. Adeline Virginia Stephen (1882–1941) British novelist and critic. She and her sister became the early nucleus of the BLOOMSBURY GROUP. She married the writer Leonard Woolf (1880–1969) in 1912; in 1917 they founded the Hogarth Press. Her best novels include *Mrs. Dalloway* (1925) and *To the Lighthouse* (1927), which uses an individual consciousness meditating on apparently insignificant events to present a whole historical period. *Orlando* (1928) takes a single

Virginia Woolf

character of changing sex from the Elizabethan era to the present day, and the radically experimental *The Waves* (1931) uses interior monologue to trace the inner lives of six characters. Such works confirmed her place among the major figures of literary modernism. Her best critical studies are collected in *The Common Reader* (1925, 1932). Her long essay *A Room of One's Own* (1929) addressed the status of women artists. Her health and mental stability were delicate throughout her life; in a recurrence of mental illness, she drowned herself.

Woollcott \'wu̇l-kət\, **Alexander (Humphreys)** (1887–1943) U.S. author, critic, and actor. He became the *New York Times* drama critic in 1914. Known for his acerbic wit, he became the self-appointed leader of the Algonquin Round Table, the informal luncheon club at New York's Algonquin Hotel that included Groucho MARX, Dorothy PARKER, and George S. KAUFMAN. He later wrote for the *New Yorker,* published such books as *While Rome Burns* (1934), and inspired the play *The Man Who Came to Dinner* (1939).

woolly bear CATERPILLAR of a tiger moth. The larva of the Isabella tiger moth (*Isia isabella*) known as the banded woolly bear, is brown in the middle and black at both ends. The width of the black bands is purported to predict the severity of the coming winter: the narrower the bands, the milder the winter.

Woolworth Co. U.S. merchandising company. Frank W. Woolworth (1852–1919) founded his first "five- and ten-cent" store in 1879. By 1904 there were 120 stores in 21 states. In 1913 in New York, the company completed its new headquarters and the world's tallest skyscraper, the magnificent Woolworth Building. By 1929 Woolworth had about 2,250 outlets. Proliferating in the U.S. and Britain, it acquired other chains dealing in sportswear, shoes, and children's wear. From 1992 it began closing down hundreds of stores; focusing on athletic footwear and apparel, in 1998 it changed its name to Venator Group, Inc., and later to Foot Locker Inc.

Worcester \'wu̇s-tər\ City (pop., 2000: 173,000), central Massachusetts. The original settlement (1673) was disbanded during KING PHILIP'S WAR (1675–76) and a later settlement was established in 1713. Textile manufacturing began in 1789; the first corduroy cloth in the U.S. was produced there. An early abolitionist center, Worcester became an important stop on the UNDERGROUND RAILROAD. It is a commercial and industrial center and the state's second-largest city. It is home to College of the Holy Cross and Clark Univ. (1887).

Worcester City (pop., 1995 est.: 91,000), county seat of Hereford and Worcester, England. Located on the SEVERN RIVER, it was an important wool town during the Middle Ages, also known for its glove making. Oliver CROMWELL routed CHARLES II in the Battle of Worcester, ending the ENGLISH CIVIL WAR. In 1751 John Wall founded the porcelain industry for which the city is now famous, and in 1838 Worcestershire sauce was introduced there by Lea & Perrins. Its noted cathedral (11th–14th cent.) contains the tomb of King JOHN.

word processing Preparation of text documents on computer. A word-processing system typically consists simply of a PERSONAL COMPUTER linked to a computer PRINTER, or a terminal linked to a MAINFRAME computer. Word processing differs from typing in numerous ways. Electronic text can be moved around at will; a misspelled term can be corrected throughout the document with a single command; spelling and grammar checkers can point out apparent errors; and the document's format and layout can be changed repeatedly. Since all editing ideally occurs on-screen, word processing can decrease paper usage and simplify editing. When the final draft is ready, the document can be printed out, sent as an E-MAIL attachment, shared on a computer NETWORK, or simply stored.

Wordsworth, Dorothy (1771–1855) English writer. An inspiring influence on her brother William WORDSWORTH, she lived with him from 1795. Her *Alfoxden Journal 1798* (1897) and *Grasmere Journals 1800–03* (1897) are intimate records of their lives. Both works are appreciated for their imaginative descriptions of nature and their perfection of

W X Y Z

style, as well as for the light they throw on her brother. In 1829 severe illness left her an invalid, and her mind was clouded in her last 20 years.

Wordsworth, William (1770–1850) English poet. Orphaned at 13, Wordsworth attended Cambridge Univ., but remained rootless and virtually penniless until 1795, when a legacy made possible a reunion with his sister Dorothy WORDSWORTH. He became friends with S. T. COLERIDGE, with whom he wrote *Lyrical Ballads* (1798), the collection that launched the English Romantic movement. Wordsworth's contributions include "Tintern Abbey" and many lyrics controversial for their common, everyday language. Around 1798 he began writing the epic autobiographical poem that would absorb him intermittently for the next 40 years, *The Prelude* (1850). His second verse collection, *Poems, in Two Volumes* (1807), includes many of the rest of his finest works, including "Ode: Intimations of Immortality." His poetry is most original in its vision of the almost divine power of the creative imagination. By the time he became widely appreciated, his poetry had lost much of its force and his radical politics had yielded to conservatism. In 1843 he became England's poet laureate. He is regarded as the central figure of English ROMANTICISM.

work In economics and sociology, the activities and labor necessary for the survival of society. As early as 40,000 B.C., hunters worked in groups to track and kill animals, while younger or weaker members of the tribe gathered food. When agriculture replaced hunting and gathering, surpluses of food allowed early societies to develop, with some members pursuing crafts. The establishment of towns led to new occupations in commerce, law, medicine, and defense. Nobles, clergy, merchants, artisans, and peasants came to pursue occupations defined largely by hereditary social class. Crafts GUILDS developed in medieval Europe, limiting the supply of labor in each profession and controlling production. The coming of the INDUSTRIAL REVOLUTION changed working life profoundly. Factories divided the work once done by a single craftsman into a number of distinct tasks performed by unskilled or semiskilled workers (see DIVISION OF LABOR). Manufacturing firms grew larger in the 19th cent., and ever more specialized positions for managers, supervisors, accountants, engineers, technicians, and salesmen became necessary. Specialization continued through the 20th cent., spawning disciplines concerned with the management and design of work, including PRODUCTION MANAGEMENT, INDUSTRIAL RELATIONS, personnel administration, and SYSTEMS ENGINEERING.

work In physics, the measure of ENERGY transfer that occurs when an object is moved over a distance by an external FORCE, some component of which is applied in the direction of displacement. For a constant force, work W is equal to the magnitude of the force F times the displacement d of the object, or $W = Fd$. Work is also done by compressing a gas, by rotating a shaft, and by causing invisible motions of particles within a body by an external MAGNETIC FORCE. No work is accomplished by simply holding a heavy stationary object because there is no transfer of energy and no displacement. Work done on a body is equal to the increase in energy of the body.

workers' compensation Social-welfare program through which employers bear some of the cost of their employees' work-related injuries and occupational diseases. It was first introduced in Germany in 1884. In Britain and the U.S. in the late 19th cent., efforts were made to secure the right of injured workers to compensation and improve working conditions through court decisions, liability statutes, and safety codes. By the mid-20th cent. most countries were offering some sort of workers' compensation. Some systems take the form of compulsory SOCIAL INSURANCE; others require the employer to provide certain benefits, with insurance voluntary. Workers' compensation serves as an economic incentive for employers to prevent accidents and illness among employees, since liability for medical costs and lost corporate income can easily exceed the costs of establishing safe working conditions.

Workers' Opposition (1920–21) Group within the Soviet Union's COMMUNIST PARTY that championed workers' rights. Formed to resist the central party's increasing con-

trol over local party units and trade unions, in 1920 it objected to Leon TROTSKY's plan to transform trade unions into state organs, insisting that the unions, as true representatives of the proletariat, should control the national economy. At the 10th Party Congress (1921), its platform was rejected and it was ordered to disperse.

workfare Form of WELFARE requiring able-bodied adults to work. In 1994 various U.S. states were already experimenting with workfare programs when Pres. William CLINTON proposed a similar national scheme. The final bill, passed in 1996, replaced the existing 60-year-old program with block grants to the states, which were to run their own programs. Most recipients were required to work within two years of receiving benefits and were limited to a lifetime maximum of five years on welfare rolls. The law provided for limited job training and child-care assistance, and denied noncitizens access to a variety of services.

working dog Any of various dogs bred as guard, herding, draft, or rescue animals. All are sturdy and muscular, intelligent and loyal. Guard breeds include the AKITA, boxer, DOBERMAN PINSCHER, giant and standard SCHNAUZERS, GREAT DANE, mastiff, and ROTTWEILER. Livestock guard breeds include the Great Pyrenees and Pyrenean mountain dogs (Britain). Herding dogs include the GERMAN SHEPHERD, SHETLAND SHEEPDOG, and Welsh corgi. Breeds developed for hauling and rescue work include the Bernese mountain dog, Newfoundland, ST. BERNARD, and sled dog.

Works Progress Administration *later (1939–43)* **Work Projects Administration (WPA)** U.S. work program for the unemployed. Created in 1935 under the NEW DEAL, it aimed to stimulate the economy during the GREAT DEPRESSION and preserve the skills and self-respect of unemployed persons by providing them useful work. During its existence, it employed 8.5 million people on the construction of 650,000 mi (1,046,000 km) of roads, 125,000 public buildings, 75,000 bridges, 8,000 parks, and 800 airports. The WPA FEDERAL ART PROJECT, Theater Project, and Writers' Project provided jobs for unemployed artists, actors, and writers. The program was terminated in 1943.

workstation Computer intended for use by one person, but with a much faster processor and more memory than an ordinary PERSONAL COMPUTER. Workstations are designed for doing large numbers of calculations or high-speed graphical displays; CAD/CAM systems were one reason for their initial development. They generally use UNIX as their operating system. An early workstation was introduced in 1987 by Sun Microsystems. The term workstation is also sometimes used to mean a personal computer connected to a MAINFRAME computer, to distinguish it from a simple terminal.

World Bank Specialized agency of the U.N. system, established in 1944. It is the principal international-development institution, with 160 member nations. The International Bank for Reconstruction and Development, its main component, lends money to middle-income and creditworthy poorer nations. Another of its five divisions, the International Development Assn. (founded 1960), makes interest-free loans to the bank's poorest member countries. The bank's International Finance Corp. (founded 1956) lends to private businesses in developing countries. Other divisions encourage foreign direct investment by offering insurance, and help settle investment disputes. See also INTERNATIONAL MONETARY FUND.

World Council of Churches (WCC) Christian ecumenical organization founded in 1948 in Amsterdam. It functions as a forum for Protestant and Eastern Orthodox denominations, which cooperate through it on a variety of undertakings and explore doctrinal similarities and differences. It grew out of two post–World War I ecumenical efforts, the Life and Work Movement (which concentrated on practical activities) and the Faith and Order Movement (which focused on doctrinal issues and the possibility of reunion). The Roman Catholic church, though not a member of the WCC, sends representatives to its conferences. The more fundamentalist Protestant denominations have refused to join.

World Court See INTERNATIONAL COURT OF JUSTICE

World Cup Any of three major international sporting competitions and their trophies. The World Cup of soccer (football) is a tournament involving the 16 best national teams. It has been held every year fourth year since 1930 (except during World War II). Followed by billions of people worldwide, it has by far the greatest audience of any single sporting event in the world. The World Cup of skiing, held annually since 1967, is an Alpine-skiing contest (downhill, slalom, and giant slalom) held at designated meets throughout the winter. The World Cup of golf (founded in 1953 as the Canada Cup) is an annual competition for two-man professional teams representing nations.

World Health Organization (WHO) Public-health agency of the U.N., established in Geneva in 1948 to succeed two earlier agencies. Its mandate is to promote "the highest possible level of health" in all peoples. It provides a clearinghouse for information on the latest developments in disease and health care, establishes international sanitary standards and quarantine measures, sponsors measures for the control of epidemic and endemic disease, and encourages the strengthening of public-health programs in member nations. Its greatest success to date has been the worldwide eradication of SMALLPOX (1980).

world heritage site Any of various areas or objects designated as having "outstanding universal value" under the Convention Concerning the Protection of the World Cultural and Natural Heritage. This convention, adopted by UNESCO in 1972, provides for international cooperation in preserving and protecting cultural and natural treasures. Among the cultural sites are many of the world's most famous buildings. The ratio of cultural to natural sites on the list is roughly three to one.

World Series Annual championship of U.S. major-league baseball, played between the top team of the AMERICAN LEAGUE and that of the NATIONAL LEAGUE. It has been held since 1903. A seven-game series has been standard since 1922.

world's fair Specially constructed attraction showcasing the science, technology, and culture of participating countries and enterprises. World fairs have often featured outstanding architectural designs and introduced significant inventions. The first was held in England in 1756; more than 300 have been held since, including the 1851 CRYSTAL PALACE Exhibition (London), the 1876 U.S. International Centennial Exposition (Philadelphia), the 1893 World's Columbian Exposition (Chicago), the 1904 St. Louis World's Fair, the 1910 Brussels World's Fair, the 1939–40 New York World's Fair, and the 1967 Montreal Exposition.

World Trade Center Former complex of seven buildings around a central plaza, near the S tip of Manhattan. Its huge twin towers (completed 1972–73) were designed by Minoru Yamasaki (1912–1986) using innovative "tube-in-tube" technology. At 1,350 ft (411 m) and 1,362 ft (415 m) tall, they crowned the New York skyline and were the world's tallest buildings until surpassed in 1974 by the SEARS TOWER. In 1993 a bomb planted in the underground garage killed several people. On September 11, 2001, the towers were destroyed in the most audacious terrorist attack in U.S. history. Two jetliners hijacked by members of the AL-QAEDA network crashed into the towers, their burning fuel melted the steel floor supports, and the concrete floors crashed down from the top to the bottom in succession, killing more than 2,800 people.

World Trade Organization (WTO) International organization based in Geneva that supervises world trade with the intention of making it flow as smoothly, predictably, and freely as possible. It was created by 104 members in 1995 to replace the General Agreement on Tariffs and Trade (GATT). Like its predecessor, it aims to lower trade barriers and encourage multilateral trade. Since 1999 its meetings have been marked by major anti-globalization protests.

World War I or **First World War** (1914–18) International conflict between the CENTRAL POWERS—Germany, Austria-Hungary, and Turkey—and the ALLIED POWERS—mainly France, Britain, Russia, Italy, and (from 1917) the U.S. After a Serbian nationalist assassinated Archduke FRANCIS FERDINAND of Austria in June 1914, a chain of threats resulted in a general war by mid-August. Germany first swept through neutral Belgium and invaded France. After the First Battle of the MARNE (1914), the Allied defensive lines

were stabilized in France, and a war of attrition began. Fought from lines of trenches and supported by modern artillery and machine guns, infantry assaults gained little ground and were enormously costly in human life, especially at the Battles of VERDUN, the SOMME, and YPRES. On the Eastern front, Russian forces initially drove deep into E. Prussia and German Poland (1914), but were forced back into Russia (1915). After several offensives, the Russian army failed to break through the German defensive lines, and Russia's enormous losses caused widespread domestic discontent that led to the RUSSIAN REVOLUTION OF 1917. Other fronts in the war included the unsuccessful DARDANELLES CAMPAIGN against Turkey; the Caucasus and Persia, where Russia fought Turkey; Mesopotamia and Egypt, where British forces fought the Turks; and N Italy, where Italian troops fought Austria. At sea, Germany's use of the submarine against neutral shipping (see LUSITANIA) eventually brought the U.S. into the war (1917). On the Western Front, the Allies were reinforced by U.S. troops in early 1918. Germany's unsuccessful offensive in the Second Battle of the Marne was countered by the Allies' steady advance, which recovered most of France and Belgium by October 1918 and led to the November ARMISTICE. Total casualties were estimated at 10 million dead, 21 million wounded, and 7.7 million missing or imprisoned. See also FOURTEEN POINTS, PARIS PEACE CONFERENCE, Treaty of VERSAILLES; Edmund ALLENBY, Ferdinand FOCH, Douglas HAIG, Paul von HINDENBURG, Joseph JOFFRE, Erich LUDENDORFF, John PERSHING.

World War II or **Second World War** (1939–45) International conflict principally between the AXIS POWERS—Germany, Italy, and Japan—and the ALLIED POWERS—France, Britain, the U.S., and the Soviet Union. Political and economic instability in Germany, combined with bitterness over its defeat in WORLD WAR I and the harsh conditions of the Treaty of VERSAILLES, allowed Adolf HITLER and the NAZI PARTY to rise to power. Secretly rearming Germany, he signed anti-Soviet alliances with Italy and Japan. Capitalizing on European reluctance to oppose him, Hitler sent troops to occupy Austria in 1938 (see ANSCHLUSS) and to annex Czechoslovakia in 1939. After signing the GERMAN–SOVIET NONAGGRESSION PACT, Germany invaded Poland on Sept. 1, 1939. Two days later, France and Britain declared war on Germany. At sea Germany conducted a damaging U-BOAT campaign against merchant shipping bound for Britain. By early 1940 the Soviet Union had occupied the Baltic states and subdued Finland. In April 1940 Germany overwhelmed Denmark and began its conquest of Norway. In May German forces swept through the Netherlands and Belgium on their BLITZKRIEG invasion of France, forcing it to capitulate in June. Germany then launched massive bombing raids on Britain in preparation for a cross-Channel invasion, but after losing the Battle of BRITAIN Hitler postponed the invasion indefinitely. By early 1941 Hungary, Romania, and Bulgaria had joined the Axis, and German troops quickly overran Yugoslava and Greece in April. In June Hitler launched a treacherous massive invasion of Russia, reaching the outskirts of Moscow before counterattacks and winter weather halted the advance. In E. Asia, Japan expanded its war with China and seized European colonial holdings. In December 1941 Japan attacked U.S. bases at Pearl Harbor and in the Philippines, and the U.S. declared war on the Axis Powers. Japan quickly invaded and occupied most of S.E. Asia, and many Pacific islands. After the crucial U.S. naval victory at MIDWAY (1942), U.S. forces began to advance up the chains of islands toward Japan. In the N. AFRICA CAMPAIGNS, the British defeated Italian and German forces by 1943. The Allies then invaded Sicily and Italy, forcing the overthrow of the Fascist government, though fighting against the Germans continued in Italy until 1945. In the Soviet Union, the Battle of STALINGRAD (1943) marked the end of the German advance. The massive Allied invasion of Western Europe began with the NORMANDY CAMPAIGN (1944), and the Allies' steady advance ended in the occupation of Germany in 1945. After Soviet troops pushed German forces out of the Soviet Union, they advanced into Poland, Czechoslovakia, Hungary, Romania, and the E third of Germany. The

WXYZ

surrender of Germany was signed on May 8, 1945. In the Pacific, an Allied invasion of the Philippines (1944) was followed by the battles at IWO JIMA and OKINAWA (1945). The war in the Pacific ended quickly after atomic bombs were dropped on HIROSHIMA and NAGASAKI in August 1945. Japan's formal surrender on September 2 ended the war. Estimates of total casualties varied from 35 million to 60 million killed, including about 6 million Jews who died in the HOLOCAUST. Millions more civilians were wounded and made homeless throughout Europe and E. Asia. See also Battles of EL ALAMEIN, the ATLANTIC, the BULGE, and GUADALCANAL; POTSDAM, TEHRAN, and YALTA conferences; DUNKIRK EVACUATION; LEND-LEASE; MUNICH AGREEMENT; NUREMBERG TRIALS; Siege of LENINGRAD; Omar BRADLEY, Winston CHURCHILL, Dwight EISENHOWER, Douglas MACARTHUR, Bernard MONTGOMERY, Benito MUSSOLINI, George PATTON, Erwin ROMMEL, Franklin ROOSEVELT, Joseph STALIN, YAMAMOTO ISOROKU, Georgy ZHUKOV.

World Wide Web (WWW) *or* **Web** Leading information-exchange service of the INTERNET. It was created by Tim BERNERS-LEE and his colleagues and introduced to the world in 1991. The Web gives users access to a vast array of documents that are connected to each other by means of HYPERTEXT or hyperlinks. A hypertext document is written in HTML or XML and is assigned an on-line address, or URL. Individual HTML files with unique electronic addresses are called Web pages, and a collection of Web pages and related files is called a WEB SITE. Users may access any page by typing in the appropriate address, search for pages related to a topic of interest by using a SEARCH ENGINE, or move quickly between pages by clicking on hyperlinks. The introduction of Mosaic, a BROWSER with a graphical interface, in 1993 led to the explosive growth in use of the Web.

World Wildlife Fund *or* **World Wide Fund for Nature** Largest privately supported international conservation organization in the world. Founded in 1961 by P.M. SCOTT and others, it raises funds and channels them to other conservation groups. It directs its efforts toward protecting endangered environments such as coral reefs, saving endangered species, and addressing global threats such as pollution. It has helped establish and manage parks and reserves, and was instrumental in saving the giant panda (whose image it uses as its symbol) and other species.

worm Any of thousands of species of unrelated INVERTEBRATE animals that typically have a soft, slender, elongated body with no appendages. The major phyla are Platyhelminthes (FLATWORMS), Annelida (ANNELIDS, or segmented worms), Nemertea (ribbon worms), Acanthocephala (spiny-headed worms), and Aschelminthes (NEMATODES and others). Length ranges from microscopic to more than 100 ft (30 m). Worms may be parasitic or free-living and are important as soil conditioners, parasites, and a link in the food chain. See also FLUKE, PINWORM, ROTIFER, TAPEWORM, TUBE WORM.

Worms \\'vórms, *Engl* 'wǝrmz\\, **Concordat of** (1122) Compromise between Pope Calixtus II and Emperor Henry V (r.1106–25) to settle the INVESTITURE CONTROVERSY, reached at Worms, Germany. It marked the end of the first phase of conflict between Rome and the HOLY ROMAN EMPIRE and made a clear distinction between the spiritual side of a prelate's office and his position as a landed magnate and vassal of the crown.

Worms, Diet of Meeting of the assembly (Diet) of the HOLY ROMAN EMPIRE at Worms, Germany, in 1521, where Martin LUTHER defended the principles of the REFORMATION. Although he had already been excommunicated, he was granted safe conduct to a hearing at the Diet. On April 17, 1521, Luther refused to recant his views. Disorder broke out, the emperor adjourned the proceedings, and Luther was obliged to go into hiding. In May the Diet issued the Edict of Worms declaring Luther an outlaw and a heretic.

Worth, Charles Frederick (1825–1895) British-French fashion designer. He left England in 1845 and worked in a Paris dress accessories shop. In 1858 he opened his own ladies' tailor shop and soon gained the patronage of the empress EUGÉNIE. A pioneer of the fashion show, he was the first man to become prominent in the field of fashion, and the first designer to create dresses intended to be copied and distributed throughout the world. He became the dictator of Paris fashion and was especially noted for his elegant Second Empire gowns. He invented the bustle, which became standard in women's fashion in the 1870s and '80s.

Wotan See ODIN

Wouk \\'wōk\\, **Herman** (b.1915) U.S. novelist. Born in New York City, he served aboard a destroyer-minesweeper in World War II. That experience provided material for *The Caine Mutiny* (1951, Pulitzer Prize; film, 1954), a drama of naval tradition. *The Winds of War* (1971) and *War and Remembrance* (1978) together represent a two-volume novel of the war. His other novels include *Marjorie Morningstar* (1955).

wound *or* **trauma** Break in any body tissue due to external action (including surgery). Blood vessels, nerves, muscles, bones, joints, and internal organs may be damaged. A closed wound can be caused by impact, twisting, bending, or deceleration; it can range from a minor bruise to a skull fracture with brain damage or a spinal-cord injury with paralysis. In an open wound, foreign matter entering through broken skin or mucous membrane may cause INFECTION; depth, surface area, degree of tearing, and structures damaged may also affect its severity. Minor wounds need only first aid. For others, after examination and perhaps diagnostic imaging and exploratory surgery, treatment may include fluid replacement or drainage, sterilization and antibiotics, TETANUS antitoxin, and repair of damaged structures. A closed wound may need to be opened or an open one sutured closed. See also BURN, COAGULATION, DISLOCATION, FRACTURE, SCAR.

Wounded Knee Hamlet and creek in SW S. Dakota, the site of two conflicts between the SIOUX Indians and the U.S. government. In 1890 the Sioux had been inspired by the GHOST DANCE movement to take up arms and reclaim their heritage, but federal military intervention quelled the rebellion. When a young brave, while surrendering, killed a trooper, soldiers fired at the Indians, killing more than 200 men, women, and children. Thirty soldiers also died. The so-called Battle of Wounded Knee is regarded as the final episode in the conquest of the N. American Indian. In 1973 some 200 members of the American Indian Movement took the reservation hamlet by force; a siege by federal marshals ended when the Indians surrendered in exchange for a promise of negotiations over Indian grievances.

Wozniak, Stephen G(ary) (b.1950) U.S. computer engineer. Born in San Jose, Cal., he designed electronic devices and games in his teens before joining Hewlett-Packard. In 1976 he and Steven JOBS founded APPLE COMPUTER, INC. Badly injured in a 1981 plane crash, he took a leave from Apple, but he returned to work on the revolutionary Macintosh computer. He left Apple for good in 1985, the year he was awarded the National Medal of Technology. He has since taught in elementary school.

WPA See WORKS PROGRESS ADMINISTRATION

WPA Federal Art Project Extensive visual-arts project, part of the WORKS PROGRESS ADMINISTRATION. It employed artists from relief rolls with a wide range of experience and styles, and had great influence on subsequent U.S. movements. At its peak in 1936, it provided work for more than 5,000 artists. Over the eight years of its existence, its employees produced 2,566 murals, more than 100,000 easel paintings, about 17,700 sculptures, and nearly 300,000 fine prints. The project also developed an audience by establishing more than 100 community art centers and galleries in regions where art was generally unknown. It was the first major attempt at U.S. government patronage of the visual arts.

W particle Electrically charged SUBATOMIC PARTICLE that transmits the WEAK FORCE that governs radioactive decay (see RADIOACTIVITY) in some atomic nuclei and the interactions between hydrogen nuclei that initiate NUCLEAR FUSION in the sun and other stars. The weak force is exchanged via three types of particles, two charged and one neutral. The charged particles are designated W^+ and W^- according to the sign of their charge, and have a mass about 90 times that of the proton, which gives the weak force a very short range. See also Z PARTICLE.

Wrangel, Pyotr (Nikolayevich), Baron (1878–1928) Russian general in the RUSSIAN CIVIL WAR. He commanded a Cossack division in World War I. After the Russian Revolution of 1917, he joined the anti-Bolshevik "White" forces of Anton DENIKIN. After capturing Tsaritsyn (now Volgograd) in 1919, he became commander of the Whites in April 1920 and tried to rally peasant and Cossack support. He launched an offensive in the Ukraine, but by November the RED ARMY had forced the Whites to retreat to the Crimea. After evacuating his troops to Constantinople, he lived in exile.

Wrangell–St. Elias National Park National park, SE Alaska. The largest U.S. national park, it has an area of 12,318,000 acres (4,987,000 hectares). At the convergence of the Chugach, Wrangell, and ST. ELIAS mountain ranges, it includes the largest assemblage of glaciers and the greatest collection of peaks above 16,000 ft (4,880 m) on the continent.

wrasse \'ras\ Any of some 300 species (family Labridae) of often brilliantly colored fishes, found in tropical and temperate seas, often on coral reefs. Species range from 2 in. to 7 ft (5 cm to 2 m) long. Wrasses have thick lips and large, often protruding, canine teeth. Most eat invertebrates; some species, called cleaner wrasses, pick off and eat the external parasites of larger fishes.

wren Any of 59 species (family Troglodytidae) of chunky songbirds, found in the Western Hemisphere. One species, *Troglodytes troglodytes,* has spread to the Old World; typical of the family, it is about 4 in. (10 cm) long and dark-barred brown, with short rounded wings and a short cocked tail. Common is the house wren (*T. aedon*). The largest U.S. species (8 in., or 20 cm, long) is the cactus wren of SW deserts. Wrens hunt insects in marshes, rocky wastes, or shrubbery, revealing their presence by chatter and loud song.

Wren, Christopher (*later* **Sir Christopher**) (1632–1723) British architect, astronomer, and geometrician. He taught astronomy at Gresham College, London (1657–61), and Oxford (1661–73). In 1662 he was engaged to design the Sheldonian Theater at Oxford. As King's Surveyor of Works (1669–1718), he had a hand in rebuilding more than 50 churches destroyed in the GREAT FIRE OF LONDON. Meanwhile, he was evolving designs for ST. PAUL'S CATHEDRAL, a work that occupied him until its completion in 1710. Other works include the classical Trinity College library, Cambridge (1676–84), additions to Hampton Court (begun 1689), and Greenwich Hospital (begun 1696). Wren was

Christopher Wren Painting by Godfrey Kneller, 1711

buried in St. Paul's; nearby is the famous inscription: "Reader, if you seek a monument, look around."

wrench *or* **spanner** Tool, usually operated by hand, for tightening bolts and nuts. A wrench basically consists of a lever with a notch at one or both ends for gripping the bolt or nut so that it can be twisted. Open-end wrenches have ends with straight-sided slots that fit over the part being tightened; box-end wrenches have ends that enclose the nut and have six, eight, 12, or 16 points inside the head. A socket wrench is essentially a short pipe with a square or hexagonal hole and a handle.

wrestling Sport in which two competitors grapple with and strive to trip or throw each other down. It is practiced in various styles, including freestyle wrestling, in which contestants can use holds above and below the waist, and GRECO-ROMAN WRESTLING, which allows only holds above the waist. SUMO is a specialized Japanese variety. U.S. professional wrestling, a highly popular spectator sport, principally involves wildly flamboyant showmanship, including such nonclassical moves as kicks to the head that would be lethal if they were not actually pulled.

Wright, Almroth Edward (*later* **Sir Almroth**) (1861–1947) British bacteriologist and immunologist. His TYPHOID immunization using killed bacteria made Britain the only country with troops immunized against typhoid at the start of World War I, the first war in which fewer British soldiers died of infection than from trauma. He also developed VACCINES against enteric tuberculosis and pneumonia.

Wright, Frank Lloyd (1867–1959) U.S. architect. Born in Richland Center, Wis., he worked for the firm of Louis SULLIVAN before opening his own Chicago practice in 1893. Wright became the chief practitioner of the PRAIRIE SCHOOL, building about 50 Prairie houses 1900–10. Early nonresidential buildings included the Larkin Building in Buffalo, N.Y. (1904) and Unity Temple in Oak Park, Ill. (1906). In 1911 he began work on his own house, TALIESIN. The lavish Imperial Hotel in Tokyo (1915–22) featured revolutionary floating cantilever construction, which permitted it to withstand the earthquake of 1923. In the 1930s he designed his low-cost Usonian houses. His most admired house, Fallingwater, in Bear Run, Pa. (1936), was cantilevered over a waterfall. His Johnson Wax Building (1936–39), an example of humane workplace design, sparked major commissions, including the GUGGENHEIM MUSEUM. Often considered the greatest U.S. architect, Wright became famous for "organic architecture," buildings that harmonize with both their inhabitants and their environment.

Wright, Richard (1908–1960) U.S. writer. Born near Natchez, Miss., he grew up in poverty. After migrating north, he joined the Federal Writers' Project in Chicago, then moved to New York in 1937. He first came to wide attention with a volume of novellas, *Uncle Tom's Children* (1938). His novel *Native Son* (1940), though considered shocking and violent, became a best-seller. The fictionalized autobiography *Black Boy* (1945) vividly describes his often harsh childhood and youth. He is remembered as one of the first African-American writers to protest white treatment of blacks.

Wright, Sewall (1889–1988) U.S. geneticist. Born in Melrose, Mass., he earned his doctorate at Harvard Univ. His earliest studies included investigation of the effects of inbreeding and crossbreeding on guinea pigs. With J. B. S. HALDANE and R. A. FISHER, he developed a mathematical basis for evolutionary theory using statistical techniques. He originated a theory that could guide the use of inbreeding and crossbreeding in livestock improvement. He is perhaps best known for his concept of GENETIC DRIFT.

Wright, Wilbur and Orville (1867–1912, 1871–1948) U.S. inventors who achieved the first powered, sustained, and controlled AIRPLANE flight. Born respectively near Millville, Ind., and in Dayton, Ohio, the brothers formed a bicycle manufacturing company, which financed their early experiments in airplane design. To test flight control, they built and flew three biplane GLIDERS (1900–2). Propeller and engine innovations led to their first powered airplane, *Flyer I* (now called the *Kitty Hawk*), which Orville flew successfully for 12 seconds and Wilbur for 59 seconds at Kill Devil Hills, N. Carolina (near the village of Kitty Hawk), on Dec. 17, 1903. Their *Flyer III,* built in 1905, could turn, bank, circle, and remain airborne for over 35 minutes. They demonstrated their planes in Europe and the U.S.; in 1908 Wilbur gave over 100 exhibition flights in France, setting a duration record of 2 hours and 20 minutes. They established an aircraft company and produced planes for the U.S. Army; it later merged with the company of Glenn CURTISS. After Wilbur's death from typhoid, Orville established a new aeronautical research company.

writ In COMMON LAW, an order issued in the name of a sovereign or court commanding a person to perform or refrain from performing a specified act. It was a vital official instrument in Old English law. Though the writ no longer governs civil pleading and has lost many of its applications, the extraordinary writs, especially of HABEAS CORPUS, mandamus (commanding the performance of a ministerial act), and prohibition (commanding an inferior court to stay within its jurisdiction), reflect its historical importance as an instrument of judicial authority.

writing System of human visual communication using signs or symbols associated with units of LANGUAGE. Its precursor was pictography, the expression of ideas through drawings. Logography, in which symbols stand for individual words, typically develops from pictography. Logography requires thousands of symbols for all possible words and names. In phonographic systems, the symbol associated with a word also stands for similar- or identical-sounding words. Phonographic systems may evolve to the point where symbols represent syllables, constituting a syllabary. An ALPHABET provides symbols for all the consonants and vowels.

Writs of Assistance See Writs of ASSISTANCE

Wroclaw \\'vrȯt-ˌswäf\\ *German* **Breslau** \\'bres-ˌlau̇\\ City (pop., 1999 est.: 638,000), SW Poland. Located on the ODER RIVER, from the 10th cent. it lay on the trade route linking the Black Sea to W Europe. In 1138 it became the first capital of SILESIA. The Tatars destroyed it in 1241. Rebuilt, it passed to BOHEMIA in 1335, and in 1526 to the HABSBURGS. In 1741 it fell to Prussia under FREDERICK II the Great, and it later became part of Germany. The city was assigned to Poland by the POTSDAM CONFERENCE of 1945. Though heavily damaged during World War II, it is now a major commercial city.

wrought iron One of the two forms in which IRON is obtained by SMELTING. Wrought iron is a soft, easily worked, fibrous metal. It usually contains less than 0.1% CARBON and 1–2% slag. It is superior for most purposes to CAST IRON, which is hard and brittle because of its higher carbon content. In antiquity, iron was smelted directly by heating ore in a forge with charcoal, which served both as fuel and reducing agent. While still hot, the iron-and-slag mixture was worked (wrought) with a hammer to expel most of the slag and weld the iron into a coherent mass. Wrought iron began to take the place of bronze (being far more available) in Asia Minor in the 2nd millennium B.C.; its use for tools and weapons was established in China, India, and the Mediterranean by the 3rd cent. B.C. In the 19th cent. STEEL supplanted wrought iron for structural purposes, and its use today is principally decorative.

wu Fundamental Taoist philosophical concept. Wu ("Not-being"), *you* ("Being"), *wuming* ("the Nameless"), and *youming* ("the Named") are interdependent and grow out of one another. Wu and *you* are two aspects of the TAO. Wu is not nothingness, but rather the absence of perceptible qualities; in LAOZI's view, it is superior to Being because it is the source of all potentialities. See also TAOISM.

Wu Chengen *or* **Wu Ch'eng-en** \\'wü-'chən-'ən\\ (c.1500–1582?) Chinese novelist and poet. Interested in bizarre stories, he used oral and written folktales as the basis of the novel *Xiyou ji* ("Record of a Journey to the West"; translated as *Monkey*), published anonymously in 1592. It relates the comic mishaps and adventures of the 7th-cent. monk Xuanzang, who traveled to India looking for sacred texts, and his entourage of three animal spirits: a monkey, a pig, and a fish. It satirizes Chinese society and government and contains elements drawn from Buddhism, Taoism, and Neo-Confucianism.

Wudi *or* **Wu-ti** \\'wü-'dē\\ *orig.* Liu Che (156–87/86 B.C.) Emperor of the Chinese HAN DYNASTY who vastly increased its influence and made CONFUCIANISM China's state religion. Under Wudi, China's armies drove back the tribes that plagued the N border, incorporated S China and N and central Vietnam into the empire, and reconquered Korea. Their farthest expedition was to Fergana (in modern Uzbekistan). Wudi's military campaigns strained the state's reserves; seeking new income, he decreed new taxes and established state monopolies on salt, iron, and wine.

Wuhan *or* **Wu-han** \\'wü-'hän\\ City (pop., 1999 est.: 3,912,000), capital of Hubei province, E central China. It is located at the confluence of the Han and CHANG (Yangtze) rivers and is a conurbation of three cities that merged in 1950: Hankou, Hanyang, and Wuchang. The chief industrial and commercial center of central China, it is a hub of maritime, river, rail, and road transportation. It has numerous industries, including iron- and steel-producing complexes. It is the seat of Wuhan Univ. and Central China Technical Univ.

Wu Hou \\'wü-'hō\\ *or* **Wu Zetian** \\'wü-dzə-'tyan\\ (625–705) Empress of China of the TANG DYNASTY. The concubine of the emperor Taizong, she later became the consort of his son, eliminated her female rivals, and became empress in 655. Because the emperor was sickly, she was able to rule in his name; after his death she ruled in the name of her sons, at last declaring herself ruler in her own name in 690. Though long vilified for her cruelty and her autocratic methods, she supported the development of a scholarly bureaucracy to replace rule by aristocratic families and she stabilized the dynasty.

Wundt \\'vu̇nt\\, **Wilhelm** (1832–1920) German physiologist and psychologist, the founder of EXPERIMENTAL PSYCHOLOGY. At the Univ. of Heidelberg in 1862, following publication of his *Contributions to the Theory of Sense Perception* (1858–62), he gave the first course in scientific psychology. At the Univ. of Leipzig (1875–1917), he established the first psychological laboratory (1879) and founded the first journal of psychology (1881). His works include *Principles of Physiological Psychology* (1873–74), *Outline of Psychology* (1896), and *Ethnic Psychology* (10 vols., 1900–20).

Wuppertal \\'vu̇-pər-ˌtäl\\ City (pop., 1998 est.: 377,000), NW Germany. It took its present name when six towns merged in 1929-30. The region was noted for its textiles as early as the 16th cent., and the modern city remains a textile center. Other products include chemicals, rubber, and machinery. It has numerous parks and public gardens and a well-known zoo.

Württemberg \\'vʏr-təm-ˌberk, *Engl* 'wu̇r-təm-ˌbərg\\ Former state, Germany. The capital was STUTTGART. In antiquity it was occupied successively by Celts, Suevi, Romans, Alemanni, and Franks. In the Middle Ages it was part of SWABIA. In 1806 it became a kingdom. A constitutional monarchy 1819–1918, it joined the WEIMAR REPUBLIC in 1919. In 1952 it was made part of Baden-Württemberg.

Wu Sangui *or* **Wu San-kuei** \\'wü-'sän-'gwā\\ (1612–1678) Chinese general. Though he had for many years battled the MANCHUS on China's NE frontier, he turned to them for aid when the MING-DYNASTY capital at Beijing fell to rebels. The Manchu forces defeated them and then set up their own QING DYNASTY, in which Wu served for many years. When he was put in charge of eliminating Ming resistance in SW China, he created his own state in Yunnan and Guizhou. With two other commanders who had set up similar states in neighboring S provinces, Wu led a rebellion (1673). After Wu's death, his grandson continued the rebellion until 1681, when it was finally crushed.

Wu-ti See WUDI

Wuwang *or* **Wu-wang** \\'wü-'wäŋ\\ (c.12th cent. B.C.) Chinese ruler and founder of the ZHOU DYNASTY. He succeeded his father, WENWANG, as king of the semibarbaric state of Zhou, formed a coalition with other border states, and overthrew (c.1122) the SHANG DYNASTY. Wuwang consolidated his rule by establishing a feudalistic form of government in which territory was bestowed on relatives and vassals willing to acknowledge Zhou suzerainty. He was regarded by later Confucians as a wise king.

Wu Zetian See WU HOU

Wyatt, Thomas (*later* **Sir Thomas**) (1503–1542) English poet. A member of the court circle of Henry VIII, he distinguished himself as a soldier and diplomat. His fame rests on his poetic achievements, especially his introduction into English literature of the Italian SONNET and TERZA RIMA verse form and the French RONDEAU. His works, unusual for their time in carrying a strong sense of individuality, include *Certayne Psalmes . . . drawen into Englyshe meter* (1549).

Wycherley \\'wi-chər-lē\\, **William** (1640–1716) English dramatist. He wrote comedies of manners that attempted to reconcile his deep-seated puritanism and ardent physical nature. *Love in a Wood* (1671) first won him favor in the Restoration court, and *The Plain-Dealer* (1676) satirized rapacious greed. In *The Country-Wife* (1675), satirical comment on excessive jealousy and complacency is blended with a richly comic and bawdy presentation. He eventually lost favor at court and spent seven years in debtor's prison until he was rescued by JAMES II.

Wycliffe \\'wi-ˌklif\\, **John** (c.1330–1384) British theologian and church reformer. He earned a doctor-of-divinity degree from Oxford in 1372. His preaching against church policies, in which he argued that the church itself was sinful and should relinquish its possessions, attracted wide attention, and in 1377 the pope called for his arrest. In 1379 he began systematically attacking the foundations of Roman Catholicism, repudiating the doctrine of transubstantiation and denying that the church hierarchy represented a line of authoritative succession from Jesus. In 1380 he became involved in a translation of the Bible into English, seeking to bypass the church in making the law of God accessible to all literate people. He was blamed by his superiors for inciting the PEASANTS' REVOLT (1381). His writings later inspired the leaders of the REFORMATION, notably Martin LUTHER. See also LOLLARDS.

Wye River River, E Wales and W England. It flows from the moorlands of central Wales southeast into the estuary of the SEVERN RIVER. It is about 130 mi (210 km) long. The ruins of Tintern Abbey (the inspiration for William WORDSWORTH's poem) are on its banks.

Wyeth \\'wī-əth\\, **Andrew (Newell)** (b.1917) U.S. painter. Born in Chadds Ford, Pa., he was trained by his father, N. C. WYETH. His subject matter comes almost entirely from the area around Chadds Ford and around his summer home in Cushing, Me. Though his technique is precise and detailed, he uses it to achieve an unreal, visionary quality. His palette is restricted largely to earth colors. His famous *Christina's World* (1948) exemplifies his mastery of unusual angles and his use of light to pinpoint time. He was the first painter ever awarded the Presidential Medal of Freedom (1963) and the first artist to receive the Congressional Gold Medal (1990). His son Jamie (b.1946) is best known for his vivid and detailed portraits and images of wildlife.

Wyeth, N(ewell) C(onvers) (1882–1945) U.S. illustrator and muralist. Raised on a farm in Needham, Mass., he studied with the master illustrator Howard Pyle (1853–1911). He first found success in depicting the American West. During his career he contributed his memorable illustrations to more than 100 books, including the children's classics *Treasure Island, Kidnapped, King Arthur, Robin Hood,* and *The Black Arrow,* and produced numerous murals in public buildings. He was the teacher of his son, Andrew WYETH.

Wyler, William (1902–1981) French-U.S. film director. He emigrated to New York in 1920. Working for Universal Pictures, he established his reputation with *Counsellor-at-Law* (1933) and went on to direct such successes as *Dodsworth* (1936), *Wuthering Heights* (1939), and *The Little Foxes* (1941). With his clear narrative style, he won Academy Awards for *Mrs. Miniver* (1942) and *The Best Years of Our Lives* (1946), and later directed such popular movies as *Roman Holiday* (1953), *Ben-Hur* (1959, Academy Award), and *Funny Girl* (1968).

Wyoming State (pop., 2000: 494,000), W U.S. It covers an area of 97,809 sq mi (253,326 sq km); its capital is CHEYENNE. It contains part of the GREAT PLAINS and the BLACK HILLS. Its ranges of the ROCKY MTNS. include the BIGHORN, TETONS, and Wind River. Wyoming's highest point is Gannett Peak, at 13,804 ft (4,207 m) tall. The CONTINENTAL DIVIDE crosses it northwest to southeast. About three-fourths of its rivers drain eastward into the Missouri-Mississippi system. Its largest lake is Yellowstone Lake. Wyoming was inhabited by Plains Indians, including the SHOSHONE, when it was first visited by white explorers during the 18th cent. The OREGON and Overland trails crossed it. Most of the area was acquired by the U.S. from France in the LOUISIANA PURCHASE (1803). Though the LEWIS AND CLARK EXPEDITION did not cross the area, a member of the group, John Colter (1775?–1813), spent time there. It was included in several U.S. territories before the organization of Wyoming Territory in 1868. It adopted women's suffrage in 1869 and in 1889 was the first state to include that right in its constitution. In the years preceding statehood, it developed a thriving cattle industry. It was admitted to the Union in 1890 as the 44th state. In 1925, it elected the first U.S. woman governor, Nellie Tayloe Ross (1876–1977). Though livestock is still important to its modern economy, mining is increasingly influential, and tourism is growing.

Wyszynski \\vi-'shin-skē\\, **Stefan** (1901–1981) Polish cardinal and primate of Poland. He founded and directed the Christian Workers Univ. (1935–39), and was later appointed primate of Poland (1948) and cardinal (1952). For refusing to consent to communist demands, he was placed under house arrest 1953–56. After his release, he reached a compromise on church and state matters with Wladyslaw GOMULKA that avoided a Soviet invasion, and he thereafter maintained the unity of the church in an uneasy coexistence with the government.

WXYZ

X

Xavier \'zā-vē-ər\, **St. Francis** (1506–1552) Spanish-French missionary to the Far East. Born into a noble Basque family, he was educated at the Univ. of Paris, where he met Ignatius of LOYOLA and became one of the first seven members of the JESUITS. Between 1542 and 1551 he engaged in missionary work in India, the Malay Archipelago, and Japan, where he was the first to systematically introduce Christianity. He died while attempting to enter China. He may have baptized about 30,000 converts; his success was partly due to adaptation to local cultures. He was canonized in 1622, and in 1927 he was named patron of all missions.

xenon \'zē-,nän\ Chemical ELEMENT, chemical symbol Xe, atomic number 54. One of the NOBLE GASES, it is colorless, odorless, tasteless, and nearly inert. Xenon occurs in slight traces in the atmosphere and in rocks. Obtained by fractional DISTILLATION of liquefied air, it is used in luminescent tubes, flash lamps, lasers, and tracer studies and as an ANESTHETIC.

Xenophanes of Colophon \zi-'näf-ə-,nēz...'kä-lə-fən\ (c.560–478? B.C.) Greek poet, religious thinker, and reputed precursor of philosophy of the ELEATICS. Though some critics consider PARMENIDES the founder of the Eleatic school, Xenophanes' philosophy probably anticipated Parmenides' views. Fragments of his poetic epics reflect his contempt for anthropomorphism and for popular acceptance of Homeric mythology.

Xenophon \'zen-ə-,fän\ (431 B.C.–shortly before 350 B.C.) Greek historian. Born of a well-to-do Athenian family, Xenophon was critical of extreme democracy and for a time was exiled as a traitor. The great experience of his life was serving with the Greek mercenaries of the Persian prince Cyrus, on which he based his best-known work, the *Anabasis*. Its prose was highly regarded in antiquity and exerted a strong influence on Latin literature.

xerography \zə-'rä-grə-fē\ Image-forming process that is the basis of the most widely used photocopiers. The process was invented in the 1930s by Chester F. Carlson (1906–1968) and developed in the 1940s and '50s by Xerox Corp. (then called Haloid). Light passing through or reflected from a document reaches a selenium-coated drum onto which negatively charged particles of ink (toner) are sprayed, forming an image of the document on the drum. As a sheet of paper is passed close to the drum, a positive electric charge under the sheet attracts the negatively charged ink particles, transferring the image to the copy paper. Applied heat fuses the ink particles to the paper. The first commercially successful xerographic copier was introduced in 1959.

Xerxes I \'zərk-,sēz\ *Persian* Khshayarsha (519?–465 B.C.) Persian king (486–465 B.C.) of the ACHAEMENIAN DYNASTY. The son of DARIUS I, he ferociously suppressed rebellions in Egypt (484) and Babylonia (482). To avenge Darius' defeat by the Greeks at the Battle of MARATHON, he raised a massive army and navy. He placed boat bridges across the Hellespont and for seven days oversaw the crossing of his army, numbering 360,000 troops. The Persians won the Battle of THERMOPYLAE and pillaged Athens, but then lost their navy at the Battle of SALAMIS (480), whereupon Xerxes returned to Asia. In Persia he began an exten-

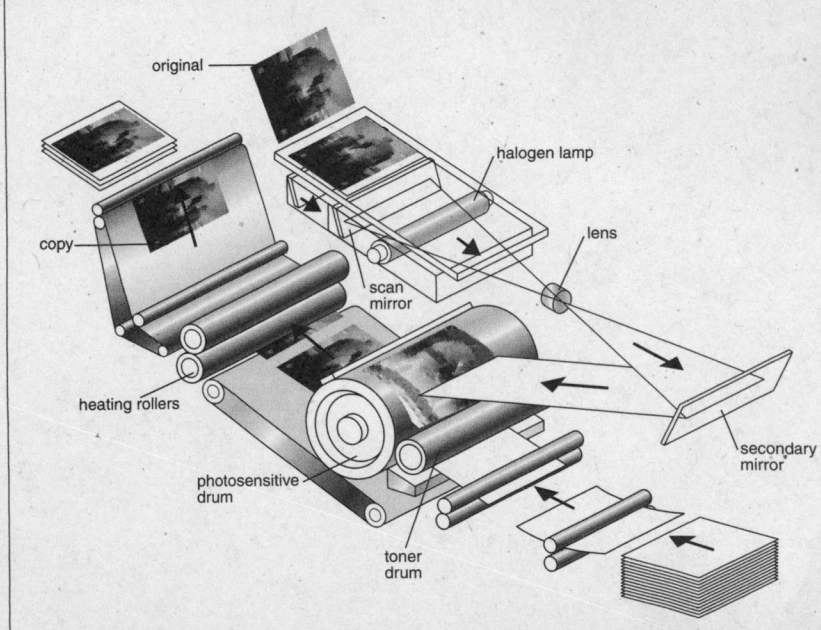

original
halogen lamp
lens
copy
scan mirror
heating rollers
photosensitive drum
toner drum
secondary mirror

Xerography Light shining on the item to be copied is reflected off a mirror, through a lens, and off a second mirror to form an image on a photosensitive (selenium-coated) drum. The drum's surface charge varies with the light and dark areas of the image. The toner drum delivers tiny black particles (toner) to the dark, charged areas of the image. The toner-based image is then transferred to paper rolled onto the drum, the negatively charged toner particles being attracted by a positive charge under the sheet, and the paper is heated to set the toner. The copy paper itself originally provided the treated surface, but the innovation of the selenium-coated drum permitted the use of ordinary paper. Light projection permits the printed image to be enlarged or reduced by any desired percentage.

sive building campaign at PERSEPOLIS. He killed his brother's family at the queen's demand, and he himself was murdered by members of his court. His setback in Greece was regarded as the beginning of the decline of the Achaemenid dynasty.

Xhosa \\'kō-sə\\ Bantu-speaking people living primarily in Eastern Cape province, S. Africa. In the late 18th and 19th cent., the series of conflicts called the Kaffir ("Infidel") Wars engaged the Xhosa against the European settlers, who eventually defeated them. During 1959–61 the government of S. Africa

Xerxes I Bas-relief, N courtyard in the treasury at Persepolis, late 6th–early 5th cent. B.C.

created the nonindependent black states of TRANSKEI and CISKEI for the Xhosa. In the 1960s many became migrant laborers. Today they number 7.4 million.

Xia dynasty *or* **Hsia dynasty** \\shē-'ä\\ Quasi-legendary first dynasty of China, preceding the SHANG DYNASTY. In Chinese histories it is said to have been founded by Yu; it supposedly lasted from about 2205 to 1766 B.C. Archaeological sites in Henan and Shanxi in NE and E China have been tentatively identified with Xia culture.

Xi'an *or* **Hsi-an** *or* **Sian** \\'shē-'än\\ City (pop., 1999 est.: 2,295,000), capital of Shaanxi province, E central China. Located on the WEI RIVER, the site served as the capital of 11 dynasties beginning in the 11th cent. B.C. It became one of the most splendid cities of the ancient world during the TANG DYNASTY (A.D. 618–907). Marco POLO visited in the 13th cent. In 1936 the XI'AN INCIDENT united the Communist-Nationalist front against Japanese invaders. It is the site of numerous temples and pagodas. It became a tourist destination with the discovery of the nearby tomb of SHI HUANGDI, with its army of 6,000 life-size terra-cotta warriors.

Xi'an Incident *or* **Sian Incident** \\'shyan\\ (Dec. 12–25, 1936) Seizure of CHIANG KAI-SHEK by one of his generals, Chang Hsüeh-liang (1901–2001), to compel Chiang to postpone his war on the Chinese Communists until the invading Japanese had been defeated. As a result of the incident, the Nationalists and Communists formed an alliance that turned its attention to the Japanese in Manchuria (see MANCHUGUO).

Xi Bo See WENWANG

Xipe Totec \\shē-pä-'tō-tek, 'hē-pä-'tō-tek\\ Pre-Columbian Mexican god of spring and of new vegetation, and the patron of precious metals. Originally a ZAPOTEC deity, he was adopted by the AZTECS. He is always depicted in art wearing a freshly flayed skin, representing the "new skin" that covers the earth in spring; in his honor, priests sacrificed human victims, flayed the bodies, and put on the skins, which were dyed yellow and called "golden clothes."

Xi River *or* **Hsi River** \\'shē, 'shi\\ *English* **West River** River, SE China. The Xi proper begins in E Guangxi Zhuangzu and flows east about 1,200 mi (1,930 km). Its volume of flow is second only to that of the CHANG (Yangtze) among Chinese rivers. It flows through the vast PEARL RIVER delta into the CHINA SEA west of HONG

Xipe Totec Pottery figure from Monte Albán, 8th–11th cent.

KONG near MACAO; the city of GUANGZHOU is also in its delta. It is the great commercial waterway of S China, linking these cities with the interior.

XML *in full* Extensible Markup Language. MARKUP LANGUAGE developed as a simplified version of SGML. It incorporates features of HTML, but is designed to overcome some of HTML's limitations. Unlike HTML, it allows the creation of customized markup tags, and it is designed to represent data by meaning rather than by layout. Introduced in 1998, it is now widely used on the WORLD WIDE WEB.

X ray ELECTROMAGNETIC RADIATION of extremely short WAVELENGTH produced by the deceleration of charged particles or the transitions of ELECTRONS in atoms. X rays exhibit phenomena associated with WAVES, but can also behave like particles (see WAVE-PARTICLE DUALITY). On the ELECTROMAGNETIC SPECTRUM, they lie between GAMMA RAYS and ULTRAVIOLET RADIATION. They were discovered in 1895 by Wilhelm RÖNTGEN. They are used in medicine to diagnose bone fractures, dental cavities, and cancer; to locate foreign objects in the body; and to stop the spread of malignant tumors. In industry, they are used to analyze flaws in structures.

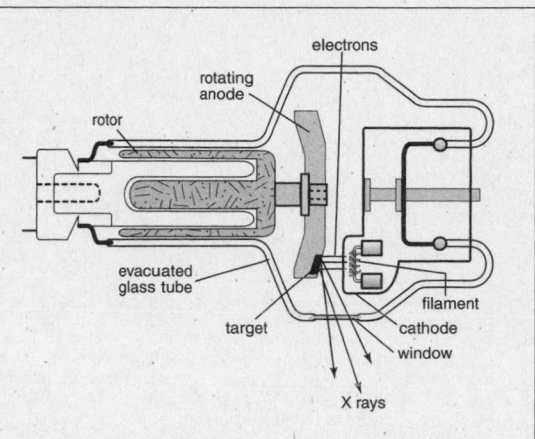

X ray An X-ray tube. Electrons "boil" off the cathode when the filament is heated by a current. A high voltage between cathode and anode causes the electrons to accelerate toward the anode, which rotates to avoid overheating of the target. When the electrons strike the anode's target area, X rays are emitted.

X-ray astronomy Study of cosmic objects that emit radiation at X-RAY wavelengths. Earth's ATMOSPHERE absorbs most X rays; X-ray telescopes and detectors must be carried above it to observe their sources. Almost all types of stars (including the sun) emit X rays, usually as a minute fraction of their output. SUPERNOVA remnants are more powerful sources. The strongest X-ray sources in the galaxy are certain BINARY STARS that probably include a BLACK HOLE; X-ray binaries can even be seen in nearby galaxies. Clusters of galaxies often contain very hot gas between the galaxies that emits strong X rays. A diffuse background of X-ray radiation, discovered in 1962, emanates from great distances and all directions; unlike the COSMIC BACKGROUND RADIATION, it appears to have multiple individual sources.

X-ray diffraction Phenomenon in which the ATOMS of a CRYSTAL, by virtue of their uniform spacing, cause an INTERFERENCE pattern of the waves in an incident beam of X RAYS. The crystal's atomic planes act on the X rays in the same way a uniformly ruled grating acts on a beam of light (see POLARIZATION). The interference pattern is specific to each substance and gives information on the structure of the atoms or molecules in the crystal.

Xuanzong *or* **Hsüan Tsung** \\shǖen-'dzun\\ *orig.* Li Longji (685–762) Sixth emperor (712–56) of the TANG DYNASTY of China, which during his reign achieved its greatest prosperity and cultural brilliance. Xuanzong reformed the bureaucracy, increased tax revenues, improved the transportation system, and established a permanent military force along

China's N frontiers. Later he withdrew from government and came under the influence of his consorts, including the notorious beauty Yang Guifei. The An Lushan Rebellion of 755 forced him to flee the capital, Changan, and he soon abdicated.

xylophone Percussion instrument consisting of a set of tuned wooden bars that are struck with mallets. A primitive xylophone may consist of logs of graded length laid across two supporting logs above a pit (serving as a resonator). Long one of the principal instruments of African music, it is also important in the Indonesian GAMELAN. The modern orchestral xylophone has bars laid out on a stand in keyboard arrangement, with vertical resonating tubes suspended under each bar. The Latin American xylophone is the MARIMBA.

XYZ Affair (1797–98) Diplomatic incident between the U.S. and France. Pres. John ADAMS sent Elbridge GERRY and John MARSHALL to France to help C. C. PINCKNEY negotiate an agreement to protect U.S. shipping from French privateers. Before the three could meet with C.-M. de TALLEYRAND, they were approached by three of his agents—referred to as X, Y, and Z—who suggested a bribe of $250,000 to Talleyrand and a loan of $10 million to France as preconditions for negotiations. Adams rejected the demands and reported the mission had failed. When the correspondence was revealed, public outrage was followed by calls for war with France. The ALIEN AND SEDITION ACTS were passed to restrict potential French sympathizers.

Y2K bug *or* **Year 2000 bug** *or* **millennium bug** Potential problem in computers and computer networks at the beginning of the year 2000. Most computer programs formerly used only the last two digits to designate the year, the first two digits being fixed at 19. As the year 2000 approached, many programs had to be partly rewritten or replaced to prevent interpretation of "00" as 1900 rather than 2000. It was feared that such a misreading would lead to massive software and hardware failures in computers, with the potential for widespread chaos on and following January 1, 2000. Up to $600 billion may have been spent to upgrade computers and application programs. Despite international alarm, few major failures occurred, partly because these measures were effective and partly because the problem was exaggerated.

yacht \\'yät\\ Sail- or motor-driven vessel used for racing or recreation. The term is popularly applied to large recreational engine-powered boats; the sailboats known as yachts and used for racing are usually light and comparatively small. Yacht design was greatly affected by the 1851 success of the *America* (see AMERICA'S CUP). After World War II, smaller racing and recreational craft became more common. See also SAILING.

yachting See SAILING

Yagoda \\yə-'gȯ-də\\, **Genrikh (Grigoryevich)** (1891–1938) Soviet politician. A leader of the Cheka secret police (1920–24) and its successor, the OGPU (1924–34), and a close associate of Joseph STALIN, he organized the Soviet Union's forced-labor camps from 1930. As head of the Commissariat of Internal Affairs, or NKVD, he prepared the first of the PURGE TRIALS. In 1937 he was replaced as police chief by Nikolay YEZHOV and himself became a victim of the purges. Accused of conspiracy, he was convicted and executed.

yak Massive OX (*Bos grunniens mutus*) of high Tibetan plateaus. Bulls grow to 6 ft (1.8 m) at the shoulder hump. The wild yak's horns spread outward and upward; the head is held low. Yaks graze on grass and require much water, eating snow in winter. Wild yaks are now endangered. Domestic yaks, which breed freely with domestic cattle, are used as pack, draft, milk, and beef

Yak *(Bos grunniens)*

animals. The hide provides leather; the tail, fly whisks; the fringe hair, ropes; the dried dung, fuel.

Yakima River \\'ya-kə-ˌmȯ, 'ya-kə-mə\\ River, S central Washington. Rising in the CASCADE RANGE, it flows southeast for about 200 mi (320 km) to join the COLUMBIA RIVER near Kennewick. The Yakima and its tributaries irrigate about 460,000 acres (190,000 hectares) in its rich valley.

Yakut \\yə-'küt\\ *or* **Sakha** SIBERIAN PEOPLE who speak a TURKIC LANGUAGE. Most were formerly seminomadic, raising cattle and horses. They lived in winter settlements of earth-covered log huts and summer camps of conical birchbark tents. Many S Yakut turned to farming, while N Yakut adopted reindeer breeding from the Evenki. They were noted for their ironwork and also made pottery; ivory and wood carving are still practiced. The Yakut number about 380,000.

yakuza \\'yä-kù-zə\\ Japanese gangsters. Yakuza, who trace their roots back to RONIN, often adopt samurai-like rituals and identify themselves with elaborate body tattoos. They engage in extortion, blackmail, smuggling, prostitution, drugs, and gambling, and they control many restaurants, bars, trucking companies, and taxi fleets in Japanese cities. Numbering over 150,000, they are organized into about 2,000 gangs, most affiliated with one of several conglomerate gangs. Yakuza gangs are rigidly hierarchical, and the price for disappointing the gang is often to be forced to cut off one's own finger.

Yale University Private university in New Haven, Conn., a member of the IVY LEAGUE. Founded in 1701, it is the third-oldest institution of higher learning in the U.S. Medical, divinity, and law schools were added in 1810, 1822, and 1824. Benjamin Silliman (1779–1864), who taught at Yale 1802–53, did much to expand its sciences curriculum, and beginning in the mid-19th cent., schools of graduate studies, art, music, forestry, nursing, drama, management, and architecture were organized. Yale's library, with more than 10 million volumes, is one of the largest in the U.S. Its extensive art galleries were established in 1832. The Peabody Museum of Natural History houses important collections. Yale is one of the most highly regarded schools in the nation; it has educated five U.S. presidents. Total enrollment is about 11,000.

Yalow \\'ya-lō\\, **Rosalyn S(ussman)** *orig.* Rosalyn Sussman (b.1921) U.S. medical physicist. Born in New York City, she developed the technique of radioimmunoassay (RIA) by combining techniques from radioisotope tracing and IMMUNOLOGY. RIA proved a very sensitive and simple way to measure tiny concentrations of biological substances or drugs in blood or other body fluids, and it soon found hundreds of applications. In 1976 she became the first woman awarded the Albert Lasker Prize, and in 1977 she shared a Nobel Prize.

Yalta City (pop., 1991 est.: 89,000), S CRIMEA, Ukraine. It faces the BLACK SEA. Yalta became a town in 1838. Its mild winters and scenic location between sea and mountains have made it one of the most popular vacation and health resorts of Ukraine. In 1945, during World War II, it hosted the YALTA CONFERENCE.

Yalta Conference (Feb. 4–11, 1945) Conference of Allied leaders at Yalta to plan Germany's final defeat in World War II. Franklin ROOSEVELT, Winston CHURCHILL, and Joseph STALIN discussed the postwar occupation of Germany, postwar assistance to the German people, war-crimes trials, the fate of Eastern Europe, and voting in the future U.N. Security Council. Stalin agreed to enter the war against Japan after the German surrender. Roosevelt died two months later, and Stalin broke his promise to allow democratic elections in Eastern Europe.

Yalu River *or* **Ya-lü River** \\'yä-lü\\ *Korean* **Amnok River** \\'äm-ˌnək\\ River between NE China and N. Korea. Some 491 mi (790 km) long, it rises on the N border of N. Korea, then flows to Korea Bay. It became a political boundary in the 14th cent. During the KOREAN WAR, as U.N. forces battled toward it in 1950, Chinese troops crossed it, in effect marking their entry into the war.

yam Any of several plant species of the genus *Dioscorea* (family Dioscoreaceae, or yam family), native to warmer regions of both hemispheres. A number of species are cultivated for food in the tropics. The edible tuberous roots,

W X Y Z

which vary in taste from sweet to bitter to tasteless, are eaten as cooked starchy vegetables. True yams are botanically distinct from the SWEET POTATO, though in the U.S. the names are commonly interchanged. *Dioscorea mexicana* contains a chemical that is used as the basis for birth-control pills.

Yama \\'yə-mə\\ In Indian mythology, the lord of death. The VEDAS describe him as the first man who died. The son of SURYA, he presides over the resting place of the dead. In the Vedas, he was a cheerful king of the departed ancestors, but in later mythology he was the just judge who punished the deceased for their sins.

Yamagata Aritomo \\ˌyä-mə-'gä-tə-ˌär-ē-'tō-mō\\ (1838–1922) First prime minister under Japan's parliamentary regime (1889–91, 1898–1900). As a SAMURAI youth, Yamagata became convinced of the need for modern armaments. After participating in the MEIJI RESTORATION, he went abroad to research military institutions. He became commander of an imperial guard of 10,000 troops, introduced conscription, and modernized the army. In politics he favored a strong executive. He served in the cabinet from 1885. As prime minister, his policies were expansionist; Japan sent the largest of all foreign forces to China to quell the BOXER REBELLION. He increased the autonomy of the military and tried to suppress an incipient social-labor movement. After retirement, he continued to wield power as a genro (elder statesman).

Yamamoto Isoroku \\ˌyä-mä-'mō-tō-ˌē-sō-'rō-kù\\ (1884–1943) Japanese naval officer. He fought in the Russo–Japanese War and thereafter rose to become commander in chief of Japan's combined fleet in 1941. When war with the U.S. was decided on, Yamamoto conceived of the surprise attack on PEARL HARBOR to cripple U.S. naval forces in the Pacific. He then sought to destroy the remnants of the U.S. fleet, principally its aircraft carriers, but the Japanese lost the resulting Battle of Midway (1942). He was killed when the U.S. broke the Japanese communications codes and shot down his plane over Bougainville island.

Yamazaki Ansai \\'yä-mä-ˌzä-kē-'än-ˌsī\\ (1619–1682) Japanese exponent of the philosophy of the Chinese Neo-Confucianist ZHU XI. A Buddhist monk, he gradually rejected Buddhism in favor of Confucianism. He reduced NEO-CONFUCIANISM to a simple moral code, which he then blended with native Shinto religious doctrines, creating a philosophical system that took on greater authority than its sources possessed alone. His thought was one of the sources of the extreme nationalism and emperor worship that developed later in Japan.

Yamoussoukro \\ˌyä-mü-'sü-krō\\ Town (pop., 1995 est.: 110,000), capital-designate of Ivory Coast. From 1960 to 1993, it served as the country's "second capital" because it was the home and headquarters of President Félix HOUPHOUËT-BOIGNY. It shares some of the functions of the former national capital, ABIDJAN. It is the site of the world's largest Christian church (1990), commissioned by Houphouët-Boigny.

Yangon \\ˌyäŋ-'gōn\\ *formerly* **Rangoon** City (metro. area pop., 1999 est.: 4,101,000), principal seaport, and capital of Myanmar. The present city was founded about 1755 by King Alaungpaya and developed into a port. After the British annexation of all of Burma (Myanmar) in 1886, Rangoon became the capital city. During World War II the Japanese occupied it and it suffered severe damage. In 1988 it was the scene of severe repression of antigovernment demonstrators by the military.

Yangshao culture \\'yäŋ-'shaù\\ (5000–3000 B.C.) Prehistoric culture of China's Huang (Yellow) River basin, represented by several sites at which painted pottery has been uncovered (see BANPO). Millet was cultivated, chipped and polished stone tools were used, silk was produced, and pottery was fired.

Yangtze Gorges Dam Project See THREE GORGES DAM PROJECT

Yangtze River See CHANG RIVER

Yanomami *or* **Yanomamö** S. American Indians of the remote forest of the Orinoco River basin in S Venezuela and the N Amazon basin in Brazil. Their reputation as "fierce people" perpetually at war has been challenged in recent

years. Because their survival was threatened by incursions of Brazilian miners, in 1991 the Brazilian government set aside an area of 36,000 sq mi (93,000 sq km) as a homeland.

Yaoundé \\yaùn-'dā\\ City (pop., 1992 est.: 800,000), capital of Cameroon. It was founded in 1888 while Cameroon was a German protectorate. The area came under French control, and it was declared the capital of French Cameroun in 1922. Briefly replaced as the capital by DOUALA, it regained capital status after Cameroon achieved independence in 1960.

Yaqui \\'yä-kē\\ American Indian people centered in S Sonora on the W coast of Mexico. They fought against first Spanish and then Mexican encroachment on their fertile lands, and were finally quelled with difficulty in 1887. Thousands were subsequently deported. In the 1930s much of their land was returned to them. Irrigation projects have led to a shift from subsistence agriculture to cash cropping. They number about 25,000 in Mexico and several thousand in Arizona.

yarn Continuous strand of fibers grouped or twisted together and used to construct TEXTILE fabrics. Yarns are made from both natural and synthetic fibers, in filament or staple form. Filament is very long fiber, including silk and the synthetic fibers. Most natural fibers are fairly short, or staple, and synthetic fibers may be cut into short, uniform lengths to form staple. Spinning is the process of drawing out and twisting a mass of cleaned, prepared fibers. Filament yarns generally require less twist than do staple yarns. More twist produces stronger yarn; low twist produces softer, shinier yarn. Knitting yarns have less twist than weaving yarns. See also THREAD.

Yaroslav \\yə-rə-'slȧf\\ *known as* **Yaroslav the Wise** (980–1054) Grand prince of Kiev (1019–54). A son of VLADIMIR I, he consolidated the state through administrative reforms and military campaigns, codified laws, and promoted the spread of Christianity. He also built many fortifications and churches in the Byzantine style, including the Cathedral of St. Sophia. Yaroslav regained Galicia from the Poles and expanded Kievan possessions in the Baltic region, but his military campaign against Constantinople was a failure (1043).

yarrow \\'yar-ō\\ Any of about 80 species of perennial herbs that make up the genus *Achillea* in the COMPOSITE FAMILY, native mainly to the N temperate zone. Some species are cultivated as garden ornamentals. They have toothed, often finely cut, sometimes aromatic leaves. Many small white, yellow, or pink flowers are often grouped into flat-topped clusters.

yaws *or* **frambesia** \\fram-'bē-zhə\\ Contagious tropical disease, caused by SPIROCHETES indistinguishable from those of SYPHILIS, which may be a subspecies. Yaws spreads mainly by discharge from skin sores, not sexual activity. It is common in children, who usually become immune. In the first stage, a sore starts as a wartlike thickening, cracks open, leaks fluid, and bleeds easily. A month or more later, multiple sores erupt. A rarely seen third stage involves destruction of skin, mucous membranes, and bones. PENICILLIN cures early-stage yaws. Prevention requires isolation and prompt treatment, and personal and group hygiene.

Yayoi culture \\'yä-ˌyòi\\ (c.250 B.C.–c.A.D. 250) Prehistoric culture of Japan. It arose on Kyushu and spread northeastward across Honshu. The Yayoi people mastered bronze and iron casting, wove hemp, and employed a Chinese method of wet-paddy rice cultivation. Yayoi pottery is unglazed; early examples have incised decorations. Chinese-style bronze mirrors and coins indicate contact with HAN-DYNASTY China.

Yazid I \\yȧ-'zēd\\ (c.645–683) Second CALIPH of the UMAYYAD DYNASTY. His victory at the Battle of KARBALA (680) led to the permanent split of Islam into Sunni and Shiite sects. He succeeded his father, MUAWIYAH I, as caliph (680–83), keeping his father's advisers and most of his policies, while reforming the financial system and improving the irrigation system of the Damascus oasis. See also ALI, FITNAH, HUSAYN IBN ALI.

Yeager \\'yä-gər\\, **Chuck** (*orig.* Charles Elwood) (b.1923) U.S. test pilot. Born in Myra, W.Va., he served as a pilot in World War II. Chosen to test-fly the secret experimental X-1 aircraft, in 1947 he became the first person to break the sound barrier in flight, with a speed of 670 mph (1,079 kph). A brash and colorful personality, he retired with the rank of brigadier general in 1975 and received the Presidential Medal of Freedom in 1985.

year Time required for the earth to travel once around the sun, slightly less than 365¼ days. This fractional number makes necessary the periodic adjustment of days in any CALENDAR that is to be kept in step with the seasons. In the GREGORIAN CALENDAR, a common year contains 365 days, and every fourth year is a leap year of 366 days.

Year 2000 bug See Y2K BUG

yeast Any of certain economically important single-celled fungi (see FUNGUS), most in the class Ascomycetes, a few in Basidiomycetes. Yeasts are especially abundant in sugary mediums such as flower nectar and fruits. The types commonly used in the production of bread, beer, and wine are from *Saccharomyces cerevisiae.* Yeast cells can ferment approximately their own weight of glucose per hour. Yeast is 50% protein and is rich in B vitamins; brewer's yeast is sometimes taken as a vitamin supplement. Some yeasts are mild to dangerous pathogens of humans and other animals (e.g., *Candida albicans,* which irritates mouth and vaginal linings; and *Histoplasma* and *Blastomyces,* which cause persistent lung infections).

Yeats \'yāts\, **William Butler** (1865–1939) Irish poet, dramatist, and prose writer. The son of a well-known painter, Yeats early developed an interest in mysticism and visionary traditions as well as in Irish peasant folklore, and both interests would continue to be sources of poetic imagery for him. In 1889 he fell in love with Maud Gonne, a brilliant, beautiful Irish patriot who inspired his involvement in Irish nationalism but did not reciprocate his feelings. With Lady Augusta GREGORY and others, he founded the ABBEY THEATRE; throughout his life he would remain one of its directors. He contributed plays to its repertoire, including *The Countess Cathleen* (1899), *On Baile's Strand* (1905), and *Deirdre* (1907). His poetry changed decisively in the years 1909–14: the otherworldly, ecstatic atmosphere of the early lyrics cleared and his work gained in concreteness and complexity, often dealing with political themes. With *Responsibilities* (1914) and *The Wild Swans at Coole* (1917) he began the period of his highest achievement. Some of his greatest verse appears in *The Tower* (1928), *The Winding Stair* (1929), and *Last Poems* (1939). He was a member of the Irish Senate 1922–28. He won the Nobel Prize in 1923, and he is regarded by some as the greatest English-language poet of the 20th cent.

Yekaterinburg \yi-ˌkȧ-ti-rən-'bủrk\ *formerly (1924–91)* **Sverdlovsk** \sfyird-'lȯfsk\ City (pop., 1997 est.: 1,275,000), W central Russia. An ironworks was established in 1721 and a fortress, named after Empress Catherine I, was founded there in 1722. Its importance increased with the building of a highway (1783) and the TRANS-SIBERIAN RAILROAD. It was where Czar NICHOLAS II and his family were held prisoner and executed by the BOLSHEVIKS (1918). In 1924 it was renamed Sverdlovsk in honor of Y. M. SVERDLOV. The city reverted to its original name after the breakup of the U.S.S.R. in 1991. It is a major Russian industrial center.

yellow fever Acute infectious tropical disease, sometimes occurring in temperate zones. Abrupt onset of headache, backache, fever, nausea, and vomiting is followed by either recovery with immunity, or by higher fever, slow pulse, and vomiting of blood. Patients may die in a week. JAUNDICE is common (hence the name). One of the world's great plagues for 300 years, it is caused by a VIRUS transmitted by several species of mosquitoes. Treatment consists of supportive care, particularly fever reduction. Control of mosquitoes near cities and vaccines—developed by Max Theiler (1899–1972)—have made yellow fever completely preventable.

yellow jacket Any of 35–40 species (genus *Dolichovespula* or *Vespula*) of social WASPS, principally of the Northern Hemisphere, named for its black-banded yellow abdomen. *Dolichovespula* species typically build exposed nests. *Vespula* species build concealed nests underground or in protected cavities; when a nest is stepped on, the colony may erupt in an angry, stinging swarm. Nests in warmer climates may weigh half a ton.

yellow journalism Use of lurid features and sensationalized news in newspaper publishing to attract readers and increase circulation. The phrase was coined in the 1890s to describe tactics employed in the furious competition between two New York papers, Joseph PULITZER's *World* and William Randolph HEARST's *Journal,* when Hearst hired away from Pulitzer a cartoonist who had drawn the popular comic strip "The Yellow Kid" and another cartoonist was hired to draw the comic for the *World.* Techniques of the period that became permanent in U.S. journalism include banner headlines, colored comics, and copious illustrations.

Yellowknife City (pop., 2000: 18,000), capital of Northwest Territories. Lying on the NW shore of GREAT SLAVE LAKE, it was founded in 1935, one year after gold was discovered in the area. Gold mining remains the chief economic activity. There are also reserves of diamonds in the region. The capital since 1967, it is the chief administrative, commercial, and educational center in the territories.

yellow poplar See TULIP TREE

Yellow River See HUANG RIVER

Yellow Sea *Chinese* **Huang Hai** \'hwäŋ-'hī\ Large inlet of the W Pacific Ocean, between NE China and the Korean peninsula. Famous for its fishing grounds, it connects with the E. CHINA SEA on the south. It has an area of 180,000 sq mi (470,000 sq km) and a maximum depth of 338 ft (103 m). It derives its name from the color of the silt-laden water discharged into it by the HUANG, CHANG, Liao, and other rivers. Leading port cities include SHANGHAI and TIANJIN in China, INCHON in S. Korea, and Nampo in N. Korea.

Yellowstone National Park National preserve, NW Wyoming, S Montana, E Idaho. The oldest national park in the world, it was established by Congress in 1872; it covers 3,468 sq mi (8,983 sq km). Its unusual geologic features include fossil forests, eroded basaltic lava flows, and 10,000 hot springs, which erupt as steam vents, fumaroles, and geysers. Old Faithful, the most famous geyser, erupts every 33 to 93 minutes. It has many lakes and rivers, including Yellowstone Lake and Yellowstone River.

Yellowstone River River, NW Wyoming and S and F. Montana. It rises in Wyoming, flows north through YELLOWSTONE NATIONAL PARK, then continues northeast across Montana into the MISSOURI RIVER on the N. Dakota boundary. It is 692 mi (1,114 km) long, and has been developed extensively for irrigation. It was first explored in 1806 during the LEWIS AND CLARK EXPEDITION.

Yellow Turbans Chinese secret society founded during a time of pestilence (2nd cent. A.D.). The rebels' yellow headdresses signified their association with the earth element. The sect was Taoist in inspiration, like the contemporaneous FIVE PECKS OF RICE sect. Its rebellion (184–204?) against the tyrannical eunuchs who influenced the emperor contributed to the fall of the HAN DYNASTY.

Yeltsin, Boris (Nikolayevich) (b.1931) President of Russia (1990–99). An ally of Mikhail GORBACHEV, Yeltsin was appointed to eliminate corruption in the Moscow party organization; as first secretary (mayor) of Moscow (1985–87) he proved a determined reformer, but his criticism of the slow pace of reform led to a break with Gorbachev. He became president of the Russian Republic in 1990 and resigned from the Communist Party. In 1991 he won the presidency again in the first popular election in Russian history. When communist hard-liners staged a coup against Gorbachev, Yeltsin faced down its leaders with a dramatic outdoor speech in Moscow. He led the establishment of the COMMONWEALTH OF INDEPENDENT STATES (1991) and began to liberalize Russia's economy. Hard-liners staged an unsuccessful coup in 1993. When Chechnya declared independence, Yeltsin sent troops to fight the rebels (1994). Reelected in 1996, he spent months recovering from a heart attack; he rejected suggestions that he resign, despite his increasingly erratic behavior, the deterioration of civil order, and rampant corruption, but continuing poor health led to his resignation on Dec. 31, 1999, in favor of Vladimir PUTIN.

Yemen \'ye-mən\ *officially* **Republic of Yemen** Country, SW Arabian Peninsula. It also includes SOCOTRA Island in the Indian Ocean and the Kamaran group in the RED SEA. Area: 203,849 sq mi (527,969 sq km). Population (2000): 17,479,000. Capital: SANAA. The population is mainly Arab. Language:

W X Y Z

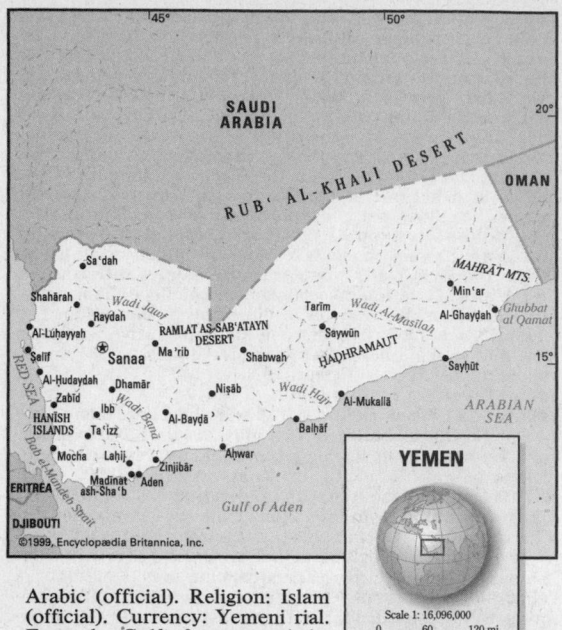

YEMEN

Scale 1: 16,096,000

©1999, Encyclopædia Britannica, Inc.

Arabic (official). Religion: Islam (official). Currency: Yemeni rial. From the Gulf of ADEN and the RED SEA, a narrow coastal plain leads to highlands that cover most of the country. The N region covers the S and SW parts of the RUB AL-KHALI. Mineral resources include iron ore, salt, oil, and natural gas, all of which are exploited. Agriculture is important; industries include food processing and salt production. It is a republic with one legislative house; its head of state is the president, and the head of government is the prime minister. Yemen was the home of ancient Minaean, Sabaean, and Himyarite kingdoms. The Romans invaded the region in the 1st cent. A.D. In the 6th cent. it was conquered by Ethiopians and Persians. Following conversion to Islam in the 7th cent., it was ruled nominally under a caliphate. The Egyptian Ayyubid dynasty ruled there from 1173 to 1229, after which the region passed to the Rasulids. From 1517 through 1918, the OTTOMAN EMPIRE maintained varying degrees of control, especially in the NW section. A boundary agreement was reached in 1934 between the NW imam-controlled territory, which subsequently became the Yemen Arab Republic (N. Yemen), and the SE British-controlled territory, which subsequently became the People's Democratic Republic of Yemen (S. Yemen). Relations between the two Yemens remained tense and were marked by conflict throughout the 1970s and 1980s. Reaching an accord, the two officially united as the Republic of Yemen in 1990. Its 1993 elections were the first free, multiparty general elections held in the Arabian Peninsula, and they were the first in which women participated. In 1994, after a two-month civil war, a new constitution was approved.

Yenisey River \yi-ni-'sā\ River, W Russia. One of the longest rivers in Asia, it rises in the borderland of S central Russia and Mongolia and flows along the W Siberian Plain to empty into the Kara Sea. Some 1,900 mi (3,000 km) of its 2,540-mi (4,090-km) course are navigable.

yerba maté See MATÉ

Yerevan *formerly* **Erivan** \,yer-ə-'vän\ City (pop., 1995 est.: 1,249,000), capital of Armenia. Fortified since the 8th cent. B.C., it developed as a center of the caravan trade. Successively ruled by Romans, Arabs, and Turks, it fell to Russia in 1827. It became the capital of independent Armenia in 1920, and remained so during Soviet rule and renewed independence. Its industries produce chemicals, aluminum, cars, and electrical machinery.

Yermak *orig.* Yermak Timofeyevich (d.1584?) COSSACK leader. Enlisted by the merchant Stroganov family to de-

fend its possessions against Siberian tribesmen, he set out with a force of 840 Cossacks and reached the central Tatar khanate of Sibir in 1582. With their firearms, Yermak and his army defeated the numerically superior forces of Khan Kuchum and occupied the capital. Considered the conquerer of Siberia, he became a hero of Russian folklore.

yeshiva \yə-'shē-və\ Academy of higher Talmudic learning (see TALMUD). The yeshiva has defined and regulated JUDAISM for centuries and is the traditional setting for the training and ordination of RABBIS. Following the destruction of the Second Temple of JERUSALEM, a series of yeshivas were set up around the Levant to codify and explain centuries of Jewish scholarship. Yeshivas flourished in medieval Europe. The first yeshiva in the U.S., Etz Hayyim (1886), later became YESHIVA UNIV. (1945).

Yeshiva University Private university in New York City. Established in 1886 as Yeshiva Eitz Chaim, in 1915 it merged with a Jewish theological seminary. Though independent, its curriculum emphasizes Jewish culture and history. Yeshiva consists of a liberal-arts college, a college for women, a college of Hebraic studies, and the Albert Einstein College of Medicine, as well as schools of Judaic studies, Talmudic studies, business, law (the Cardozo School), social work, and education, among others. Total enrollment is about 5,500.

Yeti See ABOMINABLE SNOWMAN

Yevtushenko \yif-tù-'shen-kə\, **Yevgeny (Aleksandrovich)** (b.1933) Russian poet. His small hometown is the setting of his first important narrative poem, *Zima Junction* (1956). He became the spokesman for the post-Stalin generation of Russian poets with his internationally publicized demands for greater artistic freedom, which signaled the Soviet "thaw" of the late 1950s and '60s. He revived brash, slangy language and such traditions as love lyrics and personal lyrics, and became famous worldwide for his passionate public recitals from such works as *Baby Yar* (1961).

yew Any of about eight species of ornamental evergreens in the genus *Taxus,* family Taxaceae (the yew family), distributed throughout the Northern Hemisphere. Two species are always shrubby, but the others may reach heights of 80 ft (25 m). The plants have many branches, covered with needlelike leaves. Yew wood is hard, fine-grained, and heavy. Once popular for cabinetwork, implements, and archery bows, it is used more today for articles either carved or turned on a lathe.

Yezhov \yi-'zhóf\, **Nikolay (Ivanovich)** (1895–1939?) Soviet politician. By 1927 he was a functionary for the Moscow party's central committee and a favorite of Joseph STALIN. Succeeding Genrikh YAGODA as chief of the Soviet security police, or NKVD (1936), he instituted the most severe stage of the PURGE TRIALS, known as Yezhovshchina. By 1938 he had become the object of Stalin's suspicions and was replaced by Lavrenty BERIA. He disappeared in 1939 and was probably executed.

Yggdrasill \'ig-drə-,sil\ In Norse mythology, the world tree (tree at the center of the world). One of its roots extended into the underworld, another into the land of the giants, and the third into ASGARD. At its base were three wells: the Well of Fate; the Roaring Kettle, in which dwelt a monster that gnawed the tree's roots; and Mimir's Well, the source of wisdom. After the RAGNAROK, Yggdrasill, though badly shaken, is to be the source of new life.

Yiddish drama Productions of the professional Yiddish theater. European Jewish drama originated in the Middle Ages, when dancers and jesters entertained at PURIM celebrations. By the 16th cent., elaborate Purim plays were being performed in Yiddish. The professional Yiddish theater dates from 1876, when Abraham Goldfaden (1840–1908) wrote a well-received musical sketch in Romania and organized a troupe to perform his songs and plays. In 1883 anti-Semitic laws in Russia led to emigration to England and the U.S. The playwright Jacob Gordin (1853–1909) brought new material and adaptations to the U.S. Yiddish theater, including *The Jewish King Lear* (1892), starring Jacob P. Adler, founder of a family of actors. In 1918 Maurice Schwartz founded the Yiddish Art Theatre, which trained such actors as Muni Weisenfreund (Paul Muni). World War II destroyed most Yiddish culture, and by the late 20th cent. only a few

Yiddish theaters survived in such cities as New York, London, Bucharest, and Warsaw.

Yiddish language Language of Ashkenazic Jews and their descendants (see ASHKENAZI), written in the HEBREW ALPHABET. Yiddish developed starting in the 12th cent. from Middle High German, strongly influenced by HEBREW and ARAMAIC, from which it now draws 12–20% of its lexicon. The isolation of E European speakers from High German, and their exposure to SLAVIC LANGUAGES, led to a primary distinction between W. and E. Yiddish dialects. From the late 18th cent., most Jews remaining in central Europe gave up Yiddish in favor of German. A flourishing literary language in the 19th and early 20th cent., Yiddish declined dramatically due to massive migration, assimilation, and Nazi genocide. Today Yiddish may still be spoken by 3 million people worldwide, but most of its speakers are middle-aged or older.

Yi dynasty See CHOSON DYNASTY

Yi Hwang \'ē-'hwän\ (1501–1570) Korean religious leader, the foremost Korean Confucian. He helped shape the character of Korean Confucianism through his creative interpretation of ZHU XI's teaching. His *Discourse on the Ten Sagely Diagrams* explained all the major concepts in SONG-DYNASTY learning. He elevated the level of Confucian dialogue to new levels of sophistication through his correspondence with Ki Taesung (1527–1572).

Yi jing or I ching \'ē-'jiŋ\ (Chinese: "Book of Changes") Ancient Chinese text, one of the FIVE CLASSICS of Confucianism. The main body of the work, traditionally attributed to WENWANG, contains a discussion of the divinatory system used by wizards in the ZHOU DYNASTY. A later supplementary section of "commentaries" attempts to explain the world and its ethical principles. The book's cosmology, which involves humans and nature in a single system, has made it universally popular.

Yin dynasty See SHANG DYNASTY

yin-yang In E. Asian thought, the two complementary forces or principles that make up all aspects and phenomena of life. Yin is earth, female, dark, passive, and absorbing; it is present in even numbers and in valleys and streams. Yang is heaven, male, light, active, and penctrating; it is present in odd numbers and mountains. Together they express the interdependence of opposites.

Yi Song-gye \'yē-'sùn-'gye\ *or* **T'aejo** \'tī-'jō\ (1335–1408) Founder of the Korean CHOSON DYNASTY. A military leader in the KORYO dynasty, he defeated his rivals and drove out the last king, taking the throne in 1392. He established his capital at Hanyang (now Seoul). He redistributed land, which had largely been held by a few high-ranking bureaucrats, throughout the various levels of officialdom. He made NEO-CONFUCIANISM the state religion, replacing Buddhism. Farming became the center of the economy. In foreign relations, he maintained close ties with China's MING DYNASTY.

Yi Sun-shin \'yē-'sùn-'shin\ (1545–1598) Korean admiral and national hero. He developed the *kobukson* ("turtle ship"), thought to be the first ironclad battleship. As a result of Yi's preparations, his forces alone were ready to fight when the Japanese under TOYOTOMI HIDEYOSHI invaded in 1592. His sea victories effectively undermined the Japanese troops. In 1597 he was falsely accused of disloyalty and demoted. When the Japanese launched a second invasion and largely destroyed the Korean navy, Yi was reinstated and soon restored Korea's control of the seas.

YMCA *in full* **Young Men's Christian Association** Nonsectarian, nonpolitical Christian lay movement. It originated in London in 1844 and in the U.S. (Boston) in the 1850s. YMCA programs include sports and physical education, camping, education, and citizenship activities. It also runs hotels, residence halls, and cafeterias. The World Alliance of YMCAs (established 1855) is headquartered in Geneva. The YMCA operates in dozens of countries. The Young Women's Christian Assn. (YWCA) was founded in Britain (1877) to address the needs of women from rural areas who came to the cities to find work; in the U.S. (founded 1906), it has championed racial equality. The Young Men's and Young Women's Hebrew Assn. (YM-YWHA) developed in the mid-19th cent. from Jewish men's literary societies in

the U.S. and now exists in some 20 other countries worldwide.

Ymir See AURGELMIR

Yoga One of the six orthodox systems (DARSHANS) of Indian philosophy, which has had widespread influence on many schools of Indian thought. It is better known through its practical aspect than its intellectual content. Holding that the evolution of the world occurred in stages, Yoga attempts to reverse this order so that a person reenters his or her state of purity and consciousness. Generally, the Yoga process involves eight stages, which may require several lifetimes to pass through. The first two stages emphasize morality, cleanliness, and devotion to God. The next two stages are physical preparations that make the body supple, flexible, and healthy; this aspect of Yoga has been successfully popularized in the West. In the fifth stage, the mind and senses withdraw from outward objects. The remaining three stages aim for increasingly concentrated states of awareness, with the ultimate goal of release from the cycle of rebirth. See also CHAKRA, KUNDALINI.

yogurt Semisolid, fermented, often flavored MILK food. It is traditionally made by adding *Streptococcus* and *Lactobacillus* bacteria to raw milk. In modern yogurt making, a blend of concentrated sterilized milk and milk solids is inoculated with the two bacteria; sometimes *L. acidophilus* or a lactose-fermenting YEAST is also added. The product is then incubated four or five hours at 110–112°F (43–44°C) until curd forms. Various flavors and sweetening may be added.

Yokohama Seaport city (pop., 1995 est.: 3,307,000), SE HONSHU, Japan, on W TOKYO BAY. Matthew PERRY visited in 1854 to negotiate trading possibilities; it was opened for foreign trade in 1859. It was destroyed by earthquake and fire in 1923 and severely damaged by U.S. air raids in 1945 during World War II, but was rebuilt both times. It is Japan's principal port and part of the Tokyo urban-industrial region. It produces textiles, chemicals, ships, machinery, petroleum products, and automobiles.

Yom Kippur \,yōm-kē-'pùr, ,yäm-'ki-pər\ *English* **Day of Atonement** Jewish religious holiday, observed on the 10th day of the lunar month of Tishri (in late September or early October). It concludes the 10 days of repentance that begin with ROSH HASHANAH. Its purpose is to purify the individual and community by forgiving the sins of others and by repenting one's own sins against God. Yom Kippur is marked by prayer, fasting, and abstention from sex. On its eve, the KOL NIDRE is recited.

Yongle emperor or Yung-lo emperor \'yùŋ-'le\ *orig.* Zhu Di (1360–1424) Third emperor of China's MING DYNASTY, which he raised to its greatest power. Son of the Hongwu emperor (1328–1398), founder of the Ming, he became emperor in 1403. He worked to extend China's sway and sent out ships of exploration, most notably under ZHENG HE; these returned with envoys bearing tribute to acknowledge China's overlordship. He became the only ruler in Chinese history to be acknowledged suzerain by the Japanese. His attempt to incorporate Annam (now Vietnam) into China led to years of guerrilla warfare. He five times led large armies north to the Gobi Desert, forestalling the creation of a Mongol confederation that might have threatened China. He transferred China's capital from Nanjing to Beijing. He built the FORBIDDEN CITY and repaired the GRAND CANAL. He sponsored the compilation and publication of the Confucian Classics and the 11,000-volume compendium the *Yongle dadian* ("Great Canon of the Yongle Era").

yoni \'yō-nē\ In HINDUISM, a representation of the female sexual organ and feminine generative power, the symbol of the goddess Shakti (see SHAKTI). The yoni is often associated with the phallic LINGA, the symbol of the god SHIVA. Their union represents the eternal process of creation and regeneration.

Yonkers City (pop., 2000: 196,000), SE New York. It is located on the HUDSON RIVER north of NEW YORK CITY. It was purchased from the Dutch W. India Co. from the Indians in 1639. In 1646 it was included in a grant of land made to "Jonkheer" Adriaen van der Donck. Elevator manufacturing is an important industry.

Yoritomo See MINAMOTO YORITOMO

WXYZ

York *ancient* Eboracum. City (pop., 1999 est.: 176,000), N. Yorkshire, England. It is the cathedral city of the archbishop of York and was historically the ecclesiastical capital of N England. It was also the seat of the former county of YORKSHIRE. CONSTANTINE I was proclaimed Roman emperor there in A.D. 306 During the Middle Ages it was a prosperous wool-trading town and the site of the performance of the YORK PLAYS. It has a tourist industry fostered by its medieval sites.

York, Alvin C(ullum) (1887–1964) U.S. World War I hero. Born in Pall Mall, Tenn., he was drafted into the U.S. Army after being denied conscientious-objector status. In the Meuse-Argonne offensive (Oct. 1918), his patrol was ordered to attack a German machine-gun nest. Pinned down behind enemy lines, he advanced alone, killing 25 gunners and forcing the others to surrender. As he marched them back to U.S. lines, he captured more soldiers for a total of 132 prisoners. His autobiography (1928) was the basis of the movie *Sergeant York* (1941).

York, House of Younger branch of the PLANTAGENET dynasty, descended from EDWARD III's fifth son, Edmund of Langley (1341–1402), 1st duke of York. In the 15th cent. the Yorkists took the throne from the House of LANCASTER; the Yorkist kings were EDWARD IV, Edward V, and RICHARD III. The Wars of the ROSES between the two houses continued until Richard's death at the Battle of BOSWORTH FIELD. The marriage of HENRY VII, the first Tudor king, to the daughter of Edward IV merged the House of York with the House of Tudor.

York plays Cycle of 48 plays, dating from the 14th cent., of unknown authorship, which were performed in the Middle Ages by craft guilds on pageant wagons in York, England, on the summer feast day of Corpus Christi. The cycle covers the story of the Fall of Man and his redemption, from the creation of the angels to the Final Judgment. See also MYSTERY PLAY.

Yorkshire \'york-ˌshir\ Former county, N England. Historically, it was divided into three administrative counties—N. Riding, E. Riding, and W. Riding—and the city of YORK. In 1974 Yorkshire and the ridings were divided among N. Yorkshire, W. Yorkshire, and S. Yorkshire. It was an agricultural, fishing and manufacturing center. Its main cities and towns include LEEDS, SHEFFIELD, HULL, Bradford, and WAKEFIELD.

Yorktown, Siege of (1781) American-French campaign against the British that virtually ended the AMERICAN REVOLUTION. About 7,500 British troops under Charles CORNWALLIS occupied defensive positions at the coastal port of Yorktown, Va., on Aug. 1, 1781. They were opposed by a smaller American force under the Marquis de LAFAYETTE, assisted by Anthony WAYNE and F. W. STEUBEN. From New York, George WASHINGTON and his forces, joined by French troops under Count ROCHAMBEAU, marched south. Linking up with a French fleet at Chesapeake Bay, they joined Lafayette's troops on Sept. 28, and the 14,000-man force besieged the British position. British reinforcements failed to arrive; outnumbered, outgunned, and running low on food, Cornwallis surrendered his 8,000 men and 240 guns on Oct. 19.

Yoruba \'yȯr-ə-bə\ One of Nigeria's two largest ethnic groups, numbering 22 million. The Yoruba states, including the OYO EMPIRE, were built in the 11th–16th cent. Yorubaland remains divided into politically autonomous kingdoms, each centered on a capital city or town and headed by a hereditary king (*oba*), traditionally considered sacred. Most Yoruba men are farmers or craftsmen; women control much of the complex market system. Though some Yoruba are now Christians or Muslims, belief in their traditional religion continues (see SANTERÍA). The Yoruba language has an extensive literature of poetry, short stories, myths, and proverbs.

Yosemite Falls \yō-'se-mə-tē\ Two waterfalls, YOSEMITE NATIONAL PARK, central California. The upper falls drop 1,430 ft (436 m); the lower, 320 ft (98 m). With the cascades between, the total drop is 2,425 ft (739 m), one of the world's longest cataracts.

Yosemite National Park National preserve, central California. Made a national park in 1890 at the urging of John MUIR, it encompasses 761,320 acres (308,106 hectares) in the SIERRA NEVADA range. Its many features include giant REDWOOD groves with trees thousands of years old, YOSEMITE FALLS, and huge domes and peaks; the greatest of these is El Capitan, a granite buttress 3,604 ft (1,098 m) high.

Yoshida Shigeru \'yō-shē-dä-shē-'ge-rů\ (1878–1967) Japanese prime minister after World War II. He served as ambassador to Britain in the 1930s. He first became prime minister in 1946, during the OCCUPATION, and formed five separate cabinets (1946–54). He guided Japan back to economic prosperity and set a course for postwar cooperation with the U.S. and Europe. In 1951 he negotiated the peace treaty that ended World War II; he also negotiated a security pact between Japan and the U.S.

Yoshitsune See MINAMOTO YOSHITSUNE

Youmans \'yü-mənz\, **Vincent (Millie)** (1898–1946) U.S. songwriter. Born in New York City, he started writing songs in the navy during World War I. He collaborated with such lyricists as Ira Gershwin and Oscar HAMMERSTEIN on the musicals *No, No, Nanette* (1925), *Hit the Deck* (1927), *Great Day* (1928), and *Flying Down to Rio* (1933). His standards included "Tea for Two," "More Than You Know," and "Carioca."

Young, Andrew *in full* Andrew Jackson Young, Jr. (b.1932) U.S. politician. Born in New Orleans, he earned a divinity degree in 1955 and became a pastor. He worked in the SOUTHERN CHRISTIAN LEADERSHIP CONFERENCE 1961–70, and served in the U.S. House of Representatives 1972–77. An early supporter of Jimmy CARTER, he was appointed U.S. ambassador to the U.N. (1977–79), the first black to hold the post. He served as mayor of Atlanta 1982–89. In 1999 Young became head of the National Council of Churches.

Young, Brigham (1801–1877) U.S. religious leader, second president of the MORMON church. Born in Whitingham, Vt., he was baptized into Joseph SMITH's Church of Jesus Christ of Latter-Day Saints in 1832. In 1834 he joined the Mormons in Missouri, and when they were driven out in 1838, he organized their move to Nauvoo, Ill. After Smith's murder in 1844, Young took over the church. He led the persecuted Mormons to Utah (1846–48), choosing the site of Salt Lake City for the new Mormon headquarters. He became governor of the territory of Utah in 1850. Pres. James BUCHANAN disapproved of his autocratic governance and replaced him in 1857, sending the army to assert federal supremacy in the so-called Utah War, but Young remained head of the Mormon church until his death. Having legalized polygamy, he took more than 20 wives and fathered 47 children.

Young, Coleman (1918–1997) U.S. politician. Born in Tuscaloosa, Ala., he moved with his family to Detroit in 1923. At Ford Motor Co. he became involved in union activities and civil rights activism. In World War II, he served with the Tuskegee Airmen. He later cofounded the National Negro Labor Council. He was elected to the Michigan senate in 1964, and in 1968 he became the Democratic National Committee's first black member. As mayor of Detroit from 1973, he focused on revitalizing the crime-ridden city by attracting new businesses and reinforcing the police department. He retired in 1993 after an unprecedented five terms.

Young, Cy (*orig.* Denton True) (1867–1955) U.S. baseball pitcher. Born in Gilmore, Ohio, he was a powerful 6-ft 2-in. (1-m 88-cm) right-handed thrower. He began his major-league career with the Cleveland Indians (1890–98); he later pitched principally for the Boston Red Sox (1901–8). In each of 16 seasons he won more than 20 games; in five he won more than 30. Though many early records are in dispute, he won more major-league games (509 or 511) than any other pitcher in history. Among his other records are games started (816 or 818), completed starts (750 or 751), and innings pitched (7,356 or 7,377). In 1904 he pitched the first perfect game. The annual Cy Young award honors the best pitcher in each league.

Young, Lester (Willis) (1909–1959) U.S. tenor saxophonist Born in Mississippi, Young joined Count BASIE in 1936 and was recognized as a major new stylist on the instrument dominated by the influence of Coleman HAWKINS. His small-group recordings from the late 1930s with Basie and Billie HOLIDAY are classics. Young's subtle harmonies and unconventional rhythmic independence influenced both BEBOP and cool-jazz musicians; his gentle tone and ethereal lyricism inspired an entire school of playing.

Lester Young, c.1955

Young, Thomas (1773–1829) English physicist. A doctor, he was the first to describe and measure astigmatism, and the first to explain color sensation in terms of retinal structures corresponding to red, green, and violet. He established the principle of INTERFERENCE of light, thus resurrecting the century-old wave theory of light. He explained CAPILLARITY independently of P. S. de LAPLACE. Investigating elasticity, he proposed Young's modulus, a numerical constant that describes the elastic properties of a solid undergoing tension or compression. His other work included measuring the size of MOLECULES and SURFACE TENSION in liquids, and he helped decipher the ROSETTA STONE.

Young Italy *Italian* Giovine Italia. Movement founded by Giuseppe MAZZINI in 1831 to work for a united, republican Italian nation. It was to be based on support from the Italian people, who would be educated in their political role. To propagate his ideas, Mazzini published the journal *Giovine Italia* (1832–34). The movement spread in N Italy and by 1833 included over 50,000 members. It staged revolts in the 1830s and '40s, but failed to win popular support for insurrection. See also RISORGIMENTO.

Young Men's Christian Association See YMCA

Young Turks *Turkish* Jonturkler. Coalition of college students and dissident soldiers who ended the OTTOMAN sultanate. In 1908 the group forced ABDULHAMID II to reinstitute the 1876 constitution and recall the legislature. They deposed him the following year, reorganized the government, and began modernizing and industrializing Turkish society. They joined the CENTRAL POWERS during World War I. Facing defeat in 1918, they resigned a month before the war ended. See also ARMENIAN MASSACRES, M. K. ATATURK, ENVER PASA.

Yourcenar \yür-sə-'när\, **Marguerite** *orig.* Marguerite de Crayencour (1903–1987) Belgian-French-U.S. novelist, essayist, and short-story writer. After the outbreak of World War II, she settled in the U.S. with the American woman who would be her lifelong companion and translator. Her works are noted for their rigorously classical style, their historical erudition, and their psychological subtlety. Her masterpiece is *Memoirs of Hadrian* (1951), a historical novel of the 2nd-cent. Roman empire. Other novels include *A Coin in Nine Hands* (1934), *Coup de grâce* (1939), and *The Abyss* (1968). In 1980 she became the first woman ever elected to the ACADÉMIE FRANÇAISE.

youth hostel Supervised shelter providing inexpensive overnight lodging, particularly for young people. Often located in scenic or historic areas, hostels range from simple farmhouses to hotels able to house several hundred people. Hostels place limits on the length of stay, and formerly set a maximum age limit for guests. The hosteling movement was founded by Richard Schirrmann (1874–1961), a German schoolteacher concerned about the health of young people breathing polluted air in industrial cities. Common in Germany in the early 1900s, youth hostels spread through Europe and other parts of the world after World War I. An international organization was formed in 1932; today known as Hostelling International, its membership includes national federations in more than 70 countries, comprising some 4,500 hostels. Upper age limits are no longer imposed.

Ypres \'ēpr\, **Battles of** Three costly battles in WORLD WAR I in W Flanders. In the first battle (Oct. 12–Nov. 11, 1914), the Germans were stopped on their march to the sea, but the Allied forces were then surrounded on three sides. The second (Apr. 22–May 25, 1915) marked the Germans' first use of poison gas. In the third battle (July 31–Nov. 6, 1917), also called the Battle of Passchendaele, the British were initially successful in breaking through the German lines. The seasonal rains soon turned the countryside into an impassable swamp, but Gen. Douglas HAIG persisted. On November 6 his troops occupied the ruins of Passchendaele, barely five miles from the start of the offensive. Over 325,000 British soldiers were lost in the battles.

Yuan Chiang See RED RIVER

Yuan dynasty *or* **Yüan dynasty** \yü-'än\ *or* **Mongol dynasty** (1206–1368) Dynasty established in China by MONGOL nomads. First established in Mongolia (1206) by GENGHIS KHAN, who occupied N China in 1215, it was unified in 1279 when KUBLAI KHAN took control of S China. The Mongols established their capital at Beijing (then called Dadu), rebuilt the GRAND CANAL, and restored the roads and postal stations. Paper money came to be used throughout the empire. Advances were made in astronomy, medicine, and mathematics, and trade was carried out throughout the Mongol empire from E Europe to Mongolia and China. Many foreigners came to China (notably Marco POLO) and many Chinese traveled to Iran, Russia, and even W Europe. The Chinese resented the Mongol conquerors, whose governmental system discriminated against them. Chinese artists demonstrated passive resistance by withdrawing and turning to personal expression. Disputes over succession weakened the central government from 1300 on, and rebellions were frequent, many connected with secret societies such as the RED TURBANS. The dynasty was overthrown in 1368 and followed by the MING DYNASTY.

Yuan Shikai *or* **Yüan Shih-kai** \yü-'än-'shir-'kī\ (1859–1916) Chinese army leader and first president of the Republic of China (1912–16). After serving in Korea, in 1885 he was made Chinese commissioner at Seoul; his promotion of China's interests contributed to the outbreak of the SINO-JAPANESE WAR. The war destroyed China's navy and army, and Yuan was appointed to train a new army. He played a decisive part in China's modernization and defense programs. After the overthrow of the QING DYNASTY in 1911–12, he became the first president of the new republic. Impatient with the new National Assembly, he ordered the assassination of Song Jiaoren, leader of the Nationalist Party (see GUOMINDANG) in 1913. He quelled a subsequent revolt, but his efforts to found his own dynasty (1915–16) failed. See also SUN YAT-SEN.

yuca See CASSAVA

Yucatán \yü-kä-'tän\ State (pop., 2000: 1,656,000), N YUCATÁN PENINSULA, SE Mexico. It covers 16,749 sq mi (43,380 sq km); its capital is MÉRIDA. Yucatán initially occupied the entire peninsula, but the secession of CAMPECHE (1858) and loss of QUINTANA ROO (1902) reduced its area. Long occupied by rural Maya Indians, it is the site of ancient MAYA ruins.

Yucatán Peninsula Peninsula, NE CENTRAL AMERICA. It lies between the Gulf of MEXICO and the CARIBBEAN SEA; its 76,300-sq-mi (197,600-sq-km) territory includes the Mexican states of CAMPECHE, QUINTANA ROO, and YUCATÁN and parts of Belize and Guatemala. Flat and arid, it is about 200 mi (320 km) wide, with a coastline of about 700 mi (1,100 km). It came under TOLTEC influence around A.D. 1000 and later was the seat of MAYA civilization. In 1525 Hernán CORTÉS traversed its inland part. Spanish rule was subsequently established, but the Maya have long resisted central governmental authority. Its many beaches and resorts, including CANCÚN, and its ancient archaeological sites, including CHICHÉN ITZÁ and UXMAL, are major tourist destinations.

yucca \'yə-,kə\ Any of about 40 species of SUCCULENT plants (genus *Yucca*) of the LILY FAMILY, native to S N. America. Most species lack a stem and have a rosette of stiff, sword-shaped leaves at the base and clusters of waxy white flowers. The Joshua tree (*Y. brevifolia*) has a stem more than 35 ft (10 m) high. Yuccas are commonly cultivated as ornamentals for their unusual appearance and attractive flower clusters. Yucca moths (genus *Tegeticula*) inhabit yucca bushes, each moth species adapted to a particular yucca species. The yucca can be fertilized by no

W X Y Z

other insect, and the moth can use no other plant to raise its larvae.

Yue Fei *or* **Yüeh Fei** \yǖe-'e-'fā\ (1103–1141) Chinese general and national hero. When the Juchen overran N China and captured the SONG-DYNASTY capital at Kaifeng, Yue Fei accompanied the emperor into the south, where the Southern Song was established. Yue Fei prevented the advance of the Juchen in the south and recovered some of the occupied territory in central China. His attempt to push north and recover all the lost territory was opposed by the minister Qin Gui, who had Yue executed. Yue has been extolled for his resistance to foreign domination.

Yugoslavia *officially* **Federal Republic of Yugoslavia** Federated country, W central BALKAN PENINSULA, consisting of the republics of SERBIA and MONTENEGRO. Area: 39,449 sq

©1999, Encyclopædia Britannica, Inc.

YUGOSLAVIA

Scale 1: 8,452,000

0   40   80 mi
0   60   120 km

mi (102,173 sq km). Population (2000): 10,662,000. Capital: BELGRADE. The population includes Serbian, Albanian, Montenegrin, Hungarian, and other ethnic groups. Languages: Serbo-Croatian (official), Albanian. Religions: Serbian Orthodoxy, Islam, Catholicism, Protestantism. Currency: Yugoslav new dinar. The S two-thirds of Yugoslavia is mountainous, with the Dinaric Alps in the west and the BALKAN MTNS. in the east. Rivers include the DANUBE, Ibar, MORAVA, Timis, and TISZA. The country has oil, gas, coal, copper, lead, zinc, and gold deposits. Its industries include machine building, metallurgy, mining, electronics, and petroleum products, while its agricultural products include corn, wheat, potatoes, and fruit. It is a fed-

eral republic with two legislative houses; its chief of state is the federal president, and the head of government is the prime minister. The Kingdom of the Serbs, Croats, and Slovenes was created after the collapse of AUSTRIA-HUNGARY at the end of World War I. The country signed treaties with Czechoslovakia and Romania 1920–21, marking the beginning of the Little Entente. In 1929 an absolute monarchy was established, the country's name was changed to Yugoslavia, and it was divided without regard to ethnic boundaries. Axis powers invaded Yugoslavia in 1941, and German, Italian, Hungarian, and Bulgarian troops occupied it for the rest of World War II. In 1945 the Socialist Federal Republic of Yugoslavia was established; it included the republics of Bosnia and Herzegovina, Croatia, Macedonia, Montenegro, Serbia, and Slovenia. Its independent form of Communism under TITO's leadership provoked the U.S.S.R. and led to its expulsion from the COMINFORM in 1948. Internal ethnic tensions flared up in the 1980s, causing the country to collapse. In 1991–92 independence was declared by Croatia, Slovenia, Macedonia, and Bosnia and Herzegovina; the new Federal Republic of Yugoslavia (containing roughly 45% of the population and 40% of the area of its predecessor) was proclaimed by Serbia and Montenegro. Still fueled by long-standing ethnic tensions, hostilities continued into the 1990s, when Slobodon MILOSEVIC provoked bloody conflicts with Croatia, Bosnia (see BOSNIAN CONFLICT), and Kosovo (see KOSOVO CONFLICT).

Yukaghir See SIBERIAN PEOPLES

Yukon River River, NW N. America. Formed in SW Yukon Territory, it is 1,980 mi (3,190 km) long. It flows northwest into Alaska, then southwest to the BERING SEA. It is the third-longest river in N. America; its entire course of 1,265 mi (2,035 km) in Alaska is navigable. It attracted attention following rich gold strikes in 1896 on one of its Canadian tributaries, the Klondike River (see KLONDIKE GOLD RUSH).

Yukon *or* **Yukon Territory** Territory (pop., 1999 est.: 31,000), NW Canada. Its capital is WHITEHORSE. Drained by the YUKON RIVER system, it has some of the highest mountains in N. America, notably the ST. ELIAS MTNS. and Mt. LOGAN, Canada's highest peak. It was originally settled by American Indians and the Inuit (ESKIMO). The first European visitor (1825) was John Franklin (1786–1847). The discovery of gold in the 1870s later resulted in the KLONDIKE GOLD RUSH. In 1898 it was separated from the NORTHWEST TERRITORIES and given territorial status. After the gold rush, exploitation of other minerals expanded and continued.

Yungang caves *or* **Yün-kang caves** \'yưen-'gäŋ\ Series of magnificent Chinese Buddhist cave temples, created in the 5th cent. A.D. during the NORTHERN WEI DYNASTY. There are about 20 major cave temples and many smaller ones, stretching for over half a mile. Representing the early flowering of Buddhist art in China, the predominant sculptural style is a synthesis of various foreign influences, including Persian, Byzantine, and Greek.

Yung-lo emperor See YONGLE EMPEROR

Yung-ning See NANNING

Yunnan See KUNMING

YWCA See YMCA

Z

Zacatecas \ˌsä-kä-ˈtā-käs\ State (pop., 2000: 1,351,000), N central Mexico. It covers 28,973 sq mi (75,040 sq km); its capital is Zacatecas city. Located within a central plateau, it is crossed by several mountain ranges, whose average elevation is 7,700 ft (2,350 m). Some of its mines, still worked, date from the mid-16th cent. Agriculture and livestock raising are also important.

Zadkine \zȧd-ˈkēn\, **Ossip** (1890–1967) Russian-French sculptor. Educated in England, he moved to Paris in 1909. Influenced by both Cubism and classical Greek sculpture, he developed a unique figurative style featuring concave and convex forms, lines, and parallel planes. His large bronze *To a Destroyed City* (1951–53), an homage to Rotterdam, is regarded as a masterpiece. In the 1960s he received commissions for statues in Jerusalem, Amsterdam, and elsewhere.

Zaghlul \zag-ˈlül\, **Sad** (1857–1927) Egyptian statesman. Initially cooperative with the occupying British, his attitude changed on his election to the Legislative Assembly in 1912. When Britain declared martial law during World War I, he led protests and called for abolition of the British protectorate. Widespread disorder followed and was not quelled even when Zaghlul, who had been deported to Malta, was brought back and elected prime minister in 1924 under a new constitution. He resigned after the murder of a number of British officials and Egyptian "collaborators," but later served as president of the Chamber of Deputies.

Zagreb \ˈzä-ˌgreb\ City (pop., 1998: 778,000), capital of Croatia. In 1093 a Roman Catholic bishopric was established there as Kaptol. In 1242 nearby Gradec was named a royal city. In 1850 they merged as Zagreb. Its growing industrial base brought prosperity, and the city became known for its trade fairs. In the 19th cent., it was the center of both a pan-Yugoslav movement and a Croatian independence movement. During the civil war following Croatia's secession from Yugoslavia in 1991, it sustained heavy damage.

Zaharias \zə-ˈhar-ē-əs\, **Babe Didrikson** or **Babe Didrikson** *orig.* Mildred Ella Didrikson (1914–1956) U.S. athlete, sometimes called the greatest woman athlete of the 20th cent. Born in Port Arthur, Texas, in 1930–31 she was a member of the women's All-America basketball team. In national track-and-field competition in 1930–32, she won eight events and tied for a ninth. In the 1932 Olympics she won gold medals in the 80-m hurdles and javelin throw; she was deprived of the high-jump gold medal for using a then-unorthodox method. As a golfer from 1946, she won the U.S. and British women's amateur tournaments (1946, 1947) and the U.S. Women's Open (1948, 1950, 1954); her last Open victory followed cancer surgery in 1953.

zaibatsu \zī-ˈbät-sü\ (Japanese: "financial clique") Large capitalist enterprises of pre-World War II Japan, similar to CARTELS but usually organized around a single family. One zaibatsu might operate companies in many areas of economic importance; all zaibatsu owned their own banks, which they used to mobilize capital. After the war the zaibatsu were dissolved and individual companies were freed from the control of parent companies. Many companies then began associating into enterprise groups; these differed from zaibatsu primarily in their more informal policy coordination and their limited financial interdependency. Modern-day *keiretsu* are similar.

Zaire See Democratic Republic of the CONGO

Zaire River See CONGO RIVER

Zambezi River \zam-ˈbē-zē\ River, S central and SE Africa. It rises in NW Zambia, flows south to the border of Botswana, then turns east and forms the Zambia–Zimbabwe border. It then crosses central Mozambique and empties into the MOZAMBIQUE CHANNEL. About 2,200 mi (3,500 km) long, it drains the entire S central region of the continent. Its chief landmark is VICTORIA FALLS; its many tributaries include the Kwando, Kafue, and Shire. Dams have created the huge Lakes Kariba and Cabora Bassa.

Zambia *officially* **Republic of Zambia,** *formerly* **Northern Rhodesia** Landlocked country, S central Africa. Area: 290,586 sq mi (752,614 sq km). Population (2000): 9,582,000. Capital: LUSAKA. The population is composed almost entirely of Bantu-speaking African ethnic groups (see BANTU

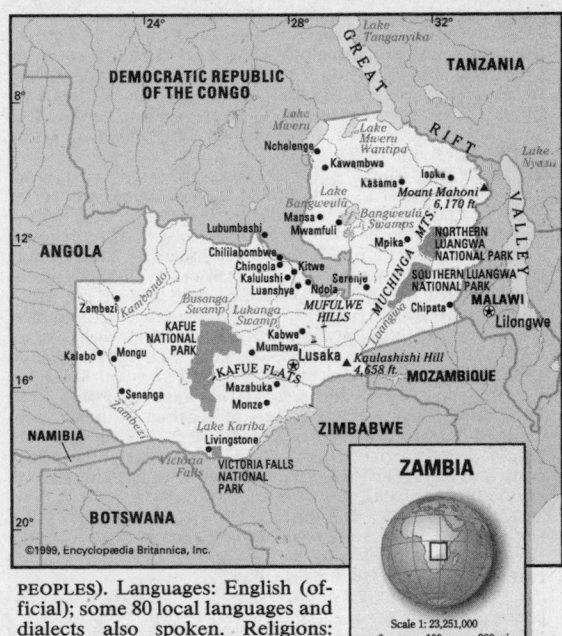

©1999, Encyclopædia Britannica, Inc.

ZAMBIA

Scale 1: 23,251,000
0   100   200 mi
0   150   300 km

PEOPLES). Languages: English (official); some 80 local languages and dialects also spoken. Religions: Christianity (predominant), indigenous beliefs, Islam, and Hinduism. Currency: kwacha. The country consists of tableland through which the ZAMBEZI (including VICTORIA FALLS), Kafue, and Luangwa rivers flow. Lake Bangweulu is within N Zambia, while lakes Mweru and TANGANYIKA touch its N boundaries. The Bangweulu Swamps form one of the largest inland wetlands in the world. The Muchinga Mtns. in the east include the highest point (7,100 ft, or 2,200 m) in the country. There are valuable forests of Zambezi teak in the southwest. Zambia's economy is heavily dependent on the production and export of copper. Other important mineral resources include lead, zinc, cobalt, coal, and gold. Agriculture also is important. It has some manufacturing. It is a republic with one

1339

W X Y Z

legislative house; its head of state and government is the president. Archaeological evidence suggests that early humans roamed present-day Zambia 1–2 million years ago. Ancestors of the modern Tonga tribe reached the region early in the 2nd millennium A.D., but other modern peoples from Congo (Zaire) and Angola reached the country only in the 17th–18th cent. Portuguese trading missions were established early in the 18th cent. Emissaries of Cecil RHODES and the British S. Africa Co. concluded treaties with most of the Zambian chiefs during the 1890s. The company administered the region known as Northern Rhodesia until 1924, when it became a British protectorate. It was part of the Central African Federation of Rhodesia and Nyasaland 1953–63. In 1964 Northern Rhodesia became the independent republic of Zambia. A constitutional amendment was passed in 1990 allowing opposition parties; the years since have been filled with political tension and economic instability.

Zangwill \'zaŋ-gwil\, **Israel** (1864–1926) English novelist, playwright, and Zionist leader. The son of Eastern European immigrants, he is remembered as one of the earliest English interpreters of Jewish immigrant life. Zangwill drew on his own experience in *Children of the Ghetto* (1892). Essays on famous Jews are collected in *Dreamers of the Ghetto* (1898). The metaphor of America as a crucible wherein various nationalities are transformed into a new race comes from his play *The Melting Pot* (1908).

Zanuck \'za-nək\, **Darryl F(rancis)** (1902–1979) U.S. film producer and executive. Born in Wahoo, Neb., he became a screenwriter for Warner Brothers and was soon a producer. He promoted the conversion to sound by producing *The Jazz Singer* (1927). In 1933 he cofounded Twentieth Century Pictures, which soon merged with the Fox Film Corp. As the controlling executive of TWENTIETH CENTURY–FOX, he produced such films as *The Grapes of Wrath* (1940) and *Gentleman's Agreement* (1947). He resigned in 1956, but returned as president (1962–69) to effect the company's financial recovery with such hits as *The Sound of Music* (1965) and *Patton* (1970).

Zanzibar Chief island (pop., 1995 est.: 457,000), Tanzania. It has an area of 637 sq mi (1,651 sq km). Zanzibar city (pop., 1988: 158,000) is the principal port and commercial center. The island probably once formed part of the African continent. Its E. African inhabitants were joined by Arab traders from the Persian Gulf from the 11th cent. The Portuguese took control in 1503; they were ousted in 1698 by Arabs from Oman. By the early 19th cent. Zanzibar was the hub of the E. African ivory and slave trade, and the world's chief source of cloves. The sultan of Oman made it his capital in 1832. In 1861 Zanzibar became an independent sultanate that included Kenya and coastal Tanzania and Somalia. In 1890 the British, having gained increasing influence, proclaimed a protectorate over Zanzibar. In 1963 the sultanate regained its independence; in 1964 it was overthrown in a coup and Zanzibar joined with Tanganyika to form the Republic of Tanzania.

Zapata \sä-'pä-tä\, **Emiliano** (1879–1919) Mexican revolutionary and champion of the rural poor. A mestizo peasant, he led his neighbors in protests against the hacienda that had appropriated their land, and eventually took it back by force. He organized a small force to help Francisco MADERO unseat Porfirio DÍAZ in 1911. Dissatisfied with the pace of LAND REFORM under Madero, Zapata led a guerrilla campaign that returned land from the haciendas to the communal Indian EJIDOS. He was instrumental in the defeat of Gen. Victoriano HUERTA after Huerta deposed Madero. With Pancho VILLA he occu-

Emiliano Zapata, 1912

pied Mexico City and began to implement land reform, but was ambushed and killed by the forces of Venustiano CARRANZA.

Zapopan \ˌsä-pō-'pän\ City (pop., 1995: 850,000), JALISCO state, W central Mexico. It is a commercial and manufacturing center for an agricultural area that produces corn, sugarcane, cotton, and honey. The 17th-cent. Basilica of Zapopan is the site of annual pilgrimages.

Zaporizhzhya \ˌzäp-ə-'ri-zhə\ *formerly (until 1921)* **Aleksandrovsk** City (pop., 1998 est.: 863,000), SE Ukraine, on the DNIEPER RIVER. Founded in 1770 to ensure government control over the nearby COSSACKS, the settlement became a town in 1806. It expanded during the construction (1927-32) of the Dnieper hydroelectric station, then the largest in the world. The dam was destroyed in World War II but was later rebuilt. The city has a major iron and steel plant; automobiles are also manufactured.

Zapotec \ˌzä-pə-'tek\ Indian population living in the state of Oaxaca, in S Mexico. Early Zapotec civilization, centered on MONTE ALBÁN (near the modern city of Oaxaca), produced the first writing in Mesoamerica and devised the 52-year round calendar later borrowed by other groups. Present-day Zapotec society is largely agricultural; major crafts include pottery and weaving. See also MESOAMERICAN CIVILIZATION.

Zappa, Frank (*orig.* Francis Vincent) (1940–1993) U.S. rock musician and composer. Born in Baltimore, Zappa grew up in California and taught himself drums and guitar. In 1964 he began working with the Soul Giants, which eventually became the Mothers of Invention. He became known for his musical virtuosity and wildly eccentric wit on such albums as *Freak Out!* (1966), *We're Only in It for the Money* (1967), *Lumpy Gravy* (1967), *Sheik Yerbouti* (1979), and *Jazz from Hell* (1988).

Zaragoza See SARAGOSSA

Zarathustra See ZOROASTER

Zatopek \'tsä-tō-ˌpek\, **Emil** (1922–2000) Czech long-distance runner. He won his first Olympic gold medal in 1948 in the 10,000-m race. At the 1952 Olympics he won gold medals in the 5,000-m, 10,000-m, and marathon. He set 18 world records.

zazen \'zä-'zen\ Sitting meditation as practiced in ZEN Buddhism. The disciple sits in a quiet room, with legs crossed, spine and head erect, and eyes open. Logical, analytic thinking is suspended, as are all desires and judgments, leaving the mind in a state of relaxed attention. The practice was brought to prominence by Dogen (1200–1253), who introduced one school of Zen to Japan. He held that, if properly experienced, meditation could constitute enlightenment. See also KOAN.

Zealand See SJAELLAND

zebra Any of three species of black-and-white-striped EQUINES that subsist almost entirely on grass. Zebras stand 47–55 in. (120–140 cm) tall. The Burchell's zebra, or bonte quagga (*Equus quagga*), of E and S African grasslands, has wide, widely spaced stripes. Grevy's zebra (*E. grevyi*), of arid areas in Kenya, Ethiopia, and Somalia, has narrow, closely spaced stripes and a white belly. The small mountain zebra (*E. zebra*), of dry upland plains in Namibia and W S. Africa, has a gridlike pattern on the rump.

zebra fish Any member of two unrelated groups of fishes: freshwater species in the genus *Brachydanio* (family Cyprinidae) and saltwater species in the genus *Pterois* (family Scorpaenidae). The zebra danio (*Brachydanio rerio*), popular in freshwater aquariums, is up to about 1.5 in. (4 cm) long and has dark-blue and silvery longitudinal stripes. The distinctive saltwater zebra fishes (*Pterois*), used in marine aquariums, have numerous extremely poisonous spines and colorful vertical stripes. Some species are known as LIONFISH and turkeyfish.

zebra mussel Either of two species of tiny MUSSELS (genus *Dreissena*) that are prominent freshwater pests. They proliferate quickly and adhere in great numbers to virtually any surface. The voracious mussels disrupt food webs by wiping out PHYTOPLANKTON, and their massive clustering on water-intake valves and pipes, bridge abutments, and other structures can cause severe commercial damage. They arrived in N. America around 1986; their invasion of all the

Great Lakes has devastated the lakes' native mussel and fish populations.

zebu See BRAHMAN

Zechariah \ˌzek-ə-ˈrī-ə\ (fl.520–518 B.C.) One of the 12 Minor Prophets of the OLD TESTAMENT, whose prophecies are recorded in the Book of Zechariah. (The work is part of a larger book, The Twelve, in the Jewish canon.) He prophesied the Jews' return to Jerusalem after the BABYLONIAN EXILE, the rebuilding of the Temple of JERUSALEM, and the world's recognition of Israel's God. The book also includes his apocalyptic visions of the end of time.

Zedillo (Ponce de León), Ernesto \sā-ˈdē-yō\ (b.1951) President of Mexico (1994–2000). He joined Mexico's ruling party in 1971 and earned a PhD in economics from Yale Univ. As a cabinet minister he controlled Mexico's huge foreign debt, reduced inflation, and balanced the budget. Elected president after the assassination of the original PRI candidate, Luis Donaldo Colosio, he undertook reforms to reduce poverty, root out corruption, and continue democratizing the electoral system. His devaluation of the peso in 1994 led to an economic crisis that was turned around with massive U.S. aid. The agrarian Zapatista rebellion in CHIAPAS plagued his administration, which was charged with human-rights abuses in that region.

Zee, James Van Der See James VAN DER ZEE

Zeffirelli, Franco \ˌze-fə-ˈre-lē\ orig. Gianfranco Corsi (b.1923) Italian director, producer, and stage designer. After serving as Luchino VISCONTI's assistant on such films as *La terra trema* (1948), he turned to stage design. His major operatic productions, noted for their visual richness, began with *L'italiana in Algeri* (1952–53); he directed films of *La traviata* (1983) and *Otello* (1986). His other films have included *The Taming of the Shrew* (1967), *Romeo and Juliet* (1968), *Endless Love* (1981), and *Tea with Mussolini* (1999).

zemstvo \ˈzemst-və\ Rural elected assembly in the Russian empire. Established by Czar ALEXANDER II in 1864 to provide social and economic services, the zemstvos became a liberal influence. Composed of delegates representing the landed proprietors and the peasant village communes, they expanded education, improved roads, and provided health care. From the 1890s they agitated for constitutional reform, and they stimulated activity in the RUSSIAN REVOLUTION OF 1905 and the RUSSIAN REVOLUTION OF 1917. They were abolished after the BOLSHEVIKS came to power.

Zen Important school of BUDDHISM that claims to transmit the experience of enlightenment achieved by the BUDDHA Gautama. Arising as Chan in China in the 6th cent. (introduced by BODHIDHARMA), Zen developed fully in Japan by the 12th cent. and had a significant following in the West by the later 20th cent. Zen teaches that the potential to achieve enlightenment is inherent in everyone but lies dormant because of ignorance. It is best awakened not by study, good deeds, rites and ceremonies, or worship of images, but by breaking through the boundaries of mundane logical thought. The practice of ZAZEN and the use of KOANS are two methods used to break through those boundaries.

Zend-Avesta See AVESTA

Zenger, John Peter (1697–1746) American (German-born) printer and journalist. He emigrated to New York at 13 and started his own printing business in 1726. In 1733 he began publishing the *New York Weekly Journal*. Arrested for libel in 1734 for his attacks on the colonial governor, he was acquitted on the ground that his charges were based on fact, in the first important colonial victory for freedom of the press.

Zeng Guofan *or* **Tseng Kuo-fan** \ˈdzən-ˈgwō-ˈfän\ (1811–1872) Chinese military leader most responsible for suppressing the TAIPING REBELLION. Having passed the highest examinations in the CHINESE EXAMINATION SYSTEM, Zeng worked successfully as a bureaucrat. In 1852 he was asked to help combat the Taiping rebels, who had reached the Chang (Yangtze) River valley and were threatening the QING DYNASTY's survival. The imperial troops being weak, Zeng and other members of the scholar-gentry organized local militias. His army seized the rebels' supply areas along the upper Chang and besieged and captured their capital, Nanjing, in 1864. In 1865 he was called on to help suppress the Nian Rebellion.

Zenobia \zə-ˈnō-bē-ə\ *in full* Septimia Zenobia (d. after A.D. 274) Queen of the Roman colony of PALMYRA (A.D. 267?–272). After her husband, a Roman client ruler of Palmyra, was assassinated, she became her son's regent but called herself queen. In 269 she seized Egypt and much of Asia Minor and declared her independence from Rome. AURELIAN defeated her armies and besieged Palmyra; she and her son were captured and taken to Rome (272), where she later married a senator.

Zeno of Elea \ˈē-lē-ə\ (c.495–430 B.C.) Greek philosopher and mathematician. He was called by ARISTOTLE the inventor of dialectic. He is best known for his paradoxes. As a pupil and friend of PARMENIDES, he defended Parmenides' monism, trying to show that the assumption of the existence of a plurality of things in time and space carried with it more serious inconsistencies.

zeolite \ˈzē-ə-ˌlīt\ Any member of a family of hydrated aluminosilicate minerals that have a framework of interconnected cavities occupied by large metal CATIONS and water molecules. The ease of movement of ions and water within the framework allows reversible dehydration and cation exchange, properties that are exploited in water softeners and molecular sieves for pollution control.

Zephaniah (7th cent. B.C.) One of the 12 Minor Prophets of the OLD TESTAMENT, traditional author of the Book of Zephaniah. (The work is part of a larger book, The Twelve, in the Jewish canon.) He prophesied in the reign of JOSIAH, denouncing the worship of foreign gods. His dominant theme is the coming time of divine judgment for Judah's sins.

zeppelin Rigid AIRSHIP of a type designed by the German builder Graf (Count) Ferdinand von Zeppelin (1838–1917). Its trussed and covered frame was supported by internal gas cells, below which hung two external cars with an engine geared to two propellers. First flown in 1900, in World War I zeppelins were used as bombers by Germany. In 1928 the *Graf Zeppelin* inaugurated transatlantic flight service; it had completed 590 flights by 1937, when the *Hindenburg* disaster halted such flights.

zero NUMBER and numeral of critical importance in mathematics. As a number, it has the property that any number added to it remains the same and any number multiplied by it becomes zero. Division by zero is undefined. As a numeral indicating an empty space, it was first used by the ancient Babylonians. The symbol 0 dates from about 150 B.C., when PTOLEMY began using the Greek letter omicron to indicate the absence of a digit at the end of a number. Zero was not widely accepted as a number in Western mathematics until the 16th cent.

Zetkin, Clara \ˈtset-kən\ orig. Clara Eissner (1857–1933) German communist leader. She joined the Social Democratic Party in 1881, and later married a Russian revolutionary exile, Ossip Zetkin (1848–1889). From 1892 she edited the Socialist women's newspaper *Die Gleichheit* ("Equality") in Stuttgart. A friend of Vladimir LENIN and Rosa LUXEMBURG, Zetkin joined the new Communist Party of Germany (1919), and was elected to the presidium of the Third International (1921).

Zeus \ˈzüs\ In GREEK RELIGION, the chief deity of the pantheon, a sky and weather god. His Roman counterpart was JUPITER. Zeus was regarded as the bearer of thunder and lightning, rain, and winds, and his traditional weapon was the thunderbolt. The son of CRONUS and RHEA, he dethroned his father, defeated the TITANS, and divided dominion of the world with his brothers POSEIDON and HADES. From his home atop Mt. OLYMPUS, he dispensed justice and served as protector. Though married to HERA, he had many love affairs with mortal and immortal women, giving rise to such offspring as APOLLO, ARES, ARTEMIS, ATHENA, DIONYSUS, HEPHAESTUS, HELEN, and PERSEPHONE.

Zeus hurling a thunderbolt, bronze statuette, early 5th cent. B.C.

W X Y Z

Zhang Yimou \'jäŋ-'yē-'mō\ (b.1950) Chinese film director. He began his film career as a cinematographer, and his work for Chen Kaige's *The Yellow Earth* (1983) helped launch the "Fifth Generation," filmmakers who brought back sensuality and emotion to Chinese movies. Zhang made his directorial debut with *Red Sorghum* (1987). Later films include *Ju Dou* (1990), *Raise the Red Lantern* (1991), *The Story of Qiu Ju* (1992), *To Live* (1994), and *Shanghai Triad* (1995).

Zhang Zhidong *or* **Chang Chih-tung** \'jäŋ-jir-'dȯŋ\ (1837–1909) Chinese classicist and reformer. A scholar and educational director (1862–82), from 1882 he rose from a provincial to a national leader. He supported the dowager empress CIXI, who in turn favored him with many promotions. He searched for a way for China to survive in the modern world that could accommodate Western knowledge but preserve traditional ways. He built a railway from Hankou to near Beijing and founded a mint, tanneries, tile and silk factories, and paper, cotton, and wool mills. In response to China's defeat in the SINO–JAPANESE WAR, Zhang turned his attention to education, encouraging study abroad for Chinese students, establishment of a school system, and translation of Western and Japanese books. He also secured the abolition of the civil-service examinations in 1905.

Zhang Zuolin *or* **Chang Tso-lin** \'jäŋ-dzȯ-'lin\ (1873–1928) Chinese WARLORD. Having organized a self-defense militia in his native district, by 1912 he was in command of a division, and he set out to dominate Manchuria, relying on the tacit support of the Japanese. He became inspector general of Manchuria's three provinces, which he ruled as a virtually autonomous state. In 1920 he pushed south into China and in 1924 took Beijing. His troops were ousted by CHIANG KAI-SHEK's 1927 NORTHERN EXPEDITION. Zhang was killed by a bomb planted by Japanese extremists who hoped his death would provoke the Japanese into occupying Manchuria.

Zheng Chenggong *or* **Cheng Ch'eng-kung** \'jəŋ-'chən-'gȯŋ\ *or* **Koxinga** \käk-'siŋ-ə\ (1624–1662) Chinese pirate leader. After the MING DYNASTY fell to the MANCHU, Zheng launched a military campaign against the new QING DYNASTY in 1659, taking a large force from his base in Fujian up the Chang (Yangtze) River. Initial success turned to failure, but undaunted, Zheng took Taiwan from the Dutch in 1662 to use as a secure rear base area. After his death, he became a cultural hero to the Chinese on Taiwan, and even the Qing court honored him as a paragon of loyalty. In Japan, CHIKAMATSU MONZAEMON celebrated him on the stage (Zheng had a Japanese mother), and in the 20th cent. both Chinese Communists and Nationalists embraced him as a national hero.

Zheng He *or* **Cheng Ho** \'jəŋ-'he\ *orig.* Ma Sanbao (1371?–1435) Chinese admiral and diplomat. A eunuch, Zheng was named commander in chief of missions to the "Western Oceans" by the YONGLE EMPEROR. He first set sail in 1405, visited Champa (S Vietnam), Siam, Malacca, and Java, then traveled through the Indian Ocean as far as Ceylon (Sri Lanka), returning to China in 1407. Subsequent voyages took him to Arabia, the E coast of Africa, S.E. Asia, and India. Chinese emigration increased in the wake of these missions, resulting in Chinese colonization of S.E. Asia and trade that lasted into the 19th cent.

Zhengzhou *or* **Cheng-chou** \'jəŋ-'jō\ *formerly (1913–49)* **Cheng-hsien** \'jəŋ-'shyen\ City (pop., 1999 est.: 1,465,000), capital of Henan province, E central China. Located south of the HUANG (Yellow) River, it is an important rail center. The SHANG Bronze Age culture (fl. c.1500 B.C.) was centered there on a walled city. ZHOU-DYNASTY tombs have also been discovered. Zhengzhou achieved its greatest importance in the 6th–12th cent., when it was the terminus of a canal that joined the Huang to the north. In the early 20th cent. it became a rail junction and a regional agricultural center. After 1949, its industrial base was greatly expanded.

Zhivkov \'zhiv-ˌkȯf\, **Todor (Khristov)** (1911–1998) Bulgarian politician. He became first secretary of the Bulgarian Communist Party in 1954, then served as premier (1962–71) and president (1971–89). He hewed closely to the Soviet line but encouraged industrialization and improved the country's living standard. When democratization reached Bul-

garia, Zhivkov resigned (1989). Convicted of embezzlement; he was sentenced to house arrest in 1992.

Zhou dynasty *or* **Chou dynasty** \'jō\ (c.1122–256/255 B.C.) Ancient Chinese dynasty that gave China its historically identifying political and cultural characteristics. The period before 771 B.C. is known as the Western Zhou; the later period is called the Eastern Zhou and includes the SPRING AND AUTUMN PERIOD (770–476) and the WARRING STATES PERIOD (475–221). During the Zhou dynasty, iron, ox-drawn plows, crossbows, and horseback riding were introduced; large-scale irrigation projects were instituted; and the great Chinese philosophers of antiquity, including CONFUCIUS, MENCIUS, and ZHUANGZI, lived and taught. Pottery and bronzework expanded on the traditions of the earlier SHANG DYNASTY, as did work in jade and lacquer. See also WUWANG.

Zhou Enlai *or* **Chou En-lai** \'jō-'en-'lī\ (1898–1976) Premier of the People's Republic of China (1949–76). Zhou became a Communist during his studies in France and was an organizer for the CHINESE COMMUNIST PARTY in Europe. Like other Communists, he worked with the Nationalists in the early 1920s and escaped capture when CHIANG KAI-SHEK purged his former allies in 1927. He joined ZHU DE and MAO ZEDONG in Jiangxi and became political commissar of the Red Army. In the 1930s he negotiated a tactical alliance with the Nationalists to resist Japanese aggression. When the Communists came to power in 1949, Zhou became premier of the new People's Republic. During the CULTURAL REVOLUTION, Zhou helped restrain Maoist extremists; with its waning in the early 1970s, he sought to restore DENG XIAOPING and other moderates to power. He is credited with arranging the meeting between Pres. Richard NIXON and Mao that led to U.S. recognition of Mao's government.

Zhoukoudian \'jō-kȯd-yən\ Cave lying 37 mi (60 km) southwest of Beijing, at which have been found fossil remains of the extinct hominid *HOMO ERECTUS*. So-called "Peking man" was identified as a new fossil human by Davidson Black in 1927 and variously classified as *Pithecanthropus* and *Sinanthropus* before being assigned to *H. erectus*. Partial remains of about 40 individuals along with over 100,000 artifacts have been uncovered. Its strata date to 460,000–230,000 years ago. Ancient hearths and other evidence indicate that the Zhoukoudian hominids had a well-developed communal culture, practiced hunting, and used fire domestically.

Zhuangzi *or* **Chuang-tzu** \'jwän-'dzȯ\ (369?–286 B.C.) Most significant early Chinese interpreter of TAOISM, and the purported author of the Taoist classic that bears his name. A contemporary of MENCIUS, he drew on the sayings of LAOZI but took a broader perspective. He taught that enlightenment comes from the realization that everything is One, the TAO, but that whatever can be known or said of the tao is not the tao.

Zhu De *or* **Chu Teh** \'jü-'de\ (1886–1976) Founder of the Chinese Communist Army. Zhu began his military career under warlords in S China. He became a Communist but hid his affiliation to become an officer in the Nationalist army. In 1927 he took part in the Communist-led Nanchang Uprising, celebrated as the birth of the PEOPLE'S LIBERATION ARMY. After its defeat, Zhu led his troops south to join MAO ZEDONG's small guerrilla forces. He became commander in chief of the Communist forces, a position he held through World War II and the subsequent civil war, only stepping down in 1954. With Mao, Zhu is credited with elevating guerrilla warfare to a major strategic concept.

Zhuge Liang *or* **Chu-ko Liang** \'jü-'gō-lē-'äŋ\ (A.D. 181–234) Celebrated adviser to Liu Bei, founder of the Shu-Han dynasty of the SIX DYNASTIES period. A mechanical and mathematical genius, Zhuge is credited with inventing a bow for shooting several arrows at once and with perfecting the Eight Dispositions, a series of military tactics. Supernatural powers are often ascribed to him, and he has been a favorite character in Chinese plays and stories. In 1724 he was made a Confucian saint.

Zhukov \'zhü-ˌkȯf\, **Georgy (Konstantinovich)** (1896–1974) Soviet army commander in World War II. As chief of staff of the Red Army, he organized the defense of Leningrad and Moscow (1941). He directed the offensive that broke the siege in the Battle of STALINGRAD (1943) and was named a marshal of the Soviet Union. After helping win the Battle of Kursk, he commanded the final assault on Berlin (1945). Zhukov's great popularity later caused Joseph STALIN to assign him to obscure regional commands. After Stalin's death he was appointed minister of defense (1955) and attempted to make the army more autonomous, but opposition from Nikita KHRUSHCHEV caused his dismissal in 1957.

Zhu Xi *or* **Chu Hsi** \ʹjü-ʹshē\ (1130–1200) Chinese philosopher and proponent of NEO-CONFUCIANISM. He was educated in the Confucian tradition and entered government service. In 1189 he began a commentary on the *Da Xue* ("Great Learning"), a text attributed to CONFUCIUS. He continued working on it all his life. Zhu Xi's commentaries on the FOUR BOOKS and on *MENCIUS* (both 1177) were enormously influential. His philosophy emphasized logic, consistency, observance of classical authority, and the value of inquiry.

Zhu Xi Ink on paper

Zia-ul-Haq \ʹzē-ə-əl-ʹhäk\, **Mohammad** (1924–1988) President of Pakistan (1978–88). He served with the British in S.E. Asia at the end of World War II; after Pakistan's independence, he held various staff and command appointments, becoming army chief of staff in 1976. In 1977 he seized power from Z. A. BHUTTO, and in 1978 he assumed the presidency. After having the popular Bhutto executed in 1979, he tightened his grip on the government, declared martial law, and worked for the Islamization of Pakistan's political and cultural life. He died in an airplane crash.

Ziegfeld \ʹzig-ˌfeld, ʹzēg-ˌfeld\, **Florenz** (1869–1932) U.S. theatrical producer. Born in Chicago, he worked as a publicist before turning to theatrical management in 1896, and his press releases promoting the French beauty Anna Held set a pattern of star-making publicity. In 1907 in New York he produced the first of his *Ziegfeld Follies*, which combined seminudity, pageantry, and comedy in an extravagant spectacle, repeating the formula successfully for 23 years while developing such talent as Will ROGERS and Fanny BRICE.

Ziegler \ʹtsē-glər\, **Karl** (1898–1973) German chemist. He was the first to explain the reactions involved in the synthesis of rubber. His most important work led to the discovery that certain catalysts permitted the fast polymerization of ethylene at atmospheric pressure to a linear polymer of high molecular weight having valuable plastic properties. His work formed the basis of nearly all later developments in the production of long-chain polymers from olefins; the resulting products came into widespread use as plastics, fibers, rubbers, and films. He shared a 1963 Nobel Prize.

ziggurat \ʹzi-gə-ˌrät\ Pyramidal, stepped temple tower characteristic of the major cities of Mesopotamia between 2200 and 500 B.C. It was built with a core of mud brick and an exterior covered with baked brick. It had no internal chambers and was usually square or rectangular. Some 25 ziggurats are known; the best-preserved is at UR, and the largest is at ELAM. The legendary Tower of BABEL has been associated with the ziggurat of the great temple of MARDUK in BABYLON.

Zimbabwe \zim-ʹbä-bwä, zim-ʹbä-bwē\ *officially* **Republic of Zimbabwe** *formerly* **Rhodesia** Landlocked country, S central Africa. Area: 150,873 sq mi (390,759 sq km). Population (2000): 11,343,000. Capital: HARARE. The Shona make up about 70% of the population, the Ndebele about 16%, and whites about 2%. Languages: English (official); BANTU LANGUAGES of the Shona and Ndebele much more widely spoken. Religions: Christianity, indigenous beliefs, Islam. Currency: Zimbabwe dollar. A vast plateau sloping southwest–northeast, whose central part lies at an elevation of 4,000–5,000 ft (1,200–1,500 m), dominates Zimbabwe's landscape.

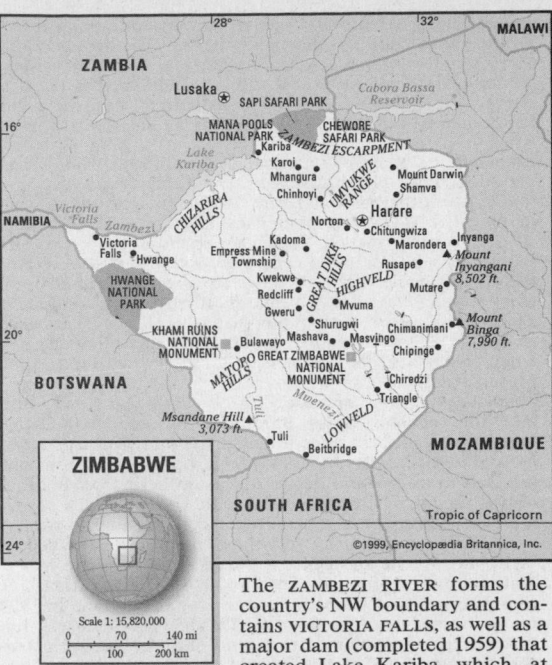

The ZAMBEZI RIVER forms the country's NW boundary and contains VICTORIA FALLS, as well as a major dam (completed 1959) that created Lake Kariba, which, at more than 2,000 sq mi (5,200 sq km), is one of the world's largest man-made lakes. The LIMPOPO and Save river basins are in the southeast. Agricultural products, raising livestock, and working the mineral reserves, including gold, are all economically important. It is a republic with one legislative house; its head of state and government is the president. Remains of Stone Age cultures dating back 500,000 years have been found in the area. The first Bantu-speaking peoples reached it during the 5th–10th cent. A.D., driving the Bushmen inhabitants into the desert. A second migration of Bantu-speakers began around 1830. During this period the British and Afrikaners moved up from the south, and the area came under the administration of the British S. Africa Co. 1889–1923. Called Southern Rhodesia (1911–64), it became a self-governing British colony in 1923. The colony united in 1953 with Nyasaland (Malawi) and Northern Rhodesia (Zambia) to form the Central African Federation of Rhodesia and Nyasaland. The federation dissolved in 1963, and Southern Rhodesia reverted to its former colonial status. In 1965 it issued a unilateral declaration of independence considered illegal by the British government, which led to economic sanctions against it. The country, which proclaimed itself a republic in 1970, called itself Rhodesia 1964–79. In 1979 it instituted limited majority rule and changed its name to Zimbabwe Rhodesia. It was granted independence by Britain in 1980 and became Zimbabwe. A multiparty system was established in 1990. The long dictatorship of Robert MUGABE has resulted in deepening poverty and government-sponsored violence.

Zimbabwe *or* **Great Zimbabwe** Extensive stone ruins, SE Africa. Located near Nyanda, Zimbabwe, it is the largest of many such ruins in S Africa. Covering 60 acres (24 hectares), it includes a hilltop fortress and walls of stone monoliths. Its oldest parts date from the 8th cent. A.D., though the site had been occupied for 600 years before that. The center of a great inland empire ruled by the Karanga people, who traded on the shores of the Indian Ocean, it flourished between the 11th and 15th cent. Its rediscovery in 1867 attracted much archaeological research. The more recent Little Zimbabwe ruins are nearby.

Zimmermann \ʹtsi-mər-ˌmän\, **Arthur** (1864–1940) German diplomat. As foreign minister of Germany 1916–17, he planned to reduce U.S. intervention in World War I by embroiling it in war with Mexico. On Jan. 16, 1917, he sent a coded telegram to the German ambassador in Mexico, proposing a German-Mexican alliance that would allow Mexico to "reconquer her lost territory in Texas, New Mexico, and Arizona." Intercepted, it was published in the U.S. on March 1. The "Zimmermann telegram" became a key factor in the U.S. declaration of war against Germany on April 6.

zinc Chemical ELEMENT, chemical symbol Zn, atomic number 30. Zinc is a bluish silver METAL, ductile when very pure but brittle otherwise. It forms BRASS (with COPPER) and many other ALLOYS. Its major use is in GALVANIZING iron, steel, and other metals. Zinc is an essential trace element, particularly in red blood cells. Zinc oxide is used as a PIGMENT, ultraviolet light absorber (to prevent sunburn), dietary supplement and seed treatment, and photoconductor. Zinc's many other compounds (usual VALENCE 2) are used in industrial and consumer applications, including as pesticides, pigments, mordants (see DYE), fluxes, and wood preservatives.

Zinkernagel \'tsiŋ-kər-ˌnä-gəl, *Engl* 'ziŋ-kər-ˌnä-gəl\, **Rolf M(artin)** (b.1944) Swiss immunologist and pathologist. Studying T CELLS in mice infected with a meningitis virus, he and Peter Doherty (b.1940) found that those from one infected mouse would destroy infected cells from another only if the mice belonged to the same genetic strain: no immune response occurs unless the T cells recognize two signals, those of the virus and those identifying the cell as "self." In 1996 he and Doherty shared a Nobel Prize.

Zinnemann \'zin-ə-mən\ **Fred** (1907–1997) Austrian-U.S. film director. In 1929 he moved to Hollywood, and in 1934 he codirected his first feature, *The Wave*, which was followed largely by documentaries and short subjects. His feature films, many of which focused on a moral crisis, include the classic western *High Noon* (1952), *From Here to Eternity* (1953, Academy Award), *Oklahoma!* (1955), *The Nun's Story* (1959), *A Man for All Seasons* (1966, Academy Award), and *The Day of the Jackal* (1973).

zinnia Any of about 22 species of herbaceous plants and shrubs that make up the genus *Zinnia* (COMPOSITE FAMILY), native mainly to N. America. Where native, they are perennial; elsewhere they are annual. Zinnias have stiff, hairy stems and oval or lance-shaped leaves arranged opposite each other and often clasping the stem. The numerous garden varieties grown for their showy, solitary flowers come from the species *Z. elegans*.

Zinovyev \zyi-'nȯf-yif\, **Grigory (Yevseyevich)** *orig.* Ovsel Gershon Aronov Radomyslsky (1883–1936) Soviet politician. He was Vladimir LENIN's close collaborator in exile (1909–17) and in the RUSSIAN REVOLUTION OF 1917, helping win public support for the Bolshevik regime. Chairman of the COMINTERN 1919–26, he helped Joseph STALIN oust Leon TROTSKY, but was removed from power by Stalin in 1926. In 1935 he was arrested for conspiracy and sentenced to prison; the next year he was retried in the PURGE TRIALS and executed.

Zinsser, Hans (1878–1940) U.S. bacteriologist and epidemiologist. Born in New York City, he isolated the bacteria that cause the European type of TYPHUS, developed the first antityphus vaccine, and, with colleagues, found a way to massproduce it. He recognized that cases of mild typhuslike symptoms in lice-free persons are recurrences after a latent period (Brill-Zinsser disease). His book *Rats, Lice and History* (1935) recounts the effects of typhus on mankind (he believed disease had destroyed more civilizations than war).

Zion Easternmost of the two hills of ancient JERUSALEM, where DAVID established his royal capital. In the OLD TESTAMENT, the name Zion frequently refers to Jerusalem as a whole; it is overwhelmingly a poetic and prophetic designation. Mt. Zion is the place where Yahweh (God) dwells. The name came to mean the Jewish homeland and thus was the source of the term ZIONISM. It is used in Christian literature and hymns in reference to the heavenly city or the earthly city of Christian faith and fraternity.

Zionism \'zī-ə-ˌni-zəm\ Jewish nationalism movement with the goal of establishing a Jewish state in Palestine. In the 16th–17th cent., a number of "messiahs" tried to persuade the Jews to return to Palestine, but interest gradually faded. POGROMS in Eastern Europe led to formation of the "Lovers of Zion," which promoted the settlement of Jewish farmers and artisans in Palestine. In the face of persistent anti-Semitism, Theodor HERZL called the first Zionist Congress in Basel in 1897. After World War I the movement picked up momentum with the BALFOUR DECLARATION. The Jewish population in Palestine increased from 90,000 in 1914 to 238,000 in 1933. The Arab population resisted Zionism, and the British tried unsuccessfully to reconcile Jewish and Arab demands. Zionism achieved its goal with the creation of Israel in 1948. See also David BEN-GURION, HAGANA, IRGUN ZVAI LEUMI.

Zion National Park National park, SW Utah. It covers an area of 229 sq mi (593 sq km); its principal feature is Zion Canyon, named by the MORMONS who discovered it in 1858. It was established as a national park in 1919. Zion Canyon was carved by the Virgin River and is about 15 mi (24 km) long and 0.5 mi (0.8 km) deep. Rocky domes dot the canyon walls, which contain an abundant fossil record. Excavation has yielded evidence of prehistoric inhabitants.

zip code System of postal-zone codes introduced in the U.S. in 1963 to improve mail delivery and exploit electronic reading and sorting capabilities. The original code, which corresponds to the postal codes used in most countries in the world, consists of five numbers. The first three identify the state and portion of the state, the last two a specific post office or zone. In 1983 a nine-digit code (created by adding a hyphen and four digits) was introduced to further speed delivery.

zipper Device for binding the edges of an opening, as on a garment or a bag. It consists of two strips of material with metal or plastic teeth along the edges, and a sliding piece that interlocks the teeth when moved in one direction and separates them when moved in the opposite direction. A slide fastener was first exhibited by Whitcomb L. Judson (d.1909) in 1893; the modern zipper began to appear on clothing in the late 1920s.

zircon Silicate mineral, zirconium silicate, the principal source of zirconium. Zircon is widespread as an accessory mineral in acid igneous rocks. It occurs in beach sands in many parts of the world, particularly Australia, India, Brazil, and Florida, and is a common heavy mineral in sedimentary rocks. Gem varieties occur in stream gravels, particularly in Indochina and Sri Lanka.

zirconium Chemical ELEMENT, one of the TRANSITION ELEMENTS, chemical symbol Zr, atomic number 40. The METAL is hard and brittle when impure, soft and ductile when highly purified. It is relatively abundant, occurring as zircon (which can be a semiprecious gemstone) and baddeleyite. Zirconium became important in the 1940s in NUCLEAR-ENERGY applications. Other uses are in ALLOYS, fireworks, and flashbulbs. Its compounds (usual VALENCE 4) are important industrial materials. Zirconia (the OXIDE) is used in piezoelectric crystals (see PIEZOELECTRICITY), high-frequency induction coils, colored glazes and glasses, heat-resistant fibers, and preparations to cure the rash of poison ivy.

zodiac \'zō-dē-ˌak\ Belt around the heavens extending about 9° on either side of the ECLIPTIC. The orbits of the moon and the major planets (except Pluto) lie within it. In ASTROLOGY, each of 12 CONSTELLATIONS along this circle is considered to occupy 1/12 (30°) of it. The positions of the sun and planets at one's birth and their motion through the zodiac are said to influence one's life, though precession of

Signs of the Zodiac

Name	Dates (traditional)
Aries, the ram	Mar. 21–Apr. 19
Taurus, the bull	Apr. 20–May 20
Gemini, the twins	May 21–June 21
Cancer, the crab	June 22–July 22
Leo, the lion	July 23–Aug. 22
Virgo, the virgin	Aug 23–Sept. 22
Libra, the balance	Sept. 23–Oct. 23
Scorpio, the scorpion	Oct. 24–Nov. 21
Sagittarius, the archer	Nov. 22–Dec. 21
Capricorn, the goat	Dec. 22–Jan. 19
Aquarius, the water bearer	Jan. 20–Feb. 18
Pisces, the fishes	Feb. 19–Mar. 20

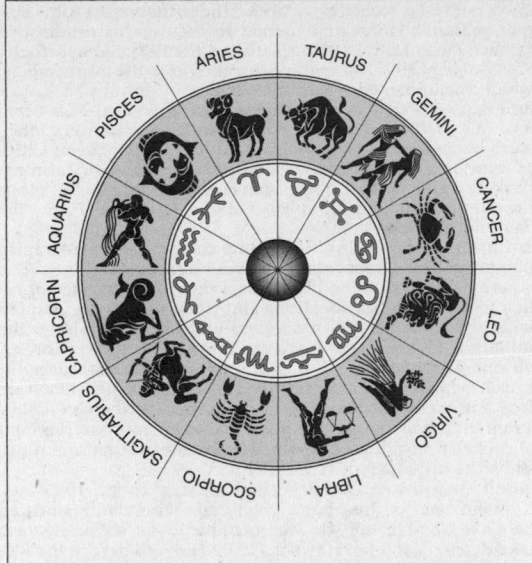

Zodiac The astrological images and symbols of the zodiac.

the EQUINOXES has shifted the constellations so the sun no longer passes through them on the traditional dates.

Zoe \'zō-ē\ (978?–1050) Byzantine empress (1042–50). The daughter of Constantine VIII, she married Emperor Romanus III Argyrus in 1028. He died in 1034, perhaps poisoned by her, and she married her lover and chamberlain, who became Michael IV. After his death in 1041, his successor, Michael V, banished Zoe to a convent; she was recalled by public outcry and Michael was blinded and exiled (1042). Zoe and her sister became uneasy corulers, and she married CONSTANTINE IX MONOMACHUS to secure her throne. Her court was known for its intellectual brilliance.

Zog I *Albanian* Ahmed Bey Zogu (1895–1961) President (1925–28) and king of Albania (1928–39). A leader of Albania's reformist Popular Party, he was elected head of the Albanian republic in 1925. Proclaimed king in 1928, he pursued a policy of close collaboration with Italy. Unable to resist Benito MUSSOLINI's increasing control of the country's finances and army, he was forced into exile when Italy invaded and made Albania a protectorate (1939). After Albania became a communist republic, Zog abdicated in 1946.

Zola \'zō-lə, *French* zō-'lä\, **Émile (-Édouard-Charles-Antoine)** (1840–1902) French novelist and critic, the founder of NATURALISM in literature. In the gruesome novel *Thérèse Raquin* (1867), he put his "scientific" theories of the determination of character by heredity and environment into practice for the first time. In 1870 he began the ambitious *Rougon-Macquart Cycle* (1871–93), a sequence of 20 novels documenting French life through the lives of the violent Rougon family and the passive Macquarts. It includes *L'assommoir* (1877), a study of alcoholism; *Nana* (1880); *Germinal* (1885), his masterpiece; and *La bête humaine* (1890). He is also notable for his involvement in the Alfred DREYFUS affair, especially for his open letter, "J'Ac-

Émile Zola Painting by Édouard Manet, 1868

cuse" (1898), denouncing the French army general staff. He died under suspicious circumstances, overcome by carbon-monoxide fumes in his sleep.

Zollverein \'tsól-ver-ˌīn\ (German: "Customs Union") Free-trade area throughout much of Germany established in 1834 under Prussian leadership. An important step in German unification, it developed from the 1818 Prussian tariff law that abolished internal customs dues and the customs union set up in 1828 in S Germany by Bavaria and Württemberg. By 1834 18 German states had joined; more joined later.

zombie In VODUN, a dead person who is revived after burial and compelled to do the bidding of the reviver, including criminal acts and heavy manual labor. It is believed that actual zombies are living persons under the influence of powerful drugs, including drugs derived from poisonous toads and puffer fish.

zoning Legislative method of controlling land use by regulating such considerations as the type of buildings that may be erected and the population density. The earliest U.S. zoning ordinances date from the early 20th cent. and were motivated by the need to regulate the location of commercial and industrial activities. Modern zoning regulations divide land use into three types: residential, commercial, and industrial. Within each designation, more specific aspects of development (e.g., building proximity, height, type) are also determined. Zoning is often used to maintain the distinctive character of a town or city; an adverse consequence of such zoning is economic segregation. The U.S. Supreme Court ruled against such zoning in 1977 when it declared the zoning regulations of one Chicago suburb discriminatory.

zoo or **zoological garden** Place where wild and sometimes domesticated animals are exhibited in captivity. Marine zoological gardens are called aquariums. Pigeons were kept in captivity as early as 4500 B.C.; other animals (e.g., elephants and antelopes) have also been kept in captivity since antiquity. Animal collections were kept by CHARLEMAGNE and other European monarchs. Hernán CORTÉS described a zoo in Mexico (1519) that required a staff of 300. Modern zookeeping started in 1752 with the founding of the Imperial Menagerie at Vienna's Schönbrunn Palace. Open-range zoos were first established in the early 1930s. There are now more than 1,000 animal collections open to the public worldwide.

zoology Branch of biology concerned with members of the animal kingdom. It originated in the works of HIPPOCRATES, ARISTOTLE, and PLINY THE ELDER. The contributions of William HARVEY (the circulation of blood), Carolus LINNAEUS (system of nomenclature), G.-L. de BUFFON (natural history), Georges CUVIER (comparative anatomy), and Claude BERNARD (homeostasis) greatly advanced the field. Since the 1859 publication of Charles DARWIN's *On the Origin of Species by Means of Natural Selection,* the study of genetics has become essential in zoological studies.

zooplankton \ˌzō-ə-'plaŋk-tən\ Small floating or weakly swimming animals that drift with water currents and, with PHYTOPLANKTON, make up the vital planktonic food supply on which almost all oceanic organisms ultimately depend (see PLANKTON). Included are many animals, from single-celled radiolarians to the eggs or larvae of herrings, crabs, and lobsters. Permanent plankton (holoplankton), such as PROTOZOANS and COPEPODS, spend their lives as plankton. Temporary plankton (meroplankton), such as young starfish, clams, and worms, live and feed as plankton until they become adults.

Zoroaster \'zōr-ə-ˌwas-tər\ or **Zarathustra** \ˌzar-ə-'thüsh-trə\ (628?–551? B.C.) Iranian religious reformer and prophet, founder of ZOROASTRIANISM AND PARSIISM. He was a priest in his polytheistic tribal religion, with which he eventually became disillusioned. Having received a vision, he began teaching that AHURA MAZDA was the only god worthy of worship, a concept that went against the polytheism of Iranian religion. He forbade the orgiastic rites that accompanied animal sacrifice, but preserved the ancient cult of fire worship. Zoroaster became the subject of legends. The Greeks regarded him as a philosopher, mathematician, astrologer, or magician; Jews and Christians viewed him as an astrologer, magician, prophet, or heretic.

Zoroastrianism and Parsiism Ancient religion that origi- nated in Iran based on the teachings of ZOROASTER. Founded in the 6th cent. B.C., it influenced the monotheis- tic religions Judaism, Christianity, and Islam. It rejects POLYTHEISM, accepting only one supreme god, AHURA MAZDA. In early Zoroastrianism, the struggle between good and evil was seen as an eternal rivalry between Ahura Mazda's twin sons. Later Zoroastrian cosmology made the rivalry between Ahura Mazda himself (by then called Or- mazd) and the evil Ahriman. Zoroastrian practice includes an initiation ceremony and various rituals of purification intended to ward off evil spirits. Fire worship, a carryover from an earlier religion, survives in the continuously burn- ing sacred fire that must be fed at least five times a day. The AVESTA is the primary scripture. Zoroastrianism enjoyed status as an official religion at various times before the ad- vent of ISLAM, but Zoroastrians were persecuted in the 8th– 10th cent., and some left Iran to settle in India. By the 19th cent. these Indian Zoroastrians, or PARSIS, were noted for their wealth and education. The few Zoroastrians remaining in Iran are known as the Gabars.

Z particle Electrically neutral carrier of the WEAK FORCE and the neutral partner of the W PARTICLE. It is nearly 100 times more massive than the PROTON and has a lifetime of only about 10^{-25} second. Measurements show that when Z particles decay to NEUTRINO-antineutrino pairs they pro- duce only three types of lightweight neutrino, indicating that there are only three sets each of LEPTONS and QUARKS.

Zuccaro \\'tsü-kär-ŏ\\, **Federico** (1540/42–1609) Italian painter and art theorist. He codified the theory of MAN- NERISM in *The Idea of Painters, Sculptors, and Architects* (1607) and in a series of frescoes in his own house in Rome. In England in 1575 he drew or painted portraits of ELIZA- BETH I and the earl of LEICESTER. He also painted the dome of Florence Cathedral (1574), a large work in the Doges' Palace in Venice (1582), and much work for El Escorial in Spain (1585–88). The central figure among the Roman Mannerists, he lived to see Mannerism become extinct.

zucchini Subspecies of *Cucurbita pepo*, dark green or yellow elongate summer SQUASH, of great abundance in home gar- dens and supermarkets worldwide. The creeping vine has five-lobed leaves, tendrils, and large yellow flowers.

Zuckerman \\'tsuk-ər-ˌmän\\, **Itzhak** *or* **Yizhak Cukierman** \\'tsuk-ər-ˌmän\\ (1915–1981) Polish-Israeli hero of anti-Nazi resistance. Active in Zionist organizations in his native War- saw, he urged the creation and arming of a Jewish defense organization after the German takeover of Poland. He used his contacts outside the ghetto to smuggle in a few arms, took command after the other leaders of the WARSAW GHETTO UPRISING were killed, and eventually led some 75 people through the sewers to safety. At war's end he helped organize transportation for Jewish refugees to Palestine.

Zuider Zee \\ˌzī-dər-'zā, ˌzī-dər-'zē\\ Former inlet of the NORTH SEA, the Netherlands. From the 13th to the 20th cent., it penetrated the Netherlands and occupied some 2,000 sq mi (5,000 sq km); it was separated from the North Sea by an arc of former sandflats that are now the W. FRISIAN ISLANDS. Frisian peoples inhabited the sandflats from about A.D. 400 and built the first seaworks, consid- ered engineering marvels, to stem rising sea levels. Control- ling water levels within the dikes developed into the recla- mation of lowland (polders). In 1927–32 a dam 19 mi (30 km) long was built across the Zuider Zee, separating it into the Waddenzee and the IJSSELMEER.

Zulu Nguni-speaking people living in KwaZulu/Natal province in S. Africa. Numbering about 9.5 million, they are S. Africa's largest ethnic group. European settlers wrested grazing and water resources from the Zulu in pro- longed warfare during the 19th cent.; with much of their wealth lost, most modern Zulu labor on farms owned by whites or work in the cities. The Zulu provide the main sup- port for the INKATHA FREEDOM PARTY. See also SHAKA.

Zululand Historical region, E Republic of S. Africa. It was the home of the ZULU people when Chief SHAKA established dominance over what is now KwaZulu-Natal. The Zulus lost territory to the Boers in the 1840s. The British annexed nearby NATAL in 1843; Zulu resistance in 1878-79 was over- come. The British made Zululand a crown colony in 1887

and annexed it to Natal in 1897. Under the APARTHEID sys- tem, a Bantu Homeland named KwaZulu was established for the Zulus in the 1970s. With the abolition of apartheid, KwaZulu in 1994 was reincorporated into Natal province, which was renamed KwaZulu-Natal.

Zuni \\'zü-nē\\ PUEBLO INDIAN people of W central New Mex- ico. When first encountered by Spanish explorers, they were living in seven separate towns, the fabled Seven Cities of CÍBOLA. The traditional occupation was corn farming; basketry and pottery were also well developed. Religious life centered on gods or spirits called KACHINAS. Today the Zuni number about 6,000.

Zurbarán \\ˌzùr-bə-'rän\\, **Francisco de** (1598–1664) Spanish painter. He was apprenticed in 1614 to a painter in Seville, where he lived most of his life as a provincial painter of re- ligious pictures. His apostles, saints, and monks are painted with almost sculptural modeling, and his emphasis on the minutiae of their dress lends authenticity to their miracles, visions, and ecstasies. This distinctive combination of natu- ralism with religious sensibility conforms to the guidelines for Counter-Reformation artists outlined by the Council of Trent. He had many commissions from monasteries and churches throughout S Spain. His late devotional paintings show the influence of B. E. MURILLO.

Zurich \\'zùr-ik\\ *or* **Zürich** \\'tsü̅e-rik\\ City (pop., 1999 est.: 336,000); metro. area pop., 935,000), Switzerland. Located on Lake Zurich, the site was occupied first by prehistoric lake dwellers and later by the Celtic Helvetii before the Ro- mans conquered the area about 58 B.C. In 1218 it became a free imperial city; in 1351 it joined the Swiss Confederation. Under Huldrych ZWINGLI it became the center of the Swiss reformation in the 16th cent. Attracting refugees from the COUNTER-REFORMATION, it established a liberal demo- cratic order during the 1830s. Switzerland's largest city, it is an industrial and financial center and a major tourist desti- nation.

Zweig, Stefan (1881–1942) German writer. His interest in psychology and the teachings of Sigmund FREUD is re- flected in his subtle portrayal of character. His essays in- clude the literary studies in *Three Masters* (1920) and *Mas- ter Builders* (1925). He achieved popularity with *The Tide of Fortune* (1928), five historical portraits. He also wrote bi- ographies, poetry, short stories and dramas. Driven into ex- ile by the Nazis in 1934, Zweig and his wife settled in Brazil, where, lonely and disillusioned, they committed suicide.

Zwicky \\'tsvik-ē\\, **Fritz** (1898–1974) Swiss-U.S. astronomer and physicist. In 1934, with Walter Baade (1893–1960), he proposed that SUPERNOVAS are a class of stellar explosion completely different from NOVAS. His search of nearby galaxies for supernovas discovered 18; only about 12 had been recorded previously in all of history. He also devel- oped (1943–46) some of the earliest jet engines. **yam** Any of several plant species of the genus *Dioscorea* (family Dioscoreaceae, or yam family), native to warmer regions of both hemispheres. A number of species are cultivated for food in the tropics. The edible tuberous roots, which vary in taste from sweet to bitter to tasteless, are eaten as cooked starchy vegetables. True yams are botanically distinct from the SWEET POTATO, though in the U.S. the names are com- monly interchanged. *Dio- scorea mexicana* contains a chemical that is used as the basis for birth-control pills.

Zwingli \\'zwiŋ-lē, *German* 'tsviŋ-lē\\, **Huldrych** (1484– 1531) Major reformer in the Protestant REFORMATION in Switzerland. He was or- dained a priest in 1506. Influ- enced by the ideas of Martin LUTHER, he began preaching reformist ideas in Zurich in 1518, actively challenging the ritualism, decadence, and hi- erarchy of the Roman Catho- lic church. The main con- tentions of his *67 Articles* (1523) were adopted by most

Huldrych Zwingli Portrait by Hans Asper, 1531

priests in Zurich. As his movement spread, he made a number of unorthodox assertions, declaring that Jesus alone is head of the church, that the mass is an affront to Christ, and that there is no biblical foundation for purgatory. He also rejected the notions of transubstantiation and priestly celibacy. He was killed in a battle while serving as an army chaplain.

Zworykin \ˈzvȯrʸ-kyin, *Engl* ˈzwȯr-i-kən\, **Vladimir (Kosma)** (1889–1982) Russian-U.S. electronic engineer and inventor. He emigrated to the U.S. in 1919. While with Westinghouse Electric Corp. (1920–29), he filed patent applications for his inventions of the iconoscope (a TELEVISION transmission tube, 1923) and the kinescope (TV receiver, 1924), which formed the first all-electronic TV system. He patented a color TV system in 1928. In 1929 he became director of electronic research at RCA. His infrared-sensitive electron image tube was the basis for devices first used in World War II for seeing in the dark.

WXYZ

Photograph Credits

Abbas I Smithsonian Institution, Freer Gallery of Art, Wash., D.C. **Abu Simbel** Air France **acropolis** T. Schneiders **J. Adams** Archive Photos **J. Q. Adams** Archive Photos **agate** B.M. Shaub **agora** Amer. School of Classical Studies at Athens **Agrippa** Musées Nationaux, Paris **Ailey** Z. Freyman **Akhmatova** Novosti Press Agency **Alamo** Greater San Antonio Chamber of Commerce **Albers** A. Newman **Albertus Magnus** Alinari/Art Resource/EB Inc. **Alcott** Louisa May Alcott Memorial Assn. **Alexander the Great** Brown Bros. **Ali** UPI Compix **alpaca** F. J. Erize, Bruce Coleman Ltd. **amanita** L. C. Moon, Tom Stack & Associates **ammonoid** L. Stunzi **anaconda** Z. Leszczynski, Animals Animals **Anderson** RCA Records **Angel Falls** G. De Steinheil, Shostal Assn./EB Inc. **anteater** R. C. Hermes, Annan Photo Features **Antony** Alinari/Art Resource/EB Inc. **Apollo** Alinari/Art Resource/EB Inc. **Arabian Desert** L. Abercrombie **arachnid** G. W. Wharton **Aristotle** Kunsthistorisches Museum, Vienna **Armstrong** AP/Wide World Photos **Arthur** Library of Congress, Wash., D.C. **Ashurbanipal** British Museum **Asturias** Camera Press **Athena** Alinari/Art Resource/EB Inc. **Auden** H. Tappe **Augustine** Alinari/Art Resource/EB Inc. **aurora** V. P. Hessler **Babbage** National Portrait Gallery, London **Bach** Brown Bros. **Bacon** National Portrait Gallery, London **Baker** H. Roger-Viollet **Baldwin** UPI/EB Inc. **Ball** Photofest **Balzac** J. E. Bulloz **Bantu peoples** Camera Press **barnacle** A. Mercieca, Root Resources/EB Inc. **Barnum** Library of Congress, Wash., D.C. **Bartók** Mrs. F. Reiner **Basie** R. Joy, Globe Pictures **Baudelaire** Bibliothèque Nationale, Paris **Becket** British Library **Becquerel** Archives Photographiques **Beethoven** Brown Bros. **Bell** Culver Pictures **Bergson** Archiv für Kunst und Geschichte, Berlin **Bernstein** Lauterwasser, Deutsche Grammophon **Bessemer** Science Museum, London; Iron & Steel Institute **bighorn** H. Engels, National Audubon Society/Photo Researchers **bird-of-paradise** M. Butler **Bizet** Bettmann Archive **Black Hawk** National Museum of Amer. Art, Smithsonian Institution, Wash., D.C. **Blackstone** National Portrait Gallery **Blake** National Portrait Gallery **Blücher** Archiv für Kunst und Geschichte, Berlin **Blum** Bibliothèque Nationale, Paris **Boccaccio** Alinari/Art Resource **Bogart** Penguin Photo, Columbia Pictures **Bolívar** Library of Congress, Wash., D.C. **bonsai** J. Groffman **Boole** J. R. Freeman & Co., Ltd.; British Museum **Borges** Wellesley College, Wellesley, Mass. **Borgia** Alinari/Art Resource/EB Inc. **Borobudur** Robert Harding Picture Library/Photobank BKK **Boulanger** EB Inc. **Bowie** Library of Congress, Wash., D.C. **Brahe** Det Nationalhistoriske Museum Paa Frederiksborg **Bramante** Anderson, Alinari/Art Resource/EB Inc. **Brandeis** Library of Congress, Wash., D.C. **Brecht** U. Bilderdienst **Brezhnev** S. Simon–K. Young **Britten** Camera Press **Brontë** National Portrait Gallery, London **Brooklyn Bridge** Devaney Stock Photos Inc. **Brunelleschi** Alinari/Art Resource/EB Inc. **Bryan** Library of Congress, Wash., D.C. **Buchanan** Library of Congress, Wash., D.C. **bugaku** To-ji, Kyoto **bullfighting** B. Conrad **Buñuel** Camera Press **Burke** National Portrait Gallery, London **Burns** National Portrait Gallery, London **Burton** National Portrait Gallery, London **G. Bush** AP Photo/Pearson **G. W. Bush** White House **Byron** National Portrait Gallery, London **cabaret** EDI Studio Barcelona **Caesar** Alinari/Art Resource/EB Inc. **Calhoun** Library of Congress, Wash., D.C. **Calvin** Museum Boymans-van Beuningen, Rotterdam **camel** G. Holton, National Audubon Society/Photo Researchers **Camões** Museu Nacional de Arte Antiga, Lisbon **Camus** H. Cartier-Bresson, Magnum **Caravaggio** SCALA/Art Resource **Cardozo** Library of Congress, Wash., D.C. **Carnegie** Brown Bros. **Carson** Library of Congress, Wash., D.C. **Carter** UPI/Bettmann Newsphotos **Caruso** Culver Pictures **cassowary** A. Mercieca, Root Resources **Castle** A. Todd **Castro** E. Erwitt, Magnum **Cavell** Syndication International Ltd. **cavy** G. Holton, Photo Researchers **centipede** E. S. Ross **Cézanne** Phillips Collection, Wash. D.C. **Chagall** A. Newman **Chanel** Chanel **Chaplin** Brown Bros. **Charles V** Bayerische Staatsgemŋldesammlungen, Munich **Charleston** Culver Pictures **Chartres** A. Perceval **Chekhov** D. Magarshack **Chiang Kai-shek** Camera Press **Chopin** Giraudon/Art Resource **Christie** UPI/EB Inc. **Churchill** Y. Karsh, J. Woodfin Camp **Cimabue** Alinari/Art Resource/EB Inc. **civet** R. C. Hermes, National Audubon Society/Photo Researchers/EB Inc. **Claudius** Alinari/Art Resource/EB Inc. **Clemente** UPI **Cleopatra** Oriental Institute, Univ. of Chicago **Cleveland** Library of Congress, Wash., D.C. **Clinton** White House **Cobb** Pictorial Parade/EB Inc. **Cody** Library of Congress, Wash., D.C. **Cohan** Pictorial Parade **Colette** C. Leirens, Black Star/EB Inc. **collie** S. A. Thompson **Colosseum** J. A. Cash **Columbus** Metropolitan Museum of Art, N.Y. **commedia dell'arte** British Museum **Comte** H. Roger-Viollet **Conestoga wagon** EB Inc. **Constantine I** Archive Photos **Constructivism** Solomon R. Guggenheim Museum, N.Y. **Coolidge** Archive Photos **Copland** Boston Symphony Orchestra **Corday** Biblioth que Nationale, Paris **Corneille** Musées Nationaux, Paris **corona** Yerkes Observatory **Cortés** Hospital de Jes's, Mexico City **cotton gin** Bettmann Archive **crane** K. B. Newman, EB Inc. **cricket** Bettmann Archive **Crockett** Rev. & Mrs. R. L. Whittenburg **Crosby** Brown Bros. **crypt** A. F. Keating **Cunningham** J. Mitchell **Curie** Granger Collection, N.Y. **curling** MALAK/Miller Services Ltd. **Custer** Mathew Brady Historical Collection, GAF Corp. **dabbling duck** L. E. Naylor, National Audubon Society/Photo Researchers **Dahshur** H. Roger-Viollet **Dalton** J. R. Freeman & Co. Ltd.; British Museum **Danilova** Penguin Photo Collection **Dante** Mansell, Alinari/Art Resource **Darrow** Chicago Historical Society **Darwin** International Museum of Photography, Rochester, N.Y. **David** Alinari/Art Resource/EB Inc. **Dean** Culver Pictures; Giant Productions, Warner Bros. **Debussy** Giraudon/Art Resource **De Forest** Culver Pictures **de Gaulle** B. Barbey, Magnum **Dempsey** UPI/EB Inc. **Descartes** Archive Photos **de Soto** Library of Congress, Wash., D.C. **Dewey** EB Inc. **Diaghilev** Dance Collection, New York Public Library **diatom** E. Grave, Photo Researchers **Dickens** Brown Bros. **Dietrich** Pictorial Parade **DiMaggio** EB Inc. **Dior** Popperfoto **Disney** EB Inc. **Doberman pinscher** S. A. Thompson **Donatello** Anderson, Alinari/Art Resource **Doria** Alinari/Art Resource/EB **double bass** EB Inc. **Douglass** Holt-Messer Collection, Schlesinger Library, Radcliffe College, Cambridge, Mass. **Doyle** National Portrait Gallery, London **Drake** National Portrait Gallery, London **Dreyfus** H. Roger-Viollet **Dryden** National Portrait Gallery, London **Duchamp** Louise & Walter Arensberg Collection, Philadelphia Museum of Art **dugong** D. C. Meighan **Dumas** Gramstorff Bros. **Dunham** Dance Collection, New York Public Library **Dürer** Blauet, Gnamm/ARTOTHEK; Alte Pinakothek, Munich **Duse** Library of Congress, Wash., D.C. **Duvalier** AP/Wide World Photos **Eames** Herman Miller Furniture Co., New York **Earhart** Culver Pictures **Easter Island** E. Manewal, Shostal/EB Inc. **Eddy** Library of Congress, Wash., D.C. **Edison** Edison National Historical Site, W. Orange, N.J. **Edward VIII** Camera Press **Egyptian art** E. Elisofon; Egyptian Museum, Cairo **Einstein** Nobelstiftelsen, Stockholm **Eisenhower** F. Bachrach **elephant seal** A. Mercieca, Root Resources **Elgin marbles** Hirmer Fotoarchiv, Munich **Eliot** National Portrait Gallery, London **Elizabeth II** Y. Karsh, Camera Press/Globe Photos **Emerson** Library of Congress, Wash., D.C. **Epicurus** Soprintendenza alle Antichita della Campania, Naples **Erasmus** Giraudon/Art Resource/EB Inc. **Erté** Sevenarts Ltd **Escher** Museum of Modern Art, New York **Essex** National Portrait Gallery, London **Evans** Pictorial Parade; Seven Pines Productions Ltd. **Fairbanks** EB Inc. **Farragut** Library of Congress, Wash., D.C. **Fauré** Giraudon/Art Resource/EB Inc. **Fellini** Paris Match, Pictorial Parade **Fichte** Deutsche Fotothek, Dresden **Fillmore** Archive Photos **Fitzgerald** Warner Bros. Records Inc. **flea** W. E. Ferguson **Foch** EB Inc. **Fonteyn** London Express **G. Ford** AP/Wide World Photos **H. Ford** Ford Motor Co. Archives **Forster** BBC Hulton Picture Library **Fourier** Giraudon/Art Resource/EB Inc. **foxglove** D. Fell **Francis I** Biblioth que Nationale, Paris **Franklin** Archive Photos **Fresco painting** SCALA/Art Resource/EB Inc. **Freud** M. Evans; W. E. Freud **frigate bird** J. & D. Bartlett, Bruce Coleman Inc./EB Inc. **Frost** Ruohamaa, Black Star **Fuller** Library of Congress, Wash., D.C. **Galileo** Alinari/Art Resource **Galton** National Portrait Gallery, London **Gama** Museu Nacional de Arte Antiga, Lisbon **Gandhi** M. Bourke-White; Time Inc. **Garbo** Culver Pictures **García Márquez** L. Ozkok **Garfield** Archive Photos **Garland** Brown Bros. **Garvey** UPI **Gauguin** Chester Dale Collection, National Gallery of Art, Wash., D.C. **gecko** A. Bannister **George VI** Keystone **Giacometti** Y. Karsh, Rapho/Photo Researchers **Gibraltar** H. Huber **Gide** Giraudon/Art Resource/EB Inc.; A.D.A.G.P. **Gillespie** UPI **Giotto** SCALA/Art Resource **Gladstone** Culver Pictures **Goethe** Neue Pinakothek; Bayerische Staatgemŋldesammlungen **golden eagle** A. & S. Carey **Goldsmith** National Portrait Gallery, London **golf** AP/Wide World Photos **Gorbachev** Colton, Picture Search/Black Star **Gorky** H. Roger-Viollet **Goya** Biblioteca Nacional, Madrid **Grange** Bettmann Archive **Grant** Library of Congress, Wash., D.C. **Grass** Authenticated News International **great auk** J. Warham **Greeley** National Portrait Gallery, Smithsonian Institution, Wash., D. C. **Greenaway** Mary Evans Picture Library, London **Gregory VII** L. von Matt, EB Inc. **Grey** National Portrait Gallery, London **Grieg** Brown Bros. **Grimm** Staatliche Museen zu Berlin **grosbeak** K. H. Maslowski **Guevara** L. Lockwood, Black Star **gyrfalcon** S. Grossman, J. Woodfin Camp **Hadrian** Anderson, Alinari/Art Resource/EB Inc. **Halley's Comet** European Southern Observatory **Hals** Rijksmuseum, Amsterdam **Hamilton** Andrew Mellon Collection, National Gallery of Art, Wash., D.C. **Handel** National Portrait Gallery, London **Harding** Library of Congress, Wash., D.C. **Hardy** EB Inc. **harlequin** H. Hintz, J. P. Ziolo; Public Art Museum, Basel **B. Harrison** Archive Photos **W. H. Harrison** Archive Photos **Hauptmann** Schiller-Nationalmuseum, Marbach **Hayes** Archive Photos **heaven** Staatbibliothek Bamberg **Hellenistic Age** Alinari/Art Resource/EB Inc. **Hemingway** Y. Karsh, Rapho/Photo Researchers; M. Hemingway **Henry the Navigator** Museu Nacional de Arte Antiga, Lisbon **Hepburn** Brown Bros. **Hesse** Wide World Photos **Hidatsa** Rare Book Division, New York Public Library **Hindenburg** U.S. Navy **Hitler** H. Hoffmann, Munich **Ho Chi Minh** M. Riboud, Magnum **Hogarth** Tate Gallery, London **Holmes** EB Inc. **Hoover** EB Inc. **hornbill** M. Boutlon, National Audubon Society/Photo Researchers **Houdini** Pictorial Parade/EB Inc. **Houston** Library of Congress, Wash., D.C. **Howe** National Hockey League **Hubble Space Telescope** Hughes Aircraft Co. **Hughes** Library of Congress, Wash., D.C. **Hugo** Archives Photographiques **Humboldt** Staatliche Museen zu Berlin **humpback whale** A. Giddings, Images Unlimited **Husserl** Archiv für Kunst und Geschichte, Berlin **Huxley** R. M. Quittner, Black Star **hyena** N. Owen-Smith, Annan Photo Features **ibis** M. P. Kahl **Ibn Saud** Camera Press **Ibsen** Universitetbiblioteket, Oslo **Iguazú Falls** R. Manley, Superstock **illuminated manuscript** Dean & Chapter of Winchester **impala** J. P. Rowan **Ingres** Giraudon/Art Resource/EB Inc. **International Style** Dr. F. Stoedtner **ironclad** J. R. Freeman & Co. Inc.; British Museum **Isabella I** Archivo Mas, Barcelona **Isis** Staatliche Museen Preussischer Kulturbesitz, Berlin **Ivan IV** Nationalmuseet, Copenhagen **A. Jackson** Archive Photos

J. Jackson D. Brack, Black Star **H. James** Smith College Archives **James I** National Maritime Museum **Janacek** Eastfoto **Janus** Larousse **Jefferson** White House Collection, Wash., D.C. **Jinnah** Pakistan Embassy, Wash. D.C. **Joan of Arc** Giraudon/Art Resource/EB Inc. **John XXIII** Keystone **A. Johnson** Archive Photos **L. B. Johnson** Archive Photos **S. Johnson** L. & F. Rothschild **Jones** Independence National Historical Park Collection, Philadelphia **Joyce** G. Freund **Juárez** Library of Congress, Wash., D.C. **judo** Kodo-Kan, Tokyo **Jung** L. Iseley, Nancy Palmer Agency **Jupiter** Jet Propulsion Laboratory/NASA **Justinian I** Giraudon/Alinari/Art Resource **kabuki** F. Watanabe; Shochiku Co.,Tokyo **Kafka** Archiv für Kunst und Geschichte, Berlin **Kandinsky** A.D.A.G.P. French Reproduction Rights, Inc.; N. Kandinsky **Kant** Marburg, Art Reference Bureau/EB Inc. **Karloff** AP/Wide World Photos **katydid** E. S. Ross **Kaunda** Camera Press **Keller** Amer. Foundation for the Blind **Kennedy** Brown Bros. **Kenyatta** J. Moss, Black Star **Kern** EB Inc. **Khrushchev** W. Wolf, Black Star **Kierkegaard** Royal Danish Ministry of Foreign Affairs **King** Archive Photos **kingfisher** Annan Photo Features **Kipling** Elliot & Fry **kite** J. A. Kern **Knossos** Greek Ministry of Culture, Archaeological Receipts Fund **koala** A. Mercieca, National Audubon Society/Photo Researchers/EB Inc. **Koch** Nobelstiftelsen, Stockholm **Komodo dragon** J. A. Kern **Kosciuszko** Polish Museum of America, Chicago **Kropotkin** Brown Bros. **Kublai Khan** National Palace Museum, Taipei **La Fontaine** J. Arlaud; Bibliothèque Publique et Universitaire, Geneva **Lagerlöf** Nobel Foundation, Stockholm **Lang** F. Lang **La Tène** Bibliothèque Nationale, Paris **Laurier** National Film Board of Canada Photothèque **Lawrence** L. Thomas & H. A. Chase **Le Corbusier** Y. Karsh, J. Woodfin Camp **Lee** Library of Congress, Wash., D.C. **Leonardo da Vinci** Alinari/Art Resource/EB Inc. **Lévi-Strauss** AP/Wide World Photos **Liliuokalani** Bernice P. Bishop Museum **lily of the valley** W. Chandoha **Lincoln** Library of Congress, Wash., D.C. **Lindbergh** Library of Congress, Wash., D.C. **Liszt** Museo Teatrale alla Scala, Milan **Livingstone** National Portrait Gallery, London **Longfellow** Historical Pictures Service, Chicago **J. Louis** EB Inc. **Louis XIV** Giraudon/Art Resource/EB Inc. **Louis XVI** Giraudon/Art Resource/EB Inc. **lovebird** T. Angermayer **Ludendorff** Archiv für Kunst und Geschichte, Berlin **Lully** Giraudon/Art Resource **Lysenko** Sovfoto **Macaulay** National Portrait Gallery, London **Machiavelli** Alinari/Art Resource/EB Inc. **Madison** Archive Photos **Mahler** Mansell Collection **Malinowski** Polish Library, London **Malraux** B. Barbey, Magnum **Mandela** C. Morris, Black Star **Manet** Courtauld Institute Galleries, London **Manzoni** Alinari/Art Resource/EB Inc. **marabou** M. P. Kahl **Marie-Antoinette** Musées Nationaux, Paris **marionette** Z. Gajda; Bil Baird Collection **Marlborough** National Portrait Gallery, London **Marshall** EB Inc. **Marx** J. R. Freeman & Co., Ltd.; British Museum **Mather** Amer. Antiquarian Society, Worcester, Mass. **Matterhorn** E. Galloway **Maupassant** Archives Photographiques **Maximilian** Albertina, Vienna **Mays** UPI **McCarthy** National Archives, Wash., D.C. **McCormick** Culver Pictures **McKinley** Archive Photos **Medici** S. H. Kress Collection, National Gallery of Art, Wash., D.C. **Mencius** National Palace Museum, Taipei **Mercury** Alinari/Art Resource **metalwork** SCALA/Art Resource **Michelangelo** Alinari/Art Resource **Mies van der Rohe** E. Stoller, Esto **Mill** Archive Photos **Milne** National Portrait Gallery, London **Miró** Y. Karsh, J. Woodfin Camp **Mistral** Library of Congress, Wash., D.C. **mobile** Museum of Modern Art, New York **Molière** Giraudon/Art Resource; Musée Condé, Chantilly, France **Monet** H. Roger-Viollet, S.P.A.D.E.M. 1971/French Reproduction Rights, Inc. **Monroe** Archive Photos **Montaigne** Giraudon/Art Resource/EB Inc. **Montessori** Publifoto **Moore** G. Freund **Morisot** Cleveland Museum of Art **mosque** M. Oppersdorff **mountain goat** E. Kubis, Root Resources **Munch** Albertina Museum, Vienna **Myron** Alinari/Art Resource **Nabokov** P. Halsman **Napoleon** Giraudon/Art Resource; S. H. Kress Collection, National Gallery of Art, Wash., D.C. **Nara** Sakamoto Photo Laboratory, Tokyo **Neruda** Camera Press **Newton** National Portrait Gallery, London **Nicholas II** Hillwood, Wash., D.C. **nightingale** H. Reinhard, Bruce Coleman Inc. **Nixon** UPI **Nkrumah** M. & E. Bernheim, J. Woodfin Camp **Nôtre-Dame** Giraudon/Art Resource/EB Inc. **Nureyev** Keystone **Nyerere** Hanos, Liaison Agency **Oakley** Bettmann Archive **O'Connell** National Portrait Gallery, London **Oedipus** Alinari/Art Resource/EB Inc. **Okapi** K. W. Fink, Root Resources **Oldenbarnevelt** Rijksmuseum, Amsterdam **Olivier** Z. Dominic **orangutan** R. Kinne, Photo Reseachers **Orwell** BBC **Osler** Osler Library, McGill Univ., Montreal **Owens** AP/Wide World Photos **Paganini** Granger Collection, New York **Paine** Thomas Paine National Historical Assn. **panda** G. Holton, Photo Researchers **panpipe** Horniman Museum, London **paper** N. Masaki **Parker** AP/Wide World Photos **Parthenon** A. Frantz **passenger pigeon** B. Reasons, National Audubon Society/Photo Researchers **Patton** U.S. Army **Pavlova** Culver Pictures **Pearson** Canadian Press **Pei** E. Stoller, Esto **Pericles** Mansell Collection **Perón** OAS; Columbus Memorial Library **Persephone** Anderson, Alinari/Art Resource/EB Inc. **Pershing** Library of Congress, Wash., D.C. **Pétain** EB Inc. **Philip II** Alinari/Art Resource/EB Inc. **phrenology** BBC Hulton Picture Library **Piaf** UPI/Bettmann Newsphotos **Pierce** Library of Congress, Wash., D.C. **Pilsudski** Culver Pictures **piranha** J. Annan, Annan Photo Features **Pissarro** Tate Gallery, London **Pitt** National Portrait Gallery, London **Plato** Staatliche Museen zu Berlin **Plisetskaya** Paris Match/Pictorial Parade **Pocahontas** Library of Congress, Wash., D.C. **Poe** J. Miller Documents, Brown Univ. Library **Polk** Library of Congress, Wash., D.C. **Polo** Columbia Univ. Libraries, New York **Pompadour** National Galleries of Scotland, Edinburgh **poodle** S. A. Thompson, EB Inc. **Pope** National Portrait Gallery, London **Porter** Culver Pictures **Potemkin** J. R. Freeman & Co., Ltd.; British Museum **Potter** Pictorial Parade/London Daily Express; Frederick Warne & Co. **Praxiteles** Alinari/Art Resource **prayer wheel** E. Fuller Memorial Collection, Seattle Art Museum **Pre-Raphaelites** Tate Gallery, London **Presley** UPI **Priestley** National Portrait Gallery, London **pronghorn** L. L. Rue III **Proust** J. E. Bulloz; S.P.A.D.E.M. 1971/French Reproduction Rights, Inc. **Ptolemy** British Museum **Puccini** Alinari/Art Resource **pygmy** H. Kanus, Rapho/Photo Researchers **Pyrenees** A.G.E. FotoStock **Qianlong** Metropolitan Museum of Art, New York **quail** W. H. Mullins, National Audubon Society/Photo Researchers **Rabelais** Musées Nationaux, Paris **Racine** Giraudon/Art Resource/EB Inc. **Raleigh** J. R. Freeman & Co., Ltd.; British Museum **Ramakrishna** Information Service of India, London **Rasputin** H. Roger-Viollet, Photo Harlingue **S. Ray** Camera Press **Reagan** Archive Photos **Redon** Archives Photographiques, Paris **Reinhardt** Theatre Collection, New York Public Library **rhinoceros** Camera Press/Pictorial Parade/EB Inc. **Rhodes** Historical Pictures Service, Chicago **rice** G. Heilman **Richelieu** Giraudon/Art Resource/EB Inc. **Richthofen** Pictorial Parade **Rimsky-Korsakov** H. Roger-Viollet **Robespierre** J. E. Bulloz **Robinson** UPI/EB Inc. **Rockefeller Center** Thomas Airviews **Rodgers** Brown Bros. **F. Roosevelt** Archive Photos **T. Roosevelt** Archive Photos **Rossetti** J. M. Cotterell; H. Rossetti **Rothschild** Historisches Museum, Frankfurt **Rouault** Giraudon/Art Resource/EB Inc. **Russell** BBC **Ruth** UPI **Saarinen** A. Newman **sadhu** J. A. Cash **Saint Basil's** R. Houser, Comstock **Sand** Musée Carnavalet, Paris **Santa Anna** San Jacinto Museum of History Assn., Texas **Sartre** G. Freund **Sauk** Library of Congress, Wash., D.C. **scarab** Oriental Institute, Univ. of Chicago **Schliemann** Deutsche Staatsbibliothek, Berlin **Schopenhauer** Archiv für Kunst und Geschichte, Berlin **Schumann** Bettmann Archive **Schweitzer** Karsh, Rapho/Photo Researchers **Scott** J. R. Freeman & Co., Ltd.; British Museum **Scriabin** Novosti Press Agency **Segovia** AP/Wide World Photos **Seleucus** J. R. Freeman & Co., Ltd.; British Museum **Senghor** United Nations **serval** C. Loke, Photo Researchers **Sèvres** W. Walter, EB Inc.; Victoria & Albert Museum, London **Shaw** Y. Karsh, J. Woodfin Camp **Shelley** National Portrait Gallery, London **Shiva** Royal Academy of Arts, London; Government Museum, Madras **Shostakovich** Novosti Press Agency **sikhara** P. Chandra **Sikorsky** Sikorsky Aircraft **Simenon** J. Bauer **Sinatra** down beat **B. Smith** C. Van Vechten; Columbia Records **D. Smith** Whitney Museum of Amer. Art, New York **J. Smith** Reorganized Church of Jesus Christ of Latter Day Saints, Independence, Mo. **Smuts** EB Inc. **snipe** I. Holmasen **Socrates** Archive Photos **Sophia** Novosti Press Agency **Soyinka** V. L. Smith **Spenser** Pembroke College, Cambridge, England **spirochete** ASM/Science Source **Staël** Giraudon/Art Resource/EB Inc. **Stalin** Archive Photos **Stanley** City Art Gallery, Bristol, England **Steichen** J. T. Steichen **Steinmetz** Union College, Schenectady, N.Y. **Stephenson** Science Museum, London **Stevenson** Brown Bros. **Stijl** Haags Gemeentemuseum **Stoss** Germanisches Nationalmuseum, Nuremberg **Strauss** Staatliche Museen zu Berlin **Strindberg** O. Vaering; Munch-Museet, Oslo **stupa** Holle Bildarchiv **Sullivan** UPI/EB Inc. **Sun Yat-sen** Brown Bros. **swan** A. A. Ambler, National Audubon Society/Photo Researchers **Swift** National Portrait Gallery, London **Taft** Library of Congress, Wash., D.C. **Tagore** EB Inc. **Taney** Library of Congress, Wash., D.C. **Taylor** Archive Photos **Temple** Brown Bros. **tern** R. W. McFarlane **Tesla** Culver Pictures **Thatcher** AP/Wide World Photos **Theodora** A. Held, J. P. Ziolo **Thorpe** Bettmann Archive **timpani** Ludwig Industries, Chicago **tobacco** J. Horace McFarland Co. **Tocqueville** H. Roger-Viollet **Tolstoy** Archive Photos **Torquemada** Biblioteca Nacional, Madrid **totem pole** B. & I. Spring **tracery** Authenticated News International **Trajan** British Museum **Trollope** National Portrait Gallery, London **Truman** U.S. Signal Corps **Truth** Burton Historical Collection, Detroit Public Library **Tshombe** AP/Wide World Photos **Turgenev** D. Magarshack collection **Turner** Tate Gallery, London **Tweed** Library of Congress, Wash., D.C. **Tyler** National Museum of Amer. Art, Smithsonian Institution, Wash., D.C. **Undset** Royal Norwegian Embassy, London **Ur** Hirmer Fotoarchiv, Munich **Valentino** Oliver Dernberger Collection, Cherokee Book Shop **Van Buren** Chicago Historical Society **Vanderbilt** Library of Congress, Wash., D.C. **van Gogh** Museum of Modern Art, New York **Vaughan** H. Snitzer **Vespucci** Alinari/Art Resource/EB Inc. **Victoria** Archive Photos **Voltaire** Archive Photos **von Neumann** A. W. Richards **Walpole** National Portrait Gallery, London **Warren** UPI/EB Inc. **Washington** Archive Photos **Watt** National Portrait Gallery, London **Westminster** A. F. Kersting **whippet** S. A. Thompson, EB Inc. **Whitman** Library of Congress, Wash., D.C. **Wilde** W. Andrews Memorial Library, UC–Los Angeles **Wilson** Archive Photos **wombat** W. Garst, Tom Stack & Associates **Woodhull** California Historical Society, San Francisco **Woolf** G. Freund **Wren** National Portrait Gallery, London **Xerxes** Oriental Institute, Univ. of Chicago **Xipe Totec** Hamlyn Group Picture Library **yak** R. Kinne, Photo Researchers/EB Inc. **Young** down beat **Zapata** Archivo Casasola **Zeus** Staatliche Museen zu Berlin **Zhu Xi** National Palace Museum, Taipei **Zola** Musées Nationaux, Paris **Zwingli** Schweizerisches Institut für Kunstwissenschaft; Kunstmuseum Winterthur, Switzerland